WORLD AUTHORS

1950-1970

Biographical Reference Books from The H. W. Wilson Company

American Reformers

Greek and Latin Authors 800 B.C.–A.D. 1000
European Authors 1000–1900
British Authors Before 1800
British Authors of the Nineteenth Century
American Authors 1600–1900
Twentieth Century Authors
Twentieth Century Authors: First Supplement
World Authors 1950–1970
World Authors 1970–1975
World Authors 1975–1980

The Junior Book of Authors
More Junior Authors
Third Book of Junior Authors
Fourth Book of Junior Authors and Illustrators
Fifth Book of Junior Authors and Illustrators

Great Composers: 1300–1900
Composers Since 1900
Composers Since 1900: First Supplement
Musicians Since 1900
American Songwriters

Nobel Prize Winners

World Artists 1950–1980

World Film Directors: Volumes I, II

WORLD AUTHORS

1950–1970

A Companion Volume to Twentieth Century Authors

Edited by
JOHN WAKEMAN

Editorial Consultant
STANLEY J. KUNITZ

THE H. W. WILSON COMPANY
New York · 1975

First Printing 1975
Second Printing 1981
Third Printing 1989

Printed in The United States of America

LIBRARY OF CONGRESS CATALOGING IN PUBLICATION DATA

Wakeman, John.
World authors, 1950-1970.

(Authors series)
"Continues the work done by Stanley J. Kunitz and Howard Haycraft in Twentieth century authors [and its first suppl.]"

1. Literature, Modern—20th century—Bio-bibliography. I. Kunitz, Stanley Jasspon, 1905- Twentieth century authors. II. Title. III. Series.
PN451.W3 809'.04 [B] 75-172140
ISBN 0-8242-0419-0

PREFACE

THIS BOOK continues the work done by Stanley J. Kunitz and Howard Haycraft in *Twentieth Century Authors*, and by Kunitz and Vineta Colby in their *First Supplement* to that volume. *Twentieth Century Authors*, published in 1942, set out to "provide a foundation-volume of authentic biographical information on the writers of this century, of all nations, whose books are familiar to readers of English." It dealt with more than 1,800 authors, many of whom provided autobiographical articles. The *First Supplement* followed in 1955, bringing all the original biographies up to date, and adding 700 more. Since these 2,500 authors have not been brought forward into the present work, it is called a companion rather than a supplement to the preceding volumes.

As it is, we deal with 959 authors, most of whom came to prominence between 1950 and 1970. We also include a number of writers whose reputations were made earlier, but who were absent from the previous volumes because of a lack of biographical information, or because their work was not then "familiar to readers of English." This criterion has now lost much of its force, thanks to the vastly increased propagation of translations since World War II.

Otherwise, this volume in the Wilson Authors Series follows the policies of its companions. Some authors are here, that is, because of their literary importance, others because of their exceptional popularity. Most are imaginative writers—poets, novelists, dramatists—but we have also included some philosophers, historians, biographers, critics, theologians, scientists, and journalists whose work seemed of sufficiently wide interest or influence.

About half of the authors in this book have provided autobiographical articles. These have been reproduced without alteration (except of course those that have been translated from foreign languages, where accuracy has been sought even at the cost of elegance).

The editorial notes on authors and their works were composed by specialists in the literatures concerned, and checked by independent researchers (most of them also specialists) with a rigor that has added years to the expected gestation period of the book. The original editorial notes have since been expanded and revised and checked again and again as fresh information has appeared. (The length of these articles, which by and large reflects the importance of their subjects, is also affected by such extraneous considerations as the quantity and diversity of their work, and the availability of information about them.) Discrepancies between our accounts and those in other books have been referred to the most authoritative sources available—to the texts or title pages of books discussed, to national bibliographies, to the authors themselves or their literary executors. Errors quite inevitably remain, but fewer, it is hoped, than are usually to be expected in a work of this scale.

Critical comment is fuller than in the earlier volumes, but abides by the same principle, attempting not "an independent appraisal but . . . a fair summation of representative critical response." Beyond this, we have quite often taken the risk of suggesting connections between an author's experience of life and the kind of books he writes. There are some artists, moreover—sometimes even quite minor ones—who achieve or suffer an emblematic status, so that their lives, no less than their books, offer clues to the social or moral or psychological mechanisms of their time and place. We have frequently gone beyond a chaste recital of events and dates to provide information or anecdotes that seem to us illuminating or suggestive in these terms.

In general, the book is intended for students and common readers (though some of the autobiographical articles, at least, will be of interest to scholars as well). We have therefore striven for simplicity in such vexed matters as pseudonyms and the transliteration of foreign names. Thus, in transliterations, we have preferred the forms made familiar by trade publishers to the daunting constructions urged upon each other by warring specialists. The bibliographies are equally utilitarian. Most of them list, with dates of first publication, all of an author's published books. In a few specified cases, however, a particularly prolific author is represented by only a selection of his titles. And on the other hand we have sometimes listed even uncollected short stories by foreign authors who have otherwise published little in English. A similar policy has been followed in the lists of writings about an author and his work: the more abundant the material, the more selective the list.

Foreign titles are usually followed by an English version of the title and a date in parenthesis. The date is that of first publication of the original work. The English title appears in roman type if we have supplied the translation; in italics if the book has actually been translated and published under that title; in quotation marks if it is a poem, story, or other short piece translated and published under that title in a magazine or collection. Dates given in the text for plays are usually specified as dates of writing or of first *production;* dates given in the bibliographies are dates of first *publication.* A necrology of authors whose deaths were reported too late for inclusion in the text will be found at the end of the book.

My warm thanks are due to the contributors, whose names are listed below. Some are already well known, and many deserve to be; some have made translations or helped with research; some have written one article and others many. There is not space to indicate the special nature and extent of my gratitude to each. However, I must single out four people who not only wrote much original matter but shared generously and companionably in the editorial drudgery: Rosalynde Ainslie, Konstantin Bazarov, John Elsom, and Susan Macdonald. And it is a particular pleasure to acknowledge the crucial contribution of the poet Stanley Kunitz, originator of the Wilson Authors Series, who, acting as Editorial Consultant in the planning and execution of this volume, made available to us an enormous body of information and wisdom about authors and books.

J. W.
May 1974

Contributors

Rosalynde Ainslie
Konstantin Bazarov
Thomas G. Bergin
Bernard Bergonzi
G. A. Campbell
B. Ciplijauskaite
Carol Clapham
Vineta Colby
John A. Coleman
Martin Collcutt
G. R. Coulthard
Arthur Curley
Dorothy Nyren Curley
Filippo Donini
Kieran Dugan
Lovett F. Edwards
John Elsom
Gavin Ewart
Andrew Field
Gerald Fitzmaurice
Averne Fordham
Gwendolen Freeman
Derek H. Gagen
David Gallagher
Isaac Goldemberg
Sarah Graham
Lloyd W. Griffin
John Guenther
Michael Hamburger
Ruth Herschberger
James A. Hodkinson
Sara Holden
Elizabeth Humphreys
Paz E. de Huneeus
Katherine Jones
Edmund Keeley
Hyman Kublin
Elias Kulukundis
Algirdas Landsbergis
Charles R. Larson
Jean P. Liddiard
Evelyn Lohr
Cora Lushington
Richard Mabey
Susan Macdonald
Joan MacLean
G. S. Manners
Kim Martin
Ruth Finer Mintz
Jennifer Mulherin

Rosemary Neiswender
Bernard S. Oldsey
Gavin Orton
Lisette Osbourn
Jean Plaister
Giovanni Pontiero
Anthony Quinton
Gregory Rabassa
Robert Regan
David Russell
Morton Seif
Martin Seymour-Smith
Henry Sloan
Emile Snyder
Evelyn Speiser
W. B. Stevenson
R. G. Surridge
Molly Tibbs
D. Tindall
Raleigh Trevelyan
Martin Turnell
Paul West
Richard Whittington-Egan
Frederic Will
John R. Willingham

WORLD AUTHORS
1950-1970

KEY TO PRONUNCIATION

ā āle
â câre
a add
ä ärm

ē ēve
e end

g go

ī īce
i ill

K German ch as in *ich* (iK)

N Not pronounced, but indicates the nasal tone of the preceding vowel, as in the French *bon* (bôN)

ō ōld
ô ôrb
o odd
oi oil
o͞o o͞oze
o͝o fo͝ot
ou out

th *th*en
th thin

ū cūbe
û ûrn; French eu, as in *jeu* (zhû), German ö, oe, as in *schön* (shûn), *Goethe* (gû′ tə)
u tub

ü Pronounced approximately as ē, with rounded lips: French u, as in *vu* (vü); German ü, as in *Gefühl* (gə fül′)

ə the schwa, an unstressed vowel representing the sound that is spelled
a as in sofa
e as in fitted
i as in edible
o as in melon
u as in circus

zh azure

′ = main accent

A NECROLOGY OF AUTHORS
WILL BE FOUND AT THE END OF THE BOOK

***ABÉ, KOBO** (March 7, 1924–), Japanese novelist, poet, and dramatist, writes: "I grew up in Mukden, in the Japanese colony of Manchuria. My father was a doctor and he taught at the medical college there. The first writer to influence me must have been Edgar Allan Poe. At junior high school, I made myself popular with my classmates by assembling them during the lunch hour and telling Poe stories. When I ran out of Poe, I had to make up similar stories of my own.

"In those days, I liked to paint pictures in imitation of the Constructivists, and to collect insects, and to solve mathematical problems, especially geometry. I was a wretched linguist. As for sports, I was required to practice *kendo*, Japanese fencing, and to run the two-thousand-meter race.

"In 1940, when I was seventeen, I returned to Japan and enrolled at Seijo High School in Tokyo. Then I got tuberculosis, and during the year I spent recuperating, I devoured Dostoevsky. That was the year the war began.

"Fascism was gradually intensified, and though I was opposed to it emotionally, at the same time my sense of isolation led me to desire assimilation, and I read as much as I could get of Nietzsche, and Heidegger, and Jaspers. Unfortunately, there were no Japanese works to give me the strength I needed and sought. Military training was compulsory, and when I was given the lowest existing military rank I began to hate school itself, though I still liked mathematics as much as ever. My teachers urged me to major in mathematics at the University, but my father was determined that I should become a doctor, and in 1943 I entered the University of Tokyo as a medical student.

"Emotionally I was very disturbed and my state of mind grew steadily worse until I was cutting classes often. I recall this period in my life very indistinctly, though I do remember being taken once to a mental hospital by a friend. Possibly I was the more normal of the two, for shortly afterwards my friend went mad. At any rate, for that two-year period I did almost nothing but read Rilke's poems on form and structure, which were an obsession with me.

"Late in 1944 I heard a rumor that Japan would soon be defeated. Suddenly, a passionate desire for action revived itself in me and, conspiring with a friend, I forged a certificate of ill health and crossed the ocean to Manchuria without a word to the University. At that time, the government had to be convinced that your reasons for wanting to travel abroad were sufficient before you could leave the country. Happily, my father had opened his own hospital in Manchuria, while my friend's father was a high-ranking official in the Manchurian government. We had heard that his official duties brought him into contact with the bandits in the Manchurian backlands, and we planned to join up with them, and why not, since Japan was soon to be defeated anyway?

* ä′ bā

KOBO ABÉ

"As it turned out, though, my life, until that day in August when the surrender came, was spent in peaceful idleness with my family in Mukden. Then, suddenly, the war was over, and a vicious anarchy reigned. The state of anarchy made me anxious and afraid, but at the same time I suspect it thrilled me too, aroused my hopes. At least that terrific wall of authority had disappeared. There was a typhus epidemic that winter and my father, who had been treating victims all over the settlement, contracted the disease and died. In this way, I was released from my obligations, first to the state, and then to my father.

"But survival itself did not become a real agony until the end of 1946, after I had shipped back to Japan. I was extremely poor and undernourished; just staying alive from day to day took all my energies. By peddling charcoal in the streets and taking whatever odd jobs I could get while I went to school, I managed somehow to graduate, but I lacked the funds to pursue a medical career further. Sometime during this period I began jotting stories down in my school notebooks, and the year after I graduated an editor happened to see one and it was published in a magazine. For the first time in my life, my own ability had earned me some money. And so I became a writer. In 1951, I received the Akutagawa Prize for Literature, and knew that I would never retrace my steps.

"I will never forget that my adolescence began amidst death and ruins."

Abé's literary career began with the publication, at his own expense, of *Mumei Shishu* (Poems by an Unknown, 1948), in which he showed his interest in the existentialism of Jaspers and Heidegger. At this stage he was attracted to communism, and he soon made a name for himself as a literary revolutionary and critic of capitalism. *Akai Mayu* (Red Cocoon, 1950) was awarded a literary prize, and in 1951 he received the highly coveted Akutagawa Prize for his novel *Kabe—S. Karuma-shi no Hanzai* (The Wall—The Crime of S. Karuma). Already evident in his work was a preoccupation with the problem of identity, which has continued to concern him, and his technique of creating a private or allegorical world against which to measure the contradictions apparent in his own society.

Of the score of plays and novels which Abé has produced, four novels have so far been translated into English by E. Dale Saunders. The first of them was *Suna no Onna* (1963, translated as *The Woman in the Dunes*), which was admirably filmed by Teshigawara Hiroshi. An entomologist looking for specimens along a remote shoreline finds shacks built in pits in the dunes and a whole strange community of people who spend their lives in an endless struggle against the engulfing sand. The young man falls into one of these pits and is trapped there. His jailer—and fellow-prisoner—is a young widow who needs his help to hold back the sand.

Out of this bizarre situation, Abé constructs a story of great narrative fascination in its account of survival techniques in an immensely specialized environment, and of the young man's ingenious escape attempts. And it is no less absorbing and convincing as a study of a developing emotional relationship which is full of universal implications —about the fragility of identity, about freedom and responsibility, fear and compassion, and about the whole nature of human societies. What so impressed the many critics who admired the book was the texture of its writing. Action is slowed almost to a standstill to permit the microscopically detailed description of physical particulars. Above all, in a way which reminded many readers of the French New Novelists, the sand itself is scrutinized with such intensity that it becomes a protagonist in the novel—sometimes a creeping, suffocating enemy, sometimes a golden film that lends beauty to the human body.

Tanin no Kao (1964, translated as *The Face of Another*) deals more directly with the identity theme. A scientist, hideously scarred in a laboratory accident, laboriously constructs a completely new face and, thus disguised, sets out to seduce his own wife. This allegory, which has a host of antecedents in both Japanese and Western literature, seemed to most critics altogether too overt. There was a warmer reception for *The Ruined Map*, a different approach to the same theme, in which a detective, searching in a corrupt and nightmarish city for a missing man, so identifies with his quarry that he *becomes* him. For many critics, *Inter Ice Age 4*, about a computer that can predict the future, confirmed the author's "mastery of the philosophical thriller."

Lewis Nichols has described Abé as "slight, engaging, with heavy, horn-rimmed glasses and an unruly mop of black hair." A former member of the Communist party, he now calls himself a Socialist. His wife Machi is an artist and has illustrated some of his books.

PRINCIPAL WORKS IN ENGLISH TRANSLATION: The Woman in the Dunes, 1964; The Face of Another, 1966; The Ruined Map, 1969; Inter Ice Age 4, 1970.

ABOUT: *Periodicals*—Encounter July 1965; The New Leader November 9, 1964; New York Times Book Review August 30, 1964; October 25, 1964; July 9, 1966; Saturday Review September 5, 1964; September 26, 1970; Times Literary Supplement March 6, 1969.

ABEL, LIONEL (November 28, 1910–), American critic, dramatist, and translator, was born in New York City, the son of Alter and Anna (Schwartz) Abelson. He attended St. John's University, New York (1926–1928), and the University of North Carolina (1928–1929). Little has been published about his early career. For some years, probably just after World War II, he lived in Paris and came to know Sartre, Camus, and other leaders of French existentialism.

Abel reached the conclusion that it is no longer possible to write dramatic tragedy, that modern man is altogether too self-conscious a creature to achieve the necessary quality of "demonic" exaltation. On the other hand, simple realism offers little satisfaction to the creative dramatist. The solution, Abel believes, is a mode which he calls "metatheatre" and which he finds not only in the work of such moderns as Pirandello, Genet, and Beckett, but also, for example, in Shakespeare and Calderón. It is a fundamentally existentialist concept which "assumes that there is no world except that created by human striving, human imagination. . . . . For metatheatre, order is something continually improvised by man." Thus the "metaplay" is about people who must consciously and deliberately invent the roles they will play in life, and Abel (as Susan Sontag says) is calling for "a theatre whose leading metaphors state that life is a dream and the world a stage."

These ideas were first advanced in essays in such magazines as *Commentary*, *Partisan Review*, and the *New Leader* and later published in book form in 1963 as *Metatheatre*. Most reviewers seemed to find Abel's theories more stimulating than convincing, but were unstinting in their praise for his practical criticism of contemporary playwrights, and especially for his essay about Jack Gelber, which had already received the Longview Award. Hostile comment centered on the bellicose and uncompromising nature of Abel's argument, and particularly on his notion that scarcely any real tragedies had been written since the Greeks (even by Shakespeare, who is allowed only *Macbeth*). Richard Gilman thought the concept of metatheatre provided an illuminating critical approach to such writers as Pirandello and Genet, but was merely "irrelevant or obfuscatory" when applied for example to Shaw and Ibsen. Susan Sontag had no such reservations, calling Abel's arguments "clean-cut, pugnacious, prone to slogans, oversimplified—and, in the main, absolutely right." She described *Metatheatre* as "the first American-style existentialist tract," and added that "no English or American writer on the theatre has done anything as interesting or sophisticated."

Abel has translated Sartre, as well as Rimbaud, Apollinaire, Ghelderode, and others, and has also sought to dramatize his theories in a number of plays of his own, most of them philosophical comedies drawn from Greek or biblical myths. The first, *The Bow and the Gun* (1947), is an attempt at verse drama. *The Death of Odysseus* (1953) is a one-acter in which the hero, failing to evade his fate by cunning, goes to certain death at the hands of Telegonus, his son by Circe. Its point, Gerald Weales thought, is that the man who lives by his wits must find in the end that a talent for survival is no preparation for dying. Saul Bellow found it "a wonderfully intelligent and exhilarating comedy."

Absalom, Abel's most successful play, is a full-length work which was produced by Theatre Artists in 1956 and which won two awards as the best off-Broadway play of the year. It centers on the struggle for the throne of David between Solomon, who has been promised the crown, and Absalom, who deserves it better but seeks God's grace as well as his justice. It is an existentialist play in that Absalom "creates" his own destiny as Orestes does in Sartre's *The Flies*. Weales found it confusing and tedious but Richard Gilman, who called it "a ziggurat of inverted conceits" enjoyed it for "a certain dash, a certain resonance."

The Pretender, which had a short off-Broadway run in 1959, is about a Negro novelist who seeks to avenge an imagined insult to his wife. Harold Clurman called it "an intellectual comedy on a subject about which it is usually considered bad taste to joke . . . a *jeu d'esprit*: mental in inspiration and almost abstract in content." *The Wives* (1965) is a metatheatrical reworking of Sophocles' *Trachiniae*, in which Herakles' wife tries to win back her husband's love with disastrous results for them both. Robert Mazzocco concluded that "Sartre is in Abel's head, and Cocteau is in his heart. Unfortunately, too often there's nothing but sawdust on his tongue." Despite the circulation of a petition to arouse interest in the play, it closed after a brief run.

Gerald Weales believes that Abel's lack of success as a dramatist is due to the fact that "despite occasionally clever lines, he has very little wit; his prose style is heavy where the genre demands polish, even elegance; he seems unwilling to use the devices of melodrama and farce that Sartre has always used to animate his philosophical discussion and, in the absence of such devices, Abel's failure to create characters becomes a fatal weakness." His critical work is quite another matter, however, and Richard Gilman has said that when Abel puts aside his theories, "there is no critic of drama who can surpass him."

Abel received a Guggenheim Fellowship in 1958, a Longview award in 1960, an award from the National Institute of Arts and Letters in 1964, and a Rockefeller Foundation grant in 1966. In recent years he has taught as a visiting professor at Columbia, Rutgers, Pratt Institute, and the State University of New York at Buffalo, where in 1970 he became professor of English. Abel was married in 1939 to Sherry Goldman, from whom he is now divorced. Their only child, a daughter, died in 1964. The author was married again in 1970, to Gloria Becker.

PRINCIPAL WORKS: *Criticism*—Metatheatre: A New View of Dramatic Form, 1963. *Plays*—Death of Odysseus *in* Playbook, 1956; Absalom *in* Artists' Theatre, 1960.
ABOUT: Weales, G. American Drama Since World War II, 1962; Who's Who in America, 1970–1971. *Periodicals*—Commentary October 1963; Commonweal June 25, 1965; New York Review of Books July 1, 1965; Partisan Review Summer 1960; Spring 1963.

ABRAHAMS, PETER (HENRY) (March 19, 1919–), South African-born novelist, memoirist, and journalist, was born in Johannesburg, the fourth child of James Abrahams, an Ethiopian, and Angelina DuPlessis, a Cape Colored woman of mixed French and Negro origin. His father died when Abrahams was still very young, and he grew up among Colored (half-caste) rather than African people in the Johannesburg slums, except for a period when he lived with an aunt in an African "location" (township) outside a white country town. He went to work before he went to school, selling firewood, working for a tinsmith, cleaning hotel rooms, carrying parcels, and doing a variety of other odd jobs.

He was still totally uneducated when, in his tenth year, a white secretary in the office where he was working read him the story of Othello from

PETER ABRAHAMS

Lamb's *Tales From Shakespeare*. This awoke in him a passion for literacy which led him, soon afterwards, to St. Peter's School, the famous Anglican school in Johannesburg which educated a whole generation of African intellectuals.

When Abrahams was fifteen he discovered, in the library of the Bantu Men's Social Centre, that black men had already created a canon of significant writing. At that moment, as he wrote in his autobiography *Tell Freedom*, "Something burst deep inside me. The world could never belong to white people only! Never again." The works of black American writers like W. E. B. DuBois, Countee Cullen, Claude McKay, Jean Toomer, and Langston Hughes convinced him that he also, a black man in South Africa, could become a writer.

From St. Peter's Abrahams went on to a teachers' training college at Pietersburg. He edited the college magazine and published his first poems in the *Bantu World*. He graduated in 1938, taught for a year in Cape Town, and worked briefly in Durban as a magazine editor. In 1939, partly because he wanted to go to England, partly because some articles he had published made him something of a political undesirable in South Africa, he signed on as a ship's stoker. "Perhaps life had a meaning that transcended race and colour," he concluded in his autobiography. "If it had, I could not find it in South Africa. Also there was the need to write, to tell freedom, and for this I needed to be personally free." For two years Abrahams traveled all over the world as a seaman but in 1941 he settled in England, earning his living as a writer and journalist.

While still at St. Peter's, Abrahams had become aware of the developing Pan-African movement, and had encountered the South African Communist party through a white couple who had befriended him. These influences are reflected in the revolutionary idealism of his first books—the volume of stories called *Dark Testament*; *Song of the City*, a novel about a young African from the country come to make his way in the urban ghetto who learns that he must overcome, through understanding, his fear of the white man; and the rather similar *Mine Boy*, the most successful of his early works.

In *The Path of Thunder* an educated African returns to his native village with ideas of reform and racial equality and inevitably clashes with the white population. *Wild Conquest* is a historical novel about the great northward trek of the Boers in the 1830s, and their running war with the Matabele. In this book Abrahams largely overcame the sentimentality and stylistic clumsiness which had marred his earlier novels, and achieved some memorable characterizations, interestingly enough succeeding better with his white characters than with the African tribesmen. Abraham's first major success was his autobiography, *Tell Freedom*, whose quiet power was warmly praised.

There followed what many consider the most effectively distanced and controlled of Abrahams' novels to date, *A Wreath for Udomo*. An educated African, after a period of study and sexual freedom in London, returns to lead his country (which some readers identified as Ghana) to independence and begins to modernize it along European lines. But political success involves Udomo in personal treachery—he betrays his friend Mhendi to the authorities of a white-ruled state and in the end is himself murdered by the tribalist, conservative wing of his party.

Though some reviewers found the book rather tract-like, "interesting rather than moving," Edmund Fuller thought it "authentic tragedy," and James Stern called it an "alternately tender and terrible story," impressive in its author's "rigid determination to be fair, to reveal the vices and virtues of both sides [white and black]." Michael Wade has pointed out that the book marks the end both of Abrahams' romantic belief in pre-European African society as a sort of golden age, and of his optimism for the postcolonial future. *A Wreath for Udomo* alienated Abrahams' political friends, but it remains his most impressive literary achievement.

Since 1955 Abrahams has lived in Jamaica, where he has worked as editor of the *West Indian Economist*, controller of the West Indian daily radio news network, and news commentator on Jamaican radio and television, writing also for the London *Observer*, *Holiday*, and other publications. In 1964 he gave up most of these activities to make more time for writing fiction, and in 1965 he published *A*

Night of Their Own, his first novel in nine years, set in South Africa during 1963–1964, when the country's underground liberation movements were dramatically smashed, at least temporarily, by the government. An exciting adventure story is set against this background of racial conflict, complicated by further tension between the black Pimpernel who is the hero, and the family of the Indian girl he falls in love with. Here as in other books Abrahams deals more convincingly with the actions of his characters than with their thought processes, represented in rather naïve interior monologues, but most reviewers admired "the clear lines of the narrative."

This Island, Now, the first of Abrahams' novels to be set in the West Indies, deals with the seizure of power on an unnamed Caribbean island by a tough young idealist, a man of the people, after the death of the benevolent old dictator who had ruled since independence. It was thought somewhat pretentious and "literary" in style, rather overschematic and, again, more perceptive in its treatment of white characters than black. Michael Wade condemned it as a sad book which exhibits "little feeling for the harsh economic and social problems" of the Caribbean, and a deep pessimism about the survival of "Western liberal values" in the Third World, but others thought it an eminently fair-minded examination of the extent to which good ends justify questionable means.

Abrahams has written in *Return to Goli* about a return visit to South Africa in the early 1950s. He has been married twice—in 1942 to Dorothy Pennington and in 1948, after that marriage was dissolved, to Daphne Miller, an artist. Abrahams has three children. His recreations, he says, include travel, gardening, tennis, walking, and "meeting and talking with people."

PRINCIPAL WORKS: *Fiction*—Dark Testament (short stories), 1942; Song of the City, 1945; Mine Boy, 1946; The Path of Thunder, 1948; Wild Conquest, 1950; A Wreath for Udomo, 1956; A Night of Their Own, 1965; This Island, Now, 1966. *Nonfiction*—Return to Goli (reportage), 1953; Tell Freedom (autobiography), 1954; (ed. with Nadine Gordimer) South African Writing Today, 1967.

ABOUT: Current Biography, 1958; Mphahlele, E. Down Second Avenue, 1959; Mphahlele, E. The African Image, 1962. *Periodicals*—Book World September 17, 1967; Commonweal July 13, 1956; Critique 1 1968; Ebony December 1967; New York Times May 20, 1956; New York Times Book Review September 24, 1967; New Yorker June 30, 1956; Times Literary Supplement March 25, 1965.

***ABSE, DANNIE** (September 22, 1923–), Welsh poet, novelist, and dramatist, writes: "I was born in Cardiff, South Wales, the youngest of four children. My father had been brought up in Bridg-

DANNIE ABSE

end and my mother was born at Ystalyfera in the Swansea valley. Initially I was very much influenced by my two elder brothers, Wilfred and Leo. Nowadays they are both rather eminent, and I am often asked, 'Are you any relation to Wilfred or Leo Abse?' Wilfred is a psychoanalyst and teaches at the University of Virginia, U.S.A. Leo is the assiduous Member of Parliament for Pontypool and happens to be, according to newspapers, one of the ten best dressed men in Great Britain, which does not surprise me since he wears my cast-offs.

"When I was a schoolboy (at St. Illtyd's College, Cardiff) I would overhear, at home, their warring discourse. There would be much talk of Karl Marx and Sigmund Freud. In short, I was exposed at an early age to the dialogue that was aired over and over by adult intellectuals in the thirties, and about this time I began to write poems, partly because of my own youthful engagement with the tragedy of the Spanish Civil War. I think, though, most of the time I lived inside my own head and made excursions into the world outside merely to swear at Franco, and to play football and cricket. A few years passed and Hitler and the noise outside came nearer and nearer to Wales, and one night this noise actually entered our house. The ceiling fell in, a wall collapsed, and I, proud of being an air raid victim, ended up in Bridgend Cottage Hospital on my back rather alarmed by the man islanded in the next bed to me who with the night-nurse regularly offered prayers to Krafft-Ebing.

"I left Cardiff, eventually, to become a medical student in war-time London, and here my education continued not so much at medical school but

* ab′ zē

in the permissive ambience of Swiss Cottage where I happened to find lodgings. Swiss Cottage, at that time, seemed to be occupied by old German-Jewish refugees, by youthful painters, deserters, budding burglars, and presentable young women. Here I discovered a gregarious café life more characteristic of Paris than moody London. Later some of the youngest café habitués became famous and sometimes I see them in Hollywood films or on television. Many of the others have ended up in jail. One young man I knew used to pilfer books from Foyles before selling them to the café habitués. The books he stole, I remember, always had titles like *Crime and Punishment* and *Thieves in the Night*. During this period my first book of poems, *After Every Green Thing*, was accepted for publication. I wish now that it had never been published.

"After qualifying at Westminster Hospital I served in the RAF and found myself in a very different milieu from Swiss Cottage. I continued to write poems, however, for then, as now, I was committed to the next poem that would 'happen' and then the next. I say 'happen' because I have never been able to will a poem into existence. Though poetry is written in the brain the brain is bathed in blood, and consequently one must wait for—to use an old-fashioned word—'inspiration.' Sometimes whilst waiting I have written novels and plays, especially since I was 'demobbed' from the RAF, for I would rather write, say, a play, than commit fine thoughts to a notebook or private diary. In any case, as I grow older, my thinking becomes more confused. I mean that the more I read and the more I experience and the more I know, the more I journey into ignorance.

"In 1951, I married Joan Mercer, whom I had met earlier in Swiss Cottage. We live now in Golders Green, London, with our three children. I am still waiting for the next poem, and if the periods of waiting sometimes become prolonged I recall my motto, which is: 'Be visited, expect nothing, and endure.'

"I have contributed to various English and American periodicals—*The New Statesman*, *Encounter*, *The Listener*, *The New Yorker*, etc., and I give poetry readings and broadcast from time to time. One of my plays won the Charles Henry Foyle Award for 1960. A compilation from my works—poems, prose, and a one-act play, *Gone*, was presented at the Lyric Theatre, Hammersmith, London, in 1964, and I have edited or co-edited several poetry anthologies, the most recent being *Modern European Verse*, which was published in the Vista paperback series. It's a lovely life."

Dannie Abse, who as a physician specializes in diseases of the chest, has always seen himself "as a poet who practises medicine, not as a doctor who writes poetry." It was in 1942 that he began his medical studies and in 1949 that his first book of poems was published. During the 1950s (to his subsequent regret), Abse was much involved in the literary civil wars of the period—notably as editor, with Howard Sergeant, of *Mavericks* (1957). This was an anthology of work by young poets who, "unafraid of sensibility and sentiment," rejected the antiromanticism which dominated English poetry at the time.

Abse's own first book, *After Every Green Thing*, was attractively youthful and eloquent, full of Socialist and humanitarian idealism, but rather woolly and generalized. *Walking Under Water* showed an advance in formal control, though at the cost of some of the freshness and exuberance of the first collection. In *Tenants of the House* Abse found his proper mode and tone, which he explored and developed with growing authority and resourcefulness in *Poems, Golders Green* and *A Small Desperation*. His *Selected Poems* were received with almost unanimous pleasure.

Roland Mathias has referred to Abse's "not-yet-defeated optimism and an anxious sensitivity, to people as to events." These qualities appear in poems on a broad and increasing range of subjects—the rival claims of art and family, Vietnam, nostalgia for the past, Ezra Pound, the nature of love, and the character of place. Quite often in his later work he turns with a scrupulous and sensible compassion to his relations with his patients. His voice now is dryer and more aphoristic—closer to Auden than to Dylan Thomas—but his easy, colloquial poems are charged with an awareness of the irrational and even the metaphysical, conveyed through allegory or more directly, as in "The Grand View": "There are moments when a man must praise / the astonishment of being alive / When small mirrors of reality blaze / into miracles: and there's One always / who, by never departing, almost arrives." Abse has contributed with great success to public poetry readings in Britain and the United States.

Although he thinks of himself as primarily a poet, it was in fact his first novel, *Ash on a Young Man's Sleeve*, which made Abse's reputation as a writer. A series of autobiographical vignettes about his childhood and early youth in Cardiff, it reminded reviewers of the prose work of Dylan Thomas and also of William Saroyan in its gaiety and lyrical spontaneity. A second novel, *Some Corner of a Foreign Field*, about a doctor doing his obligatory service in the postwar Royal Air Force, was thought rather skimpy and shapeless, but most reviewers enjoyed *O. Jones, O. Jones*, a very funny account of the adventures of a manic, disaster-prone Welsh medical student in London.

In *Medicine on Trial*, Abse discusses the present state of the art in his other profession, touching on medical training, on spectacular advances (like antibiotics) and spectacular failures (like thalidomide), and also on drug addiction, quackery, the greed of the pharmaceutical firms, the German doctors who experimented on living human beings at Auschwitz. Some readers complained of Abse's "subservience to the authority of Freud," but most found the book a capable, thoughtful, and highly readable survey.

PRINCIPAL WORKS: *Poetry*—After Every Green Thing, 1949; Walking Under Water, 1952; Tenants of the House, 1957; Poems, Golders Green, 1962; Dannie Abse: A Selection, 1963; A Small Desperation, 1968; Selected Poems, 1970; Funland, 1973. *Fiction*—Ash on a Young Man's Sleeve, 1954; Some Corner of a Foreign Field, 1956; O. Jones, O. Jones, 1970. *Plays*—Fire in Heaven, 1956; The Eccentric, 1961 (*also in* Best One-Act Plays of 1960–1961, 1963); Three Questor Plays (House of Cowards, Gone, In the Cage), 1967; The Dogs of Pavlov, 1972. *Nonfiction*—Medicine on Trial, 1968. *As editor*—(with Howard Sergeant) Mavericks, 1957; Modern European Verse, 1964.

ABOUT: Murphy, R. (ed.) Contemporary Poets of the English Language, 1970; Rosenthal, M. L. The New Poets, 1967. *Periodicals*—Anglo-Welsh Review Winter 1967; Cahiers Franco-Anglais 1, 1966; Jewish Quarterly Winter 1963–1964; Listener March 21, 1967; Poetry Book Society Bulletin Summer 1962.

***ACHEBE, CHINUA** (November 16, 1930–), Nigerian novelist, writes: "I was born in Ogidi in Eastern Nigeria of christian parents. The line between christian and non-christian was much more definite in our village thirty years ago than it is today. When I was growing up I remember we tended to look down on the others. We were called in our language 'the people of the church,' and we called the others—with the conceit appropriate to followers of a *higher* religion—'the people of nothing.'

"Thinking about it today I am not so sure that it isn't they who ought to have been looking down on us for our apostasy. But the bounties of the christian God were not to be taken lightly—education, paid jobs and other things that nobody in his right senses can look down upon. In fairness I should add that the new faith stood and stood firmly for certain civilized standards of behaviour; it said, for instance, that twins were not evil and must no longer be destroyed.

"My father joined the new faith as a young man and eventually became an evangelist and church teacher. His maternal grandfather who had brought him up (his own parents having died early) was a man of note in the village. From all accounts he had a strong sense of humour. He had received the first missionaries in his own compound, but after a few days sent them packing again for their doleful singing. Said he, 'My neighbours might think it was my funeral dirge.' But in the end he did not stop my father joining them; the old fellow also had foresight.

* ə chä′ bā

CHINUA ACHEBE

"I was baptized Albert Chinualumogu. I dropped the tribute to Victorian England when I went to university, although some early acquaintances (e.g. my mother) still call me by it. The second name which in the manner of my people is a full-length philosophical statement I curtailed into something more businesslike.

"I have always been fond of stories and intrigued by language—first my mother tongue, Ibo, and later English which I began to learn at about the age of eight.

"I did not know I was going to be a writer because I had no notion that such beings existed until relatively late. The folk stories my mother and elder sister told us had the immemorial quality of the sky and the forests and the rivers. Later at school I got to know that the European stories we read were written by Europeans—the same fellows who made all the other marvellous things like the motor-car. We didn't come into it at all. We made nothing that wasn't primitive and heathenish.

"The nationalist movement after the Second World War brought about a mental revolution which began to reconcile us to ourselves. We saw suddenly that we had a story to tell.

"At the university I read some appalling European novels about Africa (like Joyce Cary's much praised *Mister Johnson*) and realized that our story could not be told for us by anyone else no matter how gifted or well-intentioned.

"Although I did not consciously set about it in

that way my first book, *Things Fall Apart*, was an act of atonement with my past, the homage of a prodigal son.

"But things do happen fast here. I had hardly begun to bask in the sunshine of reconciliation when a new cloud appeared. Political independence had come; the nationalist leader of yesterday (with whom it was not difficult to make common cause) became today the not-so-attractive party boss—or worse. It seems I shall never know real peace."

Chinua Achebe is widely regarded as the most accomplished of the many African novelists now writing in English and is certainly one of the most successful: his first novel has sold half a million copies. His theme, as the titles of his books often suggest, is the conflict of old and new ways of life in Africa, a conflict which his own life experience typically reflects. He was educated first at the village school provided by the Church Missionary Society, where his father taught, then at the Government Secondary School at Umuahia, and at the University College of Ibadan, where he studied English literature, and became one of the first generation of graduates in 1953. In 1954 Achebe began work for the Nigerian Broadcasting Service as talks producer, and in 1961 he was appointed director of external broadcasting, a post which took him frequently abroad. In 1966 he became chairman of the Society of Nigerian Authors and a member of the Council of the University of Lagos.

At a conference on Commonwealth literature held in Leeds in 1964, Achebe commented on his motivation as an artist: "It would be foolish," he said, "to pretend that we have fully recovered from the traumatic effects of our first confrontation with Europe. . . . I would be quite satisfied if my novels (especially the ones I set in the past) did no more than teach my readers that their past—with all its imperfections—was not one long night of savagery from which the first Europeans acting on God's behalf delivered them. Perhaps what I write is applied art as distinct from pure. But who cares? Art is important but so is education of the kind I have in mind. And I don't see that the two need be mutually exclusive."

Things Fall Apart, Achebe's first—and in the opinion of many his finest—novel, deals with the traumatic encounter itself. It is set in Umuofia, an Ibo village, in the second half of the nineteenth century, and involves two intertwined tragedies: the personal tragedy of Okonkwo, who lives his life strictly according to the tribal code; and the public tragedy of his village, which hands down its collective wisdom from generation to generation but is defeated, when the white man comes, by its inability to deal with a situation without precedent.

Okonkwo is a self-made man, whose self-discipline has excluded all that is soft from his nature. He accidentally causes the death of a man at his father's funeral and is forced into seven years' painful exile. When he returns at last to the village, the white man has already built not only a church but a courthouse, where foreign justice is administered. Okonkwo's friend Obierika remarks: "The white man is very clever. He came quietly and peaceably with his religion. We were amused at his foolishness and allowed him to stay. Now he has won our brothers, and our clan can no longer act as one. He has put a knife on the things that held us together and we have fallen apart." So it proves when, at the climax of the book, a messenger from the white court insults a clan meeting. Okonkwo, acting alone, kills the intruder and then hangs himself. The white commissioner plans to incorporate the episode in a paragraph of his projected book, "The Pacification of the Primitive Tribes of the Lower Niger."

Gerald Moore wrote later that "Achebe has, as it were, gone back to that bleak little paragraph of despised and garbled history. With love, with understanding and with justice, he has drawn from it a story of people just as real and individual as ourselves, whose world had its own completeness and whose life its own dignity." Few reviewers at the time of the book's publication had Moore's insight, however, and most tended to dismiss it as a piece of innocent exotica: "an authentic native document, guileless and unsophisticated," with "no sense of plot or development."

By the time *No Longer at Ease* appeared two years later, however, reviewers had attuned themselves more successfully to Achebe's manner, and though some readers could still see only "a disarmingly ingenuous Nigerian novel," John Coleman in the *Spectator* wrote with enthusiasm that the book "moves towards its inevitable catastrophe with classic directness. Nothing is wasted and it is only after the sad, understated close that one realises . . . how much of the Nigerian context has been touched upon."

The second novel is the story of Obi, Okonkwo's grandson, educated abroad by the subscriptions of his clan members, when he returns to Lagos as Umuofia's first university graduate. He is expected to prove himself in the civil service, to uphold the dignity of his village in the places of power. At first full of determination not to succumb to the corruption of Lagos bureaucracy, Obi is eventually overwhelmed by the conflicting demands on him. He must return his study loan to the Umuofia Progressive Association, but he must also display all the trappings of success (car, house, servant, clothes); he knows he ought to feel free to marry the young nurse, Clara, but his upbringing rejects her as an *osu* (outlaw). His mother threatens suicide; he lets Clara go, accepts bribes for the scholarships he administers, is found out, tried, and imprisoned. Arthur Ravenscroft, in his study of Achebe, suggests that *No Longer at Ease* fails fully to engage us with its hero because Obi is made too naïve and self-deluded, and the cards are thus too obviously stacked against him. In any case, its tone is gray and muted compared with the tension and color of the earlier book.

Achebe's next novel, *Arrow of God*, is once more set in the past, this time around the 1920s, in a remote Ibo village. It centers on the conflicts within Ezeulu, high priest of Ulu, who as representative of the god is responsible for the safety and welfare of his clan. When the white missionaries arrive, Ezeulu must decide whether or not they represent a threat to his people—whether to resist or cooperate. It is a dilemma he is not qualified to resolve. He sends his own son to the mission school, an action which lays him open to charges of collaboration with the enemy. Thus when he does choose to resist, his elders are not behind him, and tragedy follows. Once more, Achebe has demonstrated how the inflexible traditions of African tribal life, which made that society such a stable one, also made it tragically vulnerable to alien pressures unprovided for in the tribal code.

A Man of the People is another modern urban novel, one which makes bitter fun of corrupt politicians. Ravenscroft calls it "a sparkling piece of satirical virtuosity, yet we feel throughout that deep anger, bitterness and disillusion are never far beneath the surface." Some critics have found it too savage and too despairing, but the *Times Literary Supplement* enjoyed it as "scabrous, unbuttoned, reckless—a black fabliau."

Achebe's command of language has been admired from the beginning. He is particularly skillful in the use of dialogue to differentiate character, social background, and period. In the historical books, Ibo proverbs are constantly used to express not only a sense of social stability but the spirit of inherited ideas and values. In the urban books, the same proverbs lard the speech of the city exiles but are shorn of their depth of meaning, thrown in to impress, to arouse nostalgia, to revive a sense of community. The city workers in any case speak mainly in pidgin, or assume a pompous "educated" English if they know how, emphasizing their alienation from any culture.

In 1966, after the massacre of Ibos in Northern Nigeria and the military coup in Lagos, Achebe returned to the Eastern Region, where he planned a new publishing venture with his fellow writer the late Christopher Okigbo and others. The scheme fell through when the Region declared itself independent, as Biafra, and civil war followed. With Cyprian Ekwensi and Gabriel Okara he made tours of the United States to raise funds for Biafra, and he was chairman of the Biafra National Guidance Committee, charged with traveling all over the country in order to keep the government in touch with popular opinion. There are several stories about the civil war, along with others written over the previous twenty years, in the collection *Girls at War*, published as the hundredth title in the Heinemann African Writers Series which Achebe served as editorial adviser from 1962 to 1972. *Beware Soul Brother*, a volume of poems written during the war, was joint winner of the Commonwealth Poetry Prize.

After the fall of Biafra in 1970, Achebe took up a senior research fellowship at the Institute of African Studies of the University of Nigeria at Nsukka. Since then he has been appointed first director of the Frantz Fanon Research Centre in Enugu, set up by a "group who share total commitment to the mental emancipation of the black man all over the world." The author is a director of Heinemann Educational Books (Nigeria) Ltd. and of Nwankwo-Ifejika and Company (Publishers) Ltd. He is the editor of *Okike*, a Nigerian journal of new writing. Achebe was married in 1961 to Christiana Okoli, and has four children. He has held Rockefeller and Unesco fellowships and in 1965 received the Jock Campbell *New Statesman* Award.

PRINCIPAL WORKS: Things Fall Apart, 1958; No Longer at Ease, 1960; The Sacrificial Egg and Other Short Stories, 1962; Arrow of God, 1964; Chike and the River (for children), 1966; A Man of the People, 1966; Beware Soul Brother (poems), 1971 (England, 1972); Girls at War (stories), 1972.

ABOUT: Beier, U. (ed.) Introduction to African Literature, 1967; Carroll, D. Chinua Achebe, 1970; Contemporary Authors 4, 1963; Duerden, D. and Pieterse, C. (eds.) African Writers Talking, 1972; Gleason J. This Africa, 1965; Killam, G. D. The Novels of Chinua Achebe, 1969; King, B. Introduction to Nigerian Literature, 1972; Larson, C. R. The Emergence of African Fiction, 1972; McGraw-Hill Encyclopedia of World Biography, 1972; Moore, G. Seven African Writers, 1962; Palmer, E. An Introduction to the African Novel, 1972; Ravenscroft, A. Chinua Achebe, 1969; Vinson, J. (ed.) Contemporary Novelists, 1972; Who's Who, 1972. *Periodicals*—Africa Report July 1964; March 1970; Black Orpheus June 1965; Guardian January 1, 1966; February 28, 1972; Journal of Commonwealth Literature July 1968; Modern Language Quarterly March 1969; New Statesman June 21, 1958; January 29, 1965; July 9, 1965; January 28, 1966; New York Herald Tribune Book Review April 12, 1959; New York Herald Tribune Lively Arts April 30, 1961; Nigeria June 1964; Spectator October 21, 1960; Time August 19, 1966; Times Literary Supplement June 20, 1958; February 3, 1966.

ACKERLEY, J(OE) R(ANDOLPH) (1896–June 4, 1967), English memoirist, dramatist, novelist, poet, and editor, was born at Herne Hill in Kent, the son of a wealthy banana importer whose

J. R. ACKERLEY

placid suburban life concealed a curious history. The elder Ackerley had begun his career as a trooper in the Horse Guards, had been bought out of the Army by a homosexual European aristocrat, and had eventually married a Swiss girl and made a fortune. When she died he acquired two mistresses and maintained them in separate establishments. In 1919 he married one of them—Ackerley's mother, a pretty, rather feckless actress who never learned of her husband's remarkable double life. This background, outwardly respectable, but in reality almost comically furtive, explains much about Ackerley, who was for the greater part of his life an active homosexual.

He was educated at Rossall School, fought in the trenches during World War I, and was captured. In 1918 he wrote one of the best of the plays inspired by the war, *The Prisoners of War*, a work which draws its emotional tension from an undercurrent of homosexuality which is never explicit and indeed was apparently unrecognized by contemporary critics. After the war he went up to Magdalene College, Cambridge, where he read law for a while, then English literature. He graduated in 1921 and thereafter for several years was supported by his father while he tried unsuccessfully to make a career as a writer.

From 1928 to 1935 Ackerley worked for the British Broadcasting Corporation as an assistant producer in the Talks Department. Thenceforth, until his retirement in 1959, he served as literary editor of the BBC's weekly magazine, *The Listener*. His predecessor in that post, J. A. Smith, said that he had "never known a literary editor who was so firm with less fuss, less presence in the office and less use of the typewriter." He was an exceptionally fair and eclectic editor with—ironically perhaps—a crusading zeal against all kinds of prudery and bowdlerization.

During his years with *The Listener*, Ackerley met most of the luminaries of the London literary world, and formed some intimate (but not homosexual) attachments. According to his posthumous autobiography, his sexual adventures took place in quite another milieu, among soldiers, waiters, policemen, and errand boys. Ackerley was a sad, sordid, generous man; part of his pleasure was in its furtiveness, but one sensed an underlying bitterness that this should be so. His essential loneliness and unhappiness, however, he bore stoically and privately. And for all his isolation he was capable of inspiring the warm and enduring friendship of a few exceptional people, among them E. M. Forster, whose friendship he described as "the longest, closest, and most influential" of his life.

It was through Forster that Ackerley when a young man secured his appointment as private secretary to the ruler of a small native state in India. When he got there, he found that the Maharajah needed not a secretary but a friend and confidant. It is this experience that Ackerley describes in *Hindoo Holiday*, his first prose work. V. S. Pritchett praised "a delightful tenderness" in the narrative, and called Ackerley "a man whose instinct of understanding is gentle, ready and deep. His humor is the humor of pity and love. He is an artist in understanding." Evelyn Waugh was no less impressed by what he called "a work of high literary skill and very delicate aesthetic perception."

My Dog Tulip is an account of the Alsatian (German Shepherd) bitch which entered Ackerley's life in his late forties. He wrote: "She offered me what I had never found in my sexual life, constant, single-hearted, incorruptible, uncritical devotion. . . . From the moment she established herself in my heart and home, my obsession with sex fell wholly away from me." It is a remarkable and beautifully written book, though not for all tastes. Its frankness is exemplary, but the author's morbid interest in the sexual needs of his pet, while sympathetic and loving, testifies to the barrenness of his own emotional life; it also offended the primmer reviewers, though others recognized it as "a masterpiece of empathy."

The word "masterpiece" was also applied by some critics to *My Father and Myself*. This book, which had been begun and then discarded in the 1930s, describes Ackerley's gradual unraveling as a boy of his father's strange double existence, and in this has much of the fascination of a detective story. It also gives a startlingly frank, funny, and circumstantial account of his own homosexual adventures. The book, like its author, is brave, intelligent, and elegant but, in the opinion of some readers, it denies itself the dimension of tragedy, holding back from the lyric gesture, the act of total self-confrontation and self-revelation, which might have made it a great work. Roy Fuller, for one, had no such reservations, calling it "a masterpiece of autobiography, to be ranked with Gide."

There is also a large element of autobiography (and "the same sad comedy") in Ackerley's novel *We Think the World of You.* It is narrated in the first person by a middle-aged bachelor, a civil servant, and describes in an "intimate, clear, disarming manner" his attempt to retain some place in the affections of Johnnie, a handsome young thief, while Johnnie is in prison. This pursuit of love is carried on against the greedy opposition of Johnnie's mother and his wife, and extends and develops into an attempt to win the heart of Johnnie's dog. Most critics agreed that the book was both "a superb piece of comedy" and a "beautiful and superbly executed novel."

PRINCIPAL WORKS: The Prisoners of War, 1930; Hindoo Holiday, 1932; My Dog Tulip, 1956; We Think the World of You, 1960; My Father and Myself, 1968; E. M. Forster, 1971; Micheldever and Other Poems, 1972.

ABOUT: *Periodicals*—Book World March 23, 1969; Encounter November 1968; Library Journal September 15, 1965; Listener June 8, 1967; June 15, 1967; New Republic March 29, 1969; New Statesman September 20, 1968; New York Review of Books March 27, 1969; New York Times Book Review November 21, 1965; April 27, 1969; Times Literary Supplement October 10, 1968.

ACTON, HAROLD (MARIO MITCHELL) (July 5, 1904–), English man of letters, reports: "I was born in Villa La Pietra, Florence, where I still reside. My father, Arthur Mario, was an amateur painter and art collector descended from the Neapolitan branch of Actons; my mother, Hortense Lenore, was the daughter of William Hamilton Mitchell, a veteran banker of Chicago, Illinois; so I may consider myself truly cosmopolitan. Educated at Eton and Christ Church, Oxford, I remained deeply influenced by Tuscan art and literature and evinced a precocious talent for versifying. Now I feel embarrassed by my juvenile effusions but they were deemed worthy of publication at the time. My contributions to *The Eton Candle* attracted the notice of Mr. Thomas Balston of Duckworth's who published *Aquarium* (1923) and *An Indian Ass* (1925), my first two volumes of poetry, but I was made to realize that one had to write prose to be taken seriously and produced two novels in consequence, best forgotten. Then even more than now I subscribed to Bacon's dictum that 'there is no exquisite beauty without some strangeness in the proportion,' and the rococo strangeness of the last members of the Medici family inspired me to write a study of their decline which was published in 1932.

"Discouraged by the cool reception of my writings and distressed by the progress of fascism, I

HAROLD ACTON

decided to settle in Peking in 1932. There I found a second home, for I was lucky enough to be invited to teach English literature at Peking National University, which enabled me to make many cultured Chinese friends I should not have met otherwise and I owe them some of the happiest years of my spiritual growth. Besides a predilection for Chinese landscape painting, porcelain and various crafts I was enchanted by the ancient Chinese theatre. With L. C. Arlington, a rugged old China hand of rare personality, I collaborated in the translation of some popular Chinese plays, but I translated many *K'un Ch'ü* which were lost as a result of the war. Though I studied the language I was no sinologue, but I enjoyed collaborating with my brilliant pupil Ch'en Shih-hsiang in the translation of *Modern Chinese Poetry* (1936). Other translations and a novel, *Peonies and Ponies,* were produced at this period, which eventually was overshadowed by the Japanese occupation and interrupted by the 1939 war. Returning to England, I joined the R.A.F. and was sent to India and Ceylon, humbled yet exhilarated by contact with Anglo-Saxon heroes and Oriental poets.

"My younger brother William died on active service, and I returned to a stricken home in 1945. While my memory was still green I resolved to write my memoirs. This is my apology, the most personal of my books.

"During the next years I spent much time in Naples, for which I have an atavistic affection. Convinced that the Bourbons had done more for Naples than any other dynasty, I decided to vindicate them against the accusations which had gained general currency since the Risorgimento. In *The Bourbons of Naples* and *The Last Bourbons of Naples*

I hope this aim has been accomplished. I have also written a general essay on Florence and contributed articles and reviews to *The London Magazine*, *The Oxford Companion to the Theatre*, the *Times Literary Supplement* and other periodicals, introductions to various publications, besides lecturing for the British Council and the Unione Fiorentina. My pen is apt to run away with me in unpredictable directions, and except in history I am easily wafted on the wings of fantasy. My writings are multiform and independent, and they still excite rage in the hearts of the Philistines."

When Harold Acton met Evelyn Waugh at Oxford, Acton had already produced his first book of poems and made a precocious reputation at Eton as an aesthete. He was then, Waugh said, "slim and slightly oriental in appearance, talking . . . in a peculiar vocabulary that derived equally from Naples, Chicago and Eton." What they had in common, Waugh thought, was "gusto." Acton was "vividly alive to every literary and artistic fashion, exuberantly appreciative, punctilious, light and funny and energetic. He loved to shock and then to conciliate with exaggerated politeness." Acton has acquired much learning since, but seems otherwise not much changed. He is a cosmopolitan, equally at home in London, Paris, Florence, and Peking. The first volume of his autobiography, *Memoirs of an Aesthete*, is a panorama of life in these cities from 1920 to 1940; the story is continued in *More Memoirs of an Aesthete* (published in the United States as *Memoirs of an Aesthete 1939–1969*).

No longer slim, nor particularly oriental in appearance, he retains the ironic expression of his early portraits; he is a Commander of the Order of the British Empire who advertises his recreations as "iettatura" (the evil eye) and "hunting the Philistines." And he is still an aesthete. His work, whether in prose or verse, exhibits the acute sensibility of the Edwardians. The poems have an unfashionable delicacy. His novels are traditional in form, leisurely in narrative, stately or epigrammatic in dialogue; the most recent of them, *Old Lamps for New*, is a satire on the world of modern art, its set pieces handled with "something of Ian Fleming's *panache*."

Acton's most considerable writings are those on Italian history. *The Last Medici*, a baroque account of the decline and fall of that family, has become "something of a classic . . . a wellnigh perfect treatment of a theme remarkably fascinating in itself." His two books about the Bourbons of Naples have been called "entrancing but thoroughly wrongheaded" in their defense of "this curious dynasty," but "serious and conscientious as well as humorously elegant history." Francis Haskell characterizes Acton's historical method as "a ruthless concentration on the subjects of his biography to the exclusion of wider horizons; a greater interest in their private than in their public lives; and a total absence of footnotes. But with all this goes a knowledge of the period that is unparalleled in its intimacy; a style of often dazzling brilliance and wit; and a deadpan Gibbonian approach."

PRINCIPAL WORKS: Aquarium (poems), 1923; An Indian Ass (poems), 1925; Five Saints and an Appendix (poems), 1927; Cornelian (a fable in prose), 1928; Humdrum (novel), 1929; This Chaos (poems), 1930; The Last Medici (history), 1932, revised edition 1958; (as translator with Ch'en Shih-hsiang) Modern Chinese Poetry, 1936; (as translator with L. C. Arlington) Famous Chinese Plays, 1937; (as translator with Li I-hsieh) Glue and Lacquer, 1941, reprinted as Four Cautionary Tales, 1947; Peonies and Ponies (novel), 1941; Memoirs of an Aesthete (autobiography), 1948; Prince Isidore (novel), 1950; The Bourbons of Naples, 1734–1825, 1956; The Last Bourbons of Naples, 1825–1861, 1961; Old Lamps for New (novel), 1965; More Memoirs of an Aesthete (autobiography), 1970 (U.S., Memoirs of an Aesthete 1939–1969).

ABOUT: Acton, H. Memoirs of an Aesthete, 1948; Acton, H. More Memoirs of an Aesthete, 1970; Barney, N. Traits et Portraits, 1963; Contemporary Authors 4, 1963; Waugh, E. A Little Learning, 1964; Who's Who, 1971. *Periodicals*—London Life October 30, 1965; New York Times April 5, 1971; Spectator November 21, 1958.

***ADAMOV, ARTHUR** (August 23, 1908–March 16, 1970), French dramatist, essayist, and translator, was born in Kislovodsk in the Russian Caucasus, the son of a wealthy Armenian oil-well proprietor, Sourène Adamov, and the former Hélène Bagatourov. The family left Russia when Adamov was four, settling briefly in Freudenstadt in the Black Forest. During World War I they escaped internment as enemy aliens only through the personal intervention of the King of Württemberg, a friend of Adamov's father. They moved to Geneva, where Adamov went to school. He completed his studies at Mainz, and in 1924 went to Paris.

There he was drawn into surrealist circles through his friendship with Paul Éluard and others. He wrote poetry in the surrealist manner and helped to edit the journal *Discontinuité*. During the late 1930s he suffered a severe psychological crisis which virtually disabled him for some years. In 1940 nevertheless he was interned at Argèles, and he was not released until 1943. In the mid-1940s he began to write again and completed his first plays.

Adamov was by then intellectually committed to Marxism but unconvinced that any political system could solve man's most fundamental problems. In *L'Heure Nouvelle*, a literary review which he edited after the war, he wrote: "If we turn to communism . . . it is merely because one day, when it will seem quite close to the realization of its highest aim—the victory over all the contradictions

* ä dä' môf

that impede the exchange of goods between men—it will meet, inevitably, the great 'no' of the nature of things, which it thought it could ignore."

It was this "great 'no' " that obsessed him. His own experiences, his reading of Strindberg, and his emotional collapse, had left him with an acute sense of man's "Separation." *L'Aveu*, the self-abasing autobiographical confession he published in 1946, contains this statement: "Every private fault, every individual guilt . . . transcends the individual to identify itself with the fault of all men everywhere and forever—the great original prevarication which is named Separation. . . . I do not know what name to give what I am separated from. . . . Once it was called God. Now there is no longer any name. . . . When a terrifying vision assails me and I become a prey to fear, I perform a ritual of exorcism to conquer it, and my fear diminishes. But the legions of multiform terrors all derive from a single principle: the fear of death."

This summarizes the theme of Adamov's early plays, which critics like to classify as examples of the theatre of the absurd. His first "ritual of exorcism" was *La Parodie* (The Parody), written in 1947 and produced by Roger Blin in 1952. In it are two men who desire the same woman—the contemptuous eternal whore who haunted Adamov's imagination. One man works frantically to capture her attention by a display of sheer energy, while the other simply waits to be noticed. Both approaches are equally futile and both men are rewarded only with mutilation and death. *La grande et la petite manœuvre* (1950), *Le Sens de la marche* (1951), and *Tous contre tous* (1952) similarly explore Adamov's personal preoccupations—man's total aloneness, the mechanical cruelty of society, the tyranny of parental love. Their purpose, the author said, was "the monotonous demonstration of the fact that 'whatever you do, you are crushed.' "

These plays are almost plotless—dreamlike successions of short scenes or tableaux set in some abstract country of the mind and peopled by ciphers who act out their prescribed rituals practically oblivious of each other. Under the influence of his friend Antonin Artaud, Adamov used the stage as "a space to be filled"—above all by physical movement. The impact of his early plays is primarily visual, and dialogue is deliberately reduced to platitudes counterpointing the bizarre action. Audiences naturally found it difficult to warm to these humorless and abstract constructions, which however provoked much critical argument. Jean Vilar praised Adamov for renouncing the "lacework of dialogue and plot"; others blamed him for the same achievement.

L'Invasion (1950) was a slightly more orthodox play, with real rather than allegorical characters, a plot of sorts, and touches of humor. *Le Professeur Taranne* (translated as *Professor Taranne*), written in two days in 1951, is an almost exact transcription of a dream, serving no conscious allegorical purpose. It was important for Adamov—the first time he "came out of the pseudopoetic no-man's-land and dared to call things by their names." And in *Le Ping-Pong* (1955, translated as *Ping Pong*), Adamov abandoned the determinism of his early work. In this frequently funny satire on materialism, the two young men who are so excited and obsessed by their symbolic pin-ball machine are driven not by ineluctable cosmic forces but by social and psychological ones.

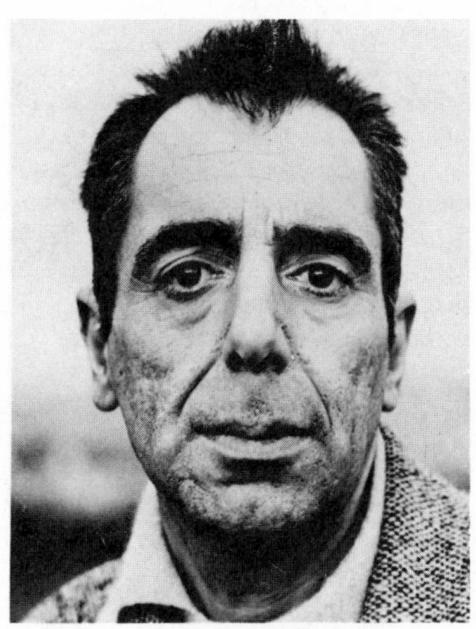

ARTHUR ADAMOV

Le Ping-Pong marks a transition in Adamov's theatre from the agonized metaphysical diagrams which preceded it to the socially conscious Brechtian epics which followed. He had come to believe that "the theatre must show, simultaneously but well differentiated, both the curable and the incurable aspect of things. The incurable aspect, we all know, is that of the inevitability of death. The curable aspect is the social one." *Paolo Paoli* (1957) is a portrait in the manner of Brecht's *Arturo Ui* of Parisian society at the turn of the century, showing the development of the state of mind which made World War I possible. The euphoria of "La Belle Époque," illustrated in the play's twelve scenes, is contrasted ironically with newspaper reports, speeches, and pictures of the period conveying a very different impression of world conditions. *Le Printemps '71* (Spring '71, 1963) attempts in similar style a panoramic history of the Paris Commune.

Adamov's early plays held for many but not all who saw them a hypnotic strangeness which derived, no doubt, from the fact that they "crudely and visibly" enact profound obsessions. His social epics lack this quality and have seemed to most critics well-intentioned but rather dull. As Martin Esslin says, "Adamov has become the main spokesman of the committed political theatre in France" and has repudiated his own contribution to the "antipolitical theatre of the soul"; but "the works inspired by Adamov's neurosis may be more profound than those of an Adamov reconciled to the world, though still determined to change its institutions."

"Slight, dark, with piercing, probing eyes in a saturnine face, no longer a ragged figure roaming Paris in abject poverty but still preferring to live in a small Left Bank hotel and holding court in his favorite *tabac* on the Boulevard Saint-Germain," Adamov, Esslin wrote in 1961, "was the embodiment of two conflicting tendencies coexisting within the same person." Adamov died in 1970 at the age of sixty-one and was survived by his wife, the former Jacqueline Austrusseau.

PRINCIPAL WORKS IN ENGLISH TRANSLATION: *Plays*—Ping Pong: A Play in Two Parts, 1959; Paolo Paoli: The Years of the Butterfly, 1959; Two Plays (Professor Taranne, Ping Pong), 1962; As We Were, *in* Evergreen Review 4, 1957. *Memoir*—The Endless Humiliation (a section of L'Aveu), *in* Evergreen Review Spring 1958.

ABOUT: Contemporary Authors 17–18, 1967; Curley, D. N. and Curley, A. (eds.) Modern Romance Literatures (A Library of Literary Criticism), 1967; Esslin, M. The Theatre of the Absurd, 1968; Grossvogel, D. I. The Self-Conscious Stage, 1958; Guicharnaud, J. Modern French Theatre, 1961; Lumley, F. Trends in Twentieth Century Drama, 1956; Pronko, L. C. Avant-Garde, 1962; Wellwarth, G. E. The Theatre of Protest and Paradox, 1964; Who's Who in France, 1969–1970. *Periodicals*—Modern Drama February 1965; New York Times March 17, 1970; Plays and Players March 1960; Yale French Studies Winter 1954–1955.

***AGNON, SHMUEL YOSEF** (July 17, 1888–February 17, 1970), Israeli novelist and short story writer and winner of the Nobel Prize, authorized before his death the following account of his life and work, written by his English translator, Misha Louvish: "Shmuel Yosef Agnon was born in the little town of Buczacz, Eastern Galicia, on July 17, 1888, the ninth of the Hebrew month of Av in the year 5648 according to the Jewish reckoning. His father, Shalom Mordecai Czaczkes, descended from a long line of Talmudic scholars, was qualified for the rabbinate and well versed in Jewish philosophy; but he did not hold a rabbinical post and earned his livelihood in the fur trade. His mother's lineage was similarly distinguished; she read widely, particularly in classical German literature.

"Besides attending the traditional Hebrew school, he studied Talmud privately with his father and the town rabbi, and of his own accord read extensively in the lore of Hasidism.

* ug non′

"He started rhyming at an early age, and his first verses in Hebrew and Yiddish were published when he was fifteen years old. He was active in the local Zionist society and wrote in Zionist periodicals. At the age of eighteen, he moved to Lvov to work on a Hebrew paper, and in 1908 set out, by way of Vienna, for the Land of Israel.

"For a time he lived in Jaffa, where he was appointed secretary of three important institutions: the Hibbat Zion (Love of Zion) committee, which maintained contact with Jews abroad; the Jewish Community Council; and the voluntary Jewish court. His first story, *Agunot*, was signed with the pen name 'Agnon,' which he adopted as his family name. This was followed by other stories, published in the foremost Hebrew literary periodicals of the time.

"In 1910 he moved to Jerusalem, where he continued with his writing, did research in the National Library, and studied all the city's Jewish communities.

"In 1913 he went to Berlin to study, living by teaching and preparing research material for scholars. During this period his stories were first published in book form and he collaborated with the late Martin Buber in collecting tales of the Hasidim. In 1919 he married Esther Marx, whom he met in Berlin. He had one daughter and one son.

"In 1924 he returned to Jerusalem and in 1927 moved to the Talpiot quarter of the city, where he still lives. In 1929, the house where he was living was pillaged during the Arab riots and he vowed to build a house of his own. However, as his wife's health had been affected by her experiences, he took her first, with their children, to live for a while with her father in Germany, while he set out on a tour of the Jewish communities in Poland and Galicia. His experiences during this visit were the basis for his novel *A Guest for the Night*, written several years after his return to Jerusalem in 1932. In 1952 he paid a visit to Norway and Sweden.

"Agnon's stories cover a wide range—from the Chmielnicki riots in seventeenth century Poland to modern life in Israel. His three full-length novels are *The Bridal Canopy*, published in 1930, a picaresque tale of eighteenth century Galicia; *A Guest for the Night*, 1940; and *Only Yesterday*, 1945, a story of the early pioneers in the Land of Israel. His numerous stories, ranging from tales of a few pages to short novels, are set in his native Galicia, Poland, Lithuania, Germany, and the Land of Israel.

"Agnon is widely recognized as Israel's foremost author. In 1936 he received an honorary doctorate from the Jewish Theological Seminary; he was awarded the Bialik Prize of Tel Aviv Municipality in 1951 and the government's Israel Prize in 1954."

When Agnon received the Nobel Prize for

Literature in 1966, he was even less well known internationally than his corecipient, Nelly Sachs. In Israel, however, visitors to his street in the Talpiot district of Jerusalem had long been accustomed to the official notice which read : "Quiet, Agnon Is Writing"—local recognition of his status as the country's greatest living novelist.

Agnon grew up in the last years of the Austro-Hungarian empire. Among the young Jews of Eastern Europe it was a time of intense intellectual activity—Zionist, anarchist, socialist. One result of this ferment was a renaissance in Hebrew literature, the emergence of a new "European spirit" in rebellion against the parochial concerns and claustrophobic traditions of the past. Ignoring the simple village themes, the simple village virtues, the young writers burst into forbidden territory—the world of nature, sexual love—invoking a passionate and romantic humanism.

And then, as Menachem Ribalow says, "Agnon appeared on the scene and began a counterrevolution. He reversed the trend from Europe homeward again, from alien ways back to the native road. . . . He said not a single word pro or contra. He simply began to write in a different manner, different from all the Hebrew writers of the time. His novelty lay in his old-fashionedness. His uniqueness consisted in his return to the old sources, to the folk-character and its traits of simplicity and sincerity, purity and piety."

Most of Agnon's early stories were set in Eastern Europe, often in Buczacz (sometimes renamed Shibbush). They were mostly folk tales with elements of fantasy, like the short novel *Agunot* (Forsaken Wives, 1909). More such traditional tales, and some similar in mood but set in modern Palestine, appeared during Agnon's years in Berlin (1913–1924).

His first major work was the two-volume novel *Ha-Khnassat Kallah* (1930, translated by I. M. Lask as *The Bridal Canopy*). It is a warmly comic account of the Galician travels of the poor, pious Reb Yudel in search of dowries for his three daughters. Some critics were reminded a little of *Don Quixote* (with Yudel's companion, Nuta the Wagoner, as his Sancho Panza). And this picaresque outline is stuffed full of stories within stories, rich in Jewish folklore, history, and Talmudic references. It is, as Arnold Band has said, "unquestionably one of the major artistic achievements of modern Hebrew prose."

Salmann Schocken, a German-Jewish businessman who was an ardent admirer of Agnon's work, had established the Schocken Verlag in 1928 primarily to publish his friend's work in Germany. Agnon returned to Berlin in 1930 to supervise the typesetting of the four-volume *Kol Sippurov* (Complete Stories), published in 1931. The

SHMUEL YOSEF AGNON

Schocken publishing house was obliged to move to Tel Aviv in 1938 and opened its New York branch, Schocken Books Inc., in 1945.

As Misha Louvish writes above, Agnon had revisited the Jewish communities in Poland and Galicia before his return to Jerusalem in 1932 and out of this experience wrote his second major novel, *Oreah Nata la-Lun* (1937, translated as *A Guest for the Night*). Arnold Band considers it "the central literary creation in Agnon's career," a work which "contains all the major themes and techniques of his other stories." Describing just such a return to native grounds as Agnon had made, it is a record of a shattering disillusionment. The visitor finds in the community that shaped him nothing but spiritual and physical decay. "It is significant," wrote Reuben Wallenrod, "that this novel is crowded with maimed people. There seems to be something defective and maimed in the community as a whole. The previous atmosphere of unity and completeness has been diffused and attenuated."

The themes of alienation and disillusionment, of severed roots, were henceforth never far below the surface of Agnon's work. He wrote less about Europe and turned increasingly to Palestine for his stories. His third full-length novel, *Tmol Shilshom* (Only Yesterday, 1945), is about a young Galicia Jew who migrates to Palestine, his life in city an kibbutz, and his premature and pointless death; a another level it is concerned with the conflict be tween old and new, with the Jew's growing (an in Agnon's mind fatal) separation from the fait and the traditions that have nourished him.

Tmol Shilshom has not yet been translated int English, but a number of other works have. *Bi-*

Levav Yamin (1933, translated by I. M. Lask as *In the Heart of the Seas*), is a joyous fable about the miraculous voyage of a group of pious immigrants from Buczacz to the Holy Land. Two long stories, "Shevuat Emunim" ("Betrothed") and "Edo ve-Enam" ("Edo and Enam") were published in English in 1966 as *Two Tales*. *Days of Awe* is a partial translation of *Yomim Noraim* (1937), a massive collection of legends and commentaries concerning the Jewish High Holy Days—one of a number of volumes of Hebrew classical material edited by Agnon.

Agnon never adopted the modern colloquial Hebrew used by most Israeli writers. Whether he wrote of the ancient past, of the East European Jewry of his youth, or of modern Israel, his language remained the language of Genesis. And his technique was that of the traditional teller of tales, meandering and intimate, full of pious exclamations, learned references, illustrative anecdotes (like his own conversation). But after the 1930s there was a powerful tension between the gentle rhythm and surface calm of his stories, and the underlying sense of disorientation and loss. This profound distress is most evident in the mysterious stories collected in *Sefer Hamasim*. It has been suggested that some of these tales, many of which are translated in the posthumous *Twenty-one Stories*, are oblique reflections of the dark night of the Jews in Hitler's Europe. Others reveal a more personal and metaphysical anguish.

This element in Agnon's work, the sense it sometimes gives of a man speaking with the gentlest possible irony of a world gone mad, has reminded many critics of Kafka, and there have been comparisons also with Joyce, Proust, Faulkner, Eliot, and Thomas Mann. Such busy labeling and categorizing Agnon (who said that his inspiration came mainly from the Scriptures and the sages) found highly entertaining. Richard M. Elman, in his review of *The Bridal Canopy* and *In the Heart of the Seas*, outraged some of his colleagues by confessing that he found the books tedious. It is probably true nevertheless that Agnon loses much in translation. His ideal reader would not only tackle him in the original, but would bring to the task a profound knowledge of Jewish history and theology.

Agnon possessed a good share of the simplicity, piety, and gentle wit with which he invested his heroes. Physically he was slight and brisk, with white hair and blue eyes. He owned a vast library of books and manuscripts on the history and traditions of Judaism, including many rare items of great value. It was the third such collection that he had assembled. The first was destroyed by fire in Germany in 1924 (when he also lost the manuscript of an autobiographical novel, never rewritten, called *Bitzror Ha-Chayyim*), the second during a riot in Jerusalem in 1929. Agnon died of a heart attack at the age of eighty-two, and was given a state funeral.

PRINCIPAL WORKS IN ENGLISH TRANSLATION: The Bridal Canopy, 1937; In the Heart of the Seas, 1948; Days of Awe, 1948; Two Tales, 1966; A Guest for the Night, 1968; Twenty-one Stories, 1970.

ABOUT: Alter, R. After the Tradition, 1969; Band, A. Nostalgia and Nightmare: A Study in the Fiction of S. Y. Agnon, 1968; Current Biography, 1967; Hojman, B. The Fiction of S. Y. Agnon, 1971; Ribalow, M. The Flowering of Modern Hebrew Literature, 1959; Twentieth-Century Writing, 1969. *Periodicals*—Book Week April 30, 1967; Israel Argosy 9, 1967; Publishers' Weekly October 31, 1966; New York Review of Books November 3, 1966; New York Times October 21, 1966; February 18, 1970; New York Times Book Review May 28, 1967.

***AKHMADULINA, BELLA (AKHATOVNA)** (1937–), Russian poet, was born of mixed Tatar and Italian origin in Moscow. In 1954 she married Yevgeny Yevtushenko, who in his *Precocious Autobiography* has described his first sight of her at a student meeting in Moscow: "At this, another eighteen-year-old girl with a round childish face and a thick red plait got up. Her slanting Tatar eyes flashing . . . . This was Bella Akhmadulina whom I married a few weeks later." Some of Yevtushenko's more intimate and personal poems, including many of his love lyrics, were written to her; but the marriage proved unhappy, and since their divorce both have remarried. Akhmadulina's second husband is Yuri Nagibin, who is well known as a short story writer and film scenarist.

She attended the Gorky Literary Institute but was expelled in 1957, so that at first she had difficulty in getting her poems published, though they achieved considerable renown when circulated in manuscript. She did, however, eventually gain membership in the Soviet Writers' Union, and her first book of poems *Struna* (The Harp String) was published in 1962 in an edition of only 20,000 copies (small by Russian standards). She has been criticized in the Soviet Union for writing poetry which is too introspective in tone; it has been compared to that of Anna Akhmatova, and echoes of Pasternak and Tsvetaeva have also been found in her work. Her style is simple and direct, and most of her early poems are short, rhymed, and traditional in form, often in quatrains, but distinguished by their startling imagery. And their subject matter is often far from traditional—she has devoted poems to a motor scooter, to catching a cold, to buying a fizzy drink from an automatic machine. J. M. Cohen, writing in 1960, placed her in the Acmeist tradition as a poet "unmetaphysically concerned with the world of appearances," a modernist "firmly anchored in the traditions of Russian poetry."

* a ʞhmä dōō′ lē nə

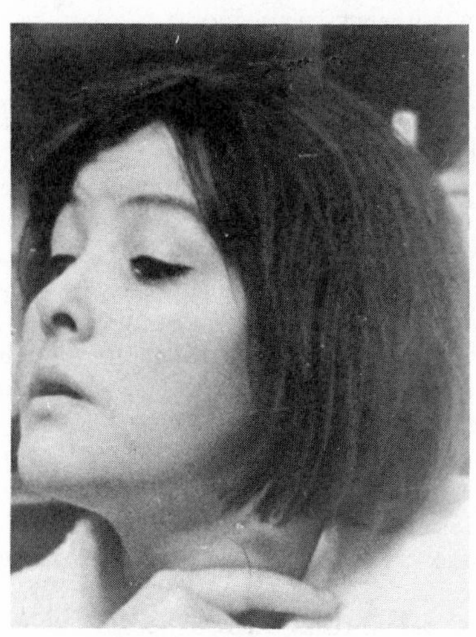

BELLA AKHMADULINA

She later published several longer poems in literary journals such as *Yunost* (Youth), and in 1968 a larger selection of her work appeared in Russian in Germany under the title of one of the poems, *Oznob* (A Chill). The outstanding long poem *Moya rodoslovnaya* (My Genealogy, 1964) derives its theme as well as its title from Pushkin's 1830 poem of the same name, and shows her widening her range of interests and experimenting with more varied forms. In another long poem, *Skazka o dozhde* (Poem About Rain), the rain is a disruptive element which enters a well-ordered home and plays with the children; some critics have seen this as an allegory in which the rain represents the irrational, life-giving spirit of poetry in confrontation with a rigid and inhibiting social order. She has also translated a considerable number of poems from Georgian and has more recently published several short prose works in magazines, three of which are reprinted in the collection *Oznob*.

Akhmadulina is generally regarded as the most brilliant woman poet of the generation of Yevtushenko and Voznesensky, and her poetry readings attract enormous audiences. Marc Slonim says of her: "Her voice has such a purity of tone, such richness of timbre, such individuality of diction, that if her growth continues she will be able some day to succeed Akhmatova . . . [as] the greatest living woman poet in Russia."

PRINCIPAL WORKS IN ENGLISH TRANSLATION: Fever, and Other New Poems, translated by Geoffrey Dutton and Igor Mezhakoff-Koriakin, 1969. *Poems in* Bosley, K. Russia's Other Poets, 1968; Obolensky, D. Penguin Book of Russian Verse, 1962; Reavey, G. The New Russian Poets, 1968.

ABOUT: Carlisle, O. Poets on Street Corners, 1969; Mihajlov, M. Moscow Summer, 1965; Slonim, M. Soviet Russian Literature, 1964. *Periodicals*—New York Times Book Review November 7, 1965; New York Times Magazine August 20, 1967.

***"AKHMATOVA," ANNA (pseudonym of Anna Andreyevna Gorenko)** (June 11 [old style, i.e., June 23], 1889–March 5, 1966), Russian poet, adopted her grandmother's name as a pen name. She was born in a suburb of Odessa, her father being a retired officer of the Russian merchant navy. Much of her early childhood was spent in the region of Petersburg, first at Pavlovsk and then at Tsarskoe Selo (now called Pushkin). She studied law in Kiev, but soon lost interest and returned to Petersburg, where she attended a course in literature given by Innokenty Annensky, who was to become a fundamental influence on her poetry, as he was on that of Pasternak. Annensky was a scholar whose poetry has a classical precision and clarity and it was these qualities which appealed to a generation of poets in reaction against the vagueness of symbolist verse.

One of these reactions was the Acmeist movement, of which Akhmatova became a leader, along with Nikolai Gumilev, whom she married in 1910, and Osip Mandelstam. Acmeism demanded the use of words in their exact logical meaning rather than musically or as symbols of some higher mystical reality. Akhmatova's own verse, consisting mainly of love poems, had begun to appear as early as 1907. Her first book, *Vecher* (Evening), appeared in 1912 with a foreword by the poet Mikhail Kuzmin, another major formative influence on post-Symbolist poetry. When her second book, *Chetki* (The Rosary), was published in 1914 it rapidly became immensely popular, especially with women, and she maintained her reputation with another collection of short lyrical poems, *Belaya staya* (The White Flock) in 1917. These intimate love lyrics of Akhmatova's early years, written in a spare, concrete, and matter-of-fact style, are intensely feminine and highly temperamental, sometimes sensuous and sometimes detached, sometimes humble and sometimes haughty. Many are what Tvardovsky has described as "miniature poetic novellas," dealing first with the birth of love and its joys, then with rejection or betrayal, which Akhmatova sees, wretchedly or ironically according to her mood, as the almost invariable lot of a woman in love. Grief and repentance follow, leading often to religious images as she seeks consolation in prayer, or at other times in nature, in solitary walks through the fields or by a deserted lake.

She divorced Gumilev in 1918 shortly after he returned from the war and married Vladimir Shileyko, an Assyriologist and himself a minor

* a KHmä′ to və

ANNA AKHMATOVA

poet. The Acmeists had little in common except a rejection of symbolism, and had gone their own poetic ways, but none of them wholly supported the Revolution. In 1921 Gumilev was shot for his alleged part in an anti-Bolshevik plot, and Akhmatova was deeply affected by the execution of the father of her only son. Her third book had already contained a series of poems dealing with Russia and the 1914 war, and her reactions to the events of the Civil War are contained in the lyric poems aptly titled *Anno Domini MCMXXI*, in which she developed a more solemn and majestic style. This collection, published in 1922, also incorporated two books which had come out during 1921, the short lyrics of *Podorozhnik* (Plantain) recording the end of her marriage to Gumilev, and *U samogo morya* (On the Same Shore), her only verse tale. This tells the story of a romantic Crimean girl whose dreamed-of lover, when he at last comes to her, is already dead. As Renato Poggioli says, she "seems to have always conceived of woman's destiny in terms of the expectation of love and of the visitation of death."

Her poetry was much criticized by the new Bolshevik rulers because of her concern with purely personal experience—often "negative" experience at that; between 1922 and 1940 she was forbidden to publish her poetry, and seems to have written very little, but she did publish in 1933 and 1936 two of her important studies of Pushkin. During the Yezhov purges in the late 1930s her third husband, the art historian N. N. Punin, was arrested and probably shot, and later her son, Lev Gumilev, was also arrested. (He was released to fight in the air force during the war, but rearrested some years after it and not finally freed until after Stalin's death.) With her friend Lidiya Chukovskaya she joined the queues outside the prisons, trying to learn his fate and to see him.

The cycle of short lyrical poems *Rekviem* (translated as *Requiem*) is a record of this experience and a great memorial to the suffering of countless others at this time: "Would you like to see yourself now, you girl so full of laughter. / The favorite of all her friends, / The gay sinner of Tsarskoe Selo, / Would you like to see what's happened to your life? / At the end of a queue of three hundred, / You stand outside Kresty prison, / And your hot tears are burning holes in the New Year ice. . . ." But if Akhmatova had no cause to love the regime, she was passionately devoted to Russia and would never emigrate, and *Requiem* begins with the declaration: "No, not under the vault of another sky, not under the shelter of other wings. I was with my people then, where my people, unhappily, were."

From 1940 onwards she was again publishing her poetry: *Iz shesti knig* (From Six Books), as its title indicates, was a selection from her five earlier books with the new poems forming the sixth collection, *Iva* (Willow), later changed to *Trostnik* (Reed). Before the German invasion she wrote two deeply-felt war poems on the bombing of London and the Nazi occupation of Paris; but then came the even greater tragedy of her own country. Her love for Russia was especially bound up with Petersburg–Leningrad and with Tsarskoe Selo, where she had grown up. She herself was evacuated from Leningrad in 1941 to Tashkent, but the terrible fate of her "granite city of glory and misfortune," where over a million people died during the three-and-a-half-year German siege, led her to write some of the most poignant poems of the war.

Akhmatova had been severely ill during the war, but in June 1944 she had recovered and was able to return to Leningrad. Two years later the repression of imaginative literature which characterized the last years of Stalin's rule began, and the continuing popularity of her poetry, especially with young people, brought her once more under attack. Stalin's cultural dictator Zhdanov, who demanded that literature should serve the state, described her as "half-nun, half-prostitute," and with the satirist Zoschenko she was expelled from the Writers' Union. During this further period of enforced silence she translated poetry from languages as diverse as Serbian and Korean and continued her studies of Pushkin. She meanwhile continued to work on her autobiographical *Poema bez geroya* (Poem Without a Hero), which she had begun in 1940 but did not finally complete until 1962 (though earlier, incomplete versions of this strange masterpiece had been published both in Russia and in the United States). After Stalin's death, however, she not only published her own poetry again but was elected to the presidium of the Writers' Union from which she had earlier been expelled, and traveled abroad to receive the Etna-Taormina prize in Italy and an honorary doctorate from Oxford University. During the last ten years of her life she produced some of her finest poems—less accessible than her earlier work, full of nostalgia and intimations of death, and of a strange kind of pantheism, but delicate, of great verbal and rhythmic beauty and remarkable visual imagery.

In her old age, very stout, and somewhat embittered by what Konstantin Paustovsky called "her hard female destiny," she nevertheless retained the "regal presence," the aquiline nose and "haughty lips" evoked in her early love lyrics. She died after a long illness in a nursing home near Moscow; an Orthodox church funeral was held though it is uncertain how far she herself was actually a Christian.

After the death of Pasternak in 1960 she was the greatest surviving representative of the so-called Silver Age of Russian post-Symbolist poetry and was widely regarded as the greatest living Russian poet and even the greatest woman poet the Russian nation had produced. Her poetry is indeed more immediately accessible than that of Marina Tsvetaeva, the other great woman poet of her generation, but it is also narrower in range and has often been compared to an intimate diary in which her sorrow and happiness are expressed directly.

PRINCIPAL WORKS IN ENGLISH TRANSLATION: Forty-seven Love Poems (tr. by N. Duddington), 1927; Selected Poems (tr. by Richard McKane), 1969; Poems (tr. by Stanley Kunitz with Max Hayward), 1973. *Poems in* Barnstone, W. (ed.) Modern European Poetry, 1966; Binyon, T. J. (ed.) A Soviet Verse Reader, 1964; Bowra, C. M. A Book of Russian Verse, 1943; Bowra, C. M. A Second Book of Russian Verse, 1948; Markov, V. and Sparks, M. (eds.) Modern Russian Poetry, 1966; Obolensky, D. (ed.) Penguin Book of Russian Verse, 1962; Atlantic February 1973, April 1973.

ABOUT: Carlisle, O. Poets on Street Corners, 1969; Poggioli, R. The Poets of Russia, 1960; Strakhovsky, L. I. Craftsmen of the Word, 1949; Zavalishin, V. Early Soviet Writers, 1958. *Periodicals*—Anglo-Soviet Journal Spring 1966; London Magazine December 1966; Oxford Slavonic Papers XII 1965; Times Literary Supplement June 9, 1966; July 10, 1969.

*AKSENOV, VASILY (PAVLOVICH)

(1932–), Russian short story writer, novelist, and dramatist, writes (in Russian): "I was born in the city of Kazan, on the Volga. In the Middle Ages, this ancient city was the center of the Tatar khanate. In the fifteenth century, after a prolonged siege, it was captured by the armies of Ivan the Terrible and became an outpost of the Russian empire in the East. In 1800 the University of Kazan, one of the first universities in Russia, was founded there.

* ak syo′ nôf

VASILY AKSENOV

"A tourist advertisement for the city might include its white walls and the towers of the Kazan Kremlin, as well as the sharp spire of the Tatar tower of Syuyumbeka, but I have my own sightseeing pleasures: the varied back streets, the tram lines, and the small cottages, which evoke memories of the difficult years of childhood, the war years, when the entire city was crusted with dirty yellow ice and overrun by starving people evacuated from Leningrad, Kiev, and Minsk.

"My mother taught at the University in the Department of History, and my father was a member of the Kazan City Council. Both were Communists, and both were victims of the 1937 purges, during the period of the 'iron' repression. I was raised by an aunt, and saw my parents again only in 1955, when justice was restored.

"During my student years I attended the Leningrad Medical Institute. I entered the Institute not because of some specific attraction toward the medical profession, but simply because I wanted to be a student, since at that time a student's status was very appealing to me. However, an inclination toward writing and a curious kind of levity prevented me from studying effectively.

"Like the majority of Leningrad students, I changed living quarters frequently, moving from apartment to apartment; and in small rooms above the canals of Leningrad I wrote poems and stories, which I never submitted for publication, but which I read to my friends in the literary section of the Leningrad District Youth Club.

"At that time I was preoccupied only with the outward appearance of things, and concentrated in my stories on bits of life which seemed to me astonishing, infinite, and most important, romantic. The stories were ineffectual, but then I had no self-delusions, and not once did it enter my head that someday I would become a writer.

"Meanwhile I finished my schooling. I became a doctor and began work at the quarantine station of the Port of Leningrad. This was an entirely new world, another life. I would go out in a cutter on the seaward canal and scramble up a Jacob's ladder to the decks of British, German, and Finnish ships. In the port I became acquainted with people who had earlier seemed to me as remote as Martians.

"Here I began to write my first novel, *Kollegi*. The book dealt with senior students at a medical institute; it contained autobiographical elements and was marked by the strengths and weaknesses typical of a first effort. In it I attempted to describe those new manifestations in the lives of our young people which appeared in Soviet society at the beginning of the post-Stalin period, at the time of the Twentieth Party Congress. The heroes are extremely talkative, and discuss at length their relationship to society, to life and death, to war and love. One of them belongs to the type later called 'the angry young men,' and the other is a so-called idealist.

"I continued to write this book while working in the rural hospital at Lake Onezhsk, and also in Moscow, where I moved after my marriage and began work in the Tuberculosis Institute.

"In 1960 my novel was published in the journal *Yunost* (Youth), and had a rousing and (for me) an unexpected success. From then on, writing has been my profession.

"At that time, *Yunost* was edited by the highly respected writer Valentin Kataev, a representative of the so-called Odessa School, which also included Babel, Olesha, and Ilf and Petrov. Kataev's principal goal was the discovery of new talent among the younger writers. His magazine published Yevgeny Yevtushenko, Bella Akhmadulina, Bulat Okudzhava, Anatoli Gladilin, and others. This was the critical turning-point in my life; from a peaceful medical environment I moved into this circle of impassioned people.

"My second book, *Zvezdny bilet*, appeared a year later, and stirred up an even noisier reaction among readers and critics. Many of the critics reproached me for celebrating nihilism and cynicism, whereas I, in my naïveté, had been striving for exactly the opposite. In addition to these two books, I wrote a story, 'Apelsiny iz Marokko,' dedicated to the inhabitants of the Far East; a novel, *Pora, moy drug, pora* (1964), which dealt with the tragic destiny of an eccentric young man, and a collection of short stories, *Na polputi k lune* (1965).

"It seems to me that my greatest success has been achieved in the genre of the short story. My literary friends are of the same opinion, although the short stories did not stir up the critical furor which accompanied my first books.

"I have recently written two satirical plays, one of which was produced at the Sovremennik [Contemporary] Theatre in Moscow. The theatre attracts me with its unrestricted possibilities for hyperbole, grotesquerie, and fantasy. However, I am presently trying to employ these qualities in my prose. Satire has now become my goal, although I occasionally think with trepidation of the spiritual crisis of Mikhail Zoshchenko, who decided toward the end of his life that satire ate away the soul like corrosion. Is there, then, no place left for lyricism and light?

"In the last three years I have traveled abroad a great deal, to Argentina, Japan, Paris, Rome, Delhi, Poland, Czechoslovakia, and Yugoslavia. The image of the world evoked by these journeys has aroused in me an intense desire to write a novel on the destiny of modern man, a subject which certain mathematicians and physicists term the search for the third model."

Aksenov's first novel, *Kollegi* (1960, translated as *Colleagues*), with its vivid depiction of young people, forthright but in the long run positive in their political and social views, was popular with both readers and critics and was quickly made into a film. It already shows some of the characteristics which emerged in his second novel, *Zvezdny bilet* (1962, translated variously as *A Starry Ticket* and *A Ticket to the Stars*). This is about a group of Moscow teenagers, three boys and a romantic young girl, who take a long vacation in Estonia before settling down to adult life. Bored by official rhetoric, irreverent and critical, they want to be left alone to discover their own principles and values. The most obvious feature of Aksenov's style is his skillful use of the racy colloquial language of modern youth. This short book was even more popular than its predecessor, but official critics attacked it bitterly, accusing Aksenov of depicting Soviet youth as beatniks, and of imitating such writers as J. D. Salinger. Aksenov has in fact made no secret of his admiration for Western writers such as Moravia, Böll, Hemingway, Faulkner, and Salinger.

In December 1961 Aksenov visited the Far East, one product of the journey being the story "Apelsiny iz Marokko" (Oranges from Morocco), published in *Yunost* in January 1963. It deals with young workers on the island of Sakhalin, which he had visited. Once again he was attacked by the conservatives, as he had been for two other stories published in *Novy Mir* in July 1962: the much-translated "Na polputi k lune" ("Halfway to the

Moon") and "Papa, slozhi!" (translated by T. P. Whitney as "Papa, What Does That Spell?" and by C. Knight as "Daddy, What Do They Say?") The first is about the truck driver Kirpichenko who, after months in an isolated lumber camp, sets out to spend his savings on a vacation. He falls in love with the stewardess on the plane which takes him four thousand miles to Moscow and thereafter flies back and forth between Siberia and Moscow in the hope of seeing her again, until his money and vacation are both used up and he has flown "half-way to the moon." It is the best, and the best known of Aksenov's stories to date.

Though to a lesser extent than Yevtushenko and Voznesensky, Aksenov was one of the main objects of attack in the 1963 conservative reaction against the liberalization of the arts. Aksenov admitted his "mistakes" in an article in *Pravda* in April, but his unrepentant creative response was the novel *Pora, moy drug, pora* (1964, translated as *It's Time, My Friend, It's Time*), which the *Times Literary Supplement* thought "by far his best to date." The novel is about the struggle for inner peace and freedom of a writer, Valya, and his actress wife Tanya, who are on the verge of divorce. She is making a film in the turreted setting of the medieval Estonian town where they had met, and he follows her there. The work is a beautifully managed account of his wanderings in the old town, recalling their former happiness. At the end of the book, after Valya and Tanya have both rather painfully matured, they are reunited, this time for good. This memorable love story is notable also for its portrayal of Kyanukuk, one of the first "outsiders" to appear in Soviet fiction—a tragic buffoon of great but unorthodox potential for whom Soviet society provides no place. Aksenov's next two books were collections of stories already published in magazines, *Katapulta* (The Catapult, 1964) and *Na polputi k lune* (1965).

Aksenov was coauthor of the film *Moy mladshy brat* (My Younger Brother), based on *Zvezdny bilet* and author of the screen version of his first novel, *Kollegi*, which was also adapted for the stage in 1961. In his first original play, *Vsegda v prodazhe* (Always on Sale), produced with great success in 1967, the central character is a young journalist who personifies the youthful Moscow cynic. The songs, which are an important feature of the play, have lyrics by Yevtushenko and music by Andrei Volkonsky. More recently, Aksenov has collaborated with Andrei Voznesensky and the *avant-garde* composer M. Tariverdiyev, in an opera called *Dlinnonogo* (Longlegs).

Aksenov continues to irritate the more reactionary Soviet critics but elsewhere is recognized as one of the best and most original Russian prose writers of his generation, admired for the beauty of his descriptive writing, his ear for the colloquial Russian of uneducated workers and of young people, and the restless and wholly contemporary spirit of search his stories convey so well. Aksenov is dark-haired, thoughtful, and, according to one interviewer, "reminds one of a youthful Jean Gabin." His mother, now active as a literary critic in Moscow, has published under her maiden name, Evgenia Ginzburg, a much-discussed account of her appalling sufferings during the eighteen years she spent in Stalinist prisons and concentration camps.

PRINCIPAL WORKS IN ENGLISH TRANSLATION: Colleagues (translated by Margaret Wettlin), 1961 (also translated by Alec Brown, 1962); A Starry Ticket (translated by Alec Brown), 1962 (also translated as A Ticket to the Stars by Andrew R. MacAndrew, 1963); It's Time, My Friend, It's Time (U.S., It's Time, My Love, It's Time) (translated by Olive Stevens), 1969. *Stories in* Bearne, C. G. (ed.) Modern Russian Short Stories, 1968; Blake, P. and Hayward, M. (eds.) Half-way to the Moon: New Writing From Russia, 1964; MacAndrew, A. R. Four Soviet Masterpieces, 1965; Reddaway, P. (ed.) Soviet Short Stories (vol. 2), 1968; Whitney, T. P. The New Writing in Russia, 1964. *Essay in* Soviet Literature 5, 1966.

ABOUT: Alexandrova, V. History of Soviet Literature, 1963; Blair, K. H. A Review of Soviet Literature, 1966; Brown, E. J. Russian Literature Since the Revolution, 1963; Hayward, M. and Labedz, L. Literature and Revolution in Soviet Russia, 1963; Hayward, M. and Crowley, E. L. (eds.) Soviet Literature in the Sixties, 1965; Whitney, T. P. The New Writing in Russia, 1964. *Periodicals*—New Statesman June 1, 1962; New Yorker September 4, 1965.

***AKUTAGAWA, RYUNOSUKE** (March 1, 1892–July 24, 1927), Japanese short story writer and novelist, was born in Tokyo into the Niihara family. He was adopted as a child by his uncle, Michiaki Akutagawa, whose surname he assumed.

Influenced by his teacher, Soseki Natsume, and another great Japanese novelist, Ogai Mori, Akutagawa accumulated a formidable knowledge not only of Chinese and Japanese, but also of Western literature. At Tokyo Imperial University he specialized in English literature, graduating with a thesis on William Morris. While still an undergraduate he joined with two classmates, Kan Kikuchi and Masao Kumé—both of whom became well-known writers—to launch a literary magazine, *Shin Shicho* (New Thought). Two of his stories, "Rashomon" (1915, translated by Takashi Kojima) and "Hana" (1916, translated by G. W. Shaw as "The Nose"), were published during his teens in student magazines of this kind, and won him immediate acclaim. He refused invitations to teach at the universities of Tokyo and Kyoto and devoted his short life almost exclusively to literature.

Akutagawa was a prolific writer, but he disdained to grind out the potboilers which have ruined so many gifted Japanese authors. In little more than a decade he produced about 150 short stories, a novel, and some poems and essays. Like Soseki and Mori, he had no use for the squalid

* ä kōō tə gä wä

RYUNOSUKE AKUTAGAWA

naturalism of the time. Indeed, Akutagawa was so completely an individual, in his writing as in his life, that it is impossible to assign him to any contemporary literary movement.

For his themes he drew on Chinese and Japanese history and on old story books like *Konjaku-monogatari.* "Rashomon," brilliantly filmed in 1951, is one of several related stories set in Japan during the Heian era (794–1185). Others reflect Akutagawa's particular interest in the sixteenth century, Japan's so-called Christian era—notably "Tabako to akuma" (1917, translated by G. W. Shaw as "Tobacco and the Devil").

At times, particularly in his charming stories for children, he was content to retell an ancient story for its own sake. More often, the original tale would be given an ironic psychological twist and made to yield a contemporary moral, as does "Rashomon," a study in the perils of subjectivity. "Jigokuhen" (1918, translated by W. H. H. Norman as "Hell Screen") is another such story and a characteristically macabre one. It is the tale of a painter who persuades his feudal master to burn a beautiful woman alive to provide a model for a painting of hell and then discovers that the girl selected for this horrible death was his own daughter.

In his style Akutagawa was a perfectionist to the point of obsession, polishing and repolishing every sentence and refusing to publish until his own standards had been met. It is not surprising that his work at times borders on the precious. The clarity and elegance of his prose is nevertheless unsurpassed in modern Japanese literature, and his profound if sardonic understanding of human frailty gives his work a peculiar relevance in this disenchanted age. He has reminded Western critics of Aubrey Beardsley and also of Swift, and his last novel, *Kappa* (1927), a political fable set in the upside-down world of the water-sprites, bears a close resemblance in tone and manner to *Gulliver's Travels.*

Sensitive, morose, and frail in health, Akutagawa committed suicide in 1927, apparently feeling, at the age of thirty-five, that the world had no more to offer him.

PRINCIPAL WORKS IN ENGLISH TRANSLATION: Tales Grotesque and Curious, 1930; Kappa, 1947; Hell Screen and Other Stories, 1948; Rashomon and Other Stories, 1952; Japanese Short Stories, 1961; Exotic Japanese Stories, 1964; Tu Tze-chun, 1964. *For children*—The Three Treasures, 1951.

ABOUT: Keene, D. Modern Japanese Literature, 1956; Morris, I. Modern Japanese Stories, 1961; Morrison, J. W. Modern Japanese Fiction, 1955; Penguin Companion to Literature 4, 1969.

***ALBEE, EDWARD (FRANKLIN)** (March 12, 1928–), American dramatist, was born in Washington, D.C. He never knew his natural parents but was adopted at the age of two weeks by Reed and Frances Albee. Reed Albee was a millionaire, a member of the family that owned the Keith-Albee Theatre Circuit. The boy grew up in a mansion in Westchester County, New York, with servants and tutors, a St. Bernard dog to pull his sleigh, and a Rolls Royce to ride in. He was a spoiled child, plump, precocious, and unhappy. His adoptive father was a silent man, a foot shorter and twenty-three years older than his wife, a hard-riding young woman who dominated the marriage. It is said that, as a child, Albee was not very close to them, and had moreover a feeling of deep resentment towards his natural parents. The only person he felt at home with was Mrs. Albee's mother, "Grandma Cotta."

Albee never took to the discipline and pomposities of school life, which began for him at Rye Country Day School. From there he went at eleven to Lawrenceville, a boarding school in New Jersey, where he interested himself in the drama and the junior newspaper, but in not much else except music. His first ambition was to be a composer, and he has not entirely abandoned it, though he is unable to play any musical instrument.

When Albee was expelled from Lawrenceville in 1943, his mother sent him in desperation to a military academy which he has referred to as the Valley Forge Concentration Camp. Expelled again after a year or so, he entered Choate School in Connecticut. Here at last, treated with humanity and intelligence, he settled down. He began to take his writing seriously, and poured out vast quanti-

* ôl' bē

ties of unexceptional verse and prose. Albee left Choate in 1946 and, after a brief and mutually unrewarding interlude at Trinity College, in Hartford, Connecticut, his formal education ended.

At the age of nineteen Albee secured his first job, writing continuity for musical programs on radio station WNYC. A year later he left home after a family argument and settled in New York City. During the next ten years, partially supported by an inheritance from Mrs. Cotta of two hundred and fifty dollars a month, he worked as an office boy, salesman, hotel barman, and Western Union messenger, and in a variety of other jobs. In 1952 he spent a few months in Italy. In his spare time he continued to write—mostly poetry at first, and then his first play, *The Zoo Story*, which was completed in three weeks. No New York producer was interested but, through the efforts of William Flanagan, a young composer with whom Albee was sharing an apartment, the play received its first performance in Berlin in September 1959.

The Zoo Story is a one-act duologue between two men who meet in Central Park. Peter, reading on a park bench, is a respectable bourgeois Everyman, outwardly contented, inwardly empty and alone. He is accosted by Jerry, a messianic outcast, who struggles, verbally and then physically, to break through Peter's reserve, and rouse him to some kind of elementary emotional contact. In the end he succeeds through an insane (or Christlike) act of self-sacrifice, handing his knife to Peter and then impaling himself on the blade.

After a successful run in Berlin, *The Zoo Story* was staged at the Provincetown Playhouse in January 1960, receiving the Vernon Rice Award and some excellent reviews for the spareness of its construction and the daring of its conception. Most critics have regarded it as an "Absurdist" play but C. W. E. Bigsby, in his extremely useful study of Albee, disagrees. Acknowledging Albee's debt to Ionesco and Genet, Bigsby suggests that he is nevertheless closer to existentialism than the Absurd—that *The Zoo Story* is not an exercise in nihilism but seeks to demonstrate the possibility of "meaningful sacrifice, and the viability of real contact."

A longer one-act play followed, *The Death of Bessie Smith* (1959). It is an impressionistic reconstruction of how the great black blues singer died after a car crash in 1937, having been refused admission to white hospitals. Around this event is built a rather unconvincing study of a white admissions nurse, whose racism is presented as a product of her personal misery, a kind of spiritual scar tissue. As many critics have pointed out, the play is less a specific attack on southern racism than a general indictment of a civilization which has substituted absurd social conventions for compassion. *The Sandbox*, also written in 1959, is a Beckett-like sketch for Albee's longer one-act play, *The American Dream* (1959–1960).

EDWARD ALBEE

In 1960 Albee complained that the American theatre audience "primarily wants a reaffirmation of its values, wants to see the status quo, wants to be entertained rather than disturbed, wants to be comforted." *The American Dream* is an expressionist onslaught on this audience and on the smugly materialistic society it represents. It is set in a "fumed oak and foamed rubber" suburban living room. Mommy and Daddy, babbling inane platitudes, await the arrival of a field worker from an adoption agency. Mommy and Daddy had adopted a child twenty years before but, finding it disobedient, Mommy had gouged out its eyes, cut off its hands, and emasculated it. When it dies, Mommy and Daddy want their money back or a more satisfactory protégé; and they receive one—an All-American Boy, handsome, brainless, spiritually dead, and ready to do absolutely anything for money. The only sane and attractive character in the play is Grandma, who retains at least a faint recollection of what the American dream once meant and who has no stomach for the ritual clichés about patriotism and togetherness voiced so piously by her family.

It is the most "Absurd" of Albee's plays, reminiscent most obviously of Ionesco's *The Bald Soprano*. It was first performed at the York Playhouse, New York, in January 1961 and, though some critics condemned it as "nihilistic, immoral and defeatist," it was by and large both a critical and popular success. Along with *The Death of Bessie Smith*, which appeared in the same program, it was voted the best play of the 1960–1961 season by the Foreign Press Association and brought Albee the Lola D'Annunzio Award. (*The Death of Bessie Smith* was added to the York Playhouse program after the failure of *Bartleby*, William Flanagan's musical adaptation of Melville's *Bartleby, the Scrivener*, for which Albee wrote the libretto in collaboration with James Hinton.)

Who's Afraid of Virginia Woolf?, the first and probably the best of Albee's full-length works, opened in New York in October 1962. It received the New York Drama Critics' Award and the Tony Award as the best play of the 1962–1963 season and ran for two years on Broadway. It has been staged in most European capitals and filmed. The setting is a cottage on the campus of a small New England college, the home of George, an unsuccessful history professor, and his stridently disappointed wife Martha, daughter of the college's president. When the play opens they are returning, already drunk, from a campus party. They launch into a relaxed and extremely funny verbal knockabout which has obviously been their principal conversational mode for years but which grows increasingly savage and damaging as the night wears on.

Shortly they are joined by a younger couple: Nick, a newly appointed lecturer in biology, and his wife, Honey. These are at first conventionally embarrassed and bewildered to find themselves drawn into a Strindbergian marital war, but they reveal themselves more and more as they become drunker. Just as George the historian-cynic takes refuge in the dead past, so Nick the greedily ambitious scientist escapes into a well-ordered future; and the brassy Martha, it emerges, fears love and conception no less than the timid Honey.

The only real difference between the two couples is that George and Martha have had time to adjust to each other's fear and sterility. Their verbal conflict is a less risky substitute for love and is complemented by their elaborate secret fantasy that they have a son. George accepts as part of the game Martha's attacks on his ability and his manhood, but when she breaks the taboo and mentions their imaginary child publicly, as if he really existed, George is shocked into action. He pretends that he has received a telegram announcing their son's death and, over Martha's hysterical pleas, insists that the fantasy is finished. The play ends on the implication that George and Martha now have some chance of achieving real emotional contact.

It is obviously a more naturalistic play than its predecessors, and was compared most widely to the work of Eugene O'Neill and Tennessee Williams. (But Martin Esslin has pointed out that George Washington, the "father of his country," was also married to a Martha, and has made the interesting suggestion that the dream child in the play represents the murdered American Dream.) Some reviewers found it morbidly pessimistic, but it is not that; it proposes that a full acceptance of reality is the path to individual salvation, and it implies that reality *can* be accepted. The play (most critics thought) is too long. But the brilliance and violence of the dialogue, the steady paring away of masks, and a mounting sense of apocalypse, sustain the tension through all the perfectly managed variations of tone and pace. It was recognized at once as the work of a major new American dramatist.

With some of the profits from *Who's Afraid of Virginia Woolf?*, Albee established a theatre workshop for dramatists and together with Richard Barr and Clinton Wilder helped to finance productions by new writers at an off-Broadway theatre, the Cherry Lane. His own next play, *Tiny Alice*, reached Broadway in December 1964. In it a young lay brother, Julian, is betrayed by his church, in exchange for a huge donation, into the hands of a group of conspirators. One of them, the mysterious woman named Miss Alice, he marries. Afterwards the conspirators find it necessary to shoot him, and he is left alone to die in Alice's great castle. The abstract God he calls upon in his extremity cannot answer him, and in the end it is Alice he prays for.

The stage is dominated by a detailed model of Alice's castle, in which tiny figures are said to repeat the movements of the actors in the real castle. If the big castle *is* the real one, that is; there are suggestions that the *small* castle is reality, and that inside it lives a Tiny Alice who is Truth. The object of the conspiracy is to rescue Julian from the illusions of faith (just as George and Martha are rescued from their secular fantasies). Human reality, Albee implies, is limited and painful, but it is what we must concern ourselves with if our lives are ever to make sense. The play is wholly absorbing, but it is seriously marred by its excessively complex imagery and its tendency to long and static monologues. It confounded most reviewers.

Like George and Martha in *Who's Afraid of Virginia Woolf?*, Agnes and Tobias in *A Delicate Balance* (1966) have made a marriage which is a bastion against reality—in this case a comfortable relationship, considerate and affectionate, which nevertheless leaves them fundamentally unloving and uncommitted. Into this alliance intrude their best friends (or *alter egos*?) Harry and Edna—people much like themselves who have suddenly been driven from home by an undefined moment of horror—an unsought glimpse of the terrible absurdity above which they precariously maintain their "delicate balance." They bring their fear with them, and the play studies its impact on Agnes and

Tobias, on their daughter Julia, who has returned from her latest marital disaster in search of reassurance, and on Agnes's alcoholic sister Claire.

During the hours of darkness, each responds in his own way to this threat—Claire resorts as usual to alcohol, and Agnes and Julia both apply for the ultimate refuge of insanity. Only Tobias brings himself to face what is really needed—absolute honesty and absolute commitment. He says to Harry and Edna: "I Don't Want You Here! I Don't Love You: But by God . . . You Stay!" But with the return of daylight the painful insights of the night are rejected—by Tobias with regret, by Agnes with relief: "We'll all forget . . . quite soon." As C. W. E. Bigsby points out, this is a long way from the routine happy ending that some reviewers thought it. *A Delicate Balance* received the Pulitzer Prize, but had a mixed press. Few critics understood it and most, with some justice, found it overburdened with ideas at the expense of action.

There was also a markedly negative and even hostile response to *All Over* (1971), set around the sickbed of a great man who himself has no part in the action but whose illness and death produce a chain of reactions and revelations from the Wife, the Mistress, the Son, the Daughter and the Best Friend. Stanley Kauffmann wrote that "the trumped-up revelations, the unproductive confrontations, retroactively reveal Albee's real bankruptcy, that he knew he had nothing to say *before he started.*" Much criticism centered on the play's deliberate formalism of style and language, which reminded some reviewers of T. S. Eliot, others of Ivy Compton-Burnett. But George Oppenheimer, one of the few critics who admired the play, saw its donnish mannerisms as part of Albee's rebellion against the "sad and shabby time we live in," and concluded: "I think Mr. Albee is struggling toward a new form, a synthesis between the naturalistic and the mystical, or the Absurd and the representational."

Albee has explored the themes that preoccupy him in other terms in his adaptations of Carson McCullers' novella *The Ballad of the Sad Café* (1963) and James Purdy's novel *Malcolm* (1966), and in *Everything in the Garden* (1967), based on a play by the English dramatist Giles Cooper. Two shorter pieces, *Box* and *Quotations from Chairman Mao Tse-tung* (1968) are experiments, the first almost totally abstract, in the application of musical form to the drama.

In Bigsby's view, "Albee's value to the American theater lies precisely in his determination to transcend the exhausted naturalism of the Broadway theater, while establishing an existential drama committed to examining the metaphysical rather than the social or psychological problems of man." It is arguable that his voice has become shriller, his message less coherent, in some of the plays that have followed *Who's Afraid of Virginia Woolf?* Nevertheless, in the power and urgency of his themes, the wit and passion of his language, he remains the most accomplished and still the most promising of the dramatists who, in the early 1960s, seemed to be bringing about a long-awaited renaissance in the American theatre.

Albee, a bachelor, is a handsome, intense man with a quiet speaking voice. He has lectured widely and written a great deal about the state of the drama in the United States. In 1965 he received the Margo James Award for encouraging new playwrights. He lives mostly in New York but is fond of travel.

PRINCIPAL PUBLISHED WORKS: The Zoo Story and Other Plays (with The Sandbox and The Death of Bessie Smith), 1960; The American Dream, 1961; Who's Afraid of Virginia Woolf?, 1962; The Sandbox, and, The Death of Bessie Smith (with Fam and Yam: An Imaginary Interview), 1963; The Ballad of the Sad Café, 1963; Tiny Alice, 1965; Malcolm, 1966; A Delicate Balance, 1966; Box, and, Quotations From Chairman Mao Tse-tung, 1969; All Over, 1971.

ABOUT: Amacher, R. E. Edward Albee, 1969; Bigsby, C. W. E. Albee, 1969; Current Biography, 1963; Debusscher, G. Edward Albee, 1967; Downer, A. S. (ed.) American Drama and Its Critics, 1965; Esslin, M. The Theatre of the Absurd, 1961; Gould, J. R. Modern American Playwrights, 1960; Kostelanetz, R. (ed.) On Contemporary Literature, 1965; Lewis, A. Plays and Playwrights of the Contemporary Theatre, 1965; Lumley, F. New Trends in Twentieth Century Drama, 1967; Rutenberg, M. E. Edward Albee, 1969; Silver, L. J. Profiles in Success, 1965; Wager, W. (ed.) The Playwrights Speak, 1967; Wellwarth, G. E. The Theatre of Protest and Paradox, 1964. *Periodicals*—Atlantic April 1965; Drama Survey Winter 1965, Spring 1966; Horizon September 1961; Life May 27, 1967; Modern Drama December 1967; Nation October 27, 1962; New Republic November 16, 1963; January 29, 1966; April 17, 1971; New York Times March 29, 1971; April 4, 1971; Newsday April 9, 1971; Newsweek October 29, 1962; February 4, 1963; January 4, 1965; October 30, 1966; May 29, 1967; March 18, 1968; New York April 5, 1971; New Yorker March 25, 1961; December 19, 1964; April 3, 1971; Paris Review Fall 1966; Reporter January 2, 1964; Saturday Evening Post January 30, 1965; Transatlantic Review Summer 1963; Tulane Drama Review Summer 1965; Twentieth Century Literature January 1968; Vogue November 15, 1962; February 15, 1966.

ALDRIDGE, JOHN W(ATSON) (September 26, 1922–), American literary critic and novelist, writes: "I was born in Sioux City, Iowa, and until the age of eleven lived a life as sane, wholesome, and predictable as any child's in that bland region of the country. My father was a business man. We had a house in a nice middle-class neighborhood. There were playmates, bicycles, cops and robbers, and regular Saturday westerns. Then the Depression came, and with it the fall, which I now think of as altogether fortunate. My father's business failed. We sold our house and furniture, loaded

JOHN W. ALDRIDGE

what we had left into the car, and went south, a ritual journey back to my father's lost Eden, where he hoped to find sanctuary for us in a world suddenly gone berserk, and perhaps recover the health or the innocence which he imagined he had left behind with his boyhood in Tennessee.

"We settled on a small farm a few miles outside a town called Tyner near Chattanooga. There I felt cast among aliens, lost in the heart of darkness. My schoolmates were mostly farm boys and girls. Many of the boys went habitually without shoes, chewed tobacco in class (the trick was to spit the juice into the ink bottle hole in the desk), wore Bull Durham tags dangling from their shirt pockets, and seemed from birth to have been expert in the use of the twelve-gauge shotgun. I made friends, was and was not accepted, learned to chew tobacco too, but never went barefoot, ingratiated myself yet remained aloof, acquired the hypocrisy of appearing to be one of the boys while cultivating a public image of insufferable goodness—neat, highminded, serious, the pet of teachers, a secret delinquent. At home there was farming to learn for all of us, how to milk, cut wood, plow, plant, and harvest. We had very little money, and we had to work hard to feed ourselves and keep warm. Through the long summers from my thirteenth to my eighteenth year I stayed on the farm, followed a mule and plow round and round a field, read what I could find to read, tried to make a world I could inhabit, remembered my friends back in Iowa who were solemnly en route to becoming lawyers, doctors, pillars of my lost community.

"After high school I received a scholarship to the University of Chattanooga. There I met some other displaced young people who had found comfort and sanity in books. I began to write poems, stories, and articles for the university newspaper and eventually became an editor. I had a lot of hostility in me and expressed it in various arrogant pronouncements on the state of the university, the caliber of the instruction, and the stupidity of the students, whose happy well-adjustedness I of course secretly envied with all my soul. But there were compensations. I was an outsider but an intellectual. By day I was Stephen Dedalus bearing my chalice above a sea of foes. By night I was Eugene Gant prowling the streets in search of the lost lane-end to Heaven. Actually, however, I was running an elevator at night at the YMCA and living as a watchman in what had once been the Municipal Library.

"In the summer of 1942, I won a fellowship to Breadloaf School of English in Vermont, and arrived on the campus by Greyhound with a ten-dollar bill pinned to the inside of my shirt. The other students all seemed to come from Harvard and Princeton, and I felt callow and very frightened until we squared off and tried to outquote one another, and I learned that the rich may be different from you and me but not necessarily better read.

"In the following year I went into the Army, was sent to England, then to Normandy a few days after D-Day. I spent more than a year sleeping on the ground in some of the dampest fields in France and Germany, and was sent home shortly after the end of the war in Europe. In 1946, I entered the University of California at Berkeley to finish work for my degree, began to write again (a collection of Hemingwayish short stories about the war), and became editor of the campus literary magazine *Occident*. A satirical article on California which I published in the magazine attracted the attention of John Fischer of *Harper's*, and shortly after I was graduated, he asked me to write something for him. It was a piece about the new postwar generation of writers. *Harper's* published it in 1947, before most people were aware that there was a postwar generation, and it attracted a good deal of attention. On the strength of the article I received a contract to write what became my first critical book, *After the Lost Generation*, and the offer of my first teaching job—at the University of Vermont.

"I stayed at Vermont seven years, with a year away to give the Christian Gauss Seminars in Criticism at Princeton. Then I went on to teach at a number of other universities, spent four years teaching and writing in Europe, married three times and fathered five sons, and have somehow managed to write what I wanted to write—books and articles about new writers and the state of the contemporary novel, as well as a novel of my own, *The Party at Cranton*, a strange, nastily funny book which angered some people and amused others. In 1964, I came back from Europe to teach at the University of Michigan, where I am now a professor of English and seem likely to remain. Another critical book, *Time to Murder and Create*, was published in 1966.

"I suppose I have had what is called a 'controversial' career. All my books have provoked argument and discussion. And I am pleased that this should be so, for I function best in an atmosphere of controversy and would very probably die if I were ever read with indifference."

After the Lost Generation provided the first serious critical consideration of the novelists who had been shaped by World War II—a generation which included Norman Mailer, John Horne Burns, Truman Capote, and Gore Vidal. Aldridge compared them with the writers who had emerged after World War I and in general found them wanting—lacking in any "distinct attitude" either toward their experience or toward the novel as a medium of expression. Other critics were quick to see the importance of their young colleague's "pioneer" work and most of them praised it, albeit with reservations and often with some condescension. Malcolm Cowley called the book "an indispensable first draft of the critical verdict that, after many revisions, will be reached in twenty or thirty years."

There was far more bad temper in the critical response to *In Search of Heresy*. This was a collection of ten essays and lectures which were mostly concerned to attack the spread of conformity in American fiction, and the way in which the academic establishment worked to perpetuate its own standards and stifle all originality. Some reviewers accused Aldridge of "literary bad manners . . . clumsy construction and inexact diction"; others, like Maxwell Geismar, were delighted by his "determination to say some things boldly, out loud, eloquently, that have badly needed to be said."

By 1966, when Aldridge published *Time to Murder and Create*, he had come to feel that the contemporary novel had reached a state of crisis; that it was increasingly an expression of "the urban and minority intelligence." There is, he wrote, "very little possibility today for the novel to achieve the kind of large, synthesizing sense of the whole culture that helped to give some of the older novels their outstanding range of emotional reference and public appeal." Robie Macauley called it "his best critical work to date" although he and others found it frequently inconsistent and excessively—almost deliberately—negative. But perhaps, as Macauley says, Aldridge's "great merit lies in being negative. . . . By his very talent, controversy, energy, and willingness to go on the high wire blindfolded, he invites a definite reaction. We need him more than we need a dozen sleepy critics of the prevalent kind." Edmund Fuller also finds Aldridge contradictory and partial as a literary theorist, but a shrewd and stimulating critic when he addresses himself to a particular writer or book.

The Party at Cranton, Aldridge's only novel, is itself a species of criticism—a satire on the literary life as it is crystallized in a faculty party at a small university. As Aldridge says, it had a mixed reception. To Paul West it seemed an outstanding exercise in the bizarre, achieving "a gorgeous urbanity" in spite of "contorted sentences, no talk, plenty of self-conscious similes and a general effect of calculated blur"; to Robie Macauley it seemed a catastrophe.

As Fulbright Professor of American Literature, Aldridge has taught at the universities of Munich (1958–1959) and Copenhagen (1962–1963). He was cofounder with Vance Bourjaily of the influential magazine *Discovery* and has contributed articles to most of the leading journals in his field. Some pieces first published in *Harper's Magazine* formed the basis for *In the Country of the Young*, a defense of "civilized," elitist values against the "pieties and pomposities of the youth movement." A very tall man, blond and blue-eyed, Aldridge has a talent for music and is an excellent speaker.

PRINCIPAL WORKS: *Criticism*—After the Lost Generation, 1951; In Search of Heresy, 1956; Time to Murder and Create, 1966; In the Country of the Young, 1970; The Devil in the Fire: Retrospective Essays on American Literature and Culture, 1951–1971, 1972. *Novel*—The Party at Cranton, 1960. *As editor*—Critiques and Essays on Modern Fiction, 1952; Selected Stories by P. G. Wodehouse, 1958.

ABOUT: Contemporary Authors 2, 1963; Current Biography, 1958; Fuller, E. Man in Modern Fiction, 1958. *Periodicals*—Book Week April 24, 1966; Critic August 1966; New Republic June 4, 1956; Sewanee Review Spring 1959.

***ALEIXANDRE, VICENTE** (April 26, 1898–), Spanish poet, writes (in Spanish): "I was born in Seville, Spain, and I spent most of my childhood in Málaga, the town and Mediterranean coast which seem to matter not a little in my poetry. Mine was a fortunate childhood; far from unhappy, it went by gently and gaily. I lived in close touch with the sea, coming to know well the people of its shores, the fishermen. Later, I made friends with the men of the country. I like to move amongst them when I go back to my land: from the Andalusian peasant I have learnt, and I still learn, more than from any other living man. My father was an engineer, and all too soon he sadly discovered my scant inclination to mathematics. I was not to follow in his steps; I read law at the University of Madrid and simultaneously took a diploma in business management. But the usefulness of those studies was to be short-lived. Many and diverse were the

* ä lāx än′ drā

VICENTE ALEIXANDRE

things I did in those days. I was a journalist with a financial magazine. For several years I lectured on commercial law at the School of Business Studies in Madrid. I worked for a railroad company. And my name first appeared in print under a series of articles in an economics magazine on the Spanish railroad problem.

"But from the age of eighteen I discovered poetry and began to write poems, almost in secrecy. It was a life I led for many years in complete solitude. I never showed anybody a line of verse before I was twenty-seven. Not out of modesty. As I came to understand later, out of fear of being hurt. Fear of adverse judgment, of being undeceived about my own ability and of never again feeling decently free to go on writing. In the meantime, a long and serious illness had taken me, at twenty-five, away from my professional tasks. I lived for two years in the countryside. And when I returned to the city, I brought with me my first book, *Ambito*, and the resolution to alter the course of my life. Ever since, my task has been that of the writer.

"I have lived mainly in Madrid. I have traveled occasionally—because of my weak health, less than I would have liked. In 1936 the Civil War broke out, and found me from its very beginning on the Republican side. My task was not too easy in the early postwar years. My first book had come out in 1928 and the last one, so far, dates from 1968.

"Not all poets know properly what they have intended. It may be that I am not very sure about it myself. But I believe there is something from which my poetry has never moved away; the inspiring principle of the unity of the poet with the whole of creation: the world, man. In my work the poet never feels himself substantially different from sensate matter. In my first period the gaze is directed towards nature, the cosmos, and man appears as part of it. In my second period (from the last part of *Sombra del paraíso*, 1944), man rises to the foreground, and, nature having drawn back, human life occupies the center.

"There is no such thing as wasted experience, and if in my youth I led a life and occupied myself in activities quite unrelated to what was my real vocation, it is possible that my vocation might not have materialized or even appeared without the contrast, and that my mature years, outwardly peaceful, though perhaps not equally so within myself, might have developed along the opposite lines, without my ever writing a word.

"By saying this I do not seek to exalt my destiny; not even to approve of it, and thus put an end to self-doubt over what would in fact have been better for me.

"On the other hand, there is no room for repentance, because among other things the writer, and more so the poet, never repents seriously, whatever he may say to the contrary. Obstinacy is one of the main features of his personality; he is himself the great culprit while being at the same time totally innocent."

Emerging like Lorca and Guillén in the brilliant decade of the 1920s, Vicente Aleixandre has never achieved their international renown. Yet in Spain his poetry has been a major influence since before the Civil War and has been the subject of brilliant exegesis by disciples and critics, notably Carlos Bousoño. No modern Spanish poet has seen his spiritual odyssey plotted with such precision.

Aleixandre's distinctive poetic vision, relentlessly established down the years, derives from a highly developed aesthetic self-awareness, from obvious influences—as disparate as Góngora and Freud—but above all from his personal circumstances. He presents an appearance—a gentle, bronzed, balding, cheerful figure—that belies his legendary ill health. The vigorous verse seems at odds with his physical frailty, as though his passions could be fulfilled only in throbbing sensual poetry, a poetry of convalescence and compensation.

Illness interrupted the composition of *Ambito* (Ambit, 1928), whose rather exclamatory delight in life evinced similarities with Guillén. Yet its traditional verse forms lack Guillén's control and Aleixandre's pursuit of the sensual soon led him to abandon regular meters. In the prose poems of *Pasión de la tierra* (Passion of the Earth, 1935) and the predominantly free verse of *Espadas como labios* (Swords Like Lips, 1932) the characteristic technique emerges, an exuberant concatenation of irrational imagery which testifies to Aleixandre's reading of both Freud and the surrealists. Greeted enthusiastically at the time, these early books have not worn well.

Written while Aleixandre was recovering from a kidney operation, and awarded the National Prize for 1934, *La destrucción o el amor* (Destruction or Love, 1935) reveals the mature poet. In this first period, as he says above, Aleixandre focuses on nature and the cosmos. The normal hierarchies are subverted, and civilized man is seen as debased; the higher creation is represented by animals and the jungle in their violence, by sensual man in his passion. Man finds his unity with the cosmos only when he relinquishes himself, his identity, to an extremity of physical sensation in love or pain or death, and the poet pleads for this unity: "Come, come, death, love . . ./Come, for I would kill or love or die."

Man is still excluded from nature in most of the poems in *Sombra del paraíso* (Shadow of Paradise, 1944), a work of major significance in Spain's postwar poetic revival. The present world is moribund, a vain imitation of a lost Paradise. Aleixandre hears not birds singing in the trees but "memories of birds." The true Paradise is the earth, the "immense mother" into which we shall all rot or, very often, the Málaga of the poet's childhood—a lost Eden of innocence and unselfconscious love.

Discussing this collection, J. M. Cohen has said that "Aleixandre's poems often open on a question, couched in uncertain rhythms, which leads to a development both thematical and musical and concludes with a resolution in more certain meters. The effect is of a poem started in perplexity that attains its own shape as it is written." Noting the similarity of Aleixandre's method to the "automatic" writing of the surrealists, the same critic points out that "the internal organization of alliteration, repetition, and sustained imagery . . . argue a more conscious guidance by the organizing intellect . . . [which is] conservative, even baroque, in its influences. A truer comparison than with Breton is with the Eliot of the *Quartets*."

In the last section of *Sombra del paraíso* certain kinds of people—lovers, peasants, poets, children—earn their place in Aleixandre's cosmos because of the directness of their sensory responses. In his next major collection, *Historia del corazón* (History of the Heart, 1954), "man rises to the foreground." For the first time Aleixandre acknowledges that, separated from the eternal as he may be, man must still live and love in the brief reality allowed to him. Some critics have seen in this change of emphasis a reflection of the new social awareness that developed in Spanish poetry in the late 1940s, and Kessell Schwartz notes that the book's "central theme concerns human solidarity and compassion for the victims of injustice." This is true, but most often the injustice is metaphysical rather than political: "We know whither we go and whence we come. Between two darknesses, a lightning flash." His lovers reach out to one another now, not in destructive frenzy, but in smiling, elegiac tenderness, aware that "it passes, / That love itself passes."

The early vision of an erotic and violent cosmos and the complementary view of man's temporality become fused in Aleixandre's most praised work, *En un vasto dominio* (In a Vast Dominion, 1962). The poetry is now more accessible, even prosaic, conveying a compassionate awareness of the unity of matter—with human relationships mirroring more infinite unions. However, *Poemas de la consumación* (Poems of Consummation, 1968) shows less serenity. A reviewer in the *Times Literary Supplement* found "these poems, for the most part of almost aphoristic brevity . . . among the bleakest which Aleixandre has written. Their treatment of old age and the passing of love is uncompromisingly honest and devoid of any kind of easy consolation. If the poet himself sees his whole work as a constant clarification of means and material . . . these new poems at last break through to the kind of difficult simplicities which are occasionally the reward for a lifetime's major work."

Such discipline had often been lacking in the earlier books. Even so, the importance of Aleixandre's influence inside Spain could hardly be exaggerated. The rebel of the 1930s, whose work was banned in his own country until after World War II, now sits in the Academy. And if the eulogies of Spanish critics are not universally echoed, his work clearly deserves some wider recognition.

The most notable of Aleixandre's few prose works is *Los encuentros* (The Meetings, 1958), a volume of affectionate portraits of his fellow writers. Writers, past and present, are also the subjects of most of the poems in his 1965 collection, *Retratos con nombre* (Portraits with Names).

Aleixandre, who lives in Madrid, spends his summers in Miraflores de la Sierra, a town which he first visited in 1932 during a period of convalescence and which appears in his poetry.

PRINCIPAL WORKS IN ENGLISH TRANSLATION: *Poems in* Barnstone, W. (ed.) Modern European Poetry, 1966; Cohen, J. M. (ed.) Penguin Book of Spanish Verse, 1956; Turnbull, E. L. Contemporary Spanish Poetry, 1945.

ABOUT: Alonso, D. Ensayos sobre poesía española, 1944; Alonso, D. Poetas españoles contemporáneos. 1965; Bousoño, C. La poesía de Vicente Aleixandre, 1969; Cano, J. L. De Machado a Bousoño, 1955; Cohen, J. M. Poetry of This Age, 1966; Díaz-Plaja, G. Poesía lírica castellana, 1948; Ley, C. D. Spanish Poetry Since 1939, 1962; Morris, C. B. A Generation of Spanish Poets, 1969; Salinas, P. Literatura española en el siglo XX, 1941; Schwartz, K. Vicente Aleixandre, 1969; *Periodicals*—Corcel (Valencia) 5–6 1944; Papeles de Son Armadans, 1958; Times Literary Supplement May 17, 1957; July 10, 1969.

ALEPOUDELIS, ODYSSEUS. *See* "ELYTIS," ODYSSEUS

ALFRED, WILLIAM (August 16, 1922–), American dramatist and scholar, was born in New York City, the son of Thomas Alfred, a bricklayer, and of Mary (Bunyan) Alfred, a telephone operator. He is by descent half Welsh and half Irish. He grew up in Brooklyn, where he attended parochial schools, served from 1943 to 1947 in the United States Army, and received his B.A. at Brooklyn College in 1948. The GI Bill of Rights took him on to Harvard University, which gave him his M.A. in 1949 and his Ph.D. in 1954. He studied playwriting at Harvard under Archibald MacLeish and has himself taught there since 1954. He became professor of English in 1963.

In 1946, at the request of a priest at Fordham University, Alfred began an English translation of the *Agamemnon* of Aeschylus. The result was rejected as being excessively "modern," but some updating seemed essential to Alfred if the play was to be viable for contemporary audiences, and with this in mind he continued to work on the theme, completing in the early 1950s a four-act verse play which retains the title and plot of the original but is wholly contemporary in its motivation. *Agamemnon*, published in 1954, seemed to Henry Rago "a fine play, with a few moments of really high distinction"—a work of "solid achievement and . . . intriguing promise."

The first of Alfred's plays to be staged was *Hogan's Goat*, also a verse play but a work very different in its inspiration. Archibald MacLeish said it was "about as close as we have yet come to a truly American theme handled in a truly American manner: which is to say, Irish-American politics practiced in Irish-American Brooklyn and presented in Irish-American cadence, the total effect being not Irish-American at all but universal, a tribute to the Republic." It opened off-Broadway in 1965, was a hit, and later moved to the East 74th Street Theatre for a long run. *Life* called it "a rowdy and tender verse hymn to the Irish who lived in Brooklyn in the 1890s, and . . . the best American play of the year."

In *Agamemnon* Alfred had kept strictly to a meter of five beats to the line; in *Hogan's Goat*, he says, "the meaning comes out in the verse paragraphs. Frequently the meter is neglected for the sake of enforcing the meaning further." Walter Kerr admired its "highly charged verse, verse with a sting in the tail," and Howard Taubman said that Alfred "is not afraid to strike for the vivid image: he can compose lines that shimmer with poetry" and is equally "capable of capturing a humorous or ironic

WILLIAM ALFRED

thought with lusty earthiness." The play fared less well at the 1966 Dublin Theatre Festival, seeming in that production stilted in its rhetoric and overripe in its metaphors. A musical version of the play, *Cry for Us All*, had a brief run on Broadway in 1970.

Alfred is a popular and busy teacher, and *Hogan's Goat* occupied his off-duty hours for nine years. His work has brought him a number of awards, including an Amy Lowell Travelling Fellowship in poetry (1956), a Creative Arts Theatre Award from Brandeis University, and a grant from the National Institute of Arts and Letters. From 1942 to 1944 he served as associate editor of *American Poet*. His translation of *Beowulf* appears in the anthology *Medieval Epics* (1963). According to the New York *Post*, Alfred is a "slightly balding, gentle-voiced but poetically articulate bachelor" who "views his success with utmost modesty." He is a Roman Catholic and a Democrat. "One of the things that I find most distressing nowadays," he has said, "is that there is a division between the theatre of entertainment and the theatre of contemplation." He believes that the solution (which he is no doubt seeking in his own work) is a theatre with "the force and attraction of television," which can yet encompass "the kind of thing that Pinter is doing."

PRINCIPAL WORKS: Agamemnon, 1954; Hogan's Goat, 1966.

ABOUT: Alfred, W. *Preface to* Agamemnon, 1954; Contemporary Authors 15–16, 1966; Who's Who in America, 1970–1971. *Periodicals*—Life April 22, 1966; New York Post January 6, 1966; New York Times November 21, 1965; January 12, 1966; New Yorker December 18, 1965.

ALLEN, WALTER (ERNEST) (February 23, 1911–), English novelist and literary critic, writes: "I was born in Birmingham, England, and educated at King Edward's Grammar School, Aston, and Birmingham University, where I read English. I graduated in 1932 and immediately became a freelance writer, as I have been, except for brief interludes, ever since. I did, in 1934, teach for six months at my old school and, a year later, had the good fortune to be invited to the State University of Iowa as a lecturer in the summer session. I began my first novel, *Innocence Is Drowned*, in Iowa City and back in Birmingham I finished it. As soon as it was accepted in 1937 I went to London, to the young writer's traditional bed-sitting-room in Bloomsbury.

"During the war I worked in the aircraft industry in Bristol and Birmingham. I found it an impossible time to write novels in, but John Lehmann encouraged me to write criticism for his magazine, *Penguin New Writing*. When the war ended, I was invited to review for the *New Statesman*, with which I was closely associated for the next fifteen years, being at various times assistant literary editor and then literary editor.

"I wanted to write from a very early age and at about fourteen became an ardent reader of novels: it seemed natural to hope to write them myself, however odd it may have appeared in the environment in which I was brought up. The only fiction we had at home was a little Scott and Dickens, though there was plenty of economics and philosophy, which indicates my father's interests. Largely self-educated, he was a silversmith; a good watercolour painter and a good amateur violinist; in his early days a passionate Socialist, in his later an equally passionate student of Plato, Spinoza, and Berkeley. He encouraged me as much as a father could. I have tried to draw his likeness in my novel *Three Score and Ten*.

"In the three novels I wrote up to 1940, *Innocence Is Drowned*, *Blind Man's Ditch*, and *Living Space*, I tried to record the conditions, as they seemed to me to be, of English working-class life at the time; but I was also fascinated, as I still am, by what might be called the terror of life. I was much influenced by Gide, Wyndham Lewis and Graham Greene, though I suspect only the last is plainly visible. When I returned to fiction after the war I tried, in *Rogue Elephant*, to write a formal comedy: it strikes me now as being pretty uncomfortable comedy.

"In my more recent novels and in those I hope to write I am after a certain complexity of theme. In *Square Peg* I tried simultaneously to give a picture of factory life in England in 1940, dramatise the changing state of factory ownership and management, evaluate the heritage of Victorianism and its consequences, and investigate the nature of personal responsibility.

WALTER ALLEN

"My ideas about the art of the novel are much less clear-cut and dogmatic than they once were; partly, no doubt, because of the years of reading that went into my critical books, *The English Novel* and *The Modern Novel*. I think now, almost against my will, that the great age of fiction, the great defining period of the novel, was the nineteenth century. I still believe that the novelist has no greater glory than to be, in F. M. Ford's phrase, the historian of his own time. But I am sure that in order to be this he has to be much more.

"I have written fewer novels than I hoped to do when younger. Largely for economic reasons—I have a wife and four children to support—most of my writing has been in criticism and literary journalism. But I value the freedom of the freelance's life. I can live wherever I like, though in England I wouldn't live willingly outside London. The nonfiction books I've written are on themes very close to me. And I have the chance from time to time of living and working in the United States: I was visiting professor at Coe College, Cedar Rapids, Iowa, in 1955-1956 and at Vassar in 1963-1964. This is especially important to me since I am as much interested in American writing as in English and have maintained, ever since I first went there, what I can only describe as a pretty intensive love-hate relationship with America, akin to that which I have with England."

Although his themes and concerns are contemporary ones, Walter Allen is a novelist in the nineteenth century tradition he so admires, an admirable "historian of his own time." The fiction he wrote in the 1930s and 1940s was shapely, observant, and solid in its characterization, but a little unexuberant, short of momentum. Kate O'Brien, reviewing *Rogue Elephant*, said, "He writes in a quiet weather of his own, of low-toned unremitting irony." Allen considers that his "first real novel" was *Square Peg*, a picture of British industry in transition praised as "a taut and gripping story, peopled with remarkably vivid characters"; John Raymond called it "a postscript to *Middlemarch*" and wrote of its author: "On the surface he is a master of that fluent and deceptively colloquial style which several writers have evolved for the purpose of describing technocracy. . . . Further down, we strike a hard, flinty stratum of psychological observation and lower still . . . there is the author's sense of the historical process." *Three Score and Ten*, Allen's portrait of his father, Charles Allen, formed a chronicle of working-class life over a period of seventy years. Paul West thought that here Allen's "solid, matter-of-fact manner" was "given a new depth and exquisitely focused intensity"; another critic prophesied that the book "may well come to be considered a small masterpiece."

As a critic, Allen is thorough, perceptive, and pragmatic. *The English Novel* and *The Modern Novel* discuss novelists rather than "the novel," and crusade for no critical theory, "no esthetic or philosophical imperatives," a fact which displeased some reviewers, but is a source of relief to the innumerable seekers after information and unbiased judgment who have found the books indispensable. The *Times Literary Supplement* called *The Modern Novel* "the rarest kind of popular book, the kind that specialists can read with profit"; and an American reviewer, considering Allen's brief academic residences in the United States, was "astonished at the intimacy and authority with which he handles dozens of American writers."

Allen's studies of individual novelists are equally admired. His critical biography of Arnold Bennett seemed to Frank Swinnerton "the best existing criticism" of that writer; Carlos Baker's only reservation concerning *George Eliot* was that "the reader may find it more fun to read Mr. Allen's account" than to take up the weighty fictions it discusses. In *The Urgent West* Allen turned his attention to the American dream as it has been revealed in American literature, arriving at conclusions about the nation's complex and often contradictory sense of itself which American critics found interesting, perceptive, but familiar.

Walter Allen is a small man, sturdily built, gray-haired, short-sighted, an excellent and vivacious conversationalist. He is a prolific contributor to British and American literary magazines and broadcasts frequently on radio and television. In 1967 he taught at the universities of Kansas and Washington, and since then he has been professor of English in the New University of Ulster, Northern Ireland, apart from a year (1970–1971) as Berg Professor of English at New York University. He is a Fellow of the Royal Society of Literature. Allen has time for few hobbies but says that he "thinks highly of eating and drinking, theatregoing and travel."

PRINCIPAL WORKS: Innocence Is Drowned (novel), 1938; Blind Man's Ditch (novel), 1939; Living Space (novel), 1940; Rogue Elephant (novel), 1946; (as editor) Writers on Writing, 1948 (U.S., The Writer and His Art); Arnold Bennett (criticism), 1948; The Festive Baked-Potato Cart and Other Stories (for children), 1948; Dead Man Over All (novel), 1950 (U.S., Square Peg); Reading a Novel, 1949 (revised edition 1963); Joyce Cary (criticism), 1953; The English Novel; A Short Critical History, 1954; The Novel Today, 1955 (revised edition, 1960); Six Great Novelists: Defoe, Fielding, Scott, Dickens, Stevenson, Conrad (criticism), 1955; All in a Lifetime (novel) (U.S., Three Score and Ten), 1955; Tradition and Dream: The English and American Novel from the Twenties to Our Time (U.S., The Modern Novel in Britain and the United States), 1964; George Eliot (criticism), 1964; The Urgent West (intellectual history), 1969; (as editor) Transatlantic Crossing: American Visitors to Britain and British Visitors to America in the Nineteenth Century, 1971.

ABOUT: Who's Who, 1971. *Periodicals*—Wilson Library Bulletin January 1960.

***ALLSOP, KENNETH** (January 29, 1920–May 23?, 1973), English novelist, critic, and television journalist, wrote some time before his death: "I was born in Yorkshire of solid North Country peasant, but deviant, stock: on my father's side were Derbyshire quarrymen and hellfire Methodist preachers; on my mother's, a blacksmith and a county cricketer. I grew up in the South of England. Curiously, it has been recently, at approaching middle age, that I have increasingly felt the tug of the Northern roots. On occasional visits to the Pennines the sense of affinity grows stronger; I confess to a deepening pleasure that the hamlet of Alsop-en-le-Dale, in Derbyshire, identifies my origins. My father was a civil servant. My education was omitted in prep and private schools of staggering crassness (which I described in *John Bull's Schooldays*). I cannot remember when I did not intend to be a writer. My imaginative life in childhood was spilled upon paper in the guise of a World War One Camel pilot (heavily influenced by American pulp magazines) and in the guise of a juvenile falconer and poacher (heavily influenced by Henry Williamson and Richard Jefferies).

"The purpose was temporarily deflected upon leaving school. My parents regarded journalism (quite accurately) as vaguely unrespectable, and I was steered into a Middle Eastern embassy in London. I rebelled and got myself hired as a trainee

* ôl′ sop

reporter on a local weekly. This I deliriously enjoyed (seeing my words in public print) until plucked away for war service. My two RAF years were dejected boredom: my real existence was in the two novels written in stolen log books but fortunately not published. During two subsequent years in hospital ending in amputation of an injured leg, I wrote nostalgic stories of birds and the countryside, later collected as a book. After the war, it was an improvised scramble back into journalism. I worked as general reporter, press officer, law courts reporter, magazine feature-writer, foreign correspondent, country columnist, jazz columnist, theatre and book critic, film scriptwriter and television interviewer and commentator, while concurrently publishing novels, short stories, literary criticism and social documentary.

"All the above reflects a prevailing melancholy dissatisfaction with my life, the knowledge of being permanently badly organized and fragmented. I am happiest in the Hertfordshire countryside where I live with my wife and three children, where swallows nest in the barns in summer and flocks of golden plover feed on the winter fields; but my job makes me a metropolitan man. Writing is almost always torment, wrung out of black coffee, cigarettes and last-minute desperation; yet if I am not writing I feel like a severed head. My greatest pleasure is to sense that I have succeeded in distilling some additional essence out of common experience; yet the glow quickly fades, and to read something I wrote last week or last year dismays and depresses me. I hanker after a more natural and harmonious life, because writing is by definition a neurotic activity, solitary self-disembowelling; yet I can work only in a state of tension, and I believe that a human being's proper function is to operate at full stretch, to extend his capacity. I think now I would rather have been a sociologist, with a quiet corner in some university department, or a forester, with a quiet corner on some wooded hillside.

"For six years I was literary editor, book critic, and comment columnist for the *Daily Mail*, and simultaneously a resident interviewer with the BBC television programme "Tonight." But the jet had to be turned down. Now I work for the "Twenty-four Hours" programme, and do less hectic reviewing for *The Spectator* and other publications. In both writing and attitude I most value individuality and scepticism. Politically I vote Labour, because this seems the nearest one can get to legislating for decency; yet distrust of authority in action, and the acceleration towards mass organisation, drives me further into a private anarchism. I suppose, now I come to think of it, what I have written, fiction and nonfiction, reveals this interest in the misfit and the maverick, the individual either embattled by society or running counter to society."

KENNETH ALLSOP

Kenneth Allsop called himself "badly organized and fragmented"; he gave no such impression on television where his compact figure, close-cropped graying hair, and hawk-like features were familiar to millions in Britain. He seemed on the contrary as buttoned-down as his shirt collars, graceful, meticulous, and slightly detached in the midst of the medium's atmosphere of well-controlled hysteria. But Allsop's recreations included jazz and bird-watching, and his career and books confirmed the impression that he was, if not "fragmented," a man of at least two worlds.

It is the contemplative world of nature which absorbed him in his first two books: *Adventure Lit Their Star* told the "imaginative yet largely factual" story of a pair of ringed plovers, from their migration to England in 1944 to the seasonal departure of one of them some years later; *The Sun Himself Must Die* contained four of the "nostalgic stories of birds and the countryside" Allsop had written in the hospital. Both books were praised for the vividness of their writing, but not widely noticed, though the first received the John Llewellyn Rhys Memorial Prize.

When these books appeared in 1949, Allsop was working as a reporter for the Press Association. From 1950 to 1955 he was a feature writer for *Picture Post*, and then for two years a reporter and commentator for British Independent Television, simultaneously writing for the *Evening Standard*. He joined the *Daily Mail* in 1957 and the following year published *The Angry Decade*, "a survey of the [British] Cultural Revolt of the 1950s," which is still being reprinted. The book was generally welcomed for the mass of information it collected about the novelists and dramatists of the period. Though it seemed to one reviewer no more than a "careful scissors and paste job," Anthony Powell called it "a splendid book for the connoisseur of literary phases," and Alan Brien wrote: "Not for the first time, it may be the journalist and not the scholar who has correctly timed the pulse of his own age."

Of Allsop's other books, the best known (and furthest removed from the world of ringed plovers) is his Balzacian study *The Bootleggers and Their Era*, which traces the rise and fall of Al Capone and the Chicago mobs in a series of studies of the neighborhoods from which they emerged. It reflected Allsop's delight in Americana, which derived from his study of jazz, and was widely and almost unanimously admired for coming to grips with the social conditions which produced the gangs, as well as for its wit, intelligence, and "sharply pictorial" style. The author's "interest in the misfit and the maverick" was equally evident in *Hard Travellin'*, his "briskly readable" history of the American hobo.

After the demise of the "Twenty-four Hours" program in 1972, Allsop divided his time between a number of documentary television programs and series, including one devoted to ecology. He moved to West Dorset in 1972, and wrote a lyrical account of the landscape and wild life of the area, *In the Country*. Allsop became rector of the University of Edinburgh in 1968 and the same year was elected a visiting research fellow of Merton College, Oxford. He became an M.A. of Oxford University (with special status) in 1969.

Allsop was found dead of an overdose of barbiturates on May 23, 1973; an open verdict was recorded at the coroner's inquest. He was married in 1942 to Betty Ashton Creak and had two sons and a daughter.

PRINCIPAL WORKS: Adventure Lit Their Star, 1949; The Sun Himself Must Die (stories), 1949; Silver Flame (for children), 1950; The Daybreak Edition, 1951; Leopard-Paw Orchid, 1954; Last Voyages of the Mayflower (for children), 1955; The Angry Decade, 1958; Rare Bird, 1958; The Bootleggers (U.S., The Bootleggers and Their Era), 1961; Scan, 1965; Hard Travellin', 1968; In the Country, 1972.

ABOUT: Contemporary Authors, 3, 1963; Inglis, B. (ed.) John Bull's Schooldays, 1961; Who's Who, 1972. *Periodicals*—Sunday Times May 27, 1973; Times (London) May 25, 1973; May 31. 1973.

ALMEDINGEN, E. M. (MARTHA EDITH VON ALMEDINGEN) (July 21, 1898–March 5 1971), Russian-born novelist, historian, memoirist, and poet, wrote: "I was born in St. Petersburg in 1898, the seventh child of a seventh son. I did not go to school until I was fifteen, and in 1916 entered the University where I read Mediaeval History. College work was interrupted in 1921 by famine relief work. In the end, I got typhus and in 1922 they let me have six months' sick leave. The British Trade Mission in Moscow got me a foreign passport. After about a year in Italy, I came to England —with eighteen pence in my pocket, and people wanted me to write on Russia but, having written one small book whilst still in Rome, I found I had nothing to say. The five and a half years of life under the Soviet were still too close in the mind to be written about from an objective angle. The Revolution could not ruin my family: we had been too poor and possessed neither estates nor fabulous jewellery. None the less, the upheaval had struck us in more ways than one, and for many years I preferred not to write about it. I came to England to write, and what ability I may have was certainly inherited rather than acquired. My great aunt, Catherine Almedingen, was virtually a pioneer in the field of children's literature in Russia. On my mother's side, I am the granddaughter of a *lettré*, Serge de Poltoratzky, whose biography is now being written by a scholar in Leningrad. My English grandmother had Robert Southey among her cousins, and my great-grandmother traced her descent from Edmund Spenser.

"It was a very long struggle—picking up odd guineas by writing little articles on every conceivable subject—from Finnish flora to Caucasian jewellery. I lived in London for eleven years—but my first book was not published until 1937 when I was living in the country. My third book, again a novel, *She Married Pushkin*, was the *Evening Standard* Book of the Month for August 1939, and my friendship with the Howard Springs dates from that year. The first 'break' came in 1941 when *Tomorrow Will Come* was awarded the Atlantic prize as the best nonfiction book of the year. In 1943, a novel, *Frossia*, went into eight editions and was later translated into several languages. I have known and loved the West Country ever since my arrival in England in 1923; I am now the owner of an old cottage standing at the head of a quiet valley. There is a trout stream and several little rills thread through the grounds. I have two friends living with me.

"My work being everything to me, I have never let it slip into a routine. Whole days may be spent without putting pen to paper—just in research. I have written novels, poetry, and historical studies. One of the latter, *An Unbroken Unity*, published in 1964, was written at the request of the late Queen Louise of Sweden. It is the study of her aunt, Grand-Duchess Serge of Russia, who was murdered in 1918.

"Critics have been more than generous to me. Personally, I feel I must stop writing for good the day I find myself satisfied with anything."

Miss Almedingen's family, hereditary counts of

the Holy Roman Empire, went from Russia to Austria in 1793. Her father, of Danish and Austrian parentage, was a professor of chemistry; her mother was half English and half Russian. Her parents were separated, and her mother had to support the family by giving private lessons. Miss Almedingen, "a lonely and studious child," was educated at home until 1913, then at Xenia Nobility College. She entered St. Petersburg University a year before the Bolshevik Revolution, earned her doctorate with a paper entitled "The Medieval Idea of Time," and in 1920 joined the university's faculty as a lecturer in English Medieval History and Literature. She made her way to England in 1923, as she says, and became a British subject in 1930. She published many articles and stories and some pamphlets and monographs in the early 1920s and 1930s, her first novel in 1937, and thereafter an unbroken stream of books in many forms, most of them about Russia.

Her four volumes of autobiography appeared between 1941 and 1952. They are remarkable for their dispassionate view of the Revolution and its effects, their apt portraits, and their unfailing optimism. "The future will picture our age through books like this, and not through the official records," wrote Storm Jameson of *Tomorrow Will Come.*

Frossia, the first of Miss Almedingen's novels to enjoy outstanding success, has been reprinted many times. It is about a girl left alone during the civil war—a story "real, convincing and exciting," and "as Russian in spirit as any piece of writing can be." Miss Almedingen excelled in natural description and in sharp and compassionate realization of character; she said: "I can't write a novel unless I become the people I write about." Even reviewers who find her novels old-fashioned admit that they are in spite of themselves enthralled by her "compelling professionalism."

Most notable among her historical studies are her biographies of the Romanovs, which are "mainly concerned with the dynasty in its personal and intimate aspect." They draw more on published work than on original scholarship, but are widely read and admired as "life-like and finely shaded" portraits of their extraordinary subjects. Miss Almedingen also published poems and a number of gentle and sensitive books for children, including several about members of her own family—imaginative reconstructions based on diaries, letters, and the like. *Young Mark* is about her great-great-grandfather, a Ukrainian peasant boy who made an adventurous journey to St. Petersburg in the eighteenth century to seek his fortune as a singer. *Fanny* deals with the author's aunt, Frances Hermione de Poltoratzky (1850–1916) and *Ellen* with her grandmother, who is also the subject of a biography for adults. *Katia* is a delightful and very skillful adaptation of *The Story of a Little Girl*, her great-aunt Catherine's famous memoir of her childhood in nineteenth century Russia. All of these books can be (and are) read by adults as well as children, and some critics consider them the most significant part of the author's large output.

E. M. ALMEDINGEN

Miss Almedingen was a lecturer in Russian Literature at Oxford University in 1951, and was elected a Fellow of the Royal Society of Literature the same year. "Except for a hundred and fifty per cent loathing of communism," she had no political commitments, but she believed firmly that the future sanity of the world depended upon the closest possible ties between the English-speaking peoples, that "a living language . . . is a weapon stronger than any nuclear missiles." Miss Almedingen could write without difficulty "in crowded trains, on top of London buses, in noisy tearooms." She was nevertheless a careful craftsman, sometimes revising a page ten times over. She was active as a lecturer and appeared occasionally on radio and television.

PRINCIPAL WORKS: The English Pope (Adrian IV), 1925; Young Catherine (novel), 1937; Lion of the North, Charles XII, King of Sweden (novel), 1938; Rus (poem), 1939; Tomorrow Will Come (autobiography), 1941; Frossia (novel), 1943; Dasha (novel), 1945; Dom Bernard Clements (biography), 1945; The Almond Tree (autobiography), 1947; The Inmost Heart (novel) (U.S., Golden Sequence), 1949; Within the Harbor (autobiography), 1950; Late Arrival (autobiography), 1952; Flame on the Water (novel), 1952; The Rock (novel), 1953; Ground Corn (novel), 1955; The Fair Haven (novel), 1956; Stephen's Light (novel), 1956; The Scarlet Goose (novel), 1957; A Life of Many Colours: The Story of Grandmother Ellen (U.S., A Very Far Country), 1958; So Dark a Stream: A Study of the Emperor Paul I of Russia, 1754–

1801, 1959; The Little Stairway (novel) (U.S., Winter in the Heart), 1960; Catherine Empress of Russia, 1961; Dark Splendor (novel), 1961; The Empress Alexandra, 1872–1918: A Study, 1961; The Emperor Alexander II: A Study, 1962; Russian Folk and Fairy Tales, 1963; Catherine the Great, 1963; The Knights of the Golden Table, 1963; The Emperor Alexander I, 1964; An Unbroken Unity: A Memoir of Grand-Duchess Serge of Russia, 1864–1918, 1964; The Ladies of St. Hedwig's (novel), 1965; The Unnamed Stream, and Other Poems, 1965; Little Katia (U.S., Katia, for children), 1966; The Romanovs: Three Centuries of an Ill-Fated Dynasty, 1966; Francis of Assisi, 1967; Young Mark (for children), 1967; My St. Petersburg (for children), 1970; Fanny (for children), 1970; Ellen (for children), 1970.
ABOUT: Contemporary Authors 2, 1963; Who's Who, 1971.

***ALSOP, JOSEPH W(RIGHT JR.)** (October 11, 1910–), American journalist and political writer, was born in Avon, Connecticut, one of the four children of Joseph W. Alsop Sr., a prosperous tobacco farmer and insurance executive. His mother, Corinne Douglas (Robinson) Alsop, was a first cousin of Mrs. Eleanor Roosevelt and a sixth cousin of President Franklin D. Roosevelt. Both of his parents were active in Republican politics and served in the Connecticut legislature. Joseph Alsop, who grew up on the family farm, took an early interest in books and was drawn equally to ancient history and the works of such contemporary writers as James Joyce, Marcel Proust, and Gertrude Stein. Alexander Woollcott once referred to him as "the only young American I have ever met who is truly educated."

Graduating in 1928 from the Groton School in Massachusetts, Alsop entered Harvard University, where he studied literature, philosophy, and the arts. He received his B.A. degree *magna cum laude* in 1932. Although he had no strong ambition to enter journalism, he did so upon the advice of his parents and from 1932 to 1935 was a reporter in the city room of the New York *Herald Tribune*. In 1936 Alsop was promoted to the newspaper's Washington bureau. In collaboration with Robert E. Kintner, Alsop wrote a column called "The Capitol Parade," which was syndicated by the North American Newspaper Alliance to some seventy-five newspapers from 1937 to 1940. The column was at first devoted mainly to domestic politics, but as the threat from Nazi Germany increased, the authors became more and more concerned with foreign affairs. They urged a vigorous anti-Axis policy and were early advocates of American lend-lease aid to Allied nations. It was "Capitol Parade" which established Alsop as a top-ranking news commentator.

His first book, *The 168 Days* (1938), written with Turner Catledge (later executive editor of the New York *Times*), is an account of the Supreme Court crisis in 1937, when President Roosevelt decided to enlarge the court. *Men Around the President* (1938), on which Alsop collaborated with Robert Kintner, is a study of President Roosevelt's inner circle of advisers. The book was described as a "vibrant action story" that was "fair without being stilted." Alsop and Kintner again collaborated on the best-selling *American White Paper* (1940), a sympathetic account of the Roosevelt Administration's semi-secret foreign policy in the period that followed the Munich crisis of 1938 and a criticism of isolationist opponents of the Administration.

Alsop's collaboration with Kintner ended in 1940, when Alsop joined the United States Navy as a lieutenant and was sent to India. In August 1941, seeking a more challenging assignment, he transferred to the American volunteer air force in China as an aide to General Claire L. Chennault. At the time of the United States entry into World War II, Alsop was in Hong Kong, where he was captured by the Japanese. In June 1942 he was repatriated in a prisoner exchange. He returned to China as a civilian official with the lend-lease mission in December 1942 and eventually became Chennault's unofficial chief of staff and ambassador to Chungking, while holding the rank of an air force captain. This experience convinced Alsop that previously he "had been writing pure drivel," and he resolved not to report any more foreign news without first-hand information. For his wartime service, Alsop received the Legion of Merit and the Chinese Order of the Cloud Banner.

In January 1946 Joseph Alsop began his collaboration with his younger brother Stewart Alsop in writing the column "Matter of Fact," which was syndicated by the New York *Herald Tribune* and eventually appeared four times a week in some two hundred newspapers. The column, one of the most highly rated and influential in the United States, featured reporting and commentary on political and military affairs, drawing on its authors' sources of information in the highest levels of government and the defense establishment. Described as "Old Testament prophets" and "disaster experts," the Alsops became noted for their pessimistic predictions, many of which—including that of the 1948 Communist coup in Czechoslovakia—proved sadly accurate.

In view of the growing challenge from the Soviet bloc, the Alsops favored a strong military establishment, including an intercontinental ballistic missile system, and advocated a firm policy toward Communist China. On the other hand, they came to the defense of persons whom they believed to be unjustly accused of subversive activities, and in the process occasionally clashed with congressional committees. Their book *We Accuse! The Story of the Miscarriage of Justice in the Case of J. Robert*

* ôl′ sup

Oppenheimer (1954) is a well-documented defense of the nuclear scientist against charges that he was a security risk. Consequently, while Communist sources branded them "Fascist warmongers" and "lackeys of Wall Street," Senator Joseph R. McCarthy referred to them as "left-wing bleeding hearts."

While Joseph Alsop traveled all over the world to the scenes of news events, Stewart Alsop generally remained close to Washington. The brothers collaborated on the book *The Reporter's Trade* (1958), which includes a collection of their columns of the previous twelve years, as well as a discussion of the journalist's profession and his role in relation to government. August Heckscher, writing in the *Herald Tribune*, called the book "a sober, highly responsible report to the public." The Alsop brothers' partnership came to an end in 1958, when Stewart Alsop became a contributing editor of the *Saturday Evening Post*. Since that time, Joseph Alsop has written the "Matter of Fact" column by himself. After the demise of the *Herald Tribune* in 1965 and of its successor, the *World Journal Tribune*, in the following year, Alsop's column has been syndicated by the Washington *Post*. By 1967, according to one estimate, it reached forty million readers.

It may be that some of Alsop's insights into current affairs, as well as some of his pessimism, derive from his lifelong study of ancient civilizations. In his book *From the Silent Earth*, he reversed the process, applying the techniques of the political analyst to the cloudy history of the Greek Bronze Age. The result was widely praised for its penetrating insights, its elegant and stimulating prose, and as "a moving account of the shadowy drama of an early civilization that ended in destruction and darkness."

Alsop was married in 1961 to Mrs. Susan Patten. They live in the Georgetown section of Washington, in a house designed for Alsop in 1949, and entertain among others former Defense Secretary McNamara. (Robert Kennedy was another notable guest.) The journalist is five feet nine inches tall and maintains his weight at 175 pounds, which cannot be easy since he is known to enjoy good food as much as he does elegant clothes. Alsop has been described as aggressive, arrogant, and gregarious, and, more kindly, as a "Renaissance man steeped in Chinese philosophy, in architecture, and in archeology." Alsop still travels far and often, generally in very considerable comfort. In recent years, Alsop has alienated some of his former admirers (but gained others) by his persistent championship of America's role in Vietnam.

PRINCIPAL WORKS: (with Turner Catledge) The 168 Days, 1938; (with Robert E. Kintner) Men Around the President, 1939; (with Robert E. Kintner) American White Paper, 1940; (with Stewart Alsop) We Accuse! 1954; (with Stewart Alsop) The Reporter's Trade, 1958; From the Silent Earth, 1964.

JOSEPH W. ALSOP

ABOUT: Current Biography, 1952; Who's Who in America, 1970–1971. *Periodicals*—Harper's Magazine June 1968; Nation January 2, 1954; Newsweek November 11, 1957; December 18, 1961; Reporter October 21, 1954; Time October 27, 1958.

ALTERMAN, NATHAN (1910–), Israeli poet and dramatist, is regarded as Israel's first *sabra* (native) poet, though he was born and spent his childhood in Warsaw. His father, a well-known Hebrew educator, emigrated with his family to Palestine in 1925, becoming superintendent of schools in Tel Aviv, where Alterman completed his secondary education at the Herzlia Gymnasium. His parents sent him to study agriculture at the University of Nancy, in France, but he spent a great deal of his time reading French literature instead and soon began to write.

His first poems were published in 1931, shortly after his return to Tel Aviv, in *Ketuvim*, the literary journal edited by Eliezer Steinman and Abraham Shlonsky. Alterman joined Shlonsky's literary group, Yahdav, devoted to making poetry out of the developing colloquial Hebrew and the changing cadences of popular speech. Soon he became editor of his own journal, *Turim*, and between 1934 and 1943 he wrote a column under the name of Agav for the daily newspaper *Haaretz*.

Alterman's first volume of poetry, *Kochavim Bahutz* (There Are Stars Outside, 1938), won him immediate recognition. In the words of Ruth Finer Mintz, the book "enchanted Israeli youth with its colorful fantasy." Echoing the simple rhythms of English ballad writers and French troubadours, these vagabond poems celebrated the

NATHAN ALTERMAN

beauty of nature and the excitement of the open road "at whose end is longing" but drew a necessary tension from certain darker images. There are autumnal tones and gallows landscapes in these poems that recall Villon, and dialogues between the living and the dead, whose shades "walk among the living in the hearts of those they love." The last theme is one that recurs repeatedly in Alterman's work.

This dark note is pervasive in *Simhat Aniyim* (Joy of the Poor, 1941), inspired by the outbreak of war. These seven cycles of songs form a single dramatic structure in which a dead poet addresses his wife, trapped in a besieged city. In this place where "the living cannot save the living," death is not an end but a deliverance: "there is no end to strength, my daughter / only the body is smashed like a shard." Out of the Gothic imagery of nightmare, Alterman fashions an urgently contemporary legend of Hitler's Europe. *Shirei Makot Mitsrayim* (1943), similarly, draws a contemporary and indeed universal statement from the biblical story of the plagues of Egypt. In these dialogues between a father and his dying firstborn, the child's death is conceived not as a punishment but as a ceremonial sacrifice, an act of grace.

By the end of World War II Alterman was recognized as a major poet, and he subsequently became the mentor of a group of young poets who gathered around him at his favorite café in Tel Aviv. With the establishment of the state of Israel, Alterman found himself in sympathy with the center Socialist party that headed the government. In 1948 he began to express his views in "The Seventh Column," a regular series of feuilletons and poems in the newspaper *Davar*. His flair for caustic political comment in verse has made "The Seventh Column" something of a national institution, and its contents have been published periodically in book form for many years.

Ir Hayona (City of the Dove), the major collection of poems published in 1957, develops the themes of alienation and return. The city where "no man living can sit under his vine and no man dead can lie under his stone" becomes the symbol of Europe and of humanity's materialist prison. Israel offers freedom and hope; its ancient and renascent literature, surviving chaos and destruction, offers both continuity and renewal.

In recent years Alterman has turned to the theatre, and his best-known plays include *Kinneret, Kinneret* (1962), *The Inn of the Winds* (1963), *The Judgment of Pythagoras* (1965), and *Esther the Queen* (1966). He himself has written the lyrics for a musical version of the latter. Alterman has also been active as a translator, preparing Hebrew versions of Shakespeare's *Merry Wives of Windsor*, Racine's *Phèdre*, Molière's *Le Malade imaginaire*, and Percy's *Reliques of Ancient English Poetry*.

Among a new generation of young poets concerned with their own innovations, some, like Nathan Zach, have found Alterman's adherence to traditional rhymed forms limiting and irrelevant. Most critics however give Alterman an important place in contemporary Hebrew poetry. By extending the ballad form into narratives of great dramatic intensity and lyric power, he has developed a unique poetry, creating a new mythology out of the tragic history of the times.

PRINCIPAL WORKS IN ENGLISH TRANSLATION: *Poems in* Birman, A. An Anthology of Modern Hebrew Poetry, 1968; Burnshaw, S. and others (eds.) The Modern Hebrew Poem Itself, 1965; Mintz, R. F. (ed. and translator), Modern Hebrew Poetry, 1966; Penueli, S. Y. and A. Ukhmani, Anthology of Modern Hebrew Poetry, 1966.

ABOUT: *Anthologies listed above. Periodicals*—Molad May–June 1962; Orot June 1966.

***ALVAREZ, A(LFRED)** (August 5, 1929–), British poet and critic, writes: "I was born into the solid Anglo-Jewish middle class. The family story is that my father's side arrived in London—ultimately from Spain—in sixteen-something-or-other; my mother's lot came about 1700. But that is just family rumour; I have never checked it.

"Certainly, they were right in the middle of the middle class, nerve-racked with respectability, but with a saving passion for music. My father cared for little else, a man of great charm but a disaster in business. I was delicate as a child, precocious and spoilt, the youngest of three children and the only son. I was given the standard 'assimilated' educa-

* al vä′ rez

tion: London prep school, boarding public school (Oundle), and Oxford. But it didn't quite work out as it should. The war started when I was just ten and we stayed in London during the Blitz. Before that I had been a diligent little schoolboy, but the air raids gave me a taste for chaos and excitement which I have never lost. Even rock climbing, which became an obsession later, and the willed uncertainties of life as a free-lance writer are no real substitute for that first blind excitement.

"All this played havoc with my education. At Oundle I was constantly feuding with the authorities and, although I was a good examination-passer, it was not until I went to Oxford that I really began to work seriously. At school I had vaguely wanted to be a scientist but my talents were obviously elsewhere, and I turned properly to literature when I was sixteen, writing bad poems and reading furiously. (Perhaps the scientific bias remains: for pleasure now I invariably read nonfiction.) At Oxford I worked hard, took a First, then stayed on with a research scholarship from my college, Corpus Christi, and the Goldsmiths' Company. At that time I also gave my first broadcast talk on the BBC Third Programme and began to publish in little magazines.

"In 1953 I went to the States on a Procter Visiting Fellowship at Princeton. This seems to have been crucial for me. I met there R. P. Blackmur and V. S. Pritchett, both of whom, in different ways, encouraged, influenced and helped me. But beyond that was a new freedom: it is, after all, difficult to be Jewish in England; however 'English' your upbringing, there is always a kind of strain and isolation. On the American East Coast, however, everyone seemed to be Jewish. I found I could relax; I also found I could write freely.

"In 1954 I went back to Oxford for another year's research and teaching. But I could no longer take it. In 1955 Blackmur got me a grant from the Rockefeller Foundation to return to the States and write a book on modern poetry. I spent half the year in Harvard, but found it too like Oxford for comfort. So I went out to New Mexico, which is as near an ideal landscape as I have found. Out there I met Frieda Lawrence; when I returned to England I met her grandaughter; we were married a couple of months later.

"That decided me against returning to Oxford, although there was a job in the offing. We scratched along for a year, very poor, living from place to place on what I could earn by writing for *The Observer*, *The New Statesman*, the BBC, and editing—for reasons I could never discover—*The Journal of Education*. In 1957 Blackmur invited me back to Princeton to give the Gauss Seminars in Criticism. Out of them came *The School of Donne*. My son Adam was born there in 1958.

A. ALVAREZ

"After a couple more years of free-lance work in London—among other things, I was drama critic of *The New Statesman*—I returned to the States for a term as a Visiting Professor at Brandeis. Around this time, my marriage began to break up. My wife and I separated in the summer of 1961 and were divorced the following year. I wrote a series of poems about all this which won the Vachel Lindsay Prize from *Poetry* (*Chicago*). In 1962 Penguin published my anthology *The New Poetry*. Meanwhile, for two or three years I was on the loose. Commissioned by the BBC, I drifted round Eastern Europe and back, briefly, to the States. Out of this came another book, *Under Pressure*. I left *The New Statesman* and began writing for *The Spectator*. I also spent a great deal of time and energy rock climbing, until, in the summer of 1964, I had a very close call in the Dolomites. This seemed to burn out some of my restlessness—though it didn't stop me climbing. I also still find it essential to make periodic sorties across the Atlantic: I work best there, and find myself more stimulated. I remarried in 1966.

"Pure literary criticism no longer much interests me. I want to try something more personal and inclusive—though what, precisely, I am still not sure. Mercifully, there are plenty of impure forms left."

Alvarez, the most influential of the younger English critics of contemporary poetry, summarized his views in the *Times Literary Supplement* for March 23, 1967. He argues that contemporary avant-garde writing, where there is any, is "largely a rewrite of that of fifty years ago . . . essentially reactionary, harmless." The arts now, he says, go through styles "as quickly as we go through socks," so that there seem no styles at all, only fashions and mannerisms. This, he believes, is because style used to be a product of shared beliefs —aesthetic, religious, or social—and all these have gone. Each artist must invent his own style, which makes his job "proportionately more difficult, tentative, compromising, risky. The reason is simple: where anything goes, a major test of originality is not a question of form but of psychic exploration, not of artifact but of the artist's identity." Therefore Alvarez is impatient with the "inert traditionalism" he sees in England, the aestheticism he finds in much American writing. He puts his faith in what he calls Extremism and attributes to Robert Lowell and his disciples. Alvarez' Extremist artist is one who has the technical skill and the personal courage to pursue "his insights to the edge of breakdown and then beyond it" until mania and hallucination "become as urgent and as commonplace as Beauty, Truth, Nature, and the Soul were to the Romantics." Now that "the traditional basis of the arts has smashed . . . internal confusion transmuted into new kinds of artistic order becomes the most possible form of coherence."

This vigorous, radical, and sometimes limiting view was reflected, more or less, in *The New Poetry*, an occasionally idiosyncratic but influential anthology which remains "the best available introduction to postwar developments" in English verse; in Alvarez' famous poetry reviews in *The Observer*; and in *The Shaping Spirit*, a much discussed and generally admired discussion of modernism in English and American poetry. "Beyond All This Fiddle," the controversial *TLS* article mentioned above, gave its title to a volume of essays on modernism, on "the literature of holocaust," and on a variety of English, East European, and American writers from Dryden and Keats to Lowell, Susan Sontag, Zbigniew Herbert, and Jan Kott. Extremist art is also a principal theme of *The Savage God*, Alvarez' "imaginative and humane" study of suicide and of the relationship between suicide and literature, which includes an account of the author's own attempt to kill himself in 1961.

Alvarez, himself a poet of some ability, is admired as a practicing critic even by those who reject his theories. He is a subjective critic, who approaches each poet, or even each poem, on its own terms, and writes with "the lucidity, the ease and the conviction of one who has devoted himself full-time and full-mind to the language of poetry." Some of his colleagues regard him as no more than a brilliant literary journalist, with no coherent critical philosophy, but Walter Allen believes that he has successfully adopted the critical formula recommended by T. S. Eliot: "The only method is to be very intelligent."

The author has a son by his 1956 marriage to Ursula Barr, and a son and a daughter by his 1966 marriage to Anne Adams. He is advisory editor of the Penguin Modern European Poets series.

Alvarez has described his stint as drama critic of *The New Statesman* as the worst two years of his life, but he is addicted to the movies, "the art of utter illusion, as purgative as a successful psychoanalysis, and far, far cheaper." He goes rock climbing regularly and has attributed to the new generation of climbers qualities which are also those he seeks in the work of contemporary poets. They have, he says, "a kind of seriousness, unromantic, hard-minded and yet, at the same time, tentative, as though searching for something: they are, I think, trying to test their own limits and resources in extreme situations." When they succeed "to the edge of the impossible" it is "a triumph, above all, of personality."

PRINCIPAL WORKS: The Shaping Spirit (U.S., Stewards of Excellence), 1958; The School of Donne, 1961; (as editor) The New Poetry, 1962; Under Pressure, 1965; Beyond All This Fiddle: Essays, 1955–1967, 1968; Lost (poems), 1968; Apparition: Poems (with paintings by Charles Blackman), 1971; The Savage God: A Study of Suicide, 1971; (with Roy Fuller and Anthony Thwaite) Penguin Modern Poets 18, 1971; Samuel Beckett, 1973.

ABOUT: Allott, K. (ed.) The Penguin Book of Contemporary Verse, 1962; Fraser, G. S. The Modern Writer and His World, 1964; Who's Who, 1972.

***ALVARO, CORRADO** (April 15, 1895–June 11, 1956), Italian novelist, short story writer, poet, and journalist, was born in San Luca, Calabria, a starkly beautiful and wretchedly poor mountainous region at the tip of the Italian boot. The son of a schoolteacher, he was educated in Naples and Rome and published his precocious first book of poems in 1911, when he was sixteen. Alvaro served during World War I as an infantry officer and in 1916 he was wounded and his face was permanently scarred. Another volume of verse, *Poesie grigioverdi* (Gray-green Poetry, 1917), deals mainly with his war experiences, as does one of his novels *Vent'anni* (Twenty Years Old, 1930).

After graduating in literature and philosophy from the University of Milan, Alvaro began his career as a journalist with the dailies *Il Corriere della Sera* and *Il Mondo*, As long as he could he openly supported the anti-Fascist cause, but he was forced to abandon political activity after the suppression of *Il Mondo* in the mid-1920s. Thereafter, as a foreign correspondent, mainly for *La Stampa*, he visited France, Germany, Russia, Greece, and the Middle East, sending back to Italy articles later

* äl vä' rō

collected in two books, *Viaggio in Turchia* (Travels in Turkey, 1932) and *I maestri del diluvio* (The Masters of the Deluge, 1935), an account of his travels in Soviet Russia. Many of these essays were attempts to open the eyes of his countrymen to the political realities from which fascism sought to insulate them. Two excellent travel books about Italy, *Calabria* and *Itinerario italiano*, also appeared during the 1930s.

Meanwhile, Alvaro had been making a separate reputation as the author of some more or less experimental novels and short stories. These revealed an interest in Freudian psychology and combined a naturalistic style with bizarre subject matter in a way reminiscent of the novels of Massimo Bontempelli. Alvaro's first novel of any importance was *L'uomo nel labirinto* (Man in the Labyrinth, 1922).

There followed a phase in which Alvaro, while retaining his interest in psychology, abandoned his youthful experiments and produced a number of stories and novellas about Calabria in a manner which has been described as "lyric regionalism." Most of his best work belongs to this period, including what is generally regarded as his masterpiece, *Gente in Aspromonte* (Folk in Aspromonte, 1930). This short novel tells the painfully familiar story of a gentle Calabrian youth driven to banditry by his family's brutally unjust landlord. Alvaro's absolute understanding of the people of the Italian South, his profound sympathy with their stubborn aspirations, and the tightly controlled lyricism of his prose, gave the book something of the quality of a myth. What Verga had done for the Sicilian poor and D'Annunzio for the people of the Abruzzi, Alvaro did for his fellow Calabrians, imposing these forgotten people on the Italian conscience. Indeed more than one critic was reminded of Verga by the intensity and compression of Alvaro's style and the underlying sense of tragedy. In 1930 *Gente in Aspromonte* received *La Stampa*'s prize as the best novel of the year, and it is still widely recognized as one of the few classics of contemporary Italian fiction. It was translated thirty years later as *Revolt in Aspromonte* and universally praised by American critics for its economy, power, and compassion.

Some readers of *Gente in Aspromonte* detected in it allegorical overtones and suggested that its concerns actually extended beyond the social and spiritual problems of feudal Calabria, embracing also a symbolic treatment of some crisis in the author's own life, or perhaps of the larger tragedy of Italy under fascism. At any rate this latter theme engaged Alvaro in another notable novel, *L'uomo è forte* (1938, translated as *Man Is Strong*). It is about a young engineer who, after some years in a democracy, returns to his own country, now a

CORRADO ALVARO

dictatorship in which love, dignity, and humanity are progressively corrupted by fear.

Alvaro here returned to the manner of his early experimental works to evoke an insubstantial nightmare country inhabited by shadows who are distorted by fear as if they were reflected in water. This vagueness tricked the Fascist censors, who allowed the book's publication under the impression that Alvaro's attack on fascism was an attack on communism. It was an immensely courageous book for an Italian to write in 1938. Whether it was also a good book is a matter of opinion. Some critics found the characters mere symbols, without life. Others thought it penetrating in its psychology and wholly successful in delineating a Kafkaesque dream world dominated by blind, irrational menace. Jerome D. Ross, reviewing the American version in 1948, called it "an imaginative analysis, unique and certainly sincere, of man's soul and spirit in modern bondage."

After the fall of fascism, Alvaro resumed his journalistic career and was a regular contributor to *Risorgimento Liberale* and the new weekly *Il Mondo*, for which he wrote film and drama criticism. The work he published in the 1940s and 1950s included new collections of poems and short stories, plays, memoirs, and a cycle of more or less autobiographical novels of which the most notable was *L'età breve* (Brief Era, 1946). In these novels, Alvaro "tried to clarify to himself all the problems facing an educated and urbanized Southerner, torn between the yearning for intellectual and sexual freedom . . . and the longing for his native land."

Alvaro was a short, stocky man, and a very modest one. He died in 1956, one of the most respected men of letters in Italy. "His life, no less than his works," wrote Thomas G. Bergin, "had reflected qualities of integrity and dedication which had brought him the affection and admiration of his fellow writers and intellectuals—a group not given normally to charitable judgments. Yet the feeling was also widespread that, viewed simply as a creative artist, Alvaro had done his best work in his early years."

PRINCIPAL WORKS IN ENGLISH TRANSLATION: Man Is Strong, 1948; Revolt in Aspromonte, 1962. *Stories*—Delicate, *in* Life and Letters August 1949, and The Wedding Journey, *in* Slonim, M. (ed.) Modern Italian Short Stories, 1954; Atlantic December 1958. *Play*—The Long Night of Medea, *in* Plays for a New Theater, 1966. *Article*—Literature and the Italian South, *in* Italian Quarterly Summer 1957.

ABOUT: Curley, D. N. and Curley, A. (eds.) Modern Romance Literatures (A Library of Literary Criticism), 1967; Dizionario enciclopedico della letteratura italiana, 1966; Dizionario universale della letteratura contemporanea, 1959; Letteratura italiana: i contemporanei, 1963; Penguin Companion to Literature 2, 1969; Riccio, P. M. Italian Authors of Today, 1938; Smith, H. (ed.) Columbia Dictionary of Modern European Literature, 1947. *Periodicals*—Annales politiques et littéraires March 10, 1935; Mercure de France February 1952; Revue des Deux Mondes June 15, 1932; Saturday Review September 4, 1948; Times (London) July 16, 1956.

***AMADO, JORGE** (August 10, 1912–), Brazilian novelist, writes (in Portuguese): "I was born on a cacao plantation in Southern Bahia, where I was brought up, the son of an immigrant from Sergipe, a neighboring state of Bahia in Northeastern Brazil. I received my secondary education in Salvador, the capital of Bahia, and during the summer holidays I returned to work on the plantation. From 1930, when I settled in Rio, I began my career in journalism and literature. My first book, *O País do Carnaval*, which aroused considerable interest on the part of the critics, was published when I was nineteen. I worked for some time as the head of the publicity department of an important publishing house and all my life I have written for newspapers and periodicals.

"My literature and my life have one characteristic trait in common: never to depart from the life and the concerns of my Brazilian people. As early as 1935, I was imprisoned for the first time for political activities and accused of being a revolutionary element. When the dictatorial regime of Vargas imposed itself on Brazil in 1937, I was forced to take refuge in the River Plate countries, from where I proceeded to Mexico, returning to Brazil after crossing the United States. Imprisoned again, I had to take refuge in exile once more in 1941, remaining this time for two years in Uruguay and Argentina. When finally allowed to return, I chose the state of Bahia as my home and there I lived, writing books and articles for newspapers, until the end of the war. I then moved to São Paulo where, in 1945, I was elected federal deputy, having collaborated in the drafting of the existing Brazilian Constitution.

"Together with the other representatives of the people elected on the nomination of the Brazilian Communist party, I had my parliamentary mandate removed in 1948, and found myself forced once more into political exile. I lived for some time in Paris, moving later to Czechoslovakia. During this period, which lasted until 1952, I traveled throughout various Western European countries and Asia, having taken an intense interest in various world movements for peace and in movements headed by European intellectuals fighting for freedom and the defense of culture. Back in my own country, I settled in Rio de Janeiro where, from 1956 until 1958, I edited a cultural periodical of wide circulation and influence which reunited the majority of Brazilian intellectuals in the defense of their national culture. Between 1955 and 1960 I made two further trips to Europe and Asia. For the last four years, I have been living in Salvador, the capital of my native state, Bahia, where I pursue my literary activities.

"After the writing of my first novel, as mentioned above, there followed those novels which form the cycle entitled 'The Novels of the Cacao Plantations,' a saga of the hardy people who cultivated this virgin territory and built a civilization there. This series of novels was followed by others, narratives of city life and the fortunes of the Brazilian man of our time. Following upon my early works, which were written with that passion and lyricism so thoroughly inherent in my Brazilian people, came my mature works which are more analytical and written with an element of humor that, sometimes, verges on the picaresque. It was possible for me to write a considerable number of works—some twenty in all—because of the support which I have always received from my readers, ever growing in number, whose stimulus has never failed me: my great satisfaction is to know that my people recognizes itself in my novels and that my writing is faithful to the most authentic reality of my country.

"Today my books are published in more than thirty countries and translated into as many languages. Their wide acceptance throughout the world gives me the tranquil assurance that my labors have not been in vain. And, I repeat, if there is any feature which distinguishes my writing and gives it exceptional value, it is the undeniable fidelity to my land and to my fellow-Brazilians, their capacity to discuss their sufferings and their happiness, to affirm their love of peace and their faith in Man."

* ə mä′ dō

Jorge Amado, the son of João Amado de Faria and Eulália Leal Amado, was born on his family's *fazenda*, Auricídia, at Ferradas, Itabuna, in Northeast Brazil. It was a turbulent time and place, to which he has returned again and again for the material of his novels. There was political violence, of which his father felt the effects; natural violence in the form of smallpox and malaria epidemics and in 1914 the disastrous flooding of the River Cachoeira, which drove the Amado family from their *fazenda* to start a new life in the seaport of Ilhéus. And in the brutal labor relations of the plantations there was social violence as well. Coffee and sugar prices were declining, and landowners were gambling desperately on cacao to recoup their fortunes—Amado's father did so in 1918.

Two teachers, the author says, profoundly affected his intellectual development. The first was Dona Guilhermina, his stern governess at Ilhéus, who appears in *Gabriela, Cravo e Canela.* The other was Father Cabral, an unconventional teacher at the Jesuit College of Antônio Vieira in Salvador, who encouraged him to read not only the Brazilian classics, but foreign writers like Charles Dickens and Jules Verne. The latter so inflamed his imagination that he ran away from the repressive college in 1926 and made his way to his grandfather's home in the Bahia backlands.

After a year of freedom, Amado resumed his education at the more liberal Ginásia Ipiranga, in Salvador. There, at the age of sixteen, he began to contribute to literary journals and newspapers, and was soon an active member of the "academy of rebels" founded by young supporters of the Modernist movement (the counterpart in Brazil of what was called Ultraism in the Spanish-speaking countries of Latin America). He wrote regularly for the group's two short-lived publications, *Meridiano* and *A Semana* and made many friends among the writers and artists who lived in bohemian squalor in the Ladeira do Pelhourinho, the Salvador slums.

In 1931, at his father's request, Amado went south to study law in Rio. There he wrote his first novel, ironically called *O País do Carnaval* (The Land of Carnival), which in spite of its technical immaturity is interesting in that it already reflects the social preoccupations that pervade his work. Influenced by his friendship with Rachel de Queiroz, Amado was increasingly drawn to left-wing politics, and this was evident in his second novel. *Cacáu* (Cacao, 1933) deals in a crude but powerful way with the exploitation of the black and mulatto workers of Southern Bahia. The novel sold out its first edition in a few weeks, but also attracted the attention of the authorities. Charged with issuing subversive propaganda, Amado was jailed for twenty-four hours, the first of many such brushes with the law.

JORGE AMADO

Four more novels followed in quick succession. *Suor* (Sweat), about the dockers, prostitutes, and waifs of the Ladeira do Pelhourinho, appeared in 1934. The same year Amado joined the newly founded publishing house of José Olympio in Rio, which published his next book. This was *Jubiabá* (1935), also set in Salvador, and centering on the struggle against injustice of its black hero Antônio Belduíno; he loses his battle, but represents the wave of the future, just as the old witch doctor Jubiabá symbolizes the African past. *Mar Morto* (Dead Sea, 1936), about the poor fishermen of Bahia, received the Graça Aranha prize of the Brazilian Academy of Letters, and was followed by *Capitães da Areia* (Beach Waifs, 1937), another study of the Bahia slums. For all their squalor and violence, these proletarian novels never fail to show the humor, vitality, and tragic poetry that were also to be found in the lives of the poor of Bahia. It was said that his lyrical but ungraceful style can impart to language "a savor as of flesh, and a rhythm almost like music."

In 1935 Amado visited Argentina and Uruguay, and in 1937 he toured North and South America, meeting many artists and writers. By then his work was available in French and Russian, and his international reputation was growing. In 1938 however the Vargas dictatorship banned his books and he went into exile. Apart from a volume of prose poems and a biography of the Communist leader Luiz Carlos Prestes, he published little until 1943.

The novel that appeared then, widely regarded

as Amado's masterpiece, was *Terras do Sem Fim* (1943, translated by Samuel Putnam as *The Violent Land*). Drawing on the scenes and memories of the author's childhood, it is an account of the struggle between Colonel Horácio and the Badaro family for the lands of Sequeiro Grande. The tale has the mythic quality of North American frontier stories, and like them is peopled by heroic figures, larger than life. Slightly flawed as it is by touches of sentimentality and archness, it is in its social and psychological observation, and its irony, infinitely more sophisticated than earlier epics of the Brazilian interior; it is, as Carlos Fuentes says, Balzacian rather than Zolaesque, "the novel of a master craftsman, richly endowed with the narrative art and the humor, distance, beauty and perceptiveness that distinguish a classic work." Subsequent novels in the cycle attracted less attention.

The novels Amado had written up to this point had established him as a master among the Brazilian "writers of the Northeast" but had not escaped censure. Critics complained that his plots and characters were manipulated to conform with Marxist ideology, and some readers disapproved of his preoccupation with sexual aberration. His later work is, as he indicates above, no less socially aware and compassionate, but it is less concerned to make political points, more picaresque. It is the novels he has produced in the late 1950s and 1960s that have won the widest international acceptance.

The first of them to appear in English was *Gabriela, Cravo e Canela* (1958, translated as *Gabriela, Clove and Cinnamon*). It is set in the 1920s in Ilhéus, where Gabriela, the amiable, beautiful, but starving migrant from the backlands, becomes in rapid succession cook, mistress, and wife to the café owner Nacib. The provincial microcosm of Ilhéus—its gossip, politics, love affairs, and bustling prosperity—is observed with warm humor, and the characters come richly to life. A best seller in its original language, and the winner of no fewer than five literary prizes, it was as kindly received in English. According to Harriet de Onís, who was to become Amado's principal translator, "one hardly knows what to admire most: the dexterity with which Amado can keep half a dozen plots spinning; the gossamer texture of his writing; or his humor, tenderness, and humanity."

Other novels in a similar vein include *Os Velhos Marinheiros* (1960, translated as *Home Is the Sailor*), *Os Pastores de Noite* (1964, translated as *Shepherds of the Night*), and *Dona Flor e Seus Dois Maridos* (1966, translated as *Dona Flor and Her Two Husbands*). These books, ribald, ironic, "full of sunshine and rum," have been compared with Sterne and with Chaucer, with Steinbeck's *Cannery Row* and Marcel Pagnol's trilogy about the Marseilles waterfront. They have been translated, as he says, into more than thirty languages, and some have been adapted for the stage, films, and radio. Apart from their immense and worldwide popularity, Amado's novels are valued in Latin America as a bridge between the stark naturalism of the regional novels of the 1920s and 1930s and the sophisticated urban fiction of such writers as Cortázar, Donoso, and Llosa.

Amado has also tried his hand at plays and film scenarios. He was married in 1945 to Zélia Gettai, a native of São Paulo, and has two children.

PRINCIPAL WORKS IN ENGLISH TRANSLATION: Gabriela, Clove and Cinnamon, 1962; Home Is the Sailor, 1964; The Two Deaths of Quincas Wateryell, 1965; The Violent Land, 1965; Shepherds of the Night, 1967; Dona Flor and Her Two Husbands, 1969; Tent of Miracles, 1971.

ABOUT: Amado, J. 30 anos de literatura, 1961; Coutinho, A. An Introduction to Literature in Brazil, 1969; Ellison, F. P. Brazil's New Novel, 1954; Oliveira, R. de. Palavras de Jorge Amado, 1966; Táti, M. Jorge Amado, 1961; Twentieth-Century Writing, 1969. *Periodicals*—Book Week July 11, 1965.

***AMIS, KINGSLEY (WILLIAM)** (April 16, 1922–), English novelist, poet, and critic, was born in Clapham, London, the only child of William Amis, an office worker, and the former Rosa Lucas. He had a lower-middle-class childhood in the southwestern suburbs of London. His parents were Baptists and Conservatives, not interested in the arts, "though not actively philistine." Amis began his literary career at the age of eleven, when his first story, "The Sacred Rhino of Uganda," appeared in the Norbury College school magazine.

The following year he went on, with a scholarship, to the City of London School. With the outbreak of World War II in 1939 the school was evacuated to Marlborough, in Wiltshire, where Amis spent the next two years. The City of London School drew boys from a wide range of social backgrounds, and Amis remembers it with gratitude for its heterogeneity and civilized tolerance. He began to write poetry there, discovered a talent for mimicry, and developed extracurricular interests in music—classical and jazz—painting, Marxism, and girls.

In 1941, another scholarship took Amis to St. John's College, Oxford University. There he read English, and made friends with Philip Larkin, John Wain, and Elizabeth Jennings. "No one who knew Kingsley at that time," Larkin says, "would deny that what chiefly distinguished him was [his] genius for imaginative mimicry. . . . He used it as the quickest way of convincing you that something was horrible or boring or absurd." (He still does.) Remembering "how much our daily exchanges were informed by Kingsley's pantomime," Larkin

* ā′ mis

goes on: "This is not to say that Kingsley dominated us. Indeed, to some extent he suffered the familiar humorist's fate of being unable to get anyone to take him seriously at all. Kingsley's 'serious side' was political. In those days of Help for Russia Week . . . he became editor of the University Labour Club Bulletin. . . . In his contentious mood he could be (intentionally) very irritating, especially to those who thought party politics should be suspended until the war was over. Sometimes he was the target of delighted laughter and violent abuse in the same evening and from the same people." (He still is.)

In 1942 Amis had to leave all this. He was commissioned in the Signal Corps (being, as he has said, "on the winning side now, because 'an Oxford man' was likely to be enough of a 'gentleman' to do all right as an officer"). He served in Normandy shortly after D Day, in Belgium, and in West Germany, and was demobilized in October 1945. He returned to St. John's, earned a first class English degree (1947), wrote an unpublished novel and some poems, and tried but failed to win a research degree with a thesis entitled "English Poetry, 1850–1900, and the Victorian Reading Public." In 1948 he married Hilary Bardwell, and the following year left Oxford.

Amis went as a lecturer in English to the University College of Swansea, where he taught for twelve years (except for one year, 1958–1959, as a Visiting Fellow in Creative Writing at Princeton). In 1961 he accepted a fellowship at Peterhouse College, Cambridge University. This arrangement ended in 1963 for reasons which he discussed, with rueful acerbity, in *Encounter* (February 1964): "What really drove me out," he wrote, "was paradoxically what made me most reluctant to leave: teaching. Nobody who has not experienced it can fully imagine the peculiar drain which this activity makes on one's energy, nor its unique rewards." About the university, as distinct from his college, he was less than complimentary, objecting in particular to the rigors of Cambridge social life and the inadequacies of the tutorial system.

Amis had published some poems in Oxford anthologies, and two or three pamphlets of verse appeared in the early 1950s. In 1953 Amis was one of the young poets featured in John Wain's BBC poetry program "First Reading." Soon afterwards two influential anthologies, D. J. Enright's *Poets of the 1950's* (1955) and Robert Conquest's *New Lines* (1956), included poems by Amis and by some of his friends: Wain, Larkin, Elizabeth Jennings, and Conquest himself. These poets, together with three or four others, constituted what journalists named "the Movement." Almost all of them, including Amis, have denied that a movement existed. For a time, nevertheless—because they were influenced

KINGSLEY AMIS

by William Empson and F. R. Leavis and each other, because of the war, because of their temperaments and circumstances—they shared certain antiromantic tendencies conveniently summarized by Anthony Hartley as "complication of thought, austerity of tone, colloquialism, and avoidance of rhetoric."

"The trouble with the newer poets, including myself," Amis wrote once, "is that they are often lucid and nothing else—except arid and bald. . . . Their great deficiency is meagreness and triviality of subject matter." It is true that Amis's subject range is small, and that he "works hard at being antiromantic," but Philip Larkin admires his "scrupulous skill" and "a style that will exasperate only those who cannot see when a poem is being funny and serious simultaneously." In recent years Amis's energies have been devoted mainly to prose, but he still produces some verse. *A Look Around the Estate* (poems 1957–1967), appeared in 1967. A sequence in it called "The Evans Country," deriding the Welsh as lecherous and avaricious, amused most reviewers, who agreed however that Amis's work in this form had not visibly developed or changed since the 1950s.

If Amis's poems connected him to a largely imaginary "Movement," his first and most famous novel placed him among the "Angry Young Men," another journalistic invention. It is clear now that *Lucky Jim* caused a furore not because Amis wrote it in anger (though it made some old men very angry indeed), but because he had identified a new British social type: the working- or lower-middle-class university graduate who has been educated out of his own class but who has no ambition to become a "gentleman"; who has been taught to relish the perquisites of power but who regards the power game, as it is played in Britain, as ridiculous and immoral.

This is the dilemma of Jim Dixon, the product of a northern grammar school, the Royal Air Force, and Leicester University. He is an inept and ignorant junior lecturer in medieval history at a provincial university. He loathes his subject, his job, and all the social and cultural affectations of university life, but knows that he is equipped for nothing better. His probationary period nearly finished, his dismissal probable, Jim tries to ingratiate himself with the head of his department, whom he regards as a pretentious buffoon, and with Margaret Peel, a neurotic but influential colleague who fills him with horrified embarrassment. His really profound, almost physical, hatred of every kind of phonyness makes the task impossible; his true feelings keep breaking through. Frustrated to the point of explosion, he dreams of outrageous revenges, risks small acts of sabotage, makes faces up his sleeve (his Edith Sitwell face, his Martian-invader face, his sex-life-in-Ancient-Rome face). At last, when he is obliged to deliver a public lecture on "Merrie England," the revolting charade becomes too much for him. The lecture turns into a drunken parody and ends with a kind of manifesto. It is only then, when his career is ruined, that a beaming *deus ex machina* steps in to present Lucky Jim with a fat job, the girl he wants, and a happy ending.

Somerset Maugham, and others like him, saw in Jim Dixon a representative of a new class which was "mean, malicious and envious" and "scum." Very many others welcomed the book as the first public expression of their own attitudes and frustrations, and thousands more enjoyed it as "the funniest first novel since *Decline and Fall.*" It was generally recognized as the work of a born novelist whose "prodigious gifts," to quote Ralph Caplan, included "a ridiculously acute ear, an eye that . . . misses nothing, and a deadly comic aim." *Lucky Jim*, a first novel which was "not promise but fulfillment," was enormously successful, was filmed, and thirteen years after its publication still had enough vitality to inspire a British television series.

The hero of Amis's second book, *That Uncertain Feeling*, is John Lewis, a happily married but restless young librarian in a small Welsh town. Like Jim Dixon he hankers after money, success, and hypergamy—the favors of a woman who is his social superior—and like Jim he despises himself for wanting such things. Unlike Jim he is not lucky. A kind of fairy godmother does emerge in the physically and socially desirable person of Elizabeth Gruffydd-Williams. He allows himself to be seduced but finds himself unwilling to be subjugated by her, and with some relief retreats into the life and values of his own class. A novel as funny as *Lucky Jim*, as rich in characterization and exact in social observation, it was admirably filmed as *Only Two Can Play*.

The Somerset Maugham Award that Amis (rather ironically) received for *Lucky Jim* paid for a trip to Portugal, the scene of his third novel. *I Like It Here* features the now familiar Amis hero—a more competent Jim Dixon—who is this time a writer on a delicate mission for his publisher. The foreign setting provides opportunities for some self-conscious xenophobia and some satirical attacks on wine and food snobbery, but the novel was thought disappointingly similar to its predecessors and sadly strained in its humor.

It was followed by *Take a Girl Like You*, which describes a philandering teacher's long campaign to seduce the delicious Jenny Bunn, an inflammatory twentieth century sex symbol with nineteenth century moral standards. He succeeds, at length, only because Jenny is too drunk to resist; and then he is ashamed. The novel offended some readers, who thought the theme an improper one for humor. L. E. Sissman, however, put it with *A Handful of Dust* as "one of the great serio-comic novels of the century." Funny as it is, the book with "great subtlety of moral observation" provokes quite serious reflections upon the relations between the sexes and between the classes in Britain. More than one critic was reminded of Fielding's *Amelia*, and of a passage in *I Like It Here* in which the hero visits Fielding's tomb in Lisbon and refers to him as the only noncontemporary novelist who had been able to make his moral seriousness "apparent without the aid of evangelical puffing and blowing." Walter Allen suggested that all of Amis's heroes could be described as Fielding does Tom Jones: "Though he did not always act rightly, yet he never did otherwise without feeling and suffering for it."

This "constant struggle between honour and inclination" was recognized again in Roger Micheldene, a sardonic snob of an English publisher who brays and troughs his way through America in *One Fat Englishman*. This "tragi-comic Iago" is also a Catholic, a vile man whose intermittently anguished awareness of his vileness enables Amis, the *Times Literary Supplement* said, to create a "picture of God the tormenter" that "equals anything in Mr. Graham Greene's books."

Though critics had observed their growing moral seriousness—what Bernard Bergonzi calls "their intermittent brooding on death . . . and the general arbitrariness of fate"—Amis's first five novels were successful because they were funny. James Gindin had noted the gradual disappearance of farce after the first two books but in 1962 still considered Amis a humorist, a master of mimicry, of word play and verbal jokes, erecting "a whole comic world through the fabric of his writing"—a world in which "the comic image or comparison is so important that it frequently interrupts a crucial scene or relationship."

Those who saw in Amis an heir to P. G. Wodehouse must have been startled by *The Anti-Death League*, which is often bitterly funny, which expertly uses some of the devices of science fiction and the spy thriller, but which could hardly be more serious in its theme. A young British army officer, engaged with others in the development of an abominable secret weapon, becomes convinced that a pattern of deaths is developing around him, threatening at last the girl he is in love with. He identifies as the source of so much undeserved suffering a nonhuman force of unlimited malignancy and wickedness which is called God. Man is morally superior to this force, and the "League" of the title is a necessary existential gesture against it. Most critics agreed that the book's thesis was of great interest, and praised the advance of this "uncertain Fielding" to "the edge of Graham Greeneland," but regretted the fact that Amis, in producing a novel of ideas, had surrendered much of his talent for characterization and humor.

Amis published a collection of short stories, *My Enemy's Enemy*, in 1962. *The Egyptologists*, intended as a comic novel, was the unfortunate result of a collaboration with Robert Conquest, with whom, for several years, Amis also edited *Spectrum*, an annual science fiction anthology. *New Maps of Hell* collects Amis's Princeton lectures on science fiction. He is also the author of an admiring study of the work of his friend the late Ian Fleming, and in 1967 had "tremendous fun" writing (as "Robert Markham") a new James Bond thriller, *Colonel Sun*. It was not a success. Nor was there much enthusiasm for Amis's next novel, *I Want It Now*, about a venal London television "personality" who sets out to bag a sexually desperate heiress and winds up redeemed, somewhat, by True Love. The sentimental plot is only partly redeemed by some characteristically violent satire, arising mostly out of the various unpleasant ways in which the rich are different from us.

A much more interesting and original book followed, *The Green Man*. The title refers to an ancient country inn near Cambridge whose owner, while contending with problems resulting from his alcoholism and lechery, and the death of his father, also has to deal with the fact that his posh pub is haunted. The ghost moreover is not the whimsical sort of apparition that might be good for trade, but the shade of a seventeenth-century diabolist who, in the end, creates and looses another kind of Green Man. L. J. Davis called it "a wonderful book, a ghost story that is scary, funny, and sad in roughly equal measure, informed by an intelligence that is both penetrating and audacious."

It is notable that, while Amis's perennial if shopsoiled hero is in this manifestation as idiosyncratically profane and as hostile to sham as ever, he does show a respect for tradition that would have embarrassed Lucky Jim. Again, though Ronnie Appleyard in *I Want It Now* is moved to a liberal outburst against racism, the same book includes a verbal swipe at "a bearded lefty"—an odd target for the former editor of the Oxford University Labour Club *Bulletin*. And few socialist intellectuals, presumably, share Amis's enthusiasm for the imperialist thug James Bond. The fact is that as early as 1957, when Amis wrote his controversial Fabian pamphlet *Socialism and the Intellectuals*, he had become a distinctly apathetic supporter of the Labour party. Thereafter he moved steadily to the right, until in 1967 he appalled the British intellectual establishment by allying himself with Robert Conquest in support of America's role in Vietnam.

He has explained his motives—his final disillusionment with communism when Russia crushed the Hungarian uprising in 1956, dissatisfaction with the Wilson government's educational policies and "the increasing power of the state over the individual," and disenchantment with the kind of intellectual he says he used to be, "who buys unexamined the abortion-divorce-homosexuality-censorship-racialism, marijuana package; in a word, the Lefty." For such reasons, he wrote in 1967, "I am driven into grudging toleration of the Conservative party because it is the party of nonpolitics, of resistance to politics." Some of the targets of his increasingly strident attacks on the Left have offered unkinder explanations of his defection, and it is interesting that James Gindin, as early as 1962, pointed out that Amis's heroes, implicitly socialist or at least antibourgeois in their attitudes, nevertheless admire the aristocracy and "are essentially conservative," characterized by "a comic and tolerant acceptance of the power structure of the contemporary world."

Girl, 20 explicitly attacks the trendy "package" itemized above, presenting for the reader's ridicule the spectacle of a famous classical musician of fifty-three, Sir Roy Vandervane, seduced by the permissive society, pop music, leftist protest, and youth—especially youth and especially young women. Most reviewers were entertained and most were also somewhat moved, finding the "pat and often facile satire" enriched by the author's refusal to see Vandervane as wholly ridiculous or wholly trivial; his story, as one critic wrote, "should excite pity and terror as well as horselaughs." Much pleasure was taken also in *The Riverside Villas Murder*, an artful resurrection of the classical British detective story, set in the 1930s (when the author was about the same age as his fourteen-year-old hero).

A few of Amis's political and autobiographical articles are collected, together with a larger number on literary and cultural themes, in *What Became of Jane Austen?* Angus Wilson, praising his "assured, graceful, and constantly controlled use of words" in these essays, regards his style as "a very important clue to the understanding of Mr. Amis's cultural and political standpoints"; he is a champion "of cultural discipline" and "the solid traditional values" of his class. Certainly his critical tone is very much the common-man, common-sense tone of his fictional heroes, by and large hostile to exotic and experimental writers, especially if they are foreign, suspicious of cult figures like Dylan Thomas and D. H. Lawrence, and drawn most to such English anti-Romantics as Fielding. These instincts, and a certain deliberate bloody-mindedness, lead him to dismiss Keats as "an often delightful, if often awkward, decorative poet," to prefer Mickey Spillane to Dashiell Hammett or Raymond Chandler, and to assert that "John D. MacDonald is by any standards a better writer than Saul Bellow."

Kingsley Amis has two sons and a daughter by his first wife. In 1965 he married the novelist Elizabeth Jane Howard, a sensitive chronicler of the emotional difficulties of the upper-middle-class. He lists his recreations as music, films, and television. Unlike Jim Dixon he likes "filthy Mozart" and was a member of the Wine and Food Society.

PRINCIPAL WORKS: *Poetry*—Bright November, 1947; A Frame of Mind, 1953; Poems, 1954; A Case of Samples: Poems 1946–56, 1956; A Look Around the Estate: Poems 1957–67, 1967. *Fiction*—Lucky Jim, 1954; That Uncertain Feeling, 1955; I Like It Here, 1958; Take a Girl Like You, 1960; My Enemy's Enemy (short stories), 1962; One Fat Englishman, 1963; The Egyptologists, 1965; The Anti-Death League, 1966; I Want It Now, 1968; (as "Robert Markham") Colonel Sun, A James Bond Adventure, 1968; The Green Man, 1969; Girl, 20, 1971; The Riverside Villas Murder, 1973. *Criticism*—New Maps of Hell: A Survey of Science Fiction, 1960; The James Bond Dossier, 1965; What Became of Jane Austen?, 1970. *Miscellaneous*—On Drink, 1972; (ed.) G. K. Chesterton: Selected Stories, 1972; (ed.) Tennyson (selected poems), 1973.

ABOUT: Allen, W. The Modern Novel, 1964; Allott, K. Penguin Book of Contemporary Verse, 1962; Allsop, K. The Angry Decade, 1958; Brophy, B. Don't Never Forget, 1966; Burgess, A. The Novel Now, 1967; Contemporary Authors 11–12, 1965; Current Biography, 1958; Fraser, G. S. The Modern Writer and His World, 1964; Gindin, J. Postwar British Fiction, 1962; Green, M. Mirror for Anglo-Saxons, 1961; Harte, B. and Riley, C. (eds.) 200 Contemporary Authors, 1969; Karl, F. R. A Reader's Guide to the Contemporary English Novel, 1962; Larkin, P. *introduction to* Jill, 1964 edition; Lodge, D. The Language of Fiction, 1966; O'Connor, W. V. The New University Wits, 1963; Rabinovitz, R. The Reaction Against Experiment in the English Novel, 1959–1960, 1967; Shapiro, C. (ed.) Contemporary British Novelists, 1965; West, P. The Modern Novel, 1963; Who's Who, 1972; Wilson, E. The Bit Between My Teeth, 1965. *Periodicals*—Books Abroad Summer 1969; Bulletin of Bibliography October 1969; Critique Spring 1966; Encounter February 1964; Guardian September 30, 1968; Harper's October 1959; Kenyon Review Fall 1959; Life March 14, 1969; Nation November 29, 1958; New Republic March 4, 1957; January 5, 1959; New Statesman January 12, 1957; September 21, 1962; November 29, 1963; July 7, 1967; New Yorker April 26, 1969; Newsweek February 17, 1958; March 2, 1964; May 8, 1967; Poetry October 1957; Saturday Review May 7, 1955; July 27, 1957; Spectator June 25, 1954; January 11, 1957; February 24, 1961; November 29, 1963; Time May 27, 1957; Times Literary Supplement March 8, 1957; September 9, 1960; September 23, 1960; February 3, 1961.

AMMONS, A(RCHIE) R(ANDOLPH) (February 18, 1926–), American poet, writes: "I was born on a farm in Whiteville Township, Columbus County, North Carolina. The nearest center of civilization was two miles away by sandroad: called New Hope, it consisted of an elementary school (an old farm building heated by pot-bellieds) and a Baptist church and cemetery (where most of my people are buried, including my mother and father, one infant sister, and two infant brothers). My father had done well on the farm (I remember musty bank statements tucked away under a bureau) before the Depression, but within my memory and until the farm was sold when I was seventeen, we were never out of debt; in fact, we were in danger from year to year of losing the farm. We grew tobacco, corn, and strawberries as money crops and had, for our own use, a vegetable garden, watermelon patch, sugar cane field, etc., plus chickens, one (usually) or more cows, pigs, a she-mule named Silver, pecan, pear, apple, and peach trees. So we were never near starvation, though never far from it.

"I attended the New Hope Elementary School for the first five grades. We walked to school. But by the time I entered the sixth grade, a new brick school had been built by a paved highway about half a mile from the old school and school buses had been invented. I didn't like the new school. It was strange: new, painted inside, with electric lights, flushing toilets and a long porcelain urinal. The move required a step into the present that I have never completed.

"But I was graduated valedictorian from the elementary school and went on to Whiteville High School, four miles away in the nearest town. The strongest memory I have of that move is of walking up stairs with other students behind me, holes in my socks, my heel-strings shining. Sometimes I had a nickel for a pack of crackers, but most often I had no lunch and would rather have starved than take a paper bag of biscuit sandwiches with me ('lightbread,' store-bought, was still a rarity). I tried boxing one year but found it impossible to go through the day without food, then work out, then walk four miles back home, and then do the chores. High school taught me that the town kids lived in a world I could never enter. Though I seldom took books home to study (we had kerosene lamps with dull yellow light) I managed to graduate sixth in a class of eighty.

"My first awareness of writing as such came in the eighth grade. We were asked to read an article in the *Reader's Digest* and then write a theme based on the reading. I did mine on a new breed of cows that were, or were to be, thirty inches high and were to eat little and give lots of milk. The teacher praised my theme to her classes, and even seniors spoke to me about what she had said. This 'attainment' stayed in the air, so that when a year or so later the class decided to do a newspaper, I was unopposed as editor-in-chief. (I don't think the newspaper ever appeared.)

"War broke out and after I graduated from high school in 1943, I went to work at the shipyards in Wilmington, North Carolina. About two weeks after I started the job, I went back home to find everybody gone and the house empty. My father had sold out and moved to Chadbourn, a town seven or eight miles away. It was a smart move for my father: he paid all his debts, got a job at the shipyard himself (later worked as a deputy sheriff), and we had money for the first time, and my mother had some rest from farmwork and anxiety for the first time.

"I served in the Navy for nineteen months, spending almost a year in the South Pacific, and found that I had nearly enough month-credits to get through college on the GI Bill. I entered Wake Forest College in 1946 and was graduated with a B.S. in General Science in 1949. I met Phyllis Plumbo at Wake Forest in 1947. She taught Spanish for one semester. After she left to do graduate work at the University of California at Berkeley, I sent her a poem about my feelings for her. She wrote back to some extent endorsing the feelings but definitely praising the poem and so lit a brush fire she has had to live with ever since. We were married November 26, 1949.

"I continued to write during 1949–1950 while I was principal of the Hatteras Elementary School in Hatteras, North Carolina. After that year, we both went to Berkeley, where I studied English and met Josephine Miles. Miss Miles encouraged me to send some of my poems to magazines. Rejections came back. But in 1953, after my wife and I had returned from Berkeley to live in south Jersey where I had taken a job, an acceptance of two poems came from the *Hudson Review*. Mr. Frederick Morgan, editor of the *Hudson Review*, continued to encourage me and through the years published most of my work.

"Other magazines printed my poems, the books finally came along, a job at Cornell University

A. R. AMMONS

(1964), a Guggenheim Fellowship (1966), and a Traveling Fellowship from the American Academy of Arts and Letters (1967).

"Writing for me has always been one way to respond to my set of absolutely insoluble problems."

As he says, Ammons's poetry began to appear in the *Hudson Review* and other magazines in 1953, and his first book, *Ommateum*, came out in 1955. It was however not until 1964, with the publication of *Expressions of Sea Level*, that critics discovered him as a poet of "originality and power." The most whole-hearted welcome for that collection came from Josephine Jacobsen, who placed Ammons at once "in the front rank of current American poets." Other reviewers praised the disciplined and confident thinking they found in these poems, the "unfettered" rhythms following "the cadence and phrasing of the reading voice," but were less happy about Ammons's fondness for coloring his generally conversational diction with esoteric words, and his "oddly spaced lines." Charles Simmons described "Nelly Myers," about a hired woman who had worked on the Ammons farm, as "one of the loveliest love poems I have ever read."

This thin but fervent chorus of critical approval swelled appreciably the following year with the appearance of *Corsons Inlet*. Donald Hall said that the volume appealed to both the ear and the eye—"to the eye that sees nature, to the eye that sees print—and to the inward eye as well." Hall concluded: "A. R. Ammons is nearly forty, and has been a modest part of the landscape of American poetry for some time; with this book he stops being modest."

Tape for the Turn of the Year is a kind of journal or commonplace book, written between December 6, 1963 and January 10, 1964—a "long, thin poem" which owes its shape and length to the fact that it was typed directly, without revision, onto a roll of adding machine tape. To Jonathan Williams the experiment seemed wholly successful, a supple and witty poem showing "an extraordinary talent for assimilation and grace in the making of language," a text that "adheres to the mind" like "the lichen whose image is central to the poem."

Another small volume, *Northfield Poems*, was followed by Ammons's *Selected Poems*, which confirmed his position as one of the most important and admired American poets of his generation. His reputation has grown with his subsequent collections and John Hollander, reviewing *Briefings* in 1971, wrote that "A. R. Ammons's work is probably to embody the major vision of nature in the poetry of our part of the century." His *Collected Poems: 1951–1971* brought him the 1973 National Book Award in Poetry.

Ammons is a pastoral poet in the transcendentalist tradition of Whitman, Emerson, and Emily Dickinson. He writes in two principal modes. One is a short lyric which may be a dialogue between the speaker and some personified element of nature—winds, mountains, trees—or a brief wry fable. David Kalstone points out that "by and large the short poems do battle against the 'periphery,' the profusion and separateness in the outside world, 'thickets hard to get around in / or get around / for an older man.'" Some of these short pieces do not escape whimsy: "I can't understand it / said the giant redwood . . ."

Most critics find Ammons's best work in long Whitmanesque interior monologues which take their shapes (as Daniel Hoffman says) "the way water flows, moving with quick runs or slow eddies along an unspoiled landscape in which is revealed the immanence of a spiritual force greater than any found in the industrial world they avoid describing." The poet describes his method in "Corsons Inlet" in which he says that, walking along the Jersey shore, "I was released from forms, / from the perpendiculars, / straight lines, blocks, boxes, blinds / of thought / into the hues, shadings, rises, flowing bends and blends of sight." In such verse the danger is a self-indulgent logorrhea ("the problem is / how / to keep shape and flow"); that Ammons generally avoids this danger is a tribute to the profundity of his perceptions and the precision of his language, which at times draws knowledgeably on scientific diction.

"What is central to this poetry," writes John Hollander, "is the figure the poet's mind makes in the midst of the landscape it is scanning. Its determining fiction is of a man motionless in the country: what moves is the interaction of his ordering mind with the givens of the world. . . . In the last, and perhaps most remarkable poem in [*Briefings*], Ammons . . . turns back to the conclusion of all the great American readers of landscape and specimen—that the search for meanings will find in the hieroglyphs over which it broods the terms of the brooding consciousness itself. At the end of this poem and of the book, 'the man stands and looks about, the / leaf does not increase itself above the grass, and the dark / work of the deepest cells is of a tune which May bushes / and fear lit by the breadth of such calmly turns to praise.'"

The job in south Jersey that Ammons mentions above was an eight-year stint as an executive vice-president of Friedrich and Dimmock, a firm which manufactures biological glassware. Ammons, "a big, quiet man," still teaches at Cornell, where he became an associate professor of English in 1969.

PRINCIPAL WORKS: Ommateum, with Doxology, 1955; Expressions of Sea Level, 1964; Corsons Inlet: A Book of Poems, 1965; Tape for the Turn of the Year, 1965; Northfield Poems, 1966; Selected Poems, 1969; Uplands, 1970; Briefings: Poems Small and Easy, 1971; Collected Poems, 1951–1971, 1972.

ABOUT: Contemporary Authors 9–10, 1964; Who's Who in America, 1970–1971. *Periodicals*—Hudson Review Summer 1967; New York Times Book Review July 11, 1965; December 14, 1969; May 9, 1971.

***ANAND, MULK RAJ** (December 12, 1905–), Indian novelist and essayist, writes: "I was born in Peshawar, on the North Western Frontier of India, educated in Punjab University, London, and Cambridge. I received a blow on the head from a stone while playing with children at the age of nine and became physically weak and oversensitive throughout my boyhood and adolescence. I began to write poetry early and my father thought that I had gone mad because of the blow on my head. The death of a girl cousin made me write prose letters complaining to God. During 1919 in Amritsar, when General Dyer machine-gunned an unarmed crowd in an enclosure in Jalianwallah Bagh, and curfew was declared, I wandered out in the evening to see what was happening. I was arrested by the police, kept in the lockup all night and given seven stripes. This made me into a political rebel, against British rule all my life. Later, I was expelled from government school for joining a procession.

"My father, who was in the British Indian army, turned me out of home, along with my mother who had also joined the Gandhi movement. I came under the influence of the great poet Iqbal in Lahore, when I was a student in the University. I told him I wanted to study philosophy and he advised me to go to Heidelberg. My mother

* un und'

pawned her jewellery and I went to London instead. Luckily I got a scholarship of three hundred pounds a year for research in English thought.

"As my formal education in India had been indifferent, my professor, the great Kantian scholar G. Dawes Hicks, sent me to North Wales, with a boxful of books, a pipe and a tobacco pouch. I read Greek and modern thought all day and climbed mountains on Sundays. Coming down from Mount Snowdon one day, I met a boy and a girl and immediately fell in love with the girl. She was the daughter of a professor and asked me home. The family was interested in India and complained how the Welsh people had been kept down by the English. And they sympathised with my anti-British feelings. The girl, named Irene, asked me to put down my life story and I began to write a confession which I used to read to her. This became two thousand pages of monologue, dialogue, dream, fantasy, comedy and nightmare. Irene said she would marry me if the book was published, and she began to type the narrative. No one would look at the amorphous mass of outpourings of a wild young rebel in London. So Irene took me to Paris to see the Louvre, then to Rome to the Sistine Chapel, on to Vienna to hear music, to Berlin to drink beer, to Brussels to eat sausages, and back to London. During the General Strike of 1926, I got beaten up, with some other students, by the Churchillians for not blacklegging. A woman called Eltie Helman, the wife of Allen Hutt, took me to a study circle to read Marx, Bakunin and Kropotkin. I could then understand Hegel and Kant more easily. So the doctoral thesis was written naturally.

"Meanwhile, I had met Bonamy Dobrée, Herbert Read and T. S. Eliot. I began to work on short notes for the latter's magazine, *The Criterion*. My differences with Eliot led me to meet D. H. Lawrence. I had begun to rediscover India, Asia and Africa, and wrote two books on Indian and Persian art. Also, I began to rewrite bits of my old confession in the form of prose poems, short stories and novels.

"On my return to India in 1929, I stayed in Gandhi's *ashram* on the River Sabarmati in Ahmedabad and finished my first novel, *Untouchable*. This was turned down by eighteen publishers, before Mr. E. M. Forster read it and wrote a preface. It was brought out by a small firm called Wishart Books. Mr. Wishart paid me so little that I had tears in my eyes. He took me to lunch and gave me an indefinite loan of a hundred pounds, which was not to be returned. I wrote my second novel, *Coolie*, which won tremendous praise from the critics and put me onto the platform of world writers at the International Intellectuals' Conference in London, 1936. Afterwards, I could do

MULK RAJ ANAND

my soul-search and write as an Expressionist without being refused by publishers.

"I went to fight in Spain in 1937 for the Republican cause. Returning to India in 1938, I worked with Jawaharlal Nehru in the anti-British struggle. Along with some other Indian intellectuals, I helped to found the Progressive Writers' Movement. For its second conference, Rabindranath Tagore gave me an inaugural address. I returned to London in the summer of 1939, in the hope of getting back a few months later, with Kathleen Van Gelder, who was an actress, as my wife. I had hoped to found a theatre with her. The second world war broke out and I was marooned in England. I was a conscientious objector and cultivated an allotment. Then, on the persuasion of George Orwell, I joined the war effort, at the B.B.C. and in the films division of the Ministry of Information.

"I returned to India in 1945 with a message from Sir Stafford Cripps for Jawaharlal Nehru that the Labour Party had decided to 'quit India.' Nehru sent me to Gandhi. Neither would believe me and asked for a message to be sent to Lord Casey, then Governor of Bengal. I settled in Lahore to found a small free school for children. India got freedom, but with the proviso that Muslims could opt for Pakistan. The partition riots broke out, in which half a million were killed. The fruits of freedom began to taste bitter. I left for Bombay and founded a publishing house and the art magazine *Marg*.

"Since then I have gone around the world working for peace against the threat of war. And I have tried to evolve a philosophy of comprehensive historical humanism which accepts the common love of all for man, even of those who may have different sanctions for their beliefs. I feel that, if there is no world war, national frontiers may ultimately break down and the process of 'one world culture' may begin. I consider creative art and literature to be the weapons of humanism. The individual cannot grow without a world in which social justice has been more or less achieved.

"I was divorced from Kathleen Van Gelder in 1948 and married Shirin Vajifdar, a classical dancer, in 1949. During the last three years I have been Tagore Professor of Fine Arts in the University of Punjab, Chandigarh. This year (1966) I have been made president of the National Academy of Art, India."

Mulk Raj Anand, the best known of all the twentieth century Indian novelists, published several books on oriental art and poetry, and even a book on curries, before he turned to fiction. Then he chose as his subject not the life of the educated and privileged, but that of the poor, exploited, and voiceless among the Indian masses: the untouchable, the coolie, the indentured laborer. In doing so he was able to draw on a personal experience unusual among Indian writers in English, for though of fairly high caste, his father (a coppersmith by trade) had joined the Indian Army, and the boy had mixed freely with the children of the servants and sweepers attached to the regiment.

But, in the turbulent atmosphere of the 1930s, writing such as his was also a political act. Srinivasa Iyengar records that "the first three novels, as they appeared, were like so many packets of dynamite: they enraged the diehard, they ruffled the bureaucracy." All three were banned by the government of India, and the third, *Two Leaves and a Bud*, had to be withdrawn from circulation in England too, under threat of prosecution for obscenity. Anand was denounced as a "Bolshevik" when in India, and harassed by the police.

Untouchable, the first novel in order of writing, is still widely regarded as the finest: "the most compact and artistically satisfying." It is a short book covering a single day in the life of Bakha, the eighteen-year-old son of the town's principal "sweeper," or cleaner of latrines. Bakha's morning round of the lavatories, his thoughts and his dreams as he works, are described in naturalistic detail; and the tension between his youth and hopefulness, and the indignity of his status, culminates in an encounter with a caste Hindu who makes sexual approaches to Bakha's sister, and, on being rejected, yells "polluted, polluted!" By evening, Bakha is desperate with frustration and misery—and he embarks on the symbolic journey which ends the book. The boy is presented with three possible solutions to his dilemma: a salvationist urges him to become a Christian and so escape his caste; he hears Gandhi at a public meeting denounce untouchability as "the greatest blot on Hinduism"; and finally he hears from the poet Iqbal Nath Sarshar of the miraculous new machine—flush sanitation—that will free the sweepers for good. He goes home to bed, hopeful that change will come. "There is a photographic fidelity about the picture that convinces at once, though it also overwhelms us by its cumulative ferocity and force of detail," comments Srinivasa Iyengar.

Coolie is not only longer than *Untouchable*, but wider-ranging both in time and space. It follows the tragic career of the hill boy Munoo—orphaned, brought up by unloving relatives, sent to serve in an unhappy, brutal household—who escapes and finds himself washed up in a strange corner of a city, loud with anger, curses, and pain. Munoo becomes a coolie in the grain market, works as a porter at the station, and finally joins a circus to reach Bombay, where he goes from degradation to degradation until he is finally defeated by work and disease.

In 1937 there followed *Two Leaves and a Bud*, a compressed and dramatic tale, this time dealing with a middle-aged contract laborer, Gangu, working on a foreign-owned tea estate. The conflict between exploiters and exploited breaks into frequent violence and comes to a crisis with the suppression of a workers' demonstration by force. Just as peace appears to be returning, a drunken British estate manager tries to rape Gangu's daughter and in his panic kills Gangu. At the subsequent trial, the criminal is found not guilty of murder and the book ends in a mood of bitter despair.

Anand's most ambitious work followed, a trilogy (*Village*, *Across the Black Waters*, and *The Sword and the Sickle*), about the youngest son of a Sikh farmer. The first volume deals with his escape from the constricting life of the village. He joins the army and is sent to France to fight alongside British troops in World War I—a war in which he can find no sense and no allegiance. Afterwards, returning to India, he throws himself into the political struggle, and the clash of ideologies provides the theme of the last volume.

Anand's later novels lack the intimacy and freshness of the early books—in *The Private Life of an Indian Prince* for example he is generally thought to have failed to identify himself with his subject. He is also the author of a number of short stories, however, in which he has created memorable characters—Chandu the barber, Dhandu the carpenter—that bear comparison with Bakha, Munoo, and Gangu. It is in fact arguable that in the short story the strengths of Anand's talent are best displayed: his eye for significant detail, his feeling for simple people, his anger at those who deny the humanity of others. As a novelist, his style is frequently undistinguished, and he possesses neither profound psychological insight nor outstanding imaginative powers. But his early stories remain moving nearly forty years after they were written. As Srinivasa Iyengar comments, "they come fresh from the flesh and blood of everyday existence."

The author retained his Tagore Professorship at the University of Punjab from 1963 to 1966. In 1967–1968 he was a visiting professor at the Institute of Advanced Studies, Simla. Since 1970 Anand has been president of the Lokayata Trust, which is working to develop a community and cultural centre in Haus Khaz village, New Delhi.

PRINCIPAL WORKS: *Fiction*—The Lost Child and Other Stories, 1934; Untouchable, 1935; Coolie, 1936; Two Leaves and a Bud, 1937; The Village, 1939; Across the Black Waters, 1940; The Sword and the Sickle, 1942; The Barber's Trade Union and Other Stories, 1944; The Big Heart, 1945; The Tractor and the Corn Goddess and Other Stories, 1947; Seven Summers: The Story of an Indian Childhood, 1951; Private Life of an Indian Prince, 1953. *Nonfiction*—Hindu View of Art (introduction by Eric Gill), 1933; Apology for Heroism: An Essay in Search of Faith, 1948; The Story of India, 1948; Lines Written to an Indian Air, 1949; Indian Theatre, 1950; Kama Kala: Some Notes on the Philosophical Basis of Hindu Erotic Sculpture, 1958; Is There a Contemporary Indian Civilisation?, 1963.

ABOUT: International Who's Who, 1972–1973; Srinivasa Iyengar, K. R. Indian Writing in English, 1962; Vinson, J. (ed.) Contemporary Novelists, 1972. *Periodicals*—Contemporary Indian Literature December 1965; Scrutiny June 1935.

ANDERSON, POUL (WILLIAM) (November 25, 1926–), American novelist and story writer, writes: "On my father's side of the family they were Danish, with rather old American connections which explain the spelling of my last name. Mostly they were sailors, though he himself became an engineer. On my mother's side they were also Danish, professional people, including the poets Henrik Hertz and Carsten Hauch. She named me for her own father, hence the spelling of my first name. (The middle one is plain William.) I was born in Bristol, Pennsylvania, but we soon moved to Port Arthur, Texas, where I grew up with my younger brother John among vacant lots, oil refineries, and Gulf Coast shipping. After my father died in 1937, we lived for a while in Europe, then around Washington, D.C., and finally for a number of years on a small farm in Minnesota.

"A hearing defect kept me out of military service, and I entered the University of Minnesota in 1944, graduating with honors in 1948. That was a purely technical education—major in physics, minors in mathematics and chemistry—and

POUL ANDERSON

whatever liberal arts I have are largely self-acquired. It occasions me small regret; science seems to be the only live enterprise these days. A long-time enthusiast of science fiction, I started writing and selling it while still in college. Afterward jobs were hard to find, so I kept alive by continuing to write, and slowly realized that this was my real vocation. Except for occasional stints elsewhere when times were lean, it's all I have done.

"In 1953 I married Karen Kruse. Our daughter Astrid was born in 1954. At present we live in Orinda, California, a hilly suburb of the Berkeley-Oakland area. Amusements include travel, camping, hiking, boating, gardening, carpentry, reading, drawing, and talk till all hours of the night. We are active in the local science fiction club, the Mystery Writers of America, and the Scowrers. Those last are the San Francisco chapter of the Baker Street Irregulars, and I am proud to have an investiture from the late beloved Edgar W. Smith himself. I also hold two Hugo trophies and won the first annual BSI and Macmillan Cock Robin Mystery Awards. Other affiliations are Science Fiction Writers of America and the American Association for the Advancement of Science.

"Mostly I do science fiction. Without being messianic about it, I think this is as legitimate a literary form as any other, with some exciting special potentialities. However, I've also published in the mystery, adventure, and historical fields, as well as nonfiction, poetry, and criticism; and not long ago I scripted a film about the American space program for USIA. Occasionally I translate, but that is for love rather than money."

Poul Anderson's arrival as one of the outstanding science fiction writers of his time is usually connected with the publication in 1960 of *High Crusade*, a remarkably plausible, mildly satirical account of the arrival of a space ship in fourteenth-century England, and the subsequent crusade to the stars by a band of British knights. *Three Hearts and Three Lions* (1961), whose ingredients include giants, witches, trolls, a search for identity, and the Danish Resistance in World War II, confirmed his reputation. H. H. Holmes, who was reminded of Tolkien and T. H. White, called it "a perfect modern romance: an exciting adventure story which is also rich in humor and poetry, in allusive wit and fantastic invention. . ." The veteran science fiction reviewer D. Schuyler Miller has spoken of Anderson's ability to look past "the play of peril and action to the psychological actions and interactions of his characters," and the *Times Literary Supplement* has praised his "para-ethnological ingenuity in inventing alien cultures appropriate to remote physical and historical conditions."

The highly successful author of over two hundred short stories, novels, and articles, Anderson is famed for his versatility. As well as such near-fantasies as *High Crusade*, he has written orthodox space operas, straight historical novels, and agreeable detective stories featuring a "Nippowegian" private detective named Trygve Yamamura. He has even combined the various genres he has mastered, as in "The Martian Crown Jewels," a synthesis of science fiction and detective story.

Usually an excellent stylist, Anderson is occasionally accused by his critics of overwriting and "shallowness"—faults endemic in pulp fiction writing. He remains, as Isaac Asimov has said, "one of the handful of serious science fiction writers who have made their segment of literature a respected field in this last generation."

Poul Anderson is the son of Anton William and Astrid (Hertz) Anderson. He has a special interest in Nordic writing and has translated Danish folk tales into English.

PRINCIPAL WORKS: Vault of the Ages, 1952; Broken Sword, 1954; Brain Wave, 1954; Planet of No Return, 1956; Star Ways, 1956; The Enemy Stars, 1959; Virgin Planet, 1959; Perish by the Sword, 1959; The High Crusade, 1960; Murder in Black Letter, 1960; Three Hearts and Three Lions, 1961; Twilight World, 1961; Guardians of Time, 1961; Murder Bound, 1962; After Doomsday, 1963; Time and Stars, 1964; Trader to the Stars, 1964; The Star Fox, 1965; Shield, 1965; Agent of the Terran Empire, 1965; The Corridors of Time, 1965; Flandry of Terra, 1965; The Troubletwisters, 1966; Ensign Flandry, 1966; The Fox, the Dog, and the Griffin (adapted from the Danish of C. Molbech), 1966; Satan's World, 1969; Seven Conquests, 1969; Tales of Flying Mountains, 1970; Beyond the Beyond, 1970; Tau Zero, 1970; The Byworlder, 1971; Operation Chaos, 1971; The Sleeping Sorceress, 1972; Un-Man, 1972; Hrolf Kraki's Saga (retold), 1973.

ABOUT: Amis, K. New Maps of Hell, 1960; Asimov, I. *Introduction to* Is There Life on Other Worlds? 1963; Moskowitz, S. Seekers of Tomorrow, 1966; Tuck, D. H. (ed.) A Handbook of Science Fiction and Fantasy, 1959. *Periodicals*—Analog October 1961; Holiday February 1965.

ANDERSON, ROBERT (WOODRUFF) (April 28, 1917–), American dramatist, writes: "I was born in New York City, but soon after my birth my family moved to the suburb of New Rochelle, where I lived until I went away to preparatory school when I was fourteen.

"At the time of my birth, my father, James H. Anderson, was an executive with The United Verde Copper Company. But he had started out as a very poor boy in New York City, his mother having died when he was a child, and his father having deserted the family. Whatever home he had was with a grandfather who ran a small newspaper stand on West Sixteenth street. My father worked from childhood on, but he managed to get some kind of education at night school. He got a job as a stenographer with William A. Clark, one of the copper kings, and gradually through dedication and determination rose to be an executive with the company. In the spring of 1929 he retired to live off his income. He was fifty-one years old. After the crash in the fall of that year, there was no income. My father, like so many men at that time, had to find a new way to earn a living. He became a life insurance salesman.

"My mother was a teacher in New York City schools at the time of her marriage. She was an extremely well-educated woman, particularly for her time, and I am grateful to her for all the trips to the theatre, museums, and concerts, and for her guarded encouragement and appreciation of my beginning talents.

"I can hardly remember a time when I wasn't doing three or four things at once. I built model ships and airplanes in the basement, miniature golf courses on the lawn, sang my head off in the living room (with the idea of becoming an opera singer or a crooner—it didn't matter which), painted portraits in the attic and wrote poetry all over the house, and sent the poetry weekly to *St. Nicholas* magazine. I also was a local kid tennis star, kept my own garden of specimen plants, and of course, attended school (a remarkable private school, Thornton-Donovan, where I was sent because it was felt I did not have enough energy to attend public school!).

"At Phillips Exeter Academy I concentrated mostly on singing and being miserably lonely. The loneliness, which I suspect is pretty common among adolescents, later found its way into *Tea and Sympathy*. I had no real reason to be lonely, since I was a member of a fraternity and the Senior Council, an officer in the musical clubs, and a letter man. But I was lonely.

"At Harvard the loneliness continued until the beginning of my sophomore year, when a friend suggested I go across the river to Boston to try out for a part in a play being put on at a girls' school (Erskine). I didn't have anything else to do that night, so I went—and met my future wife, Phyllis Stohl, who was directing the play. I didn't get the part, but I got stage-struck, and I got the girl. From then on I careered through college, acting in three shows a year for Phyllis, who also directed at Radcliffe and Harvard, writing plays in Robert Hillyer's advanced writing course, and writing book, lyrics and music for college shows. (What arrogance!) I turned Harvard into a drama school as far as I was concerned, and when I finally took my orals for my Ph.D., I countered most questions about the poetry or fiction of any Age with "I don't know much about the poetry or fiction, but I can tell you about the plays and theatre of that period." The examiners generously passed me. After all, I was entering the Navy and going off to war the next day.

"While doing my graduate work, I had taught at various schools around Boston, had assisted Harry Levin and the late Theodore Spencer in their theatre courses at Harvard, and had gone on writing very poor plays. I had also apprenticed at summer theatres, sweeping my quota of stages.

"In the war I served on board the Alaska and the Texas in the Pacific and ended up as a lieutenant attached to Admiral Nimitz's staff on Guam. I wrote a play, *Come Marching Home*, which won a contest as the best play written by a serviceman overseas. I was told at Iwo Jima that if I could write a couple more plays, I might be able to win a Rockefeller Playwriting Fellowship when, as, and if I returned from the war. After Okinawa I got down to that, and when I emerged from the Navy in 1946, I had the fellowship to study under John Gassner.

"By this time Phyllis had come to New York and was with the Theatre Guild, soon to become head of their play department and associate producer. From 1946 to 1953, the activity was intense and varied. I wrote plays in the morning, radio and later television scripts in the afternoon, and taught playwriting three nights a week at the American Theatre Wing Professional Training Program. Two plays were done at summer theatres, one at Arena Stage in Washington, D.C., and then after almost every producer in New York had turned down the play, The Playwrights Company accepted *Tea and Sympathy*. Beautifully directed by Elia Kazan, and acted by Deborah Kerr and John Kerr, it was a success and changed my life.

ROBERT ANDERSON

"A tragic pall, however, hung over this finally-won success. Phyllis had had her first operation for cancer in 1951, and I knew that her death was inevitable. She died in November of 1956, after five years of gallantly fighting and hoping and crowding as much of life and work as could be contained in whatever time was left. She had been an immense help to many young playwrights. Eight volumes have been dedicated to her, a theatre named for her, and playwriting prizes and fellowships set up in her name at Harvard and Yale.

"After Phyllis died, I wandered for some time, to Paris, where Ingrid Bergman was doing *Tea and Sympathy*, to the Congo for research for my screenplay of *The Nun's Story*, to California for other film work, and to London, where I settled down in a flat in Berkeley Square to write *Silent Night, Lonely Night*.

"In 1959 I had the great good fortune to marry Teresa Wright. We have made our home in New York City, but we have recently bought an old farmhouse in Connecticut and intend soon to leave the city and make that our permanent home.

"At present I have a play, *The Days Between*, being produced around the country by fifty college and community theatres as the first play in a new project, the American Playwrights' Theatre. The object of this group is to get plays by established playwrights to the college and community theatres before—not after—Broadway production.

"I have just completed a new play called *I Never Sang for My Father*. At forty-eight I feel I have barely begun. But the American theatre at the moment is a rough place in which to grow and experiment and develop. It is a place to make a killing but not a living. It is a place for the occasional hit but not for a body of work, which must contain good, bad, and indifferent plays. But I have a sign over my desk which reads: 'Nobody asked you to be a playwright.' "

Robert Anderson's 1953 Broadway triumph *Tea and Sympathy*, subsequently performed all over the world, is set in a boys' prep school. Its hero is a youth whose sensitivity, mistaken by his peers for evidence of homosexuality, also inhibits him from proving his virility with the campus slut. His life seems wrecked until his housemaster's compassionate wife, who is supposed to offer only "tea and sympathy," offers herself instead. Some critics objected that the play's content was slight and unoriginal, that its characters were drawn in black and white; but few denied that it was effective theatre, and there was general agreement with Louis Kronenberger's suggestion that, if it was "bad literature," it was nevertheless "a good play."

All Summer Long, first performed in 1953 at the Arena Theatre in Washington, was an adaptation of David Wetzel's novel *A Wreath and a Curse*. It attracted some critical support but did not share its famous predecessor's success at the box office. In *Silent Night, Lonely Night*, Anderson returned to the theme of sex as therapy in a drama about the chance meeting at a New England inn of two unhappy strangers. John Gassner admired the play's "quietly poetic" quality, its "personally felt rather than fabricated emotion," but others thought it lacking in incident and dull. Anderson's second popular and commercial success came in 1967 with *You Know I Can't Hear You When the Water's Running*, a program of four one-act plays which successfully combine "naturalistic pathos" and comedy. He had another Broadway hit in *I Never Sang for My Father*, a presumably semi-autobiographical study of a man's painful coming to terms with his father, a self-made tycoon in his dotage who "is never less than the ruin of a titan."

Anderson has been placed by Gerald Weales "among the leading new Pineros" of the American stage—one of those writers "so involved in the prejudices and the preoccupations of their society that their work reflects the values of its audience." According to Brooks Atkinson, he is "the sort of writer who needs illuminating staging and acting. He does not write 'actor proof' dramas."

Rex Reed interviewed Anderson in 1967, in his early nineteenth century house in Connecticut, and found him "not looking very much like Hollywood's idea of a famous playwright. More Jimmy Stewart than Reginald Gardner." Anderson has written a number of movie scripts (*Tea and Sympathy*, *The Nun's Story*, *The Sand Pebbles*, among others), and a "somber, intelligent, and . . . moving" novel, *After*, about a writer drawn into a sexual liaison with a young actress after his wife's terrible death from cancer. "The course of their affair," wrote one reviewer, "his own reliving of the past, the good and bad times in his marriage, the reappearance of the other woman in his life, all weave in and out compellingly."

PRINCIPAL WORKS: *Plays*—Tea and Sympathy, 1953; All Summer Long, 1955; Silent Night, Lonely Night, 1960; The Days Between, 1965; You Know I Can't Hear You When the Water's Running, 1967; I Never Sang for My Father, 1968. *Fiction*—After, 1973.

ABOUT: Celebrity Register, 1963; Current Biography, 1954; Gassner, J. *prefaces to* Best American Plays, fourth and fifth series, 1958 and 1963; Weales, G. American Drama Since World War II, 1962. *Periodicals*—Christian Science Monitor May 24, 1965; Life November 19, 1965; New York Times October 11, 1953; March 26, 1967; Saturday Review October 17, 1953.

***ANDRES, STEFAN** (June 26, 1906–June 29, 1970), German novelist and poet, was the ninth child of a miller. He was born in a mill in the Dhrontal, one of the tributary valleys of the Mosel, near the old Roman town of Trier. His childhood was spent in close contact with nature, but when a dam was built across the valley his parents moved to Schweich, a village near Trier, where he attended the village school. His parents had followed a pious custom by "promising him to God," that is, dedicating him to the priesthood, at his baptism. From the age of eleven, therefore, he attended various monastic schools, and the early separation from family and home, which he was able to visit for only twelve days a year, threw him onto his own resources at an early age. At twenty-two he decided against the priesthood and instead studied philosophy, German, drama, and art history, at the universities of Cologne, Jena, and Berlin.

His first novel, *Bruder Luzifer* (Brother Lucifer, 1932), is a partly autobiographical account of the steps by which an artistic young man is drawn away from the monastic life by the attractions of the world; it introduces his characteristic theme—the conflict between the spiritual life represented by Roman Catholicism and the strong appeal of the senses. After its publication, Andres traveled in Italy, Egypt, and Greece, at the same time writing the novels *Eberhard im Kontrapunkt* (Contrapuntal Eberhard, 1934) and *Die unsichtbare Mauer* (The Invisible Wall, 1934), both about young provincials making their way in the world by hard work and study. Andres returned to the conflict between Christian and worldly values in the novella *El Greco malt den Grossinquisitor* (El Greco Paints the Grand Inquisitor, 1936).

By 1937 Andres had settled in the ancient town of Positano, in southern Italy, in a self-imposed

* än′ dres

exile which reflected his love for the south as well as his distaste for the Nazi regime in his own country. There he lived and worked for thirteen years. *Der Mann von Asteri* (The Man From Asteri, 1939) tells the life story of a wealthy, self-assured Mosel winegrower whose wife commits suicide after he has become involved in an extramarital affair. *Der gefrorene Dionysus* (The Frozen Dionysus, 1941), later republished in Germany as *Die Liebesschaukel* (Love's Swing, 1951), is set in a small Italian town where a sculptor, at odds with himself and the world, is eventually reunited with his "woman of destiny," who restores meaning to his life and his desire to create.

Andres's best-known work, the novella *Wir sind Utopia* (1942, translated by G. Brooks as *We Are Utopia*), is set against the background of the Spanish Civil War. A young cleric leaves a monastery in the hope of putting his political idealism into practice—though an older priest tells him: "Nobody has yet been able to reform the world and make a Utopia of it, nobody, not even God himself! . . . He loves this world because it is imperfect." While fighting in Franco's army he is captured and imprisoned in his old monastery. The prison commandant receives orders to kill all the prisoners; the priest is in a position to assassinate the commandant before the order is passed, but he cannot bring himself to do so, and the massacre is duly carried out. The priest is one of its victims, though once again he could have escaped, since the commandant had offered him freedom in exchange for absolution. The book probes in the most direct way the question of individual responsibility in war, the moral problem involved in killing (and being killed). It was banned in wartime in Germany, though it circulated clandestinely. Graham Greene has described it as "amongst the most shattering of modern literature," and it has been compared to his own novel *The Power and the Glory*.

In the later novels *Die Hochzeit der Feinde* (The Marriage of Enemies, 1947), which treats the problem of Franco-German relationships, and *Ritter der Gerechtigkeit* (Knights of Justice, 1948), set in Italy at the time of the fall of Mussolini, Andres continued to emphasize the element of social and political criticism. This is combined with his preoccupation with man's spiritual predicament in his most ambitious work, the trilogy *Die Sintflut* (The Flood, 1949–1959), a dark (though often funny) political fantasy on the rise and fall of Nazism. Some critics thought the trilogy lacked the imaginative vitality demanded by its theme, but others agreed with H. M. Waidson, who wrote: "The plot is sustained in its many ramifications, and if the sense of its inevitability is sometimes lacking, the author jumps clean over the gap with his exuberant fantasy."

STEFAN ANDRES

Andres returned to Germany in 1950, building a house at Unkel am Rhein, near Bonn. In *Der Knabe im Brunnen* (The Boy in the Well, 1953) he recalls his own boyhood. His subsequent books include *Die Reise nach Portiuncula* (The Journey to Portiuncula, 1954), in which a prosperous middle-aged German brewer makes a journey to Italy which is also a journey into a painful but rewarding spiritual awakening; *Der Taubenturm* (The Dove Tower, 1966), the story of a German family living in Italy near the end of World War II, caught between the rival armies; and *Die Dumme* (The Dumb Girl, 1969), whose pretty and devout heroine is emotionally betrayed in West Germany by her employer and in East Germany by a middle-aged party functionary. Her two lovers are in some ways representatives of the two Germanys, the Western one selfish and corrupt, the Eastern didactic and overcerebral; disappointed with both, she returns home for "a surrealist finale revealing all the hollow, phosphorescent glitter of West Germany's affluent society," as one reviewer put it in the *Times Literary Supplement*. He added: "Andres etches the contrasting social landscape of West and East Germany with Brechtian acidity. . . . Although rooted in the complexities of the contemporary German situation, it treats of a universal theme; the incompatibility of Christian naivety with the realities of existence in West and East alike."

During the 1960s, Andres's books were consistently on the best-seller lists in Germany. He was a gifted storyteller, and his *Novellen und Erzählungen* (Novellas and Stories) have appeared in two volumes (1962 and 1964). His earlier work included several books of poetry. After the war he also turned to drama with such plays as *Tanz durchs*

Labyrinth (Dance Through the Labyrinth, 1948) and *Die Touristen* (The Tourists, 1955); the radio play *Der Reporter Gottes* (The Reporter of God, 1952); and *Gottes Utopia* (God's Utopia, 1950), a dramatization of *Wir sind Utopia*. But the only other work of his to be translated so far is his retelling of the story of the Bible, *Die biblische Geschichte* (1965, translated by M. Bullock as *The Bible Story*).

In 1961 Andres returned to his beloved Italy, settling in Rome, where he died at the age of sixty-four, of complications following surgery. He left a wife and two daughters. Andres wrote of himself: "The major formative influences on me in my youth were nature and everyday peasant life; later the village and the Catholic church, particularly in the concentrated form of monastic school and novitiate as a monk. The glory of the Eternal as temptation and consolation, commitment of the spirit, experience of discipline, obedience. After that the university: years of loosening up, of going astray, of emptiness, of seeking. Years of travel: escape into the world. First publications, even poems. All informed by naive self-assurance. Result: sheer ignorance on every page. Only in 1937, when I left Germany with my wife and children, did I find in Mediterranean solitude that atmosphere of inevitability which forced my aimlessness into stability. I am now grateful to my ill fortune for driving me onto the field of relevance, and for keeping me poor, unknown and alone for ten years."

PRINCIPAL WORKS IN ENGLISH TRANSLATION: We Are Utopia, 1964; The Bible Story, 1966.

ABOUT: Penguin Companion to Literature 2, 1969; Twentieth Century Writing, 1969; Waidson, H. M. The Modern German Novel, 1959. *Periodicals*—Times Literary Supplement January 21, 1955; May 19, 1966; January 15, 1970.

***ANDRIĆ, IVO** (October 10, 1892–), Yugoslav novelist, short story writer, and poet, winner of the 1961 Nobel Prize for Literature, was born at Docu, a village near Travnik in Bosnia, whose varied peoples and tumultuous history are the stuff of his novels. His father, a poor artisan, died when Ivo Andrić was two, and the family was brought up in Visĕgrad by the mother, a strict Roman Catholic. A Croat by birth, Andrić became a Serbian by choice. He attended secondary school in Sarajevo, the capital of Bosnia, and went on to study philosophy and history at the universities of Zagreb, Vienna, and Cracow.

While he was still in his teens, Andrić joined Mlada Bosna (Young Bosnia), an organization of South Slav patriots seeking freedom from Austro-Hungarian rule. He had already published his first essays and poems, including translations of Walt Whitman, when a member of Mlada Bosna assassinated Archduke Ferdinand of Austria. World War I followed and Andrić was arrested on political grounds and imprisoned for three years. "I grew up inside during those years," he has said.

And, indeed, the physical circumstances of his imprisonment, and his reading then of Dostoevsky and Kierkegaard, have permanently marked his work ever since. Fear, suffering, and uncertainty ruled the prose poems in *Ex Ponto* and *Nemiri* (Anxiety), published just after World War I: "There is no other truth but pain, there is no other reality but suffering, pain and suffering in every drop of water, in every blade of grass, in every grain of crystal, in every sound of living voice, in sleep and in vigil, before life and perhaps after life."

In 1918 Andrić joined the editorial board of the literary magazine *Književni Jug*, where much of his early work appeared. He subsequently completed his education at the University of Graz in Austria, receiving his doctorate in 1923 with a thesis on Bosnian intellectual life during the centuries of Turkish rule. The same year he entered the diplomatic service of the Kingdom of the Serbs, Croats, and Slovenes—Yugoslavia since 1929—and served in Rome, Bucharest, Trieste, Graz, Berlin, and elsewhere in Europe.

Andrić continued to write during the 1920s but abandoned poetry for prose, producing acutely observant stories and novellas about the full-blooded, passionate, and richly assorted peoples of Bosnia and their dark history. He was quickly established as "a master among modern Yugoslav story writers." In the 1930s, however, as his diplomatic responsibilities increased, his literary output diminished. In 1941, as Yugoslavia's minister to Germany, he left Berlin only a few hours before the Germans began their assault on Belgrade.

During the German occupation, virtually under house arrest, he sequestered himself in his Belgrade apartment and devoted himself to writing. He has described his feelings when, during the bombing of Belgrade, he saw the people fleeing past his window: "They were all trying to save something—their lives, their children, some precious possession. I had nothing to save but my life and it was beneath human dignity to run for that." The fruits of these years were the three novels published in 1945 as the Bosnian Trilogy.

The most ambitious of these, and the first to appear in English, was *Na Drini ćuprija*, translated by Lovett Edwards as *The Bridge on the Drina*. It is a chronicle of three and a half centuries of Bosnian life, ending in 1914. Its central symbol is the bridge of the title, which spans the river that divides Bosnia and Serbia, east and west, past and present, and which represents man's hunger for permanence

* an′ drēch

and balance, just as the river symbolizes the flux and chaos of history.

Some reviewers complained that the book was less a novel than a cycle of stories, but others found in it a pattern, "flowing" rather than "progressing," which was the pattern of life itself. Egon Hostovsky was reminded of "Tolstoy's monumental style," and at the same time of the "lyric tone of Turgenev." Stoyan Christowe wrote that the novel "creates its own form, style and rhythm. It reads as though it were not composed but simply grew out of the soil and the climate like a ballad to become part of the national heritage." The book was singled out for special praise by the Swedish Academy, which gave Andrić the Nobel Prize for Literature in 1961 "for the epic force with which he has depicted themes and human destinies drawn from the history of his country."

The trilogy was completed by *Travička hronika* (translated by Kenneth Johnstone as *Bosnian Story*, and also by Joseph Hitrec as *Bosnian Chronicle*), and *Gospodjica* (translated by Hitrec as *The Woman from Sarajevo*). The first is set in Travnik during the Napoleonic era and deals with the conflict there between the French and the Austrian consuls and their moral disintegration in that savagely hostile environment. Episodic in form, but more closely integrated than *The Bridge on the Drina*, it was praised especially for its masterly characterization. *Gospodjica*, a short novel about a woman "infatuated with thrift," was also admired for its direct but subtle characterization, and for the skill with which character is related to history. Comparing the trilogy with Andrić's earlier work, Joseph Hitrec found a continuing obsession with evil and guilt, but also two new elements: "One is a deliberate reaching back for myth and the healing touch of legend—the childlike folktale with its promise of innocence. The other, more important one, is the discovery of permanent values in the legacy of the past."

Prokleta avlija (1954, translated as *Devil's Yard*) is set in a prison in the last days of the Ottoman Empire and describes the conflict between the tyrannical warden of the place and an idealistic but deluded young dreamer. Both are shown to be equally the victims and the agents of a corrupt totalitarianism, and the book was widely interpreted as a parable about contemporary political systems. It remains a work of art, however, and, as R. D. Spector said of *The Vizier's Elephant*, a collection of three novellas, "Whatever [Andrić's] political views, his concerns are humanitarian; and whatever his message, his aim is art."

The Pasha's Concubine, a generous collection of Andrić's short stories translated by Joseph Hitrec, was warmly praised. "Here," wrote John Simon, "is a cross-fertilizing correspondence joining across

IVO ANDRIĆ

centuries a jaded Turkish pasha to an Austrian officer's womenfolk, a murderous Ottoman berserker to a lowly Christian monk, Eastern usurpers to Western visitors to native peasantry. All of them are physically assaulted by this fierce, barren and somehow overhuman land in which wonderful trivialities and unspeakable horrors walk side by side, as do insight and inscrutability in Andrić's darkly beautiful prose."

Since World War II Andrić has been active in Yugoslav politics and has represented Bosnia in the Yugoslav parliament. For many years he was president of the Federation of Yugoslav Writers. He is an elegant man, "modest, soft-spoken, and dignified." His wife, Milica, whom he married in 1959, is a well-known Yugoslav painter and theatrical designer. They live in Belgrade. "Having long been puzzled by what took place around me," Andrić says, "I became convinced . . . that it is futile and mistaken to seek meaning in the unimportant and yet apparently so important events occurring around us; that we should seek a meaning, instead, in the strata built up by the centuries upon the few great legends of mankind."

PRINCIPAL WORKS IN ENGLISH TRANSLATION: *Fiction*—The Bridge on the Drina, 1959; Bosnian Story, 1959 (republished as Bosnian Chronicle, 1963); Devil's Yard, 1962; The Vizier's Elephant: Three Novellas, 1962; The Woman from Sarajevo, 1965; The Pasha's Concubine and Other Tales, 1968. *Poetry in* Lavrin, J. (ed.) An Anthology of Modern Yugoslav Poetry, 1963.

ABOUT: Alvarez, A. Under Pressure, 1965; Current Biography, 1962; Kadić, A. Contemporary Serbian Literature, 1964; Penguin Companion to Literature 2, 1969; Smith, H. (ed.) Columbia Dictionary of Modern European Literature, 1947. *Periodicals*—Books Abroad Winter, 1963; Christian Science Monitor July 9, 1959;

October 28, 1962; New Statesman March 21, 1959; New York Herald Tribune Book Review, June 28, 1959; New York Times Book Review June 28, 1959; November 1, 1959; October 28, 1962; April 11, 1965; July 28, 1968; San Francisco Chronicle July 13, 1959; Saturday Review July 11, 1959; November 24, 1962; April 17, 1965; April 3, 1968; Slavic Review September 1964; Times [London] June 29, 1959; Times Literary Supplement March 20, 1959.

***ANDRZEYEVSKI, GEORGE [JERZY]** (August 19, 1909–), Polish novelist and story writer, reports: "I was born in Warsaw and resided in this city all my life with the exception of the years 1945–1952, when I lived in Cracow and Szczecin. My father was a grocer who failed in business during World War I. My mother was the daughter of a provincial doctor in the Ukraine and only by family tradition belonged to the gentry. I began to write in my early boyhood and perhaps my stubborn insistence on going on writing accounted for the fact that I was a rather average student. I left the university (where I read Polish literature) lightheartedly, before taking a degree. Luckily I was not a precocious genius and had my share of healthy disappointments before my first book—a collection of stories called *Unavoidable Ways*—appeared in 1936. The next book, a novel (*The Order of the Heart*, 1938) got the award of the Polish Academy of Literature, and some renown for the writer as well as popularity with the reading public. The collection of stories *Night* (1945) deals exclusively with Poland under German occupation. The tortuous and dramatic conflicts of postwar Poland I tried to describe in my next novel, *Ashes and Diamonds* (1948), well-known in the West mainly thanks to the success of Andrzej Wajda's film (1958). The book was several times considered in all-Poland book plebiscites as the best Polish novel in the last twenty years. Further books: an autobiographical sketch, *A Book for Martin* (1954); a collection of stories written during the "thaw," *The Golden Fox* (1955); a novel dealing with the Spanish Inquisition, *Darkness Covers the Earth* (1959); a short novel based on the Children's Crusade in the twelfth century, *The Gates of Paradise* (1960); and a contemporary novel taking place in Paris about the ironical-pathetic contradictions between youth and old age, *He Cometh Leaping Upon the Mountains* (1963).

"I consider myself a very Polish product in many ways, i.e.—and simplifying it a little—a person generally more immune to great hardships than to the petty troubles of everyday life. Two periods in my life I consider the most intense: the second World War and the period preceding the so-called 'Polish October.' I lived through two great spiritual adventures: in my youth, the Roman Catholic Church; and in my middle age the experience of Marxism. Only once did I participate in an organized political movement: from 1949 to 1957 I was a member of the Communist Party (the Polish United Workers Party).

"I am perhaps the least suitable person to speak freely about my work—that is, without any ambiguous suggestions of arrogance or modesty, faith and doubt. Therefore it might be better if I quote the Polish critic Andrzej Kijowski, who wrote in his study of my work the following words: 'J. A. is a season's writer. Please do not consider it a pejorative description. The work of this writer conforms in novelistic forms to the succession of Polish intellectual seasons. He is a writer extremely sensitive to an intellectual atmosphere. Any change in that atmosphere influences his personal attitudes. Faster than others does A. name these moods, specify these fluid ideological states; quickly does he find for them a proper artistic form. . . . Therefore people think about contemporaneity in his terms, use his pictures and metaphors. He is a writer-witness, in the meaning given to this term by the master of the generation, André Malraux. A. is beyond any doubt the writer of the intellectual elite, its *porte parole*, mandatory. . . . Anybody looking in the future for a record of what people in Poland thought during half a century . . . will have to read the novels and stories of this writer'."

The Order of the Heart, about the moral torments of a priest in a Polish village, shows the influence of the French Catholic writers in its theme, and of Conrad in its tone. This first novel earned for Andrzeyevski acclamation as his country's most gifted Catholic writer, a "Polish Mauriac." At this time, just before World War II, Andrzeyevski broke with the right-wing racist weekly *Prosto z Mostu*, which had launched him, and denounced anti-Semitism. He continued to help the Jews, at increasing risk to himself, under the German occupation, and during those years became the moral leader and "oracle" of the Warsaw writers, active as a clandestine lecturer and author, and founder of an underground literary review.

The postwar Polish government, imposed by Russia, was not the one for which the young heroes of the resistance had fought; for them the war continued. *Popiol i Diamant* (*Ashes and Diamonds*) deals compassionately with one such youth and equally warmly with the old Communist fighter whom he murders, so that the reader is left with a sense of tragic waste. The book was welcomed and rewarded by the Communist regime, and was a best seller. Andrzeyevski, who had lost faith both in Catholicism and in liberal democracy, denounced both and became a member and active publicist of the Communist party. In "Alpha the

* an dzhā ev′ ski

Moralist," an essay in *The Captive Mind* (1953), Czeslaw Milosz describes Andrzeyevski as a man of boundless ambition with a "barometer-like sensitivity to the moral opinion of his environment," and says that he was disliked and derided by his fellow writers during this period. But Milosz also acknowledges that Andrzeyevski as a young man had been a tormented seeker after truth, for whom writing was "a redemptive activity"; there are many who would accept Andrzeyevski's declaration that he was brought to Marxism by the same "search for intellectual and spiritual discipline" which had made him a Catholic.

At any rate, disillusionment with communism and with "socialist realism" was manifest in the allegorical stories Andrzeyevski published during the early 1950s. In 1957 he resigned from the party in protest against censorship and became politically disengaged. His allegorical novel *Ciemnosci Kryja Ziemie* (Darkness Covers the Earth, 1957), published in the United States as *The Inquisitors,* impressed some American reviewers with the parallels it implies between "the Holy Office and the party line" and with its subtle ironies.

More widely and enthusiastically admired in the West was *Idzie Skaczac po Górach* (1963), published in Britain as *He Cometh Leaping Upon the Mountains* and in the United States as *A Sitter for a Satyr.* It is a *tour de force* parodying a variety of literary styles and affectionately satirizing the Paris culture industry, demoralized by the return to painting after years of inactivity of a Picasso-like contemporary master. In *The Appeal,* a middle-aged paranoiac describes his delusions of political persecution, and recalls the actual persecutions that precipitated his condition. The novel, which has not been published in Poland, seemed to most critics successful both as an indictment of the police state and as a moving and accurate study of a crippled mind.

Andrzeyevski is the most widely translated Polish writer of the middle generation and internationally the best known; he has twice been nominated for the Nobel Prize. The "tall, lean figure, the ironic flash of his eyes behind his glasses," which Milosz recalls from wartime Warsaw, are today one of the main landmarks of the city's literary scene. Andrzeyevski was reportedly denied publication in Poland between 1968 and 1971, when a new "working dialogue" was established between Edward Gierek's government and the intellectuals.

PRINCIPAL WORKS IN ENGLISH TRANSLATION: The Inquisitors, 1960; Ashes and Diamonds, 1962; The Gates of Paradise, 1963; A Sitter for a Satyr (England, He Cometh Leaping Upon the Mountains), 1965; The Appeal, 1971. *Stories in* Gillon, A. and Krzyzanowski, L. (eds.) Modern Polish Literature, 1964; Kuncewicz, M. (ed.) The Modern Polish Mind, 1962; The Literary Review Spring 1967.

GEORGE ANDRZEYEVSKI

ABOUT: Gillon, A. and Krzyzanowski, L. (eds.) Modern Polish Literature, 1964; International Who's Who, 1972–1973; Milosz, C. The Captive Mind, 1953; Mutuszewski, R. Portraits of Contemporary Polish Writers (Warsaw), 1959; Who's Who in America, 1972–1973. *Periodicals*—Daedalus Fall 1966; East Europe October 1960; New York Review of Books November 11, 1965; New York Times Book Review December 11, 1960; Saturday Review November 5, 1960; July 3, 1965; Times Literary Supplement June 17, 1960; December 12, 1963; May 20, 1965.

***ANNAN, NOËL (GILROY) (Lord Annan)** (December 25, 1916–), English biographer and historian of ideas, writes: "I was born in London and brought up in the traditional style of the English upper middle class. I went to a boarding school at eight, my 'public school' at thirteen and then to the college my father had gone to at Cambridge.

"But there was a difference. My mother was an American from New York City and my father had been unhappy at his public school. So they sent me to a new public school, Stowe, which had been a vast eighteenth century country house set in a park which is the greatest example in existence of English landscape gardening. The headmaster was an original creature and a dazzling teacher, called J. F. Roxburgh, and I was lucky in that some of the teachers were young and stimulating. Thirty years later I wrote his biography.

"The college I went to at Cambridge was also different. King's is known throughout the world for the beauty of its Chapel and the fame of its choir, but it is in fact a rationalist, iconoclastic place whose most famous alumni in the first half of this

* an′ ən

NOËL ANNAN

century were Keynes and E. M. Forster, to both of whom I owe much.

"At King's I studied history and would have become a lawyer but for the war. During the war when I worked in the War Cabinet Office as an army intelligence officer, I wrote reviews for the *New Statesman*. Keynes liked them; and, since I had in fact begun some research on the history of ideas in the Victorian age, he and other dons at King's elected me a Fellow in 1944. I was in France that year, and next year in Germany I became head of a section which dealt with German political parties. But after a year in the British Control Commission, I returned to King's in 1946.

"There I settled down to write a critical study of Leslie Stephen, first editor of the *Dictionary of National Biography*, Victorian agnostic and critic, and father of Virginia Woolf. This was published in 1951 and won the James Tait Black Memorial Prize. I continued to write articles and reviews for learned journals and for the *Times Literary Supplement* and to broadcast in the Third Programme in addition to my lecturing and teaching as a don at Cambridge.

"In 1956 the newly elected Provost at King's suddenly died and to my own, and to everyone else's, astonishment, I was elected Provost in his place at the age of thirty-nine. This curtailed my writing and I got drawn into university administration. Also into the reform of higher education which at this time began to be an issue in Britain. After being made a Trustee of the new Cambridge College built in Churchill's honour, I was on the academic planning committees of three of Britain's new universities. My efforts to get Cambridge to reform itself were about as successful as trying to deflect a rhinoceros by blowing peas at it. But I suppose somebody thought these activities worthwhile as again to my astonishment I was made a life peer in 1965 and now find myself making speeches for various liberal causes in the House of Lords. As I could not envisage myself staying as Provost of King's until I was seventy, I accepted an invitation to become head of University College, London (which is a university on its own within the federal structure of London University) in 1966."

Lord Annan belongs to the radical-humanist tradition of E. M. Forster, Leonard Woolf, and John Maynard Keynes, and one of the most interesting aspects of his literary work is the extent to which it succeeds in modernizing this tradition, whose roots lie in Victorian and Edwardian rationalism.

In *Leslie Stephen* (1951), Annan made a detailed critical, biographical, and historical examination of one of the original and most distinguished of modern rationalists. His treatment of Stephen's character was sympathetic but never indulgent; a model of lucidity and skillfully deployed knowledge, it was greeted with acclaim. The book reveals that Annan's rationalism is more dispassionate than that of his acknowledged master, E. M. Forster: less imaginative, less creative, very much less tormented (one of Annan's chief characteristics as a man and as a writer is his cheerfulness), but nevertheless deeply and sincerely felt. The manner in which Stephen's thinking and character are related to his time is a model of object analysis. Henry Steele Commager thought the book "of immense value, and of immense interest, too, especially to the initiated. It is of value because it tells us so much about the English character; it is of interest because it tells us so much about interesting individuals, about the Clapham Sect, about Cambridge and Oxford, about the rationalists, and because it tells all this with such liveliness and penetration and wit."

The Curious Strength of Positivism in English Thought, Annan's Hobhouse Memorial Lecture, argues that positivism has been the dominant tradition of political thought in England for more than a century, and still has a pervasive influence. Annan's most personal book is undoubtedly his portrait of his old headmaster, J. F. Roxburgh, the snobbish, affected, and limited man who nevertheless did so much at Stowe to humanize the English public school system. "He loved intelligence, skill, enterprise, grace, breeding and beauty," Annan says, "but need was what he responded to." A reviewer in the *Times Literary Supplement* wrote: "It is the principal virtue of Lord Annan's biography that J. F.'s real quality becomes manifest." But, the critic added, "Those Old Stoics [ex-pupils of Stowe] who believe the public schools to be unjustifiable anachronisms, who think of J. F.'s modifications as helping them to prolong their existence, must read this book with mixed feelings."

Lord Annan has the capacity, not very common among authors, of being able thoroughly to enjoy public service. He has served as a governor of Stowe, on the Public Schools Commission, and as chairman of the Departmental Committee on the Teaching of Russian in Schools. He is a trustee of the British Museum and a director of the Royal Opera House, Covent Garden. Annan won the Le Bas prize in 1948, for the essay enlarged as *Leslie Stephen*, and gave the Romanes Lectures at Oxford in 1965. In the latter year he was offered the position of deputy chairman of the governors of the British Broadcasting Corporation, but he turned it down on account of his preference for academic work. Noël Annan was married in 1950 to Gabriele Ullstein, daughter of Louis Ferdinand Ullstein of Berlin; they have two daughters. His principal recreation is Mediterranean travel. His political sympathies are left-wing.

PRINCIPAL WORKS: Leslie Stephen: His Thought and Character in Relation to His Times, 1951; The Curious Strength of Positivism in English Political Thought, 1959; Roxburgh of Stowe, 1965 (U.S., The Headmaster).
ABOUT: Who's Who, 1971. *Periodicals*—Daily Telegraph October 17, 1965; Nation March 1, 1952; New Statesman October 13, 1951; New York Herald Tribune Book Review May 11, 1952; Times Literary Supplement October 19, 1951; November 18, 1965.

ANTONINUS, BROTHER (William Oliver *Everson) (September 10, 1912–), American poet, writes: "I was born in Sacramento, California, on September 10, 1912, at six in the morning. I grew up in Fresno County, in the town of Selma.

"My father was a printer and a bandmaster—far more the latter than the former. But some retrograde quirk of mentality prevented him from fully realizing his enormous charismatic potential.

"But I acquired directly from him his sense of presence on the platform. Even as a child I could spellbind.

"In high school I began to try to write, but I was twenty-three before I discovered the work of Robinson Jeffers. It was an intellectual awakening and a religious conversion in one. My father had been agnostic; Jeffers showed me God.

"In Jeffers I found my voice. From him I learned the surf-like line. Someone has said I have baptized that line but it was something other than that—something to do with compression. Someone else has said that Jeffers is a poet of 'large flaws and no weaknesses.' I removed the flaws.

* ĕ′ vər son

BROTHER ANTONINUS

"If it is arrogant of me to assert it, what else, actually, could one do, given such a master? Every disciple seeks to perfect by reduction the frame of the giant who begot him.

"When I was eighteen the first woman came into my life. I married her eight years later. She was the first of three great loves, who were to emerge as the primary vectors upon whom the periods of my life are founded.

"Each of them arrived at a time of great impasse for me. And each of them changed me in ways I could never have accomplished alone.

"It was as if it took, each time, a new and more corrosive agent to dissolve the walls of egoism and self-obsession that encased me, and shift the spiritual center of gravity to some deeper place in my soul. Each time it took more pain.

"So it was. A Swede and an Italian and a Mexican. And the last was the greatest, the most painful. Or perhaps it was only that I myself had grown greater, as life and religion are meant to make us greater. For the greater the realization the greater the need, and greatness is met in greatness.

"Be that as it may, in the end each of them failed me. Failed? In love, in passion, who fails whom? It goes without saying I loved them too much. Now I am free.

"For each delivered me, actually. This, too, was necessary. For I have learned I do not have the capacity to deliver myself, to impose my will on my life. That I have less and less capacity.

" 'When thou wast younger thou didst gird thyself and didst walk where thou wouldst. But when thou shalt be old thou shalt stretch forth thy hands, and another shall gird thee, and lead thee where thou wouldst not.'

"I entered the Catholic Church in 1949 through the hands, or better, the arms, of the Italian. I could never have done this except for one fact: the precept of Christ. Which is not to say I have any regrets. Sometimes a man has to be dragged from his greatest need in order to consummate the need of one greater than he can grasp.

"I entered the Dominican Order in 1951 as an oblate, or unvowed lay brother. Because of a canonical impediment a married man may not take vows.

" 'I live, under obedience, the life of a vowed brother,' is the way I explained it to *Time* magazine, 'only I am not vowed. I could leave any time, or they could send me away.'

"In 1960 I met the Mexican, and she it was who delivered me into my vows. When the necessary dispensation had been secured from Rome I took my novitiate and made profession on October 3, 1964, the Feast of the Little Flower. These, I have come to understand, were my true nuptials.

"And if there is blood in the nuptial bed it cannot be otherwise. In the love of woman or the love of God, it cannot be otherwise.

"Thus my most friendly critic, when he demurs before a certain 'pointlessly sadistic' element in my work, flinches from truth. Sadistic? Pointless? When violence is the agent of deliverance it can surely be neither.

"All my books are stained with my blood. Some of it is profane, some of it is holy. But I poured out my heart in them, and profane or holy, that means blood. A poet is nothing without heart. The heart has to spend itself. Profane or holy, the heart must be spent.

"I live by faith. In Christ. He alone prevails."

Brother Antoninus is one of the three children of a Norwegian immigrant, Louis Waldemar Everson, and Francelia (Herber) Everson, who grew up on a Minnesota farm. He attended Fresno State College in 1931 and in 1934–1935 but left without a degree to write verse. He has said that the two "crystallizing books of my pre-Catholic formation" were *Lady Chatterley's Lover* and *Tropic of Cancer*. An eleven-page pamphlet of poems, *These Are the Ravens*, appeared in 1935 as by Bill Everson. His first book, *San Joaquin*, composed of poems written while the author was farming in the San Joaquin Valley, appeared in 1939 with a foreword by Lawrence Clark Powell. Antoninus was a conscientious objector during World War II and spent several years (1943 to 1946) in work camps in Oregon. There he himself printed several small books of his verse, all later gathered in his first important volume, *The Residual Years*.

After the war the poet joined the San Francisco anarcho-pacifist group centered around Kenneth Rexroth, who has been his chief advocate among the critics. Antoninus entered the Catholic Church, as he says, late in 1949, and joined the Catholic Workers movement in 1950, serving in the slums of Oakland. During the San Francisco "renaissance" in 1957 he re-entered the literary scene, where he exerted an important influence.

Discussing Antoninus's work in *Sewanee Review*, James Dickey called the poems in *The Residual Years* "full of the hatred and necessity of sex, and of a very convincing and powerful, from-inside-the-thing feeling about California farmers and farming." These poems seemed to Dickey open and unforced, but he was struck "by the author's humorless, even owlish striving after self-knowledge and certainty, his intense and bitter inadequacy and frustration." In the same article, reviewing *The Crooked Lines of God* (published after Antoninus's conversion), Dickey was sorry to find what he called "learned, dry sermonizing" and an attitude "somewhat self-righteous and even self-congratulatory." Rexroth disagreed, seeing instead "simple statements about subjective experience" in "poems of stunning impact."

The Hazards of Holiness, comprising poems written between 1957 and 1960, dealt according to *Commonweal*'s reviewer with the "traditional figures of the mystical search: the tortured dialogue; the continuously dangerous journey; the fearful rebirth; the perplexed approach to mystical union" —but nevertheless seemed "confessional rather than metaphysical."

The poet's spiritual autobiography was continued in *The Rose of Solitude*. Here as elsewhere, Antoninus's theme is that man becomes man through woman; by losing himself in her he finds himself, and God: "This is my fact, / I cry out a woman's name. / And have seen God. / In that woman's face / Have known God's blaze. / Is it truly a sin / That her name is written, / Stroked in primal fire, / On my stultified heart?"

The Rose of Solitude impressed most critics with its sustained power, and sometimes overwhelming bursts of passion, though not always with its sexual theme: "A poet capable of magnificence when he deals with nature," wrote James Wright, ". . . he is also magnificent when he prays. . . . When the poet addresses God in his anguish, the poetry is fresh and alive, for all its pain. When he attempts to deal with the woman, his language becomes as abstract as she."

Brother Antoninus writes usually in short syllable-stress lines. What Rexroth admires in his work is "a gnarled, even tortured honesty, a rugged unliterary diction, a relentless probing and searching, which are not just engaging, but almost overwhelming." The poet, an exceptionally tall man, is very popular, especially with young people, as a lecturer and discussion leader, and a "dynamic, intense" reader of verse.

PRINCIPAL WORKS: *As William Everson*: These Are the Ravens, 1935; San Joaquin, 1939; The Masculine Dead, 1942; The Residual Years: Poems 1934–1948, 1948; Single Source: The Early Poems of William Everson, 1934–1940, 1966; Robinson Jeffers: Fragments of an Older Fury (criticism), 1968; etc. *As Brother Antoninus*: The Crooked Lines of God, 1959; The Hazards of Holiness, 1962; The Poet Is Dead, 1964; The Rose of Solitude, 1967; The Achievement of Brother Antoninus (selected poems), 1967.

ABOUT: Allen, D. M. The New American Poetry, 1960; Contemporary Authors 9–10, 1964; Contemporary Poets of the English Language, 1970; Duncan, R. *Introduction to* Single Source, 1966; Kherdian, D. Six Poets of the San Francisco Renaissance, 1967; Mills, R. J. Contemporary American Poetry, 1965; Rexroth, K. Assays, 1962; Walsh, C. Today's Poets, 1964. *Periodicals*—Atlantic December 1963; Commonweal October 19, 1962; Dominicana Spring 1963; Evergreen Review, no 2, 1957; Jubilee August 1959; New York Times Book Review October 8, 1967; Pacific Spectator 3 1950; Poetry January 1962; April 1963; July 1967; Publishers' Weekly November 11, 1968; Sewanee Review Autumn 1960; Spirit May 1961; Time May 25, 1959; Times Literary Supplement August 18, 1966; Virginia Quarterly Review Winter 1968.

ANTSCHEL, PAUL. *See* "CELAN, PAUL"

***ARBASINO, ALBERTO** (January 22, 1930–), Italian critic, journalist, novelist, and short story writer, was born in Voghera, Lombardy, the son of Edoardo and Gina (Manusardi) Arbasino. His parents were wealthy, and after he had taken his degree in law and political science, Arbasino was able to travel widely in Europe and America, flying from a music festival here to a film festival there, from a first night in London to another on Broadway, or off it, and making friends with innumerable artists, writers, and critics.

For some time he taught international law at the University of Milan, and he made his debut as a writer with a long story in the Milan review *Paragone* and several brilliantly original essays in *Il Verri*, the quarterly of the Milanese literary avant-garde. Then his articles began to appear in weeklies such as the highbrow *Il Mondo* and the more popular and influential *L'Espresso*. Soon the principal dailies were seeking his contributions, and there is now practically no important Italian periodical in which his signature has not appeared. Arbasino was not much more than thirty when Angus Wilson called him "the youngest and cleverest of all the Italian critics today." He now writes mainly for the leading Milanese papers *Il Corriere della Sera* and *Il Giorno*, though he no longer lives in Milan but in Rome.

Arbasino's first book, *Le piccole vacanze* (The Little Vacation, 1957), was a collection of short

* är bä zē′ nō

ALBERTO ARBASINO

stories which suggested that the author was more remarkable for his style than for his invention. The impression was confirmed when these stories were republished, with new ones, in *L'anonimo lombardo* (The Anonymous Lombard, 1959). Arbasino's characters live in a world of casual relationships and superficial (but very witty) talk, changing their partners as readily as their topics of conversation, as if life were a cocktail party.

The longest story in *L'anonimo lombardo*, "Il ragazzo perduto," was published in English as *The Lost Boy*, and serves as an example of Arbasino's work. Impatient with conventional third-person narrative, which he finds restricting and logically unacceptable, he seeks other methods of establishing a sense of reality in the reader's mind (and in his own). In *The Lost Boy* he tells the story, which is about a homosexual affair, in a series of letters. These letters are purportedly written by a novelist, who seems more interested in the book he is writing about his affair than in the affair itself. His literary problems are constantly distracting him from his emotional ones, and his narrative is choked with footnotes and esoteric quotations. This device, which for one critic created "a fascinating impression of the lack of any artificial framework," seemed to others merely an irritating kind of literary exhibitionism.

Arbasino published two novels, *Parigi o cara* and *Fratelli d'Italia*, in 1961 and 1962, and another volume of stories, *La narcisata, la controra*, in 1963. They feature much pastiche and parody of Arbasino's masters, who range from Ronald Firbank, Angus Wilson, and Mary McCarthy to Antonin Artaud and Alfred Jarry, and probably pleased fewer readers with their brilliant wit than they offended with their deliberate frivolity and determined amorality. A critic in the *Times Literary Supplement* wrote in 1965 that Arbasino's fiction "has declined into the sort of reportage acceptable to *L'Espresso*—something too close to drawing-room gossip." This impression was convincingly contradicted by *Super-Eliogabalo*, an "anti-historical" fantasy about the notably decadent Emperor Heliogabalus which was the Italian literary sensation of 1969. As one reviewer wrote in the *Times Literary Supplement*, the Emperor "gets mixed up with Mussolini and encounters all kinds of people from the Sybil and Orpheus to Nietzsche and Jean Dubuffet. There are jokes galore, delightful obscenities, satirical humour, short, witty poems and a kind of surrealist collocation of unlikely persons and things. . . . *Super-Eliogabalo* is tremendously clever, highly original and immensely amusing."

That Arbasino is immensely well read has not always benefited his fiction, but it adds much to his criticism. This literary universality, together with a disciplined talent for precise observation, and a mordant, highly personal, prose style, have made him one of the best Italian essayists of his time. The often vitriolic reviews and articles about the theatre collected in *Grazie per le magnifiche rose* (Thanks for the Magnificent Roses, 1965) have great merit, not least because the author brings to the Italian stage much-needed cosmopolitan standards and ideas. His other collections of essays and interviews, dealing with a variety of arts, include *Certi romanzi* (1964), *La maleducazione teatrale* (1966), *Le due orfanelle* (1968), *Off-Off* (1969), and *Sessanta posizioni* (1972). Arbasino, who has made a specialty of literary interviews, was nicknamed by Paolo Milano "the well-tempered tape-recorder." The name has stuck and is widely used, not always charitably.

PRINCIPAL WORKS IN ENGLISH TRANSLATION: The Lost Boy, 1964. *Story*—Giorgio versus Luciano, *in* Lehmann, J. (ed.) Italian Stories of Today, 1959. *Essay*—Figaro Up and Figaro Down, *in* Trevelyan, R. (ed.) Italian Writing Today, 1967.

ABOUT: Trevelyan, R. (ed.) Italian Writing Today, 1967. *Periodicals*—Atlas May 1966; Times Literary Supplement May 21, 1964; September 30, 1965; March 16, 1973.

ARDEN, JOHN (October 26, 1930–), English dramatist, writes: "I was born in Barnsley, Yorkshire, a northern industrial town, and educated there until the outbreak of World War II, when I was sent away to prep. school and, later, public school. On leaving the latter, I spent a year in the army (Intelligence Corps) as a conscript lance corporal stationed in Edinburgh Castle. Then I read architecture for three years at King's College, Cambridge, and completed my professional qualifications at Edinburgh College of Art. My first acted play—a romantic comedy called *All Fall Down*—was presented there by the College Dramatic Society. I was one of the cast. In the same year (1955) I wrote a radio play based on an idea by Margaret Proudfoot, a fellow-student. This was *The Life of Man*, and won a prize offered by the BBC North Region.

"As a result of this award I was contacted by Oscar Lewenstein, a member of the board of the newly formed English Stage Company, which had opened a 'writers' theatre' at the Royal Court, London, under the direction of the late George Devine. Mr. Lewenstein asked me to send them any stage plays I had written. I was now working as an assistant architect in a London office. In my spare time I wrote three plays: *To No Known Grave*, based on the Arthurian legends and rejected by the Royal Court; *Soldier Soldier*, a TV piece eventually directed by Stuart Burge for the BBC; and *The Waters of Babylon*. This last was given a Sunday night production by the Royal Court. It was based on an idea given me by an Irish architect called Tom Austin with whom I shared lodgings. He introduced me to Margaretta D'Arcy, an actress and libertarian, who has collaborated with me on my plays, and for whom I have written parts.

"George Devine offered me a part-time job at the Royal Court reading scripts and commissioned a new play. I then left my architectural work and wrote *Live Like Pigs*, which George Devine directed himself in 1958. This play was not liked. I went to live in the country, and wrote *Serjeant Musgrave's Dance*. Lindsay Anderson directed this at the Court in 1959. It was not liked, but due to Mr. Anderson's determined partisanship, survived the attacks and has been frequently performed since. I held a Fellowship in Playwriting for a year at Bristol University where (with Margaretta D'Arcy) I wrote *The Happy Haven*. Directed by William Gaskill, this play was presented first at the University and then at the Royal Court. It was a 'comedy of humours' with *commedia dell'arte* masks and was not liked at all. I wrote *Wet Fish* for television, and (with Miss D'Arcy) a nativity play called *The Business of Good Government* which she produced with a cast of local people—including myself—in a village church in Somerset. My largest play to date, *The Workhouse Donkey*, was written for the arts festival held in Coventry, to celebrate the consecration of the new cathedral there in 1962. This was rejected, apparently because of bawdiness and also because I had unwittingly galled some local sore places—it was a comedy of municipal feuds and corruptions. It was later directed by Stuart Burge for the Chichester Festival Theatre.

"I have since written *Armstrong's Last Goodnight*, a political piece set in sixteenth-century Scotland (directed in Glasgow by Dennis Carey for the

Citizens' Theatre, and later for the National Theatre by William Gaskill, John Dexter and Albert Finney —an elaborate collaboration that was well enough received); *Left-Handed Liberty*, commissioned by the City of London for the 750th anniversary of Magna Carta, and directed at the Mermaid Theatre by David William; and *Ars Longa Vita Brevis*, a play for schoolchildren, written with Margaretta D'Arcy, and deriving from work with children that she had done during an 'Entertainment' held in my house in Yorkshire in the summer of 1963. This was a gratuitous artistic free-for-all, which I assisted at first rather unwillingly, but which proved more fruitful than I had imagined. Miss D'Arcy also presented our *Happy Haven* in Dublin that year and accompanied it with a similarly anarchic programme held in a smaller theatre the following week.

"I have developed a strong interest in such apparently uncoordinated work—not necessarily strictly dramatic and not necessarily employing professional performers—as a parallel to my more formal plays written for the ordinary stage. However well acted and directed the latter have been, I have become more and more aware of the difficulty of making a genuine contact with modern audiences through the traditional methods of the theatre, and although my plays have been better liked by the public (and critics) of recent seasons than used to be the case, I am always conscious of a feeling of dissatisfaction with the results. Although the theatre (in England) has re-established itself to some extent as an artistic form worth taking seriously, it has not yet regained, nor is it likely to regain, the poetic energy that it had in, say, the late sixteenth century. Perhaps it has been trying to take *itself* too seriously, and if this is so, it can be corrected. But not, at present, within the framework of conventional management. I write for that framework because most of the available professional skills (actors, directors, designers, etc.) are to be found there: but I would like—eventually—to be able to suggest some sort of workable alternative."

Although Arden's career began, as he says, with a succession of failures at the Royal Court Theatre, many critics now place him with or above John Osborne and Harold Pinter as one of the most brilliant, original, and important British dramatists of his generation. His early plays were unpopular, John Russell Taylor suggests, primarily because they give their audiences no scope for empathy—there are no absolute heroes or villains, no cause is presented as unequivocally good or bad, and the audience is in any case never allowed to forget that it *is* an audience, able to observe but not to participate in the action. This element in Arden's work has been widely compared to Brecht's "alienation

JOHN ARDEN

effect," though Arden seems to have arrived at it more or less intuitively.

All this is very evident in the first of his Royal Court plays, *The Waters of Babylon* (1957). The central character in this complicated and overplotted play is Krank, a Polish émigré who has served as a guard at Buchenwald and is now a pimp. Far from being the villain of the piece, this elusive and ambivalent survivor is its most attractive character. What is more, the colloquial realism of the dialogue is challenged by speeches in verse and by songs in the tradition of English ballad opera. Among other things, these act as sharp reminders to the audience that they are watching a fabrication —something to be considered objectively, not identified with. Arden (like Brecht again) has continued to use verse and songs in his plays, along with ordinary prose dialogue.

In *Live Like Pigs* (1958), a disreputable family of gypsies, the Sawneys, is moved into a municipal housing project, where their way of life is an outrage to their conventional neighbors, the Jacksons. This is the most naturalistic of Arden's plays, and the one (Ronald Hayman has suggested) in which he first achieved mastery of his material: "There are no stereotypes in the characterization, no jolts in the rhythm of the action and no bad patches in the writing. The dialogue is pitched perfectly throughout, controlled, economical and richly flavoured." Once again, nevertheless, critics and audiences were puzzled, and Arden, as he wrote, "was accused by the Left of attacking the Welfare State," while some equally misguided critics treated the play "as a defence of anarchy and amorality." In fact, Arden said, "I approve outright neither of the Sawneys nor of the Jacksons. Both groups uphold standards of conduct which are incompatible, but which are both valid in their correct context." The play had a short run in New York in 1965 and has since been successfully revived in London.

In his next play Arden dealt with so controversial a theme as pacifism, and still denied his audience a clear-cut cause to embrace. *Serjeant Musgrave's Dance* (1959) is set in a wintry strike-bound town in the north of England in the 1880s. Four soldiers arrive, deserters who are sick of killing and seek recruits in their pacifist campaign. But Musgrave, their leader, is a religious fanatic, secretly planning a mass slaughter as an object lesson in the horrors of war. His plan is revealed at a meeting in the marketplace but fails because of dissension among his supporters. The dragoons arrive, the deserters are arrested, and the townspeople dance to celebrate the re-establishment of law and order, the death of unreason.

Arden himself is pacifist in his sympathies, but it would not be easy to learn this from the play, in which, as in life, every character, however admirable or abominable his motives, has both virtues and weaknesses. *Serjeant Musgrave's Dance* is in formal terms one of the most satisfactory of Arden's plays, very clear and simple (if rather slow) in exposition, and building up to a powerful climax. Its ballads and verse passages are more skillfully integrated than in earlier plays, and it had a mixed but a relatively encouraging critical reception. Though it survived only twenty-eight performances at the Royal Court (five more than *Live Like Pigs*), it was later successfully adapted for television, and subsequent revivals have made it the best known of Arden's plays. It was staged off-Broadway in 1966 and received the Vernon Rice Award.

The Happy Haven, which reached the Royal Court in 1961, is the most formalistic of his plays, using masks as well as songs and verse; it had an even chillier reception than its predecessors. It is a farcical "pantomime" set in a home for the aged whose resident physician, seeking an elixir of youth, treats his charges as so many guinea pigs. In the end the old people, disinclined to live their lives over again, inject the doctor so generously with his own elixir that he is transformed into a helpless baby. Many critics (in those gentler days) thought the play a joke in poor taste and objected to Arden's unsentimental portrayal of the greed and eccentricity of old age, summed up in Mrs. Phineus's memorable speech: "I'm an old old lady / And I don't have long to live. / I am only strong enough to take / Not to give."

In 1963 the *Workhouse Donkey*, a "vulgar melodrama" of local politics in a northern town, was enthusiastically received at the Chichester Festival. And in the following year Arden had his first major success with *Armstrong's Last Goodnight* at the National Theatre. The play is set in sixteenth-century Scotland, where King James is in conflict with his lawless border barons, particularly Armstrong of Gilnockie. Armstrong is finally caught and killed through the efforts of the king's shrewd and subtle emissary, Sir David Lindsay. The modified sixteenth-century Scots dialect in which the play is written makes it hard to follow at a first hearing, but Richard Gilman considers that in "its range and sure-handed balancing of contrarieties, its supple, muscular rhetoric and its fusion of lyric energy and reflective strength," this is Arden's masterpiece. There was also general admiration for another historical play, *Left-Handed Liberty*, written in 1965 to commemorate the signing of Magna Carta. Once more, Arden's ability to present with equal conviction two opposing viewpoints (here the king's pragmatism against the church's ideology) produced a subtle and rounded study of a complex age.

Arden's television plays include *Soldier, Soldier* (1960), one of the most equivocal of his early studies of conflict between society and anarchy, and winner of the Italia Prize, and *Wet Fish* (1962), an unusually naturalistic play centered on the further adventures of Krank, the eccentric hero of *The Waters of Babylon*. He has also made a lively and exciting adaptation of Goethe's early play *Goetz von Berlichingen*.

As he says, Arden's interest in improvisational and other free theatrical techniques has led him to do a great deal of experimental work with children and amateurs as well as professional actors. His collaborator in many of these experiments is Margaretta D'Arcy, whom he married in 1957. Among the plays they have written together are *The Business of Good Government* (1960), a radiantly simple and often funny nativity play which reflects Arden's interest in medieval stage techniques; *Ars Longa Vita Brevis*, a short and very witty play about discipline, set in a private school; and *The Hero Rises Up*, a deliberately crude deflation of the Nelson legend in the form of a ballad opera. The most ambitious of the plays written by the Ardens in collaboration is *The Island of the Mighty* (1972). It is a version of Arthurian legend, more epic than dramatic in form, and anti-imperialist in intention, which was on the whole very coolly received by the critics (and indeed by the authors, who picketed the Aldwych Theatre in protest against the Royal Shakespeare Company's interpretation of the play).

As Ronald Hayman points out, Arden is "a public playwright," concerned above all with "the business of good government"—in particular the problem of finding a proper balance between law and order on the one hand, and personal liberty on the other. It follows that he is more interested in relations between groups than between individuals, and "is alone among dramatists of today in trying to see a community as a whole. . . . His Brueghel-like canvases teem with physical life and a very warm sympathy penetrates into the oddest corners of the social scene." Arden's social concerns are not limited to his writings. He was serving as honorary chairman of the socialist-pacifist weekly *Peace News* when, in 1969, he found himself unable to support the action of an acquaintance convicted of a bomb-throwing incident. Arden was excoriated by some of his associates as a "bourgeois liberal," and shortly afterwards resigned from *Peace News*. His dilemma—the need to choose between political idealism and political action—is explicit in *The Ballygombeen Bequest* (1972), a violent vaudeville about class and political conflict in Ireland, and *The Bagman*, one of two fantastic dream-ballads published in 1971 as *Two Autobiographical Plays*. Arden's visit to India in 1970 is said to have intensified his political concern.

It remains very difficult to reach firm conclusions about Arden's achievement. He seems to write not to express his convictions so much as to discover what they are, and as a result his plays sometimes seem muddled in their ideas and inconsistent in style. He is regarded by many nevertheless as the most original, talented, and serious of the British dramatists, and perhaps the only one who is capable of real greatness.

Arden and his wife have four sons and live in a remote part of Ireland. His hobbies include architecture and antiquarianism.

PRINCIPAL PUBLISHED WORKS: Serjeant Musgrave's Dance: An Unhistorical Parable, 1960; Live Like Pigs, 1961; The Happy Haven, 1961; (with Margaretta D'Arcy) The Business of Good Government, 1963; The Workhouse Donkey, 1964; Three Plays (Waters of Babylon, Live Like Pigs, The Happy Haven), 1964; Armstrong's Last Goodnight, 1965; Left-Handed Liberty, 1965; Ironhand, 1965; Soldier, Soldier, and Other Plays (Wet Fish, When Is a Door Not a Door?, Friday's Hiding [the last in collaboration with Margaretta D'Arcy]), 1967; (with Margaretta D'Arcy) The Royal Pardon, 1967; (with Margaretta D'Arcy) The Hero Rises Up, 1969; Two Autobiographical Plays: The True History of Squire Jonathan and His Unfortunate Treasure, and The Bagman or The Impromptu of Muswell Hill, 1971; (with Margaretta D'Arcy) Three Political Plays: Ars Longa Vita Brevis, Harold Muggins Is a Martyr, The Ballygombeen Bequest, 1973.

ABOUT: Armstrong, W. A. (ed.) Experimental Drama, 1963; Brown, J. R. (ed.) Modern British Dramatists, 1968; Brown, J. R. Theatre Language, 1972; Hayman, R. John Arden, 1968; Hunt, A. Arden, 1973; Lumley, F. New Trends in Twentieth-Century Drama, 1967; Marowitz, C. (ed.) Theatre at Work, 1967; Taylor, J. R. The Angry Theater, 1962; Wager, W. The Playwrights Speak, 1967; Wellwarth, G. E. The Theatre of Protest and Paradox, 1964; Who's Who, 1972; Who's Who in the Theatre, 1967. *Periodicals*—Horizon July 1962; Plays and Players August 1963; Tulane Drama Review 2, 1966.

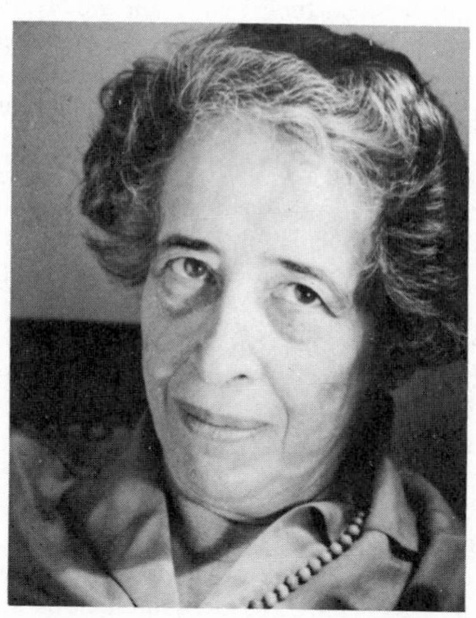

HANNAH ARENDT

ARENDT, HANNAH (October 14, 1906–), political philosopher, is prominent among the German-Jewish refugee scholars who have so greatly enriched America's intellectual life. She was born in Hanover, the only child of Paul Arendt, an engineer, and Martha (Cohn) Arendt, and was reared in Königsberg (now Kaliningrad). In East Prussian schools she began to acquire the impressive erudition and mental discipline that distinguish her work. Later, at the University of Heidelberg, she studied philosophy under Karl Jaspers, whose existentialism became part of her own thinking. For her Ph.D. degree, granted at Heidelberg in 1928, she submitted a dissertation on St. Augustine.

Quick to foresee the implications for the Jews of Nazism, Miss Arendt fled to Paris in 1933. There, while continuing to study and write, she worked for a relief organization that found homes in Palestine for Jewish orphan children. In 1940 she married Heinrich Blücher, a professor of philosophy, and soon afterward moved to the United States, of which she became a naturalized citizen in 1950. She was employed successively, from 1944 to 1952, as research director of the Conference on Jewish Relations; as chief editor of Schocken Books, Inc., one of whose publications was the Max Brod edition of the Kafka diaries; and as executive director of Jewish Cultural Reconstruction in New York City.

Her first book appeared in 1951. By then, her articles in learned periodicals had already earned her recognition as an authority on anti-Semitism. *The Origins of Totalitarianism* sought to locate the roots of both national socialism and communism in nineteenth century imperialism and anti-Semitism. It was a thesis which did not convince everyone but which received a most respectful hearing—not least because of its author's deep personal involvement in her subject. August Heckscher, who said the book left questions unanswered, thought it would nevertheless "be read as a brilliantly creative reconstruction, lit by little-known facts and unfamiliar relationships. It will stand as the measure of one person's spiritual torment and victory."

The range of Miss Arendt's learning and the power and originality of her thought emerged more clearly in her next two books, both dealing with the breakdown in Western civilization of humanism and the classical tradition. They were *The Human Condition*, comprising her Walgreen lectures given at the University of Chicago, and a volume of essays called *Between Past and Future*. According to Peter Laslett, the latter book argued that bereft of tradition and authority we are now "without the capacity to educate our children, and without standards of behavior to tackle the fundamental problems of living together." Laslett found these conclusions unconvincing and depressing but said that on the way to them Miss Arendt "reveals an originality and a suggestiveness which is difficult to parallel in any contemporary." Irving Kristol praised in particular an essay called "What Is Authority?" in which "her classical perspective and her apocalyptic sensibility unite most forcefully," making it "one of the remarkable intellectual achievements of our age." There was less enthusiasm for Miss Arendt's sometimes "impenetrable" prose style.

Proposing that revolution is even more characteristic of this age than war, Hannah Arendt in *On Revolution* draws valuable insights from a comparison between the French and American revolutions. Benjamin DeMott called it "exhilarating in its appreciations of political action, brilliant when it is engaged in psychological analysis. . . . The writing . . . is sometimes verbose and humorless, but more often is trenchant and generously demanding, and occasionally leaps high into moving tragic intensities."

The most discussed of Miss Arendt's books has been *Eichmann in Jerusalem*, based on articles about the Eichmann trial published in the *New Yorker*. Her report raised questions about the conduct of the trial and about much wider issues, including the behavior of the Jews and their leadership in the face of the holocaust. The resulting passionate controversy was no doubt inevitable, and in the course of it Miss Arendt's own views on these subjects have been misunderstood and misquoted. In the *New York Review of Books*, *Encounter*, and elsewhere, she has sought to establish that many of the critical statements attributed to her were in fact made by the Israeli prosecution. Others believe that she was attacked "not so much for what she said, but for how she said it," and that her book was "deficient in both factual knowledge and judgment." The debate on the issues raised by the book is very far from finished.

Men in Dark Times is a collection of essays and lectures about some men and women whose lives and writings had provided "light in dark times"; it was thought most valuable for its "intellectual profiles" of Rosa Luxemburg, Isak Dinesen, Hermann Broch, Walter Benjamin, and Bertolt Brecht. *On Violence* is an incisive essay in which Miss Arendt argues that power is creative, that violence is the opposite of power, and that violence appears when men are denied power.

Miss Arendt accepted a professorship in 1963 at the University of Chicago, where she became a member of the Committee on Social Thought. She left Chicago in 1967 and since then has taught at the New School for Social Research in New York. She has lectured as a visiting professor at the University of California (Berkeley), at Princeton, and at Columbia University. Her research has been supported by Guggenheim and Rockefeller fellowships, among other grants. She is a member of the Deutsche Akademie für Sprache und Dichtung and a fellow of the American Academy of Arts and Sciences.

Hannah Arendt is an attractive, dark-eyed woman of medium stature, with a calm, assured manner. She claims no religious or political affiliations, insisting rather upon independence in her outlook. Irving Kristol thinks her "one of the most brilliant and original of living political philosophers." Noting her debts to Jaspers, to classical German philosophy, and to Heidegger, as well as to the Graeco-Roman perspective, Kristol praises in her work the tension "between an almost uncanny (and exceedingly feminine) percipience and a noble, elevated (and exceedingly masculine) architectonic of ideas."

PRINCIPAL WORKS: The Origins of Totalitarianism (England, The Burden of Our Time), 1951; The Human Condition, 1958; Between Past and Future: Six Exercises in Political Thought, 1961; On Revolution, 1963; Eichmann in Jerusalem: A Report on the Banality of Evil, 1963; Men in Dark Times, 1968; On Violence, 1970; Crises of the Republic, 1972.

ABOUT: Current Biography, 1959; McCarthy, M. T. On the Contrary, 1961; Podhoretz, N. Doings and Undoings, 1964; Robinson, J. And the Crooked Shall Be Made Straight: The Jewish Catastrophe and Hannah Arendt's Narrative, 1965; Spitz, D. Essays in the Liberal Idea of Freedom, 1964; Who's Who in America, 1972–1973; Who's Who in World Jewry, 1965. *Periodicals*—American Scholar Spring 1964; Commonweal May 9, 1970; Encounter January 1964; Ethics October 1962; Journal of Modern History December 1952; Journal of Religion April 1952; National Review November 17,

1964; May 5, 1970; New Statesman March 7, 1959; New York Review of Books November 11, 1965; January 20, 1966; February 3, 1966; March 17, 1966; Political Studies October 1964; Review of Politics January 1953; Saturday Review March 24, 1951; December 7, 1968; Sewanee Review July 1951; World Politics January 1960

***ARGUEDAS, JOSÉ MARÍA** (January 18, 1911–November 28, 1969), Peruvian novelist, short story writer, and ethnologist, sent the following note (in Spanish) some time before his death: "I was born in the small capital city of a province of great antiquity, called Andahuaylas. According to the census of 1940, only three per cent of the inhabitants did not speak Quechua, the common language of the Inca Empire. As a child, I was taken to another small city called Puquio, the capital of Lucanas, a province as ancient as that of Andahuaylas. Until 1940, eighty per cent of Puquio's inhabitants were monolingual and spoke only Quechua. I lived in this city and in the towns of San Juan de Lucanas, Uteq, and Akola until I was fourteen.

"On account of the rather unusual circumstances of my father's profession, I spent the greater part of my childhood among the free Indians of the communities of Puquio and San Juan de Lucanas—free but subjected to endless social discrimination, to an absolute form of political tyranny and the economic exploitation which a human situation of this kind implies. I myself suffered with the Indians and experienced injustice, humiliation, and feelings of rebellion and resentment against landowners both great and small.

"At the same time, cared for by the natives, I was deeply nourished by their affection and felt a spirit of close solidarity with those who suffered and a vivid sense of communion with nature, which is gentle, imposing, and sometimes terrifying in the Andes. I learned to love, to hate, to think, to sing, to discover the universe in the Quechua language, whose sounds are charged with the natural language of things.

"At fourteen, I began to travel with my father through many remote regions; I visited many, many provinces on horseback (Ayacucho, Coracora, Cangallo, Huancapi, Huaytara, Huancayo, Pampas, Yauyos). In twelve days I traveled from Cuzco, the ancient capital of the Incas, to Ica on the coast near Lima. During these travels, I came to know several haciendas which had Indian serfs who belonged to the landowner and who were treated with less consideration than the animals. I lived for some months on one of these haciendas; there, in an accident in a sugar mill where the cane was crushed, I lost two fingers. I won the confidence of the serfs because I spoke the same language as they did, and I knew how to sing quite well in Quechua and the owner treated me as an undesirable intruder.

* är gwä′ thäs

JOSÉ MARÍA ARGUEDAS

"When I was nineteen I went to Lima and entered the University of San Marcos (1931). I had completed my secondary education in several cities (Ica, Huancayo, and Lima) in a somewhat haphazard fashion. Soon after I embarked upon my studies at the University of San Marcos my father died and I became an orphan.

"For several weeks I was obliged to sleep on the benches of a public park. Finally, I found work in a post office (1932–1937) and this turned out to be a reasonable job. The University was closed down for four years by a tyrannical government (that of Sánchez Cerro in 1932). In 1937 I was arrested by the police and remained in prison for thirteen months. For two hundred prisoners there was only one water tap and one lavatory. At that time I was still a student and was arrested, together with fifteen others, for having organized a demonstration against an Italian Fascist general in the main courtyard of the University. Upon my release from prison, I managed to secure an appointment to teach at the National College (Mateo Pumacahua) at Sicuani, Cuzco (1939–1941).

"In Lima, I began to read Peruvian fiction. I found myself irritated and astounded by the false and incredibly stereotyped image of the Andean peoples and their landscape which appeared in the narratives of the famous writers of the time, such as López Albújar, Ventura García Calderón, and even in younger authors who belonged to the so-called indigenous movement. The Indian was always described as a man of impassive and inscrutable countenance; the only truth to be found in this description was that these authors were unfamiliar with the people they were trying to describe. The Indian was also shown as oscillating between an inhuman ferocity and cowardice, between arrogance and servility. These authors did not know the whole Andean world and the novels which they wrote illustrated the total lack of communication between the people of the Quechua tongue and their overlords.

"But in the literature favorable to the Indian cause, the landowners, too, were always depicted as being ferocious and nothing else. I decided to write in order to reveal the highly complex and beautiful world, the cruel and tender universe, both human and natural, of Andean Peru. My book of short stories *Agua* (1935) was well received. I had written it three times before achieving a style that might give life and expression to the Quechua language and convey something of its spirit.

"Then I wrote five novels: *Yawar fiesta* (1940), which interprets the life of a province; *Los ríos profundos* (1959) which presents and interprets a specific region of the country; *El sexto* (1961); *La agonía de Rasu Ñiti* (1962); and *Todas las sangres* (1963) which studies Peruvian culture with its highly complex pattern of castes, classes and traditions, and its links with the centers of international influence.

"I have also translated songs and folk tales from Quechua into Spanish."

Arguedas was the son of a provincial traveling judge, Victor Manuel Arguedas. His mother, Doña Victoria Altamirano, died when he was three, and his stepmother relegated him to the kitchen to be raised by the Indian servants. He was later to dedicate one of his books to the old cook who gave him more affection than his own family. Arguedas learned Quechua before he could speak Spanish and grew up with a deep love and respect for the Indians of the Andes.

As a student at the University of San Marcos in Lima, Arguedas was soon active in intellectual life, and was one of the editors of the literary review *Palabra* (The Word). This was an expression of the indigenous movement—away from the intellectual domination of Europe, and towards a new appreciation of native and national cultures and concerns—that swept Latin America in the 1920s and 1930s.

A would-be writer from childhood, Arguedas doubted his ability, and as he says was moved to begin his first book chiefly by indignation aroused by the ignorance of Indian life displayed in the fiction of the time. *Agua*, begun when he was nineteen, was published five years later. It consists of three short narratives, "Agua" (Water), "Los Escoleros" (The Students), and "Waima Kuyay." These stories are all partly autobiographical and written from the point of view of an observant and sensitive child who identifies himself completely with the feelings of the Indians he describes. This is particularly telling in "Los Escoleros," set in a hacienda whose serfs are so tyrannized that they lose all humanity, throwing off their mental confusion and lethargy and recovering their identity only when their master is away.

Agua is no mere documentary. Arguedas had set out to devise a kind of speech through which his Indian characters could express not only their natural dignity and intelligence, but the whole structure of their attitudes and beliefs—their close relationship to the natural world and the spirit in which they met social injustice. He has described the long process of experiment and revision through which he arrived at a form which satisfied him, applying Quechua syntax to the Spanish language. *Agua* was recognized at once as "the quintessence of Peruvian indigenous literature."

Arguedas's first novel, *Yawar fiesta* (Blood Feast, 1940), centering on a local kind of primitive bullfight, deals in a larger sense with the expulsion of the Indians from their communal lands. It was followed by a volume of Quechua songs and legends, *Canciones y cuentos del pueblo quechua* (1948), and then by another collection of stories, *Diamantes y pedernales* (Diamonds and Gems, 1953).

A second novel, *Los ríos profundos* (The Deep Rivers, 1959), established Arguedas as one of the most notable contemporary writers of Latin America. It is a closely autobiographical account of the author's own itinerant early life and of his misery when he is separated from his beloved Indians and sent to a harsh and rigidly conventional boarding school. *El sexto* (1961), also a work of fictionalized autobiography, recalls his experiences in the infamous Lima prison he describes above.

Todas las sangres (All the Races, 1965), the most considerable of Arguedas's novels, is set in a remote Andean village and deals with the bitter competition between two brothers, one a farmer and one a mine owner. "Twined into the thread of the narrative," wrote a reviewer in the *Times Literary Supplement*, "are the deep insight into the spirit of the *serrano* [mountaineer], the inevitable tilting against corrupt local politics, and the downtreading of the Indians, the flashes of poetry and mysticism and folkloric elements of Quechua songs and customs which one has learned to expect from Dr. Arguedas."

In 1940 Arguedas was a member of the commission set up in Lima to reform secondary education. In 1945 he became head of the Department of Folklore and Popular Arts in the Ministry of

Public Education, and in 1951 he was appointed director of the Institute of Ethnological Studies in the Peruvian Museum of Culture. From 1959 onwards he was Professor of Regional Cultures of Peru in the University of San Marcos. He was also director of the Casa de la Cultura in 1963–1964 and thereafter of the National Museum of History. In 1950–1951 he gave a much discussed series of lectures, "The Problems of Peruvian Culture." He published a number of learned works on Peruvian folklore.

Arguedas was married in 1939 to Celia Bustamente Vernal. In 1943 a serious illness brought on by overwork reduced him, he said, "to one third his normal physical capacity," but he recovered and continued to write, teach, and travel for another twenty-five years until shortly before he took his own life in 1969. His unfinished last novel was published in 1971 as *El zorro de arriba y el zorro de abajo.* Its five sections, interspersed with the author's diaristic comments, reflect his agonized sense of helplessness in the face of the continued oppression and degradation of the Indians, and his obsession with the failure of his vision. A reviewer in the *Times Literary Supplement* wrote: "No writer has ever tried as hard as José María Arguedas to hold a middle ground between the Indian and the Hispanic world of Peru, between the domains occupied respectively by the two creatures who give . . . his last work its title: the Fox from Above and the Fox from Below. The effort killed him."

PRINCIPAL WORKS IN ENGLISH TRANSLATION: The Singing Mountaineers: Songs and Tales of the Quechua People, 1957.

ABOUT: Anderson-Imbert, E. Spanish-American Literature, 1963; International Who's Who, 1969–1970; Posada, M. A. La multitud y el paisaje peruanos en los relatos de J. M. Arguedas, 1939. *Periodicals*—Casa de las Américas (Havana) March–April 1966; El Comercio (Lima) November 28, 1954; September 4, 1955; Cuadernos Americanos 1962; Estudios Hispanoamericanos (Seville) 43, 1955; Hispania March 1962; Mercurio Peruano May–June 1966; La Prensa (Lima) November 9, 1954; November 14, 1954; November 15, 1954; December 18, 1961; Reseña April 1966; Revista Atenea October –December 1964; Revista Peruana de Cultura April 1965; Times Literary Supplement March 17, 1966; Visión del Perú (Lima) August 1964.

***ARKELL, REGINALD** (October 14, 1882–May 1, 1959), English writer, possessed a "whimsical and various talent as librettist, versifier, story-teller, and editor." He was born at Lechlade, Gloucestershire, the son of Daniel Arkell, a farmer, and educated at Burford Grammar School. His training was as a journalist, but he was soon drawn to the theatre. *Colombine*, his fantasy in verse, was seen in London and New York before World War I, during which he served with the King's

* är kel′ or är′ kəl

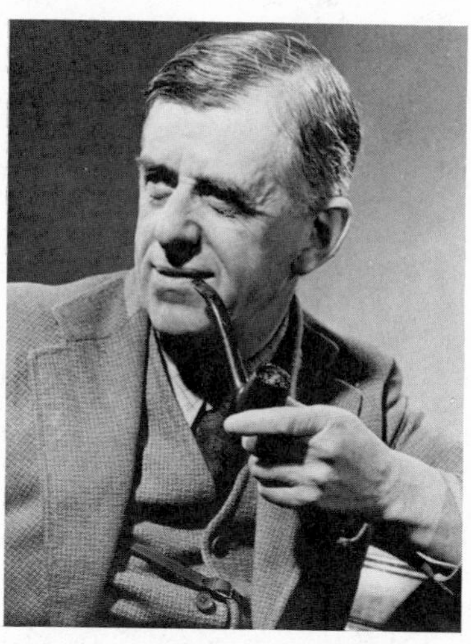

REGINALD ARKELL

Own Yorkshire Light Infantry and the Norfolk Regiment.

After the war Arkell became editor of the magazine *Men Only*, a position he retained until 1954. He continued his work as a librettist and song lyricist, and was associated in this way with many of England's most successful musical comedies and revues between the wars, from *Jumble Sale* in 1920 to *Moonshine* in 1940. His best known work in this form was his adaptation of Sellar and Yeatman's *1066 and All That* (1935).

Arkell did not confine his facility as a versifier to the theatre. *Winter Sportings* was a collection of rhymes poking fun at those who risked their necks in pursuit of sport and fashion at Swiss ski resorts. Arkell's passion for bridge inspired a "harmless handbook" in verse called *Bridge Without Sighs*, and his equal enthusiasm for the less sophisticated pleasures of gardening produced a whole series of "Green Fingers" books whose technical finesse, warm humor, and simple philosophy have made them abidingly popular.

The most notable of Arkell's prose works is the novel *Old Herbaceous*, the story of Bert Pinnegar, a retired gardener whose reminiscences about the good old days, when he was head gardener at the Manor, build up a picture of rural life in England from the 1880s almost to the present. The book is weakly plotted but wonderfully knowledgeable about gardening and country life, and the cantankerous character of Bert is explored perceptively, without sentiment and in some depth. It was a best seller both in England and the United States and was translated into several foreign languages.

Charley Moon tells the story of a comedian who tries but fails to make a career in the theatre and who eventually finds happiness in his native village with his childhood sweetheart. The story is scarcely original, but Arkell tells it with engaging simplicity and towards the end, when Charley is back at home in the country, captures some of the warmth of *Old Herbaceous*. It was adapted as a film and as a play. *The Miracle of Merriford* is a mildly satirical account of the impact upon an English village and its vicar of a nearby American air base.

Arkell died at his home in Wiltshire at the age of seventy-six, survived by his wife, the actress Elizabeth Evans, and his son. He was well known in England as a broadcaster and a frequent contributor to the BBC's "Country Magazine." He was an excellent and witty conversationalist, a mainstay of the Savage Club.

PRINCIPAL WORKS: Colombine, and Other Verses, 1912; The Tragedy of Mr. Punch, 1920; Meet These People, 1928; Winter Sportings, 1929; Richard Jefferies and His Countryside, 1933; Bridge Without Sighs, 1934; A Cottage in the Country, 1934; Green Fingers, 1934; Playing the Games, 1935; 1066 and All That, 1935; More Green Fingers, 1938; War Rumours, 1939; Green Fingers Again, 1942; And a Green Thumb, 1950; Old Herbaceous, 1951; (with A. P. Herbert) Come to the Ball, 1951; Green Fingers and Other Poems, 1952; Charley Moon, 1953; Trumpets Over Merriford, 1955 (U.S., The Miracle of Merriford); Collected Green Fingers, 1956; The Round House, 1958.
ABOUT: Who Was Who, 1951–1960. *Periodicals*—Times (London) May 2, 1959.

ARMSTRONG, CHARLOTTE (May 2, 1905–July 19, 1969), American suspense novelist, short story writer, and dramatist, wrote: "I was born, the elder of two girls, in a little iron mining town in the Upper Peninsula of Michigan, where my father was the Chief Engineer for The Company. We were surrounded by woods and lakes and hills; there was plenty of snow in the winter, and many enchantments for children. But I always knew that I would not live my grown-up life in that place. I knew that I was going to be a writer. I seem to have been born a reader. I cannot remember learning how. I scoured that library-less town for books of any kind, and gobbled them all up, thus acquiring a vocabulary of words I had never heard spoken, and many notions I did not speak about.

"But I was no misfit, not lonely, never sickly or inactive. On the contrary, I was ingenious in mischief and often led the pack, because I could dream up adventures.

"Still, I read and I wrote.

"Aged eight, I used to march around and around my father's billiard table, chanting the lines of a long ballad I was working on at the time, because, although I had never heard of meter, my ear knew when the syllables fell as they should.

"I went away to school, aged sixteen, to Ferry Hall, Lake Forest, Illinois, where I encountered academic standards I had never known before, and Girls' School rules that were hard on one who had been running as free as I had been. Miss Blair, my mentor in the editing of the school magazine that year, advised my parents to send me to a university, because—said she and bless her—I was obviously going to be a writer, and needed wider experience.

"After two years at the University of Wisconsin, I knew that I must get to New York, somehow, so I transferred to Barnard for my senior year, and, having been through the collegiate phase, I became an avid New Yorker, haunting the Village, and seeing all the plays on Broadway, from the balconies. In 1925, a college graduate with no commercial skills, I found a job in the Classified Advertising Department of the New York *Times*. A young man named Jack Lewi happened to be working there.

"After a while, I found another job as a fashion reporter, going up and down Fifth Avenue to spy out who was buying what. All this while, I kept on practicing how to write stories, whenever I could find time. Later I had a brief job in Wall Street, with a firm of CPA's, where I had nothing to do, really, so I sat high up in a skyscraper and wrote light verse, some of which was published in the *New Yorker* magazine, for pay.

"Jack Lewi and I were married in January of 1928 and promptly, in December of 1928, we had a baby boy. So gleefully I began to write plays, working two hours every afternoon while the baby napped. Speak to me not of trapped young mothers!

"John Golden took one of the plays and I rewrote it for him during two solid years. It was agony, at the time, but after that, I was no longer an amateur. The play folded up in summer try-out on Cape Cod. But I did not.

"Two plays reached Broadway eventually, one a tragedy, one a comedy. Both flopped. In the midst of all this—and by now we had three children, a girl and another boy—I more or less casually, and for fun, wrote a mystery novel. (Well, I had read and enjoyed thousands of them.) When it was published—with none of this finding myself locked up in a hotel room, away from my children, rewriting for the star, the director, the producer, the angel—I peacefully wrote two more. I changed over to suspense with the fourth book, *The Unsuspected*, and have been writing suspense ever since. Meanwhile, I helped raise, as I must in honesty declare, three very successful children.

"I have since branched off into short stories, whenever I feel like it, some suspense and some not. I have had collections of these in hard covers. I have written a couple of so-called straight novels. I have done TV-scripts and motion picture screen plays, now and then, enjoying a return to storytelling in dialogue.

"We moved to southern California in 1946, where I was an unreconstructed New Yorker for two years but have long since succumbed. We inhabit a big old white house, with pool and palms. Our three children are now delightful grown-ups. We have four charming grandchildren, characters all. I still read and write.

"I cannot here put down all the theories I have evolved about the kind of work I do. Devotees of the suspense story know that they can be good or bad and they come in variety. People who never read them tend to call them all 'mere escape'. I wonder if these people find reading a task and cannot read for fun. Or think that they ought not? If they suppose a suspense novel to be easy to do and therefore somehow 'cheap,' they should try to do one. The form is related to, and has the strictures of, drama. Therefore it *has* form—which not every novelist bothers about. The fact is, they are stories, and storytelling is an old human delight that began in the caves of antiquity.

"I do believe that if you are any kind of storyteller, you are not excused from looking all about you, as well as within. You are not let off trying to understand as many kinds of human beings as you meet, in as much depth as you are able—and yourself, besides. Boredom is forbidden you. When an occasion *is* boring, *you* must simply busy yourself figuring out why. You are not—and for this Praise Be—ever going to come to the end of what is to be seen that you might tell, or what is to be learned about how to tell it better. And you are not, if you are *my* kind of storyteller, permitted to leave your readers wondering what happened.

"I am committed to 'telling,' which is communication. As for 'self-expression,' I can't help thinking that the phrase must be imprecise. I challenge anyone *not* to express himself, no matter what he does.

"I consider *my*self a very very lucky woman. Without missing any of the dear and basic human relationships—marriage, home, children—I have also been doing all my life what my self always wanted to do. And I still may."

Charlotte Armstrong was the daughter of Frank and Clara (Pascoe) Armstrong. Her father, an inventor as well as a mining engineer, came from a long line of "covered-wagon" Yankees. Her mother's family was Cornish.

It cannot be denied that her plays "flopped" on Broadway, but it should be said that one of them, *The Happiest Days*, directed by Marc Connelly, earned the approval of Brooks Atkinson for its "simplicity and tenderness." Her first mystery stories, featuring a detective named MacDougal Duff, pleased the addicts, and were praised for their humor, freshness, and "honest detecting."

CHARLOTTE ARMSTRONG

Miss Armstrong found her *métier* when she turned to the suspense story. Howard Haycraft called *The Unsuspected* an "extraordinarily exciting surface melodrama," distinguished by "tight writing and broad, colorful delineation of character and mood." During its serialization in the *Saturday Evening Post* it so involved its readers that many of them telephoned to inquire or advise about the story's conclusion. It was when Hollywood bought this book that Miss Armstrong and her family moved to California.

In *Mischief*, published a few years later, a young couple visiting New York leave their baby with a teen-age sitter who, it then emerges, is insane. One reviewer wrote: "For sheer, crawling horror, this story beats anything of the kind I have ever read," and praised in particular the simplicity of its construction, its commonplace setting, and "almost casual, matter-of-fact air." It is, Anthony Boucher believed, "one of the finest pure terror-suspense stories ever written." It was filmed as *Don't Bother to Knock*, starring Marilyn Monroe.

Charlotte Armstrong also wrote shorter thrillers, as novellas or short stories, and in her mastery of these forms was ranked with Stanley Ellin and Roald Dahl. She was said to be "amazingly adroit at fusing action with character development, and in utilizing the most theatrical devices not only to thrill but to say something about Man and his world." Anthony Boucher, praising her ability to combine horror and human warmth, intensity and humor, called her the "long-established mistress of daylit terror-in-the-ordinary."

PRINCIPAL WORKS: *Plays*—The Happiest Days, 1939; Ring Around Elizabeth, 1942. *Fiction*—Lay On, Mac Duff,

1942; The Case of the Weird Sisters, 1943; The Innocent Flower, 1945; The Unsuspected, 1946; The Chocolate Cobweb, 1948; Mischief, 1950; The Black-Eyed Stranger, 1951; Catch-as-Catch-Can, 1953; (as "Jo Valentine") The Trouble in Thor, 1953; The Better to Eat You, 1954; The Dream Walker, 1955; A Dram of Poison, 1956; The Albatross (and 9 suspense stories), 1957; Duo: The Girl with a Secret (and) Incident at a Corner, 1959; The Seventeen Widows of Sans Souci, 1959; A Little Less Than Kind, 1963; The Witch's House, 1963; The Turret Room, 1965; A Dream of Fair Woman, 1966; I See You (short stories), 1966; The Gift Shop, 1967; Lemon in the Basket, 1967; The Balloon Man, 1968; Seven Seats to the Moon, 1969; The Protégé, 1970; Charlotte Armstrong Reader, 1970.

ABOUT: Contemporary Authors 1, 1962; Current Biography, 1946; Who's Who in America, 1968–1969.

ARNOW, HARRIETTE SIMPSON (July 7, 1908–), American regional novelist and historian, writes: "My first memories are of dark green cedar boughs, red clay mud, gray limestone rocks, and an empty house. This last meant my parents had just moved again, all early ones in Wayne County, Kentucky. Each was part of my father's search for a better livelihood. He like my mother was an ex-country school teacher, though even before marriage the low pay had forced him to try other work. Both parents were descended of Virginians and Carolinians who had settled in what was to be Wayne County shortly after the Revolution. So rooted were they in that place, I don't think they felt at home in any other, even though there was a fair handful of kin in the little town of Burnside in the adjoining county of Pulaski where they eventually settled. I was around five years old, the second in what would be a family of six, when we moved to the new home, high on a western-facing hill above the Cumberland.

"Save for two years in boarding school and the year of the great flu epidemic when I studied at home, all education through high school was had in Burnside. The site now buried under Lake Cumberland, it was then a small but busy river and lumber town, served both by steamboats and the main trunk line of the Southern Railway. Halfway between Cincinnati and Chattanooga and at the meeting point of the Kentucky Hills and the Highland Rim, it partook of many worlds.

"The Simpson home, high on its rocky hill above the town, was still another world. Life up there was hard, but never dull. The great rocks, the woods, and the wide views were eternally interesting, and early I peopled them with wondrous beings. Our debt-ridden home was an ever thickening clutter of books, children, dogs, newspapers, magazines, potted plants, often visitors, and over and under everything the sound of the human tongue—talking, singing, teaching. I learned the Beatitudes to the sound of the churn dasher in my grandmother's hands, for always the work must go forward—everything from tatting to sausage making. There are many modern words of which we had never heard—routinize was one.

"Everybody told stories of many varieties. Most often told I think were the bloody, handed-down tales of the many wars our people had survived; they began with Indian tales before the French and Indian War and came on down through The War. Most horrible of all were the tales of this war; nobody in our country of South Central Kentucky where even families were divided dared call it by the name used either in the North or South, for fear of offending a neighbor or even a relative. In addition to the ebb and flow of invading armies, the region had been almost constantly overrun by horse thieves and guerrillas. Stories of these gave me an everlasting hatred of war.

"There were of course books, listened to before we could read, but too little time for reading. So, early I began to tell myself stories; they helped along the harder chores; when I could find the time I tried to put them on paper. I was active in the family letter writing for most of our kin were elsewhere. A fourth-grade teacher read one of my efforts to my class, but at home any writing beyond that required was frowned upon as a waste of time, though the writing of other things was not unknown. One of my father's cousins owned a weekly newspaper, and a great uncle was 'working on' a family history. I only wanted to write ten books.

"The need of helping out at home forced me for many years to follow the road laid out for me: finish high school as quickly as possible—at fifteen; then attend college for two years and so be ready to teach school at eighteen. My first job was in a one-room school in a roadless, shut-away hill community. I found the life most interesting.

"I was eventually able to earn a degree at the University of Louisville, but it was not until I was twenty-five that I could get away from teaching. I went up to Cincinnati, rented a furnished room near the public library, and supporting myself by any short-houred job available—often as waitress—I began to try to learn to write.

"I was soon publishing in the little literary magazines of the mid-thirties; there was a star or so from Mr. O'Brien, a story in the old *Southern Review*, and in 1936 a novel. Three years later I married Harold Arnow, newspaperman from Chicago. Once more writing was only something to do in stolen time; more teaching while trying to survive as writers in a hill community; life in wartime Detroit; two children; it was thirteen years until my next book. I have now for many years known the unreal time and mind-consuming life of exurbia. Thus, in a sense my life as a writer stopped in Cincinnati. It was there I decided to write more or less of what I have since written, though I believe all my work so far has been colored by my very early childhood."

Harriette Arnow was born in Wayne County, Kentucky, the daughter of Elias and Mollie Jane (Denney) Simpson. She majored in science at the University of Louisville and did graduate work in mathematics, but she devoted her spare time to the literary society and to writing, mostly verse.

Her first novel, *Mountain Path* (1936), is set like most of her books on the Cumberland, where she grew up. It is the partly autobiographical story of a college girl aiming for a career in chemistry but forced, like the author, to quit school and teach in a backwoods area where, to her surprise, she gradually finds herself drawn into the life of the community. Along with her stories and reviews, it brought her the encouragement of such notables as Robert Penn Warren, Edward Weeks, and Granville Hicks. At that promising point her career, as she says above, was interrupted by marriage, children, and the war.

When at last it appeared, her second novel, *Hunter's Horn*, brought Mrs. Arnow greater success than her first: a best seller and a Fiction Club selection, it was widely translated. Set in the hills of Kentucky, it deals with a poor white farmer who becomes obsessed by his determination to kill the big red fox, King Devil, which is plaguing his farm, and almost brings himself and his family to ruin. Some reviewers seemed shocked by the novel's realism of language and action, but most were profoundly moved. F. H. Bullock praised its narrative appeal and added: "It is the underlying philosophy—the willingness to accept and present life as it is—which fits the novel into its fine, strong frame of universality." Herschel Brickell said that Mrs. Arnow "writes, or seems to write, as effortlessly as a bird sings, and the warmth, the beauty, the sadness and the ache of life itself are not even once absent from her pages." It is lucidly and most authoritatively written, and was warmly praised for its deep poetic understanding of the relationship between natural and human life.

It was followed by *The Dollmaker*, the finest of Harriette Arnow's books to date. In it, she draws on her own wartime experience of life in Detroit to contrast rural values with urban corruption. Its central character is Gertie Nevel, a countrywoman rooted in the Kentucky mountains, whose skill in carving figures from wood gives the novel its title. Gertie is totally uneducated, but she is a woman of discernment, courage, and will. The war takes her husband to Detroit and she joins him there, beginning a long and finally hopeless struggle to preserve the decency and integrity of her family. The critical response is summed up in the words of Coleman Rosenberger, who wrote: "This is a novel of extraordinary power, creating for the moment a world more real and immediate than the reader's own, extending the limits of our understanding of character, and unafraid of coming to grips with the major themes of the integrity of personality, the corrosive influences in modern society, and the tragedy of the defeat of the human spirit." Joyce Carol Oates called it "a legitimate tragedy, our most unpretentious American masterpiece."

HARRIETTE ARNOW

After *The Dollmaker*, Mrs. Arnow temporarily abandoned the novel to produce two notable historical studies. *Seedtime on the Cumberland* is an account of how men, most of them from the southern colonies, learned to live away from the sea in the late eighteenth century, and to find their necessities in the woods, gradually exploring, hunting over, and settling the Cumberland Valley. *The Flowering of the Cumberland* is a complementary volume covering roughly the same period and dealing with these same pioneers in their roles as husbands, fathers, and members of a community. These are meticulous, thorough, and loving studies which, like her novels, draw their strength from the author's highly developed sense of her roots.

Mrs. Arnow's dislike of "the unreal time and mind-consuming life of exurbia" is expressed in *The Weedkiller's Daughter*. It is an odd novel, about a teenage girl growing up in a Detroit suburb under the shadow of a xenophobic and paranoid bully of a father who is allergic even to flowers. By no means cowed, Susie creates a rich secret life for herself which her father cannot spoil, and in time comes in spite of him to self-knowledge and maturity.

Mrs. Arnow, a member of the Disciples of Christ Church and a Democrat, takes an active part in community affairs in her own exurbia, near Ann Arbor, Michigan. Her husband is publicity director of the Michigan Heart Association.

PRINCIPAL WORKS: *Fiction*—(as Harriette Simpson) Mountain Path, 1936; (as Harriette Arnow) Hunter's Horn, 1949; The Dollmaker, 1954; The Weedkiller's Daughter, 1970. *Nonfiction*—Seedtime on the Cumberland, 1960; The Flowering of the Cumberland, 1963.

ABOUT: Contemporary Authors 9–10, 1964; Current Biography, 1954; Michigan Authors, 1960; Warfel, H. R. American Novelists of Today, 1951. *Periodicals*—Chicago Sunday Tribune April 18, 1954; Detroit Times March 5, 1949; May 26, 1949; New York Herald Tribune Book Review April 25, 1954; New York Times April 25, 1954; New York Times Book Review January 24, 1971; Saturday Review April 24, 1954; Woman's Home Companion January 1956.

***ARON, RAYMOND (CLAUDE FERDINAND)** (March 14, 1905–), French sociologist, historian, and political journalist, was born in Paris, one of the three sons of Gustave Aron, a professor of law, and Suzanne (Lévy) Aron. He took his *baccalauréat* at the Lycée Hoche in Versailles in 1922, studied at the Condorcet for two years, and then entered the École Normale Supérieure, where Sartre was a fellow student. After passing his *agrégation* in philosophy in 1928, he studied for his doctorate and then began his academic career in 1930 as a lecturer at the University of Cologne, transferring in the following year to the Maison Académique in Berlin. From 1933 to 1934 he taught philosophy at the *lycée* in Le Havre and then became secretary of the Centre du Documentation Sociale at the École Normale Supérieure, where he remained until 1939.

His doctoral thesis was published in 1938 as *Introduction à la philosophie de l'histoire* (translated by G. J. Irwin as *Introduction to the Philosophy of History*). This work established the direction that his later thought was to take, with its relentless attack on such historicist doctrines as Marxism, which offer their adherents the sanction of an ultimate truth. Aron calls for a pragmatic political science in which objective analysis of the social structure leads to specific decisions; according to Professor Roy Pierce, "For Aron, the function of political thought is to determine . . . both the margin of choice that exists in the circumstances and the content of the choice itself. The political thinker must analyse the existing situation, define goals which are capable of being attained, and suggest means which have some reasonable probability of attaining the goals."

In many ways Aron belongs to the politically conscious, undogmatic, and liberal sociological tradition which he has himself identified as "the French school of political sociology, whose founder is Montesquieu and whose second great figure is Tocqueville." But his first sociological work, and in fact his first published book, was *La Sociologie allemande contemporaine* (1936, translated by M. and T. B. Bottomore as *German Sociology*), which has become the standard work on its subject.

The history of sociology has been one of Aron's constant preoccupations, and a course of lectures which he gave at the University of Paris developed into his major two-volume historical survey of sociological thought, *Les Grandes Doctrines de sociologie historique* (translated by R. Howard and H. Weaver as *Main Currents in Sociological Thought*). The first volume, published in French in 1960, centers on the Montesquieu-Tocqueville school of political sociology; the Comtean school, the basis of academic sociology, which "underplays the political as well as the economic in relation to the social"; and the Marxist school, "the one that has been most successful, not in classrooms, but on the great stage of world history." He expounds the ideas of Montesquieu and Tocqueville much more sympathetically than those of Comte, and he is particularly critical of Marx, not always convincingly. The book was, however, highly praised for conveying what is most distinctive in sociological thought, as it developed out of the attempt to grasp the complex changes of the industrial and political revolutions.

The second volume (1963) is devoted to the three great social theorists of the early twentieth century: Durkheim, Pareto, and Weber. Aron expounds their systems brilliantly and once again leaves us in no doubt about his preference: "To me, Max Weber is the greatest of the sociologists; I would even say that he is *the* sociologist. . . . The Weberian approach has been and still is fundamental for those of us who conceive of reflection on the past as a philosophical confrontation between our lives and those of other people."

Aron has himself said that "sociological teaching can never escape some degree of partiality, both in what it says and does not say, and in the way it says it." Many of his own works are quite frankly polemical and are closely related to his journalism, which began during World War II. Aron served in the French Air Force from the outbreak of war until the defeat of France in 1940, when he joined General de Gaulle in London and became editor in chief of *La France libre*. After the liberation he was appointed professor at the Institut d'Études Politiques of the Sorbonne and the École Nationale d'Administration, and he joined Sartre and Merleau-Ponty in founding the existentialist review *Les Temps modernes*, the first number of which appeared in October 1945. But it was not long before Aron split with Sartre,

* a rôN'

existentialism, and the left in general. Much of his work since then has been ideological criticism from a conservative, rationalist, and anti-Marxist point of view, or political journalism in *Le Figaro* and other journals, French, British, and American. The best known of these polemical works is *L'Opium des intellectuels* (1955, translated by T. Kilmartin as *The Opium of the Intellectuals*) which attacks some political "myths of the left" and then deals with the role of the intelligentsia. *Marxism and the Existentialists* (1969) is a translation of five essays dating from 1946 to 1964 which are specific critiques of the attempts of Sartre and Merleau-Ponty to find a *modus vivendi* between existentialism and Marxism.

Aron's criticism of the "myths of the right" in *Espoir et peur du siècle* (Hope and Fear of the Century, 1957) is less well known. The hope is for the gradual enrichment of classes and nations through economic progress, but Aron's argument is closely linked with peculiarly French problems, and only the essay dealing with fear (of annihilation by thermonuclear bombs) has been translated. Many of his other books deal primarily with the French political situation, like *Immuable et changeante* (1959, translated as *France Steadfast and Changing*) which discusses the causes of French political instability under the Fourth Republic and the changes brought by de Gaulle's return to power in 1958. *De Gaulle, Israël et les juifs* (1968, translated as *De Gaulle, Israel and the Jews*) is a collection of his newspaper articles on the Middle East question, from the viewpoint of a nonreligious French Jew critical of Gaullist diplomacy towards Israel. *La Révolution introuvable* (1968, translated as *The Elusive Revolution*) is about the student revolt that took place in France during May 1968, which seemed to Aron a "psychodrama," absurd, but also genuinely dangerous because it led to a conservative reaction and therefore produced a polarization which threatened liberal institutions.

It has been suggested in the *Times Literary Supplement* that the revival of radical criticism and radical movements in most of the industrial societies "casts doubt upon the usefulness of some of the categories which Professor Aron and others were trying to establish in the 1950s—the distinction, for instance, between industrial and developing countries, which was to take the place of the earlier distinction between capitalism and socialism. The whole debate about the industrial type of society now seems slightly dated." This distinction rested on the primacy which Aron gives to politics, seeing the political system as decisive for the social system. This is the theme of a series of three works, collectively called *Sociologie des sociétés industrielles* (Sociology of Industrial Societies), in which Aron compares Soviet and Western societies

RAYMOND ARON

on three different levels: economic, social, and political: *Dix-huit leçons sur la société industrielle* (1961, translated as *18 Lectures on Industrial Society*); *La Lutte des classes* (The Class Struggle, 1964), and *Démocratie et totalitarisme* (1965, translated as *Democracy and Totalitarianism*).

Trois essais sur l'âge industriel (1966, translated as *The Industrial Society: Three Essays on Ideology and Development*) approaches similar problems from several different angles. In *Progress and Disillusion* (1968) Aron attempts a total picture of the condition and direction of modern industrial societies, insisting throughout that industrial society has no predetermined goal, that the variety of contradictions between the ideals and the realities of industrial societies is such that change has no fixed direction. Some readers concurred with the critic who thought that "the movement towards generalization in this work turns out to be a movement towards facile and empty statement."

Aron has also written many works on international relations and on war. His major work on the subject is *Paix et guerre entre les nations* (1962, translated by R. Howard and A. B. Fox as *Peace and War*), in which Aron attempts to develop a theory of international relations, conceiving the work as a contemporary *summa* in the tradition of Plato's *Republic* and Aristotle's *Politics*. George Steiner found himself awed by the book's industry and "occasionally moved by its sober reasonableness," but thought that "these 800 pages are made almost unreadable by their gray mixture of generality and ponderous abstraction." Other critics praised Aron's style as precise and often epigrammatic, but agreed that the complexity of his ideas and the concentration of his prose made the book a very taxing one to read. Stanley Hoffman called it "the most intellectually ambitious work that has ever been written about international relations . . . [a] great and difficult book."

Aron taught at the Sorbonne from 1955 to 1968. In 1960 he became also a professor at the École Pratique des Hautes Études, and in 1970 a professor at the Collège de France. He is a Chevalier of the Légion d'Honneur. Aron married Suzanne Gauchon, a former teacher of Latin and Greek, in 1933, and they have two daughters.

Aron has been a prolific writer, and much of his work is controversial. He has, as he himself has said, "the reputation in France for being far too much pro-Anglo-Saxon," and A. J. P. Taylor has said of him: "He admires English ways—perhaps to excess; and in turn we reward him by finding him as nearly sympathetic as a French writer can be." He has perhaps been best summed up in the *Times Literary Supplement* as "an intellectual aristocrat" with "a passionate attachment to reason."

PRINCIPAL WORKS IN ENGLISH TRANSLATION: The Century of Total War, 1954; German Sociology, 1957; The Opium of the Intellectuals, 1957; War and Industrial Society, 1958; On War: Atomic Weapons and Global Diplomacy, 1958; France, Steadfast and Changing, 1960; France, the New Republic, 1960; Introduction to the Philosophy of History: An Essay on the Limits of Historical Objectivity, 1961; Main Currents in Sociological Thought: Vol. 1, Montesquieu, Comte, Marx, Tocqueville: The Sociologists and the Revolution of 1848, 1965; Vol. 2, Durkheim, Pareto, Weber, 1967; Peace and War: A Theory of International Relations, 1967; 18 Lectures on Industrial Society, 1967; The Industrial Society: Three Essays on Ideology and Development, 1967; Democracy and Totalitarianism, 1968; Progress and Disillusion, 1968; De Gaulle, Israel and the Jews, 1969; The Elusive Revolution, 1969; Marxism and the Existentialists, 1970.

ABOUT: Bottomore, T. B. Élites and Society, 1964; Current Biography, 1954; Pierce, R. Contemporary French Political Thought, 1966. *Periodicals*—American Journal of Sociology May 1968; January 1969; March 1970; American Political Science Review December 1969; American Sociological Review April 1968; October 1969; Annals of the American Academy of Political and Social Science March 1968; International Affairs January 1963; Journal of International Affairs 2, 1967; Journal of Modern History June 1961; Journal of Politics February 1963; Listener September 5, 1968; New Society May 30, 1968; August 29, 1968; October 24, 1968; New Statesman August 31, 1957; July 19, 1968; August 16, 1968; February 6, 1970; New York Times Book Review January 7, 1951; Observer April 23, 1967; Saturday Review November 23, 1957; Social Research Winter 1956; Times Literary Supplement September 16, 1955; April 12, 1957; June 16, 1961; June 25, 1964; April 7, 1966; August 25, 1966; April 4, 1968; November 28, 1968; June 19, 1969; Virginia Quarterly Review Summer 1968; World Politics January 1955; October 1958; Yale Review October 1968.

***ARRABAL (TERÁN), FERNANDO** (August 11, 1932–), Spanish dramatist and novelist authorized the following account by his wife, Mme. Luce Arrabal-Moreau: "Arrabal could not write anything but a strictly literary text and, consequently, he could not write the story of his life, which he probably considers a puzzle, a series of mysterious facts whose logic escapes him.

"He settled in Paris ten years ago, in 1955. The atmosphere of his country not being favorable to him, either from the social point of view, or from the familial, he left Spain and its capital. Who was that young man of twenty-three that arrived at Austerlitz Station carrying with him scant luggage but plenty of manuscripts? Above all a sick man, unaware of the gravity of his illness: one of his lungs was eaten up by tuberculosis. Arrabal arrived from Madrid, where he had led the triple life of a law student, an office clerk, and an up-and-coming playwright. The French Embassy had awarded him a grant to study drama in Paris, thus rewarding the efforts of a young writer who in his own country had won two prizes for his first plays.

"Nothing, in fact, destined Arrabal to this exile or to a literary career: his family never possessed more than three or four books—for the sake of appearances—and his writing was regarded with much skepticism by them.

"Arrabal was born in Melilla, a Moroccan town, at the time a Spanish protectorate. Four years later, a military insurrection broke out: it was the onset of the Civil War that was to ravage Spain and leave in her children's spirit an indelible mark. Arrabal is himself a victim of the cruel conflict that rent his country, for his parents rose against each other to take opposite political sides. His mother sought the victory of Francoism; she would not allow her son to listen to the BBC, considering the English radio 'democratic and liberal' (and therefore dangerous); his father, an officer, didn't take part in the anti-Republican rising. He was arrested a few hours after the first shots of sedition; then he was sentenced to death, curiously enough, for 'military rebellion.' Eight months later his penalty was commuted to perpetual confinement, then to thirty years' imprisonment. Overwhelmed by his wife's reproaches on the few occasions she visited him in jail, this man escaped and disappeared forever in 1941. His son's efforts to trace him have proved entirely fruitless.

"It isn't difficult to understand Arrabal when he holds that his two years in the University Sanatorium of Bouffémont, on the outskirts of Paris, calm and restful as they were, gave him a respite in which to write. Far from his family, far from his mother still burning with hatred for her husband,

* är rä bäl′

far from a country where life and survival had proved so hard, he wrote endlessly. The despair engendered by his illness remains evident in his work and doubtless contributed to its development.

"After an operation in 1957, Arrabal recovered his health. At the same time Éditions Julliard in Paris offered him employment, and his plays began to be produced. Nowadays, his work is seen in relation to the literature of the Absurd (Esslin), to the avant-garde theatre (Penguin Books), to surrealist poetry (J. L. Bédouin), to eroticism (Encyclopédie Planète), to the *nouveau roman*, to 'panic' . . . one would rather say, with A. Prullansky, that Arrabal's work 'increasingly states its originality and its unity.'

"Arrabal has been invited to attend productions of his plays (translated into more than twenty languages) in several countries: in this way he has been able to visit the United States, Cuba, Australia, etc. At the end of one of his recent trips around the world, he could enjoy the thought that the young man in a little-known North African town, who never had in his childhood more than a few books, had at last succeeded, against all expectations, in making his voice heard."

A diminutive, dark, bewhiskered dandy of a man, Arrabal belongs to that line of Spanish artists —from Blanco White to Picasso and Buñuel—who have worked abroad while remaining profoundly Spanish. Recognition has come in a comparatively short time. Since leaving Madrid in 1955 he has not only produced a substantial corpus of published work, but he had by the late 1960s become that rare phenomenon, a commercially successful avant-garde dramatist. Though he writes in Spanish, Arrabal has his work translated into French by his wife; and his success is Parisian. But he affirms his Spanishness: "I am a Spanish writer, I am known as such abroad. . . . It gives me satisfaction to see that my theatre can present a new face of Spain."

Despite a clear evolution, Arrabal's work is characterized by recurrent themes, the product of personal and national upheavals—in particular what Alain Schifres has called his "deep and weird" relationship with his mother. She had always pretended that his father was dead, and it was not until he was sixteen that Arrabal discovered this deception. For five years afterward he would not speak to her, though they lived under the same roof, while she slaved to pay for his education at what he calls "Fascist Catholic" schools. These traumas of his youth, set against the horrors of civil war, terror, torture, and betrayal in Spain, no doubt account for that quality in Arrabal's work which has led critics to categorize him as a writer of the Absurd.

FERNANDO ARRABAL

The plays collected in Arrabal's *Théâtre I* (1958) illustrate the essential features of his vision and give some clues to the heterogeneous cultural influences that have shaped his mode of expression. (Beckett, Ionesco, Adamov, Artaud, Jarry, Genet, Chaplin, the Marx Brothers, Lewis Carroll, W. C. Fields, Kafka, Goya, Dali, and Bosch have all been nominated by one critic or another, and, though some of these at least were totally unknown to him when he began to write, the list is not without interest.)

In *Le Cimetière des voitures* (translated as *The Automobile Graveyard* and in England as *The Car Cemetery*), the betrayal and murder of Emanou, trying unsuccessfully to be "good," blasphemously parodies the Passion of Christ. A characteristic touch is the prostitute Dila, who follows her profession in simple obedience to the injunction that one should love one's neighbor. Fidio and Lilbé in *Oraison* (translated as *Orison*), seated on the coffin of their child, whom they have murdered, also discuss the nature of goodness. They decide to relinquish "fun"—killing people, tearing the eyes out of corpses—and follow the example of Jesus, though Lilbé fancies that the new game will soon pall. Arrabal's characters are like murderous children; through them, Martin Esslin says, he questions "all accepted ethical standards from the standpoint of an innocent who would be only too eager to accept them if only he could understand them."

Another play in *Théâtre I*, *Les deux bourreaux* (translated as *The Two Executioners*), presents in Françoise another Arrabal type. She is the evil mother, delightedly aiding the two men who are slowly torturing her husband to death, deeply distressed by her son's unfilial wickedness when he protests. The personal background here—Arrabal's family situation is clearly mirrored—reappears in the novel *Baal Babylone* (1959, translated as *Baal Babylon*), in which the reactionary mother endeavors to eradicate the memory of the radical father languishing in one of Franco's prisons. Guy Mernier sees this novel as "a monologue overwhelming with poignant poetry." It was filmed under the author's own direction in 1970 as *Viva la Muerte*.

Arrabal's subsequent work contains fewer private references, though the naïve and troubled narrators of the novels clearly reflect his puzzled reactions to the contradictions between social and moral laws. These latter-day Candides inhabit an apocalyptic world, conveyed in the eerie prose poems of *La Pierre de la folie* (1963) and the grotesque montage of *L'Interrement de la sardine* (1962, translated as *The Burial of the Sardine*) with its theme, in J. K. Simon's words, of "the helpless passive individual incapable of interpreting and communicating the equivocal inanimate world which engulfs him." The later novel *Fête et rite de la confusion* (1967) exemplifies Arrabal's evolution towards a highly abstract and ritualistic art.

A similar development is discernible in Arrabal's plays—in such pieces as *Le Grand Cérémonial* and *Cérémonie pour un noir assassiné* in *Théâtre III* (1965). The ceremonial rites in these works are usually a playing out of sadistic fantasies, practiced on the archetypal uncomprehending protagonist. Rather than an assertion of the ritualistic violence of society, this is a demonstration of "panic" art. Panic, which Arrabal has been expounding since 1962, is not an artistic movement but " 'a manner of being,' controlled by confusion, humor, terror, chance, and euphoria." He sets up the great god Pan against the Christian God, in a gesture of revolt, derision, and deliberate blasphemy.

Arrabal's panic theories did not at first receive serious critical attention, and indeed his whole achievement has been questioned in the United States and Britain. Robert Brustein felt that the early *Pique-nique en campagne* (1959, translated as *Picnic on the Battlefield*), "though it qualifies as an Absurdist play does not qualify as art," while a reviewer in the *Times Literary Supplement* described a collection of Arrabal's plays as "the 'New Theatre' at its most pretentious." A more penetrating criticism derives from G. E. Wellworth: "The trouble with Arrabal . . . has always been an inability to sustain and work out his brilliant initial ideas." Jacques Guicharnaud feels that the plays are too static, tableaux rather than fully developed dramas. Few of these criticisms seem applicable to *L'Architecte et l'Empereur d'Assyrie*, the most admired of Arrabal's recent plays. A notable success in Paris in 1967, it was received with great interest at the Stratford (Ontario) Festival in 1970 and at the British National Theatre in 1971. It is an account of the confrontation between a "civilized" man and a "primitive" one on a desert island, a sort of symposium of all of Arrabal's themes, a festival of scatological and sadomasochistic role playing, an assault on every kind of social repression, worked out with immense verve and unfailing inventiveness.

And Arrabal has found distinguished champions. When he was arraigned before a Spanish court in 1967 for blasphemy and antipatriotism, Ionesco, Mauriac, Anouilh, Beckett, and Cela were among those who wrote to the Madrid press affirming the importance of Arrabal's work. *Et ils passèrent des menottes aux fleurs* (1969), a play derived from his conversations with political prisoners in a Spanish jail, had a *succès de scandale* in France, where it was eventually banned (as it was also in Sweden and Belgium). It brought Arrabal his first major success in the United States, where it was staged in 1971 and again in 1972 as *And They Put Handcuffs on the Flowers*. Clive Barnes wrote: "This is a shocking play, and its dramatized graffiti, extravagances, and pictures of violence are sometimes too strident, too insistent. But . . . it is very calculated, very balanced. For all his imagery and expressionist wanderings, Arrabal is a classical playwright." The author, who directed both New York productions of the play, taught during the fall semester of 1971 at the Santa Cruz campus of the University of California.

Arrabal himself denies that his concerns are political: "I am no Sartre. In my plays I put my dreams, my fears, my thoughts. I have no politics except that I am against tyrants." As for his private life, he says: "I am a married man. I have a child. I lead a completely normal life. I don't drink. I don't take drugs. I lead a chaste life. The only exception is yesterday—I wrote a woman's name on my penis."

PRINCIPAL WORKS IN ENGLISH TRANSLATION: *Plays*—The Automobile Graveyard and The Two Executioners (translated by Richard Howard), 1960; Four Plays (Orison, The Two Executioners, Fando and Lis, The Car Cemetery, translated by Barbara Wright), 1962; Guernica and Other Plays (Guernica, The Labyrinth, The Tricycle, Picnic on the Battlefield, The Condemned Man's Bicycle, translated by Barbara Wright), 1969 (England, Plays, 1967); The Architect and the Emperor of Assyria (translated by E. d'Harnoncourt and A. Shank), 1969; First Communion *in* Benedikt, M. and Wellworth, G. E. (eds.) Modern Spanish Theatre, 1968; Four Plays (Solemn Communion, Panic Ceremony, Striptease of Jealousy, Impossible Loves) *in* Drama Review Fall 1968; Groupuscule of My Heart *in* Drama Review Summer 1969. *Fiction*—Baal Babylon, 1961; The Burial of the Sardine, 1966.

ABOUT: Contemporary Authors 11–12, 1965; Current Biography, 1972; Esslin, M. The Theatre of the Absurd, 1961; Guicharnaud, J. The Modern French Theatre from Giraudoux to Genet, 1967; Penguin Companion to Literature 2, 1969; Schifres, A. Entretiens avec Arrabal, 1969; Serreau, G. *Prefaces to* Arrabal's Théâtre I and II, 1958 and 1961. *Periodicals*—Commonweal December 8, 1961; Drama Review Fall 1968; Insula March 1966, September and October 1967; New York Times August 9, 1970; April 22, 1972; May 10, 1972; New Yorker November 25, 1961; Sunday Times February 25, 1968; Times Literary Supplement January 11, 1963; Yale French Studies Spring–Summer 1962.

ARROWSMITH, WILLIAM (AYRES) (April 13, 1924–), American scholar and translator, was born in Orange, New Jersey, the son of Walter Weed Arrowsmith and Dorothy (Ayres) Arrowsmith. He went to schools in Massachusetts and Florida, and then to Princeton University, but was drafted in 1943 before he had graduated. The Army sent him to the Military Intelligence Language School to learn Japanese—a skill he put to nonmilitary use in the translation of medieval Japanese poetry.

When he was discharged in 1946, Arrowsmith returned to Princeton, which gave him his B.A. the following year. For the next three years he studied at Oxford University as a Rhodes Scholar, receiving his second B.A. there in 1951. His Oxford M.A. followed automatically seven years later. Meanwhile Arrowsmith taught classics at Princeton (1951–1953) and at Wesleyan University (1953–1954). He earned his doctorate in 1954, taught for two years at the University of California (Riverside), and then returned to Europe. From 1956 to 1958 Arrowsmith lived and studied in Italy, supported by a Bollingen grant, a Prix de Rome fellowship, and a Guggenheim Fellowship. In 1958 he joined the faculty of the University of Texas in Austin, where he became University Professor in Arts and Letters, professor of classics, and chairman of the classics department. One of a number of professors who resigned from the University of Texas in 1971 on the grounds that political considerations had become a major and damaging factor in the running of the university, he accepted an appointment to the classics department at Boston University.

Arrowsmith's reputation rests principally on his spirited contemporary versions of Euripides, Petronius, and Aristophanes. He is prominent in that school of translators which accepts the principles of "prosodic equivalence and the rejection of rhyme." His use of contemporary American idiom in his renderings of the classics has been known to upset some scholars, one of whom once complained that he had made the Phrygian Slave in Euripides' *Orestes* speak "a hair-raising amalgam of Wardour Street and hill-billy vernacular." In general, however, his renderings have been found as sensitive as they are energetic and readable. A writer in the *Times Literary Supplement*, reviewing

WILLIAM ARROWSMITH

his version of the *Satyricon* of Petronius, called it a "brilliant new translation, which at one stroke renders every other version obsolete" and which, "for the first time, gives modern Latinless readers the full impact of Petronius—allusions, puns, parodies, bawdry and all." The same reviewer praised Arrowsmith's "ironic sense of humor," his "easy-going sophistication," and said that "almost alone among classical translators, Professor Arrowsmith has an accurate ear for the subtle demands of spoken dialogue." Arrowsmith's translations of classical plays have been performed by professional as well as by college theatre companies.

The Craft and Context of Translation, which Arrowsmith edited with Roger Shattuck, included papers delivered at a symposium on translation held at the University of Texas in 1959. In his own contribution to the symposium, Arrowsmith, according to J. P. Sullivan, "attempts to define what mediation between the past and the present, between the alien and the contemporary tradition, should mean. Tact, flexibility, and judicious improvisation are his reasonable answers and his examples (like his own translations of Aristophanes) show his liberalism."

Arrowsmith has maintained his interest in Italy, where he spent the academic year 1962–1963 gathering new teaching materials. He was the editor of a special Italian issue of the *Texas Quarterly*, republished in book form as *The Image of Italy*, and selected and introduced the collection *Six Modern Italian Novellas*. Cesare Pavese's *Dialogues with Leucò*, written in 1946, appeared in 1965 in a translation by Arrowsmith and D. S. Carne-Ross.

Sources as diverse as *Time* magazine and the

Times Literary Supplement have described him in similar terms: he is, it is said, an "amiable if mercurial scholar" who "smiles often, likes to shed his tie in class, melts co-eds with his boyish good looks." He has received four awards for excellence as a teacher, and holds several honorary degrees. Arrowsmith sees no point in studying the classics "except to learn how to live better." His outspoken attacks on the sterility of much contemporary teaching and research—notably in an article called "The Shame of the Graduate Schools" in *Harper's* (March 1966)—have attracted widespread attention. He was one of the founding editors of the literary quarterlies *Chimera* and the *Hudson Review* and of the classical quarterly *Arion*. He nurses an ambition to write a novel.

Arrowsmith was married in 1945 to Jean Reiser. She describes him as "basically good natured and outgoing, with a skeptical turn of mind." They have two children. Arrowsmith is fond of music and is drawn especially to the baroque.

PRINCIPAL WORKS: (tr.) Euripides, The Cyclops *and* Herakles, *in* The Complete Greek Tragedies, Vol. 2, 1956; (tr.) Euripides, Hecuba, *in* The Complete Greek Tragedies, Vol. 3, 1958; (tr.) Euripides, Orestes, *in* The Complete Greek Tragedies, Vol. 4, 1958; (tr.) Euripides, The Bacchae *in* The Complete Greek Tragedies, Vol. 5, 1959; (tr. and ed.) Petronius Arbiter, The Satyricon, 1959; (ed.) The Image of Italy, 1961; (ed. with Roger Shattuck) The Craft and Context of Translation, 1961; (tr.) Aristophanes, The Birds, *in* The Complete Greek Comedy, Vol. 1, 1961; (tr.) Aristophanes, The Clouds, *in* The Complete Greek Comedy, Vol. 2, 1962; (ed.) Six Modern Italian Novellas, 1964; (tr. with D. S. Carne-Ross) Cesare Pavese, Dialogues with Leucò, 1965.

ABOUT: Contemporary Authors 9–10, 1964; Directory of American Scholars, 1969; Silver, L. J. Profiles in Success, 1965; Who's Who in America, 1970–1971. *Periodicals*—New York Times May 21, 1971; Time October 28, 1966.

***ARTAUD, ANTONIN (ANTOINE-MARIE-JOSEPH ARTAUD)** (September 4, 1896–March 4, 1948), French theorist of the drama, was born in Marseilles, the son of a wealthy shipfitter. His mother, Euphrasie Nalpas, was of Greek origin, and Artaud occasionally visited her family at Smyrna. When he was five he nearly died of meningitis and, though he survived, the aftereffects of the disease dominated his life.

Artaud was educated at the Collège du Sacré Cœur in Marseilles and was a good student, early attracted to symbolist poetry, drawing, and the theatre. When he was only about fourteen he founded a small literary magazine which he seems to have maintained for three or four years—until the onset of the fierce head pains which were to plague him for the rest of his life. This development coincided with the death of his Greek grandmother, who had given him a sense of security which neither his ambitious father nor his over-solicitous mother could provide. An acute attack of neurasthenia, which prevented him from taking his baccalaureate in philosophy in 1914, was treated in a local rest home. His condition improved and he returned home after a few months, but the head pains persisted, and in 1915 Artaud was given opium to alleviate his suffering. He was soon addicted. Inducted into the army in 1916 for his national service, he was released after nine months on grounds of mental instability. In 1918, suffering from alternate bouts of mystical exaltation and desperate melancholy, he entered a Swiss clinic where he remained for two years.

* är tō′

Artaud went to Paris in 1920, his health much improved, happy to be free of the restrictions and associations of family life. It had been arranged that he should stay with a Dr. Toulouse, a writer and a man of culture who guided and encouraged him. Artaud studied with Charles Dullin, the actor and theatrical director, and found work as a stage and screen actor and as a costume and set designer. Those who saw his performance as the monk Massieur in Carl Dreyer's film *La Passion de Jeanne d'Arc* (1928) will not forget his strong ascetic features. His poems began to appear in literary magazines in the early 1920s.

A slim volume of verse in the symbolist manner, *Tric trac du ciel* (Backgammon of the Sky, 1923) was followed by *L'Ombilic des limbes* (1925, translated as "Umbilical Limbo"), a collection of prose poems, letters, and snatches of dialogue which, like its successor, *Le Pèse-Nerfs* (1927, translated as "Nerve Scales"), reflected his conversion to surrealism. John Weightman, who considers Artaud's poetry in general to be not much more than "a flux of words coming from a diseased brain," does credit him with some "very graphic and moving descriptions" of his own illness. Particularly affecting is Artaud's recurrent fear of aphasia, his sense that words are slipping out of his control even as he uses them. He refers constantly to this fear, notably in the correspondence he had with Jacques Rivière in 1923. Some critics find in this condition a partial explanation for Artaud's desire for a nonverbal theatre.

Artaud had joined the surrealist movement in 1924, broke with its leader Breton in 1926, but continued to think of himself as a surrealist. He was the author of *La Coquille et le clergyman* (1927), one of the most famous surrealist films. In 1927, seeking a platform for his developing theatrical doctrines, he founded with Roger Vitrac and Robert Aron the Théâtre Alfred Jarry "to contribute by strictly theatrical means to the ruin of the theatre as it exists today in France." A small under-rehearsed company with no stage of its own, it produced innovatory plays by Vitrac, Artaud, Strindberg, and others, but at the time made little impact and survived only two seasons.

Although there were already signs of an awakening, the French theatre was then still dominated by "well-made" entertainments which stated a problem at the beginning of the evening and glibly resolved it in time for the final curtain. Such plays reflected the nineteenth century assumption that life is rational and orderly and can be benevolently controlled for the general good. In France after World War I, these comfortable assumptions seemed meaningless. Artaud was infuriated by the craven dishonesty of what he called "culture"—by a theatre which closed its eyes to the demonstrable savagery of life, the blind forces of disorder with which he himself was obliged to grapple constantly.

It was their acknowledgment of these forces that had drawn Artaud to the surrealists and to their prophet Alfred Jarry, whose *Ubu Roi* (1896) had been an outrageous insult to the well-made play and its audience. Artaud found some of the qualities he sought in the English Elizabethan theatre of violence, in Mallarmé's incantations and Rimbaud's *dérèglement*, and in the frenzied paintings of Van Gogh. His theatrical philosophy received its catalysis in 1931, when Artaud saw Balinese drama at the Colonial Exposition and felt the impact of a "total" theatre which was not merely verbal and literary, but addressed to the spectator's whole being.

Artaud's doctrines were expressed in the two *Manifestes du théâtre de la cruauté* (Manifestos of the Theatre of Cruelty, 1932 and 1933), and in the articles written between 1931 and 1938 and published as *Le Théâtre et son double* (1938, translated as *The Theatre and Its Double*). In place of a theatre dedicated to reassuring lies, Artaud called for one so terrible and excessive as to shatter the spectator's self-control, inducing trance and delirium, revealing to him his forgotten instincts, binding men together in their recognition of an inherited collective unconscious. The "cruelty" of this theatre lay not in mere sadism, but in its acknowledgment and enactment of the implacable inhumanity of life; and it was life itself which Artaud saw as the theatre's "double."

As in the Oriental theatre, speech was to be used not in communication but as incantation; an idea fully realized in words is dead. "The poetry of speech" was to be replaced by "the poetry of space," by dance, symbolic gestures, masks and apparitions, music, incoherent cries, vocal mimicry, "new and surprising objects" of all kinds. Artaud's actors were to be "animated hieroglyphics" and his *metteur en scène* an adept in an almost religious sense, contriving a simultaneous assault upon all of the spectator's senses in a "sacral" rite of magical power.

Staging was thus of central importance in

ANTONIN ARTAUD

Artaud's concepts, and during the early 1930s he badgered Dullin, Pitoëff, Jouvet, and others for opportunities to work out his ideas in production. Even those few who were interested in his theories found him personally trying, and most dismissed his views as the ravings of a lunatic. Nevertheless, he did manage to bring a handful of plays to the stage, notably, in May 1935, *Les Cenci*, a *mélange* of rape, incest, and murder which he had adapted from texts by Shelley and Stendhal. This extraordinary production, with Artaud himself in a leading role and Jean-Louis Barrault as assistant director, is said by some to have initiated "theatre in the round," designed by Artaud to establish closer contact between actors and audience, and was full of strange speech rhythms, dissonant noises, storms of light, and all the devices of the "poetry of space."

Admired by a few sympathetic critics, *Les Cenci* was otherwise a total failure. In January 1936, despairing and ill, Artaud went to Mexico where he remained for almost a year, spending several months with the sun-worshiping Tarahumara Indians. This was one of the richest and most rewarding experiences of Artaud's wretched life. It reached its climax when he was initiated into the Tarahumaras' ancient peyote ritual, which seemed to him a living enactment and justification of his conception of the "theatre of cruelty" as sacral rite. Artaud returned to France, renewed and hopeful, at the end of 1936. The following year he became engaged to a Belgian girl, Cécile Schramme, and made one of his many attempts to end his dependence on drugs. (He had previously had little to do with women, and seems to have been both fascinated and revolted by sexuality.)

This happy interlude was short-lived. In May 1937, while giving a lecture in Brussels, Artaud lost control of himself and ended by screaming invective at the audience. Cécile Schramme broke off the engagement and Artaud, always fascinated by the supernatural and the occult, was now seized by religious mania. He ended a visit to Ireland in the latter half of 1937 in a straitjacket, and descended into schizophrenia. His next nine years were spent in a succession of mental institutions.

Meanwhile, however, his theories were gaining adherents. *Le Théâtre et son double*, republished in 1944, was described by Barrault as "indisputably the most important thing written on the theatre in the twentieth century." Still under medical supervision, but free, Artaud returned to Paris in 1946 to find himself regarded by some avant-garde writers as a prophet and martyr. In January 1947 he gave a reading and lecture in Paris, binding for three hours an audience which included Gide, Breton, Camus, Adamov, and Paulhan with a performance oscillating "between genius and madness." Gide wrote: "My memory of it is indelible—atrocious, painful, almost sublime at moments, revolting also and quasi-intolerable." The following year Artaud died of cancer in a rest home near Paris.

His influence is evident in the plays of Samuel Beckett, in Ionesco's emphasis on the uncertainty of reality, in Genet's theatre of ritual, and to some extent in the work of most recent avant-garde dramatists in France. It has been traced in the plays of such American dramatists as Albee, Gelber, and the Living Theatre writers, and in the New Wave cinema of France. Peter Brook's 1964 production of Peter Weiss's *Marat/Sade* play, a major success both in London and New York, embodied many of Artaud's theories. It was preceded by the same director's "theatre of cruelty" season in London, which included Artaud's own short play *Le Jet de sang* (1927, translated variously as *Jet of Blood* and *The Spurt of Blood*). Artaud's collected works have been published by Gallimard in nine volumes, and are now being translated into English.

Artaud has many opponents. He is blamed for the meaningless violence purveyed by followers who misunderstood his views, and attacked with more justice for the vagueness of his critical vocabulary. Much of what he wrote was nonsensical, and his own few plays are scarcely stageworthy. But his importance is beyond question, as the theoretician of a vitalizing and liberating revolt against an artificial and moribund drama, and as the originator of stage techniques which have transformed the theatre. "We are not free," he wrote. "And the sky can still fall on our heads. And the theatre has been created to teach us that, first of all."

PRINCIPAL WORKS IN ENGLISH TRANSLATION: The Theatre and Its Double, tr. by Mary C. Richards, 1958 (also tr. by Victor Corti, 1970); Artaud Anthology, ed. by Jack Hirschman, 1965; The Cenci, tr. by Simon Watson Taylor, 1969; Collected Works: Volume One, tr. by Victor Corti, 1969; Volume Two, tr. by Victor Corti, 1971; Volume Three, tr. by Alastair Hamilton, 1972; Selected Writings, ed. by Susan Sontag, 1973; Jet of Blood *in* Benedikt, M. and Wellwarth, C. E. Modern French Plays, 1964.

ABOUT: Bonneton, A. Le Naufrage prophétique d'Antonin Artaud, 1961; Brustein, R. The Theatre of Revolt, 1964; Charbonnier, G. Essai sur A. Artaud, 1966; Chiari, J. Landmarks of Contemporary Drama, 1965; Fowlie, W. Dionysus in Paris, 1960; Greene, N. Antonin Artaud: Poet Without Words, 1971; Guicharnaud, J. Modern French Theatre, 1961; Hahn, O. Portrait d'Antonin Artaud, 1969; Kitchin, L. Drama in the Sixties, 1966; Knapp, B. L. Antonin Artaud, Man of Vision, 1969; Pronko, L. C. Avant-Garde, 1962; Roose-Evans, J. Experimental Theatre, 1970; Sellin, E. The Dramatic Concepts of Antonin Artaud, 1968; Sontag, S. Against Interpretation, 1966; Wellwarth, G. E. The Theatre of Protest and Paradox, 1964. *Periodicals*—American Heritage Spring 1970; Combat May 19, 1948; Educational Theatre Journal December 1967; Encounter August 1967; Evergreen Review May–June 1960; French Review February 1968; Horizon Spring 1970; London Magazine March 1964; New York Times Magazine March 6, 1966; New Yorker May 19, 1973; Saturday Review May 24, 1969; Times Literary Supplement March 18, 1965; May 8, 1969; July 6, 1969; Tulane Drama Review Spring 1965; Yale French Studies May 1964.

ASHBERY, JOHN (LAWRENCE) (July 28, 1927–), American poet, dramatist, and critic, was born in Rochester, New York, the son of Chester and Helen (Lawrence) Ashbery. He was brought up on his father's farm at Sodus, New York, and educated at Deerfield Academy and Harvard College. Originally he wanted to be a painter, but at eighteen he transferred much of his interest to music. In 1949, when he was a senior, Ashbery became editor of the *Harvard Advocate* and published some of the first writings of Frank O'Hara. The same year he met O'Hara in a bookstore and began a friendship which lasted until O'Hara's death.

In 1951 Ashbery received his M.A. in English from Columbia University. For the next four years he worked as a copywriter, first for Oxford University Press and then for the McGraw-Hill Book Company. During this period his first volume of poetry, *Turandot*, was published by the Tibor de Nagy Press, and his one-act play *The Heroes* was produced by the Living Theatre and the Artists' Theatre.

Ashbery went to Paris in 1955 on a Fulbright scholarship to work on translations of modern French poetry, some of which were published. The following year, as a Fulbright teaching fellow, he taught American studies to college students at Rennes. It was also in 1956 that *Some Trees* was published in the Yale Series of Younger Poets and his three-act play *The Compromise* was produced at the Poets' Theatre in Cambridge, Massachusetts. His plays have been thought amusing, but at a rather undergraduate level.

For ten months in 1957–1958 Ashbery studied towards a doctorate at New York University and at the same time became, like Frank O'Hara, a contributor to *Art News*, developing "much contact with modern art, friendships with artists." He went back to Paris in 1958 and in 1960 became art critic of the Paris edition of the New York *Herald Tribune*. In the mid-1960s Ashbery returned to New York as executive editor of *Art News* and soon made a new reputation there as an exceptionally able literary critic. He has also been editor of the quarterly *Art and Literature* since 1963.

Ashbery believes that "journalism is perhaps good experience in communication since my poetry, though very experimental, does try to communicate." It is this that some of his critics have seemed to doubt. His elegant, sad, inscrutable poems, so simple in their language, are often so violently surreal in their juxtapositions that he has been accused of waging a "total and furious" war *against* communication.

Nevertheless, Donald Hall credits Ashbery with "a fine ear and an honest eccentricity of diction which, used properly, excites the attention and speaks with an oblique precision." Jonathan Cott goes so far as to call him not only the foremost poet of the New York school, but also "today's most radically original American poet," who "writes of characters who operate in a drama without a story." Ashbery's verse, Cott says, "has the quality of a dream which begs to be interpreted, since we dreamt it, and yet whose most fascinating and wondrous quality is that it resists being interpreted." The meaning which exists so mysteriously in Ashbery's poems, Cott believes, is that "change is horror." Hope survives only in childhood's brief ignorance of death, and the poet's verbal disguises are to protect him or distract him from the fear of death: "And only in the light of lost words / Can we imagine our rewards."

Critics have recognized in Ashbery's work not only the influence of contemporary French poetry and of Pasternak, but also correspondences with both abstract painting and serial music. Ashbery himself has pointed out similarities between his verse and painting, and elsewhere has discussed his desire to emulate music's capacity for carrying an argument successfully to its conclusion, even though "the terms of this argument remain unknown quantities." But he also says that he often changes his mind about his poetry and "would prefer not to think I have any special aims in mind." Ashbery received an Ingram Merrill Foundation grant in 1962 and the Harriet Monroe poetry award in 1963.

The critical argument about the value of John

JOHN ASHBERY

Ashbery's poetry swung quite decisively in his favor with the publication of *Rivers and Mountains* in 1966. These poems, and in particular his long poem "The Skaters," seemed to some reviewers an arrival after years of experiment. They convinced Stephen Koch that Ashbery is "among the finest poets now writing," and brought from Howard Wamsley this prophecy: "The chances are very good that he will come to dominate the last third of the century as Yeats, also afflicted with 'this madness to explain,' dominated the first."

Ashbery tried his hand at fiction in *A Nest of Ninnies*, a novel written in collaboration with James Schuyler. It is a Firbankian fable about two middle-class American suburban families, their vacations abroad, their elaborate meals, their conversations about music and literature. Most reviewers read it as a satire on the American way of life and were mildly amused and/or bored by it, but W. H. Auden called it a pastoral, depicting "an imaginary Garden of Eden, a place of innocence from which all serious needs and desires have been excluded," and thought the book was "destined to become a minor classic."

PRINCIPAL WORKS: *Poems*—Turandot and Other Poems, 1953; Some Trees, 1956; The Poems, 1960; The Tennis Court Oath, 1962; Rivers and Mountains, 1966; Selected Poems, 1967; The Double Dream of Spring, 1970; Three Poems, 1972. *Fiction* (with James Schuyler)—A Nest of Ninnies, 1969. *As editor* (with T. B. Hess)—Academic Art, 1971; Avant-garde Art, 1971; The Grand Eccentrics, 1971; Light in Art, 1971.

ABOUT: Contemporary Authors 7–8, 1963; Kostelanetz, R. (ed.) The New American Arts, 1965; Leary, P. and Kelly, R. (eds.) A Controversy of Poets, 1965; Stepanchev, S. American Poetry Since 1945, 1965; Who's Who in America, 1970–1971. *Periodicals*—Poetry February

1957; New York Times Book Review February 11, 1968; May 4, 1969; July 5, 1970; April 9, 1972.

"ASHE, GORDON." *See* CREASEY, JOHN

ASHTON-WARNER, SYLVIA (December 17, 1908–), New Zealand teacher, novelist, and memoirist, was born in Stratford, New Zealand, and educated at small country schools and at Teachers' College, Auckland (1928–1929). She married a headmaster, Keith Dawson Henderson, and worked with him for many years, teaching mixed classes of Maori and European children in several remote back-country infant schools (two-grade kindergartens).

Miss Ashton-Warner's teaching philosophy derived from her passionate conviction that the Maori people must learn to live in fruitful symbiosis with their European neighbors. Seeking a bridge between the Maori and Western cultures, she developed her Creative Teaching Scheme. It represents an attempt—frequently successful in her hands—to overcome the child's fear and apathy in the face of culture shock, to unlock his creative energies at the expense of his destructive urges. An important element in the scheme is that the teacher should use, rather than frustrate, the child's natural drives toward self-preservation and sexual gratification. Thus Miss Ashton-Warner discarded the traditional "Janet and John" primers in favor of primers written by the children themselves, exploiting a key vocabulary of first words, some of them unpleasant by adult standards, chosen by the child in accordance with the intensity of his feeling about them. She reached the children, as Elizabeth Janeway puts it, "by listening to what was within them . . . by respecting their fears and using their strengths."

These unorthodox, unpretentious, organic methods regularly brought Miss Ashton-Warner gradings as a "low-ability teacher," but her work aroused sympathetic interest among other New Zealand teachers, if not among Education Department authorities. She left the classroom in the mid-1950s, but continued her campaign, explaining her scheme in articles published in the New Zealand journal *National Education* and elsewhere. Her ideas won international recognition when they appeared as part of her book *Teacher*, which also incorporates an absorbing diaristic account of her "trials, errors, defeats, victories" in applying the scheme. *Teacher* was warmly received in the United States in 1963, and won endorsement from many American educators, including John H. Fischer, who praised it as a significant, seminal book of far-reaching implication. Others however seemed to suspect that Miss Ashton-Warner's successes depended less on her theories than on her own personal qualities: "What a wonderful, rampageous, intolerant, gifted and compassionate woman she must be," Rumer Godden observed.

By 1963, when *Teacher* appeared, Sylvia Ashton-Warner had already established another reputation as a novelist—and one who treated the form as "fresh territory rather than exhausted terrain." *Spinster*, her strikingly original first novel, had a New Zealand schoolteacher as its heroine and briefly set forth the principles of the Creative Teaching Scheme, but it was not the book's educational ideas which impressed the critics. The narrator, Anna Vorontosov, no longer young and the victim of a hopeless love affair, is neurotic, guilt-ridden, and lonely—but a superb teacher, "alive and brave and dedicated," and a marvelously well realized character. The jerky stream-of-consciousness style has the effect of "an exuberant monolog." Virgilia Peterson called the novel "only incidentally, though beautifully, pedagogical. Primarily, without illusion, with pain unmasked, it is a eulogy to love."

Germaine de Beauvais, in *Incense to Idols*, is superficially at least an entirely different kind of woman, but no less well drawn. She is a concert pianist, beautiful, elegant, and libidinous, who comes to New Zealand from France in search of an exiled Parisian music master and falls in love with a clergyman. Max Cosman suggested that the novel studied another kind of symbiosis, this time "between saint and sinner." Again there was much discussion of Miss Ashton-Warner's "nervous, expansive, self-revelatory" style, her penchant for the historic present, and this time some reviewers were irritated. Most were not, however, and E. C. Dunn wrote: "The reader is made an active part in the unrolling of the story. What is happening and how one feels about it are inextricably bound together, simultaneous, not sequential." To an extraordinary extent in Miss Ashton-Warner's novels, "the medium is the message."

Bell Call expresses some of the novelist's views on the importance of personal freedom in a story about a woman's defiance of all authority (including her husband's) in keeping her small son out of school until he feels ready to go. *Greenstone* is a fable about the huge eccentric Considine family, who live and grow in a rich New Zealand culture of dirt and poetry, rage and love. The Considines' illegitimate granddaughter, half European, half Maori, represents, one critic thought, "the author's vision, not only of a glorious, merged New Race, but of a consciousness which skips at will between the realism of the West and the mysticism of the Maori." It seemed to some reviewers that this "at times absurdly hoked-up book" fails, "dissolves in bathos," but there was nevertheless a warm response to its author's detestation of bigotry and

SYLVIA ASHTON-WARNER

sterile provincialism, her admiration for "passionate intellect," the love and skill with which she described her country and her Maori characters.

Myself is a memoir of the years between 1941 and 1945, in which Miss Ashton-Warner returns to the setting of *Teacher* but concentrates not on her work but on the emotional cost of her struggle to resolve the "conflicting demands of the contending roles of mother, wife, lover, teacher, artist." Central to the book is the story of Miss Ashton-Warner's prolonged, but apparently unconsummated love affair with a young doctor. Most reviewers greatly disliked the book, finding it smug, sentimental, self-adulatory, and oddly out of focus. During 1971 the author taught at an experimental school in the American Rockies. *Spearpoint* describes her experiences there and expresses her deep skepticism about our society, and its future in the hands of a generation whose "native imagery" has been manufactured for it by television.

PRINCIPAL WORKS: *Novels*—Spinster, 1958; Incense to Idols, 1960; Bell Call, 1965; Greenstone, 1966; Three, 1970. *Nonfiction*—Teacher, 1963; Myself, 1967; Spearpoint: "Teacher" in America, 1972.

ABOUT: Vinson, J. (ed.) Contemporary Novelists, 1972. *Periodicals*—Landfall September 1969; New York Herald Tribune December 4, 1960; New York Times November 4, 1960; New York Times Book Review September 8, 1963; Saturday Review October 5, 1963; Time September 6, 1963.

***ASIMOV, ISAAC** (January 2, 1920–), American science and science fiction writer, was born in Petrovichi, USSR, the son of Judah and Anna (Berman) Asimov. When he was three years old the family emigrated to the United States and settled in New York City, where his parents opened a candy store. Asimov has a photographic memory and was a precocious student, but he greatly disliked physical work and sports. He was also, according to Sam Moskowitz, egocentric, introverted, and sarcastic.

Helping in the family store after school, Asimov would be drawn to the magazine rack, where "reams of fascinating blood and violence lay about me and yet were kept from me by my father's stern notions about the degenerating influence of cheap literature. . . . Then came a wonderful break. A science fiction magazine, *Amazing Stories*, passed under his eagle glance and received the august paternal nod. Science fiction, he decided, might improve my mind by interesting me in the achievements and potentialities of science. From then on I was hooked."

Asimov graduated from Boys High School in Brooklyn at the age of fifteen and went on to study chemistry at Columbia University. He received his B.S. in 1939 and his M.A. in 1941. After the United States entered World War II, he went to the Naval Air Experimental Station in Philadelphia as a chemist and later served in the United States Army, emerging in 1946 with the rank of corporal. After the war he returned to Columbia, which gave him his Ph.D. in 1948. The following year he joined the faculty of the Boston University School of Medicine, where in due course he became an associate professor of biochemistry. He still holds that title, though he now gives only one lecture a year.

His first story (The Greenville Chums at College) was produced at the age of twelve. When he was sixteen his father "dug deep into the almost invisible family savings" to buy him a second-hand typewriter. Asimov wrote his first science fiction story when he was eighteen, and took it to the great John W. Campbell, then editor of *Analog*. Campbell rejected the story but recognized its promise, and gave Asimov the encouragement he needed. "He was lean and hungry and enthusiastic," Campbell recalled. "He couldn't write, but he could tell a story. You can teach a guy how to write, but not how to tell a story." Asimov made his first sale in October 1938 to *Amazing Stories*, and thereafter contributed to virtually all of the science fiction pulp magazines.

In 1950 Asimov published his first novel, *Pebble in the Sky*, a well-plotted space thriller which was also "a nice satire on our own racial intolerance and our own militarists." The same year, the experience of working on a textbook for medical students introduced him to "the delights of nonfiction," and later on he discovered the "even greater ecstasies of writing science for the general

* az′ i mov

ISAAC ASIMOV

public." Little by little, he says, "my science writing swallowed up the rest of me." In 1958 he became a full-time writer.

Asimov is an obsessive worker. He does his own typing (at ninety words a minute), reads his own proofs, prepares his own indexes. He works up to ten hours a day, seven days a week, turning out between two and four thousand words a day. He is only rarely to be dragged "kicking and screaming" from his desk for a family vacation. In his search for new fields to satisfy his passion for elucidation, he has moved in recent years from science to history to religion to literature. In 1969 he published his hundredth book and by 1973 the total exceeded one hundred and twenty.

From the beginning, Asimov's books have been enthusiastically received by public and critics alike. H. H. Holmes was of the opinion that he has produced "some of the purest science fiction outside the Heinlein canon." Asimov has an exceptional gift for narrative and great ingenuity in plotting. These talents are both evident in his much admired novel *The Currents of Space*, a melodrama rich in Machiavellian intrigue that reminded one reviewer of a "trans-galactic" *Prisoner of Zenda. The Caves of Steel* and *The Naked Sun*, featuring a law enforcement team composed of a human being and a robot, are notable examples of a genre which Asimov pioneered, the science fiction detective story.

He also possesses a great "gift for translating scientific gobbledygook into English"—for the clear and simple exposition of highly complex scientific developments. The *Times Literary Supplement* found his encyclopedic *New Intelligent Man's Guide to Science* as good as anything of its kind currently available, and *Time* has commented that "no emissary to the nonscientific world has been more successful." Asimov himself says of his work as a popularizer: "I don't indulge in scholarly depth. I don't make creative contributions. I'm a 'translator.' I can read a dozen dull books and make one interesting book out of them. I'm on fire to explain, and happiest when it's something reasonably intricate which I can make clear step by step. It's the easiest way I can clarify things in my own mind."

Asimov's prose is clear, laconic, and sometimes extremely funny—the tool of an expositor who recognizes the value of light relief. His fiction, admired and highly successful as it is, is weak in its characterization, and indeed he steers clear of the mysteries of human personality and human relationships (except in his somewhat unexpected 1971 essay *The Sensuous Dirty Old Man*). The nearest thing to a love affair in any of his stories, he wryly admits, involved a motor car's affection for a human being. Yet he has always insisted that science fiction should be taken seriously as a literary genre: it is "a literary response to scientific change, and that response can run the entire gamut of human experience."

Asimov is five feet nine inches tall, brown-haired, and blue-eyed. He has been married since 1942 to the former Gertrude Blugerman and has two children.

PRINCIPAL WORKS: *Fiction*—Pebble in the Sky, 1950; I, Robot, 1950; The Currents of Space, 1952; Caves of Steel, 1954; The Martian Way (short stories), 1955; The End of Eternity, 1955; Earth Is Room Enough, 1957; The Naked Sun, 1957; Nine Tomorrows (short stories), 1959; Triangle (short stories), 1961; The Rest of the Robots (short stories), 1964; Asimov's Mysteries (short stories), 1968; The Early Asimov (ed. by L. P. A. Shmead), 1973. *Science*—The Chemicals of Life, 1954; Races and People, 1955; Inside the Atom, 1956; Building Blocks of the Universe, 1957; The World of Carbon, 1958; The World of Nitrogen, 1958; Only a Trillion, 1958; Words of Science (for teenagers), 1959; The Living River, 1959; Realm of Number (for teenagers), 1959; The Wellsprings of Life, 1960; Life and Energy, 1962; The Genetic Code, 1963; The Human Body, 1963; The Human Brain, 1964; Asimov's Biographical Encyclopedia of Science and Technology, 1964; The New Intelligent Man's Guide to Science, 1965; The Universe From Flat Earth to Quasar, 1966; Understanding Physics, 1966; Is Anyone There? (essays), 1967; From Earth to Heaven (essays), 1967. *History and General Works*—The Greeks, 1965; The Roman Republic, 1966; The Roman Empire, 1967; The Egyptians, 1967; Asimov's Guide to the Bible: The Old Testament, 1968; The New Testament, 1969; Opus 100 (selections from earlier books), 1969.

ABOUT: Asimov, I. Opus 100, 1969; Contemporary Authors 2, 1963; Current Biography, 1968; Moskowitz, S. Seekers of Tomorrow, 1966. *Periodicals*—Fantasy and Science Fiction October 1966; New York Daily News October 4, 1967; New York Times October 18, 1969; New York Times Book Review April 14, 1968; August 3, 1969; January 28, 1973; Newsday March 18, 1967; Publishers' Weekly August 2, 1969; Time July 7, 1967; Times Literary Supplement March 2, 1967.

***ASTURIAS, MIGUEL ANGEL** (October 19, 1899–), Guatemalan novelist, poet, and journalist, received the Nobel Prize for Literature in 1967 for his "highly colored writings, rooted in a national individuality and Indian traditions." He was born in Guatemala City, the son of Ernesto Asturias, a magistrate of the Supreme Court of Justice, and the former María Rosales, a schoolteacher. When he was about four years old his father lost his judgeship for refusing to take legal action against antigovernment student demonstrators, and the family was forced to spend several years away from the capital in Salamá. Thus Asturias' hatred of oppressive government was fostered from an early age and in the most direct and personal way.

In 1907 the family returned to Guatemala City. Asturias received his secondary education at the Instituto Nacional Central de Varones before studying law at the University of San Carlos. As an undergraduate he himself was active in the student protest movements which helped to overthrow the dictator Manuel Estrada Cabrera in 1920, and he served as secretary to the court in which Estrada Cabrera was prosecuted.

The military regime which followed was no less oppressive, however, and Asturias soon found himself once more in conflict with authority. He continued his education nevertheless, participated in the establishment of the Universidad Popular de Guatemala (which provided free evening classes for workers), and was one of the founders of and most outspoken contributors to the weekly newspaper *Tiempos Nuevos*. In 1923 he received his doctor of laws degree with a prizewinning dissertation on the social problems of the Guatemalan Indians. The same year, learning that his life was in danger, he left the country.

Asturias went first to London, intending to study economics, but changed his mind after a visit in July 1923 to Paris, where he met Georges Raynaud, a specialist in Mayan civilization. For the next five years he studied with Raynaud at the Sorbonne, supporting himself by writing for newspapers in Mexico and Central America. These years during which, far from home, he immersed himself in the ancient myths and culture of his people, were of central importance in Asturias' development. Direct results of these studies were the translations he helped to make of the *Popul Vuh* and the *Anales de Xahil*, the sacred books of the Quiché and Cakchiquel Indians, and *Leyendas de Guatemala* (Legends of Guatemala, 1930). The latter was warmly praised by Paul Valéry, won the Prix Sylla Monsegur, and has been widely translated.

In his notes to *Leyendas de Guatemala*, Asturias contrasts the rational processes of the European mind with the exuberant dream logic exemplified in the legends. It is not surprising that he made friends in Paris with André Breton, Paul Éluard, and others in surrealist circles, attracted by this deliberate expedition into the unreasoning unconscious. His first book of verse, *Rayito de Estrella* (Little Starbeam, 1925) is of some interest as a product of cross-fertilization, an attempt to marry Indian legends with surrealist forms of expression.

* ä stōō′ rē äs

MIGUEL ANGEL ASTURIAS

A rather similar process is at work in the novel *El Señor Presidente*. It was begun in 1922 as a short story, expanded into a novel, repeatedly rewritten, and completed in 1930. At the narrative level it is an account of a dictator's attempt to eliminate a political enemy. Based on the dictatorship of Estrada Cabrera, it is in its final form an indictment of all political oppression and of the corrupting power of fear, expressed partly in conventional terms, partly as a surreal and brutal fable. Brigid Brophy said of it that Asturias' writing ". . . is almost incomparably visual, its texture composed in striking and beautiful images. The very hallucinations of his characters palpably appear; and perhaps the book itself is not so much a novel . . . as a vision of hell." *El Señor Presidente* was not published until 1946 (ironically enough because of the new Guatemalan dictatorship of Jorge Ubico) and was translated into English (by Frances Partridge, under the same title) only in 1964.

Meanwhile, in 1933, following a tour of Europe and the Middle East, Asturias had returned to Guatemala. He earned his living as a newspaper and radio journalist and for about fifteen years published only some mildly satirical poems. In 1942 he was elected to the National Congress and in 1945, with the fall of Ubico, he joined Guatemala's diplomatic service. He was serving in Buenos Aires as cultural attaché (1947–1951) when he published his second novel, *Hombres de maíz* (Men of Corn, 1949). It is a fantasy, drawing on Mayan mythology to contrast the Indian's ancient marriage to the Guatemalan earth with the European's rape of it.

The liberal government of Juan José Arévalo was succeeded by the similar regime of Jacobo Arbenz in 1951. Asturias served as minister-counselor in Buenos Aires (1951–1952) and in Paris (1952–1953) and then went to El Salvador as ambassador. The Arbenz government was overthrown in 1954 in a revolution in which the American Central Intelligence Agency played an important role. Asturias lost his citizenship and went into exile in Argentina. These events are recounted in his volume of stories, *Weekend en Guatemala* (1956). Most critics thought the book had been written with more passion than art, and a similar element of rather crude communistic propaganda troubled some reviewers of the otherwise much-praised trilogy of novels in which Asturias studies the whole question of United States economic and political influence in Central America, focusing on the activities of the giant United Fruit Company. These novels are *Viento Fuerte* (1950, translated as *Strong Wind*), *El Papa Verde* (1954, translated as *The Green Pope*), and *Los Ojos de los Enterrados* (1960, translated as *The Eyes of the Interred*).

During his years in Argentina Asturias worked as a correspondent for the Caracas newspaper *El Nacional* and as adviser to the publishing house Editorial Losada. He wrote a great deal of verse and drama at this time, his plays being collected as *Teatro* (1964). In 1962, with the fall of the Frondizi government in Argentina, he moved to Genoa. *Mulata de Tal* (translated by Gregory Rabassa as *Mulata*), which many critics regard as his masterpiece, was published in 1963. It is a Rabelaisian retelling of a Guatemalan legend about a man who sells his wife to the corn god so that he may become rich and possess a voluptuous *mulata*. Retribution follows and the man, penniless again, bedeviled by the *mulata*, sets out on a journey through a nightmare world inhabited by monsters and freaks, Indian demons and Christian priests, surreal happenings and enigmatic rituals.

Alexander Coleman saw the book as an inspired exercise in free association which manages "cheerfully to exorcise the irrational and subhuman demons of a whole continent." Some critics objected that the reader is given no point of reference and is quickly lost in a maze of personal and national fantasies, but a reviewer in the *Times Literary Supplement* found a guide in "the clear dream logic" of the book. He said that Asturias' imaginings carry their own authority and "the teeming uninhibitedness of the Maya mind becomes a quality of [his] Spanish."

In 1966, when a moderate left-wing regime took power in Guatemala, Asturias returned to his country's diplomatic service, and he is now ambassador to France. In 1966 he received the Lenin Peace Prize for his trilogy on the United Fruit Company. Asturias is married to Blanca Mora y Araujo, his second wife, and has two sons. According to a friend, "a tremendous impression of force emanates from him. He looks exactly like a Mayan statue. He is relatively tall, although beginning to be slightly stooped. He is heavy set, very bronzed, and likely has both Red Indian and Negro ancestors. He has thick lips, an eagle nose, oval eyes and graying hair."

PRINCIPAL WORKS IN ENGLISH TRANSLATION: El Señor Presidente, 1963 (England, The President); Mulata (England, The Mulata and Mr. Fly), 1967; Strong Wind, tr. by Gregory Rabassa, 1968 (England, Cyclone, tr. by Darwin Flakoll and Claribel Alegria); The Green Pope, tr. by Gregory Rabassa, 1971; The Talking Machine (for children), tr. by Beverly Koch, 1971; The Eyes of the Interred, tr. by Gregory Rabassa, 1973. *Poems in* Fitts, D. (ed.) Anthology of Contemporary Latin American Poetry, 1942.

ABOUT: Anderson-Imbert, E. Spanish-American Literature, 1963; Current Biography, 1968; Guibert, R. Seven Voices, 1973; Harss, L. and Dohmann, B. Into the Mainstream, 1967; International Who's Who, 1972–1973; Who's Who in Latin America: Part 2, 1945. *Periodicals*—Américas July 1950; January 1968; Atlas December 1967; Books Abroad Spring 1968; Hispania May 1968; Hispanic Review July 1968; Inter-American Review of Bibliography April–June 1965; Nation April 13, 1964; February 17, 1969; New Republic February 22, 1969; Newsweek October 30, 1967; New York Times October 20, 1967; Symposium Fall 1968; Times Literary Supplement November 19, 1971.

***AUCHINCLOSS, LOUIS (STANTON)** (September 27, 1917–), American novelist, short story writer, and critic, writes: "With the exception of a great-uncle who published a new key to the Book of Daniel, I come of a family that, until myself, had written no books. My father was and is a member of a large corporation law firm on Wall Street; one of my grandfathers was a director of Illinois Central and the other an officer of Standard Trust Company. My parents, my four grandparents and my eight great-grandparents all lived in the City of New York. I went to Groton, to Yale and to the University of Virginia Law School. It was a background usually considered unsympathetic to the development of artistic creativity; it was too sane, too reasonable, too involved with the status quo. And indeed, I may have been hampered at the start by a sense that it was a bit indecent to put one's emotions into print. But this was as nothing compared to the value of the subject material that my life has given me.

"It has often been said that I write about a small world. If that is so, it is a defect in my art. Balzac would have reveled in it. Groton may be small, but

* aw′ kin klōs

the President of the United States, a graduate, visited there twice while I was a student, and of my own form of little more than twenty boys, we number at this writing two ambassadors, the Secretary of the Army and an Assistant Secretary of State. The New England boarding schools had a great effect on the customs of the eastern seaboard (read John O'Hara!) just as Wall Street has had an enormous impact on the economy and philosophy of the nation. To have witnessed the disintegration of an economic ruling class in the 1930s from a front-row seat was all a novelist should ask. And since then I have had a world war and sea duty in two oceans and my law practice in New York. I know that it is no longer the fashion to emphasize subject in fiction, but the more I read, the more I think it matters.

"The particular problem of my literary life has been to combine it with my career as a lawyer. This started as early as Yale when I was planning both occupations. There and at Groton I had written short stories and published them in school and college magazines, but it was not until my junior year, when I finished my first novel, that I seriously contemplated the writing of fiction as a life work. I sent it to Scribner's where it was rejected with a very kind letter, but I was so unreasonably discouraged that I left college without my degree, and enrolled in the law school of the University of Virginia, resolved to put behind me any dabbling in an art for which I had no aptitude. I kept my resolution of not writing in the law school terms, but during the summers I wrote another novel which I destroyed. I liked the law, and I thought I was settled at last.

"I had just begun to practice in New York when the war broke out and I had to spend four years in the Navy. On shipboard in the Pacific I wrote a third novel which I published after the war was over, under a pseudonym. I used the pseudonym because at the last moment I didn't like the book. Shortly after resuming my law practice I decided to abandon it and go to Yale to study for a doctor's degree in English Literature, but I was dissuaded by the late Professor Robert French who wisely pointed out that I was simply adding a third profession to solve my difficulties in dealing with two. I returned to my law firm and continued to write and to publish, now under my own name. In 1952 I embarked on the career of a full-time writer, but by 1954 I had returned again to the practice of law which I had desperately missed. It was not until the age of forty that I finally succeeded in making the two careers fit, but I now believe that it was worth all the effort. There can be great advantages to the writer of fiction in being associated with the non-literary world.

"I believe that writers today (and probably always) are too conscious of literary fashions. I

LOUIS AUCHINCLOSS

think that the habit of considering fiction by decades as, for example, fiction of the forties, or fiction of the fifties, is not in the long run instructive. I do not think that basic facts or readers change that much in such short periods, even giving consideration to the catastrophic events of our time. I find Balzac as relevant to New York today as I find Saul Bellow, in some ways more so. For years I was intensely interested in the technique of Henry James. Now I consider that his theories are relevant only to his own fiction. Nor do I see why any literary technique should ever be out of date, and I would not hesitate to write a novel in letters like *Clarissa Harlow*, if I felt the urge. I find that in writing criticism I write more and more about novelists of the past, and I never write with any other object but to induce my reader to revisit them. This is not to say that I do not read my contemporaries—I do—but I feel less division than many of them do between past and present."

Louis Auchincloss writes from within about what remains of the New York aristocracy, the subdued nostalgic heirs of those whom Edith Wharton studied fifty years earlier. His subjects, as the *New Yorker* once put it, are "people who have beautiful manners, plenty of money, and a perfectly ghastly time all around." The son of Joseph Howland Auchincloss, a lawyer, and the former Priscilla Dixon Stanton, he married Adèle Lawrence in 1957, has two sons, and lives on Park Avenue. Since 1958 he has been a partner in the Wall Street law firm of Hawkins, Delafield and Wood. He is a trustee of the New York Society Library and president of the Museum of the City of New York.

The Indifferent Children, his first book, is about a wealthy dilettante thrown into active service in World War II. It introduced a recurrent theme in Auchincloss's novels, many of which are concerned with a member of New York society who is pitched, physically or emotionally, out of his comfortable cocoon and forced to a reassessment of himself and his assumptions about life. Thus in *Sybil* and *A Law for the Lion*, his two subsequent novels, his heroines (frequently compared with those of Edith Wharton) struggle to survive in the face of scandal; in *The Great World and Timothy Colt*, a young lawyer loses his illusions; and in *Venus in Sparta* and *Pursuit of the Prodigal* rich New Yorkers cope with broken marriages. All of these books were praised for the Jamesian elegance of their style, the fastidious irony of their social observation.

The Rector of Justin is widely recognized as Auchincloss's most accomplished novel. Here he turns from the world of big business and the law to give a portrait of an eminent headmaster, the Reverend Francis Prescott, founder of Justin Martyr, an Episcopal boarding school for boys near Boston. Many reviewers assumed that Prescott was modeled on Endicott Peabody of Groton. The portrait is a composite one, built up through the eyes of both admirers and enemies of Prescott, but mostly through the diary of a shy young English teacher. According to their different lights, reviewers found the headmaster "as inspiring a character as any reader could want" or "a petrified old windbag." There was less difference of opinion about the virtues of the book itself, and most critics seemed to share Whitney Balliett's opinion that it is "a model novel," whose "poise and taste and intelligence strike one on every page, as do its unerring knowledge and literary skill."

In his short stories, Auchincloss (like Somerset Maugham) frequently employs a first-person narrator to provide unity and continuity and also a certain distance from his material. It is this emotional coldness that troubled Webster Schott in his review of *Tales of Manhattan*. He found wit, truth, and "many enjoyable things" in these stories, but concluded that Auchincloss's work is "a museum of all that American writing valued before its World War I baptism of despair." Virgilia Peterson had said something similar about Auchincloss's fiction fifteen years earlier: "This kind of satire applied to our day seems as anachronistic as the society it depicts. For all its merits, it is out of context today and, as such, curiously lacking in passion and the power to move."

Remote as he may be from the violent center of modern American writing, Auchincloss is an enjoyable writer, with something to teach about style and taste and about his own vanishing society. As a critic, he has written engagingly and perceptively about Henry James, Proust, Edith Wharton, and such contemporary novelists of manners as John O'Hara and John P. Marquand. In *Motiveless Malignity* he discusses Shakespeare's "sense of the perverse and irrational in human nature." He is a tall, slim man, a witty conversationalist.

PRINCIPAL WORKS: *Fiction*—The Indifferent Children, 1947 (published under pseudonym, "Andrew Lee," and republished under Auchincloss's name in 1964); The Injustice Collectors (short stories), 1950; Sybil, 1952; A Law for the Lion, 1953; The Romantic Egoists (short stories), 1954; The Great World and Timothy Colt, 1956; Venus in Sparta, 1958; Pursuit of the Prodigal, 1959; The House of Five Talents, 1960; Portrait in Brownstone, 1962; Powers of Attorney (short stories), 1963; The Rector of Justin, 1964; The Embezzlers, 1966; Tales of Manhattan (short stories) 1967; A World of Profit, 1968; Second Chance (stories), 1970; I Come As a Thief, 1972. *Nonfiction*—Reflections of a Jacobite, 1961; Pioneers and Caretakers, 1965; Motiveless Malignity, 1969; Edith Wharton, 1971; Richelieu, 1973.

ABOUT: The Author's and Writer's Who's Who, 1963; Benét, W. R. The Reader's Encyclopedia, 1965; Hart, J. D. (ed.) The Oxford Companion to American Literature, 1965; Newquist, R. (ed.) Counterpoint, 1965; Who's Who in America, 1972–1973. *Periodicals*—Best Sellers February 16, 1966; Book Week November 8, 1964; February 20, 1966; March 26, 1967; Christian Science Monitor April 27, 1967; Critic April 1966; Nation July 31, 1967; New Republic May 13, 1967; New Statesman October 20, 1967; New York Review of Books November 19, 1964; October 12, 1967; New York Times Book Review July 15, 1962; July 12, 1964; July 25, 1965; February 6, 1966; March 19, 1967; May 28, 1967; November 24, 1968; New Yorker August 19, 1962; August 1, 1964; Reporter July 13, 1967; Saturday Review July 14, 1962; August 17, 1963; June 5, 1965; February 5, 1966; April 8, 1967; November 30, 1968; Times Literary Supplement January 28, 1965; June 23, 1966.

***AUDIBERTI, JACQUES** (March 25, 1899–July 10, 1965), French poet, dramatist, and novelist, was born in Antibes on the French Riviera. He was the son of Louis Audiberti, a mason, and Victorine (Médard) Audiberti. A timid and solitary child, he was educated at the local *collège* and became a clerk to the justice of the peace at the Antibes Tribunal. At the age of thirty, Audiberti was drawn by literary ambition to Paris, where for many years he earned his living as a journalist, looking back on the Provençal beaches and countryside as a lost Eden.

His first volume of poetry was published in 1930, but it was not until *Race des hommes* (Race of Men) appeared in 1937 that his verse attracted much attention. Its author, influenced it was thought by Mallarmé and Rimbaud, seemed "intoxicated by nature within and without and certainly intoxicated by words, with which he juggles marvellously." Audiberti saw man as an animal who had deviated fatally from his natural course. His early work excitedly anticipated the renewed communion with

* ō dē bâr′ tē

nature which, he thought, science might bring about. This optimism did not survive his experience of life as a Paris journalist and gave way to indignant nostalgia for a paganism irretrievably lost.

This view was expressed with a somehow endearing belligerence in a variety of literary forms, but less often in poetry as Audiberti grew older. He wrote some fifteen novels, of which the first was *Abraxas* (1938) and the best known probably *La Nâ* (1944). Less important than his other work, they shared with it an exuberant richness of language and imagery, a taste and talent for the exotic and unexpected.

Though Audiberti turned late to the theatre and was not produced until after World War II, it is as a dramatist that he is now most widely discussed. Influenced, he said, by opera rather than by the realism of postwar French drama, he insisted that the theatre was an "accepted delirium," an "authorized oasis of lies." His plays mixed farce and horrific melodrama. They were rituals, full of magical transformations, parodies, songs, and incantations, in which pagan gods take their revenge on those who have abandoned them for the decorous artificialities of Christianity.

Thus in *Quoat-Quoat* (1946), the modern world and its conventions are represented by a ship and are destroyed by the power of an ancient Mexican deity. *Le Mal court* (The Evil Runs, 1947), his greatest commercial success, is another essay on the corruption and artificiality of contemporary life in the form of a "black" fairy tale. *La Fête noire* (The Black Feast, 1948) grimly celebrates the church's failure to destroy the Dionysian sexual drives it has suppressed and perverted; it made ambitious use of the devices advocated by Antonin Artaud for involving the spectator in the play by placing him in the midst of it, with leaves flying through the auditorium, "cries, groans, apparitions, surprises, theatricalities of all kinds."

La Hobereaute (The Hobby, 1958) is another richly suggestive essay on the conflict between Christianity and the old gods, but a confusing one. Indeed, Audiberti's later dramas, and particularly *Les Naturels du Bordelais* (The Natives of Bordelais, 1953) were increasingly mystical and abstruse. Although his plays were admired for their humor, fantasy, and torrential rhetoric, in many of them a delight in language and literary device was too freely indulged at the cost of dramatic effectiveness. He once said that a play is simply "words in the mouth," and many considered that he remained a poet in the theatre. He also wrote for radio, and for the cinema, to which he was addicted. His characteristically gloomy philosophy of "abhumanism" was explained in one of a number of lively essays.

Official recognition came to Audiberti only in the last year of his life, when he was created an

JACQUES AUDIBERTI

Officier de la Légion d'Honneur, received two literary prizes, and had a square named after him in Antibes. He was married and had two daughters. Audiberti was a stout, bald, untidy man, with a squashed nose and a "ferocious" chin, perpetually alarmed and astonished by everything he saw, and as loquacious and unpredictable in his speech as in his writing. He has been called "a lyric writer preserved from chaos by a strong sense of form," and a welcome relief from the austere intellectualism of his contemporaries. In his novel *Monorail* (1964) he said that all a writer can do, faced with the debacle of civilization, is "chanter le massacre." This he did, in the words of one of his friends, with "passionate innocence." His works have not been translated into English.

ABOUT: Boisdeffre, P. de. Dictionnaire de littérature contemporaine, 1962; Brereton, G. Introduction to the French Poets, 1956; Deslandes, A. Audiberti, 1964; Guicharnaud, J. Modern French Theater, 1961; Pronko, L. C. Avant-Garde, 1962; Rousselot, J. Les Nouveaux Poètes français, 1959; Smith, H. (ed.) Columbia Dictionary of Modern European Literature, 1947; Wellwarth, G. E. The Theater of Protest and Paradox, 1964; Who's Who in France, 1965–1966. *Periodicals*—Nouvelle Revue Française December 1965; Times (London) July 12, 1965; Times Literary Supplement March 24, 1966.

***AUERBACH, ERICH** (November 9, 1892–October 13, 1957), German (later American) philologist, scholar, and critic of classical and medieval literature, was born in Berlin. Before and after World War I he studied at various universities, receiving a law degree from Heidelberg in 1913 and a Ph.D. in Romance philology from Greifs-

* ou′ ər bäk

ERICH AUERBACH

wald in 1921. He began his career as librarian at the Preussische Staatsbibliothek in Berlin (1923–1929). For the next six years he was professor of Romance philology at the University of Marburg, but he was dismissed in 1935 under the Nazi racial laws. He left Germany in 1936 and settled in Istanbul as professor of Romance languages at the state university of Turkey. It was in Turkey, between 1942 and 1945, that he wrote *Mimesis*, the work which established his reputation and on which scholars of all countries have bestowed the accolade of greatness. After the war, in 1948, he emigrated to the United States. He was a visiting professor at Pennsylvania State University in 1948–1949 and spent the following year as a member of the Institute for Advanced Studies at Princeton. In 1950, he joined the faculty of Yale University where he remained, for the last years of his life as Sterling Professor of Romance Philology.

Mimesis presents a comprehensive theory of the nature of European literature. It begins with a subtle comparison between Homeric and Old Testament narrative "in order to reach a starting point for an investigation into the literary representation of reality in European culture." Concentrating on carefully selected key passages, Auerbach goes on to analyze literary methods in a number of seminal works, among them the *Chanson de Roland*, the *Mystère d'Adam*, *Gargantua and Pantagruel*, Shakespeare's *Henry IV Part 2*, *Don Quixote*, and *Le Rouge et le noir*. The book ends with a sympathetic appraisal of Virginia Woolf's *To the Lighthouse*, of which Auerbach writes: "What takes place here . . . is . . . to put the emphasis on the random occurrence, to exploit it not in the service of a planned continuity of action but in itself. And in the process, something new and elemental appeared: nothing less than the wealth of reality and depth of life in every moment to which we surrender ourselves without prejudice." This quotation gives an example of his acuteness, and of his capacity for compression.

Auerbach's great achievement in *Mimesis* was to record what he called "the complicated process of dissolution which led to the fragmentation of the exterior action" in fiction. His view was that the development of modern fiction pointed to a "common life of mankind on earth" (though he saw the process as a very slow one). "Before *Mimesis* appeared," wrote one critic in the *Times Literary Supplement*, "there were whole areas of the relations between language and life we had sensed, but not realized could be coherently understood." Delmore Schwartz spoke of the originality of Auerbach's critical method, "which is at once encyclopedic and microscopic, combining the disciplines of philology, literary criticism, and history" in a work whose "compass and richness . . . can hardly be exaggerated."

Auerbach's book on Dante, and his essays on the poet in *Scenes from the Drama of European Literature*, are full of new insights into the nature of the traditions to which Dante belonged. The most important of his posthumous works is *Literary Language and Its Public in Late Antiquity and the Middle Ages*. It shows "how, during the Middle Ages, the bases of European thought, the criteria of literary style, and the constitution of the literary audience underwent a fundamental change, the effect of which is still with us." This is a more forbidding book than *Mimesis*, prodigiously learned, and elliptical at times to the point of obscurity. Nevertheless it was recognized at once as "a fundamental text for all students of medieval and Renaissance thought," and as one in which "every new essay is a re-creation of the powerful electric charge" that *Mimesis* administered.

Auerbach's ideas about the relationship between literature and life have powerfully influenced scholars all over the world, not least in America, but have not yet had their full effect on the writing of contemporary literature (though W. H. Auden has been recommending Auerbach's work for years). And yet, as one critic has said, *Mimesis* "is not so much a source-book for academic men, which of course it is and will be for a long time, as a piece of direct speech to those who understand what literature is, or who want to understand it: the limitations and the possibilities." The masterpiece of a European scholar of great range and originality, imbued with a nobility that is specifically "a function of the circumstances of exile," it is "an enormous beacon burning against despair."

PRINCIPAL WORKS IN ENGLISH TRANSLATION: Mimesis: The Representation of Reality in Western Literature, 1953; Scenes from the Drama of European Literature, 1959; Dante: Poet of the Secular World, 1961; Introduction to Romance Languages and Literature, 1961; Literary Language and Its Public in Late Antiquity and the Middle Ages, 1965.

ABOUT: *Periodicals*—Encounter April 1966; Times Literary Supplement November 25, 1965.

AXELROD, GEORGE (June 9, 1922–), American playwright, screenwriter, and novelist, was born in New York City, the son of Herman and Beatrice (Carpenter) Axelrod. He began his Broadway career as an assistant stage manager for a revival of *Kind Lady*, and at eighteen was already writing gags and scripts for radio. Since then his radio and television scripts have totaled more than four hundred.

After the war, Axelrod tried his hand at two novels, *Beggar's Choice* (1947) and *Blackmailer* (1952), but these attracted less attention than the sketches he was writing for such Broadway reviews as *Small Wonder* and *New Faces.*

His first and greatest success came in 1952, when *The Seven-Year Itch* began its long run on Broadway. It is a "sad, hilarious fable" about a New York husband's brief adultery with the girl upstairs, during a long hot summer when his family is away in the country. The play employs some of the devices of French farce, while the husband's Walter Mittyish fantasies seemed to one critic "expressionism thoroughly domesticated." But the amiably lubricious humor is wholly American, and the story ends on a note of moral affirmation which has made it acceptable as a mainstay of suburban drama groups. It has appeared in many theatre anthologies, and was filmed.

Axelrod's second play was *Will Success Spoil Rock Hunter?*, staged under his own direction in 1955. It is a satire on Hollywood which concerns itself with the problems of George MacCauley, a writer who sells his soul to the devil, ten per cent at a time, for money, sex, prestige, and other inducements. George, however, sees the light in time for the final curtain, thus enjoying the best of both worlds. Like its predecessor, it was a success on Broadway and was filmed, though its critical reception was relatively cool.

The screen version of *Seven-Year Itch* was Axelrod's own work, and he went on to write scenarios for *Phffft!* and *Bus Stop*. In 1957 he was co-producer of Gore Vidal's satire *Visit to a Small Planet* and in 1958 directed *Once More With Feeling*. The following year he staged his own play, *Goodbye Charlie*, about a Hollywood heel,

GEORGE AXELROD

reincarnated as a woman, who has to suffer the punishment of thinking like a male while looking like a female. Reviewers found this "leering joke" both dull and distasteful.

During the 1960s, Axelrod limited his activities to Hollywood, writing scripts for such movies as *Breakfast at Tiffany's, The Manchurian Candidate, Paris When It Sizzles,* and *How to Murder Your Wife*, and co-producing several of them. He returned to fiction in 1971 with a farce called *Where Am I Now—When I Need Me?*, about a golden-hearted call girl with literary ambitions who turns the writings of the Marquis de Sade into an Oscar-winning stag movie with the help of a teacher at the Best-Selling Writers School.

George Axelrod has two children by his first wife, Gloria Washburn, whom he married when he was nineteen, and one by his second wife, Joan Stanton. He lives with his family in Los Angeles. Axelrod is a tall man, plump and youngish looking. A financial and popular success, he makes the most of it, drinks cognac for breakfast, and smokes very long cigars. "The only people I work with," he says, "are the people I like. I'm too rich, too old, my liver is too bad, to work with any other kind."

Gerald Weales regards Axelrod as "a fair example of the popular Broadway comic writer" who "plays safe in his comedies as though he wanted to titillate his audience without offending it. His verbal and visual jokes display the same tendency; in technique, as well as in idea, his work suggests imagination, but rests on the acceptable." Axelrod himself believes that "most of life today is pretend. . . . People . . . do these pretend jobs and get pretend money that they go out and spend on pretend enjoyment. . . . My own misunderstood version of existentialism is that life is all a huge practical—or rather impractical—joke, since it clearly doesn't work."

PRINCIPAL WORKS: Beggar's Choice (novel), 1947 (England, Hobson's Choice); Blackmailer, 1952; The Seven-Year Itch (play), 1953; Will Success Spoil Rock Hunter? (play), 1956; Where Am I Now—When I Need Me? (novel), 1971.

ABOUT: Weales, G. American Drama Since World War II, 1962; Who's Who in America, 1970–1971. *Periodicals*—Look May 18, 1965; Manchester Guardian Weekly May 18, 1965; Theatre Arts March 1956.

AYER, SIR A(LFRED) J(ULES) (October 29, 1910–), English philosopher, writes: "I was born in London. My father was a French-Swiss who had emigrated to England as a young man and become a British citizen. My mother, whose maiden name was Citroen, was of Dutch-Jewish extraction. I was sent to a preparatory school in Eastbourne at the age of seven, and at the age of twelve won a scholarship to Eton. There I specialized in classics and won a classical scholarship to Christ Church, Oxford in 1929. I obtained first class honors in Litterae Humaniores in 1932 and after spending a few months at the University of Vienna, returned to Christ Church as a lecturer in philosophy in 1933. Apart from the war, when I served first in the Welsh Guards and then in Military Intelligence, the whole of my career has been academic. I was a Research Student (i.e., Fellow) of Christ Church from 1935–1940, Fellow and Dean of Wadham College, Oxford, from 1945–1946, Grote Professor of the Philosophy of Mind and Logic at University College, London, from 1946–1959, and have been Wykeham Professor of Logic at Oxford University and a Fellow of New College, Oxford, since 1959. I am a Fellow of the British Academy, an honorary Fellow of Wadham College, Oxford, a Doctor *honoris causa* of the University of Brussels and an honorary member of the American Academy of Arts and Sciences.

"I first became interested in philosophy as a schoolboy, mainly as a result of reading some of the works of Bertrand Russell. At Oxford I was very strongly influenced by the writing of Ludwig Wittgenstein and subsequently by the work of Schlick, Carnap and other members of the Vienna Circle. Accordingly, my first book, *Language, Truth and Logic*, which came out in 1936, was very much a manifesto of Logical Positivism. I have since changed my views on specific questions, but still maintain the empiricist standpoint and the hostility to metaphysics and to theism which the book displayed. My main philosophical interest has always been in the theory of knowledge, and my approach has been very similar to that of Bertrand Russell. I share with him the belief that philosophical problems are capable of being solved by the technique of logical analysis.

"Apart from my academic writing, I have written a fair number of articles and reviews on political and social questions, and also taken part in numerous discussions on radio and television. I have occasionally reviewed plays and films and have written articles and radio broadcasts about Association Football. I enjoy traveling and have given lectures all over the world from China to Peru. I have lectured in Russia and twice been visiting professor at universities in the United States.

"I became actively interested in politics at the time of the Spanish Civil War and twice stood unsuccessfully as a Labour candidate for the Westminster City Council. I am still a supporter of the Labour Party but no longer so active. I am interested in social reform and have been President of the Humanist Association, the Homosexual Law Reform Society and the Marriage Reform Council. I was also a member of the Central Advisory Council which conducted an enquiry into Primary Education.

"I was married in 1932 to Renée Lees and divorced in 1940. In 1960 I married Alberta Wells (*née* Chapman), who is well known as a journalist and television commentator under the name of Dee Wells. I have a son and a daughter by my first marriage and a son by my second."

A. J. Ayer's *Language, Truth and Logic*, published when he was twenty-five, may well have been the most influential British book on philosophy of the last forty years. Much more readily intelligible than the later writings of Wittgenstein, briefer and more systematically coherent than Ryle's *Concept of Mind*, it owed its initial impact to its timeliness and to the force with which it was expressed. Its continuing influence, in the postwar period of second thoughts about its main assumptions, can be attributed to the splendid precision and lucidity with which it is written. A generation of Anglo-Saxon philosophers has cut its teeth on Ayer's lapidary sentences.

In it Ayer took the main ideas and methods circulating among the Vienna Circle of logical positivists, led by Schlick and Carnap, articulated them in an organized form, and linked them firmly to the continuing preoccupations of the British empiricist tradition from Locke and Hume to Russell and Moore. The foundation of his views is a division of thoughts or assertions into three kinds: the empirically verifiable propositions of science and common observation; the analytic or definitionally true propositions of logic, mathematics, and philosophical analysis; and the kind of

A. J. AYER

metaphysical, theological, and evaluative utterances which could serve at best to express the emotions of their users.

In *Foundations of Empirical Knowledge* (1940), a strategically crucial part of his system is developed at length: his account of the sense-perception on which all genuine knowledge of fact must be based. He presents and defends a phenomenalist theory that the significant content of all beliefs about the material world must be interpretable in terms of private, individual, sense-experiences. To talk of an objective external world is not to talk of the unobservable causes of our sensations, but is to talk of those sensations, actual and possible, themselves. The *Problem of Knowledge* (1956) is a more impersonal treatment of the main problems of epistemology in which a little ground is given to his critics but the main lines of his initial position are still held. This is also true of his three collections of essays, *Philosophical Essays, The Concept of a Person,* and *Metaphysics and Common Sense.*

Ayer's theory that religious and moral utterances are not really statements at all—true or false—but merely expressions of feeling, has seemed the most scandalous of his innovations to many readers. But it has had a revolutionary effect on both theology and ethics. It may be that in the long run his most important service to the intellectual community will be his achievement in making philosophy exciting, in showing that dedication to unconditional rationality need not be dim, stuffy, and hesitant. Ayer was knighted in 1970. The same year he visited the United States, delivering the William James lectures at Harvard and the John Dewey Lectures at Columbia.

PRINCIPAL WORKS: Language, Truth and Logic, 1936 (revised 1946); The Foundations of Empirical Knowledge, 1940; Philosophical Essays, 1954; The Problem of Knowledge, 1956; The Concept of a Person, and Other Essays, 1963; The Origins of Pragmatism, 1968; Metaphysics and Common Sense, 1969; Russell and Moore: The Analytical Heritage, 1972; Probability and Evidence (John Dewey Lectures), 1972; Russell (Modern Masters series), 1972. *As editor*—The British Empirical Philosophers (with Raymond Winch), 1952; Logical Positivism, 1959.

ABOUT: Austin, J. L. Sense and Sensibilia, 1962; Current Biography, 1964; Gilson, E. H. (ed.) Recent Philosophy, 1966; Hill, T. E. Contemporary Theories of Knowledge, 1961; Passmore, J. A Hundred Years of Philosophy, 1966; Urmson, J. O. Philosophical Analysis, 1956; Who's Who, 1972. *Periodicals*—Journal of Philosophy December 17, 1942; February 3, 1949; June 29, 1963; Mind July 1936; July 1941; October 1942; October 1948; Newsweek April 16, 1962; Observer September 15, 1957; Sunday Times February 8, 1959; March 25, 1962; Times Literary Supplement February 19, 1970.

AYRAUD, PIERRE. *See* "NARCEJAC, THOMAS"

***AZUELA, MARIANO** (January 1, 1873–March 1, 1952), the most celebrated novelist of the Mexican Revolution of 1910, was born in Lagos de Morena, a small town in the state of Jalisco, Mexico. His father, Evaristo Azuela, owned a grocery shop in Lagos and a small farm nearby. Azuela was educated at the local *liceo* until he was fourteen, and then at a school in the state capital, Guadalajara, at whose university he subsequently became a medical student. His vacations he spent at home, or traveling about the countryside, meeting and talking with the poor peasants who were later to figure as the heroes and heroines of his many novels. The principal formative reading of his youth was predictably, for his time, contemporary French fiction: Balzac, Flaubert, Daudet, the Goncourts, and above all Zola, whose work inspired his first literary endeavor, *Impresiones de un estudiante* (A Student's Impressions, 1896). He was married in 1901 to Carmen Rivera, a girl from Lagos, where he returned later as a doctor.

The condition of his patients—their abject poverty, hunger, and disease—awoke his social conscience, whose gradual development can be traced through his early novels, of which the best is *Mala yerba* (The Weed, 1909). In spite of the stereotyped naturalistic mold in which they are cast, these books show a steadily increasing air of urgency and purpose.

In 1910 Azuela was one of the founders of a Lagos political club formed in support of Francisco Madero, the liberal revolutionary who was seeking to overthrow the aging dictator Porfirio Díaz. Madero triumphed in May 1911, and Azuela was appointed "political governor" of Lagos. He found

* ä swā′ lä

MARIANO AZUELA

that political corruption in Mexico was not easily swept away. *Andrés Pérez, Maderista* (Andrés Pérez, the Maderist, 1911) expressed his contempt for those who were already exploiting the revolution.

Madero was overthrown and put to death in 1913 by the reactionary forces of Victoriano Huerta. The long years of guerrilla warfare began, and Azuela joined a revolutionary band loosely associated with the forces of Pancho Villa, serving as a doctor. After their defeat he fled to El Paso, Texas, where he wrote the most famous of his novels of the Revolution, *Los de Abajo* (1915, translated as *The Underdogs*).

This story of a revolutionary army derives from Azuela's own experiences. The guerrilla chieftain Demetrio Macías is based on an actual revolutionary leader, Manuel Coloca, whose wounds Azuela had once helped to heal. The author himself figures in the book as Luis Cervantes, a medical student and journalist whose middle-class language and sophisticated concepts are scarcely comprehensible to the guerrillas, who have barely heard of Madero, and who have only the vaguest notions of the aims of the revolution. They fight largely for themselves—first in inarticulate anger against Huerta's federal troops, then for loot, and finally, as though mesmerized by violence, because they have rifles and can think of nothing else to do.

For this novel, the only one of Azuela's books written out of the heat of the fighting itself, he—like the Mexican mural painters of the time—evolved unprecedented techniques. The violence and chaos of his subject is reflected in a style that is rapid and impressionistic. Hectic action replaces the leisurely psychological investigation then in vogue, and detailed descriptive writing is superseded by laconic dialogue. Often the revolutionary crowd is treated as other novelists treat an individual character. *Los de Abajo* was barely noticed until 1924, when a series of articles on the novel and the Revolution appeared in *El Universal Illustrado.* It has since been translated into at least eight languages and is widely recognized as the greatest novel of the Mexican Revolution.

Azuela returned to Mexico in 1916, to spend the rest of his long life practicing medicine in a humble quarter of Mexico City. He brought out a new book almost annually, over the years publishing novels, short stories, essays, and criticism. For some years he continued his cycle of novels about the Revolution: *Los caciques* (1917, translated as *The Bosses*); *Las moscas* (1918, translated as *The Flies*); *Domitilo quiere ser diputado* (Domitilo Wants to Be a Deputy, 1918). All resemble *Los de Abajo* in style and in their sympathy for the underdog.

Las tribulaciones de una familia decente (1918, translated as *The Trials of a Respectable Family*), marked a sharp change of attitude. It depicts the Revolution not from the point of view of the suffering masses but rather, as in *Dr. Zhivago*, from that of a middle-class family sacrificed to the revolutionary hordes. There followed a trilogy of experimental, expressionistic novels: *La malhora* (The Evil Hour, 1923), *El desquite* (The Revenge, 1925), and *La luciérnaga* (The Firefly, 1927). Their self-conscious distortion of language and fragmentation of chronology were later condemned by the author himself.

Disillusion with politics led Azuela in the 1930s to occupy himself mostly with historical novels and historical biographies. From time to time, however, he abandoned the pleasures of the past to attack contemporary bureaucracy (in *Regina Landa*, 1939), the union leaders (*Avanzada*, 1940), or the new revolutionary bourgeoisie (*Nueva burguesía*, 1941). Azuela spent the last decade of his life a greatly mellowed man, a member of the Mexican cultural establishment and a benign collector of literary honors: in *La Marchanta* (The Shopkeeper, 1944), the oppressed are victims no longer of government incompetence and corruption, but of their own moral flaws.

"It is curious," wrote the Uruguayan critic Emir Rodríguez Monegal, "that this writer who was one of the first to join the revolutionary movement, once it had triumphed withdrew from it more and more. The truth of the matter is that the Revolution had been withdrawing from those who began it. . . . In his early novels, such as *Los de Abajo*, he conveyed all that was noble and spontaneous in the revolution, but at the same time he pointed out . . . the medium it provided for the growth of demagogy. And as soon as the struggle came to an end and sought to establish order—even though at the cost of compromises and injustices—Azuela turned his back upon it and became the chronicler of its defects. . . . The point is that Azuela is not a reactionary but a moralist." Azuela is revered in Mexico as the originator of a native school of writing, evolved in the heat of the Revolution, that owed little if anything to foreign models. His influence on Carlos Fuentes, Juan Rulfo, and others of their generation (some of whom disparage his achievement), has been incalculable.

PRINCIPAL WORKS IN ENGLISH TRANSLATION: The Underdogs, 1929; Marcela, 1932; Trials of a Respectable Family, 1938; Two Novels of Mexico: The Flies, *and* The Bosses, 1956.

ABOUT: Spell, J. R. Contemporary Spanish-American Fiction, 1944. *Periodicals*—Hispana February 1935; New Republic October 23, 1938.

***BACCHELLI, RICCARDO** (April 19, 1891–), Italian novelist, critic, dramatist, and poet, was born into a wealthy and well-established family in Bologna, in the north of Italy. He is the son of a lawyer, Giuseppe Bacchelli, and of the former Ada Bumiller. Bacchelli has remained outside the main literary currents that have swept his homeland in this century. The stylized and neoclassical prose, the scholarly interests, the literary and political conservatism of this painstaking and highly disciplined writer contrast sharply with the introspective and neorealistic elements in contemporary Italian literature. In fact, one critic has sarcastically predicted that some future graduate student may demonstrate irrefutably that Bacchelli could not possibly have written in the twentieth century.

Although he has always been a hard-working and prolific writer, Bacchelli labored for nearly twenty years before he received widespread recognition. His first book was privately published in 1910, and a rather more notable volume of prose poems, *Poemi lirici*, followed in 1914. At the end of World War I, in which he had served as an artillery officer, Bacchelli and six other writers and critics (later known in literary circles as "the Seven Sages") founded *La Ronda*, an influential literary review published in Rome from 1919 to 1923. The Rondisti sought to establish order in the chaotic postwar world, looking back for their inspiration (over the heads of the Futurists and the *crepusculari*) to Ariosto, Leopardi, and Manzoni.

Bacchelli gave evidence of his skill in evoking the past in *Il Diavolo al Pontelungo* (1927), his first important work, translated as *The Devil at the Long Bridge*. It is a historical novel in episodic form—extremely funny in its first section—about the efforts of the aging Russian anarchist Mikhail

* bäk kel′ lē

RICCARDO BACCHELLI

Bakunin to ferment social revolution in Italy during the 1860s. Its critics thought it an ironical, charming, and sensitive study of the revolutionary mind.

The qualities so admired in *Il Diavolo al Pontelungo* are by no means typical of Bacchelli's work as a whole. Though he has tried his hand at comedy in *La città degli amanti* (1929, translated as *Love Town*) and has explored almost every fictional genre, from the gothic to the socio-psychological, his skill in description and narrative, his sense of history, and his extraordinary stamina, equip him above all for the *roman-fleuve*. His masterpiece is *Il mulino del Po* (1938–1940), first published serially in *Nuova Antologia* and then in three huge volumes totaling two thousand pages. The first two were translated by Frances Frenaye and published as one under the series title *The Mill on the Po*; the third, translated by Stuart Hood, appeared in English as *Nothing New Under the Sun*.

Il mulino del Po is a chronicle of the Scacerni family, millers in the Po Valley, from the Napoleonic Wars through the end of World War I. These people, immersed in their own everyday affairs, are only vaguely aware of the great events of their time. Yet for Bacchelli it is the common people—who "with tenacious humility have kept faith in self and refused to be crushed by the almost overwhelming burden of their history"—that constitute the true personality of a nation. But history does not spare the Scacernis. Bacchelli's book, tracing the emergence of Italy as a modern unified nation, also records the disintegration of the peasants' traditional way of life.

In Italy, as elsewhere, *Il mulino del Po* was thought ponderous, unsubtle, and old-fashioned, generally undistinguished in its characterization, but "an epic novel on the largest and most satisfying scale." Thomas Sugrue objected to its "village view of history," but Edmund Fuller called it "an Italian literary landmark . . . a majestic, tragic human chronicle." Serge Hughes wrote: "There is a place for neither smugness nor despair in Bacchelli. Only a sense of life, which is not a violent outburst or a quiet oozing away, but a purposeful movement, although not necessarily seen as such by men." That sense of life, or of history, is symbolized in Bacchelli's novel by the River Po and is his true protagonist.

Several of Bacchelli's subsequent novels have also been published in English. They include *L'incendio di Milano* (1952, translated as *The Fire of Milan*), "an interesting and thoughtful" picture of one segment of Milanese society at the time of the 1943 armistice, and *Il figlio di Stalin* (1953, translated as *Son of Stalin*), about the "grimly horrible comedy of cross purposes" that develops when Stalin's illegitimate son becomes a German prisoner during World War II. "This is a book on which every alert political mind must form its own opinion," wrote a reviewer in the *Times Literary Supplement*, "for everyone whose mind is awake should read it."

Serge Hughes has said that Bacchelli's "outlook on life, art, politics, and religion is a skillful, frequently successful attempt to perpetuate the legacy" of that other Catholic traditionalist Alessandro Manzoni. His style is slow, easy, and musical and he is, as Thomas Bergin has said, "a lover of exact words, words that have accurate concrete meaning, '*mots justes*.' One can trace to this love of words some of the more important aspects of his art." Many writers with greater gifts have died unknown. It is above all Bacchelli's industry and persistence, his determination to become a major novelist, that have brought him to his present eminence as a kind of grand old man of Italian letters. He has been mentioned as a Nobel Prize candidate, is a member of the Accademia Nazionale dei Lincei and of several other academies, and is a Grand Officer of the Italian Republic.

PRINCIPAL WORKS IN ENGLISH TRANSLATION: The Devil at the Long Bridge, 1929; Love Town, 1930; The Mill on the Po, 1950; Nothing New Under the Sun, 1955; Fire of Milan, 1958; Son of Stalin, 1956 (U.S., Seed of Steel). *Stories in* Adam, 1960; Nation October 9, 1937.

ABOUT: Curley, D. N. and Curley, A. (eds.) Modern Romance Literatures (A Library of Literary Criticism), 1967; Dizionario universale della letteratura contemporanea, 1959; Dizionario enciclopedico della letteratura italiana, 1966; Letteratura italiana: i contemporanei, 1963; Smith, H. (ed.) Columbia Dictionary of Modern European Literature, 1947. *Periodicals*—Dial May 1928; Mercure de France May 1, 1937; Nuova Antologia September 1, 1936.

***BACHELARD, GASTON** (June 27, 1884–October 16, 1962), French philosopher of science, whose later works deal with the creative imagination in literature, was born at Bar-sur-Aube, where his father, Louis, was a shoemaker. Bachelard was largely self-taught, working as a postman while he prepared for his *baccalauréat*. He then studied science at the University of Paris, gaining the *agrégation* and a *doctorat ès lettres*. After a period teaching physics and chemistry in the *lycée* of his home town, he began a brilliant university career as professor of philosophy at Dijon and from 1941 as professor of the history and philosophy of science at the Sorbonne.

His early works on the philosophy of science include *Le Nouvel Esprit scientifique* (The New Scientific Attitude, 1934), *La Formation de l'esprit scientifique* (The Formation of the Scientific Attitude, 1938), *Le Rationalisme appliqué* (Applied Rationalism, 1949), and *La Philosophie du non* (1940, translated by G. Waterston as *The Philosophy of No*). These books belong to the French "criticism of science" school developed by the mathematician Henri Poincaré and the physicist Pierre Duhem, though Bachelard was also strongly influenced by the thought of Bergson. The characteristic feature of modern science for Bachelard is that it is dynamic, constantly developing and changing, and this continuous scientific advance revolutionizes earlier conceptions of the relation between mind and nature. Science is not a matter of observing and seeking to understand an empirical world "out there"; the world itself, to the extent that it is "constructed" by the scientific mind, is changing as scientific thought changes. Therefore, "immediate reality is not an object of knowledge, but an occasion for scientific thought. . . . Scientific reality is in dialectical relation with scientific reason." In *La Philosophie du non* Bachelard shows that the postulates and principles of classical science have not been discarded by the new science, but given a place and a new meaning in a greater whole. The philosophy of the sciences is of necessity not closed but open in structure, constantly developing, like reality itself. All scientific and philosophical thought is always provisional, every phase preparing the way for a new phase.

Bachelard therefore tried to include the existential problem within the framework of the criticism of science, seeking to understand the dynamics of thought in its relationship to reality. This led him in his later work to concentrate not on rational, scientific thought but on the creative imagination. He regarded the essence of science as "malign vigilance"—a deliberate repression of the intuition and empathy through which man makes his first contacts with reality. The arts, on the contrary, depend

* bash lar′

on this constructing power of the imagination, pursuing intimacy with nature through a complex range of metaphors and myths. Bachelard believed that these constructive feats of the imagination originate in "la rêverie," daydreaming or fantasy making. It is in daydreaming that the material world penetrates man's inner life, when he allows his mind to dwell half-consciously on colors and movements, forms and textures. Then the imagination embarks on strange, liberating adventures, generating the images and metaphors from which we create the psychic worlds we live in.

Whereas Freudian psychoanalysis studies dreaming for what it reveals of private motivation, Bachelard, like Jung, was primarily interested in its revelation of collective experience. Among the primitive unconscious archetypes which constantly occur in poetic imagery are the traditional four elements of earth, air, fire, and water. They have been displaced by science as elements of nature but have retained their potency in imaginative experience. Believing that these images contain the clue to man's most fundamental instincts and drives, Bachelard embarked on a series of books showing these four mythic elements as the essential substance of the world created by poets: *La Psychanalyse du feu* (1937, translated by A. C. M. Ross as *The Psychoanalysis of Fire*); *L'Eau et les rêves* (Water and Dreams, 1942); *L'Air et les songes* (Air and Visions, 1942); *La Terre et les rêveries du repos* (The Earth and Reveries of Repose, 1945) and *La Terre et les rêveries de la volonté* (The Earth and Reveries of Will, 1948).

Bachelard begins *La Psychanalyse du feu* by pointing out that fire is linked by analogy with many other aspects of experience, being especially an image of vitality and sexuality—the "ultra-living element" because it can symbolize everything that changes quickly. He argues that in the child's knowledge of fire social prohibition comes before actual experience of being burnt, so that the problem of obtaining a personal knowledge of fire is the problem of "clever disobedience": the naughty child playing with matches is a little Prometheus, and Bachelard proposes a "Prometheus complex" to cover "all those tendencies which impel us to know as much as our fathers." He analyzes the work of E. T. A. Hoffman to show how the flaming punch bowl became a metaphor of artistic release and creativity, and explores many other aspects of the same basic image in the work of Novalis, Hölderlin, Goethe, Zola, d'Annunzio, and others. He discusses the profound sexual basis of alchemy, and ends with a chapter on "idealized fire," the fire that purifies rather than pains.

In *L'Eau et les rêves* Bachelard begins with the clear, running water in which Narcissus sees his own image, and he goes on to discuss the symbolic

GASTON BACHELARD

function of mirrors and reflections. In the narcissistic search for self, water is first the source of life, related to woman and birth, and the unchangeable nature of this profound substance in which all nature can be reflected induces feelings of security and eternity. But the reflection visible on the surface is constantly under the threat of disappearing, so that water imagery is related to death as well as to birth, especially that of deep and stagnant waters. This study of water, in which Bachelard also considers the symbolism of Leda and the Swan, Ophelia's death by drowning, and Charon's boat, seemed to Sartre so rich in "ingenious and profound insights" that he adopted it as the basis of his own existential psychoanalysis.

Bachelard similarly explores air and earth, maintaining that the mind of every great dreamer is drawn to one of four basic phantoms: the gnome (who lives in rock and earth), the salamander (inhabitant of fire), the undine (water nymph), and the sylph (immaterial spirit of the air). The human mind is drawn to one of these elemental objects and then projects its deepest interests and values on to it and thus creates an image. In later works Bachelard turns his attention to other aspects of imagery, as in *La Poétique de l'espace* (1958, translated by Maria Jolas as *The Poetics of Space*), which begins with his famous analysis of the house, from the cellar, which represents the dark subconscious forces in us, to the attic, representing our need for spiritual elevation.

Bachelard's prose is difficult and, as Leo Bersani says, "rather exotic fare for Anglo-Saxon readers," and he typifies the contemporary French critic's "neglect of the literary content of literary texts and its indifference to judgments of literary value." But Roland Barthes, one of the most influential contemporary French critics, has said that "Bachelard, starting from an analysis of substances rather than of works and tracing the dynamic distortions in a great many poets, founded a whole critical school which is, indeed, so prolific that present-day French criticism in its most flourishing aspect can be said to be Bachelardian in inspiration." Another French critic, Georges Poulet, has even proclaimed Bachelard's approach to the imagination's fundamental themes as a revolution which "was Copernican in scope. He has been the greatest explorer of the life of the mind since Sigmund Freud (although his was a very different path from Freud's)."

Bachelard was married and had one daughter. He was elected to the Academy of Moral and Political Sciences in 1955, and a year before his death he was awarded the French Grand Prix for literature.

PRINCIPAL WORKS IN ENGLISH TRANSLATION: The Psychoanalysis of Fire, 1964; The Poetics of Space, 1964; The Philosophy of No, 1968; The Poetics of Reverie, 1969.

ABOUT: Delfgaauw, B. Twentieth Century Philosophy, 1969; Farber, M. The Foundation of Phenomenology, 1962; Fowlie, W. The French Critic 1549–1967, 1968; Levin, H. Refractions: Essays in Comparative Literature, 1966; Lockspeiser, E. Debussy: His Life and Mind, Vol. 2, 1965; Sartre, J.-P. Being and Nothingness, 1957; Smith, C. Contemporary French Philosophy, 1964; Stern, A. Sartre, 1968. *Periodicals*—London Magazine April 1965; New York Review of Books April 30, 1964; Partisan Review Spring 1967; Virginia Quarterly Review Summer 1964.

***BACHMANN, INGEBORG** (June 25, 1926–), Austrian poet, short story writer, critic, dramatist, and novelist, was born in Klagenfurt, Austria. She studied both law and philosophy at Innsbruck and Graz, and received her doctorate in philosophy at the University of Vienna in 1950 with a dissertation on Heidegger's existentialism and its critical reception.

From 1951 to 1953 Ingeborg Bachmann worked with Radio-Weiss-Rot in Vienna. She made her first significant appearance in the literary world in 1952, reading her poetry at a meeting of the Gruppe 47. The same year her libretto for Hans Werner Henze's ballet *Der Idiot* was published. Her first book of verse, *Die gestundete Zeit* (Borrowed Time), followed in 1953 and received the Gruppe 47 prize. Echoing through these frequently beautiful lyrics is an implicit but unmistakable awareness of German guilt and escapism, and of man's gloomy future prospects: one critic called her "a Cassandra with a soft heart."

She lived from 1953 to 1957 in Italy, in 1955 visiting the United States at the invitation of Harvard University. In 1959–1960, as the first Dozent of the newly founded Chair of Poetics at Frankfurt University, she gave a series of lectures on Literature as Utopia that throw a great deal of light on her concerns as a writer. She interested herself there in the whole existential setting of the modern writer: his view of himself, his essential challenges and anxieties, his ways of overcoming himself through his writing. As she put it in another essay at this time, the writer has all his feelers out, "feels toward the form of the world, toward the traits of man at this moment in time." She shows a similar concern for the existential context of thought in her important essay, published in *Frankfurter Hefte*, on Ludwig Wittgenstein and the importance of neopositivism in Germany.

* bäk′ män

Ingeborg Bachmann has addressed herself to these themes in a variety of literary forms. Her radio plays *Die Zikanden* (1954), set on a Mediterranean island, and *Der Gute Gott von Manhattan* (The Good God of Manhattan, 1958), set in New York, are startling in their joining of fantasy and liberated imagination with ordinary language. Both deal with one kind or another of escapism, and assert the responsibility of human beings (including artists) for one another.

A volume of short stories, *Das Dreissigste Jahr* (1961), has been excellently translated by Michael Bullock as *The Thirtieth Year*. These stories, one or two of them virtually prose poems, were admired by some critics for their "poetry and passion," damned by others for their "tireless undisciplined ranting." The author has also translated Ungaretti and produced librettos for two operas by Hans Werner Henze, *Der Prinz von Homburg* (The Prince of Homburg, 1960) and *Der Junge Lord* (The Young Lord, 1965). Her *Gedichte*—a selection from her work, both verse and prose—appeared in 1964. The same year she received the Georg Büchner prize.

It is on her poetry that Ingeborg Bachmann's reputation rests most securely. A second collection, *Anrufung des grossen Bären* (Invocation of the Great Bear) appeared in 1956. It shows a diminished concern with the immediate political and moral climate, a growing preoccupation with language and myth, and includes more directly personal poems, including love poems, than her first volume. Some critics found a hopeless acceptance (for example in the title poem) of man's ultimate self-destruction, and accused the poet of a flight from moral engagement into personal emotion or aestheticism. The complaint (if it is one) seems born out by the cycle of poems called "Lieder auf der Flucht," whose last poem includes these lines: "Death has a triumph and love has one, / time and the time afterwards. / We have none. / Only the sinking of constellations about us. Splendour reflected and silence. / Yet the song above the dust

INGEBORG BACHMANN

afterwards / will rise above us." It may be that for Ingeborg Bachmann, who has learned from both Heidegger and Wittgenstein, linguistic integrity stands revealed as the path toward salvation. Certainly, as George C. Schoolfield has said, her poetry is "an example of contemporary lyric language at its finest, both arresting and lucid." Many of the themes which recur in the author's poetry also preoccupy her in her first novel, *Malina* (1972), in which, one critic wrote, "the process of subjective exploration is pushed to its limits."

PRINCIPAL WORKS IN ENGLISH TRANSLATION: The Thirtieth Year (stories), 1964. *Poems in* Bridgwater, P. (ed.) Twentieth-Century German Verse, 1963; Hamburger, M. and Middleton, C. (eds.) Modern German Poetry, 1962.

ABOUT: Closs, A. Twentieth Century German Literature, 1969; Holthusen, H. E. Das Schöne und das Wahre, 1958; Jens, W. Marginalien zur modernen Literatur, 1959; Kaiser, J. and others, Ingeborg Bachmann, 1963; Keith-Smith, B. (ed.) Essays on Contemporary German Literature, 1966; Krolow, K. Aspekte zeitgenössischer deutscher Lyrik, 1961. *Periodicals*—German Life and Letters 4, 1964; Texte and Zeichen 3 1957.

BAKER, CARLOS (HEARD) (May 5, 1909–), American critic, novelist, and poet, writes: "I was born in Biddeford, Maine, of Yankee and early nineteenth-century German stock, and brought up there and later in Saco, across the river. Both cities are small mill towns, with strong French–Canadian infiltrations, surrounded by rolling countryside of forests, fields, and streams which was the playground of my boyhood. In the summers there was always Biddeford Pool, on the rugged granite-basalt coast, where I became familiar with the ocean in all its moods and rhythms, and which still seems to me like a lost paradise. Education began at home, moved to the Manlius School near Syracuse, New York, where I was first sergeant in a machine gun company, and led on to Dartmouth (A.B., 1932), marriage and Harvard (A.M., 1933), and finally Princeton (Ph.D., 1940) where I began teaching in 1937 and have stayed ever since. All through school and college I wrote fiction and poetry (of sorts) and a few experimental plays. Graduate work opened into the field of criticism and the first big book, after several jobs of editing: a study of Shelley's major poetry, 1812–1822.

"From there, following the range of romanticism like a mountain trail into the modern age, it was a considerable hike to a full-length critique of the work of Ernest Hemingway, whose work I had always admired, and of whose famous story, 'The Killers,' my first serious undergraduate short story was a palpable, though crude, imitation. Most of the book was written in Tucson, Arizona, on a year's leave from teaching. Once I had accepted his interdiction against biography, Hemingway was very helpful with information, and the book was the first to be published among the various studies of his work that have come since 1952. It was because of this interest that I was asked, after his suicide, to become his authorized biographer, a task that has taken up most of my time since the fall of 1961.

"Throughout these years I wrote innumerable book reviews, essays, and poetry, seeking always to say with cogency, clarity, and force whatever seemed worth saying, and perhaps succeeding some of the time. E. M. Forster said once that literature holds a light behind the world, and for me it was one of three such lights, the others being the raising of a family, and the teaching of generations of undergraduates and graduate students.

"My first venture into full-length fiction was *A Friend in Power*, an academic novel about the selection of a university president, written in six weeks under ideal conditions at a writers' colony in Saratoga Springs, New York. The book had its origins in some committee work in which I was involved while Princeton was seeking a new president. I thought then, and still believe, that most academic fiction misrepresents the actualities of academic life, and accordingly set out to tell a version of the truth of what happens in a year's time in a representative university community. In a second novel, *The Land of Rumbelow*, with a setting in the curious desert metropolis of Tucson, I wanted to do a latter-day fable about the incursions of evil into human life. This time everything but the setting was invented; it was probably a much better novel than the first. It took the better part of two years, it attempted far more, and I'm glad to have done it, because it finally said what I wanted to say

CARLOS BAKER

about the theme, the region, and the people. At this time also a selection from twenty years of my poetry was published. It was a small harvest that I was glad to get into the barn.

"Among my favorite modern novelists are Dos Passos, Faulkner, Hemingway, James Gould Cozzens, Robert Penn Warren, E. M. Forster, James Joyce, and Evelyn Waugh; and I particularly admire Yeats, Frost, Stevens, Eliot, and Auden among the poets. But there are hundreds of others, both newer and older, who seem to me to have spoken true and lively words. These I read unremittingly while trying to speak in a voice of my own about whatever comes closest to heart and mind. It is a fascinating and absorbing process, and I would like to continue with it to the end of my life."

In *Shelley's Major Poetry*, Baker's primary concern was "to live the inner life of these poems from one end to the other and to set down the record" of this experience. Most critics welcomed the result as an enlightening study of Shelley's philosophy, not least in showing that a poet previously thought of as an atheist in fact held "unorthodox but genuinely religious beliefs." Baker's pioneer study of Hemingway (whom he never met) was called a model of its kind, the product of much "toil, patience, and responsibility." Some readers found it a little partisan in its approach, but most thought it useful and illuminating. According to *Commonweal*'s reviewer, Baker's "great virtue as a critic is that despite his warm devotion to the subject he does not fall back on rhapsodic gusto as a substitute for thought and analysis. The cards are all on the table."

A Friend in Power, though it suffered by the inevitable comparisons with C. P. Snow's *The Masters*, was generally enjoyed as a readable, agreeable, well-observed study of academic life. *The Land of Rumbelow* is, as Baker says, a more ambitious novel, a "fable" about the violence and evil just below the calm surface of everyday life. Paul Pickrel thought it altogether too schematic, and *Newsweek*'s reviewer disliked it intensely, calling it "a garden of clichés, a gallery of non-people," but other reviewers reacted more warmly, and Elizabeth Janeway found it both readable and interesting. Baker's "jotting and musings" in verse, collected in *A Year and a Day*, were praised by W. T. Scott for their "neat, epigrammatic, literary skill." R. D. Spector said that "for all his allusiveness, Baker's first volume of verse is never obscure and has a quiet and modest personal charm."

The seven-hundred-page biography of Hemingway, begun in 1961, was published in 1969 as *Ernest Hemingway: A Life Story*. It draws on letters, unpublished manuscripts, and many interviews to provide an immensely detailed chronological narrative of the external events of Hemingway's life, Critics praised the book as "a superb job of research," clear if somewhat chatty in style, and scrupulously objective, which disposes "once and for all of the legend and the lies." Vance Bourjaily, however, expressed a fairly common view when he wrote that Baker, by refusing to judge, select, or interpret the great mass of facts he had collected, had given us "the whole substance of a life, but little of its quality."

Carlos Baker is the son of Arthur and Edna (Heard) Baker. He was married in 1932 to Dorothy Thomasson Scott and has three children. At Princeton he was chairman of the English department from 1952 to 1958, and since 1954 has been Woodrow Wilson Professor of Literature. He was a Fulbright lecturer in American literature at Oxford University in 1957–1958, and at the Centre Universitaire in Nice in 1958. He received a Guggenheim Fellowship in 1965–1966 and has an honorary Litt.D. from Dartmouth College.

PRINCIPAL WORKS: *Nonfiction*—Shelley's Major Poetry: The Fabric of a Vision, 1948; Hemingway: The Writer as Artist, 1952; Ernest Hemingway: A Life Story, 1969. *Novels*—A Friend in Power, 1958; The Land of Rumbelow: A Fable in the Form of a Novel, 1963; The Gay Head Conspiracy, 1973. *Poetry*—A Year and a Day, 1963.

ABOUT: Contemporary Authors 5–6, 1963; Who's Who in America, 1970–1971. *Periodicals*—Book World April 13, 1969; Harper's Magazine May 1969; New York Review of Books June 5, 1969; New York Times Book Review April 27, 1969; Publishers' Weekly March 31, 1969; Times Literary Supplement September 11, 1969.

BALDWIN, JAMES (ARTHUR) (August 2, 1924–), black American novelist, essayist, and dramatist, was born in Harlem Hospital, the son of Berdis (Jones) Baldwin. His stepfather, David Baldwin, was a pastor from New Orleans, a bitter and paranoid man who raised his children in an atmosphere of bigotry, fear, and religious fanaticism. James Baldwin has himself attributed his sense of alienation and rejection to this man (who called him ugly to his face) rather than simply to his race.

Baldwin began his education at P.S. 24 and went on to the Frederick Douglass Junior High School, where he is remembered as "a small, bright, sad-looking boy." He was an avid reader, even though his position as the oldest of nine children meant that he often had to hold his book with one hand, a baby with the other. At fourteen he became a Holy Roller preacher at the Fireside Pentecostal Church in Harlem; he was a success and, delighted by his ability to attract bigger congregations than his stepfather, preached in neighborhood storefront churches for the next three years, until his religious faith was gone. In a sense, Baldwin has been a secular preacher ever since: a prophet, a witness, and an orator.

He completed his education at De Witt Clinton High School, where he edited the literary magazine, and graduated in 1942. His first job was on a defense project in New Jersey. When his stepfather died in 1943, Baldwin, by then determined on a literary career, left home and settled in Greenwich Village. During the next five years he earned his living as an office boy, dishwasher, factory worker, and waiter, writing in the evenings. He sold a few essays and reviews to magazines like *Nation* and *Commentary*, and began work on his first novel. In 1945, thanks to the intercession of Richard Wright, he received a Eugene F. Saxton Memorial Trust Award. Three years later a Rosenwald Fellowship paid his way to Paris. There he lived for most of the next decade, sometimes in great poverty, but safe from the grosser kinds of racial discrimination, and able to travel all over Europe. He continued to write and to read (learning most, he says, from Henry James), and in 1952 published the novel he had begun ten years earlier in Greenwich Village.

This was *Go Tell It on the Mountain*, a powerful, lyrical, and heavily autobiographical account of the religious conversion of a fourteen-year-old Harlem boy. John Grimes's terrifying stepfather is a deacon of the Temple of the Fire Baptized, and John himself faces a choice, as his mother puts it, between the church and the jail. A sensitive and gentle youth, much troubled by his recent discovery of sex, he eventually embraces the church, impelled partly by religious excitement, partly by emotional panic, partly by an intuitive realization that he can in this way vanquish his stepfather on the latter's own

JAMES BALDWIN

ground. His conversion is the climax of a brilliant account of a long late-night service, during which flashbacks reveal the past lives of John and his parents; these flashbacks throw great light on the relationship between black racial experience and black religion, and immeasurably increase the scope and density of the novel.

Stanley Edgar Hyman, who regarded Baldwin as a writer of symbolist fantasy, believed that the novel "disguised its story of a boy's conversion to homosexuality as a religious conversion." Most critics have been content to take the book at its face value, and to admire the elegance of its structure, the power and economy of its language, and its authenticity as a portrayal of a way of life. Some regard it as Baldwin's best novel.

Critical hopes that a major new talent was emerging were confirmed three years later, when *Notes of a Native Son* appeared. These ten essays, first published in such magazines as *Harper's* and the *Reporter*, were unfashionably personal reflections on black–white relationships in America and abroad, centering on the special dilemma of the northern black intellectual, inheritor of no culture, Western or African. Despairing as many of these pieces are, the best of them have an unflinching honesty combined with a grace of style that is more exhilarating than depressing. Robert F. Sayre, writing in *Contemporary American Novelists*, pointed out that "invisibly connected to this tough sincerity and delicate elegance is a quality of exact distance from his subject, whether himself, books, his society, or whatever. One of the reasons Baldwin can handle violence so smoothly is that he seems to know the emotions and hidden prejudices of his audience so well . . . he now evokes, now balances, and now hushes the response of his audience so that it provides the energy while he fingers the keys. This is the real source of Baldwin's power—his finesse and his control of his audience."

In his second novel, *Giovanni's Room*, Baldwin seems deliberately to have put aside the problem of race and turned to his other principal theme, homosexuality. The story is narrated in flashback by David, a white American student who has an affair in Paris with a young Italian bartender. David has deserted Giovanni in favor of his American fiancée and respectability, and Giovanni, in desperation, has murdered his former patron. Now, on the eve of Giovanni's execution, David spends the night in ruthless self-examination. It is, as reviewers remarked, a frank and a brave book, skillfully narrated and subtle in its perceptions, though it does not escape melodrama or self-pity.

Having published his first three books as an expatriate, Baldwin returned in 1957 to the United States. On a visit (his first) to the South he was deeply impressed by what he saw of the civil rights campaign and thereafter became fully involved in that cause. Baldwin, who has served on the national advisory board of the Congress of Racial Equality, is a compelling lecturer and television speaker, a small man giving an impression of extraordinary emotional and intellectual power. During the late 1950s and early 1960s, through his public appearances and his writings, he did as much as anyone in America to bring home to his compatriots, white and black, the full moral, historical, and personal significance of the race issue.

Another Country, the first of his novels to be completed in the United States, is his most ambitious book. It is much less perfectly shaped than *Go Tell It on the Mountain* and is seriously flawed in other ways, but it comes closest of all his novels to a full working out of his sexual and racial ideas, in particular his belief that racial discrimination is a sickness of the whites, a symptom of thwarted love and displaced self-hatred. It begins with the suicide of Rufus Scott, a gifted black jazz musician who has been embittered and finally overwhelmed by racial hatred and frustration. The rest of the book centers on the sexual and racial encounters of his sister Ida, his white friend Vivaldo Moore, and Eric, a bisexual white Southerner who had been Rufus's lover. All of them are struggling for love but are denied it by the aridity and unreality of American life. Eric discovers and frees himself through an affair with Yves, a street boy in the south of France, and is able to pass on what he has learned to some of the others. In the end Ida and Vivaldo are together with some hope of happiness.

There is some very bad writing in the novel—vulgar, unconvincing, and boring. On the other hand it takes enormous risks, and contains passages that are as perfectly achieved as anything Baldwin has ever written. The short stories collected in *Going to Meet the Man* and the subsequent novel *Tell Me How Long the Train's Been Gone* were even more roughly handled by most critics—found mechanical, artificial, or violently polemical, without the largeness of vision that distinguished *Another Country*.

Blues for Mister Charlie, the first of Baldwin's plays to reach Broadway, is a story of racial murder based loosely on the killing of Emmett Till. "Mister Charlie" is the white man and, as the title suggests, the play embodies Baldwin's conception of racial discrimination as a disease of white society. David Boroff wrote that Baldwin "has mustered all his pamphleteering skill and has written a raw, stinging denunciation of racial oppression. The play is as much a civil-rights pageant as a drama—militantly propagandistic in intent, often crudely oversimplified, but unfailingly vivid, moving, and powerful." (But a less sympathetic critic concluded that the author was in process of "exchanging creative writing for demagogic oratory.") It ran for four months in New York in 1964 and shared the Foreign Press Association's drama award for the season.

The Amen Corner, written in Paris in the early 1950s, did not reach the New York stage until 1968. It is for the most part a pleasantly nostalgic reminiscence of a boyhood spent in and around a Harlem storefront chapel. The critics generally enjoyed the portrait of the congregation and the chapel scenes, though once again many felt that the play was marred by too many long didactic speeches.

It seems increasingly clear that the artist in Baldwin has been murdered by the prophet in him, or by racial hatred itself, an implacable enemy of artistic detachment. Many now consider that, for all the brilliant promise of his novels, none of them (except perhaps the first) represents as large an achievement as his essays. His friend Norman Mailer has said that "Maybe the [novel] form is not for him. He knows what he wants to say, and that is not the best condition for writing a novel. Novels go happiest when you discover something you did not know you knew. Baldwin's experience has shaped his tongue toward directness, for urgency."

In *Nobody Knows My Name*, this directness and urgency is embodied in fifteen magazine articles and lectures dealing partly with books and writers, partly with Baldwin's return to the United States, his rediscovery of Harlem, his discovery of the South and the civil rights movement. Three of these pieces deal with Richard Wright, Baldwin's "spiritual father," whose literary and personal failings he attacks with a harshness never extended to writers who mean less to him. *The Fire Next Time* is the appropriate title of a later collection containing only two pieces, one of them the dark minatory summation of his racial views originally published in the *New Yorker* as "Letter From a Region of My Mind," perhaps the most powerful and moving of all his essays. In this form, Mailer says, "on the long continuing line of poetic fire in his essays, one knows he has become one of the few writers of our time. . . . Nobody has more elegance than Baldwin as an essayist, not one of us hasn't learned something about the art of the essay from him."

For nearly ten years Baldwin was the inspired spokesman of the silent black masses, teaching white America how it felt to be black. He preached love and understanding between the races, prophesying holocaust if the dialogue failed. Even in *The Fire Next Time*, where he cannot keep the hatred and bitterness from his own voice, his insistent theme is that "we, the black and white, deeply need each other if we are really to become a nation."

After the murder of Martin Luther King, which for him marked the death of the civil rights movement, Baldwin returned to Europe, living in Paris and Istanbul. Interviewed in 1970, he still insisted that black and white Americans are, literally, blood-brothers, and still thought it possible that racial conflict might be ended by reason and understanding. But, he said, the possibility was fading: "White people have simply raised the price, and raised it so high that fewer and fewer black people will be willing to pay it. . . . I'm optimistic about the future, but not about the future of this civilization. I'm optimistic about the civilization which will replace this one." These are very much the views he expressed also in *A Rap on Race*, a long tape-recorded conversation with the anthropologist Margaret Mead, and in *No Name in the Street*, a loosely constructed two-part autobiographical essay. *One Day, When I Was Lost* is a film script based on Alex Haley's *The Autobiography of Malcolm X.*

PRINCIPAL WORKS: *Fiction*—Go Tell It on the Mountain, 1953; Giovanni's Room, 1956; Another Country, 1962; Going to Meet the Man (short stories), 1965; Tell Me How Long the Train's Been Gone, 1968. *Plays*—Blues for Mister Charlie, 1964; The Amen Corner, 1968. *Essays*—Notes of a Native Son, 1955; Nobody Knows My Name, 1961; The Fire Next Time, 1963; Nothing Personal, 1964; No Name in the Street, 1972. *Miscellaneous*—(with Margaret Mead) A Rap on Race, 1971; One Day, When I Was Lost (film script), 1972; (with Nikki Giovanni) A Dialogue, 1973.

ABOUT: Current Biography, 1964; Eckman, F. M. The Furious Passage of James Baldwin, 1967; Gross, T. L. (ed.) Representative Man, 1970; Harper, H. M. Desperate Faith, 1967; Harte, B. and Riley, C. (eds.) 200 Contemporary Authors, 1969; Hyman, S. E. Standards, 1966; Ludwig, J. Recent American Novelists, 1962; Margolies, E. Native Sons, 1968; Moore, H. T. (ed.) Contemporary American Novelists, 1964; Who's Who, 1972; Who's Who in America, 1970–1971. *Periodicals*—Atlas March 1967; British Journal of Sociology June 1966; Christian Century August 28, 1963; March 24, 1965; Commonweal July 26, 1963; October 11, 1963; May 29, 1964; May 7, 1965; Critique Winter 1964–1965; Ebony October 1961; December 1961; June 1964; March 1970; Encounter August 1963; July 1965; Guardian July 3, 1970; Hudson Review Autumn 1964; Nation May 11, 1964; May 10, 1965; June 10, 1968; National Review May 21, 1963; June 18, 1963; July 16, 1963; December 17, 1963; September 8, 1964; April 6, 1965; Negro History Bulletin April 1967; New Republic August 7, 1961; August 27, 1962; May 16, 1964; November 27, 1965; New Statesman February 8, 1963; July 19, 1963; May 1, 1964; May 6, 1965; New York Times Book Review May 24, 1953; September 15, 1963; New Yorker November 25, 1961; April 24, 1965; Partisan Review Summer 1964; Spectator July 12, 1963; Times (London) May 4, 1965; May 17, 1965; August 24, 1965; Times Literary Supplement September 6, 1963; June 6, 1968; July 4, 1968; Tri-Quarterly Winter 1965; Twentieth Century Literature April 1967; Wilson Library Bulletin February 1959; Yale Review October 1966.

BALLARD, J(AMES) G(RAHAM) (November 15, 1930–), English novelist and short story writer, reports: "I was born in the International Settlement in Shanghai, China, of English parents. My full name is James Graham Ballard. My first sixteen years were spent in this large, polyglot city near the mouth of the Yangtze, and it seems likely that the influence of this bizarre landscape was greater than that of any emotional experiences of childhood. I was brought up largely by servants–my father was a prosperous businessman–and my memories of childhood are of wandering around the Chinese areas of the city on my own or of being driven out by the Russian chauffeur to visit the abandoned battlefields a few miles away in the countryside. Since the Sino-Japanese hostilities of 1937 the city had been surrounded by Japanese troops, and these years passed against a background of intermittent fighting and political excitement. I have a vague recollection of being introduced to Madame Sun Yat-sen.

"Immediately after Pearl Harbor the Japanese occupied Shanghai and my parents and I were interned in a camp some ten miles from the city. The camp was adjacent to a Japanese airfield, and in the last year of the war we had a close view of the continuous American bombing raids. After the Japanese capitulation we were released and returned to Shanghai. During this unusual period, an interregnum of two months or so, I made a number of visits to our camp, walking across this empty landscape where units of Japanese, American and both Kuomintang and Communist Chinese forces were busy rounding each other up. During this return to peace Shanghai was one of the most exhilarating places in the world.

"England, after this, was a great shock. I find that even after twenty years here I still regard it as a foreign country. I spent two years at the Leys School, and then went on to read medicine at King's

J. G. BALLARD

College, Cambridge. After winning the annual short story competition in 1951 I decided to give up medicine and become a writer. From the beginning it was clear to me that whatever talents I had were those of an imaginative writer and that the landscape of England would never provide me with a subject matter to which I could respond. This in fact has proved the case, and not one of my novels or short stories has been taken from the country where I have lived for the past two decades. For the social writer this would fairly be regarded as an insuperable handicap, but in my own case I feel it has been an immense advantage, because it has forced me to create the entire basis of my fiction from scratch. My novels, *The Drowned World*, *The Drought* and *The Crystal World*, have the architecture of dreams.

"From the start I have always been drawn to the visual arts, and in fact the greatest influences on me have not been writers so much as painters. The surrealists in particular, with their landscapes of the soul, provided me with a powerful compass towards that terrain which I have called 'inner space'—that zone where the outer world of reality and the inner world of the psyche meet and fuse. Most of my fiction has been concerned with the construction of the external landscapes of the mind.

"My self-evident preoccupation with time is an example of the direction I feel the novel must take if it is to remain a valid speculative force. To a large extent, the novel is still dominated by its retrospective cast of mind, excessively concerned with the roots of behaviour and character seen in moral terms, and I do not believe this tallies with the facts of people's actual experience. In an attempt to produce a genuinely prospective form of narrative fiction, I have begun recently to write what I term 'condensed novels'—non-linear structures that more accurately reflect the texture of people's lives and imaginations. Several of these have been published in periodicals such as *Encounter* and *Ambit*. In these, for the first time I have used the materials of the environment around me."

Ballard's novels can be read on several levels. They are adventure stories, full of exciting, strange, and often repellent incident; they are biological fantasies about human evolution and devolution; and they are attempts to construct a timeless world of the psyche.

In his first novel, *The Drowned World*, a radical increase in the sun's heat has melted the ice caps, swamping Europe in lagoons and jungle. An expedition sets out from the new center of civilization in Greenland, seeking to reclaim the area around London. This has reverted to Triassic conditions and the expedition's attempts to cope with this primeval world provide the novel's adventure and suspense. Gradually, however, their problems cease to have any connection with everyday reality. One by one they succumb to primitive dreams, like that of Kerans, the expedition's leader, in which the sun moves closer and closer, and enormous Triassic lizards roar at it, "the noise gradually mounting until it becomes indistinguishable from the volcanic pounding of the solar flares." This pounding becomes the hammering of his own pulse, the lake outside an extension of his own bloodstream: "As the dull pounding rose, he felt the barriers which divided his own cells from the surrounding medium dissolving, and he swam forwards, spreading outwards across the black thudding water." These "dreams" are in fact memories of the evolutionary process: "Each of us is as old as the entire biological kingdom, and our bloodstreams are tributaries of the great sea of its total memory." As conscious control sweeps away, the "neuronic psyche" takes over. One by one the victims obey the compulsion to go south towards the sun. This strange world is evoked with great skill and power, and a characteristic mastery of visual effects, sometimes weakened by a self-indulgent use of language.

The Drought is similar in structure. Here the primitive conditions result from the drying-up of the world's fresh water supplies, and it is the barriers between present and future that collapse. In *The Crystal World* Sanders, a leper-doctor, arrives in a French West African settlement to find it full of strange rumors. A body is washed downstream, one arm encrusted with exquisite crystals. Sanders sets off up-country into a jungle where "everything is transfigured and illuminated, joined together in the last marriage of space and time." None of the book's reviewers seemed to have understood the "rather vague cosmic teleology" which the novel is intended to express, but none of them greatly cared. "In this latest novel," one wrote, "which contains in its atmosphere so much of Conrad's *Heart of Darkness*, in its characters so much of Graham Greene, and in some of its situations so much of Edgar Allan Poe, his descriptive powers do not fail him."

The Four-Dimensional Nightmare contains several stories united by the theme of man's regression from an evolutionary peak, while the stories in *Disaster Area* are set in a city of the future whose inhabitants are sleepless prisoners, compulsively buying the useless goods that subliminal advertising forces upon them, able to escape only into infantilism (and in one case actually returning to the womb). *Love and Napalm*, which some reviewers treated as a novel, others as a volume of related stories, presents even more extreme examples of "the private psyche being invaded by public events," from the assassination of President Kennedy to the sexual symbolism of car crashes. Ballard's development away from fantasy and towards a savage and surreal kind of social criticism has not pleased all of his critics. *Love and Napalm* seemed to Paul Theroux "the novel as a form of abuse," and a reviewer in England (where the book was called *The Atrocity Exhibition*) complained of "a cold plodding sadism masked in jargon which soon becomes self-parody."

Ballard's attention to "inner space" has greatly influenced English science fiction. His views also "hang heavy over almost every page" of the literary journal *Ambit*. In 1967 Ballard stirred up much controversy when he offered in that magazine a prize for "the best creative work . . . written under the influence of drugs." There were also angry reactions to one of Ballard's stories (also in *Ambit*), called "Plan for the Assassination of Jacqueline Kennedy." His point, he said, was that people like the then Mrs. Kennedy and Elizabeth Taylor, rich enough "to buy mass media," have projected themselves as fictional characters and should be written about as such. The Arts Council predictably rejected Ballard's request for a grant of one thousand pounds to finance a "private advertising campaign," whose features were to include a nude on Westminster Abbey's high altar and "Princess Margaret's left armpit."

Ballard has three children by his 1953 marriage to Helen Mary Matthews, who died in 1964, and one child by his second wife, Claire Churchill. He lives with his family in Middlesex.

PRINCIPAL WORKS: The Voices of Time (short stories), 1962; Billenium (short stories), 1962; The Drowned World, 1962; The Wind From Nowhere, 1962; Passport to Eternity (short stories), 1963; The Four-dimensional Nightmare (short stories), 1963; The Terminal Beach (short stories), 1964; The Drought, 1965; The Crystal World, 1966; The Impossible Man (short stories), 1966; The Disaster Area (short stories), 1967; The Overloaded Man (short stories), 1967; The Day of Forever (short stories), 1967; The Atrocity Exhibition, 1970 (U.S., Love and Napalm); Vermilion Sands (short stories), 1971; Chronopolis (short stories), 1971; Crash!, 1973.

ABOUT: Author's and Writer's Who's Who, 1971; Vinson, J. (ed.) Contemporary Novelists, 1972. *Periodicals* —Observer January 27, 1963; Times Literary Supplement, October 19, 1967.

***BANDEIRA, MANUEL (CARNEIRO DE SOUZA)** (April 19, 1886–1968), Brazilian poet, was born in Recife, Pernambuco, the son of an engineer, Manuel Carneiro de Souza, and the former Francisca Ribeiro. His father, who gave him an early introduction to literature, had himself wanted to be an architect, and encouraged the boy to follow that career. The family moved to Rio de Janeiro when Bandeira was ten, and he entered the Colégio Pedro II. He was an average student but showed a precocious talent for poetry. His architectural studies at the Escola Politécnica in São Paulo, begun in 1903, were cut short a year later by tuberculosis. For some years thereafter he was obliged for the sake of his health to spend much of his time in the interior.

His illness gave him the opportunity to concentrate on poetry, and by 1912 he was experimenting with free verse in the manner of Apollinaire. But his condition did not improve, and in 1913 he was sent to a sanatorium near Davos-Platz in Switzerland, where he made friends with a fellow-patient, the French poet Paul Éluard. He returned to Brazil in 1914 with the outbreak of World War I.

Bandeira's first volume, *A Cinza das Horas* (The Ash of Hours), appeared in 1917. Influenced as it was by French symbolist and Parnassian models, at its best it nevertheless had something of the lyric simplicity that has always characterized Bandeira's verse. In some of these poems Bandeira allows himself a bitter acknowledgment of the disease which had still not left him: "I write poetry like one who dies." And this bitterness sometimes finds expression in the harsh irony of such pieces as "Poemeto irônico": "And your hot useless desires / Beat their wings in unreality— / What you call your passion / Is merely curiosity."

At about this time, a number of Brazilian artists and writers were tiring of the strict forms and abstract themes of the French masters who had dominated them for so long and were seeking a freer and more native utterance. Bandeira, with Mario de Andrade, was one of the originators of this movement, and his first experiments, appearing in magazines towards the end of World War I, were collected in *Carnaval* (Carnival, 1919). By

* bun dā′ rə

MANUEL BANDEIRA

1922, when Brazilian modernism emerged as a fully fledged movement, he was advocating complete technical freedom.

In his *Brief History of Brazilian Literature* (1964), Bandeira wrote: "The modernists introduced free verse into Brazil; they sought to express themselves in language free of both Parnassian rhetoric and symbolist vagueness, less bound by the dictates of logic, adhering less closely to classic Portuguese standards of vocabulary and syntax. They boldly broadened the field of poetry, taking in the most prosaic aspects of life. In its beginnings, the movement was destructive in nature and characterized by novelty of form. Later it took on a decidedly nationalistic tone, seeking to provide an artistic interpretation of Brazil's present and past."

O Ritmo Dissoluto (Dissolved Rhythm, 1924), together with his critical articles and pronouncements, established Bandeira as the "St. John the Baptist of the new poetry." In "Poetica," published in *Libertinagem* (Libertinism, 1930), he excoriated "public-servant lyricism" and declared that he would have "nothing more to do / With a lyricism which is not freedom." *Libertinagem* has been called his "most representative contribution to *modernismo*," containing "the most characteristic examples of Bandeira's lyricism—colloquial, ironic, and often infused with a tragic humor."

By this time Brazilian modernism had split into an assortment of warring camps, and many regarded the movement as dead. In Bandeira's view, however, it had merely evolved beyond the youthful excesses of its destructive first phase "towards more liberty and greater expressiveness." In his own work he simplified and refined his style, and turned increasingly for his themes to the Negro folklore of Brazil—a development that is very evident in *Estrêla da Manhã* (Morning Star, 1936). He became, according to John Nist, "the most Brazilian of all the modern poets, full of coinages from popular usage and terms from African and Indian dialects. At times his terms are so Brazilian as to be the despair of metropolitan interpreters whose vocabularies are more literary."

Meanwhile, during the 1920s and early 1930s, Bandeira had been passing through a period of great financial hardship, living on a small pension left him by his father and what he could earn as a literary critic and journalist. Gilberto Freyre and other friends helped to secure assignments for him in such publications as *Mês Modernista*, *Ariel*, and *Diário da Noite*. The situation began to improve in 1935, when Bandeira was appointed superintendent of secondary schools. A year later, on his fiftieth birthday, his stature was recognized by the publication of *Homenagem a Manuel Bandeira*, with contributions by most of Brazil's principal literary figures. In 1938 he returned to the Colégio Pedro II as professor of universal literature, and in 1943 he became professor of Spanish American literature at the University of Brazil.

Although Bandeira's work was prized principally for its critical contribution to modernism during the 1920s, he remained a major figure in Brazilian literature and an important influence on his juniors. His later poetry was distinguished by its emotional control and by the great purity and simplicity of its diction, its concern with the word for its own sake, as something unique in weight, sound, and meaning. At the same time, Bandeira remained open to new tendencies, experimenting with Concretism, for example, in the 1950s. His long struggle with tuberculosis was reflected in his preoccupation with the warring forces of life and death. "What I adore in you: is life," he says to his love in "Melancholy Madrigal." And it is this lust for life which enabled him in middle age to triumph over his disease. He died in 1968, at the age of eighty-two.

Bandeira edited several important anthologies, including *A Poesia do Brasil* (1961). His *Literatura hispano-americana* appeared in 1949 and his literary criticism was collected as *De poetas e de poesia* in 1954. Notable translations of *Macbeth* and of Schiller's *Maria Stuart*, among other works, have been successfully performed in Brazil. His modest autobiographical essay, *Itinérario de Pasárgada*, was published in 1954. Bandeira was elected to the Brazilian Academy of Letters in 1940, and received the Poetry Prize of the Brazilian Institute of Cultural Studies in 1946. He returned to Europe in 1957, after an absence of over forty years, and visited Holland, England, and France. He was unmarried.

Bandeira's complete works were published in two large volumes in 1958.

PRINCIPAL WORKS IN ENGLISH TRANSLATION: A Brief History of Brazilian Literature, 1964. *Poems in* Burnshaw, S. (ed.) The Poem Itself, 1960; Dounes, L. S. (ed.) Modern Brazilian Poetry, 1954; Fitts, D. (ed.) Anthology of Contemporary Latin-American Poetry, 1942; Nist, J. A. (ed.) Modern Brazilian Poetry, 1962.
ABOUT: Burnshaw, S. (ed.) The Poem Itself, 1960; Nist, J. A. The Modernist Movement in Brazil, 1967; Twentieth-Century Writing, 1969; Who's Who in Latin-America: Brazil, 1947. *Periodicals*—Arizona Quarterly Autumn 1962; Books Abroad Winter 1967; Hispania December 1965; Journal of Inter-American Studies October 1963; New York Times October 15, 1968.

***"BANTI, ANNA" (pseudonym of Lucia Longhi Lopresti)** (1895–), Italian novelist, short story writer, biographer, and critic, was born in Florence of Calabrian parents with northern antecedents. Her father was an *avvocato di stato*, a state lawyer. She was educated in Rome, where she obtained her degree in art, and is married to the distinguished art historian Roberto Longhi.

Her first two books were collections of short stories—the largely autobiographical *Itinerario di Paolina* (Guide to Paolina, 1937) and *Il coraggio delle donne* (The Courage of Women, 1940). Then came a novel, *Sette lune* (Seven Moons, 1941), and more stories, *Le monache cantano* (The Nuns Sing, 1942). Her work was thought labored and verbose, but showed a steady improvement—a loosening in the style, a greater command of narrative technique—from book to book. And these early writings introduced her principal theme, the low status and sense of isolation of the intelligent woman in Italy.

The war diminished her output, and it was not until 1947 that the next book appeared. This was *Artemisia*, a novel based on the life of Artemisia Gentileschi, a sixteenth century artist who was "one of the first women to . . . maintain the right to spiritual parity between the sexes." It was this book, greatly admired by Bernard Berenson among others, which established Anna Banti's reputation. It was dramatized, and later reissued. *Le donne muoiono* (The Women Die), the volume of stories which followed in 1952, received the Viareggio Prize and (according to Harold Acton) "has become a minor classic."

The next few years were highly productive, suggesting that Anna Banti's periods of silence had been spent in research. Biographies of Fra Angelico and Lorenzo Lotto appeared in 1953, one of Diego Velásquez in 1955, and one of Claude Monet in 1956. Two novels, *Il bastardo* (The Bastard) and *Allarme sul lago* (Alarm on the Lake) were published in 1953 and 1954. The first, which attracted little attention at first, is now thought by some critics to have been much underestimated; the second, which won the Marzotto Prize, is the most fiercely feminist of Anna Banti's books, the most contemptuously pitying in its attitude to men.

* bän′ tē

ANNA BANTI

It might be said that her career reached its apogee in 1957. In February of that year an issue of *Fiera Letteraria* was devoted to her, with columns of praise from such writers as Pasolini and Bassani. The latter singled out as her masterpiece a story called "Arabella e affini" (Arabella and Her Relations), published in 1956. An earlier story, "Lavinia fuggita" (Lavinia Fled) was also much admired. Later in 1957 a novel, *La monaca di Sciangai* (The Nun of Shanghai), commended for the smoothness of its style, received the Veillon Prize.

A play, *Corte Savella* (Savella Court), appeared in 1960, and a biography of the energetic Greek-Italian novelist Mathilde Serao (with whom Anna Banti has been compared) in 1964. The most ambitious of her recent books were *Le mosche d'oro* (The Golden Flies, 1962), a long, acutely perceptive "novel of modern manners" written in the cinematic style then popular in Italy, and *Noi credevamo* (We Believed, 1967). The latter is set in the years following the Risorgimento and is based on the life of Signorina Banti's grandfather, who was imprisoned for subversive activities under the Bourbons of Naples. One English reviewer called it "the kind of hefty historical novel, sprinkled with 'real' characters, from Garibaldi downwards, that never gets beyond externals." Harold Acton disagreed, however, and said the book had struck him as "a profound parable for the young Communist intellectuals of today, doomed to disillusion, frustration and despair. As such it seemed to me courageous and original, a novel of unusual value."

This earnest, prolific, and versatile writer, famous and much honored in her own country, has not yet been translated into English. Some of the reasons for this are suggested by a critic in the *Times Literary Supplement* (September 28, 1967), who wrote: "Her qualities and limitations (not surprisingly, considering the position of women in much of Italy, even today) are strikingly suffragette-like. Ambitious and well-informed, prosy and humorless, she writes with a kind of dogged fluency at inordinate length."

For some years Anna Banti has been literary editor of the Milan magazine *Paragone*, in which her husband is responsible for art criticism. She reviews books and films, and has translated Virginia Woolf. A handsome woman, always well and quietly dressed, she is said to be rather formidable and even awe-inspiring in conversation.

ABOUT: Dizionario enciclopedico della letteratura italiana, 1966; Dizionario universale della letteratura contemporanea, 1959; Robertazzi, M. Scrittori italiani contemporanei, 1942. *Periodicals*—La Fiera Letteraria February 1957; Times Literary Supplement September 28, 1967; November 9, 1967 (letter).

BARAKA, IMAMU AMIRI. *See* JONES, (EVERETT) LEROI

"BARBETTE, JAY." *See* SPICER, BART

BARNETT, LINCOLN (KINNEAR) (February 12, 1909–), American journalist, writes: "I was born on Morningside Heights, New York City, on the 100th anniversary of the birth of Abraham Lincoln, which accounts for my first name and many of my attitudes. My father, Leon H. Barnett, a graduate of Columbia University '94, was a mining engineer and inventor with a philosophical bent which, although I did not realize it for many years, would have an important influence on my later work by planting in my mind an awareness of his greatest interest: cosmology. My mother, Jessie Kinnear, was a native of Denver, the daughter of a 'grub-staker' (i.e. a provider of funds and supplies to prospectors) and the owner of a chain of Colorado mining equipment stores. They met in Rico, Colorado, where my father was engineer for the Enterprise Gold Mine. I was their only child.

"When I was growing up in New York, I was much more drawn to my mother's intellectual interests—literature, history, the theatre—than to my father's scientific and philosophic poles. She read to me constantly as soon as I was old enough to listen—with particular emphasis on mythology. Long before I went to school I knew the stories of the *Iliad* and *Odyssey*, all the principal Greek and Roman myths, and Norse and German legends. Yet it was neither my father nor my mother who steered me to my calling. It was my godfather, F. Fraser Bond, an editorial writer on the New York *Times* and a professor at the Columbia School of Journalism, who concluded while keeping an eye on my academic progress at the Horace Mann School for Boys that I could perhaps one day become a writer. He insisted, however, that before attempting fiction it would be wise for me to acquire the kind of multifarious experience that newspaper work could provide—plus the editorial attention that dries out lush, subtropical prose. Though he was tolerant of the Edgar Allan Poe type of stories and verse I wrote for the literary quarterly at school, he saw to it that I was exposed to printer's ink. He often took me to the theatre on Saturday evenings, and after the show would drop into the *Times* to pick up messages and mail. The building at midnight vibrated with the roar of the rotating presses; the city room was aglare with lights and staccato with editorial energy. It seemed foreordained that I should be a reporter for the *Times*. As it turned out, I ended up on the New York *Herald Tribune*.

"From Horace Mann I went to Princeton University where I majored in English, danced in a couple of Triangle shows, tumbled on the varsity gym team, and toyed briefly with the idea of going into show business as an acrobatic dancer—a notion that met with no enthusiasm from my family. I received my B.A. degree in June 1929. That fall, just after I had started classes at the Columbia School of Journalism, the stock market crashed and my father lost everything. For the next two years I helped pay my tuition by working in the afternoons in the physical education department at Horace Mann. I also earned a bit of extra money by giving tap dancing lessons and performing at occasional school and college parties. In the spring of 1931 I received a B.Litt. degree from Columbia along with a scholarship entitling me to another year of study to work for an M.S. At the same time I landed a job as Columbia correspondent to the *Herald Tribune*. And the following year, having received my M.S., the famous city editor of the *Herald Tribune*, Stanley Walker, asked me to come on the city staff as a full-time reporter at twenty-five dollars a week.

"I remained with the *Herald Tribune* for six years in which I covered every conceivable kind of story—floods, fires, elections, trials, ship news, night district work, theatres, cute kid stuff and crime—until I knew I had experienced the entire spectrum of metropolitan journalism. Rising tensions in Europe made me eager to go abroad as a foreign correspondent, and I made my ambitions known to the management. Suddenly in September 1937, I was faced with an extraordinary dilemma. One day the managing editor told me that an opening had occurred in the Paris bureau and asked me how soon I could pack up and go. The very next day I was offered a job on the editorial staff of a ten-months-old picture magazine called *Life*. Although the *Herald Tribune* had granted what I long had begged for, I accepted the *Life* invitation for two overriding reasons. First my wife, the former Hildegarde Harris, a graduate of the University of Toronto, whom I had married in 1935, was at that moment threatened with a miscarriage and unable to travel. And secondly, the editor-in-chief of *Life*, Henry R. Luce, after a lengthy interview offered me exactly double the salary I was earning on the *Herald Tribune*—plus the promise of an overseas assignment in the future.

"Mr. Luce kept his promise. In the next decade I worked variously as a staff writer, domestic news editor, war correspondent (in England and North Africa, 1942–43), Hollywood correspondent, and articles editor. I wrote many biographical articles about famous people in all categories of life—among them General Eisenhower, General Marshall and Ernie Pyle during the war, later on Fred Astaire, Bing Crosby, Ingrid Bergman, Richard Rodgers, Tennessee Williams and J. Robert Oppenheimer. A collection of these biographical pieces and others, together with professional notes and comment, was published under the title *Writing on Life* in 1951.

"In 1946, aged thirty-seven, I decided to retire—not from journalism but from urban living, office hours and editorial routine. I gave up the security of a monthly pay check in return for the liberty of a freelance writer, and moved 275 miles northward to Westport, New York, on the shore of Lake Champlain, where I had spent many ecstatically happy summers from the age of fourteen. It was here, looking across a six-mile expanse of blue water to the Green Mountains of Vermont that I wrote my first book, *The Universe and Dr. Einstein*. It appeared, after initial serialization in *Harper's Magazine*, in a hard-back edition, with an introduction by Dr. Einstein, in January 1948. The following year it won a National Book Award Special Citation, and it has since been translated into more than twenty languages on every continent.

"The success of *The Universe and Dr. Einstein* induced the editors of *Life* to offer me a succession of science assignments which kept me occupied throughout the entire decade of the 1950s. Each consisted of an ambitious series of articles which appeared at intervals over many months and were then revised, elaborated and brought together in book form. The first and most notable series was *The World We Live In*, for which I received the Benjamin Franklin Magazine Award and the

LINCOLN BARNETT

American Association for the Advancement of Science—George Westinghouse Science Writing Award in 1953. I received both of these awards again in 1956 for a second series, *The Epic of Man*. The third and final *Life* series on natural science described Darwin's historic voyage aboard the Beagle and the impact of his observations on human thought; it appeared as a book in 1960, entitled *Wonders of Life on Earth*. My most recent book, *The Treasure of Our Tongue*, published in 1964, recounts the story of the English language from its obscure beginnings to its present eminence as the most widely-spoken language on earth today.

"My wife and I still live in Westport on Lake Champlain. We have two sons, Timothy Lincoln, born 1940, and Robert Morgan, who was born in 1949. Our house stands on a grassy bank above a beach from which we go swimming in summer and ice skating in winter. A half hour's drive brings us to the high peaks of the Adirondacks which we have climbed many times and hope to climb many times again."

The Universe and Dr. Einstein, Lincoln Barnett's account of the post-Newtonian revolution and of Einstein's theory of relativity, was recognized as a "classic" of science popularization, comparable "in maturity, clarity and grace with the . . . works of Sir James Jeans and Sir Arthur Eddington." Einstein himself called the book a "valuable contribution" and Thomas Mann found it more interesting than "any novel I had read in a long time." Barnett's contributions to *The World We Live In* and subsequent *Life* popularizations of science subjects were also much admired and much honored.

Before he acquired his reputation as a science writer, Barnett was already well known as "a master of the alert and delicate art of the interview." Sixteen of his biographical articles are collected in his second book, *Writing on Life*, in which he also explains his working methods. Barnett believes in gathering his information from his subjects themselves, rather than from books and clippings. "He puts a special value on those small revelatory facts that the biographer must observe for himself," wrote George Genzmer. "He says that he writes only about people whom he likes, and it is evident that his subjects like him."

A lover and student of the English language, Barnett in *The Treasure of Our Tongue* traces its long history and voices his fears for its future, threatened as it is on the one hand by pedants and jargoneers, on the other by ignorance and the growth of nonverbal methods of communication. Most reviewers expressed minor reservations and disagreements; most nevertheless welcomed the book warmly for its masterly organization, its "intensely interesting style," and for Barnett's "brilliant success in conveying his own excitement and delight in learning." The *Yale Review* called it "a splendid synthesis, for the layman, of the present state of our knowledge, and . . . also a contribution to a vital debate."

PRINCIPAL WORKS: The Universe and Dr. Einstein, 1948; Writing on Life: Sixteen Close-ups, 1951; The Treasure of Our Tongue: The Story of English from Its Obscure Beginnings to Its Present Eminence as the Most Widely Spoken Language, 1964. *With the editors of Life*—The World We Live In, 1955; The Wonders of Life on Earth 1960; The Epic of Man, 1962.
ABOUT: Fadiman, C. The Lifetime Reading Plan, 1960.

BARNSLEY, ALAN GABRIEL. *See* "FIELDING, GABRIEL"

***BARRACLOUGH, GEOFFREY** (May 10, 1908–), English historian, is the eldest son of Walter and Edith Barraclough. He was educated at Bootham School in York and at Oriel College, Oxford University. In 1931 he was Bryce Research Student at the University of Munich and Rome Scholar at the British School in Rome. Barraclough was elected a fellow of Merton College, Oxford, in 1934, and two years later moved to Cambridge, initially as a fellow and lecturer of St. John's College, then as a university lecturer (1937). During the first part of World War II he was attached to the Foreign Office and from 1942 to 1945 served in the Royal Air Force. In 1945 Barraclough went to the University of Liverpool as professor of medieval history.

The books he published during the 1930s were all concerned, directly or indirectly, with the

* bar′ ə cluf

GEOFFREY BARRACLOUGH

medieval history and influence of the papacy, an influence which he deplored and which preoccupied him to some extent even in his study *The Origins of Modern Germany* (1946). Believing that Germany's "present perplexities and problems" could be understood only in the light of its medieval history, Barraclough dealt in detail with the repeated interventions in German affairs of France and Rome, which (he said) sabotaged and delayed the country's unification. Many of Barraclough's colleagues found, as they often do, some of his ideas unacceptable but his scholarship impeccable—massively thorough and brilliantly organized in a way that some thought as Germanic as Barraclough's rather ponderous style. *Factors in German History* (1946) is a simplified version of the same book.

History in a Changing World, which followed in 1955, is one of Barraclough's most important and influential books. It is a collection of essays on various themes and periods but all urging a new view of European history. Barraclough, who acknowledged his debt to both Spengler and Toynbee, argued that it was foolish to approach twentieth century history through a study of the centuries immediately preceding it, as if history were an unbroken continuum. It is rather a succession of cycles in which civilizations rise and fall, "each inspired by a different spirit and each pursuing different aims," but each passing through similar phases. Such a process, begun in 1945, "when European society swung upwards, out of its existing course, on to a new plane," polarized around the two great new powers, the United States and the USSR. He wrote: "It is only a history that is universal in spirit—a history that looks beyond Europe and the West to humanity in all lands and ages—that can serve our purpose." Even those critics who thought these ideas misguided or overstated found the book both stimulating and important, and the medieval essays included in the volume were called "masterpieces, clear, judicious and without the exaggeration of the more polemical pieces."

In 1956 Barraclough succeeded Arnold Toynbee as Research Professor of International History at the University of London, where he remained until 1962. He subsequently taught at the University of California (1965–1968) and at Brandeis University (1968–1970). In 1970 he became Chichele Professor of Modern History in the University of Oxford, and a Fellow of All Souls. He is said to be working under the auspices of the Rockefeller Foundation on a major history of the twentieth century world. He gave a foretaste of what is to come in his relatively brief *Introduction to Contemporary History*. This work, as controversial as ever, proposed that contemporary, "postmodern," history began in 1960–1961, as power in the United States and the USSR passed into new hands, the Communist monolith began to disintegrate, and the emergent nations took up their positions on the world stage. These developments, in Barraclough's opinion, point to the decline of the West and the replacement of Western traditions of liberal humanism by more efficient forms of mass democracy. Barraclough's critics seemed disturbed less by his prophecies, which many of them discounted, than by his "Panglossian" readiness to accept a world in which technology and organization mattered more than individuals.

When Barraclough followed Toynbee at London University he also succeeded him (from 1956 to 1960) as editor of *The Survey of International Affairs*, where he "powerfully impressed his own personality" on the work of his contributors. Barraclough, a stimulating broadcaster and lecturer, is a former president of the Historical Association. In 1966, addressing that body, he allied himself with the new school of demographic historians, saying that if history is to survive as more than "high-class entertainment," it must substitute science for surmise and deal in the kind of hard statistical facts available in such records as the Domesday Book.

PRINCIPAL WORKS: Public Notaries and the Papal Curia, 1934; Papal Provisions: Aspects of Church History, Constitutional, Legal and Administrative, in the Later Middle Ages, 1935; (tr.) Medieval Germany, 911–1250: Essays by German Historians, 2 vols., 1938; Origins of Modern Germany, 1946; Factors in German History, 1946; History in a Changing World, 1955; (ed.) Social Life in Early England: Historical Association Essays, 1960; European Unity in Thought and Action, 1964; An Introduction to Contemporary History, 1964; The Medieval Papacy, 1968; (ed.) Eastern and Western Europe in the Middle Ages, 1970.

ABOUT: Who's Who, 1971. *Periodicals*—Nation April 13, 1957; May 11, 1957; New Statesman March 17, 1956; New York Times Book Review May 2, 1965; Times Literary Supplement September 13, 1934; May 16, 1935; March 2, 1956; World Politics January 1957.

BARTH, JOHN (SIMMONS) (May 27, 1930–), American novelist, was born in Cambridge, Maryland, the son of John Jacob and Georgia (Simmons) Barth. He has a twin sister, Jill, and an older brother, William. Music was his first vocation, and he was a professional jazz drummer and also a "dropout orchestration student" at the Juilliard School of Music before he enrolled as a journalism major at Johns Hopkins University, where he earned his B.A. in 1951 and his M.A. in 1952.

As an undergraduate Barth earned part of his tuition by shelving books in the university's classics library. There he discovered and immersed himself in *The Thousand and One Nights*, the *Gesta Romanorum*, the *Decameron*, and the other great tale cycles. At one time he began but did not finish a cycle of a hundred stories about Dorchester County, Maryland, and he has said that his "affair with Scheherazade is an old and continuing one." In 1953 Barth joined the faculty of Pennsylvania State University as an English instructor, becoming assistant professor in 1957 and associate professor in 1960.

Barth's first book (not published) was, he says cheerfully, "a long gloomy novel about libidinous cretins." *The Floating Opera*, inspired by childhood memories of a showboat, began as an attempt to write "a philosophical minstrel show" and wound up as a profoundly pessimistic but funny novel about a nihilistic small-town lawyer, Todd Andrews, who, finding nothing preferable to anything else, can see no reason why he should not follow his father's example and kill himself. After inhabiting a variety of roles—saint, rake, cynic—and quitting each when it appears no longer tenable, he decides that "if nothing makes any final difference, that fact makes no final difference either, and there is no more reason to commit suicide, say, than not to." It is a "very neat novel," an excellent intellectual joke, which in its humor and general oddness reminded many reviewers of *Tristram Shandy*.

The End of the Road is considered the weakest of Barth's books by some critics (but not by all; each of his books has its passionate champions). It is an existentialist (or anti-existentialist) comedy which begins: "In a sense, I am Jacob Horner." The narrator is a chronically indecisive neurotic who on his witch-doctor's advice teaches prescriptive grammar at a Maryland college, and becomes involved with a campus couple who endlessly analyze their

JOHN BARTH

"love relationship." With the husband's permission Horner has the wife, who then dies of an abortion. A plea for commitment or an attack upon it, depending on which critic is heard, it contains some brilliant scenes but was thought by most fatally uneven in tone.

Barth's first two novels are more or less orthodox, at least in form and language; his third is not. *The Sot-Weed Factor* is 806 pages of impeccable eighteenth century pastiche which attempts and achieves "a more contrived plot than *Tom Jones*." It recounts the adventures in England and the New World of Ebenezer Cooke, "sot-weed factor" (tobacco merchant) and would-be poet laureate of Maryland. Cook(e) was an actual historical personage but this is scarcely relevant. The book is a bawdy subversion of written history (including for example a remarkable *Secret Historie* of John Smith's relations with Pocahontas) and at the same time "a redoing of *Candide*" and an outrageous burlesque of the creaking devices and coincidences of the picaresque form itself. Richard Kostelanetz calls the novel "one of the most eloquently written books" and "one of the funniest, most erotic, and pervasively scatological novels," and indeed "one of the greatest works of fiction of our time." Leslie Fiedler found it "closer to the 'Great American Novel' than any other book of the last decade." Terry Southern said it was "prolix and overwhelmingly tedious," but went on: "This is, of course, an integral part of the book's destructive function. . . . Mr. Barth's sense of humor, in short, is an extremely advanced one."

Perhaps for this reason, *The Sot-Weed Factor*, in spite of critical encomiums, was not at first much read. *Time* magazine reported in 1967 that Barth's first three novels "together sold fewer than 8,000 copies." Nevertheless, *The Sot-Weed Factor* and to some extent its predecessors enjoyed a healthy "underground" reputation, especially among intelligent undergraduates, to whom the general excitement which greeted Barth's fourth novel must have seemed a little belated.

Giles Goat-Boy, like *The Sot-Weed Factor*, is a very long and complex book and difficult to summarize usefully. Barth believes that "the best fantastical stories are the result of similes turned into metaphors," and in this one the world is a university divided into a West and an East campus. The coming is prophesied of a new Grand Tutor who will bring a Revised New Syllabus. This messiah may (or may not) be Giles Goat-Boy, who is perhaps part goat and was possibly fathered by Wescac, a giant computer. The book describes Giles's quest for the truth about his birth; his heroic descent into the fearsome bowels of Wescac to amend its programming; his career as a messiah in search of a message, as a husband and father, and as a scapegoat. Along the way many contemporary, historical, fictional, and typical personages are introduced in a variety of guises, and there are metaphorical references to a vast range of contemporary dilemmas. There is also a nearly full-length parody in rhymed couplets of *Oedipus Tyrannus*, and numerous other diversions. Burlesqued editorial paraphernalia at the beginning and end cast doubt on the worth, authorship, and authenticity of the entire work. It borrows its story line from the recurrent myth of the questing hero, and parodies among other things this myth, the New Testament, the Swiftian satire, and itself.

The publication of *Giles Goat-Boy* was a major literary event. The novel received long front-page reviews, was distributed by two book clubs, and became a best seller. Its critical reception was nevertheless rather mixed. One or two reviewers were excited enough to call it a great novel, and for one it confirmed Barth's standing "as perhaps the most prodigally gifted comic novelist writing in English today." But another found it cumbersome and philosophically naïve and Denis Donoghue thought it "sprightly in rare paragraphs" but "too long, too tedious, a dud." Even among its admirers, "none ever wished it longer than it is." A. Alvarez in his *Observer* review of *Giles Goat-Boy* was unable to "subscribe to the claims that Barth is saying profound things about Religion and the Human Condition" and said that "at no point does the book seem motivated by anything more profound than supreme ingenuity." Richard Poirier in *Book Week* found in it a recommendation of the simple values —peace, the pleasures of the body, love—and added: "Barth writes not so much in praise of these things but in search of them through the labyrinths that have been made of life." Another reviewer seemed to find the book's meaning in its assertion that man is and must be "committed and condemned to knowledge," which squares with Stanley Edgar Hyman's belief, drawn from his reading of *The Sot-Weed Factor*, that for Barth "ignorance of the world . . . is bad, destructive to the innocent and to those who come in contact with him."

There is, however, wide agreement that John Barth, with four novels behind him, is one of the best and most promising American novelists, a writer of great originality and erudition, the possessor of a "brilliant philosophical mind," with a marvelous command of language, an unsurpassed talent for parody, and a fine bawdy wit. He is deficient, it has been said, in psychological insight; is inclined (sometimes deliberately) to prolixity; and in his earlier novels at least sometimes failed to "hold his comic perspective." His friend Leslie Fiedler calls Barth an "existentialist comedian" and "the best, the most achieved" novelist of his generation. Others have located him in the tradition of the "anti-novel," and Richard Poirier places him, with Sterne and Joyce, as an exponent of the "novel of self-parody, which takes pleasure in exposing the limits of its own procedures" and makes "structures in order to blow them up." Barth himself, who believes that the novel "may be nearing the end of its line," admires writers like Beckett, Borges, and Nabokov who "have been able to turn this ultimacy against itself in order to produce new work." This is what he is doing most often in *Lost in the Funhouse*, a collection of pieces written for voice and tape recorder, together with other kinds of fictional experiments. Most of these stories are self-consciously concerned with "what happens when a writer writes" (and what happens when a reader reads)—with "the metaphysical plight of imagination engaging with imagination." The same is true of *Chimera*, a volume of three interconnected novellas having to do with Scheherazade, John Barth, Perseus, Bellerophon, and other mythical figures. There was much admiration for the book's structural ingenuity, though Michael Wood complained that Barth will not let his writing "loose from the safe zones of pastiche . . . as if he would rather not know where the limits of his talent lie." *Chimera* was joint winner (with John Williams's *Augustus*) of the 1973 National Book Award for fiction.

In 1965 Barth went as professor of English to the State University of New York at Buffalo. The following year he received a grant from the National Institute of Arts and Letters. Barth was married in 1950 to Harriette Anne Strickland and has three children by her, Christine, John, and Daniel. He made a second marriage in 1970, to Shelly Rosenberg. *Time* magazine says that he is "a tall, unassuming man with a prematurely bald head and an understated moustache." He brews his own beer, hunts deer with bow and arrow, and occasionally plays drums with a local jazz band. His first three novels were republished, with some revisions, in 1967.

Barth outlined some of his attitudes and opinions in *Book Week* (September 26, 1965), in an essay which begins with a plea that he never be numbered among the "black humorists," who are "in their way *responsible*." He begs to be spared from "Social-Historical Responsibility, and in the last analysis from every other kind as well, except Artistic." However, Barth says, "the use of historical or legendary material, especially in a farcical spirit, has a number of technical virtues, among which are esthetic distance and the opportunity for counter-realism. . . . In passionate, mysterious farce, it seems to me, lies also the possibility of transcending . . . the distinction between Tragedy and Mystery . . . the finest expressions respectively of the Western and Eastern spirits." At the end he returns to praising "the story of deflowered Scheherazade, yarning tirelessly through the dark hours to save her neck"—a figure for "the estate of the fictioner in general and the particular endeavors and aspirations of this one, at least, who can wish for nothing better than to spin like the vizier's excellent daughter, through what nights remain to him, tales within tales within tales."

PRINCIPAL WORKS: The Floating Opera, 1956; The End of the Road, 1958; The Sot-Weed Factor, 1960; Giles Goat-Boy, or, the Revised New Syllabus, 1966; Lost in the Funhouse: Fiction for Print, Tape, Live Voice, 1968; Chimera, 1972.

ABOUT: Contemporary Authors 1, 1962; Current Biography, 1969; Fiedler, L. A. Waiting for the End, 1964; Hyman, S. E. Standards, 1960; Kostelanetz, R. (ed.) The New American Arts, 1965; Who's Who in America, 1972–1973. *Periodicals*—Book Week September 26, 1965; August 7, 1966; Horizon January 1963; New York Review of Books August 18, 1966; New York Times Book Review May 8, 1966; August 7, 1966; September 24, 1972; Time March 17, 1967; Wisconsin Studies in Contemporary Literature Winter–Spring 1965.

***BARTHELME, DONALD** (April 7, 1931–), American short story writer, was born in Philadelphia, the eldest of the five children of Donald Barthelme and the former Helen Bechtold. He had a Roman Catholic upbringing in Houston, Texas, where his father was professor of architectural design at Houston University. It was Barthelme's father who introduced him to modern art, in all its forms, and provided his first important literary influence when he gave him an anthology of modern French poetry. At the university he relinquished Catholicism and adopted an existentialist philos-

* bär′ thul mē

DONALD BARTHELME

ophy. He served in Korea (after the war) and then returned to Houston, where he worked as a journalist, as a university public relations man, as a magazine editor, and as curator of a modern art gallery. His friend Herman Gollob came to think of him at that time as "one of the great despairers," as well as a man with "a great sense of camaraderie."

His stories began to appear in the early 1960s, mostly in the *New Yorker*. Some of them are more or less orthodox in appearance; others consist (for example) of a hundred numbered sentences or a single sentence, or masquerade as essays, or are in question and answer form. They fully enact such dicta of Barthelme's as that "the only forms I trust are fragments," and "the principle of collage is the central principle of all art in the twentieth century." He means that the optimistic assumptions and rational development of traditional prose fiction disqualify it as a mode in which to describe a mad and wicked world. Barthelme is a moralist in that all his fiction expresses, in satirical terms, his despair at this madness and wickedness. The strain that such unhealthy realities impose on *any* kind of coherent literary discourse—and hence a radical literary self-consciousness—is another central element in his work—one he shares with Joyce, Beckett, Borges, and Nabokov, as well as such younger writers as John Barth and Kurt Vonnegut.

Barthelme's first book, *Come Back, Dr. Caligari*, reduced many reviewers to something approaching incoherence: "You have to read it to believe it," one wrote. Among these "short verbal objects," as *Newsweek* gingerly called them, is one about Batman, but Batman in ignominy and failure, retrieved from disaster only by the efforts of his friends. Another is a parable about the outraged public reaction to a demonstration "against the human condition." A third considers the plight of a grown man who is obliged to spend his days in a sixth-grade classroom, and a fourth is a monologue spoken by a deserted husband who has moved into a radio station and there rehearses the history of his marriage while the transmitter plays "The Star-Spangled Banner." Some of these stories are experiments in literary pop art resembling the surrealist prose poems of S. J. Perelman—unnerving juxtapositions of "solemn absurdities from ads, comic-books, mail-order catalogs, record-blurbs, and instruction-leaflets."

On the whole, the volume impressed even those critics it confounded. There was much praise for Barthelme's word play, his mastery of the "humor of the non-sequitur," and his "outrageous imagination." The principal criticisms were of a certain monotony of tone and a tendency in the "pop" stories for "the dead voice of the found prose . . . to choke out the voice of the narration altogether." Even in Barthelme's relatively naturalistic stories, Robert M. Adams suggested, his dialogues "often resound against a curious blank wall of dead nothing . . . in a desolate landscape littered with pathetic fragments of useless speech-patterns. It is a book written as if with verbal components from a used-car graveyard." *Snow White*, the "slight, derisive" novella that followed, is a dark paraphrase of the fairy tale. Morris Dickstein said that it "mainly limited itself to fragmentary take-offs on a huge variety of rhetorical styles and verbal trash. . . . The book was all language, and the language was not good enough to carry it."

In Barthelme's next book, a second volume of stories called *Unspeakable Practices, Unnatural Acts*, most critics found both increased technical mastery and a clearer sense of purpose; as Dickstein wrote: "The fragments began insidiously to cohere, into pointed fables like 'The Balloon' and 'The Police Band,' into surreal and indirect political commentary, such as 'The President' and 'Robert Kennedy Saved From Drowning.'" One of the most admired stories in this collection, "The Indian Uprising," is an account of a Comanche attack on what might be Manhattan. Barricades are built from the emblems of the good life—wine, sex, slogans, conversation: they are useless; the savages are already within the gates. No doubt they always were. William H. Gass called this story "a triumph of style, achieving with the most unlikely materials an almost lyrical grace and beauty." He went on to say that in such stories as this "Barthelme has managed to place himself in the center of modern consciousness."

The stories collected in *City Life* represented for many readers "the maturing of a major talent."

These pieces were on the whole less topical and political, more literary and personal—meditations on Tolstoy and Kierkegaard, speculations about angels thrown out of work by the death of God. Richard Schickel suggests that Barthelme is preoccupied with the fragmentary and disjunctive because he so yearns for order and wholeness; like his angels he is searching for "a new principle," in stories which increasingly involve the reader's emotions as well as his mind. Schickel is not alone in thinking him "the most interesting writer of fiction in America."

Donald Barthelme lives in Greenwich Village with his Danish third wife, Birgit, and their small daughter. He is a red-haired, blue-eyed man who dresses conservatively, lives quietly, and dislikes publicity and literary gatherings. He attended one of the latter in 1972, nevertheless, to receive a National Book Award for his first children's book, *The Slightly Irregular Fire Engine*—and made an acceptance speech so witty that many in the audience felt that it also should get a prize. The NBA jurors described the book (which Barthelme illustrated as well as wrote) as one "of originality, wit and intellectual adventure . . . [It] is at once elegant and playful, and each re-reading discovers fresh surprises and delights."

PRINCIPAL WORKS: Come Back, Dr. Caligari, 1964; Snow White, 1967; Unspeakable Practices, Unnatural Acts, 1968; City Life, 1970; The Slightly Irregular Fire Engine, or The Hithering Thithering Djinn (for children), 1971; Sadness, 1972.

ABOUT: Contemporary Authors 21–22, 1969. *Periodicals*—Atlantic July 1968; Book Week May 31, 1964; May 21, 1967; Commonweal December 29, 1967; Critic June 1968; Nation June 8, 1964; June 19, 1967; May 27, 1968; New Republic May 2, 1964; June 3, 1967; June 1, 1968; New York Review of Books April 30, 1964; August 24, 1967; April 25, 1968; New York Times Book Review April 12, 1964; May 21, 1967; April 26, 1970; New York Times Magazine August 16, 1970; Newsweek April 13, 1964; May 22, 1967; Saturday Review April 4, 1964; Wilson Library Bulletin December 1962.

***BARTHES, ROLAND** (November 12, 1915–), French critic, was educated at the University of Paris, where he studied literature and classics and founded the Groupe Théâtral Antique. The beginning of his career was delayed by a serious and prolonged attack of tuberculosis. During World War II, he joined the Centre National de Recherche Scientifique, where he devoted himself to sociological and lexicological research. The results of these studies are evident in all his work. Barthes was a cofounder of the magazine *Théâtre populaire*. He has taught at the Sorbonne and in Egypt and Rumania, and in 1967–1968 he was a visiting professor at Johns Hopkins University. He is now director of studies in the sixth section of the École

ROLAND BARTHES

Pratique des Hautes Études, where he teaches a course in the sociology of signs, symbols, and collective representations.

Barthes is the central figure in a new critical movement which, after adding Freudian, Marxist, and existentialist theories to the "psychological intuitism" of Gaston Bachelard, has evolved in the direction of the structuralist analysis of language. His views were first adumbrated in a series of articles which appeared in *Combat* in 1947 and were enlarged and published in book form as *Le Degré zéro de l'écriture* (1953, translated as *Writing Degree Zero*).

Language, Barthes believes, is a "system of signs" reflecting the attitudes and assumptions of a particular society at a given time. Literature is a product of the relationship between language, with all its social and historical implications, and the writer's own personal vision or opinion, expressed in his *style*. Throughout the seventeenth, eighteenth, and early nineteenth centuries, there was little conflict between the writer and his society and there was in effect a "single style"; since then "the unity of the bourgeois ideology" has been shattered and the classical style has been replaced by a multiplicity of styles and experiments.

In modern poetry, since Rimbaud, "the word is no longer directed in advance by the general intent of socialized speech: the consumer of poetry, deprived of the guidance of selective associations, comes upon the Word head-on, and receives it as an absolute quality, accompanied by all its possibilities." Thus "modern poetry is an objective poetry"—one "without prevision or permanence of intent," able to exploit "the sonorous and

* bart

semantic accident" and achieve "the splendor and freshness of dreamed language." Poetry of this kind, "inhuman," unconcerned with coherence, leads towards silence, "to the doors of a world without literature about which, however, it will be necessary for the writers to testify."

An alternative is "invisible" writing—"writing degree zero"—a form of expression which would assert no ideological position, would not even bear the stamp of the author's personality, but would, with the purity of a mathematical statement, disclose "the human condition." Barthes commends examples of this kind of "blank" writing in the work of the French "new novelists," among others, and suggests that it may provide a new "common language." If it did so, not all critics would welcome the development. And indeed Barthes's theories lead him to some strange positions: he is disdainful of the great stylists, from Flaubert to Gide, and praises Sartre on the grounds that it was "never said that he wrote well."

The essays collected in *Mythologies* (1957; selection translated under same title by Annette Lavers) represent a frequently entertaining but very serious attempt to analyze the "myths" that underlie such phenomena as fashion, striptease, personality cults, advertising campaigns, and other nonverbal expressions of social attitudes—all of them, as Barthes points out, "extralinguistic languages." This book has been much admired and enjoyed, but there was less enthusiasm for *Système de la mode* (1967), in which Barthes reverts for 330 pages to the social implications of fashion, implacably applying all the paraphernalia of linguistic analysis to such magazines as *Vogue* and *Elle*. At least one critic suspected a spoof but sadly rejected the possibility.

Sur Racine (1963, translated as *On Racine*) contains three fundamentally Freudian essays on the dramatist, whose theme, Barthes asserts, "is the use of force within a situation that is generally erotic." Martin Turnell considers this book "the most lucid, as well as the most enjoyable, exercise in practical criticism that [Barthes] has so far given us." It nevertheless provoked from the distinguished scholar Raymond Picard a brilliant rebuttal which began an extremely stimulating literary controversy. Picard's essay, *Nouvelle critique ou nouvelle imposture* (New Criticism Or New Imposture, 1965), accuses Barthes of generalizing from inadequate evidence, of inventing pseudoscientific neologisms which are more or less meaningless, of inconsistency, and of "dogmatic impressionism."

Barthes's *Essais critiques* (1964, translated by Richard Howard) discuss a number of individual writers and probe the relationship between literature and criticism. Criticism in his view should concern itself neither with value judgments nor with the meaning of the work under discussion, but rather with an analysis of the system of signs by which that meaning is expressed. It is a matter of "*fitting together*, in the manner of a skilled cabinetmaker, the language of the day . . . and the language of the author." In the view of many Anglo-Saxon readers, accustomed to a less abstract procedure, this tends to be an exercise of principal interest to the critic himself.

In France Barthes's reputation has suffered, at least in academic circles, from the effects of Picard's essay and the ensuing controversy. *Éléments de sémiologie* (1964, translated as *Elements of Semiology*), an introduction to the linguistic theories of structuralism's founder, Ferdinand de Saussure, was seized upon by Leo Bersani as evidence of Barthes's "evolution toward rococo banality." Nevertheless —and whether or not his views are accepted—the very extremity and ruthlessness of his attack on all that is most literary in literary criticism has been salutary and has influenced even British and American critics raised in a very different social and intellectual ambience. An editorial in the *Times Literary Supplement* in 1966 pointed out that "for many people M. Barthes is *the* critic of the moment, the person whose difficult and often oracular pronouncements are quoted by writers and intellectuals, and who has stepped into the place left partly vacant through Jean-Paul Sartre's absorption in politics."

PRINCIPAL WORKS IN ENGLISH TRANSLATION: On Racine, 1964; Elements of Semiology, 1964; Writing Degree Zero, 1967; Critical Essays, 1972; Mythologies, 1972. *Articles in* Partisan Review Winter 1967; Times Literary Supplement September 27, 1963; September 28, 1967.

ABOUT: Doubrovsky, S. Pourquoi la nouvelle critique, vol. 1, 1966; Mauriac, C. The New Literature, 1959; Picard, R. Nouvelle critique ou nouvelle imposture, 1965. *Periodicals*—Times Literary Supplement September 30, 1965; February 3, 1966; June 15, 1967; September 28, 1967; October 12, 1967; March 24, 1972.

***BARZINI, LUIGI (GIORGIO)** (December 21, 1908–), Italian journalist, writes: "I was born in Milan. My father came from a middle-class family of Orvieto, my mother from Venice. My father was Italy's most famous journalist of his time. As a correspondent for *Corriere della Sera*, he covered most great events at the beginning of the century, including the Boxer rebellion in China (1900) and the Russian-Japanese war (he was the only European journalist at the battle of Mukden); in 1907 he took part with Prince Borghese in an automobile race from Peking to Paris, which they won. When I was a schoolboy I saw very little of him, as he was covering the Italo-Turkish war, the Balkan wars, the first World War and the subsequent peace conference.

* bär dzē′ nē

"I studied in Italy until 1925, when the family moved to the United States, where my father had founded in 1921 the *Corriere d'America*, an Italian language daily in New York. There I attended the Columbia School of Journalism, class of 1930. While studying I worked for a time as a cub reporter on the old New York *World*. Back in Italy I was hired by the *Corriere della Sera* and covered important international events of the succeeding decade: the beginning of the Roosevelt era in the United States, the conquest of Ethiopia, the Chinese-Japanese war, etc. During the Chinese-Japanese war I was on board the U.S. river gunboat Panay, which was bombed by Japanese planes on the Yangtze and sunk. In 1940, on my return to Italy after a few months in London, I was arrested by the police and sentenced to five years' house arrest for anti-Fascist activities. I spent those years mostly reading and taking notes for a book on Italy which I had in mind to write some day, if I ever could find the time and the patience to do so. I resumed my work as a journalist when the Allies entered Rome. I published and edited two dailies (*Il Globo* and *Libera Stampa*). I went back to the *Corriere della Sera* again for a few years, contributed to weeklies, wrote books and plays. I started again to write occasional articles in English for American and English magazines. In 1953 I published with Random House a survey of the United States, *Americans Are Alone in the World*, originally written in English, which was later translated into several languages.

"I had taken an active part in politics and in 1958 I was elected to Parliament for the Italian Liberal Party. I was re-elected in 1963. Yet my idea of writing a deep and accurate study of the Italian people, for which I had been gathering notes for so many years, still haunted me. A good friend, Mike Bessie of Atheneum, asked me for this book. In 1960 I had a heart attack which kept me in bed for a few months. Realizing death was nearer than I thought, I got down to work in earnest, hoping to leave a lasting book behind me. It took me three years to finish the job. *The Italians* came out in the United States in August 1964 and was on the best-seller list until the following June. It was the fruit of long observations, reflections and reading by an Italian who had been exposed to the way of life of the English-speaking world. I was trying to understand the reasons for the boastful vagaries of the Fascist regime and its subsequent complete collapse and, looking back, the tormented politics of my country through the centuries. The book has recently been translated into Italian, German, French, Spanish, Japanese and other languages.

"I have been married twice and have five children, three daughters and two sons."

LUIGI BARZINI

The three years invested in the writing of *The Italians* were, as Barzini indicates, well justified by the result. It is a "socio-psychological essay on the Italian character," seen in the light of the country's history. Barzini concludes that his countrymen's great gifts are seriously flawed, above all by their inability to face facts, their weakness for self-deluding optimism and the theatrical gesture, their fondness for "the baroque as an escape from humiliation." Along the way he touches on nearly every aspect of Italian life—the country's repeated failure to unite against foreign invaders, its political and religious extremism, its mother cult, its bourgeois snobberies, the Mafia, everyday habits, customs, and attitudes. Two of the best chapters are those on Cola di Rienzo and Benito Mussolini, two personifications of the "national reliance on make-believe as an instrument of policy."

The Italians is a work in the tradition of G. A. Borgese's *Goliath* and Leo Olschki's *The Genius of Italy*. But Borgese was a polemicist, shrewd but embittered, and Olschki a social philosopher; Barzini is an engaging, witty, and highly articulate journalist. He does not spare his compatriots in his urbane and somewhat mischievous assessment of their foibles, and the book brought anguished protests from sensitive Italo-Americans. It is fair to add that in Italy it was accepted with more understanding and, though some readers were ruffled, more were amused. It became a best seller in both English and Italian and has made Barzini's name well known throughout Europe. A number of essays and magazine articles on the same subject were published later as *From Caesar to the Mafia: Sketches of Italian Life*.

Americans Are Alone in the World, which Barzini says was "originally written in English," in fact appeared first in Italian as *Gli americani sono soli al mondo* (1952). In approach it is similar to *The Italians*, dealing quite frankly with the political innocence and moral self-righteousness of Americans, their worship of machinery and statistics, and other familiar themes. A large part of the book is concerned with America's role in world politics: its obligations, as Barzini sees them, its options and interests. In these pages the author speaks, one may say, for the general community of concerned, middle-of-the-road Europeans. The book received rather a cool reception in the United States, where one reviewer wrote that "if this is the view Europeans get of America [it is no wonder that] foreigners are paralyzed with apprehension."

Barzini has also written a play, *I disarmati* (published in *Il dramma* 256, 1958), a translation of Huxley's *The Giaconda Smile*, and several volumes of political essays and reports. Of the latter the best known is *L'Europa domani mattina* (Europe Tomorrow Morning, 1964), based on the author's conversations with statesmen and prominent personages throughout Europe. Its thesis is that the day of a truly and effectively united Europe is in the offing, and that such a solution is not only predictable but essential if the subcontinent is to survive. Here again Barzini speaks for many Europeans of his generation; if his ideas are not particularly original they are set forth with persuasive—and very readable—cogency.

There has been much praise for Barzini's mastery of English, but he himself speaks modestly of his skill. "Perhaps," he says, "it is easier to write in a language not one's own because one is always conscious of artifice. . . . I wake up in the middle of the night worrying about the place of an adjective. And perhaps my English is simply another form of Italian *virtuosismo*, an Italian *trompe-l'œil* English good enough to deceive people, like painted stucco marble."

PRINCIPAL WORKS IN ENGLISH TRANSLATION: Americans Are Alone in the World, 1953; The Italians, 1964; From Caesar to the Mafia: Sketches of Italian Life, 1971; Peking to Paris, 1973.

ABOUT: Contemporary Authors 13–14, 1965; Current Biography, 1972; International Who's Who, 1971–1972; Who's Who in America, 1972–1973. *Periodicals*—Book Week May 16, 1965; Encounter December 1964; New York Times Book Review January 3, 1954; August 23, 1964; New Yorker October 31, 1953; September 12, 1964; Times (London) September 25, 1964; Times Literary Supplement October 22, 1964; Vogue October 15, 1965.

***BASSANI, GIORGIO** (March 4, 1916–), Italian novelist, short story writer, poet, and editor, is the son of a Jewish physician from Ferrara, Angelo Bassani, and the former Dora Minerbi. He was born in Bologna and returned there to study literature at the university, but lived mostly in Ferrara until 1943, when he was arrested by the Blackshirts. He spent some time in prison before the fall of Fascism later the same year. Subsequently he took part in the Resistance, in Florence and in Rome, and he has lived in Rome ever since.

* bä sä′ nē

Bassani's first story appeared in *Letteratura* in 1938. His first book, a collection of stories and poems called *Una città di pianura* (A City of the Plain), was published in 1940 under the pseudonym of Giacomo Marchi. According to Bassani it was not until 1942 that he started writing verse seriously. A volume of his poems, *Storie dei poveri amanti* (Tales of Poor Lovers), was published in 1945 and reissued in 1946 with additional poems. Two more collections appeared in 1947 and 1951, and *L'alba ai vetri* (Dawn on the Window Panes), a selection of the poems written between 1942 and 1950, was published in 1963. Bassani's verse, not the most important part of his work, is (like his prose) classical and restrained. Before 1942 his poems were somewhat boyish and immature. Though the persecution of the Jews and his own war experiences changed that, there is still something reserved and stifled about his work in this form, and he seems to have written relatively little verse since 1950.

From 1948 to 1961 Bassani was assistant editor of Marguerite Caetani's influential multilingual literary magazine *Botteghe Oscure*, and from 1953 to 1955 he co-edited the Milanese review *Paragone*. The Milanese publishing house Feltrinelli employed him from 1958 to 1964 as a literary adviser, and in that capacity he selected a library of some eighty volumes of modern classics and contemporary works. To Bassani belongs the credit for the discovery of Lampedusa's *The Leopard*, to which he wrote a foreword. Meanwhile his own work continued to appear. He published a collection of three stories, *La passeggiata prima di cena* (Walk Before Supper) in 1953, and two years later a novella, *Gli ultimi anni di Clelia Trotti* (The Last Year of Clelia Trotti), which won the Charles Veillon prize.

It was his next book, *Cinque storie ferraresi*, that brought Bassani fame, winning the Strega Prize when it was published in 1956. It contains five novellas (all previously published elsewhere) which together present a composite picture of a large provincial town—the Ferrara of Bassani's youth—and the gradual seeping into it of the poisons of Fascism and anti-Semitism. The characters in these stories were to reappear in Bassani's later fiction. They include the rich and exclusive Jewish family, the Finzi-Continis; the valiant anti-Fascist Clelia Trotti; the young narrator, a middle-class Jewish intellectual who is at least partly Bassani himself; his brother Ernesto and sister Fanny; and several others.

Through the lives of these few individuals, a strong sense of an entire community is brilliantly conveyed, with ironic acknowledgment of its class-bound narrowness and nostalgia for its innocence. The book has been translated by Isabel Quigly as *A Prospect of Ferrara* and by William Weaver as *Five Stories of Ferrara.*

Gli occhiali d'oro, first published in *Paragone*, appeared in book form in 1958 and in Isabel Quigly's English version as *The Gold-Rimmed Spectacles* in 1960. It is another story of Ferrara, with the same narrator, in which a respected Jewish physician, Dr. Fadigati, is driven to ruin and suicide by his homosexual passion for a young thief. It was enthusiastically received by the Italian critics, who compared it with Melville's *Bartleby* and Mann's *Death in Venice*, and the American reviewers welcomed it with almost equal warmth. A. J. Guérard called it "a small triumph of controlled perspective" which "develops with minute care its counterpointed stories of sexual and political exile." He praised its total freedom from meretricious appeal, but added: "It is necessary to observe (and at last to complain) that this deliberately gray and muted novel lacks energy and vivacity . . . to a really extreme degree." All of the Ferrara stories then published, and two new ones, were collected in *Le storie ferraresi* (1960).

Bassani's first full-length novel, and his most important work to date, winner of the Viareggio Prize, was *Il giardino dei Finzi-Contini* (1962, translated by Isabel Quigly as *The Garden of the Finzi-Continis*). The setting and the characters are as in the novellas; the narrator is the same sensitive young intellectual; the time, as usual, is the late 1930s. Racial persecution is mounting in Ferrara and to escape the ugliness outside the two Finzi-Contini children are confined to the great garden of their house. There the young narrator becomes infatuated with Micòl, the Finzi-Continis' pampered daughter, and this leads to a disintegration of relationships, an end of innocence, which mirrors on a small scale the corrupting moral chaos outside. At the beginning of the book the narrator recalls the Finzi-Contini family tomb, and at the end he observes that only one of them is buried there. The rest had been deported, and no one knew their graves. The work seemed to some English and American reviewers too artful, too cultivated a treatment of its brutal theme, but Steven Marcus, among others, praised it as a work of piety, "a graceful and charming elegy" for the Jews of Ferrara, and a reviewer in the *Times Literary Supplement* thought it "a delicate and profound personal story for which it is difficult to find a comparison." In fact, critics have been most often reminded by Bassani's "cool, dry prose style" of Manzoni, Henry James, or Flaubert; while his preoccupation with things past evokes comparisons with Joyce and above all with Proust. Like Proust, Donald Heiney has suggested, "Bassani is a specialist in decadence. Decadence and nostalgia; the gradual corruption of his characters is seen always through a veil of time that lends it a curiously haunting and poetic effect." Vittorio de Sica's film version of the novel has been disowned by Bassani.

GIORGIO BASSANI

Dietro la porta (1964, translated by William Weaver as *Behind the Door*), another short Ferrara novel, attracted less attention. However *L'airone* (1968), a study of an alienated, anachronistic Ferrarese landowner during a single day's hunting, was a best seller in Italy and was warmly admired in its English translation, *The Heron*. *Le parole preparate* (Prepared Words) is a volume of literary criticism. From 1964 to 1966 Bassani was vice president of RAI, the Italian state radio and television service, and from 1957 to 1968 taught theatre history at the Rome Academy of Dramatic Art. He is a short, stocky man, dark-haired and voluble. Bassani was married in 1943 to Valeria Sinigallia and has a son and a daughter. His favorite recreation is tennis. In 1969 he received both the Campiello Prize and the Nelly Sachs Prize.

PRINCIPAL WORKS IN ENGLISH TRANSLATION: The Gold-Rimmed Spectacles, 1960; A Prospect of Ferrara, 1962 (also translated as Five Stories of Ferrara, 1971); The Garden of the Finzi-Continis, 1965; The Heron, 1970; Behind the Door, 1972. *Stories in* Commentary October 1958; Trevelyan, R. (ed.) Italian Writing Today, 1967; *Story and poems in* Caetani, M. (ed.) An Anthology of New Italian Writers, 1951.

ABOUT: Curley, D. N. and Curley, A. (eds.) Modern Romance Literature (A Library of Literary Criticism), 1967; Dizionario enciclopedico della letteratura Italiana, 1966; Dizionario universale della letteratura contemporanea, 1959; Harward, T. B. (ed.) European Patterns,

1966; Trevelyan, R. (ed.) Italian Writing Today, 1967. *Periodicals*—Comunità VI, 1952; L'Espresso 6, 1956; 26, 1958; Letteratura e ideologia, 1964; Il Mondo XII, 1945; La Nuova Europa, 1945; Nuovi Argomenti January–March 1966; Paragone VI, 1952; Reporter November 18, 1965; Saturday Review August 27, 1960; July 24, 1965; Times Literary Supplement September 2, 1965.

BASTARD, LUCIEN. *See* "ESTANG, LUC"

***BATAILLE, GEORGES** (September 10, 1897–July 9, 1962), French poet, novelist, and philosopher, was the son of a tax collector who became blind and then paralyzed. He was born in Billom (Puy-de-Dôme). He attended the *lycée* at Chartres and, after passing his *baccalauréat*, studied to become a paleographic archivist. Bataille was married and had two children. He began his career as a librarian, rising to the position of deputy keeper at the Bibliothèque Nationale in Paris, where he worked until 1942. During this time he became friendly with Michel Leiris and André Masson. He was a member of the Communist party from 1931 to 1934.

His association with the surrealists left its mark on some of his work, particularly his poetry, but at the heart of all his writing is his obsession with God, or rather with the absence of God. From his youth Bataille had made a study of mysticism. He was much influenced by the anthropologist Marcel Mauss, and admired the cultures of the Aztecs and the American Indians. He had also made a particular study of the German philosophers—Hegel, Heidegger, and especially Nietzsche, whom he regarded as his master. All these influences, together with the Catholicism which he rejected and which left his life in "disorder," played their part in shaping his ideas. He came to distinguish between a "profane" human world of reason and order, and a "sacred" world of animalism, characterized by disorder, cruelty, and excess.

Because of his position at the Bibliothèque Nationale, where his duties included the editorship of the learned journal *Documents*, the books in which he expressed his views were at the beginning published pseudonymously. The first of them was *L'Histoire de l'œil* (Story of the Eye, 1928), published as by "Lord Auch," but reissued under his own name in 1967. It is a matter-of-fact account of sexual excess involving a group of middle-class adolescents and built around a complex sequence of interrelated metaphors. Other works in the same vein include *Le Mort* (also reissued by Pauvert in 1967), turning on the relationship between death and sexuality, and *Madame Edwarda* (1937), published as by "Pierre Angélique."

It was not until 1944, after Bataille had left the Bibliothèque Nationale, that he published a novel

* ba tä' y'

GEORGES BATAILLE

under his own name. This was *Le Coupable* (The Guilty One), an altogether less erotic book. It became the most popular of his novels, and was followed the same year by *L'Archangélique*, which for a time also had a vogue. *La Haine de la poésie* (The Hatred of Poetry, 1947) is the most notable of his books of verse.

Bataille is best remembered for his philosophical essays. These include *L'Expérience intérieure* (Inner Experience, 1943), the first and only volume of a proposed "Summa Atheologica," which was greeted by a storm of protest in France, and *L'Érotisme ou la mise en question de l'être* (1957, translated as *Death and Sensuality*). *Sur Nietzsche* (On Nietzsche, 1945) is largely an intimate confession. In these and other works Bataille adumbrated a religious or mystical view that renounced all formal theologies and in particular Christianity (which, in his opinion, was nullified by its antieroticism). For Bataille, spiritual "sovereignty" was to be attained through "excess not lack"—through eroticism, laughter, and intoxication, through poetry, and ecstatic meditation. According to Maurice Blanchot, one of his most sympathetic critics, Bataille's "new theology" had "its principle and end in the absence of salvation, in the renunciation of all hope." Through despair and excess, one may hope to achieve what is variously designated as the "unknown" or "impossible," as "nothingness"—as a dazzling light which "announces the opacity of *night*; it announces only night."

Like all writers with such views, Bataille was faced with an insoluble dilemma; he was obliged to rely on language, the most rational of mediums, to express his convictions about the supremacy of the irrational—that, or be silent. He would not be silent, but he attempted to inject silence into his prose by suppressing words essential to its understanding: "I turned in the direction of . . . in the hope . . ." In *Méthode de méditation* there are whole paragraphs of ellipsis marks, indicating a failure of thought or language in face of the inexpressible. If these habits, together with an equally deliberate tendency to self-contradiction, make it difficult to grasp Bataille's thought, this is after all his intention: "What I teach (if it is true that . . .) is an intoxication, it is not philosophy: I am not a philosopher but a *saint*, perhaps a madman."

Critique, the review Bataille established in 1946, developed under his editorship into one of the foremost intellectual journals in France, and introduced many important new writers. He had always been interested in painting and in 1955 wrote two art books, one on prehistoric art and one on Manet, both of which were translated into English. He established a reputation as an incisive and intuitive art critic and enhanced his standing as a literary critic with *La Littérature et le mal* (1957, translated as *Literature and Evil*), in which he wrote of Blake, Kafka, Emily Brontë, de Sade, Proust, Baudelaire, and Genet. Nor were his interests limited to the arts: in *La Part maudite* (1949) he wrote of the danger of suppressing aggressive instincts which, if not dissipated in private life, would continue to lead to war.

Bataille became keeper of the Orléans library in 1951. He died at Puy-de-Dôme, where he was born. He will have a place, if not a major one, in the history of the century's literature. As a critic wrote in the *Times Literary Supplement*, he is one of those who (like Antonin Artaud) "challenges our pallid humanism in many fundamental ways."

PRINCIPAL WORKS IN ENGLISH TRANSLATION: Lascaux, or the Birth of Art, 1955; Manet, 1955; Death and Sensuality: A Study of Eroticism and the Taboo (England, Eroticism), 1962; My Mother (novel), 1972; Literature and Evil, 1973.

ABOUT: Boisdeffre, P. de. Une Histoire vivante de la littérature d'aujourd'hui, 1958; Marcel, G. Homo Viator, 1951; Mauriac, C. The New Literature, 1959; Nadeau, M. The French Novel Since the War, 1967; Sartre, J.-P. Situations I, 1947. *Periodicals*—L'Arc 32, 1967; Critique August–September 1963; Times Literary Supplement August 3, 1967; March 3, 1972.

BATE, WALTER JACKSON (May 23, 1918–), American biographer, scholar, and critic, writes: "I was born in Mankato, Minnesota, the second child in what was to become a sizable family. We soon moved to Richmond, Indiana, where my father became superintendent of schools. My first literary interest was in historical novels and history itself, and I hoped to become an historian. By the time I was fifteen, I had become fond of poetry, tried to write some, and used to declaim the 'Rubaiyat' and poems of Wordsworth and Keats as I walked to school or to work. Our large family was quite conscious of the Depression, and my father's health was rapidly failing. The best job I could get (bottle-washer in a dairy, sixty-five hours a week at twelve cents an hour) made the possibility of college seem very remote. But I finally showed up at Harvard and got through college and graduate school, though less time was spent on study than on other work.

WALTER JACKSON BATE

"The best thing about the Harvard of those days was its diversity. It had every sort of person, every sort of approach to literature (or to any other subject). There were disadvantages. But you had a fair chance of discovering what you valued most (and least). By my last year in college I felt I had found a vocation if I could survive the obstacle-course. The vast written record of man's experience that we call literature was beginning to seem to me, as it has more with every year, the richest source we have of general education and enlightenment; and however modest one's own qualifications might be for studying it, so varied a subject was irresistible. After writing a short undergraduate discussion of Keats, which was lucky enough to be published (*Negative Capability*, 1939), I made a bow to stylistics, in a work that now seems to me jejunely over-systematic, and then, in *From Classic to Romantic* and a series of papers, to the relation of the history of ideas to literature. I meanwhile became a member of the Society of Fellows at Harvard, where with other young men I was exposed to evenings once a week with older scientists and scholars (above all Alfred North Whitehead). In the company of such men I felt an increased admiration for approaches that could subsume the widest philosophical interests with the directly human. When I was given an appointment at Harvard as associate professor (1949), I tried to introduce a course in the criticism of literature that would be broadly humanistic, and published my *Criticism: The Major Texts* (1952) with that in mind. I also continued to teach eighteenth-century literature, considering it as the pivotal period between the literature of Shakespeare's and Milton's time and the period we may loosely call 'modern,' and wrote *The Achievement of Samuel Johnson* (1955) and a series of papers on figures and issues of the time. I was then (1955–62) caught up in a series of administrative jobs, first as chairman of History and Literature and then of the Department of English. In spare moments I worked on four volumes of the *Yale Edition of Johnson* and also returned to a book on Keats I had planned years before. In it I hoped by coalescing biography with different critical approaches especially to concentrate on the most elusive problem to the biographer of genius—what in the character and circumstances of the man permitted him to achieve what he did. This long-delayed book came out in 1963, and won some prizes, including the Pulitzer Prize for biography (1964). One of the pleasures it has brought me is the interest in it shown by poets of our own time. I hope next to turn to a general historical study of the relation of criticism to literature.

"In 1956 I became professor of English at Harvard, and later Lowell Professor of the Humanities (1962). I have never lost my liking for manual work. For several years after the war I made an avocation of farming (an unprofitable thing, as I found, in New England), and still try to keep it up on a reduced scale."

The Stylistic Development of Keats, which Bate now finds "jejunely over-systematic" and which was certainly highly technical, seemed to the poet Robert Hillyer "without parallel" in its "microscopic examination of [Keats's] prosody," and a work of "deep scholarship and impeccable taste." *The Achievement of Samuel Johnson* brought its author the Phi Beta Kappa society's Christian Gauss Award in 1956, when he also received a Guggenheim Fellowship. In this book, which deals primarily with Johnson's thought, and digs deep into his generally neglected periodical essays, Bate stresses (as he does above) his debt to Alfred North Whitehead, whose philosophy, like Bate's criticism, always goes back "to the living and concrete nature of experience." Joseph Wood Krutch, who admired *The Achievement of Samuel Johnson*, found it "closely written" and difficult, and indeed most of Bate's early work was addressed to and read by his fellow scholars and largely ignored except in learned journals.

The biography *John Keats* was quite another matter. The critical response, and then the award of the Pulitzer Prize, made it one of the literary events of 1963—a year which also saw the publication of Aileen Ward's equally remarkable but very different life of Keats. Opinions varied somewhat as to the relative merits of the two books (which appeared within a few weeks of each other), but the general feeling was that whereas Miss Ward's is the more readable, fast-moving, and speculative, Bate's is "the more comprehensive, the more 'definitive' "—Miss Ward is "essentially the biographer"; Bate "essentially the critic." Bate's treatment, it was said, "is exhaustive and integrated with every feature, past and future, of Keats's life or environment that might have some bearing." The result, in the words of the poet Howard Moss, "is one of those rare and monumental studies in which a lifetime's devotion to an artist's life and work is finally distilled."

Bate's next book was a contribution to the "Masters of World Literature" series, a critical biography of Coleridge that was called "the most sensitive short study yet to appear." This was followed by *The Burden of the Past and the English Poet*, a "deft, compact and characteristically ranging" discussion of a problem recognized as early as the Augustan era—that "there was nothing original to be written in poetry."

PRINCIPAL WORKS: Negative Capability: The Intuitive Approach in Keats, 1939; The Stylistic Development of Keats, 1945; From Classic to Romantic: Premises of Taste in Eighteenth-Century England, 1946; The Achievement of Samuel Johnson, 1955; Prefaces to Criticism, 1959; John Keats, 1963; Coleridge, 1968; The Burden of the Past and the English Poet (Alexander Lectures), 1970. *As editor*—Criticism: The Major Texts, 1952; Major British Writers, 1959; Selected Works of Edmund Burke, 1960; Keats: A Collection of Critical Essays, 1964; The Yale Edition of Johnson, vols. II–V, 1963–1966.

ABOUT: Contemporary Authors 7–8, 1963; Who's Who in America, 1970–1971.

BATESON, F(REDERICK) W(ILSE) (December 25, 1901-), English critic and scholar, writes: "I didn't start reading until I was eight years old. My mother, who was Norwegian, had a theory that too early an introduction into the other world of print retards the child's mental development. She may have been right. At any rate, when I did at last go to school—at a day-school in Lausanne (Switzerland), then at a conventional English preparatory school, and finally at Charterhouse—I collected all sorts of prizes and scholarships. But perhaps, being naturally docile, it was just that I worked harder than the others. At Charterhouse I found myself in the house Robert Graves had recently left, which he has described in all its squalor in *Good-bye to All That.* But if the Carthusian ethos was brutish, there was also a savage nobility in our war against authority. I only missed being called up for the real 1914–18 war by two years.

"At Oxford I sat at the feet of Robert Graves, a neighbour of ours on Boar's Hill, where my parents had settled when my gentle polymath of a father retired from cotton-broking in Manchester. Oxford educated me and civilized me. It had always been assumed by my unpretentious upper-middle-class family that I would go into the Indian Civil Service, but I now discovered that I could write—and in any case with the Montagu-Chelmsford reforms the I.C.S. had lost its prestige. Might there perhaps be a career for me in reviewing or even in literary criticism? Matthew Arnold, Aldous Huxley and T. S. Eliot were then my successive intellectual heroes and models.

"An Oxford thesis on early eighteenth-century comedy turned into a successful book, which was published by the University Press, and two pleasant years (1927–29) at Harvard as a Commonwealth Fellow made the critic into a scholar who soon had a string of learned articles and an edition of Congreve to his name. When I returned to England I became the editor of *The Cambridge Bibliography of English Literature*, an ambitious work of reference not completed until 1940, and in 1931 I was able to marry Jan Cancellor, the niece of a distinguished Metropolitan magistrate who is now a Justice of the Peace herself. We soon settled down with our two children in the Buckinghamshire village of Brill, where we have lived happily ever after.

"Brill gave my criticism a sense of social purpose. Though the surrounding countryside was picturesque it was then a desperately poor community, and most of my spare time was spent in organizing a strong Labour party in the constituency. In 1945 we had the satisfaction of winning the Buckingham Division for Labour, a triumph that meant more for me at the time than any of my literary successes.

"During the 1939–45 war I was an official of the Buckinghamshire War Agricultural Executive Committee and wrote two books and many articles on various aspects of agricultural reform. At the end of 1945, however, I was invited to help the Oxford English Faculty in the tutoring of the ex-servicemen who were then pouring into the University. (Oxford has the accidental advantage of being only twelve miles from Brill.) It was a stimulating experience teaching undergraduates who were already mature; disillusionment came with the discovery that the Oxford syllabus and examination system were antediluvian. In founding my quarterly *Essays in Criticism* (now in its nineteenth year) I hoped to encourage the growth of an Oxford school of criticism parallel to F. R. Leavis's group at Cambridge. Literary criticism *ought* to be both scholarly and critical. This is the ideal to which all my recent writings have, however ineffectually, aspired.

F. W. BATESON

"I am a Fellow of Corpus Christi College, Oxford, and I have been a Visiting Professor at Minnesota, Cornell, California (Berkeley) and Pennsylvania State universities."

F. W. Bateson's criticism has always illustrated two central convictions. The first is that freedom of critical interpretation should be accompanied by a historical sense of the original context in which the literary work was first composed and read. The second is that writing poetry is a rational, humane, socially oriented activity. His criticism has always shown an anti-romantic, anti-rhapsodic emphasis, with a strong bias towards the social; at the same time, Bateson, though a life-long socialist, has never been tempted by the methodological rigor of Marxist criticism.

In *English Poetry and the English Language* he attempted to show how stylistic change in English poetry was closely related to linguistic change; the book exemplified Bateson's great virtue of throwing out innumerable interesting and suggestive notions and his accompanying limitation of scarcely ever following them up and developing them.

The approach of this book was continued and expanded in *English Poetry: A Critical Introduction*, which was still concerned with the relations between poetry and language but whose main stress was on the relations between phases of English social and economic history and corresponding phases of English poetry. The English journalist Alan Brien, a onetime pupil of Bateson's, has observed: "No-one can hope to understand the inter-relation of literature and society who has not been exposed to his *English Poetry: A Critical Introduction*—a book so full of devastating insights they explode like time-bombs for the rest of your life." It is certainly a book full of insights and entertainingly provocative observations and a valuable corrective to the kind of literary study that discusses poetry entirely in terms of individual inspiration and conventional literary history. Nevertheless, it seemed to some critics that many of the socio-literary parallels are quite unconvincing. It was objected also that Bateson's illustrative chapters are too brief to allow him to establish his points.

In his book on Wordsworth, Bateson finally gave himself sufficient elbow room, and the result is a brilliant critical interpretation—or reinterpretation as he called it. It effectively brings together several disparate approaches: highly documented scholarship and psychological insights, all combined in the lucid and flexible prose of which he is a master. The result was a book that, although unwelcome to traditional admirers of the poet because of its assumptions about Wordsworth's attitude toward his sister, nevertheless gave a striking portrait of Wordsworth both as man and poet.

Bateson has always been a lonely figure in the English literary establishment. His devotion to scholarship and his urbane lack of moralizing evangelical fervor have placed him in a different camp from F. R. Leavis, for whom he nevertheless has a sincere if qualified admiration. And his strongly idiosyncratic literary criticism has set him apart from the way English studies are traditionally pursued at Oxford, where he taught until his retirement in 1969. Yet his intellectual integrity and his ability to use both the scholarly and the critical approaches to literature give his work a unique value. As his pupils can testify, Bateson has always been an outstanding teacher, and his writings show the good teacher's capacity for illuminating his subject with a casual aside rather than a dogmatic conclusion.

PRINCIPAL WORKS: English Poetry and the English Language, 1934; English Poetry; A Critical Introduction, 1950; Wordsworth: A Reinterpretation, 1954; A Guide to English Literature, 1965; Essays in Critical Dissent, 1972; The Scholar-Critic: An Introduction to Literary Research, 1972. *As editor*—Cambridge Bibliography of English Literature (4 vols.), 1940.

ABOUT: Who's Who, 1972. *Periodicals*—Modern Philology August 1935; February 1959; New Statesman August 12, 1950; January 1, 1955; December 17, 1965; Saturday Review of Literature August 31, 1935; April 2, 1955; Scrutiny June 1935; October 1953; Spectator June 23, 1950; November 27, 1959; Sunday Times June 22, 1969; Times Literary Supplement March 21, 1935; November 12, 1954; November 25, 1965; Twentieth Century January 1955.

"BAX, ROGER." *See* WINTERTON, PAUL

BAXTER, JAMES K(EIR) (June 29, 1926–October 22, 1972), New Zealand poet, critic, and playwright, wrote some time before his death: "I was born in the South Island of New Zealand, and spent my first three years at Kuri Bush, a farm close to the mouth of the Taieri river: a very bare place, with a house on a knoll surrounded by a brushwood fence, and the sea stretching out (as it does down there) towards the Antarctic or Peru. Perhaps my poems, which get simpler as I get older, indicate a wish to be back there, or at least to understand the world from some such simple point of view. My father was a socialist and a pacifist, a mainly self-educated farmer who was a conscientious objector during the First World War. My mother came from a Canterbury family—her father was a professor of English and Classics at Canterbury College, her own mother was (I think) the first woman B.A. in New Zealand; and she herself had taken a degree at Newnham College in England. I have one elder brother, who wisely chose to work as an electric welder, after spending five years behind barbed wire as a so-called military defaulter during the Second World War.

"When I was three and a half we shifted to the township of Brighton, half-way between Kuri Bush and Dunedin. There I grew up, with one interim period, a year of which was spent in Wanganui in the North Island, and nearly three years in England, where I went to a boarding school in the Cotswolds. Coming back from England at thirteen, I found that the choice loomed up which is crucial for many New Zealanders: 'Where do you belong?' One can decide to try to become an Englishman; or one can stay put as a Pig Islander. In the long run I think I made the second choice.

"I had always tended, in my own mind, to reject the process of education; and when I was eighteen, I made an actual break with it, leaving the University to take up a number of jobs—working in a range factory, labouring on a cow farm and a sheep farm, in the freezing works, in an iron works, in a sheet metal shop, as a builders' labourer, as a copyholder on a newspaper, as a porter in a sanatorium, in the Wellington abbattoir, as a postman—and then, being married, decided to 'get a ticket'—that is, to become a school-teacher. It was not entirely a wise choice. I taught for two and a half years, acquired a B.A. degree, and worked for seven years in the fog belt of the Department of Education, editing social studies bulletins for primary schools. Then I repented and became a postman again for three years. This year (1966) I am holding the Robert Burns Fellowship at the University of Otago.

"It seems likely to me that liquor has played a large part in shaping my way of thinking: as anaesthetic, Dutch courage, and symbolic second self. From the age of seventeen to the age of twenty-eight I progressed from first-stage to third-stage alcoholism, with the usual personal, domestic and social upheavals. Since twenty-eight I have found it necessary to stay away from the bottle. I think the booze was a necessary evil. It de-educated me, put me through the various hoops of calamity which are necessary if one is to understand oneself and one's neighbours, and made the circumstance of living in the modern world more tolerable. It did not seem to make my writing better or worse. Some subconscious mechanism has continued to deliver the poems on time, unconnected with internal or external crises.

"About eight years ago I became a Roman Catholic; and have not regretted this. My religion is simple, sub-literate and Marian. I find it reassuring that the Catholic Church does not make much distinction between an unsuccessful criminal and a successful businessman: both are obliged to accept the role of the Penitent or Impenitent Thief. This squares with the human condition as I see it. I have no politics, apart from a belief that militant unions are the best defence for the worker in the dehumanised conditions of modern industry, and that Government decisions are generally best left unmade.

"To write is a very haphazard vocation. One cannot live by it unless one becomes a journalist. I would tend to put family life first, writing second, and any work done for money third on the list of priorities; but money is necessary for family life, and so to write requires a strong will and a hide like that of a rhinoceros. I have acquired these, and hope to continue writing until my brains give out on me. Then I may buy a part share in a fishing launch; or give lectures about other people's writing to people who wish to be reassured that they are leading a cultured useful life."

James K. Baxter was, in the words of E. H. McCormick, "the central figure in the contemporary [New Zealand poetic] scene, mediator among writers of different ages and outlooks, focus of highest hopes for the future." As a critic and a poet he was the moving spirit in a loosely knit set of New Zealand writers known as the Auckland Group. His critical work *Recent Trends in New Zealand Poetry* (1951) is authoritative, and its groupings of poets into different schools have been widely influential. In it Baxter stated the belief, important to an understanding of his work, that "poetry should contain moral truth," that it should be "a cell of good living in a corrupt society." His socialism, emphatically humanistic rather than doc-

JAMES K. BAXTER

trinaire, was a consistent element, and it in no way conflicted with his Roman Catholicism.

He first came into prominence at the age of eighteen with the publication of his collection of poems *Beyond the Palisade* (1944), in which he appeared as the surprisingly mature disciple of such important older New Zealand poets as Allen Curnow and A. R. D. Fairburn. His *Rock Woman: Selected Poems* (1969), however, contains nothing from this first book, nor from his second, *Blow, Wind of Fruitfulness* (1948)—further evidence both of his prolificacy and his keen self-selectiveness. *The Iron Breadboard* (1957) contains excellent parodies of contemporary New Zealand poets; and *The Fire and the Anvil* (1955) and *The Man on the Horse* (1968) are collections of positive, forthright, and intelligent essays.

Baxter was a versatile but uneven poet who clearly relied on a rigid critical selection from a wealth of work. He ranged from the strident and simplistic ("We have one aim: to get men free / From fear and custom and the incessant war / Of self with self and city against city. . . ."); through the humorously pathetic, often expressed in ballad style ("Flanagan got up on a Saturday morning, / Pulled on his pants while the coffee was warming; / He didn't remember the doctor's warning, / 'Your heart's too big, Mr. Flanagan. . . .' "); and the lyrical ("Let Time be still / Who takes all things, / Face, feature, memory / Under his blinding wings. . . ."); to the conventional and descriptive, as exemplified in much of *Pig Island Letters* (1966)—for Baxter "Pig Island" is not just the South, but the whole of New Zealand.

In the preface to *Rock Woman* Baxter wrote: "If

I have at times written well, it was hardly by natural aptitude; and I must thank the man-killing Muse for the care she has taken of her idiot son." Although well endowed intellectually, he refused to tame the wildness of his poetic impulse; but his struggle to make his poetry "a cell of good living" was not an artificial one. The activity of poetry was, for him, a matter of turning bitter (and sinful) experience into something purer—but never of pretending that the human condition is other than it is. Thus, in "Tomcat," he refuses his friends' advice to get the shrieking, "terrible" animal doctored: "I think not." This is what existence is, and he affirms it: "He has no / dignity, thank God!" For Baxter, pain "is its own instruction"; he searches for the relief of simplicity in the midst of the intellectual preoccupations that he sees as distracting, and he often discovers it, particularly in his more recent poetry, in powerful and vivid descriptions of landscapes and seascapes.

Roy Fuller has written that "in the use of nature, of New Zealand life, of a retrospective view of the poet's wild youth, there is a remarkable realism underlying and sustaining the inventive and muscular language." Baxter was indeed increasingly recognized as the leading New Zealand poet of his generation; such later meditative poems as "The Waves," with its startling imagery and deeply felt spiritual optimism (in sharp contrast to the rather self-conscious bitterness of some earlier work), suggest that he may rank as the most considerable poet his country has produced. James Bertram says that "no one has more successfully assimilated the authentic flavour of the New Zealand vernacular into poetic speech. In this sense, Baxter is a genuinely popular poet, who has somehow succeeded in becoming bard, scapegoat, and moral censor to a not notably imaginative tribe."

Baxter's father, Archibald, wrote an influential book about his experiences as a conscientious objector, *We Will Not Cease*; his maternal grandfather, Professor J. Macmillan Brown, "became a legend for his energy, prejudices, utopian writings and works on Pacific ethnology." Baxter's minor works include a number of plays and the text of the picture book *New Zealand in Color*. In 1958 he went to India on a Unesco grant. Baxter died in 1972 at the age of forty-six. He was married in 1948 to Jacqueline Sturm and had a son and a daughter.

PRINCIPAL WORKS: *Poetry*—Beyond the Palisade, 1944; Blow, Wind of Fruitfulness, 1948; Poems Unpleasant, 1952; The Fallen House, 1953; In Fires of No Return, 1958; Howrah Bridge, 1961; Pig Island Letters, 1966; The Lion Skin, 1967; Rock Woman: Selected Poems, 1969. *Miscellaneous*—Recent Trends in New Zealand Poetry, 1951; The Fire and the Anvil (criticism) 1955; The Iron Breadboard (parodies), 1957; New Zealand in Color, 1961; The Man on the Horse (criticism), 1968; Aspects of Poetry in New Zealand, 1968.

ABOUT: Contemporary Poets of the English Language, 1970; Curnow, A. (ed.) Penguin Book of New Zealand Verse, 1960; McCormick, E. H. New Zealand Literature, 1959; Smithyman, K. A Way of Saying, 1965. *Periodicals*—Meanjin Summer 1952; New Zealand Monthly Review December 1966; New Zealand News November 1972; Review of English Studies 1959; Scotsman October 8, 1966; Times Literary Supplement December 15, 1966.

***"BAZIN, HERVÉ" (pen name of Jean-Pierre Marie Hervé-Bazin)** (April 17, 1911–), French novelist, writes (in French): "I was born at Angers into a middle-class family which remained loyal to its royalist ancestors and rooted in the Anjou soil. Nephew of René Bazin, an ultra-Catholic novelist and member of the Académie Française, I am also the grandson, on my father's side, of a monarchist writer, and, on my mother's, of a conservative politician. This explains the atmosphere in which I grew up and how I had to react against an anachronistic milieu, to revolt against my family.

"Undoubtedly this revolt was encouraged by circumstances: my mother detested me. If I was not a neglected child, I was a child who knew no tenderness and was marked by that for life. I spent my childhood getting myself expelled from the religious schools in which I was placed. When I was eighteen years old, a *bachelier*, I wanted to go to journalism school. But my father, a magistrate, made me enter a Catholic law school and then a military academy. It was only after breaking with my family that I got a degree in literature, working at night as a head waiter to earn my living. This experience also marked me: it put me once and for all on the side of those who have to make it alone; it also cleared my head of the preconceptions, of the ready-made ideas, and of the orthodoxies which young men often cling to instead of thinking for themselves.

"I was married soon after, for the first time, to a typist, who gave me a son. Our life was very difficult at first. By turn I tried being a salesman, an actor, and the representative of a vacuum cleaner company. At the same time I tried to write. Without success. It is true that at this time I published mostly poems.

"It was only after the war and after overcoming some very grave health problems (the results of a skull fracture) that my literary life really began. In 1947 my book of poems, *Jour* (Day), despite the Prix Apollinaire, passed unnoticed. But the following year, with *Vipère au poing*, a novel about my childhood, I gained a wide public, shocking it, I fear, more than I touched its heart. Indeed it took nearly twenty years to eradicate my reputation as one who had had the audacity to speak ill of his mother, to make my readers understand that, if I am indeed the novelist of family problems that they say I am, it is to bring people back again to

* ba zaN'

the study of love. By my second wife I have four children and I know what I am talking about . . .

"There are of course other subjects for a writer and the books I am planning will be of broader inspiration, more deliberately social. Politics is not my specialty. But we live in a dangerous age when one must involve oneself with what matters, that is to say, in the fight against imperialisms—red or white—against the atomic bomb, and against the choice they offer us between a world which pretends to justice and a world which pretends to freedom. Four literary prizes, a seat in the Académie Goncourt, five million copies of books printed (most in France though some in foreign countries) . . . this is first of all a responsibility. I scorn success if, even at the risk of losing my readers, I do not feel I am serving them by proposing to them a worthwhile interpretation of this world and of the dignity of man."

Bazin is the son of Jacques Hervé-Bazin and of the former Paule Guilloteaux. He received his law degree from the Faculté Catholique in Angers and his degree in literature from the Sorbonne. He was active in the Resistance during World War II and after it established a poetry review with a group of friends. He has published three volumes of poetry, a book of short stories, and a humorous essay on the perils of logic, *Plumons l'oiseau* (1966). But it is on his novels that his reputation rests.

The first of these, *Vipère au poing* (1948, translated as *Viper in the Fist*), was a resounding success, critical and popular. Jean ("Firebrand") is one of the three sons of Madame Rezeau, a female monster dedicated to the persecution of her children. They respond in kind, at one point attempting to drown her. For Jean, his rebellion is "my viper duly strangled but forever coming to life again, I still brandish it and I shall always brandish it, whatever name you want to give it: hate, despair, the cult of evil, or the taste of misfortune." The novel was awarded the Prix des Lecteurs and was received by critics in France and abroad as the work of a born writer. Many were reminded of Jules Renard's minor classic *Poil de Carotte*, the story of another boy who regretted that "everyone can't be an orphan." Even reviewers who found the book distasteful admired the verve of Bazin's prose and his merciless anatomy of provincial Angers. The *Atlantic's* reviewer wrote: "M. Bazin has wrested from this grim subject a curiously exhilarating tale, glowing with ferocious humor and executed with superb artistry." The fearsome Madame Rezeau reappears in *Cri de la chouette* (Cry of the Owl, 1972).

La Tête contre les murs (1949, translated as *Head Against the Wall*) is another savage portrait of bourgeois parents, in which a delinquent boy is

HERVÉ BAZIN

committed to a succession of appalling French mental hospitals to avoid a scandal and in the end is destroyed, physically and mentally, by these dreadful institutions. *Lève-toi et marche* (1952, translated as *Constance*) is a powerful and moving character study of a beautiful girl, dying of a paralytic disease, who tries to live vicariously through others and ruthlessly dissects her own ambiguous motives as her growing bitterness spreads havoc among those she tries to help. *La Mort du petit cheval* (Death of the Little Horse, 1950); *L'Huile sur le feu* (Oil on the Fire, 1954), and *Qui j'ose aimer* (1956, translated as *A Tribe of Women*) are all bitterly misanthropic studies of family life, particularly venomous in their portrayal of women. In the last-named book Bazin articulates his distrust of logic, his belief in a philosophy of cumulative coincidence: "Things don't happen *just like that*, clearly and neatly, for definite, unambiguous reasons. They bunch together, they slide, they happen by themselves . . . coming to a conclusion that you learn to accept little by little."

Au nom du fils (1960, translated as *In the Name of the Son*) showed a marked change of tone, a new capacity for compassion as well as hatred. It examines the relationship between a widower (the narrator) and his youngest son, who he suspects is not his own. His relationship with this difficult boy nevertheless becomes the central factor in his life. Some critics found this story considerably less interesting than its predecessors, but a reviewer in the *Times Literary Supplement*, who thought the translation deplorable, said that in its original form the book was "in its modest way one of the most perfect novels to have appeared in any country since 1945." In *Le Matrimoine* (1967), Bazin returns to his earlier manner. Marc Slonim says that his "word play, witty maxims, facetious similes and idiomatic inversions give a very special flavor" to this ferocious satire on marriage in Angers, and the monstrous regiment of women who support the institution. *Les bienheureux de la désolation* (1970), translated as *Tristan*, is an absorbing fictionalized account of what happened when the inhabitants of Tristan da Cunha, a remote South Atlantic island devastated by a volcanic eruption, were forced to spend four years in Britain, and were thus translated from a pastoral utopia to a highly developed industrial society which, on the whole, they greatly disliked.

Bazin works for Grasset, the publishing house, and as a reviewer for *L'Information*, among other journals. He has served as vice president of the Association of Writers and president of the Association of Western Writers, and is a member of P.E.N. His work has brought him many honors: apart from his membership in the Académie Goncourt, he is a Chevalier des Arts et des Lettres and a Chevalier des Palmes Académiques, and he has received the Grand Prix Littéraire de Monaco. His first marriage was to Odette Danigo and his second to Jacqueline Dussolier, whom he married in 1948. He made a third marriage in 1967, to Monique Serre-Gray.

PRINCIPAL WORKS IN ENGLISH TRANSLATION: Grasping the Viper, 1950 (U.S., Viper in the Fist); Head Against the Wall, 1952; Constance, 1955; Tribe of Women, 1958; In the Name of the Son, 1962; Tristan, 1971.

ABOUT: Anglade, J. Hervé Bazin, 1962; Boisdeffre, P. de. Dictionnaire de littérature contemporaine, 1962; Boisdeffre, P. de. Une Histoire vivante de la littérature d'aujourd'hui, 1958; International Who's Who, 1972–1973; Peyre, H. French Novelists of Today, 1967; Ullman, S. Style in the French Novel, 1957. *Periodicals*—Livres de France May–June 1956; New York Herald Tribune Book Review April 29, 1951; June 8, 1952; May 11, 1958; New Yorker May 26, 1951; Nouvelles Littéraires February 2, 1957; Saturday Review April 14, 1951; June 21, 1952; Times Literary Supplement August 31, 1962.

"BEACHCOMBER." *See* MORTON, JOHN (CAMERON ANDRIEU) BINGHAM (MICHAEL)

BEDFORD, SYBILLE (March 16, 1911–), English novelist, writes: "I was born in Charlottenburg, Germany. I left Germany as a small child, and was privately educated in England, Italy and France. I was put down for the Sorbonne, thought of Oxford and also possibly of reading law; nothing came of either of these. I began writing at the age of sixteen or seventeen, chiefly literary essays and criticism and several (unpublished) novels. In 1935 I married Walter Bedford. I have lived chiefly in England, France, Italy and the United States.

SYBILLE BEDFORD

"During the last ten years or so, my life has been divided between writing fiction and doing my own brand of law reporting. I have written, for instance, about the trials of D. H. Lawrence's *Lady Chatterley's Lover*, and Stephen Ward in London, Jack Ruby in Dallas and the Auschwitz trial in Frankfurt, West Germany.

"At present I am living partly in the South of France, partly in London, and working chiefly on a novel."

Both as a novelist and as a reporter, Sybille Bedford has a devoted and distinguished following among critics who find that in her writing "nothing is obvious, everything is new." John Davenport used these words of her Mexican memoir *The Sudden View*, reissued in 1960 as *A Visit to Don Otavio*; many said similar things of her second and most admired book, *The Legacy*. This is a novel about the interweaving of two wealthy families, one Jewish and one Catholic, in pre-1914 Germany. It contains, beneath its glossy surface, "an evolving character portrait of a society and, finally, a morality as well." The book's most enthusiastic advocates included Nancy Mitford, Evelyn Waugh, Aldous Huxley, and Christopher Sykes, who thought it "written with genius" and said: "No novelist could convey with more decisiveness a vision of how life moves in certain conditions."

Mrs. Bedford's second novel, *A Favorite of the Gods*, is a nostalgic evocation of the upper reaches of Italian society in the late 1920s, and a study of three remarkable women: Anna Howland, an American heiress who married an Italian prince at the turn of the century, her Italian daughter

Constanza, and Constanza's English daughter Flavia. The novel is brought into focus by—and explains—an apparently casual decision made by Constanza which changes her life and Flavia's. The book illustrates the author's preoccupation with the whole question of free will and "the interaction of character and events," which is also the theme of her next and related novel, *A Compass Error*. Here the scene has changed to the 1930s and a French coastal town where the plain and bookish Flavia has gone to study for university entrance, and where she is seduced by a ruthless lesbian into a situation in which she betrays those she most loves. Mrs. Bedford's fiction is consistently admired for the detailed precision of her descriptive writing, but some reviewers find it hard to penetrate the "solidly enamelled" surfaces of her novels and to sympathize fully with the moral dilemmas of her characters in their remote and Jamesian world.

No such reservations seem applicable to Mrs. Bedford's lucid reports on the administration of justice. *The Trial of Dr. Adams*, "an exposition of human justice at its careful best," is "a masterpiece of objective yet sensitive reporting," as readable as a good thriller. *The Faces of Justice*, describing, illustrating, and comparing criminal court procedures in England and four European countries, managed to be both objective and compassionate. It was praised for its brilliant *pointilliste* style, and said by one English reviewer to "bring home to us, as no abstract argument could, the virtues and the defects of legal traditions and ways of doing justice other than our own."

Sybille Bedford writes on the law, and also on food and travel, for a number of magazines in England and the United States. For many years she was a friend of Aldous Huxley, and she has been selected by his family as his official biographer. She is spare in figure, with dark hair and blue eyes, and is reserved about her private life.

PRINCIPAL WORKS: The Sudden View: A Mexican Journey, 1953 (re-issued as A Visit to Don Otavio, 1960); A Legacy (novel), 1956; The Best We Can Do: An Account of the Trial of Dr. John Bodkin Adams, 1958 (U.S., The Trial of Dr. Adams); The Faces of Justice (nonfiction), 1961; A Favorite of the Gods (novel), 1963; A Compass Error, 1968.

ABOUT: Hoffman, H. R. The Reader's Adviser, 1964; Vinson, J. (ed.) Contemporary Novelists, 1972. *Periodicals*—Nation May 4, 1963; New Statesman January 11, 1963; Publishers' Weekly April 7, 1969; Saturday Review February 9, 1957; Spectator April 13, 1956; Times Literary Supplement October 24, 1968.

***BEHAN, BRENDAN (FRANCIS)** (February 9, 1923–March 20, 1964), Irish dramatist, memoirist, novelist, and journalist, was born in a Dublin tenement, one of several owned by his grandmother, into a genteel family which had "come down in the world." His father, Stephen Behan, a Dublin character, housepainter, union leader, and soldier of the Irish Republican Army, first saw Brendan through the bars of Kilmainham Prison after the civil war. As a young man, Stephen Behan had been trained for the priesthood. He read French and Latin and after tea in the evenings would act out extracts from Dickens, Zola, Maupassant, Pepys, Marcus Aurelius, and Boccaccio for the pleasure and instruction of his family. Brendan Behan's uncle Peadar Kearney wrote the "Soldier's Song," which became the Irish national anthem. Another uncle managed a Dublin music hall which Brendan and his brothers attended regularly as boys, and relations on both sides of the family were associated with the Abbey Theatre. But perhaps the most important family influence was that of his passionate and powerful mother, Kathleen (Kearney) Behan, who is said to have sung over his cradle Connolly's famous song: "Come workers sing a rebel song / A song of love and hate . . . ."

* bē′ hən

BRENDAN BEHAN

Behan had two stepbrothers, a sister, and three brothers (two of whom, Brian and Dominick, followed him into the writing trade). He himself learned to read when he was three. Precocious, handsome, and spoiled, he was an arrogant, tough, and bookish boy with a nervous stutter, soaked in Irish history and legend, and a contributor from the age of twelve to republican magazines. His parents, devout if anticlerical, sent him to Catholic schools until he was thirteen. At fourteen he was expelled from the Christian Brothers' School and apprenticed to his father's trade. The same year he graduated from the youth organization Fianna Eireann to the I.R.A.

In 1939, when he was sixteen, Behan was arrested in Liverpool with a suitcase full of homemade explosives. The boy spent two grim months in Walton Prison before he was sentenced to three years at a comparatively enlightened Borstal (reform school). Six months after his return to Dublin in 1942, Behan was arrested again for shooting at two policemen. It was while he was serving his sentence, this time in an Irish prison, that Behan began seriously to write. Released in 1945, he worked as a housepainter, as a seaman and, increasingly, as a freelance journalist. After the war he became associated with a bohemian group loosely based at McDaids, a Dublin pub. There he met Alan Simpson, founder of the tiny Pike Theatre, where in 1954 *The Quare Fellow* made its triumphant provincial debut.

What the play lacked in professional expertise was supplied by Joan Littlewood, who then bought it for her Theatre Workshop in East London and, with Behan installed in a pub across the road, argued and acted it into shape. It opened in May 1956, bringing Theatre Workshop its first major success, and going on to win further laurels in New York two years later. "Quare fellow" means "condemned man," and the play involves the audience in the tension and sickening sense of justice gone mad which grips a prison when a man is to be hanged. Behan's tape-recorder ear for dialogue and the impartial generosity of his characterization, which allows humanity to warders as well as prisoners, makes *The Quare Fellow* more potent than any tract against capital punishment. Brilliantly orchestrated rather than tidily plotted, its stark theme is set off by graveyard humor so richly comic as to remind some critics of Sean O'Casey.

The Hostage, a slighter play dashed off in two weeks, was built around the predicament of a young Cockney soldier, held in a Dublin brothel as surety for the life of a condemned I.R.A. man, and killed at last in a pointless accident. Originally written in Gaelic and first produced in Dublin in 1958, it later enjoyed long runs in London and New York. In *The Hostage* Behan satirized even the I.R.A., in which the "laughing boys" of the great days have been replaced by the "earnest religious-minded ones." Behan revised the play repeatedly, loading onto its slim story line so many ribald songs, dances, and asides that it finished as a kind of bawdy revue, These highly entertaining accretions, attributed by some critics to a Brechtian influence, more probably derived from the *commedia dell'arte* traditions of Theatre Workshop, and even more from Behan's temperament. His heritage made him a rebel and pride made him a good one, but at some level he hated conflict and he would do almost anything for a laugh. *The Hostage* and *The Quare Fellow* have both been filmed.

Most critics agreed that the fertile characterization and marvelous exuberance of the plays was marred by a lack of shape and discipline. The same charges were leveled at the autobiographical *Borstal Boy* (1959)—with equal justice but less conviction, since few reviewers seemed able to resist the book's vitality and warmth. One critic said, "It belongs with the world's great prison literature" and another reviewer, in the *Times Literary Supplement*, wrote: "Beneath the surface of this lewd and riotous book lies an essential charity which is altogether moving and memorable. . . . [It] remains a work of unique authority in its confident evocation of the very breath and being of life under captivity."

Behan's only novel was *The Scarperer* (1964), an "artfully constructed" thriller first published under a pseudonym in 1953 as a serial in the *Irish Times*. *Brendan Behan's Island* (1962), a talkative ramble through Ireland, included two good short stories and a play, *The Big House*, which has since been produced. *Brendan Behan's New York* (1964) was a similar jaunt; *Hold Your Hour and Have Another* (1964) collected some of the columns Behan wrote for the *Irish Press* (1954–56). Behan translated Marlowe's verse into Irish, taking a craftsman's pride in scholarship as he did in housepainting. A sequel to *Borstal Boy*, based largely on tape recordings Behan made shortly before his death, was published in 1966 as *Confessions of an Irish Rebel*, and there have been one or two other posthumous compilations, listed below. A play begun in 1963, *Richard's Cork Leg*, was completed from a rough draft by Alan Simpson and staged in 1972. Set partly in a Dublin graveyard, and dealing with a riotous company of whores, beggars, puritans, and politicos, it was found even more tenuous in plot and characterization than *The Hostage*, but was enjoyed nevertheless as an excellent entertainment, studded with jokes and good songs.

No lean and hungry revolutionary, Brendan Behan was five feet eight inches tall and towards the end of his life was fat. He had gray-green eyes and tousled dark hair. He loved the sea and swimming and travel, and sang and talked as well as he wrote, in English, French, and Gaelic. He drank far too much and was a splendidly unpredictable interviewee on television. From time to time he would interrupt performances of his plays to harangue or entertain the audience. And yet Behan's roistering public performance as a professional Irishman concealed what Frank O'Connor called "a shuddering sensibility and the innocence of an acolyte." His friend Kate O'Brien said he had a "a Franciscan grace of soul" and was "generous to madness."

Brendan Behan died of diabetes, drink, and jaundice at the age of forty-one. He left a widow, the painter Beatrice ffrench-Salkeld, and a daughter. His brother Brian attributes his death, in part at least, to bitter disillusionment, an uncaring self-indulgence which amounted to self-destruction. "Brendan loved humanity; he believed heart and soul in its causes . . . but his causes crumbled and his very success drove away his true friends and left him prey to the flatterers and spongers. Fame and success became his twin headstones."

PRINCIPAL WORKS: *Plays*—The Quare Fellow, 1956; The Hostage, 1958. *Prose*—Borstal Boy, 1958; Brendan Behan's Island, 1962; Hold Your Hour and Have Another, 1963; Brendan Behan's New York, 1964; The Scarperer (novel), 1964; Confessions of an Irish Rebel, 1965; The World of Brendan Behan (ed. by Sean McCann), 1966; The Wit of Brendan Behan (ed. by Sean McCann), 1968.
ABOUT: Atkinson, B. Tuesdays and Fridays, 1963; Behan, Brendan. Borstal Boy, 1958; Behan, Brendan. Confessions of an Irish Rebel, 1965; Behan, Brian. With Breast Expanded, 1964; Behan, Dominick. My Brother Brendan, 1965; Current Biography, 1961; Jeffs, R. Brendan Behan, Man and Showman, 1966; McCann, S. The World of Brendan Behan, 1966; O'Connor, U. Brendan Behan, 1970 (U.S., Brendan); Simpson, A. Beckett and Behan and a Theatre in Dublin, 1962. *Periodicals*—Atlantic Monthly June 1959; Esquire February 1962; Hudson Review Winter 1960–1961; Kenyon Review Winter 1965; Modern Drama February 1966; National Review July 14, 1966; New Statesman March 27, 1964; August 31, 1970; Newsweek February 23, 1959; March 30, 1964; New York Times March 24, 1964; Publishers' Weekly March 30, 1964; Redbook March 1966; Sewanee Review Spring 1966; Spectator March 27, 1964; Time March 27, 1964; Times (London) December 8, 1958.

*"**BELY, ANDREY" (pseudonym of Boris Nikolayevich Bugaev)** (October 14 [old style, i.e., October 26], 1880–January 8, 1924), Russian poet, novelist, critic, and theoretician of symbolism. He was born in Moscow, the son of a professor of mathematics who was renowned for his absent-mindedness and eccentricity as well as his erudition and of a beautiful but neurotic and hysterical woman thirty years younger than her husband. Bely's memoirs give a vivid picture of the family conflict that raged around him, and he soon turned away from this quarrelsome world to the truer realities (for him) of romantic music and German romantic poetry. He did, however, study under his father and graduated in both natural sciences and philosophy at the University of Moscow before devoting himself to literature. Some critics have seen Bely's life as a constant conflict between the shy and charming science graduate and the vain and quarrelsome poetic genius, and his greatest works are arguably those which most successfully fuse the scientist and the artist in his makeup.

Bely belonged, like Alexandr Blok and Vyacheslav Ivanov, to the second generation of Russian symbolist poets, for whom symbolism was not just an aesthetic movement but a metaphysical philosophy or even a mystical religion of which the poet was the high priest. Though the three poets drew

* byā' lûi

ANDREY BELY

their doctrines from many different sources they were all profoundly influenced by the mystical philosophy of Vladimir Solovev, whom Bely knew well through his great friendship with the family of Mikhail Solovev, the philosopher's brother.

According to Solovev the whole creation is ruled by a single, all-embracing feminine principle, which can be identified with nature or personified into a mystical and divine feminine being to which he gave the Gnostic name Sofia, the Divine Wisdom. She is also the Muse who inspires poetry, which is a visionary experience, for the tangible world is but the shadow of another world, the ultimate reality revealed to poets in moments of creative inspiration. The duality of spiritual and material will ultimately be overcome, for Christ's incarnation shows that man can be redeemed and become divine, but the period before the coming of Sofia's City of God will be one of wars, tribulations, and the temptations of Antichrist.

These apocalyptic expectations are part of a long tradition of Russian messianic futurism, but the feelings of impending catastrophe also reflect the social and political ferment of the time, which was driving towards the explosion of 1917. In his brilliant philosophical and critical articles, which were later collected in *Simvolizm* (Symbolism, 1910), *Lug zeleny* (The Green Meadow, 1910), and *Arabeski* (Arabesques, 1911), Bely developed these ideas and gave the movement its theoretical basis. Many of his essays first appeared in the journal *Vesy*, which he coedited with Valery Bryusov from 1904 to 1909.

Music was for Bely, as for many other symbolists, the art which best expressed the true essence of life, and his earliest works were a series of "symphonies" which, with only a loose narrative thread, used lyrical prose in an attempt to achieve compositional effects analagous to music. The first of these, published while he was still an undergraduate, was the *Dramaticheskaya simfoniya* (1902). It is a prophetic vision of Sofia, and this mystical expectation is also the main theme of Bely's first volume of lyric poems, *Zoloto v lazuri* (Gold in Azure, 1904) in which, as the title indicates, Sofia is seen in much more gorgeous colors than the creature embodied in *Beautiful Lady*, Blok's earliest collection, published the same year. Indeed a youthful delight in extravagant imagery and flamboyant language gives many of the poems a certain gaudiness and preciosity which conflicts with their serious intentions.

The poems in Bely's second collection, *Pepel* (Ashes, 1908) are completely different, and far more mature. They deal realistically and satirically with social themes—satirically because for Bely people were shadows and caricatures of the ideal, leading coarse and stupid lives on the vast plains of Mother Russia, here personified as a monstrous female figure. The book shows the literary influence of Nekrasov and the political impact of the unsuccessful 1905 revolution—Bely later described the period 1906–1909 as a journey through a "spiritual morass." Nevertheless the poems in *Pepel*, with their subtly orchestrated folk rhythms, colorful language, concrete imagery, and passionate verse have an immediate appeal which has earned them widespread popularity.

In Bely's third book of verse, *Urna* (The Urn, 1909), the dominant mood is the intense despair born of his unrequited passion for Blok's wife Lyubov. The two poets were born in the same year and were closely linked in a tempestuous relationship for almost twenty years, from their first correspondence in 1903 until Blok's death in 1921. Blok regarded Lyubov as his Beautiful Lady; Bely saw her in a romantic light even before he met her, and when he did he fell in love with her immediately. When Blok's disillusion with her became apparent, Bely began a crusade to save Lyubov from her husband. The fervor and intensity of the triangular relationship continued, with several challenges to duels, until Bely at last in 1910 found his "soul-companion" in Asya Turgeneva. By that time the crisis of symbolism had led to the movement's collapse as a coherent force, and Bely's search for an acceptable faith led him in other directions. All his life he remained an ardent and hopeful seeker after new truths and a bold experimenter and innovator.

During the decade following the completion of *Urna* Bely abandoned poetry and wrote his three most important novels. The first two end with the destruction of the rational order by the forces of chaos, for he was acutely aware of how the patterns of order which man has imposed on experience are threatened by irrational passions. In *Serebrany golub* (The Silver Dove, 1909), his first novel, the rational is identified with the West and the irrational with the East. Daryalski, the protagonist, a young poet with much in common with Bely, becomes dissatisfied with his fashionable life and classical studies and turns to the Russian people in search of spiritual rebirth. He joins the White Doves, a peasant sect whose orgiastic rites remind him of the Eleusinian mysteries. But he finds that their world is ruled not by the spirit but by the flesh, and their sacraments are erotic and sadistic. Chaos is as unsatisfactory by itself as the cold and sterile rationalism from which he had originally turned, but he learns this too late and is murdered by the forces of unreason.

In his second and greatest novel, *Peterburg* (1913, translated by John Cournos as *St. Petersburg*), the same conflict is extended to the political sphere, for the rational order is now the autocratic government, threatened by the rising revolutionary tide. Nikolai Ableukhov's search for truth has led him to join the revolutionaries, and the central action is his inadequate attempt to assassinate a representative of the traditional bureaucracy—his own father—by means of a time bomb in a can of sardines. But both revolution and reaction are aspects of the same Russian nihilism; father and son share the same Tatar blood, both are moved by the same dark Asiatic forces. While the son hopes to impose an ideological system on the Russian wilderness, the father strives to control it through strict regulations, just as the geometrical avenues of the capital city were imposed on the Baltic marshes.

It was Vyacheslav Ivanov who insisted that *Peterburg* was the only possible title for the book, since Bely develops the historical and political myth of Petersburg as it is found in Gogol and Dostoevsky, and the city itself is the dominant character. Peasant superstition predicted that Peter's artificial city would be destroyed by a new deluge, and this apocalyptic threat haunts Bely's book. The unreality of this center of rationalized order is reflected in the constant shifting between the different planes—real, symbolic, and ideological—on which the novel is written; the bizarre humor and fantastic imagery; the stream-of-consciousness and other psychological techniques; and the magical, liberating use of language, which permanently extended the resources of Russian prose. Western critics have often compared it with the work of James Joyce and of Kafka, and F. D. Reeve calls it "a turning point in the development of the Russian novel."

In 1910 Bely had traveled with Asya Turgeneva through Italy, North Africa, and Palestine, and in the following year they were married in Switzerland. More than ever Bely felt that mankind faced a grave crisis and stood at the watershed of a new era, and Asya's inclination towards mysticism reinforced his thirst for a new infallible faith. He found it in Rudolf Steiner's anthroposophy, and from 1914 to 1916 Bely and Asya lived in the anthroposophical community at Dornach and took part in the building of the Goetheanum. Here he wrote *Kotik Letaev*, an autobiographical novel of infancy which, starting with the chaos of the womb, traces the gradual emergence of consciousness in the child. In places of straightforward narrative its structure is derived from music, the unordered images of early life being arranged contrapuntally but slowly giving way to more rational interpretation.

By 1916 Bely was longing for Russia and returned. Like Blok he gave an enthusiastic welcome to the Revolution, and each of them wrote a long poem on it, both being influenced by the messianic ideas of Ivanov-Razumnik. Bely's poem *Khristos voskres* (Christ Is Risen) lacks the power of Blok's *Dvenadtsat'* (The Twelve) and is far inferior to the other long poem Bely himself wrote in these years, *Pervoe svidanie* (First Meeting, 1921), which many critics have regarded as his outstanding poetic achievement. It resembles the long poems that the other symbolists, Blok and Ivanov, also produced in their later years, built up out of fragmentary autobiographical episodes, recreating the cultural environment and the spiritual atmosphere of the early days of symbolism in which they grew up.

Bely's enthusiasm for the Revolution soon faded, and his attempt to resurrect the symbolist aesthetic with his magazine *Zapiski mechtateley* (1919–1922) proved a failure. After Blok's death in 1921 Bely felt the need to leave Russia; but the deep roots of his work were there, and after two years as an émigré in Berlin he returned. His later novels, such as the series of three under the general title *Moskva* (Moscow, 1926) do not match his earlier ones, and the sequel to *Kotik Letaev* is a relatively conventional work, though it has considerable autobiographical interest. The most important products of this last decade of his life are his literary reminiscences, starting with *Vospominaniya o Bloke* (Recollections of Blok, 1922), a fascinating account of their friendship. The incomplete series of memoirs runs only up to the Revolution, comprising the trilogy *Na rubezhe dvukh stoleti* (On the Border of Two Centuries, 1930), *Nachalo veka* (The Beginning of the Century, 1933) and the unfinished *Mezhdu dvukh revolyutsi* (Between Two Revolutions, 1934), in which he recreates with characteristic verbal brilliance and irony the intellectual ferment of those years. Among his critical works of this period two in particular stand out—the statistical analysis of Pushkin's meters in *Ritm kak dialektika: 'Medny vsadnik'* (Rhythm as Dialectic: The Bronze Horseman, 1929), and *Masterstvo Gogolya* (The Craftsmanship of Gogol, 1929). In these and other pioneering studies Bely laid the foundations of the Russian formalist school of criticism.

Bely also had a great influence on poets such as Blok and Pasternak and on both the style and ideas of later novelists, such as Zamyatin and Pilnyak. Though as a poet he is inferior to Blok, the originality and variety of his work make him the most typical product of the age of symbolism, a restless searcher and experimenter in an unstable, transitional time of cultural crisis. And two of his novels, *Serebrany golub* and *Peterburg*, along with Sologub's *Melky bes* (Petty Demon), are regarded by many critics as the masterpieces of twentieth century Russian prose.

PRINCIPAL WORKS IN ENGLISH TRANSLATION: St. Petersburg, 1959. *Excerpt from* Kotik Letaev *in* Slonim, M. and Reavey, G. (eds.) Soviet Literature, 1933. *Poems in* Bowra, C. M. (ed.) Book of Russian Verse, 1943; Lindsay, J. Russian Poetry 1917–1955, 1957; Obolensky, D. Penguin Book of Russian Verse, 1962.

ABOUT: Cournos, J. *introduction to* St. Petersburg, 1959; Grigson, G. (ed.) Concise Encyclopedia of Modern World Literature, 1963; Maslenikov, O. A. The Frenzied Poets, 1952; Mochulsky, K. Andrey Bely, 1955; Poggioli, R. The Poets of Russia, 1960; Reavey, G. *foreword to* St. Petersburg, 1959; Zavalishin, V. Early Soviet Writers, 1958. *Periodicals*—Times Literary Supplement March 21, 1968.

BENCHLEY, NATHANIEL (GODDARD) (November 13, 1915–), American novelist, humorist, and journalist, writes: "I was born in Newton, Massachusetts. My father, Robert Benchley, was about to be fired from his job as editor of the house organ for a paper company, and when he was offered a job as a reporter on the New York *Tribune*, our family moved to New York. Both he and my mother, the former Gertrude Darling, had been born and brought up in Worcester, Massachusetts, and the move represented the first time that either of them had been out of New England for any length of time. I was brought up in Crestwood, New York, and then Scarsdale, from which base I attended the Roger Ascham School, a progressive (for then) day school in White Plains; the Phillips Exeter Academy; and Harvard. I graduated from Harvard in 1938 as a bachelor of science, for although I had majored in English my Roger Ascham training in Latin was so shaky that I couldn't muster the Latin credits required for a bachelor of arts. I got into writing because it seemed the only thing I could do; I had been president of the Harvard *Lampoon* and as such had had to do a certain amount of drawing, but my

NATHANIEL BENCHLEY

art work was nowhere near professional caliber and there was nothing else for it but to write.

"Having been told that any writer should start as a reporter I presented myself to the New York *Herald Tribune*, but they were unimpressed, and I went to work instead writing feature pieces for Heywood Broun's weekly newspaper, *The Connecticut Nutmeg*, at a salary of thirty-five dollars a week. Finally, and reluctantly, the *Herald Tribune* agreed to take me on, and I became a city reporter at a ten-dollar weekly pay cut. About the only distinguished thing I did as a reporter was, through a misreading of the press release, to close the Grand Central Flower Show one day early, and narrowly missed being fired. The rest of my time was spent doing feature stories and obituaries, and reporting such events as Girl Scout cherry-pie-baking contests, American Paper and Pulp Association conventions, and the minor exhibits at the New York World's Fair. In the summer of 1941 I became an ensign in the Public Relations Office of the Third Naval District; although my naval knowledge was nil, I was considered eligible for a commission because I was a reporter, and the burgeoning Navy Public Relations Office needed reporters. In the course of time I wearied of public relations and applied for sea duty, and after extensive schooling wound up as executive, and later commanding, officer of a submarine chaser.

"Early in 1946 I went to work at *Newsweek* magazine as assistant editor of the Entertainment Department, and for nearly two years reviewed plays and motion pictures and tried to supplement my salary by writing articles for other magazines on the side. This finally caught up with me, and in November of 1947 I was fired, along with twenty-one researchers and secretaries who were declared redundant. (*Newsweek's* explanation was that they had taken on too many people after the war, but nobody was really fooled.) By this time I had built up enough contacts among the magazines so that I felt I could take a fling at freelancing, and I have been doing it ever since. At first I did only articles, then an editor friend suggested I try fiction, so I veered off into the short-story field and later into light novels, which have probably been most accurately referred to as 'hammock reading.' I am always intending to write a serious book, but it somehow never seems to work out that way when I'm through with it.

"At one point, about 1951, I decided to have a fling at the theatre and started work on what turned out to be a two years' playwriting project. The result, *The Frogs of Spring*, appeared at the Broadhurst Theatre for fifteen performances, and I had dug myself into a financial hole that took a year of working in Hollywood to climb out of. Since then, I have concentrated almost entirely on the short stories and novels, which as a way of making money is something like diving for sunken treasure.

"In 1939 I married Marjorie Bradford, whom I had met six years earlier, and we have two sons. One of them, God help him, is a born writer and is at present the Radio-TV editor at *Newsweek*, through, it should go without saying, no help from me. The other is still in college, and isn't quite sure what he wants to do. But whatever it is, he doesn't think it will be writing."

Finding it a mixed blessing to be the son of a famous humorist, Nathaniel Benchley has sought to avoid the kind of writing associated with his father (whose portrait he has drawn in a remarkably objective and widely praised biography). His own manner has been called "a delightful blend of understatement and satiric insight." According to William Barrett, "his comedy aspires to no metaphysical or social profundities; and these days it is a pleasure to encounter a humorist who takes neither himself nor his material too solemnly."

Benchley's entertaining and inventive satires, many of them set in New England, have hit a wide variety of targets, including business conclaves, spies, amateur theatre groups, and haunted houses. These books, rich in outrageous situations and improbable characters, lend themselves organically to film adaptation. A notable case in point is *The Off-Islanders*, about what happens when the crew of a Russian submarine, beached on an island resembling Nantucket, is mistaken for the spearhead of a full-scale invasion. Reviewers were delighted by the novel's combination of excitement and preposterous farce, and there was no less praise for the resulting movie, called *The Russians Are Coming, The Russians Are Coming*.

Benchley, whose novels have been translated into several languages, has also written movie scripts and a number of excellent books for young readers. He has named Thurber, Wolcott Gibbs, and E. B. White as the writers who have influenced him most. He likes to relax by doing "landscape paintings of amateur quality" which, to his surprise, find buyers. A horrifying novel, *Jaws*, about a man-eating shark, was written by Benchley's son Peter and published in 1973 with enormous success.

PRINCIPAL WORKS: *Fiction*—Side Street, 1950; One to Grow On, 1958; Sail a Crooked Ship, 1960; The Off-Islanders, 1961; Catch a Falling Spy, 1963; A Winter's Tale, 1964; The Visitors, 1965; A Firm Word or Two (stories), 1965; The Monument, 1966; Welcome to Xanadu, 1968; The Wake of the Icarus, 1969; Lassiter's Folly, 1971; The Hunter's Moon, 1972. *Nonfiction*—Robert Benchley (biography), 1955.

ABOUT: Contemporary Authors 4, 1963; Current Biography, 1953; Who's Who in America, 1970–1971. *Periodicals*—Publishers' Weekly October 2, 1972.

GOTTFRIED BENN

BENN, GOTTFRIED (May 2, 1886–July 7, 1956), German poet, was born at Mansfeld, Brandenburg, the son and grandson of Lutheran pastors, His mother was a French Swiss. Benn attended elementary schools at Sellia, Neumark, where his parents had moved in 1887, and the *Gymnasium* at Frankfurt on the Oder. To please his father, whom he revered, he studied theology for two years at the University of Marburg. Benn's relations with his father were strained by his mother's agonizing death from cancer. He settled on a medical career and entered the Kaiser Wilhelm Academy in Berlin, which trained medical officers for the Prussian Army. After qualifying, Benn began an obligatory period of army service but was released on medical grounds in 1912 after only a few months.

For the next two years, Benn worked in pathological laboratories, in a sanatorium, and on cruise ships, writing poetry in his spare time. He came to know the Mediterranean, entered avant-garde literary circles in Berlin, and wrote for their magazines. His first short collections were *Morgue* (1912) and *Söhne* (Sons, 1913), which established Benn as an expressionist *enfant terrible*. In fact, these books shared the disgust and rebellion, but not the stylistic innovations, of the early expressionists. *Morgue* was dominated by Benn's response to his work: by shockingly clinical descriptions of sickness and death on the one hand, fantasies of escape from them on the other.

In August 1914, Benn was recalled by the army and sent to occupied Belgium. There he was in medical charge of an army jail and of the Brussels prostitutes. It was these experiences, Ian Hilton suggests, which shattered Benn's "trust in reality." The stories he wrote at this time were published by Kurt Wolff in *Gehirne* (Brains, 1916). In them, his style developed past realism to the freedom and dynamism associated with expressionism; thematically, they laid the foundations of all Benn's later work. Rönne, the young doctor in the book, who could make no real contact with others and "who could not bear any reality . . . who knew only the rhythmic opening and closing of the ego," is clearly Benn himself. Michael Hamburger has said that Benn's development after 1914 "was a perpetual struggle between his ego and the external world. Total reality had been disposed of; all that remained was the isolated fact and the autonomous fantasy, the two components of his later poetry and prose."

In 1914 Benn had married Edith Osterloh and adopted her son, who died at the age of eighteen. Benn's daughter Nele was born in 1915. After his return to civilian life in 1918, he settled in Berlin as a specialist in skin and venereal diseases. His wife died in 1922, and his daughter was entrusted to foster parents in Denmark, where she grew up and married. The poems Benn wrote in the 1920s remain his best work. Though scientific terms are a striking component of their diction, the concepts for which these terms stand are introduced only to be dissolved in a flood of feeling. In such volumes as *Spaltung* (Fission, 1925), dispensing with verbs and almost with syntax, Benn sought and sometimes came close to distilling an "absolute poetry" —incantatory lyrics no more functional (or translatable) than music. Similarly, in his critical essays, he attempted a kind of "absolute prose" which at times, and effectively, borrowed the language and rhythms of poetry.

Prolific as he was throughout the 1920s, Benn's literary earnings, as he was fond of pointing out, amounted to almost nothing. His readers were few but enthusiastic, liberal intellectuals who admired his stylistic experiments and seemed unaware of the direction of his thought. Influenced by Nietzsche and Spengler, and his own embattled egocentricity, Benn had arrived at a nihilism which he supposed must be shared by every intelligent European but which might be transcended or sidestepped by denying reason and invoking subconscious and primitive instincts—the "primal vision." These views, which sometimes seem closer to French surrealism than to German expressionism, filled Benn's poetry with fantasies of a return to the prerational sources of life: images of the primeval lushness of the South. Politically, they warmed him to the mindless tribalism of National Socialism.

In 1932, to his immense satisfaction, Benn was elected to the poetry section of the Prussian Academy of Arts. In the same year, he profoundly shocked the majority of his devotees by proclaiming his sympathy with the ascendant Nazi party. When most eminent German writers chose to emigrate, Benn was left at the head of the poetry section of the Academy and defended his position in *Der Neue Staat und die Intellektuellen* (The New State and the Intellectuals, 1933). But it was soon made clear to him that the new state promised not an artistic renaissance but the suppression of such "degenerate" art as his own. He opted for what he called "the aristocratic form of emigration," in 1935 joining the army again as a medical officer. He did garrison duty in Hanover until, in 1937, he was transferred to the Ministry of Defense in Berlin. His work was attacked in the Nazi press and he was forbidden to publish. In 1938 he was expelled from the Reichsliteraturkammer, and he spoke without conviction of suicide. The same year he married Herta von Wedemeyer.

Benn worked in Berlin for five years, writing for himself and a few friends poetry and prose which included increasingly scathing attacks on the Nazi regime. In 1943 his section of the Ministry was evacuated to what is now Gorzow, in Poland. There, with his young wife, he spent the "quietest and happiest" months of his life. Towards the end of the war, Benn returned to Berlin, where the need for doctors was desperate, and sent his wife to a village on the Elbe. She committed suicide there shortly after the end of the war.

Later in 1945 Benn wrote to a friend: "I've no more plans, no hope, no longings." By then fifty-nine, he continued to practice medicine in the ruins of Berlin, and things got better. In 1947 he married again, a young dentist named Ilse Kaul. The following year he published, in Switzerland, his first book for a decade: *Statische Gedichte* (Static Poems). Like its successors, it contained not only expressionist poems but some in a more sober neoclassical style, From 1949 until his death, and posthumously, all his works, old and new, were issued in volume after volume. "The comeback is under way," he said, and so it was, in spite of attacks from those who resented his associations with National Socialism and from those who resented the extremity of his disenchantment with it.

Benn had become the sole prominent survivor of a generation of innovators whom their successors reverenced. His insistence that art and form were the only values worth preserving—a new attempt to transcend nihilism—was argued in Benn's very influential lecture *Probleme der Lyrik* (Problems of Lyric Poetry, 1951). It appealed to a younger generation disillusioned by the collapse of Nazi power and ideology, while Benn's political apologia, *Doppelleben* (Double Life, 1950) seemed to speak for an entire people. Among the prose works of this last period are two conversation pieces, *Drei alte Männer* (Three Old Men, 1949) and *Die Stimme hinter dem Vorhang* (The Voice Behind the Curtain, 1952); they seem to suggest that, if Benn had failed to transcend his nihilism, he had found a stoic courage with which to face it: "when night comes, we shall endure it." He continued his medical practice in Berlin until 1955 and died there the following year.

Michael Hamburger has suggested in *Reason and Energy* that Benn's "chief limitation as a poet and critic is that nearly all his thinking is determined by a reaction against [other views]"; that his "best poems succeed in spite of his theories," inducing "a euphoria of infinite possibilities, which results from the total release of energy from the bonds of reason." Since the late 1950s, the new moral and political preoccupations of the younger German writers have diminished the influence of Benn's "soliloquy art," which however continues to be widely read and studied, in Germany and elsewhere. Although T. S. Eliot quoted him, there has been relatively little interest in Benn in England and the United States, perhaps because of the difficulty of translating his most characteristic work. But Benn's eminence among the twentieth century innovators is secure.

PRINCIPAL WORKS IN ENGLISH TRANSLATION: Primal Vision (selected poetry and prose by various translators), 1960.

ABOUT: Buddeberg, E. Gottfried Benn, 1961; Hamburger, M. From Prophecy to Exorcism, 1963; Hamburger, M. Reason and Energy, 1957; Hilton, I. Gottfried Benn *in* Natan, A. (ed.). German Men of Letters, vol. III, 1964; Lohner, E. Passion und Intellekt, 1961; Nef, E. Das Werk Gottfried Benns, 1962. *Periodicals*—German Quarterly 26 1953; Poetry 80 1952.

***BERGENGRUEN, WERNER** (September 16, 1892–September 4, 1964), German novelist and poet. The following note was supplied (in German) by his widow, Charlotte Bergengruen: "He was born in Riga, Latvia, the son of a physician. His father sent him and his brothers to Germany when they were still very young, in order to remove them from the intensifying Russification of the Baltic region. Werner Bergengruen described this transplantation as one of the deepest woundings of his life. At the universities of Marburg and Munich he studied theology, German literature, and art history. In the First World War he served on the German side in the East, then fought in the Baltic infantry under Colonel Alexander, later Governor of Canada, against the Bolsheviks in the Baltic region.

"He earned his living subsequently as a journalist specializing in Eastern questions, and as a translator; during this period he was living with his family chiefly in Berlin, and was already devoting himself intensively to his own creative efforts. His first book, a collection of *novellen*, appeared in 1923, and from that time on, in quick succession, novels, *novellen*, poems. His growing reputation as poet and novelist suffered a serious setback with the upsurge of National Socialism, against which he fought from the first moment. With his novel *Der Grosstyrann und das Gericht* (1935) he became famous overnight. In 1937 he was excluded from the Writers Council of the Reich, but then received special permission—thoroughly restricting though it was—to exercise his profession, so that his second great novel, *Am Himmel wie auf Erden* (1940), could appear in print, even though shortly afterwards it was banned. Both novels are decidedly documents of the Resistance, and as a writer of the Resistance he acquired a high reputation during the twelve years of National Socialism. In 1942 his house in Munich was destroyed in a bombing raid. The family moved to a small mountain village in the Tyrol, and from there emigrated in 1946 to Switzerland. Here he remained for twelve years, exercising a continuing influence in Germany through extensive lecture tours. In 1958 he settled down in a house which he had built for himself in Baden-Baden, where on September 4, 1964 he died.

"The two great poles in the work of Werner Bergengruen are on the one hand his lost Baltic homeland and old Russia, and on the other hand Italy. In the year 1936 he became a convert, with his family, to the Catholic faith, finding in the Church a new homeland as a substitute for his lost homeland. Religious content, along with a deep knowledge of history, is a further element in his creative work. He spent a half year in Rome in the winter of 1948–49, and there wrote his *Römisches Erinnerungsbuch* (Roman Book of Memories, 1949) which portrays, through all its deep layers of centuries, this city which had become his spiritual homeland.

WERNER BERGENGRUEN

"In addition to the two novels already discussed, mention must be made of the historical *Herzog Karl der Kühne* (Duke Charles the Bold, 1930), and the novel-trilogy *Der letzte Rittmeister*, the history of a Russian émigré who ended his life in Tessin after the First World War.

"As a lyric poet Werner Bergengruen is best known for his book of poetry *Die heile Welt* (1950), which contrasts the inviolable, indestructible core of human nature with the fragmented quality of our time; but he is known also for his cycle of poems *Dies Irae*, poems which—like many others by him and by his close friend Reinhold Schneider—circulated secretly during the Third Reich.

"Werner Bergengruen is considered a master of the *novelle*. This form, which he viewed as his own narrative field, gave him the opportunity to create art works of an extraordinary concision and pregnancy. Especially worth mentioning here are *Der spanische Rosenstock* (*The Spanish Rosebush*, 1940), and *Die drei Falken* (*The Three Falcons*, 1937).

"His translations of Tolstoy's *War and Peace* and Dostoevsky's *Crime and Punishment* are considered to be unexcelled.

"Werner Bergengruen won the Wilhelm Raabe prize in the year 1948. In 1958 he was elected to the order Pour le Mérite, in which there are at any time only thirty representatives of German cultural life, chosen from the arts and sciences. In 1962 he received the Schiller Memorial Prize of the State of Baden-Württemberg."

* ber′ gen grün

As Charlotte Bergengruen writes, her husband, after the publication during the 1920s of a succession of fundamentally religious historical novels, became famous overnight with the appearance in 1935 of *Der Grosstyrann und das Gericht* (translated by Norman Cameron as *A Matter of Conscience*). Set in Renaissance Italy, it is at once a meditation on justice and an allegory about Nazi Germany—about the "temptations that beset the mighty and . . . the corruptibility of the unmighty and the threatened." The sin of the Grand Prince, who argues that justice must be tailored to the needs of the community, is "lunatic pride." By putting the interests of the state above all else, he brings social and moral chaos to his city. Only the Christ-like self-sacrifice of a humble man is able to bring people and ruler to their senses.

Some reviewers of the English version found Bergengruen's allegorical and philosophical concerns rather intrusive, weakening his narrative and imposing an abstract quality upon his characters, as in a morality play. The novel was nevertheless very warmly admired, both for the nobility of its theme and the technical perfection of its structure. John Raymond found it "brilliant and profoundly moving," and Serge Hughes called it "the work of a master writer, one of the most impressive to have come from a modern German novelist." In the opinion of many readers it is Bergengruen's best book.

Am Himmel wie auf Erden (In Heaven as on Earth, 1940), deals in a similar fashion with a similar theme: the corrupting and disintegrating effect of fear. The setting is Berlin in 1524, when the state astrologer prophesies a new Deluge, but much of what Bergengruen demonstrates of the relationship between fear and power was equally applicable to Nazi Germany (as Goebbels, belatedly, realized).

Bergengruen's *novellen* tend to be less overtly philosophical than his full-length works, and at their best show him to be a master storyteller, polished, inventive, and eminently readable. An element of macabre humor in some of his tales reflects the influence of E. T. A. Hoffmann, of whom he wrote a study. A group of stories, all supposedly related by an old Czarist officer, form one of Bergengruen's most likable books, *Der letzte Rittmeister* (1952, translated by Eric Peters as *The Last Captain of Horse*). Whimsically ironic and entertaining as they are, these stories convey a nostalgia for a vanished code of chivalry which is only another aspect of Bergengruen's central preoccupation with the conflict between morality and power. The book forms a trilogy with *Die Rittmeisterin* (1954) and *Der dritte Kranz* (1962).

The best known of Bergengruen's poems is the cycle published in 1945 as *Dies Irae*, but written at Achenkirch in the Tyrol during the war and recited at clandestine meetings of the German Resistance. Traditional in form but apocalyptic in tone, they saw in the allied bombing of Germany a divine punishment, calling for a moral renaissance in all men. Of his other collections of verse, the most notable are the mainly religious poems collected in *Die heile Welt* (The Intact World, 1950), and *Lombardische Elegie* (1951). In the latter Bergengruen devotes himself to the contrasts—physical and metaphorical—between the beloved northland of his Baltic and patrician childhood and the southern regions of his equally beloved Italy.

Bergengruen was an immensely prolific and professional writer who consistently addressed himself to the crucial issues of his time, albeit with a Christian certainty and a reliance on traditional forms that now seem out of fashion. Hermann Kunisch has spoken of his feeling for that point "where the boundaries between inner and outer are unimportant, and unity produces itself in love." He published his best work when his courage, his affirmation of divine and human values in the face of chaos, were most needed.

PRINCIPAL WORKS IN ENGLISH TRANSLATION: A Matter of Conscience, 1952; The Last Captain of Horse, 1953; Four Tales, 1966.

ABOUT: Bänziger, H. Werner Bergengruen, Weg und Werk, 1950; Bergengruen, W. Schreibtischerinnerungen, 1961; Bithell, J. Modern German Literature, 1959; Closs, A. Twentieth Century German Literature, 1969; Hoffmann, C. W. Opposition Poetry in Nazi Germany, 1962; Kampmann, T. Die Welt Werner Bergengruens, 1952; Klemm, G. Werner Bergengruen, 1954; Kunisch, H. Der andere Bergengruen, 1958; Penguin Companion to Literature 2, 1969; Sobota, E. Das Menschenbild bei Bergengruen, 1962; Waidson, H. M. The Modern German Novel, 1959; Weber, M.W. Zur Lyrik Werner Bergengruens, 1958. *Periodicals*—German Life and Letters 1949; New Statesman May 17, 1952; New York Herald Tribune Book Review March 21, 1954; New York Times April 20, 1952; Saturday Review June 7, 1952; Spectator April 25, 1952.

BERGER, THOMAS (LOUIS) (July 20, 1924–), American novelist, writes: "I was born at noon on a hot Sunday in Cincinnati, Ohio, and grew up in Lockland, a nearby suburban community of some five thousand souls. My father was business manager of the same public school that I attended from kindergarten through high school. My parents live still in the same town, in the same house.

"In high school I ached to get away to a university, but hated college once there and enlisted in the Army, in which I was happy and which I have always since defended as the purest version of moral democracy.

"For years, without ever having written a line on my own initiative, except some wisecracks for a students' periodical, I had thought of myself as a writer. After returning from the war and completing my formal education, I had no further excuse for delay. I moved to New York, enrolled in a 'writers' workshop' at the New School for Social Research, and began to produce simple-minded short stories. I got married and for a few years held nine-to-five jobs, in my third and last serving as copy editor on a magazine and so learning a trade which in my subsequent practice as a freelancer for book publishers, was to sustain me through the many years in which my own writing brought little income.

"It was my wife who encouraged me to leave full-time employment, stay home at our house on the Hudson River in Rockland County, New York, where living was inexpensive, and begin a novel. My first book took four years to write. In the course of this labor I discovered my inability to see at any time beyond the sentence under composition. I work without plot or plan, and I foresee few characters. I start with nothing to say, and proceed by what I think of as a series of revelations. Sometimes these prove to be spurious, leading me off the highway into the trackless wastes, and when I eventually get my bearings, I must destroy the work of months. Early on, as if I were making a forced march and were determined to pass an arbitrary number of telephone poles before falling out, I found it necessary to set for myself a daily quota of one page. Too often, through the years, this has proved a maximum rather than the minimum intended; but if one works as I do, six days a week, he produces some three hundred pages per annum.

"The income from my third novel enabled me to give up the freelance copy editing and manuscript revision which, added to the labor of my vocation, often kept me at the desk ten hours a day, and, moving five times in two and a half years, I realized various fantasies of residence in London, at Malibu Beach and elsewhere. I settled finally in a penthouse in Manhattan.

"Since 1950 I have been married to Jeanne Redpath, a painter and an extraordinarily patient woman. Because my style of life is as extemporaneous as that in which I work, I believe in a personal God who would never be recognized by the institutional faiths. I have no politics whatever, and while I am superficially sympathetic to almost any cause, I fundamentally wish it ill.

"I admire animals and therefore approve of blood sports which are pursued according to the established rituals. Being by nature a man of mind I am more impressed by physical bravery than by intellectual courage. To things I react instantly; to abstractions, with reluctance. In general I am bored by opinions, but fascinated by tastes; indifferent to what a man thinks, but enthralled by an account of what he eats. I especially abhor what is current and try strenuously to remain ignorant of it. I worship the English language.

"My characteristic endeavor is to lose my self, and then to find it, in the creation of an extended fictional narrative. For me, writing can be distinguished from living only in the respective materials employed, and like living it progressively, and rightly, destroys the practitioner thereof."

THOMAS BERGER

Thomas Berger seems to subscribe to the contemporary view that life is absurd but to believe at the same time that this absurdity is intolerable—that it cannot and must not be allowed to be true. His comic and picaresque novels explore this paradox with high linguistic energy and creative zest.

His first book, *Crazy in Berlin*, seemed to W. J. Smith among others "one of the finest and funniest to come along since the war." It introduced Carlo Reinhart, an oversized GI attached to an Army hospital in occupied Germany at the end of World War II. Reinhart likes the Army, "where the petty decisions were provided and the major ones ignored"; indeed he loves everyone and everything and is therefore constantly at odds with loveless society.

Reinhart in Love takes this Reichian hero home to the Midwest after the war and records his struggles to preserve a little humanity, to walk unspotted through the grubby world of real estate salesmanship, to remain loyal to his inadequate wife. Reinhart's disillusionment is completed in *Vital Parts*, in which he is put down for his old-style liberalism by his wife and children and taken up only by the self-made entrepreneur Bob Sweet, who wants Reinhart frozen into immortality as an advertisement for cryobiology. The Reinhart books are relished for the extravagance of their fantasy, the brilliance of their language, and the murderous accuracy of their dialogue. Written "without plot or plan," they have spontaneity and gusto but lack shape and control, rambling at times into dullness.

In *Little Big Man*, with history to discipline his imagination, Berger produced what is undoubtedly his best book so far, at once a loving parody of the mythology of the American West and an important contribution to it. It is the picaresque story of one-hundred-and-eleven-year-old Jack Crabb, a former frontiersman whose memories encompass the rise of the Old West and its fall, and who has lived alternately as a white man (by birth) and as a Cheyenne (by adoption). There is no better account in fiction of the life and attitudes of the plains Indians and no more tragic expression of what America has lost by its extinction of their strangely direct perception of life. In the course of his life Crabb meets Wyatt Earp, Wild Bill Hickock, and most of the other notables of the frontier, and is the only white survivor of Custer's last stand (which is brilliantly and poignantly described).

R. V. Cassill, in his review of *Little Big Man*, wrote: "In about the same way that Faulkner delivers the old South to the ken of jaded but renewable imagination, Berger delivers the West . . . finding, by a prophetic leap, the common ingredients our regressive dreams of the West shared with the dreams of those vanished Indians and a boy kidnapped from a wagon train. And oh, that Wild West dream is funny, magically and marvelously funny as Berger recreates it." The novel earned its author the Rosenthal Award for Fiction and the Western Heritage Award in 1965, and a few years later was filmed. Many critics consider it the best novel ever about the American West.

That Berger delights in paradox is evident even in his brief note above, and paradox is a dominant element in *Killing Time*, which turns the traditional detective story on its head. Many critics were delighted by the central character, an irresistibly sane mass-murderer called Joseph Detweiler, but the book seemed to some readers excessively didactic and sometimes dull. Berger is also the author of a play, *Other People*, performed for the first time in 1970 in Stockbridge, Massachusetts. The three nine-to-five jobs he mentions above were as a librarian at the Rand School of Social Science (1948–1951), as a staff member of the *New York Times Index* (1951–1952), and as an editor of *Popular Science Monthly* (1952–1953).

PRINCIPAL WORKS: Crazy in Berlin, 1958; Reinhart in Love, 1962; Little Big Man, 1964; Killing Time, 1967; Vital Parts, 1970; Regiment of Women, 1973.

ABOUT: Who's Who in America, 1970–1971. *Periodicals*—Books and Bookmen October 1965; Bookweek October 25, 1964; Commonweal November 20, 1964; New York Times Book Review September 17, 1967; March 29, 1970; Saturday Review April 14, 1962; October 10, 1964; September 23, 1967; Times Literary Supplement June 21, 1963; September 9, 1965.

***BERGMAN, HJALMAR (FREDRIK ELGÉRUS)** (September 19, 1883–January 1, 1931), Swedish novelist, story writer, and dramatist, was born in Örebro, the capital of a mining province in central Sweden. He was the son of a domineering and extrovert banker, Klas Fredrik Bergman, and of the former Fredrique Elgérus. Fat, clumsy, and hypersensitive, Bergman had a wretched childhood, developing in consequence a rich fantasy life and a defensive sense of humor. He read history and philosophy for a time at the University of Uppsala and continued his studies during a long visit to Italy in 1901. Italy—particularly Florence—was to be one of his favorite halts in a restless life spent largely in hotels. Personal relationships outside his immediate circle were always painfully difficult for him, and not even his marriage in 1908 prompted him to settle down, though he did acquire a summer cottage in the Stockholm archipelago which, after 1917, served as a kind of home base.

His wife, Stina Lindberg, was a member of a prominent theatrical family and, partly for that reason, Bergman wrote plays as well as fiction from the beginning of his literary career. His early works display diversity rather than originality but have in common a disillusioned and pessimistic view of life. His first major book was the novel *Hans nåds testamente* (The Baron's Will, 1910), a story of improbable complications based on the author's childhood memories of the mining and foundry country of Bergslagen, near Örebro, but translated into a world of caricature and farce. The novel was recognized by some critics, though not by the general public, as the work of an original comic genius of the first order.

It was followed by a series of works about Bergslagen. The three parts of *Komedier i Bergslagen* (Comedies of Bergslagen, 1914–1916) are particularly striking examples of the great range of Bergman's work at this time: realistic events imperceptibly acquire symbolic force or undergo fantastic distortions, while elements of tragedy and farce mingle without incongruity. "The situations are often mad," writes Alric Gustafson, "the characters eccentric, the dialogue apparently a mere crazy-quilt of alternately gay and macabre indirections. So utterly brilliant indeed are the surface features of Bergman's art that they tend in some of the Bergslagen novels to obscure somewhat the author's more serious purposes . . . his central concern with the tragic drift of character in a world of petty, directionless, meaningless conflict."

Bergman probed ruthlessly into his characters' most deeply repressed impulses—their jealousies, fears, and secret desires—and was particularly fascinated by the contrast between active extroverts and hopeless dreamers. This is the basis of the conflict

* bâr' y' man

between father and son in *En döds memoarer* (Memoirs of a Dead Man, 1918), an extraordinary novel that is part family chronicle, part horror story, and part allegory. The narrator belongs to a family doomed to murder and treachery, whether they seek to escape their fate through frenetic activity or yield to it like the narrator, the "dead man." Man may propose, but God (or fate, or subconscious impulse) disposes: "Let us then humbly confess that our thoughts and our wills flutter like moths about the flame. And therein lies our power and our security—that we are powerless."

The Swedish reading public was not ready for Bergman's disturbing views or methods, and with his next novel, *Markurells i Wadköping* (The Markurells in Wadköping, 1919, translated as *God's Orchid*), he made deliberate concessions to popular taste, moderating the macabre and fantastic elements in his work, and making his ethical intentions more explicit. The book is a broadly satirical account of the scandals and intrigues of Wadköping (Örebro). It centers on the innkeeper Markurell, who experiences a moment of hubris when he seems to hold supreme power over the town but plunges forthwith from the heights to the depths when he discovers that his adored son is not his. Markurell's story is constructed like Greek tragedy, and his sufferings are explicitly compared to those of Job, but—in a way that is thoroughly characteristic of Bergman's work—these elevated parallels are drawn in a context of broad farce. Somewhat similar is the brilliantly realized novel *Farmor och Vår Herre* (Grandmother and Our Lord, 1921, translated as *Thy Rod and Thy Staff*), in which a despotic old woman, accustomed to speaking on equal terms with God, is put firmly in her place.

Bergman's life ended in a dark period of increasing personal disintegration, exacerbated by illness and a short stay in the unnerving atmosphere of Hollywood, where he had hoped to continue a fruitful collaboration with the producer Victor Sjöström. The novel *Chefen fru Ingeborg* (Madame Directress Ingeborg, 1924, translated as *The Head of the Firm*) is the story of a middle-aged widow who becomes the victim of a repressed passion for her prospective son-in-law, a characterless man whose motto is: "Nothing really matters much." Ultimately she can recover her self-respect only by sacrificing herself.

Bergman's last novel also reveals a concern with merciless self-judgment. In *Clownen Jac* (Jac the Clown, 1930), a famous clown condemns himself for prostituting his art and his emotions—particularly fear—for the sake of popular success. This was Bergman's final judgment on his own career; he died in a hotel room in Berlin shortly after completing the novel.

While Bergman did his most important work

HJALMAR BERGMAN

as a novelist, he also made a considerable contribution to Swedish drama. In such highly successful plays as *Swedenhielms* (1925, translated as *The Swedenhielms*), a gay comedy about a Nobel Prize winner and his family, and the dramatized version of *Markurells i Wadköping*, Bergman is undoubtedly playing to the gallery. Earlier, he had seen the failure of his dreamy and hypnotic *Marionettspel* (Puppet Plays, 1917). At least one of these, *Herr Sleeman kommer* (translated as *Mr. Sleeman Is Coming*), in which an otherwise lively young girl submits somnambulistically to an ugly old man, is now recognized as a classic of the form. Indeed Bergman's intensely personal world is ultimately one of puppets, of people animated by forces, internal or external, over which they have no control. Their antics may seem comic, but they are inspired by fear or anguish.

PRINCIPAL WORKS IN ENGLISH TRANSLATION: God's Orchid, 1924; The Head of the Firm, 1936; Thy Rod and Thy Staff, 1937; Four Plays (The Markurells in Wadköping, The Baron's Last Will, Swedenhielms, Mr. Sleeman Is Coming), 1968.

ABOUT: Ek, S. R. Varklighet och vision, 1964; Gustafson, A. A History of Swedish Literature, 1961; Linder, E. H. Sju världars herre, 1962; Penguin Companion to Literature 2, 1969; Smith, H. (ed.) Columbia Dictionary of Modern European Literature, 1947. *Periodicals*—Scandinavian Studies February 1965; Tulane Drama Review 2, 1961.

BERLIN, SIR ISAIAH (June 6, 1909–) is a British philosopher who, in the words of A. J. P. Taylor, "dwells in that strange borderland, the history of ideas, especially of ideas displayed in literature; and one sometimes feels that he has more

ISAIAH BERLIN

ideas than all the historical authors whom he sets out to illuminate." He was born in Riga, the capital of Latvia, then part of the Russian Empire. His parents were Jewish. His father, Mendel Berlin, was a successful timber merchant. His mother was the former Marie Volshonock.

Isaiah Berlin spent most of his early life in Russia. But in 1920 his family emigrated to England, where he attended St. Paul's School in London. From an early age he showed the predisposition towards learning that his colleagues later referred to as "subconscious osmosis," for it seemed impossible that one man could have read all the books that he cites, quotes, and criticizes. He went with a scholarship to Corpus Christi College, Oxford, and graduated in 1931 with first class honors both in humane letters and in Modern Greats (philosophy, politics, and economics). In the following year he was appointed lecturer in philosophy at New College and a Fellow of All Souls College.

Oxford at that time was in the throes of the linguistic revolution that has transformed philosophy. Berlin grasped the new ideas with as much relish as the other young philosophers, writing articles during the 1930s on the logical problems of induction and the positivist criterion of meaning. He learnt most of his philosophy from J. L. Austin of All Souls where, according to Stuart Hampshire "they used to sit around in the Common Room and talk philosophy day and night."

In 1938 Berlin was elected a Fellow of New College, and he continued as Fellow and lecturer there until 1950. His first book was published in 1939 and the title alone indicated that he was moving away from logical positivism: *Karl Marx: His Life and Environment.* This short biography is an objective and scholarly presentation of Marx as "an overbearing and aggressive theorist" who revolutionized social and historical thought. It concentrates on Marxism as a system of philosophy, almost totally ignoring its economic theories. Berlin justified this by claiming that the two subjects were independent in Marx's thought, and, in general, critics found the book invaluable.

During the war Berlin worked for the British Ministry of Information in New York (1941) and was first secretary to the British Embassy in Washington from 1942 until 1946, when he received a C.B.E. for his wartime services. Berlin's diplomatic dispatches were widely admired and eventually attracted the attention of Winston Churchill himself. The Prime Minister invited this prodigy to dinner and passed a bewildering evening until it was learned that his invitation had gone astray; his guest was the American songwriter Irving Berlin.

In 1947 Berlin returned to his New College lectureship, but he was now no longer what Oxford considered a "philosopher." Berlin spent a year lecturing at Harvard in 1949 and on his return to Oxford in 1950 went to All Souls College as a research fellow. The same year he published a translation of Turgenev's *First Love* and in the following year his celebrated essay *The Hedgehog and the Fox: An Essay on Tolstoy's View of History* appeared in Volume II of the Oxford Slavonic Papers. It was published in book form in 1953.

The title refers to a saying of Archilochus: "The fox knows many things, but the hedgehog knows but one big thing." Berlin adapts this to fit classes of thinkers: the hedgehogs, like Dante and Lucretius, who relate everything to a single central vision; and the foxes, like Aristotle and Montaigne, who pursue many theories often unrelated and sometimes contradictory. Tolstoy, says Berlin, "was by nature a fox but believed in being a hedgehog." His point is that literary critics, by dismissing Tolstoy's historical theories as mere crankishness, had thrown away an important key to *War and Peace*. Like Kutuzov in that novel, Tolstoy believed in a "universal explanatory principle," but he could not hope to discover it because it was his nature to see not one-ness but multiplicity —"always with an ever-growing minuteness, in all its teeming individuality, with an obsessive, inescapable, incorruptible, all-penetrating lucidity which maddens him."

This is the Berlin rhetoric that so exercises the critics: "The target is accurately located and is then assailed by a stream of . . . tracer bullets," says one, while, according to A. J. P. Taylor, "The divine *afflatus* descends upon him. The sentences get longer and longer, the thought soars higher and higher, and what had begun as an essay in literary criticism ends as an utterance of the Delphic Apollo." Nevertheless, all were agreed that this was a brilliant, exciting, and important analysis of Tolstoy's thought and personality, even if, as some critics felt, Berlin's procedure did not take him to the roots of the despairing and destructive qualities in Tolstoy.

Berlin's 1953 Auguste Comte Memorial Trust Lecture was published in 1955 as *Historical Inevitability*. (It is characteristic of him that many of his most-discussed works are of pamphlet length and were originally presented as lectures.) His purpose in *Historical Inevitability* is to show that the doctrine of determinism, which asserts that every event is in some sense shaped by theoretically predictable forces, is incompatible with the notion of human responsibility. He does not claim that determinism is necessarily false, only that it is irrelevant to the study of history inasmuch as "we neither think nor speak as if it were true." Conceding that the social sciences have shown human choice to be "a good deal more limited than we used to suppose," he insists that a real area of human freedom remains.

Historical Inevitability is undoubtedly, as one critic said, "one of the most brilliant and provocative studies in the philosophy of history to have appeared in many years." It has occasioned some very heated criticism, notably from E. H. Carr, the Cambridge historian, who described Berlin's preoccupation with the notions of freedom and responsibility as the dead horse he had "flogged into life."

This animal was resurrected to run a different race in Berlin's inaugural lecture on his appointment as Chichele Professor of Social and Political Theory at Oxford, a post he held from 1957 (when he also received his knighthood) until 1967. *Two Concepts of Liberty* begins with the statement "There are two sorts of notions of the word 'liberty'—negative and positive—in the history of thought." Berlin defines the positive concept of liberty as a desire to be the active instrument of one's own will and not the will of others; it is, he says, the refuge of ambiguities and inconsistencies. Negative liberty is passive—a freedom from coercion: He thinks it is this that people refer to when speaking of social or political liberty. He believes his distinction is clear if the two concepts are compared historically, though not all of his critics were convinced. Even Berlin's opponents cannot deny, however, that the lecture is a remarkable *tour de force*, and, as one reviewer wrote, "in its indirect, hypothetical way *Two Concepts of Liberty* is as forceful and as emotional a plea for individuality and independence and human variety as its predecessor [John Stuart Mill's *On Liberty*] of a hundred years ago."

Berlin has produced several less important works. *The Age of Enlightenment* consists of selections from writings of the British empiricist school of the eighteenth century, with an extremely useful introduction to the thought of that period. Berlin's 1957 Herbert Samuel Lecture, *Chaim Weizmann*, is an appraisal of the first president of Israel, who was a close friend of Berlin's. *The Life and Opinions of Moses Hess* is a "scintillating and deeply-felt essay" on the German-Jewish revolutionary who played a critical role in the development of both communism and Zionism. Berlin is a regular contributor to such various journals as *Mind*, *Foreign Affairs*, *Encounter*, *Twentieth Century*, and the *Spectator*.

In 1966 Isaiah Berlin became president of Wolfson College, Oxford, a controversial choice for a new college whose emphasis was to be on technology. In the same year he became associated with the Graduate Center of the City University of New York, serving successively as Professor of Humanities, as Visiting Professor, and (since 1971) as Distinguished Professor of Humanities. He has also lectured at Harvard, Chicago, Princeton, Bryn Mawr, and elsewhere.

Berlin married Aline Elizabeth Yvonne de Gunzbourg in 1956. His powers of conversation, in several languages, are legendary. In English he talks at four times the speed of normal people in an accent which retains a slight trace of his native Latvian, producing according to one of his colleagues a "noise like bath water running." He slows down his delivery somewhat for his famous lectures and broadcasts, which have nevertheless been described as "rapid, vivid, torrential cascades of rich, spontaneous, tumbling ideas and images." Berlin is equally renowned for his charm and his intolerance of stupidity. He received one of Britain's highest honors in 1971, when he became one of the twenty-four members of the Order of Merit.

PRINCIPAL WORKS: Karl Marx: His Life and Environment, 1939; The Hedgehog and the Fox: An Essay on Tolstoy's View of History, 1953; Historical Inevitability, 1955; (ed.) The Age of Enlightenment, 1956; Two Concepts of Liberty, 1958; Chaim Weizmann, 1958; The Life and Opinions of Moses Hess, 1959; Mr. Churchill in 1940, 1964; Four Essays on Liberty, 1968; Fathers and Children (Romanes Lecture), 1972.

ABOUT: Current Biography, 1964; White, M. G. Religion, Politics, and the Higher Learning, 1959; Who's Who, 1971. *Periodicals*—American Scholar Fall 1959; Ethics January 1967; Nation February 23, 1957; New York Times February 8, 1966; New Yorker September 25, 1954; Spectator January 1, 1954; January 14, 1955; Sunday Times (London) March 31, 1957; Time August 13, 1945; Times Literary Supplement November 20, 1953; December 17, 1954; February 20, 1959.

***BERNAL, J(OHN) D(ESMOND)** (May 10, 1901–September 15, 1971), Irish scientist and writer on the philosophy and history of science, was born at Nenagh, Tipperary, of Roman Catholic parents. Educated at Bedford School and Stonyhurst, a Jesuit

* ber nal'

J. D. BERNAL

College in Lancashire, he went with a scholarship to Emmanuel College, Cambridge. Bernal stayed on after his graduation to do research in crystallography under Sir William Bragg at the Davy–Faraday Laboratory (1923–1927). He became a lecturer and then assistant director of research in crystallography at Cambridge (1934–1937), and was soon recognized as a major authority in his field.

C. H. Waddington discussed Bernal and his work in an informative article in the *New York Review of Books* (February 29, 1968). According to Waddington, Bernal always defined his subject very broadly, taking crystallography "to involve an attempt to discover and understand the spatial arrangement of any assemblage of repeated units, however complex these units might be. He was one of the great pioneers, along with W. T. Astbury and Linus Pauling, in the application of X-ray crystallography to the complex substances found in living things"—work which has been central to the tremendous advances made since then in the development of molecular biology. He was elected a Fellow of the Royal Society in 1937.

The brilliance and originality of Bernal's work was never in doubt. If he left it to others to cultivate the ground that he cleared (and to reap the Nobel prizes) it was because he lacked their single-mindedness. Cambridge science in the 1920s and 1930s was in a state of intellectual ferment and Bernal, relinquishing his Catholicism in favor of Marxism, involved himself in "almost every living and growing aspect of science except pure nuclear physics." Bernal is remembered in the Union Library at Cambridge carrying immense piles of books on a staggering range of subjects; in scientific circles he was known as "the Sage." "Not only did he know more facts about more subjects than anyone else," Waddington says, "but he had an outstanding ability both to generalize an observation so that its broad relevance became apparent, and to focus precisely what was the real issue in a complex tangle of problems." He was as active on the political as on the scientific scene. During the Spanish Civil War he was serving at one time on over forty anti-Fascist committees, and he was a familiar figure at the great political rallies of the time.

Bernal's first book, *The World, the Flesh, and the Devil*, appeared in 1929 and expressed his convictions about the scientific waste that takes place in a capitalist society. The *Social Function of Science*, perhaps his most important book, followed ten years later. It is a comprehensive survey from the Marxist position of the role of science in human life, contrasting the chaotic manner in which scientific investigation proceeds with what might be achieved by a major reorganization of scientific teaching and research. C. P. Snow in his review said that "no other book of this range and vision is going to appear for many years. It is the testament of one of the few minds of genius in our time." The book has become, according to Waddington, "the acknowledged source of what is nowadays known as the Science of Science, and of much technological forecasting besides."

When World War II came Bernal made no secret of the fact that, though he thought the war essential, he had no time for the government of the day. Sir John Anderson nevertheless brought him into the Ministry of Home Security as scientific adviser, saying that he would have him "even if he is as red as the flames of hell." Later, as adviser to the Chief of Combined Operations (1942–1945), Bernal applied his knowledge of soil structures to the problems of landing vast quantities of men and equipment on the Normandy beaches for D Day, characteristically employing such unexpected sources of information as a medieval manuscript. In 1945 he received the Royal Medal of the Royal Society.

Two years before the war, Bernal had left Cambridge and gone to Birkbeck College, in the University of London, as professor of physics. He returned to that post after the war and in 1963 became Birkbeck's professor of crystallography. After a serious illness he retired in 1968 as emeritus professor. Bernal published a number of books after the war, some of them extremely valuable and important. *The Freedom of Necessity* has been called "probably the first major study in what is now called science policy." *The Physical Basis of Life* is a brief exposition of the way in which life may have emerged spontaneously, and without divine agency, from nonliving matter—a theme which is developed and brought up to date in *The Origin of Life. Science in History* is, according to Waddington, "a major, though controversial, source from which much of the modern study of the history of science has sprung." *World Without War* examines the causes of war and calls for a gigantic program of worldwide industrialization to end the dangerous disparity between the rich nations and the poor.

Bernal was a member of a number of European academies of science and an honorary professor of the University of Moscow. He received the Lenin Peace Prize in 1953 and the Grotius Medal in 1959. He served as vice president of the World Federation of Scientific Workers and as chairman of the World Council for Peace. In 1965–1966 he was a member of the British government's Advisory Committee for Scientific and Technical Information.

C. P. Snow regarded Bernal as "the most learned scientist of his time . . . [with] enormous imaginative sweep and deep insight." Snow said: "I have not in my life met anyone who more passionately, or with more knowledge or imagination, wanted to be of some use to his brother men." Ilya Ehrenburg had a story about Bernal waiting for a plane at the Moscow airport in pouring rain and receiving from this uncomfortable source an inspiration about the structure of water, a thesis later developed in a scientific paper. Ehrenburg thought him a typical man of science, "always forgetting or losing something . . . [but] he remembers everything [that really matters]." A tall, mop-haired man, Bernal was married in 1922 and had two children.

PRINCIPAL WORKS: The World, the Flesh, and the Devil: An Enquiry into the Future of the Three Enemies of the Rational Soul, 1929; The Social Function of Science, 1939; (with M. C. Cornforth) Science for Peace and Socialism, 1949; The Freedom of Necessity, 1949; The Physical Basis of Life, 1951; Marx and Science, 1952; Science and Industry in the Nineteenth Century, 1953; Science in History, 1954; World Without War, 1958; A Prospect of Peace, 1960; Science for a Developing World: Account of a Symposium Organized by the World Federation of Scientific Workers, 1963; The Origin of Life, 1967; The Extension of Man: A History of Physics Before 1900, 1972.

ABOUT: Ehrenburg, I. Postwar Years, 1945–1954, 1966; Goldsmith, M. and Mackay, A. Society and Science, 1965; Who's Who, 1971. *Periodicals*—Hibbert Journal April 1956; New Statesman March 6, 1954; May 6, 1960; New York Review of Books March 3, 1966; February 29, 1968; New York Times June 18, 1939; Scientific American August 1960; March 1966; Scientific Monthly December 1945.

BERRIAULT, GINA (January 1, 1926–), American novelist and short story writer, writes: "The youngest of three children, I was born in Long Beach, California, to Russian-Jewish immigrant parents. My father was a writer and ad solicitor, poorly paid, for trade journals, and, in his youth, a marble cutter; my mother lost her sight when I was an adolescent. My formal education stopped after high school. Working as clerk, waitress, news reporter, and at other numerous and forgotten jobs, I wrote nights if I worked days, or days if I worked nights. I began writing when very young, and feel that I am still serving a long apprenticeship.

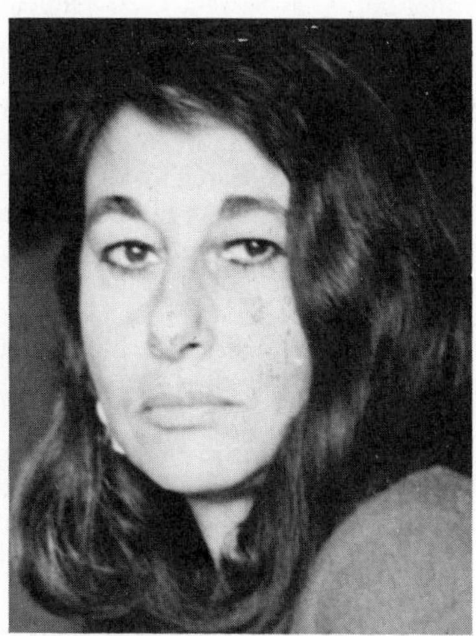

GINA BERRIAULT

"My work is an investigation of reality which is, simply, so full of ambiguity and of answers that beget further questions that to pursue it is an impossible task and a completely absorbing necessity. It appears to me that all the terrors that human beings inflict upon one another are countered to a perceptible degree by the attempts of some writers to make us known to one another and thus to impart or revive a reverence for life. The nineteenth century Russian writers; Samuel Beckett; Italo Svevo speak most clearly to me.

"I am divorced from J. V. Berriault, a musician, and have one child, Julie Elena, born in 1955. I received an appointment as scholar to the Radcliffe Institute for Independent Study, Cambridge, Massachusetts, in 1966. In 1963 I lived in Mexico on a fellowship from the Centro Mexicano de Escritores, Mexico City. My work has been included in the O. Henry and Best American Short Stories collections and has been awarded two *Paris Review* fiction prizes."

Gina Berriault first attracted critical attention in 1958, when seven of her stories, somber studies in alienation and frustration, were collected as "The Houses of the City" in *Short Story I.* Her first book was *The Descent,* a brief fable about a midwestern professor who is imported into a future Washington administration as Secretary for Humanity. A good man in a thankless post, he soon learns that the professional politicians who control the country and its terrible nuclear capacities are not merely venal and incompetent but dangerously insane. This "smarting satire" was admired for the characterization of the professor and as a forceful plea for disarmament, but found rather patronizing in its tone and unsophisticated in its manner.

There were mixed reactions to *Conference of Victims*, which examines the effects of a suicide upon the dead man's wife, mother, sister, brother, and mistress, and to *The Son*, a study in incest. Some reviewers of these novels seemed depressed by Mrs. Berriault's pessimism about human nature, her flat and inelegant style, and her failure to build her plots to a climax; they found the results "more gloomy than tragic"—"just one damned thing after another." But no one has denied the authenticity of Mrs. Berriault's dialogue and her remarkable ability "to develop character and to write beneath the surface of people"; this is quite enough for the many critics who admire her work wholeheartedly.

If she has not so far wholly mastered the complex interactions which go to make a successful novel, her short stories have been widely and warmly praised. Fifteen of them were collected in *The Mistress* which, while it did not escape charges of dreariness and prolixity, convinced Richard Kostelanetz of Mrs. Berriault's "extraordinary capacity to empathize with a wide variety of isolated people and then to convey in fiction her knowledge of their minds." This same ability to go to "the core of the human problem" left Hiram Haydn feeling "downright reverent." He wrote: "It is about time that Gina Berriault's extraordinary talent should achieve the recognition and the audience it deserves . . .; [she can] wrench the heart as few living story writers can."

Gina Berriault lives across the bay from San Francisco and sets many of her stories there and elsewhere in northern California. According to a note which accompanied one of her stories in *Esquire* in 1965, she "is rather remote and difficult of approach. She knows no critics, has no 'interesting anecdotes' to relate, and retains the privacy of her life."

PRINCIPAL WORKS: The Houses of the City, *in* Short Story I, 1958; The Descent, 1960; Conference of Victims, 1962; The Mistress, and Other Stories, 1965; The Son, 1966.

ABOUT: *Periodical*—Library Journal June 1, 1960.

***BETOCCHI, CARLO** (January 23, 1899–), Italian poet and editor, writes (in Italian): "I was born in Turin. In our family we were two brothers and a sister. When I was six years old we came with our parents to live and study in Florence. My father's family was of Cento di Ferrara, the native land of Guercino, and my mother's from San Giovanni in Valdarno, fatherland of Masaccio. I like to think about this now and again, as I like also to recall that under the sign of Aquarius, which is mine too, such spirits as Manet, Pergolesi, Mozart, Schubert, and Chopin were born and also such prophets of the future as Wells, libertarians like Marivaux and Voltaire, and free and ardent spirits such as Stendhal or pioneer scientists like Volta and Mendeleev. This satisfaction has its source in the double pleasure I feel in the idea of destiny and in its unpredictability. All of which however remains confined within the vague zone of imaginary delights which I sometimes need to distract myself from truth. I am not really disposed to accept these notions into my spiritual being, which rebels against them, nor into my faith and manner of living, which quickly replace them with my sense of certainty and desire to be free of every determinism precedent to my own choice, for which I like to consider myself solely responsible.

"Indeed my mind and my conscience, which are the sources of my poetry, take pleasure in acknowledging the formative influences on my character as of the humblest: the fervid and silent religious devotion of my mother and her obedience, by no means passive but consciously devoted, even when it was difficult for her, to that which gave her life; I love the obscurity of the information I have concerning my father, who died when I was still a child; the poverty in which we were left at that time, which was happy just the same; the life of the people and the peasants that I had ample leisure to learn of in the long free times of summer, and the seasons of the city; the countryside of Tuscany which in every possible way I studied, saw, heard and smelled. A great help to me in coming to know all of the people of Italy from north to south was offered by the 1915–1918 war which I entered in 1917. I served as an infantry officer and often in the front line: I was lucky enough never to be obliged to fire on any man. I am sure that the country wherein he has lived for a long time in infancy and youth is significantly formative for any poet, and, in one way or another, always recognizable in his works to any good reader. I do not like Petrarch but I like Dante, with all the consequences of judgment and choice which follow as a reader's preference and a writer's choice: I don't like Mallarmé but I like Villon and Rimbaud, and better than the latter Baudelaire; however, among French writers I prefer the moralists to the poets; of the poetry of the whole world I like best that of the English language and spirit; I prefer the empirical attitude

*bā tŏk′ kē

of the English to the systematic thought of the Germans. I hold that the great and true Italian philosopher is Giambattista Vico. Next to the reading of the good poets I prefer the reading of the best historians. By the time I was eighteen I had already read three histories of the French Revolution: those of Michelet, Thiers and Carlyle, all of Dante, most of Shakespeare, and the majority of the Italian authors of the thirteenth, fourteenth, and fifteenth centuries. The formation of my character is based on that reading. In the retreat from Caporetto (1917) I lost my barracks bag with the only three books of poetry I had with me: Dante, Shelley and Keats.

"I am a Catholic. I recognized my shepherd in John XXIII and in Vatican II I witnessed the opening of the Church to my hopes. Pascal, Manzoni and the *Apologia* of Cardinal Newman have shown me the ways of truth through which the intellect reveals to the spirit the substantial greatness of the Catholic faith. I have a son, Marcello, and a daughter, Silvia, children of successive marriages. I began to write poetry in 1928. I believe that for good poetry assiduous exercise in prose, which gives substance to thought, is essential. In 1955 I won the Viareggio Prize for poetry and in 1961 the Montefeltro Prize. Among the poets of the twentieth century I admire principally Eliot, Dylan Thomas (but ahead of them Hopkins and Emily Dickinson), Apollinaire, Machado, Cavafy, Yesenin, and Attila József. Among Italians my preferences are Campana, Rebora, Ungaretti, Montale and among the younger ones Sereni and Luzi. In America my poems have been translated by I. L. Salomon, a very good poet and friend who has made an excellent selection from my principal books."

Betocchi, who has lived in Trieste and Bologna as well as Turin and Florence, trained and practiced as a surveyor before settling down to a career in journalism and editorial work. He played a prominent role in the editing of *Il Frontespizio*, a lively review of the late 1930s.

His early poems, collected in *Realtà vince il sogno* (Reality Conquers the Dream, 1932), introduced his principal themes—children, plain and rugged landscapes, and the simple people who inhabit them. These quasi-Franciscan subjects persist throughout such later volumes as *Poesie* (Poems, 1955), which received the Viareggio Prize, *Cuore di primavera* (Heart of Springtime, 1959), and *L'estate di San Martino* (Saint Martin's Summer, 1961), winner of the Montefeltro Prize.

From the beginning, his work has shown a kind of passionate and all but polemical commitment to the instinctive and simple as against the sophisticated, coupled with a basic and almost uncritical

CARLO BETOCCHI

Catholicism. These qualities have suggested to some critics a link with Clemente Rebora, though Betocchi is certainly more artful and more polished in expression.

If his first poems contained lingering echoes of the *crepuscolari*, these soon gave way to the virtually irresistible influence of the hermetics. Yet there has always been perceptible in Betocchi's verse a posture which is fundamentally anti-hermetic and which has become increasingly evident. Without being self-consciously confessional, he seeks to communicate his vision more powerfully—and perhaps with a wider public in mind—than most of his contemporaries. His rhythms, which occasionally have the simple cadence of folk measures, disclose the same urgency to identify with the unsophisticated, the uncomplicated, and—as the poet would no doubt add—the enduring.

In one sense of the word, Betocchi is a poet of patriotism; Gianni Pozzi speaks of the "unifying and popular poetic vision of Italian nature and Italian society which the poet achieves in his most mature and independent work, *The Coachman of Cosenza*." Sidney Alexander, reviewing I. L. Salomon's English version of the *Poems*, wrote: "In the constellation of contemporary Italian poetry, Carlo Betocchi shines with a light all his own: a luminous lyricism compounded of resignation, Christian faith and a muted joy in natural things."

PRINCIPAL WORKS IN ENGLISH TRANSLATION: Poems, 1964.

ABOUT: Bo, C. Otto studi, 1939; De Robertis, G. Altro novecento, 1962; Macrì, O. Esemplari del sentimento poetico contemporaneo, 1941; Macrì, O. Caratteri e figure della poesia italiana contemporanea, 1956; Mazza, M. S. Not For Art's Sake: The Story of "Il Frontespizio,"

1948; Pozzi, G. La poesia italiana del novecento, 1965; Volpini, V. Letteratura italiana, 1963; *Periodical*—New York Times Book Review April 12, 1964.

***BETTI, UGO** (February 4, 1892–June 9, 1953), Italian dramatist, was born at Camerino in the Italian Marches. The son of Tullio and Emilia (Mannucci) Betti, he was reared in Parma, where his father in 1900 became superintendent of the municipal hospital. Since his elder brother Emilio had been left in Camerino in the care of his grandparents, Ugo Betti was brought up in Parma as an only child, pampered and doted upon. He was educated in the classics and, despite a passionate devotion to sport—as a young man he played soccer for two leading clubs—found time to translate Catullus's *Marriage of Thetis and Peleus*, published when he was only eighteen.

Like his brother, a distinguished jurist, and in spite of his literary leanings, Betti was educated in the law. There was no faculty of letters at the University of Parma and his father in any case considered literature too precarious a career. It is interesting that Betti's doctoral thesis, only peripherally concerned with the law, was an attempt to interpret human history in terms of man's essential egoism—a theme to which he was subsequently to return in his plays.

During World War I, which turned Betti into a pacifist, he was commissioned in the artillery, captured at Caporetto, and sent to a prison camp in Germany, where he began to write the poems later published as *Il re pensieroso*. After the war he became a police magistrate and then a judge in Parma. In 1930, the year of his marriage, he was transferred to Rome as a judge of the high court. During the period of fascist rule, although he never endorsed the dictatorship in his writings, Betti had expressed some support for the government in newspaper interviews, and with the Liberation in 1943 he was deposed from the bench, serving for some years as an archivist in the Rome Palace of Justice. He was reinstated in 1950 as an appeals judge, serving in that capacity until shortly before his death.

Betti began his literary career with the poems collected in *Il re pensieroso* (The Thoughtful King, 1922). The romantic folklorism of these early lyrics, burned away perhaps by what he saw of human misery and corruption in the courts, was gradually replaced by a kind of bewildered realism. Though some critics found Betti's poetry marred by artificiality, others believed that his third collection, *Uomo e donna* (Man and Woman, 1937), played an important part in returning Italian poetry to human and social concerns. Some of the poems collected in the posthumous *Ultime liriche* (Last Lyrics, 1937–1953) are also greatly admired. Betti also wrote short stories and a novel of some distinction, *La piera alta* (The Tall Stone, 1948).

* bāt′ tē

UGO BETTI

It is, however, on his plays that Betti's reputation stands. He wrote nearly thirty, and critics have detected in them evidence of an extraordinary assortment of influences, from Maeterlinck to Ibsen. Certainly Betti learned much from Pirandello, whereas the discipline and tragic inevitability of his best plays clearly reflect his classical training. But Betti remained his own man, adapting to his own purposes whatever devices would best elucidate his singular vision of a world on trial.

His first play was *La Padrona* (The Mistress, 1926). It won a Rome dramatic competition and exhibited, already fully formed, the symbolism and driving concentration of Betti's dramatic manner. His central theme, which is the problem of human guilt, emerged clearly in his fifth play, *Frano allo scalo Nord* (1936, translated as *Landslide*). It is about an inquiry into the causes of an industrial disaster, and shows that an entire community shares responsibility for the tragedy.

Frano allo scalo Nord established Betti's claim to recognition as a major dramatist, and popular success came with the agreeable and observant comedies, like *Il paese delle vacanze* (1937, translated as *Summertime*), to which he unexpectedly turned in the late 1930s. There remained many critics who considered Betti's work literary rather than truly theatrical.

In 1941, however, he was seized by what his English translator, the poet Henry Reed, has called one of the "greatest creative outbursts in dramatic literature." Between 1941 and his death in 1953, Betti wrote thirteen plays, including much of his finest work. To this period belong *Corruzione al Palazza di Giustizia* (Corruption in the Palace of Justice, 1949), the most pointed of his several attacks on judicial corruption; *Delitto al'isola delle capre* (1950, translated as *Crime on Goat Island*), about the revenge taken by three lonely women upon the man who has revealed to them their sexual needs; and *La regina e gli insorti* (1951, translated as *The Queen and the Rebels*), a powerful if rather melodramatic study of the conflict in modern man between a God-given desire for justice and peace and his defiant egoistic drive towards revolution and power.

Betti was a religious dramatist and indeed a specifically Christian one. Original sin is the true protagonist in his plays; human beings its despairing tools. He himself said that all of his plays "sought to demonstrate the existence of God"—even when his experience of sin and corruption as a young magistrate placed heavy strains upon his own faith. But the pessimism of his early work was replaced in the last plays by a new faith in the possibility of expiation and redemption. Thus, in *L'aiuola bruciata* (1953, translated as *The Burnt Flower-Bed*), a group of revolutionaries plan assassination and war almost helplessly, bound together in an evil dream of fear and habit and guilt. It is the martyrdom of a passionately religious young recruit which releases them from the nightmare in which, Betti implies, most men spend their lives.

It is the most frequent criticism of Betti's work that he is more concerned to discuss morality than to investigate personality. He himself has said that "the facts of life are basically uninteresting," and that what concerned him was "the human predicament." Indeed, as G. H. McWilliam has pointed out, "Betti's art, like Dante's, is allegorical, and . . . stylization is as natural within its context as the stylization of medieval paintings or sculpture." Nevertheless, most American reviewers have seemed bored and mystified by the handful of Betti's plays staged in the United States. In England and throughout Europe, however, Betti's stock is high, and in Italy he is regarded as the leading playwright of the generation that followed Pirandello.

PRINCIPAL WORKS IN ENGLISH TRANSLATION: Three Plays (The Queen and the Rebels, The Burnt Flower-Bed, Summertime), 1957; Crime on Goat Island, 1961; Three Plays on Justice (Landslide, Struggle Till Dawn, The Fugitive), 1964; Three Plays (The Inquiry, Goat Island, The Gambler), 1966.

ABOUT: Cologni, F. Ugo Betti, 1960; Curley, D. N. and Curley, A. (eds.) Modern Romance Literatures (A Library of Literary Criticism), 1967; De Michelis, E. La poesia di Ugo Betti, 1937; Dizionario universale della letteratura contemporanea, 1961; Grigson, G. (ed.) Concise Encyclopedia of Modern World Literature, 1963; Lumley, F. New Trends in Twentieth Century Drama, 1967; McWilliam, G. H. *Introduction to* Three Plays, 1966; Penguin Companion to Literature 2, 1969; Reed, H. *Introduction to* Three Plays, 1957; Smith, H. (ed.) Columbia Dictionary of Modern European Literature, 1947; Twentieth-Century Writing, 1969. *Periodicals*—Drama Winter 1964; Italica March 1960; Modern Drama May 1968; Poetry August 1959; Tulane Drama Review Winter 1960, Fall 1963; World Theatre Summer 1962.

BEVINGTON, HELEN (April 2, 1906–), American verse writer and memoirist, who declines to be called a poet, writes: "I was born in a Methodist parsonage in the upstate village of Afton, New York. Soon after my birth my parents were divorced, and I failed to make the acquaintance of my father, about whom I have written in a book called *Charley Smith's Girl*, until I was four years old. My mother and I lived in a small town in New York State, where she taught music in the public school, taking me along with her each day from class to class because there was nothing else to do with me. Thus my formal education began almost as soon as I could hold her hand and march into a classroom. I learned there to mind, to sit still, and before long to read. As a result of this early habit of attending school, I seem to have spent most of my life in classrooms, as student, teacher, and eventually college professor.

"I was graduated from the University of Chicago, where at nineteen I had really nothing to my name but three sudden ambitions that appeared at the time unlikely of fulfillment: to fall in love, to earn a graduate degree, and to take a trip around the world. Soon after, I enrolled in the graduate school at Columbia University and, so kind is fate, managed to accomplish all three wishes in orderly succession. For the next dozen years my husband, Merle Bevington, and I lived and taught in New York City, where our two sons were born. In 1942 we came to Duke University in Durham, North Carolina, and there until his death in 1964 we taught together in the same department, he as a professor of English, I as an associate professor. I cannot imagine a happier solution to existence. Now I go on teaching alone, and my two sons have themselves become college professors, David at the University of Virginia, Philip at Stanford University.

"Years ago I began writing light verse, much as one would practice the piano or grow camellias. It was a modest undertaking with words, not the making of poetry but of verse, which requires a degree of deftness and order and arrangement but certainly not passion, never high seriousness. I have therefore declined to be called a poet, especially a poetess. My verses are a kind of notation, often the elaborating of a quotation from something I have read, like for example Aunt Mary Emerson's imperious command: 'Be still. I want to hear the men talk.' Or like Thoreau saying: 'Do what you love.

HELEN BEVINGTON

Pursue your life.' Without the power of invention or the imagination of a poet, I write as a notetaker, not of the disasters and folly of the world that needs no memorandum from me, not to be a preserver of grief, but to remember something delightful I have read or seen or heard. I want only to have a talent for such experiences.

"From the beginning this was private entertainment. It did not occur to me to submit such pieces for publication. One day my husband wrapped up a notebook of my verse and sent it off to a poetry contest being conducted by the publishers Houghton Mifflin. My manuscript was, of course, highly inappropriate to the occasion, being lighthearted and frivolous by nature. But two of the judges, an editor of the *New Yorker* and the editor of the *Atlantic Monthly*, invited me to become a contributor to their magazines, and Houghton Mifflin, while wisely bestowing the prize elsewhere on a more serious work, accepted the whole volume for publication and asked for more. This is the simple story of an undeserved stroke of luck. I have with a sense of amazement been a writer ever since.

"Such occupation combines well, I think, with the teaching of English literature, where one's mind is forever on words and the shaping of words into patterns of meaning. More or less accidentally, I have found a way of life, even a lifework, that seems to me not work at all: to read books, to talk about books, and occasionally to write books. It turns out to be the pursuit of pleasure, one which actually has no end."

The Methodist parsonage in which Mrs. Bevington was born was her grandfather's. Her parents were Charles Wesley Smith, also a Methodist preacher, and Elizabeth (Raymond) Smith. She received her Ph.B. from the University of Chicago in 1926 and her M.A. from Columbia in 1928, the year of her marriage. She taught at Bedford Academy in Brooklyn, New York, from 1929 to 1931, and was a librarian at New York University from 1936 to 1942, when she went to Duke University.

Dr. Johnson's Waterfall, her first collection of verse, appeared in 1946. The reviewers liked it, as they have liked its successors. Mrs. Bevington writes about writers, books, travel, and humanity's more attractive foibles, including love. "She has," according to Morris Bishop, "a seeing eye, a hearing ear, and a sense of the weight, taste and inner music of words. It takes a good deal to be a minor poet." Bishop is one of those who have been unwilling to accept her own modest estimate of her work, finding beneath her urbane humor and wordplay much learning and sharp perceptions. Phyllis McGinley, who should know, agrees: "What Helen Bevington writes, in the main, is poetry and I trust I am not ruthlessly cutting down her royalties when I admit it. . . . Her intent is serious, just as the intent of every other light verse writer worth his salt, from Horace to Ogden Nash and including Mr. Eliot, is serious." She received the Roanoke-Chowan poetry award in 1956 for *Change of Sky* and again in 1962 for her "commonplace book" *When Found, Make a Verse Of.*

Helen Bevington's childhood and youth were not happy. Her mother, divorced from a philandering husband, was too busy supporting her to have much time for loving her. This bred a resentment which led in adolescence to open rebellion. The girl's relationship with her father, whom she saw occasionally as a child, ended in a violent quarrel when she was at college. *Charley Smith's Girl*, Mrs. Bevington's memoirs of those years, was seen by reviewers as an act of contrition, written when she had come to understand that her parents "did as well as they knew how." Perhaps for this reason, her "even-tempered, objective, often gay account" seemed to Virgilia Peterson, among others, to bring the parents more vividly to life than the author herself. "My mother and my father—one was strong and brave and indomitable, and one withdrew in utter despair," she wrote at the end of her book. "Neither of them ever discovered how to be happy. There must be a third way. I am not sure, but I think there must a third way."

That Mrs. Bevington herself "discovered how to be happy" is abundantly clear from *A Book and a Love Affair*, her warmly praised account of her idyllic married life from 1927 to 1942 (when the Bevingtons went to Duke University) and its sequel *The House Was Quiet and the World Was Calm*, which carries the story forward to 1956.

PRINCIPAL WORKS: Dr. Johnson's Waterfall, and Other Poems, 1946; Nineteen Million Elephants, and Other Poems, 1950; Change of Sky, and Other Poems, 1956; When Found, Make a Verse Of (a "commonplace book" in verse and prose), 1961; Charley Smith's Girl: A Memoir, 1965; A Book and a Love Affair, 1968; The House Was Quiet and the World Was Calm, 1971.
ABOUT: Bevington, H. Charley Smith's Girl, 1965 (and its sequels); Contemporary Authors 15–16, 1966.

"BEYNON, JOHN." *See* "WYNDHAM, JOHN"

***BIALIK, CHAIM NACHMAN** (January 9, 1873–July 4, 1934), Hebrew poet, short story writer, essayist, philologist, translator, and editor, was born in the Ukrainian village of Radi in the Volynia district, the youngest of seven children of Reb Yitzhok Yoissef Bialik and Dinah (Priveh) Bialik. His father, a pious scholar of Hasidic background, was an unsuccessful member of a prosperous timber-trading family and made a meager living managing some of the family business interests. A gifted, imaginative boy, Bialik attended the traditional Jewish *heder* (elementary school), where his early education was devoid of modern Western European or Slavic influences. According to Israel Efros, who edited the standard English edition of his poems, "Bialik was subjected in his childhood to three influences that shaped his entire being: learning, poverty, and nature."

In 1879 Bialik moved with his family to the outskirts of Zhitomir, the provincial capital. His father died the following year and the family broke up. Bialik, then six years old, entered the stern religious and scholarly household of his grandfather, Reb Yaakov Moishe Bialik, in another Zhitomir suburb. There he sought comfort in his grandfather's extensive library. By the time he was eleven he was reading the Cabalistic literature of the Middle Ages, the philosophical works of Moses Maimonides, and the poetry of Yehuda Halevi. At the age of thirteen he began of his own accord to study the Talmud and spent many hours in the *beth hamidrash*, the traditional house of learning. At the same time, he secretly bought and studied "forbidden" books, including modern poetry, philosophy, and novels; and he began to question some of the rigid principles and practices of traditional Jewish life.

Determined to move beyond his narrow home environment, Bialik, at the age of fifteen, with the reluctant consent of his grandfather, went to Volozhin in the Vilna district, to attend the noted yeshiva (Hebrew seminary) there. While continuing his Talmudic studies at Volozhin, he also acquainted himself with the sciences and with modern Hebrew and Russian literature. He joined a secret Zionist society at the seminary and helped draft its program.

* byä' lik

CHAIM NACHMAN BIALIK

Among the chief influences on Bialik during this period were the works of the noted Hebrew essayist Ahad Ha-Am (Ascher Ginzberg). In 1890, after one and a half years at Volozhin, Bialik went on his own to Odessa, then a center of modern Hebrew letters. There he made friends with such noted literary figures as Moshe Leib Lilienblum and J. H. Ravnitzky and met Ahad Ha-Am, who became his lifelong friend and mentor. It was through Ahad Ha-Am that he published his first poems, which from the beginning were characterized by a great and impetuous lyric power.

Returning to Zhitomir in 1892, Bialik married into a family of lumber merchants who set him up in business in Kiev province. This enterprise failed and in 1897 he moved to the Polish town of Sosnowice, where he worked as a teacher and again failed in business, this time as a coal merchant. Meanwhile, he continued to write poetry, and by the end of the nineteenth century he was recognized as a leading Hebrew poet. In 1900 his friends rescued him from want and isolation, arranging for the Society for the Improvement of Jewish Education to invite him back to Odessa. There he was soon established, with Ahad Ha-Am and the novelist Mendele Mokher Seforim, as a principal architect of the Hebrew literary renaissance, which, steeped in the Jewish tradition of the ages, was at the same time committed to the growing Zionist movement for the establishment of a Jewish homeland in Palestine.

Bialik's first volume of poems was published in Warsaw in 1901, and most of his poems were written before 1908. He visited Palestine in 1904 and 1908 and wrote poems and essays about his impressions. For a time he was coeditor of the monthly journal *Hashiolah*, which had been founded by Ahad Ha-Am. In 1905 Bialik, in cooperation with J. H. Ravnitzky, established the world-famous Odessa publishing house Moriah, which issued Hebrew classics, biblical texts, and rabbinical texts for schools and seminaries. After the Bolshevik Revolution, Bialik's efforts on behalf of the Hebrew language and culture were looked upon with disfavor by Soviet authorities, and the Moriah publishing house was forced to close. In 1921, as a result of the intercession of Maxim Gorky, Bialik was permitted to emigrate; he moved to Berlin, where he established the Dvir publishing house.

In 1924 he settled in Tel Aviv, where he spent the last decade of his life. In 1925 he delivered the address that marked the opening of Hebrew University in Jerusalem and became a member of its board of governors. He visited the United States in 1926 on behalf of the Palestine Foundation Fund and was awarded honorary degrees by the Jewish Theological Seminary and the Jewish Institute of Religion. In 1927 he toured Poland, and on his return he founded the weekly philosophical and literary discussions in Tel Aviv which he called *Oneg Shabbat* (Enjoyment of the Sabbath), since initiated in many other parts of the world.

Although Bialik's output was limited, he is honored as the greatest Hebrew poet of modern times. As a Jewish national poet, he reflected in his work the ancient traditions of his people, the suffering of ghetto Jews of his day, and the hope for freedom in a revived Jewish homeland. Speaking to his people as a prophet, Bialik sometimes chastised them for their weakness and, as one critic noted, acted as "a surgeon who most cruelly dissects the soul of the modern Jew." In the early poem *Ha-Matmid* (The Talmud Student), reflecting his own youthful experiences, he depicted the scholar as a heroic and ascetic figure and as the mainstay of the strength of Judaism. In *Methe Midbar* (The Dead of the Wilderness) he called for a reawakening of the Jewish people after a long sleep.

The 1903 pogrom in Kishinev inspired Bialik's poem *Be-Ir ha-Haregah* (In the City of Slaughter), in which he foretold the horrors of the Nazi era and raged against the passivity of the Jewish people. The poem was said to have inspired Jews in Russia to form the first armed defensive units, the Haganah. His masterpiece is the eight-part allegorical epic poem *Megillath Ha-Esh* (Scroll of Fire), set in the time of the destruction of the first temple in Jerusalem. It forms a profound, often puzzling, and strangely beautiful vision of the whole of Jewish history.

In a number of his poems, Bialik dealt with less specifically Jewish and more universal themes, as in the love poems *Im Dimdumey* (At Twilight) and *Where Art Thou?* His nature poems, in which he delineates a mystical communion between man and the natural world, include *Misirey Hahoref* (A Twig Fell). His later poems reflect a withdrawal from the world, a preoccupation with death, and finally, a return to childhood. Ruth Finer Mintz sees in Bialik's childhood the principal source of his imagery, and suggests that his orphanhood and exile from his early home came to symbolize for him the fate of the Jewish people and of modern man in general.

Bialik's poems have been translated into some twenty-five languages, and are included in many anthologies. He was also noted as an essayist and short story writer. A collection of his earthy and generally humorous stories was translated as *Aftergrowth and Other Stories* (1939). During his years in Odessa, Bialik, in collaboration with J. H. Ravnitzky, published a three-volume edition of *Sefer ha-Agadah* (Book of the Legend, 1922), collecting the folk tales and proverbs scattered through the Talmud. Later he was to make his own creative use of legend, retelling many tales in new and contemporary terms, as in *Agadat Shelosha ve-Arbaah* (Legend of the Three and the Four, 1941), a story about King Solomon based on biblical sources but extended by Bialik into a plea for peace, symbolized by the love of a Jewish boy and the daughter of his non-Jewish enemy. Bialik also published a four-volume collection of Yiddish legends, *Di yidishe agode* (1948). Among European literary classics translated by Bialik into Hebrew are Schiller's *Wilhelm Tell*, Shakespeare's *Julius Caesar*, Cervantes' *Don Quixote*, S. Ansky's *Dybbuk*, and the poetry of Heinrich Heine. Collections of Bialik's works include *Kol Kitve* (4 vols., 1924–1935) in Hebrew, and *Shriften* (1946) in Yiddish. His letters, including his love letters to his wife, have also been published.

Bialik died in Vienna at the age of sixty-one, following surgery. He was survived by his wife, the former Mania Averbach. His death was mourned not only in Palestine, but throughout the world. His home, on what is now Bialik Street in Tel Aviv, has been opened to the public as a museum. He is remembered as an unassuming man, noted for his friendliness and wit. His role as a central figure in the Zionist movement and his scholarly contributions to the Jewish tradition are universally recognized. More than any other individual he was credited with the revival and modernization of the ancient Hebrew language. Bialik has been called "the greatest Hebrew poet in a thousand years" and "the soul of his generation." Abraham Karib says that he was "the last of the poets of the old, and the first of the poets of the new generation."

PRINCIPAL WORKS IN ENGLISH TRANSLATION: *Poetry*—Poems from the Hebrew, 1924; Selected Poems, 1926;

Knight of Onions and Knight of Garlic (humorous verse), 1939; Complete Poetic Works, 1948; Selected Poems, 1965. *Prose*—Law and Legend, 1923; And It Came to Pass, 1938; Far Over the Sea (stories for children), 1939; Aftergrowth and Other Stories, 1939.

ABOUT: Birman, A. (ed.) An Anthology of Modern Hebrew Poetry, 1968; Burnshaw, S. and others (eds.) The Modern Hebrew Poem Itself, 1965; Efros, I. Chaim Nachman Bialik, 1940; Halkin, S. Modern Hebrew Literature, 1950; Jewish Book Annual, 1959–1960; Lipsky, L. Gallery of Zionist Profiles, 1956; Ribalow, M. The Flowering of Modern Hebrew Literature, 1959; Waxman, M. A History of Jewish Literature, 1960.

***BILLETDOUX, FRANÇOIS (-PAUL)** (September 7, 1927–), French dramatist, novelist, and journalist, was born in Paris, the son of Paul and Adrienne (Vidal) Billetdoux. His father, who taught French and classical literature at a Paris school, encouraged his natural aptitude for writing, and he received a far-ranging arts education—at the Lycée Condorcet in Paris, at the Sorbonne, at the Charles Dullin school of dramatic art (1944), and the Institut des Hautes Études Cinématographiques (1945). In 1946, when he was only nineteen, he became a writer and producer with Radiodiffusion Française, the national radio service, and a year later was appointed director of that institution's variety services, where he discovered and promoted many artists who are now stars. In 1949 he went to Fort de France in Martinique as artistic director of the newly opened radio station there. He returned to Paris in 1951 and for the next few years worked as a journalist with *Opera*, *Arts*, and *Combat*; as a disc jockey; and as a radio actor and cabaret performer. In 1957–1958 he was director of overseas broadcasting for Radiodiffusion Française.

This experience in radio no doubt helped Billetdoux to develop his subtle gifts for dialogue, argument, and characterization. His concern has always been with human relationships—with his characters' struggles to escape from the prisons of their own personalities, and to love and communicate with each other.

Billetdoux's first play was the one-act *À la nuit la nuit*, produced under his own direction at the Théâtre de L'Œuvre in 1955. It aroused considerable critical interest, as did one or two other early pieces. Real success came in 1959, when *Tchin-Tchin* was staged at the Théâtre de Poche in Montparnasse, with the author playing the principal male role. The play studies the strange relationship between Pamela Puffy-Picq, who is English, houseproud, and inhibited, and Césaréo Grimaldi, an intensely emotional Italian businessman. This disparate couple meet to discuss the fact that their respective spouses are having an affair. At first they dislike each other but, having no one else who will listen to their problems, they continue to meet and, increasingly, turn for comfort to alcohol. Césaréo gives up his business; Pamela abandons her housekeeping; both become helpless alcoholics. Their degradation is such that when Pamela finds her own son lying drunk in the gutter, she takes his wallet and leaves him there. Paradoxically, however—and this is the point of the play—the wretched couple discover in their squalor a free response to life which was denied them in their days of material security. The play has been translated by Mark Rudkin as *Chin-Chin*. In its London production it seemed to the British critic Harold Hobson a Christian parable, and Billetdoux himself has spoken of its "Christian optimism."

* bi yā dōō′

FRANÇOIS BILLETDOUX

Tchin-Tchin depended for its success on the characterization of the two principals, but in his subsequent plays Billetdoux has tended to rely more on philosophic or social argument. *Le Comportement des époux Bredburry* (The Behavior of the Bredburry Couple, 1960) was based on an actual advertisement in an American newspaper in which a woman offered her husband for sale for thirty thousand dollars—a perfectly natural development, Billetdoux suggests, in a capitalist society. *Va donc chez Törpe* (1961, translated by Rudkin as *Chez-Torpe*) concerns a hotel where an epidemic of suicides leads to a police inquiry. The investigating detective finds the cause of the outbreak when he meets the hotel's owner—a woman whose impatience with pretense impels her to burst the pathetic bubbles of hope and fantasy which are her clients' only defense against despair. In the end the inspector has to battle against his own impulse to suicide. The play, widely discussed and variously interpreted, in both theological and political terms, made Billetdoux "the great revelation" of the 1961–1962 Paris season. It was followed in 1964 by *Comment va le monde, Môssieu? Il tourne, Môssieu*, a somewhat Brechtian piece about the struggle for survival of two escaped prisoners of war.

Billetdoux, who says that he writes in order "to attain silence," has always delighted in paradox and mystification; Paul Mankin maintains that his originality "resides precisely in the spectator's inability to come to terms" with his plays. The couple in *Tchin-Tchin* relate to each other only when all relationship has become irrelevant, and the two escaped prisoners in *Comment va le monde* are bound together by their mutual exploitation. Claire, the heroine of *Il faut passer par les nuages* (One Must Go by Way of the Clouds, 1964) achieves fulfillment only when she gives away to her family the property she has spent her life accumulating. This play, staged by the Barrault-Renaud company, and using abstract sets, fragmentary scenes, disconnected monologues, and many of the techniques of the theatre of the Absurd, seemed to some critics to establish Billetdoux as the "leader of the French avant-garde."

There is a characteristic paradox also at the heart of Billetdoux's novel *Brouillon d'un bourgeois* (1961, translated by Ralph Manheim as *A Man and His Master*), about a respectable Parisian *père de famille* psychologically enslaved by a drunken profligate. The implication that true happiness is to be found in a state of abject bondage was unattractive to many reviewers, but there was a great deal of critical respect for this "short, difficult, and fearsome study."

Billetdoux has written two other novels, and a great variety of work for radio, television, and the cinema. Perhaps his most spectacular achievement was the 1967 television play *Pitchi-Poï*, a tragic story about a man and a waif wandering across Europe after World War II in search of the child's family. It was filmed with the collaboration of seventeen television companies, and was shown throughout Europe. Billetdoux won the Grand Prix du Disque in 1957 for his work as a recording editor and has also received the Prix Georges Colin, the Prix Triomphe, the Prix Ibsen, and the Prix Lugné-Poë. The author is a heavy-set man whose shaven head, thick black eyebrows, and "large dark humorous eyes" put one interviewer in mind of "a highly intelligent Italian-American cab driver." He was married in 1947 to Evelyne Colin, and has two children.

PRINCIPAL WORKS IN ENGLISH: A Man and His Master (novel), 1963; Two Plays (Chin-Chin, Chez-Torpe), 1964.
ABOUT: Corvin, M. Le théâtre nouveau en France, 1963; International Who's Who, 1971–1972; Penguin Companion to Literature 2, 1969; Who's Who in France, 1971–1972. *Periodicals*—Book Week April 19, 1964; Educational Theatre Journal March 1963; Hudson Review Spring 1961; Spring 1963; Nation November 17, 1962; New Statesman November 12, 1960; January 5, 1962; New Yorker January 21, 1961; November 3, 1962; April 11, 1964; January 23, 1965; Newsweek November 5, 1962; Saturday Review November 10, 1962; Spectator November 11, 1960; Theatre Arts February 1962, December 1962; Time November 2, 1962; Yale French Studies April 1962.

BISSELL, RICHARD (PIKE) (June 27, 1913–), American novelist and stage and screen writer, was born in Dubuque, Iowa, on the Upper Mississippi River, a fact which he says has been the biggest single influence on his life and writing. He is the son of Frederick Ezekiel Bissell, a businessman of English descent who had edited the *Crimson* at Harvard, and of Edith (Pike) Bissell, whose family included Pennsylvania Dutch and French-Canadian strains. Richard Bissell graduated from Phillips Exeter Academy in 1932 and went to Harvard, where he majored in anthropology, receiving his B.S. in 1936.

A place awaited him in the H. B. Glover Company, the shirt and pajama factory which his great-grandfather had established at Dubuque, but first Bissell wanted to see something of the world. A stint in the Venezuelan oil fields was followed by two years as an ordinary seaman with the American Export Lines. In 1938 he went into the family business as factory superintendent and stayed until the beginning of World War II. Rejected by the Navy because of poor vision, Bissell spent most of the war on the inland waters of the Midwest, earning his license as a mate and pilot of the Central Barge Company's towboats. In 1944 he returned to a vice presidency at the H. B. Glover Company, where he remained as superintendent and stylist until 1952.

Bissell's first published work, a short story called "Coal Queen," won a one-thousand-dollar prize in the *Atlantic Monthly* "I Personally" series. Other stories followed and, in 1950, his first novel. *A Stretch on the River* was welcomed as a work of "casual, vernacular effectiveness" possessing some of "Mark Twain's own feeling for the rugged, easy-going river hands." It was followed by *The Monongahela*, an informal and charming contribution to Rinehart's Rivers of America series, and then by *7½ Cents* (1953), the novel which led to Bissell's first fame. The story concerns a strike at the Junction City plant of the Sleep Tite pajama company. What pleased the critics and the reading public, and made the novel a Book-of-the-Month Club selection, was "the natural talk, the sure feeling for the pace of midwestern life, the shrewd humor of such scenes as the union picnic," adding up to "an oddly likable piece of Americana." Several critics were reminded of Ring Lardner, and one credited Bissell with a "satiric eye as sharp as Sinclair Lewis's."

Although the success of *7½ Cents* enabled Bissell

to leave the family factory and become a full-time writer he had by no means finished with the pajama industry. With George Abbott he turned his novel into the hit musical *Pajama Game*, which won both Antoinette Perry and Donaldson awards, and a few years later he went to Hollywood to turn the musical into an equally successful movie. And the cycle was still not complete. Bissell's first experience of Broadway inspired an approximately autobiographical novel, *Say, Darling* (1957), which seemed to some reviewers "just about the funniest novel of the year," and which in turn was parlayed by Bissell, his wife, and Abe Burrows into another highly successful musical, described by Walter Kerr as "a smart, sassy and wonderfully funny romp."

This immensely profitable chain reaction did nothing to alter Bissell's conviction that he is basically a novelist who finds it "hard to work in the theatre." *High Water* (1954), a story about a towboat trip up the Mississippi during a flood, evoked more comparisons with Mark Twain and seemed to Maurice Dolbier "further evidence that Richard Bissell is one of the sharpest and surest" of contemporary American novelists. *Good Bye, Ava* (1960), narrated by a Mississippi houseboat owner who refuses to make way for a fertilizer plant, also pleased most reviewers, and David Dempsey called Bissell "a good runner-up" to Ring Lardner "in catching the high-spirited, satiric nonsense of plain people." There was far less enthusiasm for *Still Circling Moose Jaw* (1965), a "resolutely funny novel" about a middle-aged millionaire's last fling which seemed to strain too hard for laughs. *Julia Harrington* (1969) was an experiment and a successful one, a nostalgic scrapbook novel about life in Winnebago, Iowa, in 1913, as it seems to a twelve-year-old girl, using colored advertisements, valentines, book jackets, and Christmas cards to recall the naïve, nationalistic, optimistic mood of that golden era.

You Can Always Tell a Harvard Man is "a sort of grab bag" about the college attended by Bissell, his father, and at least one of his sons—a mixture of history, commentary, and autobiography which pleased even the Harvard graduates among its reviewers. Bissell was married in 1938 to Marian Van Patten Grilk, and has three sons and a daughter. Lewis Nichols has described him as "a shortish chunk of a man with a twang, glasses and a pallor suggestive of Broadway rather than the Mississippi," though "his weskit and haircut maybe do suggest the . . . riverboat gambler type." Bissell, who has been president since 1958 of his own Mississippi tugboat company, likes boating, mountaineering, and history, and regards travel as "life's greatest luxury." His travels with his family in various parts of North America are engagingly described in *How Many Miles to Galena?*, based partly on articles first published in *Holiday* and other magazines.

RICHARD BISSELL

PRINCIPAL WORKS: A Stretch on the River (novel), 1950; The Monongahela (topography), 1952; 7½ Cents (novel), 1953 (England, A Gross of Pyjamas); High Water (novel), 1954; (with George Abbott) The Pajama Game (play), 1954; Say, Darling (novel), 1957; (with others) Say, Darling (play), 1959; Good Bye, Ava (novel), 1960; You Can Always Tell a Harvard Man, 1962; Still Circling Moose Jaw (novel), 1965; How Many Miles to Galena? or, Baked, Hashed Brown or French Fried, 1968; Julia Harrington: Winnebago, Iowa, 1913 (novel), 1969.
ABOUT: Biographical Encyclopedia and Who's Who of the American Theatre, 1966; Contemporary Authors 4, 1963; Who's Who in America, 1970–1971; *Periodicals*—Business Week June 5, 1954; Life May 12, 1958; New York Times Book Review October 23, 1960; November 23, 1969; Newsweek April 14, 1958; Wilson Library Bulletin January 1963.

BLACKBURN, THOMAS (February 10, 1916–), English poet, critic, novelist, and memoirist writes: "I was born in a Cumbrian vicarage. Although my father was a Church of England parson he was born in Mauritius. My grandfather was an Anglican missionary on that island and had married a woman of French extraction whose family had been there since they left France at the time of the Revolution. From his upbringing on that haunted little island my father derived a profound dislike of Eurasians and Roman Catholics and a capacity to believe both in the 39 Articles and Black Magic. I mention this since I believe that, given a certain capacity to handle words, it is childhood experience, often of a rather disastrous kind, that determines the poetic vocation. Certainly I was profoundly influenced by the curious nurture of my clerical father; a man who saw his own extremely

THOMAS BLACKBURN

bizarre fantasies in other people, and with a singular clarity! My mother, on the other hand, came from a family of north country landowners who had farmed in the same valleys for many generations and preserved their property and gingery bloodhound appearance by judicious intermarriage. I believe that a great deal of my earlier poetry came from an attempt to exorcise the ghosts wished upon me by my father and solve the contradictions between the Anglo - Franco - (possibly) - Indo - Blackburn stock and the thoroughly 'English' Fenwicks.

"I was educated at a Cumbrian 'prep' school, run by a woman who smelt of sanctity and fish. Her secular arm, a brawny Latinist, administered corporal punishment with gusto. The process was continued at a minor public school, which fostered poetry by ignoring its existence. The exceptional achievement of England in this art may not be unrelated to its profound discouragement by our schools. Certainly although concerned now with 'Education' I have little belief in Courses of Creative Writing. I remember my almost mystical ecstasy when I discovered for myself Shelley's 'Ode to the West Wind' at the age of fourteen. I think the experience might have been nipped in the bud by a well-meaning teacher expatiating on the beauties of the poem.

"At Durham University I took an English Degree and, more important, was introduced to the sport of rock-climbing by a very remarkable don, the late A. P. Rossiter. Mountaineering is still a main interest of my life—perhaps because it makes life significant by bringing it as close to death as one's feet and fingers.

"Then war service, and I began to write or try and write poetry at the age of thirty or so. I suspect what started me off was the discovery that Yeats, for whom I have a profound admiration, had not said certain things I felt a need to say. But I knew great swathes of his work by heart and it has taken a long time to get his wonderful rhythms and attitudes out of my work and try and find my own way of writing. At first I relied on myth a good deal; Oedipus, Pasiphae, one could talk through these personae, and they seemed to make a bridge between oneself and that rare bird, the reader of modern verse. Then in later books I have tried to express very ordinary human situations, a quarrel, a child observing its parents quarrelling, personal understanding, misunderstanding, and show how they shade off into areas of unlimited significance and mystery.

"I have also written a book about modern poetry and recently a study of the work of Robert Browning. The latter because I lecture at a Teachers' Training College and when they put Browning on the Degree Syllabus I could find no study of his works that I could 'crib' from—with any conviction. So I had to read him for myself and discovered what a tremendous poet he is when one gets through an unusually thick rind of nonsense.

"I am married and have a daughter."

Blackburn's disastrous childhood and youth are described in *A Clip of Steel*—the title is a reference to the device which his father expected him to clip onto his penis to prevent nocturnal emissions. Blackburn was an alcoholic in his early twenties, was sent down from Cambridge, and began to be able to cope with life only after three years of psychiatric treatment. He has earned his living as a schoolteacher, except for two years (1964–1966) as Gregory Fellow of Poetry at the University of Leeds. He is considered a "better poet than critic," and *The Price of an Eye*, his study of modern poetry, was received without very much enthusiasm. The kind of poetry he admires and writes is suggested by his assertion that poets "are attempting to understand, clarify and make articulate the dark processes of human life."

As he indicates, Blackburn at first worked a great deal through myth, spoke in the very accents of Yeats, and seemed possessed by his father's simultaneous commitment to Christianity and to older, darker faiths. Jung, and the painter Francis Bacon, have also been important influences. His early poetry has been called "weird stuff," decadent and overripe, mixing religious themes and bizarre erotic myths and including a sequence dedicated to Aleister Crowley, the seedy prophet of black magic.

But, as John Press has shown, each succeeding collection of Blackburn's verse has marked an advance in the direction of control and lucidity and "a Christian longing for grace." In *A Smell of Burning*, Blackburn had found his own voice, in which he was able to speak directly, and sometimes with a savage jocularity, of personal preoccupations which previously he had been able to approach only in terms of myth.

In *A Breathing Space*, finding his subject in his divorce and remarriage, Blackburn moved further toward direct, confessional verse—too far, indeed, and too clumsily in the opinion of most critics, who hoped for a return to the manner of *A Smell of Burning*. There was also a mixed reception for the restless and uneven poems in *The Fourth Man*. Blackburn has also tried his hand at fiction, and *The Feast of the Wolf* was thought an interesting and sometimes powerful study of the relationship between psychosis and demonic possession.

PRINCIPAL WORKS: The Outer Darkness (poems), 1951; The Holy Stone (poems), 1954; In the Fire (poems), 1956; The Next Word (poems), 1958; (as editor) 45–60: An Anthology of English Poetry, 1960; The Price of an Eye (criticism), 1961; A Smell of Burning (poems), 1961; A Breathing Space (poems), 1964; Robert Browning: A Study of His Poetry, 1967; A Clip of Steel (autobiography), 1969; The Fourth Man (poems), 1971; The Feast of the Wolf (novel), 1971.

ABOUT: Allott, K. (ed.) The Penguin Book of Contemporary Verse, 1962; Murphy, R. (ed.) Contemporary Poets of the English Language, 1970; Orr, P. (ed.) The Poet Speaks, 1966; Press, J. Rule and Energy, 1963.

***BLAIS, MARIE-CLAIRE** (October 5, 1939–), French-Canadian novelist, writes: "I was born in Québec City in 1939 and was educated at convent schools where, as a boarder, I was subject to stricter discipline than the day students. I began to write stories at about the age of ten but since I was discouraged from it and even punished for it, I felt guilty about my imaginary world, and I sensed already the loneliness of the literary vocation.

"In my teens, I wrote novels, poems, and plays, and in 1959, *La Belle Bête*, a novel, was published by l'Institut Littéraire de Québec; it was received with a mixture of praise and vituperation. A year later, I published *Tête Blanche*, a novel, and in 1961, *Tête Blanche* and *La Belle Bête* were published in English by Little, Brown and McClelland. Meanwhile, I wrote two plays, *Eleonor*, which was produced in the summer of 1962 by the Théâtre de l'Estoc in Québec City, and *La Roulotte aux poupées*, produced in the winter of 1962 by the Théâtre de Mme. de Vienne Blanc in Montréal. I obtained a fellowship from the Conseil des Arts du Canada, and spent the year 1960–1961 in Paris. (My first book had also been published in Paris by Flammarion.) It was a lonely and difficult but fruitful year, for I wrote novels and poems, and when I came back to Québec, a novel was published, *Le Jour est noir*, by Les Editions du Jour, Montréal. A volume of poems was also published by Librairie Garneau in Québec. Also a short novel, *Les Voyageurs sacrés*, in *Les Écrits du Canada Français*.

* ble

MARIE-CLAIRE BLAIS

"In 1963, I received a fellowship from the Guggenheim Foundation and came to live in the U.S.A. where I have been ever since. After publishing a second book of poems in Québec in 1964 (*Existences*, Librairie Garneau, Québec), I obtained a second fellowship from the Guggenheim Foundation in June 1965. My novel, *Une Saison dans la vie d'Emmanuel*, was published by les Éditions du Jour in Montréal in June 1965. I live in the country (Wellfleet, Massachusetts) and besides my own work, have time to do a good deal of reading. My favorite writers are: Proust, Balzac, Gide, Kafka Virginia Woolf, Faulkner, T. Mann."

After leaving her convent school, Mlle. Blais studied literature and philosophy at Laval University, Quebec. There she showed the manuscript of her controversial first novel to Père Lévesque, the enlightened and influencial founder of the university's School of Social Sciences, who helped to secure its publication in 1959 as *La Belle Bête*. It is a dark fable—almost an inversion of *Beauty and the Beast*—about a vain young widow whose physical beauty is destroyed (and spiritual ugliness symbolized) by cancer of the face; her ugly and unloved daughter, who marries a blind man but loses him when he regains his sight; and her adored, handsome, but half-witted son, who kills his mother's lover and, eventually, himself.

In the cultural microcosm of Canada this gothic tale was greeted with a mixture of outrage and acclamation, though it naturally caused less of a stir elsewhere. Translated by Merloyd Lawrence as *Mad Shadows*, it seemed to most English-language reviewers an often extravagant adolescent romance which nevertheless showed great promise. Harding Lemay went further, speaking of a legendary quality, a "vigor of precision and . . . velocity of imagination" which made this brief book a "remarkable *tour-de-force*." *Tête Blanche* (translated under the same title by Charles Fullman), is another study of isolation and lovelessness, told mostly in letters by an embittered boy who is neglected by his actress mother and separated—apparently forever—from his girl.

The men and women in *Le Jour est noir* show a similar inability to sustain relationships or even, it seems, to bear for long the pain of life itself. Like *Les Voyageurs sacrés*, *Le Jour est noir* partakes of the nature of a prose poem in which language at times assumes the imagery and cadence of verse and dialogue the formality of ritual responses. These two novellas were published together in English translations by Derek Coltman as *The Day Is Dark* and *Three Travelers*. In his review, the Canadian novelist and critic Robertson Davies said that Mlle. Blais "is interested in the exploitation of a world of her own, in which people of uncommon sensibility, lacking in will and, in the Anglo-Saxon term, 'doom-eager,' submit to a romantic destiny. They do not struggle. They feel, and we are allowed to feel with them."

Edmund Wilson's notes on Canadian culture, first published in the *New Yorker*, appeared in book form as *O Canada* in 1965. His account of Mlle. Blais as "a true 'phenomenon' " and "possibly . . . a genius" did much to make her known to non-Canadian readers, and this process was accelerated by the publication in 1966 of her best and best-known novel, *Une Saison dans la vie d'Emmanuel*. It won the Prix Médicis in France and was translated into English by Derek Coltman as *A Season in the Life of Emmanuel*.

It describes the struggle for survival of a huge and impoverished French Canadian family presided over by a domineering grandmother and a brutish father. There are fifteen or sixteen children and life is spiritually and physically degraded—even the priests in this world prey on their charges. One daughter escapes into mysticism; the cleverest child is packed off to a seminary and dies there of tuberculosis. The story is narrated by one of the children, Emmanuel, and his viewpoint is beautifully sustained, as in the account of the image that dominates his vision of the room in which he is growing up—the unequivocal image of his grandmother's feet: "They lay there like two quiet, watchful animals, scarcely twitching at all inside their black boots, always ready to spring into action; two feet bruised by long years of work in the fields."

Edmund Wilson in his introduction called this the most naturalistic of Mlle. Blais's novels, but few other critics agreed, and there were comparisons with such assorted writers as Virginia Woolf, Henry James, Louis Hémon, and even Kafka—a tribute, as Melvin Maddocks said, both to the quality of her achievement and its originality. It was the gentle lyricism with which Mlle. Blais described the sordid horrors of her story that impressed most reviewers. Denis Donoghue said, "Reading it as a romance, we see why the most vivid chapters are dreams and reveries, where the prose is lyric, unrooted in fact. . . . [This is] an exceptional book; vulnerable between success and failure, it is a beautiful thing."

Manuscrits de Pauline Archange (1968) and *Vivre! Vivre!* (1969) were translated by Derek Coltman as a single work: *The Manuscripts of Pauline Archange*. In its manner and "inner milieu," Donoghue says, it resembles *Une Saison dans la vie d'Emmanuel*. It describes the childhood of a girl so starved of love at home and in her convent school that she becomes a monster, who "can only love by devouring the beloved." Donoghue calls it "a story recited from a great distance in the history of human feeling. . . . It lives upon ancestral memories, natural laws, primitive needs. The world it invokes is indeed temporal, but haggard with the weight of centuries, and wise after the experience of death."

According to Edmund Wilson, Mlle. Blais's poetry, collected in *Pays voilés* (1963) and *Existences* (1964), contains the same kind of "bold and beautiful" imagery as her later fiction. "What all of her works . . . more or less have in common are the familiar Canadian themes of the fugitive or exile from society and the dislocated love affair. . . . Yet her work has more than local interest. It is the refinement to a purer kind of poetry than that of the professional patriots or the desperate cry that arises from the poverty, intellectual and material, the passionate self-punishing piety and the fierce defeated pride of Quebec."

Marie-Claire Blais, to quote Edmund Wilson again, "has almost the appearance of a schoolgirl, with fine little features and hands and feet." She received the Prix de la Langue Française in 1961 and the Prix France Québec in 1964.

PRINCIPAL WORKS IN ENGLISH TRANSLATION: Mad Shadows, 1960; Tête Blanche, 1961; A Season in the Life of Emmanuel, 1966; The Day Is Dark, and Three Travelers, 1967; The Manuscripts of Pauline Archange, 1970.

ABOUT: Oxford Companion to Canadian History and Literature, 1967; Tougas, G. History of French Canadian Literature, 1966; Wilson, E. O Canada, 1965. *Periodicals*—Book Week June 18, 1967; New York Review of Books June 9, 1966; New York Times Book Review February 4, 1962; August 21, 1966; April 30, 1967; Publishers' Weekly February 27, 1967; Saturday Review April 29, 1967; Times Literary Supplement February 16, 1962; March 30, 1967.

BLAKE, ROBERT (Baron Blake) (December 23, 1916–), English biographer and historian, was born in Brundall, Norfolk, the elder son of William Joseph Blake and the former Norah Daynes. He attended the King Edward VI School in Norwich from 1926 to 1935 and went on to Magdalen College, Oxford University, where in 1938 he gained a first class honors degree in Modern Greats (politics, economics, and philosophy). Blake stayed on at Oxford as Eldon Law Scholar until the outbreak of World War II in 1939, when he joined the Royal Artillery. He served in the North African campaign and in Italy, where he was captured. He was a prisoner of war for two years but escaped in 1944.

ROBERT BLAKE

After the war Blake became tutor in politics at Christ Church College, Oxford, where he remained until 1968. He served as his college's censor in 1950–1955 and its senior proctor in 1959–1960. His work is in the Christ Church tradition of scrupulous scholarship but avoids the rather chill detachment which is also associated with that college. In 1967–1968 he gave the Ford Lectures in English History, and in the latter year he left Christ Church and went to the Queen's College, Oxford, as provost. A political activist, Blake represented the Tory party on the Oxford City Council from 1957 to 1964 and, according to Noël Annan, is "leader of the conservative cause in the academic politics of Oxford."

Blake began his literary career in 1952 as editor of *The Private Papers of Douglas Haig*, a selection said to be "of very high interest," providing "a new and even startling picture of Haig." His reputation was established by equally revelatory biographies of two Tory prime ministers, Bonar Law and Disraeli, who had nothing in common except that both rose to power in the teeth of all probability. In a sense, Blake has transferred some of the gilt from Disraeli's golden image to Bonar Law's neglected one.

Andrew Bonar Law, a scholarly and conscientious former businessman, entered politics out of a sense of duty and died in 1923, a year after he had come to power. He was quickly forgotten and dubbed, by Asquith, "the unknown prime minister." Adopting this phrase as the title of his official biography, Blake set out to contradict it. In this he was greatly aided by formerly inaccessible documents in the Royal Archives and in the possession of Lord Beaverbrook, who was Bonar Law's friend and was widely supposed to be his master. Blake was able to show that Bonar Law was nobody's puppet and to paint a convincing and affectionate portrait of his subject as an "ordinary man writ large." The book was universally praised as "one of the best biographies of the year," scholarly, readable, and written in "a clear and unobtrusive style." Even Socialist reviewers commended Blake's objectivity, and a reviewer in the *Times Literary Supplement*, who did not announce his politics, wrote that "as a biography it is exhaustive and discerning, as a record it is indispensable, and as a monument of painstaking research it need fear no comparison."

Disraeli is a far more ambitious study of a far more ambitious man—one about whom remarkably little of value had been written since the completion of a monumental official biography in 1920. Like Blake's first book, it is a reappraisal in the light of new evidence, especially that contained in the Disraeli papers at Hughenden. The Disraeli who emerges from Blake's biography is no less fascinating but considerably less noble than the dedicated savior of party and country proposed by the history books. Blake's Disraeli is motivated almost entirely by his greed for power, a man not to be trusted with money, women, or political ideals, whose great enemy was not Tory snobbery or anti-Semitism but himself and whose famous reforms were the work of others. But this Disraeli is also a political magician, who climbed "the greasy pole" in spite of everything he and others could do to stop him, a brilliant wit, a man of unquenchable courage, a scandalous romantic genius in an age of pedestrian rectitude.

There was some feeling that Blake had not paid sufficient attention to Disraeli's novels or to his superb oratory—and more generally that Blake's magnificently lucid book could not of its nature quite contain a subject so untidily self-contradictory and irrational. Otherwise there was general recognition that *Disraeli* was a masterpiece of political biography. A. J. P. Taylor called it "a solid achievement of the first order. It is a fine piece of scholarship and . . . a delight to read. Blake is as far from Disraeli in temperament as anyone could be. . . . This is all to the good. After the romance and allusiveness with which Disraeli has usually been treated, it was time for daylight and cool prose."

Blake's 1968 Ford Lectures, considerably edited and supplemented, were published in 1970 as *The Conservative Party From Peel to Churchill*—that is from 1830 to 1955. It was as warmly praised as its predecessors, and a reviewer in the *Times Literary Supplement* wrote: "To have depicted so lucidly the essential character of a party which prides itself on having no definable philosophy and no precise constitution is a challenge which could probably have been successfully met only by Mr. Blake—the biographer of Disraeli and Bonar Law, and, one hopes, one day of Peel."

Robert Blake was married in 1953 to Patricia Waters and has three daughters. He is a regular book reviewer for the *Sunday Times* and writes also for the *Spectator* and the *Illustrated London News*. He received a life peerage in 1971, and is a Fellow of the British Academy and a Justice of the Peace.

PRINCIPAL WORKS: (ed.) The Private Papers of Douglas Haig, 1914–1919, 1952; The Unknown Prime Minister: The Life and Times of Andrew Bonar Law, 1858–1923, 1955 (U.S., Unrepentant Tory, 1956); Disraeli, 1966; The Conservative Party From Peel to Churchill, 1970.
ABOUT: Who's Who, 1971.

***BLANCHOT, MAURICE** (September 22, 1907–), French man of letters, was born at Quain, Saône-et-Loire, and now lives in Paris. After completing his university education, in which philosophy was presumably one of his major interests, he began the career—as literary journalist, editor, essayist, and novelist—that has earned him an important place and a great influence in French literary circles. Very little is generally known about his life, and his work, too, presents many obscurities. Geoffrey Hartman has called him "the most esoteric writer of contemporary France."

Blanchot's preoccupation with the problematic nature of literature unifies his work to an extent that sometimes makes the distinction between his criticism and his fiction hard to maintain. It is as a critic that he is most widely known, however, and none of his fiction has appeared in English. His literary essays are collected in *Faux pas* (1943); in *La Part du feu* (The Fire's Part, 1949), which includes pieces on Kafka, Malraux, Sartre, and others, as well as expounding his general critical views; in *L'Espace littéraire* (The Literary Space, 1955), the most explicit statement of his aesthetic; and in *Le Livre à venir* (The Book to Come, 1959), which includes a notable study of Beckett. Blanchot also writes regularly for *La Nouvelle Revue Française* and has contributed to *Critique* and *L'Arche*. Instead of judging a work of art on its face value, he considers that what should be examined is the artist's intentions, regarding the act of writing as an attempt by the author to become "more real." In France, and in other countries where his work is known, many regard him as one of the two or three most profound and original critics of his generation.

* blän shō

In both his fiction and his criticism, Blanchot is concerned with the problem of the artist, which is seen as a hopeless but essential quest for a reality beyond consciousness, an impossible but constantly renewed attempt to transcend the self without ceasing to be. The artist, fragmented by this task, haunted by his alienated self, is condemned and privileged to seek his reality in a kind of limbo between existential being and transcendent Being, unable wholly to live or wholly to die. In this *espace littéraire*, aware that the tools of his craft serve their own purposes, not his, he must nevertheless, lacking alternative means, employ them, reaching through language towards silence and death.

These fundamentally romantic ideas are dramatized in Blanchot's novels: *Thomas l'Obscur* (Thomas the Obscure, 1941, revised 1950), *Aminadab* (1942), and *Le Très-Haut* (The Almighty, 1948). Sartre points out the resemblance between these books and Kafka's, finding "the same minute and courtly style, the same nightmare politeness, the same preposterous and studied ceremoniousness, the same vain quests that lead nowhere, the same exhaustive and futile discussions, the same sterile initiations that initiate into nothing."

In a sense, as Geoffrey Hartman says, these novels have themselves as their subject. The hero is the novelist, his dialogue is with himself, the world he lives in is his book. Here the logic of narrative and characterization is mocked as in a dream, symbols are shown to symbolize nothing but themselves, language itself turns upon its creator. In *Thomas l'Obscur* the hero feels himself "bitten or struck, he did not know which, by a thing that seemed to be a word, but resembled rather a giant rat, with piercing eyes, pure teeth, an all-powerful animal. . . . He threw himself on it and, digging his nails into its entrails, tried to make it his own."

In *L'Arrêt de mort* (Death Arrested, 1948), *Au Moment voulu* (At the Required Time, 1951), *Celui qui ne m'accompagnait pas* (He Who Didn't Accompany Me, 1953), and *Le Dernier Homme* (The Last Man, 1957), Blanchot turns to a different form, the *récit*. In these confessional monologues, halfway between novel and philosophical discussion, the ideas illustrated in the novels are made more explicit. (And at the same time the viability of the *récit* form is questioned: who is the "I" of whom the narrator speaks? where is the "here"? when is the "now"?)

Blanchot's novels and *récits* call for great intellectual exertion in an extremely rarefied atmosphere, and it is unlikely that they will ever be popular in so pragmatic a place as the United States. Some critics nevertheless regard him as the most seriously underrated writer of his time. A reviewer in the *Times Literary Supplement* credits him with one of the most original minds of our day and suggests that in reading him "it is possible to feel the pangs of a language struggling to be born afresh. . . . It is less the task of the reader to understand than to follow as far as he can into the heart of a new experience."

PRINCIPAL WORKS IN ENGLISH TRANSLATION: *Essays in* Flores, A. and Swander, H. (eds.) Franz Kafka Today, 1962; Kostelanetz, R. (ed.) On Contemporary Literature, 1964; Lewis, R. W. B. (ed.) Malraux: A Collection of Critical Essays, 1964; René Char's Poetry, 1957. *Periodicals*—Horizon August 1949; December 1949.

ABOUT: Boisdeffre, P. de. Dictionnaire de littérature contemporaine, 1900–1962, 1962; Boisdeffre, P. de. Une Histoire vivante de la littérature d'aujourd'hui, 1938–1958, 1958; Hartman, G. Maurice Blanchot, *in* Cruickshank, J. (ed.) The Novelist as Philosopher, 1962; Le Sage, L. The French New Novel, 1962; Nadeau, M. The French Novel Since the War, 1967; Pingaud, B. Écrivains d'aujourd'hui, 1940–1960, 1960; Sartre, J.-P. Literary and Philosophical Essays, 1955. *Periodicals*—Mercure de France April 1952; Times Literary Supplement May 27, 1955; Yale French Studies 16 1955–1956.

BLISH, JAMES (BENJAMIN) (May 23, 1921–), American science fiction writer, writes: "I was born in Orange, New Jersey. My mother was a pianist and teacher; my father an advertising space salesman, chiefly for *True Story* but later also for *Esquire*. They were divorced when I was about seven. I spent my childhood in Chicago and my teens in northern New Jersey suburbs, in comfortable middle-class circumstances.

"I graduated from Rutgers University in 1942 and was almost immediately drafted, emerging from the Army—where I had been a medical laboratory technician—in 1944. After two years of graduate school at Columbia University, I became successively a reader for a literary agency, a trade-journal editor, and finally a public relations counsel specializing in technological or science-related accounts, which I still am.

"Up until about 1946 I thought of myself as a fledgling limnobiologist; but I had begun to read science fiction when I was nine, and sold my first story in 1939 after a good many misses. By 1946 I was convinced that I had no vocation as a scientist, and in the meantime had published at least twenty stories, so I switched fields.

"As of 1967 I have written 27 books and about

JAMES BLISH

175 other pieces of various kinds. The books are mostly science fiction novels, one of which (*A Case of Conscience*) won the 'Hugo' award as the best science fiction novel of 1958. I was also guest of honor at the Eighteenth World Science Fiction Convention (Pittsburgh, 1960); one of the three founders, in 1955, of the Milford (Pennsylvania) Science Fiction Writers' Conference; and the first vice president of the Science Fiction Writers of America.

"However, the books also include a historical novel, several short story collections, a volume of critical essays, and a spy novel for teen-agers. My other writings include poetry and criticism for the little magazines, short stories, stage plays, motion picture scripts, television plays, and magazine articles, as well as scores of unsigned fugitive pieces. My work has appeared in some fifty anthologies and in eighteen different countries.

"Though more than a third of my output is *not* science fiction, this is the genre I prefer and in which I am chiefly known. For the writer, it has the advantage of allowing him to place characters in stress situations which he can completely design, as well as giving him the fun of speculating on the effects of technological change on human behavior and beliefs. For the reader it is essentially a branch of romance, but it may also have the function of preparing him for some of the changes he may shortly have to live through. I know no other branch of fiction which pays any attention to technology at all.

"I still hold a regular daytime job, and write at night and sometimes on lunch hours. At present I live near and work in Washington, D.C.

"I was married in 1947 to Virginia Kidd, also a writer, by whom I have two children. We were divorced in 1963, and in 1964 I married Judith Ann Lawrence, an artist and illustrator. My other interests are concert music, amateur theatricals, private flying, and cats."

The highest and best sustained flight of Blish's restless imagination is the tetralogy Cities in Flight, about self-propelled nomad cities of the future that leave the earth to look for a new life among the stars. The volumes of the tetralogy, in the order of the story they tell, are: *They Shall Have Stars*, *A Life for the Stars*, *Earthman, Come Home*, and *The Triumph of Time*. A reviewer in the *Times Literary Supplement* has called Blish one of the few masters of that kind of science fiction "in which speculative philosophical ideas can be explored on an Aeschylean scale," and says that the Cities in Flight series has "probably carried the concept of space travel a multiplicity of light years further than anyone else has been able to contemplate."

A Case of Conscience, considered Blish's masterpiece, was one of the first science fiction novels to tackle a religious theme. It places a Roman Catholic priest on a distant planet whose reptilian inhabitants are, it seems, free of original sin, and sends him back to earth with a fertilized egg containing what might be a monstrous new savior. This story, originally published in *IF* (September 1953), was greatly extended for book publication and suffered in the process but was nevertheless sufficiently well regarded to bring Blish his Hugo award in 1959.

Both "ingenious and careful" in his use of technological detail, Blish is highly appreciated by readers qualified to judge his scientific plausibility. Kingsley Amis has credited him with "variety that goes beyond mere rearrangement" and has singled out his kind of writing as "the way of escape for those who feel that the novel is bogged down in contemporaneity and self-repetition."

"The science fiction writer chooses, to symbolize *his* real world, the trappings of science and technology," writes James Blish, "and in so far as the reader is unfamiliar with these, so will the story seem *outré* to him. . . . Yet it is not really the ideas that are 'crazy' but the trappings; not the assumptions, but the scenery. . . . The absolutely essential honesty, however, must lie where it has to lie in all fiction: honesty to the assumptions, not to the trappings."

PRINCIPAL WORKS (*all fiction*): Earthman, Come Home, 1955; They Shall Have Stars, 1956; The Frozen Year, 1957; The Triumph of Time, 1958; A Case of Conscience, 1958; A Life for the Stars, 1962; Doctor Mirabilis, 1964; Best S-F Stories of James Blish, 1965; Black Easter, 1968; Anywhen, 1970; The Day After Judgment, 1971; Midsummer Century, 1972; And All the Stars a Stage, 1972.

ABOUT: Contemporary Authors 3, 1963. *Periodicals*—Times Literary Supplement June 10, 1965; December 9, 1965.

***BLOCH-MICHEL, JEAN** (April 1912–), French novelist and essayist, writes (in French): "I was born in Paris. My father, Louis Bloch, was a doctor. My two grandfathers, Gustave Bloch and Henry Michel, were professors at the Sorbonne and my father's brother, Marc Bloch, had also been a professor at the Sorbonne. I therefore spent all my childhood in a milieu at the same time very bourgeois and very intelligent. Perhaps one should say very intellectual. My grandparents' friends, some of whom I knew during my childhood, included Jaurès, Bergson, Lévy-Bruhl, Gustave Lanson. We belonged to that very intimate society which is the Jewish intellectual bourgeoisie, a society which was harshly disrupted by the Dreyfus affair, of which I heard a good deal while still young. And, since he was our neighbor, people often pointed out Captain Dreyfus to me in the street, walking along with little steps, pince-nez riding on his nose, holding his wife's arm.

"I studied in Paris, then in Strasbourg. Mediocre studies. Then, after a law degree, I registered myself as an advocate. It was, all in all, a quite boring profession and I hardly think I would have succeeded in it despite the fact that I had been accepted by a probationary body, the Concours de la Conférence du Stage, and named secretary of this Conférence in 1938, if I remember correctly. Besides, during those years in Europe men of my age could scarcely imagine that the troubled times would let them live a normal life.

"I have never been a member of a political party, but I have always been passionately interested in politics and have always taken part. I remember the Front Populaire marches in which I participated and the riots, even in the halls of the Palais de Justice, by those on the extreme right.

"In 1939 I was called up as an infantry sergeant. Three months at the outpost in the Warndt Forest, then some cold country places between Bar-le-Duc and Sedan: it was the 'phony' war. Suddenly the real war came, at least what we thought was war. I took part in confused battles in the middle of a retreating army. And I found myself a prisoner among thousands of others.

"It happened that I was able to escape very quickly. In October 1940 I was back in Paris and thanks to my friend Léon-Maurice Nordmann, who was to be one of the first Frenchmen shot by the Nazis, I began to make contact with the beginnings of the Resistance movements. Until the Liberation, I did nothing but work in these movements. In Paris at first, then in the south, in an

* blôk mē shel′

information network; next in Nice with the *Combat* group and then in Lyon in the united Resistance groups.

"I was arrested in March 1944 and repeatedly tortured by the Gestapo. But I was freed in June a few days before the Allied landing. Returning to Paris I participated in August 1944 in the publication of the first issues of *Combat* with a group of newspapermen including Albert Camus, whom I met then for the first time and to whom I became attached by a friendship which grew more and more close. Since then I have been principally engaged in journalism, and, fortunately, not at all in war. It's a business that ages one.

"In 1945 I married Vivette Perret who is also a novelist. We have a son and a daughter.

"I began writing in 1949 and my first novel, *Le Témoin*, was published by Albert Camus in his series Espoir, published by the NRF. Since then I have continued to write novels and essays. I left journalism and my only activities in that area are as literary editor of the review *Preuves*, and the essays in literary criticism I write for *La Gazette de Lausanne*.

"I don't know how to define myself as a writer. However, the only one of my books which has had much success—the others have never earned me more than the esteem of some of my colleagues, never the least public notice—the only one of my books, then, which has had some success is *Le Présent de l'indicatif*. It is a polemic against the French New Novel. What is certain, therefore, is that I do not belong to that school. I continue to believe, contrary to those who adhere to the new group, that a writer is not a man who has nothing to say."

Le Témoin (1949), Bloch-Michel's first and best-known novel, is an investigation into the sources of courage and cowardice. It reminded some critics of Conrad's *Lord Jim* (because of its theme), others of Camus's *The Fall* (because of its form and mood). It is a long confession of failure by a young man whose cowardice reaches its peak when he sees his wife arrested by the Gestapo and cannot bring himself to aid or even acknowledge her. He concludes that his weakness stems from the fact that he has cut himself off from society: "Solitude has the same effect on the soul as fasting and flagellation have: at first it exalts it, and then it makes it die, for lack of nourishment." Translated by Eithne Wilkins as *The Witness*, it had a respectful reception from American and British critics, though some found the introspective style of this "lengthy suicide note" somewhat tedious.

La Fuite en Égypte (1952, translated by Francis Fresnaye as *The Flight into Egypt*) describes the efforts of a small-town French family, refugees

JEAN BLOCH-MICHEL

from the German invaders, to make a new home in a deserted mountain area. Characterization and narrative are deliberately subordinated to the book's philosophical concerns, expressed through the family's need to create a society for itself, an outer reality. It had a rather mixed press; some readers found it tedious in its abstraction, others were moved by its poignancy.

Besides his journalism, and some translations of English-language books, Bloch-Michel has also written a number of other novels and several volumes of essays. The first of these, *Les Grandes Circonstances* (1949), is a collection of laconic and understated sketches of the author's work with the Resistance. For him, these were "the important times. . . . We now have ordinary life. Right now is when men know what they are made of." The same theme is taken up in *Un Homme estimable* (A Respectable Man, 1956), a novel which explores the problems of adapting to the flat perspectives of postwar life after the challenges and excitements of the occupation. Those terrible but enlarging times are revisited almost nostalgically in *Le Visage nu* (The Naked Face, 1959), containing three short stories about the war and involving characters who also appear in *Un Homme estimable*.

Several of the essays in *Journal du désordre* (Diary of a Confused Mind, 1955) deal with aggressive nationalism and its products, attacking among other things French policy in Indochina and the harsh treatment meted out to collaborators after World War II. Bloch-Michel goes on to question his own motives, wondering whether his moral attitudes can bear objective scrutiny, whether he was right to bring children into the world, and whether he can continue to endure the banalities of peacetime life. The same humanity and scrupulous honesty are evident in the essay he contributed to *Réflexions sur la peine capitale* (Reflections on Capital Punishment, 1957), edited by Camus and Arthur Koestler. *Le Présent de l'indicatif* (Present Indicative, 1963) is a discussion of the French New Novel, a literary phase or fashion which Bloch-Michel regards as an interesting failure.

PRINCIPAL WORKS IN ENGLISH TRANSLATION: The Witness, 1949; Flight into Egypt, 1955.

ABOUT: Peyre, H. French Novelists of Today, 1967. *Periodicals*—Chicago Sunday Tribune August 21, 1955; Christian Science Monitor October 6, 1949; Commonweal September 30, 1949; New York Herald Tribune September 25, 1949; August 21, 1955; New York Times Book Review September 25, 1949; August 21, 1955; New Yorker November 19, 1949; Saturday Review November 12, 1949; Time August 29, 1955.

BLOOMFIELD, ANTHONY (JOHN WESTGATE) (September 8, 1922–), British novelist, writes: "I was born, and now live, in London, but as my father—a Civil Servant—moved from place to place at regular intervals I spent my boyhood and was educated in provincial towns, in England and Scotland. I retain a preference for smaller places and regret the circumstances which at present oblige me to live in an increasingly uncomfortable and inhuman metropolis.

"Aside from cricket, 'English' was the only school activity for which I had a real aptitude, and I think from the age of twelve or less I developed the assumption that I would be some kind of a writer. (I believe, incidentally, that as reader I can detect those writers who were similarly early in their formation, although this is not necessarily a mark of merit.)

"I left school shortly before the Second World War and early in 1940 I joined the Royal Air Force, from which I was not discharged until 1946. I spent four years in the Middle East—Iraq, Trucial Oman, Palestine, Egypt—in various unheroic capacities, and it was during this time and immediately after the war that I began to have short stories published in the little magazines that flourished then. On discharge I worked on various small-town newspapers until I joined the British Broadcasting Corporation as a television scriptwriter in 1954. I am, at time of writing, still employed by the BBC, in charge of the day-to-day production of television news programmes. As I am married and have a school-age son—and as also I have in middle-age no taste for 'attic' life—I am obliged, like most novelists, to earn money additional to that which my books earn. I regret, and fear, the demands on time and energy that my television work entails, for I have no doubt that my vocation is that of fiction-writer; on the other hand, I enjoy the semi-creative co-

ANTHONY BLOOMFIELD

operation with other people in television and also reluctantly welcome the escape from the painful solitariness of one's desk. As I work a shift system, I have—at least, in theory—half my week for my own writing.

"My first novel was published by the Hogarth Press in 1955; I have since published three others and am at present working on another with the provisional title of 'Love in Exile,' set in part in England and in part in the United States. All four completed books have been published in paperback as well as hardcover; three of the four in the United States; and there have been translations into French, Swedish and German. They have in the main been critically as well received as I could have expected, without making a large public impact—possibly, in part, because their sociological content being slight, they have not been in the fashion of the past decade.

"I am not a quick writer: my method, once I have formed a generalised conception of the book I want to write, is to lead myself on from word to word, from page to page. This necessarily involves a good deal of discarding and a good deal of re-writing in the final shaping. While I am sure that a writer's cast of mind—mine is reactionary, ironic, un-intellectual, pessimistic—must colour his work and that the objective or 'absent' author is an impossibility, I regard the writing of a book as, in the last analysis, the creating of a self-contained object, rather than as a vehicle for ideas, for influencing people or as a means of self-expression. Other than that, I find it hard to describe the nature of my books, partly because I do not care to analyse their sources too closely and partly because I find it absolutely necessary to try to make something different each time. In writing, it is the craftsmanship that gives me the greatest satisfaction. I believe that the naturalistic novel, however expertly done, is no longer worth doing, and, in common with the contemporary novelists whom I most admire (chiefly American), I am trying to find new ways of blending reality and unreality. I would also like my books to be funny or, at least—please God—un-solemn."

———

Russian Roulette was a much praised "study of self-destruction" set in a seedy English seaside town where Carr, a middle-aged journalist, becomes obsessively involved in the affairs of a youth who is connected with the murder of a prostitute. Similar themes have recurred in Bloomfield's subsequent novels. *The Delinquents* was another study of moral decay set in a seaside town. *The Tempter* was a fable in which a pornographer assumes the role of scapegoat for the secret vices of the world; it seemed to some labored in its symbolism, but greatly impressed other reviewers, one of whom called it a "somberly beautiful book."

In *Throw*, a clerk seeking to punish the man whose car killed his son begins an escalating campaign of reprisal which becomes a compulsive and vicious end in itself. The novel was called a "chillingly convincing picture of schizophrenic disintegration . . . subtly and illuminatingly written." A fifth novel, *Life for a Life*, appeared in 1971. It is another account of psychological breakdown, in which Laurence Carpenter, a London businessman, unheroically saves from drowning a professional assassin, who then proposes to show his gratitude by killing any one of his rescuer's enemies. Carpenter insists that he has none but finds himself reacting to the ordinary stresses of life in increasingly violent ways under the pressure of his deeply hidden wish for the killing. Martin Levin called it "a beautifully engineered thriller" reminiscent of Simenon, with "a more concentrated texture and a splash of wit."

Bloomfield says that his novels are not intended as vehicles for ideas, but it is clear that he is preoccupied in them with moral questions—most often the susceptibility to corruption of those whose emotional lives are empty. Because of this, and because of his extraordinary capacity to evoke spiritual and physical squalor, he is often compared to Graham Greene. Anthony Boucher believed that his "rich-textured, allusive, sometimes dazzling prose may suggest William Sansom."

Bloomfield continues to enjoy cricket (though "not of the literary variety"). He loathes the automobile, which he says is "the symbol and the cause of the isolation and anguish in the Western World."

PRINCIPAL WORKS: Russian Roulette, 1955; The Delinquents, 1958; The Tempter, 1961; Throw, 1965; Life for a Life, 1971.

ABOUT: Contemporary Authors 1–4 (first revision), 1967. *Periodicals*—Encounter June 1955.

BLY, ROBERT (ELWOOD) (December 23, 1926–), American poet, editor, and translator, was born in Madison, Minnesota, the son of Jacob Thomas Bly, a farmer, and the former Alice Aws. He served during World War II with the United States Naval Reserve (1944–1945) and, after a year at St. Olaf College (1946–1947), went to Harvard, where he received his A.B. *magna cum laude* in 1950. Further study at the State University of Iowa brought him his M.A. in 1956. The same year he went with a government grant to Norway, where he translated contemporary Norwegian poetry.

Returning to his native Madison, Bly settled on the farm where he and his family still live. There in 1958 he founded his magazine *The Fifties*, which has survived to become, successively, *The Sixties* and *The Seventies*. From the beginning it has been characterized by the large amount of space it gives to contemporary European and Latin American poetry in translation and by the distinctive quality of the American poetry it favors and fosters, notably in the work of James Wright, Donald Hall, Louis Simpson, and Bly himself.

The *Fifties* poets, who acknowledge the influence of such poets as Lorca, Neruda, Trakl, and Breton, seek in their work what they call the deep image. Donald Hall believes that they are drawing upon "a new kind of imagination." He says: "This imagination is irrational yet the poem is usually quiet and the language simple; there is no straining for apocalypse and no conscious pursuit of the unconscious. There is an inwardness to these images, a profound subjectivity." And yet, Hall says, this is not the subjectivity of confessional poetry: "This new imagination reveals through images a subjective life which is *general*, and which corresponds to an old objective life of shared experience and knowledge."

Bly's own verse had begun to appear in *Poetry*, *Paris Review*, *Hudson Review*, and other magazines in 1950. His first volume was *Silence in the Snowy Fields* (1962), containing mostly pastoral poems about Minnesota. Their most obvious quality was an extreme bareness and simplicity of diction, which seemed to some critics indistinguishable from "bald statement" but which greatly impressed others. Richard Howard thought that Bly had been able "to confer upon even the simplest words a weight and consequence as of new things . . . to invest his seasons and spectacles, however dull or even dreary, with so much felt life that even the simplest monosyllables speak to him, and to us."

ROBERT BLY

On the whole reviewers paid less attention to the "gently surrealistic perceptions" that produced, from sleep or reverie, such unexpected images as "The bare trees more dignified than ever, / Like a fierce man on his deathbed"; or snow flakes "like jewels of a murdered Gothic prince"; or lamplight that "falls on all fours in the grass." Ian Hamilton thought that Bly, in his best poems, "can achieve a genuinely rooted kind of imagery that is resistant to the dissolving invitations of his fancy, but more often than not he is happy to muse off into the pretty, the diminutive, the vacuously sentimental. . . . 'How beautiful to walk out at midnight in the moonlight / Dreaming of animals.' "

A specifically surrealistic use of imagery occurs more often in Bly's second collection, *The Light Around the Body*, which contains poems of two kinds. The most admired of them are mystical poems, similar to and often, many thought, better than Bly's earlier work. There are also many poems of political protest, most of them opposing the Vietnam war in a manner which one English critic has called "loose, lengthy and presumptuous, and reeking with moral vanity." Another anonymous writer, in the *Virginia Quarterly Review*, suggested that "Bly is an innocent; his mysticism springs in part from that innocence and its purity of insight; his political verse springs almost wholly from that innocence and its childishness."

This judgment would not be acceptable to the jury of three poets—Donald Hall, Harvey Shapiro, and Theodore Weiss—who gave Bly the National Book Award for poetry in 1968. It seemed to them that "Bly is writing about the most important subjects—the great events of the spirit and of the day, and of the American past. He reveals the invisible but real psyche of our nation." At the NBA ceremony Bly received a standing ovation for the bitter attack he made there on America's role in Vietnam; he gave his one-thousand-dollar check to the Resistance, an antidraft organization. The previous year he had for similar reasons refused a grant of five thousand dollars to the Sixties Press from the National Endowment for the Arts. He has also canceled subscriptions to his magazine held by universities doing research in support of the war. Bly has received Fulbright, Guggenheim, and Amy Lowell fellowships. The Seventies Press specializes in small volumes of poetry in translation, many of them the work of Bly himself.

Bly was married in 1955 to Carolyn McLean and has four children. He is much in demand as a poetry reader on American campuses.

PRINCIPAL WORKS: Silence in the Snowy Fields, 1962; The Light Around the Body, 1967; Sleepers Joining Hands, 1972. *As Translator*—The Story of Gösta Berling (Lagerlöf), 1962; Forty Poems of Juan Ramón Jiménez, 1967; Hunger (Hamsun), 1967; (with James Wright) Twenty Poems of Pablo Neruda, 1968; (with Christina Paulston) I Do Best Alone at Night: Selected Poems of Gunnar Ekelöf, 1968 (In England, Late Arrival on Earth, 1967); Selected Poems by Yvan Goll, 1968; Neruda and Vallejo: Selected Poems, 1971; Lorca and Jiménez: Selected Poems, 1973. *As Editor*—(with David Ray) A Poetry Reading Against the Vietnam War, 1962; The Sea and the Honeycomb, 1966; Forty Poems Touching on Recent American History, 1970.

ABOUT: Contemporary Authors 5–6, 1963; Hall, D. *Introduction to* Contemporary American Poetry, 1962; Murphy, R. (ed.) Contemporary Poets of the English Language, 1970; Ossman, D. The Sullen Art, 1963; Rosenthal, M. L. The New Poets, 1967; Stepanchev, S. American Poetry Since 1945, 1965; Who's Who in America, 1972–1973. *Periodicals*—Library Journal April 1, 1968; Nation March 25, 1968; New York Review of Books October 21, 1967; Publishers' Weekly March 18, 1968; Times Literary Supplement July 17, 1969.

***BOILEAU, PIERRE (LOUIS)** (April 28, 1906–), French crime novelist, writes (in French): "I was born in Paris, at the foot of Montmartre, a stone's throw from Pigalle, and I have always lived in this district. My father, who was a departmental manager in a shipping agency, had studied in a school of commerce. Naturally, I attended this same school, where I spent several years without succeeding in being initiated into the secrets of accounting. My vocation had already been decided: I wanted to be a writer of detective stories. Unfortunately, there were certain immediate needs and, my studies finished, I made equally unsuccessful beginnings in the most diverse fields, going from the textile industry to the food industry, and trying advertising and architecture in passing.

"Meanwhile, in my spare time, I wrote some short stories to get my hand in. These were well

* bwä lō′

received. Encouraged, I then attempted novels and published in this order: *La Pierre qui tremble*, *La Promenade de minuit*, and *Le Repos de Bacchus*, which was awarded the Prix du Roman d'Aventures in 1938. I could at last live by my writings.

"I lived by them . . . until September 1939. In 1942, I returned from captivity. There was no question of my contributing, under any circumstances, to the journals then being published. Until the Liberation, I worked for a special Welfare Department concerned with helping political prisoners and criminals. In this way I was able to visit most penitentiary establishments . . . and I met some remarkable people there.

"After the war, I published a few more novels and a very great number of novellas. One day, a book in a shop window attracted my attention: *Esthétique du roman policier*. Author: Thomas Narcejac; a name unknown to me. I bought the book and devoured it. I found discussed in it problems concerning the evolution of the detective novel and its future that had been troubling me for some time; suggestions with which I immediately agreed; definitions that I would never forget. I wrote to Narcejac, who immediately answered; it was the beginning of a long correspondence in which we tried to find remedies for the ills of a literary genre which escaped the sclerosis of the traditional problem novel only by foundering in the excesses of the 'black' novel.

"In June 1948 we met, at the luncheon for the Prix du Roman d'Aventures, which had been awarded to Narcejac. Hardly had we started discussing our favorite topic, when Narcejac said to me: 'It's all very well to exchange theories, but wouldn't it be much more effective to put them into practice?' 'You mean?' 'To write the novel we should like to read.' So we wrote our first novel together: *Celle qui n'était plus . . .*; a novel so far removed from the usual concepts that all the 'specialist' publishers to whom we submitted our manuscript refused it. It was finally accepted by Denoël who, appropriately, didn't publish detective novels.

"Thinking that our attempt might interest him, we sent our book to the director Georges Clouzot. Two days later, he bought the film rights. He made a film from it, *Les Diaboliques*.

"The following year, it was Alfred Hitchcock who brought one of our other novels to the screen, under the title *Vertigo*. We had therefore every reason to think that we were on the right track, and we have persevered. We have now published our thirteenth novel. We have written film scripts and dialogues; sketches for radio and television. We are finishing a play."

By 1938, as he says, Pierre Boileau was already

PIERRE BOILEAU

well established in France as a highly capable technician of the detective novel. The international reputation he has achieved since the war is a product of his association with "Thomas Narcejac" (Pierre Ayraud), a philosophy teacher fascinated by abnormal psychology and the theory of suspense fiction. Their success derives from the fact that, as Narcejac puts it, Boileau is "interested in the hows and I [am] interested in the whys of a story."

Their first book, *Celle qui n'était plus* (1952), was translated as *The Woman Who Was No More*. It is an appallingly ingenious murder story in which a sudden reversal at the end reveals the would-be murderer as actual victim. The grim, compelling mood of the story is established with a skill and economy reminiscent of Simenon, and the reader is drawn so thoroughly into the tale, so teased with faint and almost subliminal hints and doubts, that the shatteringly unexpected conclusion is immediately and terrifying believable, in terms of both plot and character. One finishes the book with a sense of escaping from the horrible logic of a nightmare. It was brilliantly filmed in 1954 as *Les Diaboliques* (released as *Diabolique* in the United States and as *The Fiends* in Britain).

None of Boileau and Narcejac's subsequent novels has quite matched the almost physical impact of the first, but all are characterized by the same preoccupation with the morbid and macabre, the same ingenuity and skill in building atmosphere and suspense. *D'entre les morts* (1954, translated as *The Living and the Dead*) provides a "shocking and brilliant" explanation of a man's apparent rediscovery of his former mistress, long since a suicide. *Les Louves* (1955, translated as *The Prisoner*) is about an escaped convict who finds himself imprisoned in the grim past of the man he is impersonating.

Several other stories turn on physical disabilities of one kind or another. Blindness is the theme of *Les Visages de l'ombre* (1953, translated as *Faces in the Dark*) and a new level of medical nastiness is achieved in *Et mon tout est un homme* (1965, translated as *Choice Cuts*), which won the Grand Prix de l'Humeur Noir in France. It is about what happens when portions of a gunman's corpse are distributed among seven different people by "spare-part" surgery. "It is the authors' remarkable achievement," wrote one reviewer, "that they make suspension of disbelief quite easy, and they weave a mystery, the brilliantly horrifying solution of which few readers will foresee."

Boileau, the son of Léon and Maria (Guillaud) Boileau, was married in 1939 to Josette Baudin.

PRINCIPAL WORKS IN ENGLISH TRANSLATION (*all in collaboration with "Thomas Narcejac"*): The Woman Who Was No More, 1954 (England, The Woman Who Was); Faces in the Dark, 1955; The Living and the Dead, 1956; The Prisoner, 1957; The Evil Eye [and] The Sleeping Beauty, 1959; Heart to Heart, 1959; The Tube, 1960; Spells of Evil, 1961; Who was Claire Jallu?, 1965; Choice Cuts, 1966; The Victims, 1967.

ABOUT: Who's Who in France, 1971–1972. *Periodicals*—New York Herald Tribune Book Review April 11, 1954; New York Times May 9, 1954; May 5, 1957; New York Times Book Review November 6, 1966; Saturday Review May 22, 1954; Spectator July 2, 1950; Times Literary Supplement August 5, 1955; May 4, 1956; August 16, 1957; January 30, 1959; October 9, 1959; November 25, 1960; December 29, 1961; August 18, 1966.

***BÖLL, HEINRICH** (December 21, 1917–), German novelist and short story writer, received the 1972 Nobel Prize for Literature for his contribution "to a renewal of German literature." He has spent most of his life in the Catholic city of Cologne, where he was born the sixth and youngest surviving son of a cabinetmaker and woodcarver of British descent. After graduating from his Gymnasium, Böll began his career as an apprentice in a Cologne bookshop and then was conscripted into the German army. He served throughout the war, mainly on the Russian front, was wounded four times, and emerged with the modest rank of corporal. In 1945 he returned from an American prisoner-of-war camp to Cologne and eventually found work in the city government's statistical department. At the same time he began to write, and since 1951 he has supported himself in this way.

In a short essay called "Über mich selbst" (Concerning Myself, 1958), Böll describes the inner history of his early years. His first memory is of Hindenburg's returning army, "gray, orderly, offering no hope." Then there were the smell and look of his father's workshop, the strong Teutonized names of the streets in his city, the poverty of his schoolmates, and the inflation that was drowning them all; finally his own ambitions: "I always wanted to write, and I tried it from the beginning, but I didn't find the words until later."

The first words, it seems, were poems and stories written at school. These were destroyed during the war but the loss is not regretted by Böll, who thinks "they would have been frightful." He made his reputation with three books about the war: the short stories of *Der Zug war pünktlich* (1949, translated as *The Train Was on Time*); the stories of *Wanderer, kommst du nach Spa* (1950, translated as *Traveler, If You Come to Spa*), and the novel *Wo warst du, Adam?* (1951, translated as *Adam, Where Art Thou?*). The latter has also been published, together with *Der Zug war pünktlich*, as *Adam and the Train*, in a new translation by Leila Vennewitz, Böll's exclusive translator since 1965.

In these books the war is seen nearly always from the point of view of the common soldier—as a mindless waste, a pointless idiocy, an infectious disease. All three were generally successful and are interesting now because in them Böll was forging his characteristically simple, laconic, and serviceable style, strongly reminiscent at first of Hemingway. Together with the other writers of the now famous Gruppe 47, which he had joined in 1950, Böll believed that the German literary tradition had to be purged and reborn after the war, morally and linguistically. Morally, German society had not accepted its full burden of guilt and was ready to march without self-examination from defeat to "economic miracle." And the German language itself, tainted by Nazi use, had to be remade. Böll and Gruppe 47 sought simplicity—short words and short sentences, scorning the complex rules of classical German prose.

Most of the work Böll produced during the 1950s dealt with the immediate aftermath of war—the physical and spiritual rubble, the growing materialism. *Und sagte kein einziges Wort* (1953, translated as *Acquainted With the Night*) is about a returned soldier reduced by the war to alcoholic apathy and rescued from total moral disintegration only by his wife's unshakable Catholic faith. There is another study of postwar alienation in *Haus ohne Hüter* (1954, translated as *Tomorrow and Yesterday* in the United States, and more literally in England as *The Unguarded House*). The people in these novels look back nostalgically to the prewar past and acknowledge the gray present, but they try to ignore the war, the dreadful limbo in between. As W. E. Yuill puts it, in his valuable essay on Böll in *Essays on Contemporary German Literature*, "Reminiscence is the characteristic dimension of Böll's writing. He is fascinated by the counterpoint of time and place and by the changes worked through time and circumstance."

* bûl

The truth of this is evident in Böll's most complexly structured novel, *Billard um halb-zehn* (1959, translated as *Billiards at Half-Past Nine*). The action of the book is confined to a single day, during which however the history of the Faehmels family—and of Germany—over half a century is reconstructed in the recollections of the principal characters. The history of the family, and of the class and faith they represent, is linked with the abbey of St. Anton, built by Robert Faehmel's father, destroyed by Robert during the war as an anti-Nazi protest, rebuilt with the help of Robert's son. The book makes explicit what is implicit in all of Böll's writings: the distinction he makes between "buffalo" people—the materialistic, powerful, and soulless exploiters—and their victims, the "lambs"—the dreamy misfits with whom Böll identifies himself.

Another experiment with time is conducted in *Ansichten eines Clowns* (1963, translated as *The Clown*). The narrator is Hans Schnier, the misfit son of a rich manufacturer. Disgusted by his family and class, he runs off with a Catholic girl and makes a name for himself as a clown and a satirist of postwar German society. His girl leaves him in favor of her church, needing the "abstract principles of order" that he loathes. Schnier's efforts to get her back, and then to resume contact with his family and former friends, end in failure and despair: time is not reversible. The novel is both funny and moving and asks some searching questions about the role of Catholicism during and after the war. Daniel Stern warmly praised Böll's command of his material in this book and the simplicity of its structure, finding it "dense with realized and felt experience."

Some critics believe that Böll is most at home in the short story, where he can create "satiric close-ups of unsurpassed power." The element of sardonic humor that has always distinguished his short fiction has become increasingly prominent in his novels also, and it dominates *Entfernung von der Truppe* (1964, translated as *Absent Without Leave*) and *Ende einer Dienstfahrt* (1966, translated as *End of a Mission*).

In the short novel *Absent Without Leave* the hero, Schmölder, becomes "a Jew by being bellowed at" as a soldier during the war. Even assignment to latrine duties fails to make a man of him, and he deserts in order to marry his girl. Schmölder has opted out and recommends this course to others: "Defection and desertion I would advise in favor of rather than against, for as I said: there are idiots who aim to hit, and everyone ought to realize the risk they are running. Firearms are instruments completely lacking in humor." Schmölder's young wife is killed in a bombing raid and in the end it is clear that he will always be a misfit. E. M. Potoker in his review said that Böll's style "has now become an instrument of striking subtlety, maintained intricately on several levels, artfully moving back and forth in time and making use of symbols and parables both poignant and absurd."

HEINRICH BÖLL

"I write about [the contemporary world]," Böll says, "because I am an engaged and contemporary writer, but I write because I love it." His many essays reflect his passion for *Wirklichkeit*—reality—and the same concern is evident in his fiction and radio plays. Reality in his work is apprehended subjectively through the eyes and ears of his characters, and very often through their sense of smell. But his is a poetic realism—he is, as W. E. Yuill writes, very much aware of "the intrinsic strangeness of familiar things," and often "invests objects with symbolic significance and employs them in thematic patterns." At the root of his view of the world is a Christian compassion, an anti-establishment, antibourgeois charity reminiscent of Graham Greene's. In his early work this was sometimes softened by sentimentality into what one critic has called "allegorical confectionary" but the sweetness has increasingly been "neutralised by the acid of satire."

Satire, tinged with humor and sadness, predominates in *Gruppenbild mit Dame* (1971, translated as *Group Portrait With Lady*), which is generally regarded as his best book to date. It is a portrait of Leni, a florist in her late forties, and of her teachers, family, lovers, and enemies. Leni is an anachronism in postwar Germany, a mysterious alien in the consumer society. Motivated by instinct rather than greed, she is a kind of Earth Mother, intensely erotic and at the same time wholly innocent. The novel has something of the character of a detective story, in which the author describes his pursuit of the truth about his characters, and passes on to the reader his growing store of information about their activities and motivations. And as Leni and the people around her come gradually into focus, the reader finds that he is receiving also a profoundly ironical panorama—and indictment—of German society from prewar days to the present. As one reviewer wrote, "It is difficult to do justice to a work so rich in characters and scope. [It] has a thick texture into the fabric of which are woven some remarkable vignettes. It is from these that we piece together a world of great emotional complexity. The characters are inextricably interrelated, and as their subtle interplay is explored, the author subjects his countrymen to harsh and clear illumination, [though he] criticizes and investigates with humaneness."

A *Guardian* interviewer has described Böll as "a large, saggy, calm man with a pitted, veined face, sea-colored eyes and bushy eyebrows," and as "a hedonist, a sociable, bucolic café man . . . tortured by deep personal uncertainties." Böll lives with his wife and the youngest of his three sons in a village just outside Cologne. He has collaborated with his wife, the former Annemarie Cech, on German versions of Brendan Behan, J. D. Salinger, and Patrick White, among others. He has remained a Catholic, though one who "elevates conscience above dogma," and a socialist—he participated in Willy Brandt's successful campaign in the 1972 elections. He loves Ireland, where he owns a house, and has published an account of his travels there, *Irish Journal*. Böll is chairman of the International PEN Club. Among the many honors he has received are the René Schickele prize (1952), the German Critics' prize (1953), the French Prix du Meilleur Livre Étranger (1955), the Swiss Charles Veillon prize (1960), and the Georg Büchner prize (1967). Ernst Pawel has called him "Germany's best as well as best selling author," as popular in Eastern Europe as in the West, who owes his universal appeal to his "utter, uncompromising integrity," and who is "both profound and eminently readable."

PRINCIPAL WORKS IN ENGLISH TRANSLATION: Acquainted With the Night, 1954; Adam, Where Art Thou?, 1955; Traveler, If You Come to Spa, 1956; The Train Was on Time, 1956; The Unguarded House (U.S., Tomorrow and Yesterday), 1957; The Bread of Our Early Years, 1957; Billiards at Half-Past Nine, 1961; Absent Without Leave, and Other Stories, 1965; The Clown, 1965; Eighteen Stories, 1966; Irish Journal, 1967; End of a Mission, 1968; Children Are Civilians Too (stories), 1970; Adam and the Train, 1970; Group Portrait With Lady, 1973.

ABOUT: Closs, A. Twentieth Century German Literature, 1969; Current Biography, 1972; Daniels, K. Zur Problematik des Dichterischen bei Heinrich Böll, 1966; Hatfield H. Modern German Literature, 1966; Käufer, H. E. Das Werk Heinrich Bölls, 1963; Keith-Smith, B. (ed.) Essays on Contemporary German Literature, 1965; Lettau, R. Die Gruppe 47, 1967; Melius F. Der Schriftsteller Heinrich Böll, 1962; Moore, H. T. (ed.) Twentieth-Century German Literature, 1967; Penguin Companion to Literature 2, 1969; Reich-Ranicki, M. (ed.) in Sachen Böll, 1968; Schwarz, W. J. Heinrich Böll, 1969; Stresau, H. Heinrich Böll, 1964; Thomas, R. H. and Will, W. van der. The German Novel and the Affluent Society, 1968; Waidson, H. M. The Modern German Novel, 1959; Wirth, G. Heinrich Böll, 1968. *Periodicals*—Guardian June 3, 1968; New York Times October 20, 1972.

BOLT, ROBERT (OXTON) (August 15, 1924–), English dramatist and screen writer, was born at Sale, near Manchester, the younger of the two sons of Ralph and Leah (Binnion) Bolt. His father kept a small shop, selling furniture, glass, and china; his mother taught at a primary school. Bolt has described the ruling atmosphere as one of "northern nonconformity." There was "much emphasis on education, social responsibility and progressive politics; a good deal of Chapel and Sunday School in early years . . . the *Manchester Guardian* and no alcohol . . . and all much better fun than it sounds because of the vigour and seriousness."

Nevertheless, looking back, Bolt thinks of his childhood as a "very dark one . . . very gloomy, fraught, self-doubting, self-contemptuous, lots of petty delinquency, very bad behavior at school, cordially disliked by my teachers" (especially in contrast to his successful elder brother). Bolt left Manchester Grammar School in 1940 with a profound sense of failure. Unqualified for admission to a university, he drifted into an insurance office and hated it. Fortunately, a teacher friend found him a place at Manchester University under a special wartime entry scheme. His first year there was "really the opening of the gates of paradise for me. . . . I was more or less drunk the whole year on freedom and ideas and new things and oh! everything." He studied history, became a Marxist and joined the Communist party; when he left it five years later it was because he had concluded that it had "nothing to do with democracy and freedom."

Bolt was drafted into the Royal Air Force in 1943 and for the first time left "home"—for London, then South Africa. But he developed air sickness and was transferred to the Army and officer training at Sandhurst, by which time he was "partly repelled and partly seduced" by the military ethic. He served with the West African Frontier Force on the Gold Coast (now Ghana), leaving the Army in 1946 with the rank of lieutenant. Bolt resumed his studies at Manchester University, graduating with an honors degree in history in 1949, and going on to secure a teaching diploma at Exeter University. He began his career in 1950 at a village school in Devon, moving on in 1952 to the Millfield School, a progressive school in Somerset, where he taught English until 1958.

Although Bolt had written stories since childhood, he came to the drama almost by chance, when in 1950 he was asked to write a nativity play for his pupils. This "was an astonishing turning point. . . . [I knew] that this was what I was going to do and that I was going to succeed or fail by this." In the following eight years, Bolt wrote eight radio plays for adults and seven for children, the latter mostly concerned with the exploits of a dim but beguiling knight named Sir Oblong Fitz-Oblong. *The Master*, a play about wandering scholars in the Middle Ages, was broadcast in February 1953; *Fifty Pigs* in the same year; and an early version of *A Man for All Seasons* in July 1954. *Ladies and Gentlemen* followed; *The Last of the Wine* (which has no connection with the novel by Mary Renault); *Mr. Sampson's Sundays*, *The Window*, and in 1958 *The Drunken Sailor*, about seamen in the eighteenth century navy. Several of these, including *The Last of the Wine* and *A Man for All Seasons*, were later adapted for the theatre.

The Critic and the Heart, the first of his plays to reach the stage, was produced in 1957 at the Oxford Playhouse. Subsequently rewritten as *Brother and Sister*, it deals with the relationship between a dying painter and his sister. She has sacrificed her own life and happiness to his art but, it emerges, he has been exploited no less selfishly by the crassly commercial art world, represented here by the critic Reeves, who steals his private letters for publication. Whether the paintings (or art in general) are worth so much human sacrifice is left open.

Bolt's first important success was *Flowering Cherry*, which opened in London in November 1957. It is about a middle-aged dreamer, Jim Cherry, trapped in an office job he hates but sustained by the fantasy that he will one day escape to the country and plant an orchard. But he is so enmeshed in his sense of failure that, when a legacy makes it possible for him to realize his dream, he is unable to accept the chance. The play, warmly praised for its maturity and honesty, received the *Evening Standard*'s award as the most promising play of the year and ran for over four hundred performances in London (though it subsequently failed in New York).

The best and most successful of Bolt's plays to date is *A Man for All Seasons*, a study of the martyrdom of Sir Thomas More. More was Chancellor of England when the Vatican denied Henry VIII permission to divorce his first wife and marry Anne Boleyn. Henry responded by smashing the power of the Roman Catholic Church in England and putting himself at the head of an autonomous Church of England. More, torn between loyalty to Catholicism and loyalty to his king, said nothing. This was not enough for Henry, who wanted the active support of his most respected minister. In the end More, a wise, moderate, and earthly man, with no taste for martyrdom, found that he valued his principles more than his life. More's reluctant but

ROBERT BOLT

unshakable nobility is brilliantly counterpointed in the play by the character of the Common Man, venal, vulgar, and often irresistibly comic, who acts as chorus to the tragedy.

A Man for All Seasons opened in London in July 1960 and played there for over nine months before beginning an even longer run in New York in November 1961. It won awards from the American Theatre Wing and the New York Drama Critics Circle, has been repeatedly revived by amateurs and professionals, and became an award-winning film. Walter Kerr summed up the critical reaction when he wrote that the play was "as remarkable in its restraint as in its ultimate fire. . . . What is colloquial falls on the ear with a humorous grace . . . and what is formal is so precisely, trenchantly phrased as to build a reservoir of suppressed power toward an eventual explosion of intelligence and emotion. . . . What Mr. Bolt has done is to make the human mind shine. The glare is dazzling, the experience exhilarating."

A crucial moral dilemma rather like More's is the theme of *The Tiger and the Horse*, launched in London a month after *A Man for All Seasons*. In it a successful academic is asked to sign a ban-the-bomb petition which will cost him the vice chancellorship of his university. His ultimate decision is made on emotional rather than intellectual grounds, in accordance with Blake's apothegm: "The tygers of wrath are wiser than the horses of instruction." The theme was clearly an important one for Bolt, an active member of the Campaign for Nuclear Disarmament who in 1961 went to prison for his beliefs. Some critics however found the play's conclusion unconvincing, emotionally satisfying though it is, and it had a relatively cool reception.

In 1962 Bolt scored a notable success in another medium with his scenario for the Oscar-winning film *Lawrence of Arabia*. He has since written screenplays for *Dr. Zhivago*, *A Man for All Seasons*, and *Ryan's Daughter*. His next stage play, *Gentle Jack*, though it was a failure, was an interesting attempt to break away from the tradition of the realistic "well-made" play. It is an allegorical fantasy in which the god Pan (or Jack-in-the-Green) lends his magic to the gentle hero Jacko. Jacko uses his new power to resolve the conflicts around him through love but finds that the price of passion is violence. "If you want the rush of spontaneous physical tenderness and emotional fulfilment," Bolt explained in an interview, "with it, as a necessary concomitant, goes the rush of aggression and physical destruction." *Vivat! Vivat! Regina*, which followed in 1970, is something of a historical pageant, a brilliantly contrived mosaic of short scenes built around the careers of Elizabeth I and Mary Stuart, "and finding them equal, mirror-images of each other. Mary fails as a queen to succeed as a woman, Elizabeth as a woman to triumph as a queen." A children's play, *The Thwarting of Baron Bolligrew*, was produced by the Royal Shakespeare Company in 1965.

Bolt's plays seldom have distinct "heroes" and "villains"—he says that he *is* all his characters and that what he is interested in is the complexity of human conflict. This complexity, he believes, must be reflected in the structure of the play—hence his deep concern with form. The construction of his plays has always been admired, as has the exemplary technique by which every speech, every incident, every image, is made to promote the action. This concern for craftsmanship and coherence, together with Bolt's generous compassion and fundamental optimism, have made him seem something of an anachronism in the age of the Absurd, and critics have tended to take him less seriously than the general public has. Thus Ronald Hayman, in his study of Bolt, is able to find encouragement in the fact that some of the later plays show a less perfect formal mastery than the early ones, whose absolute control, Hayman feels, tended to operate as an inhibiting factor.

Bolt remains a deeply moral writer but one who describes himself as passionately attached to moderation and the traditional values. His pleasures include talking, eating, walking, and sailing. He has three children by his first wife, the painter Celia Roberts, and a son by Sarah Miles, the actress, whom he married in 1967. Sarah Miles starred in the London production of *Vivat! Vivat Regina!*, and in the film *Lady Caroline Lamb*, which Bolt wrote and also directed. The author received a CBE in 1972.

PRINCIPAL WORKS: Flowering Cherry, 1958; A Man for All Seasons, 1960; Three Plays (Flowering Cherry, A Man for All Seasons, The Tiger and the Horse), 1964; Gentle Jack, 1965; Dr. Zhivago (screenplay), 1966; The Thwarting of Baron Bolligrew, 1966; Vivat! Vivat Regina!, 1971.

ABOUT: Contemporary Authors 17–18, 1963; Current Biography, 1963; Harte, B. and Riley, C. 200 Contemporary Authors, 1969; Hayman, R. Robert Bolt, 1969; Who's Who, 1971; Who's Who in the Theatre, 1967. *Periodicals*— Catholic World September 1962; Commonweal December 15, 1961; Contemporary Review October 1960; Educational Theatre March 1962; English Spring 1961; Hudson Review Spring 1961; Spring 1962; Modern Drama September 1967; New Statesman July 9, 1960; September 3, 1960; December 6, 1963; New Yorker October 31, 1959; December 2, 1961; Saturday Review December 16, 1961; September 15, 1962; December 29, 1962; Spectator July 8, 1960; September 16, 1960; December 6, 1963; Theatre Arts December 1959; February 1962; May 1963; Tulane Drama Review Winter 1962; World Theatre Summer 1964.

***BONHOEFFER, DIETRICH** (February 4, 1906–April 9, 1945), German theologian, was born in Breslau, the former capital of Silesia, Prussia, now part of East Germany. He was the son of Karl Bonhoeffer, a noted psychiatrist, and the former Paula von Hase. His great-grandfather was the theologian Karl August von Hase, and he was the nephew of a pastor. At sixteen, Bonhoeffer decided to study for the ministry and was accepted in 1924 at the University of Berlin. Three years later he received the licentiate of theology with his thesis *Sanctorum Communio* (1927, translated by R. G. Smith and others as *The Communion of Saints*), described by Karl Barth as "a theological miracle." Bonhoeffer studied Barth's dialectic theology as well as the modernism of his teachers, Adolf von Harnack and Reinhold Seeberg.

After graduating, Bonhoeffer studied in Barcelona and then at Union Theological Seminary in New York. One of his American friends, Paul Lehmann, recognized even then Bonhoeffer's "contagious humanity," and found him a perfectionist in his attitude toward anything he undertook. Indeed, Bonhoeffer excelled in sports as well as in the academic realm. Eberhard Bethge, Bonhoeffer's close friend and best biographer, recalls that Bonhoeffer was tall and heavily built and "always gave the impression that he was savoring good food." Elsewhere he has been described as "a man of enormous fortitude and intelligence, physically strong, proud but not vain, rather lonely, with a touch of innocence which almost at times merges into naïveté."

In 1931 Bonhoeffer returned to Germany as a lecturer at the University of Berlin, where he wrote his doctoral thesis *Akt und Sein* (1931, translated by B. Noble as *Act and Being*). This work, like his earlier thesis, stresses the importance of linking revelation theology with sociology. The Church,

* bôn′ hû fər

as part of the community, must reflect both the transcendental and social aspects of human life. *Act and Being* was written during Hitler's rise to power, to which Bonhoeffer was violently opposed from the beginning. He did not wait (like most of the prominent Christian opponents of Nazism) for the Church itself to come under attack; Hitler's anti-Semitism was enough for him.

In 1933 he went to England as pastor of the German Church in South London, where began his friendship with Bishop G. K. A. Bell, to whom Bonhoeffer became the chief representative of the "Other Germany"—the anti-Nazi Germany for whose recognition both Bell and Bonhoeffer campaigned throughout World War II. In 1935 Bonhoeffer returned to Germany as head of an underground seminary at Finkenwalde. There he wrote the most influential book he published in his lifetime, *Nachfolge* (1937, translated by R. H. Fuller as *The Cost of Discipleship*). Based on the struggle of the Confessing Church in Germany (which broke with the Nazi-dominated official church), this work stresses the distinction between "cheap" and "costly" grace. Real grace can only be obtained by suffering in this world after the example of Jesus Christ. While at Finkenwalde, Bonhoeffer also wrote *Gemeinsames Leben* (1938, translated by J. W. Doberstien as *Life Together*), describing community life at the seminary.

In danger because of his political views, Bonhoeffer went to New York in 1939. He soon felt, however, that his duty was in Germany, and returned to participate in the struggle. Bonhoeffer then decided that his pacifism could not be maintained against Hitler, and he joined the resistance movement. For him, true patriotism was to mean nothing less than treason. He took a post in German Intelligence, which was also the center of the Canaris resistance group, and under this cover was free to travel, communicate with foreigners, and pass on information in the plot against Hitler. At the same time, from 1940 to 1943, Bonhoeffer worked on his *Ethik* (1949, translated by N. H. Smith as *Ethics*), which he called his most important work. *Ethics* reflects Bonhoeffer's political involvement and his distress at the apathy of other German Christians. It insists that Christ and the world must not be considered opposites; that the Church must fight for the salvation of the world. To obtain grace, the Christian, like Christ, must involve himself in the alleviation of hunger, injustice, and all other worldly miseries. Bonhoeffer does not offer a systematic guide for ethical behavior. He holds that only some decisions involve an ethical choice, and that these must be judged by the particular circumstances. This is the theory of "situation ethics," later developed and popularized by others, notably by Joseph Fletcher. For Bonhoeffer, "the contemporary Christian must be a man who sees reality as

DIETRICH BONHOEFFER

it is and who acts responsibly, basing his action upon a clear vision of this reality."

Before he was able to complete *Ethics*, Bonhoeffer was arrested by the Gestapo and imprisoned at Tegel on April 5, 1943, for his part in the conspiracy to assassinate Hitler. In February 1945 he was removed to Buchenwald, then to Schönberg, and lastly to Flossenburg. Bonhoeffer spent his final weeks with fellow prisoners from various countries. One was Payne Best, an English officer, who writes of Bonhoeffer in *The Venlo Incident*: "He was one of the very few men that I have ever met to whom his God was real and close to him. . . . Sunday, the 8th April 1945, Pastor Bonhoeffer held a little service and spoke to us in a manner which reached the hearts of all." The following day Bonhoeffer was hanged. "Death," he had said, "is the last great festival on the road to freedom."

Bonhoeffer's prison writings were compiled by Bethge and published in 1951 as *Widerstand und Ergebung* (translated by R. H. Fuller as *Prisoner for God*). These "modern classics of the spirit" deal with a wide range of subjects, including thoughts on marriage, baptism, and friendship. His letters reveal his close relationship with his family and his engagement to Maria von Wedenmeyer-Weller. Most significant is his development of the theme of "religionless Christianity" in his letters to Bethge. To Bonhoeffer, religion is merely a garment cloaking true faith. Christianity has been made into a religion of salvation, and the hope of salvation hinders worldly life. Like Feuerbach, Bonhoeffer finds religion an escapist device, an appeal to weakness. A *deus ex machina* is superfluous in today's "world come of age." The Christian must say Yes to the twentieth century and learn to live in a godless world. The world must be responsible for its own problems and concern itself not with theology but the shape of human life. In his letter of January 23, 1944, Bonhoeffer wrote: "To renounce a full life and all its joys in order to escape pain is neither Christian nor human."

Ethics and *Prisoner for God* form "a watershed in contemporary theology." Bonhoeffer has greatly influenced the modern "death of God" school, as can be seen in John Robinson's *Honest to God* and the works of Paul van Buren. Priests and ministers working in city slums are following Bonhoeffer's example. Reinhold Niebuhr said, "The story of Bonhoeffer . . . belongs to the modern Acts of the Apostles."

PRINCIPAL WORKS IN ENGLISH TRANSLATION: The Cost of Discipleship, 1948; Letters and Papers from Prison, 1953 (U.S., Prisoner for God); Life Together, 1954; Ethics, 1955; Temptation, 1955; Creation and Fall, 1959 (*also published with* Temptation, 1965); Act and Being, 1962; The Communion of Saints: A Dogmatic Inquiry into the Sociology of the Church (England, Sanctorum Communio), 1963; No Rusty Swords (letters, lectures, and notes, 1928–1935), 1965; The Way to Freedom (letters, lectures, and notes, 1935–1939), 1966; Christ the Center (England, Christology), 1966.

ABOUT: Bethge, E. Dietrich Bonhoeffer, 1970; Bosanquet, M. The Life and Death of Dietrich Bonhoeffer, 1968; Godsey, J. D. Preface to Bonhoeffer, 1965; Godsey, J. D. Theology of Dietrich Bonhoeffer, 1960; Hamilton, K. Life in One's Stride: A Short Study in Dietrich Bonhoeffer, 1968; Harper, H. V. Profiles of Protestant Saints, 1968; Kuhns, W. In Pursuit of Dietrich Bonhoeffer, 1967; Leibholz-Bonhoeffer, S. The Bonhoeffers: Portrait of a Family, 1972; Marlé, R. Bonhoeffer: The Man and His Work, 1968; Marty, M. E. (ed.) The Place of Bonhoeffer, 1962; Mehta, V. P. The New Theologian, 1966; Pearman, D. G. and Marty, M. E. (eds.) Handbook of Christian Theologians, 1965; Phillips, J. A. D. Christ for Us in the Theology of Dietrich Bonhoeffer, 1967; Reist, B. A. The Promise of Bonhoeffer, 1970; Robertson, E. H. Dietrich Bonhoeffer, 1966; Smith, R. G. (ed.) World Come of Age, 1967; Two Studies in the Theology of Dietrich Bonhoeffer, 1967; Vorkink, P. (ed.) Bonhoeffer in a World Come of Age, 1968; Woelfel, J. W. Bonhoeffer's Theology, 1970; Zimmerman, W. D. and Smith, R. G. (eds.) I Knew Dietrich Bonhoeffer, 1966. *Periodicals*—Christian Century April 20, 1960; September 20, 1961; April 7, 1965; Commonweal September 17, 1965; Ecumenical Review July 1965; Life May 7, 1965; Nation April 19, 1965; Newsweek December 4, 1967; New Yorker November 27, 1965; Religious Life Autumn 1961; Saturday Review March 18, 1967; Time May 9, 1960; May 27, 1966; December 1, 1967; Times Literary Supplement November 20, 1953.

***BONNEFOY, YVES** (June 24, 1923–), French poet, critic, and scholar, was born in Tours. He was educated there and at Poitiers, and received his *licence* in philosophy from the University of Paris. Between 1945 and 1947 he traveled in Italy, Spain, Greece, England, and the United States, pursuing studies in the history of art. His first books were collections of essays, reflecting his friendships and early affinity with the Surrealists: *Traité du pianiste* (Treatise on the Pianist, 1946) and *Anti-Platon* (Anti-Plato, 1947).

* bun fwä′

A single poem sequence, *Du Mouvement et de l'immobilité de Douve* (*On the Motion and Immobility of Douve*), appearing in *Mercure de France* in 1953, established Bonnefoy as a major poet, and provided the title of his first volume of poems, published the same year. The starting point of all of Bonnefoy's mature work, critical and poetic, is summed up in the epigraph to *Douve*, Hegel's paradox: "Now the life of the spirit does not cringe in front of death nor keep itself pure from its ravages. It supports death and maintains itself in it." Douve represents this notion, that life exists only in the presence of death, and further that light needs dark to define it, that motion can be conceived only in relation to its opposite, that all such "polarizations exist only in function of each other." Douve appears in the poem half-real, half-mythical, as a woman and a symbol, as a forest or a river, as love or as the principle of poetry. She is sought and is present, she dies and is reborn. Through her, and through other such images elsewhere in his work, the poet pursues, as one critic says, "a dialogue between his mind and his spirit."

Douve, it has been said, had an impact in French literary circles comparable to that achieved by Valéry's *La Jeune Parque* in 1917. There is evidence in the poem of Bonnefoy's apprenticeship to the Surrealists, but it is traditional enough to employ recognizable (if unorthodox) metrical and stanza forms. By virtue of these qualities, and its gravity and eloquence, the poem according to Mario Maurin "effortlessly inserted itself in the body of French poetry and secured the backing of tradition without the least evidence of retrogression." Galway Kinnell's translation of *Douve* won the Cecil Hemley Award for 1967.

Bonnefoy's next collection of poems, *Hier régnant désert* (1958) received the Prix de l'Express and was hailed as the work of "a great metaphysical poet." *Pierre écrite* (of which the title sequence was published separately in 1959) followed in 1965 and includes a number of essays on poets and poetry which show how clearly Bonnefoy's verse is the application of his theory. One of these essays is an act of homage to his acknowledged master, Baudelaire. C. A. Hackett calls Bonnefoy "a *déchiffreur* [decoder] of the visible world and a *témoin* [witness], in the line of Baudelaire, Rimbaud, and Jouve. . . . His poetry, like theirs, is a poetry of search and exploration, conflict and anguish; but there is something new here. The struggle to achieve what Bonnefoy calls a '*sagesse de vivre*' has, to a great extent, replaced protestation and revolt." A writer in the *Times Literary Supplement* carries this further, suggesting that Bonnefoy, returning

YVES BONNEFOY

like Baudelaire to the original orphic myth of the death of the poet, has gone beyond his master: "For Bonnefoy now the 'act' of poetry is more than the act of dying, it is equally the act of being reborn."

There is growing recognition, in France and abroad, of Bonnefoy's right to be considered "one of the most significant French poets writing today," and he is equally well known as a critic and scholar. His most important essays on literature, art, and architecture have been collected in *L'Improbable* (winner of the Prix de la Nouvelle Vague in 1959) and *Un Rêve fait à Mantoue* (1967). These two volumes form, it has been said, "an ongoing *art poétique*" embodying "the myths that the rites of his poems enact." He has also written a much-praised study of Rimbaud and a sumptuously illustrated one of Miró. Bonnefoy is a most perceptive critic, in that recent French tradition which is more concerned to relive the artist's experience than to analyze its products.

He is in addition one of the most original of the younger French Shakespearian scholars, and his versions of *Henry IV, Part 1, Hamlet, Julius Caesar,* and *The Winter's Tale* have established him, in the opinion of some authorities, as "the best translator of Shakespeare France has yet produced." His interest in English culture is not limited to Shakespeare: he is drawn to the music of the Shakespearian period, the Metaphysical poets, and Yeats. In 1962–1964 Bonnefoy was a visiting professor at Brandeis University, Massachusetts, and in 1969–1970 he taught at the University Center at Vincennes. He was married in 1968 to Lucille Vine. In 1971 he received the Prix des Critiques for his work as a whole.

PRINCIPAL WORKS IN ENGLISH TRANSLATION: On the Motion and Immobility of Douve, translated by Galway Kinnell, 1967; Miró, 1967; Selected Poems, translated by Anthony Rudolf, 1969. *Poems in* Barnstone, W. (ed.) Modern European Poetry, 1966; Gavronsky, S. (ed.) Poems and Texts (includes an interview with Bonnefoy), 1969; Marks, E. (ed.) French Poetry From Baudelaire to the Present, 1962; Taylor, S. W. French Writing Today, 1968. *Poems or articles in* Atlantic Monthly June 1958; Critical Quarterly Autumn 1962; Hudson Review Winter 1960–1961; Poetry September 1952; July 1962 (complete issue); Times Literary Supplement March 3, 1966.

ABOUT: Boisdeffre, P. de. Dictionnaire de littérature contemporaine, 1900–1962, 1962; Hackett, C. A. An Anthology of Modern French Poetry, 1965; Kostelanetz, R. (ed.) On Contemporary Literature, 1964; Paris, J. Anthologie de la poésie nouvelle, 1956; Pingaud, B. Écrivains d'aujourd'hui, 1940–1960, 1960; Who's Who in France, 1971–1972. *Periodicals*—Critique May 1961; La Nouvelle Revue Française August 1958; Lettres Nouvelles November 1953; Mercure de France December 1953; Preuves No. 104; Times Literary Supplement May 27, 1965; September 28, 1967; February 13, 1969; Yale French Studies 21, 1958.

BOORSTIN, DANIEL J(OSEPH) (October 1, 1914–), American historian and critic, writes: "When I was only two my family moved from Atlanta, Georgia, to Tulsa, Oklahoma. In the 1920s in that self-styled 'Oil Capital of the World' optimism was the established religion. My father, an energetic lawyer, was full of civic spirit. My mother, who had been born in New York City (like my father, of recent Russian-Jewish immigrant parents) had not been to college, but was extremely ambitious for me, and was largely responsible for my going to Harvard in 1930.

"Harvard was an adventure, a travail, and in most ways a welcome shock. I had hardly heard of many of the people and movements—Pericles, Talleyrand, Beethoven, the Renaissance—familiar to boys from Andover and Exeter. I had never seen a copy of the *Nation*, the *New Republic*, or the *New Yorker*. I worked overtime, determined to get a start on a career (still undefined) by being near the top of the class. Majoring in English history and literature, I came under the spell of F. O. Matthiessen, who was a great teacher. Though he lacked clarity of thought or flamboyance of phrase, he had an overpowering talent to impress you with the dignity and importance of any subject, and with the possibilities in you. Stirring experiences were the months of competing and writing editorials for the undergraduate daily, the *Crimson*, and reading and rereading Gibbon's *Decline and Fall.* My first extended writing was my senior honors essay on Gibbon, which brought me my degree (1934) *summa cum laude* and the Bowdoin Prize, and which encouraged me to think I might go on writing.

"A Rhodes Scholarship sent me to Balliol College, Oxford, where I spent three years (1934–1937),

DANIEL J. BOORSTIN

romantic in retrospect, which at the time were lonely and disoriented. Unsure about returning to the U.S.A., I wanted to prepare myself for a profession in England. Urged on by Harold Laski, I read law, first the B.A. in jurisprudence and then the B.C.L., securing first class honors in both degrees. Meanwhile I 'ate dinners' and took the examinations to become a barrister, finally being called by the Inner Temple. I read superficially lots of miscellaneous philosophy and in the long vacations got to know Italy.

"After a dreary year as Sterling Fellow at Yale Law School (where I secured the J.S.D.) I was recalled by F. O. Matthiessen to Harvard where I taught American history and literature in the college and legal history in the law school. The great gain of these years was the discovery of my wife, Ruth Frankel, who was the sister of my research assistant, and whom I married in 1941. Ever since, she has been the principal inspiration and editor of all my writing. We have three sons.

"I practiced law briefly in the Government as attorney for the lend-lease administration during the war. At first amused, I soon became astonished and then dismayed at the buccaneering spirit of Government lawyers. After two years teaching European history at Swarthmore College, in 1944 I was invited to the University of Chicago, where I have remained—with an enviable freedom to do my writing, enriched by a constant flow of bright students, in a community of lively colleagues. A stimulus and a source of ideas have been my extended intervals abroad, usually on lecturing assignments: at the University of Rome (1950–1951), the University of Puerto Rico (1955), the University of Kyoto, Japan (1957), round-the-world (1959), the University of Paris (1961–1962), and Cambridge University, England (1964–1965). These travels have reminded me that the U.S.A.—like every other place—is quite odd.

"Lacking professional training as a historian, I have been both an amateur (pursuing the subject for the sheer love of it, or more precisely from obsession with it) and an outsider (staying out of some professional ruts simply from not having been instructed in how to stay in them). Gibbon remains my model. To be a writer means to risk oneself: not to be plagued by professional respectability, by the etiquette of 'soundness,' or by the compulsion to talk about what everybody has already talked about too much before. One should write only if he can't help it. I rewrite frequently, and take pleasure and pride in cutting. I write partly to dispose of a stage in my thinking, so I can move on to another; therefore I am not haunted by the specter of consistency, which is only another name for the ghost of one's past.

"The work to which I have devoted much of my writing time for the last twenty years is *The Americans*, eventually to be three volumes, a historical interpretation of American civilization along my own peculiar lines. In between I have written several small volumes on irresistible subjects. When I finish *The Americans* I hope to be obsessed by another big subject. I think writing is a vocation in the original sense of the word. A writer has to be called, and if he sees too many good practical reasons for writing a particular book, it probably had better not be written."

Daniel Boorstin differs from many of his colleagues not only in the breadth and variety of his learning and experience, but in his pragmatic approach to American social history; he believes that the uniqueness of the nation's social and political institutions derives not from abstract conceptions and ideas, but from the practical response of the American people to the realities of their environment.

After two books on legal subjects, Boorstin in 1948 published *The Lost World of Thomas Jefferson.* Here he examines the intellectual attitudes of Jefferson, Benjamin Franklin, Thomas Paine, and their contemporaries to show how European thought-patterns and preconceptions had been modified or eradicated by the unique circumstances obtaining in the New World. Similarly, *The Genius of American Politics*, a revision of Boorstin's 1952 Walgreen Lectures, argues that American democracy is a product of "the unprecedented opportunities of this continent" and of "a peculiar and unrepeatable combination of historical circumstances." One English reviewer of this work referred to its author as "the Burke of the Wabash," and J. W. Lukacs called Boorstin one of a "small but honorable group of principled, liberty-loving American thinkers who aim to restore American conservative cornerstones."

In 1958 appeared the first volume of Boorstin's *magnum opus*. *The Americans: The Colonial Experience* examines colonial life in Massachusetts, Georgia, Virginia, and Pennsylvania. It suggests that the first three of these colonial experiments succeeded because ideology was abandoned in favor of a pragmatic approach to environmental conditions, while the Quakers of Pennsylvania largely failed in the business of government because of a "preoccupation with the purity of their own souls and a rigidity in all their beliefs." Maurice Dolbier wrote that Boorstin "makes his points tellingly, with wit and logic and a wealth of illuminating quotations from the correspondence, the books and newspapers of the period." In *The Americans: The National Experience* Boorstin shows how his thesis may be applied to the period between the Revolutionary War and the Civil War and the story is brought up to date in *The Americans: The Democratic Experience*. The first volume received the Bancroft Prize and the second the Francis Parkman Prize.

Lawrence Grauman, Jr., writing in the *New Republic*, puts Boorstin at the head of the "lumpers" among American historians: "Boorstin has a gift for synthesis, a faculty for discovering the most provocative relations underlying seemingly disparate phenomena," and a willingness to draw on psychology, sociology, political science, economics, and literature to supplement historical data. The arguments of his critics are those generally leveled against synthesizers: "foreshortening of history," and a fondness for sweeping generalizations and for absolutes. Boorstin's massive bibliographies are one of his trademarks. He writes better than most historians, and his style has been praised for its fluency and momentum, its wit and gaiety.

Boorstin's other books include *America and the Image of Europe*, a volume of essays, and *The Image*, a much-discussed polemical work which argues that because of the power of the mass media, contemporary Americans live in a world of "pseudo-events," increasingly remote from the realities which shaped the nation. There was also a mixed and often heated reception for the essays collected in *The Decline of Radicalism*, one of which, "The New Barbarians," attacks the New Left, Black Power, and other movements of dissent with great vehemence. At Harvard in the 1930s, Boorstin himself had been a left-wing radical and, for a brief, "boringly instructive" period in 1938–1939, a member of the Communist party. Since then he has come to feel that while *disagreement* with society is healthy, *dissent* from generally accepted values is a threat to the nation's sense of community.

Boorstin left the University of Chicago in 1969 to become director of the Smithsonian's National Museum of History and Technology in Washington. From 1951 to 1955 he served as American history editor of the *Encyclopaedia Britannica*. He is editor of the Chicago History of American Civilization series and author of an excellent account for children of the first 150 years of American history, *The Landmark History of the American People*. Boorstin is a member of Phi Beta Kappa, the International House of Japan, and of a number of historical associations. In 1968 he received an honorary Litt.D. from Cambridge University. His recreations include tennis, walking and exploring in the woods.

PRINCIPAL WORKS: The Mysterious Science of the Law, 1941; The Lost World of Thomas Jefferson, 1948; The Genius of American Politics, 1953; The Americans: The Colonial Experience, 1958; America and the Image of Europe (essays), 1960; The Image: What Happened to the American Dream, 1962; The Americans: The National Experience, 1965; The Decline of Radicalism: Reflections on America Today, 1969; The Sociology of the Absurd, or, The Application of Professor X, 1970; The Americans: The Democratic Experience, 1973. *As editor*—Delaware Cases, 1792–1830, 1943; An American Primer, 1961; American Civilization, 1972. *For children*: The Landmark History of the American People: From Plymouth to Appomattox, 1968.

ABOUT: Current Biography, 1968; Noble, D. W. Historians Against History, 1965; Skotheim, R. A. American Intellectual Histories and Historians, 1966; Who's Who in America, 1970–1971. *Periodicals*—Book Week September 19, 1965; Journal of Social History August 1962; Journal of Modern History December 1960; Nation May 9, 1970; New Republic October 2, 1965; Newsweek February 26, 1962; New York Review of Books November 11, 1965; New York Times Book Review April 8, 1962; Saturday Review January 17, 1970; Time October 1, 1965; Times Literary Supplement April 20, 1962.

BOOTH, PHILIP (October 8, 1925–), American poet, writes: "I was born and brought up in the simple world of Hanover, New Hampshire, where I disliked school, built model airplanes, and managed at the locally late age of fifteen to go off the Dartmouth ski jump. I began to grow up only after frustrated pilot-training in 1944–1945, when I returned to Dartmouth to read rather than ski, to marry the Georgia girl I'd met in the Air Corps, and to find myself as more than a faculty son. Save for long Maine summers at my mother's family home, where I hung around wharf-talk, messed with boats, and sailed to explore some near first islands, my boyhood was sheltered and lonely.

"I fell out of Eden during the second summer of my early marriage, when my mother began those seven years of depressive breakdowns which were to end in her death in a mental hospital. During that time I gravitated toward teaching by way of an M.A. year at Columbia, and taught Freshman English at Bowdoin, only to discover there that I distrusted my teaching-talk, and wanted to write down what few words felt like my own. I wrote myself into, and out of, a bad first novel in a sum-

PHILIP BOOTH

mer's realization that my characters were less deeply interrelated than my words; moved to Norwich, Vermont, and there began poems, encouraged (by such former teachers as Mark Van Doren and Robert Frost) to explore my own bent. I wrote hard and read widely for three years (newly the father of two daughters), working variously as a college admissions officer, a carpenter's helper, a ski-book salesman, a tutor to foreign students, and finally, as the part-time teacher of a Dartmouth writing course. That job, and the luck of good publication, returned me to full-time teaching at Wellesley, where I fell publicly in love with the whole student body, was privately suspect in the Victorian mind of the matriarchy, and learned that the difficult art of teaching is subject neither to colleagues nor students. I have taught in the Creative Writing Program at Syracuse since 1961, glad of my part in this emerging university.

"If my father taught me respect for words, my mother's imagination intuitively made real to me the world that words reach for. But I might never have chanced the gap between language and image had it not been for the courage critically lent me in Norwich by Dilys and Alexander Laing, and by John Holmes when I moved my family to Lincoln, Massachusetts. We there brought home our third daughter, to an orchard once surveyed by Thoreau. My long verse letter to Thoreau became the title poem of my first book, which was awarded the 1956 Lamont Prize of the Academy of American Poets. Become known as 'a poet' by that publication, I began those public readings which, perhaps requisite to certain careers, still seem to me to have little to do with poetry; the only muse I ever slept with refused to be publicly bearded. I continue to believe that protective coloration best suits a poet who hunts to bring home to readers the marginal stake each has in this world of shared backyards.

"Whatever the imagery of my poems, my sense of language is rooted in metaphors native to Maine-talk, where each word counts. I have a strong sense of place (given the freedom of two Guggenheim Fellowships, I wrote my second book in Lincoln, and completed my third in Maine), but I mean my poems to be read on margins beyond my own. Between inland winters and littoral summers, I'd like to think that my poems now range to make metaphorical (as well as literal) sense of the tidal edges that most of us experience and all of us inhabit. My books are structured, and my poems revised, toward that end; but my life is unresolved; my poems aren't yet the poem I mean to write."

The long title piece in *Letter From a Distant Land* is an autobiographical monologue in blank verse which impressed Louis Simpson with its honesty, conviction, and colloquial ease. The poems in *The Islanders* set out, according to John Holmes, "to demonstrate that from youth to middle age the movement must be from Eden to acceptance of the world as it is." A similar development was recognized in *Weathers and Edges*: "from land to sea, from the artificial complexities of contemporary society to the self's confrontation with its elemental destiny."

Thus, if Booth's poems are, as they have been called, "more Maine than Maine," he is clearly in his intentions not simply a regional poet of the New England coast. James Dickey has found his "water-locked rugged world of love and uncertainty and responsibility a valuable one," and thinks it "very much to Mr. Booth's credit that he shows us that this world, in its symbolic implications, is as real as it is in its own brute and terrifying fact. That is, I take it, the task of his kind of poet." Booth's own statement suggests that he sees his task as rather larger—to explain as well as to make real.

Opinions differ about the quality of Booth's performance so far. John Ashbery, for example, considers him merely "the archetype of the conservative younger poet," deriving both his matter and his manner from Robert Frost. Ashbery and others have thought some of his poems lacking in immediacy and necessity, "written merely for the sake of writing some poem." Perhaps so; Booth himself says, "There are days when I'm short of courage when I selfishly write to hear my own voice."

Most critics are happy enough to find the qualities summarized by A. J. Gelpi in his review of *Weathers and Edges*: "These sad and elegiac poems are written with a terse, tight-lipped New England quality stripped of dramatics or histrionics. The images are clearly and sharply sketched; the lines are hard-packed with sound; the diction is effective in its directness, so that seemingly flat statements resonate. Granite-gray and granite-strong, the best of these poems have a resistant and resilient compactness which dares the sea's weathers as it mourns the sea's inescapability."

The poet is the son of Edmund Hendershot Booth, a professor at Dartmouth College, and the former Jeanette Challis Hooke. He was married to Margaret Tillman in 1946. Columbia gave him his M.A. in 1949 and Booth subsequently taught at Bowdoin College (1949–1950), then moved to Dartmouth (as college admissions officer in 1950–1951 and as English instructor in 1954), and to Wellesley College (1954–1961). In 1962 he was Phi Beta Kappa Poet at Columbia. Since 1961, as he says, he has taught at Syracuse University. He received the Bess Hokin prize for poetry in 1955, *Saturday Review's* poetry award in 1957, and a twelve-thousand-five-hundred-dollar grant in 1967 from the National Institute of Arts and Letters.

Philip Booth is a member of the Castine (Maine) Yacht Club and was its commodore in 1963.

PRINCIPAL WORKS: *Poetry*—Letter From a Distant Land, 1957; The Islanders, 1961; Weathers and Edges, 1966; North by East, 1967; Margins: A Sequence of New and Selected Poems, 1970.

ABOUT: Contemporary Authors 5–6, 1963; Martz, W. J. (ed.) The Distinctive Voice, 1966; Who's Who in America, 1970–1971. *Periodicals*—Christian Science Monitor September 1, 1966; Hudson Review Autumn 1957; New York Times Book Review December 24, 1961; Twentieth Century Literature January 1959.

***BORCHERT, WOLFGANG** (May 20, 1921–November 20, 1947), German prose writer, dramatist, and poet, was born in Hamburg, the son of Fritz Borchert, a teacher, and of his wife Herta, a writer. He left secondary school without completing his final year and in 1939 was apprenticed to a book dealer. An aesthetic and noncomformist youth, with some ability as a painter, he was regarded by authority as an eccentric outsider. In 1940 he had his first brush with the Gestapo on the strength of rumors of his "homosexual" attachment to the poet Rilke (who died in 1926). In 1939–1940 Borchert studied acting, leaving the bookshop at the end of 1940. The few months he spent in 1941 as an actor with a touring company were perhaps the happiest of his life.

The same year he was conscripted into the army and sent to the Russian front, where he contracted jaundice and diphtheria and was wounded. Accused of inflicting the wound himself, he was sent to Nuremberg under the threat of a death sentence,

* bôr′ kərt

WOLFGANG BORCHERT

but he was acquitted and returned to the Russian front. His deteriorating health brought his release from the army in 1943. Borchert was denounced for parodying a Goebbels speech, spent nine months in prison, and in September 1944 was sent back into action near Frankfurt, where he was captured by Allied troops.

Released, Borchert made his way home on foot, reaching Hamburg in May 1945. He founded a cabaret in the city and helped to launch a small theatre, but became too ill to continue his career. For most of his last two years he was bedridden, writing feverishly until his death, at twenty-six, in a hospital in Basel, Switzerland. His was, Stephen Spender has suggested, "the life of a perfect victim of our times."

Borchert began to write at fifteen—lyric poems, of which some of the later ones were collected in *Laterne, Nacht und Sterne* (Lantern, Night and Star, 1946). They were for the most part apprentice pieces in the manner of Rilke and the Expressionists. After January 1946, Borchert abandoned verse, and concentrated on the short stories which some critics consider his best work and which were collected in *Die Hundeblume* (The Dandelion) and *An diesem Dienstag* (On That Tuesday) both published in 1947. Mostly dealing with the war and its immediate aftermath, they combined an extraordinary poetic talent for evoking concretely the appearance, feel, and smell of *things*, with an extreme detachment toward his human characters and their concerns. The first quality is seen most purely in prose poems Borchert wrote about his native and beloved city Hamburg, and about its river, the Elbe.

The stunned nihilism of Borchert's stories is

heard in shriller tones in the radio play *Draussen vor der Tür* (Outside the Door) first broadcast in February 1947. Beckmann, a half-dead human scarecrow home from the Eastern front, attempts to drown himself in the Elbe, but is persuaded by his hopeful *alter ego* that there is still a place for him in postwar Germany. Obediently wandering the ruins of Hamburg, Beckmann finds nothing and no one worth living for—even God is senile and helpless. Stylistically a mixture of expressionist allegory and savage caricature, the play is in the tradition of the *Heimkehrer* (homecoming) plays written after World War I. It echoed the self-pitying disillusionment which was the prevailing mood of postwar Germany and was an immediate and sensational success. A stage version had its premiere the day after Borchert's death, and the work was subsequently widely performed and also filmed. In a report on sales between 1950 and 1965 the Hamburg publisher Rowolt noted that a paperback version of the play was the most successful item on his list, selling during that period over half a million copies.

Borchert's work has received belated recognition abroad. His collected works (*Das Gesamtwerk*, 1949) were much translated—into English by David Porter as *The Man Outside* (1952). In his introduction, Stephen Spender wrote: "What Borchert does do most memorably, is create the doomed, horrible reality of the victims who are just nothing but victims . . . whose widest sense of humanity is a feeling that on the other side of the barbed wire fence which surrounds them, there are other victims." Borchert called himself a nihilist, but one whose "No is a protest," who believed that "into nothingness we must again build a Yes."

Borchert's influence on the younger generation of German writers seems to have been short-lived. Perhaps he will be remembered longest not for the strident bitterness of *Draussen vor der Tür*, but as the poet of Hamburg, the city in which, too briefly, he found "the smell of life."

PRINCIPAL WORKS IN ENGLISH TRANSLATION: The Man Outside, 1952; Selected Short Stories, 1964.

ABOUT: Garten, H. F. Modern German Drama, 1964; Hamburger, M. From Prophecy to Exorcism, 1965; Popper, H. Wolfgang Borchert *in* Natan, A. (ed.) German Men of Letters vol. III, 1964; Rühmkorf, P. Wolfgang Borchert, 1961; Spender, S. *Introduction to* The Man Outside, 1952; Urban, C. Wolfgang Borchert: Ein bibliographischer Versuch, 1958; Waidson, H. M. The Modern German Novel, 1959. *Periodicals*—Books Abroad Winter 1951; German Quarterly May 1960; Modern Language Quarterly June 1956.

***BORGES, JORGE LUIS** (August 24, 1899–), Argentinian short story writer, poet, and man of letters, is considered by many critics the greatest living writer in Spanish. He was born in Buenos Aires, the son of Jorge Borges and Leonor Acevedo de Borges, and comes from a long line of Argentinian soldiers and patriots. His lifelong Anglophilia is easily traced to his half-English father, a lawyer and talented amateur of the arts—linguist, psychology teacher, translator, and author of a forgotten novel, *The Caudillo*. His father enchanted the young Borges and his younger sister Norah, now a well-known painter, with incantatory recitations of Keats and Swinburne.

*bôr′ hās

Borges, a timid, brilliant child, was educated at home, or more exactly educated himself in his father's library, until he was nine. By then he had read Dickens, Kipling, Mark Twain, Poe, and H. G. Wells, the Arabian Nights and some Greek mythology, as well as Cervantes, *El Cid*, and much Argentinian gaucho literature. Soon he was to add to his literary pantheon Dr. Johnson, Henry James, De Quincey, Chesterton, and Robert Louis Stevenson, the last two being special addictions. He began to write stories at six or seven, and when he was nine made a Spanish translation of Oscar Wilde's "The Happy Prince" which was published and taken for the work of his father. The latter began to go blind when his son was a boy and, Borges says, "it was tacitly understood that I had to fulfill the literary destiny that circumstances had denied [him]. . . . I was expected to be a writer."

His early school days were miserable. Bespectacled, and dressed in an Eton collar, he was jeered at and bullied. World War I broke out while the family were on a tour of Europe. They took refuge in Switzerland for the duration of the war. Borges completed his secondary education at the Collège de Genève, acquiring French and Latin and receiving his baccalaureate in 1918. He also taught himself German, making his first acquaintance of Schopenhauer. From 1919 to 1921 Borges traveled in Spain, becoming associated with Rafael Cansinos-Asséns and the *ultraístas*, who, influenced by the French symbolists, advocated free verse and sought to reduce the lyric to its "first element," the metaphor. On his return to Buenos Aires, Borges took a leading part in importing ultraist ideas into Latin America through a succession of short-lived magazines—*Prisma*, *Proa*, and the renowned *Martín Fierro*. In Buenos Aires these ideas become integrated with the nationalistic literary currents of the time, the effort to throw off the cultural dominance of Europe and to express the individual character of Argentina through a concentration on local themes and local speech forms. Among his friends and colleagues at this time were Norah Lange, Ricardo Güiraldes, Eduardo Mallea, Alfonso Reyes, and two brilliant eccentrics, Macedonio Fernández and Alejandro Xul-Solar.

At the same time, Borges' own first books began to appear: two volumes of poetry, *Fervor de Buenos Aires* (1923) and *Luna de enfrente* (Moon Across the

Street, 1925), and two volumes of essays, *Inquisiciones* (Inquiries, 1925) and *El tamaño de mi esperanza* (The Size of My Hope, 1926). This early verse, often dealing romantically with the old quarters of Buenos Aires or the pampas of the gauchos, is intensely rhetorical and mannered. It shows a preoccupation with history, time, and death, and also at times an inflamed patriotism and indigenism that Borges later ruefully described as "exercises in apocryphal local color."

In 1928 he published his essay *El idioma de los Argentinos*, calling for the liberation of language from academicism. Another volume of poetry, *Cuaderno San Martín*, followed in 1929, and then a book on the Buenos Aires poet Evaristo Carriego. In 1931 Victoria Ocampo founded *Sur* (South), the most important "little magazine" in Latin America, and Borges became a frequent contributor as short story writer, film and book reviewer, and translator (of, among others, E. E. Cummings, Hart Crane, John Peale Bishop, Wallace Stevens, and Delmore Schwartz). A volume of his essays and film reviews was published in 1932 as *Discusión*. Borges wrote in 1970 that "this productivity now amazes me as much as the fact that I feel only the remotest kinship with the work of these years."

Historia universal de la infamia, containing pseudo-portraits of a bizarre gallery of slave traders, gangsters, impersonators, and forgers (originally contributed to the yellow-press daily *Crítica*), appeared in 1935 as a foretaste of Borges' interest in narrative technique and his fascination with some aspects of evil. *Historia de le eternidad* (1936), a volume of essays, explores the varying concepts of eternity which man has fabricated over the centuries.

Up to this point, Borges had contributed to his support only the proceeds of various minor editorial tasks, but in 1937, shortly before his father's death, it became necessary for him to earn his living. He found a modest post as cataloger in a branch of the municipal library in Buenos Aires. It was at this time—a deeply unhappy one for him—while convalescing from an accident, that he began to write the speculative tales for which he is best known, publishing the first collection of them in 1941 as *El jardín de senderos que se bifurcan* (The Garden of Forking Paths). *Ficciones*, now considered his most important single volume, brought him the grand prize of the Argentine Writers' Association in 1946.

During World War II Borges had antagonized many of his countrymen with his anti-Nazi views, and he and his family were equally frank in their opposition to the Perón dictatorship that began in 1946. In that year he was dismissed from his library post (and contemptuously offered "promotion" to the position of poultry inspector in the municipal market). Thanks to a friend, he secured a teaching post. Later, overcoming his acute shyness, he be-

JORGE LUIS BORGES

came a popular and successful lecturer, speaking on a great range of literary subjects to adult and student audiences. In 1950 the Argentine Writers Society, defying the Perón regime, made Borges its president. His mother and sister were arrested and he himself was shadowed by a detective (whom he eventually befriended). Of the books he published during these difficult years the most important is *El Aleph* (1949), a third volume of his totally unique stories.

It is on Borges' twenty or thirty brief "fictions" that his enormous reputation depends, and they are finally indescribable. It should be said first of all that Borges' passions are wholly of the mind—books are the only protagonists and dynamic elements in his spiritual life. What he said of Valéry may be said of him: "He always prefers the lucid pleasures of thought and the secret adventures of order." He delights in verbal trickery, elaborate conceits, sly and bewildering allusions, puzzles, mirrors, labyrinths, the convoluted algebra of the mind. The real world of feeling, greed, rebellion, evil—this interests him, perhaps frightens him—but it is not here that he looks for order.

Instead he creates a solipsistic world, something like our own, and perfectly logical and realistic in its own terms, whose values derive from the "magic realism" of his literary style. "Typically," says Ronald Christ, his tales "tell of makers, authors, or wizards who invent artificial creatures only to discover the sadness of a being who is unreal, yet unaware of the fact; typically they conclude with the humiliating revelation that the maker is himself the creation of still another imagination." Marianne Kesting writes that "for Borges, the world is a chaotic labyrinth of mirror images, which gains a kind of order only through the recurrence of identities, through repetition."

An early example of Borges' literary "duplicity" is "Tlön, Uqbar, Orbis Tertius," where he blithely describes the imaginary world of a fictitious planet, known to us only through a spurious reprint of the *Britannica* which has been underwritten by a maniacal southern segregationist—an exercise in pseudo-reality which assumes the imaginative grandeur of reality itself. In "Pierre Menard, Author of the Quixote," the life of an imaginary writer is described by a devoted biographer, complete with highly diverting bibliographical entries. The writer, Pierre Menard, takes on the task of reinventing *Don Quixote*, word for word, by abandoning the present and immersing himself in the relics of Cervantes' world. "The Library of Babel" contains a literary cosmos: "Everything is there: the minute history of the future, the autobiographies of the archangels, the faithful catalogue of the Library, thousands and thousands of false catalogues, a demonstration of the fallacy of the true catalogue . . . the truthful account of your death, a version of each book in all languages, the interpolations of every book in all books."

Borges' fictions do not appeal to everyone. His friend and collaborator Adolfo Bioy Casares maintains that his work is "deprived of every human element, whether pathetic or sentimental," and is written for "intellectuals, lovers of philosophy and specialists in literature." Some of his compatriots complain that Borges shows no interest in political or moral concerns. That his stories nevertheless compel devoted admiration and an eager suspension of disbelief in so many readers is an achievement above all of style. "Borges' prose," says Keith Botsford, "is a prose of statements and definitions; it is not a prose of description or ambiguity. . . . It is so *sure* of itself, so unqualified in its declarations! Brief, clear, and dense, it seems almost legal in intent, so that its own laws, as the laws of the Borges world it describes, seem immutable, codified, and complete."

Critics have also drawn attention to a peculiarly evocative and allusive quality in Borges' style, the sense it gives that the author knows far more than he is saying. Borges himself has spoken of his stories as notes on unwritten books; Octavio Paz calls him a "writer who has discovered that all books are in fact the same book and that, 'abominable as mirrors,' they reiterate one and the same word. . . . Borges interrogates mirrors and watches the slow disappearance of their images. His work aspires to the refutation of time; yet it is perhaps no more than a parable of how vain are the eternities that we men seek to create." "Through the years," Borges says, "a man peoples a space with images of provinces, kingdoms, mountains, bays, ships, islands, fishes, rooms, tools, stars, horses, and people. Shortly before his death he discovers that the patient labyrinth of lines traces the image of his own face."

In 1955, after the fall of Perón, Borges became director of the National Library of Argentina and was elected to the National Academy. A year later he was also appointed Professor of English and North American Literature at the University of Buenos Aires. His literary output diminished for a time thereafter, but he began once more to write poetry, in an increasingly classical mode. Botsford says that these later poems "are among the most skilled and immaculate in Spanish. Strict in their rules and sober in their imagery, gentle in tone, recollected in tranquillity, they are elegiac, formal, symmetrical: as one critic pointed out, they are in every sense of the word *conventional*. The true Borges is now elsewhere." Some of these poems are collected in *Elogio de la sombra* (In Praise of Darkness, 1969).

El hacedor (1960), a collection of his later prose and poetry, has been translated by Mildred Boyer and Harold Moreland as *Dreamtigers*, and *Antología personal* (1961), Borges' own selection of the stories, sketches, parables, poems, and essays he most wants to preserve, is available in English as *A Personal Anthology*. His complete works (*Obras Completas*, ten volumes, edited by José Edmundo Clemente) were published between 1953 and 1967. A new collection of "modest experiments in straightforward storytelling" was published in 1970 as *El informe de Brodie* (translated as *Doctor Brodie's Report*). Borges' collaborations with Bioy Casares range from satirical detective stories to film scenarios. Their *Chronicles of Bustos Domecq*, a volume of bombastic essays on an assortment of imaginary avant-garde artists, Borges claims to like better than any of his own writings. He is now at work on stories, essays, and films, and is collaborating with Norman Thomas di Giovanni in the translation of his work into English.

As a result of an inherited eye disease, Borges' sight has been failing ever since he was a child, and it deteriorated radically in the 1950s. He has nevertheless traveled widely in recent years. In 1961–1962 he was a visiting professor at the University of Texas, lecturing during this period on many American campuses, and in 1967–1968 he was Charles Eliot Norton Professor of Poetry at Harvard University. He lectured at the University of Oklahoma in 1969 and has also visited Britain, Scandinavia, and Israel. Borges has received a number of honorary degrees and literary awards, and in 1961 shared the ten-thousand-dollar Prix Formentor with Samuel Beckett.

Borges is now almost totally blind. He is a wisp of a man, with finely sculptured features, bushy eyebrows, erect and Olympian bearing. He radiates a calm and gentle fragility. John Updike has referred to his "voracious and vaguely idle learning," which ranges from Old English and Old Norse literature to contemporary metaphysics, from history to philosophy. When he lectures or recites he can call forth in sonorous English whole poems of Wordsworth, Coleridge, Browning, Keats—he is at his most imposing at these bardic moments. He married in 1966 but remains close to his mother, now in her nineties. She has been his lifelong companion and mentor, reading to him in all the European languages, transcribing his writings, and guiding him through all the trials of his failing sight. Borges has the impish disposition of the practical joker and can be pithy and acerbic in conversation. He has enrolled in the Conservative Party, out of "skepticism," and has defined politics as "one of the forms of tedium." Borges says that "life and death have been lacking in my life," and that "few things have happened to me . . . or rather, few things have happened to me more worth remembering than Schopenhauer's thought or the music of England's words."

In 1970, in a long and notable autobiographical article in the *New Yorker*, Borges wrote: "I suppose my best work is over. This gives me a certain quiet satisfaction and ease. And yet I do not feel I have written myself out. In a way, youthfulness seems closer to me today than when I was a young man. I no longer regard happiness as unattainable; once, long ago, I did. Now I know that it may occur at any moment but that it should never be sought after. As to failure or fame, they are quite irrelevant and I never bother about them. What I'm out for now is peace, the enjoyment of thinking and of friendship, and, though it may be too ambitious, a sense of loving and of being loved."

PRINCIPAL WORKS IN ENGLISH TRANSLATION: Labyrinths: Selected Stories and Other writings, 1962; Ficciones, 1962 (England, Fictions); Dreamtigers, 1964; Other Inquisitions (essays), 1965; A Personal Anthology, 1967; (with Margarita Guerrero) The Book of Imaginary Beings, 1969; The Aleph and Other Stories 1933–1969, 1970; Doctor Brodie's Report, 1972; Selected Poems, 1923–1967, 1972; Borges on Writing, 1973.

ABOUT: Anderson-Imbert, E. Spanish-American Literature, 1963; Barrenechea, A. M. Borges the Labyrinth Maker, 1965; Burgin, R. Conversations with Jorge Luis Borges, 1969; Christ, R. The Narrow Act: Borges's Art of Allusion, 1969; Contemporary Authors 21–22, 1969; Current Biography, 1970; Harss, L. and Dohmann, B. Into the Mainstream, 1966; Murillo, L. A. The Cyclical Night: Irony in James Joyce and Jorge Luis Borges, 1968; Stabb, M. S. Jorge Luis Borges, 1970; Wheelock, C. The Mythmaker, 1969. *Periodicals*—Antioch Review Fall-Winter 1970; Atlantic January 1967; Book World January 12, 1969; Kenyon Review Autumn 1964; Nation March 30, 1963; August 3, 1970; New York Review of Books November 19, 1964; November 20, 1969; October 19, 1972; New Yorker September 19, 1970; Paris Review Winter–Spring 1967; Publishers' Weekly May 17, 1971; Times Literary Supplement September 28, 1967; November 14, 1968; Tri Quarterly Fall 1972 (special Borges issue).

BORLAND, HAL (pen name of HAROLD GLEN BORLAND) (May 14, 1900–), American writer about country life, memoirist, journalist, and novelist, writes: "I was born in Sterling, Nebraska, son of a country editor, grandson of Midwest pioneers of Scotch-Irish, German, and English ancestry. My father had dreams of being a ranchman so in 1910 we moved to a high plains homestead in eastern Colorado. I grew up there in the last days of the big ranches. In 1915 my father gave up the ranch dream, bought a weekly newspaper in Flagler, Colorado, and there I learned the printer's trade. At the University of Colorado I cut my journalistic teeth as campus reporter for the Denver *Post*. After two years studying chemical engineering at Boulder I spent a year as coeditor of my father's paper, then came East and worked as a New York newspaperman while I took my degree at the Columbia School of Journalism. Before I was graduated I wrote my first book.

"For the next few years I barnstormed all over the U.S. as a linotype operator and a copyreader. Then, with money from the sale of short stories, I bought a Colorado weekly, ran it for a year, sold out and came East for good. Eleven years on the Curtis papers in Philadelphia, as news editor, daily book reviewer, editorial writer, were followed by seven years on the New York *Times* Sunday magazine. In 1943 I quit the *Times* to become a free-lance magazine writer. During my newspaper years I wrote six books and several dozen short stories.

"From 1943 to 1956 I wrote on assignment for various magazines. During the last ten of those years I also collaborated with my wife, Barbara Dodge Borland, on fiction for the major magazines here and abroad. We wrote about fifty short stories and eight short novels for them. During that time I wrote only one book.

"We turned from full-time magazine work to books in 1956. Since then I have written thirteen books, all but one of which are still in print and selling. I have also written occasional magazine articles, continued the series of weekly outdoor editorials I began in 1942 for the New York Sunday *Times* (about thirteen hundred of them to date), since 1957 have written a weekly column for the Pittsfield (Massachusetts) *Berkshire Eagle*, and since 1958 have written a series of countryman essays for *The Progressive*. I have collected selections of the *Times* editorials in two books, and I have adapted material from the editorials and the columns in two other books. The essays, columns, and editorials have been reprinted in I don't know how many textbooks and anthologies.

HAL BORLAND

"I have always been a prolific writer, but I am not a first-draft writer. My books are revised four or five times before I let them go, and my *Times* editorials are sometimes rewritten half a dozen times before they satisfy me. This means four or five hours at the typewriter almost every day of the year (I can't think the way I want to in longhand). I also spend a part of every day in the woods, the fields, or on the riverbank of our hundred-acre farm, hunting, fishing, studying the natural world around me. Since boyhood I have been interested in nature and the outdoors and over the years have become a self-trained naturalist and ecologist. This background seems to be a part of almost everything I write, as it is of me.

"Over the years I have written in many forms—documentary movies, radio scripts, plays, poetry, lyrics for songs, folklore, articles for *Collier's Encyclopedia*, book reviews, editorials, philosophical essays, as well as fiction. Early engineering training taught me to respect facts and logic. Newspaper years taught me to write straight sentences and build logical paragraphs, and fostered my work habits. A bent toward poetry gave me a sense of words and language that helped shape my style. Besides natural history, my particular interests include American history and folklore, archaeology and natural philosophy. I have taught writing courses, one year at Temple University, one summer at the University of Colorado.

"I served a brief hitch in the Navy in 1918, in the heart of the Rocky Mountains. In World War II, I was for a time a magazine correspondent with the Air Corps. I have traveled all over the U.S. on foot, on horseback, by car, bus, train and plane.

"Honors and awards include: B.Litt. (honorary) from the University of Colorado, 1944; the Westerners' Buffalo Award, 1957; the Secondary Education Board Award, 1957; the Housatonic Valley Regional Award, 1959; the Columbia Journalism Alumni Award, 1963.

"My manuscripts, work papers and related materials are on deposit in the Beinecke Rare Book and Manuscript Library at Yale University, in the Hal and Barbara Borland Collection."

Borland's father, Will A. Borland, was of pre-Revolutionary Scotch-Irish stock, one of a family of sixteen children that had arrived in Nebraska by covered wagon. Borland's mother, the former Sarah Clinaburg, was of German-English birth. The part of eastern Colorado where the boy grew up was "an island of isolation . . . an arid, treeless, short-grass upland with few live streams" where he saw "the tag-end of the big cattle ranch and sod-house days."

After his two years at the University of Colorado (1918–1920) he was (to fill out his own account a little) associate editor of his father's *Flagler News* in 1920–1921 before moving to New York City. There he attended Columbia (B.Litt., 1923) and wrote for the Brooklyn *Times*, King Features, and United Press. His barnstorming years followed, taking him to Utah, Nevada, California, Texas, and North Carolina. In 1925 he was a publicity writer for Ivy Lee, in 1925–1926 published his own *Stratton Press* in Colorado, and from 1926 to 1937 worked for Curtis Newspapers in Philadelphia. He joined the staff of the New York *Times* Sunday magazine in 1937, leaving to freelance in 1943.

Borland's first book, *Heaps of Gold* (1922), was a verse collection. A later volume of poems, *America Is Americans*, appeared during World War II and was called "a collection of swinging patriotic chants, exhortations, and narratives—all well geared to today's national mood." During the 1930s he wrote two or three entertaining westerns as "Ward West." The novels published under his own name have also dealt with western themes, but in more serious terms. *The Amulet* is an absorbing story of Plains life during the Civil War, with a rich "awareness of natural things" and "the texture . . . of homespun, both tough and comely." *The Seventh Winter*, which brings to life the early years of the cattle industry, centers on one man's struggle to save his herd in the face of a savage winter and his own fierce emotional conflicts. It was called "a mature, ably written and highly interesting picture of . . . pioneer life." Reviewers also enjoyed *When the Legends Die*, about the adventures and eventual self-realization of an Indian youth at the turn of the century.

The most admired of all of Borland's books was

High, Wide and Lonesome, his account of the frontier life he had known as a child in Colorado. Ralph Moody said that "it tells, without a word of self-pity, the story of hardship, courage, honesty and determination which have made America," and Gerald Carson called it "a narrative of rare charm and a living document in the history of the last days of the open range." It was this book that received the Buffalo Award of the Westerners and the education award. Borland's life story is continued in *Country Editor's Boy*, which was received with almost equal enthusiasm.

Most of Borland's other books have dealt with country life on and around his farm in northern Connecticut. *An American Year*, a collection of leisurely essays on the changing seasons, seemed to William du Bois "a book that yields truth, beauty, and sustenance," and a later, similar volume, *This Hill and This Valley*, struck William Hogan as "a quiet, dignified, honest appeal for reason, and often Thoreau-like contemplation of the earth about him that is expressed with a rare masculine poetry." *Sundial of the Seasons* collects some of Borland's New York *Times* editorials, and *Hill Country Harvest* reprints columns which first appeared in the *Berkshire Eagle*. The latter won the John Burroughs Medal as the year's best book in the field of natural history. David McCord in his review of it said that Borland, "more than escapist, less than farmer . . . is an insatiable cross-examiner of life."

Borland habitually rises at dawn and is often at work by six A.M. He had two sons by his first marriage and has a stepdaughter by his 1945 marriage to Barbara Ross Dodge.

PRINCIPAL WORKS: *Poems*—America Is Americans, 1942. *Fiction*—Rocky Mountain Tipi Tales, 1924; The Amulet, 1957; The Seventh Winter, 1959; When the Legends Die, 1963. *Nonfiction*: An American Year: Country Life and Landscapes Through the Seasons, 1946; How to Write and Sell Nonfiction, 1956; High, Wide and Lonesome, 1956; This Hill, This Valley, 1957; The Enduring Pattern, 1959; The Dog Who Came to Stay, 1961; Beyond Your Doorstep: A Handbook to the Country, 1962; Sundial of the Seasons: A Selection of Outdoor Editorials from the New York Times, 1964; Countryman: A Summary of Belief, 1965; Hill Country Harvest, 1967; Homeland: A Report From the Country, 1969; Country Editor's Boy (essays, articles, and autobiographical material), 1970.

ABOUT: Borland, H. High, Wide and Lonesome, 1956; Borland, H. Country Editor's Boy, 1970 (*also his collections of essays and articles*); Contemporary Authors 4, 1963; Who's Who in America, 1972–1973. *Periodicals*—Audubon Magazine May 1964; Newsweek April 6, 1964; Wilson Library Bulletin March 1960.

***BOSCO, HENRI (FERNAND JOSEPH MARIUS)** (November 16, 1888–), French novelist, writes (in French): "I was born in Avignon (Vaucluse), the old city of the popes, to Louis Bosco, lyrical artist, and Louise Faléna. Both were natives of Provence and spoke Provençal fluently. The Sign of the Scorpion was then in the Zodiac.

* bôs cō′

HENRI BOSCO

"I didn't leave Avignon until the age of eighteen. I lived exclusively in the country between the Durance and the Rhône.

"I studied in my native town, particularly at the *lycée*. These studies were beneficial. But at the same time I took a course in music at the Conservatoire. For I was destined for a musical career. Circumstances obliged me to choose another, teaching.

"In 1907 I enrolled in the Faculty of Arts at Grenoble and the French Institute in Florence. There I obtained the necessary diploma for the *Agrégation*. Then I worked as a teacher (Classics) in Secondary and Higher Education from 1912 to 1945, in other words for thirty-three years. But wanting to know countries other than my own, I held only two posts in France, Avignon, Bourg-en-Bresse. On the other hand I held many others outside France, in Algeria, in Serbia, in Italy, in Morocco. That is the outline of my career.

"Interrupted by World War I (1914–1918), I was mobilized in a regiment of Zouaves, the Fourth, and sent to the Middle East (the Dardanelles, Serbia). When World War II broke out (1940), I was teaching in Morocco (Rabat). I was mobilized on the spot in my profession, because of my age. I retired in Morocco, in 1945, but remained there a further ten years, until 1955.

"Then I left North Africa and settled in Nice where I now live.

"From my early childhood I had a desire to write. At the age of seven I composed a short adventure novel. Forty years later this became *L'Enfant et la rivière*. But at first I was attracted to poetry. A literary prize at thirteen guided me in that direction. I therefore wrote numerous poems which resulted in a vast trilogy: *Les Poèmes de l'espoir* (Poems of Hope). They showed the influence of Dante and the great French Romantics. But towards the age of thirty I realized the insufficiency of these monumental compositions. I gave them up. Out of spite and in reaction, I turned to the prose then in fashion and wrote three novels. They are influenced by the so-called avant-garde writers of the period: Max Jacob, Cocteau, Apollinaire, Giraudoux, etc. They were no more than artificial and acrobatic exercises in style. They quickly disappointed me. This was not my true nature, nor my vocation. I looked for and finally found what I should do to express myself most fully in writing *Le Sanglier*.

"From this novel dates a second and definitive manner of writing. My principal works are: *L'Âne Culotte*, *Le mas Théotime*, *Hyacinthe*, *Malicroix*. Altogether there are twenty novels which established my reputation.

"This has been confirmed by a number of literary prizes: Grand Prix National des Lettres Françaises, Prix Renaudot, Ambassadeurs.

"To the novels must be added some essays (*Des Sables à la mer*, *Sites et mirages*); some childhood memories (*Un Oubli moins profond*, *Le Jardin des Trinitaires*); some poems (*Le Roseau et la source*); the life of a saint (*Don Bosco*), etc.

"A large proportion of these works have been translated into English, German, Spanish, Italian, Dutch, Polish, Japanese, etc.

"To date, twenty-two university theses on my work have been undertaken in France and abroad.

"Every work of some importance is the expression of a nature, that of its creator. His forces give it life.

"I recognize three in my life: my blood, my native country, my experience of the world.

"My blood is Italian and Provençal, purely Mediterranean. Hence my love of the concrete, of forms, of life, of action, of craft and of lucid thought. But with this is the presentiment that everything, and even thought, is only a perceptible manifestation of an imperceptible reality. Hence the presence in everything of a mystery, its attraction, and the approach one can attempt through dreams. In these dreams reminiscences build up, of ancient myths and of the forgotten dead of the race. This is a real world which I attempt to explore in my fictional writing. This is the part that my blood plays in my work.

"The effect of my country is no less powerful. The country is Provence and particularly the illustrious city of Avignon; a river, the Rhône; and a mountain. The town is a powerful link with the past, a past that is continued in one's own life. The river is knowledge, fear, obsession with water and the revelation of the universal flow of things. From this came *Malicroix*, a *récit* which is the struggle between man and the river.

"But another force has also worked upon me strongly, a mountain in Haute Provence, the Luberon. There I have experienced most powerfully the presence of an indefinable mystery at the heart of all created things. There are born the most hallucinatory dreams, turned into people, dramas, poetic fictions. There lie the spells essential to the communication of these dreams. Through them, every thought becomes magic, every enchantment can be worked in the most ordinary words.

"These attitudes of mind, which may be a little strange, are not only the products of race and of country. Life has also made its contribution.

"And first of all culture—entirely Mediterranean: Greek, Latin, French, Italian. I loved the great classical poets: Hesiod, Homer, Aeschylus, Virgil, and the Platonic philosophy. Later Dante and most of the French classic and romantic writers. And I didn't forget Mistral. All these writers were not just scholarly figures for me. I have known them as one knows the living. They were my intimates. While still a youngster I construed Theocritus with my teacher in open fields under the olive trees. Life already permeated my learning. My learning was life. It has remained so.

"Learning therefore mingled easily with my way of life, since for half a century I lived only in the countries of the ancient Mediterranean civilization: Italy, Greece, Egypt, North Africa, Provence. My natural inclinations and all I learned were strengthened by this.

"Thus the origins of my work can be explained, at least those which are definable. But the attention I have always paid to the mystery present in all things makes me believe that here as elsewhere what can be explained is not what is essential. There is also the secret of the King."

In his excellent study of Henri Bosco, R. T. Sussex writes that "Bosco's Provence is a land of brooding midsummer heat and storm, and his characters creatures of passion and violence." His stories have "a contained strength, pent up and menacing. Action is phenomenally slow, and dialogue only subsidiary: visible forms are subordinated to invisible by the dominion of the dark, which is peopled with presences that can only be sensed. . . . Over everything hangs the stillness that is the characteristic background of Bosco's work."

Bosco's novels made little impression until the publication in 1945 of *Le mas Théotime* (translated as *Farm in Provence*), winner of the Prix Renaudot. It tells the story of the farmer Pascal, the quiet rhythm of whose life is abruptly destroyed by the arrival of his married cousin Geneviève. He takes her into his house without a word, and as mutely falls in love with her. There follows a series of mysterious events—mysterious principally because none of the characters explain themselves to one another—culminating in murder. Geneviève finally leaves and Pascal gradually finds peace again in the healing cycle of plowing, sowing, and harvesting. The charged and precarious quiet of Bosco's Provençal landscape, with its undercurrent of menace, is evoked with a poet's skill, and the book brought him immediate fame in France. The English translation was more doubtfully received, some critics finding the story rather static and naïve.

In some of Bosco's novels, "the indefinable mystery at the heart of things" is manifested in fantasy. *L'Âne Culotte* (The Donkey Culotte, 1937) is about two children, Hyacinthe and Constantin, who follow Culotte to the mysterious realm of his master Cyprien. He possesses the power that Adam was given—mastery over the earth and its creatures—and loses it as Adam did. In the end Cyprien leaves his Eden to roam the earth with Hyacinthe. Germaine Brée, reviewing this powerful fable, wrote: "What is peculiar to Bosco is the secrecy that shrouds their ventures and the rapt wonder in which they live." *Le Jardin d'Hyacinthe* (Hyacinthe's Garden, 1946), a sequel in which Hyacinthe returns to the ordinary world, was found equally strange and haunting.

Bosco's novels are often about children. In *L'Enfant et la rivière* (1945, translated as *The Boy and the River*), Pascalet falls under the spell of the river and, following it, meets the gypsies and the boy Gatzo—fulfilling, as one critic said, "the lonely boy's dreams of a powerful friend, the sheltered child's dream of the wide world." The river also plays a central role, as Bosco says, in *Malicroix* (1948), winner of the Prix des Ambassadeurs, in which the fierce intransigence of the hero is gradually eroded and mellowed by the quieter and greater power of the Rhône beside which he lives. *Le Sanglier* (The Boar, 1932) is one of several novels dominated by the brooding presence of Mount Luberon.

Un Oubli moins profond, the volume of childhood reminiscences which Bosco published in 1961, achieves the same poetic evocation of people, scenes, and events that distinguishes his novels.

Bosco was married in 1930 to Marie-Madeleine Rhodes. He is an Officer of the Légion d'Honneur and holds a number of other decorations, including the Croix de Guerre and the Grand Prix de Littérature de l'Académie Française.

PRINCIPAL WORKS IN ENGLISH TRANSLATION: *Fiction*—Farm in Provence, 1947 (England, Farm Théotime); The Dark Bough, 1955; Monsieur Carre-Benoît in the Country, 1956; The Boy and the River, 1957; The Fox in the Island, 1958; Barboche, 1959. *Nonfiction*—Don Bosco, 1967.

ABOUT: Brée, G. and Guiton, M. An Age of Fiction, 1957; Peyre, H. French Novelists of Today, 1967; Primault, M. and others. Terres de l'enfance, 1961; Sussex, R. T. Henri Bosco, Poet-Novelist, 1966; Who's Who in France, 1971–1972. *Periodicals*—Books Abroad Winter 1965; France Illustration April 26, 1952; French Review January 1960; January 1965; Mercure de France May 1952; Modern Language Notes April 1958; Times Literary Supplement December 21, 1946.

***BOSMAN, HERMAN (CHARLES)** (February 5, 1905–October 14, 1951), South African short story writer and poet, was born at Kuils River, near Cape Town, but brought up on the Witwatersrand. His father was killed in a mining accident there while Herman Bosman was still a boy. With his younger brother, he was educated at Fairview Junior School and Jeppe Boys' High School, where he excelled at languages and made a name for himself as a contributor to the school magazine. He was a precocious writer—at sixteen, he was already publishing stories in a Sunday paper, under the pseudonym "Ben Eath"—and a voracious reader. While still in his teens, he was converted to atheism (a highly independent stand in his conventional Afrikaner society) by the writings of Robert G. Ingersoll. At the same time he fell under the spell of writers who were to be the most important literary influences on his creative life: the American short story writers of the nineteenth and early twentieth centuries, from Edgar Allan Poe (with whom he seems to have felt a special affinity) to O. Henry, and the French symbolist poets Baudelaire, Rimbaud, and Verlaine.

He studied at the University of the Witwatersrand, Johannesburg, and then at the Normal College. There he qualified as a teacher and became an enthusiastic demonstrator and slogan painter for various left-wing youth organizations which flourished in the aftermath of the 1922 miners' strike, when Prime Minister Smuts had ordered the bombing of white miners' homes. While still a student, he married Vera Sawyer. The marriage was doomed. Vera refused to leave her mother to accompany him to his first teaching post in the Groot Marico, in the bushveld of the North-Western Transvaal.

Bosman's single year in this derelict, famine-ridden district near the Bechuanaland border turned out, as his compatriot William Plomer has remarked, to be a most fortunate thing for him. In the reminiscences and lore of a small frontier community he found a rich source of material perfectly suited to his talents; he drew on it for the rest of his life.

After this happy interlude came disaster. Bosman

* bŏss' mən

HERMAN BOSMAN

returned on holiday to the Rand. His mother had remarried, to a Scots widower with children of his own. In the course of a domestic quarrel Bosman fired a hunting rifle and killed his stepbrother. He was condemned to death and then, at twenty-one, reprieved to serve four years' hard labor. While he was in prison he began to write his "Voorkamer" (front room) sketches, first published in the Johannesburg *Forum*, and the stories of *backveld* life narrated by an old Boer farmer and trekker "Oom" (Uncle) Schalk Lourens.

It is on these stories that Bosman's reputation rests most securely. This excerpt from "Makapan's Caves" is a good example of his manner: "We had a difficult task, that time [said Oom Schalk Lourens], teaching Sijefu's tribe of Mtosas to become civilised. But they did not show any appreciation. Even after we had set fire to their huts in a long row round the slopes of Abjaterskop, so that you could see the smoke almost as far as Nietverdient, the Mtosas remained just about as unenlightened as ever."

Through Bosman's laconic, ironical prose emerges, as one critic has said, "a singularly vivid, objective portrait of a remote Afrikaner community" and a frank but generally affectionate picture of its inhabitants—ignorant but shrewd, tough but prudent, generous but without illusions. Bosman's stories have earned comparisons with Maupassant and "Saki"; his pupil and editor, Lionel Abrahams, prefers to place him in the line of Mark Twain, Bret Harte, Ambrose Bierce, and O. Henry —those "whom Bosman considered to be the Elizabethans, the true Golden Age *poets* of American literature."

After his release from prison, Bosman joined with a group of other writers and journalists who bought a printing press and became their own publishers. He published a little verse and was involved in editing a series of literary journals—*The Touleier, The New Sjambok, The New L.S.D.*—which gained a certain notoriety for lurid sensationalism. His poetry was unremarkable—direct in diction and form, and very much in the romantic tradition, as befitted a rebel in a conformist society.

Bosman married again, this time a young pianist named Ella Manson. For her sake they spent nine years in Europe, trying without success to find a teacher and a career for her. Living in London, Paris, and Brussels on what little Bosman could earn as a writer and drama critic, they were often destitute. Towards the end of this period he met W. W. Jacobs in London and founded with him the Arden Godbold Press.

After World War II began in 1939, Bosman returned to South Africa, working as a journalist and advertising space salesman. In 1943 he went to Pietersburg, as editor of the local newspaper, and met and married his third wife, Helena Stegman, a teacher. The following eight years were the most fruitful of his life. In 1944 he became literary editor of the journal *South African Opinion*. He made an Afrikaans translation of *The Rubáiyát* of Omar Khayyám. In 1946 he published a novel, *Jacaranda in the Night*, a strange and difficult work which Lionel Abrahams thinks has not yet received the attention due its "extraordinary literary and visionary qualities." In 1947 came *Mafeking Road*, a collection of the Marico stories, now recognized as a minor masterpiece. It was followed in 1949 by *Cold Stone Jug*, a sardonic and often immensely funny account of Bosman's years in prison. At about this time Bosman and his wife moved to Cape Town. Two years later they bought a house in Johannesburg, where Bosman died of a stroke on the day after their housewarming party. He was forty-six.

Lionel Abrahams, who knew him well in his last years, writes of the enchantment of Bosman's unpredictable personality, and of his kindliness. Another friend, the writer William Plomer, has described him as someone "unsure of himself, at odds with society, unanchored and not always lucky," who was nevertheless one of South Africa's three greatest short story writers, with Pauline Smith and Nadine Gordimer. As Plomer says, "An imaginative man who has been sentenced to death and has survived to write so winningly of his fellow-beings (about whom his remaining illusions can be few), deserves much wider appreciation than he was able to enjoy in his lifetime." There are signs that this appreciation is coming at last. The first of his books to appear outside South Africa, a volume of stories called *Unto Dust*, was published in 1963. *The Best of Bosman*, another selection, edited like the first by Lionel Abrahams, followed in 1967.

PRINCIPAL WORKS: Jacaranda in the Night, 1947; Mafeking Road, 1947; Cold Stone Jug (autobiography), 1949; A Cask of Jerepigo, 1957; Unto Dust, 1963; Bosman at His Best, 1965. *As editor* (with C. Bredell)—Veld Trails and Pavements: South African Short Stories, 1949. *Poems in* Penguin Book of South African Verse, 1968.

ABOUT: Abrahams, L. *introduction to* Bosman's A Cask of Jerepigo, 1957; Grigson, G. (ed.) The Concise Encyclopedia of Modern World Literature, 1963; Plomer, W. *introduction to* Bosman's Unto Dust, 1963. *Periodicals*—Standpunte May–June 1958.

***BOULLE, PIERRE (FRANÇOIS MARIE LOUIS)** (February 20, 1912–), French novelist and short story writer, was born in Avignon, the son of Eugène Boulle, a lawyer, and Thérèse (Seguin) Boulle. He attended the local *lycée*, studied science at the Sorbonne, and received his *licence* in 1931. Boulle spent the following year training as an electrical engineer at the École Supérieure d'Électricité but followed his profession for only two years, in 1936 becoming a rubber planter in British Malaya. At the outbreak of war in 1939, he enlisted in the French army in Indochina. After the collapse of France he went to Singapore and joined the Free French, who trained him as an intelligence agent and saboteur. There followed several months of fruitless efforts to infiltrate Indochina, then held by Vichy forces. In 1942, after a hair-raising descent of the wild Nam-Na River on a flimsy bamboo raft, Boulle entered Indochina and was promptly captured. He escaped in 1944 and spent the rest of the war with Special Force, Calcutta. After the war he went back to Malaya, but with diminished enthusiasm for the rubber industry. It was then that Boulle began to write. In 1948 he decided abruptly that writing was to be his life, returned forthwith to Paris, and began his first novel.

Boulle has given a modest and often very funny account of his wartime adventures in *Aux Sources de la Rivière Kwai*, admirably translated, like most of his books, by Xan Fielding. It appeared in the United States as *My Own River Kwai*, and in England as *The Source of the River Kwai*, a title which refers of course to the best-selling novel which brought Boulle world fame. This was *Le Pont de la rivière Kwai* (1952, translated as *The Bridge Over the River Kwai*, 1954).

The novel is set in a Japanese prisoner-of-war camp in Siam, where the prisoners, forced to build a bridge of military value to their captors, are doing so with maximum delay and inefficiency. To the unbending British Colonel Nicholson however, it becomes a point of honor, and then an obsession, that his men shall erect a bridge beyond reproach. The climax comes just as the bridge is finished,

* bo͞ol

PIERRE BOULLE

when the Colonel confronts an equally honorable man determined to destroy it. The novel received the Prix Sainte-Beuve in France and was warmly praised abroad. An English reviewer called it a "fascinating taut narrative, rich in irony and accurate observation of the British character." The warmest praise was reserved for Boulle's portrait of Colonel Nicholson, who "overshadows everyone else in the book. Superbly set down with great sympathy and respect, he is the archetype of much that is admirable in military life." The book was made into an award-winning motion picture.

More than one reviewer was reminded of the stories of Rudyard Kipling, not only by the novel's setting but by its "brisk yet laconic style, the unforgettable character sketches, the technical details, the storytelling magic." It is a comparison which has frequently been made since, especially of course in connection with Boulle's Malayan novels. These have included *L'Épreuve des hommes blancs* (1955, translated as *The Test*), about a French girl who during the war becomes the child bride of a Malayan fisherman and is then thrust back into the rigors of the French educational system; *Voies du salut* (1957, translated as *The Other Side of the Coin*), a sort of reversed Cassandra story; and *Le Sacrilège malais* (1951, translated as *S.O.P.H.I.A.*), an attack on big business.

Boulle has also written several books concerned with espionage and some science fiction. An admirable example of the former is his first novel, *William Conrad* (1950, translated as *Not the Glory*), an ingenious and exciting spy story set in wartime England which is also a "penetrating, ironic, but deeply sympathetic study of the British national character." Of his speculative fictions, the best known (if only because it has inspired a series of successful films) is *La Planète des singes* (1961, translated as *Planet of the Apes*, 1963) a grim fable about a pair of space travelers who discover a planet where human beings are subservient to gorillas and chimpanzees. *La Face* (1953, translated as *The Face of a Hero*), one of the few novels Boulle has set in France, is also one of his most admired books. This work, which probes the motives of a public prosecutor who risks his reputation and career in pursuit of the death penalty for a man he secretly knows to be unjustly accused, was called "a dramatically tight story, effectively told with parable-like directness, a fine character study in the classic French tradition."

Boulle's novels are regularly praised for their clear and vigorous prose and for the author's skill in devising ingenious and often exciting plots and situations. Readable as they are, however, his books are never merely entertainments but are intended to illustrate Boulle's ironic yet fundamentally uncynical views on human behavior. His principal weakness is one to which the novelist of ideas is particularly liable—a tendency for his characters to become no more than mouthpieces for his opinions. Colonel Nicholson, William Conrad, and the prosecutor in *La Face*, however, show that he is capable of extremely acute and convincing characterization when he does not allow his argument to overwhelm his craftsmanship.

Pierre Boulle is a bachelor. He says that his favorite authors are Joseph Conrad and Edgar Allan Poe, his chief relaxation fencing.

PRINCIPAL WORKS IN ENGLISH TRANSLATION: *Fiction*—The Bridge Over the River Kwai (England, The Bridge on the River Kwai), 1954; Not the Glory (England, William Conrad), 1955; The Face of a Hero (England, Saving Face), 1956; The Test (England, White Man's Test), 1957; The Other Side of the Coin, 1958; S.O.P.H.I.A. (England, Sacrilege in Malaya), 1959; A Noble Profession, 1960 (England, For a Noble Cause); The Executioner, 1961 (England, The Chinese Executioner); Planet of the Apes, 1963 (England, Monkey Planet); The Garden on the Moon, 1965; Time out of Mind, and Other Stories, 1966; The Photographer (England, An Impartial Eye), 1968; Because It Is Absurd (stories), 1971; Ears of the Jungle, 1972. *Autobiography*—My Own River Kwai (England, The Source of the River Kwai), 1967.

ABOUT: Boisdeffre, P. de. Dictionnaire de littérature contemporaine, 1900–1962, 1962; Contemporary Authors 11–12, 1965; Who's Who in France, 1971–1972. *Periodicals*—France Illustration October 18, 1952; New Statesman January 5, 1962; New York Times Book Review November 9, 1960; Partisan Review Winter 1959; Saturday Review October 8, 1955; November 23, 1957; Time October 15, 1956; Wilson Library Bulletin December 1960.

***BOURJAILY, VANCE (NYE)** (September 17, 1922–), American novelist, was the third of the seven children of Monte Ferris Bourjaily, a Lebanese-born journalist who became manager of the United Features Syndicate and a newspaper editor and publisher. His mother came from a New England family and wrote popular romances under her maiden name, Barbara Webb. Bourjaily was born in Cleveland, Ohio, but the family split up while he was still a child and he grew up on the small dairy farm, at Winchester, Virginia, run with his help by his mother and stepfather. His vacations were spent at his father's house in the North, where he encountered such glamorous public figures as Heywood Broun, Deems Taylor, and Eleanor Roosevelt. Bourjaily remembers his youth as less discontented than "tentative."

In 1939 he graduated from Winchester's Hadley High School, and when World War II began he was at Bowdoin College. He joined the American Field Service in 1942 as a volunteer, and like Skinner Galt in his first novel served as an ambulance corpsman in Egypt, Libya, Syria, and Italy, before entering the U.S. Army (1944–1946). After the war he returned to Bowdoin, where he received his B.A. in 1947. *The End of My Life* was published the same year.

Bourjaily's novels form a kind of autobiography of his generation as it has been shaped, wounded, numbed, or destroyed by this century's cataclysms. The first of them, *The End of My Life*, traces the progress of Skinner Galt and his friends from college to that experience of war which was their brutal rite of passage. "We were war-born," Galt says at the end. "Listen, the war made us. Let the bad joke of the past die decently, along with the clowns who tried to make it funny." The book was received with no great enthusiasm by the reviewers, some of whom were shocked by so much youthful disillusionment, rough language, and sexual frankness. It sold poorly and was little noticed until John W. Aldridge devoted a chapter to it in *After the Lost Generation* (1951). He conceded its callowness but called it "in many ways the most promising" of the war novels of the 1940s. "No book since *This Side of Paradise*," he wrote, "has caught so well the flavor of youth in wartime, and no book since *A Farewell to Arms* has contained so complete a record of the loss of that youth in war."

After he left Bowdoin, meanwhile, Bourjaily had begun a career in journalism, working for the San Francisco *Chronicle*, among other papers. Aldridge's interest in his work led to a meeting in 1951, and the same year Aldridge and Bourjaily founded the periodical anthology *discovery*, which the latter edited throughout its brief, useful life. Six issues appeared between 1953 and 1955, containing

* bōr zhā′ lē

work by Bourjaily himself and by such contemporaries as Mailer, Styron, Bellow, and Malamud. In 1954, with the last two issues of the magazine more or less complete, Bourjaily turned to the theatre. That year his play *The Quick Years* was produced off-Broadway, and he became the first drama critic of the *Village Voice*, supporting his family by writing for television.

Bourjaily's second novel, *The Hound of Earth*, is a whimsical but sometimes moving story about a young physicist who discovers his unwitting contribution to the Hiroshima tragedy and tries—in the end unsuccessfully—to opt out of society. It was followed by *The Violated*, a much more ambitious novel, covering forty years and involving more than fifty characters. The book focuses on four members of the New York cocktail-party set, once rich in promise, whose crime is that they "have grown up into zombies instead of adults." Norman Mailer, for whom Bourjaily is one of "my crowd," called it "a good long honest novel filled with an easy sense of life and detail about pieces and parts of my generation, a difficult book to do." It fared less well with other reviewers, who in general thought it overly earnest and indigestible, though with flashes of brilliance and a saving vitality.

Confessions of a Spent Youth again divided the critics: some of them dismissed it as dull and salacious, but many welcomed it as fulfilling the promise of Bourjaily's first novel. It describes an odyssey from college to war rather like Skinner Galt's (or Bourjaily's), but from the viewpoint of a different hero, significantly named U. S. D. Quince. Quince speaks for those who left behind in the war "part of [their] ability to feel," but unlike Galt, who believes that he has come to the end of his life, Quince decides finally that he had "better open up some possibilities for [himself], find a direction, make a commitment." Those who liked the novel liked it very much, as an unwaveringly honest and original attempt to disentangle the truth, pursued in a vivid and flexible style with touches of De Quincey-like rhetoric; many think it Bourjaily's best book.

In 1967, after a long silence, he carried his history of the war-born generation into the 1960s, where it had encountered the terrible psychic shock of President Kennedy's assassination, an inescapable reminder of the power of unreason. *The Man Who Knew Kennedy* is about Dave Doremus, another of Bourjaily's fallen angels, a man of great ability and charm whose promise is never fulfilled and who takes his life in a pointless suicide. His fault, Bourjaily seems to imply, lies not in himself but in his stars (as Webster Schott suggests), in a society which is "[not] safe for good men." The book, a Literary Guild selection, is an acknowledgment perhaps that it has become hard or impossible to "find a direction, make a commitment." There is a more hopeful conclusion to *Brill Among the Ruins*, in which the boozy, nature-loving lawyer hero, Bob Brill, who opts out of American society in his fantasies about the past and more literally on an archaeological trip to Mexico, eventually goes home to see what can be salvaged in the morally and physically poisoned environment of Rosetta, Illinois.

VANCE BOURJAILY

Ernest Hemingway, shortly before his death, spoke of Bourjaily as "the most talented writer we have under fifty." His novels are carefully constructed, with close attention to such models as Hemingway himself, Fitzgerald, Sinclair Lewis, and Henry Miller. He is extremely gifted "in catching characters in action," and his dialogue is often perfectly rendered and brilliantly employed—sometimes against the speaker, so that "ironies are lightly established and implied judgments made." He writes now with increasingly poignant regret of the wasted promise of his generation, its "loss of the ability to feel," but never without humor and balance. All in all, it is difficult to understand why his work has received so little serious critical attention. It may be, as some critics have half implied, that Bourjaily is above all a reporter, accurate, tough, nostalgic, and often brilliant, but without the transforming vision that would make his chronicle of a generation into high art.

Bourjaily teaches at the University of Iowa's Writers' Workshop and lives with his family on a farm near Iowa City. He was married in 1946 to Bettina Yensen. They have had three children: a daughter, who died in childhood, and two sons. Bourjaily has lectured for the State Department in

Latin America and has paid several prolonged visits to Mexico. He enjoys archaeology, fishing, and hunting, and celebrated the latter in his first nonfiction book, *The Unnatural Enemy*.

PRINCIPAL WORKS: *Fiction*—The End of My Life, 1947; The Hound of Earth, 1955; The Violated, 1958; Confessions of a Spent Youth, 1960; The Man Who Knew Kennedy, 1967; Brill Among the Ruins, 1970. *Nonfiction*—The Unnatural Enemy, 1963; Country Matters (essays and articles), 1973.

ABOUT: Aldridge, J. W. After the Lost Generation, 1951; Contemporary Authors 2, 1963; Who's Who in America, 1970–1971. *Periodicals*—Commentary April 1961; Publishers' Weekly August 4, 1958; February 6, 1967; Saturday Evening Post February 15, 1964; Wilson Library Bulletin November 1960.

"BOURNE, GEORGE." *See* STURT, GEORGE

***BOUSOÑO, CARLOS** (May 9, 1923–), Spanish poet and critic, writes (in Spanish): "I was born in Boal, Asturias. As a consequence of my birth, my mother became so ill that she had to live apart from all her family in a sanatorium. I believe that the absence of my mother and her early death (I was ten years old at the time) were the events that had the greatest influence on me as a writer and as a man. From the age of ten until I was eighteen, my only brother and I lived in the home of one of our great-aunts, a woman whose disposition was disagreeable, harsh, and intolerant and who made my childhood and adolescence the opposite of what those ages are for most people. Furthermore, those years coincided with the Spanish Civil War and the first years of the postwar period, two events that have left a deep imprint on all the Spaniards of my generation. While still very young I made the close acquaintance of human pain, injustice, and death, and my eyes became accustomed to seeing life in all its streaked and changing coloration. Changing, indeed. The mutability of the world, its essential transitoriness and historicity, is perhaps the primary intuition to be found in the depths of all my poetry, and it throbs implicitly or explicitly in all my poetic works. But in a complex manner, for if to me the world is more or less a 'springtime of death' (the title of one of my books and of my complete works), it means also that I attribute a great value to life ('springtime'), even though that life may be anything but paradisiacal, and although as seen from the outside it may indeed add up to nothing—'the nothing that is' (death). My early experiences in a hostile family environment and an inimical social climate opened my eyes to the negative side of living, while at the same time it impelled me to love life itself, both dark and luminous, and the sole source of possibilities. As long as I am here and for whatever time I am here, the world exists; it has value. Hence to realize that the world is changeable is not to object to it. We must accept that historic condition for all that there is in Creation in the name of its present values, which are not diminished by our awareness of its future vacuity. By so doing, we can spare ourselves anguish without falling into the optimism of innocence. The keynote of all my poetry might be said to be optimism 'in spite of everything,' something I learned very quickly while I was still a child, when I saw death in all its horror and life going gallantly side by side with death, bubbling up like a fount of limpid water. During that terrible war, springtime came punctually every year.

"In 1945 I completed a course in philosophy and literature in Madrid and published my first book, *Subida al amor*. The following year, my second book appeared, *Primavera de la muerte*. In September of that same year I left Spain for Mexico where my father had been living for years. From Mexico I entered the United States as a professor. In 1948 I went back to Spain. I took a doctorate and joined the faculty of the University of Madrid where I gave some courses on poetry. Since then I have alternated teaching with the composition of works of poetry and literary theory and criticism. It may be said that the dual vocation of poet and theoretician has made me see with greater clarity what art and science have in common. Before anything else whatsoever, poetry is to me an exercise in conscious understanding, and it differs from science only in the object to which such understanding applies. Science knows the relationships among things, whereas art knows things themselves and our reaction to them, that is, to the particular thing as such. But without art, without poetry, the human experience of life, always private and unique, would perish with each man. Thanks to the novelist, the poet, the musician, or the painter, we are able to know something about ourselves and about others as concrete individuals. Hence aesthetic pleasure does not differ in any essential from that which science achieves. My two vocations have taught me this much, and their conjunction has shaped my calling as a poet. Today I conceive of a poem as a verbal object which helps us to investigate and to recognize and know the mystery that we are and the mystery that the world is to us. To me, then, poetry stands as an intelligent questioning charged with emotion; not at all as a dream or an unreality. Although the man who does not write may permit himself the luxury of being a sleepwalker, the poet cannot. The poet must be a lucid consciousness in this world without lucidity."

Bousoño is probably the most celebrated poet-critic of postwar Spain. Educated at the University of Madrid, where he obtained a Ph.D. and where

* bō sō′ nyō

he still lectures, he won respect as a poet while still a student. Soon after arriving in Madrid in 1942, he began to frequent the *cénacle* of Vicente Aleixandre, the most influential of the Republican poets who had survived the War and remained in Spain. Aleixandre's circle became a center of poetic fertility amid the dry formalism of the pro-Franco poets of the time; Bousoño found in him a master, and a source of warm and indeed hyperbolic encouragement. Bousoño in his turn was to produce what is generally regarded as the definitive study of Aleixandre's lyric poetry, in his *Poesía de Vicente Aleixandre* (1950).

Bousoño's poetic style, however, is very different from that of the older man. He writes in regular meter, while Aleixandre worked in free verse, and his poetry is "pure" and elegant where Aleixandre's is often dense and difficult. C. D. Ley suggests Gustavo Adolfo Bécquer and Espronceda as more direct influences on Bousoño's work—Bousoño has expressed admiration for both poets—adding, however, that Bousoño's use of allusive imagery, verbal ambiguities, and surrealist metaphor lead to the conclusion that while "Bousoño may not write free verse like Aleixandre's . . . they both admire energy and violence for its own sake."

Bousoño sees his own work in terms of paradox. He has said, "All my poetry, compounded of opposites that are not mutually exclusive, flows from these two poles—value and valuelessness, being and nothingness, springtime and death." His first volume, *Subida al amor* (Ascent to Love, 1945), concerns the poet's desperate struggle for religious faith, now frustrated, now successful. In his second, *Primavera de la muerte*, he descends into death-obsessed doubt and despair, a mood still unresolved in *Noche del sentido* (Night of Feeling, 1957). J. M. Cohen finds in this volume a fusion of the two dominant styles in contemporary Spanish poetry, the romantic and the religious baroque: "Bousoño has effectively brought the two styles together. His poetry both reasons and sings; it can be both wiry and tender, as in his metaphysical love poem "Tu y yo" (You and I): "You and I, two, beneath the light of day. . . . And here we two, looking at one another without seeing. Here we two, speaking without hearing one another. Groping towards one another without taking hold. And time, already impelling us towards an unending departure. We can never be ourselves, for we are always entering into death."

The *Times Literary Supplement* critic too found *Noche del sentido* a high point in Bousoño's poetic development, demonstrating both "loss of faith and a toughening metaphysical curiosity"—until then, he had "seemed strangely uncommitted to his poetry. It was a critic's exercise." But *Invasión de la realidad* (Invasion of Reality, 1962), claims, accord-

CARLOS BOUSOÑO

ing to the same critic, "an experience of reality that is not evident in his poems." Stock attitudes reappear, and "reality is obscured by a splendid imprecision." Spanish opinion, however, rates Bousoño's verse consistently high. A recent volume of poems, *Oda en la ceniza* (Ode in the Ash, 1967), in which Bousoño focuses on his fellow men and their anguish, was awarded the *Crítica* prize. Ana María Facundo described the book as "not an Ascent to Love but a descent into the darkest recesses of being . . . in search of an answer to so much mystery." And most critics can agree with J. M. Cohen that "of all contemporary Spanish poets he has the greatest variety of technical accomplishments, the widest store of digested reading among foreign authors. He cites Shelley, Keats and Leopardi as among his favorite poets."

Bousoño's major critical work is his *Teoría de la expresión poética* (Theory of Poetic Expression, 1952). The *Teoría* was awarded the Fastenrath Prize, and has gone through a number of editions. Its method resembles that of the German exponents of "the science of literature." Bousoño enunciates laws of poetry, and his demonstrations aim at the tone and elegance of scientific proof. He builds on Aleixandre's definition of poetry as communication, and patiently analyzes the means by which the poet conveys his meaning to the reader. He shows how many literary devices—telescoped imagery, for example—depend for their effect on the existence of a received literary tradition. He thinks that the force of modern poetry—the poetry of what he calls "the revolt against Reason"—depends to an important degree on substituting the unexpected phrase for the expected. Once, he says, it was only the humorists who juggled with expression in this way; now irony, paradox, and bathos are instruments of serious poetry. Yet, while he associates himself with this revolution, he foresees a time when it will have destroyed the shared inheritance on which the poets of the past have depended. Even those who find Bousoño's critical methods laborious, or challenge his general theories, find him a precise and perceptive analyst of other poets' work.

PRINCIPAL WORKS IN ENGLISH TRANSLATION: *Poems in* Cohen, J. M. (ed.) Penguin Book of Spanish Verse, 1968; Wohl Patterson, H. (ed.) Antología bilingüe, 1965.

ABOUT: Ley, C. D. Spanish Poetry Since 1939, 1962; Olivio Jiménez, J. Cinco poetas del tiempo, 1964; Penguin Companion to Literature 2, 1969. *Periodicals*—Encounter February 1959; Insula September 1969; Papeles de Son Armadans February 1962; Times Literary Supplement July 19, 1963.

BOWEN, JOHN (GRIFFITH) (November 5, 1924–), English novelist and dramatist, writes: "I was born in India, where my father was the Works' Manager of a tar plant. It was the custom then for English families in India to send their children 'home' to be reared, so that I was packed off at the age of six to the care of an uncle in Cumberland, and spent much of my childhood shuttling between uncles and aunts, my grandparents and two boarding schools. This is a sort of upbringing I share with Kipling and Saki, but whereas they hated the aunts in whose care they grew, most of mine were pleasant, and my grandmother spoiled me. It did mean, however, that during school holidays I was often a lonely child, more in the company of adults than of other children, and that at one time I was reading three books a day.

"I returned to India in 1940, wasted two years acquiring a useless degree of Calcutta University, and in working for a shipping firm, and joined the Army in 1943. I was commissioned, worked on the Lines of Communication and never saw an enemy, and was demobilised in 1947. I wanted to go to Oxford, but my Indian degree was no sort of qualification, and in any case the universities were crowded with applicants. Eventually Pembroke College, Oxford, which was in those days a little eccentric and refused to hold any kind of entrance examination, accepted me for the fall of 1948, so I spent a year teaching in a Primary School (children between seven and eleven years old) before I could continue my own education.

"I read Modern History, and wanted to be an actor. I had begun to write stories, but it seemed to me that this was something easy to do. I acted and directed plays for my college, and played small parts in University productions, and spent two of the long summer vacations acting for a small professional repertory company at a seaside resort in North Wales. Then I took my degree, and was told that, if I wished to return to undertake a piece of graduate research, I might expect a University Exhibition. I had discovered that I was neither a very good nor a very bad actor; I had no money: I gave up the idea of acting, accepted the Frere Exhibition in Indian Studies, and returned to Oxford to undertake a piece of research (still uncompleted) on the Educational Policy of the East India Company.

"A year at St. Antony's College, Oxford, then a year in the U.S.A. (1952–3), first at the Ohio State University, then three months hitch-hiking, then at the University of Indiana, where the Kenyon School of Letters gave me a scholarship. While at Oxford, I had been first Literary Editor, then Editor of the student magazine, *The Isis*, and had played about with some experimental writing. Now, while hitch-hiking, the beginning of my first novel came to me; scenes and dialogue began to form, and I had to stop where I could to write them down.

"I left the U.S.A. with the book unfinished, returned to Oxford, and found that I had not enough money to complete my research and the University Exhibition was not renewable after two years. I took the first job which offered, as the Assistant Editor of *The Sketch*, a fortnightly glossy magazine. The job was ill-paid but the duties were not arduous. I had spare time to finish my novel, *The Truth Will Not Help Us*. It was snapped up by the first publisher to whom I showed it, appeared, made no mark whatever, and was remaindered. But I had begun to be a novelist.

"I wrote other novels, left the ill-paid job for better pay at an advertising agency, became within eighteen months the Head of the Copy Department of another agency, then gave it up to live as a writer. I wrote criticism in what are called 'the serious Sundays' and the *Times Literary Supplement*, appeared on radio and television as a critic, wrote television plays and (in 1964) a play for the theatre, *I Love You, Mrs. Patterson*. In 1965 I went back to acting for a short while, with another repertory company, believing that, if one is to write for the theatre, one should have practical experience from the inside.

"I am unmarried. I live in London. My friends are actors, directors, a few writers: I believe that a writer should not know too many writers, but I acknowledge a debt to Angus Wilson who has helped and encouraged me ever since he read my second novel in manuscript. I do not regard myself as a novelist only. I believe that the image one makes as a writer—the 'imaginative object'—can be expressed in various forms, and I regard it as a challenge to be able, if I can, to use a number of forms. To write for the theatre is one of the most exasperating undertakings known to man, but I intend to continue with it, though I intend to continue as a novelist also."

In 1705 three English sailors were hanged in Scotland after a travesty of a trial, ostensibly for "piracy," actually because they were English. John Bowen had already recognized the literary possibilities of the incident when he went to the United States and encountered McCarthyism. *The Truth Will Not Help Us*, bringing out the parallels between the two situations, began Bowen's career as a novelist. It is not a very good book—less a novel than notes for one, as Bowen acknowledges—but it set the tone of his subsequent work, reflecting an ironical and orderly mind, classical rather than romantic, quick to see the contrasts between appearance and reality, the parallels between history or myth and the present.

After the Rain imagines a scientifically-induced Deluge and a handful of survivors on a raft, their lives efficiently ordered by an agnostic Noah. It is this superrationalist who introduces the forces of unreason when, inflamed by power, he shyly proclaims himself God, invents ritual, and assumes authority over life and death. *The Center of the Green*, which won the James Tait Black Memorial Prize, examined the loneliness and isolation of four members of a middle-class family in short, deftly linked scenes, each "completely realized and visually memorable." In *A World Elsewhere*, the attempts of a discredited political party to woo back its untarnished "Grand Old Man" are related to the Greek myth of Philoctetes, wounded like the old man, and like him necessary. Discussing this novel in the *Times Literary Supplement*, a reviewer wrote: "Mr. Bowen has a command of prose, an ear for simple fluency and conciseness, which put him at once above the ordinary run of novelists. And he is very good at making his characters real . . . but Mr. Bowen . . . appears to have a Jonah whom he would do well to throw overboard: a Jonah of parallel narratives." This tendency to "structural overloading" in his novels has troubled a number of Bowen's critics, but by no means all of them. "Few modern fabulists," says Paul West, "have tied allegory so cleverly to reportage. . . . Bowen seems to have it all in his hand: a passion for symbol, a tenacious regard for the everyday world, and a scalpel wit."

John Bowen has emerged since 1960 as one of the most accomplished of Britain's television playwrights—one of the few whose work for that medium (a serious one in England) has appeared in book form. His first stage play made no great stir, but his dramatization of *After the Rain* was a major critical success. Ronald Bryden wrote: "The conception grips with brilliant theatricality, and the

JOHN BOWEN

writing's always witty, chilling and finely intelligent."

Little Boxes, two one-act plays about people living isolated lives in city apartments, confirmed Harold Hobson in his belief "that a major talent, disturbing, brooding and despite its humour, essentially tragic, has come into the British theatre." *The Disorderly Women*, produced in 1970, is a powerful transplantation to the present day of *The Bacchae*, giving a contemporary significance to Euripides' warning of the dangers of ignoring the forces of unreason. Bowen's other plays include a musical version of *The Corsican Brothers*, and *The Fall and the Redemption of Man*, adapted from medieval mystery plays. He is also the author of a number of books for children, including the Garry Halliday series, written in collaboration with Jeremy Bullmore under the joint pseudonym of Justin Blake.

James Gindin sees in Bowen's work a stoic code similar to Hemingway's, a belief that "in a world where he has no control over the central issues of life, death, and truth, man must try to live with as much exterior grace and dignity as he can muster." For Bowen, the novel is "an image of an attitude to life" but he believes that the writer must always remember that he is "telling a story to other people and must use every device of toy and game to keep them listening."

PRINCIPAL WORKS: The Truth Will Not Help Us (novel), 1956; Pegasus (for children), 1957; After the Rain (novel), 1958; The Mermaid and the Boy (for children), 1958; The Center of the Green (novel), 1959; Storyboard (novel), 1960; The Birdcage (novel), 1962; The Essay Prize, with A Holiday Abroad and The Candidate (television plays), 1962; I Love You, Mrs. Patterson (play), 1964; A World Elsewhere (novel), 1965; After the Rain

(play), 1967; Little Boxes, 1968; The Fall and the Redemption of Man (play), 1968; The Disorderly Women, 1969; The Corsican Brothers (with music), 1971; The Waiting Room, 1971.
ABOUT: British Broadcasting Corporation. Writers on Themselves, 1964; Contemporary Authors 4, 1963; Gindin, J. Postwar British Fiction, 1962; Vinson, J. (ed.) Contemporary Novelists, 1972; West, P. The Modern Novel, 1965; Who's Who, 1972. *Periodicals*—Books and Bookmen October 1965; Guardian August 6, 1971.

BOWERS, EDGAR (March 2, 1924–), American poet, was born in Rome, Georgia, the son of William Edgar Bowers, an agronomist, and the former Grace Anderson. Bowers served in the Army from 1943 to 1946, for the last part of the time as a technical sergeant with counterintelligence in occupied Germany. He subsequently attended the University of North Carolina, receiving his B.A. in 1947. Stanford University gave him his M.A. in English in 1949 and his doctorate in 1953.

Bowers has been an English teacher since 1952: at Duke University (1952 to 1955); at Harpur College (1955 to 1958); and thereafter as associate professor of English at the University of California at Santa Barbara. He is fluent in German, Latin, and especially French, and has a detailed and profound knowledge of French and English poetry and critical theory.

The Form of Loss, Bowers' first book, was published in 1956. David Ignatow wrote that these poems, "treating of war, death and religion, address themselves to common experience with an earnest elegiac appeal." Ignatow admired Bowers' craftsmanship, his "fine sobriety of phrase and tone," and suggested that his "curable fault" was overcautiousness, a tendency towards "regularity, monotony and vagueness." William Meredith heard "echoes not only of the Elizabethans but of Allen Tate and Yvor Winters," and like Ignatow missed "the impetuousness of a new poetic conviction."

Yvor Winters himself had a quite different reaction. Noting that Bowers had been raised as a Presbyterian, and now showed a certain sympathy for Roman Catholic doctrine and civilization, he guessed that the poet was in fact no longer a Christian, but combined a Calvinistic tendency toward mysticism "with an inability, both temperamental and intellectual, to delude himself." Bowers, Winters wrote, was "involved intellectually and emotionally—and quite consciously—in the history of Western religion and philosophy, and . . . in the predicament of the post-Christian intellectual." It was this involvement, and a related concern with the decline of Western civilization, which provided Bowers' themes. His style reflected these preoccupations, and was "at once as modern and as rooted in history as his subject matter." Yvor Winters found some of Bowers' poems imperfect, a little clumsy and obscure, and thought that six or seven of the thirty-three in the book could probably be dispensed with. But the rest seemed to Winters "among the best American poems of this century, and nine or ten of them among the very great poems."

Bowers' admirers had to wait nine years for *The Astronomers*, his second book, which contained only fourteen lyrics and a ten-part autobiographical poem. These few poems were thought to have been worth waiting for nevertheless. Once again there was much praise for Bowers' craftsmanship, his ruthlessly pared and disciplined lyrics, rich in strong Anglo-Saxon monosyllables, sparing in their use of adjectives. This time there were no charges of overcautiousness. Carol Johnson spoke of Bowers' "apprenticeship to the impossible" and wrote: "This is not poverty of emotion but emotion more abundant than is readily borne by most, converted to enduring shape in words." Joseph Bennett said that some of Bowers' "compressed forms accomplish more in a single poem than many poets do in a lifetime," praising in particular the "power, grandeur and discipline" of "The Astronomers of Mont Blanc"; the "Valéry-esque densities of the freighted 'Adam's Song to Heaven,' his nudging among the blind roots of Christian belief in 'An Answer,' the stately explicitness of the first poem of 'Autumn Shade.' " William Jay Smith has called Edgar Bowers "one of the best poets to have emerged in the 1950s."

Bowers has received Fulbright, Guggenheim, and *Sewanee Review* fellowships, among other awards. His poems have appeared in such magazines as the *Paris Review*, the *New Statesman*, *Poetry*, and the *Sewanee Review*, as well as in the anthologies *The New Poets of England and America* (1957) and *Five American Poets* (1963). He is a member of the American Civil Liberties Union.

PRINCIPAL WORKS: The Form of Loss, 1956; The Astronomers, 1965.
ABOUT: Contemporary Authors 7–8, 1963; Winters, Y. Forms of Discovery, 1967. *Periodicals*—Commonweal September 24, 1965; Harper's Magazine August 1965; Saturday Review August 18, 1956; Sewanee Review Fall 1956.

BOWLES, JANE (SYDNEY) (February 22, 1917–May 4, 1973), American novelist, short story writer, and dramatist, wrote: "I started to 'write' when I was about fifteen and was obliged to do composition in school. I always thought it the most loathsome of all activities, and still do. At the same time I felt even then that I had to do it. Like most adolescents I read a great deal, and had very snobbish tastes. I thought Aldous Huxley wrote only pot-boilers. Since I always had had French governesses, and had spoken French before I spoke English, the books I read were in that language.

"The year I was fifteen I went to Switzerland to be cured of tuberculosis of the bone. It was then that I read all of Proust and Gide. They were my classics. I also read Louis-Ferdinand Céline. Later I met him on a ship going to New York and fell in love with him. In New York I had an unsuccessful operation on my knee, and remained with my leg in a heavy cast for eight months. I used to explore Greenwich Village on foot, wearing the cast. Since I was only sixteen, I was allowed to wander only during the day, and accompanied by my cousin Bobby, who was several years younger than I. At that time I was supposed to be taking dramatic lessons at Reginald Goode's. I was neither talented nor determined, and soon failed. For a while I went to a typing school, and started a novel which I hated, but which I made a point of finishing. It was in French, and was called *Le Phaéton Hypocrite*.

"Then I met John Latouche. Instead of a belt he wore a necktie to hold up his trousers. My mother was very nervous about me because I was not looking for a husband. She would try to frighten me with threats of being taken to live at the poor farm. My father had died when I was fourteen, and my mother had spent what money he had left. Like all mothers she hoped I would marry a man who would take care of me. By the time I was twenty she had become extremely nervous, because she wanted to get married herself.

"That winter Latouche and I used to go every Sunday afternoon to E. E. Cummings's in Patchin Place. One day Paul Bowles was there with a Dutch surrealist painter, Tonny, and his wife Marie-Claire. I had met Paul before, in Harlem. He wrote music and was mysterious and sinister. The first time I saw him I said to a friend: He's my enemy. He and the Tonnys were about to go to Mexico for several months. I got up and went into the other room and telephoned my mother. I told her I was going to Mexico with Paul Bowles. She asked me to put him on the wire, and they arranged it between them. It was not a successful trip for me, as I was very ill in Mexico City and had to fly back to Arizona and recuperate. Then I went back to my mother in New York.

"The next winter, on the day before my twenty-first birthday, Paul and I were married. We got on a Japanese ship and went to Costa Rica. Later we went to Eze-Village on the Grande Corniche above Monaco and rented a small house there. That was where I learned to cook. Back in New York I started to write *Two Serious Ladies*. The work was interrupted by our moving to New Mexico. Finally we settled in Mexico definitively, and I completed the novel there.

"It was only after the end of World War II that I came to Morocco. Paul had come ahead of me and bought a house in Tangier. From the first day, Morocco seemed more dreamlike than real. I felt cut off from what I knew. In the twenty years that I have lived here I have written only two short stories, and nothing else. It's good for Paul, but not for me."

JANE BOWLES

Jane Bowles was born in New York, the daughter of Sydney and Claire (Stajer) Auer. She was educated at Stoneleigh and, during her two years at Leysin in Switzerland, by tutors. It was in 1938 that she married the writer and composer Paul Bowles. For a time at the end of World War II she lived with him in a boarding house whose other tenants included Richard Wright and his wife, Oliver Smith, Gypsy Rose Lee, Carson McCullers, Benjamin Britten, W. H. Auden, and an animal trainer and his chimpanzee. After the war she traveled again—the Sahara, Paris, Ceylon—before settling in Tangier in 1952.

Her chief work, the novel *Two Serious Ladies*, was completed and published in 1943, and attracted an enviable "underground" reputation, augmented by its extreme rarity—in the end, not even the author had a copy. When it was reissued by the British publisher Peter Owen in 1964, it immediately achieved a *succès d'estime* on a wider scale and led to a belated rediscovery of the author. Owen published her short stories, *Plain Pleasures*, in 1966, and the same year Farrar, Straus in America brought out her *Collected Works*, containing the novel, seven stories, and a play, *In the Summer House*.

Two Serious Ladies is difficult to classify. John Ashbery has suggested that "if one can imagine George Ade and Kafka collaborating on a modern version of Bunyan's *Pilgrim's Progress* one will have a faint idea of its qualities." Perhaps the most useful comparison of all is with Ivy Compton-Burnett, whom Mrs. Bowles resembled in her plain but profoundly idiosyncratic style.

But, unlike Ivy Compton-Burnett, Jane Bowles rejected all of the kind of logic that is implied in *plot*; in this most of all she was (in 1943) an innovator. In her novel, Miss Goering, rich and domineering, advances confidently towards sainthood as hostess for or mistress to a succession of loafers and failures; Mrs. Copperfield, weak and sensuous, bullied by her husband, finds self-fulfillment with a native prostitute during a Panamanian vacation: "I have gone to pieces," she remarks to Miss Goering, "which is a thing I've wanted to do for years." And the book ends with the other woman's shocked response: " 'Certainly I am nearer to becoming a saint,' reflected Miss Goering, 'but is it possible that a part of me hidden from my sight is piling sin upon sin as fast as Mrs. Copperfield?' This latter possibility Miss Goering thought to be of considerable interest but of no great importance."

The activities of the two women are described in parallel; they actually meet only twice. But one pursues virtue and the other sin, and each in a sense achieves the opposite; it is their contrapuntal moral ballet that gives the book its shape. Conventional critics found it "difficult to see what *Two Serious Ladies* is about," and Geoffrey Wagner thought it "incredibly bad." The English novelist Alan Sillitoe on the other hand called it "a landmark in twentieth century American literature," and it is no doubt an early emergence of the nihilistic sensibility that produced the gothic humor of the 1960s. It is a beautifully controlled and realized exercise in style, a novelist's novel which however lacks the sustained imaginative vigor of a major work.

The danger for such a writer as Jane Bowles is that when the creative momentum falters, preciosity and mere whimsy may intervene. These failures are more readily avoided within the smaller scope of the novella or short story, and some of the short pieces in the *Collected Works* are very nearly perfect examples of the form. Like the novel, they are about the conflict between control and sensuality, centering most often upon a domineering woman with a misguided sense of mission who is in the end undone by the "terrible strength" of the weak. This is also the theme of Jane Bowles's two-act play, *In the Summer House*, which enjoyed a critical but not a popular success when the play was staged in New York in 1954 with Judith Anderson, Mildred Dunnock, and Jean Stapleton. A short puppet play, *A Quarreling Pair*, was published in *Mademoiselle* in December 1966.

John Ashbery has called Jane Bowles "one of the finest modern writers of fiction, in any language. . . . In all her work, it is impossible to deduce the end of a sentence from its beginning, or a paragraph from the one that preceded it, or how one of the characters will reply to another. And yet the whole flows marvelously and inexorably to its cruel end; it becomes itself as we watch it. No other contemporary writer can consistently produce surprise of this quality."

Jane Bowles, a frail and diminutive woman, fond of cooking and mimicry, died in 1973 after a long illness. Truman Capote in 1966, remembering her in 1946, says that "even then she had seemed the eternal urchin, appealing as the most appealing of non-adults, yet with some substance cooler than blood invading her veins, and with a wit, an eccentric wisdom, no child . . . ever possessed."

PRINCIPAL WORKS: Two Serious Ladies, 1943; In the Summer House (play), 1954; Plain Pleasures, 1966; The Collected Works of Jane Bowles, 1966.

ABOUT: Contemporary Authors 19–20, 1968. *Periodicals*—Book Week May 16, 1943; February 12, 1967; Commonweal February 3, 1967; Mademoiselle December 1966; New York Times May 31, 1973; New York Times Book Review May 9, 1943; January 29, 1967; February 12, 1967; New York Review of Books December 15, 1966; Saturday Review January 14, 1967; Times Literary Supplement February 4, 1965; June 30, 1966.

BRADFORD, ERNLE (DUSGATE SELBY) (January 11, 1922–), English historian and writer of books about the sea, writes: "I was born at Cole Green in Norfolk and call myself 'English'—which means that I am a mixture of Norman, Irish and North Country Anglo-Saxon ancestry. My father was a regular army officer turned journalist, and my mother's family have sat around the same area in Norfolk since the Norman conquest. Designed to go into the Guards and marry a county girl with a good seat on a horse, I naturally went into the Navy and married a painter. Educated at Uppingham, where I studied classics under A. R. Burn and philosophy under the headmaster John Wolfenden, I left in 1939 and went into the Navy as an ordinary seaman on my eighteenth birthday. After two years as a sailor I got a commission, and spent three and a half of the war years in the Mediterranean theatre. It was during this unlikely period that my love affair with the Mediterranean began; something that has now turned into a permanent marriage. I have spent most of the past fifteen years living in or sailing around that area of the world.

"I have never intended being anything else but a writer, except for a brief period after the war when I thought I was going to be a painter. Pictures still mean as much to me as books and it is probably this visual part of my nature which at one time and another has drawn me to an interest in antiques and particularly antique jewellery. I was founder-editor of the *Antique Dealer and Collectors' Guide* in 1946 and subsequently edited the *Watchmaker, Jeweller and Silversmith*. Finding it difficult to live within the constrictions of post-war England, I sold up everything in 1950, bought a boat and set off with my wife to sail the Mediterranean. During the next five years I never had a house, lived aboard boats, and explored the Mediterranean from the Levant to the shores of Spain. Later I moved further afield and sailed to the West Indies, crossing the Atlantic three times under sail during the 1950s.

"Married again (to another painter), I went back to the Mediterranean and have subsequently lived in Malta, Sicily and Greece, with a now permanent base in England's New Forest. For the past fifteen years I have lived by writing books and freelancing, including a certain amount of radio and television work. Recently I have been lucky enough to be able to dispense with most of the freelancing and devote myself almost entirely to history, and to the attempted imaginative reconstruction of past events that fascinate me. I love cities, particularly London and New York, but prefer to live aboard a boat in a warm climate or in the country in England."

Ernle Bradford's first book about sailing was *The Journeying Moon*, recalling a journey through the canals of France, tunny fishing in the Mediterranean, and a number of his other postwar voyages. It showed a notable talent for evoking clearly a great variety of places and people, and had "a real poetry to it." Reviewers welcomed it as the work of a cultivated and well-read man, free of the false heartiness which sometimes disfigures such accounts. Similar qualities have distinguished his subsequent books, all of which take a special authority from Bradford's own knowledge and experience of the sea. *The Mighty Hood* is a "graceful and colorful" biography of a famous battleship. *The Great Siege*, with "almost as much drama and suspense as a first-rate historical novel," describes the attempt of Suleiman the Magnificent to wrest Malta from the Knights of St. John in 1565.

In *Ulysses Found*, Bradford sought to bring to life the mythical hero who had fascinated him since adolescence by reconstructing Ulysses' journey with, as it were, tiller in one hand and Homer in the other. Some reviewers thought the attempt succeeded, establishing "the whole voyage as factually possible, day by day, knot by knot, cave by cave"; most were unconvinced but thought the attempt as entertaining as a detective story, and full of the "water-level slap and tang of the open sailing boat." *The Great Betrayal*, an account of the sack of Constantinople by the Crusaders in 1204, conveys a similar excitement. Cyril Connolly called it a "clear and most readable book," and said of Bradford that "he can tell a story and unravel the politics of a long-vanished age in a way that brings events and people to life without seeming superficial."

ERNLE BRADFORD

PRINCIPAL WORKS: Contemporary Jewellery and Silver Design, 1950; Four Centuries of European Jewellery, 1953; The Journeying Moon, 1958; English Victorian Jewellery, 1959; The Mighty Hood, 1959; The Wind off the Island, 1960; Wind from the North: The Life of Henry the Navigator, 1960 (England, Southward the Caravels); The Great Siege, 1961; The Touchstone (novel), 1962; Antique Collecting, 1963; The Companion Guide to the Greek Islands, 1963 (U.S., The Greek Islands); Dictionary of Antiques, 1963; Ulysses Found, 1963; The America's Cup, 1964; Three Centuries of Sailing, 1964; Drake (U.S., The Wind Commands Me), 1965; Wall of England: The Channel's 2000 Years of History, 1966 (U.S., Wall of Empire); The Great Betrayal, 1967; The Sultan's Admiral: The Life of Barbarossa, 1968; Mediterranean: Portrait of a Sea, 1971; Gibraltar: The History of a Fortress, 1972.

ABOUT: Bradford, E. The Journeying Moon, 1958; Bradford, E. The Wind off the Island, 1960. *Periodicals*—Country Life February 20, 1964; New York Times January 9, 1966; New York Times Book Review February 23, 1964; Times Literary Supplement December 5, 1963.

BRAINE, JOHN (GERARD) (April 13, 1922–), English novelist, writes: "The house where I was born in Bradford, Yorkshire, is opposite St. Patrick's Church, which was built for the first wave of Irish immigrants at the time of the Great Famine. My mother, though she was born in England—as indeed her parents were—always thought of herself as Irish. ('If you're born in a stable,' she'd say, 'that doesn't make you a horse.') My father was English Noncomformist, though after the 1914 War he rejected organised religion, for which I can't entirely blame him.

"My mother was a librarian; in consequence I

JOHN BRAINE

was always encouraged to read and grew up in a house full of books. My father was a works superintendent for the Bradford Council; we were never rich, but we owned our house and always had enough to eat. There was no fear of unemployment hanging over us; I look back to my childhood as a time of absolute security.

"Eventually we moved to Thackley, a village north of Bradford. Strictly speaking, it's a suburb, having long since been taken over by Bradford, but it still retains a certain individuality. There are woods and fields and a river and a canal and a few seventeenth-century houses; it's far from being a beauty spot, but much of it is undeniably beautiful.

"I lived in Thackley until 1951, when I resigned my job as Chief Assistant Librarian at Bingley, a small town nearby, to live on my earnings as a writer in London. This was absolutely the most stupid action of my whole life. I had behind me a handful of articles in *Tribune* and the *New Statesman*, and an unsuccessful verse play, *The Desert in the Mirror*. I had very little money, poor health, and no journalistic experience. I didn't even have a university degree, which might have secured me some sort of foothold in publishing. Before 1939 it might have been possible for me to have earned a living by free-lance journalism; in 1951 the magazines and newspapers I could have contributed to had gone out of existence.

"In November 1951 my mother was killed in a road accident. I went home to Thackley; after the funeral I felt over and above my grief an unaccountable fatigue, a sense of something being physically broken. The tuberculosis which had invalided me out of the Navy in 1943 had returned, and in January 1952 I became a patient at Grassington Sanatorium. I spent eighteen months at Grassington, and it was there that I began *Room at the Top*.

"Looking back, I see this as being one of my few wise decisions. I had no job, no prospects, and not even my health; I couldn't retreat any further. All that was left was for me to go forward; slowly and painfully I went to work. I remember thinking that it wouldn't really matter if I died after it had been finished; what was important was that it should be known that I had been alive, that I shouldn't vanish without trace.

"After I left the hospital I spent a miserable and frustrated year in Thackley, my time divided between ill-paid journalism for the local papers and *Room at the Top*. In September 1954 I took up a post with the Northumberland County Library and was able to finish the novel in October 1955, just before my marriage to Helen Patricia Wood. In 1957, after having been rejected four times, *Room at the Top* was published; in June of that year I was able to resign my job as a librarian and become a full-time writer again. I should really say *novelist*, because though I have tried every other literary form, this is the only one which really suits me.

"I suppose that *Room at the Top* is my best-known novel, but my own favourite is *The Vodi* (*From the Hand of the Hunter* in the U.S.A.). The Vodi is an organization dedicated to the perpetration of injustice; I see it at work everywhere and, although I'm not sure how to defeat it, I did learn in Grassington Sanatorium how to fight it.

"I remain a practising and believing Catholic though not, I hope, a complacent one. I'm not by nature religious, being too much in love with the material world, with what can be seen and touched and smelled and heard; but I'm always aware that at the centre of things there is a mystery. Religion is the acknowledgement of this mystery.

"This sounds all too tidy. In fact I'm always intoxicated by what the poet Louis MacNeice called 'the variousness of things.' If I didn't put them into some sort of order, they would overwhelm me. I couldn't cope with my impressions of the material world if I had at the same time to work out my relationship with God.

"I'm never wholly satisfied with anything that I've ever written, nor even remotely satisfied with myself. But I am now reasonably content to live quietly in a small town earning my living by writing what I want to write. Let this be my epitaph: as a writer, I never tried to please anybody except myself."

John Braine, who was educated at St. Bede's Grammar School, Bradford, had a variety of jobs before he became a librarian—selling furniture and books, working in a factory and a laboratory, and serving as a telegraphist in the Royal Navy.

Room at the Top, his spectacularly successful first novel, was about a working-class Yorkshire boy who wants "an Aston Martin, three-guinea linen shirts, a girl with a Riviera suntan." It costs him his humanity, but Joe Lampton gets what he wants. Presumably because of his hero's social class (and the cultural climate of the 1950s), Braine was labeled an "angry young man." The critics admonished Braine for his "copywriter's English" and occasional sentimentality but praised the book as a forceful moral fable about ambition; the general public read it by the thousands and flocked to see the excellent film version, because *Room at the Top* was a well-plotted, sexually explicit, and wholly contemporary version of the irresistible "rags-to-riches" theme. Its sequel, in which Lampton reaps as he has sown, had a relatively cool reception.

The Jealous God, which some thought his best novel to date, concerns a mildly intellectual Catholic in a seedy Yorkshire town who, finding the local Catholic girls socially unacceptable, falls in love with a Protestant one and nearly loses her when he finds that she is divorced. The book, entirely traditional in form, was greatly admired for its subtle characterization, its vivid evocation of a community in which, as Wilfred Sheed wrote, "Hell is nothing worse than the prying relatives who notice that you haven't been going to Communion lately." Braine has moved to the right in his political thinking, and this is reflected in his later novels, which most reviewers have found readable but "defiantly perverse" in their enthusiastic materialism and rather crude contempt for the "Progs" (progressives). There was, however, a relatively warm reception for *The Queen of a Distant Country*, about a successful but disenchanted novelist's return to his North Country home town and to Miranda, the failed writer whose literary protégé he had once been. One reviewer wrote: "After some dreadful pot boiling, John Braine has produced a novel of real unforced style and feeling," whose virtue "lies in the absolutely distinct recreation of a time and place and the way it felt to be one particular person."

John Braine appears often on radio and television. He retains his Yorkshire accent and is proud of it. He travels as much as he can, enjoys walking, and is interested in Victoriana and the American Civil War. Braine is five feet ten inches tall, dark, and blue-eyed. He says he weighs between two hundred and two hundred and twenty pounds, "according to who is winning." He lives with his wife and four children in Woking, Surrey.

PRINCIPAL WORKS: Room at the Top, 1957; The Vodi, 1959 (U.S., From the Hand of the Hunter); Life at the Top, 1962; The Jealous God, 1964; The Crying Game, 1968; Stay With Me Till Morning (U.S., The View From Tower Hill), 1970; The Queen of a Distant Country, 1972.

ABOUT: Allsop, K. The Angry Decade, 1958; Contemporary Authors 2, 1963; Ford, B. (ed.) The Modern Age (Pelican Guide to English Literature), 1963; Fraser, G. S. The Modern Writer and His World, 1964; Karl, F. R. A Reader's Guide to the Contemporary English Novel, 1963; Lee, J. W. John Braine, 1968; West, P. The Modern Novel, 1963; Who's Who, 1971. *Periodicals*—Encounter June 1965; New York Times March 7, 1965; New York Times Book Review April 19, 1959; July 10, 1962; March 11, 1965; Saturday Review October 6, 1962; March 6, 1965; Time and Tide October 4, 1962; Wilson Library Bulletin November 1963.

***BRANCATI, VITALIANO** (July 24, 1907–September 25, 1954), Italian novelist, dramatist, and critic, was born in the Sicilian village of Pachino, in the province of Syracuse. His father was also a novelist and critic, and his grandfather was a minor poet. Brancati was a serious child, timid and sensitive, and the places he knew in his early years impressed themselves vividly upon his memory—especially the city of Catania, in eastern Sicily, where the family moved when he was seventeen, and where he studied literature and began his career as a teacher. It was in Catania that he decided to become a writer, and the life of that city provided him with the raw material for more than twenty years of work.

His first work, the poetic drama *Fedor* (1928), reveals a youthful infatuation with the vigor of rising fascism, and the same is true of a second play, *Piave* (1932), and an early novel, *L'amico del vincitore* (The Victor's Friend). But from the beginning there were signs of a developing internal crisis in the fact that *Fedor* was dedicated to Giuseppe Borgese, a well-known anti-Fascist, in an introductory statement proclaiming an ideal of universal love.

In 1933 Brancati became an instructor at the Istituto Magistrale in Rome. His grandfather, a man of great wisdom and warmth, died the same year, and Brancati felt his loss deeply. This, combined with the influence of Borgese and other liberal intellectuals, seems to have altered the course of Brancati's development. His comedy *Don Giovanni involontario* (Don Juan in Spite of Himself), staged in 1933, showed that his literary method as well as his ideas had taken an entirely new course. This play about a man incapable of feeling or arousing real love was widely recognized as a satire on the political regime and was soon suppressed by the censors.

Brancati's first considerable novel, *Singolare avventura di viaggio* (Strange Travel Tale, 1934) was also banned by the censors as a thinly veiled political satire. There followed the three novels for which

* brän cä′ tē

VITALIANO BRANCATI

Brancati is best known, *Don Giovanni in Sicilia* (1941), *Il bell'Antonio* (1949, translated as *Antonio, the Great Lover*), and *Paolo il caldo* (Paolo the Hot, 1955). They are set principally in Catania and satirize Sicilian bourgeois and upper-class mores—in particular the South Italian phenomenon of *gallismo*. This refers to the amorous posturing of the frustrated male, to whom strict convention denies sexual fulfillment either within marriage or outside it but whose pride demands a display of aggressive eroticism. In each of these stories, the inheritors of this tradition are shown as its ludicrous and pathetic victims, intellectually, emotionally, and spiritually crippled by their obligatory commitment to sensuality. All three books can also be read as critiques of D'Annunzio's glorification of sexual freedom.

Il bell'Antonio, the only one of these novels so far translated, tells the tragicomic story of a handsome youth who is the son of a distinguished lecher. Antonio's own glorious reputation for venery is thrust upon him unsought and maintained only by a succession of exhausting strategems. The eventual discovery of his total impotence is a devastating blow to the good name of Catania and even to the Fascist party, which has honored Antonio for his achievements, now shown to be as spurious as the party's own. English-language critics, unfamiliar with the tradition against which Brancati wrote, gave the translation a mixed reception. George D. Painter found Antonio himself a folk hero rather than a person and seemed most impressed by Brancati's "astonishing flow of language, as molten as lava, as harsh, heady, and vulgar as wine jetting from a goatskin."

Gli anni perduti (The Lost Years, 1941), was another notable caricature of the provincial bourgeoisie. The novella *Il vecchio con gli stivali* (The Old Man With the Boots, 1945), a particularly bitter satirical attack on fascism, was filmed by Luigi Zampa in 1948 as *Anni difficili*. Brancati was a prolific contributor to a number of periodicals and newspapers, including *Il Mondo* and *Corriere della Sera*, for which he wrote a regular column.

In 1945 Brancati was able to give up teaching and devote himself exclusively to writing. He spent his last ten years in Turin with his wife, the former Anna Proclemer, and his young family. *Paolo il caldo*, on which he was working when he died at the age of forty-seven, was the first of his novels to be set in Rome. It seemed to many critics to show a moral sophistication and a subtlety of style lacking in Brancati's earlier work, which nevertheless had established him as a moralist who "illuminated the erotic aspects of the human comedy with enlightened irony and compassionate humor."

PRINCIPAL WORKS IN ENGLISH TRANSLATION: Antonio, the Great Lover, 1952.

ABOUT: Curley, D. N. and Curley, A. Modern Romance Literatures (Library of Literary Criticism), 1967; Dizionario enciclopedico della letteratura italiana, 1966; Dizionario letterario Bompiani, 1956; Dizionario universale della letteratura contemporanea, 1959; Penguin Companion to Literature 2, 1969. *Periodicals*—Books Abroad Summer 1957; New Statesman and Nation May 24, 1952; New York Times September 28, 1952.

***BRANNER, HANS CHRISTIAN** (June 23, 1903–April 24, 1966), was the leading Danish novelist and short story writer of his generation and a notable dramatist. He was born in Ordrup, a suburb of Copenhagen, the son of Christian Branner, a schoolmaster, and the former Fanny Frederiksen. He graduated in 1921 from the Ordrup *gymnasium* and then studied philology at the University of Copenhagen. Branner began his career as an actor with a touring company but abandoned this to work in publishing from 1923 to 1932, when he impulsively resigned his position to become a full-time writer. Branner said: "A slow organic development brought me irresistibly to that which I had always wished to avoid. I did not know whether I could write; but I knew that in the long run there was nothing else I could do."

Legetøj (Toys), the novel with which Branner made his debut in 1936, is in the tradition of the social realism of the 1930s. Its chief character is not a person but a business organization, Kejserboderne, within which he pictures an avid struggle, skillfully creating a microcosm of contemporary Europe in which assertive Fascist and Nazi movements were flexing their muscles.

Branner retained his interest in man's lust for

* brän′ ər

power but quickly came to see it in psychological rather than political terms, as a product of human fear and loneliness. The destructive, mutilating character of fear—fear of the unknown, fear of life itself—is the theme of his second novel, *Barnet leger ved Stranden* (The Child Plays on the Beach, 1937), which demonstrated his special and profound understanding of the child's mind.

Branner's unique quality emerged most distinctively in his short stories, collected in *Om lidt er vi borte* (In a Little While We Are Gone, 1939), *To Minutters Stilhed* (Two Minutes of Silence, 1944), *Bjergene* (The Mountains, 1953), and *Vandring langs Floden* (A Stroll Along the River, 1956). They established him as the most accomplished of a generation of Danish writers who rejected the social and literary dogmas of the 1930s and assigned a pre-empting value to characterization and psychological insight. A selection of the stories was translated by Vera Lindholm Vance and published in 1966 as *Two Minutes of Silence* (which has the same title story as Branner's 1944 volume but is not an identical collection).

In his stories, Branner usually writes about ordinary people in unremarkable situations, isolating some single telling moment of pain or pleasure. At his best, his method affords astonishing glimpses of reality transformed to the level of myth. This is achieved through a prose style rather reminiscent of Hans Christian Andersen's in its apparent naïveté. In fact, Branner learned much from Freud. His sentences are usually lucid and uninvolved, his metaphors not particularly striking in a literary way. They are however very carefully and skillfully chosen, evoking patterns of thought which obliquely explain the often puzzling and irrational behavior of his characters.

In time, Branner came to regard sexual desire and frustration as important keys to an understanding of the problems that most concerned him—fear, loneliness, and the power complex. This is evident in his later novels. They include *Drømmen om en Kvinde* (Dream About a Woman, 1941), set in Denmark on the eve of war, and *Historien om Børge* (The Story of Børge, 1942), a lyrical, bittersweet description of a child's troubled everyday life.

He is probably best known abroad for the short novel *Rytteren* (1949), which also enjoyed great success in play form. It has been widely translated—into English, by A. I. Roughton, as *The Riding Master*. This story of a woman torn between two men—the primitive, violent riding master, who exerts a power over his friends even after his death, and a gentle, idealistic doctor—poses an urgent contemporary problem: the choice between unrestrained force and guilt-laden humanism. *Ingen kender Natten* (1955), translated as *No Man Knows the Night*, is an extension of the same theme, an

HANS CHRISTIAN BRANNER

apocalyptic vision of Copenhagen under German occupation, full of sexual frenzy. Branner's affirmation of faith in man's ultimately healthy instincts is personified in a bankrupt, dissolute writer whose life acquires a direction and meaning when he risks it to help a member of the Resistance.

Branner's plays express similar concerns. In *Søskende* (1952, translated as *The Judge*), three siblings meet at their stern father's deathbed and, in their conversation about him and their childhood, succeed briefly in recapturing a dream of harmony which each of them has lost. In *Thermopylae*, which enjoyed a sensational first night at the Royal Theatre in Copenhagen in 1958, the hero's optimistic belief in reason wanes as he sees his life's work crumble and his children perish, but a drunken artist in search of Christ strikes a characteristic note of hope. Branner also wrote a number of radio plays, of which the most notable are *Natteregn* (Rain in the Night, 1937), *Hundrede Kroner* (A Hundred Kroner, 1949), *Jeg elsker dig* (I Love You, 1956, filmed 1957), and the lyrical drama *Et Spil om Kaerligheden og Døden* (A Game of Love and Death, 1961).

Branner became a member of the board of the Danish Authors' Union in 1940 and a recipient of an annual state grant in 1941. He served as an editor of the review *Perspektiv* from 1953 to 1955 and received the Holberg Medal in 1954. He translated many English and American novels, and also Kafka, into Danish, and the influence of Virginia Woolf and James Joyce on his style has often been remarked. Branner, it is said, was a humanist, who wrote "of landscape, objects and animals only as they affect human existence," and who was "undoubtedly the most important psychologist of his generation" in Denmark.

PRINCIPAL WORKS IN ENGLISH TRANSLATION: *Prose*—The Riding Master, 1951; No Man Knows the Night, 1958; Two Minutes of Silence (stories), 1966. *Stories or extracts in* Modern Danish Authors, 1946; Contemporary Danish Prose, 1958; Adam, June 1948; The Norseman, July–August 1949. *Play*—The Judge, *in* Contemporary Danish Plays, 1955.

ABOUT: Bredsdorff, E. and others. Introduction to Scandinavian Literature, 1951; Fonsmark, H. H. C. Branner, 1951; Kraks Blå Bog, 1964; Kristensen, S. M. Digtning og Livssyn, 1959; Mitchell, P. M. History of Danish Literature, 1957; Penguin Companion to Literature 2, 1969; Vosmar, J. H. C. Branner, 1959; Vowles, R. B. *introduction to* Two Minutes of Silence, 1966.

BREAN, HERBERT (December 10, 1907–May 7, 1973), American detective story writer and journalist, wrote: "I was born in Detroit, Michigan of middle-class, reasonably honest parents. When I was about five we moved to northern Vermont, St. Albans being the home region of my father's family, and there I received some highly formative experiences. These included being given *Huckleberry Finn* to read when I was nine (I somehow sensed it to be better than *The Rover Boys on Land and Sea*, although the part where Huck simulates his own murder puzzled me) and part of the Sherlock Holmes saga, which kindled a lifelong devotion. I came to love popular music, buying small ten-cent records at Woolworth's, and learned that Vermont is not too comfortable if you are physically slighter than the other kids in school and your family is proudly Democratic, Catholic and Irish (the name originally was O'Briean).

"My father's death returned my mother and me to Detroit where I learned at the University of Detroit High School that I could write fast and expressively and that this was somehow enjoyable; otherwise I was an upper-middle student and a tolerable football player. An ardent sports page reader, I began to long to write newspaper stories, especially since I also came to love baseball and ice skating. One brilliant June day I met Ty Cobb, then in the latter stages of his career, on his way to the ball park for the day's game; he stopped and smiled and talked to me, and then waved goodbye. I sometimes think nothing at all happened in my life up to then, and very little since.

"While I was an undergraduate at the University of Michigan I got, through a happy accident, a part-time job with the United Press and found it a curious experience. My introduction to a news room was like coming home, but to a place I had never been in before.

"After graduation (A.B., 1929, a great year for wines but rather bad for people) I went to work for the U.P. in the main office in New York as reporter and rewrite man, was transferred to

HERBERT BREAN

Detroit as assistant bureau manager, moved to the Detroit *Times* and there presently began to write the by-line news stories I'd wanted to write as a high school junior.

"So I developed a new ambition: writing slick-paper magazine stories, and began producing and selling detective stories to pulp magazines, then in high newsstand favor. I also became part-time correspondent for *Time*, *Life* and *Fortune* magazines. These, with a full-time newspaper job of increasing importance, marriage and a growing family made for a busy life.

"After almost ten years on the *Times* I left to be *Time* and *Life* news bureau chief in Detroit and in late 1944 was moved to New York as a *Life* editor and, later, staff writer. Now I could and did write articles for top magazines and so a new goal developed: a book. A mystery novel, it appeared in 1948 and holding it for the first time brought back a June afternoon and Ty Cobb. Like another, later, one it was nominated for that year's 'Edgar,' the Mystery Writers of America's equivalent of Hollywood's Oscars for mysteries in various categories.

"There have been thirteen books in all and writing them has served to deepen my conviction that the good and intelligent book (this is no self-reference) is a workmanlike job that is a pleasure to read, not a wild, unsteered experimental flight nor a test of the reader's decoding skill. Which leads me to regret (this *is* a self-reference) that mystery authors must so often submit to the indignity of being asked 'What name do you write under?' in the same tone one might ask 'What name do you give when caught in a police raid?' In the hands of a skilled practitioner (Hammett, Ambler, Le Carré) the mystery becomes an art form that far outstrips, in character, style, background and originality, the 'serious novels' of many brash aspirants.

"Over the years my tastes have not greatly changed, but they have deepened and multiplied. I still like good jazz music, but I also love 'serious' music. I love good food and wine (cooking is a major hobby), early American furniture, sports cars and the Caribbean islands. I believe in journalism as a vital public service and as a private avenue to, as it has been for me, experience with life, travel and close-up observation of people.

"And I still love to write. That's where things stand now."

The intelligent craftsmanship which Brean advocated was demonstrated in everything he wrote—in his journalism, in his witty and realistic guides to the renunciation of life's more pernicious pleasures, and in his detective stories, which were regularly praised for the authenticity of their settings, the excellence of their characterization and dialogue. The first of these, *Wilders Walk Away*, made no great stir when it was published but is now regarded by some connoisseurs as a "classic in modern crime fiction." *The Clock Strikes Thirteen*, published in 1952, impressed reviewers as a detailed study of the development of biological weapons, then a new and terrifying theme. One of the most admired of Brean's mysteries, and an outstanding example of his "beautiful sleight-of-hand" plotting, is *Traces of Brillhart*, a sophisticated puzzle about a supposedly dead Broadway playboy, with a lively and well-realized background in popular music and broadcasting, and characteristically witty dialogue. "If it falls just short of the Carr-Christie-Queen standards of rigorous demonstration," wrote Anthony Boucher, "this is still a who-, how- and whydunit in the classic grand manner."

Brean lectured on mystery writing at Columbia, at New York University, and for the Mystery Writers of America, Inc., whose national president he was. He was optimistic about the future of the mystery story, which he believed has unique recreational qualities, and is winning "ever wider acceptance." He was married in 1934 to Dorothy Skeman and was the father of two daughters. Brean, who lived on New York's East Side and had a house in the Virgin Islands, died at the age of sixty-five, apparently of a heart attack.

PRINCIPAL WORKS: *Fiction*—Wilders Walk Away, 1948; The Darker the Night, 1949; Hardly a Man Is Now Alive, 1950; The Clock Strikes Thirteen, 1952; A Matter of Fact, 1956 (England, Collar for a Killer); The Traces of Brillhart, 1960; The Traces of Merrilee, 1966. *Nonfiction*—How to Stop Smoking, 1951; How to Stop Drinking, 1958; (ed.) Mystery Writer's Handbook: A Handbook on the Writing of Detective, Suspense, Mystery and Crime Stories, 1956; The Only Diet That Works, 1965.

ABOUT: Who's Who in America, 1970–1971. *Periodicals*—New York Times May 9, 1973.

***BRÉE, GERMAINE** (October 2, 1907–), American scholar and critic, writes: "I was born at Lasalle, Gard, a village in the Cévennes mountains in Languedoc, where my father, a Channel-islander and a British citizen, was the rather impecunious pastor of a small Huguenot church. My mother, who had married in her late thirties, was a well-traveled woman from Lorraine and had twice visited Australia, where one of her sisters had settled. Of my father's three brothers, one lived in England, the other two in Argentina and India. The Franco-British background of the family—both my parents were bilingual—and their dispersal in space, gave me the sense of a world unknown and yet within reach, fostering no doubt a love of travel which I later indulged, in spite of a chronic lack of funds. I have traveled in the British Isles, Western Europe, and Greece; Algeria, Morocco and Tunisia; the U.S.A., Canada and Australia, visiting all too briefly along the way Malaya, Ceylon, India, Iran and Turkey, and I still look forward to further forays abroad. Better still perhaps my background gave me a double perspective and a double education. When I was five the family—which eventually numbered eight children—moved to the Channel Islands (a haven during World War I), first to Guernsey, then to Jersey. When I was fifteen, we returned to the Cévennes, thence, a few years later, to Brittany. The Cévennes and the Channel Islands, different though they be, were both ideally suited for a happy childhood, and it was there I acquired my taste for a country décor and for walking, swimming and the simpler forms of boating. When I was nine, I attended an English school in Jersey as weekly boarder, and at fifteen was suddenly transferred to a school in France, an experience more profitable than pleasant. Following the course of French studies, I subsequently went to Paris, where I studied at the Sorbonne while earning my living. I took my degree—*l'agrégation*—in English literature in 1932 after having spent a memorable year as graduate student at Bryn Mawr College. I then taught for four years in Algeria, returning as lecturer in French to Bryn Mawr in 1936 where I remained except for a couple of years during World War II, until 1953.

"The thirties I remember as unsettling years, overshadowed by the threats of fascism and war, culminating in the scandal of the Spanish Civil War. But they were also years in which I experienced the exhilarating quality of life by the sea and in the sun of Algeria, and the beauty of the land, an experience which later made the universe of Albert Camus of great significance to me. It was

* brā

GERMAINE BRÉE

Bryn Mawr, with its tradition of careful scholarship, that oriented me toward writing, an activity in which I had previously only sporadically indulged. Toward 1942, I joined an ambulance unit which, in 1943, left the United States for Morocco. I spent a little over two years in the French Army, was transferred first to Algiers, then to Dijon, and later to continental Advance Section, an American supply headquarters for the First French Army. I returned to Bryn Mawr College in 1945. My academic life since then has been uninterrupted. It was immediately after the war that I decided to become an American citizen, completing my naturalization in 1953. The same year New York University invited me to become chairman of the French Department at Washington Square College, then to head the University Department of Romance and Slavic Languages. In 1960 the University of Wisconsin's Institute for Research in the Humanities offered me life membership and a chair as Vilas Professor of French. I now live in Madison, an urbane city of great charm and vitality.

"It was after the war that I started to work on the books of criticism I have since published. From English, I had moved to the teaching of French, more particularly, though not exclusively, to the twentieth century literature. I do not consider myself a writer, and should probably be classed among the 'academic' critics, a generally unpopular group. Writing has become for me a discipline, a way of clarifying my own reactions to the books I value and that it is my professional business to discuss with my students. I have no particular critical method and am, in fact, an eclectic. Each writer seems himself to suggest to me the method of approach I should use as I attempt to elucidate the kind of book he has written. A good deal of literary criticism seems to me preparatory to the understanding of literature rather than directly involved in it. I attempt, with a good deal of difficulty, to communicate what seems to me essential about each writer, rather than to prove, attack or praise."

Germaine Brée's critical intention is, she says, to elucidate rather than to judge, and this was evident in the first of her books to appear in English, *Marcel Proust and Deliverance From Time*. One reviewer finished it "not only with a much deeper awareness of the true range and significance of Proust's achievements (and, for that matter, of his limitations), but with something of the same exhilaration one feels in reading the original." The book has become well known as one of the most necessary of the numerous guides to Proust's novel, "illuminating both the complex ramifications of its individual relationships and the solidity of the underlying structure." It was supplemented by *The World of Marcel Proust*, found "particularly useful on the implications of the new material published since 1950."

It is scarcely possible to imagine a writer more different from Proust than Camus, and Miss Brée's study of the latter showed that she is indeed an eclectic, and one of exceptional range and ability. Paul West called the book a "thorough, discerning and unlabored study" which "extracts a steady Camus from the mosaic of his own inconsistencies and hyperboles," and most critics agreed that Miss Brée had produced the "clearest and most comprehensive" account of Camus which had yet appeared, "admirably balanced as well as arranged." Her ability to hold in clear focus even the most elusive of writers, brushing aside inessentials, was demonstrated again in *Gide*, an English version of *André Gide, l'insaisissable Protée* (1953). *An Age of Fiction*, later republished under its subtitle, *The French Novel from Gide to Camus*, is a brief and stimulating survey of the period.

It is clear that Germaine Brée has elucidated her own work, in the sketch above, as usefully as she has that of others. These notes can do little more than document her self-assessment, except in one respect: few critics would accept her assertion that she is simply an academic, and no writer. Her prose is regularly praised, and R. M. Adams is specific in his admiration: "She writes well, not merely in the sense of turning a neat phrase now and then, but strategically; she marshals her information carefully, maintains good impetus, avoids the excesses of jargon, and focuses her ideas with a distinct and wiry energy worthy of Camus himself."

Germaine Brée is the daughter of Walter and Lois (Andrault) Brée. Her intelligence work with the French Army during World War II brought her a number of decorations, including the Bronze Star, the Army Commendation Medal, and a Citation à l'Ordre de la Division. She is a Chevalier de la Légion d'Honneur. Miss Brée serves on the advisory board of the American Council of Learned Societies and is a member of several other scholarly societies. In addition to the books listed below, she has edited a collection of critical essays about Camus and translated Jules Romains's *Seven Mysteries of Europe*, among other such assignments.

PRINCIPAL WORKS: Marcel Proust and Deliverance from Time (tr. from the French by C. J. Richards and A. D. Truitt), 1956; (with M. O. Guiton) An Age of Fiction: The French Novel from Gide to Camus, 1957; Camus, 1959; Gide, 1963; The World of Marcel Proust, 1966; (with A. Y. Kroft), Twentieth Century French Drama, 1969; Women Writers in France, 1973.

ABOUT: Contemporary Authors 1–4 1st revision, 1967; Who's Who in America 1970–1971.

***BREIT, HARVEY** (November 27, 1909–April 9, 1968) American poet, novelist, dramatist, and journalist, wrote the following note shortly before his death: "I was born and raised in New York City and had no formal education to speak of, my fragmented two years at New York University being altogether somnambulistic. Class cuts and quarrels forced the dean to drop me, and drop out I did from everything, including baseball and family.

"I began working immediately, and waking up too, with a job on the Puerto Rican Lines where life was dominated by rats as big as bulldogs; in fact I never slept at sea except when weather permitted bunking on deck. My first land job was with an ambiguous publishing house ('Musk, Hashish and Blood') where I packaged books and helped write the catalog copy and for which house the late Alexander King did some of the illustrations.

"I came to young manhood at the tail-end of the bootleg era and drank raw applejack and beer chasers in a Saugerties roadhouse where Jack 'Legs' Diamond supplied the booze. I got a job on the Writers Project of the WPA but obviously I wasn't lasting at anything. Kenneth Patchen, on a Guggenheim in Arizona, found employment for me in Santa Fe, but after a month I was jobless again. Nevertheless, living in an adobe in a small Mexican community outside Santa Fe, I found I could just make it by writing. I stayed three years, wrote lots of stories, some of which I sold, all of which were muck, and I was maddeningly hungry for at least two of those years. (Since that time I always try to have a full fridge.)

"But Patchen, on a visit, suggested I was more a poet than a writer of prose, and perhaps for that time it was true: I felt easier and obsessive both. I would write with a pad on my lap, staying that way

* brīt

HARVEY BREIT

for six or eight hours at a clip and time did stop; and when I left the poem, say for a slab of cheese, I would move (I remember the sensation) as though made of glass, not shaking myself up as it were, so that I could come back to the poem just as I'd left it. I only wish the poems reflected that experience and derangement! Wallace Stevens wrote me a hilarious letter about those poems.

"Anyway, marriage meant an end to poetry because the precondition for me was complete silence for days and nights at a time. I took a job on the New York *Times*, Sunday Division, where I edited and wrote for more years than I care to count, and though it was a good discipline and a beneficial experience, I should have gotten away sooner. I escaped in small ways: a two-day-a-week leave to teach for a year at Sarah Lawrence College; a solid leave to go to India for the Ford Foundation. Together with Budd Schulberg, I dramatized his novel *The Disenchanted*, and when the play became a reality, that is to say when I was needed to go on the road with it, I resigned from the paper. It was like another divorce with all the contrary emotions inherent in the breakup of a protracted relationship. Though I always required solitude, the loss of the fantastic social life of a newspaper was terribly difficult to adjust to.

"I am more bored with myself now, more turned inward, more silent, more remote. I remember, with something of a shock, how 'interesting' I used to be. In prose, I admire most Melville. I would like to achieve a modicum of what he accomplished in *Moby Dick*. Every word of that novel gives me continuous pleasure. I feel closest to Rilke in poetry. My oldest, very pretty, sister, now dead, went to

Dayton, Tennessee, as the secretary of Clarence Darrow for the Monkey Trial. My uncle, Max Beer, wrote *The History of British Socialism*. Those are my family influences, if my being a writer isn't altogether an accident. I have four children and two ex-wives, none of whom live with me, so I should be writing poetry again, but when you neglect an art you are forfeit. For pleasure, I wish I had developed into a smooth three-cushion billiard player. For truth, I wish I had been a great opera singer, like Bjoerling or Fischer-Dieskau. Whenever I listen to a Mozart or Verdi opera I hear sublimities and subtleties of communication I have never heard in all literature except possibly Shakespeare."

Harvey Breit, one of the most universally well-liked of literary men, died suddenly of a heart attack in his New York apartment at the age of fifty-eight. He had had an operation to replace part of an artery a year previously.

He was the son of Jack and Sarah (Beer) Breit and was educated at Franklin K. Lane High School in Brooklyn before beginning his "fragmented two years at New York University." To his own account of his career it can be added that he wrote for *Time* magazine for a year in 1933 and was with the New York *Times* from 1943 to 1957. He also did some editorial work for the publishing firms of Viking and Simon and Schuster. His first marriage was to Alice Morris, a literary journalist, and his second to Mrs. Patricia Rinehart Campbell, granddaughter of Mary Roberts Rinehart; he had a son and a daughter by each marriage.

It is difficult to understand why Harvey Breit never fulfilled his undoubted literary potential. The poems in *There Falls Tom Fool*, his only collection, are not completely realized, but they are full of integrity, rich in experience, and often finely wrought. It was perhaps Breit's fatal though endearing humility, rather than lack of time or opportunity, that made him neglect this most promising branch of his creative activity.

Of his abilities as a literary journalist there can be no doubt, and some of the interviews he did for the New York *Times* have fortunately been preserved in *The Writer Observed*. Breit was an admirable interviewer, combining shrewdness and honesty with real modesty and friendliness. His short appraisals of such writers as Eliot, Hemingway, Frost, and Mailer are genuinely revealing—much more so than their sometimes rather journalistic tone suggests. And there is reason to believe that Breit was capable of a larger contribution to literary criticism; his essay on James Baldwin in *The Creative Present* (1963, edited by Nona Balakian and Charles Simmons) is more developed, suggestive, and profound than anything in *The Writer Observed*, and shows what he could do when he had time to think and room to work out his ideas.

Harvey Breit's novel, *A Narrow Action*, is set on a Caribbean island and is clearly a fictional account of Castro's Cuba. R. D. Spector said that Breit "has a good sense of narrative pace, a perceptive eye for detail, a sharp ear for dialogue," but thought the book a deliberate attempt to manufacture a best seller. Others agreed that this highly readable novel was marred by a certain superficiality and slickness and also by the excessive influence of Hemingway. It nevertheless enjoyed a considerable popular success, and this appears in some measure to have restored Breit's creative confidence. At the time of his death he was working on a second novel and had arranged to write a film version of *A Narrow Action*. After that he was to prepare a screen treatment of Malcolm Lowry's *Under the Volcano*. (In 1965, he had edited, with Lowry's widow, a selection of his letters.)

Breit's 1959 stage adaptation (with the author) of *The Disenchanted*, Budd Schulberg's novel about Scott Fitzgerald, was highly successful; he fared less well with *The Guide*, a play which he and his second wife based on R. K. Narayan's novel and which failed on Broadway in 1961. Both adaptations were very skillful but, by their nature, less original and personal than the work Breit might have accomplished if he had been able to gamble more heavily on his own creative imagination. When he died, Norman Mailer said of him: "He was one of the warmest people I ever knew. I thought he was a talented man. He knew a lot about boxing and poetry. He was a marvelous story teller about literary figures."

PRINCIPAL WORKS: There Falls Tom Fool (poems), 1940; (ed.) Perspectives of India (anthology), 1952; The Writer Observed (interviews), 1956; (with Budd Schulberg) The Disenchanted (play), 1959; (with Patricia Rinehart) The Guide (play), 1961; A Narrow Action (novel), 1964; (ed. with Margerie Bonner Lowry) The Selected Letters of Malcolm Lowry, 1965.

ABOUT: Contemporary Authors 5–6, 1963; Roskolenko, H. When I Was Last on Cherry Street, 1965. *Periodicals*—Commonweal March 9, 1956; New York Times April 10, 1968; Saturday Review February 18, 1956; Time April 22, 1968.

BRENNAN, CHRISTOPHER (JOHN) (November 1, 1870–October 5, 1932), Australian poet, was born in Sydney, the eldest child of Christopher Brennan, a brewer, and Mary Ann (Carroll) Brennan. Both parents were of Southern Irish descent. Brennan was educated in Catholic primary schools and in 1885 went with a scholarship to St. Ignatius' College, Riverview. He had been intended for the priesthood, but lost his faith. In 1888 he entered the University of Sydney, earned a degree in classics and philosophy, and was awarded a two-year traveling scholarship.

Brennan went to Berlin, where he read prodigiously in English, French, German, and Italian literature, but did not bother to take his doctorate.

He returned to Sydney in July 1894, was unsettled for a time, and in 1895 joined the staff of the Sydney Public Library. There he eventually became chief cataloger, characteristically spending weeks reading for pleasure "and then making up in a day or two what would have taken another more time than he had lost."

In December 1897 Brennan was married in Sydney to Anna Werth, the daughter of his former landlady in Berlin. There were to be four children, two sons and two daughters; but the marriage steadily deteriorated, until in 1925 Anna Brennan sought and obtained a judicial separation.

Meanwhile, Brennan had begun to teach in the University of Sydney as a relief lecturer, and in 1909, confirmed as a lecturer in French and German, he resigned his library post. He became associate professor of German and comparative literature in 1920, and for five years (to quote his friend J. Le Gay Brereton) he "enlarged his students' horizons . . . gave new impulses to their humanity. They revered him and loved him." The breadth of Brennan's learning is suggested by the fact that at different times he substituted for professors of Greek, Latin, French, and German literature and languages.

By 1925 these good days were over. His mistress, Violet Singer, was killed in a tramway accident, and her death shattered him. The liaison was exposed to public censure and the revelations of his wife precipitated his dismissal from the university. There followed a period of acute distress, but gradually he managed a living by a little teaching and some writing, and was also awarded a small literary pension. He died of cancer at the age of sixty-one in Lewisham Hospital, Sydney, having become reconciled to the Church.

Brennan was "a huge man in a huge flapping mantle, with a huge nose and a huge pipe . . . and a black felt hat, like a wandering scholar out of some German film." As H. M. Green has said, "There was about him a breadth and depth, a loftiness, almost a magnificence, that persisted through and behind the atmosphere of beer and tobacco and bawdry and huge humour that surrounded him in his more social moods." But the Brennan cult did not long survive his death. His poetry, which seemed obscure and foreign in the enthusiastic nationalism of the period, went out of print, and for many years he was almost forgotten. Brennan's rehabilitation seems to have begun about the end of World War II. His verse was collected and republished in 1960. His collected prose, mostly critical and occasional essays which still read easily, with a modern ring, followed in 1962.

The corpus of Brennan's poetry is meager. All that is likely to endure was written by the time he was thirty-three, and the best of it is in *Poems 1913*, a collection of one hundred and five poems, seven-

CHRISTOPHER BRENNAN

teen of them revised from earlier volumes. The book is a deliberately shaped poetic edifice. Individual lyrics, written in isolation, are fitted more or less successfully into a pattern that culminates in the sequence called "The Wanderer," evoking a lonely journey at night, under trees, near the sea, and magnifying it into a spiritual pilgrimage.

This pilgrimage pervades Brennan's thought and poetry. The mind, grown separate from what it contemplates, has surrendered its "primal consciousness": "I am shut out of my own heart." But "Man the wanderer is on his way to himself," and the way lies through self-knowledge; the lost Eden is to be found in the individual unconscious. Hence the engrossed subjectivity of Brennan's verse—what A. G. Stephens called his "didactic sonorous spectacular comments on I, Mine, Me." His poetry is a personal saga conceived as myth, an attempt to discover in his own spiritual experience a complete allegory of the human search.

The sense of loss in Brennan's poetry, whether it reflects modern man's loss of spiritual values, as Judith Wright suggests, or a prerational Celtic nostalgia, is expressed in the grand manner. His diction is elevated, studded with archaisms, sometimes grandiose. His style is elaborate, ponderous, often clumsy. There are occasions when his inspiration collapses under the weight of learning it is made to bear, and his poetry has been found derivative of the German Romantics, the English Romantics, and the French Symbolists, among others. At its best, nevertheless, there is a solemn, plangent inevitability about his work which no other Australian poet has equaled. Brennan saw in himself "two half-souls that struggle and mix" and certainly there are two voices in his poetry. One is the "trumpet of romantic traditionalism" with which he sometimes achieves real grandeur and sometimes, as A. A. Phillips has said, "blares flat." The other, heard most often in opening lines, speaks with a heart-moving lyric simplicity which is quite his own. Brennan is widely regarded as the least Australian and also the most eminent of Australian poets.

PRINCIPAL WORKS: XVIII Poems, 1897; XXI Poems (1893–1897): Towards the Source, 1897; A Mask (verse drama written in collaboration with J. Le Gay Brereton), 1913; Poems 1913, 1914; A Chant of Doom, 1918; Twenty-three Poems, 1938; The Burden of Tyre, 1953 (first issued in typescript in 1906); The Verse of Christopher Brennan, ed. by A. R. Chisholm and J. J. Quinn, 1960; The Prose of Christopher Brennan, ed. by A. R. Chisholm and J. J. Quinn, 1962; Poems, 1966.

ABOUT: Chisholm, A. R. Christopher Brennan, 1946; Chisholm, A. R. and Quinn, J. J. *introduction to* The Verse of Christopher Brennan, 1960; Green, H. M. Christopher Brennan, 1939; Green, H. M. History of Australian Literature, 1961; Hughes, R. C. J. Brennan, 1934; McAuley, J. C. J. Brennan, 1963; Stephens, A. G. Christopher Brennan, 1933; Stone, W. W. and Anderson, H. Christopher John Brennan: A Comprehensive Bibliography, 1959; Wilkes, G. A. New Perspectives in Brennan's Poetry, 1952. *Periodicals*—Southerly vol. 10 no. 4 1949.

***"BŘEZINA, OTOKAR" (pseudonym of Václav Ignác Jebavý)** (September 13, 1868–March 25, 1929), Czech poet, was born in the town of Počátky in southern Bohemia, the son of a shoemaker. He was educated at a secondary school in Teltsch, and thereafter was a teacher in various parts of Moravia. In 1901 he settled in the town of Jaroměřice (or Jarmeritz), where he spent the rest of his life.

Březina began to write poems while still at school. As a young man he was identified for a time with the small group of Czech "decadent" poets centered around Arnošt Procházká's *Moderne Revue*. Their romantic pessimism and the stylistic influence of Baudelaire is reflected in Březina's first book of poems, *Tajemné dálky* (Secret Distances, 1895), which was somewhat more personal than his later work, touching for example upon the early death of his parents and containing such melancholy assertions as: "My memories are colorless and parched," and "Poverty's acid savour did I taste betimes. . . ." But even this preliminary volume showed its author's originality in its intricate imagery, often drawn from Roman Catholic liturgy, and in "the strangely farfetched, extremely effective rhymes."

In fact Březina was the product of no literary school, but a solitary thinker and mystic. He immersed himself in the study of languages and of the religious and philosophical writings of the past and present, East and West. He recorded this spiritual search in a few very short books of poems (or

* bər zhe′ zi nä

OTOKAR BŘEZINA

hymns, as they have been called), and then was silent.

There are intimations of his mature style and philosophy in *Svítání na západě* (Dawn in the West, 1896), in which Březina seemed to embrace suffering as a means to understanding and which contained at least one great poem, the dithyrambic "Morning Prayer." But it was in his third book, *Větry od pólů* (Polar Winds, 1897), that he found his true voice. These dithyrambs, meditations, and prayers, written in free verse with many dactyls and anapaests, were distinguished by enormously long lines and "clusters of magnificent metaphors which seem to burst one from the other." Their imagery was drawn from the natural sciences rather than from the church, but these were religious poems in the broadest sense, expressing a cosmic optimism which saw all creation as part of a divine pattern, and envisaged the ultimate fusion of all things, beings, and ideas into a single harmony.

In *Stavitelé chrámů* (Temple Builders, 1899), Březina seemed to have lost his way, to feel bearing down upon him the weight of all suffering. With *Ruce* (Hands, 1901), his last and greatest collection of poems, all doubts had gone. The whole book is an exultant paean of praise to every aspect of creation, postulating a "cosmic brotherhood" which would encompass the living, the dead, and the yet unborn. The "hands" of the title are those, visible and invisible, that will carry out the will of God and the laws of the universe. *Hudbá pramenů* (Music of the Springs, 1903) was a collection of essays which had appeared in periodicals between 1897 and 1903. These "meditations in prose" complement the poems, developing for example Březina's notion of art as a form of service to God;

ornate in style, they do not bear comparison with his verse. With this volume, having apparently said all that he wanted to say, Březina ended his literary activities.

Living at Jaroměřice an uneventful life of almost monastic seclusion, Březina avoided publicity even after his reputation was established. He refused a professorship at the University of Brno, but accepted an honorary doctorate from the University of Prague. He continued to teach until 1925, and after his retirement worked as a gardener. In spite of his humanism and social idealism, he never became involved in the political movements of the time. Towards the end of his life, visitors reported that his cosmic philosophy had dwindled to a "disgruntled provincial nationalism."

The Christian mysticism Březina expressed in his poems was not specifically Roman Catholic and at times approached pantheism. He nevertheless remained a Catholic, and indeed inspired a Catholic literary movement which produced several talented poets. Stylistically, Březina's "wonderful cascades of metaphors and majestic free verse . . . his rare and sublime art" have had and could have few imitators. He is generally regarded as the greatest of the Czech symbolists, and by many as his country's greatest modern lyric poet.

PRINCIPAL WORKS IN ENGLISH TRANSLATION: *Poems in* Chudoba, F. A Short Survey of Czech Literature, 1924; Ginsburg, R. A. (ed.) The Soul of a Century, 1942; Selver, P. (ed.) A Century of Czech and Slovak Poetry, 1946; Selver, P. Otokar Březina, 1921.

ABOUT: Chudoba, F. A Short Survey of Czech Literature, 1924; Selver, P. Otokar Březina, 1921; Smith, H. (ed.) Columbia Dictionary of Modern European Literature, 1947.

"BRIDIE, JAMES" (pseudonym of Osborne Henry Mavor) (January 3, 1888–January 29, 1951), Scottish dramatist, was born in Glasgow. He was the eldest of three sons of Henry A. Mavor, a gifted electrical engineer and inventor, and Janet (Osborne) Mavor. He was educated at Glasgow Academy and at Glasgow University where, over a leisurely eight years, he acquired a medical degree, qualifying in 1913 at the age of twenty-five. During World War I, as Captain Osborne Mavor, he served with the Royal Army Medical Corps (1914–1919) in France, Mesopotamia, Persia, India, Turkey, and Russia. He was later to draw on these journeys for the backgrounds of his biblical plays and to describe them in *Some Talk of Alexander*.

In 1919 he resumed his civilian medical career in Glasgow, subsequently becoming a consulting physician to the Victoria Infirmary and professor of medicine at Anderson College. Increasingly successful as a dramatist, in 1938 he abandoned his medical career to devote himself to the theatre, although during the early part of World War II he again served with the R.A.M.C.

JAMES BRIDIE

Bridie's literary horizons were shaped in childhood by his father's readings from such diverse sources as the Bible, Darwin, Shakespeare, and the *Arabian Nights*. His activities as editor of school and university magazines and as author of undergraduate plays show early evidence of his literary talent. Bridie was first drawn into the professional theatre as a reader and dramatist for the Scottish National Players. He was almost middle-aged when, in 1928, his short play *The Sunlight Sonata*, written under the pseudonym of "Mary Henderson," was produced by Tyrone Guthrie at the Lyric Theatre, Glasgow.

The Anatomist, in 1931, successfully introduced his work to the London stage. This play, inspired by the nineteenth-century Burke and Hare body-snatching scandal, together with such later works as *The Switchback* (1929), *A Sleeping Clergyman* (1933) and *Dr. Angelus* (1947), enabled Bridie to exploit his medical background to good dramatic effect. *The Anatomist* was followed by *Tobias and the Angel*, one of his best and most successful plays, in which Tobias is presented as "a kind of apocryphal Charlie Chaplin" and the author's delight in and affection for his characters is perfectly communicated. Bridie's talent for suggesting the follies of modern society by reference to the remote past is also evident in two subsequent biblical plays, *Jonah and the Whale* (which was twice rewritten) and *Susannah and the Elders*, neither of them as successful as *Tobias*.

A Sleeping Clergyman (1933) was described by Bridie (though not by his critics) as "the nearest thing to a masterpiece I shall probably ever write." Its theme is the mysterious working of heredity, which is shown producing a genius out of generations of abject failure. The play's London success was not repeated in New York, where Brooks Atkinson praised the authenticity of the medical background but wrote: "Mr. Bridie has not learned enough from Dr. Mavor about writing up a case."

In *Mr. Bolfry* (1943), a witty discussion piece about the conflict of the powers of darkness with those of light, Bridie unites their representatives, a devil and a clergyman, in a temporary alliance against youthful skepticism. In *Daphne Laureola* (1949), which gave Edith Evans one of her finest roles, Bridie, ever an experimenter, was working towards a combination of poetic and realistic drama which achieved its fullest expression in his last play, *The Baikie Charivari* (1952), a restatement of the Punch and Judy legend in a modern context.

Bridie was tall and massively built. "His head," wrote Winifred Bannister, "was bulbous, his face far from handsome, but his wide expressive mouth, tight and dour when he was withdrawn, was full of diablerie and charm when he smiled, fully revealing his large capacity for enjoyment. He had a high, scholarly forehead, emphasised by receding hair and sometimes gaily challenged by an adventurous-looking trilby on the back of his head." Shy by nature, he disliked pomposity and pretense. He was a registered Rationalist but this did not inhibit his delight in singing psalms at the top of his voice. He was an accomplished artist and when literary inspiration flagged he found recreation in drawing and painting.

Bridie was married in 1923 to Rona Bremner and had two sons. He died of a vascular ailment in the Edinburgh Royal Infirmary at the age of sixty-three.

His plays are witty, sometimes brilliant in their language, and full of the clash of ideas, but finally a little too cozily optimistic. They inevitably inspired—but suffered from—comparison with Shaw. Winifred Bannister suggests that Bridie's frequent lack of discipline in construction stemmed partly from an attempt to avoid this comparison. Bridie himself wrote, in a letter to James Agate: "It is true, of course, that most of my last acts are bad; but they are bad with good intention and may become good in time. The tidy last act maddens me and I am trying to find a new formula without deserting the old shape."

Bridie was an indefatigable worker in the interest of dramatic art in Scotland and was largely instrumental in the foundation, in 1943, of "the first significant Scottish drama stage," the Glasgow Citizens' Theatre. In 1946 he was made a Commander of the Order of the British Empire. Besides bringing a vitalizing talent to Scottish drama, Bridie also, to quote Frederick Lumley, "came to the rescue of the English theatre when there was no one left . . . who could write the polished and witty conversation pieces which English audiences had grown to admire." The words of his character Mr. Gillie provide an apt comment on his work: "If I've done nothing else in my life, at least I've unsettled one or two people."

PRINCIPAL PUBLISHED WORKS: *Plays*—The Switchback, [with] The Pardoner's Tale, The Sunlight Sonata, 1930; The Anatomist [with] Tobias and the Angel, The Amazed Evangelist, 1931; Jonah and the Whale, 1932; Colonel Wotherspoon [with] What It Is to Be Young, The Dancing Bear, The Girl Who Did Not Want To Go To Kuala Lumpur, 1934; A Sleeping Clergyman and Other Plays (*including revised editions of* The Anatomist, etc.), 1934; The Black Eye, 1935; Moral Plays (*including revised editions of* Marriage Is No Joke, etc.), 1936; The King of Nowhere [with] Babes in the Wood, The Last Trump, 1938; Susannah and the Elders [with] The Golden Legend of Shults, The Kitchen Comedy, What Say They?, 1940; Plays for Plain People (Mr. Bolfry, Lancelot, Holy Isle, Jonah 3, The Sign of the Prophet Jonah, The Dragon and the Dove), 1944; Daphne Laureola, 1949; John Knox [with] Dr. Angelus, It Depends What You Mean, The Forrigan Reel, 1949; Mr. Gillie, 1950; The Queen's Comedy, 1950; The Baikie Charivari, 1953; Meeting at Night, 1956. *Other Works*—Some Talk of Alexander (autobiography), 1926; Mr. Bridie's Alphabet for Little Glasgow Highbrows, 1934; One Way of Living (autobiography), 1939; The British Drama, 1945.

ABOUT: Bannister, W. James Bridie and His Theatre, 1955; Linklater, E. The Art of Adventure, 1947; Luyben, H. L. James Bridie: Clown and Philosopher, 1965; Priestley, J. B. *introduction to* Bridie's Meeting at Night, 1956; Weales, G. Religion in Modern English Drama, 1961; Williamson, A. Theatre of Two Decades, 1951; Wittig, K. The Scottish Tradition in Literature, 1958; Worsley, T. C. The Fugitive Art, 1952. *Periodicals*—British Medical Journal February 10, 1951; Drama Autumn 1952; Listener September 27, 1956; New Statesman December 31, 1955; Newsweek February 12, 1951; Scotland's Magazine September 1958; Scots Magazine March 1951; August 1951; Spectator February 2, 1951; Theatre Arts July 1950; November 1951; Time February 12, 1951.

BROAD, C(HARLIE) D(UNBAR) (December 30, 1887–March 11, 1971), English philosopher, was born at Harlesden, in Middlesex, the only child of Charles Stephen Broad, a vintner, and the former Emily Gomme. Family attachments were strong, and Broad was raised in a tight-knit circle of uncles and aunts whose idiosyncrasies are delightfully described in his introduction to the volume devoted to him in the Library of Living Philosophers. In 1894 his father moved to Sydenham and Broad attended a preparatory school there, later going to Bexhill as a boarder. At thirteen he transferred to Dulwich College, where he specialized in science subjects. He entered Trinity College, Cambridge, in 1906.

Broad at first read Natural Sciences but switched to the Moral Science Tripos. He held the Arnold Gerstenberg studentship in philosophy, won the Burney Prize, and graduated with first class honors with special distinction in 1910. The following year his college elected him to a fellowship, but by then he had already accepted a post as assistant to the professor of logic at St. Andrews University in Scotland. He saved his Trinity College fellowship dividends and, as he put it, so started "that course of saving and investment which has been one of my main sources of interest and satisfaction in life. All my experience had impressed on me the importance of having private means." From St. Andrews, Broad went to a lectureship at University College, Dundee, and in 1920 he was called to the chair of philosophy at Bristol University. Two years later he returned to Trinity College as fellow and lecturer in Moral Science. He remained at Cambridge, becoming the university's Knightbridge Professor of Moral Philosophy in 1933. Broad was a visiting lecturer or professor at Trinity College, Dublin (1929), at the University of Michigan (1953–1954), at the University of California at Los Angeles (1954), and at Columbia (1960).

Broad described his role as a philosopher in these terms: "If I have any kind of philosophical merit, it is neither the constructive fertility of an Alexander, nor the penetrating critical acumen of a Moore; still less is it that extraordinary combination of both with technical mathematical skill which characterises Whitehead and Russell. I can at most claim the humbler (yet useful) power of stating things clearly and not too superficially." This very characteristic statement, excessively modest in its terms, is nevertheless fundamentally true.

His first book was a revision of his fellowship thesis, *Perception, Physics and Reality*. It is an inquiry into the information that physical science can supply about the reality of objects which perception presents to us. In its method it is largely analytic, based on what Broad had learned from G. E. Moore and Bertrand Russell. Russell himself commended the work for appraising "with extraordinary justice and impartiality and discrimination, the arguments which have been advanced by others on the topics with which it deals." *Scientific Thought* followed, showing how traditional concepts in mathematics and physics have to be modified in the light of fresh discoveries, and concluding that all scientific concepts are ultimately dependent on sensory experience. This notion—that things like colors and sounds are immediately apprehensible through the senses—was a major preoccupation in the philosophy of the period, and it was in this field that Broad made his most distinctive contribution.

Broad's analytic approach was employed to excellent effect in *The Mind and Its Place in Nature*. It enumerates seventeen theories on the relation between mind and matter, demolishing many of them but attaching most weight to a theory of "emergent materialism." The book caused a considerable stir by taking seriously the evidence of psychical re-

C. D. BROAD

search for human survival after death. Broad, whose interest in psychic phenomena began in childhood, joined the Society for Psychical Research in 1920 and was its president in 1935–1936 and 1959–1960. He visited a number of mediums and was inclined to explain their powers in terms of telepathy. He gave an interesting discussion of this and related themes in the essays collected in *Religion, Philosophy and Psychical Research*, advocating serious consideration of the possibility that each person's experience sets up modifications in the substratum which can in some way affect the subsequent experience of others. His principal book on the subject, *Lectures on Psychical Research*, was enthusiastically received. As one critic wrote: "Its admirable clarity of thought, its detailed precision of treatment, and its exact and impartial examination of all that is meant, involved and implied by psychical research could hardly be bettered."

Broad also wrote two books on ethics and a three-volume study of J. M. E. McTaggart, his former teacher at Cambridge. It gives a clear and closely reasoned exposition of McTaggart's work, much of which is extremely complicated, and also elucidates Broad's own position, containing in his own opinion "about the best work of which I am capable in philosophy."

By 1953, when Broad relinquished his Knightbridge professorship, the work of such philosophers as Austin had reduced the question of sense-perception to one of merely historical interest. Broad retired, he said, with "great positive pleasure. No longer need I occupy the ambiguous position of an unbelieving Pope, or the invidious one of the veteran who lags superfluous on the stage." He remained a Fellow of Trinity and, being unmarried, lived in college. Since, as he said, "the kind of philosophy which I have practised has become antiquated without having acquired the interest of a collector's piece," his reputation must rest for the present on his acute and pellucid analytical assessments of the work of others. Broad was president of the Aristotelian Society in 1927–1928 and again in 1954–1955. He was a Fellow of the British Academy and of the American Academy of Arts and Sciences and held several honorary degrees and fellowships.

PRINCIPAL WORKS: Perception, Physics and Reality, 1914; Scientific Thought, 1923; The Mind and Its Place in Nature, 1925; Five Types of Ethical Theory, 1930; Examination of McTaggart's Philosophy (3 vols.), 1933–1938; Ethics and the History of Philosophy (essays), 1952; Religion, Philosophy and Psychical Research (essays), 1953; Lectures on Psychical Research, 1962; Broad's Critical Essays on Moral Philosophy (ed. by David Cheney), 1972.

ABOUT: Lean, M. Sense Perception and Matter: A Critical Analysis of C. D. Broad's Theory of Perception, 1954; Muirhead, J. H. (ed.) Contemporary British Philosophy, 1924; Passmore, J. A. A Hundred Years of Philosophy, 1966; Ratner, S. (ed.) Vision and Action, 1953; Schilpp, P. A. (ed.) The Philosophy of C. D. Broad (The Library of Living Philosophers), 1960; Who's Who, 1970. *Periodicals*—International Journal of Ethics October 1923; Mind October 1925; April 1934; January 1938; April 1939; October 1939; Monist January 1935; Philosophical Review November 1941; Philosophy of Science April 1943; Times (London) March 15, 1971.

*BRODSKY, JOSEPH ALEXANDROVICH

(May 24, 1940–), Russian poet of Jewish origin, was born in Leningrad, the son of a commercial photographer. He left school at fifteen but studied languages at home, especially Polish and English, and acquired a wide knowledge of Russian as well as foreign literature. He did some work as a translator but was unable to find regular literary employment because he was a sensitive young man who attended a psychiatric clinic and had a reputation as a "hysterical youth" (*isterichnyi paren*). Brodsky was kept under surveillance because of a brief adolescent involvement with an "anarcho-individualist" circle in Leningrad. His poems appeared mainly in the underground magazine *Sintaksis* (Syntax), one of several publications produced by SMOG, a circle of young writers and artists who were later attacked as "a bunch of loafers."

On November 29, 1963, Brodsky was attacked in a Leningrad newspaper as "a semiliterary parasite," who corrupted young people with his "pornographic and anti-Soviet poetry," while refusing to work and living off the labors of others. On February 18, 1964, a Leningrad court heard charges against him of *tuneyadstvo* (parasitism and idleness), One of the main prosecution witnesses was "a worker, an ordinary member of society" whose son, because of Brodsky's evil influence, refused to work; Brodsky was not merely a parasite but a "militant" one.

Defense witnesses, mostly professional writers and translators, praised his talent both as a translator and as a poet in embryo, and stressed the enormous amount of solid work needed to produce his translations alone. But the judge, a woman, wanted to know who gave Brodsky the authority to call himself a poet, how he had qualified himself for such a career. Brodsky did nothing to help his case when he asked ironically who had given him "the authority to enter the human race." He went on to say that he didn't think poetry was a matter of learning and, when pressed, said in confusion that he thought it was "a gift from God." Brodsky, it was clear to the court, was not a poet; instead of fulfilling the duties of a Soviet citizen he "[had] refused to work and [had] continued writing his decadent poems and reciting them at private evening parties."

Brodsky was condemned to five years of forced labor on a state farm near Archangel, in the extreme north of Russia, where he worked as a carrier of manure. But, unlike the court, Shostakovich, Akhmatova, Chukovsky, Marshak, and other prominent cultural figures thought he *was* a poet. After eighteen months, thanks to their efforts, he was pardoned and set free, and obtained a job in a Moscow publishing house. In June 1972 it was reported that Brodsky had in effect been exiled from the Soviet Union. It was said that he intended to settle in the United States, where he would become poet in residence at the University of Michigan in Ann Arbor. Brodsky appealed to Leonid Brezhnev, the Communist party leader, for the right to return eventually to the USSR: "I belong to Russian culture," he wrote, "I feel a part of it."

The Russian texts of Brodsky's early poems, and a few written in 1964 after the trial, were published in the United States in 1965, and selections translated into English by Nicholas Bethell appeared in 1967. The *Selected Poems* published in 1973 in translations by George L. Kline include a number of more recent poems. The accusation of pornography was clearly completely unfounded, and his poems are antisocial only in the negative sense, common to many young artists in both Russia and the West, that their concerns are not those of the masses or of organized society. "I am not a rebel," Brodsky says, "I am a poet. And I do not write political poems."

In fact Brodsky's published work shows him as a lyric poet, rather wryly preoccupied with his own sense of loneliness, nostalgia, and isolation—a critic in the *Times Literary Supplement* found his early verse "depressed, sometimes confused, sometimes

* brôt′ ski

martyr-conscious, sometimes élitist in its views." His work has from the beginning exhibited a surprising interest in religious themes and a frequent use of Christian imagery, and this tendency has developed in his more recent verse: W. H. Auden commended his "extraordinary capacity to envision material objects as sacramental signs, messengers from the unseen." His technical control and inventiveness are exceptional, and he has a remarkable talent for evoking atmosphere and a sense of place. This may be seen in "Elegy for John Donne" (1963), a somber and powerful long poem which is his best-known work. It begins with a vivid evocation of Donne uneasily asleep on a snowy London night with the whole world sleeping round him, and develops into a long meditation on death, the soul, and unfulfilled human longing.

Brodsky's preoccupation with human suffering and with the possibility of salvation are even more evident in another long poem, "Gorbunov and Gorchakov" (1967), a version of the Christ/Judas theme, set in a mental hospital. George L. Kline has drawn attention to a passage in Canto V of this poem in which the Russian verb *skazal* ("he said"), inflected like a noun, "becomes almost a thing." Kline believes that "for Brodsky, as for Rilke and Eliot, poetic language has the same degree of 'reality' as the world: words regularly interact with things. In 'Isaac and Abraham' (1963) the transformation, in Isaac's dream, of the word *kust* ('bush') into the word *krest* ('cross'), which takes place painfully, letter by letter, symbolizes the transformation of a part of nature into the altar on which Isaac is to be sacrificed." If, as Brodsky writes in "Gorbunov and Gorchakov," "life is but talk hurled in the face of silence," his own poetic diction is of a caliber to give silence pause.

Brodsky is tall and well built, with reddish hair, and sharp gray-green eyes. He has given some visitors an impression of youthful arrogance, especially when he expresses his generally contemptuous opinions of other contemporary Russian writers. He himself seems most influenced by the Bible, and by Blok, Mandelstam, and his patroness Akhmatova. Among American poets he most admires Robert Frost and Edwin Arlington Robinson, John Berryman, and Robert Lowell. Because of his persecution by the Soviet authorities, his work has probably been rather overestimated, but many critics believe that he "is destined to become one of Russia's true poets."

PRINCIPAL WORKS IN ENGLISH TRANSLATION: Elegy to John Donne (selected poems), 1967; Selected Poems, 1973. *Poems in* Bosley, K. (ed.) Russia's Other Poets, 1968; Carlisle, O. Poets on Street Corners, 1969; New Leader May 10, 1965.

ABOUT: Carlisle, O. Poets on Street Corners, 1969. *Periodicals*—Encounter September 1964; New York Review of Books April 5, 1973; New York Times Magazine August 20, 1967; New Yorker September 11, 1965; Times Literary Supplement July 20, 1967.

JOSEPH ALEXANDROVICH BRODSKY

***BRONOWSKI, JACOB** (January 18, 1908–), English philosopher, scientist, scholar, and dramatist, writes: "I was born in Poland, but when I was three years old my family moved to Germany, and when I was twelve we came to England. Before I put pen to paper, then, I had changed my mother tongue twice. At the time the changes distressed me, of course, but now I think that they helped to form me. I fell in love with the clear depth, the concise richness of the English language. I became interested in the philosophic relation between experience, thought and language. And I grew up to be indifferent to the distinction between literature and science, which in my teens were simply two languages for experience that I learned together.

"So when I went to Cambridge in 1927 as a mathematical scholar, I did not feel it out of character to help to found and edit a literary magazine—which characteristically we called *Experiment.* All intellectual life was exhilarating and on the move in the six years that I spent there. Quantum physics was transformed by Dirac and others; Cockcroft split the atom, and Chadwick discovered the neutron. At the same time, literature and painting were made over by the shock of surrealism; and the film (and later the radio) grew to an art. I duly became a Wrangler in mathematics at Cambridge, but when the University Press published my first book, it was called *The Poet's Defence.*

"I wrote another book about literature during the war, because I discovered (and was fascinated

* bro nof′ skē

JACOB BRONOWSKI

by) the deep base of realism under the mystic poems of William Blake. But naturally (if that is the right word) my official business as a scientist in war time was with the work of destruction. This is how I came to be sent by the Chiefs of Staff to Japan at the end of the war, to assess how well we had done our dreadful work. I wrote the report on *The Effects of the Atomic Bombs at Hiroshima and Nagasaki*, and broadcast my summary of it on the night of the test at Bikini in 1946, when ten million listeners straining their ears could hear nothing but me. Thus I discovered by chance that what I had to say was as clear and as urgent to intelligent people who were not scientists as it was to my colleagues.

"From that time my ambition has been to create a philosophy for the twentieth century which shall be all of one piece. One part of that is to teach people to command science—to have command of the basic ideas of modern science, so that they can take command of its use. I think that readers are drawn to my exposition because I show not the wonders but the concepts of science, and they turn out to be wonderful. For me science is an expression of the human mind, which seeks for unity under the chaos of nature as the writer seeks for it in the variety of human nature.

"There cannot be a philosophy, there cannot even be a decent science, without humanity. I have never forgotten the ruins of Nagasaki—nor that they would have been the ruins of the holy city of Kyoto if someone had not overruled the military men who planned the bombing. This is why I also write about human motives, for example in *The Face of Violence*. It is also why I left my work first in mathematics and then in industrial technology, and now work in an Institute for Biological Studies.

"When I look at my life, I count myself lucky to have had access to more varied forms of knowledge than most men. I was lucky to learn English after other languages. I was lucky to be at Cambridge during the revolution in physics about 1930. Now I count myself lucky again to be present at the new revolution in biology. Here, if anywhere, lies the hope that our discoveries in nature will guide us also into the special character of living things, and so of man. I see now that the problem of man's status between the world and himself has haunted me since the difficult days of my boyhood. All that I have written, though it has seemed to me so different from year to year, turns to the same centre: the uniqueness of man that grows out of his struggle (and his gift) to understand both nature and himself."

Jacob Bronowski is "not one man but a multitude," wrote Laurence Thompson. Originally, Bronowski was a mathematician; his own research has been in algebraic geometry and he began his career in 1934 as senior lecturer in mathematics at University College, Hull. In 1942 he left Hull to join J. D. Bernal's team at the Ministry of Home Security, supervising studies in the physical and economic effects of bombing and making, in passing as it were, a reputation as a pioneer in the development of operational research method. His "brilliantly illuminating" and influential book on William Blake belongs to this period, breaking important new ground by placing the poet in his political context and thus for the first time making sense of his "prophetic" works. This short, packed, and highly original piece of scholarship is at the same time so lucidly written that it remains "the best introduction to Blake for the general reader."

In 1945, as scientific deputy to the British chiefs of staff, Bronowski saw what science had done to Hiroshima and Nagasaki, an experience which as he says determined his subsequent intellectual direction. His career has continued to be as various as ever. During the years 1946–1950 he was a scientific adviser to the Ministry of Works, applying himself to statistical research into the economics of building and of other industries and taking a brief leave of absence (1948) to head the projects division of UNESCO. For the next fourteen years, apart from a year (1953) as Carnegie Visiting Professor at the Massachusetts Institute of Technology, he was with the National Coal Board, first leading the search for an economic smokeless fuel, then bringing this to the production stage. In 1964 he went to the Salk Institute for Biological Studies in California as senior fellow, trustee, and director of the Council for Biology in Human Affairs.

Bronowski has written four radio plays of which

one, *The Face of Violence*, won the 1951 Italia Prize as the best radio drama broadcast in Europe in 1950. He is also without question "one of the most effective popularizers of science in English." In his search for "a philosophy for the twentieth century which shall be all of one piece," Bronowski introduced the "two cultures" debate (later associated with Lord Snow) as early as 1953. He has developed the theme in most of his subsequent books, notably in *Science and Human Values*, which argues that creativity, whether in science or the arts, springs from the same source. The book was called a "credo for a new liberalism, a new humanism," and Snow said of it: "If I were trying to select six works in order to explain to an intelligent non-scientist something of the deepest meaning of science, Bronowski's would be one of them." *The Identity of Man* collects lectures (delivered in 1965 at the American Museum of Natural History in New York) of which the central theme, in his own words, was "the crisis of confidence which springs from each man's wish to be a person, in the face of the nagging fear that he is a mechanism." Among Bronowski's many other writings are numerous papers on mathematics—and an opera libretto. *The Ascent of Man*, an important television series written and presented by Bronowski under the joint auspices of the British Broadcasting Corporation and Time Inc., is an account of man's struggle to gain control over his environment. It was first broadcast in 1973 and appeared the same year in book form.

Bronowski's father Abram was a "staunchly orthodox" man; his mother, Celia, was an "ardent Leftist." He himself has been married since 1941 to the sculptor Rita Coblentz (known professionally as Rita Colin). They have four daughters. Bronowski is "a short nut-colored man" with extremely broad shoulders. He has wiry black hair and wears horn-rimmed spectacles. His eyes are brown, variously described as "twinkling," "penetrating," and "piercing" (but in any case remarkable). He speaks deliberately, in a deep baritone. Bronowski was a popular member of the British television panel "The Brains Trust" but resigned when he felt that the program had deteriorated into an "entertainment." In 1957–1958 he served as president of the Library Association in Britain, and believes that "the printed word and the public library remain for others, as they were for me . . . the most powerful means for self-education." In that connection he tells the story of how, as a boy of twelve, knowing little English, he asked a librarian for a book he could read with pleasure and from which he could learn good English. He was given *Masterman Ready*, and has "thought it a perfect choice ever since." Bronowski's recreations are chess and squash racquets; his greatest delight, according to the *New Scientist*, "lies in sharing his thoughts."

PRINCIPAL WORKS: The Poet's Defence, 1939; Spain 1939: Four Poems, 1939; William Blake, 1757–1827: A Man Without a Mask, 1943 (*revised as* William Blake and the Age of Revolution, 1965); The Common Sense of Science, 1951; The Face of Violence (play), 1954; The Dilemma of the Scientist, 1955; Science and Human Values, 1956 (revised with a new dialogue, 1965); (with Bruce Mazlish) The Western Intellectual Tradition: From Leonardo to Hegel, 1960; Insight, 1964; The Identity of Man, 1965; The Ascent of Man, 1973.

ABOUT: Contemporary Writers 2, 1963; Current Biography, 1958; Thompson, L. Portrait of England, 1952; Who's Who, 1971; Who's Who in World Jewry, 1965. *Periodicals*—Library Association Record March 1957; October 1957; Nature April 22, 1950; New Scientist November 23, 1961; New York Times March 13, 1965; New Yorker April 3, 1965; Scientific American February 1963; Yorkshire Post March 28, 1956.

BROOKE-ROSE, CHRISTINE (1926–), English critic and novelist, writes: "I was born in Geneva. My mother was herself half Swiss, half American, and married an Englishman, but separated from him early in my childhood, so that we went to live with my grandparents in Brussels, where I was brought up. I was bilingual, but French was my first language. After my father's death I was sent to an English school and remained in England throughout the war, after which I went to Oxford. There I read English Philology, specializing in mediaeval literature, and then worked for four years on a thesis for a Ph.D. at London University. This was a grammatical analysis of metaphor in Old French and Middle English poetry, comparing methods of expression in both at a time when French had considerably influenced the development of English.

"While still at Oxford I married Jerzy Peterkiewicz, a Polish poet, then a Ph.D. student at London University, and later Lecturer, now Reader, in Polish literature at the School of Slavonic Studies there. During these early years we were very poor. In 1953 my husband, having, like Rimbaud, given up poetry, started (unlike Rimbaud) writing novels, but in English.

"I had always wanted to be a writer. But I was a slow developer. I think that bilingual children often are. During my teens, when girls who want to write are scribbling diaries and reading voraciously, I felt neither in one language nor in another. Certainly my later urge to study both thoroughly was due to this feeling of uncertainty, and although I never pursued Pure Philology or Pure Linguistics professionally, I have never regretted this grounding and have remained deeply interested in language. Nor do I regret my French upbringing, which has given me a constant, and often devilish hunger for Gallic precision in style.

"When I finished my thesis, in 1954, a publisher from Secker & Warburg, whom I met by chance, got interested, and commissioned me to write a

CHRISTINE BROOKE-ROSE

similar book for them, that is, a study of metaphor using the same grammatical analysis, but not a comparative study, and not on mediaeval texts. The result, published in 1958, was *A Grammar of Metaphor*, which analyses the metaphoric language of fifteen selected poets from Chaucer to Dylan Thomas.

"By then, however, I had regained linguistic confidence. In 1956 my husband fell very ill, and nearly died, and the worry of it caused me to drop my serious work and to write—with incredible speed—my first novel (*The Languages of Love*), a light-hearted satire about philologists. To my astonishment my publishers took it, and it appeared in 1957. I also started reviewing, to earn extra money, chiefly in the *Times Literary Supplement*, but gradually elsewhere as well.

"From then on I wrote three more novels in fairly quick succession (*The Sycamore Tree*, 1958; *The Dear Deceit*, 1960; *The Middlemen*, 1961). But I was somehow dissatisfied with them. Wit and satire seemed to me too easy, not just technically but morally. Humour has always been an important ingredient in my writing, but real humour does not consist of laughing at people, even at oneself; rather with people, with oneself.

"Self-criticism which makes one suffer can be a neurosis, but it can also arise quite honestly out of critical faculties, and these I was developing rapidly. I had been reviewing a great many novels, which left me as unsatisfied as my own. The only novels I could whole-heartedly admire were those of Jerzy Peterkiewicz, and—laying aside possible bias—for obvious reasons I did not want to imitate him, indeed could not, for our talents are very different.

"The crisis came in 1962, when I fell desperately ill for two years—oddly enough in France, where I first remained for six months. It was like a return to my essential self. Already before this I had, as a critic, become extremely interested in the experiments of certain French novelists, especially Nathalie Sarraute and Alain Robbe-Grillet, both of whose critical essays on the problems of the novel were a revelation to me, although their individual solutions were not, in any direct way, to be mine. Also influential was Samuel Beckett, as a novelist rather than as a playwright—much though I admired his plays. *Watt*, an early novel, about which I had written in the *London Magazine*, was a turning-point for me. The almost mathematical precision of language, the humorous play with all possible permutations of the simplest situation, as if each had its own philosophical existence, the mock-'scientific' but also in some essential way truly scientific attitude behind the poetry, all these delighted me, and seemed to me the only possible way of dealing with both inner and outer reality in this age of the uncertainty principle in physics, an age of undermined causality, an age in which subjective and objective have almost merged through the strange colloidal chemistry of psychic and physical energy.

"At any rate, during my long illness, I found that I couldn't read novels, good or bad, about love-affairs, class-distinctions and one-upmanships, or portraits of society on any scale from parochial to professional: the sort of novel, in fact, that I had been writing. I devoured scientific books, which bred their own curious poetry: 'Each molecule can expect five thousand million collisions per second.' 'Weight consists of the attraction between two bodies.' 'In this kind of communication the echo decreases with the fourth power of the distance, rather than with the square.' Such phrases, of precise significance to the scientist, fired my imagination as poetic metaphors for what happens between people, and people are and always will be the stuff of the novel.

"I started to write *Out*, still very ill, achieving at first no more than a few sentences a day. It was finished in 1963. My publishers turned it down. They couldn't understand it. But Michael Joseph took it and it appeared in 1964. I had at last found what I wanted to do, even if it took me four novels to learn; one has to learn one's craft, learn to draw before one can do abstracts. I was immensely excited by the challenge. Since then I have written *Such* (1966), and have three more in my head."

Christine Brooke-Rose, described by those who know her as beautiful, modest, and entertaining, began as a poet. *Gold* (1955), a long and abstruse poem in an idiom half archaic and half modernistic, was followed by a number of poems in magazines which have never been collected. The difficulties inherent in *Gold* foreshadow those found by a number of readers in her second and more important group of novels, (*Out, Such, Between*). The main one of these difficulties is that Miss Brooke-Rose is to some extent the prisoner of her formidable intellect. Again, her scientific approach—which denies, as one critic has put it, "the comfort of a 'hidden heart' to things"—and her devotion to "the new" have perhaps tended to inhibit as much as to animate her very considerable creative powers. Because of her cleverness, as genuine and as substantial as that of any writer of her generation, critical reaction to her work has been overcautious and even intimidated—not at all an effect she has ever intended to create.

Her first nonfiction work, *A Grammar of Metaphor* (1958), is a brilliant book but forbiddingly dry in its presentation; however, despite Miss Brooke-Rose's failure to humanize her highly revealing analyses of various poets' use of metaphor, it has been reprinted in paperback and now seems likely to stay in print.

Her first four novels are relatively lighthearted affairs. *The Sycamore Tree* (1958), her second novel, concerns two couples who live in the anxiously fashionable world of Chelsea. One critic wrote that she "plays the expected variations on the theme of their relationships with a light and original touch," but added that when she tried to add psychological depth to her novel "Miss Brooke-Rose [seemed] only to have succeeded in getting her characters thoroughly bogged down." Her best novel of this period, and the most ambitious one, is *The Dear Deceit* (1960). This is almost certainly nearer to the French *nouveau roman* than anything in English before it: it is told (effortlessly, and with point) in reverse, and its purpose is antirealistic in the old-fashioned sense in which realism is regarded as "keeping to ordinary appearances." It searches for the truth about a character called Alfred Northbrook Hayley, the description of whose adventures might be called picaresque were it not for the lumber of seemingly recondite and irrelevant detail with which Miss Brooke-Rose accompanies her more straightforwardly zestful account.

Out (1964), the first of her novels in a markedly new manner, comes even nearer to the *nouveau roman*, chiefly in its employment of an underlying science fiction concept. No English writer has so thoroughly absorbed the spirit (if not the exact letter) of the critical messages of Alain Robbe-Grillet and Nathalie Sarraute. The *Times Literary Supplement*, while suggesting that it was "very hard to be certain if one has grasped the point," acknowledged that "Miss Brooke-Rose's intelligence is shiningly visible from beginning to end . . . and, on the evidence . . . a whole range of new matter is within her grasp." In *Out* it is the nameless hero who is "out": he is a "Colorless" in a world unobtrusively but masterfully ruled by "Coloreds" (the distinction in this world of the future arose originally from the differing reaction of two groups to radiation). Despite its remarkable science fiction component, *Out* is perhaps most distinguished for its savage and yet sensitive parody of racial discrimination as it exists today.

Such (1966) begins with the awakening into consciousness of a three-day dead physicist-psychiatrist called Lazarus; the description of his mental processes as he struggles towards reality, while not easy to read, is a *tour de force*. In the latter half the author inventively struggles with fundamental problems of existence, again using a brilliantly ingenious science-fiction framework. For this novel Miss Brooke-Rose was joint winner (with Aidan Higgins) of the James Tait Black Memorial Prize.

Between (1968) is concerned with linguistics: a woman's whole life—her career (she is an interpreter), her marriage, her divorce—is seen in terms of language. The words she calls upon define her experience and are themselves "heavy with associations, challenges, temptations." Life is comically and subtly tested for the adequacy with which it fulfills the infinite possibilities of language.

Miss Brooke-Rose was educated at the Cours d'Éducation, Brussels, and at St. Stephens' College, Folkestone. Before going to Somerville College, Oxford, she worked as an intelligence officer with the British Women's Auxiliary Air Force. In 1968–1969, she taught at the experimental university at Vincennes in France, and during this period, made her translation of Alain Robbe-Grillet's novel *Dans Le Labyrinthe* (*In the Labyrinth*), which won the Arts Council prize for translation. Since 1969 she has been a lecturer in English at the University of Paris.

PRINCIPAL WORKS: *Fiction*—The Languages of Love, 1957; The Sycamore Tree, 1958; The Dear Deceit, 1960; The Middlemen, 1961; Out, 1964; Such, 1966; Between, 1968; Go When You See the Green Man Walking (short stories) 1970. *Poetry*—Gold, 1955. *Nonfiction*—A Grammar of Metaphor, 1958; A ZBC of Ezra Pound, 1972.

ABOUT: Who's Who, 1971. *Periodicals*—Guardian November 7, 1964; New Comment November 2, 1964; Scotsman April 17, 1965; Times Literary Supplement September 30, 1965; October 20, 1966; October 31, 1968.

BROPHY, (ANTONIA) BRIGID (June 12, 1929–), Anglo-Irish novelist, dramatist, and critic, writes: "I began writing two or three years after I was born—which latter happened on 12 June, 1929 and, though I am mainly Irish, in London (where, with only enforced interruptions, I have lived ever since). At eight I was an experienced playwright and producer. But though I was a precocious I was

BRIGID BROPHY

by no means a prodigious child, my youthful works being remarkable for my age but not at all in themselves—which remained true of the first book I published, a volume of stories written when I was twenty-two.

"My basic education consisted of the elements of the craft of prose, which I picked up from my father, the novelist John Brophy, and the principles of English and Latin syntax, which I learned painlessly (i.e. before I was old enough to know I was learning) from my mother, Charis (*née* Grundy), a teacher by both profession and inspiration. My idyllic childhood was disrupted in 1939 by the war, thanks to whose exigencies I was shifted from school to school. This, if it did little to educate me directly, at least gave me an unrivalled view of the varieties of educational practice. I have been on the receiving end of a dozen separate educational establishments, including a secretarial college and an art school in which, since I was irremediably ahead of schedule, I filled in a few years before I won a scholarship in Classics to Oxford. There I acted on the belief that I had more to learn by pursuing my personal life than from textual emendation, with the result that the authorities could put up with me for only just over a year; I came down at nineteen without a degree and with a consequent sense of nudity which I have never quite overcome, and earned my living as a shorthand-typist.

"In my twenty-fifth year, I sat down to write a narrative poem and rose a fortnight later (a fortnight of which I have no memory) having written instead a brief novel called *Hackenfeller's Ape*, which is probably the best I shall ever write and which already displays at its most intense the violently romantic feeling in a precisely classical form to which most of my fiction aspires. (Critics sometimes disparage my type of novels as 'artificial,' which offends me not at all since art is by definition artificial.) In 1954 I married (which turned out to be a matter of serene happiness) Michael Levey, art-historian and now Deputy Keeper at the National Gallery, London. Since 1957 we have had a daughter, Kate. The responsibility of becoming this person's mother obliged me to pause and define my own convictions, accounting to myself for how I could be both an artist and a rationalist, and both a Freudian and a Shavian Evolutionist. The result was a colossal work of non-fiction, *Black Ship to Hell*, in writing which I found that the classical learning which had eluded me at Oxford, where it was expected of me, came fluently to my fingers now that I wanted it for its own sake and that in making a psychoanalytical exploration of the Death Instinct I was also, between the lines, psychoanalysing myself. This book led to my being invited (by its assistant editor, Charles Osborne) to contribute to the *London Magazine* and by that route I entered journalism, becoming a critic and a propagandist of libertarianism (including liberty for animals) in the papers (most regularly the *Sunday Times* and the *New Statesman*) and from time to time on television. I continued to write nonfiction (my study of Mozart's operas is detested by music critics but, happily for me, liked by composers) and novels; the latter include *Flesh*, an almost distressingly cold-blooded little story which reads better in the French translation than in English (and which in paperback was the first of my books to have a numerical as distinct from a highbrow success), *The Finishing Touch*, an entirely pleasant lesbian fantasia much of which *is* in French, and *The Snow Ball*, whose heroine is in love with death and which attempts to transcribe in literature the erotic perspectives and the chilling effects of a baroque tomb. I have just prepared a collection and selection of my criticism, to be published under the title *Don't Never Forget*, and am now [1965] contemplating taking up again my original vocation of dramatist."

Miss Brophy was educated mainly at St. Paul's Girls' School, and her abortive time at Oxford was spent at St. Hugh's College, to which she had previously won the Jubilee Scholarship in Classics.

Her first book, a collection of short stories, *The Crown Princess* (1953), is prentice work; but *Hackenfeller's Ape* is that rare thing, a perfectly executed piece of fantasy. It tells the story of Percy, a laboratory ape who becomes passionately attached to a human being and, to his mate's distress, acquires a set of human inhibitions. It is Miss Brophy's most successful piece of fiction perhaps because in it she has kept her creative purpose absolutely separate from her not always unaggressive intellectual predilections. The book received the Cheltenham Festival's first prize for a first novel in 1954.

The King of a Rainy Country was, like many successors to brilliant first novels, a comparative failure; but *Flesh*, "a powerful piece of sophistication" (as one critic called it), attracted much praise for its satirical sharpness and acute observation. It is about the transformation, by a knowing girl, of a thin and self-effacing man into a chubby lover of food and sex, and paints a "brilliant portrait of bourgeois Jewish life."

The Finishing Touch is less elegant and assured but *The Snow Ball*, which was thought too carefully contrived, "too cold and hard to be entirely sympathetic," is not so easily dismissed. It is a seriocomic novella designed to exploit the author's views on the death instinct (and her delight in the operas of Mozart). The setting is a masked ball in twentieth century London, and this scene is so skillfully evoked, the heroine's vanity is depicted with such Swiftian savagery, that the reader is left in no doubt of the author's potentialities as a mature novelist. *In Transit* is narrated by a person who is certain of nothing, even his/her sex, and who, waiting in the transit lounge of an anonymous airport, participates in or observes a series of charades representing familiar contemporary dilemmas in a variety of pastiche art and journalistic forms. The language moreover is disrupted by puns, jokes, rhymes, and other devices, which are themselves discussed and often ridiculed by the author. It had a mixed reception, some critics finding it full of interest and linguistic flair, others dismissing it as a depressing failure.

Miss Brophy's qualities—and faults—as a journalist may be assessed from the reviews and radio broadcasts collected in *Don't Never Forget*. Provocative when they are encountered week by week, her essays read badly in volume form: they seem to attack, too stridently, what had already been defeated sixty years before they appeared—Christian complacency, sexual prudery, male supremacy. And the debunking book Miss Brophy wrote with her husband and Charles Osborne, *Fifty Works of English and American Literature We Could Do Without*, was universally condemned. Most critics thought that some of the "classics" pilloried here deserved oblivion, but found nothing but "damp impertinence" and "creaking wit" in the attacks on such works as *Hamlet*, *Wuthering Heights*, and *Huckleberry Finn*.

As a psychoanalytic critic of Mozart (in *Mozart the Dramatist*), of things-in-general (in *Black Ship to Hell*), of Aubrey Beardsley (in *Black and White*), and of Ronald Firbank (in *Prancing Novelist*), Miss Brophy is less deliberately provocative. The chief criticism of her procedures in these books is that she shows little heed of post-Freudian developments, preferring to make her interpretations in too rigidly classical a manner. And she seems unable wholly to avoid the "hectoringly superior" tone that infuriates so many critics. Nevertheless her own insights are valuable and deserve more attention, perhaps, than they have received.

The Burglar, a Shavian play about a puritanical thief shocked by the sexual depravity of his social betters, ran at the Vaudeville Theatre in London for seven performances in 1967. It was published—with a long Shavian preface—in 1968.

Brigid Brophy received the *London Magazine* prize for prose in 1962. In herself she is unaffected, engagingly honest (she confessed on television that she picked her nose, a habit of which she does not approve), and passionately fond of animals (she is vice president of the National Anti-Vivisection Society of Great Britain). Of her talent there can be no question, and her admirers continue to expect from her a fictional performance that will be not merely clever, but masterly.

PRINCIPAL WORKS: *Fiction*—The Crown Princess (stories), 1953; Hackenfeller's Ape, 1953; The King of a Rainy Country, 1956; Flesh, 1962; The Finishing Touch, 1963 (published in the U.S. *with* The Snow Ball); The Snow Ball, 1964; In Transit, 1969. *Nonfiction*—Black Ship to Hell, 1962; Mozart the Dramatist, 1964; Don't Never Forget: Collected Views and Reviews, 1966; (with Michael Levey and Charles Osborne) Fifty Works of English and American Literature We Could Do Without, 1967; Black and White: a Portrait of Aubrey Beardsley, 1968; Prancing Novelist: A Defence of Fiction in the Form of a Critical Biography in Praise of Ronald Firbank, 1973. *Play*—The Burglar, 1968.

ABOUT: Brophy, B. *preface to* The Burglar, 1968; Contemporary Authors 7–8, 1963; Vinson, J. (ed.) Contemporary Novelists, 1972; Who's Who, 1972. *Periodicals*—Book Week April 16, 1967; New York Times Book Review May 21, 1967; Saturday Review June 12, 1954; Times Literary Supplement December 1, 1966.

BROWN, FREDRIC (October 29, 1906–March 11, 1972), American novelist, detective story and science fiction writer, was born in Cincinnati, Ohio, the son of Karl Lewis Brown and Emma Amelia (Graham) Brown. He attended public schools in Cincinnati and went on to Hanover College in Indiana. Brown began his career as a journalist, working for some time on the Milwaukee *Journal*, but became a full-time writer in the late 1940s.

His first novel, *The Fabulous Clipjoint*, introduced Ambrose and Ed Hunter, an uncle-and-nephew detective team based in Chicago that has enlivened many of Brown's books. The story attracted an unusual amount of interest and won the Edgar Allan Poe award of the Mystery Writers of America. Reviewers found it rather naïve, and faulty in its construction but "refreshingly unhackneyed" and "touching and convincing" in its

FREDRIC BROWN

manner, the work of a writer with "something of his own." Brown's next four books established him as a craftsman capable of great ingenuity in plotting, distinguished from his peers by an ability to mix his often very violent stories with wry humor.

The same qualities were welcomed in *What Mad Universe*, Brown's first full-length venture into the science fiction field. It was an inventive and extremely funny account of the adventures of an earth man knocked sideways in time into a different universe, a "skillful blend of fantasy and suspense novel." By the end of the 1940s, Brown was noted "in both detective stories and science-fantasy . . . for sharp melodrama and offbeat humor."

Brown retained his reputation and impressed some critics as a writer whose abilities were not confined to the production of able entertainments. *Here Comes a Candle* (1950) incorporated movie, radio, stage, and television scripts to study from a variety of angles the obsessive fears and eventual death of a small-time criminal. Most reviewers thought it an interesting though not entirely successful experiment, a psychological novel rather than a thriller; in one critic's opinion it was "a brilliantly written biography of frustration." H. H. Holmes, reviewing *Lights in the Sky Are Stars*, found it outstanding even in 1953—"the best year to date for serious and intelligent science fiction novels"—distinguished by "a warm blend of simplicity and sincerity." *The Office* (1958) was a novel of character, perhaps partly autobiographical, about life during the early 1920s in a Cincinnati office. The story, recalled thirty-five years later by the former office boy, was thought a little monotonous but "human and plain and believable."

Fredric Brown was married in 1948 to Elizabeth Charlier and had two children by a previous marriage. He lived in Tucson, Arizona.

PRINCIPAL WORKS: The Fabulous Clipjoint, 1947; Dead Ringer, 1948; Murder Can Be Fun, 1948; Screaming Mimi, 1949; What Mad Universe, 1949; Here Comes A Candle, 1950; Far Cry, 1951; We All Killed Grandma, 1952; Lights in the Sky Are Stars, 1953 (England, Project Jupiter); Mostly Murder (stories), 1953; Angels and Spaceships (stories), 1954; The Wench Is Dead, 1955; The Lenient Beast, 1956; Rogue in Space, 1957; The Office, 1958; Late Lamented, 1959; The Murderers, 1961; The Five-Day Nightmare, 1962; Mrs. Murphy's Underpants, 1963; Daymares, 1968.
ABOUT: Who's Who in America, 1970–1971.

BROWN, NORMAN O(LIVER) (September 25, 1913–), American philosopher and scholar, was born in El Oro, Mexico, while his father was working there as a mining engineer. He was educated partly in England, where he received his B.A. from Oxford University in 1936, and partly in the United States, at the universities of Chicago and Wisconsin. In 1942, when Wisconsin gave him his doctorate, he became professor of languages at Nebraska Wesleyan University, but a year later was drawn into war service as a research analyst with the Office of Strategic Services. In 1946 he joined the faculty of Wesleyan University, Connecticut, where he became an associate professor of classics. He is now Wilson Professor of Classics and Comparative Literature at the University of Rochester. Brown was married in 1938 to Elizabeth Potter and has four children.

Hermes the Thief (1947) was a highly technical study of the Hermes myth in Greece between the Homeric age and the fifth century B.C. It sought to correlate the evolution of the myth with the economic, social, and philosophical revolution which took place in Athens over the same period.

It was Brown's second book which brought him to the startled attention of the general reader. In 1953, aided by a Ford Foundation grant, he had begun a deep study of Freud, undertaken, he says, because he felt "the need to re-appraise the nature and destiny of man." The result was *Life Against Death: The Psychoanalytic Meaning of History*. It drew not only on Freudian and post-Freudian psychoanalytic theory, but also on literature, philosophy, sociology, theology, economics, linguistics, and anthropology. It is not this breadth of reference alone which makes it a difficult book. As Herbert Marcuse pointed out, Brown's argument is developed in short paragraphs and aphorisms which flow and are organized in a manner "more musical than conceptual," so that "in its best parts, this book is a poem and a song."

In *Life Against Death*, Brown has analyzed in Freudian terms not a man but mankind, and he has concluded that "everything is a metaphor." Man, divided from himself and from reality, acts out gigantic and terrible charades. His political parties "are conspiracies to usurp the power of the father." War is a sexual perversion. Sex itself is symbolic, an attempt to re-enact the sexual life of the father, a vicarious act. All that we think real and important, all the Apollonian assumptions of Western man, are murderous and enslaving lies. According to Marcuse, *Life Against Death*, moving "along the limits of communication," seeks to convey a "new non-repressive interpretation of the old repressive symbols." Brown believes that man needs a rebirth, a Dionysian transubstantiation, which will overcome by fusion "the distinction between inner self and the outside world, between subject and object."

"With humor, scholarship, and philosophic speculation," wrote Alan W. Watts, Brown "proposes the outrageous thesis that Freud's diagnosis be taken seriously, and that we actually face the practical possibility of doing without repression." Philip Toynbee called it "a difficult but very important book . . . a major contribution to man's study of himself." Lionel Trilling was equally impressed, and a reviewer in the *Times Literary Supplement* praised Brown's willingness "to follow a line of inquiry to its final conclusion, no matter how disturbing or even mad this may appear to the contemporary ethos." Other critics, it must be said, were unconvinced or irritated, called the book facile, rash, or biased, or found Brown's conclusions "muzzy."

Love's Body, which Brown called a "continuation of a voyage," is a "loosely organized series of jottings . . . sparked by readings in Freud, Marx, Durkheim, Whitehead, William Blake . . . and a couple of hundred others." Eliot Fremont-Smith, writing in the New York *Times*, said it was "an illustration or evocation of what Mr. Brown's earlier work has led him to, a radically unsettling view of utopia . . . an Eden, innocent and androgynous" in which all the barriers are down "between inside and outside . . . real and imaginary, physical and mental." To Fremont-Smith, Brown had "attempted in a most interesting and far-reaching way to force a coalition of Freud and Nietzsche, man and nature, intellect and instinct," and the result was "provocative, original, and richly imaginative." To other critics, like Brigid Brophy, Brown seems to propose only a reduction of man to his "lowest common denominator, the pre-rational, pre-realistic and pre-individual layer in everyone's unconscious."

Life Against Death, though apparently it sold slowly at first, has according to one source "led an increasingly vigorous underground existence," and according to another has had an incalculable influence, particularly in America. Fremont-Smith

NORMAN O. BROWN

calls Norman O. Brown an "astronomer of the psyche" and compares him to Marshall McLuhan in his "spine-tingling" originality of thought, and also in his "campus popularity among the intelligent, disaffected, with-it young"; both men, he goes on, are deeply influenced by oriental concepts, and both, ultimately, reject the practical and ethical values of logical systemization."

PRINCIPAL WORKS: Hermes the Thief: The Evolution of a Myth, 1947; Life Against Death: The Psychoanalytic Meaning of History, 1959; Love's Body, 1966; Closing Time, 1973.

ABOUT: Directory of American Scholars, 1964; Who's Who in America, 1970–1971. *Periodicals*—Commentary February 1967; March 1967; New York Times July 15, 1966.

BRUSTEIN, ROBERT (SANFORD) (April 21, 1927–), American critic, writes: "I was born in Brooklyn, New York, the second son of Max Brustein and the former Blanche Haft. My childhood was happy and uneventful, but my adolescence was troubled, and it was during these morose years that a discontented spirit developed—superimposed, as it were, on a nature basically peaceful and settled. I was educated in New York public schools, and having developed a passion for music, I went for two and a half years to the High School of Music and Art, leaving that institution for the Columbia Grammar School, from which I was graduated in 1943 at the age of sixteen. I went from there to Amherst College—a stay interrupted by World War II, and by my two-year stint at sea and at the Merchant Marine Academy (this discipline I hated intensely). Returning to Amherst, I was graduated from that placid New England college in

ROBERT BRUSTEIN

1948, Phi Beta Kappa and *magna cum laude.* My major had been medieval history but I was really attracted more by the stage; and after a few false starts in other graduate programs, I ended up at the Yale Drama School, majoring in directing.

"Yale was intensely disappointing because it was primarily concerned with preparing its students for the commercial theatre; and after one fruitless year at the place, I transferred to the graduate school of Columbia University, where I received an M.A. in 1950 and a Ph.D. in 1957—my work was done in dramatic literature. Throughout these years, I remained torn between the intellectual life and the theatre. I continued to act and direct during the summers with a classical stock company called Group 20, operating at Theatre on the Green in Wellesley, Massachusetts; but during the academic year, I pursued my studies. A Fulbright Fellowship brought me to the University of Nottingham in England in 1953–1955; and when I returned to the United States, my dissertation on the Stuart drama partially completed, I began to teach—first at Cornell, then at Vassar, and finally at Columbia where I have been ever since.

"I had been writing fiction and plays since late adolescence; I published two critical articles on non-theatrical subjects in the early fifties; but it was not until 1957 that I began to write in earnest, particularly on theatrical subjects, for such magazines as *Harper's*, *Commentary*, *Partisan Review*, *Encounter*, *Hudson Review*, and *Tulane Drama Review*. In 1959, I was invited to become the theatre critic of the *New Republic*, a post I have held ever since; the only other organ to which I contribute more than intermittently is the *New York Review of Books*, which publishes my articles on movies, books, and general cultural subjects. In 1961, I received a Guggenheim grant to begin work on a book, *The Theatre of Revolt*, which was published in 1964; in 1964 I received a Ford Foundation grant to visit American and European theatre companies. I received the George Jean Nathan award for the best dramatic criticism of 1962, and the George Polk Memorial award for Best Criticism of 1964. In 1965, I collected my theatre reviews and essays together in a volume called *Seasons of Discontent*.

"In 1962 I married the former Norma Cates (born Ofstrock), a lovely girl of New Bedford Jewish stock who had been both an actress and a playwright; I have lived very happily with her ever since. I have a charming stepson of thirteen named Phillip Cates, and a two-year-old son named Daniel Anton Brustein—both children are the source of immense pride and pleasure. I am now a full professor at Columbia and am continuing my criticism at the *New Republic* and elsewhere; I spend my summers at Martha's Vineyard, fishing, swimming, and writing. I have been richly rewarded in my life and my career seems settled—but since it is always at such moments that some imp goads me into new directions, I would not be surprised if, within the next few years, I branched off into something as yet untried and unknown. I continue to be suspended between the theatre and teaching, between action and contemplation, and though I seem to have achieved some kind of synthesis at present, I suspect the balance may some day be upset again. The only thing that remains constant in my life is a profound disappointment over what I think to be a serious deterioration in the American spirit, reflected in our institutions, official representatives, and foreign policy. It is this that continues to feed my discontent, even in the face of the pleasures and rewards of my approaching middle age."

Soon after Robert Brustein wrote the autobiographical statement above, he did indeed branch off in a new direction, in July 1966 becoming dean of the Yale School of Drama, which had so disappointed him as a student. He assumed the post with the intention of settling "for nothing less than changing the whole face of the theatre" in America, and he has made an excellent start, introducing at Yale a tough new professionalism, an openness to every kind of theatrical experience, which soon brought Broadway producers and critics to the campus, and generated both rage and excitement. It is a necessary revolution whose effects will in years to come spread far beyond the university.

Brustein's work at Yale seems the logical culmination of a progress which began when he "edged cautiously into a reviewing career, curious to see if a declining theatre could still be subjected to the same rigorous tests that were currently being applied" to the other arts. Brustein's was soon a highly audible voice in the wilderness, denouncing or dismissing the "tripe and treacle" that filled Broadway, slashing away with no less violence at "fashion-mongering and cultural opportunism" off-Broadway, and speaking up almost alone for Jack Gelber's *The Connection* and other rare signs that life still flickered in the American theatre.

Opinions of Brustein's work for the *New Republic* emerged in reviews of *Seasons of Discontent*, a selection of the notices he had written between 1959 and 1965. Philip Roth called him "the most important drama critic in America," praised his intellectual clarity and deep knowledge of dramatic literature, and concluded that his distinction "is not that he possesses all this equipment; rather that it is employed in the service of a strong moral concern for the quality of the lives we live." An English reviewer saw him as an "austere figure descending the mountain to break up the party round the Golden Calf and recall the tribe to the true faith," commended his unwavering dedication to the highest standards, but objected at the same time to his "pharisaical style" and a tone of "grating self-righteousness." (As he amiably admits, Brustein was raised in the "Jewish Messianic tradition.") A further selection of essays and reviews was published in 1969 as *The Third Theatre*.

In *The Theatre of Revolt* the critic discusses eight major modern dramatists, attempting to show that each was in his way a revolutionary, and that his rebellion stemmed from conflicts within himself. Most reviewers seemed unconvinced by Brustein's general thesis and treated the book not as a monograph but as "a thoughtful and well-informed series of essays." G. S. Fraser called it "a book by a man immersed in the living theatre" and praised in particular a brilliantly illuminating article about Strindberg; Norris Houghton thought that Brustein wrote with special insight about Brecht, O'Neill, Artaud, and Genet; and there were other testimonials to the catholicity of his critical sensibility.

Robert Brustein is the son of a wool-yarn merchant. He has been described as "lanky and gangling in shapeless green tweeds; more boyish looking than some of his students," one of whom has detected in him "a refreshing kind of rational madness." According to Philip Roth, he is "combative as an intellectual, but as a person . . . quite gentle." He spent the 1972–1973 drama season in England, as theatre critic of the London *Observer*.

PRINCIPAL WORKS: The Theatre of Revolt, 1964; (ed.) Strindberg, J. A. Selected Plays and Prose, 1964; Seasons of Discontent: Dramatic Opinions 1959–1965, 1965; The Third Theatre, 1969; Revolution as Theater: Notes on the New Radical Style, 1971.

ABOUT: Brustein, R. *Foreword to* Seasons of Discontent, 1965; Who's Who in America, 1970–1971. *Periodicals*—Commentary October 1953, February 1958; February 1965; Commonweal March 11, 1960; New Republic November 13, 1961; New York Review of Books October 22, 1964; New York Times February 20, 1966 (Section 2); New York Times Magazine May 21, 1967; Partisan Review Fall 1959; Summer 1965.

BUCHWALD, ART(HUR) (October 20, 1925–), American humorist and journalist, was born in Mount Vernon, New York, the son of Joseph Buchwald, who was a curtain manufacturer, and the former Helen Kleinberger. Art Buchwald's mother died when he was six, and he and his three sisters grew up in an orphanage and a succession of foster homes in New York City. He was a poor student and left high school without a diploma. "Out of the foster homes, the odd jobs, the schools and the city streets came a hard-eyed attitude," according to *Newsweek*, which quotes Buchwald as saying: "The world may look all right to you, but it looks crazy to me. My book—I tell you, *my* book—is *Catcher in the Rye*."

The family was reunited for a time in Queens, New York City, but at sixteen Buchwald ran away and joined the Marines, lying about his age. He spent most of World War II with a fighter squadron on a lonely Pacific atoll, editing his outfit's newspaper, and was a sergeant when he was discharged in 1945. Buchwald enrolled under the GI Bill in a liberal arts course at the University of Southern California. There he was managing editor of the college humor magazine, wrote a column for the campus newspaper, and, it seems, recognized his vocation. In 1948, without waiting to graduate, he took his two-hundred-and-fifty-dollar veteran's bonus and sailed for France.

Art Buchwald began his career in Paris—humbly enough, as a legman for *Variety*. In 1949 he proposed a column, "Paris After Dark," to the European edition of the New York *Herald Tribune* and was hired. A second column, "Mostly About People," was added in 1951, and a year after, the two were amalgamated as "Europe's Lighter Side," later usually called "Art Buchwald in Paris."

Buchwald's first book, *Paris After Dark* (1950), was a highly successful "lighthearted guidebook." It is not to be confused with *Art Buchwald's Paris* (1954), a selection of his *Herald Tribune* columns which happily mixed humor, gentle satire, and offbeat information about Paris people and places, and which delighted reviewers with its "loose, mocking style." Other, similar, collections followed during the late 1950s and early 1960s. Buchwald's column was syndicated in an ever-growing number of newspapers, and his fame spread, aided by an engaging manner and a talent for public clowning, and apparently unhampered by "a meager command of the French language." According to *News-*

ART BUCHWALD

week, Buchwald "had the cushiest newspaper job in Europe—a celebrity interviewing celebrities, clowning in gondolas in Venice and wryly cross-examining stars like Ingrid Bergman."

By 1963, nevertheless, Buchwald was back in the United States, embarked on a new career as a political humorist. "I figured I needed a change of scenery," he told *Time*. "And I decided to live in Washington because I don't like New York." Washington, though doubtless grateful, must have felt some misgivings since then, for Buchwald rapidly emerged as "one of the nation's sharpest political satirists." His column is probably the most widely read in the business, syndicated by 1966 to over three hundred newspapers in the United States and elsewhere. His books, collecting the best of the columns, regularly sell twenty thousand copies in hard covers, one hundred to one hundred and fifty thousand in paperback.

In June 1965 Art Buchwald made the cover of *Newsweek*, in a Herblock cartoon which envisaged a Washington entirely populated by Buchwald. "With his indifferent clothes, his amiable panda face peering from behind thick, horn-rimmed glasses, a six-inch Bering Coronet cigar in his mouth," *Newsweek* said, "he looks the part of the court jester. But for all the funnyman props, Buchwald is basically a serious person." Walter Lippmann called him "one of the best satirists of our time," and Arthur Krock found him "as capable of classical political satire as anyone now writing," at his best not inferior to Trollope. (Buchwald returned the compliment when he said: "There are only four of us writing humor from Washington these days—Drew Pearson, David Lawrence, Arthur Krock and myself.") Buchwald does not revise his columns for book publication, and reviewers have occasionally accused him of "sloppy syntax and grammar," and of using "old chestnuts." Some find his humor heavy-handed. Robert J. Manning, reviewing *Son of the Great Society*, says that Buchwald "is no Thurber, gliding tellingly through human fancy and foible, nor a Perelman sending spirals of nonsense into happy orbit. . . . His forte is the cartoon brought to life, the campus skit or vaudeville blackout raised to a certain . . . maturity and social relevance." Buchwald has written for most of the media at one time or another, and has even produced a novel, "an unpretentiously funny charade" about a deported racketeer called *A Gift from the Boys*.

Art Buchwald was married in 1952 to Ann McGarry, an American whom he met in Paris when she was doing public relations for Pierre Balmain. They have three adopted children: Joel, Conchita, and Jennifer, born respectively in Ireland, Spain, and France. Buchwald (who cannot drive), commutes daily by taxi from his large stone house in Washington's Wesley Heights to his office on Pennsylvania Avenue, spends the morning reading the newspapers and writing letters, and disposes of his column in an hour or two after lunch. He is an excellent poker player—"impossible in victory and insufferable in defeat" according to a regular victim—and also enjoys chess, gin rummy, and his work. He is a popular and expensive lecturer. "Some of his most consistent fans," according to Robert J. Manning, "are the Washingtonians whose manners, or sacred cows, or personalities he most likes to mimic or satirize. This is because he writes without malice. . . . He's a funny man and who doesn't want to have a funny man around?"

PRINCIPAL WORKS: Paris After Dark, 1950; Art Buchwald's Paris, 1954; The Brave Coward, 1957; I Chose Caviar, 1957; A Gift from the Boys, 1958; More Caviar, 1959; Don't Forget to Write, 1960; How Much Is That in Dollars?, 1961; Is It Safe to Drink the Water?, 1962; I Chose Capitol Punishment, 1963; . . . And Then I Told the President, 1965; Son of the Great Society, 1966; Have I Ever Lied to You?, 1968; The Establishment Is Alive and Well in Washington, 1969; Getting High in Government Circles, 1971; I Never Danced at the White House, 1973.
ABOUT: Current Biography, 1960; Lewis, Mildred and Lewis, Milton, Famous Modern Newspaper Writers, 1962; Who's Who in America, 1970–1971. *Periodicals*—Book Week October 23, 1966; Look March 13, 1962; Newsweek February 13, 1956; December 4, 1961; June 7, 1965; Time November 23, 1953; October 3, 1960; June 22, 1962.

BUCKLEY, WILLIAM F(RANK), JR. (November 24, 1925–), American political writer and editor, wrote in 1965: "I was born in New York City, the sixth of ten children, to WFB Sr. and Aloise Steiner Buckley, respectively a Texan and Louisianan. My mother's ancestors, back before the Civil War, were French, German, and Swiss. My father's parents were Canadian, and before that Irish and Welsh.

"My early schooling was in France and England, where my father lived as a peripatetic businessman engaged as an independent oil man, and there never was a more independent oil man. Our permanent home, to which we returned in 1933, was in Sharon, Connecticut, and there we were tutored for five years, going back again to school in England (because my father thought our elocution abominable). Then Millbrook school (1943), a half-year at the University of Mexico; the Army; and Yale (1950).

"At Yale, I took a divisional major (economics, political science, history), was elected chairman of the *Yale Daily News* (it was a spirited year, and I used to collect cancellations from prominent faculty members gleefully, remarking the inevitable correlation between their public endorsements of toleration, and their own dogmatism), was elected to respectable organizations (Fence Club, Torch Honor Society, Elizabethan Club, Skull & Bones), and was named Class Orator, giving me, technically speaking, the very last word in my extensive dialogue with the faculty and administration of Yale.

"My book on Yale was written during that summer and fall, I having meanwhile married Patricia Aldyen Austin Taylor of Vancouver, B.C., on the same day that Elizabeth Taylor married No. 1, and began her program of learning by doing. The Yale book was badly received, on the whole, though here and there a critic seemed to be saying that he expected more books. I repaired to Mexico on an assignment, and returned at the urging of the amiable William Bradford Huie as his assistant on the *American Mercury*, which association lasted three months, at the end of which my patience, and Mr. Huie's funds, wore out. I bought a house in Stamford, Connecticut (where I still live) and undertook, in collaboration with my brother-in-law who was studying law at Yale, *McCarthy and His Enemies*, which gravely displeased my erstwhile friend Dwight Macdonald, and is otherwise of no historical importance save for those who wish to know exactly something about what it was that generated the big fuss.

"In 1955 I founded *National Review*. My original collaborators included William Schlamm, James Burnham, Brent Bozell, Frank Meyer, John Chamberlain and, a little later, Whittaker Chambers. The magazine has grown and now (1965) has a circulation of about one hundred thousand, which is not bad for an anti-establishment journal of opinion. During the whole period, I also lectured extensively. I wrote another book in 1959, edited one in 1962, and published a collection in 1963. In 1962 I began a weekly syndicated column, which went three-times-a-week in 1964, and now has about three hundred clients.

WILLIAM F. BUCKLEY, JR.

"That, if you count Christopher Taylor Buckley, born 1952, brings me up to date. As regards my craft, I strive to please myself, and very rarely succeed. I doubt that I am a born writer, since I am miserable when I write and could conceive myself perfectly contented, and vast numbers of people even more so, if I never wrote again. I envy those who are happy while writing; though I do confess that, like Whittaker Chambers, I like to have written; a sensation which, however, is undoubtedly related to liking to have dug a ditch. I do love to read, though I confess that this may be pure addiction, rather than any intellectual tapeworm within me. I have a dreadful memory, which is one reason why I do not hammer away at more of the basic books (sample: St. Thomas Aquinas) whose contents I would dearly love to have always at my disposal. The critics, on the whole, have not been unfriendly to me as a writer, though they are horrified, mostly, at what I say, but then I have many opportunities to be horrified at their horror, and I comfort myself that, *sub specie aeternitatis*, I am on the side of the provoked, rather than the provokers.

"I am happily married, a practicing Catholic, and have known in my lifetime only the single personal tragedy of the premature death of my beloved sister, Maureen."

According to Dan Wakefield, Buckley inherited from his father, as well as a large fortune, "a rigid ideology based on free enterprise and the survival of the fittest." He showed his polemic bent at the age of six, when he wrote to the King of England urging him to pay his war debts, and he has established himself more recently as the most articulate of America's conservative intellectuals.

In 1944 Buckley went into the Army as a private, emerging in 1946 as a second lieutenant. At Yale he quickly made his name as an orator, a "brilliant journalist," and/or as "the most dangerous undergraduate Yale has seen in years." He received his B.A. with honors in 1950 but stayed on at Yale for another year as an instructor in Spanish.

God and Man at Yale, published in 1951, examines the university's curriculum and concludes that in general it opposes religion and favors economic collectivism. Read as an assault on liberal education as a whole, it caused a furore, delighting the right wing and outraging not only freethinking liberals but also many nonextremist Catholics and conservatives. While William Fulton called it important and brilliant, McGeorge Bundy, writing as "a believer in God, a Republican, and a Yale graduate," described it as "dishonest in its use of facts, false in its theory, and a discredit to its author."

There has been a similarly partisan response to most of Buckley's subsequent books. *McCarthy and His Enemies*, which Buckley wrote with his brother-in-law, L. Brent Bozell, identified McCarthyism as "a movement around which men of good will and stern morality can close ranks." *Up From Liberalism* undertakes the vivisection of American liberals and their journals of opinion and proposes that "we must bring down the thing called Liberalism, which is powerful but decadent; and salvage a thing called conservatism, which is weak but viable." *Rumbles Left and Right* collects essays and lectures about "troublesome people and ideas," and there have been three more general collections of occasional pieces, *The Jeweler's Eye*, *The Governor Listeth*, and *Inveighing We Will Go*. *Cruising Speed*, a journal of one week (late in 1970) in Buckley's life, appeared in two parts in the *New Yorker* (August 21 and 28, 1971) and was published in book form later the same year.

Whereas his supporters liken him to Hilaire Belloc, Buckley's opponents accuse him of blindness to the contradictions in his own opinions, of "a masterly use of the hatchet, the innuendo, the *ad hominem* argument." Over the years, nevertheless, there have been signs of a thaw in the liberal attitude toward Buckley. Norman Mailer, for instance, has remarked that "Mr. Buckley writes in a logical, lovely and lucid style, which I have studied very closely." Daniel Callaghan, reviewing *Rumbles Left and Right* in *Commonweal*, confessed: "I have become 'soft' on Mr. Buckley." Even those who abominate the authoritarianism which is central to Buckley's political philosophy acknowledge, as Irving Kristol has done, that he is personally "gay, witty, candid, intelligent, and unassuming."

From time to time, on the other hand, Buckley's weekly, the *National Review* contrives to upset his adherents by finding fault with Republicanism, by attacking the encyclical *Mater et Magistra* of Pope John XXIII, or by denouncing Robert Welch, founder of the John Birch Society, as a danger to the right-wing movement. Buckley's views are expressed also in his highly successful syndicated column, in major periodicals of all political persuasions, in many debates, interviews, and lectures. Since 1966 he has been host of a weekly television show, *Firing Line*, on which his guests have ranged from Richard Nixon to Norman Thomas, from Muhammad Ali to Enoch Powell, and which in 1969 brought him the "Emmy" award for outstanding program achievement. He is a most plausible and eloquent speaker, highly popular with campus audiences, and has been called the spiritual leader of the right-wing Young Americans for Freedom.

In 1965 Buckley was the Conservative party candidate for the mayoralty of New York City. His unsuccessful campaign is described in *The Unmaking of a Mayor*, which many reviewers found wryly witty, original, and interesting, especially in its account of the way in which newspapers distorted the author's speeches and statements. In 1967–1968 he lectured on municipal government at the New School for Social Research, and in 1969 he was appointed by President Nixon to the five-member Advisory Commission of the United States Information Agency. He holds a number of honorary degrees.

Buckley, "tall, trim, and debonair," has pale blue eyes and brown hair. He races a forty-two-foot cutter called the Panic, plays the piano and clavichord, and also enjoys gliding, swimming, riding, and skiing. Conservatism he defines as "the tacit acknowledgment that all that is finally important in human experience is behind us. . . . Certain questions are closed: and with reference to that fact the conservative orders his life and, to the extent that he is called upon by the circumstances to do so, the life of the community."

PRINCIPAL WORKS: God and Man at Yale: The Superstitions of Academic Freedom, 1951; (with L. B. Bozell) McCarthy and His Enemies, 1954; Up From Liberalism, 1959; (with the editors of National Review) The Committee and Its Critics: A Calm Review of the House Committee on Un-American Activities, 1962; Rumbles Left and Right: A Book About Troublesome People and Ideas, 1963; The Unmaking of a Mayor, 1966; The Jeweler's Eye: A Book of Irresistible Political Reflections, 1968; The Governor Listeth: A Book of Inspired Political Revelations, 1970; Quotations from Chairman Bill (comp. by David Franke), 1970; Cruising Speed: A Documentary, 1971; Inveighing We Will Go, 1972; Four Reforms, 1974.

ABOUT: Buckley, W. F. Cruising Speed, 1971; Cain, E. They'd Rather Be Right, 1963; Current Biography, 1962; Forster, A. and Epstein, B. R. Danger on the Right, 1964;

Markmann, C. L. The Buckleys: A Family Examined, 1973; Tucille, J. It Usually Begins With Ayn Rand, 1971; Who's Who in America, 1970–1971. *Periodicals*—Atlantic November 1951; Commonweal December 23, 1966; Esquire January 1961; January 1968; National Review May 7, 1963; New Yorker August 21 and 28, 1971; Time November 3, 1967.

BUCKMASTER, HENRIETTA, American novelist and historical writer, writes: "I was born in Cleveland, Ohio, but came to New York City almost immediately when my father became foreign editor of the New York *Herald Tribune*. It was assumed that my interests would be 'artistic' and so they were, shifting ingeniously until I was twelve when my first short story was published. By eighteen I was reviewing books for the New York *Times* and my first novel had been published.

"I identify myself to myself as a novelist, though I have done two books of nonfiction, *Freedom Bound*, a history of the Reconstruction Period, and *Let My People Go*, a history of the antislavery movement in the United States. On this basis I received a Guggenheim Fellowship, a few modest regional literary awards, and a deep commitment to civil rights.

"Writing is the most demanding of all the arts, and the one requiring the greatest discipline. Yet what is more magnificent, subjective, cathartic? For a while my novels appeared to have historical backgrounds. I say 'appear' because in fact they were exercises in immediacy. Certain subjects seemed to yield their points more readily if tackled tangentially. And historical knowledge has persuaded me that perspective brings hope. No crisis seems overwhelmingly decisive when seen from the distance of a hundred years.

"My first two historical novels had an American background. Both dealt with the opposition to slavery within the southern states. I knew that the present unfinished business of civil rights was inextricably entangled with our misinformation about the Negro before and after the Civil War.

"I suppose moral issues have always interested me most of all. By moral I mean 'responsible.' After my exhausting twenties had been relinquished, I grew more reflective, more realistic, more optimistic, more committed to the moral point of view, and more unsurprised.

"At the end of the war, in 1945, I was sent to Germany to do a series of articles on the adults and children who had survived concentration camps. Of those who had survived, many looked forward to life with sharpened insights. Many did not. Yet when life has tossed you up you are no longer complacent. I did not need to go to concentration camps to find this out, but the violently incontrovertible nature of concentration camps made moral exigencies inescapable, moral defeat unthinkable.

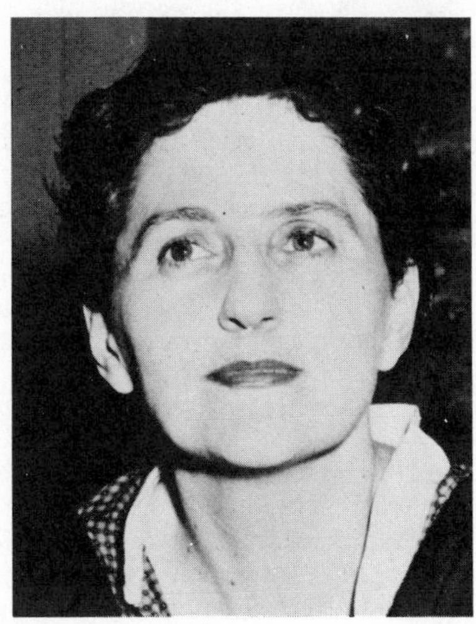

HENRIETTA BUCKMASTER

My novel *Bread From Heaven* was written after coming back from Germany.

"I went to a Quaker school (and then to a fashionable school for girls!). My books have always come out of questions: how and why people *are*, individually, collectively, in terms of their own self-concepts, in terms of social change.

"After *Bread From Heaven* I did two more historical novels but with a new purpose in mind. In *And Walk in Love* (Ephesians 5:2) I brought my wonder to bear on Paul of Tarsus and asked myself what makes a spiritual genius. As far as I was concerned Paul had been a living sacrifice to theologians, and sacrifices of this kind seemed to me strikingly anti-life. I was also anxious to say some things about the metamorphosis of Sauls into Pauls.

"Then I wondered what made a humane genius. This time around I did a novel on Shakespeare, one year of his life, *All the Living*. No one really wanted me to do the book. My English publisher thought I had lost my wits. Apparently you can bring a free imagination to bear on any two-legged phenomenon in the world with impunity, but not on Shakespeare. However I am glad to say that everyone—about a dozen people—whom I wanted to like the book (and my English publisher stood high on the list) responded as I had hoped. The only bad reviews were written by college professors who could not square something with Bradley or Sir Sidney Lee.

"I am poor at languages—when I reach Paris I am in a panic; when I move farther east my reason is affected—so I travel mostly to England. I married an Englishman. I love England, Wales, Scotland, and Ireland as if they were my own. I drove alone to that mysterious northern tip of Scotland near Cape Wrath where the sea is as blue as the Aegean. I like the slower pace, the orderliness and regard for law. I like the feeling that all this began a long time ago and will continue a long time after. And yet my final conclusion is that I am indisputably American.

"I feel we must all surrender old ways of thinking, nations as well as individuals. Wars and rumors of wars, killing of men and beasts, must someday become obsolete. As we move out into space we will begin to grasp various meanings of the fourth dimension. Right now this responsibility for change concerns me very much."

Henrietta Buckmaster is the daughter of Rae and Pearl (Winterunte) Henkle, and comes of a family which settled in the South in the early eighteenth century. Miss Buckmaster attended the Friends Seminary in New York and went on to the Brearley School in the same city and others in Europe. She has said, however, that the strongest influence on her early life was that of her father. She contributed the autobiographical statement above on the understanding that it would not include her birthdate: "This is not vanity," she says; "it is a one-woman fight (although I am discovering many adherents) against this sort of labeling and classifying which can do such damage to people—not artists, but those who suffer arbitrarily from time-decisions." It is an attitude characteristic of a writer who is and has been since adolescence most profoundly concerned with civil liberties.

The first of her novels to deal directly with civil rights was her third, *Deep River*, set in Georgia in the 1850s and centering on the work of a young abolitionist who is married to the daughter of a slave owner. It shares to some extent the weakness attributed to her first two novels—a tendency to make her characters mouthpieces for the expression of admirable but abstract sentiments—but is at the same time full of action and excitement and contains some excellent dialogue. *Bread From Heaven*, a considerably more interesting book, is an allegorical "sermon on prejudice" studying the reactions of a New England village to a young woman who brings her maimed child to live there. It was called a "richly concerned, sound, and absorbing novel," written with a poet's "sympathy and insight."

Miss Buckmaster's first major success, and her best novel, was *And Walk in Love*, "the most important novel about St. Paul since Sholem Asch wrote *The Apostle*," a monumentally "ambitious and broad-canvassed" study, and a "truly magnificent character study." Edmund Fuller found in it both beauty and majesty, and Robert Peel said that it was "enormously, vividly alive and . . . blessed with a degree of spiritual insight rare in the modern novel." The novelist produced another, nonfictional, study of St. Paul in *Paul: A Man Who Changed the World*, which was generally well received.

All the Living is another large-scale historical novel, this time about Shakespeare, who is pictured in 1600, heavily involved with the "Dark Lady" and also with political intrigue The book was found a little slow, but praised for its scholarship and "its determination to see man and society at their broadest and deepest." There was a respectful reception also for *The Lion in the Stone*, a long and complex account of a fictional international crisis narrated by a fictional Secretary General of the United Nations. There are convincing portraits of a huge international cast, and most readers thought the book a subtle, assured, and instructive dramatization of our contemporary fears and aspirations.

Let My People Go, Miss Buckmaster's history of the antislavery movement, was admired both for its scholarship and its vitality, and one reviewer found in it "the tonic katharsis of true tragedy." *Freedom Road*, about Reconstruction, drew to a greater extent than most such studies on black sources. It troubled some critics with its avowed partiality but was said by Ralph Ellison "to redeem American historical writing," ridding it of "myths and stereotypes."

Miss Buckmaster, who lives in Greenwich Village, says that her only recreation is reading thrillers. In 1972 she surprised her readers by producing an example of the form herself, an action-filled story called *The Walking Trip*, set in London and Scotland.

PRINCIPAL WORKS: *Novels*—Tomorrow Is Another Day, 1934; His End Was His Beginning, 1936; Deep River, 1944; Fire in the Heart, 1948; Bread From Heaven, 1952; And Walk in Love, 1956; All the Living, 1962; The Lion in the Stone, 1968; The Walking Trip, 1972. *Nonfiction*—Let My People Go, 1941 (England, Out of the House of Bondage, 1943); Freedom Bound, 1965; Paul: A Man Who Changed the World, 1965.

ABOUT: Contemporary Authors 9–10, 1964; Warfel, H. R. American Novelists of Today, 1951. *Periodicals*—Christian Science Monitor August 2, 1956; Wilson Library Bulletin March 1946.

***BUECHNER, (CARL) FREDERICK** (July 11, 1926–), American novelist, writes: "I was born in New York City. My father was of almost entirely German descent. My mother (born Katherine Golay Kuhn) came from a mixed background including Pennsylvania Dutch, French, English, Welsh and Irish strains. I have one younger brother. During the Depression years, my father moved from one minor executive job to another so that I spent my childhood in a number of differ-

* bēk′ nər

ent places along the Eastern seaboard—New Jersey, Westchester, Pennsylvania, Washington D.C., North Carolina—and until I went away to boarding school at Lawrenceville, New Jersey, in the fall of 1940, I attended a different school every year. Graduating from Lawrenceville in 1943, I entered Princeton, where I received an A.B. in English in 1948 after two years in the Army. I returned then to Lawrenceville and taught English there until 1953 when I resigned in order to make what turned out to be an unsuccessful attempt at being a full-time writer. In 1954 I was awarded a Rockefeller Brothers Theological Fellowship for a year's study at Union Theological Seminary. At the end of the year I decided to continue my studies there, and in 1958 I received the B.D. degree and was ordained a minister in the Presbyterian Church. Since that time, I have served as School Minister and Chairman of the Religion Department at Phillips Exeter Academy. In 1956 I married Judith Friedrike Merck, and we have three daughters, Katherine, Dinah, and Sharman.

"Aside from my mother and brother (my father died in 1936, and the only memories I have of him are very fragmentary, blurred, haunting), the dominant figure in my life up through adolescence was my maternal grandmother, who appears as a character in my first novel, which I dedicated to her. She had great serenity of spirit, great elegance of diction, and a wry Gallic wit which she must have inherited from her father, a French Swiss who came to this country as a young man to fight for Negro freedom in the Civil War. She had read quite widely in French and English literature, had contributed some stories to *St. Nicholas* as a young woman, and to her as much as anyone I owe the interest that I have always had in books and writing. Two of my teachers at Lawrenceville, Gerrish Thurber and Richard Martin, did much to direct and encourage that interest and at Princeton R. P. Blackmur and John Berryman carried on from where they had left off. In this regard I should also mention my friend James Merrill. From the start of our friendship at Lawrenceville in 1940 and on through our college years, there was much competition between us as writers, and I believe that this had a good deal to do not only with the way that we came to write but with the fact that we kept on writing at all whereas so many others our age simply gave it up for other things. The early reading that had most influence on my whole way of seeing the world consisted of the Oz books (at the age of six, sick in bed for almost a year with pneumonia, I virtually lived in Oz and eventually came to know well the entire Baum-Thompson canon), *Sketches by Boz*, *The Picture of Dorian Gray*, and Chesterton's *The Man Who Was Thursday*. From a more narrowly literary point of view, I am

FREDERICK BUECHNER

still conscious of the later influence of *The Brothers Karamazov*, *Moby Dick*, *Religio Medici*, *The Wings of the Dove*, Ford's *The Good Soldier*, and Warren's *All the King's Men*.

"The first book that I published was a series of poems entitled 'The Fat Man's Prescriptions,' which appeared in *Poetry Magazine* in 1946, and it was out of them, or more particularly out of the character of the Fat Man himself, that *A Long Day's Dying* gradually evolved, the novel that I began as a junior at Princeton. On the rare occasions when I can bring myself to look back at that book, I cringe with embarrassment at most of what I find (the labyrinthine style, by the way, had little or nothing to do with Henry James, as most critics maintained, but came straight out of my grandmother's epistolary and conversational style and Sir Thomas Browne), but at the same time I recognize in embryo there most of the themes that have concerned me since both as a writer and as a human being: the isolation of the individual, and his need to be known, the failure of communication, the reality of the unseen, the subterranean presence of grace.

"A writer turned minister is often asked to explain how it happened, and part of what I was trying to do in *The Final Beast* was to give some answer to that question. It was a process rather than an event although I see the significance of certain events more clearly now than I did when they occurred. A writer of the kind that I have tried to be looks beneath the surface of things, and the deeper I looked, the more aware I became of a reality that I eventually found myself unable any longer merely to describe; I finally reached the point where there was little real choice but to commit myself and serve. As a novelist my aim continues to be no different from that of any other serious member of the trade: to try to describe as fully as possible a vision of the world. Like many of my generation, I have seen darkness and pain and ambiguity enough to turn the heart to stone, and I see and describe it still. But I take this to be the penultimate thing about the world, the next to the last thing. It is what I have found to be the last thing of all, its joy and its power, that as a teacher, preacher, novelist, I spend my life trying to body forth somehow in words."

A Long Day's Dying is an "extremely contorted" reworking of the Philomela myth, set in and around a contemporary American university. Buechner was only twenty-three when he wrote this novel, which now so embarrasses him. It nevertheless attracted a great deal of very respectful attention when it appeared, although some critics then and more since have expressed impatience with its mannered and mandarin style, "charged in every sentence with ambiguities and ironies to produce the appearance of significance." John W. Aldridge, among others, maintained that while the young author had employed the fashionable devices of myth and religious symbolism, the dilemma of his characters was neither moral nor significant. There were similar complaints about *The Seasons' Difference*, which examines the impact upon a small cast of characters of the news that one of them has seen a vision.

Buechner's third novel received the Rosenthal Award and an altogether warmer press. *The Return of Ansel Gibbs* investigates the strains placed upon a decent cultivated man by contemporary public life. It showed the same skill in the handling of relationships and the same mastery of language which had impressed some critics in Buechner's earlier books, but none of the self-conscious overwriting which marred them, and was welcomed as "the firmest and clearest of his works." Elizabeth Janeway, who thought it "sincere, vigorous and serious" but not wholly successful, added that it was "worth half a hundred 'successful' and superficial novels that pretend to deal with matters of ethics and religion."

The Final Beast tells the story of a small-town pastor, whose attempt to bring back a parishioner's runaway wife, scandalously misinterpreted, leads to a murder and a martyrdom—a grim sequence from which, nevertheless, Buechner seeks to extract an affirmation of human goodness and Christian joy. The book seemed precious and whimsical to some readers but impressed others. Gerald Weales, reviewing it in *The Reporter*, acknowledged its weaknesses but thought it "Buechner's most ambitious novel to date," demonstrating "his intellectuality and his compassion; his delight in and his seriousness about images, a habit of mind derived from the seventeenth-century writers he so admires; his recognition that the spiritual world must take shape—particularly for his secular readers—in the material world of children's swings and picture postcards."

The theme of most of Buechner's work, Weales believes, is the possibility of spiritual rebirth. This is no doubt true at one level of *The Entrance to Porlock*, in which the octogenarian Peter Ringkoping has decided to leave the New England mountain he owns not to his family but to Hans Strasser, a mystic who runs a community for retarded adults. Ringkoping visits the community with his two sons and his grandson, and the novel studies the effects of their journey and of their confrontation with Strasser and his charges. Some readers were irritated by Buechner's "highly self-conscious" prose; others were puzzled but moved by a book that seemed to one reviewer "more poem than prose, more parable than story." *Lion Country*, a grotesque and sometimes bawdy comedy about a skeptical writer's investigation of a theological diploma mill in Florida, is even more obviously a parable, though reviewers seemed reluctant to attempt an exegesis. Once again opinion was divided, some readers complaining of the author's "tiresomely clever voice," others praising the book as a work in the manner of Flannery O'Connor, "beautifully written with the mastery of a craftsman." The story is continued in *Open Heart.*

Some of Buechner's convictions are expressed more directly in *The Magnificent Defeat*, a collection of sermons grouped about the ideas of surrender, love, and grace, and in three volumes of meditations, *The Hungering Dark*, *The Alphabet of Grace*, and *Wishful Thinking*. Buechner has also written poetry and short stories and has indeed won awards for both. He left Phillips Exeter Academy in 1967 to devote his full time to writing, apart from occasional preaching missions. He and his family live (like the Ringkopings in *The Entrance to Porlock*) on a mountain in Vermont.

PRINCIPAL WORKS: *Novels*—A Long Day's Dying, 1950; The Seasons' Difference, 1952; The Return of Ansel Gibbs, 1958; The Final Beast, 1965; The Entrance to Porlock, 1970; Lion Country, 1971; Open Heart, 1972. *Nonfiction*—The Magnificent Defeat, 1966; The Hungering Dark, 1969; The Alphabet of Grace, 1970; Wishful Thinking: A Theological ABC, 1973.

ABOUT: Aldridge, J. W. After the Lost Generation, 1951; Allen, W. The Modern Novel, 1964; Contemporary Authors 13–14, 1965; Current Biography, 1959; Who's Who in America, 1970–1971. *Periodicals*—Publishers' Weekly March 29, 1971; The Reporter September 9, 1965; Saturday Review February 17, 1951.

BUGAEV, BORIS NIKOLAYEVICH. *See* "BELY, ANDREY"

***BULGAKOV, MIKHAIL (AFANASEVICH)** (1891–March 10, 1940), Russian novelist and dramatist, was born in Kiev, where his father was a professor at the theological academy. He studied medicine at the University of Kiev, qualified in 1916, and for a short time worked as a doctor during the disturbed period of war and revolution. His first publication in 1919 was in a provincial paper, but by 1921 he was in Moscow earning a living as a journalist and writer of satirical and grotesque short stories.

The turning point in his career came in 1925 with his novel *Belaya gvardiya* (The White Guard) which began serialization in the April and May issues of the magazine *Rossiya.* Only these two installments appeared before the magazine failed, but Bulgakov dramatized the novel as *Dni Turbinykh* (translated in 1938 by R. Acland, in 1963 by F. D. Reeve, and in 1972 by Carl and Ellendea Proffer as *The Days of the Turbins*), which was enormously successful when it was produced at the Moscow Art Theatre by Stanislavsky in 1926. Its theme is the civil war between the Bolsheviks and the Whites, but unlike the many other contemporary works on the same subject, it describes the war from the White side. Its central characters, the Turbin brothers, are members of the White Guard, and it gives a sympathetic but objective account of their resistance to the occupation of Kiev successively by the Germans, Petlyura's Ukrainian Nationalists, and finally by the victorious Reds, with whom they eventually make peace not out of any sympathy with Bolshevism but because of the need for Russian reunification.

The play was carefully nonpolitical, but Bulgakov's treatment of the Whites as patriots and idealists, his refusal to glamorize the revolutionary proletariat, and the playing on the legendary opening night of the old Russian national anthem, struck a chord of deep nostalgia in the audience, members of which wept themselves into hysteria. A storm of controversy followed.

After this naturalistic work Bulgakov reverted to his early fantastic and satiric vein in a volume of stories, very much in the manner of Karel Čapek, which also appeared in 1925. The most famous of them is "Rokovye yaytsa" (translated as "The Fatal Eggs"), clearly an allegorical attack on Marxism. It is about a scientist who invents a red ray which will increase the growth rate of living organisms. A commissar orders its immediate practical application to poultry breeding on state farms, but the government department has sent crocodile and anaconda eggs by mistake, and the monsters hatched from them lay waste the countryside, which is saved from total destruction only by an early frost.

* bōōl gä′ kôf

MIKHAIL BULGAKOV

Sobacheye serdtse (translated as *The Heart of a Dog*) was also published in 1925 and is also about a scientist, this time a surgeon specializing in sexual rejuvenation techniques like Serge Voronoff's then fashionable experiments with monkey glands. The professor picks up a stray dog and transplants the testicles and pituitary gland of a human cadaver. The dog Sharik thus turns into the Soviet bureaucrat Sharikov, who demonstrates his humanity by whining, swearing, stealing, and a great variety of disgusting habits until the professor manages to turn him back into a dog. Two English-language versions, one by Mirra Ginsburg and the other by Michael Glenny, appeared in 1968 and both were warmly received. Maurice Friedberg said that the book "firmly establishes Bulgakov as one of the few truly great writers produced by the Soviet Union," and others praised his mordant humor and direct and powerful style.

Bulgakov followed these satirical stories with two satirical plays, *Zoykina kvartira* (1926, translated as "Zoya's Apartment") set in a brothel catering to the needs of the new class of Soviet officials, and *Bagrovy ostrov* (1928, translated as "The Crimson Island"), an attack on theatre censorship. The censors retaliated by banning not only these two plays but *Dni Turbinykh* as well, and the earlier play was not restored to the repertoire until 1932, when Bulgakov appealed directly to Stalin. Much of Bulgakov's work after 1928 dealt indirectly with the persecution of the artist by bureaucrats and tyrants.

In 1930 Bulgakov became assistant producer and *dramaturg* (resident dramatist) in the Moscow Art

Theatre. He was very much a man of the theatre, and one of his great literary heroes was Molière, of whom at this time he wrote a highly original biography, *Zhizn gospodina de Molyera* (1932–1933, published in 1962), and also in 1932 a tragedy called *Kabala svyatosh* (translated as "A Cabal of Hypocrites"). This deals with the last months of Molière's life, when he had lost the favor of the court. Stanislavsky fell ill and rehearsals of the play lasted four years; when a bowdlerized version finally reached the stage in 1936, it ran for only seven days. The parallel with Bulgakov's own treatment by the censors was obvious, and the play was fiercely criticized by the press. Bulgakov blamed Stanislavsky for the failure and resigned from the theatre full of rage.

Another play, written in 1934–1935, *Poslednie dni* (The Last Days), deals similarly with the end of Pushkin's life, when the poet was maneuvered into a duel and in effect murdered. Gogol was another writer with whom Bulgakov had a special affinity and he made a very scrupulous and successful dramatization of *Dead Souls* (1934); in an earlier story, *Pokhozhdeniya Chichikova* (translated as "The Adventures of Chichikov"), Gogol's hero is transplanted to the modern Soviet Union (finding the country as dirty and dishonest as ever). He later wrote a dramatization of *Don Quixote*, and a not very successful sequel to *The White Guard.* After his resignation from the Moscow Art Theatre Bulgakov became librettist for the Bolshoi Theatre and wrote at least three opera libretti. In 1938 he became ill with sclerosis, went blind in 1939, and was in constant pain until his death the following year.

Shortly before he died he took his revenge on Stanislavsky, dictating to his wife the novel *Teatralny roman* (translated by Michael Glenny as *Black Snow: A Theatrical Novel*). It was not published until 1965 in *Novy Mir* and was an immediate success, all one hundred fifty thousand copies being sold on the first day. The novel is a lightly fictionalized account of the production of his first play. Stanislavsky is mercilessly satirized as a vain, attitudinizing tyrant, and the whole enclosed world of the theatre with its jealousies and feuds is brilliantly captured.

Since 1928 Bulgakov had been working on a major allegorical novel, *Master i Margarita*, of which an abridged version finally appeared in the magazine *Moskva* in 1966. This was translated by Mirra Ginsburg in 1967 as *The Master and Margarita.* A fuller version was translated the same year and under the same title by Michael Glenny. This bizarre phantasmagoria weaves together three main themes. The first is a satire on human greed and pomposity, in which the devil arrives in Moscow in the 1930s, thinly disguised as a visiting professor, and accompanied by various familiars including a huge black cat, Behemoth, which walks upright, talks, smokes cigars, and is a crack shot. The climax of their visit is a performance of magic at the Variety Theatre in which they shower money on the hysterically greedy audience and the world goes mad. Two people, the prophetic artist called the Master, and his delightful mistress Margarita, remain uncorrupted. The Master, "a madly comic Faust," is the author of a great novel about the Crucifixion and has been driven into a lunatic asylum by those who would silence him. Margarita frees him by sacrificing her soul (and much else) to the devil. The third element in the book is the Master's novel itself, "an oddly touching" if unorthodox account of Pilate's dealings with Jesus. In the end the two lovers find peace through divine intervention. The book was warmly praised by English-language critics; it was called a masterpiece, a brilliant political and social satire, and a "perfect balance of hallucination and contrivance."

At the time of Bulgakov's death, most of his work was still unpublished, and until the appearance of *Teatralny roman* in 1965 his reputation was based largely on his plays, eleven of which had appeared. But since the sensational success of that novel, more of his work has been brought out by a literary committee under Konstantin Simonov and the author's widow, and even in the Soviet he is increasingly recognized as one of the few prose masters to have emerged in Russia since the Revolution. English versions of his work have continued to appear, and 1972 saw the publication of *The Early Plays*, translated by Carl R. and Ellendea Proffer, and also of *Diaboliad and Other Stories*, translated by Carl R. Proffer.

PRINCIPAL WORKS IN ENGLISH TRANSLATION: The Days of the Turbins, 1938, *also in* Lyons, E. (ed.) Six Soviet Plays, 1934 and Reeve, F. D. (ed.) Anthology of Russian Plays, 1963; The Master and Margarita (two versions), 1967; Black Snow, 1967; The Heart of a Dog (two versions), 1968; The Early Plays of Mikhail Bulgakov, 1972; Diaboliad and Other Stories, 1972. *Stories in* Reeve, F. D. (ed.) Great Soviet Short Stories, 1962; Ginsburg, M. (ed.) The Fatal Eggs and Other Soviet Satire, 1965.

ABOUT; Penguin Companion to Literature 2, 1969; Piper, D. G. B. *introduction to* Belaya gvardiya, 1969; Rudnitsky, K. Voprosy Teatra, 1966; Smith, H. (ed.) Columbia Dictionary of Modern European Literature, 1947; Struve, G. Soviet Russian Literature, 1951; Zavalishin, V. Early Soviet Writers, 1958. *Periodicals*—Commentary March 1968; Nation January 22, 1968; Newsweek October 23, 1967; New York Review of Books July 11, 1968; New York Times Book Review October 22, 1967; Saturday Review April 27, 1968; Times Literary Supplement December 7, 1967.

***BULTMANN, RUDOLF (KARL)** (August 20, 1884–), German theologian and New Testament scholar, was born in Wiefelstede, in the

* (bo͞olt′ män)

grand duchy of Oldenburg in northern Germany. He is the eldest son of Arthur Bultmann, a Lutheran pastor, and Helene (Stern) Bultmann, and is descended from clergymen and missionaries on both sides of the family. One of his brothers was killed in World War I; another died in a Nazi concentration camp. Bultmann spent a happy childhood in Rastede, where his father had taken over a pulpit. From 1895 to 1903 he attended the Humanistisches Gymnasium in Oldenburg, where his favorite subjects were the study of religion, German literature, and Greek.

In 1903 Bultmann embarked on theological studies at the University of Tübingen, and after three semesters there he studied for a time at the University of Berlin. In 1906–1907, after passing his first theological examination, he taught at the Gymnasium at Oldenburg, and in the fall of 1907 went on with a scholarship to the University of Marburg, a world-famous center for theological studies. He received his degree in theology in 1910.

Bultmann began his career as a university teacher in 1912, as a *Privatdozent* for New Testament exegesis at Marburg. From 1916 to 1920 he was an assistant professor at the University of Breslau, and in 1921, after a short period at the University of Giessen, he returned to Marburg, where he remained until his retirement in 1951. For a time, Bultmann was associated with Martin Rade in the publication of *Die Christliche Welt*, then the leading organ of Protestant liberalism in Germany. Later he was editor of *Theologische Rundschau* and *Neue Theologische Grundrisse*. One of the most profound influences on Bultmann during his early years on the Marburg faculty was his association with the existentialist philosopher Martin Heidegger. For his view of history, Bultmann is greatly indebted to the works of the British historian and philosopher R. G. Collingwood.

As an exponent of radical biblical criticism, Bultmann represents a school of thought that had its antecedents in the eighteenth century Enlightenment. Along with Martin Dibelius and Karl Ludwig Schmidt, Bultmann was a pioneer of form criticism, which seeks to assess the historical validity of New Testament stories and sayings by studying the literary forms in which they are expressed. In *Die Geschichte der synoptischen Tradition* (1921), translated as *History of the Synoptic Tradition*, Bultmann applied the method of form criticism to the synoptic Gospels. He found some parts of the Gospels more reliable than others and was severely criticized for his skepticism by more orthodox scholars. In his book *Jesus* (1926), translated as *Jesus and the Word*, Bultmann contended that the historical Jesus was mythologized by primitive Christians and that little could be ascertained about his actual

RUDOLF BULTMANN

life. The important thing, Bultmann concluded, was not Christ's nature, but his message.

Although Bultmann is essentially nonpolitical in his outlook, he took a firm stand against the Nazis as early as 1933, when he criticized their exclusion of non-Aryan Christians from the ministry. In 1934 he became a member of the Confessing Church (Bekennende Kirche), based on the theology of Karl Barth, which claimed to represent true Christianity while rejecting the pagan tendencies of the Nazi-dominated state church. In 1935, when Hitler's government barred theological faculties from taking sides in the church controversy, Bultmann declared in a letter that as a theological scholar he could not stand aside on issues of vital concern to the church. A number of his essays also contain explicit criticism of the Nazis.

In 1941 Bultmann presented the lecture "Neues Testament und Mythologie" (New Testament and Mythology) before the Gesellschaft für Evangelische Theologie. In it he sought to draw a distinction between the Christian Gospels, whose truth is timeless, and the mythological world view prevalent in the early days of Christianity. Bultmann called for the demythologization of the New Testament message and for its interpretation in existential terms—that is, in terms that would have genuine meaning in the light of present-day experience. He maintained that if the Christian message was to have influence in the modern world it would have to be separated from the form in which it is presented in the Gospels. Bultmann's essay brought him into the center of the field of systematic theology and gave rise to a great controversy within the church. It was attacked not only by the orthodox but also by some liberal theologians, and it led some critics to accuse him of near-heresy. The documents of the demythologization controversy, including Bultmann's essay, are contained in the five-volume *Kerygma und Mythos* (1948–1955), published in English as *Kerygma and Myth*.

Bultmann's three-volume *Theologie des Neuen Testaments* (1953), published in English translation as *Theology of the New Testament*, is regarded by some as his most important work. In it he sought to reconstruct and analyze the thought processes that underlie the surviving Christian literature of the first century of church history. Although the work was criticized for its "arrogant dogmatic skepticism" and for alleged distortion of the historical background of the New Testament, it also drew praise as a first-rate work of scholarship, both in Germany and in the English-speaking world. Bultmann is also noted for his absorbing, simple, and often moving sermons, some of which have appeared in English in *This World and the Beyond: Marburg Sermons*. In 1951 he spent eight weeks in the United States, where he delivered the lectures collected in *Jesus Christ and Mythology*. Some of Bultmann's shorter writings have been collected in *Existence and Faith* (which includes an autobiographical sketch), in *The Theology of Rudolf Bultmann*, and in *Faith and Understanding*.

Bultmann was married in 1917 to Helene Feldmann and has three daughters; the warmth and stability of his family life in Marburg has been of the greatest importance to him. He is a member of the academies of Oslo, Heidelberg, and Göttingen, and he holds honorary doctorates from the universities of Marburg, St. Andrews in Scotland, and Syracuse, New York. Bultmann's work has had a major influence on Protestant theology for more than four decades and has been a dominant one in the postwar era. His views have had some impact on Roman Catholic and even Jewish theological scholarship. Some scholars find his pioneering studies on the historical validity of the New Testament too negative and destructive; others believe that no one has done more to establish the relevance of the Christian message in a skeptical age. Ernst Wolf has spoken of "the stubborn relentlessness of his critical inquiry and of his loyalty to his own truth, as well as a sly humor and tempered bluntness in his dealings with his fellows"; even his critics have acknowledged his vast erudition. There is no doubt that he is one of the very greatest of contemporary theologians.

PRINCIPAL WORKS IN ENGLISH TRANSLATION: Jesus and the Word, 1934; Theology of the New Testament, 1951–1955; (with others) Kerygma and Myth, 1953–1962; Essays: Philosophical and Theological, 1955; Primitive Christianity in Its Contemporary Setting, 1956; Presence of Eternity (England, History and Eschatology), 1957; Jesus Christ and Mythology, 1958; This World and Beyond: Marburg Sermons, 1960; Existence and Faith: Shorter Writings, 1960; History of the Synoptic Tradition, 1963; (with Karl Jaspers) Myth and Christianity: An Inquiry into the Possibility of Religion Without Myth, 1958; The Theology of Rudolf Bultmann (ed. by C. W. Kegley), 1966; Gnosis, 1967; Faith and Understanding, Vol. I, 1969; The Gospel of John, 1971.

ABOUT: Braaten, C. E. and Harrisville, R. A. (eds. and trs.) Kerygma and History, 1962; Cairns, D. S. Gospel Without Myth?, 1960; Current Biography, 1972; Fries, H. Bultmann-Barth and Catholic Theology, 1967; Henderson, I. Rudolf Bultmann, 1966; Jones, G. V. Christology and Myth in the New Testament, 1956; Ladd, G. E. Rudolf Bultmann, 1964; Macquarrie, J. The Scope of Demythologizing: Bultmann and His Critics, 1960; Macquarrie, J. Rudolf Bultmann, 1965; Malet, A. The Thought of Rudolf Bultmann, 1971; Miegge, G. Gospel and Myth in the Thought of Rudolf Bultmann, 1960; Oden, T. C. Radical Obedience, 1964; Ogden, S. M. Christ Without Myth, 1961; Owen, H. P. Revelation and Existence: A Study in the Theology of Rudolf Bultmann, 1957; Peerman, D. G. and Marty, M. E. (eds.) A Handbook of Christian Theologians, 1965; Ridderbos, H. Bultmann, 1960; Robinson, J. M. New Quest for the Historical Jesus, 1959; Schmithals, W. An Introduction to the Theology of Rudolf Bultmann, 1968; Smart, J. D. The Divided Mind of Modern Theology, 1967; Wolf, H. C. Kierkegaard and Bultmann: The Quest of the Historical Jesus, 1965.

BUNTING, BASIL (March 1, 1900–), English poet, writes that he was born in Scotswood-on-Tyne, Northumberland, and had a Quaker upbringing. He was, he says, "educated at Ackworth, Leighton Park, Wormwood Scrubs Prison and the London School of Economics. Successively music critic, idler, soldier, diplomat and journalist. Travelled much. Read much in several tongues."

It is a summary that needs some amplification. He is the son of a doctor, T. L. Bunting, and the former Annie Cheesman. Near the end of World War I, when Bunting was eighteen, he was called up for military service. As a Quaker he refused the draft and was imprisoned until 1919. His experiences were grim, as "Villon" and some other poems suggest, and were once cited in a campaign to reform British prisons.

After his release from Wormwood Scrubs he studied at the London School of Economics and began to write verse, strongly influenced by T. S. Eliot and Ezra Pound, and imagist in manner. In 1923 he visited Paris and in 1924–1925 stayed in Rapallo with Pound, who became his close friend. In Rapallo he met his first wife, Marian Culver, an American, by whom he had three children before their divorce in 1935.

Bunting's first volume of poems, *Redimiculum Matellarum*, was published privately in Italy in 1930, and in 1931 he edited with Pound the *Active Anthology*, which included a good deal of Bunting's early work, Poundian in its concentration and concrete imagery, and in its range of references to oriental poetry, classical myth, and modern politics.

His friend Louis Zukofsky noted at this time that "Mr. Bunting's poetic care is measure. He is aware that quantity has naturally to do with the tones of words."

In 1928 Bunting spent some time in England as music critic of the magazine *Outlook*, but throughout the 1920s and 1930s he lived a great deal abroad, in France and Italy and Madeira. From 1937 to 1939 he earned his living as captain of a private yacht, sailing in the Mediterranean and across the Atlantic to America. In 1939 the threat to civilization posed by Hitler overcame his pacifism, and he returned to England and joined the Royal Air Force.

Bunting rose to the rank of wing commander and spent much of the war in Iran, where his rapid grasp of languages, and his interest in Iranian literature and thought, earned him many friends. After the war he stayed on in Iran with the British Consulate, acting also as Middle Eastern correspondent of the London *Times*. Bunting spent ten years in Persia in all, and in 1948 married an Iranian woman, Sima Alladadian, as his second wife. His feeling for the Middle East is expressed in *The Spoils*, a long poem written in 1951, and interesting as a transitional work between his early Poundian manner and his later unique style. A volume of his poems was published in 1950 by a small press in Galveston, Texas.

Iranian government changes in 1951 brought Bunting home to an England where his poetry was scarcely known. He was out of work for months and finally took a job as subeditor on a Newcastle newspaper. Very gradually, mostly through the efforts of a few such admiring critics as Michael Hamburger and Edward Lucie-Smith, the climate of opinion warmed. In 1965 Migrant Press published *The Spoils* in book form, and Fulcrum Press, another small publishing house, brought out *Loquitur*, containing most of the other poems Bunting wanted to preserve up to that time. These made no great stir, being dismissed in most quarters as mere Poundian pastiche. However, the long poem *Briggflatts*, published by Fulcrum Press in 1966, was greeted with considerable excitement and led to something of a reassessment of Bunting's work, notably in the Autumn 1966 issue of the magazine *Agenda*. Bunting's *Collected Poems* appeared in 1968.

Briggflatts is an autobiographical poem in five movements. A celebration of the poet's return from travel, it is also the poem in which he claims his inheritance and speaks at last in his own and native voice. Several critics have found in it the tone and manner of Anglo-Saxon poetry—the same concentration and immediacy and the same stoic sense of tragedy, along with an incomparably greater richness of technical resource. Others have been reminded of Wordsworth, not least by the

BASIL BUNTING

oral nature of Bunting's poem; it needs to be read aloud, and to be read moreover in the accent of Northumbria, with broad soft vowel sounds, and sharply enunciated consonants: "Rain rinses the road, / the bull streams and laments. / Sour rye porridge from the hob / with cream and black tea, / meat, crust and crumb. / Her parents in bed / the children dry their clothes. / He has untied the tape / of her striped flannel drawers / before the range. Naked / on the pricked rag mat / his fingers comb / thatch of his manhood's home. // Gentle, generous voices weave / over bare night / words to confirm and delight / till bird dawn. / Rainwater from the butt / she fetches and flannel / to wash him inch by inch, / kissing the pebbles / . . ."

Reviewing Bunting's *Collected Poems*, Allan Brownjohn wrote "this is a stark, powerful and chastening poetry, but [Bunting's] refusal of easy effects and preference for the bold and elliptical leads to some coldly impenetrable writing. . . . The poems mostly have a remote, hard quality that comes of marrying dour, arresting imagery with suggestive abstractions. . . . It is a poetry of barren magnificence and no ease."

Bunting is a short man with thick gray hair and a wiry moustache. He is direct in conversation and impatient of critical fads and fashions. Bunting, who now teaches at the University of Durham, lives with his wife and two of his children in Northumberland, but still travels as much as he can. He believes very firmly that "poetry, like music, is to be heard," that it seeks "to make not meaning, but beauty."

PRINCIPAL WORKS: (ed. with Ezra Pound) Active Anthology, 1931; Poems, 1950; The Spoils, 1965; First

Book of Odes, 1965; Loquitur, 1965; Briggflatts, 1966; What the Chairman Told Tom, 1967; Two Poems, 1967; Collected Poems, 1968; Descant on Rawley's Madrigal (Conversations with Jonathan Williams), 1968.
ABOUT: Murphy, R. (ed.) Contemporary Poets of the English Language, 1970; Who's Who, 1972. *Periodicals*—Agenda Autumn 1966; National Review October 31, 1967; New York Times August 3, 1969; Poetry November 1966; Sunday Times July 25, 1965; Times Literary Supplement February 17, 1964.

BURDICK, EUGENE (LEONARD) (December 12, 1918–July 26, 1965), American novelist, short story writer, and political scientist, was born in Sheldon, Iowa, one of the three sons of Jack Burdick, an itinerant painter, and the former Marie Ellerbroek. After his father's death his mother worked for a time as a waitress and later married Fritz Gaillard, a cellist with the Los Angeles Philharmonic. Burdick grew up in Los Angeles, and in 1936 entered Stanford University, where he was a Phi Beta Kappa psychology student, and graduated with a B.A. in 1942. War service as a Naval Reserve officer took Burdick to the South Pacific, a region which immediately and permanently fascinated him. He was decorated for his part in an action near Guadalcanal and discharged in 1945 as a lieutenant commander. Burdick, who had begun to write while he was still in the Navy, published his first story in 1946 and the following year won the O. Henry prize.

In 1948 Burdick went as a Rhodes Scholar to Magdalen College, Oxford University, where he read philosophy and earned his Ph.D. in 1950. Back in the United States, he received a fellowship from the Center for the Advancement of the Study of the Behavioral Sciences at the University of California (Berkeley). In 1952 he joined the Berkeley faculty as an assistant professor of political theory, becoming an associate professor in 1958.

Burdick's first novel, *The Ninth Wave* (1956), on which he worked for nine years, deals with the rise of a completely amoral California politician from poverty to great power. It was a Book-of-the-Month Club selection, praised by some reviewers for its realistic portrayal of the machinery of politics, damned by others as a cynical caricature which "seems bent on providing shock rather than enlightenment." It won for Burdick a Houghton Mifflin literary fellowship.

The Ugly American (1958), which Burdick wrote in a long-distance collaboration with William J. Lederer, brought him almost instant fame and was later filmed. Set in a fictitious country in Southeast Asia, it describes the ignorance, cynicism, and arrogant estrangement from the native population of American officials administering the U.S. foreign aid program. Contrary to what is generally supposed, the "ugly American" of the title is not one

EUGENE BURDICK

of this sort; he is a physically ugly but morally attractive engineer who, by meeting some of the real needs of the people, tries to undo some of the damage inflicted by foreign service officials. The book provoked a major controversy, prompted a congressional review of the foreign aid program, and is said to have helped to inspire the Peace Corps program. Criticized as it was for its stereotyped characters and "*Reader's Digest* prose," few contemporary novels have had a greater political impact.

Burdick's next novel was also a collaboration—this time with Harvey Wheeler—and also more effective as a political tract than as a work of literature. *Fail-Safe* (1962) was a "cosmic horror story" showing how easily a nuclear war could be touched off by accident. It was the result of a massive program of research and consultation with experts; reportedly prompted a Defense Department review of safeguards against accidental nuclear war; and had movie producers bargaining for it even before it was published. Some reviewers, even those who were unconvinced by its thesis or its wooden characters, praised it as a fast-paced suspense story, a "cleverly contrived melodrama."

There was a harsher press for *The 480* (1964), about a group of behavioral scientists who seek to use their slide rules, their computers, and their cynical expertise to sell their presidential candidate to the American voters (classified for this purpose into 480 groups). Critics described it as pulp fiction, and "an appalling libel of the social sciences, democracy, and its politics." *Nina's Book* (1964), the story of a heroine of the French resistance in World War II, fared no better, and was condemned for its "meretricious philosophizing," its "undistinguished jog-trot prose." The following year, Burdick died of a heart attack on a tennis court at San Diego, at the age of forty-six.

Two books appeared posthumously. *Sarkhan*, the result of a second collaboration with Lederer, was published in 1965. It was a sequel to *The Ugly American*, a novel "as artlessly conceived as a war propaganda poster" which nevertheless struck at least one reviewer as having "a more engrossing story line" than its famous predecessor. Burdick published two collections of shorter pieces: *Blue of Capricorn*, a notably interesting, original, and engaging mixture of essays and stories reflecting his profound feeling for the South Pacific; and the posthumous selection of "short and readable" adventure stories called *A Role in Manila*. He also wrote for television and films.

Eugene Burdick was a tall man, soft-spoken and mild in manner. He lived in Berkeley with his wife, the former Carol Warren, and his son and three daughters, and he also owned a house and some land on an island near Tahiti. He liked surfing and skin diving, and was known in Berkeley as an active Democrat. He will be remembered as an effective reformer with a talent for dramatizing his ideas in fictional form.

PRINCIPAL WORKS: The Ninth Wave (novel), 1956; (with William J. Lederer) The Ugly American (novel), 1958; (ed. with A. J. Brodbeck) American Voting Behavior, 1959; Blue of Capricorn (essays and stories), 1961; (with Harvey Wheeler) Fail-Safe (novel), 1962; The 480 (novel), 1964; Nina's Book (novel), 1965; (with William J. Lederer) Sarkhan, 1965; A Role in Manila: Fifteen Tales of War, Postwar, Peace, and Adventure, 1966.

ABOUT: Contemporary Authors 5–6, 1963; Hook, S. The Fail-Safe Fallacy, 1963; Who's Who in America, 1966–1967. *Periodicals*—New York Times July 28, 1965; Newsweek October 22, 1962; Publishers' Weekly August 9, 1965; Saturday Review October 20, 1962; Wilson Library Bulletin April 1961.

"BURGESS, ANTHONY" (pseudonym of John Anthony Burgess Wilson) (February 25, 1917–), English novelist and critic who also writes as "Joseph Kell," writes: "My full name is John Anthony Burgess Wilson: Anthony is my confirmation name; Burgess my mother's maiden name. When I began to write professionally, I was still an officer in Her Majesty's Overseas Civil Service, and it was thought better that I should use a name not generally known: there is a taboo on a colonial officer's revealing too much of his true attitudes, especially to the country he serves and wants, at the same time, to write about. My first published novels make up what is known in England as the *Malayan Trilogy* and in America as *The Long Day Wanes*. I wrote them at a later age than most authors choose to publish their first work—in my late thirties. I had had artistic ambitions since my earliest days, but no one talent had managed to

ANTHONY BURGESS

assert itself before Malaya acted as a midwife to a wordy gift that had had an inordinately long gestation. I had at first wished to be a pictorial artist, and I had, by the age of twelve, had drawings accepted by national newspapers. Then, at fourteen, I taught myself the piano and musical composition and, almost till the time of my first novel, I wrote full-length serious musical works—two symphonies, two concertos, sonatas, songs, incidental music for plays. I think that a triple apprenticeship of this kind (inevitably, I also wrote verse and short stories) is a good thing for a novelist.

"Invalided out of the Colonial Service in 1959, I had to take to full-time writing in order to earn a living. In my first year I wrote five novels, several stories, a couple of plays, and various radio scripts. This over-fecundity was, perhaps rightly, frowned on by critics, but I feel that, if one is going to write, one ought to write all the time, since re-priming a dormant engine is difficult. In recent years I have written one novel a year, though usually a non-fiction book—on philology or music or literature—acts as a whetstone or foil to the more creative activity. I also appear on television, which I like, and write television scripts, which I'm not sure whether I like or not. I review books for *The Guardian*, *The Listener*, *The Spectator*, *Encounter*, the *Times Literary Supplement*, and various American periodicals, and I have done a two-year stint as a television critic. But I get worried if anything prevents my writing a novel every year.

"Of the quality, or even purpose, of these novels I am not really qualified to speak. They are usually intended primarily to entertain, but a fairly serious element creeps into them, often against my will. I doubt if the novels I have already written comprise a homogeneous corpus as do, say, the novels of William Golding or Muriel Spark. I have written about the future, about William Shakespeare, about contemporary Russia, about espionage, about the London underworld, about Gibraltar. I plan a mock-biography of a great composer, a comic *Divina Commedia*, a delirious diary of a tour of the English countryside, a political allegory set in France. If there is a common theme to both the written and projected, it is perhaps the failure of liberalism, or rather the need to expiate the sin of liberalism. I was brought up a Catholic and have a cousin who is an archbishop, but I have long belonged to the wearisome fraternity of the renegades. Nevertheless, the older, pre-liberal philosophy which accepts the primacy of evil and the necessity of suffering permeates, I think, most of what I write.

"The novel-form itself (whatever it is; it is undergoing so many changes) seems to me to be the only viable imaginative form. If I were capable of it, I should like to write a novel that has the surface of pure entertainment (capable of being taken as easily as an Ian Fleming thriller) but, underneath, essays all the new-wave devices imaginable, getting away with them because of the solidity of the surface structure. In other words, I want the novel to be Shakespearian. It is dangerous for it to close in, as is happening in France, on the intellectual level, and to open out into the mere sex-and-violence-glorifying best seller. We have two fictional extremes at present; I want the extremes to meet in the single work of universal appeal, compact of action, psychology, ideas, as well as symbolism and poetry.

"In some ways, my own appreciation of the novel as an art-form is limited, even crippled, by a lifelong devotion to the work of James Joyce, who seems to me to have done more with the novel than anyone, with the possible exception of Laurence Sterne. To write in his shadow is humbling. In him I see the fusion of the fragmentary talents which, along with renegade Catholicism, I exhibit in my own work. He may not be the best model to a novelist, but he is certainly the best example. To achieve that self-martyring devotion to art is what I would wish, but I know I'm not big enough."

Anthony Burgess comes, he says, "of an old though not particularly distinguished Lancashire Roman Catholic family, one that held to the faith through the Reformation, and had its quota of undistinguished martyrs." He was born in Manchester, the son of a pianist, Joseph Wilson, and the former Elizabeth Burgess, a musical comedy performer billed as "Beautiful Belle Burgess." The great influenza epidemic of 1918 killed both his mother and his sister when he was a year old, and his father was soon married again, to a woman who reportedly inspired the portrait of a slatternly stepmother in *Enderby*.

After a Roman Catholic education at Bishop Bilsborrow School and Xaverian College in Manchester, Burgess received his B.A. with honors at Manchester University in 1940. The same year he went into the army, serving for six years with the Education Corps, in which he became musical director of a special services unit, entertaining troops in Europe. He worked for some time at Gibraltar, an experience which inspired *A Vision of Battlements*, his first novel in order of writing. He was married in 1942 to Llewela Jones. Leaving the army as a sergeant-major in 1946, Burgess spent the next two years lecturing in Birmingham University's extramural department. From 1948 to 1950 he was a Ministry of Education lecturer in phonetics, and from 1950 to 1954 he was a grossly underpaid teacher in a grammar (secondary) school in Banbury, near Oxford. This experience provided him with a theme and setting for *The Worm and the Ring*, written in 1954 but not published until 1961 (when it was withdrawn and pulped shortly after publication as the result of a libel action). In the end, disgusted by the meanness of his salary as a teacher, he applied (while drunk, so he claims) for a Colonial Office post in Malaya. He spent the next five years there and in Brunei, Borneo, as an educational officer.

In the East, Burgess settled down to write, completing and publishing his first three books, *Time for a Tiger*, *The Enemy in the Blanket*, and *Beds in the East*. They attracted little attention at the time—the *Times Literary Supplement* found them amusing and perceptive, but rather flippant and contrived—but they were much more warmly received when they were republished in 1964 as the *Malayan Trilogy* (and appeared in the United States as *The Long Day Wanes*). The trilogy deals with the career and marital disasters of Victor Crabbe, a British teacher in Malaya just before independence who, abandoned by his second wife, overcome by his general inadequacy, ends the story by killing himself. Bernard Bergonzi called it "a fairly unsophisticated piece of writing," casual and episodic in organization, which "in a general way is reminiscent of an older master of black humor, Evelyn Waugh." Other critics have been more enthusiastic, praising the work above all as a detailed and vivid evocation of the twilight of British colonial rule.

In Brunei, Burgess and his wife preferred the company of local anticolonialists to that of their peers. And it did nothing to endear Burgess to the Colonial Office when his wife, accosting Prince Philip at a garden party, told him frankly and publicly what she thought of British policy. One day, Burgess collapsed while lecturing. After tests he was told that he had a brain tumor but might live for a year or more if he returned at once to the temperate climate of Britain. Back in England, Burgess set himself to make some provision for his widow—hence the great creative outburst of 1959–1960, which he mentions above. The year passed, he did not die, and the brain tumor apparently vanished—Burgess wonders now if his political unsuitability in Brunei was not an element in the original diagnosis.

More than any other English novelist who has emerged in the last twenty years, Burgess has a truly fantastic energy and inventiveness. Joyce is, as he says, his chief mentor, and he has also acknowledged the influence of Sterne, Henry James, and Evelyn Waugh. Burgess is not, in the usual sense, an avant-garde writer; his linguistic experiments often go with a fairly conventional approach to character and construction, and this can produce a disproportionate effect whereby the manner seems rather too much for the matter. He has retained from his abandoned Catholicism a nagging concern with evil and a deep skepticism about the usual ideals of humane liberalism. At the same time, his expatriate years have given him an unusual angle of vision on English life.

This was spendidly evident in *The Right to an Answer*, which shows England through the eyes of a businessman who is home on leave from Japan and who observes with mounting distaste a purposeless, amoral provincial society that seems to take all its values from the mass media. Norman Shrapnel wrote that "there is a portentous air about this writer which makes him a sort of music-hall Graham Greene . . . but he has a wickedly accurate ear and eye." Most critics thought the book uneven but found in its style, characterization, and narrative vigor signs of exceptional originality and promise.

The Doctor Is Sick, a satirical picaresque based on Burgess's own tragicomic encounter with the medical profession, was followed by *Devil of a State*, another sad farce in the manner of early Waugh about love and politics in an imaginary East African caliphate. Then came what is perhaps the most admired of Burgess's books, *A Clockwork Orange*, reportedly inspired by an assault on the author's wife which resulted in the loss of an expected child, and from which she never fully recovered. It is set in England in a near future when gangs of adolescents roam the streets and countryside, looting, raping, and murdering for pleasure. One such youth is the narrator, Alec, who speaks in a brilliantly conceived and rendered slang, drawing heavily on Slavic words, which the reader is able to master as he goes along. Daniel Talbot said of this *patois* that "Burgess combines an acute ear for the onomatopoeic aspects of language with an intuitive sense of the ambiguity of words, and his artificial slang has an emotional impact which transcends specific word meanings."

Alec is cured of his taste for violence by aversion therapy—he is conditioned like a laboratory animal until the very thought of violence makes him physically sick. The novel implies that this destruction of a personality is a worse crime than Alec's revolting cruelty, since it is better to do evil than to be spiritually dead (a view which also underlies some of Graham Greene's novels, notably *Brighton Rock*). Some critics mistook Burgess's painful wit in this book for frivolity, but many recognized its quality and several were reminded of George Orwell's *1984*. Bernard Bergonzi described it as a penetrating exploration of the problems of guilt and responsibility, and one of the finest English novels of the 1960s. It has always had a large following, especially among young people, and this was vastly increased in 1971–1972 by the controversy aroused by Stanley Kubrick's film version.

Burgess took up another science fiction theme in *The Wanting Seed*, in which homosexuality, war, and cannibalistic dining clubs are invoked against the population explosion. Brigid Brophy called it "half-baked," but another critic, in the *Times Literary Supplement*, thought it "wildly and fantastically funny," with "all the usual rich exuberance of Mr. Burgess's vocabulary, his love of quotations and literary allusions . . . his fantastic dream and nightmare sequences, and his little digs at other literary figures." Similar pleasures were found in *Honey for the Bears*, about an Englishman who sets out to sell twenty dozen dresses on the Russian black market. Along the way he discovers, with only mild regret, that he is a homosexual. Christopher Ricks, pointing out that Russia emerges here as a society disconcertingly like the United States, called the novel politically and sexually subversive, and one of Burgess's best books.

The author's most audacious virtuoso performance, *Nothing Like the Sun*, tells "a story of Shakespeare's love-life." It is in effect a reading of the sonnets and to some extent the plays in terms of their motivation, which is represented as deeply sexual. Not everyone accepted this, but the critics were full of praise nevertheless for Burgess's impersonation of genius, his verbal ingenuity, and his convincing portrait of Shakespeare's England. *The Eve of Saint Venus*, originally an opera libretto, is an erudite farce, set in an English country house, which delighted most reviewers, and *Tremor of Intent* is an "eschatalogical spy novel" that pleased some readers as a thriller and some as theological speculation but few as both.

Enderby, an expanded version of *Inside Mr. Enderby* (published in 1963 as by "Joseph Kell"), is about a scruffy middle-aged poet who likes to write in the lavatory, and his long and finally successful struggle to escape rehabilitation by women and psychiatrists. Guy Davenport wrote: "There are novelists who could have created Enderby; there are fewer novelists who could have created Enderby's poetry for him—poetry that we aren't quite certain isn't parody; there are very few novelists who could have topped this and invented a Muse who reels off top-notch textual criticism of the densest of Enderby's poems . . . . The category in which we can place Mr. Burgess seems to contain Mr. Burgess alone." This judgment was substantiated by *MF*, a serious and intricately structured comedy, whose rich young hero flees to the Caribbean to escape an unwelcome marriage. There he discovers that he was incestuously conceived, meets and murders his double, marries his sister, and accomplishes much else. Stephen Donadio, noting that the book "affords all the pleasures of language at work and play," also spoke of its "intellectual aggressiveness and underlying somber power."

The best known of Burgess's nonfictional works is *Here Comes Everybody*, published in the United States as *Re Joyce*. It is a commentary on *Ulysses* and *Finnegans Wake* invented "to help the average reader who wants to know Joyce's work but has been scared off by the professors." Most reviewers thought it did more than this, and one wrote: "Whatever faults the book has are minor and hardly detract from its eloquent style, rich good humor, and, more important, its illumination of Joyce's contribution to twentieth century literature."

There was also a warm reception for *Language Made Plain*, which discusses grammar, phonetics, semantics, the physiology of speech, and other aspects of language, including the pleasure of words for their own sake. *The Novel Now* is a rather breathless survey of modern English and American fiction, with even sketchier treatment of Continental, Asian, and African novels. There is much more solid and useful criticism in *Urgent Copy*, a collection of book reviews and literary essays which are full of good sense and insight. Burgess's biography of Shakespeare was praised in the *Times Literary Supplement* as "a narrative well-informed to the point of gossip, and as boldly colored as the gorgeous Elizabethan portraits that lavishly deck this volume." Burgess's rhymed version of Edmond Rostand's *Cyrano de Bergerac*, translated and adapted for the modern stage, was performed very successfully in 1971 at the Tyrone Guthrie Theater in Minneapolis. *Cyrano*, a musical with a book based on Burgess's adaptation, music by Michael J. Lewis, and lyrics by Burgess, opened at the Palace Theatre in New York in 1973.

According to Walter Clemons, Burgess is "a big man of sturdy, ramshackle appearance, with a blunt disarming manner." For many years after his return to England, Burgess divided his time between a cottage in Etchingham, Sussex, and a semidetached house in the gloomy and unfashionable suburb of Chiswick—no great hardship for him, since he is extremely shortsighted, is quite unconcerned with his visual surroundings, and has moreover no taste for London literary society. Working seven days a week, he was content to devote what little spare time he allowed himself to music and painting, cooking and language study, relying for his social life on local pubs. His first wife died in 1968; after her death Burgess made a second marriage to Liliana Macellari, a young Italian philologist (and translator of Thomas Pynchon) with a small son by a previous marriage. Burgess is deeply attached to England, but distressed by its loss of vigor and purpose, and in particular by its inhospitality to the arts; these feelings, and Burgess's increasing tax burden, drove him and his wife to Malta, which they disliked, and then to the United States and to Italy, where they have a small house. They spent 1969 in Chapel Hill, North Carolina, and 1970–1971 in Princeton, where Burgess taught creative writing. In 1972 Burgess signed a three-year contract as playwright-in-residence at the Tyrone Guthrie Theatre, and the same year accepted a post as Distinguished Professor of English at New York's City College.

Burgess has continued to produce reviews and essays for a number of English and American periodicals; he also writes for radio and television and has tried his hand at film scenarios. But, although he remains a quite remarkably prolific writer, the great outburst of creativity that began his career as a full-time writer (and stunned the reviewers) has long since passed, and he is tired of being discussed as a prodigy rather than as a writer. He says: "I call myself a professional writer in that I must write in order to eat. . . . But primarily I call myself a serious novelist who is attempting to extend the range of subject-matter available to fiction, as also a practitioner who is anxious to exploit words as much as a poet does."

PRINCIPAL WORKS: *Fiction*—Time for a Tiger, 1956; The Enemy in the Blanket, 1958; Beds in the East, 1959 (all republished in 1964 as The Malayan Trilogy; U.S., The Long Day Wanes); The Right to an Answer, 1960; The Doctor Is Sick, 1960; The Worm and the Ring, 1961; One Hand Clapping, 1961 (published originally as by "Joseph Kell," republished under his own name, 1964); Devil of a State, 1961; A Clockwork Orange, 1962; The Wanting Seed, 1962; Honey for the Bears, 1963; Inside Mr. Enderby, 1963 (published as by "Joseph Kell," expanded as Enderby Outside [England] and as Enderby [U.S.], 1968); Nothing Like the Sun: A Story of Shakespeare's

Love Life, 1964; The Eve of Saint Venus, 1964; A Vision of Battlements, 1965; Tremor of Intent, 1966; *MF*, 1971. *Nonfiction*—Language Made Plain, 1964; Here Comes Everybody: An Introduction to James Joyce for the Ordinary Reader (U.S., Re Joyce), 1965; (ed.) A Shorter Finnegans Wake, 1966; The Novel Now: A Student's Guide to Contemporary Fiction, 1967; Urgent Copy, 1969; Shakespeare, 1970; Cyrano de Bergerac, by Edmond Rostand (tr. and adapted for the modern stage), 1971; Joysprick: An Introduction to the Language of James Joyce, 1973.

ABOUT: Bergonzi, B. The Situation of the Novel, 1969; Contemporary Authors 3, 1963; Current Biography, 1972; Dix, C. M. Anthony Burgess, 1972; Kostelanetz, R. (ed.) On Contemporary Literature, 1964; Solotaroff, T. The Red Hot Vacuum, 1970; Vinson, J. (ed.) Contemporary Novelists, 1972; Who's Who, 1972. *Periodicals*—Book Week February 9, 1964; September 20, 1964; October 9, 1966; Guardian October 10, 1964; November 16, 1966; Life October 25, 1968; Listener June 6, 1968; London Magazine February 1964; Massachusetts Review Summer 1966; New Republic October 15, 1966; New Statesman April 5, 1963; April 24, 1964; June 6, 1968; New York Review of Books January 23, 1964; May 20, 1965; June 9, 1966; New York Times Book Review January 9, 1966; April 10, 1966; November 29, 1970; New York Times Magazine November 3, 1968; New Yorker April 8, 1961; Saturday Review July 15, 1967; November 25, 1967; June 8, 1968; Times (London) January 16, 1964; August 24, 1968.

BURFORD, ELEANOR. *See* HIBBERT, ELEANOR BURFORD

BURNS, JAMES MAC GREGOR (August 3, 1918–), American biographer, political scientist, and historian, was born in Melrose, Massachusetts, one of the three sons of Robert Arthur and Mildred Curry (Bunce) Burns. His father was a businessman specializing in sales and advertising. Burns grew up in rural Massachusetts and was educated at Lexington High School, but traveled a good deal with his family in Europe and Mexico. In 1935 he began as an undergraduate his long and brilliant career at Williams College, where he was a Phi Beta Kappa student majoring in political science, edited both the student newspaper and the student magazine, won prizes for his undergraduate thesis, and graduated *magna cum laude* (1939). In 1941, after a year's study at the National Institute of Public Affairs in Washington, he went back to Williams as an instructor in political science.

Burns's first wartime assignment was as executive secretary of the Nonferrous Metals Commission (1942–1943). In 1943 he joined the Army as a combat historian, and thereafter fought and recorded the fighting at Guam, Saipan, and Okinawa, ending the war as a master sergeant. Burns received his M.A. and Ph.D. degrees from Harvard in 1947 and then returned to Williams College. There he has remained, apart from a year at the London School of Economics (1949), sorties into political action, and participation in the Salzburg Seminars in

JAMES MAC GREGOR BURNS

American Studies (1954 and 1960). "The sage of Williams College" is James Phinney Baxter Professor of History and Public Affairs and also chairman of the college's department of political science.

Congress on Trial (1949) discusses the conflict between national and local pressures which plagues and obstructs the Congress and proposes a solution in the development of more powerful and monolithic political parties. The need for strong political leadership is the recurrent theme in Burns's work and underlies even *Government by the People*, the much-used college textbook he wrote with J. W. Peltason. This was originally published as two volumes, one devoted to "the dynamics of American national government," the other to "the dynamics of American state and local government." Reviewing the first volume, S. G. Brown wrote: "The tacit assumption throughout is that big government and big power, as means for advancement of the general welfare, are inevitable and that the administrative process is the characteristic development of modern democracy."

The same views are reflected in Burns's absorbing assessment of Franklin D. Roosevelt in *Roosevelt: The Lion and the Fox*, a work which focuses in particular on FDR's career during the New Deal years, from 1933 through the election of 1940. August Heckscher called it a book "on a big scale, solid, penetrating, honest," and a number of reviewers thought it the most careful and objective study of Roosevelt so far published. It received awards from both the Woodrow Wilson Foundation and the Tamiment Institute. No less frank and balanced is Burns's "political profile" *John Kennedy* (1960), which was praised also for its stylistic grace and for conveying "a sense of inner life, pressures, tensions, conflicts, and the directions taken by the subject in the course of his . . . development."

Returning in *The Deadlock of Democracy* to his central preoccupation, Burns argued that each of the two principal political parties is itself divided into two groups, and traces the growth of "four-party politics" back to the clash between the presidential philosophies of Madison and Jefferson. This "engrossing, readable and challenging" book was followed by *Presidential Government*, which proposes, as a solution to "weak coalition government," a strong presidency balanced by a "loyal opposition" on the Hamiltonian model. It was in general less favorably received than its predecessor, striking some reviewers as a "muddled" book, and alarming others with its emphasis on an extension of presidential powers.

Roosevelt: The Soldier of Freedom completes the study begun in *Roosevelt: The Lion and the Fox*, providing a highly critical but vivid and convincing account of FDR's life and work during World War II. It received both the National Book Award and the Pulitzer Prize for biography. G. W. Johnson wrote: "About James MacGregor Burns as a literary craftsman there can be no two opinions. . . . To style he adds the rare gift of ability to sort out from a tangled skein the significant threads. . . . As historiography, also, the book commands admiration. Its documentation is ample and invariably apposite. . . . He has written a very fine book. If it falls short of greatness the reason, in this reader's opinion, is that Burns is too dedicated a logician." Most critics agreed that the two volumes formed the first substantial scholarly biography of the President.

Burns, who believes that the scholar has an important role to play in politics, was a member of the Massachusetts delegation to the Democratic Convention in 1952, 1956, 1960, and 1964. In 1958 he ran for Congress in the 1st District of Massachusetts (unsuccessfully, in spite of Kennedy's support). He is a contributor to such magazines as *Atlantic Monthly* and the *New Republic*, and a member of the American Civil Liberties Union, Americans for Democratic Action, and the American Political Science Association, among other organizations. He is married to a teacher, the former Janet Thompson, and has four children. Burns, a Congregationalist, has brown hair and hazel eyes, and is six feet tall. His recreations include tennis and skiing.

PRINCIPAL WORKS: Congress on Trial: The Legislative Process and the Administrative State, 1949; (with J. W. Peltason) Government by the People: The Dynamics of American National Government, 1952, *and* Government by the People: The Dynamics of American State and Local Government, 1952 (both volumes published as one in 1954); Roosevelt: The Lion and the Fox, 1956; John Kennedy: A Political Profile, 1960; The Deadlock of Democracy: Four-Party Politics in America, 1963; Presidential Government: The Crucible of Leadership, 1966; Roosevelt: The Soldier of Freedom, 1970.

ABOUT: Current Biography, 1962; Who's Who in America, 1970–1971. *Periodicals*—New Republic September 29, 1958; New York Times Book Review September 13, 1970; New York Times Magazine August 31, 1958; Times Literary Supplement March 5, 1971.

BURNSHAW, STANLEY (June 20, 1906–), American poet, critic, and translator, writes: "I was born in New York on the shores of the Hudson in an orphans' home which my father had recently been asked to direct. Though trained as a philologist, he had given up teaching Greek and Latin for the hope of making real his private educational dream. And he succeeded: with the erstwhile aid of several philanthropists, he established (1912), in a Westchester County cottage home, a year-round curriculum that combined academic with manual learning to produce his special version of the contemporary Renaissance Man. Throughout its six-year life, the experiment achieved fame; and I was one of its beneficiaries, though the playing-fields interested me more than studies, the countryside more than books. It wasn't till my fifteenth year that I discovered reading and writing.

"In 1925, bearing a B.A. in English, I hunted a job and found one as an advertising apprentice in a huge steel-products mill in a Pittsburgh suburb. But my thoughts were on literature, and though spare time did not exist, I managed to issue a little magazine (*Poetry Folio*, which was little enough for me to set up in type by hand). I was also writing a book-length poem against the steel mill and its work of human destruction. Five sections were taken for publication in the first *American Caravan*, and with such assurance, I set off for Europe in May 1927.

"Six months later my writing plans were overturned by a lecture at the Sorbonne on André Spire. To my absolute amazement, I met the poet himself that very evening—and my fate was sealed. I would, with his assistance, translate his verse into English and write the 'true' account of *vers libre*. The book did not appear until 1933 and by that time I had put in four years writing advertising in New York and two semesters taking an M.A. at Cornell. But teaching jobs were scarce—and the Revolution, unlike Prosperity, was just around the corner. Having by this time published parts of my steel-mill poem in left-wing journals I gravitated naturally to the *New Masses*, which was about to become a weekly. For almost three years I worked as a full-time editor, spending most of my energy in reviewing plays and books. My piece on Wallace Stevens' *Ideas of Order* brought a reply from the poet himself: 'Mr. Burnshaw and the Statue'—to which I replied twenty-five years later in the *Sewanee Review* (Summer 1961).

"Bored with journalism and unable to write advertising, I joined some textbook men in a publishing venture, only to found an imprint of my own in 1939. For twenty years I directed the Dryden Press, editing and designing books and catalogues by day and writing my own poems, a novel, and a play by night. With Dryden's acquisition by Henry Holt, I became a half-time publisher. At last I had the chance to write new poems, to teach a world-literature seminar at N.Y.U., to edit a volume of criticism. Almost as important: I could now put into book-form a new approach to translation which I had embarked on mainly to make the wonderfully difficult poems of Mallarmé 'available' to my young daughter (*The Poem Itself*). At the same time, the Holt job was enabling me, among other things, to reestablish an old (1929) relationship with Robert Frost and to reissue a neglected classic by Christina Stead (*The Man Who Loved Children*, 1965).

"I am now trying to complete a play, a book tentatively called 'A Dissenting View of Poetry,' and such poems and other writings as keep coming."

Stanley Burnshaw is the son of Ludwig and Sophia (Kievmann) Burnshaw. He received his B.A. in 1925 at the University of Pittsburgh and in 1927–1928 studied at the universities of Poitiers and Paris. His four years in advertising in New York (1928–1932) were followed by study at Cornell (M.A., 1933) and then three years on the *New Masses*. Burnshaw was a vice president of the Cordon publishing company from 1936 to 1939, and thereafter served as president and general manager of his own Dryden Press until Henry Holt took it over in 1958. He stayed with Holt for some years—as a vice president until 1965 and then as adviser to the company's president until he left to write full time in 1967.

Social conditions, the intellectual climate of the 1920s and 1930s, and Burnshaw's own temperament and family background combined to make him in his first books more concerned with social reform than with self-expression. *The Iron Land*, published in 1936 when he was with the *New Masses*, was begun ten years earlier in the Pittsburgh steel mill. It is a group of poems about life in the mill, forming an indictment of "the slavery of men under modern industrialism," and it was more warmly praised for its social intentions than for its "deft" and "competent" performance. *The Bridge*, an allegorical play in blank verse, and *The Sunless Sea*, an equally allegorical fantasy in the shape of a novel, were also damned with faint praise for their social idealism.

Other considerations, personal and aesthetic, have been allowed a place in his more recent work,

STANLEY BURNSHAW

which has benefited greatly from his long involvement as translator and teacher with European literature. James Dickey said that in his 1963 book of poems *Caged in an Animal's Mind*, Burnshaw had "fused the European daring and total surrender to the unconscious . . . to an idiom eminently English," producing "some remarkable poems." Kenneth Rexroth, approaching the book from a different direction, was moved by its "exceptional emotional integrity and lucidity"—the result, he thought, of "the kind of life this poet has lived . . . out in the world of men and affairs, which has also given him definite attitudes toward his subject matter and his verse certain immediacies uncommon on the current scene." There was also much praise for Burnshaw's collected poems, published as *In the Terrified Radiance*.

The Poem Itself deals with verse by forty-five major European and South American writers. Each poem is printed in its original language and followed by a line-by-line literal translation and an analysis of the poem's construction, metaphors, meanings, and allusions. In effect, the reader ignorant of the language of the poem is provided with a do-it-yourself translation kit, which he can use as successfully as his intelligence and sensibility allows. Some critics remained glumly unconvinced that there is *any* way in which poetry can be effectively translated, but others, like John Ciardi, were delighted: "Anyone who will read the explication with care should soon find himself ready to read the original poem . . . . Mr. Burnshaw and his associates have fathered a new school of translation."

The Seamless Web has been described as "a

natural history of the poetic process," which Burnshaw investigates in terms of biochemistry, anatomy, zoology, anthropology, psychology, linguistics, metrics, aesthetics, and literary criticism. His conclusion has been well summarized by a writer in the *Times Literary Supplement*: "The artist, mankind's most sensitive representative, profoundly alienated and self-conscious, feels from time to time within him an excessive psychophysical pressure; his self-release from this burden, his creativity, manifests itself in the exterior world as his art, which is in effect the register of a desire to achieve again the natural state, prior to alienation, self-consciousness and culture—infantile, innocent, sensible only of an Adamic harmoniousness and integrity." Hilton Kramer called the book "a defense of poetry that . . . places it pre-eminently among [man's] instruments of survival"; Philip Toynbee believes that it "may well turn out to be a major work of theoretical criticism."

Burnshaw is a founder and editor of the magazine *Adult Leadership* and has served on the board of the American Institute of Graphic Arts and as a National Book Awards judge. He was married in 1943 to Lydia Powsner and has two daughters.

PRINCIPAL WORKS: *Poetry*—The Iron Land: A Narrative, 1936; Early and Late Testament, 1952; Caged in an Animal's Mind, 1963; In the Terrified Radiance, 1972. *Play*—The Bridge, 1945. *Novel*—The Sunless Sea, 1949. *Nonfiction*—(tr. and ed.) André Spire and His Poetry: Two Essays and Forty Translations, 1933; (ed. with others) The Poem Itself: Forty-five Modern Poets in a New Presentation, 1960; (ed. with others) The Modern Hebrew Poem Itself—From the Beginnings to the Present: Sixty-nine Poems in a New Presentation, 1965; The Seamless Web, 1970.

ABOUT: Burnshaw, S. *Preface to* Early and Late Testament, 1952; Contemporary Authors 9–10, 1964; Gassner, J. *Introduction to* Burnshaw, S. The Bridge, 1945; Who's Who in America, 1970–1971.

BURROUGHS, WILLIAM S(EWARD) (February 5, 1914–), American novelist, was born in St. Louis, Missouri, the son of Perry and Laura (Lee) Burroughs, and grandson of the man who, as he puts it, "invented the gimmick which made the adding machine possible." He studied English literature at Harvard, then did graduate work in ethnology and archaeology. During World War II, apart from three months of military service, he held a variety of jobs in New York City: bar attendant, private detective, "exterminator," journalist, advertising copywriter, and factory worker. At this time Burroughs presided over a kind of permanent literary salon on 115th Street where he entertained Allen Ginsberg, Jack Kerouac, and their friends, acting as both midwife and father-figure to the Beat generation. In 1944 he became addicted to heroin, and moved first to Texas and then to Mexico. He was married in 1945 to Jean Vollmer and has one son, William, whose first novel appeared in 1971. There was reportedly an earlier marriage to a German-Jewish refugee.

A friend suggested to Burroughs that he should record his experience as an addict, and while still in Mexico he wrote his first book, *Junk*, under the pseudonym of William Lee. In the process, he said later, "I found out that I was more interested in writing [than in drugs] and that addiction was interfering. I could never have written *The Naked Lunch* on drugs. Certain kinds of writing you can do: straight prose, editing. But not poetic writing; there are less and less images as someone gets more heavily addicted." Burroughs' years in Mexico ended when he accidentally shot and killed his wife. He traveled in Colombia, in Peru (where he experimented with the mescaline-like drug *yage*), and in Ecuador, then lived for several years in Tangier, Morocco. After undergoing a number of unsuccessful "cures" for his addiction, Burroughs went to London in 1957 to receive the apomorphine treatment, which is banned in the United States. Since then, apart from two relapses immediately dealt with, he has never used heroin again.

The Naked Lunch, first published in Paris in 1959, is an accumulation of short scenes, some of them episodes from the life of the addict-narrator, "William Lee," others records of his hallucinations during withdrawal from the drug. Chronology, logic, and character development are all ignored; the book is an impressionistic vision, Swiftian in its savagery, of a nightmare totalitarian city peopled by pathetic, zombie-like addicts and their demonic exploiters (like the evil scientist Doctor Benway, who is in charge of "interrogation, brainwashing and control" and who has a taste for human blood).

The book rapidly acquired an immense underground reputation. In 1962 it was published in the United States by Grove Press and caused a furor, the critics disagreeing violently about the justice of its attacks on authority, the acceptability of its explicit and often homosexual eroticism, and its literary worth. Edith Sitwell, Victor Gollancz, and some other contributors to a very long correspondence in the *Times Literary Supplement* denounced the book as "bogus, highbrow filth" by a "dirty-minded neurotic." John Wain condemned its "owlish seriousness" and said that "from the literary point of view, it is the merest trash, not worth a second glance." Mary McCarthy on the other hand admired its humor, "peculiarly American, at once broad and sly," and Anthony Burgess praised Burroughs' "uninhibited prose, his ability to attack the nerves." The author was described by Norman Mailer as "the greatest writer of graffiti who ever lived"—inasmuch as graffiti constitute "the language of hatred unencumbered by guilt, hesitation, scruple, or complexity."

The themes and some of the characters introduced in *The Naked Lunch* have recurred in Burroughs' subsequent fiction. What interests him above all, as the real object of life, is the untrammeled pursuit of self-knowledge and self-fulfillment. What he opposes is any form of interference with the individual's freedom to explore his own "inner possibilities." He abominates materialism, marriage, and all other kinds of social conditioning; the machinery and agents of law and order; and every kind of limiting addiction—to drugs, power, sex, and also to logic, which he regards as a trap from which Western man must learn to escape.

Burroughs' literary manner is an expression of this thoroughgoing anarchism, and in all of his fiction since *The Naked Lunch* he has experimented with "precisely how word and image get around on very, very complex association lines." He will, for example, "take a page of text, [his] own or someone else's, and fold it lengthwise down the middle and place it on another page of text, [his] own or someone else's, lining up the lines. The composite text is then read across, half one text and half the other." Advertising copy, magazine articles, and other nonliterary matter may be introduced in accordance with this and other aleatory techniques and superimposed on "plots" borrowed most often from pulp science fiction. Burroughs is a perfectionist within his own terms, and some of his books have been augmented, revised, and issued more than once.

Nova Express, one of the most successful of his experiments, has to do with the interplanetary escapades of the Nova Mob, whose members include Izzy the Push, Hamburger Mary, the Subliminal Kid, and Mr. and Mrs. D. (alias Mr. Bradly Mr. Martin). These "cosmic thugs," who reappear in other Burroughs romances, are "tracked from planet to planet by Inspector Lee of the Nova Police." When apprehended, they are turned over ("for the indicated alterations") to the Biologic Courts, which however are every bit as corrupt as the mob itself.

Burroughs' methods produce prose like the following, quoted from another science fiction epic, *The Ticket That Exploded*: "Wooden pegs in another room forgotten memory controlling the structure of his Scandinavian outhouse skin—The man flicked Ali's clothes—Prisoner pants with wriggling movement stood naked now in green mummy flesh, hanging vines and deflated skin—Death kissed him."

In such works as these, Anthony Burgess says, "Burroughs seems to revel in a new medium for its own sake—a medium totally fantastic, spaceless, timeless, in which the normal sentence is fractured . . . and the author shakes the reader as a dog shakes a rat. . . . It is literature as a total release

WILLIAM S. BURROUGHS

from the bondages of gravity and inhibition alike, sometimes baffling, often exhilarating." This is a minority view, however, and most critics, even when they commend Burroughs' experiments in principle, seem to find them unjustifiably hard to read. Richard Rhodes, reviewing a much-revised version of *The Ticket That Exploded* in 1967, commented with satisfaction that Burroughs "is progressing toward fewer experiments and greater control of his complex medium. He is filling in his grand comedy . . . [and] the comedy ultimately wins the reader."

Burroughs has also published *The Yage Letters*, his correspondence with Allen Ginsberg. He is much interviewed as a spokesman of the avant-garde, although in appearance he more resembles a conservative businessman. He is tall, slim, polite, and serious, and wears grey suits, white shirts, and dark ties. He is much liked, as a warm and pleasant man, by those who know him well. He has lived abroad for many years, in Tangier, London, and elsewhere. Burroughs is or was attracted to Scientology, and refreshes himself in a Reichian box. His extreme misogyny has led him to postulate an all-male community in which reproduction would be confined to test tubes.

PRINCIPAL WORKS: (as "William Lee") Junk, 1953 (repub. under author's own name as Junkie, 1964); The Naked Lunch, 1959; The Exterminator, 1960; The Soft Machine, 1961; The Ticket That Exploded, 1962; Dead Fingers Talk (selections from The Naked Lunch, The Soft Machine, and The Ticket That Exploded), 1963; The Yage Letters (correspondence), 1963; Nova Express, 1964; The Last Words of Dutch Schulz, 1970; The Wild Boys, 1971; Exterminator!, 1973.

ABOUT: Burgess, A. The Novel Now, 1967; Burroughs, William, Jr. Kentucky Ham (autobiography), 1973; Contemporary Authors 9–10, 1964; Current Biography, 1971; Kostelanetz, R. (ed.) The New American Arts, 1965; McCarthy, M. The Writing on the Wall, 1970; Odier, D. The Job: An Interview with William Burroughs, 1970; Vinson, J. (ed.) Contemporary Novelists, 1972; Writers at Work III, 1968. *Periodicals*—Guardian July 5, 1969; Harper's July 1967; Life November 30, 1959; Massachusetts Review Autumn 1967; New Republic December 1, 15, 29, 1962; January 12, 1963; New Statesman February 8, 1963; March 4, 1966; New York Times Book Review September 16, 1962; December 27, 1964; Paris Review Fall 1965; Partisan Review Fall 1966; Saturday Review June 27, 1959; Spectator July 29, 1960; Time November 30, 1962; Times Literary Supplement November 14, 1963–January 30, 1964 (correspondence); August 6, 1964; Twentieth Century Literature October 1965; July 1966.

***BUTOR, MICHEL (MARIE FRANÇOIS)** September 14, 1926–), French novelist and essayist, has had the warmest reception, both from critics and common readers, of all the writers associated with the so-called *nouveau roman*—the French "new novel." He was born at Mons-en-Barœul, a suburb of Lille, in northern France. He is the third of the seven children of Émile Butor, a railroad inspector, and the former Anna Brajeux. His father was transferred to Paris in 1929 and Butor was educated there, in Catholic schools and at the Lycée Louis-le-Grand, where he complained of poor teaching and was unhappy. At the Sorbonne he began by studying literature but switched to philosophy, gaining his *licence* in that subject in 1946 and an advanced diploma the following year.

Although he failed to qualify for the *agrégation* he found a post as a philosophy teacher at the *lycée* in Sens and thereafter held a variety of teaching jobs, mostly abroad. He taught French at Al Minya, in Egypt, from 1950 to 1951, and has written at length of this experience in *Le Génie du lieu* (The Spirit of Place, 1958). Two years followed in England, at the University of Manchester, during which he wrote his first novel, *Passage de Milan*. In 1953–1954 Butor worked in Paris on his translation of Aron Gurtwitsch's study of phenomenology, *The Field of Consciousness*, published in 1957 as *Théorie du champ de la conscience*. During 1954–1955 he taught in Salonika and in 1956–1957 in Geneva. At that point the success of his third novel, *La Modification*, made it possible for him to abandon full-time teaching.

Butor seems not to have been much influenced by his contemporaries and had arrived at his characteristic manner before he read either Robbe-Grillet or Nathalie Sarraute. Mallarmé, Proust, Gide, and Beckett have all been important to him, as have Kafka, Faulkner, and Joyce. Leon S. Roudiez, whose valuable monograph on Butor suggests that he came to the novel as a "meeting ground" that might accommodate both "his rational quest in the domain of philosophy" and the parallel but nonrational investigations pursued in his early (and largely unpublished) poetry. At any rate, his novels combine a charged and even lyrical use of language with a profound interest in structure—in structure as a means by which experience can be organized and profitably studied: taken apart and reassembled, run through at different speeds, examined in different contexts and from different angles.

* bü tôr′

Passage de Milan (1954) has not yet been translated and the title, indeed, is untranslatable in its ambiguities. It is an account of the groupings and regroupings, the events and social rituals, that take place in a Paris apartment house over a twelve-hour period. The house represents and indicts a lonely and joyless society in which mechanical forms have replaced the realities of emotional contact. The interior monologues of its innumerable residents are blended and counterpointed in an ambitiously symphonic manner but are not always successfully differentiated. The result bored and confused many readers who nevertheless recognized its promise.

The far more accomplished novel that followed was *L'Emploi du temps* (1956, translated by J. Stewart as *Passing Time*), which won the Prix Fénéon. Jacques Revel, a young French businessman, is to spend a year in the dreary British city of Bleston (Manchester), where he is puzzled and alarmed by a series of mysterious events and encounters. Seven months after his arrival, in an attempt to understand his situation, he begins a retrospective diary of his visit. But his interpretation of events that took place early in his stay are constantly being called in question by fresh developments. When this happens, Revel conscientiously makes another attempt to set the record straight. His diary becomes an increasingly worthless tangle of past and present versions of "objective reality."

The novel is packed with rather Joycean echoes from pagan and Christian mythology which hint at Revel's identification with (among others) Theseus in the labyrinth (of Bleston), the murderer Cain, and Oedipus. Roudiez suggests that Revel, like the author himself, "writes in order to give meaning to his life; his effort results in a partial failure, not because he chose the wrong means but because he must preserve the freedom of the reader in order to allow him, too, to seek a meaning for his own life. The hero fails so that the novel may succeed." Henri Peyre found this book "the richest, the most musically orchestrated and the most poetical novel of the last ten years."

It was, however, Butor's next novel that achieved the greatest popular success. This was *La Modification* (1957, translated by J. Stewart as *A Change of Heart*). It is a record of the thoughts of a businessman as he travels by train from Paris to Rome. At the beginning he is planning to abandon his wife in favor of his mistress; but the memories, reflections, events, and dreams of the journey bring him to an understanding of his nature and the negative but (for him) honest and appropriate decision to stay with his family. Butor's skillful management here of a second-person narrative form is reminiscent of Faulkner; the reader sometimes has the guilty feeling that he is the "you" addressed. The book was warmly praised for its mastery of a complex form, through which "a whole life is revealed"; it received the Prix Renaudot.

Degrés (1960, translated by Richard Howard as *Degrees*) is an attempt to record what happens, and the meaning of what happens, in the course of an hour's lecture in a French *lycée*. This impossible task eventually involves three narrators (not to mention Butor himself, and his readers). The book reflects the author's constant preoccupation with the relativity of time and the relativity of truth, and with the role and responsibility of the artist. Beyond this, Leon Roudiez points out, there is an indictment of an educational system and the society it serves. The novel is unobtrusively divided according to an exceedingly complex system into sections and subsections, and various other patterns are worked out within its structure. In its style it is intentionally less resonant, more precise, than Butor's earlier books. Some critics regard *Degrés* as a failure, and others as a deliberate failure that is also a masterpiece.

A French critic once defined the novel as "a prose work of a certain length"; it is only in this sense that any of Butor's subsequent books can be regarded as novels. *Mobile* (1962) makes use of typographical conventions, bizarre verbal juxtapositions, homonyms and other correspondences, to construct a kind of prose poem, or surrealist collage, or moving verbal sculpture of America; *Où* deals in a rather similar fashion with later journeys to New Mexico and the Far East. *Réseau aérien* (Air Network, 1962) is a radio play assembling the conversations of passengers traveling between various airports all over the world to form what one critic called a "choral song of mankind." *Description de San Marco* (1963) alternates between a description of Saint Mark's in Venice, the author's comments upon it, and snatches of the trivial remarks of other tourists. *Votre Faust* (1962–1965), an opera whose development is guided by the audience, has music by the serial composer Henri Pousseur—both an opera on the Faust theme and an investigation of the problems faced by the creator and the audience of such a work.

Another work, *6,810,000 litres d'eau par seconde* (1965, translated by Elinor S. Miller as *Niagara*) is an evocation of Niagara Falls and of the society that has vulgarized them. *Portrait de l'artiste en jeune singe* (Portrait of the Artist as a Young Monkey, 1967) is a relatively light-hearted "caprice" in which, as a guest of alchemists in a Bavarian castle, the author

MICHEL BUTOR

cultivates his own marvelous dreams and turns gradually into a monkey.

Butor's modest, persuasive, and highly original essays on literature, music, and painting are collected in *Répertoires* (1960), winner of the Prix des Critiques Littéraires, *Répertoires II* (1964), and *Répertoires III* (1968); some of these have appeared in English in *Inventory*, edited by Richard Howard. *Illustrations* (1964) and *Illustrations II* (1970) contain *récits*, or prose poems, inspired by various works of art. The author is employed by Gallimard as an advisory editor; he was a visiting lecturer at Bryn Mawr and Middlebury in 1960, at the University of Buffalo in 1962, at Evanston in 1965, and at Albuquerque in 1969–1970. He also teaches at the University of Paris center at Vincennes. In 1964 he visited West Berlin on a Ford Foundation grant. Married in 1958 to Marie-Josèphe Mas, he has four children. He is a Chevalier de l'Ordre National du Mérite and a Chevalier des Arts et des Lettres.

Roudiez sees Butor as a writer dedicated to understanding the life of his time so that he may help to transform it, and a critic in the *Times Literary Supplement* speaks of him similarly as "a surprising writer whose elaborate concern with technical experiment ought to be seen as a sign of his moral fervour." Henri Peyre believes that his is "the finest mind among those who have undertaken to renovate the novel since 1950—the only one . . . whose universal intellectual and artistic curiosity grants him a place in the literature of the last third of our century comparable to that of Sartre at mid-century."

PRINCIPAL WORKS IN ENGLISH TRANSLATION: Passing Time, 1960; A Change of Heart, 1959 (England, Second Thoughts); Degrees, 1961; Mobile: Study for a Repre-

sentation of the U.S., 1963; Niagara, 1969; Histoire Extraordinaire (essay), 1969; Inventory (essays), 1971.
ABOUT: Albérès, R.-M. Michel Butor, 1964; Boisdeffre, P. de. Dictionnaire de littérature contemporaine, 1900–1962, 1962; Contemporary Authors 9–10, 1964; Charbonnier, G. Entretiens avec Michel Butor, 1967; Le Sage, L. The French New Novel, 1962; Moore, H. T. Twentieth-Century French Literature Since World War II, 1966; Nadeau, M. The French Novel Since the War, 1967; Peyre, H. French Novelists of Today, 1967; Pingaud, B. Écrivains d'aujourd'hui, 1960; Ricardou, J. and Van Rossum-Guyon, F. (eds.) Nouveau Roman, 1972; Roudat, J. Michel Butor, ou le livre futur, 1964; Roudiez, L. S. Michel Butor, 1965; Sturrock, J. The French New Novel, 1969; Will, F. (ed.) Hereditas: Seven Essays on the Modern Experience of the Classical, 1964; Who's Who in France, 1971–1972. *Periodicals*—Archivum Linguisticum 1961, 1962; Bucknell Review March 1962; Critique (Paris) February 1958; July 1960; October 1962; Critique: Studies in Modern Fiction Winter 1963–1964; Esprit July–August 1958; French Review December 1961; October 1962; February 1965; Nation April 25, 1959; Symposium Summer 1965; Yale French Studies 24, 1959; Yale Review June 1959.

***BUZZATI, DINO** (October 16, 1906–January 28, 1972), Italian novelist, short story writer, journalist, and dramatist, was born in northern Italy at Belluno, a small city south of the Dolomites, where the Arde and Piave rivers meet. He was the son of Giulio Cesare Buzzati, a professor of international law, and the former Alba Mantovani. Buzzati earned a law degree in Milan and spent most of his adult life there as a writer and journalist. Beginning in 1928 he worked for the *Corriere della Sera*, first as a reporter and later as an editor and foreign correspondent. He was also one of the founders of the *Corriere Lombardo*.

His whimsical first novel, *Barnabò delle montagne* (Barnabò of the Mountains), was published in 1933. The hero's solitude in the Alps, where he is assigned to guard a deposit of explosives, and his failure to cope with life, can be seen as a preliminary statement of Buzzati's principal themes. The book is also notable as a lyrical expression of the author's love for the fierce beauty of the north Italian mountains, a quality which recurs in his next book, *Il segreto del bosco vecchio* (The Secret of the Old Wood, 1935).

It was Buzzati's third novel that made him famous. *Il deserto dei Tartari* (1940, translated as *The Tartar Steppe*), which won the award of the Italian Academy, is Buzzati's most powerful statement of his major themes: man's loneliness and absurdity in the face of death, the ludicrous devices he adopts to blunt his awareness of the inevitable. The novel tells the story of a young lieutenant, Drogo, stationed at a fortress on the northern borders of his homeland to await the invasion of the Tartars. The threatened attack is delayed and the young officer, hungry for glory, grows impatient. The weeks of waiting become months, the months years. When at last the invasion does come, Drogo is too old to fight and is invalided out, defeated in his only real battle, the hopeless one against time.

* bōōt tsä′ tē

Il deserto dei Tartari has frequently been compared to Kafka's allegories of irrational menace, though Buzzati's novel is more reflective and philosophical and his impeccable prose communicates a more subdued sense of terror. In it, as Gian-Paolo Biasin wrote in the *Italian Quarterly*, man is brought "face to face with his destiny—a destiny of tardiness, of death, momentarily obscured by delusions of glory. Kafka's castle, in comparison, is an inward nightmare; Buzzati's fortress, on the contrary, looks outside, over a wasteland." Stanley Edgar Hyman suggested that Buzzati's gift is more "wryly comic" than Kafka's, "more closely related to Svevo."

Buzzati published no more novels for twenty years, but a number of volumes of short stories appeared during the 1940s and 1950s, the contents of which were collected in 1958 in *Sessanta racconti* (Sixty Stories), which received the Strega prize. Other volumes followed, and a selection of Buzzati's stories was published in English in 1966 as *Catastrophe*. Like his novels, they are preoccupied with fear—"fear of death, first of all; fear of the mysterious, of the unknown, of natural catastrophes, of revolutions, of the unforeseen, of what transcends man." They are often allegorical, admirably humorous and ironical, but rather lacking in intensity, "like a faded photograph of someone screaming."

A fourth novel, *Il grande ritratto* (1960, translated by Henry Reed as *Larger than Life*), is about a giant machine, Number One, which is equipped with superhuman intelligence and then, disastrously, with an extremely imperfect human soul. Most critics found the plot thin and the characters superficial. *Un Amore* (1963), translated by Joseph Green as *A Love Affair*, deals with an aging man's obsessive passion for a young call girl and her casual destruction of him. Helene Cantarella wrote: "In his explicit realism, in his insistence on gratuitous erotic details, in the catapulting stream-of-consciousness confession that serves Dorigo to vent his frantic jealousy, Buzzati has strayed far afield from the elegant, chaste, disciplined understatement which has characterized him until now. Could it be that *A Love Affair*, admittedly autobiographical in some of its elements, represents an irrepressible search for catharsis?"

Buzzati also wrote opera librettos and several plays, of which the most notable, *Un caso clinico* (A Clinical Case), has been performed in Milan, Berlin, and Paris. It is based on his short story "I sette messaggeri," translated in *Catastrophe*, and is an allegorical account of the decline and death of a man who seems invulnerable in his strength and wealth. Mildly troubled in his spirit, he enters a private clinic and is assigned to the seventh floor, reserved for people who are not really ill at all. Gradually, steadily, he is moved down towards the first floor, "the antechamber of death." At first he fails to realize what is happening; finally he refuses to believe it. Martin Esslin has called the play "a remarkable and highly original work" and says that "in the hospital, with its rigid stratification, Buzzati has found a terrifying image of society itself . . . distant, rule-ridden, incomprehensible, and cruel." Another of his plays, *Un verme al ministero* (A Worm at the Ministry), is a political satire.

If *Il deserto dei Tartari* is the most admired of Buzzati's books, the most widely known and best loved of them is a fable for children called *La famosa invasione degli orsi in Sicilia*, translated as *The Bears' Famous Invasion of Sicily*. It tells how, once upon a time, the bears came down from the mountains to escape the cold winters and found so much corruption among men that they were glad to return to their caves. The story has been warmly praised for its "delicacy, humor, and richness of detail" and for the author's splendid illustrations.

A bachelor, Dino Buzzati led a quiet life, removed from political and literary debate. His principal recreations were skiing and mountaineering in the Dolomites, and he was also a painter of some ability. His work in this form is reminiscent of De Chirico's surrealistic cityscapes, and of the bleak, metaphysical atmosphere of *Il grande ritratto* and *Un amore*. Buzzati drew on this talent in a surprising and impressive way in *Poema a fumetti* (1969), a pop-art strip cartoon version of the myth of Orpheus and Eurydice, set in some city of the future. The illustrations, some of them in color, are accompanied by "balloons" or captions, often in rhymed verse, showing a characteristic preoccupation with death, evil, and sex. The result is a sophisticated, striking, and often frightening poem that has been very popular in Italy, especially with young people.

Biasin has provided a description of the author at a lecture: "Buzzati, dressed entirely in severe black, with a white, rigid, round collar, was attentive, motionless. The meaning and force of his sharp features, crowned by short dark hair, were concentrated in his eyes, always restless, alert, inquisitive."

PRINCIPAL WORKS IN ENGLISH TRANSLATION: The Bears' Famous Invasion of Sicily, 1947; The Tartar Steppe, 1952; Larger Than Life, 1962; A Love Affair, 1964; Catastrophe (short stories), 1966.

ABOUT: Chi è?, 1961; Dizionario enciclopedico della letteratura italiana, 1966; Dizionario universale della letteratura contemporanea, 1959; Esslin, M. The Theatre of the Absurd, 1962. *Periodicals*—Books Abroad 25, no. 1, 1951; Italian Quarterly 22, 1962; New York Times August 24, 1952; New York Review of Books July 30, 1964; New Yorker March 26, 1955; Time August 25, 1952.

DINO BUZZATI

***CADOU, RENÉ-GUY** (February 15, 1920–March 20(?), 1951), French poet, was born at Sainte-Reine-de-Bretagne. When he was a child, the family moved to Nantes where Cadou attended the *lycée*. He was successful in the first part of his *baccalauréat* but had little interest in formal education and did not pass the final stage. (The French government decided in 1966 that the *baccalauréat* should become a single examination whereas previously it had been taken in two parts.)

Cadou had a very happy childhood, and his father, who had himself wished to be an author, encouraged his interest in literature. His mother died when the boy was twelve and his father eight years afterwards. Cadou had been deeply attached to his parents and in his poetry he refers despondently to their early deaths and speaks of the joy shared with them amidst the countryside which he loved. In the bitterness which he was to experience later he sought refreshment in the places where he had been brought up with such tender care.

There had hardly ever been any doubt in Cadou's mind that he must be a poet. Before he was eighteen and while still at school he published his first book, *Les Brancardiers de l'aube* (The Stretcher-bearers of the Dawn, 1937), which, though immature, is astonishingly competent technically. *Forges du vent* (Works of the Wind) in 1938 and *Retour de flamme* (Return of the Flame) in 1940 gave evidence of improved craftsmanship.

* ka dōō'

RENÉ-GUY CADOU

France was now at war, but nevertheless Cadou was able to publish three further books in 1941—*Années-Lumière* (Light Years), *Morte-Saison* (Dead Season), and *Porte d'écume* (Gate of Foam). He had a stern struggle and speaks of his cold attic and the privations he had to endure during the German Occupation. Nevertheless he worked unremittingly. To learn to write, he said, one must learn to live, and suffering was part of his apprenticeship. Sustained by his fervent religious faith, he produced books quickly—perhaps, he admitted, too quickly. Cadou believed that he would die young, a conviction that was to prove true, and he felt a need to complete what he considered his duty as well as his pleasure. In his writing life of only fourteen years he wrote over thirty books.

After the war *Pleine Poitrine* (Full Voice, 1946) and *Les Visages de solitude* (The Faces of Loneliness, 1947) appeared, and in the following year the passionate love poems—*4 Poèmes d'amour à Hélène* (Four Love Poems for Hélène). No year passed without at least one new book, and when in 1950 he published a collection of his work, *Poèmes choisis*, 1944–1950, his reputation, already high with other poets, began to grow with the general public.

Cadou never liked town life, though in his last years he lived in Paris. He was something of a lonely figure. He felt most relaxed with simple friends in simple surroundings and shunned the fashionable drawing rooms and the literary salons. He had come under the influence of the surrealists but he complained that surrealism had taken the wrong road and developed into a kind of Morse telegraphy.

Cadou is at his finest as a lyrical and romantic poet, sometimes narrowly avoiding the oversentimental. He sought significance in everything, in the day-to-day routine of the common people as much as in the majesty of the heavens and the changing of the seasons, and at his best he expressed it in what became incantations remarkable for their emotional intensity.

After the publication of his collected poems in 1950, Cadou had little more than a year to live, but in this short period he was at his most prolific. *Les Biens de ce monde* (The Joys of This World) was published in 1951 and, after his death, in 1952 and 1953, appeared Parts 1 and 2 of *Hélène ou le règne végétal* (Hélène or the Vegetable Kingdom) which many regard as his most important work.

Some writers demand close concentration from their readers before providing any satisfaction. Though there are depths of meaning in his work which repay study, Cadou has an immediate and straightforward appeal: he repeated that he wanted to give his verse the odor of white bread and the perfume of flowers. He believed that everyone could understand good poetry. It was René-Guy Cadou's achievement, said a critic, to open the world of imagination to the ordinary man.

PRINCIPAL WORKS IN ENGLISH TRANSLATION: *Poems in* Aspel, A. and Justice, D. (eds.) Contemporary French Poetry, 1965; Hartley, A. (ed.) The Penguin Book of French Verse: Twentieth Century, 1959.

ABOUT: Boisdeffre, P. de. Dictionnaire de littérature contemporaine, 1900–1962, 1962; Boisdeffre, P. de. Une Histoire vivante de la littérature d'aujourd'hui, 1938–1958, 1958; Manoll, M. René-Guy Cadou: Une Étude, 1954; Rousselot, J. Panorama critique des nouveaux poètes français, 1952.

CALDER, (PETER) RITCHIE. *See* RITCHIE-CALDER, BARON, OF BALMASHANNAR

CALDER-MARSHALL, ARTHUR (August 19, 1908–), English novelist, memoirist, and biographer, was born in a suburb of London, the younger son of Arthur Grotjan Calder-Marshall and the former Alice Poole. His father, a consulting engineer and merchant, traveled a great deal abroad, and the family lived in a succession of rented suburban houses until, when Calder-Marshall was fifteen, they settled in the isolated Sussex market town of Steyning. He and his brother went to St. Paul's School in London, living partly in Steyning, partly in Bloomsbury, where their father had rented a town apartment.

Calder-Marshall's admirable memoir *The Magic of My Youth* describes his friendship in Steyning with Victor Neuburg, a "Mauve Decade" poet known to his friends as "Vickybird." It was said that Neuburg had once been turned into a zebra by the notorious black magician Aleister Crowley. Neuburg denied this and subsequently earned a somewhat less equivocal reputation as the poetry editor of the *Sunday Referee*, the first publisher of Dylan Thomas and Pamela Hansford Johnson, among others. Influenced by the temper of the times, by "Vickybird," and by the lively cultural ambiance of Bloomsbury and Soho, Calder-Marshall was caught up in the "war between the artists and the Philistines . . . [and] enlisted enthusiastically in the ranks of the artists, swallowing modernism at a gulp."

From St. Paul's, Calder-Marshall went on to Hertford College, Oxford University. There he edited *Oxford Outlook*, studied ritual magic, and was falsely accused of celebrating a Black Mass. He was also secretary of the university's poetry society, securing such varied guest speakers as Walter de la Mare and Wilhelmina Stitch. Aleister Crowley, however, was banned by the university authorities. Calder-Marshall, meeting "the Great Beast" at this time, was rapidly and permanently disillusioned with "the magic of his youth."

Calder-Marshall had published some stories in the Manchester *Guardian* while still at the university, but his search for literary work when he came down was unsuccessful. With his father's financial support, he wrote a novel—seventy thousand words at the rate of one thousand words a day—but destroyed it after a single rejection. He says: "The book wasn't a novel at all, it was an exercise book; and there was no need to keep it because I knew all those lessons by heart." Dejected, but still determined to be a novelist, Calder-Marshall went off to teach at a minor and very bad public school.

His first published novel, *Two of a Kind*, appeared when he was twenty-five. He was credited by his reviewers with "a talent for graphic description and an understanding of the emotion underlying apparently irrational conduct." *At Sea*, about a young married couple adrift in an open boat, was welcomed as the work of "one of those young and vigorous writers who are determined to have no respect for ordinary conventions." *About Levy* was even less conventional—a series of forty-four sketches of its central character, a man on trial for murder. *Pie in the Sky*, the novel which established his reputation, was much wider in scope than its predecessors, involving a relatively large cast of characters in a story about emotional and industrial conflict in a Midlands mill town. It was called "almost fiercely contemporary, and often political" though "rarely partisan," and praised for the vividness of its characterization, its "sustained veracity and variation in dialogue and event." Calder-Marshall wrote another admired novel, a political thriller called *The Way to Santiago*, before he volunteered for the army in 1940.

After a year in the army, Calder-Marshall went to the Films Division of the Ministry of Information, where he remained until the end of the war. *The Watershed* describes some of his experiences there. He has written relatively little fiction since the war, but has instead produced a number of excellent biographies. They include among others *No Earthly Command*, about Alexander Woods, DSO, who during the Battle of Jutland, "received an interposed message telling him to serve God"; *The Innocent Eye*, about the documentary film director Robert Flaherty; and *Wish You Were Here*, about Donald McGill, creator of picture postcards of splendid vulgarity. The author's best-known biography is *Sage of Sex*, his life of Havelock Ellis. Cyril Connolly said of Calder-Marshall that "it must be a pleasure to have one's life written by him."

ARTHUR CALDER-MARSHALL

Calder-Marshall has also written travel books, short stories, screen plays, and books for children. He is a frequent contributor to a variety of periodicals, and to radio and television, and his editorial assignments have included the four-volume Bodley Head edition of the works of Jack London. The author has been called "compact, with closely cut grey hair, serious in mien, but with an engaging sense of humor . . . a man of deep Christian principles and advanced social views." He was married in 1934 to Violet Sales and has two daughters. One of them, Anna, is a stage and television actress.

PRINCIPAL WORKS: *Fiction*—Two of a Kind, 1933; At Sea, 1934; About Levy, 1934; A Crime Againt Cania, 1934; Dead Centre, 1935; A Pink Doll, 1935; A Date With a Duchess (stories), 1937; Pie in the Sky, 1937; The Way to Santiago, 1940; A Man Reprieved, 1950; Occasion of Glory, 1955; The Fair to Middling, 1959; The Scarlet Boy, 1961. *Nonfiction*—Glory Dead, 1939; The Watershed, 1947; The Magic of My Youth, 1951;

No Earthly Command, 1957; Havelock Ellis, 1959 (U.S., Sage of Sex); The Enthusiast, 1962; The Innocent Eye, 1963; Wish You Were Here, 1966; Lewd, Blasphemous and Obscene, 1972. *As editor*—Selected Writings of Tobias Smollett, 1950; The Bodley Head Jack London (4 vols.), 1963–1966; Prepare to Shed Them Now: The Ballads of George R. Sims, 1968.
ABOUT: Who's Who, 1971.

***CALISHER, HORTENSE** (December 20, 1911–), American short story writer and novelist, writes: "A writer's life, unless chronicled for itself, is tangential to his work. All that he is, significant or not, and whether he likes it or not, is there.

"I was born in New York City, grew up and was schooled there, married and lived in various places elsewhere in the United States, until returning to a small Hudson River town in 1946, and to Manhattan in 1959. So, though my friends here are from many places and all sides, I do not live here as a member of a literary set, or as an émigré to the lodestar, but in the continuity of my birthplace, under all the associative weight this bears anywhere. Continuity like this gives the writer his dynasts and a seat for his reflections, no matter what the region is, Wessex or the city world.

"My parents were Hedwig Lichtstern and Joseph Henry Calisher. My mother came here as a young girl around the turn of the century, from Oberelsbach to family already residents of Yorkville, the German community in New York. They were middle-class German Jews. My father, old enough to be hers, was born in Richmond, Virginia, during the Civil War. His father, Henry Jacob Calisher, an English émigré, is listed in the 1830s as an elder of the Spanish-Portuguese synagogue there. Many German Jews were. There is a town of Kalisch on the oft-disputed German-Polish frontier. In England some Calishers had become Curtises or even Campbells; the tradition that they were originally Sephardic Spanish persists, plus a few stray patronymics to support it. Berthe Bendan (ben Dan), whom my grandfather married in 1852, was from Dresden, the daughter of a rabbi and sister of a professor of philosophy at the university, who later was a visiting professor at New York University. After the Civil War, the family moved to New York, first to 'brownstone' living, later to apartments. My grandmother, widowed matriarch of eight, of which Joseph was the youngest son, was known to me in her nineties. My parents met at Saratoga, at the races.

"There were thus many influences in the household—longer than normal gaps between the generations, conflicts of interest between the mercantile and the scholarly, the 'American' and the émigré. Jews have a pride of heritage, tradition and tragedy. So have Southerners, with different subject matter. Both are often anecdotalists, of humors peculiar to each—and run to large family gatherings. My father's family saw no contradiction in being both; my mother's were far more German than they seemed Jews. The combination was odd all round, volcanic to meditative to fruitfully dull, bound to produce someone interested in character, society, and time. Outside in school and street was all polyglot New York.

"My first stories of the 'Elkin' family, five published in the *New Yorker*, were variously hailed—as adding a new 'environment' to American letters, and protested by rabbis and other Jews—just as later, Southerners would protest what I wrote of them. A few other 'family' stories were published elsewhere in the early years; later came a second wave of first-person stories like 'May-ry' and 'Time, Gentleman!,' which are more memoir, and to which I occasionally add, as with 'Gargantua.' But I deserted the autobiographically traceable story early, perhaps because though I had written since the age of seven, I was thirty-six when published. I have regretted none of these facts, though taking so long was hard. When 'In Greenwich There Are Many Gravelled Walks' came out, an editor asked whether the people were 'real' ones, and when I answered 'No—not in that sense' said, 'Congratulations—you've just written your second novel.' The *New Yorker* published this and three other non-family stories (the last in 1956), to a total of nine out of thirty-six stories, four novellas and three novels; my oft-dubbed '*New Yorker* writer' status is therefore not fair to them.

"*In the Absence of Angels* (story collection) was published in 1951; *False Entry*, the first novel, ten years later; in between, I wrote stories as well, brought up two children, held brief jobs, taught in colleges. As a novel, *False Entry* has been called Dickensian in England and Proustian here; it is of course both an 'inward' and an 'outward' novel which scorns neither events nor psyches, violent action nor soliloquy. The style is almost as much the narrator's as mine; my pen has always changed its voice with its subject matter. The long chapter on the Ku Klux Klan trial was thought to be a 'flight of the imagination,' by those who demand that a novel's social concerns be thumpingly plain and functionally separate from character; though history has now authenticated that chapter in the very pages of the New York *Times*, I should hope that in the book it still is freed into the imagination. *Textures of Life*, a smaller, more contained novel, is written in an 'oblique' voice, concerned as it is with the dailiness which subtly pushes our lives on while we wait for the overt event. In *Journal From Ellipsia*, which deals with outer space, I found my pen straining a new way to make meaning clear—which is what style is. If 'The Railway Police' and

* kal′ ish ər

'The Last Trolley Ride' have subtly different idiom, it is because their worlds are so apart. But I have no interest in language experiment as such. As a child I was steeped in the Old Testament and Thackeray, among much else. Form I must have in some sense; to me each manuscript to a degree makes its own. Most writers go from short works to long ones, and sometimes back again if they live long enough; I am interested in any way a writer can give form to experience. At best one is not a Jew or Buddhist artist, a Congo Black or Virginia-ham pink one, or even male or female, but ultimately humane, intense and particular; it is all a dancing before the ark of the Lord."

Her autobiographical stories about "Hester Elkin" provide a detailed and affectionate picture of Hortense Calisher's childhood and adolescence. Hester lived, as William Peden has written, in "a comfortable world of middle-class Manhattan apartment-dwellers in the first quarter of the twentieth century, a bustling active world of a large family with many cousins, uncles, and aunts 'so close-knit that all its branches lived within round-the-corner call of each other.' " Miss Calisher received her bachelor's degree from Barnard College in 1932, her master's from Columbia. Soon afterwards, in 1935, she married Heaton Bennet Heffelfinger, an engineer. They traveled a great deal in the following years, and in 1946 settled in Nyack. They had two children, a son and a daughter.

Her first book, *In the Absence of Angels*, placed Miss Calisher at once among the major American short story writers of her generation, admired for her great narrative skill, the grace and economy of her prose, and the Proustian subtlety of her insights into character. Her themes (except in the Hester stories) are dark. Her concern is with the "knell of sadness for something that had been, that had never quite been, that now had almost ceased to be." And this "singular concern," according to Gloria Levitas, "often involves her in a melancholy sentimentalism that blurs the acuity of her vision by reducing all of life's problems to the lack of communication between human beings. . . . If Hortense Calisher's intimate vignettes seem strangely static in a world mad with motion . . . she has at the same time created some of the most discomfortingly vivid writing of this decade."

The critical response to her novels has been more mixed and uncertain. The first, *False Entry*, was an investigation of the problem of identity. A. S. Morris thought it a "brave and major book, with many of its scenes drawn to the measure of a masterpiece," and Brigid Brophy called its author "an American of European sympathies, taut artistry and stupendous talent." But other critics

HORTENSE CALISHER

had reservations. Melvin Maddocks found "an unevenness in Miss Calisher's attention to her subject. . . . She has compact scenes next to overblown episodes, weakly integrated. She shows a spare, sure sense of compassion, then allows it to spread into sentiment or melodrama or aimless erotica. Brilliant phrases easily become mere overwriting. The reader's final impression may be that he is witnessing an excellent minor writer stretching beyond her natural range."

Miss Calisher's subsequent novels and novellas have had a similarly ambivalent reception—wholehearted praise from some, but suggestions from others that her dense, idiosyncratic, and sometimes precious prose style obscures meaning, and that prolonged moral or psychological investigations are allowed to clog the narrative pace: as the author herself once wrote, "reality decamps while the philosopher strives to define it."

Miss Calisher writes slowly, after much thought and preparation, and seldom finds it necessary to change what she writes. She received Guggenheim Fellowships in 1952 and 1955, and a grant from the National Institute of Arts and Letters in 1967. In 1958 she visited Southeast Asia. She has taught as a visiting lecturer at several universities, and from 1968 to 1970 was an adjunct professor at Columbia. She remarried in 1959, her husband being the novelist Curtis Harnack. Emily Hahn has described Miss Calisher as "a tall, graceful woman with an individual type of beauty, much humor, and tremendous vitality." She enjoys art, opera, the theatre, walking, and the domestic arts.

PRINCIPAL WORKS: In the Absence of Angels (stories), 1951; False Entry (novel), 1961; Tale for the Mirror (a novella and other stories), 1962; Textures of Life (novel), 1963; Extreme Magic (a novella and other stories), 1964; Journal from Ellipsia (novel), 1965; The Railway Police, and The Last Trolley Ride (novellas), 1966; The New Yorkers (novel), 1969; Queenie (novel), 1971; Standard Dreaming (novel), 1972; Herself: An Autobiographical Work, 1972; Eagle Eye (novel), 1973.

ABOUT: Brophy, B. Don't Never Forget, 1966; Contemporary Authors 4, 1963; Peden, W. H. The American Short Story, 1964; Vinson, J. (ed.) Contemporary Novelists, 1972; Who's Who in America, 1972–1973. *Periodicals*—Book World April 27, 1969; Christian Science Monitor November 2, 1961; Library Journal October 1, 1951; New York Herald Tribune Books November 4, 1962; New York Times Book Review March 28, 1971; Saturday Review February 16, 1952; October 28, 1961; Wilson Library Bulletin March 1963; Wisconsin Studies in Contemporary Literature Summer 1965.

***CALVINO, ITALO** (October 15, 1923–), Italian novelist and short story writer, was born in Santiago de Las Vegas, Cuba. Both parents, Mario and Eva Calvino, were botanists. A bookish boy, Calvino was brought up on the Italian Riviera at San Remo, where his father was curator of the botanical gardens. Although his parents were not able to interest him in a scientific career, Calvino's intense feeling for natural scenery and his passion for precise description are clearly as much scientific as poetic, and in recent years he has come to see that the problems of science, literature, and philosophy are inseparable.

In 1940, as a compulsory member of the Young Fascists, Calvino participated in the Italian occupation of the French Riviera. Three years later, when he was nineteen, he joined the Italian Resistance and from 1943 to 1945 fought the Germans in the Ligurian mountains. At the end of the war he settled in Turin, where he graduated in literature and joined the publishing firm of Einaudi. A friend of Cesare Pavese and Elio Vittorini, he actively supported their attempt at a Communist renovation of Italian society, contributing to Vittorini's periodical *Il Politecnico* and other leftist papers.

His first novel, *Il sentiero dei nidi di ragno* (1947, translated by Archibald Colquhoun as *The Path to the Nest of Spiders*), was based on his experience as a partisan. Appearing at a time when Italian opinion of the resistance movement was still divided, it was a sort of challenge both to the detractors and the apologists, an effort to reestablish the truth. Indeed this story of a boy who joins the partisans and discovers, all at the same time, the excitement of war and the joys of love and the fear of death, the ways and the language of the poor, the charm and cruelty of nature, discipline and freedom, is an orgy of truth. Or, if truth is not so easily had, an orgy of that neorealism which expressed the harsh, crude, violent postwar mood of the Italian partisans. What distinguished Calvino's voice from the neorealistic chorus was an oblique, irrepressible, anarchic streak of poetry, a fairy-tale quality, which Pavese recognized even before Calvino did. *Il sentiero* received the Premio Riccione and was acclaimed by most Italian critics, who in their search for influences mustered not only Pavese and Vittorini and the nineteenth century Italian novelist Nievo, but also Robert Louis Stevenson and Hemingway, Babel and Fadeev.

* kal vē' nō

ITALO CALVINO

Calvino retained his realistic, politically conscious manner into the 1950s, drawing mostly on recent Italian history and often on his own experiences for the themes of the short stories collected in *Ultimo viene il corvo* (Last Comes the Crow, 1959), and *L'entrata in guerra* (Entry into War, 1954). Many of these stories were translated, with the novella *La formica Argentina* (The Argentine Ant, 1952), in *Adam, One Afternoon*. "The Argentine Ant" also appears, with two later stories, in *The Watcher*.

But at the same time Calvino's lyrical-fantastical streak was pulling him in quite another direction—a development that was accelerated by the left wing's serious if generally unsuccessful attempt to give a "political direction" to Italian literature. It was his distrust of such tendencies, his refusal to draw anything resembling a Communist hero, which had given *Il sentiero* some of its polemical thrust. Calvino was greatly affected by Pavese's suicide in 1950, and from that moment his socialist ardor diminished, until in 1957 he left the Communist party.

His changing attitude was evident in the publication in 1956 of *Fiabe italiane*, a large collection of popular fables retold in modern Italian with scrupulous philological care. There followed three remarkable novels in the tradition (as Calvino acknowledged) of *Orlando Furioso*. These were *Il visconte dimezzato* (1952), *Il barone rampante* (1957), and *Il cavaliere inesistente* (1959)—highly entertaining allegories recounting the adventures of three unlikely heroes, one split in half by a cannonball, one so alienated that he has taken triumphantly to the trees, and one totally nonexistent. Each continues to enjoy life in his fashion, and all three lend themselves very well to an ironical interpretation of life in postwar Italy. These stories were translated in two volumes by Archibald Colquhoun as *Baron in the Trees* (1959), and *The Non-Existent Knight and the Cloven Viscount* (1962). Some English-language critics thought them too slight to bear the weight of their metaphysical intentions, but most were delighted by their wit and charm and the quality of their prose. Calvino's "gay, beautifully detailed images," wrote one reviewer, "have the confidence of poetry and the color of an early Renaissance painting."

Thereafter for a time Calvino swung back to a new kind of political and sociological realism. *La speculazione edilizia* (1957) and *La giornata di uno scrutatore* (1963) are discussion novels in which the author appears to be working out the problems he encountered in leaving the uneasy haven of the Communist party.

The Italian critic Renato Barilli, reviewing the massive collection of Calvino's stories published in 1958 as *I racconti*, found a fundamental unity in Calvino's preoccupation with the precise observation and description of *things*—objects, plants, actions. It is because Calvino's talent is basically descriptive, Barilli suggested, that his work is so various and eclectic; he is seeking "a mold, a blueprint, a framework to help him organize the diffuse, detailed material that his eye catches." It may be that Calvino has now found such a framework. In the *Times Literary Supplement* for September 28, 1967, Calvino called for "a literature which breathes philosophy and science but keeps its distance and dissolves, with a slight puff of air, not only theoretical abstractions but also the apparent concreteness of reality." Such a literature, he said, exists so far only in "that extraordinary, indefinable region of the human imagination from which have issued the works of Lewis Carroll, of Queneau, of Borges."

And, he might have added, of Calvino, for he too was then penetrating that region with the stories in *Le cosmicomiche* (1965, translated as *Cosmicomics* by William Weaver, who received a National Book Award for this work). These "evolutionary tales," featuring the protean and ageless creature Qfwfq, are assaults on the frontiers of literature, scientific fairy tales, mathematical fables, suspense stories about the origin of life and the birth of language itself. And all this, as one reviewer wrote in the *Times Literary Supplement*, "at a high level of comedy that, with extraordinary lightness, sees contemporary happenings, sharply observed and socially exact, in terms of infinitely ancient experience." Thus, the story of Qfwfq's reprobate old uncle, who shames his family by remaining a fish when all fashionable creation is scrambling onto the land, can be read as ironic comment on a number of modern movements and attitudes. Often Calvino overcomes the reader's logical reservations by sheer effrontery; in one story, for example, Qfwfq remarks that his sister, who disappeared when the planets were solidifying, turned up "much later, at Canberra in 1912, married to a certain Sullivan, a retired railroad man"—and adds disarmingly that she was then "so changed I hardly recognized her." There are more stories in this mode, not all of them about Qfwfq, in *Ti con zero* (1967, translated by William Weaver as *t zero*.

Le città invisibili (Invisible Cities, 1972) is a novel, or assemblage of prose poems, in which Marco Polo discourses to Kubla Khan on fifty-five cities that are not so much places as states of mind. For one reviewer the work confirmed that Calvino is a master of the *conte philosophique*, who literally "confounds the actual and the fanciful," and who "makes his moral and philosophical points without for a moment spoiling the beauty or weakening the impact of his fables." The same year, 1972, Calvino received the Italian equivalent of a Pulitzer Prize, the Premio Feltrinelli per la Narrativa.

Although he has left the Communist party, Calvino has continued to write for *Il contemporaneo*, the mouthpiece of Italian Marxist intellectuals, and was associated with Vittorini in the founding of a new literary magazine, *Il Menabò*. He is now a director of Einaudi's. He lectures a great deal in Italy and abroad, and makes a special contribution to the quality of Italian culture as a kind of importer of new ideas and exporter of native talent. He was married in 1964 to Chichita Singer, and has a daughter.

PRINCIPAL WORKS IN ENGLISH TRANSLATION: The Path to the Nest of Spiders, 1956; Adam, One Afternoon (stories), 1957; Baron in the Trees, 1959; (comp.) Italian Fables, 1959; The Non-Existent Knight and the Cloven Viscount, 1962; Cosmicomics (stories), 1968; t zero (stories), 1969 (England, Time and the Hunter); The Watcher and Other Stories, 1971. *Stories in* Trevelyan, R. (ed.) Italian Writing Today, 1967; Trevelyan, R. (ed.) Italian Short Stories, 1965; Reporter January 5, 1961. *Articles in* Italian Quarterly Spring–Summer 1960; Times Literary Supplement September 28, 1967.

ABOUT: Arbasino, A. Sessanta posizioni, 1972; Dizionario enciclopedico della letteratura italiana, 1966; Dizionario universale della letteratura contemporanea, 1959; Pacifici, S. A Guide to Contemporary Italian Literature, 1962; Pescio-Bottino, G. Calvino, 1967; Trevelyan, R. (ed.)

Italian Writing Today (includes translation of R. Barilli's review of I racconti, partial translation of Calvino's preface to 1964 edition of Il sentiero dei nidi di ragno); Woodhouse, T. R. Italo Calvino, 1968. *Periodicals*—Atlas July 1966; Italian Quarterly Spring–Summer 1960; New York Review of Books November 21, 1968; Times Literary Supplement April 18, 1968; February 9, 1973.

CAMERON, (JOHN) NORMAN (1905–April 20, 1953), Scottish poet and translator, was born in India of Scottish Presbyterian parents who sent him home to school in Edinburgh, at Fettes College. He went on to Oriel College, Oxford, where he read languages, played rugby for his college, became president of the Oxford English Club, and published his first verses in *Oxford Poetry*. His friendship with Robert Graves began at Oxford and lasted until his death. Cameron left the university with an undistinguished degree and in 1929 went out to Nigeria as an education officer. He liked Nigeria and the Nigerians but found his fellow colonials unrewarding companions, their way of life idle and boring. He left in 1932, intending to return to Europe and devote himself to literature. However, after a short stay with Robert Graves in Majorca, he realized that he needed settled employment, emotionally as well as financially, and returned to England. He joined the London advertising agency of J. Walter Thompson and stayed there as a copywriter until the outbreak of World War II.

His poems began to appear during the early 1930s, mostly in Geoffrey Grigson's *New Verse*. His first book, *The Winter House*, was published in 1935 and widely admired for its wit and verbal precision, its eschewal of fashionable stylistic tricks, its humanity and dramatic tautness. During the war Cameron was engaged in "political warfare" in England, Italy, and Austria, receiving an MBE for his services. He returned to advertising in 1947, and subsequently earned his living, or part of it, as a translator.

Norman Cameron destroyed far more poems than he published, and was in any case far from prolific. He called himself an occasional poet, and there are no more than sixty pieces in his posthumous *Collected Poems*. Nevertheless his verse affected not only his contemporaries but also younger postwar poets. Cameron was interested in but not involved in the poetic trends of the 1930s and 1940s—surrealism, political engagement, neo-romanticism. John Press found in his work "a quizzical irony, self-scrutiny, and calm acceptance of life's absurdity" which places him in a "line of wit" descending from Eliot and Empson through Graves and Auden and on to Philip Larkin and the so-called "Movement." Press heard this characteristic tone of voice in Cameron's "The Compassionate Fool," in which the speaker visits his

NORMAN CAMERON

enemy, knowing that the welcome he receives is false: "I made pretence of falling in his plot, / And trembled when in his anxiety / He bared it too absurdly to my view. / And even as he stabbed me through and through / I pitied him for his small strategy."

The strength of Cameron's poems, it has been said, lies in their stories. They are legends in small space, like the one quoted above. "The Compassionate Fool" was thought by some contemporaries to refer to the weakness of England's response to Nazi aggression in the 1930s, but in fact Cameron rarely wrote politically. Most of his poems are introspective—a working out of some personal problem which he contrives to raise to a universal level, aiming at myth rather than polemics. These terse allegories draw much of their power and tension from their ambiguities, which are left to the reader to resolve, "like a modern *Pilgrim's Progress* or spiritual obstacle race." In Frederick Grubb's opinion, "Cameron stakes everything on his story; when he fails, it is because the story is too unprovocative to intrigue us and generate the meaning which transcends the story; then his poems suffer from a low-pressure discursive monotony and an over-staid tone . . . at best, he declares a whole reverberant judgement in terms of one focal image; it is his exhaustive dauntless pursuit of this image's potentialities which makes the meaning reverberate."

Cameron was not drawn to technical experiments, maintaining instead a consistent clarity of expression and a surefooted mastery of traditional rhythmic forms. Critics have drawn attention to his passionate verbal fastidiousness, and Graves says he never used an unfamiliar word without first checking the dictionary for respectable precedents. This quality accounts in part for the excellence of his translations, from Russian, German, and especially from French. In his version of *Candide*, for example, he refused to use words which would have been unfamiliar to Voltaire's English contemporaries. His translations of Villon and of Rimbaud are also highly regarded, and one French critic wrote: "If I knew the English language better, I might dare to affirm that *Le Bateau ivre* is more beautiful in Norman Cameron's translation than in the original."

In 1950 Norman Cameron published a volume of poems, *Forgive Me, Sire*, which reflected a growing sense of personal guilt and intimations of death. He was indeed already suffering from the disease which killed him three years later. At about the same time he underwent psychoanalysis and became a convert to Roman Catholicism. He seems to have written no poetry during the last three years of his life.

Robert Graves described Norman Cameron as "tall, pale, never very strong, with a stutter in his voice, gentle, witty, clumsy, shrewd, over-generous and utterly reliable." He was, Graves said, "a divided character—alternately a Presbyterian precisian and moralist, and a pagan poet and boon-companion . . . he never became a schizophrene, but learned to watch the internal drama and politely introduce the irreconcilable characters."

PRINCIPAL WORKS: *Poetry*—The Winter House, 1935; Work in Hand (containing poems also by Alan Hodge and Robert Graves), 1942; Forgive Me, Sire, 1950; Collected Poems, 1957. *Translations*—Rimbaud, A. Select Verse Poems, 1942; Voltaire, F. Candide, 1947; Constant de Rebecque, B. The Red Note-Book, 1948; Murger, H. Vie de Bohème, 1949; Rimbaud, A. A Season in Hell, 1949; Balzac, H. de. Cousin Pons, 1950; Kerenyi, K. The Gods of the Greeks, 1951; Ivanov, V. I. Freedom and the Tragic Life, 1952; Triolet, E. Inspector of Ruins, 1952; Villon, F. Poems, 1952; Bergengruen, W. A Matter of Conscience, 1952; Stendhal Letters, 1952; Deleuze, B. Vagabond of the Ashes, 1953; (with R. H. Stevens) Hitler's Table Talk, 1941–1944 (U.S., Secret Conversations), 1953.

ABOUT: Allott, K. Penguin Book of Contemporary Verse, 1962; Graves, R. *introduction to* Cameron's Collected Poems, 1957; Grigson, G. (ed.) The Concise Encyclopedia of Modern World Literature, 1963; Grubb, F. A Vision of Reality, 1965; Press, J. Rule and Energy, 1963; Reeves, J. The Modern Poet's World, 1957. *Periodicals*—New York Times April 23, 1953; The Review Autumn-Winter 1971–1972; Times (London) April 23, 1953; Transatlantic Review August 1958.

***CAMPANA, DINO** (August 20, 1885–March 1, 1932), Italian poet, was born at Marradi, near Florence, in the mountains of central Italy. The son of a schoolmaster, he possessed great intellectual gifts, but in his early teens he began to show signs of mental instability. He was educated at a school near Turin and studied chemistry at the University of Bologna but failed to graduate. At that point he began a life of aimless wandering, driven, he said, "by a kind of vagabond mania."

* käm pä′ nä

DINO CAMPANA

He was jailed for brawling in Switzerland, and elsewhere was more than once arrested for being without papers. In 1906, suffering from dementia praecox, he spent some months in a mental hospital in Imola, the first of many such confinements. His wanderings took him to Latin America where he was a bandsman in the Argentine navy and subsequently, in Buenos Aires, a doorman at a nightclub, a policeman, and a fireman. He returned to Europe, apparently as a stoker on a cargo ship, and joined a gypsy fair in Odessa, traveling with it as a vendor. The poet Camillo Sbarbaro described a visit from Campana: "My family barely tolerated him because of his lice. In the evening he had an almost maidenly modesty about taking off his clothes. Hospitality was quickly irksome to him, and by the third day he would have no more of it. I watched him go off, stubborn, with his vagabond's gait, toward Sottaripa. For his only baggage he had in his pocket *Leaves of Grass*."

A powerfully built man, with red hair and a ruddy complexion, Campana is said to have greatly resembled the painter Rubens. The flamboyance and intensity of his personality were all the more remarkable in Italy, where poets were mostly respectable academics. His close friend, the critic Bino Binazzi, remembered him in Florence: "He would go from table to table, making the rounds of the best-known cafés, to sell his poems. And he would often make fun of those who bought them. He would look hard at their faces, making out their philistine natures; then, he would burst out laughing with that laugh of his that seemed to belong to some comely, bronzed faun . . . tearing out pages from the book he had just sold, upon the specious and hardly flattering pretext that the buyer would never have understood them."

The attitudes reflected in Campana's poetry were disordered and contradictory. He was associated with the group of progressive and socially conscious poets who contributed to *La Voce*, but he was fascinated by the brutality of the Hohenzollern empire and dedicated his poems to Wilhelm II; Peter M. Riccio called him "a subversive and a reactionary, an anarchist and an imperialist." His religious views were similarly divided between Christian and pagan ideals. And the gypsy girl who is so often the central figure in his poems is treated now with love, now with contempt, sometimes with fear, sometimes with pity. He could not, or would not, coordinate his ideas into a coherent structure.

What Campana sought to convey was the direct unmodified impact of intense emotional experience, free from any kind of intellectual or formal restraint. His lyrics are fragmentary, hallucinatory, pervaded with an elegiac nihilism. They move between and merge dream and reality, image and object, sound and color, as if all life were a dream, breaking "the chains of matter" as if they did not exist. "It is necessary to sweep over life," Campana wrote, "it is the only art possible." And for him it was.

At times Campana's verse resembles the automatic writing of the surrealists, and seems "only a harmony of words and a race of images," mere rhetoric. His best poems, written perhaps when the lyrical impulses coincided with a period of mental stability, have an exactness, a visionary lucidity, without equal in modern Italian poetry: "I watch the white rocks, the mute fountains of the winds, / . . . And the swollen rivers that flow weeping / And the shadows of human labor bent there over the cold hills" ("La Chimera").

Campana's only book of poems, *Canti orfici* (Orphic Songs), was first published in 1914, when it attracted little attention. The same year he enlisted as a volunteer in the Italian army and he had reached the rank of sergeant before he was discharged as mentally deranged. He wrote no poetry after 1916. *Lettere* (1958), his correspondence between 1916 and 1918 with Sibilla Aleramo, provides a moving record of his decline into madness and despair. "I was a writer once," he told his doctor some years later, "but had to give up, being of unsound mind. I don't connect ideas. I don't follow . . . ." On January 28, 1918, at the age of thirty-two, Campana was committed to the asylum of Castel Pulci, in Florence, where he remained until his death.

Dino Campana's life, as well as his poetry, has put many critics in mind of Rimbaud, and of the Austrian poet Georg Trakl. As Edward Williamson said, however, "the luminous landscapes which are glimpsed through the broken architecture of his verse are purely Italian: they are peaceful landscapes where archaic figures stand in attitudes of immemorial rite." Campana's influence has been seen in the work of poets as widely different as Ungaretti and Montale, and in a general loosening of the forms of Italian poetry, a new sense of its musical and pictorial possibilities. *Canti orfici* was expanded posthumously and reissued in 1952 and 1960. An English translation by I. L. Salomon appeared in 1968.

PRINCIPAL WORKS IN ENGLISH TRANSLATION: Orphic Songs, 1968. *Poems in* Barnstone, W. (ed.) Modern European Poetry, 1966; Golino, C. L. (ed.) Contemporary Italian Poetry, 1962; Kay, G. (ed.) Penguin Book of Italian Verse, 1958. *Periodicals*—Italian Quarterly Summer 1958.

ABOUT: Barnstone, W. (ed.) Modern European Poetry, 1966; Bonalumi, G. Cultura e poesia in Campana, 1953; Burnshaw, S. (ed.) The Poem Itself, 1960; Cohen, J. M. Poetry of This Age, 1960; Costanzo, M. Studi critici, 1955; Curley, D. N. and Curley, A. (eds.) Modern Romance Literatures (A Library of Literary Criticism), 1967; Dizionario enciclopedico della letteratura italiana, 1966; Dizionario universale della letteratura contemporanea, 1959; Falqui, E. Per una cronistoria dei 'Canti Orfici,' 1961; Gerola, G. Dino Campana, 1955; Golino, C. L. (ed.) Contemporary Italian Poetry, 1962; Grana, G. (ed.) Letteratura italiana: I Contemporanei, 1963; Grigson, G. (ed.) Concise Encyclopedia of Modern World Literature, 1963; Riccio, P. M. Italian Authors of Today, 1938; Smith, H. (ed.) Columbia Dictionary of Modern European Literature, 1947. *Periodicals*—Italian Quarterly Summer 1958; Poetry Magazine December 1951.

CAMPBELL, DAVID (WATT IAN) July 16, 1916–), Australian poet and short story writer, writes: "I was born in a brass bed on a sheepstation in New South Wales not far from Gundagai, the town most often celebrated in the early songs and ballads of shearers, bullockies and bushrangers. We had our own legends too. There was my father's boast, 'Though I wouldn't tell everyone,' that his great-grandfather, who farmed near Ayr, used to drink with Robert Burns; and that his maternal grandfather, Captain Campbell, survived shipwreck by catching and eating flying-fish. My mother, not to be outdone, spoke of her great-grandfather, Samuel Blackman, who as the family well knew, crossed the Blue Mountains a jump ahead of Blaxland and party (Lawson and Woolworths as a younger member put it*); and however this may be, there is an obelisk to him in the town of Mudgee which he founded. She was full of tales of Northwest horsemen who compared in our

* Gregory Blaxland's companions in his 1813 crossing of the Blue Mountains were Lieutenant Lawson and William Charles Wentworth (not Woolworths).

young minds very favourably with the biblical characters she read about each Sunday and led me to an early liking for Banjo Paterson's ballads. In my book of stories, *Evening Under Lamplight*, I tried to recapture the lonely yet imaginative life we led at Ellerslie, but the characters changed in the telling so that only the atmosphere is as I remember it.

"In the tradition of the King's School, I played football seriously in my teens, and at night on a Crimea bed, when thoughts of suburban girls on islands became too tropical, I would return them to the sidelines and play whole matches through my head. These flights, with a flair for divinity and geometry—I still prefer poems with the economy and completeness of a theorem—were probably as good an imaginative training as any; but going up to Cambridge, it was forced upon me that there were some gaps in my background. While in this bewilderment, on the strength of a couple of rough ballads and a half-finished history paper, Dr. E. M. W. Tillyard swung me over to English (I had read *The Forsyte Saga*) and tutored me with the greatest patience and encouragement; John Manifold asked me round for DOM and Mozart (I had discovered Roy Campbell and the Elizabethan lyrists); and word came from the great 'Q' [Sir Arthur Quiller-Couch] that I was a poet. It seemed I was made—and for four years I could write nothing, by which time I was a pilot in the Pacific, married and reading Yeats.

"Yeats saw me through the war and my first poems. These were usually gifts: the first line or phrase given, and the sense of bringing to light something already there rather than of a conscious making. The results surprised me even more than my friends and I kept my methods very dark, thinking them a kind of cheating, until I found them common to most poets—not that there was not a lot of sweat and waiting. At this time Douglas Stewart did more for me than was reasonable to expect from any friend or editor.

"After the war, I tried journalism—nothing given there; then with my wife and two children (now three) took over the family farm looking across Canberra to the winter snowfields. The land, with its white trees stripping to grass-gold in summer, I loved; at times I had the sense of riding around my own world of the imagination, my own creation. There hard work and harsh seasons which kept me, I claimed, from writing, provided the tensions from which no doubt my best work has come. It has meant, however, that my output so far has not been large. Recently we moved to a high pleasant valley east of Canberra where larks sing above the drought and frost and my search for time at the right time continues."

David Campbell, the son of a doctor, is one of the

DAVID CAMPBELL

two or three most important of his generation of Australian poets. As he says, he was educated in Sydney at the King's School (of which he was captain in his time), and in England at Cambridge University. A distinguished athlete, he was a football "Blue" at Cambridge, and played for England against Ireland and Wales. He returned to Australia in 1938. In World War II he was a pilot in the Royal Australian Air Force, rising to the rank of wing commander, and winning the DFC and bar. His poems began to appear during the war in the Australian review *The Bulletin*, edited by Douglas Stewart, and in England in *The Listener*. His first book, *Speak With the Sun*, was published in 1949 by the London firm of Chatto and Windus—evidence that he is better known in England than most Australian poets.

Like Douglas Stewart, whose poetry Campbell's in some ways resembles, he springs from a non-intellectual, predominantly lyrical tradition; the influence of Roy Campbell has been greater than the influence of Yeats. But David Campbell appears to some Australian critics to be speaking for his country in a unique way. As Enid Moodie Heddle put it: "Campbell is expressing an Australian vision which in a strange, dream-like fashion recalls the timeless land within time which all Australians hold somewhere hidden in memory"; he writes of "his country in poetry . . . accurately and exactly in the words of dream and symbol." Celebrated lines illustrative of this are: "The Murray's source is in the mind / And at a word it flows."

Vincent Buckley has commented from a different viewpoint upon the vision of Australia which Campbell shares with such poets as Douglas

Stewart and Judith Wright—of an endless desert of stripped bones and circling hawks, where people "seem hardly to matter at all, except as objects in a whimsical drama whose action is doomed from the start." Buckley finds this "inadequate as a creative reflection of Australian life and aspirations," and so it may be, though it is difficult to see what Campbell can be expected to do about it.

Brought up as he was in "Banjo" Paterson country, David Campbell has been much influenced by the old bush ballads. He writes easily in ballad rhythms, though his longer and more ambitious narrative poems tend not to be very well sustained. He is essentially a lyric poet, and his peculiar strengths, which can produce poetry of great purity and power, are a Housman-like capacity for epigram and an even more unusual ability to evoke and wryly comment upon the cruelties of nature. The first quality is well illustrated in "Mothers and Daughters": "The cruel girls we loved / Are over forty. / Their subtle daughters / Have stolen their beauty; / And with a blue stare / Of cool surprise, / They mock their anxious mothers / With their mothers' eyes." The second quality emerges, for example, in "Among the Farms," which asks God to "look twice on animal and man / Caught in the narrow ways of blood," and ends by describing the "country man" who stripped the marauding fox of "the russet pelt for prize / And set the living creature loose." Campbell's short stories, a little too easy and lacking in tension, are gracefully written.

The author was married in 1940 to the former Bonnie Lawrance, and has two sons and a daughter.

PRINCIPAL WORKS: *Poetry*—Speak With the Sun, 1949; The Miracle of Mullion Hill, 1957; Poems, 1962; Selected Poems 1942–1968, 1968. *Short stories*—Evening Under Lamplight, 1959. *As editor*—Australian Poetry, 1967.

ABOUT: Australian Writing Today, 1968; Buckley, V. Essays in Poetry, 1957; Green, H. M. A History of Australian Literature, 1962; Heddle, E. M. Australian Literature Now, 1949; Who's Who in Australia, 1969.

CAMPBELL, JOHN W(OOD) (JR.) (June 8, 1910–July 11, 1971), American science fiction writer and editor who also wrote as "Don A. Stuart" was science fiction's acknowledged father-figure. He was born in Newark, New Jersey, and was named for his father, an electrical engineer who had married Dorothy Strahern, like him a native of Ohio. Campbell's childhood seems to have been an unhappy one. His father, according to Sam Moskowitz's *Seekers of Tomorrow*, was an unbending disciplinarian; his mother was self-centered and unpredictable. The boy, "precociously intellectual, interested in everything around him," was almost friendless except for his younger sister Laura, and immersed himself in scientific experiments and in books. By the time he was eight he had discovered

JOHN W. CAMPBELL

Jeans and Eddington, and he went on to read widely, enjoying in particular mythology, folklore, and anthropology.

At fourteen Campbell was sent to Blair Academy in Blairstown, New Jersey, where he annoyed his instructors by correcting their errors, did well in physics and Spanish, but left in 1928 without a diploma. The same year he enrolled at the Massachusetts Institute of Technology, majoring in physics. Already an avid reader of science fiction, at MIT he began to write it. His first published story, "When the Atoms Failed," appeared in *Amazing Stories* in January 1930, when Campbell was nineteen. It featured one of the first computers in science fiction history, a circumstance which perhaps owes something to Campbell's friendship with MIT's professor of mathematics, the cybernetician Norbert Wiener. More stories appeared in 1930 and 1931, including Campbell's first full-length novel, *Islands of Space*, published in *Amazing Stories Quarterly* for spring 1931. The same year he married Dona Stuart and failed at MIT. Campbell switched to Duke University, graduating a year later with a bachelor of science degree.

During the Depression years, science fiction magazines paid one half cent per word, and that not very promptly; to support himself and his wife Campbell was forced to take a variety of jobs. He continued to write, nevertheless, specializing in violent cosmic epics like "The Mightiest Machine," full of superscientific know-how, which established him as one of the most popular living writers in the field. But Campbell was not content to churn out space operas. He set out "to write a story in which mood and characterization would predominate and science would play a secondary role." The result was "Twilight," about the "perfect, ceaseless machines" which work on forever, though their creators are dead, the earth cold. Editors were at first unanimous in rejecting the story but F. Orlin Tremayne, taking over *Astounding Stories*, accepted it enthusiastically.

Campbell adopted a pseudonym derived from his wife's maiden name, and "Twilight" appeared as the work of "Don A. Stuart" in November 1934. According to Moskowitz, "Don A. Stuart bid fair to eclipse Campbell in popularity as a result of this single story. . . . Its appearance was to alter the pattern of science-fiction writing."

During the mid-1930s, Campbell continued to write superscience epics under his own name, and such serious speculative fiction as "Night" and "Who Goes There?" under his pseudonym, in both manifestations inspiring innumerable imitators and disciples. In 1937 he joined the Street & Smith pulp empire and in 1938 became sole editor of *Astounding Stories*, changing its name to *Astounding Science Fiction* and later to *Analog*. Thereafter he produced little original work of his own. This is not to say that his influence diminished; on the contrary, as the paternalistic editor of the leading magazine in its field, he probably did more to shape modern science fiction than any other man. (He was, indeed, so prolific of ideas, advice, and opinions that *Analog* was sometimes referred to by initiates as "Monolog.") Some of his ideas were too good to be used, like the atomic bomb fuse mechanism he devised for one of his writers in 1944; it was so close to the one being developed at Los Alamos for use at Hiroshima that worried FBI men turned up to investigate the security leak.

Campbell was a tall, powerfully built man with hawklike features. Reviewing a collection of his magisterial and deliberately provocative *Analog* editorials in 1967, Anthony Boucher wrote that it was Campbell and his "truly astounding stable of writers . . . who brought science fiction out of the era of gadgetry and converted it into a vehicle for mature speculation, not only about science but about people." But Campbell was not content to rest on his laurels: he believed that "the province of science fiction is both the ridiculous and the sublime"—that "new philosophies are coming" and that "science fiction can help evaluate [them]." He was elected in 1970 to the Science Fiction Hall of Fame. A year later, at the age of sixty-one, he died of a heart disease. He was survived by his wife and three daughters.

PRINCIPAL WORKS: The Atomic Story (nonfiction), 1947; Who Goes There?, 1948; The Incredible Planet, 1949; The Moon Is Hell!, 1951; Cloak of Aesir, 1952; The Black Star Passes, 1953; Invaders from the Infinite, 1961; Collected Editorials from Analog, 1966; The Best of John W. Campbell, 1973; John W. Campbell Anthology, 1973. *As editor*—Astounding Science Fiction Anthology, 1952; Modern Science Fiction: Its Meaning and Its Future, 1953; Prologue to Analog, 1962; Analog 1–2 (2 volumes), 1963–1964; Analog 3, 1965; Analog 4, 1966.

ABOUT: Moskowitz, S. Explorers of the Infinite, 1963; Moskowitz, S. Seekers of Tomorrow, 1966. *Periodicals*—New York Times July 13, 1971; New York Times Book Review February 19, 1967; Sunday Times (London) Magazine October 3, 1965.

CANADAY, JOHN (EDWIN) (February 1, 1907–), American art critic who writes detective stories as "Matthew Head," was born in Fort Scott, Kansas, the son of Franklin and Agnes (Musson) Canaday. He received his B.A. from the University of Texas in 1929 and his M.A. in the history of art from Yale (1933), where he also studied painting. There followed several years of study in Paris, at the École du Louvre and elsewhere.

Canaday began his career in 1938, as a teacher of art history in the University of Virginia's department of architecture. The war soon intervened. In 1942 Canaday went to the Congo with the Bureau of Economic Welfare, and after a year there joined the United States Marine Corps, finishing the war in the South Pacific as a first lieutenant in an air warning squadron. He returned to his old post at the University of Virginia, teaching there until 1950 when he went to Newcomb College, Tulane University, as head of the school of art. He left in 1952 to become chief of the division of education at the Philadelphia Museum of Art.

While he was still in that post Canaday was engaged to write the text for the *Metropolitan Seminars in Art*, a self-study guide to the history and appreciation of art published in twenty-four portfolios between 1958 and 1960 by the Metropolitan Museum of Art in cooperation with the Book-of-the-Month Club. Canaday's *Mainstreams of Modern Art*, surveying the major trends in European art since the French Revolution, won the Athenaeum Award and was well received by most critics. However, Katharine Kuh pointed out that while Canaday "surveys the nineteenth century expansively yet in penetrating detail . . . he merely summarizes art of the last sixty years."

Mainstreams of Modern Art appeared in 1959. In September of the same year Canaday became art critic of the New York *Times*. The first article he wrote in that capacity caused a furor. It was an attack on abstract expressionism, then firmly established as the dominant school of painting in the United States. Canaday expressed his admiration for de Kooning, Jackson Pollock, and Philip Guston but, pointing out that "the nature of abstract expressionism allows exceptional tolerance for incompetence and deception," went on to condemn "the freaks, the charlatans, and the misled who surround this handful of serious and talented

JOHN CANADAY

artists." It was the first of many such attacks on the abilities and motives of "action" painters, and on the cynicism or stupidity of the critics, dealers, and buyers who supported them. Unmoved by editorial rebuttals in *Art News* and angry letters to the New York *Times*, Canaday published *Embattled Critic* (1962), giving permanent form to thirty-nine of his articles and some of the resulting correspondence. Reviewers were, predictably, divided. Some found the book reactionary, ponderous, and feeble in its attempts at satire; others thought it "sane and refreshing." John Richardson in the New York *Times Book Review* concluded that Canaday had failed to make his case against the abstract expressionists, but pointed out that the book contained less controversial articles "on individual painters and general topics which the idle reader as well as the informed gallery-goer will return to with pleasure because they are stimulating, free of jargon and wide in their appeal."

Keys to Art, with captions and commentary by Canaday's wife, was a kind of montage of illustrations arranged so as "to reveal formal and expressive contrasts and similarities in the arts of all ages." The *Saturday Review* said: "The appearance of Ingres's Bather of Valpinçon of 1808 opposite Lipchitz's stone Bather of 1917 adds an unexpected classic element to Cubism. But often the confrontations seem capricious or dictated by chance resemblances alien to the understanding of the object as a work of art." The book was first published in France in 1962, with a text by Luc Benoist. *The Lives of the Painters*, Canaday's four-volume exercise in art history-through-biography, was warmly welcomed by most reviewers.

As "Matthew Head," Canaday is the author of seven Inner Sanctum mystery novels published between 1943 and 1955. He has been praised (by Anthony Boucher) for his ability "to combine the formal detective story with a wittily literate novel of character perception," and called "one of the subtlest, at once the most artistic and most artful of American murder writers." Canaday has said that his books on art "pay better than mystery novels."

Mrs. Canaday is the former Katherine S. Hoover, an editor before she married John Canaday in 1935. They have two sons. Brooks Atkinson has described the author as "a slender, handsome man."

PRINCIPAL WORKS: *Nonfiction*—Mainstreams of Modern Art, 1959; Embattled Critic, Views on Modern Art, 1962; (with Katherine S. Canaday) Keys to Art, 1963 (England, Look, or The Keys to Art); The Lives of the Painters, 1969; Culture Gulch: Notes on Art and its Public in the 1960s, 1969; The Artful Avocado, 1973. *As "Matthew Head"*—The Smell of Money, 1943; The Devil in the Bush, 1945; The Accomplice, 1947; The Cabinda Affair, 1949; The Congo Venus, 1950; Another Man's Life, 1953; Murder at the Flea Club, 1955.

ABOUT: Atkinson, B. Tuesdays and Fridays, 1963; Current Biography, 1962; Who's Who in America, 1970–1971. *Periodicals*—New York Times Book Review May 6, 1962; New Yorker January 4, 1964; Newsweek April 16, 1962; Saturday Review December 7, 1963.

CANETTI, ELIAS (July 25, 1905–), was born at Ruschuk, Bulgaria, of Spanish-Jewish descent. He is the son of Jacques Canetti, a businessman, and the former Mathilde Arditti. His first language was Spanish. When he was six his parents settled in England, but after the early death of his father his mother moved to Vienna. It was his third tongue, German, in which he began to write.

Canetti went to school in Zurich and Frankfurt, going on in 1924 to study at the University of Vienna, where he obtained his doctorate in 1929 with a dissertation in chemistry. He first saw mass street demonstrations in Frankfurt, at the time of the inflation, and his preoccupation with the behavior of crowds was confirmed on July 15, 1927, when the Palace of Justice in Vienna went up in flames. Canetti lived mainly in Vienna, as a writer, until 1938, emigrating in that year to England where he still lives. Canetti was married in 1934 to Venetia Toubner-Calderon, who died in 1963; they had no children.

Soon after a visit to Berlin in 1929 Canetti planned a series of eight novels that was to be a "*comédie humaine* of madness." Of this period Canetti has written: "It seemed no longer possible to me to get to grips with the world by means of conventional realistic fiction. The world had fallen too much apart, as it were, in all directions." Only one of the eight novels was ever written: *Die Blendung* (The Deception, 1935). It concerns a pure scholar, a Sinologist for whom words are the only reality, whose life is contained in the great library which fills his Vienna apartment. Peter Kien marries his housekeeper, and this spiderish creature conspires with the brutish caretaker Pfaff to oust Kien from his apartment and his library. An abstract man, helpless in the jungle of the real world, Kien sinks into the nightmare underworld of Vienna and at last, cut off from his life source, destroyed, returns to burn his library and himself.

In its form, which reflects the fragmentation of reality, and in its perception of the triumphant bestiality to come, the book was ahead of its time. A quarter of a century passed between its first appearance and its full acceptance by German readers. It was translated by C. V. Wedgwood and published in England as *Auto-da-Fé* (1946), in the United States as *Tower of Babel* (1947). Reviewers of this version complained of its "dreadful morbidity" and insane humor, and thought it "rigid with symbolism." But some appreciated its quality even then. Kate O'Brien wrote that Canetti, "with desiccated, pedantic caution . . . reflects fantasy against fact, merges nightmare with routine, cupidity with fanatical innocence, and so establishes all his forces as one great hell that the exhausted reader cannot after a few pages tell light from dark, or hell from hope. . . . A mad, magnificent work which we are not able to endure . . . but of which we dare not deny the genius or the justification." Since then the book's underground reputation has grown steadily, and it has influenced writers in a number of countries. In 1964 it was republished in the United States as *Auto-da-Fé*, and in 1966 Canetti received the Literature Prize of the City of Vienna.

The other seven novels Canetti had planned to illustrate the fracture of reality were never written. When he had finished *Die Blendung*, at the age of twenty-six, he felt that this one case included and subsumed all the others. The novel can be read as a study of the conflict between culture and the mass mind. In the preface to his diaries, *Aufzeichnungen* 1942–1948 (1965), Canetti wrote: "The problem of masses had occupied me since 1925, and that of power had become associated with it only a little later. But until shortly before the war they were not my only concern." Like Hermann Broch, another novelist who had set out to diagnose the sickness of the modern world, Canetti felt that only scientific studies qualified a writer to deal with such questions. He resolved to devote himself to research in the psychopathology of power, to make "a desperate attempt to undo the division of labor and to think about everything myself, so that it comes together inside one head and so becomes one thing again. It is not all knowledge that I want, but the re-integration of that which had disintegrated. . . . The very slight prospect that [this endeavor] might succeed makes every kind of effort worthwhile."

ELIAS CANETTI

Canetti's sense of crisis was such that for a time he forbade himself to continue his literary work. When in the 1930s he began to write the plays collected in *Dramen* (1964), they were intimately connected with his studies. *Hochzeit* (The Wedding, 1932) powerfully depicts "a group of human monsters vying for possession of each other and of the house in which they live." *Die Komödie der Eitelkeit* (Comedy of Vanity, 1934) deals with a case just as extreme as that of Peter Kien, though its subject is the attempted suppression of vanity—and of mirrors—in a whole community. *Die Befristeten*, which Canetti has called a "textbook of death," was performed in England in 1956 as *The Numbered*. Canetti's dramatic characters are types rather than individuals, though each is distinguished by what he calls an "acoustic mask," a peculiar way of speaking. The farcical element in his plays, which anticipated the so-called theatre of the absurd, has not yet led to a revival as successful as that of *Die Blendung* after its third publication in German.

Masse und Macht (1960, translated as *Crowds and Power*) was the first direct product of Canetti's decades of research, a study of the origins, nature, and symbolism of crowds, the paranoia of despots. It was thought unscientific in its generalizations, and sometimes preposterous, but original, highly stimulating, and written in a strangely compelling style. Canetti has published two volumes of selections from his notebooks, *Aufzeichnungen* 1942–1948 (1965) and *Alle vergeudete Verehrung: Aufzeichnungen* 1949–1960 (1970). *Der andere Prozess* (1970), his short study of Kafka's letters to Felice Bauer, has been called "perhaps the most revealing essay on Kafka ever published." Canetti has also written a monograph about his friend the sculptor Fritz Wotruba.

Die Blendung places Canetti in the company of those novelists who have attempted nothing less than the portrayal and interpretation of a whole world—novelists like Robert Musil and Broch, to whom Canetti has paid tribute. That the world so portrayed in his novel ends by being "a world in the head" is no accident, given his awareness of a disintegrating society and culture that could no longer be rendered realistically. In order to be true to his vision and interpretation of the modern world, Canetti had to resort to allegory, nightmare, and farce—or, alternatively, to a treatise on sociology and psychopathology. Canetti's reputation, which has always stood high with an informed minority, spread more widely during the late 1960s, and in 1972 he received the most coveted of German literary distinctions, the Georg Büchner prize.

PRINCIPAL WORKS IN ENGLISH TRANSLATION: Auto-da-Fé, 1946 (U.S., Tower of Babel, 1947; Auto-da-Fé, 1964); Fritz Wotruba, 1955; Crowds and Power, 1962.

ABOUT: Canetti, E. Aufzeichnungen 1942–1948, 1965; Canetti, E. Alle vergeudete Verehrung, 1970; Contemporary Authors 21–22, 1969; Fried, E. *introduction to* Canetti's Welt im Kopf, 1962; Grigson, G. (ed.) Concise Encyclopedia of Modern World Literature, 1963; Parry, I. Elias Canetti's Novel Die Blendung *in* Norman, F. (ed.) Essays in German Literature I, 1965. *Periodicals*—Times Literary Supplement January 15, 1971; January 22, 1971 (letter).

CANNING, VICTOR (June 16, 1911–), English novelist and adventure story writer, was born in Plymouth, Devon. His flair for creating suspense was no doubt nurtured by his boyhood enjoyment of cliff-hanger serials at the local movie theatre. By the time he was fourteen Canning was working in Oxford, earning starvation wages as a clerk and trying to write in his spare time. His first sale was to a boys' magazine. In 1934 he published his first novel and became a full-time writer. For a time he was a feature writer for the London *Daily Mail*, but he was soon earning an excellent living as a freelance, writing short stories for leading magazines both in England and in the United States.

Most of the novels Canning wrote during the 1930s are set against an affectionately described background of the English countryside, like the amiably picaresque series about Mr. Finchley, and *Polycarp's Progress* (1935), described by Howard Spring as "a readable, swift-moving novel, an extravaganza peopled by folk you don't believe in at all, but joyous, happy and incurably optimistic." Wider in range are the novels written pseudonymously during the same period as by "Alan Gould." The first of these, *Two Men Fought*, is a powerful

VICTOR CANNING

account of an inherited feud, set in Cornwall during the first two decades of this century. The reviewers were impressed, and A. G. Macdonell wrote: "He has emerged full-fledged. His writing is strong and unpadded. His characters are leaping with vitality. His sense of plot is flawless."

From 1940 to 1946, Canning served with the Royal Artillery in North Africa, Italy, and Austria, ending the war with the rank of major. His first postwar novel was *The Chasm*, set in an Apennine village isolated by the collapse of a bridge and describing the struggle for survival between an emotionally scarred architect and a wartime traitor. D. S. Savage wrote of it: "If you can imagine *For Whom the Bell Tolls* as it might be written by Charles Morgan, you will have a good notion of what *The Chasm* is like." *The Golden Salamander*, one of a number of Canning novels to have been filmed, established him as a highly skilled and professional exponent of "the neo-Buchan and post-Ambler school" of adventure story writers.

Since then, a succession of ingeniously plotted entertainments have confirmed Canning's reputation as "one of Britain's most resiliently successful storytellers." He has been credited with "a wonderful sense of background"—an ability to bring to life settings as varied as Venice (in *Bird of Prey*), Holland (in *The House of the Seven Flies*), Somaliland (in *The Burning Eye*), and the Caribbean (in *A Delivery of Furies*). Admirers of the Ian Fleming school of thriller writing have sometimes found Canning's work rather slow-paced and thoughtful but recently, as Maurice Richardson noted, "Canning has toughened up his writing a bit and given it a shot or two of sex." Canning has written serials for

British television, and has been a scriptwriter for both American and English film studios.

Victor Canning was married in 1934 to Phyllis McEwen and has two daughters. He leads a squire-like existence in an Elizabethan farmhouse near Brenchley, in Kent, where he fishes, grows carnations, and plays golf. His favorite author is William Faulkner. Canning regards himself as "not a Hepplewhite or a Sheraton, but a good journeyman carpenter." Not all critics would accept this modest assessment; Francis Iles has said: "He is a writer of delicate sensibility who would have made his mark in any branch of fiction. That he can, in addition, compose an exciting plot, full of unexpected twists, is so much the more to his credit."

PRINCIPAL WORKS: *Fiction*—Mr. Finchley Discovers His England, 1934 (U.S., Mr. Finchley's Holiday); Polycarp's Progress, 1935; Fly Away Paul, 1936; Matthew Silverman, 1937; Mr. Finchley Goes to Paris, 1938; Fountain Inn, 1939; Mr. Finchley Takes the Road, 1940; Green Battlefield, 1944; The Chasm, 1947; Panther's Moon, 1948; The Golden Salamander, 1949; A Forest of Eyes, 1950; Venetian Bird (U.S., Bird of Prey), 1951; The House of the Seven Flies, 1952; The Man From the Turkish Slave, 1954; Castle Minerva, 1955 (U.S., A Handful of Silver); His Bones Are Coral (U.S., Twist of the Knife), 1955; The Hidden Face (U.S., Burden of Proof), 1956; The Manasco Road, 1957; The Dragon Tree, 1958; Young Man on a Bicycle (short stories) (U.S., Oasis Nine), 1959; The Burning Eye, 1960; A Delivery of Furies, 1961; Black Flamingo, 1962; The Limbo Line, 1963; The Scorpio Letters, 1964; The Whip Hand, 1965; Doubled in Diamonds, 1966; The Python Project, 1967; The Melting Man, 1968; Queen's Pawn, 1969; The Great Affair, 1970; Firecrest, 1971; The Rainbird Pattern, 1972; The Runaways, 1972; Flight of the Grey Goose, 1973. *As "Alan Gould"*—Two Men Fought, 1936; Mercy Lane, 1937; Sanctuary from the Dragon, 1938; Every Creature of God Is Good, 1939; The Viaduct, 1940; Atlantic Company, 1941.

ABOUT: Contemporary Authors 13–14, 1965; Who's Who, 1971. *Periodicals*—Evening Standard (London) June 6, 1935; The Observer November 6, 1966.

CARETTE, LOUIS. *See* "MARCEAU, FÉLICIEN"

CARNAP, RUDOLF (May, 18, 1891–September 14, 1970), American philosopher, was born at Ronsdorf, a town which has now been swallowed up by the city of Wuppertal, in northwestern Germany. He was the son of Johannes Carnap, a manufacturer, and the former Anna Dörpfeld. He and his sister were educated at home by their mother, a former teacher who gave them only an hour's tuition a day, intending in this way to develop their ability to think for themselves. This, together with her exceedingly enlightened and tolerant attitude towards most subjects, had an influence on Carnap which showed to advantage in his later work. His father died in 1898 and the family moved to Barmen, where Carnap attended the Gymnasium and

RUDOLF CARNAP

showed a precocious interest in the logical structure of mathematics and of language. The family moved again in 1909 to Jena.

From 1910 to 1914 Carnap studied physics, mathematics, and philosophy at the universities of Jena and Freiburg im Breisgau. It is said that he had great difficulty in deciding whether to specialize in physics or philosophy; his real interest was in formulating scientific and philosophical concepts in symbolic terms, an activity for which the physics professor recommended him to the philosophy department and vice versa. At Jena, Carnap was one of the very few to appreciate the teaching of the great logician and mathematical philosopher Gottlob Frege.

Carnap's studies were interrupted by war service from 1914 to 1918. He was at the front until 1917, and then in a scientific establishment. He subsequently resumed his studies, obtaining his doctorate with a thesis on space. It was published in 1921 and, like Bertrand Russell's comparable first publication, showed a degree of Kantian influence that was later overcome.

It was, indeed, Russell's writings on the theory of knowledge that had the greatest formative influence on Carnap at this time. Russell was attempting to make philosophy a genuinely scientific discipline by applying to it the new logic that he and Frege had independently developed. Carnap, even more than Russell, made this project his own. All of his many writings are characterized not just by his preoccupation with the concept and findings of modern formal logic but by a splendidly impersonal lucidity of expression, an unwaveringly constructive readiness for cooperation and willingness to recognize the value of different philosophical approaches.

In 1926 Carnap went to the University of Vienna, where he worked under Moritz Schlick, leader of the Vienna Circle and a founder of logical positivism. Other influential figures encountered at this time were Otto Neurath, Hans Reichenbach (with whom from 1930 he was joint editor of the Circle's periodical *Erkenntnis*), Alfred Tarski, and Karl Popper. In the late 1920s he joined with other members of the Vienna Circle in discussions with Ludwig Wittgenstein, being wholly convinced by his uniquely profound substantiation of the theory that all logical truth is analytic. After publishing various essays on the philosophy of science, Carnap brought out his first major treatise, *Der logische Aufbau der Welt* (1928, translated in 1967 as *The Logical Structure of the World*). It is a most thorough and detailed attempt to analyze systematically, in terms of modern logic, the whole conceptual apparatus of ordinary and scientific discourse.

From 1931 to 1935 Carnap worked, in comparative isolation, in Prague. In 1936 he went as professor of philosophy to the University of Chicago, remaining there until 1952 and acquiring American citizenship in 1941. In 1954, after two years at the Princeton Institute for Advanced Study, he went as professor of philosophy to the University of California at Los Angeles, a chair rendered vacant by the death of his friend and collaborator Hans Reichenbach. He remained at UCLA after 1962 as a research professor.

Carnap has been by far the most productive, and in many ways the most typical, of the philosophers of the Vienna Circle, subscribing without reservation to its scientific attitude toward the world. In the 1930s he expounded in a mass of publications, of all levels of technicality, three main theses: the analytic nature of logical and mathematical truth, the meaninglessness of metaphysical and theological utterances, and the unity of science. He preferred, but without dogmatic insistence, to take statements about observable physical things as the foundations of scientific knowledge. This obliged him to give a "physicalist" interpretation to statements about the subject matter of psychology, the topic of a number of his influential writings.

His main work during the 1930s was his difficult but influential *Logische Syntax der Sprache* (1934, translated as *The Logical Syntax of Language*). Its intention was to demonstrate (as against the skepticism of Wittgenstein on this point) that language could be discussed as a system of meaningful expressions, and in particular to define the main concepts of logic. At this time Carnap believed he could do this without considering more than the strictly formal properties of language, but he soon came to agree with his critics that syntax must be supplemented with semantics—that the meaning of expressions is related to their use in ordinary discourse. He published a revised theory of language—a semantic one—in 1947 in his *Meaning and Necessity*.

During the latter part of his life, Carnap's main interest lay in the field of inductive logic, the theory of valid scientific inference. His principal publication on the subject, *The Logical Foundations of Probability*, was recognized as a landmark in its field.

Carnap was a somewhat dry but magnificently lucid writer who seems to have taken as a stylistic model the most orderly kind of mathematics textbook. His complete openness, his readiness at all times to consider and accept criticism, were attractive features of his dedication to the ideal of philosophy as a science. He did not give birth to any profoundly original ideas of his own but his precise, systematic, and vigorous presentation of the philosophy of the Vienna Circle has done much to secure its widespread acceptance, and Carnap is largely responsible for the transplantation of neopositivism to America. He was married in 1933 to Elizabeth Ina von Stöger, who died in 1964.

PRINCIPAL WORKS IN ENGLISH TRANSLATION: The Unity of Science, 1934; Philosophy and Logical Syntax, 1935; The Logical Syntax of Language, 1937; Foundations of Logic and Mathematics, 1939; Introduction to Semantics, 1942; Formalization of Logic, 1943; Meaning and Necessity: A Study in Semantics and Modal Logic, 1947 (enlarged ed., 1956); The Logical Foundations of Probability, 1950; The Continuum of Inductive Methods, 1952; Introduction to Symbolic Logic and Its Application, 1958; Logic and Language, 1963; Philosophical Foundations of Physics: An Introduction to the Philosophy of Science, 1966; The Logical Structure of the World [and] Pseudo-Problems in Philosophy, 1967.

ABOUT: Bentley, A. F. Inquiry into Inquiries, 1954; Black, M. Problems of Analysis, 1954; Carnap, R. and Jeffrey, R. C. (eds.) Studies in Logic and Probability, vol. 1, 1972; Cohen, M. R. Preface to Logic, 1944; Gilson, E. H. (ed.) Recent Philosophy: Hegel to the Present, 1966; Hill, T. E. Contemporary Theories of Knowledge, 1961; Schilpp, P. A. (ed.) The Philosophy of Rudolph Carnap (The Library of Living Philosophers), 1963; White, M. G. (ed.) Age of Analysis, 1955; Who's Who in America, 1970–1971. *Periodicals*—International Philosophical Quarterly March 1967; Journal of Philosophy January 16, 1936; June 6, 1940; August 12, 1948; November 9, 1967; Journal of Symbolic Logic June, September 1955, September 1958, March 1960; Mind October 1935, July 1944, April 1945, April, October 1949, January 1950, April 1952; Philosophy of Science January, October 1946, April 1952, July 1956, January, April 1963; Philosophical Review November 1941, May 1943, May 1949, July 1951; Review of Metaphysics March–June 1966.

***CARPENTIER (Y VALMONT), ALEJO** (December 26, 1904–), Cuban novelist, journalist, and musicologist, was born in Havana of mixed French and Russian parentage. His father, Jorge Julian Carpentier, an architect who had emigrated to Cuba in 1902, had a passionate love for all things

* kär pen tyer′

Hispanic and an equally inflamed hatred of Europe. In Carpentier's words, "he always wanted to live in a young country where everything was still to be done." Carpentier received from him a cosmopolitan and skeptical upbringing. He attended the Candler College and the Colegio Mimo and then entered the University of Havana to study music and architecture. Carpentier began writing in his early teens, all the while cultivating a musical talent which would remain a constant in his future work. (He is a passable pianist, a distinguished musicologist, and the librettist of several operas.)

Carpentier's first writings showed him to be heavily influenced by Anatole France, a veritable cult in Cuba at that time. After abandoning his university studies, he began in 1921 a minor career as a commercial journalist—he wrote a history of the shoe for the shoemakers' union, edited the fashion section of a local magazine (as "Jacqueline"), and from 1924 to 1928 was editor in chief of the magazine *Carteles*. He made the first of many trips to Mexico in 1926 at the invitation of the Mexican government, meeting Jaime Torres Bodet, José Clemente Orozco, and Diego Rivera. Jailed in 1927 for signing a manifesto against the dictator Machado, Carpentier began his first novel, *Ecué-yamba-o* (1933), an exercise in nativistic folklore patterns which the author now dismisses as a flawed attempt at American regionalism, written under a "false conception of what was national which everyone in my generation shared." He went into voluntary exile in 1928 with the aid of the French poet Robert Desnos, who generously lent him his identity papers so that he could board the ship for France.

Carpentier's eleven years in Paris were essential to his artistic formation. He met André Breton and contributed to the surrealist review *Révolution Surréaliste* with Louis Aragon, Tristan Tzara, and others. However, Carpentier's sympathy with surrealism was short-lived, and he later complained of its "bureaucracy of the marvelous." He adds: "My surrealist attempts seemed to me vain efforts, but it did show me how to see aspects of American life which I had not seen before, drowned as I was in the wave of *nativismo* exemplified by such authors as Ricardo Güiraldes, Rómulo Gallegos, and José Eustasio Rivera." A man of inexhaustible energy, Carpentier was active in innumerable ways during this period. He was the director of the Foniric Studios in Paris, which produced records and radio programs of poetry and drama readings, and was also the editor of the literary review *Imán*, which published many distinguished contemporary French writers in Spanish translation. His own book of verse, *Poemas de las Antillas*, appeared in Paris in 1932.

He returned in 1939 to Havana, where he earned

ALEJO CARPENTIER

his living by writing and producing radio programs on station CMZ. In 1941 he was appointed Professor of the History of Music at the Conservatorio Nacional. Two years later he accompanied the French director and actor Louis Jouvet on a personal appearance tour of Haiti, which gave Carpentier the fantastic setting for his first mature novel, *El reino de este mundo* (1949, translated by Harriet de Onís as *The Kingdom of This World*). This short, beautifully composed novel provides a bizarre and brilliant version of Haitian history as a cyclical but never hopeless process of revolution. One critic described it as a series of tableaux, "alive as the stone frozen into perpetual movement in some elaborate but ordered rococo edifice."

Some autobiographical elements are evident in *Los pasos perdidos* (1953, translated by Harriet de Onís as *The Lost Steps*), a fictional journal by a dispirited musicologist who has, in the author's words, "lost the key to his authentic existence" and who seeks to regain it. His Conradian quest takes place on a voyage up the Orinoco—an allegorical journey back through time to the lost Eden. There he lays down the burden of civilization, exchanging his sophisticated mistress for the mestizo Rosario, in whom "had fused . . . the great races of the world, the most widely separated, the most divergent." Some critics have found the novel a little simplistic in its symbolism, but in France it received the Prix du Meilleur Livre Étranger, and in England it was described by J. B. Priestley as "a work of genius, a genuine masterpiece." The elegantly, almost musically structured *El acoso* (The Pursuit, 1956), about a victim of the Machado dictatorship, was also greatly admired.

Carpentier spent much time in Europe and the Americas during the 1940s and 1950s, but returned to Cuba in June 1959 at the outbreak of the Castro revolution, carrying with him the manuscript of his next novel *El siglo de las luces* (1962, translated by John Sturrock as *Explosion in a Cathedral*). Ostensibly it is a historical novel, a fictional account of events in the life of Victor Hugues, agent of the French Revolution in the Antilles, conqueror of Guadeloupe. In fact, like all of Carpentier's mature work it demonstrates that revolution is followed by dictatorship and by revolution again; that history and time itself is cyclical and unreal; that (to quote Mario Vargas Llosa), "the poetic reality of surrealism, a product in Europe of the imagination and the subconscious, could be an objective reality in America."

Carpentier's concern with time and its workings, which reminds some critics of Jorge Luis Borges, is most explicit in his book of short stories *Guerra del tiempo* (1958, translated by Frances Partridge as *The War of Time*). He has written a major history of Cuban music, and is now at work on a three-volume history of the Castro revolution, serving meanwhile as cultural attaché in the Cuban embassy in Paris. The author is married to the former Andrea Esteban.

At once visionary and ecumenical in his approach to Latin America, Carpentier nowadays eschews regional realities and literary chauvinism. His novels present American man within formative environmental "contexts," a Sartrian word appearing frequently in Carpentier's theoretical writings. He generally forgoes the subjective and concentrates instead on the exemplification of issues and roles forced upon individuals by society and by time. Carpentier speaks disdainfully of "the little psychological novel," and it is usually of unindividualized and unheroic characters that he writes with that magic realism which he evokes through a style that is slow, sensual, and mythopoeic. Carpentier is at once a militant historicist and a generous and exalted humanist. His faith in revolution is unshaken: "Men may fail, but ideas continue to make headway until the time comes for them to be fully realized."

PRINCIPAL WORKS IN ENGLISH TRANSLATION: The Lost Steps, 1956; The Kingdom of This World, 1957; Explosion in a Cathedral, 1963; The War of Time (stories), 1970.

ABOUT: Harss, L. and Dohmann, B. Into the Mainstream, 1967; International Who's Who, 1970–1971; Rodríguez Monegal, E. Narradores de América, 1966; Who's Who in Latin America, VII, 1951. *Periodicals*—Américas (Pan American Union) February 1950, July 1954, February 1957; Books Abroad Spring 1959; Commonweal November 23, 1956; Cuadernos Hispanoamericanos February 1965, October 1966; Encounter September 1965; Hispania (Appleton, Wisconsin) March 1965; Insula January, September 1965; PMLA September 1963; Symposium Fall 1964; Times Literary Supplement February 15, 1963; November 14, 1968; Yale Review Winter 1957.

***CARRUTH, HAYDEN** (August 3, 1921–), American poet, novelist, and critic, writes: "My grandfather, Fred Hayden Carruth, started the first newspaper in the Territory of Dakotah in 1883 at the age of twenty. A fact; I am, evidently for no good reason, very proud of it. Five years later he went to New York and on the strength of his work in Dakotah became a 'literary man,' as they were called then; he was, actually, an old-style humorist in the tradition of frontier hyperbole. He had one or two good jobs, including several years as daily comic editorialist for Whitelaw Reid's *Tribune*, and several bad ones, and several periods without any job at all. He published four books, hundreds of magazine sketches and stories, a fair amount of verse, using various pseudonyms; but his books and most of his later work were signed simply 'Hayden Carruth'—and that's where I got my name. His second son, Gorton Veeder, was my father, a journalist and rather old-fashioned poet. When I was born in Waterbury, Connecticut, he was a reporter on the city's morning daily (the *Republican*); soon after that he became editor, but in the mid-depression was fired over a matter of conscience, whereupon the family moved to Westchester County, New York, where my grandfather had originally established us in the 1890s. My father's people were Scotch-Irish, descendants of two brothers who emigrated from King James's Plantation in 1720, thereby elevating themselves from starvation to bare subsistence. Before me, they were socialists for generations; I know no political label in the present world that fits me, but you can say I approach most public questions from a standpoint combining attitudes of abolitionism and radical nonalignment.

"My mother, Margery Dibb, came from an English family that emigrated to the United States in the late nineteenth century.

"I was 'educated' in public school and the University of North Carolina, chiefly in subjects thought useful to a newspaperman. During the war I served in Italy for two years, as ingloriously as possible; then, scrapping journalism, enrolled in the University of Chicago Graduate School under the G.I. Bill. For the first time I became acquainted with modern poetry and criticism, and in great excitement began producing both. A couple of years later I became editor of *Poetry*, but the connection terminated before I could make the changes I had intended. I worked for the University of Chicago Press and, in New York, for Intercultural Publications, Inc. In 1953 I entered a mental hos-

* kə ro͞oth′

pital, suffering from alcoholism and an acute psychoneurotic and phobic breakdown. This lasted for seven years, though I left the hospital after about a year and a half.

"During my illness, as an aid to recovery, I read philosophy and worked out a crude, creaky, but complex sort of Kantean-pragmatic conceptualization of things and people, which I found later was coincidental with parts of the radical secular existentialism that had emerged in Europe during the 1940s. My writing since then has been chiefly an attempt to extend these themes imaginatively. Critics say that much of my poetry is too formal, austere, even academic—though really, by temperament and accomplishment, I am the worst academic imaginable. I suppose fundamentally my answer—vague and unsatisfactory, I know—is that the poems spontaneously took the forms they have and that considering the circumstances of their inceptions they would not have been writable in any other way. I have published seven books, chiefly poetry, though one is a novel and another a book about Albert Camus; also some hundreds of reviews and articles, and a few short stories.

"I live in semi-seclusion in a remote part of the Green Mountains. I earn my living by ghost-writing and hack editing. My pastimes are painting, playing the clarinet, driving and maintaining sports cars, raising poultry (which is a little more than a pastime actually), keeping records, birdwatching, silviculture (ditto). I have been married three times; first to Sara Anderson of Honolulu; second to Eleanore Ray of Paterson; third and presently to Rose Marie Dorn of Parchwitz, near Liegnitz, Silesia. I have two children, Martha Hamilton from my first marriage and David Barrow from my present one.

"Finally, as is no doubt evident in the foregoing, I am embarrassed at being asked to write about myself in this manner. This is not a virtue but a defect; yet a common one, even among writers. Hence I question the desirability of a reference work based on the principles that govern this one."

Reviewers of *The Crow and the Heart* (1959), Carruth's first book, were impressed by the author's versatility, his easy mastery of many moods and styles, but moved, if at all, only occasionally. James Dickey, for example, found much "ordinary, jargoning stuff" but also "The Asylum," which seemed to him the finest sonnet sequence he had read by a contemporary poet, and evidence that Carruth was one of the few living American poets capable of producing a really good long poem. Dickey was not alone in believing that Carruth achieved this in *Journey to a Known Place* (1961), "a beautifully conceived and imagined poem, into which Carruth blends his tremendous and sensitive

HAYDEN CARRUTH

vocabulary (surely the largest and most precise since Hart Crane's) with a mixture of cold, steady fury and nightmarish passion in the presence of which I can do little more than record my amazement and gratitude."

In 1961 Carruth spent a summer in the Berkshires, producing in response to this new environment work published the following year as *The Norfolk Poems of Hayden Carruth*. The poems in this and in *North Winter* (1964) seemed direct, simple, and conversational after the richness and complexity of his earlier work. Whatever their themes—the New England landscape, Hindu mythology, the Eichmann trial—they are like all of Carruth's verse basically autobiographical, self-obsessed, self-denunciatory. But in these two relatively minor volumes the poet could be seen struggling towards "a peace and reconciliation" and securing "a rested and quietly restrained verse by which both his anguish and his genius are transfigured into something new and beautiful."

Nothing for Tigers is a selection of the poems produced between 1959 and 1964. Richard Howard called it "a Yeats-haunted volume which represents a kind of progress-report on Carruth's condition, with samples of all his modes jostling for preeminence." Here as in the past, the deftness of his technique both impressed and disturbed some readers, who regarded an excessive facility as the principal cause of his "strange and terrifying shifts in quality." Later volumes include *The Clay Hill Anthology*, a collection of 142 "jottings" in haiku form which were admired for their "variety, tensility, toughness and genuine music," and *For You*, containing five long poems (including "The

Asylum" and "North Winter"). Adrienne Rich wrote of the latter: "I think there is no poetry being written now in which anger and pity for the wasting of man by man are more melded with love for the possibilities for the earth and man upon it."

Carruth's novel *Appendix A* reminded one reviewer of *Herzog*—and not only in its use of Chicago "as a mirror and emblem of the disparate self." It concerns a well-meaning but ineffectual husband, his wife, and the narrator, who is the husband's friend and the wife's lover. The book was thought seriously flawed in its structure, but perceptive in its characterization, precise in its language, and elegantly witty in some of its set pieces. The author's interest in "the radical secular existentialism" of which he writes above appeared most overtly in *After the Stranger*, a work of "uncompromising ambiguity" which sets within a novel-like framework a series of imaginary dialogues with Albert Camus.

Carruth received his B.A. from the University of North Carolina in 1943, his M.A. from the University of Chicago in 1948. He has received many prizes and awards, among them the Bess Hokin Prize (1954), the Vachel Lindsay Prize (1956), the Harriet Monroe poetry prize from the University of Chicago (1960), a Bollingen Foundation fellowship in criticism (1962), a Guggenheim Fellowship (1965), and a ten-thousand-dollar literary award from the National Council on the Arts (1966). He serves on the editorial board of the *Hudson Review*.

PRINCIPAL WORKS: The Crow and the Heart, 1946–1959 (poems), 1959; Journey to a Known Place: A Poem, 1961; The Norfolk Poems of Hayden Carruth, 1962; Appendix A (novel), 1963; North Winter (poems), 1964; After the Stranger: Imaginary Dialogues with Camus, 1965; Nothing for Tigers: Poems, 1959–1964, 1965; For You, 1970; The Clay Hill Anthology (poems), 1970; From Snow and Rock, From Chaos: Poems 1965–1972, 1973.

ABOUT: Contemporary Authors 9–10, 1964; Murphy, R. (ed.) Contemporary Poets of the English Language, 1970; Who's Who in America, 1972–1973. *Periodicals*—Minnesota Review Spring 1962; Nation February 15, 1965; New Leader March 1, 1965; New Republic February 15, 1964; New Yorker January 4, 1964; Poetry August 1963; Sewanee Review Autumn 1960; Time November 22, 1963; Virginia Quarterly Review Autumn 1961.

CASH, W(ILBUR) J(OSEPH) (May 2, 1901–July 1, 1941), American journalist and historian, was born in Gaffney, South Carolina, to John William and Nannie Lutitia (Hamrick) Cash. He grew up and went to school not in the romantic South of stately homes and plantations but in a drab cotton-mill town where his father ran a company store. A sensitive and sickly boy, "nearsighted from secret reading," young Cash went through a period of anxious religious fervor inspired by Bible-belt Baptist preachers. He studied for a year

W. J. CASH

at Wofford College in Spartanburg, then moved on to Wake Forest College in North Carolina, where he received his B.A. in 1922. He spent the following year at the Wake Forest law school but did not take a law degree. After a brief period in 1923 on the Charlotte (North Carolina) *Observer*, he taught English and French at Georgetown College in Kentucky and at the Blue Ridge School for Boys in Hendersonville, North Carolina.

By 1925 Cash was launched on his career in journalism. He worked briefly in Chicago on the *Post* and as a freelance, then returned south to the *Charlotte News* in 1926. From 1929 to 1937 Cash freelanced, contributing articles to various southern newspaper syndicates, to the *American Mercury*, the *Nation*, and other magazines. He was back on the *Charlotte News* as associate editor from 1937 until 1941 when he published *The Mind of the South.* In that same year he received a Guggenheim Fellowship for work on a novel. He went to Mexico to write, and there, in a hotel room in Mexico City, hanged himself. The explanation offered by his biographer, Joseph L. Morrison, is that he was in the grip of a fear psychosis induced, at least in part, by the toxic effects of a hyperthyroid condition. Cash was survived by his wife, Mary B. Ross Northrop, whom he had married in 1940.

Cash left only one book but it was a memorable one. At the time of its first publication, *The Mind of the South* was overshadowed by international crises and World War II, but twenty-five years later, especially in the light of the civil rights struggle in the 1960s, it was recognized as a classic of its type.

The Mind of the South is a profoundly personal,

though not autobiographical, work, full of both love and loathing for the region. Its genesis goes back at least a dozen years, to a series of articles Cash contributed to H. L. Mencken's *American Mercury*. In one article called "The Mind of the South" (October 1929), Cash sketched the thesis he was to develop in his book: "There *is* a new South to be sure. It is a chicken-pox of factories on the Watch-Us-Grow maps; it is a kaleidoscopic chromo of stacks and chimneys. . . . But I question that it is much more. For the mind of that heroic region, I opine, is still basically and essentially the mind of the Old South. It is a mind . . . of the soil rather than of the mills—a mind, indeed, which, as yet, is almost wholly unadjusted to the new industry."

In this same richly flavored style, full of Southern rhetoric, the book traces historically and psychologically the roots and the development of the modern South. Cash saw those roots in the 1830s–1860s—in the harsh life of the cotton planter of comparatively humble birth and breeding who struggled to make a living out of the land. The Civil War, destroying the old economy, created new and greater stresses. Defensive myths were cultivated about a romantic and aristocratic past, and men clung to and demanded conformity to these illusions. But the coming of modern industry offered new hope as well as new problems for the South, and Cash concluded his book on a note of cautious optimism.

Some critics, thirty years later, find his views naïve—especially his hope that industrial unionization would prove a panacea. Others object to his generalizations—what a fellow Southerner, Donald Davidson, called "his attempt to apply a purely rhetorical definition to a stubborn and unwieldy body of facts." Nevertheless, the continuing popularity of the book, its wide circulation in paperback edition on college campuses, its influence upon later, more elaborately documented studies of the South, demonstrates that Cash's work is of lasting fascination and importance. A number of his editorials from the *Charlotte News*, together with some book reviews, are republished in Joseph Morrison's "biography and reader."

PRINCIPAL WORK: The Mind of the South, 1941.
ABOUT: Davidson, D. Still Rebels, Still Yankees and Other Essays, 1957; Morrison, J. L. W. J. Cash: Southern Prophet: A Biography and Reader, 1967. *Periodicals*—Harper's September 1965; New York Review of Books December 4, 1969; Time February 24, 1941.

***CASSILL, R(ONALD) V(ERLIN)** (May 17, 1919–), American novelist and short story writer, writes: "I was born in Cedar Falls, Iowa, while my father was attending college there, preparing him-

*kas′ əl

R. V. CASSILL

self for the teaching career that he always followed. As he moved at the whim of schoolboards from one small Iowa town to another, I grew up in a totally non-urban environment. My adolescence was typically conditioned by the Depression—that is, I hitch-hiked over the country and rode the freights to Canada and California in search of summer employment, but up through high school I was a pretty well-adjusted kid with no real impulse toward art.

"College changed that mysteriously and firmly. I thought of myself as a painter and lithographer when I graduated, and indeed spent two years teaching these subjects in WPA art centers. After four years service in the Army Medical Department (highest rank 1st Lt. MAC) I began compulsively and in desperate search for a meaningful career to write fiction. Within a couple of years I'd won an *Atlantic* 'First' prize and had published some stories elsewhere in literary magazines.

"When my first novel flopped in 1950, I had been teaching at the Writers Workshop at the University of Iowa for two years. I left there for a year on a Fulbright scholarship in 1952. During that year in France I wrote a second novel, which was subsequently published as a paperback 'original.' For the remainder of the 1950s I supported myself as a writer in New York, partly by writing more paperback novels (totaling eleven), partly by editorial work, partly by writing short stories. In France again in 1956 I began work on my novel *Clem Anderson*, which absorbed the best and most of my efforts until 1960. Since its publication in 1961 I have begun again to write stories as well as novels.

"The fundamental trait of my nature is a kind of inertia of the heart. The circumstances of my life show one fracture of relationship after another and a very great deal of moving from one place to another. And between these external circumstances and my rooted emotions there has always been a bitter tension. My simple emotional patriotism and identification of myself as a Midwesterner have been in conflict throughout my adult life with the swift historic alterations I have lived through. And maybe this split accounts for the fact that my most successful work is usually built on a pattern of two disparate, though fatally linked, central characters.

"My first marriage was to Kathleen Rosecrans of Primghar, Iowa. In 1956 I married Karilyn Adams in Rome. We have three children—Orin, Erica, and Jesse—who provide the dearest anchorage of my life.

"Perhaps closest to my heart of all quotations by writers I cherish is Thomas Mann's: 'I was born to bear witness in tranquility.' I have not had a tranquil life, nor do I foresee personal tranquility; but I long for it for my own sake and the sake of such talents as remain with me."

Cassill was educated at the University of Iowa and taught there in 1948–1952 and 1960–1966. He went in 1966 to Brown University, where he is president of the Associated Writing Programs. His first novel, *The Eagle on the Coin* (1950), dealt with the personal and political problems of a black campaigning for election to a school board in a small town; in some respects this remains Cassill's most obviously objective book; but the writing, while professional, lacks confidence.

The paperback novels Cassill wrote to support himself, either under his own name or as "Owen Aherne" or "Jesse Webster" (*Dormitory Women*, 1954, is the title of one) need not be regarded as part of his corpus—yet in some of these books he appears, if casually and hurriedly, to be seeking to express something, a statement about the proper nature of erotic love not yet fully formulated.

Clem Anderson (1961) is an almost Dreiseresque study of the disintegration, disgrace, and final death of a promising young author. One senses in it a certain creative despair; some of the writing is thin, but as always in Cassill there is a sense of an energy and power that have not been fully or wholly efficiently harnessed. Reviewers saw in this tragic hero elements of Thomas Wolfe, Dylan Thomas, and Cassill himself, but not all of them found the character convincing.

Pretty Leslie is a novel patterned after *Madame Bovary*. Leslie Daniels, haunted as an adolescent by fears of obesity, is terrified that her masochism will annihilate her womanhood. Ben, her gentle doctor husband, sometimes made impotent by the furious desire to be humiliated that he senses in her, is finally driven to kill her lover—tragically repeating a killing of which he had been guilty in his childhood, and with which he has been almost able to come to terms. Primarily *Pretty Leslie* is the story, spiced with much somewhat mechanically used psychoanalysis, of two people who love each other but are no good for each other.

Some of the sexual sensationalism of Cassill's money-spinners seeps into this book, and the style does not always avoid pretentiousness; but the main protagonists do come alive, and an appropriately febrile atmosphere is generated. Most successful of all in this uneven but at times powerful novel, however, is the character of Leslie Daniels' lover, the sadistic painter Don Patch. This destructive, suffering personality is delineated with great care, and quite without the faint vulgarity that sometimes mars even Cassill's best work. Robert Alter called it "a moving novel honest in its conception and skillful in its execution," and David Boroff, who described Patch as "an absolutely brilliant creation," concluded that Cassill was "a writer of the first rank."

The President is another carefully worked out psychoanalytical study, this time of a power-hungry college president. In *La Vie Passionée of Rodney Buckthorne* the sexual sensationalism of the potboilers reemerges as pure fun à la Terry Southern. Buckthorne is a "fraudulent professor of classics" from Wyoming and a sexual athlete of Olympic prowess. In this account of Buckthorne's last stand in Greenwich Village Cassill's clearly admirable intentions get submerged in total confusion. Some critics nevertheless found it full of "mirth and life," and some of the social satire certainly works, particularly the splendidly comic description of "The End of the World Show," an art "happening" in a decaying hotel which one reviewer thought "worth the price of the book."

Doctor Cobb's Game is a less manic and more successful attempt at the big, sexy, picaresque novel now almost obligatory for all serious American novelists. Michael Cobb, a British osteopath, artist, and mystic, sets out to rescue his fading country through a kind of politico-sexual revolution, selecting as his hapless agent the current minister of war. The result, as James R. Frakes wrote, is Cassill's "most ambitious novel, encompassing as it does both white and black magic, bureaucratic labyrinths, the jagged pulse of swinging London, Russian defectors, diabolic possession, hermaphroditism" and many varieties of sexual experience. A few critics thought the novel (clearly inspired by the 1963 Profumo scandal) shoddy in conception and style, but most admired it as a wholly sincere and brilliantly achieved investigation of the Dionysian spirit, "profound, disturbing, and compellingly readable."

PRINCIPAL WORKS: *Fiction*—The Eagle on the Coin, 1950; (with Herbert Gold and James B. Hall) Fifteen x Three (stories), 1958; Clem Anderson, 1961; Pretty Leslie, 1963; The President, 1964; The Father and Other Stories, 1965; The Happy Marriage and Other Stories, 1966; La Vie Passionée of Rodney Buckthorne, 1968; Doctor Cobb's Game, 1970. *Nonfiction*—Writing Fiction, 1963; In an Iron Time (essays), 1969.

ABOUT: Contemporary Authors 9–10, 1964; Graham, J. The Writer's Voice: Conversations With Contemporary Writers, 1973; Robinson, W. R. (ed.) Man and the Movies, 1967; Who's Who in America, 1970–1971. *Periodicals*—Book Week May 24, 1964; April 25, 1965; Book World October 11, 1970; Library Journal April 1, 1968; New York Herald Tribune Books May 19, 1963; New York Review of Books July 9, 1964; New York Times Book Review June 4, 1961; May 26, 1963; April 4, 1965; November 15, 1970; Saturday Review June 3, 1961; December 19, 1970; Time June 16, 1961.

CARLO CASSOLA

***CASSOLA, CARLO** (March 17, 1917–), Italian novelist, writes: "I am considered to be a Tuscan writer because most of my stories and novels are situated in Tuscany. Actually I was born in Rome, and of my parents only my mother was a Tuscan; my father came from the North. Though I was born in a great city, of an intellectual middle-class family, I have nevertheless been attracted, ever since I was a child, by the little provincial towns of Tuscany and by the simple people who live in them. In these little places I later had the most important experiences of my life, including that of partisan struggle. That is why they have become the favorite background of my stories.

"In order to earn my living I have been a teacher and journalist. Thanks to the success of my recent books I am now able to live on my literary earnings.

"I began to write immediately before the war. At that time I tried to create a purely existential narrative, one, that is, which gave a sense of existence. In other words I aimed at expressing the flow of time, stripping objects of every cognitive, ideological, psychological, practical or ethical attribute in order to use them simply as existential symbols. It was an attempt at the limits of the impossible (and in fact I called it 'the film of the impossible'): the facts, even the least of them, which I had perforce to put into this time always seemed to run the risk of assuming too much importance, of becoming the reason for the story as in traditional narrative; and the psychological connotation, however vague, which I was bound to give my characters also ran the risk of coming into the foreground, thus constituting the reason for the story as in traditional narrative.

"However, since I was not moved by any of the reasons which moved the traditional writer, since I had no story to tell, no theory to prove, nor did I intend to psychologize, space given to imagery and story was reduced to a minimum. Very few images sufficed to give the sense of a fact, indeed of an entire life. Every traditional detail ran the risk of impoverishing and canceling out the existential emotion instead of reinforcing it. If my first stories covered few pages, the last ones covered few lines. I completely lost my narrative breath. I stopped writing.

"Silence was the logical conclusion of a literary search directed solely towards the existent symbol. Moreover these brief stories were unknown or half understood, and could in fact be understood rather within the circle of European experience than in the more restricted one of a national literature. Therefore I was very pleased that in a book published in 1958, *Le Roman italien et la crise de la conscience moderne*, the French critic Dominique Fernandez should have recognized that I had anticipated by many years the aim of the *nouveau roman* to give life to a completely new narrative.

"I did no writing for five years. I began again after the war. The War and the Resistance had not altered me; rather, after so many changing events did I feel more strongly than ever the need to take refuge in my own little private world. I was therefore in complete disagreement with the literature of *engagement* then in the ascendant. I believed (and I still believe today) that a writer must express only his own nature and only his own personal story. In this state of mind I wrote several long stories, such as 'Rosa Gagliardi' and 'Il taglio del bosco.'

* käs sō′ lä

Later I tried to give life to a more complex narrative, to include psychology, set subjects, affections, passions. In this way was born the novel *La ragazza di Bube* which gave me the Premio Strega and public success. In my latest novels I have gone back to the position of my youth."

As his foregoing remarks indicate, Cassola began writing with a definite program. Inspired by Joyce and particularly by the technique of *Dubliners*, he aimed at reproducing only the essentials of experience, shorn of any thesis, political or social, with a minimum of the ornamental or descriptive, and with no concern for plot—a program, as has been remarked, more suited to a hermetic poet than to a novelist. Cassola furthermore had from the beginning a preference for the "peripheral" background, the undramatic life of the suburb or small town, indeed even the suburb of the small town. This, with the cast of characters inevitably associated with such a milieu, makes him a kind of Pascoli in prose. The early stories collected in *La visita* (The Visit, 1947) illustrate this original and austere commitment, anticipating as Cassola says the "zero degree" writing of the French "New Novelists."

With the publication of *Fausto e Anna* (1952, translated by Isabel Quigly as *Fausto and Anna*), a modification of the author's original intent became evident. This novel, published under the auspices of Vittorini, has in fact an old-fashioned "story line" and a great deal of the collateral descriptive material that we might fairly associate with the style of the older regional writers. It is an account of the frustrated romance of the sophisticated urban young revolutionary Fausto and the conventional country girl Anna; the second part of the novel owes much of its vitality to the background of the partisan struggle, in which Fausto plays a prominent part. Yet in the unpretentious style, the eschewal of gratuitous commentary and analysis, one may see a certain fidelity to the author's earlier program.

La ragazza di Bube (1960, translated by M. Waldman as *Bébo's Girl*) is cut of much the same cloth, presenting another star-crossed romance, this time between the girl Mara and Bube, a nineteen-year-old ex-partisan who becomes involved in the killing of a policeman. At the end of the book Bube has been in prison for seven years, and Mara faces seven more years of waiting. Here too the skillful evocation of characters moved by impulses they do not quite understand and are certainly unable to express, against a soberly drawn background of provincial life, produces a work of true originality of tone if not of substance; the climate of the times (the unsettled postwar period) suffices in itself to provide the spice of excitement.

The two short novels, *Storia di Ada* and *La maestra* (Ada's Story and The Schoolteacher, published together in 1967 under the title of *Storia di Ada*) are lacking in this ingredient: Ada is a simple farm girl who loses her hand in an accident and, searching for some resolution of her rather pointless life, eventually marries an illiterate soldier who is hospitalized with what may be an incurable malady; the schoolteacher Fiorella struggles hard for existence in a small town and finds the answer to her crisis in an illicit relation with the provincial doctor. These fumbling, inarticulate personalities are presented in such a way as to arouse our compassion and understanding if not always our sympathy, and the hard and monotonous life of the small town and rural community is unobtrusively but effectively depicted.

In *Un cuore arido* (1961, translated by William Weaver as *An Arid Heart*), Anna, the protagonist, almost perversely chooses lonely self-sufficiency in her native village rather than follow her fiancé to America; more clearly than her sisters in Cassola's stories she exemplifies the almost programmatic resignation of his heroines; in almost all of his novels it is the women who make the crucial decisions and incidentally carry the burden of the narrative. Helene Cantarella wrote: "If Anna chooses solitude, it is because she no longer wishes to be 'expendable' in terms of her own world, but determines to be herself. Woven out of the minutiae of everyday life, this chronicle achieves its point . . . through an almost unbroken dialogue punctuated by long silences. . . . The sinuous rhythm of the tranquil prose, the limpid clarity of Tuscan colloquial speech . . . intensify Cassola's muted, poetic picture of those quiet, remote Italian towns in which life, for all its secret turbulence, seems as if arrested in time and space."

Since the immense popular success of *La ragazza di Bube*, Cassola's novels have almost automatically become best sellers in Italy. Nevertheless some critics find his recent work in this form—much of it developed from themes and characters first explored in the early stories—too monotonously undiscriminating in its tape-recorder objectivity; their preference is for Cassola's more selective shorter pieces, such as "Il taglio del bosco" (Woodcutting, 1954) and "Il soldato" (The Soldier, 1958).

PRINCIPAL WORKS IN ENGLISH TRANSLATION: Fausto and Anna, 1960; Bébo's Girl, 1962; An Arid Heart, 1964.

ABOUT: Alberto, A.-R. Scrittori e popolo, 1966; Ferretti, G. Letteratura e ideologia, 1964; Grillandi, M. Letteratura italiana: i contemporanei, 1969; Macchioni-Jodi, R. Cassola, 1967; Mariani, G. La giovane narrativa italiana tra documento e poesia, 1962; Penguin Companion to Literature 2, 1969; Pullini, S. Il romanzo italiano del dopoguerra, 1960; Russo, L. I narratori, 1958. *Periodicals*—Nuova Antologia September 1963; Le Ragioni Narrative September 1960.

CASTILLO, MICHEL DEL. *See* DEL CASTILLO, MICHEL.

***CAU, JEAN** (July 8, 1925–), French novelist and journalist, writes (in French): "The village where I was born, in 1925, is called Bram. It is situated close to the frontier of the Pyrenees in the South of France. When I was born, it had a population of three thousand souls, as they say in Russian novels. Now it has three thousand inhabitants. Because of the progress of television and cars, I daren't call them 'souls' any longer. My parents were poor. One day, they decided that instead of being poor in the country, they would be poor in the town. We went to live in Carcassonne, a town famous for its medieval center. I began my studies there. I continued them in Paris where I still live. I like Paris very much. For a long time, I felt like a black there: I was poor and was born in the provinces. I have become more and more white. For better or for worse.

"When I was little, I dreamt of one day becoming a writer. As one dreams of being a bird and having wings, or of walking through walls. It was indeed a dream for I believed that one could not be a writer until one was dead. In fact, at school, all the writers we were told about had been dead for a long time, and, most often, wore wigs. One of my greatest surprises was to discover that one could be a writer and alive. All at once, I started to write. But I don't know why people write, I mean *serious* people. I think all writers are children who are afraid of the dark and that is why they tell their stories. As for those called 'intellectuals,' maybe they become so because their teachers dazzled them and they hoped one day to resemble this Sun.

"In France, it is quite fun to be a writer. The French believe that it is because of Voltaire and J. J. Rousseau that they made the Revolution, learned to read, to write, to live and, today, to be tourists in Spain and to own a television. This national superstition gives great prestige to writers. They are asked about everything and, usually, they answer even when they don't understand the question.

"If I had not been a writer, I would have liked to be a dancer, a torero, a boxer, or a lion tamer, but, all things considered, I regret nothing."

Jean Cau, the son of Étienne Cau, a laborer, and the former Rosalie Olivier, was educated at the *lycée* in Carcassonne, the Lycée Louis-le-Grand in Paris, and the Arts Faculty of the Sorbonne, where he gained his *licence* in philosophy.

He began his career as secretary and general factotum to Jean-Paul Sartre, joining in the famous literary and philosophical discussions at 42, rue Bonaparte, and modeling himself closely on his master. It was therefore a matter of considerable surprise in French literary circles when, after some

* kō

JEAN CAU

years, evidently disenchanted with the intellectual life, Cau left the Sartrean ménage and joined *L'Express* as a reporter. He rapidly established himself as a brilliant and versatile journalist, writing with equal authority on social problems, the arts, and the entertainment industry. According to a note in the *New Statesman*, Cau's "style is sometimes violent (*L'Express* is often threatened by writs in consequence), but it has a rare element of convincing objectivity. Some of his articles have become journalistic classics and—perhaps more important—have been followed by action." In 1971 Cau was described in the *Times Literary Supplement* as "a spokesman for the fanatic Right in the French press."

Cau's first novel was *La Coup de barre* (The Blow, 1950), a rather flimsy satire that attracted little attention. *Les Paroissiens* (The Parishioners, 1958) is a kind of contemporary *éducation sentimentale*; *Mon Village* (1958, translated as *My Village*) is a volume of short stories; and *Les Oreilles et la queue* (The Ears and the Tail, 1961) is an essay on bullfighting.

His most successful book to date was the novel *La Pitié de Dieu*. Four convicts, imprisoned together for life, ruminate endlessly about their past lives, the murders they may or may not have committed, punishment and mercy. Their narratives are interwoven rather than consecutive, and the substance of their confessions changes at each retelling (though each version gains equal acceptance from the other inmates). Each prisoner—and, Cau implies, we are all prisoners—creates his own truth and builds his own prison.

The novel, which inevitably evoked comparisons with Sartre's *Huis-Clos*, received the greatly esteemed Prix Goncourt and became a best seller in France. Translated by Richard Howard as *The Mercy of God*, it had a rather mixed reception from British and American critics. Anthony West thought it a thoroughly silly "excursion into the arbitrary," but Hans Koningsberger was impressed: "It is the measure of Cau's great skill that these doubts [about the truth of the men's stories] . . . do not make the book itself nebulous; on the contrary, the ultimate mosaic is sharply defined, powerful, and extremely frightening."

Cau has written several plays and screenplays, and has translated Edward Albee's *Who's Afraid of Virginia Woolf?* Apart from his work for *L'Express*, Cau has been on the staff of *Les Temps Modernes* and contributed regularly to *Figaro Littéraire*, *Candide*, and *France-Observateur*. He has traveled widely in the course of his work—in North and South America and North Africa as well as all over Europe.

PRINCIPAL WORKS IN ENGLISH TRANSLATION: *Fiction*—My Village, 1961 (with drawings by Siné); The Mercy of God, 1963. *Nonfiction*—(with Jacques Bost) Brazil (Nagel Travel Guide), 1955.

ABOUT: International Who's Who, 1970–1971; Nadeau, M. The French Novel Since the War, 1967; Peyre, H. French Novelists of Today, 1967; Who's Who in France, 1971–1972. *Periodicals*—Commonweal October 4, 1963; New Statesman November 24, 1961; New York Times Book Review May 26, 1963; Saturday Review June 1, 1963.

CHARLES CAUSLEY

CAUSLEY, CHARLES (STANLEY) (August 24, 1917–), English poet, writes: "I was born in the market-town of Launceston, just on the Cornish side of the River Tamar that divides Cornwall from Devon. My father was born in Ontario, Canada, but returned to his family's native Devon while still a small child. He served as a driver in the Royal Army Medical Corps (22nd Wessex) in France in the First World War, left the army as a permanent invalid, and died in 1924. His name (spelt wrongly: an extra 'e' has crept in) is on his village war-memorial at Trusham in Devon. My mother, Laura Bartlett, was born in the village of Langore, near Launceston. My father's family were mostly agricultural workers. My maternal grandfather was a quarryman, killed at work by a fall of slate. I am an only child, and—I think—the first writer in the family.

"I grew up in the long after-shadow of the First World War. Its songs, jokes, terrible stories, were familiar to me as a boy from the men who returned. In the early thirties in Britain there were huge general unemployment figures throughout the country. I left school in 1933 and took a job in the office of a building firm; later I worked for an electricity corporation. I found the work stiflingly boring, and felt I was doomed for life.

"I read the war-writers Blunden, Graves, Owen. I was influenced particularly by the writings of Siegfried Sassoon, who helped crystallise my attitude towards war, and showed me that poetry could be written not only in a classical/romantic style, but also in a simple, terse, and entirely personal manner of one's own.

"In 1940 I joined the Royal Navy as a lower-decker, and emerged as a petty officer in 1946. I was a poor sailor, often seasick, and almost as apprehensive of the sea (which I knew well, from my background in North Cornwall) as of the enemy mine, bomb and torpedo.

"Since the age of sixteen, I had written plays, poems, stories, but with little success. A play was broadcast in 1939. But in 1943 I felt a real certainty, at last, of theme and form. I began concentrating on poetry, but made no serious attempt at magazine-publication until 1947. I discovered that poetry could be written in the head; when ostensibly working at other jobs, pretending to be asleep in a hammock, leaning on a bar. It could be written down, like some magic formula, on a bit of paper the way a play or novel or short-story couldn't. Provided that one had something to say, it could be written at any time, anywhere.

"After leaving the Navy I went to Peterborough Training College and trained as a teacher. Since then, I have been teaching and writing in my home-town. In 1951, the year I published my first collection of poems, I also published a book of short-stories. While trying to write in two such distinct forms, I sensed a disagreeable and debilitating conflict: one form, as it were, extracting essential juices from the other, to mutual disadvantage. I have since worked mainly at poetry.

"In 1954 I was awarded a Travelling Scholarship by the Society of Authors, which I spent in Spain. I have travelled widely in Europe, including the USSR. In 1958, I was elected a Fellow of the Royal Society of Literature.

"The companion who left home with me for the Navy on that same day in 1940 was later drowned in a convoy to Archangel. The words in the twenty-fourth chapter of St. Matthew were inescapable: 'Then shall two be in the field; the one shall be taken, and the other left.' This has something to do with how my writing really began."

Causley was seven when his father died, and his mother thereafter did domestic work to support them, managing to provide "plenty of books, food, warm dry clothes, and a good home." Causley now lives with his mother in a house not far from the one in which he was born, and teaches in a little primary school in Launceston, where indeed he is better known as the teacher than as a poet. A modest and methodical man with a slight Cornish accent, Causley writes for about ninety minutes every evening. From 1953 to 1956 he served as literary editor of two radio "magazine" programs broadcast by the BBC's West Region, and from 1962 to 1966 was a member of the Arts Council's poetry panel. His verse anthologies for children are greatly admired. His recreations include travel, the theatre, and playing the piano "with expression."

It is Causley's achievement to have revitalized the ballad form in English poetry. Beginning his serious work during World War II, he wrote from the beginning in the accents of the ordinary seaman about "the inevitable wartime subjects of separation, love, death in far and lonely places," and has also, he says, "been obsessed by the theme of lost innocence." If his forms are traditional ones, his matter is often urgently contemporary, and informed, Elizabeth Jennings says, "with a sharply intelligent nostalgia." Causley's technical skill and precision of language have been very widely praised, and have been claimed (by Anthony Thwaite) as an influence on the popular poetry of the 1960s—"a poetry intended to be read aloud, to be grasped immediately and cheerfully by a mass audience." Cyril Connolly has called him "a topographical poet" whose "ballads have passed through Auden." He received the Queen's Gold Medal for Poetry in 1967 and the Cholmondeley Award in 1971.

PRINCIPAL WORKS: Farewell, Aggie Weston (poems) 1951; Hands to Dance (short stories), 1951; Survivor's Leave (poems), 1953; (ed.) Peninsula (verse anthology), 1957; Union Street (poems), 1957; Johnny Alleluia (poems), 1961; Penguin Modern Poets 3 (with George Barker and Martin Bell), 1962; (ed.) Dawn and Dusk (verse anthology for children), 1962; (ed.) Rising Early, 1964 (U.S., Modern Ballads and Story Poems); (ed.) Modern Folk Ballads, 1966; Underneath the Water (poems), 1968; Figure of 8 (poems), 1969; Figgie Hobbin (poems for children), 1970; The Tail of the Trinosaur (poem for children), 1973.

ABOUT: Contemporary Authors 9–10, 1964; Currey, R. N. Poets of the 1939–1945 War, 1960; Finn, F. E. S. (ed.) Poets of Our Time, 1965; Jennings, E. Poetry Today, 1961; Murphy, R. (ed.) Contemporary Poets of the English Language, 1970; Who's Who, 1971. *Periodicals*—Guardian January 15, 1965.

***CAYROL, JEAN** (June 6, 1911–), French poet, novelist, essayist, and film writer was born in Bordeaux, the son of Antoine Cayrol and Marie Armanda (Berrogain) Cayrol. He was educated at the *lycée* and the *facultés de droit et des lettres* in Bordeaux. After obtaining his *licence* in law, he worked as a librarian in his native city from 1936 to 1942. During the Occupation he was an active member of the Resistance, and he holds the Médaille de la Résistance and the Croix de Guerre. He was captured by the Gestapo in 1942, imprisoned for a year at Fresnes in Paris, then deported to the concentration camp of Gusen, near Mauthausen in Austria, where he was held for nearly three years. Since 1950 he has been on the selection committee of Éditions du Seuil, now his publishers, and since 1956 he has been a director of *Écrire*. He is a Chevalier des Arts et des Lettres.

Cayrol published three volumes of verse in the 1930s, all of them strongly influenced by surrealism. The poetry he has written since the war includes *Et Nunc* (And Now, published with *Miroir de la rédemption*—Mirror of the Redemption—in 1944), which contains some moving poems written while he was imprisoned at Fresnes; *Poémes de la nuit et du brouillard* (Poems of Night and Fog, 1946), described by Carlos Lynes as a "searing record of the poet's inner experience in the concentration camp," and *Passe-temps de l'homme et des oiseaux* (Pastimes of Man and Birds, 1947), reflecting the poet's return to ordinary life.

It is principally to his fiction, however, that Cayrol owes his considerable and growing reputation. He made his debut as a novelist in 1947, winning that year's Prix Renaudot with the first two volumes of his trilogy *Je vivrai l'amour des autres* (I Will Live the Love of Others). The novel which begins the sequence is a long monologue called *On vous parle* (Someone Is Speaking to You)—the "someone" being an anonymous tramp returned from a concentration camp. This Lazarus has risen from the dead to find himself homeless, friendless, and alone in a ruined and disordered city. For him —who must "talk in order to know"—the only reality is in words, which gush from him endlessly, and in objects, which are described with a poetic intensity that makes them seem alive. Nothing else

* kā rōl′

JEAN CAYROL

is solid or certain, least of all the narrator and his remote and nebulous fellow exiles in the city.

But even in this nightmare world hope is possible. In the second volume of Cayrol's trilogy, *Les premiers jours* (The First Days), his hero acquires a name, Armand, and a certain humanity, and even love, at first vicarious, then personal. He nevertheless retains a poignant sense of deprivation and in *Le Feu qui prend* (The Fire That Takes Hold, 1950) glimpses the possibility of a fuller reality, a richer harmony, which is, no doubt, the love of God. Cayrol is, as he says, "a Catholic who writes" rather than "a Catholic writer"; the religious element in his novels is never more than implicit and he is, in any case, too sophisticated an artist to end his trilogy with a convenient conversion. But there is, as Carlos Lynes wrote "a spiritual affirmation in the last pages of *Le Feu qui prend* . . . which reveals a deep and grave optimism about the irreducible value of the human person."

Cayrol returns again and again to the same themes in his subsequent novels, which include among others *La Noire* (The Dark Water, 1949); *L'Espace d'une nuit* (1954, translated by G. Hopkins as *All in a Night*); *Le Déménagement* (The Removal, 1956); *Les Corps étrangers* (1959, translated by Richard Howard as *Foreign Bodies*); *Le Froid du soleil* (The Chill of the Sun, 1963), and *Midi-Minuit* (Midday-Midnight, 1966). The imagery of the concentration camps and the war, so vivid in the first trilogy and *La Noire*, becomes less marked in the later books. But Cayrol's "Lazarean hero" is always a person confined in a situation as secure and as stifling as the grave, who is then released into a chaotic world of infinite possibilities—to endure, and perhaps to begin to find grace.

In his vision of life it is evident that Cayrol has been influenced by his Catholic faith, by his wartime experiences, and by surrealism. The style and manner of his dreamlike, incantatory, and strangely resonant stories is, it has been suggested, more an incarnation of his unique vision than the product of any literary school or fashion. Cayrol is nevertheless often categorized as a rather early exponent of the "new" or "anti-" novel, and it is easy to see why. Carlos Lynes wrote: "With Cayrol and the figures moving in his fictions we enter a 'space' which becomes a 'world' only as we become aware of its *presence*, as we begin to 'structure' our perceptions with no regard for a priori notions of reality. 'I write as one walks,' Cayrol says. 'I invent my psychology in proportion as I advance in an *inattentive* world. . . . I know nothing beyond what the inhabitants of my books know, I do not go ahead of them.' "

Cayrol has discussed his literary views and intentions in a number of lectures and essays, notably in the two essays published in *Lazare parmi nous* (Lazarus in Our Midst, 1950). *De l'espace humain* (1968) is another volume of essays, appealing for an element of human irrationality in the gaunt algebra of city planning. Cayrol is much involved with the cinema. He wrote the commentary for Alain Resnais's great film about the concentration camps, whose title *Nuit et brouillard* was borrowed from his own volume of poems on the same theme, and also wrote the screenplay of Resnais's *Muriel*. Cayrol is the author with Claude Durand of a theoretical work on the cinema, *Le Droit du regard*, and in 1965 directed his first film, *Le Coup de grâce*.

PRINCIPAL WORKS IN ENGLISH TRANSLATION: All in a Night, 1957; Foreign Bodies, 1960.

ABOUT: Blanchet, A. La Littérature et le spirituel, 11, 1960; Boisdeffre, P. de. Dictionnaire de littérature contemporaine, 1900–1962, 1962; Boisdeffre, P. de. Une Histoire vivante de la littérature d'aujourd'hui, 1938–1958, 1958; Fritz, W. H. Jean Cayrol's "lazarenische" prosa, 1967; Hatzfeld, H. A. Trends and Styles in Twentieth Century French Literature, 1957; Le Sage, L. The French New Novel, 1962; Lynes, C. Jean Cayrol, *in* Cruickshank, J. (ed.) The Novelist as Philosopher, 1962; Nadeau, M. The French Novel Since the War, 1967; Oster, D. Jean Cayrol et son œuvre, 1968; Pingaud, B. Écrivains d'aujourd'hui, 1960; Rousselot, J. Panorama critique des nouveaux poètes français, 1952. *Periodicals*—Esprit March 1952; Yale French Studies 24, 1959.

"CECIL, HENRY" (pseudonym of Henry Cecil Leon) (September 19, 1902–), English novelist, dramatist, and writer on legal subjects, was born in Middlesex, the youngest son of J. A. Leon. It is said that he wrote his first poem at the age of five and was turning out socially conscious verse in great profusion by the time he was eight. He was educated at St. Paul's School in London and at King's College, Cambridge University, where he read law, edited an undergraduate magazine, and was one of the authors of a May Week "Footlights" revue. No one doubted that he would be a writer, and it is surprising only that he was in his mid-forties before his first book appeared.

A distinguished legal career and World War II account for the delay. He was called to the bar in 1923 at the age of twenty-one and had developed a successful practice when the war came. He served as an infantry officer, winning a Military Cross for bravery in 1942. After the war, in 1949, he became a county court judge and remained one until 1967.

Cecil's first book, *Full Circle*, was based on stories he had invented for the entertainment of his battalion during the war. It attracted little attention but was followed by an "ingenious, witty, and charming" mystery story which was far more successful. This was *No Bail for the Judge*, about an eminent jurist in imminent danger of getting himself hanged. One reviewer called it an "anthology of wry observations held together by a sufficient webbing of plot." *According to the Evidence*, equally entertaining if somewhat shaky in its legal ethics, centers on the outrageous defense in court of a man who impulsively pushes a dedicated sex murderer off a cliff.

In *Brothers in Law*, Cecil temporarily abandoned crime for unadulterated comedy, describing the private pleasures and professional pitfalls of a young barrister's first year in practice. The story line was said to be thin and the romantic interest sketchy, but no one seemed to mind very much, these limitations being distinctly outweighed by the story's humor and the absorbing interest of the court scenes. Cecil's delight in deflating the more pretentious aspects of the British legal process has fortunately never concealed his affection and respect for it. Roger Thursby, the hero of *Brothers in Law*, reappears as an established barrister in *Friends at Court*, and as a high court judge in *Sober as a Judge*.

Cecil has continued to produce a steady stream of legal novels, some of them thrillers, some of them romantic comedies, and some of them, like *A Child Divided*, serious examinations of the painful human problems which the law must try to resolve when less public methods fail. None of his fiction has been found less than witty, humane, and intelligent, though he is sometimes accused of a weakness for sermonizing, and his characters are seldom much more than mouthpieces for their creator's wit and wisdom. As a reviewer put it in the *Times Literary Supplement*, "Mr. Henry Cecil's characters are like the families in the medicine columns of some Sunday papers. As the latter exist only to contract certain ailments, so his laymen and women have only sufficient being to exemplify certain legal difficulties."

HENRY CECIL

Among Cecil's other books are several nonfictional works about the law, including a learned study of the case of Lord Cochrane, accused of connivance in the 1814 stock exchange fraud. *Brothers in Law* was adapted for the theatre by the author and Ted Willis, became a successful film, and provided the basis for popular television and radio series. *Alibi for a Judge*, turned into a play with the help of Felicity Douglas and Basil Dawson, ran for years in London's West End; the same team dramatized *According to the Evidence*. Cecil collaborated with William Saroyan on a stage adaptation of *Settled Out of Court*, has made his own stage versions of *No Fear or Favour* and *A Woman Named Anne*, and has written a number of radio plays.

Cecil was married in 1935 to Lettice Apperly, who died in 1950. He was married again in 1954 to Barbara (Blackmore) Ovenden and has a stepson by that marriage. Dame Edith Sitwell, one of Cecil's admirers, wrote: "His prose and his invention run as quickly as a hare. One never tires of reading him, and each time one rereads a novel or short story of his, one discovers some fresh brilliance to admire."

PRINCIPAL WORKS: *Fiction*—Full Circle, 1948; The Painswick Line, 1951; No Bail for the Judge, 1952; Ways and Means, 1952; Natural Causes, 1953; According to the Evidence, 1954; Brothers in Law, 1955; Friends at Court, 1956; Much in Evidence (U.S., The Long Arm), 1957; Sober as a Judge, 1958; Settled Out of Court, 1959; Alibi for a Judge, 1960; Daughters in Law, 1961; Unlawful

Occasions, 1962; Independent Witness, 1963; Portrait of a Judge (stories), 1964; Fathers in Law, 1965; The Asking Price, 1966; A Child Divided, 1966; A Woman Named Anne, 1967; No Fear or Favour, 1968 (U.S., The Blackmailers); Tell You What I'll Do, 1969; The Buttercup Spell, 1971; The Wanted Man, 1972; Brief Tales From the Bench: Eight Courtroom Vignettes, 1972. *Nonfiction*—Brief to Counsel, 1958; Not Such an Ass, 1961; Tipping the Scales, 1964; A Matter of Speculation: The Case of Lord Cochrane, 1965; The English Judge (Hamlyn Lectures), 1970.
ABOUT: Who's Who, 1971.

***CELA, CAMILO JOSÉ** (May 11, 1916–), Spanish novelist and travel writer. The following account is based partly on a statement prepared on Cela's behalf by the critic Antonio Fernández Molina.

Cela was born in Iria-Flavia, in the province of La Coruña. His father, a customs official and part-time writer, was Spanish, his mother English, and one of his grandmothers was Italian. His early childhood was spent in Galicia, and this first phase of his life played a very important role in his development as a writer. While still a child he moved to Madrid, where he became steeped in the atmosphere of the city. He himself says, "I was educated in the schools of the Jesuits, the Escolapians, and the Marists, but my sensibility was formed on the streets."

He embarked on studies in medicine, the arts, and law at the University of Madrid, which he attended from 1933 to 1936 and from 1939 to 1943. His literary career began at about the same time, and his work was published for the first time by the Argentinian magazine *El Argentino* in 1935—an autobiographical sketch and some poems. A book of poetry appeared in 1936: *Pisando la dudosa luz del día* (Treading the Dubious Daylight). Cela fought with Franco's rebel army in the Civil War, during which his already low opinion of humanity was amply confirmed by what he saw of man's brutality.

Cela's bitterness and revulsion went into his novel *La familia de Pascual Duarte*. Published in 1942, it was an overnight sensation and, most critics agree, established the harsh tone of the postwar Spanish novel. It purports to be the confession, written in the death cell, of a peasant who has committed several murders. Pascual describes in horrible detail his squalid upbringing and early acts of violence, culminating in the murder of his wife's lover, then of his own mother. His monologue and the dialogues he reports are charged with grotesque imagery that at times achieves a kind of perverse and surrealistic poetry.

Pascual Duarte was already recognized in Spain as a modern classic and had appeared in nearly twenty foreign versions before Anthony Kerrigan's excellent translation, *The Family of Pascual Duarte*, reached the United States in 1964. Some American reviewers responded with nothing more than "amazed distaste and revulsion," but most thought it a masterpiece of naturalism, and something more—the expression of a nihilism closer to Céline than to Zola.

The repentant Pascual attributes his downfall to destiny and his inherent wickedness, but he is clearly more a victim of his society than its aggressor, the product not only of poverty and social injustice but of an absolute spiritual bankruptcy and chaos—"a lack of belief in anything not immediate," as Kerrigan said in his introduction, "the myth unraveled, the absurdity of chance." Emile Capouya wrote: "One could offer sociological or psychological accounts of Pascual Duarte's life that would be adequate on their own terms, but these terms are not really relevant to the abasement and prostration he represents. As children of the Enlightenment, we are quite firm about wanting to change the conditions that produce a Pascual Duarte. But there is that in him that suggests a condition anterior to all 'conditions,' and evokes in us a superstitious terror that the humanization of man may be unrealizable." An earlier English version by John Marks had appeared in Great Britain in 1947 as *Pascal Duarte's Family*.

Cela's next two novels were generally less well received. *Pabellón de reposo* (1943, translated by Herma Briffault as *Rest Home*) comprises the letters, diaries, and reflections of seven inmates of a tuberculosis sanatorium, while *Nuevas andanzas y desventuras de Lazarillo de Tormes* (1944) is an attempt to update the picaresque. More significantly, Cela over the next few years published several books of short stories, sketches, and travels, and in them evolved a technique of close observation, allied to a richly redundant and mannered style, which owes much to Baroja and Valle Inclán. This discipline bore fruit in the most admired of his novels, *La colmena* (1951, translated by J. M. Cohen and Arturo Barea as *The Hive*).

La colmena is an account of three days in the lives of some one hundred and sixty people, all patrons of a seedy café in a working-class district in postwar Madrid. Lacking plot and characterization in the usual sense, it snaps rapidly from one squalid life to another in highly convoluted patterns of repetition, building up a brilliant, ugly, *pointilliste* portrait of a society in which poverty and oppression have bred both extreme sexual license and extreme hypocrisy. Cela had set out to record "a slice of life, narrated step by step, without reticence, without strange tragedies, without charity, exactly as life itself rambles on"; the result is a triumph of neorealism. Saul Bellow pointed out that Cela differs from both the French naturalists and the French

* thā′ lä

existentialists in that he "has no existential, sexual, or political message to deliver." And again, as with *Pascual Duarte*, critics seemed uncertain whether Cela believes "that society perverts man or whether man is perverted *ab ovo*."

Between 1951 and 1969 Cela published thirty-four books, none of which received widespread acclaim. Among the better-known novels of this period, *Mrs. Caldwell habla con su hijo* (1953, translated as *Mrs. Caldwell Speaks to Her Son*) is a study of an incestuous passion, and *La catira* (The Blond, 1955) presents a somewhat guignolesque picture of life on the Venezuelan *llanos*. Cela's output during the 1950s and 1960s also included travel books, sketches, reminiscences, and sundry ephemera. The sardonic vision and distinctive style of Cela's early travel book *Viaje a la Alcarria* (1948, translated as *Journey to the Alcarria*) had reestablished a *genre* neglected since Azorín and Ortega. In Cela's later travelogues, as D. W. McPheeters remarked, one "becomes conscious of repeated formulas, personal quirks, recurrence of favorite words, which can become a little annoying at times."

Cela's talent seemed to be on the wane. Novels of increasing formal complexity and in a great variety of modes interested only the writers of doctoral theses—D. W. Foster confesses that "Cela's novels are a critic's delight in that the author has followed so many different procedures." In 1969, however, Cela published another major work with wide appeal. *San Camilo, 1936*, is set in Madrid on the eve of the Civil War. A patently autobiographical account of the three days centering on the feast day of Cela's patron saint, it uses interior monologue and extracts from newspapers and radio bulletins to build up a picture of a doomed community. The minute tabulation of brothel life in the first part—rather more than another display of the erudite bawdry in which Cela specializes—provides a backdrop to the strife. This long and impressive novel ends with an epilogue in which the narrator's uncle recommends love, humility, and promiscuity as the threefold path to national regeneration, the antidote to a self-destructive violence in the Spanish temperament which Cela obviously attributes in large measure to sexual repression and hypocrisy.

Cela has explored every part of Spain, often on foot, and has visited most of the European countries, Africa, South America, and the United States. In 1955 he left Madrid and settled in Majorca. There he founded and still edits the review *Papeles de Son Armadans*, with hand-set type and illustrations from old engravings. Cela's press also publishes books in fine editions, with illustrations by such artists as Picasso and Miró. He became a member of the Spanish Academy in 1957 and has an honorary doctorate from Syracuse University.

CAMILO JOSÉ CELA

He was married in 1944 to María del Rosario Conde Picavea and has a son. Cela is a collector of stamps and of literary myths. In 1968 he began to publish his massive *Diccionario secreto*, in which are assembled synonyms for, jokes about, phrases based on, and ideas associated with the testicles (Volume One), urine and penis (Volume Two), with further volumes promised on the female parts, the buttocks, and the breasts. A reviewer in the *Times Literary Supplement* of the second volume wrote that "one must marvel at the breadth and perverse detail of his erudition, the tenacity and magnificent scurrility of his labours. . . . Cela's mission is unique: he is a sort of conservative pornographer out to destroy modern sexolatry and return us to the golden age of bawdy and snigger."

In spite of his early identification with falangism and a seat in the Academy, Cela's indictment of Spanish society has earned him the enmity of establishment critics in Spain; and, while his novels and travel books have undoubtedly influenced the younger committed writers, the latter, as Gil Casado says, "reject Cela's work because of his tendency to avoid the real essence of social problems." *Persona non grata* with both the old establishment and the new, Cela is nevertheless and beyond doubt the most important Spanish prose writer to emerge since the Civil War.

PRINCIPAL WORKS IN ENGLISH TRANSLATION: Pascual Duarte's Family (tr. by John Marks and published in England only), 1947 (also tr. by Anthony Kerrigan as The Family of Pascual Duarte, 1964); The Hive, 1953; Rest Home, 1961; Journey to the Alcarria (travel), 1964; Mrs. Caldwell Speaks to Her Son, 1968.

ABOUT: Contemporary Authors 21–22, 1969; Curley, D. N. and Curley, A. (eds.) Modern Romance Literatures

(Library of Literary Criticism), 1967; Entrambasaguas, J. de (ed.) Las mejores novelas contemporáneas, vol. X, 1966; Foster, D. W. Forms of the Novel in the Work of Camilo José Cela, 1967; Gil Casado, P. La novela social en España, 1968; Ilie, P. La novelística de Camilo José Cela, 1963; Kerrigan, A. *introduction to* The Family of Pascual Duarte, 1964; Kirsner, R. The Novels and Travels of Camilo José Cela, 1963; McPheeters, D. W. Camilo José Cela, 1969; Nora, E. G. de. La novela española contemporánea, 1962; West, P. The Modern Novel, 1963; Zamora Vicente, A. Camilo José Cela, 1962. *Periodicals*—America November 7, 1964; Books Abroad Spring 1953; Nation November 14, 1953; New Republic July 12, 1954; New York Herald Tribune Book Review September 27, 1953; New York Times Book Review September 27, 1953; Revista Hispánica Moderna 2–4, 1962; Saturday Review November 28, 1964; Times Literary Supplement April 2, 1970.

***"CELAN, PAUL" (pseudonym of Paul Antschel)** (November 23, 1920–May 1, 1970), German poet, was born at Cernowitz (or Chernovtsy), in the Bukovina region of Rumania. He came of a Jewish family—German-speaking because Bukovina had been part of the Austrian Empire before becoming Rumanian. It was, he has recalled, "a region in which men and books lived." Paul Celan was educated at the Chernovtsy Gymnasium until his matriculation. In December 1938 he went to France to study medicine in Tours, but returned the following summer and entered the local university, studying Romance languages and literature. In 1940 the region was occupied by the USSR. Celan remained at the university until 1941, when Chernovtsy was occupied by German and Rumanian troops and a ghetto was established. In 1942 Celan's parents were deported to an extermination camp. He escaped, but had to serve for some time in a Rumanian labor camp. He returned to Chernovtsy at the end of 1943, and the following year resumed his studies there. In 1945 Celan left the Soviet Union to live in Bucharest as a translator and publisher's reader. In 1947 he went to Vienna and in 1948 to Paris, where he studied German and linguistics, receiving his *licence ès lettres* in 1950. In the same year he married Gisèle Lestrange, a graphic artist. Celan became a French subject, earning his living as a writer and translator, mainly of French and Russian poetry, and also lecturing at the École Supérieure of the University of Paris.

Paul Celan's poems began to appear in periodicals in 1947, and his first collection was published (under his own name) in 1948. But it was his second book, *Mohn und Gedächtnis* (Poppy and Memory, 1952) that established his reputation in the German-speaking countries. His most famous poem, "Todesfugue" (Death Fugue), was included in both books. It is a poem about the Nazi death camps, or about Germans and Jews: a mad and broken song of indescribable strangeness and power: "Coal-black milk of morning we drink it at sundown / we drink it at noon and at dawning we drink it at night / we drink it and drink it / we'll shovel a grave in the heavens there's no crowding there / A man's in the house he plays with his serpents he writes / he writes back home when the dark comes your golden hair Margareta / he writes it and then leaves the house and the stars are atwinkle he whistles his dogs to come near / he whistles his Jews to come here and shovel a grave in the earth / he commands us to play sweet now for dancing . . ." (Translated by Donald White)

* sā län′

The influence of French surrealist and post-surrealist poetry may have helped Celan at an early stage of his development, and he learned also from the linguistic improvisations of Rilke's later period. At the core of his work is his experience of the torture and extermination of the Jews under Nazism; the "surrealist genitive" was one of the devices which enabled him to transmute this experience into poems, like "Todesfugue," that not only aspire to but approximate the "condition of music." The purity and intensity of his diction may also have something to do with his remoteness from the mainstream of German usage; and his austere, uncompromising, almost religious attitude to the art of poetry set him apart from most of his German contemporaries.

The dark images of exile and loss persist in Celan's subsequent collections, but in *Von Schwelle zu Schwelle* (From Threshold to Threshold, 1955) the genitive metaphors are used less freely, and the poems in *Sprachgitter* (1959, translated as *Speech-Grille*) are altogether more spare, their rhythms stifled and contained. Celan wrote of the Nazi years: "In the midst of all losses one thing remained within reach and not lost: language." Siegbert Prawer has suggested that in his later poems Celan sought, like Hölderlin, to find in poetry itself a "home"; to construct "a landscape of language." *Sprachgitter* ends with the astonishing and triumphant poem "Einführung": "Nothing, nothing is lost. / Hosanna."

As J. C. Middleton has pointed out, Celan worked "in terms less of entities than of relations. His idiom is evasively figurative. . . . Syntax and imagery make few concessions to the audience." Yet Celan was very much concerned with communication—on his own terms, with readers capable of responding to his music and to his silences. "The poem," he said, "being a manifestation of language and therefore essentially a dialogue, can be a message inside a bottle, sent out in the not always secure belief that it could be washed ashore somewhere, some time, perhaps on a land of the heart. . . . A place that is open, habitable, perhaps a 'you' that can be addressed, a reality that can be addressed."

Increasingly, this mode of address dispensed with rhetoric and even with the syntax of discourse; the message in the bottle was made up of ciphers, blank spaces, strange new coinages. Celan admitted that poems of our time "show a marked tendency to fall silent"; many do in his 1963 collection *Die Niemandsrose* (The No Man's Rose). Poems, he said, are solitary: "They are solitary and on their way"; and he insisted that true poets communicate despite, and even because of, this solitude. "The poem wants to reach something other than itself, it needs that otherness, it needs a confrontation." But the beauty and originality of his later poems are inseparable from Celan's refusal to make them easily accessible.

In 1958 Celan was awarded the Literature Prize of the City of Bremen, in 1960 the Georg Büchner Prize. His work has been widely translated and many critics regarded him as the most distinctive and distinguished of the postwar German poets. A reviewer in the *Times Literary Supplement* of *Atemwende* wrote in 1967 that the volume "conveys the tragedy, as well as the hard-won, ever-menaced triumph, of a poet deprived of a society (even a linguistic ambience) in which he can feel at home, and a profoundly religious temperament that cannot identify itself with any creed. It shows a poet projecting his breath into emptiness and feeling it return, on the wind or in the snow, charged with a numinous power. No other German writer of Celan's generation has so powerfully conveyed the *mysterium tremendum* which the mystics experienced as divine; and it is therefore no paradox to assert that, for all his doubts, unorthodoxies and near-blasphemies, he has shown himself to be one of the few great religious poets of our time." Celan committed suicide at the age of forty-nine, but had written, in "Fadensonnen": "Thread-suns / over the gray-black wasteland. / A tree- / high thought / strikes the note of light: there are / still songs to sing beyond / mankind."

PRINCIPAL WORKS IN ENGLISH TRANSLATION: Speech-Grille (tr. by Joachim Neugroschel), 1971; Nineteen Poems (tr. by Michael Hamburger), 1972; Selected Poems (tr. by Michael Hamburger and Christopher Middleton), 1972. *Poems in* Barnstone, W. (ed.) Modern European Poetry, 1966; Bridgwater, P. (ed.) Twentieth-Century German Verse, 1963; Hamburger, M. and Middleton, C. (eds.) Modern German Poetry 1910–1960, 1962; Middleton, C. (ed.) German Writing Today, 1967; Schwebell, G. C. (ed.) Contemporary German Poetry, 1964; Rothenberg, T. (ed.) New Young German Poets, 1959.

ABOUT: Prawer, S., Paul Celan *in* Keith-Smith, B. (ed.) Essays on Contemporary German Literature, 1966; Szondi, P. Celan-Studien, 1973; Wagenbach, K. *Introduction* to Celan's Gedichte, 1961. *Periodicals*—Books Abroad Summer 1962; Germanic Review January 1964; New York Times Book Review July 18, 1971; Times May 23, 1970; Times Literary Supplement December 7, 1967; September 18, 1970.

PAUL CELAN

"CERAM, C. W." *See* MAREK, KURT W.

***CERNUDA (Y BIDÓN), LUIS** (September 21, 1902–November 6, 1963), Spanish poet and critic, was one of the most distinguished if controversial members of the so-called "Generation of 1927," an astonishing array of talent: Rafael Alberti, Federico García Lorca, Vicente Aleixandre, and others. Born in Seville, Cernuda endured a conservative Catholic upbringing under his father, a colonel in the Corps of Engineers. His was evidently an unhappy childhood and adolescence, exacerbated by his hypersensitive spirit; his family appears in his writings only to be excoriated. He wrote his first poem in 1916, just before beginning his secondary education. As a young law student, he enrolled in a course taught by Pedro Salinas, but did not introduce himself to the older poet until much later. Salinas remembers him as "difficult to get to know. Delicate, extremely modest, retaining his intimacy for himself alone . . . his way of being, the impeccable tailoring, sharply combed hair, perfectly knotted tie, all were nothing more than the desire to hide himself, the wall of the timid youth, mocker of the bad bull of public attention."

Cernuda received his doctorate in law at the University of Madrid, and went on to study at the Centro de Estudios Históricos. But it was his association with Salinas that was decisive. It was Salinas who urged Cernuda to study French litera-

* ther nū′ dhä

LUIS CERNUDA

ture, who lent him essential texts: Baudelaire, Mallarmé, Rimbaud, Reverdy, Lautréamont, and Gide above all—"I met Lafcadio (of Gide's *Les Caves du Vatican*) for the first time, and fell in love with his youth, humor, liberty, and daring." Salinas also helped arrange for the publication of Cernuda's first book, *Perfil del aire* (1927), an exercise in refined sensibility, imbued with an appropriately Andalusian languor.

If the influence of Jorge Guillén was occasionally discernible in Cernuda's first book, a measured and lucid classicism is evident in *Égloga, Elegía, Oda* (1927–1928), which marks the culmination of Cernuda's Petrarchan tendencies. This ecstatic pagan world of the pastoral was to be shattered by surrealism. For Cernuda the movement was a liberation from both poetic and social traditions; a perfect vehicle for the sometimes acrimonious individualism which characterized the poet and his relations with the world. Surrealism is most evident in *Un rio, un amor* (1929), written while he was teaching in France at the University of Toulouse; and *Los placeres prohibidos* (1931). Both *Donde habite el olvido* (1934) and *Invocaciones* (1934–1935) represent a full assimilation of surrealism along with an intensely personal utterance, an ironic and resigned realization of the failure of love. *Invocaciones* (Invocations) is a key book. During its composition, just before starting to compose the "Himno a la tristeza," Cernuda began an intensive study of the work of Friedrich Hölderlin and translated a selection of some of his poems. Hölderlin's ethical grandeur and simple gravity made a decisive impression upon Cernuda. In 1936 he collected published and unpublished books into one volume entitled *La realidad y el deseo* (Reality and Desire), a work which was to be successively amplified and altered in later editions dated 1940, 1958, and 1965.

Cernuda had returned from France in 1930 to work with a pedagogical committee, but subsequently served for a while in his country's embassy in Paris. During the Spanish Civil War he met and formed friendships with many of the Spanish and Spanish-American poets who thronged to the Republican cause, and he contributed to many literary magazines published within the Republic such as *Ahora, El Luchador,* and *Hora de España.* In February 1938, an English friend arranged with the government of Barcelona for Cernuda to lecture in England. The absence from Spain was to last a month; in fact, it lasted twenty-five years. He taught at a secondary school in Surrey, and was a reader at Glasgow and Cambridge during World War II. In 1947 he accepted a professorship of Spanish at Mount Holyoke College in Massachusetts, but in November 1952 took up permanent residence in Mexico, where he died eleven years later.

"I conclude," Cernuda wrote, "that exterior reality is a mirage and that the only thing certain is my desire to possess that reality. Thus I feel that the essential problem in poetry is the conflict between reality and desire, between appearances and truth." The unifying theme throughout Cernuda's mature poetry is man's mortality and his thirst for eternity, the tragic impulse to return to the world of childhood, love, and nature—"gestures of nostalgia for a lost Eden," in Philip Silver's words. Cernuda has been called a Romantic lyricist, but his expressive dilemma is much more complex than such a simplistic description would indicate, for he is at the same time a poet of profoundly philosophical and ethical motivation whose poetry is as devoid of aestheticism as it is of unbridled personal revelation.

The depersonalization of his Romantic impulses might be ascribed to the circumstances of his exile. While in England, Cernuda read voraciously in English poetry of all periods, and found there a distinctive "meditative" tone which coincided with his instinctive desire for an unadorned verbal unity of thought and feeling. He is the only Spanish poet of his generation to undergo the decisive stylistic influence of English poetry. Cernuda's love poetry recalls Donne and the Shakespeare of the sonnets, which is not surprising, since he translated both. Cernuda's meditations on nature bring to mind his beloved Wordsworth and Coleridge. Browning, Yeats, and Eliot taught him the use of the dramatic monologue, which he used to magnificent expressive effect in such long poems as "Silla del rey" and "Quetzalcóatl." The *persona* has never been more artfully used in Spanish literature. The quality of Cernuda's verse is soberly objective, with a colloquial and plain diction which often has a Latinate sublimity of tone unique in his time. He has had a signal influence on the younger generation of poets now writing in Spain.

He was also a superb prose stylist, and wrote some of the most original and provocative books of literary criticism in contemporary Spanish letters.

PRINCIPAL WORKS IN ENGLISH TRANSLATION: The Poetry of Luis Cernuda (ed. by Anthony Edkins and Derek Harris), 1972. *Poems in* Cohen, J. M. The Penguin Book of Spanish Verse, 1956; Texas Quarterly Spring 1961.
ABOUT: Chandler, R. E. and Schwartz, K. A New History of Spanish Literature, 1961; Macrì, O. Poesia spagnola del novecento, 1961; Muller, E. Die Dichtung Luis Cernuda, 1962; Muñoz, J. (ed.) Homenaje a Luis Cernuda, 1962; Olivio Jiménez, J. Cinco poetas del tiempo, 1964; Paz, O. Cuadrivio, 1965; Salinas, P. Literatura española siglo XX, n.d.; Silver, P. "Et in Arcadia Ego": A Study of the Poetry of Luis Cernuda, 1965; Tentori, F. Poesie di Luis Cernuda, 1962. *Periodicals*—Índice February 1964; Ínsula November 1948, February 1964, March 1964; Papeles de Son Armadans February 1959, June 1960, April 1963, October 1964, December 1965; Revista de Occidente March 1964; Revista Hispánica Moderna January–April 1960.

AIMÉ CÉSAIRE

***CÉSAIRE, AIMÉ** (June 25, 1913–), West Indian poet, dramatist, and essayist, who writes in French, was born in Martinique of a poor family. He grew up in "a tiny, cruel house" presided over by an emotionally unstable father and an overworked mother. Césaire was educated first at the Victor Schoelcher School in Martinique, and in 1931 went to Paris to attend the Lycée Louis-le-Grand, the École Normale Supérieure, and ultimately the Sorbonne, where he studied Latin, Greek, and French literature.

It was at this time that young Negro intellectuals in Paris, inspired by the anthropologists' rediscovery of the forgotten cultural richness of ancient Africa, were challenging the role assigned to them by the white man. Césaire met and formed a lasting friendship with the Senegalese poet Léopold Sédar Senghor—later president of Senegal—and with him became deeply involved in this ferment. Together with Senghor and the French Guiana poet Léon Damas, Césaire helped to promote the concept of *négritude* through the magazine *L'Étudiant noir* as well as in his own writings.

By *négritude*, Césaire understood the "simple recognition of the fact of being black and the acceptance of this fact and of its cultural and historical consequences." Since then the movement has come to stand for a variety of other things and is now virtually exhausted, but it began by rejecting the rationalism of Western civilization, which for centuries had denied a history to the black man. It follows that for Césaire, at any rate, the task of the Negro intellectual was to rehabilitate the African cultural heritage and to manifest the unique genius of the black race.

His feelings were first fully expressed in *Cahier d'un retour au pays natal* (Notebook of a Return to the Native Land), which many critics still regard as his masterpiece. This is a poem, or a sequence of poems, in verse and in prose, and in three movements. The first movement, written in Paris, is a recollection of the physical and moral squalor which colonialism visited upon Martinique. The second, composed after Césaire had returned to Martinique in the late 1930s, records his conscious attempt to purge himself of his acquired and alien preoccupation with reason and technology, and to recover his *négritude*. The third movement is a celebration, in tropical torrents of language and drumming rhythms, of unreason, of primitiveness, of passion, of blackness. For André Breton, the French Communist and surrealist poet, this work was "nothing less than the greatest lyrical monument of our time." Not everyone would accept this, but it is certainly one of the finest long lyrical poems in contemporary French literature. The *Cahier*, completed in 1939, was not published in full until 1947, when it appeared with Breton's blessing. There was a definitive edition in 1956. Emile Snyder's English translation, *Return to My Native Land*, was published by Présence Africaine in 1968. Another version, by John Berger and Anna Bostock, appeared the following year.

It was during World War II, when Césaire was working in Martinique as a teacher, that he met Breton. Césaire and René Menil were publishing a magazine, *Tropiques*, ostensibly concerned with West Indian folklore, actually a vehicle for their

* sā zâr′

political and cultural ideas. It was this review that attracted the attention of Breton, then a refugee in Martinique from occupied France. With Breton's encouragement, Césaire began to make surrealism his own, turning it into a political weapon as well as a literary technique. As Hubert Juin has pointed out, surrealism permitted Césaire to "liberate himself" from the French language—to use the violence which surrealism did to that language to attack "the *colon* who lies behind the language." "In Césaire," wrote Jean-Paul Sartre, "the great surrealist tradition is achieved, takes its definite sense, and destroys itself. Surrealism, a European poetic movement, is stolen from the Europeans by a black who turns it against them."

Poems written in the surrealist tradition are collected in *Les Armes miraculeuses* (The Miraculous Weapons, 1946), *Soleil cou coupé* (Sun Severed Neck, 1948), and *Corps perdu* (Lost Body, 1950). Characteristic of the "carefully controlled destructiveness" of Césaire's work in this mode are the following lines, translated by S. Akanji: "Clouds derail on a straw! Rain, violent girl unravel your bandages! Wounds of the sea settle down whistling! Crater and volcano, into the drift with you! Stampede foolish gods! Burst your brains! Let the trident tear out the fields and thrust the pearl-divers into the sky."

In 1956 Césaire turned to the stage with the poetic drama *Et les chiens se taisaient* (And the Dogs Were Quiet). Surrealist in style, it criticizes the apathy of the Caribbean people and extols the courage of their lonely leaders. With *La Tragédie du roi Christophe* (The Tragedy of King Christophe, 1963), Césaire began a dramatic cycle depicting in more conventional forms the long struggle of his people for freedom from white oppression. The hero of the first play is Henri Christophe, King of Haiti from 1811 to 1820. This was followed by *Une Saison au Congo* (A Season in the Congo, 1967), based on the martyrdom of Patrice Lumumba. Césaire planned to complete the cycle with a play about the slain Black Muslim leader, Malcolm X. His prose works include *Discours sur le colonialisme* (Discourse on Colonialism, 1950), *Lettre à Maurice Thorez* (1956, translated as *Letter to Maurice Thorez*), and a study of Toussaint L'Ouverture (1961).

Césaire's work during the 1960s suggests that he no longer finds surrealism a suitable tool for his purposes. The volume of selected poems published in 1961 as *Cadastre* excludes his surrealist poems, and his recent verse is direct and laconic.

Since the war Césaire has divided his time between Paris, where he represents Martinique in the French Assembly, and Martinique itself, where he is mayor of Fort-de-France. A former Communist, he left the party in 1956. He is a well-known figure at international conferences of intellectuals and artists. Césaire was married in 1937 to Suzanne Roussi, and has six children. He received the Viareggio-Versilia literary prize in 1968.

PRINCIPAL WORKS IN ENGLISH TRANSLATION: Letter to Maurice Thorez, 1957; Return to My Native Land, 1968 (new translation under same title, 1969), Cadastre, 1973. *Poems in* Literary Review Spring 1961; Chelsea June 1963; Poetry Northwest Autumn–Winter 1963–1964.

ABOUT: Beier, U. (ed.) Introduction to African Literature, 1967; Boisdeffre, P. de. Dictionnaire de littérature contemporaine, 1962; Kesteloot, L. Aimé Césaire, 1962; Sartre, J.-P. Black Orpheus, 1963; Wauthier, C. The Literature and Thought of Modern Africa, 1966. *Periodicals*—Comparative Literature Studies Fall 1963; Times Literary Supplement September 16, 1965.

***CÉSPEDES, ALBA DE** (March 11, 1911–), Italian novelist and journalist, was born in Rome. She is the granddaughter of Carlos Manuel de Céspedes, liberator and first president of the Cuban Republic. Her father, also Carlos Manuel, was another president of Cuba, and at various times his country's ambassador in Rome, Washington, London, and Madrid. Her mother, however, was an Italian, Laura Bertini, and Alba de Céspedes herself acquired Italian nationality through her first and very early marriage to Count Antamoro, a *guardia nobile* to the Pope. She has a son and grandchildren by this marriage. Her second husband is Franco Bounous, an Italian diplomat. A hardworking and prolific writer, Alba de Céspedes is well known in Italy as a journalist whose signature has appeared regularly in *Il Piccolo*, *Il Roma*, *Il Giornale d'Italia*, *L'Ora*, *Epoca*, and *La Stampa*.

Her first three novels, published between 1935 and 1937, were not much esteemed, and neither was *Prigonie* (Captivities, 1936), a book of poems. Success came with the novel *Nessuno torna indietro* (1938), which sold over two hundred thousand copies in Italy and was translated into twenty-four languages (into English as *There's No Turning Back*). It explores in some depth the characters and problems of eight women, focusing particularly on a girl torn between the guilt she feels for bearing her dead fiancé's child, and her longing to forget the past and begin life afresh. *Fuga* (Flight, 1940) is a volume of stories which, if they are most interesting as exercises in various forms of expression, also reveal the author's skill in depicting the kind of middle-class provincial milieu which figures in some of her novels.

Nessuno torna indietro was banned by the Fascists in 1940, and *Fuga* was withdrawn soon after publication. With the fall of fascism, Alba de Céspedes escaped from Rome and crossed the German lines into free Italy, where she broadcast for the partisans under the name Clorinda. It was at this time that she founded *Mercurio*, the monthly review of

* chās′ pā dās

politics, art, and science which she edited from 1944 to 1948.

Her war experiences—the German occupation of Rome, the hopes and ideals of the partisans—inspired her ambitious novel *Dalla parte di lei* (On Her Part, 1949), translated into English by Frances Frenaye as *The Best of Husbands*. Its theme, to which Alba de Céspedes returns repeatedly in her later novels, is one which almost inevitably preoccupies writers of her sex in Italy—the rights of women in marriage, and in particular their spiritual and intellectual rights. As Thomas G. Bergin wrote of this novel, Alessandra wants from her husband "not so much protection as comradeship, not so much privilege plus disregard as respect and interest. Tragedy comes about not because the best of husbands doesn't understand her but because he simply doesn't see that there is anything to understand." It seemed to Virgilia Peterson that "this tale of an unresigned Cinderella . . . moves towards its climax of violence with emotional power and a certain genuine sensitivity. But the climax itself is somehow incredible."

This "female knight-errant" continued her work in the novel *Quaderno proibito* (1952) and the novella *Prima e dopo* (1955). Both were translated by Isobel Quigly, the one as *The Secret*, the other as *Between Then and Now*. Each in its different way examines the dilemma of a woman who wants to be a wife and mother, but also an individual in her own right, and who finds that the price of self-realization is loneliness. *Il rimorso*, translated by William Weaver as *Remorse*, is about another such woman, who exchanges her apparently enviable life, her apparently admirable husband, for the possibility of fulfillment with a penniless young architect.

Alba de Céspedes' novels regularly find their way onto the best-seller lists in Italy and nearly always receive respectful attention from the critics. However, some intellectuals, troubled perhaps by her financial success, are mildly disdainful of her work, maintaining that she has all the trappings of the serious writer, including a cause, but is incapable of true profundity. Elsewhere in Europe, and particularly in France, she is very highly regarded. Indeed in its elegance and lucidity her work seems almost more French than Italian. W. L. Webb, reviewing *Between Then and Now*, wrote that she "combines the finest sort of purely feminine sensibility with a not so feminine, almost classical talent for organising her sensitive perceptions and reactions into a strong, complex, and wonderfully lucid novel." These qualities have put some critics in mind of Colette, but the English reviewer Maurice Richardson would have none of this comparison, and said: "Though her writing touch is light she is full of lofty ideals, like one of the noble souls that so delighted Stendhal when he first arrived in Italy."

ALBA DE CÉSPEDES

La bambolona (The Big Doll, 1967) was something of a departure for Alba de Céspedes, a novel more concerned with people than with "messages," and with a male protagonist, a middle-aged, middle-class man who loses his head over a much younger girl from a lower point on the Italian social scale and is ruined. The story moves swiftly, unimpeded by philosophical digressions, the dialogue is lively and revealing, and the girl is particularly well drawn, rather reminiscent of similar characters in Moravia's stories. If the author's previous novels evoked the Italy of Antonioni and Fellini (for whom she has written film scripts) *La bambolona* suggests the simpler and more zestful Italy of De Sica. It has indeed been successfully filmed, and was admirably translated (under the Italian title) by Isobel Quigly.

Alba de Céspedes has written a three-act comedy, *Gli affetti di famiglia* (Family Affections), in collaboration with A. Degli Espinosa, and is the author of an adaptation of *Quaderno proibito* which was staged in Paris. After the war she ran a kind of salon in Rome, and she remains a popular figure in literary circles there. Her Spanish antecedents are evident both in her appearance and in her character. Her favorite sports are swimming and skiing.

PRINCIPAL WORKS IN ENGLISH TRANSLATION: There's No Turning Back, 1941; The Best of Husbands, 1952; The Secret, 1957; Between Then and Now, 1959; Remorse, 1967; La Bambolona, 1969.

ABOUT: Curley, D. N. and Curley, A. (eds.) Modern Romance Literatures (Library of Literary Criticism), 1967; Dizionario universale della letteratura contemporanea, 1959. *Periodicals*—Il Corriere della Sera November 9, 1949;

Epoca May 1958, August 1963; L'Europa October 23, 1949; Italiani e Stranieri 1957; Nuova Antologia July 1967; Piccolo della Sera December 15, 1938; January 23, 1941; July 8, 1947; Quadrivio VII September 1937; Time December 29, 1952; Uomini e Tempi 1957.

CHALLANS, MARY. *See* "RENAULT, MARY"

CHAMBERS, (DAVID) WHITTAKER (April 1, 1901–July 9, 1961), American memoirist, journalist, and translator, was born in Philadelphia, one of the two sons of a middle-class Quaker family of Dutch, German, French, English, and Scottish background. His father, Jay Chambers, was a staff artist with the New York *World*. His mother, the former Leah Whittaker, had been an actress. He grew up in Lynbrook, Long Island, and was educated there, at high school showing a special aptitude for languages. The most important literary influence on his life was Victor Hugo's *Les Misérables*, which he called "the Bible of my boyhood," and which taught him "two seemingly irreconcilable things—Christianity and revolution."

Chambers' early home life was unstable, emotionally and economically. His father left the family for a time, and later his brother committed suicide. When he finished high school Whittaker Chambers went on the road, traveling through the South, working occasionally as a laborer or farmhand, and living for some time in a New Orleans slum. In 1920 he returned to New York and entered Columbia University. There he read Lenin and was attracted to communism, a tendency strengthened when he visited Europe in 1923. The following year Chambers left Columbia without graduating, joined the Communist party, and became an editor of the *Daily Worker*. He also wrote fiction for *New Masses*, achieving a certain reputation as a "proletarian" writer, and translated a number of French and German books (beginning in 1928 with Felix Salten's *Bambi*).

During the early 1930s, Chambers became a courier in the Soviet espionage apparatus in Washington, D.C., moving into the higher echelons of the party. However, his faith in communism, already weakened by news of the Soviet purges, was further eroded by the party's materialism and stringent discipline. He made his painful break with the party in April 1938, renewing his earlier Quaker connections. The following year, impelled by the Nazi-Soviet nonagression pact, he told the State Department what he knew of the Soviet spy apparatus in the United States.

Chambers' revelations were not acted upon until ten years later. In April 1939, meanwhile, he had taken his first real job as a book reviewer with *Time* magazine. As he worked his way up through

WHITTAKER CHAMBERS

the Time-Life editorial hierarchy, Chambers became known as one of the organization's most brilliant and controversial writers, the author of a number of editorial articles for *Life* and cover stories for *Time*. During World War II he became senior editor of *Time*'s foreign news section, and his writings took on a strongly anti-Soviet flavor. He also edited a series of articles on great philosophers that appeared in *Fortune* in 1942 and 1943, and contributed to *Life's Picture History of Western Civilization* (1947). By 1948, Chambers' salary as one of Time-Life's seven senior editors was thirty thousand dollars a year.

In August of that year Chambers was called upon to testify before the House Committee on Un-American Activities about his earlier Communist connections. It was at these hearings that Chambers identified Alger Hiss, a former State Department official, as one of his Communist party associates, whom he had known since 1935 and who had allegedly supplied him with State Department documents to be turned over to Soviet agents. When Hiss denied the charges and sued Chambers for slander, Chambers produced microfilm copies of the documents in question—the so-called "pumpkin papers." Hiss was indicted for perjury and eventually convicted and imprisoned. The case and Chambers' role in it have ever since been the subjects of violent controversy, passionately debated in an apparently endless stream of books and articles.

Chambers left Time-Life in December 1948 and retired to Carroll County, Maryland, where he worked the farm he owned there and prepared his autobiography, *Witness* (1952). The book, which is marked by strongly religious overtones and a pessimistic view of Western civilization and its prospects, dwells at length on the Hiss trial and on Chambers' motives in entering, and ultimately denouncing, the Communist party. It gave fresh impetus to the Hiss controversy and divided reviewers mostly along ideological lines, although there was fairly widespread praise for its author's swift, powerful prose. Sidney Hook called *Witness* "one of the most significant autobiographies of the twentieth century," and Irving Howe referred to it as a confession of almost classical stature.

In the mid-1950s, Chambers moved to a more secluded farm in the same part of Maryland. From 1957 to 1959 he was a senior editor and writer for the right-wing magazine *National Review*. During the last two years of his life, in declining health, Chambers studied languages and science at West Maryland College. He died of a heart attack at the age of sixty and was survived by his wife, the former Esther Shemitz, and a son and daughter.

A posthumous selection of letters, notes, and excerpts from his diary, edited by Duncan Norton-Taylor, was published in 1964 as *Cold Friday* (named after one of Chambers' fields, a kind of haven to him). Noting the book's "prevailing tone of melancholy and despair," its author's "total recoil from the twentieth century," *Newsweek* listed among "its obsessively recurrent themes . . . the fatality and anguish of history, the inadequacy of man." Sidney Hook wrote: "A religious attitude, already apparent in *Witness*, here dominates every theme." There was much praise for Chambers' "wonderfully sensitive description of the natural scene," even from Irving Howe, who was otherwise appalled by "his grandiose solemnity, his stunning pretentiousness, his oracular incompetence."

Whittaker Chambers seemed to Conor Cruise O'Brien a "veteran liar," and to Rebecca West "a Christian mystic of the pantheist school." Arthur Koestler suggested that he might be both—a man who, "when he testified . . . knowingly committed moral suicide to atone for the guilt of our generation."

PRINCIPAL WORKS: Witness, 1952; Cold Friday, 1964.

ABOUT: Andrews, B. and P. A. A Tragedy of History, 1962; Chambers, W. Witness, 1952; Chambers, W. Cold Friday, 1964; Cook, F. J. The Unfinished Story of Alger Hiss, 1958; Cooke, A. A Generation on Trial, 1950; De Toledano, R. and Lasky, V. Seeds of Treason, 1950; Hiss, A. In the Court of Public Opinion, 1957; Jowitt, W. A. The Strange Case of Alger Hiss, 1953; Weyl, N. Treason, 1950; Zeligs, M. A. Friendship and Fratricide, 1967. *Periodicals*—National Review July 29, 1961; New York Times July 12, 1961; Reader's Digest May 1952; Saturday Evening Post November 15, 1952.

CHANG, EILEEN (**Chang Ai-ling**) (September 30, 1920–), Chinese novelist, writes: "I spent most of my life in Shanghai where I was born, the child of a blind marriage that ended in divorce. My father was a 'gentleman of leisure,' my mother a painter who traveled and stayed in Europe. However, they both believed in an early acquaintance with Chinese classics and I had long hours of tutoring since the age of seven. I went to a large Episcopalian school for girls for six years and discovered that my family was not as different as I had thought, if more extreme. The Chinese family system was falling apart, generally held together only by economic factors. I was going to London University over my father's objections but was prevented by the Second World War. My mother sent me to the University of Hong Kong instead. The Pacific War caught up with me there in my junior year, so I went back to Shanghai. I made a living by writing stories and film scripts and became increasingly engrossed in China. It took me three years to make up my mind to leave after the Communist takeover.

EILEEN CHANG

"After I got to Hong Kong I wrote my first novel in English, *The Rice-Sprout Song*, which was published in the U.S. I have lived in the U.S. for the last ten years, largely occupied with two unpublished novels about China before the Communists, a third that I am still working on, and translations, film and radio scripts in Chinese. The publishers here seem agreed that the characters in those two novels are too unpleasant, even the poor are no better. An editor at Knopf's wrote that if things were so bad before, then the Communists would actually be deliverance. Here I came against the curious literary convention treating the Chinese as a nation of Confucian philosophers spouting aphorisms, an anomaly in modern literature. Hence the dualism in current thinking on China, as just these same philosophers ruled by trained Communists. But there was decay and a vacuum, a need to believe in something. In the final disintegration of ingrown latter-day Confucianism, some Chinese seeking a way out of the prevalent materialistic nihilism turned to communism. To many others Communist rule is also more palatable for being a reversion to the old order, only replacing the family with the larger blood kin, the state, incorporating nationalism, the undisputed religion of our time. What concerns me most is the few decades in between, the years of dilapidation and last furies, chaos and uneasy individualism, pitifully short between the past milleniums on the one hand and possibly centuries to come. But any changes in the future are likely to have germinated from the brief taste of freedom, as China is isolated by more factors than the U.S. containment policy.

"The Chinese experience predates the problems of Southeast Asia, India and Africa where the family in its larger sense is just as much of a system, said to be at the root of government corruption, as in China. The trend is for the West to be tolerant, even reverential, without a closer look at the pain inside the system, a field that has been thoroughly explored by modern Chinese literature in its eternal attacks on what was called 'the man-eating old ritualistic teaching,' to the extent of flogging a dead horse. A common reversal of verdict is the vicious adulterous woman represented as a desperate rebel against the scheme of things—Freudian psychology juxtaposed with *chinoiserie*. The realistic tradition persists, sharpened by the self-disgust that came from national humiliations. By comparison the occidental nonhero is still sentimental. I myself am more influenced by our old novels and have never realized how much of the new literature is in my psychological background until I am forced to theorize and explain, having encountered barriers as definite as the language barrier."

Although Eileen Chang is little known except among specialists in Chinese literature, she is regarded in some quarters as possibly "the greatest Chinese writer since the May Four Movement" of 1919. Most of her short stories, novels, and novellas have been written in Chinese, but she has also published two books in English. Her tales, with few exceptions (*Rice-Sprout Song* is one), are set among the ruling and rich merchant families in the years before the 1948 revolution. They present a society in the last stages of decay, paralyzed by traditions and conventions that corrupt the men and stifle the women.

This is the world, both authoritarian and decadent, in which Eileen Chang herself grew up. Her good fortune was a mother who refused to be broken by the system. When her father, already an opium addict, took a concubine, her mother left to study in France. When she returned she divorced her husband. Eileen Chang spent as much time with her mother as she could. Her father retaliated by locking her in the house for months on end, and she passed through a period of mental and physical breakdown until she was able to escape to live permanently with her mother. As she says, she was sent to study at the University of Hong Kong during the war, then returned to Japanese-occupied Shanghai. She began to make a living by writing romances for popular magazines, gradually developing what C. T. Hsia calls an "intimate boudoir realism" quite new in Chinese fiction, combining the social and moral concerns of the Chinese tradition with a psychological sophistication drawn from her Westernized education.

After the war, the Communist regime looked askance on writers who had continued to publish during the Japanese occupation, and Eileen Chang limited herself for a while to working on film scripts. In 1952 she decided to leave China for Hong Kong, and in 1955 she arrived in the United States, where she now lives. She has been a writer in residence at Miami University, Oxford, Ohio, and associate scholar at the Radcliffe Institute for Independent Study, Cambridge, Massachusetts, holding a scholarship to translate a novel from Old Chinese, *Hai Shang Hua*.

Eileen Chang's constant theme is the crushing of the individual by the family until he no longer even wants to escape. Widely regarded as the finest of her stories is the novella *The Golden Cangue*. The spirited girl Ch'i Ch'iao, daughter of shopkeepers, is married to the weakling son of the rich Chiang family. Her husband fills her with disgust; her tyrannical mother-in-law rules the household from her opium couch. Ch'i Ch'iao's passion for a wastrel brother-in-law is rejected, and all her sensitivity dries up. When her husband and mother-in-law die at last, she is ready to take on the mantle of the old woman, her only passion money and the family property, which she uses to ruin her own son and daughter, turning them both into addicts like herself, driving her daughter-in-law to suicide, and destroying her plain daughter's only love affair.

C. T. Hsia comments that these tales are frequently gay and satirical in tone, but that below the surface is always a "profound, impersonal sorrow." Her tragic revelations come not in dramatic crises, but in moments when the self finds itself "unpropped by its usual stays of vanity or desire." He adds that her prose is "the richest in imagery of any modern Chinese writer."

The Rice-Sprout Song was Eileen Chang's first novel written in English. Sparer in style than her earlier work, it is an account of life in a village, just after the 1948 revolution. Gold Root is a model farmer, and his wife, Moon Scent, who has been working in the city, is returning home. Instead of the social transformation she has been led to expect, she finds starvation, and envy and suspicion of the savings she has brought home with her. Comrade Wong, the Party administrator, asks the peasants for donations for the families of soldiers of the Liberation Army, but they refuse because they do not have enough for themselves, and instead ask for loans to carry them through the coming New Year celebrations. Wong refuses, and riots follow, bloodily suppressed. Gold Root's little daughter is killed, and he is seriously wounded. Rejected even by his beloved sister, who dares not nurse a wanted man, he drowns himself. Moon Scent dies setting fire to the village granary, and the book ends with the villagers dancing to the rice-sprout song as they bear their gifts to the soldiers. The book was sympathetically reviewed when it appeared. The New York *Herald Tribune Book Review* called it "moving and unassuming," the *Yale Review* found it "both very funny and very sad," and *Time* "mordant if melodramatic." In 1967 appeared *The Rouge of the North*, an English adaptation of *The Golden Cangue*, with some of the more harrowing scenes omitted. Though partly emasculated, it remains a richly evocative picture of a dying social system and the havoc it wreaks upon human beings.

Eileen Chang's work has no doubt been overpraised by those who regard it as fuel for the cold war, and too little regarded by those who see no task for the contemporary Chinese novel but to serve the political needs of the revolution. Her pictures of prerevolutionary China, however, achieve at their best a universality that transcends their time and place.

PRINCIPAL WORKS IN ENGLISH: The Rice-Sprout Song, 1955; The Rouge of the North, 1967.

ABOUT: Hsia, C. T. A History of Modern Chinese Fiction, 1917–1957, 1961. *Periodicals*—New York Herald Tribune Book Review April 17, 1955; New York Times Book Review April 3, 1955; Saturday Review May 21, 1955; Time April 25, 1955; Yale Review Summer 1955.

***CHAPIN, KATHERINE GARRISON** (September 4, 1890–), American poet, writes: "I was born on the Connecticut shores of Long Island Sound of a New England father, whose ancestor, Deacon Samuel Chapin of Springfield, Massachusetts, has been immortalized as 'The Puritan' in the statue by St. Gaudens, and a mother whose ancestors were Dutch descendants of Nieuw Amsterdam and the English of the Hudson River. I was a native New Yorker and grew up in that city, where I went to private schools. I had a postgraduate year of study at Columbia University, when Max Eastman, assistant to John Dewey, was writing his significant book *The Enjoyment of Poetry* and teaching a course in aesthetics.

KATHERINE GARRISON CHAPIN

"Poetry came into my life first as drama. My mother, who could have had a career on the stage, constantly read aloud to us, and took us as small children to every Shakespearean performance available. We also went to the opera when I was eight, in the old Metropolitan opera house three blocks away from where we lived on 37th Street. My sister and I studied acting and ballet, music and pantomime, and acted in a small theatre group.

"I began to write poetry when I was still at school, and I graduated just before the American poetry renascence which began about 1912. Robert Frost was coming back from England with his first volume; Yeats was saying, 'Poetry should be as simple as a cry of the heart,' and Ezra Pound had started his long embattled career. John Masefield came to New York in the beginning of the first World War and read aloud his 'Sea Fever' to a small group in a studio near Carnegie Hall—an unforgettable experience.

"For the next ten years I absorbed a great deal of poetry, classic and contemporary, and some poetic criticism. I did not attempt to publish until 1925. For ten years my poems appeared fairly regularly in the monthly magazines, *Scribner's*, *Harper's*, and others. I reviewed books of poetry and wrote a few critical essays. For many years I have been giving talks on poetry with readings.

"Among the definitions of poetry two remain with me as essential: a poem is never something which could just as well be said in prose—it is a thing in itself; and as the Chinese say, 'Poetry is the sound the heart makes.'

* chā′ pin

"My own poetry, though traditional in form, is contemporary in feeling. I do not find many direct influences, though my poetic thinking has been widened and stimulated by my association with the French Nobel Prize poet, St. John Perse.

"At the request of a composer, Harl McDonald, I wrote my first ballad poem for the music of women's voices, and the Philadelphia Orchestra, *Lament for the Stolen*. Later I wrote a ballad for Negro and white voices called *And They Lynched Him on a Tree* for music by the Negro composer William Grant Still. Grant Still also made a musical setting for my poem *Plain-Chant for America*, which was widely performed during the war.

"Several years later I returned to my interest in drama and wrote a three-act play called *Sojourner Truth*, the story of the great Negro woman evangelist, which was produced in New York by the American Negro Theatre (1948).

"In 1918 I married Francis Biddle and moved to Philadelphia where we lived for twenty years. We came to Washington in the Franklin Roosevelt Administration where my husband was successively Solicitor General, Attorney General during the Second World War, and American judge-member of the International Tribunal at Nuremberg after the War.

"We had two sons. The elder is now professor of English at Pennsylvania Military College, having received his doctorate from the University of Pennsylvania (1964). Our younger son, a vivid child, died at the age of eight. It was not until two years later that I was able to feel that my burden of sorrow could be a weight on such a free spirit, and that I must let him go. It was then I wrote my poem 'Bright Mariner,' which has been often reprinted, bringing I believe solace to others.

"We live in Georgetown in the District of Columbia in the winter and a house that dates from the end of the eighteenth century on Cape Cod in the summer."

Miss Chapin is the daughter of Lindley Hoffman Chapin and the former Cornelia Garrison Van Auken. Her precocious enthusiasm for writing and the theatre was encouraged at Miss Eleanor Keller's school in New York City, where her English instructor was the playwright Rachel Crothers, and she later studied music with Kurt Schindler, founder of the Schola Cantorum, New York. The small theatre group with which she and her sister Cornelia acted was the Washington Square Players, the original Theatre Guild School. Cornelia Chapin went on to develop in a different direction, achieving some prominence as a sculptor.

Time Has No Shadow (1936) was the first considerable collection of Miss Chapin's poems, which eschewed immediate sensuous appeal to convey a fine distillation of emotion in well-controlled traditional forms. In 1937 and 1938 she gave several radio talks about and readings of contemporary poetry, including her own, and in the latter year, during the Spanish War, contributed an anti-Fascist poem to the League of American Writers' anthology, *Writers Take Sides*.

Among Miss Chapin's thoughtful and lucid literary essays is "The Quality of Poetry"; it was first published in *Poetry*, whose editor, George Dillon, called it "one of the finest poets' credos I have read." It states Miss Chapin's belief that the poet has a duty to contribute, through his verse, to the conduct of society, and not least "in a time of chaos, of social upheaval, or war." This conviction has found its most successful expression in three major choral ballads, a form for which Miss Chapin is admirably equipped by an instinctive concern for clarity of expression and by her training in music and drama. *Lament for the Stolen* was first performed in December 1938 by the Philadelphia Orchestra under Eugene Ormandy, with a chorus of two hundred and fifty women's voices. Two years later an audience of thirteen thousand attended the première at Lewisohn Stadium of *And They Lynched Him on a Tree*, which movingly reflects Miss Chapin's hatred of mob violence and racial intolerance. *Plain-Chant for America*, Miss Chapin's second collaboration with William Grant Still, was written after a prolonged argument with some Fascist-minded Americans, which left the author "good and mad." She says: "I thought it important that Americans get together to state their democratic faith and defy the rest of the world on it." The poem, written for baritone and orchestra, was first performed at Woodstock, New York, in September 1939, and several times repeated elsewhere.

A selection of Miss Chapin's poems, new and old, appeared in 1959 as *The Other Journey*. Their themes are the "perilously usual" ones of "woman's universal destiny"—love and grief, the birth and loss of children, the loneliness and the consolations of old age. *Poetry's* reviewer commended an expert management of sound but found neither tension nor personal impact. Other critics—a majority—disagreed, saying that Miss Chapin had marked her familiar material with her own stamp, "delicate, serene, assured."

The poet's husband, Francis Biddle, who died in 1968, was not only a jurist of the first importance but the author of a life of Oliver Wendell Holmes, and of two volumes of memoirs, *A Casual Past* (1961) and *In Brief Authority* (1963), which were greatly relished for their "flair, gusto, and distinction."

PRINCIPAL WORKS: Outside of the World, 1930; The Bright Mariner, 1933; Time Has No Shadow, 1936; Lament for the Stolen: A Poem for a Chorus, 1938; Plain-

Chant for America: Poems and Ballads, with an Essay, The Quality of Poetry, 1942; The Other Journey: Poems New and Selected, 1959.

ABOUT: Contemporary Authors 5–6, 1963; Current Biography, 1943. *Periodicals*—New Republic May 9, 1960; Poetry December 1960; Saturday Review of Literature August 15, 1952.

CHAPMAN, GUY (PATTERSON) (September 11, 1889–June 30, 1972), English memoirist, historian, and biographer, wrote: "So far as I can remember I have always had a passion for books and their content, even before I could read. One of my great-uncles, Edward Chapman, was Charles Dickens's publisher, and I was brought up on *The Pickwick Papers*, of which my father used to explain the illustrations, along with those of La Fontaine's Fables, every Sunday. I was brought up to love books, their appearance and their feel. My father was a senior government official. We lived in London and I went to Westminster School and after that to Christ Church, Oxford. At that time my mother intended me for the Church, my father for the Civil Service. I wanted to become a publisher. This was forbidden. I wasted three years in a barrister's chambers. In 1913, my father died and I rushed into a publishing house, only to be once more frustrated by the outbreak of war. From August 1914 to February 1920 I served in the army, from July 1915 until 1920 in France and Germany. Of what happened to me during those years, much is related in my book *A Passionate Prodigality*, published in London in 1933 and in New York in 1966. It had been a maturing experience. I had had more than three years with the infantry and was lucky to have escaped unwounded. I was twice decorated.

"On leaving the army I went back to publishing and between 1924 and 1926 squandered what money I possessed in producing books ill-calculated to make my fortune. In 1926 I married the novelist Margaret Storm Jameson and have lived happily ever since.

"During these years, as a result of publishing an edition of *Vathek*, I became deeply interested in the author of that unique grotesque novel, William Beckford of Fonthill, edited three of his books, produced a bibliography of his writings and eventually a biography of him. At the same time I was editing and designing a series of special books for Eyre and Spottiswoode under the general title of the King's Printers' Editions. And also I had decided that my true bent was for history and had rejuvenated myself by becoming an undergraduate at the London School of Economics at the age of forty-three. After this, at the approach of war, I found myself in the editorial office of Jonathan Cape. Between 1930 and 1940 I produced my *Beckford* and wrote a study of the social influences on the British birth-rate, *Culture and Survival*. This

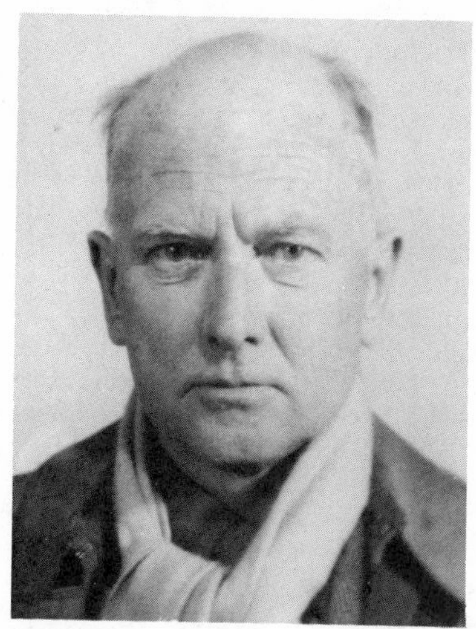

GUY CHAPMAN

was a good book and was praised by reviewers, but its publication coincided with the defeat of France. At this point I threw up publishing and went back to the army, unemployable except as a chair-borne officer. Having wasted another four years or so, I came back to civilian life and was elected to the chair of Modern History at the University of Leeds. I stayed here for eight years, one of which I spent in the splendid and exciting city of Pittsburgh at the University. I threw in my hand in 1953, retired, and went to live in France in order to write modern history. I came back a year later and after various trials, settled in Cambridge. In 1957 I spent some months at the Institute for Advanced Study in Princeton.

"I am passionately interested in the history of our own times, not so much in what happened as how and why. One watches with dismay men of good intentions blindly leading the ignorant from error to error, wholly unaware of the forces afflicting them. I don't enjoy writing, which I do with pain and difficulty, but I am spurred by curiosity. If I write about France, it is because, in spite of my fondness for it, I am not involved in it as I am in my own country. So far I have been engaged in clearing lumps of obtrusive matter out of the way. In 1955, I published *The Dreyfus Case: A Reassessment*, of which I hope to produce a new edition shortly. In 1962, there came *The Third Republic of France: the First Phase*, covering the period up to the Dreyfus case. I have just completed a history of the French Army from the Treaty of Versailles up to the defeat of June, 1940."

Guy Chapman was born in Cookham Dean,

Berkshire, the only son of George Chapman, Official Receiver in Bankruptcy. He himself qualified as a barrister and was called to the bar in 1914. He served during World War I in the Royal Fusiliers, fighting with them through the battles of the Somme and, after a period on the staff, returning to what remained of his battalion for further fighting. He was twice mentioned in dispatches, received an OBE and the Military Cross, and left the army with the rank of major.

Chapman's early books were remarkable for their variety and their ill fortune. The first was a novel, *A Painted Cloth* (1930), a "spirited and ironic" picture of the inside workings of a great publishing house. Chapman's "stoic radiant memoir" of the war, *A Passionate Prodigality*, appeared a few years later. Its quality was recognized at once by the critics but its publication was ill-timed and it was allowed to go out of print. A totally different sort of book followed, Chapman's biography of William Beckford, the brilliant, decadent, enigmatic builder of Fonthill Abbey. Beckford had complained that "not an animal comprehends me"; most critics thought that Chapman's study, the product of ten years' research, was the best attempt yet made to do so. Another sharp change of direction produced *Culture and Survival*, "a book of fascinating interest and great importance" which had nothing like the impact it deserved simply because, as Chapman says, its publication coincided with the fall of France.

The author's four years (1941–1945) as "a chair-borne officer" in World War II were spent in the Army Educational Corps, and for part of this time he served as commandant of the Army School of Education, with the rank of lieutenant colonel. His postwar books include what is now regarded as the standard account of the Dreyfus case, a work which achieves both scholarly impartiality and some of the excitement of a detective story; the first volume of Chapman's history of modern France; and his detailed study of the French army's defeat in 1940.

In 1965, no doubt in recognition of a revival of interest in World War I, *A Passionate Prodigality* was republished in England, appearing for the first time in America a year later. It was then, fifty years after the events it described, thirty years after its first publication, that it found its audience. It is a personal account of the destruction of a generation between 1915 and 1918. Ignoring strategy and politics, it concentrates always on individual soldiers, the way they lived in the trenches, what they said and felt, and the way they died. "It is not only a singularly concrete picture of the war," wrote Thomas Lask, "but also one that captures the mixture of exaltation and despair, of comradeship and alienation of the men who fought it. His book has the quality of poetry. Full of overtones, it expands and fills the mind, and engages the heart and intellect together." Many critics placed the book among the few masterpieces written about the Great War. George Steiner thought it better than Robert Graves's *Goodbye to All That*, "more professional, more detached and technical in focus." Many reviewers were much affected by Chapman's acknowledgment that the war brought not only horror and death but a heightened sense of life: "the central persuasion of the book," Steiner said, "is one of beauty and, in a paradoxical sense, of joy," and it is this Homeric spirit which assures the book of "a lasting place in the history of modern English prose."

PRINCIPAL WORKS: A Painted Cloth (novel), 1930; A Passionate Prodigality: Fragments of Autobiography, 1933 (U.S., 1966); Beckford: A Biography, 1937; Culture and Survival, 1940; The Dreyfus Case: A Reassessment, 1955; The Third Republic of France: Vol. 1, The First Phase 1871–94, 1962; Why France Collapsed, 1968. *As editor*—Travel Diaries of William Beckford of Fonthill, 1928; Vathek, 1930; (with J. Hodgkin) A Bibliography of William Beckford of Fonthill, 1930; Vain Glory, 1937.

ABOUT: Who's Who, 1971. *Periodicals*—New Statesman March 20, 1937; April 23, 1955; New York Review of Books October 6, 1966; New York Times July 25, 1937; April 19, 1966; New York Times Book Review April 10, 1966; Reporter November 3, 1966; Spectator March 12, 1937; April 29, 1955; Times Literary Supplement March 13, 1937; April 29, 1955; Washington Post Book Week May 15, 1966.

***CHAR, RENÉ** (June 14, 1907–), French poet, has authorized the following note, prepared (in French) on his behalf by a friend: "René Char was born at L'Isle-sur-la-Sorgue, Vaucluse, the son of Émile Char, a manufacturer, mayor of L'Isle-sur-la-Sorgue, and of Marie-Thérèse Rouget of Cavaillon. His grandfather, a public ward, had been given the name Charlemagne, which he changed to Char-Magne, a name which his son Émile shortened to Char.

"René Char spent his childhood at L'Isle-sur-la-Sorgue and was very much affected by his acquaintance with men from the area, chiefly craftsmen and peasants, men who fished the Sorgue, rebels of all sorts. From this early stage in his life he acquired a taste for and a profound love of nature; in the same way he developed a strong love for freedom. His father died in 1918. The child studied at the public schools, then at the *lycée* at Avignon until he received his *baccalauréat*. René Char stayed for a while in Tunisia in 1924, acquiring strong anticolonial feelings. In 1925 he pursued, not very diligently, the course at the École-de-Commerce at Marseilles, then did his military service at Nîmes in 1927 and 1928.

"In 1929 René Char published *Arsenal* and sent a copy to Paul Éluard. Éluard came to L'Isle-sur-la-Sorgue; the two poets formed a strong and lasting

* shar

friendship. Char made his first visit to Paris in 1929; Éluard introduced him to friends, including André Breton; Char became an associate of the surrealists in the second period of the movement from 1930 to 1934 and published, notably, *Ralentir travaux* (Works Slowed Down, 1930) in collaboration with Breton and Éluard. In 1933 he married Georgette Goldstein, whom he divorced in 1949. He lived sometimes in L'Isle-sur-la-Sorgue, sometimes in Paris, and made several trips to Spain. In 1934 he published *Le Marteau sans maître* (The Hammer Without a Master). In 1935 he became manager of the chalk pits of Vaucluse from which he resigned some years later because of incompatibility.

"In 1936 René Char became ill with blood poisoning, was in a serious condition for three months at L'Isle-sur-la-Sorgue, and spent a year convalescing near Cannes. He published *Placard pour un chemin des écoliers* (Sign for a Bypath) in 1937 and *Dehors la nuit est gouvernée* (Somewhere Night Is Ruled) in May 1938. This period of the life of the poet and, inevitably, his work, should be considered in relation to the social strife in France, the beginning of the Front Populaire, the developments in the Spanish war, the anguish created by European fascism, and the presentiment of great world catastrophes. Mobilized in 1939, he fought in Alsace and was demobilized in July 1940.

"At L'Isle-sur-la-Sorgue the Vichy police investigated René Char, who was called a Communist because of his surrealist activities. The poet escaped with his wife to the Alps; the underground activity of the Resistance began. Char, under the name of Captain Alexandre, became the departmental commander of the Parachute Landing Division of the Second Region of the Free French Forces, and deputy to the regional commander of the operations network. From his mobilization in 1939 until the liberation of France, Char did not publish any work. In June 1944 he was wounded in action against the Germans and was cared for by the doctors of the *maquis*. Nevertheless, he was able to go to Algeria in July 1944 when he received a summons from the North Africa Allied Council to which he was assigned. On his return he was parachuted into France, participated in the battles which liberated Provence, and held various responsible posts until 1945 when he was demobilized, the holder of important decorations for his war service.

"The appearance of *Seuls demeurants* (The Only Ones Left) in 1945 and of *Feuillets d'Hypnos* (Leaves of Hypnos) in 1946 contributed decisively to spreading the fame of the poet. Char again was able to live part of the year in Paris and part in the Vaucluse and to devote himself to poetry. Indeed, so few significant exterior events occurred in Char's life after 1945 that one can summarize them as follows:

RENÉ CHAR

"René Char abstained henceforth from all official literary life and refused the honors that were offered him in civilian life, feeling that poetry was not to be considered as a career or livelihood. He also refused to answer any of the entreaties for political action such as French society was, and still is, likely to address to a famous author, a man of the left and one, especially, who had been a notable *Résistant* from the beginning. He explains his feelings on these matters in his book *Recherche de la base et du Sommet* (Inquiry Into the Base and the Summit). But, while René Char hardly ever took a public position on political problems, not even on the Algerian war, feeling on each occasion that these problems arose too superficially and unilaterally, it is impossible not to see in Char's books since 1945 that closely linked to the poetic act is a profound engagement with the great problems of our time.

"In the course of these years the audience for his work kept growing both in France where critical comment increased, and abroad where his poetry was translated into most of the living languages of the Western world, as well as in Eastern Europe. As for René Char's circle after the war, one can say that it was made up for the most part of old friends, fellow countrymen from Provence, Resistance workers, and literary contemporaries, as well as young poets whom he encourages with the greatest kindness. It should be noted at the same time that Char was one of the closest friends of Albert Camus and that he kept up a correspondence with Boris Pasternak; he also maintained close contact with Martin Heidegger.

"Finally one may add that in the last twenty

years the poet has seen his works published in very beautiful editions, illustrated by the greatest painters of the twentieth century, whose work he has always followed very closely; he was particularly associated with Nicolas de Staël and Georges Braque."

Char's early poetry suffered, it has been suggested, from its subservience to external events. Like many surrealists, he associated the poetic dislocation of language with a commitment to the transformation of society, and his work in the 1930s reflects the political urgencies of the period, especially the Spanish Civil War. His years in the *maquis* transformed both the content and the form of his work, as was evident at once when he began to publish again after the war.

Feuillets d'Hypnos is a volume of verse and prose poetry describing and reflecting on his war experiences—a notebook exalting "the resistance of humanism aware of its duties, discreet about its virtues, wishing to keep in reserve the inaccessible as a free field for the fantasy of its suns, and resolved to pay the price for this." These poems are laconic but richly suggestive in their language, startling in their imagery and, for all their painful experience of loss and chaos, hopeful. In Char's postwar poetry, as Pierre de Boisdeffre put it, the word becomes an instrument not for abolishing the world, but for buying it back; he has achieved the optimism of one who had "lived through the absurd and passed beyond it."

Some of Char's best poems are contained in *Fureur et mystère* (1948), and other important collections are *Les matineaux* (1950), *La Parole en archipel* (1962), and *Le Nu perdu* (1971). His *Poèmes et prose choisis* appeared in 1957, and *Commune présence* (1964) is also a selection of poems, arranged by theme and mood. Char has published several volumes of essays, including *Recherche de la base et du sommet* (1955) and *Sur la poésie* (1958), and has also written on the work of Joan Miró and Georges Braque. *Le Soleil des eaux* (1949) is a play.

René Char has been placed with Camus "among the most convincing defenders of human values in our times." His poems are full of the praise of human love and liberty and aspiration, expressed and illustrated through images and anecdotes drawn from the natural and domestic life of Provence and its austere and burning landscape. His poetry itself grows increasingly austere and impersonal. More and more it is written in prose—a matter of radically compressed images, paradoxes, aphorisms, and maxims: "The purpose of poetry being to make us supreme by impersonalizing us, we reach by grace of the poem the plenitude of what was only hinted at, or travestied, in the rantings of the individual. / Poems are those bits of incorruptible being we toss into the repugnant jaws of death, arching them high so that they ricochet and fall into the formative world of unity." (From "The Rampart of Twigs," translated by Jackson Mathews)

Poetry to Char is a kind of religion, and he accepts the priest's role, announcing the unknowable but guarding its mystery in lean flashes of perception: "The bird tills the soil, / The serpent sows, / Death, enriched, / Praises the harvest. // Pluto in the sky! // . . . . Suddenly love, the equal of terror, / With a hand I had never seen, puts an end to the fire, straightens the sun, reshapes the beloved. // Nothing had heralded so strong an existence." ("Lightning Victory," translated by W. S. Merwin)

Camus, who considered Char "our greatest living poet," wrote: "Ancient and new as it is, his poetry is both subtle and simple. It carries daytime and night on the same impulse. In the brilliant landscape where Char was born, the sun, as we know, is something dark. At two in the afternoon, when the land is fagged with heat, a black breath blows over it. And so, when Char's poetry appears to be obscure, it is because a furious condensation of imagery, an intensification of light, removes it from that degree of abstract transparency which we all too often demand only because it makes no demand on us. But at the same time, that point of darkness, as in the sun-soaked landscape, creates around it vast reaches of light in which the human face is laid bare."

Char holds the Croix de Guerre and the Médaille de la Résistance, and is a Chevalier de la Légion d'Honneur. He received the Prix des Critiques in 1966. For René Char, "a poem is the fulfillment of a desire which remains desire . . . that instant when beauty, after keeping us waiting a long time, rises out of common things, binds everything that can be bound, lights up everything that needs lighting in our bundle of shadows."

PRINCIPAL WORKS IN ENGLISH: Hypnos Waking (sel. and tr. by Jackson Mathews and others), 1956; Leaves of Hypnos, 1973. *Poems in* Barnstone, W. (ed.) Modern European Poetry, 1966; Hartley, A. Penguin Book of French Verse (Twentieth Century), 1959.

ABOUT: Aspel, A. Contemporary French Poetry, 1965; Balakian, A. Surrealism, 1959; Berger, P. René Char, 1951; Blanchot, M. and others René Char's Poetry, 1956; Boisdeffre, P. de. Une Histoire vivante de la littérature d'aujourd'hui, 1958; Clouard, H. and Leggewie, R. French Writers of Today, 1965; Contemporary Authors 15–16, 1966; Curley, D. N. and Curley, A. Modern Romance Literatures (Library of Literary Criticism), 1967; Fowlie, W. A Guide to Contemporary French Literature, 1957; Grigson, G. (ed.) Concise Encyclopedia of Modern World Literature, 1963; Guerre, P. René Char, 1961; Hackett, C. A. Anthology of Modern French Poetry, 1952; La Charité, V. A. The Poetics and the Poetry of René Char, 1968; Lely, G. René Char, 1946; Mounin, G. Avez-vous lu Char?, 1946; Rau, G. Rene Char, 1957; Richard, J.-P. Onze études sur la poésie moderne, 1964; Who's Who in France, 1971–1972.

Periodicals—Chicago Review Autumn 1961; New Republic September 17, 1956; New York Times August 5, 1956; New Yorker October 6, 1956; Poetry October 1953; Time August 27, 1956; Times Literary Supplement October 21, 1965; May 15, 1969; Yale French Studies Spring–Summer 1958.

CHARLES, GERDA, English novelist, writes: "I was born and brought up in Liverpool but have lived in London since the war. An only child with only one parent since I was twelve months old, my mother and I endured long periods of acute poverty before managing to achieve a precarious security by running small hotels and boarding houses. As we moved about a great deal my education was scanty and disorganised—I went to nine different schools—and this, together with the fact that I worked domestically and never went out to a job, has made me a very slow writer. I have never been trained to think and consequently have to 'work through' to the essence of my material; a slow, fumbling process.

"Though my Lithuanian forebears were highly cultured my own early environment, lower middle class, provincial, Orthodox Jewish was appallingly narrow. I consider myself fortunate however in one respect. I have escaped being torn apart by conflicts about my Jewishness and indeed find myself able to accept many of the disciplines of Orthodox Judaism though they are not easy disciplines to uphold in contemporary society (whether Jewish or Gentile) since the temper of our time is against them.

"I find this bearable. What I find unbearable is lower-middle-classness. I believe, though it is a dangerous thing to say at this moment of inverted-snob value, the mental climate of that particular social strata to be even now one of suffocating limitations, of required inarticulacy, of realities constantly befogged and diminished to clichés. I disliked this small-horizoned quality of my class so much that I spent most of my early life trying to avoid it by a sort of willed sleep of my own sensibility. This was a difficult thing to wake myself out of and accounts for my very late development as a writer.

"I was helped out of this fog and towards creativity by attending evening classes at various London colleges. These classes don't—can't—teach you to 'write.' But, if you're lucky, they do bring you into contact with lively, intelligent minds all *interested* (this is the important thing) in writing. It was through them that an agent happened to come across a little article of mine, wrote to me, induced me to let him read the first forty thousand words of a novel I had been slowly toiling over and in his enthusiasm sent this fragment to a publisher who promptly took an option on it. It had taken me five years to write forty thousand words. With

GERDA CHARLES

this encouragement it took me five months to write the further eighty thousand words of what turned out to be my first novel. This, when eventually published (though by another publisher!), was well received, being given first place by reviewers in the *Observer*, the *New Statesman*, etc., but it was my second book, *The Crossing Point*, a study of Anglo-Jewish life, which really established me. I then edited a selection of modern Jewish short stories which I enjoyed doing and in the same year published my third novel, *A Slanting Light*, which was awarded one of the major literary prizes in this country, the James Tait Black Award for the best British novel of the year. I also received a good many invitations to lecture, many of which I accept and mostly enjoy, and I have done a lot of literary criticism for various journals, including the New York *Times Book Review* plus a period as novel reviewer on the *New Statesman*.

"I am apolitical, indolent, trusting and touchy. I write not because, as I have heard other writers say, I wish to create a work of art; or to teach; or preach; or for self-aggrandisement. I have no theories about 'beauty.' I write for one purpose only: to be understood. I want it to be known what it is like to be me. I want my situation as a product of my class, my experience, the particular pressures which have acted upon me, to be *known* . . . not because I think myself unique but on the contrary because I believe there to be so many like me whose situations have never been either properly explored or properly comprehended.

"Perhaps it is because I believe that I would be better understood in America that that country has haunted my imagination all my life and Americans haunt my books. I have never been there but hope to go one day."

Gerda Charles, one of the few women among the Anglo-Jewish writers, is steadily consolidating a reputation as a novelist of exceptional talent, perception, and courage. *The True Voice*, with its high and clearly defined moral values, was about Lindy, a girl inarticulately rebelling against her lower-middle-class background. *The Crossing Point*, a long and rich account of a rabbi's search for a wife both suitable and passionate, was called a "hard-hitting yet compassionate commentary on Jewish character," and praised for its impeccable dialogue and lively irony. *A Slanting Light* is told in the form of letters from a woman hired as housekeeper to Bernard Zold, an American playwright visiting London. A novel whose flaws were called the product of "the confident recklessness of a first-rate writer with a lot to say," it remained in spite of them "a memorably deep and disturbing revelation of our time's greatest anguish: the struggle of 'goodness' to keep its head above water."

Miss Charles's fourth novel, *A Logical Girl*, was even more warmly received. It is set in 1943 in an English seaside town where the narrator, Rose, a shy and unattractive girl, learns during the influx of American GIs that her intelligence and honesty will never win her "any of the prizes." Irving Wardle called it "a work of classic quality" in that it contained "a world of its own, a sense of the ordinary external world, and the moral imagination to translate a story into a parable." Rose seemed to Wardle not only a Cinderella figure but "the symbolic Jew . . . persistently robbed of identity by those around her." *A Logical Girl*, Wardle concluded, "is the first novel I have come across that applies post-Auschwitz morality to the inhumanities of daily life." *The Destiny Waltz* centers on Jimmy Marchant, once a famous band leader, who becomes involved as adviser and link man in a television program about his friend Paul Saloman, a poet who had died in his thirties. A struggle develops between the production company's reverential approach to Saloman, Jew and Artist, and Marchant's wish to tell the unsentimental truth about the poet's mean and lonely existence. The book was thought admirable if rather humorless in the explicitness of its moral concerns, and was praised for its wholly convincing accounts of "strained encounters between people of different worlds." It received the Whitbread Award for Fiction.

Brian Glanville, discussing the problems of Anglo-Jewish writers, said that among those doing serious work only Gerda Charles has remained within the Jewish community, and that she differs from most of her literary contemporaries also in her Orthodoxy. "She has never concealed the fact that her position in the community is a difficult, at times an embattled one. . . . Yet one has an idea that Gerda Charles, if only she can stick it out, may be luckier than any of us." Miss Charles, a tall, handsome woman, is an excellent conversationalist and public speaker and broadcasts occasionally on radio and television.

PRINCIPAL WORKS: The True Voice, 1959; The Crossing Point, 1960; (ed.) Modern Jewish Stories, 1963; A Slanting Light, 1963; A Logical Girl, 1967; The Destiny Waltz, 1971.
ABOUT: Contemporary Authors 1–4, 1st revision, 1967; Who's Who in Europe, 1965; Who's Who in World Jewry, 1965. *Periodicals*—Critique Winter 1963; Jewish Chronicle May 29, 1959, January 13, 1961; Jewish Quarterly Winter 1963; Menorah April 1965; New York Times Book Review April 17, 1966.

CHARTERIS, HUGO (FRANCIS GUY) (December 11, 1922–December 20, 1970), English novelist, journalist, and television dramatist, wrote that he "was born in London, brought up by grandparents and cousins in Gloucestershire, the Highlands . . . and Wales (Glamorgan)." He was the son of the Honourable Guy Lawrence Charteris, a London investment registrar and amateur naturalist. Hugo Charteris was educated at Eton, which he remembered gratefully "for never having tried to impose any kind of mystique—say, of rugby or even of snobbery."

At the beginning of World War II Charteris tried but failed (on medical grounds) to join the Royal Air Force as a fighter pilot. Instead he served from 1941 to 1947 with the Scots Guards. He was twice wounded in Italy and earned the Military Cross. Later he worked as a public relations officer in Malaya and Java with South East Asia Command, leaving the army with the rank of major.

Thus, from the age of seventeen to twenty-four, Charteris's education was limited to war, and he "suffered from a hideous innocence as regards a main motive of society—the making of money." He spent four terms at Oxford University in order "to have time to find out what I wanted to do. By then I'd had some short stories published in the *Cornhill* and so read English. In fact I read almost nothing—but had affairs, looked for a mate and a job. The latter I got through a relation—journalism—simply because it was the quickest way to one thousand, five hundred pounds—the minimum which I thought necessary for marriage (I was engaged by then)." He joined the staff of the *Daily Mail* and the same year married Virginia Adam. In 1951, after four very successful years of journalism in London and Paris, a small inheritance made it possible for him and his wife to "retire to what we thought would be a cheap life" in the Scottish Highlands.

It took him fifteen years to reach the salary of three thousand, five hundred pounds he gave up as a journalist in Paris. A large part of that income came from television plays and from the ten weeks a year he used to give to the *Daily* and the *Sunday Telegraph* as a feature writer. At first, less came from his novels, which are not of a fashionable sort. Charteris was not a social realist, an existentialist, or a Freudian, though he was certainly a social critic. Nevertheless, his novels have won increasingly close and enthusiastic critical attention in England, and were warmly received in the United States when, in 1970, he was first introduced to American readers.

His first book, *A Share of the World* (1953), is about John Grant, who as an army officer comes into conflict with a private called Bright. Bright later reappears as a butler serving the beautiful, difficult, and passionless girl that Grant is to marry. The conflict between these two, the author hinted, symbolized a real struggle between himself and his personal obsessions and hallucinations. For Charteris the novel must always deal with a moral conflict, leading to greater self-knowledge, just as his characters must always be something more than accurate portraits of credible people. "They [must] spark off in me the kind of projections about life in general . . . which are the basis of my wish to write."

Charteris set many of his novels in Scotland, preferring it to other milieux that he knew well. It provided him with a provincial (if generally patrician) background against which he could define his characters in relation to the freedom and danger of the larger world outside. In *Marching With April*, a young London publisher, seeking to wind up an unwanted estate that he has inherited in the Highlands, is reluctantly drawn into the affairs of a small, ruthless, and eccentric society. *The Lifeline* is an exuberant satire about a failed television personality who takes over a Scottish pub and throws himself too enthusiastically into his new role.

The River-Watcher is a much more ambitious book, a subtle and powerful study of a former fascist politician in retirement, and an analysis of the fascist mentality. "The possibility is implied," wrote one reviewer, "that to defy moral attitudes, whether for motives of power or honesty, may be in itself a kind of nobleness which society lacks and needs." A similar theme is explored in *The Indian Summer of Gabriel Murray*, whose hero is caught between his need for an honorable retreat from contemporary pollutions to the Highlands, and his desire for the lost, beautiful wife of a neighbor there. David Rees called it "an exemplary parable of a hero of our time . . . caught irreversibly in the rat trap of his own character," and a memorable portrayal "of an exceptional man in a society where

HUGO CHARTERIS

the old truths can no longer give meaning even to those who believe most devoutly in them."

All of these novels contain passages of precisely observed and lyrically expressed natural description. Animals have an important place in Charteris's Highland landscapes, their undissimulated passions being used to counterpoint or symbolize the masked feelings of human beings in a way that makes Charteris's acknowledged admiration for Jung (whom he met shortly before Jung's death) of particular interest. Several critics have referred to an element of subdued violence in his books, a preoccupation with hunting, death, and mutilation which is more overt in *The Coat*. This is one of several Charteris novels that is not set in Scotland, an account of upper-middle-class decadence contrasted with the horrible realities of England during the blitz.

"Mr. Charteris," wrote one critic, "attacks the business of writing a novel rather in the manner of a sculptor savagely starting to chip a huge piece of stone. He moves all round his subject, hacking chunks off it and sending splinters flying at all angles. His prose is tortuous, allusive, disjointed—a kind of complex, sometimes witty, sometimes poetic stammer." This is a perceptive account of Charteris's early work, but is less applicable to his later novels, which were relatively direct both in approach and style.

In 1968 the novelist left Scotland and settled with his wife and four children in Yorkshire. He had visited Africa, the setting of *Picnic at Porokorro*, where he spent some time with an animist tribe in French Guinea and made a tour of the West Coast by Land Rover. His hobbies were photography, gardening, and shooting. He made several translations from the French.

PRINCIPAL WORKS: A Share of the World, 1953; Marching With April, 1956; Picnic at Porokorro, 1958; The Lifeline, 1961; Clunie (for children), 1963; Pictures on the Wall, 1963; Staying With Aunt Rozzie, 1964; The River-Watcher, 1965; The Coat, 1966; The Indian Summer of Gabriel Murray, 1968.

ABOUT: Who's Who, 1971. *Periodicals*—London Magazine November 1965, October 1968; New York Times Book Review February 22, 1970.

***CHAYEFSKY, "PADDY" (SIDNEY CHAYEFSKY)** (January 29, 1923–), most successful of the writers to emerge during the "golden age" of American television drama, was born in the Bronx, New York City. He is one of the three sons of Harry and Gussie (Stuchevsky) Chayefsky, both Russian-born Jews, largely self-educated, who emigrated in their teens and met at Coney Island. The family lived in the Bronx, experiencing "some rough times" when Harry Chayefsky, who had founded the Dellwood Dairy in Yonkers," went broke in 1934.

Chayefsky graduated from De Witt Clinton High School, New York, in 1939, went on to City College, and later studied languages for a time at Fordham University. While he was at college he played semiprofessional football with the Kingsbridge (Bronx) Trojans, and enlisted in the United States Army Reserve. After City College gave him his bachelor's degree in social science in 1943, the army sent him overseas as a machine gunner. In Germany he stepped on a land mine. While recovering in an army hospital in England he wrote the book and lyrics for a GI musical comedy called *No T.O. for Love*, which was produced in London. Later he worked on *The True Glory*, a movie made for the army, and was briefly a gag writer for Robert Q. Lewis. Chayefsky was nicknamed "Paddy" by a dubious lieutenant when he requested relief from KP duty to attend Mass.

Back in New York after the war, he worked briefly in his uncle's print shop on West Twenty-eighth Street and—according to his own account—"sold some plays to men who had an uncanny ability not to raise money." He wrote for radio and then churned out many mystery shows for television. Chayefsky's first television play, *Holiday Song*, was about synagogue life and was produced in 1952 with such success that it was repeated two years later.

Chayefsky's best-known television script was *Marty*, a profoundly compassionate and touching story about two lonely people, neither of them exceptional, both of them hurt by life, and their hesitant reaching out for love. It won a Sylvania Television Award, and the author's triumphant movie translation, which followed in 1955, was heaped with honors, including an Oscar. In *Marty*, Chayefsky had set out "to write . . . the most ordinary love story in the world," but at the same time, he says, "ventured lightly into such values as the Oedipal relationship, the reversion to adolescence by many 'normal' Americans, and the latent homosexuality of the middle class." It was not these "values" but the shock of recognition which moved and delighted the thousands of ordinary people who saw *Marty*. In Chayefsky and such other television playwrights as Horton Foote and Tad Mosel, critics saw the pioneers of a new realism.

* chī ef′ skē

PADDY CHAYEFSKY

Marty established a formula which has recurred in most of Chayefsky's subsequent work. There is a preoccupation with loneliness, often the result of emotional damage which is explained in rather simplistic Freudian terms and repaired or alleviated at last by love. This is the situation in *Middle of the Night*, Chayefsky's first stage play, which suggests what poignant realities may lie behind grubby jokes about middle-aged businessmen with youthful mistresses. A Broadway success in 1956, it was based on a 1954 television play and later filmed. In *The Bachelor Party*, a television play which became a movie in 1957, the hero is persuaded that a married life is better than a "free" but sterile one. The prizewinning original screenplay *The Goddess* is a case history showing how the absence of love in childhood has wrecked the life of an apparently successful movie star. All three works were widely admired for the tape-recorder accuracy of their dialogue, but none had quite the success of *Marty*, and there was a growing critical realization that Chayefsky's "intentional cultivation of the average and the obvious has its own limitations."

The Tenth Man, a Broadway success in 1959, was at least superficially a departure from this pattern. A dramatic comedy set in a shabby Orthodox synagogue, it concerns two young people of whom one is possessed by a *dybbuk* (or only, perhaps, by a neurosis). The play, which combines "demonology and Freud, fantasy and realism," was, according to Allan Lewis, "an attack on present-day intellectual cynicism and advocates redemption through love." Gerald Weales thought it excessively sentimental, "a Jewish *Going My Way*"; Robert Brustein reached a similar conclusion, but nevertheless enjoyed the play's exoticism and humor, and welcomed a break from Chayefsky's "morbid preoccupation with the mediocre and the banal."

Visiting Israel in 1959, Chayefsky found himself much moved by a sense of the past. One result was his biblical play *Gideon*, produced in 1961 by Tyrone Guthrie and representing another long step away from naturalism. *The Passion of Josef D*, a "morality with music" staged in 1964, concerned a turning point in the career of Stalin. Critics praised some individual scenes but most of them found the play "at times puckish and at times rather embarrassingly highfalutin' in its prose." *The Latent Heterosexual* (1968) tells the story of a homosexual poet who writes a best seller, falls into the clutches of a tax evasion expert, and is transformed successively into a loving husband, an inhuman machine for making money, and a suicide. This black and often very funny fairy tale about the contemporary worship of money and sex provided a notable vehicle for Zero Mostel and was generally admired for its "grim wit and melancholy shrewdness."

The Americanization of Emily (1964), a film written by Chayefsky, based on William Bradford Huie's novel of the same title, was welcomed as "a spinning comedy that says more for basic pacifism than a fistful of intellectual tracts." It was another movie, *The Hospital* (1971), which brought Chayefsky his greatest recent success. The author, who said that he had turned to the film because he is "a playwright who has no theatre," acted as "collateral producer" as well as scenarist. The film is set in a huge New York City hospital center, where the callousness and incompetence of the staff represents the collapse of a whole society. It focuses on the dilemma of the hospital's director, a middle-aged liberal at the end of his tether, who must choose between personal salvation and social responsibility. It was called a "black comedy of the highest order, a splendidly savage and funny film."

The author married Susan Sackler in 1949, and has a son, Dannie. Chayefsky is dark-haired, rather short, and powerfully built. Whether or not his break with realism is permanent remains to be seen, but he has said: "I'm rather fond of that stuff, philosophy, metaphysics. And I suspect the age of reason is over and this is the age of unreason."

PRINCIPAL WORKS: Television Plays, 1955; The Bachelor Party (film scenario), 1957; Middle of the Night, 1957; The Goddess (film scenario), 1958; The Tenth Man, 1960; Gideon, 1962; The Passion of Josef D, 1964; Marty *in* Sheratsky, R. E. and Reilly, J. L. (eds.) The Lively Arts, 1964; The Latent Heterosexual, 1967.

ABOUT: Biographical Encyclopedia & Who's Who of the American Theatre, 1966; Chayefsky, P. *Introduction and author's notes in his* Television Plays, 1955; Contemporary Authors 11–12, 1964; Current Biography, 1957; Lewis, A. American Plays and Playwrights of the Contemporary Theatre, 1965; Weales, G. American Drama Since World War II, 1962; Who's Who in America, 1970–1971.

CHEEVER, JOHN (May 27, 1912–), American novelist and short story writer, was born in Quincy, Massachusetts, one of the two sons of Frederick Lincoln Cheever and the former Mary Liley, an Englishwoman. He remembers them as "kindly and original people." Cheever, who began to write at the age of ten or eleven, was educated at Thayer Academy in South Braintree, Massachusetts. That institution, by expelling him when he was seventeen, provided him with the theme of his first published story, which appeared in the *New Republic* in 1930. "I was some kid in those days," Cheever said once, "hair down to my shoulders and I wore a big ring."

Leaving Quincy, Cheever continued to contribute to the *New Republic*, *Collier's*, *Story*, *Atlantic*, and especially the *New Yorker*, which has published the majority of his stories. During the 1930s he lived mostly in New York and did a variety of jobs, for a time teaching advanced composition at Barnard College. Cheever served throughout the war in the army. He was married in 1942 to Mary Winternitz and published his first collection of stories, *The Way Some People Live*, in 1943.

After the war Cheever became a television scriptwriter, working for a while on the *Life With Father* series. His reputation (and income) as a short story writer however gradually eclipsed the other aspects of his career. He received a Guggenheim Fellowship in 1951, the Benjamin Franklin Short Story Award in 1954, the O. Henry Award in 1955, and in 1956 an award from the National Institute of Arts and Letters which helped to finance a visit to Italy. *The Enormous Radio*, Cheever's second volume of stories, appeared in 1953 (and its title story, about a super-efficient radio which received and broadcast the scandals and miseries of its owner's apartment house, has since become one of the most anthologized of contemporary American stories). Three more collections of stories followed.

Some of Cheever's stories derive from his 1956 visit to Italy and other such excursions, but the vast majority deal with well-heeled New England sub-

JOHN CHEEVER

urbanites like himself and like so many of his readers. From the beginning critics admired the tolerant irony in these stories, their humor and "sad, licked lyricism." F. J. Warnke called Cheever "the master of a prose style as natural, clear, and luminous as any currently to be found among our writers," and said: "He has the quality of invention without which fiction becomes merely documentation."

No one, moreover, has ever made more precisely pointed use of the artifacts and sad emblems of our civilization, as in this passage about an American Ophelia in a supermarket (which appears in fact not in a short story but in Cheever's second novel): "No willow grows aslant this stream of men and women and yet it is Ophelia that she most resembles, gathering her fantastic garland not of crowflowers, nettles and long purples, but of salt, pepper, Bab-o, Kleenex, frozen codfish balls, lamb patties, hamburger, bread, butter, dressing, an American comic book for her son and for herself a bunch of carnations. She chants, like Ophelia, snatches of old tunes. 'Winstons taste good like a cigarette should. Mr. Clean. *Mr. Clean,*' and when her coronet or fantastic garland seems completed she pays her bill and carries her trophies away, no less dignified a figure of grief than any other."

Some reviewers of Cheever's more recent stories have complained of his continuing preoccupation "with essentially the same character types and situations within the self-imposed boundaries of his world." Others however have come to see him as a writer of obsession, and one who sees far beneath the surface of the life he records so graphically—as a J. P. Marquand with more than a trace of Kafka in his makeup. J. H. Kay spoke of "the sense of some perverse or capricious power" which "underlies the mounting meanings of story after story"; Melvin Maddocks believes that Cheever "is working with some desperation . . . to confront with tragic values a way of life whose chief genius, he believes, is for evading the tragic."

Cheever has also published three novels, similar in content (and some would say in shape) to his stories. The first, *The Wapshot Chronicle*, which brought its author the National Book Award and an international reputation, is an exuberant history of a rich Massachusetts family, the Wapshots of St. Botolphs. It focuses on Aunt Honora, the family's unpredictable despot "who will only pay bus fares by annual check"; on her brother Leander, a retired sea captain married to a do-gooder and reduced to writing his Rabelaisian memoirs; and on Leander's sons Moses and Coverly. The story moves abruptly from St. Botolphs to Clear Haven (a crumbling estate ruled by another eccentric Wapshot), from New York to the Pacific (following Coverly's activities), to Washington, Boston, and elsewhere. The story is continued in *The Wapshot Scandal*, in which it emerges that Aunt Honora has never in all her life paid any income tax. She dies in cheerful and impoverished disgrace, and Moses, cuckolded by his wife Melissa with Emile, a grocery boy, takes no less scandalously to drink.

Most reviewers agreed that both novels are wonderfully funny and observant, possessing indeed all the virtues of Cheever's stories, and containing, in Honora and Leander, two memorable and full-scale comic creations. Criticism centered on inconsistencies of character and tone and on the episodic nature of the books. They are packed with incident and rich in splendid anecdotes and set pieces, but this material, some readers thought, never coheres into a novel. Not everyone felt this, however, and it seemed to Glenway Wescott, for example, that the author's own "strong and graceful and original" narrative mentality imposed a kind of unity on his material. Whether or not he succeeds, it is clear that Cheever is pursuing in his novels a private and largely intuitive notion of form. He has described *The Wapshot Scandal* as "an extraordinarily complex book built around non sequiturs." And he says of his third novel, *Bullet Park*, that it had been "almost like shaping a dream . . . to give it precisely the concord you want . . . the arch, really. It's almost the form of an arch."

The fearsome shapes of chaos and unreason which so often heave themselves up through the glistening surface of suburban life in Cheever's short stories appear again in *Bullet Park*. These dark powers are represented by Paul Hammer, a rebellious misfit who sets out to destroy Tony Nailles, son of a rich suburbanite, as a vaguely defined social protest. The story turns on the efforts of Eliot Nailles, an amiable man ashamed of his wealth, to save the life of his son. Many readers were puzzled by the content and the shape of the novel—Benjamin DeMott for example found it not much more than "a grand gatherum of late twentieth century weirdos," broken-backed in structure and sluggish and perfunctory in manner. Others, however, thought it the most satisfactorily integrated and sustained of Cheever's novels, and the *Times Literary Supplement*, seeing Hammer and Nailles as the two "halves of the cruelly over-burdened American psyche," called it a remarkably convincing fantasy.

Cheever himself has said that he wanted in *Bullet Park* to describe a love like William Tell's for his on, "a love that could be implemented." He regards all three of his novels as love stories: "*The Wapshot Chronicle* is my love for Leander . . . a posthumous attempt to make peace with my father's ghost . . . what I remember of him." *The Wapshot Scandal* is about Melissa's love for Emile, and *Bullet Park* "is simply Nailles' love for Tony. Anything else is all in the nature of a variation."

John Cheever and his wife have two sons and a daughter, and live in Ossining, New York. Cheever likes fast cars and most kinds of sport—"practically everything except big game."

PRINCIPAL WORKS: *Short stories*—The Way Some People Live, 1943; The Enormous Radio, 1953; The Housebreaker of Shady Hill, 1958; Some People, Places and Things That Will Not Appear in My Next Novel, 1961; The Brigadier and the Golf Widow, 1964; The World of Apples, 1973. *Novels*—The Wapshot Chronicle, 1957; The Wapshot Scandal, 1964; Bullet Park, 1969.

ABOUT: Contemporary Authors 7–8, 1963; Harte, B. and Riley, C. (eds.) 200 Contemporary Authors, 1969; Hyman, S. E. Standards, 1966; Oxford Companion to American Literature, 1965; Who's Who, 1971; Who's Who in America, 1970–1971. *Periodicals*—Commentary May 10, 1953; Commonweal May 17, 1957; Critique Spring 1963; Library Journal February 1, 1957; Life April 18, 1969; Nation February 8, 1965; New Republic June 3, 1957; May 15, 1961; Newsweek January 13, 1964; April 28, 1969; New York Times Book Review April 11, 1953; March 23, 1957; September 13, 1958; January 5, 1964; April 27, 1969; October 24, 1971; Time March 27, 1964; Times Literary Supplement September 10, 1964; May 6, 1965; October 30, 1969; Twentieth Century Literature January 1969; Wilson Library Bulletin December 1961.

CHIN-YANG LI. *See* LEE, C. Y.

CHITTY, SIR THOMAS WILLES. *See* "HINDE, THOMAS"

"CHRISTOPHER, JOHN." *See* YOUD, SAMUEL

LIDIYA CHUKOVSKAYA

***CHUKOVSKAYA, LIDIYA** (1907–), Russian novelist, biographer, and editor, born in St. Petersburg, is the daughter by adoption of "Uncle" Kornei Chukovsky, whose books for children have sold more than forty million copies in the Soviet Union alone, and who was also an eminent literary scholar and translator. The family name is actually Korneichuk, from which he derived the pen name which his daughter has inherited.

She is well known in the Soviet Union, though more perhaps as Kornei's daughter than for her own books, which apart from *V laboratorii redaktora* (In the Editor's Laboratory), a technical book about her work as an editor in a publishing house, have been mainly biographies. These include one of a Soviet children's author, Boris Zhitkov, and several about nineteenth century Russian explorers, such as the travels of the geographer N. N. Miklukho-Maklai in New Guinea, the exploration of Siberia by various Decembrists who had been exiled there after the failure of their abortive revolt, and the travels in Mongolia of another Decembrist, Nikolai Bestuzhev.

But the book for which she became famous in the West arose out of tragic personal experience: in 1937 her husband, a distinguished scientist, was arrested in Leningrad during the Stalinist purges and shot as an "enemy of the people." She did not learn of his death until later, and like thousands of others she joined the queues in front of the prisons and the prosecutor's office for fruitless interviews with the indifferent officials of the NKVD. A frequent companion in these vigils was her great

* chōō kôf′ ska yə

friend the poet Anna Akhmatova, whose son had also been arrested. So these two eminent women found themselves caught up in the Kafkaesque nightmare of Stalin's arbitrary political tyranny, and both subsequently wrote about their experience, though Chukovskaya's *Opustelyi Dom* (translated by Aline B. Werth as *The Deserted House*), like Akhmatova's poem *Requiem*, has never been published in the Soviet Union.

The Deserted House, written in the winter of 1939–1940 shortly after the purge, is the story of a woman caught up by external events which destroy her world of established certainties. Chukovskaya makes her tragedy representative of thousands of similar ones by choosing as her central figure a very ordinary woman, a doctor's widow who supports her adored only son by working as head of the typing pool in a publishing house. As the purges begin she reads of political arrests in the papers, including that of an old doctor friend of her husband; then the director of her own publishing house is arrested; and at last her son, now a highly respected engineer, is taken. She joins the queues of women waiting for news of husbands and sons, and even then thinks of them as the relatives of criminals, believing her son the victim of a unique mistake which will soon be rectified. Then a friend and colleague is dismissed and eventually driven to suicide for typing "*Krysnaya Armiya*" (Rat Army) instead of "*Krasnaya Armiya*" (Red Army), a one-letter error which is interpreted as a piece of anti-Soviet activity. The widow finds herself ostracized both at work and in her flat. Finally her son "confesses" and is sent for ten years to a labor camp, from which he smuggles a letter begging her to save him. But she has at last learned enough to know that she can do nothing for him, and will only endanger her own life; she burns the letter.

This story of the purges could not of course be published at the time, and the manuscript was hidden in Leningrad when Chukovskaya left the city a month before the German invasion. After Stalin's death it circulated in typescript, and she was anxious to see it published "to help to reveal the reasons for and the consequences of the great tragedy my country had suffered"; after the publication of Solzhenitsyn's *Ivan Denisovich*, however, the authorities decided to release no more stories of the camps or the purges. A Russian edition eventually came out in Paris in 1965 (without the author's knowledge) and was quickly translated into other languages, including English in 1967. The *Times Literary Supplement* ranked it among the classics of purge literature for its movingly direct and simple account "of how the 'purge' suddenly broke into the life of a perfectly ordinary, loyal and law-abiding family." Saul Maloff found in it "the quality of folk tale . . . its transparent clarity acting as a perspective on the horror of its substance." At the same time, since it lacks any account of the woman's psychological disintegration, "the tale remains external; and so, finally, it remains a document, a note from underground, an impressive and humanly valuable one." There was a similar if rather more muted welcome for a second novel, *Going Under*, set during the 1949 purge of the intellectuals, but looking back obsessively to the great purges of the 1930s in which the heroine, a woman much like the one in *The Deserted House*, had lost her husband.

In 1966 she published *'Byloe i Dumy' A. I. Gertsena* (Herzen's "My Past and Thoughts"), a study of one of the most famous Russian autobiographies and of its author. Since Anna Akhmatova's death she has, though herself ill and half blind, been working on a book of reminiscences about her friend; few people knew Akhmatova so well, and this memoir, if published, may prove to be of great literary and historical importance.

PRINCIPAL WORKS IN ENGLISH TRANSLATION: The Deserted House, 1967; Going Under, 1972.

ABOUT: *Periodicals*—Book World November 5, 1967; New York Review of Books January 4, 1968; Reporter January 11, 1968; Times Literary Supplement February 16, 1967; September 7, 1967.

***CHUKOVSKY, KORNEI (pseudonym of Nikolai Ivanovich Korneichuk)** (March 19 [old style, i.e., March 31], 1882–October 28, 1969), Russian children's writer, was also a leading authority on the Russian Language and on Russian and English literature. He was born in St. Petersburg and educated at the Nikolaev Gymnasium. In 1901 he began his career as a journalist with *Odesskie novostie*, and in 1903 he went to London as a correspondent for that newspaper, returning in 1905, when he became editor of the satirical magazine *Signal*. That venture came to an end in 1908 and Chukovsky thereafter earned his living as a writer, critic, and journalist, apart from five years (1916–1921) in publishing. It was during World War I, when he was working as children's editor of the Parus publishing house, that he produced his own first books for children.

Chukovsky grew up during the symbolist period of Russian literature, and though he himself did not belong to any literary movement he knew almost all the important writers of the time. One of his earliest books, *Leonid Andreev bolshoy i malenky* (The Great and Small Leonid Andreyev, 1908), was the first of many on Russian contemporaries in which he combined personal reminiscence with literary criticism; later memoirs were on Chekhov, Gorky, Blok, Bryusov, Mayakovsky, Kuprin, and Korolenko. But his most important literary criti-

* chōō kôf′ ski

cism reflects a lifelong interest in the nineteenth century populist poet Nikolai Nekrasov, on whose work he wrote a series of papers culminating in 1952 in the authoritative study *Masterstvo Nekrasova* (The Craftsmanship of Nekrasov).

In an interview, recalling his days in London, Chukovsky insisted that he was a failure as a newspaperman, spending his time in the British Museum library instead of covering sessions of Parliament. It was in the course of these truancies that he started to develop another of his major interests, the translation of English into Russian. He began working on his versions of Walt Whitman during several months spent in jail after the abortive revolution of 1905. A small volume of these early efforts appeared in 1907 as *Poet anarkhist Walt Whitman* and, perfectly mirroring the revolutionary spirit of the time, had a great success. Chukovsky always felt a particular affinity for his "beloved poet," and throughout his life continued to revise his earlier translations of Whitman and make new ones; he likewise continually revised and expanded his famous study of Whitman's life and poetry, taking account of the most recent American research. His translations also included works by Dickens, Mark Twain, Kipling, Wilde, and Chesterton, and the seriousness with which he always regarded translation is indicated by the title *Vysokoye iskusstvo* (The High Art, 1941) which he gave to his book on the subject, a discussion and comparison of translations from numerous languages.

All of Chukovsky's work, whether as critic, translator, or writer for and about children, reveals his deep interest in the Russian language and how words are formed and used. His fascination with the free and creative way in which young children use language led to his great classic on children's speech, *Ot dvukh do pyati* (translated by Miriam Morton as *From Two to Five*). It is a collection of surrealist remarks like "Put your glasses on. You'll catch cold," and of illuminating stories by or about children, with Chukovsky's perceptive and enlightened comments. The book was repeatedly revised and new editions produced as parents and teachers from all over the Soviet Union sent him fresh quotations and observations.

His best-known works are his children's tales in verse, which have sold millions of copies in the Soviet Union and have entered the Russian consciousness like folktales, so that many adults as well as children can recite long passages from them by heart. Among the best known are *Krokodil* (translated by Babette Deutsch in 1931, and by Richard Coe in 1964, as *The Crocodile*), about the adventures of a crocodile who comes to town; *Kradenoe solntse* (translated by Dorian Rottenberg as *The Stolen Sun*), about how the sun is rescued by a hippopotamus from a crocodile which has seized

KORNEI CHUKOVSKY

it; and *Moydodyr*, in which bedclothes, clothes, and breakfast all flee from an unwashed child who, after being chased by the Great Washstand, the famous *Moydodyr*, is eventually only too glad to have a good scrubbing. The prose tale *Doktor Aibolit* is an adaptation of Hugh Lofting's *Dr. Dolittle*, but has itself been readapted into English by Richard Coe (*Doctor Concocter*, 1967).

In 1962, when Chukovsky was eighty years old, he was awarded an honorary Oxford doctorate for his translations from English, as well as the Order of Lenin for his work on Nekrasov. Criticism of him has come mainly from bureaucrats who objected to the "irrationality" of his children's verse, and complained (for example) that he aroused compassion for flies and mosquitoes "when we are conducting a systematic war against insects and parasites." He in turn attacked his "puritan" critics in *Zhivoy kak zhizn* (As Alive as Life), the phrase which Gogol used to describe the Russian language. This discusses the whole range of modern Russian usage, welcomes a healthy influx of foreign words, and prefers slang to "officialese." About half the book consists of a devastating attack on the use of worn-out clichés and official jargon instead of the living speech of the people.

"Uncle" Kornei Chukovsky was a tall and slender man, warm in manner, alert and humorous, the much-loved father figure of Peredelkino, the writers' colony just outside Moscow. Two of his four children, Nikolai (who died in 1965) and Lidiya, also became writers. All his life he maintained an extensive correspondence with foreign authors, and in his late seventies spoke admiringly to a visitor about the work of James Baldwin, J. D.

Salinger, and Bernard Malamud. He was, as a critic wrote in the *Times Literary Supplement*, "an eminent literary scholar" and "a great master of the Russian language."

PRINCIPAL WORKS IN ENGLISH TRANSLATION: *Nonfiction*—Chekhov the Man, 1945; From Two to Five, 1963. *For children*—The Crocodile (tr. by Babette Deutsch in 1931, and in 1964 by Richard Coe); The Stolen Sun, 1962; Doctor Concocter, 1967.
ABOUT: Contemporary Authors 7–8, 1963; Penguin Companion to Literature 2, 1969; Petrovsky, M. Kornei Chukovsky, 1962; Who's Who in the USSR, 1960–1961. *Periodicals*—New York Times Book Review January 30, 1966; Times Literary Supplement January 16, 1964; November 30, 1967.

***CIORAN, E(MILE) M.** (April 8, 1911–), Rumanian-born philosopher and essayist, writes: "I was born in Rasinari, a village in the Carpathians, where my father was a Greek Orthodox priest. From 1920 to 1928 I attended the Sibiu grammar school. From 1929 to 1931, I studied at the Faculty of Arts at Bucharest University. Postgraduate studies in philosophy until 1936. In 1937, I came to Paris with a scholarship from the French Institute in Bucharest and have been living here ever since. I have no nationality—the best possible status for an intellectual. On the other hand, I have not disowned my Rumanian origins; had I to opt for a country, I would still opt for my own. Before the war I published various essays in Rumanian of a more or less philosophical nature. I only began writing in French in about 1947. It was the hardest experience I have ever undergone. This precise, highly disciplined and exacting language seemed as restrictive to me as a straitjacket. Even now I must confess that I do not feel completely at ease with it. It is this feeling of uneasiness which has led me to ponder over the problem of style and over the very *anomaly* of writing.

"As all my books are more or less autobiographical—a rather abstract form of autobiography, admittedly—I feel it is pointless to dwell on my preferences or my difficulties, be they theoretical or practical."

"I write to rid myself of my obsessions, of my anguish," says E. M. Cioran. "But I believe in nothing." His nihilistic philosophy was evident in his first book, *On the Summits of Despair*, published when he was only twenty-two. It received the Prize for Young Rumanian Writers.

Four years later, he went to France. Looking back on his origins, he takes a masochistic delight in denigrating them in his characteristically witty and biting style: "The paradox of being . . . [a Rumanian] is a torrent one must know how to exploit. . . . Hating my people, my country, its timeless peasants enamored of their own torpor

* chi o ran′

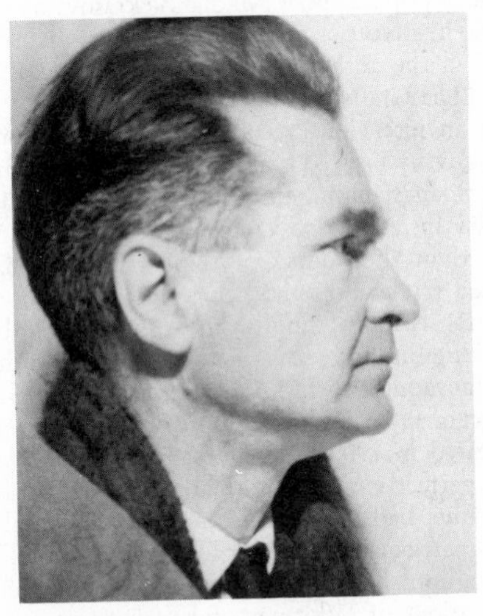

E. M. CIORAN

and almost bursting with hebetude, I blushed to be descended from them. . . . Unable to shove them aside, or to animate them, I came to the point of dreaming of an extermination." This statement appears in "A Little Theory of Destiny," published in *La Tentation d'exister* (1956, translated by Richard Howard as *The Temptation to Exist*). Later in this essay he discusses the advantages of his background: "Would I have been able, without my country, to waste my days in so exemplary a manner?. . . To spoil one's life . . . takes a tradition, long training, the labor of several generations. . . . The certainty of Futility then forms part of your inheritance."

Cioran's elegant expression of despair appealed to intellectual France and his first work published there, *Précis de décomposition* (Summary of Decay, 1949), established him at once. Many regard him as "the greatest French prose stylist since Valéry," as well as "the most original living French thinker." Among his other books in French are *Syllogismes de l'amertume* (Syllogisms of Bitterness, 1952); *La Tentation d'exister*; *La Chute dans le temps* (1964, translated by Richard Howard as *The Fall Into Time*); and *Histoire et Utopie* (History and Utopia, 1960), winner of the Prix Combat—all of them collections of essays. He has also published a selection from the work of Joseph de Maistre (1957).

Cioran believes that modern Western civilization is in a state of paralysis; Western man has achieved sufficient sophistication to realize that every action will negate itself eventually, and every profound idea give rise to another refuting it. His answer is not the surrender of consciousness, but total self-consciousness: "The only free mind," he says, is "the one that, purged of all intimacy with being or objects, plies its own vacuity." ("Thinking Against Oneself")

He writes about impossible states of being, about unthinkable thoughts. He sees writing as a form of waging existence, for words constitute a move away from reality and "to exist is to profit by our share of unreality." Since all life for him is futile, the decision to exist is the most irrational act of all—irrational but not impossible: "*To exist* is a habit I do not despair of acquiring."

Cioran's thought is in essence Nietzschean, though highly relevant to the literary climate in modern France. His works provide a basic commentary on those of Beckett or Camus, for instance. And they are essentially books for an intellectual élite: "His is the kind of writing that is meant for readers who . . . have traversed these vertiginous thoughts for themselves," said Susan Sontag. "Cioran doesn't make any of the usual efforts to 'persuade,' with his oddly lyrical chains of ideas, his merciless irony, his gracefully delivered allusions to nothing less than the whole of European thought since the Greeks. An argument is to be 'recognized,' and without too much help. Good taste demands that the thinker furnish only pithy glimpses of intellectual and spiritual torment. Hence, Cioran's tone—one of immense dignity, dogged, sometimes playful, often haughty. But for all of what may appear arrogance, there is nothing complacent in Cioran, unless it be his very sense of futility and his uncompromisingly élitist attitude toward the life of the mind."

Cioran is a shy, retiring, middle-aged bachelor, who shuns Parisian literary circles and rarely gives interviews. He lives in an attic flat on the Left Bank and works part time as a translator and manuscript reader: "I don't make a living," he has said, "I eke one out. But I don't wish to be well off." He spent his first thirteen years in Paris studying at the Sorbonne, but refused to acquire an advanced degree. He maintained his interest in the university during the May Revolt of 1968, when each night he listened to the youthful revolutionaries denouncing human history as irrelevant. Possibly none of them had read his works, or even heard his name, for he is little known even in his own country. But fame for Cioran would only be a burden, even though he admits in "The Ambiguity of Fame": "If we all confessed our most secret desires, the desire behind all our schemes and all our acts, we would say: 'I want to be praised.' "

PRINCIPAL WORKS IN ENGLISH TRANSLATION: The Temptation to Exist, 1968; The Fall Into Time, 1970. *Essays in* Hudson Review Winter 1962–63, Spring 1964, Summer 1965, Winter 1966–67, Summer 1967, Spring 1968; "A Little Theory of Destiny" *in* Partisan Review Fall 1966.

ABOUT: Boisdeffre, P. de. Dictionnaire de littérature contemporaine, 1962; Mauriac, C. The New Literature, 1959; Pingaud, B. Écrivains d'aujourd'hui, 1960; Sontag, S. *Introduction to* The Temptation to Exist, 1968. *Periodicals*—New Republic May 18, 1968; Nouvelle Revue Française August 1960; Preuves December 1956; Time August 9, 1968; Times Literary Supplement February 11, 1969.

CLEARY, JON (STEPHEN) (November 22, 1917–), Australian novelist, dramatist, short story writer, and scenarist, writes: "I was born in Sydney, New South Wales, in one of the tougher, poorer districts. My father was a worker, socially and by temperament; there is some of him in me, but diluted. My mother, of necessity, always had to make one penny do the work of two; there must be some of her in me, because my wife and daughters tell me I am tight-fisted. I have never wanted to be rich, but from even my teens I have wanted a comfortable old age—which is a hell of an ambition in the young. But the older I get, the more I appreciate it.

"I left school just after my fifteenth birthday, at the depth of the Depression in Australia. Up till 1939 I had more jobs than I can now remember, only a few of which I did not find boring. I had shown some talent for sketching at an early age, and till the war art looked like the career I would follow—commercial art, that is, because money was always needed at home (I am the eldest of seven children) and I never even thought of art for art's sake. I did some writing for amateur revues, but never entertained the idea of writing for a living.

"But I started writing in the army in 1940 and I've been at it ever since. I had five-and-a-half years in the army, in the Middle East and New Guinea, distinguishing myself in no way at all; when I came out I at last knew what I really wanted to do. I had sold some stories to American magazines and I had enough of a stake to give me two years to see if I could make it. I left Australia and spent the next eight years abroad, working, travelling and learning. After twenty years I am still following the same pattern.

"I am not as good as I should like to be and I doubt if I shall ever be; but I keep trying. I write a novel a year, partly to live and partly because I have to: I'm too restless when doing nothing. Not all my themes excite me, but I can't sit around waiting for the exciting theme to turn up. I get one story in three which really gets me steamed up, and that's a pretty good average, I think. But I don't just dash off the in-between books: I work on them as hard as on the others (my father coming out in me). I am not entirely pleased by any of my books, but some parts of them give me pleasure, though I rarely open my books after they have been published. I am sometimes asked which is my favourite

JON CLEARY

book and I truthfully answer: 'My next one.' When it isn't, then the urge to write will have died.

"I enjoy writing and I can't understand authors who complain that their work is a chore. My father was not the fictional type beloved by writers, always given to spouting gems of wisdom; but he did once tell me, 'A good craftsman enjoys his work.' I try to be a good craftsman. I look on myself as primarily a storyteller, but I labour over my style and my dialogue. It may not be good, but it's as good as I can do; and no more should be expected of any workman. I am not interested in 'messages', but I do like to sneak in comments so long as they don't hold up the narrative. My recurring themes are of people set against action in remote regions, and I make a point of never writing about a place I haven't visited. But one day I should like to write a good social novel about Australian urban life.

"I met Joy Lucas, a Melbourne girl, on a ship coming to England in 1946 and we were married two weeks after disembarking; the result could not have been happier. We have two teenage daughters. The younger is not yet particularly interested in reading; the elder prefers Dostoevsky to Dad. All I can do is remind them whose books are keeping them.

"I belong to no political party, but I lean a little to the Left, without being doctrinaire. I am a practising Catholic who would welcome more liberality in the Church; I have done enough travelling in Asia and Africa to know that Rome isn't always right. I am a restless traveller who spends more time out of Australia than in it, but still calls it home. I meet people easily, but am not gregarious as many seem to think. I value friendship so much that I do not use the word 'friend' cheaply; my closest friend I met when I was five years old. I despise hypocrisy, bigotry and jingoism; and despise myself when I occasionally find myself guilty of thoughts of all three. I walk a lot, play cricket and squash racquets and hope to remain active till it's time to go. I talk too much, but with more care for other people's feelings than I used to. I am not sentimental in my behaviour, yet sentiment is always there in my writing.

"Several pieces have been written about me, but I couldn't tell you where or when. My first novel, when published in the USA, was hailed as both 'on the edge of greatness' and 'if this is a prizewinner, God help the rest of Australian writing'. I realised then, at that very early stage, that a writer really has to find his own way. And I don't mind at all. In fact, I enjoy it."

Jon Cleary says that when he was thirty-five, already an established novelist, "I stood aside and examined myself. I knew I did not have the mental equipment to be the Great Writer I had started out to be, so I totted up my assets. I had a gift for narrative, for conveying atmosphere, and for writing dialogue, and I decided then to employ these gifts to the best of my ability." That is what he has done, in the process making a great deal of money for himself and providing a great deal of pleasure for others.

Most (but not all) of Cleary's novels have been adventure stories, like *Back of Sunset*, about a young doctor who gives up a fashionable Sydney practice to join the flying doctor service; *The Green Helmet*, which draws its razor-edge excitement from the world of motor racing; and *The Long Pursuit*, describing the efforts of an adroitly assorted party of refugees to fight their way from Singapore to freedom in 1942. But even Cleary's highly professional and readable entertainments are likely on occasion to strike a deeper note; *Justin Bayard*, called an Australian Western, was praised for its honest anger against the absentee landlords of the Outback, and prompted one reviewer to wish that the author "would set his sights higher . . . and turn out a novel more obviously in line with his unmistakable talents."

In fact Cleary, who is an admirer of J. P. Marquand, once spent eighteen months on a long political novel about Sydney between 1930 and 1955, only to have it rejected by his publisher. But he has not forgotten the theme, and may yet produce the "good social novel about Australian urban life" he speaks of. Meanwhile Cleary's best and most successful novel is *The Sundowners*, which is neither a political novel nor an adventure story but the account of a year in the nomadic life of Paddy Carmody and his family as they drift across Australia in a horse-drawn wagon. The book, written with an unsentimental nostalgic warmth, traces the growth to maturity of Paddy's son Sean, but leaves Paddy himself as irresponsible at the end of the story as he is at the beginning, a piece of honest observation praised by the many critics who enjoyed this "fine, true, and moving" novel.

The Sundowners, which sold over a million copies, became an excellent film, and there were screen versions also of *The Green Helmet* and *Justin Bayard*. Cleary has also written scenarios for M.G.M., Warner Brothers, and Ealing Studios; television plays for English and American programs; stage plays and short stories. He won the Australian National Play Award in 1944, the Crouch Gold Medal for the best Australian novel of 1950, and was co-winner of a New York *Herald Tribune* World Story contest. Bearded, blue-eyed, and stocky, Cleary, according to one journalist, is "one of those people who almost interview themselves, they are so easy to talk to."

PRINCIPAL WORKS: *All fiction*—These Small Glories (stories), 1946; You Can't See Around Corners, 1947; The Long Shadow, 1949; Just Let Me Be, 1950; The Sundowners, 1952; The Climate of Courage, 1954; Justin Bayard, 1955; The Green Helmet, 1957; Back of Sunset, 1959; North From Thursday, 1960; The Country of Marriage, 1962; Forests of the Night, 1963; Pillar of Salt (stories), 1963; A Flight of Chariots, 1963; The Fall of an Eagle, 1965; The Pulse of Danger, 1966; The High Commissioner, 1966; The Long Pursuit, 1967; Season of Doubt, 1968; Remember Jack Hoxie, 1969; Helga's Web, 1970. The Liberators, 1971 (England, Mask of the Andes); The Ninth Marquess, 1972; Ransom, 1973.

ABOUT: Contemporary Authors 4, 1963; Green, H. M. A History of Australian Literature, 1962; Hetherington, J. Forty-two Faces, 1962. *Periodicals*—Books and Bookmen March 1964; Saturday Evening Post May 15, 1954.

***COCKBURN, (FRANCIS) CLAUD ("James Helvick," "Frank Pitcairn")** (April 12, 1904–), Scottish journalist, memoirist, and novelist, was born in Peking, where his idiosyncratic father, Henry Cockburn, was Chinese Secretary to the British Legation.

Originally he subscribed to the staunch Conservative views of his mother, the former Elizabeth Stevenson, but despite a conventional upper-middle-class education at Berkhamsted School and Keble College, Oxford, he moved eventually to the Left. This process owes something to what he saw in Berlin, where he went in the late 1920s with a Queen's College Travelling Scholarship. It was then that his journalistic career began. Cockburn became an unofficial Berlin correspondent of the London *Times*. After a highly successful period as official correspondent for the same newspaper in New York and Washington (1929–1932) he published his first book, *High Low Washington* (1933), an "inside" exposure of Washington politics.

* kō′ bərn

CLAUD COCKBURN

In 1933, returning to London, Cockburn joined the Communist party and in March of the same year launched his famous newssheet *The Week*. It consisted of half a dozen foolscap pages duplicated in brown ink, but thanks to Cockburn's wit and journalistic brilliance and his willingness to publish informed gossip as well as hard news, it achieved immense influence. It was read and discussed at every level of society, including the highest—King Edward VIII was a subscriber and at one point almost a contributor. Its principal concern was with foreign affairs, especially the growing brutality and greed of the Nazis (similar developments in the USSR were of course not reported). At home it found evidence of political and financial corruption, and bitterly attacked those who sought to appease Hitler. *The Week* became one of the sharpest thorns in the side of the British Establishment, and led Philip Toynbee to canonize Cockburn as "the patron saint of the 1930s."

In 1936 Cockburn went to Spain to fight on the Republican side in the Civil War; he has described the experience in *Reporter in Spain*. After an early marriage to an American journalist he was married again in 1940 to Patricia Arbuthnot, who worked with him on *The Week*, wrote its history (*The Years of the Week*, 1968) and bore him three sons. The non-aggression pact between Hitler and Stalin was a blow from which *The Week* never really recovered. In 1941 it was suppressed, along with the *Daily Worker* (for which Cockburn had worked as "Frank Pitcairn"), and its postwar revival was short-lived.

After the war Cockburn took his family to live in an ancient country house at Youghal, near Cork,

Ireland. Here, in spite of periods of acute financial difficulty, he has remained. He "retired" fairly amicably from the Communist party in 1948 and, as he says, seemed to have "come to the end of a literary as well as a political tether—though it was hard to tell whether political dissatisfaction had promoted dissatisfaction with my writing, and a sharp longing for new fields of writing, or whether it was the other way round."

Since then, besides contributing to journals as diverse as the *New Statesman* and the *Daily Telegraph*, *Private Eye* and the *Saturday Evening Post*, Cockburn has indeed explored a variety of new literary fields. As "James Helvick" he has written a number of entertainments in the manner of Graham Greene or Eric Ambler. The best known of them is *Beat the Devil*, a quietly cynical comedy, embellished with a romance and a few murders, about an extraordinary gallery of con men and adventurers in search of uranium in the Belgian Congo. It provided the basis for an excellent movie. *Ballantyne's Folly*, published under his own name, is an amiably nihilistic novel about its hero's attempt to buy a stately home as a youth center, the dubious means he adopts to further his good ends, and the almost total depravity of everyone he comes into contact with in the process.

Cockburn was a regular contributor to *Punch* during Malcolm Muggeridge's editorship, and has collected these essays in *Nine Bald Men* and *Aspects of English History*. Muggeridge has spoken of his friend's ability to "see in life's inherent absurdity an image of its mystery and grandeur. . . . Cockburn is a clown, with a clown's serious, watchful eyes set in a wide expanse of face."

It seems likely that Cockburn will be best remembered for his autobiography, which began to appear in the mid-1950s. In general it is, as he says, concerned more with the "characters, scenes and incidents" of his life than with "cogitations and internal monologues"; for Cockburn "that is a way of approaching a true impression. So long as the people talk and act, the reader can form his own estimate of them and their environment, and of the author." The first volume, *In Time of Trouble* (called *Discord of Trumpets* in America), covers his early life from childhood to 1938; *Crossing the Line* deals with the war years, the break with communism, and his life in Ireland; and *View From the West*, the most subjective volume, movingly describes his youngest son's long struggle with poliomyelitis and his own with tuberculosis. *I, Claud* combines all three volumes in a revised edition.

Some critics have suggested that Cockburn's autobiography is a record not precisely of what happened but "of how Mr. Cockburn saw the events he described or, on occasion, of how he wished he had seen them." It remains, as one reviewer said, "the most brilliantly amusing and invigorating modern autobiography that any of us is likely to get his hands on." Malcolm Muggeridge pointed out that it was in any case not intended as an exact record: "It is a work of art—funny, enthralling, gay, shrewd, zestful," which "vitally conveys the flavor of those strange times." Muggeridge concluded that "above everything, Cockburn is a journalist; perhaps the most perfect specimen of the genus ever to exist, certainly the most accomplished I have known. He loves the trade, and has practised it in the manner of a maestro, realising that news is life's drama, not its data."

PRINCIPAL WORKS: *As Claud Cockburn*—In Time of Trouble (U. S., Discord of Trumpets), 1956; Nine Bald Men, 1956; Aspects of English History, 1957; Crossing the Line, 1958; View From the West, 1961; I Claud, 1967; Ballantyne's Folly, 1970; The Devil's Decade: The Thirties, 1973. *As "Frank Pitcairn"*—Reporter in Spain, 1936. *As "James Helvick"*—Beat the Devil, 1951; Overdraft on Glory, 1955; The Horses, 1961.

ABOUT: Cockburn, C. I, Claud; Cockburn, P. The Years of the Week, 1968; Muggeridge, M. Tread Softly, for You Tread on My Jokes, 1966; Who's Who, 1971. *Periodicals*—New Republic June 25, 1956; New Statesman March 10, 1956; September 29, 1961; New York Herald Tribune Book Review September 4, 1960; New Yorker September 22, 1956; Spectator February 24, 1956.

"COLLINS, HUNT." *See* HUNTER, EVAN

***COLQUHOUN, ARCHIBALD** (November 16, 1912–March 22, 1964), English translator and critic, was born in Yorkshire. He was educated at Ampleforth College and Christ Church, Oxford, which he left to enter the Royal College of Art. He began his career as a watercolorist and decorative painter in a style reminiscent of Rex Whistler.

Before the war Colquhoun lived on Ischia, and in 1940 was made acting director of the British Institute in Naples. The same year he left Italy and joined the British Army, serving as an intelligence officer in the Western Desert and later in the Sicilian and Italian campaigns. He accompanied the divisions making the Salerno landings and showed great skill in the interrogation of Italian refugees and the organization of anti-Fascist resistance. In 1944 he was appointed Civil Liaison Officer to the Eighth Army, building up an effective intelligence service in cooperation with Italian partisan units. He himself led an expedition across the German lines to assist the Garibaldi Brigade at Ravenna, a service for which he subsequently received the freedom of Ravenna.

After the war Colquhoun became director of the British Institute at Seville, but was later obliged to leave Spain on account of his left-wing sympathies.

* kō ho͞on′

ARCHIBALD COLQUHOUN

From 1951 to 1954 he lived at the Torre del Monticello in Lerici, near Spezia, which he subsequently bought. After 1954 he worked for the Oxford University Press, editing the Oxford Library of Italian Classics. In 1963 he established the John Florio Prize for English translations from the Italian.

It is as a translator that Colquhoun is best known. His ability was first recognized in 1951 with the publication of *The Betrothed*, his version of Manzoni's great novel *I promessi sposi*. Colquhoun's subsequent translations were no less cordially received. He was drawn most often to contemporary novels reflecting his own sense of disenchantment and desolation, among them Mario Tobino's *Women of Magliano*, set in an asylum for the insane; Italo Calvino's savagely poetic novel *The Path to the Nest of Spiders*; two of Mario Soldati's psychological studies, *The Capri Letters* and *The Real Silvestri*; and Italo Svevo's story of provincial drudgery and suicide, *A Life*. One of Colquhoun's last and most important translations was of Giuseppe di Lampedusa's rich historical novel of the Risorgimento *Il Gattopardo*, which appeared in English in 1960 as *The Leopard*. E. M. Forster wrote that Colquhoun's version "does not flow and glow like the original—how should it?—but it is sensitive and scholarly." For many readers this translation captured "the noble voice of what seems at times to be that of Western European literature itself."

Although he had planned a war novel and a history of the Risorgimento, Colquhoun actually completed only one original work, a thorough and scholarly study of Manzoni which was the first major critical study of that writer in English. The book was welcomed as a well rounded portrait of Manzoni and admired for its grasp of the political and religious circumstances which influenced him.

Colquhoun's temperamental instability was reflected in the alternation of his sympathies between communism and Roman Catholicism. He never faltered however in his love and understanding of Italy and the Italians, and did all he could after the war to rehabilitate them in the eyes of the world. Often poor himself, he had a profound sympathy for the under-privileged. Colquhoun was married to Joan Holford and had a daughter, Gianna, born on Ischia. He died suddenly at the age of fifty-one.

PRINCIPAL WORKS: Manzoni and His Times, 1954. *As translator*—Manzoni, A. The Betrothed, 1951; Jovine, F. Estate in Abruzzi, 1952; Tobino, M. Women of Magliano, 1954; Soldati, M. The Capri Letters, 1955; Calvino, I. The Path to the Nest of Spiders, 1956; Calvino, I. Adam, One Afternoon, 1957; Pirro, V. Camp Followers, 1958; Calvino, I. Baron in the Trees, 1959; Pomilio, M. Witness, 1959; Soldati, M. The Real Silvestri, 1960; Lampedusa, G. di. The Leopard, 1960; Montalto, S. Voice From the Cell, 1960; Lampedusa, G. di. Two Stories and a Memory, 1962; Svevo, I. A Life, 1963.

ABOUT: Times (London) March 24, 1964.

COMBER, ELIZABETH. *See* "HAN SUYIN"

CONDON, RICHARD (THOMAS) (March 8, 1915–), American novelist, writes: "I was born in the City of New York. Everything seems to have happened to me by fortuitous accident. This has affected my plotting, although my character writing continues to reflect the defiance of a long-time stutterer covered with a quite thick aplomb, something any stutterer will understand. Unconsciously, stuttering led to writing just as surely as the deep need to express oneself with grace must be resolved by anyone denied that pleasure. It could also have begun with the determination and the need to learn more synonyms than other people might because I had to have a reserve for words sharing the same meanings in that I could not frequently say the first word which came to mind. That led to a blood brotherhood with words and it also led to a better understanding of character. I knew at an early age that when people laughed at the stuttering they immediately felt badly and sought any means to make right something which I hadn't seen as wrong on their side in the first place. Although I did not know it at the time, I was on my way to achieving the comfort of the last of the *flaneurs'* professions, this side of politics. Too, the love affair with words has given me thirty-eight publishers of seventy-four editions of books, in sixteen languages and Braille which could have made for a lot of stuttering if read aloud.

"I went around the world as a waiter on the Dollar Line when I was eighteen, after a high

RICHARD CONDON

school 'education'—there were over four thousand boys in my graduating class. Back in New York, I became a writer of 'package inserts,' those minutely printed exhortations upon exquisitely folded sheets with which are wrapped toothpaste and deodorants before being boxed. As a less inhibited copy writer in an advertising agency, I wrote an alphabet book, illustrated by the late George Anrig. Although nothing happened for the book, it unaccountably landed me the job as Eastern Publicity Director for Walt Disney Productions.

"I had not liked the advertising business. As I went on into the 'live' (as opposed to the 'animated') film world, working with beautiful actresses, ugly actors, and talking dogs, I liked publicity work much less. To get 'over the wall' I began to write at night. I wrote one novel out of which only the title was salvaged later, two children's record albums, a thousand-odd pages of not immediately useful notes; and a play. When the play was produced on Broadway in 1953, I resigned as a vice president of RKO–Radio Pictures. The play ran four performances and the family joke, still cherished by us as a genuine tear-jerker, was that if it had opened on a Monday night we could have doubled the run. I and my family—wife, two daughters—moved to Paris that year and since then we have moved to a new country every two years, living in Paris, Madrid, New York, Mexico City and Geneva, but breaking the spell in Geneva where we stayed for four years and hope to stay longer.

"I am considered a compulsive writer because I spend a seven-hour day and a seven-day week at the typewriter. I am an automated writer with a microfilm reader, an electrostatic copying machine, and an electric typewriter. I get pleasure and satisfaction from writing but it was not until I had written two hours a day for eleven years, while not recognizing myself as a professional writer because I could not have reached my present weight had I depended on calories from that output, I turned out my first to-be-published novel at forty-two. I have decided since then that, for a story teller, it is all a matter of getting the first paragraph right because it is connected to the last paragraph by unseverable cables, for better or worse. If I had found that out sooner I would have written many, many more books."

Richard Condon's first novel, *The Oldest Confession*, is about a young man who, sickened by the accepted corruption of the financial world, finds more honest employment as an art thief. A sardonic commentary on business ethics, it is also a bravura performance with "the thrust and speed, the sudden shocks and surprises, the high excitement of superior melodrama." *The Manchurian Candidate*, an equally ingenious and breathtakingly suspenseful thriller, doubles as a very funny and often very savage political satire.

This combination of humor, "messianic exasperation," and irresistible narrative momentum has recurred in all of Condon's later books, along with his Rabelaisian capacity for wild picaresque invention and the Condon prose style. Whitney Balliett, under the temporary influence of this last instrument, described it as "a tough, unique, mock-Mandarin prose, which lies in between the glistening plumbing of Hemingway and the baroque weather vanes of the Sitwells"; Orville Prescott has called it "a thing of wonder and a source of consternation forever."

There is, not surprisingly, a large and growing Richard Condon cult, which appears to include a number of prominent reviewers. Some of his fans are content to enjoy him as a unique and brilliant entertainer; others see him as a serious moralist all the more effective for being compulsively readable. Condon himself regards it as the novelist's duty to reflect himself—"not necessarily his times"—entertainingly. The book reviewer's job, he believes, is "to obscure the enjoyment of novels"; it is up to posterity to decide what is art.

The Manchurian Candidate has been filmed, and Condon has written several original screenplays. The son of Richard and Martha (Pickering) Condon, he was married to Evelyn Hunt in 1938 and has two daughters and a granddaughter. It is said that "in person, as in his novels, Condon surprises, entertains, disquiets." His enjoyment of food, wine, books, travel, and life is generously mirrored in his books. He and his family are currently living in Ireland.

PRINCIPAL WORKS: *Fiction*—The Oldest Confession, 1958; The Manchurian Candidate, 1959; Some Angry Angel, 1960; A Talent for Loving; or, The Great Cowboy Race, 1961; An Infinity of Mirrors, 1964; Any God Will Do, 1966; The Ecstasy Business, 1967; Mile High, 1969; The Vertical Smile, 1971; Arigato, 1972.
Nonfiction—And Then We Moved to Rossenara, Or the Art of Emigration, 1973.

ABOUT: Celebrity Register, 1963; Contemporary Authors 1, 1962; Who's Who in America, 1970–1971. *Periodicals*—Books and Bookmen July 1963; New Yorker April 2, 1960; Time July 6, 1959.

CONNELL, EVAN S(HELBY), JR. (August 17, 1924–), American novelist and short story writer, writes: "I was born in Kansas City, Missouri. Attended Southwest High School and then went to Dartmouth College until entering the Navy as an aviation cadet. After graduation from Pensacola on VE day I was assigned to duty as a flight instructor. When the war ended I entered the University of Kansas on the GI Bill and graduated with a degree in English. I studied fiction writing under Ray B. West. Then went to Stanford University for a year and studied under Wallace Stegner. Then to Columbia for a course with Helen Hull. After that I lived for a while in Los Angeles, and in Santa Cruz, and then went to Europe for a couple of years. From Europe I moved to San Francisco. While here I took a course in fiction writing with Walter Van Tilburg Clark.

"Most of the time spent at these different schools was in the art department. I was interested in graphic arts before I thought about writing, and given different circumstances earlier in life I would probably have become a sculptor. At Columbia I studied modeling with Oronzio Maldarelli and felt a greater affinity to this than to anything else, but I was by that time in my twenties and had decided on writing.

"None of the arts seemed actually possible as a way of life to a boy in the Midwest during the thirties. Thomas Hart Benton lived and worked in Kansas City, and Curry and Grant Wood were, of course, household names; however it was understood and accepted without question by everybody I knew that one had a choice of becoming a lawyer, a doctor, or a businessman. While at Dartmouth I was planning to become a doctor, as my father is, and as his father was. I think that if there had not been a second World War I might have continued that direction for at least another year or so.

"I don't know exactly how or when I decided on writing but it must have been toward the end of the war when some sort of decision became necessary; so I made use of the GI Bill to the full extent. Becoming a writer seemed slightly less impossible than becoming a sculptor.

"My attitude toward writing is not complex. I enjoy doing it, and don't mind the long hours.

EVAN S. CONNELL, JR.

I am irritated by the effusions of certain authors who claim that writing is some sort of agony. It isn't. It can be very very tedious, discouraging, profitless, senseless, and many other things, but there is no more agony involved in going to work at the typewriter than there is in trying to sell somebody an insurance policy. The myth of the 'artist' as a special form of being is too much with us; painters, poets, novelists, composers, jewelers, potters and whisk broom makers are all craftsmen working at their trade with varying degrees of skill and sensibility. One art may seem more significant than another, but this is a judgment of rank, not of kind.

"Authors who seem to have the most meaning for me are Proust, Mann, Chekhov, and Tolstoy. Such a list of course could be extended almost endlessly, but these would be among the first names. I don't read much contemporary fiction. In the United States today there are some excellent stories being written, and probably some excellent novels, but usually these are concealed by the cataract of drivel. If there is one defect prevalent among American writers it is their inability or disinclination to metamorphose their experiences. A novel or a story is as different from a transcript of life as a painting is from a photograph, and what is published as fiction usually isn't.

"I have had stories in various magazines, textbooks, and anthologies, including *Stories of Modern America*, *Fiction of the Fifties*, *Best Stories From the Paris Review*, *Best Stories From the Saturday Evening Post*, *Writing Fiction*, *Writers in Revolt*, *Prize Stories* of 1949 and 1951, *Best American Short Stories* of 1955 and 1957."

Evan S. Connell is a product and a justification of the American belief that creative writing can be taught, a writer whose high professionalism has not kept him from a series of increasingly ambitious and valuable experiments. His first book was *The Anatomy Lesson*, a very able and entertaining but entirely conventional volume of short stories. It was followed by the novel *Mrs. Bridge*, a series of precisely pointed sketches of a Kansas City matron between the wars which add up to a wonderfully thorough and perceptive portrait. Mrs. Bridge is the woman Helen Hokinson used to draw for the *New Yorker*, but she is no mere caricature: "Vulnerable in her innocence, funny and touching in her hapless cultural aspirations," she is at once "a triumph of ironic characterization" and a figure of real pathos. For *The Patriot*, a rather less shapely book which nevertheless contains some excellent writing, Connell drew upon his own experience as a U.S. Navy flyer. It traces the passage to maturity of an idealistic young cadet who ultimately finds the courage to dissent from his father's militarism.

It was followed by the remarkable prose epic *Notes From a Bottle Found on the Beach at Carmel*, assembling "some of the most resonant anecdotes, legends, horrors, and local color our earthly annals have preserved." The theme is the physical, intellectual, and spiritual explorations of mankind, endlessly rewarded by disaster and despair, endlessly renewed. Some reviewers found the book uneven in quality and flawed in structure, and many questioned Connell's presentation of these prose notes in a typographical pattern suggestive of free verse. But as many critics were profoundly impressed. Hayden Carruth, in spite of his reservations about the book, called it "a work of art, even a work of high art." George Garrett, who testified to its "growing underground reputation," had no doubt that it was in fact a poem, and one "of the size and scope of Pound's *Cantos*."

Connell's reputation was further enhanced by the publication of *At the Crossroads*, another volume of spare, assured, and ironic short stories. Discussing Connell's work in this form, Warren Bower wrote: "His best stories flow in a rhythm of their own, with a high correspondence to what transpires within a subtle mind. His worst are without structure, and flow turgidly because of the heavy burden of private comment and extraneous detail carried by the stream of the narrative. . . . Mr. Connell is an interesting and resourceful experimenter with freer form in the short story."

Up to this point, as Roger Shattuck has said, Connell had steadily increased his range. In *Diary of a Rapist* he reversed himself, limiting his point of view to "one obsessed mind as it reveals itself to us and to itself in a diary." The diary is that of Earl Summerfield, a young man bored and humiliated by life, who becomes fascinated with newspaper accounts of sexual violence, and decays slowly into madness. It is a study both of a diseased spirit and of the society that created it. Totally and sometimes even monotonously convincing, the novel has been called "a triumph of art over case history"; and it is a triumph in that it compels the reader, as one critic said, "to face that in himself that makes him brother to the diarist, to yield up to the madman the kind of painful compassion which purges and cleanses."

Mr. Bridge, considered by some to be Connell's most thoroughly realized novel, is, like its companion volume *Mrs. Bridge*, a mosaic of short vignettes which assemble themselves into a profound portrait of a man stunted by his full acceptance of the standards of a stunted society. Referring to Connell's ability to achieve wonders through "the patient piling up of tiny particles," one reviewer of "this subtle, most beautifully composed novel" called him "the coral insect among novelists."

Connell is a big man, brown-haired and brown-eyed, and wears a moustache. He is unmarried and has no religious or political affiliations. He enjoys drawing and painting, "not as recreation or hobby but as an avocation." From 1959 to 1965 he was editor of *Contact* magazine.

PRINCIPAL WORKS: The Anatomy Lesson (stories), 1957; Mrs. Bridge, 1958; The Patriot, 1960; Notes From a Bottle Found on the Beach at Carmel, 1963; At the Crossroads (stories), 1965; The Diary of a Rapist, 1966; Mr. Bridge, 1969; Points for a Compass Rose, 1973.

ABOUT: Vinson, J. (ed.) Contemporary Novelists, 1972; Who's Who in America, 1972–1973. *Periodicals*—Book Week June 5, 1966; Nation June 15, 1963; New Mexico Quarterly Summer 1966; Newsweek April 25, 1966; New York Review of Books June 23, 1966; April 24, 1969; New York Times Book Review April 20, 1969; Saturday Review July 17, 1965; Times Literary Supplement June 8, 1967; December 4, 1969; Wilson Library Bulletin April 1965.

CONQUEST, (GEORGE) ROBERT (ACWORTH) (July 15, 1917–), English poet, novelist, editor, and writer on Soviet affairs, was born at Great Malvern, in Worcestershire. His father, R. F. W. Conquest, was American by descent and lived on a small private income, occasionally writing for *Punch* and other magazines, and traveling a great deal with his wife, the former Rosamund Acworth, and their three children. Robert Conquest went to a preparatory school in Great Malvern and afterwards to Winchester College, but much of his childhood was spent in the south of France, where his parents encouraged him to live a tough and independent life. "From the age of about eight," he says, "my two sisters and I would be thrown out of the house in the morning with a couple of francs, and expected to fend for ourselves during the day."

His father, with whom he was not on good terms, nevertheless fostered his intellectual curiosity, which extended to science as well as to poetry and history. His schooldays at Winchester were reasonably happy, and after a year at the University of Grenoble (1935–1936), he won a History Exhibition to Magdalen College, Oxford, where he read politics, economics, and philosophy.

Leaving the university in 1939, Conquest went directly into the Army, serving in Italy and the Balkans with the Oxford and Buckinghamshire Light Infantry until 1946. Although he resented the boredom and waste of army life, he found the experience a useful antidote to the "easy" pacifism of the 1930s. In 1946 Conquest went into the Foreign Office, serving first with the legation in Sofia, then in New York with the British Delegation to the United Nations. He found the diplomatic life congenial but underpaid.

Conquest has written poems for as long as he can remember and some of them began to appear in magazines early in the war. His elegy for Drummond Alison received the Brazil prize in 1945 and in 1953 he coedited *New Poems*, a PEN anthology, in this and other ways coming to know a number of poets whose work he admired. *Poems*, his own "elegantly vertebrate" first collection, appeared in 1955 and was warmly welcomed. William Van O'Connor saw him as a poet "searching for a balance between the Apollonian and Dionysian," and found throughout the book "the suggestion of a sensitive cosmopolitan mind searching out a sense of order, and asking, over and over, how the poet contributes to order." It might be said that in one form or another, this concern for order pervades Conquest's work. It is evident in *A World of Difference* (1955), a rather thinly characterized science fiction in which totalitarian revolutionaries seek to subvert the rule of law and are fought by cruisers named the *Amis*, the *Gunn*, the *Larkin*, the *Enright*.

These same names are, of course, to be found on the title page of Conquest's famous anthology of contemporary British poetry, *New Lines* (1956). It includes work by Philip Larkin, Thom Gunn, Kingsley Amis, Elizabeth Jennings, Donald Davie, John Holloway, John Wain, and Conquest himself, who also provided a pungent and influential introduction. These writers, at one time assembled in the public mind as "the Movement," shared for a while a tone which, as one critic said, was or seemed "humanistic rather than religious, liberal rather than radical, cool rather than fervid, pragmatic rather than systematic, sceptical rather than enthusiastic, empirical rather than transcendental." After the romantic and surrealistic excesses of the "New Apocalypse," Conquest believed that such coherent, well-crafted poetry represented the re-

ROBERT CONQUEST

covery of a central tradition in English verse. To others it seemed a deliberate, chauvinistic jettisoning of all that had been painfully learned from European poetry. In any case, the importance of *New Lines* as a catalytic agent in the recent history of English poetry is undeniable.

Conquest left the Foreign Office in 1956 to become a freelance writer and part-time academic —at first as a research fellow in Soviet politics at the London School of Economics. After three years there he went as an English lecturer to the University of Buffalo (1959–1960). In 1958 he published a valuable anthology of "thaw" poetry from Eastern Europe, *Back to Life*, and in 1960 his serious, scholarly and dispassionate study *The Soviet Deportation of Nationalities* (revised and largely rewritten in 1970 as *The Nation Killers*). *Common Sense About Russia* (1961) is a brief introduction but *Power and Policy in the U.S.S.R.*, published the same year, is a much more important book, a "study of Soviet dynastics" that established Conquest as a bold and original practitioner of "Kremlinology"—the art of reading between the lines of Soviet official documents with the intention of making informed guesses about the realities such documents seek to conceal. The sobriety and scholarly care he brought to this work were widely praised, though some critics felt that "his critical attitude towards Soviet evidence is sometimes carried to extremes." Reviewing *Courage of Genius*, an account of the persecution of Boris Pasternak, Geoffrey Grigson asked if Conquest was "illuminating genius or having a cold swipe at Moscow?"

After a year as a senior fellow at Columbia

University's Russian Institute (1964–1965), Conquest became editor of an important series of Soviet studies published in the United States by Praeger and in Britain by The Bodley Head. His own recent work in this field includes *Russia After Khrushchev* (1965) and *The Great Terror* (1968). The latter is the most complete and well-documented account to date of the Stalinist purges of the 1930s, a masterpiece of historical detection. *Where Marx Went Wrong* (1971) is a characteristically deft and lucid account of the non-Marxist nature of both the Russian Revolution and subsequent Soviet governments.

Another of Conquest's extraordinarily diverse interests is represented by *Spectrum*, the annual science fiction anthology he used to edit with his friend Kingsley Amis. Conquest once said that he would rather read the *Scientific American* than any literary magazine, and his feeling for science, both as an intellectual discipline and as a source of wonder, is often evident in his poems, collected in *Between Mars and Venus* (1962) and *Arias From a Love Opera* (1969). Both books were found rather determinedly and excessively cerebral, only occasionally achieving the fusion of passion and reserve he attempts. *The Egyptologists* (1965), the satirical novel Conquest wrote with Kingsley Amis, was not well received, but illustrates his dislike of cant, jargon, and every kind of affectation. So does "Christian Symbolism of Lucky Jim," a very clever parody of contemporary critical procedures published in *Critical Quarterly* (Spring 1965).

Robert Conquest lives in Battersea, London, but travels a great deal in France and the United States. He has two sons by his marriage to Joan Watkins, from whom he was divorced in 1948. His second marriage to Tatiana Mihailova also ended in divorce and in 1964 he married Caroleen Macfarlane. From 1962 to 1963 he was literary editor of the *Spectator* and he has contributed widely to British and American periodicals—never more controversially than in 1968 when he, Amis, and others, in a letter to the London *Times*, pledged their support for American policy in Vietnam. He has been a member of the British Interplanetary Society since 1946. Conquest lives "a moderately social life" and is "relieved to find" that he can now earn his living solely by writing. He has an OBE.

PRINCIPAL WORKS: *Poetry*—Poems, 1955; Between Mars and Venus, 1962; Arias From a Love Opera and Other Poems, 1969. *Fiction*—A World of Difference, 1955; (with Kingsley Amis) The Egyptologists, 1965. *Nonfiction*—The Soviet Deportation of Nationalities, 1960 (revised as The Nation Killers, 1970); Common Sense About Russia, 1961; Courage of Genius, 1961 (U.S., The Pasternak Affair); Power and Policy in the U.S.S.R., 1961; Russia After Khrushchev, 1965; The Great Terror, 1968; Where Marx Went Wrong, 1971; Lenin, 1972. *As editor*—New Lines, 1956; Back to Life, 1958; New Lines II, 1963; (with Kingsley Amis) Spectrum I–V, 1961–1966; The Soviet Studies Series, 1967–.

ABOUT: Allott, K. (ed.) Penguin Book of Contemporary Verse, 1950; O'Connor, W. V. The New University Wits and the End of Modernism, 1963; Orr, P. (ed.) The Poet Speaks, 1966; Who's Who in America, 1970–1971. *Periodicals*—Commonweal June 8, 1962; Essays in Criticism April 1957; London Magazine November 1964; Nation August 12, 1961; August 11, 1962; New Statesman November 24, 1961; May 18, 1962; October 15, 1965; New York Review of Books August 5, 1965; New Yorker August 19, 1961; Observer August 8, 1965; Saturday Review October 13, 1962; Spectator June 2, 1961; August 16, 1963; Sunday Times July 22, 1956; September 22, 1968; Times Literary Supplement September 30, 1955; February 5, 1960; June 10, 1960; June 9, 1961; December 1, 1961; October 5, 1962; December 14, 1962; June 10, 1965; October 14, 1965; Yale Review October 1962.

CONRAD, BARNABY, JR. (March 27, 1922–), American artist, novelist, memoirist, and authority on bull fighting, writes: "I was born and brought up in Hillsborough, a suburb of San Francisco inhabited by wealthy commuters. My father, an investment banker, a trade I've never quite been able to understand, was not as rich as the other millionaires around us but my older brother and I had total security at least until we got through college. My mother was, and is, an attractive musician who was always interested in the arts. She was born in Helena, Montana, where her father was a Supreme Court Judge, but then he was named Governor of Puerto Rico and she lived eight years there. Judge Hunt, my grandfather, whose father was Secretary of State, met every President of the U.S., except one, from Lincoln to FDR. My mother is inordinately proud of the fact that Martha Dandridge Custis Washington was her great-great-great grandmother. I take far more pleasure in a distant kinship with Fletcher Christian and my wife's antecedent, Lizzie Borden (whom Alexander Woollcott described so nicely as 'unfilial').

"My mother felt I had artistic leanings so I was sent to special art classes at an early age. I continued drawing at Taft prep school in Connecticut and illustrated my own stories in the school magazine.

"My brother's loss of a leg in a Montana Rodeo accident upset me emotionally yet somehow drew me toward violent sports. As a freshman at the University of North Carolina, I was captain of the boxing team, though in truth I believe I forced myself into it because of my innate fear of bodily violence. As Thomas Fuller wrote over a hundred years ago: 'Many would be cowards if they but had the courage.'

"The University of Mexico sounded glamorous so I studied painting there in the summer. However, I soon became fascinated by the bullfights. One day, full of youth and tequila, I jumped into the arena using my raincoat as a cape and somehow emerged alive. I was taken under the wing of some professional matadors and was coached for several months. During one afternoon's session, I was severely injured by a half-breed animal and, my teacher having been gored, I left Mexico on crutches. The commercial plane crashed at Los Angeles upon landing, but though several people were injured, I was not one of them.

"After a leg operation, I went to Yale and was graduated in two years due to the wartime speed-up schedule. Since, because of my leg injury, I was unable to go into the services, I joined the State Department, and was sent to Spain as a Vice Consul at Vigo, later serving at Málaga, Sevilla, and Barcelona. I met Juan Belmonte, probably the greatest matador who ever lived, and he took an interest in me. When my leg got better I began fighting bulls on his ranch and three years later appeared on the same program with him with some success. Two weeks later another injury caused me to give up any ideas of becoming a professional. I quit the Consular Service and went to Peru for a year where I played the piano in Lima's best night club, did thirty-five portraits of the elite, and worked on a novel. The following year I met Sinclair Lewis, was hired as his secretary, and, in Massachusetts, finished my first novel, *The Innocent Villa*, which Random House published. It was not good, one reviewer calling it 'Mr. Conrad's passport to oblivion.' A short story of mine appeared in *Collier's* magazine, won several awards, and appeared in the *O. Henry Collection Prize Stories* 1949 as 'Cayetano, The Perfect'. In 1952, Houghton Mifflin Company published *Matador* which became a 'runaway' bestseller with universally good reviews, selection by Book-of-the-Month, movie sale, etc. It is in its thirteenth printing, has been translated into fifteen languages, is said to have sold two million copies in all versions, and is still selling.

"I have written some nine books since, one on Tahiti, where I have lived, one on San Francisco, where I now live, a novel based on Sinclair Lewis, and the rest on bullfighting.

"I opened a saloon in 1953 in San Francisco's Barbary Coast called El Matador and ran it for ten years until I sold it. It was fun in the beginning—more of a salon than saloon with Saroyanesque characters around (and Saroyan himself)—but then it grew to be a chore and a bore.

"I fought last in 1958 in Spain and was gored almost fatally. I go every other year to Spain but am content in between to stay home with my wife and many children, paint portraits, and write articles and stories for magazines. I also do occasional work for TV and motion pictures and translations."

BARNABY CONRAD, JR

Barnaby Conrad, once awarded the bull's ears for his performance on the same program as Juan Belmonte, has gone on to greater fame as bard, chronicler, and encyclopedist of bullfighting.

His outstanding literary achievement is *Matador*, a novel about Manuel Rodríguez, the great matador known as Manolete, who was driven to his death in the ring by the taunts and blandishments of the aficionados and the press. *Matador* was called authentic, convincing and exciting, and widely compared—not always unfavorably—with Ernest Hemingway's books about bullfighting and with a novel by another artist-writer, Tom Lea's *The Brave Bulls*. Riley Hughes wrote that the book's tragic conclusion "has the authority and inevitability of a painting by Goya."

Conrad tells the same story straight in *The Death of Manolete*. It was observed that the book's two hundred and fifty photographs lent a cinematic quality to the text, and in 1957 Conrad created from still photographs the notable documentary film *The Day Manolete Was Killed* which he wrote, directed, produced, and narrated, and for which he composed the music. Conrad has returned repeatedly to this event, so charged for him with beauty and terror, courage and squalor; in 1956 he produced a television documentary about it and in 1957 made it the subject of a television play. *La Fiesta Brava* is a history of bullfighting; *The Gates of Fear* a collection of bullfighting stories, some true, some legendary.

Dangerfield, Conrad's second novel, is another fictionalized account of a great man's last bid for immortality. It shows Winston Dangerfield (Sinclair Lewis), after years of alcoholism and decline, waiting hopefully to hear that his last novel has won him the coveted literary award which will re-establish his reputation. The novel was praised for its realism and its spare, dry humor, but suffered a little from the fact that it appeared in the same year as Mark Schorer's splendid biography of Lewis, although some critics found the novel's impressionism no less illuminating than the biography's patient detail. Conrad's own modest and engaging autobiography, *Fun While It Lasted*, has according to David Dempsey "a pleasantly anachronistic air about it, as though the author had been set apart, or set back, in an era when it was possible to live a legendary life without being a legend."

There seem to be no limits to Conrad's versatility. He has illustrated a number of his own books, including *Matador* and *Fun While It Lasted*, and is an accomplished painter and sculptor. He has also been active as a teacher, as a film producer, and as an editor and translator. Conrad has been married twice, to Dale Cowgill in 1949 and to Mary Slater in 1962; there are three children by the first marriage, one by the second. He is Protestant and Republican. His facial features—large nose, wide mouth—and his muscular frame still suggest the grace, power, and determination of "Bernabé Conrad, el Niño de California."

PRINCIPAL WORKS: The Innocent Villa (novel), 1948; Matador (novel), 1952 (England, Death of a Matador); La Fiesta Brava: The Art of the Bull Ring, 1953; The Gates of Fear (stories), 1957; The Death of Manolete, 1958; San Francisco, 1959; Encyclopedia of Bullfighting, 1961; Dangerfield (novel), 1961; Tahiti (travel book), 1962; How to Fight a Bull, 1968; Fun While It Lasted (autobiography), 1969.
ABOUT: Contemporary Authors 9–10, 1964; Current Biography, 1959; Who's Who in America, 1970–1971. *Periodicals*—Newsweek July 14, 1958.

COOK, ALBERT S(PAULDING) (October 28, 1925–), American critic, scholar, poet, dramatist, and translator, writes: "I was born in Exeter, New Hampshire, and grew up in the cities of my father's sales territory: Wakefield and Springfield, Massachusetts; Albany and Utica, New York. Moving around taught me to treasure and distrust roots, and may have induced a comparable pattern; I have lived in eight cities since marrying.

"Going to a public high school acquainted me with a range of feelings and purposes in people, and my awareness thereof was intensified by a stint in the wartime Infantry, where I also was brought up short at the anonymity bred under the brute force we fall back on, and at the terror of the limit in human purpose. Returning to Harvard soon, I carried out my twofold plan already shaped in high school: to grow as a writer, and to steep myself in as much of the world's literature as I could. The atmosphere of high civilization at Harvard inspired me to exactly the same degree that its impenetrable self-worship exasperated me. In that atmosphere, and on the heels of my bad contribution to a just war, I was converted to Anglo-Catholicism.

"I had begun to write poetry first from six to eleven, and I began again, almost unwittingly, to compose long poems in my head while delivering newspapers up Prospect Street hill in Utica at dawn. Then I was a sophomore in high school; within a year I had covered lots of paper with everything from short stories to the beginnings of a bad epic poem. At college I kept writing and published in *Wake* under a pseudonym. In graduate school I edited *Halcyon* and emerged as a poet, and as an uneasy but committed literary critic. After a three-year term of free development afforded by the Society of Fellows at Harvard, I determined to break free of academic life and to devote myself as totally to literature as I could. I moved with my wife and young son to New York and lived a lean but productive year first at determinedly non-literary jobs, including accountancy in an art school, then as a technical editor. Thereby I discovered my deep inner inertia (or stability) as an academic, and after a year in France on a fellowship returned to the university, where I have remained. This situation, together with the inner disposition that adjusted it, has kept me a critic in much of my public life, and at my writing desk, where I try to work out the problems that lie behind my own practice in various genres: poetry, fiction, and drama. These do not converge into one, though I imagine them to be merging into a final, common vision.

"I have been Chairman (1963–66) of the Department of English at the University of Buffalo, where I remain Professor of English and Comparative Literature (1963–). I married Carol Sarah Rubin on June 19, 1948, and have three sons, David, Daniel, and Jonathan, born respectively on June 26, 1949; February 19, 1952; and April 14, 1954. I am a member of the Third Order of St. Francis (Anglican) and of the Modern Language Association."

Cook is an extremely versatile and erudite academic critic who, not content to examine the performance of individual writers, has sought to disentangle the linguistic, stylistic, and philosophical roots of literature, ancient and modern American and European. *The Dark Voyage and the Golden Mean* sets out to analyze the difference between comedy and tragedy. *The Meaning of Fiction* seeks and finds, in the work of novelists from Cervantes to Faulkner, evidence that fiction is best to be defined not in terms of language and form, but in terms of content and meaning. In Cook's opinion, almost the opposite is true of the epic, and in *The Classic Line* he is concerned to mitigate the critical tendency to focus so closely on the meaning of the great epics that their character as poems is almost overlooked. An even more fundamental consideration engages the critic in *Prisms*, which studies the philosophical views implied by the use of language in literature, and specifically the way in which these have been revealed and extended in the work of modern writers.

All of these books have been praised for their intelligence and insight, and found both learned and provocative. Criticism has tended to center on a habit of abstraction in Cook's thought, and on his style. *The Meaning of Fiction* in particular was harshly reviewed—even by critics who thought its argument convincing—for its prose, which at times becomes quite "impenetrably gnomic and quirky," and its lack of "even a rudimentary . . . sense of humor."

Three of Cook's verse plays have been performed or broadcast: *Double Exposure*, *Night Guard*, and *Open Palm*. He is also the author of a libretto for an opera, *Seawrack*, composed by David Diamond. Cook's translation of Sophocles' *Oedipus Rex* has been performed many times by college and other drama groups, and his version of *The Odyssey*, which attempts to follow the original very closely as a work in the oral tradition, was said to "scan easily and move rapidly, thus reproducing one of the special delights of Homeric style."

In his introduction to *Progressions*, containing eighty-one poems, Richard Eberhart remarked that Cook's "poems are multifarious, showing many ways and styles of his poetic approach to life," but that "the feeling of the whole work is some kind of abstraction from life." Several critics, including Eberhart, detected the influence of William Empson in these poems, which were found rather unmusical and forbidding in their intellectual austerity, but astringent, thoughtful, and worthy of the close study they demand.

The writer is the son of Albert and Adele (Farrington) Cook. He received his A.B. in 1946 and his A.M. in 1947, both from Harvard, where he was a Junior Fellow from 1948 to 1951. In 1952–1953 he was a Fulbright Fellow at the University of Paris, and for the next ten years, until he went to the University of Buffalo, taught at the University of California (Berkeley) and at Western Reserve University. He has also lectured as a visiting professor at the universities of Munich (1956–1957) and Vienna (1960–1961).

PRINCIPAL WORKS: *Poetry*—Progressions, 1963. *Criticism*—The Dark Voyage and the Golden Mean: A Philosophy of Comedy, 1949; The Meaning of Fiction, 1960; The Classic Line: A Study in Epic Poetry, 1966; Prisms: Studies in Modern Literature, 1967. *As translator*—Sophocles, Oedipus Rex: A Mirror for Greek Drama, 1963. (*Also in* Lind, L. R. [ed.] Ten Greek Plays, 1957); Homer, The Odyssey: A New Verse Translation, 1967.

ABOUT: Contemporary Authors 1–4, 1st revision, 1967; Directory of American Scholars II, 1964; Eberhart, R. *Introduction to* Cook, A. S. Progressions, 1963. *Periodicals*—Commonweal March 29, 1957.

ALBERT S. COOK

COON, CARLETON S(TEVENS) (June 23, 1904–), American anthropologist, writes: "My birthplace was Wakefield, Massachusetts, where my Cornish great-grandfather settled in the 1830s. Shortly after my birth my grandfather, William Lewis Coon, went blind. Until I was eight he was my baby-sitter and informal teacher. Among other stirring tales he told me of his adventures in the Civil War, of his travels in the Near East, and of the explorations of Livingstone and Stanley, whose accounts he had apparently memorized. Every morning he shaved with a straight-edged razor, and never cut himself.

"When I was fifteen my parents sent me to Phillips Academy, Andover, where I studied Greek with Allen 'Zeus' Benner. In class he had me read passages from the *Iliad*, chosen at random. For such an exhibition I was once beaten after class by other students who claimed that I had been tipped off.

"Because Andover filled me with zeal for ancient history, I decided to become an archaeologist. There I taught myself to read Ancient Egyptian hieroglyphs, and as a freshman at Harvard I studied Egyptology with George A. Reisner. As a sophomore I was admitted to Charles T. Copeland's graduate course in English composition. Copey let me in, he said, because I was of Cornish descent and therefore a born writer. My first assignment was to read the works of another Cornishman, George Borrow.

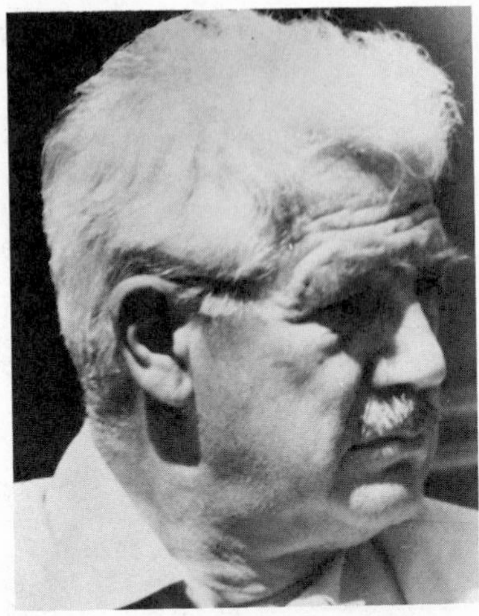

CARLETON S. COON

"That same year a course in anthropology with Earnest A. Hooton influenced me to move from classics and Egyptology into the broader field of general anthropology, including physical and cultural anthropology as well as archaeology. Since then I have tried to maintain a grasp of this vast panorama, but the emergence of many splinter disciplines has made the coverage difficult.

"In 1926 I was married. My sons Carleton S. Coon Jr. and Charles A. Coon were born in 1927 and 1931. My oldest grandson, William Putnam Coon, is now at Andover.

"At various times from 1924 through 1928 I conducted field work in Morocco, concentrating on the Riffians. In the winter of 1929–30 I walked through the snowy mountains of Northern Albania, studying the Ghegs, and in 1933–34 worked in Ethiopia and southern Arabia.

"My teaching at Harvard began in 1935 and continued until Pearl Harbor, after which I volunteered in General William J. Donovan's special services and was sent to North Africa well before the TORCH landings on November 8, 1942. Later, in uniform, I fought in Tunisia and Corsica. In these enterprises I was but one of many anthropologists, for in those days it was still considered patriotic and honorable for men of my profession to offer to their country their special knowledge and their lives. After a head wound, a medical discharge, and a divorce, I remarried.

"Following three years of teaching freshman courses at Harvard and Radcliffe I moved on, in 1948, to the University Museum of the University of Pennsylvania. For that institution I did field work and also appeared in their television program, *What in the World?*, an anthropological quiz-show that lasted fifteen years. Before my retirement in 1963 and after, my wife and I have traveled widely for the University Museum, principally to dig caves in Asia and Africa. Our most recent excavation was a cave in Sierra Leone, in the fall of 1965.

"Although my career has consisted principally of exploration, field studies, warfare, and teaching, I have found time to write over a hundred and fifty articles, reviews, and scientific monographs, as well as fourteen books. A few of the latter are novels and travel books, but my principal product has been a series of comprehensive works directed at the layman and scholar alike. Among these are *The Races of Europe*, *Principles of Anthropology* (which I helped Eliot D. Chapple write), *Caravan: The Story of the Middle East*, *The Story of Man*, *The Origin of Races*, and *The Living Races of Man*. All of those named have appeared in both American and British editions, and some have been translated into several languages.

"In these books and in my own way I have tried to make sense out of history—to fit the human experience into the vast sweep of life and of cosmic events in an orderly and meaningful manner. Although, in recent years, my interest in human evolution and in explaining why *Homo sapiens* is divided into races has drawn partisan misrepresentation and personal abuse, I shall continue to write what and as I choose."

Carleton S. Coon is the son of John and Bessie (Carleton) Coon. He received his A.B. (*magna cum laude*) in 1925, his A.M. and Ph.D. in 1928, all from Harvard University, where he was elected to Phi Beta Kappa. He describes his career above, but does not mention that he left the U.S. Army in 1945 with the rank of major, and Harvard in 1948 as professor of anthropology. From 1948 until 1963 he was curator of ethnology and professor of anthropology at the University Museum, Philadelphia. During these years he led many archaeological expeditions under the auspices of the museum, and the Hall of Man he installed there is famous all over the world. Coon retired in 1963 but continues to serve the museum as research curator in anthropology.

His first books grew out of his field trips (1924–1928) to Morocco, where he lived among and studied the Riffs, an extraordinary tribe of Berber mountaineers. *Flesh of the Wild Ox*, a chronicle of several generations of Riffian life, was enthusiastically praised for the vast amount of information it conveyed and as a piece of folk literature written in a clear, unsentimental, vivid style. Coon's admiration for the Riffs, a warrior people of great courage, cunning, and stoicism, found a different kind of expression in *The Riffian*, an absorbing picaresque novel about the adventures and philosophy of a Riffian Ulysses named Ali the Jackal. Subsequent works, readable, entertaining, and often funny, described later travels elsewhere. Some of Coon's expeditions are famous, such as the one in 1939 to North Africa, where he discovered fossilized human remains fifty thousand years old, and the Iranian cave dig of 1951 which turned up the fossils of three human beings who died some seventy-five thousand years ago.

But as Coon says, his most important writings have been large-scale synoptic works which "have tried to make sense of history," and which have established him as "a leading exponent of the sound and welcome theory that natural science . . . can and should be written as interestingly and understandably as any other topic." *The Races of Europe*, *Caravan*, and *The Story of Man* were all warmly and almost unanimously praised by laymen as well as scholars for their originality and scholarship, their pace and humor, their "forthright common sense and wisdom." *The Story of Man* was called "the first anthropological account of human history which is both readable and authoritative," and "a magnificent, very personal, highly stimulating, provocative shout in favor of the future of mankind."

The "partisan misrepresentation and personal abuse" of which Coon complains have centered on *The Origin of Races* and its sequel *The Living Races of Man*. The first draws on evidence from genetics, zoogeography, human physiology, archaeology, and other sciences to trace the descent of man, and seeks to show that mankind divided into races before, not after, reaching the *Homo sapiens* stage. Theodosius Dobzhansky praised Coon's achievement in creating "order and a system in a field of study that has traditionally suffered from an accumulation of disconnected and undigested observations," but regretted "some unfortunate misstatements" that make his work "susceptible to misuse by racists [and] white supremacists." F. S. Hulse likewise commended it as "a serious attempt to arrange the fossil evidence of human evolution in a meaningful way," comprehensive and thoroughly up to date, but noted many "highly speculative" conclusions, a number of methodological weaknesses, and other "unnecessary blemishes in a work which is in many ways a major contribution to our knowledge of the evolutionary history of the human stock." Other anthropologists reacted more harshly, dismissing the book as a racist tract. Lay opinion divided along predictable lines.

The Living Races of Man presents further "findings and conclusions concerning race origins, distribution, biochemical and pathological peculiarities, as well as behavioral patterns of man." Edmund Leach in the *New York Review of Books* found it "a mine of heavily interpreted (or misinterpreted?) information," which supported Coon's thesis "that Caucasoids are a more developed subspecies of humanity than are Congoids [Negroes]." Leach thought it "to Professor Coon's discredit that he should seek to support his purportedly scientific classification with . . . photographs in which the *Caucasians* are posed in shirt sleeves . . . whereas most of his other categories appear as bare-arsed savages." But a reviewer in the *Times Literary Supplement* was satisfied that Coon "keeps partisan emotion out of his book," and Coon himself denies adherence to "any dogma, cause, emotion, personal interest or preconceived idea."

Coon was awarded the Legion of Merit in 1945 and the Viking Medal in Physical Anthropology in 1952. After his divorce from Mary Goodale, he was married to Lisa Dougherty Geddes, a cartographer who has drawn the maps for many of his books. He belongs to the Congregational Church.

PRINCIPAL WORKS: Tribes of the Rif, 1931; Flesh of the Wild Ox: A Riffian Chronicle, 1932; Riffian, 1933; Measuring Ethiopia, 1935; The Races of Europe, 1939; Mountains of Giants, 1951; Caravan: The Story of the Middle East, 1951; The Story of Man, 1954 (England, History of Man); The Seven Caves: Archaeological Explorations in the Middle East, 1957; The Origin of Races, 1962; The Living Races of Man, 1965; The Hunting Peoples, 1971.

ABOUT: Current Biography, 1955; Who's Who in America, 1970–1971. *Periodicals*—American Anthropologist June 1963; Archaeology Summer 1951; New York Review of Books February 3, 1966; March 17, 1966; Saturday Review January 5, 1957; Scientific American February 1963; Times Literary Supplement December 22, 1966.

"COOPER, WILLIAM" (pseudonym of Harry Summerfield Hoff) (August 4, 1910–), English novelist, writes: "My name is Harry Hoff. I was born in Crewe, a small Midlands town which owed its entire existence to a large railway locomotive works, an existence uniformly petty bourgeois/working-class, adorned, so far as I recall, by none of the graces that bloom on money and privilege: unbeautiful, unappealing, unmarked by the slightest distinction, it provides an object-lesson to people who yearn over 'the old home-town.' They should just have mine!

"Both my parents were teachers in what were then called public elementary schools; and on both sides of my family I sprang from generations of Dissent; on my father's side, Baptists, on my mother's side, Wesleyans. The heritage is a difficult one to get away from: I would not do so if I could. Although when I became adult I took off into religious disbelief, I stayed, with equal conviction, by the ethic in which I had been brought up. The social condition of the greater part of mankind is still far from being a credit to us; and it behoves us, if only for the sake of our self-respect, to do something about it. The means for doing it, generally

WILLIAM COOPER

provided by technology, are to hand: I should like to see them applied radically.

"At the age of eighteen, having been educated at a public elementary school and secondary school, I went to Cambridge University—nobody from my family, my school, or possibly even the town, had gone to Cambridge before. I went on the strength of my winning a scholarship and my parents raising a loan. I cannot account for my taking it into my head that it was Cambridge I must go to. I read Science, on the advice of my father, who thought a boy educated in science would never be out of work—the year was 1928, and how right he was! With hindsight I should say that if I have an academic talent, it is for languages. At the time I already had intimations of being an artist. But I emerged from Cambridge as a physicist—never to regret it, partly because physics is interesting, mainly because it spared me, as an artist, from ever feeling in conflict with the scientific-technological culture.

"I have always had two careers, at the beginning not from choice. When I went down from Cambridge the first thing I wanted to do in life was to write novels—it has remained the first thing. But I could not then expect to make a whole living out of it. The choice that actually was open to me was to make the second half of my living by a job that did not confine me to literary society, in fact a job which kept me in scientific society. Before the war I taught physics, and during it I moved into a career in which I have specialised in trying to match individual research scientists and engineers with the jobs in research most appropriate to them. Altogether I have personally interviewed over fifty thousand of them in the last twenty-five years. I now hold part-time personnel consultancies with the United Kingdom Atomic Energy Authority and the Central Electricity Generating Board.

"So far as my literary career is concerned, my novels should speak, I think, for themselves. Writing is to me some kind of internal necessity: my threshold of reluctance to begin is high—rather than pick up my pen I will stoop to any chore, such as straightening the pictures on the wall or trimming my moustache. But, once over the threshold, I fall into an obsessive state, in which I can be visualising scenes, hearing dialogue, even forming sentences, while sitting at meals with my wife and two young daughters.

"On the whole I write novels about people I know, in parts of society I have lived in—they are what have interested me, and what I want to interest my readers in. I think novels should above all be interesting; and for me they are interesting especially in what they reveal about human beings, on their own, in isolation, and in their relationships with each other, with society. And that, as an assignment, is so overwhelming that I never got down as far as interest in words for their own sake, in 'fine writing,' verbal 'experimentation,' and suchlike.

"Under my real name I published three novels before the war and one after. I then wrote *Scenes From Provincial Life,* which combined being seemingly autobiographical with being scarcely the sort of novel to be expected from a senior civil servant who was going round the universities advising the young what to do. To spare embarrassment to my friends on the one hand and to my employers on the other, I adopted a pseudonym and took pains to keep it secret. The secret is now out, but I shall stick to the pseudonym. Cooper is a family name, and William seems right for the sort of writer I think I am."

William Cooper has been called "the pathfinder for the provincial school" of contemporary English novelists. The narrator of his best novel, *Scenes From Provincial Life,* is Joe Lunn, a part-time novelist teaching (as Cooper did) in a provincial secondary school just before World War II. Lunn is educated and intelligent but anti-intellectual; vaguely humanitarian and good natured, but totally unprincipled in his attempts to avoid marrying the girl he is sleeping with. Walter Allen called this very funny novel "an exact impression of one aspect of provincial life," narrated in "an extremely adroit approximation to colloquial speech." Lunn was a new kind of hero in modern English fiction (though he has characteristics reminiscent of William Gerhardie and H. G. Wells); many critics have seen him as the forerunner of Kingsley Amis's picaresque heroes.

Joe Lunn's career continued to parallel his creator's. His progress to a senior post in the Civil Service, marriage and fatherhood, are recorded in *Scenes From Married Life*, thought an excessively relaxed and shapeless book, sometimes rather arch. (It replaced one called *Scenes From Metropolitan Life*, suppressed as the result of a libel suit.) Of Cooper's other novels, the most admired were *The Struggles of Albert Woods*, an amusing and affectionate study of a young chemist; *Young People*, about life in a provincial university during the early 1930s; and *You Want the Right Frame of Reference*, an observant if rather extravagant satire on the various literary and cultural fashions that have flourished in England since the war. Cooper has dramatized Lady Murasaki's novel *The Tale of Genji* for radio.

Cooper taught at Alderman Newton's School in Leicester in 1933–1940 and from 1940 to 1945 was in the Royal Air Force, emerging as a Squadron Leader. His personnel work in the RAF led him into similar work as an assistant commissioner on the Civil Service Commission (1945–1958). "Interviewing," Cooper has said, "provided a realistic basis for an analytical sympathy towards the few individuals I have known well enough to write about." This sympathy with his characters leads Cooper to a degree of moral tolerance which at least one critic, G. S. Fraser, has found "almost alarming." At the same time, Fraser has said, he is "a fine craftsman, a most acute observer, and a writer who always conveys vitality." Cooper's novels have been thought in some respects the comic counterparts of C. P. Snow's. Snow is a friend and colleague of Cooper's, and figures in some of his novels. When the two books about Joe Lunn were published together in the United States as *Scenes From Life*, Snow said the book had "an undislodgable place in the recent history of the English novel"—that "underneath a facade of innocent knowingness" it was "both strong and wise."

Apart from occasional broadcasts, Cooper is not much in the public eye. Small, dapper, with silver hair and moustache, he is a man who radiates confidence. "My private life is very unriotous but very comfortable," he says, "somewhat different, as is my accent, from what I was born with. I seem to have turned not into a member of a different class, but a man independent of both." He lives, with his family, in the South London middle-class suburb of Putney.

PRINCIPAL WORKS: *As Harry Hoff*—Trina, 1934 (U.S., It Happened in Prk); Rhea, 1935; Lisa, 1937; Three Marriages, 1946. *As "William Cooper"*—Scenes From Provincial Life, 1950; The Struggles of Albert Woods, 1952; The Ever-Interesting Topic, 1953; Disquiet and Peace, 1956; Young People, 1958; C. P. Snow (*pamphlet in* Writers and Their Work series), 1959; Prince Genji: A Play, 1960; Scenes From Married Life, 1961; Scenes From Life, 1961; Memoirs of a New Man, 1966; You Want the Right Frame of Reference, 1971; Shall We Ever Know? The Trial of the Hosein Brothers for the Murder of Mrs. McKay, 1971; Love on the Coast, 1973.

ABOUT: Allen, W. The Novel Today, 1960; Allen, W. Tradition and Dream, 1964; Allsop, K. The Angry Decade, 1958; Contemporary Authors 4, 1963; Fraser, G. S. The Modern Writer and his World, 1964; West, P. The Modern Novel, 1963; Who's Who, 1971. *Periodicals*—Books and Bookmen February 1961.

CORNWELL, DAVID JOHN MOORE. *See* "LE CARRÉ, JOHN"

***CORTÁZAR, JULIO** (August 26, 1914–), Argentinian novelist and short story writer, was born in Brussels, Belgium, of Argentinian parents, Julio and Mariá (Descotte) Cortázar. The family, comfortably middle class, soon afterwards moved back to Argentina, and from the age of four Cortázar grew up in Banfield, a residential suburb of Buenos Aires. He attended the Buenos Aires Teachers' College from 1926 to 1936.

As a young man Cortázar belonged to a generation in Argentina whose ideas were almost exclusively derived from France and England. At the age of eighteen, with a group of friends, he made an abortive attempt to sail on a cargo boat to Europe—an experience on which he draws in his novel *Los Premios*. He failed to reach Europe itself, but compensated for this by digesting a vast amount of contemporary English and French literature at home. Much of his youthful cosmopolitan reading in fact follows that of his compatriot and master Jorge Luis Borges, and his interest in turn-of-the-century English literature closely coincides with Borges' critical interests of that time. He began his career in the literature department of the University of Buenos Aires.

Cortázar published a forgettable volume of Mallarméan sonnets under a pseudonym in 1941. His first book of any importance was *Los Reyes* (The Kings, 1949), a sequence of dialogues revolving around the theme of the Cretan Minotaur. In 1951, with a group of short stories called *Bestiario* (Bestiary), he launched himself, after Borges, into one of the domains that he has made his own, the literature of fantasy. Two other collections of short stories, *Final del juego* (End of the Game, 1956) and *Las armas secretas* (The Secret Weapons, 1959), followed in similar vein.

Usually in Cortázar's stories fairly ordinary events slip almost unobtrusively into fantasy. A healthy citizen of Buenos Aires may suddenly vomit a small fluffy rabbit. Another, half conscious after a motorcycle accident, may dream that he is being offered up in an Aztec ritual sacrifice—only

* kôr tä' zär

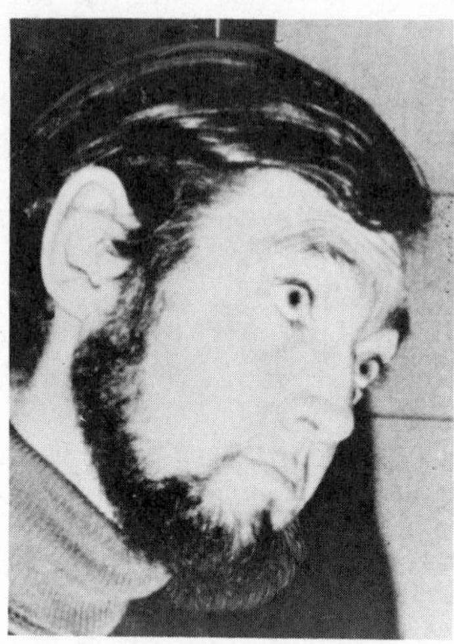

JULIO CORTÁZAR

to realize, as the axe falls, that he is no longer certain what is dream, what reality. (What could be more absurdly unreal, after all, than the idea of traveling through "an astonishing city . . . on an enormous metal insect that whirred away between his legs"?)

Los Premios (1960), Cortázar's first novel, is very much in the same mode as his short stories. The winners of a Buenos Aires municipal lottery are to receive a luxury voyage to a secret destination. Once aboard, however, they find themselves restricted to certain parts of the ship and cut off from communication with any of the officers. The ship leaves harbor but stops not far out. The passengers are told that some of the crew have typhus. For some this is enough; others, more aggressive or more curious, are driven to explore the forbidden and unknown. Their invasion of the crew's quarters ends in murder.

This novel, admirably translated by Elaine Kerrigan as *The Winners*, established Cortázar's international reputation. Though some reviewers thought the book intellectually condescending and too overt in its symbolism, it was generally found both stimulating and readable. William Goyen called Cortázar "a dazzling writer" who, in the *persona* of the eccentric and philosophical proofreader Persio, "creates a language and rhythm and sensuality as mysterious and terrible as Melville's, but all in his own voice."

The work for which Cortázar is best known, however, is *Rayuela* (1963, translated by Gregory Rabassa as *Hopscotch*), which is regarded in some quarters as the finest novel yet to have come out of Latin America. Its central character, Oliveira, is an Argentinian living in Paris. He is one of a circle of exotic, Durrellesque expatriates who devote themselves to intellectually exhibitionist conversation about Argentinian and European culture and society, and to love affairs, like Oliveira's with the conveniently telepathic girl called La Maga. Persio in *The Winners* had sought by occult means to trace a cosmic pattern in things; Oliveira on the contrary is a wholehearted existentialist, fascinated by the absurd arbitrariness of life, an enemy of cohesion.

This ephemeral world dissolves for Oliveira at the first touch of reality; with the death of La Maga's child his circle breaks up and he returns to Buenos Aires. There he encounters Traveler and Talita, the stolid provincial doubles of himself and La Maga, and with them gains employment in a mental hospital. He seduces Talita in the hospital morgue and then barricades himself in his room, hoping to keep out the vengeful Traveler and all he stands for—Argentina, convention, order.

But this is not necessarily the end of the story. Having read through the book from chapter 1 to chapter 56, the reader may then begin again, following a different pattern, and this time including the numerous short "expendable" chapters at the end of the book, some of which are relevant to the story, others passages of "found" prose—letters, law reports, and the like. In the recommended alternative sequence the first ten chapters, for example, are those numbered 73, 1, 2, 116, 3, 84, 4, 71, 5, 81.

This ambitious attempt to discover a kind of metaphysical order in things was very widely admired, even by critics who disliked the book's intellectual pretensions. Latin American critics in particular have praised its anarchic humor, still a rarity in their literatures, and its enlarging and liberating experiments with the Spanish language. English-language critics have naturally been less impressed by these Joycean innovations, and on the whole their enthusiasm has been more moderate. A characteristic response was that of Emile Capouya, who wrote: "Detail, poetic and random, takes the place of texture in this novel, and it proliferates with a violent fecundity that goes far to make it an acceptable substitute. . . . At first, from moment to moment, the reader has the conviction that he is in the hands of a master artist. It is only after some time that he finds the art to have been improvisation only. . . . I offer the opinion that *Hopscotch* is 'too odd to do very long,' half hoping, for the sake of the author's evident talent, to be proved . . . wrong."

Since *Rayuela* Cortázar has written another volume of short stories, some fantastic, some realistic, called *Todos los fuegos el fuego* (1966, translated by Suzanne Jill Levine as *All Fires the Fire*), an eccentric miscellany called *La vuelta al día en 80 mundos* (Around the Day in Eighty Worlds, 1967), and another novel, less ambitious than *Rayuela* and to some extent an appendix to it, *62, modelo para armar* (1968, translated by Gregory Rabassa as *62: A Model Kit*). Fifteen of his short stories have been translated by Paul Blackburn in *End of the Game*, which includes the piece used by Antonioni as the basis for his film *Blow-Up*.

Blackburn has also provided a translation of *Historias de cronopios y de famas* (1962), an engaging self-improvement manual, which includes surrealistic advice on How to Be Afraid, How to Dissect a Ground Owl, and other important matters. The author distinguishes between *cronopios*—who are disorganized optimists, and *famas*—cautious pessimists, clearly preferring the former. This lightweight work offers an interesting gloss on *Rayuela*, whose hero is obviously a dedicated *cronopio*. *Pameos y meopas*, a volume of deliberately flat and antiromantic poems about purity, nostalgia, time, and other romantic themes, was published in 1972.

Cortázar settled in 1951 in Paris, where both he and his wife, the former Aurora Bernárdez, work as freelance translators for Unesco. He is a tall, slim, reticent man, astonishingly boyish in appearance. He likes jazz and himself plays a trumpet.

PRINCIPAL WORKS IN ENGLISH TRANSLATION: The Winners, 1965; Hopscotch, 1966; End of the Game (U.S., Blow-Up and Other Stories), 1967; Cronopios and Famas, 1969; 62: A Model Kit, 1972; All Fires the Fire, 1973.

ABOUT: Guibert, R. Seven Voices, 1973; Who's Who in America, 1972–1973. *Periodicals*—Book Week April 4, 1965; May 1, 1966; Commentary October 1966; Encounter September 1965; Mundo Nuevo March 1967; Nation September 18, 1967; New Republic April 23, 1966; July 15, 1967; New York Review of Books April 28, 1966; New York Times Book Review March 21, 1965; April 10, 1966; July 9, 1967; Saturday Review March 27, 1965; July 22, 1967; Times April 29, 1966; Times Literary Supplement September 30, 1965; February 9, 1967; March 9, 1967; March 14, 1968; November 14, 1968.

COTTERELL, (ALAN) GEOFFREY (November 24, 1919–), English novelist, writes: "I was born at Southsea, Hants, where my father was a Naval dentist. I had one brother, Anthony, b. 1916. When my father was demobilised he went first to Lowestoft to be an assistant to a dentist called Britten. (My pram was pushed on occasion by the latter's small son Benjamin.) He moved to London and bought a practice at Wanstead, an east London suburb. From the age of eight I was a passionate reader and an equally passionate player of ball games, especially the less rough ones. When I was sixteen I took an opportunity of leaving school—Bishop's Stortford—and going off to Berlin to learn German. I did learn German, so that in Hamburg after the war I was able to broadcast as The Voice of Military Government, but I didn't get very far with economics, which I took up on

GEOFFREY COTTERELL

my return to England from Berlin. Luckily I sold a story to a pulp magazine and, if you exclude six years spent in the army, I've done nothing but write ever since.

"When I went to Berlin my brother Anthony had just succeeded in making the transition from being a student at Guy's Hospital to being on space in the features department of the *Daily Express*. He was a precocious success in Fleet Street. During the war he wrote two brilliant personal accounts of army life: *What! No Morning Tea?* and *An Apple for the Sergeant*. He was charming, witty, kind and brave. He was taken prisoner at Arnhem in September, 1944, and then was wounded by a trigger-happy S.S. man; whatever happened to him after that he did not come back.

"At this moment I am recovering from my ninth novel. I re-write incessantly and am apt to juggle with a paragraph for days; so it takes me some time to write a book. Anything from eight months to three years. I write to entertain but I can only do it on the basis of some sort of obsession either with a real character or with some revealed truth about success and failure or happiness and unhappiness. Without this nothing happens at all. Sometimes travel supplies it. For instance I had a long trip in the winter of 1950–51 in the U.S.A., driving an old Chev from coast to coast and back. It was a time when the World War II G.I. brides were settling in. I met several of them and was deeply impressed by their unanimity about the English social scene. They gave me or forced on me *Westward the Sun*. The thought behind my intentions may be superficial, and well-qualified persons have said so, though I prefer not to think so; but it is the obsession that matters. Aside from satisfying this I like recreating atmospheres and trying especially to get the right nostalgic overtones, time past always in time present, in a mixture of irony and sentimentality."

As a prewar writer for the pulps, Cotterell "lived in a gale of rejection slips," but learned his trade. He served during World War II in the Royal Artillery, rising to the rank of major, and afterwards was in Hamburg with the Control Commission. *Then a Soldier* and *Randle in Springtime*, arising from these experiences, brought him recognition if not fame. *Strait and Narrow*, a Book Society choice in England, established his reputation and introduced him to American readers. It was about an Englishman driven by political and social ambition into an unhappy marriage, and was praised as the work of a "devastatingly competent writer with a flair for authenticity that is little short of ventriloquism."

As he points out, some of Cotterell's material is acquired through travel, like *Westward the Sun*, which was called "featherweight" in its approach to the problems of GI brides but "worth more than volumes of set pieces about Anglo-American relations." It was a Book-of-the-Month Club selection. A voyage to Australia and the Pacific preceded *Errand at Shadow Creek* and *Tiara Tahiti* (which was successfully filmed from a script by the author). *Go, Said the Bird* was "a solidly constructed work of fiction which is also a useful bit of social history." Like several of Cotterell's earlier novels, it was concerned with the emotional and social damage still inflicted by the English class system. Class, indeed, has been called the focal point of Cotterell's "study of contemporary British society as it appears in his novels." Cotterell admires Somerset Maugham and J. P. Marquand, and has been compared to both writers—to Marquand in his "gifts of observation, wit, irony and narrative skill." He is a very accomplished professional novelist of a kind no longer fashionable, but still popular and necessary.

Cotterell is Conservative in his politics, a member of the Church of England, and is addicted to golf, which he plays near his seaside home at Eastbourne, Sussex.

PRINCIPAL WORKS: Then a Soldier, 1944; This Is the Way, 1947; Randle in Springtime, 1949; Strait and Narrow, 1950; Westward the Sun, 1952; The Strange Enchantment, 1956; Tea at Shadow Creek, 1958 (U.S., Errand at Shadow Creek); Tiara Tahiti, 1960; Go, Said the Bird, 1966; Bowers of Innocence, 1970; Amsterdam (history), 1973.

ABOUT: Contemporary Authors 7–8, 1963; Current Biography, 1954; Who's Who, 1971. *Periodicals*—Books and Bookmen October 1956, November 1960; New York Times February 14, 1961.

LEONARD COTTRELL

COTTRELL, LEONARD (ERIC) (May 21, 1913–), English journalist and writer about archaeology and ancient history, is the son of William and Beatrice (Tootell) Cottrell. He was born at Tettenhall, Staffordshire, and educated at King Edward's Grammar School in Birmingham. Cottrell began his career as an advertising copywriter but freelanced in his spare time for the British Broadcasting Corporation and in 1942 joined the BBC as a radio scriptwriter in the features department. In 1944–1945 he was attached to the Royal Air Force as a war correspondent. He returned to the BBC in 1946 as a senior producer and thereafter created many memorable programs about flying.

His first book was *All Men Are Neighbours* (1947), a much-praised account of air travel across the Atlantic which uses many of the techniques of the radio writer to bring life and immediacy to its subject. It was, however, not this wholly modern story but his excursions into the remote past which made Cottrell's literary reputation, beginning in the early 1950s with *Lost Pharaohs* and *The Bull of Minos*. The former is a highly readable and informative compression of the archaeological history of Egypt, a subject which has fascinated Cottrell since his boyhood. *The Bull of Minos* describes the achievements of two dissimilar men whose work carried our knowledge of Greek history back to the third millenium B.C.: the romantic Heinrich Schliemann and the scholar Sir Arthur Evans. E. B. Garside, one of many reviewers who gave the book an enthusiastic welcome, said that Cottrell "is at his best when communicating that fresh and fateful sense of life which must have prevailed in very ancient times when gods walked the earth like men. It is this feeling of epiphany . . . which makes Mr. Cottrell's book a most worthwhile popularization of its subject."

In 1951–1953 Cottrell had been assigned by the BBC to study and report on the work which Unesco was doing in the Middle East. He produced a number of radio programs on the subject, and later described his eight-week tour of the region in *One Man's Journey*. After this hectic interlude he returned to the BBC, and in 1956 switched to the same organization's television service as a writer-producer in the drama department. He left the staff of the BBC in 1960 to devote himself to travel and writing, but has continued to make freelance contributions to radio and television.

His most notable books since *The Bull of Minos* include a biography of Hannibal, "brightly written and ingenious in speculation"; *The Tiger of Ch'in*, a vivid account of the early history of China; and *Realms of Gold*, called a "popularization at a very high level" of what little is known about the Myceneans and Minoans, charting "a careful voyage through the perilous seas of Homeric debate." The author has also written a number of excellent introductory studies in his special fields for children and young people.

Part of the vividness and immediacy, the sense of "warm understanding and personal involvement," which distinguish Cottrell's books springs from his practice of going to see for himself the sites and relics of the events he describes. Before he wrote *Hannibal*, for example, he drove along the conqueror's route, over the Alps from Spain to Italy, in a small bus. He is sometimes accused of excessive enthusiasm in his imaginative reconstruction of forgotten events, and of the occasional errors and misunderstandings which amateur historians can never entirely avoid; but he is unquestionably one of the most perceptive, scrupulous, and entertaining popularizers in his field. As Rex Warner wrote, "He infects the reader with his own enthusiasm, and gives us the pleasure not only of learning something new but of finding the whole process as exciting as a detective story. He has the gift of infusing both the background and the details with life."

Leonard Cottrell was married in 1940 to Doris Swain. That marriage was dissolved in 1960 and in 1965 he married Diana Randolph. His recreations include reading, listening to music, and driving fast cars.

PRINCIPAL WORKS: All Men Are Neighbours, 1947; Lost Pharaohs: The Romance of Egyptian Archaeology, 1950; Madame Tussaud, 1951; The Bull of Minos, 1953; One Man's Journey, 1955; Life Under the Pharaohs, 1955; Two Thousand Years of Pyramid Exploration, 1956 (U.S., Mountains of Pharaoh); Lost Cities, 1957; Seeing Roman Britain, 1957 (U.S., A Guide to Roman Britain); Anvil of Civilization, 1958; The Great Invasion, 1958; Wonders of the World, 1959; Enemy of Rome, 1960 (U.S., Hannibal: Enemy of Rome); The Tiger of Ch'in, 1962; Realms of Gold, 1963; The Quest for Sumer, 1965; Crete, Island of Mystery, 1965; The Land of Shinar, 1965; The Lion Gate: A Journey in Search of the Myceneans, 1966; Egypt, 1966; Queens of the Pharaohs, 1966; The Warrior Pharaohs, 1968; Reading the Past, 1969. *As editor*—Concise Encyclopedia of Archaeology, 1960.
ABOUT: Contemporary Authors 5–6, 1963; Who's Who, 1971; Who's Who in America, 1970–1971.

COX, WILLIAM TREVOR. *See* "TREVOR, WILLIAM"

COXE, GEORGE HARMON (April 23, 1901–), American detective story writer, was born in Olean, New York, the son of George and Harriet (Cowens) Coxe. He went to school in Olean and at the nearby Elmira Free Academy, and after a year at Purdue University (1919–1920) and another at Cornell he went to California to work as a newspaperman for the Santa Monica *Outlook*. That was in 1922, and over the next five years Coxe worked for the Los Angeles *Express*, and, back in New York, for the Utica *Observer-Dispatch*, the New York *Commercial*, and the Elmira *Star-Gazette*. He left newspaper work in 1927 and spent a further five years in advertising with the Barta Press of Cambridge, Massachusetts.

Since 1932 Coxe has earned his living as a writer of detective stories. In his early years as a freelance he wrote stories and novelettes for the pulps—*Argosy*, *Black Mask*, *Blue Book*, etc.—later graduating to magazines of the caliber of *Collier's*, *Cosmopolitan*, and the *Saturday Evening Post*. His first book, *Murder With Pictures*, was published in 1935, and the following year he was hired as a scriptwriter by Metro-Goldwyn-Mayer. Coxe returned permanently to freelancing in 1938 and since then has published over fifty books.

In his first novels, Coxe introduced the jazz-loving Boston news photographer and part-time detective Kent Murdock, and immediately won the approval of the critics for his excellent characterization, crisp dialogue, and ingenious, action-filled, "medium-tough" plots. Thirty years later Murdock was still talking, thinking, and battling his way in and out of trouble, and nothing much had changed except that he had been joined in the Coxe cosmogony by a great many other indestructible heroes. These have included—among others—a clever and agreeable young lawyer named Gary Marshall; the fat professional detective Sam Crombie; and Dr. Paul Standish. Coxe's settings are equally varied, ranging from Boston to Havana, Barbados to New Orleans.

Erle Stanley Gardner called him "one of the few authors that have a knack of hitting a fast pace [and]

GEORGE HARMON COXE

keeping it up from chapter to chapter and book to book," while Anthony Boucher spoke with a connoisseur's pleasure of the inimitable skill with which the conclusion of a Coxe story is invariably constructed. James Sandoe, who at times has found Coxe's work a little underwritten and lacking in savor, has praised his "dedication to the formal mode of detection with a liberal salting of clues, his meticulous interest in details of physical setting and his workmanlike assembly of a cast."

Coxe, who spent a year as a war correspondent in 1945, has sold his stories to radio, television, and the movies. He is a member of the Authors' Guild and the Republican Club and is a past president of the Mystery Writers of America, which in 1964 gave him its Grand Master's Award. Coxe was married in 1929 to Elizabeth Fowler and has two children, Janet and George III.

PRINCIPAL WORKS: Murder With Pictures, 1935; The Glass Triangle, 1940; The Jade Venus, 1945; Lady Killer, 1949; Inland Passage, 1949; Eye Witness, 1950; Death at the Isthmus, 1954; Top Assignment, 1955; Suddenly a Widow, 1956; Man on a Rope, 1956; The Last Commandment, 1960; Moment of Violence, 1961; Mission of Fear, 1962; One Hour to Kill, 1963; Deadly Image, 1964; With Intent to Kill, 1965; The Ring of Truth, 1966; The Candid Imposter, 1968; An Easy Way to Go, 1969; Double Identity, 1970; Fenner, 1971; Woman With a Gun, 1972.

ABOUT: Who's Who in America, 1970–1971.

COXE, LOUIS (OSBORNE) (April 15, 1918–), American poet and dramatist, writes: "I was born in Manchester, New Hampshire, but my family moved not long after to Salem, Massachusetts, where the Osbornes, my mother's forebears, had lived. My father's people were mostly upstate New Yorkers, and there were clergymen on both sides of my family as well as lawyers and merchants. I grew up in Salem but went away to school at thirteen to St. Paul's, in Concord, New Hampshire, thence to Princeton University, from which I graduated in 1940. I taught briefly, then joined the Navy and served in small ships in the Caribbean and Pacific. After the war I returned to teaching, first at the Lawrenceville School, next for a year at Harvard, on to the University of Minnesota for six years, and in 1955 I came to Bowdoin College, where I am now. I have had visiting jobs, one for a year at Princeton, another at Trinity College, Dublin, on a Fulbright fellowship. I was married in 1946 to Edith Winsor, and we now have three sons and a daughter.

"My childhood was, I suppose, rather conventional for the time, place and milieu; I should describe it as Victorian. At any rate I do not recall it as either unhappy or frustrating, as no doubt I should. It was sheltered, serene, rather stuffy, but very literary in the sense that I read a great deal—which by no means interfered with the activities typical of boys I knew. Poetry took hold of me early. I read a great deal of romantic verse all through my early days, and in college came up against Auden and Eliot with a sense of shock and amazement. I suppose I always knew I would be a poet, in the same way that I always knew my name: it was Me. I wrote poems very early in life and have never stopped, for good or ill or neither. College proved exciting, vivid, full of discovery and exploration. I learned from contemporaries and teachers and can never repay the debts I then contracted. Those four years and the four in the Navy, or at any rate those of seagoing, seem now to have made me finally a poet. Though I have taught without a break (having a family to support) since 1946, I have no doubt which is vocation and which is breadwinning, though I would not teach at all if I found it either repugnant or tedious.

"I used to do some criticism and reviewing but have given up both, partly out of disinclination and partly on principle: no poet is reliable or disinterested when it comes to judging the work of his peers and contemporaries. I like what I like and what I can use; the rest is for others. I have written a number of plays and along with Robert Chapman achieved a small success with the dramatization of Melville's *Billy Budd*. Apart from that, my work in both poetry and drama remains obscure—a state perhaps preferable to that of being prematurely or foolishly praised and rewarded, at least as far as one's own balance is concerned. I would like to have many people read and like my work but they do not and perhaps never will. I have the poetry and the plays to write, and as Eliot says, 'The rest is not our business.'

"I write with some regularity in the sense that I have, luckily, never known a really long 'dry' period. In the past fifteen years or so I have been interested in the possibility of the long narrative poem and how one might use novelistic techniques poetically. One result of such interest has inevitably been a preoccupation with subject and symbolic action; my best hope would be to tell a poem so well that the very narrative would convey its own meaning or significance in the telling, with no asides, explanations or recourse to abstraction. It remains an ideal. And meanwhile I enjoy my family life, being outdoors a lot, looking at as much of my world as I can imagine.

"In the 1960s poetics and style are vexed, obscured matters. Coteries abound, each off-limits to any other, all intolerant, many destructive. I have stayed clear of all such, not out of any special virtue, but simply because neither inclination nor circumstance has brought me close to many poets or poetic circles. I regret the fact in many ways, yet perhaps this very isolation, apart from being all-American, has at least not interfered with the finding of my own kind of poetry, if in fact I have found it. I should like to be a Power and a Celebrity, as who would not, but I hope I can manage to do without. My family contrives to keep me more or less human and my job to place me in the 'real' world."

As he says, Coxe's greatest single success was his prose dramatization with Robert Chapman of *Billy Budd*, produced on Broadway in 1951. John Mason Brown called it an enthralling play which deserved even larger audiences than it received. John Gassner, on the other hand, was dissatisfied, finding in it not tragedy but "undischarged pathos." Gerald Weales regretted that the authors had made Melville's setting more realistic, his characters on the other hand more overtly symbolic, but went on: "By comparison with Melville, whose characters twist and turn as you hold them, changing symbolic value with each new light, Coxe and Chapman are as neat as the writers of ancient morality plays. It is this neatness that is their greatest virtue. . . . They are at their best when they let their philosophical play speak as directly as the morality play has always done."

Coxe's poems have for the most part provoked less discussion and enthusiasm. They are praised for their tautness, their exactness, their fastidious avoidance of verbal and emotional clichés, but censured, often by the same critics, as dull and humorless, unenticing. It is his long poems which have attracted most attention, like *The Middle Passage*, a three-thousand-line narrative about a whaling ship turned slaver which on another level is a poem about America herself. Philip Booth called it an ambitious and demanding work, a

LOUIS COXE

"major poem . . . which nobody who didn't risk minor failures could write."

"In what is supposedly the heyday of the persona poem and the loose style," wrote one critic "Louis Coxe chooses to write about heroes. What's more, he employs a tightly rhymed quatrain more often than not, and his metaphor is traditional and highly charged." Coxe's work has suggested comparisons with Melville and, more often, with Edwin Arlington Robinson, about whom he has written an excellent critical biography (1969) as well as a briefer account in the University of Minnesota's Pamphlets on American Writers series (1962).

Louis Coxe is the son of Charles Shearman Coxe and the former Helen Osborne. He won the Vachel Lindsay prize in 1960 and has also received a *Sewanee Review* fellowship and Brandeis University's Creative Arts award. At Bowdoin he is Pierce Professor of English. He also serves as a trustee of the New York School of Interior Design.

PRINCIPAL WORKS: The Sea Faring, and Other Poems, 1947; (with R. H. Chapman) Billy Budd: A Play in Three Acts, Based on a Novel by Herman Melville, 1951 (in England, with authors' introduction, glossary and notes, 1966); The Second Man, and Other Poems, 1955; The Wilderness, and Other Poems, 1958; The Middle Passage, 1960; Edwin Arlington Robinson (criticism), 1962; The Last Hero, and Other Poems, 1965; Nikal Seyn [and] Decoration Day: A Poem and A Play, 1966; Edwin Arlington Robinson (critical biography), 1969.

ABOUT: Brown, J. M. As They Appear, 1952; Coxe, L. O. and Chapman, R. H. Notes on the Play *in* Billy Budd, 1951, 1966; Contemporary Authors 13–14, 1965; Gassner, J. Theatre at the Crossroads, 1960; Weales, G. American Drama Since World War II, 1962; Who's Who in America, 1970–1971. *Periodicals*—Poetry October 1960; Yale Review Summer 1959.

CRAYENCOUR, MARGUERITE DE. *See* "YOURCENAR, MARGUERITE"

CREASEY, JOHN (September 17, 1908–June 9, 1973), English crime novelist, sent the following memoir: " 'CREASEY,' said my headmaster, after reading my essay on 'an imaginary conversation between Marshal Foch and the Kaiser,' 'if you ever want to, I believe you could earn a living by writing.' It was 1918. Since that day (apart from a few spasmodic longings to put the world to rights) I never wanted to do anything else. There were difficulties—in the shape of seven hundred and forty-three rejections between the ages of ten and seventeen, for instance; leaving school at fourteen, and having twenty-five jobs from office-boy to counter-hand, warehouse-clerk to vacuum-cleaner salesman; sceptical relatives would say: ' . . . wasting your time writing when you can go down to the shop at the corner and buy Edgar Wallace for sixpence . . .' (score E. W. 156, J. C. 451). But after being told never to write on a subject of which I knew nothing, I wrote, in desperation, a story about a Japanese boy and a Chinese girl falling in love in the mountains of Tibet—although I'd never been more than thirty miles from London; nor in love. It was my first sale—three guineas (eight dollars).

" 'CREASEY,' said my first book publisher, 'you may be able to write twelve books a year, although I doubt it. But I can only publish two a year by the same author.' 'What about pen-names?' I inquired. He laughed. Question and laughter carried me on to an average of fifteen books a year for thirty years, twenty-three in one year (1949); thirteen pen-names, of which seven are still thriving—(thriving? Well, producing some fifty million words); some sixty million copies sold throughout the world, and recently, five or six million sales a year—more titles published in France and the U.S.A. than anywhere else in the world except England. (N.B. Every American publisher I saw on my 1948 (first) visit to the U.S.A. said how sorry he was that I would never be able to sell in America, and has been laughing with me about it ever since.) Oh—translations into twenty-five languages, over three thousand editions, two major television series (seven more to come, I hope, as there are nine series of books as well as individual titles), and a few movies.

" 'CREASEY,' said Dorothy L. Sayers, 'is the kind of writer who, when he cannot think of the right word, believes that anything approximate in sound will do.' Five years later, when I could bear to hear her name without reaching for an axe, I read the maligned book; she was right. Thus I learned that, while I could write fast, I needed others to read me 'cold' and to report dispassionately—(although I can still growl when anyone suggests that, writing at such speed, I cannot possibly revise). I hope that, today, only the right word will do. Each book is written (now) by hand, revised 'hot,' read by my secretary, revised 'cold,' typed, sent to a male reader whose report is often ten folios and a hundred queries long, revised by me, partly retyped, read again by my secretary for grammar and syntax plus, yet again by another reader who has a positive genius for spotting the wrong word . . . sent to the publishers, reported on, re-read by the original male reader, and given a final reading by me. Whenever asked the secret of this phenomenal output and effort, I answer truthfully: 'Organised concentration.' (My astrologist friends point out that I am a Virgo—born Southfields, Surrey, England, 17th September, 1908.)

" 'CREASEY,' said the Assistant Commissioner of the Criminal Investigation Department of New Scotland Yard, 'why don't more authors get the atmosphere of the Yard as accurately as you?' I don't know. I do know that I've been in and out of the Yard for thirty-odd years, been readily helped there time and time again, and come to see a policeman as a human being first—I see a criminal that way, too. As one lives, of course, one researches unthinkingly about those things which most interest one. I have accumulated a vast store of incidental knowledge of police work, court work, judges and juries, police surgeons, pathologists, forensic medicine, prisons, ballistics, fingerprints, hair (nine different kinds on the human body), and life in general. I write out of this storehouse, and research only after the book is done to fill in gaps or statements open to suspicion and pointed out by my ever-zealous MS. readers. (Not to mention a few book readers, like the man who sent me ten pages on why the automatic lift which nearly killed a character couldn't have crashed down the shaft the way mine did. Mine won't again.)

" 'CREASEY,' said the intellectual (from whom heaven preserve me), 'don't you ever feel like writing a *real* book?' I have learned to explode quietly. He wilted as I claimed (with Bertrand Russell among others) that the crime story is (almost) the only novel worth reading today, it having a beginning, a middle, and an end, and being preoccupied with the conflict of good and bad (evil), the fundamental conflict of mankind. That the crime story at its best is the morality play of our age. That—I could go on and on; in fact I have gone on and on, from writing 'yarns' to believing with absolute certainty that crime is a reflection less on criminals (punished though they must be) than on society as a whole. That we haven't yet very much to boast about as human beings, for there must be something drastically wrong with a world which has been nominally

Christian, Mohammedan, Buddhist, Hindu, Humanist, *et al.*, for so many centuries, yet in which we still kill each other (with weapons and on highways), strike to get our own way and be damned to the next man (or woman or child), have colour bars and racial bitterness, democracy which misses on five out of six cylinders, famine, fear, pestilence, and hatred among fellow men.

"It's a crime. But life in society is too often avoidable crime. We could avoid it if we tried. This could be a near-perfect world. I try to say so, clearly, in every book I write."

John Creasey was the most prolific writer of crime novels in the history of the genre: his output reached 560 before he died. He was an excellent storyteller and, though he produced no masterpieces, maintained a remarkably high level of competence. The seventh of nine children of a poor coachmaker, Creasey was almost crippled with polio at the age of two. He sold his first story in 1925 when he was seventeen, and his first crime novel, *Seven Times Seven*, in 1932. Beginning in 1935 he was able to support himself as a writer and by the mid-1960s he had an estimated annual income of one hundred thousand dollars. His most admired books were those (by "J. J. Marric") about Commander Gideon of Scotland Yard, a well-drawn and believable police officer modeled on Creasey's friend Commander George Hatherill. *Gideon's Fire* was awarded the Edgar of the Mystery Writers of America in 1962. Creasey also wrote (as "Anthony Morton") a series about the art dealer detective called the "Baron") more successful in England than in the United States); stories (under his own name) about the "Toff" and about Inspector West; and the series (by "Gordon Ashe") about Pat Dawlish. He wrote westerns (under three different pseudonyms) and science fiction stories under his own name. To Creasey, writing was a business like any other, and he had no patience with writers who suffer from mental blocks, which he called "nothing but laziness."

But Creasey was more than a writing machine. He owned a literary agency and had been co-publisher of *John O'London's Weekly* and the *New Strand* magazine. He founded the Crime Writers Association in England and in 1966 was elected president of the Mystery Writers of America. During World War II, unfit for military service, he earned an MBE by his efforts in the National Savings Movement. Thereafter he was active in the social service work of Rotary and the Round Table, and became a candidate for Parliament, first as a Liberal and subsequently on his own platform, the All Party Alliance. Tall, thickset, bespectacled, he was calm, matter of fact, outgoing in personality, enjoyed cricket and motoring, and traveled twice

JOHN CREASEY

round the world. He lived with his family in a Wiltshire country house. Creasey was married four times—most recently, only three weeks before his death, to Mrs. Diana Farrell, who had nursed him after a heart attack in 1972. At the time of his death, Creasey was working on his most ambitious project, a fictional history of the London Metropolitan Police, seen through the lives of several generations of several families. Creasey had two sons and always hoped that they would "come into the business, so to speak. We've a nice little thing here, good for a hundred years, and it would be a pity for it to stop with me."

PRINCIPAL WORKS: *Crime novels*—(as John Creasey) Department Z, Inspector West, "Toff" series; (as "Gordon Ashe") Pat Dawlish series; (as "J. J. Marric") Commander Gideon series; (as "Anthony Morton") "Baron" series; other stories under pseudonyms "Norman Deane," "Michael Halliday," "Kyle Hunt," "Peter Manton," "Richard Martin," "Jeremy York." *Science fiction*—(as John Creasey) Dr. Palfrey series. *Westerns* (under pseudonyms "Ken Ranger," "William K. Reilly," "Tex Riley"). *Nonfiction*—(with Jean Creasey) Round the World in 465 Days, 1953; Let's Look at America, 1956; Optimists in Africa (with supporting chapters by Jean, Richard, and Martin Creasey), 1963; Good, God and Man: An Outline of the Philosophy of Self-ism, 1967.

ABOUT: Contemporary Authors 5–6, 1963 (includes a bibliography); Current Biography, 1963; Who's Who, 1971. *Periodicals*—Life April 27, 1962; Newsweek February 2, 1959; New York Times June 10, 1973; New York Times Book Review November 23, 1958; March 18, 1962; January 31, 1965; New Yorker July 16, 1960; Rotarian December 1957; Times June 11, 1973.

CREELEY, ROBERT (WHITE) (May 21, 1926–), American poet, short story writer, novelist, and essayist, writes: "I was raised in Massachusetts for the most part, having been born in

ROBERT CREELEY

Arlington, son of a physician who died when I was four. That and the loss of my left eye when I was a little younger mark for me two conditions I have unequivocally as content, but which I have neither much bitterness about nor other specific feeling. I did miss my father certainly. With him went not only the particular warmth he might have felt for me, but also the whole situation of our life as we had apparently known it. He had got a house in the country, in West Acton, while he continued his practice in Watertown, and so we were left there, when he died, to manage as we could. My mother became, first, town nurse for Stow, then later for the Actons, West, East, North, South, and Center. But Concord was always a qualification, in terms of sophistications of all kinds. I remember being very pleased that Captain Isaac Davis was among those present at the battle in Concord, having brought there a contingent of Acton farmers.

"But my upbringing was in that respect small pickings, happily so. Having no father, I was dependent upon an uncle whose nervous ambitions for his own children I never really trusted, and a grandfather, my mother's father, a Nova Scotian, French, who had gone to sea at the age of twelve to support five younger brothers after the death of his father. He didn't like girls, and so my sister got little from him, but for me he was the one measure of literal *man* I had for those early years.

"We lived first on what had been a farm, though we never used it as such, but its upkeep and general costs became too much for my mother to manage. So we left it, happily having found a buyer, and moved to a smaller place but there were still woods and a sense of much space. I used to like animals very much. I wanted to be a veterinarian until I went to college, at which time I disposed myself toward writing, with much hope, due to the sympathetic teachers at the school to which I had gone.

"So my childhood was happy, as I remember it. I loved the possibility of the woods, and went with friends into them constantly. We had trails it seemed halfway to Canada. I can remember literal battles employing everything from slingshots up to BB guns and an occasional .22—one time my cousin took my stocking cap off with a spear as I went running through a clearing. Somehow it was a lovely moment of precision for all concerned.

"Then, when it came time for me to start my freshman year in high school, my sister who had got a scholarship to Northfield, having a friend who had a brother at Holderness in New Hampshire, persuaded my mother to apply for my entrance there. I got a scholarship and so went off, very tentatively—in fact, I brought my pigeons with me so generous was that school then in its understanding of boys as myself. Yet I had much indeed to learn. The 'sports coat' bought at Grover Cronin's in Waltham turned out to have cardboard buttons so that they dissolved the first time I sent that coat to the cleaners. It was all a new world for me, but I was decently treated—very much so, in fact, and count the most relevant part of my schooling to be the four years spent there. They did not misuse my idealism.

"Subsequently I went to Harvard, where I found little place despite the various friendships I made. Only one teacher, Fred McCreary, gave me any sense that I might have possibility as a writer. I left college for a time to join the American Field Service and drove an ambulance in the India-Burma theater. Then back to college, an early marriage at the age of twenty, leaving Harvard in the last half of my senior year, and a son born shortly after.

"The time from then to now consists of much travel, a closer and increasingly helpful rapport with writers as Charles Olson, Robert Duncan, and Allen Ginsberg, a most incisive time as an instructor at Black Mountain in the middle fifties (for which college I also edited *The Black Mountain Review*), divorce, subsequent remarriage which proved an equal revelation, and presently I live in Bolinas, a small town on the coast of California, with my wife and two daughters.

"But the point is, for me, that words have given me a use of myself I might otherwise not have known. The New England environment, as I knew it, does not easily make emotions evident. I wanted to learn how to articulate that which I felt in words —as poems, as stories, as the novel *The Island*. The 'divorce' which Williams speaks of in *Paterson*, and his sense of the possibilities of writing more generally, were very valuable instruction for me. I have also believed deeply in Pound's statement, 'Peace comes of communication.' I trust to words."

Robert Creeley is the son of Oscar Slade Creeley and Genevieve (Jules) Creeley. He left Harvard in 1947 and lived until 1950 in Littleton, New Hampshire. It was then that his literary career began in earnest. One Saturday night when he was in Boston (showing chickens at the Boston Poultry Show), he read some poems on Cid Corman's radio program *This Is Poetry*. At about the same time he began to publish in Corman's magazine *Origin*, through which he met Charles Olson, Paul Blackburn, and Denise Levertov.

Then began the years of travel he mentions above. He and his family spent a year or so at the beginning of the 1950s in France, near Aix-en-Provence, and then lived for a while in Majorca (the setting of his novel *The Island*) where he founded the Divers Press. In 1954 Charles Olson brought him to Black Mountain College in North Carolina, where he wrote and taught writing, received his B.A. (1954), and edited the *Black Mountain Review* (1954–1957). Subsequently he taught at a boys' school in Albuquerque, earned his M.A. at the University of New Mexico (1959), and taught there (1961–1962 and 1963–1966). He has also taught in Guatemala, at the University of British Columbia, and at the State University of New York at Buffalo, where he was appointed a professor of English in 1967. Creeley received a D. H. Lawrence fellowship in 1960, a Guggenheim in 1964–1965, and a Rockefeller Foundation grant in 1966.

Black Mountain College no longer exists, but the school of poetry associated with it survives in the work of Creeley, Robert Duncan, Charles Olson, and others. Olson, the movement's principal theoretician, had learned from Ezra Pound and William Carlos Williams, and was influenced in particular by Williams's preoccupation with natural speech rhythms. In his famous essay "Projective Verse" (1950), Olson describes a poem as a "high energy construct." This energy, received by the poet, must be transmitted to the reader with no loss of power or immediacy and in the poet's true voice, modulated from moment to moment by what he has to say. The poem must be shaped not according to traditional measures but by "the breathing of the man who writes."

Creeley shares and has contributed to this view of poetry. He believes that "form is never more than an extension of content," and this was evident in all of the small volumes of wry, laconic, sometimes poignant love poems that began to appear in 1952. Thus his first books were characterized by a "short, seemingly broken line," which came he says from "the somewhat broken emotions that were involved in them." The more lyrical line that emerged in *A Form of Women* (1959), published two years after his second marriage, reflected his sense of being "more settled, more at ease in my world."

Most of the work Creeley had done between 1950 and 1960 was collected in *For Love* (1962), which established him as a prominent figure among the poets of his generation. Paul Carroll called them "close-to-the-bone, fiercely personal poems" and said that Creeley "is, above all, a poet of immediate, concrete, personal relationships—between lovers, friends, a man with himself." M. L. Rosenthal, indeed, found these poems too limitingly personal, too self-concerned and reticent; others, like R. W. Flint, applauded this "concentration on one experience." And there was no doubt of Creeley's technical skill: William Carlos Williams credited him with "the subtlest feeling for the measure that I encounter anywhere except in the verses of Ezra Pound."

Subsequent collections have suggested that Creeley's direction is towards an even greater verbal and emotional economy—what Charles Philbrick called "a terseness that tends to abstraction, in which statement has been stripped of reverberation or even of significance." An example is the poem "A Night Sky": "All the grass / dies / in front of us / The fire / again / flares out. / The night / such a large / place. Stars / The points / but like / places no / depth, I see / a flat— / a plain as if the / desert / were showing smaller / places." Critics welcomed or deplored this tendency according to their lights, some feeling that Creeley's verse lacked sufficient profundity and complexity to support further reduction, others praising his efforts to avoid any kind of falseness, and to extend himself.

The Gold Diggers and Other Stories, first published privately in 1954, was republished by Scribner's in an extended edition in 1965. It seemed very much a poet's book, concerned less with character or narrative than with language; with the ability of words "to chart the flux of consciousness the way iron filings indicate the sweep of a magnetic field." Rather similar comments were made about Creeley's novel *The Island*, a partly autobiographical study of a young American writer on Majorca, struggling for self-knowledge as his marriage collapses around him. Benjamin DeMott, one of a number of critics who admired the book, said that "its author writes like a man crossing a minefield—every word a grim step, an act of difficult trust—but genuineness is the effect. As he edges patiently into the character of the husband and wife . . . a contemporary kind of marriedness springs up from the page."

The personal and critical essays collected in *A Quick Graph* are interesting for the light they throw on Creeley's poetry, but their prose seemed to some reviewers humorless, unattractive, and gratuitously obscure.

As a poet, according to Hayden Carruth, "Creeley's personal influence on other writers has been widespread. What was his individual manner has become a public property; one sees it everywhere in the work of younger poets. His writing has been studied with an intentness seldom accorded the works of living poets, and he himself is much in demand as a public reader and teacher."

PRINCIPAL WORKS: *Poetry*—Le Fou, 1952; The Immoral Proposition, 1953; The Kind of Act of, 1953; All That Is Lovely in Men, 1955; If You, 1956; The Whip, 1957; A Form of Women, 1959; For Love: Poems 1950–1960, 1962; Poems, 1950–1965, 1966; Words, 1967; Pieces, 1969; The Charm: Early and Uncollected Poems, 1969; The Finger: Poems 1966–1969, 1970; St. Martin's, 1971; A Day Book, 1972. *Fiction*—The Gold Diggers and Other Stories, 1954; The Island, 1963. *Essays*—A Quick Graph, 1970. *As editor*—Selected Writings of Charles Olson, 1966; (with Donald Allen) The New Writing in the USA, 1967; Mayan Letters, by Charles Olson, 1953 (Majorca), reissued, 1968; Whitman, 1973.

ABOUT: Allen, D. M. (ed.) The New American Poetry, 1960; Contemporary Authors 1st revision 1–4, 1967; Leary, P. and Kelly, R. (eds.) A Controversy of Poets, 1965; Murphy, R. (ed.) Contemporary Poets of the English Language, 1970; Ossman, D. The Sullen Art, 1963; Rexroth, K. Assays, 1961; Rosenthal, M. L. The New Poets, 1967; Stepanchev, S. American Poetry Since 1945, 1965; Who's Who in America, 1970–1971. *Periodicals*—New Mexico Quarterly Autumn and Winter 1962–1963; New Republic October 11, 1969; New York Times Book Review November 19, 1967; Poetry August 1966; The Review 10 1964; Times Literary Supplement November 25, 1965; Yale Review December 1969.

CREIGHTON, DONALD GRANT (July 15, 1902–), Canadian historian and biographer, writes: "I was born in Toronto, Ontario, Canada. My father, William Black Creighton, was of Ulster Irish stock and my mother, Laura Harvie, came of a Lowland Scottish family. Both my parents were born in Canada; but both grandfathers were immigrants from the United Kingdom. I was brought up among strong literary influences. When my sister and I were quite small, my mother began reading nineteenth-century English classics aloud to us. My father was the editor of a church weekly, which gave a good deal of space to current affairs and general literature, and he used to bring home a wide variety of books and periodicals to read and review. In the autumn, when the publishing season was at its height, the parcels of books became larger and more interesting, and it was one of my greatest pleasures to open them as soon as my father had arrived. I suppose that, as a result, I acquired a greater knowledge of contemporary books and authors than most boys of my age.

"I went to public and high school in Toronto, and then to Victoria College, in the University of Toronto, where I took the honours course in English and History. For the first two years my interests were about evenly divided between the two subjects; but in my third year a very gifted and stimulating young lecturer tipped the balance in favour of history. At the end of my undergraduate course at Toronto, I won a scholarship which took me to Balliol College, Oxford University, where I read the History Schools. I was then offered a post as a lecturer in the Department of History at the University of Toronto, and I have taught there ever since. From 1954 to 1959 I was Chairman of the Department; but I soon tired of the administrative work involved in the chairmanship of a large department in a modern university, and I was extremely glad when I could resign this post and give all my spare time to research and writing.

"I always hoped and believed that I would be a writer. At school and college I wrote short stories and parts of novels; but after I discovered that my main interest seemed to lie in historical studies, I gave up all attempts at what is called 'creative' writing and tried to find satisfaction for my literary impulse in histories and biographies. At first I wanted to be an historian of the French Revolution; but I could not afford to go to France every year and, as no assistance to historical scholarship was then available in Canada, I soon decided that I must seek my subjects nearer home. My first book, *The Empire of the St. Lawrence*, was published in 1937, and since then I have continued to find themes in Canadian history that appealed to me. I have written general histories, biographies, and special studies, two of which have won Canadian medals and awards. The Molson Prize, established by the Canada Council in 1964, was awarded for the first time to me.

"I enjoy reading the classic English narrative historians, Gibbon, Macaulay, and Parkman, for example; but other literary influences have been equally important in my work. I owe much to the English and French realistic novels of the nineteenth and twentieth centuries, particularly to those which deal with large casts of characters and a broad social scene. My books are carefully documented; but I believe that once an historian has gathered all the relevant material available, he is free to use the appropriate literary technique in its presentation.

"My life as a teacher has been spent at the University of Toronto; but I have travelled a good deal, largely to gather material for my books and occasionally to visit and lecture at other universities. I have been interested in the history and problems of federal countries, particularly those within the British Commonwealth. Before the Second

World War, I served as a research assistant to a Royal Commission on Canadian federal relations; and I am at present a member of the Advisory Committee on Confederation appointed by the government of the Province of Ontario. I was also a member of the Monckton Commission established by the British government to advise it on the revision of the constitution of the ill-fated Federation of Rhodesia and Nyasaland."

Donald Creighton has been described by Max Beloff as "one of the half-dozen best historians now writing in the English-speaking world." His first book, *The Commercial Empire of the St. Lawrence* (1937), was already generally recognized as a classic of North American history when it was republished twenty years later as *The Empire of the St. Lawrence.* Each of its successors has been warmly praised for a characteristic combination of density of fact with stylistic grace and great readability. The critical superlatives seem to have fallen most thickly upon Creighton's two-volume biography of John A. Macdonald, Canada's first prime minister. Canadian reviewers called it "an intensely intimate, moving and exciting story," "the greatest biography of a Canadian ever written," and "the greatest biography ever written by any Canadian." Foreign critics were scarcely less impressed, and one in the *Times Literary Supplement,* who thought that Creighton "exercises an over-generous poetic licence in dealing with natural scenery," concluded that "such momentary descents into the florid cannot detract from the power and scholarship of this absorbing narrative."

W. A. Mackintosh, presenting the Tyrrell Medal of the Royal Society of Canada to Creighton in 1951, summarized his achievement thus: "It is the contribution of his generation of historians to have righted the balance in this country between the older constitutional and political history and the newer economic and social history and to have achieved a new and significant synthesis. In this achievement, he has a notable share. It is the particular personal contribution of Mr. Creighton that by his sound research, his creative imagination, and his graceful and forceful prose he has made the development of Canada a chapter in history absorbing and significant in itself and as full of meaning for the understanding of our contemporary world. *The Commercial Empire of the St. Lawrence,* his report on *British North America at Confederation,* and *Dominion of the North* are books which will always hold a distinguished place in any library of Canadian history and many of the interpretations set forth in them have already become part of the common stock of Canadian thought."

Creighton received his B.A. from the University of Toronto in 1925 and a B.A. (1927) and M.A.

DONALD GRANT CREIGHTON

(1929) from Oxford. He joined the Toronto faculty in 1927 and became a full professor there in 1945, University Professor in 1967. He holds honorary degrees from a dozen Canadian universities and has received a number of foundation fellowships. He has twice been awarded the Governor-General's Medal for Academic Non-fiction (1952 and 1955), and received the University of British Columbia's Medal for Biography in 1955, and the University of Alberta's National Award in Letters in 1957. He has been a fellow of the Royal Society of Canada since 1946 and in 1956–1957 was president of the Canadian Historical Association. He was named a Companion of the Order of Canada in 1967. Creighton was married in 1926 to Luella Sanders Browning Bruce and has a son and a daughter.

PRINCIPAL WORKS: The Commercial Empire of the St. Lawrence, 1760–1850, 1937 (republished as The Empire of the St. Lawrence, 1956); Dominion of the North: A History of Canada, 1944 (U.S., revised and enlarged ed., A History of Canada: Dominion of the North, 1958); John A. Macdonald: The Young Politician, 1953; John A. Macdonald: The Old Chieftain, 1955; Harold Adams Innis: Portrait of A Scholar, 1957; The Story of Canada, 1959; The Road to Confederation: The Emergence of Canada, 1863–1867, 1964; Canada's First Century, 1867–1967, 1970.

ABOUT: Royal Society of Canada Proceedings and Transactions, 1951; Who's Who, 1971.

"CRISPIN, EDMUND" (pseudonym of Robert Bruce Montgomery) (October 2, 1921–), English detective-story writer and anthologist, writes: "My real name is Robert Bruce Montgomery, and under the name of Bruce Montgomery I've done all my musical work—compos-

EDMUND CRISPIN

ing, mostly. My mother was Scottish and my father an Ulsterman; I myself was born in England. My upbringing was in the twenties and thirties, conventionally middle-class, and I look back on it with pleasure and gratitude. The middle-class standards demonstrated to me then still seem to me worth serious consideration. They were kindness, politeness, strictness in money matters, conscientiousness in work, marital fidelity and a regular (in all senses) life. Religion was there too, but was an option—i.e., up to the age of fourteen or so some small acquaintance with it was obligatory, but after that one was left to choose for oneself. Since children are at their happiest when bombinating inside a framework of unoppressive but definite rules and conventions, I was happy, and although I have often failed to live up to those *bourgeois* standards, I've always regretted my failures. For all its limitations, decent *bourgeoisisme* seems to me not at all a bad or unreasonable code to live by—or to write by, either.

"The start of my writing and composing was, I think, a matter of compensating for the lameness which at school (Merchant Taylors') prevented me from taking part in games and athletics. Overdoing it, I became a prig and an intellectual snob. At Oxford, however, these dislikeable characteristics were to some extent modified when I met various fellow undergraduates whose minds seemed to me much better than my own: just in my own College, for example, there were Kingsley Amis, Philip Larkin, Alan Ross and John Wain. In that sceptical generation, with its distaste for pretentiousness and humbug, I found many of my best friends, losing at least some of my own pretentiousness and humbug in the process. And after twenty years we are still, I think, to some extent a homogeneous group, as strict now about leaving the capitals off the words Creative Artist as we were then.

"Where writing was concerned, my own line was lightweight, almost all of it detective fiction: up to now the score is eight novels, fifty short stories, four radio scripts, two film scripts, eleven anthologies (science fiction, mostly) and the usual oddments. The anthologies apart, most of this work was done between the ages of twenty and thirty. I then veered over to composing, the chief part of this, quantitatively but not only quantitatively, being background music for some fifty films. Now, however, I'm getting back to writing again.

"Much contemporary fiction seems to me too predictable—too modish, in fact—and I wish that everyone, myself included, could write more recklessly, more variously, more anachronistically even; in any event, a good deal less self-consciously: 'more matter with less art.' But this is perhaps a reader's opinion, rather than a writer's. And even if it isn't, I still have half a ton of beams to get out of my own eye before I can excusably start censuring the motes in other people's."

"Edmund Crispin" is the son of Robert Ernest Montgomery, an official in the Indian Civil Service, and of the former Marion Jarvie. He is descended from "various Earls of Arundel, Shrewsbury, and Eglinton." A "timid, lazy, daydreaming child with nice manners," he was brought up with his older sisters at Chesham Bois, in Buckinghamshire, and educated at the Merchant Taylors' School. From there a modern languages scholarship took him to St. John's College, Oxford, where in due course he became president of the University Music Club and conductor and organist to its choir, pianist to the University Ballet Club, and organist and choirmaster to his college.

The poet Philip Larkin has described this austere wartime Oxford and his friendship there with Bruce Montgomery, who at first overawed him: "He had a grand piano; he had written a book called *Romanticism and the World Crisis*, painted a picture that was hanging on the wall of his sitting room, and was a skilled pianist, organist and even composer. . . . Beneath this formidable exterior, however, Bruce had unsuspected depths of frivolity, and we were soon spending most of our time together swaying about with laughter on our bar stools."

In 1943, encouraged by another friend, the novelist Charles Williams, Montgomery spent two weeks of his Easter vacation writing, "with his J nib and silver pen-holder," a detective story called *The Case of the Gilded Fly*. It was published the following year under the pseudonym "Edmund Crispin" and reached the United States in 1945 as

Obsequies at Oxford. The reviewers welcomed a promising new talent in the urbane tradition of Michael Innes and, though some found Crispin's literary allusions rather recondite and overwhelming, most thought the book lively and amusing.

The Case of the Gilded Fly introduced, as its brilliant and agreeably eccentric amateur investigator, an Oxford don named Gervase Fen (who also writes detective stories in his spare time). Fen reappears in each of Crispin's subsequent novels, usually investigating mysterious crimes involving his personal friends. In *Love Lies Bleeding*, for example, the setting is a public school, and the plot turns on the discovery of a "lost" Shakespeare play. Reviewers found the setting nicely observed and commended "some pleasant wit, great talent for bringing interesting characters vividly to life, a good plot with an exciting climax."

A. E. Murch has said that Crispin is "as devoted as Michael Innes to the polysyllabic adjective, the abstruse noun, and whimsical proper names." Some readers find both his style and his social attitudes a little precious, and wince when he attempts to render proletarian characters and their speech patterns, but most agree that, as James Sandoe once wrote, Crispin's "charm and facility . . . make his books, in spite of their fairly striking limitations and flaws, lively and dependable diversions."

Crispin taught from 1943 to 1945 at The Schools, Shrewsbury. Since then he has earned his living as a writer and anthologist, and as a composer—mostly, as he says, of film music, but also of choral works, including the ballad opera *John Barleycorn.* He lives in Devon, is a bachelor, and enjoys conversation, reading, the cinema, and swimming. He is a Conservative and a member of the Church of England. Some years ago he reported that his friends consider him to be "lazy, tolerant, politically apathetic, extravagant over food, drink, books, and cigarettes, good-humoured, garrulous, and very occasionally witty, much attracted by the other sex, terrified of children, a cat-lover, and a person temperamentally requiring a good deal of solitude."

PRINCIPAL WORKS: *Novels*—The Case of the Gilded Fly, 1944 (U.S., Obsequies at Oxford); Holy Disorders, 1945; The Moving Toyshop, 1946; Swan Song (U.S., Dead and Dumb), 1947; Love Lies Bleeding, 1948; Buried for Pleasure, 1948; Frequent Hearses (U.S., Sudden Vengeance), 1950; The Long Divorce, 1951; Beware of the Trains (stories), 1953. *As editor*—Best Detective Stories, 1949 and 1964; Best S. F., 1955, 1956, 1958, 1961, 1963, 1966; Best Tales of Horror, 1962; Best Tales of Terror, 1962 and 1965.

ABOUT: Current Biography, 1949; Larkin, P. *Introduction to* Jill (1964 edition); Murch A. E. Development of the Detective Novel, 1958; Symons, J. The Detective Story in Britain, 1962.

***CROMMELYNCK, FERNAND** (November 19, 1885–), Belgian dramatist writing in French,

FERNAND CROMMELYNCK

was born in Brussels to a Flemish father and a French mother. His father came of a theatrical family, his uncle was a noted Flemish vernacular actor, and Crommelynck himself received a complete stage training at a very early age. His academic schooling on the other hand was sketchy, and indeed he seems to have been largely self-educated. Crommelynck began his career as an actor. His first plays were written while he was still in his early twenties, and three of them had been produced in Belgium with some success before World War I. One of these, *Le Sculpteur de masques* (The Sculptor of Masks), written in 1905, was seen in Paris in 1911 but had no great impact there. It was a one-act verse play which already hinted at Crommelynck's skill in drawing bizarre characters in strange and vaguely ominous settings.

Crommelynck's best play, *Le Cocu magnifique* (The Magnificent Cuckold) was presented in Paris by Lugné-Poë in December 1920, and took France by storm. It is a lyrical farce about a husband who becomes so obsessively uncertain of his devoted wife's fidelity that, finding continued doubt intolerable, he forces her into repeated adulteries. In the pungency of its language, the extravagance of its imagery, and its unpredictable mingling of tragedy and low comedy, the play reminded some critics of the Elizabethan dramatists, others of the bawdy vitality of the Flemish *kermess* or of Crommelynck's contemporary and countryman Michel de Ghelderode.

Le Cocu magnifique quickly took its place in the European repertory, and was widely regarded as "the greatest play Belgian literature has ever produced." Ashley Dukes saw it in 1924 and on the

* crōm′ lank

strength of it placed Crommelynck among the three greatest living dramatists. He said that Crommelynck, "who abandons the plane of realism and seeks for the ludicrous essentials of his situation, escapes at the same time from the urbanity and the lassitude of [his] contemporaries. His *reductio ad absurdum* of the sexual motive imparts a new vigor to the theme. His comedy is cruel and grandiloquent but it is elemental." The play has been repeatedly revived, notably by Georges Marchal in December 1945, and a film version with Jean-Louis Barrault was released in 1946.

The huge success of *Le Cocu magnifique* permitted Crommelynck to abandon acting and become a full-time writer. He went to live at Saint-Cloud, near Paris, in a house that had belonged to Émile Verhaeren and that he and his family shared with the poet's widow. Although he has never quite repeated his first triumph, Crommelynck established himself during the 1920s and 1930s as a major figure in the French theatre.

Les Amants púerils (produced in 1921 but written in 1913), a tragic farce about passion and disillusion, was called a "poetic nightmare," as full-blooded as *Le Cocu magnifique*. *Tripes d'Or* (1926) is a grotesque satire on capitalistic greed which also had much success (particularly in Moscow). *Carine* (1929) is a lyrical piece about a girl who prefers death to the ugliness of reality, and *Chaud et froid* (1934) returns to the themes of cuckoldry and self-delusion. Indeed it can be argued that all of Crommelynck's plays are concerned in one way or another with the tragic and ludicrous disparity between fantasy and reality.

Crommelynck himself has been called a *sculpteur de masques*—"a creator of dramatic masks, outsize and highly colored, rather than of normal dramatic characters." This has seemed a fault to some of his critics, who have also accused him of "carnal obsession," and attacked him for the coarseness as well as the extravagance and artificiality of his language and imagery. His defenders deny that these are faults in a dramatist who is above all a master of atmosphere. The passions of his characters, says D. I. Grossvogel, "are intensified to such an extent that at the final curtain they escape from the physical framework of the drama. . . . It is by this uprooting, by cutting the individual adrift from all reserve, all modesty, all worldly conventions that might conceal a fragment of the true self, that Crommelynck analyses the ravages of an emotion upon the individual possessed." He is, in the opinion of the same critic, a pioneer among those dramatists who have been "able to free the French stage of naturalism by creating a language—as well as a world—of the theater."

During his years in Paris, Crommelynck had sometimes disclaimed his Flemish heritage. However, during the German occupation of France he returned to Brussels as codirector of the Galéries theatre, and was enthusiastically received by his countrymen. He has written relatively little since the war, but his early plays continue to be revived in Paris and to provoke keen reactions. He is also the author of two amusing novels.

PRINCIPAL WORKS IN ENGLISH TRANSLATION: The Magnificent Cuckold *in* Two Great Belgian Plays, 1966.
ABOUT: Grossvogel, D. I. The Self-Conscious Stage in Modern French Drama, 1958; Knowles, D. French Drama of the Inter-War Years, 1918–1939, 1967; Lilar, S. The Belgian Theatre Since 1890, 1950; Seymour-Smith, M. Guide to Modern World Literature, 1973; Smith, H. (ed.) Columbia Dictionary of Modern European Literature, 1947. *Periodicals*—Books Abroad October 1945; Romanic Review December 1954; Theatre Arts September 1932.

CROSSMAN, RICHARD (HOWARD STAFFORD) (December 15, 1907–), English politician and journalist, writer on politics and philosophy, is the son of Sir Charles Crossman, a High Court Judge, and the former Helen Howard. Like his father, he went with a scholarship to Winchester, the most intellectually demanding of England's leading public schools, and from there with another scholarship to New College, Oxford, where (again like his father) he earned first class honors in Greats. In 1931, after studying for a year in Frankfurt and Berlin, he took up a fellowship at New College and tutored there in philosophy and politics until 1937.

During his years as a don, Crossman quickly established a far more than local reputation as a writer and as a Labour party intellectual. His articles began to appear in British journals in the early 1930s, and in 1934, when he became leader of the Labour group on Oxford's City Council, he also published his first book, a volume of essays about Buchmanism. *Plato Today* (1937) gave clearer evidence of Crossman's ability. After a brief introduction to Plato's political ideas, the book goes on to speculate about the likely Platonic reaction to various twentieth century ideologies. Not everyone accepted Crossman's extrapolations, but a majority of his reviewers found the exercise stimulating and witty.

At this point Crossman astounded his colleagues by relinquishing his immensely promising academic career for the dust and heat of practical politics. In 1937 he was an unsuccessful Labour candidate for Parliament in the West Birmingham constituency and the same year he joined the staff of the *New Statesman*, the voice and conscience of the British intellectual left wing. He became Kingsley Martin's assistant editor in 1938 and remained in that post until 1955. In 1938–1940 he was also a part-time lecturer for the Workers' Educational Association and in Oxford's Extra

Mural Studies program. *Government and the Governed* (1939) was a history of political thought since the Renaissance, showing how ideology is molded by the pressure of events. Harold Laski found it a brilliant and attractive essay, and D. W. Brogan delicately noted another Crossman characteristic, "an absence of formal respect for eminent persons."

In World War II, Crossman served first in the Ministry of Information, then in the Foreign Office, for which he directed BBC propaganda broadcasts to Germany. In 1943 he went to Algiers as deputy director of psychological warfare at Allied Headquarters there, and in 1944 returned to similar duties in England.

The Labour landslide of 1945 brought Crossman into Parliament as the member for Coventry East, which he has represented ever since. He quickly made his mark as the leader of an unsuccessful but memorable back-bench crusade against Attlee's domestic and Bevin's foreign policies, seeking among other things the creation of a European alliance as a buffer between the United States and the USSR. In 1946 Crossman became a member of the Anglo-American Palestine Commission, investigating the postwar situation and prospects of what remained of European Jewry. *Palestine Mission* was his "personal record" of the Commission's deliberations, which converted him to a belief that Palestine should be partitioned and one hundred thousand Jews admitted. It seemed to some reviewers a coldly analytical book, explaining the Arab, Jewish, British, and American viewpoints with almost improper objectivity. Other readers recognized that the detachment was hard-won, and found a searching, lucid, and very frank "record of an honest man's tussle with a problem almost insoluble"—"the most illuminating book about Palestine" published for years.

In *The God That Failed*, Crossman assembled a very powerful and significant indictment of communism in the shape of six essays by prominent, articulate, and bitterly disillusioned former Communists: Arthur Koestler, Ignazio Silone, Richard Wright, André Gide, Louis Fischer, and Stephen Spender. In 1955 Crossman caused a mild sensation when he left the *New Statesman* in order to write a regular political column for the mass-circulation *Daily Mirror*—presumably in pursuit of the masses. *Planning for Freedom*, published in the United States as *The Politics of Socialism*, was a volume of essays concerned among other things with the long process of "re-thinking socialism" which took place between Labour's fall from power in 1951 and its return to government in 1964.

Crossman has spoken ruefully of his reputation as an intellectual, "the kiss of death for a Labour politician in Britain today." His willingness to

RICHARD CROSSMAN

change his mind when an opposing argument seems to him convincing has blurred his public image and has been interpreted variously as evidence of scrupulous integrity and of "Double-Crossmanship." He is probably, as he has been called, "the last nineteenth-century Liberal left in the House of Commons." At any rate, his career gathered momentum after Labour came to power in 1964, and he served in Harold Wilson's government successively as Minister of Housing (1964–1966) and as Leader of the House of Commons (1966–1968), in 1968 becoming Secretary of State for Social Services. When the Labour government was ousted in 1970, Crossman returned to the *New Statesman* as editor. He resigned in March 1972 when the board of the magazine found his "preoccupation with Westminster politics" excessive; the board also referred to "his age, his health, [and] his manner, which some of the staff found hectoring."

A tall man, powerfully built, bespectacled, and untidy, Crossman was married in 1954 to Anne McDougall and has a son and a daughter. He served on the Labour party Executive from 1952 to 1967.

PRINCIPAL WORKS: (ed.) Oxford and the Groups: The Influence of the Groups Considered by G. F. Allen (and others), 1934; Plato Today, 1937; (with N. M. H. Mitchison) Socrates, 1937; Government and the Governed: A History of Political Ideas and Political Practice, 1939; Palestine Mission: A Personal Record, 1947; (ed.) The God That Failed, 1950; (ed.) New Fabian Essays, 1952; The Charm of Politics, and Other Essays in Political Criticism, 1958; A Nation Reborn: A Personal Report on the Roles Played by Weizmann, Bevin and Ben-Gurion in the Story of Israel, 1960; Planning for Freedom, 1965 (U.S., The Politics of Socialism); Inside View: Three Lectures on Prime Ministerial Government, 1972.

ABOUT: Current Biography, 1947; Who's Who, 1971. *Periodicals*—New Republic December 16, 1946; November 22, 1954; New Statesman September 10, 1960; Newsweek May 26, 1947; New York Herald Tribune Weekly Book Review April 6, 1947; New York Review of Books June 9, 1966; Saturday Evening Post January 3, 1948; Spectator October 7, 1955; Times Literary Supplement June 7, 1947; October 7, 1960; Twentieth Century July 1952.

CUNNINGHAM, J(AMES) V(INCENT) (August 23, 1911–), American poet and scholar, writes: "J. V. Cunningham was born in Cumberland, Maryland. He grew up in Billings, Montana, and Denver, Colorado, where he graduated from a Jesuit high school in 1927. Subsequently, he spent one semester in 1928 at St. Mary's College, St. Mary's, Kansas, and worked for a number of companies in Denver. In 1930 and 1931 he traveled through the Southwest, writing articles for trade journals. Through the kindness of Yvor Winters he was enabled to come to California, where he entered Stanford University in 1932. He received the bachelor's degree from Stanford in 1934, and the doctorate in 1945. From 1934 to 1937 he was a teaching assistant in English at Stanford, from 1937 to 1945 an instructor. He was assistant professor of English at the University of Hawaii, 1945–1946; at the University of Chicago, 1946–1952; at the University of Virginia, 1952–1953. He came to Brandeis University in 1953 and is now the Paul E. Prosswimmer Professor of English. He has been at various times chairman of the department of English and of the council of the school of humanities at Brandeis. He has been a visiting professor at Harvard University (1952), the University of Washington (1956), Indiana University School of Letters (1961), and the University of California, Santa Barbara (1963). He was a Guggenheim Fellow in 1959–1960.

"He is married to Jessie Campbell Cunningham and lives in Sudbury, Massachusetts. He has one daughter, Mrs. Marjorie Ann Lupin of Highland Falls, New York, and four grandchildren."

Cunningham's parents were James Joseph and Anna (Finan) Cunningham. From his Irish Catholic background he has retained, according to G. E. Powell, "the habit of solving personal problems through the traditional categories of Thomistic psychology." At Stanford University he at first studied the classics, switching to English literature for his doctorate. His dissertation served as the basis for his book *Woe or Wonder: The Emotional Effect of Shakespearean Tragedy*. He spent most of the war years teaching mathematics at an Air Force base in Southern California.

During his years at Stanford as a student, teaching assistant, and instructor, Cunningham was a member of the literary group which centered around the poet and critic Yvor Winters. There is much evidence of their mutual influence. Cunningham, who in his early work had pursued "modern feeling . . . shadows and blunted light," had by the early 1940s abandoned this romantic mode and turned to his present epigrammatic style.

J. V. CUNNINGHAM

This at first attracted little attention, though there were always a few critics, including Winters, who recognized the quality of Cunningham's work and considered him a major poet. This view gained greater currency with the publication in 1960 of *The Exclusions of a Rhyme*, collecting all of Cunningham's verse and including some translations from the Latin. Donald Justice said that he was "within his limits, the most expert craftsman we have today"; Thom Gunn that he must be "one of the most accomplished poets alive, and one of the few of whom it can be said that he will still be worth reading in fifty years' time." A reviewer in the *Times Literary Supplement*, noting that Cunningham's gift is essentially epigrammatic, wrote: "His epigrams are sometimes uncannily like Ben Jonson's, not only in their weightiness but in their frank coarseness. Sometimes he seems frigidly formal, sometimes almost repellently harsh. But the central attitude . . . is . . . crystallinely coherent. And the reader who wishes to dismiss Mr. Cunningham's volume as primarily an exercise in scholarly *pastiche* will be puzzled at the difficulty of finding an unsatisfactory poem in it."

Cunningham has constantly analyzed his own work, as in *The Quest of the Opal* and *The Journal of John Cardan*. In his preface to *The Exclusions of a Rhyme*, he wrote: "I have no special way of seeing.

I think of poetry as a way of speaking, a special way of speaking. As a poet I speak in meter, and sometimes in rhyme; I speak in lines. . . . A poem . . . on this view is metrical speech, and a good poem is the definitive statement in meter of something worth saying." Cunningham is "committed by temperament and habit" to brevity, but he has experimented with ways in which his short poems can be provided with "context, reference, and resonance"—extending them in narrative sequence in *To What Strangers? What Welcome?* and, in *The Quest of the Opal*, surrounding a group of them (from *The Helmsman*) with prose commentary and paraphrase. According to Donald Justice, Cunningham's characteristic meter is the iambic, his characteristic stanza form the difficult dimeter quatrain.

In 1961 Yvor Winters described Cunningham as "the most consistently distinguished poet writing in English today, and one of the finest in the language." His principal limitation, Winters thought, was his tendency to exclude "sensory detail," to draw "abstraction from the experience" and discard the experience itself: "All in due time: love will emerge from hate, / And the due deference of truth from lies. / If not quite all things come to those who wait / They will not need them: in due time one dies." Grosvenor E. Powell suggested in *Poets in Progress* that Cunningham's achievement "has been that of knowing where he is. The value of this poetry lies in its total honesty to the experience it describes. The mind builds within itself heaven and hell: 'I am the idea that informs my experience.' In arriving at this position, and in exploring beyond it, Cunningham has written some very great poems."

PRINCIPAL WORKS: The Helmsman, 1942; The Judge Is Fury, 1947; Doctor Drink, 1950; The Quest of the Opal, 1950; Woe or Wonder: The Emotional Effect of Shakespearean Tragedy, 1951; The Exclusions of a Rhyme, 1960; Tradition and Poetic Structure, 1960; To What Strangers? What Welcome?, 1964; The Journal of John Cardan, 1964; The Resurgent Neighborhood, 1965; (ed.) The Renaissance in England, 1966; (ed.) The Problem of Style, 1966; Some Salt, 1967; Collected Poems and Epigrams, 1971.

ABOUT: Contemporary Authors 1, 1963; Donoghue, D. Connoisseurs of Chaos, 1965; Powell, G. E. The Poetry of J. V. Cunningham *in* Hungerford, E. B. (ed.) Poets in Progress, 1962; Who's Who in America, 1970–1971. *Periodicals*—Arizona Quarterly Summer 1950; Commonweal May 14, 1965; Poetry October 1947, December 1960, January 1965; Twentieth Century Literature April 1960; Yale Review Autumn 1960.

CURNOW, (THOMAS) ALLEN (MONRO) (June 17, 1911–), New Zealand poet, editor, and critic, was born at Timaru, the son of Tremayne Curnow, a clergyman in the Anglican church who also wrote poetry. His mother was born in England, but on his father's side his New Zealand ancestry

ALLEN CURNOW

goes back to a great-grandfather born in North Auckland early in the nineteenth century. Curnow was educated at Christchurch Boys' High School and at the universities of Canterbury and Auckland. From 1931 to 1934 he studied for the Anglican ministry at St. John's College, Auckland, but he decided against the church and began his career as a journalist, working from 1935 to 1948 for the Christchurch *Press* and then for a year in London on the *News Chronicle*. After a stay of some months in the United States in 1950—the first of several visits to America—he returned to New Zealand and joined the faculty of Auckland University as a lecturer in English, becoming a senior lecturer in 1955 and an associate professor in 1967.

As he has said, he had "for so many years two vastly different kinds of employment (from night sub-editing to university teaching)" that his original writing has always been a spare-time occupation. He has emerged nevertheless as one of the most prolific and versatile of those New Zealand poets who had their start in the left-wing magazine *Phoenix* in the early 1930s. He has never allowed himself the luxury of waiting for inspiration, but is a dedicated and highly professional craftsman, who has worked his way through a long apprenticeship to his present high position among the best of his country's poets.

His early books, as he himself has pointed out, are strongly derivative. *Valley of Decision* echoes (rather weakly) the self-lacerating gloom of R. A. K. Mason's early work; and the satirical attacks on the banality and materialism of New Zealand life in *Enemies* reflect his association with Denis Glover. A more personal voice was heard in

Not in Narrow Seas, a poetic sequence with prose commentary which is not less critical of New Zealand than *Enemies,* but more thoughtfully so. Curnow, writes E. H. McCormick, "had found in the New Zealand past a theme worthy of his maturing talent . . . [and] now wrote of a lost or mis-shapen destiny, of a petty race in sublime surroundings." His country's past has become a continuing preoccupation in Curnow's poetry, and very often he will approach the theme through some scrupulously observed New Zealand scene, which then "becomes the vehicle for often intricate reflections on mutability and memory and human transience." A notable example is the title poem in *At Dead Low Water.*

Fifty of Curnow's best poems, showing how his work has developed over the years, were collected in *The Small Room With Large Windows* (1962). The "small room" is New Zealand, from which Curnow views the world; it is also more largely the human mind, from which man peers out to apprehend the landscape of experience. The poet and critic C. K. Stead called this book "the most impressive single collection yet put out by a New Zealander," and found in it "a preoccupation with a conflict between Imagination, which comprehends, encompasses and reconciles, and the Rational Will, which creates or destroys blindly, and which understands only by exclusion and simplification." Stead has called Curnow a traditional poet whose verse "has already achieved the fullness and coherence of a major work," and who has "earned his place in the tradition by studying that which is central, and therefore permanent and unchanging, in human life." Other reviewers were equally impressed by Curnow's technical subtlety and vivid imagery, and the "superbly moulded shapes" of his more recent poems, but complained of "the confusion within"—a lack of lucidity arising from disorder in the engendering thought. A writer in the *Times Literary Supplement* found this weakness particularly regrettable because "in plenitude of response and variety of technique Mr. Curnow is eminent among New Zealand poets and there are few poets writing in English today who surpass him as an artist."

Curnow has also experimented with verse drama. *The Axe,* staged at Canterbury College in 1948 and adapted for radio in 1961, depicts the collapse of Maori culture on Mangaia, one of the Cook Islands, under the impact of Christianity early in the nineteenth century. It lacks dramatic cohesion and the dialogue was thought inadequate, but the play remains an original and interesting piece of work, and its Eliot-like choruses include some of Curnow's most memorable verse. Three more radio plays have followed.

In his criticism as in his poetry, Curnow places content above form, life above art, and looks for "the common experience of which the poems he values are the visible record." His *Book of New Zealand Verse, 1923–1945* is of the first importance, bringing together a great deal of work previously scattered in ephemeral magazines and pamphlets and making it possible for the first time "to appreciate the range and quality of the poetry written in the previous twenty years." Curnow's introduction to this anthology and to his later *Penguin Book of New Zealand Verse* stand together, it has been said, "as the most substantial critical account of [New Zealand] poetry so far written."

Allen Curnow was married in 1936 to Elizabeth J. Le Cren, by whom he has two sons and a daughter, and is now married to Jenifer Tole. He has received grants from the New Zealand State Literary Fund, the Carnegie Endowment, and the British Council, and had a Fulbright Travel Award in 1961.

PRINCIPAL WORKS: *Poems*—Valley of Decision, 1933; Enemies: Poems 1934–1936, 1937; Not in Narrow Seas: Poems, with Prose, 1939; Island and Time, 1941; Sailing or Drowning, 1943; Jack Without Magic, 1946; At Dead Low Water, and Sonnets, 1949; Poems, 1947–1957, 1957; A Small Room with Large Windows: Selected Poems, 1962. *Plays*—The Axe: A Verse Tragedy, 1949. *As editor*—A Book of New Zealand Verse, 1923–1945, 1945; The Penguin Book of New Zealand Verse, 1960.

ABOUT: Baxter, J. K. The Fire and the Anvil, 1955; McCormick, E. H. New Zealand Literature, 1959; Murphy, R. (ed.) Contemporary Poets of the English Language, 1970; Reid, J. C. Creative Writing in New Zealand, 1946; Who's Who in New Zealand, 1968. *Periodicals*—Landfall March 1960, March 1963.

***CURTIUS, ERNST ROBERT** (April 14, 1886–April 19, 1956), German scholar, critic, and philologist, was born at Thann, Alsace, and received his early education at the Protestant Gymnasium in Strasbourg. He went on to study at the universities of Berlin and Heidelberg. With three Strasbourg friends—Albert Schweitzer, Ernst Stadler, and Kurt Singer—he early developed a lifelong interest in French history and culture. In 1913, he began his teaching career at Bonn University, where he became a professor in 1919. In 1920, after a period at the Front in World War I, he went to a professorship at Marburg University, and in 1924 to another at Heidelberg.

Early in his career, Curtius dedicated himself to the task of bringing together scholars and humanitarians from all countries. His central field of studies was the Romance languages and literatures, and after the divisive cataclysm of World War I he began his self-appointed task with *Die literarischen Wegbereiter des neuen Frankreich* (1919)—an attempt "to make modern France understood in Germany through studies of Rolland, Gide, Claudel, Péguy." Three separate studies—of Barrès, of Balzac and

* kur′ tyo͞os

Proust, and of Valéry and Larbaud—followed between 1922 and 1925. Much of his time during the next five years was spent in an exhaustive investigation of French culture which resulted in *Einführung in die französische Kultur* (1930, translated as *The Civilization of France*).

Curtius, like T. S. Eliot, regarded all cultures as parts of one vast culture, and now turned to the literature of the English language. A study of Eliot was published in 1927 together with Curtius's translation of *The Waste Land* (still said to be in many respects the most faithful German version). His book on Joyce followed in 1929. In that year he accepted the coveted chair of Romance Literature and Language at Bonn University, where he remained until 1951. His studies of twenty-five years, including essays on Virgil, Goethe, Unamuno, Eliot, and Toynbee (a characteristically wide range), were collected in *Kritische Essays zur europäischen Literatur* (1950, translated by Michael Kowal as *Essays in European Literature*).

In 1932 Curtius attacked what he called "the barbarization of education and the nationalistic frenzy which were the forerunners of the Nazi regime" in a polemical pamphlet, *Deutscher Geist in Gefahr.* He spent the next fifteen years in a study of the Latin literature of the Middle Ages. This was his reaction to the "intellectual chaos" of Nazism—an affirmation of faith in the ultimate authority of human reason which bore fruit in his monumental *Europäische Literatur und lateinisches Mittelalter* (1948). This, his most important work, was translated by Willard Trask and published in 1953 as *European Literature and the Latin Middle Ages.* His intention was to demonstrate the unity of Western culture, tracing the exact nature of the debt owed by the Middle Ages to classical Latin literature, and showing that all modern European literature is still securely based on classical foundations.

Ernst Robert Curtius believed that "the accidental truths of fact can only be established by philology. Philology is the handmaid of the historical disciplines." In his masterpiece he supported this thesis not only through his sweeping studies of different European literatures—he was at home in seven languages—but also through a wealth of detailed insights. He pointed out for example that "All the world's a stage . . ." is a close translation of the Latin motto above the door of Shakespeare's Globe Theatre: "*Totus mundus agit histrionem*"—itself a quotation from a work written by John of Salisbury in 1159. A trick of versification in Calderón (1600–1681) was shown to have a common form with the work of the Carolingian Walafrid Strabo (808–849). *European Literature and the Latin Middle Ages* has been said to reflect the influence of Edward Kenneth Rand's *Founders of the Middle Ages* and of Jung's psychology, but it is a work unique in its sweep and scope, surveying its vast subject with something of the revelatory effect of an aerial photograph, and with a nobility of tone and vision that proceeds from its fundamentally humanitarian aims. Curtius, who had honorary doctorates from the Sorbonne and from the University of Glasgow, died in Rome in 1956.

ERNST ROBERT CURTIUS

PRINCIPAL WORKS IN ENGLISH TRANSLATION: The Civilization of France, 1932; European Literature and the Latin Middle Ages, 1953; Essays in European Literature 1973.

ABOUT: Dizionario Universale della Letteratura Contemporanea, 1959; Handbuch der Deutschen Gegenwartzliteratur, 1965. *Periodicals*—Cambridge Journal September 1950, May 1951; German Life and Letters July 1966; Times Literary Supplement December 4, 1953.

DAHL, ROALD (September 13, 1916–), British short story and screen writer, was born in Llandaff, South Wales. His father was Harald Dahl, who had left the family farm near Oslo in his teens and built a new life and a successful business as a shipbroker in Wales. His mother, also Norwegian, was the former Sofie Hesselberg, daughter of a noted meteorologist and Greek scholar. Harald Dahl died of pneumonia when Roald was four years old, leaving four girls and two boys to be educated. However, Dahl has written, "there was always enough money for good private education and there were good-sized houses to live in and large gardens—in the countryside of South Wales until I was nine, then in the countryside of Kent, both beautiful. We are a very close family." Roald Dahl was educated at Repton, in Derbyshire, where he excelled at sports. He left school at sixteen and joined an expedition which explored Newfoundland.

ROALD DAHL

Unattracted by the idea of a university education, Dahl joined the Shell Oil Company of East Africa in 1932 and after a training period was stationed at Dar es Salaam in Tanganyika (now Tanzania). He was still there in 1939 when World War II began, and he drove a thousand miles to Nairobi to volunteer for the Royal Air Force. Dahl became a fighter pilot. He was seriously wounded over the Libyan desert and was hospitalized for four months. He caught up with his squadron in Greece in time to be driven out again by the advancing Germans, escaped by air, and went on to fly against Vichy forces in Syria.

In 1942 Dahl was invalided home and from there posted to Washington as assistant air attaché to the British Embassy. He began his writing career when the novelist C. S. Forester asked him for an account of his most exciting RAF experience and sent the result to the *Saturday Evening Post*, which published it. A number of other magazine stories followed, as did the Walt Disney film script published in 1943 as *The Gremlins*. Dahl, who had meanwhile exchanged his diplomatic posting for one in intelligence work, ended the war with the rank of wing commander.

Over to You, Dahl's first book, contained stories mostly about flyers and flying. Reviewers thought they showed an "original turn of mind and considerable perceptiveness" and that their irony and brevity caught the mood of the young airmen they describe, but the book attracted little attention. *Sometime Never*, which followed, was a fantasy about a world taken over by the gremlins and fifinellas, the mythical goblins blamed by RAF pilots for inexplicable mishaps. Its critical reception was generally chilly.

Dahl's reputation was established by his third book, *Someone Like You*, collecting stories which had originally appeared in the *New Yorker*, *Harper's*, *Collier's*, and elsewhere. These fourteen stories, many of them describing skirmishes in the war between the sexes, are "gamey, and macabre, and satirical by turns." They have in common a terse and vivid style and "a demonic vision reminiscent of Saki," as well as what some readers saw as "morbidity and a certain irresponsible cruelty." Several of them have become familiar anthology pieces, and the book itself was enlarged and republished in 1961. *Kiss, Kiss* was another and almost universally admired collection of stories in which Dahl's "macabre realism stretches the intellectual nerve almost beyond bearing."

Roald Dahl owes part of his large American following to his CBS-TV series *Way Out*. He is also the author of several much-admired cautionary tales for bad children, and of a number of screenplays, including those for Ian Fleming's *You Only Live Twice* and *Chitty-Chitty-Bang-Bang*. *Charlie and the Chocolate Factory*, his second children's book, has been filmed as *Willy Wonka and the Chocolate Factory*. His play, *The Honeys*, about the energetic attempts of two wives to kill their husbands, was staged in New York in 1955 but failed quietly after unfavorable reviews.

Dahl remains best known as a short story writer —one, according to a critic in the *Times Literary Supplement*, who "knows how to steer an unwavering course along the hairline where the gruesome and the comic meet and mingle. He thinks of a story as of a staircase up which the reader is to be lured and finally coaxed into taking that confident last step which, breathtakingly and deliciously, isn't there." Some reviewers of *Kiss, Kiss* saw in his "caricature of human weakness" signs of a "social satirist and moralist at work behind the entertaining fantast." He has been compared to Angus Wilson as well as to Saki and Salvador Dali.

In 1953 Dahl was married to the American actress Patricia Neal. They have had more than their share of tragedy—the death of one child, the nearly fatal accident of another, and then the desperate illness of Patricia Neal herself. Barry Farrell has given in *Pat and Roald* an account of Miss Neal's illness and remarkable recovery—a victory in which her husband played an important part. The Dahls live in a Buckinghamshire village with their four children. The author is six feet six inches tall and has brown hair and gray-blue eyes. According to one interviewer, he has "a serious mien and a gift for anecdote." He speaks Swahili and Norwegian. His recreations include buying antiques, restoring old paintings, and growing species roses. He also likes "drinking wine and all forms of gambling, especially on horses."

PRINCIPAL WORKS: *Fiction*—Over to You, 1946; Sometime Never, 1948; Someone Like You, 1953, expanded edition, 1961; Kiss, Kiss, 1960; The Selected Stories of Roald Dahl, 1968; Twenty-nine Kisses (collected stories from Someone Like You and Kiss, Kiss), 1969. *For children*—James and the Giant Peach, 1961; Charlie and the Chocolate Factory, 1964; The Magic Finger, 1966; Fantastic Mr. Fox, 1970; Charlie and the Great Glass Elevator, 1972.
ABOUT: Farrell, B. Pat and Roald, 1969; Vinson, J. (ed.) Contemporary Novelists, 1972; Who's Who in America, 1972–1973. *Periodicals*—Times Literary Supplement March 31, 1961; Wilson Library Bulletin February 1962.

DANGERFIELD, GEORGE (October 28, 1904–), British-born American historian, writes: "I was born at Newbury, Berkshire, England. My father, George Dangerfield, was born George Bubb—the Bubbs are, or were then, a large Gloucestershire family—but changed his name to Dangerfield, in accordance with the wishes of an aunt of that name, who had sent him to school and to Oxford. He was a priest in the Church of England, and at the time of his death was Rector of Finmere-cum-Mixbury in the Diocese of Oxford. My parents' marriage was a very happy one. My mother's maiden name was Tyrer: her father was a schoolmaster in Cheltenham, Gloucestershire. My paternal grandfather was a Cheltenham lawyer, who died very young: while at Oxford, he won first class honors both in classics and mathematics.

"At the age of seven—such was the custom in those days—I was sent away to a 'prep' school in Wiltshire, where I received a loving and fine education; thence I proceeded to Forest School, Walthamstow, Essex, where I was most unhappy; thence to Hertford College, Oxford. Here I took two years of Latin and Greek, and two years of English language and literature, graduating in 1927. After that I taught English at Prague and at Hamburg, but seeing no future whatsoever in this kind of endeavor, I emigrated to the United States in January 1930. In New York, I was lucky enough to get a job with the publishing house of Brewer, Warren & Putnam; and when this concern collapsed—chiefly because of the prevailing hard times—I joined the staff of *Vanity Fair*, then under the editorship of that entirely charming and remarkable man, Frank Crowninshield. *Vanity Fair's* circulation was steadily increasing, but its advertising revenue just as steadily diminished: under these fatal circumstances it had no choice but to go the way of all flesh. Nobody regretted its death more than its assistant editors, who had enjoyed themselves enormously. After that I took to lecturing as a chief means of livelihood.

"In 1942 I was inducted into the army; and in 1943, I became an American citizen, while serving with the 102d Infantry Division. I remained with the Division, in America and Germany, until my discharge in the fall of 1945.

GEORGE DANGERFIELD

"Since then, my life has been lived between New York and California, and has been spent in writing of various kinds, chiefly historical. I have been married twice: (1) to Helen Mary Deey Spedding, who died in 1935; (2) to Mary Louise Schott, by whom I have three children. We now live in Santa Barbara.

"I cannot remember *not* wanting to be a writer; but the kind of writer I really wanted to be was a poet. I continued to want to be a poet until I was twenty-five or so. I had then published two poems, one in Paris and one in New York. They were not good poems, and it was probably seeing them in print that decided me to give up poetry as a vocation. The writing of poetry, however, is extremely hard work; and I feel that I owe a good deal to that discipline. As a prose writer, I am sure that I should be grateful for an early training in the classics: indeed I cannot help thinking, rightly or wrongly, that for such prose style as I have I am especially indebted to a youthful fascination for Cicero. All writers, I believe, must serve an apprenticeship also to some contemporary: and I acknowledge, with gratitude, the influence of Lytton Strachey.

"I got my start as a writer of books through George Palmer Putnam, one of the partners in Brewer, Warren & Putnam, who asked me to do something on the Indian Mutiny. I wrote a little book after the minimum of research and at some speed. It was a grisly book; I succeeded in horrifying myself while working on it; and, once it was published, I was never able to open it again. But it had one good result; it received a devastating review in a New York newspaper, in which I was accused of social irresponsibility. I thought this review had great force and justice; and I was determined never, if possible, to incur such a rebuke again.

"From that time onward, I found my imagination becoming more and more engaged with the writing of history. Two of my books, *The Strange Death of Liberal England* (1935) and *The Era of Good Feelings* (1952), one dealing with the collapse of Liberalism in 1910–1914, the other with the administration of James Monroe and John Quincy Adams, illustrate the kind of approach that has most moved me. That is to say, I started on each venture without having the least idea of what I was going to find; and in each case my interpretation developed as the research proceeded. *The Era of Good Feelings* won the Bancroft Prize and the Pulitzer Prize in American History. Nowadays, I find I must have some kind of a working hypothesis before I can begin at all. That may be the effect of wisdom, or of a respect for methodology: but it is more probably due to advancing age."

Dangerfield's "grisly" first book, *Bengal Mutiny*, pleased most of its reviewers far more than its author. Edward Thompson in *The Spectator* called it vivid, sympathetic, and accurate, "the best popular account of the Mutiny," and this opinion was very nearly unanimous. *The Strange Death of Liberal England*, centering on the four years between the death of Edward VII and the beginning of World War I, concluded that by the end of 1913 "true pre-war Liberalism . . . was killed, or it killed itself." This thesis was not accepted by all of the book's reviewers but most, like William MacDonald, enjoyed Dangerfield's "jaunty manner and sparkling style . . . his unforgettable pictures of stirring episodes." The portrait of the young Edward VII in *Victoria's Heir* impressed most critics with a lucidity and a sardonic wit reminiscent of Dangerfield's master, Lytton Strachey.

Since World War II the author has turned his attention to American history, most notably in his much honored study *The Era of Good Feelings*. It is "essentially a description of some of the personalities and experiences, American and European, which assisted in or were necessary to the political transition from Jeffersonian democracy to Jacksonian democracy"—that is, from 1817 to 1829. It seemed to Richard Hofstadter "one of the solidest works of historical writing in years . . . a general synthesis of the history of the period that is almost certain to endure as a standard work." J. H. Powell found it "full of people, conflicts, ideas, and color" and wrote: "It is a learned book, and witty and skillful; on every page it is thoughtful, clever, and original." Dangerfield re-examined the same period in *The Awakening of American Nationalism*, a volume in the New American Nation series which was as warmly praised as its predecessor.

History, Dangerfield once said, "is a combination of taste, imagination, science, and scholarship; it reconciles incompatibles, it balances probabilities; and at last it attains the reality of fiction, which is the highest reality of all." The writer is a handsome man, tall and blue-eyed. He is a Democrat and enjoys reading and spectator sports. Since 1968 he has been a lecturer in history at the University of California at Santa Barbara.

PRINCIPAL WORKS: Bengal Mutiny: The Story of the Sepoy Rebellion, 1933; The Strange Death of Liberal England, 1935; Victoria's Heir: The Education of a Prince, 1941; The Era of Good Feelings, 1952; Chancellor Robert R. Livingston of New York, 1746–1813, 1960; The Awakening of American Nationalism, 1815–1828, 1965; Defiance to the Old World (for children), 1970.
ABOUT: Contemporary Authors 9–10, 1964; Current Biography, 1953; Who's Who in America, 1970–1971. *Periodicals*—New York Times April 21, 1953; May 5, 1953.

***DANINOS, PIERRE (CHARLES)** (May 26, 1913–), French novelist, humorist, and journalist, is the son of Maurice and Andrée (Ranovitz) Daninos. He was born in Paris and educated at the Lycée Janson-de-Sailly. Daninos began his career in 1931 as a journalist, and during the next few years he covered tennis tournaments in France, England, and the United States. During the early part of World War II he fought in Flanders and as a liaison officer with a British battalion survived the retreat from Dunkirk. Thereafter he traveled in South America and Mexico, publishing his first novel, *Le Sang des hommes* (The Blood of Men, 1940), in Rio de Janeiro.

Daninos returned to France in 1942 and supported himself by contributing to French and English magazines. A second novel, *Méridiens* (Meridians), appeared in 1945, and a third, *Eurique et Amérope*, in 1946. Neither had much impact and in 1946 Daninos joined the staff of *France-Soir* as feature editor. He went on writing novels in his spare time, however, and had his first critical success with *Les Carnets du Bon Dieu* (The Notebooks of God, 1947), which gained him the Prix Interallié.

It was Major Marmaduke Thompson who brought Daninos real financial, popular, and critical success. The Major, invented by Daninos during the 1940s, is a red-faced caricature of a retired British Army officer who has married a Frenchwoman and settled in her country. He is thus in a position to compare the French temperament, and the society it has produced, with their equally peculiar English counterparts. His essays, first appearing in *Le Figaro*, were so much enjoyed that a collection of them in book form was published in 1954 as

*da nē nôs′

Carnets du Major Thompson (translated the following year as *The Notebooks of Major Thompson*). It was a selection of book clubs in both France and England and became a global best seller. A sequel presenting the Major's reflections during visits to England and the United States was called *Secret du Major Thompson* (1956). By 1957 Daninos was able to resign from *France-Soir* and devote himself full time to his own writing.

Daninos' approach is comparative: "The American pedestrian who sees a millionaire going past in a Cadillac dreams secretly of the day when he will be driving it; the French pedestrian . . . dreams of the day when he'll get him out of it and make him walk *comme les autres*." The French critics were delighted, and in his own country Daninos has been compared to André Maurois and even Voltaire. Gilbert Sigaux credits him with the instincts of a moralist and ironist and calls him a "remarkable observer, who draws the everyday lives of men and women of his time with accuracy and humor." English and American critical reactions have been more mixed. Some have praised his "devastating humor," his "barbed malice overlaid with unflinching analysis," but a majority have been more muted in their enthusiasm. There is a feeling that Daninos tends to satirize the clichés rather than the realities of national behavior—that in fact his social comment is out of date.

Daninos has been married twice—to Jeanne Marrain in 1942 and to Marie-Pierrette Dourneau in 1968. For literary purposes, however, he has provided himself with an imaginary wife, Sonia. Daninos' rueful stories of his life with this charming but formidable creature, introduced like Major Thompson in *Le Figaro*, have been collected in three volumes: *L'Éternel Second* (The Eternal Second, 1949); *Sonia, les autres et moi* (Sonia, the Others and I, 1952), winner of the Prix Courteline; and *Comment vivre avec (ou sans) Sonia* (How to Live With [or Without] Sonia, 1953). A selection of these stories appeared in English as *Life With Sonia* in 1958 and was thought moderately amusing but not very original. *Un Certain Monsieur Blot*, a novel about a self-effacing insurance salesman who becomes a celebrity when he is selected as "the average Frenchman," attracted an excellent press in France in 1960, but like its predecessors fared less well with Anglo-Saxon critics when it was translated as *A Certain Monsieur Blot* (1962). The *New Yorker* described it rather ambiguously as a "silly, funny book," while a reviewer in the *Times Literary Supplement* found it "sad, facetious stuff."

Pierre Daninos describes himself as the possessor of brown eyes and black and white hair and says that his favorite recreation is silence. Several of his books have been filmed or dramatized. He has three children by his first marriage.

PIERRE DANINOS

PRINCIPAL WORKS IN ENGLISH TRANSLATION: The Notebooks of Major Thompson, 1955 (England, Major Thompson Lives in France and Discovers the French); The Secret of Major Thompson, 1957 (England, Major Thompson and I); Life with Sonia: or, That's Not How Things Happen to Me, 1958; A Certain Monsieur Blot, 1961; Major Thompson Goes French, 1971.

ABOUT: Boisdeffre, P. de. Dictionnaire de littérature contemporaine, 1900–1962, 1962; International Who's Who, 1970–1971; Who's Who, 1971; Who's Who in France, 1971–1972. *Periodicals*—New York Times Book Review October 27, 1957; Wilson Library Bulletin February 1963.

DAVIDSON, BASIL (RISBRIDGER) (November 9, 1914–), English novelist, journalist, and historian, writes: "My mother, whom I dearly loved, came from a family that was partly northern English and partly southern Scots. She used to say that our Scottish side was related to the family of Robert Louis Stevenson, but I rather think she dreamed this up out of the goodness of her heart when she knew that I meant to be a writer if I could. Her mother had furiously quarrelled with all the relations, so I was never able to find out. My father, Charles Risbridger, died six months after I was born: he came from southern England, but the family quarrelling had severed all connexions on that side too. Altogether we seem to have been a disputatious lot; and when my mother, left with three small children, married again in 1920 it was decided that I, who was the youngest, should take my step-father's name. Thomas Davidson was a southern Scot of dour and passionate nature who could never really get on to terms with life. I can understand him now, which makes a difference, but I still remember him with a mixture of uncer-

BASIL DAVIDSON

tainty and deep dislike. All this gave me a rather solitary and mistrustful childhood that didn't make for happiness. Then came the Great Depression during which I left school at sixteen, and went from one more or less haphazard employment to the next until, finally, I surfaced in London not long before 1939. I'd gone on meaning to be a writer, and I'd written a great deal of which very little, quite rightly, had been published. I took to journalism as the next best thing.

"The war, to put it mildly, was an interruption; I served in the British Army for five and a half years, almost entirely overseas and for nearly three years in enemy-occupied territory, a curious but highly educational experience, and emerged in 1945 as a lieutenant-colonel with the Military Cross and the U.S. Bronze Star. Like millions of others, I had to start all over again. I went to work for the London *Times* in Paris and then in London; but I also published my first book, a volume of war memoirs, and soon after my first novel, a rather obscure and poetical affair for which I reserve some affection. Since then I have written a vast amount of journalism of one kind or another, reportorial and polemical, and have travelled enormously in order to do it; very enjoyable, but enough is enough, and since the late fifties I have been able to give more and more time, helped by some success, to writing books.

"Several of these books have been novels. Others have been about Africa. I began looking at Africa in 1950 and have never since ceased visiting this grand hospitable continent. At first I wrote about contemporary events, trying to reflect the profoundly dramatic stirrings of political renaissance then in movement up and down that colonised mass of land and people. But gradually I saw that this wasn't enough. I found myself driven into thinking about historical Africa. What, after all, had happened before the Europeans came? In 1958 I began writing a series of historical studies which have brought me friends and readers in many languages, not least in the United States. All this has given me much enjoyment and satisfaction, and there are times now when I count myself as someone upon whom the gods have smiled: no doubt they're making up for all those dirty tricks they played me long ago. In 1960 I was given the Anisfield-Wolf Award. In 1964 I was invited to the University of California at Los Angeles as a visiting lecturer. Very pleasant things. I also go on with some journalism because I like it. As to technique, I write very fast but try to compensate for this by an enormous amount of rewriting. I invariably write my books two or three times over. In 1943 I married Marion Ruth Young, in which I was very fortunate. We have three sons, and we live in London. I feel, so far as putting words on paper is concerned, as if I'd only just begun. It's not a bad feeling, as a matter of fact."

Basil Davidson's World War II service with the partisans of both Yugoslavia and Italy brought him many distinctions and a fund of experience on which he drew for his first book, *Partisan Picture*, and his first novel, *Highway Forty*. The latter, "almost an adventure story" about a band of Communist Italian partisans, was said to owe much to the influence of Hemingway. His best-known novel, *The Rapids*, was a "thoughtful, considerate and admirable" book in which, however, character development seemed unduly influenced by the author's hatred of apartheid.

Davidson's characteristic championship of the oppressed is most evident in his historical books about Africa. These opened up a field previously reserved to specialists, demonstrating that the continent nourished highly developed cultures long before the white man came and insisting upon the African's ability to govern himself. The author has been called "more of a publicist than a professional historian," sometimes partial in his arguments. But his research, drawing mostly upon printed sources, is wide ranging and authoritative, and his work is well organized, deftly written, and highly readable.

An outstanding journalist, Davidson is also well known as a broadcaster. A tall, muscular man, he lives with his family in the London suburb of Barnes.

PRINCIPAL WORKS: *Novels*—Highway Forty, 1949; Golden Horn, 1952; The Rapids, 1956; Lindy, 1958 (U.S., Ode to a Young Love); The Andrassy Affair, 1966. *Non-fiction*—Partisan Picture, Yugoslavia 1943–44, 1945; Germany—What Now?, 1950; Report on Southern Africa, 1952; Daybreak in China, 1953; The African

Awakening, 1955; Turkestan Alive: New Travels in Chinese Central Asia, 1957; Old Africa Rediscovered, 1959 (U.S., The Lost Cities of Africa); Black Mother, 1961 (repub. as The African Slave Trade, 1965); Guide to African History, 1963; Which Way Africa?, 1964; (ed.) The African Past: Chronicles from Antiquity to Modern Times, 1964; (with F. K. Buah) The Growth of African Civilization, 1965 (revised as A History of West Africa, 1966); (with eds. of Time-Life Books) African Kingdoms, 1966; Africa: History of a Continent, 1966 (revised as Africa in History, 1968); (with J. E. F. Mhina) A History of East and Central Africa to the Late Nineteenth Century, 1967; The Liberation of Guiné, 1969; The Africans, 1969 (U.S., The African Genius); In the Eye of the Storm: Angola's People, 1972.

ABOUT: Contemporary Authors 1, 1962; Who's Who, 1971. *Periodicals*—Books and Bookmen March 1956; Saturday Review December 9, 1961; Times Literary Supplement February 17, 1956; June 4, 1971.

DONALD DAVIE

DAVIE, DONALD (ALFRED) (July 17, 1922–), English poet and critic, writes: "I was born in Barnsley, Yorkshire, the son of a businessman in a small way in that coal-mining town on the slopes of the Pennines. Absurd as it seems in the case of a country so small as England, I believe there is a real anthropological difference between north and south, and though I have lived for a quarter-century in southern England I think I shall never lose my sense of being in important ways a stranger there. The surprisingly wild and unpeopled stretch of Pennine moorland at my back-door through my boyhood has never ceased, for example, to be very important to me. As the son of a petty-bourgeois in a community of only two classes, petty-bourgeois and proletariat, I have never found a political home in the British two-party system; so far as I can see, if I had not had a strong dose of humanitarianism early on (for instance by way of the nonconformist Christianity I was brought up in), I might have drifted into *poujadisme* or some other semi-Fascist allegiance. As it is, my friends and associates have been predominantly of the Left, and I agree with them on many issues yet seldom with enthusiasm and never without private reservations. This makes me seem apolitical, but it is circumstances not conviction that make me so. And yet this inability to strike roots may go deep, for I have turned out to be a very eclectic person, shifting and swaying not just in political allegiances but among various schools of writing and even among countries as places to live in. It seems to me that I was born short on *esprit de corps*, able to give loyalty and affection to individuals, but not to institutions or groups.

"I served with the Royal Navy from 1941 to 1946, and the best thing this did for me was to send me for eighteen months at a very impressionable age to North Russia. I was already a literary person, for I had been writing poems since I was fourteen if not earlier (my mother, who had been a schoolmistress, was widely read in English poetry), and I had already (1940–41) studied English for a year at Cambridge. So my imaginative involvement with Russian people and Russian landscapes naturally led to voracious reading of Russian literature—an interest which has never left me, though my command of Russian is very imperfect. My Russian interests have broadened so as to comprehend other parts of Eastern Europe; and I have visited Poland and Hungary.

"In 1945 I married Doreen John of Plymouth, and our first son was born the same year. I returned to my studies in Cambridge, and did not leave until 1950, when I had completed my studies for Ph.D. My years in Cambridge I suppose trained me as a critic and less certainly as a scholar. Criticism always came easily to me, and just for that reason, though I dare say I have a better reputation as critic than as poet or scholar, I have never thought that a critic was a particularly fine or important thing to be. I have spent my adult life teaching literature in universities (in Dublin and Cambridge and now in the University of Essex, with briefer periods in California and Iowa), and have suffered in consequence from having the label 'academic' tagged on my poetry. Academicism *is* one of the enemies of literature but nowadays it is the critic-pedagogue, not the scholar, who is the danger. (I believe that the poet and the scholar are natural allies.) In 1964 I turned myself into a university administrator so as to help produce an academic milieu in which the critic shall not be elevated above the creator, nor the two misleadingly lumped together as 'the literary intelligence'; but I shall not continue with this self-sacrifice for more than a few years.

"I am always having revelations about what poetry is, and discarding in my own mind poems I wrote before the latest revelation came. Therefore I will defend the poems I am writing now but not those I wrote in the past. Some people are annoyed to find me changing my mind like this. I admire American poets of this century more than most British ones, and I try to learn from the Americans, and yet I think that in theme and style alike the two traditions are, and should continue to be, distinct."

Donald Davie emerged from the Navy a sub-lieutenant. He was a lecturer in English at Trinity College, Dublin, from 1950 to 1957 (becoming a Fellow of the college in 1954). In 1958, after a visiting professorship at the University of California, he went to Cambridge University as a lecturer in English, and from 1959 to 1964 was a Fellow of Gonville and Caius College, Cambridge, in 1963 visiting the University of Cincinnati, Ohio, to give the George Elliston Lectures. He was professor of literature in the University of Essex in 1964–1968, and pro-vice-chancellor in 1965–1968. After a year as Bing Professor of English and American Literature at the University of Southern California (1968–1969), he became professor of English at Stanford University, California, in 1969. He includes "literary politics" among his recreations.

A thoughtful and sensitive critic, Davie has been credited with helping "to rediscover the eighteenth-century poets" for his generation. He feels acutely the European poet's responsibility to his literary and linguistic inheritance, and is suspicious of the romantic imprecision of postsymbolism. In his first two critical books he advocated an Augustan purity of diction and syntax, and in his richly complex book on Pound emphasized the neoclassical objectivism he found in that poet's work. *Thomas Hardy and British Poetry* explores the thesis that the deliberately limited range, moderate tone, and metrical elaboration of much recent British verse is "part of an inheritance from Hardy, an attempt to work out problems, especially social and political problems, which Hardy's poetry has posed for the twentieth century."

Davie's poetry reflects these concerns and also his brief but "exciting and reassuring" association with "the Movement," that postwar revulsion against the romantic incoherence of some British poetry of the 1940s. His verse has been praised most for its formal elegance, its "lapidary care," its compressed energy. Davie once called himself, ironically, "a pasticheur of late-Augustan styles," and reviewers of his first poems, *Brides of Reason*, agreed. His later work has been less reticent and coldly intellectual, sometimes employing longer lines and looser forms. Bernard Bergonzi believes that in recent years Davie has "succumbed to the strange magnetic attraction that symbolism has for those who attempt to study it in a spirit of detachment," and critics have detected in *Events and Wisdoms* evidence of the unexpected influence of such confessional poets as Robert Lowell. A reviewer of *Essex Poems*, 1963–1967, suggested that Davies' poetic poise "seems maintained against the pressure of an isolation and rootlessness too undermining to be effectively transmuted in the poetry itself," and another critic, discussing the *Collected Poems* (1972), suggested that Davies' candor and "conscious integrity" led him at times into "a defiant bathos, as if to say: It happened so, and so you must take it." Kenneth Allott wrote that the "intelligence and sensibility" of Davie's work "rest on a more equable disposition than most poets are lucky enough to possess," and praised his "eagerness to experiment . . . to enlarge, even at some risk, the boundaries of his art."

PRINCIPAL WORKS: Purity of Diction in English Verse (criticism), 1952; Articulate Energy: An Inquiry into the Syntax of English Poetry, 1955; Brides of Reason (poems), 1955; A Winter Talent (poems), 1957; (ed.) The Late Augustans, 1958; The Forests of Lithuania (adaptation of Mickiewicz's Pan Tadeusz), 1959; New and Selected Poems, 1961; The Heyday of Sir Walter Scott, 1961; A Sequence for Francis Parkman (poems), 1961; The Language of Science and the Language of Literature, 1700–1740, 1963; Ezra Pound: Poet as Sculptor, 1964; Events and Wisdoms (poems), 1964; (trans.) The Poems of Dr. Zhivago, 1965; Essex Poems, 1963–1967, 1969; Six Epistles to Eva Hesse, 1971; Collected Poems, 1950–1970, 1972; Thomas Hardy and British Poetry, 1973.
ABOUT: Allott, K. (ed.) Penguin Book of Contemporary Verse, 1962; Murphy, R. (ed.) Contemporary Poets of the English Language, 1970; Press, J. Rule and Energy, 1963; Rosenthal, M. L. The New Poets, 1967; Thwaite, A. Contemporary English Poetry, 1961; Who's Who, 1971; Who's Who in America, 1970–1971. *Periodicals*—Critical Quarterly Winter 1962; Listener March 1, 1973; New York Times Book Review February 6, 1966; Poetry May 1962; The Review December 1964; Times Literary Supplement November 13, 1969; November 27, 1970; Western Humanities Review Winter 1965.

DAVIES, HUGH SYKES (1909–), English novelist, poet, and critic, has allowed the publication of almost no information about his early life, apart from some unspecific reminiscences in Allen Tate's 1966 symposium on T. S. Eliot. Here Davies speaks of Eliot's influence on his own schoolboy poems which "were, of course, full of desert scenery, red rocks, and rats' feet slithering over broken glass." He went up to St. John's College, Cambridge University, "with a fair stock of verses in this manner." He was a brilliant student and graduated with first class honors in both classics (1930) and English (1931).

During his undergraduate years Davies became a regular visitor to London (being provincial enough, he says, "to believe that there must be a metropolis somewhere, some kind of centre for the world of letters and culture"). He frequented Harold Munro's Poetry Bookshop, where he met Eliot, Herbert Read, and the imagist poet F. S. Flint. When, through what he calls "a curious series of improbable accidents," Davies was elected a Fellow of St. John's in 1933, he was able to return Eliot's hospitality by inviting him to college banquets. Much later they found themselves together in a different place when Davies—to illustrate some remark on Machiavelli—took Eliot to the Oxford-Cambridge Rugby match at Twickenham. A university lecturer as well as a Fellow of his college, Davies has taught English at Cambridge for the better part of forty years, excepting five wartime years in the Ministry of Food. In recent years he has also become well known in England as a broadcaster.

Davies's first book, *Realism in the Drama*, won the Le Bas Essay Prize in 1933 and was soon followed by *Petron*, a long prose poem about a bizarre pilgrimage. It is one of the very few notable products of surrealism in England and has been described by Paul West as a daunting "mixture of Swiftian fantasy and Freudian obsession." Davies went on to publish, either as separate monographs (like his studies of Trollope and De Quincey) or as essays in symposia, a distinguished series of papers on English literature. Of wider popular interest are two books that reflect the pains and delight of a career devoted to the English language and its literature. *Grammar Without Tears*, calling for "a more lively and living English," enjoyed a considerable success on both sides of the Atlantic, while the two-volume anthology *The Poets and Their Critics*—revised from a wartime Pelican "special"—was welcomed as "the sort of reference book that every student will find valuable."

No Man Pursues, about a simple-minded deserter who becomes involved with black marketeers and is eventually killed, was called "a highly literary and pretentious thriller," but there was a warmer reception for Davies's second novel, *Full Fathom Five*, an allegory about a deep-sea diver. Its reviewer in the *Times Literary Supplement* found it "unusual and interesting," and called the diver's final confession, from a wreck on the sea-bed, "a triumphant if tragic close."

The most widely admired of Davies's novels so far is *The Papers of Andrew Melmoth*. Melmoth, a brilliant young scientist studying the genetics of rats, has mysteriously disappeared. A friend (who signs himself "H. S. D."), looking for an explanation, pieces together Melmoth's life story from his diaries and notebooks and the recollections of friends, proceeding rather as A. J. A. Symons did in *The Quest for Corvo*. It emerges that Melmoth's researches in the sewers of London had convinced

HUGH SYKES DAVIES

him that radioactive fallout was affecting the development of the rats—that they were rapidly evolving a civilization while mankind faced a hideous doom. In the end he had opted for the rats and gone down into the sewers to join them. The book was read variously as science fiction, as a terrifying study in the macabre, and as "a striking fable, full of ideas and erudition," about the dangers of atomic testing. "The special grace of the book," wrote a reviewer in the *Times Literary Supplement*, "lies in the quality of the style. It is bare, voluble and beautifully free from extravagance. . . . [Davies] is concerned with moral values and it is to his credit as a novelist that 'message' has not taken precedence of plot and character. The people of the story linger, curiously memorable, when the book is laid aside."

PRINCIPAL WORKS: Realism in the Drama, 1934; Petron, 1935; No Man Pursues, 1950; Grammar Without Tears, 1951; Full Fathom Five, 1956; The Papers of Andrew Melmoth, 1960; The Poets and Their Critics (2 vols.), 1960–1962; Thomas De Quincey, 1964; Anthony Trollope, 1965.

ABOUT: Tate, A. (ed.) T. S. Eliot: The Man and His Work, 1966; Tindall, W. Y. Forces in Modern British Literature, 1956; West, P. The Modern Novel, 1963. *Periodicals*—Eagle May 1965; Library Journal August 1961; Nation September 2, 1961; New Republic October 9, 1961; New Statesman November 5, 1960; New York Times Book Review September 3, 1961; Saturday Review September 30, 1961; Spectator November 11, 1960; Times Literary Supplement November 25, 1960.

DAVIES, (WILLIAM) ROBERTSON (August 28, 1913–), Canadian novelist, dramatist, and critic, writes: "I was born in Thamesville, Ontario, and as my family moved several times I went to

ROBERTSON DAVIES

many schools, ending at Upper Canada College, which in my day was run on lines that would have delighted Dr. Arnold. My mother's family came to Canada in 1796; my father was a latecomer from North Wales, arriving in 1894. He was a newspaperman and a demon grammarian; if any prizes for writing were offered at school, I was expected to take them, and I did.

"It was impossible for me to take a degree at a Canadian university, because I was a fool at mathematics. I did honours B.A. work at Queen's, in Kingston, then went to Oxford (Balliol '36–'38) and got a B.Litt. for Shakespeare studies. I had done a lot of work with the O.U.D.S., so I went on the stage, and worked at the Old Vic as a literary handyman for Tyrone Guthrie, who was director at that time, and as an actor. I played idiots, drunkards, pedants and the fathers of more important characters, principally in Shakespeare.

"My job blew up with the war, but as I had married an Australian girl named Brenda Mathews, who was stage-manager, and as this was one of the great decisive acts of my life, my stage career must be accounted a triumphal success. Several doctors and boards decided that as a soldier I would make a low-grade clerk. (This accorded with the judgement of the only IQ test I ever had, which ranked me as 'one who, in the army, would never rise to the rank of corporal.') So my wife and I returned to Canada, and I became book editor of *Saturday Night*, a political and literary weekly. In 1942 I became editor of the Peterborough *Examiner*, a provincial daily paper, and remained on the job until 1962. During this twenty-year period, as well as writing a good deal of editorial and critical work every day, I wrote eight long plays, a great many short plays, two books of essays, four books of criticism, three novels, and an introduction to Shakespeare for schools. I also did a weekly job as principal book reviewer for *Saturday Night* and later for a newspaper syndicate. This work was done during evenings and at weekends. I do not write this vaingloriously, but only to show that I know what I am talking about when I say that it is possible to write and do another job as well, and that in my case the daily work provided the experience which gave rise to the nightly work.

"My success has been variable. The plays are acted a good deal in Canada, occasionally in the U.S., and now and then abroad, in Norway, Switzerland, Australia and Britain. My most recent play, *Love and Libel*, was produced in 1960 by the Theatre Guild, directed by Tyrone Guthrie, and after a tour went to Broadway, where it expired after five performances. I am still delighted to think that it had a splendid false dawn in Boston, where the critics and the audiences liked it greatly. My novels have been much more successful. All three have appeared in the U.S. and Britain as well as Canada, and have had some translations.

"The label 'humorist' was put on me very early, and has stuck. Naïve people are disappointed when they meet me, because I am not remorselessly funny. I am in fact a very serious man, and am surprised that people should be so deceived by the exuberance and high colour of my writing as to suppose my first and only desire is to make them laugh. I make them laugh in the hope that the exercise will air their heads and persuade them to think and, even more, to feel.

"In 1960 I was asked to be the head of a college for graduate students at the University of Toronto, and overseeing the building and organization of that institution has kept me busy—so busy that my writing has been confined to occasional articles. But I am at work on a novel which will be in a vein markedly different from anything I have done before, and most certainly it will be serious. Which is not, of course, the same as saying that it will be solemn."

Robertson Davies, "the *enfant terrible* of Canadian letters," in fact began his literary career at the age of eight, when he reported a lantern-slide lecture for the *Renfrew Mercury*. His first book was his thesis on Shakespeare's boy actors; the next two collected the opinions of "Samuel Marchbanks," a dyspeptic commentator on the Canadian scene who had made his appearance in the Peterborough *Examiner* and who loathes above all the stifling conformity and hypocrisy of Canadian life. Hugo McPherson, writing in *Canadian Literature* (Spring 1960), has suggested that the central theme in all

Davies's work is "the plight of the imagination" in the "chilly cultural climate" of Canada.

Thus, Davies's first full-length play, *Fortune, My Foe*, turns on the dilemma of a young intellectual who feels that he must emigrate to the United States or abandon his artistic ambitions. The "Canadian problem" is at the core of all of Davies's plays, and it is perhaps for this reason that they have made no great impact abroad. In Canada, however, they are highly esteemed for their craftsmanship and the "comic spirit which pervades them," and some critics regard Robertson Davies as his country's leading playwright.

Davies's international reputation rests mostly on his novels, the first three of which were set in the hide-bound university town of "Salterton" (Kingston), Ontario. *Tempest-Tost*, about the pettiness and infighting which accompany the casting and production of an amateur performance of *The Tempest*, ironically measures the cream of Salterton society against the characters they play. *Leaven of Malice* (later dramatized as *Love and Libel*) is another comedy of Salterton manners, examining the consequences of a spurious engagement announcement.

The most serious criticism made of Davies's plays and novels is that he had seemed unable to create characters who existed in their own right (rather than as mouthpieces for his opinions). This weakness was overcome in *A Mixture of Frailties*, about a working-class Salterton girl born with the capacity to become a great singer. The growth of this delightful heroine, as an artist and as a person, first in Salterton and later in London, symbolizes according to Hugo McPherson the growth to maturity of the Canadian imagination. If this is so, most foreign critics missed the point, but nevertheless welcomed the book with almost unanimous enthusiasm. Edmund Fuller had "never read a better novel about the training and rise of an artist" and Dan Wickenden wrote: "Mr. Davies's wry yet tolerant view of human nature, his dry humor, his ability to enlist the reader's sympathy, is as refreshing in *A Mixture of Frailties* as in *Leaven of Malice*. But he has built, this time, a far more solid and coherent narrative, and one possessing rather more specific gravity. In the happiest sense . . . an old-fashioned novel, comfortable, leisurely, continuously and quietly engrossing."

Davies writes above about a forthcoming novel "in a vein markedly different from anything I have done before." This eventually appeared in 1970 as *Fifth Business*, which describes in the form of a 300-page letter how a snowball, carelessly thrown by the narrator as a small boy in 1908, had changed the course of five lives. The results of this action had included a premature birth, a damaged mind, and lifelong remorse on the part of Dunstable Ramsey, the Canadian schoolmaster who tells the story. His account ranges across sixty years, three continents, and two wars, and embraces a very large cast of characters. Through symbolism and the introduction of what he calls "twice-born" characters, the author is also concerned to deal with the "oddly recurrent themes of history which are also the themes of myth," and with religion as "psychological truth." L. J. Davis called it "a mature, accomplished and altogether remarkable book, one of the best of this or any other season, and it simply cannot be ignored. . . . [It] achieves a richness and depth that are exceptional in a modern novel and rare at any time. On its simplest and most obvious level it is a remarkably colorful tale of ambition, love and weird vengeance. At its deepest, it is a work of theological fiction that approaches Graham Greene at the top of his form." The same concerns are pursued in a sequel, *The Manticore*.

As a reviewer and critic Robertson Davies writes not for academics but for "the clerisy"—those "who love books but do not live by books." His work in this field, long admired in Canada, reached a wider audience with the publication of *A Voice From the Attic*, a collection of essays about the pleasures of words and books. It was comprehensively praised by Carlos Baker for its "wit, satirical touches, firm indignations, sound sense, good taste, judiciousness, cosmopolitan breadth of view, urbanity, sanity, unexpected eccentricities, educated humanism." Among Davies's aphorisms in this book is one which suggests that his students at Massey College will receive from him an admirably disquieting education: "Of what use is a university education to a young man, unless he comes under the influence of instructors who will astonish him?"

Robertson Davies dislikes sports, hobbies, and travels; enjoys music, theatre, food and drink. In his politics he is a Liberal. He is a tall man, lean, with white hair and a faintly diabolical beard. In 1961 he was awarded the medal of the Royal Society of Canada for his distinguished contribution to Canadian letters and he has also received the Leacock Medal (1955) and several honorary degrees.

PRINCIPAL WORKS: Shakespeare's Boy Actors, 1938; Eros at Breakfast and Other Plays, 1949; Fortune, My Foe (play), 1949; At My Heart's Core (play), 1950; Tempest-Tost (novel), 1951; A Masque of Aesop (play), 1952; Leaven of Malice (novel), 1954; A Jig for the Gypsy (play), 1955; A Hunting Start (play), 1955; A Mixture of Frailties (novel), 1958; A Voice From The Attic (essays), 1960; The Personal Art: Reading to Good Purpose, 1961; A Masque of Mr. Punch (play), 1963; Fifth Business (novel), 1970; The Manticore, 1972. *As "Samuel Marchbanks"*—The Diary of Samuel Marchbanks, 1947; The Table Talk of Samuel Marchbanks, 1949; Marchbanks' Almanack, 1967.

ABOUT: Canadian Who's Who, 1969–1970; Herzberg, M. J. (ed.) The Reader's Encyclopedia of American Literature, 1962; Klinck, C. F. Literary History of Canada, 1965; Smith, A. J. M. Masks of Fiction, 1961.

Periodicals—Canadian Literature Spring 1960, Winter 1961; Publishers' Weekly April 5, 1971; Wilson Library Bulletin February 1962.

***DAVIN, DAN(IEL) (MARCUS)** (September 1, 1913–), New Zealand novelist, short story writer, critic, and historian, writes: "I was born in Invercargill, New Zealand. My father had emigrated from County Galway. My mother was born of Irish emigrant parents—her father from Cork and her mother from Galway. I was educated by the Marist Brothers in Invercargill until I was sixteen. A scholarship in 1930 took me to the Sacred Heart College, Auckland, where I won a scholarship to Otago University in Dunedin.

"My childhood was Irish Catholic in ambience—a numerous, clannish and hospitable household. At university I found myself in a more secular setting. The years 1931–1935 in Dunedin loosened my ties with my childhood religion. These were the years of the Depression and the rise of fascism; and, although I was not politically active, my own working-class background proved to have a stronger claim on my loyalties and to be more tenacious than the religion in which I had been brought up.

"I had long intended to be a writer and I now began to write stories and verse, publishing a little in the university journals. But quickness to learn, combined with addiction to the classics (particularly Catullus, Lucretius, and Tacitus) and to the traditional English literature, made me put my main effort into conventional scholarship. I was also fond of games and naturally gregarious.

"In the autumn of 1936 I came to Balliol College, Oxford, as a Rhodes Scholar, and read Greats (Literae Humaniores). By this time the great issues of the day were the Spanish War, the Moscow Trials, and the coming war with Hitler. My sympathies were to the left but I was unable to become a member of any political party: I had ceased in principle to be a Catholic, having long ceased to be one in practice, and I would not replace a religious faith with a political one.

"A sense of guilt at not fighting in Spain was controlled by the expectation that the main battle against fascism was still to come and the assumption that one would be killed in France. When appeasement could hold the blanket over its head no longer, and war began, I volunteered for the British Army and served as a private and cadet until I was commissioned in 1940. I then transferred to the New Zealand Division. I went as a platoon commander to Greece and was wounded in Crete. After some months in hospital I was seconded to military intelligence in Cairo. I rejoined the N.Z. Division just before Alamein, and spent the rest of the war in staff appointments, close enough to the guns for conscience but not close enough for serious danger.

"After the war, I had to determine how I was to be a writer. I had married in 1939 a fellow New Zealander whose own, and greater, literary gifts I have to reproach myself for cannibalizing. We already had two children and were expecting a third. I was temperamentally averse to the precarious life of the free lance. I gambled on having the energy to work eight hours a day in a job and still write. One novel written in great haste before and during the war had already been published and I was ashamed of it. Another novel set in the war I was already writing. And during the war I had from time to time written short stories.

"In the autumn of 1945 I joined the Clarendon Press where I am now Assistant Secretary to the Delegates. Out of piety to the New Zealand Division and curiosity about historical form, I agreed to write the History of the Battle of Crete for the New Zealand Government and this took me seven years. But somehow I also found time to write novels, at first with comparative ease. The novel which I am now finishing, however, originally planned in 1939, has taken me seven years. It may be my last. The critical faculty hypertrophies with age, the creative faculty declines. An exacting professional life develops a logic of brevity in writing which is disastrous to the logic of association on which the creative writer depends. Being continually exposed to the vanity of authors, one loses the confidence of one's own. Along with a scepticism about facts, there develops an excessive respect for those that can be established and this happens at the expense of the power to create fiction. As one grows older one becomes more interested in what is the same in people and sees the repetitions in their behavior at the expense of delight in their variety. The philosopher overcomes the gossip, and thought kills life. The abstracting faculty gains ascendancy and one cannot see the fly or the spider because one is looking at the geometry of the web. But for the novelist the web should be important only because it is indispensable to the struggle of the spider and the fly.

"Nor can the expatriate draw indefinitely on a past which is not renewed. So the end of my work-in-progress, completing the New Zealand cycle to which my first novel was a penny-farthing, will confront me with some major problems."

Dan Davin had a brilliant academic career at Otago University (first class honors in English in 1934, in Latin in 1935), and at Oxford (first class honors in Greats, 1939). Despite his modest account of his war record, he was mentioned in dispatches during the Crete campaign and again, twice, during

* da' vin

the Italian campaign of 1943–1944. In 1945 he received the MBE for his work as New Zealand Intelligence representative at the Control Commission.

His first, hastily written, book was the novel *Cliffs of Fall* (1945). It is a clearly autobiographical exercise in rather bitter self-probing and is seriously marred by a melodramatic plot. This was followed in 1947 by a volume of short stories, *The Gorse Blooms Pale*. These beautifully realized vignettes evoke the South Canterbury area the author knew as a child and his experience of war in Greece and North Africa. It is in these stories and in the novel *For the Rest of Our Lives*, published the same year, that Davin's art can be seen at its most brilliant and least inhibited.

For the Rest of Our Lives is unsurpassed as an account of the war in North Africa. Like Davin's first novel, it is to some extent an act of unflinching self-appraisal by the author, who figures as the introspective intellectual Frank Fahey. Some critics thought that this character lacked definition and that others were drawn rather mechanically, but there was nothing but praise for the book's finely authentic dialogue and the sense it achieves of "the Kiwi, the collective New Zealander, as the collective hero." The battle accounts are physical in their impact, written with "the immediacy of the journalist, and the conscience of an historian."

Roads From Home is an account of the Irish Catholic community in which Davin grew up. Like E. M. Forster, whose humanism he shares, Davin's essential message in this book is "only connect," and here, with more optimism than this author usually shows, people are to some extent seen as connecting. *The Sullen Bell* continues the cycle; set in London, it deals with New Zealand expatriates, most of them war veterans. As much a social document as a novel, its chief interest lies in its meticulous observation of the postwar scene through colonial eyes. Davin's "antipodean *Bildungsroman*," *Not Here, Not Now*, centers on a New Zealand youth from very much the same background as the author himself, and studies his career at Dunedin University, where his half-justified reputation as a womanizer almost costs him his Rhodes Scholarship to Oxford. It was thought that Davin had told his story "with considerable subtlety but at too great length," in a novel which is "agreeably and appropriately" old-fashioned.

Not Here, Not Now, which completes the New Zealand cycle, was no doubt the novel Davin was working on when he wrote the note above, and it was not, after all, his last. *Brides of Price*, which followed two years later, concerns an Oxford anthropologist who has reached a double crisis in his life. He must choose between the chairmanship of his department and the freedom to complete his magnum opus, a study of social attitudes toward death. And at the same time he must come to terms with the death of the woman he loves, and with his wife's desertion. In spite of a rather unconvincing plot, the novel was greatly enjoyed for its remarkable handling of moods and of characters—"their combination of complexity and clarity, and the empathy one feels for them."

DAN DAVIN

Davin is married to the former Winifred Gonley, who has edited a volume of the *Oxford Junior Encyclopedia* and is the literary editor of Joyce Cary's posthumous works. They have three daughters. Davin is now Deputy Secretary and Oxford Publisher to the Delegates of the Clarendon Press (the imprint of Oxford University Press). He lives in Oxford and is a Fellow of Balliol. Davin says that his recreations have declined "from Rugby and athletics through squash and swimming to chess, walking, and talking."

PRINCIPAL WORKS: *Fiction*—Cliffs of Fall, 1945; For the Rest of Our Lives, 1947 (reissued 1965); The Gorse Blooms Pale (stories), 1947; Roads From Home, 1949; The Sullen Bell, 1956; No Remittance, 1959; Not Here, Not Now, 1970; Brides of Price, 1972. *History*—Crete (New Zealand Official War History), 1953. *Criticism*—(with John Mulgan) Introduction to English Literature, 1947; (with Winifred Davin) The New Zealand Novel, 1956. *As editor*—New Zealand Short Stories, 1953; Katherine Mansfield's Short Stories, 1953; English Short Stories of Today, 1958.

ABOUT: Cassell's Encyclopedia of Literature, 1953; McCormick, E. H. New Zealand Literature, 1959. *Periodicals*—Landfall September 1970; Times Literary Supplement December 23, 1965.

DAVIS, DOROTHY SALISBURY (April 26, 1916–), American mystery writer and novelist, writes: "I have been told I was born in Chicago. I

DOROTHY SALISBURY DAVIS

cannot prove it. I was raised an only child with much love and a discipline which crumbled into indulgence if I held out long enough. Like many another child in moments of rebellion I dreamt I had been adopted, but unlike most I discovered, at the age of seventeen, that it was so. I was more than a year telling anyone, including my parents, that I knew. In that year I developed a sense of loneliness which I have never entirely lost. With it came a great yearning to belong, not merely to join but to become integrated into the families of friends, into the life of a religious community, then much later, into an alien culture.

"When I finally began to write professionally I did not want to write about myself. I felt I had nothing in me to write about, which I think is why I chose the mystery: escape into escape. I have not escaped of course. I am in the darkest fantasies of my reluctant villains and, hopefully, in my heroes who seem to have in common their resolute refusal to judge others—which makes also for reluctant heroes.

"The father I knew was born in Dorset, England, Thomas Hardy country, my mother in Belfast, Ireland. The lore they gave me from their childhoods was rich and warm and I have adopted it as they adopted me. My mother loved the city, but a city of anonymous people: she had few friends. My father loved the farm and the farmers' grange, his church, lodges, veterans' organizations. He had served in the Spanish-American War and World War I. I was throughout childhood torn between their disparate interests. My mother encouraged the student in me, my father the hoyden. I grew up on farms in Wisconsin deep in wilderness, then in Illinois, a few miles from Chicago. I went to Holy Child High School in Waukegan and Barat College of the Sacred Heart in Lake Forest. My mother died before I finished school and I was on my own, graduating at the taggle end of the Great Depression with an excellent taste in books and music and a ha'penny in my pocket.

"I worked in adult education, then in the Historical Research section of the WPA Writers' Project. My mother once said there wasn't a lazy bone in my body, and it is probably true. I know I gobbled up in a month the work on the Project which was supposed to have lasted me the summer. I quit when I was reprimanded for it. I then discovered that there was virtually no other work for me anywhere. For a year and a half I traveled much of the country promoting a magic show. Finally, through the help of the dean at Barat College, I got a job in the research library of Swift and Company. I reveled in security, six years of it, going from the library to industrial relations, to advertising. My only gesture of dissent was to wear a Roosevelt button. I know I wanted to write because I remember a friend's saying to me: 'You and I will never write. We read too much.' I thought he wrote beautifully, he thought I wrote miserably. I suspect we were both right. I was trying to write in a straitjacket.

"In 1945 I met Harry Davis, an actor in Chicago at the time with the play *Jacobowsky and the Colonel*. A year later we were married in New York, and at the age of twenty-nine I began to grow again. My husband encouraged me to write and to keep at it. Hunger, he said, comes of eating. So. Writing came of writing.

"After more rejections than I knew, my first book was accepted by Scribner's. It was a legended house even to me who knew more then about what was in books than of the legends in their writing. Today, fourteen books and many visits later, my every trip to 597 Fifth Avenue has a touch of pilgrimage in it.

"Of the fourteen books three are straight novels, the other criminous. I have come to know many writers, most of them in the mystery field. I have been president of the Mystery Writers of America. Yet to me the greatest mystery in life is why men kill, and it is only a little less of a mystery why people read of killing with such avid pleasure. I do it myself, which mutes the question but does not answer it."

Mrs. Davis's first book was *The Judas Cat*, an excellent, well-controlled story about a small-town crime which was welcomed as one of the best mystery stories of the year. *The Clay Hand*, published in 1950 and republished in 1963, confirmed the arrival of a notable new talent. A harsh, strange, tragic book, too grim to be regarded as simply an entertainment, it was found "delicate and unsentimental" in its understanding of character, "quietly but surely impressive." *A Gentle Murderer*, in which a man's quest for absolute beauty and goodness leads him to destruction and disaster, showed a capacity for subtle irony and compassion which convinced the *New Yorker*'s reviewer that the author was equipped to write "really serious and even distinguished fiction."

In fact, Mrs. Davis has made three excursions into straight fiction, most notably in *Men of No Property*, which follows the American fortunes of a group of Irish immigrants who arrive in New York in 1848. Fanny Butcher called it a major historical novel, and it was credited with almost every novelistic virtue except a sound structure, many critics finding it too long and too shapeless. There were similar reservations about the organization of a later novel, *The Evening of the Good Samaritan*, but a generally favorable response to *God Speed the Night*, written in collaboration with Jerome Ross—a story which combines great suspense with a searching and vivid study of the costs and rewards of religious faith, set in occupied France during World War II. All the same, it may be that Mrs. Davis works best within the tight framework and rigid conventions of the thriller genre, even though her novels seem always on the point of breaking free of such limitations.

At any rate, after *Men of No Property*, Mrs. Davis invented in *Death of an Old Sinner* a story quite unlike her earlier mysteries or anyone else's, but with a flavor reminiscent of Edwin O'Connor's *The Last Hurrah*. It combines Irish politics, an absorbing mystery, and offbeat humor in "a rare and charming bit of blarney" dominated by Major General Ransom Jarvis, the irresistibly engaging old sinner of the title. The regular reviewers of mystery stories, surfeited with cardboard characters and mechanical plots, have always welcomed Mrs. Davis's books with special gratitude and warmth, and they outdid themselves in their tributes to *Death of an Old Sinner*, "a joyous and unqualified success." There was no less enthusiasm for *Old Sinners Never Die*, a similar mixture of melodrama and Mack Sennett farce in which Jarvis rides again.

But Mrs. Davis has not abandoned her earlier mode, and in the opinion of some reviewers produced her best suspense story in *The Pale Betrayer*, which has a New York university background. "This delicate yet warm novel," wrote Anthony Boucher, "combines solid characterization, credible police work . . . and a prevailing mood which is surprisingly rare in the novel of death: sadness." It is a judgment applicable to many of Mrs. Davis's remarkable and memorable novels.

PRINCIPAL WORKS: The Judas Cat, 1949; The Clay Hand, 1950; A Gentle Murderer, 1951; A Town of Masks, 1952; Men of No Property, 1956; Death of an Old Sinner, 1957; A Gentleman Called, 1958; Old Sinners Never Die, 1959; The Evening of the Good Samaritan, 1961; Black Sheep, White Lamb, 1963; The Pale Betrayer, 1965; Enemy and Brother, 1967; (with Jerome Ross) God Speed the Night, 1968; Where the Dark Streets Go, 1969; Shock Wave, 1972; The Little Brothers, 1973.

ABOUT: Boucher, A. *introduction to* The Clay Hand, 1963; Who's Who in America 1970–1971.

***DAYAN, YAËL** (February 12, 1939–), Israeli novelist and journalist, writes: "I was born in Nahalal, a village near Nazareth, where I lived for thirteen years. During the Israeli war of independence the family moved to Jerusalem which was commanded by my father (Moshe Dayan, later Commander in Chief of the Israeli forces during the Sinai Campaign). I have attended schools in Jerusalem, Haifa, and Tel Aviv and, when sixteen, graduated, left home, decided I wanted to be a writer, and did some writing for local newspapers. I studied in the Hebrew University of Jerusalem, faculty of political science, for two years.

"Restlessness, laziness, and curiosity about subjects other than Hobbes's theories prevented me from completing the course and I enlisted in the army before my conscription was due. Serving for two years as a recruit, a cadet, and as an officer (first lieutenant) training recruits supplied some of the material for my first novel, *New Face in the Mirror*, which I wrote while still in the army. It was published in 1959 when I was twenty and won me early fame and independence not totally deserved. Coping with both proved difficult and I found the early success frightening and committing. For a few years I traveled in Africa, the Far East, and the U.S.A. The discovery of new places, the first contact with a foreign scenery, a new city, with new smells, colors, tastes, fill me with pleasure unequaled by other recreations.

"When not traveling I worked. I work in rather a spasmodic way, three or four months a year, every day to exhaustion, letting my story shape itself and carry me away impatiently and mysteriously—that is for me the pleasure of writing: the surprise, the unknown that the next page holds. Between books, when I do not travel—and there is a limit to new places—I enjoy working with film director Michael Cacoyannis, having adopted Greece as a second home. I am active in politics in Israel (Ben-Gurion's socialist party, RAFI); I write for Israeli newspapers; and am single.

"More than with any other factor I am involved with my county's life. I believe in nationalism, or rather patriotism. I am able to move and be free because I do not take the term 'home' for granted. The special quality of the State of Israel is some-

* da yan′

YAËL DAYAN

thing I have been trying to express in my novels, using it always as background—criticized, analyzed, but always loved.

"Moments of relaxation take me to the sea, to Dostoevsky, and to the poets Alterman (Hebrew) and Cavafy (Greek). I speak several languages and my novels are published in many.

"My frustrations outnumber my achievements. I would have liked to study medicine, I would have liked to give my family and my country as much as I keep taking from them, and I would like to think that my intolerance of stupidity and boredom will be modified by the years.

"My mother heads the Israeli Home Industries. It is her trust and pride in me that pull me out of my insecurities. I have two brothers, one a farmer and the youngest a talented writer. I own a house on the slopes of Mount Carmel, a garden with fifty vines and pomegranate trees, and the desire to achieve an equilibrium between the pain and agony my work requires—and its final quality."

Since early 1966, when she wrote the note reproduced above, Yaël Dayan has fought a war, married, and seen her "second home," Greece, fall under a dictatorship.

Her first novel, *New Face in the Mirror*, is narrated by a young Israeli, daughter of a professional soldier, who at first rebels against her compulsory military training but emerges from it a better and more mature person. The book's precocity caused a great deal of excitement and this, together with its freshness and astringency and its sexual frankness, persuaded some journalists that Miss Dayan was the Françoise Sagan of Israel. Other reviewers, alarmed perhaps at the prospect of a worldwide epidemic of Sagans, attacked the book with undeserved violence for its "pompous introspection," complaining that it conveyed almost no information about its narrator's country. Anne Duchêne's more balanced appraisal acknowledged these faults but pointed out that the author's narcissism was of a youthfully innocent variety and that she "often touches a true nerve of feeling in her nervous, tangential relationships and her progress towards some compassion."

Yaël Dayan's subsequent novels, all (like the first) written in her second language, English, have dealt with the growing pains of her country and in particular with the postwar conflict in values there between the old-world Jews of the pogroms and Hitler's "final solution," and the hard young sabras who have known no country but Israel. *Envy the Frightened* advances in fictional form the thesis that the sabras, purged of old-country fears and self-doubts, have also been purged of tenderness and the capacity to love. *Dust*, the best received of her recent novels, describes one girl's attempt to bridge the gap between herself and a death camp survivor, while they and other present-day Israeli pioneers work to build a new city in the desert. *Death Had Two Sons* shows how a failure to bridge this gulf, widened by a hideous Nazi joke, may even separate father and son.

In these novels, far more than in her first, Miss Dayan has succeeded in conveying the look and feel of her country, and proved that she "can evoke the physical world with striking and sensitive immediacy." Her subject, moreover, is an important and absorbing one. For some readers this is enough, and Edmund Fuller, for example, has praised her work for its depth and wisdom. Many reviewers, however, have so far found Miss Dayan's literary means inadequate to her theme and have complained in particular about the unevenness of her style and the thinness of her characterization.

In June 1967, serving as a morale officer in Sinai during the six-day Arab–Israeli war, Yaël Dayan met Colonel Dov Sion, who in peacetime teaches at the National Defense College. They were married on July 22, 1967. The journal which Lieutenant Dayan kept during the war, published later the same year, gives a spare and personal account of what she saw in her sector. Howard Junker wrote in *Newsweek* that the book was most fascinating as "a laboriously disguised love story," and went on: "Israel needs a cultural star, a bright young sensibility at home in the old world as well as the new. Yaël Dayan has seized this obvious opportunity. Someday she may settle down and stop playing the impetuous, ravishing mouthpiece. If she then disciplines her talent, she might yet render the life of young Israel with the skill and power that nation deserves." "Ravishing" Miss Dayan is—black-haired, "sulkily attractive," and a little like Joan Baez. She is said to resemble her famous father in her bluntness, impatience, and reckless courage, but she has a mind and opinions of her own and an excellent sense of humor. She is a crack rifle shot.

PRINCIPAL WORKS: *Novels*—New Face in the Mirror, 1959; Envy the Frightened, 1961; Dust, 1963; Death Had Two Sons, 1967. *Nonfiction*—Israel Journal: June 1967, 1967 (England, A Soldier's Diary). *As editor*—Pioneers in Israel, by Shmuel Dayan, 1961 (England, The Promised Land: Memoirs).

ABOUT: Dayan, Y. Israel Journal, 1967. *Periodicals*—Life September 14, 1959; New York Times Book Review August 23, 1959; Newsweek November 20, 1967; Saturday Review August 22, 1959; Time November 17, 1967; Vogue September 1, 1967.

***"DAZAI, OSAMU" (pseudonym of Shuji Tsushima)** (June 19, 1909–June 13, 1948), Japanese novelist, was born in Aomori Prefecture, northern Japan. He was the sixth son and the youngest child of ten in one of the wealthiest landowning families in the prefecture. In *Omoide* (Recollections), published while he was a university student, Dazai presents himself as an intelligent and extremely sensitive child, physically weak and fearful but precociously mature, resorting to lying and deliberate clowning to forestall any hostility from schoolfellows or family.

In 1923 his father died, and the same year Dazai entered Aomori Prefectural Middle School. He was a brilliant, bookish student and in 1927, at the age of nineteen, went on to Hirosaki High School (now Hirosaki University). Dazai was deeply affected by the suicide in that year of Ryunosuke Akutagawa, whose pessimism he shared. While at Hirosaki he became interested in *Gidayu* (Japanese ballad drama) and began to frequent Japanese restaurants and geisha houses. He became involved with a geisha, Hatsuye Koyama—a liaison which waxed and waned over the years and which set Dazai at odds with his family. By 1929 he was himself seriously considering suicide.

In April 1930 he entered the Department of French Literature of Tokyo Imperial University, not because he knew or wished to know French, but because the department had a bohemian aura which appealed to him. He later boasted that he did not attend a single lecture in five years. At this time he made friends with the novelist Masuji Ibuse, one of the very few people whom he wholeheartedly admired. With Ibuse's encouragement he published several stories in literary magazines. The autobiographical *Omoide* appeared in 1933. In 1934 "Romanesque," a farce about the artist's isolation from society, appeared in the magazine *Aoi Hana* (Blue Flower) which Dazai was editing with friends.

* dəz ä ē'

OSAMU DAZAI

Tokyo exacerbated his latent instability. In 1930 he became involved with a café waitress, a married woman, with whom he attempted a double suicide. They threw themselves into the sea at Enoshima: he failed; she died. This event earned Dazai considerable notoriety. He had been attending Communist meetings and later said that one reason for his misery was a fear that he was intellectually betraying the movement, though he was also generally uneasy about family difficulties and his studies. His political enthusiasm reflected his desperate desire "to escape from my own shadow—being an aristocrat." But he found that it was not so easy to obliterate his origins. "I became coarse. I learned to use coarse language. But it was half—no, sixty per cent—a wretched imposture, an odd form of petty trickery. As far as the 'people' were concerned I was a stuck-up prig who put them all on edge with my affected airs."

Dazai was not really satisfied by the left-wing vision: "I felt sure that something more obscure, more frightening lurked in the hearts of human beings. Greed did not cover it, nor did vanity. Nor was it simply a combination of lust and greed. I wasn't sure what it was, but I felt that there was something inexplicable at the bottom of human society which was not reducible to economics." Alienated from one group, unable to commit himself to the other, he "soon came to understand that drink, tobacco and prostitutes were all excellent means of dissipating (even for a few moments) my dread of human beings."

During the 1930s Dazai's literary reputation and personal notoriety increased. In 1936 his novel *Gyakko* (Retrogression) was runner-up for the

Akutagawa Literary Prize. In 1935 he withdrew from the university without taking a degree. He tried to join the staff of a daily newspaper, the *Miyako Shimbun*, but failed the entrance examination and a few days later made another attempt at suicide. He was by this time addicted to morphine and on the verge of emotional and physical collapse. Dazai's writing was always subjective, but the work of the late 1930s was full of personal agony, self-pity alternating with contemptuous self-mockery.

In March 1937 he again tried a double suicide—this time with Hatsuye Koyama, the Aomori geisha, who had been living with him since 1931. Having failed yet again to kill himself, he made a determined effort to break with drugs and reconstruct his life on more normal lines. His friend Ibuse encouraged him to consider marriage, found a suitable candidate, and arranged the meetings. The girl, Miwako Ishihara, was a high school teacher. They were married in 1939 after two months' engagement. Dazai, who suffered from tuberculosis, was exempted from military service during the war. He continued to write, moving from place to place to avoid the bombing. His work showed signs of becoming brighter and healthier, partly no doubt because of his marriage—partly, perhaps, because of the exigencies of government censorship.

Real fame came after the war, when for a few years Dazai's personal nihilism coincided with a more general anguish. He became an almost legendary figure, the idol of young people, a type of *poète maudit*. His acceptance of this role is evident in the story "Villon no Tsuma" (1947, translated as "Villon's Wife"), in which he writes from the point of view of a woman who has unreservedly bound her life to that of an artist. Her simple struggle to survive is movingly counterpointed with his monstrous will to self-destruction. "There's nothing wrong with being a monster, is there," she asks, "as long as we stay alive?"

Dazai's masterpiece is the short novel *Shayo* (1947, translated by Donald Keene as *The Setting Sun*). One of the results of Japan's defeat in World War II was the destruction of its aristocracy, and *Shayo* studies the abrupt dispossession of one such family. The most objective and unself-conscious of Dazai's books, it was admired equally for the delicacy of its characterization and for its powerful evocation of the nature and mood of the postwar scene. So great was its impact that the "new poor" became known as *shayo-zoku* (The Setting Sun People), and it is generally regarded as one of Japan's greatest postwar novels. The English translation had a more equivocal reception. Some reviewers found it a "hideous distortion of life," while Kenneth Rexroth complained of Dazai's "exasperating eclecticism." But as many reviewers were profoundly impressed, and Earl Miner wrote: "[Dazai's] triumph in bringing Western intellectuality and coherence to the Japanese novel without losing its traditional lyric depths was purchased at the cost of self-sacrifice. It is this heroism of weakness as well as the depravity of tenderness which makes the novel so moving."

In *Ningen Shikkaku* (1948, translated by Donald Keene as *No Longer Human*), Dazai returned to the directly personal and autobiographical, tracing his own total social retrogression and the ultimate alienation implied in the title. In the year of its publication, on June 13, 1948, he and his mistress threw themselves into the Tamagawa reservoir and were drowned. Dazai's body was recovered six days later, on his thirty-ninth birthday.

PRINCIPAL WORKS IN ENGLISH TRANSLATION: The Setting Sun, 1956; No Longer Human, 1958. *Stories in* Keene, D. Modern Japanese Literature, 1956; Morris, I. Modern Japanese Stories, 1961; Encounter 1 1953; Japan Quarterly October–December 1958; The Reeds 4 1958.
ABOUT: Grigson, G. (ed.) Concise Encyclopedia of Modern World Literature, 1963; Keene, D. Modern Japanese Literature, 1956; Penguin Companion to Literature 4, 1969; Usui, Y. Dazai: The Man and His Work (in Japanese), 1964. *Periodicals*—Commonweal October 12, 1956; Nation September 29, 1956; New Republic September 15, 1958; New York Herald Tribune Book Review June 29, 1958; New York Times October 7, 1956; July 27, 1958; Saturday Review September 29, 1956; August 2, 1958; Yale Review Winter 1957.

DE CAMP, L(YON) SPRAGUE (November 27, 1907–), American novelist and writer on science and history, reports: "I was born in New York City, the son of Lyon de Camp, an upstate New York businessman of remotely French descent, and Beatrice Sprague de Camp, daughter of Colonel Charles Ezra Sprague, a Civil War hero, professor, banker, linguist, mathematician, and inventor. Being named Lyon Sprague de Camp, I could not, for obvious reasons, be called either 'Lyon' or 'Junior'; hence the use of my middle name, which rhymes with 'plague.' At least it saves me the trouble of thinking up pen names, since my name sounds more like a pseudonym than most pseudonyms do.

"Receiving my early education in New York City and the South, I attended high school and college in southern California. Although by temperament I was cut out to be a professor and had an intense interest in the biological sciences, I was persuaded that an engineering course would be more 'practical.' Receiving my B.S. from California Tech in 1930 and my M.S. from Stevens Tech in 1933, I found myself shut out of the engineering profession by the Great Depression. Therefore I drifted into technical writing, teaching, editing, and patent consultation.

"In 1937, I was principal of the School of Inventing and Patenting of the International Correspondence Schools of Scranton, Pennsylvania, and putting the finishing touches on a textbook called *Inventions and Their Management*, by Alf K. Berle and myself. This book was published by the International Textbook Company, has run through a number of revisions and one complete rewriting, and has been cited in a decision of the U.S. Supreme Court.

"At this time, a former college roommate of mine was unemployed in New York. To eat, he wrote (with some help from me) a couple of stories for the science fiction magazines. To the surprise of all, he sold them. Thinking that if he could do it, so could I, I also wrote a few and sold them. Some months later, when an editorial job in New York fell victim to an economy purge, I tried full-time freelance writing. I found that I could make about as much money as, and have a lot more fun than, I had been doing as a salaried employee.

"Except for a few short excursions into editing, technical writing, public relations, and uranium prospecting, I have been a freelance ever since. The main excursion was the Second World War, when I was an officer in the Naval Reserve, assigned to engineering duty at the Naval Air Material Center in Philadelphia. For three and a half years, along with my colleagues Isaac Asimov and Robert A. Heinlein, I fought the foe with a slide rule and requisitions in quintuplicate.

"I have collaborated with several other writers, notably P. Schuyler Miller, Willy Ley, and most of all the late Fletcher Pratt, with whom I wrote a number of fantasy stories from 1939 to 1953. I learned much about writing techniques from Pratt; from John W. Campbell, editor of *Astounding Stories* (now *Analog*); and from Bernard De Voto and other speakers at the Bread Loaf Writers Conference. I have also been influenced by the writings of Edgar Rice Burroughs, Alfred Duggan, Lord Dunsany, E. R. Eddison, Robert Graves, Ernest Hemingway, Robert E. Howard, Thorne Smith, and P. G. Wodehouse.

"In 1939, I married Catherine A. Crook. We live in the suburbs of Philadelphia with two stalwart sons. In recent years, my wife has done a great deal of work on editing and rewriting my manuscripts. Her name appears on two books as a collaborator and could with justice have been placed on several others.

"For the first decade of my full-time writing, I wrote almost entirely for magazines specializing in imaginative fiction. That is, I wrote science fiction, fantasy, and articles on borderline scientific subjects. Then, with the opening up of other markets, I gradually withdrew from science fiction and have not written any since 1956. I have, however, continued active as a science fiction fan and a fantasy anthologist. My writing during the last decade has consisted mainly of: (*a*) popularizations of science; (*b*) historical novels laid in the Mediterranean region in classical times; and (*c*) juvenile picture books on scientific and historical subjects. My total production to date is as follows: books—forty-three published, four in press, four in preparation; magazine stories—one hundred and three published, one in preparation; magazine articles—one hundred and forty-four published, two in press; anthologies and symposia to which I have contributed—thirty-six. I have also written about seventy-five radio scripts and numerous fugitive pieces such as verse and book reviews. My writings have been translated into at least six foreign tongues.

L. SPRAGUE DE CAMP

"I enjoy my work immensely and work long hours. I work fairly fast but revise extensively; most copy goes through three drafts. I research strenuously, using the facilities of nine or ten major libraries and traveling about the country to interview people with shorthand and tape recorder. For a typical nonfiction book, I read one hundred to three hundred source books and articles.

"My spare time, what there is of it, goes into reading; study of subjects that interest me, such as history, languages, and archaeology; gardening; and travel. I have been fortunate in being able to visit considerable parts of Europe, Asia, Africa, Latin America, and the Pacific, often with my wife. I am also active in several professional and literary clubs and societies. Altogether, while I have had my ups and downs, I have been on the whole far luckier than I deserved."

Sam Moskowitz has described de Camp as "the

funniest writer in science fiction," whose "fantasies were based on a rare degree of scholarship," and who "pointed the way to a lighter, less self-conscious tone in science fiction." According to Moskowitz, de Camp had a wretched childhood. A thin, awkward, stubborn boy, precociously intellectual, he spent ten years at a military school in North Carolina where he was persistently bullied and humiliated. He was nevertheless good at his studies and escaped at last to the California Institute of Technology, where he began to come into his own as editor of the college paper and a member of the fencing team.

De Camp sold his first science fiction story in 1937 and by 1939 was famous in the field. His best novel, *Lest Darkness Fall*, first appeared in *Unknown* in December 1939 and was published in hard covers in 1941. It is an astringent and exciting story about an archaeologist sent back in time to ancient Rome in its decadence, and is clearly modeled on Mark Twain's *A Connecticut Yankee in King Arthur's Court*. "In its grasp of the welter of peoples and religions that filled the peninsula of Italy," wrote Basil Davenport, "it is as sound a historical novel as many that are more pretentious. And in taking a strange but definite problem and attacking it realistically, it shows itself a work of real and stimulating imagination." Published the same year and also well received was *The Incomplete Enchanter*, a basically similar story about the wanderings in time of a bored psychologist, written in collaboration with Fletcher Pratt.

The most successful of de Camp's postwar science fictions was *Rogue Queen*, set on a planet whose inhabitants reproduce themselves much as bees do. It was notable as a "successful combination of stirring action, scientific thinking and witty commentary," with the rather daring addition of an erotic element seldom admitted into science fiction at that time.

In general, however, de Camp's interests have turned away from science fiction since World War II. His swashbuckling historical novels have attracted less attention than his nonfiction (though the first of them, the ingenious historical travelogue *An Elephant for Aristotle*, won the 1958 fiction award of the Philadelphia Athenaeum). De Camp's *Science Fiction Handbook*, notable for its "vigorous, colloquial prose" and characteristic flashes of humor, has been used as a college text. *Lost Continents*, which explores the Atlantis theme in history, science, and literature, is also a basic guide to its subject, and there was much praise for *The Ancient Engineers*, a history of early technology. The *Times Literary Supplement*, reviewing *Ancient Ruins and Archaeology*, found it thoroughly researched and skillfully written, with "more than a hint of scholarly humour." *The Great Monkey Trial* also pleased reviewers, one of whom called it the definitive account of the famous Darrow-Bryan courtroom battle.

A tall, handsome man, de Camp gives occasional lectures and has spoken on radio programs. His club memberships reflect his wide-ranging interests and include associations devoted to literature in general and science fiction in particular, philology, and the history of science and technology. He is a Democrat. De Camp is a collector of the works of R. E. Howard, Lord Dunsany, and C. A. Smith. Some of his very large output has appeared pseudonymously as by "Lyman R. Lyon" or "J. Wellington Wells."

PRINCIPAL WORKS (a representative selection): *Science fiction*—Lest Darkness Fall, 1941; (with Fletcher Pratt) The Incomplete Enchanter, 1941; Rogue Queen, 1951. *Historical fiction*—An Elephant for Aristotle, 1958; The Arrows of Hercules, 1965. *Nonfiction*—(with Alf K. Berle) Inventions, Patents, and Their Management, 1937 (frequently rev.); The Science Fiction Handbook, 1953; Lost Continents, 1954; The Ancient Engineers, 1963; (with Catherine C. de Camp) Ancient Ruins and Archaeology, 1964; The Great Monkey Trial, 1968.

ABOUT: Contemporary Authors 2, 1963; Moskowitz, S. Seekers of Tomorrow, 1966; Tuck, D. H. (ed.) A Handbook of Science Fiction and Fantasy, 1959; Ward, M. E. and Marquardt, D. A. Authors of Books for Young People, 1967. *Periodicals*—Amazing Stories February 1964; Chester (Pennsylvania) Times June 15, 1955; Delaware County (Pennsylvania) Times May 21, 1958; January 4, 1960; Everybody's Weekly January 11, 1948; Fantasy and Science Fiction January 1963.

DE GHELDERODE, MICHEL. *See* GHELDERODE, MICHEL DE.

DEIGHTON, LEN (February 18, 1929–), English novelist, was born in Marylebone, London, the son of a chauffeur and an Irish hotel cook. He entered the Royal Air Force at eighteen, and did his national service with the RAF Special Investigation Branch. Deighton is a graduate of the Royal College of Art in London and for some years worked as a commercial artist and photographer in London and New York. His career has also included brief stints as a railway lengthman, a waiter, an assistant pastry cook, an airline steward, the manager of a London gown factory, a fashion artist, and a teacher in Brittany. His hobbies are cookery and military history.

In 1962 these oddly assorted elements began to come together in highly profitable ways. In that year the London Sunday newspaper *The Observer* began to publish Deighton's "cookstrips"—recipes in which both the ingredients and the way in which they should be used are very clearly illustrated in cartoon-style action drawings with a minimum of verbal instruction, so that (as Deighton says) "even a moron can follow the directions." This excellent idea, executed with much knowledge, skill, and humor, had an immediate success and the cook-strips have been collected into several books.

The Ipcress File, Deighton's first novel, was written on vacation in 1960 and 1961 and published in 1962. The story is narrated with sardonic wit by an anonymous British espionage agent, a cynic who nevertheless takes a certain stoical pride in his grubby, dangerous, and thankless work. The extremely complicated plot centers on the mysterious abduction of a number of British biochemists and involves a bewildering web of double and triple agents. It is adroitly seasoned with violence and a touch of romance and moves in a rapid succession of short, vivid episodes from London to the Near East, to a nuclear testing site in the Pacific, to a brainwashing hideout purportedly behind the Iron Curtain.

It was recognized at once that the book was not only an exciting thriller but also a debunking parody of the romantic spy fantasies of Ian Fleming, and many British critics welcomed it with enthusiasm. Deighton's spy is the very antithesis of James Bond. He is no gentleman amateur but a professional—brash, fallible, insolent to his superiors, with "three months' back pay outstanding from the War Department, a slight weight problem, glasses, and a trench coat with a Smith and Wesson, several packs of Gauloises, a garlic sausage and some Normandy butter in its pockets." G. W. Stonier, reviewing the book in the *New Statesman*, wrote: "There has been no brighter arrival on the shady scene since Graham Greene started entertaining."

Deighton's nameless narrator has since been featured in a number of stories written to a similar formula, of which the most admired were *Funeral in Berlin* and *An Expensive Place to Die*. He devotes about a year to each book, and half of this time is spent traveling to the locations he intends to use, taking photographs, making sketches, and in general insuring that his settings are absolutely authentic. All of his books are scrupulously researched and reflect an impressive range of knowledge concerning tactics, weapons, military aircraft and vehicles, and modern espionage systems. Much of his more esoteric information seems to come from military journals, and some of it finds its way into the documentary or pseudodocumentary footnotes and appendixes which adorn his novels. Deighton's interest in cookery is also exploited in his stories, and the villain in *The Ipcress File* is taken while basting a lobster with butter and champagne.

A reviewer in the *Times Literary Supplement*, discussing Deighton's work in general, points out that "his successes have been achieved by circumstantial documentation on the one hand and oblique narration on the other" and speaks of his style as cinematic—"the presentation of the mere image,

LEN DEIGHTON

explication largely depending on the gradual accumulation of images." The American critic Richard Schickel has also considered the Deighton novels at some length (in *Book Week* May 1, 1966). Deighton, he says, shares "Raymond Chandler's taste for overcomplicated plotting and occasionally overstrained metaphors"; Ian Fleming's predilection for grotesque villains and his air of knowledgeability about the techniques and gadgets of espionage; and John Le Carré's distaste for the moral implications of spying and of patriotism." But, Schickel believes, "Mr. Deighton never manages to cross the shadow line that separates his genre from the rest of literature—something, it seems to me, Chandler and Le Carré, at their best, do."

In his sixth novel, *Only When I Larf*, Deighton abandoned his familiar recipe to write an extremely ingenious story about the professional activities and emotional problems of a trio of high-powered confidence tricksters. Like most of its predecessors, it has been filmed.

Deighton changed gear again in *Bomber*, subtitled "events relating to the last flight of an RAF bomber over Germany on the night of June 31, 1943." The story is told alternately from the point of view of the flyers and of their enemies. Deighton, for whom the spy thriller has lost some of its fascination, says that *Bomber* is closer to what he wants to do than anything else he has written. It is a long book, embodying a huge amount of research (coordinated with the help of a computerized typewriter). Most reviewers admired Deighton's moral intention, which was to make the reader experience, through detailed and dispassionate reporting, the full horror of the air war. However, as Paul

West said, while "half of the book is first-rate imaginative reporting . . . the other half is homework done with obsessive care and worked into the text redundantly." In *Close-Up*, a novel about the film world, centering on an aging star, it seemed to one reviewer that Deighton had settled down to what he does best: "reporting, lucidly and readably, on what his imagination sees."

Deighton's concern for accuracy in research is matched by his meticulous care in composition. It is said that he revises each sentence about eight times, though he claims not to be a writer but someone "interested in narration and the pattern of events." He is married to Shirley Thompson, an illustrator, and lives on a remote farm in Ireland.

PRINCIPAL WORKS: *Fiction*—The Ipcress File, 1962; Horse Under Water, 1963; Funeral in Berlin, 1964; The Billion Dollar Brain, 1966; An Expensive Place to Die, 1967; Only When I Larf, 1968; Bomber, 1970; Declarations of War (stories), 1971; Close-Up, 1972. *Cookery*—Action Cook Book, 1965; Où est le garlic: or Len Deighton's French Cook Book, 1965; Cookstrip Cook Book, 1966. *As editor*—London Dossier, 1967; Continental Dossier, 1968.

ABOUT: Contemporary Authors 11–12, 1965. *Periodicals*—Book Week May 16, 1965; May 1, 1966; Book World September 27, 1970; Life March 25, 1966; New York Times Book Review April 18, 1965; November 15, 1970; Newsweek December 24, 1962; January 31, 1966; Observer Colour Supplement December 8, 1968; Times Literary Supplement June 1, 1967; Vogue July 1965; Wine and Food Autumn 1964.

DELANEY, SHELAGH (November 25, 1939–), English dramatist, was born in Salford, an industrial suburb of Manchester, the daughter of Joseph and Elsie (Twemlow) Delaney. Her father was a transport worker and a great reader and storyteller. She was a late developer and was consigned to Broughton Secondary School rather than to the academically oriented local grammar school. She was lucky all the same, since a perceptive teacher at Broughton recognized her literary ability and encouraged it. Shelagh Delaney left school at seventeen and worked variously as a salesgirl, as a clerk, in a factory, and as a movie theatre usherette.

What she wanted to do, though, was to write. She had already started work on a novel when she went to the theatre one evening and saw Terence Rattigan's *Variations on a Theme*. Disliking it and convinced that she could do better, she rewrote her novel as a play and sent it to Joan Littlewood's Theatre Workshop. The class revolution in the English theatre was then at its height, and Miss Littlewood in particular was searching for "grand, vulgar, simple, pathetic plays." *A Taste of Honey* went into rehearsal within two weeks. It tells the story of Jo, a caustic, sensitive, awkward teen-ager growing up too fast in Salford. Neglected by her sluttish mother, Jo turns for romance and affection to a transient black seaman who leaves her un-

SHELAGH DELANEY

romantically pregnant. Her mother remarries and Jo is taken over by a gentle young homosexual who looks after her until the baby is almost due. It is their odd, affectionate, quarrelsome ménage which supplies Jo's "taste of honey." It lasts only until her mother returns, bristling with parental indignation, and ousts the homosexual.

The play opened at the Theatre Royal, Stratford, in May 1958 and was an immediate success, later continuing its run in London's West End. Shelagh Delaney, then nineteen, was promptly and for no good reason labeled an "Angry Young Woman," and there were protests—especially from the Manchester area—that her play was sordid. But most English critics welcomed it enthusiastically for its vitality and humor, the authority of its female characterizations, and its wry, unaffected honesty. Graham Greene said that it had the freshness of John Osborne's *Look Back in Anger* and a greater maturity. The New York drama critics saw it in 1960 and were equally impressed. They chose it as the best foreign play of the season, adding this award to the Charles Henry Foyle New Play Award and the Arts Council Bursary it had already brought its author in England. It ran on Broadway for nearly four hundred performances. The vexed question of how much Joan Littlewood had altered and improved the play in rehearsal has been resolved by John Russell Taylor, who compared the original and the amended texts and found much pruning and tightening but no fundamental difference. *A Taste of Honey* has been staged in many countries and was rewritten by the author as a prize-winning film.

Miss Delaney's second play, *The Lion in Love*,

was less successful. It is a study of a hopeless marriage between a vital, aggressive woman and a discontented and frustrated man, and takes its title from an Aesop fable about the futility of ill-matched marriages. Most reviewers found it wordy, shapeless, and diffuse, but Kenneth Tynan praised its "authenticity, honesty, restraint and . . . prevailing sense of humour," and John Russell Taylor thought it in certain respects an advance over the first play, especially in its handling of the principal male character.

Sweetly Sings the Donkey is a collection of autobiographical reminiscences, some of them no doubt partially fictionalized. It had mixed reviews but there was almost universal praise for the title piece, an account of the author's stay in a Roman Catholic convalescent home written, according to Marion Magid, "in that same arresting voice—dry, entirely without literary pretension, honest to the point of brutality—that made Miss Delaney's first work so striking."

Shelagh Delaney, who has a daughter, is slim, poised, and very tall. She has dark hair. Her father died in 1958 and since then, although she has an apartment in London, she has spent much of her time with her mother in Salford. Her television study of Salford was screened by the British Broadcasting Corporation in 1962. More recently she wrote the award-winning script for Albert Finney's film *Charlie Bubbles*.

PRINCIPAL PUBLISHED WORKS: A Taste of Honey, 1959; The Lion in Love, 1961; Sweetly Sings the Donkey (memoir), 1963.

ABOUT: Contemporary Authors 19–20, 1968; Current Biography, 1962; Taylor, J. R. Anger And After, 1963; Who's Who, 1971; Who's Who in America, 1970–1971; Who's Who in the Theatre, 1967.

***DEL CASTILLO, MICHEL** (August 3, 1933–), Spanish-born novelist writing in French, was born in Madrid. His early life is the subject of his first book, *Tanguy* (1957, translated by Peter Green as *Child of Our Time*). It is a very lightly fictionalized account of how Del Castillo and his pro-Republican mother escaped from Spain after the Civil War and went to join his bourgeois and unsympathetic father in France, where the two refugees were arrested and put into a concentration camp in the Midi. Separated from his mother, who was smuggled back to Spain, the boy went from camp to camp in France and Germany, and after World War II was sent to a brutal orphanage in Spain. He escaped in 1949. In 1953, just before his twentieth birthday, he joined his father in Paris, where he received his long-delayed education at the Lycée Janson-de-Sailly and at the Sorbonne. He has lived in France ever since, though he has returned to his native country for visits.

* del cäs tē′ lyō

MICHEL DEL CASTILLO

Perhaps the most moving section of *Tanguy* describes Del Castillo's relationship with an older boy in a German prison camp and his friend's eventual death in the gas chamber. But the whole book is a record of a child's deep and unrelieved suffering, described with an innocent objectivity and reticence that give it, as one critic said, the quality of "a parable of the collapse of civilization." Another reviewer wrote: "He has no complaints, although his life has been one of incessant suffering; no demands, although he has nothing, and no expectations because he has seen everything. . . . The refusal of the author to express a condemnation he has every right to pronounce, and the extraordinary poignancy of his voice, make our failure still harder to bear."

The excellence and importance of *Tanguy* are scarcely that of fiction; *La Guitare* (1957, translated by Humphrey Hare as *The Guitar*) showed that Del Castillo's talent extended to purely imaginative writing. This *récit*—"a book of absolute despair," as the author calls it—is set against the savagely superstitious background of Galicia. It is narrated by a hideously ugly hunchbacked dwarf, who is shunned by the peasants he lives among. Hoping to communicate his great capacity for love through music, he learns to play the guitar. This achievement seems to the peasants an act of witchcraft and they stone the dwarf, who is brought to such a depth of despair that he can only hope the stones will disfigure him a little further. The book is a small, painful triumph of cool and lucid writing.

Le Colleur d'affiches (1958), about the Spanish Civil War, has been translated as *The Disinherited* (and in England, more literally, as *The Billsticker*).

Once again a mood of almost total nihilism is evoked with extreme detachment. It centers on a youth from the slums of Madrid, his excited discovery of communism, and his gradual disillusionment as the war drags on. The book is not an attack on any one ideology however, but "a denunciation of human brutality in all its forms."

Del Castillo's subsequent books have attracted less serious critical attention. *La Mort de Tristan* (1959, translated as *The Death of Tristan*), set in Paris at Christmas time, deals with its hero's emotional coming of age, the growth of his love from adolescent self-indulgence to maturity. It is interesting for the author's attempt to achieve both a lightness of touch and a Gallic grasp of amorous psychology, but was found superficial in its characterization and intellectual content. *Le Manège espanol* (1960, translated as *Through the Hoop*) is a bitter portrait of social injustice, venality, and religious hypocrisy in contemporary Spain, introducing a satirical note reminiscent of Camilo José Cela. The most fascinating aspect of the book, the hero's claim to have been visited by Christ, is disappointingly neglected. A similar criticism—that the author fails to explore "provocative possibilities for further development"—was made by Edmund Fuller of *The Seminarian*, an excessively brief and schematic study of the homosexual relationship between two lonely students in a Spanish seminary.

At his best Del Castillo has powerfully and poignantly conveyed his profound sympathy for the oppressed innocents, the victims of history. His attempts to widen his range have lacked the authority of his first two books, but this is a fault that a writer with such a background can overcome.

PRINCIPAL WORKS IN ENGLISH TRANSLATION: Child of Our Time (England, Tanguy), 1958; The Guitar, 1959; The Billsticker, 1959 (U.S., The Disinherited); The Death of Tristan, 1961; Through the Hoop, 1962; The Seminarian, 1970.

ABOUT: Curley, D. N. and Curley, A. (eds.) Modern Romance Literatures (Library of Literary Criticism), 1967; Peyre, H. French Novelists of Today, 1967; Twentieth Century Writing, 1969. *Periodicals*—America March 9, 1963; Commonweal October 17, 1958; Guardian August 26, 1958; New Republic November 3, 1958; New Statesman October 3, 1959; Newsweek February 11, 1963; New Yorker April 27, 1963; New York Herald Tribune Book Review April 17, 1960; New York Times Book Review March 1, 1970; Saturday Review December 20, 1958; April 16, 1960; March 2, 1963; Times Literary Supplement September 5, 1958; November 9, 1962.

DE LIMA, SIGRID (December 4, 1921–), American novelist, writes: "I was born in New York City, the only child of Andrew L. Lang and Agnes de Lima, both of whom were professional writers, and I have some small, irrelevant memories of being a very young city child. But by the time my consciousness really begins, my parents' marriage had broken up and I was living up in Rockland County, New York, in a pre-Revolutionary house where my mother was boarding half a dozen children and running a creative nursery school for them.

"When I was six, we went to Mexico City to stay with my grandfather and two uncles who had settled there some years earlier. My grandfather, at that time president of the Bank of Mexico, was dying and we lived forlornly but grandly in his official residence on the Paseo de la Reforma.

"Next we moved to Palo Alto, California, a small university town, girt about by orchards that bloomed sweetly in the spring over carpets of wild flowers. Above these were marvelous bare hills, softly rounded and forever changing color: from green to a magnificent yellow gold as the wild grass ripened under unvarying blue skies.

"Summers, we went up to the high Sierras or down to the white, rocky, dazzling, empty beaches of the Pacific. Then as I grew older, we began to take long automobile trips, crossing the continent several times and once down to Mexico City and back. Finally when I was fifteen, we returned to New York for good. The summer I was seventeen we went abroad.

"This was not the usual Europe that a young girl visits, however: we traveled from a gray England where our friends huddled over their wireless sets to listen to Chamberlain speaking of peace in our time; to France, where I saw Chartres Cathedral without its glass; to Norway, which was unaccountably filled with German 'tourists' of military age. Finally we reached Switzerland to visit my godmother, Alyse Gregory, formerly managing editor of *The Dial*, and her husband, Llewelyn Powys, the well-known writer, who were living in a tiny, oddly familiar Alpine town—familiar because it was similar to and only a few miles separated it from the setting of Thomas Mann's *Magic Mountain*. This was where I found myself in the early days of September, 1939.

"I spent the next years in college, graduating from Barnard in 1942 and the Columbia School of Journalism in 1944, and then until 1946 I worked in the financial news department of the United Press in New York. There followed a year or two when I freelanced, writing feature stories principally for the Sunday section of the Philadelphia *Inquirer* about financial wizards and lurid murder cases, the cotton industry or curious facts about nails, whatever was wanted at the time. But presently I began to devote full time to writing fiction. In 1948 I published a short story, 'Room With Mirrors,' in the magazine *Tomorrow*.

"That year I enrolled in Hiram Haydn's novel workshop at the New School for Social Research, and the book I began there, *Captain's Beach*, was subsequently published by Scribner's in 1950. This was followed in 1952 by *The Swift Cloud* (published in paperback as *A Mask of Guilt*) and in 1954 by *Carnival by the Sea.*

"In 1953 I was awarded a Prix de Rome—a fellowship in literature at the American Academy in Rome by the American Academy of Arts and Letters. There I met Stephen Greene, the artist (also a Prix de Rome Fellow), and we were married in Rome's Campodoglio, designed by Michelangelo, on Christmas Eve, exactly ten weeks afterwards, going to North Africa for our honeymoon. I now entered quite a different world than I had known previously, for the artists who ventured into the company of the young writers and editors whom I knew best, were few and far between.

"We returned to the United States and lived for two years in the Rockland County home where I spent part of my childhood. In 1956, we moved to Princeton, New Jersey, where my husband was artist-in-residence at the University, and where our daughter Alison was born. I also managed in Princeton to complete my fourth novel, *Praise a Fine Day* (1959). Since then we have lived alternately in New York City and in Rockland County, where I am presently putting the finishing touches on my fifth novel, *Oriane.*"

Captain's Beach is about a seedy rooming house near the New York waterfront and the unhappy people who live there, among them a crippled young book agent, the family he lives with, and a pathetic trio of old ladies. The novel aroused considerable critical interest and, though some reviewers found it almost unbearably gloomy, there was no doubt that it marked the debut of a writer of exceptional promise. Nelson Algren called it "a very real achievement in tenderness, in understanding, and in earnestness," and there was much praise for the prose style, thought notably graphic and articulate. *The Swift Cloud*, concerned with a man falsely accused of murdering his mentally defective son, was similarly praised for its style and sharp observation, but seemed to some readers overwritten and too "dirgelike."

By the time they came to her third book, reviewers were beginning to appreciate the distinctive flavor of Miss de Lima's novels, which Sylvia Stallings compared to a prickly pear, "difficult to penetrate" but full of "a surprising tart sweetness." *Carnival by the Sea* is a tour de force which, mostly through a skillful interweaving of flashback and monologue, pieces together the story and character of a crippled woman coming to the end of her life in a fantastic house in a California resort town. "She has taken what Freud has called the *Familienroman* of the neurotic," wrote Doris Grumbach,

SIGRID DE LIMA

"organized it on her own special terms, placed it in the singular, nightmarish atmosphere of a cold California sun, and made a really good story of it all."

Praise a Fine Day is narrated by an artist who, stranded and penniless in Rome, had contracted to marry the stateless and pregnant mistress of a wealthy Egyptian. As always, wrote Edmund Fuller, the author "is drawn to the strange and peripheral in human experience," and here "continues her advance as one of the most deft, accomplished stylists among our younger writers." The visual quality of the writing, the excellent dialogue, and Miss de Lima's "feeling for subtleties and ambiguities," were particularly admired. Her fifth novel, *Oriane*, disappointed most of its critics, and indeed was not widely reviewed.

PRINCIPAL WORKS: *All novels*—Captain's Beach, 1950; The Swift Cloud (published in paperback as A Mask of Guilt), 1952; Carnival by the Sea, 1954; Praise a Fine Day, 1959; Oriane, 1968.
ABOUT: Current Biography, 1958.

"DELVING, MICHAEL." *See* WILLIAMS, JAY.

DE MOTT, BENJAMIN (HAILE) (June 2, 1924–), American novelist and essayist, writes: "I was born in Rockville Centre, Long Island, New York—the third child of five. My father's family had lived and farmed thereabouts since before 1700 (there are nice uncomplimentary bits about the family in Kenneth Roberts's *Oliver Wiswell*). My mother's family—she was formerly Miss Janet Sanders—is southern, lived for generations in Col-

BENJAMIN DE MOTT

umbia, South Carolina, and once was a shade fancier (in social level) than my father's.

"I was educated in local public schools and in 1940 went to work in New York as a clerk. Three years of mindless jobs in the city (all I could find) and then the Army (I served for the duration as a noncommissioned infantryman). Thereafter I worked in Washington as a reporter and freelance writer, and finally in the late forties managed to get to college, part time, at George Washington University. My teachers—G. W. Stone, Calvin Linton, the late Fred Tupper—were able, overworked, uncommonly generous men; they turned life around for me. Part of what they gave was a nomination for a John Harvard scholarship, which I won, and this enabled me and my family—I had married Miss Margaret Craig of Westbury, Long Island, in 1946, and we had had the first of our four children—to move to Cambridge, Massachusetts, where I became more nearly a genuine student. I studied English literature, tutored Harvard undergraduates and continued to do freelance writing from 1949 to 1951, and then became an instructor at Amherst College. I've moved about a little since then, as teachers do—a period in Portugal, a period as a TV writer and consultant, some jobs as columnist for magazines, Fulbright lecturer in England, etc.—but this town has remained my home.

"I don't remember having had another ambition except to write, and I remember being good with big words in school and relishing the writing even of book reports. Always, as they say, I 'read a lot.' Was the boyish dream of writing merely a dream of coming to notice, being visible, famous and so on? It certainly was. And nowadays when I'm not working, just looking on at myself with a despising eye, I think the usual poisonous writerly thoughts —about vanity, about the puerility of wanting to be known, wanting to be a voice, wanting to be regarded as an interesting type. I can, in short, depress myself about my motives.

"But when I'm writing—at a story or a novel or a piece of reporting or even a review—self-laceration seems wrong. The work is hard, to begin with—practically impossible to cheat at it. Nothing comes easy, the expenditure of effort is constant, the mind actually tires itself. . . . Then too the work produces its own satisfactions—pleasures of discovery—occasional exhilarations at a surprising turn of argument or lucky breeze of livingness suddenly-quietly pushing open the door of a scene. And when something is finished, not possible for me to improve it (now and then, even under deadline, I've had that amazing feeling)—at such moments I tell myself that after all this is my work, it's what I do best (whether I do it well or badly), it's what I am most myself in. The father in my nature, the husband, the teacher—the sailor, the piano player, the gardener, the visiting lecturer, nonpartygoer, department chairman—often these characters talk and act with seeming authority. None is, I hope, a faker through and through. But the least spurious world of confidence I know is a writing world. 'This is the one right way'—I like saying these words and not feeling obliged to step on them instantly with meaching rationalization, explanation, apology.—So it comes out to: this Author loves his work? he has only a sunny commonplace to offer? I *believe* in the work, put it that way. I believe in writing as an arena of self-evident things, a place where rules of truth and feeling are known to me and where I find rules make sense, an act in which pleasure and self-satisfaction are not invariably ambiguous. And I admit I doubt that anyone but a fool would trade off the likes of all this cheap."

Hells & Benefits and *You Don't Say* are two volumes of essays, some of which were first published in magazines, about the contemporary American scene, social, political, and cultural. Both books reflect the generous scope of DeMott's interests and draw a certain unity from the consistency of his point of view. This emerges most clearly in *You Don't Say*, which is concerned with the kind of reductive inhibitions which nowadays forbid, for example, the direct expression of idealism or moral commitment, and which tend to create "a crowd of spectators conscious of experience only as a show not to be interrupted."

DeMott finds the agents of the new orthodoxy in the mass media—in a *Playboy* mentality which offers "a vision of the whole man reduced to his private parts"—and also in an educational and critical apparatus which is "against interpretation" to the extent that this involves moral judgments. Dan Wakefield in his review of *You Don't Say* seemed irritated by the "hopefully hip terms" which sprinkled and jarred with DeMott's "otherwise civilized and often graceful prose," but most reviewers were glad of these essays. R. V. Cassill was reminded by DeMott's "judicious and militant" attitude of Péguy, and thought his book "distinguished by its beauty as by its wisdom," his language "as lucid as it can be while he follows close on the track of obscurantism." *Supergrow* and *Surviving the 70's*, two later volumes of essays, pursue similar themes, concentrating in particular on the failure of imaginative sympathy—the inability and often the refusal to try to understand another from within—which seems to DeMott an increasingly divisive element in American life: "It is a matter simply of a general, culture-wide dimming of the lights of inward life."

The Body's Cage, DeMott's first novel (and first book), examines the divided loyalties of a youth whose younger sister is dying of tuberculosis, denied medical attention by a bogus faith healer who dominates the parents. It was generally well received, admired for its "fluid narrative prose" and a "strong natural talent for characterization," and found powerful if a little portentous. Reviewers detected echoes of both Faulkner and Robert Penn Warren. *A Married Man* is a very short novel about a casual adultery which becomes a cruel trap for the three people involved. Some reviewers thought it unoriginal and limited, but R. V. Cassill called the story "a legend of our times" in which "fate speaks in the banal small-talk of the middle-class sufferers doomed to enact it."

DeMott has taught at Amherst since 1951 and has been professor of English there since 1960, receiving a Harbison award for distinguished teaching in 1969. His special interests include English and American literature and the history of science. In 1962–1964 he wrote a regular column for *Harper's Magazine*.

PRINCIPAL WORKS: *Novels*—The Body's Cage, 1959; A Married Man, 1968. *Essays*—Hells & Benefits: A Report on American Minds, Matters & Possibilities, 1962; You Don't Say: Studies of Modern American Inhibitions, 1966; Supergrow, 1969; Surviving the 70's, 1971.

ABOUT: Contemporary Authors 5–6, 1963; Directory of American Scholars II, 1964; Who's Who in America 1970–1971.

DENNIS, NIGEL (FORBES) (January 16, 1912–), English novelist and dramatist, was born at Bletchingley, Surrey, the son of Lieutenant-Colonel M. F. B. Dennis, DSO, and the former Louise Bosanquet. His father, an officer in a Scottish regiment, died in 1918 and the family moved to

NIGEL DENNIS

Southern Rhodesia, where Nigel Dennis attended the Plumtree School. At fifteen he joined his uncle, a British consular official, in Austria. Dennis completed his education in Europe and returned to England in the Depression.

His literary career had begun when he was fourteen, with short stories written for *The Boy's Own Paper*. During the Depression years he supported himself by "selling silk stockings and tweed suits from door-to-door" and as a versatile contributor to *Time and Tide*, for which he wrote stories and book reviews and devised crossword puzzles.

In 1934 Dennis went to New York for a "brief visit" which lasted fifteen years. He helped to translate into English the works of Alfred Adler, reviewed films as secretary of the National Board of Review of Motion Pictures (1935–1936), and in 1937–1938 was assistant editor and book review editor of the *New Republic*. In 1940 he became a staff book reviewer for *Time* magazine, and remained with Time Inc. until 1958—in New York until 1949 and thereafter with the organization's London bureau. He has served since 1960 as drama critic of *Encounter* (and has collected some of his articles in *Dramatic Essays*), and since 1961 as a staff book reviewer of the *Sunday Telegraph*. He was joint editor of *Encounter* from 1967 to 1970.

Dennis wrote his first novel at eighteen. It was published during World War II but was, he says, "mercifully obliterated from the human scene" when a German bomb disposed of the remainder copies. Other novels, unpublished, "died the lingering death they deserved in damp cabin trunks and forgotten cupboards."

The Sea Change (1949), the first book for which

Dennis is "prepared to take responsibility," won the Anglo-American Novel Contest. It is devoted mainly to Max Divver, an American journalist and left-wing Freudian, who serves his creator as a mouthpiece for disquisitions on identity, psychoanalysis, politics, literary life, the war of the sexes, and a variety of other topics. As satire the book evoked comparisons with Peacock and Aldous Huxley, but critics were more or less in agreement that Dennis's talent for "theoretical *reductio ad absurdum*"—the "unnerving" high spirits of an ingenious mind ruminating, for example, on the future of three hundred eggs or the proceeds of an Evacuation Fund misdelivered to a Polish lunatic asylum in September 1939—is entirely his own and achieves consummate form in his celebrated comic masterpiece, *Cards of Identity*.

"This long, rambling, loosely constructed tale" studies a conference of the Identity Club, whose members seek to rule the world by manipulating the personalities of others. Their success is due less to their brainwashing techniques than to the eagerness of contemporary man—uncertain who or what or why he is—to embrace any unequivocal identity that offers. The novel is in three parts. In the first, three members of the club appropriate an empty country mansion and casually translate a harrassed doctor, a nostalgic Tory, and other local residents into servants, complete with new personalities and appropriate memories. In the second section, the Identity Club, in conference, considers notable case histories: the story of a Communist converted to Catholicism (and making a fortune from his memoirs); an idealistic reformer withdrawn from social struggle to officiate at a ludicrous Olde English ritual. The novel ends with a pseudo-Shakespearean entertainment, full of disguises and identity confusions, a murder, and a raid by the police (who capture no one but the bemused "servants").

Cards of Identity still divides its critics. Some object to its "tasteless" satire on such institutions as law, religion, homosexuality, and the British class system, and find the book's jokes repetitious, its stylistic parodies uneven. Others delight in the " 'bad taste' Dennis so uproariously sloshes about" and add that *Cards of Identity*, for all its limitations and "intellectual tomfoolery" is a virtuoso achievement, a satire of a scope and power not seen in England since the days of Wyndham Lewis, a "Pirandello plot narrated by Chesterton, with dialogue by Evelyn Waugh and Ivy Compton-Burnett."

Dennis adapted the novel for the stage in 1956. A second play, *The Making of Moo*, records the development of a new religion in Africa. Devised by a British engineer to replace an ancient river cult inadvertently destroyed by a new dam, the worship of Moo originates as a rational code of ethics, acquires a liturgy and hierarchy and, as it gathers momentum, embraces prophecy, myth, and human sacrifice. Moovianism finally goes into a polite decline reminiscent of the present state of the Church of England. After a bold opening the play weakens, some thought, "as the characters gradually turn into abstractions." It remains, nevertheless, pungent and engaging, a devastating attack on religion. Both plays were welcomed by George E. Wellwarth for their "innate and intuitive sense of the theatre," and as the work of "an unabashedly intellectual dramatist" who is "a worthy, direct-line descendant of Shaw." They were published together in 1958 with a brilliantly witty preface. Dennis has written a third but inferior play, a political farce called *August for the People*.

A House in Order, Dennis's fourth novel, appeared eleven years after the third. Set during an unnamed war, it opens with its anonymous narrator trying desperately to be captured by the enemy. Denied official imprisonment, he incarcerates himself in the prison greenhouse, cares for the plants there, and with them survives the dreadful hardships of winter. His unwilling captors, discounting his protestations of cowardice, assume him to be a spy of great cunning and courage. At length he is returned to the perils of freedom in his native land, where he is hailed as a hero—an irony similar to that in *The Sea Change*, where Max Divver dies attempting murder and is mourned as a martyr. *A House in Order*, which utterly confounded some of its reviewers, was read by others as a morality play against war, an allegory of "the artist's present peripheral relation to society," and/or as a rebuttal of existentialist philosophy. It was agreed only that Dennis, eschewing in this book his gifts for comedy and parody, had lost none of his originality.

For his biography of a fellow satirist, *Jonathan Swift*, Dennis received an award from the Royal Society of Literature. He has also published a volume of rather prosy poems about the Mediterranean and the Middle East, past and present, called *Exotics*. It includes a version of the Sumerian "Epic of Gilgamesh," and translations of the Italian satirical poet Giuseppe Giusti.

Cards of Identity was first seen at the Royal Court Theatre in July 1956, immediately after John Osborne's *Look Back in Anger* had launched there a new era in the British theatre. For this reason, perhaps, Dennis was at one time bracketed with Osborne as an "Angry Young Man." He is, on the contrary, said to be diffident and shy and, according to Osborne, "the most charming, kindest and mildest of men." Dennis is the father of two daughters by his first marriage and lives in Malta with his second wife, the former Beatrice Matthew.

PRINCIPAL WORKS: Boys and Girls Come Out to Play (novel), 1949 (U.S., A Sea Change); Cards of Identity (novel), 1955; Two Plays and a Preface, 1958; Dramatic Essays, 1962; Jonathan Swift, 1964; A House in Order (novel), 1966; Exotics (poems), 1970; An Essay on Malta, 1972.

ABOUT: Allen, W. The Modern Novel, 1964; Allsop, K. The Angry Decade, 1958; Contemporary Authors 25–28, 1971; Gindin, J. Postwar British Fiction, 1962; Karl, F. R. A Reader's Guide to the Contemporary English Novel, 1962; Wellwarth, G. E. The Theater of Protest and Paradox, 1964; Who's Who, 1971. *Periodicals*—London Magazine November 1963; Times Literary Supplement October 27, 1966.

"DENNIS, PATRICK." *See* TANNER, EDWARD EVERETT

***DERMOÛT, MARIA** (June 15, 1888–June 27, 1962), Dutch memoirist, novelist, and short story writer, whose full name was Helena Antonia Maria Elisabeth Dermoût-Ingermann, was born at Pekalongan, on the island of Java, in the Dutch East Indies (now Indonesia). Her father's family, which included merchant marine officers and newspaper publishers, had been connected with the East Indies since her great-grandfather first went to the islands in the service of the Dutch East India Company. As a child, Maria Dermoût lived with her parents on a sugar plantation in central Java. Before she was six she had made two visits to the Netherlands, and at the age of eleven she went to Holland for her education, attending a girls' *gymnasium* in Haarlem. She was married at eighteen to Abraham Dermoût and returned with him to the East Indies. Maria Dermoût remained in the East for twenty-seven years, traveling widely in the islands with her husband and living at various times in the Moluccas, the Celebes, and Java. Her children and grandchildren were also born in the East Indies.

It was not until she was in her sixties that she began her literary career. Her first book, *Nog pas gisteren* (1951, translated as *Yesterday*), was a fictionalized memoir of her childhood in Java. It recreates an orderly colonial society of carriages and gaslight and plentiful servants, strangely superimposed on a country of lush primitive beauty, still haunted by ancient and barbaric beliefs and rituals. The book, which evokes the cruelty and fear in this world as well as the beauty, was said to "resemble a poem in its unity and sustained intensity." One reviewer called it "a brilliant batik of heliotrope and scarlet orchids and cockatoos," and another observed that the author writes as if "with a peacock's feather upon a rice-paper scroll."

Nog pas gisteren, the first of Maria Dermoût's books in order of writing, was preceded in English translation by *De tenduizend dingen* (1955). It appeared in the United States as *The Ten Thousand Things*, superbly translated, like *Yesterday*, by the novelist Hans Koningsberger. A woman sits in her garden on a spice-growing estate in the Moluccas and thinks back over the people, places, sights, events, that have made up her life. Reviewers were divided as to the nature of the book—describing it variously as a novel, a memoir, and a volume of short stories—but in absolute agreement as to its quality. Whitney Balliett thought it "a primitive work in the best sense," with passages of such "startling, unadorned, three-dimensional clarity" that "one can almost touch what she describes." Phoebe Adams called it "a tough-minded pagan statement . . . a great paean of admiration for the beauty of the world and a lament that all this life and beauty must end in death." The book has an elusive quality of mystery which reminded some reviewers of the work of Isak Dinesen, while Maria Dermoût's spare but marvelously evocative and sensual prose evoked comparisons with Thoreau and the early Hemingway.

MARIA DERMOÛT

Other works by Maria Dermoût include a book of sketches, *Spel van Tifagong's* (1954) and the collections of short stories *De juwelen haarkam* (1956) and *De kist; en enige verhalen* (1958). Her posthumously published works include *De sirenen* (1963), *Donker van uiterlijk* (1964), and *Zo luidt het verhaal: de goede slang; de oliftanen; het kanon* (1964).

Although Maria Dermoût wrote with great nostalgia of the colonial past, there is no bitterness in her work for the passing of that era, idyllic as it was for her and her peers. One of her favorite quotations was from a poem by Sacheverell Sitwell: "I have lived to see what I was born to see / It is not 'une pauvre terre' after all / It has splendours as well

* dâr mōōt′

as miseries to recommend it." During her last years she withdrew from the world, doing much of her work in a house she owned at Ascona, in Switzerland. She was a writer quite outside the literary mainstream but was by no means ignored. Among the honors accorded to her were a special prize of the Jan Campert Foundation in 1952; the Cultural Prize of the Municipality of Arnhem in 1955; and the Tollens Prize in 1957. She died in the Hague at the age of seventy-four, a little more than a decade after she had begun her literary career.

PRINCIPAL WORKS IN ENGLISH TRANSLATION: The Ten Thousand Things, 1958; Yesterday, 1959 (England, Days Before Yesterday).
ABOUT: Lexikon der Weltliteratur, 1963; Moderne Encyclopedie der Wereld Literatuur, 1964; Winkler Prins Boek van het Jaar, 1963.

***DÉRY, TIBOR** (October 18, 1894–), Hungarian novelist, writer of short stories, poet, and critic, writes (in German): "As I consider it a folly and nonsense for artists to comment on themselves, I shall restrict myself to dates and facts. Anything else the reader can best learn from my books.

"Born in Budapest, Hungary, into a lawyer's family, I fell ill at the age of four or five with tuberculosis of the bones, which in Hungary is called 'the English disease,' and was confined to bed for four years. After having been treated by numerous native and foreign doctors, I eventually arrived at a German sanatorium by the North Sea where I recovered completely. My schooling I completed somewhat behind time, first at the Lateinische Gymnasium, then the Handelsakademie, followed by two years at a Swiss *Collegium*, from which—driven by the physical and psychological constraint exercised there—I bolted twice, trying to reach Budapest on foot without any money, being unsuccessful on both occasions.

"Working in the office of a large timberworks and sawmill, of which my uncle was managing director, I soon lost all enthusiasm for business life. I was still spending my days in this way when my first literary work was published with a double success: amazed frowns from the literary world and a severe court sentence for an offense against morality. The high fine, ten times my remuneration, was paid by the begrudging publishers.

"In the first World War I was, as an employee of the strategically important sawmill, exempted from military service, but when I organized a strike against my uncle in 1918, I was called up again. Fortunately, the war soon came to an end, but it was followed in Hungary by two revolutions—a democratic one and a Communist one—in both of which I took part, if not with saber and shotgun and not in an official position, at least with youthful commitment and enthusiasm, which was dampened only by my father's tragic suicide. When Admiral Horthy crushed the Reds and I had fallen several times into the hands of White terror groups, I eventually had to emigrate. I spent seven years in Austria, Germany, France, and Italy with my first wife, most of the time in very poor circumstances, as laborer, journalist—there was never a worse one —as agent, stamp dealer, language teacher, etc. Even after returning to Hungary I couldn't much further my literary career; my surrealistic works did not catch on with the publishers, nor did my politically notorious name, which was blacklisted by the police. I don't think that in the first twenty years of my literary life I earned more than one week's living per year. When, apart from that, the political conditions in the country were not to my liking, and I was also separated from my wife, I again—this time supported by friends—went on long journeys abroad, to (among other countries) Spain and Yugoslavia, spending a year in each. Here I succeeded in writing my first tolerably good books.

"Despite that, however, I still had to wait for years to find publishers—until the end of World War II, which I spent at home as unfit for active service. I earned my living by translating books which were mostly bad, the publishers trusting me for my knowledge of languages. During the last months of the war I was several times carried off by the Hungarian National Socialists, but managed to escape every time; not so my brother, who ended in the gas chambers of Auschwitz.

"After the end of World War II my books were published in quick succession until the moment when, after initial agreement and collaboration, I fell into ever increasing opposition to Rákosi's regime. Only the overthrow of the dictator saved me from another arrest—which, as I learned afterwards—had already been decided upon. Shortly after that I was nevertheless arrested as a party to the October Revolution of 1956 and sentenced to nine years at hard labor. Worth mentioning is the fact—which figures among the memorable occasions of my life—that international protest actions were staged in Europe as well as in America against my sentence and that of my codefendants—protests in which not only politicians took part but also writers of all nationalities, including those of the English tongue, like T. S. Eliot, E. M. Forster, W. Somerset Maugham, Charles Morgan, J. B. Priestley, Bertrand Russell, C. P. Snow, Stephen Spender, etc.

"I was given an amnesty after three years' imprisonment, during which time my ninety-six-year-old mother died without my seeing her again. At first I had to earn my living once again by translating, which increased the number of books trans-

* dā′ rē

lated by me to between forty and fifty. Since 1963 I have, however, had my own works published again, among others a novel written in the three years of my imprisonment.

"Today I can, despite my critical temperament, write and publish freely. The work gives me as much pleasure as it did in my younger years, if not more."

As he says, the books which established Déry as a major and even a patriarchal figure in Hungarian literature did not find publishers until the end of World War II, when he was in his fifties. This was part of the price he has had to pay for the chronic nonconformity imposed upon him by his country's recent history and his own integrity. For his books reveal a skeptical and inquiring element in his nature which would make it difficult for him to commit himself unreservedly to any totalitarian system.

Some critics have detected an occasional detached and ironic note even in the pro-Communist enthusiasm of his first major novel, *A befejezetlen mondat* (The Unfinished Sentence), written during the 1930s but not published until 1945, after the fall of the Horthy regime. And *Felelet* (The Answer) caused a major controversy in 1952 by implicitly questioning the ability of the Communist regime to solve the country's problems. *Niki*, published a few years later, and ostensibly the story of a fox terrier bitch, was an even harsher indictment of the regime's inhumanity. It is a touching story, without the turgidity of Déry's longer novels. Translated under the same title by Edward Hyams, it was warmly received by English language reviewers. Norman MacKenzie wrote: "*Niki* is a fable, moving, beautifully conceived, its texture firm and splendidly simple. . . . The force of *Niki*, for an English reader, may lie in its gentle understatement, its ability to convey the atmosphere of fear through the simple relationship of a man, a woman and a dog."

Most critics agree, however, that in general Déry is at his best in his short stories. Although his themes are often political, a study of his work in this form suggests that his interest is not in ideologies, but in the effects of political interference in the lives of ordinary people. His themes are isolation and loneliness, and the destruction of personality under repression, but also the resilience of human beings, and their capacity for comradeship and love even in despair.

Thus, most of the stories collected in translations by Kathleen Szasz in *The Portuguese Princess* are about life in Budapest at the end of World War II, when the city was under Russian siege. These are wry, understated studies of waifs, doomed lovers, and bewildered old people poised between the past and an unknown future—of all those, as Keith

TIBOR DÉRY

Kraus wrote, "who grope towards 'the gentle, inward order of resignation.' " Sometimes grotesque, sometimes poignant, often a characteristic blend of burlesque and tragedy, these tales, another critic said, achieve at their best "the force and beauty of a parable." Such a story is the title piece, in which three orphaned children, refugees wandering in the Hungarian lowlands, chance upon a performance by traveling players of the drama of *The Portuguese Princess* and are enchanted and altered by this taste of fantasy.

Déry's more recent work includes another collection of short stories, old and new, called *Szerelem* (Love, 1963), and the satirical Utopian novel *G. A. ur X-ben* (Mr. G. A. in X, 1964). These books express the sense of freedom of which Déry writes above, but many critics found his memoirs, which began to appear in *Magyar Nemzet* in 1968, altogether too outspoken. They were subsequently published in book form as *Itélet nincs* (No Verdict). Partly because he exhumes an old political controversy, partly because of a startlingly frank account of an adulterous love affair of the 1930s, the author found himself at the age of seventy-four once more at the center of violent controversy. But the book is far more than a *chronique scandaleuse*. As one reviewer wrote in the *Times Literary Supplement*, it "reveals Déry's marvellous powers of observation and his dazzling use of metaphor" and "an almost Proustian subtlety of association." It "confirms Déry among the few outstanding writers in Hungarian of our times, and certainly as the greatest writer now writing in Hungary."

Déry was married in 1955 to Elisabeth Hulman. He lives in Budapest.

PRINCIPAL WORKS IN ENGLISH TRANSLATION: Niki: The Story of a Dog, 1958; The Giant (stories), 1965; The Portuguese Princess, 1967. *Stories in* Duczynska, I. and Polányi, K. The Plough and the Pen, 1963; New Hungarian Quarterly IV 10.
ABOUT: Klaniczay, T. and others. History of Hungarian Literature, 1964; Konnyu, L. Modern Magyar Literature, 1964; Twentieth Century Writing, 1969; Who's Who in America, 1970–1971. *Periodicals*—Nation June 1, 1957; New York Times November 5, 1968; Time November 25, 1957; October 5, 1962; Times Literary Supplement February 2, 1967; February 12, 1970.

***DESNOS, ROBERT** (July 4, 1900–June 8, 1945), French poet, was born near the central market in an ancient section of Paris called Saint-Merri. His father kept a small café. After elementary school and commercial college, Desnos began to earn his living as a clerk. A natural writer whose first poem was published before he was sixteen, he soon found a foothold in journalism as literary columnist of *Paris-Soir*. Compulsory military service took him to Morocco, but during a leave he met André Breton who, after Desnos's release from the army, became his close friend. Breton was then building surrealism and recruited Desnos to the new movement in 1922.

In the surrealists' experiments with automatic writing, Desnos proved a perfect medium. Breton wrote of him that he had come closest of them all to the surrealist truth, that he could "read in himself as in an open book." Desnos was making a scanty living as a journalist and had broken with his family, but he wrote and drew and painted, throwing himself into the artistic life of the capital with delighted enthusiasm. He was a thin man with hollow cheeks and bright eyes, his hair constantly flopping over his forehead. Subject to fits of melancholy, he was for the most part of sanguine temperament, with a fanciful sense of humor which made him one of the best-loved members of his circle. Desnos sought to live as surrealistically as he wrote. His sexual adventures were notorious, he drank and gambled heavily, and though not an addict, turned to drugs at times of stress.

Desnos's first book of poems was published in 1924. Another early work, *La Liberté ou l'amour!* (Liberty or Love, 1927), was to his astonishment condemned by the courts as pornographic. It was at about this time that he met Youki Foujita, who brought some order into his life, whom he married, and who remained his inspiration until the end of his life. Their studio on the rue Blomet became a center for surrealist gatherings, and the dance hall next door thumped with the rumba records Desnos brought to Paris from a journalists' convention in Havana.

In 1930 appeared *The Night of Loveless Nights* (of which only the title is in English). A despairing

* dā nō′

ROBERT DESNOS

modern epic on the Don Juan theme, it explored the loneliness and emptiness of the life of erotic adventure and is one of Desnos's best known poems. *Corps et biens* (With All Hands), also published in 1930, collected the verse written between 1919 and 1929. Some critics have been repelled by what they saw as a "crawling accumulation of filth" but most have found much beauty in the bizarre dream imagery of these poems, their hypnotic repetition of words and rhythms, their power to wring wonder from the banal. These early lyrics are generally considered Desnos's best work.

His break with surrealism came in the same year, 1930, when he contributed to a rebellion against Breton and was excommunicated. Desnos, whose "necessary and unforgettable" role in the movement had just been acknowledged by Breton, retained many friends who were surrealists and continued to be influenced by the movement's theories. In 1932 he became a radio writer, and between then and the beginning of the war his output, income, and reputation soared. He poured out radio scripts, songs, sketches, articles, and poems in vast numbers and wrote a number of film scenarios. During 1936, as an experiment, he wrote a poem every day of the year. He and Youki lived on the rue Mazarine, and his great talent for friendship brought there Barrault and Madeleine Renaud, Picasso and Hemingway, Éluard, Artaud, and Dos Passos.

Desnos was recalled to the army in 1939 but returned to Paris after the capitulation and continued his career. During the occupation he played a part in the Resistance, and under the pseudonyms of Guillois and Cancale wrote poems, some of them in the Parisian argot, which delighted French readers with their hidden tilts at the invaders. In 1942 he published his only novel, *Le Vin est tiré* (The Wine Is Drawn), a story about drug addiction marred, like much of his later work, by signs of haste and an excessive facility. Soon afterwards he completed *La Place de l'Étoile*, a play begun many years earlier which its translator, Michael Benedikt, praised for its "lyrical delicacy" and called "the first masterpiece produced by surrealism in the theatre."

On February 22, 1944, Desnos was arrested by the Gestapo and denounced while in custody by a French collaborator. He was sent to Auschwitz and Buchenwald, and later made the terrible journey to the international ghetto at Terezin in Czechoslovakia, where he caught typhoid. He was still alive when the camp was liberated in May 1945 and was recognized by Josef Stuna, a young Czech medical student who struggled in vain to save his life. Stuna found on him a poem beginning "*J'ai rêvé tellement fort à toi*"—a revision of one written twenty years before to Youki. Desnos's ashes were brought by a delegation of Czech writers to Paris and honored there with civil and religious ceremonies. His *Choix de poèmes* was published in 1946. Much of Desnos's later work was ephemeral, but his permanent poems place him, Wallace Fowlie has suggested, with Breton, Éluard, and Artaud, as "one of the four authentic surrealist poets."

PRINCIPAL WORKS IN ENGLISH TRANSLATION: *Poems in* Barnstone, W. (ed.) Modern European Poetry, 1966; Fowlie, W. Mid-Century French Poets, 1955; La Place de l'Étoile *in* Benedikt, M. and Wellwarth, G. E. Modern French Plays, 1964.

ABOUT: Berger, P. Robert Desnos, 1949; Bucholе, R. L'évolution poétique de Robert Desnos, 1960; Desnos, Y. Les Confidences de Youki Desnos, 1957; Fowlie, W. Mid-Century French Poets, 1955; Hackett, C. A. Anthology of Modern French Poetry, 1952; Huguet, G. *introduction to* Desnos's Choix de poèmes; Lemaitre, G. From Cubism to Surrealism, 1947; Peyre, H. Contemporary French Literature, 1964; Raymond, M. From Beaudelaire to Surrealism, 1957; Rousselot, J. Les Nouveaux Poètes Français, 1959.

***DEUTSCHER, ISAAC** (April 3, 1907–August 19, 1967), Anglo-Polish author, journalist, and historian of modern European affairs, wrote the following note shortly before his death: "I was born near Cracow, Poland's medieval capital, into an orthodox Jewish family, in which some of the traditions of medieval Judaism still lived on. The first act of my self-determination was to renounce religious orthodoxy, to write poetry in Polish, and to translate Hebrew, Yiddish, German and Latin poetry. (I began to publish my writings at the age of sixteen.) The next act of my self-determination was to renounce my bourgeois environment and become a member of the outlawed Communist party of Poland. From poetry I moved to literary criticism, from this to philosophy, from that to history, and then to economics. These were the successive stages of my renunciation of the bourgeois *Weltanschauung* and of my study and acceptance of Marxism and Leninism, which opened my eyes to the pure poetry of class struggle and socialist revolution.

* doich′ ər

ISAAC DEUTSCHER

"In the course of six years, from 1926 till 1932, I fought in the heroic ranks of the Polish Communists; conducted, as an ordinary soldier, revolutionary agitation in Marshal Pilsudski's army; edited many periodicals and wrote scores of pamphlets and masses of leaflets. I did also some large-scale historical and political studies, which never had any chance of passing the Polish censorship of those years.

"In 1931, with three or four comrades, I founded the first anti-Stalinist opposition in the Polish Communist party. We tried to arouse the party and the Communist International to the dangers of rising Nazism; we demanded joint action with the Socialists against Hitler and Pilsudski; and we denounced Stalin and his henchmen for leading European communism to catastrophe and denying us freedom of expression and policy-making. In June 1932 I was expelled from the party; and the official motive of my disgrace was that I had 'exaggerated the danger of Nazism and was spreading panic.' After that I was active in anti-Stalinist groups on the Left, but mainly as a political freelance, strongly influenced by the ideas and fate of Leon Trotsky. Like my comrades, I was persecuted simultaneously by the Pilsudskist political police and by the Stalinists; but as Poland had an anti-Communist government at that time, no decent person in the West protested in the name of 'cultural freedom.'

"In April 1939 I emigrated to England and began to learn English and to write in it. In the same year I became a contributor to *The Economist* (London); and from 1942 till 1947 I was its expert on Soviet affairs and chief European correspondent. In the meantime I still joined the Polish army which had, in 1940, escaped under General Sikorski from Nazi-conquered France, and re-assembled in Scotland. But I spent most of my time there in a kind of a punitive camp for criminals—in this way I was punished for my protests against the anti-Semitism that was rampant in that army. Released, I re-joined *The Economist* and joined also the staff of *The Observer* (London), for which I was, *inter alia*, a roving European correspondent (pen name 'Peregrine').

"At the end of 1946, jaded with journalism and unwilling to wage the cold war, I withdrew from Fleet Street and regular journalism. I wrote *Stalin: A Political Biography*, published by Oxford University Press in 1949, and described as 'the most controversial political biography of our time.' The book has been re-printed many times and translated and re-translated in a dozen languages. My *Trotsky* trilogy (*The Prophet Armed, The Prophet Unarmed, The Prophet Outcast*) appeared in the years 1954, 1959, 1963, arousing not less controversy on both sides of the Atlantic, and in every language into which it has been translated. This biographical series is to be concluded with a study of Lenin. These works will, I hope, eventually be seen as a single essay in a Marxist analysis of the revolution of our age and perhaps also as a triptych of some artistic unity. I have written and published more articles, treatises and collections of essays than I can mention here. My great teachers are Spinoza and Hegel, Marx and Herzen, Engels and Heine, Rosa Luxemburg and Kautsky, Lenin and Trotsky. I have sat at the feet of the classical French historians of the Revolution and Freud's wisdom has deeply impressed me. Indebted beyond all measure to the poetry of my native country, I was careful not to try and emulate my famous countryman, Joseph Conrad, in bringing the Polish literary idiom into the English language. I have tried instead to learn a little English from Gibbon and Macaulay. If my work does something to free a few minds from the fetishes of bourgeois ideology and from the lingering idiocies of Stalinism, I shall have achieved something; and the day on which Russians are at last free to read my *Trotsky*, *Stalin* and *Lenin* will be a great day for me and perhaps not only for me."

Isaac Deutscher was born in Chrzanów into a respected family of orthodox Jews, the eldest of three children of Jacob Deutscher, a printer and publisher, and his second wife, the former Gustawa Jolles. Deutscher attended the local *heder* (elementary Jewish school), where he was immediately recognized as an infant prodigy, the possessor of "a fantastic memory, capacious mind and an uncommon ability for abstract thinking." At the age of thirteen, after delivering a learned discourse on the qualities of the Kikiyon, a mythical bird, he was received as a rabbi. But even then he felt "an unexpected sense of embarrassment, of unease," and he quickly rejected "all this pseudo-knowledge [which] cluttered and strained my memory, took me away from real life." Deutscher studied simultaneously at the *Gymnasium* and went on as an extramural student to the Yagellon University in Cracow. His early poetry, written in Polish, attempted a fusion of "Polish romanticism with Jewish lyrical folklore."

When he was eighteen Deutscher went to Warsaw, where he studied philosophy and economics. A year later, in 1926, he joined the outlawed Polish Communist party in which he was soon an important figure as an editor and pamphleteer. In 1931 he visited the Soviet Union and saw for himself the rigors of Stalinism. Declining academic positions in Russia, he returned to Poland to organize the work against Stalinism that led to his expulsion from the Communist party and his migration to England. As he says, Deutscher reached London in April 1939, began to learn English, and the same year became a contributor to *The Economist*, an astonishing feat. He was a brilliant journalist, distinguished by his wide personal knowledge of Eastern Europe, his direct and trenchant style, his passion for facts, and above all, his ability to convey the human importance of the events he described.

Deutscher's first major work was his political (as distinct from personal) biography of Stalin. Reinforcing his argument with close historical analysis and many telling anecdotes, he presented a very different picture of Stalin from the one currently accepted in the West—of a man uncertain and clumsy, constantly forced to contradict himself, and unable to control the forces he sets in motion. The book was widely recognized as one of the finest political biographies of our time and in 1966, when a revised version appeared, one critic said that this "brilliant summing-up of the grandeurs and miseries of Stalin's achievements . . . is still valid today."

For his biography of Trotsky, Deutscher had access to the Trotsky Archives at Harvard University, including the so-called Closed Section. This contains Trotsky's political correspondence during his time of exile and provides an exceptionally wide and detailed picture, not just of his own activities but of the internal politics of the Soviet

Union and the Communist movement during the years between the wars. The biography, intended as a one-volume work, extended to three: *The Prophet Armed*, covering the years of Trotsky's rise to great power (1879–1921); *The Prophet Unarmed*, about his fall (1921–1929); and *The Prophet Outcast*, about his exile (1929–1940).

This trilogy, superbly researched, clearly and energetically written, provides one of the most absorbing accounts of the history of modern communism and a magnificent "monument to one of the most remarkable historical figures of the present century." Deutscher, said a reviewer in the *Times Literary Supplement*, "is an exceedingly vivid writer with a sense of style and a warm and understanding sympathy for his hero: this makes him a first-rate biographer. But he also has the passion for analysis of the true historian, the eternal search for the answer to the question: why? And his answers are always based on wide knowledge and acute observation."

Deutscher's death, from a heart attack in Rome, prevented him from completing his biography of Lenin; its first chapter has been published as *Lenin's Childhood*. His widow Tamara, whom he married in 1947 and who had helped him greatly in his work, published in 1968 a collection of Deutscher's essays called *The Non-Jewish Jew*. In it he analyzes certain traits shared by such Jewish "heretics" as Spinoza, Heine, Marx, Trotsky, and Freud. They all rejected the "too narrow, too archaic" boundaries of Jewry, and all matured at times and in places where the most diverse cultural influences fertilized each other. Each lived in intellectual exile on the periphery of his society and thus was able to rise above and beyond its received ideas and attitudes. It was in this tradition that Deutscher worked.

Other essays have been collected in *Russia After Stalin*, which centers on the Stalinist "cult of personality" and its disintegration; *Russia in Transition* and *The Great Contest*, about the "thaw" under Khrushchev and the Cold War; *Ironies of History*; and in two posthumous volumes, *Russia, China, and the West* and *Marxism in Our Time*. *The Unfinished Revolution: Russia 1917–1967*, contains Deutscher's G. M. Trevelyan Lectures, given at Cambridge in 1966–1967.

PRINCIPAL WORKS: Stalin: A Political Biography, 1949; Soviet Trade Unions, 1950; Russia After Stalin, 1953 (U.S., Russia: What Next?); The Prophet Armed: Trotsky 1879–1921, 1954; Russia in Transition, 1957 (republished as Heretics and Renegades, 1969); The Prophet Unarmed: Trotsky 1921–1929, 1959; The Great Contest: Russia and the West, 1960; The Prophet Outcast: Trotsky 1929–1940, 1963; Ironies of History, 1966; The Unfinished Revolution: Russia 1917–1967, 1967; The Non-Jewish Jew, 1968; Russia, China, and the West: A Contemporary Chronicle, 1953–1966, 1970; Lenin's Childhood, 1970; Marxism in Our Time, 1972.

ABOUT: Deutscher, T. *introduction to* The Non-Jewish Jew, 1968; Goldsmith, S. J. Twenty Twentieth Century Jews, 1962; Horowitz, D. (ed.) Isaac Deutscher: The Man and His Work, 1971; Who's Who, 1968. *Periodicals*—Nation March 15, 1971; New York Review of Books April 20, 1967; New York Times August 20, 1967; Newsweek August 28, 1967; Publishers Weekly August 28, 1967; Saturday Review October 1, 1949; Times (London) August 21, 1967; Times Literary Supplement August 28, 1953; October 2, 1959; July 8, 1960; November 7, 1963; June 23, 1966; August 3, 1967; October 23, 1968; December 5, 1968; July 10, 1969; August 4, 1970; November 20, 1970.

DEVLIN, DENIS (April 15, 1908–August 21, 1959), Irish poet and translator, was the eldest son of a prosperous Irish businessman who lived in Greenock, Scotland. Devlin was born in Greenock and spent his early childhood there until, when he was ten, the family returned to Ireland. Their house was a meeting place for such political leaders as Michael Collins and Éamon de Valera, and Devlin's home life was a happy and lively one.

He was educated by the Christian Brothers and at Belvedere College, Dublin (Joyce's college). There followed a year at All Hallows College as a clerical student. Although Devlin was very brilliant and passionately religious, he found that the priesthood was not for him and left the seminary to study languages at University College, Dublin. Mervyn Wall met him at Belvedere in 1924 and says: "There was a strangeness about him . . . a courtesy and a charm unusual in schoolboys. . . . He had a notable, sometimes self-deprecatory, sense of humour of a quizzical kind and a self-conscious humorous habit of standing with his arms hanging loosely on either side of his open overcoat. I remember a cartoon in our University College days which depicted him as a penguin with cherrywood pipe stuck in his mouth." At University College Devlin was one of the founders of the dramatic society, and in those philistine days caused something of a sensation there when in 1930 he and his friend Brian Coffey jointly published a small volume of verse.

After taking his degree in languages Devlin paid his first visit to the Blaskets, remote islands off the coast of Kerry, to improve his knowledge of the Irish language. Later he collaborated with Niall Montgomery in translating poems by Verlaine, Baudelaire, and Rimbaud into Gaelic, though these remarkable experiments were never published. In 1930–1931 he studied at Munich University and then at the Sorbonne in Paris. After a brief visit to Spain in 1932 he returned to University College where he taught for a time and wrote a thesis on Montaigne which earned him his M.A. (1933).

Devlin entered the Irish diplomatic service in 1935 as a cadet. A book of poems, *Intercessions*, appeared in 1937, and was notable for the richness of its vocabulary, its technical assurance, and the

DENIS DEVLIN

wide acquaintance it reflected with European literature. Some critics found Devlin's religious fervor unacceptable however, and one dismissed it as "more intoxicated than intelligent."

In 1938 Devlin became first secretary to the Irish legation in Rome and the following year went to New York as consul. From 1940 to 1947 he was first secretary to his country's legation in Washington. Robert Penn Warren read Devlin's poem "Lough Derg" early in World War II and published it in *Southern Review* in 1942. He thought it "a beautiful poem, calm and poised but glowing with feeling . . . in a peculiar contrast to most of the poetry of that period, outside of schools and trends." Warren met Devlin two years later at Katherine Anne Porter's house in Washington. "It was then," Warren recalls, "that I first got a real sense of Denis's quality—the easy wit without malice or egotism, the flashes of learning, the gaiety that was apt to burst into song, and most of all, the gift of making other people break away from their preoccupations and discover their own gaiety."

At the end of the war Devlin published a series of translations from St. John Perse. A collection of his own, *Lough Derg and Other Poems*, came out in 1946. Again there was a preponderance of religious poems, but these were not the fevered lyrics of *Intercessions*. The models here were Perse and Yeats, not Rimbaud and Baudelaire, and the results were subtle and complex in thought, exact and classical in manner. They seemed to Babette Deutsch more learned than accomplished, but Marguerite Young found them, for all their abstract intellectuality, fundamentally Romantic.

Devlin went home in 1947, becoming counselor to the Irish High Commission in London and then to the Ministry of External Affairs in Dublin. From 1950 until his death he lived mostly in Italy, first as minister plenipotentiary and from 1958 onwards as Ireland's first ambassador in Rome. A visit to Turkey in 1951 as minister plenipotentiary is remembered in "Memoirs of a Turcoman Diplomat," published in *Botteghe Oscure*.

Thanks to Devlin the Irish Embassy in Rome became a place where, as Ignazio Silone said, "Italian writers and poets could come together, including many commonly rather restive of the social round and diplomatic residences." Silone, who admired above all Devlin's "absolute lack of pose," detected in him during these last years an "habitual sadness"—an instinctive foreknowledge perhaps of the still undetected disease that was to kill him. During this period, at any rate, Devlin published no books of verse, though some poems continued to appear in magazines. He occupied himself a great deal with translations of Goethe, Apollinaire, Quasimodo, and others. Many of these translations remain unpublished, as does Devlin's unfinished autobiography. He died in Dublin at the age of fifty-one and was survived by his wife, the former Marie Caren Radon, whom he had married in 1946, and his son Stephen. His friend Niall Montgomery spoke of him as "a secret, special fellow . . . crystalline, passionate, unquestionable," whose speech and presence "seemed to proliferate metamorphoses" in those around him.

Devlin's *Collected Poems*, edited by Brian Coffey, was published posthumously in Dublin in 1963, and the same year a *Selected Poems* appeared in the United States, edited by Allen Tate and Robert Penn Warren. It was, Ray Smith wrote, "a special poetry of personal shorthand and telescoped syntax —compressed, dense, hermetic, with occasional vivid imagery." Tate and Warren in their introduction said that Devlin had written "many good poems and perhaps three great ones." The three they meant included two long religious poems, "The Passion of Christ" and "Lough Derg," and one political one, "From Government Buildings." Some critics would add a fourth, "The Heavenly Foreigner," but Hayden Carruth was doubtful if any of them were quite good enough to be called great. For him, he said, "they lack the strength of vision, rhythm, and feeling . . . which would be required to sustain them as whole poems." Yet he saw that this was an important book: "It contains nothing cute, stereotyped, facile, or merely debonair. It is hard-wrought work, and like other such its surface appeal is overborne by its deeper urgencies; but this does not mean we may not ultimately come to prize it."

PRINCIPAL WORKS: (with Brian Coffey) Poems, 1930 (Dublin); Intercessions, 1937; Lough Derg and Other

Poems, 1946; Collected Poems (ed. by Brian Coffey), 1963 (Dublin); Selected Poems (ed. by Allen Tate and Robert Penn Warren), 1963. *Translations of St. John Perse*—Rains, 1945; Snows, 1945; Exile, 1949.

ABOUT: Coffey, B. *introduction to* Devlin's Collected Poems; Tate, A. and Warren, R. P. *introduction to* Devlin's Selected Poems, 1963. *Periodicals*—Ireland (weekly bulletin of the Irish Department of External Affairs) September 5, 1960; Nation August 10, 1946; New York Times August 22, 1959; Times (London) August 22, 1959.

DE VRIES, PETER (February 27, 1910–), American novelist and satirist, writes: "I was born in Chicago into a Dutch immigrant community of Christian Reformed Calvinists who were so determined to preserve their special identity, and who so resisted Americanization, that my origins would have been little different had my parents never come to America at all, but remained in Holland. I still feel somewhat like a foreigner wherever I go, and not alone for ethnic reasons. Our insularity was twofold, being a matter of religion as well as nationality. In addition to being immigrants, and not able to mix well with the Chicago Americans around us, we were these Calvinists who weren't supposed to mix—who, in fact, had considerable trouble mixing with one another. The principle of the Elect requires you to 'come out from among them and be separate,' to remain unspotted from the world, and so on. Worldliness was a specifically named sin among us. And I suppose that the simultaneous pursuit of worldliness and its satirization, in my books and stories, is some kind of uneasy reconcilement of contradictory elements within me —a way of eating my cake and having it too. A sop is thrown to household gods even while they are being flouted.

"The gods who disallowed worldliness were rigid. I wasn't allowed to go to the movies, to dance, to play cards, go to the regular public schools, or do anything much that was secular, even on weekdays. On Sundays we went to church, usually three times, and in between Dutch as well as English sermons we sat around the kitchen table drinking coffee and engaging in doctrinal disputation ourselves. We became quite adept at hairsplitting at a very early age. It was said about us, 'One Dutchman a Christian; two Dutchmen, a congregation; three Dutchmen, heresy.' We accepted and repeated this without any apologies or any thought that there was anything wrong with such religious pugnacity. We were the product of a schism, and we produced schisms. Even now when I hear that a man is an orthodox Christian the term is meaningless to me. I want to know whether he is a premillennialist, a postmillennialist, or an amillennialist.

"I became ultimately, in a society of dissenters, a splinter group of one. But I did attend the de-

PETER DE VRIES

nominational school, Calvin College, and after graduating from it took a variety of jobs in order to support myself while writing. I ran a taffy apple route in Chicago, serviced vending machines, worked as a freelance radio actor, and became an editor of *Poetry* magazine. There I met and married one of our contributors, Katinka Loeser, who continues to write under her own name. We moved east in 1944 when I took a job on the *New Yorker*, with which I'm still a part-time editor. We have four children and live in Westport, Connecticut."

De Vries is the son of Joost De Vries, who went into the furniture removal business on Chicago's South Side with a "one-horse outfit which he gradually built up to a sizable warehouse business." His mother was the former Henrietta Eldersveld. He attended a Reformed Calvinist high school in Chicago, where he played basketball and struggled to overcome a childhood stammer by participating in debating and public speaking. His determination was such that in 1931, at Calvin College in Grand Rapids, he won the Michigan intercollegiate championship contest for extemporaneous speaking.

Graduating in 1931, De Vries began to write, mostly poetry at first, surviving the Depression in a variety of part-time and freelance jobs, including a six-year stint as a part-time associate editor of *Poetry* magazine. His first three novels, appearing between 1940 and 1944, attracted little attention. In 1943 he met the humorist James Thurber at a *Poetry* benefit program, and through him was invited to join the staff of the *New Yorker*.

It was not until 1952 that his next book appeared.

This was *No, But I Saw the Movie*, a collection of his *New Yorker* pieces that was warmly received on both sides of the Atlantic. These "anecdotes of domestic, marital and convivial embarrassment," together with some knowledgeable and very funny parodies of contemporary novelists, persuaded a *Punch* reviewer that De Vries was "a much better writer than most humorists and a much better humorist than most writers of short stories."

Popular success came with his next novel, *The Tunnel of Love*, about the adventures in exurbia of an unsuccessful cartoonist. One critic wrote that De Vries "uses his puns and fantasies to mask a sometimes frighteningly keen observation." The book became a best seller and, adapted by the author and Joseph Fields, was equally successful as a stage play in 1957. It was filmed in 1958.

More sharp but not unaffectionate reports on exurbanite motives and morals followed. W. J. Smith, reviewing *Through the Fields of Clover* in 1961, was moved to describe De Vries as "the greatest living American comic novelist . . . and beyond any doubt the greatest punster the world has ever known." At about the same time critics were beginning to realize that De Vries was more than simply a humorist. Clifton Fadiman spoke of him as a serious moralist, a man who knew that the times were out of joint and who "expresses his knowledge, not by caterwauling, but through farce, parody, language-play, and a kind of *commedia dell'arte* manipulation of absurd characters and situations."

With *The Blood of the Lamb* De Vries turned openly to tragedy (or some say to pathos). It is an account, narrated by himself, of the life of a Chicago Dutch Calvinist called Don Wanderhope whose young daughter dies—as De Vries's daughter did—of leukemia. In one characteristically ambivalent scene Wanderhope, drunk after a visit to the hospital, throws a cake meant for his dying daughter into the face of a statue of Christ. In De Vries's hands this is an action of ambiguous religious significance and also a moment of slapstick comedy. Some critics were puzzled or offended by this "more or less hilarious short novel about death"; many were moved. A critic in the *Times Literary Supplement* said that De Vries had here overcome "a somewhat alarming susceptibility to literary influences . . . [and now] commands a fine lyrical voice that he has the courage to call his own . . . [along with] resources of deep compassion and tenderness."

In his subsequent books De Vries has continued to probe, more or (usually) less directly, the connection between religion, suffering, and comedy. In *Let Me Count the Ways*, for example, the young hero experiences religious conversion as the result of a miraculous sickness acquired, of course, at Lourdes. *The Cat's Pajamas & Witch's Milk*, two obliquely connected short novels, deal respectively with a spiritual pilgrimage that ends in a ludicrous death, and a ludicrous marriage that ends in tragedy.

Joe Sandwich's wife in *The Vale of Laughter* says to him: "These practical jokes. Isn't there an element of cruelty behind them?" It is a question often asked of De Vries's endless and sometimes apparently involuntary joking. Joe's characteristic answer is: "It's the tale that dogs the wag"; later, more soberly, he suggests that tragedy and comedy, properly considered, are indistinguishable.

Another frequent criticism of De Vries's novels is that they tend to be shapeless and erratic, lacking the control essential to a serious work of art. The author himself once told an interviewer: "I don't think I pursue any conscious 'purpose' or 'motivation' so much as an unconscious instinct of, and for, the absurd. I simply follow a comic scent where it leads, and if I seem occasionally to meander, I do it like the beagle who rambles in a strict attention to the trail." And for Melvin Maddocks, at least, "It is when things run away from Mr. De Vries' studied control that his genius, almost against his will, makes itself felt. For his humor has a kind of headlong compulsiveness to it. . . . Farce snowballing with a kind of attendant horror—Kafka crossed with the Keystone Kops—this is what one reads Mr. De Vries for. . . . He is a punster thunderstruck at his own puns, a moralist whose homilies, to his distress, go amok."

De Vries prefers life outside the city, and describes himself as "rather stodgily" engaged in civic and Democratic political activities in Westport, Connecticut. Blue-eyed and brown-haired, he is six feet two inches tall. His favorite author is Anthony Powell and he finds it difficult to enjoy any but contemporary literature.

PRINCIPAL WORKS: But Who Wakes the Bugler? (illustrations by Charles Addams), 1940; The Handsome Heart, 1943; Angels Can't Do Better, 1944; No, But I Saw the Movie (stories), 1952; The Tunnel of Love, 1954 (published as a play in 1957); Comfort Me With Apples, 1956; The Mackerel Plaza, 1958; The Tents of Wickedness, 1959; Through the Fields of Clover, 1961; The Blood of the Lamb, 1962; Reuben, Reuben, 1964; Let Me Count the Ways, 1965; The Vale of Laughter, 1967; The Cat's Pajamas & Witch's Milk, 1968; Mrs. Wallop, 1970; Into Your Tent I'll Creep, 1971; Without a Stitch in Time: A Collection of the Best Humorous Short Pieces, 1972; Forever Panting, 1973.

ABOUT: Current Biography, 1959; Jellema, R. Peter De Vries (Contemporary Writers in Christian Perspective), 1966; Newquist, R. (ed.) Counterpoint, 1965. *Periodicals*—Christian Science Monitor July 22, 1965; November 21, 1968; College English April 1967; Newsweek February 17, 1964; New Yorker February 25, 1961; New York Times Book Review April 29, 1956; February 12, 1961; February 16, 1964; Saturday Review March 24, 1962; Studies in the Novel Fall 1969; Time March 10, 1958; Times Literary Supplement June 23, 1961; May 18, 1962; March 7, 1968.

***DHÔTEL, ANDRÉ** (September 1, 1900–), French novelist, was born at Attigny in the Ardennes, the scene of many of his books, to Charles Dhôtel, an auctioneer, and the former Marie Cartulat. He studied at the Collège d'Autun and began writing poetry at the age of fifteen. After receiving his *licence* in philosophy at the Sorbonne he taught at schools in Greece and in France—for many years at the secondary school at Coulommiers, near Paris.

Le Village pathétique (The Pathetic Village, 1943) was the first of his many novels. He was especially prolific between 1948 and 1952, when five books appeared in rapid succession, among them *David* (1948), winner of the Saint-Beuve Prize. Widespread critical and popular recognition, however, came only with the publication of *Le Pays où l'on n'arrive jamais* (The Country Where One Never Arrives, 1955), winner of the coveted Prix Fémina. This strange lyrical story describes the adventures of a boy and a girl in their search for the latter's family. Published in the United States as *Faraway* (1957), it was well received by the American critics. Judith Quehl thought that it existed on two levels—as a "lighthearted fantasy adventure impregnated with that special sort of beauty and imagination found in fairy tales and the mind of a child," and also as a "hopeful morality play, a modern Everyman in search of himself." Many reviewers noted its resemblances to Alain-Fournier's classic *Le Grand Meaulnes*, and others compared it with James Stephens' *The Crock of Gold* or Robert Nathan's *Jenny*. In its blend of "magic and homely realism, of irony and wistfulness," and in its wanderlust, the novel seemed to one critic more closely related to early German romanticism than to the dark mainstream of contemporary French fiction.

Most of what was said about *Le Pays où l'on n'arrive jamais* is equally applicable to the majority of Dhôtel's novels. His heroes are always young, dreamers and idealists who refuse to grow up, who reject and in their innocence sometimes transform the ugly realities of life. Their mysterious adventures take place beside misty rivers or in shadowy forest glades in a world—which Maurice Nadeau calls "Dhôtelland"—floating between the forest of Ardennes (the Arden of *As You Like It*) and the seaports of Bohemia. In these stories, love and purity are everything, reason nothing at all. ("There is nothing in thought," says one of his characters. "I realized this while looking at plants. They are quite similar to the constellations.")

"The surrealist adventure of the 1920s," wrote Henri Peyre, "left [Dhôtel] with a passion for mystery and for the marvelous inserted into daily life. He surrounds his half-real characters with a halo of poetry and an obstinate elusiveness, which bewilder most readers. There is no structure, no solidity whatever to his stories, no progression, only gratuitous fireworks of tender poetry amid rolling layers of clouds." The same critic considered Dhôtel the finest painter of nature in French fiction since Giono and Bosco.

ANDRÉ DHÔTEL

Among Dhôtel's recent novels are *Les Voyages fantastiques de Julien Grainebis* (The Fantastic Journeys of Julien Grainebis, 1958), *La Tribu Bécaille* (The Bécaille Tribe, 1963), and *Le Mont Damion* (Mount Damion, 1964). He has written interestingly about Rimbaud, whom he greatly admires, and is the author of a biography of Saint Benoît Labre and of many short stories. Dhôtel was married in 1932 to Suzanne Laurent and has one child, François. He is a chevalier of the Legion of Honor. As his stories suggest, Dhôtel is an ardent amateur botanist.

PRINCIPAL WORKS IN ENGLISH TRANSLATION: Faraway, 1957.

ABOUT: Nadeau, M. The French Novel Since the War, 1967; Peyre, H. French Novelists of Today, 1967; Schneider, M. La Littérature fantastique en France, 1964; Who's Who in France, 1971–1972. *Periodicals*—Mercure de France March 1949; November 1953; New York Herald Tribune Book Review September 1, 1957; New York Times Book Review September 1, 1957; Saturday Review September 28, 1957; Time September 9, 1957.

* dō tel'

DICKENS, MONICA (ENID) (May 10, 1915–), English novelist, memoirist, and journalist, writes: "I was born in London, in a Victorian house in Kensington, where my parents still live. My grandfather, the judge, Sir Henry Fielding Dickens, was Charles Dickens' eighth child and

MONICA DICKENS

sixth son. My father, Henry Charles Dickens, barrister-at-law, now retired, is his eldest son.

"I went to a small private school in London. Then to St. Paul's School for Girls, where I won two scholarships, because I had the knack of passing examinations. I was not especially drawn to writing, perhaps because family pride in our ancestor was so stultifyingly strong that there was an unstated feeling that Charles Dickens had done it for all time, and no one else should have the nerve to try.

"Sickening of school before I was eighteen, I destroyed my uniform and got myself expelled. Fat and gauche, I was presented resentfully at Court in pink satin and feathers, and after one debutante dance, where my best friend stole my escort, I rebelled against a wallflower fate and was sent to Paris to be 'finished.'

"Back in London, still unfinished, I went to the Central School of Speech Training and Dramatic Art, from which I was expelled for not being able to act. I wanted a job, but was trained for nothing. A few esoteric cooking lessons at the Cordon Bleu had left me still unable to boil an egg or make that staple of middle class diet, blancmange, but I decided to be a cook. A domestic agency gave me the job of cooking a six-course dinner for twelve people, and although it was a nightmare, for the diners as well as for me, I was so fascinated by life 'below stairs' that I plunged down and took a variety of jobs as cook-general, house-parlormaid, nanny, waitress—I had twenty jobs in two years, on the principle that nothing is boring if you don't stay with it too long.

"Then I met a young man called Charles Pick, who had just started with Michael Joseph, Ltd., the London publishers. He suggested that I should write a book about my kitchen experiences. I bought a pencil and notebook, wrote my first book, *One Pair of Hands*, in three weeks (now it takes me five to six months). It was untidy, naïve, undisciplined, but the very fact that I knew nothing about writing techniques gave it a certain spontaneity that carried it through. It was a success then, in 1938, and still sells about twenty thousand copies in paperback every year, for which I am grateful though baffled, since it is quite gauche, and servants are ancient history anyway.

"I wrote a novel, *The Moon Was Low*, about my own childhood and growing up, but then World War II started, so I stopped being a writer and joined a hospital in Windsor, Berkshire, as a student nurse.

"By this time, I was intrigued enough with writing not to be able to see the comic, dramatic and startling experiences of nursing go to waste. I wrote a book called *One Pair of Feet*, and had to leave the hospital, because a nurse in those days was a cross between a nun and a slave, and not allowed to be articulate. Later, when the book began to sell, the matron of my old hospital banned it as subversive.

"The Battle of Britain was on, and I worked for a year in an aircraft factory repairing Spitfire fighters. Out of that, came a novel: *Edward's Fancy*, about a factory foreman. I was beginning to realize that if you have the luck to be able to write, every experience has double value, since it can all be used. Also the writer's secret treasure and escape of being able to lead this second life of your own creating.

"I went back to another hospital for three years until the war ended, and got two more books out of it, one of which, *The Happy Prisoner*, was made into a play, which has been popular with amateur groups since it has a static hero with one leg, simple humor and only one set.

"James Drawbell, editor of the *Sunday Chronicle*, which had helped to launch my first book, was starting a weekly, *Woman's Own*, in the new format for women's magazines, young and colorful and stimulating, instead of cosy. I joined it with a column 'The Way I See It,' which I have written every week since for nearly twenty years, for what grew to nine million readers.

"I lived alone in the country and kept horses, and wrote all night and slept all day, if I wanted to, and would have turned into the local freak, but with my usual luck, I met an American Navy Commander, Roy Stratton, and we were married in 1951 and went to the United States, where I have lived most of the time since, in an old house on Cape Cod. We have two daughters and a lot of animals, and it is an ideal place to write, because you see a lot of people in the summer, and no one at all in the winter, except your typewriter.

"I write a novel every other year, and spend the year between researching and planning the next book. I write for about six hours a day, when the children are at school, and I still have the same publisher, Charles Pick, now with William Heinemann, Ltd., whose consistent encouragement and flair for what is right for me to do can't be overemphasized as a factor in whatever success I have had. Far better writers than I fail for lack of an enthusiastic publisher.

"My aims? With seventeen books, I figure I'm about halfway through my life's output. I want to entertain, to tell the truth, to try to help people understand other people. I think they already understand themselves better than the psychiatrists give them credit for, so I don't want to write subjectively, introspectively, but rather objectively, and, I hope, with humor, as long as I can stay sane enough to go on finding things funny."

Monica Dickens, one of England's most popular writers, was described in her youth as "undisciplined, but real, vivid and individual." The same could be said of her books, episodic and disorganized, but "alive, witty and fun to read." In her family, the "feeling that Charles Dickens had done it for all time" was so strong that *One Pair of Hands*, her first book, almost remained unpublished. When it was, it became an immediate best seller. *One Pair of Feet* and *My Turn to Make the Tea* were subsequent exercises in autobiography, the latter about her experiences on the staff of a provincial newspaper. They were funny, unaffected, sometimes touching, and immensely successful, full of characters so exactly observed as to give "the impression of photographs." Her novels, light and unfashionably readable, are praised for their "acute portrayal of relationships and episodes in domestic life," for their warmth and quiet humor, and for their "refreshing acidity" in exposing pretension and fatuity. In recent years she has also written some excellent books for children.

Rebecca West has said of Monica Dickens that "she undertakes too much and in what she does is not sufficiently attentive to form. In her works . . . a multitude of personages and an over-abundance of incidents are crowded. Her haste is often abominable, but it is life itself which is caught up in the pages of her books." Miss Dickens' virtues as a writer are in fact Dickensian.

Monica Dickens, still "vivid," slim and sociable, says she hates all clubs and politicians indiscriminately. Her chief recreations are travel and horseback riding.

PRINCIPAL WORKS: *Autobiographical Works*—One Pair of Hands, 1939; One Pair of Feet, 1942; My Turn to Make the Tea, 1951. *Novels*—Mariana (U.S., The Moon Was Low), 1940; The Fancy (U.S., Edward's Fancy), 1943; Thursday Afternoons, 1945; The Happy Prisoner, 1946; Joy and Josephine, 1948; Flowers on the Grass, 1949; No More Meadows (U.S., The Nightingales Are Singing), 1953; The Winds of Heaven, 1955; The Angel in the Corner, 1956; Man Overboard, 1958; The Heart of London, 1961; Cobbler's Dream, 1963; Kate and Emma, 1964; The Room Upstairs, 1966; The Landlord's Daughter, 1968; The Listeners, 1970 (U.S., The End of the Line). *For Children*—The House at World's End, 1970; The Great Fire, 1970; The Great Escape, 1971; Follyfoot, 1971; Summer at World's End, 1972; World's End in Winter, 1972; Dora at Follyfoot, 1972; Spring Comes to World's End, 1973.

ABOUT: Catholic Authors, 1948; Chambers, P. Women and the World Today, 1963; Drawbell, J. W. The Sun Within Us, 1963; Leasor, J. Author by Profession, 1952; Who's Who, 1971. *Periodicals*—Books and Bookmen November 1956; March 1961; Newsweek December 27, 1965; Wilson Library Bulletin June 1963.

DICKEY, JAMES (LAFAYETTE) (February 2, 1923–), American poet, novelist, and critic, writes: "I was born in Atlanta, Georgia. My mother's family were Confederates, but my father's were Union sympathizers, and took no part in the Civil War. Fannin County, Georgia, in the Appalachian foothills, is the scene of a good many of my poems, and is the place I consider my spiritual home, though most of my family's connections there have long been severed. I renewed my acquaintance with the North Georgia landscape and people only after a long interval which included two wars, and when I went back there it seemed to me that I had been born again out of my own elements. It was from this date that the first of the poems I wish to preserve were written, out of long day-and-night walks, canoeing trips and endless conversations with the mountain people. Oddly enough, it was through the resensibilizing effect of these experiences that I was finally able to write about the wars, and also about love, family, and other things I had never been able to come to terms with insofar as writing was concerned.

"My early life had nothing in it that seemed favorable to my becoming a poet. Since I was big and fairly fast, it seemed more or less natural to everyone—and to myself—that my main activity would be sports. My father wanted me to be a baseball player, but, though I could hit well enough, I had no arm, and so I drifted over into football and track, where legs were more important. I was a good journeyman high school player, and later went on to Clemson College, in South Carolina, where I played my one season of college football just before I went into the service in 1942.

"I went through Air Force cadet training, and later served with the 418th Night Fighter Squadron in the Pacific Theatre, moving from Milne Bay, New Guinea, all the way up through the Philippines and Okinawa to occupation duty in Japan

JAMES DICKEY

after the war. During much of this time I read whatever I could find, and in some kind of obscure but very natural-feeling process I still can't explain, gravitated slowly but steadily toward poetry. I remember when, in the great October hurricane on Okinawa just after the war, how terribly excited I was when the island library was blown into splinters and the books scattered everywhere, and I picked out of the mud beside a road a copy of the poems of Yeats, and realized that under the circumstances, under the fortunes of wind and war, I could keep it.

"It has been a peculiarity of my temperament that I have never been interested in a thing, an activity, without wanting to see if I could do it myself. It was the same with poetry, and during the occupation duty in Japan I began to try to write a little, influenced by the widest and wildest diversity of writers possible: Roy Campbell and Keats, Robert Service and Milton, John Crowe Ransom and George Barker and Dylan Thomas. Language was magical to me at that time, and alchemical combinations of words—of the poor words I was trying to put together—were things I had been looking for all my life, without knowing it. Success or failure mattered relatively little: it was the *doing* of it that held me, the possibilities.

"When I left the service in 1946 I went to Vanderbilt University on the GI Bill, graduated there, took a master's degree, and went to teach at Rice University in Houston, Texas. I was almost immediately recalled into the service and served for two years in the Korean conflict. After that I took various small teaching jobs and finally, disgusted with them and with my humiliatingly low earning capacity, I went into the advertising business, first in New York with McCann-Erickson, then in Atlanta as copy chief with Liller, Neal, Battle and Lindsey and then as creative director with Burke Dowling Adams. Meanwhile my first book of poems had come out, I was given a Guggenheim Fellowship, and I was able to get out of business, take my family to Europe, and then able to get back into teaching in a capacity which suited me better than formerly. I have been writer in residence at Reed College in Portland, Oregon, at San Fernando Valley State College in Northridge, California, at the University of Wisconsin and at Hollins College in Roanoke, Virginia.

"I work slowly, and when I work I mean it. Some poems I carry around with me for years, for I have found that working on poems over a very long period of time is an integral part of my method. The poems change as different things happen to me, as I read different things and meet different people: all material that I couldn't have known about when I first began to write the poems.

"I am married to Maxine Syerson, and we have two boys, Christopher and Kevin. We have no permanent home, but plan presently to end up in North Georgia, where, my wife tells me, as though it were her fondest hope, we have the best chance of becoming 'magnificent, witty old people.' "

James Dickey is the son of Eugene Dickey, a lawyer fond of reading aloud the speeches of Robert Ingersoll, and of the former Maibelle Swift. He has been a considerable athlete, and at Vanderbilt University (in addition to graduating *magna cum laude* and Phi Beta Kappa) won the Tennessee state championship in the one-hundred-and-twenty-yard high hurdles.

The *Sewanee Review*, which published Dickey's first poems in 1951, three years later gave him a thirty-five-hundred-dollar fellowship. This bought him an unsettling year of freedom in Europe, and it was after this, and a brief return to academic harness at the University of Florida, that he switched in 1956 to advertising. For nearly six years, Dickey devoted his days, with growing success but growing distaste, to celebrating Coca Cola, fertilizers, and Delta Airlines. In August 1961 he quit his job and went on relief. His five-thousand-dollar Guggenheim grant came six months later.

"Sweating out" an artillery barrage in the South Pacific, Dickey had been struck by the great expressiveness of that phrase; he "eased into poetry," he says in *Poets on Poetry*, in pursuit of this kind of "correlation between lived time—experience—and words." At the same time he discovered a subject—his own life, or rather his memories of "those times when I felt most strongly and was most aware of the intense reality of the objects and people I moved among." Beyond this, he found that he was attracted to the narrative mode and also that he "worked most fruitfully in cases in which there was no clear-cut distinction between what was actually happening and what was happening in the mind of a character in a poem. I meant to try to get a fusion of inner and outer states, of dream, fantasy, and illusion where everything partakes of the protagonist's mental processes and creates a single impression."

Disliking the artificiality of rhyme and of most prosodic effects, Dickey nevertheless recognized his need for a strong declaratory rhythm which he found, eventually, in the anapaests that dominate his first three books, *Into the Stone*, *Drowning With Others*, and *Helmets*. The second collection contained "The Lifeguard," a moving, much anthologized, and characteristic example of his early manner, in which a summer camp lifeguard, after one of his charges has drowned, imagines that he has walked out across the lake and called the dead child up from the water: "I wash the black mud from my hands. / On a light given off by the grave / I kneel in the quick of the moon / At the heart of a distant forest / And hold in my arms a child / Of water, water, water."

Critics found in these early poems what James Schevill called "a unique unmistakable tone, an awareness of the physical forces of the world that flow beyond time, beyond history." One source of this awareness in Dickey's work is his sense of himself as a survivor. This comes partly from his experience of war—he flew one hundred combat missions in the South Pacific—partly from the loss of a brother who died of typhoid before James Dickey was born: "I look in myself for the being / I was in a life before life . . . ."

This is why Dickey's poetry is (usually) more than mere autobiography. He intently scrutinizes his own experience and, as Peter Davison says, "penetrates deeper and deeper beneath the guises of reality," seeking evidence of order and permanence; he "ransacks through obsession, through trial and error, changes of costume and skin, through transformation of personality and the accidents of experience, to discover some sort of relation between the human and animal worlds, a bridge between the flesh and the spirit, and, more than these, a link between the living and the dead." Dickey's themes grow out of these concerns—the continuity of the family and of the seasons, the recurrence of love and of violence, the mysterious simplicities of death and return, the bond between man and beast, hunter and hunted, the alternative realities of dream, fantasy, and magic.

Some critics found signs of strain in *Helmets* and complained of monotonous rhythms, synthetic mysteries, and a laborious spelling out of moral messages. Dickey himself wanted to move forward, and did so in *Buckdancer's Choice*, aiming for what he calls "the conclusionless poem, the open or ungeneralizing poem, the un-well-made poem," which would involve the reader in a series of experiences instead of offering him a finished and polished object for contemplation. A more personal and flexible use of rhythm and a fuller confrontation of his experience of war also emerged in the new collection, along with a device Dickey calls the "split line," in which typographical gaps between words replace punctuation or even line breaks: "Enemy rivers and trees / Sliding off me like snakeskin, / Strips of vapor spooled from the wingtips / Going invisible passing over on / Over bridges roads for night-walkers / Sunday night in the enemy's country absolute / Calm the moon's face coming slowly / About . . ." ("The Fire Bombing").

Buckdancer's Choice received the National Book Award as the best book of poetry published in 1965 and seemed to Joseph Bennett "one of the remarkable books of the decade." And this new urgency and technical range was maintained in the later works included in *Poems 1957–1967*. That collection was criticized by William Meredith for Dickey's tendency to "drag out a poem," for a certain "bardic vulgarity," and "an unevenness that seems inextricably bound up with the kind of generosity required to by-pass the limits of intellectual and academic audiences." But to a number of reviewers, the book seemed evidence that Dickey was potentially a major poet.

He is also a quite remarkably popular one, with a very wide and mixed readership—a literary celebrity whose public readings draw crowds. In 1966 Dickey's standing was recognized by his appointment as Consultant on Poetry in English to the Library of Congress, a distinction which may be compared to that of poet laureate. He was reappointed in 1967 for a second year. Dickey's fame appeared to several critics to have had an adverse effect on his work. *The Eye-Beaters, Blood, Victory, Madness, Buckhead and Mercy* contains some brilliant poems, but some also that seemed "public," depersonalized, or synthetic. It may simply be that he is coming to the end of his present mode, and preparing for another move forward.

Good poets are almost never successful as novelists, but Dickey is an exception to that rule as he has been to so many others. His first and so far his only work of fiction, *Deliverance*, had a generally enthusiastic critical reception, and was a best seller. It is an adventure story about four Georgia businessmen, amateur archers, who set off one weekend on a canoeing and hunting trip in a remote part of the state. Only one of them is physically or temperamentally fit for life in the wilderness, and this becomes terribly clear when they are attacked without reason or warning by a pair of murderous and perverted mountaineers. They manage to kill one of the men, and then begin a long, tense struggle against the other man and against nature itself. In the course of this ordeal, the amateur woodsmen find themselves capable of quite unexpected feelings and actions, and for some of the survivors the experience is a renewal, a "deliverance."

A reviewer in the *Times Literary Supplement* complained of "an annoyingly onomatopoeic muscularity" in the style, "a verbal ruggedness redolent of Hemingway, which slips too easily into unintentional self-parody." Christopher Ricks found "a moral insensitivity comparable to the stylistic," and others called the characterization weak, the dialogue unconvincing. Most reviewers all the same enjoyed the book as a splendidly exciting thriller, "a double-clutching whopper," "a monument to tall stories." Dickey himself wrote the screenplay for John Boorman's film version of the novel, and played a small part in it.

Dickey's reviews of contemporary poets have been collected in *The Suspect in Poetry* and *Babel to Byzantium.* Both volumes had a rather mixed press, some critics liking the directness of Dickey's response to what he read and his refusal to apply the fashionable criteria of the literary establishment, others finding his judgments interesting and entertaining, but "wildly unreliable." There are more of Dickey's frequently unorthodox opinions—on literary and other matters—in *Self-Interviews*, which contains his tape-recorded replies to written questions devised by Barbara and James Reiss, and in *Sorties,* containing entries from his journals, together with six new essays.

Since February 1969, Dickey has been professor of English and writer in residence at the University of South Carolina, Columbia. He also serves as poetry editor of *Esquire* magazine. His honors and awards, apart from those already mentioned, include the Vachel Lindsay Prize (1959), the Longview Foundation Award (1960), and the Melville Cane Award (1966). He also received a grant from the National Institute of Arts and Letters in 1967.

Dickey, who exercises with weights and bow and arrow, is six feet three inches tall and massively built. Although he suffers from diabetes, he is said to exude "formidable physical energy and enthusiasm." He is a gregarious and affable man who speaks in a soft Georgia accent. Dickey writes his poems anywhere, "late at night, early in the morning, at home, on street-cars or buses." For relaxation he plays the guitar.

Dickey has been associated with the "Sixties" group of poets, some of whom write rather strident protest poetry. He has no use for such "tracts," and his own war poems are very different, acknowledging the excitement as well as the guilt of combat. Dickey's talent for celebrity has irritated some of his contemporaries, and he has been sourly described as "the jock-strap poet of our day," and "Superpoet." All the same, no serious critic has denied his talent or the extraordinary speed of his development. His position is secure in the front rank of contemporary American poets, and some think him capable of greatness.

PRINCIPAL WORKS: *Poetry*—Into the Stone, 1960; Drowning With Others, 1962; Helmet, 1964; Two Poems of the Air, 1964; Buckdancer's Choice, 1965; Poems 1957–1967, 1967; The Eye-Beaters, Blood, Victory, Madness, Buckhead and Mercy, 1970. *Novel*—Deliverance, 1970. *Nonfiction*—The Suspect in Poetry, 1964; Babel to Byzantium, 1968; Self-Interviews (recorded and edited by Barbara and James Reiss), 1970; Sorties: Journals and New Essays, 1972.

ABOUT: Contemporary Authors 11–12, 1965; Current Biography, 1968; Graham, J. The Writer's Voice: Conversations With Contemporary Writers, 1973; Lieberman, L. The Achievement of James Dickey, 1968; Martz, W. J. (ed.) The Distinctive Voice, 1966; Nemerov, H. (ed.) Poets on Poetry, 1966; Rosenthal, M. L. The New Poets, 1967; Walsh, C. Today's Poets, 1964; Who's Who in America, 1970–1971. *Periodicals*—Antioch Review Winter 1964–1965; Atlantic October 1967; Hudson Review Summer 1964; Library of Congress Information Bulletin January 20, 1966; Life July 22, 1966; Nation April 24, 1967; New York Review of Books June 25, 1964; New York Times September 10, 1966; New York Times Book Review August 23, 1964; January 3, 1965; March 16, 1966; Partisan Review Summer 1965; Summer 1966; Publishers' Weekly March 28, 1966; Sewanee Review Winter 1965; Summer 1966; Shenandoah Spring 1965, Autumn 1966; The Sixties Winter 1964; Times Literary Supplement August 20, 1964; October 29, 1964; January 27, 1966; May 18, 1967; Washington Post October 9, 1966; Yale Review Winter 1965.

DICKEY, WILLIAM (December 15, 1928–), American poet, writes: "I was born in Bellingham, Washington, and brought up in Washington and Oregon. I studied at Reed College, Harvard University, and at the Writers' Workshop of the University of Iowa. I had written both poetry and fiction since childhood. My bachelor's thesis at Reed was a novel, but at Iowa I began to work exclusively in poetry, and to publish it in magazines. I continued this work at Cornell University, where I became an instructor in English in 1956. In 1959 I was married, my first book of poems was accepted by W. H. Auden for the Yale Series of Younger Poets, and I received a Fulbright scholarship to Jesus College, Oxford. After a year in England I returned to the United States to teach at Denison University, and then at San Francisco State College, where I am now an associate professor of English, teaching eighteenth century English literature, the history of English poetry, and directed study in the writing of poetry. I have continued to publish poems in periodicals, and my second collection was published at the end of 1963.

"My parents are intelligent and literate people to whom the writing of poetry seemed a natural occupation; both this background and this encouragement have been of value to me. I have been influenced by matters of family history and family geography: my mother's family crossed to Oregon by covered wagon in 1851, and I myself remember interviewing, when I was seventeen or eighteen, a woman in her eighties who had been the first white child born in the Skagit Valley of Washington. The briefness of white civilization in the Pacific Northwest, and the sense of great areas of wilderness very near at hand, have formed a continuing contrast in my mind with the sense of long settlement and tradition I find in England and in English poetry. I have been more curious about the relation between the newness and the tradition than I have been about the poetry or philosophy of other cultures—a subject with which many of my contemporaries have been closely concerned.

"I enjoy studying and teaching eighteenth century English literature because I prefer neoclassic attitudes to romantic ones—the latter seem to me often exaggerated and untrue. I am more interested in writing poems that concern themselves with man in society than I am in dealing with introspective isolation. And I hope to be able to write more poems than I have yet done which can use the eighteenth century sense of a fruitful and exciting balance between opposites as a figure through which the nature of the world and of our experience in it can be understood."

Auden selected *Of the Festivity* for the Yale Series of Younger Poets because "the lines speak, something has been noticed, and speech and observation have become the servants of a personal vision." Dudley Fitts was also impressed; he called Dickey "skillful and engaging" and "also witty, in a donnish sort of way, and very successful in establishing an air of casual inconsequence that turns out, upon reflection, to be anything but inconsequential."

Interpreter's House was less warmly received. Where Auden had judged from Dickey's first book that his "speciality is nightmare worlds described in the simplest possible diction," the *Times Literary Supplement* found in the second collection much "speculative meandering"—a "casting around for curious subject matter"—and an "abstract and circuitous" vocabulary. Indeed, the "simplest possible diction" for Dickey's "closely textured thought" was never very simple; he himself has said that some of his early poems are not clear enough, and consequently unfair to readers.

Among the poets who have influenced his work, Dickey has said, are Paul Engle, John Berryman, W. D. Snodgrass, Philip Levine, Donald Justice, and Paul Petrie. Reviewers have suggested other names

WILLIAM DICKEY

that might be added to the list, including Auden's and Yeats's, and there is a general feeling that Dickey has not yet found his own voice, or has mislaid it in the stony labyrinths of modern prosody.

Judson Jerome, writing in the *Antioch Review* in 1963, called Dickey "a spare, long-figured fellow with a rusty beard and genteel manner, [and] a lovely wife." She is the former Shirley Ann Marn, a psychiatric nurse. Dickey is the son of Paul C. and Ann (Hobart) Dickey. He was for a time managing editor of the *Western Review*. He belongs to Phi Beta Kappa and the Society for Italic Handwriting, among other organizations. Dickey considers much contemporary poetry to be "deficient in sound values, prosy, flat," and would "like a few more touches of opulence about the place."

PRINCIPAL WORKS: Of the Festivity, 1959; Interpreter's House, 1963; Rivers of the Pacific Northwest, 1969.

ABOUT: Auden, W. H. *foreword to* Of the Festivity; Contemporary Authors 9–10, 1964; Murphy, R. (ed.) Contemporary Poets of the English Language, 1970. *Periodical*—Antioch Review Spring 1963.

***DJILAS, MILOVAN** (1911–), Yugoslav memoirist and political writer, was born at Kolašin in Montenegro, one of the seven children of Nikola Djilas, an army officer of the peasant class who owned a small farm. He attended local schools and at eighteen went on to the University of Belgrade, where he studied law and literature, discovered Marx, and was prominent as an organizer of left-wing student activities. In 1933, soon after he received his law degree, he joined the illegal Communist party. Arrested for demonstrations against the monarchy, he was jailed for three years at

* jē′ läs

MILOVAN DJILAS

Sremska Mitrovica prison. In 1937 he met Josef Broz, known as Tito, leader of the Yugoslav Communist party, and became his friend and collaborator.

During World War II, in which his father, two brothers, and two sisters were killed, Djilas led the Yugoslav partisans against the German invaders in Montenegro. After the war he held a series of Cabinet posts in Tito's government and was in charge of Communist party propaganda. Tito broke with the Cominform in 1948 and Djilas, who in 1944 had criticized the behavior of Russian troops in Yugoslavia and later complained bitterly about Soviet interference in Yugoslav affairs, was made the focus of Russian attacks on Yugoslav "deviations."

In January 1953 Djilas became one of his country's four vice presidents and often represented Yugoslavia abroad. By then, however, Djilas was falling out of step with his colleagues in the Communist hierarchy. In 1953 and 1954, with characteristic courage, he expressed his views in newspaper and magazine articles attacking the snobbery of party leaders and their wives and calling for a liberalization of the regime. Some of these articles were later published in book form in New York as *Anatomy of a Moral*. Kingsley Martin said of them: "He wrote without clarity, and he sometimes vacillated under attack because he could not bear to cut himself off from his comrades. He emerges as an able, brave, rather naïve Socialist of an old-fashioned type."

In December 1953 Djilas was named president of the Yugoslav legislature but never took up this important post. The following month he was stripped of all his Communist party positions and in April 1954 he resigned from the party. His subsequent interviews with foreign journalists led to his arrest. He was charged with propaganda hostile to the government and given a suspended sentence, but ignored this warning and continued his campaign. In December 1956 he was sentenced to three years' imprisonment at Sremska Mitrovica, reportedly in the same cell that he had occupied in the 1930s.

Before his arrest Djilas had sent the manuscript of *The New Class* to New York. It was published there in the summer of 1957 and earned its author an additional seven-year sentence. The book described the emergence of a privileged and parasitic class within the supposedly egalitarian Communist system. Banned in Yugoslavia, it has been translated into more than a dozen languages. It was a best seller in English, regarded as one of the most damaging indictments of communism ever written, and widely praised for its objectivity and thoroughness, its "proud impersonality." Jack Raymond said that Djilas "never wrote so informatively as a Communist propagandist; among other things, this volume is a fine example of how lucid a man's thoughts can be when they reflect his true convictions."

Land Without Justice appeared in 1958. It is an account of Djilas's family, rebels for more than a century, and of the author's own youth. Montenegro, formerly an independent state, in 1918 became part of what was later called Yugoslavia. Recalling the bloody feuds and religious warfare which followed, Djilas wrote: "It seems to me that I was born with blood on my eyes. My first sight was of blood." Of less political importance than *The New Class*, the book attracted almost unanimous enthusiasm for the beauty of its style and imagery, seasoned with the sayings and aphorisms of Montenegro. The *New Yorker* thought it "something close to a folk epic" and was not alone in prophesying that it would take its place as a classic of Balkan literature. None of Djilas's later books has been so warmly praised.

In 1961 Djilas was released on parole, having served less than half of his sentence. In May 1962, in spite of Yugoslav attempts to prevent its publication, *Conversations With Stalin* appeared in New York. That same month Djilas was rearrested and sentenced to nine years' imprisonment for allegedly divulging official secrets. In fact the book, which reported Djilas's meetings with Soviet leaders in the 1940s, contained very little that was not known. Most reviewers nevertheless found it of absorbing interest, if somewhat turgidly written; some specialists questioned its accuracy and one critic called it "an unbalanced, not to say silly, book."

Three books followed which Djilas had written in prison between 1956 and 1961 and sent to New

York before his rearrest. *Montenegro* is a violent, lyrical, semifictional account of recent Montenegrin history. According to J. C. Campbell, it contains "passages that gleam with the poetic fire that Djilas can give to striking landscapes and passionate human beings," but lacks "the simple and sustained eloquence and genuineness" of *Land Without Justice. The Leper* is an uneven collection of short stories, most of them fictionalized memoirs and many of them dealing with partisan conflict during World War II. The title story, a political parable about the author's relations with Tito, was thought of particular interest; others were weakened by didacticism or their "socialist realist" manner. *Njegoš* (1966) was a generally admired study of the great nineteenth century Montenegrin ruler and poet.

At the end of 1966 Djilas was unexpectedly released once more, having spent nine years and twenty-five days in prison since 1956. Richard Eder, who interviewed him for the New York *Times* in the spring of 1967, reported that Djilas's political aspirations, "while they do not exclude the idea of personal power, center mostly on putting his thinking and writing to work to support the most liberal elements of the Communist party that are working to democratize Yugoslavia." Djilas himself said: "We cannot think of a revolution for democracy here. I would put it this way: society must go nervously forward." Eder found that Djilas's black hair had grayed during his years in captivity and that his temperament, once distinguished by "a certain sharpness of manner, a kind of intolerant brilliance, has been replaced by a milder, more deliberate way of talking and moving."

Djilas has continued to publish abroad since his release. *The Unperfect Society*, subtitled "Beyond the New Class," draws in part on the author's own career in an attempt to show that Communism is a dying faith based on unacceptable premises. The result, one reviewer wrote, is both "a fresh critique of the entire Marxist legacy and a spiritual biography of a heretic whose struggles are wider and deeper than those of cold war politics or revisionist philosophies. . . . [Djilas] now looks to Gandhi more than Lenin, and rejects remote goals and utopian illusions of all kinds in favor of 'a new, undoctrinaire, unidealized existential humanism.' " *Under the Colors*, a historical novel about the Montenegrin struggle against Turkish rule in the nineteenth century, seemed to many reviewers disappointingly long-winded and melodramatic. An account of the author's youth, and his early years in the then outlawed Communist party, was published in 1973 as *Memoir of a Revolutionary*. The same year, according to the New York *Times*, articles that Djilas had published in Western journals brought him once more under attack in several Yugoslav publications.

Djilas has also made a Serbian translation of Milton's *Paradise Lost*. In 1968 he visited England and the United States, and for a few months held a fellowship in international affairs at Princeton University. His first marriage, to Mitra Mitrović, ended in divorce. He and his second wife, Stephanie, live in Belgrade. Djilas has two children, one by each of his marriages.

PRINCIPAL WORKS IN ENGLISH TRANSLATION: The New Class, 1957; Land Without Justice, 1958; Anatomy of a Moral, 1959; Conversations With Stalin, 1962; Montenegro, 1963; The Leper and Other Stories, 1964; Njegoš: Poet, Prince, Bishop, 1966; The Unperfect Society: Beyond the New Class, 1969; Under the Colors, 1971; The Stone and the Violets (stories), 1972; Memoir of a Revolutionary, 1973.

ABOUT: Current Biography, 1958; Djilas, M. Memoir of a Revolutionary; International Who's Who, 1972–1973; Jovanovich, W. Now, Barabbas, 1964; Who's Who in America, 1972–1973. *Periodicals*—New York Times April 2, 1967; June 21, 1973.

***DODERER, HEIMITO VON** (September 6, 1896–December 23, 1966), Austrian novelist, was born at Weidlingau near Vienna, the son of a railroad engineer. He had just matriculated when war was declared. "At nineteen," he wrote in an autobiographical note, "he wore what has long ago become an historical costume, with its gay colors, red and blue: the uniform of an Imperial Austrian officer of the Dragoons." A year later Doderer was a prisoner of war in Russia. He said that "at twenty-three he was a lumberjack deep in the virgin forest of Siberia; at twenty-four a printer; at twenty-five he wandered through the Kirghiz Steppes on foot; still in the same year he became a student of history in Vienna."

In 1925 Doderer received his doctorate in history, a subject that continued to be of the utmost importance to him. After an early book of poems, two novels, and a monograph on the painter and writer A. P. Gütersloh, whom Doderer regarded as his master, he published little for a time. But—again in his own words—"already he had made what remains his most important discovery, bearing both on the mechanics of the mind and on outward events: that of the indirect way; that of making thought conform to life, as opposed to the attempts, apparent all around him incessantly, to make life conform to thought; attempts that inevitably led to dogmatism, to reformism, and ultimately to the totalitarian state." This perception underlies all Doderer's subsequent work, including his magnum opus, the long novel *Die Dämonen*. Begun in 1931, it was not to be published until a quarter of a century later.

Meanwhile World War II came and went.

* dō′ də rər

HEIMITO VON DODERER

Doderer served during the war in the German Air Force—on the Eastern Front again, and elsewhere. For a time he had sympathized with the pro-Nazi and pro-Anschluss factions in Austria, and his diaries of the war years, published in the volume *Tangenten* (Tangents, 1964), record his change of heart. After the war Doderer settled in Vienna as a writer. In 1950 he became a member of the exclusive Institut für Geschichtsforschung (Institute for Historical Research) and in 1958 received the Grosse Österreichische Staatpreis.

Die Dämonen was published in 1956, on Doderer's sixtieth birthday, and translated in 1961 by Richard and Clara Winston as *The Demons*. It is a vast novel set in Vienna, covering the nine months ending with the burning of the Austrian Supreme Court building by a mob on July 15, 1927. There are some thirty major characters and innumerable minor ones, whose interrelationships and personalities are explored in separate but connected episodes; the book is a major feat of literary engineering and much more than that. Into *Die Dämonen* and its somewhat shorter but related predecessor *Die Strudlhofstiege* (1951) Doderer put all his experience of recent history, his thinking about human behavior, and his observation of Austrian society. His perception of the dangers of making "life conform to thought" is central to the book. The "demons" which possess his characters he calls "second realities"—obsessions of one kind or another which gradually unbalance their personalities, making them less than whole, less than real. For some of them comes a moment of self-discovery which enables them to break free and recover reality.

In the German-speaking countries *Die Dämonen* was hailed as the greatest Austrian novel of the century, and Doderer was spoken of in the same breath as Thomas Mann, though many might now think such praise excessive. The English version in any case had a more mixed reception, some critics accusing Doderer of "middle-class prejudices and intellectual clichés." But Thornton Wilder found it "many-sided: at times powerful, macabre, touching, charming, illuminating." Frederic Morton spoke of its "moral grandeur" and called it "an intricate, passionately conservative, magnificent book."

If Doderer had written no more than *Die Dämonen* and *Die Strudlhofstiege*—and together they fill some twenty-three hundred pages—his status as a major Austrian novelist would be assured. In fact he produced other novels less ambitious but not less accomplished, covering very different ground—*Die Merowinger* (The Merovingians, 1962), for example, is an exercise in grotesque fantasy. His other work embraces short stories and anecdotes, poems and epigrams, and essays, like *Grundlagen und Funktion des Romans* (Principles and Functions of the Novel, 1959), that complement his imaginative works. At the time of his death he was working on a projected tetralogy, akin to *Die Dämonen* in that it would have dealt with a whole historical period, the years between 1880 and 1960. The first volume, *Die Wasserfälle von Slunj* (1964), was translated in 1966 as *The Waterfalls of Slunj*, and rather coolly received in the United States.

If Doderer has had little influence on younger Austrian and German writers, it is mainly because he was a traditionalist, both in outlook and in his practice as a novelist. He was a careful and fastidious stylist capable of the utmost delicacy, but his manner has an elaborate formality which is far from congenial to most of the postwar writers or to their younger readers.

PRINCIPAL WORKS IN ENGLISH TRANSLATION: The Demons, 1961; Every Man a Murderer, 1964; The Waterfalls of Slunj, 1966.

ABOUT: Closs, A. Twentieth Century German Literature, 1969; Hamburger, M. From Prophecy to Exorcism, 1965; Hatfield, H. Modern German Literature, 1966; Waidson, H. M. The Modern German Novel, 1959; Weber, D. Heimito von Doderer: Studien zu Seinen Romanwerk, 1963. *Periodicals*—Times Literary Supplement April 20, 1973.

DODGE, DAVID (FRANCIS) (August 18, 1910–), American travel and detective story writer and humorist, was born in Berkeley, California, the son of an architect, George Dodge, and of the former Maude Bennett. He and his three older sisters were raised mostly in California, where Dodge attended the Lincoln High School in Los Angeles but left without graduating. During the

Depression years, Dodge says, he "scrabbled for a living, as everyone did, at odd jobs, temporary employment, relief." For a time he was a bank clerk in Los Angeles, and then he shipped out as a merchant marine fireman on the South American run—an experience which no doubt stimulated his passion for travel. There followed a period as a social worker in San Francisco, where he discovered an interest in amateur theatre and wrote some one-act plays for the Macondray Lane Theatre and the Bohemian Club.

In 1935 Dodge took a job as a public accountant and eventually, through self-education, qualified as a certified public accountant. His specialty was income tax, and this provided the theme of his first book, written to convince his wife that he could turn out a detective story and a good one. *Death and Taxes* (1941) won five dollars from Mrs. Dodge and much praise from the reviewers, who found the book fast and easy reading, hard-hitting and well knit. *Time* called it the "find" of the month. *Shear the Black Sheep*, another thriller with a tax theme, followed in 1942. At that point World War II intervened, and Dodge spent the next three years in uniform as a Naval Reserve lieutenant.

"Some writers travel to gather material to write about," Dodge says; he on the other hand writes "so as to gather money to travel [with]." After his Navy discharge in 1945 he found a way to combine these operations. He set out with his wife and daughter to see the world via the Pan American Highway, and described the first leg of their journey in his first best seller, *How Green Was My Father* (1947). The Dodges, traveling by car down through Mexico to Guatemala, collided on the way with the language barrier, the technology barrier, and obstacles yet unnamed. But if it was not an easy trip it was, in his account, a very funny one: "His predicaments are so absurd and mostly so unnecessary," wrote Carleton Beals, "his telling of them so infected with humor, with clever *bon mots* and gags, that laughter bubbles from every page."

How Lost Was My Weekend (1948) described the Dodge family's long stay in Guatemala and Honduras, and *Crazy Glasspecker* (1949) gave an account of their year in Peru. Subsequent travels have inspired a whole series of serio-comic travel books, full of information cunningly disguised as entertainment. Rather more orthodox is *The Poor Man's Guide to Europe* (1953), a handbook which has proved its value through several editions and has been joined by companion guides to the Riviera and the Orient.

Dodge's travel books have alternated over the years with detective stories, many of which also have exotic foreign settings. His best-known thriller is *To Catch a Thief*, a cleverly original story about a Raffles of the French Riviera, praised for its

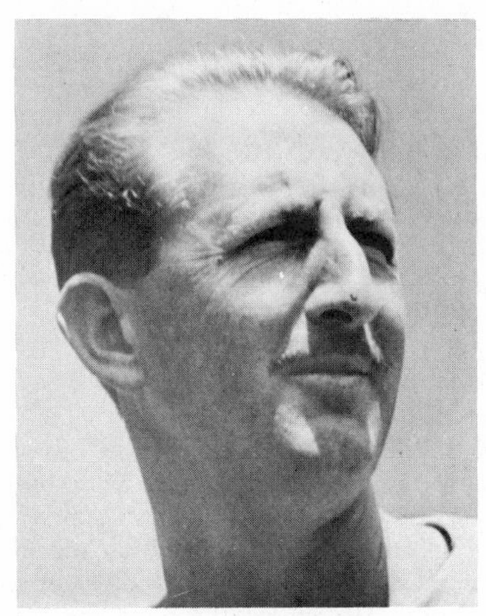

DAVID DODGE

"sprightly characterization, swift and deft movement, and surprise climax," and later filmed by Alfred Hitchcock. Dodge has made a kind of speciality of the chase theme which in his hands combines the pleasures of suspense and travelogue. As L. G. Offord wrote, reviewing the pursuit novel *Carambola*, "Dodge readers already know that this author's apparent ease of writing makes for unusually good narration and pace, and that his people take on reality from the first word. They may also expect a fine scenic background and a light touch on serious situations." *Loo Loo's Legacy*, not a suspense story but a "warm-hearted, slightly crazy comedy," was received with pleasure on both sides of the Atlantic.

David Dodge is a little over six feet tall, has hazel eyes and brown hair. He was married in 1936 to Elva Keith, then a Macmillan editor. Dodge speaks French and Spanish (but not so well as his much traveled daughter Kendal, who is completely trilingual). When they are not traveling, the Dodges live in Princeton, New Jersey.

PRINCIPAL WORKS: *Fiction*—Death and Taxes, 1941; Shear the Black Sheep, 1942; Bullets for the Bridegroom, 1944; It Ain't Hay, 1946; The Long Escape, 1948; Plunder of the Sun, 1949; Drug on the Market, 1949; Red Tassel, 1950; To Catch a Thief, 1952; Lights of Skaro, 1954; Angel's Ransom 1956 (England, Ransom of the Angel); Loo Loo's Legacy, 1961; Carambola (England, High Corniche), 1961; Hooligan, 1969; Hatchetman, 1970. *Travel*—How Green Was My Father: A Sort of Travel Diary, 1947; How Lost Was My Weekend: A Greenhorn in Guatemala, 1948; Crazy Glasspecker; or, High Life in the Andes, 1949 (England, High Life in the Andes); 20,000 Leagues Behind the 8 Ball, 1951 (England, With a Knife and Fork Down the Amazon); The Poor Man's Guide to Europe, 1953; Time Out for Turkey (England, Talking Turkey), 1955; The Rich Man's Guide to the

Riviera, 1962; The Poor Man's Guide to the Orient, 1965; Fly Down, Drive Mexico, 1968 (republished as The Best of Mexico by Car, 1969).
ABOUT: Wilson Library Bulletin March 1956.

***DOLCI, DANILO (BRUNO PIETRO)** (June 28, 1924–), Italian social reformer, was born in the village of Sesana, near Trieste. He is the son of Enrico Dolci, "a skeptical, moody" man employed by the Italian State Railways, and of "a devoutly Catholic, Slovenian mother, Mely Kontely." Dolci acquired very early an intense interest in music, especially Bach, and in books, reading so voraciously that his parents feared for his health. He attended primary schools in a number of northern Italian towns where his father's work took the family, but settled in Milan for his secondary education. Shortly before the fall of fascism in Italy, when he was nineteen, he was drafted for service in the army. He refused the draft and was imprisoned but escaped the same year, crossing the Allied lines in the Abruzzi.

By the end of the war Dolci had decided on a career in architecture and town planning. He entered the architecture department of the University of Rome, at the same time studying the piano at Rome's Conservatorio di Musica, and then returned to Milan where he continued his architectural studies, eking out his income by teaching geometry at the Milan Politecnico. His first publications appeared at this time, monographs on the science of construction. In 1950, when he was on the point of taking his finals, he says, he realized that he was about to bury himself "in a materialistic society which glorified intellect to the point where it killed feelings. . . . Better to be penniless and in shirtsleeves and a nobody, merely alive in the midst of life."

Forthwith Dolci abandoned his studies, left his home, and went to Nomadelphia in Sicily, a Catholic community for destitute orphans run by Don Zeno Saltini, whose adherence to Christian principles of love and service had earned him the title of "the mad priest." Dolci served as Saltini's secretary, started a small orchestra, did manual labor, and discovered his mission. In 1951 some of the poems he had written at Nomadelphia and earlier were collected in *Voci della città di Dio* (Voices From the City of God, 1951). At that point Dolci was obliged to do his national service in the army, where he refused a commission. While he was away the church and political authorities managed to close Don Zeno's community, which had embarrassed them.

When he left the army, Dolci went to western Sicily, the poorest and most hopeless part of that tragic island. He went first to Trappeto, a fishing village which he had first visited when his father was stationmaster there. He arrived in February 1952 and in December of that year made his first impact on the world. After watching a child die of starvation, Dolci fasted for a week, suffering a mild stroke but forcing the government to at least a semblance of responsible action. (Since then Dolci's public fasts have become an annual event, said to be responsible for the construction of at least three dams.) At Trappeto he built the Borgo di Dio, a refuge for the homeless, and in 1954 he married one of its first occupants, Vincenzina Mangano, widow of a murdered Trappeto fisherman. Dolci has five children of his own, five from his wife's first marriage, and several others whom he has adopted.

* dōl′ chē

DANILO DOLCI

In 1955 Dolci moved on to the farming town of Partinico, which has become his headquarters, and the following year organized his famous "strike-in-reverse," in which two hundred jobless men set to work, unpaid, to rebuild an impassable road outside Partinico. The police stopped the work; Dolci received a light sentence for interfering with public property, but also much valuable publicity.

Meanwhile he had found another way to awaken the public conscience. His first book was *Fare presto (e bene) perche si muore* (Act Quickly and Well Because People Are Dying, 1953). It was followed by a similar but more effective work, *Banditi a Partinico* (1955, translated as *Outlaws*); by *Inchiesta a Palermo* (1956, translated as *Report From Palermo*), the most admired of Dolci's books, and winner of the Viareggio Prize; *Spreco* (1960, translated as *Waste*); and *Chi Gioca Solo* (1966, translated as *The Man Who Plays Alone*). All of these books mix "statistics that seem like those of concentration camps" and some account of Dolci's work with autobiographical statements written or spoken in their own words by the people of western Sicily. They form anthologies "of moral and physical horror, of anguished desperation, of hatred, brutality and callousness." Hurried and sometimes poorly organized as they are, they are propaganda masterpieces, the work of "an interviewer of genius" with an "unerring capacity to discover not merely the facts but the typical and crucial facts." It is a gift which has reminded American critics of the sociologist Oscar Lewis. If such men "reach, touch and persuade people," Robert Coles has suggested, "perhaps they are not *only* gifted and effective authors, but men who are on the right track, who live close to what is real and important without feeling any need to disguise or blunt their feelings."

With the twenty-five thousand dollars he received in 1957 as a Lenin Peace Prize winner, Dolci has established centers in Partinico and in several smaller towns, and maintains them with funds raised by national committees in Italy and many foreign countries. The government money which is at last being spent in Sicily will be useless, Dolci believes, unless the peasants can be taught to throw off the resignation and fatalism they have learned from centuries of misery. Hence his search for a philosophy which can provide a basis for hope in a world without religion. He explores this problem in *Verso un mondo nuovo* (1964, translated as *A New World in the Making*) which also includes accounts of the community planning and development schemes he has studied in Russia, Yugoslavia, Senegal, and Ghana.

In March 1970, arguing that proper communication with the people of Sicily was impossible through conventional media, Dolci established an independent radio station at Partinico. After a few hours of transmission it was closed down by the police. The same year Dolci published *Il limone lunare* (The Moon Lemon), a volume of passionately humanitarian poems which he had intended to broadcast "so as to be understood by the people who often express themselves in proverbs, in unconscious meters and in a language that is often both classical Italian and dialect."

Dolci has many enemies, not only in the Church and the government which he has shamed, and in the Mafia, which seems powerless to resist his attacks, but even among his own volunteer helpers, many of whom have left him "because of his vagaries, his autocracy, his interference in their plans." An athlete in his youth, Dolci is a tall, ruddy-complexioned man with glasses, who looks more like a sales manager than a saint, and whose clothes (like his companions) always look too small for him. He seems never to relax or take vacations, but can talk knowledgeably about a wide range of subjects from television to Vivaldi. Robert Coles has said that he is a grave and stubborn man who will not think of defeat: "We cannot afford the luxury of losing." Aldous Huxley called him "the ideal twentieth century saint."

PRINCIPAL WORKS IN ENGLISH TRANSLATION: Report From Palermo, 1959 (England, To Feed the Hungry); The Outlaws of Partinico, 1960 (U.S., The Outlaws); Waste: An Eye-witness Report on Some Aspects of Waste in Western Sicily, 1963; A New World in the Making, 1965; For the Young, 1967; The Man Who Plays Alone, 1969.

ABOUT: Current Biography, 1961; Dizionario enciclopedico della letteratura italiana, 1966; Dizionario universale della letteratura contemporanea, 1959; Ganachaud, G. Les Bandits de Dieu, 1957; Harcourt, M. Portraits of Destiny, 1966; McNeish, J. Fire Under the Ashes, 1965; Steinmann, J. Pour ou contre Danilo Dolci, 1959. *Periodicals*—Christian Century August 19, 1959; November 25, 1959; September 9, 1964; Commentary February 1961; Commonweal August 2, 1957; March 20, 1964; Nation April 29, 1961; June 30, 1969; New Republic March 20, 1961; May 29, 1961; August 19, 1967; New Statesman March 8, 1958; New York Review of Books October 9, 1969; Saturday Review April 8, 1961; July 29, 1967; Time February 20, 1956; April 9, 1956; January 13, 1958; September 21, 1962; April 8, 1966.

DONALD, DAVID (HERBERT) (October 1, 1920–), American historian, was born in Goodman, Mississippi, one of the six children of Ira Unger Donald, a farmer, and Sue Ella (Belford) Donald, a teacher. He graduated from Holmes County Agricultural High School in 1937 and from Holmes Junior College in 1939. Donald, whose maternal grandfather had fought with the Vermont Cavalry in the Civil War, and who was raised on a plantation employing more than a score of black field hands, grew up with a profound interest in race relations. This led him to a special concern with the Reconstruction period, fostered by excellent teachers at Millsaps College in Jackson, Mississippi, where he received his B.A. in 1941.

From 1941 to 1947 Donald was engaged in postgraduate research, mostly at the University of Illinois, which gave him his M.A. in 1942 and his Ph.D. in 1946. Thereafter, until 1959, Donald taught history at Columbia University, becoming a full professor in 1957. His years at Columbia were interrupted by teaching excursions to Smith College, to Amherst, and in 1953–1954 to the University College of North Wales as Fulbright professor. Donald left Columbia in 1959 to spend a year as Harmsworth Professor of American History at Oxford University, where he delivered a course of lectures on "Slavery and Secession." In 1960 he went to Princeton University and in 1962 to Johns Hopkins University, where he is now Harry C. Black Professor of American History.

Donald's first book was a biography of William Henry Herndon, Lincoln's friend and biographer.

DAVID DONALD

David C. Mearns called it "a masterful achievement of sound scholarship, enlightened exposition and absorbing interest." *Lincoln Reconsidered*, a collection of essays, provides, according to R. E. Danielson, "a gentle assessment, a common-sense, witty, and erudite analysis of certain unrealities . . . in the average American's thinking about Lincoln and the Civil War. It is a book which had to be written and it could not have been written with more wisdom, better documentation, or more charm."

In 1960 Donald published his third and best-known book, *Charles Sumner and the Coming of the Civil War*, an account of the prewar life and career of the powerful and in many ways disagreeable antislavery senator from Massachusetts. The book, which received the Pulitzer Prize in 1961, was universally praised for its scholarship, for its "supple and vivacious" narrative style, and for the discernment and patient objectivity with which Donald approached his complex and controversial subject. Allan Nevins wrote: "In what promises to be one of the enduring American biographies, Dr. Donald . . . gives us a picture of the times which is full of new illumination, and a study of the man which presents him as a convincing human being." Donald completed his "magisterial and moving portrait" in *Charles Sumner and the Rights of Man*.

The Politics of Reconstruction, 1863–1867 borrowed the statistical methods of the social scientists to show how the voting records of Republican congressmen during Reconstruction could be related to the security of their seats. Donald's fellow scholars showed much interest in his technique, though not all were convinced that he had mastered it or that he had proved his case.

During his postgraduate years at the University of Illinois, Donald had served for a time as research assistant to the great Civil War historian James Garfield Randall. In 1961 Donald published his revised edition of Randall's 1937 classic *The Civil War and Reconstruction. The Divided Union*, revising only that portion of Randall's book relating to the war, appeared as a separate volume, also in 1961. Donald followed his master's example by giving close attention to the nonmilitary aspects of the conflict, but otherwise rewrote drastically, adding much new knowledge, many fresh insights. Donald has edited or coauthored a number of other books about the Civil War and contributes to scholarly and other periodicals. In 1961 he became general editor of Hill and Wang's six-volume history, The Making of America, intended to meet the need for a popular history which would steer a middle course between the journalistic and the excessively academic.

David Donald was married in 1955 to Aida DiPace, also a historian. They have one son, Bruce Randall. Gray-haired and brown-eyed, Donald is five feet ten inches tall. He is an independent in his politics and an Episcopalian. Donald was a member of the Institute for Advanced Study at Princeton in 1957–1958 and belongs to a number of learned societies, including Phi Beta Kappa. In 1969–1970 he was a fellow of the Center for Advanced Study in the Behavioral Sciences, and in 1971–1972 a senior fellow of the National Endowment for the Humanities. He is an honorary M.A. of Oxford University.

PRINCIPAL WORKS: Lincoln's Herndon, 1948; (ed.) Inside Lincoln's Cabinet: The Civil War Diaries of Salmon P. Chase, 1954; Lincoln Reconsidered, 1956; (ed.) Why the North Won the Civil War, 1960; Charles Sumner and the Coming of the Civil War, 1960; (with J. G. Randall) The Civil War and Reconstruction, 2d ed., 1961; (with J. G. Randall) The Divided Union, 1961; (ed. with Aida DiPace) The Diary of Charles Francis Adams (two vols.), 1964; The Politics of Reconstruction, 1863–1867, 1965; (comp.) The Nation in Crisis, 1861–1877, 1969; Charles Sumner and the Rights of Man, 1970.
ABOUT: Contemporary Authors 11–12, 1965; Current Biography, 1961; Directory of American Scholars, 1963; Who's Who in America 1970–1971. *Periodicals*—New England Quarterly Summer 1964; Journal of Southern History August 1959.

***DONLEAVY, J(AMES) P(ATRICK)** (April 23, 1926–), American-born Irish novelist, dramatist, and short story writer, was born in Brooklyn, the son of a New York City civil servant, and grew up in the Bronx. Both of his parents had come to the United States from Ireland. Donleavy passed in and out of several New York prep schools, served in the U.S. Navy during World War II, and in 1946 went to Trinity College, Dublin, on the GI

* don lē′ vē

Bill. He spent three and a half years there, majoring in microbiology and (according to *Time* magazine) "wenching, pubcrawling, and street fighting" in the company of his "close enemy" Brendan Behan.

Leaving Trinity without a degree, he lived for a time on a farm in County Wicklow. He was a painter before he was a writer and did his first serious writing for catalog introductions to his painting exhibitions in Dublin. Donleavy later settled for several years in London. With his English wife and two children, he now lives at Bective in County Meath, Ireland. He has been an Irish citizen since 1967.

Donleavy's first novel was *The Ginger Man*, which is regarded by some critics as a comic masterpiece. It was first published in Paris by Maurice Girodias' Olympia Press in 1955. Expurgated versions appeared in England in 1956 and in the United States in 1958. It was only in the more permissive climate of the 1960s that complete editions were published in England (1963) and in America (1965).

"The Ginger Man" is Sebastian Dangerfield, an impoverished expatriate American who is supposed to be reading law at Trinity College. In fact his energies are all consumed in his desperate battle against a hostile universe—a battle in which he feels obliged to cheat, steal, bully, booze, brawl, and womanize; to drive away his chilly wife and their child; and to exploit anyone who can be charmed into trusting him. Through it all, mustering an army of fantasies to protect his delusions of dignity, Dangerfield rages against the desperate loneliness of man's condition.

Donleavy was at first categorized as an "angry young man," but he rejects this and all other labels. Indeed, although there are similarities between Dangerfield and the alienated antiheroes of Kingsley Amis and John Osborne, Donleavy's concerns seem fundamentally different. Gerald Weales has argued plausibly that the "peace" which Sebastian pursues with such demonic energy is death; that like the maddened and vicious horses he remembers at the end of the book, Dangerfield is "running out to death which is with some soul."

It has been generally agreed that Dangerfield, whatever makes him run, is a major comic creation, and that Donleavy had developed a unique prose voice in which to describe him. This rapid, telegraphic, alliterative style accommodates windy rhetoric and pure lyricism as readily as bawdry and bathos, savors of Mr. Jingle as well as of Joyce and Henry Miller. Dangerfield describes his actions in the third person, his thoughts in the first person—a narrative device much admired by critics, which enables him to speak both as sufferer and observer.

This same idiosyncratic and marvelously flexible voice has been heard in all of Donleavy's subsequent novels, but none of them so far has equaled

J. P. DONLEAVY

the success of *The Ginger Man*. They have seemed to most critics variously interesting but variously inferior approaches to the same theme. This theme, Donleavy says, is Donleavy himself, inasmuch as all his work draws on his "dreams and inner desires . . . is all a kind of emotional autobiography."

A Singular Man is about George Smith, mysteriously rich, mysteriously threatened, a more quietly desperate Sebastian Dangerfield with a comparable repertoire of disguises and defensive tactics to outmaneuver despair. His limousine is bulletproof, he lives in an office with a door like a bank vault, and plays an applause machine when he is depressed. His enemies are never identified and are quite probably himself. David Daiches found in the book "a wry, shrugging, half-comic and half-sad awareness of the frustrations, absurdities, and compulsions of contemporary business life"; Gerald Weales regarded it as an extremely neat study of "the relationship between the fantasies society imposes and the ones we invent to escape from it." What most critics missed, perhaps unreasonably, was the exuberant energy and momentum of *The Ginger Man*.

The Saddest Summer of Samuel S. presents the roaring boy come forlornly to the end of his tether. Sebastian Dangerfield had moments when he yearned for domestic peace; Samuel S. is beginning to want nothing else but lacks the qualifications. He is a writer nearing forty, in his fifth year of psychoanalysis in Vienna, yearning for a wife, children, and his own hearth and receiving nothing but exotic propositions. Samuel's dilemma is "explored, not solved," according to Alan Pryce-Jones, but "the process is wonderfully witty and compassionate." *The Beastly Beatitudes of Balthazar*

B. and *The Onion Eaters*, two later novels, seemed to most critics labored and repetitive. *Meet My Maker, the Mad Molecule* is a collection of short stories and sketches, containing early versions of many of the incidents in the novels and plays.

Donleavy's first play was an adaptation of *The Ginger Man*, which stripped the long novel down to a more or less satisfactorily dramatic skeleton. The play was well received when it opened in London in September 1959 but was closed down by the unofficial censors in Dublin—an incident described by Donleavy in a scathing satirical essay called "What Happened in Dublin." *Fairy Tales of New York* draws on several of Donleavy's stories and evokes four episodes in the life of Cornelius Christian, another slightly saddened and damaged version of Donleavy's perennial hero. Kenneth Tynan thought it was "rather like a program of vintage Chaplin two-reelers." There was a generally enthusiastic welcome also for *A Fairy Tale of New York* (1973), a novel derived from the play. Brandeis University gave Donleavy its 1961–1962 Creative Arts Award for his first two plays. *A Singular Man* has also been dramatized, becoming in the process "a string of sparkling, flimsy sketches." Ronald Bryden regretted that the novel's brilliance of tone had been lost but said that enough "wit and originality survive . . . to make a funny, touching evening."

Donleavy's heroes, according to Arland Ussher, "have the sense of the Absurd, which is despair refusing to take itself seriously." He himself says that he is a storyteller, with no message to deliver, but adds that the principal influence on his work is Kafka's. Richard Gilman has described Donleavy as "an extremely good writer, in some ways a remarkably original one. . . . One of the true forerunners and legitimizers of a new hurtfully comic sensibility . . . he remains, along with John Barth, John Hawkes, and Donald Barthelme . . . one of the handful of contemporary Americans who continue to make it new but also good."

PRINCIPAL WORKS: *Fiction*—The Ginger Man, 1955 (Paris); A Singular Man, 1963; Meet My Maker, the Mad Molecule (stories and sketches), 1964; The Saddest Summer of Samuel S., 1966; The Beastly Beatitudes of Balthazar B., 1968; The Onion Eaters, 1971; A Fairy Tale of New York, 1973. *Plays*—The Ginger Man, 1961 (published in England with introductory essay "What They Did in Dublin"); Fairy Tales of New York, 1961; A Singular Man, 1965; The Plays of J. P. Donleavy, 1972. ABOUT: Contemporary Authors 9–10, 1964; Moore, H. T. (ed.) Contemporary American Novelists, 1964; Vinson, J. (ed.) Contemporary Novelists, 1972; Who's Who in America, 1972–1973. *Periodicals*—Book Week March 13, 1966; Books and Bookmen May 1964; Commonweal January 10, 1964; Nation December 21, 1963; New Republic December 21, 1963; New Statesman April 17, 1964; New Yorker December 7, 1963; Newsweek December 2, 1963; Saturday Review May 10, 1958; December 7, 1963; Times Literary Supplement July 26, 1963.

DONNADIEU, MARGUERITE. *See* "DURAS," MARGUERITE

DOUGLAS, KEITH (CASTELLAIN) (January 24, 1920–June 9, 1944), English poet, was born in Tunbridge Wells, Kent, the only son of Keith Sholto Douglas and the former Marie Castellain. His father, a civil engineer, left his mother when Douglas was eight. The boy never saw him again. At the age of eleven Douglas went to Christ's Hospital School, and thereafter won scholarships to pay for his education, distinguishing himself not only academically but in school sports and theatricals. He wrote his first poems while still at Christ's Hospital, and at sixteen sold one of them to *New Verse*. Even this very early work was extraordinarily original and underivative.

In 1938 Douglas went up to Merton College, Oxford, where he read English with Edmund Blunden as his tutor, made many friends, and joined the university's officer training corps. Douglas quickly established a reputation as a poet at Oxford, distinguished from his contemporaries by the directness and assurance of his work. He was for a time editor of *The Cherwell*. With Alexander M. Hardie he compiled the undergraduate miscellany *Augury* (1940) and contributed to this as well as to the *Anthology of Eight Oxford Poets* (1941). In the poems he wrote just before he left the university, Ted Hughes has noted "a sharpening to realism, as if, after considering possibilities and impossibilities, he has stood up to act."

Douglas went into the Army late in 1940, before he graduated. The following year he was posted to the Middle East with the Sherwood Rangers' Yeomanry. He was given a staff job at headquarters, disliked it, and absconded to rejoin his regiment in time for the Battle of El Alamein and Montgomery's subsequent advance. Thereafter, apart from a brief interval in hospital when he was wounded, Douglas fought his Crusader tank all the way to Wadi Zem Zem in Tunisia. At the end of 1943 he was posted home to train for the invasion of Europe.

Douglas's informal journal of these years of tank warfare in the Western Desert was published posthumously in 1947 as *Alamein to Zem Zem*. Its "brutal vividness" was combined with great detachment. "I observed these battles partly as an exhibition," he wrote. "I went through them like a little child in a factory." G. S. Fraser has ranked the book with the prose classics of World War I. A reviewer in the *Times Literary Supplement* found in it evidence of "a hotly combative spirit" and wrote: "He was a good soldier, to the extent not only of enjoying the comradeship and excitement of war, but to the extent of enjoying his sense of mastery over machines and men."

KEITH DOUGLAS

His letters showed that Douglas returned from the Alamein campaign with an awareness that his life and his poetic career were nearly ended. The same presentiment is apparent in some of his last poems, notably the much quoted "Simplify me when I'm dead." Death, indeed, and its power to strip away all human pretensions was the theme or motivation of very many of Douglas's poems. He was killed on a Normandy beach, shortly after D Day. Just before his death he managed to bring back information from behind enemy lines, and was mentioned in dispatches. Fraser called him a "cavalier . . . an aloof, gay, and passionate man" who "loved risk."

Douglas's mature poetry appeared in magazines —most of it in *Poetry London*; the *Collected Poems* was not published until 1951. By then the poetic climate favored a kind of neoromanticism and Douglas's poetry struck stark and chill, stripped to the bone. The collection, though well received, seemed soon forgotten, and its author's reputation was overshadowed by that of his contemporary, Sidney Keyes.

In recent years, however, there have been signs of a reawakening of interest in Keith Douglas's poetry, a growing admiration for the directness and honesty of its diction, the subtlety and economy of its technique. A writer who was also a man of action, capable of enjoying and understanding battle, as well as measuring its cost, he is now placed by many critics above Keyes and Alun Lewis as the finest poet of his war. Ted Hughes, who edited a new volume, *Selected Poems* (1964), saw Douglas as "a renovator of language" in whose work language "reposes at a point it could only have reached, this very moment, by a feat of great strength"—one able to speak his mind "with a flexibility and nonchalance that contrasts hypnotically with the ritual intensity, the emblematic density, of what he says." Keith Douglas, Hughes believes, produced "a more inexhaustibly interesting body of poetry than any one of his generation has produced since, in England or America."

PRINCIPAL WORKS: Alamein to Zem Zem, 1946; Collected Poems, 1951; Selected Poems, 1964.
ABOUT: Currey, R. N. Poets of the 1939–1945 War, 1960; Fraser, G. S. Keith Douglas *in* Publications of the British Academy, 1956; Robson, J. (ed.) Modern Poets in Focus 2, 1973. *Periodicals*—Critical Quarterly Spring 1963; Listener June 21, 1962; Poetry London X 1944.

DRESSER, DAVIS. *See* "HALLIDAY, BRETT"

***DRUON, MAURICE (SAMUEL ROGER CHARLES)** (April 23, 1918–), French novelist, was born in Paris, the son of René and Léonilla (Samuel) Druon de Reyniac. He was educated at the Lycée Michelet and the École Libre des Sciences Politiques in Paris, and when France fell in 1940 was a cadet at the Saumur cavalry school. He escaped from France via Spain and worked for the Free French information services in London from 1942 to 1944. It was during this period that his first play, *Mégarée*, was produced, and he wrote, in collaboration with his uncle, Joseph Kessel, the words of the French Resistance song "Le Chant des Partisans." From 1944 to 1945 Druon was a war correspondent, and after the war, until 1947, he remained in journalism. His first novel, *La Dernière Brigade*, was published in 1946 and translated in 1957 as *The Last Detachment: The Cadets of Saumur*, 1940.

Druon's first important literary success came in 1948 when he received the Prix Goncourt for *Les Grandes Familles*. It is the first in a trilogy of three novels known collectively as *La Fin des hommes* (1948–1951), and published in a one-volume English edition as *The Curtain Falls* (1959), translated (like most of Druon's work) by Humphrey Hare. It chronicles the decline during the 1920s and 1930s of two great families which are linked by marriage: the de la Monneries, ancient and aristocratic, and the Schoudlers, a Jewish banking family. Instrumental in their decline is a young man of peasant origin, Simon Lachaume, who rises to political and literary success at their expense. It is, Druon says, "a matter of reciprocity, a labor of human spiders, in which each one, to manufacture his own web, must allow his feet to be caught in the webs of others." Druon's skill in evoking the ambiance of the period, a sense of a society in decay, reminded some reviewers of Proust; others, impressed by his ability to weave together a score of

* drü ôN′

MAURICE DRUON

diverse subplots, spoke of Dumas *père*. The trilogy fails finally, most critics thought, because of the author's contempt and hatred for his own characters, who are seen without warmth or kindness or understanding—not as people but as "symbols of a decaying civilization."

The critics gave a rather warmer welcome to Druon's next book, *La Volupté d'être* (1954, translated as *Film of Memory*), which pursues on a smaller scale a theme similar to that of *The Curtain Falls*. Here a dying courtesan, once famous, passes on the key to at least transient power and wealth to a young servant in a squalid Rome hotel. There are pathos and an element of fantasy, as well as mordant social criticism, in this sordid Cinderella story; above all there is Druon's extraordinary ability to involve the reader in the atmosphere of a time and place.

The novelist's special talents are seen to their best advantage in the sequence called *Les Rois maudits*, translated as *The Accursed Kings* (1956–1962). These six rather short novels recreate with meticulous care the royal history of France from 1285 to the beginning of the Hundred Years' War, and find in the reigns of Philip the Fair and his successors a confirmation of the life view expressed in *The Curtain Falls*: "Days lived, whether full or empty, whether busy or serene, are but days gone by, and the ashes of the past weigh the same in every hand."

Druon employed researchers to gather the facts on which these novels are based, and himself visited the places in which they are set in order "to see the shape of fields, feel the earth under [his] feet, learn what the reactions of a man would be in [the] place." His care was well rewarded by the critics. Isabel Quigly reviewed *The Iron King* in terms applicable to the entire series: "A book without heroes or even precise villains, the portrait at various levels of an age almost unbelievably brutal, its main quality is urgency and immediacy: you feel the texture of the crowded days, the whole grain of thought and outlook, and how it felt to live each moment so close to danger, violence, unspeakable misery and, in a very few cases, . . . passionate hope."

A versatile writer, Druon has also written plays, film scripts, history, short stories, an appreciation of Bernard Buffet, and a book of maxims on the subject of power (*Le Pouvoir*, 1965), as well as two novels set in ancient Greece. A satirical fable about an arms manufacturer who fathers an angel was translated as *Tistou of the Green Thumbs*. Druon's books are available in over twenty different languages. He has been a member of the French Academy since 1966, when he also received the Prix de Monaco. Druon was married in 1968 to Madeleine Marignac. His recreations include riding and travel.

In April 1973 Druon joined Pierre Messmer's Cabinet as Minister of Culture. A few weeks later he announced that he had no intention of giving government subsidies to subversives, pornographers, or "intellectual terrorists," thus at a stroke uniting against himself an extraordinarily wide range of French artists, intellectuals, and Socialist politicians, who regard him as an "intellectual dictator." On May 13, 1973, thousands of enemies of Druon's policies staged in Paris a funeral march for "the mortal remains of free expression."

PRINCIPAL WORKS IN ENGLISH TRANSLATION: *Fiction*—Film of Memory, 1955; The Accursed Kings Series: vol. 1, The Iron King, 1956; vol. 2, The Strangled Queen, 1956; vol. 3, The Poisoned Crown, 1957; vol. 4, The Royal Succession, 1958; vol. 5, The She-Wolf of France, 1960; vol. 6, The Lily and the Lion, 1961; The Last Detachment: The Cadets of Saumur: 1940, 1957; Tistou of the Green Thumbs, 1958 (England, Tistou of the Green Fingers); The Curtain Falls: A Modern Trilogy, 1959 (published in one vol.; Book 1 originally tr. as The Rise of Simon Lachaume, 1952); Alexander the God, 1960; The Black Prince and Other Stories, 1962 (U.S., The Glass Coffin and Other Stories); The Memoirs of Zeus, 1964. *Nonfiction*—Bernard Buffet, 1965; The History of Paris, 1969.

ABOUT: Boisdeffre, P. de. Dictionnaire de littérature contemporaine, 1962; Boisdeffre, P. de. Une Histoire vivante de la littérature d'aujourd'hui, 1958; Contemporary Authors 13–14, 1965; International Who's Who, 1970–1971; Who's Who in France, 1971–1972. *Periodicals*—New Republic September 15, 1952; New York Herald Tribune August 25, 1957; February 29, 1960; New York Times February 28, 1960; May 17, 1964; May 26, 1973; Saturday Review April 6, 1957; September 28, 1957; April 7, 1966; Time April 2, 1956; April 7, 1966; Times Literary Supplement November 20, 1959.

DRURY, ALLEN (STUART) (September 2, 1918–), American journalist and novelist, was born in Houston, Texas, the son of Alden Monteith

Drury, a real estate broker and insurance agent, and of Flora (Allen) Drury. He grew up in California and received his liberal arts B.A. in 1939 from Stanford University.

At the university Drury had been on the staff of the Stanford *Daily* and had contributed to local newspapers. He began his career as editor (1939–1941) of the Tulare *Bee*, winning a national award for his editorials in the weekly. A year followed as county editor of the Bakersfield *Californian*. After service in the United States Army from 1942 to 1943, he went to Washington, D.C., as a United Press correspondent. Drury was a member of UP's Senate staff from 1943 to 1945, freelanced in 1946–1947, and from 1947 to 1953 was national editor of *Pathfinder* magazine. A brief stint followed with the Washington *Evening Star*, and then five years (1954–1959) on the congressional staff of the New York *Times*. He became political contributor to *Reader's Digest* in late 1959, and a year later acquired a weekly newspaper serving Groveland and Clermont, Florida. Drury's work as a journalist had a right-wing and anti-Communist orientation.

His first and best-known novel was *Advise and Consent*. He had begun it in 1950 and then laid it aside until 1957 when he resumed work on it under contract to Doubleday and Company. It was published in 1959 while he was on the staff of the New York *Times*. *Advise and Consent* grew directly out of Drury's experiences as a Washington correspondent; he said later that "writing this book was like breathing—it practically wrote itself." The novel centers on a Senate struggle over the confirmation of a presidential nominee for Secretary of State who is favored by the liberals. Its basic message is that American democracy "represents, usually with success, a compromise between idealism and workaday realities."

The book became the subject of great controversy, and critical opinions of it differed sharply. William V. Shannon, for example, called it a "right-wing comic strip," while Senator Richard L. Neuberger of Oregon thought it would "stand as one of the finest and most gripping novels of our era." Even some of those who enjoyed it found it too long and unselective. It was, however, widely agreed that the story was highly readable and brilliantly constructed, and that it provided one of the most vivid portraits of the Senate in print, taking the reader behind the scenes of that institution into the thick of its political intrigues, power plays, ideological and personal clashes, and occasional manifestations of idealism. Patrick O'Donovan wrote: "It joins the select company of good bad books, along with the works of Marie Corelli and Hall Caine." *Advise and Consent* headed the best-seller lists for many months and won the 1960 Pulitzer Prize for fiction. It was a selection of the Book of the Month Club and of the Reader's Digest Condensed Book Club, reached Broadway in an adaptation by Loring Mandell, and was filmed by Otto Preminger.

ALLEN DRURY

Five sequels to *Advise and Consent* have so far appeared. *A Shade of Difference* involves a black American congressman and an African politician in an attempt by the UN's Afro-Asian bloc to discredit the United States for racism. It was a Literary Guild selection and, like its predecessor, a best seller. *Capable of Honor* has as its villain an influential liberal columnist who attempts to prevent the President's intervention in two foreign crises. The liberal menace threatens a presidential nomination in *Preserve and Protect*, the American space program in *The Throne of Saturn*, and much else in *Come Nineveh, Come Tyre*. All of them divided the reviewers, frequently along political lines, striking some readers as simplistic melodrama written in "graceless prose," others as absorbing and illuminating political novels. *That Summer* is a love story set in an exclusive California vacation colony. Lacking Drury's political expertise to distract attention from his limitations in style and characterization, it failed. One reviewer received the impression that it had been written by a computer, but found a certain fascination in "wondering just how bad it can get."

Allen Drury has also written a number of nonfiction books. The first was *A Senate Journal*, composed between 1943 and 1945 when he was a UP reporter, but not published until 1963. Many reviewers, especially those who rejected its political attitudes, thought it dull and dated, but some found its detailed observations of the Senate and senators valuable. *Three Kids in a Cart* is a collection of Drury's news articles written mostly between 1946 and 1954. *A Very Strange Society* recorded "a journey to the heart of South Africa," and seemed to Tom Hopkinson a generally balanced picture of that country and its "intensely complicated social problem," seen mostly from "the standpoint of [a] thoughtful and fair-minded white man."

Drury, a tall, rangy Texan, has remained a bachelor, although he has on occasion expressed an interest in marriage. He lives in Florida and in 1961 received an honorary Litt. D. from Rollins College in that state. His goal, he says, is to be the "kind of writer who says a little something valid about the human experience, and who illuminates also something of his times so that his contemporaries and those who come after may find their understanding a little better for what he has done."

PRINCIPAL WORKS: *Novels*—Advise and Consent, 1959; A Shade of Difference, 1962; That Summer, 1965; Capable of Honor, 1966; Preserve and Protect, 1968; The Throne of Saturn, 1971; Come Nineveh, Come Tyre, 1973. *Nonfiction*—A Senate Journal, 1943–1945, 1963; Three Kids in a Cart: A Visit to Ike, and Other Diversions, 1965; A Very Strange Society: A Journey to the Heart of South Africa, 1967; Courage and Hesitation: Notes and Photographs of the Nixon Administration, 1971.
ABOUT: International Who's Who, 1970–1971; Who's Who, 1971; Who's Who in America, 1970–1971. *Periodicals*—New York Times May 3, 1960; New York World-Telegram & Sun March 25, 1960; Saturday Review August 15, 1959.

***DUDINTSEV, VLADIMIR (DMITRIEVICH)** (June 29, 1918–), Russian novelist, was born in Kupyansk, near the Ukrainian city of Kharkov, into an intellectual and musical family: his mother had been an opera singer and his father was a surveyor who in his youth had hoped to become a singer. Dudintsev was in love with literature from an early age; he first published a poem when he was thirteen, and in 1933 he was asked to contribute poems and stories to the children's newspaper *Pionerskaya Pravda.* Despite this he chose to study law, believing that a legal career would provide material for his writing, and he graduated from the Moscow Law Institute in 1940. During World War II he was wounded in action near Leningrad in 1942, and for the rest of the war worked as a military lawyer in Siberia. After the war he became a journalist on *Komsomolskaya Pravda* where many of his poems and stories appeared, and by the 1950s his work was appearing in many other periodicals, including the magazine *Novy Mir.*

Dudintsev's first book, *U semi bogatyrey* (With the Seven Heroes, 1952), was a collection of stories, very much within the limits of Soviet inspirational literature, about the lives of a team of road blasters in Central Asia. A later story, "Na svoem meste"

* dōō dēnt' sef

VLADIMIR DUDINTSEV

(In Its Proper Place), published in 1953 in *Novy Mir,* takes place in a phosphate works in a remote area of Siberia and turns on the contrast between Vasya, a young worker who values money above everything, and Fedya who believes that the important thing is to be a "real human being." This story was a forerunner of Dudintsev's novel *Ne khlebom edinym* (1956, translated by Edith Bone as *Not by Bread Alone*) which was a literary sensation when it appeared as one of the principal works of the Thaw, the period of liberalization in the arts which followed the death of Stalin.

The novel begins in the little Siberian town of Muzga, where the director of the local factory, Drozdov, has become completely dehumanized by ambition and greed. The inventor Lopatkin, who also lives in the town, is a lonely idealist completely obsessed with his design for a pipe-casting machine. When Lopatkin's design is submitted to Moscow it is rejected because the Ministry expert on such things happens to be the designer of the less efficient machine currently in use. Drozdov, whose indifference and hostility constantly hamper and frustrate Lopatkin, is promoted to a post in Moscow where Lopatkin also goes to try to further his cause. He does succeed in interesting the military in his project, but this provides an excuse for his bureaucratic enemies to have him arrested and exiled for "divulging state secrets." After Stalin's death Lopatkin is rehabilitated and returns to Moscow, but although his machine is at last accepted by the army, his enemies are still entrenched in power and Drozdov is about to become deputy minister.

As it was serialized in *Novy Mir* the novel became the subject of furious controversy. Its theme

—the conflict between creative individuality and a self-serving official bureaucracy—made it immensely popular. It also brought charges from literary conservatives of "individualism," and early in 1957 the book was being attacked in the Writers' Union for concentrating on the dark side of Soviet life and blackening reality. Much of the argument turned on whether officials like Drozdov were typical or exceptional. The liberal writer Konstantin Paustovsky claimed that "there are thousands of Drozdovs," forming a new and arrogant caste; he linked them with the Stalinist personality cult and said: "If it weren't for the Drozdovs, such people as Meyerhold, Babel and many others would still be living among us. They were destroyed by the Drozdovs." These political implications also made the book a sensation in the West, despite the fact that, from a literary point of view, it tends to be pedestrian in style and two-dimensional in characterization.

The severe official criticism silenced Dudintsev for three years, until January 1960, when "Novogodnaya skazka" (translated as *A New Year's Tale*) appeared in *Novy Mir*. This is a fable, set on a distant planet, about the importance of making the best and most creative use of our brief lives. "If we eliminate the story's somewhat ponderous embellishment of fantasy," says Vera Alexandrova, "we can easily discern in it the values that Dudintsev has cherished from his earliest youth: selfless dedication to the good, and even a kinship with the Kantian dictum about the stars: the starry sky above me, and inner law within me." Despite its emphasis on creative individuality it was, as Max Hayward pointed out in introducing his own translation, calmly accepted by the official critics.

Dudintsev lives in Moscow with his wife and three daughters. According to Mihajlo Mihajlov, Dudintsev is "a short man with a big oval head and clever, lively eyes behind thick glasses. He is as gay and direct as a child." During the 1960s he published several articles on biology and genetics, subjects which he was studying while writing a novel on the controversy between Lysenko and more orthodox geneticists. Whatever he produces in the future, he will be remembered as the author of one of the most important works of the Thaw—one of those, as Edward Crankshaw has said, "who, without being great creators, mark with their work a turning-point or a new beginning."

PRINCIPAL WORKS IN ENGLISH TRANSLATION: Nina and Other Stories, tr. by E. Kretova, 1954; Not by Bread Alone, tr. by Edith Bone, 1957; A New Year's Tale, tr. by Gabriella Azrael, 1960 (also tr. under the same title by Max Hayward, 1960, and as New Year's Fable by George Reavey *in* Partisan Review Spring 1960).

ABOUT: Alexandrova, V. A History of Soviet Literature, 1963; Brown, E. J. Russian Literature Since the Revolution, 1963; Gibian, G. Interval of Freedom, 1960; Hayward, M. and Crowley, E. J. (eds.) Soviet Literature in the Sixties, 1965; International Who's Who, 1970–71; Mihajlov, M. Moscow Summer, 1965; Simmonds, G. W. (ed.) Soviet Leaders, 1967; Slonim, M. Soviet Russian Literature, 1964; Swayze, H. Political Control of Literature in the USSR, 1946–1957, 1962. *Periodicals*—America March 23, 1957; Catholic World November 1967; Life May 2, 1960; Nation December 21, 1957; New Republic April 22, 1957; New Statesman April 22, 1957; New York Times Magazine March 24, 1957; Newsweek May 2, 1960; Saturday Review October 19, 1957; December 11, 1965; Spectator October 4, 1957; Time October 21, 1957.

DUGAN, ALAN (February 12, 1923–), American poet, was born in Brooklyn, New York. His father worked, so Dugan's ironic poem "Coat of Arms" tells us, at "odd sales jobs." Dugan began his college education at Queens College, New York, but World War II service in the Army Air Corps interrupted his studies. After the war he matriculated at Olivet College in Michigan and subsequently transferred to Mexico City College, where he received his B.A. in 1950. He worked for a time in advertising and publishing; his poem "On Trading Time for Life by Work" suggests why he did not remain in those fields. He turned next to making plastic molds for a medical supply house, and since 1967 has taught at Sarah Lawrence College, New York. His wife Judy is a daughter of the painter Ben Shahn.

Dugan began placing his poems in magazines and anthologies in the late 1940s, but he did not publish a book until 1961, when *Poems* appeared in the Yale Series of Younger Poets. It received both the National Book Award and the Pulitzer Prize in 1962, and also won Dugan the Rome Fellowship of the American Academy of Arts and Letters for 1962–1963. In his introduction to *Poems*, Dudley Fitts wrote: "I am moved chiefly by the plainness of Mr. Dugan's themes and by his nuances of imagery, phrasing, run and rhythm. The cast of mind is hard, yet the detail is wonderfully ingenuous and tender." Philip Booth welcomed *Poems* as "clearly the most original first book that has appeared on any publisher's poetry list in a sad long time."

The book contains fifty poems, most of them short, spare, and unornamented. They explore subjects, or conceits, which include the life cycle of the conch, an episode of ancient history, the virtues of cows, marriage, military life, working in an office, being unemployed. Whatever the subject, the tone remains the same: dry, caustic, conditional. Dugan is learnedly but unsentimentally aware of the past, especially the Greek past. He writes with rage or resignation of the present and of his own unheroic role in it, is thankful for small mercies, and sees no reason to hope for larger ones: "I have: / a money making job, time off it, a wife / I still love / . . . and my new false teeth." Some of the poems are experi-

ALAN DUGAN

mental either in their prosodic or rhetorical structure but the best of them are in unrhymed short lines, usually of six or eight syllables, with a terminal emphasis.

Poems 2 (1963) was similar in form and content, and again there was much praise for Dugan's force and originality. G. S. Fraser said that he "writes in prose syntax and mainly in tight, though unobtrusive iambics; the bare diction, the syntactical poise, and the harsh emotional thrust remind me at times . . . almost of Catullus." Other critics have mentioned resemblances to Donne, Empson, and William Carlos Williams.

Poems 3 was published in 1967, and *Collected Poems* in 1970. Dugan's work has not developed; one critic has remarked that all his poems could be drawn together as one long poem. At his worst, according to Alan Brownjohn, his poems seem to "suspend themselves from elaborate cryptic titles and dance a routine of metaphysical ingenuity around nothing in particular." But, as Denis Donoghue says, "in the best poems Mr. Dugan has worked up steam before the poem begins, and the first lines release it; thereafter the power drives through the language, nothing is allowed to rest until the whole work of syntax is accomplished." In spite of his limited emotional and technical range, the critical excitement that greeted Dugan's first book has not much diminished, and his popularity and influence continue to increase.

PRINCIPAL WORKS: Poems, 1961; Poems 2, 1963; Poems 3, 1968; Collected Poems, 1970.

ABOUT: Martz, W. J. The Distinctive Voice, 1966; Murphy, R. (ed.) Contemporary Poets of the English Language, 1970; Who's Who in America, 1970–1971. *Periodicals*—Approach 64 1963; Hudson Review Autumn 1961; New York Review of Books November 23, 1967; May 7, 1970; Poetry March 1964; Times Literary Supplement March 19, 1964.

***DUMITRIU, PETRU** (May 8, 1924–), Rumanian novelist, short story writer, essayist, and playwright, was born in Bazias on the Danube. He writes: "My father was a Rumanian Army officer, a sensualist, an agnostic, and a worshiper of his wife. My mother was born in a family of the Hungarian country gentry in Transylvania; she was very proud of her Calvinistic ancestors and of her beautiful self. He wanted me to learn languages and to be a scholarly man; he hired teachers and bought lots of books for me. She wanted me to be a renowned author. It happened that I had a gift for languages; I read and speak, with various degrees of proficiency, five languages, and my mother tongue, and some school Latin. And I have read many books. My mother's wishes were fulfilled too: I wrote my first story at the age of thirteen, verse at fourteen, my first play at sixteen. At seventeen, I studied philosophy at the University of Munich, Germany. I saw no point in getting a degree, and have made a living as a writer since about the age of twenty-three. I was a very well-known author in Rumania after World War II and my novels and short stories were translated from East Germany to Korea and from the Soviet Union to Albania and North Vietnam.

"With maturity, I became more and more impatient with the limitations imposed upon creativity by the contemporary Eastern European societies. I believed, and still do, that progress and liberalization are due to come, are in effect under way. But the progress is too slow for one single life, and I felt that I had and have too many and too fascinating tales to tell and that it would have been a pity for me to lose my best years waiting for something to come, which could come too late for my creative purposes. So I left the country of my birth and have lived in Western Europe since 1960. I write my novels in French now, essays and short stories in German. (My first story, at the age of thirteen, was written in French and called 'Les trois combats avec l'hydre'; I only afterwards wrote in Rumanian, and my *Boyars*, by the way, may have their place in the history of the Rumanian novel.) My later novels, written in French, are now being translated into the more prominent Western languages: English, German, Spanish, Italian, the Scandinavian languages. I consider it as a great piece of good luck—for which I paid the adequate price—to have intimately known two different worlds and to be able to seek some elements common to both, within myself and within the groups to which I belong. And so to help heal

* dōō mi tri′ yōō

to some extent the wounds within myself and—even more—around myself.

"I'm six feet two inches tall and have a deceivingly athletic appearance. I used to do a lot of swimming, rowing, and fishing but stopped long ago. Now I confine myself to writing. I like thrillers and movies, especially Rex Stout and Hitchcock. I like to dance Latin American dances, especially with my wife. I understand, like, and admire women more readily than men, particularly my wife. The most important women in my life are my two small daughters."

When in February 1960 Petru Dumitriu and his wife Irene escaped to the West from a "cultural mission" in East Berlin, Communist Rumania lost its most prominent young author. During the 1950s he had served as chief editor of the literary review *Viata Romaneasca,* as director (1953–1955) of the Union of Writers and the State Literary Society, as manager (1955–1958) of the State Publishing House for Literature and Art, and as chairman (1958–1960) of the Rumanian Ministry of Culture's Council of Publishing Houses. He held the Rumanian Order of Labor, and received his country's State Prize for Literature in 1950, 1952, and 1954.

The best known of the socialist-realist works Dumitriu wrote in Rumania is his trilogy "The Boyars," which was widely published throughout the Communist world. It traces the history of a totally corrupt, vicious, and irresponsible family of aristocrats, the Cozianos, from its feudal heyday in the mid-nineteenth century to its destruction a hundred years later. Two volumes of the trilogy have appeared in English, *Family Jewels* and *The Prodigals.* Edgar Reichman has suggested that "The Boyars" is not what it seems, that Dumitriu is himself a "crypto-Boyar" who has "always indentified himself with the classes he was called upon to condemn." If so, this hidden meaning has escaped both Rumanian officials and most Western critics. The latter, indeed, have tended to feel that the Cozianos are represented as too unrelievedly evil, their peasant victims too unbelievably virtuous. Nevertheless, "The Boyars" has been much praised in the West, where Olivia Manning, an old Bucharest hand, compared *The Family Jewels* to Lampedusa's *The Leopard* "in its brilliance, ease of manner and ironical humor."

Since his escape, Dumitriu has sought to reevaluate both East and West in the light of his experiences, most notably in *Incognito.* The novel is narrated by a Rumanian who, anxious to defect to the West, is forced to spy upon a deposed Communist leader suspected of deviation. This is Sebastian Ionescu, whose discovered autobiography occupies much of the book and traces his development from a boyar childhood, through Communism, to a kind of Christian pantheism. *Meeting at the Last Judgment* records the brutal struggle for personal power in the upper reaches of Communist officialdom, while *The Extreme Occident* reflects, through the eyes of a Rumanian couple who flee to the West, Dumitriu's discovery that corruption, brutality, and social malaise are not confined to the Communist bloc. *The Sardinian Smile,* about a Swedish family settled in a remote Sardinian village, centers on the wife's destructive passion for her son, and the father's primitive revenge.

PETRU DUMITRIU

Opinions of Dumitriu's technical ability vary greatly, partly perhaps because of variation in the ability of his translators. Most Western critics would agree that his characterization is skillful, his use of language competent, and that he possesses at his best great narrative power. Some readers have complained of a lack of originality in his thought and a weakness for sermonizing. In France Dumitriu has been called "the Rumanian Pasternak"; George Steiner, reviewing *Incognito,* thought a comparison with Sholokhov's *And Quiet Flows the Don* more appropriate, since Dumitriu "is neither poet nor metaphysician." What he can do, Steiner suggested, is to give "dramatic shape to a complex, savage sweep of history." In the Rumanian literary tradition, Dumitriu stands close to Panait Istrati's exalted social criticism.

An imposing, heavyset man, Dumitriu has settled in Germany with his family after a stay in Paris. From 1963 to 1967 he was employed by the publishing firm of S. Fischer Verlag in Frankfurt, where he still lives. His older daughter was kept as a hostage in Rumania until the Dumitrius' desperate efforts to secure her release were successful in 1966.

PRINCIPAL WORKS IN ENGLISH TRANSLATION: *Novels*—Stormy Petrel (Rumania), 1956; Family Jewels (vol. 1, The Boyars), 1961; The Prodigals (vol. 2, The Boyars), 1962; Meeting at the Last Judgment, 1962; Incognito, 1964; The Extreme Occident, 1966 (England, Westward Lies Heaven); The Sardinian Smile, 1968.
ABOUT: International Who's Who, 1970–1971. *Periodicals*—New Statesman September 15, 1961; New York Times Book Review September 13, 1964; New York Review of Books September 24, 1964; Survey October 1965; Time January 1, 1965; Times Literary Supplement September 10, 1964.

DUNCAN, ROBERT (January 7, 1919–), American poet, was born in Oakland, California, and named originally after his father, Edward Howard Duncan, a day laborer. His mother, Marguerite (Wesley) Duncan, died at the time of his birth, and he was adopted on March 10, 1920, by Edwin Joseph Symmes, an architect, and Minnehaha (Harris) Symmes, who named him Robert Edward Symmes. In 1941 he took the name Robert Duncan.

It was a high school teacher, Edna Keough, who gave him his first understanding of the rewards and responsibilities of the writer, but he has chosen not to preserve his juvenilia or the poems he wrote during his two years at the University of California at Berkeley (1936–1938). When he brought some of his early work back into print in *The Years as Catches* (1966), he included only poems written between 1939 and 1946. They seemed to John Perreault extraordinarily varied in their influences, drawing on Milton, Swinburne, Hopkins, Pound, Lorca, and George Barker. Perreault admired their virtuosity and the frankness with which they dealt with the poet's homosexuality, but thought them often too personal and marred at times by "mellifluous sentimentality" and Duncan's "rather overblown attempts at grandeur, his mindless love-hate relationship with Christianity, and his unsuccessful attempts to cancel its influence by counter-magic and counter-myth."

After the war, from 1946 to 1950, Duncan lived in San Francisco, where his "mentor, censor and peer" was the younger poet Jack Spicer. Duncan learned also from Ernst Kantorowicz's classes at Berkeley in the civilization of the middle ages. These helped to confirm him in his belief that, since "to form is to transform," art is a kind of magic, a ritual invoking perceptions that are revelations to the artist as much as to his audience. Some of the work of this period appeared in *Medieval Scenes* (1950).

Duncan is remarkably widely read, not only in poetry but in history, science, mythology, and the occult, among other fields. During the late 1940s and early 1950s he encountered a whole range of new influences, from modern music and painting and, very markedly, from the poems of Denise Levertov, Robert Creeley, and Charles Olson. Creeley and Olson both subsequently taught at Black Mountain College in North Carolina, as Duncan himself did in 1956, and these three are now regarded as the most considerable of the poets guided by Olson's concept of "projective verse."

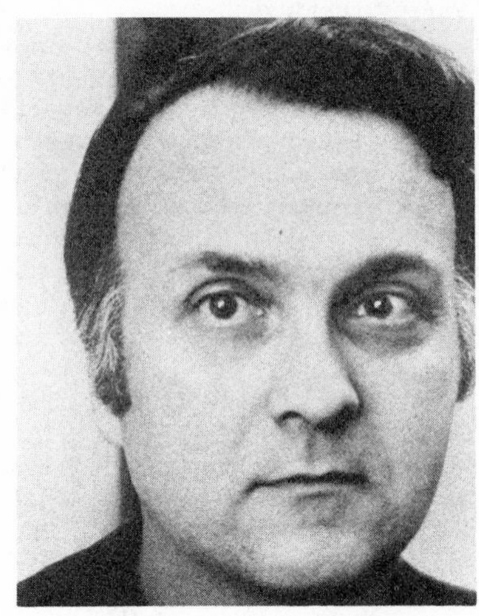

ROBERT DUNCAN

All of Duncan's work since about 1951 has reflected this influence in a number of ways. As Stephen Stepanchev has said, "He shapes his lines irregularly, to accord with leaps and changes of feeling and thought." Moreover, in accordance with Olson's theory of "composition by field," he allows into a poem not only what is relevant to the development of his theme but whatever reflections or perceptions or private associations occur to him while he is writing. He is, he says, convinced "that the order man may contrive or impose upon the things about him or upon his own language is trivial beside the divine order or natural order he may discover in them."

It is a method that makes heavy demands upon the reader, who may be further bemused by Duncan's fondness for the occult and his sometimes idiosyncratic spellings, and irritated by his tendency to portentousness. Even admirers of his "four-dimensional" technique find him one of the most difficult of contemporary poets, and Jim Harrison has said that Duncan's poetry is not to be read in a linear fashion but as something closer to "a block of weaving" or a piece of serial music. For Duncan, "the poem is not a stream of consciousness, but an area of composition in which I work with anything that comes into it."

Many critics seem to value Duncan as it were in spite of himself. M. L. Rosenthal, for example, who thought his was "the richest natural genius among the Black Mountain poets," found his work "to some extent self-defeating." Warmly praising his "exquisite workmanship," he has suggested that he is fundamentally "a modern romantic whose best work is intensely engaging by the standards of the purest lyric traditions." Rosenthal quoted in evidence part of the first poem in *The Opening of the Field*, a poem whose first line is also its title: "Often I am permitted to return to a meadow / as if it were a scene made-up by the mind / that is not mine, but is a made place, / that is mine, it is so near to the heart, / an eternal pasture folded in all thought / so that there is a hall therein / that is a made place, created by light / wherefrom the shadows that are forms fall. . . . / Often I am permitted to return to a meadow / as if it were a given property of the mind / that certain bounds hold against chaos."

Besides his major collections of verse, Duncan has published numerous books through small presses, including two plays, *Faust Foutu* and *Medea at Kolchis; Writing Writing*, a book of poems and essays; and other volumes of poems and drawings. He edited the *Experimental Review* in 1938–1940 and the *Berkeley Miscellany* in 1948–1949. Duncan worked on a Ford Foundation grant as assistant director of the Poetry Center at San Francisco State College in 1956–1957, was associated with the Creative Writing Workshop at the University of British Columbia in 1963, and lectured in the Advanced Poetry Workshop at San Francisco State College in the spring of 1965. He received the Harriet Monroe Prize in 1961 and the Levinson Prize in 1964, and held a Guggenheim Fellowship in 1963–1964. He lives in San Francisco.

PRINCIPAL WORKS: Heavenly City, Earthly City, 1947; Medieval Scenes, 1950; Selected Poems, 1959; The Opening of the Field, 1960; Roots and Branches, 1964; The Years as Catches: First Poems (1939–1946), 1966; Bending the Bow, 1968; The First Decade: Selected Poems 1940–1950, 1968; Derivations: Selected Poems 1950–1956, 1968.

ABOUT: Allen, D. (ed.) The New American Poetry, 1960; Contemporary Authors 11–12, 1965; Murphy, R. (ed.) Contemporary Poets of the English Language, 1970; Nemerov, H. (ed.) Poets on Poetry, 1966; Rosenthal, M. L. The New Poets, 1967; Stepanchev, S. American Poetry Since 1945, 1965; Who's Who in America, 1970–1971. *Periodicals*—Nation October 24, 1959; January 14, 1961; December 7, 1964; New York Times Book Review November 19, 1967; September 29, 1968; Poetry April 1960; September 1965; Times Literary Supplement May 1, 1969.

***DUPIN, JACQUES** (March 4, 1927–), French poet and art critic, writes (in French): "I am quite unable to write, in the first person, an autobiographical text conforming to the models you offer me, to the very substance of your undertaking. In fact poetic activity is for me no continuation or expansion of my private life, but is rather in a certain sense its negation or contradiction. In any case poetic activity is located on another plane, where I am not the only person involved, where I am even the last person involved. Poetry is the word of all men, or of no one, before it is my own word. For me the personality of the poet is only the vehicle of a word which comes from beyond him, which uses him, which passes through him but does not express him. The poet is only the instrument by which language casts itself, verifies itself, and daily reconstitutes itself. The episodes of my existence are of virtually no importance in the eyes of poetry. Hence my repugnance and difficulty, within the framework of your project, in relating my real life to the practice of poetry on which I am being questioned. I can only offer you the following dates and facts which I am in no position to interpret.

JACQUES DUPIN

"I was born on March 4, 1927, at Privas (Ardèche) in the southeast of France. My mother was a native of Picardy, from which region the German invasion had driven her in 1916. My father, Pierre Dupin, was a doctor in the Psychiatric Asylum of Privas. He came from a family of old Ardèche stock, the men of the family having been village notaries since the seventeenth century. He died when I was four years old. After his death I lived for several years in the north of France and returned to Ardèche in 1939. I had my secondary schooling at the Collège de Privas. What essentially marked my adolescent years in Ardèche was on the one hand the war—the second World War—and on the other the country in which I was living.

* dü paN′

"The war, which caused me no direct suffering, meant this: the presence of German troops, the closeness of the *maquis*, a sense and then a revelation of the monstrous character of Nazism and of war itself, a shaking and overturning of my sense of values, a situation which readily called into question bourgeois education and bourgeois society, the intoxication and terror of the *tabula rasa*.

"Nature was the only recourse, the only tangible reality. A country of stones, of volcanoes, of sharp cliffs, of denuded mountains. Granite and basalt. Chestnut groves and pine woods. Torrents, often dried up, and crater lakes. But also, rapid and all powerful, the Rhône.

"The Liberation coincided with the end of my secondary studies. Then I went in for the study of law and political science in Paris. A front which allowed me to write poetry. The main happening for me was my meeting with René Char in 1947—the discovery through him of contemporary poetry, his encouragement, his friendship. I published my first poems in 1949 in the review *Cahiers d'Art*. I worked as an editorial secretary on the review *Empédocle*, then with *Cahiers d'Art*. René Char wrote a preface for my first pamphlet of poems, *Cendrier du voyage*, published in 1950 by G.L.M. In 1951 I married Christine Rousset. We have two daughters, Élisabeth and Hélène. Then I began writing articles on contemporary art for the *Cahiers d'Art* and other reviews. Since that time I have continued to express my interest in modern art and in contemporary painters in articles, prefaces, and books, as well as in my professional activity at the Galérie Maeght, where I have been the publications editor since 1954.

"Several friendships have mattered, and still matter, a great deal to me: that of René Char, which I have mentioned, those of Alberto Giacometti, Francis Ponge, and André du Bouchet. My opacity to foreign languages has kept me from reading foreign writers except in translation; in this way I have read especially Hölderlin and Kafka. Thus the influences on me have come essentially from French poetry, from the whole French poetic tradition since François Villon; and it is banal to cite the names of Baudelaire and Nerval, of Rimbaud and Mallarmé. Among my contemporaries, besides the poets I have named, I am especially in debt to Antonin Artaud, Georges Bataille, Maurice Blanchot."

As he says, the war swept Dupin's mind clear of the values inculcated by a "bourgeois education and bourgeois society" and turned him towards "the only tangible reality"—an overwhelmingly powerful natural world. These elements have been reflected in his poetry from the beginning, expressed in an aphoristic and enigmatic style which at first owed a great deal to his association with Réne Char. The poems in his first book, *Cendrier du voyage* (Ashtray of a Journey, 1950) were, according to a critic in the *Times Literary Supplement*, "solidly, even passionately, based in a reality of *things*, elementary things in all their relative solidity, durability and immobility." And the permanence of nature was contrasted, defiantly rather than despairingly, with human transience.

Dupin's poetry has continued to illustrate "that almost apocalyptic vision of the human spirit striving impossibly towards light and space through an arid mental landscape dominated by night and stone." The publication of the retrospective collection *Gravir* (To Climb, 1963), showed how Dupin had gradually freed himself of mannerisms learned from René Char, ascending towards a manner increasingly bare and precise in its originality. Some of this quality is evident in "L'air" (translated by William Brown as "Air"): "The body and the dreams of the lady / For whom the hammers whirled / Are lost together, and return / Retrieving from the storm clouds / Only the tattered rags of the lightning / With the dew to come." Dupin's 1969 volume, *L'Embrasure*, gave its title also to the collected poems of 1971.

The poet has written important studies of the work of the sculptor Giacometti and the painter Miró, and some critics have seen in Dupin's intensely visual poetry something of "the asperity of Giacometti's taut figures, or of the sharp outlines of Miró's elementary shapes."

PRINCIPAL WORKS IN ENGLISH TRANSLATION: Joan Miró, 1962; Alberto Giacometti, 1964. *Poems in* Aspel. A. and Justice, D. R. (eds.) Contemporary French Poetry, 1965; Hartley, A. (ed.) The Penguin Book of French Verse: Twentieth Century, 1966 ed.; Taylor, S. W. (ed.) French Writing Today, 1968. *Periodicals*—Paris Review Winter–Spring 1968.

ABOUT: Richard, J.-P. Onze études sur la poésie moderne, 1964. *Periodicals*—Reporter June 6, 1963; Times Literary Supplement February 19, 1970.

***"DURAS," MARGUERITE (pseudonym of Marguerite Donnadieu)** (April 4, 1914-), French novelist, dramatist, and screen writer, was born in Giadinh, in what was then French Indochina, not far from Saigon. She is the daughter of Henri Donnadieu, a professor of mathematics, and of the former Marie Legrand, also a teacher. Her father died when she was four and she went with her mother and two brothers to France, returning a few years later to Indochina, where her mother bought a ruinously salt and barren strip of land near the Siam border. Marguerite Duras was educated at the Lycée de Saigon and at nineteen went back to France to study law, politics, and mathematics at the Sorbonne. From 1935 to 1941 she worked in

* dü rä'

the French Colonial Affairs Ministry. She was a member for ten years of the Communist party, leaving it because "we were told one day we should burn Sartre's books. . . . And I wasn't even an admirer of Sartre! But the intrusion of political commitment into literary creation is, for me, the beginning of a moral position which is incompatible with literature."

An unremarkable first novel, *Les Impudents* (1941), was followed by *La Vie tranquille* (1944), a *récit* narrated by a naïve country girl, and then by *Un Barrage contre le Pacifique* (1950, translated by Herma Briffault as *The Sea Wall* and by Antonia White as *A Sea of Troubles*). The latter is at least partly autobiographical, the story of an impoverished white family in Indochina—the mother's stubborn struggle to prevent the sea's encroachment on her land, her lazy son, her daughter's obstinate rejection of a wealthy but stupid suitor. These poor whites and their situation evoked comparisons with the novels, then popular in France, of Erskine Caldwell and John Steinbeck, though the story is told with Gallic objectivity. It was generally admired for its vigor and precise observation.

Even these early books show a particular interest in the limits of human freedom, and contrast those who rebel against their situations with those who passively accept them. These concerns are central in *Le Marin de Gibraltar* (1952, translated by Barbara Bray as *The Sailor From Gibraltar*). A young man succeeds with great effort in freeing himself from an unrewarding job and an unrewarding love affair, and ships aboard a yacht owned by the rich and beautiful Anna. The development of their relationship is frustrated by Anna's yearning for her former lover, the "sailor from Gibraltar," whom she seeks across the seven seas. In the end the young man comes to realize that their uncommitted relationship is the best they can hope for, that it is their pursuit of the unattainable which binds them together, and arms their temporary and conditional love against the ordinary ravages of time. The book was warmly praised for its "sharp visual sense and delicacy of feeling," and Adele Silver thought that in it "the symbolic elements are so deeply embedded in the characters, events and style that the novel stands by itself."

Les Petits Chevaux de Tarquinia (1953, translated by P. DuBerg as *The Little Horses of Tarquinia*) is a subtle study of the obstacles to real human communication, illustrated through a characteristically "exterior" account of a holiday love affair. Another chance encounter is the subject of *Le Square* (1955, translated by Sonia Pitt-Rivers and Irina Morduch as *The Square*), in which the characters' conversation is brilliantly shown to be not an expression of their real feelings, which are intuitively understood, but an almost irrelevant social ritual.

MARGUERITE DURAS

Anna Desbaresdes, the central figure in *Moderato cantabile* (1958, translated by Richard Seaver under the same title), is the young class-bound wife of a wealthy industrialist. She is profoundly stirred by the sight of a man hugging the body of a woman he has just killed, and begins to haunt the café where the murder occurred, drinking with a man she meets there and obsessively rehearsing with him the details of the crime. Germaine Brée has pointed out how often Mlle. Duras's characters are "living vicariously events which they both retell and relive in another key." The story follows a musical structure, that of a sonatina by Diabelli which Anna's child is learning. Working almost exclusively with dialogue, the author creates an intense atmosphere of masochistic carnality. One critic spoke of the book as a kind of contemporary *Madame Bovary*.

Mlle. Duras's books are admired above all for their dialogue. As Laurent Le Sage has said: "The novels are full of conversation—a bumbling, inexplicit flow of words that through its very incoherence and fortuity reveals the pathos of these starved lives." Or, to quote Philippe Sénart: "The word, with Mlle. Marguerite Duras, is not communication but solitary incantation; it fills silence like the most hopeless cry for help."

This mastery of a particular kind of dialogue and her strong visual sense make her novels peculiarly suitable as bases for both films and plays. It was in fact an original scenario which first brought her to the attention of a wide public. This was Resnais's *Hiroshima mon amour* (1959), about a brief love affair in postwar Hiroshima between a French film actress and a Japanese businessman. Both have traumatic memories of the war and they try to exorcise these for each other in a hopeless but generous and splendid assault upon the barriers of loneliness and isolation. The film was universally acclaimed and won several major awards. *Une aussi longue absence*, another film written by Marguerite Duras, won the Grand Prix at the Cannes Film Festival in 1961, and at about the same time Peter Brook's film version of *Moderato cantabile* achieved its international success. *Un Barrage contre le Pacifique* and *Le Marin de Gibraltar* have also been filmed, and the author has made her own screen versions of her play *La Musica* and her novel *Détruire, dit-elle*. The short story "Des journées entières dans les arbres" was adapted for the French stage in 1965, and had considerable success in English as *Days in the Trees*. *Le Square* has also been dramatized and performed in English both as a radio and a stage play. The 1970 play *Suzanna Andler* studies a modern marriage and the isolation and frustration imposed by that institution. Splendidly translated by Barbara Bray, it was brought to London in 1973 thanks to the determined championship of the actress Eileen Atkins, who achieved a personal triumph in the title role.

The novels Marguerite Duras wrote during the 1960s include among others *Dix heures et demie du soir en été* (1960, translated as *Ten-thirty on a Summer Night*), about the impact of a violent crime on a trio of respectably repressed French tourists in Spain; *L'Après-midi de Monsieur Andesmas* (1962, translated by Anne Borchardt as *The Afternoon of Mr. Andesmas*), in which time itself is the protagonist; and *L'Amante anglaise* (1967, translated by Barbara Bray under the same title and based on the author's prize-winning play, which has itself been staged in English as *The Viaduct* and also as *The Lovers of Viorne*). In it an investigator is presented with several equally mysterious accounts of a monstrous crime which was in fact probably inspired by nothing more than boredom—another victory for time. *Détruire, dit-elle* (1969, translated by Barbara Bray as *Destroy*), studies the maneuvering of a handful of characters in a hotel. The translator has provided an extremely useful introduction stressing the author's revolutionary political views and their oblique presentation in this and other works.

Mlle. Duras's work grows increasingly austere, stripped of authorial omniscience, suspense, action, plot, psychological explanation, and most of the other traditional supports of the novel. Some critics have claimed her as an exponent of the *nouveau roman*, and certainly she has much in common with the movement, though she rejects the label. Henri Peyre has written that "the author, obsessed by the impossibility of communication, sketches a fiction of silence and of the slow lapse of time engulfed in vacuity which recalls the 'theatre of silence' of the 1920s and is destined to be forgotten just as fast." Germaine Brée, on the other hand, has praised the "unique, elusive, poetic quality" of her work and her ability "to shape a story so that it achieves an emotional intensity and unity that goes beyond the limits of the outer events related."

Marguerite Duras lives in Paris and has another house just outside the city and an apartment at Trouville. She has a grown son but has never married, believing that marriage "is the best situation yet invented for killing love." Mlle. Duras, according to one interviewer, speaks of herself with a scrupulous and "endearing" honesty, and "is small-boned, pale, with the olive and brown coloring of a Courbet portrait."

PRINCIPAL WORKS IN ENGLISH TRANSLATION: The Sea Wall (also tr. as Sea of Troubles), 1953; The Square, 1959; The Little Horses of Tarquinia, 1960; Moderato Cantabile, 1960; Hiroshima Mon Amour (film scenario), 1961; Ten-thirty on a Summer Night, 1962 (new tr. 1966); The Afternoon of Monsieur Andesmas *and* The Rivers and Forests, 1965; Four Novels (containing The Square, Moderato Cantabile, Ten-thirty on a Summer Night, The Afternoon of Monsieur Andesmas), 1965; Hiroshima Mon Amour *and* Une Aussi Longue Absence, 1966; The Ravishing of Lol Stein, 1966 (also tr. as The Rapture of Lol V. Stein, 1967); The Sailor From Gibraltar, 1966; Three Plays (The Square, Days in the Trees, The Viaducts of Seine-et-Oise), 1967; L'Amante Anglaise, 1968; The Vice-Consul, 1968; Destroy, 1970.

ABOUT: Berger, Y. Marguerite Duras, 1960; Brée, G. Introduction to Four Novels, 1965; Chapsal, M. Quinze Écrivains, 1963; Contemporary Authors 25–28, 1971; Curley, D. N. and A. (eds.) Modern Romance Literatures (A Library of Literary Criticism), 1967; Hatzfeld, H. A. Trends and Styles in Twentieth Century French Literature, 1966; International Who's Who, 1971–1972; Le Sage, L. The French New Novel, 1962; Penguin Companion to Literature 2, 1969; Peyre, H. French Novelists of Today, 1967; Who's Who in France, 1970–1971. *Periodicals*—Cahiers Renaud-Barrault December 1965; Encounter February 1963; Le Figaro littéraire March 12, 1958; Kenyon Review January 1967; Mercure de France June 1958, June 1962; Theatre Arts November 1963; Vogue April 15, 1966; Yale French Studies Summer 1957; Spring-Summer 1961.

***DURRELL, GERALD (MALCOLM)** (January 7, 1925–), English naturalist, was born in Jamshedpur, India. He is the youngest son of Lawrence Durrell, a civil engineer of Irish descent who built some of India's most important bridges and steel works, and of Louisa (Dixie) Durrell. He has two brothers, of whom the elder is the novelist and poet Lawrence Durrell, and a sister.

When Gerald Durrell was three, he and his family returned to England, moving on again five years later to Europe. The boy was educated by private tutors in France, Italy, Switzerland, and Greece. His delight in animals seems to have been first noticed when he was two, and hopefully dismissed by his brother Lawrence as "just a phase."

It was a phase, however, that lasted throughout

* dur′ əl

his boyhood and gathered fresh momentum in 1935, when the family began a five-year residence on the island of Corfu and Gerald Durrell studied natural history with Dr. Theodore Stephanides of Athens. The house, Lawrence Durrell complained, became a death-trap: "Every conceivable nook and cranny is stuffed with malignant *faunae* waiting to pounce. . . . First, I was attacked by a scorpion, a hideous beast that dropped venom and babies all over the place. Then my room was torn asunder by magpies. Now we have snakes in the bath and huge flocks of albatrosses flapping round the house, making noises like defective plumbing." These years on Corfu—the island, its animals, and its eccentric people—are evoked with a mixture of "sharp, delicate and exquisite precision" and "charming ribaldry" in *My Family and Other Animals*, one of the most successful of Durrell's books, and its companion volume *Birds, Beasts, and Relatives*. In 1939, when the family went back to England, a frontier official unsmilingly listed them as "one traveling circus and staff."

In 1945–1946 Durrell worked in England as a student keeper at Whipsnade Zoo; he has described his experiences there in *A Bevy of Beasts*. In 1946, when he was twenty-one, he received an inheritance which enabled him to begin his chosen career as a collector of wild animals. He has since supplied specimens to zoos and museums all over the world, and contributed more than twenty new species to the collection of the Zoological Society of London.

Durrell's first expedition (1947–1948) was to the British Cameroons in West Africa, and his experiences there are described in his first book, *The Overloaded Ark* (1953). He discovered that, contrary to romantic expectations, "You do not spend your time on a trip risking death twenty times a day from hostile tribes or savage animals. . . . Ninety per cent of your time is spent tending your captures, and the rest of your time in tramping miles through the forest in pursuit of some creature that refuses to be caught." Reviewers of his light-hearted and often funny account nevertheless found it full of "zest and enthusiasm and courage and the impact and freshness of first contact with a new continent."

There has been similar praise for his descriptions of subsequent travels: *The Bafut Beagles*, about a second trip to the Cameroons, notable for its portrait of a local potentate, "the monstrous, many-wived, drunken and entirely amiable Fon of Bafut"; *Three Tickets to Adventure*, about a 1950 journey to British Guiana; *The Drunken Forest*, describing Durrell's adventures in Argentina and Paraguay, this time accompanied by his wife, the former Jacqueline Rasen, whom he married in 1951. Return trips to the Cameroons and to Argentina were evoked in *A Zoo in My Luggage* and *The Whispering Land*.

GERALD DURRELL

The logical consummation of such a career is a zoo of one's own. In 1959 Durrell founded on one of the British Channel Islands the Jersey Zoological Park, of which he is now Honorary Director. The zoo has given him an opportunity to further what has become his central concern—the breeding of rare and threatened species of animals. In 1964 he established the Jersey Wildlife Preservation Trust. *Menagerie Manor* is the story of the creation of the zoo and trust.

There must be many young naturalists in the world who have caught their enthusiasm from Durrell's "intense, poetic, intrigued and intriguing" descriptions of animal life. His books show a similar affectionate understanding of human beings. Durrell's funny, warmhearted style has occasionally been found a little whimsical and consciously charming, and some reviewers think him guilty of "colorful exaggeration" in his stories of eccentric beasts and improbable humans. No doubt the problem of financing his various projects has led him to write more and more rapidly than he should. At his best, however, he writes, as William Hogan once said, "like a young Evelyn Waugh who has found out about chimpanzees, tree frogs and bald-headed birds." There has been much praise for the drawings by Ralph Thompson which have illustrated most of the books.

Durrell has written several books for children, contributed to many magazines, and lectured widely. He has also given a number of radio talks (collected in *Encounters With Animals*) and made several documentary television series with the BBC's Natural History Unit. His first novel, *Rosy Is My Relative*, is a fantasy about an alcoholic elephant which seemed "arch" to some reviewers, "splendidly comic" to others. The author, brown-haired, blue-eyed, sometimes bearded, is nearly six feet tall. His hobbies include sailing, swimming, riding, photography, drawing, and reading poetry. Almost all of his books have been selected by one or more book clubs.

PRINCIPAL WORKS: The Overloaded Ark, 1953; Three Singles to Adventure, 1954 (U.S., Three Tickets to Adventure); The Bafut Beagles, 1954; The Drunken Forest, 1956; My Family and Other Animals, 1956; Encounters With Animals, 1958; A Zoo in My Luggage, 1960; The Whispering Land, 1961; Menagerie Manor, 1964; Two in the Bush, 1966; Rosy Is My Relative, 1968; Birds, Beasts and Relatives, 1969; Fillets of Plaice, 1971; Catch Me a Colobus, 1972; Beasts in My Belfry, 1973 (U.S., A Bevy of Beasts). *For children*—The New Noah, 1955; Island Zoo, 1961; Look at Zoos, 1961; My Favorite Animal Stories, 1962; The Donkey Rustlers, 1968.

ABOUT: Contemporary Authors 7–8, 1963; Durrell, J. Beasts in My Bed, 1967; Who's Who, 1971. *Periodicals*—Guardian May 6, 1951; Mademoiselle July 1955; Natural History January 5, 1957; Saturday Review September 26, 1953; Wilson Library Bulletin January 1961.

DÜRRENMATT, FRIEDRICH (January 5, 1921–), Swiss dramatist and novelist, was born at Konolfingen, Canton Berne. He is the son of Pastor Reinhold Dürrenmatt and Hulda (Zimmermann) Dürrenmatt, and grandson of Ulrich Dürrenmatt, well known as a writer of satirical and polemical verse. Dürrenmatt went to school in Berne and, originally intended for the church, studied theology at the city's university. Deciding instead on a career as a painter, he went on to the University of Zurich, concentrating on art and philosophy, but did not complete his studies. He worked for a time as a graphic artist, and also wrote lyrics for cabaret songs and drama criticism for Zurich's *Die Weltwoche*, at the same time beginning himself to write for the theatre. In 1947 Dürrenmatt married Lotti Geissler, a former actress. The same year his first play was produced in Zurich.

Es steht geschrieben (It Is Written, 1947), about the suppression of the Anabaptists, was a study in the corrupting tendencies of power, a theme which has preoccupied Dürrenmatt in many of his plays. The controversy provoked by its unorthodox theology established Dürrenmatt's reputation, and the play won him the first of many literary prizes. *Der Blinde* (The Blind Man, 1948) was a parable play set during the Thirty Years' War but reminiscent of the Job story. These early practice pieces, excessively rhetorical and imperfect in form, were tragedies, but already marked by the grotesquerie, the love of a Shavian and shocking twist in the argument, which characterize Dürrenmatt's work. Both plays show the influence of the German expressionists, and especially of Georg Kaiser, who had emigrated to Switzerland.

It was in his third play that Dürrenmatt achieved command of his own style and tone. *Romulus der Grosse* (translated as *Romulus the Great*) was first performed in 1949 and remains the "sunniest" of Dürrenmatt's plays. Ostensibly concerned with the decline of the Western Roman Empire, the play's historical setting is treated freely and sometimes farcically to bring out parallels with Dürrenmatt's own time. Romulus has made himself emperor with the sole purpose of liquidating an empire which he regards as a corrupt anachronism, but is denied the martyrdom he expects at the hands of the German invader, who turns out to be as idealistic as himself.

Dürrenmatt has been nicknamed the "Helvetian Aristophanes" and, less charitably, accused of making sport of critically serious problems. His answer is given by Romulus, who says: "Whoever is on his last legs, as all of us are, can no longer understand anything but comedies." The theory that tragic drama is impossible in an age without moral standards is developed in Dürrenmatt's *Theaterprobleme* (1955, translated as *Problems of The Theatre*). In the same essay he writes: "It is my not always happy passion to want to render the wealth, the complexity of the world in the theatre. So my plays often become ambiguous and seem to confuse people." Dürrenmatt insists that he does not "start from a thesis, but from a story"; and that it is the duty of the critic to discover "the world in my possible worlds."

Dürrenmatt strikes no moral attitudes in his plays, and it is this refusal to take sides, as much as his reluctance to lay "the egg of explanation," which has puzzled the audiences of such plays as *Die Ehe des Herrn Mississippi* (1951, translated as *The Marriage of Mr. Mississippi*, produced in New York in 1958 as *Fools Are Passing Through*) and *Ein Engel kommt nach Babylon* (1953, translated as *An Angel Comes to Babylon*). The former is nevertheless interesting in several ways and was the work which established his popularity in Europe. It is a bizarre and violent fantasy of considerable complexity, interpreted by some critics as a recommendation of single-minded idealism, by others as a warning against it. (*Romulus* had divided reviewers along similar lines.) The first of Dürrenmatt's plays to use a modern setting, it is remarkable for the variety of theatrical devices it employs. These include inverted time sequences, "alienation effects," and a steadily disintegrating set.

Der Besuch der Alten Dame (1956, translated by Patrick Bowles as *The Visit*) is generally regarded as Dürrenmatt's masterpiece. Its success in the German-speaking countries was followed by many foreign performances. Its subject is the visit of an immensely powerful and wealthy old creature to the small town where, as a girl, she had been seduced and abandoned. Her intention is that the impoverished but eminently respectable townspeople should murder her seducer, himself now equally respectable, in exchange for a large check. And this, protesting piously, they do. Some critics were shocked by the play's relish for the macabre detail but most American reviewers enjoyed both its savage humor and its moral implications. It has been made into an opera by Gottfried von Einem.

The most notable of Dürrenmatt's recent plays are *Die Physiker* (1962, translated as *The Physicists*) and *Der Meteor* (1965, translated as *The Meteor*). Both have been staged internationally and *Die Physiker* has already enjoyed great success. It is set in a mental institution where a physicist has taken refuge from the greater insanity outside, vainly hoping to hide the evidence of a discovery with which, he fears, man might destroy himself. Some critics have found in the play an excessive flippancy which robs it of some of its credibility, and have preferred *Der Meteor*, a sardonic inversion of the Lazarus story in which a great painter, snatched unwillingly from the jaws of death, struggles to regain that blessed state. Both plays have been thought to lack the brutal impact of *Der Besuch*, but to surpass it in technical skill.

Dürrenmatt wrote in 1970 that he was "abandoning literature in favor of theatre"—that he had become more interested in stage effects than in words, and was no longer writing plays *for* actors but "composing them *with* actors." Since the mid-1960s, he has drawn upon the entire repertoire of contemporary theatrical techniques, mostly in adaptations of existing plays. These include Shakespeare's *King John* and *Titus Andronicus; Play Strindberg* (adapted from *The Dance of Death*); and *Die Wiedertäufer* (adapted from his own early play *Es steht geschrieben*). *Porträt eines Planeten* (1970), an original work in this new manner, is a complex and highly formalized "montage of cameos" in which humanity, on the verge of extinction, shows that it can behave as greedily, brutally, and stupidly as ever in the midst of cataclysm. Staged in England in 1973 as *Portrait of a Planet*, in a translation by James Kirkup, it seemed to most reviewers shallow, dull, and arid.

Dürrenmatt has been a prolific writer of radio plays, most of which have been collected in *Gesammelte Hörspiele* (1961), and has also published a number of novels. Some of these have been precisely logical detective stories, including *Der Richter und sein Henker* (1952, translated as *The Judge and His Hangman*) and *Das Verdacht* (1953, translated as *The Quarry*). *Das Versprechen* (1958, translated as *The Pledge*) was subtitled "Requiem auf den Kriminalroman";—the detective story, Dürrenmatt suggests, is a form as obsolete as tragedy when truth and justice become ambiguous. Of his other novels, *Die Panne* (1956, translated as

FRIEDRICH DÜRRENMATT

Traps), has been successfully adapted as a television play. *Grieche sucht Griechin* (1955) was translated in 1965 as *Once a Greek . . . .* It is about a poor and virtuous Greek who becomes a tycoon when he stumbles into marriage with an influential courtesan. This fatalistic fable delighted some American critics and disappointed others.

A stout, stocky man, witty and amiable in conversation, Dürrenmatt lives with his wife and three children at Neuchâtel. His recreations include painting and astronomy. It is generally accepted that Dürrenmatt's principal limitation as a dramatist is that his characters remain spokesmen for his own ideas, taking on no life of their own. And yet the energy and quality of his thought and the brilliant theatricality of his plays have won him a reputation equaled in the German-speaking theatre only by his compatriot Max Frisch. George E. Wellwarth has suggested that Dürrenmatt sees life as "a long futility working up to an ultimate futility," which is death—a point made most explicitly in *Der Meteor*. And yet Dürrenmatt's response is not nihilistic despair but a stoic unillusioned courage which is fundamentally classical and which is illustrated throughout his work. Thus Knipperdollinck in *Es steht geschrieben*, finding religious fulfillment in his last agony was, H. F. Garten said, "the first of a long line" of Dürrenmatt characters "who refute the absurdity of the world by accepting it." For Dürrenmatt, as he himself has said, "The World . . . stands as something monstrous, an enigma of calamity that must be accepted but to which there must be no surrender."

PRINCIPAL PUBLISHED WORKS IN ENGLISH TRANSLATION: *Plays*—The Visit, 1958; The Physicists, 1964; Four Plays

(Romulus the Great, The Marriage of Mr. Mississippi, An Angel Comes to Babylon, The Physicists), 1964; Romulus the Great, 1966; Play Strindberg, 1972. *Novels*—The Judge and His Hangman, 1954; The Pledge, 1959; Traps (England, The Dangerous Game), 1960; The Quarry, 1962; Once a Greek . . . , 1965. *Essay*—Problems of the Theatre *with* The Marriage of Mr. Mississippi, 1966.

ABOUT: Baenziger, H. Frisch und Dürrenmatt, 1960; Brock-Sulzer, E. Dürrenmatt, 1960; Current Biography, 1959; Garten, H. F. Modern German Drama, 1959; Jauslin, C. M. Friedrich Dürrenmatt, 1964; Jenny, U. Dürrenmatt: A Study of his Plays, 1971; Peppard, M. B. Friedrich Dürrenmatt, 1969; Waidson, H. M. Friedrich Dürrenmatt *in* Natan, A. (ed.) German Men of Letters, Vol. III, 1964; Wellwarth, G. E. The Theater of Protest and Paradox, 1964; Who's Who, 1971. *Periodicals*—Nation January 9, 1960; Times Literary Supplement January 11, 1963; October 27, 1972; Tulane Drama Review May 1960.

"EAST, MICHAEL." *See* WEST, MORRIS

EASTLAKE, WILLIAM (DERRY) (July 14, 1917–), American novelist and short story writer, writes: "I was born in New York and grew up in New Jersey where I attended a boy's farm boarding school near Liberty Corners, called Bonnie Brae. Instead of going to college I wandered around this country and traveled with the Mexican Army in Old Mexico. I ended up selling books in Stanley Rose's bookstore in Los Angeles. Stanley had a good literary business and there I became acquainted with Nathanael West, Theodore Dreiser and Clifford Odets, and I realized that writers were only human beings and I could become a writer too. Stanley was helpful, but just as I was getting started war was declared and I went into the army for four years, ending up in the infantry and finally being wounded at the Battle of the Bulge. This war experience went into a book published by Simon and Schuster, *Castle Keep*.

"When I got out of the army I went back to California, but it all looked fake now, so I found a ranch in northern New Mexico and began punching cows, and this is the material out of which many of my books have come. My ranch is in a high, dry, beautiful mesa country between the Apache and the Navajo Reservations. This is a handy location because I am able to arbitrate the differences between the Apaches and the Navajos. There has been no serious war between the tribes since I settled here; both seem content to steal what they can from me.

"My parents were both from England. My father was a Cornishman. He gave me a love for the outdoors. My love of animals is best expressed in my novel, *Portrait of an Artist with Twenty-six Horses*. My relations with the Indians I explored in a novel called after a Navajo phrase, *Go in Beauty*. The local cowboys I took care of in *The Bronc People*.

"I live near Cuba, New Mexico, in a Spanish-speaking community with a girl I met at Stanley Rose's who can type. We are also close to the pueblos so we have six or seven languages going here, and myriad cultures. Other attractions that keep me here are the high clean blue air, the long pyrotechnic mesas, and several horses I am in love with. My original reason for coming to New Mexico was that the American West has never been written about. A great many illiterates, beginning with the dime novelists in the 1840s, then the pulps, then the slick writers have tried it, but never any artists. Our Melvilles and Twains, our geniuses, were not interested, although Twain gave it a brief try in *Roughing It*. Stephen Crane did some short stories on it, but outside of that, and until our time, the West has been neglected by our artists, so I have moved in and staked it out. Our great West, the American promise, has been waiting for two hundred years to be discovered, and that has been my dedication and delight, my Seven Cities of Cibola.

"I live here too because New Mexico is the last silent sanctuary where I can enjoy the splendid isolation that is the imperative of art, where you can contemplate eons of time in the violent riot of the varicolored mesas and man as his primitive and original self in my friends the Navajos, and the animals other than man in all their wild beauty—the elk, mountain lion, the coyotes that howl at midnight at the mysteries of my ranch. The West—promise and dream, legend and myth, the West that has not only escaped the painter, the poet and the movie makers, but because of this has escaped reality itself, has failed to exist—what greater challenge than to make the American dream an alive, a fulfilled promise?"

Though parts of it are set in Europe, Eastlake's first novel, *Go in Beauty*, is dominated by the New Mexico ranch where it begins and ends. Its hero is George Bowman, who owns the ranch and an Indian trading post and is a man at peace with himself, his Indian friends, and the "splendid isolation" he shares with them. He is contrasted with his rootless older brother Alex, who represents the fraudulent world of the new urban America, the parasitic exploiters and "communicators," and who runs off with George's restless wife Perrette. Eastlake's direct and simple style reminded some critics of Hemingway, and the book was welcomed as thoughtful, well-written, and entertaining.

There was an even more favorable response to his second novel, *The Bronc People*. This continues the story of the Bowman family, focusing in particular on the relationship between Sant Bowman (George's son) and his black foster-brother. The book was warmly praised for its "wonderful, mad, ironic conversations," and for "small scenes . . . which are better than anything for which the word 'Western' now stands." One reviewer thought that "no other novel written about the Southwest has told so original a story."

Portrait of an Artist with Twenty-six Horses is an altogether less conventional work. Sant's brother, Ring Bowman, has fallen into an arroyo and, trapped in the quicksands at the bottom, is sinking slowly to his death. His Navajo friend Twenty-six Horses hears his cries for help but rides on, fearing evil spirits. The book intersperses its account of George Bowman's search for his son with Ring Bowman's memories, moments of despair, and flashes of self-knowledge. The young man's recollections form a kind of anthology of New Mexico stories, many of them bizarrely funny. Oliver La Farge described Eastlake's characters as "small, remote, yet very clear, presented through a reversed telescope that yet brings them right to the reader." Other reviewers commended his control of an original and demanding form, and "the spare beauty" of his prose.

Nevertheless, and in spite of his devotion to the idea and the reality of the American West, Eastlake has had his greatest success in dealing with a very different world. *Castle Keep* is about a detachment of American troops holed up in an ancient château in the Ardennes on the eve of the Battle of the Bulge (in which Eastlake himself was wounded). Its primary qualities are its impressionistic vividness and its high fantastic comedy. Each chapter is narrated by a different character, among them the castle's hereditary master, his lady, and the gallant lunatic who commands the American troops. The château, a symbol of a vanishing civilization, means something different to each of them. Some are prepared to defend it and its art treasures to the end; others are equally certain that it should be handed intact to the attacking Germans.

The brashness of the narrators is occasionally annoying—this is likely to happen in any Eastlake novel, when the "simple" tone suddenly becomes self-consciously false—but the book is never dull and provoked strong though divided critical reactions. Emile Capouya, for example, was disappointed that so lighthearted, deft, and considerable a writer should permit himself so many errors of tone, but Anthony Burgess thought it "one of the really good American war books." It was subsequently filmed.

The Bamboo Bed is another blackly humorous war novel, set this time in Vietnam, where the insanity of war is demonstrated in a series of improbable vignettes and absurd conversations between such as Ho Chi Minh, Disraeli, and Karl Marx. Robie Macauley thought it no more than a fashionable but unsuccessful pastiche of Joseph Heller's *Catch-22*, "a small-scale literary disaster" by "an author who has done better things," but

WILLIAM EASTLAKE

other reviewers were less totally damning, finding individual scenes mordantly and hysterically funny.

Eastlake studied for a time after the war at the Alliance Française in Paris. He has lectured at the universities of New Mexico, Southern California, and Arizona, and at writers' conferences, and has received Ford and Rockefeller grants. He now lives in Tucson, Arizona. His wife, whom he married in 1942, is the former Martha Simpson.

PRINCIPAL WORKS: Go in Beauty, 1956; The Bronc People, 1958; Pilgrims to the Wake (short stories), 1961; Portrait of an Artist with Twenty-six Horses, 1963; Castle Keep, 1965; The Bamboo Bed, 1969; A Child's Garden of Verses for the Revolution (poems and essays), 1970.

ABOUT: Contemporary Authors 5–6, 1963; Who's Who in America, 1970–1971. *Periodicals*—Book Week April 4, 1969; Chicago Sunday Tribune October 26, 1958; Commonweal January 4, 1957; December 26, 1958; June 21, 1963; Nation September 20, 1958; New York Herald Tribune Book Review June 2, 1963; New York Review of Books June 3, 1965; New York Times Book Review April 28, 1963; March 28, 1965; November 30, 1969; Times Literary Supplement March 3, 1966; Virginia Quarterly Review Summer 1965.

EDDISON, ERIC RUCKER (November 24, 1882–August 18, 1945), English fantasist, was the elder son of Octavius and Helen (Rucker) Eddison, of Adel in Yorkshire. He was educated at Eton (where he contrived to study Icelandic) and at Trinity College, Oxford University, where he read classics and literature. In 1906 he entered the civil service. He became private secretary to the president of the Board of Trade (1915–1919) and thereafter served in a number of other increasingly important capacities, retiring in 1938 as deputy

ERIC RUCKER EDDISON

controller general of the Department of Overseas Trade. Eddison was named a Companion of the Order of St. Michael and St. George in 1924, and a Companion of the Order of the Bath in 1929. He was married in 1909 to Winifred Henderson and had a daughter, Jean. Eddison died at Marlborough at the end of World War II. He was sixty-three.

In his books, Eddison "recklessly" brought together all he admired—Homer, the Norse sagas, the Elizabethan drama, the Italian Renaissance, the court of Frederick II. *The Worm Ouroboros*, which has been compared to William Beckford's *Vathek*, is a full-blooded tale of feasting, fighting, and magic on Mercury, a planet ruled by a wizard king hungry for conquest and infested with such horrors as the Mantichore, a man-headed lion-porcupine. *Styrbiorn the Strong* is a retelling (with some additions) of a Viking saga, written with "a kind of skaldic fury," and possessing the same "rough-hewn directness and economy" as Eddison's translation of *Egil's Saga*. It was followed by *Mistress of Mistresses, A Fish Dinner in Memison*, and *The Mezentian Gate*—the three volumes (the last incomplete) of the Zimiamvian trilogy.

Zimiamvia is an imaginary country of "Renaissance richness, where action and intrigue, philosophy and love, mingle in scenes of lavish colour and brilliance." It is a fantasy world conceived in as much detail and as completely realized as Cabell's Poictesme and Tolkien's Gondor. Zimiamvia's scenery is said to resemble that of the English lake district, with features borrowed from Iceland and the Lofoten Islands. In this Renaissance Valhalla, this barbarous Olympus, move men and women of superhuman splendor and nobility—some of them incarnations, in fact, of Aphrodite and Zeus. Notable among them is Lessingham, who had been introduced in *The Worm Ouroboros*, and who is "a very Odysseus of wiles, warrior, poet and diplomat," and Lord Horius Parry, vicar of Rerek, "a villain of grand Elizabethan stature." Their adventures are recounted, as James Stephens said, in prose of heroical magnificence. Eddison's narrative style reflects the hard, clear light of the sagas; his dialogue is "clipped and forcible, more archaic than the narrative"; his descriptive writing is rich, elaborate, and sensuous, reveling in the colour and texture of fabrics, the sumptuous furnishings of hall and palace. Through all of Eddison's work, wrote his *Times* obituarist, "runs a passionate belief in the supreme principle of beauty, the spiritual revealed in the physical."

Eddison is said to have been a man of great generosity and exuberant vitality, who combined "a firm conviction of the value of his writings with a real personal modesty." His literary executor, G. Rostrevor Hamilton, wrote: "Eddison has obvious faults—incongruities, lapses of taste, mannerisms. . . . On the other hand, in his towering fantasy, the sweep of his invention and the grandeur of his style, I find something more than high talent—a vein of genius, setting him apart as one of the most remarkable writers of our age." *The Times Literary Supplement*, reconsidering Eddison's work in 1958, found in it "a compelling power, due largely to his own intense conviction and concentration," and said that he had "added a new province to the imagination." *The Worm Ouroboros* has been several times reprinted, and *Mistress of Mistresses* and *A Fish Dinner in Memison* have also been republished.

PRINCIPAL WORKS: (ed.) Poems, Letters and Memories of Philip Nairn, 1916; The Worm Ouroboros (novel), 1922; Styrbiorn the Strong (novel), 1926; (tr.) Egil's Saga, 1930; Mistress of Mistresses (novel), 1935; A Fish Dinner in Memison (novel, introd. by James Stephens), 1941; The Mezentian Gate (uncompleted novel), 1958.

ABOUT: Hamilton, G. R. The Prose of E. R. Eddison, *in* English Association, English Studies, 1949; Who Was Who, 1941–1950. *Periodicals*—Times (London) August 24, 1945; Times Literary Supplement December 5, 1958.

***EDEL, (JOSEPH) LEON** (September 9, 1907–), American biographer and man of letters writes: "I was born in Pittsburgh and was taken, as a small boy, to Saskatchewan when that Canadian territory was a fading frontier. Yorkton was a town of wooden sidewalks, muddy streets, hitching posts and a polyglot Central European farm population in addition to the settlers from the British Isles. A daily train came westward across the endless prairieland in the morning; in the evening it returned to the east. The grain elevators

* ā′ dl

changed and shifted on the skyline as we approached the town by horse and buggy along curving dirt roads. Years later, reading Proust's description of cathedrals shifting in the angle of vision on the French landscape, I remembered the farmland elevators. My boyhood was spent cycling, swimming, fishing, camping; I went to public and high school where we studied a well-organized curriculum in the British tradition. There was also a tradition of culture in my home, and I studied music. But the town had no library. I read the big family Bible and anything else that came to hand: Shaw or Dickens, Wells or Louisa Alcott. What I later recalled was the hunger of some of the transplanted people who had known the culture of the east or of Europe. Later, writing the life of Willa Cather, I was to recover these memories.

"In this way, I had a sense of the Old World from the first. When I went to Montreal at sixteen to attend McGill University I discovered the life of French Canada. I found myself at McGill in a group that read Yeats, Eliot, Joyce, James; from the provincial prairies I was thus inducted into an advance guard of letters; and I was the one 'critic' and reviewer in a group of poets which founded a fortnightly review (now known in Canada's literary history as the 'Montreal Group'). On graduation in 1928, I went to Europe on a traveling scholarship, lived in Paris and wrote letters on the arts abroad for the *Montreal Star*. In the French capital I moved on the periphery of the Joyce circle and *transition*; I explored surrealism, went to Stravinsky's concerts, grew a beard, wore a beret, and read Gertrude Stein. I had become interested in the Joycean 'stream of consciousness' and laid the foundations for my future studies of the psychological novel. In Vienna in 1930 I encountered the new psychology. Pursuing the trail of Henry James, I was befriended by Edith Wharton, and met Bernard Shaw, Granville-Barker, Logan Pearsall Smith during occasional visits to England. I was in Joyce's claque at the opera on behalf of an Irish tenor. I absorbed much of the café life of Montparnasse.

"In 1932 I received a doctor of letters degree at the Sorbonne and returned to the American Depression. I tutored, wrote music and movie reviews, did much hack work until 1936 when I was given a Guggenheim Fellowship to edit James's unpublished plays. I returned to Paris; then went to New York. And then came the war and more journalism. In 1943 I entered the army as a private. A year later, as a sergeant, I was at the liberation of Paris. During the Battle of the Bulge I won a field commission, and the Bronze Star medal. I have five battle stars. In the German Occupation I helped set up a news agency in the American Zone.

"After the war I was able to return to my original career in letters, and began to bring out a series of

LEON EDEL

volumes of literary history, criticism and editions of various kinds. In 1950 I started to write the life of Henry James; the first volume appeared three years later, at the same time as a life of Willa Cather, originally begun by E. K. Brown and completed by me on his death; two subsequent volumes of the James appeared in 1962 and won the Pulitzer Prize and National Book Award. Since 1947 I have seen some forty volumes through the press and written numerous reviews and articles. I have taught at Princeton, Harvard, Indiana, Hawaii, but mainly at New York University where in 1955 I became professor; in 1966 I was given the newly-created Henry James Chair of English and American Letters. I continue to divide my time between writing, teaching, lecturing and research, with long leisurely summers on Martha's Vineyard to collect my thoughts and recover the prairie-sense, in a sea-setting of space, distance and unpolluted air. I tend to write slowly. My aim in biography is to achieve tightness of synthesis and a clear narrative 'line.' In criticism I like directness and lucidity."

Leon Edel is one of the two sons of Simon Edel, a merchant and entrepreneur, and the former Fannie Malamud. His younger brother Abraham must have shared his "longing for the things of the mind and spirit in a community busy with pioneering"—he also became an author, and a professor of philosophy.

The literary review that Edel helped to found at his university was the *McGill Fortnightly Review*, which is said to have launched modernism in Canadian writing. He received his B.A. in 1927, his M.A., with honors in English, in 1928. Edel was already fascinated by Henry James, who was the subject of his two Sorbonne dissertations. Both were published in Paris in 1932, the year that he returned to the United States and began the difficult decade which he describes above, and which was followed by his distinguished career in the army. Apart from two years at Sir George Williams University in Montreal in the early 1930s, he did not begin to teach until 1950, when he went to New York University.

Although Edel was thus well into his forties before his academic career was properly begun, he was by no means unknown in the world of scholarship. His Sorbonne thesis on James's plays had so impressed the Master's family that they had granted Edel priority of access to James's papers. He had never abandoned his researches or let "the trail of Henry James" go cold. His edition of *The Complete Plays of Henry James* appeared in 1949 and has been followed by many other editions of James's work, all of them notable for their scrupulous scholarship and bibliographical rigor.

The first volume of Edel's biography of Henry James appeared in 1953, rediscovering as Alfred Kazin said "that long-buried world of James's childhood and youth," restoring "the extremely vulnerable, shy, and ambitious young person James was, while constantly confronting [him] with the retrospective, voracious, and still secretly troubled artist he was to become." Kazin found in the book "the ease and naturalness and shape of a work of art," and other critics agreed that Edel had in hand the definitive biography of James, and a masterpiece. The second and third volumes followed in 1962, bringing Edel the Pulitzer Prize in biography and the National Book Award for nonfiction. Edel's psychological speculations were thought not invariably convincing, and George Steiner, who called Edel "the most erudite Jamesian alive," found his work lacking in objectivity and inclined to excessive praise. But the critical response was overwhelmingly favorable and full of admiration for Edel's tact and subtlety, his narrative skill and sense of character, his scholarship and his "unobtrusive blending of his sources." There was, if anything, even warmer praise for the fourth volume. When the fifth and final volume appeared in 1972, Hilton Kramer wrote that "it brings to a close one of the most extraordinary literary labors of our time. So far as the art of literary biography is concerned, it may well be the *most* extraordinary. The greatest of American writers . . . has at last been rendered his due in a 'Life' that is itself a first-class work of art."

The work which Edel did in completing E. K. Brown's life of Willa Cather was universally praised, as was his influential study *The Psychological Novel.* Centering on the stream of consciousness in the work of Joyce, Proust, and Dorothy Richardson, it was written "simply and warmly . . . with a delectable abundance of appropriate quotations," no jargon, and much good sense.

Edel gave his views on the qualities of the ideal literary biographer in a lecture published in 1957, which John K. Hutchens has summarized in these terms: "He is . . . a sensitive critic as well as a scrupulous collector of facts, searches a writer's work not only for its own esthetic sake but for what it says about the writer's inner life, uses the psychoanalyst's techniques but is not confined by them, and by-passes the orthodox biographer's subservience to chronology in favor of grouping for dramatic emphasis outside a fixed-time schedule."

Edel has received Guggenheim and Bollingen fellowships, among other such awards, is a Fellow of the (British) Royal Society of Literature, and has several honorary degrees. In 1969 he became Citizens Professor of English at the University of Hawaii and in 1973 he retired as Henry James Professor at New York University and moved to Hawaii. At the same time it was announced that he had been appointed editor of the diaries and journals of his friend the late Edmund Wilson. The journals, maintained from 1919 to 1972, were to be published in five or six volumes at intervals of about eighteen months. Edel, who was married in 1950 to Roberta Roberts, has been described as a trim man of medium build, five feet six inches tall, with gray hair and brown eyes, "unostentatious, dedicated, scrupulous, reticent, soft-spoken." He is a Democrat, and enjoys music, book collecting, and beachcombing.

PRINCIPAL WORKS: James Joyce: The Last Journey, 1947; Henry James, vol. 1: 1843–1870: The Untried Years, 1953; (with E. K. Brown) Willa Cather: A Critical Biography, 1953; The Psychological Novel, 1900–1950, 1955 (rev. as The Modern Psychological Novel, 1959); Literary Biography, 1957; Henry James, vol. 2: The Conquest of London, 1870–1881 (1870–1883 in English ed.), 1962; Henry James, vol. 3: The Middle Years, 1882–1895 (1884–1894 in English ed.), 1962; Henry James, vol. 4: The Treacherous Years, 1895–1901, 1969; Henry James, vol. 5: The Master, 1901–1916, 1972. *As editor*—The Complete Plays of Henry James, 1949; The Ghostly Tales of Henry James, 1949; Selected Fiction [of Henry James], 1953; Selected Letters of Henry James, 1955; The Future of the Novel, 1956; The American Essays [of Henry James], 1956; (with I. D. Lind) Parisian Sketches, 1957; (with others) Masters of American Literature (2 vols.), 1959; Five World Biographies, 1961; The Complete Tales of Henry James (12 vols.), 1962–1965.

ABOUT: Contemporary Authors 1st revision 1–4, 1967; Current Biography, 1963; Kendall, P. M. The Art of Biography, 1965; Who's Who, 1971; Who's Who in America, 1970–1971. *Periodicals*—New York Herald Tribune May 7, 1963; New York Times May 7, 1963; January 18, 1973; New York Times Book Review May 3, 1953; June 13, 1965; February 6, 1972; New Yorker March 13, 1971; Saturday Review May 9, 1953.

EDELMAN, MAURICE (March 2, 1911-), English novelist and journalist, was born in Cardiff, Wales, the son of Joshua Edelman, an artist, and the former Ester Solomon. Edelman, who was one of four children, left Cardiff High School in 1929 and went as an exhibitioner in modern languages to Trinity College, Cambridge. There he read widely in French and German literature and was much influenced by both—in particular, he thinks, by Heine. Graduating in 1932 during the Depression, he found congenial employment hard to come by. He went to work for a timber company which manufactured plywood.

Edelman's literary career was foreshadowed by a volume of verse published just after his graduation; his parliamentary career by the spare-time political journalism which engaged him increasingly during the 1930s. His first factual book was *GPU Justice*, an account of a German engineer's experience in a Moscow prison. *Production for Victory, Not Profit* followed in 1941—an antiprofiteering tract which, Edelman says, "wasn't very popular in the circles in which I moved" and "the direct occasion for my leaving my plywood job." By this time, however, Edelman had established his reputation as a journalist. He joined the staff of *Picture Post* and in 1943–1945 served as a war correspondent in Algeria and France, developing a close acquaintanceship with both countries, and making many friends in French political circles. Out of this experience he wrote *France: The Birth of the Fourth Republic*. In 1945, covering Britain's first postwar election, Edelman found himself selected by the Labour party as its parliamentary candidate for Coventry West. He has represented one or other of the Coventry constituencies in Parliament ever since.

A Trial of Love, Edelman's first novel, was about a journalist who seeks self-realization in the experience of combat, and it drew on his own knowledge of wartime Algeria. It was generally praised, principally for its wit and pace. It was followed by *Who Goes Home?*, which concerns a politician whose career is wrecked when he accepts a loan that has the appearance of a bribe. This novel set the pattern for *Minister of State*, in which a single offensive witticism about Africans almost ruins a colonial secretary, and for *The Prime Minister's Daughter*, where a rumor that the prime minister has induced the police to drop charges against his daughter nearly unseats him.

A similar formula operates in almost all of his work—in *A Dream of Treason*, where the alcoholism of a civil servant's wife forces him to "leak" a Cabinet secret; in *The Happy Ones*, where the hazard is a divorce scandal; in *A Call on Kuprin*, an excellent political thriller in which the Russians exploit a long-forgotten homosexual incident.

MAURICE EDELMAN

Edelman is one of a surprisingly small number of novelists to have written about Parliament from the inside, and he has been called the best political novelist since Disraeli (the subject of one of the most admired of his books). But he is not an ideological writer. He writes about Parliament because it is the world he knows best and "a place where one can study human nature very closely." What fascinates him above all, he says, is "the contrast—indeed, the conflict—between the private and public personalities of politicians who must present a certain standard face to the world no matter what [their] private inner conflicts." This conflict provides Edelman with stories which, in his best books, achieve the dimensions of tragedy. His less ambitious novels are highly entertaining "politico-moral melodramas," fascinating and illuminating in their delineation of the British political scene. In *The Fratricides* he wrote with similar authority of the Algerian struggle for liberation, and in *Shark Island* of the Caribbean. Edelman possesses "a polished style, a way with atmosphere and the ability to move a plot along through clipped and relevant dialogue." His work never falls below a level of craftsmanship which has earned him comparison with Nigel Balchin and Constantine FitzGibbon.

Edelman's work also includes a lively biography of David Ben-Gurion, television plays, and much journalism. His principal interest in Parliament (apart from the special concerns of his constituents) is in European cooperation, and he is a frequent delegate to the Council of Europe. He served from 1951 to 1967 as vice-chairman of the British Council, and is an officer of the Légion d'Honneur. Edelman was married in 1933 to Matilda Yager and has two daughters. He is a dark, handsome man of above-average height, whose recreations include tennis and amateur painting. An American journalist once described him as "one of the best-dressed men I have ever interviewed."

PRINCIPAL WORKS: *Novels*—A Trial of Love, 1951; Who Goes Home?, 1953; A Dream of Treason, 1954; The Happy Ones, 1957; A Call on Kuprin, 1959; The Minister (U.S., Minister of State), 1961; The Fratricides, 1963; The Prime Minister's Daughter, 1964; Shark Island, 1967; All on a Summer's Night, 1969; Disraeli in Love, 1972. *Nonfiction*—GPU Justice, 1938; Production for Victory, Not Profit, 1941; France: The Birth of the Fourth Republic, 1945; Ben-Gurion, 1964 (U.S., David); The Mirror, 1966.

ABOUT: Current Biography, 1954; Newquist, R. (ed.) Counterpoint, 1965; Who's Who, 1971.

***EICH, GÜNTER** (February 1, 1907–), German poet and radio dramatist, was born in the small town of Lebus on the Oder, and grew up in the province of Brandenburg. He was educated at the University of Leipzig and at universities in Paris and Berlin, studying economics and Chinese. His early poems appeared in *Anthologie Jüngster Lyrik* (1927) under the pseudonym Erich Günter, and in his *Gedichte* (1930). They showed affinities with the new nature poetry of Oskar Loerke and Wilhelm Lehmann, as well as with that of Eich's contemporary Peter Huchel. In 1929 Eich wrote his first radio play. He settled in Berlin in 1932 and thereafter earned his living as a writer, especially for radio, until the outbreak of World War II. Eich served with the army, was captured, and was an American prisoner of war until 1946. It is with the poems written then that Eich struck a new note which was to establish him as one of the foremost German poets of the postwar period.

As a poet, Eich has been preoccupied with the relation of man to nature, or with the relation of historical to unhistorical time. Even if one discounts his prewar poems, most of which have not been reprinted, what is most striking about his poetry is its range both of theme and manner. Beginning with strict and conventional forms, Eich introduced a new laconic and deliberately casual diction in *Abgelegene Gehöfte* (Remote Homesteads, 1948), as in the much-anthologized poem "Inventur," which merely lists the possessions of a prisoner of war, refraining from any appeal to sentiment or judgment. In the next two collections there was a development towards free, organic, and deliberately modulated rhythms. Thematically, the collection *Botschaften des Regens* (Messages of the Rain, 1955) was dominated by those "messages" conveyed by natural phenomena which cannot be deciphered in human terms, though their relevance and importance are felt to be decisive. "I write poems to orient myself in reality," Eich has written.

* īk

GÜNTER EICH

"I regard them as trigonometrical points or as buoys that mark out my course over an unknown plane. Only by my writing do things attain reality for me. Reality is not my premise, but my goal. I have to find and establish it."

An element of mystery, then, is essential to all of Eich's work. His more recent poems, as collected in *Zu den Akten* (For the Record, 1964) and in *Anlasse und Steingärten* (Occasions and Stone Gardens, 1966), are more cryptic and condensed than those written in the late 1940s and the 1950s; their imagery has become less realistic, their syntax more elliptical. The prose poems of *Maulwürfe* (1968) are if anything even more hermetic.

Eich's radio plays appear quite different, investigating human institutions and human destinies with ingenuity, subtlety, and wry humor. But the difference is superficial, imposed by the medium; the true function of these plays is to explore a mystery akin to that in which Eich's poems are rooted. One question that recurs again and again in the radio plays, despite their great diversity of setting and period, is the need to come to terms with death, the irony of the fact of death and of human attempts to evade it.

This theme was explicit in *Träume* (Dreams), the play which established Eich's reputation with a far larger audience than his poems could reach. It was first broadcast in 1951, caused a sensation and much protest, but has been called "the birth of the German radio play." In five scenes, linked by verse passages, it evokes the subconscious fears and horrors locked beneath the comfortable surface of modern life. In *Die Mädchen aus Viterbo* (The Girls from Viterbo) a Jewish girl, by bearing in her imagination a different tragedy, is brought to a calm acceptance of her own murder by the Gestapo. At least two of Eich's radio plays evolved from a purely linguistic nucleus. In *Die Brandung von Setúbal* (translated as *The Rolling Sea at Setúbal*) it is a common German idiom which Eich took literally, building his plot and characters on so seemingly trivial a foundation, but using language to "orient himself in reality." Similarly, *Das Jahr Lazertis* (translated as *The Year Lacertis*) is held together by the associations and possible meanings of a single half-heard word.

Only a medium permitting great imaginative freedom and intended mainly for the ear has enabled Eich to extend his essentially poetic sensibility to the wide range of subjects and characters rendered in his radio plays. These have been published in several collections and separate volumes, most recently in *Fünfzehn Hörspiele* (Fifteen Radio Plays, 1966), Eich's own selection. These plays have been as widely read as listened to, and their quality is unimpaired on the page, though Eich is rightly regarded as a master of effects peculiar to radio. In recent years he has also experimented with puppet plays for television; these show a development parallel with that in his poems, towards a manner more cryptic and surrealist. Five of Eich's radio plays have been broadcast in English versions in England, and a number have been published in English and American periodicals. They would be more widely known already but for a tendency to exclude radio drama from consideration as literature to be read, as well as heard. Günter Eich has contributed more than any other German writer to a reversal of this attitude.

Since the war, Eich has lived in Bavaria and Austria, traveling widely in Europe and Africa. He was married in 1953 to the writer Ilse Aichinger, and they have two children. Eich was a founder-member of Gruppe 47, and in 1952 was the first recipient of its annual prize. Among many other honors he has also received the Georg Büchner Prize (1959). The address he delivered at that time is a radical, and most characteristic, examination of the proper attitude of writers to political power and to what he calls "controlled language"; his insistence on the freedom of writers to oppose both made Eich a spokesman for most of the prominent postwar writers in West Germany.

PRINCIPAL WORKS IN ENGLISH TRANSLATION: Journeys (containing The Rolling Sea at Setúbal *and* The Year Lacertis), 1968. *Poems in*—Bridgwater, P. (ed.) Twentieth-Century German Verse, 1963; Hamburger, M. and Middleton, C. (eds.) Modern German Poetry 1910–1960, 1962; Schwebell, G. C. (ed. and tr.) Contemporary German Poetry, 1964.

ABOUT: Donath, A. Günter Eich *in* Schriftsteller der Gegenwart, 1963; Fowler, F. M. Günter Eich *in* Keith-Smith, B. (ed.) Essays on Contemporary German Literature, 1966. *Periodicals*—Books Abroad Summer 1962.

LOREN EISELEY

***EISELEY, LOREN (COREY)** (September 3, 1907–), American anthropologist, and historian and philosopher of science, writes: "I was born in Lincoln, Nebraska, the grandson of pioneers who had drifted west with the frontier into the Nebraska Territory. My mother was stone deaf and my childhood, part of which was spent in obscure western towns, was largely solitary. Perhaps there is something symbolic in the fact that Robinson Crusoe was the first adult book I ever read. As a consequence of that book and my own experience as a kind of social castaway I find it difficult to this day not to pick up a length of rope or a piece of machinery dropped in the street, under the impulse that these castoffs might sometime prove useful like the iron of Crusoe's ship.

"Since my first experience with Daniel Defoe I have had an enormous appetite for books. I could read before I entered grade school and, in the early, lonely years, I was an incessant haunter of public libraries. I read everything from the dime novels swapped by farm boys in the western towns, to treatises on the farms of Africa, borrowed from more erudite collections. Long before I entered college I was an avid maker of aquaria and an intense observer of nature at all seasons. I took walks in winter blizzards or the heat of midsummer. Doubtless these absences from home offered escape from a somewhat oppressive family atmosphere but they also intensified my attachment to the Plains country, which has persisted into my adult writing.

"I first became vividly aware of the fossil past when visiting, as a child, the old red brick museum which used to house the paleontological collections

* īz′ lē

of the University of Nebraska. Later I attended the University and served several seasons with fossil collecting parties in the Badlands. It was a time when traces of early man were first being discovered in the West.

"My college years were variously and successively interrupted by my father's death, the Great Depression, and long periods of common labor. During this unseasonably lengthy driftage my interests shifted through English literature, biology and philosophy, to anthropology. Eventually I obtained my B.A. and came east to graduate school at the University of Pennsylvania in Philadelphia. Here I worked under the late Frank G. Speck who, besides being an ethnologist of note, was no mean naturalist. To him I owe my introduction to the eastern woodlands and my final professional degree in anthropology.

"Finishing my doctorate in 1937 I went west to teach at the University of Kansas (Lawrence) and in 1938 married Mabel Langdon. I never expected to see Philadelphia again. Ten years later I was teaching at Oberlin College when the call came to succeed Frank Speck, then in his last illness, as chairman of the Department of Anthropology at Pennsylvania. The old days of Speck's naturalist's paradise on the top floor of College Hall were ending. Gone were his box turtles wandering about underfoot, his snakes in sacks, or stalking, eccentric Indians appearing unbidden at the door. Anthropology was no longer the haunt of rebels from other disciplines. Professional students were multiplying. The staff moved to new quarters.

"Teaching and administration led on eventually to the provostship of the University, and then to the conferring of a special professorship which I continue to hold. I have always found some time to write. I had published verse while still an undergraduate and later had written essays, not all scientifically oriented, for many magazines. Anthologies of English literature have published my work and certain of my books have received awards from unexpected sources. Insomnia, a painful affliction from the troubled past, has secured me at some cost, a little extra time. I write slowly in longhand, revising as I go. As an insatiable reader I rather begrudge the time spent on my own compositions.

"Though from far inland I love the sea and the islands of the West Indies. It may be that Robinson Crusoe has imprinted my memory too strongly to be forgotten. At all events I am known to come home from far coasts with such old treasures as the voice of the sea contained in a conch shell. My wife contends that I have all along secretly anticipated the fall of civilization, and am only waiting the proper moment to use the conch shell, the bit of rope, and an old bolt picked up in the street, in some necessary primitive contrivance. I have to admit that I can batter out of flint a reasonable fascimile of a Stone Age handax. Furthermore, I seem, at times, to be searching for an island whose compass bearings are lost."

Loren Eiseley is the son of Clyde Eiseley, a hardware salesman, and the former Daisy Corey. It was not until 1933, when he was twenty-six, that he received his B.A. in anthropology at the University of Nebraska, and it is perhaps surprising that he managed, even then, to choose between science and literature. During his college years he had become closely associated with the University of Nebraska's *Prairie Schooner*, where he published poems, stories, and reviews, and edited a poetry page. As early as 1930 he was recognized as a young poet of unusual promise, and he had a story in the *Best Short Stories of 1936* and a sonnet in *Best Poems of 1942*.

Once his decision was made, however, he soon showed exceptional ability in his chosen field. From Nebraska a Harrison Scholarship took him to the University of Pennsylvania (M.A., 1935). He returned to Nebraska for a year and then went back to the University of Pennsylvania, this time with a Harrison Fellowship, for his Ph.D. The same year, 1937, he joined the faculty of the University of Kansas, where he taught until he went to Oberlin College in 1944 as chairman of the department of sociology and anthropology. Since 1947 he has been at the University of Pennsylvania, where he is now University Professor of Anthropology and the History of Science.

Eiseley's special interests include human evolution, paleo-archaeology, and the life of early man in America, and since 1931 he has participated in many paleological expeditions all over the North American continent. His articles, essays, and lectures about his work began to appear during the 1940s, not only in learned journals but in such publications as *Harper's Magazine* and *Reader's Digest*. All of his work, from his early poems and stories to his scientific articles and books, have shown a "taste for the marvelous," a capacity for "discerning in the flow of ordinary events the point at which the mundane world gives way to quite another dimension."

The Immense Journey is a splendid account for the layman of the history of life on this planet. Man, in Eiseley's view, is not life's "perfect image" but is nevertheless unique, having "escaped out of the eternal present of the animal world into a knowledge of past and future." Eiseley believes that "the most enormous extension of vision of which life is capable is the projection of itself into other lives. This is the lonely, magnificent power of humanity." The book was enthusiastically praised, both for its inspiring vision of history and for its style, "compelling in impact and poetic in its imagery."

Darwin's Century, which received the first Phi Beta Kappa science prize in 1959, describes the development of evolutionary thought, demonstrating according to one scholarly reviewer "a thorough command of the scientific concepts, an independent and original turn of mind, and a gift for writing vigorous, lucid prose." It was followed by *The Firmament of Time*, containing six lectures given at the University of Cincinnati in 1959, and showing how man's relationship with the natural world has changed. This "irresistible inducement to partake of the . . . excitements of reflection" received the medal of the John Burroughs Memorial Association and the Lecomte du Noüy award. Eiseley's John Dewey Society lecture, *The Mind as Nature*, is a discussion of the teaching process which includes "a brief and painful account" of the author's own childhood (republished with other essays in *The Night Country*).

Eiseley fears that we are losing sight of the humane values which should control and direct scientific research, and in *Francis Bacon and the Modern Dilemma* urges Bacon's view that a scientist should be "a man of both compassion and understanding." *The Unexpected Universe* is a volume of lyrical-philosophical musings about patterns of life and meaning in the universe which reminded some readers of Teilhard de Chardin. Most reviewers confessed that they found Eiseley's meaning obscure but were nevertheless charmed by his style; at least one critic, however, thought the book virtually meaningless—"prose-poetry . . . overlaid with an insufferable air of mystery and ineffable wisdom." *The Invisible Pyramid* expresses Eiseley's growing distress at the way in which Space Age man is devouring and polluting the environment.

He has been active in many scientific societies and organizations, including the National Research Council and the American Anthropological Association, and has been a visiting lecturer at Columbia, Berkeley, Harvard, and elsewhere. He has received a number of fellowships and honorary degrees. In 1966–1967 he was the host and narrator of an NBC-TV educational series. Eiseley is a grave and courteous man, fairly tall, with brown hair and brown eyes. In religion, he is a Protestant. His wife is assistant director of the Pennsylvania Academy of Fine Arts.

PRINCIPAL WORKS: The Immense Journey, 1957; Darwin's Century: Evolution and the Men Who Discovered It, 1958; The Firmament of Time, 1960; The Mind as Nature, 1962; Francis Bacon and the Modern Dilemma, 1963 (revised and enlarged as The Man Who Saw Through Mirrors, 1973); The Unexpected Universe, 1969; The Invisible Pyramid, 1970; The Night Country, 1971; The Innocent Assassins, 1973.

ABOUT: American Men of Science, 1962; Contemporary Authors 1st revision 1–4, 1967; Current Biography, 1960; Eiseley, L. The Mind as Nature, 1962; National Cyclopaedia of American Biography Current Volume J, 1960–1963, 1964; Who's Who in America, 1970–1971. *Periodicals*—Esquire March 1967; Time October 12, 1962; Wilson Library Bulletin June 1964.

***EKELÖF, (BENGT) GUNNAR** (September 15, 1907–March 16, 1968), Swedish poet, wrote (in Swedish): "I was born in Stockholm, Sweden, in September 1907, under the sign of the Virgin, on a Sunday, and with a caul. This is not meant as a boast, since I wish now it had happened by Caesarean operation. My father was a self-made man, but not without idealism and a certain education; my mother was from the petty nobility. My father died when I was eight years old, of a 'secret' illness. Victorian prudery, or what we call Oscarianism, was still strong in Sweden, and the disease was, then, incurable. I have some idea of the nature of his last mad affairs and more than an idea of how my mother succeeded in getting through her share of the money. My own portion vanished in speculation round about 1930.

"I should not mention this were it not my experience that most artists, and poets in particular, have had a wretched and largely loveless childhood as a spur to their later activity. All who know how an author becomes something more than an entertainer also know that there is always a skeleton in the cupboard, a childhood trauma that the author in question tries all his life to explain to himself from different angles, by different means, with different results: escapism, aggressiveness, pride, arrogance, humility.

"I hated school and had, in my opinion, detestable teachers. Because of conditions at home, where I lived with my insane father who in his last years was a living corpse, I had stomach ulcers when I was still in the higher classes at school. That is also part of the anamnesis that pursues me. At school I learned some Latin and Greek which still lingers in my mind, and, because so few speak Scandinavian languages, something of and about the world languages: firstly French, then English, and some German. I studied in London and Uppsala without taking any degrees because I was after something else. Then, in the 1920s, I came to the great university that is Paris, which offers quite other than academic degrees, with the intention of studying music. But I had the misfortune to end up in an apartment with such paper-thin walls that I did not dare to have an instrument because of the neighbors. So I began to devote myself to the silent arts: writing, and to some extent drawing. I can say, then, that I am in effect self-taught.

"Since early childhood I have traveled a good deal, and since I have eyes and ears I have also seen a good deal and felt a good deal that is ineradicable. In 1920, when I was twelve, I saw Unter den

* ā′ kel uv

GUNNAR EKELÖF

Linden full of waxen shell-shock victims who could not control their reflexes; the same year I saw the battlefields, which had not then been cleared. In Rheims only one house survived unscathed, a kind of inn. Later, as a young student, I remember a night in a hotel when I was drugged and robbed. But I also remember a lot that was good.

"My strength on various occasions has been that I possess a fund of naïveté, combined with a certain intellectualism. So I cannot forget the final exchange between the young ladies: 'Hasn't he got a checkbook as well . . .' But they were in a hurry. It was long ago, and yet it seems relevant even today.

"Since then I have progressed through all the odd jobs in literature, even ghosting, and yet I have succeeded in preserving my eyes and ears and a heart of a mild grubbiness that perhaps might still pass for a white shirt in its second or third day of wearing. I rarely go out; I live with my books. I make one or two journeys—short ones—every year, chiefly to Greece or the Near East to visit museums and above all to see the lovely, poor, denuded terrain where one is still, sometimes, received as a guest and a friend. Paris with its hard economic features is nowadays too far west.

"I am sometimes called a learned man, *un érudit*, but that is not my intention. I have only studied, unsystematically, things which could have some importance for my work as a poet. For the work of a poet is vision and form, and I praise the particular God who has made me capable of translating even dull facts in thick tomes into vision."

Gunnar Ekelöf's "wretched and largely loveless childhood" was spent in affluent surroundings; his father, John Gerhard Ekelöf, had been a stockbroker. But Ekelöf refused to exploit his advantages and preferred to go his own way, "an outsider's way": "It was a long and adventurous odyssey before I had succeeded in avoiding possibilities open to me." Early studies in Oriental languages in London and Uppsala came to nothing academically, as he says above, but later made their mark on his poetry; similarly, though his musical ambitions remained unrealized, he has said that "it is music that has given me most in life." Ekelöf made his first literary contacts in the early 1930s among the writers around the radical journal *Spektrum*, who shared an interest in Freud and psychoanalysis. In 1933, with Artur Lundkvist, he founded a short-lived surrealist journal, *Karavan*.

It was while he was in Paris that Ekelöf wrote his immensely influential first book of poetry, *Sent på jorden* (Late on Earth, 1932). Written in deep depression, to the accompaniment of records of Stravinsky, it is a series of dreamlike visions of emptiness and desolation in a world nearing its end. In this "suicide book" Ekelöf set out to shatter the conventional structures of language and literature: "Crush the alphabitch between your teeth yawn vowels." Hailed as the first Swedish surrealist, Ekelöf in his early verse also owed much to Rimbaud, whose assertion that the poet should make himself into a prophet by a deliberate derangement of his senses provides the epigraph to the collection *Dedikation* (Dedication, 1934).

Ekelöf deliberately cultivated abrupt changes of style in his work. *Dedikation* was followed by two melodious, somewhat romantic volumes: *Sorgen och stjärnan* (Grief and the Star, 1936) and *Köp den blindes sång* (Buy the Blind Man's Song, 1938). In 1940 he formally announced his break with surrealism, "a completed chapter." A more philosophical and intellectual note emerges in *Färjesång* (Ferry Song, 1941) and *Non serviam* (1945). Here, instead of attacking poetic conventions, Ekelöf attempts to destroy accepted patterns of thought to reveal what lies behind them. He explores the teeming confusion of impulses and desires concealed by the apparent unity of the ego. He adopts a position between opposite extremes, writing as an observer on the ferry between life and death, at a point between good and evil, truth and falsehood, for "Those who can still see that grey is grey, / who know that life has a multitude of shades: / The relativity of all truths and lies." This more meditative phase has been attributed to the influence of T. S. Eliot, but Ekelöf's work retained a passionate, ecstatic note that has little to do with Eliot and has suggested comparisons with Hölderlin, Shakespeare, and the Swedish mystics Stagnelius and Almqvist.

Om hösten (In the Fall, 1951) is something of a review of Ekelöf's work, containing poems and various drafts of poems produced over a period of many years. In this collection Ekelöf develops a technique introduced in earlier books of employing structures derived from music—another influential innovation. Ekelöf's eclectic but fundamentally original virtuosity is also illustrated in *En Mölnaelegi* (A Mölna Elegy, 1960), parts of which were first published in 1946. The poem explores in depth a single fragment of time in the poet's consciousness, showing how the preoccupations of the moment are mingled and compounded with personal and ancestral memories. Into the carefully constructed framework of the elegy Ekelöf empties the unsorted jumble of a poet's soul; part of the poem is contrasted with Latin and Greek graffiti—similarly crude and spontaneous fragments of consciousness.

Artlessness was the goal to which Ekelöf seemed at this time to aspire. In *Strountes* (Nonsenses, 1955) he writes: "When you have come as far as I have in meaninglessness, / every word is interesting again. / Finds in the earth / you turn up with an archaeologist's spade." Ekelöf published further examples of what he strenuously denied was poetry in *Opus incertum* (1959) and *En natt i Otočac* (A Night in Otočac, 1961), where he reduces verbal communication to minimal statements shorn of all artistic decoration.

Possibly Ekelöf's most lasting work of this type will prove to be his Byzantine triptych *Dīwān över Fursten av Emgión* (Divan of the Prince of Emgión, 1965), *Sagan om Fatumeh* (The Story of Fatumeh, 1966), and *Vägvisare till underjorden* (Guide to the Underworld, 1967), based on oriental and Greek themes. Each part is built around a passionate relationship—between the blinded, imprisoned Prince of Emgión and an ikon of the Madonna; between a noble lord and his "shadow," the prostitute Fatumeh; between the Devil and a young novice nun. These relationships also have a symbolic significance: the familiar theme of the meeting of light and darkness, good and evil. *Partitur* (Score, 1969), a posthumous collection published by his wife, contains some harrowing expressions of Ekelöf's suffering during his final illness.

Ekelöf's poetry, sometimes simple and direct, sometimes mystical and esoteric, is difficult to translate, and English versions of his work have had a mixed reception. He is nevertheless generally recognized as the most original and influential Swedish poet of his generation. He was an extreme individualist, contemptuous of Sweden's welfare state and its materialist preoccupations, immersed in his own visions. His attitudes are elegantly and clearly expressed in his essays, in such collections as *Promenader och utflykter* (Walks and Excursions, 1963) and *Lägga patience* (Laying Patience, 1969). Ekelöf was also influential as a translator and adapter of foreign poetry, both classical and modern. He was elected to the Swedish Academy in 1958.

PRINCIPAL WORKS IN ENGLISH TRANSLATION: Selected Poems (tr. by Muriel Rukeyser and Leif Sjöberg), 1967; I Do Best Alone at Night: Selected Poems, 1968 (tr. by Robert Bly and Christina Paulston; published in England as Late Arrival on Earth, 1967); Selected Poems (tr. by Leif Sjöberg and W. H. Auden), 1972. *Poems in* Fleisher, F. (ed.) Seven Swedish Poets, 1963; Swenson, M. (ed.) Half Sun, Half Sleep, 1967.

ABOUT: Bäckström, L. and Palm, G. (eds.) Sweden Writes, 1965; Ekner, R. I den Havandes Liv, 1967; En bok on Gunnar Ekelöf, 1956; Gustafson, A. A History of Swedish Literature, 1961; Penguin Companion to Literature 2, 1969. *Periodicals*—American-Scandinavian Review 2, 1965; American Swedish Monthly July 1965; Books Abroad Summer 1967; Germanic Review March 1965; January 1969; Literary Review Winter 1965–1966; New York Times March 22, 1968; Partisan Review Spring 1966; Scandinavian Studies November 1963, November 1965, May 1967; Scandinavica 2, 1966.

***EKWENSI, CYPRIAN** (September 26, 1921–), Nigerian novelist, writes: "In 1918 my father, who had been educated in a Catholic mission primary school in Nkwelle near Onitsha, decided that Eastern Nigeria would not give him enough scope for the adventurous life. With my mother, he traveled on a riverboat up the Niger from Onitsha to Lokoja, Baro, and thence to Minna in Northern Nigeria, where I was born. As a carpenter, he found employment in the Public Works Department, and as a hunter, he found plenty of game in the savannahs of Northern Nigeria.

"We lived in many parts of Northern Nigeria—Zaria, Kano, Gusau and finally Jos where my two surviving brothers and two sisters were born. The mining town of Jos, with its high altitude and cool climate, gave me my primary school education. Here, in 1927, my father built our mud and pan-roof house which we still own today.

"My primary education at the Government School, Jos, was free. Here I won a prize for 'Proficiency in English.' The book was called *Highroads of Literature* and it contained extracts from John Ruskin, Charles Dickens, Lord Tennyson, Jonathan Swift, etc. This book laid the early foundation of my interest in literature; an interest which was to grow at the Government College, Ibadan, in Western Nigeria, where I received my secondary education. Here under English lecturers I was exposed to the writings of Alexandre Dumas, Charles Dickens, Marie Corelli, Jonathan Swift, John Milton. Nigeria was then a British colony. There was no future for creative African writers until many years later—after further education at the Higher College, Yaba, Lagos, and Achimota College, Gold Coast—when the Public Relations Department of Nigeria during World War II began to produce a monthly paper entitled *Nigeria Digest* in which my

* ek wen′ zē

CYPRIAN EKWENSI

first short stories were published. Publication followed in the *West African Review* and *Wide World Magazine*. In 1947 I produced, in three days, a novelette entitled *When Love Whispers* which mesmerised the whole of Nigeria by the magic of its triangle love affair. Nearly twenty years later, this story is still on sale.

"In 1951, I wrote *People of the City*. I was then a student of pharmacy, having tried my hand at teaching and forestry. From my forestry experience, I wrote *Burning Grass*. It was in the 1950s that I wrote most of the stories based on my experience as a young man living in the center of Lagos. A scholarship to England to study pharmacy widened my horizon, and while in England I became intimately associated with various media of mass communication: press, radio, television (which was then in its infancy). Publication of *People of the City* took place in England in 1954; after which no further long pieces from me appeared until *Jagua Nana* was published in 1961. From then on, other works have appeared, notably *Burning Grass* and *Beautiful Feathers*. The shorter novels, which are used mainly in schools as supplementary readers, were published from 1960 (*Passport of Malam Ilia*; *Drummer Boy*; *An African Night's Entertainment*; *Trouble in Form Six*). *Burning Grass* has been translated into Russian, *Passport of Malam Ilia* into Dutch, *People of the City* into Czech, *Jagua Nana* into Italian, German, Serbo-Croat, Portuguese.

"Most of my writing has been done outside newspaper offices, but I have produced practically every form of writing from television plays (which have been broadcast) to press releases. My life in government and quasi-government organizations (like the Nigerian Broadcasting Corporation) has prevented me from expressing any strong political inclination, but I am as much a nationalist as the heckler standing on the soapbox but with the added advantage of objectivity in considering every critical situation on its own merits.

"I am married with children and for my hobbies, I shoot game, swim, and play about with weights sometimes."

Apart from Amos Tutuola's *The Palm-Wine Drinkard*, which is not really an orthodox novel at all, Ekwensi's *People of the City*, published in 1954, was the first Nigerian novel to make an international impact. It is a picaresque story, packed with incident, about the career and downfall in Lagos of Amusa Sango, a young crime reporter. He wants money, status, and power; so does Beatrice, a young beauty from the provinces; and so do all the prostitutes, thieves, hustlers, politicians, civil servants, and wheeler-dealers who throng the city and the novel. Colonialism has destroyed the old tribal morality, leaving in its place Western materialism, individualism, and greed.

Some critics complained of structural weaknesses in the novel, and pointed out that the author himself had no consistent set of values to offer—only a sometimes extreme sentimentality. What saves the book is the vitality of its descriptive writing, the Breughelesque vision it imparts of a corrupt society which is nevertheless bursting with life. The same brutal city dominates *Jagua Nana*, a novel about a life-loving prostitute and her hopeless struggle to free herself from her history and background through her love affair with a young teacher. Some critics thought that Ekwensi had made a genuinely tragic character out of his golden-hearted prostitute; others found her no more than a competently handled fictional cliché, and were more impressed by the portrayal of Uncle Taiwo—crass, gross, amorous, and vicious, but enormously alive. John F. Povey called him "the most sure and powerful creation of modern African fiction."

A very different book followed. As he says, Ekwensi grew up in Northern Nigeria, in Hausa country, and it is this experience on which he draws in *Burning Grass*, about the wanderings of a family of Cow Fulani, a nomadic tribe of the region, which is ruined and scattered after the father buys a disturbingly beautiful slave girl. Some reviewers found an almost Arabic quality in its fable-like structure and spare, austere prose, and one wrote that it conveyed an "exciting sense of a people and a place, unmarred by [Ekwensi's] weakness for sentimentality and melodrama."

Beautiful Feathers returns to an urban setting. It deals with the attempt of Wilson Iyeri, a young Lagos pharmacist, to form a Pan-African political party, and the tension that results between his public and domestic life. Growing success as a politician leads to increasing inadequacy as a husband and father, until his son's death and his wife's infidelity show him the falseness of the path he has chosen. Tauter construction, a restraint in Ekwensi's narrative style, and the effectiveness of his political satire were widely admired; though the book is marred by a contrived and unconvincing happy ending, it is widely regarded as his finest achievement to date. Walter Allen read it as "a tract for his fellow-Africans against the dangers of naïve idealism." *Iska*, about an Ibo girl from Northern Nigeria seeking liberation from tribal conventions in the big city, is another Lagos picaresque.

Ekwensi regards himself as "a writer for the masses." He began to write when, as a schoolteacher, he found there were no books on local, familiar themes to interest his students in English language and literature. He has written a number of books for children which, as he says, are used as supplementary readers in schools. Ekwensi's own youthful reading ran to storytellers rather than stylists—Dickens, H. Rider Haggard, H. G. Wells, Edgar Wallace—though when he discovered Hemingway "something new happened. The skeletal directness was invigorating." Ekwensi's style, cliché-ridden and derivative in his early books, has steadily improved; he says that he has sought to use "the medium of English to translate the speech rhythms" of his own country. Though Ekwensi has not entirely overcome his taste for sentimentality and melodrama, John F. Povey believes that he has it in him to "write a full-scale political satire of present-day Nigeria; vicious, sardonic and pointed."

The author began his career as a lecturer in science and English at Igbogi College (1947–1949). He subsequently taught at the Lagos School of Pharmacy (1949–1956) and practiced as a pharmacist with the Nigerian Medical Service. His growing reputation as a writer and journalist then took him to the Nigerian Broadcasting Corporation as head of features (1956–1961), and on to the Federal Ministry of Information as director of information (1961–1966). He left that post shortly before the outbreak of the Nigerian Civil War and threw in his lot with his fellow Ibos in the Eastern region, serving the secessionist Biafran government as Director of Information. After the fall of Biafra he found it difficult to obtain a professional post, and for a time was reportedly working as a salesman in Enugu. He became chairman of the East Central State Library Board, Enugu, in 1971. A tall, urbane man, he visited the United States in 1964 and has traveled widely in Africa and Europe.

PRINCIPAL WORKS: People of the City, 1954; Jagua Nana, 1961; Burning Grass: A Story of the Fulani of Northern Nigeria, 1962; Beautiful Feathers, 1963; The Rainmaker and Other Stories, 1965 (Lagos); Lokoland and Other Stories, 1966; Iska, 1966.

ABOUT: Gleason, J. This Africa, 1965; International Who's Who, 1971–1972; King, B. (ed.) Introduction to Nigerian Literature, 1972; Larson, C. R. The Emergence of African Fiction, 1972; Palmer, E. An Introduction to the African Novel, 1972; Vinson, J. (ed.) Contemporary Novelists, 1972. *Periodicals*—Book Week August 15, 1965; Critique Fall 1965; Observer August 28, 1966; Punch August 17, 1966; Spectator August 26, 1966; Times Literary Supplement June 4, 1964; August 25, 1966; Twentieth Century April 1959; West Africa July 28, 1962; August 25, 1962.

***ELIADE, MIRCEA** (March 9, 1907–), Rumanian-born philosopher, historian of religion, and novelist, writes: "I was born and brought up in Bucharest, Romania. While still in the *lycée* I began writing and publishing essays and short stories. At that time I thought that I would study natural science or chemistry, but during the last years of college my interests shifted to philosophy, oriental languages, and history of religions. I entered the University of Bucharest in 1925 and took my M.A. degree in 1928, with a dissertation on Italian philosophy from Ficino to Giordano Bruno. While in Rome I came across *A History of Indian Philosophy* by S. N. Dasgupta. In the preface the author had acknowledged his debt of gratitude to the Maharajah Sir Manindra Chandra Nundy of Kasimbazar, whose financial support had made the research possible. To study Sanskrit and Indian philosophy was my fervent desire. Nowhere could I accomplish my goal better than at Calcutta. I wrote to the Maharajah, asking if he would grant me a scholarship for study with Dasgupta. The Maharajah replied that he would, not just for one or two years, as I had asked, but for five years. Thus I was able to live in India from 1928 to 1932. After three years of study with Dasgupta and six months in the āshram of Rishikesh, Himalaya, I prepared my Ph.D. dissertation on yoga.

"Meanwhile, my first novel, *Isabel*, had been published in Bucharest in 1930. After returning to Romania, I resumed my collaboration with literary magazines and newspapers. In 1933 I was appointed assistant professor of philosophy at the University of Bucharest. I taught primarily history of religions and Indian philosophy. During the same year my second novel, *Maitreyi*, became a best seller almost immediately after its publication. This undreamed-of popularity somehow annoyed me—and for many years thereafter I tried to publish only rather difficult novels and scholarly works. Among the novels, two volumes from an uncompleted trilogy, *The Return from Paradise* (1934–45), and also *The Serpent* (1937) and *Marriage in Heaven* (1938) were well received both by the public and by the critics. But I was personally more deeply attached to the

* el ē äd′

MIRCEA ELIADE

volumes of critical and philosophical essays and to the monographs on Indian religions, Asiatic alchemy, and mythical thought. In 1938 I began to publish *Zalmoxis*, an international journal for history of religions; but it was soon interrupted by the war.

"In March 1940 I was sent to the Romanian Legation in London as cultural attaché. I thought that I was going for just a few years and that I would soon resume my teaching at the university and my writing in Romanian. As a matter of fact, I did continue to publish books in Bucharest during the war, after being transferred to the legation in Lisbon (1941–1945). When I went to Paris in 1945 as a visiting professor at the École des Hautes Études of the Sorbonne, I had behind me more than twenty volumes published in Romanian. But from that time on I was obliged to write in French. And of course I began to write about the problems which had obsessed me from my youth: yoga and Indian philosophy, history of religions, the structure of myths and religious symbolism. Some of those books (e.g., *Le Mythe de l'eternel retour*, 1949; *Traité d'histoire des religions*, 1949) were well received and have been translated into many languages. For ten years I lived the life of a scholar in Paris. I lectured at the Sorbonne from 1946 to 1948, and afterwards in many European universities. During the autumn of 1956 I was invited to deliver the Haskell lectures at the University of Chicago; in 1957 I became a regular professor of History of Religions and in 1962 I was appointed the Sewell L. Avery Distinguished Service Professor at the same university.

"In 1950 I married Christinel Cottesco. My wife was, and still is, more interested in my literary activity than in the historical and philosophical research—and I believe that she is right. But for me all these instruments of expression—history, philosophy, fiction—are complementary. Sometimes my ideas on myth, time, or religious symbolism can be presented in more cogent form in fiction than in scientific treatises. Of course I have continued to write novels and short stories in Romanian; *Forêt interdite*, which I consider to be my *chef d'œuvre*, was translated from the manuscript and published by Gallimard in 1955. But I think that my best books are those as yet unpublished or in the process of being completed: an autobiography and a journal, written in Romanian; and a history of religions which I am writing in French."

According to Edmund Leach, Eliade's fundamental concern is with "the symbolic modes through which communication is established between the sacred and the profane." He is particularly interested in such interdependent polarities as good and bad, violence and passivity, life and death.

Although Eliade, as he says, had published a score of books in Rumanian by 1945, it was the appearance of *Le Mythe de l'eternel retour* in 1949 which established his international reputation, and its translation in 1955 as *The Myth of the Eternal Return* that made him known to British and American readers. It is a study of human attitudes towards history in which Eliade argues that all archaic religions are fundamentally similar, sharing a cyclical view of the cosmos, a belief that man enters the profane world at birth from some sacred realm to which he returns at death. "Archaic man acknowledges no act which has not been previously posited. . . . His life is the ceaseless repetition of gestures initiated by others." Eliade contrasts this denial of history with the eschatological, chronologically oriented, historical nature of Judeo-Christianity. He himself favors a Hegelian view of historical events as the products of man's freedom to "make himself," but believes that human freedom is illusory unless it is identified with Christianity.

Certain symbols for the sacred that recur in many archaic religions are analyzed in *Patterns in Comparative Religion*. This "important and quite beautiful book" shows how the gap between "being and becoming," which so obsesses modern thinkers, was readily reconciled by the primitive imagination. *The Sacred and the Profane* discusses the "tragedy" of modern nonreligious man, whose "camouflaged myths and degenerated rituals" show that he can never completely "desacrilize" himself and should not try: "Do what he will he is an inheritor. He cannot utterly abolish his past, since he is himself the product of his past." *Yoga*, subtitled "immortality and freedom," is one of the most substantial and authoritative studies of its subject, written with "a masterly combination of sympathy and detachment."

Birth and Rebirth deals with the religious meaning of initiation ceremonies. *Myth, Dreams and Mysteries* and *Myth and Reality* both argue the validity of primitive religious beliefs for modern man. Eliade, a Christian and a Jungian, believes that "every primordial image is the bearer of a message of direct relevance to the condition of humanity, for the image unveils aspects of ultimate reality that are otherwise inaccessible." Some of his books, like *The Forge and the Crucible*, an account of myth and ritual in the work of the miner, the metalworker, and the alchemist, are based on much earlier writings originally published in Rumanian.

In *Mephistopheles and the Androgyne* and in his periodical, *History of Religions*, Eliade has attacked the timidity of colleagues who limit their studies to one small area of their field. But his own ambitious attempt "to assimilate culturally the spiritual universes" of Asia and Africa has not escaped criticism. Edmund Leach devoted a long article in the *New York Review of Books* (October 20, 1966) to a comprehensive attack on the quality of Eliade's scholarship, thought, and methodology (which is compared to the notoriously inadequate procedures of Sir James Frazer). Leach accuses Eliade of grandiose and "Shamanic" generalizations, of "exposition by citation," of inconsistency, and of an "abysmal" ignorance of recent developments in anthropology. Leach's opinions are by no means generally accepted. Mircea Eliade's work has had much influence, and he is widely regarded as a great and creative scholar, unequaled as an analyst of religious imagery and symbolism. His novels, none of which has so far appeared in English, have been called "long and complex and heavy with Eastern European motifs."

PRINCIPAL WORKS IN ENGLISH TRANSLATION: The Myth of the Eternal Return, 1955 (republished as Cosmos and History); Patterns in Comparative Religion, 1958; Yoga: Immortality and Freedom, 1958; Birth and Rebirth, 1958 (republished as Rites and Symbols of Initiation); The Sacred and the Profane, 1959; (ed. with J. M. Kitagawa) History of Religions, 1959; Myths, Dreams and Mysteries, 1960; Images and Symbols, 1961; The Forge and the Crucible, 1962; Myth and Reality, 1963; Shamanism: Archaic Techniques of Ecstasy, 1964; Mephistopheles and the Androgyne, 1966 (England, The Two and the One); (ed.) From Primitives to Zen: A Thematic Sourcebook of the History of Religions, 1967; The Quest: History and Meaning in Religion, 1969; Patanjali and Yoga, 1969; Two Tales of the Occult, 1970.

ABOUT: Altizer, T. J. J. Mircea Eliade and the Dialectic of the Sacred, 1963; Kitagawa, J. M. and Long, C. H. (eds.) Myths and Symbols: Studies in Honor of Mircea Eliade, 1969; Who's Who in America, 1970–1971. *Periodicals*—Acta Philosophica et Theologica II, 1964; Cahiers du Sud 316, 1952; Christian Century February 5, 1964; Christian Scholar Winter 1962; Commentary March 1966; Hudson Review Autumn 1959; New York Review of Books October 20, 1966; Religion in Life Spring 1967; Review of Metaphysics September 1961; Review of Religion November 1957; Spectator April 1, 1955; Time February 11, 1966; Times Literary Supplement February 10, 1966; June 8, 1967; La Torre 1, 1953.

ELLIN, STANLEY (BERNARD) (October 6, 1916–), American novelist and short story writer, reports: "I was born in the Bath Beach section of Brooklyn, New York, and spent my early childhood there at a time when the last gas street lamps and horse-drawn fire-engines were still part of the local scene along with frame houses and quiet, tree-shaded avenues. These symbols of the past are associated in my mind with an extremely happy childhood, one I sometimes feel apologetic about in the company of normally neurotic acquaintances. My parents were intensely devoted to each other and to me, an only child, and practiced, without preaching, a simplicity and integrity in living which they still maintain after fifty years of marriage. My father also idolized Mark Twain and introduced me to him almost as soon as I had learned to read. I think it is the combination of all these elements which makes me what I am today: a social reactionary, mourning the shapes and sounds and smells of a comfortable past (which exists, admittedly, largely in my imagination), and a political radical, looking forward to the day, a few millennia from now, when every man is assured the necessities of life without having to cut his neighbor's throat for them.

"I graduated from Brooklyn College in 1936, Depression time, married immediately afterward, and worked at various jobs—teaching at a small college, covering a route for a magazine distributing company, running an upstate dairy farm for its absentee owner—until, through the help of a friend, I was admitted into a boilermakers' union, and, after serving a hard apprenticeship, settled down to what I then thought was a permanent career as journeyman and later foreman in metal-working plants, shipyards, and construction jobs around New York. I liked the work and the men I worked with, and whatever vague thoughts I had of becoming a writer were at their vaguest in those years.

"But near the end of the war I served briefly in the army, and on my discharge my wife suggested that I use whatever income I could get from the 52–20 Club, the veteran's unemployment allowance, plus her earnings as a freelance editor, to try my hand at professional writing. We estimated we could make do this way for a year, and before the year was up I had sold my first story, "The Specialty of the House," to *Ellery Queen's Mystery Magazine* where it made something of a splash, and then my

STANLEY ELLIN

first novel to Simon and Schuster. From that time on, 1946, I have made a more or less precarious living as a writer of short stories and novels.

"My work is generally regarded as fitting into the recently expanded bounds of the mystery *genre*, which, since this *genre* is not quite top drawer in America, has led to my having a somewhat larger reputation in Europe than here, something I once supposed happened only to aspiring American opera singers. I did not deliberately set out to write mystery and suspense fiction. However, because I believe that crime and punishment offer the most potent material for fiction, and am inclined to plan a story structure carefully, I am evidently writing mysteries. Fortunately for my freedom of action, I deal with only two editors, Frederic Dannay of *Ellery Queen's Mystery Magazine* and Lee Wright of Random House, both of whom give me *carte blanche* to write what I will and how I will, so I am not confined to the traditional forms of the *genre*.

"My wife, still a freelance editor, and I today live a thoroughly enjoyable life in a seedy apartment house in the Flatbush district of Brooklyn, almost completely detached from the literary world nested across the river in Manhattan. We have lived here for twenty-five years; our world consists largely of old neighbors and friends, of acquaintances at the local bowling alley, of our daughter who has her own flat nearby. We work hard most of the day, find in each other the best possible company. If there is anything in my life I would wish to change, it is my abysmally slow pace at writing. It takes me a year or two for a novel, at least several weeks for a short story, and each novel or story seems to require more time than the last to do as I want it to be done."

Stanley Ellin's first novel, *Dreadful Summit*, was a psychological study of a youth compulsively driven to avenge his father's brutal murder; it was widely praised, and filmed as *The Big Night*. *The Key to Nicholas Street*, which followed, examined family relationships in a small town and was called "the best mystery, in simple truth, for some years past." *The Eighth Circle*, as much a philosophical novel as a thriller, seemed to some reviewers a little slow, but nevertheless brought Ellin the third of his three Edgar Allan Poe Awards.

At the root of Ellin's preoccupation with crime lies a serious moral concern which is quite overt in, for example, *The Winter After This Summer*, a novel about the slow moral and emotional development of a youth almost shattered by guilt when he fails to save a friend from accidental death by fire. *The Panama Portrait*, a skillful suspense story at one level, seemed to some reviewers marred by "a good deal of palaver about the symbolism of hanging *à la* Santo Stefano." On the other hand, *The Valentine Estate* was generally enjoyed as a contrived but exciting and light-hearted entertainment.

If there are critical reservations about some of Ellin's novels, there seem to be none about his short stories, which have been written slowly, at the rate of about one a year, and collected into two notable volumes. Cecil Hemley compared Ellin's stories with those of Saki and said, "His greatest gift is his grasp of structure." Dorothy B. Hughes called Ellin "today's foremost writer of the new weird story, one which has macabre logic and peppercorns of humor as leaven for unpalatable horrors." Anthony Boucher regarded him as "one of the modern masters" of the macabre whose stories, "dazzlingly clever in plot and technique," are "also deeply human and disturbingly meaningful."

Numerous translations, especially into German and Italian, have earned Ellin a worldwide reputation. The son of Louis and Rose (Mandel) Ellin, he was married to the former Jeanne Michael in 1937. They have one daughter. Brown-haired, brown-eyed, and rugged, Ellin lists chess, bridge, bowling, baseball, writing, and travel as his hobbies.

PRINCIPAL WORKS: Dreadful Summit, 1948; The Key to Nicholas Street, 1952; Mystery Stories, 1956; The Eighth Circle, 1958; The Winter After This Summer, 1960; The Panama Portrait, 1962; The Blessington Method and Other Strange Tales, 1964; House of Cards, 1967; The Valentine Estate, 1968; The Bind, 1970; Mirror Mirror on the Wall, 1972.

ABOUT: Contemporary Authors 3, 1963. *Periodicals*—Books and Bookmen June 1961; New York Times Book Review May 20, 1956; The Reporter January 1961; Saturday Review September 12, 1964; Wilson Library Bulletin June 1961.

ELLIOTT, GEORGE P(AUL) (June 16, 1918–), American man of letters, writes: "I was born on a farm near Knightstown, Indiana, a small country town. My father's family had been Quaker farmers for several generations. My mother's family was Methodist; her father had been a teacher and school principal, her maternal grandfather a dentist. My father did not succeed in making a living from farming, and in 1928 we moved to Southern California, near Riverside. There, a schoolteacher cousin of my mother's mother had bought into a carob plantation, one of those fantastic schemes which flourish off and on in Southern California, and my father worked her share of it. In the mid-1930s it failed. After some hard times, my father got work as an irrigator in large orange groves, and stayed with that work until his retirement. My mother was active in women's clubs, amateur theatricals, PTA, and similar matters until her last illness. I have two younger brothers, and a younger sister.

"When I was twelve I read 'The Rime of the Ancient Mariner' and decided I would spend my life writing stories and poems. I immediately began to write them and have never stopped since, except under the pressure of circumstances.

"Being studious and loving books, I did well in school and worked my way through college. I went to the Riverside Junior College and then to the University of California in Berkeley, where I got my M.A. in English in 1941, the year in which I married a native Berkeleyan, Mary Emma Jeffress. During the war, being exempted from military service for medical reasons, I worked in war jobs. Our only child, Nora, was born in 1943.

"From the time I graduated from high school in 1934 until after the war, I held a variety of jobs—farm hand, service station attendant, gardening, house-cleaning, assistant in a botany lab, chauffeuring, copy-typing, teaching in a private high school, shipfitting, making blueprints, wage rate analyst for the War Labor Board, labor union business agent, real estate broker, surveyor's helper, taxi driver, correcting exam papers, reporter for a labor paper—and one year I stayed home tending the baby and writing a novel while my wife worked. In 1947 I began teaching English at St. Mary's College, near Oakland, and since then have earned my living in that profession. I taught for eight years at St. Mary's, one year each at Cornell University and the University of Iowa (The Writers Workshop), one semester at Berkeley, three years at Barnard College, and since 1963 at Syracuse University. Even if I did not have to teach to earn a living, I think I would continue to teach one literature class for pleasure. (I enjoy helping younger writers when I can, but I dislike doing so when

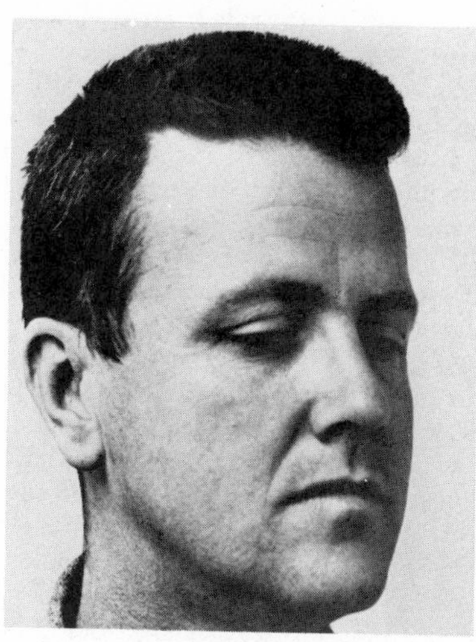

GEORGE P. ELLIOTT

grades and degrees are at stake, in creative-writing classes.)

"I write poems, stories, novels, plays, and informal and literary essays, turning from one to another as I feel inclined. I have no program of ideas or themes which I see as controlling what I write, no large plan for my writing. A few times I have tried to write for money—ghostwriting, journalism, stories on assigned topics—but with little success, except for book reviews. At first my writing consisted chiefly of deadly naturalism, conventional versification, and bloodless fantasy. My dominant literary aim has come to be to infuse poetic fantasy with the blood of life.

"With few exceptions, my writings are known and spoken well of only in the American literary-intellectual world, and I have published verse, fiction, essays, and reviews in many literary magazines. I have received five fellowships which have given me productive years or half-years off from my teaching duties: Albert Bender Award in fiction, fellowship from the Fund for the Advancement of Education to study poetic drama, Hudson Review Fellowship in Fiction, Guggenheim Fellowship in creative writing, and a Ford Fellowship to write in connection with a theater.

"In my writing, I rely on the advice and assistance of others for making revisions and occasionally for original ideas. My wife's severe, particular, and acute criticisms have diverted me from egregious error innumerable times; and the first autobiographical-literary-speculative essay I wrote, 'Getting Away from the Chickens,' owes its genesis in idea to her suggesting some similarities between

The Princess Casamassima and *Tarzan of the Apes*. That essay owes its genesis in form to a book review by Herbert Gold—to whom I also owe specific criticisms over ten years. James Schevill set me looking for a new prosody. Josephine Miles for fifteen years pruned away at my poems, teaching me economy; and a remark she made in 1957—'I think your best poems are narrative'—changed the course of my poetry and also helped me begin writing essays which are constructed poetically and narratively rather than logically and expositorily. Since 1956, W. D. Snodgrass has given me suggestions in matters of tone and structure in all my writing which I have benefited from, and one big nudge which has helped me see things differently. To Sigurd Burckhardt I owe at least half my ideas. My debts to friends and editors for ideas and specific criticism—sometimes for words and whole lines—are too many to pay here. Some whose advice has been most important are: Daniel Dixon, Brother S. Robert, Timothy Pember, Dean Jeffress, Christina Page Gardner, Robert Pack, Thomas Bledsoe, Joseph Fox, Frederick Morgan, Aaron Asher, Johann Hannesson, Robert Brustein, Bernard Taper, Alan Friedman, Philip Booth, Arlene Heyman, and David Segal. But such listing is unsatisfactory. The real way I express my gratitude is by offering similar help to others as and when they can use it, for them to pass on as and when they will."

Elliott is the son of Paul Revere Elliott and the former Nita Gregory. When he was twelve, his parents bought him a five-dollar fountain pen (out of a monthly income of eighty-five dollars). One evening the pen fell down the outhouse hole. Later on, his father went out without a word and dug it up again. After that, Elliott pretty much had to be a writer, he thought, and he used the pen for twenty years. Many such anecdotes are scattered through the essays in *A Piece of Lettuce*, and they add up to an excellent picture of a good, loving, rural childhood in the 1930s. They also support, as Stanley Edgar Hyman said, "a fascinating new form of literary and cultural criticism . . . criticism by autobiography and parable."

Criticism by autobiography: because the standards by which Elliott judges the world—and literature—were formed on the farm rather than at college, from life rather than from books. The example of his father (who "believed and didn't believe" in the transcendent and irrational) was supported by experience. The farm taught him to keep his feet on the ground, however messy it was. But milking a three-titted goat gave him an affection for the imperfect, so he says, and having a hen's egg laid in his mouth acquainted him with the likelihood of the fantastic.

Criticism by parable: Elliott went through an ascetic Shelleyish phase when he rejected his father's irrational Christianity and thought Yeats, for example, both fey and coarse, unpoetically ribald about sex and excrement; in the end he came to see, as his father had, that the muck was there and his fountain pen in it. That is how he came to find himself lying down, with Yeats, "where all the ladders start, / In the foul rag-and-bone shop of the heart." And lying down, also, with Blake, Dante, Sophocles, and others for whom man is "the uncontrollable mystery on the bestial floor." What he will not tolerate is the "blasphemers" (he cites Norman Mailer and Henry Miller), the nihilists who deny the mystery, who are "up to the eyebrows in muck," and advertising their position. Stanley Edgar Hyman believed that Elliott was his critical opposite, an affirmer of life and love more concerned with content than form, a fantast and a Christian; but, Hyman concluded, "It is far too long since we have heard such a voice in American criticism." Most other critics agreed, even those who found *A Piece of Lettuce* at times "too chummy," or self-consciously naïve and provincial. A similar collection of essays, reviews, and reminiscences was published in 1972 as *Conversions*.

Elliott has explored his fundamentally religious convictions in a number of novels and short stories. Oddly enough, while essays like "A Brown Fountain Pen" are as complex in their symbolism and as cunning in their organization as good stories, Elliott's novels are essayistic. Because he asks important questions about the quality and conduct of contemporary life, and is intelligent and readable and technically adroit, his novels have all aroused a great deal of interest and discussion. But reviewer after reviewer has found book after book static and undramatic. "In the end," wrote one reviewer of *David Knudsen*, "Elliott's ideas and perceptions have greater force of reality than his characters."

His short stories are often more successful. Some of them are fables, like the title story of his first collection, *Among the Dangs*, about an anthropologist caught between today's world and the ancient, holy world he is studying. Others by contrast show a very special and rare talent for revealing what is important and unique about the lives of quite ordinary people; an example is "Words, Words, Words" in *An Hour of Last Things*, a love story which shows how large and generous an imaginative achievement it is to acknowledge fully the reality of another person.

Fever and Chills, a long poem about a suburban adultery, is a characteristic attack upon Freud, science, mere rationalism, which deprive the couple of joy, dignity, and even guilt, leaving only blind sexual avarice. This and other narrative poems, as well as shorter pieces, appear in Elliott's first collection of poems, *From the Berkeley Hills*. Victor Howes said of them that "their philosophical concerns function beneath the surface like the bones of a fine face. . . . These are serious poems, demanding and rewarding, Donnean poems to be chewed and digested, read and reread."

Elliott's wife is an editor of *Hudson Review*. His recreations include chess, touring, and looking at pictures.

PRINCIPAL WORKS: *Novels*—Parktilden Village, 1958; David Knudsen, 1962; In the World, 1965; Muriel, 1972. *Short stories*—Among the Dangs: Ten Short Stories, 1962; An Hour of Last Things, 1968. *Poetry*—Fever and Chills, 1961; From the Berkeley Hills, 1969. *Essays*—A Piece of Lettuce: Personal Essays on Books, Beliefs, American Places, and Growing Up in a Strange Country, 1964; Conversions: Literature and the Modernist Deviation, 1971. *As editor*—Fifteen Modern American Poets, 1956; Types of Prose Fiction, 1964.

ABOUT: Contemporary Authors 1, 1962; Elliott, G. P. *in* Gold, H. (ed.) First Person Singular, 1963; Elliott, G. P. A Piece of Lettuce, 1964; Hyman, S. E. Standards, 1966; Rahv, P. The Myth and the Powerhouse, 1965; Who's Who in America, 1970–1971. *Periodicals*—Commonweal December 3, 1965; Hollins Critic December 1968; New Republic November 27, 1965; Saturday Review April 4, 1964; Wilson Library Bulletin June 1965.

ELLISON, RALPH (WALDO) (March 1, 1914–), American novelist and essayist, was born in Oklahoma City, the son of Lewis Ellison, a construction worker and tradesman, and the former Ida Millsap. His father died when Ralph Ellison was three, and his mother worked as a domestic servant to support herself and her son. Ellison developed an early interest in music and books, fed by the discarded magazines and phonograph records his mother brought home from the white households where she worked.

Growing up in Oklahoma City, where caste lines were still relatively fluid, he was aware of racism but had no sense of racial inferiority. He became an ardent movie- and theatregoer, as well as a friend and devotee of such local jazz musicians as Hot Lips Paige and Jimmy Rushing. He himself played trumpet in his high school band. At the same time he took an important step towards becoming a writer: "I began to look at my own life through the lives of fictional characters. When I read Stendhal, I would search until I began to find patterns of a Stendhalian novel within the Negro communities in which I grew up. I began, in other words, quite early to connect the worlds projected in literature . . . with the life in which I found myself."

In 1933, Ellison entered the Tuskegee Institute in Alabama, where for the next three years he studied music. He went to New York in 1936, studied sculpture for a time, worked with the Federal Writers' Project, and met Langston Hughes

RALPH ELLISON

and Richard Wright. Like many other now prominent black writers, Ellison owes much to Wright's encouragement and guidance, including the discovery that "writing must be done consciously." In 1939 Ellison's short stories, essays, and reviews began to appear in the *New Masses*, the *Antioch Review*, and elsewhere. For a time during 1942 he edited the *Negro Quarterly*. Ellison served from 1943 to 1945 with the United States Merchant Marine, and after the war, aided by a Rosenwald Fellowship, settled down to work on the novel that was published in 1952 as *Invisible Man*. The book opens with a Prologue set in a secret basement room where the (nameless) young hero has holed up, surrounded by 1,369 electric lights that blaze night and day to remind him that he exists and is visible. Here he relives his experiences and tries to make sense of them.

His grandfather had told him how to deal with whites: "I want you to overcome 'em with yeses, undermine 'em with grins, agree 'em to death and destruction." A bemused and innocent Candide, he does as he is told so successfully that he is chosen to give his high school's valedictory address (on the desirability of humility) at a white smoker. First, however, he and nine other black boys are obliged to watch the performance of a blonde belly-dancer, and then are blindfolded and set to fight each other for the amusement of the white spectators.

His optimism dented but intact, he goes off to a southern Negro college which in due course is revealed as only another device for keeping white consciences peaceful and black men invisible. This episode includes a powerful and significant scene in which Norton, a visiting white philanthropist, meets a black sharecropper locally notorious as the father of his daughter's child and, listening to the black man's story, vicariously fulfills his own secret incestuous urges. Jonathan Baumbach wrote: "Underlying Norton's recurrent platitude that 'the Negro is my fate' (he means that they are his potency) is the same prurience that motivates the sadism of the white citizens in the preceding scene."

Suspended for excessive obedience, the hero then goes to New York. After various ordeals he is taken up by the Brotherhood (the Communist party), but is disillusioned again. An episode follows in which the increasingly embittered narrator takes on the role of Rinehart, a Harlem gambler, lover, priest, and seer—a black man who has relinquished anything as limiting as an identity. This desperate disguise is stripped away during a riot in Harlem, in the course of which the hero is hunted by both blacks and whites, and goes to earth in his basement room.

He realizes at last that all along he has been playing out a succession of stereotyped roles forced on him by the facts of Negro history. These masks are the only identity that the world has allowed him; he himself has remained "invisible," to blacks as well as whites. But telling his story has taken him a long way towards self-knowledge. At the end he is preparing to leave his well-lighted basement womb and to be born again into the world.

This long novel is full of symbolic patterns and allusions, and it forms a kind of condensed history of the black man in America. Some critics go further, and see it as an allegory of universal scope about man's quest for identity. In form, as Ellison says, it moves from naturalism to expressionism to surrealism—too abruptly for some tastes—in a way that led Jonathan Baumbach to suggest that Ellison has more in common with Joyce, Kafka, and Melville than with, say, James Baldwin or Richard Wright. There were complaints about the uneven quality of the book's style, but by and large its profound originality, imaginative richness, and savage humor were recognized at once. Irving Howe wrote: "Ellison has an abundance of that primary talent without which neither craft nor intelligence can save a novelist; he is richly, wildly inventive; his scenes rise and dip with tension, his people bleed, his language sings. No other writer has captured so much of the confusion and agony, the hidden gloom and surface gaiety of Negro life. His ear for Negro speech is magnificent . . ." *Invisible Man* received the National Book Award for fiction in 1953 and in 1965 a *Book Week* poll singled it out as the most distinguished novel published during the preceding twenty years.

Shadow and Act, Ellison's second book, is a collection of personal essays about literature and folklore, jazz, and the author's life and work. Here, as in the novel, the style is uneven—sometimes eloquent, sometimes clumsy or pompous. One critic suggested that Ellison's fundamental theme is "his attempt to find humanity beneath the categories, abstractions, and legends through which our thought forms." These essays make it clear that the author, though he is acutely conscious of the situation of his race in contemporary America, is an artist before he is a black. As Philip Larkin wrote, "Ellison was 'freed' not by the Negro Freedom Movement but by Marx, Freud, T. S. Eliot, Pound, Gertrude Stein, and Hemingway." He has been much abused by black activists and even some white ones who feel that a black writer has no choice but to commit himself unreservedly to the cause; but he believes, like Kenneth Burke, that "the work of art is a social action in itself." Ellison has also published a number of short stories, and some excerpts from the novel on which he has been working since the 1950s.

Ralph Ellison has lectured, or taught as a visiting professor, at Yale, Chicago, and many other American universities and colleges, and made a lecture tour of Germany in 1954. In 1970 he went to New York University as Albert Schweitzer Professor of Contemporary Literature and Culture.

Ellison serves or has served as honorary consultant in American Letters at the Library of Congress, as a trustee of the John F. Kennedy Center for the Performing Arts, as a member of the council of the National Institute of Arts and Letters, and on the editorial board of the *American Scholar*. He is a member of the American Academy of Arts and Sciences and of P.E.N. He held the Rome Fellowship of the American Academy of Arts and Letters in 1955–1957, received the United States Medal of Freedom in 1969, and has honorary doctorates from Tuskegee Institute, Rutgers University, the University of Michigan, Williams College, and Grinnell College. Ellison was married in 1946 to Fanny McConnell. They live quietly in New York City in an apartment on Riverside Drive. Ellison's hobbies are photography, tinkering with his hi-fi equipment, and playing the recorder.

PRINCIPAL WORKS: Invisible Man, 1952; Shadow and Act, 1964.

ABOUT: Baumbach, J. The Landscape of Nightmare, 1966; Bigsby, C. W. E. (ed.) The Black American Writer, 1970; Breit, H. The Writer Observed, 1956; Chester, A. and Howard, V. Ralph Ellison, 1963; Current Biography, 1968; Gottesman, R. (ed.) Studies in Invisible Man, 1971; Gross, S. L. and Hardy, J. E. (eds.) Images of the Negro in American Literature, 1966; Harte, B. and Riley, C. (eds.) 200 Contemporary Authors, 1969; Klein, M. After Alienation, 1964; Kostelanetz, R. Master Minds, 1969; Margolies, E. Native Sons, 1968; Parks, G. Camera Portraits, 1948; Pearce, R. A. Stages of the Clown, 1970; Rubin, L. D. Jr. (ed.) Bibliographical Guide to the Study of Southern Literature, 1969; Who's Who in America, 1972–1973. *Periodicals*—American Mercury June 1952; Atlantic July 1952, December 1970; Chicago Review 2, 1967; Commentary November 1953; May 1965; Commonweal February 19, 1965; Contemporary Literature Summer 1969; Winter 1970; English Journal September 1969; Harper's Magazine March 1967; Life August 25, 1952; May 8, 1970; Modern Fiction Studies Winter 1969–70; Nation May 10, 1952; February 7, 1953; November 9, 1964; Newsweek August 12, 1963; October 26, 1964; New York Times Book Review May 4, 1952; New York Times Magazine November 20, 1966; Partisan Review September–November 1961; Reporter March 25, 1965; Saturday Review April 12, 1952; February 7, 1953; March 14, 1953; November 16, 1957; Sociological Quarterly Autumn 1965; Twentieth Century Literature October 1969.

ELLMANN, RICHARD (March 15, 1918–), American biographer and critic, writes: "I was born in a small and comparatively quiet enclave of Detroit called Highland Park, and attended public schools there. Both my father, a lawyer, and my mother read widely and encouraged me to do the same. My two brothers went into the law, whereas I made the eccentric choice of teaching English literature.

"As a senior at Yale I learned from Andrews Wanning about W. B. Yeats, and in graduate school I thought of a dissertation on him even though Yeats, who had just died, seemed at that time a subject suspiciously and brazenly modern. Half-way along with it when war came, I served haphazardly in the Seabees, the Navy, and the Office of Strategic Services. The last of these deposited me in London, and soon after the German surrender I took a leave in Dublin, then newly tolerant of military visitors. Mrs. Yeats received me kindly and encouraged me to return. During a year in Dublin (1946–47) I wrote a biography of Yeats which dwelt upon some insistent connections of his life and his poems and plays. After it was published in 1948, when I was teaching at Harvard, I felt I should deal with his poetry more in its own terms, and wrote *The Identity of Yeats* (1954).

"Although the war was no patron of letters, the generation to which I belong inevitably began writing during those years. While with the Navy in Paris in 1944–45 I came to know the prose poems of Henri Michaux and then to know him as well. Being subversive of all organized concepts, and unpretentious in the most ironical way, Michaux offered a counter to Yeats, who except in his last poems was elevated and eager for firm outlines. I translated *L'Espace du dedans* of Michaux and it was published in 1951 under the title of *Selected Writings*.

"When one day in 1947 I asked Mrs. Yeats in Dublin about the notorious first meeting of Yeats with James Joyce, which occurred in 1902, she dug up a summary of the encounter that Yeats had made. Joyce's impudence with his distinguished and much older contemporary led me to attempt

RICHARD ELLMANN

in 1951 an article on the relations of the two writers, and then to begin a year later (by which time I was teaching at Northwestern) a biography of Joyce. Faithful to his own principle that random gestures might be as characteristic of the mind as its more formal behavior, I thought to present his life with a little of the density of actual experience, yet always with at least covert reference to certain ruling passions and to his writings. This biography was published in 1959.

"The feeling that modern writers, for all their variety, were in some sense engaged in a communal enterprise of an imaginative kind, led me to propose to my friend from college days, Charles Feidelson Jr., that we undertake a book together on the intellectual backgrounds of modern literature. This appeared in 1965 under the title *The Modern Tradition*. Since that large experience I have felt drawn to the most specific topics, and am now writing a biography of Oscar Wilde.

"In 1949 I married Mary Donahue, of Newburyport, Massachusetts, who had also taken a doctoral degree at Yale. We have three children: Stephen, Maud, and Lucy Ellmann."

Ellmann's two books about Yeats were both well received. One critic thought that *The Identity of Yeats* gave disproportionate and therefore misleading attention to what is abstruse in the poet's work, but there was otherwise little but praise for Ellmann's frankness and detachment, his decorous, cool, quick-witted scholarship.

In his first book Ellmann conducts an illuminating investigation into the relationship between Yeats's life and his work. He uses the same method in his critical biography of Joyce, and with superb effect—"translating James Joyce's books," Stephen Spender said, "back into his life." What Ellmann did was to pile upon the ordinary processes of scholarly research innumerable interviews with Joyce's surviving friends and relations. Far from being overwhelmed by the resulting mountain of data, his immensely detailed narrative "absorbs the reader like a great novel." What it shows, T. E. Cassidy said, is that Joyce "experienced every line he wrote, that he filled his books with the events, mostly little, of his own life, with the people he had met and known, and with the words they spoke."

James Joyce earned Ellmann a National Book Award in 1960, among other honors, and was everywhere praised for its judgment and tact, its elegant prose, and its apt sense of comedy. The book was almost generally recognized as the definitive biography of Joyce and seemed to Mark Schorer "one of the great literary biographies of this century." The qualities which distinguish Ellmann's masterpiece—and not least his "pawky" sense of humor—are also evident in his edition of Joyce's letters. Another important contribution to Joyce's studies was Ellmann's persuasive explication of *Ulysses*, based on his 1971 Eliot Memorial Lectures at the University of Kent, and published as *Ulysses on the Liffey*.

The Modern Tradition, which Ellmann edited with Charles Feidelson, is a brilliant mosaic of passages from the work of about a hundred authors who, between the eighteenth century and the present, constructed the pattern of ideas which shape modern literature. *Eminent Domain* studies with clarity, grace, and wit the social and literary interactions between Yeats and a number of his eminent contemporaries, achieving a kind of literary history which Kevin Sullivan called "select, essential, personal, at times almost intimate."

Richard Ellmann received his B.A. in 1939, his M.A. two years later, and his Ph.D. in 1947, all from Yale. His year in Dublin was spent at Trinity College, which gave him a B.Litt in 1947. Ellmann taught English at Harvard for five years (1942–1943 and 1947–1951), and joined the faculty of Northwestern University in 1951, becoming Franklin Bliss Snyder Professor of English there in 1963. He was professor of English at Yale from 1968 to 1970, when he went to England, as Goldsmith's Professor of English Literature at Oxford University. His extramural assignments have included a lecture tour of Europe and England in 1961–1962 under the auspices of the United States Information Services, and a visiting professorship at the University of Chicago in 1959. Ellmann has received Rockefeller, *Kenyon Review*, and three Guggenheim fellowships, and grants from the American Philosophical Society and the Modern Language Association. He is a member of the editorial boards of the *Publications of the Modern Language Association* and the *American Scholar*, and a Fellow of the American Academy of Arts and Sciences.

PRINCIPAL WORKS: Yeats: The Man and the Masks, 1948; The Identity of Yeats, 1954; James Joyce, 1959; Eminent Domain: Yeats Among Wilde, Joyce, Pound, Eliot, and Auden, 1967; Ulysses on the Liffey, 1972; Golden Codgers: Biographical Speculations, 1973. *As editor*—My Brother's Keeper, by Stanislaus Joyce, 1958; (with Ellsworth Mason) The Critical Writings of James Joyce, 1959; (with Charles Feidelson) The Modern Tradition: Backgrounds of Modern Literature, 1965; Letters of James Joyce, vols. 2–3, 1966; Giacomo Joyce, by James Joyce, 1968; The Artist as Critic: Critical Writings of Oscar Wilde, 1970. *As translator*—Selected Writings of Henri Michaux, 1951.

ABOUT: Connolly, C. Previous Convictions, 1963; Contemporary Authors 1, 1962; Kermode, F. Puzzles and Epiphanies, 1962; National Cyclopaedia of American Biography, Current Volume J, 1964; Who's Who, 1971; Who's Who in America, 1970–1971. *Periodicals*—Newsweek October 26, 1959; New Yorker April 2, 1960; Saturday Review November 13, 1948, March 26, 1960.

***"ELYTIS," ODYSSEUS (pseudonym of Odysseus Alepoudelis)** (November 2, 1911–), Greek poet, writes: "My family came originally from the island of Lesbos (commonly called Mytilene), but I was born in Heraklion, Crete, where my father, a soap manufacturer, had set up his first factory. Later on, however, we moved to Athens, where I was brought up, went through high school, and, finally, studied law at the University of Athens. Nevertheless, I always spent my summer vacations in the islands—Hydra, Spetsai, Tinos, Mykonos, or Mytilene—and this was later to have a deep influence on my work as a poet. When my interest in poetry was first awakened, round the age of seventeen, I found myself in possession of a fund of experience acquired from my life in the islands; my imagination had developed among the rocks and the *caïques*—the small island boats—among the rectangular, whitewashed houses, and the windmills. The Aegean had indelibly stamped my consciousness.

"Thus provided, I could easily have started on a poetic career the sole aspiration of which would have been to reveal the Greece of sun and sea, and would have contented myself with that. But it so happened that, at this crucial moment, I became aware of the theories and the works of the revolutionary French movement of surrealism. I read with passion all the books and magazines which came from Paris, and soon found myself knowing all about, as well as sharing in the beliefs of, all those writers and artists, many of whom were in later years to become my personal friends. True, even at that time, I never accepted uncritically all

* e lē′ tis

the premises of surrealism, nor did I follow their methods in a strict or literal way. What was much more important for me was the possibility which suddenly struck me, of adapting at least some of the more positive elements of surrealism to the long, rich, and flexible Greek tradition—the only one to have lasted uninterruptedly for twenty-five centuries—yet a tradition, which, I now decided, was badly in need of renewal. The belief, for instance, in a superior type of reality, as distinct from the common, everyday one, or the method, adopted from psychoanalysis, of the dream-like free association of images, and the boldness of image-making—these, combined with my Aegean consciousness, helped me to discover new forms with which to express my poetic world.

"Then came the war years. As a second lieutenant, I fought in Albania against the Fascists. This was a totally new experience for me, and, along with that of the Nazi occupation of Greece, it helped to shape inside me that special ethical freedom which, I believed, corresponded to my poetic vision. During the period immediately following the war, I went to live in Paris, and spent four years there studying literature at the Sorbonne, and forming permanent friendships with many leading poets and painters. From there I traveled to other countries—Italy, Spain, Switzerland and England—and later on, as a guest of their respective governments, I visited the USA and the Soviet Union. On my return to Greece, I worked as a director of the Broadcasting Section of Athens Radio, and as adviser to the National Theatre. I have never married, and live alone in a small apartment, where I continue to write poetry, and essays on contemporary poetic and artistic problems.

"Today, my requirements from poetry are much more exacting than they used to be: a kind of second life within the conventional everyday one—this is what I am trying through my works to bring into the light of consciousness, expressed in forms which, while not akin to traditional forms, will nevertheless possess their solidity. Objectivity, myth-making, and synthesis, are, I believe, those elements which constitute my ties with the true Greek tradition, while at the same time they align me with the avant-garde writers of our time."

Elytis belongs to the generation of poets which emerged during the 1930s and included D. I. Antoniou and Nikos Gatsos. They centered on the review *Ta Nea Grammata*, edited by George Katsimbalis and Andreas Karantonis.

His first collection, *Prosanatolismoi* (Orientations, 1940), reflects the life and landscape of the Aegean Islands which, as he says, had so "indelibly stamped my consciousness." These joyous early lyrics are full of the subjective and boldly fanciful imagery

ODYSSEUS ELYTIS

Elytis had learned from his surrealist reading: ". . . On plains where the naked girls awake, / When they harvest clover with their light brown arms / Roaming around the borders of their dreams—tell me, is it the mad pomegranate tree, / Unsuspecting, that puts the lights in their verdant baskets / That floods their names with the singing of birds—tell me / Is it the mad pomegranate tree that combats the cloudy skies of the world?" ("The Mad Pomegranate Tree," translated by Edmund Keeley and Philip Sherrard).

The poet has described the personal mythology which underlies his work as one of "repeated metamorphosis—the girl that becomes fruit, an idea that becomes incarnate in a human form"; surrealism thus became for him a means of exploring this ancient theme of the mystery of change. The poems in *Ilios o Protos* (Sun the First), published in 1943, responded to the Nazi occupation by evoking in a similar style the spirit and values embodied in the Greek landscape. Elytis's long elegy for a young Greek officer killed in Albania, published in 1945, is one of the most poignant and beautiful poems inspired by the war.

Elytis was silent throughout the civil war and the recovery, and began to publish again only in 1958. *Axion Esti* (Seemly It Is, 1959), his finest and also his most difficult work to date, follows the pattern of Byzantine liturgy, alternating prose and verse, and employing also a variety of typographical effects. It begins with the poet's vision of Genesis, a time of "green blood and bulbs golden in the soil," and goes on to interweave these images of the Creation with those of the present day, achieving an even greater density of effect by addressing both conditions, on occasion, in liturgical or biblical language. According to S. J. Papastavrou, the poem succeeds in evoking "the 'genesis' and growth of a poet's consciousness projecting itself into the history, tradition, nature and life of Greece. . . . It is by any standards a major poem." *Axion Esti* received the National Prize in Poetry in 1960.

Another small volume of poems, more sober and profound than Elytis's earlier work but still surrealistic in style, was published in 1960 as *Exi Kai Mia Typseis Ghia Ton Ourano* (Six and One Regrets for the Sky).

PRINCIPAL WORKS IN ENGLISH TRANSLATION: *Poems in* Barnstone, W. (ed.) Modern European Poetry, 1966; Keeley, E. and Sherrard, P. Six Poets of Modern Greece, 1960, *and* Four Greek Poets, 1966; Trypanis, C. (ed.) Penguin Book of Greek Verse, 1971; Accent Summer 1954; Poetry 1, 1964.

ABOUT: International Who's Who, 1970–1971; Keeley, E. and Sherrard, P. Six Poets of Modern Greece, 1960; Penguin Companion to Literature 2, 1969. *Periodicals*—Books Abroad Spring 1971.

PIERRE EMMANUEL

***"EMMANUEL, PIERRE" (pseudonym of Noël Jean Mathieu)** (May 3, 1916–), French poet, was born at Gan, a market town in the Béarn region of southwest France. He is the son of Émile and Maria (Boulogne) Mathieu. His parents had migrated to the United States at the beginning of the century but his mother returned periodically to Béarn for the birth of her children. Apart from three early years in America, Emmanuel was raised in Gan by his maternal grandmother until he was ten, and thereafter by his father's brother, a teacher in Lyons. The boy wanted to stay in Béarn and study Latin; instead he was uprooted and "condemned to become an engineer" in a narrowly puritanical society that he hated.

In his autobiographical preface to Alain Bosquet's 1959 study of him, Emmanuel wrote: "Though I showed all the outward signs of affection, I was an introverted boy. I loathed the family code of conduct, yet I submitted to it passively. From the age of ten to the age of eighteen, I had not a single friend." He took refuge from the tedium and loneliness of his life in an increasingly rich imaginative life, and began to write poetry at college after his mathematics teacher read him Valéry's *La Jeune Parque*. At twenty he visited his father in America, realized that they were strangers to one another, and decided that henceforth he must make his own way in life. Returning to France, he began his career as a teacher.

Emmanuel, a Catholic poet, has been greatly influenced by Pierre Jean Jouve. In 1937 he visited Jouve in Paris and showed him his early poems, all of which were later destroyed except "Christ au Tombeau" (Christ at the Tomb). Here for the first time he used the pseudonym "Pierre Emmanuel," which symbolizes for him the whole drama of creation. The publication of Emmanuel's first collection, *Élégies* (1940), coincided with the German invasion of France. Bombed out of his house at Pontoise, he made his way (with Jouve's help) to Dieulefit, on the edge of Provence. Here he stayed throughout the war, working with the Resistance and writing the books that established him.

* e ma nü el'

His first major volume was *Tombeau d'Orphée* (The Tomb of Orpheus, 1941). The title poem is a Christian interpretation of the Orpheus myth, in which Orpheus, bound to the earthly cycle of birth and death by his sexuality, frees himself to live in Christ by his rejection of Eurydice. Here, as in much of Emmanuel's early work, the influence of Jouve is very strong, not only in the theme but, as C. A. Hackett pointed out, "in the rhetorical style, the prophetic tone, and in the mingling of erotic and religious images."

The years at Dieulefit were a watershed in Emmanuel's life and work. The landscape entered his poetry and his thought: "its comparative aridity, its austere lines, its gentleness lying beneath the surface harshness." He says that "this relationship between gentleness and rigor" taught him much about poetry and more about mysticism. And the war itself awoke him to a new spiritual sensitivity and self-awareness. *Jour de colère* (Day of Wrath, 1942) and *Combats avec tes défenseurs* (Battles with Your Defenders, 1942) contain some of the most moving and profound poems of the Resistance. They were written, Emmanuel says, "to express suffering, to raise it to an absolute . . . and to point to the spirit of Evil which inflicts it."

Emmanuel has produced about twenty volumes of verse, several critical studies, and an autobiography, *Qui est cet homme?* (1947, translated as *The Universal Singular*), a stern, difficult, but often eloquent "record of a spiritual search." His ambition is "to understand the present and the eternal, the inner man and man in the universe, the torturer and the saint, the hell of suffering and the heaven of praise, in a continuous thought-process to which my poetry endeavors to bear witness." He finds his subjects and imagery most often in biblical stories and the pagan myths, and writes most readily in alexandrines, usually unrhymed. No doubt he has written too much, and his work is often marred by a diffuse and facile rhetoric. At his best, however, he achieves a noble eloquence. The Miltonic epic *Babel* (1951), one of the most admired of his poems, showed him, according to Joseph Chiari, "not only as a poet of apocalyptical vision but as a maker of striking images and majestic music which can conjure up in a background of metaphysical *Angst* the vision of man, the problems of his destiny and the complexity of feelings which they produce."

Emmanuel says that in recent years he has "acquired a truer sense of the exacting nature of language," and this is reflected in *La Nouvelle Naissance* (The New Birth, 1963) and in *Jacob* (1970), another biblical epic conceived in the light of a modern, and sexually tormented, consciousness; it is the most ambitious of his long poems, and is regarded by many as his masterpiece. Emmanuel goes on: "The question of language is now central in my poetry. I must learn to use words in such a way that I can serve them, for language is not an instrument: it is the very Being of man, and of the world which he has made his abode by naming it and imposing order on it through words."

Since the war, Emmanuel has worked for the French radio, directing the English service from 1945 to 1947, the North American service from 1947 to 1959. He has lectured in many parts of the world, including the United States, where he has been a visiting lecturer at Johns Hopkins University, Harvard, Brandeis, and elsewhere. For a time he was attracted to communism, but was disillusioned by a visit to East Europe. He was married in 1952 to France Loo, who is his second wife. Emmanuel was elected to the Académie Française in 1968. He received the Grand Prix de Poésie de l'Académie Française in 1963, is a Chevalier of the Légion d'Honneur, and has an honorary doctorate from Oxford University. From 1969 to 1971 he was president of P.E.N. International.

PRINCIPAL WORKS IN ENGLISH TRANSLATION: The Universal Singular (autobiography), 1951; The Mad Poet (poems in memory of Friedrich Hölderlin), 1956. *Poems in* Fowlie, W. Mid-Century French Poets, 1955; Marks, E. French Poetry From Baudelaire to the Present, 1962; Strachan, W.J. Apollinaire to Aragon, 1948. *Articles in* Atlantic January 1951, August 1954, June 1958.

ABOUT: Boisdeffre, P. de. Dictionnaire de littérature contemporaine, 1962; Boisdeffre, P. de. Une Histoire vivante de la littérature d'aujourd'hui, 1958; Bosquet, A. Pierre Emmanuel, 1959; Brereton, G. An Introduction to the French Poets, 1956; Chiari, J. Contemporary French Poetry, 1952; Fowlie, W. Mid-Century French Poets, 1955; Hackett, C. A. An Anthology of Modern French Poetry, 1965; International Who's Who, 1970–1971; Marks, E. French Poetry From Baudelaire to the Present, 1962; Moore, H. T. Twentieth Century French Literature Since World War II, 1966; Pingaud, B. Écrivains d'aujourd'hui, 1960; Rousselot, J. Panorama critique des nouveaux poètes français, 1952; Who's Who in France, 1971–1972. *Periodicals*—Books Abroad 20 no. 1, 1946; Mercure de France August 15, 1939; New Statesman and Nation July 7, 1951; New Yorker November 12, 1949; Times Literary Supplement June 4, 1970.

ENGLE, PAUL (HAMILTON) (October 12, 1908–), American poet, novelist, and editor, was born in Cedar Rapids, Iowa, the son of Hamilton Allen Engle and the former Evelyn Reinheimer. His father was a horse trainer and trader, as *his* father had been before him. Paul Engle entered Coe College, Cedar Rapids, during the Depression, when students were paying their tuition with calves, pigs, and potatoes. He graduated *magna cum laude* in 1931, and received his M.A. a year later from the State University of Iowa, where his thesis was a collection of poems, *Worn Earth*. Engle believes that this was the first advanced degree ever granted in the United States for a piece of imaginative writing. In 1932 the volume was published in the Yale Series of Younger Poets, and called sound and promising, if rather humorless. The same year Engle was awarded a fellowship to Columbia, where he did graduate work until, in 1933, he went to England as a Rhodes Scholar. At Merton College, Oxford University, Engle studied under the poet Edmund Blunden, played cricket and baseball, and rowed both for his college and for the university.

American Song was published while Engle was still at Oxford. This volume of poems, affirming his faith in America, was very widely and fully reviewed and became a best seller. William Rose Benét praised it, and J. Donald Adams prophesied that it would become "a literary landmark." But the book encountered as much hostility as enthusiasm. E. L. Walton acknowledged that Engle had a certain power and wrote with abandon and exultation, but found his blank verse "often very blank," his lyrics "completely undistinguished by beauty of phrase or image." Malcolm Cowley said that he was not a poet at all, but an orator.

Engle was a contemporary at Oxford of W. H. Auden, Stephen Spender, and Cecil Day Lewis,

PAUL ENGLE

but felt "out of line" with them. "They think they are Marxists," he said, "but it is both funny and painful to imagine some of them going into a pub and standing a working man to a beer." It may be that Engle did not greatly enjoy his years at Oxford. At any rate, the poems collected in *Break the Heart's Anger* reflected a total if temporary disillusionment both with Europe and America, and at least a flirtation with left-wing attitudes. Ben Belitt found the volume technically as "slovenly" as ever, and Cowley said that Engle was still an orator, but one who "delivers his oration on May Day now, instead of the Fourth of July."

Break the Heart's Anger appeared in 1936. The same year Engle left the university and was married at the Oxford registry office to Mary Nomine Nissen of Cedar Rapids. Their honeymoon took them to Scandinavia, Poland, and Russia and lasted into 1937, when they went home. Engle began his teaching career at the State University of Iowa, where he has remained. *Corn* (1939), it was said, contained the poems of a "defeated expatriate," back at last where he belonged, and *West of Midnight* (1941) showed Engle "shifting back completely into his early affirmation of America." The most widely admired of Engle's volumes of verse was *American Child*, a sonnet sequence for his first daughter, Mary, which was published in 1945. There was warm praise for the "tolerance, courage, and gayety that live everywhere in these honest and supple poems."

For a time in the 1940s Engle's optimistic Whitmanesque verse made him one of the most popular and widely read American poets of his generation but, though even his most stringent critics have noted a steady growth in his metrical range and control, there are many who believe that he has never fully mastered his craft. Paul Fussell, reviewing *A Woman Unashamed* (1965), suggested that he is "too nice a man to write very good poems. His reactions to experience are always decent and occasionally even complicated; but, alas, however humane his general stance, the poems he constructs are sentimental, with little distinction of language or image and without sufficient emotional dynamics to provide many delights of structure."

At any rate, Engle's verse output has dropped considerably in recent years, and he has turned to other forms. His novel, *Always the Land*, about Iowa farmers and horse traders, had a mixed reception but was well liked by many for its intimate, easy, natural manner. His memoir, *Prairie Christmas*, was called a little masterpiece, full of "the very taste and smell and happy tension of old-time Christmases." Engle has written the libretto for an opera by Philip Bezanson—a kind of American frontier version of the Christmas story performed on television as "Western Child," and published in 1962 as *Golden Child*. He is also active as an itinerant lecturer, and as an editor and anthologist.

It may be that Paul Engle will be best remembered for his work at the State University of Iowa, where he is director of the Program in Creative Writing. It has grown under his leadership into the best-known writers' workshop in the world. Henry Rago, editor of *Poetry* magazine, said that "no poet in the United States has done as much for young poets as Paul Engle" and called the Iowa Workshop "a high honor to the Middle West, important for what it does here among us and important for what it represents to the rest of the country and the whole international world of letters."

Engle received Guggenheim Fellowships in 1953, 1957, and 1959, and holds several honorary degrees. He is a member of the advisory committee for the John F. Kennedy Cultural Center in Washington, D.C., and a member of the National Council of the Arts. He was at one time editor of the annual *O. Henry Prize Stories*. Engle, who now has two daughters, Mary and Sara, is tall and lanky, with a strong chin, penetrating blue eyes, and "an awesome store of energy."

PRINCIPAL WORKS: *Poetry*—Worn Earth, 1932; American Song: A Book of Poems, 1934; Break the Heart's Anger, 1936; Corn: A Book of Poems, 1939; West of Midnight, 1941; American Child: A Sonnet Sequence, 1945; The Word of Love, 1951; American Child: Sonnets for My Daughters with Thirty-six New Poems, 1956; Poems in Praise, 1959; A Woman Unashamed, and Other Poems, 1965. *Fiction*—Always the Land, 1941; Golden Child, 1962. *Nonfiction*—A Prairie Christmas, 1960; Who's Afraid?, 1963; An Old Fashioned Christmas, 1964. *As editor*—(with others) Midland: Twenty-five Years of Fiction and Poetry Selected from the Writing Workshops of the State University of Iowa, 1961; (with B. T. Langland) Poet's Choice, 1962; On Creative Writing, 1964.

ABOUT: Cowley, M. Think Back on Us, 1967; Contemporary Authors 1st revision 1–4, 1967; Current Biography, 1942; Who's Who in America, 1970–1971. *Periodicals*—Life August 17, 1959; Look June 1, 1965; Time June 3, 1957.

ENRIGHT, D(ENNIS) J(OSEPH) (March 11, 1920–), British poet, critic, memoirist, and novelist, writes: "I was born in Leamington, Warwickshire. My father was an Irishman, obliged early in life to enlist in the British Army as a result of the premature death of his father, a Fenian. Demobilised in England after the First World War, my father, a Catholic, married an Anglo-Welsh Wesleyan Methodist. These circumstances deprived me pre-natally of the ability to comprehend religious or political ideologies, race, nationality and nationalism—phenomena which one needs to have a firm grasp of if one is to lead a stable and balanced life.

"Thanks to scholarships I was enabled to read English at Cambridge, as a member of Downing College, where F. R. Leavis presided over English studies. I contributed to the review *Scrutiny*, mainly articles on German literature, during the last ten years of its existence. My profession is the teaching of English literature, which I first practised in Alexandria, at what was then known as Farouk I University. (For further details see *Academic Year.*) After four years in Egypt I returned to England and taught in the Extra-Mural Department of Birmingham University. In 1953 I went to Japan and taught at Kōnan University (near Kobe) and elsewhere for the next three years. I then spent a year as *Gastdozent* at the Free University of West Berlin, under the auspices of the British Council, and then went East again, to Bangkok, as British Council Professor of English at Chulalongkorn University. My stay in Thailand was cut short by an unsuitable happening outside a brothel, involving myself and my wife on one side and some fifteen brave policemen on the other. The result was a moral victory for myself and wife, and after being released from the lock-up, I was ordered out of the country. (For further details see *Figures of Speech.*) In addition it seemed that some carelessly worded poem of mine had wounded the feelings of Marshal Sarit (Prime Minister and a well-known anti-Communist of the day). With tempered regret on both sides, the British Council and I decided to part company.

"In 1960 I was appointed to the Chair of English in the University of Singapore, which I was almost obliged to vacate at once on account of a misunderstanding arising out of my inaugural lecture. I had spoken of 'culture' in the sense of the production of works of art, whereas to the Singapore government it signified the reduction of race riots. Students demonstrated in favour of academic freedom, and the fuss died down as it became plain that the professor was neither a colonialist nor a Communist but merely rather simple.

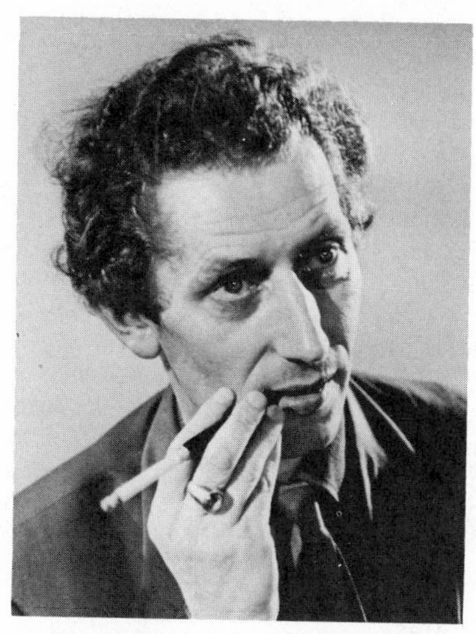

D. J. ENRIGHT

"Poetry and criticism I have struggled with from an early age, but gratitude to the publisher of my first collection of poems betrayed me into writing a novel for him. Typically, he declined it. But unhappily it was published by someone else and so I was led on to write further novels, four in all, all about what to the British reviewers were very foreign parts, all quite remarkably non-successful. Heading a university department in a 'new country' is no sinecure and I am now largely a Sunday writer, dependent on the day traditionally reserved hereabouts for combing the beaches. My writing mostly consists of reviews for the *New Statesman*, with occasional contributions to *Encounter*, the *London Magazine* and the *New York Review of Books*, among others. I like to think that I would like some kindly Foundation to subsidize me for a whole year of doing nothing but write poems. But since I am one of those people who work under pressure or not at all, it seems better to have a full-time job, if only as an alibi. I am married to a Frenchwoman and we have one daughter."

Urgently conscious that "we are all indebted to other human beings for love and pity," Professor Enright seeks but perhaps scarcely expects to see a new humanism, free of posturing and cant. He is a restless, quick-witted man, who looks more the poet than the professor.

Believing that modernism is an exhausted convention in literature, Enright published in Japan his anthology *Poets of the 1950's*, exhibiting a new English poetry of "chastened commonsense." Intended to steer the Japanese "between the rock of Wastelanditis and the whirlpool of Dylanitis," it accidentally helped to persuade English readers of the existence of what became known as "the Movement."

Enright's own poetry at its best achieves "that special tone" described in one of his poems: "Wholly truthful, intimate / And utterly unsparing, / A man communing with himself . . ." He writes of the exotic places he has known, most often to contrast the romance that art finds in them with the tragically squalid reality, and extends his irony to flay the hypocrisy or uselessness of such idealists as himself. Marius Bewley praises above all the decorum of Enright's poetry, the marriage in it of literary form and moral meaning, "celebrated in one of the most unassertively personal rhythms possessed by any contemporary poet." William Walsh thinks that, of all the Movement poets, Enright is "the most individual in character and the most representative of the times."

As a critic and frequent reviewer, Enright is unusually well-informed about foreign literatures. As befits a disciple of F. R. Leavis, he seems often more interested in a writer's social intentions or originality of mind than in his literary means, and he can be savagely sardonic about cultural pretension and academic cant (in students as well as in teachers). His satirical novels are often very funny, and full of good characterizations. William Van O'Connor thought that Enright had great capacities as a novelist but did not "sufficiently respect the nature of his medium." Enright seems in all his writing to be inhibited by a Puritan's guilty sense that, in the face of human suffering, words are not enough, and deliberately wrought literary effects slightly contemptible.

Enright's account of his exotic career, *Memoirs of a Mendicant Professor*, includes along with much else of interest lively descriptions of his widely discussed brushes with authority in Bangkok and Singapore. The *Times Literary Supplement* found it "a fascinating book, witty and elegant and full of observations about life in both East and West which merit more than a casual thought." Enright left his University of Singapore professorship in 1970, becoming joint editor of *Encounter*. He spent two years in that post, also teaching at Leeds University (1970–1971) and acting as literary adviser to the publishing house of Chatto & Windus. In 1973 he became chief editor of Chatto & Windus. He lists his recreations as reading, writing, films, and listening to music. He is a Fellow of the Royal Society of Literature.

PRINCIPAL WORKS: *Poetry*—The Laughing Hyena, 1953; Bread Rather Than Blossoms, 1956; Some Men Are Brothers, 1960; Addictions, 1962; The Old Adam, 1965; Unlawful Assembly, 1968; Selected Poems, 1969; The Typewriter Revolution (new and selected poems), 1971; Daughters of Earth, 1972; The Terrible Shears: Scenes From a Twenties Childhood, 1973. *Novels*—Academic Year, 1955; Heaven Knows Where, 1957; Insufficient Poppy, 1960; Figures of Speech, 1965. *Criticism*—A Commentary on Goethe's Faust, 1949; The Apothecary's Shop, 1957; Conspirators and Poets, 1966; Shakespeare and the Students, 1970; Man Is an Onion, 1972. *Travel*—The World of Dew: Japan, 1955. *Autobiography*—Memoirs of a Mendicant Professor, 1969. *As editor*—Poets of the 1950's, 1955; (with Takamichi Ninomiya) The Poetry of Living Japan, 1957.

ABOUT: Allott, K. (ed.) Penguin Book of Contemporary Verse, 1962; Enright, D. J. Memoirs of a Mendicant Professor, 1969; Murphy, R. (ed.) Contemporary Poets of the English Language, 1970; O'Connor, W. V. The New University Wits, 1963; Press, J. Rule and Energy, 1963; Walsh, W. A Human Idiom, 1965; Who's Who, 1972. *Periodicals*—New York Review of Books March 31, 1966; Times (London) February 27, 1964; Times Literary Supplement July 29, 1965; February 20, 1969; May 21, 1970.

***ENZENSBERGER, HANS MAGNUS** (November 11, 1929–), German poet and critic, was born in Kaufbeuren, Bavaria. He was brought up in Nuremberg, undergoing bombing and temporary evacuation, until in the winter of 1944–1945 he was enlisted in Hitler's desperate Volkssturm. This experience presumably lies behind his subsequent reluctance to take part in any group movements, and no doubt also explains much of his political extremism. After the war he completed his undergraduate studies, working on the side as an interpreter and bartender, and graduating in 1948. Further studies followed at Erlangen, Hamburg, Freiburg, and the Sorbonne—in languages, philosophy, and the history of literature. He traveled throughout Europe at this time, and worked with student theatre projects for three years. In 1955 he received his doctorate *summa cum laude* at Erlangen with a dissertation on Clemens Brentano's poetic theory.

Thereafter Enzensberger worked for a time as an editor for the South German Radio in Stuttgart, then as a guest *Dozent* at the Hochschule ür Gestaltung in Ulm. In 1957 he visited the United States and Mexico, and settled for the first time in Norway, which since then has served as his home base. Since 1960 he has worked as a reader for his publisher, Suhrkamp. Much subsequent travel—in Italy, the United States, and Cuba—has not prevented him from producing a distinguished body of work which has brought him important literary prizes, including the Critics' Prize for Literature (1962) and the Georg Büchner prize of the German Academy for Language and Poetry (1963). He is married to the former Maria Makarova, and has a daughter.

* ents' ənz berg ər

His first book of poems, *verteidigung der wölfe* (defense of the wolves, 1957) was followed by *landessprache* (landspeech, 1960), the Suhrkamp *Gedichte* (Selected Poems, 1962), and *blindenschrift* (braille, 1964). The first two collections came complete with "directions for use," and from the beginning the function of poetry for Enzensberger has been social or political rather than aesthetic. Like Brecht, he believes that "a conversation about trees is almost a crime / because it includes a silence about so many wrongs." And, like Brecht, he cultivates a kind of talking-in-poetry which, while ostensibly casual, is in fact carefully structured (in his essay "Die Entstehung eines Gedichts" he draws a careful analogy between the poet and the scientific technician, each with his "tools"). The general tone, of broadly humanitarian cynicism, is expressed fairly typically in a poem like "to a man in the streetcar": in that man, of whom the poet "wants to know nothing," he sees almost despite himself a "*stinkender Bruder*"—"a stinking brother."

There has never been any doubt of Enzensberger's cleverness, but his early work sometimes had little else to recommend it. The poems in his first two collections seemed brilliantly, venomously, but indiscriminately angry. As D. J. Enright wrote: "Rilke and Dior, branflakes and bombs . . . all feature as expletives in a lengthy curse, all of equal weight apparently or, in the end, of equal weightlessness." According to Patrick Bridgwater in *Essays on Contemporary German Literature*, "the very diversity of his imagery and vocabulary sometimes seems to replace poetic form . . . the images, ideas or slogans are strung together in an uncritical manner, resulting in . . . a pre-poetic statement rather than a poetic enactment."

Enzensberger, most readers thought, found his own voice for the first time in *blindenschrift*, which contains a few poems in the old manner, some notable experiments in "open-field" verse of the sort associated in the United States with the Black Mountain poets, and some in which a startling lyric note presses itself forward. Critics welcomed a new concern with "truth rather than provocation," a "new richness and suggestiveness of texture" and "subtlety and precision of language." The collection includes what many consider Enzensberger's best poem to date, "lachesis lapponica," which is, significantly, a debate between the poet (as singer) and the politically conscious "bird" shrieking inside his head: "i'll cut off your head, bird. (*it's your own! / viva fidel! better dead than red! have a break! ban the bomb! / über alles in der welt!*) don't say that. (*you are all that,* / says the bird, *imagine, you have been that, you are that.*) / how do you mean? (*in all seriousness,* says the bird and laughs.) / a curlew can't laugh. / (*it's yourself,* it says, / *who are laughing, you'll regret it. i know who you are, / death's head on*

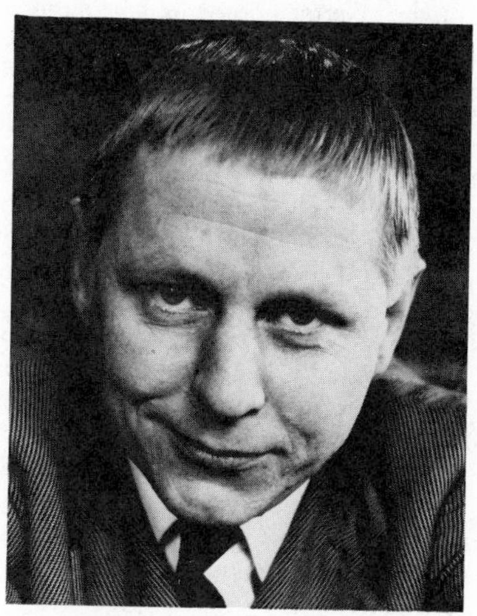

HANS MAGNUS ENZENSBERGER

the kurfürstendamm.) on the moor. / white, dusky, gray, there are no victories here. / that is the moor sedge, those are the gray willows, / that is the bright bird against the dusky sky."

Enzensberger is a sensitive and prolific translator, and a critic of formidable range and intelligence. He has translated (among others) John Gay, Jacques Audiberti, William Carlos Williams, and César Vallejo; in his *Museum der modernen Poesie* (Museum of Modern Poetry, 1960) he assembled a vast anthology, in German with original texts included, of what he considered the best poetry of the century. His preface to this volume explains his notion of poetry as being in some sense a universal language, with an important role to play in the struggle for human freedom.

His belief in the political function of poetry is one of the themes elaborated in *Politik und Verbrechen* (Politics and Crime, 1964), a series of essays on the relationship between public and individual crimes. Other aspects of Enzensberger's literary-social concerns are discussed in *Einzelheiten* (Particulars, 1962). In 1965 Enzensberger became editor of *Kursbuch*, a review seeking "to create connections, but not to give directions." *Allerleirauh* (1961) is a collection of children's poems and songs rather like the *Oxford Dictionary of Nursery Rhymes.* In January 1968 Enzensberger resigned a fellowship at the Center for Advanced Studies at Wesleyan University, feeling that it compromised his position as an opponent of the United States government and its foreign policy.

A small pamphlet of Enzensberger's poems, in translations by Michael Hamburger, appeared in 1966. These translations, with others by Jerome

Rothenberg and the author himself, were published alongside their German originals in *poems for people who don't read poems* (1968). The same volume was also published without the German texts by Penguin as *Selected Poems*.

In his introduction to the latter, Michael Hamburger speaks of the conflict in Enzensberger's work —so evident in "lachesis lapponica"—between his social conscience and his personal and metaphysical concerns. Attempts to resolve this conflict by resort to a collage technique had failed, and "his recent work suggests that the antagonism between public purpose and private impulse has become a deadlock." In fact, Enzensberger is one of several German authors who in 1968 announced that they were done with writing, or at any rate with Literature—a system, as Enzensberger has explained, which allows a hearing only to the specialist (the author): "My proposition is that other people may well have something more important to say and that the writer . . . should place himself at the service of these people." Enzensberger has turned away from high art to such popular and proletarian forms as radio and television, and to the documentary mode of *Das Verhör von Habana* (The Interrogation of Havana, 1970), based on the transcripts of public interrogations conducted by pro-Castro journalists of counter-revolutionaries captured in the Bay of Pigs invasion. His first "novel," *Der kurze Sommer der Anarchie* (1972), was in fact a documentary montage of the life and death of the Spanish anarchist Buenaventura Durruti, interspersed with the comments of the author (who has also made a television film about Durruti).

PRINCIPAL WORKS IN ENGLISH TRANSLATION: Poems, 1966; poems for people who don't read poems, 1968; Selected Poems, 1968.

ABOUT: Hamburger, M. *Introduction to* Selected Poems, 1968; Holthusen, H. E. Kritisches Verstehen, 1961; International Who's Who, 1970–1971; Keith-Smith, B. (ed.) Essays on Contemporary German Literature, 1966. *Periodicals*—Belfagor 1966; Die Zeit August 5, 1960, September 15, 1961; Frankfurter Hefte February 1958; German Life and Letters October 1967; Guardian April 18, 1970; Merkur 1963; Times Literary Supplement September 3, 1964; May 28, 1970.

ESENIN, SERGEI. *See* YESENIN, SERGEI

***"ESTANG, LUC" (pseudonym of Lucien Bastard)** (November 12, 1911–), French poet, novelist, and critic, was born in Paris, the son of Lucien Bastard, watchmaker and jeweler, and of the former Marie-Eugénie Peyroux. He was educated in religious colleges at Artois and in Belgium and returned to Paris in 1929. After holding several jobs, he joined the staff of the Catholic newspaper *La Croix* in 1934, eventually becoming its literary

* es tän′

LUC ESTANG

editor and drama critic (1940–1955). Since then he has been one of the directors of the publishing house Éditions du Seuil. He reviews new novels regularly for *Figaro Littéraire* and contributes to a number of other literary magazines. He also writes for radio and is a member of the jury of the Prix Renaudot.

Estang first became known as a poet. *Au-delà de moi-même* (Beyond Myself) appeared in 1938 and a second collection, *Transhumances* (Moving the Flock) a year later. His other volumes of verse include *Puissance du matin* (Power of Morning, 1941); *Les Béatitudes* (1945), *Poème de la mer* (Poem of the Sea, 1950) and *Les Quatres Éléments* (The Four Elements, 1956). Estang is a religious poet, influenced by Claudel and Péguy, but not a pietistic one. Jean Rousselot has called his verse "a dialogue between man and his creator" in which the man "has his eyes fixed continuously on reality and its miserable grandeur." Gilbert Sigaux has put it a little differently, speaking of a poetry which is as much of the body as of the spirit, which regards both the creation and the Creator as "at the same time enigmas and inexhaustible sources. In a certain sense, original sin is the starting point of his poetry, and, in his eyes, of all poetry." Estang's verse is neoclassic in its melodious unity of form, though in his later poems there is a tendency for melody to give way to metaphysics and rhetoric.

It is as a novelist that Estang is best known—and specifically as a novelist in that tradition of personal, nonconforming, agonized Catholicism associated with Graham Greene and François Mauriac. His first novel, *Les Stigmates* (The Stigmata, 1949), was also the first work in a trilogy whose general title is *Charges d'âmes* (Cure of Souls, 1949–1954). It disturbed orthodox Catholics by proposing that a depraved man might not be totally without grace even in the depths of corruption. *Cherchant qui dévorer* (Seeking Whom He May Devour, 1951) is set in a religious seminary whose future priests seem to draw from their faith not hope and inspiration but guilt-ridden negativism, while *L'Interrogatoire* (The Interrogation, 1957) examines the contrasting claims of communism and Roman Catholicism.

In all of Estang's novels, more overtly than in his poetry, he is concerned with the Christian's need to identify and come to terms with what is, for him, good and what is, for him, evil; to reconcile his own worldly needs with his ultimate responsibility to God. This is the dilemma of Octave Coltenceau in *Le Bonheur et le salut* (1961), the only one of Estang's novels to appear in English, translated by Denise Folliot as *The Better Song* (1964). It tells the story of a middle-aged law clerk who drifts into an adulterous affair which provides him with the first rich human relationship, the first real happiness, of his life; he learns that it is nevertheless destructive for others and therefore evil. Few American reviewers could accept the novel's patly tragic ending (and Anthony West called the book "sanctimonious fudge") but most readers were impressed by its skillful organization and fascinated by Estang's exact observation of "every shift of Octave's agonized mind." A reviewer in the *Times Literary Supplement* concluded that Estang "has not François Mauriac's gift of making tragic actions seem inevitable"; that the novel's strength "lies in its lucid and sympathetic understanding of the religious temperament."

Estang has written studies of Bernanos (a major influence on his work) and of Saint-Exupéry, and has published essays on religious and literary subjects. He has received several important literary prizes and is a Chevalier of the Légion d'Honneur. Estang was married in 1939 to Suzanne Bouchereau-Boisgontier. He is an amateur art collector, and enjoys swimming and gardening.

PRINCIPAL WORKS IN ENGLISH TRANSLATION: The Better Song (novel), 1964. *Poems in* Strachan, W. J. Apollinaire to Aragon: Thirty Modern French Poets, 1948; Poetry September 1952.

ABOUT: Boisdeffre, P. de. Une Histoire vivante de la littérature d'aujourd'hui, 1938–1958, 1958; Boisdeffre, P. de. Dictionnaire de littérature contemporaine, 1900–1962, 1962; Chalecka, M. E. Luc Estang, 1952; Peyre, H. French Novelists of Today, 1967; Rousselot, J. Panorama critique des nouveaux poètes français, 1952; Who's Who in France, 1971–1972. *Periodicals*—France Illustration March 18, 1950; New York Times Book Review January 26, 1964; Times Literary Supplement March 26, 1964.

EVANS, ABBIE HUSTON (December 20, 1881–), American poet of Welsh descent, was

ABBIE HUSTON EVANS

born in Lee, New Hampshire, the daughter of Lewis Darenydd Evans and the former Hester Huston. She was educated at Radcliffe College, receiving her B.A. in 1913, her M.A. in 1918. In 1923 she joined the staff of the Settlement Music School in Philadelphia, where she was to teach for thirty years.

Her first book, a small volume of lyrics called *Outcrop*, appeared in 1928, when she was in her late forties. A similar volume, *The Bright North*, was published ten years later. The response to both was favorable but unenthusiastic. Miss Evans was docketed as a New England nature poet, competent, perceptive, and moderately original in her imagery, and then she was forgotten.

Only one critic of any weight seemed to find more in these poems, and that was Edna St. Vincent Millay, who provided a preface for *Outcrop*. "Read these poems too swiftly," she warned, "or only once, and your heart may still be free of them. Read them again, with care, and they will lay their hands upon you." What she had found was a special fragrance, delicate, subtle, and unexpected, and an inseparable mixture of music and meaning in verses that "sing partly to the ear and partly to the mind."

Because Miss Evans is a traditional poet, and one who has allowed little of her work into print, it was more than twenty years before Edna Millay's judgment was vindicated. At last, at the age of eighty, Miss Evans published another book of lyrics, *Fact of Crystal*, and the critics vied with each other to honor her. Babette Deutsch praised above all "the joy and courage" she found in these poems, and wrote: "It is her intense delight in the sensual world, a delight deeply tinged with a feeling for its awfulness, that links this perceptive octagenarian with such other poets as Traherne and Emily Dickinson. . . . The strength of her verbs, the freshness of her adjectives, the liveliness of her nouns, derive as much from her responsiveness to life as from the love of language for its own sake." Louise Bogan, suggesting comparisons with Emily Dickinson and also with Hopkins, added that these poems "include work of such profound inspiration that small modern categories and classifications fall in confusion before them." Odell Shepard spoke of the title poem as "a work of unquestionable grandeur, produced by a woman whom it is high time we recognized as a major poet of our day."

In 1953 Miss Evans left the Settlement Music School, but spent four more years on the staff of the College Settlement Farm-Camp. She received the Guarantor's Prize from *Poetry* in 1931, a Loines award from the National Institute of Arts and Letters in 1960, and an honorary doctorate from Bowdoin College in 1961. Since 1940 she has served on the advisory board of *Contemporary Poetry*. She is also a member of Phi Beta Kappa, Americans for Democratic Action, and the American Civil Liberties Union.

PRINCIPAL WORKS: Outcrop, 1928; The Bright North, 1938; Fact of Crystal, 1961; Collected Poems, 1971.
ABOUT: Millay, E. St. V. *Foreword to* Evans, A. H. Outcrop, 1928; Who's Who in America, 1970–1971. *Periodicals*—Nation April 1, 1961; Poetry March 1939.

EVANS-PRITCHARD, SIR E(DWARD) E(VAN) (September 21, 1902–), English anthropologist, was born in Crowborough, Sussex, the second son of the Reverend Thomas Evans-Pritchard. After attending Winchester College and Exeter College, Oxford, he went on to study anthropology under Professor C. G. Seligman at the London School of Economics. Seligman was so impressed by his student's ability that when ill health forced him to abandon the ethnographical survey he was conducting for the Sudanese government, he suggested that Evans-Pritchard should complete the work.

Evans-Pritchard made his first expedition to Zandeland in the Southern Sudan in 1926, and during the next four years lived there for a total of twenty months. From 1930 to 1933 he was professor of sociology at the Egyptian University, Cairo, and by 1939 had made six major expeditions to the Sudan. This work formed the foundation for a lifetime's study of the people of that region, particularly the Nuer and the Azande, on whom he was to become one of the world's foremost authorities.

His investigations among the Azande set a new standard for ethnographical field work. He lived

E. E. EVANS-PRITCHARD

for long periods at a time with the tribe, learning their language, adopting their customs, and constantly trying to reach beyond the outward appearances of their rituals and social relationships to the *meanings* which these held for them. He claims that he even found it expedient (and frequently helpful) to order his daily affairs by constant reference to oracles, as the Azande did themselves. When he published his first book *Witchcraft, Oracles and Magic Among the Azande* (1937), Seligman was moved to write: "No one who reads this book will doubt that it is one of the leading works standing to the credit of British anthropology during the past few years."

Between 1935 and 1940 Evans-Pritchard was a research lecturer at Oxford, and in 1940 published *The Nuer*, which the *Times Literary Supplement* described as "probably the most seminal work in the social anthropology of politics that has yet appeared." During the war years he was engaged on active service, and produced for the British Military Administration in Cyrenaica a number of papers and monographs on the tribes of northeastern Libya. In 1946, after one year as reader at Cambridge, he was appointed professor of social anthropology at Oxford, a position he held until his retirement in 1970.

In recent years he has been able to devote more time to theoretical writing. The radio talks published in *Social Anthropology* and the lectures collected in *Theories of Primitive Religions* express his well-known and immensely influential views about the overall aims and methods of social anthropology. Evans-Pritchard sees no reason to suppose that human society is subject to universal laws, and believes that anthropology has more affinity with the humanities than with the natural sciences: "Social anthropology is a kind of historiography, and therefore ultimately of philosophy or art . . . it studies societies as moral systems and not as natural systems . . . it is interested in design rather than in process, and . . . it therefore seeks patterns and not scientific laws, and interprets rather than explains." Thus, he argues, religions are most usefully studied in their own particular ethnographic contexts, not as clues to some universal source which would explain all religious phenomena. His writing is elegant and scholarly, and reveals a deep and respectful knowledge of the whole tradition of European and American writing in philosophy, history, and the social sciences. In his recent books, it has been said, Evans-Pritchard breaks no new ground and "makes no attempt to resume a position of innovating leadership," a fact "which in no way reduces his significance for the history of his subject."

Evans-Pritchard was president from 1949 to 1951 of the Royal Anthropological Institute, and is life president of the Association of Social Anthropologists. He is a Fellow of the British Academy, holds several honorary degrees, and is an honorary member of American and French learned societies. He was married in 1939 to Ioma Nicholls, who died in 1959, and has three sons and two daughters. He lives at Oxford, and lists his recreations as gardening and bird watching. Evans-Pritchard was knighted in 1971.

PRINCIPAL WORKS: Witchcraft, Oracles and Magic Among the Azande, 1937; The Political System of the Anuak, 1940; The Nuer, 1940; The Sanusi of Cyrenaica, 1949; Social Anthropology, 1951; Kinship and Marriage Among the Nuer, 1951; Nuer Religion, 1956; Essays in Social Anthropology (1932–1961), 1962; Social Anthropology and Other Essays (combining Social Anthropology *and* Essays in Social Anthropology), 1964; Theories of Primitive Religion, 1965; The Position of Women in Primitive Societies (essays, 1928–1963), 1965; The Zande Trickster, 1967; The Azande: History and Political Institutions, 1971.

ABOUT: Kuper, A. Anthropologists and Anthropology, 1973; Who's Who, 1973. *Periodicals*—American Anthropologist December 1963, December 1966; Geographical Journal January 1942; Nature August 3, 1946; Times Literary Supplement September 20, 1963; May 13, 1965; December 16, 1965; December 3, 1971.

EVERSON, WILLIAM OLIVER. *See* ANTONINUS, BROTHER

EVTUSHENKO, EVGENY. *See* YEVTUSHENKO, YEVGENY

EWART, GAVIN (BUCHANAN) (February 4, 1916–), British poet and critic writes: "W. H. Auden has given it as his opinion that no poet should ever write an autobiography; and it is certainly true that the work is more important than the life.

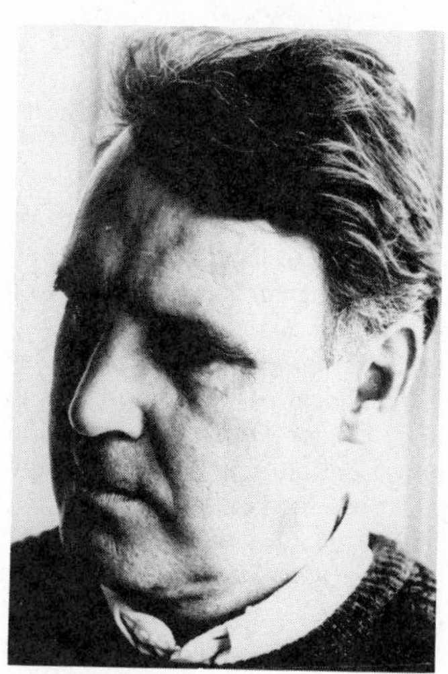

GAVIN EWART

"However, the few facts that follow perhaps do not do great violence to this wise general rule. I was born in London, of a Scottish father and an Anglo-Scottish mother; and, apart from war service I have lived in London all my life. My father was a surgeon at St. George's Hospital, and my mother also came from a medical family; but no pressure was put on me to become a doctor. My education was conventional. At the age of eight I went to what in England is called a Preparatory School—Wellesley House at Broadstairs—and from there at the age of thirteen to Wellington College in Berkshire. From the age of about eleven I had written poetry, but it was not until I was seventeen, in the summer of 1933, that my first poems were published in *New Verse*, Geoffrey Grigson's famous 'little magazine.' My English master at Wellington was T. C. Worsley, later well known as a dramatic critic; and to him I owed my introduction to the poetry of Auden, the criticism of F. R. Leavis, and the writers of the 'modern movement' in general.

"From Wellington I went in 1934 to Christ's College, Cambridge; where I 'read' first Classics and then English. My supervisor in English was Dr. F. R. Leavis, and I was an enthusiastic attendant at the lectures of Dr. I. A. Richards. I left Cambridge in 1937 and worked as a travelling salesman (lithographs) and a research worker on behalf of the Brewers' Society, until the outbreak of war in 1939. In 1938 my first collection of poems, *Poems and Songs*, was published.

"I served in the Royal Artillery during the war,

writing very little. In 1946 I came back to England from Italy and worked first for a publisher under the aegis of Tambimuttu, the Editor of *Poetry London*, and then on the home staff of the British Council. In 1952 I became a copywriter in an advertising agency, and I have done this kind of work ever since.

"During the 1950s I wrote mainly light verse, and not very much of that; but at the beginning of the Sixties, with the encouragement of Alan Ross, the Editor of *The London Magazine*, I began to write more, and more seriously. Since then I have written a great deal of poetry, as well as critical articles and reviews. A book of topographical poems about London, called *Londoners*, appeared in 1964; and in the same year a small collection covering the fifties—*Throwaway Lines*. A new book of poems, *Pleasures of the Flesh*, was published in 1966. I consider that this book contains my best verse to date (even allowing for the fact that with all writers the latest is usually the greatest)."

Gavin Ewart went to his first literary party in 1933, when he was seventeen, and at Geoffrey Grigson's house in Hampstead met Auden, Spender, and MacNeice. Eliot had been his model, but Ewart "took up the light verse side of Mr. Auden's talent with resource and precocity," writing agreeable satirical poems about his social class and education. The class war seemed less relevant when the real one began and Ewart, as he says, thereafter wrote little until the 1960s. He broke his silence with *Londoners*, Betjemanesque light verse which prompted Cyril Connolly to call him "a cartoonist in verse," and *Throwaway Lines*, praised for its "refreshing impact," its "odd juxtaposition of sprightly grotesqueness and bland hymn-metres." With *Pleasures of the Flesh*, it was clear that Ewart had found his new theme; now, according to a writer in the *Times Literary Supplement*, "his position is that of the married man of fifty whose erotic desires are at once made sharp and ludicrous by their improbability of fulfilment." Most reviewers welcomed this volume of what one called "poems of personal situation, usually so fertile in their use of the properties of civilization, so true in their oblique feeling, so unobvious in the matter of metre, punch-lines, poetic logic."

PRINCIPAL WORKS (all poetry): Poems and Songs, 1938; Londoners, 1964; Throwaway Lines, 1964; Pleasures of the Flesh, 1966; Two Children, 1966; The Deceptive Grin of the Gravel Porters, 1968; The Gavin Ewart Show, 1972.

ABOUT: Symons, J. The Thirties, 1960. *Periodicals*—London Magazine February 1966; Times Literary Supplement November 19, 1964; April 14, 1966.

FAIRBURN, A(RTHUR) R(EX) D(UGARD) (February 2, 1904–March 25, 1957), New Zealand poet and journalist, was born in Auckland and educated at Auckland Grammar School. He was the son of Arthur Fairburn, for many years music critic of the *Auckland Star*. "I am a New Zealander of the fourth generation," Fairburn wrote. "My grandfather was born in this country in the year 1827. This is my country, and I am very glad to belong to it—in spite of everything." Like his father, who was well known as a cricketer, he was a brilliant sportsman, excelling at league Rugby, golf, competitive swimming, riding, and sailing. "Much of his verse," according to Allen Curnow, "is coloured by a romantic nostalgia for the athletic delights of youth in Auckland's warm latitudes, among the bays and inlets of the Hauraki Gulf."

After leaving school Fairburn went to work as an insurance clerk, writing poetry, painting, and designing textiles in his spare time. In New Zealand during the 1920s there was little interest in cultural things and few opportunities for young writers. The country had no major publishing house, no influential literary magazine, no literary traditions except those borrowed from England, which was still thought of as home.

The kind of writing which resulted from these conditions is perfectly exemplified in Fairburn's first book, *He Shall Not Rise*, which was, significantly, published in London. The poems it contained, though they had been written in New Zealand, were wholly English in inspiration and composed in emulation of Rupert Brooke and the "Georgians," showing "a pagan but generally decorous delight in nature and the physical senses, a gentle, melancholy lyricism, and some slight facility in turning epigrams." However, the last poem in the collection is a specific rejection of all this genteel lyricism and marks the end of Fairburn's prolonged literary adolescence: "Tonight I have taken all that I was / and strangled him that pale lily-white lad. . . ."

Thereafter, Fairburn, together with his friend R. A. K. Mason and a few other Auckland writers, began the task of creating a national literary tradition. The New Zealand writer, he said, "must be willing to partake, internally as well as externally, of the anarchy of life in a new place and, by his creative energy, give that life form and consciousness." He suggested that New Zealand writers should seek their models not only in England but in America: "We can understand Huck [Finn], the true colonial, where we can only pretend to understand Tom Brown, the English public-school boy." The short-lived but influential magazine *Phoenix*, which Fairburn wrote for and Mason edited, was an important beginning, and Fairburn pamphleteered, talked, argued, and worked for the development of an indigenous cultural consciousness for the rest of his life.

In 1931 meanwhile, after a year in England, Fairburn had married Jocelyn Mays and settled with her in Auckland. He became a lecturer in the history and theory of art at the Elam School of Fine Arts, a versatile and prolific journalist, and a very successful broadcaster—a role for which he was splendidly equipped by his conversational talents, his wit, and the warmth and vigor of his personality. He produced some amusing prose (collected in *How to Ride a Bicycle*), wrote radio scripts, became a popular football commentator, and for twenty years, according to Charles Brasch, was at the center of intellectual life in Auckland. But the diversity of his activities left him little time for poetry and, though he published one or two collections in the 1940s, his reputation rests principally on two volumes published in 1952. *Strange Rendezvous* collected the shorter poems he had written since 1929, many of them love poems. "Sensuous, passionate, profound, these love poems," wrote E. H. McCormick, "are unique in our literature. Death, equally pervasive and equally protean, is refuge, foe, the source of honour, the gate to a qualified immortality." The volume also contained a number of satiric poems, directed against the worldly and wealthy, and distinguished by a sharp deflationary wit. *Strange Rendezvous* showed that the romantic "lily-white lad" of *He Shall Not Rise* was not after all quite dead but had gained enormously in maturity and vigor.

Of Fairburn's longer pieces, collected in *Three Poems*, the most notable is the last, "To a Friend in the Wilderness." This elegiac poem is regarded by many as Fairburn's finest work, in which he records his "mature reflections on the material of his earlier work," and in which the lyricism which runs through all his verse finds a new suppleness and freedom of utterance. "Of no poem," writes McCormick, "can it be said more truly that it gives form and consciousness to the anarchy of life in New Zealand."

Fairburn was for some time assistant secretary of the Auckland Farmers' Union, and for the last six years of his life lectured at Auckland University. He died suddenly at the age of fifty-three, leaving four children. Rex Fairburn, a big, robustly handsome pipe-smoking man, was one of those, like Rupert Brooke, who seemed singled out by providence for special favor. Allen Curnow called him "a vigorous, versatile, wholly unaffected poetic personality: one who reconciled in a singular way, in his lyric style, the English and the traditional with the modern, the regional, and the personal." Charles Brasch says that Fairburn "loved living and lived fully, sometimes extravagantly" and wrote poetry which "has the generous largeness of the man himself."

A. R. D. FAIRBURN

PRINCIPAL WORKS: *Poetry*—He Shall Not Rise, 1930; Poems 1929–1941, 1943; The Rakehelly Man and Other Verses, 1946; Strange Rendezvous, 1952; Three Poems, 1952; The Disadvantages of Being Dead, 1958. *Prose*—How to Ride a Bicycle, 1947; The Woman Problem and Other Prose (essays), 1967.

ABOUT: Curnow, A. (ed.) The Penguin Book of New Zealand Verse, 1960; Johnson, O. A. R. D. Fairburn: Bibliography and Monograph (University of Auckland, 1958); McCormick, E. H. New Zealand Literature, 1959. *Periodicals*—Auckland Star March 26, 1957; New Zealand Herald March 27, 1957; Times (London) April 10, 1957.

FALKNER, JOHN MEADE (May 8, 1858–July 22, 1932), English novelist and scholar, was born at Manningford Bruce, Wiltshire, the eldest son of the Reverend Thomas A. Falkner and the former Elizabeth Grace Meade. He was educated at (but expelled from) Marlborough College, and at Hertford College, Oxford University, graduating in modern history in 1882. After leaving Oxford he went as tutor to the sons of Sir Andrew Noble, head of the armaments firm which became Armstrong, Whitworth & Company. Noble liked Falkner, a "tall, gaunt, voluble, charming man," and engaged him first as his own secretary, then as secretary of his company. Noble lived at Newcastle, and Falkner at first disliked the region, spending his spare time walking and cycling in Oxfordshire and Berkshire. He wrote excellent guides to both counties.

It is often said that Falkner was a poor businessman, but according to Sir William Haley there is no evidence of this. He had at any rate a talent for languages and a great capacity for friendship, and his company benefited from both. Falkner traveled widely on its behalf in Europe, South America, and the Far East. In 1901 he was made a director of

JOHN MEADE FALKNER

Armstrong, Whitworth, and from 1915 until his retirement in 1921 was its chairman.

Falkner was a learned medievalist, especially in paleography and liturgiology, and the antiquarian riches of northeast England had soon overcome his initial dislike of the region. He had settled in Durham, in a house on the Cathedral Close which he filled with choice antiques and his collection of missals. He served during his retirement as honorary librarian of the Dean and Chapter's Library at the cathedral, and as honorary reader in paleography at Durham University.

A collection of Falkner's poems, most of which had appeared first in such journals as *The Spectator*, was published by his friends after his death, but as a poet he was unremarkable. It is his novels which have survived. The first, *The Lost Stradivarius*, is a ghost story—one more instructive than alarming, packed with thinly disguised lectures on music, heraldry, and the occult. (It was nevertheless dramatized in 1965 for British television.) Falkner's second novel, *Moonfleet*, is altogether different—a story of smuggling in a Dorset village which V. S. Pritchett called "a brilliant *pastiche* of eighteenth-century adventure," and "a novel which has the sustained excitement, if not the richness of character, of the best work of Stevenson." The book was immediately recognized as a minor masterpiece, and in England has sold steadily ever since its publication. There was no American edition until 1951, but since then *Moonfleet* has been several times reprinted in the United States. The American historical novelist Walter D. Edmonds said of it: "It has the quality of books stumbled on in boyhood of completely transporting the reader into its own world."

The Nebuly Coat is "an imaginative romance" drawing heavily on Falkner's knowledge of heraldry and church history and architecture, about the wicked Lord Blandamer's efforts to conceal his bastardy and keep his inheritance. Blandamer (whose coat of arms gives the book its title), is a magnificently unscrupulous villain in the great romantic tradition. A "strange but beautiful tale" called "Charalampia" was published in the *Cornhill* magazine in 1916. The incomplete manuscript of a fourth novel was lost by Falkner, or stolen from him, at Newcastle railroad station.

Falkner died at his home in Durham at the age of seventy-four, and was survived by his wife, the former Evelyn Adye. He was buried at Burford, in Oxfordshire, whose small historic church he had "adopted" many years before. He was noted for his patience, dignity, and generosity, and was an excellent conversationalist—a man who enjoyed society but pretended to be a recluse. Falkner was honored by the governments of Japan, Italy, and Turkey, not for his work as a writer or antiquarian but for the services of his company to war.

PRINCIPAL WORKS: The Lost Stradivarius (novel), 1895 (U.S., 1955); Moonfleet (novel), 1898 (U.S., 1951); Oxfordshire (topography), 1899; Berkshire (topography), 1902; The Nebuly Coat (novel), 1903 (U.S., 1955); Bath, Its History and Social Tradition, 1918.

ABOUT: Dictionary of National Biography, 1931–1940; Grigson, G. (ed.) The Concise Encyclopedia of Modern World Literature, 1963; Pritchett, V. S. The Living Novel, 1946; Royal Society of Literature, Essays (new series) Vol. XXX, 1960; Who Was Who, 1929–1940. *Periodicals*—Times (London) July 25, 1932.

FALL, BERNARD B. (November 11, 1926–February 21, 1967), French historian, political scientist, and journalist, was born in Vienna the son of Léon and Anne (Selignan) Fall, and brought up in France, where his father sold engineering materials and the rest of the family was in the book trade. In World War II his father was a *maquisard* and was tortured to death by the Gestapo. His mother was deported as a hostage and never seen again. Bernard Fall himself joined the French Resistance at the age of sixteen and fought as a guerrilla in the Savoie mountains. At the end of the war he received the Medal of Liberated France.

From 1946 to 1948 Fall was a research analyst for the Nuremberg War Crimes Tribunal, and then began a hectic decade of work, study, and travel. He was enrolled at the University of Paris in 1948–1949 and the University of Munich in 1949–1950, combining his studies with work for the International Tracing Service and as assistant district manager of *Stars and Stripes*. At the end of 1950 he went to the United States as a Fulbright student at the University of Maryland. It was then that he began to specialize in Indochina, at the suggestion of a teacher who thought he should capitalize on his French background.

Fall was a graduate student at Johns Hopkins University in 1952 and the same year received an M.A. in political science from Syracuse University. In 1953 he made his first visit to Indochina, where he traveled with French forces in the field and prepared his doctoral thesis—presumably the work published in 1954 as *Viet-Minh Regime*. In 1954–1955 Fall was a research assistant at Cornell. His Ph.D. came from Syracuse at the end of 1955, and in 1955–1956 he taught and studied at American University in Washington, D.C. He went to Howard University in the same city in 1956, initially as associate professor and from 1962 until his death as professor of international relations. During his years at Howard he served as a consultant on Southeast Asian affairs and on guerrilla warfare to several government agencies.

Fall made half a dozen visits to Indochina (or, as it became, Vietnam) and often expressed his contempt for those who wrote of the struggles there from the safety of the United States. He was of medium height, but well built and, according to the New York *Times*, "cut a dashing figure" at the battlefront, "dressed in shorts and a sports shirt open to the middle of his chest and wearing specially tinted sunglasses." He was "a man of enormous enthusiasm as well as powerful intellect," whose ambition was nothing less than "to be the foremost military writer" of his generation. He became a fine journalist, the author of over two hundred and fifty articles in learned and popular magazines, and winner in 1966 of the George Polk Memorial award for outstanding interpretive reporting. His essays and books made him perhaps the most influential academic critic of American policy in Vietnam. Fall brought to his writing much learning, a workmanlike style, and the courage, patience, and skill to find the telling details which give such life to his reports. As a Jew—a member of an oppressed people—and as a guerrilla fighter, he wrote with a profound empathy for the Vietnamese and for Ho Chi Minh in particular. Fall spoke French, English, Polish, Russian, German, and some Vietnamese.

Street Without Joy, his account of key events in Indochina's successful struggle to oust its French masters between 1946 and 1954, takes its title from the name of a famous battleground, a desolate stretch of seacoast near Hué. The book was warmly admired, especially those sections based on Fall's own observation of the fighting, and is considered by some a minor classic of military reporting. (One reviewer complained that the author wrote "in not always very elegant American, while thinking in French." Fall's characteristic reply was that in fact he also *thought* "in not very elegant American. . . . It is a lovely language not to be elegant in.")

BERNARD B. FALL

A very clear and complete history of Indochina followed, *The Two Viet-Nams*. It provides an invaluable background to an understanding of the conflict there, and includes an unsurpassed portrait of Ho Chi Minh. Like most of Fall's books, it seemed to American reviewers biased in favor of the French and ungenerous in its view of the United States' role in Vietnam, but thoughtful, informed, and for the most part eminently sensible. The twenty-six articles collected in *Viet-Nam Witness* had been written between 1953 and 1966. They showed that Fall had sometimes changed his mind and had often been wrong, but confirmed his right to be considered "the most substantial student of the war in any language."

The last of Fall's books to appear during his lifetime was *Hell in a Very Small Place*, an account of the siege of Dien Bien Phu, which destroyed French power in Indochina. Fall had consulted secret French files and had interviewed hundreds of survivors of the battle in both Vietnams, France, and Algeria. His book, according to Paul Mus, is "a monument of accurate and vital information, written so directly and grippingly that one relives the drama with its actors, and one is happily surprised to find, after reading of so many moving episodes, that the Postface contains a list of those who survived the trial of combat and captivity. They have become, for the reader, real people." Such criticism as there was centered on Fall's discussion of America's failure to intervene in the battle—some thought his comments unjust and some found them inconclusive. To David Schoenbrun, among others, the book seemed "destined to be a classic."

Fall went to Vietnam for the last time in December 1966 on a Guggenheim Fellowship. He was delighted to find his books on the shelves of senior American officers and in the tents of many GIs. On February 21, 1967, he accompanied American marines into action in "the Street Without Joy." His last tape recording ends as he says: "It's a little bit suspicious . . . could be an amb—" At that point his jeep hit a Vietcong mine. The recording is transcribed in *Last Reflections on a War*, a collection of articles, tapes, and talks selected by his widow. She is the former Dorothy Winer, an American art designer whom he had married in 1954. Fall left four children. He had retained French citizenship, which gave him more freedom of movement than an American passport, but had been on the point of applying for United States papers. According to the *New Republic*, no one understood the war in Vietnam better than Fall, "or exposed more clearly or as early the danger of the deepening American military involvement. Vietnam was an agony to him. He lived with it wherever he was every day for more than a decade." Paul Mus wrote that he "was uncompromising in his commitment to his vision of history, and he insisted on describing it, and living it, to his last minute."

PRINCIPAL WORKS: Viet-Minh Regime: Government and Administration in the Democratic Republic of Vietnam, 1954; Street Without Joy: Indochina at War, 1946–54, 1961; The Two Viet-Nams: A Political and Military Analysis, 1963; (ed. with M. G. Raskin) The Viet-Nam Reader, 1965; Viet-Nam Witness, 1953–66, 1966; Hell in a Very Small Place: The Siege of Dien Bien Phu, 1966; Last Reflections on a War: Preface by Dorothy Fall, 1967; Anatomy of a Crisis: The Laotian Crisis of 1960–1961 (ed. by Roger M. Smith), 1969.

ABOUT: Contemporary Authors 4, 1963; Who's Who in America, 1966–1967; Who's Who in France, 1965–1966. *Periodicals*—Commonweal March 10, 1967; New Republic March 4, 1967; New York Times February 22, 1967; New York Times Book Review December 10, 1967; Newsweek April 11, 1966; March 6, 1967; November 20, 1967; Publishers' Weekly January 2, 1967; Time March 3, 1967.

***FANON, FRANTZ** (July 20, 1925–December 6, 1961), West Indian born philosopher of social revolution, was born in Martinique, French Antilles, and educated in Martinique and France. In 1944 he volunteered for the French army, fought in the war in Europe, and afterwards studied medicine and qualified as a psychiatrist at Lyons in 1951. As a student, he edited a newspaper for black students, called *Tom Tom*. Fundamental to his development was his encounter with the black intellectuals grouped around the cultural and political Paris review *Présence Africaine*, through which he came under the crucial influence of Aimé Césaire, the Martinican poet, and Jean-Paul Sartre. Césaire was to disappoint him, when as mayor of Port-de-France he was prepared to accept de Gaulle's plan for the French colonies in 1958. Sartre remained the most important intellectual influence of his life.

Fanon's first book, *Peau noire, masques blancs* (later translated as *Black Skin, White Masks*), was published in 1952. It is a study of the psychology of racism. Like other black intellectuals brought up in the French colonies, Fanon had been educated to regard French language and culture as his own. And like nearly all his fellows, he had also encountered racism. The contradiction between the explicit humanism of white civilization, and the implicit racism of white behavior, was the central experience of his youth. He learned that even academic distinction could not erase the stigma of a black skin: "When people like me, they tell me it is in spite of my color. When they dislike me, they point out that it is not because of my color. Either way, I am locked into the infernal cycle."

In *Peau noire, masques blancs* he sets out to analyze the psychological basis of racism. A myth of black sexual potency, he found, haunts white and black alike. He shows how this myth, while denying the black man the ability to assert his manhood through political or economic power, confers on him a stereotype which he either embraces by acting it out, or seeks to escape through assimilation—by adopting a "white mask." Either course, Fanon claims, is a kind of emasculation. The black man's dream is to possess a white woman (or to kill his desire once and for all by raping or murdering one); the black woman's image of herself is as rejected, undesirable, and her dream is to become white. The book showed that "from the very beginning," (as A. R. Zolberg wrote), Fanon "displayed a brilliant knack for transforming clinical insights into political poetry."

In 1953 Fanon married a young French woman and was appointed director of the Psychiatric Department of the Blida-Joinville Hospital in Algeria, just a year before armed revolution broke out. His experience in that hospital, treating the casualties of the struggle that followed, changed Fanon's ideas, and his life. Increasingly, he began to concentrate on the socio-economic causes of mental stress. Where he had at first attacked the myths of color as the main source of racist oppression, he began to see not a psychological aberration but a political phenomenon—colonialism based on technological power—as the enemy. He concluded that his aim as a psychiatrist—to "prevent man from feeling a stranger in his own environment"—could not be achieved by treating the man. It was the environment that must be changed.

Colonialism during the Algerian war showed its ugliest face. French soldiers and policemen became

* fä nôN′

systematic torturers. Algerians became informers against their families and comrades. Both tortured and torturers came to Fanon for treatment and he repeatedly risked his freedom and his career to shelter the former. He quotes the example of a European police inspector involved in torture sessions, who eventually found himself striking his own wife and children at home: "He asked me without beating about the bush to help him go on torturing the Algerian patriots without any prickings of conscience, without any behavior problems and with complete equanimity." Even French doctors, the men whose professional ideals he had adopted as his own, he found to be involved in the practice of torture. His bitter disappointment with the 1956 Mollet government, elected to end the war, and then with the French Communist party, which voted in favor of special powers for the Mollet government in Algeria, completed Fanon's disillusion with France. "When I search for man in the technique and style of Europe," he wrote, "I see only a succession of negations of man, and an avalanche of murder."

In 1956 he resigned his post, and put himself at the service of the Algerian liberation movement, the FLN. He became an editorial writer for the party's underground newspaper, *El Moudjahid*, published in Tunis; attended the First Congress of Black Writers and Artists, called by *Présence Africaine* in Paris in 1956; and the All African People's Conference in Accra in 1958. In 1960 he was appointed Ambassador to Ghana by the Algerian Provisional Government. Throughout this period he was regularly traveling in and out of Algeria. In 1959 he was badly injured when his jeep struck a mine on the Algerian border, and at least two attempts were made on his life soon afterwards, apparently by a French terrorist organization, the Red Hand. In 1960 he undertook a hazardous journey through Mali to explore possible supply routes to Algeria across the Sahara and barely escaped a French kidnapping attempt. The same year he contracted leukemia.

Fanon went to the Soviet Union for treatment, and then, reluctantly, to Washington, where he spent the last months of his life working furiously on his masterpiece, *Les Damnés de la terre* (1961, translated as *The Wretched of the Earth*). When he died, soon after its publication, his body was flown back to Algeria for burial. The following year Algeria won its political independence.

Les Damnés de la terre is the work which has established Fanon's reputation as a major contributor to the revolutionary philosophy of the Third World. In it, he develops his thinking on racism (expressed in *Peau noire, masques blancs*) and colonialism (expressed in essays collected in 1959 and 1964) into a philosophy of revolution. The

FRANTZ FANON

Algerian struggle had convinced him that the colonial victim could free himself of oppression only by socialist revolution; that revolution must be achieved by violence; and that the instrument of revolution would not be the urban proletariat, as traditional Marxists assert, but the poor peasants, the wretched of the earth.

He reached these conclusions along a number of paths. His medical experience, he maintained, taught him that the victim of colonialist violence could win back his manhood and his emotional wholeness only by using violence himself; that what his patients needed was not psychiatric treatment, but guns in their hands. His travels to independent African states taught him that negotiated independence changes only the skin color of the masters, not the way of life. And his disillusionment with the French Left convinced him that the solidarity of the workers of the world was a myth. Instead, he argued that the developed countries as a whole, working classes included, benefit from colonial exploitation, that indigenous black middle classes do the same, and that even black urban workers have something to lose. Only the poor peasants (like the Algerian *fellaheen*)—the very bottom of the exploitative heap—have nothing to lose and are the only class uncorrupted by the individualistic values of Western materialism. According to Fanon, they are the authentic revolutionary class of the Third World, and indeed of the whole world.

Fanon's theories on the "healing" properties of violence (which have much in common with those of Georges Sorel), and on the role of the peasantry, have been seriously challenged by other revolutionary thinkers. David Caute, author of the first full study of Fanon in English, finds contradictions in his arguments for violence, and even in the psychiatric evidence he advances, and points out that Fanon generalizes from his experience in Algeria, with little knowledge of the rest of Africa and less of Asia and Latin America. His program is vague and his doctrine incomplete, and his qualities indeed are those of a poet and prophet rather than a theorist. Yet the importance of his contribution to social philosophy is acknowledged even by his critics. Building on Marxism, and on Sartre's *Critique of Dialectical Materialism*, he drew from his experience as a psychiatrist and his exacerbated creative imagination a new vision of the sources of racism, colonialism, and revolution. Though he is still better known in the West than in his adopted continent, his ideas are increasingly quoted by black militants in the United States and debated in radical publications throughout the world, and their full consequences are yet to be seen.

Much of Fanon's work has been published posthumously in English. A. R. Zolberg has spoken of his "hallucinatory imagery, which links him with Rimbaud and Jean Genet"; Saul Maloff says that "he surrounds, overpowers and evokes his subject as a poet might; but, as he was also a scientist, he employs all the weapons at his disposal, especially his wide and deep learning in psychoanalysis, philosophy and literature. The result is a strange, haunting mélange of existential analysis, revolutionary manifesto, metaphysics, prose poetry and literary criticism—and yet the nakedest of human cries." *Black Skin, White Masks* was described by Robert Coles as the product of "a brilliant, vivid and hurt mind, walking the thin line that separates effective outrage from despair," and *The Wretched of the Earth* has been called "a rock thrown through the windows of the West."

PRINCIPAL WORKS IN ENGLISH TRANSLATION: The Damned, 1963 (republished as The Wretched of the Earth, 1964); Studies in a Dying Colonialism (essays), 1965; Toward the African Revolution (essays), 1967; Black Skin, White Masks, 1967. *See also* Présence Africaine June–November 1956 (special issue on the First Congress of Negro Writers and Artists).

ABOUT: Beauvoir, S. de. Force of Circumstances, 1964; Caute, D. Fanon, 1970; Cranston, M. W. (ed.) The New Left, 1971; Geismar, P. Fanon, 1971; Gendzier, I. L. Frantz Fanon: A Critical Study, 1973; Howe, I. (ed.) Beyond the New Left, 1970; Rose, P. I. (ed.) Americans From Africa, vol. 2, 1970; Woddis, J. New Theories of Revolution, 1972. *Periodicals*—African Affairs January 1969; America November 1, 1969; Choice December 1967; Encounter November 1966; Esprit April 1962; Horizon Winter 1972; Journal of Modern African Studies 4 1968; Monthly Review May 1969; Nation June 21, 1965; New Society January 4, 1968; New York Times Book Review April 30, 1967; Newsweek April 24, 1967; La Pensée February 1963; Présence Africaine 40, 1962; Quatrième Internationale 15, 1962; Revue de l'Institut de Sociologie 2–3, 1967; Saturday Review April 24, 1965; July 17, 1971; Studies on the Left May–June 1966; Time April 30, 1965.

***FARGUE, LÉON-PAUL** (March 4, 1876–November 24, 1947), French poet and essayist, was born and spent his life in Paris. He was the son of a stained-glass and ceramics maker, a descendant of the Renaissance architect Pierre Lescot and the seventeenth century philosopher Pierre Bayle. The marriage of Fargue's parents, opposed by his paternal grandmother, did not take place until he was thirty. He felt his illegitimacy keenly, but was nevertheless devoted to his parents and seems to have had a happy childhood. He was educated at the Collège Rollin (where Mallarmé was his English teacher), at the Lycée Janson-de-Sailly, and at the Lycée Henri IV (where he and his classmate Alfred Jarry studied philosophy under Henri Bergson). Fargue was intended for a teaching career but rejected this prospect in favor of literature.

He was a precocious poet and *Ludions*, published in his old age, contains some extremely clever poems written when he was twelve. While still in his teens he was a cofounder of the review *Le Centaur* and when he was eighteen his poem sequence "Tancrède" was published in *Pan*. At about this time Fargue, whose work was already known and liked by the Symbolists, became a regular visitor at Mallarmé's famous "Tuesdays" on the rue de Rome, where he met among others Verlaine, Renoir, and Debussy. In 1896 *Mercure de France* devoted almost an entire issue to his poetry, though it was not until many years later that his work became widely known and appreciated.

His father died in 1899, to Fargue's great grief, but the glassworks continued to provide him with an income, though one scarcely large enough for his prodigal way of life. This "great bear with the eyes of a Persian prince," a cigarette always drooping from his lips, wandered Paris endlessly, especially at night, and was at home in every part of his city, from the fashionable salons to the cafés of St.-Germain and the lowest bars of Montmartre. He despised and dined off the aristocracy, was "adored by duchesses, petted by girls." His judgment in literature, music, and painting was shrewd and advanced, and he numbered among his close friends Ravel and Stravinsky, Cézanne, Picasso, and Braque, and many major writers of the period. His acquaintances believed that he lived in bars and taxis, and accepted his assurance that his only ambition was "to enjoy my sensuous life lazily, and any laziness sensuously."

In fact, this pose masked, as André Beucler said, Fargue "the man of letters, hard-working, cultured, and conscientious." A fastidious craftsman, he published relatively little poetry and is remem-

* färg

bered principally as a link between symbolism and surrealism. The first edition of his *Poèmes*, said to resemble in their condensed and close-packed imagery the work of Rimbaud, did not appear until 1912. It attracted little attention, though it greatly influenced a small circle of admirers. After a long silence, this collection was reissued in 1918 with much greater impact. In 1919 Fargue contributed to the first issue of the surrealist review *Littérature*, and in 1924 he was associated with Valéry Larbaud and Paul Valéry in the direction of another review, *Commerce*. Two collections of poetry appeared in the late 1920s, *Espaces* and *Sous la lampe*. The first includes "Vulturne," a fantastic vision of the primeval world, and the dreamlike "Épaisseurs"; the second contains "Suite familière," a notable statement of Fargue's artistic opinions.

From the beginning his poetry, like Fargue himself, half-concealed behind a gay and witty façade an acute sensibility, a deep melancholy. Most of his poems are in prose, "a fusion of the colloquial and the mysterious," and seek through lyrical daydreams and memories of childhood an escape from the harshness and banality of real life. Dreams fascinated him and this, together with his experiments in sound and imagery, his respect for and delight in the power of words, links him with surrealism. Fargue admired the Surrealists but was too much the son of his father—too devoted and deliberate a craftsman—to share their enthusiasm for "automatic" writing. In fact, though Fargue was a member of no school, it is possible to find intimations of many literary modes in his work: Robert Kemp, for example, has called him "the real father of Dadaism . . . who invented it without saying so, perhaps without knowing it . . . and who remains the most exquisite and enchanting of the image jugglers." Others have sought to define the elusive quality of his poetry through musical comparisons —most helpfully, perhaps, with the études of Chopin. Valéry, who valued his work highly, wrote: "His invention is limitless, so prompt, so fecund and frequent, that it gives an impression of stasis, and of infinitely sustained scintillations . . . [combined with] the most simple and sad tenderness."

After about 1930, Fargue wrote little poetry, perhaps because of his delighted discovery that some newspapers, unlike the literary quarterlies, paid on receipt—perhaps for less mercenary reasons. At any rate, he devoted himself during the last part of his life mostly to newspaper columns about Paris restaurants and nightclubs, to radio talks, memoirs, and the superbly evocative essays about Paris collected in *Le Piéton de Paris* and elsewhere. At least half his writings are about Paris, and he has been called "the poet of the melancholy of cities." In 1939 he married the painter Chériane.

LÉON-PAUL FARGUE

Four years later he was partially paralyzed by a stroke and he died, after a long illness borne with much fortitude, in 1947. Always unsure of himself, he had coveted public recognition. Election to the Académie Française eluded him, but he achieved membership in the Académie Mallarmé, the Prix de la Renaissance and, shortly before his death, the Grand Prix of the City of Paris.

PRINCIPAL WORKS IN ENGLISH TRANSLATION: The Magic Lantern, 1948. *Poems in* Fowlie, W. (ed.) Mid-Century French Poets, 1955; Hartley, A. (ed.) Penguin Book of French Verse 4, 1959; Strachan, W. J. Apollinaire to Aragon, Thirty Modern French Poets, 1948.

ABOUT: Beucler, A. The Last of the Bohemians: Twenty Years with Léon-Paul Fargue, 1954 (England, Poet of Paris); Chonez, C. Léon-Paul Fargue, 1950; Fowlie, W. (ed.) Mid-Century French Poets, 1955; Hackett, C. A. An Anthology of Modern French Poetry, 1965; Smith, H. (ed.) Columbia Dictionary of Modern European Literature, 1947. *Periodicals*—Horizon May 1949; Mercure de France December 1, 1935; April 15, 1936; New York Times November 26, 1947; Sewanee Review April 1933.

"FARLEY, RALPH MILNE." *See* WEINBAUM, STANLEY GRAUMAN

***FEDIN, KONSTANTIN (ALEKSANDROVICH)** (February 24, 1892–), Russian novelist, was born in Saratov, on the Volga. His father, the son of a serf, had built up a small business of his own as a stationer; he was a self-taught man who collected religious books and had tried to write poetry. Fedin's mother, the daughter of a village schoolteacher from a remote part of the Penza district, had been educated by her grandfather, a priest, and "brought the customs of a Russian

* fye′ dēn

KONSTANTIN FEDIN

clerical family into our home." From the age of seven until he was fourteen Fedin studied the violin. His childhood was unhappy because "our life was strictly ordered, according to rules made by my father once and for all, like a calendar. There was a sense of compulsion in everything. By the time I was fifteen I felt unbearably fettered at home, and was doing very badly in my studies, and in December 1907 I pawned my violin and ran away to Moscow." His father soon found him and brought him back, and after another attempt to run away in 1908, Fedin settled down for three years in a commercial school in Kozlov (now Michurinsk); it was here that he first dreamed of becoming a writer.

He continued to write during the three years he spent at a Moscow commercial college, his first publications appearing in the Petersburg magazine *Novy Satirikon* in 1913. In the spring of 1914 he went to Germany to improve his knowledge of the language and was interned when war broke out, though he was able to travel around Saxony and Silesia giving Russian lessons, singing and acting in the Zittau and Görlitz theatres, and meanwhile writing a novel which he subsequently destroyed. In the autumn of 1918 he was sent back to Moscow in a prisoner-of-war exchange, and after a period of editing a magazine in Syzran on the Volga he was mobilized into the Red Army and sent to Leningrad late in 1919. Here in 1920 he struck up a friendship with Gorky, and a year later became one of the founders of the "Serapion Brothers," a movement established under Gorky's patronage in reaction against "compulsion and boredom," and the exclusive preoccupation of the literature of the period with social and contemporary themes.

Fedin's first book was *Pustyr* (The Wasteland, 1923), a collection of seven stories set for the most part in prerevolutionary times and imbued with the poetic and melancholy flavor of Bunin's or even Chekhov's Russia. In his first major work, the novel *Goroda i gody* (1924, translated by M. Scammell as *Cities and Years*), Fedin introduces the themes which were to preoccupy him for the next thirty years: the relationship of Russia and Europe, the psychological impact of the Revolution, the role of art, and the search for a more positive hero to replace the "superfluous man" who had been a major character in previous Russian literature. *Goroda i gody* is the tragedy of Andrey Startsov, a typical member of the Russian intelligentsia who tries but fails to commit himself wholeheartedly to the Revolution. Caught in Germany by the 1914 war, Startsov returns to Russia after the Revolution and encounters his friend Kurt, a German artist who has become a dedicated Communist. Hamlet-like doubts and hesitations lead him to betray both the girl he loves and the Red cause in the Civil War, and Kurt kills him, thus doing for him "all that should be done by a comrade, a friend, and an artist."

It was in this novel that the liberating Serapion influence on Fedin first appeared, and it is an altogether more complex, mannered, and experimental work than *Pustyr*. This is most evident in its organization: it begins with Andrey's death and thereafter ranges back and forth between Germany and Russia, between 1914 and 1922, between "cities and years," ignoring chronology and following instead the pattern of Andrey's recollections. There are humorous touches reminiscent of Laurence Sterne, and long digressions that are virtually autonomous stories within the novel. The book provoked heated debate because of its fusion of realistic narrative with new stylistic devices, and also of course because of its frankly ambiguous attitude to the Revolution. Critics accused Fedin of having too much sympathy with his weak-willed, vacillating hero, even though this "superfluous man" is eventually killed. As one critic observed: "To diagnose your own sickness does not mean that you have been cured of it," and Professor E. J. Simmons believes that Fedin's struggle to overcome his doubts about communism—to accept that its ends justify its means—is the central factor in his emotional and creative life. Many Western critics, however, regard the book as one of the half dozen outstanding Soviet novels, and at least one thinks it superior to Pasternak's *Dr. Zhivago*.

Fedin's experience of living in a village in the Smolensk region between 1923 and 1926 resulted in the stories of peasant life which appeared in book form in 1927 as *Transvaal*. The title story, the longest and best, is a strange and psychologically profound study of a strong-willed and hypocritical Estonian of Boer extraction who despises his fellow peasants and exploits them to build up a private village empire.

In his second novel *Bratya* (The Brothers, 1928), Fedin returns to the problem of the intellectual, this time the composer Nikita Karev, who tries to escape from the revolutionary struggle into the realm of pure art. The early, prerevolutionary life of the Karev family is brilliantly depicted in the manner of nineteenth century Russian realistic fiction. Returning to postrevolutionary Russia Nikita finds his father and his younger brother Rostislav, an intransigent Bolshevik, on opposite sides in the Civil War. Rostislav is killed, and afterwards Nikita tries to serve in his own way the cause for which his brother died, trying to communicate by means of a symphony not only his own torments and aspirations but those of his whole generation. In this way Fedin strove to blend the humanitarian traditions of the past with the new demands of a new society, and this novel was more favorably received by Soviet critics than his earlier one.

Fedin at this time became seriously ill with tuberculosis. He spent most of the next seven years, 1928–1934, in a Swiss sanatorium and traveling throughout Western Europe. The impact of this experience on his work, as well as on his ambivalent social and political views, is clearly apparent in his fiction. These were the years of the Depression, and his next book contrasts the deteriorating social and economic conditions of the West with the economic advance in the Soviet Union: the two-volume *Pokhishchenie Evropy* (The Rape of Europa, 1933 and 1935) is however usually regarded as his weakest book. The short novel *Sanatorii Arktur* (Arcturus Sanatorium, 1940) is a psychological study of illness in the patients, and indeed in some of the doctors, in a Swiss sanatorium.

The years of the Nazi invasion of Russia were among Fedin's busiest and most productive, during which he began a trilogy of historical novels and published two volumes of *Gorky sredi nas* (Gorky Amongst Us, 1943–1944), a valuable account of Russian literary life which grew out of his extensive correspondence with Gorky in the 1920s and early 1930s. The first volume was widely praised, but the second was just as widely condemned, expressing as it does Fedin's own belief in the unconscious (and nonpolitical) springs of artistic creation. The projected third volume did not appear, though Fedin was reportedly working on it during the 1960s.

Fedin was also criticized for remaining outside politics at a time when his country was fighting for its life, but in fact he spent much time as a reporter at the front, witnessing the terrible destruction and loss of life in the invasion. A deep feeling of patriotism helped him to resolve his ideological uncertainties, and he turned away from his preoccupation with the West to purely Russian material in the huge historical trilogy *Pervye radosti* (1944, translated by H. Kazanina as *Early Joys*), *Neobyknovennoye leto* (1947–1948, translated by M. Wettlin as *No Ordinary Summer*), and *Koster* (1961–, translated in part as *The Bonfire*). The trilogy has its champions, but many critics consider that Fedin's style has lost its earlier distinction, and complain of some historical falsification in the trilogy.

Slonim described Fedin as "a highly civilized writer whose stature may not be great, but whose aspirations to link the Soviet novel with the traditions of nineteenth-century Russian realistic narrative have been not without success, and whose sincerity, good faith, and profound humanism make him one of the most attractive, if not most original, representatives of Soviet prose." Fedin's novels have received many awards and prizes, and since 1959 he has been secretary general of the Union of Soviet Writers, where he has avoided extremes of literary policy and, in the words of Max Hayward, "proved to be an excellent exponent of the policy of 'consolidation.' "

PRINCIPAL WORKS IN ENGLISH TRANSLATION: Early Joys, 1948; No Ordinary Summer, 1950; Cities and Years, 1962; The Orchard *in* Great Soviet Short Stories, 1962; The Bonfire *in* Soviet Literature 1 and 2, 1962, 8, 1965; Carp *in* Soviet Literature 11, 1963. *Essays in* Atlantic June 1960; Soviet Literature 1, 1962.

ABOUT: Alexandrova, V. A History of Soviet Literature, 1963; Blum, J. M. Konstantin Fedin, 1967; Braynina, B. Konstantin Fedin, 1962; Brown, E. J. Russian Literature Since the Revolution, 1963; Hayward, M. and Labedz, L. (eds.) Literature and Revolution in Soviet Russia 1917–62, 1963; International Who's Who, 1970–1971; Reavey, G. Soviet Literature Today, 1946; Simmons, E. J. Russian Fiction and Soviet Ideology, 1958; Slonim, M. Modern Russian Literature, 1953; Slonim, M. Soviet Russian Literature, 1964; Struve, G. 25 Years of Soviet Russian Literature (1918–1943), 1944; Swayze, H. Political Control of Literature in the USSR 1946–1959, 1962. *Periodicals*—The New Leader February 18, 1963; Slavonic Review April 1937.

***FEIS, HERBERT** (June 7, 1893–March 2, 1972), American economist and historian, was born in New York City to Louis J. and Louisa (Waterman) Feis. Specializing in economics at Harvard University, he took his B.A. degree in 1916 and, after World War I service in the Navy, received his Ph.D. in 1921. His primary interest at this time was labor relations, which he made the subject of his earliest books, including *The Settlement of Wage Disputes* (1921). For several years after leaving Harvard he acted as an adviser at the International Labor Office of the League of Nations in Geneva.

* fīz

HERBERT FEIS

Eugene Burdick once observed that Feis wrote "with the sure-footedness of an intellectual who has been within the Establishment of both government and the academy." He began in the academy, teaching economics during the 1920s at the University of Kansas and the University of Cincinnati. Then while employed in 1931 on the staff of the Council on Foreign Relations in New York, he accepted an appointment as economic adviser in the State Department in Washington. Surviving the transition between the outgoing Republican administration of Herbert Hoover and the incoming Democratic administration of Franklin D. Roosevelt, he remained with the Federal Government until 1947, at the State Department for about a dozen years and at the War Department for the following three. From 1949 to 1962 he was intermittently a member of the Institute for Advanced Study in Princeton, New Jersey.

Feis's experience in Washington during a crucial period of American history gave him an insider's view of many of the occurrences that he recorded as a historian. *Seen from E.A.: Three International Episodes* (1947) and *1933: Characters in Crises* (1966) are among his books that deal with salient events at home and abroad in the 1930s, and most of his accounts, especially those involving economic affairs, bear the special authenticity and directness of an eyewitness.

In 1950 Feis began his five-volume diplomatic history of World War II with *The Road to Pearl Harbor*, a chronicle of events leading up to the United States entry into the war. He ended it in 1961 with *Japan Subdued*, in which he explored, among other issues, the complex problems involved in the American decision to drop the atom bomb. The fourth volume in his series, *Between War and Peace* (1960), a comprehensive account of the Potsdam Conference, won him the Pulitzer Prize in history.

Although Feis's direct and indirect participation in many of the world-shaking developments of his time often animates his narrative, he was seldom accused of partiality. On the other hand, his standing as "court historian" earned him privileged access to important source materials not available to other historians. This did not apply when he was gathering material for the most important of his subsequent books, *From Trust to Terror*, a summary and analysis of the breakdown in relations between the victorious allies after World War II. With the postwar archives still closed, Feis wrote to some extent as a "shackled historian," and the result was a valuable but controversial interim report on the sources of the Cold War.

A sharp and practiced analyst, Feis brought an unsurpassed capacity for organization to a tangled bulk of conflicting points of view and contradictory information on exceedingly intricate matters. He could write eloquently, but usually preferred to sacrifice the colorful and dramatic for a tone which is characteristically humane, sober, and exact, though not lacking in sometimes mordant humor.

Soon after completing his graduate work at Harvard, Feis married Ruth Stanley-Brown, on March 25, 1922; they had one daughter, Mary Felicia. For many years he made his permanent home in York, Maine, where he had room to keep at hand his sizable collection of books, letters, and other documents. His research often took him elsewhere. He also left Maine to lecture occasionally and to garner such honors as the Liberty and Justice Award of the American Library Association (1958) and an honorary Litt.D. degree from Princeton University (1961).

PRINCIPAL WORKS: The Settlement of Wage Disputes, 1921; Europe, the World's Banker, 1870–1914, 1930 (2nd ed., 1964); The Changing Pattern of International Economic Affairs, 1940; Sinews of Peace, 1944; Seen from E. A.: Three International Episodes, 1947; The Spanish Story: Franco and the Nations at War, 1948; The Diplomacy of the Dollar, 1950; The Road to Pearl Harbor, 1950; The China Tangle, 1953; Churchill-Roosevelt-Stalin, 1957; Between War and Peace, 1960; Japan Subdued, 1961 (rev. as The Atomic Bomb and the End of World War II, 1966); Foreign Aid and Foreign Policy, 1964; 1933: Characters in Crisis, 1966; Contest Over Japan, 1967; The Birth of Israel: The Tangled Diplomatic Bed, 1969; From Trust to Terror: The Onset of the Cold War, 1970.

ABOUT: Contemporary Authors 9–10, 1964; Current Biography, 1961; Who's Who in America, 1970–1971. *Periodicals*—American Historical Review October 1961; Book Week March 27, 1966; Book World December 6, 1970; New York Review of Books June 15, 1967; New York Times May 2, 1961; New York Times Book Review August 21, 1960; April 30, 1961; January 17, 1971; Saturday Review October 1, 1960; June 24, 1961.

FERLINGHETTI, LAWRENCE (March 24, 1919?–), American poet, novelist, dramatist, and publisher, was born (according to his own account in *Contemporary Poets of the English Language*), in Yonkers, New York. He is the son of Charles Ferling, an auctioneer who had emigrated from Italy at the turn of the century, and the former Clemence Monsanto. (The family name, shortened by his father to Ferling, was restored by Lawrence Ferlinghetti when he came of age.) His father died shortly before he was born, and his mother was committed to an asylum shortly afterwards. He spent his early childhood in France with a member of his mother's family, Emily Monsanto. She subsequently brought him back to the United States. Ferlinghetti says that after an interlude in an orphanage at Chappaqua, New York, he "spent many years in a mansion of a branch of the Lawrence family which founded Sarah Lawrence College in Bronxville, New York," where Emily Monsanto had obtained a post as a French governess. After a time she left him there and, Ferlinghetti says, "later died in an asylum at Central Islip, Long Island, unknown to LF. . . . Little else is known. . . ."

In fact a great deal more is known or at any rate generally reported about Lawrence Ferlinghetti: that he has a B.A. from the University of North Carolina, where he wrote unpublished prose in emulation of Thomas Wolfe and Ernest Hemingway; that he served from 1941 to 1945 in the United States Naval Reserve, taking part in the Normandy invasion as a lieutenant commander; that he subsequently earned a Columbia M.A. (1948) with a thesis on Ruskin and Turner; and that he studied for four years at the Sorbonne on the GI Bill, receiving a doctorate in 1950. He was for a while during this postwar period an employee of *Time* magazine.

The early history of Ferlinghetti's famous City Lights Bookstore in San Francisco is rather less clear. Peter Collier, whose interview with the poet appeared in the New York *Times Book Review* on July 21, 1968, says that Ferlinghetti went to San Francisco in 1951, and at first earned his living by teaching French to adult education classes. Ferlinghetti is quoted as saying that he opened City Lights in a vacant store in 1953. A letter from F. W. Howton, published in the *Times Book Review* on September 8, 1968, claims that City Lights was established in 1951 by Peter Martin, and sold to Ferlinghetti in 1953 as a going concern.

It was in any case Ferlinghetti who gave City Lights its place in American literary history. It is at 261 Columbus Avenue, in San Francisco's North Beach section, which in the early 1950s was just beginning to replace the International Settlement as the city's bohemian quarter. The store, open seven days a week until midnight or later, is on

LAWRENCE FERLINGHETTI

three floors, packed with American and foreign paperbacks, avant-garde periodicals, broadsheets, posters, and pamphlets. It became an informal reading room and salon for the young writers who formed what is remembered as the Beat Movement, and soon it became their champion, midwife, and publisher.

The first publication in the City Lights "Pocket Poet" series was Ferlinghetti's own first book of poems, *Pictures of the Gone World* (1955). Allen Ginsberg's *Howl*, which launched the Beat Movement as an international literary phenomenon, was published as Number Four in the series in October 1956. Ferlinghetti appeared as defendant in the celebrated trial of *Howl* for obscenity, a transcript of which has been published as *The Howl of the Censor* (1961). He won his case, and the sales of *Howl* benefited greatly from the resultant publicity. Also on the City Lights list are Gregory Corso, Jack Kerouac, Alan Watts, Michael McClure, William Burroughs, and others who were leading figures among the beats, or their heirs the hippies, or both.

Most of Ferlinghetti's own books, apart from the first, have been published by New Directions. They have enjoyed great popular success but on the whole have had only a moderately enthusiastic critical reception. Ferlinghetti wants "to get poetry out of the inner esthetic sanctum and out of the classroom into the street," and his work has the faults and virtues of oral poetry. His second and best-known book, *A Coney Island of the Mind,* appeared in 1958. Harvey Shapiro thought it "a grab bag of undergraduate musings about love and art, much hackneyed satire of American life and some real and wry perceptions of it." Hayden Carruth could detect in it no trace of "respect for the capacities of language," no "sensitivity to its sounds and speeds." *Starting from San Francisco*, published with the author's recording of three of the poems, was admired for its "gusto and surreal inventiveness" and its "mastery of spoken rhythms" but seemed to some reviewers vulgar and superficial. However, James Schevill thought that "the phrasing, which often seems repetitious and oversimplified on the page, takes on a new color and dimension in terms of the dramatic intent of his voice."

Ferlinghetti's novel, *Her*, is an almost plotless account of the narrator's pursuit of the woman who represents for him all women, the female principle itself. One reviewer called it "a highly romantic throwback to surrealist experiments" which occasionally "achieves a fizzing rhetorical (and scatological) wit." The author has also published two volumes of experimental short plays, and a volume of translations from the *Paroles* of Jacques Prévert (1959).

Ferlinghetti has been active as a book designer, graphic artist, and painter, as well as a writer. He is a socialist and calls himself a "*Catholique manqué*." In 1960 he and Allen Ginsberg participated in the Pan American cultural conference in Chile, and he has traveled a great deal in South and Central America, the Far East, and Europe. He was married in 1951 to Seldon Kirby-Smith and has two children. Peter Collier described him as a gaunt and balding man with very blue eyes. When Collier interviewed him, he was just recovering the grizzled beard he surrendered over Christmas 1967, when he was jailed for participating in a peace demonstration at the Oakland Army Induction Center.

After the hippies installed themselves in Haight-Ashbury, the City Lights Bookstore ceased to be San Francisco's intellectual center, but Ferlinghetti has no regrets. "The fifties were good," he says, "but what's going on today is much more exciting as far as I'm concerned. . . . The Beat generation has been gone a long time now, but what isn't gone are the things it began." Ferlinghetti has expressed an interest in making films: "Publishing just isn't that exciting any more. Like everybody is saying, the written word seems a little obsolete." All the same, Allen Ginsberg remarked in 1969 that Ferlinghetti deserved "some sort of Nobel Prize for publishing" because of the extent to which his work has enriched the culture.

PRINCIPAL WORKS: *Poetry*—Pictures of the Gone World, 1955; A Coney Island of the Mind, 1958; Starting from San Francisco, 1961; An Eye on the World: Selected Poems (England only), 1967; The Secret Meaning of Things, 1969; Tyrannus Nix, 1969; Open Eye, Open Heart, 1973. *Plays*—Unfair Arguments with Existence: Seven Plays for a New Theatre, 1963; Routines: Short Plays, 1964. *Novel*—Her, 1960. *Nonfiction*—The Mexican Night: Travel Journal, 1970.

ABOUT: Allen, D. M. (ed.) The New American Poetry 1945–1960, 1960; Contemporary Authors 7–8, 1963; International Who's Who, 1972–1973; Murphy, R. (ed.) Contemporary Poets of the English Language, 1970; Stanford, D. E. (ed.) Nine Essays in Modern Literature, 1965; Who's Who in America, 1972–1973. *Periodicals*—Nation October 11, 1958; New York Times Book Review July 21, 1968; September 8, 1968; Poetry November 1958, July 1964; Reporter December 12, 1957; Saturday Review October 5, 1957; September 4, 1965.

FERMOR, PATRICK (MICHAEL) LEIGH

(February 11, 1915–), Anglo-Irish travel writer and novelist, is the son of a distinguished geologist, Sir Lewis Leigh Fermor, and the former Eileen Ambler. He was educated at King's School, Canterbury, but then, instead of preparing for the military career his parents had intended for him, elected to spend four years traveling in Europe, the Near East, and the Greek archipelago.

In 1939, with the outbreak of World War II, Fermor enlisted in the Irish Guards. He fought in Greece with the British Military Mission of 1940, and was later liaison officer at Greek headquarters in Albania. Between 1942 and 1944, disguised as a shepherd, he worked with the resistance movement in German-occupied Crete. It was during this time that he led the guerrilla force which captured General Kreipe, commander of German forces on Crete, and delivered him to British authorities in Cairo. This exploit, one of the most audacious of the war, was described by Fermor's partner, W. Stanley Moss, in *Ill Met by Moonlight* (1950). Major Fermor, who received an OBE in 1943 and a DSO in 1944, was later made an honorary citizen of Heraklion, capital of Crete. He finished the war in northern Germany, as a team commander in the Special Allied Airborne Reconnaissance Force.

After the war, Fermor spent a year as deputy director of the British Institute in Athens and then resumed his travels. His first book, *Traveller's Tree*, is a record of his wanderings in the Caribbean in 1947 and 1948. In England it won him the Heinemann Foundation Prize and the Kemsley Prize, and was immediately and universally recognized as the work of "a born writer." The *Times Literary Supplement* called it "a picture in which the historical, social and visual elements are beautifully combined" and said that Fermor's "range of interest is so wide and his fund of knowledge so heterogeneous that, almost in spite of himself, he gives a picture . . . of far more than temporary interest."

A Time to Keep Silence contains Fermor's "meditations" on the value that he, an unbeliever, finds in occasional monastic retreats. It reflects a quality present in all of Fermor's best work—an acutely

PATRICK LEIGH FERMOR

sensitive response to and imaginative sympathy with ways of life whose ruling beliefs are unfamiliar or even unacceptable to him. This short lucid book was followed by a novel, *The Violins of Saint-Jacques*, about a remote and feudal Caribbean island. It was praised for its evocative power but thought more successful as a splendid spectacle than as a work of fiction; it nevertheless provided the basis for Malcolm Williamson's successful opera of the same name.

Mani and *Roumeli* are both travel books about regions seldom visited and scarcely known, the southern Peloponnese and northern Greece. Together they confirmed Fermor's reputation as one of the finest living writers in the tradition of Richard Burton, Doughty, and T. E. Lawrence—a traveler to desolate and intractable places and peoples which he has the skill to record in superbly vivid prose, and the learning to comprehend through all the resources of history, myth, and folklore. Thus in *Mani* a caïque captain's shouted order evokes thoughts on "the demotic nomenclature of Aegean winds" and other incidents inspire asides on, for example, Greek mysticism, Phanariot headgear, and early Christian saints. It is this "interplay between a culture as remote as Homer's and his own civilised mind" which gives his books their unique density. Those who object that Fermor's "passion for words [and] greed for detail" encumber his narrative are outnumbered by readers like Freya Stark, who relish "the felicitous profusion, the exuberance of learning and information" in his books.

Fermor is a Fellow of the Royal Geographical Society and of the Royal Society of Literature, and is a contributor to *Atlantic Monthly* and *Holiday*, among other magazines. He has translated Colette's *Julie de Carneilhan* and *Chance Acquaintances*, and *The Cretan Runner*, an account of the German occupation of Crete by G. Psychoundakis. Fermor was married in 1968 to the Honorable Mrs. Joan Rayner, daughter of the first Viscount Monsell.

PRINCIPAL WORKS: The Traveller's Tree, 1950; A Time to Keep Silence, 1953; The Violins of Saint-Jacques (novel), 1953; Mani: Travels in the Southern Peloponnese, 1958; (with Stephen Spender) Ghika—Paintings, Drawings, Sculpture by N. Chatzekuriakos-Grikas, 1964; Roumeli, Travels in Northern Greece, 1966.

ABOUT: Current Biography, 1955; West, P. The Modern Novel, 1963; Who's Who, 1971. *Periodicals*—Times Literary Supplement December 19, 1950.

***FEYDEAU, GEORGES (LÉON JULES MARIE)** (December 8, 1862–June 5, 1921), French dramatist, was born in Paris into a prosperous middle-class family of aristocratic antecedents. His father, Ernest Aimé Feydeau, was a stockbroker and an amateur archaeologist; he was also a friend of Flaubert and Gautier and a writer of some reputation during the Second Empire, whose realist novel *Fanny* (1858) achieved considerable notoriety. His mother, Lodzia Zelewska, was a well-known Polish beauty whose classical features her son inherited. The Goncourt brothers mention the boy's exceptional charm and prettiness in their famous *Journal*.

Feydeau was first taken to the theatre at the age of six or seven and enjoyed the experience so much that he sat up overnight to write his first play. When his governess called him to study early the following morning, his father ordered her to leave him undisturbed. Thus, Feydeau always claimed, he discovered that the theatre could be a refuge from the governesses of this world, and chose his profession out of laziness.

A dramatic monologue called *La Petite Révoltée* (1880) was the first of Feydeau's works to be professionally performed. A number of other monologues, most of them comic, were recited with great effect in the Paris cafés and music halls during the early 1880s, and his first one-act play, *Gibier de Potence*, was produced when he was twenty-three. A number of full-length comedies followed during the next few years, and Feydeau's first major success, *Champignol malgré lui*, ran for six hundred performances at the Théâtre des Nouveautés in 1892–1893. For the next fifteen years his farces, often starring Marcel Simon or Germain, dominated light comedy in Paris.

The famous French actor Lucien Guitry once asked Feydeau if he had a part for him. The dramatist replied after some thought that there were only two important roles in his plays, he who kicks and

* fā dō′

GEORGES FEYDEAU

he who gets kicked; the second was the starring role, an unsuitable one for Guitry. There is an element of truth in this courteous reply, but there is more to Feydeau's plays than simple slapstick.

Marcel Achard has identified three phases in Feydeau's work, characterized by the nature of his heroines. His first plays, much influenced by Labiche, feature timidly immoral bourgeois wives and are pure bedroom farce, complex, implausible, governed by a wild logic of their own. They include such famous comedies as *L'Hôtel du Libre-Échange*, which ran for five hundred performances in France in 1894 and was revived with great success fifty years later in London as *Hotel Paradiso*.

The plays of Feydeau's middle and greatest period, according to Achard, are closer to the English comedy of manners. Their heroines are gay, determined, and emancipated young women, and their plots show a degree of simplification to allow the author more room for witty social observation. Many of Feydeau's most memorable plays belong to this period: *Le Dindon* (1898), produced in New York as *There's One in Every Marriage* in 1972, when it was also staged in England, in a different translation, as *Ruling the Roost; La Dame de Chez Maxim* (1899), which had a long run in London as *The Lady from Maxim's; La Puce à l'oreille* (1907), staged in London in 1968 as *A Flea in Her Ear*, in a version by John Mortimer which was also filmed; and *Occupe-toi d'Amélie* (1908). The latter, considered by many to be Feydeau's masterpiece, was adapted (not very successfully) by Noël Coward as *Look After Lulu* (1959).

Among Feydeau's later plays are *Mais n'te promène donc pas toute nue!* (1912), *On purge Bébé* (1910), *Hortense a dit: 'J'm'en fous!'* (1916), and the posthumous *Cent millions qui tombent* (1923). Less successful than his earlier work, the plays of this period are notable for their shrewish heroines, and are comedies of character rather than farces.

For twenty years after his death Feydeau was dismissed as a trivial entertainer, but in the years since World War II he has been increasingly recognized as a master of theatrical technique and elegantly economical dialogues. His plays have entered the repertory of the Comédie-Française and Jean-Louis Barrault and have been widely translated. Jacques Guicharnaud said that Feydeau, "in applying the rules of *vaudeville* with the intransigence of a mathematician, arrived at a kind of formal perfection, a theatricalism which places him far above his predecessors, his contemporaries, and particularly his successors." Marcel Achard (who is the best known of those successors) thinks Feydeau the greatest French comic dramatist since Molière.

Feydeau's vast output and long years of success brought him great wealth, much of which he squandered on unfortunate speculations. He was a brilliant conversationalist, knew everyone, but had only a few close friends. Robert de Flers described "his elegance, his physical distinction, his smiling and detached manner. . . . He was very friendly but with a certain coldness . . . ambitious but modest, hardworking but nonchalant, good-humored but sad." As a young man Feydeau had been much in demand as an actor, and nearly made that his career—he reportedly abandoned the idea when a producer called him to an audition and then kept him waiting. He was married to a daughter of Charles Durand (Carolus-Duran), the portrait painter. Feydeau was a Chevalier of the Légion d'Honneur and an officer of the French Academy—an extraordinary honor for a light-comedy writer.

PRINCIPAL WORKS IN ENGLISH TRANSLATION: Hotel Paradiso, 1957; Look after Lulu, 1959; A Flea in Her Ear, 1968; Cat Among the Pigeons, 1970; Four Farces (Par la Fenêtre, Le Mariage de Barillon, Un Fil à la patte, On purge Bébé), 1971.

ABOUT: Penguin Dictionary of the Theatre, 1966; Skinner, C. O. Elegant Wits and Grand Horizontals, 1962. *Periodicals*—Nation December 13, 1952; New Yorker April 20, 1957; March 18, 1961; Saturday Review December 13, 1952; October 13, 1956; April 6, 1957; Spectator March 20, 1959; Theatre Arts April 1957, June 1957, March 1958; Times (London) June 6, 1921; Times Literary Supplement June 18, 1971.

FIEDLER, LESLIE A(ARON) (March 8, 1917–), American literary critic and novelist, writes: "I was born in Newark, New Jersey, on March 8, 1917, and lived in and around Newark for the next twenty-one years, which is to say, through the period of the Depression which was exactly contemporaneous with the making of my mind. I like to think that there was no better place for enduring the melancholy of the thirties; but it is probably only inverted chauvinism which makes me believe that there are not scores of other cities equally drab and undistinguished. 'But who ever came out of Newark?' we used to ask each other in those days, possessed as we were by an undefined kind of ambition and a somewhat more sharply focused conviction of the inevitability of failure. And when someone had answered, 'Well, there's always Stephen Crane,' we would stare at each other in silence, since that just about did it.

"Still, I managed to get educated in Newark, not so much by the schools themselves, though even there an occasional idea would glimmer briefly and die—but chiefly in the Public Library, in Military Park and at various radical meetings which possessed in those days a life not less vivid for being rather unreal. The books on the open shelves of the library, the bums and hoboes in the Park eager to tell lies to one young enough to believe them, the street-corner speakers yelling over the hecklers: all these suggested to me the difficulty and allure of communication, created for me an image of the writer-speaker (even what I write for print is silent speech) trying to be heard over the roar of traffic and the whispered jokes of a hostile audience.

"And all the while I was being brainwashed by a school system aimed at depriving me of the vulgar authentic speech of my childhood, the speech of a second-generation city Jew, and substituting for it an imaginary WASP non-language proper to the spiritual descendants of Dick and Jane. Yet after a while I became convinced that the way into the great libraries which contained the books that spoke a living language lay through the schools; and so I committed myself to the business of earning degrees (B.A. at New York University in 1938, M.A. in 1939 and Ph.D. in 1941, both at Wisconsin) as a method of preparing myself for a lifetime of teaching, i.e., of talking about the books I loved to those learning to love them. A soft touch it seemed to me, and infinitely preferable to the careers I had dreamed of earlier of journalism (à la *Front Page*) or acting or defending the guilty in Courts of Law whose premises I despised.

"The East, however, came to seem to me finally unendurable—partly because of its physical ugliness, partly because of the high visibility in its streets and shops of all the good things a poor and greedy boy could not have. Graduate school in Wisconsin turned out to be the first stage of my trek West—or more properly, of my flight from the East; since I did not know what I was pursuing, had not even a myth much less a real notion of the West in my head, only a desire to get the hell out of wherever the hell I was. But I hardly lived in Madison, Wisconsin, as a place, too busy getting

LESLIE A. FIEDLER

degrees and a wife and my first child and the job which took me to a more ultimate West, to Missoula, Montana.

"From 1941 to 1964, Montana State University was my home base, and in a crazy way it is Montana which has made me, city-boy that I basically am. Certainly it is a Montana landscape I see when I close my eyes, its people I imagine understanding, or more often misunderstanding me. And in this sense, I have to think of myself as a Western writer. In Western space, at any rate, I defined myself and my career, began to bring up my six children, conceived most of my books, articles, stories, poems; came to be known (first nationally, then locally—which is the Montana way) as a 'wild man of literature,' though I have always considered myself as more reasonable than wild, a good bourgeois, eminently cautious, though passionate, too. But the book reviewers in New York and the legislators of Montana agreed with each other in disagreeing with me—chiefly, I suppose, because being a Westerner by adoption (at one point I was even inducted into the Blackfoot tribe) I was able to perceive the true nature of that peculiarly 'Western' brand of love which bound Huck to Jim on the raft, and Natty Bumppo to Chingachgook in the virgin forest.

"I never quite had to flee Montana, though I traveled a lot from time to time (sometimes at what struck me as being especially appropriate moments to get out) for a little while. It was, I suppose, the enforced tourism of World War II which first taught me to be a traveler, taking me to Honolulu, Iwo Jima, Guam, eventually China. During that War I was an interpreter of Japanese—

another exercise in communicating between hostile sides and being only approximately understood by both. But I was also forced (in a series of letters to my wife) to become an interpreter of my absent self and of the world of my wanderings, which I experienced as utterly unreal but felt the obligation to render real.

"After the War, my own impulses plus a Rockefeller Fellowship took me to Harvard where I began writing stories in earnest; since the world I returned to seemed to me no more real than the one from which I had returned, and the obligation I had learned in exile persisted at home. I had thought of myself initially as a poet, and have continued to write verse all my life—but from the late forties on fiction has intrigued me more. Criticism I stumbled into, beginning with reviews and articles suggested to me by my editors, not quite willing to accept my stories but somehow eager to have me work out on certain notions of their own. Suggestions from the outside have, as a matter of fact, most often seemed to me preferable to those I cooked up myself; since I am superstitious enough to believe that the pattern of my life ought to be given from moment to moment rather than invented.

"Next to editors, the officers of Foundations have helped most to shape my fate. A Fulbright Fellowship, for instance, removed me to Italy for two years (1951–1953), where I acquired the nearest thing to a second language I have ever achieved (Japanese I forgot with much more joy than I had ever experienced learning it); and I was forced for the first time in my life to lecture on American literature. I had always before felt our own books an improper subject for the classroom, finding in them too much private pleasure for public exploitation. But explaining them and our character and fate as reflected in them—has seemed to me ever since a part of my destiny, as necessary and unchosen as being a Jew. The final fruit of my Italian lectures was *Love and Death in the American Novel*, though I did not actually publish that fat, complex book until 1960; by which time I had committed myself permanently to wandering about the world (Greece and Yugoslavia, England and Israel and Turkey) as well as up and down our country—looking for cues and responding to invitations, talking, talking, talking as I never grow weary of doing.

"Still Montana remained my home—the place from which I started and to which I returned (happy always to leave it again, but just a little happier to come back)—until 1964 when I moved to the State University of New York at Buffalo, for reasons I do not yet entirely understand. Perhaps I was only trying to prove to myself that I was still young enough to leave home for a second time. In Buffalo, I completed my second novel, *Back to China*, revised *Love and Death* and put the finishing touches on a collection of short fiction called *The Last Jew in America*, and in Buffalo I stubbornly continue to teach, as has always been my practice, what I do *not* write about: Shakespeare, Renaissance lyric poetry etc. But asked abroad where I come from, I find myself still saying, 'Montana.' To my children, too, it has remained somehow home, though they move about as restlessly as I to places like Florence, Tokyo, Paris, San Francisco and the Fiji Islands. I guess it is a mythic home I long for and which Montana seems, as I longed for it in my quite un-mythic Newark thirty years ago.

"To be a writer anyhow these days is to enact a role mythological enough, sometimes too patly mythological to bear. But it is not the myths of the literary life—the customary talk of 'alienation' or 'commitment,' both of which finally separate the writer from his audience—for which I yearn. What intrigues me is the communal dream which writer and audience both dream below the level of all customary lies, of politics and piety and public speech: the American dream of mutual betrayal and endless flight, which readers consider it scandalous to be reminded of but can never forget; and which I have committed myself to pursue as critic and poet, in prose and in verse, into the absolute West which is its proper home."

Leslie Fiedler emerged as a passionate, exciting, and often deliberately provocative critical essayist in the early 1950s. His first two books, *An End to Innocence* and *No! In Thunder*, were both collections of pieces originally published in magazines and had a lively reception. Fiedler's interests are at least as much social and psychological as literary, and his approach is fundamentally Marxist and Freudian. What infuriates his critics is not his often startling ideas, or even his habit of lapsing at times into incomprehensible academic jargon, but his need (as Irving Howe puts it) "to dazzle and display, to thrust his ego between the reader and his ostensible subject to remain—all else failing—brilliant, brilliant, brilliant to the last bitter and anxious word." For all that, as most of his reviewers have conceded, Fiedler often *is* brilliant, and brilliantly illuminating.

The fullest exposition of his views is the one he gives in the vast, diffuse, ill-organized, and consistently entertaining *Love and Death in the American Novel*. It is less a work of conventional criticism than an exploration of the mythic dimensions of American cultural history, and a spiritual autobiography. It seeks to define what the dominant themes and patterns of American fiction reveal about the American consciousness. What preoccupies Fiedler is "the absence of vivid or convincing female characters in our greatest novels; the odd love affair, pure and physical at once, between males, colored and white . . . ; our tormented ambivalence towards the natural world," and, above all, "the predominance of the Gothic tradition, of terror and death and violence, in the works we love best." With characteristic panache, Fiedler has claimed that *Love and Death* is itself as much a novel as a work of criticism, and a Gothic novel at that: "My long, darkly comic study is a Gothic Novel or it is nothing."

The reviewers of this study were not prepared to say that it was nothing. Some found it nasty, tasteless, effusive, and violently partial, but few denied its fascination, and V. S. Pritchett wrote that "his lack of interest in literary values does not detract from the perspicacity of Mr. Fiedler's anthropological words on Gothic romance." Since then the book has gradually been recognized as the major work of a critic who at his best is (as Saul Maloff says) "wonderfully suggestive, not in the way of most criticism, but in the way of imaginative literature."

Fiedler resumed his argument in *Waiting for the End*, which looks at the development of American literature from Hemingway to James Baldwin in a spirit of jaunty apocalypticism (and sometimes unfortunately at the level of literary gossip). *The Return of the Vanishing American*, the third and final volume in Fiedler's "venture in literary anthropology," sees resurgent in the national subconscious a notion of anarchic savagery associated once with the American Indian, now with the hippies and dropouts, the inhabitants of a "New West" of the spirit. Fiedler's *Collected Essays*, published in two volumes in 1971, show that he has recently, as he says, "been willing to cross the border which once separated High Art from Pop." He believes that it is "necessary to develop a really new criticism, free of all vestiges of . . . elitism and the Culture Religion," and now discusses movies, comic books, pop songs and Japanese prints as well as such academically respectable subjects as the plays and poems of Shakespeare (whose latent dread of women, Jews, and other alien archetypes is scrutinized, often convincingly and with "astonishing virtuosity" in *The Stranger in Shakespeare*).

According to their lights, the critics have found Fiedler's fiction deliberately nauseating or "ruthlessly honest" in its portrayal of a diseased society. Most agree that Fiedler is capable of highly effective set pieces, but that his fiction as a whole is uneven in style and technical accomplishment, and that he tends to analyze his characters to death. Maloff, reviewing the three novellas that make up *The Last Jew in America*, points out that Fiedler's fiction is peopled with the same archetypal figures—Jew and Goy, Negro and Indian—that occupy him in his criticism: "We keep expecting them to spring to new and surprising life in his fiction—leap free of all fetters, sprung free by an imagination answerable to no text, to nothing but itself. But nothing much happens."

In 1967 Fiedler found himself the center of a new, nonliterary debate when he and other members of his family were arrested and charged with "maintaining a premise" where marijuana was smoked. Fiedler denied this charge. He had agreed to act as faculty adviser to a student organization campaigning for the legalization of marijuana and believes that, on this account, and because of his progressive and "permissive" attitude toward young people, he was victimized, persecuted, and spied upon. A national controversy developed. Fiedler received much support from liberals and intellectuals, but also death threats, and he was subjected to a variety of economic and social sanctions. He has described his arrest and its sequel in *Being Busted*, which is also a partial autobiography and a statement of his educational views. In 1970 he returned from a year in England to face trial, and with his wife, the former Margaret Shipley, was found guilty. Fiedler, sentenced to six months in the penitentiary, appealed his conviction, which was struck down in 1972 by the New York Court of Appeals. The court concluded that "it was never contemplated that the criminal taint would attach to a family home should members of the family on one occasion smoke marijuana or hashish there," and that therefore "no crime was charged or proven." In 1970–1971 he taught at the University Center at Vincennes, in France, on a leave of absence from Buffalo.

PRINCIPAL WORKS: *Fiction*—Pull Down Vanity (stories), 1962; The Second Stone, 1963; Back to China, 1965; The Last Jew in America (3 novellas), 1966; Nude Croquet (collected stories), 1969. *Nonfiction*—An End to Innocence, 1955; No! In Thunder, 1960; Love and Death in the American Novel, 1960 (rev. ed., 1966); Waiting for the End, 1964; The Return of the Vanishing American, 1968; Being Busted, 1970; Collected Essays (two vols.), 1971; The Stranger in Shakespeare, 1972.

ABOUT: Bergonzi, B. (ed.) Innovations, 1968; Bryden, R. The Unfinished Hero, 1969; Current Biography, 1970; DeMott, B. Hells and Benefits, 1962; Malin, I. Jews and Americans 1965; Schulz, M. F. Radical Sophistication, 1969; Simon, J. The Acid Test, 1963; Sutton, W. Modern American Criticism, 1963; Vinson, J. (ed.) Contemporary Novelists, 1972; Who's Who in America, 1972–1973. *Periodicals*—Book Week May 17, 1964; Chicago Review Autumn 1960; Christian Science Monitor April 25, 1968; Commentary January 1967; National Review July 28, 1964; New Republic December 5, 1960; May 11, 1968; New York Herald Tribune Book Review April 10, 1960; New York Review of Books July 9, 1964; July 13, 1967; New York Times April 30, 1967; May 6, 1967; August 23, 1967; April 10, 1970; July 7, 1972; New York Times Book Review March 27, 1960; May 31, 1964; July 31, 1966; March 17, 1968; December 10, 1972; Saturday Review March 19, 1960; May 23, 1964; March 30, 1968; Times (London) April 18, 1960; March 15, 1968; Yale Review June 1960.

GABRIEL FIELDING

"FIELDING, GABRIEL" (pseudonym of Alan Gabriel Barnsley) (March 25, 1916–), English novelist and poet, writes: "My mother, Katherine Mary Fielding Barnsley, recently wrote to me from her home in Melbourne, Australia. She said: 'I am now re-reading *Greenbloom* and have got as far as poor little Victoria's murder. I remember the case you took that from; but it left little impression on me, whereas your writing has haunted me. I can think of few other writers who have had your gift. I think Bulwer Lytton came nearest to it and perhaps one or two others; but they, like Scott and Fielding, are all inclined to be too wordy and haven't your gift of spell.'

"I quote this letter because it reminds me of those evenings in my earliest childhood when my mother was writing. I see her vulcanite and gold fountain pen, already green with age, as in her small hand it rushed over the paper in the hall of the dark north country vicarage where I spent my boyhood. At these times her face was bright and girlish. She would bully us all six out of her excitement and conviction. From the landing upstairs I would sometimes watch her unseen as, nowadays, I have occasionally found my own children spying on me.

"Although, even before this, after reading my first book, I had secretly decided that I was going to be a storyteller myself, I now know that it was her ardour and longing—not for me but for her own work—that contributed to my determination. When I grew older I even became jealous of her confidence and excitement, occasionally wishing that she might fail so that I could take over. For in those later days of my adolescence I was her chief confidant and audience—the cheer-leader who kept her at it when publishers, editors and theatre managers let her down.

"I think there may be two kinds of writers, those to whom it is an escape, narcissistic and solitary, and those who are over-busy and greedy. My mother and I belong to the second group; our writing is neither an escape nor a fulfilment; it is not an emotion recollected in tranquillity because we are never tranquil. We are both of us people who are simultaneously in the audience and on the stage: we talk and tell out of an intense and ceaseless activity, totally engaged in being 'here.' We write only in order that we may ourselves realise what's been going on.

"When it came to it, my mother's own disappointments went against me. She persuaded me to take up medicine so that I should have my bread and butter and be of some use to people. Though she was excited when I had some small success as an undergraduate litterateur at Trinity College, Dublin, she was always afraid of encouraging me too much in later life. She would say, 'If only you knew how much it has hurt me.' And we would quarrel over the telephone and the three hundred and fifty miles that then separated us.

"Eventually, an illness caused by the stresses of my medical work and the feeling that I had never really started my life, gave me the chance to write in earnest: first, some verse and later my stories.

"I published my first novel, *Brotherly Love*, in 1954. It was followed by the remainder of the trilogy and one intervening book in which I tried to record the inner experiences of my conversion to Roman Catholicism.

"In 1959 I decided that I had finished an apprenticeship to the novel and that it was time to attempt a less subjective approach to fiction. I chose a theme which, though it was at a great distance from myself, was one which had long obsessively concerned me as a European. I started work on *The Birthday King* at that time; a study, from the inside, of people born and living in the Germany of Hitler. Published in 1962, the book was a success and went into paperback both in my own country and in the United States. Although it is still discussed it has not brought me much money and I never expected that it would."

Gabriel Fielding was born at Hexham, Northumberland, the fifth of six children of George Barnsley, a well-to-do "sporting" parson of the Church of England. His mother, by whom he has remained fondly fascinated, was a commercially unsuccessful playwright and a successful breeder of whippets—a combination such as Fielding the novelist always enjoys; she has been described by Evelyn Cavallo as the "scourge and stimulus" of his early life. Fielding remembers his childhood as "a beautiful golden blur," then "a terrible separation when I was sent away at the age of eight to a snob preparatory school in the south of England, where everything and everyone, from the masters to the hens, seemed hostile. I think that this, in a sense, was the beginning of the pain out of which I write."

Fielding went on to St. Edward's School, Oxford, and in due course began his medical studies at Trinity College, Dublin, graduating in 1939, and completing his training at St. George's Hospital, London. Wartime service in the Royal Medical Corps followed, and Fielding left the army in 1946 with the rank of captain. After the war he built up a varied general practice as a physician in Maidstone, Kent, where among other things he attended the inmates of Maidstone Prison (an experience on which he has drawn in his fiction). As he says, it was not until he was nearly forty that his literary career began in earnest, though after the success of his first novel he steadily reduced his medical commitments.

In *Brotherly Love*, John Blaydon observes the conflict between his domineering mother and his eldest brother David, who is forced against his will and nature to enter the church and is driven to gradual self-destruction. Reviewers pointed out that the book's ten chapters each deal with a dramatic episode complete in itself, but still subtly integrated with the rest, and embodying a sense of mounting drama that makes the novel compulsively readable. "Despite the sombre depths of the book," Dan Wickenden wrote, "its surface is lively, glittering with humor and a somewhat acrid wit. . . . And the characterization is brilliant, especially of the doomed, philandering, increasingly alcoholic David himself, and of his appalling, forceful mother."

John Blaydon's adolescence is the subject of *In the Time of Greenbloom*. His girl friend Victoria is raped and murdered, and he descends into a mood of terrible grief and irrational guilt from which he is gradually rescued by the patient friendship of Horab Greenbloom. Paul Pickrel thought it "one of the finest novels to come out of England since the second world war." *Through Streets Broad and Narrow* deals with Blaydon's medical studies in Dublin, and seemed to some reviewers overplotted —"a brilliant, infuriating, awkward novel—rather like Blaydon's own character." Whitney Balliett said of the trilogy that "all three books are episodic and fragmentary, and yet, they are unbreakable wholes. . . . The reader sinks right into these dark, leisurely, disquieting, old-fashioned books, where the bears bite and death really stings."

Evelyn Cavallo, in her informative article on Fielding in *The Critic*, said that "through the character of John Blaydon, Fielding was trying to understand himself; to seize, with a sense of exact location, the moods and masks of his former existence." The same might be said of the character of William Chance in *Eight Days*, a religious thriller about a prison doctor, a recent convert to Roman Catholicism, whose faith is tested during a North African vacation. *The Birthday King* is, as Fielding says above, deliberately a less subjective book. It follows the fortunes of a part-Jewish Catholic family of armament manufacturers in Nazi Germany during World War II. It was much praised for its compassion, restraint, and "sad lucidity," and received the W. H. Smith Award.

In *Gentlemen in Their Season*, Randall Coles, an agnostic who produces religious broadcasts for the BBC, has an affair with Betty Hotchkiss, whose Catholic husband is in prison for murdering her lover. Hotchkiss escapes, catches Coles with his wife but, instead of killing him, forces him at gunpoint to say the Lord's Prayer. Frightened back into the cool security of his own marriage, Coles is trapped by his nature into a cowardly betrayal that leads to Hotchkiss's death. This witty and often very funny book has what one critic called "odd, unconsummated leanings towards allegory" which puzzled those who noticed them. A few reviewers thought it Fielding's best book to date, but most were mildly dissatisfied by a certain unevenness of tone, and what to some seemed like a deliberate weighting of the scales in favor of the Catholic characters—the only ones who are allowed to take full responsibility for their actions.

Fielding is widely admired as a serious, skillful, but entertaining writer who, like Graham Greene, uses melodramatic plots to express his metaphysical paradoxes. His black depressive humor, however, more closely resembles that of Evelyn Waugh. His poetry, published in two early volumes, is conventional in form and somewhat inhibited in expression. In 1966 Fielding was invited to Washington State University, where he has remained, and is now professor of English. He has been married since 1943 to the former Edwina Cook, and they have five children. Fielding is a tall, elegant-looking man, a gifted conversationalist of great warmth and charm. He gives his recreations as "televised news, competitions, space, theology, walking."

PRINCIPAL WORKS: *Poetry*—The Frog Prince and Other Poems, 1952; XXVIII Poems, 1955. *Fiction*—Brotherly Love, 1954; In the Time of Greenbloom, 1956; Eight Days, 1958; Through Streets Broad and Narrow, 1960; The Birthday King, 1962; Gentlemen in Their Season, 1966; New Queens for Old: A Novella and Nine Stories, 1972.

ABOUT: Contemporary Authors 13–14, 1965; Current Biography, 1962; Newquist, R. (ed.) Counterpoint, 1964; Vinson, J. (ed.) Contemporary Novelists, 1972; Who's Who, 1973; Who's Who in America, 1972–1973. *Periodicals*—Book Week May 1, 1966; Catholic World June 1963, September 1966, February 1967; Chicago Sunday Tribune March 1, 1959; Commonweal June 28,

1957; October 13, 1961; Critic December 1960, January 1961; Harper's February 1962, April 1963; New Statesman July 7, 1956; November 29, 1958; New York Herald Tribune Book Review July 24, 1960; New Yorker September 23, 1961; Publishers' Weekly May 23, 1966; Saturday Review June 29, 1957; June 4, 1960; March 9, 1963; Time June 10, 1957; Times Literary Supplement November 28, 1958; July 8, 1965; June 23, 1966; July 27, 1967.

FINLAY, IAN HAMILTON (October 28, 1925–), Scottish poet, short story writer, and dramatist, writes: "I was born, quite inappropriately, in Nassau, Bahamas. My father was involved in bootlegging. My parents are both Scottish, and my father's father was head forester on a Scottish estate. My earliest memories are of hurricanes, the little Nassau sponge-boats, fishing, and the sea.

"When I was still quite wee I was sent to boarding-school in Scotland. But then my father, having lost his money farming in Florida, came home; we stayed in a poor part of Glasgow. When the war began I was about thirteen; I was sent to the country and this was the end of my formal education—I spent most of my time fishing in the wee highland burns.

"I spent almost four years in the army. After this I got married and worked as a shepherd; but I had a dream of young men engaged in learned discourse while strolling on lawns. I gave up being a shepherd and while I tried to live off trout and snared rabbits, I studied philosophy from library books.

"I started to write—first, little 'descriptions' of 'nature,' and after a time short stories, some of which were published. My very first published work was a little 'nature essay' (not the customary beginning for an 'avant-garde' writer), which I submitted to a newspaper under a pseudonym. It was rejected, but when I accidentally re-submitted it to the same paper under my own name, it was published at once. In time, my stories began to have less description and more and more dialogue, finally turning into plays. Several were broadcast. A collection of my stories was eventually published, and perhaps twelve years later some of the plays were published in Vienna, in German translation.

"I had great difficulty in writing these stories and plays. For one thing I was often hungry; for another, I was puzzled as to how to put the words together so that the result would be what I then called 'pure'—neither working nor middle class, but 'human,' like the writing of Chekhov.

"I knew almost no other writers as friends. My chief friend at that time was the village thief, who often gave me soup in his low-ceilinged smoke-blackened kitchen. I also worked now and then as a casual labourer.

"I soon began to suffer from nervous anxiety. This is, of course, unpleasant. However, it is perhaps of no more general interest than toothache. I went to the city for treatment; my marriage came slowly to an end.

"As soon as possible I went to stay in Orkney, on a small heart-shaped island where the sea seemed higher than my low bed with its straw-mattress set against the whitewashed wall. I started to write poetry, puzzled by the old problem of how to put words together—essentially the problem of 'syntax,' the radical treatment of which was to be such a feature of 'concrete poetry.' A collection of my poems (which found little favour in Scotland) was eventually published by Migrant Press, Ventura, California. Through this I came to know other poets by letter: Jonathan Williams, Robert Creeley, Cid Corman (editor of *Origin*).

"Later, when I had to return for a while to the city, I started a small press, the Wild Hawthorn Press, which introduced such poets as Louis Zukofsky, Lorine Niedecker, and Augusto de Campos (of the Brazilian 'concrete' movement). I found that Scotland's 'internationalists' were strangely hostile to modern lyric poetry written by foreigners.

"I am now settled (I hope) on the Scottish mainland. We live in a farmhouse and have a wee boy; I work at concrete poetry.

"It is hard to describe concrete poetry—still a controversial subject—in a few sentences. For my part, I am pleased by its concern with intelligence, clarity, and order, as opposed to 'thought' and *fuss*. I am not personally excited by 'experiment' but rather by avant-garde work which will step backwards as well as forwards, finding links with the past. I consider that random experiment in *all* fields is quite out-of-date.

"I have become interested also in concrete poetry in relation to architecture and to out-of-door settings. This is not, I think, a whim, but a logical development of earlier concrete poetry—from the poem as an 'object' on the printed page to the poem as an actual object, properly realised in sandblasted glass, wood, stone, or even concrete itself. I see in such poems the possibility of a quiet assertion of reasonable values—something very different from both 'experimental' and 'confessional' aims.

"I also—though much more wearily now—go on publishing. In respect of literature I feel that Scotland has no need to be different from other nations. There are no good reasons why we should be exempt from 'culture' values or why we should not have an intelligent contemporary literature like almost everywhere else."

Concrete poetry has been called (in the *Times Literary Supplement*) "the most international and perhaps also the most distinctive and closest-knit literary movement of our day." For a long time poets have realized that the effect of their verses depends not only on the meanings and associations and sounds of the words they choose, but to an unknown extent on their appearance—on the way they are written, or typed, or printed. This realization is evident in all good book design as well as in the typographical experiments of the Dadaists and Futurists and their heirs.

What is generally called concrete poetry is a development of this concern with visual effect—with the poem as a two- or three-dimensional object, "in and by itself." A concrete poem may be so shaped as to suggest visually the object, mood, or movement it is about. Phrases or words or parts of words may be repeated, permuted, isolated, or typographically emphasized. The effect may be to bring out latent associations or resonances, to make a pattern, or to show a relationship between these functions.

Because the movement has attracted graphic artists, musicians, mathematicians, and architects, as well as poets, some experiments of this kind are purely abstract visual constructs. These are not recognized as concrete poems by Ian Hamilton Finlay, who is Britain's leading exponent of the form. For him at least, concrete poetry "is essentially concerned with the conventional notation of the alphabet. It is entirely removed in origin from the indeterminate signs and forms that occur in abstract painting."

Finlay's early poems were gentle, tender, and whimsical lyrics in which hindsight discovers a strong visual element, as in "Bi-lingual Poem" in his first collection, *The Dancers Inherit the Party*: "Christmas, how your cold sad face / Leans on the city where everything glows. / Far in the fields stands the gentle animal. / Quel a pity il so seldom snows." An enlarged edition of this collection was published without the author's approval in 1969 by the Fulcrum Press. Finlay responded by issuing an extremely funny pseudo-announcement of "Several New First Editions" of the book, offering as a special bargain 'A complete set of First Edition editions" at three thousand pounds.

In 1962 Finlay received from Augusto de Campos of the Noigandres group of experimental poets in Brazil their *Pilot Plan for Concrete Poetry*, and recognized his own association with the movement. At about the same time he was much influenced by the theories of the Russian painter Malevich, who in 1913–1915 attempted to replace cubism with an absolutely pure geometrical abstract art called "suprematism." In a letter written in 1963 Finlay said: "I approve of Malevich's statement, 'Man distinguished himself as a thinking being and removed himself from the perfection of God's creation. Having left the non-thinking state he strives

IAN HAMILTON FINLAY

by means of his perfected objects to be again embodied in the perfection of absolute non-thinking life.' That is, this seems to me, to describe approximately my own need to make poems." In the same letter (to Pierre Garnier) Finlay speaks of his art as "a model of order even if set in a space full of doubt," and elsewhere he has said that "art can create an order and clarity not attained in life by most people."

The effect of these ideas can be seen in a poem like "Homage to Malevich," published in *Rapel* (1963). Properly, this is printed in large boldface type:

lackblockblackb
lockblackblockb
lackblockblackb
lockblackblockb
lackblockblackb
lockblackblockb
lackblockblackb
lockblackblockb
lackblockblackb
lockblackblockb
lackblockblackb
lockblackblockb
lackblockblackb

Mike Weaver, who is one of Finlay's most capable interpreters, says that this poem is "analagous to a retinal, optical or, as I believe it should be, neural painting. Its structural principle is an additive binary system . . . the eyes, not the voice should be doing the work." Against this, it might be argued that the arrangement is merely ingenious and mechanical, and that any such system may be reduced to "retinal" or to "binary" elements, since the former is common to all seeing and the latter to many arrangements in nature. Much critical comment upon Finlay consists simply of generally "structuralist" remarks about life itself, and is philosophical rather than literary in nature. But he is also capable of such charming picture poems as this one, printed in green and weaving down the page: "this is the little burn that plays its mouth organ by the mill."

Finlay's world of boats, fish, sailors, trawlers, and clear streams is a coherent one, and emerges with a fresh and oddly stark simplicity from all his work, which is most successful when it refers to that world rather than to abstract ideas. In recent years Finlay, as his note above suggests, has concerned himself primarily with what he calls "free-standing poems" —sculptures incorporating words, or poems incised in glass, so that the reader can look through a poem to the living scene beyond. It is probably true that the intellectual content of Finlay's verse is rather slight but, as Weaver says, he is Britain's "only genuinely experimental poet." Hugh Kenner says of him that "he fishes no one's waters, and no one else can fish his, or even arrive where they are. What would be whimsy from an Englishman, Finlay invests with bleak and casual panic, as though on the edge of the world." There was an exhibition of his concrete poems in 1968 at the Axiom Gallery in London.

The stories collected in *The Sea-Bed* reminded Weaver of the work of J. D. Salinger, "but without the baroque Freudianism." His plays are said to be "both funny and varied in a style somewhere between Synge and Ionesco." As editor of *Poor. Old. Tired. Horse.* and proprietor of the Wild Hawthorn Press, both founded in 1960 and devoted to avant-garde and especially concrete poetry, Finlay has been influential. His correspondence, when it is collected, will be seen to contain all his critical ideas expressed in a highly coherent form. As a man he combines great sweetness with great egotism, which in the past has led him to make melodramatic semipublic gestures; both spring from his essential simplicity. His nervous anxiety, which makes travel almost impossible for him, has not been allowed into his work. Finlay received Scottish Arts Council poetry bursaries in 1966–1967 and 1967–1968, and was awarded $1,000 for his concrete poetry in 1968 by an American oil company, Atlantic-Richfield.

PRINCIPAL WORKS: *Poetry*—The Dancers Inherit the Party, 1960 (unauthorized ed., 1969); Glasgow Beasts, an a Burd—Haw, an Inseks, an, aw, a Fush, 1961; Concertina, 1962; Rapel, 1963; Telegrams from My Windmill, 1964; Canal Game, 1967; Poems to Hear and See, 1971. *Stories*—The Sea-Bed, 1958. *Plays*—(in German) . . . Und Alles Blieb Wie Es War, 1966.

ABOUT: Bann, S. (ed.) Concrete Poetry, 1967; Kinetic Art: Concrete Poetry (special issue of Image), 1965; Murphy, R. (ed.) Contemporary Poets of the English Language, 1970; Rosenthal, M. L. The New Poets, 1967; Williams, E. (ed.) An Anthology of Concrete Poetry, 1967. *Periodicals*—Architectural Review April 1966; Arts in Society Summer 1966; Encounter January 1966; Extra Verse Spring 1965; Journal of Typographical Research July 1967; London Magazine May 1967; Origin 6, 1965 (Tokyo); Spectator September 6, 1968; Typographica December 1963.

FITZGERALD, R(OBERT) D(AVID) (February 22, 1902–), Australian poet, was born in the Sydney suburb of Hunter's Hill, where he now lives in retirement. He was named for his father, a surveyor, and his grandfather, also a surveyor and author of a monumental study of Australian orchids. On the maternal side, his uncle was J. Le Gay Brereton, friend and collaborator of Christopher Brennan. Fitzgerald was educated at Sydney Grammar School and at the University of Sydney, where he studied science for two years but left without taking a degree. He qualified as a land surveyor in 1925, and spent five years in Fiji, fixing tribal boundaries for the Native Lands Commission. During World War II Fitzgerald made engineering surveys for airports in New South Wales. He became senior surveyor in the Commonwealth Department of the Interior, from which post he retired in 1965.

In the early 1920s Fitzgerald was a contributor to *Vision*, which preached a Dionysian cult of art and beauty, but in his first books he rejected the hedonism of the "Australian Renaissance." *The Greater Apollo* (1927) and *To Meet the Sun* (1929) affirmed instead a strenuous stoicism in poems, sensible and direct, which however made no great impact. He published nothing more until 1938, when a competition marking the one hundred and fiftieth anniversary of the settling of Australia was won by his "Essay on Memory." This long and intricate poem was a meditation on the transience of life, which yet defiantly insisted that man must act, venture, build, "though we guess not to what skies." Cecil Hadgraft called it "one of the most considerable poems in our literature."

"Essay on Memory" was republished in *Moonlight Acre* (1938), for which Fitzgerald received the gold medal of the Australian Literature Society as well as general recognition as the finest and most influential Australian poet of his generation. These poems, conventional in form and rather old-fashioned in diction, owe something in style and tone to Christopher Brennan, and are not always free of Brennan's tendency to prosiness and over-elaborate imagery. But Fitzgerald's conclusions are his own: to a constant awareness of death and the depredations of time he opposes a faith in the continuity of consciousness through memory; an almost existentialist faith in the need for commit-

R. D. FITZGERALD

ment which gives his verse at its best a stubborn strength and nobility—"Time is a fool if he thinks to have ended / One splendid single thing that has been."

This Night's Orbit (1953), collecting nineteen poems written over a period of some twelve years, shows a sparer style and a freer use of conversational idiom. It contains two poems on historical themes, "Heemskerck Shoals" and "Fifth Day," which have persuaded some critics that such narratives are Fitzgerald's true métier. Altogether more remarkable in form and content is "The Face of the Waters," a vision of the creation and perpetual recreation of the universe which is free in form, unrhymed, and contains dark dream images quite remote from the deliberate realism of Fitzgerald's other work. It is a successful experiment which has not so far been repeated.

In an article written for *Southerly* in 1948, Fitzgerald said he believes "in a return to the passionate and sincere in art . . . to re-establish order and forcefulness and high adventure in the hearts of men." He received the OBE in 1951 but, temperamentally withdrawn and averse to publicity, remains a little-known figure. He was married in 1931 and has four children. Judith Wright said of him in 1965: "Though his theme is still, as it always has been, the justification of man to man, his later short poems in particular have expressed it in terms much more epigrammatic and moving than those of his middle period. . . . There is about them a quality of sculpture—sculpture well and truly made, that will stand up to time and weather. They are poems that form a kind of monument to man."

PRINCIPAL WORKS: The Greater Apollo, 1927; To Meet the Sun, 1929; Moonlight Acre, 1938; Heemskerck Shoals, 1949; Between Two Tides, 1952; This Night's Orbit, 1953; The Wind at Your Door, 1959; Southmost Twelve, 1962; Of Some Country, 1963; The Elements of Poetry (lectures), 1963; Selected Poems, 1963; Forty Years' Poems, 1965.

ABOUT: Buckley, V. Essays in Poetry, 1957; Green, H. M. History of Australian Literature, 1961; Hadgraft, C. Australian Literature, 1960; Johnston, G. (ed.) Australian Literary Criticism, 1962; Moore, T. I. Six Australian Poets, 1942; Murphy, A. Contemporary Australian Poets, 1950; Murphy, R. (ed.) Contemporary Poets of the English Language, 1970; Stewart, D. The Flesh and the Spirit, 1948; Wright, J. Preoccupations in Australian Poetry, 1965.

FITZGIBBON, (ROBERT LOUIS) CONSTANTINE (LEE-DILLON) (June 8, 1919–), Irish-American novelist, biographer, and historian, writes: "I was born in my grandfather's house, in Lenox, Massachusetts. My nationality, at one time a source of confusion to me, has now become a matter of complete equanimity. Like those children of divorcing parents who are told—hopefully and, alas, usually incorrectly—that they will henceforth have two homes instead of one, I have at least two, probably three, and perhaps four countries that I can call home. My father was an Irishman, educated in England, a British naval officer: when I cross the Irish Sea, I am home again, and when that splendidly eccentric body, the Irish Academy of Letters, honoured me with the chair of the late Eugene O'Neill I was flattered as I have seldom been. When I arrive in New York, where I spent my early years and with which my mother's family have been connected ever since it was New Amsterdam, there, too, it is home again and those people are my people. In England, where I mostly live these days, I feel foreign—until I have been away, and come back, and been embraced by grimy London and lovely Dorset and walked the streets and lanes where I meet myself, as I once was, coming out of almost forgotten pubs at closing time (time 1937, time 1940, time 1951) or collecting horsechestnuts (time 1928) or kissing on a summer's evening, timelessly. And, finally, there is France, which still smells to me, as it has done for a third of a century, of fresh bread, fresh linen and fresh love. Oh, and coffee in the morning . . .

"I am an American citizen, but an English writer. I am proud, yes anachronistically and unashamedly proud, to have 'served' in the armies of both those two fine countries during the period 1939–1945, three years in each; I am equally astonished that I was court-martialled in neither. I was, once upon a time, a major. That also surprises me in retrospect.

"Briefly a schoolmaster, like almost all the rest of us, I have lived by writing for twenty years now, and by translating, in the early days: twenty German, a dozen French, one Italian (to show off). I

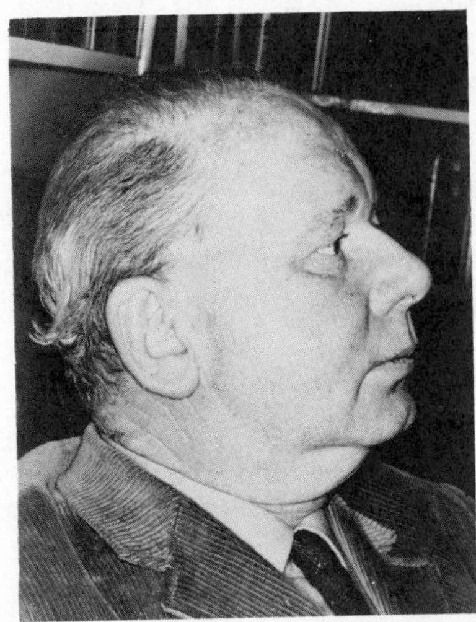

CONSTANTINE FITZGIBBON

think of myself principally as a novelist, though they tell me now that I am better at history and biography.

"My views on the novel are that it should never be referred to in the singular. Its joy as a form of art, and its nightmare, too, to its writer, is that it has no set form. A man who sits down to write a novel can do whatsoever he likes *provided he does it well*. But the point is that it must be what *he* likes, not what the critics or the academics or even the other, better, novelists like. And that is why it is so difficult to write good novels.

"History is an exhausting relaxation, like mountaineering, which I do not do; and eventually one is forced to choose a route that no one else has taken, which one hopes is the true route. Biography is also exhausting, but in quite another way, rather like poker, which I do play, in which one has to back one's own intuitions or even inhibitions. It is, however, a great mistake to bluff too much in either pastime.

"I do not believe that politics and writing are connected save in so far as no stupid man can write well and no man who is not stupid can ignore the world about him. Politics are like traffic, and we all have to cross the road from time to time."

Constantine FitzGibbon's background, Philip Toynbee says, "reads like something invented by some iridescent novelist of the twenties. On his mother's side very gentlemanly American tycoons and eccentrics; on his father's side very well-born Irishmen; and bizarre expatriates on every side." His parents were divorced during his infancy and he lived with his mother in America until, when he was seven, she re-married. There followed five years in France. In 1933 he was sent to Wellington College in England, where the school's anti-semitism, jingoism, and middle-class ethics soured him on these qualities, and made him a rebel and atheist Marxist. Two years (1935–1937) in Germany did nothing to change his views.

His education continued in London—where in the Soho pubs he met all the famous and notorious ornaments of those seedy salons of the 1930s—and briefly at Oxford. His concerns became less political; more aesthetic and romantic. He served with the British Army from 1939 to 1942, then with the U.S. Army until 1946—among other things researching into documents for use at Nuremberg. He was sufficiently shocked by the use of the atomic bomb on Japan to attempt to resign his commission. For three years after his release from the Army he lived in Bermuda and Capri, eking out his income by teaching until he was able to live by his writing and translating.

FitzGibbon had begun to write his first novel during the war. He says it was "the relationship between men and women that preoccupied me above all, the still unsolved mysteries of why we love one another and why love sometimes dies . . . But politics kept creeping in." *The Iron Hoop* was a faintly Kafkaesque study of "the lasting evils, for the victors as well as the vanquished, of military occupation . . ." *Dear Emily* was a portrait of a ruthless and domineering woman; *The Fair Game*, a "sprightly" exercise in the "amorous-picaresque"; but politics took over again in FitzGibbon's best-known novel, *When the Kissing Had to Stop*.

Translating Manès Sperber's trilogy *The Wind and the Flame*, FitzGibbon was persuaded that Communism is "an extremely dangerous and well organized anti-social movement." *When the Kissing Had to Stop* reflects this opinion, imagining an England which, thanks to a Labour Government's self-serving idealism, becomes a Soviet colony. The book had its supporters, who approved of its politics, or simply enjoyed it as a rapid and absorbing narrative. Patrick O'Donovan wrote: "The novel is based on the premise that there is something soft and perverted and dishonest and traitorous in the essential idea of liberalism," but conceded that "Even if you loathe its ideas, the book still has not only the strange fascination of its subject, but is technically a brilliant performance and it is damnably difficult to ignore." An even greater furore greeted a television adaptation of the novel, and one viewer called FitzGibbon a "fascist hyena." The writer answered this charge with a collection of his essays called *Random Thoughts of a Fascist Hyena*, convincing Conor Cruise O'Brien that he was "no more a fascist than he is a hyena. He is something . . . more harmful than either: an intellectual propagandist with a gift for blurring distinctions."

Notable among FitzGibbon's nonfictional works are *The Twentieth of July*, a scholarly and readable account of the German generals' attempt to assassinate Hitler, and his *Life of Dylan Thomas*, widely regarded as his best book. W. R. Rodgers called it "a good book and a deeply concerned one, just, frank, easy, modest in approach, impeccably compassionate, uncompromisingly careful: and it gives a picture of the man that could not, within its limits and intention, be much bettered." The author has also tried his hand at the theatre, and a fantasy called *The Devil at Work* was produced (not very successfully) at the Abbey Theatre, Dublin.

FitzGibbon's work has been much translated in Europe. He is a broad-browed man of medium height with graying hair. His fourth marriage, to Marjorie Steele Hartford Sutton, took place in 1967, and he has two children. Philip Toynbee speaks of FitzGibbon's "free-booting Poujadism," and calls him a romantic and "a great admirer of style in life," with "a warm heart" and "occasional gusts of common sense." FitzGibbon, impatient of all restrictions imposed by "them," says: "Our best . . . defence is to dismiss all their claptrap about loyalties, countries, ideologies and above all about humanity, and to love one another. The best way to start that is by loving one other person, preferably of the opposite sex."

PRINCIPAL WORKS: The Arabian Bird (novel), 1948; The Iron Hoop (novel), 1949; Cousin Emily (novel) (U.S., Dear Emily), 1952; Norman Douglas: A Pictorial Record, 1953; The Holiday (novel), 1953; Miss Finnigan's Fault (travel), 1953; In Love and War (novel) (U.S., The Fair Game), 1956; The Shirt of Nessus (history) (U.S., The Twentieth of July), 1956; The Blitz, with drawings by Henry Moore, 1957 (U.S., The Winter of the Bombs); Paradise Lost, and More (short stories, essays and a play), 1959; Watcher in Florence (novel: privately printed), 1959; When the Kissing Had to Stop (novel), 1960; Going to the River (novel), 1963; Random Thoughts of a Fascist Hyena (essays), 1963; The Life of Dylan Thomas, 1965; (as editor) Selected Letters of Dylan Thomas, 1966; Through the Minefield (autobiography), 1967; Denazification, 1969; High Heroic (novel), 1969; Out of the Lion's Paw: Ireland Wins Her Freedom, 1969; London's Burning, 1970; Red Hand: The Ulster Colony, 1971; In the Bunker (novel), 1973.

ABOUT: Contemporary Authors 4, 1963; FitzGibbon, C. Random Thoughts of a Fascist Hyena, 1963; FitzGibbon, C. Through the Minefield, 1967; O'Brien, C. C. Writers and Politics, 1965; Who's Who, 1972; Who's Who in America, 1972–1973. *Periodicals*—Observer March 26, 1967.

FLANNER, JANET ("GENÊT") (March 13, 1892–), American journalist and novelist, was born in Indianapolis, the daughter of Francis Flanner and the former Mary-Ellen Hockett. She and her sisters, of whom one became a concert pianist and one a poet, had a semi-Quaker upbringing. Janet Flanner, who knew from the age of six that she wanted to be a writer, attended Tudor Hall, a preparatory school in Indianapolis. When she was seventeen the family went to Berlin so that her sister could study the piano with Ossip Gabrilovitch, and spent a year and a half in Germany and in Britain. Back in the United States, she was a student for two years at the University of Chicago, which "was cheap and excellent, especially strong in writing."

JANET FLANNER

In 1922 Janet Flanner went to Paris, where she settled, and wrote a novel called *The Cubical City*, about a luscious blonde from Ohio who comes to New York to be a stage designer. When it was published in 1926 it was greatly admired for its vitality and for "a broad, unhurrying sense of character," though some reviewers found it unpleasantly frank and cynical by the standards of the day, and there was a difference of opinion about its style, which seemed witty and original to some, rather mannered to others. The warmest praise was for Miss Flanner's portrait of the Broadway producer Goldstein, "ugly, bestial, vulgar . . . yet capable of deep emotion and a sentimentality which makes him pathetic and almost lovable."

Meanwhile, Miss Flanner had been writing long letters about her new life in France to friends in America. One of these friends was Jane Grant, who in 1925 asked her to write a regular Paris letter for the magazine launched that year by Harold Ross, Jane Grant's husband. The first Paris letter appeared in the *New Yorker* in September 1925, and when Miss Flanner received her copy she found that it was signed "Genêt." She asked Ross if the pseudonym was meant to refer to the yellow weed called genestra in English or to the female of the ass family. He never answered the question, but Miss

Flanner's Paris letter continued to appear with the same signature, and still does.

By 1940 Genêt was already something of an institution. In that year she published *American in Paris*, a collection of her articles from the *New Yorker* and *Vanity Fair* on subjects ranging from murder to fashion, and including portraits of an assortment of famous people, among them Adolf Hitler, Queen Mary of England, Isadora Duncan, and Edith Wharton. Almost every reviewer used the word "brilliant" to describe those essays. Katherine Woods said that "behind the cool, bright light there is a profound competence, thorough, selective, unagitated. Her writing is mordant but not venomous. She is humorous and polished and wise."

Janet Flanner's long *New Yorker* profile of Pétain appeared in book form in 1944 and was called a superb impressionistic portrait which included a marvelously condensed account of France's recent history. *Men and Monuments*, containing profiles of Matisse, Picasso, Braque, and Malraux was also almost universally praised, especially the "affectionate, gentle study" of Matisse. John Berger alone found behind the candid facts and *savoir-faire* of these portraits "no thought, no questioning and no real understanding of the subjects discussed."

American in Paris was subtitled "Profile of an Interlude between Two Wars" and evoked what Miss Flanner calls "the most brilliant modern epoch of taste and modernistic creation"; her *Paris Journal*, published twenty-five years later, forms a record of a much darker time. It is drawn from the letters she contributed to the *New Yorker* between 1944 and 1965, from the Liberation, through the wretched confusions of the Fourth Republic and the agonies of Indochina and Algeria, to the ambiguous new dawn brought by de Gaulle, whom Janet Flanner called "unexpected and insoluble" but "the father of resuscitated hope for France." In his review Glenway Wescott wrote that "her great quality is her immediacy and candor of impression." Some critics spoke of gaps in her comprehension, but it seemed to Wescott that she "has seen and evidently understands everything, and shows us the enjoyments and entertainments and fine arts of her adoptive country like a rainbow," while her criticism of its politics and public morality "is severe, compassionate, and fearful of the future." Donald Keene found in her work the "suitably French virtues" of intelligence, clarity of style, and a passion for analysis, and says that she "calls herself a journalist, and . . . is a good one." *Paris Journal* received the 1966 National Book Award in the category of Arts and Letters. A second volume, covering the years 1965–1971, had an equally warm welcome from the critics. *New Yorker* letters first published between 1925 and 1939 (including some which had appeared in *Americans in Paris*) were collected in 1972 as *Paris Was Yesterday*.

Janet Flanner holds an honorary Litt.D. from Smith College and is a member of the Légion d'Honneur. She has translated a number of books from the French, including two by Colette. Miss Flanner is a scrupulous writer who reads "enormously," devours ten newspapers a day, and takes four or five full days, some of them extending to twelve hours of work, to complete a twenty-five-hundred-word Paris letter. She says: "I adore to write, but I suffer." Miss Flanner, who speaks English almost as elegantly and simply as she writes it, does so with a faint hint of a French accent. She lives in a hotel overlooking the Tuileries, "a view quite superior to anything I might have found in Indiana."

PRINCIPAL WORKS: The Cubical City (novel), 1926; American in Paris: Profile of an Interlude between Two Wars, 1940; Pétain: The Old Man of France, 1944; Men and Monuments, 1957; Paris Journal, 1944–1965 (ed. by William Shawn), 1965; Paris Journal: 1965–1971 (ed. by William Shawn), 1971; Paris Was Yesterday, 1925–1939 (ed. by Irving Drutman), 1972.

ABOUT: Newquist, R. Counterpoint, 1964; Who's Who in America, 1970–1971. *Periodicals*—Publishers' Weekly March 28, 1966; June 12, 1972; Time April 12, 1948.

FLEMING, IAN (LANCASTER) (May 28, 1908–August 12, 1964), creator of James Bond, Agent 007 of the British Secret Service, was born into a wealthy family of London merchant bankers, though his grandfather, who built the family fortune, had started life in the poorest part of Dundee, Scotland. Fleming's father, Major Valentine Fleming, D.S.O., was Conservative Member of Parliament for South Oxfordshire, a country gentleman rather than a man of affairs, a sportsman, a man of convention and courage, who was killed in action in 1917. His mother, Evelyn Beatrice (born St. Croix Rose) was beautiful, gifted as a hostess and musician, with an exacting and powerful personality. Ian was the second of four sons, less than a year younger than Peter, who became a distinguished explorer and writer.

As a boy, Fleming was handsome, intelligent, and charming, but restless and solitary. His years at Eton, distinguished by a fine athletic record, ended discreetly but prematurely when his fondness for girls and automobiles conflicted too conspicuously with school restrictions. Private coaching led to Sandhurst Military Training College, where he made his reputation as a notable rifle shot, but where again his high spirits and impatience with authority spilled over. He was under reprimand and resigned before taking up his commission.

The next year was both a happy and a crucial one for him. He was sent to Austria to study languages with an English couple, the Forbes Dennises, and Mrs. Forbes Dennis (Phyllis Bottome, the novelist) encouraged Fleming to write. He read a great deal, worked hard, skiied, swam, and climbed. To his many girl friends he seemed gay, fearless, and entirely charming; to the Forbes Dennises he was clearly a very complex and troubled young man.

Fleming went on to prepare for a diplomatic career at the universities of Munich and Geneva, but failed the Foreign Office examination and decided to try journalism instead. He joined Reuters and worked for them in London, Moscow, and Berlin. After four years he felt the need for more money (the Fleming wealth was tightly held), and joined first a merchant bank, then a firm of London stockbrokers, where he remained until the outbreak of World War II in 1939.

From 1939 to 1945 Fleming served with the Royal Naval Volunteer Reserve, becoming personal assistant to the director of naval intelligence. He had not yet started to write, but the fund of material was building up, and some of Fleming's wartime activities were very much in the Bond tradition. On one occasion, for example, encountering German agents in a Portuguese casino, Fleming hit on the idea of ruining them at chemin de fer. Fate, notoriously unpredictable, sent him out of the game penniless but saw to it that he recovered his investment with interest when he used the incident in his first novel. In 1945 Fleming became foreign manager of Kemsley Newspapers, a post he retained until 1959.

It was during the war that Fleming discovered Jamaica. He bought a small estate on the north shore and built his house, Goldeneye. It was not a luxurious place, but it was surrounded by beauty, and was a perfect setting for the sort of vacations Fleming enjoyed: long periods of peaceful hedonism followed by bursts of hectic activity. Here, in 1952, Fleming married Anne, Lady Rothermere. Here, in the same year, he conceived James Bond. The juxtaposition is not cynical, for the relationship between Fleming and his creation was to be as binding as a marriage, and possibly more exacting.

Fleming's first book was *Casino Royale* (1953). With it he established a regime of work (a morning's writing, with another short spell in the evening, continued for two months) and discovered a successful formula that was to need only slight variation throughout the series. Against the background of a French resort the book describes Bond's destruction of the French branch of SMERSH, the Soviet espionage ring. The climax of the story is a tense game of baccarat in which Bond ruins the leader of the ring, Le Chiffre. The girl in the case is a compliant Soviet agent named Vesper Lynd, and there is much closely described violence.

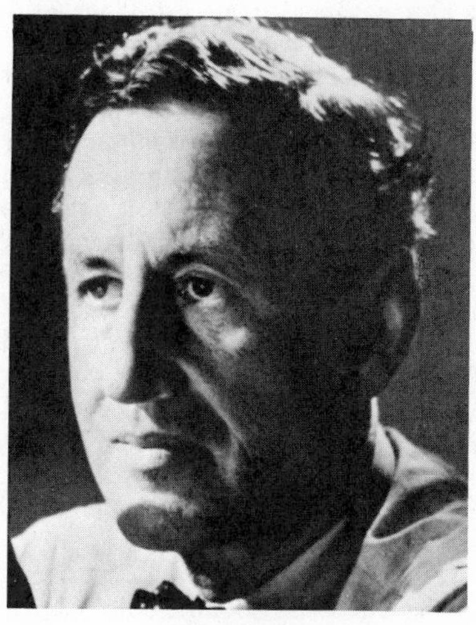

IAN FLEMING

The books that followed—one a year for the rest of Fleming's life—all had cosmopolitan and exotic backgrounds that the author knew at first hand. The action moved from first-class hotels to ingeniously appointed torture chambers, from luxury and self-indulgence to dreadful hardship and danger. There was a fiendish new villain for each adventure, and one or more new girls, all limber, beautiful, and generous. And always there was "M," the masterful father figure who assigned Bond his ordeals and incidental pleasures.

There was only moderate enthusiasm at first for the Bond novels. The reviewers praised Fleming's sense of place and atmosphere, and his journalist's skill in conveying an impression of great knowledgeability, real or assumed, about an immense variety of skills and sports. It was agreed that he could describe action very clearly and convincingly and could build suspense, but also that he had no talent for plotting or characterization. Anthony Boucher described *Live and Let Die* as a mixture of Oppenheim and Spillane, and others were reminded of Buchan by Fleming's unquestioning patriotism. The first four Bonds sold well, but not fantastically well.

The breakthrough seems to have come with *From Russia, With Love* (1957), in which some particularly memorable psychopaths and even more girls than usual are involved in a SMERSH attempt to assassinate its most formidable enemy, 007. The book is no doubt Fleming's "tautest, most exciting and most brilliant tale," as one critic said, and it earned comparison with the work of Eric Ambler.

The critical reaction to *Dr. No* (1958) made it clear that Fleming had become a literary phenomenon to be reckoned with. This story, in which Bond is pitted against a maniacal master criminal in the West Indies, delighted James Sandoe as "the astutest of elegant leg-pulls . . . the most artfully bold, dizzyingly poised thriller of the decade." But back at the *New Statesman* Paul Johnson called it "the nastiest book" he had ever read, a combination of schoolboy sadism, adolescent sexual fantasies, and suburban snobbery, skillfully and deliberately exploited for profit, but socially dangerous and without literary merit. Fleming equably accepted these charges, pointing out only that Bond satisfied a contemporary hunger for epic heroes, and was "fun." Bernard Bergonzi developed the argument, suggesting that Bond succeeded as the antithesis of the welfare state, and Kingsley Amis, in *The James Bond Dossier*, discovered in 007 an incarnation of the Oedipus myth.

Fleming himself never made much secret of the fact that he wrote the Bond books because he wanted to make a lot of money, and this he did. His sales, already large, became astronomical after 1961, when Harry Saltzman and Albert Broccoli released the screen version of *Dr. No*, the first of a series of Bond movies introducing 007 to a huge new audience. But according to Fleming's biographer, John Pearson, "the runaway success of his last years . . . never brought him anything like the pleasure with which he had dreamed of it all." His alternately indulgent and rigorous way of life, the strain of supporting what had become a one-man industry, began to tell on him; his health suffered and the later Bond books showed a decline in ingenuity. As Fleming himself told an interviewer in 1963, "One can't go on forever having blondes and guns and so forth in the same old mixture." In 1964, after an anxious year of increasingly serious ill health, Fleming died of a coronary thrombosis. At that time over forty million copies of his books had been sold.

Fleming was survived by his wife and his son, Caspar. In addition to the Bond books he produced a factual account of smuggling in South Africa, *The Diamond Smugglers*, and a collection of *Sunday Times* travel articles, *Thrilling Cities*. His children's stories about Chitty-Chitty-Bang-Bang, the magical car, had a posthumous success almost comparable to that of the 007 books.

Tall and lean, with high cheekbones and an aquiline but broken nose, Fleming was as saturnine and finally as inscrutable as his hero, with whom also he shared a passion for gambling, fast cars, and sports, especially golf, at which he had a handicap of six. Fleming was also an expert on first editions and published the bibliophile magazine the *Book Collector* as a hobby. Bond's obituary (he was missing, believed killed, on a mission to Japan in *You Only Live Twice*) was laced with similarities to Fleming's own career, and some observers have been at pains to suggest that Bond was to a marked and important degree an expression of Fleming's private fantasies—an *alter ego* who came to dominate his creator's life and eventually, in a sense, to end it. According to John Pearson, Fleming was, in spite of his gifts and opportunities and eventual success, an unhappy man, dissatisfied with his achievements and with something like contempt for the millions who bought his books. At any rate, when Kingsley Amis tried to continue the Bond series (he published *Colonel Sun* in 1968 under the pseudonym of "Robert Markham"), neither his own skill as a novelist nor his faithful observance of the Fleming formula could persuade his readers that Bond lives.

PRINCIPAL WORKS: *Fiction*—Casino Royale, 1953; Live and Let Die, 1954; Moonraker, 1955; Diamonds Are Forever, 1956; From Russia, With Love, 1957; Dr. No, 1958; Goldfinger, 1959; For Your Eyes Only (short stories), 1960; Thunderball, 1961; The Spy Who Loved Me, 1962; On Her Majesty's Secret Service, 1963; You Only Live Twice, 1964; The Man With the Golden Gun, 1965; Octopussy, and The Living Daylights, 1966. *Non-fiction*—The Diamond Smugglers, 1957; Thrilling Cities, 1963. *For children*—Chitty-Chitty-Bang-Bang, the Magical Car, 1964.

ABOUT: Amis, K. The James Bond Dossier, 1965; Boyd, A. S. The Devil With James Bond!, 1967; Current Biography, 1964; del Buono, O. and Eco, U. The Bond Affair, 1966; Gant, R. Ian Fleming: The Fantastic 007 Man, 1967; Pearson, J. The Life of Ian Fleming, 1966; Snelling, O. F. Double O Seven, James Bond, 1964; Starkey, L. M. James Bond's World of Values, 1966; Tanner, W. The Book of Bond, 1965; Who's Who, 1965; Zeiger, H. A. Ian Fleming, 1965.

FOOTE, HORTON (March 14, 1916–), American dramatist, screen and television writer, and novelist, writes: "I was born in Wharton, Texas, a river town surrounded by rich farmlands, forty miles from the Gulf of Mexico. My paternal great-grandparents came to this part of the Gulf Coast in the 1830s from Alabama, acquiring a large plantation of cotton and sugar cane, part of which is still held by a branch of my family. My maternal great-grandparents came from Virginia to Texas in the 1840s. They settled in East Columbia, a then thriving port on the Brazos River, twenty-eight miles from Wharton. I am one of the few members of my family on either side to have left the state.

"A great part of my family has been involved with the farming of cotton from their first arrival in Texas to the present day. When I was growing up, cotton was the center of our universe. It seemed to me everything depended on how the crop came out. It still does, more or less, for my immediate family, and invariably, one of the first questions I ask when returning is 'How's the crop?' As a boy, I had nightmares worrying over the havoc to be wrought when cotton-picking machines were introduced.

"My maternal grandfather's house in town was surrounded by ten acres of land. He gave an acre of this to my parents and built them a house on it next to his. The remaining acreage he had planted in cotton, corn, and sugar cane, and as children, we played our games in these fields. One of my first memories as a boy was the beauty of a cotton field in its various stages of growth. They were our flowering gardens.

"At ten, I went to work in the afternoons after school and on Saturdays in my father's store. There were never a great many customers, except on Saturdays during the cotton season, but my father had been forced to work to help sustain himself as a child, and he seemed anxious that I have some understanding of what making a living meant. I never minded this, really. Occasionally I would have preferred being other places, but I enjoyed talking to the people that came into the store and listening to my father and his friends discuss politics, religion, and their acquaintances.

"I finished high school when I was just past sixteen and convinced my family to let me go to dramatic school and prepare for a career as an actor. I studied first at the Pasadena Playhouse and then in New York City with Tamara Daykarhanova at her School for the Stage. I got some professional jobs as an actor in stock, on and off Broadway, but mostly supported myself by ushering, running an elevator, waiting on tables, and clerking in a bookstore.

"With a group of other students at Daykarhanova's, I helped form the American Actor's Company, an off-Broadway company. It was during the second year of the Company, after meeting playwrights Lynn Riggs, Ramon Noya, Tennessee Williams, and Arnold Sundergaard, that I first became interested in writing.

"I wrote a short play which was produced by the Company and the following year I went back to Texas to spend the summer there working on a full-length play. From then on, part of every day of my life has been given to writing or struggling with the problems of the writer. I had two more plays produced off-Broadway by the American Actor's Company. The latter, *Only the Heart*, was rewritten, recast, and taken briefly to Broadway.

"I married Lillian Vallish in 1945. After our marriage, my wife and I went to Washington where I taught acting and playwriting and managed a semi-professional theater company. I directed and produced the plays of Sartre, Lorca, Ibsen, Chekhov, Williams, and Saroyan. I did a great deal of studying and experimenting as a writer while there, returning to New York in 1950.

"In the 1950s, I had three plays produced on Broadway—*The Chase*, *The Trip to Bountiful*, and *The Traveling Lady*, and eight short plays produced on television by Fred Coe.

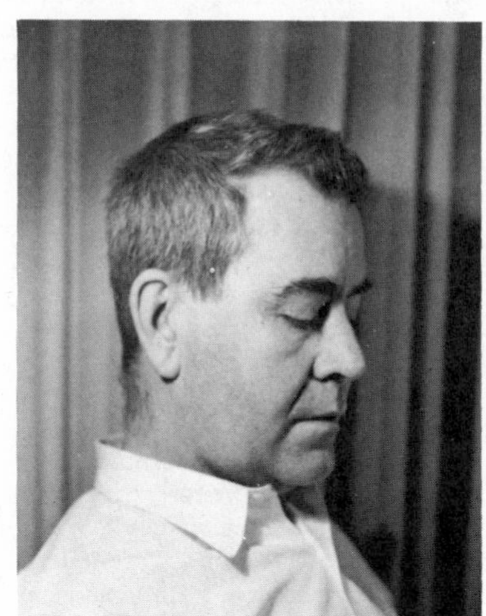

HORTON FOOTE

"I was displeased by my final work on *The Chase* as seen on Broadway, and redid it as a novel, which was published in 1956. On the same day, *Harrison, Texas*, a collection of eight of my short plays, was published. *The Chase* and *The Traveling Lady* have been made into films, and I did the screenplay for *The Traveling Lady*.

"I am at present at work on three plays—*The Indian Fighters*, *The Habitation of Dragons*, and *Beginning Again*, related to each other in time and place.

"From the beginning, most of my plays have taken place in the imaginary town of Harrison, Texas, and it seems to me a more unlikely subject could not be found in these days of Broadway and world theatre, than this attempt of mine to recreate a small Southern town and its people. But I did not choose this task, this place, or these people to write about, so much as they chose me, and I try to write of them with honesty.

"I live now in Nyack, New York, another river town, with my wife and four children."

As Foote transfers his stories from one medium to another—television, theatre, novel, film—they retain certain constants: their locale, a Gulf Coast town resembling his native Wharton; a scrupulous, understated realism in dialogue and behavior; and a concern most often with characters who are neither very young nor quite old, whose problem is "an acceptance of life or a preparation for death." In a typical Foote play, Gerald Weales says, the protagonist is made aware of a situation that has long existed but now must be faced and understood, a process which leaves him a better or a stronger person.

It may be that Foote's detailed realism is to some extent the product of his work in television, a medium notoriously most hospitable to the documentary manner. Although his first full-length play, *Texas Town*, was written as early as 1941, and several had been staged before he turned to television, it was his association with Fred Coe's Philco-Goodyear Television Playhouse that made his reputation. For a few years in the mid-1950s, it seemed possible that Foote, Chayefsky, Tad Mosel, and others had launched on television the long-awaited renascence in American drama.

In 1956, eight of Foote's television plays, all of them produced during 1953 and 1954, were published in a collection called *Harrison, Texas*. "If the plays have a serious fault," wrote Anthony Boucher, "it is an extension of their virtues; they seem over-subtle, tenuous, as they deliberately avoid theatricality and even drama—more suggestive of short stories written for a limited 'quality' audience than of mass-medium entertainment." To a more sanguine critic in *Saturday Review*, it seemed that "Television is in redemptive hands as long as it can work with art like this." The hoyden, alas, ordered her redeemers out, and the brief golden hour of television drama was soon done.

Some of Foote's stage plays have been well received by the critics, though none has enjoyed any resounding success. *The Trip to Bountiful*, originally written for television, reached Broadway in 1953, and seemed to Harold Clurman arresting in its theme and authentic in its feeling and observation, "a sensitive voice communicating something honestly felt." Eric Bentley identified Foote as one of the new school of playwrights who "when successful seem modest, fastidious, compassionate, lyric; when unsuccessful, cagey, gauche, spineless, tongue-tied."

The Chase, staged in 1952 by José Ferrer, was something of a departure for Foote, a "psychological melodrama" which examines his fictional Texas community's responsibility in the making of a criminal. Rewritten as a novel, it was much praised for its perceptive characterization, fast and suspenseful action, and taut plotting. Foote's scenario from Harper Lee's novel *To Kill a Mockingbird* received an Oscar for the year's best screenplay derived from another medium.

PRINCIPAL WORKS: *Plays*—Only the Heart, 1944; Young Lady of Property: Six Short Plays, 1955; Harrison, Texas, 1956; Three Plays, 1962; To Kill a Mockingbird (screenplay), 1964. *Novel*—The Chase, 1956.

ABOUT: Nathan, G. J. Theatre in the Fifties, 1953; Weales, G. American Drama Since World War II, 1962; Who's Who in America, 1970–1971. *Periodicals*—Commonweal March 16, 1956; Life October 25, 1954.

"FORD, HILARY." *See* YOUD, SAMUEL

***FORT, PAUL** (February 1, 1872–April 20, 1960), French poet, was born in Rheims and moved with his family to Paris in childhood. As a boy he wanted to be a soldier and devoured such martial reading as the *chansons de geste* and histories of the Napoleonic Wars. He studied at the Lycée Louis-le-Grand in Paris with a view to going on to the École St. Cyr, the military academy, but two factors intervened. One was the Luxembourg Gardens, where he often lingered dreamily on his way to school. The other was his friend Pierre Louÿs, who abetted his truancy in the Gardens and whetted his appetite for the literary life.

With Louÿs, Fort, then seventeen, began to frequent the Café Voltaire, the gathering place of such symbolists as Jean Moréas, Henri de Régnier, and Verlaine. Fort embraced symbolism immediately, less for ideological reasons than because he equated the movement with liberty and *joie de vivre*. At eighteen he published a one-act comedy in prose and the same year, 1891, founded the Théâtre d'Art. It survived for three years, presenting "unstageable" poetic plays by Verlaine, Remy de Gourmont, Laforgue, and Maeterlinck, among others, with Fort acting in some of the productions. Later ridiculed, it served its purpose as one of the first manifestations of a much-needed revolt against the bourgeois complacency of late nineteenth century French theatre. After its demise, Fort founded the magazine *Livre d'Art* with Louÿs, Léon-Paul Fargue, and Alfred Jarry, and later contributed to *Mercure de France* and *L'Ermitage*.

Fort's poetry began to appear in 1894 and was collected in a volume called *Ballades françaises* (1897), the generic title borne by all his subsequent books of poetry. Further collections soon followed, and Fort became leader of one of the numerous schools of poetry then flourishing, with headquarters in a café, the Closerie des Lilas. In 1905 he founded the influential symbolist review *Vers et Prose*, and was its editor until 1914. For most of this time he lived in Montmartre, with his second wife Marguerite, hobnobbing with the novelist Alain-Fournier and the painters Picasso, Braque, Utrillo, and Gino Severino (who married Jeanne, the first of Fort's numerous children). These were Fort's years of glory, culminating in his election in 1912 as "prince of poets."

In World War I Fort served in the French army; afterwards he traveled in the United States and elsewhere, lecturing on French literature. Returning to France in 1921, he settled with his third wife, Germaine Tourangelle, at Montlhéry, where he and his family became fruit farmers. His attraction to Montlhéry is partly explained by its associations with Louis XI, who had fascinated him from childhood. He devoted the third volume of his *Ballades*

* fôr

PAUL FORT

to a lighthearted history of the king, and this was adapted and staged as one of the handful of dramatic chronicles he produced during the 1920s.

Definitive editions of the *Ballades françaises* began appearing in 1922, and ran eventually to some forty volumes. Fort generally employed rhyme and alexandrines, always with great freedom and suppleness, demonstrating his confidence in these devices by printing his poetry in continuous paragraphs, like prose. If he chose to, indeed, he would slip into true prose, or a rhythmic compromise. This relatively sophisticated manner expressed an inspiration of the greatest simplicity, drawn from old folk songs, French history (especially of the Middle Ages), French people and landscapes, and all the colorful themes of popular poetry. He greatly admired the English Romantics, and sought, he said, "to realize, in French, a poetry like theirs."

His precocious taste for revolution apparently satisfied, Fort's work seemed untouched by the great literary movements which swept France between the wars, and his ballads, with their "slightly affected innocence of outlook," lost favor. By the beginning of World War II, he was publishing so little that his friends issued anthologies of his earlier work in an attempt to relieve his extreme poverty. In 1956, however, he was awarded the Grand Literary Prize of the City of Paris, making one of his last public appearances there to receive it, his long white hair surmounted by the familiar black beret. Fort was an Officer of the Legion of Honor. He died near Montlhéry at the age of eighty-eight.

At his best, Fort sang with the irresistible exuberance and mastery of form that caused Mistral to describe him as "the cicada of the North." But he was a facile and uneven writer, sometimes repetitive, not always saved from sentimentality and preciousness by his agreeable irony. His patriotism is by contemporary standards objectionably boastful. Alan Pryce-Jones has suggested that his rustic and tender ballads brought something of the Virgilian spirit to French poetry, and calls his a charming minor talent.

PRINCIPAL WORKS IN ENGLISH TRANSLATION: Selected Poems and Ballads, 1921.

ABOUT: Cazamian, L. A History of French Literature, 1955; Cornell, K. The Post-Symbolist Period, 1958; Fort, P. Mes Mémoires, 1944; Lowell, A. Six French Poets, 1915; Smith, H. (ed.) Columbia Dictionary of Modern European Literature, 1947. *Periodicals*—New York Times April 22, 1960; Nineteenth Century and After January 1915; Times April 22, 1960.

FOURNIER, PIERRE. *See* "GASCAR, PIERRE"

***FOWLES, JOHN** (March 31, 1926–), English novelist, writes: "I was born in a town at the mouth of the Thames, a small town dominated by conformism—the pursuit of respectability. The rows of respectable little houses inhabited by respectable little people had an early depressive effect on me, and I believe that they partly caused my intense and continuing dislike of mankind *en masse*. I like sparse populations and sparse meetings. This isn't misanthropy; but it has always seemed to me that the crowd (and a crowd begins whenever two people are joined by a third) distorts the individual.

"In boyhood my own counter-totem to people —and to respectability—was nature, in which I found the mystery and beauty that the human environment lacked. However, I wasn't born, like so many writers and natural historians, a particularly shy or sensitive child. At any rate I was given some facility with masks. When I was younger this ability to think and feel very differently from my outward appearance and speech puzzled and shamed me; now I am happily resigned to being a schizophrenic. I enjoy pretending to be what I am not, especially with people who bore me. I pretended so well at boarding-school that I became head boy. It was one of those schools where a clique of senior boys are given complete licence to discipline (i.e. tyrannise) the rest. I was chief of a Gestapo-like network of prefects, and each day I was both judge and executioner of a long queue of criminals. Even then only half of me believed in this beastly system; but it was a fortunate experience. By the age of eighteen I had had dominion over six hundred boys, and learnt all about power, hierarchy, and the manipulation of law. Ever since I have had a violent hatred of leaders, organisers,

* foulz

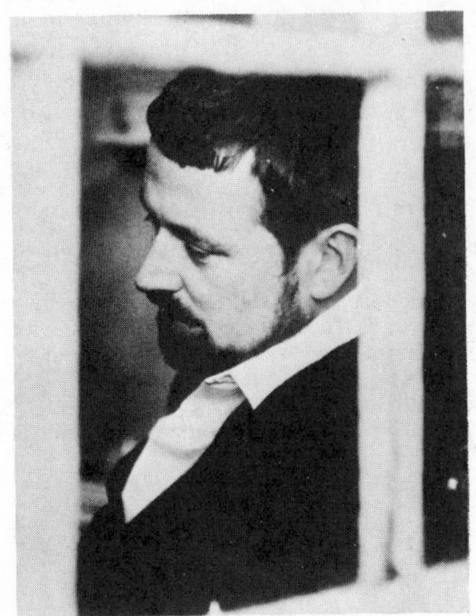

JOHN FOWLES

bosses: of anyone who thinks it good to get or have arbitrary power over other people.

"After military service I went to Oxford and studied French. I love French culture, and France, though the French themselves often irritate me. Later I worked in France, and in Greece. I think Greece is the most beautiful country in the world, and the Greeks, still today, the most human (because the most individualistic) of all races. I feel I have roots in these three countries—France, Greece and England. A great deal of what I like in humanity—especially the fight to maintain a freedom of the individual—resides in that triangle of cultures. I feel much more European than British.

"I didn't begin to write until I was nearly twenty-five. There is no literary tradition in my family. I began partly because I have always found it easy to fantasise, to invent situations and plausible dialogue; partly because I have always rejected so much of the outward life I have had to lead. For twelve years that outward life took me through a variety of educational establishments. In one way at least teaching is a good profession for a writer, because it gives him a sharp sense of futility. I am sure this is a principal drive in all artists: the effort not to waste what one is.

"I now live with my wife on a remote and derelict farm in Dorset. Day and night the sea roars on the reefs below our fields, which are slowly, sadly, but remorselessly crumbling away into the sea. *Nihil manet* . . . we live symbolically. The farm adjoins one of the last primeval wildernesses in Southern England. I have only to walk a hundred yards to disappear into the trees. Nowhere is the age easier to forget; and I find it often needs forgetting."

John Fowles was born in Essex, and it was at Bedford School that he ran his "Gestapo." After national service as a lieutenant in the Royal Marines (which he hated) he went to New College, Oxford (1947–1949), where he "came deeply under the influence of French existentialist writers." He taught for a year in France at the University of Poitiers, then at a boys' school in Greece, then in England until, in April 1963, he became a full-time writer.

Fowles had begun seven or eight novels before he found the story he wanted and wrote *The Collector*, a study of destructive obsession in which an insignificant Caliban kidnaps and seeks to possess his Miranda, a young art student. It was recognized at once as an agonizing and brilliant first novel, the work of "a master storyteller." Though some journals "shocked" Fowles by reviewing it as a crime thriller, the *Times Literary Supplement* identified this "haunting and memorable book" as one "that is trying to make a serious moral statement and making it seriously and well." It became a best seller and was filmed.

We live, Fowles believes, in a society where a few authentic spirits are dominated and suffocated by "the Many." *The Collector* is an allegorical expression of this view in extreme terms and Miranda "an existentialist heroine . . . groping for her own authenticity." Having stated the problem in his first novel, Fowles sought "a direct existentialist answer" in *The Aristos*, "a self-portrait in ideas" consisting of numbered aphoristic statements about a great range of contemporary problems. The "Aristo" is Fowles's term, borrowed from Heraclitus, for the "authentic," self-realized man. Fowles believes that the struggle between the Aristos and the Many, between order and chaos, is the essence of life—a permanent conflict which neither side must win. Reviewers, expecting a second novel and presented with *The Aristos*, reacted variously—most of them favorably, but some in England seeming upset by such seriousness. Julian Mitchell, however, although he found Fowles's views often conventional, praised his "orderly mind and . . . admirable determination to work things out for himself" and called the book "a brave attempt to look at the world and to decide what an intelligent man should think about it."

The Magus, Fowles's second novel, confounded many reviewers but is perhaps an account in mythological terms of how one of the Many acquires the self-knowledge to become one of the Few. A young English schoolteacher, a greedy moral illiterate, goes to teach on a remote Greek island, where a contemporary Prospero makes him the victim of a "savage and rococo" rite of passage, a "hoax or experiment in illusion and reality." J. D. Scott thought it "an extraordinary literary feat . . . a sumptuous firework exhibition of fantasy upon themes of personal identity, sexual love and moral awareness." Some critics attempted to explain the novel in terms of *The Tempest*; Frederic Raphael was reminded rather of an Orpheus whose journey through the underworld "is emblazoned with brutal metaphors and its images . . . reflected in a thousand distorting mirrors until all hope of simple solutions is lost and the labyrinth becomes its own justification, neither stating nor concealing but, as Heraclitus put it, 'indicating.' " It has been filmed.

Fowles thinks that "English is a naturally empirical language" and hopes for "a return to the great tradition of the English novel—realism." This is a part of his achievement in *The French Lieutenant's Woman*, which received the W. H. Smith literary award for 1970. The story opens in Lyme Regis in Dorset (where Fowles himself lives). There Charles Smithson, a gentlemanly amateur scientist, heir presumptive to a baronetcy and a fortune, becomes interested in and then obsessed with Sarah Woodruff. She is a farmer's daughter, educated above her station, who by her own admission has been the mistress of a French naval officer, a married man who could offer her nothing. For much of its length the novel is a Victorian love story, written in the style of Thackeray, and complete with historical footnotes and omniscient comments by the Author. It ends with Charles mastering his infatuation and settling doggedly down with his respectable fiancée Ernestine.

But this Victorian conclusion occurs not far past the middle of the book, and is promptly rejected. Instead, Charles jilts Ernestine and seduces Sarah, finding in the process that she had in fact been a virgin. Sarah vanishes and, after two years of wandering, Charles finds her again in London, where she has become the emancipated secretary of Dante Gabriel Rossetti. The Author (who is sometimes Fowles and sometimes his narrator and butt) then offers the reader his choice of two endings, one happy, one sad.

The novel is brilliantly plotted and immensely and compulsively readable, and it is no doubt primarily for that reason that it became a major international best seller. It is also a splendid piece of Victorian pastiche, which at the same time raises important questions about the role of the author in contemporary fiction: "The novelist is still a god, since he creates . . . what has changed is that we are no longer the gods of the Victorian image, omniscient and decreeing; but in the new theological image, with freedom our first principle, not authority." James Price wrote that the book's primary objective was "to pinpoint an historical change in consciousness. Charles's odyssey is the process, in miniature, in which nineteenth-century man becomes twentieth-century man or fails to." So, if Fowles writes here like Thackeray, it is, as one reviewer put it in the *Times Literary Supplement*, "a Thackeray who has considered the works of Freud, Marx and recent historians, and feels free to discuss their conclusions. . . . John Fowles has found a way, in this tour de force, to emulate the great Victorians, to supplement them without patronage."

John Fowles, a broad and bearded man, is married to the former Elizabeth Whitton. They have left the farm outside Lyme Regis that he mentions above, and have moved into an old house in the town, overlooking the English Channel. Contemptuous of London literary society and ignored by "the clannish Tories" of Lyme Regis, Fowles according to an interviewer "leads a life of utter privacy and solitude." This "exile" has been deliberately achieved, and seems essential to the health of his very rich imaginative life. His chosen recreations are all solitary—book collecting, reading, gardening, walking.

PRINCIPAL WORKS: The Collector (novel), 1963; The Aristos, a self-portrait in ideas, 1965; The Magus (novel), 1966; The French Lieutenant's Woman (novel), 1969.

ABOUT: Contemporary Authors 7–8, 1963; Newquist, R. (ed.) Counterpoint, 1965; Vinson, J. (ed.) Contemporary Novelists, 1972; Who's Who, 1973; Who's Who in America, 1972–1973. *Periodicals*—Books and Bookmen June 1963; Book World January 4, 1970; Life May 29, 1970; New York Times Book Review January 9, 1966; November 9, 1969; The Sunday Times June 13, 1965; May 1, 1966; Texas Quarterly Autumn 1964.

FRAME (CLUTHA), JANET (PATERSON) (August 28, 1924–), New Zealand novelist, short story writer, and poet, writes: "I was born in Dunedin, New Zealand. I'm a mixture of third and fourth generation New Zealander with forebears that include a minister of religion, a doctor (whose casebook bore the name of a patient, Elizabeth Barrett), whalers, seacaptains, blacksmiths, and one great grandfather who was a pubkeeper, politician, and newspaper editor. My father was a railway worker, also a Union Secretary, and the early years of my life were spent in railway houses and huts in small towns in Southland with the railway station, the goods and engine sheds, trucks, trolleys and the turntable as a playground. My mother had poetic ambitions and a neatly handwritten copy of her grandmother's poems to inspire her; my father's mother who could make only a cross on her marriage certificate had a vast store of Scottish and American folk tales and songs; and I and my three sisters and one brother were brought up in an atmosphere of fictional and real drama coloured by poverty, religion, poetry; by picnic enjoyment of rivers and beaches, my father's dancing and bagpipe-playing; and always there were the trains whistling, panting, shunting, and the sheep and

JANET FRAME

people (the two species distinguishable, I thought then but I'm not sure now) going away and arriving.

"I was educated at Waitaki Girls' High School, Otago University and Dunedin Teachers' Training College. I left teaching before the end of my first year and wrote a book of stories in the linen-cupboard-bedroom of the boardinghouse where I worked. Then after spending eight of the next ten years in hospital I continued my writing, was awarded a travel grant, lived in the United Kingdom, Ibiza, Andorra, and seven years later returned to New Zealand and after spending a year in Auckland and a year at Otago University as Burns Fellow I have made my home in Dunedin in a cottage overlooking the bushcovered hills.

"My main interest is writing. I write from obsession, habit, and because I have a thorn in my foot, head and heart and it hurts and I can't walk or think or feel until I remove it. When I was a child and I used to ask my father why he worked, I could not understand the answer he gave—'To keep the wolf from the door.' I understand now, though it's a different kind of wolf that writing keeps at bay and the writer has no hope of keeping it from the door: the important task is to stop it from getting in!

"Though I am regarded as a novelist I do not look on myself as such. I look on my writing as exploration in no favourite form. It is hard work: it is easier to write about it than to write. One must be an apprentice to solitude and silence with the terrible realisation that the term of apprenticeship may never end and if it does one may meet a locked door, one may be denied the final silence and solitude, or find it only in death when one cannot speak or make sentences in writing."

Janet Frame began to write as soon as she was literate, finding in her imagination a refuge from "a background of poverty, drunkenness, attempted murder, and near-madness." She began a novel in high school, and had a story published in *The Listener* while still at college. By the time she began her brief teaching career it was becoming difficult for her to reconcile the differences between the world she imagined and the world she lived in, and one day she walked out of the school where she was teaching and never went back. Breakdown and a suicide attempt followed, and then the years in mental hospitals. From time to time there were brief periods of freedom during which Janet Frame condemned herself to menial labor in hotels and boardinghouses, wrote obsessively, and tried to obey medical instructions to "mix and conform" until the next breakdown came, and the next hospital.

The first break in this cycle came after ten years, when she was befriended by the writer Frank Sargeson in Auckland. In an army hut in his garden she wrote *Owls Do Cry* and then, penniless, went to work once more as a cleaner in an Auckland hotel. Sargeson rescued her again, helping her to secure the Literary Fund grant which enabled her to travel in Europe and England. In London, ill once more, she found a doctor who refuted all previous medical advice, confirming her own instinctive conviction that survival for her lay not in conformity but in writing, in "making designs from my dreams." She has done this ever since.

Some of her early stories had been published in 1951 in a collection called *The Lagoon*, written in "a free, colloquial, intimate prose and developed by an ostensibly casual method of association." Remarkable as some of them are, given the time and place of their writing, they seem in retrospect no more than exercises for her first novel.

Owls Do Cry assembles the interior reflections and recollections of three members of a family, contrasting the gentleness and sensitivity of one girl, who escapes into private madness from the insane realities of her life, with the idiocy of her "well-adjusted" sister. The novel's achievement, E. H. McCormick said, is to give "imaginative form not merely to a family, the Witters, but to an entire town, Waimaru; and Janet Frame has accomplished this feat of synthesis while discarding the structural props of conventional fiction. In their place she has used an elaborate—perhaps over-elaborate—system of recurring themes, symbolic cross-references, echoing words and phrases, so that the work resembles an intricate poem rather than a novel in the usually accepted sense." The book was greeted with great excitement in New Zealand, where many regarded it as the country's first important novel. Foreign critics have tended to agree, but have drawn attention to Miss Frame's debt, in the symphonic structure of her first novel, to Virginia Woolf's *The Waves*. There have also been more or less ritual comparisons with the work of Katherine Mansfield, though Richard Mayne found "a raw edge and a controlled bitterness much sharper" than hers, and guessed at American influences (with some justification, perhaps, since Janet Frame feels a particular affinity with the United States). However it was nourished, *Owls Do Cry* is a very good and moving novel, and a landmark in New Zealand literature—the first but not the last or even the best which Miss Frame has erected.

In a rapid succession of novels and stories she has gone on "making designs" and developing her capacity "to organize into a harmonious whole an immense, intractable mass of human experience and physical detail." *Faces in the Water*, presented as the documentary memoir of a cured mental patient, is "a view into the madwoman's view out"—"a long and completely successful poem in prose, lyric, touching, and deeply entertaining." *The Edge of the Alphabet*, an experiment whose effect is close to surrealism, ventures perilously out from autobiography into the limbo between illusion and reality, where words crumble and communication fails.

Janet Frame's unique talent, still only half recognized, is nowhere more evident than in her fourth novel, *Scented Gardens for the Blind.* In successive chapters it records the interior monologues of Vera Glace, a middle-aged New Zealand woman; of her absent husband; and of her daughter Erlene, who is dumb and, like many of Miss Frame's characters, obsessed with death. Near the end of the novel it is revealed (to the annoyance of some readers) that all three wonderfully distinct voices belong to Vera Glace, a spinster who has spent thirty years in an asylum, and is dumb. When she recovers her speech a fresh revelation is made which throws the novel into yet another perspective, shaping it into a general rather than a particular comment on the human condition. Stanley Edgar Hyman said it was "the most remarkable novel that I have read in many years." Conceding its passages of whimsy, of pseudo-profundity, of labored imagery, he concluded that in its "intellectual complexity, ornate and figurative language, and intense moral seriousness," it "remains a unique and unclassifiable work." A reviewer in the *Times Literary Supplement* said of the same book what is applicable to all of Janet Frame's fiction: "There is no mistaking the power of Miss Frame's imagination and the anguish of her concern for suffering and for beauty. The collision between her sensibility and the reality it encounters creates a world which it is a memorable experience to enter, though one it would be a martyrdom to inhabit." Miss Frame's poems, surprisingly, are direct and agreeable, abounding in "neat, topographical observation," concerned for the most part with "ordinary household things like bread and peaches, Sunday afternoons and bereavements."

The writer is the daughter of George and Lottie (Godfrey) Frame. She has legally adopted the surname "Clutha," but seems not to use it, at any rate in her writing. She is a small woman, dark-haired, meditative, fond of chess and of reading.

PRINCIPAL WORKS: *Novels*—Owls Do Cry, 1957; Faces in the Water, 1961; The Edge of the Alphabet, 1962; Scented Gardens for the Blind, 1963; The Adaptable Man, 1965; A State of Siege, 1966; The Rainbirds (U.S., Yellow Flowers in the Antipodean Room), 1968; Intensive Care, 1970; Daughter Buffalo, 1972. *Short stories*—The Lagoon and Other Stories, 1952; The Reservoir: Stories and Sketches, and, Snowman, Snowman: Fantasies and Fables (two vols.), 1963; The Reservoir, and Other Stories, 1966. *Poems*—The Pocket Mirror, 1967.

ABOUT: Hoffman, H. R. The Reader's Adviser, 1964; Hyman, S. E. Standards, 1966; McCormick, E. H. New Zealand Literature, 1959; Vinson, J. (ed.) Contemporary Novelists, 1972; Who's Who in New Zealand, 1971. *Periodicals*—Cornhill Spring 1966; Guardian November 16, 1962; Times Literary Supplement June 4, 1964.

FRANK, JOSEPH (December 20, 1916–), American critic and scholar, writes: "I was born in Chicago at the end of 1916 into a prosperous and challenging household. My father was a rare combination of a liberal and successful stockbroker, my mother a pretty intellectual, and my two older sisters fiercely competitive—with each other and with me. Childhood and adolescence were, as I remember them, easy and pleasant: a progressive private school, summers in Michigan or Canada, a couple of trips to Europe, and, despite the Depression, my own car when I was a senior in high-school. Then, from 1935 to 1939, Harvard, from which I emerged with a BA and a superficial knowledge of English literature. College, too, was gay and stimulating, but the gaiety was perforated by a sense of guilt that I was having fun in Cambridge instead of suffering in Madrid, and by a sense of urgency that a decent world, or an apparently decent world, was coming to an end.

"After graduation I worked briefly, restlessly, and not very effectively for a Chicago tabloid, a small advertising agency, and a large corporation. Then late in 1941 I joined the American Field Service and spent a year driving an ambulance with the British Eighth Army in North Africa. This was followed by a short stint as an economist with the War Labor Board, then by two years in the American Army, the second in India and Burma. It was

JOSEPH FRANK

during this depressing year that I decided to become a teacher, an ambition that I had long, if not entirely consciously, held. So, early in 1946, I returned to Harvard and for two years I labored and learned in an atmosphere very different from that of pre-War days. In 1948 I came to the University of Rochester, where I've remained. I'm now a professor of English, having climbed the appropriate rungs in the academic ladder, en route receiving a Ph.D. from Harvard. I love teaching, tolerate my share of committee work, keep an open door, enjoy politicking for progressive causes, and play adequate middle-aged golf and tennis.

"I also like to write. So far I've published two scholarly books: *The Levellers* (Harvard University Press, 1955) and *The Beginnings of the English Newspaper* (Harvard University Press, 1961); and I've edited two books for college students: *Literature from the Bible* (Little, Brown, 1963) and *Modern Essays in English* (Little, Brown, 1966). In addition, I fairly regularly turn out scholarly articles and reviews, mostly pertaining to seventeenth-century English literature, and I'm associate editor of a journal dramatically entitled *Seventeenth-Century News*. Much of this professional productivity has been aided by fellowships from the Huntington Library, the Folger Shakespeare Library, and—twice—the John Simon Guggenheim Memorial Foundation.

"I'm now working on a study of minor English poetry during the Cromwellian period, after which I intend to skip a couple of centuries and indulge in a critical appreciation of George Bernard Shaw. Some day, too, I may attempt a novel."

Frank left the University of Rochester in 1967 and, after two years as chairman of the Department of English at the University of New Mexico, became head of the Department of English at the University of Massachusetts, Amherst.

The Levellers: A History of the Writings of Three Seventeenth-Century Social Democrats is a scholarly account of a short-lived but important movement in English democratic reform during the mid-seventeenth-century, approached through an analysis of the writings of its leaders—John Lilburne, Richard Overton, and William Walwyn—and their followers and opponents. John J. Murray found the work "artistic and informative," a book of "intrinsic value for the student of seventeenth-century political thought and party warfare." The *Times Literary Supplement*, though skeptical about the "overdone" political cult of the Levellers, who were "religious fanatics more than 'social democrats,'" nevertheless viewed Frank's study as "amply justified," adding that "if the Levellers are regarded not in terms of modern political propaganda, but as seventeenth-century eccentrics, they are not tedious at all," and pointing out that Frank has "a firm grasp of the historic setting and . . . can write with terse vigour and with wit." Another reviewer noted that Frank "has emphasized those ideas which are contemporary to the Twentieth Century, quite sensibly avoiding any too easy identification."

The Beginnings of the English Newspaper, 1620–1660 is an equally valuable work of scholarship in the field of seventeenth-century literary and political history. Frank's study of minor poetry of the Cromwellian period was published in 1968 as *Hobbled Pegasus: A Descriptive Bibliography of Minor English Poetry, 1641–1660*. The work lists more than eight hundred poetic publications, each analyzed to place it in political, religious, or intellectual context; illustrative, often very amusing, quotations supplement most of the titles.

In 1941 Joseph Frank married Margery Goodkind; they had three children. In 1969 he married Florence Stanton Clark Zartman. He was a Huntington Library Fellow in 1955–1956, a Guggenheim Fellow in 1958–1959 and 1961, and a Folger Shakespeare Library Fellow in 1962. He is a Democrat.

[Ed. Note: Joseph Frank has often been confused with another writer and scholar of the same name, Joseph (Nathaniel) Frank, professor of comparative literature and author of *The Widening Gyre: Crisis and Mastery in Modern Literature* (1963).]

PRINCIPAL WORKS: The Levellers: A History of the Writings of Three Seventeenth-Century Social Democrats, 1955; The Beginnings of the English Newspaper, 1620–1660, 1961; Hobbled Pegasus: A Descriptive Bibliography of Minor English Poetry, 1641–1660, 1968. *As editor*—Literature From the Bible, 1963; Modern Essays in English, 1966; The New Look in Politics, 1968.

ABOUT: Contemporary Authors 1, 1962; Who's Who in America, 1972–1973.

FRASER, G. S. (November 8, 1915–) Scottish critic and poet, writes: "I was born in Glasgow. My father, like myself called George Sutherland Fraser, was at that time a captain in the Highland Light Infantry. He saw service both on the Western Front and in Italy and one of his elbows was shattered by a sniper's bullet. He was a member of a large family, of Highland origins, that had been settled in Glasgow for about one generation. My paternal grandfather made a good deal of money, but had lost it before he died, in the wholesale clothiery business. Two of my aunts on my father's side were prominent suffragettes, and one later a Lloyd George Liberal candidate in Glasgow. Most of my uncles emigrated to Canada or Australia after the First World War. My father, the only one of them who had chosen to go to a university, worked as a legal adviser in the Glasgow municipal offices and when I was about eight became first deputy Town Clerk, then Town Clerk, of Aberdeen. There I went to Aberdeen Grammar School, which has some literary associations, as Byron's first school before he inherited his title and his fortune. At sixteen, according to the Scottish custom of sending boys to university very young, I went to St. Andrews and had taken my M.A. there before I was twenty-one. I then spent two or three years training as a reporter on the Aberdeen *Press and Journal*, but after enlisting and being called up at the end of 1939 I was rarely, after my training period, to see Scotland again.

"I had been publishing occasional poems and literary articles since my late 'teens and during the war I wrote and published a good deal of poetry, my first volume of poems, *Home Town Elegy*, coming out in 1944. I served in the Middle East, doing work on military newspapers and magazines in Cairo and Asmara, and latterly for the M.O.I. [Ministry of Information] in Cairo. Discharged in 1945, I settled in London where my mother, now widowed, had taken a flat in Chelsea. I married Eileen Lucy Andrew in August of 1946, and we have now three children. Between 1945 and 1958 I earned my living as a free-lance writer, reviewer, broadcaster, anthologist, translator, in London, with the exception of three months which I spent on a cultural mission in South America in 1946 and about eighteen months as Edmund Blunden's successor with the U.K. Liaison Mission in Japan in 1950 and 1951. My longest prose book, *The Modern Writer and His World*, was originally written for Japanese students.

"My reviewing and broadcasting was mainly for the *Times Literary Supplement*, *The New Statesman*, and the Third Programme. My main topic was

G. S. FRASER

modern poetry and this interest was reflected also in British Council pamphlets on Yeats and Dylan Thomas, anthologies of modern poetry, *Springtime* (1954) and *Poetry Now* (1956), and a collection of critical essays, *Vision and Rhetoric* (1959). I have also published a short monograph on Ezra Pound (1961).

"In 1958, I became a lecturer in English literature at what was then the University College and is now the University of Leicester. My teaching duties have cut down the amount of time I have to spare for writing, though I still review occasionally and sometimes produce critical essays. I have been busy recently as one of the editors of the forthcoming edition of the verse and prose of Keith Douglas (1920–1944), whose first *Collected Poems* I helped to edit in 1951. I am under contract, also, to produce a short book on Lawrence Durrell, an old friend of my Middle East years, and am hoping also some time to collect and work into unified shape a number of essays and lecture notes on current American poetry.

"I am, I suppose, typical of many writers who set out with the ambition of doing mainly imaginative work and found themselves instead busy with teaching and criticism. The more one goes on criticising, of course, the more fastidious one becomes about one's original work. I find I write or, at least, publish about one new poem a year. I keep my hand in by translating verse, and was a contributor to the Third Programme's recent series of versions from the *Inferno* and the *Paradiso*. Outside criticism, I have written mainly travel and topographical books, on South America and Scotland. I enjoy travel, and had a delightful year as a visiting professor at Rochester, U.S.A., in 1963–64, and an adventurous seven weeks camping in Greece in the summer of 1965. In many ways a teacher's life relieves one of the financial anxiety which dogs most writers, except the very successful, but it also makes it difficult to work with concentration on anything much longer than the short poem and the essay. If I pride myself on anything in my career it is more on having been generally helpful to the profession of letters, and particularly to the appreciation of poetry, than on the lasting value of anything I myself have achieved in prose or verse."

G. S. Fraser was one of the poets associated in the 1940s with the "New Apocalypse," which attempted a poetry, as Fraser said, "more florid, more savage, more lavishly ornate" than the Audenesque mode then current. But the movement "existed more as a concept than a reality." Fraser scarcely knew many of his fellow Apocalyptics, and believes they were all simply "writing the sort of poetry we would write anyway, but were pleased to be anthologized and too naïve, then, to realize the disadvantages of being given a label." In fact Fraser's early poetry, which was "both finely woven and richly wrought," seemed closer in spirit to Yeats than to the New Apocalypse. Alexander Scott has praised the forthright passion of "poems on his Scottish background which were sometimes as remarkable for their sensuous expression of love of place ('Home Town Elegy') as for their savage attack on the place's limitations ('Lean Street')." Later came the long reflective verse epistles written from the Middle East during the war which Fraser thinks of as his best work (though not all critics agree). He writes little verse nowadays, as he says, and what there is has seemed to most reviewers intelligent but rather donnish and lacking in intensity.

In the mid-1950s, before he turned to teaching, Fraser was, according to Martin Seymour-Smith, the chief poetry reviewer in Britain. *The Modern Writer and His World* was warmly welcomed as the best available general introduction to contemporary British writing. *Vision and Rhetoric*, a collection of magazine articles, was "unified by Fraser's astute comparison of the romantic and counter-romantic complexes." Frank Kermode thought it "not only a record of some of the best literary journalism of our time but an excellent introduction to modern poetry."

Some critics have complained of what one called a "lack of any personal urgency of judgment or commitment" in Fraser's work, but most have commended his hospitality and generosity. A writer in the *Times Literary Supplement*, praising his "gift of hitting off the essence of a writer or work in one brief, pregnant phrase," said: "He is equally at home with imagistic and metrical analysis, contextual or historical criticism, philosophical illustration and aesthetic judgment. . . . This critical breadth and knowledgeability, this sturdy refusal to be pegged down by any one fashionable discipline, is what gives all Mr. Fraser's work its peculiarly idiosyncratic value."

PRINCIPAL WORKS: The Fatal Landscape (poetry), 1943; Home Town Elegy (poetry), 1944; The Traveller Has Regrets (poetry), 1948; News from South America (travel), 1949; (joint-ed.) The Collected Poems of Keith Douglas, 1951 (rev. 1966); Leaves Without a Tree (poetry), 1956 (Japan); Keith Douglas (the British Academy Chatterton Lecture), 1958; Vision and Rhetoric (criticism), 1959; Ezra Pound (criticism), 1960; The Modern Writer and His World (criticism), rev. ed., 1964 (originally published in Japan, 1951); Conditions (poetry), 1969; Lawrence Durrell (Writers and Their Work Series), 1970.
ABOUT: Deutsch, B. Poetry in Our Time, 1956; Fraser, G. S. The Modern Writer and His World, 1964; Murphy, R. (ed.) Contemporary Poets of the English Language, 1970; Skelton, R. The Poetic Pattern, 1956; Thwaite, A. Contemporary English Poetry, 1961. *Periodicals*—Times Literary Supplement April 10, 1959.

FRAYN, MICHAEL (September 8, 1933–), English novelist and humorist, writes: "I was born over an off-licence (a liquor store) in Mill Hill, on the northwestern edge of London. My father was a sales representative for an asbestos company; his family were small shopkeepers who had moved to Holloway, in North London, from the West Country, after failing in business in Plymouth. My mother had been an assistant in various London department stores, and her father was a linen salesman who also failed—partly through an inordinate addiction to chess, which kept him away from his business for days at a time. As a young man he used to take his samples to the Palace, and sell to Queen Victoria. Later he traveled America for the Irish Linen Company. My grandmother went out to marry him, at City Hall in New York. My mother was born while they were in Chicago, on a long straight avenue way down on the South Side which is now half obliterated by the Chicago Skyway. My grandfather was a strong swimmer, and a good amateur watchmaker, and until late in life he used to ride immense distances on a bicycle which looked as if it were made of solid iron, sucking a pebble to stop his mouth getting dry. He played the violin, and so did my mother, who studied it at the Royal Academy, and almost became a professional musician instead of a shop assistant. They both died while I was a child. I've inherited their passion for music (my father's, too—he sang as a boy), but not their skill. I regret my musical impotence more bitterly than any other failing.

"When I was eighteen months old my family moved to a quiet residential district near Epsom, on the southwestern edge of London, and it was here that I grew up. I was sent to a nearby grammar school, at Kingston-on-Thames. When I left school I was conscripted into the Royal Artillery for my National Service, sent on the army's Russian interpretership course at Cambridge, and eventually commissioned into the Intelligence Corps. After my release from the army, in 1954, I returned to Cambridge to read Moral Sciences (philosophy) at Emmanuel College.

"The origins of humour are often defensive. I first began to write humorous bits and pieces when I was quite small, but I turned increasingly to the techniques of mockery when I was fourteen and fifteen, and found that I could earn the approval of the class by making jokes at the expense of the master. I sometimes wonder if this isn't an embarrassingly exact paradigm of much that I've done since. At Cambridge humour seemed the most natural form of expression. The tradition of A. A. Milne and the Footlights was strong. Jonathan Miller was at the height of his undergraduate fame when I came up, and Peter Cook wrote his first and highly successful West End show while he was still *in statu pupillari*, a year or so after I came down. The art-forms most passionately aspired to were musical comedy, revue, jazz, singing to a guitar, posters—anything that was predominantly entertaining and stylish. Our brand of humour was what was then called by its admirers 'off-beat,' which meant whimsical; carefully artless sub-Thurber cartoons, fantasies based, in what was hoped to pass for the style of Paul Jennings, upon archaic railway regulations and the like. I wrote stories, humorous articles, and a rather overweening column in the undergraduate newspaper, after one particularly intolerant instalment of which I was thrown into the Emmanuel pond. In my last year I wrote most of the Footlights May Week Revue; it was one of the few unsuccessful May Week shows that the club ever did.

"When I came down in 1957 I joined the *Manchester Guardian*, and worked for two years in the Reporters' Room in the Manchester office. Then I moved to the paper's London office and took over the Miscellany column. My intention was to fill it with *off-beat* reporting, but since I had to do it three times a week, without assistance, I soon discovered, like C. P. Scott, that comment was a freer form than fact. So, by sheer force of gravity, it declined into a conventional humorous column. After it had been going for about a year in this form, *Beyond the Fringe* opened in London. And what all of us were doing was now no longer off-beat or whimsical—simultaneously, it seemed, we had all become interested in something not totally unlike the real world. The strange satirical spasm of the early sixties was under way.

"In 1962 I moved to the *Observer*, the London

MICHAEL FRAYN

Sunday paper, where I have been writing a weekly column ever since. I have also written three novels. What can one say about one's own books? Nothing; the books themselves are what one wants to say, or at any rate the nearest one has ever managed to get to it. Any afterthoughts or explanations can only make things worse."

Michael Frayn no longer writes regularly for the *Observer*, but his satirical columns for that newspaper and the *Guardian* are not forgotten, and many of them are preserved in book form. His usual method was to select some new manifestation of social progress—the insolent television interviewer, Frozen Pea Week—and to extend the notion to its insane conclusion. In this, and in his talent for parody and fantasy, he resembled J. B. Morton ("Beachcomber") or, at times, an extremely English S. J. Perelman. Elsewhere, especially in his later pieces, he turned no less wittily and often more perceptively to less obvious targets; he became, the *Times* said, the unrivaled analyst of "the foibles, rationalizations and self-deceptions of confused, liberal, urban, middleclass man."

His first novel, *The Tin Men* (1965), is a high-spirited and extremely funny account of the preparations for a royal visit at the William Morris Institute of Automation Research. It received the Somerset Maugham Award and was an immediate success as a sociotechnological satire along the lines of a Frayn *Guardian* column, but seemed to many readers a failure as a novel, clumsy in its construction and thin in its characterization.

The suspicion that Frayn was "an unclassifiable who does not fit easily into the department of fiction" was removed by his second novel, *The Russian Interpreter*. It is set in Moscow, to which Frayn has paid two brief visits, first (like his central character) as a student at Moscow University, then as a *Guardian* correspondent. The *Times Literary Supplement* called it "a most skilful and polished short book, with a cast of live characters quite unlike the cardboard personalities of *The Tin Men*." Funny as it is, the novel is basically "a serious, rather mournful story about the shabby half-world of deceit that surrounds dealings, on even the most personal level, between East and West." It brought Frayn the Hawthornden Prize and seemed to Anthony Burgess "one of the best ever evocations of what it is like to live in Moscow." *Towards the End of Morning* (published in America as *Against Entropy*) is a flawed but interesting satirical novel set in a London newspaper office.

The diversity of Frayn's talents was demonstrated again in his next book, *A Very Private Life*, which is neither a satire nor a novel of character, but a Huxleyan fable about a future in which the English class system has reached its apotheosis. The best people (the "deciders") have achieved the absolute privacy that the best people have always sought. They live forever in windowless houses where three-dimensional television provides them with selected companions, drugs induce whatever mood appeals to them, and they are connected to the near-bestial workers outside only by wires and tubes. *Time* concluded that this "enigmatic little fable confirms Frayn's position as one of the few worthwhile novelists writing in Britain today," and its reviewer in the *Times Literary Supplement* seemed to agree, calling it "an outstanding short book which nobody else could have written, and which ought to be put in the classic modern repertoire alongside *Animal Farm*."

In 1964 Frayn edited with Bamber Gascoigne a collection of the drawings and cartoons of Timothy Birdsall, a Cambridge contemporary of great wit and skill who died tragically young. His first television play, *Jamie on a Flying Visit*, was broadcast in 1968 with considerable success. There was also a generally delighted welcome for *The Two of Us*, a group of four very witty and original playlets staged in 1970 in London's West End. *The Sandboy* (1971), a play about a man whose capacity for happiness is constantly challenged by his puritanical guilt feelings, was enjoyed for its excellent jokes but thought "badly over-extended."

The cadence of Frayn's prose has reminded several readers of the work of Evelyn Waugh, but he himself is disinclined to discuss influences on his work or any other aspect of it. In a letter accompanying the autobiographical note above he expressed his feeling that writers "should be as *transparent* as they can; so that their readers look right through them, and see not the author, but the outside world through the author's eyes. Gossip about authors—whether it's about their hobbies or their (frequently inaccurate) ideas about their own work —is really a distraction from this." Michael Frayn was married in 1960 to Gillian Palmer and has three daughters. He still contributes from time to time to the *Observer* and other newspapers, and received the National Press Award in 1970.

PRINCIPAL WORKS: *Collected newspaper columns*—The Day of the Dog, 1962; The Book of Fub, 1963 (U.S., Never Put Off to Gomorrah; U.S., paperback ed. with original title); On the Outskirts, 1964; At Bay in Gear Street, 1967. *Novels*—The Tin Men, 1965; The Russian Interpreter, 1966; Towards the End of Morning (U.S., Against Entropy), 1967; A Very Private Life, 1968; Sweet Dreams, 1973. *Play*—The Two of Us, 1970. *As editor*—The Best of Beachcomber, 1963; (with Bamber Gascoigne) Timothy, 1964.

ABOUT: Vinson, J. (ed.) Contemporary Novelists, 1972; Who's Who, 1973. *Periodicals*—Listener January 21, 1965; Observer June 11, 1967; Times Literary Supplement March 31, 1966; June 8, 1967; October 3, 1968.

FREELING, NICOLAS (1927–), English crime novelist, writes that he "was born in London in 1927, and spent early years in France, England and Ireland. A solitary childhood was made more so by his father's early death and his mother's heart disease. An unguided and uninstructed boy—a series of schools taught him nothing whatever—made the common mistake of the adolescent: thinking the 'education of the world' better than going to a university. After military service (1946–8), which did teach him something, he took to beachcombing, another banal and stupid notion. What such a life teaches one is turned to no proper use, for the boy lacks standards and values. Instead of being 'freed' he is retarded; he is stunted and brutalised by the lack of self respect and lack of contact with any genuine reality. What he takes for reality is an illusion; what he imagines to be philosophy is an adolescent cynicism, pretty cheap and very crude.

"The boy did read anything that came his way: poetry, fiction, even history—as long as it was sufficiently easy. One lacks the self discipline needed for any real study.

"One of the few jobs open to the beachcomber is the hotel business. After some years, he became, at least, a competent craftsman. He would certainly have been a complete failure, and most probably a criminal, but for the good fortune of marrying a woman of unusual character and talent.

"During these years, he often thought about writing, in a bemused and foggy way. He finally got to it at the age of thirty-five, through a lucky accident (caught redhanded lifting hotel food to bring home, and being slapped in jail. In jail one has leisure both to think and to write.) The first pages of a largely autobiographical first novel were written on wrapping paper (one is given simple chores, like packing soap) in the town jail of Haarlem, Holland. It was another two or three years, however, before *Love in Amsterdam* was finally written, typed, and sent to an agent.

"A writer needs a good deal of luck, and he was extremely lucky in his agent. The book was unlike other crime novels; publishers hesitated over it. Not only did the agent sell it, but set the young man to work on a second, and it is the second book that starts a writer's career.

"The same London literary agent sold the first two books, within a year, to a dozen other countries and for filming. Freed from hotels, the young man went back to Holland, where life was cheaper, and wrote ten books in five years, nine of which were published. At half-time, he moved to France, where he now lives and where his children go to school.

"Ten books form an apprenticeship. At the end of these five years, aged forty, he has learned the basic rules of English (he spoke three languages, none well) and the rudiments of how to tell a story.

"The novel is not as dead as people think; the 'crime novel' indeed has barely been scratched. We know next to nothing about human behaviour; we are rethinking all our systems relating to the part crime and other human departures from the norm play in society. Our sense of responsibility is defined by each person according to his scale of values, and these are as fluid as ever they have been. The novelist tries to keep pace with this society in perpetual flux.

"Freeling has been compared often to Simenon. The comparison is only valid in that the two men have some thoughts and several habits in common. He does try to look at society from the viewpoint of its victims. He also alternates conventional crime tales based on a policeman with the type of novel called by Simenon 'hard.'

"His novels are at present published in fifteen languages. Most have appeared in paperback and been chosen for filming. But to keep the ripples widening one must keep throwing stones. One must progress. Becoming self-satisfied is a deadlier disease to writers than to most men—it is deadly to all. As a group, they are peculiarly vulnerable to this kind of moral leprosy."

It took Nicolas Freeling only a few years to establish himself as one of the finest living crime novelists, and this is scarcely surprising, since he seems to possess all the narrative skills of the popular storyteller, together with many of the talents of the serious novelist, including acute insight into character and an excellent command of atmosphere.

Love in Amsterdam is a study of a happily married writer suspected by the police—and at times by

NICOLAS FREELING

himself and by the reader—of having murdered his former mistress. It attracted immediate attention for its depth and subtlety, and introduced Inspector Peter Van der Valk of the Amsterdam Police Central Recherche, the likable and unorthodox detective who has appeared in most of Freeling's books. Van der Valk, according to his creator, "is moral, serious, doesn't sleep with anyone else's wife, looks rather stupid, but isn't really. He is rather disrespectful of anyone pompous or self-important and tries to humiliate people like that. To anyone downtrodden, he is sympathetic. Basically he is very kind-hearted." Freeling's second novel, *Because of the Cats*, was admired even more than the first. It is set in a rich Dutch suburb where Van der Valk is sent to investigate the depredations of a teen-age gang. Dorothy B. Hughes called the book "scrupulously honest and intelligent" and said: "There has been no more important writing on the problem of juvenile delinquency." *Gun Before Butter*, the smuggling story which followed, received a Crime Writers Award in England in 1963 and the Grand Prix du Roman Policier in France in 1965.

One of the most admired of Freeling's Van der Valk novels is *King of the Rainy Country*, in which his hero's search for a millionaire dropout leads him into a nearly fatal ambush. Critics, who noted deliberate echoes of the Mayerling story (as well as of the Baudelaire poem which gives the book its title), were particularly impressed by Freeling's tantalizing unfinished portrait of the missing man. The book received the Edgar Award of the Mystery Writers of America as the best suspense novel of the year.

There have been several Freeling novels in which Van der Valk does not appear. *Valparaiso*, originally published in England under the pseudonym "F. R. E. Nicolas," is not a crime story at all but a novel about a beachcomber on the Côte d'Azur who dreams of sailing his boat to Valparaiso. It struck reviewers as "a nice blend of irony and romance," terse, literate, and distinguished by the same wry sympathy that makes Freeling's detective novels so attractive. Reviewers of *The Dresden Green* were more inclined to regret Van der Valk's absence, and found the book intellectually rather pretentious, but still a quietly compelling thriller with "an up-to-standard supply of bleak internationalist wisdom as well as the usual flourish of scarred, aphoristic insights into what makes people love and hate the way they do."

Freeling believes that every crime novel must center around "a moral problem for which you do not know too easily or quickly what the solution will be." This is most evidently the case in *This Is the Castle*, an extremely funny novel which offers the reader the choice of two endings. Does the best-selling novelist Dutheil shoot his teen-age daughter's boyfriend to death, face trial, welcome punishment, but escape it? Or does he never pull the trigger at all? A reviewer in the *Times Literary Supplement* suggests that Freeling is hesitating himself—that "his novel is really about the writer's choice—and his own choice?—between facile invention and hard seriousness." According to the same critic, "Mr. Freeling's humorous gift has been put to use in a series of marvellously grotesque situations, his ear for inconsequential dialogue is beautifully acute, and his deft handling of half-serious satire marks a promising extension of his scope as a novelist."

However, there are many devoted Freeling readers whose interest in his work is limited to the Van der Valk stories. It was therefore an act of considerable courage when Freeling, finding that the Van der Valk formula had no more to offer him, killed off his hero in *A Long Silence* (1972). The novel ends as a study of a woman's character, when Arlette, the Inspector's wife, sets out to bring to justice those responsible for his death. But Van der Valk's real murderer was also his creator, and he is still at large.

Kitchen Book is an account of Freeling's earlier career as a hotel cook in France and England, an unsurpassed record of an immensely intricate craft which, one reviewer wrote, succeeds in "presenting a strange kind of life, with its values and standards, its hatreds and friendships, and making these not only credible but as worthy of respect as any lives his readers are likely to be leading." It was ranked with Orwell's *Down and Out in London and Paris*.

One of Freeling's favorite writers is Joseph Conrad, a set of whose novels, left him by his father, has accompanied him on all his travels. The writer lives in France with his Dutch wife, the former Cornelia Termes, and their five children. Van der Valk was resurrected in 1973 in a new British television series.

PRINCIPAL WORKS: Love in Amsterdam, 1962; Because of the Cats, 1963; Gun Before Butter (U.S., A Question of Loyalty), 1963; Double Barrel, 1964; Valparaiso (by "F.R.E. Nicolas" in England), 1964 (under own name in U.S.); Criminal Conversation, 1965; The King of the Rainy Country, 1966; The Dresden Green, 1966; Strike Out Where Not Applicable, 1967; This Is the Castle, 1968; Tsing-Boum, 1969; Kitchen Book (nonfiction), 1970; Over the High Side, 1971 (U.S., The Lovely Ladies); A Long Silence, 1972 (U.S., Auprès de Ma Blonde); Cook Book (nonfiction), 1972.

ABOUT: Freeling, N. Kitchen Book, 1970; Vinson, J. (ed.) Contemporary Novelists, 1972; Who's Who, 1973. *Periodicals*—New Statesman August 12, 1966; New York Times April 22, 1967; New York Times Book Review October 11, 1964; November 27, 1966; Publishers' Weekly May 29, 1967; Times Literary Supplement December 10, 1964; January 20, 1966; September 19, 1968.

***FRÉNAUD, ANDRÉ** (July 26, 1907–), French poet, writes (in French): "I was born in Montceau-les-Mines, a small mining town in central France, where my father was a pharmacist. My family was middle class. One of my ancestors, who had left Pons in Charente in 1787 to make his 'tour de France' as an itinerant carpenter, had a thorough experience of the French Revolution as he traveled from city to city perfecting his art, and finally ended up in Burgundy where he established himself at Tournus in 1792. On my father's side my family was fond of remembering its former affiliation with the painter Greuze, and a distinguished relationship—even though illegitimate—with a general of the Empire, Jean-Claude Petit, who was killed at Presburg in 1818. (He was my great-great-great-grandfather.)

"After my secondary studies in a religious college in Dijon, I studied philosophy and law in Paris. For a year, in 1930, I was a lecturer in French at the University of Lwow, which is now in the Ukraine but was then Polish, and I have made sundry trips in Europe, including one to the USSR in 1935, and one to Spain shortly before the Civil War.

"My family was Catholic in its opinions, and conservative. In my youthful revolt against my family I was seduced for a little while by the simplistic aggressiveness of Action Française; that was before I realized that Maurras's reactionary sectarianism represented a position totally contrary to my nature. Learning to be myself, I was inspired by the Russian Revolution and its promise of a human fulfillment which, along with many intellectuals of my generation, I tried to discern through

* frā nō′

its craggy features—Hegel, Marx, Rimbaud helping in the interpretation, as is well known—to transform the world . . . to change life. . . . The Moscow trials, the great purges of the Stalin period showed sadly—and not for me alone—that we had not been without our lyrical illusions. . . . Age has made me less revolutionary than I once considered myself, but I remain a socialist in my way, and a democrat, my heart in any case set well over to the left.

"When the War broke out, though I had sketched and then abandoned a large novel, and had dreamed about what to myself I called a socio-psychoanalysis, I had not yet published anything. All the same I had just been writing, rather feverishly during the previous year, some hundred poems. This late productivity in poetry (at the age of thirty-one) is rare. No doubt it was the case that my childhood difficulties and conflicts, my unhappy love affairs, all those things, had for a long time blocked all my channels of creative expression. In any case poetry came all of a sudden, in an eruption of words, unforeseen and irresistible. Secret and meaningful words, yes. For a long time I was afraid that the source would dry up as suddenly as it had opened; today I hope it will continue up to the end.

"I took part in the war. As a prisoner I passed two years in Brandenburg, at Lückenwald. With forged papers I was able to get back to France in 1942, as a medical corpsman. After my return I became acquainted with Aragon and Seghers, and published *Les Rois-Mages* in 1943.

"I participated in the Resistance. Close to Éluard and involved in his undertakings. On my return from captivity I returned to my administrative position in the Ministry of Public Works. I retired in 1963. Since then I have nothing to do except write poems. It is the only thing that interests me, or nearly.

"I write no prose. It is hard and arduous enough to write poems, even if they happen to be *inspired*. And one also has to see and to live! Sometimes I say that prose will come when the poetic inspiration has stopped, stopped for good. But that's an illusion; it will be too late, I'm afraid, and I won't know. Too bad!"

Les Rois-Mages (The Magi, 1943), published with the blessings of Aragon, Char, and Malraux, collected the poetry Frénaud had written between his late beginning in 1938, and 1942. The book made a great stir. It appeared at a time of intense patriotism, and part of its appeal lay in the nostalgia for France expressed in the poems Frénaud had written as a prisoner of war in Germany. Since then his standing has steadily increased, but mostly in intellectual circles. Indeed it can now be seen that the sense of exile conveyed in, for example, "Plainte du

ANDRÉ FRÉNAUD

Roi-Mage," is not merely patriotic, but also a metaphor for Frénaud's permanent feeling of spiritual or psychological isolation. "Pays perdu," a poem written as early as 1938, expresses a similar sense of loss: ". . . Where is my country? / Who will lead me there?"

In "Epitaphe," his first important poem, he wrote "my numbers are not false / they add up to pure zero"—a statement of futility that would not seem out of place in any of his later works. Nevertheless, Frénaud's hard, pure, almost metallic poetry is far from being meaningless. He has no philosophical or religious formula to offer, nor very much hope of one, but like the wise men in "Les Rois-Mages" and "Plainte du Roi-Mage," he is journeying after an answer; unlike them he puts his trust in man rather than God.

Meanwhile, as C. A. Hackett has said, Frénaud provides "with complete integrity . . . a stoical commentary on his own searchings." Notable among the many volumes that have followed *Les Rois-Mages* are *Poèmes de dessous le plancher* (Poems From Under the Floor, 1949); *Source entière* (Total Source, 1952); *Agonie du Général Krivitski* (The Agony of General Krivitski, 1960); each of them has marked an important stage in his development, which has been towards an increasing simplicity of utterance, a more direct pleasure in landscape and nature. In 1962 he published his collected poems in a volume called *Il n'y a pas de paradis* (There Is No Paradise). Since then the purity of Frénaud's poetry, its care for fresh language and startling metaphor, has prompted an increasing amount of critical attention. He remains very much a poet's poet—and a painter's: he numbers many artists among his friends and has written knowledgeably about their work; attracted by his vivid visual imagery, they have responded by illustrating his poems. Dubuffet, Villon, Bazaine, Fautrier, and Ubac have all done so.

PRINCIPAL WORKS IN ENGLISH TRANSLATION: *Poems in* Aspel, A. and Justice, D. (eds.) Contemporary French Poetry, 1965; Gavronsky, S. (ed. and tr.) Poems and Texts: An Anthology of French Poems, Translations and Interviews, 1969; Taylor, S. W. (ed.) French Writing Today, 1968; Partisan Review 1946; Poetry September 1952; Yale French Studies 21, 1958.

ABOUT: Clancier, G.-E. André Frénaud, 1963; Hackett, C. A. An Anthology of Modern French Poetry, 1964; Pingaud, B. Écrivains d'aujourd'hui, 1960; Rousselot, J. Panorama critique des nouveaux poètes français, 1952; Who's Who in France, 1971–1972. *Periodicals*—Critique February 1963; Esprit September 1947; Les Lettres Nouvelles March 1967; Les Temps Modernes February 1964; Poésie 22, 23, 1945; Yale French Studies 21, 1958.

***FREYRE, GILBERTO (DE MELLO)** (March 15, 1900–), Brazilian sociologist, anthropologist, and novelist, was born in Recife, Pernambuco, one of the four children of Dr. Alfredo Freyre, a teacher, and Francisca de Mello. On both sides he is descended from slave-owning plantation families. As a small child, educated at home by tutors, Freyre was interested in nothing but drawing. He was so long in acquiring literacy that his parents at one time thought him mentally retarded. In due course, however, he learned French and English, developing a particular passion for English literature. He wrote his first poem at the age of eleven.

In 1917 Freyre finished his secondary schooling at the American Colégio Gilreath in Recife and left for the United States, where he entered Baylor University in Texas. Graduating in 1920, he went on to Columbia University for his master's degree in anthropology. Two of the greatest influences on Freyre's life and thought were people he met in the United States—the anthropologist Franz Boas, his professor at Columbia, and H. L. Mencken, who encouraged him to expand his dissertation into what became his masterpiece, *Casa-Grande e Senzala.*

After a year of travel, Freyre returned in 1923 to Brazil, where the modernist movement was beginning to take hold. An important feature of Brazilian modernism was its ardent cultural nationalism, expressed most vividly in various regionalist movements. Freyre became the leader of the principal movement in the Northeast, which was characterized by a strong revival in the novel and the emergence of such writers as José Lins do Rêgo and Jorge Amado. At this time Freyre was working as secretary to the governor of Pernambuco, a post he retained for four years. From 1928 to 1930 he was professor of sociology at the Escola Normal de Pernambuco, and in 1931 he was a visiting professor at Stanford University. There followed a period of travel and research in Brazil, Europe, and Africa, culminating in the publication in 1933 of *Casa-Grande e Senzala* (translated by Samuel Putnam as *The Masters and the Slaves*).

This seminal work centers on the relationship in the sixteenth and seventeenth centuries among the conquering Portuguese plantation owners, their imported African slaves, and the aboriginal Amerindians. The prevailing view had been that large-scale miscegenation between the inhabitants of the *casa grande* (the great house) and the *senzala* (slave hut) had produced an inferior mongrel race. Freyre claimed that the Brazilian mestizo was on the contrary ideally adapted to the Brazilian climate and way of life, a triumph of natural selection. His book lent the authority of scholarship to the emerging national pride in Indian and Negro culture, and more than any other single work provided the Brazilian people with a sense of identity.

It is moreover a work of tremendous fascination, drawing not only on the traditional documents of history, but on travel accounts, novels, cookery and etiquette books, advertisements, and illustrations. Its critics complain with truth that it is poorly organized, that it focuses almost exclusively and misleadingly on the Northeast, that it ignores the more vicious aspects of Brazilian slavery and fosters the legend of racial tolerance in Portuguese colonialism. It remains a pioneering classic of modern sociology, written with great force and stylistic skill, and "a major landmark in Brazil's intellectual coming of age."

Freyre's masterpiece brought him the Filipe d'Oliveira Award in 1934, when he also organized the first Afro-Brazilian Congress. The same year he was imprisoned briefly for his political activities. In 1935 he taught at the law school of the University of Recife, and from 1935 to 1938 he was professor of sociology and founding professor of social anthropology in the University of Brazil. In 1937 he served as technical adviser to the government department responsible for the care of historical documents, and in 1938 as adviser to the national geography council. In 1938 and 1939 he also lectured in Portugal, England, and the United States.

Meanwhile Freyre had published, as a companion volume to *Casa-Grande e Senzala*, a study of the slow breakdown of the rural society he had depicted in that work, and the rise in the nineteenth century of an urban society. This was *Sobrados e Mucambos* (1936, translated by Harriet de Onís as *The Mansions and the Shanties*). It is a more limited work than its predecessor, and even less coherent in its organization, though still a book of

* frā′ rē

great interest. A third volume in the series, *Ordem e Progresso* (1959, translated by Rod Harton as *Order and Progress*), examines Brazil's transition from a slave to a free economy.

Freyre has also produced a great many technical books and articles and a number of works of more general interest. These include his "sentimental" guides to various cities of the Northeast; a volume of lectures given in English at Indiana University and published as *Brazil: An Interpretation* (1945), and his first long work of fiction. This "semi-novel," as he calls it, is *Dona Sinhá e o Filho Padre* (1964, translated by Barbara Shelby as *Mother and Son*). Set in Brazil in the late nineteenth century, it attempts to illustrate the great currents of social, religious, and political change then sweeping the country in the story of a boy condemned willy-nilly to the priesthood by his suffocating mother. Some critics thought the narrative line too frail to sustain so great a weight of ideas, but enjoyed it nevertheless as a subtle psychological study. Alexander Coleman called it "a portrait in depth of the unconscious homosexual, a hero-victim of what Freyre calls 'the middle sex.' . . . It is delicate, immensely touching, generous in its comprehension of sexual ambivalence."

Freyre was a member of the Brazilian parliament from 1946 to 1950. In 1949 he founded in Recife the Joaquim Nabuco Institute for social and educational research, and since 1957 he has been supervisor of the North East Brazil Social and Educational Research Center. Freyre was a Brazilian delegate to the United Nations General Assembly in 1949 and 1964, and served on the United Nations committee on race relations in South Africa in 1954. He is a member of the Federal Council of Culture in Brazil, and of various historical, anthropological, philosophical, scientific, geographical, and sociological societies in America and Europe. He is a director of *Diogène* and *Cahiers Internationaux de Sociologie* in Paris. Freyre's work as a scholar, writer, and statesman has been widely recognized. He is an honorary professor of literature in the University of Baía, and has honorary degrees from universities in America, England, France, and Germany. He lectures all over the world, and in 1967 received the Aspen Prize for accomplishment in the humanities.

Married in 1941 to Magdalena Guedes Pereira, Freyre has a son and a daughter. He lives in Apipucos, a suburb of Recife, in a former plantation house rich in antique furniture and colonial tilework. "The man is very like his house," Keith Botsford has written in *Encounter*. "His mind is lofty, and also exotic; his temperament aristocratic but tolerant. The knowledge, especially the *love* of Brazil that fills his conversation—itself a sonorous and stylized speech—is choked, generous, and rich, like carving or mosaic."

GILBERTO FREYRE

PRINCIPAL WORKS IN ENGLISH TRANSLATION: Brazil: An Interpretation, 1945; The Masters and the Slaves: A Study in the Development of Brazilian Civilization, 1946; New World in the Tropics: The Culture of Modern Brazil, 1959; The Mansions and the Shanties: The Making of Modern Brazil, 1963; Mother and Son: A Brazilian Tale, 1967; Order and Progress: Brazil from Monarchy to Republic, 1970.

ABOUT: International Who's Who, 1970–1971; Who's Who in Latin America (Brazil), 1948. *Periodicals*—Américas (Pan American Union), May 1949; Encounter November 1962; Hispania (Appleton, Wisconsin) May 1964; New York Herald Tribune Book Review May 12, 1963; New York Times August 26, 1945; October 6, 1946; April 12, 1959; New York Times Book Review May 12, 1963; May 7, 1967; Political Science Quarterly December 1946; Quarterly Journal of Inter-American Relations July 1939; Review of Politics April 1947; Times Literary Supplement September 22, 1966.

FRIAR, KIMON (November 18, 1911–), American poet, translator, and editor, is of Greek descent and was born on the island of Emir Ali, off the coast of Turkey. He is the son of Dimitrios and Hrisoula (Hadjikostandi) Friar. He was brought to the United States when he was still a small child. Friar is an honors graduate of the University of Wisconsin (1935). He also studied at the Chicago Art Institute, under George Pierce Baker at the Yale Graduate School of Drama, at the State University of Iowa, and at the University of Michigan, where he won the Avery Hopwood Major Award for an essay on Yeats, and received his master's degree in 1940.

From 1940 to 1945 Friar taught at Adelphi College, and since then he has served for shorter periods on the faculties of the University of Minnesota, Amherst, and New York University. From 1943 to 1946 he directed the famous Poetry Center at the

KIMON FRIAR

YM-YWHA in New York City, and in 1952–1953 ran the Theatre Circle at New York's Circle in the Square Theatre. In 1951–1952 he presented a weekly radio program, "Magic Casements of Poetry and Prose," in New York, and in 1958–1959 he broadcast in Greek over Voice of America on American cultural subjects. He has spent much time in Greece and lived for a while on the island of Poros.

Friar has published his poems, translations, and articles in the *Atlantic*, the *New Republic*, and *Poetry*, among other magazines, and has himself edited *The Charioteer* (1960–1962) and *Greek Heritage* (1963–1965), quarterly magazines dealing respectively with modern Greek culture and with Greek culture as a whole. He is no doubt best known as the translator of Nikos Kazantzakis' verse epic *The Odyssey: A Modern Sequel.*

Kazantzakis' poem, originally published in 1938, is 33,333 lines long. It takes up the story of Odysseus where Homer leaves off, introduces the hero to Buddha, Faust, and Don Quixote among others, and expresses the poet's fierce romantic humanism. As Friar wrote in his introduction to the translation, "the poem was filled with disturbing innovations and seemed to depart from tradition in every conceivable way, for the poet had chosen to publish it in a form of simplified spelling and syntax which he had long advocated, analogous in English to the experiments of Robert Bridges in *The Testament of Beauty*." Kazantzakis had also used ancient words and phrases still employed by Greek shepherds and fishermen, but so unfamiliar to metropolitan intellectuals that the poet had had to supply a lexicon of almost two thousand words.

Friar's translation, begun in 1951 and done in close collaboration with the author, was published in 1958, with Friar's invaluable introduction, synopsis, and notes. John Ciardi said it was "not a book of the year, nor a book of the decade, but a monument of the age," and this was typical of the critical acclaim which the book received, not least for its translation. Anne Fremantle thought that Friar had at times become "entangled in the author's plethora of complex double adjectives" but that "where he has used short, strong, Anglo-Saxon words he has succeeded in producing a magnificent language." Dudley Fitts called it a translation which "reads magnificently" and "enters the region of glory." A number of readers, it must be said, remained marvelously unimpressed by *The Odyssey*, and the poet Winfield Townley Scott called it "at best a freak and at worst a thumping bore."

In 1960 Friar published his translation of another book by Nikos Kazantzakis. This was *Savior of God*, a sequence of free verse soliloquies, first published in 1927, in which the author attempted a more direct expression of his philosophy. "Once again," wrote one reviewer, "the English-speaking world owes thanks to Mr. Friar for expertly and lovingly bridging the great linguistic gulf fixed between us and modern Hellas." Friar's version of Kazantzakis' play *Sodom and Gomorrah* was staged in 1963.

Kimon Friar serves as Greek editor of *The Charioteer* and of *Books Abroad*, and in 1967 became *Saturday Review*'s correspondent for Greece and the Middle East. A fine anthology, *Modern Greek Poetry From Cavafis to Elytis*, published in 1973, was the product of twenty-five years of work. It contains Friar's translations of more than four hundred poems by some thirty authors, together with a long introduction on the historical background, critical biographies of the poets, notes on Greek metrics and pronunciation, and an illuminating essay on the art of translation.

PRINCIPAL WORKS: (ed.) The Poetry Center Presents, 1947; (ed., with John Malcolm Brinnin) Modern Poetry: American and British, 1951; (tr.) Kazantzakis, N. The Odyssey: A Modern Sequel, 1958; (tr.) Kazantzakis, N. Saviors of God, 1960; (tr.) Sahtouris, M. With Face to the Wall: Poems, 1968; (tr.) Modern Greek Poetry, 1973.

ABOUT: *Note in* Engle, P. (ed.) Midland, 1961; International Who's Who in Poetry, 1972–1973; *introduction to* Kazantzakis, N. The Odyssey: A Modern Sequel, 1958.

FRIED, ERICH (May 6, 1921–), Austrian-born poet, translator, novelist, and librettist, was born in Vienna, the only son of Jewish parents. His father, Hugo Fried, was a haulage contractor who, after his business failed, made a modestly successful new career for himself as a hypnotist; his mother, the former Nellie Stein, was a fashion designer. His parents were not Orthodox Jews and sent their son to state schools. When he was only five, Erich Fried was "discovered" as a child actor, and learning parts in plays and acting them gave him a precocious social confidence, and also helped him for the first time to feel the power of language. On July 17th, 1927—"Bloody Friday"—he witnessed the violent political disturbances on the streets of Vienna, during which eighty-three people were shot by the police; later in the same year, when he was asked to recite before his school, he refused to do so, saying that it was wrong to waste time with poetry when surrounded with violence and social injustice. It was his first political stand, taken at the age of six.

During the 1930s the Fried family had to face financial difficulties, as well as the growing pressure of Nazi anti-Semitism. Shortly before he left school at seventeen, Fried had patented two lamp bulbs which a local manufacturer was going to market in France. The venture failed because of the French slump, and this disappointment, together with the effects of an unhappy early love affair, caused a deterioration in his health. He was sent to a sanatorium in the mountains and met there a girl who converted him to socialism and also convinced him of his potential as a writer, so that he returned home with his health and confidence restored. The same year, 1938, his father was arrested by the Gestapo, sent to a concentration camp, and released only on the day of his death. Erich Fried fled with his mother to London, where he has remained. During World War II, he helped seventy-three other Jews to escape from occupied Europe.

In England, during the war, Erich Fried earned his living as a chemist analyzing milk for United Dairies, as a librarian, and as a glass-factory worker. But he continued to write in his spare time, and before the end of the war published his first collections of verse: *Deutschland* (Germany, 1944) and *Österreich* (Austria, 1945). In 1946 he gave up his other jobs to concentrate on writing, and in 1950 he became the joint editor of the periodical *Blick in die Welt*. In 1952 he joined the German language section of the British Broadcasting Corporation, where he stayed until 1968 and acquired a brilliant reputation as a translator, particularly of Dylan Thomas and T. S. Eliot, of Shakespeare, and of contemporary British playwrights.

In 1960 Fried published his novel *Ein Soldat und ein Mädchen* (A Soldier and a Girl), on which he had been working since 1946. The girl of the title had been a guard at Belsen and is awaiting execution for her crimes. The soldier is her prison guard at Nuremberg, a German Jew now in the United States Army. The girl has fallen in love with the soldier, and asks to spend her last night with him. His response to this appeal—as a man, as a Jew, as an unsuccessful writer, etc.—is the subject of the novel. It has been called a "mosaic" of prose fragments, juxtaposing past and present, fact and fiction.

ERICH FRIED

Most critics admired it warmly for its humanity—"a humanity that sees and searches for a human being even in the last SS-trooper and Stalinist NKVD officer." Julian Exner wrote: "There can be little doubt that this slender volume . . . is in form and content one of the weightiest works of modern German literature."

Between the end of the war and the early 1960s, Erich Fried concerned himself in his poetry with a variety of abstract linguistic experiments. As one critic wrote in the *Times Literary Supplement*, his "exploration of verbal affinities, homonyms and near-homonyms, has the desperate seriousness of a man clinging to all that remains to him of his heritage, a language that has been divorced from people and things. . . . Words are weighed and turned over, fondled and mishandled, arranged this way and that, in the hope that they will yield a meaning inherent in them, perhaps the material for a world. . . . Since Erich Fried has a prodigious sense of style, an almost infallible ear, his variations never fail to salve something valuable from the inarticulate." Poetry of this kind is the principal content of *Reich der Steine* (Realm of Stones, 1963), *Warngedichte* (Poems of Warning, 1964), and *Überlegungen* (Reflections, 1964).

More recently Fried has begun to put his verbal inventiveness at the service of his political and social concerns, and most critics welcomed the development. Once his work had acquired content and direction, wrote one, "his formal brilliance quickly turned him into one of the most considerable poets writing in German." Poems in this new manner have been collected in the much-translated *Und Vietnam und . . .* (And Vietnam and . . ., 1966), in *Anfectungen* (Arguments, 1967), and in *Befreiung von der Flucht* (Deliverance from Flight, 1968).

Kinder und Narren (Children and Fools, 1965) is a volume of prose pieces—stories, parables, prose poems—which in their themes and often in their forms closely resemble his verse. Alexander Goehr's opera *Arden muss sterben*, for which Fried wrote the libretto, is based upon the English Elizabethan play *Arden of Faversham*. It was produced in 1967 at the Hamburg Opera House and, in spite of neo-Fascist demonstrations on opening night, was a notable success—an almost Brechtian synthesis of an old play with its modern Marxist interpretation.

Although Fried is a disciple of Marx, he has pointed out that "Marx insisted that we must question everything"—including communism. Fried is a member of the important German writers' association Gruppe 47. In 1967 he shared the Schiller prize with Martin Walser. Fried has become one of the most prolific of living German poets and, in the opinion of many critics, one of the best of them. His verbal experiments have already had a great deal of influence on the work of his contemporaries. Although he travels frequently to Germany and Austria, Fried still lives in London. He resigned from the BBC in 1968, in spite of the freedom that institution had given him to express his views, for reasons explained in the *Listener* (January 25, 1968). He has been married three times, to Maria Marburg (in 1944), to Nan Spence (in 1951), and to Katherine Boswell (in 1965). He has two sons and two daughters.

PRINCIPAL WORKS IN ENGLISH TRANSLATION: Last Honours (poems, tr. by G. Rapp), 1968; On Pain of Seeing (poems, tr. by G. Rapp), 1968. *Poems in*: Bridgwater, P. (ed.) Penguin Book of Twentieth-Century German Verse, 1963; Hamburger, M. (ed.) Modern German Poetry, 1962; Middleton, C. German Writing Today, 1967; Encounter August 1966; Times Literary Supplement April 8, 1965.

ABOUT: *Periodicals*—Listener January 25, 1968; February 1, 1968; February 8, 1968; February 15, 1968; Times Literary Supplement January 16, 1964; January 7, 1965; November 4, 1965; January 19, 1967; January 4, 1968; February 2, 1969.

FRIEDMAN, BRUCE JAY (April 26, 1930–), American novelist and short story writer, was born in the Bronx, New York City, the son of Irving Friedman, a garment industry executive who once provided the piano accompaniment for silent movies, and the former Molly Liebowitz. He attended the DeWitt Clinton High School in New York, where he first became interested in writing, and the University of Missouri, which gave him his Bachelor of Journalism degree in 1951. After two years with the Air Force as a lieutenant, Friedman became an editor with the Magazine Management Company in New York City, publisher of men's adventure magazines, where he worked until the summer of 1966, at the same time selling short stories to *Playboy*, *Esquire*, the *Saturday Evening Post*, and other journals.

His first novel, *Stern* (1962), was called "a delight, at once uproarious and heartbreaking." Stern is a flabby neurotic in his thirties, ashamed of his Jewishness, obsessed by his fears of anti-Semitism, possessed by pathetic, ludicrous, and sometimes charming fantasies. When he buys a house in the suburbs, and his wife is insulted, Stern nurses the incident into a monstrous attack upon his race and manhood, but cannot find the courage to fight back. In his frustration he develops an ulcer, is cured, has a nervous breakdown, and at last confronts his tormentor, making a small, doomed, but nevertheless real gesture of protest. Flashbacks into his childhood and youth establish the reasons for his sense of sexual and racial inadequacy.

There was general agreement that Friedman had invented a memorable comic character and written a first novel of great originality, "delightful, moving, and sometimes quite beautiful." Stanley Edgar Hyman called Friedman "the most unselfconscious Freudian novelist I have ever read," was reminded also of James Joyce, Joseph Heller, and Peter de Vries, but concluded that no page of *Stern* could have been written by anyone but Friedman.

Far from the City of Class, which followed, was an uneven collection of short stories, some of them rather flashily written, all of them about contemporary Jewish life "viewed with understanding and occasional distaste." The best of them, according to Richard Kostelanetz, are "portraits of neurotic behavior or reactions, like 'The Good Time,' which tells of a young man's traumatic discovery of all the complicated underwear under his mother's dress."

This story, Kostelanetz says, provided the basis for Friedman's second novel, *A Mother's Kisses*. When Joseph fails to get into Columbia his promiscuous, wildly over protective caricature of a Jewish momma carries him off to a midwestern college, where she looks out for his interests to the extent of attending his classes and fraternity parties. The novel tells the story of Joseph's emancipation from this monster. Nelson Algren called it a major success, and *Newsweek*'s reviewer dismissed its flaws as "those of a marvelously gifted novelist—the excesses of an exuberant imagination." Most critics however were guarded in their praise, admiring Friedman's minor character sketches and the "nervous, crackling vitality" of his prose, but finding Joseph's mother "too wildly exaggerated in too many different directions," so that she "keeps canceling herself out." *A Mother's Kisses*, adapted as a musical, was staged in New Haven, Connecticut, in 1968.

Black Angels (1966) collects sixteen stories, most

BRUCE JAY FRIEDMAN

of them reprinted from *Esquire*, *Playboy*, *Transatlantic Review*, and elsewhere, most of them grotesque cartoons of the way we live now. A man's erratic temperature readings follow precisely the fluctuating fortunes of his stock market holdings; a boxer urged to knock his opponent's head off does so; suburban status hunger continues in the grave. Webster Schott called Friedman "the Prince of Black Humor," who disarms by laughing at them "death, erotic disloyalty, matrimonial doom." Friedman himself said that "A new Jack Rubyesque chord of absurdity has been struck in the land," which "can only be dealt with by a new one-foot-in-asylum style of fiction."

Friedman calls himself a "worrier," and he has continued to explore, in a mood of deadpan farce, the profound racial and sexual anxieties which have risen to the surface of the modern consciousness. These are treated very directly in his play *Scuba Duba*, which opened Off Broadway in July 1967 and at once became a runaway success, critical and financial. In it Harold Wonder, a quintessential Jewish victim, spends an agonized night wondering if his inconstant wife has finally left him for good with a black scuba diver. During the night he receives his man-eating landlady, a xenophobic French burglar, a hastily summoned psychoanalyst, and other more or less bizarre visitors. And in the end he does lose his wife. Most critics found it a coarse-grained but uproariously funny farce, though some recognized that, as Friedman says, "it's also a straight, serious play about a guy in a terrifying situation." It received a Drama Desk–Vernon Rice Award.

The same themes are resumed in *The Dick*, a novel which introduces a vein of rather obvious and often ribald symbolism, and had a mixed critical reception—admired by some for its "wild wit" and "bravura figures of speech," attacked by others as a "monotonously bad" piece of self-parody. There was also a rather mixed press for *Steambath* (1970), a play in which God is portrayed as a Puerto Rican steambath attendant whose random distribution of rewards and punishments is explained by his extreme ethnic touchiness. The commonest criticism of Friedman's work is that his view of life is limited and obsessive, and that he has become an increasingly crude caricaturist who owes his success to the exploitation of the current broadening of the bounds of taste. Friedman's reply to this charge is simply that he writes as he must: "I like literature of compulsion or obsession. . . . I like guys who go after the unmentionable stuff, who get as naked and as close to the bone as possible. . . . As for my own stuff, I'm not a kid. I'm aware it's strange, not funny. . . . I'm aware it's uncomfortable and that's why it bugs people. But as long as I feel honest, I know it's all right."

He was married in 1954 to Ginger Howard, an actress and model. They have three sons and own a large house on the North Shore of Long Island, New York. Friedman says that he likes "good friends, good talk, theatre, books, films, music." He is a big man (six-feet tall) and dark-complexioned. He works out regularly at a local gymnasium, and in the evening reads, goes to the movies, or plays poker with Mario Puzo and other former colleagues from the Magazine Management Company.

PRINCIPAL WORKS: Stern, 1962; Far From the City of Class, and Other Stories, 1963; A Mother's Kisses, 1964; Black Angels, and Other Stories, 1966; Scuba Duba (play), 1968; The Dick, 1970; Steambath (play), 1970.

ABOUT: Contemporary Authors 11–12, 1965; Current Biography, 1972; Hyman, S. E. Standards, 1966; Kostelanetz, R. (ed.) The New American Arts, 1965; Who's Who in America, 1972–1973. *Periodicals*—Book Week July 18, 1965; Nation September 21, 1964; New Republic October 8, 1966; New York Times Book Review October 2, 1966; New York Times Magazine January 14, 1968.

FRIEL, BRIAN (January 9, 1929–), Irish dramatist and short story writer, writes: "I was born in 1929, outside the town of Omagh, County Tyrone. My father was principal of a three-teacher country school, and I remember living in three homes, each slightly bigger than the previous one and closer to father's school. Those first ten years made me solidly rural by inclination; I am never fully at ease in a city. In 1939 we moved to Derry [Londonderry] where father was appointed principal of a much larger school. And until April 1967 I lived there, first with my parents, and then, after I married, in my own home. Because my father was

BRIAN FRIEL

determined to make me a good scholar (he taught me in school and after school) I resisted all book learning and had an uneven passage through my primary and secondary school career. At seventeen I went to Maynooth, a seminary for the priesthood, and left there after two years. Then, because I was academically equipped for nothing else, I took up teaching and taught for ten years (1950–1960) in various schools in and around Derry. I liked the work very much.

"I began writing when I was nineteen; mostly short stories. Then I did some radio plays. Then, with considerable temerity because my knowledge of theatre was nil, stage plays. Now, at thirty-eight, I am completely tied up in theatre; but I prefer to work in the short story form and hope to return to it.

"Ireland is recklessly encouraging to the young dramatist—for the simple reason that it is still relatively inexpensive to mount a fully professional production; no one is going to make or lose a fortune. So all my plays—even the early ones that I want to forget—were done competently. And when *Philadelphia, Here I Come!* was first produced at the Dublin Theatre Festival, I expected it to have the usual run of five or six weeks and then to be dropped. I stopped teaching in 1960 and took up full-time writing. This was possible because of the encouragement and generosity of the *New Yorker*. In that year they offered me their First Reading Agreement. That was the first act of official recognition and confidence I had got.

"In 1963, immediately prior to its opening season, I went to the Tyrone Guthrie Theatre in Minneapolis, and there for the first time I observed at close quarters exciting acting and exciting direction. This was a memorable experience. And when after six months I was about to return home to Ireland, broke, I learned that the Irish Arts Council had awarded me a thousand-pound Fellowship.

"I am now back in the country again, with my wife, and three daughters, in a house that overlooks the River Foyle."

Eighteen stories, seven of them from the *New Yorker*, made up Friel's first book, *The Saucer of Larks*. These low-keyed stories, set in rural Ireland, acquire an air of objectivity—almost of impersonality—from their heavy reliance on dialogue, but are very affectionately and exactly observed. They are often moving and often funny, in a mood (as one critic said) of "slightly dotty recollection." Many of them are concerned with family relationships, or with recapturing incidents from the past—and some do both, like "Among the Ruins," in which a man, visiting with his family the now derelict house where he had grown up, finds the dead past alive again in the happiness of his children playing where he had played. Children are featured often and sympathetically in these stories, as are their grandparents (but parents occupy an awkward and unmagical realm apart). Another collection of similar stories appeared in 1966, *The Gold in the Sea*. "His talent . . . is for the bittersweet aspects of life, and he excels at evoking them," wrote one critic; another, however, said that "we do not, finally, have much sense of a searching or transforming view of life behind these tales."

Friel's first and so far his greatest success in the theatre was *Philadelphia, Here I Come!* Originally produced in 1964 during the Dublin Theatre Festival, it subsequently played in London and in New York, where it was a major hit. It tells the story of Gareth O'Donnell, a small-town Irish youth drudging in his father's shop, his sweetheart lost through his own timidity, despised and rejected by all, until his American aunt offers him escape to Philadelphia. The play shows him on the eve of his departure, surrounded by those he loves but has never managed to communicate with, still longing for someone (preferably his father) to ask him to stay. The dialogue between Gareth the familiar inarticulate underdog, and the dynamic free spirit within, is spoken by two actors, a device which Friel uses with great success. The *New Yorker*'s critic thought that the play showed something of Sean O'Casey's "ability to draw three-dimensional characters with warmth, wit and sympathy," while a London critic described it as "intelligent, humane, touching, comical and extremely well done." It has been filmed.

The Loves of Cass McGuire, produced without

much success on Broadway in 1966, is about an indomitable old Irishwoman who returns home after fifty years in America to find that her "penniless" brother, whom she has been helping for years to support, is in fact a successful businessman who doesn't need or want her—yet another of the many people in her life who have loved her less than she loved them. The critics found touches of poetry and humor in the play, but thought it for the most part strained, clumsy, and shapeless.

They were on the whole kinder to the two one-act plays staged together as *Lovers*. These are *Winners*, which draws its tension from the audience's knowledge that the two happy young lovers are about to die; and *Losers*, about a late-marrying carpenter whose life is wrecked by his mother-in-law's sentimental piety. Though some thought these plays rather contrived, Friel's mastery of theatrical effect was widely praised. *The Freedom of the City*, a "bitterly ironic documentary" about the political turbulence in Northern Ireland, was staged in Dublin and in London in 1973. Desmond Rushe expressed a common critical response when he wrote that Friel "is sincere, concerned and noble in his intentions, [but] is not altogether successful in giving them impact."

The author is the son of Patrick and Christina (MacLoone) Friel. He was married in 1954 to Anne Morrison, and now has a son and four daughters. He says that he likes reading, trout-fishing, and "slow tennis."

PRINCIPAL WORKS: *Short stories*—The Saucer of Larks, 1962; The Gold in the Sea, 1966. *Plays*—Philadelphia, Here I Come!, 1965; The Loves of Cass McGuire, 1967; Lovers, 1968; Crystal and Fox *and* The Mundy Scheme, 1970.

ABOUT: Who's Who, 1971. *Periodicals*—Guardian October 8, 1964; New Yorker February 26, October 15, 1966; August 3, 1968; Saturday Review March 5, October 22, 1966; August 10, 1968.

FRISCH, MAX (RUDOLF) (May 15, 1911–), Swiss dramatist and novelist, was born in Zurich, the youngest of the three children of Franz Frisch, an architect, and Lina (Wildermuth) Frisch. From 1924 to 1930 he attended the Kantonale Realgymnasium of Zurich, and then began to study German philology at the University of Zurich. Forced by his father's death to abandon his studies after two years, he earned his living for the next three as a freelance journalist, writing mostly about sports, and traveling widely in Italy and the Balkans. At the age of twenty-five he began to study architecture at the Technische Hochschule in Zurich, qualifying in 1941. The following year he married Anna Constance von Meyenberg.

During World War II Frisch served in the Swiss army. After his release he won an architectural competition, opened his own office, and thereafter

MAX FRISCH

until 1955 divided his time between architecture and writing. During this period Frisch traveled in the United States and Mexico with a Rockefeller Fellowship, and lived for a time in a Negro ghetto in San Francisco. In 1953 he separated from his wife, by whom he has three children, and a divorce followed in 1959. When the success of his plays enabled Frisch to give up his architectural practice, he settled in Uetikon, near Zurich, but in recent years has lived mainly in Rome.

Frisch wrote his first play at sixteen, and had already published two novels before the war began—the autobiographical *Jürg Reinhart* (1934) and a romance, *Antwort aus der Stille* (1937). But the turning point in his literary development came at the end of the war, when he was able to leave Switzerland and see what the war had done to the rest of Europe. Their country's neutrality did not prevent Frisch and some of his Swiss contemporaries from feeling a passionate and even guilty sense of involvement in a conflict from whose physical effects they were immune. Also important in Frisch's development was his friendship with Bertolt Brecht, whom he met in 1947. Frisch's experiences and reflections during and just after the war are recorded—and often digested to form the plots and themes of much of his later work—in his remarkable diaries: *Blätter aus dem Brotsack* (Leaves from the Breadsack, 1940), *Tagebuch mit Marion* (Diary with Marion, 1947), and *Tagebuch* 1946–1949 (1950). In all his work since that time, beginning with the play *Nun singen sie Wieder* (Now They're Singing Again, 1945), Frisch has grappled with the moral issues bound up with the war and the rise of totalitarian creeds.

At the heart of these issues Frisch places the question of "real" and potential identity. This question was broached in the romance *Santa Cruz* (1944; his first play in order of writing), and is central to Frisch's thought. Again and again Frisch shows us that society is irrational, perverse, and suicidal, and asks us why its individual members neither resist nor resign. Again and again he gives the same answer: it is too late. Each man is infected by society's corruption, and is afraid; each man shuts his eyes, denies reality, and plays to the death the role society assigns him.

Thus, in *Die Chinesische Mauer* (1946), the great conquerors of history are brought together at a party and dwell lovingly on battles past and future. "Contemporary Man's" appeal for reason in the shadow of the hydrogen bomb is unheard, and he himself joins his potential destroyers as court jester. Frisch called this play a farce, and so it is—a grim and disturbing one. Translated in 1961 as *The Chinese Wall*, it is one of the most admired of Frisch's plays.

Graf Öderland (1951, translated as *Count Oederland*) is the name adopted by a highly respectable public prosecutor who breaks free—or dreams that he breaks free—from his social identity. He becomes an outlaw, is involved in a successful revolution, but finds, as head of state, that he cannot escape his conditioning. He has placed himself in a new society as rigid as the old. Only death offers true freedom. The play was produced in 1973 at Washington's Arena Stage as *A Public Prosecutor Is Sick of It All*. A similar theme is explored in less somber terms in *Don Juan oder die Liebe zur Geometrie* (1953, translated as *Don Juan or The Love of Geometry*), which considers the plight of a man who seeks only the lonely pleasures of mathematics, but whose unsought reputation as a murdering voluptuary condemns him to endless lechery.

Biedermann und die Brandstifter (1958) was produced in New York in 1963 as *The Firebugs*. The bourgeois Biedermann, alarmed by an outbreak of arson, nevertheless in a fit of moral flatulence gives shelter to two sinister thugs. These, patently, are the arsonists. Biedermann, averagely corrupt and cowardly, seeks to placate them—finally handing them the matches with which they destroy him, his household, and his city. An ironic verse chorus is provided by the fire brigade, ready to save the situation if only someone will call them. It is a subtle, brilliant, and often very funny parable in which can be found parallels with Hitler's assumption of power in Germany or of the Communists in Czechoslovakia, and with the general world situation in the age of the nuclear bomb.

The imposition of identity by external pressure is quite explicitly studied in *Andorra* (1960, translated 1964). "Andorra" is a mythical country, small and mountainous, exhibiting the pettiness and complacency Frisch scorns in his native Switzerland. The illegitimate son of an Andorran schoolteacher, called a Jew to conceal his real parentage, begins to think and behave as others expect a Jew to think and behave. When "Andorra" is threatened by a neighboring country which is both powerful and anti-Semitic, the youth is persecuted as a Jew and finally chooses to die as one. This despairing play is notable technically for its masterly use of Brecht's "alienation effect" and is regarded by some critics as Frisch's most accomplished work for the theatre. Joseph Chiari considers it "one of the most important plays of our time" and is not alone in this opinion.

Of Frisch's novels, the most widely read has been *Stiller* (1954). It has been translated into all major European languages and into English as *I'm Not Stiller* (1958). It is the story of a sculptor who, feeling that he has failed both as an artist and a husband, seeks to cast off his old identity and start life afresh. The attempt is defeated by official inertia and the sentimental pressures applied by family and friends. Stiller, too uncertain of his potentialities to go on fighting for them, is condemned for life to a role in which he has already failed. Martin Esslin has called this a "great novel . . . brilliantly conceived" and "deeply serious." The short novel *Homo Faber* (1957) is a version of the Oedipus myth placed in the context of the technological age, with the vagaries of machinery playing the role of fate. It was in general warmly received in the United States and was thought to resemble Camus's *The Stranger* in its mood and manner.

Doubts about identity become most acute in *Mein Name sei Gantenbein* (1964). This novel, translated in 1966 as *A Wilderness of Mirrors*, is the most radically experimental of all Frisch's work to date, an ingenious, witty, but exasperating book, which deliberately refuses to engage the reader's sympathy.

Frisch's novels have been far more successful in the United States than his plays. *Andorra* was misinterpreted in its American production as a simple tract against anti-Semitism and *The Firebugs* struck Howard Taubman of the New York *Times* as thin and transparent. It has been suggested that Frisch's essentially European disillusionment is unpalatable to Americans. Both plays were staged in New York in 1963 and both failed, though they were major successes in Germany and throughout Europe. Frisch has received many honors and awards, including the Wilhelm Raabe Prize in 1955 and the Georg Büchner Prize in 1958. Together with his rival, Friedrich Dürrenmatt, Frisch is generally regarded as the most eminent dramatist to emerge in the German-speaking countries since World War II.

Comparisons with Dürrenmatt are indeed difficult to avoid: both writers are Swiss and have been conditioned by that fact; both write disillusioned morality plays in the shape of intellectual fantasies; and both show the influence of Brecht. But Dürrenmatt writes from above the fight, describing the idiocies he sees with a stoic objectivity; Frisch, as George E. Wellwarth has said, is "a human being like everyone else." The questions he asks are directed to himself, as much as to his audience.

Some of the questions that most exercise Frisch are asked directly in the latest volume of his diaries, *Tagebuch 1966–1971* (1972). Indeed this *Tagebuch*, like its predecessors, is something much more than the title suggests, including uncomfortable questions ("Would you like to be your wife?"), notes concerning the establishment of a Suicide Society, revealing (and sometimes infuriating) quotations from a variety of sources, several short stories, and a jumble of generally fascinating jottings on places visited and people encountered. The book was an immediate best seller.

PRINCIPAL WORKS IN ENGLISH TRANSLATION: I'm Not Stiller (novel), 1958; Homo Faber (novel), 1959; The Chinese Wall, 1961; Three Plays (The Fire Raisers, Count Oederland, Andorra), 1962; The Firebugs, 1963; Andorra, 1964; A Wilderness of Mirrors (novel), 1966; Three Plays (Don Juan or The Love of Geometry, The Great Rage of Philip Hotz, When the War Was Over), 1967; Biography, 1969; Four Plays (The Great Wall of China, Don Juan, Philipp Hotz's Fury, Biography), 1969.

ABOUT: Baenziger, H. Frisch und Dürrenmatt, 1960; Current Biography, 1965; Esslin, M. Max Frisch *in* Natan, A. (ed.) German Men of Letters, Vol. III, 1964; Frisch, M. Tagebuch 1946–1949, 1950; Garten, H. F. Modern German Drama, 1959; Stäuble, E. Max Frisch, 1960; Weber, W. Tagebuch eines Lesers, 1965; Weisstein, U. W. Max Frisch, 1967; Wellwarth, G. E. The Theater of Protest and Paradox, 1964; Who's Who in America, 1972–1973; Ziskoven, W. Max Frisch *in* Geissler, R. (ed.) Zur Interpretation des modernen Drames, 1960. *Periodicals*—Tulane Drama Review Spring 1962; Yale French Studies 29, 1962.

FRYE, (HERMAN) NORTHROP (July 14, 1912–), Canadian critic, writes: "I was born in Sherbrooke, Quebec, Canada, in 1912, and grew up in Moncton, New Brunswick, where I received my primary and secondary education, along with some training in music and a year at business college. I entered the University of Toronto, Victoria College, in 1929 and was graduated in the Honour Course in Philosophy and English in 1933. I then did three years of theology at Emmanuel College, Toronto, along with some graduate work in English, and was ordained in the United Church of Canada in 1936. I realized by then that my vocation was for university training, and went to Merton College, Oxford, to read the school in English, and got my M.A. from there in 1940. I joined the Department of English at Victoria College as lecturer

NORTHROP FRYE

in 1939, became a full professor in 1947, and Principal of the College in 1959.

"For a long time I published very little, except for reviews of Canadian music, art and literature in the *Canadian Forum*, a magazine of which I later became editor. This was because I had been completely absorbed in the symbolism of the Prophetic Books of William Blake. My study of Blake, *Fearful Symmetry*, appeared in 1947, and, because his poems are mythical, I became perforce a critic of the 'mythical school.' So I looked into the implications of being that, and the result, ten years later, was *Anatomy of Criticism*. This book attempts to provide a rationale or schema for the various contemporary approaches to criticism, and has had a good deal of influence. Its starting point is the principle that primary criticism is descriptive and categorical, and that evaluative criticism gives us no real knowledge of literature. It goes on to consider such terms as symbol, archetype, genre, myth, and the like, and, in particular, tries to show that myth is a structural principle of literature.

"What I have written since then has been mainly amplification of these principles, and the applying of them to different authors: most of the results of this are incorporated in *Fables of Identity* (1963), a collection of my essays, some theoretical, some ranging over various authors from Spenser to Wallace Stevens. I have been asked to give a number of public lectures on various foundations, and some of these have resulted in books: *The Well-Tempered Critic* (1963), the Page Barbour Lectures in Virginia; *The Educated Imagination* (1963), the Massey Lectures for the Canadian Broadcasting Corporation; *A Natural Perspective* (1965), the

Bampton Lectures at Columbia, on Shakespearean comedy; *The Return of Eden* (1965), the Centennial Lectures at Huron College, Western Ontario, on Milton. Three other series are in course of publication. Since I became Principal of Victoria College, my attention has been increasingly taken up with educational matters, and my interest in the relations between literary criticism and the teaching of English, at all levels, is reflected in the first two books mentioned above. A fair number of teachers are now working on my critical principles with a view to applying them to a curriculum sequence in English teaching.

"I have been involved a good deal in Canadian cultural affairs, have worked with the CBC and the National Film Board, have been a member of the Royal Society of Canada since 1951 and won its Lorne Pierce Medal for services to Canadian letters in 1958, have served on the Governor-General's Awards Committee for Canadian writers, of which I was Chairman in 1962–64, and was Rapporteur of the Atlantic Congress of 1959. From 1950 to 1960 I wrote the annual critical survey of Canadian poetry in the *Letters in Canada* section of the *University of Toronto Quarterly*. I have a number of honorary degrees.

"At present I plan to retire soon from the Principalship and devote myself more completely to writing and teaching. I should like to consider, in particular, the relations of criticism and society and the total social context of the theoretical study of literature, a huge subject still almost entirely unexplored."

Anatomy of Criticism has been called "the most scintillatingly provocative . . . of the classics of modern criticism," and is certainly a book easier to read than to describe. It proposes that literary criticism is ideally a kind of science, which should therefore eschew value judgments, moral and aesthetic, concerning itself not with opinions but with knowledge. Aristotle approached poetry "as a biologist would approach a system of organisms, picking out its genera and species"; the modern critic should do the same, and *Anatomy of Criticism* attempts to provide suitable methods of classification and an appropriate terminology. These instruments are derived from "an inductive survey of the literary field," which is systematically divided, subdivided, and further subdivided into modes, genres, and phases. In this way, as he acknowledges, Frye "attempts to annotate" Eliot's fundamental premise in *The Function of Criticism* that "the existing monuments of literature form an ideal order among themselves, and are not simply collections of the writings of individuals."

The longest of the essays that make up *Anatomy of Criticism* is called "Archetypal Criticism: Theory of Myths." This makes an ingenious classification of Western literature from the Middle Ages to the present, using biblical symbolism and classical mythology as a "grammar of literary archetypes." From this study Frye derives his theory that there exists in all literature one central unifying myth, which he identifies with the Jewish-Christian myth of quest and salvation.

In his "Tentative Conclusion," he suggests that perhaps the "verbal structures of psychology, anthropology, theology, history, law and everything else built out of words have been informed or constructed by the same kinds of myths and metaphors that we find, in their original hypothetical form, in literature." And he concludes that a fundamental purpose of criticism should be to repair "the broken links between creation and knowledge, art and science, myth and concept."

Walter Sutton, in *Modern American Criticism*, finds Frye's key terms "diffuse and interchangeable," and questions his claim to a distinterested scientific method; the attempt to integrate "the total universe of Western literature" seems to him closer to the apocalyptic vision of a religious mystic than to "the limited view of the scientist." Equally partisan and unscientific, in Sutton's view, is Frye's specific concern with Western literature and with "the Christian version of the rebirth archetype." Others have centered their objections on Frye's rejection of value judgments, without which the critic must presumably regard, say, Shakespeare and Tennyson as of equal significance.

But *Anatomy of Criticism* remains a remarkable achievement of learning and exposition and an extremely influential one; Frye is undoubtedly the most able systematizer of his time. And, whatever one's reaction to its central argument, a book that so lucidly and intelligently re-explores the fundamentals of critical theory is valuable and important if only because it obliges others to do the same. Its "Polemical Introduction" includes what is probably the most moderate and yet effective refutation of the "critic as parasite" theory, arguing that criticism is essential because "criticism can talk, and all the arts are dumb." Moreover, as Walter Sutton acknowledges, "Frye is a perceptive reader, and his work is full of original insights and unsuspected relationships brought to light by his interest in archetypes."

The sixteen critical essays collected in *Fables of Identity* are intended to illustrate the application of Frye's theories to individual authors, but not all reviewers seemed sure that they do so. "When Professor Frye goes in for practical criticism," said G. S. Fraser, "he seems to me excellent on a poet like Spenser, who might, indeed, have been writing to his prescriptions; much less good on a poet like Yeats, who talked a great deal about mythology, but whose permanent interest lies in the force of his personal reaction to a very concrete and actual world around him." Martin Price, similarly, wrote: "It is because he is so very brilliant and yet robust a critic, so sensible, vigorous, free, and even unsystematic at his best, that one digs in all the harder to resist the encyclopedist, the system-builder, and the astrologer who seems to lie in ambush within his work."

Frye's other books are, as he says, mostly based on lectures. *The Well-Tempered Critic* was called a "graceful repetition and extension of earlier accomplishments." *The Educated Imagination* proposes that literature, like every other art, is (as one reviewer put it) "a device through which man copes with his experiences of what is different from himself, reconceives his environment in less alien and more manageable ways, and defines for himself a place in it." *A Natural Perspective*, which suggests that Shakespearian comedy "represents a deliberate departure from the conventions of reality," was thought "so unobtrusively well organized and so alluringly readable that its hard substance may actually be overlooked." It is complemented by *Fools of Time*, which sets out to define three recurrent patterns in Shakespearian tragedy. According to a critic in the *Times Literary Supplement*, Frye's categories, as he himself concedes, "merge into and emerge from each other with extreme indistinctness. . . . What transpires is a kind of fluid myth-map of Shakespeare's historical and tragical plays, drawn up in a series of cool and choice epigrams, definitions, generalizations, and off-hand profundities. . . . Professor Frye makes up the rules of his game."

Northrop Frye, who lives in Toronto, was married in 1937 to Helen Kemp. He received the Canada Council Medal in 1967 for his services to literature. Frye left his post as Principal of Victoria College in 1967 to become a professor in the college's parent institution, the University of Toronto.

PRINCIPAL WORKS: Fearful Symmetry, 1947; Anatomy of Criticism, 1957; Fables of Identity, 1963; The Developing Imagination, 1963; The Well-Tempered Critic, 1963; T. S. Eliot, 1963; The Educated Imagination, 1964; The Return of Eden, 1965 (England, Five Essays on Milton's Epics); A Natural Perspective, 1965; Fools of Time, 1967; The Modern Century, 1967; A Study of English Romanticism, 1968; The Stubborn Structure: Essays on Criticism and Society, 1970.

ABOUT: Kermode, F. Puzzles and Epiphanies, 1962; Krieger, M. (ed.) Northrop Frye in Modern Criticism, 1966; Story, N. (ed.) Oxford Companion to Canadian History and Literature, 1967; Sutton, W. Modern American Criticism, 1963; Who's Who in America, 1970–1971. *Periodicals*—Cambridge Quarterly Spring 1967; Hudson Review Winter 1965; Listener May 9, 1968; Yale Review June 1964.

***FUENTES, CARLOS** (November 11, 1928–), Mexican novelist, short story writer, and essayist, is today the most distinguished exponent of the militant social conscience which first appeared in the literature of the Mexican Revolution. His biography, however, does not at all suggest the formation of a politically engaged writer. Born in Mexico City, the son of a career diplomat, he attended the best schools in several of the major capitals of the Americas. He learned English at the age of four in Washington, D.C., and lived subsequently in Santiago, Chile, and in Buenos Aires, before returning to study law at the University of Mexico. Subsequently he spent some time at the Institut des Hautes Études Internationales in Geneva.

* fwen′ tās

CARLOS FUENTES

From 1950 to 1952 Fuentes was a member of the Mexican delegation to the International Labor Organization in Geneva. Returning to Mexico he became in 1954 assistant head of the press section of the Ministry of Foreign Affairs, serving subsequently in a similar capacity at the University of Mexico (1955–1956) and as head of the department of cultural relations at the Ministry of Foreign Affairs (1957–1959). For much of this time, from 1954–1958, he was also editor of *Revista mexicana de literatura*, and later edited or coedited *El espectador*, *Siempre*, and *Política*. Since 1959 he has devoted himself to writing—novels, book reviews, political essays, travel pieces (written in English for *Holiday*), film scripts (for Luis Buñuel among others), and plays.

Fuentes is a realist by nature, but his search for the essence of Mexican reality often brings him to its roots in a variety of mythologies. For him, the Aztec, Christian, or revolutionary past is not simply a literary theme, but an atavistic force which must be reckoned with in describing today's society. Above all he is concerned with the Mexican Revolution and the failure of its promises, and this alone has earned him the hostility of the Mexican establishment and the fervent admiration of a new generation of freethinkers, who look to him for ideological leadership.

He began his literary career with a book of short stories, *Los días enmascarados* (Masked Days, 1954), in which he excoriates the vestigial customs and primitive modes of life that burden modern life in Mexico. This theme is developed in *La región más transparente* (1958), translated as *Where the Air Is Clear* by Sam Hileman (who has been responsible for all the English versions of Fuentes' books except *Aura*). In this extraordinary and influential first novel he attempts both a "biography of a city" and a "synthesis of present day Mexico." As Mario Vargas Llosa said, it "is a mural painting, pullulating and populous, of Mexico City" in the early 1950s, full of acrid insights into a country whose social revolution ceased to be truly revolutionary much too soon. Everyone is represented—oppressors and oppressed—in rapid cinematic flashes, a technique which Fuentes himself ascribes to his reading of Dos Passos. Through this spectrum of characters, he seeks the essence of modern Mexican man among a welter of formative influences and finds nothing—no shared philosophy or sense of purpose, nothing to prevent the strong preying endlessly upon the weak.

The stifling of the revolutionary instinct is the subject of *Las buenas conciencias* (1959, translated as *The Good Conscience*) a more conventional novel intended as the first volume in a planned tetralogy since abandoned. It is set in Guanajuato, the bastion of provincial conservatism, and shows how an exalted young liberal finally capitulates to the false values of his bourgeois family. Paradoxically it is at this moment, when he accepts and acknowledges his essential weakness and traditionalism, that Fuentes credits him with honesty and a kind of courage: "[It] is the only time he is absolutely sincere with himself. The one time he admits the truth."

La muerte de Artemio Cruz (1962, translated as *The Death of Artemio Cruz*), is a richly orchestrated historical tour de force depicting once again the failure of the revolution, this time through the ruminations of the dying robber baron Artemio Cruz as he recalls scenes in his life from the horrors of the revolution to the present. Here, as in *La región más transparente*, Fuentes attempted a panorama of recent Mexican history, and many critics thought he had succeeded. Others, however, like a reviewer in the *Times Literary Supplement*, considered that Fuentes had dealt more successfully with physical detail and atmosphere than with character or history: "What remains when the book is over is not an impression of wide stretches of history or landscape but pleasing small pictures of moments or moods."

The technique of second person narrative, which Fuentes uses at times in *Artemio Cruz*, is employed throughout his Jamesian novella *Aura* (1962, translated by Lysander Kemp under the same title). This relatively slight work was followed by *Cambio de piel* (1967, translated as *A Change of Skin*), which at the narrative level describes the pilgrimage of five characters from Mexico City to Vera Cruz for Holy Week. The book's more fundamental concern is with man's primitive but indestructible notions of vengeance and atonement—with what Anthony West called our "astonishing capacity for rationalizing blood sacrifices at every level of cultural development and under every form of social organization." Some found the book overburdened by its symbolism, or were irritated by Fuentes' use of so many fashionable devices (including a capricious narrator toying with reality). And in Spain the novel was described as "pornographic, communistic, anti-Christian, anti-German and pro-Jewish"—terms which must no doubt be regarded as pejorative in intent. For many readers however, *Cambio de piel* seemed in its scope and energy, and in the skill with which Fuentes recreates the varied backgrounds of his characters, a work close to greatness. *Cumpleaños* (Birthday), a short novel reminiscent of the work of Jorge Luis Borges, appeared in 1969.

Apart from his novels, Fuentes has also published a volume of admirable short stories, *Cantar de ciegos* (Tales of the Blind, 1964), several collections of essays, and the plays *Todos los gatos son pardos* (All Cats Are Gray, 1970) and *El tuerto es rey* (The One-Eyed Man Is King, 1970). An interviewer in the New York *Times* has described Fuentes as "a taut, handsome man with wavy chestnut hair, a thick mustache and long sideburns." His political views have made him *persona non grata* in the United States, and the decision to forbid him to enter Puerto Rico in February 1969 led to a spate of liberal attacks on United States immigration policy. For a time he was also excluded from his own country, as a result of his denunciation of the Mexican government's brutal repression of student demonstrations during the 1968 Olympic Games. He spent his exile in Paris—where he witnessed the events he describes in *Paris: La revolución de Mayo* (1968)—but has now returned to Mexico City. In September 1971 Fuentes acted as spokesman for a group of leftist intellectuals and labor leaders who created a new informal political organization to challenge by non-violent means the one-party rule of the dominant Institutional Revolutionary party. Fuentes was married to the actress Rita Macedo in

1959 and has a daughter. The marriage ended in divorce in 1969. Anthony West thinks him "perhaps the only living Latin American writer who . . . [can] make the passion of the land's rebirth and repossession comprehensible to the outsider."

PRINCIPAL WORKS IN ENGLISH TRANSLATION: Where the Air Is Clear, 1960; The Good Conscience, 1961; The Death of Artemio Cruz, 1964; Aura, 1965; A Change of Skin, 1968.

ABOUT: Current Biography, 1972; Harss, L. and Dohmann, B. Into the Mainstream, 1967; International Who's Who, 1972–1973; Langford, W. M. The Mexican Novel Comes of Age, 1971; Schwartz, K. A New History of Spanish American Fiction, 1971; Who's Who in America, 1972–1973. *Periodicals*—Book Week November 7, 1965; Books Abroad Summer 1966; Commonweal February 10, 1961; Commentary February 1965; Encounter September 1965; Hispania May 1967; Nation April 21, 1962; June 1, 1964; January 3, 1966; New York Review of Books June 11, 1964; New York Times November 17, 1968; February 28, March 3, December 3, 1969; New York Times Book Review February 4, 1968; New Yorker March 4, 1961; June 8, 1968; Publishers' Weekly March 10, 17, 1969; Revista Iberoamericana July-December 1965; Saturday Review January 27, 1968; Times Literary Supplement September 30, 1965; November 2, 1967; March 7, 1968; November 14, 1968.

EDMUND FULLER

FULLER, EDMUND (MAYBANK) (1914–), American novelist, critic, memoirist, and editor, has taught at Columbia University, at St. Stephen's School in Rome, and at the South Kent School, an Episcopal preparatory school in Connecticut. He has also been a senior editor in a New York publishing house, and reviews regularly for the *Wall Street Journal.*

Fuller began his literary career in the early 1940s as editor of a series of thesauri—of quotations, of anecdotes, and of epigrams and *bons mots.* His first novel was *A Star Pointed North* (1946), a fictionalized biography of Frederick Douglass which was generally well received. *Brothers Divided* tells the very different stories of two brothers who come to maturity during the 1930s. One is an artist who dies, after a short colorful life, in the Spanish War; the other, a Presbyterian minister, is left to pick up the pieces, care for his brother's illegitimate son, and comfort his widow. Reviewers found much in the book that was inept, and complained about its complex and sometimes improbable plot, but were almost unanimous in agreeing that the novel's "power and urgency," its "intensity of conviction," outweighed its technical weaknesses. Donald Harrington called it "sincere, warm, and always absorbing, an unusual portrait of a generation. . . ."

In Fuller's third novel, *The Corridor* (1963), a husband waits in a hospital to know whether his wife will live or die, and is driven to examine his "ideal marriage" and what it means to him—its guilts and angers, as well as its joys. Although the story first appeared in *Good Housekeeping*, it avoids "most of the soap-opera clichés of the *genre*," and for Virgilia Peterson was lifted "above mere adequacy [by] the author's underlying, passionate belief in married happiness as the greatest boon on earth." One or two reviewers seemed to find the book a little dull, and David Dempsey, who liked it, was nevertheless troubled by its "terrible moral earnestness" and didacticism. In a later novel, *Flight*, the middle-aged narrator sets out to help two adolescents who have absconded to Venice. Haskel Frankel thought the book rather too much like a television discussion program, but admired the author's willingness to tackle some difficult contemporary problems, while eschewing the sensationalism of the "generation-gap" novel.

To many readers Fuller is best known as the author of *Man in Modern Fiction* (1958), which attacks those trends in contemporary American writing that conflict with or ignore the image of man deriving from the Judeo-Christian moral tradition. He deals critically with such questions as the treatment of women and sex in modern fiction, the influence of Joyce, the prevalence of an amoral and clinical viewpoint, and the compassionate treatment, on the other hand, of the bum, the brute, and the hipster. Fuller's "minority opinions" divided his reviewers along predictable lines. Some praised his "wit and devastating gift for demolishing popular idols," and echoed his "air of Christian outrage"; others as fervently disagreed. "When one is seriously invited to slam the door on Algren and Bellow," one critic wrote, "and to make room for the estimable Nancy Wilson Ross, something inward rebels." Fuller continued his argument in *Books With Men Behind Them* (1962), a companion volume which discusses some contemporary books not simply in aesthetic terms but as projections of their authors, on the theory that "a good book will have a good man behind it." He singles out seven writers who have, as one reviewer put it, "a significant vision of experience and a unique artistic medium for its revelation": Thornton Wilder, Gladys Schmitt, Alan Paton, C. P. Snow, C. S. Lewis, J. R. R. Tolkien, and Charles Williams.

In 1948, in an attempt to escape the tensions of New York life, Fuller bought a ramshackle farm in Vermont and moved there with his wife Ann, his three children, and his mother-in-law, Virginia Graham. A fourth child was born during their four-year struggle to restore the farm to working order—a struggle abandoned in 1952 when the physical difficulties of the task and the farm's cultural isolation proved unbearable. Some years later, looking back on this adventure with a mixture of wry amusement and nostalgia, Fuller wrote an admirable account of it in *Successful Calamity*.

Edmund Fuller is the author of *A Pageant of the Theatre*, a fascinating panorama of the art from its prehistoric beginnings to Samuel Beckett. He has written a biography of Milton for teenagers, a "shrewd and witty" study of Shaw, histories of Vermont and of the Yankee inventors, and an account of what happened when Prudence Crandall opened a school for black girls in nineteenth century Connecticut. He is prolific as an editor in a number of fields.

PRINCIPAL WORKS: *Novels*—A Star Pointed North, 1946; Brothers Divided, 1951; The Corridor, 1963; Flight, 1970. *Nonfiction*—A Pageant of the Theatre, 1941 (rev. 1965); John Milton, 1944; George Bernard Shaw, Critic of Western Morale, 1950; Vermont: A History of the Green Mountain State, 1952; Tinkers and Genius: The Story of the Yankee Inventors, 1955; Man in Modern Fiction, Some Minority Opinions on Contemporary American Writing, 1958; Books With Men Behind Them, 1962; Successful Calamity: A Writer's Follies on a Vermont Farm, 1966; Prudence Crandall: An Incident of Racism in Nineteenth-Century Connecticut, 1971.

ABOUT: Fuller, E. Successful Calamity, 1966; Vinson, J. (ed.) Contemporary Novelists, 1972.

FULLER, J(OHN) F(REDERICK) C(HARLES) (September 1, 1878–February 10, 1966), English military historian, was born in Chichester, Sussex. He was the son of Alfred Fuller, a clergyman, and of the former Selma de la Chevallerie. Fuller attended a "dame school" in Chichester and then went with his family to Lausanne, where, as he wrote, he "attended various schools, fought big and little Swiss boys; paid twopence . . . to see a cannibal bite heads off rabbits; ran several miles . . . to watch a murderer have his head off with a broadsword and, to my despair, arrived there a few minutes too late."

Back in England, Fuller attended a preparatory school in Hampshire and then Malvern College, which he detested. In 1898, after a year at Sandhurst, he joined the Oxfordshire and Buckinghamshire Light Infantry as a subaltern. He enjoyed a roving commission as an intelligence officer during the Boer War, then did a tour of duty in India, contracting a lifelong interest in Yoga and also a fever which sent him back to England. In 1904 he was married to Sonia Kainatzki, daughter of a Warsaw doctor. In these early years Fuller found soldiering "intensely boring." He seems to have changed his mind when he entered the Staff College in 1913. At any rate, it was at about that time that he began to write the articles and books which quickly earned him a reputation within the British army as a brilliant heretic.

From the beginning, Fuller showed a lack of faith in cavalry tactics, an ungentlemanly interest in the new hardware of war. During World War I he found his niche as a staff officer with the newly formed tank units, and developed his flair for fitting tactics to the capabilities of the new weapons. He fought in France and Flanders and won a DSO in 1917. After the war Fuller served as chief instructor at the Staff College, as military assistant to the chief of the Imperial General Staff, and as commander of the 13th Infantry Brigade. Promoted to major general in 1930, but highly unpopular with his colleagues, he was offered an inadequate post in India, refused it, and in 1933 was retired.

Throughout his military career, and especially during World War I, Fuller had with good reason been appalled by the ignorant dogmatism of the British high command, the "medieval witchcraft" that passed for tactics, the blind resistance to new ideas and new weapons. In support of his campaign for mechanization and preparedness, he began a profound inquiry into the causes, conduct, and effects of war. Fuller became a Fascist in the 1930s, and his philosophy of history is neither attractive nor convincing. He put his faith in "Great Men" and "Great Ideas," had little use for the mass of humanity, and came to the conclusion that war was a product of easy living and immorality.

Fuller was a polemical writer, and most of his books are to some extent marred by his views. Even his great *Decisive Battles* is weakened, it is said, by his blindness "to the values of that very society of the West whose conflicts he has set himself to describe." But the *Military History of the Western World*, a three-volume revision and expansion of *Decisive Battles*, seemed to some critics more mellow and more mature, and is widely regarded as his masterpiece. And as a narrative historian, as distinct from an interpretive one, Fuller was superb. He believed that "truth is courage intellectualized," and was so thorough in research that *Decisive Battles* was announced as a work based on "a thousand books." He always preferred, he said, "to consult

J. F. C. FULLER

the writings of participants in and eyewitnesses of events. . . . They bring their readers into closer contacts with the emotions, sentiments, and feelings of their day." His style has been called "clear, vivid, and colorful . . . punctuated by keen metaphors," and in his understanding of the conduct of war he had no contemporary superior. David H. Zook, writing in *Military Affairs*, said: "There is good reason to treat him as the greatest historian, in his field, that the English world has produced. This judgement can be supported by the great breadth of his scholarship, the vast body of material he has mastered, the brilliance and originality of his conclusions, the uniqueness of his method and the unquestioned depth of his mind."

Fuller wrote about thirty books. They have been widely translated and have had a decisive influence on the evolution of tactics, notably in Germany, whose blitzkrieg technique owes much to Fuller's thought, and in Russia, which adopted his concept of combined tank-air operations in World War II. *Memoirs of an Unconventional Soldier*, Fuller's autobiography, is outspoken in its criticism of the military clique, reticent about his own life, but generous to his friends. He was a Fascist who wrote knowledgeably about Yoga and *The Secret Wisdom of the Qabalah*, and a soldier who hated war and brutality. Liddell Hart called him "one of the most remarkable men I have known in any sphere."

PRINCIPAL WORKS: Foundations of the Science of War, 1926; Warfare, 1928; The Generalship of Ulysses S. Grant, 1929; Operations Between Mechanized Forces, 1932; War and Western Civilization, 1832–1932, 1932; Generalship: Its Diseases and Their Cure, 1933; Grant and Lee: A Study in Personality and Generalship, 1933; The Army in My Time, 1935; Memoirs of an Unconventional Soldier, 1936; Decisive Battles (2 vols.), 1940; Decisive Battles of the U.S.A., 1942; The Second World War, 1948; The Decisive Battles of the Western World, and Their Influence Upon History (U.S., A Military History of the Western World) (3 vols.), 1954–1956; The Generalship of Alexander the Great, 1958; The Conduct of War, 1961; Julius Caesar, 1965.

ABOUT: Contemporary Authors 15–16, 1966; Crossman, R. H. S. The Charm of Politics, 1958; Higham, R. The Military Intelligence in Britain, 1966. *Periodicals*—American Journal of Economics April 1960; Atlantic November 1949; Commonweal November 9, 1945; Infantry Journal December 1945; Military Affairs no. 4 Winter 1959–60; New Republic March 14, 1949; April 8, 1967; New York Times August 5, 1923; December 29, 1929; February 11, 1966; Publishers' Weekly February 21, 1966; Reader's Digest February 1953; Spectator February 2, 1951; Time November 30, 1942; Times (London) February 11, 1966; Times Literary Supplement July 20, 1956; November 14, 1958.

FURNAS, J(OSEPH) C(HAMBERLAIN) (November 24, 1905–), American biographer, historian, novelist, and journalist, writes: "I was born in Indianapolis, Indiana. Somehow I learned to read at the age of three. Both my grandfathers were farmers a few miles outside town; so while my rearing was basically urban, I had much time in summer among barns and woods and country cooking. There and everywhere else I read and read—junk and more nourishing stuff mingled higgledy-piggledy. In the same month, for instance, on a farmhouse-porch scratching chigger-bites and listening to the quail whistling in the field across the road, I read *Vanity Fair* and Bertha M. Runkle's *The Helmet of Navarre*. Both came from the same small, glass-lined bookcase in the sitting-room. In the overheated, boxy-square house in town I read all the books in the elaborate sets that book-agents sold my mother, which, fortunately, included Scott, Kipling, Stevenson, Dickens, and an arty series of translations from European virtuosos of the short story such as Mérimée and Daudet. In the overheated big white house on the huge fruit farm that my great uncles operated outside town another glassed bookcase supplied me with *The Virginian* and Lemprière's *Classical Dictionary*. Behind the bookcase-glass in my aunt's overheated square house in a suburb of Chicago I found *Three Men in a Boat*, from which I first learned that the mere printed page could make me laugh till my belly-muscles ached.

"At that same age of three they put me into glasses. Wearing them was then a handicap in athletics, at which I'd have been no good anyway. I was oppressively bright in the local public school, which was vapid in spite of being run by an experiment-minded disciple of John Dewey. I was also oppressively bright in a local high school. Its school paper led to school-notes for the Indianapolis *News*, revenue from which paid for my first

J. C. FURNAS

typewriter, a three-shift Corona. The *News* offered me a cub's job on one of its small-town, upstate newspapers, but I had been accepted at Harvard and thought I should go straight on there—a decision that I am now in two minds about. At Harvard the Corona kept busy on college publications as well as academic chores. Sporadic and then absolute lack of money made it advisable for me to work at odd jobs summers and during all of my senior year. Thanks to complications therein involved, I am probably the only member of Phi Beta Kappa ever elected while on disciplinary probation.

"The impulse to write was always there, sometimes specific, sometimes rather generalized. After college I had several years of highly educational and penurious floundering in New York. Just as the depression was bearing down hard I had the luck to be put in touch with the Brandt & Brandt literary agency through which non-fiction magazine-work, e.g., for the *Saturday Evening Post*, began to come my way. In 1935 I did a piece for the *Reader's Digest* on deaths in traffic accidents that came at just the right moment and caused a nation-wide furore that was excellent promotion for me. For the next nine years I worked intensively at reporting for slick magazines, learning much, traveling much, prospering; and in intervals writing two novels that were well reviewed and meagerly bought. A third novel, interrupted half-written by World War II, I picked up again in 1961 and finished it over twenty years later. Nobody can tell where the joint occurs, which may mean that I had not grown any in the interval.

"During the war my reporting was largely confined to this country with the exceptions of a North Atlantic convoy cruise with a Royal Canadian Navy corvette in the crucial winter of 1942–3 and a correspondent's stretch in the South Pacific in 1945. As soon as possible I returned to that area for legwork on a large book about it that won the 1948 non-fiction Annisfield-Wolf award for contribution to good inter-racial relations. That led to a biography of Robert Louis Stevenson, using new material then just come to light. Heightening interest in racial problems put me on a book about the American Negro that, coming soon after the Supreme Court decision on educational facilities, was a widely noticed Book-of-the-Month; its sequel dealt with the implications of John Brown. Consequent interest in the crusader-personality resulted in a book on the American Temperance and Prohibition Movements.

"In 1931 I married Helen Winthrop Levinson of Chicago; our first date was financed by my pawning the Phi Beta Kappa key. In 1940, after years in New York, we built a simple 'modern' house on thirty wooded acres in rural New Jersey. I do the vegetable-gardening, wood-chopping and other strong-back-and-weak-mind chores as physical and mental conditioning. You can do a lot of thinking and working-off of professional strains while spading a vegetable patch or felling a tree with an axe, not a power-saw.

"Obviously writing and good reading are the medium I live in as a fish lives in water. For me the best place to do a piece of writing is on board ship, preferably a freighter, on a long voyage, the fewer ports the better."

Furnas's prize-winning *Anatomy of Paradise*, about life in the South Seas before and after the white man came, was followed by *Voyage to Windward*, another major success. David Daiches called it "the definitive life" of Robert Louis Stevenson, "accurate, perceptive, understanding, drawing on much unpublished material, the product of indefatigable research and clear intelligence."

J. C. Furnas is a humanist who dislikes fanaticism of every kind, and has always been happy to say so. Thus, in *Goodbye to Uncle Tom*, he sets out to demolish the anthropological and cultural fallacies that have relegated the black to an inferior place in American society, sparing the sentimental condescension of Harriet Beecher Stowe and her like no more than the vicious lies of the racialists. His "odd, pugnacious" book *The Road to Harper's Ferry* extends his attack on the Abolitionists, arguing that their fanaticism was largely responsible for the Civil War, and in *The Life and Times of the Late Demon Rum* he turns his attention to the Temperance Movement, telling "the story of the unavailing effort to make the American man over in the image of the American woman" with wit, grace, and vigor. *The Americans* is a rather undisciplined account of the development of national attitudes and practices from 1587 to 1914—less a considered analysis than an anthology of fascinating facts and anecdotes. It was a Book-of-the-Month Club selection.

The touch of the documentary writer is evident in his fiction. *The Devil's Rainbow*, for example, develops in the form of a novel Bernard de Voto's suggestion that Joseph Smith, founder of the Mormon faith, was a paranoiac who brought about his own destruction. There was a feeling that in spite of its "richly dramatic material" (which of course offended many readers), the book never quite came alive.

Gerald Carson has called Furnas "an accomplished scholar-journalist and a man of the Enlightenment." His scholarship is extensive and dependable, if not quite impeccable, but he is at times inclined to weaken his thesis by overstatement. His highly individual style pleases some and irritates others; it has been called "sometimes jaunty, sometimes pretentious, occasionally epigrammatic, given to odd and archaic words and hyphenated phrases." At his best, as in *The Life and Times of the Late Demon Rum*, he writes "with a brio that recalls the great days of the *American Mercury*."

Furnas is the son of Isaiah and Elizabeth (Chamberlain) Furnas. He credits his wife with assisting him "as researcher, editor and whetstone to an extent that amounts practically to collaboration."

PRINCIPAL WORKS: *Nonfiction*—Anatomy of Paradise: Hawaii and the Islands of the South Seas, 1948; Voyage to Windward: The Life of Robert Louis Stevenson, 1951; Goodbye to Uncle Tom, 1956; The Road to Harper's Ferry, 1959; The Life and Times of the Late Demon Rum, 1965; The Americans: A Social History of the United States, 1587–1914, 1969. *Novels*—The Prophet's Chamber, 1935; Many People Prize It, 1937; The Devil's Rainbow, 1962; Lightfoot Island, 1968.

ABOUT: Who's Who in America, 1970–1971. *Periodicals*—New York Herald Tribune Book Review October 28, 1951; New York Times Book Review October 14, 1951; Saturday Evening Post June 1, 1957.

GADDA, CARLO EMILIO (November 14, 1893–May 21, 1973), Italian novelist, was born in Milan, "two weeks before the fall of the first Giolitti ministry," as he chose to put it himself. His father, who died when Gadda was a child, came of a distinguished family of considerable means, lost in a series of industrial speculations. His mother, of German origin, was a cultivated woman, forced to bring up her family alone and under great financial difficulty, yet still ambitious, and vainly striving to keep up appearances beyond her means.

Gadda studied at the Milan Polytechnical Institute, qualified as an industrial engineer, and practiced that profession for many years. He fought in World War I and was taken prisoner, an experience recorded in his greatly admired *Giornale di guerra e di prigionia* (Journal of War and Imprisonment), which was not published in full until 1955. Gadda's tormented relationship with his mother, his almost pathological attachment to a brother who was killed in World War I, and his jealousy because this brother was their mother's favorite, are all reflected in *La cognizione del dolore*, which also had to wait many years for publication in book form. Gadda lived in Argentina, France, Germany, and Belgium, as well as in various parts of Italy; after the end of World War II he made Rome his permanent residence.

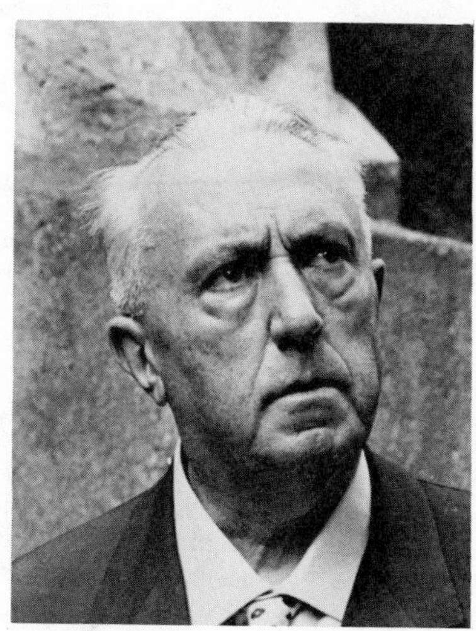

CARLO EMILIO GADDA

His first two books were published under the aegis of the Florentine review *Solaria. La Madonna dei filosofi* (The Philosophers' Madonna, 1931) provides a fairly typical example of his substance and his manner; the "stories" it tells serve primarily as a basis for commentary of a philosophical-lyric nature on the human adventure. In *Il castello di Udine* (The Castle of Udine, 1934), the second of the *Solaria* publications, the narrative element is somewhat more robust and the book is notable for strong characterizations and realistic military accounts. *L'Adalgisa* (1944) is essentially an evocation of the life of Milan, somewhat satirical in tone. Of similar content and color are the stories and vignettes that compose the *Novelle del ducato in fiamme* (Tales of the Duchy in Flames, 1953—the "duchy" being Mussolini's Italy); here too narrative and satire are sometimes reinforced and sometimes strangled by an irresistible tendency to digress.

Gadda's masterpiece is *Quer pasticciaccio brutto de*

via Merulana (1957), generally known in Italy as *Il pasticciaccio* (The Pastiche), and translated by William Weaver as *That Awful Mess on Via Merulana*. In outline it is a detective story, describing the investigation into a grotesque crime of violence on the Via Merulana (or, as some critics hold, into the roots of fascism in Italy). The mystery is in any case never solved, but along the way it serves to introduce a baroque gallery of pimps, porters, whores, petits bourgeois, and others—the bizarre components of a monstrous society.

The incomparable richness of the book is in its language, which moves, as Harold Brodkey says, "from high-euphuistic Latino-rhetoric through philosophico-theological jargon and gaudy Italian journalese, through . . . a large number of dialects" —mostly Roman, but also Neapolitan, Milanese, and the sophisticated Italian of the educated classes. It is indeed an immense anthology of pastiche which ransacks the Italian language, past and present, for its models, and when these are exhausted invents new ones. It forms a radical assault upon the Italian character through its linguistic and literary assumptions. This Joycean "anti-epic" is widely regarded as the work with which Italian fiction reenters the mainstream of contemporary European literature.

An equally extraordinary work is *La cognizione del dolore* (1963, translated by William Weaver as *Acquainted With Grief*). Written between 1938 and 1941, during the last days of fascism, it is set in a fictional South American state, Maradagàl, which is nevertheless transparently Italy. An evocation rather than a tale, it centers on the relationship between Gonzalo, a middle-aged engineer, and his mother, the mistress of an impoverished country estate. They live together but alone, unable to communicate either with each other or with the peasants among whom they live. The novel begins satirically, Gadda using all his wit and linguistic ingenuity to make bitter fun of the petty vices and vanities of his society. But the appearance of the haunted, raging Gonzalo dispels the humor, and the mood darkens into violence. At the end of the book there is an apparently successful attempt to murder the mother—in fact by an employee of the sinister Nistitúo (which represents fascism), but in a sense through the agency of the tragic Gonzalo himself. So painfully personal is this book that Gadda did not allow its publication in Italy until 1963, and only then without its lacerating and incomplete final section, which Gadda referred to as a "self-inflicted wound." A further fragment of this section appeared in the English translation of 1969, and two more chapters in a new Italian edition in 1970.

Like *Il pasticciaccio*, the book is remarkable for its linguistic virtuosity, and its brilliant use of Italian dialect. Richard Howard referred to it as "a discourse of scatological obsession, brutal self-confidence . . . and pathetic self-loathing; a text deliberately fashioned to appear inadequate, contesting the very means by which its stunning victories over silence are gained, and gainsaid—is this a novel? It will be one, perhaps—when the canon is closed. For now, it is a voice sounded, a passion discharged." Gadda's first novel, *La meccanica*, written in 1924 and in 1928–1929 but (characteristically) never completed, was published for the first time in 1970. It is a study of lower- and middle-class life in Milan during World War I, relatively mild in its humor and orthodox in its language, but worth reading according to one critic "not only for its own sake but because in it we can find the seeds of Gadda's later masterpieces." Three more interesting fragments, begun between 1928 and about 1932, but never completed, were published in 1973 under the title *Novella seconda*.

Gadda was not much interested in narrative, and his habit of digression irritates some readers. Others are offended by his fondness for (or fascinated disgust with) Rabelaisian grossness. Gianfranco Contini, however, sees him as the savior of Italian letters and many would agree with that and with Vittorini's description of him as "the greatest Italian novelist, indeed the only great one." He greatly influenced, among others, Pasolini, Arbasino, and Sanguinetti. Among his awards were the Prix Formentor (1957) and the Prix Internationale de Littérature (1963). In 1967 Gadda published *Eros e Priapo*, an essay on, more or less, the psychology of fascism. A reviewer in the *Times Literary Supplement* called it "a brilliantly impressionistic and often extremely funny account of attitudes, of feelings, of tensions and absurdities, of all kinds of Italianness, fascist or not specifically so, seldom unearthed let alone discussed; written in the most extreme form of Gadda's endlessly inventive language, which seems to spin itself, rather than be spun by Gadda, so totally are style and subject one, so completely does Gadda persuade one of the exactness, the inevitability even, of his extraordinary method." A shy and courtly man, he chose to live in a cheap apartment house in Rome and to work amid the clatter of dishes and yelling of children.

PRINCIPAL WORKS IN ENGLISH TRANSLATION: That Awful Mess on Via Merulana, 1965; Acquainted with Grief, 1969.
ABOUT: Contini, G. Letteratura dell'Italia unita 1861–1968, 1968; Devoto, G., Studi di stilistica, 1950; Pacifici, S. (ed.) From Verismo to Experimentalism: Essays on the Modern Italian Novel, 1969; Penguin Companion to Literature 2, 1969; Robertis, G. de. Scrittori del novecento, 1940; Roscioni, G. C. La disarmonia prestabilita, 1970; Seroni, A. C. E. Gadda, 1969; Weaver, W. *introductions to* That Awful Mess on Via Merulana, 1965, and Acquainted with Grief, 1968; Who's Who in Italy, 1957–1958. *Periodicals*—Book Week September 5, 1965; London Magazine October 1963; Nation November 1, 1965;

New York Times Book Review September 29, 1963; August 29, 1965; Saturday Review September 4, 1965; Times Literary Supplement September 30, 1965; May 26, 1966; September 25, 1970.

GADDIS, WILLIAM (December 29, 1922–), American novelist, writes: "Born in Manhattan, boarding school in Connecticut age five till about thirteen, public school on Long Island, Harvard College 1941–1945, a year or so on a New York magazine and the next five in Central America and the Caribbean, Europe mainly Spain, and briefly North Africa before returning to complete the partially written novel finally published in 1955, later issued in paper, and ground for a National Institute of Arts and Letters award in 1963, a sequence, significant only in any transmutations its details may find in my work, which has offered too many temptations to take myself instead of my work seriously, one of concern only to those whose good faith goes long unrewarded, and possibly of some eventual uncontrollable meaning to the son and daughter by whom I set such store, even as they prosper from beginnings that have redeemed more recent years unproductive of any accomplishment but getting a living, and groping in the tangle of apparently disparate projects which continue their struggle to devour, and develop, and illuminate one another, to escape whole the limitations of my own mind."

WILLIAM GADDIS

The Recognitions, William Gaddis's first and only novel, was begun in 1947 and published in 1955. It has been a subject of controversy from the beginning. The book takes its title from a religious work usually attributed to Pope Clement I. Its central character is a painter who forges old masters, but its real concern is a religious one with the uglier and commoner kinds of misrepresentation—emotional hypocrisy and moral cheating. Gaddis says: "People will disdain no . . . ruse at all to prove their own existence." He finds evidence to support this conviction in settings which include New England, Greenwich Village, Paris, Spain, Italy, and Central America. His testimony, presented with unflagging imaginative vitality and comic invention, occupies more than 950 pages.

In 1955 most critics seemed impressed by the book's sheer size and energy but irritated by its young author's audacity in tackling so vast a theme and also by his erudition, which many of them found too insistently evident. Milton Rugoff called it "easily the most exasperating *mélange* of genuinely scathing and merely random satire, of shrewd and of merely grotesque characterization, of clever dialogue and chaotic fragments, of apt allusion and pretentious display, of suggestive prose and turgid outpourings that this reader has come upon." Some reviews were considerably harsher.

The Recognitions was not forgotten, however. Its "underground" reputation grew steadily. One admirer even launched a periodical which was wholly devoted to praising and explaining the novel. When a paperback edition appeared in 1962 there was an altogether more respectful critical reception for it. The comparisons with Joyce's *Ulysses* suggested by its theme and scope were now made less invidiously. Philip Toynbee was reminded in addition of *The Waste Land*, of Gide's *Les Faux Monnayeurs*, of Mann's *Dr. Faustus*, of Dostoevsky's *The Idiot*—and also, by the book's style and organization, of Firbank, Norman Douglas, Conrad, and Faulkner, among others. At times, he said, it seemed to him like "a vast *summa* of the modern novel; an elaborate, semi-comic proof that all is over except for the iridescent sheen of parody and pastiche."

In fact, Toynbee believes, Gaddis wrote his book with multiple intentions—seeking to construct a satirical panorama of the modern world and also to write "the latest Christian novel as *The Recognitions* of Clement had been the earliest." Toynbee, acknowledging that the novel is too long and sometimes tiresomely mystifying, thought that Gaddis's "galloping excess of energy" had also contributed "a really astonishing richness of imagination . . . a depth of aesthetic experience; a deftness of fantasy" which make *The Recognitions* "a very important and a very impressive novel—among . . . the dozen most impressive novels in English which have appeared since the war."

PRINCIPAL WORK: The Recognitions, 1955.
ABOUT: Tanner, T. City of Words, 1971; Vinson, J. (ed.) Contemporary Novelists, 1972. *Periodicals*—Atlantic April

1955; Critique Winter 1962–1963; New York Herald Tribune Book Review March 13, 1955; New Yorker April 9, 1955; Newsweek March 14, 1955; Observer (London) September 9, 1962; Village Voice November 1, 1962; Wisconsin Studies in Contemporary Literature Summer 1965.

***GAISER, GERD** (September 15, 1908–), German novelist and short story writer, poet, essayist, and art historian, was born at Oberriexingen in Württemberg, the son of Hermann Gaiser, a Protestant minister, and the former Julie Lachenmann. He was influenced from earliest childhood by the Bible, which was read aloud daily at home, and the folk tales he heard from his governess, as well as by Cervantes' *Novelas Ejemplares*. As a schoolboy he studied classical languages and literature and came to admire Hölderlin and Stefan George. Like most young Germans of his generation Gaiser was involved in the youth movements of the 1920s, and he has retained a powerful nostalgia for the Spartan ideals and the comradeship he learned around the campfires. His parents intended him for the church, and Gaiser attended two theological seminaries before he decided that his vocation was for the creative arts. He studied at art academies in Stuttgart, Königsberg, and Dresden and traveled all over Europe before entering the University of Tübingen to work for his doctorate, which was granted in 1934 for a thesis entitled "Renaissance and Early Baroque Plastic Art in New Castile."

In 1935 Gaiser began his career as an art teacher in a secondary school. World War II intervened in 1939, and Gaiser, who had qualified as a glider pilot at the university, joined a fighter squadron of the Luftwaffe. His first book appeared in 1941, a volume of poems, full of idealistic patriotism, called *Reiter am Himmel* (Riders in the Sky). Another collection, *Gesang von Osten* (Song from the East), appeared in 1943. Gaiser ended the war in a British P.O.W. camp in Italy. After his release he earned his living as a laborer while he tried his luck as a freelance artist. In 1949 he returned to teaching as a drawing instructor and student counselor at the Gymnasium in Reutlingen, the city in Württemberg where he still lives.

In 1949 Gaiser published *Zwischenland* (The Land Between), containing seven related stories about rootless, homeless individuals in a shattered society. One of these, "Brand im Weinberg," is a sketch for what became his first published novel, *Eine Stimme hebt an* (A Voice Is Raised, 1950). It is an account of the return of a war veteran to his home town, which has become monstrously artificial and materialistic, and to his wife, who has cuckolded him. Oberstelehn (the name indicates his peasant descent), at first numbed by suffering and shock, comes to realize that he must try to rescue something of value from the flux and superficiality of the postwar world, and he sets out at last to repair his marriage.

This book, which established Gaiser's reputation, also introduced his principal themes and his unique style. He believes that nature—immortal, endless, ineluctable—is man's source and his salvation, which he ignores at his peril. Gaiser's heroes are those inevitably lonely individuals who understand this, who have not lost contact with nature, or their sense of continuity with the past. They speak out bravely against the greed and self-indulgence that possesses postwar Germany, and generally they are punished for their wisdom and courage. But they do not despair, knowing that history repeats itself forever and better times will surely return. These somewhat Nietzschean views are reflected in Gaiser's extraordinary style, which modulates from the chatty triviality he associates with the antics and speech of the new bourgeoisie, to the archaic constructions and biblical or epic simplicity of tone he applies to natural description. *Eine Stimme hebt an* brought Gaiser the Fontane Prize in 1951.

Die sterbende Jagd, which appeared in 1953 as Gaiser's second novel, was in fact begun during the war, when parts of it were published. Relatively direct in its style, it makes a characteristic distinction between the camaraderie and resigned heroism of its squadron of Luftwaffe pilots, fighting on in Norway in the face of disillusionment and death, and the moral squalor of the civilians who have betrayed them. Though some critics found the book a little diffuse, most admired the "aerial dance of death" of the final battle, and some thought it the finest German novel of World War II. It was translated as *The Last Squadron* (1956) and was generally well received in the United States.

Gaiser's clearest statement of his mystical attachment to nature and the heroic past is made in *Das Schiff im Berg* (The Ship in the Mountain, 1955). It tells the story of a fictitious mountain in southern Germany from its geological origins to the present day. The power and permanence of the mountain is contrasted with the triviality and transience of the men who live upon it and seek to exploit its caves as a tourist attraction. A boy, exploring the caves, is trapped and dies: "Of course he screamed a few more times, but there was not much noise left in him, and he became less and less conscious of himself." So much for man, who, for all his presumptuous scheming, is no more than "grass and dust."

Schlussball (1958) is set in a prosperous industrial town, Neu-Spuhl, thriving under the *Wirtschaftswunder*, Germany's "economic miracle." The people of Neu-Spuhl, softened and corrupted by success, are obsessed with materialism and the

* gī′ zər

crassest kind of snobbery. These reach their height as the final ball of the season approaches. The schoolmaster Soldner intervenes, insuring that the dance shall be open to all, but losing his job for his pains. (Gaiser is opposed to class distinction on the basis of income but favors an elite chosen for its ability and moral worth.) In *Schlussball*, utilizing some of the motifs, and even some of the characters, from his earlier books, Gaiser unfolds his story kaleidoscopically, in a series of monologues—by the living and the dead—which perfectly convey his vision of a society technologically brilliant but spiritually dead. On the basis of this novel the critic Günter Blöcker described Gaiser as "the most talented prose-writer in postwar German literature." *The Final Ball*, Marguerite Waldman's English version, also impressed some American reviewers with its careful construction and "poetically precise style"; others however found it somewhat gloomy and heavy-handed, overloaded with symbolism.

Gaiser's short stories, though they are sometimes more experimental in form, are concerned with similar themes. He has also written a number of books on the history of art, and an interesting travel book, *Sizilianische Notizen* (Sicilian Notes, 1949), full of his theories about nature.

Since 1962 Gaiser has been a *Dozent* (lecturer) in art education at the Pädagogische Hochschule, a teachers' training college, in Reutlingen. He has been married twice, to Elisabeth Schmidt in 1935, and to Irene Widmann in 1959. Gaiser has received a number of literary awards, including the Wilhelm Raabe prize of Brunswick (1956 and 1960). The Academy of Arts in West Berlin elected him to membership in 1956.

Some German critics have compared Gaiser's idyllic and brilliantly visual descriptions of nature to the work of the late Elisabeth Langgässer, and his "revolutionary conservatism," which puzzles and disturbs some readers, incorporates many ideas associated with Nietzsche, Hofmannsthal, and Ernst Jünger. His style, which so impresses like-minded writers such as Günter Blöcker, has been called "wretched" by those who dislike the views it expresses. He came to writing late and, as Ian Hilton has pointed out, retains in his work "a mixture of old and new, thereby creating a kind of ambivalence in form as much as he does in content through his seeming unreadiness to wholesale commitment."

PRINCIPAL WORKS IN ENGLISH TRANSLATION: The Last Squadron (England, The Falling Leaf), 1956; The Final Ball (England, The Last Dance of the Season), 1960. *Nonfiction*—The Present Quandary of German Novelists (essay) *in* Heitner, R. R. (ed.) The Contemporary Novel in German, 1967.

ABOUT: Handbuch der deutschen Gegenwartsliteratur, 1965; Gaiser *in* Keith-Smith, B. (ed.) Essays on Contemporary German Literature, 1966; Hohoff, C. Gerd Gaiser, 1962; International Who's Who, 1970–1971; Lennartz, F. Deutsche Dichter und Schriftsteller, 1963; Soergel, A. and Hohoff, C. Dichtung und Dichter der Zeit, 1963; Thomas, R. H. and Will, W. van der. The German Novel and the Affluent Society, 1968; Wer ist wer, 1969–1970; Wilpert, G. von. Deutsches Dichterlexicon, 1963.

GERD GAISER

***GALBRAITH, JOHN KENNETH** (October 15, 1908–), American economist, was born to William and Catherine (Kendall) Galbraith on a farm at Iona Station, on the north shore of Lake Erie in Ontario, Canada. The area had been settled by emigrants from Scotland, and Galbraith's memoir *The Scotch* gives a relaxed, anecdotal account of the country life and customs of the clansmen as he had observed them in his youth.

His own early experience of manual farm labor led Galbraith, as an economist, to doubt the supposed hostility of workers toward mechanization. Agriculture was his major subject at the University of Toronto, where he earned his B.S. in 1931. A research fellowship in economics at the University of California (Berkeley) ended in 1934, when Galbraith received his doctorate and began his teaching career at Harvard University. Apart from a year in England as a social science research fellow at Cambridge University, he taught at Harvard until 1939, when he went to Princeton as assistant professor of economics.

Even before the United States entered the war, Galbraith went to Washington to help the defense effort. The most important of his wartime assignments was the violently controversial and unpopu-

* gal brāth′

JOHN KENNETH GALBRAITH

lar one of establishing price controls. Galbraith did this so thoroughly that by 1943, as he says, his enemies outnumbered his friends, and he was obliged to resign from his post as deputy administrator of the Office of Price Administration. He spent the next five years on the board of editors of *Fortune* magazine, but continued to accept government appointments, directing studies of the effects of air attacks upon the German and Japanese economies, and later, after the war, of the progress of European economic recovery.

In 1949 Galbraith returned to Harvard as the Paul M. Warburg Professor of Economics, the post he has retained ever since. He had by no means withdrawn from public affairs, however. A liberal Democrat, he was a key figure in the presidential campaigns of Adlai Stevenson in 1952 and 1956. Harvard was also the base from which he wrote many of the books which made him a leading spokesman for a new economic philosophy. Galbraith's views are said to be basically Keynesian, but he is a pragmatic and therefore unorthodox thinker; if he regularly outrages conservatives (who have gone so far as to accuse him, with total inaccuracy, of Communist sympathies), he also offends Keynes's less flexible disciples.

American Capitalism, for example, while accepting the common view that the market is self-regulating, offers in the theory of "countervailing power" a highly unconventional explanation of the phenomenon. This much-discussed book also laid the cornerstone of Galbraith's reputation as the wittiest and most elegant stylist among American economists. His account of the Depression, *The Great Crash: 1929*, enhanced that reputation, and *The Affluent Society* made Galbraith's name a household word—not simply because of its great readability, but because it slaughtered a whole herd of cows sacred to traditional capitalist thought. In particular it pointed out how dangerously little was being spent on public services, how much on the consumer goods for which advertising created a wholly artificial demand.

In recent years Galbraith has made a number of excursions from the Harvard campus. *Journey to Poland and Yugoslavia* describes his 1958 tour of those countries as the first westerner to lecture on capitalist economics there since the Russian Revolution. A far more important assignment followed when Galbraith, an early supporter of and close adviser to President Kennedy, went as United States Ambassador to India (1961–1963). His contributions to Indian economic development, and his part in bringing about a cease-fire during the 1962 Chinese invasion, earned Galbraith the public thanks of Prime Minister Nehru. He has described the experience in his incisive, frank, and often amusing *Ambassador's Journal.*

Galbraith's special interest in the economic problems of underdeveloped nations is reflected in his Harvard seminar on that subject, which has attracted students from all over the world; in his work as economic adviser to the governments of India, Pakistan, and Ceylon; and in his writings. Some important and influential lectures he gave in India in 1961 were published the following year as *Economic Development in Perspective.*

In his 1966 Reith lectures for the British Broadcasting Corporation, Galbraith returned to another of his abiding concerns, the search for a realistic approach to the problems of corporate power in America. *The New Industrial State*, containing his Reith lectures, argues that the gradual institutionalization of the great corporations is blurring the distinctions between public and private enterprises and altering the entire economic structure in ways which may be either beneficial or dangerous to society, depending upon the nature of governmental reactions to the situation.

Among Galbraith's other writings are several technical books and pamphlets, which are not listed below, and *The Liberal Hour*, which is. This is a collection of lectures and magazine articles distinguished by his "barbed and witty style, a malicious joy in puncturing the orotund profundities of Conventional Wisdom, an outrageous propensity to call spades spades." A *jeu d'esprit* by "Mark Epernay" called *The McLandress Dimension* is generally credited to Galbraith, and describes the political uses of a system for measuring the average time in which an individual's thoughts "remain diverted from his own personality"—three seconds in the case of Richard Nixon, for example, three minutes in the case of Miss Elizabeth Taylor. Published in 1963, it was relished by critics as a "highly sophisticated spoof . . . of the pretensions of scientific management and sociometrics."

Reviewing *The New Industrial State* in the *New York Review of Books* (June 29, 1967), Robert L. Heilbroner described Galbraith as "an economist . . . who seeks to infuse economics with a social relevance that is, on the whole, egregiously missing from most of its current output." Because of his unorthodoxies, Heilbroner says, Galbraith "has not enjoyed the regard of his fellow economists to anything like the degree that he has enjoyed the acclaim of the public," although even his peers admire his literary style. Heilbroner shares this admiration, but finds in Galbraith's style—"aphoristic, terse, above all mocking"—a certain danger, a tendency to substitute "mocking irony" for "a clear moral commitment." The fact remains that Galbraith's "moral commitment" has been clear and forceful enough to make his name, as Heilbroner says, "very nearly anathema" to conservatives.

Galbraith usually spends his winters at Harvard, his summers at a farm in Vermont. In 1970–1971 he went to England as a Visiting Fellow of Trinity College, Cambridge. He married Catherine Atwater in 1927 and has three sons, Alan, Peter, and James. His interests range from skiing to Indian painting, and in 1968 he published his first novel, *The Triumph*, a satirical fable about the unexpected and unwelcome outcome of American interference in the affairs of a small Latin American republic. It had a generally favorable reception, though some reviewers found it "loftily condescending and relentlessly witty" in its style, and a little obvious in its message. Galbraith, who has been described as "whimsically Lincolnesque" in appearance, is six feet eight inches tall. He holds the President's Certificate of Merit and the Medal of Freedom, and has honorary doctorates from a number of universities. He became chairman in 1967 of Americans for Democratic Action.

PRINCIPAL WORKS: American Capitalism, the Concept of Countervailing Power, 1952 (revised 1956); The Great Crash: 1929, 1955; The Affluent Society, 1958; Journey to Poland and Yugoslavia, 1958; The Liberal Hour, 1960; Economic Development in Perspective, 1962 (expanded as Economic Development, 1964); The Scotch (England, Made to Last), 1964; The New Industrial State, 1967; The Triumph (novel), 1968; Ambassador's Journal, 1969; A Contemporary Guide to Economics, Peace and Laughter (essays), 1971; A China Passage, 1972; Economics and the Public Purpose, 1973.

ABOUT: Current Biography, 1959; Hession, C. H. John Kenneth Galbraith and His Critics, 1972; Sharpe, M. E. John Kenneth Galbraith and the Lower Economics, 1973; Strachey, J. The Strangled Cry, 1962; Who's Who, 1973; Who's Who in America, 1972–1973. *Periodicals*—Harper's Magazine December 6, 1961; New York Review of Books June 29, 1967; April 25, 1968; New York Times March 20, 1967; New York Times Magazine December 18, 1966; Time January 12, 1962; Times Literary Supplement October 30, 1969.

GALLANT, MAVIS (August 11, 1922–), Canadian short story writer and novelist, writes: "I was born in Montreal, Canada, and, although I have lived there only a few years of my life, it remains my favourite city. It is unique and unclassifiable. Most of the writers it has produced, in English and in French, reflect its climate, its racial tensions, and its mixture of elegance and ugliness. Few English-Canadians (fewer than two percent) are bilingual. I was extremely fortunate in that my father, who was British-born, knew nothing whatever about the local situation, still less that French was supposed to be an inferior language, and had me taught French almost from the time I could speak: I simply learned two words for everything. At the age of four, I was sent to a French convent school. Although my origins are English, German, Breton, and Roumanian, I was, and remained, 'Anglaise' to the nuns who taught me. They were extremely strict. Toys were forbidden, we dressed in black, and our sole recreation consisted of walking up and down a wooden platform in the garden. I was permitted some of my books from home (no other parents had ever made such a request, so that there was no precedent for refusal). These books were in English, which seemed to me the language of freedom and of an open world. It was also the language of *stories*, and the choice between writing in French or in English must have been made then. I began writing poems when I was about five. They were simply variations of English nursery songs and Christmas carols. I wrote only poems until I was about nineteen. Prose was limited to descriptions of people and their dialogue, not what could happen to them. I do not remember any period of childhood and adolescence when I was not writing something: I wrote some curious letters addressed to my future self—to myself as a writer, so to speak—reminding that person not to forget certain places and times. When I was thirteen, and no longer a child, I wrote, and kept in a sealed envelope for many years, a solemn promise that I would never forget what childhood had been like and would describe it accurately; however, like everyone else, I have forgotten. I do not remember what I expected to become or how I meant to spend my life, but there must have been an idea at work, for a friend who was at school with me in New York has told me that I have lived as I told her I wanted to when we were both fifteen. I began writing stories, plays and novels when I was nineteen, without attempting to have anything read or published. After a few years I destroyed a hamperful of manuscripts and began from scratch writing

MAVIS GALLANT

stories, one of which I eventually sent to the *New Yorker*. With rare exceptions the *New Yorker* has published nearly everything I have written since then. As far as my activities are concerned, I worked for a newspaper in Montreal for a few years, and then came to live in France. I have discovered that writers' lives tend to fall into a pattern, and mine is no different. They are often the product of a solitary childhood, and have known, early, the shocks of violent change. The vocation exists, and so does the gift; but vocation and gift are seldom of equal proportions, and I suppose that the struggle to equate them is the true and secret tension."

Eight of the twelve stories in *The Other Paris*, Miss Gallant's first book, were about Americans in Europe after World War II—people who, "lacking in either maturity or a sense of humor . . . can never distinguish between the trivial and the significant." William Peden, among others, admired the "sureness, grace and understanding" of Miss Gallant's writing. *Green Water, Green Sky*, which followed, seemed to some readers less a novel than a cluster of four short stories about the emotional breakdown of an American adolescent, who is exiled in Europe with her mother, a selfish and self-pitying divorcée. Another novella, "Its Image on the Mirror," appeared with a number of short stories in the collection called *My Heart Is Broken*.

Miss Gallant's first three books had a mixed reception. Edmund Wilson praised her "descriptions, amusing and acutely observed, of middle-class Scottish Canadian households," and indeed her gift for "evoking, by dialogue and detail, a variety of milieux." However, the lack of incident and emotional substance in her work displeased some critics, as did her frequently negative themes and sleazy characters. Chad Walsh said that in her work "external events are less important than inner drama," and that she "often understates to the point where the reader must supply most of the emotions, guided by subtle clues." It may be, as Edmund Wilson suggested, that she had not "found her form and her stance," and "that there may here be involved a difficulty of national identity which makes her orientations uncertain."

There were no such reservations about Mavis Gallant's next novel, *A Fairly Good Time*. It is set in Paris, where Shirley, a Canadian working as a professional translator, helplessly watches the breakdown of her marriage to Philippe, a French journalist and television personality. Isolated in a foreign country, immobilized by memories of her first husband's meaningless death and of her mother's insanity, she herself comes close to emotional collapse until she is returned to herself by her mother's death and the need to reorder her life. Elizabeth Janeway found a Dickensian gift for character and a prose which is "a serious delight," concluding: "Here are some facts about a world where the capacity for sympathy is a burden to its possessor, a deformity to others and, at the same time, represents the compassion we so desperately long for." Judith Rascoe praised "a talent, virtually unequaled, for the riveting detail," and said, "The story is haunting, almost a mystery in the religious sense: an event that moves us, has a meaning but no logical description. . . . Sometimes it seems that Mavis Gallant knows everything."

The author contributes a "Paris Letter" on literary and cultural affairs to the New York *Times Book Review*, and still writes from time to time for the *New Yorker*, among other journals.

PRINCIPAL WORKS: The Other Paris (stories), 1956; Green Water, Green Sky (novel), 1959; My Heart Is Broken (stories and a novella), 1964 (England, An Unmarried Man's Summer); A Fairly Good Time (novel), 1970; (with Raymond Jean) The Affair of Gabrielle Russier, 1971.

ABOUT: Author's and Writer's Who's Who, 1972; Vinson, J. (ed.) Contemporary Novelists, 1972; Wilson, E. O Canada, 1967.

GANN, ERNEST K(ELLOGG) (October 13, 1910–), American adventure story writer and memoirist born in Lincoln, Nebraska, writes: "Educated in various schools, with emphasis on military schools. No college, but spent two years at Yale Drama School.

"I began writing so long ago I cannot remember just when it was, but it was many years before I sold anything at all. Meanwhile, I worked at a variety of occupations including general managing a New York musical (Broadway).

"I learned to fly at a relatively early age when airplanes were still made of fabric, spruce, and glue. This skill in time became my true love and led me into innumerable adventures which I have since recorded in books and on film. I continued to fly professionally for over twenty years—all the while scribbling away on books which were astonishingly successful.

"Then for about eight years I eased slightly away from flying and took to sailing all over the world in various boats I had either purchased or built. So I am half sailor, half flyer, and it was only last summer, 1966, that I returned to flying professionally during the summer months from this island where I live.

"Although I still fly my own twin-engined amphibian from this island to any place on the North American continent that may intrigue me, I rather think that I will now swallow the professional anchor and propeller as well. I own a rather large farm here in a lovely green valley, and it is my hope to control my travel-worn feet a little better than I've been able to in the past.

"Here I work in a little house which was aptly enough the former chicken 'brooding' house. Here I brood over what the next sentence on the next page will be. I suppose I will continue to write as long as I can think—which is of questionable duration."

Ernest K. Gann, "the dean of American flying writers," is the son of George Kellogg and Caroline (Kupper) Gann. He grew up in St. Paul, Minnesota, where his father was an executive of the local telephone company. In his teens, photography and flying appealed to him more than academic studies. He began his career during the 1930s as a news photographer and, as soon as he could, became an airline pilot. Gann entered the U.S. Army Air Transport Command in 1942 and left it in 1946 as a captain and the holder of the Distinguished Flying Cross.

Gann's articles and stories had begun to appear before the war in pulp and aviation magazines, and his first books, nonfictional works about flying, were published in the early 1940s. His first novel, at any rate under his own name, was *Island in the Sky*, in which an Army transport plane crashes in the wastes of northern Canada. The book studies the behavior under stress of the carefully differentiated crew of five—a familiar formula which Gann handles, as one reviewer said, "with an economy of words and emotion that mark the poet of the air."

Many of Gann's subsequent novels have been mixed to a similar recipe, including his first best seller, *The High and the Mighty*. Here he worked with a larger cast of characters and a smaller stage,

ERNEST K. GANN

telling the story of a crippled airliner en route from Honolulu to San Francisco in which twenty people are confronted with the probability of imminent death. Reviewers found both the situation and the characters stereotyped, but they were fascinated by the detailed information about airline operations and flying technique which Gann wove into his narrative and impressed by his masterly building of suspense. Another major success, critical as well as popular, was *Twilight for the Gods*, about the epic voyage across the Pacific from Tahiti of an ancient barquentine. V. P. Hass called it "an absorbing tale of human beings at a moment of supreme crisis," and "a love letter to a way of life now virtually extinct." *The Antagonists* was a departure from Gann's usual themes, an absorbing fictional account of the last stand of the Zealots at Masada in 73 A.D. against the overwhelming might of Rome.

The most admired of all of Gann's books is not a novel but the autobiographical *Fate Is the Hunter*, "an episodic log" of his ten thousand flying hours in peace and war and an expression of his belief in the phenomenon of luck—his conviction that "the pattern of anyone's fate is only partly contrived by the individual." It is this idea, and the evidence that Gann provides in support of it, that raises the book above the ordinary and evoked so many critical comparisons with the work of Antoine de St. Exupéry. V. S. Pritchett in his review called Gann "a writer saturated in his subject" and said "he has the skill to make every instant sharp and important and we catch the fever to know that documentary writing does not often invite." Others praised the way Gann draws the reader "so intimately into the shielded sanctum of the cockpit," and his laconic tributes to so many lost comrades. The *Times Literary Supplement* found it "the best and most complete account of how an airline pilot grows up." The brig Albatross, and an extraordinary assortment of smaller craft that he has owned or sailed, from a Chinese junk to a Brazilian balsa raft, are evoked in another successful memoir, *The Song of the Sirens*.

Gann has been a movie buff since childhood, and most of his novels have been filmed from his own scenarios. According to Emmet Watson, he "is a man of immense personal dignity, a short, energetic fellow with a strong, friendly voice, a sense of humor, a zest for living, an eye for minutiae." His most serious diversion is painting; his favorite dress, the flyer's dishabille. Gann was first married in 1933 to Eleanor Michaud, by whom he has three children, and remarried in 1966 to Dodie Post, who often flies as his copilot when he ferries passengers from island to island in the Puget Sound area. His home is on San Juan Island, Washington.

PRINCIPAL WORKS: *Fiction*—Island in the Sky, 1944; Blaze of Noon, 1946; Benjamin Lawless, 1948; Fiddler's Green, 1950; The High and the Mighty, 1953; Soldier of Fortune, 1954; Twilight for the Gods, 1957; The Trouble With Lazy Ethel, 1958; Of Good and Evil, 1963; In the Company of Eagles, 1966; The Antagonists, 1971. *Nonfiction*—Fate Is the Hunter (autobiography), 1961; The Song of the Sirens, 1968.
ABOUT: Contemporary Authors 4, 1963; Who's Who in America, 1970–1971. *Periodical*—Flying June 1967.

***GANZO, ROBERT** (August 22, 1898–), French poet and archaeologist, writes (in French): "Born in Caracas, Venezuela, but a poet of the French language. Came to France as an adolescent and settled in Paris. While retaining his Venezuelan nationality he remained in France during the German occupation and took part in the Resistance.

"He published *Orénoque* [Orinoco] in 1938, and the critics immediately hailed him as one of the greatest poets of his time, 'un mallarméen cosmique' [a cosmic Mallarméan] as Jean Rousselot called him in his *Panorama critique des nouveaux poètes français* (1952). He added: 'There is not merely one question, for each of Ganzo's stanzas raises hundreds of this sort, so perfectly does he fuse all the means which language puts at the disposal of the spirit, and by means of which it itself becomes spirit.'

"One of his poems, *Lespugue*, published in 1939, shows its author's deep vocation for prehistoric research. By means of his poem he changes our conception of prehistoric man and at the same time makes us know and understand the oldest sculpture which we possess, a carving in fossil ivory discovered in 1922 by René de Saint-Perier at Lespugue (Haute-Garonne), which Ganzo obtained for the Musée de l'Homme in Paris.

"In his *Poètes contemporains* (Cahiers du Sud, 1951) Léon-Gabriel Gros wrote of *Lespugue* that it is '. . . a poem which is a glorification of poetry and also becomes a monument to the idol which gave rise to it. *Lespugue* is a mental tomb in which the primitive Venus is preserved forever in aromatic words, where a perpetual vigil is kept by a light which has every chance of lasting as long as the language which Ganzo uses. . . . The poetry of this century has not, since [Valéry's] *Le Cimetière marin*, produced a work at the same time so rich in content and so dazzling in form. It is the greatest poem of religious eroticism written in our time.'

"Ganzo has for many years devoted himself to the study of excavations in the caves and prehistoric strata of the Dordogne and elsewhere. It used to be thought that with the disappearance of the reindeer from Western Europe about fifteen thousand years ago the last Magdalenian [Upper Paleolithic] men also disappeared. But some important protohistoric burial sites which Ganzo discovered in 1958 in the Massif of Fontainebleau, at Villeneuve-sur-Auvers and at Huison, belong to the earliest stage of population settlement on land stretching from the Mediterranean to the Atlantic newly uncovered by the last phase of withdrawal of the northern glacier. The first really settled inhabitants of these regions, after thousands of years of nomadism and migration, are called Campigniens (after the type locality of Le Campigny, at the mouth of the River Seine, where in 1968 the Morgan brothers discovered new stone tools) and are the founders of our village and agricultural civilization. In the graves discovered by Robert Ganzo, Magdalenian and Campignien tools were deposited together, which means that with the possibility at last of greater domestication of animals and cultivation of cereals these men who belonged to the last stage of prehistory were able to advance and settle near the Atlantic.

"In addition Robert Ganzo discovered in these interments numerous beautiful sculptures representing humans and animals, as well as tablets with engraved characters on them, much older than the cuneiform writing of Sumer. However, the tablets of the Massif of Fontainebleau and the oldest Hittite hieroglyphs are clearly related. In 1963 Robert Ganzo published an account of these discoveries in *Histoire avant Sumer* (History Before Sumer).

"He has been a guest of honour at Trinity College, Cambridge, and is a chevalier of the Legion of Honor."

Ganzo began to publish poetry only at the age of forty, when *Orénoque* appeared, and his work is

* gan zō′

ROBERT GANZO

small in volume though dense in texture. He is above all a skillful, meticulous craftsman, an impeccable artist who understands the classical ode and of whom Gaëtan Picon has said, "All his effort consists in making the interior universe enter the weft of the poem, in such a manner that nothing constrains the precise arrangement of the strophes and the perfect movement of the verse"—though Picon suggests that this can sometimes lead to academicism.

Most of his work consists of long philosophical poems such as *Lespugue* or the later *Domaine* (Domain, 1942), which has been described by Wallace Fowlie as "a remarkably achieved poem on a jellyfish as a symbol of the poet's conscience reflecting all appearances." His *Œuvre poétique* (Poetic Works, 1958) includes in one volume all his poems written before that time.

Ganzo's poetry contains surrealist elements, and his affinity with Valéry and especially with Mallarmé has often been pointed out. André Bourin and Jean Rousselot have said of him that "he has put into his musical, rigorously classical strophes a world of questions and of cosmic and metaphysical propositions, a bold imagery, in short, which makes of him an eminently 'modern' poet."

ABOUT: Fowlie, W. A Guide to Contemporary French Literature, 1957; Gros, L.-G. Poètes contemporaines, 1951; Rousselot, J. Panorama critique des nouveaux poètes français, 1952.

***GARCÍA MÁRQUEZ, GABRIEL** (March 6, 1928–), Colombian novelist, short story writer, and journalist, was born in Magdalena province, near the Caribbean seacoast of Colombia, in the remote small town of Aracataca. He is the oldest of the twelve children of Gabriel Eligio García, a telegraph operator, and Luisa Santiaga Márquez Iguarán. His parents lived in considerable poverty in the coastal town of Riohacha, but the boy was raised in Aracataca, in the great gloomy house, thronged with relatives and memories, of his maternal grandparents. His childhood impressions of Aracataca's isolation and heat and decay, combined with the stories he heard from his grandparents, gave birth in his imagination to the mythical town of Macondo, the quintessential Latin American provincial limbo, a place that "God had declared unnecessary and had thrown into a corner where towns that have stopped being of any service to creation are kept." The colonel who appears in so many of his stories is modeled on his grandfather, who had fought in the bloody Colombian civil war of 1899–1903 and whom García Márquez has described as the most important influence in his life.

* gar sē' a mär' kes

At the age of eight, García Márquez was sent to the Liceo Nacional at Zipaquirá, near Bogotá, from which he graduated in 1946. A writer from childhood, he published his first stories in 1947, while he was studying law at Bogotá University. The following year, an assassination in the city began *la violencia*, a state of something close to civil war which sputtered on for over ten years, costing hundreds of thousands of lives. *La violencia*, which has powerfully affected García Márquez's writing, closed Bogotá University in 1948. He went to Cartagena where (in spite of his dislike for the law) he continued his studies, and began his career as a journalist. In 1950 he moved on to Barranquilla, where he wrote a column for the daily *El Heraldo*, lived in a four-story brothel called "the Skycraper," read voraciously, and wrote an apprentice version of the novel later rewritten as *La hojarasca.*

In 1954 he returned to Bogotá to work as a reporter and film critic for *El Espectador*, writing short stories in his spare time. In 1955 he achieved celebrity with a series of articles in *El Espectador* giving a true account of the wreck of a Colombian naval destroyer, as recounted to him by the sole survivor, Luis Alejandro Velasco. This young man, glorified as a national hero by the government press, revealed to García Márquez that the destroyer had been sunk not by a great storm but by contraband cargo, incompetently stored on deck. This *Relato de un naufrago* was published in book form in Barcelona in 1970, and praised as a "thornily independent" work of anti-journalism, which "exposes the patriotic chest-beating of the Colombian press." In 1955 it profoundly embarrassed the Rojas dictatorship (which tried but failed to refute it),

GABRIEL GARCÍA MÁRQUEZ

causing a furor which greatly increased the sales of *El Espectador*.

It was in 1955 also that García Márquez published his first short novel, *La hojarasca* (translated by Gregory Rabassa as "Leaf Storm"). It is set in Macondo, where an eccentric old doctor, hated because he had once refused to treat some wounded revolutionaries, hangs himself in an empty house. In the turmoil which follows, the colonel defies the vengeful hostility of the townspeople to secure for the dead man a decent burial. The colonel, his daughter, and his grandson tell the story alternately, in intertwined interior monologues that evoke the past history of the ruined town. This device, and the rich dense style, reminded many readers of William Faulkner, whose influence García Márquez has acknowledged. Even this early work, however, is far from being merely derivative, containing along with the realism characteristic touches of the fabulous (like the doctor's fondness for boiled grass).

After the publication of *La hojarasca*, according to the American novelist William Kennedy (*Atlantic* January 1973), García Márquez was wooed by the Bogotá Communists and went through "a flurry of party militancy" before leaving for Europe as a roving correspondent for *El Espectador*. After some months in Rome (where he studied at the Experimental Film Center), he moved on to Paris and learned that the Rojas dictatorship had closed down *El Espectador*, putting him out of work. He remained in Paris for two or three years, most of the time in great poverty, and there wrote two more short novels. These are less Faulknerian than the first book, more staccato in style, with dialogue playing a larger part. In general they show a greater concern with communication, less with artistry—a development, Kennedy suggests, that reflects the influence of his Communist friends as well as his own dissatisfaction with *La hojarasca*.

El coronel no tiene quien le escriba (translated by J. S. Bernstein as "No One Writes to the Colonel") appeared in the Colombian magazine *Mito* in 1958 and was published in book form in 1961. The setting is not Macondo but a similar steamy backwater called El Pueblo. Here the old soldier waits endlessly for his army pension, long after he and his war have been forgotten by the government, scrabbling to survive without quite relinquishing his dignity. In this story, wrote Mario Vargas Llosa, "he had written a small masterwork, but not only did he not know it, he also experienced the same sensation of failure as when he finished *Leaf Storm*." The other short novel written at this time was *La mala hora* (The Evil Hour), about political oppression in the same dusty town during *la violencia*. It received the Colombian Premio Literario Esso when it was published in 1961. In 1958, meanwhile, García Márquez had returned to Colombia to marry his fiancée, Mercedes Barcha Pardo, before going on to work as a journalist in Caracas, Venezuela, during the last days of the Pérez Jiménez dictatorship. In Caracas he worked for the magazine *Momento* and the gossip sheet *Venezuela Gráfica*, and wrote the short stories later published as *Los funerales de la mamá grande* (1962, title story translated by J. S. Bernstein as "Big Mama's Funeral").

García Márquez eagerly welcomed the Cuban revolution and, beginning in 1959, worked for Castro's news agency Prensa Latina in Colombia and Havana, briefly becoming its assistant bureau chief in New York in 1961. At the end of 1961 he made his way to Mexico and began a new career as a screenwriter, collaborating for a time with the novelist Carlos Fuentes, and eking out his income by working from time to time as a journalist and publicist. He went through a period of severe self-criticism and dissatisfaction with all of his earlier work and wrote virtually no fiction for five years, until he began his masterpiece *Cien años de soledad* (1967, translated by Gregory Rabassa as *One Hundred Years of Solitude*). He and his wife and small son lived in Mexico City, largely on borrowed money, for the eighteen months it took to complete the book.

Jack Richardson wrote of *Cien años de soledad* that the reader immediately "senses in its style a simple audaciousness which alerts him to the premise . . . that he is being presented . . . with a work that presumes nothing, that starts from a beginning both in literary and historical time." Alfred Kazin was perhaps referring to the same quality when he said that "as with Emerson, Poe, Hawthorne, every sentence breaks the silence of a vast emptiness, the famous New World 'solitude' that is the unconscious despair of his characters but the sign of [García] Márquez's genius."

At the most obvious level, the novel is an account of the rise and fall of the town of Macondo, and of the Buendía family which founded it. Macondo is at first a nearly perfect community, carved out of the swamp by José Arcadio Buendía, patriarch of the clan—a "spiritual conquistador" who is finally overwhelmed in his Adamic pursuit of knowledge, and who ends chained to a chestnut tree, babbling in Latin the arguments against the existence of God. His son Colonel Aureliano brings Macondo out of its isolation into political conflict, revolution, and civil war. A period of development and exploitation by a giant American fruit company leads to strikes and then to an appalling secret massacre, after which Macondo slides into its final decline. The matriarch Úrsula, having struggled for some hundred and thirty years to save the family's soul, surrenders her grip on life and gradually the town is reclaimed by the jungle. In the end the two surviving Buendías succumb to the family curse and sink into a delirium of incest, the curly-tailed product of which is eaten by ants on the first day of his life. Thus are fulfilled all the prophecies of the Promethean gypsy Melquíades, who long before had written down (in Sanskrit) the history here presented.

The novel is both a family saga and a history in microcosm of Colombia—even of the entire continent. Beyond that it is an epic (but also deeply comic and ironic) myth of all human experience, from the innocence of Eden to apocalypse. A vigorous and highly readable account of the ordinary joys and sorrows of life, it describes with equal gusto and conviction the fabulous and the surreal—ghosts grow old along with the living; a plague of insomnia plunges the whole community into progressive amnesia; Mauricio Babilonia is followed everywhere by a host of yellow butterflies; Remedios the Beauty, in her maddening and immaculate purity, ascends to heaven still clutching the bedsheets she had been hanging on the line. And this is to say nothing of the innumerable local and literary jokes and allusions which make the book a particular joy to Latin American readers.

Cien años de soledad received the French Prix du Meilleur Livre Étranger and the Italian Premio Chianciano and indeed has been recognized all over the world as a great comic masterpiece. Carlos Fuentes said of it that "all 'fictional' history coexists with 'real' history, what is dreamed with what is documented, and thanks to the legends, the lies, the exaggerations, the myths . . . Macondo is made into a universal territory, in a story almost biblical in its foundations, its generations and degenerations, in a story of the origin and destiny of human time and of the dreams and desires by which men are saved and destroyed." Pablo Neruda called it "perhaps the greatest revelation in the Spanish language since the *Don Quixote* of Cervantes."

In 1972 García Márquez published a new collection of stories, *La increíble y triste historia de la cándida Eréndira y de su abuela desalmada* (The Incredible and Sad Story of Innocent Eréndira and Her Heartless Grandmother). The title piece derives from an episode in *Cien años de soledad*—the story of the fairground girl who has accidentally burned down her grandmother's house and has to pay off the gigantic debt by prostituting herself to endless queues of men. "Like Don Quixote, García Márquez's characters find themselves in a hybrid world in which the imaginary and the marvellous are weighted down by drab and sordid reality," wrote a reviewer in the *Times Literary Supplement*. "So, although Eréndira's lover kills the wicked grandmother, he does not win the prize, for she runs off alone with the plunder, leaving him with the crime and the guilt. In the seven stories of this collection, corrupting forces of money or power invade the world of the imagination and only occasionally . . . does imagination triumph."

García Márquez has been working for a number of years on a major new novel centering on an almost immortal Latin American dictator. In 1972 he received the huge Caracas Prize, and donated the entire award to a small Venezuelan left-wing group, the Movement Towards Socialism. The same year he was awarded the ten-thousand-dollar Books Abroad-Neustadt International Prize. He lives in Barcelona with his wife and their two sons, Rodrigo and Gonzalo. His principal recreation is listening to recorded music, which he does with a passionate and obsessive intensity worthy of one of his own characters.

PRINCIPAL WORKS IN ENGLISH TRANSLATION: No One Writes to the Colonel, And Other Stories, 1968; One Hundred Years of Solitude, 1970; Leaf Storm, and Other Stories, 1972. *Stories in* Cohen, J. M. (ed.) Latin American Writing Today, 1967; Harss, L. Into the Mainstream, 1967.
ABOUT: Arnau, C. El mundo mítico de Gabriel García Márquez, 1971; Cohen, J. M. (ed.) Latin American Writing Today, 1967; Current Biography, 1973; Guibert, R. Seven Voices: Seven Latin American Writers Talk to Rita Guibert, 1973; Gullon, R. García Márquez o el olvidado arte de contar, 1970; Harss, L. Into the Mainstream, 1967; Ludmer, J. Cien años de soledad: una interpretacíon, 1972; Mejía Duque, J. Mito y realidad en Gabriel García Márquez, 1970; Vargas Llosa, M. García Márquez: historia de un deicidio, 1971. *Periodicals*—Atlantic January 1973; Books Abroad Winter 1973, Summer 1973; Commonweal March 6, 1970; Harper's February 1972; Nation December 2, 1968; May 15, 1972; New Statesman June 26, 1970; February 9, 1973; New York Review of Books March 26, 1970; April 6, 1972; New York Times Book Review March 8, 1970; January 20, 1972; Saturday Review December 21, 1968; March 7, 1970; Times Literary Supplement November 9, 1967; September 29, 1972.

HELEN GARDNER

GARDNER, DAME HELEN (LOUISE) (February 13, 1908–), English scholar and critic, was educated at the North London Collegiate School and at St. Hilda's College, Oxford, where she gained first class honors in the English School in 1929. She became M.A. in 1935 and a Doctor of Literature in 1963.

Helen Gardner began her career in 1931 as an assistant lecturer at the Royal Holloway College in the University of London. In 1934 she went as a lecturer to the University of Birmingham, leaving there in 1941 to return to Oxford as tutor in English literature at St. Hilda's (1941–1954), then as reader in Renaissance literature to the university (1954–1966). In 1966 she became Oxford's Merton Professor of English Literature.

Both as editor and interpreter, Dr. Gardner is one of England's most distinguished academic critics. Her most important work is contained in her two editions of John Donne: *The Divine Poems* (1952) and *The Elegies and the Songs and Sonnets* (1965). In these Dr. Gardner, making the fullest use of H. J. Grierson's edition of 1912, established a new text and a new canon. She also provided a fuller and more exhaustive and learned commentary to the poems than had previously existed. As is inevitable in so controversial a field, her editions have attracted vigorous criticism; what is notable are the high level of the argument and the respect accorded to Dr. Gardner. Even scholars who disagree with her have paid tribute to the scrupulous fairness and shrewdness of her reasoning, her "unrivalled knowledge of the conditions in which Donne's poems were transmitted in manuscript and in print," her complete familiarity with "the life and thought and literature of his age." The critical consensus, in so far as one has emerged, leans to the view that Dr. Gardner is at her best when determining the canon; that her "severe and economical" commentaries sometimes give an impression of dogmatism, if only because she is more ready to give her opinion than to explain the processes by which it was reached.

It is an indication of Dr. Gardner's range that her first book was an introduction to the work of her friend T. S. Eliot—a crisp and lightly written study, balanced and sensitive, which has long been established as a standard college text. In the lectures collected in *The Business of Criticism* she has expressed her dissatisfaction with the New Criticism and with all absolute and authoritarian systems, calling instead for a humane and tolerant approach which recognizes that the critic's task is not to influence but to elucidate: "The beginning of the discipline of literary criticism lies in the recognition of the work of art's objective existence as the product of another mind." Reviewing her prodigiously learned (and controversial) *A Reading of Paradise Lost*, a critic in the *Times Literary Supplement* wrote "Any book by Helen Gardner is a promise of certain virtues: lucidity, moderation, downrightness in places where it is needed and an absence of inconsequential learning."

The New Oxford Book of English Verse, which had occupied Helen Gardner intermittently for ten years, was published in 1972. It naturally differs quite radically from Sir Arthur Quiller-Couch's *Oxford Book of English Verse* (1900), reflecting the poetic revolutions of half a century and the editor's own special enthusiasms, including her taste for satire and her concern to show the reactions of great poets to great events. It includes no poems written after 1950.

In 1954 Dr. Gardner spent a year as visiting professor at the University of California, Los Angeles, where she is said to have achieved the miraculous conversion of the captain of the UCLA football team to an interest in modern poetry. In 1962 she delivered the Alexander lectures at the University of Toronto. She gave the Ewing lectures in California in 1966, was the Messenger Lecturer at Cornell University in 1967, and the T. S. Eliot Memorial Lecturer at the University of Kent in 1968. The Ewing lectures, on religious poetry, and the Eliot lectures, on tragedy, have been published together as *Religion and Literature*. She is an excellent lecturer and has given many radio talks on the BBC. She has also appeared on the television program *The Critics*, speaking warmly and knowledgeably about children's books. Dr. Gardner has been a Delegate since 1959 on the board of the Oxford University Press and served on the Robbins Committee on Higher Education (1961–1963) and the Council for National Academic Awards (1964–1967). She was awarded the CBE in 1962, has received several honorary degrees, and in 1967 was named a Dame Commander of the Order of the British Empire. She is a Fellow of the British Academy and of the Royal Society of Literature.

An interviewer in the *New Yorker* has described Helen Gardner as "a woman of great wit, learning, and charm," with "an immense fund of energy and a lively interest in art." She likes travel and gardening, plays the recorder, is a connoisseur of food and wine, and an excellent chess player. Dr. Gardner is a short, finely featured woman with gray hair and gray-blue eyes. She is a firm believer in classical studies, and, according to the *New Yorker*, was instrumental in securing the defeat of a proposal that Latin be dropped as a requisite for entrance to Oxford. She is a devout member of the Church of England and has edited *The Faber Book of Religious Verse*.

PRINCIPAL WORKS: The Art of T. S. Eliot, 1949; The Business of Criticism, 1959; A Reading of Paradise Lost, 1965; Religion and Literature, 1971. *As editor*—Donne: The Divine Poems, 1952; The Metaphysical Poets, 1957; (with G. M. Story) The Sonnets of William Alabaster, 1959; (with Herbert John) Elizabethan and Jacobean Studies, 1959; John Donne: A Collection of Critical Essays, 1962; Donne: The Elegies and the Songs and Sonnets, 1965; (with Timothy Healy) Donne: Selected Prose, 1967; Shakespearian and Other Studies by F. P. Wilson, 1969; F. P. Wilson, Shakespeare and the New Bibliography, 1971; The Faber Book of Religious Verse, 1972; The New Oxford Book of English Verse, 1972.
ABOUT: Who's Who, 1971. *Periodicals*—New Yorker January 9, 1960; Times Literary Supplement April 6, 1967.

GARDNER, ISABELLA STEWART (September 7, 1915–), American poet, writes: "I was born in Newton, Massachusetts, and brought up in Boston. I have three brothers and two sisters and innumerable first cousins. All of us spent our summers in Bristol, Rhode Island, and the month of September on an island off the northernmost coast of Maine.

"I had conventional and inadequate schooling. I read voraciously and wrote verses from the time I was eight until I was eighteen. At eighteen I decided against college. I read Dante and Chaucer with Edith Kennedy in Cambridge. At that time I wrote short stories which were neither good enough nor bad enough. I decided that my verse was too glib and facile. I went to dramatic school in London (the Embassy School of Acting directed by Sybil Thorndike's sister, Eileen). For the next few years I acted professionally in summer stock, in touring companies, on the subway circuit and briefly on Broadway. I invariably played character comedy parts. I stopped acting because I was married and had a daughter. I was divorced and married again and had a son. I was very much *engagé* politically, very much on the left, in the early forties.

ISABELLA STEWART GARDNER

"I began to write poetry again around 1950. Oscar Williams, whom I met by chance at a friend's house, urged me to send them to magazines. When Karl Shapiro became editor of *Poetry* magazine I submitted seven poems. He accepted five and asked me to stop in at the office. I then joined the staff of *Poetry*, first as assistant editor, then as associate editor. Karl Shapiro was infinitely helpful in his encouragement, support and advice.

"I have been married to and divorced from Harold A. Van Kirk, Maurice Seymour, Robert McCormick, and Allen Tate. My children are Rose Van Kirk who lives in Spain and is a Flamenco dancer and Daniel Seymour who is a photographer. I now live at the Chelsea Hotel in New York City.

"I write each poem in the form which *it* seems to demand. My techniques are therefore extremely varied but my tone is recognizable as my own, and consistent. Due to sloth and the erratic pattern of my personal life and the fact that, as Allen Tate once remarked, I live by my sensibilities. I have some wit and too much imagination and no intellect. I have faith (not religious faith) and no confidence. Like most poets I have been aware of death and feared it since I was a small child.

"I do not think that I rebelled against my Proper Bostonian background. My opinions, values and needs differed from the beginning and there was no resentment or animosity involved. I am fortunate in having a patient and loving family. I could not do other than follow the dictates of my willful, stubborn and vulnerable nature.

"Currently I find that I am more concerned with equal rights in every area of human existence for Negro citizens and with the cessation of all aggressive action in Vietnam than I am with writing poetry."

Isabella Gardner is the daughter of George Peabody Gardner, a Boston investment broker, company director, and keen sportsman who wrote several books about travel and sailing. Her mother was the former Rose Phinney Grosvenor of Providence, Rhode Island. Miss Gardner attended private schools in Massachusetts and Virginia. Her acting career lasted from 1939 to 1943 and included stints with both the Chicago and the New York companies of Noël Coward's *Blithe Spirit.* She says: "I like to swim in the ocean. I like to climb rocks beside the ocean. I like mountain streams and waterfalls. I like to ride horses, or used to like to. I like sea voyages. I like Greece, Italy, and Ireland. I care about mythology, folk lore, fairy tales, ballads and nursery rhymes."

Reviewers of her first collection of lyrics, *Birthdays From the Ocean*, recognized it at once as the debut of a natural poet of exceptional originality and charm, already the master of "a highly individual and accomplished technique." Edith Sitwell made the point that her poems "arise from her personality," and it is this that distinguishes her from those of her contemporaries who think it their duty to make anonymous records of objective reality. Isabella Gardner "is a conjurer, a believer, a maker." She writes, as one Italian critic has said, with "an elementary, magical faith in the power of poetry," out of a world of feeling which "swings between the dominion of love and the terrible fact of death." The effect can be incantatory, partaking of myth. *Birthdays From the Ocean* was nominated for a National Book Award and warmly praised by poets as various as William Carlos Williams, Elizabeth Bishop, Delmore Schwartz, and Wallace Stevens, who said it was "the freshest truest book of poetry that I had read for a long time."

The Looking Glass was also considered for a National Book Award and would have been nominated for a Pulitzer Prize, Karl Shapiro said, if he had had anything to do with it: "The present volume though small is even better than the first. What 'echoes' there are (Marianne Moore, Sitwell, Skelton) are not mannerisms, but part of the grammar of her style. . . . Nearly every poem in the book deserves applause: a sonnet (of all forms!) on Little Rock, 1957; a marvellous monologue on failing to become an actress; a brilliant one on the ever-unlikely theme of writing poetry." Paul Carroll was particularly taken by Miss Gardner's skill in delineating "the odd, sometimes beautiful twists in a relationship between people," while B. A. Robie called her both a "musician" and a "magician."

Work from both of these volumes, but only two new poems, appeared in *West of Childhood.* It seemed to Robert Huff that Miss Gardner's poetry was unified by that awareness of death of which she speaks above: "The confrontation of death in a variety of appearances, often at once fearsome and humorous, creates the tone of this collection of poems concerned with childhood, loss of innocence, age." Maurice English, discussing the book in *Tri-Quarterly*, suggested another (perhaps related) characteristic: what Max Jacob called a sense of "loyalty to the universe." A selection of Isabella Gardner's poems, translated by Alfredo Rizzardi, was published in Italy as *Un Altra Infanzie* (Another Childhood, 1959).

PRINCIPAL WORKS: Birthdays From the Ocean, 1955; The Looking Glass, 1961; West of Childhood: Poems, 1950–1965, 1965.

ABOUT: Carroll, P. The Poem in Its Skin, 1968; Mills, R. J. Contemporary American Poetry, 1965; Who's Who in America, 1970–1971. *Periodicals*—New England Quarterly December 1966; Poetry December 1962, October 1966; Sewanee Review 1956; Tri-Quarterly Fall 1966.

GARRETT, GEORGE (PALMER) (June 11, 1929–), American poet, novelist, short story writer and dramatist, writes: "Born in Orlando, Florida. Son of an extremely fine and gifted and honest lawyer of mixed southern and New England ancestry. Mother's side all pretty much from late seventeenth century Charleston and Low Country, South Carolina stock. Born into what was already the deep Depression in Florida. Depression stayed long enough in those parts so I thought it was a Way of Life. Only people around then who had money or 'security' were crooks. So I remain baffled and amazed in so-called affluent society. Went to public schools, did poorly but learned to fight my way to and from school every day. Later got a chance to go to small military school, Sewanee Military Academy, in Tennessee. Did poorly. Seventy-five was passing. Graduated with seventy-six average. But played football and was on boxing, swimming and track teams. Was dedicated jock. Went to the Hill School to play another season of football. Got hurt and started reading books. Had been *writing* since before I learned alphabet, but now discovered I enjoyed to read other people's things too. From Hill went to Princeton University. Played a little football, halfhearted and taped up like a mummy. Read and wrote more. Dropped out of school a couple of times. Held the usual various and sundry jobs—bartender, truck driver, boxing instructor, member of Geophysical Exploration Crew for Texaco. Finally graduated. Served total of six years in

Army, active reserve and active duty. Served in Field Artillery in Trieste, Italy, Austria, and Germany. Emerged as Sergeant First Class and Chief of Gun Section. Which is next to Battery Commander who, in turn, is next to God. Meanwhile was married to Susan Parrish Jackson of Philadelphia and ended up in *Social Register* on her good name. Which I call poetic justice. In return she acquired umpteen southern cousins and multitudinous relatives who are lively and active and always dropping in. And who don't buy books and if they did I'd be a best seller. Finally gave up on Real Life as source of income. Went back to grad school at Princeton and squeaked an M.A. Went to work teaching and ready to enjoy academic life because a wise old lady told me: 'Academic people go through life so gently.' (She was wrong.) Started teaching at Wesleyan University where I doubled on the football coaching staff until one day I said, 'Gimme the ball,' to demonstrate something. Woke up in hospital with busted leg. Had epiphany. Realized I'm not and never was a legit jock. Bye-bye to all that. Still writing and reading, but no luck publishing anything until in 1957 Mr. John Hall Wheelock picked my book of poems for the Scribner's Poets of Today series. That wasn't exactly a turning point because I still collect bales of rejection slips on everything. But was a beginning and point of no return. Since then have taught at Rice, Princeton and the University of Virginia. Like to teach. Have continued to read and write. Have applied for many fellowships and goodies and never got one I applied for. On other hand, ones I didn't apply for but got anyway are Sewanee Review Fellowship in Poetry, Rome Prize of American Academy of Arts and Letters, and Ford Foundation Grant in Drama. Which sent me to wonderful Alley Theatre in Houston, Texas, and left me so stage struck I'll never be the same. Have written plays for adults and children. None successful, all pure joy to do. Have also made ends meet and had some fun (not joy) doing screenplays. Continue to write stories, novel(s), verses, plays etc. Hope to as long as I breathe. Many people have helped me with words or deeds. Among them especially Babette Deutsch, John Hall Wheelock, Marianne Moore, William Peden, Richard Wilbur, David Slavitt. Writing is lonely but not lonesome. More than influence, William Faulkner (whom I never met) is Example. Of professionalism, courage, integrity, broad mind and good humor. Meanwhile I enjoy Real Life as much as possible. Have three wonderfully eccentric and deeply alive children. My wife plays superb classical guitar and keeps me out of trouble. I like to shoot guns, take pictures, dance and play games. Still occasionally send off letters and telegrams to astonished football coaches and players telling them how to win. Some guys never quit. As a writer I enjoy the pleasures of unsuccess. Principally Freedom. Freedom to write what I please, when I please, without regard to cash or kudos. In all fairness, others are free not to publish it and not to read it. Philosophically I'll go along with Faulkner who's reported to have replied to a lady who asked him for his 'philosophy of life': 'Fear God, women, and the po-lice. Next question.' Politically I'm a Democrat because I learned how to read. Theologically I'm an Episcopalian, an indifferent churchgoer, but willing to witness and to say without doubt or question that 'I believe in the resurrection of the dead and the life in the world to come.' "

GEORGE GARRETT

George Garrett finds his poetic themes in the people and occasions of his daily life, in travel, and sometimes in mythology and the Old Testament. He favors free verse and a diction that is said to be "relaxed, conversational, not intended to astonish." Critics have noted at times a certain lack of tension in his verse, and at others an imposed note of violence, but his best work is, in its humanity and vitality, "alive beyond mere technique." Babette Deutsch, reviewing *Abraham's Knife*, called it "the work of a man going his own gait and speaking in an individual voice. And if he is intensely conscious of the plight that he shares with his fellows, he is clean of self-pity, and quick to acknowledge the joys, as well as the big and little jokes, that relieve our anxiety, our ennui, our griefs."

King of the Mountain, Garrett's first volume of short stories, had a considerable critical success on both sides of the Atlantic. It was praised for its intelligence and technical "cunning" and was said to stress character and atmosphere rather than plot, "in the Eudora Welty tradition." The more obvious comparison with Faulkner has been made often. One reviewer, discussing the title novella in *Cold Ground Was My Bed Last Night*, said that with one or two possible exceptions, "no American story of this length since Faulkner's 'The Bear' has exhibited such dramatic intensity and technical skill." The same collection included the much-translated story "The Wounded Soldier." *In the Briar Patch* was also admired, especially for a number of excellent stories about children and young people. Garrett's is "an unsentimentalized rural South," wrote R. C. Healey, "seen clearly and sharply," without melodrama or "fuzziness of intention."

Garrett's first novel, *The Finished Man*, is an investigation of Florida politics. Some reviewers seem to have found it a very unattractive book, others a savagely honest one, skillfully paced, clear and deep in its characterization. Subsequent novels have also dealt with people who do ugly things—a black marketeering GI in Italy, a troupe of spurious revivalists in the South—and without special pleading revealed their pathos and humanity. In Garrett's fiction, as William Robinson wrote in *Red Clay Reader*, "man never becomes something more than man, is never reborn into a transcendent state nor allowed to diminish into a mechanism. He is doomed to be himself, simultaneously free and responsible, empowered but moral." Some critics, recognizing Garrett's "professionalism, courage, integrity, broad mind and good humor," believe that his work has been sadly undervalued. He had his first popular success with *Death of the Fox*, "an immense and immensely learned" novel about Sir Walter Ralegh. Writing with a verbal energy and exuberance worthy of the Elizabethan giants he describes, Garrett "creates a labyrinthine world of speculation and inference filled out with a staggering amount of factual, literary, imaginative and sensual detail." One reviewer called it one of the finest novels he had ever read.

George Garrett is the son of George and Rosalie (Toomer) Garrett. He taught at the University of Virginia from 1962 to 1967, except for a year (1964–1965) as a resident fellow of Princeton University. From 1967 to 1971 he was professor of English and director of the writing program at Hollins College, Virginia, where he was also co-editor of *The Hollins Critic*. Since 1971 he has been professor of English and writer-in-residence at the University of South Carolina. A classroom exercise at Hollins, in which students were asked to write a story or poem involving a girl in a black raincoat, developed into a game played by Garrett's friends, among them Babette Deutsch, Leslie Fiedler, Shelby Foote, and William Meredith. Their "variations on a theme" are collected in *The Girl in the Black Raincoat*, which was received by reviewers with interest but only moderate approval. From time to time Garrett has worked for CBS television and for Hollywood. He was U.S. poetry editor of *Transatlantic Review* from 1958 to 1971.

PRINCIPAL WORKS: *Poems*—The Reverend Ghost *in* Poets of Today, IV, 1957; The Sleeping Gypsy, and Other Poems, 1958; Abraham's Knife, and Other Poems, 1961; For a Bitter Season: New and Selected Poems, 1967. *Short stories*—King of the Mountain, 1958; In the Briar Patch: A Book of Stories, 1961; Cold Ground Was My Bed Last Night, 1964; A Wreath for Garibaldi, 1969; The Magic Striptease, 1973. *Novels*—The Finished Man, 1959; Which Ones Are the Enemy?, 1961; Do, Lord, Remember Me, 1965; Death of the Fox, 1971. *Play*—Sir Slob and the Princess (for children), 1962. *As editor*—The Girl in the Black Raincoat: Variations on a Theme, 1966; The Writer's Voice: Conversations With Contemporary Writers, 1973.

ABOUT: Contemporary Authors 2, 1963; Red Clay Reader II, 1965; Vinson, J. (ed.) Contemporary Novelists, 1972; Wheelock, J. H. *introduction to* Poets of Today, IV, 1957; Who's Who in America, 1972–1973. *Periodical*—Princeton University Library Chronicle Autumn 1963.

"GARVE, ANDREW." *See* WINTERTON, PAUL

***GARY, ROMAIN** (May 8, 1914–), Russian-born French novelist, short story writer, and memoirist, was born Romain Kacew in Tiflis, Georgia. He was raised by his mother, the former Mina Josel, daughter of a Jewish watchmaker. This fantastic woman had been an actress and a great beauty, and was twice married (the first time at sixteen) and twice divorced. She was abandoned with her son when he was seven at Vilna (then in Poland, now in the Soviet Union), where by fair means and foul she built up a successful hat business.

From the beginning it was understood between Gary and his mother that he was to be nothing less than magnificent—in what field was not important. He was taught riding, fencing, shooting, languages, and the polite arts until, when he was fourteen, the hat business failed and his mother took him to Nice. There he became a French citizen and attended the *lycée* while Madame Kacew hawked the "family jewels" from hotel to hotel, gave beauty treatments, and told fortunes, nearly starving herself (as he eventually discovered) so that he could eat steak every day.

It became painfully clear, Gary recalls, that he lacked genius as an actor, singer, dancer, painter, or violinist (though he was Ping-Pong champion of Nice in 1932). But it did seem that he might have literary talent, and he certainly possessed great pride and spirit, reckless courage, and an intense feeling of dedication. His mother went on

* ga rē′

searching with unquenchable optimism for the "secret bonanza of genius that would lead us both to some supreme triumph, greatness, and material success." Gary meanwhile attended the universities of Aix-en-Provence and Paris, where he obtained a *licence* in law, and returned to Poland for a diploma in Slavic languages.

His chance came with the outbreak of World War II in 1939. Gary served with the French Air Force until his country's capitulation, and then escaped to England. He subsequently fought with the Royal Air Force and the Free French Air Force in several countries, including Africa and Russia, and was three times wounded in action. After the war, to his mother's satisfaction but scarcely to her surprise, he received the Croix de Guerre. He is also a Companion of the Liberation and an Officer of the Légion d'Honneur.

Gary's first novel, *Éducation européenne*, was published originally in England, as *Forest of Anger* (1944). It is a series of vignettes, alternately tender and brutal, about a group of partisans in Poland. At the core of the book is the story of a boy and a girl, scarcely more than children, who in spite of their "education" in death, rape, and every kind of atrocity, manage to love one another. When the book was published in France in 1945 it was recognized at once as one of the most moving and memorable novels of World War II, and was awarded the Prix des Critiques, another trophy for Madame Kacew. Foreign critics were equally impressed, and an American one called it "a terrible parable for our times." Gary subsequently revised the book, and it has been much translated in both versions.

At the end of the war, thanks to his mother's tireless machinations, Gary was to his great surprise invited to enter the French diplomatic service. In 1945 he joined the French Embassy at Sofia, and during the next ten years served in the French Foreign Office, at Berne, and as First Secretary of the French Delegation to the United Nations. Literary activity has always flourished in the French government service, and Gary has continued this tradition.

Tulipe (1946), is an allegory and, according to Henri Peyre, a "pretentious" one. More successful was *Le Grand Vestiare* (1948, translated as *Company of Men*), about adolescents in postwar Europe—a book which mixes compassion and humor, satire and sentimentality, and evoked comparison with the great Italian film *Shoeshine*. Three years later a chorus of critics praised *Les Couleurs du jour* (1952, translated as *The Colors of the Day*), an uproariously funny novel about Nice in carnival which is, nevertheless (and characteristically), centered upon an entirely serious moral problem—its hero's need to choose between personal fufillment and participa-

ROMAIN GARY

tion in the ancient and endless struggle for human liberty.

Gary's best known novel, and the one that most completely expresses his view of life, is *Les Racines du ciel* (1956, translated as *The Roots of Heaven*). The author has said: "I was quite ill after the war, unable to walk the earth for fear of treading on an ant . . . and then I wrote *The Roots of Heaven*, urging human beings to take the protection of nature into their own hands." During the war, in a German concentration camp, its hero Morel had found an almost mystical pleasure and comfort in thinking about the freedom of the wild life of Africa, and especially of the great herds of elephants which become for him the very symbol of liberty. After his release, finding that the elephants are threatened by ivory hunters, he seeks to end the slaughter, at first by legal means, and then by leading his own extraordinary force of fanatics and adventurers in an insane guerilla campaign against the hunters.

It is an imperfect novel, clumsily constructed, not always believable in its characterization, occasionally turgid in its prose. But these weaknesses are overwhelmed by the book's great passion and dramatic power, the vividness of the descriptive writing. In France it received the Prix Goncourt, and critics all over the world recognized it as a flawed masterpiece, an allegory of the scope if not the achievement of *Moby Dick*.

It is some indication of Gary's range that his next novel, *Lady L.*, was a lucid satirical fantasy of great charm and wit, set not in the forests of Africa but in the drawing rooms of England. His other fictional works—novels, stories, and plays—have shown an equal variety in theme and mood. Gary has been described as a chameleon of a writer, and over the years critics have compared him with Prévost, Rousseau, and Maupassant, with Shelley, Melville, and Conrad. He has been called "a deep and bitter seer who also happens to be a superb romantic poet" and "the most American of French novelists," a cynic, a farceur, and a sentimentalist. No doubt he is all of these things. It is his unfashionable insistence on mixing laughter with tragedy that confuses his critics, his delight in the variety of life. These qualities are nowhere more evident than in *The Dance of Genghis Cohn*, a novel whose protagonist is a *dybbuk*—the ghost of a Jewish music-hall comedian who has taken possession of the former S.S. officer who murdered him. This "incredible carnival of symbolic interplay, cynical historiography and stand-up comedy" offended some readers but delighted others, including André Malraux, who called it "one of the rare contributions of our time, both to mythology and to great comic literature."

In 1955 Gary went from the United Nations to a post at the French Embassy in London, and from 1956 until 1960, when he asked to be placed on the inactive list of the diplomatic corps, he served as French Consul General in Los Angeles. Gary subsequently became *chargé de mission* in the department of Georges Gorse, minister of information in the 1967–1968 government of Georges Pompidou. At about the same time he directed his first film, *Les Oiseaux vont mourir au Péru* (1968). He has been married twice, to the English writer Lesley Blanch and, in 1963, to the American-born actress Jean Seberg, by whom he has a son.

Gary's "imaginative" exercise in autobiography, *La Promesse de l'aube* (1960, translated as *Promise at Dawn*), is in effect a tribute to his mother. During World War II, when Gary had to leave her behind in France and death seemed imminent, she wrote two hundred letters to be mailed at regular intervals, so that he would not be troubled by fears for her. In fact she survived the war to see her impossible ambitions realized in the wartime hero, the world-famous novelist, the successful diplomat. "Ludicrous, pathetic, cagey, magnificently heroic," wrote Charles Rolo, "Madame Kacew comes brilliantly to life as a fusion of lunatic romanticism and indomitable resourcefulness." Henri Peyre called *Promise at Dawn* "one of the few entertaining and vigorously healthy books written in France since World War II."

PRINCIPAL WORKS IN ENGLISH TRANSLATION: *Fiction*—Forest of Anger, 1944 (tr. of Éducation européenne; rev. and re-tr., U.S., A European Education; England, Nothing Important Ever Dies, 1960); Company of Men, 1950; The Colors of the Day, 1953; The Roots of Heaven, 1958; Lady L., 1959; The Talent Scout, 1961; Hissing Tales (short stories), 1964; The Ski Bum, 1965; The Dance of Genghis Cohn, 1968; The Guilty Head, 1969; White Dog, 1970; The Gasp, 1973. *Autobiography*—Promise at Dawn, 1961.

ABOUT: Boisdeffre, P. de. Dictionnaire de littérature contemporaine, 1962; Peyre, H. French Novelists of Today, 1967; Spivey, T. R. Religious Themes in Two Modern Novelists, 1965; Who's Who, 1971; Who's Who in America, 1970–1971; Who's Who in France, 1971–1972. *Periodicals*—Life January 12, 1962; New York Times April 27, 1970; New Yorker December 15, 1956; April 27, 1960; Newsweek January 20, 1958; October 16, 1961; Time October 12, 1953; October 20, 1961.

***"GASCAR, PIERRE"** (March 13, 1916–), French novelist and short story writer, writes (in French): "My legal name is Pierre Fournier. When I began to write I took the pseudonym of Pierre Gascar, which refers to my Gascon origins. Although I was born in Paris, in 1916, my family came originally from the southwest of France. Circumstances led to my being sent for my education to my uncles, who still lived in Gascony. That is how it happened that I had the childhood of a little peasant. Deprived of my own parents and treated with some coldness by those to whom I was entrusted, I learned very young to rely on nature: earth, plants, trees, animals, which gave me a sort of consolation. That explains the subject and tone of several of my books.

"I completed my secondary studies thanks to scholarships, for my parents were poor. When I was seventeen and a half I had to find a job. I was then back in Paris. I was employed successively in a bank, as a space salesman, a traveling salesman, etc. Then I was drafted into the army. That was in 1937. They sent me to the Maginot Line. I began to write, driven by a need which I had felt even as a child. War broke out. In 1940 I volunteered for the forces going to Norway, where the Germans had just landed. It was too late. My battalion had to retreat to Scotland. Three weeks later I found myself on the Somme front where I was taken prisoner.

"Eventful imprisonment. Escape attempts, one taking me right up to the French border, earned me internment in the punishment camp at Rawa-Ruska (now in the Ukraine). Since I spoke German, I became the interpreter for the camp's crew of gravediggers. The French cemetery which I and my comrades created is still there and is kept up carefully by the schoolchildren of that Soviet village. I was freed by the Red Army in 1945.

"When I got back to France, I became a newspaperman. At first a reporter, I soon was managing the book section of the paper *France-Soir*. I took care of literary criticism for *La Gazette de Lausanne* too. At the same time I published short stories in several magazines.

"In 1946 I married a newspaperwoman, Jacque-

* gas car′

line Salmon. I had two children by her, sons, born respectively in 1951 and 1954.

"In 1953 I received the Prix des Critiques and, the same year, the Prix Goncourt. I left journalism to spend all my time on literature. In 1954 I was invited to China by the government of that country. There I met Alice Simon, whom I was to marry a little later.

"In 1956 and 1957 I made several trips to Asia and Africa for the World Health Organization, which wanted a book written on the work it carried on around the world.

"Returning from all this traveling, I became somewhat involved in journalism again and published articles in *Le Monde* and various European newspapers. I soon returned to literature (which I had never really left). I had a play staged in Paris in 1958. I published a book almost every year. Quite often it was translated: in the U.S.A., Great Britain, Germany, Japan, etc.

"Since then my life, professional and private, has changed very little. Literature, in its narrower definition, is still my chief occupation. But I do still write for some newspapers (*Le Figaro* and *Le Figaro littéraire*); sometimes I work for the movies (collaborating with H. G. Clouzot); for television (my play "Les Murs" in 1964); for radio and for cultural relations projects (conferences in Belgium, Holland, Germany, England, Sweden).

"Divided between a private, a secret world, and the outer world of my fellow men, in everything I write I accept this dualism and find in it a sort of equilibrium. From this comes the diversity of my work which gives almost equal weight to reality and to the dream."

Gascar received the Prix des Critiques for *Les Bêtes* (The Beasts), a collection of stories about the "flat alien meeting" of men and animals. It was published in 1953 in a volume which also contained *Les Temps des morts* (The Time of the Dead), a short novel based on Gascar's atrocious experiences in Rawa-Ruska. It was this double volume which was awarded the Prix Goncourt and was subsequently translated as *Beasts and Men*. It describes a world in which man subjugates and exploits both the beasts and his own kind, and is no less brutish and pitiful than the animals. The helpless isolation of man from nature and man from man in these dark symbolic stories, and the "prismatic strangeness" of Gascar's style, reminded many readers of Kafka. The book was as much admired in Britain and America as it had been in France, and Phoebe Adams said that Gascar wrote brilliantly, "balancing details which suggest, in their precision and plausibility, literal reporting, with images and metaphors that have the unexpected, shocking rightness of poetry."

PIERRE GASCAR

Gascar's novel *La Graine* (1955, translated as *The Seed*), also draws poetry and meaning from his experience of life—this time from his youth in a southern factory town, where he once planted seeds and waited, too impatiently, for trees to grow. Another, happier, part of Gascar's childhood exile in the south is recalled in *Le Meilleur de la vie*, admirably translated like most of his books by Merloyd Lawrence and published in the United States as *The Best Years*. Here, writing of the years he spent in rural Aquitaine, Gascar seems to invoke against the grim chaotic life view of *Les Bêtes* an orderly natural world of abundance, love, and fertility. It was called a "neoclassical pastoral," a prose poem in which the only action is the slow turning of the seasons.

Of Gascar's other novels, the most widely known is *Le Fugitif* (1961, translated as *The Fugitive*). It tells the story of a young Frenchman's search in the dark underworld of postwar Germany for a refugee girl and, in another sense, for himself. For some American critics it seemed to succeed better as an extremely exciting suspense novel than in its philosophical speculations. The stories in *Women and the Sun*, selected from the volumes published in France as *Les Femmes* and *Soleils*, persuaded most reviewers that Gascar is at his best in the short form.

Beasts and Men was an unqualified success and *The Seed* was also generally admired. Gascar's books since then have tended to divide the critics, at least in Britain and America. He is a brilliant stylist, a master of concrete imagery which conveys the very look and feel of life, but too conscious and deliberate a virtuoso for some tastes. Henri Peyre nevertheless ranks him "among the most original talents of contemporary France and . . . among the best authors of *récits* and short stories since Maupassant." Gascar himself says that he views literature "as not just literature: it represents primarily a moral life, it stands for exigencies which I do not fulfill. . . . To write is a strange malady, a need to prove one's existence to oneself . . . a self-punishment, a desire for redemption." In 1969 he received the Grand Prix de Littérature de l'Académie Française.

PRINCIPAL WORKS IN ENGLISH TRANSLATION: Beasts and Men (stories), 1956; The Seed, 1959; The Coral Barrier, 1961; The Fugitive, 1964; Women and the Sun (stories), 1964; Lambs of Fire, 1965; The Best Years, 1967.

ABOUT: Boisdeffre, P. de. Dictionnaire de littérature contemporaine, 1962; Boisdeffre, P. de. Une Histoire vivante de la littérature d'aujourd'hui, 1958; Brée, G. An Age of Fiction, 1957; Curley, D. N. and Curley, A. (eds.) Modern Romance Literatures (A Library of Literary Criticism), 1967; International Who's Who, 1970–1971; Pingaud, B. Écrivains d'aujourd'hui, 1960; Who's Who in France, 1971–1972.

GASCOYNE, DAVID (October 10, 1916–), English poet and translator, was born in Harrow, Middlesex, and educated at the Salisbury Cathedral Choir School. His parents were members of the prosperous middle class and were both proud of and slightly dismayed by their son's astonishing precocity as a poet. David Gascoyne published his first book at the age of sixteen. This was *Roman Balcony*, a collection of poems which already showed an "interest in hallucinatory obsessive symbolism." A novel, *Opening Day*, appeared a year later. David Wright remembers Gascoyne as an "intensely nervous" young man, "tall as a pylon, beautiful as a derelict archangel escaped from the illuminated margin of an anglosaxon psalter." He was the "wonderful boy" in a group which centered around the poet and film maker Humphrey Jennings, one of the earliest exponents in England of French surrealism. Gascoyne completed his education at the Regent Street Polytechnic in London and then made his first visit to Paris, where he formed lasting friendships with Paul Éluard, Pierre-Jean Jouve, and other writers and artists. Philippe Soupault once said that Gascoyne is not an English poet, but a "French poet writing in English."

For a time Gascoyne was an active proselytizer for surrealism. He wrote *A Short Survey of Surrealism* (1935), contributed to the influential surrealist issue of *Contemporary Poetry and Prose* (1936), argued the surrealist case and translated surrealist poetry in many literary magazines. His own poems in *Man's Life Is This Meat* (1936) illustrated for his generation the emotional energy that could be generated by the juxtaposition of apparently irrational and unrelated images: "The afternoon scrambles like an asylum out of its hovel / The afternoon swallows a bucketful of chemical sorrows. . . . " It is generally agreed that Gascoyne's are the only English poems of any real power inspired by surrealism.

Gascoyne, however, was not an orthodox surrealist of the Freudian kind. He lacked the narcissism of many of his colleagues who raptly looked no further than their own psyches for the strange images and bizarre associations which floated up into their minds and poems. Gascoyne inveighed against automatic writing as early as 1934, saying (at eighteen): "I no longer find this navel-gazing activity at all satisfying." At this time he seems to have shared with Humphrey Jennings and Charles Madge a rather sociological approach to surrealism. These three, writing in England at a time of intense and revolutionary social awareness, saw in the trappings of civilization—buildings and clothes, the daily visual and spoken clichés of urban life—an expression of the unconscious needs of the entire community. Surrealism in their view should tap not merely the private fantasies of the poet, but the collective dreams of society.

By 1938 in any case, when Gascoyne published his translations of the poems of Hölderlin's madness, it was clear that surrealism had more or less ceased to serve his purpose. Most of Gascoyne's verse translations are fairly strict paraphrases, informative and influential, but seldom very successful as poems in their own right. His versions of Hölderlin are much freer, resembling Robert Lowell's imitations: "deeply imagined and intellectually alive." Extended by the inclusion of four of Gascoyne's own poems into a kind of dialogue, this work (one critic wrote) "enlarges the scope of translation." There followed for Gascoyne a time of great ordeal. Humphrey Jennings' early death caused him much suffering, and his own shyness and introversion ruled out the comforts of marriage or work. He wandered in poverty and despair from London to Paris and back. For a time during the war he was an actor. Gascoyne was horrified by the war and sickened by the materialism he saw on every hand. Increasingly he turned to Christianity—not to any church, but to the example of such mystics as Boehme, Kierkegaard, and William Blake.

The work collected in *Poems, 1937–1942*, brilliantly illustrated by Graham Sutherland, show these influences and also that of Pierre-Jean Jouve. These poems retain much of the hallucinatory strangeness of his surrealist verse and continue in a different context his pursuit of an ultimate truth beneath the surface of everyday appearances. Many of them show an obsession with the discovery of the fact of death, and a resulting sense "of dislocation, of panic, of abrupt unfamiliarity and questionableness of everything hitherto regarded as certain." The Christ of these poems is not the King of

DAVID GASCOYNE

Heaven but the suffering son of man, a "Christ of Revolution and of Poetry."

Another book of verse, *A Vagrant*, appeared in 1950, and six years later the BBC broadcast Gascoyne's long poem *Night Thoughts*. It is a vision of contemporary London, which sees the great buildings and endless streets as symbols and portents of man's loneliness and despair. Some consider it his finest poem and certainly, as one critic wrote, "it states his prophetic message with an eloquence and coherence of symbolic landscape appropriate to the dignity of [his] theme."

Gascoyne's collected poems were published in 1965. They seemed to some critics marred by a tendency to rhetoric, a fondness for archaic and poetical words, but greatly impressed their reviewer in the *Times Literary Supplement*. He found these poems remarkable above all for their oracular quality, suggesting that Gascoyne resembled Blake in the nature and degree of his sensitivity, and that "like Blake he sees the holy spirit accompanying man into whatever depths he may travel; he is the poet of the world-long crucifixion to which mankind subjects that indwelling presence."

The *Collected Verse Translations* of David Gascoyne appeared in 1971 and was welcomed especially for its republication of Gascoyne's versions of Hölderlin, "an event of some importance." With one or two exceptions, the more recent works collected in *The Sun at Midnight* were received with less enthusiasm. Mostly prose poems, exploring Christianity in terms of alchemy, they seemed to lack both urgency and control, and were called "quirky rather than eccentrically wise." David Gascoyne, who calls himself "a spiritually displaced person," visited the United States and Canada in 1951–1952, and lived in France from 1954 to 1965, when he returned to Britain and settled on the Isle of Wight. He is a Fellow of the Royal Society of Literature.

PRINCIPAL WORKS: *Poetry*—Roman Balcony, 1932; Man's Life Is This Meat, 1936; (tr.) Hölderlin's Madness (includes four original poems), 1938; Poems, 1937–1942, 1944; A Vagrant, 1950; Night Thoughts, 1958; Collected Poems, 1965; Collected Verse Translations (ed. by Alan Clodd and Robin Skelton), 1971; The Sun at Midnight, 1971. *Novel*—Opening Day, 1933. *Nonfiction*—Short Survey of Surrealism, 1935.

ABOUT: Allott, K. (ed.) Penguin Book of Contemporary Verse, 1962; Jennings, E. Every Changing Shape, 1961; Morgan, K. Christian Themes in Contemporary Poets, 1965; Murphy, R. (ed.) Contemporary Poets of the English Language, 1970; Press, J. Rule and Energy, 1963; Raine, K. Defending Ancient Springs, 1967; Stanford, D. The Freedom of Poetry, 1947. *Periodicals*—Life and Letters Today September 1944; London Magazine July 1957, November 1965; Poetry September 1956; Times Literary Supplement August 12, 1965; October 1, 1971; Twentieth Century June 1959.

GASS, WILLIAM H(OWARD) (July 30, 1924–), American philosopher, short story writer, novelist, and critic, writes: "Though I was born in Fargo, North Dakota, before I was six months old I had, like Moses, floated away in a woven wicker laundry basket to Ohio where my father had taken a job teaching engineering drawing in the Warren High School. Thus I grew up in a dirty, tense, industrial city, my family moving, as rents and renting went, from house to house—I, from school to school—throughout the Depression. Of that economic affliction, I had the dimmest understanding. My eyes seemed to open only in the summer when my parents returned to North Dakota—to Larimore and Devil's Lake—where they still had many relatives and friends and my father could make some summer money playing semi-pro ball. These were the dust bowl years, too; grasshoppers ate even the daylight; yet these towns were everything that Warren wasn't: small, quiet, full of other smells than oil and metal; people stayed put, the pace of life was slow (and consequently quick for children), and when the dust wasn't blowing, summertime seemed heaped up in the sky for miles.

"By the time I was perhaps seven or eight I had determined to be a writer. The choice was inexplicable since my parents were not particularly 'literary,' and there were no writers among their friends or relatives; yet it was equally irrevocable, and it enabled me, quite early, to plan my life with a determination and certainty about what had to be done which chills me now as much as it must have warmed me then. I soon decided, for example, that the kind of writing I hoped to do would never purchase me a living. I imagined teaching would be satisfying and provide the most leisure.

WILLIAM H. GASS

Philosophy was also intensely interesting to me, and shortly I chose that. My college education, which I began at Kenyon, was interrupted by World War II, and I found myself in the Navy where I played sailor for three years. As a consequence I spent a little time in Japan and China at the end of the war. My parents were politically conservative and so, vaguely, was I, but the war woke me up, I began to move left, and recent events have accelerated that move until it is now a hurtle.

"I finished my undergraduate work at Kenyon and went on to Cornell for my Ph.D. in philosophy, postponing any thought of writing seriously until I had obtained my degree. Instead I worked on sentences and paragraphs for several years, seeking a perfection of form and intensity of effect which I tried to transfer to my fictions. It is not surprising, I suppose, that philosophical ideas, used as a painter might use pigment, have always colored, if not clouded, my work.

"I began teaching at the College of Wooster where I met and married my first wife, wrote a few short stories, and began the novel *Omensetter's Luck*. Teaching never gave me the leisure I had hoped for, raising three children took energy and time, I turned out to be a slow, stubborn, and lazy writer, and the novel dragged on for years, was frequently rewritten, the manuscript once stolen, and when finally completed, was many times rejected.

"I left Wooster for Purdue in 1955 and became a full professor there in 1966. Since I have always believed that to be a 'man of letters' in the European sense was the highest calling, I have spent much of my time and energy, recently, badly imitating one: lecturing and reading, reviewing and writing essays in esthetics and criticism. I received a Longview Foundation Award for fiction in 1959, in 1966 a grant from the Rockefeller Foundation, and in 1969 a Guggenheim. I am now married to Mary Henderson, working on a novel called *The Tunnel* (from which two excerpts have appeared in magazines), and teaching philosophy at Washington University in St. Louis."

Omensetter's Luck begins with an old man's perambulations and musings at an auction in Gilean, a quiet river town on the Ohio. People present and absent, and the objects to be sold, lead back to the day in the 1890s when Brackett Omensetter drove into town with his wife and two daughters. Omensetter's remarkable good fortune springs from his goodness and innocence; he is a man at one with the cosmos. And such amazing grace is an affront to Gilean's lustful and ambitious spiritual leader, the Rev. Jethro Furber. When Omensetter's landlord is found mysteriously hanged, Furber hints at diabolism and Omensetter is almost lynched. The greater part of the book is devoted to "Jethro Furber's change of heart," which leads him at the last to confess himself a false witness. Omensetter, now stained by the world, his luck gone, moves on, and Gilean resumes its pettiness and torpor.

The novel is long and, at a first reading, difficult. This is partly because of the density of Gass's prose, partly because his story, though it is pieced together from the conversations and reflections of many observers, dispenses with quotation marks. The result, Roger Shattuck thought, "is that distinctions of character and act and attitude are at first submerged beneath the landscape of sheer style." In the end it is Furber, agonized and fallible, who dominates the book; Omensetter himself is always a little beyond the reader's reach, more an idea than a person. These reservations apart, most reviewers seemed to share the view of *Newsweek*, in which the book was called a "vastly rewarding and very beautiful first novel"—one that becomes "an intense debate on the nature of life, love, good and evil, and finally, of death. Full of incident and echo, reverberating sentences and accumulating conviction [this] . . . is an important contribution to the literature of our time."

Gass believes that fiction has been replaced as a form of entertainment by television and other media, and that psychiatrists and sociologists in their new literacy have usurped the other traditional functions of novels and short stories. At a National Book Award seminar in 1969 he said that the chief concern of contemporary fiction writers is with words themselves—that they are "as interested in exploring the range of their medium as in the nature of the world."

That this is true for Gass himself is evident in *Omensetter's Luck*, and no less in the two novellas and three short stories which make up *In the Heart of the Heart of the Country*. The title story, set in a small Indiana town where the poet-narrator has gone "in retirement from love," is in effect a series of prose poems evoking with wry precision the pathos and seediness of life in the Middle West. The other pieces are monologues in which the narrator—a semiliterate boy, a lonely bachelor, a small-town gossip—is revealed through his own attitudes and fantasies and through his use of language. Eliot Fremont-Smith spoke admiringly of Gass's technical accomplishment—"the variations of cadence, the telescoping cinematic focus, the splendid use of metaphor"—and above all the authority of his voice. "These stories," he concluded, "scrape the nerve and pierce the heart. They also replenish the language. They are told sparely, hauntingly, with compassion and a remarkable exploratory courage."

Willie Masters' Lonesome Wife is a novella which makes enterprising and often witty and pointed use of a variety of typographical and other visual devices. It is the monologue of Mrs. Masters, a former stripper who, in bed with a friend, muses upon her loneliness, her past life, language, and literature. She speaks, it is clear, for the lonesome writer (who must also strip and tease in his humiliating need for attention and love). Michael Wood thought that "behind the fussiness of much of the book there is a real urgency, a powerful vision of the loneliness inherent in writing."

A volume of Gass's reviews and critical articles has been published as *Fiction and the Figures of Life*. A unifying theme is the author's defense of the purity and autonomy of art, which is to be apprehended on its own terms, and not interpreted or judged politically, or psychologically, or in other irrelevant contexts. Robert Kiely wrote that "nearly all of these essays . . . are a pleasure to read and some . . . are works of beauty. . . . The unlikely combination of criticism, philosophy and metaphorical inventiveness has resulted in a kind of poetry."

PRINCIPAL WORKS: Omensetter's Luck, 1966; In the Heart of the Heart of the Country, 1968; Willie Masters' Lonesome Wife, 1972 (first published as supplement to TriQuarterly, 1968); Fiction and the Figures of Life, 1971. ABOUT: Contemporary Authors 19–20, 1968; Vinson, J. (ed.) Contemporary Novelists, 1972; Who's Who in America, 1972–1973. *Periodicals*—Nation May 9, 1966; New Republic May 7, 1966; May 18, 1968; New York Review of Books June 23, 1966; New York Times March 29, 1968; New York Times Book Review April 17, 1966; Newsweek April 18, 1966; Saturday Review March 2, 1968; Southern Review Spring 1967.

GELBER, JACK (April 12, 1932–), American dramatist and novelist, was born in Chicago, Illinois. His father, Harold Gelber, was a Chicago-born sheet-metal worker, son of an ironworker who had emigrated from Rumania. Like his two younger brothers, Mike and David, Jack Gelber attended the local public schools. At John Marshall High School he played tuba in the band and was on the basketball team.

JACK GELBER

He began at the University of Illinois as a chemistry major, intending to be a chemist or a chemical engineer, but changed his major and earned a B.S. in journalism in 1953. Working in the university library, Gelber came across books that were important to him—works on Greek philosophy and on Buddhism, and the Egyptian and the Tibetan Books of the Dead. He says: "I was in a conducive state. I wanted to know."

Two weeks after graduation Gelber got a lift in a friend's car to San Francisco. He lived in pre-hippie North Beach from 1953 to 1955, working as a shipfitter's helper or living on unemployment insurance. He met Jack Kerouac once but didn't know he was a writer.

In 1955 Gelber moved to New York City. "I always wanted to come to New York," he says. "When I got here, I never felt, as some people do, that I was an outsider. . . . My first nine months here I spent just going to movies and walking the streets." He went to New York with a three-year-old beard but shaved it off, realizing that people were looking at him when what he wanted was to be looking at them.

During his first years in New York, Gelber earned his living as a nightshift mimeograph operator at the United Nations. On December 23, 1957 he married Carol Westenberg. They have two children, Jed Randall and Amy.

Shortly after his marriage Gelber began to write seriously. His first play, *The Connection*, was written rapidly, in fifteen- or sixteen-hour bursts. A friend suggested he submit it to Julian Beck of the Living Theatre. Gelber took the subway to Beck's apartment and left the manuscript. A week later it was accepted, and Gelber plunged into the work of helping to build his play into a production.

Richard Kostelanetz has traced the birth of what he calls "the New American Theatre" to *The Connection*'s opening at the off-Broadway Living Theatre in July 1959. The play begins with the "producer" introducing himself and the "author" to the audience. On stage is a group of "real" drug addicts who, it is explained, have been assembled to improvise on the author's themes. The result is to be filmed. During the first act, while they wait for their "connection" to arrive with a fix, the junkies talk aimlessly, gradually revealing themselves and the nature of their emotional problems. In the second act the heroin is delivered and administered, the addicts get high, and the author and one of the movie photographers are hooked. The play's argument seems to be that life is painful and absurd and that drugs offer a form of escape no different in quality from the audience's more respectable addictions—to religion, to alcohol, to "the next dollar, the next new coat."

At first coldly received or ignored by most critics, *The Connection* survived to run for four years off-Broadway. It was subsequently performed in many other American and foreign cities, published in several languages, and made into an award-winning film. It received the Vernon Rice award, the *Village Voice* Obie award as a contribution to off-Broadway theatre, and the French *Théâtre des Nations* best play award. Gelber won the *Variety* critics' poll as the most promising playwright of 1959–1960.

Part of *The Connection*'s explosive impact upon the moribund American theatrical scene no doubt derived from the quality of its production—the brilliance of its direction by Judith Malina, the resourcefulness of its actors, the excellence of the jazz interludes (used to replace speech when the characters are high). Indeed, as Henry Hewes has pointed out, the play in its form closely resembles a jazz performance "where the individual soloists take turns improvising upon an agreed-upon theme." Nevertheless, and in spite of its Pirandellian gestures towards audience involvement, *The Connection* is fundamentally in the tradition of naturalism. Its characters are observed honestly and unsentimentally, but not very profoundly. Its language, though it includes some "sharp and funny lines," is unexceptional. But for all its faults, it does somehow succeed in posing some pointed moral questions without weighting the evidence, leaving the audience free to seek its own answers. Robert Brustein was struck above all by the play's honesty: "Constantly tripping over the boundary between life and art, stripped of significant form, antagonistic to all theory or morality which does not accord with practice, *The Connection* is probably not a 'good' play by any standard we now possess to judge such things; but it forms the basis for a brilliant theatrical occasion, and it lives in that pure, bright, thin air of reality which few of our 'good' playwrights have ever dared to breathe."

Gelber's second play, *The Apple*, is an amorphous imitation "happening" which was found neither spontaneous nor illuminating. *Square in the Eye* is a realistic play enlivened by complicated switches in time and an enterprising use of film backgrounds. Perhaps the message of all three plays is simply that we must accept what is chaotic in life and look for the satisfaction it offers.

On Ice, Gelber's novel, presents the same *milieu*, New York, and a similar thesis. This time it is embodied in the story of a young man who is driven to accept work as a detective, pretending that he is a salesman but in fact spying upon his fellow-employees. Richard Kostelanetz thought it an ambitious but unsuccessful "attempt to pattern a novel after the structures of serial music." If so, the pattern eluded most reviewers, who found it surprisingly and disappointingly naturalistic and conventional. William Barrett, however, called it "one of the best, if understated portraits of what the beat generation was really like," and another reader said it was a convincing statement of Gelber's view of things, and a quiet plea, not for doing good, but for leaving well enough alone.

The author applies his philosophy to his own life: "I don't want to do anything different. I don't want a whole bunch of aggravation. I'm selfish. I don't need anything except to eat and pay rent. . . . I don't see myself climbing." All the same, there was obvious political commitment in Gelber's first Broadway play, *The Cuban Thing* (1968), which deals with the Castro revolution. It outraged anti-revolutionary Cuban exiles, and provoked numerous bomb scares, but was called "dramatically and politically turgid." Gelber, who teaches at Columbia, received Guggenheim fellowships in 1963–1964 and 1966–1967.

PRINCIPAL WORKS: The Connection (play), 1960; The Apple (play), 1961; On Ice (novel), 1964; Square in the Eye (play), 1966; The Cuban Thing (play), 1969.

ABOUT: Abel, L. Metatheatre, 1963; Brustein, R. Seasons of Discontent, 1965; Contemporary Authors 4, 1963; Kostelanetz, R. (ed.) The New American Arts, 1965; Weales, G. American Drama Since World War II, 1962; Wellwarth, G. E. The Theatre of Protest and Paradox, 1964; Who's Who in America, 1970–1971. *Periodicals*—New Yorker July 9, 1960; Newsweek December 18, 1961.

"GENÊT." *See* FLANNER, JANET

***GENET, JEAN** (December 19, 1910–), French dramatist, novelist, and poet, was born in Paris. Abandoned by his mother, he was at first brought up in public institutions: "as a ward of the Assistance Publique it was impossible for me to know anything about my background." Only at the age of twenty-one, when he was able to obtain a birth certificate, did he discover that he was the illegitimate son of Gabrielle Genet and an unknown father, born at 22 rue d'Assas. When he went to that address he found that it was a public maternity hospital.

At the age of seven Genet was placed with foster parents in Le Morvan, a country district in the northeast of the *massif central.* According to Jean-Paul Sartre, he was a pious and docile child until, at the age of ten, he was accused of stealing. Called a thief, he became one, and was eventually sent to a reformatory, the *maison correctionnelle* at Mettray. Far from reforming him, it confirmed him in a total defiance of society and its standards. "Abandoned by my family," Genet wrote in *The Thief's Journal,* "I found it natural to aggravate this fact by the love of males, and that love by stealing, and stealing by crime. . . . Thus I decisively repudiated a world that had repudiated me." Prison and crime formed the basis of his experience for the next twenty years or more, though the exact details are uncertain from Genet's accounts, and as Philip Thody has pointed out, even his most precise dates are not always trustworthy. He seems to have been at Mettray for three years, from January 1926 until 1929, when he escaped, joined the Foreign Legion to gain the enlistment bonus, and then deserted, stealing luggage belonging to his African officers as he did so.

During the 1930s he led the life of a criminal vagabond, which took him over much of Europe and into the prisons of many countries: as a beggar and homosexual prostitute in Spain, a pickpocket in Italy, a cattle thief in Albania. He was arrested in Poland for passing forged banknotes, and in Holland for drug smuggling. In Hitler's Germany, however, he felt out of place: "I had a feeling of being in a camp organized by bandits. . . . If I steal here, I accomplish no special act that could help me to realize myself. I merely obey the habitual order of things."

In France during the German occupation, Genet was in and out of various prisons, and it was at Fresnes Prison in 1942 that, for a dare, he wrote his first poem, the long incantatory elegy "Le Condamné à mort" (translated as "The Man Condemned to Death"). It is dedicated to the memory of Maurice Pilorge, a homosexual who was executed at twenty for murdering a client. The same quality of solemn incantation is present in the autobiographical novels Genet wrote during the 1940s, which indeed some critics regard as prose poems rather than novels. All of them mingle memory and fantasy in their accounts of love and violence, power and humiliation, in a homosexual criminal underworld. It is a world whose values are deliberate inversions of those of the bourgeois world that had rejected Genet—a world where perversion and crime are normal, murder and betrayal heroic, and the way to the sublime is through absolute self-degradation, abasement, and despair.

* zhə nā'

JEAN GENET

The rogue males and pretty queens who prowl this underworld speak their own argot. But Genet describes them, and transfigures them, in a sumptuous and ceremonial prose which, as John Weightman says, "turns prison yards into courts of love, condemned murderers into holy martyrs, and tattooed thugs into Lancelots and Guineveres." How Genet learned to write this elegant and sometimes almost precious French, and where he acquired the knowledge of literature and art that he displays, remain intriguing mysteries; his prison reading scarcely seems a sufficient explanation.

The first of his novels, *Notre Dame des Fleurs* (1943, translated as *Our Lady of the Flowers*), was written at Fresnes Prison on brown paper intended for making paper bags. It was avowedly composed to stimulate, and preserve for future reference, the author's masturbatory fantasies, here attributed to Divine, a male prostitute who recalls his former lovers as he lies dying in a Paris garret. The beautiful young hoodlum known as Notre Dame des Fleurs, whose career and execution figure largely in the book, is modeled no doubt on Maurice Pilorge, one of the three worthies (the others are a mass murderer and a traitor) to whom the novel is dedicated. It was admirably translated, like nearly all of Genet's work, by Bernard Frechtman.

Alfred Chester called it "the greatest novel Genet or probably anyone else has produced during the past twenty years"; it is an extreme book, evoking extreme reactions. In fact, as several critics have pointed out, it shares with Genet's other fiction weaknesses which are perhaps functions of its masturbatory nature—it is highly episodic, showing little concern for overall structure and, since it is entirely (and sometimes boringly) self-absorbed, interested in others only as instruments, its characterization is rudimentary. But, as Jean-Paul Sartre says in his introduction, "no other book, not even *Ulysses*, brings us into such close physical contact with an author." And Susan Sontag wrote: "Only a handful of twentieth-century writers, such as Kafka and Proust, have as important, as authoritative, as irrevocable a voice and style."

Miracle de la Rose (1946, translated as *Miracle of the Rose*) is a rapturous confession of betrayal and degradation, set this time in the reformatory at Mettray and in Fontevrault prison—a book, according to John Weightman, which "gives one of the most convincing and moving visions of psychological distress to be found in contemporary literature." The critic Claude Bonnefoy regards death as the central theme in Genet's work, but only *Pompes funèbres* (1947, translated as *Funeral Rites*) deals with this theme in the context of his other preoccupations with crime and homosexuality. The death celebrated is that of Jean Descarnin, a young Resistance fighter who had been Genet's lover before he was killed in street fighting. Genet discovers that he loves Jean *because* he is dead, and unable to intrude upon Genet's fantasies about him. Thus Genet can imagine himself eating Jean's corpse, or enter lovingly into the sadistic fantasies of Jean's Nazi murderers: Jean, dead, is Genet's creature. If, Leo Bersani says, "evil is the totalitarian freedom of the imagination, a brutal violation of reality by fantasy," this brilliant and horrible book "proposes a view of literature as the Hitlerism of the spirit."

Querelle de Brest (1947, complete version 1953, translated as *Querelle of Brest*) is about a criminal young sailor ("my wife is the sea; my mistress is my captain"). This "ideal and heroic personage" murders an accomplice but manages to lay the blame on a friend. That Genet was beginning to progress beyond the total subjectivity of his earlier books is shown here by his first portrayal of a woman as a major character, the brothel-keeper Madame Lysiane. As Sartre wrote in his massive critical-biographical study *Saint Genet* (1952), "By infecting us with his evil, Genet delivers himself from it. . . . With each book this possessed man becomes a little more the master of the demon that possesses him. Ten years of literature are equivalent to a psychoanalytic cure."

In 1948, in spite of his growing literary reputation, Genet, arrested and found guilty for the tenth time of theft, became automatically liable to a sentence of life imprisonment. Thanks to a petition signed by many influential writers, including Sartre, Gide, Claudel, and Cocteau, Genet was granted a free pardon (and even invited to dinner at the presidential palace). The same year he published his most directly autobiographical prose work, *Journal de voleur* (translated as *The Thief's Journal*), a detailed account of the various humiliations he had chosen to endure in pursuit of satanic sanctity during his wanderings in the 1930s.

As he mastered his obsessions, Genet turned from poetry to prose, and then from prose to drama—a progression, as Martin Esslin has pointed out, from the most subjective to the more objective forms of writing. The transforming power of words in Genet's fiction had led other writers to speak of him as a "black magician," "an enchanter of the first order"; he brought the same quality to the drama, and found there the perfect medium in which to work out his obsessive sense of ritual. Genet's theatre has the scrupulous perversity and hieratic authority that is aimed at in a Black Mass. It has indeed the same inspiration as the Black Mass—the Christian Mass itself. As Genet wrote in 1958: "The highest modern drama has found expression through two thousand years and every day in the sacrifice of the Mass. . . . No doubt it is one of the functions of art to replace religious faith by the effective ingredient of beauty. At least this beauty must have the power of a poem, that is to say of a crime."

His first play, *Haute surveillance* (translated as *Deathwatch*), is a dramatized form of the kind of story told in his novels. The setting is a prison cell containing three prisoners, who form a hierarchy. At the top is the idolized Yeux-Verts (Green Eyes), who by murdering a prostitute in a sadistic frenzy has fulfilled his destiny ("I didn't want it. It chose me," he says). Inspired by this example, Lefranc, one of his cell-mates, ambitiously throttles the other. It is not enough: the murder is a self-conscious act of the will, not the natural response of a great criminal, and cannot admit him to Genet's pantheon. (A character resembling Lefranc —an introspective outcast among outcasts—recurs in Genet's work and, some critics maintain, represents the author himself.)

Haute surveillance, a kind of transitional work between Genet's fiction and his plays, was not staged until 1949, two years after *Les Bonnes* (translated as

The Maids). In this, his second play in order of writing, Genet is more confidently in possession of his natural genius for the theatre—has fully realized that he is no longer addressing a solitary reader but a congregation, society in the flesh, paying to witness the antisocial fantasies of Genet the thief. As the play opens, an elegant lady is being dressed by her maid; the lady is arrogant, the maid patient and obsequious until, suddenly, she can stand no more and slaps her mistress. An alarm clock ends the charade, and we learn that both characters are actually servants, who act out this never-completed ritual of domination, abasement, and rebellion whenever their real mistress is out. Impelled by the mixture of hate and love that they feel for their employer, the maids betray her criminal lover to the police. He is released, and in fear or jealousy they decide to poison their mistress. This fails, and the maids resume their game, which this time reaches its proper conclusion when one of them, in the role of mistress, calls for and drinks the poisoned tea.

Martin Esslin argues that "the revolt of the maids against their masters is not a social gesture, a revolutionary action; it is tinged with nostalgia and longing, like the revolt of the fallen angel Satan against the world of light from which he is forever banished. That is why this revolt finds its expression not in protest but in ritual." Though the play has female characters, "we are back in the daydream of the prisoner, the fantasy of the outcast who makes futile efforts to reach the world of acceptance and belonging." Oreste Pucciani has shown that in technical terms, *Les Bonnes* is "a nearly perfect tragedy in the French tradition . . . Racine turned inside out."

Liberty and fame produced an inner crisis in Genet, and he wrote no more for six years, until he at last freed himself from purely autobiographical subject matter and embodied his vision of the world in a brilliant new metaphor, the brothel of illusions in *Le Balcon* (1956, translated as *The Balcony*). The play begins with a discourse by a magnificently robed bishop. Then, just as in the opening of *The Maids*, the audience is made sharply aware that things are not what they seem. We are watching not a bishop in his palace but a randy gas man in a brothel, acting out his daydreams of sex and power. Others in Madame Irma's dream palace play out the roles of a dying Foreign Legionary, a leper miraculously healed by the Madonna, a judge, a general.

Outside the brothel, a revolution is in progress which eventually rids the country of its monarchy and ruling hierarchy—and of all its ceremonies and communal illusions. Knowing that people need the ancient rituals and symbols of power, the tottering government appeals in despair to Madame Irma, who agrees to act as substitute queen, while the travesty bishop, general, and judge assume their roles in earnest. The revolution has failed, and its disillusioned young leader comes to the brothel; he dresses up as a police chief and punishes himself (and by proxy the real police chief) by castrating himself. Outside the brothel, a new revolution begins.

The Balcony dramatizes Genet's belief that the rulers of the society which rejected and punished him are as criminally corrupt as he is; the only difference is that they have been more successful in fulfilling their dreams of power (which for Genet always means sexual dominance). It is no doubt a simplistic and vindictive view of the establishment, but one with no lack of adherents at a time when the individual is being made increasingly aware of his impotence in the face of the intricate and mysterious machinery of power in the modern state. More than its predecessors, *The Balcony* is a fantasy about fantasies—a ritual playing out (and ritual deflating) of rituals by symbolic figures that never take on the semblance of real people, and are not meant to: the point of the play is that nothing at all is real. Its strengths are its magnificent theatricality and the splendor of its language; its principal weakness is the flimsy plot structure linking the ceremonial passages.

Plot is virtually dispensed with in *Les Negrès* (1957, translated as *The Blacks*), which is presented as a *clownerie* (clown show). Genet's persistent search for self-definition through opposition is here worked out in racial terms. The play is performed entirely by black actors. One group, wearing grotesque white masks, represents the colonial hierarchy—queen, governor, judge, missionary; these are the Whites, who sit in judgment at the back of the stage, a distorted reflection of the real spectators in the auditorium. The rest of the company act out, for the benefit of both audiences, their racial revenge fantasies, including the ritual rape-murder of a white woman.

We are then informed that all this is only a diversion from the real subject of the play—the trial and execution, offstage, of a black traitor to the Black cause. (But, Martin Esslin has asked, what is more "real" in fact—the fantasies we have seen enacted, or the actuality we have only been told about?) In the end the Whites leave their seats and are trapped, mutilated, and murdered by the Blacks, one of whom explains: "We are what they want us to be. We shall therefore be it to the very end, absurdly." Or again: "On this stage we are like guilty prisoners who play at being guilty." At the very end of the play a suggestion emerges that real human contact is possible through love—the first gleam of optimism in Genet's work.

Les paravents (1961, translated as *The Screens*)

again sides with the outcasts and victims of the world against the powerful, this time in the context of the Algerian war. It is meant to be performed in the open air, on a vast four-tier stage, in front of screens that are to be rolled on and off as the scenes change. The difficulty of staging the play, its enthusiastic anal eroticism, and above all its political implications, kept it from French stages until 1966, when it was produced under Roger Blin's direction, with Jean-Louis Barrault and Madeleine Renaud leading the huge cast. Far from causing the national scandal that had been predicted, it was a major success. Tom F. Driver has said of it that "the play, in spite of its massiveness, soars and wheels like some giant bird. It is Genet's most sordid play, a work one has to say is conceived in filth, and at the same time it is exalted, a mystic vision of the spiritual truth of the dispossessed."

It remains Genet's last work, though his views on every aspect of its staging have been published as *Lettres à Roger Blin* (1966, translated together with other reflections on the theatre as *Letters to Roger Blin*). Genet's film *Un Chant d'Amour* (A Song of Love), a celebration of homosexuality made in the 1940s, has not been widely shown because of censorship difficulties. There is a film version by Joseph Strick of *The Balcony*, and Genet also wrote the scenario filmed in 1966 by Tony Richardson, with Jeanne Moreau in the lead, as *Mademoiselle*.

Genet's incantatory language and imagery seizes and excites his audiences emotionally rather than intellectually; this, and the "cruelty" of his theatre, has led some critics to identify him as a disciple of Antonin Artaud. Others, like Martin Esslin, have claimed him as a practitioner of the "theatre of the absurd." And there are many who share the feelings of a *Times Literary Supplement* critic who has described his works as products of "a formalist, sterile, Fascist-oriented art, which only the feverish and spectacular fireworks can save." Tom F. Driver believes that Genet's work is pervaded by "the myth of the dying king or [a related] myth of perverse sexuality"; he says that "Genet, who had pledged himself as a child to the pursuit of evil, created dazzling and sometimes beautiful works out of the insistence that evil is superior to good because it is nothingness expressed as pure form. . . . The books and the early plays contained much genuine passion, which Genet betrayed, in both senses of the word. He revealed it and at the same time turned it into charade. . . . Genet wrote in artistic form a phenomenology of sin."

Driver finds in *The Blacks* and *The Screens* indications that the world racial struggle had captured and modified Genet's imagination; he remained considerably less than an engaged writer, but began to "conceive of a reality transcending human imagination." Sartre had noted a similar development much earlier: "In willing himself to be a thief to the utmost limit, Genet plunges into dream; in willing his dream to the point of madness, he makes himself a poet; in willing poetry to the final triumph of the word, he becomes a man; and the man has become the truth of the poet, just as the poet had been the truth of the thief."

PRINCIPAL WORKS IN ENGLISH TRANSLATION: *Plays*—The Maids, and, Deathwatch, 1954; The Balcony, 1958; The Blacks: A Clown Show, 1960; The Screens, 1963. *Fiction*—Our Lady of the Flowers, 1963; The Thief's Journal, 1964 (also published in English translation in Paris, 1954); Miracle of the Rose, 1965; Querelle of Brest, 1966; Funeral Rites, 1969. *Poetry*—The Man Condemned to Death (limited edition), 1965. *Miscellaneous*—Letters to Roger Blin: Reflections on the Theater (England, Reflections on the Theatre), 1970.

ABOUT: Abel, L. Metatheatre, 1963; Bataille, G. La Littérature et le mal, 1957; Beauvoir, S. de. The Force of Circumstance, 1965; Brustein, R. The Theatre of Revolt, 1964; Coe, R. N. C. The Vision of Jean Genet, 1968; Driver, T. F. Jean Genet, 1966; Esslin, M. The Theater of the Absurd, 1968; Fletcher, J. New Directions in Literature, 1968; Fowlie, W. Climate of Violence, 1967; Grossvogel, D. I. The Blasphemers: The Theater of Brecht, Ionesco, Beckett, Genet, 1964 (originally published as Four Playwrights and a Postscript, 1962); Guicharnaud, J. Modern French Theatre From Giraudoux to Genet, 1967; Jacobsen, J. and Mueller, W. R. Ionesco and Genet: Playwrights of Silence, 1968; Laing, R. D. and Cooper, D. H. Reason and Violence, 1964; McMahon, J. H. The Imagination of Jean Genet, 1963; Nadeau, M. The French Novel Since the War, 1967; Pronko, L. G. Avant-Garde, 1962; Sartre, J.-P. Saint Genet, Actor and Martyr, 1963; Sontag, S. Against Interpretation, 1966; Styan, J. L. The Dark Comedy, 1962; Sypher, W. Loss of the Self in Modern French Literature and Art, 1962; Thody, P. Jean Genet, 1968; Tynan, K. Curtains, 1961; Tynan, K. Tynan Right and Left, 1967; Wellwarth, G. E. The Theater of Protest and Paradox, 1964; Williams, R. Drama From Ibsen to Brecht, 1968. *Periodicals*—Antioch Review Fall 1964; Atlantic April 1967; Christian Century November 20, 1963; Commentary April 1964; Commonweal October 28, 1960; October 28, 1968; Critical Quarterly Autumn 1964; Encore July–August 1963; Encounter May 1968; French Review October 1962, November 1965; Modern Drama December 1965; Nation March 20, 1954; June 12, 1967; New Republic March 28, 1960; New Society November 20, 1969; New Statesman May 4, 1957; March 13, 1964; July 16, 1965; January 7, 1966; New York Review of Books August 24, 1967; New York Times Book Review September 29, 1963; November 15, 1964; February 19, 1967; June 15, 1969; New Yorker November 4, 1967; Partisan Review April 1949; Saturday Review March 11, 1967; Sewanee Review Fall 1959; Temps modernes June 1960; Time February 3, 1967; Times Literary Supplement February 10, 1961; April 8, 1965; May 13, 1965; February 3, 1966; December 15, 1966; May 4, 1967; September 12, 1968; October 9, 1969; Tulane Drama Review September 1960, Spring 1963; Wisconsin Studies in Continental Literature Autumn 1965; Yale French Studies Spring–Summer, 1962.

***GEYL, PIETER (CATHARINUS ARIE)** (December 15, 1887–December 31, 1966), Dutch

* kāl

historian, wrote: "Born Dordrecht; high school at The Hague; Leyden University 1906; final examination in history 1911; doctoral thesis 1913. Married December 1911. First six months of 1912, traveling scholarship in Italy; then history master in a Schiedam high school.

"I did not dislike high school teaching, but what a relief when I was appointed, as from January 1914, the London correspondent of a well-known Rotterdam newspaper. Introduced into the cultural life and the politics of a big country, a member of the National Liberal Club, at home in Fleet Street, soon the drama of the war; it was indeed something very different from the atmosphere of a small provincial town, tied down to the regular time scheme of school classes. The work—long articles, apart from telegrams, on all imaginable subjects (politics of course obligatory)—I found delightful and inspiriting. The historian in me benefited from it, I am sure.

"I had never abjured history, and in 1919 I was appointed to the chair of Dutch studies newly founded in the University of London (I soon had it transformed into a chair of Dutch History). The journalistic episode was not completely closed either. I became, unofficially, but in fact, press attaché to the Dutch Legation. My connections with Fleet Street came in very usefully: indeed, I added to them considerably in these years. I talked with leading journalists on controversial subjects and wrote articles, often in the form of letters to the editor. My activities were on the whole appreciated by my principals in Holland and the Dutch Legation, but my dragging in of the Flemish question, which I generally did anonymously, was regarded as the sign of an unrealistic, and at times dangerous, personal hobby.

"Flemish is the language spoken in various dialectical forms in the northern half of Belgium. Its official name is 'Netherlandish,' and in its cultivated form it is identical with the language of Holland. Flemish is however, and was even more a generation ago, in a bad way in Flanders, where the leading class had adopted French for polite and cultural purposes.

"It was in 1911, at a Flemish Students Congress in Ghent, that I first came into contact with the movement to restore the language of the people in Flanders. The impressions I gathered there were never effaced and they inspired an important part of my life's work. I came to understand that these students, who were at that time still being educated in a foreign language, were animated by sound social sentiments. Flemish intellectuals were by the prevailing system artificially estranged from the people, who were largely ignorant of French. Unless the university were 'flemified'—only one of many reforms needed, of course—Flanders was to remain backward and culturally sterile.

PIETER GEYL

"When in the following years I threw myself into the struggle, the battle I waged was on two fronts: against the indifference, misconception and ignorance prevailing in Dutch public opinion; and against the anti-Belgium, 'Great-Netherlands' extremism to which Flemish nationalists and the small group of their Dutch supporters often resorted. My great contribution to the controversy was a new conception of our common Dutch and Flemish history. The split of the seventeen Netherlands in the late sixteenth century used to be represented as due to an innate difference between the North and the South. I showed, in the first part of my *History of the Netherlands People* (the part translated as early as 1932 and still being reprinted as *The Revolt of the Netherlands*) that the event is to be explained by the geographical factors dominating the war with Spain.

"It was among other things my close connection with the Flemish Movement which led me in the early thirties to hope for an appointment to a chair in Holland, but that same 'hobby' of mine was played off against me when the modern history chair at Utrecht fell vacant. After a bitter fight, I was appointed as from January 1, 1936 and, once there, came to be warmly accepted.

"A strong polemical strain does run through my *œuvre*, and it is by no means only the Dutch-Belgian question that gave occasion to it. The menace of National Socialism, and the rise of a National Socialist party in our own country; the spectacle of 'appeasement' in England, which was applauded by many on our side of the sea, roused me to passionate opposition. More than once in the years before we were dragged into the war, I testified to my abhorrence at mass meetings of 'Unity Through Democracy' and in outspoken newspaper articles.

"On October 7, 1940, I was arrested and sent to Buchenwald as a hostage, under a regime that must be called mild in comparison with that of the prisoners. As a boy I had written poetry, and in my early days in London had translated into rhymed English verse a lovely medieval Flemish play, *Lancelot of Denmark*, which was several times performed and warmly reviewed. At Buchenwald this poetic strain woke up, and I wrote sonnets, a volume of which were published after the liberation, and also a detective novel.

"In November 1941 our group was transferred to a camp in Holland and in February 1944 I was released. Afterwards I came into contact with an underground group, writing occasional articles in their 'illegal' newspaper and hiding arms and munitions in my cellar. In April 1945 the Germans invaded our house. Fortunately my wife (my second wife, 1934) had taken shelter just in time with friends in another part of the town. Our house was ransacked and one of my own hand grenades exploded in our sitting room.

"During my year at home I had written a book, *Napoleon: For and Against*. Events had caused me, although I was still hoping to complete my voluminous *History of the Netherlands People*, to take a wider interest in the problems of historiography. After *Napoleon: For and Against*, the English translation of which proved a great success, I dealt with Toynbee, very critically; also with the Dutch Marxist historian Romein. The volume in which these and other theoretical essays were collected, *Debates with Historians* (1955), also went through several paperback editions. Invitations from American colleges and universities, membership of national academies, honorary doctorates, paperback editions, gave me a feeling, after the opposition I had met with in my younger years, of having arrived. In the Netherlands, too, my interpretation of the sixteenth century split and other controversial subjects has won wide acceptance.

"I have remained active in my old age, although it does not seem that I shall ever finish my large *History of the Netherlands People*. In English, *The Revolt of the Netherlands* was followed by *The Netherlands in the Seventeenth Century*, carrying the history down to 1715; and in Dutch a volume covering 1751–1798 appeared in 1959. I am afraid I shall stick there."

Geyl's first publication was his doctoral thesis on Christofforo Suriano, Venetian Resident at The Hague (1616–1623). It was the beginning of a life-long interest in seventeenth century Netherlands history, as well as of a life-long habit of exhaustive investigation of primary sources. In the archives, he wrote, one can escape for a moment "all the generalisations and conventions" of historical abstraction, and join in the life of "a jumble of people, diplomats, merchants and officers, skippers, shipowners and bankers"—but only for a moment, because "as soon as the time comes for giving back what one has taken, choice, judgment and organization reassert their invincible rights."

Geyl's next book, written while he was living in England, was on William of Orange (*Willem IV en Engeland*, 1924), and this book H. H. Rowen describes as bearing "the marks that henceforth characterise Geyl's historical writing: the dominance of analysis over story-telling; the deep personal involvement with the issues at stake; and a readiness to evaluate persons and movements with devotion to the evidence and a sense of fair play." His work on the theme of Anglo-Dutch relations was continued in the masterly *Oranje en Stuart, 1641–1672* (1939, translated as *Orange and Stuart*), of which C. R. Boxer said it "shows Geyl at his best, and Geyl at his best is unsurpassable."

These books were in a sense by-products of what Geyl saw as his major work (unfortunately never completed)—his *History of the Netherlands People*. The first volume was published in 1930 and translated two years later as *The Revolt of the Netherlands, 1555–1609. The Netherlands Divided, 1609–1648*, followed in 1936, and was reprinted in 1961 as Part I of *The Netherlands in the Seventeenth Century*. Part II of this work (1648–1715) appeared in 1964. He took as his subject the Dutch-speaking peoples, including the Flemish. The book's keystone is the primacy of language as a national bond, and its central concern is to establish how and why the Low Countries were ever divided. The generally accepted view was that the separation had taken place on religious and national lines during the period of revolt against Spanish rule. Geyl's revolutionary thesis was that Spain had lost control of what became Holland not because of special qualities in the people of the northern Netherlands, but for geopolitical reasons—and fundamentally because the Spanish army could be, and was, halted at the natural barriers formed by the Rhine and the Meuse. As A. J. P. Taylor says, the simplicity of this argument, now an accepted historical dogma, "at last made sense of what had been a confused, almost incomprehensible picture. It was a triumph of common sense."

Geyl's belief in the unity of the Dutch-speaking peoples had its roots in his passionate interest in Flemish nationalism. In 1925 he had published a highly controversial book, *De Groot-Nederlandshe Gedachte* (The Greater Netherlands Idea). Flemish nationalism was at that time suspect both in Holland and Belgium, and in the late 1920s Geyl was twice arrested in Brussels. In 1935 the fact that Nazi sympathizers were to be found in the Flemish movement nearly cost him his chair at Utrecht, in spite of the outspoken opposition to Hitlerism which led to his detention in Buchenwald.

Napoleon: For and Against, written during the last year of the war, examines the contrasting views of Napoleon presented over a period of one hundred and fifty years by various French historians. The point of the book is that the vision of any interpreter of historical events is colored by his own attitudes and those of his time. Alan Bullock thought it "an illuminating chapter in the intellectual history of France" and H. S. Hughes called it "a historian's book for historians, the best single volume on Napoleon in the English language." It was also Geyl's first venture into historiography, a major concern in the latter part of his life, and the source of some notably stimulating controversies, though some of his colleagues regret the fact that he devoted so much energy to debate on the methods of other historians, leaving his own major work unfinished.

Geyl maintained that historians may be objective about facts but that they are and should be subjective in interpreting those facts: "The study even of contradictory conceptions can be fruitful. . . . History is indeed an argument without end." Thus he found himself in permanent opposition to those who sought universal historical laws or philosophies. This point of view emerges repeatedly in *Use and Abuse of History*, which studies the methods and attitudes of historians since Augustine, and in *Debates With Historians*, a volume of essays on European scholars including Ranke, Macaulay, Carlyle, Michelet, and Arnold Toynbee. With Toynbee Geyl conducted a public controversy for the rest of his life. Geyl accused him of imposing an artificial pattern on history, of misreading or ignoring empirical data, of abandoning history for "prophecy." Toynbee in turn complained that Geyl confined his view too narrowly to Western civilization, that he accepted too readily the convention that the "study of human nature and experience should be carved up into a number of separate disciplines," and especially that he excluded philosophy from the study of history.

All the same, when Geyl died, Toynbee spoke of his running argument with him as "a life-long course of adult education" and the source of many of the reassessments of his own ideas published in *Reconsiderations*. Many who knew Geyl paid tribute to what Toynbee called a "spiritual gift": "Geyl could and did hit out at his human targets with all his might, but this always without any touch of malice or uncharitableness." Others paid tribute to Geyl's exceptional command of English—some of his books indeed were first published, or given as lectures, in that language, and others he translated himself. He was widely regarded as one of the greatest historians of his time, and A. J. P. Taylor (whose book *The Origins of the Second World War* Geyl once described as "dreadful") said of him: "He is one of the few living men whose writings make me feel that Western civilization still exists."

PRINCIPAL WORKS IN ENGLISH: The Revolt of the Netherlands, 1555–1609, 1932; Netherlands Divided 1609–1648, 1936; (with Arnold Toynbee) Can We Know the Pattern of the Past? (U.S. The Pattern of the Past), 1949; Napoleon: For and Against, 1949; From Ranke to Toynbee: Five Lectures on Historians and Historiographical Problems, 1952; Use and Abuse of History, 1955; Debates With Historians, 1955; Encounters in History, 1961; The Netherlands in the Seventeenth Century: Part I, 1609–1648, 1961; Part II, 1648–1715, 1964; History of the Low Countries, Episodes and Problems (the Trevelyan Lectures, 1963), 1964; Orange and Stuart, 1641–1672, 1970.

ABOUT: Mehta, V. Fly and Fly Bottle, 1963. *Periodicals*—American Historical Review October 1949, July 1959, January 1965; Atlantic April 1954; Encounter May 1965, May 1967; English Historical Review July 1960; History Today December 1957, March 1967; Illustrated London News January 29, 1949; Journal of the History of Ideas January 1948, April 1955; Journal of Modern History March 1965; Nation February 23, 1957; April 13, 1957; April 14, 1966; New England Quarterly June 1951; New Statesman February 26, 1949; New York Review of Books April 8, 1965; New Yorker December 8, 1962; Saturday Review November 19, 1955; Spectator February 25, 1949; March 9, 1956; Times Literary Supplement January 9, 1964; May 28, 1964; Virginia Quarterly Review October 1950.

***GHELDERODE, MICHEL DE** (April 3, 1898–April 1, 1962), Belgian dramatist of Flemish origin who wrote in French, was little known outside his own country until 1949. In that year Jean-Louis Barrault produced *Fastes d'enfer* (Chronicles of Hell, 1929) in Paris. The play is set in medieval Flanders, just before the funeral of the Bishop of Lapideopolis. The Bishop, murdered by one of his own unspeakably corrupt and bestial clergy, is able to die only when he has spat out the Host, which is choking him. *Fastes d'enfer* shocked Paris. Ghelderode was said by some to be an unfrocked priest and was even accused of lycanthropy. In 1951 he gave a series of radio interviews, themselves a work of art, which contain most of what is known of his life. They were published in 1956 as *Les Entretiens d'Ostende* (Ostend Interviews).

"Michel de Ghelderode" adopted that name legally in 1929. He was born in Brussels, where his father, Adolphe Martens, was principal clerk at the Archives Générales. Ghelderode grew up amongst ancient books and manuscripts and "fell in love with things of the past." His mother, a woman of great simplicity, believed literally in the devil, whom "she had seen many a time," and from her he derived his taste for the supernatural.

* gel′ də rōd

MICHEL DE GHELDERODE

Daunted by his father's intention that he should enter the civil service, Ghelderode took refuge in "the realm of dreams to which, alone, [he] had found the magic keys." He read widely, relishing in particular the adventures of Eulenspiegel and Quixote, all that was fantastic, macabre, and extreme. He studied painting, and later music, with lasting effect but little immediate success. Eventually he adopted his father's profession and for twenty years earned his living as an archivist.

Ghelderode had produced his first poems and stories at sixteen, during his convalescence from a nearly fatal illness. At this time he haunted the Brussels marionette plays, writing down and preserving the texts, which were to have a great influence on his own work. In 1918 he wrote, for a literary group to which he belonged, a play in the manner of Poe. Thereafter, though he continued to write prose, he was a man of the theatre. "The nail in the scenery that had made a tear in my jacket had likewise scratched my flesh."

Four more short pieces were written during the next few years, and his first considerable play, the "music hall tragedy" *La Mort de Docteur Faust*, was completed in 1925. A year later the director of the Flemish Popular Theatre commissioned from him a play about Saint Francis of Assisi, and gave him a free hand. Ghelderode borrowed from the popular arts to make a play in which miracles were expressed through pantomime, angels swung on trapezes, and the saint danced. Many Catholic critics were outraged but Ghelderode, thinking it good that a saint should praise God dancing, saw no blasphemy. Neither did the unsophisticated rural audiences of the Popular Theatre. *Saint François d'Assise* (1927) was a success which heralded a short but fruitful association with the Theatre, from which Ghelderode learned much.

Between 1927 and 1930 he wrote a great number of plays. Some of them were vehicles for Renaat Verheyen, who had played Saint Francis. Several reflected Ghelderode's preoccupation with the appearance-reality enigma, notably the modern morality play *Don-Juan* (1928) and the greatly admired wry comedy *Pantagleize* (1929), about a Chaplinesque "little man" who is the cheerful and unwitting catalyst of a revolution. *Christophe Colomb* and *Escurial*, both written in 1927, were two of the most successful of the plays Ghelderode based on historical themes, the first proposing a Columbus for whom America was "too easy to discover." Two biblical plays written in 1928, both offering a grossly human view of the Crucifixion, were *Barabbas* and *Les Femmes aux tombeau* (*The Women at the Tomb*).

When Renaat Verheyen died in 1930, Ghelderode mourned him in the somewhat melodramatic *Sortie de l'acteur* (Actor's Exit, 1930), and thereafter severed his connection with the Flemish Popular Theatre—returning as he said, to his "ivory tower." All the plays he wrote between 1931 and 1937 were set in medieval or renaissance Flanders. They included among others, *Magie rouge* (Red Magic, 1931); *La Balade du Grand Macabre* (The Grand Macabre's Stroll, 1934); *D'un diable qui prêcha merveilles* (Of a Devil Who Preached Marvels, 1934); *Sire Halewyn* (Lord Halewyn, 1934); *Hop Signor!* (1935); and *L'École des bouffons* (School for Jesters, 1937). After the beginning of World War II Ghelderode, an asthmatic, became a virtual recluse, living alone in a room full of marionettes. dolls, and puppets whom he considered his friends. He wrote only one play after 1937: *Marie la misérable* (1952). By 1962, when he died, he was recognized as a master of the theatre, and his plays were being produced all over the world.

Ghelderode wrote in all over fifty plays, some of them for radio, some for marionettes, but most of them brilliantly exploiting all the resources of the theatre. He was above all a poet, using words with Rabelaisian pungency or a desperate incantatory lyricism which dismisses reason and invokes myth. He loved music and employed sound to superb effect. Many of the plays begin before the curtain rises, with music, bells, or the voice of crowds—devices which may impose their atmosphere throughout the performance. And when the curtain does go up, it is on sets that proclaim Ghelderode's devotion to the visual arts: dimly lighted stages, thick with shadows, glowing with rich colors and faded pomp. It is a "total theatre" of which Antonin Artaud would have approved.

Ghelderode acknowledged his debt to Poe and

the "gloomy writers," and to the English Elizabethan dramatists who taught him to "free himself from the rules" and showed him "men of great size and powerful voice." But he "discovered the world of shapes before he discovered the world of ideas," and his true masters were the Flemish painters—his plays themselves four-dimensional paintings after James Ensor and Pieter Breughel. Many of the plays were set in "Breugellande" or "Brugelmonde" and some were actually dramatizations of Breughel paintings—*La Pie sur le gibet*, for example, and *Les Aveugles*. Together, Ghelderode's works form a great fresco of a medieval Flanders, ruled by the Flesh and the Devil, crowded with carousing and deformed puppets, who lust and blaspheme through feasts, and seedy fairs, and baroque ceremonies until Death himself steps on stage, and the laughter, for a moment, is stilled. Of all the large characters in his plays, Death is the greatest. For Ghelderode, it was the "fear of the night" which "gives value to our days," and it was to "fix that fear" that he wrote.

Ghelderode is called anticlerical but called himself a Catholic. Nor was he totally cynical, though few of the plays allow a victory to innocence. "Men are not lovely," he said, "not often, and it's very well that they are not even more ugly; but I believe in *Man*, and I think that this can be felt in my work." David Grossvogel has suggested that, for Ghelderode, "the tragedy of man is that, try as he may, he can never be quite an animal. Some residual spark of consciousness always stirs . . . to defeat him." Ghelderode himself said: "I have an angel on my shoulder and a devil in my pocket"; it is the struggle between these two that gives his plays their enormous life.

PRINCIPAL WORKS IN ENGLISH TRANSLATION: Escurial *in* Bentley, E. The Modern Theater, Series V, 1937; Seven Plays (The Women at the Tomb, Barabbas, Three Actors and Their Drama, Pantagleize, The Blind Men, Chronicles of Hell, Lord Halewyn; *with* selections from the Ostend Interviews), 1960.

ABOUT: Francis, J. Michel de Ghelderode, 1949; Grossvogel, D. The Self-Conscious Stage, 1958; Guicharnaud, J. Modern French Theatre, 1961; Iglesis, R. and Trutat, A. Michel de Ghelderode: Les Entretiens d'Ostende, 1956; Pronko, L. C. Avant-Garde, 1962; Wellwarth, G. E. The Theater of Protest and Paradox, 1964. *Periodicals*—Tulane Drama Review Autumn 1959, Fall 1963, Summer 1965.

"GIBB, LEE." *See* WATERHOUSE, KEITH

GIBSON, WILLIAM (November 13, 1914–), American dramatist, memoirist, poet, and novelist, was born in New York City, the son of George and Florence (Doré) Gibson. His father was a bank clerk, and both parents were amateur musicians. Gibson graduated in 1930 from Townsend Harris Hall, New York City (which he has called "a school for three-foot geniuses") and attended the City College of New York from 1930 to 1932, when he found he could no longer tolerate academic discipline. After leaving school he did some acting with the Barter Theatre in Virginia and for a time worked in bars as a jazz pianist. In 1940 he married Margaret Brenman, a psychoanalyst who was to work in the Menninger Clinic in Topeka; they moved there shortly after their marriage.

WILLIAM GIBSON

Gibson had his first literary success in 1943, when his one-act verse play *I Lay in Zion* was staged by the Topeka Civic Theatre, with the author as a member of the cast. In 1947 *A Cry of Players* had an amateur production at the University of Kansas. This play, which deals with three days in the life of Shakespeare before he leaves Stratford for London, was revived many years later at Lincoln Center in New York.

In 1945 Gibson had received the Harriet Monroe Memorial Prize for a group of poems in *Poetry* magazine, and his first volume of poetry, *Winter Crook*, appeared in 1948. Reviewers were impressed and, though some found Gibson's verse rather derivative (most obviously of Gerard Manley Hopkins), at least one critic thought that these influences had been "transmuted into something new and beautiful and extraordinarily personal." There was also a generally favorable reception for Gibson's novel *The Cobweb*, which is set in a midwestern mental hospital and focuses on the heated but pathetic quarrel between four inmates over who should choose the drapes for the community room. Charles Lee wrote of Gibson: "He is a master of dialogue. His characters, remarkably alive, are viewed with clarity and charity; he sees them moving through life with ironical unawareness of the disaffections they often inspire in those nearest them, and at the same time he stirs the reader to pity for them all." The novel was filmed in 1957.

Gibson is best known as the author of two enormously successful Broadway plays: *Two for the Seesaw* and *The Miracle Worker*. *The Miracle Worker*, he says, "was written as a television script while *Two for the Seesaw* was languishing for a producer, but it existed in a prior form. Three years earlier I had first read Annie Sullivan's letters recounting her work with the child Helen Keller, and been so smitten with love that I turned them into a narrative intended to accompany a solo dancer. The dance evaporated, and I was left with twelve pages of narration on my hands." Gerald Weales writes of *The Miracle Worker*: "If the effects are often stagy, they at least work in the way the playwright seems to intend. . . . It is Gibson's neatness that is finally defeating because his characters become not the complicated persons that they obviously were, but sentimental stereotypes . . . who perform expectedly in standard scenes."

The engaging two-character tour de force *Two for the Seesaw* was received with almost universal acclaim and pleasure. In it a Nebraska lawyer, seeking a divorce in New York, has a brief, bittersweet affair with a warm-hearted girl from the Bronx and, healed by this experience, returns to pick up the threads of his marriage. Of no less interest than the play itself was Gibson's *The Seesaw Log* (1959), an account of his tribulations during the stage production, particularly of the changes that were required of him during rehearsals. He found that "the theatre, in this country, in this decade, was primarily a place not in which to be serious, but in which to be likable." The critic Allen Lewis, who liked *Two for the Seesaw* rather less than some of his colleagues did, has suggested that Gibson should have resisted more fiercely the commercial pressures that led him to alter the play's original conception. It became a successful musical in 1973.

Dinny and the Witches, originally performed at the Topeka Community Theatre and produced in New York in 1959, was a far less successful play, but the author preferred it, as did Gerald Weales, who called it "an often inventive, occasionally funny, play about the acceptance of death as a fact of life and the consolations of love; it suggests Saroyan to some extent, not only in its elaborate eccentricity but in its finally enervating sense of its own significance."

Gibson, who wrote six songs for *Dinny and the Witches*, also supplied the book for the successful musical *Golden Boy*, based upon Clifford Odets' play. *A Mass for the Dead* is an account of Gibson's childhood and youth and more particularly an act of homage to his mother and father—good but ordinary people whom he came to love and value only when his own two sons began to grow away from him. The book becomes an attempt (as Jack Richardson said) "to bind together through the memory of birth, love, and death Gibson's intermediary position between past and future"—an attempt to conquer time and death through art. Some reviewers thought the book was defeated in its high intentions by an artificial structure and a clumsily rhetorical style, but most were profoundly moved. Granville Hicks wrote: "The sections of the book are named for portions of the mass, and though he broke long ago with his mother's Catholicism, the work is a sustained meditation in a spirit that can only be called religious on life and love and death. . . . It is a strong book, written out of compunction, love, and hope."

Gibson and his family live in Stockbridge, Massachusetts. The author is a tall Irishman, writes Jerry Tallmer, "long, lean, and rugged, with huge hands, a craggy jaw, two black forests for eyebrows, faraway hazel eyes, a sober grin."

PRINCIPAL WORKS: I Lay in Zion (verse play), 1947; Winter Crook (poems), 1948; The Cobweb (novel), 1954; The Miracle Worker: A Play for Television, 1957; Two for the Seesaw: A Comedy in Three Acts, 1958; The Seesaw Log: A Chronicle of the Stage Production, *with* the text of Two for the Seesaw, 1959; Dinny and the Witches, *and* The Miracle Worker, 1960; Golden Boy: The Book of a Musical (based on the play by Clifford Odets), 1965;A Mass for the Dead (memoirs), 1968.

ABOUT: Contemporary Authors 9–10, 1964; Encyclopedia and Who's Who of the American Theatre, 1966; Gassner, J. Theatre at the Crossroads, 1960; Gibson, W. The Seesaw Log, 1959; Kerr, W. The Theater in Spite of Itself, 1963; Lewis, A. American Plays and Players of the Contemporary Theatre, 1970; Tynan, K. Curtains, 1961; Weales, G. American Drama Since World War II, 1962; Who's Who in America, 1970–1971. *Periodicals*—Cosmopolitan August 1958; New York Herald Tribune Book Review March 21, 1954; New York Post February 17, 1958; November 4, 1959; New York Times October 26, 1959; June 18, 1967; New Yorker February 15, 1958; Newsweek March 16, 1959; Theatre Arts October 1959; Tulane Drama Review May 1960; Village Voice November 18, 1959.

"GILBERT, ANTHONY." *See* MALLESON, LUCY BEATRICE

GILBERT, MICHAEL (FRANCIS) (July 17, 1912–), English detective story writer, novelist, and dramatist, was born in Billinghay, Lincolnshire, the son of Bernard and Berwyn (Cuthbert) Gilbert. He was educated at private schools and at London University, where he received a law degree in 1937. A year with a London firm of solicitors was followed by service throughout World War II with the Royal Horse Artillery. Gilbert spent some time in an Italian prison camp, earned a mention in dispatches, and left the Army with the rank of major. In 1947 he joined Trower, Still, and Keeling, a London legal firm, and the same year published his first book. Since then he has pursued a dual role as a successful writer and a successful lawyer, becoming a partner in his firm in 1952.

From the beginning, Gilbert's detective stories have benefited from his professional knowledge of court and legal procedure, police practice, and criminology. His first novel, *Close Quarters*, was set in an English cathedral town and called "a first-rate, highly formal whodunit . . . with admirable detection by Chief Inspector Hazlerigg and an entertaining view of the private life of the Church of England." Hazlerigg is one of several Gilbert characters—the lawyer Macrae is another—who play important subsidiary parts in a number of his stories.

Gilbert's first few books were all warmly received, earning praise for their suspense and ingenuity, the realism of their characters and settings, the humor and irony which characterized their style. It was Gilbert's fifth novel, *Death Has Deep Roots*, that established him as a master of the genre. A French girl is on trial in England for murder. While the brilliantly handled court drama grinds towards its conclusion, one of the girl's lawyers is scouring London for evidence of her innocence, and another is doing the same in Paris. Somewhat to Hazlerigg's chagrin they succeed, and not a moment too soon. The three story lines are brilliantly integrated in what one critic called "a technical *tour de force* of fusion."

Unlike most writers in his field, Gilbert has never been content to settle for a proven formula, and many of his books are nothing like the traditional whodunits that made his name. *Death in Captivity* for example draws on his own war experiences, combining suspense, adventure and detection in an Italian P.O.W. camp, where the British prisoners seek the traitor who is threatening their escape plans. *Fear to Tread*, which followed in 1953 and was called "one of the year's most credible, exciting and delightful thrillers," has as its unorthodox and highly successful detective the headmaster of an east London secondary school. Other stories, including *Be Shot for Sixpence* and *After the Fine Weather*, both set on the Continent, are novels of suspense in the manner of Eric Ambler.

Some of Gilbert's recent books are so exact in their observation of place and character that reviewers have seemed uncertain whether to treat them as thrillers or as straight novels. *Crack in the Teacup* is about a young English solicitor who blunders into the web of crime and political intrigue being drawn around his seaside town and rashly tries to unravel it. Anthony Boucher, who found it tense, exciting, and "rich in the suggestion

MICHAEL GILBERT

of oppressive evil," said that "the detailed creation of the history, culture, and politics of Sandling, Kent, becomes a major character in itself." *The Dust and the Heat*, published in America as *Overdrive*, examines twenty years in the life of a ruthlessly ambitious businessman, so perceptively and vividly that one reviewer suggested that it could be read either "as a straight novel utilizing certain techniques of suspense or as a suspense novel of unusual substance." The stories collected in *Game Without Rules*, about the work of two middle-aged counterespionage agents, were called "short works of art in social realism."

Four of Gilbert's ingenious plays have been staged in London's West End, and he has also written for radio and television. *The Claimant* is a factual account of the Tichborne case, a celebrated nineteenth century case of imposture, and *Crime in Good Company* is a volume of essays by various hands on the art and craft of thriller writing.

Michael Gilbert was married to Roberta Marsden in 1947 and has two sons and five daughters. He lives in Cobham, Kent, and does most of his writing on the train between there and London. Gilbert is a founder member of the Crime Writers Association and of the Screen Writers Guild. He has served as legal adviser to the government of Bahrain, as a member of the Arts Council Committee on Public Lending Right, and as a member of the Royal Literary Fund. His recreations include archery, walking, and contract bridge.

PRINCIPAL WORKS: *Fiction*—Close Quarters, 1947; They Never Looked Inside, 1948; The Doors Open, 1949; Smallbone Deceased, 1950; Death Has Deep Roots, 1951; Death in Captivity (U.S., Danger Within), 1952; Be

Shot for Sixpence, 1956; Blood and Judgement, 1959; After the Fine Weather, 1963; The Crack in the Teacup, 1966; Game Without Rules (short stories), 1967; The Dust and the Heat, 1967 (U.S., Overdrive); The Etruscan Net, 1969 (U.S., The Family Tomb); Stay of Execution (stories), 1971; The Body of a Girl, 1972. *Plays*—The Bargain, 1961; A Clean Kill, 1961. *Nonfiction*—The Claimant, 1957; (comp.) Crime in Good Company, 1959.
ABOUT: Contemporary Authors 1, 1963; Who's Who, 1971.

***GILBOA, AMIR** (September 30, 1917–), Israeli poet, writes: "On a cold winter night towards the end of 1937, a small Greek vessel, the S.S. Poseidon, unloaded its illegal living cargo, sixty-five members of the Polish youth organisation *Hehalutz*, at a certain distance from the beach of the northern Sharon Plain. Wet to the skin, we were led by members of the Hagana, by paths hidden from the eyes of the British police, to the citrus-house of a near-by kibbutz (collective settlement), where we spent our first night in Eretz-Israel (Palestine).

"While I made my way for the first time through a citrus grove, I felt as if I distinctly remembered this way from days far back, and the orange scent—this was the picking season—seemed to me well known since time immemorial.

"Next morning, we were divided into groups and sent to various kibbutzim in the country. I myself, however, disappeared the same day and toured the whole country on foot for several weeks, putting names to the various places I saw, without asking anybody, but sure within myself that my identifications were correct.

"Then I settled down for about a year in a kibbutz, where I did all kinds of jobs. But my aspiration to become a writer, an aspiration I carried with me since childhood, drove me out of the kibbutz. Being alone and without means, I had to take any kind of work offered. World War II was drawing near and the general situation made itself felt in this country too.

"It was at that time that I began to write poetry. The first poem I sent in 1941 to a newspaper in Tel Aviv was published immediately, and in 1942 I published my first volume of poetry, *La'oth* (To the Sign).

"A short time afterwards, I volunteered for the British Army and was sent to Egypt to a transport unit composed of Palestinian Jews. With this unit I went to Libya, Malta and Italy and, after the end of the war, to Belgium and the Netherlands. While we were stationed in northern Italy, near the Austrian and Yugoslav borders, I had the privilege of being among the drivers who transported, without the knowledge of the military authorities, Jewish survivors from D.P. camps in Austria and Germany to ports in southern Italy, from where they proceeded to Palestine on board the famous illegal ships.

"During my military service, I wrote almost nothing, except during two short periods. The events and the feelings they aroused were too powerful, and I felt that whatever I could write would hardly give them adequate expression. Sometimes I jotted down a few lines on a piece of paper or on the back of a packet of cigarettes. Those poems which survived the vicissitudes of military life, were included in the volume *Sheva Reshuioth* (Seven Realms), published in 1949.

"It seems to me that the most fruitful period in my life as a poet were the years 1950–1952. The poems written in this period were published in 1953 in a volume called *Shirim baboker-baboker* (Songs in the Early Morning).

"Since then I have been obliged to work as an editor in a commercial publishing company, in order to earn a living for my family (wife and two girls). This is a full-time job, which leaves little time for writing poetry. When however a Tel Aviv publishing house approached me with the proposal to republish all my poems, I could not resist the temptation to accept, particularly as I saw in this proposal a new challenge. Indeed, the volume *Blues and Reds* (1963) (of four hundred pages) included about fifty pages of new poetry.

"My childhood and youth were spent in a forlorn little place in Volhynia, in the Polish Ukraine, today within the boundaries of Soviet Russia. The majority of the inhabitants were Jews, but there were also Ukrainians, Russians and some Czechs. The only Poles were those brought from central Poland to serve as local government officials. The villages round about were inhabited by Ukrainians, but there was also a German village. At school too, all the peoples were represented in my class, and there were even some Gypsy boys. A beautiful Polish teacher, in one of the higher forms, was the first to prophesy that I was to become a writer, after she read some stories I had written.

"My inclination to writing was, perhaps, due to the influence of the teacher who taught me, in my childhood, Hebrew and the Bible. He used to write on the blackboard stories which he composed extempore. At least this was what his pupils thought. I also liked to sit near him and watch him drawing animals, birds and initials in wonderful colors on the front pages of registers which religious and other societies ordered from him. From that time on, white paper and pencil never left me indifferent. I was a dreamy, musing child, and the songs which my father used to sing by night with his beautiful voice, songs from the sunny South where he had spent his youth, aroused in me a longing for a distant and marvelous world. Our little town, open to all the winds in the Volhynian

* gil bō' ə

steppe, seemed to me a desolate place and I felt attracted by the world abroad. A country I used to dream of was Palestine, the Land of Israel.

"I attempted my first escape at the age of six or seven, but peasants found me and brought me back to my parents next day. The real escape occurred years later. This was the fateful one, owing to which I did not share the gruesome doom reserved to my parents, brothers and sisters, a few years later. After having wandered, worked and learned for a while, I came home for the last time to see my people, but without telling them that it was in fact a leave-taking and that I had found a possibility of illegal immigration to Palestine. The illegal immigrants were forbidden to disclose their plans to their family or to anybody else. This was the last time we saw each other."

AMIR GILBOA

Throughout his poetry Gilboa has maintained a steady consistency of language: one is, as Ruth Mintz says, "immediately aware of a wholly individual tone." And she adds that "his poetry moves closer to life than to literature, and reveals the intellectual's will to comprehend, as well as to perceive, relationships."

The vehicle of those perceptions is, in Gilboa, a special meditative surrealism. He is at his best in collapsing the time between Old Testament events and the immediate present. In "Moses" he begins: "I approached Moses and said to him: / Arrange the camps thus and so. / He looked at me / Arranged them as I bid." Thereupon the poet makes plans for the building of a city, taking pride, as he does so, in the admiration of former girl friends: of "the long-legged ones from the girls' farm," of "Melvina from Rabbat in Malta," or "Dinah from the Italo-Yugoslav border." Finally the poet confesses his fatigue at his whole undertaking. He falls back into the persona of a little boy, as he had in the poem "Isaac," or in "Birth," in which as a child he declares: "Oh my God, how embraced we have been." In all these major lyrics the traditional Hebrew world is made sharply contemporary, brought into the center of today's life; yet Gilboa's life, as he presents it, is itself meditative, poetic, and not without distinct elements of verbal play.

Gilboa takes his place with other Israeli poets of his generation whose lives have been largely shaped in the turbulent new Israel of the last twenty years. These poets, for serious historical reasons, have insisted on bringing poetry close to life. Thus Gilboa has turned away from the generation of Shlonsky and Alterman, poets for whom "the metric scheme of iambs and anapests" was sacred: his verse is free, built on internal rhyme, alliteration and repetition —whole phrases may be condensed into single words. At the same time he has remained true to the past in a deeper sense. "The personality of Gilboa is unique in our modern poetry," asserts the critic L. Goldberg. "This is autonomous poetry expressing itself in a way very different from the accepted and usual aesthetic conventions, even if its roots are in the old and ever new tradition of Hebrew poetry. Whoever tries to discover here influences, will finally be obliged to recognize its originality."

Perhaps more than any other established Hebrew poet, Gilboa was adopted as the celebrator of post-independence Israel—"Suddenly a man rises in the morning and feels that he is a nation and starts walking," he wrote at the time of independence. He was the poet of the immense confidence of the first years of freedom. Lately, however, his mood has changed, and Miriam Arad wrote of his collection *Ratsiti Liohtov Siftei Yeshenim* (To Write the Lips of Those Asleep, 1968): "There is little pure joy in Gilboa now—except in poems about Jerusalem. His poems used to glow so, be filled with a kind of secretive, hugging delight, of which only a little lingers now." She comments on an increasing bitterness in his writing, on a sense of urgency in the face of approaching death, a tendency to withdraw into himself, and quotes the lines: "I press the muzzle of the pen to paper like the barrel of a gun to temple / Now in one shot to discharge all the days and nights." "I have no answers," he laments elsewhere; and again, "I wanted more. I wanted something. Hope. / To write hope. She might still be there / Why is my only one asleep?" Gilboa received the Bialik Prize in 1971.

PRINCIPAL WORKS IN ENGLISH TRANSLATION: *Poems in* Burnshaw, S. and others (eds.) The Modern Hebrew

Poem Itself, 1965; Mintz, R. F. (ed.) Modern Hebrew Poetry, 1966.
ABOUT: Burnshaw, S. and others (eds.) The Modern Hebrew Poem Itself, 1965; Mintz, R. F. (ed.) Modern Hebrew Poetry, 1966. *Periodicals*—Jerusalem Post October 6, 1968; New York Times Book Review May 2, 1965.

GINSBERG, ALLEN (June 3, 1926–), American poet, was born in Newark, New Jersey, the son of Louis and Naomi (Levy) Ginsberg. Louis Ginsberg, a high school teacher, is himself moderately well known as a poet. With his brother Eugene, now a lawyer, Ginsberg grew up in Paterson, New Jersey, in a household where, during the Depression, poverty was exacerbated by his mother's decline into madness. A bright, idealistic Marxist in her youth, she became violently paranoid during Allen Ginsberg's childhood and died in 1956 after long confinement in a mental hospital.

Ginsberg attended high school in Paterson, then went to Columbia University. There he achieved an A-minus average, won the Woodbury Poetry Prize, was president of the Philolexian Society, edited the *Columbia Jester*, and belonged to the debating team. During his sophomore year (1945) he was suspended for tracing obscenities on the dusty windows of his room—an activity he undertook in the earnest hope that it would stimulate the cleaning staff to greater efforts. Then, and during more orthodox Columbia vacations, Ginsberg held jobs as a dishwasher at Bickford's, as a seaman on various cargo ships, as a spotwelder in the Brooklyn Navy Yard, and as a night porter at a store in Denver. He was reinstated at Columbia after a year on condition that he accept psychiatric aid. However, as Diana Trilling recalls, he continued to get into a great deal of trouble "and had to be rescued and revived and restored; eventually he had even to be kept out of jail." This last incident came about through his friendship with Herbert Huncke, a thief and mystic whom he met, along with Jack Kerouac and others later prominent in the Beat movement, at William Burroughs' apartment near Columbia. Ginsberg says that Burroughs taught him far more than the university did, introducing him to the Mayan codices, and to Proust, Yeats, Céline, Spengler, Korzybski, and many other writers who were important in his development.

In the summer of 1948, his graduation year, Ginsberg was visited by a series of mystical experiences—apprehensions of "a totally deeper real universe than I'd been existing in" inspired by certain of Blake's poems. These experiences, at first beatific, became fearful and brought him close to madness. He spent eight months then in a mental hospital, where he met Carl Solomon, to whom "Howl" is dedicated.

For three or four years thereafter Ginsberg worked at various jobs, notably as a book reviewer for *Newsweek* and as a market research consultant in New York and San Francisco. In San Francisco in 1954 he met the poet Peter Orlovsky, who has been his companion ever since, and with his psychotherapist's blessing decided to give up his job and devote himself to "writing and contemplation, to Blake and smoking pot, and doing whatever I wanted." Although he had written much poetry while in college, it was in San Francisco that his style first achieved the free-swinging exuberance which reminds his admirers of Vachel Lindsay, Carl Sandburg, and above all of Whitman.

San Francisco itself was a liberating influence, but two other specific factors which were to prove profoundly important should be noted: the use of drugs, and the disciplines of Oriental religions, particularly Zen Buddhism. San Francisco also gave him a publisher. *Howl and Other Poems* (1956) was the fourth book in the Pocket Poets series published by Lawrence Ferlinghetti, owner of the City Lights Bookshop. William Carlos Williams, whose lyric simplicity is echoed in some of Ginsberg's shorter poems, supplied an introduction.

"Howl" is an apocalyptic vision of the physical, mental, spiritual destruction of a whole generation of young Americans on the altars of war and greed, a furiously obscene cry of outrage uttered in what Ginsberg calls his "Hebraic-Melvillian bardic breath": "I saw the best minds of my generation destroyed by madness, starving hysterical naked." In 1957 the San Francisco police arrested Ferlinghetti for publishing a "filthy" book. The ensuing trial, in which Kenneth Rexroth, Mark Schorer, Walter Van Tilburg Clark and other noted literary figures testified for the defense, gave the book immense publicity. By the time Judge Clayton W. Horn delivered his verdict that *Howl* was not obscene, the Beat movement had its poetic manifesto, and Ginsberg was a famous man, the shaman and superstar of poetry readings and anarchic literary happenings all over the United States.

Kaddish and Other Poems was published by City Lights Books in 1961. The title poem, "Kaddish for Naomi Ginsberg (1894–1956)," is a prayer and lament for his mother which is widely regarded as his masterpiece. It gives an apparently quite factual account of her tragic journey through life, which took her, a frightened yet expectant Russian child, to America and onward "toward education, marriage, nervous breakdown, operation, teaching school, and learning to be mad." Ginsberg's traumatic memories of her frenzied paranoia are the substance of "Kaddish," yet its spirit, after the protests, after the blasphemies, after the self-abasements, is one of acceptance, even one of celebration. A powerful and moving "mixed media" stage version of the poem has been made by Robert Kalfin, artistic director of the Chelsea Theater Center of Brooklyn, from a script by Ginsberg, and was first produced by the Chelsea Center in February 1972.

Pull My Daisy, a spontaneous film in which Ginsberg appeared in 1961 with Kerouac, Orlovsky, and other friends conveys something of the spirit of the Beat movement (and shows that celebrity had done nothing to diminish his sense of humor). He subsequently acted in several other underground movies. In 1962 and 1963 Ginsberg, with Orlovsky, toured the Far East. He later reported that "experience in Benares with mantra chanting (short magic formulae sung or repeated aloud as invocation to inner divinity) and in Kyoto with Zen belly-breathing delivered my accustomed voice (and center of self) from upper chest and throat to solar plexus and lower abdomen. The timbre, range and feeling-quality of the physical voice was thus physiologically deepened till it actually approximated what I'd youthfully imagined to be the voice of rock."

Ginsberg returned to the United States in the spring of 1963 changed in other ways also. He had decided to renounce mystical aspirations in favor of "direct vision, sense perception contact with the now of life," and he preached the superiority of yoga and meditation over drugs. In a tour of American universities subsidized by a Guggenheim grant, and in later talks to student groups, he has expressed concern over the addictive drugs, though he continues to believe that marijuana, peyote, and occasionally LSD have their uses, particularly in writing poetry. And in testimony before a Senate judiciary subcommittee on narcotics he asserted that LSD offered one of a number of paths towards an ideal society based on universal love, and had in fact enabled him to stop hating President Johnson as a criminal and to pray for him.

In 1965 Ginsberg went to Cuba as a correspondent for the *Evergreen Review* but was deported when he spoke against the government's persecution of homosexuals at Havana University. He journeyed on to the Soviet Union, Poland, and Czechoslovakia, and was shortly deported from Czechoslovakia also because, as he put it, the authorities were embarrassed by the welcome accorded by the young people of Prague to "a bearded American fairy dope poet," whom they crowned King of the May on May Day 1965.

Later the same year, back in the United States, Ginsberg invented "flower power," first used by antiwar demonstrators in California to combat harassment by police and the Hell's Angels motorcycle gang. Armed with LSD and chanting mantras, he entered the headquarters of the Hell's Angels and won them over. Ginsberg was also the moving spirit behind the Gathering of the Tribes for a Human Be-In, the first of the hippies' evangelical picnics, held in Golden Gate Park in San Francisco in January 1967. Later the same year he was arrested with Dr. Benjamin Spock and others for his part in a New York City antiwar demonstration. During the 1968 Democratic Convention in Chicago he was tear-gassed while chanting "om" at the Lincoln Park Yippie Life Festival. More recently he has been an eloquent champion of ecological sanity.

ALLEN GINSBERG

Less sensational but no less important is his work as "the central casting office of the underground." He maintains an enormous correspondence with people at every level of American society and all over the world, and goes to considerable trouble to put like-minded acquaintances in touch with each other, or with sympathetic and influential Establishment figures who might be helpful to them. In this and other ways he has become, as Jane Kramer says, not only "the philosopher-king of a seminal hippiedom," but "the most practically effective drop-out around."

A volume of Ginsberg's early poems was published as *Empty Mirror* in 1962 and followed a year later by *Reality Sandwiches*, collecting poems written between 1953 and 1960. *Planet News*, *T.V. Baby Poems*, and *Ankor Wat* all appeared in 1968. None of these volumes has been received with anything like the excitement that greeted *Howl* and *Kaddish*. Thomas Lask, discussing Ginsberg's recent work in 1969, thought that the lines had become firmer, but that the poetry had "the same juxtapositions and the frequent lists" that appeared in earlier works, "as if he wanted to be sure that no bit of experience would be left out"; Lask suggested that Ginsberg's work had become "a running editorial on current affairs." Karl Shapiro has called him "the hair stylist of a generation; a poor poet who never learned the trade; a weak thinker who settles most questions with a homemade brand of mushy Hinduism, a deacon in the crusade for drugs, a minor Marxist scoutmaster leading his rabble to the fountain of youth." Kenneth Rexroth continues to regard Ginsberg as "a great literary artist," who "deprovincialized American verse and returned it to the mainstream of modern international literature," but acknowledges the difficulty of disentangling his literary achievement from his reputation as a social phenomenon and as a religious leader: "Allen Ginsberg is in the direct line of the *nabis*, those wild men of the hills, bearded and barefoot, who periodically descended upon Jerusalem, denounced king and priesthood, and recalled the Chosen People to the Covenant."

Ginsberg lives in a cheap, cluttered apartment on New York City's Lower East Side with Orlovsky and (as Jane Kramer says) "any congenial being who wants to camp there and is willing to help with the cleaning up." For peace and quiet he often retreats to the farm he owns in Cherry Valley, New York. Apart from the little he retains to meet his own modest financial needs, his nowadays quite large income, most of it from poetry readings, goes to the Committee on Poetry, the foundation which Ginsberg established in 1966 to help less affluent artists. The poet wears a full beard, a droopy moustache, "and long black ringlets, hanging like a thatch corona from his bald spot." Jane Kramer calls him "a rumpled, friendly looking man with a nice, toothy face, big brown owl eyes behind the glasses, and a rather affecting weary slouch."

PRINCIPAL WORKS: Howl and Other Poems, 1956; Kaddish and Other Poems, 1961; Empty Mirror (early poems), 1961; Reality Sandwiches (poems 1953–1960), 1963; Yage Letters (with William Burroughs), 1963; Planet News (poems 1961–1967), 1968; T.V. Baby Poems, 1968; Ankor Wat; photographs by Alexandra Lawrence, 1968; Indian Journals, March 1962–May 1963: Notebooks, Diary, Blank Pages, Writings, 1970; The Fall of America: Poems of These States, 1965–1971, 1973.

ABOUT: Carroll, P. The Poem in Its Skin, 1968; Cook, B. The Beat Generation, 1971; Current Biography, 1970; Dowden, G. (comp.) A Bibliography of Works by Allen Ginsberg, October 1943 to July 1 1967, 1971; French, W. G. (ed.) The Fifties: Fiction, Poetry, Drama, 1970; Gross, T. L. (ed.) Representative Men, 1970; Howard, R. Alone with America, 1969; Kostelanetz, R. Master Minds, 1969; Kramer, J. Allen Ginsberg in America, 1969 (England, Paterfamilias: Allen Ginsberg in America, 1970); Martz, W. J. The Distinctive Voice, 1966; Merrill, T. F. Allen Ginsberg, 1969; Rosenthal, M. L. The New Poets, 1967; Stepanchev, S. American Poetry Since 1945, 1965; Who's Who in America, 1972–1973; Writers at Work: The Paris Review Interviews, 3rd Series, 1967. *Periodicals*—America March 4, 1972; Book World May 25, 1969; Commentary January 1970; Commonweal April 21, 1967; Esquire December 1965; Evergreen Review July–August 1961; Harper's October 1966; Horizon Winter 1969; Library Journal June 15, 1966; Life May 27, 1966; Nation November 16, 1957; November 8, 1965; March 10, 1969; February 28, 1972; New Leader July 31, 1961; New Republic July 25, 1970; New York Times Book Review August 14, 1966; April 4, 1971; January 2, 1972; New York Times Magazine July 11, 1965; New Yorker August 17, August 24, 1968; Newsweek February 21, 1972; Paris Review Spring 1966; Partisan Review Spring 1959; Poetry August 1962, July 1969, September 1969; Publishers' Weekly June 23, 1969; Reporter December 12, 1957; Saturday Review April 22, 1972; Sunday Times April 13, 1967; Time August 8, 1969; Times (London) July 13, 1967.

GINZBURG, NATALIA (July 14, 1916–), Italian novelist, writes (in Italian): "My name is Natalia Levi. My father, Giuseppe Levi, was a scientist and taught anatomy at the university. My mother's name was Lidia Tanzi and she came from Milan; my father was from Trieste. Both were Socialists and friends of Kuliscioff and of Filippo Turati. I was born in 1916 at Palermo, where my father was teaching at that time. When I was three, my father was transferred to the University of Turin and I spent my childhood and adolescence in that city. I have told the story of my family in my book *Lessico famigliare.*

"I began to write in my adolescence and my first stories appeared in 1934 in the review *Solaria*, which was published in Florence. In 1938 I married Leone Ginzburg, professor of Russian literature and himself of Russian origin, who had come to Italy in his childhood and was an active anti-Fascist. From 1940 to 1943 we spent three years in compulsory residence in a district of the Abruzzi. We had three children.

"Leone Ginzburg was arrested in Rome in November 1943 when working in a clandestine press and was handed over to the Germans, who were in charge of the Regina Coeli prison. He died in the infirmary of the Regina Coeli on February 5th, 1944.

"After the liberation I returned to Turin with my children and worked there as a consultant with the publishing firm of Einaudi. Einaudi had published my first novel, *La strada che va in città*, in 1942 while I was still in compulsory residence. I used the pseudonym 'Allessandra Tornimparte.' The book had a moderate success.

"In 1947 I published *È stato così.*

"In 1950 I married again. My second husband was Gabriele Baldini, professor of English literature, and we went to live in Rome. We lived in London, for three years, from 1959 to 1962. My husband was then head of the Italian Institute of Culture in London.

"In 1962 we returned to Rome.

"In 1961 I published *Le voci della sera* and in 1962 *Le piccole virtù*, a collection of essays, and in 1963 *Lessico famigliare*, a sort of autobiographical novel which won the Strega prize and has since been published in English. I do some work for newspapers (*La Stampa, Il Giorno*), but only occasionally and not regularly."

It is unnecessary to add anything of a biographical nature to Signora Ginzburg's own summary; her report is of the same nature as her creative works in its straightforward, understated tone, with its precise details and avoidance of editorial comment. Such elements are already visible in her first short novel, *La strada che va in città* (1942, translated by Frances Frenaye as *The Road to the City*), which is the story of a girl who is almost passively led into marriage to a man for whom she feels only a superficial attraction and who ultimately deserts her. It is not clear what leads the protagonist on her illogical path; her motivation seems to be compounded of boredom with her surroundings, a certain sense of fatality, and an abdication of the will in the face of events.

The heroine of what may well be Signora Ginzburg's best novel, *È stato così* (1947, translated as *The Dry Heart*), is of the same stamp; in this case, however, we are given the story of the disintegration of a marriage: Giovanna, despairing of drawing her husband away from his mistress and, what is worse, failing to find a level of true communication with him, finally kills him, almost, as she seems to imply, against her will—because it had to "happen this way."

Tutti i nostri ieri (1952, translated by Angus Davidson as *A Light for Fools*) is a novel of more ambitious scope; in this work, significantly, the novelist abandons the first-person narrative and adopts the more conventional and objective third-person approach. The book is an attempt to reconstruct the history of the author's generation, which had come of age under fascism and subsequently experienced the war and the resistance, through the vicissitudes of a small cast of characters. Although the intellectual Cenzo Rena, who heroically sacrifices himself for a friend, is at the center of the action, he is not alone in carrying the burden of the tale, which does successfully convey the impression of group response to historical events. And as the background is richer than that of the earlier novels, moving from the city to the countryside, so too the author attempts to give a more coherent philosophical interpretation to the events she chronicles: here the characters are not merely passive observers and sufferers but conscious and critical witnesses of history and, within limits, participants in its action. There is also something of a "moral" in the overtly expressed hope that the harsh experiences of the generation depicted in the story may illuminate those who will come after.

Le voci della sera (1961, translated by D. M. Low as *Voices in the Evening*), is another chronicle of the

NATALIA GINZBURG

Fascist era, centering on a Piedmontese family of Socialist-minded factory owners. It was followed by *Lessico famigliare* (translated by D. M. Low as *Family Sayings*), a similar but this time a factual work. It is a volume of autobiography, making use of the same techniques as Signora Ginzburg's fiction, and characteristically telling the reader less about the author than about her family and friends, who include Adriano Olivetti and Giulio Einaudi. "These characters," wrote one reviewer, "wander in and out of the story only when they are wanted, as in a novel. . . . The whole book is comedy of a high, sad sort, in which themes and people recur in a musical way; nothing is wasted, nothing stressed. It seems to give biography a new dimension, new possibilities, and the tired old form of the family chronicle an aspect that is entirely new."

This same reviewer, writing in the *Times Literary Supplement*, has described Natalia Ginzburg's most obvious characteristics as "a curious technique of omission, of felicitous gaps. . . . She writes conversationally (some say chattily), with an apparent simplicity that is in fact dense and suggestive. . . . It is in this capacity to mean much while saying little—a kind of poetic compression, or metaphorical outlook, using the plainest, most 'anti-poetic' language—that her quality and above all her originality lie." *Mai devi domandarmi* (1970), a collection of essays and occasional pieces on many topics, has been translated by Isabel Quigly as *Never Must You Ask Me*.

PRINCIPAL WORKS IN ENGLISH TRANSLATION: The Road to the City (published with The Dry Heart), 1949; A Light for Fools (England, Dead Yesterdays), 1956; Voices in the Evening, 1963; Family Sayings, 1967; Never Must You Ask Me (essays), 1973.

ABOUT: Manacorda, G. Storia della letteratura italiana contemporanea, 1967; Pacifici, S. A Guide to Contemporary Italian Literature, 1962. *Periodicals*—Belfagor 3, 1953; Il ponte 4, 1953; Times Literary Supplement February 23, 1967.

GIPSON, LAWRENCE HENRY (December 7, 1880–September 26, 1971), American historian, wrote: "I have lived long enough to be a part of history—to have spent my formative years during a period when the British Empire was at its height, to have been a Rhodes Scholar at Oxford in the Edwardian Age, and to have reversed Horace Greeley's adage to go West (which my ancestors, descendants of the Elder Brewster, had followed, even to helping to found the 'Union Colony' of Greeley, Colorado, of which my grandfather was President for many years and where I was born, before my parents moved on to settle in Caldwell, Idaho).

"After finishing my studies at the University of Idaho, I went as far East as England as a member of the original group of Rhodes Scholars who entered the University of Oxford in 1904. There I was a student at Lincoln College (which recently topped off my Oxford career by making me an Honorary Fellow). After taking my degree at Oxford I returned to Idaho, but soon headed East again to teach in the Middle West and to take my Ph.D. at Yale University. There I studied under that great authority on the American colonies, Charles McLean Andrews, and wrote my dissertation on a notable Loyalist fellow, Jared Ingersoll (a biography fortunate enough to be published by the Yale University Press and to win several prizes.)

"When I came to Lehigh University in 1924 as head of the Department of History and Government I had in hand an outline for writing what later became my series: *The British Empire Before the American Revolution* (a title I would now prefer to see as 'The British Empire before the Declaration of American Independence,' for I believe that the American Revolution, in the sense that I use the term, was completed with the Declaration of Independence). In launching my project I conceived that it would be proper to limit it to the years 1763–1775, but saw the necessity of writing an introductory chapter to deal briefly with the period before 1763. Thirty years later that chapter had become eight volumes long. Now, with twelve volumes of my series in print (bearing the distinguished Alfred A. Knopf 'Borzoi' colophon) and the thirteenth complete, except for the bibliography, I can reflect that the germination of the idea for my project began during my first year at Oxford as the result of a disastrous debate.

"It was in the spring of 1905 when, in an unguarded moment, I was persuaded by some upper classmen of my college to propose the resolution and open the Sunday night quadrangle debate on the subject: 'Resolved, that it would be to the best interest of Great Britain if her overseas possessions would secure their independence.' There were not only most devastating attacks on my speech from those present—who, representing as they did many parts of the British Empire, taught me something of the intense pride in which that Empire was held at the turn of the century—there were further repercussions. With Rudyard Kipling present as a special guest of honor at the first of the great Rhodes Scholar banquets, which took place soon after the Lincoln College debate, the toastmaster referred to it with the icy comment that certainly Cecil Rhodes had not established these scholarships for the purpose of liquidating the British Empire! These incidents were undoubtedly instrumental in leading me to undertake a serious study of the history of that Empire in order to account for the loss of the thirteen American Colonies. This study is now nearing completion, thanks to the support across the years of Lehigh University, the Rockefeller Foundation and other foundations that made grants-in-aid, and especially, of my wife, Jeannette Reed Gipson, who has rejoiced with me as various volumes in the series have received, among other recognitions, the Loubat Prize, the Bancroft Prize, and the Pulitzer Prize in History, perhaps as a tribute to my now more sophisticated view of part of the history of the British Empire."

Gipson was the son of Albert Eugene and Lina Maria (West) Gipson. He grew up in Caldwell, Idaho, where his father edited the *Idaho Odd Fellow* and the *Gem State Rural and Live Stock Farmer.* Gipson himself learned the printing trade before entering the University of Idaho, and to a great extent met his expenses there by working as a newspaper reporter. He received an A.B. from Idaho in 1903 and the following year, as he says, went to England as one of the original Rhodes Scholars. This prototype "Yank at Oxford" from the Wild West, where he had actually driven a stagecoach, must have seemed a colorful and romantic figure to the undergraduates of Lincoln College. Oxford gave him his B.A. in 1907 and he returned to the United States, where he earned his Ph.D. at Yale in 1918 and taught at the University of Idaho, the College of Idaho, and Wabash College, Indiana, before joining the Lehigh University faculty in 1924. Gipson was head of Lehigh's Department of History and Government until 1946, when he moved to the Lehigh Institute of Research as research professor of history. After his retirement in 1952 he held the title of professor emeritus of Lehigh University. In 1951–1952 he returned to Oxford as Harold Vyvyan Harmsworth Professor of American History and in 1965 became an Honorary Fellow of Lincoln College.

The first three volumes of *The British Empire Before the American Revolution* were published in 1936 by Caxton Printers, a Gipson family enterprise in Caldwell, Idaho; these three books were later revised and were reissued by Knopf in a format uniform with the later volumes. Gipson's monumental series, "one of the major works of American history in the twentieth century," runs to fifteen volumes and occupied him for over forty years.

"The Gipson series," wrote Richard B. Morris in *The William and Mary Quarterly*, "has constituted a massive assault upon the old-line nationalist interpretation of the period, a critical questioning of patriotic assumptions about our Revolutionary past, combining the most recent researches of the imperial school of historians and the followers of Sir Lewis Namier." Morris adds: "It is clear from the start that Gipson is sympathetic to the British Empire and its imperial administrators in the year 1750." However, "he does not exculpate British statesmen of all blame. He concedes their failure to realize that the old system of imperial control was no longer applicable to so advanced, so populous and highly cultivated a society." Michael Kraus has termed the series "the most comprehensive of the imperial school of colonial history."

It was the tenth volume, *The Triumphant Empire: Thunder-Clouds Gather in the West, 1763–1766*, that won Gipson the Pulitzer Prize. While praising the book, the *New England Quarterly* found it "history for historians," and suggested the general reader turn to "the author's more concise and somewhat more popular *The Coming of the Revolution*." Crane Brinton described Gipson's approach in his review of the eighth volume, which had "the virtues we have come to associate with his work—careful, unhurried piling up of detail sifted through careful research, thorough exploration of byways neglected by more general historians, the whole put together in a narrative rather deliberately undramatic, but—for the real lover of history—never dull."

Gipson was married to Jeannette Reed, a teacher, in 1909; she died in 1967. He was "a warm-hearted, generous human being" who, despite his great achievements, had "a becoming modesty, a readiness to accept suggestions as well as to give them." He was a member of Phi Beta Kappa and of many historical societies, and he held seven honorary degrees. He was a Republican and a Congregationalist. Gipson died in his sleep at the age of ninety, a few months after the publication of the final volume of his masterpiece.

LAWRENCE HENRY GIPSON

PRINCIPAL WORKS: Jared Ingersoll: A Study of American Loyalism in Relation to British Colonial Government, 1920; Lewis Evans, 1939; The Coming of the Revolution, 1763–1775, 1954; The British Empire Before the American Revolution—Vols. 1–3, The British Isles and the American Colonies, 1748–1754, 1936; Vol. 4, Zones of International Friction: North America, South of the Great Lakes Region 1748–1754, 1939; Vol. 5, Zones of International Friction: the Great Lakes Frontier, Canada, the West Indies, India, 1748–1754, 1942; Vol. 6, The Great War for the Empire: The Years of Defeat, 1754–1757, 1946; Vol. 7, The Great War for the Empire: The Victorious Years, 1758–1760, 1949; Vol. 8, The Great War for the Empire: The Culmination, 1760–1763, 1954; Vol. 9, The Triumphant Empire: New Responsibilities, 1763–1766, 1956; Vol. 10, The Triumphant Empire: Thunder-Clouds Gather in the West, 1763–1766, 1961; Vol. 11, The Triumphant Empire: The Rumbling of the Coming Storm, 1766–1770, 1965; Vol. 12, The Triumphant Empire: Britain Sails into the Storm, 1770–1776, 1965; Vol. 13, The Triumphant Empire: The Empire Beyond the Storm, 1770–1776; Summary: Historiography, 1967; Vol. 14, A Bibliographical Guide to the History of the British Empire, 1748–1776, 1969; Vol. 15, A Guide to Manuscripts Relating to the History of the British Empire, 1748–1776, 1970.

ABOUT: Contemporary Authors 7–8, 1963; Current Biography, 1954; Directory of American Scholars 1, 1963; Kraus, M. The Writing of American History, 1953; Who's Who, 1971; Who's Who in America, 1970–1971; Wish, H. The American Historian, 1960. *Periodicals*—New York Times May 27, 1948; January 12, 1951; September 27, 1971; William and Mary Quarterly April 1967.

GLANVILLE, BRIAN (LESTER) (September 24, 1931–), English novelist and short story writer, writes: "Born at Golders Green, North West London. My father, a Dubliner, was a dentist. I was sent through the usual upper-middle class educational mill; a prep. school, evacuated to cold country houses in the Midlands, which despite its traumas was stimulating and encouraging, and Charterhouse which, despite its claims and reputation, was neither.

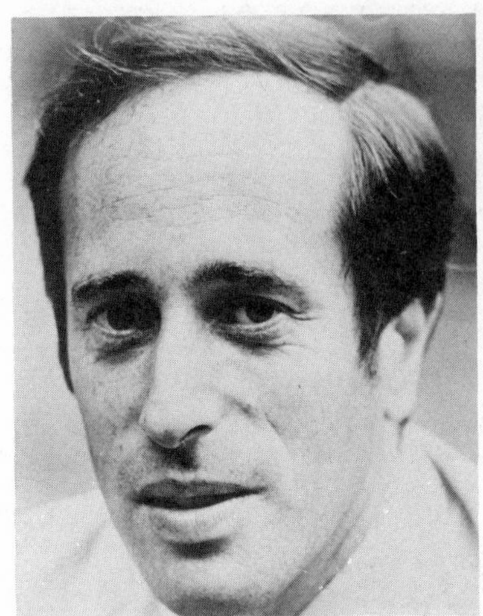

BRIAN GLANVILLE

"I wrote my first novel, *The Reluctant Dictator*, an extravaganza set in a mythical South American dictatorship, at eighteen; it was published when I was twenty, and was very properly ignored. At twenty-one, I went to live in Florence, and spent much of the next three years there and in Rome. My relationship to Italy remains powerful and ambivalent; I feel restless if I cannot get back there at least once a year, dissatisfied when I do. It was in Florence, in 1954, that I wrote my novel *Along the Arno*, the first to gain any serious recognition, and my first to be published in the United States.

"At the same time, I was making a living from journalism, much of it about football, a game with which I had become passionately caught up from the age of eight, though it was not until 1958 that I began to realise its possibilities for fiction. Watching football, writing about football and playing it —which I still do, with my Chelsea Casuals club— have always been for me a distraction and a therapy. There has never seemed to me the least conflict between this interest and being a serious writer of fiction; indeed, the fact that I was eventually able to combine the two was reassuring.

"Though there are obvious limitations to the world of professional football as subject matter for fiction, there are equally clear advantages in its vigour of language and behaviour, its self-perpetuating drama. It has also, in my case, done something to counteract the almost mandatory isolation of the novelist in the present age.

"In 1960, the *Sunday Times*, whose soccer correspondent I was, sent me to Rome to cover the Olympic Games, and presented me afterwards with a sports column. Though I still would not voluntarily cross the road to see any sporting event but a football match—better still, to play in one—the travel and the variety of the job have been helpful and stimulating.

"In 1958, I published a novel about a London Jewish family, *The Bankrupts*, the echoes of whose controversy have pursued me ever since; up to and beyond a second, less inflammatory, "Jewish" novel, *Diamond*, published in 1962. Though I had to fight, and luckily win, an unpleasant High Court case about both books, in 1964, I feel it hard now to become involved with either; they are written, published and behind one. Like any other author, I tend to hope and think that whatever was last is best.

"My first collection of short stories, most of them written between 1958 and 1960, appeared in *A Bad Streak* in 1961 and probably had a better press than they deserved; largely, I suspect, on account of the novelty of the football stories. In 1962, I published a football novel, *The Rise of Gerry Logan*, though doubtful whether a middle-class writer could really hope to bring off what was, when all was said and done, properly a branch of the proletarian novel.

"I'm aware of the fact that writing in different genres about so many different backgrounds—*A Second Home* is a novel wholly narrated in the first person by an actress—has its dangers. Probably it tends to dissipate any impact one might hope one's work to have, but this can hardly be a serious consideration for anyone who is trying to write seriously. Fiction, in fact, is for me the *only* serious writing; anything one does in cinema, television or journalism must by definition be peripheral, though one has proper deference for one's betters, the poet and the dramatist.

"I'm married, with four children, and live in one of those great, rambling Victorian houses in Holland Park."

Brian Glanville has recalled his arrival, aged thirteen, at Charterhouse, to find not only anti-Semitism but an alien and shocking emotional coldness. He was thus early confronted with the need to decide whether he was a Jew or an Englishman—a tension, he says, which faces all Anglo-Jews and may be either destructive or fruitful. It has been fruitful in his case, although his Jewish novels have earned him the bitter enmity of what he calls the "lunatic fringe" of Jewish critics. *The Bankrupts* and *Diamond*, "pitilessly direct" studies of the claustrophobia and hysteria he saw in middle-class Jewish life, were warmly praised by objective critics as moving and unmistakably authentic novels. *A Second Home*, narrated in the first person by a young Jewish actress, was called a double *tour de force*—in its evocation of theatrical life, and as a "self-portrait" of "one of the very few women characters successfully created in this way by a man."

But Glanville is not only or even predominantly a "Jewish writer"; he deals as familiarly and convincingly with two other worlds. In *Along the Arno, A Roman Marriage, A Cry of Crickets*, and in many short stories he writes about Italy, Alan Ross says, "very much as contemporary Italians do," with a mixture of irony and tenderness, and a *rapport* hardly ever achieved by foreign writers. His stories about the world of the professional soccer player have been called an "exciting extension of the usual territories of English fiction," exploring a tight-knit and unfamiliar society in depth "without either satirizing or cheapening it." A frequent theme is the danger to human relationships of imposing upon them any kind of abstract purpose or generalized conception. Glanville's suspicion of abstractions is matched by a concentration on the particular in his manner of writing. He is credited with an ear and eye almost uniquely "sensitive to gradations of feeling as they are revealed by inflections and gestures," and with "perceptions which are sharp, biting, immersed in the actual."

Glanville is an admirer of Ring Lardner, with whom he has been compared in his ear for dialogue and feeling for professional sportsmen. He enjoys journalism, and is one of the best of a generation of newspapermen who write about sport not simply for its own sake, but for what it reveals about the people involved in it. Glanville is of medium height, small-boned, with hazel eyes. He is a witty and uninhibited speaker, equally at ease on radio, on television, at a football ground, at a literary party.

PRINCIPAL WORKS: *Fiction*—The Reluctant Dictator, 1952; Henry Sows the Wind, 1954; Along the Arno, 1956; The Bankrupts, 1958; After Rome, Africa, 1959; A Bad Streak (stories), 1961; Diamond, 1962; The Director's Wife (stories), 1963; The Rise of Gerry Logan, 1963; Goalkeepers Are Crazy (stories), 1964; The King of Hackney Marshes (stories), 1965; A Second Home, 1965; A Roman Marriage, 1966; The Artist Type, 1967; A Betting Man (stories), 1969; The Olympian, 1969; A Cry of Crickets, 1970; Goalkeepers Are Different (for children), 1971; The Financiers, 1972 (U.S., Money Is Love); The Thing He Loves (stories), 1973. *Nonfiction*—Arsenal, 1952; Soccer Nemesis, 1955; Soccer Round the Globe, 1959; People in Sport, 1967.

ABOUT: Contemporary Authors 7–8, 1963; Walsh, W. A Human Idiom, 1964; West, P. The Modern Novel, 1963; Who's Who, 1971. *Periodicals*—London Magazine April 1961; Newsweek March 23, 1964; New York Times Book Review April 17, 1966; Times Literary Supplement September 29, 1966.

JON GODDEN

GODDEN, JON (August 3, 1906–), English novelist, writes: "I was born in India, the eldest of four sisters, the second of whom is Rumer Godden, and made the first of many voyages between India and England when I was six months old. My childhood was spent chiefly in Bengal where my father worked for the steamer companies that managed the navigation of the Ganges and Brahmaputra. Our life in the big house and garden by the river was free, easy and happy, and mostly play although my parents tried to educate us themselves. My sisters and I all wrote books, not magazines or attempts at short stories as most children write, but long books which we bound and which I illustrated; some of these have survived but they do not show any promise. Every hot weather we were taken to a different hill-station, even as far as Kashmir; these journeys often took several days and at an early age we learned something of the vastness and variety of India. We were undisciplined children and when we were sent back to school in England we found life difficult and could not settle down. I never stayed long at any school, was never properly educated, and have often wondered if I would have written better novels, or no novels at all, if I had had regular schooling instead of those Indian childhood years. At sixteen I went to an art school; it had always been understood that I was to be a painter and my sister a writer. I worked hard, meaning to take my diploma as a teacher of art, but went out to India for what was to be a short holiday and married there.

"When my husband died after a year, I came back to Europe to study in art schools in England and Paris and then worked for some time as a commercial artist in India. I married again in 1936 and lived for the next twenty-one years in Calcutta except for holidays in England or in fishing camps in the Indian jungles; my husband and I also travelled a great deal in Europe, Africa and Japan. I never drew or painted after I was thirty although my interest in other people's painting has stayed with me all my life. I first started to write seriously soon after my second marriage, perhaps because I was bored with Calcutta's social life, or perhaps because some kind of creative work was necessary to me. A short story of mine was published just before the war but during the war years there was no time for writing as I worked as an auxiliary nurse in military and civil hospitals. My first novel was written when I spent a few months' sick leave in Kashmir with my sister Rumer, but it was not published until 1947.

"Since then I have written, and had published, seven novels, often written at long intervals. I work very slowly and for many years had to run a large house and entertain a great deal. Writing soon became necessary to me but all my life I have allowed myself to be diverted by many other interests: travel, reading, fishing, riding, and an absorbing interest in animals, tame and wild; some of the happiest days of my life were spent in the great game reserves of Africa and India. My husband and I were divorced a few years ago and I now live in Kent, in sight of the English Channel and France. I know though that I shall never be able to live in England permanently, and that I must go back to India one day."

Jon Godden's novels are delicate and fragile, written with a "serene natural fluency." Solitude, sometimes of claustrophobic intensity, is often a theme. *The House by the Sea* is about an American army deserter who takes refuge in a spinster's cottage; *The City and the Wave* examines the loneliness of an Anglo-Indian in a Calcutta tenement; and *Seven Islands* is a *tour de force* with only one character—a holy man on an island in the Ganges. In *A Winter's Tale*, two men, a woman, and "a great, sleekly beautiful" Alsatian dog are snowbound in a remote English country house. Fanny Butcher called this "strange but delightful" story "a crafty satire on human passion, on the urgencies and demands of the born writer" in which there is "a deep understanding of the interdependence between a dog and its humans." Jon Godden and her sister Rumer have described their childhood in *Two Under the Indian Sun*, and in a subsequent collaboration produced *Shiva's Pigeons*, a wonderfully evocative portrayal of India and its people, accompanying photographs by Stella Snead.

The solitude in Miss Godden's novels is reflected in her life in Kent. She prefers landscapes and animals to crowds and parties, but is deeply interested in the "things human beings make: paintings and music and books." Intimidated by a blank sheet of paper, she drafts her strange and subtle novels in pencil on envelopes and scraps of paper.

PRINCIPAL WORKS: *Novels*—The Bird Escaped, 1947; The House By The Sea, 1947; The Peacock, 1950; The City and the Wave, 1954; The Seven Islands, 1956; Mrs. Panopoulis, 1959; Told in Winter (U.S., A Winter's Tale), 1961; In the Sun, 1965; Kitten With Blue Eyes, 1971 (U.S., Mrs. Starr Lives Alone). *Nonfiction*—(with Rumer Godden) Two Under the Indian Sun, 1966; (with Rumer Godden) Shiva's Pigeons: An Experience of India, 1972.

ABOUT: *Periodicals*—Saturday Review July 21, 1956.

"GODFREY, WILLIAM." *See* YOUD, SAMUEL

GÖKCELI, YASA KEMAL. *See* "KEMAL, YASHAR"

GOLD, HERBERT (March 9, 1924–), American novelist, short story writer, and critic, writes: "I was born and raised in Lakewood, Ohio, a suburb of Cleveland. My father is a Jewish immigrant from Russia who poured his considerable restless creativity into various forms of business. My mother is a lively, talkative woman for whom the world is never too much. I seem to have inherited many of their faults along with their virtues, but I am particularly grateful for their examples of unabashedness before the darkness of the human fate. I have tried to suggest some of these family qualities in the book entitled *Fathers*.

"At seventeen the middle-class, middle-everything life of Lakewood seemed out of the question to me. For a time I lived away from home, finishing high school, and then took to the road as a boy bum, hitchhiking to New York and then southward, employing myself in minor con ways. For a time I worked as a shill in a gambling joint on Key Largo. After swimming among barracuda and ladies from Miami Beach, I decided to return home, clean up, and go to college. I attended Columbia College for a few months, enlisted in the Army, and served three and a half years, doing not very much except learning Russian for use in liaison with our gallant Soviet allies. Since there was not very much liaison, we Russian experts were shipped around and played volleyball in many posts from the Atlantic to the Pacific.

"In 1946 I returned to Columbia to take a B.A. and then an M.A. in Philosophy. I intended to be a Philosopher and find Answers. I got married, went to Paris on the GI Bill, got a Fulbright grant, had a child, gave up formal philosophy, indulged my secret vice of writing poetry and stories, wrote a first novel, *Birth of a Hero*, which was published in 1951. After two years in Paris I began to feel the weight of family responsibilities and returned to Cleveland and various jobs: manager of a hotel, regional planner, part-time philosophy instructor. I wrote another novel, *The Prospect Before Us*, while working over fifty hours a week in a hotel. I was interested in Haiti, and also in not working so much, and managed to get a grant to go live and write in Port-au-Prince. I wanted to be like Huck Finn, floating down the river, but found myself instead involved in the passionate dream life of that place. By this time I had two daughters.

"Then again I bethought myself of my responsibilities and took a job in Detroit at Wayne University, teaching English and writing. In 1956 I was divorced and went to live in New York City. I began to discover what is called the literary life, and for a time it amused me. Shortly the power game appalled and palled, but it was probably a useful experience, like KP. Also like KP, it dries the hands and stupefies the brain.

"Since 1960, I have traveled a good deal, but learned to be at home in San Francisco and feel as if I am settled there. I try to scratch an itch to be effective in the world by doing certain kinds of political journalism and reportage. The writing of novels and stories, for me at least, needs to be fed by direct experience of efficacity. I keep looking for more difficult tasks as a writer and as a human being. 'What bars the way only increases our need to travel along it.'

"At age forty-one I have accumulated many regrets, but expect to have the time to make up for some of my errors. Cleaning my desk today I came upon this note to myself: 'If I cease to make love, there will still be lovers. If I die, there will still be growing things. But if I do not write what I have to say, no one else can write it.' "

In 1951 Herbert Gold published in *Hudson Review* a memorable short story called "The Heart of the Artichoke," an autobiographical piece about the adolescent rebellion of "Daniel Berman" against his father, the tough, vigorous, earthy immigrant grocer. Even then, before the vogue for the "Jewish novel," the theme was familiar; what was new, as Theodore Solotaroff has said, "was the color and bounce of the language, the full range of feeling that enabled Gold to do justice to the father's vitality as well as the son's sensitivity." Gold says it was "my most personally crucial story because, by writing it, I learnt to be a writer. I had a sense of mastering my experience. Not just examining, not just using, but *riding* my world, with full sense of my faculties in the open air." It appears in *Love and Like* (1960), a collection which includes several other stories that are obviously based on the author's own experiences.

Gold's first novel, *Birth of a Hero*, appeared the same year and was a much more muted performance. It is about a middle-aged lawyer, unrealized as a human being, who discovers his potentialities through a brief adulterous love affair. In form the

HERBERT GOLD

book is derivative and conventional, but its concern with self-discovery is Gold's own, and central in his work. The theme recurs in melodramatic form in *The Prospect Before Us*, in which an unheroic hotel owner in the Cleveland honky-tonk district becomes involved in the civil rights movement and dies trying to rescue a Negro girl from his burning hotel.

The Man Who Was Not With It is an altogether better book. It is an account of the passage to maturity of Bud Williams, a young carnival worker who becomes addicted to drugs, is cured by the carnival barker, and eventually grows up enough to realize that being "with it" is not an adequate life philosophy. Gold makes brilliant use of the carnie slang in which Bud tells his story and most reviewers were moved by the compassion and humanity with which his violent and degraded world is presented. Some critics consider this to be Gold's best novel. *The Optimist* is a kind of negative treatment of Gold's central theme, studying the career through college, the army, law, and politics of an ambitious man who, through greed and haste, fails to come to terms with himself.

Therefore Be Bold, which occupied Gold intermittently for many years, is another affectionate autobiographical memoir of adolescence during the 1930s in Cleveland. Gold himself called it "a piratical, lying map of boyhood," which expresses very well the tone of this "witty, cunningly wrought, nervous piece of writing." *Salt* is about two young men in New York, their work, friendships, and love affairs in a society in which "people [have] everything, yet don't get the good out of it." It had a mixed reception, some critics finding it disagreeably slick and "brittle."

In *Fathers*, "a novel in the form of a memoir," Gold assembled into a single narrative many of the incidents already described in his short stories, including "The Heart of the Artichoke." The novel moves from Russia, where his father was born, to San Francisco, where the author now lives, charting "the continuities of character and fortune that underlie their seemingly divergent careers." Theodore Solotaroff, concluding that the book's style is uneven, and that accounts of Jewish family life have become a little thin and predictable, admired the book primarily for Gold's portrait of his father, in which he "seizes upon every expression, mannerism, material detail of this coarse and canny man to create a character who is as bright and sturdy on the page as he is in life." *The Great American Jackpot* is a sardonic study of the San Francisco hippie scene, centering on the ultimately impossible friendship between Al Dooley, a Berkeley student who seeks to relieve his ennui and sense of betrayal by attempting a bank robbery, and Jarod Howe, a brilliant black sociology professor who turns to the Muslims and militancy. It had a mixed reception, as did *The Magic Will*, a collection of essays and stories written during the 1960s.

"My writing," Gold says, "is an effort to master experience and to communicate some sense of mastery. I mean to make a vision not just of reality as it is, but as it should be." As Granville Hicks puts it, "In the work of many of Gold's contemporaries, the world is closing in on the characters. In Gold's novels the world is open." It is this "existentialist" optimism, together with his unquestioned technical ability, that has provoked so much critical interest in Gold's work—and so much frustration when each book falls a little short of the major work that many critics believe him capable of. Maxwell Geismar expressed this feeling very well in his review of *The Age of Happy Problems*, a collection of Gold's essays on writing and society which he found "curiously flat." Geismar said that Gold "is bright, sophisticated, well-informed; his values as artist and critic are sound; his prose is sharp and witty. . . . As a social critic, this writer is particularly sharp in describing the surface-tone of our period whose central problem is that we appear to have no central problem. . . . Perhaps part of [his] trouble is his sheer talent and facility. He can do, apparently, almost everything; and in the end, everything, in this volume at least, appears to be more or less the same."

The author has received Guggenheim and *Hudson Review* fellowships, an award from the National Institute of Arts and Letters, and a Ford Foundation Theatre Fellowship to work at the San Francisco Actors' Workshop. Theatre fascinates him, but so far the only tangible result of his interest has been a play based on his story "Love and Like," staged in Los Angeles.

Gold has black hair and brown eyes and is a little under six feet tall. According to one interviewer he gives an impression of "complete physical containment. . . . His handshake is muscular, he is tanned and trim and looks younger than he is. . . . He does not drink and smokes only an occasional cigar." Tennis, ice skating, and walking are among his favorite diversions. Gold has two children by his first (1948) marriage to Edith Zubrin, and three by his second wife, Melissa Dilworth, whom he married in 1968. He has taught as a visiting professor at Cornell, Berkeley, Harvard, and Stanford.

PRINCIPAL WORKS: Birth of a Hero, 1951; The Prospect Before Us, 1954; The Man Who Was Not With It, 1956; The Optimist, 1959; Love and Like (stories), 1960; Therefore Be Bold, 1960; The Age of Happy Problems (essays), 1962; Salt, 1963; Fathers, 1967; The Great American Jackpot, 1970; The Magic Will (stories and essays), 1971; My Last Two Thousand Years (autobiography), 1972.

ABOUT: Allen, W. Tradition and Dream, 1964; Balakian, N. and Simmons, C. (eds.) The Creative Present, 1963; Current Biography, 1955; Hassan, I. Radical Innocence, 1961; Moore, H. (ed.) Contemporary American Writers, 1964; Peden, W. The American Short Story, 1964; Vinson, J. (ed.) Contemporary Novelists, 1972; Who's Who in America, 1972–1973. *Periodicals*—Life April 7, 1967; Nation October 6, 1951; April 25, 1959; New York Herald Tribune Book Review June 24, 1962; April 9, 1967; New York Times April 14, 1954; Saturday Review April 20, 1963; Yale Review Summer 1956.

GOLD, HORACE L(EONARD) (April 26, 1914–), Canadian-American story writer, writes: "I was born in Montreal, Canada, raised in Providence, Rhode Island, educated and live in New York City. Except for wanting to be a Mountie, I was an ordinary enough child—until thirteen, when I found *The War of the Worlds* on a library shelf and resolved to be another H. G. Wells. That goal I have achieved so qualifiedly that you might suppose it was easy, unless you also got out of school into the Depression and had to try so hard to get started. To compress seven bitter years into one paragraph, I worked when I could find work, at all the usual Depression jobs—and such bizarre ones as faking drownings for lifeguards about to be laid off because their safety records were too good; and in between working and looking for work, I managed to get some things written and sold somehow, making enough of a reputation to land me an assistant editorship on a string of pulps in 1939.

"There was a lot to be lost working on pulps and I promptly lost it—style and ideals and devotion to characterization—but there was as much to be learned about literary carpentry. Most important, shifting from mystery to romance, western to adventure at each deadline, I learned diversification and in 1941 I put in a year of writing true-detective cases—four stories a week, a million words in twelve months, filling two magazines from cover to cover under an assortment of pseudonyms and selling the overflow to the competition. From there I went into radio, comics, slicks, anything that could be published or broadcast, and I was just climbing into the upper brackets when I was drafted early in 1944.

"Maybe the fact that I was sent to the Pacific as a combat engineer explains my breakdown in the service. Despite that, I finished out the war, even being given the privilege of refusing a field commission. I returned home in 1946 to my little son Eugene, a doomed marriage, starting my career all over again and, a year later, the second of a series of breakdowns. In 1950, completely housebound, I established *Galaxy* magazine, was divorced at last in 1957, and stopped editing in 1961 to be hospitalized by the Veterans Administration. During my eleven years on *Galaxy* and two of my four years in the hospital, books under my byline came out regularly in trade and paperback editions.

"Discharged and ambulatory once more, free from magazine deadlines and money hunger, I was living in lonely anonymity when *Newsweek* decided to do an item on me. The response it provoked included book and movie interest—and a note in a pretty hand from someone nicknamed Nicky, whose small children had played with my son nineteen years before. She too was divorced, she wrote, and we were married a few months later.

"To listen to my story, you wouldn't believe I have had every important wish granted, but I have. I lived through the Depression, lived through the war, lived through my first marriage, lived through being housebound and hospitalized and alone, and now I'm through living through things. A happy marriage has opened my writing pores as a wretched one never did and the steam I am giving off will condense into books, for I've seen so many of my magazine and broadcast words, millions of them, evaporate that I want some momentary immortality. Of all the things I've done, only my science fiction and fantasy have had survival value—many of my stories written as far back as the thirties are still being reprinted—and so I plan to stay in those fields.

"I am working simultaneously on two novels, *None But Lucifer* and *The Enormous Room*, and collecting some of my science fiction articles under the title *Squeamish People Turn My Stomach*, and I hope at least one will end up near Wells's on lists of books to read while cast away on a desert island."

As editor of over twenty-four magazines and the author of acres of confession, detective, science fiction stories, radio scripts, and comics, Horace L. Gold has left a distinct mark on American popular writing. Frederick Pohl, who succeeded him as editor of *Galaxy Science Fiction*, has described him as one of the "giants in the field," who "changed the whole shape of science fiction" in the 1950s.

HORACE L. GOLD

What Gold brought to *Galaxy* was a preoccupation with the psychological and sociological effects of technological progress. "His gargantuan optimism, and the deeper pessimism that lies under it," writes Damon Knight, "have helped to make *Galaxy* the brilliant and sometimes bewildering magazine it is. His scorn of clichés has been a major influence in the modern growth of science fiction; his indifference to questions of content and conviction has done as much to vitiate the field." Gold's own writing shows similar qualities; vigorous and inventive, it is also burdened by artificial plots and characters. The stories collected in *The Old Die Rich* form a representative sampling of his work.

Gold has been characterized as "amiable, prowling, interested, alert, alarmed, skeptical, ironic, anxious." "Few things," he says, "reveal so sharply as science fiction the wishes, hopes, fears, inner stresses and tensions of an era, or define its limitations with such exactness."

PRINCIPAL WORKS: The Old Die Rich (short stories), 1955; Five Short Novels, 1958; The World That Couldn't Be, 1959; Bodyguard, 1960; Mind Partner, 1961. *As editor*—The Galaxy Readers (numbers 1 to 6), 1952–1962.

ABOUT: Amis, K. New Maps of Hell, 1960; Knight, D. In Search of Wonder, 1956; Moskowitz, S. Seekers of Tomorrow, 1966; Tuck, D. H. (ed.) A Handbook of Science Fiction and Fantasy, 1959. *Periodicals*—Business Week October 20, 1951; Newsweek July 26, 1965.

HARRY GOLDEN

GOLDEN, HARRY (LEWIS) (May 6, 1902–), American essayist and journalist, was born in Austria-Hungary in 1902 (1903 according to some sources), one of the five children of Leib and Anna (Klein) Goldenhurst or Goldhirsch. When he was two the family migrated to the United States, where Golden's father eventually became a member of the editorial staff of the *Jewish Daily Forward* in New York. Golden was graduated in 1918 from the East Side Evening High School, and from 1919 to 1922 studied English at the College of the City of New York, leaving without a degree. During the next four years he worked at a variety of jobs in New York—as, among other things, a blocker of women's straw hats, a hotel clerk, and a reporter. He was also active as a speaker and pamphleteer for the Socialists and the Henry George single-tax movement. By 1928 he was running a bucket-shop on Wall Street—an illegal but common enterprise that the law winked at in the Roaring Twenties until District Attorney Tuttle cracked down on gambling in stocks. In 1929 he was convicted of using the mails to defraud in connection with stock purchases on margin, and he served more than three years of a five-year prison sentence.

When he was released, Harry L. Goldhurst, as he was then known, began his life again as Harry L. Golden. Many years later Adlai Stevenson wrote: "I suspect that this experience deepened Harry Golden's understanding, lengthened his vision, and enlarged his heart. His subsequent life and work is best evidence of this." During the 1930s Golden worked for a time as a teacher and then returned to journalism, writing for the New York *Post* and the New York *Mirror* among other newspapers until 1939, when he moved to North Carolina as a reporter first for the Charlotte *Observer* and then for the Hendersonville *Times-News*. In his spare time he wrote pamphlets and articles for Zionist, New Deal, and Socialist groups.

In 1941 Golden launched the *Carolina Israelite*. "I wanted to publish a liberal newspaper in North Carolina," he says, "but I was a Jew . . . and a Northerner. The odds were too much. So I insulated myself. I called the paper the *Carolina Israelite*. My critics could say, 'This is another Jew paper,' and perhaps, I thought, sooner or later the non-Jews would get acquainted with it." This is what happened, but slowly. The paper, published six times a year, was a sixteen-page tabloid in the honorable tradition of personal journalism. It consisted mainly of editorial comment on race, trade unionism, and other contemporary southern issues, lightened by agreeably nostalgic reminiscences of life on New York's Lower East Side in the early years of the century.

Golden says that he started the paper with two assets: "One was a memory which recalled to me the faces of men to whom I sold a newspaper as a boy . . . and recalled as well all the sights and sounds of a world long vanished. The second was an inventory of nearly half-a-century of uninterrupted reading." He might have added a few more, as Joseph Wood Krutch has done: "an agile, wide-ranging mind, a good deal of information, much good humor as well as much humor . . . and a fresh, easy free-flowing style." His "Yiddish newspaper translated into English" grew steadily from an initial circulation of eight hundred. By 1958 it had sixteen thousand paid subscribers and by 1963 it had forty-five thousand, in every state of the union, and in some foreign countries—among them Harry S. Truman, Earl Warren, Adlai Stevenson, Thomas E. Dewey, and William Faulkner.

During the 1950s Golden published two books, *Jews in American History* (1950), an account of the Jewish contribution to American life—from 1492 to 1950—written in collaboration with Martin Rywell, and *Jewish Roots in the Carolinas* (1955). What brought Golden to national attention, however, was a series of Swiftian proposals put forward in the mid-1950s, all of them ingenious illustrations of the absurdity of southern racism. His "out-of-order" plan, for example, was based on the fact that white Southerners seemed prepared to use Negro drinking fountains when their own were broken, and he pointed out that this aspect of segregation could be abolished by making the white facilities permanently nonfunctional. The "Golden Vertical Negro Plan," similarly, depended on the southern white's apparent willingness to stand but not to sit beside Negroes.

These amiable suggestions, published in the *Carolina Israelite*, were widely reported and discussed and led to the publication of a collection of Golden's essays, *Only in America* (1958). The book went immediately onto the best-seller lists, where it remained for a year. Maurice Dolbier summed up the general reaction when he said of Golden: "It's nice to live in the same country with him." *For 2c Plain*, another volume of essays, appeared in 1959 and was also a best seller. Subsequent collections include *Enjoy, Enjoy!*, *You're Entitle'*, *So What Else Is New?*, and *Ess, Ess, Mein Kindt* (*Eat, Eat, My Child*). R. L. Duffus, reviewing the latter, thought that Golden had grown a little more serious over the years, but was otherwise unchanged: "Mr. Golden glories in his Jewish culture, yet is at home in all our cultures. . . . He is up to his ears in causes that may injure him financially. He is tolerant of everything but intolerance. Courage and insight are his stock in trade. He may be more bitter than he was, but he keeps his sense of humor."

But in the end, even Golden's sense of humor failed him. *The Carolina Israelite* ceased publication in 1968, and Golden has explained why in his admirable autobiography, *The Right Time*, and in a later collection of relatively somber essays, *So Long as You're Healthy*. His reason—apart from ill health, declining vigor, and rising costs—is simply that "nothing is funny any more." In particular, the civil rights conflict, which had engaged Golden so completely and so fruitfully, had escalated far beyond the range of his kind of genial satire. "When satire no longer penetrates," wrote Gerald W. Johnson, "Golden is a Roland disarmed."

Golden's study of his friend Carl Sandburg was thought a little careless and repetitive, but warm and vivid. *Mr. Kennedy and the Negroes* is an account of the civil rights movement and of John F. Kennedy as "the second Emancipator President." *A Little Girl Is Dead* examines the case of Leo Frank, a white man who was tried and lynched in Georgia for the murder (in 1913) of a teen-age girl. Golden spent a year in Israel after the Six-Day War, and *The Israelis* is an entertaining collection of sketches, interviews and vignettes written out of this experience. It was followed by *The Greatest Jewish City in the World*, a "warmly personal" history of the Jews in New York.

In 1926 Golden was married to Genevieve Gallagher, a former schoolteacher. They had four sons, one of whom died in 1957. Golden has been separated from his wife for many years. He has been described as "a short, bulbous moon-faced man . . . fond of strong cigars, starchy dishes and bourbon." He includes two honorary doctorates among his many awards, and he is a member of the board of the American Jewish Congress.

PRINCIPAL WORKS: (with Martin Rywell) Jews in American History, 1950; Jewish Roots in the Carolinas, 1955; Only in America, 1958; For 2c Plain, 1959; Enjoy, Enjoy!, 1960; Carl Sandburg, 1961; You're Entitle', 1962; Forgotten Pioneer, 1963; Mr. Kennedy and the Negroes, 1964; So What Else Is New?, 1964; A Little Girl Is Dead, 1965 (England, The Lynching of Leo Frank); Ess, Ess, Mein Kindt (Eat, Eat, My Child), 1966; The Right Time (autobiography), 1969; So Long as You're Healthy (Abee Gezundt), 1970; The Israelis, 1971; The Greatest Jewish City in the World, 1972; Travels Through Jewish America, 1973.

ABOUT: Current Biography, 1959; Golden, H. The Right Time, 1969; Levin, M. (ed.) Five Boyhoods, 1962; Who's Who in America, 1970–1971; Who's Who in World Jewry, 1965. *Periodicals*—Commentary January 1961, March 1961; Coronet September 1958; Life October 6, 1958; New York Herald Tribune May 31, 1958; New York World-Telegram September 13, 1958; Saturday Evening Post September 27, 1958; Time April 1, 1957; September 29, 1958.

GOLDING, WILLIAM (GERALD) (September 19, 1911–), is one of the very few contemporary English novelists for whom greatness has ever been seriously claimed. He was born in St. Columb Minor, a village near Newquay in Cornwall. Golding comes of a long line of schoolmasters, of whom one of the most distinguished was his father, Alec Golding, a polymath of whom he says, "I have never met anybody who could do so much, was interested in so much, and who knew so much. . . . He inhabited a world of sanity and logic and fascination."

The autobiographical passages in *The Hot Gates*, a collection of Golding's essays, evoke a rather isolated boyhood with his parents and nurse in a gloomy house in Marlborough. There was a graveyard next door, which came to hold for him all his desperate hidden fears of death and the unknown, and a chestnut tree in the garden where he sat to read and to spy on the world outside. He developed very early a passionate interest in words, which he says he collected "like stamps or birds' eggs." And he had an equally precocious and romantic love of history, which led him at the age of seven to begin to learn hieroglyphics so that he could write a play about Ancient Egypt. Later, at Marlborough Grammar School, his favorite extracurricular reading included not only Verne, Henty, and Ballantyne, but also medieval romances and ancient epics from the curriculum itself.

At nineteen Golding went up to Brasenose College, Oxford University. For two years, in accordance with his parents' wishes, he read Natural Science, then switched with relief to English, discovering and rejoicing in Anglo-Saxon literature, which has continued to be important to him. A volume of poems appeared in 1934 but, to his subsequent relief, soon went out of print. Leaving Oxford the following year with a B.A. and a diploma in education, Golding began his career as a

WILLIAM GOLDING

social worker, in his spare time writing, acting, and producing for a small London theatre.

Golding was married in 1939 to Ann Brookfield, an analytical chemist, and, bowing to family tradition, became a teacher of English and philosophy at Bishop Wordsworth's School in Salisbury. The following year the Royal Navy claimed him. He saw much action in ships of all kinds, from cruisers to the rocket launching craft which he commanded at the end of the war and which he had taken to Normandy for the D Day invasion. The war, which gave him time to read and reread the Greek classics, was also he believes a turning point for him, its evidence of man's brutality the prime source of his extreme pessimism.

When in 1945 Golding resumed his post at Bishop Wordsworth's School, he also began writing again, publishing some reviews and essays and completing several novels, none of which found a publisher. He persevered, "haunted by this desperate, cruel, bloody business of believing I can write." *Lord of the Flies*, his first published novel, appeared in 1954 in England, where its success was immediate. Published the following year in the United States, it at first made little impact, though it found and retained an influential minority audience. It was reprinted with great success in 1959, found its way onto many school reading lists, and became a best seller, rivaling in its popularity with young people J. D. Salinger's *The Catcher in the Rye*. In 1961, at the age of fifty, Golding was able to leave his teaching post and, after a year as writer-in-residence at Hollins College in Virginia, became a full-time writer.

His first two novels are carefully worked-out allegories in which man is presented as a creature irredeemably fallen from grace. *Lord of the Flies* describes the apparently inevitable degeneration into murderous savagery of a party of "decent" English schoolboys, marooned without adult control on a Pacific island. The result is a deliberate rebuttal of the optimistic assumptions underlying *Coral Island*, the Victorian classic of boyish adventure in the South Seas—a rebuttal which nevertheless retains some of the narrative fascination of Ballantyne's innocent tale. This story about the ascendancy in man of the powers of darkness can be read variously as a political, psychological, or religious fable: all three interpretations have their advocates. Its unrelieved pessimism is shocking because it is convincing, and it convinces, as one critic said, because of its "dense and often poetic verbal texture, in which metaphor and image work as they do in poetry." The book was filmed by Peter Brook in 1963.

The Inheritors (1955), which reached the United States only in 1962, repeats the message of *Lord of the Flies*. It is a moving and brilliant *tour de force*, inhabiting the near-animal consciousness of Lok, a Neanderthal man, and describing in his clumsy terms and with great pathos the casual destruction of his species by *Homo sapiens*. The reader is shown his ancestors, already armed, arrogant, murderous, and corrupt—not superior to the Neanderthalers, only more clever and more evil. Some critics believe that we are meant to see in Lok, the bemused innocent, Adam before the Fall. In this book, and repeatedly in Golding's work, knowledge and science are equated with evil, faith and poetry with good.

These first two novels observed man in society; the third, *Pincher Martin*, is, as Samuel Hynes put it, "a novel with a single character, who dies on page two." After his ship is torpedoed "Pincher" Martin, a British naval officer and former actor, is flung upon a molar-like rock in mid-Atlantic and begins a desperately courageous and ingenious struggle to preserve his life. It has been, one learns, a depraved, grabbing, loveless life, but Martin will not let it go, for a time preferring even madness to the finally irrefutable truth. The truth is that he is already drowned; his long battle for life on the rock was a fantasy sustained by his will, a "ravenous ego's" self-imposed purgatory, a frantic refusal to "die into heaven." Martin himself emerges as an archetype rather than a character, but the details of his ordeal are very vividly and engrossingly imagined, and the book is a superbly organized realization of a splendid theme.

Man's wickedness is convincingly illustrated in these early books, but not explained. Nor is the sinner offered much hope of salvation. The boys in *Lord of the Flies* corrupt their Eden, Pincher Martin struggles against God's mercy—not from choice but because that is their nature. *Free Fall* is a considerably more optimistic book which posits both free will and the possibility of grace. It is also the first of Golding's books to be set in contemporary society. Sammy Mountjoy, a successful painter, facing torture in a Nazi prison camp, is searching back and forth through his memories to find the point in his life where, by making a Faustian error of judgment, he surrendered forever the ability to choose. Sammy is a complex and well-drawn character, if not exactly a memorable one, and the world in which he lives is admirably realized. Critics praised these new elements in Golding's work, but found the structure of the book confusing and its argument opaque. The conflict between science and faith is central to the novel, though Sammy seems to achieve grace by *not* choosing between them, but accepting both. Or perhaps he achieves grace for no reason—simply because he does: "the difference between being alive and being an inorganic substance," Golding said in 1958, "is just this proliferation of experience, this absence of pattern." In *Free Fall*, he went on, "I want to show the patternlessness of life before we impose our patterns on it."

In *The Spire* Golding returned to a relatively remote and enclosed society, a cathedral close in medieval England. Dean Jocelin, after a vision, has vowed to raise a great spire upon his church, a "prayer in stone." His builder tells him that the foundations cannot support it but Jocelin, instructed by God, forces his spire upwards, at the cost of friendship and health, at the cost of other men's lives, at the cost of sacrilege. And when it is finished and he is dying, he no longer knows if he built it for God's sake or his own, whether the work is blessed or damned, sacred or obscene—only that the spire is there. "One might hazardously conjecture that this novel, like its predecessors, is as much about Golding writing a novel as about anything else," Frank Kermode said. "But one need not believe that to agree that it is deeply personal. . . . It is remote from the mainstream, potent, severe, even forbidding. And in its way it is, quite simply, a marvel."

The Pyramid is a novel in three episodes about life during the 1930s in "Stilbourne," a small town near Salisbury. The narrator is Oliver, son of the doctor's dispenser. The first episode is an account of his successful but destructive campaign to "have" the town trollop Evie Babbacombe; the second describes a ludicrous production of the Stilbourne Operatic Society; in the third, returning to Stilbourne in middle age, Oliver visits the grave of his old music teacher, "Bounce" Dawlish and recalls the tragedy that drove her to insanity. Almost all of the novel's reviewers received it, with some surprise, as "a low-keyed realistic novel of growing up in a small town," quite without allegorical overtones. Some welcomed this departure and some regretted it, but most agreed that the book was sharp in its social observation, unusually solid and convincing in its characterization, often funny, and generally agreeable.

In fact it *is* an allegory, a subtle but very complex one, resuming the themes of free will, and the conflict between science and art, that have always occupied Golding. The novel's title is a reference to (among other things) science, which (as Golding says elsewhere), delightedly builds its "pyramid of information," forgetting less measurable things, and "has begotten this lame giant we call civilization as Frankenstein created his monster." Oliver abandons music to make poison gas and "has" Evie Babbacombe instead of loving her because these are rational and expedient actions in a society where love is stillborn; for similar reasons the mechanic Henry Williams ruins the music teacher and with her money builds his garage where the town's music shop had stood. These people fall from grace but not because they choose to fall; the choice is made for them by the "lame giant" which cripples its children. And in that sense *The Pyramid* is the most humane and forgiving of Golding's novels. If, as he said, his first book was "an attempt to trace the defects of society back to the defects of human nature," this one does the opposite, completing the cycle.

William Golding is an original, a member of no contemporary literary school, who believes "that there is really very little point in writing a novel unless you do something that either you suspected you couldn't do, or which you are pretty certain that nobody has tried before." His novels, Samuel Hynes says, are "unusually tight, conceptualized, analogical expressions of moral ideas," in which "the form itself carries meanings apart from the meanings implied by character or stated . . . by the author." Or, as Frank Kermode said of *The Spire*, "you live along the lines of the book and feel, in its pattern, a total explanation."

Perhaps the most serious and persistent criticism of his books has been that his characters, selected to illustrate certain ideas, generally fail to live memorably in their own right. Some critics are irritated by the "gimmick" endings which, in his early books, force the reader to review and reassess all that has gone before. Against this must be set his "great gifts of imagination and narrative," the richly suggestive poetic density of his prose, and what R. W. B. Lewis calls "the genuine beauty, the harmony of movement," in the structure of his novels. Stanley Edgar Hyman found Golding's touch unsure, but said "he is the most interesting British writer today, and he baits his hook for

Leviathan." Hynes places his work "with the important symbolic novels of our century." Angus Wilson and Kermode have both referred to him as a great writer.

The Brass Butterfly, Golding's only play, was based on his short story "Envoy Extraordinary." It is an assertion in comic terms of his distaste for science. A Roman emperor, offered a variety of twentieth century devices by a Greek inventor of genius, sees no virtue in any of them except a pressure cooker. The play was produced in 1958 but had only a short run. "Envoy Extraordinary" was republished, along with two new long stories, in *The Scorpion God*. The title story is set in an ancient Egyptian kingdom, "Clonk Clonk" in a more primitive society, and both are very deft and distinguished studies of the interraction between man and the social rituals and institutions he creates.

Golding became a fellow of the Royal Society of Literature in 1955 and a CBE in 1966. He is a man of middle height, blue-eyed, with a grizzled beard, said to look like "an astute, well-feasted Viking," and to be "shy, courteous, blunt in response," a person of "sensitive bluffness . . . true privacy." Golding is a "disillusioned ex-liberal" who calls himself an "incompetently religious man." His recreations include archaeology, sailing, and the study of Greek. He is a talented amateur musician, and plays the piano, the violin, the viola, the cello, and the oboe. Golding and his wife, who have a son and a daughter, live in Wiltshire, near Salisbury.

PRINCIPAL WORKS: Poems, 1934; Lord of the Flies, 1954; The Inheritors, 1955; Pincher Martin, 1956 (U.S., The Two Deaths of Christopher Martin); Envoy Extraordinary (novella) *in* Sometime Never (by William Golding, John Wyndham, and Mervyn Peake), 1956; The Brass Butterfly (play, based on Envoy Extraordinary), 1958; Free Fall, 1959; The Spire, 1964; The Hot Gates (essays), 1965; The Pyramid, 1967; The Scorpion God, 1971.

ABOUT: Allen, W. The Modern Novel, 1964; Babb, H. S. The Novels of William Golding, 1973; Baker, J. R. William Golding, 1965; Contemporary Authors 7–8, 1963; Current Biography, 1964; Gindin, J. Postwar British Fiction, 1962; Hynes, S. William Golding, 1964; Karl, F. R. A Reader's Guide to the Contemporary English Novel, 1962; Kermode, F. Puzzles and Epiphanies, 1962; Kinkead-Weekes, M. and Gregor, I. William Golding, 1967; Oldsey, B. S. and Weintraub, S. The Art of William Golding, 1965; Steiner, G. Language and Silence, 1967; Vinson, J. (ed.) Contemporary Novelists, 1972; Who's Who, 1973. *Periodicals*—Atlantic May 1965; College English January 1961, March 1965; Commonweal March 18, 1960; Dalhousie Review Summer 1960; English Spring 1964; Guardian December 20, 1971; Kenyon Review Fall 1957; Literature and Psychology Autumn 1961, Winter 1962; Manchester Guardian Weekly April 16, 1964; Nation May 21, 1960; New Statesman August 2, 1958; New York Herald Tribune Books November 4, 1962; New York Times Book Review October 15, 1967; Spectator April 10, 1964; Times Literary Supplement August 7, 1959; October 23, 1959; June 1, 1967; Transactions and Proceedings of the Royal Society of Literature 32, 1963.

***"GOLL, YVAN"** or **"IWAN" (pseudonym of Isaac Lang)** (March 29, 1891–February 27, 1950), Franco-German poet and dramatist, also used the pseudonyms Iwan Lassang, Tristan Torsi, Tristan Thor, and Johannes Thor. He was born in Saint-Dié in the Vosges region of France. His father was from Alsace, his mother from Lorraine. Goll attributed the rootlessness which shaped him to the fact that he was "Jewish by destiny, French-born by chance, designated a German by a piece of stamped paper." At home he spoke French, but he was taught in German at Metz, where he went for his secondary education. Goll went on to study jurisprudence at the University of Strasbourg and received his doctorate of philosophy there in 1912. The same year he published an ode to the brotherhood of man and a collection of the folk songs of Lorraine.

The war began two years later and Goll, unwilling to take up arms against France, went into exile in Switzerland. There he associated with the circle of French pacifists around Romain Rolland and with the dadaists, and there he met the poet Claire Studer, who later became his wife. In Zürich Goll founded the Rhein Verlag, which was to publish the first German edition of Joyce's *Ulysses*. Goll's own verse during this period was written in German. His requiem for Europe's dead (1916) was a lyric cantata, dedicated to Rolland. Six more volumes followed between then and 1920, containing verse mainly expressionist and dithyrambic, notably rich in its imagery, and strongly pacifist and humanitarian.

In 1919 Goll settled in Paris, where his friends included Picasso and Chagall, Breton and Éluard. The influence of the dadaists and surrealists is evident in the poetry of *Le Nouvel Orphée* (The New Orpheus, 1923) and *Der Eiffelturm* (The Eiffel Tower, 1924), and in his plays. Goll was one of the first surrealist playwrights and pioneered the use of film in the moving and poetic *Die Chaplinade* (1920) and in other plays, including *Methusalem* (1919, first published in 1922). This was Goll's most ambitious play, designed to illustrate his belief in a "theatre of enormity" similar to Artaud's "theatre of cruelty," which would shatter the audience's complacency and probe "into a world beyond the senses." A flat exchange of nonsensical clichés in *Methusalem* anticipated Ionesco by many years. Martin Esslin has suggested that in spite of the play's surrealist tamperings with logic, it remains a "witty and charming" but fundamentally conventional antibourgeois satire. It was Goll's mistake, Esslin believes, that "he, who was a great and sensitive lyric poet . . . in subordinating his imagination to the demands of masks and film . . . failed to transmute his material into the new poetry of the

* gôl

Absurd, which he had so clearly foreseen and so effectively formulated in theory." Nevertheless, the handful of plays Goll wrote in the 1920s stand as a link between Jarry and Ionesco.

During the 1930s, when he was influenced by the poet Paula Ludwig, Goll turned away from the Parisian literary coteries and produced work increasingly subjective and autobiographical. Between 1933 and 1948 he wrote exclusively in French, publishing among other things the love lyrics *Chansons malaises* (1935), translated by Clark Mills as *Songs of a Malay Girl* (1942).

Goll had abandoned his German citizenship and in 1939 settled in New York. There he completed *La Chanson de Jean sans Terre* (Landless John, 1936–1944), a cycle of fifty-nine poems. It was the autobiographical epic of a homeless wanderer, in which Goll related his own life to world events in mythical terms, combining "medieval mysticism with an observation modern in the extreme." Louise Bogan saw in "Jean" the prototype of "the guiltless Jew dispossessed." An English version, published in 1944, included translations by Lionel Abel, William Carlos Williams, Clark Mills, and John Gould Fletcher; a complete edition, with translations by many hands, illustrations by Eugène Berman, Chagall, and Dali, critical notes by Louise Bogan, Clark Mills, Jules Romains, and Allen Tate, and a preface by W. H. Auden, appeared in 1958. In New York, Goll founded the literary journal *Hémisphères*, which he edited from 1943 to 1946 and which included among its contributors St. John Perse, Breton, and Henry Miller.

Goll's work during the 1940s was increasingly influenced by occult and cabalistic mysticism. His discovery in 1944 that he was fatally ill with leukemia combined with his dark view of the world situation to turn his thoughts more and more to death—and to love, which he saw as man's only refuge. These were the themes of his final testament, *Traumkraut* (Dream Plant), completed in a hospital during the five weeks of his last illness, when he was kept alive with blood donated by fellow-poets from five countries. These visionary poems, in which he reverted to German, were free of all rhetoric, "astonishingly lucid." They were the distilled essence of all that he had learned from the modern movements of Europe, and all that he had learned as a man. Some critics place *Traumkraut*, posthumously published in 1951, among the most significant works of poetry in German. Goll himself was aware of its importance, and it is said that he asked his wife to publish these poems and destroy all the rest. He had returned to France in 1947 and died there, at Neuilly, near Paris.

Goll also wrote the opera *Royal Palace* (1928), with music by Kurt Weill, as well as essays, and a number of novels and *récits*, of which the best

YVAN GOLL

known was *Die Eurokokke* (1927; published in French as *Lucifer vieillissant*, 1934).

Several volumes of poetry and the play *Mélusine* were published after his death by his wife. The two-volume *Gesammelte Dichtungen* appeared in 1959, *Dichtungen* in 1960, and the complete works in four volumes during the 1970s, with illustrations by Matisse, Dali, Chagall, and Léger among others. Yvan Goll seems to defy all attempts to classify him. Despite the surrealist and mystical elements in his verse, his imagery was sharply clear and his diction "startlingly simple." Richard Exner has called him "the tragic poet, *par excellence*," and a "romantic nihilist" who rejected all secular and spiritual authority and who "died the death of the whole world."

PRINCIPAL WORKS IN ENGLISH TRANSLATION: Songs of a Malay Girl, 1942; Jean sans Terre (Landless John), 1944; Love Poems, 1947; Four Poems of the Occult, 1962; Methusalem (tr. A. S. Wensinger and C. J. Atkinson *in* Plays for a New Theater, 1966; also tr. by J. M. Ritchie *in* Seven Expressionist Plays, 1968).

ABOUT: Carmody, F. J. The Poetry of Yvan Goll, 1956; Esslin, M. The Theater of the Absurd, 1962; Handbuch der deutschen Gegenwartsliteratur, 1965; Müller, J. Yvan Goll im deutschen Expressionismus, 1962, *Periodicals*—German Life and Letters July 1955.

***GOMBRICH, SIR E(RNEST) H(ANS) J(OSEF)** (March 30, 1909–), Austrian-British art historian, writes: "I was born in Vienna on March 30, 1909. My father was a respected lawyer who much disliked litigation; his father had come to Vienna from Offenbach, his mother from Frankfurt am Main. My mother (still alive at the time of writing) is a pianist who had been assistant to the

* gom′ brik

E. H. J. GOMBRICH

famous Leschetitzky and a member of the circle of Gustav Mahler. Her father came from Prague, her mother's family from Bratislava. My four grandparents were Jewish. There always was much music-making in our house and my parents' friendship with the great violinist Adolf Busch belongs to my formative influences (he disliked modernism and so do I). Like most middle-class families ours was hard hit by the post-war shortages and during the worst period I was sent to Sweden under the scheme arranged by the Save the Children Fund. The only school ready to take me on my return was the Theresianum, a very conservative Gymnasium concentrating on the classics. Like most reasonably bright children I was much bored at school but I was treated well by my teachers and passed the *Matura* with special distinction. At that time regulations also demanded a minor dissertation for that examination; my choice was the subject of 'Changes in the Appreciation of Art' and I find that after forty years I am still at work on this topic.

"From 1928 till 1935 I attended Vienna University, taking courses in the history of art and in classical archaeology under Julius von Schlosser, Emil Reich and Emanuel Loewy and also attending lectures on psychology and philosophy. My first publication (before graduation) was on an early medieval ivory pyx, my Ph.D. thesis on the architecture of Giulio Romano (only partially published).

"I had the good luck to be asked by an elder colleague, Ernst Kris, an art historian and member of Freud's circle, to assist him in writing a book on caricature; though the main manuscript remained unpublished I learnt a great deal in the process. At the age of twenty-six I offered, half in earnest, to write a 'World History' for children within eight weeks. The resulting book proved a success and was translated into five languages. Otherwise chances of employment were dim in Austria and since the Nazi menace grew more urgent it was a real deliverance for me to be invited to the Warburg Institute (which had emigrated from Hamburg to London), to work there as from 1936 on the papers left by its founder. On these slender chances I married Ilse Heller, a pupil of my mother. We finally settled in England in 1937 where a son was born to us.

"Though we were spared the horrors of a flight from the Nazis, the catastrophe that engulfed our homes has darkened my memory of these years. When the war broke out I joined the Monitoring Service of the BBC, which operated first near Evesham and then near Reading. Listening for six years to foreign (mainly German) broadcasts and supervising their translation was strenuous work but it helped me to keep sane and to learn English.

"After the war I returned to my work at the Warburg Institute, where I wrote papers on Botticelli's symbolism and on other topics linking the history of philosophy and that of art. A popular introduction to the history of art which I had started before the war was published by the Phaidon Press in 1950. It caught on, was translated into twelve languages and, most surprisingly, procured me the Slade Professorship at Oxford (1950–1952).

"Nothing succeeds like success and so I was invited to teach at Harvard, to give the Mellon lectures at the National Gallery of Art in Washington, subsequently published as *Art and Illusion*, to become Durning-Lawrence Professor at University College, London, then Director of the Warburg Institute and also Slade Professor of Fine Art in Cambridge (1961–1963). Most surprising of all, I was even awarded a literary prize for a collection of my essays entitled *Meditations on a Hobby Horse* (the W. H. Smith Literary Award for 1964). It is to this I suppose that I owe the honour of being included among WORLD AUTHORS, though I regard myself rather as a historian with philosophical and psychological interests."

E. H. Gombrich is the son of Karl B. Gombrich, who served as vice-president of the Disciplinary Council of the Vienna Lawyers' Chamber, and of Professor Leonie (Hock) Gombrich. As he says, apart from the war years, he has been on the staff of the Warburg Institute at London University ever since 1936, and has retained a Special Lectureship there even during his three years (1956–1959) as Durning-Lawrence Professor of the History of Art at University College. In 1959 he was Unity

Professor of Fine Art at Harvard, and in October of the same year he became Director of the Warburg Institute and London University's Professor of the History of the Classical Tradition.

The talent for popularization which Gombrich had first shown in his epitome of world history, *Weltgeschichte für Kinder* (1935), was applied with great success to his own field in *The Story of Art.* The book was intended for teen-agers, but is written and illustrated with so much clarity, perception, and wit that it has achieved immense success as one of the finest available introductions to the history of art.

However, it is Gombrich's Mellon Lectures, given in 1956 at the National Gallery of Art and published as *Art and Illusion*, that his fellow scholars are likely to think of as his major work. The book is "a study in the psychology of pictorial representation." A baby, psychologists maintain, has no means of choosing between the multitude of visual stimuli it receives when its eyes begin to function and at first sees only a chaotic blur. Slowly perception becomes more selective and better organized, but also more prone to illusion, since we tend to see what reason and experience have taught us to expect. Thus, when we look at a picture, we participate with the artist in the creation of the images we see. Gombrich shows that artists have always exploited this fact, conjuring three dimensions out of two by the use of shadow and perspective, persuading us to agree that an impressionist blob of paint is a horse, a smudge of green is a tree in leaf. Eric Newton gave the book warm praise as the work of "a philosopher thinly disguised as an *enfant terrible*." Frank Getlein called it "one of those rare, prolonged delights for the mind that result from immense erudition being channeled by a sharp intellect into a fairly narrow inquiry."

Meditations on a Hobby Horse, which followed, is a volume of lectures and essays on a wide range of subjects, from the writings of André Malraux to the art of the cartoonist. Many of these pieces explore in one context or another the author's belief that, as Frank Kermode puts it, "all communication involves prior understanding between transmitter and receiver." Most reviewers—even when they opposed some of Gombrich's opinions—admired the book for its iconoclastic curiosity and wit. Richard Wollheim suggested that Gombrich's "supreme merit as a theorist of art" is "not his erudition, nor his sensibility, nor his wit—though he has all these things: what really distinguishes his work and sets it apart from the mass of somnambulistic writing that ordinarily passes for comment on art is his capacity to make a point."

Norm and Form collects papers and articles written between 1942 and 1963 on various aspects of the art of the Italian Renaissance—its sources, aesthetics, and patronage, and the reactions to it of a number of modern art philosophers. It is a learned work, not intended for the general reader, but characteristically rich in stimulating insights and written in a style which, if it is rather elaborate and sometimes difficult, is often "colorful, instructive, amusing and . . . memorable." Gombrich has also written an "intellectual biography" of the founder of the institute he directs, the great art historian Aby Warburg.

Gombrich was Lethaby Professor at the Royal College of Art in 1967–1968 and Andrew D. White professor-at-large at Cornell in 1970. He holds honorary degrees from a number of universities and is an honorary fellow of Jesus College, Cambridge. He is a Fellow of the British Academy, a Fellow of the Society of Antiquaries, and a Fellow of the Royal Society of Literature, as well as an honorary member of several foreign academies. Gombrich received a CBE in 1966 and was knighted in 1972.

PRINCIPAL WORKS: (with E. Kris) Caricature, 1940; The Story of Art, 1949; Art and Illusion: A Study in the Psychology of Pictorial Representation, 1960; Meditations on a Hobby Horse, and Other Essays on the Theory of Art, 1963; Norm and Form: Studies in the Art of the Renaissance, 1966; Aby Warburg: An Intellectual Biography, 1970; Symbolic Images: Studies in the Art of the Renaissance, 1972; (with others) Art, Perception and Reality, 1973.

ABOUT: Who's Who, 1973. *Periodicals*—Encounter May 1964, May 1967; Journal of Philosophy October 21, 1965; New Statesman January 3, 1964; New York Review of Books February 20, 1964; March 9, 1967; New York Times Book Review April 23, 1967; Partisan Review Spring 1964; Spectator April 8, 1960; Times Literary Supplement January 27, 1950; April 8, 1960; July 30, 1964; August 31, 1967; Yale Review June 1960, June 1967.

***GOMBROWICZ, WITOLD** (August 4, 1904–July 25, 1969), Polish novelist, short story writer, and dramatist, was born in Maloszyci, Poland, the son of Jan and Marcela (Kotkowski) Gombrowicz. His father was a wealthy lawyer. Gombrowicz entered Warsaw University in 1922, graduating in 1927 as master of law. From 1927 to 1929 he studied philosophy and economics in Paris.

His first book, a collection of short stories called *Pamiętnik z okresu dojrzewania* (Memoirs of Immaturity, 1933), made no great impact, but his first novel did. This was the "anarchic, fantastic, surrealist, existentialist" *Ferdydurke*, which began its long and complex publishing history as the literary sensation of Warsaw in 1937. The novel's thirty-year-old hero is magically turned back into an adolescent schoolboy. Around this theme, Gombrowicz erects a dense and dazzling but apparently casual structure, mingling social satire, some of it bitter, much anecdotage and "a measure of deliberate and cheerful absurdity." The novel

* gôm brô′ vich

WITOLD GOMBROWICZ

expresses the author's tragi-comic view of man as a creature who, while he exists only, or most fully, in his relations with other people, yet struggles constantly to be "himself," free of the disguises and distortions imposed upon him by his involvement with others. *Ferdydurke* also foreshadowed another, related theme that was to recur in Gombrowicz's work—the preoccupation of grown men, set in their ways, with unformed, spontaneous youth.

Ferdydurke, in its confident and sophisticated use of surrealism and its existential preoccupations, was ahead of its time. So was *Iwona, księzniczka Burgunda* (1935, translated as *Princess Ivona*), a four-act comedy which anticipated many of the typical themes and attitudes of the theatre of the absurd. It was produced in the 1960s and 1970s in Paris, Berlin, London, Stockholm, and elsewhere, as was another play, *Ślub* (translated as *The Marriage*), written during the war and published in Paris in 1953. Gombrowicz's interest in the distorting effects of interpersonal relationships lends itself very readily to theatrical expression, and his plays effectively dramatize the way in which social situations and rituals determine both the characters and the actions of the participants (so that, in *The Marriage*, a boorish simpleton begins to speak like a king merely because his adoring son treats him like one).

When the Nazis invaded Poland in 1939, Gombrowicz was in Buenos Aires. There he was obliged to stay, working for a time at the Polish Bank. *Ferdydurke*, by then banned in Poland, was translated into Spanish with the help of a whole committee of South American writers. This version appeared in 1947, but, according to Gombrowicz, was "drowned in the sleep-walking immobility of South America." In the anonymity of exile, he continued to write in Polish—although he learned to speak Spanish fluently—and to grapple with the problems which had occupied him before the war. Romanticism and the dangerous cult of heroes were the principal targets of his satire and he developed an entire language of "demythization," most noticeable in his second novel, *Trans-Atlantyk* (1953), which was published in German and Polish.

The postwar Communist regime in Poland maintained the ban on Gombrowicz's novels, and only a few copies circulated from hand to hand. However, a brief thaw followed the "Polish October" of 1956, and in 1957 *Ferdydurke* was republished in Warsaw. The well-known Polish critic Arthur Sandauer hailed Gombrowicz as the "greatest living Polish writer," and ten thousand copies of the novel sold out in a few days. Gombrowicz's plays appeared on Polish stages and drew comparisons with Beckett and Ionesco.

The freeze was soon reimposed by the Gomulka regime, and in 1958 Gombrowicz's name disappeared once more from print and the theatres. Meanwhile, however, he was being discovered in Western Europe, England, and the United States. The French version of *Ferdydurke* (1958) was received with enthusiasm as a work of "capital importance," and its author was called the "greatest unknown writer of our time." Gombrowicz had invited readers who enjoyed the book to touch their right ears, the rest to touch their left ears, or their noses, to show that they did not like it or were not sure. The British and American reviewers of Eric Mosbacher's brilliant English translation obediently divided themselves into three variously gesticulating groups of more or less equal size. The "right-ears" admired the novel's "outrageous humor," its political satire, its word play and poetry, its absurdity; the "left-ears" disliked its "whipped-up Pantagruelistic fantasy" and its absurdity; the "noses" looked both ways, and a few creative reviewers reached, as it were, for the organs of the others. Comparisons were made with Beckett and the "anti-novel" and with *Tristram Shandy*.

In 1963 a Ford Foundation grant enabled Gombrowicz to leave Argentina for the first time since 1939. In Poland he was still regarded as an enemy of the regime, and his chronic asthma drove him south. After an interlude in West Berlin, he settled in Vence, in the south of France.

Pornografia, his third novel, was completed in 1957, published in Polish in 1960, and in English in 1966. It resumes the theme of *Ferdydurke*: the conflict and the symbiosis between youth and age. Two old men, Warsaw intellectuals, share a passion for "immaturity, nonachievement, youth." Visiting the countryside during the German occupation, they attempt—for their own vicarious pleasure—to maneuver two adolescents into a mating. Several deaths later, it is no longer clear which are the puppets, who pulls the strings. The novel reminded D. J. Enright of Nabokov's *Lolita*: "One realizes and admires Gombrowicz's sensitiveness and subtlety, but would like to know what he is being sensitive to and subtle about." Others found the book chilling and compelling, "for all its originality, a novel in the classical tradition."

Pornografia missed the International Literary Prize by only one vote; his next novel, *Kosmos* (1965), carried off that rich prize. It is about two young men who become friends and share a room for a time in a hot, lonely country village outside Warsaw. "Born as we are out of chaos," Gombrowicz says, "why can we never establish contact with it? No sooner do we look at it than order, pattern, shape is born under our eyes." What the narrator perceives as a pattern of clues—a half-strangled sparrow, the deformed lips of a girl, the mysterious behavior of his friend—may indeed be part of a cosmic design or entirely random and meaningless. This increasingly frustrating uncertainty creates its own tension and is brilliantly exploited. As one critic wrote in the *Times Literary Supplement*, "To charm with monotony, with deliberate irritation, is a rare ambition, rarely achieved. The sensation of reading Witold Gombrowicz's surrealistic novel recalls that of being tickled by someone who doesn't know when to stop." Other reviewers, it must be said, were merely bored. In general there is a sharp division of critical opinion about Gombrowicz's work, some regarding him as the greatest living Polish novelist, others as a "polyartist who uses the novel to express philosophical fantasies."

Gombrowicz's asthmatic condition deteriorated until he was almost speechless, and in the end his heart was also affected. He died in 1969. Shortly before his death he had married his French-Canadian secretary. His "Fragmenty z dziennika" (Fragments From a Journal) appeared serially in the Paris *Kultura*, and has since been published in book form. *Bakakai* (1958) is a volume of short stories. Gombrowicz was also the author of a satirical operetta, a form whose "monumental stupidity" appealed to him as particularly appropriate to a consideration of "the monumental pathos of history." This work (naturally called *Opérette*) is of course about a libidinous aristocrat's assault upon the virtue of a simple peasant maiden. The problem is that the count's ambition is to imprison his victim in layer upon layer of clothes, while she dreams only of nudity. (As well she may, for nudity undermines the stifling conventions and discriminations of society, and "is in fact plain socialist.") *Opérette* was published in Polish in 1966 and in French in 1969, and has been translated into English as *Operetta*. Staged in Paris in 1970, it was welcomed by Pierre Schneider as "the most successful as well as the best stage work of the season." In 1969 the Institut Littéraire in Paris began the publication of Gombrowicz's collected works in Polish.

Gombrowicz's novels have already been lightly dug over for submerged moral and political meanings and will doubtless be more thoroughly worked in the years to come. His own public reaction to questions about the meaning of his books was boredom. "Come, come," he said, speaking of *Ferdydurke*, "be more sensuous, less cerebral, start dancing with the book instead of asking for meanings. Why take so much interest in the skeleton if it's got a body?"

PRINCIPAL WORKS IN ENGLISH TRANSLATION: Ferdydurke, 1961; Pornografia, 1966; Cosmos, 1967; Princess Ivona (play), 1969 (U.S., Ivona, Princess of Burgundia); The Marriage (play), 1969; Operetta (play), 1971.

ABOUT: Gillon, A. and Krzyzanowski, L. Modern Polish Literature, 1961; Gombrowicz, W. A Kind of Testament (1968 interview with Dominique de Roux), 1973; Jelenski, C. and Roux, D. de. Gombrowicz, 1972 (Paris); International Who's Who, 1969–70. *Periodicals*—Guardian June 23, 1961; New Statesman February 7, 1961; October 28, 1966; New York Review of Books June 15, 1967; New York Times March 9, 1970; New York Times Book Review July 30, 1961; Saturday Review September 9, 1961; Times (London) May 3, 1967; May 5, 1967; November 18, 1967; June 11, 1969; August 14, 1969; Times Literary Supplement November 3, 1966; November 30, 1967; September 25, 1969; February 11, 1972.

***GONZÁLEZ MARTÍNEZ, ENRIQUE** (April 13, 1871–February 19, 1952), Mexican poet, is regarded as the bridge between the so-called modernist movement of Latin American poetry that flourished between 1890 and 1910, and the movements that followed. He was "the last modernist" and "the first post-modernist" poet.

He was born in Guadalajara, Mexico, where he attended the Seminario Conciliar, a clerical school, before moving to the School of Medicine at the University of Guadalajara. There he graduated with a doctor's degree at the early age of twenty-two, soon moving on to practice medicine in Culiacán, where his father had been appointed headmaster. For fifteen years he worked as a physician in the state of Sinaloa, and during this time was married to Luisa Rojo, by whom he had three children.

It was then also that he published his first volumes of verse—*Preludios* (Preludes, 1903) and *Lirismos* (Lyricisms, 1907)—books which revealed a close involvement with the modernist ethic of pure, idealized beauty, sensual contours, and insinuating melody: an art, in short, of exquisite forms derived

* gôn sä′ lās mär tē′ nās

ENRIQUE GONZÁLEZ MARTÍNEZ

largely from the French Parnassians and symbolists. González Martínez indeed subsequently published a volume of translations of French poetry, *Jardines de Francia* (Gardens of France, 1915), including works by Baudelaire and Verlaine.

A considerable change in tone was evident in the poems collected in *Silénter* (1909). Here, for the first time, the poet's own voice was to be heard clearly amidst the modish rhetoric. According to Max Henríquez Ureña, in his distinguished *Breve historia del modernismo* (1954): "From *Silénter* there begins to prevail a profoundly modified attitude to life: as has often been said, his poetry now becomes . . . a record of his spiritual biography, with a sort of pantheist philosophy to guide it."

It is clear that the objective and coldly formal Parnassian aesthetic has given way to something more subjective and emotional. And this departure is described in a famous sonnet, "Wring the Swan's Neck," written in 1910 and included in *Los senderos ocultos* (The Secret Paths, 1911). The swan had symbolized the modernist ideal of formal, statuesque beauty. Far better than the swan with its "false plumage," says González Martínez, is "the wise owl" who, although without the swan's grace, "interprets / the mysterious book of the night's silence." The swan "just parades his gracefulness, but does not feel / the soul of things and the voice of the landscape."

Armed with his new, spiritually intuitive poetry, González Martínez moved to Mexico City in 1911. There he earned his living as a teacher, and was respectfully received into a group of young novelists and poets which, founded in 1907, had been known successively as the Sociedad de Conferencias, the Ateneo de la Juventud, and, finally, as the Ateneo de México, of which González Martínez was immediately elected president.

At the same time he joined the editorial staff of *El Imparcial*, a newspaper which, in 1911, was in hectic opposition to the newly triumphant regime of the liberal revolutionary leader Francisco Madero. Throughout the Mexican civil war, González Martínez supported the forces of reaction, and during the presidency of the counterrevolutionary General Huerta he served his government in the ministry of education. He was nevertheless given diplomatic posts by subsequent revolutionary regimes—in Chile, Argentina, and finally Spain, where he was minister plenipotentiary from 1924 to 1931. He then retired from diplomacy and resettled in Mexico, a much honored national figure until his death in 1952.

Poets are often best remembered for their innovations. González Martínez published twelve new volumes of poems after *Jardines de Francia*, the last of which, *El nuevo Narciso y otros poemas* (The New Narcissus and Other Poems), appeared in 1952, but none of these are read today as eagerly as his earlier volumes. Indeed there is not much in them that had not already been more freshly done in *Silénter* and *Los senderos ocultos*—except that in some of these books, and particularly *Ausencia y canto* (Absence and Song, 1937), and *Bajo el signo mortal* (Under the Mortal Sign, 1942), there is an impressive candor in the poet's depiction of personal emotions, for instance of his grief at the death of his wife and of one of his sons, Enrique Carlos. Gonzáles Martínez also wrote two books in prose, *El hombre del buho* (The Owl Man, 1944), and *La apacible locura* (The Quiet Madness, 1951). Mostly autobiographical, they include reminiscences of his literary past.

Octavio Paz says that "in fact González Martínez was not opposed to modernism; he stripped it and laid it bare. In depriving it of its sentimental and Parnassian trappings, he redeemed it, made it aware of itself and of its hidden meaning. González Martínez confers upon modernism a Mexican originality, that is to say, he gives it consciousness and links it to the tradition."

PRINCIPAL WORKS IN ENGLISH TRANSLATION: *Poems in* Caracciolo-Trejo, E. (ed.) Penguin Book of Latin-American Verse, 1971; Fitts, D. (ed.) Anthology of Contemporary Latin American Poetry, 1942; Paz, O. (ed.) An Anthology of Mexican Poetry, 1958.

ABOUT: Englekirk, J. E. Outline History of Spanish-American Literature, 1965; González Peña, C. History of Mexican Literature, 1968; Paz, O. *introduction* to An Anthology of Mexican Poetry, 1958; Who's Who in Latin America, Part I: Mexico, 1946.

"GOPALEEN, MYLES NA." *See* O'NOLAN, BRIAN

GORDIMER, NADINE (November 20, 1923–), South African novelist and short story writer, writes: "I was born in a small town on a high plateau in Africa. It was one of the towns that had grown up along the gold reef that has made South Africa the richest country on the continent. Around me were streets of bungalow houses, my horizon was flat veld, the natural features of my landscape were mine headgear and man-made hills of yellow sand from the mines. This was not the Africa I read about and saw pictures of in books: when I was a child it seemed to me that I lived in the most ignored and therefore what must be the most uninteresting part of the whole world. I wrote from the age of nine or ten but it was only when I was about twenty that I realized that what I was writing about was exotic—the life of the mining towns scratching the marks of a thin European identity above the wealth dug from the earth by strange-looking, half-naked black men brought from all over Africa to do it. The children of my generation—and their fathers and even grandfathers, some of them—had never seen the European civilisation whose shabbier conventions we were taught to reproduce, and the black men of the mines, familiarly seen walking from their compounds to the shaft-head with their clay-dressed hair, anklets and blankets, were to us no more than the Sakabula birds with their long tails, whose calls, like the speech of the men, we didn't expect to understand. We had black nannies and servants at home, of course, of the tame canary breed, but they—in our presence, anyway—gave back a third-hand reflection of the genteel 'European' ways we ourselves had second-hand.

"I am the daughter of a Jewish watchmaker who emigrated to Africa from a Baltic town when he was thirteen, and my mother was born in England. I had a scrappy and uninspiring minimal education and a deadly dull colonial social background, and at an early age turned to books for all that that background did not offer me. Life was prefigured in them; without knowing quite how I should bring this about, I felt that I should live it for myself someday. I began, quite unconsciously, through writing; passing from the passive act of reading to the creative act of writing brought me to life. Walls fell down; one of the biggest was the colour-bar. I discovered that although the law of my country and the custom of the white people kept them huddled together with their skirts drawn up away from what Africa really is, I in myself was free of their prejudices and their fears. I was not merely part of a suburban white life aping Europe; I lived with and among a variety of colours and kinds of people. This discovery was a joyous personal one, not a political one, at first; but, of course, as time has gone by it has hardened into a sense of political opposition to abusive white power. The core of it remains a personal freedom, to me.

NADINE GORDIMER

"I wrote stories long before I began to write novels, and continue to write both. Out of the sixty or more stories I have written, there are some that satisfy me, but I have not written, yet, the novel I should like to write and perhaps may never be capable of. I am not interested in repeating, with variations, what I know I can do as a writer; with each book I want to attempt to grasp what has eluded me before. I never discuss work in progress and am inarticulate in discussion of literary theory as applied to my own writing. But I have written elsewhere and will repeat: I think that a writer's purpose is to make sense of life. Even the most esoteric of linguistic innovations, the wildest experiments with form, are an expression of this purpose. The only dictum I always remember is André Gide's—'Salvation, for the writer, lies in being sincere even against one's better judgement.' The ideal way to write is as if oneself and one's readers were already dead.

"I married in 1949 and have a daughter; I married again in 1954 and have a son. My husband and I live in Johannesburg and during the last twelve years have travelled a great deal."

Nadine Gordimer, the daughter of Isidore Gordimer and the former Nan Myers, was born and brought up at Springs, near Johannesburg. She attended a convent school among others, and was a good student, with a "bossy vitality" which made her popular with other girls, but restless and a frequent truant. Study at the University of Witwatersrand took her into the broader social and cultural life of Johannesburg, and her own precocious talent laid open the larger world beyond. She acknowledges many guides along the way, among them D. H. Lawrence, who influenced her way of looking at the natural world; Henry James, from whom she acquired a consciousness of form; and Hemingway, who taught her to hear what was essential in dialogue. Nadine Gordimer, who is small, slim, and very attractive, is married to Reinhold Cassirer, a company director.

Her early stories, many of which had appeared in the *New Yorker*, *Harper's*, and other American magazines, were first collected in *Face to Face* (1949) and *The Soft Voice of the Serpent* (1952). Reviewers were quick to recognize in her verbal dexterity, her "mercilessly accurate" sensory responses, the arrival of a "potentially major writer." William Peden was reminded of James Joyce by the preoccupation in these stories with the themes of "exile, alienation, and aloneness" and with people who are "eternal foreigners" in their own country.

Miss Gordimer's first novel was *The Lying Days*, an account of the first twenty-four years in the life of its narrator, Helen Shaw—a somewhat disguised Nadine Gordimer growing up in Springs. It is a narrative as intimate as a diary, written with a warmth and a sensuous vividness in description that at times imposes upon the reader an impression of physical participation in the novel. James Stern found it "in many respects as mature, as packed with insight into human nature, as void of conceit and banality, as original and as beautifully written as a novel by Virginia Woolf"; he could "think of no modern first novel superior to Miss Gordimer's."

Of the several volumes of short stories which have followed, most have been set in Africa, and most have been praised for their faultless *New Yorker* style of prose, their implicit compassion, and the "extreme precision and delicacy" with which nuances of human relationships are perceived and recorded. *The Soft Voice of the Serpent* brought her the W. H. Smith Literary Award in 1961. There is, as Honor Tracy has said, "no living writer of short stories more interesting, varied and fertile than Miss Gordimer at her best." When she is not at her best her humanity, it has been said, can "degenerate into motherliness," and on the other hand her stories can at times shrink so fastidiously from stating the obvious that the point of them is scarcely visible at all. For the most part Miss Gordimer's short stories are perfectly achieved, immaculate.

It may be for this reason that some reviewers seem more interested in her novels, where she is still experimenting and still, at times, reaching beyond her competence. In *A World of Strangers* the narrator is a young Englishman (a feat of impersonation in which Miss Gordimer is very nearly successful). Assigned to Johannesburg, he is faced with a choice between the obvious appeals of an opulent white society and the harsher path of commitment to the cause of black nationalism. The same bitter choice is placed before white middle-class South Africans in two subsequent novels which weigh precisely the cost of either decision.

It has been objected that Miss Gordimer uses South Africa's racial conflict as a device to illuminate character—that her own belief in racial equality is only implicit. Her reply, given in a *London Magazine* interview in 1965, is that political or religious commitment involves a limitation of vision which the artist has no right to accept: "The temptation to put one's writing at the service of a cause . . . is a betrayal. . . . My method is to let the general seep up through the individual." (But her customary objectivity seemed less evident in *The Late Bourgeois World*, published in 1966 but banned in South Africa, of which one reviewer said it "bristles openly with angry frustration.") Miss Gordimer herself has described better than anyone else the direction her work has taken. It has, she told her *London Magazine* interviewer, grown more intellectual, more complex in its organization, preoccupied with "why" rather than "how"; a recent influence has been that of Camus. What she has lost, she said, is sensuousness, nervous tension, "the eye that sees everything as if for the first time"; and these "I shan't find again."

In the late 1960s, Nadine Gordimer traveled a great deal through the new nations of Africa, lecturing on African literature. This experience bore fruit in what many critics consider her best novel, *A Guest of Honour*. The honored guest is James Bray, a former colonial official who returns to the newly independent African state from which he had once been expelled for supporting the black nationalists. Back in the district he had once ruled, he is at first optimistic for the new country, then disquieted by rumors of corruption and police state methods. In the end he has to choose—between loyalty to his old friends in the government and blind faith in a revolutionary future, and also between his wife and the Kenyan girl who has become his mistress. In this book, wrote one reviewer, "Miss Gordimer has consolidated all her achievements in a long, weighty, and magnificent novel which not only reflects the mature political awareness that has always been implicit, but which also shows her special gift of patient and painstaking honesty as a writer to its fullest advantage." The book was awarded the James Tait Black Memorial Prize.

Miss Gordimer has lectured at a number of American universities, and in 1971 went to Columbia as adjunct professor of writing.

PRINCIPAL WORKS: *Novels*—The Lying Days, 1953; A World of Strangers, 1958; Occasion for Loving, 1963; The Late Bourgeois World, 1966; A Guest of Honour, 1970. *Short Stories*—Face to Face, 1949; The Soft Voice of the Serpent, 1952; Friday's Footprint, 1960; Not for Publication, 1965; Livingstone's Companions, 1971.
ABOUT: Contemporary Authors 5-6, 1963; Current Biography, 1959; Nell, R. J. Nadine Gordimer (bibliography), 1964; Who's Who, 1973; Who's Who of South Africa, 1966. *Periodicals*—Guardian May 30, 1969; London Magazine May 1963, May 1965.

GORENKO, ANNA ANDREYEVNA. *See* "AKHMATOVA," ANNA

***GORTER, HERMAN** (November 26, 1864–September 15, 1927), Dutch poet and critic, was born at Wormerveer, the second son of Simon Gorter, a clergyman and author, and the former Johanna Catharina Lugt. In 1870, the family moved to Amsterdam, where Simon Gorter became a newspaper editor. He died a year later at the age of thirty-two, leaving the responsibility for the children's upbringing in their mother's hands. Gorter at first inclined to the study of theology, but in 1883 matriculated to study classical literature at the University of Amsterdam.

Gorter was deeply influenced in his youth by Milton, the novels of "Multatuli," and his father's sermons and essays. But the most crucial encounter of his formative years was with Willem Kloos, the leader of the literary movement known as the Tachtigers (the Generation of 1880) who, inspired principally by the English romantic poets, sought to break away from the cliché-ridden "parsons' poetry" of the day towards a more lofty utterance, a "note of ecstatic singing."

In 1889 Gorter obtained his doctorate with a dissertation on Aeschylus and then worked as a teacher in Amersfoort for several years. He married Wies Cnoop Koopmans in 1890. Three years later they settled in Bussum, where Gorter thereafter devoted his life to his two great concerns, literature and politics. In appearance, Gorter was robust and upright, with close-cropped head and intense eyes behind pince-nez spectacles. He was a cricket enthusiast and a member of the first Dutch team to compete in England.

In 1889, when he was twenty-five, Gorter published his masterpiece, the three-thousand-line lyrical epic *Mei* (May). It is recognized not merely as the apogee of the Tachtiger movement but as one of the supreme achievements of Dutch poetry. Mei, personifying sensual, pastoral, physical beauty, seeks to perpetuate herself in a union with the blind god Balder, symbol of the soul world. To the extent that the poem is a myth, she fails, and dies, because Balder cannot join himself with what is

* gôr′ tər

HERMAN GORTER

physical and mortal. But *Mei* is also a spiritual autobiography, or artistic confession—the poet's desperately sad acknowledgment that the absolute and ineffable cannot be captured in words. The poem had immense influence. Its freedom of form and startling imagery, its melancholy yearning for spiritual fulfillment, inspired many imitators.

The pursuit of absolute beauty through a distillation of the poet's own feelings and sensations was carried further in *Verzen* (Poems, 1890), a cycle of vividly sensual, intensely personal fragments of experience which has been compared to the later paintings of Van Gogh; Kloos called them "the most individual expression of the most individual emotion." The violence of these assaults upon the limitations of language brought Gorter to a state of emotional exhaustion. He began to feel that poetry itself was deserting him, and with it his hopes and his youth.

Then began the radical change of direction that explains the current revival of interest in Gorter's career—the evolution of this intensely personal poet into a public one. Seeking beyond himself for the truth, he turned to philosophy, especially Spinoza, whose *Ethics* he translated in 1895, and Marx. He rejected his earlier works as "bourgeois" and became a Socialist. This political awakening is already evident in *De School der Poëzie* (School of Poetry, 1897), along with a scrupulous adherence to conventional forms, especially the sonnet, quite remote from his earlier practice.

In 1897 Gorter joined the S.D.A.P., the Dutch Social Democratic party. He played an important role as a propaganda speaker, and from 1898 onwards as coeditor of the S.D.A.P. monthly, *De*

Nieuwe Tijd (The New Age), in which he published many of his own political and literary essays. Among them was a memorable demolition of the theories of Kloos and the Tachtigers, although he remained their friend and admirer.

In 1909, seeking a more radical socialism, Gorter broke away from the S.D.A.P. and became a founding member of the new left-wing S.D.P., a party which exerted little practical influence on political life. At about this time he retired to his cottage in the dunes near Bergen aan Zee, where he lived for long periods quite alone after his wife's death in 1916. His health began to decline.

In 1912 Gorter attended the International Socialist Peace Congress in Basel, and, on repeated visits to Switzerland for health reasons, he met Russian political exiles, became an ardent supporter of the October Revolution of 1917, and one of the founders of the Communist International. During 1918 and 1919 he worked closely with radical elements in the German Communist party, and in the fall of 1920 traveled from Berlin via Stettin to Russia as a stowaway. He futilely debated the course of revolutionary tactics, particularly in regard to the West, privately with Lenin and publicly at Comintern committee meetings. He broke with the party leadership, and the next year set up in the Netherlands the K.A.P., a small party which advocated workers' councils as the only just basis of a free, Socialist society. During a return journey from Switzerland in September 1927, Gorter suffered a heart attack in the train and died some hours later in a hotel in Brussels.

Gorter considered himself a pioneer in the task of molding the greatness of the Socialist idea through poetry. For him socialism meant a renewal of society which would also free poetry from its middle-class limitations and return it to classical heights. *Een klein heldendicht* (A Little Heroic Poem, 1906) was a not entirely successful attempt to create a Socialist epic based on a strike, but Gorter's artistic stature should by no means be measured solely by the achievement of his pre-Socialist period. The monumental twelve-thousand-line epic *Pan*, published in 1912 and in an expanded edition in 1916, is a remarkable Marxist vision of the liberation of humanity. *De groote dichters* (The Great Poets), published in 1935, is a penetrating historical-materialist study of the relationship between the writer and society as seen in Homer, Vergil, Dante, Shakespeare, Goethe, and Vondel. A standard edition of the *Verzamelde werken* (Collected Works) in eight volumes, including many unpublished poems, was published under the editorship of Garmt Stuiveling between 1948 and 1952.

PRINCIPAL WORKS IN ENGLISH TRANSLATION: Poems *in* Barnouw, A. J. Coming After, 1948; Columbia University Course, The Great Literature of Small Nations, Volume VIII, 1929; Snell, A. L. Flowers From a Foreign Garden, 1902; Weevers, T. Poetry of the Netherlands in Its European Context, 1960.

ABOUT: Cassell's Encyclopaedia of Literature, 1966; Corstius, J. C. B. Herman Gorter, 1934; Holst, H. R. Herman Gorter, 1933; Penguin Companion to Literature 2, 1969; Ravesteijn, W. van, Herman Gorter, 1928; Russell, J. D. Dutch Romantic Poetry, 1961; Smith, H. (ed.) Columbia Dictionary of Modern European Literature, 1947; Weevers, T. Poetry of the Netherlands in Its European Context, 1960.

"GOULD, ALAN." *See* CANNING, VICTOR

***GOVER, ROBERT** (November 2, 1929–), American novelist, writes: "My father came from farm country in south-central Kentucky; he went North to study medicine on the dregs of the family money, went to a dance, became a father, then got killed in an auto accident. I was raised by my maternal grandparents (he was a factory worker) till age seven, then put into Girard, an endowed home and school in Philadelphia for 'poor, white, male orphans.' Where I probably would have grown up thinking of myself as not much more than the number they gave me if my mother hadn't put me on a bus and sent me to Kentucky for the summer. There, my father's people un-numbered and individualized me by giving me their version of who I am and what my relationship to the land is. They had what was called 'Neighborliness': when you see a neighbor out building a house or barn, you hike on over and get to work helping. Lunch on whatever's handy—watermelon and moonshine, maybe—and take a storytelling siesta and work till dark. I learned that things can get done pleasantly and well by this cooperative or socialistic method, and it was good to remember this while coming of age during the McCarthy repressions.

"Girard has a wall around it, like a prison, and much of the surrounding neighborhood is a Negro ghetto, and some of my childhood adventures came from roaming into 'their' territory. Inside the wall there was 'discipline,' which my instincts and summers in Kentucky put me into a running battle of wits against. And this—bucking authority—has for better or worse become a lifelong habit. Some of my childhood pals were sent to reform school and I came close to going that route, but was re-routed when offered athletic scholarships for swimming. I chose the University of Pittsburgh because it was reputed to have an outstanding writing course.

"I was a storyteller for as far back as I can remember. Used to sit through movies, then re-tell them, making everything happen the way I wanted it to—this was both an amusement and a way to try

* gō′ vər

to figure out what's really going on—and I spent many a study period writing little sagas for the diversion of my buddies. By the time I was let out of Girard at age eighteen, I assumed I was destined to be a recognized Writer by age twenty—clearly, I was not ready for what lay ahead.

"It took me several years to get oriented to non-institutional, civilian life. My own personal values clashed with the values of students from middle-class or upper-middle-class backgrounds, and I felt absurd and apathetic, and drifted through four years on a 'free ride,' dropping classes and sleeping through finals. Then, when I got to the writing class, I did all the wrong things: I showed up with a big stack of stories and was promptly told that only four were required for the course; I found myself among the anti-athlete arty set, and since I wrote most of the stories 'discussed' I ended up feeling like a worn-out flintstone for the sharpening of 'critical faculties.'

"When my four years of eligibility ran out, I still had another year's worth of credits to get for a degree and since I couldn't think of anything else to do, I got 'serious'—a job 4 P.M. to midnight in a mill. This settled me down so much I did blunder my way to enough credits, whereupon the university withheld the roll of paper called a Diploma; I have vague plans to someday find out why.

"Anyhow I was soon holed up nicely in an apartment, collecting Unemployment Compensation and writing short stories and one-act plays, reading them to fellow outcasts Saturday nights and trying to get published. Then the girl I was fond of up and married a psychoanalyst and people began shaking a finger at me, telling me I should stop being a bum and get a job. I gave up trying to get published and decided on suicide, chickened out and got a job.

"Several jobs and many a drunken funk later I wrote a novel, six hundred pages long and, in structure, 'loose' to say the least. Some literary lights encouraged me, said I should move to Paris or New York and 'make friends' with the 'right people.' So, given my old habit of the running battle, I steadfastly stayed put and wrote more novels, blunderfully figuring that writing was what I wanted to do, and I would make it writing or make it not at all.

"The fourth novel I wrote, *One Hundred Dollar Misunderstanding* (1959), drew the usual rejections from U.S. publishers, so I had it sent overseas. Marcel Duhamel translated and *La Table Ronde* published it in French, Henry Miller talked Grove Press into bringing out an American hardback edition and it made the best-seller list just in time for the 1961 New York newspaper strike.

"While living in Vero Beach, Florida, I became involved in the nearby Negro ghetto of Gifford trying to help get the Change. Until the local reactionaries became attentive, then I found it most politic to flee like a thief in the night and go—now seemed the ripe time—to New York, where I completed *Poorboy at the Party*."

ROBERT GOVER

Robert Gover is a literary cartoonist whose subject is the gap in America between poor and rich, black and white, and whose special talent is for dialogue. His theme is most directly and successfully illustrated in his first published novel, *One Hundred Dollar Misunderstanding*, which introduces Kitten, a fourteen-year-old black prostitute, and J. C. Holland, a nineteen-year-old white college sophomore. J. C., with one hundred dollars in his pocket, visits a brothel in search of "experience." Kitten thinks him rich and invites him to her apartment, a tactic which he regards as a personal tribute. Their irreconcilably different views of the bawdy weekend that follows are expressed in alternate monologues which brilliantly reveal Kitten as an honest child of nature, J.C. as a pompous, hypocritical, moral illiterate. Some critics found the book offensive but most were deeply amused and impressed. Nat Hentoff called Kitten's monologues, which dominate the book, "as richly individualized a curve of spoken rhythms as has appeared since the equally unique and equally believable ruminations of Holden Caulfield." Other reviewers echoed his enthusiasm for Gover's skill at dialect but were less appreciative of his attempts at dialectic, finding Kitten's untutored spontaneity sentimental and her adversary's pieties too simple a caricature of Wasp mores.

The novels in which Gover has managed without Kitten and J.C. have not been successful. *The*

Maniac Responsible is a Faulknerian interior monologue spoken by a young newspaperman whose sense of guilt towards his frigid, teasing girl friend leads him to confess to the rape-murder he is reporting. Though it was Gover's second published book, it seemed to Anthony Boucher "like a fumbling and amateurish first attempt, dug out of the trunk to follow up a success." *Poorboy at the Party* is about a poor-white swimming star who hustles his way into an upper-class party and, effectively if unwittingly, precipitates an orgy which tears away the moral facade of his hosts and leaves their property in ruins. It was generally disliked as a "blending of stag-movie action with pseudo-profound comment."

There have been two sequels to Gover's first novel. In *Here Goes Kitten*, which has all of the faults and little of the charm of *One Hundred Dollar Misunderstanding*, Kitten is hustling in a more sophisticated setting, while J.C. is making his "ratfinkish" way in local politics. Their next reunion occurs in *J. C. Saves*, a funnier and somewhat more optimistic book in which J.C., now a public relations man for a city threatened with race riots, abandons all for love of Kitten, who responds by introducing him to marijuana ("Turkish cigarettes") and LSD ("Mah own hangover cure"), leaving him an altogether better man. Here, as in *Poorboy at the Party*, Gover's message seems to be that (as Robert Detweiler puts it), "erection stimulates destruction, and out of the orgasmic chaos a kind of fresh world emerges."

Gover worked spasmodically as a reporter for various small dailies in Pennsylvania and Maryland until his first book was published, and then became a full-time writer. His 1955 marriage to Mildred Vitkovich, a nurse, ended in divorce in 1966. He was married again in 1968 to Jeanne-Nell Gement, and has one child.

PRINCIPAL WORKS: One Hundred Dollar Misunderstanding, 1961; The Maniac Responsible, 1963; Here Goes Kitten, 1964; Poorboy at the Party, 1966; J. C. Saves, 1968.

ABOUT: Contemporary Authors 11–12, 1965; Moore, H. T. (ed.) Contemporary American Novelists, 1964; Vinson, J. (ed.) Contemporary Novelists, 1972; Who's Who in America, 1972–1973.

GOWERS, SIR ERNEST (ARTHUR) (June 2, 1880–April 16, 1966), English rhetorician, was born in London, the youngest son of Sir William Gowers, a famous neurologist, and Mary (Baines) Gowers. He was educated at Rugby and went on with a scholarship to Clare College, Cambridge, where he graduated in classics with first-class honors. Gowers began his distinguished career in Britain's apolitical Civil Service in 1903, when he entered the Internal Revenue Department. He transferred to the India Office in 1904, undertook legal studies, and became a barrister in 1906. His abilities were soon recognized, and in 1911 he became principal private secretary to Lloyd George, who was then Chancellor of the Exchequer. A succession of increasingly important posts followed during and after World War I. From 1920 to 1927 he served as Permanent Under-Secretary for Mines and for three years thereafter was chairman of the Board of Inland Revenue. He was knighted for his public services in 1926, and retired from the Civil Service in 1930 to accept the chairmanship of the Coal Commission, a post he held until 1946.

ERNEST GOWERS

His literary career began during World War II, when he became London Regional Commissioner for Civil Defence. One of his concerns in that critical post was morale, and the program of concerts and lectures arranged by his headquarters included an extremely amusing and pointed talk by Sir Ernest himself on the writing of good English. It was so successful that after the war Gowers was asked to write an instructional booklet on the same subject for the benefit of civil servants. This was published in 1948 as *Plain Words* by Her Majesty's Stationery Office. The problem of accurate communication is not confined to civil servants, and it was soon evident that HMSO had a best seller on its hands. This introductory essay was followed by a reference book, *The ABC of Plain Words* (1951), and the two works were published together as *The Complete Plain Words* (1954).

Although a little space in Gowers' book is "reluctantly" devoted to grammar and punctuation, it is concerned mainly with "the choice and arrangement of words in such a way as to get an idea as exactly as possible out of one mind into another." Invaluable as a guide to simple and direct English, it is also a very entertaining anthology of various kinds of failure in communication. "To be told that the Minister 'is not in a position to approve,'" Gowers said, "may excite a desire to retort that he might try putting his feet on the mantelpiece and see if that does any good."

The Complete Plain Words, which has sold over a million copies in Britain alone, persuaded the Oxford University Press that Sir Ernest should be entrusted with the revision of H. W. Fowler's standard but dated *Dictionary of Modern English Usage*. This monumental task, begun in 1957, occupied Gowers for eight years. The result, published in 1965, was another best seller, both in Britain and the United States.

Gowers' revision adhered to Fowler's principle that "there is a proper and orderly way of placing words . . . to make the whole relationship perfectly clear." Sir Ernest was rather more flexible than Fowler in his attitude to grammar, pronunciation, and the acceptance of new words, inclining to the view that usage establishes correctness. But Gowers was far from being totally permissive and complained for example about the "hideous and unnecessary words now being spawned" by the addition of *-ize* to nouns to create new verbs. One reviewer called the book a "decorous, decent, often witty but already old-fashioned revision," but most authorities were far more enthusiastic. F. W. Bateson thought Gowers easier to use than Fowler and said "he has been remarkably successful, in my opinion, in retaining Fowler's *ipsissima verba* while making the minor corrections and qualifications that time has made necessary."

Gowers' literary career did not interfere with his public one. He was chairman in 1945 of the commission on the admission of women to the senior branch of the Foreign Office, and subsequently chaired or participated in several other inquiries, including the important Royal Commission on Capital Punishment (1949–1953). This last assignment made a convinced abolitionist of him, and he explained his views in *A Life for a Life*, published in 1956, shortly before Britain abandoned capital punishment. He served on the development corporation of Harlow "new town" (1947–1950), was chairman of the National Hospitals for Nervous Diseases (1948–1957), and president of the English Association (1956–1957). From 1952 to 1960 he was active in court life as Gentleman Usher of the Purple Rod. He was a Knight Grand Cross of the Bath (1953), held an honorary doctorate from Manchester University, and was an honorary fellow of Clare College.

When his public duties permitted, Gowers lived the life of a country gentleman on his Hampshire estate, reading Dickens and Homer, venturing into the "exhausting" world of James Bond, on Sundays playing the organ at the village church. He was a tall man, very upright, with a humorous mouth and piercing blue eyes, much liked and respected for the energy, kindness, and firmness which had made him so excellent a chairman and "one of the greatest public servants of his day." He was already ill with cancer when his revision of Fowler appeared, and he said, "It gives me rather a sensation of going out not with a whimper but a bang." Sir Ernest's wife Constance had died in 1952; he was survived by a son and two daughters.

PRINCIPAL WORKS: Plain Words, 1948; The ABC of Plain Words, 1951; The Complete Plain Words, 1954; A Life for a Life? The Problem of Capital Punishment, 1956; H. W. Fowler: The Man and His Teaching, 1957; (ed. and rev.) H. W. Fowler's Dictionary of Modern English Usage, 1965.

ABOUT: Who's Who, 1966. *Periodicals*—Newsweek May 17, 1965; May 2, 1966; New Yorker August 14, 1965; New York Times April 18, 1966; Time April 29, 1966; Times (London) April 18, 1966.

GOYEN, (CHARLES) WILLIAM (April 25, 1915–), American novelist, short story writer, and dramatist, was born in Trinity, a railroad and sawmill town on the Trinity River in East Texas. He is the son of Charles Provine Goyen and the former Mary Inez Trow. In a statement published in *Contemporary Novelists*, Goyen writes: "We lived in Trinity until I was seven. The world of that town, its countryside, its folk, its speech and superstition and fable, was stamped into my senses during those first seven years of my life; and I spent the first twelve years of my writing life reporting it and fabricating it in short fiction." The family moved in Goyen's seventh year to Shreveport, Louisiana, and then to Houston, Texas, where the boy completed his education. "As a child," he says, "I was quick and scared; serving; secretly unsettled; imaginative and nervous and sensual." By the time he reached Sam Houston High School he was convinced that he would be a composer, actor, or singer and, in spite of his parents' distrust of these exotic ambitions, contrived secretly to study musical composition, dancing, and singing. Discovered, he turned to writing as a less noticeable form of artistic expression.

At Rice University, Goyen was unhappy both with his courses (especially mathematics) and with his fellow students, until in his junior year he discovered the pleasures and excitements of literature, and immersed himself in the English, French, and American classics, reading and writing furiously, and taking all the college prizes for both stories and plays. He received his B.A. in 1937 and his M.A. (in comparative literature) in 1939. Later the same year, after teaching briefly at the University of Houston, he was drafted into the Navy, joining as

WILLIAM GOYEN

an enlisted man and after a year going on to Midshipman School for officer training at Columbia University in New York. Goyen served with the Navy throughout the war, mostly on an aircraft carrier in the South Pacific.

After the war Goyen went to New Mexico and settled down to write. At El Prado, near Taos, he met Dorothy Brett and Frieda Lawrence, and built an adobe house on land given him by the latter. There he worked for two years on his first novel, *The House of Breath*, which he finished a little later in London.

Goyen wants, he says, "to make splendor," and at his best has done so. *The House of Breath*, published in 1950, is "an incantation which conjures up the narrator's small home town in Texas . . . in the years of his childhood and adolescence." Katherine Anne Porter wrote of it: "Here are the most extravagant feelings, the most absurd recklessness of revealment, at times there is real danger of the fatal drop into over-pathos. . . . To balance this fault, the writing as a whole is disciplined on a high plane, and there are long passages of the best writing, the fullest and richest and most expressive, that I have read in a very long time—complex in form, and beautifully organized, shapely as a good tree, as alive and substantial." Jean Garrigue thought that "prose wants to do here what poetry does. And it succeeds."

In a Farther Country, Goyen's second novel, resembles his first. It was called "a captivating fantasy" in which, by a kind of literary sleight of hand, the writer continued to sustain his "fragile world of super-reality." *The Fair Sister*, although it retained an element of fantasy, was something of a departure—a satirical account of the adventures in the wicked world of Ruby Drew, a dedicated black evangelist. Most reviewers thought it extremely funny, though one called it a "witless exercise" and none seemed to think it more than "a refreshing interlude for an important writer."

Most of Goyen's short stories are set in or allude to Texas. Discussing them, William Peden suggests that his theme is "a never-ceasing conflict between the present and the past, between the visible and the invisible," in which his characters, torn between the two worlds, struggle to make the best of both of them. This theme, Peden says, is presented "with considerable variety of mood, method, and subject matter," ranging from the realistic to "the grotesque and masquelike." Goyen's preoccupation with the violent and bizarre has persuaded some critics that he can be conveniently pigeonholed as a "southern writer," but he himself vehemently rejects the classification. And Peden, who was troubled by the "cloudy metaphysics, florid rhetoric, and emotional intensity" of Goyen's early stories, finds his more recent work purged of "Gothic excesses."

Goyen's books have been translated into French, German, and some other languages; his stories have appeared in major magazines in Europe as well as in America. He has written a number of plays, including a stage adaptation of *The House of Breath*, and *The Diamond Rattler*, which was premiered in Boston in 1960. Goyen has taught writing and literature at New York's New School for Social Research (1955–1960) and at Columbia (1964–1965), and was a critic and reviewer for the New York *Times* from 1950 to 1965. From 1966 to 1971 he was a senior editor in the trade books department of McGraw-Hill. He has received a number of ASCAP awards for musical compositions as well as two Guggenheim fellowships and a Ford Foundation grant. He was married in 1963 to Doris Roberts, an actress. Some critics, in the United States and elsewhere, believe that William Goyen is a major writer whose unique style and vision have not yet received due recognition.

PRINCIPAL WORKS: The House of Breath (novel), 1950; Ghost and Flesh (stories), 1952; In a Farther Country (novel), 1955; The Faces of Blood Kindred (stories), 1960; The Fair Sister (novel) (England, Savata, My Fair Sister), 1963; A Book of Jesus, 1973.

ABOUT: Bachelard, G. The Poetics of Space, 1964; Contemporary Authors 7–8, 1963; Gossett, L. Y. Violence in Recent Southern Fiction, 1965; Nin, A. The Novel of the Future, 1966; Nyren, D. (ed.) A Library of Literary Criticism: Modern American Literature, 1961; Peden, W. The American Short Story, 1964; Vinson, J. (ed.) Contemporary Novelists, 1972; Who's Who in America, 1970–1971. *Periodicals*—Nation October 22, 1955; New York Times Book Review September 10, 1950; August 7, 1960; Southwest Review Summer 1971; Time February 25, 1952.

GOYTISOLO, JUAN (January 5, 1931–), Spanish novelist, writes (in Spanish): "I was born into a comfortable and somewhat indolent middle-class environment in Barcelona. My father's family is of Basque origin and my mother's Andalusian and Catalan. My paternal great-grandfather accumulated a fortune in Cuba; my grandfather, however, settled in Barcelona after it became clear to him that he had no choice but to sell his two sugar mills as a consequence of the war with the United States—the Spanish-American war. During the first third of the century, the family lived on its income; in addition, my father was the manager of a small industrial firm. At the moment of the military uprising against the Republic, this entire conventional middle-class world collapsed like a house of cards. For some time my father was imprisoned by the Anarchists. My mother died in the streets of Barcelona, victim of a raid by Mussolini's airplanes. My brothers and sisters, my father, and I lived as refugees in a small village in the north of Catalonia where we remained until the conclusion of the hostilities.

"From 1939 until 1947 I endured the education customarily given to children of well-to-do families in Spain, an experience which engendered in me a deep-seated spirit of rebellion against all the pillars of old Spanish society. Between 1948 and 1952 I studied law in the universities of Barcelona and Madrid, but my studies bored me beyond measure, and one fine day I abandoned them ingloriously with no regret. Since 1956 I have been living in Paris where I am employed as a planning adviser to an important publishing house, although I make frequent trips back to Spain, preferably to the South. I have traveled, too, over almost all of Europe, the north of Africa, and some of the Latin American countries.

"My vocation as a writer got off to an early start. At the age of eight I was writing poems and stories, and between my twelfth and sixteenth years I wrote at least a dozen novels on such themes as life in the Far West, Guana de Arco, the exploration of the Amazon River, and the French Revolution. As I completed each of them, I would seek out some younger and weaker child than myself to serve as an audience, and would shut myself into a room with him and read them to him from start to finish. I wrote a play, too; fortunately, it was never staged.

"My first real venture dates from my twenty-first year, the age at which I began to write the novel *Juegos de Manos* (*The Young Assassins*) which was published in Spain in 1954. Its critical reception in Spain was poor, but it turned out to be a great success in its French version and was translated straightaway into more than ten languages. Since then I have devoted myself entirely to literature.

"Two of my brothers also write: José Agustín,

JUAN GOYTISOLO

the older, is a poet; Luis, the younger, a novelist. Perhaps the source of our vocation may be traced to a great uncle on our mother's side who produced several written works in Castilian and Catalan and translated some of the Persian poets into the latter language. I believe, however, that the determining factor for us was the brutal impact of the war on our sensitive childhood. In 1954 I wrote in answer to a survey of the writers of my generation in these words: 'Many young novelists of today were children at the time of the Civil War. Their young eyes witnessed impassively some terrible things. But as they grew up there came a moment when they remembered them. And this memory became increasingly urgent as their bones hardened and their blood quickened. Then they began to write novels, not in order to forget these things—which would have been impossible—but to be free from them. After the first surge, a wave of brief duration marked by a kind of journalism that described the crimes committed and collected statistics on ruined homes and the men shot down, came the second wave, slower and more powerful, which reports what was destroyed and what was awakened in our consciousness.'

"Since *Juegos de Manos*, I have published seven novels, two volumes of short stories, two collections of essays, and two books on my travels through the south of Spain. Owing to the censorship still existing in Spain, some of my books could not be published in my own country, for which reason they made their first appearance in France and in several countries of Latin America."

Juan Goytisolo is the most prolific of the Spanish

novelists—baptized "the new wave" by Eugenio de Nora—who began publishing in the 1950s. He early won international recognition and is widely regarded as the best Spanish novelist of his generation.

In *Juegos de Manos* (1954, translated by John Rust as *The Young Assassins*), some middle-class student intellectuals plan to assassinate a minor politician; they call themselves anarchists but, as Kessel Schwartz has pointed out, what really motivates them is the urge to commit "some irrevocable act that will cut their parental ties forever." David, the sensitive youth chosen to perform the assassination, has no stomach for it and is murdered for his failure by the leader of the gang. It is significant that David accepts the justice of this sentence and makes no resistance; as Schwartz says, the murder "constitutes a kind of guilt atonement for their own, their companions', and their parents' shortcomings in a meaningless world." Paul West found the novel initially slow moving and occasionally awkward, but wrote: "The last seventy pages, in which climax and anticlimax force maturity, self-denial, conscience and stark terror into the hermetic world of the well-heeled delinquents, are almost Dostoevskian; the characterization is steady throughout, the writing harsh and agile."

Duelo en el Paraíso (1955, translated by Christine Brooke-Rose as *Children of Chaos*), weakened by confusingly abrupt transitions in time and place, nevertheless shows greater imaginative power. It describes the reign of terror instigated by a group of refugee children when public order collapses at the end of the Civil War, and has reminded some critics of William Golding's *Lord of the Flies*. Violent forces and violent figures pervade Goytisolo's early novels, notably the trilogy "El mañana efímero" (The Ephemeral Morrow, the title of a celebrated poem by Antonio Machado).

The trilogy's best volume is *Fiestas* (1958, translated by Herbert Weinstock under the same title). In it a boy becomes involved in the dangerous excitements of the Barcelona waterfront through his friendship with Gorila, a huge man strangely compounded of tenderness and mindless brutality; a little girl sets out for Italy in search of her father; an old teacher dreams of establishing a school in Barcelona's squalid shanty town: each pursues an illusion more palatable than the bleak realities of Franco's Spain; each illusion leads only to disaster.

Ramón Sender called the novel "a model of harmony, sharpness, love of things and beings. . . . *Fiestas* is a brilliant projection of the contrast between Spanish official and real life." Isabel Quigly drew attention to Goytisolo's use of selective "close-ups," rapid cutting from scene to scene, and other cinematic techniques, and concluded: "As in his other novels Goytisolo puts his people into a present-day situation, politically and morally explicit . . . without the use of a single 'political' expression. The satire is oblique, delicate: in fact the whole of *Fiestas* is a satire, the whole situation, in which people go about their daily lives preparing for an enormous religious congress, comments on the Spanish mentality today."

The trilogy's other two novels are less successful. Utah, the central character in *El circo* (1957)—a painter who commits an absurd fraud before paying, equally absurdly, for a murder he did not commit—is an overliterary creation, though the hypocrisy and harshness of Catalonian life is effectively captured. *La resaca* (1958) is set in working-class Barcelona and exemplifies Goytisolo's view that "in Spain the novel performs a documentary function that in France and other European countries falls to the Press."

Campos de Níjar (1960) and *La Chanca* (1962) are literally documentaries. They deal respectively with the countryside around Almería and the slums of the city itself, revealing through description and interviews the appalling conditions under which the poor live and die, taking the "travel book" into the age of political commitment. In his fiction at this time Goytisolo was examining, with a similar documentary realism, the other side of the coin: the aimless lives of the Spanish middle class. In two novels, *La isla* (1961, translated by José Yglesias as *Island of Women*) and *Fin de fiesta* (1962, translated by Yglesias as *The Party's Over*) he focuses on members of the affluent and degenerate bourgeoisie, at play on the Mediterranean coast. In the process, as one critic said, he ran the risk "that any novelist who writes on stupid people must run, that his novel will be stupid."

In *Problemas de la novela*, a volume of essays published in 1959, Goytisolo had called for a socially aware realistic novel. However, none of the work he himself had produced in this mode had been entirely satisfying, and critics by then were attacking his political one-sidedness, his lack of psychological penetration, and above all the unreality of his characters, who seemed to owe more to the novelist's imagination than to his observation. Not surprisingly, Goytisolo has impressed most when combining his documentary technique with autobiographical material, as in some of the short stories collected in *Para vivir aquí* (1960), and to great effect in *Señas de identidad* (1966, translated by Yglesias as *Marks of Identity*).

In this novel Álvaro, who spends an evening and night in August 1963 in a monumental self-analysis that is both national and personal, is largely Goytisolo himself. The book becomes a compelling indictment of the author's "own upper middle class, the eternal bosses" who, more than Franco or any other single leader, are responsible for Spain's "eternally hopeless, helpless poor." According to a reviewer in the *Times Literary Supplement*, "The narrator's memories are related in a cleverly ordered variety of styles. Aspects of the past are reconstructed in an ingenious kind of collage of direct observation, fragments of newspaper articles, police reports, isolated conversations and incidents, and some interior monologue in a free verse form. A rich interplay of suggestion makes commentary superfluous." The result is "a fine and moving novel, in a class apart from even the best of Señor Goytisolo's previous work." The collage technique is extended in *Reivindicación del Conde Don Julián* (1970), a dense and bizarrely poetic meditation on exile and betrayal.

PRINCIPAL WORKS IN ENGLISH TRANSLATION: The Young Assassins, 1959; Children of Chaos, 1959; Fiestas, 1960; Island of Women, 1962 (England, Sands of Torremolinos); The Party's Over, 1966; Marks of Identity, 1969.

ABOUT: Buckley, R. Problemas formales de la novela contemporánea, 1968; Curley, D. N. and Curley, A. Modern Romance Literatures (Library of Literary Criticism), 1967; Curutchet, J. C. Introducción a la novela española de postguerra, 1966; Gil Casado, P. La novela social española, 1968; Nora, E. G. de. La novela española contemporánea, 1962; Schwartz, K. *introduction to* Laurel Language Library edition of Fiestas, 1964; West, P. The Modern Novel, 1963. *Periodicals*—Guardian March 3, 1961; Insula January 1967; La Torre January–March 1961; New Statesman April 30, 1960; New York Times Book Review March 18, 1962; Papeles de Son Armadans February 1964; Saturday Review February 14, 1959; June 11, 1960; Times Literary Supplement April 3, 1959; September 28, 1967.

"GRAAF, PETER." *See* YOUD, SAMUEL

GRAHAM, W. S. (November 19, 1918–), Scottish poet, writes: "W. S. stands for William Sydney and I was born in a set-in bed in a high tenement kitchen that looked out over Greenock and the noisy shipbuilding Firth of Clyde. My father was a turner in one of the yards, a good fiddler and ran a concert-party. My mother was partly Irish (Greenock has a good bit of Irish in it) and I was the first of two sons.

"For a boy maybe Greenock was more wonderful than most towns to grow up in. A town of distilleries, humming sugar-houses and ships. From our topflat kitchen you could see shipyards bristling with derricks and winking with welding lights and hear the riveters. Across the firth the mountains and lochs of Argyll began and farther away Ben Lomond. So, as a town to start a poet from, Greenock was not wanting.

"At school I was well belted by the masters and many a time in the summer I was off gallivanting the high moors above the town. Although I got on well enough with my chums I liked being on my own. I began to really like poetry then and Nature

W. S. GRAHAM

and Solitude (those overtones of what the poetry really was) were the qualities which gave me pleasure. Keats, Burns, Blake and the Georgians, with special poets like W. J. Turner and Edward Thomas. I was fourteen and began writing some poems which I know didn't have the slightest bit of originality or talent. I went off to Glasgow then to be an engineer but never took to it. I think my dislike of engineering helped to drive me into writing poetry (the exercise book hidden under the drawing-board) as an escape.

"I wrote more and read more and became more singly and self-consciously interested in verse. When my verse began to be accepted in periodicals it made a difference to me. I wasn't just speaking in front of a mirror. I was being listened to. I realised that whatever subjective kick I was getting out of the act of writing my poem, it should be 'made' as well and as consciously as possible. In this way it would be a more successful mechanism for the reader to use to find out something about himself. That was my beginning as a writer.

"Since then I have spent two years in America (where I taught Literature at New York University and gave Poetry Readings in various cities) and have travelled in Italy, France and Greece. In this country I have read at various universities and on the BBC. I was granted an Atlantic Award in Literature in 1947."

It was at Greenock High School that W. S. Graham was "well belted." At nineteen, his five-year apprenticeship completed, he became a journeyman engineer, and then went with a bursary to Newbattle Abbey College, near Edinburgh. There he continued the studies in literature and philosophy he had begun at university night classes. Graham worked during World War II as a precision engineer in a Clydeside torpedo factory, and subsequently as a casual laborer, crofter, and fisherman in Cornwall, where he still lives.

Graham's poetry is characterized by its sea imagery, used often symbolically rather than descriptively; by the "Scottishness" of his "hard, massive" diction; and by syntactical dislocations reminiscent of Dylan Thomas. Graham also resembles (and sometimes echoes) Thomas in the romantic obscurity of much of his early verse—which, even when apparently meaningless, is often strangely moving and memorable. *The Nightfishing* was thought a notable advance towards a more personal and disciplined style, and the title poem, a long meditation, was compared by one critic to "a northern *Cimetière marin*."

Critics hostile to neoromanticism accuse Graham of "preconceived attitudinizing in singing robes," but Vivienne Koch has found in his work evidence of "a radical and uncompromising moral intelligence" and Anthony Hartley praises the power of his descriptive passages "with their subtle alliteration and balance within the lines" and "the quality of stillness he produces in his verse at moments of meditation."

PRINCIPAL WORKS (all poetry): Cage Without Grievance, 1943; The Seven Journeys, 1944; 2nd Poems, 1945; The White Threshold, 1949; The Nightfishing, 1955; Malcolm Mooney's Land, 1970; Penguin Modern Poets (with David Gascoyne and Kathleen Raine), 1970.

ABOUT: Allott, K. (ed.) Penguin Book of Contemporary Verse, 1962; Blackburn, T. The Price of an Eye, 1961; Ford, B. (ed.) The Modern Age (Pelican Guide to English Literature), 1963; Murphy, R. (ed.) Contemporary Poets of the English Language, 1970. *Periodicals*—Nine May 1960; Sewanee Review October 1948.

***GRASS, GÜNTER (WILHELM)** (October 16, 1927–) is the most widely discussed writer to emerge in Germany since World War II. He was born in the Free City of Danzig, the Baltic seaport which is now the Polish city of Gdánsk, and has been the setting of three of his novels. His father was a grocer and a minor official. His immediate home environment is evoked in *The Tin Drum* and in the autobiographical poem "Kleckerburg." On his mother's side Grass is descended from Kashubians, a Slavonic-Pomeranian people of the Danzig region. He attended primary and secondary schools in Danzig, and at an early age began to draw and paint. Grass wrote his first novel at thirteen, for a competition organized by a school newspaper. Danzig was annexed by the Nazis immediately after the outbreak of World War II. At sixteen, before he had graduated from secondary school, he was drafted as a Luftwaffe auxiliary, wounded, and sent to an American prisoner-of-war camp in Bavaria. Released in the spring of 1946, but far from home, he worked as a farm laborer and potash miner in West Germany.

*gräs

In 1947 he resumed his schooling in Göttingen, but soon lost interest and apprenticed himself to a stonemason in Düsseldorf, for whom he made tombstones. In 1949 he entered the Düsseldorf Academy of Art, where he studied painting and sculpture, working at night as a jazz drummer and writing poetry and dramatic sketches in his spare time. In 1951 he traveled in Italy, and he visited France the following year. Disliking the postwar materialism of Düsseldorf, Grass in 1953 went to West Berlin, where he studied sculpture with Karl Hartung at the Berlin Academy of Art. In 1954 he married Anna Schwarz, a Swiss dancer.

A year later some poems, submitted by his wife without his knowledge, won a prize in a competition sponsored by a radio station. Grass's work began to appear in literary magazines, and he became a member of Gruppe 47. *Die Vorzüge der Windhühner*, his first book of poems, was published in 1956; another collection, illustrated like the first with his own drawings, followed in 1960. Poems from both collections were translated by Christopher Middleton and Michael Hamburger in Grass's *Selected Poems* (1965). Surrealist in technique but satirical in intention, full of puns and wordplays, Grass's verse was placed in "the great Anglo-German tradition of (serious) 'nonsense' poetry." A. Alvarez wrote: "In his erratic, joky way he catches whatever bad dreams still haunt modern Germany and gives them a certain threatening coherence."

Beginning in 1956, a number of Grass's plays were produced in avant-garde theatres in Germany. He was regarded at first as a dramatist in the "Absurd" tradition, and Martin Esslin compared his "violent and grotesque" plays to paintings by Bosch or Goya. His best-known plays in this mode are *Onkel, Onkel* (1957, translated as *Mister, Mister*), about a would-be murderer who fails miserably to inspire fear; and *Die Bösen Köche* (1957, translated as *The Wicked Cooks*), an interesting if mystifying religious allegory in the form of a poetic tragicomedy.

It was however Grass's first novel which established his reputation in Germany and abroad. *Die Blechtrommel* was written in Paris, where Grass and his family lived from 1956 to 1958 on a small allowance from his publisher, Hermann Luchterhand. Grass's reading of extracts from the book won him the Gruppe 47 prize in 1958, and more honors followed its publication in December 1959. *Die Blechtrommel* has been translated into most major languages and was a best seller in Germany,

France, and the United States. Its much-praised English version, *The Tin Drum*, was by Ralph Manheim, who also translated Grass's subsequent novels. *Die Blechtrommel* is a huge and exuberantly grotesque picaresque novel, mixing fairy-tale fantasy and detailed realism, in the tradition of Grimmelshausen and Rabelais. It surveys the Nazi era through the eyes of Oskar Matzerath, who grows up in Danzig with a background much like Grass's own, and who contemplates the horror and wickedness of his time and place with the playful air of astonishment which distinguishes Grass's verse. Oskar is not Grass, however, but a precocious, demoniacal, and sometimes pathetic dwarf who deliberately stopped growing at the age of three, who can precisely evoke the past by pounding on his toy drum, who has many magical talents, and a special but ambiguous relationship to the Christ child. The publication of *Die Blechtrommel* established Grass as a major writer, but a controversial one. In Germany and abroad, some critics were daunted by the sheer bulk of the book, and more disliked Grass's irreverent treatment of religion, political ideology, and romantic love. Grass is a Roman Catholic, brought up "between the Holy Ghost and photographs of Hitler," who cannot forgive his church its failure to make an unequivocal stand against National Socialism; his blasphemies are inseparable from his incomparably rich and vivid evocation of the Nazi era. As for ideology, his deflation of the semireligious pretensions of National Socialism has served, as he says, to "de-demonize" it. In all of his novels, Grass excels at the imaginative recreation of childhood, and this includes those curious erotic fantasies, cruelties, and perversities which offend some of his readers.

Katz und Maus (1961, translated as *Cat and Mouse*) was a shorter, neater, and less ambitious work, a *novelle* about a Danzig boy set apart from his peers by his grotesquely large Adam's apple. Joachim Mahlke becomes an athlete and a hero, but even as "the Great Mahlke" cannot win acceptance by his small-minded contemporaries.

Grass's third novel was on the scale of his first, and covered roughly the same historical period. *Hundejahre* (1963) was translated as *The Dog Years.* Michael Ratcliffe wrote that it leaves the reader feeling "he has read a history of modern Germany when in fact he has read a history of young people and dogs." The young people are Walter Matern and the half-Jewish Eddi Amsel, a creator of marvelous scarecrows. Their relationship, alternating between brotherhood and betrayal, is traced from 1917 to 1957. At the same time the book follows the fortunes of a line of Alsatian dogs, culminating in Prinz, Hitler's favorite. John Simon and others have shown that

GÜNTER GRASS

Hundejahre is also "about the German language," full of parodies of many different kinds of linguistic attitudinizing—of Heidegger and Nazi German, for example, in the magnificent scene in which a great military operation is launched in an attempt to recover Prinz, who has defected in disgust from the bunker. The book lacks a cohesive central figure of the caliber of Oskar, but was thought a technical advance over *The Tin Drum*, harnessing Grass's prodigious comic inventiveness more effectively to his satirical purpose. One section of the novel has been adapted by Grass as the scenario for a ballet, *The Scarecrows*, with music by Aribert Reimann.

In the West German elections of 1965 Grass emerged as a tireless, forceful, and brilliant campaigner for Willy Brandt and the Social Democratic Party. *Über das Selbstverständliche*, a collection of Grass's political speeches and writings, has been translated as *Speak Out!* This decisive political commitment has affected all of his subsequent work in ways which have been welcomed by some critics, deplored by others.

Ausgefragt (1967), a collection of poems written mostly in 1966, was translated by Michael Hamburger as *New Poems*, and found considerably less witty and playful than his earlier verse—a bitterly ironical "poet's diary throughout a year of self-inquiry and reaction to personal and political perplexities." Grass's play *Die Plebejer proben den Aufstand* (1966, translated as *The Plebeians Rehearse the Uprising*) is a controversial but more or less naturalistic attack on Bertolt Brecht's ambivalent attitude during the East German workers' uprising of 1953. Brecht is pilloried as an equivocating intellectual, failing to give the workers the voice and leadership they desperately need, and instead picking their brains for ideas that will lend authenticity to his adaptation of *Coriolanus*; most critics thought that the play embodied but never fully enacted a brilliant theatrical idea.

Another play, *Davor*, which had an unsuccessful production in Berlin in 1969, introduced a theme explored more thoroughly in the novel *Örtlich betäubt* (1969, translated as *Local Anaesthetic*). It is set in West Berlin in the complacent present. Starusch is a high school teacher, a decent liberal whose prize pupil Scherbaum proposes to douse his pet dachshund with gasoline and immolate him outside a café popular with bourgeois ladies. The dog-loving ladies are to be made to gag on their cream cakes and perhaps to think a little about the propriety of burning human beings in Vietnam. Starusch's problem—what to do about the proposed demonstration—is compounded by his relationships with his war-obsessed fiancée, a guilt-obsessed female colleague, and his dentist, a formidable amateur dialectician and a champion of the new technology. The story is told through Starusch's reflections and fantasies as he sits in his dentist's chair, his thoughts darting from place to place and person to person, merging with what he sees on the dentist's television set, and counterpointed by an imaginary dialogue with the dentist himself. Some readers missed the Rabelaisian imagination and linguistic exuberance of the earlier novels, while acknowledging that Grass had gone on, as one critic wrote, "to tackle problems which evidently and perhaps necessarily hamper his performance"; others welcomed the clean and sharp language of *Local Anaesthetic*, and had nothing but praise for a book which, as one wrote, "gives a new dimension to the old stream of consciousness device" and in which, "as in music, every part modulates every other part." A stage version by Grass of the story (it is not clear whether this is *Davor* or a different treatment) has been translated by A. Leslie Wilson and Ralph Manheim, and was produced in 1972 by the Arena Stage in Washington, D.C., as *Uptight*. This has been published as *Max*. Another adaptation, drawing on both *Davor* and the novel, and made by Christopher Holmes, was broadcast the same year by the BBC in England as *Local Anaesthetic*.

Günter Grass lives in West Berlin with his wife and four children. He has received many literary awards including the Büchner Prize (1965) and the Theodor Heuss Prize (1969). Soft-spoken and mild in manner, he is broad-shouldered and square-jawed, with dark eyes and a notable moustache. He has given lectures and readings in universities and elsewhere in Germany and in many foreign countries including the United States, and there have been exhibitions of his graphic work in Bremen, Berlin, and New York. Grass is *persona non grata* in East Germany, and also has many enemies among right-wing elements in West Berlin, who alternately threaten his life and seek to ban his works. George Steiner has said of him that he "has had the nerve, the indispensable tactlessness to evoke the past [and] has rubbed the noses of his readers in the great filth . . . of their time." Grass campaigned for the SPD as devotedly in the 1969 German elections as in 1965, and afterwards published *Aus dem Tagebuch einer Schnecke* (1972, *From the Diary of a Snail*), in which, addressing himself to his children, he discourses and fantasizes (at times a little self-consciously) about himself, his family, his electioneering experiences, and much else, including the unavoidably snail-like pace of the progress of democracy.

PRINCIPAL WORKS IN ENGLISH TRANSLATION: *Fiction*—The Tin Drum, 1962; Cat and Mouse, 1963; The Dog Years, 1965; Local Anaesthetic, 1970. *Poetry*—Selected Poems, 1965; New Poems, 1968. *Plays*—The Plebeians Rehearse the Uprising: A German Tragedy, 1966; Four Plays (Flood; Mister, Mister; Only Ten Minutes to Buffalo; The Wicked Cooks), 1967; Max, 1972. *Miscellaneous*—Speak Out! Speeches, Open Letters, Commentaries, 1969; From the Diary of a Snail, 1973.

ABOUT: Arnold, H. L. and Gortz, F. J. (eds.) Günter Grass: Dokumente zur politischen Wirkung, 1971; Cunliffe, W. G. Günter Grass, 1969; Current Biography, 1964; Enzensberger, H. M. Einzelheiten, 1962; Esslin, M. The Theater of the Absurd, 1962; Hamburger, M. From Prophecy to Exorcism, 1965; Loschütz, G. (ed.) Von Buch zu Buch: Günter Grass in der Kritik, 1968; Schwarz, W. J. Der Erzähler Günter Grass, 1969; Who's Who, 1972; Who's Who in America, 1972–1973. *Periodicals*—Commentary May 1964; New York Times Magazine May 8, 1966; Observer January 2, 1966; Times Literary Supplement January 20, 1966; September 25, 1969; December 22, 1972.

GRAU, SHIRLEY ANN (July 8, 1929–), American novelist and short story writer, writes: "What can I say about myself? I dislike intensely having to say anything. I am not introspective, first of all. And secondly I don't regard myself as an object of particular interest. Background? My grandfather fled Prussia and came to this country in time for the Civil War; he apparently never said why he left and made no attempt to keep in touch with his family. Some political reason, I suppose. The other side of my family is the classic American mixture of English, Scotch and Irish. We were in North Carolina in the 1740s and Virginia in the 1720s. We were, in another branch, in Massachusetts and Rhode Island a couple of generations earlier. My mother could have told you much more; I frankly have never paid any attention to family, since none of them were very interesting. I grew up with the usual family stories of births and wars and killing, of Indians and feuds. I have the two strains—New England and southern—that were careful to preserve a sense of family continuity.

"I lead a completely conventional, and very comfortable life. I'm married to a teacher in New Orleans. I have three children, two boys and a girl, a large house, steady streams of visitors. I spend my summers on Martha's Vineyard because my husband likes the ocean. I myself like to swim and walk and play tennis and sail. I hate cards and other pastimes, because I have no time to waste.

"I regard writing as a craft, as something to be worked at very hard. I think I have something to say, though I would be hard put to express it in abstract words. I have a world view that I can express in terms of my fiction, if you care to put it that way.

"My future plans? I hope to go on writing novels and short stories and perhaps an occasional piece of reporting. I hope to have another child or two. In any case I look for the future eagerly, because it seems to me that each succeeding year of my life has been more interesting, more exciting. Simply put, I am a happy and contented woman, and that's rather dull, I'm afraid—at least for other people, not for me."

Shirley Ann Grau, one of the two daughters of Adolph and Katherine (Onions) Grau, was born in New Orleans. She was educated at the Booth School in Montgomery, Alabama, and at Newcomb College, Tulane University, in her native city, where she played no games and joined no organizations but had "a splendid, if not intellectual time." It was intellectual enough, nevertheless, for Miss Grau to receive her B.A. in 1950 with honors in English. After a year's graduate work at Tulane, she settled down to writing.

Her first book was the collection of stories about white and black bayou people called *The Black Prince*. It was greeted by *Time* magazine as "the most impressive U.S. short story debut between hard covers since J. D. Salinger's *Nine Stories*," and with scarcely less enthusiasm by other reviewers. Several of them expressed relief that these stories about the South had "no truck with Southern Gothic"—that they recorded "frustration and violence and death" but also "serenity, achievement, and life." Riley Hughes wrote in *Catholic World* that Miss Grau had "caught the authentic slur of speech, the slant of shadow on a blue night, and the random, spiraling movement of life."

Discarding her first novel, Miss Grau published her second, *The Hard Blue Sky*, a long book about a Franco-Spanish island community at the mouth of the Mississippi. Virginia Kirkus found in this "island world . . . a somnolent fascination" and thought that "the vitality and violence" of its people had been "retained and reflected with a very

SHIRLEY ANN GRAU

realistic but unquestionable lyricism." Many critics, however, called the novel shapeless and plotless and recommended a return to the short story. This advice was wasted on Miss Grau, who does not read her reviews and persisted in writing novels. *The House on Coliseum Street* examines the effects of an abortion upon a young woman living with her family in New Orleans—her "slow withdrawal from bewilderment into silence and hatred." It was received with even less enthusiasm than its predecessor—praised indeed for its plotting and for its style, which enfolds the reader in "the sights and smells, the heat, humidity and decay of New Orleans," but dismissed by most reviewers as melodramatic, contrived, and insignificant.

Undaunted by all this, or unaware of it, Miss Grau obstinately wrote another novel and won the Pulitzer Prize. *The Keepers of the House*, set in the southern Delta country, centers on a segregationist politician's ambitious wife whose grandfather, it emerges, had contracted an interracial marriage. There was almost universal praise for the novel's dramatic force, its vigorous characterization, and what F. C. Crews called Miss Grau's "lucidity, her narrative directness, her reliance on the bare details of her plot instead of on ponderous philosophizing." Granville Hicks said that "all the virtues of Miss Grau's earlier books are here, together with a new power. I think it is her best novel."

The Condor Passes, which followed after a longish interval (and the birth of a fourth child), is a Louisiana family chronicle spanning three generations. It records the accumulation and eventual disposal of a great fortune, built on brothels and bootlegging by the ancient patriarch whose death gives the book its focal point. It was generally admired, especially for the author's ability to write with equal authority from the viewpoints of a very large and assorted cast of characters, but seemed to some reviewers an unaccountable expenditure of talent on an overly familiar theme.

Miss Grau is a meticulous stylist who says that she rewrites everything at least three times but has no cause and no message: "I've always thought writing was lots of fun, and I still do." Miss Grau, who is of medium height, has green eyes and black hair. She is a Democrat and a Unitarian. Her husband, whom she married in 1955, is the writer James Kern Feibleman, professor of philosophy at Tulane University, and she shares with him "a fair record collection" and a better one of modern painting and sculpture. They now have three sons and two daughters.

PRINCIPAL WORKS: The Black Prince and Other Stories, 1955; The Hard Blue Sky, 1958; The House on Coliseum Street, 1961; The Keepers of the House, 1964; The Condor Passes, 1971; The Wind Shifting West (stories) 1973.

ABOUT: Contemporary Authors 1, 1962; Current Biography, 1959; Gossett, L. Y. Violence in Recent Southern Fiction, 1965; Vinson, J. (ed.) Contemporary Novelists, 1972; Who's Who in America, 1972–1973. *Periodicals*—Mademoiselle January 1955.

GREEN, F(REDERICK) C(HARLES) (February 25, 1891–March 23, 1964), Scottish scholar and critic, was born in Aberdeen, the only son of James and Jessie (Mathieson) Green. He attended Harris Academy in Dundee and went on to the universities of St. Andrews, Paris, and Cologne, earning advanced degrees at all three. With the outbreak of World War I in 1914, Green enlisted in the 11th Royal Scots, subsequently serving with the Royal Artillery, Trench Mortars, and the Intelligence Corps. He was wounded and won the Military Cross. In 1916 Green married Mary Gilchrist, who was to bear him two sons and two daughters. After the Armistice he remained in the Army to serve as First Intelligence Officer with the Rhine Forces in 1919–1920.

Resuming his career, Green taught for a year at Armstrong College, University of Durham, and in 1921 went to Canada as assistant professor at the University of Manitoba. His first books were published at this time. In 1925–1926 Green taught in the United States at the University of Rochester and in 1926 he became professor of French at University College, Toronto.

During his nine years at Toronto, Green established his reputation with three books of the first importance. *French Novelists, Manners and Ideas: From the Renaissance to the Revolution* discusses the evolution of the modern French novel and the two

F. C. GREEN

tendencies which have most affected its course, romanticism and realism. There was nothing but praise for the book's scholarship and its entertaining style. A reviewer in the *Times Literary Supplement* called it "a remarkable little book" which owed its distinction to the fact that Green had "grasped his subject as a whole" and was thus enabled to avoid received generalizations "and to make new and more adequate generalizations of his own." Its sequel, *French Novelists: From the Revolution to Proust*, showed the same combination of "profound knowledge" with the willingness and ability to "conceal all traces of labour." Apart from one earnest reviewer who seemed shocked by Green's "astonishingly casual and playful manner," the critics were unanimous in their praise of his erudition and enthusiasm, his "balanced mind and personal sensitiveness." *Minuet*, Green's "masterful" survey of French and English literary ideas in the eighteenth century, is one of his best-known works, a searching piece of criticism and a source to its readers of much "intelligent delight."

Green returned to England in 1935 and went to Cambridge as Drapers Professor of French and a Fellow of Magdalene College. With the outbreak of World War II in 1939 he was, though now nearing fifty, recalled by the Army. Assigned to special duties, he served, with the rank of major, until 1945. The succession of impeccable editions of French texts which Green had begun to publish in the mid-1930s continued during the war years and included Rousseau's *Discours sur l'inégalité* (1941), Prévost's *Manon Lescaut* (1942), Maupassant's *Quinze Contes* (1943), and the *Maximes* of La Rochefoucauld (1945).

After the war Green resumed his chair at Cambridge. In 1949 tribute was paid to the eminence he had now attained with his election as first president of the Association Internationale des Études Françaises. The same year he published *The Mind of Proust*, his notable study of *A la recherche du temps perdu*, which was called "a mine of information, subtle observation, and interpretation."

In 1951 Green accepted the professorship of French literature at Edinburgh University. His last major work, as deft and illuminating as his earlier publications, was his study of Jean-Jacques Rousseau. Leon Edel wrote: "The biographer is in complete command at every point. Professor Green marshals his facts with a freshness of narrative and a continual lucidity that makes him a delight to read."

Green retired from Edinburgh as Emeritus Professor of French in 1961 and died three years later at the age of seventy-three. A history of the French novel of the Second Empire, completed shortly before his death, remains unpublished. He was a Chevalier de la Légion d'Honneur, and held a number of other decorations and honors. For all his devotion to the written word, Green was never "bookish" in the sense that he substituted literature for life. On the contrary, he is remembered as a man of uncommonly shrewd insight into human behavior, an amusing companion, and an excellent raconteur. The postwar trends in criticism and literature generally had no appeal for him. He remained essentially an Edwardian, whose style, literary and personal, was deeply rooted in the modes and manners of a more urbane era.

PRINCIPAL WORKS: Robert Fergusson's Anteil an der Literatur Schottlands, 1923; La Peinture des mœurs de la bonne société dans le roman français de 1715 à 1761, 1924; French Novelists, Manners and Ideas: From the Renaissance to the Revolution, 1928; Eighteenth Century France: Six Essays, 1929; French Novelists: From the Revolution to Proust, 1931; Minuet: A Critical Survey of French and English Literary Ideas in the Eighteenth Century, 1935 (republished as Literary Ideas in Eighteenth Century France and England, 1966); Stendhal, 1939; The Mind of Proust: A Detailed Interpretation of A la Recherche du Temps Perdu, 1949; Jean-Jacques Rousseau: A Critical Study of His Life and Writings, 1955; A Comparative View of French and British Civilization (1850–1870), 1965.

ABOUT: *Periodicals*—New Statesman February 28, 1931; February 16, 1935; Saturday Review February 11, 1956; Times (London) March 26, 1964; Times Literary Supplement February 7, 1929; February 26, 1931; March 7, 1935; March 16, 1956.

GREEN, GERALD (April 8, 1922–), American novelist, memoirist, and television journalist, was born in the Brownsville section of Brooklyn, the son of Dr. Samuel Greenberg and Anna Ruth (Matzkin) Greenberg, Russian immigrants. Dr. Greenberg had worked as a stenographer and

GERALD GREEN

physical education instructor while studying at Bellevue Hospital in New York. Receiving his M.D. shortly before World War I, he opened a general practice in Brownsville and worked there for forty years as it deteriorated into a "savage" slum.

After graduating from Samuel Tilden High School in Brooklyn (1938), Gerald Green entered Columbia University, majoring in English literature and the social sciences. He edited the campus humor magazine, *The Jester*, and was elected to Phi Beta Kappa. Following graduation in 1942, he spent four years with the United States Army in England and Germany, first as an ordnance sergeant, then as a writer and director for the Armed Forces Radio Network in Bremen.

Returning after the war to Columbia, Green received an M.S. from the School of Journalism in 1947. From 1947 to 1950 he worked as night editor with the International News Service, where he met and married a fellow-employee, Marie Pomposelli. In 1950 he went to the National Broadcasting Company as one of the country's first television news writers. Apart from three freelance years (1957–1961), he has been with NBC Television ever since and has been associated as a writer, director, or producer with Dave Garroway's *Today* show, *Chet Huntley Reporting*, *Wide, Wide, World*, and many documentaries, some of them involving much travel.

Most of Green's books have been written in his spare time as an NBC employee. The first, done in collaboration with Lawrence Klingman, was *His Majesty O'Keefe*, a fictionalized biography of a swashbuckling American fugitive who became the wealthy "king" of a Micronesian island in the late nineteenth century. It was admired as "a fast, stirring narrative" and for the accuracy of its historical and anthropological detail. *The Sword and the Sun* is an equally colorful and exciting story of the conquest of Peru.

It was followed by Green's most successful novel, *The Last Angry Man*, based on his recollections of Brownsville and in particular of his father, who appears lightly disguised as Dr. Sam Abelman. Abelman is an ill-tempered, overworked, irreverent Schweitzer of the slums, who astounds the slick producers of a "Typical Americans" television series by his embarrassing refusal to conform or compromise, his intransigent adherence to an unfashionable code of ethics. Though some reviewers thought the book too wordy, and at times rather clumsily written, it was warmly praised as a rich character study and as a telling attack on contemporary values. It was selected by the Book-of-the-Month Club, condensed by *Reader's Digest*, and filmed.

In 1957, encouraged by this success, Green left NBC to freelance. *The Lotus Eaters*, an angry if rather brassy satire on the operators, publicists, and fixers of Miami Beach, was followed by another and more memorable onslaught on the communications industries. *The Hidden Light* focuses on the blind, irresponsible greed for news of the press and television reporters covering a kidnapping. This excessively long book was commended for its moral attitudes, its striking if superficial sketches of a large and mostly unsavory cast of characters, and its well-handled suspense.

In 1958, at a cocktail party on Long Island, someone called Green a "square." Conceding that the charge might be justified, Green set off with his wife and three children for the unsquare Italian Riviera. *The Portofino P.T.A.* is a rather sour but frequently very funny memoir of this jaunt. As one critic put it, the Greens found "high prices, bad wine, Ezra Pound, seedy representatives of the international set, a lack of social justice—and no P.T.A." In 1961 Green went back to NBC.

His next novel, *The Legion of Noble Christians*, is the least "square" of his books. It describes the efforts of an Irish veteran to track down, for the record, and on behalf of a rich Jewish friend, some of the Europeans who had put their lives at stake by helping Jews during World War II. Some reviewers were unimpressed by the novel's excursions into black humor, but Charles Dollen thought it "an absorbing volume that will disturb the consciences of many." *To Brooklyn With Love* is a closely autobiographical story about a middle-aged suburbanite's visit to and recollections of the Brownsville of his youth. Once again it is the complex figure of the author's father who dominates a book which the critics found uneven but moving and immensely likable. *Faking It*, a comedy about the adventures of a minor Jewish novelist at a world conference in Paris, was thought very funny and successful as a satire on the American literary establishment, less so as a parody of the spy thriller.

Gerald Green is a tall man, brown-haired and gray-eyed. He is a Democrat and belongs to the Overseas Press Club and the American Anthropological Association, among other organizations. His interest in archaeology took him in 1969 to Israel, where he visited a number of digs, interviewed famous archaeologists, and wrote a very readable and personal diary of his observations published as *The Stones of Zion*.

PRINCIPAL WORKS: *Fiction*—(with Lawrence Klingman) His Majesty O'Keefe, 1950; The Sword and the Sun, 1953; The Last Angry Man, 1957; The Lotus Eaters, 1959; The Heartless Light, 1961; The Legion of Noble Christians, or, The Sweeney Survey, 1965; To Brooklyn With Love, 1968; Faking It, 1971; Blockbuster, 1972; Tourist, 1973. *Nonfiction*—The Portofino P. T.A.,1962; The Artists of Terezin, 1969; The Stones of Zion, 1971.

ABOUT: Contemporary Authors 15–16, 1966; Who's Who in America, 1970–1971. *Periodicals*—Publishers' Weekly March 25, 1968; Wilson Library Bulletin June 1962.

GRIFFIN, (ARTHUR) GWYN (1922(?)–October 12, 1967), British novelist and short story writer of Welsh extraction, was generally considered "one of the finest storytellers of this generation." He resented and resisted personal publicity and there are conflicting versions even of his date of birth. He was born in Egypt, probably in 1922. Sent to England for his education, he returned at the age of eighteen to become a cotton planter in the Sudan. The following year, 1941, he joined an African regiment and became an intelligence officer, serving for a time in Abyssinia as cipher officer to Orde Wingate.

After the war Griffin knocked about the world in a variety of more or less adventurous occupations, as a police officer in the Sudan, for example, and as a ship's pilot in the East African port of Assab. At one point in the mid-1950s he toured southern England in a decrepit gypsy caravan, and in the course of this journey he met and married the daughter of Sir Reginald Dorman-Smith, minister of agriculture in Chamberlain's government and wartime governor of Burma. He settled down for a while and in 1956 was running an English country pub. He soon moved on again to Sydney, Australia, where he began his career as a novelist, then sampled life in the Canary Islands, and finally settled in Italy.

All of these experiences are reflected in Griffin's books, along with the violent misanthropy which drove him around the world in search of a tolerable way of life and which both animated and weakened his books. "The special quality of a Griffin novel," wrote Orville Prescott, "is its combination of three factors, each of them magnified to a superlative degree. The first is old-fashioned narrative power, a gift for storytelling which defies one not to be engrossed, defies one with almost insolent assurance. The second is a satirical distaste for most human beings and their institutions, which makes Mr. Griffin's novels seem harsh and even cruel. . . . The third is Mr. Griffin's Kiplingesque ability to soak himself in the local atmosphere of particular places and in the technical lore of particular occupations."

At first Griffin's dislike of his fellow creatures seemed to be limited to those of them who happened to be English. His first novel, *The Occupying Power*, is set in an Italian colony, "Berissa," occupied during World War II by British troops under Colonel Lemonfield, a model of integrity and rectitude. In a variety of subtle and often very funny ways, the Italian captives undermine Lemonfield's moral authority until, in an "altogether believable, if shocking, denouement," he is finally destroyed. Some characteristically bizarre touches apart, this was the most light-hearted of Griffin's novels. *By the North Gate*, set in an African colony fighting for independence, is an altogether more violent anti-British tract, "an epitaph to Colonialism, harsh in its reproof and often savage in its demonstration." The same could be said of *Sons of God*, published in America as *Something of an Achievement.*

Shipmaster was the first of Griffin's novels to attract widespread critical attention in the United States (where it was called *Master of This Vessel*). The setting is a ship carrying British immigrants to Australia. Its second-in-command is Ciccolanti, a young officer from the slums of Naples, able, ambitious, but tactless and unpopular. The crisis comes when the captain falls ill and Ciccolanti, assuming command, is faced by a kind of uprising of his stupid and vicious passengers as the ship drives into a cyclone. Many reviewers were reminded of Conrad, and there was much praise for Griffin's skill in building his complex plot to an almost unbearably powerful climax. Though some reviewers found the author's "unsparing portrayal of the ugly side of the British working class" excessively harsh, to the point of distortion and melodrama, the book was universally recognized as the work of "a born storyteller." *Freedom Observed*, another "tremendous story," is also somewhat marred by melodrama and Griffin's bigotry, directed this time against the French. *A Significant Experience*, which investigates sadism and perversion in a British army officers' training camp in Egypt, offended Honor Tracy as "a grievous libel" on the British officer class, but one which "describes with great brilliance and a tension marvelously sustained an act of sickening brutality." Six of Griffin's wonderfully taut and economical short stories, all about colonialism in Africa, were collected in *A Scorpion on a Stone.*

GWYN GRIFFIN

By the time Griffin wrote *A Last Lamp Burning* (1966), his hatred of humanity had extended to the Italians, of whom he had written so indulgently in the past. Griffin spares neither the old aristocracy of Italy, nor the greedy new bourgeoisie; the wretched poor have his pity but not his respect. Granville Hicks found the novel as thoughtful as it was readable, but some readers were less impressed, finding the story perplexing and diffuse. One wrote: "The violence is so abundant and so bizarre that at times it is hard to believe in Mr. Griffin's seriousness." There was a less equivocal critical reception for *An Operational Necessity*, about the sinking of a French freighter by a U-boat in World War II and the subsequent trial of the German officers for murdering survivors. Edward Weeks found no central character in whom "one can repose one's sympathies," but most reviewers were content with the book's realism, suspense, and intelligence, and it became a best seller.

Gwyn Griffin died in 1967 from an infection of the blood contracted in Introdacqua, the village in central Italy where he lived.

PRINCIPAL WORKS: The Occupying Power, 1956; By the North Gate, 1958; Sons of God (U.S., Something of an Achievement), 1960; Shipmaster (U.S., Master of This Vessel), 1961; Freedom Observed, 1963; A Significant Experience, 1963; A Scorpion on a Stone (stories), 1965; A Last Lamp Burning, 1966; An Operational Necessity, 1967.

ABOUT: *Periodicals*—Literary Guild Preview May 1966;

New Republic September 28, 1963; New York Times Book Review April 17, 1966; September 29, 1968; Saturday Review April 16, 1966; July 29, 1967. Times (London) October 3, 1967.

GRIFFIN, JOHN HOWARD (June 6, 1920–), American novelist, writes: "I was born in Dallas, Texas, spent my early years in Texas, my adolescence in France, war years in France and the Pacific, postwar years in Texas, Europe, Mexico. My parents are of Pennsylvania Dutch and Georgia backgrounds. My mother studied to be a concert pianist, so we grew up with good music in our lives.

"Sometime in my fourteenth year, the famed pianist Moritz Rosenthal gave a concert in our area. My interests were largely oriented toward science —I wanted to study medicine eventually. Reading a newspaper account of Rosenthal's background, however, opened me up to a far more fascinating horizon. I learned that he, like Schweitzer, had got degrees in medicine and philosophy and was in addition an eminent musician. I decided simply to devote my life to learning and let later developments come as they would in the way of a career or vocation.

"My parents allowed me to go to France to finish my high school and future educational work. There I attended the Lycée Descartes in Tours and the École de Médecine de Tours. I read voraciously in literature, the sciences and philosophy. In medicine, my interests drifted toward psychiatry. I became assistant to Dr. Pierre Fromenty at the Asylum of Tours and did my extern work under him, specializing in the development of therapy based on the physics of sound.

"With the beginning of World War II in 1939, all doctors were conscripted into the French army. I found myself, with no degrees, and 'unconscriptable' as an American citizen, placed in charge of the Asylum. I also became involved in smuggling Jewish refugees from Germany, through France, to England. We were poorly organized and often unsuccessful. The tragedy of our failures, the human tragedy of families whose lives touched mine and who were then caught and sent back to Germany to the extermination camps. I discovered man, after years of dealing with man only in an intellectual context. I think I was fortunate in discovering man so early.

"I returned to the U.S., into the Air Force and to the Pacific for thirty-nine months. At the point of embarkation I left my clothing and filled my duffel bags with books on philosophy and musicology and with musical scores for analysis. My years overseas were years of study.

"After the war, with severely impaired vision from head wounds, I went back to France to continue my studies. With a prognosis of total blindness in the near future, I abandoned my medical studies and concentrated on musicological ones, working with Nadia Boulanger and Abbé Pierre Froger in Tours and Paris, then proceeding to the famed Benedictine Abbey of Solesmes, seat of Gregorian learning, where I worked in the Paléographie Musicale on Gregorian Chant and early keyboard music. There, too, I began much more formalized studies of philosophy, with specialized attention to anthropology.

JOHN HOWARD GRIFFIN

"With total loss of sight, I left the Benedictines of Solesmes and returned for training at the schools for the blind in America. Here, I was able to continue my studies in philosophy with the Discalced Carmelites, and with the special help of Jacques Maritain.

"I continued these studies for eleven years with the help and guidance of the Basilian Fathers in Canada, and began writing books. My hope was to treat in the form of the novel the great philosophical themes that escape most men who do not read the language of philosophical and theological speculation; but to do this only as the framework and to avoid the 'message' novel or *roman à thèse*.

"In 1953 I married Elizabeth Ann Holland of Mansfield, Texas. We had two children when, in 1957, my vision was partly restored. I saw my wife and children for the first time, and I saw the world for the first time in eleven years. We have since then had two more children.

"As a southerner, I became increasingly tormented by the similarity of our racist attitudes and rationalizations to those I had encountered in Nazi Germany. I began to do studies dealing with the problems and patterns of racism. In 1959, convinced that we were making little progress in resolving the terrible tragedy of racism in America—a tragedy for the white racist as well as for the Negro (and other) victim groups, I had myself medically transformed into a Negro and lived in the states of Louisiana, Mississippi, Alabama and Georgia. The journals of this devastating personal experience were published as the book *Black Like Me*. Since that time, my life has become more deeply involved in the problems of racism and most of my lecturing, writing and teaching have dealt with these problems."

Griffin's first novel takes its title from a French proverb: "The devil rides outside monastery walls." It is in effect an account of an exorcism, in which a young American, studying Gregorian music in a French monastery, obsessed and possessed by sex, is brought slowly and painfully to redemption by the influence and example of the dedicated celibates around him. The novel, which obviously draws on the author's own life, became in turn an important part of his experience, since, as he says, "in the course of it I wrote my way into the Church." Crudely written and poorly organized as it is, *The Devil Rides Outside* is "brutal in its intensity, visceral in its images of flesh." Full of faults, it has "the power of life itself."

Nuni, which followed four years later, is a product of Griffin's wartime studies in the Pacific. It is about an American college professor, "a typical family man" who is deposited by a plane crash on a remote Pacific island. The novel describes his struggle, as much spiritual as physical, to come to terms with a tribal society so formalized and ritualized that the capacity for love has almost been destroyed. As one critic pointed out, it is "an allegory really, of man's struggle to fulfill himself in the largest sense that religious faith allows." Some reviewers thought it overwritten, and many were irritated by the fact that it is narrated throughout in the present tense. Once again, however, praise outweighed blame, and most critics seemed fascinated by the book's anthropological content and gripped by its "immense narrative interest." In Maxwell Geismar's opinion, it established Griffin as "the most original young American writer today."

In 1959, as he says, two years after he recovered his sight, Griffin undertook an extraordinary assignment for *Sepia* magazine, disguising himself as a Negro and traveling for six weeks in the Deep South. His experience of hostility and racial discrimination, first recorded in *Sepia*, attracted international attention (and led to Griffin's being burned in effigy in his home town). His articles were published in book form as *Black Like Me*, which received *Saturday Review*'s 1961 Anisfield-Wolf award. Griffin's flat and artless account, it was said, "carried a shock and a poignancy which statistics obscure." A film version was released in 1964.

The John Howard Griffin Reader, published in 1968, includes short stories, articles, and excerpts from all his books. It is illustrated with the author's own photographs. In his introduction Maxwell Geismar, who has championed Griffin's work from the beginning, spoke of him as "a Texas Balzac" and said: "There is nothing of the safe, the innocuous, the formalistic or the mediocre in John Howard Griffin's work, or in him."

PRINCIPAL WORKS: The Devil Rides Outside, 1952; Nuni, 1956; Land of the High Sky, 1959; Black Like Me, 1961; The John Howard Griffin Reader, 1968; The Church and the Black Man, 1969; (with others) A Part of Space: Ten Texas Writers, 1969; (as compiler) A Hidden Wholeness: The Visual World of Thomas Merton (selection of Merton's photographs), 1970.

ABOUT: Contemporary Authors 1st revision 1–4, 1967; Current Biography, 1960; Geismar, M. American Moderns, 1958; Who's Who in America, 1970–1971. *Periodicals*—Time January 21, 1957; March 28, 1960; Wilson Library Bulletin May 1963.

***GUILLÉN, JORGE** (January 18, 1893–), Spanish poet, was born in Valladolid, Castile, and received his secondary education there. He subsequently studied with the French Fathers of the Oratory in Freiburg and at the universities of Madrid and Granada. In 1917 he left Spain to continue his studies and begin his teaching career at the Sorbonne in Paris. His first poems were written in 1919. ("Why had I never written before that? Because I never dared. But from time to time I would say to my friends, 'I'd give anything to write a book of verse.' Even then I was thinking about a single work with an organic unity.")

In 1923 Guillén returned to Spain. His poems began to appear in reviews, and his promise was soon recognized. At the same time he was making a career for himself as a specialist in Spanish literature, and he has since taught or lectured in Spain, Germany, Italy, England, Mexico, Chile, Puerto Rico, the United States, and Canada. He was Professor of Spanish Literature at Seville from 1931 to 1938 when, with the fall of the Spanish Republic, he left Europe and settled in the United States. He taught for seventeen years at Wellesley before his retirement in 1957, and he has also lectured at Middlebury, Harvard, Berkeley, Ohio State, and Yale.

Guillén belongs to the great Spanish literary generation that included Lorca, Cernuda, and Alberti. He has written that, coming of age in the 1920s, "all of us turned out to be, quite unintentionally, as up-to-date as our contemporaries in Europe and America. Our strongest feelings were

* gē lyen′

JORGE GUILLÉN

in tune with the general atmosphere of the 1920s, though at the same time we echoed a purely Spanish tradition." Many critics have noted the example of Juan Ramón Jiménez in Guillén's concern to achieve by distillation a poetry of total purity, but they also see in his classical Spanish rhythms and packed metaphors the influence of Góngora and his contemporaries. No doubt Guillén also learned from Paul Valéry, whom he knew, and of whose "Le Cimetière marin" he made a fine translation.

At any rate, these influences were already assimilated to the service of a unique vision by the time he published his first book in 1928. This was *Cántico* (Song), a volume of seventy-five lyrics which had been the product of a decade of painful labor. There was an expanded edition of *Cántico* in 1936, and another in 1945. The final edition of 1950 contained 334 lyrics, the later poems indistinguishable in style and mood from the earliest.

The subtitle and theme of *Cántico* is "affirmation of life." These poems are full of the archetypal images of opening, awakening, flowering, union, harmony, and light. The life the poet celebrates is that of the real world—of human love, and the beauties of nature, of man at one with a well-made universe. All that is dark and disordered is ignored. J. M. Cohen has spoken of the "deceptive transparency" of these poems: "white seems to be laid on white, mirror to reflect mirror"; Ernst Robert Curtius called them "cataracts of light"; and F. A. Pleak writes of "the serenity of Jorge Guillén's contemplation of limited units of space, his feeling for structural content, for density and outline, oriented with exactness in space."

Guillén's concern is not to describe the objects of his delight, but rather to seize and fix forever the moment of apprehension. Blake wrote: "He who bends to himself a Joy / Doth the wingèd life destroy; / But he who kisses the Joy as it flies / Lives in Eternity's sunrise." Guillén, on the contrary, seeks to "live in Eternity's sunrise" by capturing Joy on the wing.

It follows that Guillén's poetry (like Valéry's) makes great use of the present tense. Some of his lyrics are almost verbless exclamations of pleasure, as in this poem, translated by Patricia Terry as "Beyond," in which (again like Valéry), the poet watches himself awakening from sleep to the apprehension of beauty: "(Now to the body the soul / Returns, moving toward the eyes, / Makes contact.) Light! I by my whole / Being invaded. Wonder! // Intact it is, enormous, / Prowling time . . . Abruptly, / Noises. How they leap / Over the not yet // Sharp-bladed yellows / Of a sun now gentle / With its dawning rays / Through the room diffused, // While the substantial / Begins to appear / Which, disposed in things, / Will limit, center me! // And the chaos? Far away / From its source, I receive / Out of the turbulence of light / These chips of coolness. Day! . . ."

In 1949 Guillén revisited Spain and there conceived the darker poems which complement *Cántico* and were eventually published in *Maremágnum* (Pandemonium, 1957), *Que van a dar en la mar* (That Flow Into the Sea, 1960) and *A la altura de las circunstancias* (To Rise to the Occasions, 1963). In this trilogy, whose overall title is *Clamor*, the poet deliberately turns away from the absolute and timeless to acknowledge the existence of "chance and disorder, evil and pain, time and death." He writes specifically of the Spanish war, of his own flight from Europe, of the violence he found in the New World. The note of hope remains, but joy is now to be perceived only through a cloud of obstacles and pain. Even here, however, there is no loss of control. As in *Cántico*, to quote a critic in the *Times Literary Supplement*, "The language is purified to the point of being univocal. Strong verbs and nouns shoulder out weak adjectives and pronouns. Feeling is concentrated in exclamations."

Homenaje (Homage, 1967) represents the union of life's darkness and light. It is in part a literary voyage through history, paying homage to the world's great writers. The enthusiastic affirmation that had paled in *Clamor* re-emerges. The ordinary realities are accepted into these poems, but life is so fully lived that there remains no margin for the fear of death, which is accepted without grief or bitterness. The volume contains a section of new and marvelously fresh love lyrics addressed to Guillén's second wife, whom he married in the early 1960s.

Guillén celebrated his seventy-fifth birthday by bringing all his work together in a single volume, *Aire nuestro* (1968). He continues to write and to lecture as a visiting professor. Among his critical works, the most notable is *Language and Poetry*, an expanded version (in English) of his 1957–1958 Charles Eliot Norton lectures at Harvard. Since the death of Jiménez, Guillén has been widely regarded as the greatest living Spanish poet.

PRINCIPAL WORKS IN ENGLISH TRANSLATION: *Poetry*—Cántico: A Selection, ed. by Norman Thomas di Giovanni, 1965; Affirmation: A Bilingual Anthology, 1919–1966, tr. by Julian Palley, 1968; Luminous Reality: The Poetry of Jorge Guillén, ed. by I. Ivask and J. Marichal, 1969. *Poems in* Barnstone, W. (ed.) Modern European Poetry, 1966; Burnshaw, S. (ed.) The Poem Itself, 1960; Cohen, J. M. (ed.) Penguin Book of Spanish Verse, 1956; Turnbull, E. L. Contemporary Spanish Poetry, 1945. *Criticism*—Language and Poetry: Some Poets of Spain, 1961.

ABOUT: Casalduero, J. Cántico de Jorge Guillén, 1953; Cohen, J. M. Poetry of This Age, 1966; Curley, D. N. and Curley, A. Modern Romance Literatures (A Library of Literary Criticism), 1967; Darmangeat, P. Jorge Guillén, 1958; Dennin, E. Cántico de Jorge Guillén, 1969; Gil de Biedma, J. El mundo y la poesía de Jorge Guillén, 1960; González Muela, J. La realidad y Jorge Guillén, 1962; Gullón, R. and Blecua, J. M. La poesía de Jorge Guillén, 1949; Ivask, I. and Marichal, J. (eds.) Luminous Reality: The Poetry of Jorge Guillén, 1969; Lind, G. R. Jorge Guillén's Cántico, 1955; Pleak, F. A. The Poetry of Jorge Guillén, 1942; Trend, J. B. Jorge Guillén, 1952. *Periodicals*—Books Abroad Winter 1969; Comparative Literature Summer 1961; Hispanic Review July 1962, April 1966; Modern Language Quarterly March 1963; New York Times Book Review June 20, 1965; August 18, 1968; Poetry May 1957, January 1962; Publication of the Modern Languages Association October 1966; Times Literary Supplement April 22, 1965; September 12, 1968; Virginia Quarterly Review Autumn 1965.

***GUILLÉN, NICOLÁS** (July 10, 1902–), Cuban poet, was born of mixed Spanish and Negro blood in Camagüey, Cuba. His father, a veteran of the Cuban war of independence of 1898, had entered politics and journalism and was eventually to become a liberal senator (1908–12) and finally a liberal martyr, the victim of political assassination in 1917.

In order to help his widowed mother, Nicolás Guillén took odd jobs from the age of fifteen and attended evening classes in Camagüey. In 1920 he traveled for the first time to Havana in order to read law at the university, and for the next few years he experienced a life of often adventurous bohemian poverty. A few of his early poems appeared in magazines.

In 1928 he was commissioned to write articles for the *Diario de la marina* which, although a conservative paper, allowed him to express his views about the need for the racial and cultural integration of Cuba. The time was one of growing interest

NICOLÁS GUILLÉN

in Negro culture in the Caribbean, just as it was one of increasing concern for the disappearing Indian cultures in mainland Latin America. In Cuba, the phenomenon of *negrismo*, or Afro-Cubanism, seems to have had literary rather than social and political roots and to have been inspired in part at least by the European vogue for African and primitive art. A great deal of the *negrismo* poetry of the 1930s accordingly stressed the primitive, the sensual, and the exotic in Negro dance and ritual, rather than the Negro's humanity, or his needs. To this rule Guillén, the greatest of the Afro-Cuban poets, was an exception, partly no doubt because of his own mixed blood: "Shadows that only I can see / my two grandfathers go with me, / . . . Federico / Fecundo. They both embrace. / They both sigh. They both / raise their proud heads / under the high stars; / both of the same stature."

In 1930, stimulated by the visit to Cuba of the black North American poet Langston Hughes, Guillén sat down to write in one hectic session a cycle of poems called "Motivos de son" (*Son* Themes), in which the rhythms and mood of an Afro-Cuban dance known as the *son* were reproduced in poetic descriptions of life in the poor quarters of Havana. By capturing the rhythms of Africanized Spanish and allowing them freely to blend into his verse, Guillén created a new type of throbbing, hallucinated poetry in Spanish which was soon to make him famous.

Not quickly enough, though, to have his first collection of verse, *Sóngaro cosongo*, published in orthodox fashion: the publication in 1931 of this, his most famous book, was financed solely by his opportune winning of three thousand pesos in

* gē yän'

the lottery. In *Sóngaro cosongo* (which included the "Motivos de son" cycle), he couched, in the African rhythm and Africanized vocabulary of the *son*, a fervent appeal for the mulatto, the man of black and white descent who, with his "Cuban color," should be the future hero of the island. Many of the poems are purely descriptive—of Negro dances and customs—and many rely entirely on onomatopoeic effects and rhythm. The naïve, beautiful, nonsensical imagery of *Sóngaro cosongo* has often been compared to the poetry of Federico García Lorca.

With the advent of the brutal Machado dictatorship in the early 1930s, Guillén's work became increasingly political and militant. *West Indies Ltd.* (1934) and *Cuentos para soldados y sones para turistas* (Stories for Soldiers and *Sons* for Tourists, 1937), though again in the rhythms of Negro music, were solidly anti-imperialist in content. "Take your bread, do not beg for it," he says to the Negro; "Take your light, take your definite hope / Like a horse by the bridle."

In 1937, too, he published his *España* (Spain), a long elegiac poem inspired by the Spanish republic. The same year, he attended, at the invitation of Pablo Neruda, the Second International Congress of Writers held in Valencia and Madrid. Like his friend Neruda, he was led by the experience of the Spanish Civil War to join the Communist party. During World War II Guillén lived in Cuba, but in 1945 he embarked on a long odyssey around Latin America, staying months in each country, writing prolifically, and eventually including in *El son entero* (The Entire *Son*, 1947—a vast anthology of his works to date) many new poems in celebration of what he saw.

Batista came to power in Cuba in 1952 and Guillén, still abroad, was not able to return. The next six years were a time of bitterness, the last three of them spent in Paris. His poems of this time, in particular those of *La paloma de vuelo popular* (1958), were almost exclusively dedicated to political protest against the dictatorship. He received the Lenin Peace Prize in 1954.

Nicolás Guillén returned to Cuba on January 20, 1959, nineteen days after the triumph of Fidel Castro. In 1961 he was elected president of the Cuban Union of Writers and Artists (UNEAC), and since then he has played the role of cultural father to the Cuban people.

Guillén is the most widely known of Cuban poets, and his decades of commitment have been handsomely recognized by the revolution. Curiously, however, although he is revered by most Cuban writers, his influence on the younger generation of poets has been unexpectedly slight.

PRINCIPAL WORKS IN ENGLISH TRANSLATION: Cuba Libre, ed. by Langston Hughes and B. F. Carruthers, 1948; Man-making Words: Selected Poems, tr. by Robert Márquez and David McMurray, 1972; Patria o Muerte: The Great Zoo and Other Poems, ed. and tr. by Robert Márquez, 1972. *Poems in* Caracciolo-Trejo, E. (ed.) Penguin Book of Latin-American Verse, 1971; Cohen, J. M. (ed.) The Penguin Book of Spanish Verse, 1956; Fitts, D. (ed.) Anthology of Contemporary Latin American Poetry, 1942; Hays, H. R. (ed.) Twelve Spanish American Poets, 1943.
ABOUT: Anderson-Imbert, E. Spanish American Literature, 1963; Augier, A. Nicolás Guillén, 1962; Coulthard, G. R. Race and Colour in Caribbean Literature, 1962; International Who's Who, 1973–1974; Moore, G. Seven African Writers, 1968.

GUIMARÃES ROSA, JOÃO. *See* ROSA, JOÃO GUIMARÃES

***GÜIRALDES, RICARDO (GUILLERMO)** (February 13, 1886–October 8, 1927); Argentinian novelist, short story writer, and poet, was born in Buenos Aires into a wealthy and distinguished family of Spanish origin. His father, Don Manuel Güiraldes, was at one time mayor of Buenos Aires. Most of the writer's short life was divided between the family ranch (La Porteña), Buenos Aires, and Paris. He was first taken to Europe at the age of two, and when he returned four years later he spoke French and German as fluently as Spanish. He had his early education from governesses and tutors and attended the Colegio Lacordaire in Buenos Aires from the age of twelve. A complement to his early reading in French was the work of the innovating Nicaraguan modernist poet Rubén Darío.

In his early twenties Güiraldes made a two-year journey around the world and settled for a time in Europe. It was his notable achievement to introduce the tango into Parisian society (where his tall, handsome figure found much favor). He returned to Buenos Aires in 1912 and married Adelina del Carril, who was later to become the wife of the Chilean poet Pablo Neruda.

In Paris Güiraldes had been much influenced by Jules Laforgue and numbered Léon-Paul Fargue and Valéry Larbaud among his close friends. The latter was one of the first to distinguish the two strains that dominate Güiraldes' work, the aesthetic and the pastoral, and Güiraldes, in a letter to Larbaud, wrote: "In Europe the problem consists in seeing things through the prism of an interesting temperament. Many writers torture their wits looking for new forms. But here [in Argentina] the secret would be to forget all about European research and allow the native themes themselves to create in your writing the natural and adequate forms to express them."

The dichotomy in Güiraldes' work is exemplified in the two books he published in 1915: *El cencerro de cristal* (The Glass Cowbell), a volume of

* gwē räl′ dās

poetry in the manner of Laforgue; and *Cuentos de muerte y de sangre* (Tales of Death and Blood), which deal mainly with Argentinian ranch life. In "Al rescoldo" (Embers), the gaucho Don Segundo Sombra appears for the first time to narrate a tall tale of the pampas. But storytelling is less important in this book than the metaphorical and rhythmical poetic prose in which it is written.

Güiraldes' three novels all deal with members of the ranch-owning family of Galván, based no doubt on his own. *Raucho* (1917) is clearly autobiographical, an account of the experiences on the ranch, at school in Buenos Aires, and then in Paris, of Raucho Galván, son of the wealthy Don Leandro. The destructive pleasures and alluring sophistication of Paris are contrasted with the placidly simple and salutary life of the Argentinian plains. *Xamaïca* (Jamaica, 1923) records Marcos Galván's impressions on a voyage to Jamaica, during which he falls in love with a fellow-passenger. It is in fact less a novel than a lyrical travel memoir.

All of these early works are principally of interest for the light they shed upon Güiraldes' masterpiece, *Don Segundo Sombra* (1926). He retired to La Porteña to write it in 1925 and worked on it daily, perched in the branches of a large *ombú*, a tree peculiar to the pampas. By the time it was finished he was ill with cancer. He returned to Paris for treatment and died there at the age of forty-one.

The gauchos, the nomadic cattle-drivers of the pampas, were even then a vanishing breed, displaced by the railroads and the fencing of the plains, but Güiraldes has assured them of immortality in *Don Segundo Sombra,* the greatest of the many novels and stories they have inspired. Don Segundo himself is based on a gaucho whom Güiraldes had hero-worshiped as a boy; he is, as Arturo Torres-Ríoseco says, "not so much a human being of flesh and blood as a myth—the ideal gaucho, the symbol of the pampas. Above everything else, this Don Segundo is a complete man, master of himself in every situation, possessor of his soul. His nobility derives from his concept of liberty, which compels him to lead a life of solitude and anarchic individualism, and to wander ceaselessly across the plains."

Güiraldes sees this epic figure mainly through the worshiping eyes of young Fabio Cáceres, who, ignorant of his identity as the illegitimate son of a wealthy ranch owner, escapes the confining atmosphere of his aunts' town house to follow Don Segundo. For five years he roams the pampas with his master, learning the skills and sports and folklore of the gauchos, and absorbing their code, a product of the pampas themselves. In all that flatness, where the only points of reference are the distant horizon and the sun, moon, and stars, the mundane problems of town dwellers fall into perspective. Don

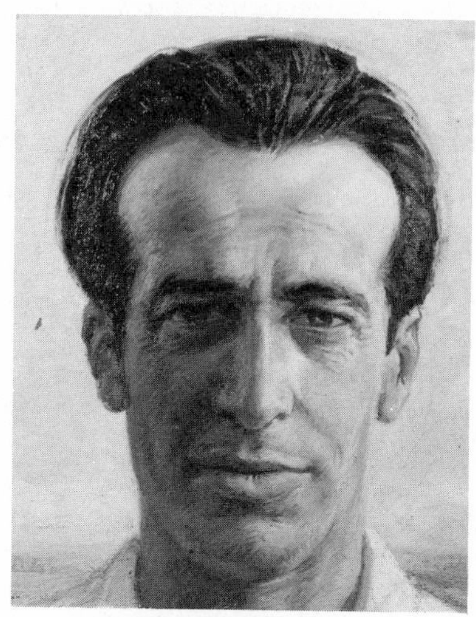

RICARDO GÜIRALDES

Segundo teaches his protégé to face the rigors of life with stoicism and to confront its dangers and problems with the grand equanimity of the landscape itself. Fabio's freedom is brought to an end when he inherits his father's estates and enters upon a new stage in his education at the hands of Don Leandro and Raucho Galván. Don Segundo rides away, his duty done. Fabio's regret as he watches him go is for the loss not only of his friend, but of a symbol of Argentina's irrecoverable past.

The novel has been compared to *Captains Courageous*, *Huckleberry Finn*, and *Don Quixote*, among other works. It was an immediate success, received the Argentinian National Literature Prize, and is now generally regarded as a classic. Over the years it has had its detractors, who object to the Gallicisms that occasionally invade the dialect or, who, more often, simply find the novel's hero too good to be true, as he undoubtedly is. And it is this very fact which insures that "the shadowy figure of Don Segundo will forever stretch across the pampas . . . as a legendary symbol of a heroic type that was."

Güiraldes' other works include the novella *Rosaura* (1922), a tragic story about a village girl hopelessly in love with a young aristocrat, and a number of posthumous collections of prose and poetry, among them *Poemas solitarios* (Solitary Poems, 1928), *Poemas místicos* (Mystical Poems, 1928), *Seis relatos* (Six Stories, 1928), and *Pampa* (1954). He was co-director of the short-lived Buenos Aires review *Proa* in 1924–1925. *El sendero* (The Path, 1932), is a work of Tolstoyan mysticism written in illness during the last months of his life.

PRINCIPAL WORKS IN ENGLISH TRANSLATION: Don Segundo Sombra, 1935. *Stories in* Frank W. (ed.) Tales From the Argentine, 1930; Onís, H. de (ed.) The Golden Land, 1948; Torres-Ríoseco, A. (ed.) Short Stories of Latin America, 1963.
ABOUT: Bordelois, I. Genio y figura de Ricardo Güiraldes, 1966; Ghiano, J. C. Ricardo Güiraldes, 1961; Kovacci, O. La pampa a través de Ricardo Güiraldes, 1961; Magill, F. N. Cyclopedia of World Authors, 1958; Onís, H. de (ed.) The Golden Land, 1948; Previtali, G. Ricardo Güiraldes, 1963; Spell, J. R. Contemporary Spanish-American Fiction, 1944; Torres-Ríoseco, A. The Epic of Latin American Literature, 1961. *Periodicals*—Commonweal May 17, 1946; Comparative Literature Winter 1959; Hispania (Baltimore) November 1951, March 1957; Hispania (Wallingford, Conn.) May 1958, March 1959, September 1960, March 1963, September 1963; Hispania (Washington, D.C.) May 1942; Hispanic Review January 1948; New Mexico Quarterly Autumn 1951; New York Times Book Review February 13, 1966.

GUNN, THOM(SON) WILLIAM (August 29, 1929–), English poet, writes: "I was born in Gravesend, Kent. My father, a journalist, was the son of a merchant seaman, and my mother was the daughter of a tenant farmer. I have one brother, Alexander, a photographer. First because of my father's profession and later because of the Blitz, my brother and I went to a variety of schools before living in Hampstead, where we went to University College School. I did two years' national service in the army, which was probably good for me, in that it gave me practice in resisting boredom. After this, when I was twenty, I spent six months working in Paris, where I wrote my third and last unfinished novel. In 1950 I went to Cambridge, and it was at the end of my first year that I had my first poem published in an 'anti-war' issue of a student magazine. The encouragement I received as a result of this, combined with a certain maturing of attitudes and an intensive reading of good poets, was what started me off, I think. While I was at Cambridge I wrote the poems that made up my first book, *Fighting Terms*. In the vacations I did a lot of hitch-hiking in France and Italy, and when I left I spent six months in Rome on a scholarship. In 1954 I came to the United States on a writing fellowship to Stanford, where I worked under Yvor Winters for a year. I have lived in the U.S. ever since, mostly in San Francisco or nearby, though I spent a year in San Antonio (1955–56), a few months in Berlin on a Somerset Maugham Award in 1960 and a year in London (1964–65). I taught at the University of California, Berkeley, from 1958 to 1966.

"I was poetry reviewer for the *Yale Review* from 1958 to 1964. I have now given up reviewing, because I have come to find it distasteful to sit in judgment on my contemporaries, but I intend to write essays on poets I like, from time to time, essays which I hope will end up as a book on American poetry.

"Most of my poetry has been metrical, but I have experimented with syllabics for some years and latterly with free verse. My principal problem—and it is probably that of most of my contemporaries—is that I need to find a kind of poetry which will combine the virtues (in tone and subject matter as well as in rhythm) of free verse with those of metrical verse. Robert Lowell is about the only man who has managed to do this.

"I have a considerable fear of the public role, partly superstitious and partly well justified. The life of literary conferences, cocktail parties and poetry readings not only bores me but sabotages my poetry. One's writing is intended for other people ultimately, but the process of doing it is private and lonely, and most poets benefit from being able to slip around anonymously. This I expect to continue doing."

While he was still at Cambridge, early in the 1950s, Thom Gunn was recognized as one of the best and potentially most important English poets to have emerged since World War II. In those days he found himself associated for a time with "the Movement"; in fact, as he says, he writes in the tradition, "lasting from Chaucer to Hardy, that a poem should balance the emotion with the intellect." Gunn, most often described as a metaphysical poet, is credited with a Donne-like passion and lucidity and wit, a mastery of metaphor and compression.

His first books contained poems about sexual warfare, about the search for an identity, about the conflict between will and energy. Some of them were allegories, borrowing from history and legend, and they were metrically strict and traditional. Many of these poems were defiant celebrations of violence and danger, passionately callous; seeing around him "the crowded, broken and unfinished," Gunn "would not have the risk diminished." His heroes were the intellectual toughs of history, or such contemporary substitutes as motorcycle gangs (in the much discussed "On the Move"), pop singers, and dance-hall thugs—those, as John Press says, who "impose their hard wills upon the natural world." (Gunn likes cities for the same reason.)

In *My Sad Captains* there were a number of gentler and altogether more exact and "transparent" poems in the loose syllabic form to which Gunn refers above. They disappointed some admirers but reassured critics who had distrusted his earlier commitment to unmotivated violence. Bernard Bergonzi welcomed the poems in the new manner as "extremely subtle and delicate organisms of language," and Frank Kermode thought that "there is every reason in the world to applaud this volume, in which a chaste and powerful modern poet goes about his . . . business of arranging words to reveal a world."

These developments in Gunn's work have been attributed to the influence of his friend Yvor Winters. But, if Winters taught him to "keep both Rule and Energy in view," his principal theme, Gunn said in 1965, was still the conflict between the two.

This fruitful tension was evident also in *Touch*, a collection of poems gathered around the theme of rebirth. Again there are both metrical and syllabic poems, and the book includes a sequence of seventeen lyrics called "Misanthropos"—a kind of post-holocaust fantasy, written for radio, in which "the final man walks the final hill / without thought or feeling." Judson Jerome called it "a poem of almost liturgical dignity and gravity, strict in form and moving slowly through its series of disciplined meditations. . . . It is a tiny epic, one of grandeur and faultless technique."

Gunn has consciously sought in his work a way to immerse himself in experience—to "live experience through in detail" and simultaneously to be sufficiently detached to control his subject-matter. The problem was a technical one to the extent that metrical verse committed him (he found) "to a particular kind of rather taut emotion, a rather clenched kind of emotion," while syllabic verse, much more suited to "the casual perception," was not appropriate to the kind of complex moral statement of which Gunn is capable.

In *Moly*, it was thought, he had gone far towards achieving the balance he sought. One critic wrote in the *Times Literary Supplement*: "The sharp disjunctions between controlling mind and chaotic matter of the early volumes are here superseded: it is by rooting himself responsively in the flow of natural forces, not by fending them off, that man can master them. . . . The moly plant, whose black roots shade upwards into a white flower, itself images this division-within-unity. Human consciousness sinks its tentacular roots into the earth . . . and at its most intensified (some of the poems were written under LSD) it acknowledges the dependency of its sharpened perceptions on an amorphous undertow of mindless natural merging: 'In looking for the words, I found / Bright tendrils, round which that sharp outline faltered: / Limber detail, no bloom disclosed / I was still separate on the shadow's ground / But, charged with growth, was being altered / Composing uncomposed.' " In these poems "a spare, precise verbal economy is maintained, but a complex sensuousness is allowed to emerge through it. . . . *Moly* lacks much of the metaphysical drama of the earlier Gunn; but it represents a mature distillation of some of the major issues which he has pursued so ambitiously throughout his work."

THOM WILLIAM GUNN

The poet's father, Herbert Gunn, was editor of the London *Daily Sketch*. In a 1965 interview in *The Observer*, Thom Gunn suggested that "the sources of a writing talent are something like Freud's theory of sexuality. Things happen in childhood to make you more aware of certain aspects of the world." Gunn, a powerful swimmer, has been said to resemble "a lumberjack in dress and build." He lists his recreations as reading, drinking, going to films. He has lived as a freelance writer since 1966, eking out his income with an occasional teaching or editorial job.

PRINCIPAL WORKS: (ed.) Poetry from Cambridge, 1953; Fighting Terms, 1954 (revised 1962); The Sense of Movement, 1957; My Sad Captains, 1961; Selected Poems (by Thom Gunn and Ted Hughes), 1962; (ed. with Ted Hughes) Five American Poets, 1963; (with Ander Gunn) Positives (photographs, with verse captions), 1966; A Geography, 1966; Touch, 1967; Poems 1950–1966: A Selection, 1969; Moly, 1971 (republished with My Sad Captains, 1973).

ABOUT: Allott, K. (ed.) Penguin Book of Contemporary Verse, 1962; Grubb, F. A Vision of Reality, 1965; Mander, J. The Writer and Commitment, 1961; Murphy, R. (ed.) Contemporary Poets of the English Language, 1970; O'Connor, W. V. The New University Wits, 1963; Press, J. Rule and Energy, 1963; Who's Who, 1971. *Periodicals*—London Magazine November 1964; Observer March 7, 1965; Times Educational Supplement August 3, 1956; Times Literary Supplement July 29, 1965; October 5, 1967; April 16, 1971.

***HADAS, MOSES** (June 25, 1900–August 17, 1966), American scholar, regarded himself as a steward of the legacy of classical literature and made it his task to propagate that legacy as a teacher and as the author, translator, or editor of more than

* had' as

MOSES HADAS

thirty books. He was born to David and Gertrude (Draizen) Hadas in Atlanta, Georgia, where he attended Emory University. Graduating in 1922, he went to New York for his rabbinical training at the Jewish Theological Seminary, at the same time doing graduate work at Columbia University. Hadas received his M.A. in 1925 and taught at Columbia and the University of Cincinnati until he had earned his doctorate in 1930. His thesis was *Sextus Pompey*, his first original published work. Returning to Columbia, Hadas taught there with few interruptions for the rest of his life.

He made one of his excursions from the classroom in World War II when from 1943 to 1946 he served as a civilian with the OSS in Greece and North Africa. It was then, faced with "a choice between a cup of tea and a shave," that Hadas acquired his splendid beard and mustache. He was of medium height, vehement in speech, jaunty in appearance. At Columbia he advanced steadily through the academic ranks to become Jay Professor of Greek in 1956. His reputation was that of a vigorous, stimulating teacher who related the literature of the ancients to the concerns of his students, and was not above linking Aristophanes' humor with that of the Marx Brothers, whom he adored. He made "blood run through the classics."

Believing that each age should "put down the classics in its own language," Hadas translated and in many cases edited works by Euripides, Xenophon, Julius Caesar, and Seneca, among other Greek and Roman writers, as well as a number from Hebrew and German, including Joseph ben Meir Zabara's *Book of Delight* (1932) and Jakob Burckhardt's *Age of Constantine the Great* (1949).

Hadas's own studies of the classics, recognized as standard works, revealed a learning "both deep and delightful." *A History of Greek Literature* (1950) surveyed the literary forms and ideas of writers from Homer to Lucian. Its companion volume, *A History of Latin Literature* (1952), covered every important work from the beginnings of Latin literature to the sixth century A.D. Both works were widely praised and the mild criticism that writers had not been clearly related to their times was fully met in *Ancilla to Classical Reading* (1954), which discussed in close detail the backgrounds against which the classics were written.

Hellenistic Culture: Fusion and Diffusion (1959) was probably his most ambitious book. It examined the process of amalgamation between Greek and Oriental cultures from which Western civilization emerged and upset some reviewers, who protested that Hadas had overemphasized Jewish sources in illustrating the transmission of cultural elements. But in praising Hadas for not trying to "strait-jacket" the Hellenistic period "into any rigid theory of history," W. B. Stanford commented in the *Guardian* that "he is content to describe, compare, and explain, with a sober eloquence of style and a warm brilliance of thought and sympathy."

Hadas's 1926 marriage to Ethel J. Elkus ended in divorce, and in 1945 he married Elizabeth M. Chamberlayne. He had two children by each marriage. Hadas was an occasional guest on television, admired for his "wise and puckish performances," and held several honorary doctorates. He died of a heart attack in Colorado, where he had gone to participate in a program of the Aspen Institute for Humanistic Studies. The most notable of his posthumous works was *The Living Tradition*, an account of the Greek notion of the primacy of man which Hadas saw as the essential ingredient in the humanistic tradition. Jacques Barzun, Provost of Columbia University, said of him that "he belonged to that ancient time when scholars loved to teach, knew how to write, and developed personalities without effort."

PRINCIPAL WORKS: A History of Greek Literature, 1950; A History of Latin Literature, 1952; Ancilla to Classical Reading, 1954; Hellenistic Culture, 1959; Humanism: The Greek Ideal and Its Survival, 1960; Old Wine, New Bottles, 1962; (with Morton Smith) Heroes and Gods: Spiritual Biographies in Antiquity, 1965; The Living Tradition, 1967.

ABOUT: Current Biography, 1960; Who's Who in America, 1966–1967. *Periodicals*—Newsweek March 14, 1960; New York Times August 18, 1966.

HAGIWARA, SAKUTARO (November 1, 1886–May 11, 1942), who has been described as "the father of modern Japanese poetry," was born in Maebashi, Gumma Prefecture, where he received his early education. He was the eldest son of a doctor. He started writing while at school under the influence of Akiko Yosano's collection of verse, *Midare Gami* (Disheveled Hair, 1901).

Hagiwara's later schooling was repeatedly interrupted and outwardly not very successful. He entered the English Literature Department of the Fifth High School (now Kumamoto University) in September 1907 but failed his first year final examination and left. In September 1908 he entered the Department of German Law of the Sixth High School (now Okayama University). He withdrew from the school in the summer of 1910 after an attack of typhus. In May 1911 he entered the present Keio University in Tokyo but again withdrew after six months to give more time to opera and the theatre and to the study of the mandolin. His academic setbacks and the criticism they aroused at home, poor health, and his lack of any definite ambition or career prospect contributed to the spiritual distress which he suffered during these years. He felt, he said, a sense of disgust and revulsion against his parents, politics, and society at large. From childhood, extreme sensitivity had made it difficult for him to enter into or sustain friendships, and a sense of loneliness and nervous introspection is characteristic of his poetry. While a student he read Dostoevsky, Poe, and Nietzsche, and later Herbert Spencer, Schopenhauer, and Baudelaire. Whatever he owed to these writers, his poetry remains very much his own.

In 1911 Hakushu Kitahara published a collection of verse, *Omoide* (Recollections). Hagiwara was impressed and sent some of his own work to Hakushu, who encouraged him to take poetry more seriously. In 1914 he returned to Maebashi where he established a school for teaching the mandolin and started a circle for the study of poetry, religion, and music. He showed some interest in Christianity and some critics have tried to detect Christian feeling in his work.

In 1916 he started a literary magazine, *Kanjo* (Emotion), a title which deliberately flaunted its anti-Naturalist bias. In 1917 he published what has since become a landmark in the history of modern Japanese poetry, *Tsuki ni Hoeru* (Barking at the Moon). This lyrical, symbolist collection, praised by Ogai Mori, showed strong originality in its sensuous imagery and in Hagiwara's sensitive, rhythmical use of colloquial language—a startling departure from the conventions of the time. Unfortunately Hagiwara's use of rhythm is untranslatable but some idea of his use of extremely simple language and disturbing imagery can be gained from "The Death of a Frog" (he writes frequently about animals in his poems): "A frog has been killed, / The ring of children raise their hands, / All together raise / Childlike, / Blood-stained hands, / The moon appears, / On the hill a man is standing. / Under the hat a face."

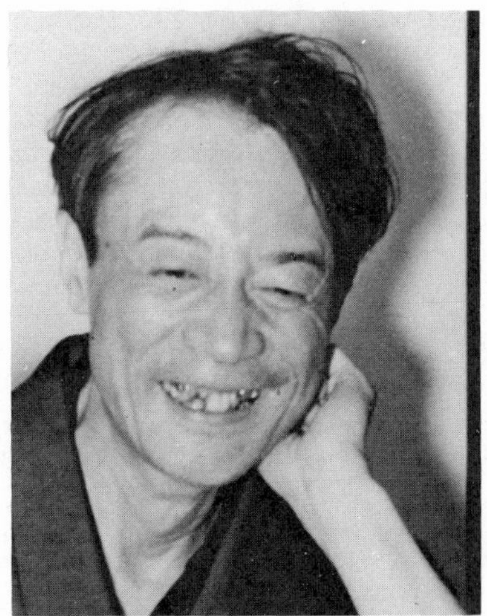

SAKUTARO HAGIWARA

Not all the poems in *Tsuki ni Hoeru* are as simple as this. Besides trying to raise colloquial speech to the level of poetry, Hagiwara introduced psychology—Spencer's idea of "nervous shock"—into his verse in order to express his vision of man's loneliness and mental and spiritual dislocation: "From the pain of a long disease / The face is enmeshed in a spider's web, / From the hips down clothed in shadow, / From the hips up a thicket sprouts, / The hands are rotten, / The whole body utterly in disorder, / Ah, again today the moon appears, / The morning moon appears in the sky, / Under that lantern-dim glow, / A deformed white dog is howling. / Near daybreak, / On a lonely road—a howling dog." ("Daybreak") Hagiwara has provided his own commentary for this poem: "The dog howls because he suspects and fears his own shadow. To the dog's sick heart, the moon is a pale, ghost-like, ominous mystery. I too, wish to nail my gloomy shadow to the moonlit earth lest it pursue me eternally."

The sense of world-weariness and introversion is even more noticeable in the collection entitled *Aoneko* (Blue Cat, 1923). *Tsuki ni Hoeru* and *Aoneko* established Hagiwara's reputation as a poet and a sensitive, if somewhat morbid, thinker. He continued to write prolifically until his death, publishing not only poetry but also a collection of aphorisms, *Atarashiki Yokujo* (New Desire, 1922); a work on the theory of poetry, *Shi no Genri* (Principles of Poetry, 1928) and essays on literature and civilization. He was a member of the group centered around the journal *Shiki* (Four Seasons), which opposed naturalism and advocated lyricism in modern Japanese poetry. He also had some interest in physiology and for a time edited a magazine on that subject.

Later collections, like *Hyoto* (Ice Island, 1934), show that Hagiwara's nihilism became more pronounced, aggravated perhaps by his friendship with Ryunosuke Akutagawa and the shock of Akutagawa's suicide in 1927; partly perhaps by the break-up of his marriage. He divorced his wife in 1929. Hagiwara's poetry is the justification of his influential theories, which he summed up in two sentences: "The expression of poetry should be simple—I would wish the scent to be pure"; and "Poetry is something that grasps the emotional nerves—it is living, working psychology."

PRINCIPAL WORKS IN ENGLISH TRANSLATION: Face at the Bottom of the World and Other Poems (tr. by Graeme Wilson), 1969. *Poems in* Keene, D. Modern Japanese Literature, 1956.

ABOUT: Seymour-Smith, M. Guide to Modern World Literature, 1973. *Periodicals*—Times Literary Supplement July 2, 1971.

HALL, DONALD (ANDREW) (September 20, 1928–), American poet, memoirist, editor, and critic, writes: "I was born in Hamden, Connecticut, where my father helped to run the family business, a dairy. Summers I spent in New Hampshire with my mother's parents who were farmers. There, I read and wrote in the mornings, and hayed in the afternoons. I always preferred New Hampshire to Connecticut. After grammar school, and two years of Hamden High, I went to Exeter which I found grueling but intellectually useful; when I was seventeen I lost a year of school through illness, but there was no permanent escape. I went back to Exeter the next year when I was eighteen, and to Harvard at nineteen. There, I was on the *Advocate* with Robert Bly, and met a number of poets and talked poetry with them: Richard Wilbur, John Holmes, John Ciardi, Robert Frost, Theodore Spencer, Archibald MacLeish and Richard Eberhart. I went up to Oxford (Christ Church) on a Henry Fellowship in 1951, and in the summer of 1952 returned to the United States to marry Kirby Thompson, whom I had known at Radcliffe. I took a B.Litt. (my subject was theoretical prosody, typical of my interests at that time) in 1953, and spent 1953–4 at Stanford as a Creative Writing Fellow under Yvor Winters. My son Andrew was born there that spring. From 1954–7 I was a Junior Fellow in the Society of Fellows at Harvard, and did nothing for three years but read and write; I am continually grateful for that long episode of freedom. I came to teach at the University of Michigan in 1957. In 1959 my daughter Philippa was born, and I spent the year 1959–60 in England writing, and again the year 1963–4, when I had a Guggenheim. Since then I have been able, by using whatever money I could make from prose and from poetry-readings, to take frequent leave, though I have remained in Ann Arbor. In recent years I have taught only a quarter of the time.

"I started writing when I was twelve, and became intense about it when I was fourteen. When I was sixteen I published some poems in small magazines. I wrote fiction at that time, as well as poetry, but the fiction was particularly bad. I gave it up when I was twenty, and between twenty and thirty wrote virtually no prose except to argue about poetry. My early poetry concentrated on form entirely. I was concerned that poetry should *be* only technique, and perfectly finite. I now regard this attitude as self-defensive, but I suspect that I learned some skill by putting all my trust in it. By 1954 I had begun to distrust the vanity of technique; and I began to learn that what I called technique covered small ground. Working with syllabics and free verse—abandoning gradually the metric I had learned—I tried to extend my range, and to make poems which were more expressive and imaginative. My first book was the old world. My second book was the book of my father's death, and largely examined the outward details of the life of the American suburbs; but partly it looked into an alternative to that life. In my third book I tried to explore that alternative, and now my interest in writing poetry lies in what it can reveal: poetry as exploration of the inward continent of the spirit.

"At thirty I began to write prose again, first a memoir of the New Hampshire summers and later some stories. I doubt that I will ever prefer prose to poems, but I enjoy it as an alternative. I did a biography of Henry Moore, and learned about poetry from the study of sculpture. In England I enjoy talking on the BBC, and have done perhaps forty broadcasts in the past five years. I enjoy editing too—trying to impose my taste on the world, even though that taste keeps changing. I edited poetry for the *Paris Review* for nine years, and have done a number of anthologies, and was on the poetry board of the Wesleyan University Press for five years. At present I am a consultant for Harper and Row. I made a play out of Robert Frost's poems and letters which ran Off-Broadway in 1965–6. If there is anything I like more than writing, it is reading my poems to audiences."

Since Donald Hall was at first "concerned that poetry should *be* only technique," it was quite naturally the formal qualities of his early work that were most praised in *Exiles and Marriages*, which won the Newdigate Prize and was the Lamont Poetry Selection in 1955. Even then though, some critics saw more than virtuosity and wit in these poems, in which, as D. G. Hoffman put it, Hall traced "the record of his own growing," giving "grave and affectionate tribute to ancestors and places that have shaped his life," writing "unabashedly of his love and marriage." Louise Townsend Nicholl heard in the book "the good crunch of new talent biting into life." Hall's preoccupation with an "icily witty and beautiful" technique was still evident in *The Dark Houses*, and troubled critics who saw that his talent was really lyrical rather than satirical.

More recently, as he says, Hall has relinquished "the vanity of technique" and begun an "exploration of the inward continent of the spirit." His approach to this exploration resembles that of several American poets who, like himself, have been associated with the magazine *The Sixties*: Robert Bly, Louis Simpson, James Wright, James Dickey. These poets, who have learned from Lorca and Neruda as well as from each other, favor a new simplicity and directness of statement but combine this with a taste for surrealist imagery. They exhibit, as Hall said in his Penguin anthology *Contemporary American Poetry*, "a new kind of imagination." Its impulse "is irrational yet the poem is usually quiet and the language simple; there is no straining for apocalypse and no conscious pursuit of the unconscious. . . . This new imagination reveals through images a subjective life which is *general* (not confessional and particular), and which corresponds to an old objective life of shared experience and knowledge. . . . What I am trying to describe is not a school or a clique but a way of seeing and a way of feeling, and I believe they have grown by themselves from the complex earth of American writing and American experience."

Some of the fruits of this imagination as it has worked in Hall's poetry were collected in *A Roof of Tiger Lilies*. Many of these poems, as the publisher suggested, "seem to consist wholly of direct actions and sensuous images; they often deal with magical transfiguration or metamorphosis, with the experience of *breaking out*." Robert Mazzocco thought they were Hall's most impressive aesthetic achievement, though they "do not fulfil themselves" psychologically. M. L. Rosenthal found in the book evidence that Hall "has slowly evolved from a poet whose work was derivatively intellectual and verbose into one able to make a poem move in a single, self-creating curve." There was more verse of this kind in *The Alligator Bride*, a volume of "poems new and selected," and in *The Yellow Room*, a series of short lyrics forming an account of a love affair.

Hall's delight in reading his poems aloud has also helped to change them, as he explained in an article in the New York *Times Book Review* (December 11, 1966). He finds, he says, that he no longer wants to write essayistic poems in syllabics whose appeal is to the eye, but poems rather "in which the sound

DONALD HALL

itself keeps the listeners intent," which can be enjoyed as sensual objects without having to be understood intellectually. He quotes as an example: "Then the knee of the wave / turned to stone. / By the cliff of her flank / I anchored, / In the darkness of harbors / laid-by."

String Too Short to Be Saved, Hall's gentle and sometimes beautiful prose reminiscences of his New Hampshire boyhood, was generally admired, as was his "intimate biography" of Henry Moore. The poet has also written a thorough and often acute critical biography of Marianne Moore, and a children's book, *Andrew the Lion Farmer* (1959). He and his wife were divorced in 1969. Hall has been a full professor at the University of Michigan since 1966.

PRINCIPAL WORKS: *Poetry*—Exiles and Marriages, 1955; The Dark Houses, 1958; A Roof of Tiger Lilies, 1964; The Alligator Bride: Poems New and Selected, 1969; The Yellow Room: Love Poems, 1971; The Gentleman's Alphabet Book (limericks, with drawings by Harvey Kornberg), 1972. *Prose*—String Too Short to Be Saved (autobiography), 1961; Henry Moore: The Life and Work of a Great Sculptor, 1966; Marianne Moore: The Cage and the Animal, 1970. *As editor*—(with Louis Simpson and Robert Pack) New Poets of England and America, 1957; (with Robert Pack) New Poets of England and America: Second Selection, 1962; A Poetry Sampler, 1962; Contemporary American Poetry, 1963; (with Warren Taylor) Poetry in English, 1963; (with Stephen Spender) The Concise Encyclopaedia of English and American Poets and Poetry, 1963; Faber Book of Modern Verse (revision), 1965; The Modern Stylists: Writers on the Art of Writing (for teenagers), 1968; A Choice of Whitman's Verse, 1968; Man and Boy: An Anthology, 1968; American Poetry: An Introductory Anthology, 1969; The Pleasures of Poetry, 1971.

ABOUT: Contemporary Authors 7–8, 1963; Hall, D. String Too Short to Be Saved, 1961; Murphy, R. (ed.)

Contemporary Poets of the English Language, 1970; Who's Who in America, 1970-1971. *Periodicals*—Chicago Review Summer 1956; The Fifties 3, 1959; New York Times Book Review December 11, 1966; Saturday Review February 18, 1956; Virginia Quarterly Review Winter 1960.

"HALLIDAY, BRETT" (pseudonym of Davis Dresser) (July 31, 1904–), American detective story writer, is the son of Justus and Mary Dresser. He was born in Chicago but grew up in Texas. At the age of fourteen he ran away from home and spent two years in the Army. Discharged, he returned briefly to high school, disliked it, and at sixteen became a wanderer. During the next few years he worked in construction camps as a mule skinner, dug graves, sailed on oil tankers, and in general saw more of life, death, and the world by the time he was twenty-one than most writers ever hear about.

At some time during the 1920s Dresser settled down in Indiana long enough to secure his Civil Engineering certificate, and thereafter worked as an engineer and surveyor. By 1927, however, he was broke and jobless in Los Angeles. It was then that he began to write, stimulated first by hunger and the Dodd Mead Red Badge contest, then (though he didn't win the contest) by a conviction that he could put together saleable fiction. Publishers at first disagreed, but by the early 1930s Dresser was churning out and selling quantities of "drug store fiction"—love stories, sex stories, westerns, and mysteries—under a dozen pseudonyms.

The first Michael Shayne detective novel by "Brett Halliday" appeared in 1939. It was called *Dividend on Death* and had been rejected twenty-two times. A New York *Times* reviewer said prophetically if rather sniffily that, though it was the work of "an inexpert storyteller," it seemed possible "that Brett Halliday may become popular with readers whose first demand is for nonchalant rough stuff." The second Brett Halliday story, *The Private Practice of Michael Shayne* (1940), sold to the movies and in effect, Dresser says, "started Shayne on his long career."

Since then the redheaded private detective has battled, boozed, and plotted his way through fifty novels and armies of gamblers, murderers, bribed bartenders, and gorgeous dames. Shayne's faithful secretary Lucy, the obliging reporter Timothy Rourke, the antagonistic Miami policeman Peter Painter have become household names, figuring in a highly entertaining succession of movies, a radio series, and (less successfully) on television. No one has ever suggested that Brett Halliday is a literary figure of any particular importance, and he has been accused on occasion of turning out "sub-average tough stuff." But Anthony Boucher, a respected critic of the genre, generally relished the

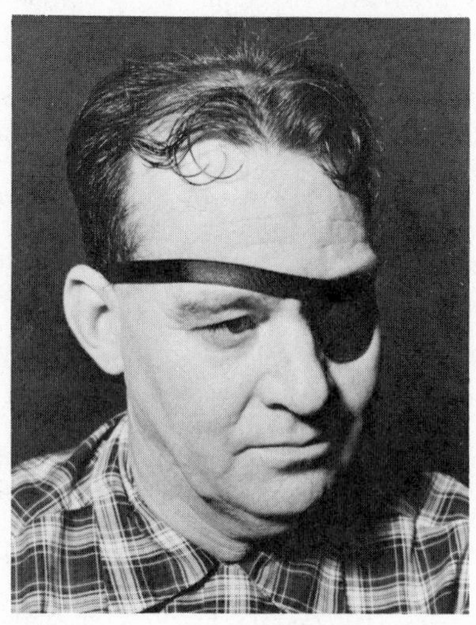

BRETT HALLIDAY

twists, puzzles, and complexities of the Shayne books, and a vast number of common readers have enjoyed the "satisfying amount of shooting, slugging, cognac swilling and shrewd sleuthing" they invariably provide.

Dresser's own favorites among his books are *Charlie Dell* (1952), a novel in the James M. Cain tradition written under the pseudonym "Anderson Wayne," and *Before I Wake* (1949, by "Hal DeBrett"). He has used more than a dozen pseudonyms and written over a hundred novels.

Dresser is a founding member of the Mystery Writers of America and belongs to the Western Writers of America and the National Writers' Club. He was married in 1961 to Mary Savage. Mrs. Dresser is also a writer, as is Dresser's former wife, Helen McCloy. He has a daughter, Chloe. Dresser, a husky man an inch or two under six feet tall, wears a patch over one eye as a consequence of a childhood riding accident.

PRINCIPAL WORKS (a representative selection): *As "Brett Halliday"*—Dividend on Death, 1939; A Taste for Violence, 1949; Stranger in Town, 1955; Murder by Proxy, 1962. *As "Anderson Wayne"*—Charlie Dell, 1952. *As "Hal DeBrett"*—Before I Wake, 1949.

ABOUT: *Periodical*—Wilson Library Bulletin October 1963.

HAMBURGER, MICHAEL (PETER LEOPOLD) (March 22, 1924–), English poet, critic, and translator, writes: "I was born in Berlin and educated there up to the age of nine, when my family emigrated to Britain—at first to Edinburgh, where my father, a medical specialist and professor of medicine, had to qualify for the second time before building up a new practice in London. I began to write poems at Westminster School, and by the age of sixteen I knew that I wanted to be a writer. Though my poems were in English from the start, my early German background made me something of a freak. At school, too, I began to translate poems from the German, finishing my first book, *Poems of Hölderlin*, at the age of eighteen. When it was published in the following year I had just become an infantry-man after four precocious but stimulating terms at Christ Church, Oxford, to which I had won an Exhibition in Modern Languages soon after my father's early death in 1940. Four years of military service took me all over the British Isles, as far as the Shetlands, then to Italy and Austria. I acquired a smattering of many skills and idioms, laid cables on North Lancashire moors and unloaded sheep in the harbour of Naples, worked as an interpreter with German prisoners of war and as the headmaster of a co-educational school for the children of British 'personnel' in Austria. Those were decisive years, at once formative and disruptive of any sort of unified personality.

"In 1947 I returned to England and hurriedly completed my studies at Oxford, impatient to be free of courses and corporative life at last. Four years as a free-lance writer and odd-job man in London cured me of all illusions about that freedom. My first book of poems appeared in 1950, followed by new translations. In 1952 I became a lecturer in German, first at University College, London, then at the University of Reading, where I taught for nine years, till 1964. Meanwhile I had been awarded a Bollingen Foundation Fellowship, also two prizes in Germany for my work as a translator of German poems. In 1964 I resigned my Readership at Reading, so as to have more time for writing. In the following year I was awarded a second Bollingen Fellowship.

"I had also married—in 1951—and become the father of three children. I had continued to write and publish poems, criticism and translations, with rare and not very strenuous excursions into prose fiction. Though I have written essays on English and French writers, and am now preparing a study of modern poetry that will touch on many literatures, both inner and outer pressures made Germany my constant and primal concern. My critical books *Reason and Energy* and *From Prophecy to Exorcism* deal with German writers. The poet Hölderlin remained of special importance to me. I have only recently finished what I hope will be the definitive edition of my translations from his work, after recasting them and adding to them for twenty-five years. Another writer to whom I devoted research, critical studies and translations is the Austrian poet and dramatist Hugo von Hofmannsthal; and I have translated poems, prose and radio plays by living German writers.

MICHAEL HAMBURGER

"It is not for me to judge how the freakishness of my circumstances has affected my own work, though I am well aware of certain problems of style and diction bound up with the dilemma of being very nearly bi-lingual. Language—in poetry and imaginative prose—lives by its associations with immediate experience. English is the language in which I feel at home; but it will always remain a second home, lacking in childhood associations on which my poems would otherwise draw. In recent years I have written some reminiscent prose in German, only to find that words fail me precisely at the point where English became my every-day language. Most of the time I forget these special difficulties, happy enough to struggle with them and cope with them if I can."

Jon Silkin has described Michael Hamburger's verse as "a poetry of ideas made as sensuous as possible by being passed through images of nature, tinged very frequently with a decent uncloying melancholy." His early poems were praised for their often successful fusion of emotion and thought, but found lacking in tension; Hamburger himself has said that he at first "used the traditional forms to protect myself from the pressure and intensity of my feelings."

Since then, beginning with the poems in *Weather and Season* (1963), rhyme and traditional meters have been discarded. He writes directly now, conversationally but exactly, in staccato rhythms, of his strong moral and emotional concerns—as a Jew, as an enemy of technology and the madness of cities, or simply as a man fearful and nostalgic in the face of change and death. A reviewer in the

Times Literary Supplement of *Travelling* (1969) noted that Hamburger's effects are "carried within the careful texture of his language: a language which is dexterously selective without a show of craft, drawing on a subdued yet inventive pattern of metaphor which sometimes comes closer to imagism than the tersely observant tone of realist reportage would suggest." Alan Brownjohn, discussing the same volume, wrote that its "cumulative effect is of a determined intelligence achieving, rather against the odds, a poetry of power and simplicity by rejecting the easy answers."

At the same time, Hamburger has achieved an unequaled reputation as a contemporary translator and interpreter of German poetry for English readers. The essays collected in *Reason and Energy* and *From Prophecy to Exorcism* were called fresh and penetrating, full of insights, and the books have become standard works. As a translator, Hamburger sets out "to get under the original poet's skin, rather than exhibit the effects on my own skin of exposure to his work." The result is said to be "at the furthest possible remove from the now fashionable 're-creations' or 'metaphrases' of foreign-language poems." His schoolboy obsession with Hölderlin culminated in the 1966 bilingual *Poems and Fragments*, universally recognized as the best conceivable English version of Hölderlin and described by one critic as "one of the most accomplished works of creative translation ever to appear in the field of German–English literary relations." There has also been much praise for Hamburger's translations of such contemporary figures as Nelly Sachs, Günter Eich, Günter Grass, Hans Magnus Enzensberger, and Paul Celan, and for his two important anthologies, *Modern German Poetry 1910–1960* (edited with Christopher Middleton) and *East German Poetry*.

Hamburger's devotion to poetry is not limited to verse in German and English. He reads French and Italian as well, and is familiar at least through translations with Spanish, Portuguese, Greek, Russian, and East European poetry. He draws on all these literatures in the most ambitious of his critical works, *The Truth of Poetry*, subtitled "Tensions in Modern Poetry from Baudelaire to the 1960's." There are chapters on "Lost Identities," on "Masks," on anti-poetry, on the connections between absolute poetry and extremist politics, and on a number of other themes. The result is a survey, full of interest and insight, but a little haphazard in organization and uneven in the quality of its perceptions—a work more successful as an encyclopedic introduction to modern poetry than as a thesis.

The author's marriage to the actress Anne File, who as Anne Beresford is also a poet, was dissolved in 1970. His younger brother is the publisher Paul Hamlyn. Apart from the two German prizes for translation he mentions above, he received in 1969 the Translation Prize of the Arts Council of Great Britain. Hamburger was the Florence Purington Lecturer at Mount Holyoke College in 1966–1967, a visiting professor at the State University of New York at Buffalo in 1969, and at Stony Brook in 1971, and a visiting fellow at Wesleyan University's Center for the Humanities in 1970. He likes music, plants and animals, walking, riding, swimming, and tennis.

PRINCIPAL WORKS: *Poetry*—Flowering Cactus, 1950; Poems 1950–1951, 1952; The Dual Site, 1958; Weather and Season, 1963; In Flashlight, 1965; Feeding the Chickadees, 1968; Travelling, 1969; Penguin Modern Poets 14 (with Alan Brownjohn and Charles Tomlinson), 1969; Ownerless Earth: New and Selected Poems, 1973. *Nonfiction*—(as ed.) Beethoven: Letters, Journals and Conversation, 1951 (U.S., 1960); Reason and Energy, 1957 (rev. and expanded, 1970; rev. ed. published in U.S. as Contraries); (as ed.) Hugo von Hofmannsthal: Poems and Verse Plays, 1961; (as ed. with Christopher Middleton) Modern German Poetry 1910–1960, 1962; (as ed.) Hugo von Hofmannsthal: Selected Plays and Libretti, 1964; From Prophecy to Exorcism, 1965; (as tr.) Hölderlin, F. Poems and Fragments, 1966 (first published as Poems of Hölderlin, 1943; new eds. 1952, 1961); The Truth of Poetry, 1969; Hugo von Hofmannsthal: Three Essays, 1970; (as ed.) East German Poetry: An Anthology in German and English, 1972; A Mug's Game (autobiography), 1973.

ABOUT: Blackburn, T. The Price of an Eye, 1961; Contemporary Authors 7–8, 1963; Murphy, R. (ed.) Contemporary Poets of the English Language, 1970; Who's Who, 1971. *Periodicals*—Guardian January 27, 1970; Poetry Chicago 101 1962; Times Literary Supplement March 9, 1967.

HAMPSHIRE, STUART (NEWTON) (October 1, 1914–), English philosopher, writes: "I was born in 1914 in Healing, Lincolnshire, England. I was educated at a boarding school, Repton, where I had studied Greek and Latin literature and history. In 1933 I went to Balliol College, Oxford with a history scholarship, but also with the firm intention of becoming a philosopher. I therefore studied Greats at Oxford, which is a combination of Greek and Roman history with philosophy. In 1933 logical positivism was just becoming known in England, and I, unlike my Oxford tutors, became intensely interested in its polemics against traditional philosophy. My tutors viewed this interest with distaste, and my early philosophical training was principally argument with contemporaries who shared my interest in the new philosophy. We used to read the periodical *Erkenntnis* and other foreign journals. At that time the center of philosophical interest was Cambridge, England, where G. E. Moore and Wittgenstein were teaching. I met and heard Moore, but I never had any first-hand contact with Wittgenstein. Only after the war did his philosophical position become accessible to me in any clear form. The only formal instruction in philosophy that I received at Oxford, and that was profoundly enlightening, was a class given jointly by the late J. L. Austin and by Isaiah Berlin on C. I. Lewis's 'Mind and the World Order.' This was, I believe, the first class to be given at Oxford on a book which was not yet recognized as a philosophical classic. The two teachers made the occasion memorable.

"During my undergraduate years political discussion, arising from the slump of 1931 and from the rise of Fascism in Europe, was a principal interest of mine, as of many of my contemporaries at Oxford. The issue was the validity of Marxism as the only adequate instrument for understanding the situation, and several of my friends became Communists in those years. But Marxism and the new analytical philosophy were plainly incompatible. I became, and have remained, a member of the British Labour Party and have retained an interest, both philosophical and political, in Socialist politics.

"During the war I was in the army and after the war was in the British Foreign Office as Personal Assistant to the Minister of State. In this capacity I came to America in the early days of the United Nations meetings in Ne ⁄ York. I also participated in the European meeting in Paris in the summer of 1947 which drafted the proposals for the Marshall Plan. Thereafter I returned to the teaching of philosophy at University College, London, and set myself to writing a book on Spinoza, which I hoped would show that a classical metaphysician might still be intelligible and useful, even if his methods of argument were in many respects unlike those of contemporary analytical philosophers. Spinoza had been since my school days a philosopher who seemed to me central and who was personally sympathetic to me in style and attitude. Also I had always intended to work on the problem usually called the problem of the freedom of the will. I had been elected in 1936 to a Fellowship at All Souls College, Oxford, which offers the opportunity of research and which is an institution without students; but after the war I taught at New College, Oxford as well as University College, London, and, even when I returned to All Souls for a period of five years in the fifties, I still continued to teach students. During these years I had gradually come to believe that the new rigour in argument, which the new analytical philosophy had introduced, might still be compatible with recovering the connections between different areas of philosophy which had been lost. In particular I was convinced that moral philosophy was a much more intellectually complex subject than the prevailing logical analysts in England had allowed. Soon after the war I had published an article 'Fallacies in

STUART HAMPSHIRE

Moral Philosophy,' and I wrote my second book, *Thought and Action*, with a view to showing some connections between philosophical ethics and the philosophy of mind. In these postwar years I had written a number of articles and reviews, in popular or semi-popular periodicals, which tried to relate philosophy to literary criticism and political argument. I had also been continuously encouraged by the British Broadcasting Corporation to explain the significance of recent advances in philosophy to laymen. I am rather horrified now to think of the number of words that I must have uttered on these topics in these years; but I still think that analytical methods in philosophy can be made intelligible and relevant to non-philosophers. In recent years, and before coming to America, I also became interested in a philosophical criticism of Freud's hypothesis of the unconscious mind, which seems to me an interest continuous with my interest in Spinoza. I have continued, and will continue, to think about the definition of human freedom, and I have published a set of lectures under the title *Freedom of the Individual* which were originally given in New Zealand. I intended this title to indicate that all questions of freedom in society had been neglected in the lectures. Plainly an adequate treatment of this subject would need to include freedom as a problem of individual psychology with freedom as a social problem. But at this time I am still far away from such synthesis.

"I believe that aesthetics, ethics, and political philosophy are parts of a single inquiry, now often called the philosophy of mind. I want to hold them together, as far as this can be done without altogether losing the precision, and the attention to detail in analysis, which are characteristic of the best contemporary philosophy. These areas of philosophy will always, I think, be less rigorously impersonal and objective, and more tentative, than the philosophy of science and logic. Reasoned opinions, and some imaginative accuracy, are the best that one can hope for. I do not doubt that the greatest intellectual achievements in our time, within the general area of traditional philosophy, have been in mathematical logic. But discoveries can also be made in the philosophy of mind, even if they are not discoveries that can be proved."

Stuart Hampshire was revealed by his first publications as an independent-minded analytic philosopher, distinguished from his more or less like-minded contemporaries at the universities of Oxford and London by the breadth of his interests outside philosophy in politics and literature and by a certain aesthetic resonance of style, very different from the colloquialness or mathematical severity favored by most of his fellow philosophers. In a number of essays he drew attention to the extravagances of Ryle's behaviorism. Agreeing that there is an essential connection between thought and behavior, Hampshire dissented from Ryle's effective identification of the two.

His first book, *Spinoza* (1951), was a compact and authoritative exposition which concluded that although Spinoza's project of a purely deductive theory of the nature of the world could not be validly carried out, the attempt was full of incidental interest. He was particularly attracted by Spinoza's thesis that freedom is not the opposite to causal determination but rather the outcome of self-knowledge—of rational understanding, and thus control, of the forces that move a man to action.

These early writings gave only a mild foretaste of the boldness and originality of *Thought and Action*, which Hampshire published in 1959. It starts from a reasoned rejection of the implicit belief of most theorists of knowledge—that knowledge is something achieved by the detached spectator, thinking about the impressions of which he is the passive recipient. Hampshire insists that human knowledge is the outcome of action—of the formation and attempted fulfillment of intentions in face of an obstructive external world. Knowledge is more a product of manipulation than of contemplation. It is a view that has much in common with existentialism, which greatly interests Hampshire. Another leading theme is the extent to which our understanding of the world and ourselves is influenced by our historically varying interests and circumstances.

In the latter part of the book Hampshire lays much stress on two kinds of knowledge a man has about his personal future. "I shall do so-and-so" can be a prediction, but it can also be the expression of a resolve. Self-knowledge of the predictive sort, as yielded, for example, by Freudian psychiatry, can increase freedom by contributing to the effectiveness of intentions. This theme is explored further in *Freedom of the Individual* (1965).

Thought and Action is a very difficult book, differing from most of the philosophy done in England in that it brings philosophy into close relation with human and social schemes, and seeks to establish connections between philosophical topics that are usually treated in isolation. As A. J. Ayer wrote, "The breadth of his approach makes it difficult for him to be meticulous over details. . . . But the attempt at what he calls a more general survey was well worth making." P. F. Strawson said of the first part of the book: "The treatment is highly general, and some of the transitions are difficult to follow. But many interesting and suggestive things are said and the total effect is both brilliant and persuasive."

Since World War II, as he says, Stuart Hampshire has lectured at University College, London (1947–1950), been a Fellow of New College, Oxford (1950–1955), and a research fellow (and domestic bursar) of All Souls (1955–1960). He went to London University as Grote Professor of the Philosophy of Mind and Logic in 1960, and after three years there went as Professor of Philosophy to Princeton University (1963–1970). Since 1970 he has been warden of Wadham College, Oxford. He was married in 1961 to Renée Lees, formerly the wife of A. J. Ayer. Hampshire became a Fellow of the British Academy in 1960, and has been a member of the Arts Council since 1972.

PRINCIPAL WORKS: Spinoza, 1951; (ed.) The Age of Reason: The Seventeenth-Century Philosophers, 1956; Thought and Action, 1959; The Freedom of the Individual, 1965; (ed.) Philosophy of Mind, 1966; Modern Writers and Other Essays, 1969; Freedom of Mind and Other Essays, 1971.

ABOUT: Who's Who, 1971; Who's Who in America, 1970–1971. *Periodicals*—Encounter July 1966; New York Times February 21, 1970; Review of Metaphysics June 1960; Spectator August 21, 1959; Times Literary Supplement September 11, 1959.

"HAN SUYIN" (pseudonym of Elizabeth Comber) (September 12, 1917–), Eurasian novelist, memoirist, and political writer, was christened Rosalie Chow but hated her first name and later changed it to Elizabeth. She is one of the four surviving children of eight born to Y. T. Chow and his wife, the former Marguerite Denis, a Belgian of the upper bourgeoisie. Her father, a member of the Chinese landed gentry, was a scholar who made his living as a railroad engineer. Han Suyin was born in China, at a station along the Lunghai railway line or, according to some accounts, in Peking.

In accordance with her mother's wishes she was reared as a Roman Catholic and attended a convent school in Peking until 1930. The suffering she saw in a land devastated by warlords had made her determined from early childhood to become a doctor. After working as a clerk at Peking Union Medical College and taking courses for two years at Yenching University, she obtained a fellowship for study in Belgium, where she attended the Université Libre of Brussels from 1935 to 1938.

Throughout her early life she had felt alienated as a half-caste, fragmented by the disparities between her Chinese and European backgrounds. But in Europe in mid-1938, as the Sino-Japanese War worsened, she became passionately convinced that she belonged to China. Returning home she was married the same year to Tang Paohuang, a general in Chiang Kai-shek's Nationalist army. This first part of her life was recorded in her first book, *Destination Chungking*, which was generally praised as "an absorbing, beautifully written book." From the beginning her work has reflected her love for the English language, "that rich and inexhaustible treasure of moods and music, feeling and thought, endless ambrosia, a firm enchantment, lifelong." It is a description which exemplifies very well her own adorned and highly personal prose style.

In 1947 General Tang was killed in action against the Communists. With her daughter, Yingmei, the young widow went to England, a country to which she is greatly attached, and completed her medical training at London University, graduating with honors in 1948.

Han Suyin's best-known book, *A Many-Splendored Thing*, is an account, to some extent fictionalized, of her love affair with a married British newspaper correspondent in Hong Kong. Counterpointing this passionate story is the heroine's inescapable sense of her Eurasian ancestry, influencing everything she does and feels. Most reviewers were profoundly moved, and one wrote: "This book must have been written in great agony and great joy, for only a book so written can tear the emotions of the reader and break the heart with tragedy and triumph." It was a best seller, was much translated, and was successfully filmed as *Love Is a Many-Splendored Thing*.

In the early 1950s Han Suyin practiced medicine in Malaya as Dr. Elizabeth Comber, the wife of a British official, Leonard Comber, whom she married in 1952. Malaya provided the setting for her second novel, *. . . And the Rain My Drink*, depicting with warmth and compassion the struggle between colonialism and the new Asian nationalism. Anne Duchêne wrote that it had "the ring of close, perceptive reporting" by "a clever, sensitive,

HAN SUYIN

and loving woman." *The Mountain Is Young* is a love story set in Nepal; *The Four Faces*, bitterly anti-Western, "pokes some pointed fun" at the ideological warfare which wrecks a neutralist writers' congress in Cambodia. None of these novels had quite the success of her first. Some readers thought them overly explicit in their sexual scenes, others found Han Suyin's style at times florid and mannered, or her ideological preoccupations excessively intrusive. There has however been general agreement that as a novelist she "can catch the intense feeling of a moment, the passion of one of her characters, the beauty of the natural world. And she can write love scenes of strength and depth."

In recent years Han Suyin seems, at least temporarily, to have abandoned fiction. *The Crippled Tree*, *A Mortal Flower* and *Birdless Summer* were the first volumes of a series combining autobiography with "a sort of subjective history of China in her time." Vincent Sheean wrote that she "often overstates her case and makes startling statements which are not susceptible to proof," but that her "own story is vitality itself, and . . . holds us intent from beginning to end." There have been similar complaints from many other western critics about the pro-Communist (and anti-Kuomintang) bias in these volumes, which nevertheless provide a vivid and revealing account of the great events which have touched her life. *China in the Year 2001*, a non-Marxist "apologia for Maoism," seemed to a reviewer in the *Times Literary Supplement* "the least unconvincing and most easily readable of this genre," notable for the author's "uncanny ability to convey Chinese sentiment to a European reader" and, "for all its lacunae and idiosyncrasies," an important book.

Han Suyin's admiration for Mao and his regime is no less evident in her autobiography and in the lectures she gives in many foreign countries. Her Sir Edward Beatty Memorial lectures, given at McGill University in Montreal, have been published under the title *Asia Today*. She holds dual British and Chinese citizenship and visits China for a few months each year, although she is not a Communist and her own books are reportedly banned in the country she defends so passionately. In 1963 she gave up her medical practice to devote herself entirely to writing and lecturing. She is a slender and handsome woman, candid, defiant, witty, and compassionate. Her recreations include botany, riding, and swimming.

PRINCIPAL WORKS: Destination Chungking (autobiography), 1942; A Many-Splendored Thing (novel), 1952; . . . And the Rain My Drink (novel), 1956; The Mountain Is Young (novel), 1958; Two Loves (England, Cast But One Shadow and Winter Love), 1962; The Four Faces (novel), 1963; The Crippled Tree (autobiography), 1965; A Mortal Flower (autobiography), 1966; China in the Year 2001 (politics), 1968; Birdless Summer (autobiography), 1968; Asia Today (essays), 1969; The Morning Deluge: Mao Tse-tung and the Chinese Revolution 1893–1953, 1972.

ABOUT: Current Biography, 1957; Han, S. Birdless Summer, 1968; Han, S. The Crippled Tree, 1965; Han, S. Destination Chungking, 1942; Han, S. A Mortal Flower, 1966; Who's Who, 1972; Who's Who in America, 1972–1973. *Periodicals*—Guardian May 11, 1965; Holiday December 1954; Newsweek October 20, 1958; Reporter January 20, 1953; Saturday Review October 18, 1958; September 24, 1966.

HANSBERRY, LORRAINE (May 19, 1930–January 12, 1965), an American playwright who rejected stereotypes in both her life and work, maintained that she was not a black playwright but a playwright who happened to be black. She was born in Chicago, the youngest of four children of Carl Augustus and Nannie (Perry) Hansberry. A well-to-do real estate broker, her father successfully fought a civil rights case on restricted covenants all the way to the Supreme Court.

Although her father bought a home in a white neighborhood when she was eight years old, Lorraine Hansberry was a product (she said "victim") of Chicago's segregated half-day elementary schools. At Englewood High School, from which she graduated in 1948, she was attracted to the theatre, but she also attended classes at the Art Institute of Chicago, and painting fascinated her even more. During her two years at the University of Wisconsin she majored in art, and she later studied painting in Guadalajara, Mexico. Eventually she decided that she was a "lousy painter," but her courses at Wisconsin in literature and stage design helped provide a substitute: "the feeling that the theatre embraces everything I like all at one time."

LORRAINE HANSBERRY

Moving to New York in 1950, Miss Hansberry worked briefly at a series of odd jobs. For a time she was a waitress and cashier at a Greenwich Village restaurant operated by the family of Robert Nemiroff, a music publisher, whom she married on June 20, 1953. During the latter years of a literary apprenticeship that included the writing of several unpublished short stories and three unfinished plays, she found an audience in her husband and a small group of friends.

It was at such a gathering in the fall of 1957 that she felt her play, *A Raisin in the Sun*, begin to take on "a life of its own." It deals with an episode in the life of a black family in Chicago, when they receive a windfall of insurance money and decide to buy a house in a white neighborhood. Miss Hansberry had written it in protest against the black "cardboard characters" that she had seen on the stage, and one of her objectives was to show "the many gradations in even one Negro family." The play's title is from Langston Hughes's "Harlem": "What happens to a dream deferred, / Does it dry up like a raisin in the sun . . .?" It opened on Broadway in 1959 and delighted the New York critics. Walter Kerr praised its "relieving and wonderfully caustic comedy." Brooks Atkinson wrote: "She has told the inner as well as the outer truths about a Negro family in Chicago. The play has vigor as well as veracity and is likely to destroy the complacency of anyone who sees it." *A Raisin in the Sun*, the first play by a black woman to be produced on Broadway, ran for nineteen months in New York and won the New York Drama Critics Circle Award as the best American play of 1959. Miss Hansberry's film adaptation was released by Columbia Pictures in 1961.

Miss Hansberry's second venture on the Broadway stage, *The Sign in Sidney Brustein's Window*, which had its premiere in October 1964, scarcely touches on the race question at all, but is concerned with the moral problems of a Jewish intellectual in Greenwich Village, a man of mind who has to learn painfully that people are more important than abstractions. "The silhouette of the Western intellectual poised in hesitation before the flames of involvement," she once said in discussing the play, "was an accurate symbolism of my closest friends." Illness prevented her from working on changes in the script during rehearsal, and Gerald Weales has suggested that in Sidney Brustein the author "has drawn a character more complicated than the commitment she demands from him—that the play is marred by Miss Hansberry's confusion "between her concept of drama as . . . social statement and drama as an examination of character." It drew only mixed notices, but nevertheless deeply impressed many people in the theatre, clergy, and other professions who helped keep it running until the death of Miss Hansberry, from cancer, about three months after its opening.

The Movement (1964), a notable collection of photographs of the black struggle for equality, owed much of its success to the savage deadpan wit of her text. At the time of her death she was occupied with several literary projects, including a study of Toussaint L'Ouverture and a play, *Les Blancs*, which probed the conflicting interests of black and white inhabitants of a young African republic. These subjects belong to the main currents of her life, which she said were based on her "awareness of the political force of the American Negro and African people." Her pride in being part of that force also gave her the courage to overcome a certain shyness when she spoke before civil rights and other groups. She had been raised as a Methodist, but came to regard herself as a nonbeliever.

Some years after her death, Robert Nemiroff assembled a program of excerpts from her plays, journals, speeches, and letters, forming a kind of biography of the author. It was presented off-Broadway in January 1969 as *To Be Young, Gifted and Black*, given as a series of dramatized readings by friends of both races. "Its main impression," wrote Ronald Bryden, "was of a warm, humorous, typically American college-girl intelligence, battering with impatience, but a good deal of wit, at the wall of prejudice dividing her from her peers." The program had a long run in New York and subsequently toured all over the United States. In 1972 there was a revival in New York of *The Sign in Sidney Brustein's Window*, with songs by Gary William Friedman and Ray Errol Fox. *Raisin*, a musical based on *Raisin in the Sun*, was a major Broadway success in 1973.

A slim, attractive, articulate, and cheerful woman, Lorraine Hansberry enjoyed her short life. She delighted in skiing, cooking, theatregoing, reading (especially biography), and talking with her friends.

PRINCIPAL WORKS: A Raisin in the Sun, 1959; The Movement, 1964 (England, A Matter of Colour); The Sign in Sidney Brustein's Window, 1965; To Be Young, Gifted and Black: Lorraine Hansberry in Her Own Words, 1969.
ABOUT: Cherry, G. S. Portraits in Color, 1962; Current Biography, 1959; Phelps, R. H. (ed.) Men in the News II, 1960; Weales, G. The Jumping-Off Place, 1969; Who's Who in America, 1964–1965. *Periodicals*—New York Times October 11, 1964; January 13, 1965; January 3, 1969; January 27, 1972; New Yorker May 9, 1959; Theatre Arts October 1960.

HARDWICK, ELIZABETH (July 27, 1916–), American novelist, short story writer, and essayist, writes: "I grew up in Lexington, Kentucky, among a large family of brothers and sisters. When I graduated from the University of Kentucky, I immediately made my way to New York City, feeling I am afraid like some provincial in Balzac, yearning for Paris. That feeling was common among Southerners of an artistic or intellectual bent. Indeed so great, at that time, was my interest in New York that I did not think of myself as a 'Southerner' and it has turned out that an urban life, mixed populations, diversity have continued to be of special interest and importance to me. I went to Columbia for a few years and then settled down to writing. My earliest desire was to write fiction and I wrote, over the years, two novels and many, many short stories. But I was also very much interested in intellectual matters, tended to be opinionated about politics, social problems, and the general cultural scene in America. These considerations led me inevitably to the essay. I have a great affection for the form and have given to it everything and more than would be required of fiction, that is, everything I possibly could. Indeed I have always written essays as if they were examples of imaginative writing, as I believe them to be. I received a Guggenheim fellowship after my first novel came out and also at that time I began to write for *Partisan Review*, the very peak of my ambition at that time. Around that magazine, in the work it published and the issues it cared about, I feel that I learned much that was essential to me. I wrote also for many other magazines, reviewing books, and writing essays on many topics. In 1949 I married Robert Lowell, and we traveled about a bit, lived for a time in Boston, and then came back to New York, with our daughter. During the time

ELIZABETH HARDWICK

we were in Boston I became interested in the enchanting William James and edited an edition of his letters. In 1963, I was with some friends one of the founders of the *New York Review of Books*. I am still advisory editor of this literary paper and write a great deal for it."

The Ghostly Lover explores, through the eyes of a young girl, the complex relationships within a large Kentucky family, presumably modeled on Miss Hardwick's own. The quality and promise of this first novel were widely recognized. Gertrude Buckman thought it lacked "structure and decisiveness," but called it a book "of the quietest kind of excellence" whose author "recognizes our evasions, the hints and revelations we give one another, the sudden conjunctions and isolations of the spirit." Diana Trilling said its general tone was "a twilight tone of sensibility; yet it has a way of every now and then suddenly bursting into the full crude light of a rare imaginative intensity." At such moments, "Miss Hardwick passes beyond, say, Eudora Welty at her beginning best, to come close to the slashing courage of D. H. Lawrence."

Her second novel, *The Simple Truth*, is an account as by two interested but detached observers of the trial of an Iowa college student, accused of murdering his wealthy sweetheart. The *New Yorker*'s reviewer was happy enough with the way the trial itself dwindles in importance as the novel emerges as "a study of several characters by a gifted writer who never fails to perceive the moment that reveals the whole personality." For this critic, Miss Hardwick succeeded in creating "an atmosphere of almost dazzling intimacy and involvement," but not all of her readers were so caught up. What seemed to some "finely shaded language" struck others as "stilted and mannered rhetoric." There was some feeling that the book's dialogue was too often overburdened with ideas, and in general it seemed admired as much as but enjoyed rather less than *The Ghostly Lover*.

There was however little but praise for *A View of My Own*, collecting seventeen "essays in literature and society," most of which had first appeared in *Partisan Review*. Even critics who disagreed with her opinions commended the prose style in which she expressed them—the "dry, almost matter-of-fact elegance" which Gerald Sykes christened "Bloomsbury-on-the-East River." And beyond this many reviewers were moved by the selflessness of Miss Hardwick's involvement with her subjects. Her concentrated awareness of and pleasure in the work of other writers seemed to Alfred Kazin so intense as to be actually creative, while Melvin Maddocks, speaking no doubt of her social concerns, found in the essays an engagement beyond compassion. He wrote: "Here is an unpalpitating kind of love, as a requirement of justice and plain accuracy. In this purified balance of sympathy, it is just possible, Miss Hardwick may be discovering the special function of the woman writer even as she superbly exemplifies it."

Elizabeth Hardwick is the daughter of Eugene and Mary (Ramsey) Hardwick. She received her A.B. from the University of Kentucky in 1938, her M.A. there the following year, and did postgraduate work at Columbia between 1939 and 1941. In 1967 she became the first woman to receive the $4,000 George Jean Nathan award, presented for her drama criticism in the *New York Review of Books*. She is an adjunct professor of English at Barnard College.

PRINCIPAL WORKS: The Ghostly Lover (novel), 1945; The Simple Truth (novel), 1955; (ed.) The Selected Letters of William James, 1961; A View of My Own: Essays in Literature and Society, 1962.

ABOUT: Contemporary Authors 7–8, 1963; Who's Who in America, 1970–1971. *Periodicals*—Christian Science Monitor August 23, 1962; Nation May 5, 1945; Reporter October 11, 1962.

HARRIS, JOHN WYNDHAM PARKES LUCAS BEYNON. *See* "WYNDHAM, JOHN"

HARROD, SIR ROY (FORBES) (February 13, 1900–), English economist and biographer, writes: "The keynote of my childhood was intense poverty. My mother (born Forbes-Robertson), a writer and painter, had been of beauty and brilliant promise in her youth, and was a great friend of Oscar Wilde, George Meredith and Henry James, and knew most of the eminent literary figures of the 'nineties. My home was one of high literary and artistic culture. My father, the son of a very distinguished antiquary, had once been affluent, but went broke when I was an infant. There was no twist or turn of poverty that I did not learn about; what cost money just could not be had. They managed, however, to send me as a day boy scholar to Westminster School, which I dearly loved; two masters there, Sargeaunt and Smedley, had a permanent influence on my life, a greater one than did any don at Oxford. I was intensely happy through all those years of stringent poverty.

"But then a shadow fell. When I was eighteen, my father died (aged sixty), leaving my mother with thirty-eight years still to live. There was not a penny in the bank. Always inclining to melancholy, she had been largely cut off from her early friends, and she was unable to adapt her writing or her mind to the post-1914 world. She struggled courageously, but her life was sad. I was the only child.

"From the earliest age my interest was in things of the mind. I went to New College, Oxford, where I had many stimulating contemporaries like Jack Haldane, Stephen Tomlin and Maurice Bowra. I have spent my life as a tutor of economics at Christ Church, Oxford, this being interrupted only by the Second World War (I was an officer cadet in the First), when I served directly under Lord Cherwell, who was Winston Churchill's principal aide.

"Before the war I made some specific contributions to economics, but also spent a great deal of time on college and university administration, which I later abandoned.

"Of my writings, the one I believe to be the best is *The Foundations of Inductive Logic*, but its tenets are grossly out of fashion. It could one day gain recognition, but it may not do so. I wrote two biographies, one of Maynard Keynes and one of Lord Cherwell. In the post-war period I have been a very voluminous writer on economics, both in books and for the press. At times I have had an itch to enter politics, and stood as Liberal candidate for Huddersfield in 1945.

"After the early shadows, my life has been an exceedingly happy one. Christ Church is a very wonderful place, unique. I have had many dear friends. I married at the age of thirty-eight and have two sons.

"In the last ten or fifteen years I have had an entirely unexpected bonus. The profession of economics has taken me all over the world, to give lectures or attend conferences. Of foreign countries, the one that I think I love most is Japan."

Sir Roy has been called "a don who can com-

ROY HARROD

municate the pleasures of college life, a liberal . . . and a cultivated economist who shares his master's view that economics are not an end in themselves but designed to promote the good life." That master is John Maynard Keynes, whose liberal and positive philosophy is at the basis of all of Harrod's influential and sometimes revolutionary economic theories.

To other economists, Sir Roy is said to be best known for his contributions to dynamic theory and the theory of imperfect competition, enunciated in technical articles and books which even his peers have sometimes found difficult reading. The general public know him better for his "bubbling and sometimes boiling" attacks on the economic policies of both Labour and Conservative postwar governments—essays, lectures, and letters stressing in particular the dangers of what he regards as excessive capital expenditure. These lively tracts, collected in such works as *Are These Hardships Necessary?*, *And So It Goes On*, and *Policy Against Inflation*, possess "in an eminent degree the virtue of putting fundamental issues as clearly, simply, and authoritatively as the subject allows."

Sir Roy's masterpiece is his life of Keynes. It was inevitably a controversial book, containing "irritating mannerisms, lapses in style and taste, and minor inaccuracies which appear magnified into major blemishes in the eyes of some of Keynes's intimate friends." Yet "it is a great book"—not merely a biography but "a great document in the history of twentieth century Britain; at once a study in the history of ideas, a survey of the development of economics and a portrait of the outstanding intellectual of the age." It is a book "full of excitement and vitality," its prose "exceptionally lucid; though it is neither elegant nor melodious."

The book, it was said, interprets Keynes's life as an expression of "Cambridge civilization"—"the encounter of a Cambridge intellectual with the world." It was an achievement all the more remarkable in that Harrod—though he worked briefly under Keynes at Cambridge as a young graduate—has spent most of his life at Oxford. He earned brilliant degrees there in Literae Humaniores (1921) and modern history (1922) at New College, and thereafter, until his retirement in 1967, served as a tutor at Christ Church, with two periods (1929–1937 and 1946–1952) as his university's lecturer in economics, and a longer one (1952–1967) as Nuffield Reader in Economics. He is an honorary student (i.e., fellow) of Christ Church and an honorary fellow of Nuffield College. Sir Roy has served as president of Section F of the British Association for the Advancement of Science (1938), as joint editor of the *Economic Journal* (1945–1961), and as a member of important national and international commissions. He is a fellow of the British Academy and a former president of the Royal Economic Society. His knighthood came in 1959, and he has honorary doctorates from the universities of Aberdeen, Poitiers, Pennsylvania, Glasgow, and Warwick. Sir Roy is a man of great personal charm and brilliance, as Sir Maurice Bowra testified in his *Memories*. A writer in the *Times Literary Supplement* (October 26, 1967) has called him "the most distinguished economist writing at Oxford since Edgeworth," but one whose reputation "has never quite matched his achievement. This is desperately unfair, because his work has been of a kind that entitles him to a major status as an originator of ideas and an acute analyst of the economic scene."

PRINCIPAL WORKS: International Economics, 1933 (revised 1957 and 1962); The Trade Cycle, 1936; Are These Hardships Necessary?, 1947; Towards a Dynamic Economics, 1948; The Life of John Maynard Keynes, 1951; And So It Goes On, 1951; Economic Essays, 1952; The Dollar, 1953 (revised 1963); Foundations of Inductive Logic, 1956; The Pound Sterling, 1951–1958, 1958; Policy Against Inflation, 1958; The Prof: A Personal Memoir of Lord Cherwell, 1959; Topical Comment, 1961; The British Economy, 1963; Reforming the World's Money, 1965; Towards a New Economic Policy, 1967; Dollar-Sterling Collaboration, 1968; Money, 1969; Sociology, Morals and Mystery (1970 Chichele Lectures), 1971.

ABOUT: Bowra, C. M. Memories, 1966; Contemporary Authors 9–10, 1964; International Who's Who, 1970–71; International Year Book and Statesmen's Who's Who, 1971; Who's Who, 1971. *Periodicals*—Times Literary Supplement February 23, 1951; October 26, 1967.

HART-DAVIS, SIR RUPERT (CHARLES)

(August 28, 1907–), English biographer and editor, is the only son of Richard Vaughan Hart-Davis and the former Sybil Mary Cooper. He was educated at Eton and at Balliol College, Oxford, where he made his mark as an actor. He left the university in 1927 to study at the Old Vic, and the following year worked as an actor at the Lyric Theatre, Hammersmith. Hart-Davis abandoned acting for publishing in 1929, when he joined William Heinemann Ltd. His first book appeared in 1930, an anthology of work by contemporary writers called *The Second Omnibus Book*. He left Heinemann's in 1931, was manager of the Book Society in 1932, and from 1933 to 1940 worked as a director of Jonathan Cape Ltd. His career was interrupted at that point by World War II, during which he served in the Coldstream Guards. In 1946 he founded his own publishing house, Rupert Hart-Davis Ltd.

RUPERT HART-DAVIS

His first book under the Hart-Davis imprint was *The Essential Neville Cardus* (1949), a selection from the books and articles of a distinguished music critic and cricket lover in which the predominance of cricketing items reflects Hart-Davis's own predilections. A kind of companion volume appeared the following year when Hart-Davis put together *Cricket All His Life* from the writings of E. V. Lucas.

Hart-Davis's first important book, and so far his only original one, was his biography of the novelist Hugh Walpole. In "poor Hughie" he had found a fascinating subject—a man who owed his great if temporary literary success more to his skill as a publicist than to any real talent as a novelist; a snob whose many friends were selected from among the literary and social leaders of his time, but who remained unhappy, unfulfilled, and lonely. Hart-Davis quotes at length from Walpole's correspondence with such figures as Henry James, Arnold Bennett, and Virginia Woolf, so arranging his material as to impart to the book "much of Hugh Walpole's own nervous boyish enthusiasm." The biography was universally praised, and it was said that the author had "painted in detail not only the picture of a success but the successful portrait of an age."

Three volumes of literary letters followed, of which the most important is Hart-Davis's edition of *The Letters of Oscar Wilde*. In the absence of a definitive biography of Wilde this, the first major collection of his letters, was recognized as a work of the greatest possible value. It was called "definitive both in scope and execution" and "a masterly piece of scholarship," and there was particular praise for Hart-Davis's succinct footnotes which, with his "intelligent and amusing index," provided "a fascinating Who's Who and panorama of the society out of which the letters sprang." According to a reviewer in the *Times Literary Supplement*, "the editor has performed a Herculean labour with faultless efficiency, an imaginative understanding of Wilde, and an unfailing awareness of what the reader needs to be told about him and his background."

Rupert Hart-Davis, who was knighted in 1967 for his services to literature, lives in Marske-in-Swaledale, near Richmond, Yorkshire. He remained a director of his publishing house, now a part of Granada Publishing Ltd., until his retirement in 1968. His first two marriages, to the actress Peggy Ashcroft (1929) and to Catherine Borden-Turner (1935) were dissolved. In 1964 he married Winifred Ruth (Ware) Simon who died in 1967. He made a fourth marriage in 1968 to June (Clifford) Williams. Hart-Davis has three children by his second marriage. His chairmanship of the committee of the London Library (1957–1969) and his membership of the Middlesex Cricket Club reflect his primary interests, collecting books and watching cricket.

PRINCIPAL WORKS: Hugh Walpole: A Biography, 1952. *As Editor*—The Second Omnibus Book, 1930; The Essential Neville Cardus, 1949; E. V. Lucas: Cricket All His Life, 1950; George Moore: Letters to Lady Cunard 1895–1933, 1957; The Letters of Oscar Wilde, 1962; Sir Max Beerbohm, Letters to Reggie Turner, 1964; More Theatres, 1898–1903, by Sir Max Beerbohm, 1969; Last Theatres, 1904–1910, by Sir Max Beerbohm, 1970; A Peep Into the Past and Other Prose Pieces by Sir Max Beerbohm, 1972.

ABOUT: West, A. Principles and Persuasions: The Literary Essays of Anthony West, 1957; Who's Who, 1971. *Periodicals*—New York Herald Tribune Book Review August 24, 1952; New Yorker August 23, 1952; Spectator June 29, 1962; Times Literary Supplement March 7, 1952; June 29, 1962.

CHRISTOPHER HASSALL

HASSALL, CHRISTOPHER (VERNON) (March 24, 1912–April 25, 1963), English biographer, poet, dramatist, and librettist, was born in London to John Hassall, a well-known painter and illustrator, and Constance Brooke-Webb. His parents sent him to St. Michael's College, Tenbury Wells, a choice that played a decisive part in his development as a poet and lyricist, since music formed an important part of the curriculum there and Hassall sang twice daily in the choir, unconsciously absorbing the phrasing and imagery of the hymns and acquiring the ability to fit speech patterns to music. He visited the college as an adult and realized while listening to the intoning of the Lord's Prayer how large a debt he owed to his early training.

He later attended Brighton College and then Wadham College, Oxford, where he read music and English literature. His love of poetry and desire to be a poet were already strongly developed. He had in fact previously sent some poems to Walter de la Mare and received a letter of encouragement. At Oxford his ambitions crystallized under the influence of his tutor, Lord David Cecil, but his undergraduate career was cut short by a financial crisis at home. He had acted with the Oxford University Dramatic Society, playing Romeo in John Gielgud's 1932 production of *Romeo and Juliet*, and when he left the university he embarked upon a theatrical career.

This took him in 1933 to Egypt and Australia with a touring company led by Nicholas Hannen. Back in England he was playing in *Henry VIII* at the Old Vic when he was invited to join the cast of *Proscenium* as Ivor Novello's understudy. It was an assignment which decided the course of Hassall's career. In 1935 Novello read Hassall's first volume of verse, *Poems of Two Years*, and asked him to write the libretto for the musical which became famous as *Glamorous Night*. Thereafter Hassall was Novello's chief lyricist, collaborating with him on five more shows that included *The Dancing Years* and *King's Rhapsody*. Nor was Hassall's skill as a librettist confined to romantic musicals. He wrote English versions of a number of foreign operas and collaborated on new works with such composers as William Walton (*Troilus and Cressida*), Arthur Bliss (*Tobias and the Angel*), and Antony Hopkins (*The Man From Tuscany*). Hassall also wrote several verse dramas, including *Christ's Comet*, performed in 1938 at Canterbury Cathedral, and *Out of the Whirlwind* (1953), commissioned by the Dean and Chapter of Westminster Abbey to mark the coronation of Elizabeth II. His plays were thought a little static, but excellent in their characterization and often eloquent.

At the beginning of his career, Hassall had met Sir Edward Marsh, patron of the arts and for many years private secretary to Winston Churchill, who knew virtually everyone of social and literary importance in England. Marsh liked Hassall's verse, took him up, and introduced him to others of his friends and protégés. The plain, georgic kind of verse fostered by Marsh has long been out of fashion, and Hassall's reputation as a poet has no doubt suffered by the association. In fact, if he was not a great poet, he was a very able one, sometimes rather imprecise in his language and prone to clichés, but witty and zestful, with a real talent for descriptive writing and the striking image. He received the Hawthornden Prize and the A. C. Benson medal in 1939 for his narrative poem *Penthesperon*, and his later volumes, *The Slow Night*, *The Red Leaf*, and *Bell Harry*, were all generally admired. The latter is the most successful of his longer poems, a sonnet sequence in memory of his friend Frances Cornford built around the single symbolic image of the central tower of Canterbury Cathedral.

Nevertheless it may be that Hassall's biographies comprise the most lasting part of his varied output. His life of Sir Edward Marsh appeared in 1959 and brought him the James Tait Black Memorial Prize. Most reviewers thought it too long, too unselective and gossipy, but enjoyed it nevertheless as a lively and zestful portrait of an extraordinary individual and of one whole layer of English society during a period of rapid change. The *Times Literary Supplement* praised its "vivid, easy English prose which . . . is also scrupulously correct."

Hassall's study of Rupert Brooke, dealing with the same society and often the same people that figured in the Marsh biography, had a similar reception. It was enjoyed both as "a rich pageant of English life" and as an "entertaining, touching, and illuminating biography," but accused of prolixity and "genteel evasiveness"—a refusal "to come to grips with the central issues of Brooke's personality and psychic history." All the same it seemed to Harold Hobson "a book which will destroy romantic illusions about Brooke, but will raise the stature of his poetry."

Hassall served during World War II in the Army, mostly with the Education Corps and in the War Office. He was released in 1946 with the rank of major. From 1947 to 1949 he served as director of voice at the Old Vic Theatre School, and in 1950 as poetry editor of the BBC's Third Programme. Hassall returned occasionally to the stage as an actor, and for many years was a poetry reader for the Apollo Society. He was a Councillor and Fellow of the Royal Society of Literature and a Governor of the London Academy of Music and Dramatic Art. Hassall was a talented composer and himself wrote the music for *Christ's Comet*. Renowned for his cordiality, his ability to disseminate enthusiasm and to iron out petty disputes and jealousies, he was described by Leonard Clark as "an amateur in the best sense of the term." He died suddenly, on a train in Chatham, Kent, and was survived by his wife, the former Evelyn (Chapman) Lynett, and their two children.

PRINCIPAL WORKS: *Poems*—Poems of Two Years, 1935; Penthesperon, 1938; The Slow Night, and Other Poems, 1940–1948, 1949; The Red Leaf, 1957; Bell Harry, 1963. *Plays*—Christ's Comet, 1937; The Player King, 1953; Out of the Whirlwind, 1953. *Libretti for Ivor Novello*—Glamorous Night, 1935; Careless Rapture, 1936; Crest of the Wave, 1937; The Dancing Years, 1939; Arc de Triomphe, 1943; King's Rhapsody, 1949. *Libretti etc. for others*—(for Antony Hopkins) The Man From Tuscany, 1951; (for Wilfrid Mellers) Voices of the Night (cantata), 1952; (for William Walton) Troilus and Cressida, 1954; (for Arthur Bliss) Tobias and the Angel, 1960. *Nonfiction*—The Timeless Quest: Stephen Haggard (biography), 1948; Notes on Verse-Drama, 1948; Words by Request: A Selection of Occasional Pieces in Verse and Prose, 1952; Edward Marsh: Patron of the Arts (U.S., A Biography of Edward Marsh), 1959; Rupert Brooke: A Biography, 1964; (with Edward Marsh) Ambrosia and Small Beer: The Record of a Correspondence, 1964.

ABOUT: Enright, D. J. Conspirators and Poets, 1966; Leasor, J. Author by Profession, 1952; Who's Who, 1963. *Periodicals*—New Statesman May 29, 1964; New Yorker October 10, 1964; Southern Review 5 No. 3, 1940; Spectator June 12, 1959; Times (London) April 27, 1963; Times Literary Supplement June 3, 1949; June 12, 1959; November 28, 1963; May 28, 1964.

HAWKES, JOHN (CLENDENNIN BURNE)

(August 17, 1925–), American novelist, writes: "I was born in 1925 in Stamford, Connecticut, and spent my early childhood a few miles south of that city in the town of Sound Beach (now Old Greenwich) which I best remember for its large houses, old-fashioned grocery and candy store filled with the violent monologue of an ancient green parrot, a meat market where the butchers still wore straw hats, and the stable (Rennie's Riding Academy) that existed just beyond the trees at the edge of my grandmother's property. My first teacher was Mr. Rennie, a stern little bow-legged Cockney who was already old when I knew him, and all my childhood seems to have consisted of working in Mr. Rennie's gardens to pay for my hours atop his horses, or, since I suffered from asthma, of wheezing away at dusk in my bedroom from which I could hear the kicking and thumping of the nearby horses as they settled down for the night. In those days my mother undertook my education, so that properly speaking she rather than Mr. Rennie was my first teacher. But whereas in reading and arithmetic I was a poor student, in the world of horses I displayed a natural talent. This world, which was soon gone, continued to exist for me in the imagination, and much of my fiction is based on it. However, about thirty years later, during a brief visit as writer-in-residence at the University of Virginia, I was able to ride horseback in the fields beyond Charlottesville, and so had the pleasure of discovering that the ambitions of childhood can sometimes be fulfilled after all in the life of the man.

"Thanks to my father, who was a natural storyteller and re-created family lore (a political murder in New York, a golden wedding anniversary in Ireland) with energy and vividness and a kind of brilliant nostalgia, and who was also a true adventurer and pursued his dream with courage and idealism but never ruthlessness, I spent my early adolescence in Alaska where I acquired a permanent preoccupation with the alien nightmare landscape of darkness, rain, high wind, mountains, fragments of glaciers, distant bears, wild strawberries, one-legged Indians and the terrifying ruins of abandoned mining towns. In Juneau I wrote my first story (about death in an abandoned gold mine), listened to Hitler's maniacal speeches on a dusty ornate radio, and made up my mind to spend my life, if possible, in the East.

"By 1940 we had in fact returned to the East and I had begun to write poetry. I wrote mordant poetry for brief periods in Trinity School in New York City and Pawling High School in the upper part of the state, briefly at Harvard (where I was encouraged by Robert Hillyer and later by Theodore Spencer), briefly in Italy and Germany where I drove an ambulance with the American Field Service and developed, suddenly, a detached sympathy for the corrupted and deteriorated landscape more appropriate to fiction than to poetry. In 1947 I gave up poetry for fiction, married Sophie Tazewell from Norfolk, Virginia, returned to complete my last two years at Harvard and met Albert J. Guerard in whose writing class I wrote my first visionary novel, *The Cannibal.*

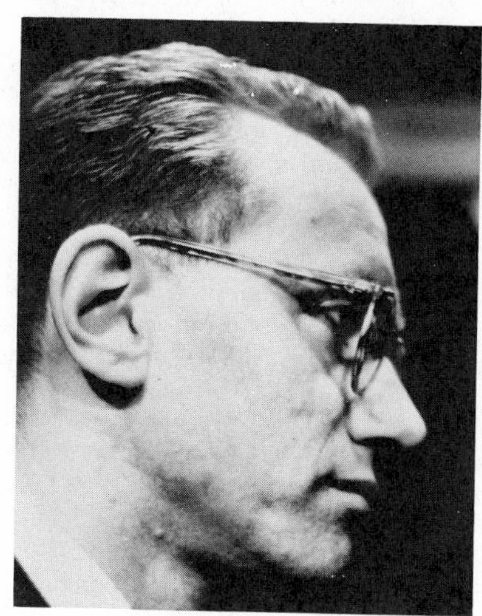

JOHN HAWKES

"As the father of four children and as a teacher (at Harvard and thereafter at Brown University) I have continued to live in the pleasantly remote and fading world of New England. But we have still been fortunate enough to discover more 'mythical' landscapes (the West Indies on a Guggenheim Fellowship, San Francisco on a Ford Foundation Fellowship) and despite my nostalgic temperament and some moments of serenity and personal satisfaction, I find that in fiction I am still committed to the nightmare world and comic treatments of violence."

Even before he turned his attention to the novel, at a time just after World War II when he was principally interested in the theatre, Hawkes was speculating about the possibilities of the kind of "unsympathetic" art that deliberately alienates its audience. "This was important," he said in *Book Week* (May 30, 1965), "in that it served in a way as a basis for my fiction, which, in the beginning, was intended to keep the reader at a distance. I'm a very detached writer, interested in the absolute creation of pure vision. . . . My [earlier] books were intentional smashing of conventional forms, but I'm not interested in mere indulgence or chaos. I believe my books to have form and genuine coherence; there's always conscious control."

This was evident even in Hawkes's first books, which were attempts to create purely verbal structures, unsupported by the usual girders of plot and character. The first and best of these nearly abstract novels was *The Cannibal*, a repellent vision of "the corrupted and deteriorated landscape" of postwar Germany, inhabited by people who retain no vestige of hope or love or humanity, but prey upon each other like beasts. Time is dislocated and narrative logic ignored, and monstrous scenes are described with a loving and witty precision reminiscent of Hieronymus Bosch. Many readers were confused or disgusted, but a few recognized its quality from the beginning. Paul Engle called it "one of the most brilliant books to be published in this country in a long time. In imaginativeness of phrasing, poised rhythm of prose, richness of detail, it surpasses any such book I can recall." It has been reprinted several times, and has become something of a classic of the avant-garde. Reviewers were reminded of Faulkner, Kafka, and Nathanael West, and though Hawkes had read none of these authors at that time, he agrees that his work "shares a birthmark" with them and also with Djuna Barnes and Flannery O'Connor.

Another violated country, the gaunt and arid landscape of the American West, was the setting and to some extent the inspiration of *The Beetle Leg*. Here the land has been raped to make a dam, but has claimed a sacrifice, burying one construction worker alive. The novel is built around this incident and its effects, but with as little regard for narrative conventions as *The Cannibal*. The extreme authority and concentration of Hawkes's prose was admired, but it remains the least known of his major books, though he himself cherishes it as the work that "comes closer than anything I have written to creating reality out of language itself." It was followed by two short novels, *The Goose on the Grave* and *The Owl*, both gothic fantasies set in Italy. They were republished in 1969, together with an earlier novella, "Charivari," and six short sketches, in a collection called *Lunar Landscapes*.

The Lime Twig is superficially quite different from its predecessors in that it possesses a coherent and even suspenseful plot and consistent characterization. It is set in London during World War II and centers on William Hencher and a married couple, Michael and Margaret Banks, who move into his house and become the objects of his devotion. The respectable Banks become involved in a criminal attempt to steal a famous racehorse, thus entering the half-real world of their unconscious fantasies. In the outcome Hencher is crushed to death by this animal, Margaret Banks is beaten slowly to death by the sadistic gangster Thick, and her husband seeks atonement under the hoofs of the racehorses he worships.

Hawkes's adoption of a sequential narrative in no way modified the radical originality of his vision. He seeks to write, he says, in "a climate of pure and immoral *creation*." A. J. Guerard, one of the first and most loyal of his champions, has spoken of the "demonic sympathy" that Hawkes extends equally in his novels to the corrupters (whose sins go unpunished), and to the corrupted (who generally pay a horrible price for their fall from grace, and often rather enjoy it). Hawkes's preoccupation with sexuality and violence is not moral but rhetorical; as S. K. Oberbeck says in *Contemporary American Novelists*, "His is a disturbingly resonant and precise language, expression urged from an intense clash with our deepest obsessions." Thus, during the fatal beating of Margaret Banks, "one feels a quickening in the prose, a tensing of cadences, almost a rhetorical sense of jubilation: Here is something about which one can write!"

For Flannery O'Connor, the intensity and compression of Hawkes's prose made a reading of *The Lime Twig* a profound but suffocating experience that one "suffers like a dream." Peter Brooks spoke of the novel's final effect as "a sense of overwhelming lucidity about our relations to others and to ourselves, a monstrous clarity about our passions." And with this book, for the first time, Hawkes found a readership that was not limited to an avant-garde minority. A Guggenheim Fellowship and a grant from the National Institute of Arts and Letters took him to the West Indies, where he wrote his next novel.

In *Second Skin* Hawkes writes for the first time in the first person. His narrator is a retired naval officer, Skipper, who offers the "naked history" of his life as evidence that he is a man of "love and courage." The reader quickly discovers that he is no such thing. In one appallingly comic scene, while his daughter is repeatedly raped under a cactus in the desert, Skipper holds her hand and murmurs, "Courage." He is a soft man who breeds failure and death. Peter Brooks thought that *Second Skin* lacked "the stark and horrifying lucidity of *The Lime Twig*" but has "its own clarity: a clarity of the senses, a clarity of emotional landscapes rendered in full sensuous dimension. Hawkes's success is a question of total style; his senses and his imagination are alive, and his control of language—the choice of word and of intonation, the rhythms and the coloring—is remarkable. The brilliance of the moment found in *The Cannibal* has been shaped into an overall vision that we accept as coherent and intelligent."

After *Second Skin* Hawkes spent some time on a Ford Foundation Fellowship with the San Francisco Actors' Workshop, and wrote a number of one-act plays. Four of these were published in *The Innocent Party* and were thought on the whole rather pretentious and unsatisfactory, though often very funny.

Another change of landscape, this time a sabbatical in Greece and the south of France, produced *The Blood Oranges*. A cultivated American couple, Cyril and Fiona, live in "Illyria" a life dedicated to leisure, beauty, and sexual "aesthetics." The book is an account of their seduction and eventual destruction of another couple who come to stay in their village, narrated by Cyril in an effete and mannered style through which his selfishness and vanity are progressively exposed. It seemed to one reviewer "the work of a contemptible imagination"; to another "a fabric of unfolding ironies, an impressively artful book" in which, however, Hawkes's "earlier experimental interests seem to have become a scrupulous concern for the art of writing itself."

"My prose may be radical," Hawkes says, "but my habits are quite ordinary." And indeed Herbert Blau has described him as "crew-cut, garrulous . . . about as gothic as a fraternity pledge." He received his A.B. at Harvard in 1949 and from then until 1955 was assistant to the production manager of the Harvard University Press. He remained at Harvard for another three years as an English teacher, and went to Brown University in 1958 as an assistant professor, earning his M.A. with honors there in 1962 and becoming a full professor in 1967. In 1971–1972 he was visiting distinguished professor of creative writing at the City College of New York.

PRINCIPAL WORKS: The Cannibal, 1950; The Beetle Leg, 1951; The Goose on the Grave *and* The Owl, 1954; The Lime Twig, 1961; Second Skin, 1964; The Innocent Party: Four Short Plays (The Innocent Party, The Wax Museum, The Undertaker, The Questions), 1967; Lunar Landscapes, 1969; The Blood Oranges, 1971.

ABOUT: Contemporary Authors 4, 1963; Graham, J. (ed.) The Merrill Studies in "Second Skin," 1971; Guerard, A. J. *introduction to* The Cannibal (1962 ed.); Malin, I. New American Gothic, 1962; Moore, H. T. (ed.) Contemporary American Novelists, 1964; Scholes, R. The Fabulators, 1967; Vinson, J. (ed.) Contemporary Novelists, 1972; Who's Who in America, 1972–1973. *Periodicals*—Book Week May 30, 1965; Encounter June 1966; Massachusetts Review Summer 1966; Nation September 2, 1961; New York Review of Books July 13, 1967; New York Times Book Review April 5, 1964; May 29, 1966; Time February 6, 1950; Wisconsin Studies in Contemporary Literature Summer 1965.

"HEAD, MATTHEW." *See* CANADAY, JOHN

HEARNE, JOHN (February 4, 1926–), West Indian novelist, dramatist, and critic, was born of Jamaican parents in Montreal, Canada, and educated at Jamaica College. After serving with the Royal Air Force during World War II (1943–1946), he studied philosophy and history at Edinburgh University and holds the degree of M.A. (Econ.). From 1950 to 1952 he taught in Jamaica and subsequently lived in London, Paris, and the south of France. Returning in 1956, he traveled throughout the Caribbean and Guiana. In 1962 he served for a time in the information department of the government of Jamaica. Since then he has taught at the University of the West Indies—as resident tutor (1962–1967) in the department of extra-mural studies, and since 1968 as head of the university's creative center. In 1967–1968 he taught as visiting professor of Commonwealth literature at the University of Leeds, and in 1969–1970 was O'Connor Professor in Literature at Colgate University, New York. He has been married twice and has two children.

JOHN HEARNE

Unlike some other established West Indian writers, Hearne has always returned to the Caribbean where, as George Lamming has said, there is hardly any such thing as a firm reading public. The vehemence of Hearne's loyalty was revealed on one occasion in his review in *The Caribbean Quarterly* of V. S. Naipaul's travel book *The Middle Passage* (1963). Identifying the book's "fundamental weakness" as "the fact that people embarrass Mr. Naipaul, Caribbean people, that is," he went on: "He finds man under this sky to be raw, untidy, vulgar and as yet only a pass degree student in the great examinations set by Europe, Asia and Africa."

Hearne's own findings have sent him beyond straightforward chronicling into sensuous, sometimes visionary, metamorphoses of the local scene—almost as if (to paraphrase some of his critics) he were countering remoteness with myth, lack of size with a *bel canto* grandeur, and backwardness with fastidious suavity. In the opinion of the Barbadian critic Barrie Davis, this heightened and "unremitting" vision of Hearne's, which provides "masses of data about the quality and density of the Caribbean experience," is sometimes too greedy and unselective: "When description gives way to narrative, one has the sense of a brake being let off a high-powered car."

Hearne's first novel, *Voices Under the Window* (1955), is a rather excessively neat moral fable in which a white Jamaican lawyer, who has devoted himself to the poor of his island, reviews his past as he lies bleeding to death from machete wounds. In subsequent novels the setting is Cayuna, an imaginary West Indian island which greatly resembles Jamaica. *Stranger at the Gate* (1956) was welcomed as "a taut, nervous, muscular book" by a "born writer." "Characters and actions," wrote Peter Green, "cohere with rare fidelity against their sun-scorched, garish background, and the final tragedy reaches an almost Stoic height of self-sacrifice." In *The Faces of Love* (1957) Hearne switched from third-person narrative to first, from the tragedy of a wanted alien to the equally tragic fortunes of Jojo Rygin, a building contractor, on his return from prison. "Yet the book," as John Davenport insisted, "is not swamped by its drama: it is the evocation of the whole island, its birds, beasts, flowers and humans that remains with one unforgettably at the end. It would be worth reading for the descriptions of the hurricane alone."

Of the next Cayuna volume, *The Autumn Equinox* (1959), Hearne himself has said, "I took a chance with this one, and there were times, after it was finished and at the printers, when I wondered if I hadn't maybe gone out too far." The novel reads as verbal chamber music for three highly individual voices taking turns to soliloquize: Nicholas Stacey, twice a widower, now retired to Cayuna after a turbulent life; Eleanor, his adopted daughter, awakening to womanhood while running the Stacey general store; and Jim Diver, a young pro-Castro American. Each of the three, taking his turn to ruminate, lays bare the others. They think and speak in a prose both elegant and idiomatic that seems, wrote Paul West, "like an heraldic echo of the ripe commotion of the island itself."

Land of the Living (1961) brings to Cayuna a Jewish biologist, Mahler, who has lost his family in extermination camps. By far the most ratiocinative of Hearne's major characters (although by no means the least sensual of them), he seeks to re-establish his identity in an exotic limbo in which he himself is exotic too. Barrie Davis believes that Mahler represents Hearne's first triumph over "the moral determinism that deadened his earlier characters." Priapic, fiercely self-analytical, and given to high-strung outbursts of sheer euphoria, he seemed to several reviewers Hearne's most intricate, most interesting creation.

Placed by the *Times Literary Supplement* among "the mandarins and technical innovators" of Commonwealth literature, Hearne has also something of Mahler's "capacity for making an enormous moral drama out of the most ordinary material." "Perhaps his greatest gift," wrote John Davenport, "is his ability to create sensuous harmonies between men and nature, the poetic quality one finds in Hemingway. . . . His personages never get lost in the background; they are distinct, boldly and clearly drawn . . . they belong to the Caribbean as Hardy's men and women belong to Egdon Heath."

Hearne's next book was a considerable departure. *Fever Grass*, published in 1969 after a long silence, is a suspense novel set in Jamaica—the result of a collaboration between Hearne and another Jamaican novelist, Morris Cargill, published pseudonymously as by "John Morris." Reviewers found it an exciting if amoral and ruthless mixture of "interracial relations, Caribbean terror, and international espionage," and one critic thought it better than anything Hearne had written in a weightier vein.

PRINCIPAL WORKS: Voices Under the Window, 1955; Stranger at the Gate, 1956; The Faces of Love, 1957 (U.S., Eye of the Storm); The Autumn Equinox, 1959; Land of the Living, 1961; (with Morris Cargill, as "John Morris") Fever Grass, 1969; (with Morris Cargill, as "John Morris") The Candywine Development, 1970.

ABOUT: Coulthard, G. R. Caribbean Literature, 1966; Dathorne, O. R. Caribbean Narrative, 1966; Howes, B. From the Green Antilles, 1966; James, L. The Islands in Between, 1967; Ramchand, K. West Indian Narrative, 1966; Vinson, J. (ed.) Contemporary Novelists, 1972; Who's Who in Jamaica, 1966. *Periodicals*—Caribbean Quarterly December 1962; English Spring 1967; New Statesman November 14, 1959; November 3, 1961; New York Times Book Review November 19, 1961; New Yorker September 15, 1962; Spectator April 26, 1957; Times Literary Supplement May 3, 1957; September 16, 1965.

***HÉBERT, ANNE** (August 1, 1916–), French-Canadian poet, novelist, short story writer, and dramatist, was born and brought up in her parents' country house at Sainte-Catherine-de-Fossambault, near Quebec. An invalid for a long time as a child, she was educated at home, where the atmosphere was intellectually a highly stimulating one. She is the daughter of a distinguished literary critic, the late Maurice-Lang Hébert, and the former Marguerite Marie Taché, who numbered among their friends some of the liveliest minds in Quebec.

With her cousin, Hector de Saint-Denys-Garneau, and her two younger brothers and sisters, Anne Hébert explored and grew to love the countryside around her home. But her natural tendency to loneliness and introspection seems to have been reinforced rather than dissipated by the constant presence of a closely knit family. She began to write poetry in adolescence, benefiting greatly from the advice of her father and of her cousin, himself a poet.

She was slow to publish, but her first collection,

* ā bâr′

Les Songes en équilibre (Dreams in Equilibrium, 1942), aroused great critical interest and received Quebec's Prix David. These harsh, dry poems, written in a free verse not far from prose, record a slow and painful pilgrimage from the innocent delights of childhood to the acceptance of a bleak spiritual duty. In "Mort" the poet sees the last of her youthful fancies depart and is "left alone / With a noble Christ / In my arms." Henceforth there is a total renunciation of earthly pleasures and the pursuit through lonely self-abnegation of spiritual and poetic fulfillment.

Gradually Anne Hébert came to see that the nun-like life she had chosen was stifling her poetry, and this bitter realization pervades her second book, *Le Tombeau des rois* (The Tomb of the Kings, 1953). These remarkable poems resemble her earlier work in manner, but express a tightly controlled anguish with absolute technical assurance, free of the slackness that sometimes marred the first collection. Pierre Emmanuel in his introduction compares this poetry to tracings made in bone with the point of a dagger. Here poignant memories of childhood and freedom are mixed with dark poems full of the imagery of claustrophobia, groping, and blindness. Anne Hébert's cousin, Saint-Denys-Garneau, underwent a similar spiritual struggle, which silenced him as a poet and ended with his death at the age of thirty-one. Mlle. Hébert was more fortunate, and at the end of *Le Tombeau des rois* celebrates the end of her dark night as her groping hands "part the day like a curtain," and her blind bird flies.

Poèmes (1960) reprints *Le Tombeau des rois* and contains a number of new poems which, though still packed with painful imagery, lament not the poet's suffering but the world's. And there is a new note of hope, as in "La Ville tuée" (The Murdered Town), in which the crushed and tormented inhabitants overthrow their oppressors. Anne Hébert has come to regard it as the poet's task to work in the world for man's redemption, as the spokesman between man and God. This conviction is expressed in a new freedom and confidence of style, with longer lines and bolder imagery, though she still writes with a cold and abstract purity that produces in Edmund Wilson, for example, "a mortal chill." Other critics have reacted very differently to her work and many, like André Rousseaux, regard her as "one of the greatest contemporary poets in the French language."

Anne Hébert's reconciliation with life has been reflected in many ways. In January 1953 she accepted a demanding post, involving much travel, with the Canadian National Office for Film and Television. In 1954 she received a grant which enabled her to spend three years in Paris, where she wrote her first novel, *Les Chambres de bois* (The Wooden Rooms, 1958), a poetic, symbolically autobiographical work in which a young woman, stifling in her husband's morbid dream world, is freed by a young locksmith.

ANNE HÉBERT

Returning to Canada in 1957, Mlle. Hébert found herself famous. In that year she was honored by the Association France-Canada, and a year later accepted the Prix Littéraire Duvernay. *Les Chambres de bois* was awarded Quebec's Prix Littéraire in 1958. In 1960 she received the poetry prize of the Canadian Council of Arts and was elected to the Société Royale du Canada. The Council of Arts gave her another grant in 1961–1962.

Meanwhile, Anne Hébert had turned her attention to such public media as the film and the theatre. Her film scenario *La Canne à pêche* (The Fishing Rod, 1959) recaptured her own love of nature in a story about a little girl's first discovery of the countryside. In 1960 she wrote a scenario for a film about Saint-Denys-Garneau. *Le Temps sauvage* (The Savage Time, 1963) is a play about a mother who, seeking to protect her children from life, cages them in love. It was thought "theatrically unconventional" but "without doubt a text of a richness little known in Canadian literature." *Kamouraska* (1970) is a novel, based on fact, in which Elisabeth Rolland, dutifully watching at her husband's deathbed, remembers the time twenty years earlier when her brutal first husband, Seigneur of Kamouraska in the frozen north, had been murdered with her approval by her young American lover. This elegant romance, somewhat over-long, was admired for the clear picture it gives of the stifling conventions of nineteenth-century provincial Canada. Mlle. Hébert has also written television plays and a collection of short stories, *Le Torrent* (1950), which in their themes and intensity resemble her early poetry.

PRINCIPAL WORKS IN ENGLISH TRANSLATION: [Selected Poems of] Saint-Denys-Garneau [and] Anne Hébert (ed. and tr. by F. R. Scott), 1962; Kamouraska, 1973.
ABOUT: Marcotte, G. Une Littéraire qui se fait, 1962; Oxford Companion to Canadian History and Literature, 1967; Pagé, P. Anne Hébert, 1965; Robert, G. La Poétique du songe: introduction à l'œuvre d'Anne Hébert, 1962; Sylvestre, G. and others (eds.) Écrivains canadiens, 1964; Tougas, G. History of French-Canadian Literature, 1966; Wilson, E. O Canada, 1967. *Periodicals*—Canadian Literature Fall 1961; Cité Libre April 1961; Le Devoir October 3, 1953; L'Enseignement Secondaire March–April 1963; Liberté September–October 1959.

HECHT, ANTHONY (EVAN) (January 16, 1923–), American poet, was born in New York City, the son of Melvyn Hahlo Hecht and the former Dorothea Holzman. His brother Roger is also a poet. Anthony Hecht received his B.A. at Bard College in 1944 and then went into the Army as an infantry rifleman, serving in the United States, Europe, and Japan. He began his teaching career in 1947 at Kenyon College, moving on to the State University of Iowa in 1948, and New York University in 1949. He earned his M.A. at Columbia University in 1950.

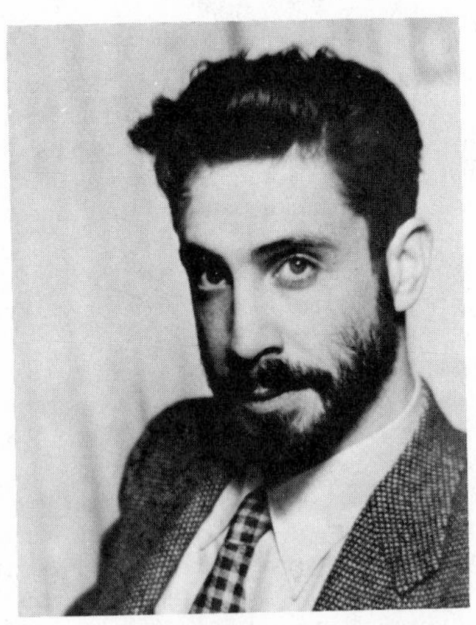

ANTHONY HECHT

By this time Hecht's poems were appearing in such magazines as the *Kenyon Review*, the *Hudson Review*, *Furioso*, and *The New Yorker*. In 1951 the American Academy of Arts and Letters awarded him its Prix de Rome. During the resulting year in Rome, Hecht's translations from Rilke were set to music by the composer Lukas Foss as the cantata *A Parable of Death*.

Hecht's first book of poems, *A Summoning of Stones*, appeared in 1954. In his review—a fairly representative one—Richard Wilbur wrote: "Anthony Hecht has much of every virtue except passionate simplicity. His characteristic performance is an extended and ornate essay-poem, full of ingeniously linked materials from art, literature and travel; the form is commonly intricate; the execution is excellent." The collection contained much "delightful pastiche"—poems which have the effect of "thank you" notes to Wallace Stevens, Auden, Ransom, and others of Hecht's many masters. There were critics however who admired even in some of these early poems a "knobbly personal rhythm," a wittiness which "only preludes or contains a tough earnestness."

Two long poems, *The Seven Deadly Sins* and *Struwwelpeter*, appeared in 1958, both in limited editions. It was not until 1967 that Hecht published his second major collection, *The Dark Hours*. Most reviewers thought it an important step forward, containing a number of poems in which Hecht had found his own voice and spoke with a new urgency out of "a deeper vein of feeling." Ian Hamilton, who previously had found it difficult to locate in Hecht's work "any central, unifying personality," was impressed by "a handful of pieces," laconic, intense, and flexible, "which finally distinguish [him] from the ruck of slick, fiftyish academics whom he so frequently seems to typify." Chad Walsh spoke in similar terms of Hecht's discovery of "a personal and poetic center of gravity permitting him to move with freedom through varied forms and subjects"—from the tightest verse forms to "the multi-part architecture of 'Rites and Ceremonies,' a majestic poem on the destiny and endurance of the Jewish people, concluding on a tone of prayer that very few living poets could bring off." This volume brought Hecht both the Pulitzer Prize and the Loines Award, and was a Poetry Book Society choice in England. *The Seven Deadly Sins* was reprinted in *The Hard Hours*, with Leonard Baskin's woodcuts from the original edition.

In 1951, inspired it is said by a heavy Roman meal, Hecht had invented a new light verse form which begins with a double-dactyl nonsense line and proceeds according to rules as strict as those for the clerihew or the *haiku*. For example: "Higgledy-piggledy / Titus Andronicus, / Fitting himself to the / Classical clime, / Covered his belly with / Decalcomanias / Picturing passionate / Sexual crime." *Jiggery-Pokery: A Compendium of Double Dactyls*, edited by Hecht and John Hollander, was published in 1967 and much enjoyed as a "good instance of donnish humor." *Time* called the form "as rhythmically insidious as the clack of rails under a train," and said that it had already infected Eastern campuses.

Hecht, who believes that poetry and the classroom "involve the same kind of living and thinking," taught from 1956 to 1959 at Smith College, from 1961 to 1967 at Bard College, and since then at the University of Rochester. He has received two Guggenheim fellowships (1954 and 1959), a *Hudson Review* fellowship (1958), a Rockefeller Foundation fellowship (1967), two Ford Foundation fellowships (1960 and 1968) and a Brandeis University Creative Arts Award (1965). In 1971 he was Hurst Professor at Washington University. His 1954 marriage to Patricia Harris ended in divorce in 1961 and he was married again in 1971, to Helen D'Alessandro. He has two sons by his first marriage, Jason and Adam. Hecht's interests include music and architecture.

PRINCIPAL WORKS—*All poetry*: A Summoning of Stones, 1954; The Seven Deadly Sins, 1958; Struwwelpeter, 1958; The Hard Hours, 1967; (as editor with John Hollander, and co-author) Jiggery-Pokery: A Compendium of Double Dactyls, 1967.

ABOUT: Contemporary Authors 11–12, 1965; Grigson, G. (ed.) Concise Encyclopedia of Modern World Literature, 1963; Murphy, R. (ed.) Contemporary Poets of the English Language, 1970; Who's Who in America, 1970–1971. *Periodicals*—Mademoiselle August 1953.

***HEIBERG, GUNNAR (EDVARD RODE)** (November 11, 1857–February 22, 1929), the most important Norwegian dramatist after Ibsen and a notable essayist, was born in Kristiania (now Oslo) and grew up there. His father was Edvard Omsen Heiberg, scholar, teacher, lawyer, and journalist. His mother was Augusta Rode, daughter of a Danish college president. Heiberg attended an exclusive private school where his father taught history and, matriculating in 1874, went on to Kristiania University. There he associated with a group of young radical intellectuals and writers and soon came to share their literary ambitions, and their atheism. He left the university after a year and began to write. His first success came in 1878, when he published two poems expressing his faith in man's revolutionary spirit and unconquerable mind.

Shortly afterwards Heiberg made the acquaintance of Ibsen during a stay in Rome, and was greatly impressed. His ambitions now turned towards the theatre, though his unprepossessing appearance frustrated him in his first intention, which was to become an actor. In 1882–1883 he studied literature and the drama in Copenhagen and Munich, and in 1883 he completed his first major play, *Tante Ulrikke* (Aunt Ulrikke). The title character is modeled on the Norwegian feminist Asta Hansteen and the play deals with the struggle between the dawning socialism of the period—the new passion for justice and equality—and the

* hā′ berg

GUNNAR HEIBERG

narrow prejudices of the established bourgeoisie. Strongly influenced by Ibsen both in theme and style, it is nevertheless far more than mere pastiche —a witty and forceful piece of work, surprisingly mature in its technique. It was produced in 1891 and earned its author an annual government stipend.

In 1884 Heiberg was appointed director of the National Theatre in Bergen. The following year he married an actress there, Didi Tollefsen. Unfortunately she was as individualistic and obstinate as her husband and their unhappy marriage ended in divorce. Meanwhile, in 1888, after a period of study in Berlin, Heiberg left the National Theatre, where his championship of modern plays had brought him much criticism. Thereafter he devoted himself to writing. *Kong Midas* (King Midas), his next play, was written in 1888 in less than a month, and published in 1890. It is a defense of the human right to happiness, and a sharp attack on the hypocrisy and cant of those who find moral reasons for restricting that right. The play, regarded as an attack on the revered dramatist Björnson, caused a furor.

Kong Midas marked the end of Heiberg's allegiance to realism and the "well-made play." During the 1890s, his most prolific period, he wrote a succession of plays that were a new and unique combination of savage satire and exalted lyricism. They are celebrations of the lonely and dedicated individual, uncompromisingly commited to some cause or passionately in love. In these plays there is relatively little action or characterization; what counts are the stylized dialogues between Heiberg's romantic men and his earthy and primitive women.

Kunstnere (1893) and *Gerts have* (1894) are light and witty examples of this manner, but are less well known than the relatively heavy-handed *Balkonen* (1894, translated as *The Balcony*), which raised another storm because it portrays an adulterous woman evidently enjoying her situation.

After his divorce in 1896 Heiberg lived in Paris until 1907. The influence of French prose is evident in the directness and lucidity of his excellent essays, which to some extent won back for him an audience alienated by some of his plays. *Pariserbreve* (Letters from Paris, 1900) deals mostly with the Dreyfus affair. His essays on literature and the theatre are collected in *Ibsen og Björnson paa Scenen* (1918), *Norsk Teater* (Norwegian Theatre, 1920), and other volumes. The best of his later plays was *Kjaerlighetens Tragedie* (1904, translated as *The Tragedy of Love*), in the same impressionistic and lyrical-erotic style as *Balkonen*. No doubt inspired by his own unhappy marriage, it is a poignant play which tries to show that love without fellowship is not enough.

Heiberg has been called his country's "first really professional man of letters . . . an assiduous, serious craftsman." A sophisticated and cosmopolitan man, described by Helge Krog as "the first trueborn European in Norwegian literature," he nevertheless "always had something of the special tone of the Oslo man, a tendency to conceal a warm heart behind a reserved exterior." His friendships, particularly with Hans Jaeger, lasted long and were not easily broken. He was less successful in his relations with women, however, and his second marriage, to Bergit Bleht in 1911, ended like the first in divorce.

PRINCIPAL WORKS IN ENGLISH TRANSLATION: The Tragedy of Love, *in* Dickinson, T. H. (ed.) Chief Contemporary Dramatists Series 2, 1921; The Balcony, *in* Poet-Lore XXXIII 1922.

ABOUT: Bach, G. The History of Norwegian Literature, 1938; Beyer, H. A History of Norwegian Literature, 1956; Downs, B. W. Modern Norwegian Literature, 1966; Jorgenson, T. History of Norwegian Literature, 1933; Penguin Companion to Literature 2, 1969; Skavlan, E. Gunnar Heiberg, 1950; Smith, H. (ed.) Columbia Dictionary of Modern European Literature, 1947.

***HEINRICH, WILLI** (August 9, 1920–), German novelist, writes: "There is nothing more uninteresting in the world than my family history. At least, I cannot imagine that any rational person would be interested to know that I was born in Heidelberg, that I attended a public—and commercial—school, that I completed a trade apprenticeship in a grocery business, and that I became a soldier at the age of eighteen. If it had not been for the war, I would perhaps have written my first novel at eighteen; it is difficult to judge that today. It was probably just as well that I did not write this first novel at that time. At the age of fifteen I wrote my first poems. They were just as mediocre as my school reports. When I finally wrote my first novel, I was thirty-five. Some critics think that if it had not been for the war I would never have begun to write, but some critics always know such things better than the author himself: why the author writes and what his intentions are when he writes his novel—all this the author finds out for the most part from newspapers. Of course, there are authors who pursue a goal with their work, whether they wish to change the world or simply to entertain their readers. As far as I am concerned, after the war I began for the first time in my life to contemplate seriously my fellow human beings, stupidity in general, and the stupidity of war in particular. For eight years, I contemplated these things, and busied myself—since one cannot make a living from contemplation alone—in various civil occupations that hardly interested me: I again sold groceries, and later lottery tickets, and after I had spent enough time contemplating and selling groceries and lottery tickets, I began my first novel in my free time. At that time I made a surprising discovery—that writing is the only occupation in which I am not bored, and because this was so, I immediately wrote a second novel, and then my third one. And after my third novel I had the feeling that I would be able to write at least another dozen novels. So I decided to remain a writer. Had I felt as little bored with another occupation, I might perhaps have become a taxi-driver or a civil servant. I believe that the important point is not what occupation one practices, but that one feels that it is the right occupation. There may be people who envy the writer his profession, but I think that they should rather not do so. For the past few years, I have lived in the Black Forest. From the window of my workroom, I can see the woods turn green in the spring and change color in the fall. In the winter, the fir trees are covered with thick snow, and often we are cut off from the outside world for days; and when I say 'we,' I mean my wife, myself, and our two four-legged creatures, a dog and a cat. We have company only rarely: we live in an isolated wooded valley, where only our best friends can find us. Sometimes we are visited by a deer from the nearby edge of the forest. Many of our acquaintances find it dreadful to live as solitarily as we do; they prefer to live in the city. A writer, I believe, should never feel lonely. Not even if he lived at the end of the world. He always lives in the great company of the characters of his novels, who fill out his life, keep him busy and hold dialogues with him. Perhaps the occupation of the writer is actually a lonely one, similar to that of the President of the United States. But with the latter I would not want to trade places under any circumstances."

* hin′ rik

Willi Heinrich fought during World War II as an infantry corporal on the Eastern Front. He marched eight thousand miles across Russia, was wounded five times, and survived to draw from his ordeal one of the most moving German novels of the war. This was *Das geduldige Fleisch* (1954), which records the sufferings of a German platoon whose implacable enemies include not only Russian troops but hunger, cold, and the cruel geography of the country they have invaded. The book's furious cynicism evoked some controversy in Germany, but the critical reaction was overwhelmingly enthusiastic. Translated by Richard and Clara Winston as *The Cross of Iron*, it earned comparisons with James Jones's *From Here to Eternity*, and became a best seller. Corporal Steiner, the taciturn, violent, Schiller-loving platoon leader, was the subject of much discussion: one critic thought him "the most exciting character to come alive in German war fiction"; another called him "both a ridiculous and revolting figure." Most American reviewers agreed that Heinrich seemed less an artist than a craftsman—an average German soldier who had acquired the skill to put down a powerful, tense, and relentlessly realistic account of what he had seen and felt. As one critic wrote, Heinrich "makes the private inferno of his war roar all over again, but as if for the very first time and for all men."

The success of *Das geduldige Fleisch* released Heinrich from the financial insecurity and hardship of the postwar years. He was married in 1955 to Erika Stocker, bought his isolated farmhouse in the Black Forest, and produced a second novel, *Der goldene Tisch* (1956, translated as *Crack of Doom*), which deals in short cinematic sequences with the destruction of a German division in Slovakia.

In *Die Gezeichneten* (1958, translated as *Mark of Shame*), Heinrich for the first time looked beyond the war to its aftermath in Germany. The result was "a portrait of a society part paranoid, part manic-depressive, still so infected that Hitler recedes into a symptom of a national disease." A central character is an ex-Nazi who becomes a high official in the Fourth Reich—and then finds himself blackmailed and threatened by men less successful but no less corrupt than himself. The book has an air of moral outrage in keeping with Heinrich's reputation as Germany's "angry young man," but was thought by some rather facile in its cynicism and marred by passages of sentimental heart-searching.

Heinrich's subsequent books include, among others, *Alte Häuser sterben nicht* (1960, translated as *The Crumbling Fortress*), a wartime adventure story about a mixed bag of refugees hiding in an old fortress in the French Alps; *Rape of Honor* (1961, apparently unpublished in German), another attack on postwar corruption in Germany; and *Gottes zweite Garnitur* (1962, translated as *The Lonely Conqueror*), the story of a love affair between a black GI and a German student. Reviewers of Heinrich's recent novels have tended to complain of routine erotic passages, stereotyped characterization, and vague rhetoric, and none of the books has achieved the passionate intensity of *Das geduldige Fleisch*—the sense it gave "of a man plucking shell fragments out of his own memory." Heinrich's later works are by and large written on a different level but are nevertheless enjoyed by many as highly readable entertainments.

WILLI HEINRICH

PRINCIPAL WORKS IN ENGLISH TRANSLATION: The Cross of Iron (England, the Willing Flesh), 1956; Crack of Doom (England, The Savage Mountain), 1958; Mark of Shame, 1959; Rape of Honor, 1961; The Lonely Conqueror, 1962; The Crumbling Fortress, 1964; The Devil's Bed, 1965.

ABOUT: Wer Ist Wer, 1970. *Periodicals*—Book Week July 26, 1964; Nation July 14, 1956; Saturday Review April 28, 1956; July 11, 1964; Time April 23, 1956.

HELLER, JOSEPH (May 1, 1923–), American novelist and dramatist, was born and raised in the Coney Island section of Brooklyn. Heller did combat service during World War II with the U.S. Army Air Force, part of the time in Italy, and left the service with the rank of lieutenant. He was a Phi Beta Kappa student at New York University and received his B.A. in 1948. The next year he took his M.A. at Columbia University, and then with a Fulbright scholarship went to England, where he studied at Oxford in 1949–1950.

Heller's first success as a writer came with the publication in *Story* and *Atlantic Monthly* of some short stories. Notable among them are "I Don't

JOSEPH HELLER

Love You Anymore" and "Castle of Snow" (which was reprinted in Martha Foley's *The Best Short Stories of 1949*). The former resembles one of Ernest Hemingway's stories of conflict between the sexes, in which the male protagonist discovers he has reached the end of an affair or a marriage that is no longer any "fun," and the dialogue is dominated by repetitive phrases of rejection that are nearly sadistic in their accuracy. "Castle of Snow," on the other hand, displays a sensibility bordering on sentimentality. It is an account of an immigrant Jewish family living in the United States during the Depression, and centers on an old man who finally sacrifices his most cherished possessions, his books. It reads a little like the work of an American Chekhov.

A varied career lay between these stories and *Catch-22*. Preceding John Barth by a year, Heller taught English composition at Pennsylvania State University in 1950–1952. Then he returned to New York and for the next eight years, while writing his novel, earned his living as an advertising writer for *Time* (1952–1956) and *Look* (1956–1958), and as promotion manager for *McCall's* (1958–1961). The opening chapter of his novel appeared in *New World Writing* in 1955 under the title of "Catch-18." (The subsequent appearance of Leon Uris's *Mila 18* made it necessary for Heller to change his title.)

Catch-22 is set on the tiny Mediterranean island of Pianosa, where the 256th bombing squadron of the U.S. Air Force is stationed during the Italian campaign in World War II. The fanatical and ambitious Colonel Cathcart constantly increases the flyers' quota of missions, the death toll soars, and the colonel's tame psychiatrist accuses the exhausted survivors of "a morbid aversion to dying." The carnage is such that a stock letter is prepared for the benefit of next of kin: "Dear Mrs., / Mr.,/ Miss, / or Mr. and Mrs.———: Words cannot express the deep personal grief I experienced when your husband, / son, / father, / or brother was killed, / wounded, / or reported missing in action." Other characters include Doc Daneeka, whose job is to keep the men alive so that they can be killed; Major Major Major, who is distinguished by his unimpressiveness; and the central character, Captain Yossarian, who retains his sanity—exemplified by a life-affirming randiness and pusillanimity—and demonstrates it in the end by a heroic act of cowardice when he deserts and sets out for Sweden in a rubber dinghy.

The looking-glass world from which Yossarian drops out is ruled by "Catch-22" and its corollaries: "Orr would be crazy to fly more missions and sane if he didn't, but if he was sane he had to fly them. If he flew them he was crazy and didn't have to; but if he didn't want to he was sane and had to. Yossarian was moved very deeply by the absolute simplicity of this . . . and let out a respectful whistle. 'That's some catch, that Catch-22,' he observed. 'It's the best there is,' Doc Daneeka agreed."

Julien Mitchell called the novel "a surrealist *Iliad*, with a lunatic High Command instead of gods, and a coward for a hero. . . . Epic in form, the book is episodic in structure. Each chapter carries a single character a step nearer madness or death or both, and a step, too, into legend." Heller's literary resources range from satire to slapstick, from fantasy to farce, from parody to puns. The book's seriousness and savagery become more evident as it proceeds, and it includes a Roman street scene of apocalyptic grimness.

It is not surprising that many readers were offended by *Catch-22*, but far more—especially young people—were delighted with it, and it became a major best seller. The critical response was also mixed. Whitney Balliett wrote that Heller "wallows in his own laughter and finally drowns in it. What remains is a debris of sour jokes, stage anger, dirty words, synthetic loneliness, and the sort of antic behavior the children fall into when they know they are losing our attention." Other critics agreed that the novel was undisciplined and repetitive but many nevertheless shared Nelson Algren's opinion—that it was "not merely the best American novel to come out of World War II; it is the best American novel that had come out of anywhere in years." Robert Brustein said that "Pianosa has become a satirical microcosm for many of the macrocosmic idiocies of our time," and Heller agrees that he was concerned to attack not only the absurdity of war but, in general, "the humbug, hypocrisy, cruelty and sheer stupidity of our mass society." The novel has been filmed by Mike Nichols.

Heller's play *We Bombed in New Haven* is a Pirandellian essay on war in which the "actors play actors" who are rehearsing a tragicomedy similar in mood and theme to *Catch-22.* The author, "heavy-set, dark and brooding," is married to the former Shirley Held and has a son and a daughter. He says: "The things I write are funny only up to a point. Actually I am a very morbid, melancholy person. I'm preoccupied with death, disease and misfortune." He writes occasionally for television and the movies, and is at work on a second novel. In 1971 Heller became distinguished visiting writer at the City College of the City University of New York.

PRINCIPAL WORKS: Catch-22, 1961 (dramatized version, 1971; critical edition, ed. by Robert M. Scotto, 1973); The American Novel: Two Studies (criticism), 1965; We Bombed in New Haven (play), 1968.

ABOUT: Burgess, A. The Novel Now, 1967; Contemporary Authors 7–8, 1968; Current Biography, 1973; Kazin, A. Bright Book of Life, 1973; Kostelanetz, R. (ed.) The New American Arts, 1965; Moore, H. T. (ed.) Contemporary American Novelists, 1965; Vinson, J. (ed.) Contemporary Novelists, 1972; Whitbread, T. B. (ed.) Seven Contemporary Authors, 1966. *Periodicals*—Atlantic January 1962; Comparative Literature Summer 1968; Critique Winter 1964–65; Guardian June 15, 1962; Life January 12, 1968; Nation November 4, 1961; New Republic November 13, 1961; New York Times December 3, 1967; New York Times Book Review October 22, 1961; September 9, 1962; March 3, 1968; The Realist November 1962; San Francisco Chronicle May 3, 1962; Saturday Review October 14, 1961; August 31, 1968; Spectator June 15, 1962; Times Literary Supplement June 15, 1962; Twentieth Century Literature January 1967.

"HELVICK, JAMES." *See* COCKBURN, (FRANCIS) CLAUD

HENSON, HERBERT HENSLEY (November 8, 1863–September 28, 1947), English theologian and memoirist, was born in London, one of the eight children of Thomas Henson and the former Martha Fear. When he was two the family moved to Broadstairs, a Victorian seaside resort. His mother died a few years later and her husband, a retired tradesman, became in Henson's words "wholly possessed by religion." He married again nevertheless and it was the German stepmother who insisted that Hensley Henson should go to a Broadstairs private school and on to Oxford. He entered the university as a member of no college, and with his father's proviso that the "expenditure should be as small as possible" and his academic career brief. Poor, living in lodgings, he was cut off from the social life of the university and absorbed himself in his work. He obtained a first class degree in modern history and at the age of twenty-one was elected a Fellow of All Souls.

HERBERT HENSLEY HENSON

Already committed to a career in the church, Henson remained at Oxford for three years after his graduation, except for a brief interlude as a tutor in Birkenhead. He read theology and ecclesiastical history, lectured, and began to make his mark as a controversialist. In 1887 he became a deacon of the Church of England, and soon after went to Bethnal Green, one of the poorest quarters of London, as director of a church mission called Oxford House. What he saw there strengthened his disgust with industrialism and formed the "respect and affection for the poor" that was to remain with him all his life. He nevertheless remained unshakably opposed to socialism, strikes, and other industrial action.

In 1888 Henson was ordained a priest and became vicar of Barking. From Barking he went in 1895 as chaplain to St. Mary's Hospital, Ilford. He became chaplain to the bishop of St. Albans (1897–1900), canon of Westminster Abbey (1900–1912), dean of Durham (1912–1918), bishop of Hereford (1918–1920), and ultimately bishop of Durham (1920–1939).

From the beginning of his career, Henson was at the center of every church controversy of his day, and many of the political ones. "I do not care one straw for popularity," he said, "for I know that it is generally purchased by a sacrifice of the truth." Henson dismissed many of the church's doctrines and attitudes as obsolete, advocated Christian unity and preached to nonconformist congregations, denied that Christians must accept the Virgin Birth, denounced the theory of apostolic succession, and came to believe that the Church of England should be disestablished as a state religion. At first drawn to Anglo-Catholicism, he soon reversed his position and opposed it. He also attacked Frank Buchman's Oxford Group, and called the kind of religion offered by the British Broadcasting Corporation "a Christianized humanism which patronizes God and advertises man." The popularity he never sought came to him nevertheless, and he was much liked, inside and outside the church, for his courage, wit, and warmth. Sir William Anson described him as "a Jacobin lacquered over to look like a Tory."

After about 1900 Henson's views were published in a steady stream of books, pamphlets, essays, lectures, and sermons, all of them distinguished by an Augustan lucidity of style and clarity of thought. T. S. Eliot, a theological opponent, said of Henson that "for vigour and purity of controversial English he has no superior today, and his writing should long continue to be studied by those who aspire to write well." (Henson, unmoved, commented: "Controversial English is an odd expression. What can it properly mean?") Even *Retrospect of an Unimportant Life*, Henson's three-volume autobiography, is full of his vehemently controversial views; those who did not welcome it for its opinions did so for the personality it revealed, for "with the personality it would not be easy to find oneself at variance."

Henson's conversation, like his letters, was brilliantly witty, "with flashes of gentle malice and shrewdest observation." His sermons are models of the form, and he has been called "the last of the great preachers." The author of an article about Henson in *The Concise Encyclopedia of Modern World Literature* describes him as "a man impossible to meet in public dispute, and impossible to resist in private converse." His long and happy marriage to Isabella Dennistoun began in 1902.

PRINCIPAL WORKS: Cross-Bench Views on Current Church Questions, 1902; Studies in English Religion in the 17th Century, 1903; The National Church, 1908; The Liberty of Prophesying (Lyman Beecher lectures), 1909; Westminster Sermons, 1910; The Road to Reunion, 1911; The Creed in the Pulpit, 1912; Puritanism in England, 1912; War-Time Sermons, 1915; Anglicanism, 1921; Notes on Spiritual Healing, 1925; Church and Parson in England, 1927; Disestablishment, 1929; The Oxford Groups, 1933; Christian Morality (Gifford Lectures), 1936; Ad Clerum, 1937; The Church of England, 1939; Last Words in Westminster Abbey, 1941; Retrospect of an Unimportant Life: Vol. 1, 1942; Vol. 2, 1943; Vol. 3, 1950; Bishoprick Papers, 1946; Letters: Chosen and Edited with an Introduction by Evelyn Foley Braley, 1950; More Letters: A Second Volume Chosen and Edited with an Introduction by Evelyn Foley Braley, 1954; Theology and Life, 1957.

ABOUT: Begbie, H. Painted Windows, 1922; Dictionary of National Biography 1941–1950, 1959; Grigson, G. (ed.) Concise Encyclopedia of Modern World Literature, 1963; Jones, E. D. Royalty of the Pulpit, 1951; Who Was Who, 1941–1950. *Periodicals*—Antiquaries Journal July 1948; English Review February 1929; Hibbert Journal April 1944; New Statesman March 6, 1954; New York Times September 29, 1947; Spectator October 3, 1947; Time October 6, 1947; Time (London) September 29, 1947; Times Literary Supplement July 25, 1942; December 18, 1943; May 5, 1950.

HEPPENSTALL, RAYNER (July 27, 1911–), English novelist, critic, and poet, writes: "My full name is John Rayner Heppenstall, and I was born at Huddersfield in the West Riding of Yorkshire. My parents were on the borderline between the 'working' and 'lower-middle' classes, my father being the first man on either side of the family to work in collar and tie. On the other hand, the standard of free education in Huddersfield was such that I easily got to university (I was at Leeds), with periods at school in Calais and at the university of Strasbourg. I took a poor degree in Modern Languages and taught for a matter of months in a senior elementary school. I have never had a penny of private income or inheritance, and this has meant either that I was extremely poor or that I had to work too hard. For the past twenty years, I have worked as a producer in broadcasting. I have a wife and two children. My daughter is married, but does a little university teaching in French and is still at work on her doctoral thesis for St. Andrews: on Valéry Larbaud. My son, aged twenty-one, is an architecture student and still lives at home. Their names are respectively Lindy and Adam.

"I arrived in London at much the same time as Dylan Thomas, and we were pretty thick for some years. I also shared a flat for a while, in 1935, with George Orwell. Older men to whom I was variously attached during the pre-war decade were John Middleton Murry, Herbert Read, Eric Gill, Rev. Fr. M. C. D'Arcy, S.J., Max Plowman and John Macmurray, all of whom must have exercised some influence on me, though it does not seem to have stuck. In those days, I thought of myself as primarily a poet. At the beginning of the war, I had a success with my first novel, *The Blaze of Noon*, and began to think of myself as a novelist, but was unfortunately swept into the Army not long afterwards. I spent four-and-a-half years in the ranks and was psychiatrised out a month before the lights came on again in Europe. My gratuity was £27. I had a family to keep, and in those days, once you had a book written, it took at least a year-and-a-half to get it out. I went to the B.B.C., meaning at first to stick it for no more than two years. I have been there twenty, enjoying it part of the time.

"For some years, I published little. My Army novel, *The Lesser Infortune*, appeared at about the time of the Coronation in 1953 and did not in the least match the mood of the second-Elizabethan moment. I was almost forgotten. In the late 1950s, I made a violent effort to hold down the radio job with one hand, while writing with the other. At the beginning of 1960, I published *The Greater Infortune*, a recension of what had appeared in war-time in a limited edition as *Saturnine*, and during the next three years put out, first, *Four Absentees*, my reminiscences of Orwell, Dylan Thomas, Gill and Murry; then a substantial volume of criticism, *The Fourfold Tradition*; then two linked novels, *The Connecting Door* and *The Woodshed* (with the latter, i.e., on the same day, appeared a new edition of *The Blaze of Noon*); and finally an autobiographical volume, *The Intellectual Part*. For the past two years, I have labored in vain, my condition during that time being one verging almost continuously on nervous and general breakdown.

"I see myself as very much a European and feel especially close to France, from which, after all, only twenty miles of water separate this country. Most of the writers I admire today, including Sam Beckett, are French. I do not admire any living American writer, except Nabokov, who is not an American writer, and Borges, who writes in Spanish and lives well outside the United States. Among my own books, the ones I still like best are *The Greater Infortune*, *The Connecting Door* and, in its very slight way, *Four Absentees*. I have never been much esteemed as a poet, but may take up verse again in my last years. Most of my life, I inclined to the Left in politics, but now see that what is most wrong with the world is progressivism gone rotten. The ultimate horror would be world government, of which so many dream. There would be no escape then for those who did not totally conform. They could not even go to another planet, since all the space-ships would be controlled by the one gang of administrators, doubtless functioning from the old United Nations building in New York."

Rayner Heppenstall, whose novels are often quite closely autobiographical, gives a clear impression of what his childhood was like in *The Woodshed*. In his "prodigiously upright and nonconformist family," according to his friend Bernard Wall, "truth was always told, even if extremely unpleasant and contentious (Mr. Heppenstall has remained this way)." Wall has described how he met Heppenstall, who was then scraping a living as a freelance writer, in a *London Magazine* article on which this note draws heavily. Heppenstall was short of food and had just moved out of the flat he shared with Orwell, who, after a row, had hit him with a shooting stick. At that time Heppenstall was greatly attracted by Catholicism, and went off to stay at Eric Gill's "ideal" colony in Buckinghamshire.

RAYNER HEPPENSTALL

Heppenstall never did enter the Church, but his religious preoccupation is reflected in his poems, most of them short, honest and adroit, but often excessively private in their imagery "and without much rhythmical compulsion." It was the novel *Blaze of Noon*, about a blind masseur, which brought Heppenstall his first and greatest success. Credited with "poultry-yard morals" by a popular London newspaper, it sold out on publication day. It is in fact an austere, conventional, and highly accomplished novel, as other critics soon pointed out, giving Heppenstall "a *succès d'estime* as well as a *succès de scandale*." As he says, the book has been reprinted, and in 1966 earned its author a £1,000 Arts Council Award.

More "Heppenstallian," according to Bernard Wall, and presenting "a world quite unlike anybody else's," are *The Greater Infortune* and *The Lesser Infortune*. The first, a revised version of the work originally published in 1943 as *Saturnine*, was called "an avant-garde or case-history picaresque" about the adventures in London Bohemia, just before World War II, of Leckie, who is "first and foremost a projection of the author's personality." The bitterest of Heppenstall's books, it describes a world, Wall says, "in which there is no beauty and very little hope, a decayed, valueless society." *The Lesser Infortune* is a rather more lighthearted account of Leckie's wartime experiences. *The Connecting Door*, in which a man is confronted by his past selves, has been called an "anti-novel," but one "told with exquisite skill, and as much humor as beauty." Some of the reductive techniques of the French "New Novelists" are employed also in *The Shearers*, a "cold, strange book" about a trial for incest and murder which some reviewers read as a comment on the connection between public and private morals.

Heppenstall's novels are generally written, revised, and rewritten over a long period of time. He writes prose in "clipped dour sentences" and his "rapid nervous story-telling makes most other novelists look like crawling removal vans." It has been said that "we feel near to the French in all Mr. Heppenstall's writings," and that he is probably "the best ally in the English-speaking world" of the French anti-novelists. In *The Fourfold Tradition*, he argues that England never has been able to live without France, and that the two countries have shared "a literary common market for almost 1,000 years." The book irritated some critics, and V. S. Pritchett called its author "an eccentric with a keen eye for literary politics . . . always on the look out for intrigue and manipulation" but attractive in "his bursts of gaiety, his intelligence, his edge and his pleasure in literature." Bernard Wall calls him a literary "lone wolf" who is for that reason far less widely known and read than he deserves to be. Apart from his literary essays and reminiscences, Heppenstall has written some highly sophisticated and original studies in the criminal history of France.

The author has translated works from the French, and encouraged others to do so. His many contributions to magazines include a number of the famous middle articles in the *Times Literary Supplement*. In his long association with the BBC's Third Programme as feature writer and producer (1945–1967), Heppenstall through his work and influence did much to make that institution unique in world radio. He has described his years at the BBC, and the circumstances leading to his dismissal, in *Portrait of the Artist as a Professional Man*. "In the end," wrote a reviewer in the *Times Literary Supplement*, "a portrait of the author can be seen through the gossiping heads that tend to impede the view. It is, in one light, of a man demanding, suspicious, vain, and concerned with money. . . . In another light there appears a man grateful for kindnesses, loyal to his family and benefactors, wilfully opposed to received opinion, amusing, catty, often witty, sometimes perceptive, and always obstinately his own man and courageous in defence of his eccentricities." Heppenstall lives with his wife, the former Margaret Edwards, in a flat in London's Notting Hill Gate.

PRINCIPAL WORKS: *Novels*—The Blaze of Noon, 1939; Saturnine, 1943, (*rev. as* The Greater Infortune, 1960); The Lesser Infortune, 1953; The Connecting Door, 1962; The Woodshed, 1962; The Shearers, 1969. *Poems*—Patina, 1932; First Poems, 1935; Sebastian, 1937; Blind Men's Flowers are Green, 1940; Poems 1933–1945, 1946. *Nonfiction*—John Middleton Murry, a Study in Excellent Normality, 1934; Apology for Dancing, 1936; The Double Image, 1947; (ed.) Imaginary Conversations: Eight Scripts of the Broadcasts in the Third Programme, 1948; Léon Bloy, 1954; My Bit of Dylan Thomas, 1957; Four Absentees: Candid Reminiscences of Dylan Thomas, George Orwell, Eric Gill and J. Middleton Murry, 1960; The Fourfold Tradition: Notes on the French and English Literatures with Some Ethnological and Historical Asides, 1961; The Intellectual Part, 1963; Raymond Roussel: A Critical Guide, 1966; Portrait of the Artist as a Professional Man, 1969; A Little Pattern of French Crime, 1969; French Crime in the Romantic Age, 1970; Bluebeard and After: Three Decades of Murder in France, 1972; The Sex War and Others, 1973.

ABOUT: Contemporary Authors 4, 1963; Heppenstall, R. Four Absentees, 1960; Heppenstall, R. The Intellectual Part, 1963; Heppenstall, R. Portrait of the Artist as a Professional Man, 1969; Vinson, J. (ed.) Contemporary Novelists, 1972; Who's Who, 1973. *Periodicals*—London Magazine March 1963; La Nef July 1948; New Republic December 4, 1961; Times Literary Supplement November 14, 1963.

***HERBERT, ZBIGNIEW** (October 29, 1924–), Polish poet and dramatist, writes (in Polish): "According to a tradition in my family, my father's ancestors were religious emigrants from England who married Germans, Austrians, Czechs and Armenians. I stress this fact because I feel myself to be a Polish writer—even an unfashionably patriotic one—although I have no genealogy which would substantiate this.

"I was born in Lwów, a multinational and multireligious town in southeast Poland, where my father was a prosperous lawyer and classicist. But my personality was really formed during the Second World War, in which I took part as a member of the anti-Nazi resistance movement. I think that the war created almost all the problems of my writing: what a man is in the face of death, how he behaves in the presence of a totalitarian threat, what moral values can and should be saved.

"After the war, in which I lost my best friends, and which ended with the physical destruction of my home, I studied economics, law, and philosophy, and also earned my living as a bank clerk, as a commercial journalist, as a manual worker, and when there was no other means of livelihood, as a blood donor. Without any hope of publication, I also wrote poems, essays and plays, in which I tried to bear witness not only to my personal experience, but to the fate and problems of my generation.

"I published my first book of poetry in 1956, the year of the Thaw, after fifteen years of writing for the drawer, which however, I don't regret. On the contrary, I regard it as fortunate for me personally, since this long period of fasting gave me the opportunity to crystallize my attitudes without external pressures and the need to conform to the obligatory ideology.

"During the period 1958–1971 I visited Western

* hâr′ bert

countries: France, England, Italy, Greece, Austria, Germany and the United States.

"I have published four books of poetry, a book of plays, and a book of essays on art, principally ancient and medieval, under the title *Barbarzyńca w Ogrodzie* (A Barbarian in the Garden, 1962). In this I also considered the theme of people blotted out from history, the Cretans and Etruscans, and also the problems of the heresies of the Albigensians and the Templars.

"Politically I belong neither to the right nor to the left. I think that the place of the writer is on the side of the individual, who suffers on either side of frontiers, walls or curtains. What worries me most in the modern world is the downfall of traditional Judaeo-Graeco-Christian standards, which have not been replaced by new values. This means that in the future we shall be unable to converse with Dantesque man and Homeric man."

Lwów (Lvov), where Herbert was born as a Polish subject, is now a part of the Ukraine, and hence of the USSR. As he indicates above, he came all too soon to maturity during the German Occupation. The Nazis were nowhere more barbaric than in Poland, where one in five of the population died and whole villages were massacred. Herbert completed his secondary education at an underground school, attended an underground university and (to quote A. Alvarez) "served a peculiarly savage apprenticeship in the underground resistance."

After the war Herbert took a degree at a commercial college in Cracow and went on to study civil law at Toruń University and philosophy at Warsaw. He also read very widely and deeply in the Greek and Roman classics and in history, as his work shows. Herbert began to publish his poems in 1950 in a Catholic weekly which, however, was suppressed in 1953, as part of the general Stalinist repression of the time. Twenty poems were included in an anthology published in Warsaw in 1954 and his first book, *Struna Światla* (The Chord of Light) appeared in 1956, when the "thaw" was well under way and he was able to join the Polish Writers' Union. *Hermes, Pies i Gwiazda* (Hermes, Dog and Star) followed in 1957 and *Studium Przedmiotu* (Study of the Object) in 1961. *Selected Poems*, in English, translated by Czeslaw Milosz and Peter Dale Scott, was published in 1968 with an introduction by A. Alvarez, who has been Herbert's principal champion in the West. Herbert's latest collection is *Napis* (The Inscription, 1969).

In his restraint, balance, and quiet irony, Herbert is a classical poet, but one who is deeply aware that he writes in an age of barbarism. Some of his poems and prose poems are wry political allegories, illustrations of the horrors of tyranny and the triviality

ZBIGNIEW HERBERT

of tyrants. More often his political iconoclasm is implicit in his tone of voice, his guarded but persistent affirmation of the values of humanism and humanity.

When he was about fifteen Herbert wrote a poem ("Two Drops") about a man and a woman who make love as the bombs fall and the forests catch fire: "When it got very bad / they leapt into each other's eyes / and shut them firmly." But these two die all the same, and it is part of Herbert's tough-minded classical rigor to acknowledge that brute reality has its claims, which are often overwhelming and never to be ignored: "The predictions of poetry are incorrect / Everything happened differently / The fire in the poem was one thing / A town in flames was another" ("Farewell to September").

The tension between humanity's splendid or wistful dreams and our savage or abject realities is at the center of Herbert's poetry and provides many of his themes. It is also the source of his irony, which is, however, never merely defensive or destructive. There is something very reassuring in his steady voice: he acknowledges our shortcomings (and his own, and poetry's), but gives us our due. In a poem called "Silk of a Soul" a man watches his girl asleep and tries to read her dreams: "I was expecting / branches / I was expecting / a bird / I was expecting / a house / by a lake great and silent / but there / on a glass counter / I caught sight of a pair / of silk stockings." That could be the cynical end of the poem, but Herbert's speaker adds a modest affirmation: "My God / I'll buy her those stockings / I'll buy them." And then he goes further: "but what will appear then / on the glass counter / of the little soul / / will it be something / which cannot be touched / even with one finger of a dream."

There is a similar tension in Herbert's style. Many of his poems are thoughtful interior monologues. His diction is generally laconic, understated, and conversational, his rhythms subdued. But, as one critic has pointed out in the *Times Literary Supplement*, "there is also a haunting visionary element in his poetry, offered though it is with caution and often with grief for its fancifulness." For example: "in the shadow of one hexameter lie down / wolves and roedeer goshawks and doves / and the child goes to sleep on the lion's mane / as in a cradle / Look how the animals are smiling / People are living on white flowers / and everything is just as good / as it was in the beginning."

One of the best known and most characteristic of Herbert's poems is "Elegy of Fortinbras," in which the soldier-administrator takes leave of the dead Hamlet, of poetry and tragedy, and commits himself to the world's dull and necessary work: "Adieu prince I have tasks a sewer project / and a decree on prostitutes and beggars / I must also elaborate a better system of prisons / since as you justly said Denmark is a prison / I go to my affairs This night is born / a star named Hamlet We shall never meet / what I shall leave will not be worth a tragedy / It is not for us to greet each other or bid farewell we live on archipelagos / and that water these words what can they do what can they do prince." As Alvarez puts it: "For all this fine classical yearning [Herbert] never tries to betray or even to escape the unredeemed obduracy of things and people and situations."

Many of Herbert's poems like "Elegy of Fortinbras," "Apollo and Marsyas," and "The Return of the Proconsul" quarry ancient literature or mythology for contemporary meanings. Similarly *The Philosopher's Den* (1957), the best known of his half-dozen plays, is a discussion of Herbert's central theme—the relative claims of thinking and acting, the ideal and the real—worked out in terms of the death of Socrates. The volume of essays, *Barbarzyńca w Ogrodzie*, centers on the pathos and beauty of our own historical experience of the ancient Mediterranean world.

In 1965 Herbert received the Austrian Nicholas Lenau prize for his contribution to European literature. He has traveled more than most Polish writers of his generation, visiting as he says most of Europe and in 1970–1971 teaching for a time at California State College at Los Angeles. An account in the *Guardian* of the 1972 Polish Writers' Congress, the first to be held since Edward Gierek came to power, noted signs that "Poland's writers were emerging from the shell that was thrust down on them in 1968," and reported that Herbert was one of seven or eight liberals elected to the new central board of the Congress. The author is coeditor of *Poezja*.

PRINCIPAL WORKS IN ENGLISH TRANSLATION: Selected Poems, 1968; The Philosopher's Den (play) *in* Mayewski, P. (ed.) The Broken Mirror, 1958. *Poems in* Gillon, A. and L. Krzyżanowski (eds.) Introduction to Modern Polish Literature, 1964; Milosz, C. (ed.) Postwar Polish Poetry, 1965; Wieniewska, C. (ed.) Polish Writing Today, 1967.

ABOUT: Alvarez, A. Under Pressure, 1965; Alvarez, A. *introduction to* Selected Poems, 1968; Gömöri, G. Polish and Hungarian Poetry, 1966; Milosz, C. The History of Polish Literature, 1969. *Periodicals*—Guardian February 9, 1972; Times Literary Supplement May 9, 1968.

HERLIHY, JAMES LEO (February 27, 1927–), American dramatist, short story writer, and novelist, writes: "I was born in Detroit, Michigan, and raised there and in Chillicothe, Ohio. My grandfathers had been in horse professions (Herlihy, a blacksmith; Oberer, a harness-maker) and though I don't remember either of them, I think of them often, in awe of that earlier, simpler time they connect me with.

"I held my first position in the literary world at the age of seven: as door-to-door salesman for the *Literary Digest*, I scored a success so unspectacular the publication was soon defunct. Delivering groceries proved to be more lucrative (four cents an hour) in those Depression years. By the time World War II began I'd moved on to dispensing sodas, and by the end of it I was in the Navy.

"I'd written fiction all through childhood, but received no official discouragement until 1948 when, on the basis of my first novel, Isaac Rosenfeld, during a summer writing seminar at Black Mountain College in North Carolina, pronounced me hopeless. With the assistance of other career guidance specialists, I found my way to Pasadena Playhouse, where I was to study acting. There I met Bill Noble, a successful young screenwriter who was teaching playwriting. He put out a lot of good advice, including the almost fanatic injunction that I avoid experts of all kinds and at all costs. So much for education.

"The next few years were painfully lean ones. My teeth always seemed to hurt in those days, and I was always making journeys with insufficient funds. But I wrote a number of plays that were done in summer stock and off-Broadway; and I'd begun to publish short stories in the little magazines. In 1952, I met Bill Noble again in New York. We holed up in a cold, dirty, wonderful flat in the West 70s, embarked upon a collaboration that resulted in a Broadway success, *Blue Denim*. I was thirty at the time.

"Marriage has always been out of the question for me. I have an unfaithful nature and, although I'm fond enough of women, I prefer the companionship of men. Besides, by the time I could afford marriage, the life I'd lived had made me too selfish to submit to a rigid moral, economic and social system policed almost exclusively by the stronger sex; and I wasn't man enough (is anyone, I wonder?) to buck it effectively.

"With my Broadway winnings I built a home in Key West; and as soon as it was landscaped and furnished and comfortable enough to be lived in, I abandoned it—along with any hope that I could ever settle down or even stay in one place very long. Now I spend my life as I had learned to spend it: writing, packing suitcases, inventing voyages.

"Fond of displaying myself, I sometimes act. In 1963, I starred as Jerry in the Paris production of Edward Albee's *The Zoo Story*, and was featured in a movie with Jean Seberg.

"Politically I used to lean heavily to the Left—but that was when the world was threatened by the Right. Now I don't lean at all, I just look for a candidate who seems kind—and crooked enough to make it stick.

"I'm drawn to persons and places that engender true religious feeling, and opposed to priests and churches, all of them, because of the evils engendered by them *in the name of* true religious feeling, e.g., moral systems instead of simple morality.

"My preference in art tends to be for works by men who have found some beauty and order and truth in a world that seems often to be ugly, chaotic and meaningless.

"Finally, I think Americans are crazy. And for this reason, I'm pro-American. I trust our great collective neurosis. I'm even convinced that it's the most noble disease ever suffered by man. It's the banner of our considerable victory over the lower orders of human misery, the more distinctly physical ones, and it betokens our acceptance of a call to battle with the greatest dragon of all—freedom."

James Leo Herlihy is of German-Irish descent, the son of William and Grace (Oberer) Herlihy. His father was a construction engineer and inspector for the city of Detroit. In the course of his own career Herlihy has been, among other things, a farm hand, foil for a carnival medicine man, snake exhibitor, bookseller, editor, and inspector of guided missile instruments.

The first of his plays to be produced was *Streetlight Sonata*, staged in 1950 at the Pasadena Playhouse, where Herlihy acted in some fifty roles between 1948 and 1952. In 1953 a fantasy called *Moon in Capricorn* reached an off-Broadway theater in New York, where it was praised by Brooks Atkinson among others. Several more plays were staged in various parts of the country until, in 1958, *Blue Denim* began its immensely successful run on Broadway. Naturalistic in style, the play deals compassionately with adolescent sexuality and its results, and probes intelligently into the lack of understanding between parents and children. It was translated into several European languages and filmed. Herlihy has also adapted two of his short stories as the plays *Crazy October* and *A Breeze from China*, and published three one-acters in the 1970 collection *Stop, You're Killing Me*. Of these, two are essentially monologues revealing their speakers' total isolation and despair, and the third is a shocker about a popular movie writer, a purveyor of profitable ghoulishness whose creations come horribly to life in his own living room. None of these later plays has been particularly successful, and most critics doubt that the theatre is Herlihy's métier.

JAMES LEO HERLIHY

His novels and stories similarly but more compellingly evoke "a peripheral world of loners and exotics," the gaudy, rootless America of motels and drive-ins. *All Fall Down*, his first published novel, traces the painful progress through adolescence of Clint Williams, who achieves maturity at the price of disillusionment with his beloved older brother. Stanley Kauffmann called it "one of the best of the post-Salinger . . . novels whose theme is that growing up means to be corrupted." Another powerful emotional attachment, grasped as a defense against loneliness, is the theme of *Midnight Cowboy*, about a would-be professional stud from Albuquerque who fails to make his fortune in New York but finds instead, though briefly, a friend. This novel, which discovers poetry in squalor, and the true voice of feeling in the patois of hustlers and vagrants, inspired John Schlesinger's equally remarkable film, and made Herlihy famous.

A much more ambitious novel followed. *The*

Season of the Witch, written it is said out of a seven-year immersion in the "youth culture," describes the adventures in New York and Canada of two young drop-outs, a high school girl named Gloria Random, who is in search of her father (and her identity), and her homosexual friend and guru, who is evading the draft. The story is narrated by Gloria, now calling herself Witch Gliz, and seemed to most critics to provide "the first full . . . and reliable renderings of the new consciousness," which, "with all its in-group fads, nonce words, and distortions, is still an essentially humane and attractive one." A few reviewers, it must be said—writing perhaps as guardians of a threatened culture—found the book an intolerably coy and simple-minded revelation of what one called "the love-generation in full gush."

Herlihy's short stories, like his novels, are thronged with "derelicts, misfortunates, and grotesques," their inarticulate pathos starkly counterpointed by his "hard and imaginative prose." Granville Hicks has praised his ability to draw character "sharply, with none of the blurring so often found in the work of Sherwood Anderson's followers," and Stanley Kauffmann has commended his unerring and witty ear for dialogue. Some readers have disapproved of Herlihy's preoccupation with the bizarre and the unnatural, but a *Time* reviewer has suggested that what is important about his characters "is not their oddness but their kinship to humanity."

Herlihy is six feet tall, brown haired, and blue eyed. His favorite authors include Sherwood Anderson, Hemingway, Gertrude Stein, and Carson McCullers. He enjoys reading, conversation, swimming, and painting. An interviewer has described him as "genuine, outgoing in his feeling for others . . . and understanding of them." Herlihy believes that there is "only one essential problem in human life: to sustain one's faith in the mysteries, in love."

PRINCIPAL WORKS: (with W. A. Noble) Blue Denim (play), 1958; The Sleep of Baby Filbertson (stories), 1959; All Fall Down (novel), 1960; Midnight Cowboy, 1965; A Story That Ends With a Scream (stories), 1967; Stop, You're Killing Me (plays: Laughs, etc., Terrible Jim Fitch, Bad Bad Jo-Jo), 1970; The Season of the Witch (novel), 1971.

ABOUT: Current Biography, 1961; Vinson, J. (ed.) Contemporary Novelists, 1972; Who's Who in America, 1972–1973. *Periodicals*—Christian Science Monitor August 10, 1967; Nation January 31, 1959; New York Review of Books November 11, 1965; New York Times Book Review August 15, 1965; Saturday Review April 10, 1971; Time January 12, 1959; August 15, 1960.

***HERNÁNDEZ, MIGUEL** (October 30, 1910–March 28, 1942), Spanish poet and dramatist, was born into a peasant family in Orihuela, in the province of Alicante. As a boy he worked as a goatherd, receiving only two years of formal education and some instruction from the Jesuits. Nevertheless he read as much as he could and soon began to write lyrics of his own, most often expressing his delight in nature: "After love, then the earth, / After the earth, no one."

MIGUEL HERNÁNDEZ

These early poems, influenced most noticeably by Góngora, began to appear in local papers in 1932 and were collected in *Perito en lunas* (Expert in Moons, 1933), which brought the young "peasant poet" immediate fame. Hernández had visited Madrid in 1931 and he settled there in 1933 as secretary to the scholar and art critic José María de Cossío. With his friend Ramón Sijé, Cossío continued Hernández's education in the classical traditions of Spain's Golden Age, encouraging him to discipline his talent without sacrificing its earthy vitality. Hernández also received support and encouragement from some of the older generation of poets, particularly Antonio Machado and Juan Ramón Jiménez.

In 1934 he completed a religious play, inspired by Calderón, called *Quien te ha visto y quien te ve . . .*, which means something like "Alas, poor Yorick." He subsequently wrote a number of other plays in verse and in prose, including the four satirical one-act pieces collected in *Teatro en la Guerra* (1937). Meanwhile, in 1936, Hernández published *El rayo que no cesa* (The Ceaseless Lightning), a volume of poems, mostly sonnets, of great classical purity. It includes the superb elegy for Ramón Sijé, and many love poems addressed to Josefina Manresa, whom he had loved for years and married at about this time. These poems are full of the imagery of

* er nän′ deth

the bullfight, used sometimes darkly, as when the poet seems to invoke death in the form of a bull, sometimes wryly when he sees himself as a bull tormented and emasculated by love: "A bull stands by the stream, apart. / Its huge face, tragic, wet, / forgets it is a bull, and virile."

With the outbreak of the Spanish Civil War in 1936 Hernández, with his close friends Pablo Neruda and Vicente Aleixandre, joined that brilliant company of writers and artists who gathered to the defense of the Republic. In the Loyalist troops he found the popular audience he had always sought, and wrote for them the fierce and stirring poems in *Viento del pueblo* (1937): "The poets are the winds of the people. We were born to be blown into their pores and to lift their eyes and their senses to the summits of beauty." But in the later war poems of *El hombre acecha* (The Ambushed Man, 1939) this optimism and sense of mission had given way to weariness, bereavement, and loss.

After the Republican defeat Hernández returned to Orihuela, where he was arrested in September 1939. Imprisoned in a concentration camp he escaped, was recaptured, and sentenced to death. Only strong international protests to the Franco government saved him from the firing squad. He was freed but rearrested almost immediately and sentenced to life imprisonment, later commuted to thirty years. Hernández survived three of them, shifted from prison to prison, each more wretched than the last. In the end he was protected against the winters only by rags he stitched together himself. It is said that no one ever heard a word of self-pity from him. "His final attitude was stoical, his last poems buoyant, without religious belief." Weakened by exposure and malnutrition, he died of tuberculosis at the age of thirty-one.

Cancionero y romancero de ausencias (Songs and Ballads of Absence), published posthumously, contains the poems he wrote between 1937 and 1941 for his wife and son, themselves starving. To his son he wrote: "I awoke from being a child: / Don't you awake! / My mouth is sad: / Laugh forever! / In your cradle / defend laughter / feather by feather."

Hernández's complete works were published in Buenos Aires in 1960. The Mexican poet Octavio Paz has described him as a man with "nut-brown eyes, a large mouth, like his hands and his heart, and like them, simple and wise," with a fine bass voice in which he loved to sing the popular songs of the Republic. Vicente Aleixandre said, "He was trusting, and never expected to be hurt. He believed in men and hoped for them." Chandler and Schwartz, in their *New History of Spanish Literature*, wrote that Hernández "fused the two eternal currents of Spanish literature, the popular and the *culto*"; and that "he, more than any other poet of his generation, had the potential to equal the great names of Spanish literature."

PRINCIPAL WORKS IN ENGLISH TRANSLATION: *Poems in* Barnstone, W. (ed.) Modern European Poetry, 1966; Cohen, J. M. (ed.) The Penguin Book of Spanish Verse, 1960.

ABOUT: Ballesta, J. C. La poesía de Miguel Hernández, 1963; Chandler, R. E. and Schwartz, K. A New History of Spanish Literature, 1961; Couffon, C. Orihuela et Miguel Hernández, 1964; Díaz-Plaja, G. Poesía lírica española, 1948; Penguin Companion to Literature 2, 1969; Romero, E. Miguel Hernández, 1958; Zardoya, C. Miguel Hernández, 1955. *Periodicals*—Ideas de México January–April 1955.

HERVÉ-BAZIN, JEAN-PIERRE MARIE. *See* "BAZIN, HERVÉ"

HIBBERT, ELEANOR BURFORD ("JEAN PLAIDY," "VICTORIA HOLT," etc.) (September 1, 1906–), English novelist, writes: "I was born in London. Father was no good as a business man and believed that the most important thing in life was Literature. Mother thought the most important thing in life was Father. Hence, although there was little money, there were always plenty of books. Nothing was forbidden, everything encouraged, and I learned to read at the age of four and by the time I was seven had started on Dickens, and by eleven had come to Hugo and Tolstoi. Having learned, too, the useful art of skipping, I found no difficulty with the classics which so many young people want to have read but not to read; and although this habit might be considered deplorable at least it gave me some understanding, if at this stage superficial, of most of the classics of English literature, and while I skimmed lightly over Thackeray and George Eliot, I devoured every word of the Brontë sisters.

"I went to a school run by the church at which the fees were very low indeed and from there gained a scholarship to what was called in those days a secondary school. My stay here was cut short—money again—and when I was seventeen I set out to earn a living, first in a restaurant in the shadow of St. Paul's where I attempted to act as interpreter to French customers and then in Hatton Garden among the precious stones and pavement dealers.

"Meanwhile I was trying to write. My heart was with the classics and my style Victorian and I was producing long verbose imitations which naturally failed to achieve publication. There were eight of these—but the effort was not entirely wasted as I did use quite a large amount of material from them in later years.

"I married and then found the time and encouragement I needed. I stopped writing unsaleable novels and started short stories with which I was immediately successful. Writing took posses-

ELEANOR BURFORD HIBBERT

sion of me. I wrote regularly every day and was reading at the same speed which I had kept up since the age of four; and I found writing not only stimulating but necessary. It rarely wearied me and almost always exhilarated me. My stories were published regularly in London newspapers and on the Continent and as soon as my work began to be published I was able to earn an income which, although in the beginning not large, was always adequate.

"I experimented with all kinds of work, feeling my way towards the novel which I intended to appeal to a large number of people and thus be a best seller. I became fascinated by history and wrote historical novels which have become very successful in England and some Continental countries. These are history in novelized form with no concessions to romance and prejudice; they are a reconstruction of facts set out to instruct while they entertain. At this stage of my career, as Jean Plaidy, I became well known with over forty books in print and still selling. I was then approached by an American agent, Patricia Schartle, who descended on me like the Fairy Godmother and asked me if I wanted to be a best seller, because if I did, I could, having the necessary talents. All I needed was a wave of the magic wand. I listened to this attractive proposal and as a result produced *Mistress of Mellyn* which did all that she had prophesied it would: serialization in *Ladies' Home Journal* and almost every country in the world, Reader's Digest Book Club Selection, film rights sold to Paramount, and a world best seller. This I followed with *Kirkland Revels, Bride of Pendorric* and *The Legend of the Seventh Virgin,* all of which have been best sellers."

Mrs. Hibbert is the daughter of Joseph and Alice (Tate) Burford. She married very young—her husband was a leather merchant—but had no children. She has written well over a hundred novels under at least seventeen pseudonyms, including "Jean Plaidy," "Eleanor Burford," "Ellalice Tate," "Elbur Ford," and "Kathleen Kellow." By far the most successful of these for many years were the historical romances she began to produce in 1945 as "Jean Plaidy." These are generally accounts of the lives of famous historical personages, making use of colorful invented dialogue but accurate in outline and highly readable. The critics have for the most part been well disposed towards these instructive entertainments. Martin Levin, reviewing *Madame Serpent,* the first volume in her trilogy on Catherine de Medici, thought her characters insufficiently well motivated to be much more than historical puppets, but the *Times Literary Supplement* considered that the author "does succeed in arousing for the unfortunate young girl a sympathy which gradually changes into repulsion for the woman she became," and others enjoyed the book as a historical thriller of the first rank.

As Mrs. Hibbert indicates, the very considerable popularity of the Jean Plaidy books was as nothing compared to the sensational success, especially in America, of the Gothic novels she writes as "Victoria Holt." These books, which reportedly earn the author about $300,000 each, were rumored to be the work of Daphne du Maurier until Mrs. Hibbert declared herself in 1967. She says that while the Plaidy novels are written for "a very special, very loyal public, who want to learn something," Victoria Holt "is for the housewife in the mid-west of America who has never heard of Louis XV and doesn't want to, thank you."

These books turn most often on the ordeals of young brides immured in remote manor houses which are stuffed to the creaking beams with family skeletons. The tradition is that of *Jane Eyre, Wuthering Heights,* or *Rebecca.* The characterization is strong and clear, and there is always a skillful balance between suspense and romance. Genevieve Casey, reviewing *The Legend of the Seventh Virgin,* wrote that "among the clamor of novels by angry young men . . . among the probings and circumlocution of psychological novels, the works of Victoria Holt stand out, unpretentious, sunny, astringent, diverting."

Mrs. Hibbert works for five or six hours a day, in this time turning out an average of about five thousand words. Now a widow, she is a delicate woman with dark auburn hair, orderly by nature, and, thanks to her large income, able to indulge her fondness for fashionable clothes and travel. She lives part of each year in a flat in Kensington, London, spends her summers at Deal on the Kent coast, and her winters traveling abroad, partly for pleasure, partly to collect material and promote her novels. She is the first to point out that her books are not "literature," but doesn't much regret the lack of serious critical interest in them: "I've got my lovely, big public panting for my next novel."

PRINCIPAL WORKS: *As "Jean Plaidy"*—Together They Ride, 1945; Beyond the Blue Mountains, 1947; Murder Most Royal (U.S., The King's Pleasure), 1949; The Goldsmith's Wife, 1950; Madame Serpent, 1951; The Italian Woman, 1952; Daughter of Satan, 1952; Queen Jezebel, 1953; The Spanish Bridegroom, 1953. *As "Victoria Holt"*—Mistress of Mellyn, 1960; Kirkland Revels, 1962; The Bride of Pendorric, 1963; The Legend of the Seventh Virgin, 1965; Menfreya in the Morning, 1966; The King of the Castle, 1967; The Queen's Confession, 1968; The Shivering Sands, 1969; The Secret Woman, 1970; The Shadow of the Lynx, 1971; On the Night of the Seventh Moon, 1972; The Curse of the Kings, 1973.

ABOUT: Contemporary Authors 17–18, 1967; Twentieth Century Writing, 1969; Who's Who, 1971. *Periodicals*—Atlanta Journal April 4, 1966; Best Sellers February 1, 1965; Chicago Sunday Tribune January 14, 1962; Library Journal March 15, 1966; New York Times Book Review April 17, 1966; January 8, 1967; Time May 13, 1966.

PATRICIA HIGHSMITH

HIGHSMITH, (MARY) PATRICIA (January 19, 1921–), American novelist writes: "I was born in Fort Worth, Texas, only child of Mary Coates and Jay Bernard Plangman. My mother is English-Scots by descent, from an Alabama family; my father is German by descent, of a family that has been in Texas for a few generations. My father's name is on my birth certificate, but my parents were divorced a few months before I was born. I began school under the name Highsmith (my mother married Stanley Highsmith when I was three), and I did nothing about this incorrect name until I was twenty-three, when I had myself adopted by Stanley Highsmith in order to secure a passport. This manoeuvre changed my name legally. Both my parents are commercial artists, my father more a teacher than a free-lancer. My stepfather is also a commercial artist. I was strongly drawn toward art-work when I was in my late teens and early twenties, and it was hard for me to make a choice, but I do not regret having chosen writing. Writing has moral and intellectual scope, which of course painting has, too, but in writing this can be made plainer, I think, than it can in painting.

"As my mother was working when I was small, my grandmother more or less raised me, in Texas, till I was six. She was a Scot, very practical, though with a great sense of humor, and very lenient with me. She had for many years let rooms in her house, by way of making both ends meet. It was in this house that I was born. At the age of six, my mother and stepfather took me to New York, where I began my education in an ordinary public school. My accent was so southern, I had a hard time making myself understood, or understanding anyone else, and my mother relates that on my first day at school, when she came to fetch me at 3 p.m., I was walking hand in hand with a little Negro boy, because we could at least understand each other. After high school at Julia Richman, I went to Barnard College, Columbia University, and graduated in 1942. I had been writing short stories, as well as drawing, since sixteen or before. One of my stories, written in college but not published in the college magazine because it was considered too horrifying, was "The Heroine," published in *Harper's Bazaar* when I was twenty-four, and then included in the O. Henry Prize Stories of 1946.

"Meanwhile, on almost no money, I had gone to Mexico in late 1943 to write a book. I had amassed a sum of $350 by working for a year writing comic books of the Superman and Batman variety. Back from Mexico, broke, my book at 365 pages and still unfinished, I continued to work on comics by way of earning my living, but on a free-lance basis, which earned me about three times as much as a salaried job doing the same thing would have done. Evenings and weekends, I wrote 'fiction.' I thus laid by enough to go to Europe in 1949. This was my ambition: to write a book, then go to Europe. The book I wrote was *Strangers on a Train*, which had the good luck to be bought by Hitchcock soon after publication. I then abandoned my hack writing, though I was by no means affluent, merely proud.

"I returned to Europe in early 1951, and remained there more than two years. Occasionally, I sold a short story to the States, and I was beginning a book called *The Blunderer*. This was followed by

The Talented Mr. Ripley, my favorite book, which was made into the film called *Purple Noon.*

"Since 1953, when I had to give up my adequate little apartment on East 56th Street, New York, I have had a rocky time geographically. But the fact is, I do like traveling and making acquaintance with new scenes. I always use them. If one loses possessions, becomes physically ill, that's part of life. It is not always a bed of roses.

"Sometimes I am inspired to write a book by a surprising, hardly believable incident which I intend to include in the plot, and sometimes I am inspired by a moral dilemma around which I create a plot. I used to make three drafts of all my novels, and now perhaps it is two-and-one-half. I often overwrite and have to cut. I am not in the least interested in 'style.' I aim at clarity. I have always written exactly what I wish to write, that is, what interests me and pleases me. I never think about where I may be able to sell something, and still less of whether it will make a good film. I think I've had good luck with films (six books out of twelve bought for films, though only three made so far), because my story ideas are often unusual, and because my settings are attractive—or at least they are to the people who buy the books for films. I am at present writing a book set in Tunisia, which will be called *The Tremor of Forgery*.

"In all my novels, I am concerned with guilt. I am interested in whether certain people have or have not a sense of guilt under certain circumstances. I think this is not always apparent to American reviewers, but it is to the French and English. I am treated as a rather serious novelist in Europe, more so than in the United States, where my books were so long eschewed also by the paperback firms because there was not enough sex in them, and because they were too psychological.

"Recently, I bought a house in France, in the country. This after nearly four years of living in a cottage in Suffolk, which was very good for working, but rather lonely. I have one Siamese cat, Samantha, who comes from England.

"I never think about my 'place' in literature, and perhaps I have none. I consider myself an entertainer. I like to tell a fascinating story. But every book is an argument with myself, and I would write it whether it is ever published or not."

In *Strangers on a Train* a young psychopath desperate to be rid of his father meets a man anxious to end his marriage, and proposes murder on an exchange basis. One reviewer called it "a horrifying picture of an oddly engaging young man" and the book was admired as a subtle examination of character and as "a sort of parable of good and evil" as well as a chilling suspense story. Alfred Hitchcock made from it one of his finest films.

This first novel introduced Miss Highsmith's theme, which as she says is guilt, and also her method, which frequently involves a confrontation between a charming but depraved man and an innocent but weak one. J. M. Edelstein has shown that her books can be divided into those that focus on a victim figure (like *The Blunderer, A Game for the Living, The Cry of the Owl*) and those centering on a dangerously unstable drifter (*The Talented Mr. Ripley, Deep Water, This Sweet Sickness*, etc.).

The talented Mr. Ripley is a young American expatriate in Italy who finds it expedient to murder and then to impersonate a wealthy friend. It is an extraordinary novel in a number of ways—not least in the fact that Ripley is never brought to justice and seems at the end spiritually enlarged by his unpunished crime. The *New Yorker*'s reviewer found him "one of the most repellent and fascinating characters to come along for quite a while" and called the book a "remarkably immoral story very engagingly told." A sequel, *Ripley Under Ground*, was received with equal pleasure.

Most members of the growing Highsmith cult would list *Strangers on a Train* and *The Talented Mr. Ripley* among the author's triumphs; some of them would add *The Blunderer, The Two Faces of January, The Glass Cell*, and *Those Who Walk Away*. The latter is the most admired of her later novels. Its setting is Venice out of season, where an American painter commits himself to the murder of his son-in-law, whom he blames for his daughter's suicide. The young man, himself possessed by ambiguous feelings of guilt and sorrow, at first hides from his pursuer and then turns on him. Neither man succeeds in his murderous intent but suspense is nevertheless superbly maintained. J. M. Edelstein called it a "low-key, subtle, and profound" novel which "in its deliberateness, in the genuineness with which the vagueness of motivation is conveyed, in its perception of evil . . . succeeds as a compelling psychological study. . . . The book is a study of things moving out of control."

To some reviewers the dark subconscious motives which propel Miss Highsmith's characters are quite incomprehensible, and some who like their murders made palatable call her vision of the world "sickening" and "nasty." But a growing number of critics find it astonishing that she is not more honored in her own country. Edelstein calls her "superb . . . a master of the suspense novel" whose work "should be among the classics of the genre." Brigid Brophy thinks that Miss Highsmith and Georges Simenon are alone in writing books which transcend the limits of the thriller genre without breaking its rules, and Francis Hope regards her as the only modern crime writer who might possibly be allowed to "walk in the same street" as Dostoevsky. In the opinion of Maurice Richardson "she reigns as the justly acknowledged queen of the intelligent thriller and any survey of crime fiction, however random, must pay its tribute to her."

One of Miss Highsmith's novels, *The Price of Salt*, was published pseudonymously as by "Claire Morgan." In *Plotting and Writing Suspense Fiction* she explains her own way of writing, describing by way of illustration the composition of *The Glass Cell*. Anthony Boucher found it fascinating and stimulating in its detail, and "a full and true picture" of "what it's like to be a professional writer." Patricia Highsmith is a slender, attractive woman who lives alone and is "always, compulsively, on the move." She has never studied or even to her knowledge met a criminal, but says that she finds it a great deal easier to understand abnormal people than ordinary ones. Perhaps, she told a *Guardian* interviewer, this is because of her family background. "I feel like an outcast, as does the criminal. . . . Like him I have had to come to terms with society as best I can. . . . I have a lurking liking for those who flout the law." She enjoys drawing, painting, and playing the piano, and also lists carpentering and snail-watching among her recreations.

PRINCIPAL WORKS: *Fiction*—Strangers on a Train, 1950; (as "Claire Morgan") Price of Salt, 1952; The Blunderer 1954; The Talented Mr. Ripley, 1955; Deep Water, 1957; A Game for the Living, 1958; This Sweet Sickness, 1960; The Cry of the Owl, 1962; The Two Faces of January, 1964; The Glass Cell, 1964; The Story-Teller, 1965 (England, A Suspension of Mercy); Those Who Walk Away, 1967; The Tremor of Forgery, 1969; The Snail Watcher and Other Stories (England, Eleven) 1970; Ripley Under Ground, 1970; A Dog's Ransom, 1972. *Nonfiction*—Plotting and Writing Suspense Fiction, 1966.
ABOUT: Brophy, B. Don't Never Forget, 1966; Contemporary Authors 3, 1963; Highsmith, P. Plotting and Writing Suspense Fiction, 1966; Vinson, J. (ed.) Contemporary Novelists, 1972; Who's Who, 1973. *Periodicals*—Guardian May 1, 1968; New Republic May 20, 1967; New Statesman October 29, 1965; Times Literary Supplement December 8, 1966; June 1, 1967; September 24, 1971.

HIMES, CHESTER (BOMAR) (July 29, 1909–), American novelist, was born in Jefferson City, Missouri, the son of Joseph and Estelle (Bomar) Himes. Both parents were teachers, and the father's career took the family during Himes's childhood from Missouri to Ohio, from Mississippi to Arkansas, and back to Ohio. The boy attended high school in Cleveland and studied at Ohio State University in 1926–1927. He began his writing career in the Ohio State Penitentiary, where he served time for armed robbery from 1929 to 1936. His account of the terrible fire in the Penitentiary in 1930, which killed over three hundred men, appeared in *Esquire* in 1932. During the depression Himes gained experience of a variety of milieus—

CHESTER HIMES

two years with the Ohio State Writers' Project, a spell as a feature writer with the Cleveland *Daily News*, involvement with the labor movement and the Communist party. He was married in 1937 to Jean Johnson.

In 1941, when America entered World War II, Himes and his wife, a social worker, moved to California. During the war years he worked in Los Angeles and San Francisco as a shipfitter, sheet-metal mechanic, and riveter in shipyards and aircraft plants. In 1944 he received a Julius Rosenwald fellowship, and the following year he published his first novel, *If He Hollers Let Him Go*. Much influenced by Richard Wright, it is a short, bitterly realistic account of the wartime experiences of an educated black defense worker and his mounting rage and frustration against the prejudice he meets every day wherever he goes. The awkward prose only adds to the power and authenticity of the narrative, and many critics consider this the best of Himes's books. "The hero is race-mad," writes David Littlejohn, "almost to the point of hysteria, packed with dry high explosive, waiting for the match. He eases the almost unbearable tension of being black by speeding a powerful car down the freeways or by insulting his lighter-colored, educated, upper-middle-class fiancée and her friends." In the end he is driven to throw up his job, leave his girl, and go off to war.

Two years later *Lonely Crusade* appeared, another story of racial oppression with a tragic denouement. This time the hero is a union organizer, whose political differences with the Communist party are interwoven with his personal struggle to regain his lost manhood—the metaphoric emasculation of the black man in a racist society is one of Himes's major themes. Some reviewers were reminded of Steinbeck's *In Dubious Battle*, though many thought that the book contained too many tedious pages of political theory.

Cast the First Stone, a naturalistic account of prison life, is the only one of Himes's novels to deal principally with white characters, and the first to show glints of the sardonic humor that has come to characterize his work. It was followed by *Third Generation*, the last novel he wrote in America. This is the most ambitious of Himes's books, the history of a black family from slavery to the prosperous present, showing them still bent and distorted under the weight of psychological fetters. The novel's raw power was recognized, as was the author's passionate concern to understand and explain his characters, but it had no more popular success than its predecessors.

The hero of *If He Hollers Let Him Go* had said: "If I couldn't live in America as an equal in the minds, hearts, and souls of all white people, if I couldn't know that I had a chance to do anything any other American could, to go as high as American citizenship would carry anybody, there'd never be anything in the country for me anyway." It must have been with some such feeling that Himes left the United States for good.

By the summer of 1954, at any rate, he was "living with a white woman socialite, graduate of Smith College, descendant of the Pilgrims, in a state of near destitution in the House of the Bleeding Jesus on the hot, dirty square at the foot of the steps in Deya, Mallorca." It was there that he wrote *The Primitive*, which is indeed about an affair between an unsuccessful black novelist and an elegant white career woman. He projects on her his sense of racial humiliation; she punishes him for her wretched sexual experiences: the end is murder. It is a book that, as Himes wrote in the New York *Times Book Review*, he recalls with particular pleasure: "Being largely autobiographical (I did not kill the white woman, however gladly I might have), the book acted as a catharsis, purging me of all the mental and emotional inhibitions that restricted my writing."

Himes has lived in Europe ever since, much of the time in Paris, where he became a close friend of Richard Wright and made a place for himself in French intellectual circles. It was in France that he began to publish the Harlem thrillers for which he is nowadays best known. These stories, fast moving and far more sophisticated than Himes's earlier books, center around a pair of black detectives, Coffin Ed Johnson and Grave Digger Jones. Their mordant humor, frequently deriving from racial ironies, delighted the French critics, and Himes in 1958 received the coveted Grand Prix Policier.

It was nevertheless not until 1965 that the first of his Harlem stories achieved hardcover publication in the United States. This was *Cotton Comes to Harlem*, in which the two detectives are involved in a hectic hunt for eighty-seven thousand dollars swindled from Harlem residents in a fake back-to-Africa scheme. The gallows humor, violence, and sexual explicitness disturbed some reviewers, but most were delighted with the book, as they have been with its successors; there was a very popular film version in 1970. Maurice Richardson has called Himes "the greatest find in American crime fiction since Raymond Chandler."

Violence is what links Himes's early novels and his thrillers—violence very often as the mindless product of fear. "A friend of mine," he writes in his preface to *Blind Man With a Pistol*, ". . . told me this story about a blind man with a pistol shooting at a man who had slapped him on a subway train, and killing an innocent bystander. . . . And then I thought of some of our loudmouthed leaders urging our vulnerable soul brothers on to getting themselves killed, and thought further that all unorganized violence is like a blind man with a pistol."

In an earlier Coffin Ed story, *Run Man Run*, it is a drunken white detective who shoots a black porter by accident, and then to cover his tracks commits another murder and attempts a third. This story illustrates another recurrent motif in Himes's books—an ironic reversal of racist myth in which it is the white man who is shown as the true "primitive." Himes says that "it has always been my opinion that we American Negroes are one of the most sophisticated people in the history of mankind. . . . We always know what white people are doing to us and what they are thinking while doing it. We are amused, in a masochistic sort of way, by their various rationalizations and justifications." As the black protagonist of *The Primitive* says to himself after he has been driven to murder and disaster: "Don't cry, son. It's funny really. You just got to get the handle to the joke." The first volume of Himes's autobiography, describing his life until 1954, was published in 1972 as *The Quality of Hurt*. The author now lives in Spain.

PRINCIPAL WORKS: If He Hollers Let Him Go, 1945; Lonely Crusade, 1947; Cast the First Stone, 1953; The Third Generation, 1954; The Primitive, 1955; For Love of Imabelle, 1957 (repub. as A Rage in Harlem, 1965); The Crazy Kill, 1959; The Real Cool Killers, 1959; The Big Gold Dream, 1960; All Shot Up, 1960; Pinktoes, 1961 (Paris), 1965 (U.S.); Cotton Comes to Harlem, 1965; The Heat's On, 1966; Run Man Run, 1966; Blind Man With a Pistol, 1969; The Quality of Hurt (autobiography), 1972.

ABOUT: Bone, R. The Negro in America, 1965; Himes, C. The Quality of Hurt, 1972; Hughes, J. M. C. Negro Novelist, 1953; Littlejohn, D. Black on White, 1966; Margolies, E. Native Sons, 1968; Nyren, D. Modern American Literature (A Library of Literary Criticism), 1969; Vinson, J. (ed.) Contemporary Novelists, 1972;

Warfel, H. R. American Novelists of Today, 1951; Who's Who in America, 1972–1973; Williams, J. A. Flashbacks, 1973. *Periodicals*—Atlantic October 1947; Book Week January 18, 1953; January 10, 1954; October 11, 1964; March 28, 1965; August 8, 1965; April 27, 1969; New Republic December 31, 1945; New York Times Book Review December 2, 1945; September 27, 1959; February 7, 1965; February 23, 1969; March 12, 1972; April 30, 1972; Saturday Review January 17, 1953.

***"HINDE, THOMAS" (pseudonym of Sir Thomas Willes Chitty)** (March 2, 1926–), English novelist, writes: "I was born in the East Coast seaside resort of Felixstowe where my father ran a small boarding school for boys. To this I was sent from the ages of six to twelve, and I don't doubt that the impossible conflict it produced inclined me towards a writer's escape into the manageable conflicts of fiction. But inclination is not achievement, and both at this school and at Winchester I was only distinguished, if at all, as a gymnast. This talent, and the War, made my parents and school-masters decide that the Royal Navy would best suit me for life and I was easily persuaded. As a result I spent three unhappy years resenting naval discipline and writing letters of resignation, till at last I'd convinced the Admiralty that they'd made a mistake. Looking back on this disagreeable experience, I am grateful that it forced me to learn science till I was eighteen—a subject which still interests me.

"In hot revolt, I went to Oxford, to read the most useless of university subjects: modern history. But everything else there was educational in the best sense and I idled away three pleasant years talking, play acting, drinking, getting a third class degree and writing a number of bad short stories of which only two were published and I doubt if those deserved to be.

"Looking back, it seems that in the following years I became a writer as much by default as by anything else. There seemed no other way I wanted to spend my time or jobs I wanted to do—and subsequent experience has shown that at least about the jobs I was right. I wrote my first novel while tutoring two children on a farm and was lucky enough to have it taken at once.

"For the next nine years I worked first as a rating officer, measuring the houses of Willesden, then in an oil company's public relations department, discovering for myself the novelist's dilemma, that a job leaves no time for writing and a remote country cottage provides nothing to write about. I still don't know the answer. My last two years with the oil company were spent in Nairobi, Kenya, where I was lucky enough to have some longish periods of glandular fever, and these were the best compromise I've ever discovered.

* hind

THOMAS HINDE

"In England my home is now in Sussex, but for the last three years (1964–7) I've been attached to two universities, the University of York where I was awarded a Granada Arts Fellowship, and the University of Illinois where I teach writing and modern British literature. I am glad to have been temporarily provoked into taking an academic view of literature, and at present enjoy teaching.

"Writing, however, remains my real and compulsive interest, so much so that I don't often bother to wonder, for instance, whether there'll be any novels in fifty years' time. In this sense I write for myself, but in a wider sense a selected and idealised audience is essential. I have of course written unpublished poems. And for money I have written reviews, travel articles and even a household encyclopedia but I don't much enjoy these. I would like to write a play, but have always had a novel I wanted to write more.

"In 1951 I married Susan Hopkinson, who writes as Susan Chitty, and we have four children. Thomas Hinde is a pen-name, which I took for personal reasons when my first book was published. My real name is Thomas Willes Chitty, but I increasingly prefer the pen-name because it is an easy way to avoid a title which I inherited in 1955 and which I find chiefly an embarrassment, creating expectations which I can't fulfill."

Thomas Hinde's first novel, *Mr. Nicholas*, was described by Kenneth Allsop as being in its "acute discernment and the understated power of its prose one of the few really distinguished post-war [British] novels . . . by the highest standards, a brilliant and beautifully written book, controlled exact and illuminating." Mr. Nicholas is a retired businessman living, slightly beyond his means, in an expensive suburb—"a middle-class incubus," Allsop calls him, greedily dominating and exploiting "a family of strangers imprisoned under one roof, strangled by their inhibitions." The narrator is Peter, dimly artistic and rebellious, who is home on vacation from Oxford and whose deep conflict with his father and all he represents comes with dreadful slowness to crisis in the course of a long, hot tennis-playing summer. For Walter Allen, who was reminded of the early Christopher Isherwood, the novel's strength lay in "the exactness of the observation of one section of middle-class life in transition."

Social change and its impact on the individual can be seen as the theme of all of Hinde's novels—of *Happy as Larry*, an almost surrealistic search for values in postwar London which shocked some reviewers with its nihilism; of *For the Good of the Company*, in which another of Hinde's helpless young men is crushed in the machinery of a giant corporation; certainly of *A Place Like Home* and *The Cage*. These last are both set in East Africa, and each shows how "the wind of change" seizes a limp expatriate, shakes him, and sets him down again with a better (though scarcely a comforting) understanding of his own nature.

The most notable of Hinde's recent books—and some believe his best novel to date—is *The Day the Call Came*, narrated by a genteel fruit farmer who becomes convinced that he is a secret agent. Hinde makes of this, according to the *Times Literary Supplement*, "not a brilliant joke or a clinical study of insanity, but an extraordinarily complex allegory about . . . the nature of perception," achieving "that perfect fusion of form and content to which all his other novels aspire. . . . The impersonal movement of the novel—logical in its progression and exact in its detail—is never jeopardized. Mr. Hinde seems to respect what he is doing too much to admire himself for being able to do it." *The Village*, Hinde's most ambitious book, was thought by most reviewers a brave failure. Taking as its theme the forthcoming demolition of an English village and the effect of this upon the villagers, it sets out to explore in great depth not one or two but a whole cast of characters, and founders—most thought—in the attempt.

Anthony Burgess admires in particular the extreme economy of Hinde's work, which, he says, "gains its effects from ellipsis rather than expansiveness." A perceptive essay in the *Times Literary Supplement* (October 27, 1966) suggests that Hinde's "distinctive mark is his impersonality. . . . Almost alone among interesting contemporary novelists, he seems to have a Jamesian faith in his medium, and an almost Jamesian determination to confront the problems of that medium directly. He . . . has brought to the rural-suburban world he knows so well the gifts of mimicry and irony, has studied its manners and detected its comedy; and most importantly he has been able to render it in such a way that . . . he has made it stand for more than itself. But such achievements seem to be almost incidental to Mr. Hinde's vision of the real issue—the internal organization, the independence and aesthetic value of the completed whole. There are times . . . when we have felt that the intensity of his artistic conviction has made him the one *pure* novelist of today."

Thomas Hinde is the son of Sir (Thomas) Henry Willes Chitty, the second baronet, and the former Ethel Constance Gladstone. As he says, he inherited the baronetcy when his father died in 1955. Hinde lives with his family in the Sussex village of West Hoathly. He and his wife, the author of some engaging light novels, devote their mornings to writing, the rest of the day to their children. Hinde was a visiting lecturer at the University of Illinois in 1965–1967, and a visiting professor at Boston University in 1969–1970. He has drawn on his American experiences in two interesting if not entirely successful novels, *High* and *Generally a Virgin*.

PRINCIPAL WORKS: *Novels*—Mr. Nicholas, 1952; Happy as Larry, 1957; For the Good of the Company, 1961; A Place Like Home, 1962; The Cage, 1962; Ninety Double Martinis, 1963; The Day the Call Came, 1964; Games of Chance, 1965; The Village, 1966; High, 1968; Bird, 1970; Generally a Virgin, 1972. *Nonfiction*—(comp.) Spain: A Personal Anthology, 1963.

ABOUT: Allen, W. The Modern Novel, 1964; Allsop, K. The Angry Decade, 1958; British Broadcasting Corporation. Writers on Themselves, 1964; Burgess, A. The Novel Now, 1967; Contemporary Authors 7–8, 1963; Debrett's Peerage, Baronetage, Knightage and Companionage, 1971; Gindin, J. Postwar British Fiction, 1962; Vinson, J. (ed.) Contemporary Novelists, 1972; Who's Who, 1972. *Periodicals*—Books and Bookmen October 1963; Times Literary Supplement October 27, 1966.

HIRAOKA, KIMITAKE. *See* "MISHIMA, YUKIO"

***HLASKO, MAREK** (January 14, 1934–June 14, 1969), Polish novelist, was born in Warsaw. He began to work at the age of thirteen and received very little formal education. Once, when he was a truck driver, he reluctantly accepted an assignment as "worker correspondent"—not realizing, as he said later, "that actually this would be the beginning of a new work in my life."

Meanwhile, Hlasko tried his hand at a variety of other occupations but began to put down on paper his thoughts and impressions. "I did it without any sort of faith or conviction—just in order to better

* hlä′ skô

my fate," he said. Hauling timber in the mountains provided him with the plot for his novella *Next Stop—Paradise*. He also learned much while driving a taxi and listening to the conversation of his fares. Work on a barge that moved at three miles an hour convinced him that "Hell is when nothing happens and you can't even hit anybody." It was then that he began to write seriously, learning gradually that "one must always begin at the very beginning, that every sentence and every story is unique and each must be told from the beginning and once only."

Hlasko's first stories were published in 1955 in Polish literary periodicals, and reflect his gradual progression away from the arid official doctrine of "Socialist realism" towards a romanticized naturalism. Collected in *Pierwszy krok w cmurach* (First Step in the Clouds, 1956), their freshness and honesty were received with delight—especially by the young, desperately bored by physical and intellectual austerity. The Polish magazine *Twórczość* serialized his novella *Ósmy dzień tygodnia* (1956, translated as *The Eighth Day of the Week*), about an assortment of people who are waiting for Sunday to transform their drab lives. When Sunday comes it is cold and rainy, and solves no problems. "There should be an eighth day in the week," Hlasko wrote, "a day when everyone can be happy." The book was filmed with immense success in a joint West German-Polish production directed by Alexander Ford.

The Polish "thaw" had begun, but as Hlasko's popularity and influence grew, the Communist authorities found it increasingly difficult to swallow his remorseless criticism of the quality of Polish life. In 1957 Hlasko was named the "most popular contemporary Polish writer" in a poll of young people. At about the same time *The Eighth Day of the Week* and a new novella, *Glupcy wierzą w poranek* (Fools Believe in Dawn), were rejected by the state-controlled publishing houses. In 1958 Hlasko went to Paris as a tourist and arranged for the Polish emigré publishing house Kultura to bring out the latter work under a new title, *Następny do raju* (translated as *Next Stop—Paradise*). When his visa expired, he did not return to Poland.

Hlasko's harsh portrait of life under communism gained, through translation, ever wider currency. The displeasure of the Polish and Soviet authorities grew accordingly, and they began a critical campaign against this "disciple of Orwell, that classical master of anti-Communist pamphleteering." Their animosity was strengthened by the publication in Paris of Hlasko's novella *Cmentarze* (1958, translated as *The Graveyard*), his only direct polemic against communism, portraying the progressive disillusionment of a once ardent party member. Hlasko was also attacked by Polish Catholic critics

MAREK HLASKO

and literary traditionalists, who found his work violent and scatological.

"A writer without his country is nothing," Hlasko once said, and indeed his writing appears to have declined after 1958 in inventiveness and intensity. After a brief stay in West Europe, he went to Israel, and in 1960 settled in Munich. His wife was the German actress Sonia Ziemann, who played the lead in the screen version of *The Eighth Day of the Week*. He dramatized his novels for West German television, and in 1964 published in Paris a collection of stories and sketches.

In the United States Hlasko's books, translated by Norbert Guterman, were in general favorably received. They were praised most often for their power and their sharp impressionistic style. Their grotesque humor, their preoccupation with horror and decay, offended some critics but put others in mind of Gogol, Kafka, and Dostoevsky (whom Hlasko admired above all other writers). The Polish critic M. J. Krynski, on the other hand, found in Hlasko's work a reflection of Hemingway's "code of behavior, his mixture of sentiment and brutality and, to a certain degree, the characteristics of his stylistic economy of means." A critic in *Encounter* suggested that he might "be described summarily as a peculiarly Polish mixture of Hemingway, Françoise Sagan, and James Dean." Like James Dean, he had a tragically short life, dying in Wiesbaden, Germany, at the age of thirty-five.

PRINCIPAL WORKS IN ENGLISH TRANSLATION: The Eighth Day of the Week, 1958; The Graveyard, 1959; Next Stop—Paradise, 1960 (also published with The Graveyard, 1961); On the Day of his Death *in* Odyssey Review June 1963.

ABOUT: Gillon, A. and Krzyzanowski, L. Modern Polish

Literature, 1961. *Periodicals*—Encounter June 1958; Mademoiselle September 1958; Polish Review Autumn 1961; Saturday Review September 5, 1959.

***HOCHHUTH, ROLF** (April 1, 1931–), German dramatist, was born in Eschwege/Werra in Hesse. His parents, Walter and Ilse (Holzapfel) Hochhuth, were Protestants, members of the German Evangelical Church. His father, who owned a shoe factory, sent him to the local Realgymnasium. In 1941, as was customary, Rolf Hochhuth joined the Deutsches Jungvolk, a Hitler youth organization. He left school in 1948, studied bookkeeping at a vocational college, and worked for a time as a bookseller. A protracted paralytic illness delayed his university education, but eventually he studied history and philosophy at the universities of Heidelberg and Munich (1952–1955). In 1955 he became a reader for Verlag C. Bertelsmann, a large German publishing firm which also ran a book club.

Rolf Hochhuth had started to write poems and short stories at school, and in 1956 began a more ambitious project, a novel (still unpublished) about the American occupation of Germany. Studying accounts of the Nuremberg trials and related documents, he was particularly fascinated by Gerald Reitlinger's *The Final Solution* (1953), which gives a circumstantial account of Hitler's Jewish extermination policy. Hochhuth's reading also uncovered the stories of three remarkable men: Kurt Gerstein, a German who joined the SS and led a double life to inform the Allied Powers of Nazi genocide; Father Maximilian Kolbe, who voluntarily took the Star of David and became Prisoner 16670 in Auschwitz; and Provost Bernhardt Lichtenberg of St. Heldwig's Cathedral, Berlin, who publicly defended the Jews and applied to the Nazis for permission to accompany them to the death camp. In 1959, after extensive research in Paris, London, and Rome, Hochhuth began to write what became the verse play *Der Stellvertreter* (*The Deputy*), in which Father Riccardo Fontana, S.J., a fictional character modeled on Kolbe and Lichtenberg, pleads with Pope Pius XII to act against the slaughter of the Jews; and the Pope, mindful of the fate of other Roman Catholics in Germany and also of papal business interests, refuses to do so.

The response to *Der Stellvertreter* was immediate, highly charged, and overwhelming. It was published on February 20, 1963, and opened the same day under Erwin Piscator's direction at his new theatre, the Freie Volksbühne in Berlin. The play shared the Gerhard Hauptmann Prize for 1962, and also won the Young Generation Playwright Award of the 1963 Berliner Kunstpreis. Productions quickly followed in Paris; in London (where it was presented by the Royal Shakespeare Company as *The Representative*), and in New York (where it was produced at the Brooks Atkinson Theatre as *The Deputy*). Jerome Rothenburg adapted the play for New York, and a translation by Richard and Clara Winston was published there in 1964. Passionate controversy flared up wherever *Der Stellvertreter* went. Riots, rotten eggs, and cheers greeted the Paris production; pickets marched outside the theatre in New York: in Berlin, the New York *Times* reported, "At the final curtain, the audience [was] too drained to applaud. It [filed] out in utter, painful, bitter silence."

Part of the controversy was caused perhaps by the fact that the original eight-hour script, radically shortened for public performance, was inevitably oversimplified, particularly with regard to the role played by the Pope. Hochhuth says that "the most comprehensive version was shown in Vienna, the shortest in Berlin, the most modern in Paris." But in all the versions, the spokesman and leader of the largest Christian church in the world, in tormented doubt, rejects a clear moral imperative for reasons of expediency; afterwards, he washes his hands. There was a storm of Roman Catholic protest. Cardinal Montini (now Pope Paul VI) accused Hochhuth of caring less for historical fact than for dramatic effect. Other Catholics pointed out that the Church under Pius XII helped many Jews to escape, and that the Pope did speak out, however obliquely, against Nazi oppression, notably in his Christmas Message of 1942 and in the 1943 speech to the Cardinals. On the other hand, Albert Schweitzer, in his preface to the American adaptation, described the play as "a clarion call for our time" and Pastor Martin Niemöller said that he was "glad and grateful" that the play had been published and "that it has caused such a furor." *Der Stellvertreter* set off a global debate on moral and historical responsibility and guilt, and because of this has been compared with Zola's *J'Accuse* and Remarque's *All Quiet on the Western Front*.

Opinion was no less divided as to the theatrical and literary merits of the play. It is not an experimental work, except in its sheer size and scope, and owes more, dramatically, to Schiller than to Brecht. It was called a "social document rather than a play," "a diatribe," "a sprawling immature first effort," written in "the ponderous heroic style of Schiller." Some critics blamed the adaptation: Albert Bermel thought the Broadway version "a heap of disconnected fragments . . . a reduction in every sense of what Hochhuth had written." But John Simon said that *Der Stellvertreter* was "the only major religious play written since the last war . . . a valid tragedy," and H. F. Garten, praising its "dramatic power and concentration,"

* hôk hōōt

called it "the most striking dramatic work to be written in Germany since the war."

After the extraordinary impact of *Der Stellvertreter*, Rolf Hochhuth turned his attention in *Die Soldaten* (*The Soldiers*) to the Allied bombing of Dresden in World War II. First performed at the Volksbühne Theatre in October 1967, it is basically a discussion play (written like its predecessor in free verse) about the ethics of the mass bombing of civilians, in which Winston Churchill, torn between Lord Cherwell's arguments for bombing Dresden and Bishop Bell's arguments against it, concludes: "I can justify Gomorrah politically."

What made the play almost as controversial as its predecessor, especially in England, was Hochhuth's suggestion that Churchill had contrived the assassination of the Polish leader General Sikorski as a sop to the Russians. Sir Laurence Olivier, artistic director of the National Theatre, was prevented by his governing board from producing the play on the grounds that it maligned Churchill's memory on insufficient evidence. *The Soldiers* was eventually staged elsewhere in London, receiving mixed reviews as it had for its world premiere in Berlin in October 1967. Most critics have found the play confusing in its attempt to deal with two separate themes—the moral implications of bombing attacks on civilians and the Sikorski incident. In the play and in a newspaper article, Hochhuth suggested that Sikorski's pilot had deliberately crashed the plane in which the General died. The pilot sued Hochhuth for libel, and in the English High Court in 1972 was awarded damages of £50,000.

Hochhuth's third play, *Guerillas* (1970), is not a documentary but an account of an imaginary and unsuccessful *coup d'état* in the United States. Planned to take place just before the nomination of Richard Nixon as a candidate for the presidency, the *coup* is intended to avert a new American civil war by overthrowing the capitalist oligarchy and substituting a socialist regime. At the last minute the attempt is frustrated by the CIA murder of one of the conspirators but, the play implies, it is only a matter of time before another and more successful revolution will be mounted.

Like all of Hochhuth's plays, *Guerillas* is buttressed by a great deal of factual information—in this case statistical and other evidence intended to prove the corruption and militarism of American government and the poverty and social injustice that result. The play has been criticized on much the same grounds as its predecessors—it is too long, covers too much ground, is written for no appreciable reason in free verse, and is, in general, melodramatic and unconvincing in its characterization. What Robert Brustein wrote of *The Deputy* is still true: "If Hochhuth has not entirely proven himself yet as either a historian or a dramatist, he has certainly proven himself as a man of discriminating moral intelligence and outstanding courage, and this alone makes him a rare and valuable figure in the modern world." As the chief instigator of the documentary mode of the 1960s, he is already assured of an important place in the literary history of the period. A number of his passionately controversial essays have been collected in *Krieg und Klassenkrieg* (War and Class War, 1971).

ROLF HOCHHUTH

Rolf Hochhuth is married to the former Marianne Heinemann, whom he met as a boy, and has two sons. He and his family live in Switzerland, where Hochhuth is resident dramatist at the Basel Municipal Theatre. He has been described as "surprisingly shy and diffident . . . a slender man with a look of pain on his face, the physical residue of partial paralysis compounded by some inner struggle." Hochhuth lives very simply, for example using a bicycle rather than a car to visit the theatre. He has written a number of unpublished works, including short stories and poems, and is essentially modest about his work: "If you measure the writing of a book against the murder of only one child, it is, of course, nothing."

PRINCIPAL WORKS IN ENGLISH TRANSLATION: The Representative, 1963 (U.S., The Deputy); Soldiers, 1968. ABOUT: Bentley, E. (ed.) The Storm Over The Deputy, 1964; Clurman, H. The Naked Image, 1967; Contemporary Authors 7–8, 1963; Garten, H. F. Modern German Drama, 1964; Schmidt, D. B. and Schmidt, E. R. (eds.) The Deputy Reader: Studies in Moral Responsibility, 1965; Wer Ist Wer, 1970. *Periodicals*—America October 12, November 2, November 9, 1963; Atlas March 1965; August 1967; Christian Century September 18, 1963; October 16, 1963; Commentary March 2, 1964; Commonweal February 28, 1964; Contemporary Review December 1966; Drama Spring 1968;

Hudson Review Summer 1964; New Statesman October 13, 1967; Newsweek March 2, 1964; New York Times April 28, 1963; February 28, 1964; November 19, 1967; Partisan Review Summer 1964; Reporter January 30, 1964; Saturday Evening Post February 29, 1964; Time November 1, 1964; Times (London) October 12, 1967; Times Literary Supplement September 27, 1963; April 27, 1967; November 9, 1967; May 28, 1970.

***HOCHWÄLDER, FRITZ** (May 28, 1911–), Austrian dramatist, writes (in German): "I was born in Vienna, still in the era of the monarchy, which disintegrated seven years later. My childhood years in the old Austria were enough to bind me for life to the cultural sphere of the Danube states: I regard myself as a dramatist of the German language and of non-German outlook. As the son of a petty bourgeois craftsman I attended the lower level of a Gymnasium, but since my accomplishments as a student were more than modest, I turned to the upholstering trade of my father, and after completing the journeyman and master examinations I lived exclusively by my trade. In addition I furthered my education by taking evening courses at the public high school and began about 1930 to write plays for my own private pleasure. Out of these early and defective products, two plays were presented, in 1933 and 1936, in little theatres in Vienna, without causing any excitement. Since early youth I have been influenced above all by the Austrian dramatist Ferdinand Raimund (1790–1836), and in general, my manner of writing plays is inseparable from the tradition of the Viennese Volkstheater, which reaches back some two hundred and fifty years.

"If it had been up to me, I never would have left Vienna. I felt myself so closely bound to this city that I feared that elsewhere my fate would be that of a fish on dry land. But, as is well known, it was not up to me. I too was among those who became homeless on 'racial' grounds after the annexation of Austria, and so, in August 1938, after months of futile waiting for an entrance visa to any country in the world, I had no recourse but to cross the border into neighboring Switzerland illegally. From 1938 to 1945 I lived in Zurich as an emigrant; after the end of the war I received permission as an Austrian citizen to settle there. I have never given up my Swiss domicile and do not intend to do so in the future.

"Up to 1938 I had regarded my early efforts as a dramatist more as a hobby than as something to be seriously considered as an occupation. This attitude changed, of necessity, during emigration. Since in Switzerland any kind of occupational activity was forbidden to me, as it was to most of those who shared my fate, I had no other recourse than to continue my present hobby in the form of an unprofitable full-time occupation. To be sure, I was as poor as a churchmouse, yet the meager subsidy that I was forced to accept kept me barely above water. Since my playwriting was not bound to any practical demands, and since I knew also that my work—because of the impossibility of its utilization during wartime—would not bring in any profit, I found myself, though totally without means, actually in the position of a wealthy gentleman of leisure, who could afford the luxury of writing that which pleased him. This peculiar state of affairs was improved still further in the spring of 1942, when friends made available to me a small cottage in Ascona on Lake Maggiore for the duration of my leave of absence from the refugee camp. There I sat utterly alone, gazed into the blue sky of the south, and wrote in barely two months *Das heilige Experiment* (The Sacred Experiment), the play whose profits are still paying me dividends today. It was not until the spring of 1946 that my work began to have an international effect, with a presentation of the comedy *Hôtel du Commerce* in Prague.

"In my view, my work is marked by two creative periods: from 1938 to 1954 I wrote mainly historical dramas, in which the costume served for the objectification of present-day relationships; in 1954 there emerged—so to speak, as a transitional work—*Die Herberge* (The Shelter), a dramatic legend that is not set in a specific place or time; subsequently I turned exclusively to contemporary themes; my most recent work of this orientation is *Der Himbeerpflücker* (The Raspberry Picker, 1965). I have not known much of a private life; in 1951 I married Ursula Büchi, a native of Switzerland; this childless marriage ended in divorce in 1957. In 1960 I married Susanne Schreiner of Vienna; in 1961 our daughter Monique came into the world, which thereby became a markedly more friendly place.

"Where my road as a playwright will lead me, I cannot foretell with any certainty. The only thing that is certain is that the calling, which I continue to feel within myself, is nourished by a fruitful contrast: my indestructible roots in the heritage of the Austrian theatre, and, equally, the physical distance from the homeland that I am conscious of in the Western location to which the fate of our time has consigned me."

"Theatre is by no means literature," Hochwälder once wrote; it "comes from the depths," and is primarily a popular art. Many critics have felt that his work is (or was) deliberately and almost perversely old-fashioned in form, though it deals with such urgently contemporary themes as totalitarianism, persecution, and guilt. Most of his best-known plays turn upon a strong internal conflict,

* hōk vel′ dər

which is often resolved when the protagonist experiences a shock of self-realization, a crisis of conscience, and a moral transformation.

His first international success was *Das heilige Experiment* (The Holy Experiment, 1942), still his most famous play. It is set in eighteenth century Paraguay, where a Jesuit community has established a nearly perfect society, founded on principles of love and brotherhood. The King of Spain sends a commission to confiscate the rich territory. The Jesuits' armed resistance to the dissolution of their "Kingdom of God on earth" is ended by an emissary from the head of their order, who recognizes in the literal application of Christ's teachings a threat to the international power structure of which his Church is a part. The core of the play is the conflict between this worldly man, himself divided between admiration for the Jesuit utopia and his sense of the realities of power, and the Jesuit Father Provincial, torn between compassion for the poor and his vows of obedience. The play is a study of the corrupting tendencies of power, a cogent indictment of all totalitarian ideologies, and much else—a moving, memorable, and richly stimulating work which escapes the oversimplification that weakens some of Hochwälder's other plays.

Das heilige Experiment was first performed in Biel, Switzerland, in March 1943, and subsequently played with great success all over Europe. The German critic Bernhard Diebold hailed it as the work of a new master of contemporary tragedy, and it ran for 400 performances in Paris. It reached Broadway in 1953 as *The Strong Are Lonely* but was a failure, partly because Eva Le Gallienne's translation was made at secondhand, from the French version. The play marked a turning point in Hochwälder's life—the end of the wretched years of isolation in refugee camps, the real beginning of his literary career, contact and friendships with other writers.

One of these was the German Expressionist Georg Kaiser. Shortly before Kaiser's death in 1945 he and Hochwälder collaborated on a theme which the latter afterwards completed as the play *Der Flüchtling* (The Fugitive, 1945). The central character is a frontier guard, one of those ordinary, decent men who, exchanging their conscience for a uniform, place themselves as tools in the hands of the power-hungry and corrupt. Driven to self-examination when his wife aids a refugee, the guard recognizes that he shares the guilt of his masters, and gives his life so that the fugitive can escape. The play was subsequently filmed.

At first, as he says, Hochwälder found it easier to deal objectively with contemporary problems when he placed them in historical settings. *Esther*, for example, an early piece written in 1940, uses the Biblical story as an allegory of the rise of Hitler.

FRITZ HOCHWÄLDER

The problem of guilt and responsibility, to which Hochwälder constantly returns, is examined in *Meier Helmbrecht* (1946), a drama based on a medieval verse tale, and in *Der öffentliche Anklager* (*The Public Prosecutor*, 1947). The latter, set during the French Revolution, has its cold-blooded prosecutor conducting a case against an unknown "enemy of the people" whose name, kept during the trial in a sealed envelope, is revealed when the case is proven as the prosecutor's own. Another moral transformation is the theme of *Donadieu* (1953), set in seventeenth century France during the Huguenot persecution.

Hochwälder's "transitional" play *Die Herberge* was followed by a number of works with contemporary settings, most of them dealing with one aspect or another of the problem of guilt. *Der Unschuldige* (The Innocent One, 1958) is a sharp comedy turning on the deceptiveness of circumstantial evidence. *Donnerstag* (Thursday, 1959), written for the Salzburg Festival, is a modern version of the Faust legend using the stock figures of the Viennese popular theatre. Hochwälder had always opposed experiment in the theatre, the "destruction of form" which in his opinion debased contemporary drama. *Donnerstag* marked his first departure from the classical tradition, and *1003* (1963) went further, using tape recordings and other modern devices in a rather Pirandellian play about identity and the nature of creativity. The television play *Der Befehl* (*The Order*), commissioned by Austrian TV for Eurovision presentation, is more orthodox in style. It was given in English over the BBC in 1967, and staged in Vienna in 1968. In theme it rather resembles *The Public*

Prosecutor, dealing with a German police inspector who, ordered to investigate the long-forgotten murder of a Dutch child by a Nazi field policeman, grimly pursues his inquiries back into his country's dark past and his own, discovering at last that he himself was the murderer.

PRINCIPAL WORKS IN ENGLISH TRANSLATION: The Strong Are Lonely, 1954; The Public Prosecutor, 1958.
ABOUT: Bithell, J. Modern German Literature, 1959; Foster, J. R. *introduction to* Das heilige Experiment, 1958, *and to* Der öffentliche Ankläger, 1962; Garten, H. F. Modern German Drama, 1964; International Who's Who, 1971–1972; Thieberger, R. *introduction to* Donadieu, 1967; Wellwarth, G. E. The Theater of Protest and Paradox, 1964; Who's Who in Austria, 1969–1970; Who's Who in Switzerland, 1968–1969. *Periodicals*—America June 9, 1956; Nation October 7, 1953; Saturday Review October 17, 1953; Theatre Arts December 1953.

HODGINS, ERIC (March 2, 1899–January 7, 1971), American humorist, editor, and memoirist, wrote: "My father had the distinction of being the first editor ever to publish Stephen Leacock. This was when both these young men were undergraduates at the University of Toronto and my father was editor of *The Varsity*. My paternal grandfather was the author of innumerable suffocating works of history and biography; with this heredity I suppose it was foreordained that I was to write for my living and that my efforts to do something else were to be unsuccessful.

"My birthplace was the once quiet city of Detroit, Michigan. Since both my parents were born in Canada and all four of my grandparents in Ireland, I am a first-generation American. I am not, however, a mid-Westerner, and don't very much like the mid-West speech or outlook. My own speech and outlook were formed by a boyhood in Philadelphia, an education in Boston and a professional life lived mostly in New York. I am thus Northeastern Provincial, educated at Episcopalian Church schools and in 1922 graduated from the Massachusetts Institute of Technology. My first job was as editor of *The Technology Review*, the official magazine of M.I.T. Here I gained invaluable experience for I was also make-up man, circulation manager, staff writer, office boy and, occasionally, advertising director.

"After five years of this I crossed the Charles River to 8 Arlington Street, Boston, in those days the home not only of *The Atlantic Monthly* but of the Atlantic Monthly Group of Publications, of which Ellery Sedgwick managed to be proprietor while at the same time being the *Atlantic's* great editor. These were exciting days at 8 Arlington Street for Mr. Sedgwick was at the height of his editorial powers, which were considerable, and a young man could learn much—of how, for example, to get Al Smith to write an article, in 1927, on Why a Catholic Can Be President of the U.S. (titled "Catholic and Patriot") in answer to an attack, yet unmade, which Mr. Sedgwick commissioned as soon as he had Al Smith in the bag. I was editor of *The Youth's Companion*, which Mr. Sedgwick had come to own against all his instincts and his wishes; he was correspondingly anxious to unload it on somebody else.

"In August, 1929, he succeeded. With an instinct unimpaired by civilization he saw the crash and depression coming and sold the *Companion* to *The American Boy*, which, in the course of ingesting the *Companion*, itself later expired. When I discovered that Mr. Sedgwick had sold "my" magazine after letting me make editorial commitments for the coming fall and winter which would now be dishonored I said something impolite about Beacon Street and, I think, even about Louisburg Square. Ten years of life in Boston ended for me then.

"Before that, Edward Weeks, in those days a pale young curate in charge of Atlantic Monthly Press books, had thought that I could write a simple, popular book about the history of aviation. The year being 1927, such a book was a fine idea, for Charles Augustus Lindbergh had just flown the Atlantic. So I started out with some of Leonardo da Vinci's predecessors and followed the path that led to what was then the present. *Sky-High* came out in 1929 (Little, Brown-Atlantic) and did quite well. It was nice to have written a book.

"Back to New York, I fetched up as an advertising salesman for *Redbook*, which had just been bought by the McCall Corporation and was firmly dug into third place in a field of three. It was tough, getting thrown out of assistant buyers' offices all day long five and a half days a week, and the reason I stuck it out for three years was very odd: when I called up my boss one night to resign because I couldn't take it any more, I was met with the message that he had been taken to the hospital with a whole flock of peptic ulcers. Obviously, then, his life was no bed of roses either. My chance to resign was lost and I never regained it. And after a while I got to be Promotion Manager for *McCall's-Redbook*; then, still later, I was made an associate editor of *Redbook* and was back on an editorial course.

"Late in 1933 Daniel Longwell mentioned my existence to his friend Henry R. Luce, who thereupon called me up. '*Fortune* has needed two managing editors for the last year, and I'm getting tired of being the other one,' he said when we met at lunch. A quarter-century of associations with Time Inc., mostly with *Fortune* as writer, managing editor or publisher, began shortly after. I got to be a vice president of the company in 1937 and only later realized that I was once more off course; I *was* an editorial character.

"In 1946 I resigned my vice presidency to get back to writing again. Next year Simon & Schuster published my first novel, *Mr. Blandings Builds His Dream House*. Everything pleasant happened to this effort; this has caused me many times to reflect on the total disrelation between struggle and reward. The book almost wrote itself; I was mostly the stenographer for my unreeling unconscious. It wrote itself not only easily but swiftly: about two and a half months saw the whole thing done. It made me pots of money; twenty years later it is still well remembered and will probably go on my tombstone. The critics thought its successor, published four years later, was a better book, and so did I. *Blandings' Way* sold quite well, but today nobody knows it was ever written.

"In 1950 I was tapped to be a presidential commissioner. Harry Truman created the President's Materials Policy Commission and named William S. Paley (of CBS) as chairman. Our job was to report on the adequacy of raw materials in the Western world for the quarter-century that then stretched forward to 1975, come peace, come war, and what the U.S. as a nation might want to do or have to do to insure that its colossal needs and wants as a consumer would not go unfulfilled. In eighteen months of work the P.M.P.C., with a staff of a hundred-odd, succeeded in producing a five-volume report, *Resources for Freedom*, of which I was supervising editor. It was a tremendous experience but I wouldn't like to go through it again. There's small likelihood I'll have to.

"In 1960 I had a stroke. Eventually I wrote about that, too (*Episode*, 1964) and this has involved me in a strange and interesting sub-career of talking to medical societies, health forums and the like about illness as the patient perceives it, and of being on the Public Education Committee (1965–67) of the American Heart Association.

"At age 67, I am collaborating with Vannevar Bush, wartime head of the Office of Scientific Research and Development and Honorary Chairman of the Corporation of M.I.T., in a book that will discuss the past and possible future of our Technological Society."

Mr. Blandings, Eric Hodgins' best-known hero, is a successful New York advertising man whose innocent dream it is to build himself an ideal country retreat. The dream costs him $56,000 and does not survive his encounters with bankers, architects, realty agents, and legal counsel. Instead Mr. Blandings acquires a new dream—a recurrent happy fantasy in which his house burns to the ground. This is the theme of *Mr. Blandings Builds His Dream House*. The house refuses to burn down and Mr. Blandings, his idealism resurgent, ventures into community politics. *Blandings' Way* describes the results, and ends with its hero and his wife back in the relative safety and sanity of a Manhattan apartment. Both books were received with critical and popular delight, though the second was recognized to be the better novel. J. H. Jackson wrote of it: "This is a wonderfully amusing book, as witty, as sly, as deflating . . . as the 'Dream House' story ever was. But it's a sad-funny book, too; the irony is clearer and deeper." Other critics agreed that in spite of its unembittered but telling satire of the "pomposity and egocentricity" of the advertising world, "it is fundamentally an incisive and rather serious book."

ERIC HODGINS

Reviewing *Episode*, which Hodgins subtitled "a report on the accident inside my skull," Marya Mannes observed that "it is not the least of Eric Hodgins' impressive accomplishments that he can make a stroke . . . as funny to read about as it is frightening." Hodgins' stroke, which cost him some $22,000 in medical bills, left him able to see, read, speak, and write, but otherwise almost immobile. Besides being an astringent and unselfpitying record of personal courage, the book formed a powerful indictment of American medical practices. Elmo Roper thought it illustrated the best qualities of Hodgins' writing: a "charming sense of humor" and an unusually exact sense of language; the book received the Blakeslee Award of the American Heart Association.

Hodgins' parents were the Reverend Frederic and Edith (Bull) Hodgins. The writer's first wife, the former Catherine Carlson, died in 1933 and in 1936 he married Eleanor Treacy. He had a son, Roderic, by his first marriage, and a daughter, Eleanor Patricia, by the second. Hodgins, who never used his engineering degree, received a Litt. D. in 1939 from Bates College.

PRINCIPAL WORKS: Sky-High, 1929; Mr. Blandings Builds His Dream House, 1946; Blandings' Way, 1950; Episode, 1964; Trolley to the Moon (autobiography), 1973.
ABOUT: Who's Who in America, 1970–1971. *Periodicals*—Book Week March 1, 1964; New York Herald Tribune Book Review October 15, 1950; New York Times Book Review December 29, 1946; October 8, 1950; Saturday Review January 4, 1947; Time March 6, 1964.

HOFF, HARRY SUMMERFIELD. *See* "COOPER, WILLIAM"

HOFFER, ERIC (July 25, 1902–), American aphorist and essayist, was born in the Bronx, New York City, the only child of Knut Hoffer, a German immigrant cabinetmaker, and of the former Elsa Goebel. He was raised in the Bronx by his parents and, after the early death of his mother, by his father's housekeeper, a woman called Martha, of Bavarian peasant background. Hoffer, who had learned to read in English and German by the time he was five, was blinded in an accident at seven. Convinced by Martha that his death was imminent, Hoffer spent eight years in a kind of nightmare. When he regained his sight, at fifteen, he began to read every book he could find, in German and in English, with a passionate and indiscriminate hunger.

In 1920, when his father died, Hoffer went to California with a basket of books and almost starved before he found a job as a dishwasher. For three years he worked in a Los Angeles box factory, and for the next twenty was a migrant worker on the West Coast, picking fruit, prospecting for gold, washing dishes, working in lumber camps and on railroads. Wherever he went he carried books, and he used a dozen public libraries. Once, snowbound in the Sierra Nevada mountains, he read a volume of Montaigne's essays over and over again, and it is Montaigne's style, many critics believe, that has most influenced his own.

Montaigne was something of a snob, and it is salutary to imagine some gem of his, rendered in Hoffer's thickly accented American English, inspiring postprandial conversation around the fire in a Californian shanty town. For Hoffer liked to pass on the fruits of his reading, and in time began to write down and organize his ideas. In 1943 he settled in San Francisco as a longshoreman and, his material needs being small, was able to spend half of each week reading and writing. In this he was encouraged by Margaret Anderson, editor of a now defunct New York magazine for foreign-born citizens called *Common Ground*.

The True Believer, Hoffer's first book, was completed in 1949. Miss Anderson typed the manuscript and sent it to Harper and Brothers, which published it in 1951. The book is subtitled

ERIC HOFFER

"Thoughts on the Nature of Mass Movements" and is a historical analysis of fanaticism. The "true believer," Hoffer says, is a person suffering some emotional deprivation in his individual life who therefore submerges himself in a cause which seems to offer a sense of hope or meaning. This surrender of individualism gives him license to "hate, bully, lie, torture, murder, and betray" in the name of some corporate entity and therefore without shame or remorse. Ironically, this "malady of the soul" is also "a miraculous instrument for raising societies and nations from the dead—an instrument of resurrection."

This short aphoristic book was universally praised. Arthur Schlesinger called it "a brilliant and original inquiry"; Neil Martin said it was the product of a "vast, amazing" range of reading; and Cleveland Amory welcomed it as a classic, "the most extraordinary book to be published in recent years." There was as much praise for its spare, lucid, and highly quotable style as for its content. President Eisenhower referred to the book often and recommended it enthusiastically. Half a million copies of the work had been sold by 1967.

Hoffer has since published *The Passionate State of Mind* and *Reflections on the Human Condition*, which are collections of aphorisms, three volumes of essays, and *Working and Thinking on the Waterfront*, a diary of the year June 1958–May 1959. He has been called "almost wholly a product of the tensions of the 1930s," and all of his books have shown a preoccupation with the problems of that period. He has great faith in the proletariat and in adult education; none in the intelligentsia, in revolution, or in mass political movements. His views, expressed in his books and—sometimes more rashly—in articles and interviews, occasionally seem simplistic and inconsistent, and are frequently controversial. In 1967 on CBS television he said that President Johnson was a man of the people, and therefore preferable to President Kennedy, "a European." This upset many people but pleased President Johnson, who invited Hoffer to the White House for a chat. There have been strong reactions to his charges that black leaders lack faith in their own masses, and to his expressed doubts about the blacks' ability "to create a genuine community." Nor can his critics find much historical justification for his faith in the working class as an instrument of progress.

In fact, as Melvin Maddocks has said, "There is very little stock or standard about the way Hoffer's mind operates. Like the best self-made philosophers, he combines a relish—even a passion—for generalization with a hard-nosed sense for the particular. . . . A Hoffer essay is more like a free-association monologue than an essay. . . . Hoffer's *forte* is intuition; his weakness is intuition extended beyond its base." He is, it has been suggested, "an idealist without illusions" whose mind "inclines to the wry epigram and the icy aphorism as naturally as did that of the Duc de La Rochefoucauld."

Hoffer, who retired as a longshoreman in August 1967, is unmarried and lives alone in a two-room, eighty-dollar-a-month apartment on Clay Street in San Francisco. He writes painstakingly, in longhand, and because of his "commitment to a fine sentence" rejects all deadlines. His writing is punctuated by long periods of solitary reflection, often coinciding with the walks which are his favorite recreation. Hoffer is a big man, six feet tall and barrel chested, with blue eyes and a fringe of white hair. In 1964 he received an award of twenty-five hundred dollars from the National Institute of Arts and Letters.

PRINCIPAL WORKS: The True Believer: Thoughts on the Nature of Mass Movements, 1951; The Passionate State of Mind, and Other Aphorisms, 1955; The Ordeal of Change, 1963; The Temper of Our Time, 1967; Working and Thinking on the Waterfront, 1969; First Things, Last Things, 1971; Reflections on the Human Condition, 1973.

ABOUT: Current Biography, 1965; Koerner, J. D. Hoffer's America, 1973; Tomkins, C. Eric Hoffer: An American Odyssey, 1968; Who's Who in America, 1970–1971. *Periodicals*—Christian Century May 29, 1963; Life March 24, 1967; Look June 12, 1956; New York Post September 23, 1967; New York Times March 19, 1956; October 8, 1967; New York Times Book Review April 1, 1956; New Yorker April 28, 1951; January 7, 1967; Reporter February 21, 1957; Time March 14, 1955; March 15, 1963; Wall Street Journal September 13, 1967.

HOFFMAN, DANIEL (GERARD) (April 3, 1923–), American poet and scholar, writes:

"Born in New York, N. Y., grew up in Larchmont and New Rochelle, New York. Parents, Daniel and Frances (Beck) Hoffman; one sister. Attended local schools, entered Columbia College in 1940; Army Air Force, 1943–46; returned to Columbia and was graduated in 1947. M.A. 1949, Ph.D. 1956 from that university.

"Without knowing how or why, I started writing verse early, and by the age of twenty-five a long apprenticeship had produced a few pages I didn't mind showing to friends. Slowly I discovered a style, and in 1954 my first book of verse, *An Armada of Thirty Whales*, was chosen by W. H. Auden for publication in the Yale Series of Younger Poets. *A Little Geste* appeared in 1960, and my third book, *The City of Satisfactions*, in 1963.

"I am possessed by the need to redefine amid contemporary circumstance the feelings that give worth and resonance to an individual life. Technology daily reduces nature to mechanism, and an insistent mass society produces our present while extirpating what it can of our past; yet the inner self remains what it always was, or was always capable of becoming. Does the rock or the ripple make the shape of the rapids? I try to accept as much as possible of the turbulence of contemporary life into my poems, where, in love, in dismay, in humor—in anything but resignation—it must find whatever shapes its collisions with what is permanent make necessary. The hope is for an unanticipated order, a revelation. I have made no manifestoes for my work and resist all movements which reduce to one or another technical innovation the practice of an art as capable of unexpected variety as is our language. I'd reject no resource of rhythm or presentation, whether familiar or yet untried, which might help me toward the discoveries I try to make.

"Ballads, myths, and folklore have intrigued me as the most durable record of how our passions and occasions are organized. While a contemporary poet must find new equivalences for what such archaic forms may seem no longer able to provide, as a critic I've explored the uses made of these traditions by American and British authors of the past two centuries. The justification of literary criticism, it seems to me, is the analysis of the order extant in the works discussed so as to demonstrate the author's achievement and inform the reader's delight. With this intention I've tried to practice an inclusive critical method, thematic, formal, historical, and I hope discriminating.

"My principal teaching has been at Columbia, Swarthmore, and since 1966 at the University of Pennsylvania where I am professor of English. I've also been a visiting professor at the Faculté des Lettres, Dijon; a Fellow in the School of Letters, Indiana University; Elliston Lecturer in Poetry at

DANIEL HOFFMAN

the University of Cincinnati, 1964; and lecturer at the Sixth International School of Yeats Studies, Sligo, Ireland, 1965.

"I am married to Elizabeth McFarland of Harrisburg, Pennsylvania. We have two children, Kate and Macfarlane, and live in Swarthmore, Pennsylvania, and on a farm on Cape Rosier, Maine."

John Ciardi, reviewing *An Armada of Thirty Whales*, called it the year's best book of verse, the work of a writer who had "language, perception, passion and intellect," and only needed to wear his poetic attitudes "more naturally." Howard Nemerov, who also found the book weakened by an inhibiting fear of sentimentality, was struck by Hoffman's extremely detailed observation of nature and his ability to make "his clams and snails and pears and whales yield intricate parables by being so closely inspected."

A similar parabolizing tendency was recognized in reviews of *A Little Geste*. The title poem, for example, discovers in the story of Robin Hood and Maid Marian "a passionate conflict between instinctual life and the claims of order," while "In the Beginning" starts by observing the poet's small daughter by the sea, announcing the presence of an imaginary boat, and leads into speculations about the nature of perception. Philip Booth wrote of this volume: "Mr. Hoffman's mind is a familiar of abstractions, but his eye and ear are equally at home in the here-and-now of sensory experience."

Hoffman's technique, it seems agreed, is beyond reproach, and his use of language in particular is both elegant and surprising, "a thesaurus of the existing varieties of diction in modern verse." There has been a tendency for some reviewers of his recent work to label him an academic, self-conscious poet, the victim of his own dexterity. But Richard Eberhart values him very highly, believing that "from his strong restraints burst dazzling powers." Marianne Moore said: "He is an observer; and what he finds, the rhythm does not contradict."

In his criticism as in his poetry, Hoffman "explores the reality of existence and the reality of the fable, of the ways in which truth is adumbrated by coping with the past—the past of one's ancestors, or of one's own childhood." In particular, he has investigated the uses made of myth and folklore by Irving, Hawthorne, Melville, and Mark Twain (in *Form and Fable in American Fiction*), and in the poetry of Yeats, Graves, and Muir (*Barbarous Knowledge*). The former was rather coldly received but *Barbarous Knowledge* seemed to William Sylvester, who reviewed it at some length in *College English*, "a beautiful accomplishment." What Hoffman says of Edwin Muir, Sylvester would say of Hoffman: "He compels our assent not by the force of an argument but by the clarity with which he has illuminated a part of the deepest truth our culture can give us." Hoffman's book on Stephen Crane benefits from his use of the Crane papers acquired in 1952 by Columbia, and was called judicious, balanced, and "a very considerable advance" over earlier biographies.

His study of Edgar Allan Poe is a very different kind of book. John Hollander called it "personal, aggressively casual in diction and tone, sometimes annoyingly flip, often pungent," employing "reverie, allusion, invective, and even such nineteenth-century belletristic devices as anecdotal accounts of first encounters with particular tales and poems in particular editions." None of this disguises the breadth and subtlety of Hoffman's knowledge and understanding of his subject, and "what emerges is a very exciting reading of Poe, truly serious and liberated from many traditional critical and scholarly solemnities."

During World War II Hoffman was managing editor of the Army Air Force's *Technical Data Digest*, and since then, as he says, has earned his living as a teacher. He has served as review editor of *Midwest Folklore* (1952–1956) and on the executive committee of the American Folklore Society (1953–1954). In 1961–1962 and in 1966–1967 he held research fellowships from the American Council of Learned Societies. In 1967 he received a grant from the National Institute of Arts and Letters and in 1971–1972 a poetry grant from the Ingram Merrill Foundation. He was elected chancellor of the Academy of American Poets in 1972, and in 1973 was named Consultant in Poetry to the Library of Congress.

PRINCIPAL WORKS: *Poems*—An Armada of Thirty Whales, with a foreword by W. H. Auden, 1954; A Little Geste, and Other Poems, 1960; The City of Satisfactions, 1963; Striking the Stones, 1968; Broken Laws, 1970. *Nonfiction*—Paul Bunyan: Last of the Frontier Demigods, 1952; The Poetry of Stephen Crane, 1957; Form and Fable in American Fiction, 1961; Barbarous Knowledge: Myth in the Poetry of Yeats, Graves, and Muir, 1967; Poe, Poe, Poe, Poe, Poe, Poe, Poe, 1972.

ABOUT: Auden, W. H. *Foreword to* Hoffman, D. An Armada of Thirty Whales, 1954; Bode, C. The Half-World of American Culture, 1964; Contemporary Authors 3, 1963; Directory of American Scholars II, 1964; Howard, R. Alone with America, 1969; Murphy, R. (ed.) Contemporary Poets of the English Language, 1970; Rexroth, K. Assays, 1961; Who's Who in America, 1970–1971. *Periodicals*—College English October 1967.

HOFFMAN, FREDERICK J(OHN) (September 21, 1909–December 24, 1967), American scholar and critic, wrote: "I was born in Port Washington, Wisconsin, in 1909; it is a town a few miles north of Milwaukee, a city in which I now live. After eighteen years of routine education, I went westward, to California, where I changed both my residence and my convictions. My college education includes a B.A. from Stanford University (1934), where I first acquired a jargon but also a style and a way of looking at life. Other degrees were an M.A. in philosophy at the University of Minnesota (1936) and a Ph.D. (1942) at the Ohio State University (dissertation on Sigmund Freud's influence upon modern literature). The dissertation became *Freudianism and the Literary Mind* (1945; second edition, 1957). This was the beginning of an active career, which included teaching at Harvard, in France and Italy, but chiefly at the University of Wisconsin, Madison (1948–1960).

"My career has been mostly a matter of writing, co-authoring, and co-editing books. The total is huge, but there are many others in the making. I have tried to alternate substantial books with short studies, though the rationale remains consistent. I consider the following books essential to my career, because they were breakthroughs in modern literary scholarship: *Freudianism and the Literary Mind*; *The Little Magazine* (1946, 1947), done with two other authors; *The Twenties* (1955, 1962); and *The Mortal No: Death and the Modern Imagination* (1964). In addition to such publications, I have published books on Gertrude Stein, William Faulkner, Samuel Beckett, Conrad Aiken, et al. I hope to stay healthy enough to write a number of other books. The *Beckett* and *The Mortal No* form two-thirds of a kind of trilogy concerning the changes and shifts of literary and philosophical metaphors. The other third will be a series of four lectures at Notre Dame University. Modern literature has changed to contemporary literature; and I am concerned to keep abreast of the contemporary (as distinguished from the modern) literary dispositions.

FREDERICK J. HOFFMAN

"I am dedicated to twentieth century literature and shall discuss it and write on it so long as I am able. The relevance of *all* literature has to do with its reference to our times; and I propose to explore this reference, so long as I shall remain in the century."

Besides the places he mentioned above, Hoffman taught at Pasadena Junior College (1936–1938), the University of Chicago (1938–1940), Ohio State University (1942–1947), the University of Oklahoma (1947–1948) and the University of California at Riverside (1960–1965). At the time of his death he was Distinguished Professor of English at the University of Wisconsin. Hoffman was a Rockefeller Fellow in 1945, held a visiting professorship at Harvard in 1953, and was a Fulbright professor in France and Italy in 1953–1954. He was married in 1936 to Eleanor Thompson and had a daughter.

Hoffman's dissertation *Freudianism and the Literary Mind* outlines Freud's theories and the mixture of sympathy and misunderstanding with which they were received, and goes on to study the work of Joyce, Lawrence, Kafka, Mann, and others who were indebted to Freud. The book, less than "exhilarating" in its style, was nevertheless welcomed as a "sound, sensible, and scholarly study." *The Twenties*, the product of a decade of research, analyzes the major writers of the period within a framework of Hoffman's own deductions and conclusions. This framework seemed to Leon Edel "artificial and highly arbitrary," but most reviewers were content with what seemed to them a full and sensitive examination of the period.

The "kind of trilogy" in which Hoffman studied the evolution in modern writing of "literary and philosophical metaphors" will no doubt be regarded as his principal monument. It begins with *Samuel Beckett: The Language of Self*, in which a history of modern introspective literature, showing for example how views of the self were affected by nineteenth century religious doubt, is followed by an analysis of Beckett's work conceived as "a special variant of the drama of self" and as an example of contemporary doubt. *The Mortal No* is a long study of the treatment of death and the self in modern writing, while *The Imagination's New Beginning*, containing Hoffman's four Notre Dame lectures, concentrates mainly on Joyce, Dostoevsky, and Kazantzakis to investigate the relationship between literature and theology.

No critical consensus has yet emerged as to the value of these three books, whose reception was extraordinarily mixed. Even Hoffman's admirers have generally conceded that he wrote without grace or humor, lapsing often into jargon. Some of his critics have virtually dismissed his books as anthologies of book digests, "interspersed with obscure generalized assertions."

Other critics have felt very differently, especially about *The Mortal No*. In a discussion of Hoffman's work in the *Massachusetts Review*, Melvin J. Friedman says that *The Mortal No*, which draws its insights not only from literature but from psychology, anthropology, theology, and painting, is "probably the most original literary study—in design, approach, and content . . . since the *Anatomy of Criticism*." Ihab Hassan, conceding that the book "describes more than it analyzes" and is written without distinction, calls it nevertheless "a work of vast range and considerable urgency, moving easily over the dark landscape of modern intellectual history, reclaiming the sense of life from the facts of outrage and death in the literature of many tongues."

PRINCIPAL WORKS: Freudianism and the Literary Mind, 1945 (2nd ed. 1957); (with others) The Little Magazine: A History and Bibliography, 1946; The Twenties: American Writing in the Postwar Decade, 1955 (rev. ed. 1962); Samuel Beckett: The Language of Self, 1962; The Mortal No: Death and the Modern Imagination, 1964; The Imagination's New Beginning: Theology and Modern Literature, 1967; The Art of Southern Fiction, 1968.

ABOUT: Contemporary Authors 1st revision 1–4, 1967; Directory of American Scholars II, 1964; Fiedler, L. A. No! In Thunder, 1960; Friedman, M. J. and Vickery, J. B. The Shaken Realist: Essays in Modern Literature in Honor of Frederick J. Hoffman, 1970; Sutton, W. Modern American Criticism, 1963. *Periodicals*—Massachusetts Review Autumn 1965.

***HOFSTADTER, RICHARD** (August 6, 1916–October 24, 1970), American historian, was born in Buffalo, New York, to Emil A. Hofstadter, a Polish-born furrier, and Katherine (Hill) Hofstadter. At the University of Buffalo, where he was elected to Phi Beta Kappa, he majored in history and philosophy, taking his B.A. degree with high honors in both subjects in 1937. Urged by his parents to emulate his uncle, Samuel H. Hofstadter, a New York Supreme Court justice, he then entered New York University Law School.

* hōf′ sta tər

Before the end of the first semester Hofstadter discovered that law put him to sleep, and that history did not. He therefore enrolled in history courses at Columbia University, where he completed requirements for his Ph.D. degree in 1942. By that time he had also served out an apprenticeship in teaching (as an instructor at Brooklyn College and at the City College of New York) and had spent a year as William Bayard Cutting Traveling Fellow (1941–1942). After four years as assistant professor of history at the University of Maryland, he returned to Columbia in 1946 and began the steady climb through the academic ranks that in 1959 brought him to his final post as DeWitt Clinton Professor of American History.

In the classroom Hofstadter became known as a stimulating and challenging teacher and as "a hard marker." He also early acquired a similar reputation as a rewarding though demanding writer of history. His first book, *Social Darwinism in American Thought*, 1860–1915, a publication of his doctoral dissertation, surveyed the use of Darwin's theories in explaining social phenomena in the United States—the application, for instance, of the doctrine of the survival of the fittest to justify *laissez-faire* policies and imperialism. It was followed by *The American Political Tradition and the Men Who Made It*, containing a dozen essays on such figures as Jefferson, Wilson, Hoover, and the Roosevelts. These two books established Hofstadter as a versatile historian of ideas—able to support his interpretations with evidence from the whole sweep of American history, as well as from such varied fields as politics, economics, education, and psychology—and as the master of a notably lucid and readable prose style.

These qualities brought him the Pulitzer Prize in History for *The Age of Reform*, which was offered not as a substantive account but as a "new analysis from the perspective of our own time" of major American reform movements between 1890 and 1940. J. P. Roche called it a superb book, which entitled Hofstadter "to rank with C. Vann Woodward as a master of creative synthesis, as an interpreter of the past who can add to cold data an empathetic insight that transforms history from a book of the dead into a chronicle of life."

Hofstadter received a second Pulitzer Prize, this time in the category of general nonfiction, for *Anti-*

intellectualism in American Life, which also won the Emerson Award of Phi Beta Kappa and the Sidney Hillman Award. The book's thesis is that "throughout most of our political history the intellectual has been for the most part either an outsider, a servant or a scapegoat." Its publisher described it as "an extended personal essay which explores various features of the American character" rather than a formal history of an idea. Robert Peel found in it something of the intellectual versatility and humane spirit of the eighteenth century, and for Harold Taylor it contained "exactly what is needed in order to place contemporary intellectual and political history in full perspective."

Rather similar concerns underly *The Paranoid Style in American Politics*, which collects essays and articles about the McCarthyites, the Birchites, the Goldwater movement, and other manifestations of the conspiratorial view of the world which has characterized American politics at intervals since the eighteenth century. It was warmly received by most reviewers, and was described by one critic as "the most balanced and authoritative analysis we have of a formidable and apparently permanent force in American politics." *America at 1750*, published posthumously, is the opening section of what was planned as a massive history of America from 1750 to the present.

David M. Potter has said that Hofstadter sought in all of his writing "to define the nature of American society as it has expressed itself politically." He was essentially liberal in his own views, but also a natural skeptic, incapable of the fuzzy-minded optimism and complacency often associated with liberalism. In *The Age of Reform* he wrote: "I find that I have been critical of the Populist-Progressive tradition . . . critical, but not hostile, for I am criticizing largely from within." On the other hand, as C. Vann Woodward wrote, he "seemed to have a solid understanding, if not a private affection," for "the odd, the warped, the zanies, and the crazies of American life—left, right, and middle."

During his more than twenty years of teaching at Columbia, Hofstadter often lectured at other universities. He was a visiting professor at Princeton in 1950 and lectured at University College, London, in 1955 (when he was in England to participate in the Fulbright Conference on American Studies and Institutions). He returned to England in 1958–1959 as Pitt Professor of American History and Institutions at Cambridge, and again in 1963 as Herbert Spencer Lecturer at Oxford. In 1962 he gave the Haynes Foundation lectures at the University of Southern California, and in 1966 he was the Jefferson Memorial Lecturer at Berkeley.

Hofstadter was married in 1936 to Felice Swados, sister of the novelist Harvey Swados; she died in 1945. He made a second marriage in 1947 to

RICHARD HOFSTADTER

Beatrice Kevitt, a fashion writer, and had a son by his first marriage, a daughter by his second. Hofstadter died of leukemia in 1970 at the age of fifty-four. A former student called him "a blue-eyed, graying, almost nondescript man" who wore clip-on bow ties and who "was continually hitching up his sagging trousers." He was "an intensely private man" who, in his unrelenting dedication to hard work and his scrupulous self-discipline, seemed dull and often melancholy. In fact he was a notable mimic with a mischievous wit, and a man with a great talent for friendship. Woodward thought him "a figure of pivotal significance in the history of American history. More clearly than any other historian he marked the transition from the Progressive to the post-Progressive era of historiography. As symbolically as any he signified the shift from the province to the metropolis. And more fully and magnificently than any he exemplified the break from the tradition that bound the professional historian to a restricted period or region and a specialized reading public."

PRINCIPAL WORKS: Social Darwinism in American Thought, 1860–1915, 1944 (revised 1955); The American Political Tradition and the Men Who Made It, 1948; (with C. DeWitt Hardy) The Development and Scope of Higher Education in the United States, 1952; (with Walter P. Metzger) The Development of Academic Freedom in the United States, 1955 (Hofstadter's contribution to this volume reprinted separately as Academic Freedom in the Age of the College, 1961); The Age of Reform: from Bryan to F.D.R., 1955; Anti-intellectualism in American Life, 1963; The Paranoid Style in American Politics and Other Essays, 1965; The Progressive Historians: Turner, Beard, Parrington, 1968; The Idea of a Party System, 1969; America at 1750: A Social Portrait, 1971.

ABOUT: Current Biography, 1956; Who's Who in

America, 1970–1971. *Periodicals*—New York Review December 3, 1970; March 8, 1973; New York Times May 5, 1964; October 25, 1970; Saturday Review October 22, 1955.

HOGGART, RICHARD (September 24, 1918–), English scholar and critic, was born in Leeds, Yorkshire, one of the three children of a house-painter, Tom Longfellow Hoggart, and the former Adeline Long. His father died when he was two and his mother when he was eight, and thereafter Hoggart was raised by his grandmother. He says that "she retained in the vitality of her spirit, in the vigour of her language, and in the occasional peasant quality of her humour, a strength which her children had not." (She admired D. H. Lawrence, Hoggart recalls, but said of his preoccupation with sex: " 'E makes a lot of fuss and lah-de-dah about it.")

Hoggart went to elementary schools and Cockburn High School in Leeds, and on with a scholarship to the city's university, graduating with first class honors in English in 1939. A further year at Leeds with a Parkinson Graduate Scholarship brought him his M.A. in 1940. The same year he enlisted in the Royal Artillery as a gunner. He was soon commissioned and served with the Artillery as an education officer in North Africa and Italy. In Italy he founded an arts club for allied troops, edited several anthologies of writing by servicemen, and was a part-time lecturer at the University of Naples. He left the Army at the end of the war as a staff captain.

In 1946 Hoggart began his teaching career as a tutor in the University of Hull's adult education department. There he remained until 1959, becoming senior staff tutor in 1957. His first book was *Auden*, subtitled "An Introductory Essay" but in fact the first full-length critical study of the poet. It was warmly welcomed and has become a standard work. V. S. Pritchett said it was "a clear, thoughtful, orderly exposition of the technique and progress of Auden's work; its appreciation is serious and its criticisms are severe but precise."

The Uses of Literacy, which had occupied Hoggart's spare time for five years, followed in 1957. This study of "changing patterns in English mass culture" is an unclassifiable work, a combination of nostalgic autobiography, social history, and cultural criticism. It begins with a restrained but "lovingly vivid" account of the working-class traditions, habits, and entertainments Hoggart had known as a child, and goes on to show how this rich culture is being debased and emasculated by the "hollow brightness" of the mass media. This second section is enlivened by exact and appalling parodies of popular journalism, pulp fiction, and the like. It was everywhere recognized as a work

RICHARD HOGGART

of great value and originality, scholarly, likable, and as readable as a novel.

In 1959 Hoggart went to the University of Leicester as senior lecturer in English, and in 1962 he became professor of English in the University of Birmingham, where in 1964 he founded the Centre for Contemporary Cultural Studies. The Centre, which Hoggart directs, is a postgraduate research institution dedicated to extending in many directions a field of study which is roughly the same as that defined in *The Uses of Literacy*. Hoggart believes that the Centre has an important contribution to make, most distinctively in "the development of critical-evaluative studies of contemporary culture, and a proper understanding of this culture in its social setting." In 1970 he began a three-year leave of absence from the Centre, serving as assistant director-general of Unesco.

It has been said that the publication of *The Uses of Literacy* established Hoggart "as a national voice —a new sage for the working class, an anthropologist among his own people." This is demonstrably true. Hoggart was a member of the Albemarle Committee on Youth Services (1958–1960) and of the Pilkington Committee on the future of British broadcasting and television (1960–1962). He has served on the BBC's General Advisory Council, on the Youth Service Development Council, on the Books Overseas Committee of the British Council, and as a governor of the Royal Shakespeare Theatre and the Birmingham Repertory Theatre. His evidence in the trial for obscenity of *Lady Chatterley's Lover* was memorable and decisive; he described D. H. Lawrence as "a British non-conformist Puritan" and held to that view "with firmness, patience and total conviction" in the face of all that the eminent counsel for the prosecution could do to fluster him.

Hoggart is "a fluent and exciting" speaker, much in demand in England, Europe, and the United States, and on radio and television. In 1956–1957 he was visiting professor at the University of Rochester, New York. He is also active as a book reviewer and as a contributor on a wide range of subjects to magazines and symposia. All this leaves him little time for writing, but in 1970 he published *Speaking to Each Other*, a two-volume collection of his social and literary essays. A principal theme in these essays, as might be expected, is the British class structure and the effect upon it of mass media and the increased accessibility of education. Literature he discusses both as an irreducible object in its own right and as a cultural symbol. "His uniqueness of tone, his irony and depth," wrote one critic, "result from the double perspective of being at once a full participant in British culture and at the same time the member of a group which until quite recently had very little access to it."

A dark-haired man of medium height, Hoggart was married in 1942 to Mary France, a former teacher. They have two sons and a daughter. Hoggart is devoted to his family, and enjoys "pottering about" in his house and garden. He has described himself, only half ironically, as a "basic provincial Honest Joe"; others have applied to him the phrase he once used of D. H. Lawrence—"a British non-conformist Puritan."

PRINCIPAL WORKS: Auden: An Introductory Essay, 1951; The Uses of Literacy, 1957; W. H. Auden: A Selection, with Notes and a Critical Essay, 1961; Teaching Literature, 1963; (as ed.) Your Sunday Newspaper, 1967; Speaking to Each Other (essays, in 2 vols.), 1970; Only Connect: On Culture and Communication (1971 Reith Lectures), 1972 (U.S., On Culture and Communication).
ABOUT: Contemporary Authors 9–10, 1964; Current Biography, 1964; Mander, J. The Writer and Commitment, 1961; Who's Who, 1971. *Periodicals*—New Statesman and Nation August 4, 1951; March 2, 1957; Spectator March 1, 1957; Times Literary Supplement July 26, 1963; March 5, 1970.

***HOLAN, VLADIMÍR** (September 16, 1905–), Czech poet. The following note is based in part on material supplied on Holan's behalf by Dr. Vladimír Justl: Holan was born in Prague. His childhood was passed in the country of Karel Hynek Mácha, the great Czech poet of the early nineteenth century whose masterpiece was the Byronic epic *Máj*; this fused the Czech baroque poetic tradition with European romanticism, and was a major influence on Holan. Since 1919 Holan has lived in Prague; he did not enter the university but worked as a civil servant in the Institute of Pensions. He published his first book of poetry in the same year, and in 1933 became a full-time writer. Since 1938 he has edited the art magazine *Život* (Life), and has also worked in the avant-garde theatre.

* hô′ lən

VLADIMÍR HOLAN

The interwar years, following the achievement of national independence in 1918, were a period of intense creativity in Czech literature, and during the 1920s a number of important lyric poets began to publish their first books. This new poetry showed two main tendencies, the first of which was proletarian and socialist. By the second half of the 1920s, however, this group was challenged by poetism, a school of pure poetry led by Nezval and joined by Seifert and others, which was related to dadaism and futurism, emphasizing fantasy, the imagination, and free mental association. Holan associated himself with the "pure poets." He produced six collections of highly introverted lyric poetry in the years up to the beginning of the war: *Blouznivý vějíř* (The Delirious Fan, 1926); *Triumf smrti* (Triumph of Death, 1930); *Vanutí* (Breezes, 1932); *Oblouk* (The Arch, 1934); *Kameni přicházíš* (Stone, You Draw Near); and *Záhřmotí* (The Noise of Thunder, 1940).

Holan's poetry is essentially metaphysical, but these early poems are especially difficult, exploring the relationship between the reality of the world and the mystery of the universe, between tangible appearance and nothingness, between the transient and the eternal, and each poem is a complex structure of interrelated ideas. Alfred French has said that "the phantoms of phantoms, and abstractions of abstractions, which haunt his verse, have given Holan the reputation of being among the 'purest' and most withdrawn of Czech poets"; French describes the breezes of *Vanutí* as those "which waft the poet, without conscious will or thought, into the dark recesses of Being—he is a sleepwalker in a mysterious land." Holan has always displayed great technical skill and originality, and apart from their bold and surprising metaphors these early poems are full of grotesque neologisms and deformed syntax.

But though Holan's work is timeless, and concerned above all with the philosophical essence of objects and phenomena, from the early 1930s onwards it becomes less hermetic and more concerned with contemporary events. In the volumes *Odpověď Francii* (The Answer to France) and *Září 1938* (September 1938) the facts of the political situation of the time—the rise of fascism, the Spanish Civil War, Munich, and the German occupation of Czechoslovakia—are made into symbols, so that this great European catastrophe is generalized into myth. This mythopoeic vision of contemporary events is continued in *Sen* (The Dream) and *Zpěv tříkrálový* (Twelfth Night Song), with their protests against the German occupation and atrocities.

In the immediate postwar period Holan published four books of lyric poetry in which there is less use of allegory and linguistic experiment. In *Dík Sovětskému svazu* (Thanks to the Soviet Union, 1945) and *Panychida* (Requiem, 1945) he welcomes the liberation and sums up the German occupation; *Rudoarmějci* (The Red Army Soldiers, 1947) is a series of portrait poems exploring the "complex simplicity" of these ordinary soldiers in their dusty tanks who eagerly respond to Holan with quotations from Pushkin, Mayakovsky, Yesenin, and Pasternak. These three books, along with the short collection of political lyrics *Tobě* (To You, 1947), were republished together in 1949 under the title *Dokument.*

During the war years Holan had written several verse tales in strict classical meter, including *První testament* (First Testament, 1940) and *Terezka Planetová* (Terezka Planetová, 1943), which is set in the impoverished countryside of the Moravian Highlands and deals with the lives of its simple inhabitants. Between 1948 and 1960 he produced the twelve large compositions written in free verse, but built on the principle of atonal harmony, which were collected in 1961 as *Příběhy* (Stories); these apparently simple stories of human suffering and tragedy together make up a modern epic, for Holan again gives them the character of mythical generalizations.

In the 1960s Holan published several more collections of short lyric poems, but many of these had been written much earlier, during the Stalinist years, including *Bez názvu* (Nameless, 1963, written 1939–1942) and *Na postupu* (In Progress, 1964, poems from the years 1943–1948). Other collections delayed until, or written during, the sixties include *Bolest* (Pain, verses from the years 1949–1955), *Trialog*, *Mozartiana*, and *Na Sotnách* (In Sotna, 1967, verses from the year 1961–1965). The majority of these poems are in free verse, in contrast to the early lyrics from the prewar years; and many of them are very short—masterpieces of compression in which Holan raises and illuminates universal problems and unexpected aspects of reality.

The impressive poem *Noc s Hamletem* (A Night With Hamlet, 1969), written between 1949 and 1956, is in many ways a synthesis of the whole of Holan's work, once again exploring the fundamental philosophical questions which he raised in his essays *Torzo* (Torso, 1933) and in the prose diary from the years 1934–1938, published in 1940 as *Lemuria*, which are basic works for the understanding of the poet. *Noc s Hamletem* is partly a testimony of the Stalinist years when it was written, in which the poet was unable to publish; but above all it reflects Holan's desire for a general philosophical conception of life, yet also his skepticism, which constantly makes him doubt that any single view is a complete one, so that the poem becomes a dialogue of the poet with himself.

Holan has produced an extremely large and impressive body of poetic work, and has become increasingly recognized as one of the greatest Czech poets of the twentieth century. In his early work especially he was influenced by Rilke, Mallarmé and Valéry, as well as by Czech poets such as Mácha and the Symbolist Otokar Březina. Nevertheless, both as a man and as an artist, his character is essentially solitary, and he has always remained uniquely himself. As Alfred French points out, "Holan wrote in riddles, and the breakdown of understanding between himself and the reader has always restricted his popularity." It has also restricted knowledge of his poetry in other countries, for it is extremely difficult to translate, and it was not until the late 1960s that his books began to appear in other languages, at first mainly in Italian and French. A volume of *Selected Poems* in English, translated by Ian and Jarmila Milner, appeared in 1972. In 1965 Holan received the title of National Artist, and in 1967 he was awarded the Sicilian Etna-Taormina Prize. He himself has made numerous translations from German, French, Spanish, Russian, and Chinese. These will occupy four of the volumes of his collected works, which commenced publication in Prague in 1965 under the editorship of Vladimír Justl.

PRINCIPAL WORKS IN ENGLISH TRANSLATION: Selected Poems, 1972. *Poems in* French, A. (ed.) A Book of Czech Verse, 1958; Otruba, M. and Pešat, Z. (eds.) The Linden Tree, 1964; Theiner, G. (ed.) New Writing in Czechoslovakia, 1969.

ABOUT: French, A. The Poets of Prague, 1969; International Who's Who, 1973–74.

HOLBROOK, DAVID (KENNETH) (January 9, 1923–) British poet, novelist, educational writer, and critic, writes: "I was born in lodgings over a chemist's shop in Norwich, the mediaeval capital city of Norfolk. Both my grandfathers were wheelwrights. My father sold bicycles and spare parts for motor cars. My mother came from a crab-fishing village near Cromer, and her mother's family were Huguenot potters at Beccles.

"As a boy I watched urban sprawl around Norwich beginning to destroy the old life of the English countryside. I spent most of my boyhood in the country, on farms and on the coast—that is, when I wasn't at school. I went to a state primary school, and from there gained a scholarship to a grammar school. At school I remember having very good English teachers all along, who used to encourage us to make up stories, and would read us James Joyce and T. S. Eliot. My mother read a great deal (she named me after David Copperfield) and wanted me to be a writer. My literary interests were deepened by being sent down to act, as a boy, at the Maddermarket Theatre—an amateur theatre built on the lines of the Elizabethan theatre, and directed, with very high standards, by the late Nugent Monck. There I played parts in several of Shakespeare's plays, and in mediaeval and modern drama.

"From the atmosphere of the Maddermarket (which Shaw and Yeats both visited), my father's educational ambitions for me, and my mother's interest in music and Dickens, I had already decided by the time I was in the Sixth Form to be a writer.

"The road to becoming an adult writer seemed, however, interminable. I had a practical sense of the Arts from my Maddermarket experience. The problem seemed to me that a writer needed a private income—and I hadn't got one. So I didn't expect to achieve anything before I was forty, and was relieved to find that Conrad didn't really start before that age either, so there was hope. I won an Exhibition to Downing College, Cambridge, in 1941, and there I read English under F. R. Leavis for a year. Then I had to go into the Army, and spent three years in a tank regiment in Normandy, Holland and Germany. In 1945 I was demobilised early to complete the Tripos, by now feeling (at twenty-four) rather behind-hand in the struggle to solve the problem of how to earn my living and become a writer.

"I drifted to London, and worked for a magazine called *Our Time*. The Editor was an elderly poet and critic of the twenties called Edgell Rickword, who once edited *The Calendar of Modern Letters*. Later I went into educational publishing. After a year or so, however, I began to yearn for touch with genuine people in a real community. I found London so tiring and distracting that I couldn't really think, write or feel. But by now I had a wife and child, so the problem of earning enough to live on was growing.

DAVID HOLBROOK

"We lit out to Suffolk, and I worked in adult education, free lancing. I lectured in the evening and wrote in the mornings. In this way I trained myself to do a full day's writing at home, and in all the other necessary self-disciplines and chores of writing.

"I also gained from my work in the local community as lecturer and teacher a sense of the relevance of imaginative creativity to the lives of ordinary people. This sense became the driving force behind my work. It also provided the clue to my financial problems. I came to teach for a while in a secondary school, and found the English work dull and ill-thought-out. So, I set out to write a book on the teaching of English, trying to apply what I had learnt from Leavis, and what I knew of children and imaginative writing, to the secondary school child's needs. Out of this work came a whole programme of books for school use which began to bring us in enough to live on, by 1964, after about twelve years' work.

"At the same time I began to write poetry and short stories. In 1954 I moved to Cambridgeshire, to become Tutor for adult education, and school teacher, at one of the village colleges there. In 1961 I was given a Writing Fellowship by Cambridge University Press and King's College, to enable me to write a book on teaching English to backward children. In 1963 this was extended, and in 1964 I was awarded a Leverhulme Senior Research Fellowship.

"In the four years of this fellowship I wrote and

published two volumes of verse, a novel about the war, two critical books, three books on education, and about fifteen books for school use. This has established me as a fully self-supporting author at last—and at last I feel I can *begin*. My wife, after bearing the brunt of the tough and hopeless years, has now settled down to produce our fourth baby in comfort. I am now working on a book on psychoanalytical theories and their bearing on creativity, a new novel, and various other projects lying here on the shelf."

The books David Holbrook has published since the early 1960s have earned him a reputation in British educational and literary circles rather similar in some ways to that of Paul Goodman in the United States. Influenced by such post-Freudian psychoanalysts as Melanie Klein, he has, according to an *Economist* reviewer, "worked out for himself a generous and compassionate set of convictions about the intrinsic goodness of humanity and the essentially creative nature of love" which underly all his work.

These convictions illuminate *English for the Rejected, The Secret Places*, and his other books and essays about the teaching of English—especially in nonacademic secondary schools—in which Holbrook argues that the teacher's first concern should be not to instill the rules of spelling and grammar but to tap the child's innate creative instincts, to unlock the "secret places" of his mind. Similarly, in his widely used school texts and anthologies, Holbrook seeks to put into the hands and hearts of schoolchildren not the usual moralizing tracts but "the rich torment of popular life with all its agony, excitement and teeming warmth."

As a literary critic, Holbrook values above all moral integrity and a "mature" approach to love and life. In his 1962 book on Dylan Thomas he uses F. R. Leavis's methods of verbal analysis to show how much meaningless rhetoric is in Thomas's poetry, and psychoanalytic arguments to convict him of infantile emotional attitudes. Some who found the book "honest and courageous" regretted that it was also "excessively self-righteous . . . priggish and uncouth." *The Quest for Love*, discussing in similar terms works by Chaucer, Shakespeare, and D. H. Lawrence, had a similarly mixed reception.

Holbrook's first book of verse, *Imaginings*, was a Poetry Book Society choice in England. His poetry has been called autobiographical, sometimes prosy in its language and "wonky" in its rhythms, but always alive and original, the product of "a most clear eye for details in the natural scene and an ability to take a straight look at his own feelings." His novel, *Flesh Wounds*, reflects his own experiences as a tank officer in the Normandy invasion. It is a realistic and sometimes brutal book, warmed by lyrical descriptions of nature and love. The general reaction was expressed by one critic who wrote that it succeeded "brilliantly in making real the apparent haphazard pointlessness of war."

Holbrook's fellowship at King's College ended in 1965, but he returned to Cambridge University in 1968–1970 as a part-time lecturer in English at Jesus College. In 1970 he received grants from the Arts Council and the Elmgrant Trust, and the same year he went as writer-in-residence to Dartington Hall, the experimental school in Devon. Since then a fresh spate of books has appeared. The study of "psychoanalytical theories and their bearing on creativity" mentioned above is perhaps *Human Hope and the Death Instinct*. It attacks Freud, Sartre, and R. D. Laing, among others, for their contributions to the present climate of nihilism, and finds a new basis for optimism about mankind in general and creativity in particular in the "object-relations" psychology of W. R. D. Fairburn and Harry Guntrip, and in the work of D. W. Winnicott, Melanie Klein, and others.

At the same time, Holbrook has achieved a measure of fame as an extremely vocal opponent of the permissive culture, and especially of sexual explicitness in the arts, attacking not only pornography but the frankness of such writers as Harold Pinter and Iris Murdoch. Unlike many campaigners against pornography, Holbrook's objections are not religious (he is an atheist). He attacks it rather as an outgrowth of that nihilism which, he maintains, has destroyed our faith in the values of our culture and left us "schizoid," alienated from our warmest, gentlest, and most loving instincts. Holbrook calls pornography "the philosophy of hate," believing that it is fundamentally sadistic, embodying various kinds of hostility—most often a desire to degrade women. The author has expressed his views in *Sex and Dehumanization, The Masks of Hate*, and *The Pseudo-Revolution*, as well as in many articles and lectures, and in a collection of pieces by various writers published under his editorship as *The Case Against Pornography*.

A frequent contributor to *The Guardian* and *The Spectator* among other journals, Holbrook has also written a number of songs and libretti. Most of his work exhibits "those tendencies and habits of mind which," as a reviewer wrote in the *Times Literary Supplement*, "his critics are so quick to designate hysterical, self-righteous, tendentious, narcissistic." But, the same writer went on, others "may on the contrary find the same tendencies exhilarating, relevant, morally fervid, and unanswerably just. Mr. Holbrook's plea is for wholeness of living . . . too often the writing is hasty, repetitive and diffuse. . . . But when all the objections have been made, much remains as inspiriting and illuminating." Holbrook has been called "loquacious, tubby, red-faced and likeable." His one recreation is oil painting.

PRINCIPAL WORKS: *Poetry*—Imaginings, 1961; Against the Cruel Frost, 1963; Object Relations, 1967; The Quarry (children's opera), 1967; Old World, New World, 1969. *Fiction*—Lights in the Sky Country (stories), 1962; Flesh Wounds, 1966. *Nonfiction*—English for Maturity, 1961; Llareggub Revisited, 1962 (U.S., Dylan Thomas and Poetic Dissociation); The Quest for Love, 1964; English for the Rejected, 1964; The Secret Places (essays), 1964; English in the C.S.E., 1964; The Exploring Word, 1967; Human Hope and the Death Instinct, 1971; (ed.) The Case Against Pornography, 1972; The Pseudo-Revolution: A Critical Study of Extremist "Liberation" in Sex, 1972; Sex and Dehumanization in Art, Thought and Life in Our Time, 1972; The Masks of Hate, 1972; Dylan Thomas: The Code of Night, 1972; English in Australia Now, 1973. *Anthologies, etc:* Children's Games, 1957; Iron, Honey, Gold: An Anthology of Verse (4 vols.), 1961 (rev. ed., 1965); People and Diamonds: An Anthology of Short Stories (4 vols.), 1962–1966; Thieves and Angels: An Anthology of Dramatic Pieces, 1962; Visions of Life: An Anthology of Prose (4 vols.), 1964; I've Got to Use Words, 1966; Children's Writing, 1967; (with E. Poston) The Cambridge Hymnal, 1967; Plucking the Rushes (anthology of Chinese poetry), 1968.

ABOUT: Contemporary Authors 9–10, 1963; Murphy, R. (ed.) Contemporary Poets of the English Language, 1970; Orr, P. (ed.) The Poet Speaks, 1967. *Periodicals*—Economist January 2, 1965; Times Literary Supplement October 1, 1964; January 25, 1965; December 10, 1971; November 3, 1972.

HOLLANDER, JOHN (October 28, 1929–), American poet and scholar, writes: "I was born in New York City on the bad Monday preceding a worse Tuesday. My parents were professional people, not hit too hard by the Depression; my mother being a high-school teacher and my father a research physiologist, from whose commitment to science I have never been immune. His family were Jews from Eastern Europe; my mother's, from Prague and Hamburg, although settled in New York since 1848. In any event, my modestly comfortable childhood, in a home that buzzed with ideals and enlightenment, lacked all but a tincture of the raw, Yiddishized culture shared by so many of my contemporaries. I went to Hunter Model School, Bronx High School of Science, and Columbia College, which I entered at the age of sixteen among a class full of war veterans. It was perhaps the most exciting moment in history to be at an American university. I studied English literature and art history; I had Mark Van Doren and Lionel Trilling as formal teachers, and older contemporaries like Allen Ginsberg as my earliest critics. After graduating from college, I traveled in Europe for a bit, worked part-time at various editorial jobs, wrote program notes for classical record liners and enrolled in graduate school at Columbia. At the same time, I began studying harmony, counterpoint and the history of music, and started to teach myself to play the lute. After taking a master's

JOHN HOLLANDER

degree at Columbia, I went to Indiana University on a teaching assistantship, married Anne Helen Loesser of Cleveland, Ohio, completed work for a Ph.D. in English save for the dissertation, and published my first poems in *New Directions 14* and *Discovery*. I was elected to the Society of Fellows in Harvard in 1954, and spent three years in Cambridge, during which I read a lot, wrote a lot and played a lot of medieval, renaissance and baroque music with small chamber groups. In 1958 my first book of poems was published in the Yale Younger Poets series, and my scholarly study of music and poetry in the renaissance was finished. I have taught at Connecticut College for Women and, since 1959, at Yale. I have never wanted to be a writer in residence, but to teach as a regular academic member of an English department. The price for not teaching creative writing under such an arrangement is a high one, though; I tend to envy some of my friends their free time. I feel that I don't write enough. I like writing for children, and wish to do more of it. I have written for the theatre (I did the lyrics for a musical, with Jerome Moross and Ben Hecht, that almost got into rehearsal) and would like to do more of that. But more and more I am jealous of the time I have for poetry. I live in New Haven with my wife and two daughters, go abroad occasionally, and look forward to moving to New York City to live some time soon."

Since he wrote that, John Hollander has indeed moved to New York City, where he is professor of English at Hunter College. His first book, *A Crackling of Thorns*, appeared with an introduction by W. H. Auden, then editor of the Yale Series of

Younger Poets. It was praised by Auden and others above all for its technique, and from that point of view seemed to Hayden Carruth "the best first book of poems I have read in a good many years"—the "ultimate flowering" of the metaphysical tradition in modern American verse. Some critics thought the book too literary, too derivative of the light verse of the seventeenth century. Thom Gunn was one of those who realized that for Hollander "the seventeenth century is a serious preoccupation, not a conscious piece of preciosity." Gunn found in the volume poems in which Restoration gallantry reacts in an interestingly odd way with "a more modern sense of the grotesque," and some in which Hollander uses what he had learned from seventeenth century verse to deal with entirely contemporary preoccupations.

Movie-Going and Other Poems seemed to Dudley Fitts one of the signal events of the season. Hollander's first book had established him as "a poet of technical virtuosity," Fitts wrote, and his second confirmed this, but also revealed "a deeper insight, at once astringent and tender, into the predicament of the displaced urban agonist." *Visions from the Ramble* is a sequence of poems about Hollander's childhood in New York in which, as Donald Hall said, "phrases which seem all appropriate to elderly reminiscences of My Boyhood in Roseville take on a weird sophistication." Hall liked the book as a memoir but not so much as poetry, finding it too slack and lacking in intensity for his taste. W. T. Scott, however, was impressed, and praised Hollander's ability to "manage a long, flowing line with musical consistency and emotional overtones." *Types of Shape*, a collection of poems whose shape on the page—bells, car keys, umbrellas—reflect their themes was followed by *The Night Mirror*, a more general collection. *Selected Poems*, which introduced Hollander to British readers in 1972, was received there with pleasure. *Town and Country Matters: Erotica and Satirica* was among the 1972 nominations for the National Book Awards.

A Book of Various Owls is a collection of nonsense poems for young children. *The Quest of the Gole*, a mock epic for older children or adults, complete with mock scholarship, was found amusing but rather insubstantial. Hollander contributed to and was the coeditor with Anthony Hecht of *Jiggery-Pokery*, an anthology of amusing light poems written to a strict double-dactylic formula. The poet's doctoral thesis was published as *The Untuning of the Sky: Ideas of Music in English Poetry, 1500–1700*.

Hollander was a visiting professor at Indiana University's Linguistic Institute in 1964, and an overseas fellow of Churchill College, Cambridge University, in 1967–1968. From 1969 to 1971 he was a contributing editor of *Harper's Magazine*.

PRINCIPAL WORKS: *Poetry*—A Crackling of Thorns, 1958; Movie-Going and Other Poems, 1962; Visions from the Ramble, 1965; (with Anthony Hecht and others) Jiggery-Pokery, 1967; Types of Shape, 1969; The Night Mirror, 1971; Selected Poems, 1972; Town and Country Matters: Erotica and Satirica, 1972; An Entertainment for Elizabeth (masque; English Renaissance Monographs series), 1972; Selected Poems, 1973 (England). *Nonfiction*—The Untuning of the Sky: Ideas of Music in English Poetry, 1500–1700, 1961; Images of Voice, 1969. *For children*—A Book of Various Owls, 1963; The Quest of the Gole, 1966; The Immense Parade on Supererogation Day and What Happened to It, 1972. *As editor*—Selected Poems of Ben Jonson, 1961; (with H. Bloom) The Wind and the Rain: Anthology of Poems for Young People, 1961; Poems of Our Moment, 1968; Modern Poetry: Essays in Criticism, 1968; American Short Stories Since 1945, 1968; (with Frank Kermode) The Oxford Anthology of English Literature, 1973.

ABOUT: Auden, W. H. *Introduction to* Hollander, J. A Crackling of Thorns, 1958; Contemporary Authors 4, 1963; Hollander, J. Visions From the Ramble, 1965; Murphy, R. (ed.) Contemporary Poets of the English Language, 1970; Ward, M. E. and Marquardt, D. A. Authors of Books for Young People, 1967; Who's Who in America, 1972–1973.

HOLLOWAY, JOHN (August 1, 1920–), English poet, critic, and prose-writer, says: "As a boy I lived in a number of houses in the south-east fringes of London: a little terrace house, a rustic cottage, a secluded bungalow, and a semi-detached villa. The earlier years are described in *A London Childhood*. At various times I read everything I could about motor-racing, was a keen bird-watcher, and was a violinist of sorts in the best school orchestra in the country. My mother was a very clever woman and my father was all right. I liked English best, went to Oxford as a history scholar (the headmaster's choice), studied mainly philosophy, and while waiting to go into the army worked as assistant to a social scientist. During the war I was commissioned as an anti-aircraft gunner, and seconded to Intelligence. I had a safe, dull war, but I got a lot out of it including proficiency in German, and my wife.

"On returning to Oxford and teaching philosophy (late 1945), I soon decided that a life-time of that would leave me bone dry. I changed to English, but just at that time got a philosophy Prize Fellowship to All Souls College—where I spent several interesting years, though never harder-up. Most of my friends thought I was insane to leave Oxford for an English lectureship at Aberdeen (1949); but it meant my chosen subject, a beautiful little seventeenth-century house, lively and varied companions, and for the first time in my life a city and a region where I could grow roots. By now I was regularly publishing verse in established periodicals; the stimulus largely came from where I lived—spectacular, iron-hard, humanly real all at once. At the same time, I finished my second book (on Victorian prose-writers), wrote a good many critical articles which were later collected, and in 1951 read the sole paper at the first English Lecturers' Conference, now a well-established annual event.

"I moved to Cambridge in 1954 in expectation of wider scope and richer intellectual environment. But I have come to realize that I am something of a northerner by temperament. My writing now became less directly descriptive, and more reflective and symbolic in content: leading up to the book-length terza-rima poem, The *Landfallers* (1962), which I see as my best work so far. In part, but only in part, it reflects ideas developed in a book, which I was writing at the same time, on Shakespearean tragedy.

"In these years I was also rescuing a fine eighteenth-century house from dilapidation and neglect, reviewing, broadcasting, writing criticism, and travelling widely. I was Francis E. Powell Travelling Fellow in the USA in 1952, visited France, Italy or Spain several times, and in 1958 spent three months travelling and lecturing in the Indian subcontinent: a visit profoundly rewarding to me. From 1961 to 1963 I was seconded to hold the Byron Chair at Athens, and besides being a perhaps troublesomely active Professor, I travelled throughout Greece, visited Turkey, the Balkans, the Near East and Egypt, and wrote a long essay on modern poetry and the modern world (*The Lion Hunt*).

"My daughter was born in 1961 in Cambridge, my son in 1965, while we occupied the centuries-old Suffolk vicarage which has been among my chief recreations since I returned to Cambridge in 1963. I find no clash between living in a remote village, following new verse and movements in art, going frequently to London, reading in several foreign languages, broadcasting and reviewing, and travel (to Persia and the Middle East in 1964, and to a visiting Chair at Chicago in 1965). In this varied life I also find a base from which to contemplate the problems of the contemporary poet, and to move consecutively forward in my own writing. Much contemporary verse strikes me as too near to intelligent and sensitive *reportage*. I believe that poetry must keep the dimension of mystery if it is to remain itself, and I am especially interested in intricacies of structure, rich and re-vitalized language, and the interweaving of reality with the imaginative. My verse tends always to be close-packed and closely-considered, and has not been found easy. But it is now being received in terms such as I should wish. I like to see myself as a life-loving man, thoughtful but with go."

A London Childhood describes the secure and happy working-class world in which John Holloway grew up. His mother, Evelyn Astbury, was the daughter of a country schoolteacher. His father, George Holloway, had little education but lifted the family into the "speculative-builder middle-class." Holloway graduated from Oxford in 1941 with first class honors in Modern Greats (politics, philosophy, and economics), and subsequently received a doctorate in philosophy (Oxford, 1947) and two doctorates in literature (Aberdeen, 1954 and Cambridge, 1969). He held his English lectureship at Aberdeen from 1949 to 1954, and was university lecturer in English at Cambridge from 1954 to 1966, when he became university reader in modern English. Since 1972 he has been the university's professor of modern English. He was married in 1946 to Audrey Gooding, and has a son and a daughter.

JOHN HOLLOWAY

In *The Charted Mirror*, Dr. Holloway expressed his reservations about the "new criticism," pointing out that "*any guiding idea* with which the critic may equip himself . . . is likely to open up parts of his subject, *but certain parts only*." Discussing Shakespeare's tragedies in *The Story of the Night*, he reminded his readers of the intellectual climate in which Shakespeare wrote, providing what was often "a salutary antidote to creative, modern readings of the plays." Literary criticism has greatly benefited from Holloway's training as a philosopher and historian, but critics have not; Frank Kermode has accused him of going among his colleagues like "one who enters to an unruly company and sternly asks what all this is about." Yet it was Kermode also who said of *The Story of the Night*: "After much thought I feel willing to say that these are the best essays on the tragedies I have ever read."

In the mid-1950s in Aberdeen, when he had still

published little verse, Holloway was invited to contribute to *Poets of the 1950's* and *New Lines*, the two "Movement" anthologies. He came to know some of his fellow contributors, but was always "right on the edge of the group." As a poet, Holloway admires and is indebted to Edwin Muir, and has the same concern for form, pursues the same "radical honesty and directness." He believes a poet must "achieve a unique speech that still has a massive tap-root in the inexhaustible soil of common speech." *The Landfallers*, which he calls his best work to date, is a very long narrative poem which earned its author praise for his stamina and immense technical vocabulary, but was thought sometimes obscure and shadowy. "And yet," wrote Donald Davie, "I suspect that with this venture Holloway has come to terms with himself; in his verse, as long ago in his elegantly weighty prose, he now takes for his own the pre-modern world of Matthew Arnold."

PRINCIPAL WORKS: *Poetry*—The Minute, 1956; The Fugue, 1960; The Landfallers, 1962; Wood and Windfall, 1965; New Poems, 1970. *Nonfiction*—Language and Intelligence, 1951; The Victorian Sage, 1953; The Charted Mirror, 1960; The Story of the Night, 1961; The Colours of Clarity, 1964; The Lion Hunt, 1964; Widening Horizons in English Verse, 1966; A London Childhood (autobiography), 1966; Blake: The Lyric Poetry, 1968. *As editor*—Poems of the Mid-Century, 1957; Selected Poems of Percy Bysshe Shelley, 1960.

ABOUT: Allott, K. (ed.) Penguin Book of Contemporary Verse, 1962; Holloway, J. A London Childhood, 1966; Jennings, E. Poetry Today, 1961; O'Connor, W. V. The New University Wits, 1963; Who's Who, 1971. *Periodicals*—Irish Times June 1962; Mind April 1952; New Statesman April 6, 1962; Times Literary Supplement April 6, 1962.

HOLMES, JOHN (ALBERT) (January 6, 1904–June 22, 1962), American poet and teacher, was born in Somerville, Massachusetts, the son of John Albert and Mary (Murdock) Holmes. He graduated from Tufts College in 1929 and was a student at Harvard in 1929–1930. Holmes began his teaching career in 1930 at Lafayette College, and in 1934 returned as an instructor to Tufts, where he taught for the rest of his life, becoming a full professor in 1961.

His verse is unassuming and readable, and its best lines have an "endearing grace." In its forms, in its philosophy, and in its "quiet delight" in the New England scene, it strongly resembles the work of Holmes' great friend Robert Frost. Holmes was at the same time a very personal poet who, as he said, wrote about himself for himself. His poems range from "chapters of autobiography in free verse and loose rhythms to more concentrated, usually metrical pieces on single incidents"—"little dramas" that were important to him as a teacher, father, husband, or New Englander. When his *Selected Poems* appeared posthumously in 1965, Philip Booth said: "John Holmes was that rare man who wrote as if 'being a poet' was simply one prime way of being a human being. . . . The result, in this final book, is poems that are scaled, with the greatest emotional accuracy, to how one man got his life said. . . . Inside the slow rhythms which pattern these poems with John Holmes' own speech, there lives a poetry of hurtfully earned wisdom."

JOHN HOLMES

Elsewhere (and speaking from experience), Booth wrote: "No poet has ever been more generous to young poets." Holmes taught at the New Hampshire Writers' Conference from 1940 to 1947 and from 1954 until his death. Between 1947 and 1952 he directed the Chautauqua Writers' Workshop and, beginning in 1952, the Tufts College Writers' Workshop. The "critical insight and demanding encouragement" that marked his teaching is preserved in *Writing Poetry*, which contains five essays by Holmes, and others by poets of the caliber of W. H. Auden, Robert Frost, and Marianne Moore.

John Holmes was the Phi Beta Kappa poet at Tufts in 1935 and 1960, at Brown University in 1950, at William and Mary College in 1955, and at Harvard University in 1956. He received the William Rose Benét Poetry Prize in 1958. For some years he was the poetry critic of the Boston *Evening Transcript*, and he reviewed for the New York *Times*, *Poetry*, and the *Atlantic*. Holmes had one son by his marriage in 1934 to Sara Ludlow, who died in 1947, and a son and a daughter by his second wife, Doris Kirk, whom he married in 1948.

When Holmes died, John Ciardi, his former student, wrote that he "was not an intellectual, nor a yea sayer, nor a defender or castigator of the age, nor a purveyor of messages. . . . His poetry is local, personal, and, if anything, intellectually timid. . . . This poetry is a low-keyed and relatively unagonized acceptance of the small truth in an age given to a higher-keyed engagement with the Big Truth, the Big Disaster."

PRINCIPAL WORKS: *Poetry*—Address to the Living, 1937; Fair Warning, 1939; Map of My Country, 1943; The Double Root, 1950; The Fortune Teller, 1961; The Selected Poems of John Holmes, 1965. *Nonfiction*—Writing Poetry, 1960.

ABOUT: Ciardi, J. *Introduction to* The Selected Poems of John Holmes, 1965; Who's Who in America, 1962–1963. *Periodicals*—Literary Review Summer 1966; New York Public Library Bulletin May 1967; New York Times June 23, 1962; New York Times Magazine March 25, 1950; Saturday Review July 8, 1961; August 11, 1962; Writer January 1946, September 1962.

"HOLT, VICTORIA." *See* HIBBERT, ELEANOR BURFORD

HANS EGON HOLTHUSEN

***HOLTHUSEN, HANS EGON** (April 15, 1913–), German poet and critic, writes (in German): "The eldest son of a Lutheran minister, I was born in the small city of Rendsburg, in Schleswig-Holstein. My father had, so to speak, inherited the ministerial profession; all of his direct ancestors, far back into the eighteenth century, had been pastors. I spent the most impressionable years of my childhood in a village on the lower Elbe and in the old episcopal city of Hildesheim, famed for its late Gothic architecture; a city founded in the seventeenth century; on March 22, 1945, almost completely destroyed; and since then 'built up again' in a monstrously misconceived way. My earliest notion of the world was thus determined by the landscape of Lower Saxony, the atmosphere of the 1920s, and the life style of a north German minister's home, with its characteristic mixture of music, humor, middle-class ease and ceremonial solemnity.

"Naturally I was driven into opposition to all this, almost as soon as I had puberty behind me, and at seventeen I was reading—besides Dostoevsky—mainly pacifist and Communist literature, and I raved about Lenin. But when—after 1933—my father identified himself with the struggle of the 'Witnessing Churches' for the freedom of the evangelical ministry and against the ideological terror of those days—when he involved himself through the boldness of his preaching, in exhausting and finally fatal conflicts with the National Socialist authorities—he died of a heart attack at Christmas, 1938—then I went over to his side. Under the influence of Jaspers' *Existentzphilosophie*, and of the 'dialectical theology' which was much discussed at that time, I had found my first coherent and ideologically adequate world view. I still regard the world of Christian tradition as my spiritual home. Even though I am generally 'on a journey' and maintain only a loose and sometimes downright skeptical relationship to that spiritual home; still that home remains, emotionally an incarnation of loving protectiveness, intellectually a challenge of unsurpassable distinction.

"For five years I studied in German universities—mostly German literature, history, and philosophy. When I was twenty years old I discovered Munich, and made it the 'home of my choice': a city which fascinated me with its 'southern' charm, its baroque-Catholic and at the same time cosmopolitan atmosphere: I apprehended it as an ideal counter-world to the North German Protestant province of my origins and childhood. During the Second World War I was a soldier for almost six years on different eastern and western fronts, including three years in Russia; I collected experiences which I have not yet, to this day, worked through; and, almost miraculously, I remained unwounded. Several days before the end of the war I found myself involved, as a junior officer in an interpreter corps, in a local uprising against the Nazi regime in Bavaria. Since that time I have lived as an independent writer in Munich, except when I have been traveling and investigating possible new homes in other countries. I have come to know almost all the countries of Europe, the Near East, the U.S.A. and Mexico. I have been a guest professor three times in American universities, and from 1961–1964 I was Director of the German-American Cultural Institute in New York, the Goethe-Haus.

"What does it mean, for a human being's self-

* hōlt′ hōō zən

knowledge, when he feels that the tension between 'home' and 'foreignness' exists for him as a leitmotif, and that travel is for him a paradigm of the way in which he experiences the world? My journeys can be interpreted in various ways: that which in theological terms conceives of man as being 'in the condition of a traveler'; or in mundane language designates simply a totally erotic disposition; in terms of the aesthetic imagination the changing appearances of the world are precisely so many hieroglyphs for the Puzzle of the World: every station is an 'inwardness raised to the condition of secrecy' (Novalis). In my eyes the precise factuality of the experienced world is so fantastic, so adventuresome, so breathtakingly inventive—example: the destruction of a more than thousand-years-old city, which one loves—that I find myself in no position, as an inventor of stories, to compete with reality. All that I have written, including the few attempts at fiction, is 'nonfiction.' All of it is commentary: either on the reality I have myself experienced or on literature, especially on contemporary literature.

"The geometrical region of literary production is that distinctive triangular area formed by scholarship, criticism, and poetry, an area where the sons of German ministers have always carried out their existence, where joy in 'the problem' bears its blossoms. Since my first essay collection, *Der unbehauste Mensch* (The Homeless Man, 1951), the title of which served for a long time as a kind of catchphrase in literary discussions, many literary, philosophical, and political problems have provided my themes. I have dismissed each of these problems finally, without having solved it, as a temporary opportunity to bear witness to one's own contemporaneity. He who does not confuse his personal, more or less fluctuating, convictions, with the truth, will find an open problem, if only it is correctly posed, more attractive than a solved problem. For me, in any case, the openness of 'my' problems has always been a source of vital energy, a supporting strength, indeed a formula of hope, even though it is formulated in contradictions.

"My literary wish-dream: a comprehensive autobiography."

The religious background of Holthusen's writing was clear from the start, testifying to the influence of his father's ministry and of the city of Hildesheim itself. Holthusen went to the *Gymnasium* in Hildesheim, then on to study at the universities of Tübingen, Berlin, and Munich, where he graduated in 1937 with a study of Rilke's *Sonnets to Orpheus*. His concern with Rilke involved many of the preoccupations of his subsequent criticism.

Der unbehauste Mensch (The Homeless Man, 1951) illustrates most of these preoccupations. The book discusses contemporary man's sickness, cruelty, loss of values, philosophical failure, and lack of existential orientation as they reflect themselves in the best twentieth century literature. Hemingway, Kafka, Rilke, are all discussed, as are many others. In some ways the analysis seems dated, for many of the perspectives are to us fairly commonplace—partly as a result of Holthusen's own influential book. But the learning and sensitive analysis in it remain extraordinary.

Das Schone und das Wahre (The Beautiful and the True, 1958) carries many of Holthusen's preoccupations into a more philosophical dimension. The chief essay of that book concerns truth and beauty in poetry as they are understood by T. S. Eliot and Gottfried Benn. The argument leads to certain formal conclusions: that since Kant we have to agree to the autonomy of the experience of the beautiful; that, however, we are unable to ignore the importance of the world that the beautiful subsumes into itself; therefore that we must live with an aesthetic which though "pure" yet accounts for the containing of the world, the material of truth, in the work of art. Once again these points play back into Holthusen's main concern: to discover a way in which the meaninglessness of the experienced world can be transcended (or resumed).

His *Rainer Maria Rilke* (1959) picks up earlier essays of his on that poet, and is at its strongest in discussing Rilke's attempt to transcend "the world" through poetry. The only one of Holthusen's books to have been translated into English, it was recognized by British and American critics as an indispensable study. Michael Hamburger, while commenting on the "absolute theological criteria" by which Holthusen judges his subject, praised his "brilliant analysis of the un-Christian character of the 'inwardness' to which many of Rilke's innovations can be ascribed." *Kritisches Verstehen* (Critical Understanding, 1961) brings Holthusen's critical concerns back into direct focus on practical criticism. The chief essay is on Brecht. But again the canvas of modern figures studied here is large: from Marx and Engels to René Wellek.

The most realized, and most influential, body of Holthusen's work has been criticism, but he has written poetry and fiction. The apocalyptic poems in *Hier in der Zeit* (Here in Time, 1949) and *Labyrinthische Jahre* (Labyrinthine Years, 1952) take up the preoccupations of his criticism, with particular stress on man's threatened need to communicate with his fellow men through love, or even through a bare being-together. Precisely this need dominates Holthusen's novel *Das Schiff* (The Ship, 1956), the fictional journal of an Atlantic crossing from America to Europe. His fiction draws perhaps too explicitly on his broadly philosophical concerns.

The critical reception of Holthusen has been

varied. It has been generally felt that his fiction and even his poetry are ultimately pointed toward a philosophy which he has best rendered in his essays. Yet at the same time some critics have insisted that Holthusen's prose is too 'fictional' or too metaphorical. Peter Demetz doubtlessly struck the most judicious note when he wrote: "Holthusen was . . . from the beginning of his critical work a passionate son, not a slave, of his time," and when he praised Holthusen's determination, in a skeptical world, to "continue inquiring into the meaning and task of the German spirit." Conservative in temperament, Holthusen has little time for "those intellectuals of the so-called left" who "wander about between fronts."

In September 1968 Holthusen became Permanent Professor of German Literature at Northwestern University, Evanston, Illinois. He enjoys hiking, swimming, and music. He has been married twice, and has a son and a stepdaughter.

PRINCIPAL WORKS IN ENGLISH TRANSLATION: Rainer Maria Rilke, 1952. *Poems in* Bridgwater, P. (ed.) Penguin Book of Twentieth Century German Verse, 1963; Hamburger, M. and Middleton, C. (eds.) Modern German Poetry, 1962.

ABOUT: Bridgwater, P. (ed.) Penguin Book of Twentieth Century German Verse, 1963; Hock, E. Interpretationen moderner Lyrik, 1968; International Who's Who, 1973–74; Penguin Companion to Literature 2, 1969; Wer Ist Wer, 1970. *Periodicals*—Frankfurter Allgemeine Zeitung August 30. 1958; German Life and Letters II 1949, IX 1950–51; Merkur 1951, 1960; New Statesman August 2, 1952; New York Herald Tribune Book Review July 27, 1952; Poetry 1953.

"HOLTON, LEONARD." *See* WIBBERLEY, LEONARD (PATRICK O'CONNOR)

***HOLUB, MIROSLAV** (September 13, 1923–), Czech poet and travel writer, writes: "I was born in Pilsen, Czechoslovakia. My mother is a high school teacher of French and German, my father a railway clerk. I am the only child.

"Between my sixth and eighth years I wrote poems and had whooping cough. Later I turned to nature and science and collected butterflies, caterpillars and plants. I was a little lonely and, consequently, I was also a good pupil, and retarded in practical matters. My education included the classical Gymnasium kind of high school, with Latin and Greek. This was associated with the most consistent reading of poetry and aesthetic thinking I ever did.

"From 1942 until the liberation of Czechoslovakia from German occupation in 1945, I worked on railways. In addition to butterflies I tried to collect poems which I occasionally wrote. Altogether there were about five surrealistic poems, one third of a novel after Saroyan and some short stories after Zoschenko.

MIROSLAV HOLUB

"After 1945 I studied science and worked in the Institute for the Philosophy and History of Science. After 1946 I studied medicine at the Medical School of the Charles IV University in Prague, where I have lived ever since.

"In 1947 my first poem was published and I received two awards in a national student contest for an essay on the problems of the 'Present Time' and for a collection of remarkably weak poems. Another collection was accepted by a publisher but it disappeared together with the publisher's firm in 1948. This gave me a long time for so-called maturation, very common among writers of my generation. Without much haste I finished my medical studies, working as a volunteer in a department of child psychiatry. I got my M.D. degree in 1953 and worked for one year as a clinical pathologist in a Prague hospital. This was the best place in which I ever worked.

"In 1954 I joined the Immunological Department of the Institute of Microbiology of the Czechoslovak Academy of Sciences in Prague, doing basic medical research. I defended a thesis on the 'Experimental Morphology of Antibody Formation' in 1958 and got the scientific degree C.Sc., equaling the Ph.D. Since 1964 I have headed the Department's Experimental Cytology Unit. In the years 1965–1967 I worked as a visiting investigator in New York. So far I have published some thirty-six scientific papers on the lymphocytes and their functions.

"For more than fifteen years I have been editing a journal for the popularization of science, *Vesmír*,

* hô′ lo͞op

founded in 1871. This is the least rewarding job I have ever done and a somewhat difficult one in the years of dogmatism of all kinds. Anyway, I still believe very firmly in the importance of science to the spirit and orientation of modern humanity. I recognize only one culture and one kind of human creativity.

"Since 1955 my poems have appeared in Czech journals. In 1958 my first book appeared and I was labeled by a high-ranking official a 'weed of Czech poetry'; this brought immediate popularity to the book and to my subsequent volumes of poetry. However, the broadest interest was gained by a book of 'lyric reportage' about the United States, written after my first visit there in 1962. Some of my books of poetry and this one of reportage obtained publishers' awards.

"Since 1957 I have been connected with the so-called 'everyday poetry' movement, and with the 'polemic generation,' editing the magazines *Květen* (May), discontinued in 1961, and *Orientace*.

"I think that the most important literary influences in my work were the young Polish poets Różewicz and Herbert, Prévert, William Carlos Williams and Lawrence Ferlinghetti. I tried to make a poetry of facts and of ideas intimately connected with them. My program is not the traditional 'lyrical,' soft-centered, antiscientific one, but derives from the new realism of science, pursuing the energy, tension and illumination contained in the fact itself. I hate superstitions about the 'basically human' and about the prophetic functions of poetry.

"I prefer chains of poems—short, condensed poems—centered on one idea to 'collections of poems.' I like mixing poems with philosophic quotations, jokes, graffiti and *aperçus*.

"Since 1963 I have been a member of the Central Committee of the Czechoslovak Writers Union and have to appear, in the role of the amphibian pathologist-poet, in different mass media—a soul-destroying activity.

"I am married and believe, in addition to science and poetry, in sports and fair play."

Holub's first collection of poems, *Denní služba* (Day Duty), appeared in 1958. Nine or ten more volumes have followed, some of them with titles which suggest very well the astringency and terse directness of his verse, like *Jdi a otevři dveře* (Go and Open the Door, 1962); *Zcela nesoustavná zoologie* (A Completely Unsystematic Zoology, 1962); *Tak zvané srdce* (The So-Called Heart, 1963); *Anamnéza* (Anamnesis, 1964); and *Ačkoli* (Although, 1969).

The poet says above that he recognizes "only one culture and one kind of human creativity." Certainly his poetry is as likely to deal with the implications of a laboratory observation as with a human emotion or a landscape. And certainly, as A. Alvarez says, he tends to write verse in the "tentative, empirical, alert" manner of a scientist—a manner which is deliberately "anti-literary." But Holub does not ignore the division between the "two cultures." Instead, speaking now from the scientific camp, now from the humanist, he exploits the "cultural gap" for ironic or emotional effect. Typically, a Holub poem consists mainly of a list of verifiable facts or phenomena, and draws its "energy, tension and illumination" from the sometimes surrealistic juxtaposition of these items and the subtly organized introduction of more speculative or emotionally resonant material.

Thus, in "Wings," he writes: "We have / a map of the universe / for microbes, / We have a map of a microbe / for the universe.// We have / a Grand Master of chess / made of electronic circuits.// But above all / we have / the ability to sort peas, / to cup water in our hands, / to seek / the right screw / under the sofa / for hours.// This / gives us / wings." Or, "In the Microscope," he finds that "Here too are dreaming landscapes, / lunar, derelict. / Here too are the masses / tillers of the soil. / And cells, fighters / who lay down their lives / for a song.// Here too are cemeteries, / fame and snow. / And I hear murmuring, / the revolt of immense estates."

Holub says that he likes "writing for people untouched by poetry. . . . I would like them to read poems as naturally as they read the papers, or go to a football game." Perhaps for this reason, he is attracted to what he calls "synthetic" art—"poetry plus music plus pictures plus I know not what." He has gone so far as to fit poems to the hospital and surgical photographs of Jan Pařik, "not describing the photograph but going on from the photograph; I hope going further than the photographs, or behind them."

Within the ardently lyrical Czech tradition, Holub's tough-minded and laconic verse seems to some coldly analytical and skeletal. He has acquired a growing following and influence nevertheless, and is now widely regarded as the leading Czech poet of the "middle generation"—the one which reached maturity during the Nazi occupation.

In 1968–1969 Holub worked at the Max Planck Institute of Immunobiology at Freiburg, Germany. He left the Czech Institute of Microbiology in 1971, and went to the Institute of Clinical and Experimental Medicine. He was a member of the central committee of the Union of Czechoslovak Writers from 1963 to 1969, and a member of the central committee of the Union of Czech Scientific Workers from 1969 to 1971. He was editor of *Vesmír* from 1952 to 1965. The author, who in 1968 was an active supporter of the reformist Dubček government, and who in 1972 signed a petition on behalf of political prisoners, astonished his friends in August 1973 by issuing a long statement repudiating these activities, presumably in order to make peace with the Czech regime and its literary bureaucrats.

Holub has been married twice—in 1948 to the actress Vera Koktová, and in 1963 to Marta Svikruhová, an editor. He has two sons. As a scientist he has traveled widely on both sides of the Iron Curtain, and he is the author of three notable travel diaries: *Anděl na kolečkách* (Angel on Wheels, 1963); *Tři kroky po zemi* (Three Steps on the Earth, 1965); and *Zít v New Yorku* (To Live in New York, 1969).

PRINCIPAL WORKS IN ENGLISH TRANSLATION: Selected Poems (tr. by Ian Milner and George Theiner), 1967; Although (selected poems, tr. by Ian and Jarmila Milner), 1972. *Poems in* Theiner, G. (ed.) New Writing in Czechoslovakia, 1969; Times Literary Supplement July 29, 1965; September 30, 1965; Tri-Quarterly Spring 1967.

ABOUT: Alvarez, A. Under Pressure, 1965; Alvarez, A. *introduction to* Selected Poems, 1967; Contemporary Authors 21–22, 1969; International Who's Who, 1972–1973. *Periodicals*—New Scientist January 26, 1967; Times (London) August 22, 1973; Times Literary Supplement April 27, 1967; August 25, 1972.

EDWIN HONIG

HONIG, EDWIN (September 3, 1919–), American poet and critic, writes: "I was born in Brooklyn, New York, where I was educated through high school. I lived through the Depression there on the strength of my paternal grandmother's beans and rice and the Automat's rolls and catsup until 1938, when leaving New York for the second time, I 'made' the W.P.A. Writers' Project in Madison, Wisconsin, lying about my age in order to get on, then saving enough money to get back into college. I graduated from the University of Wisconsin in 1941 and went directly to Washington D.C. There I worked as a minor library assistant for almost a year in the stacks of the Library of Congress, contracting from book dust a continuing case of rhinitis and a severe distrust of libraries.

"Herbert J. Muller, the critic-historian, helped me to get my first teaching job (at Purdue), which I held for six months; during the next six, while I was 'a dangling man' waiting to be drafted, I wrote a book on García Lorca. New Directions accepted it just as I was going off with an infantry regiment to France in 1943. After getting through the war I found myself engaged in a struggle to make sense to myself trying to teach subjects I had never studied while writing poems, stories, and essays, and being hopeful of getting to Spain to see if it still existed. Living in the southwest, near Albuquerque, for two years (1947–49), was the nearest I came to feeling at home anywhere. In 1958, when I first visited Spain, something of the same sense (of a place that mattered or could matter to me) vividly recurred. But I lacked the hard talent to live as an expatriate; besides, I felt that in gaining more fluency in Spanish I was somehow losing hold of English as a language to write in. By that time I had already taught at many colleges, including New York University, Claremont, New Mexico, and Harvard—although my sense of these schools now is simply that I found myself living near them for a certain period and then left. During the past nine years I have been a professor of English at Brown University.

"Matters that may have influenced my becoming a writer (though perhaps this is nothing but a nice rationalization) were an early sense of exclusion owing to my being blamed for my younger brother's accidental death when I was five, and a severe, nearly fatal bout with nephritis when I was nine. A positive influence was my illiterate grandmother, who spoke Spanish, Arabic and Yiddish (but no English); I lived with her and my grandfather for a few years after my parents were divorced when I was twelve. Experiences of this sort urged certain necessities upon me; one was to write instead of choking; another, to make sense of the world around me—but sense that would not be bereft of my own fantasy. Both my poetry and my criticism seem to rise out of such a need: the criticism that creates—Spain (Calderón and García Lorca) as well as allegory—and the poetry that criticizes persons and places I have loved and distrusted—'moral circuses' and 'gazabos.'

"My best poems are either unfinished or still merely notes in a notebook. Some poems got away (were printed in periodicals) but have since been excluded from my books because they did not seem substantial enough or true. In the same way I quarrel constantly with the poems written by contemporaries old and young. No poet writing in English in the last sixty years has mastered his art or has resisted the nervous need to keep changing his style; and so none has been able to write as a complete human being. Perhaps Rilke and Lorca succeeded in a few poems. I have taken to translating and to writing plays out of impatience with poetry and criticism; but I go on writing poetry—to stop would be a self-betrayal.

"My first wife, Charlotte Gilchrist, died in 1963. Subsequently I married Margot Dennes; we have an infant son, Daniel."

Lorca, though it was thought less than profound, was welcomed as the first detailed study of the writer in English, and as a "conscientious, systematic and scholarly" monograph. *Dark Conceit* is a discussion of allegory—a piece of literary and intellectual history which impressed even those who were unable to accept its premises. A. Alvarez, reviewing the book, called Honig "a tenacious arguer" with "a great range of reference" but regretted, as did others, that "polysyllabic swaddling . . . muffles what might otherwise have made a considerable impact."

Honig's first book of verse, *The Moral Circus*, mixes "dream and reality" in poems which "look simple [but] are usually complex," and which were praised for their "invigoration of smooth forms by a sharp, bitten vocabulary." D. J. Hughes, reviewing *The Gazabos*, called it a varied collection "as befits a marked poetic maturity," and said "the variety of forms and the exploration of many moods without ever losing that mysterious signature and blessed quiddity we call *voice* testifies to the presence of a major talent." Other reviewers admired the vigor, force, and "bounce" of Honig's "condensed and masculine" verse. *Survivals* was praised in similar terms by, among others, W. T. Scott, who wrote that Honig's "lean, muscular style, his way of lifting a small thing into significance—these are no mean gifts." There was at the same time some feeling that too much of the work collected in *Survivals* was inaccessibly private. Many thought that all that was best in the volume had been consigned to a final section, containing "poems of love and death" which Scott called "moving with an eloquence beyond rhetoric." A fourth collection, *Spring Journal*, also much preoccupied with death, seemed to some readers rather too relaxed in tone and form, lacking in intensity.

Honig has edited and translated plays by Calderón. The best-known of his own verse plays, *The Widow*, has often been performed. The writer now has a second son, Jeremy. He held Guggenheim Fellowships in 1948 and 1962, in 1966 received a grant from the National Institute of Arts and Letters, and in 1968 an Amy Lowell Traveling Fellowship. Honig has said that he read Eliot, Auden, and Hart Crane at the age of twelve, and that of these Crane has come to have the greatest influence on his poetry.

PRINCIPAL WORKS: *Criticism*—García Lorca, 1944; Dark Conceit: The Making of Allegory, 1959; Calderón and the Seizures of Honor, 1972. *Poetry*—The Moral Circus, 1955; The Gazabos: Forty-one Poems, 1959; The Gazabos: Forty-one Poems *and* The Widow: A Verse Play in One Act, 1962; Survivals, 1965; Spring Journal, 1968. *As translator*—Calderón de la Barca, P. Four Plays, 1961; Calderón de la Barca, P. Life Is a Dream, 1970; Pessoa, F. Selected Poems, 1971.

ABOUT: Contemporary Authors 7–8, 1963; Who's Who in America, 1970–1971. *Periodicals*—New Statesman March 26, 1960; Times Literary Supplement March 25, 1960; Voices January–April 1961.

HOPE, A(LEC) D(ERWENT) (July 21, 1907–), Australian poet and critic, writes: "I was born at Cooma, New South Wales, and grew up in Tasmania and Bathurst, New South Wales, where I went first to a school conducted by members of the Society of Friends and then to a country high school. From Bathurst I went to Sydney University where I graduated B.A. in 1928 and won a travelling scholarship which took me to Oxford. At Sydney I specialised in English and Philosophy, at Oxford I took the Language Schools in Old and Middle English. I returned to Australia in 1931, was for some time unemployed in the great economic depression of those years, and spent some part of that time living in a tent and writing verse which had been my main interest since the age of eight. In the next few years I was successively school teacher, public servant and vocational guidance officer in Sydney, Newcastle, and Canberra where I had charge of a trade school. The rest of my life since 1937 or so has been spent in academic teaching, first as a lecturer in Sydney Teachers' College, then at Melbourne University, Canberra University College and the Australian National University. I am married and have three children and have visited Canada, the United States, England, Ireland, Portugal, Spain, Italy and Greece in the last ten years. Although I have written a certain amount of literary criticism, I have never regarded myself as a scholar, but as a poet living on the fringe of the educational process and picking up from it the living I could not hope to earn by poetry. I made little attempt to publish any verse until I was in my thirties and did not publish any book of verse till I was nearly fifty. My interests are in poetry, and in the world in general as material for poetry, but in Australia in the last thirty years I have become involved to some extent in a sort of guerrilla warfare over the so-called modern movements in poetry, in which I have engaged in polemics against movements such as Imagism and surrealism and all the varieties of the 'pure poetry' heresy. I have consistently attacked the influence of men like T. S. Eliot, while admiring the man, and shown irreverent contempt for New Criticism and Old Balderdash alike. The result is that I am regarded in my own country as a controversialist. In fact, like Gallio, I care for none of these things very much, and am interested only in the writing of poetry—the rest I regard as the ephemeral journalism of ideas. As a professor of English I am concerned mainly with seventeenth and eighteenth century poetry."

A. D. Hope, whose poetry is better known and more appreciated in America than that of any other Australian, is the odd man out of Australian letters. If Slessor and Fitzgerald, and some poets of a younger generation, speak for the peculiarly Australian predicament, in his poetry Hope appears to speak not at all as a member of an English tradition but as a lonely independent, who humorously rejects all forms of modernism, and firmly roots himself in the solid virtues of the seventeenth and eighteenth centuries.

When he first began to write, Hope enjoyed his role as Swiftian satirist and "public literary nuisance" and thus attracted the ire of academic historians of Australian literature such as H. M. Green. But he successfully hid under this largely self-defensive bushel his dedication to the craft of poetry, and took a decade to establish himself as one of the most talented poets his country has produced—many would say the most talented, and the most important.

Hope is a romantic, particularly in his sexual attitudes, operating in a severely limited classical tradition of his own choosing. His critical dogmatism does not allow him to relax or to experiment with form—he firmly believes in "the well-made poem"—but within these self-imposed limitations his distinction is beyond dispute. No Australian poet (with the possible exception of Kenneth Slessor) can produce or has produced, within the tradition, so many lines of high poetic quality and power; and this capacity may well be the result of the tension set up between Hope's formally classical preoccupations and his romantic wildness. Certainly he has impressed the leading critics of his own country, who have discovered in him the positive intellectual virtues that they had hoped for in Kenneth Slessor.

"Standardization" is a characteristic (and famous) poem of Hope's. Summarized, it might well appear to consist of little more than an over-elaborated celebration of nature's superiority over wayward man; actually it is an extremely complex and ironic poem, worthy even of the kind of close analysis which Hope himself affects to despise, in which wit

A. D. HOPE

combines with rhetoric to produce a genuinely inspired and profound poetry: "She does not tire of the pattern of a rose, / Her oldest tricks still catch us by surprise. / She cannot recall how long ago she chose / The streamlined hulls of fish, the snail's long eyes." Here the apparently rhetorical "She cannot recall" is fully accounted for within the unobtrusively ironic structure of the poem. The subtlety with which Hope implies man's inconsistency—his impatience with beauty, his capacity for surprise—in this stanza is typical of his writing at its best.

Hope's awareness of his Australian predicament is nowhere better expressed than in his savage and yet tender poem called "Australia," whose ". . . five cities, like five teeming sores / Each drains her, a vast parasite robber-state / Where second-hand Europeans pullulate / Timidly on the edge of alien shores . . ." And yet he turns back home "gladly," hoping that in this primitive as well as pseudo-civilized country, there is ". . . some spirit which escapes / The learned doubt, the chatter of cultured apes / which is called civilization over there."

Hope's sexuality, or carnality—Vincent Buckley has called it "beastishness"—has seemed to some critics irrelevant to the themes of his most powerful work; to have originally arisen from the same defensive impulses that led him to shock his contemporaries. Essentially, in Buckley's words, "we see him alternating between a controlled affirmation of the physical and a less firmly controlled revulsion from it." He is celebrated for his explosions of sexual disgust, but what his poetry searches for above all is lucidity; it misses when it attacks or exhibitionizes too intensely but occasionally attains it midway between the absolutes of formal perfection and violent emotionalism.

The Collected Poems of 1966 was followed by *New Poems, 1965–1969,* a volume which further extended and enlarged Hope's reputation, and was greeted by Daniel Hoffman in the United States as the work of "one of the master conservative poets in English in this century." *Dunciad Minor* is a long mock-heroic poem which begins as a defense of Pope against a modern detractor and develops into a general (and often tedious) attack on modern critics in general—from "envious Leavis" to "torpid Blackmur," from the "cumbrous frolics" of Northrop Frye to the "ecstatic squeals" of Wilson Knight. Judith Wright has spoken of Hope's great "civilising" influence on younger poets, evident in the postwar movement in Australian verse away from landscape and balladic themes and towards urbanity, scholarship, and traditional forms.

As a critic, Hope is probably at his best when he is not trying to be provocative. As one reviewer wrote of his volume of critical essays, *The Cave and the Spring,* he can range from "the coarse and the inept" to "powerful, blunt, argumentative statement"; "brisk, informal, sometimes rash and petulant," Hope, continued the same writer, is always spirited in a way reminiscent of Dryden. *A Midsummer Eve's Dream* is an extended commentary on a strange poem by the sixteenth century Scottish Chaucerian William Dunbar, "The Tretis of the Tua Mariit Wemen and the Wedo." Hope calls his book a wild goose chase in which "the pleasure is in the chase." Dunbar's poem, by turns courtly and bawdy, is interpreted by Hope as a work of revolutionary literature for a women's liberation movement looking back to the ancient fertility cults. The result is a learned and curious study reminiscent of Robert Graves's *The White Goddess.*

Hope spent his boyhood in Tasmania, where his father was a Presbyterian minister. He was married in 1938 to Penelope Robinson and has three children. The poet retired as professor of English at the Australian National University, Canberra, in 1968, and has been Library Fellow of the University since 1969. In 1958 he went to the United States where he lectured with great success on a grant from the Carnegie Foundation. He was co-winner in 1965 of the Encyclopaedia Britannica Award for Literature, for "outstanding contributions in Australia."

PRINCIPAL WORKS: *Poetry*—The Wandering Islands, 1956; Poems, 1961; Collected Poems, 1930–1965, 1966; New Poems, 1965–1969, 1969; Dunciad Minor, 1970; Collected Poems 1930–1970, 1972. *Criticism*—The Cave and the Spring, 1965; A Midsummer Eve's Dream, 1970. *As editor*—Australian Literature, 1950–1962, 1964.

ABOUT: Buckley, V. Essays in Poetry, 1957; Press, J. Rule and Energy, 1965; Wright, J. Preoccupations in Australian Poetry, 1965. *Periodicals*—Australian Quarterly March 1964; Meanjin June 1962; New York Times Book Review February 5, 1967; February 21, 1971; Poetry October 1968; Quadrant Spring 1961; Times Literary Supplement August 18, 1966; September 9, 1971.

***HORIA, VINTILA** (December 18, 1915–), Rumanian novelist, poet, and essayist writes (in French): "I was born in Segarcea (Rumania), where my father held the post of agronomic engineer for Crown lands. I lived in the country, in nearly all the provinces in Rumania, until the age of eight, when we settled in Bucharest, where I received my education (*baccalauréat, licence* in law, studies in philosophy and literature). From the beginning of my existence, I was influenced by my life in the country and by exile. In my book *Journal d'un paysan du Danube* (Diary of a Danubian Peasant, 1966) I envisage my predestination thus: 'I am a man of autumn, born a few days before the winter solstice, in the country, in the midst of World War I. This is my first real point of contact with the claws of time and the rough bark of things. Thus I entered life, in its visible aspect, at a time when autumn had not yet finished its cycle, in a village in the southwest of my country, surrounded by vague hills, while war had been bloodying the Earth for more than a year. A few months after my arrival in this world, Rumania also entered the game, the enemy invaded our province and my mother fled with me to the inaccessible depths of the country, my father finding himself duties at the front from the outbreak of hostilities. My exile starts at the age of eight months. This fact is clearly inscribed in my history.'

"I wrote my first novel at eleven, my first poems at thirteen. I continue to adore trees in the midst of the town, and to spend my holidays in the country, at the edge of a little river which I called 'Le Ruisseau salé' (The Salt Stream) in my later novels. I owe my real education to this uninterrupted contact with nature and with the harmonious beauty of the Rumanian hills, where man lives in friendship and understanding with all around him. The "classical" balance which critics have not failed to reveal in my novels is no more than the style of life and the everyday philosophy of the men of my country, which I reflect unconsciously, as a river reflects the countryside surrounding it.

"I took an active part in nearly all the pre-war Rumanian literary publications and, between 1939 and 1941, founded and directed the review *Mesterul Manole,* the aim of which was to introduce foreigners to the young lions of our literature and to establish contact in depth with Western writers of the same generation.

"Between 1936 and 1942, I published, in Rumanian, one novel and four volumes of poetry.

* hô′ rēə

Sent as press attaché to Rome (1940) and Vienna (1942), I was interned in 1944 by the Nazis and freed in May 1945 by English troops of the Eighth Army. After this my exile started. Interned by the Nazis, then condemned by the Communists, I was obliged to lead a wandering life, living in Italy, the Argentine, Spain, France and then Spain again, earning my living as a bank clerk, then as journalist and writer, writing in Italian, in Spanish, and then in French my essays, poems, tales, lectures and novels.

"It was in this atmosphere of a Lost Promised Land that I wrote in Madrid, in 1957–1958, my first novel, published in Paris two years later: *Dieu est né en exil*, where I describe the poet Ovid's existence in exile in Tomis and his death among the Dacians, ancestors of the Rumanians. This novel gained the Prix Goncourt, which I chose to refuse after a press campaign organized against me by the Communist Rumanian Embassy in Paris, which tried in vain to approach me. My novel had an immediate world-wide success and was translated into twelve languages. Never having been an active politician, I have been a victim of politics, or of History, like so many of my contemporaries—a pretty thoroughgoing image of the times we live in.

"My books bear witness to that independent view which renounces, at the same time, the concept of '*zoon politikon*,' man considered as a 'political animal,' and of literature conceived of as a simple reflection of the visible. If I think of it, I am much closer to St. Augustine and Dante than to any modern writer. It is because of this that Ovid, the Pythagorean poet, and Plato, have become my best known characters. The novel is for me a *gnoseology*, I mean a technique of knowledge, rather than a *representation*, in that the religious element in my view overrides the social and everything else. The artist for me is only valid as an introduction to the true understanding of the world, which can only be of a spiritual order."

Horia's reputation rests principally upon *Dieu est né en exil* (1960, translated as *God Was Born in Exile*). A bitter controversy followed the announcement that it was to receive France's most coveted literary award, the Prix Goncourt. Two Paris newspapers alleged that Horia's previous literary career had been as a writer of Fascist propaganda—that he had hailed Hitler as "a political genius" and referred to the defeat of France as "a sad necessity" because of her cultural decadence. Pressure from various quarters resulted in Horia's renouncing the prize, in spite of the Goncourt jury's insistence that the prize was above politics.

Nor were the book's literary merits universally acknowledged. It recounts in the form of a private journal Ovid's experience of exile in Tomis, on the Black Sea, where he was banished after the publication of *Ars Amatoria* (The Art of Love). In Tomis he continues to live the sensual life he had known in Rome, until he inadvertently brings disaster upon a friend. From then on his exile becomes a period of revelation as he passes through experiences that lead him from hedonism to Christianity.

VINTILA HORIA

The book is concerned more with ideas than with action, but Moses Hadas found Horia's philosophy and theology "rather naïve," and his erudition "more than a little pretentious." Hadas thought the author "at his best in lyrical descriptions of landscapes in the region of the Black Sea, which he obviously knows and cherishes." The *Times Literary Supplement* found little to praise, condemning the book's "improbable characterization" and "pretentious mysticism." But some reviewers were enthusiastic, among them Stephen Spender: "Above all, it is a significant document of our time, skillfully and imaginatively disguised as a document coming from another time. It adds to our understanding of today through showing us that we still belong to yesterday."

Of Horia's other works, the best-known is *Le Chevalier de la résignation* (1962), another historical novel with a contemporary message. Set in Transylvania in the seventeenth century, it is an account of Radu Negru's guerrilla war against the Turks and the indifference of the Venetian republic to the plight of the Transylvanians.

PRINCIPAL WORKS IN ENGLISH TRANSLATION: God Was Born in Exile, 1961.

ABOUT: Twentieth Century Writing, 1969. *Periodicals*—New York Herald Tribune Books September 3, 1961; New York Times Book Review September 10, 1961; New Yorker December 10, 1960; Times Literary Supplement June 2, 1961; Yale Review December 1961.

EGON HOSTOVSKY

***HOSTOVSKY, EGON** (April 23, 1908–May 6, 1973), Czech-born American novelist, wrote: "I was born in a small industrial town, Hronov, in northeastern Bohemia, which was once an independent kingdom and later belonged to the Austro-Hungarian Empire; then it was a part of the Czechoslovak Republic, and still later of a German protectorate; and finally it became a portion of the Popular Democracy of the Czechoslovak Socialist Republic.

"Fifty-seven years before I first saw the light of day, there was born in Hronov a popular Czech author, Alois Jirasek, a national hero and some kind of Czechoslovak Walter Scott. He wrote an astronomical number of patriotic historical novels. Because I was born in the same locality, I was forced to read Jirasek from my childhood, in order to be on good terms with my teachers and later with my professors of literature at the university. In other words, from my early years I hated not only my famous compatriot but also writers in general. When I was ten, I wanted to be an engineer. When I was sixteen, I wanted to be a physician. My father, who owned a small textile factory, tried to make an industrialist of me. God knows how it came about that finally I turned into a writer. Perhaps it was under the indirect influence of Stefan Zweig, who was my very distant relative and with whose fame I was bothered again and again by dozens of aunts, uncles and cousins, as I had been bothered before by my teachers about Alois Jirasek. Maybe I decided to prove that I could do something similar to Stefan Zweig and the Czechoslovak Walter Scott.

* hos′ tof ski

"My first book, a collection of incomprehensible short stories, was published when I was still a student. Critics who didn't know that the author was seventeen years old compared me to Luigi Pirandello, but I published the book mainly to provoke my teachers, who knew all about the author. My parents were desperate, and I promised my mother on her fiftieth birthday that I would never write anything again. And when, in 1932, I was awarded a major literary prize (not only a medallion but also money), my father declared an armistice with me.

"I tried to make my living decently from the very beginning. This means not only through literature. From 1930 to 1937 I was an editor of various Czechoslovak publishing houses. Then I longed to see foreign countries, so I started a new career in 1937 as an employee of the Ministry of Foreign Affairs. When Hitler occupied my country in 1939, I was by chance lecturing in Belgium. This was the beginning of my odyssey. I was in France in 1940, and after the collapse of that country, I succeeded in escaping into Portugal. After eight months in Lisbon, I went to the United States, where I worked at the Czechoslovak Consulate in New York until the end of the war. In 1947 I was recalled to Prague, but soon I was sent as *chargé d'affaires* to the Czechoslovak embassy in Norway. In 1949 I resigned from that post and went to the United States, of which I am now a citizen.

"My books have been published in fifteen languages, but I have never been on the best-seller lists, which means that my father, were he still alive, would again be angry with me. I love children and old people, from whom I have learned much, and I dislike experts of literature and publishers, from whom I have not learned anything. During my lifetime I have witnessed activities of great personalities, and I have been touched by great historical events. I am able to talk about Josef Stalin and Billy Graham; I saw in person Nikita Khrushchev shoulder to shoulder with President Eisenhower, and I saw and even heard Elvis Presley; I can talk about the astronauts and the Beatles, about war in South Asia and the remarriage of Elizabeth Taylor. Haunted by all these experiences, I have been trying, independently of psychiatrists, to find the key to our troubled times and to build in my literature a place of spiritual security for myself and my readers.

"About women whom I have loved and sometimes married, I wrote discreetly and symbolically in my novels and short stories, so I don't see any reason for writing about them in this autobiographical sketch."

The first of Hostovsky's novels to attract attention in the West, though it has still not been translated, was *Případ profesora Körnera* (The Case of

Professor Körner, 1937). It is a closely observed study of a Jewish intellectual whose response to anti-Semitism and all the threats of daily life is to retreat into illness. When his wife cuckolds him with his friend Osvald, he becomes a chronic invalid. Körner makes a desperate effort to overcome his neurosis, his wife promises fidelity, and gradually, by an act of will, he recovers his health and self-respect. He is then killed in a road accident, and the relationship between Osvald and his widow is resumed. In spite of this abrupt and (for some critics) melodramatic ending, the novel conveys with chilling conviction the sense of isolation and despair among European Jews in the 1930s, without turning Körner into a merely symbolic figure, or losing sight of the fact that his particular troubles are exaggerated by neurosis.

It was only after the fall of Czechoslovakia, when Hostovsky was in exile, that his novels began to appear in English. The first of them, *Letters From Exile* (1942) and *Seven Times the Leading Man* (1945), both deal with the misery of the refugee, who feels impotent to help his fallen country and also guilty that it should have fallen. They were received with interest, but seemed to most reviewers marred by a variety of formal defects, including what one reader called "rather wild rhetorical symbolism."

Hostovsky's later books were much more tautly and effectively constructed. They continued to deal with the psychological and moral problems of the refugee intellectual, but these concerns were embodied in highly readable and often exciting narratives. Thus *The Black Band* and *The Hideout*, two short novels published together in 1950 as *Hide and Seek*, read like good thrillers. Similarly, *Missing* (1952), is a suspenseful firsthand account of a *coup d'état* in a society where fascism and communism are equally power-hungry and corrupt, and any friend may be an informer. The honest journalist who is the story's hero learns that "we must be neither good nor bad, we must only be careful." A review in the *Times Literary Supplement* called it a "bitter, hopeless book . . . written with great insight." The loneliness of the honest man in a corrupt society is also the common theme of the five novellas collected in 1951 as *Lonely Rebels*.

The Midnight Patient is Hostovsky's most ambitious treatment of a theme which recurs in his work—the connection between individual illness and a diseased society. A Czech psychiatrist in New York is drawn into the psychological war between West and East, a kind of warfare which he particularly detests. He is divided in his loyalties between his adopted and his natural country, and between his professional ethics and his desire for an easy, comfortable life; he is not comforted to discover that the mental disorders he is trying to cure are the products of similar divisions. The novel is successful on several levels: as a thriller, as a political allegory, and as a psychological study of a man caught in a maze of dilemmas. The tone is one of compassionate irony, a quality that came to characterize Hostovsky's books, and which extends at times into wild farce.

This is so in *The Charity Ball*, which has been described as "a blend of the Marx Brothers and Pirandello, with a dash of comic melancholy." It concerns a ball organized in New York for the benefit of European political refugees. What emerges all too clearly is that the refugees are deeply divided from each other by language and background, and moreover that they have brought with them to their new home all of the lost causes and ancient grievances which ruined the societies they left behind, and drove them into exile. At the ball which has been planned to help them take their places in the new world, "this peculiar group, drawn together ostensibly by a common desire and a single aim, continually broke up into groups and little knots, shouting in their many languages, and torn apart by every possible centrifugal force: like people who have made up their minds in advance that after this meeting they will part company for good."

Hostovsky's subsequent books did not attempt such broad comic effects, though they were ironically amusing in their descriptive passages, and included elements of fantasy—sometimes very dark fantasy—in their portrayal of the private worlds of their displaced and alienated heroes, as they struggle to preserve their sanity and integrity in a mad world. There is some justice in William Walsh's description of Hostovsky as "a small comic Kafka." He published nothing in English after 1964, but his literary memoirs appeared in Czech in Canada, and three of his novels made their first appearance in Czechoslovakia between 1967 and 1970.

The author became an American citizen in 1963. He was married to the former Regina Weiss and had two daughters and a son.

PRINCIPAL WORKS IN ENGLISH TRANSLATION: Letters From Exile, 1942; Hideout, 1945; Seven Times the Leading Man, 1945; Hide and Seek, 1950; The Lonely Rebels, 1951; Missing, 1952; The Midnight Patient, 1954; The Charity Ball, 1957; The Plot, 1961; Three Nights, 1964. ABOUT: Penguin Companion to Literature 2, 1969. *Periodicals*—New York Times February 3, 1961; May 8, 1973; New York Times Book Review February 18, 1945; Times Literary Supplement February 2, 1933; June 2, 1945; September 26, 1952; August 5, 1955; January 25, 1957.

***HOUGH, GRAHAM (GOULDER)** (February 14, 1908–), English scholar, critic, and poet, was

* huf

GRAHAM HOUGH

born in Great Cosby, Lancashire, the son of Joseph and Clara Hough. He was educated at Prescot Grammar School, at the University of Liverpool, and at Queens' College, Cambridge. Hough began his career in 1930 as a lecturer in English at Raffles College, Singapore. During World War II he served as a volunteer with the Singapore Royal Artillery, and he spent three of the war years as a prisoner of war of the Japanese in Siam. In 1946 he was appointed Professor of English in the University of Malaya. He went to the United States in 1950 as a visiting lecturer at Johns Hopkins University; the same year he returned to England as a fellow and subsequently as a tutor (1955–1960) of Christ's College, Cambridge. He became praelector of Darwin College, Cambridge, in 1964 and has been his university's professor of English since 1966.

Hough had with him in his Japanese prison a copy of Yeats's poems. Repeated reading of them sent his mind back over the vast changes of the past century in religious and social ideas, and the way these changes had been reflected in the arts and canalized through Yeats. This was the subject of *The Last Romantics*, which was warmly welcomed both for its careful scholarship and its richly stimulating speculations. Hough's second book was the fruit of similar meditations, which led him to the conclusion that "the only recent English writer besides Yeats to break into new spiritual territory outside the Christian boundaries was D. H. Lawrence and that his vitalism had had something of the same disruptive and fertilising effect in our century as aestheticism did in the nineteenth." *The Dark Sun* is Hough's remarkable account of Lawrence as writer and thinker, an important and original study in spite of its acknowledged debt to F. R. Leavis, which generates real excitement without ever surrendering its critical balance.

Image and Experience collects a number of essays of which the most important is called "Reflections on a Literary Revolution." It is a book which, Frank Kermode has said, "absolutely requires to be read by anyone who claims an interest in modern literature." Hough's theme is that the modernism of Eliot, Pound, and Joyce (which he calls Imagism) is not after all a watershed in the mainstream of European literature but a fascinating backwater opened by "a few very powerful talents." Eliot's criticism "was not a considered re-direction of the literary sensibility; it was a by-product of the development of his own poetry" and "the peculiar light that seemed to shine from criticism in those days was a borrowed light; its source was . . . in a stormy sun-burst of new creative work." Hough's "counter-revolutionary" essay is amiable in tone and written with a "placid, rather donnish, wit" which, as Kermode implies, half conceals its "almost explosive importance." It is explosive because, while it does not question the talent of "the men of 1914," it does rigorously question their absolute importance, their right to continue to dominate contemporary literature without critical reservations.

Hough's own reservations center on the clinical horrors of what is usually called "the new criticism," and the esoteric and irrational poetry it has tended to encourage. His concern is partly on behalf of the bemused common reader, and he gave some of his reasons for this in a series of BBC lectures published as *The Dream and the Task*. "For a great and increasing number of people in our time," he wrote, "the active agent in shaping their view of life is not religion or philosophy but imaginative literature." He goes on to discuss ways in which literature can be taught, and criticized, so as to help it satisfy "the human need for order."

Hough returns to this theme in his *Essay on Criticism*, which argues that criticism must not be solely moral, or solely concerned with form, but should establish a kind of dialogue between the two considerations. He favors, as he wrote in the *Times Literary Supplement* (July 26, 1963), "the kind of biographical criticism that can see a work in relation to the whole mental and spiritual life of its author." He recognizes the need for "a myth to give coherence and another dimension to daily experience," and believes that such a myth cannot be created out of whole cloth but must be erected upon a fresh understanding of the myths of the past. Without "some such idea" presiding over our imaginative activities, he does not feel that either literature or the criticism of it "can amount to much."

Hough has written instructively and with "extreme clarity" on both Spenser and the romantic poets, and is the author of a number of pleasing and well-made poems, collected in *Legends and Pastorals*. A colleague in the *Times Literary Supplement* wrote of him in 1966: "Mr. Hough, with his wide range of reading in several languages, and his fairness to contrasting points of view, belongs to . . . a tradition that produced such encyclopedic critics as Saintsbury or Ker and, more recently, C. S. Lewis, though Mr. Hough's tone of pleasantly subacid brisk commonsense is quite his own."

In 1958 Hough was visiting professor at Cornell University. He received a Litt.D. from Cambridge in 1961, and is also an honorary D.Litt. of the University of Malaya (1955). He has been married twice, in 1942 to Rosamund Oswell, by whom he has a son and a daughter, and in 1952 to Ingeborg Neumann. His chief relaxation is travel.

PRINCIPAL WORKS: The Last Romantics, 1949; The Romantic Poets, 1953; The Dark Sun, 1956; Image and Experience: Studies in a Literary Revolution, 1960; Legends and Pastorals (poems), 1961; (ed.) Selected Poems of George Meredith, 1962; A Preface to the Faerie Queene, 1962; The Dream and the Task: Literature and Morals in the Culture of Today, 1963; (ed.) Poems of Samuel Taylor Coleridge, 1963; An Essay on Criticism, 1966; Style and Stylistics, 1969.

ABOUT: Kermode, F. Puzzles and Epiphanies, 1962; Who's Who, 1971. *Periodicals*—Times Literary Supplement November 17, 1966.

HOUSE, (ARTHUR) HUMPHRY (May 22, 1908–February 14, 1955), English scholar and critic, was the son of William and Eleanor (Neve) House. Much loved and admired as a man, he also has a very high posthumous reputation as a scholar of exceptional versatility. He was educated at Repton and at Hertford College, Oxford, where he showed brilliant ability from the beginning. In 1929 he received a first class honors degree in *literae humaniores*, and a year later second class honors in modern history.

His career began with a virtual retracing of his educational footsteps: he taught for a year at Repton and in 1931 returned to Oxford as a fellow and lecturer in English at Wadham College. He was ordained the same year in the Church of England, but in 1932 retired into lay life. In 1936, after three years as special assistant lecturer in classics at University College, Exeter, House went to India. He spent a year as professor of English at Presidency College, Calcutta, and then moved to the University of Calcutta as lecturer in English (1937–1940).

In 1940 House returned to England to become William Noble Fellow at Liverpool University, but the same year joined the Royal Armoured Corps as a trooper. It is said that House had no mechanical aptitude, but that he forced himself to

HUMPHRY HOUSE

understand tanks well enough to become an excellent instructor. He was invalided out in May 1945 with the rank of major, having held several staff appointments. After the war House became director of English studies at Peterhouse College, Cambridge. He subsequently returned to Oxford, and was senior university lecturer in English there when he died at the early age of forty-six.

House's field was nineteenth century English literature, where his interests ranged from Coleridge to Gerard Manley Hopkins. Arthur Calder-Marshall has called him "one of the most remarkable men I have ever known for his combination of knowledge and intelligence in literary criticism." He had a passion for detail and organization, but also a great capacity for emotional sympathy with an extraordinary variety of writers. According to Calder-Marshall, he "accepted nothing at second hand, if he could avoid it, going always as close as possible to the original sources, thinking himself back into the mind and mood of the author at the moment of creation."

His unsparing perfectionism, his unwillingness to record an opinion before he had studied every possible source of information and enlightenment, made for a small but extremely valuable literary output. His edition of Hopkins's *Notebooks and Papers* is an indispensable source. His Clark lectures on Coleridge, published in 1953, provide a "thrilling, wise and scholarly examination" of the development of the poet's mind through his notebooks and early drafts; this brief, packed book has had an influence which can scarcely be overestimated.

Even more impressive was House's contribution

to Dickens scholarship. *The Dickens World*, according to John Butt, "was the first serious attempt to examine the novels in the context of Victorian social and economic history, a task to which he brought an immense fund of minute and accurate learning." In 1949 House began the planning and organization of a complete edition of Dickens's letters, a vast enterprise. He was also committed to write a biography of Hopkins, and at the time of his death was overworking desperately in an attempt to complete the lesser project so that he could concentrate on the greater. He left characteristically detailed plans for the Pilgrim Edition of the Dickens letters, and work has continued under the direction of his widow and others. The first of twelve volumes was published in 1965 and greeted as "a model of patient investigation" which "bids fair to be one of the most thorough, scholarly and valuable undertakings of its kind."

House's temperament and learning fused most rewardingly in his annotations. Calder-Marshall says that he "carried the writing of notes to the level of art, a wonderful combination of wit and scholarship." But House could wear his learning lightly, as he did in his articles for such magazines as the *New Statesman* and the *Spectator*, and in his radio talks on literary subjects, which had the warmth, wisdom, and humor of what used to be called "familiar essays." House broadcast frequently, on All India radio in the late 1930s and subsequently on the BBC. In 1948 he became a member of the executive committee of the Radiowriters' Association, and in 1949 joined the committee of management of the Society of Authors. House was married in 1933 to Madeline Church, and had a son and two daughters.

PRINCIPAL WORKS: (ed.) Notebooks and Papers of Gerard Manley Hopkins, 1937 (revised and completed by Graham Storey as Journals and Papers of Gerard Manley Hopkins, 1959); The Dickens World, 1941; Coleridge (the Clark Lectures), 1953; All in Due Time: The Collected Essays and Broadcast Talks of Humphry House, 1955; Aristotle's Poetics: A Course of Eight Lectures, 1956.
ABOUT: Who Was Who, 1951–1960. *Periodicals*—The Listener November 24, 1955; New Statesman March 5, 1955.

HOWARD, ELIZABETH JANE (March 26, 1923–), English novelist, is the daughter of David Liddon and of Katherine M. Howard, who had danced with the Diaghilev ballet. Miss Howard was educated at home. During the war years, after training at the London Mask Theatre School, she acted in repertory in Devon and at Stratford-on-Avon, made use of her blonde and aquiline good looks as a model, and worked in radio and television. In 1947–1950 she was secretary of the Inland Waterways Association, and since then has earned her living as a writer, as a publisher's reader and

ELIZABETH JANE HOWARD

editor, and as a frequent reviewer—from 1959 to 1961 as book critic of *Queen*, the English debutante's vade mecum. She has also contributed to *Encounter*, the *New Yorker*, *Vogue*, and *Town and Country*. In 1962 she was honorary artistic director of the Cheltenham Festival of Contemporary Literature.

Miss Howard won the John Llewellyn Rhys Memorial Prize for her first novel, *The Beautiful Visit*, published when she was twenty-seven. It was a "delicately introspective and vividly photographic" exploration of a young girl's passage to maturity, in which Antonia White found "true imagination and a kind of sensuous power." Miss Howard's theme in this as in her subsequent novels was, according to a writer in the *Times Literary Supplement*, "the flux of relationships at a level of intimacy which demands the most delicate investigation if we are to discover truth, and the most intricate selection of situations that will appear both complete and natural." The situation Miss Howard selected in *The Long View* was the failure of a marriage, which is traced back to its roots in the wife's vulnerable adolescence. In *The Sea Change* a playwright's secretary, by "being her unequivocal and touchingly honest self," rescues her employers from their own moral flabbiness. *After Julius*, organized rather like an English country-house comedy in which the guests' lives "jumble and crystallize in ritual couplings," is (in Miss Howard's own words) "about people who think that by adopting public responsibilities they need not worry about their immediate private ones." Another novel of manners, *Something in Disguise*, contains rather more social comedy than its predecessors, and a touch of skullduggery reminiscent of Agatha Christie. *Odd Girl Out*, which followed in 1972, has been adapted for the stage by Ronald Miller.

The value and importance of Miss Howard's work is very much a matter of opinion. Reviewing *After Julius* in 1965, Kay Dick wrote: "Progressively, over the last decade, Miss Elizabeth Jane Howard has established her position among the women novelists of her generation which is, I suggest, comparable to that of Elizabeth Bowen in the Thirties." The same book's reviewer in the *Times Literary Supplement* also found much to admire, but was irritated by the novel's "jarring artificiality," its "snobbish, over-feminine colouring," the "cliché-ridden sentimentality" of its love scenes. The earlier novels produced similar disagreements. Miss Howard is, as the late Virgilia Peterson pointed out, one of the most accomplished of "those British women writers whose trade mark is their exacerbated sensibility"; it is no doubt for this reason that she is admired more by women than by men, praised more by English critics than by Americans.

Miss Howard's novels, in which the point of view shifts from character to character, require careful planning. Some of her admirers think that she is sometimes in danger of letting "the fascination of perfect technique dominate feeling"; she herself believes that a novel must have "a bone structure, a skeleton that fits and works and can be taken to pieces." She says: "I write straightforward novels in the English tradition, am passionately against obscurity in any form." Miss Howard does not much like to be called a "woman-novelist," but she has been quoted as saying that "women don't know enough to write about men's professions." She says that she does not write about people she knows or things that have happened to her: "That would be too nerve-wracking."

Miss Howard has a daughter, Nicola, by her first (1942) marriage to Peter Scott, the naturalist. She was married again in 1959 to James Douglas-Henry, and for a third time in 1965 to the novelist Kingsley Amis, who contributed some unidentifiable pages to *After Julius*. Miss Howard enjoys all the arts, and also gardening, traveling, and natural history.

PRINCIPAL WORKS: The Beautiful Visit, 1950; (with Robert Aickman) We Are for the Dark: Six Ghost Stories, 1951; The Long View, 1956; (with Arthur Helps) Portrait of Bettina (biography of Bettina von Arnim), 1957; The Sea Change, 1959; After Julius, 1965; Something in Disguise, 1969; Odd Girl Out, 1972.

ABOUT: Burgess, A. The Novel Now, 1967; Contemporary Authors 5–6, 1963; Vinson, J. (ed.) Contemporary Novelists, 1972; Who's Who, 1973. *Periodicals*—Times (London) March 20, 1972.

RICHARD HOWARD

HOWARD, RICHARD (October 13, 1929–), American poet, critic, and translator, was born in Cleveland, Ohio. He attended Columbia University, where he edited the *Columbia Review*, receiving a B.A. in 1951 and an M.A. in 1952. He studied at the Sorbonne on a fellowship in 1952–1953. From 1954 to 1958 he worked as a lexicographer, and since then has earned his living principally as a translator and reviewer.

His first book, *Quantities*, seems to have been admired more than it was enjoyed, for its austere intelligence, exact diction, and strict meters. D. J. Hughes found "many poems that muse on objects of weather and weal in a kind of sour neo-classic manner," and thought the best pieces "those in which a firm narrative or descriptive situation is carried through."

There was a warmer reception for the more intimate and self-revealing poems in *The Damages*. A tentative title for the book had been "Internal Complications," and this suggests very well Howard's method in these poems—a polished surface control contested by a deep interior violence. Lawrence Liberman was especially taken with the longer poems in this collection—"fortresses of poetic structure," he called them, which seemed "capable of sustaining limitless amplification without losing the essential rhythm of experience that is set in motion at the start of each poem."

Thus it was not altogether a surprise that Howard's first unequivocally important book of verse, which brought him a Pulitzer Prize in 1970, should be made up of long poems that are themselves related and unified by a common theme. *Untitled Subjects* (1969) consists of fifteen monologues spoken by Victorian figures, great and small, like Ruskin, Mrs. William Morris, Scott, Gladstone's secretary, and Rossini. "There is," wrote David Kalstone, "a deeper plot which makes this book exhilarating to read whole rather than as detached or detachable poems: its awareness of the evasions and rigidities of history."

What critics found so remarkable was that each of these disparate characters is expressed from within, in a language and tone of his own which is perfectly sustained throughout his monologue. Moreover it is not the public figure or public event that is recorded, but the revealingly intimate recollection or reflection, as when Jane Morris receives from Ruskin a sealed packet of Rossetti's drawings, musing: ". . . and what / he regretted was that he could not bear / to destroy these drawings he would give me / on the condition that I never look at them in my life. / They must be naked / drawings of me, beautiful / indeed if Mr. Ruskin could not burn / what he bought to keep the world and William / from seeing . . ." "These fifteen long poems," wrote a reviewer in *Harper's*, "in the scrupulous yet totally flexible stanzaic and linear forms that pure syllabic verse allows, are inspired blends of the historical and the wholly invented."

Alone With America, published the same year, contains studies of forty-one contemporary poets—not always the most famous but those who deserve attention "because they have achieved, to my sense of it, great things for themselves, for us all." Howard pays little attention to biography, or to schools and movements; his interest is in "free-standing creative figures," and his concern (as in *Untitled Subjects*) is not to judge but to present each of his subjects in his own terms: "What Howard does with each poet," says John Thompson, "is to give himself to each in turn with all the sympathy and with all the understanding he can muster."

This generous and courageous project was greatly praised, as was the overall insight into the state of American poetry that Howard has drawn from it. He believes that American poets set out to achieve absolute mastery of technique and did so, only to find, like King Midas, that wishes come true can be dangerous—that they had become imprisoned in technique. Now, Howard says, they are trying to rid themselves of their accomplishment, striving for open forms, colloquial speech, and a direct relationship with reality—often a more intimate and personal reality than had previously been made the subject of poetry. Hilton Kramer wrote that Howard had brought to this book "a vocabulary of praise far larger, less inhibited, and more illuminating than any we have had from a critic of contemporary poetry."

Richard Howard has been an able, adventurous, and prolific translator from the French; no one has done more to introduce to English readers the work of Butor, Robbe-Grillet, Claude Simon, Barthes, Arrabal, and other influential figures in the French literary avant-garde. In 1970 he became editor of the Braziller Poets series.

PRINCIPAL WORKS: *Poetry*—Quantities, 1962; The Damages, 1967; Untitled Subjects, 1969; Findings, 1971. *Criticism*—Alone With America: The Art of Poetry in the United States Since 1950, 1969.

ABOUT: Murphy, R. (ed.) Contemporary Poets of the English Language, 1970. *Periodicals*—Library Journal November 1, 1962; September 1, 1967; Nation January 5, 1963; November 17, 1969; New Republic December 20, 1969; New York Times Book Review January 25, 1970; Partisan Review Fall, 1959; Publishers' Weekly June 1, 1970; Yale Review Summer 1968.

HOWES, BARBARA (May 1, 1914–), American poet, writes: "Brought up in Chestnut Hill, a suburb of Boston, I attended the Beaver Country Day School. Aside from this rather settled existence, though, I did spend three summers in the West, and traveled moderately. My background was externally at least well ordered and conventional, though I felt, from an early age, at some remove from the situation in which I found myself.

"On the other hand, one of the chief early aids to imaginative development was that for a number of years my mother read aloud to me, thus introducing me to the *sound* of literature and to books I could not have coped with myself. This aural training was of the greatest importance, for poets must refine the ear to catch the shades and nuance of language.

"At the age of eight, I set out to write the story of Robin Hood, not realizing that this had already been done rather thoroughly. After that I continued sporadically to compose stories and verse, but it was not until I attended Bennington College that the thought and desire came to me to work seriously on poetry. Encouraged by the teaching of Genevieve Taggard, who really did open up the eyes of the imagination, and by the fine critical sense of William Troy, I came to understand something of the dimensions of poetry, and also of the complexity of the field. Writing gradually came to be for me not a pastime but a way of keeping up with and dealing with my experience.

"After graduating in 1937, and also after spending two summers with the American Friends Service Committee Work Camps in the South, and one fall in Memphis working for the Southern Tenant Farmers Union which was going through a hazardous period, I came to live in New York. I had by then realized that, whatever my sympathies, the social field was not one in which my imagination operated usefully, and I turned again to my own work. This soon led to my taking over the editorship of the literary quarterly *Chimera*, whose former editors were drafted, and which I ran from 1943 to 1947, when for various reasons I was forced to suspend publication.

"In that year I married the poet William Jay Smith, and we lived first in Oxford where he was studying on a Rhodes Scholarship, and subsequently for two years outside Florence. There also our first son was born. This was an extremely valuable part of my life, as I had never *lived* abroad before, but merely floated through. The physical beauty of Florence and all that I could take in of its spirit made a great impression on me. Though with very little visual sense, and introverted by nature, I am much influenced by *place*, and aware of the special experiences that occur to one because of being in a special location.

"Subsequently we returned to Pownal, Vermont, where we now live, but from time to time went forth and stayed awhile in Haiti, Le Lavandou in the south of France, and Florence once more, when our second son was a baby. Needless to say the family occupied a good deal of my time, but this is as it should be, and I managed to keep in touch with my work as well.

"In 1955 I received a Guggenheim Fellowship, and in 1958 a Brandeis University Creative Arts Poetry Grant.

"I have no special theories about writing, except perhaps that as one never knows what one is going to do, it is boundlessly fascinating to find out. Talent, in so far as one has any, is both a great boon and a great responsibility."

Barbara Howes' poems had been appearing in magazines for ten years before *The Undersea Farmer* was published, and it contained few of the faults usual in first collections. It received nearly universal praise for its freshness and control, and for its "observation, insight, [and] a command of technique beyond competence." Rolfe Humphries recognized a talent manifesting itself in two apparently quite different ways—the "sub-aqueous, soft-green type of lyric" suggested by the book's title, and also in "sharp, incisive satirical comment." Dudley Fitts, whose praise was mixed with reservations about "syntactical confusion" and a certain preciosity of diction in this first book, could find no failures in its successor, *In the Cold Country*, which Louise Bogan announced without hesitation as the work of "the most accomplished woman poet of the youngest generation—one who has found her own voice, chosen her own material, and worked out her own form."

Subsequent works have consolidated Miss Howes' reputation as one of the best poets of her generation (though it must be said that a few critics remain blind to her virtues, regarding her as no more than a competent versifier). The warm and almost un-

BARBARA HOWES

qualified admiration she exacts from so many critics and fellow poets centers upon the tension in her work between a wholly contemporary sensibility, acquainted with pain and confusion, and a classical elegance of expression, often in the most rigid of metrical straitjackets. She is, according to a reviewer in the *Virginia Quarterly Review*, "an intense and coldly controlled poet, even when she is most emotional and most lyrical. Her warmth is always the warmth of hard and multifaceted jewels, catching the light and shivering it into rainbows." The same writer, who was reviewing *Looking Up at Leaves*, called it her best book, "for in it she best forms words into music, hurt into love, and in these poems moves from the shadow of a bad time, 'Leans into and joins' the light."

In *Contemporary Poets of the English Language* (1970) Barbara Howes notes the special influence on her work of Emily Dickinson, Yeats, Frost, and Hopkins. She says that she is interested in the possibilities of free verse, in trying to adapt Old French and other forms to modern or contemporary subjects and emotions, and in "the fascinations and complexities of translation." Miss Howes is the daughter of Osborne Howes, a stockbroker, and of the former Mildred Cox. She received the Bess Hokin Prize in 1949, the Eunice Tietjens Memorial Prize ten years later. *From the Green Antilles*, her selection of writings from the Caribbean, was called a first-rate anthology.

PRINCIPAL WORKS: *Poetry*—The Undersea Farmer, 1948; In the Cold Country, 1954; Light and Dark, 1959; Looking Up at Leaves, 1966. *As editor*—Twenty-Three Modern Stories, 1963; From the Green Antilles: Writings of the Caribbean, 1966; (with Gregory Jay Smith) The Sea-Green Horse: Short Stories for Young People, 1970; The

Eye of the Heart: Short Stories From Latin America, 1973. ABOUT: Bogan, L. Selected Criticism, 1955; Contemporary Authors 9–10, 1964; Howes, B. A View of Poetry *in* Nemerov, H. (ed.) Poets on Poetry, 1966; Murphy, R. (ed.) Contemporary Poets of the English Language, 1970; Untermeyer, L. Modern American Poetry, 1962.

HOYLE, SIR FRED (June 24, 1915–), English astronomer and science fiction writer, was born in Bingley, Yorkshire, the son of Ben and Mabel Hoyle. His mathematical ability and his interest in astronomy were precociously evident, and encouraged by his parents. He taught himself the multiplication tables before he was six, received a three-inch telescope when he was thirteen, and sometimes stayed up all night with it. Hoyle was educated at Bingley Grammar School and Emmanuel College, Cambridge, where he took the mathematical tripos in 1936, winning the Mayhew Prize. He stayed on at Cambridge after his graduation, was the Smith's Prizeman in 1938, and became a Fellow of St. John's College in 1939.

During World War II Hoyle worked for the Admiralty on radar development, squeezing in a little astronomy "under the desk." In 1945 he returned to Cambridge as university lecturer in mathematics, a post he held for thirteen years, and resumed the controversial work he had begun there before the war. Hoyle and his associate Raymond Arthur Lyttleton were seeking nothing less than a new theory of the origin and nature of the universe, and were prepared to bring to bear on the problem all the resources of modern mathematics and physics. Other scientists involved themselves in the work, forming a group who became known as "the Cambridge cosmographers." In the late 1940s they published their "steady-state" theory, which proposes that new stars and galaxies are constantly being formed and constantly retreating farther out into space, but that the universe itself has no beginning and no end, no center and no circumference, but is endlessly expanding, infinite in both time and space. Some discoveries since its formulation have appeared to throw doubt on the steady-state theory; others have tended to justify it: it remains one of several current hypotheses.

Hoyle explained his theories in a series of BBC lectures which were published in 1950 as *The Nature of the Universe* and which caused a heated scientific controversy. Astronomers committed to different opinions complained that he had not distinguished sufficiently between what was proven fact and what was merely the doctrine according to Hoyle. But the "oversimplification" which so enraged his professional opponents made the book "one of the finest pieces of scientific exposition for the layman which has appeared in recent years." It became a best seller, and was called a worthy successor to the work of James Jeans and Arthur Eddington. If "Hoyle and those modern astronomers who share his thinking are wrong," wrote one critic, "they have at least made a magnificent guess." *Frontiers of Astronomy*, describing the whole evolution of inanimate matter, had a similar reception—negative from those who found Hoyle's "dogma" unacceptable and felt that his lively, lucid, and persuasive prose only compounded his guilt; enthusiastically positive from those to whom the book seemed, as one critic wrote, "a turning-point in our understanding of the physical universe" and "one of the most remarkable books in the story of modern science."

FRED HOYLE

In *Man and Materialism* Hoyle has given his views on politics, religion, and a number of other topics which are outside his specialized field but by no means outside the scope of his wide-ranging speculative intelligence. *Of Men and Galaxies*, reprinting Hoyle's John Danz lectures at the University of Washington, argues that man has little left to learn on this planet and must look to the universe as his laboratory if human culture is to advance. *Encounter With the Future*, which includes an autobiographical essay, foresees calamity if the population explosion continues unchecked, but also prophesies that the fittest will survive to rebuild civilization. The five Columbia University Bampton lectures collected in *Man in the Universe* "blast away" at established social and scientific ideas with Hoyle's customary gusto.

Attracted no doubt by a field in which he could pursue his conjectures unrestrained by academic sobriety, Hoyle turned in 1957 to science fiction. The first of his several works in this genre, and perhaps the best of them, was *The Black Cloud.*

This "frolic," as Hoyle called it, is about a gas cloud which invades the solar system, threatening universal darkness, and which is imbued with a vision of the universe so inconceivably strange that it is the death of scientists who are exposed to it. The critics thought it rudimentary in its characterization but greatly enjoyed its "lively logic." G. S. Fraser found "a largeness, generosity, and jollity about the whole spirit of the book that reminds one of the early Wells at his best." *Ossian's Ride*, a mixture of spy thriller and science fiction, was called a "romantic adventure in the true grand manner," rather like a combination of *The Thirty-nine Steps* and *The Man Who Was Thursday*. Hoyle has also written a play for children, *Rockets in Ursa Major*, and—in collaboration with John Elliott—two well-received television serials, *A for Andromeda* and *Andromeda Breakthrough*. A number of his novels have been written in collaboration with his son Geoffrey.

In 1958 Hoyle became Plumian Professor of Astronomy and Experimental Philosophy at Cambridge, and in 1965 he established and became the first director of the university's Institute of Theoretical Astronomy. A dispute over another university appointment in the astronomy department led to his resignation from Cambridge in 1972. Hoyle has been professor of astronomy at the Royal Institution of Great Britain since 1969 and is also on the staff of the Hale Observatories in the United States. He was elected a Fellow of the Royal Society in 1957 and became its vice-president in 1970 (gold medallist 1968, president 1971–1973). He is also a fellow of the Royal Astronomical Society, a member of the British National Committee on Space Research, a member of the Science Research Council, and a foreign associate of the American National Academy of Sciences. He is a firm believer in the popularization of science and in 1968 received the Kalinga Prize for his work in this field. He was knighted in 1972.

Hoyle's work has benefited from two attributes not commonly found in a single individual, an "outstanding gift of physical intuition" and the self-confident individualism which has enabled him to pursue his intuitions, often in the face of widespread opposition. He looks as pugnaciously determined as he is. Hoyle married Barbara Clark in 1939 and has two children, Geoffrey and Elizabeth. He enjoys listening to music, climbing mountains, and playing cricket.

PRINCIPAL WORKS: *Nonfiction*—Some Recent Researches in Solar Physics, 1949; The Nature of the Universe, 1950; A Decade of Decision, 1953; Frontiers of Astronomy, 1955; Man and Materialism, 1956; Astronomy, 1962; Of Men and Galaxies, 1964; Encounter With the Future, 1965; Galaxies, Nuclei, and Quasars, 1965; Man in the Universe, 1966. *Fiction*—The Black Cloud, 1957; Ossian's Ride, 1959; (with John Elliott) A for Andromeda, 1962; (with Geoffrey Hoyle) Fifth Planet, 1963; (with John Elliott) Andromeda Breakthrough, 1964; October the First Is Too Late, 1966; Element 79 (short stories), 1967; (with Geoffrey Hoyle) Rockets in Ursa Major (based on play of the same title), 1969; (with Geoffrey Hoyle) Seven Steps to the Sun, 1970; (with Geoffrey Hoyle) The Molecule Men (two short novels), 1971; (with Geoffrey Hoyle) The Inferno, 1973.

ABOUT: Contemporary Authors 7–8, 1963; Current Biography, 1960; Vinson, J. (ed.) Contemporary Novelists, 1972; Who's Who, 1973. *Periodicals*—Nature October 20, 1945; March 15, 1958; Newsweek February 23, 1959; Science September 15, 1967; Science Newsletter September 1, 1956; July 11, 1959; Scientific American September 1954; Time November 20, 1950; April 21, 1952; September 3, 1956; November 2, 1959; Times (London) February 2, 1968; April 24, 1972; May 18, 1972.

HUGHES, TED (pen name of EDWARD JAMES HUGHES) (August 17, 1930–   ), English poet, is the youngest of the three children of William Henry Hughes, a carpenter, and Edith (Farrar) Hughes. He was born at Mytholmroyd, a mill town in a West Yorkshire valley. Hughes grew up there, roaming the moors and farms under the shadow of a cliff called Scout Rock, which, he says, dominated his childhood: "All that I imagined happening elsewhere, out in the world, the rock sealed from me." And yet: "The mood of the moorland is exultant, and this is what I remember of it."

Hughes was fortunate in his English teachers at Mexborough Grammar School, and with their encouragement began writing poetry at fifteen. About the same time he discovered the work of D. H. Lawrence with a powerful shock of recognition. After two years' compulsory "vegetation" as an RAF mechanic, he took up the scholarship he had won at Pembroke College, Cambridge. There he at first read English, found it pointless, and switched in his final year to anthropology and archaeology, at the same time reading much folklore and poetry—particularly Yeats, whose *Collected Poems* he once knew by heart. Hughes wrote nothing at Cambridge, and thought it "a most deadly institution unless you're aiming to be either a scholar or a gentleman."

After his graduation, he worked at odd jobs—rose gardener, night watchman, and reader for the Rank film studios—and began once more to write. In 1956 he met the American poet Sylvia Plath, married her on Bloomsday (June 16) that year, and spent two years with her in the United States, where both of them taught and wrote, living in Northampton and Boston, and finally made a slow tour of the continent before returning to live in London. Of his life with Sylvia Plath, Hughes has said, "We would write poetry every day. It was all we were interested in, all we ever did. We were like two feet, each one using everything the other ever did." Sylvia Plath committed suicide in 1963. There

TED HUGHES

is an account of this tragedy, some of it disputed by Hughes, in A. Alvarez' *The Savage God* (1971).

Ted Hughes's first volume of poems, *The Hawk in the Rain*, appeared in 1957. It was acclaimed by both British and American critics and won the New York City Poetry Center's First Publication Award and first prize in the 1958 Guinness Poetry Awards. In 1959 Hughes received a Guggenheim Fellowship. More honors, including the Somerset Maugham Award (1960) and the Hawthornden Prize (1961), followed the publication in 1960 of *Lupercal*. Many critics began to speak of him as the most significant English poet to have emerged since World War II.

It was the violence in Hughes's work which exercised his critics and distinguished him from his more academic contemporaries—human violence sometimes, but the violence most often of the beasts and birds of his Yorkshire childhood, captured with "verbal belligerence" in "hectoring physical images." The hawk's path "is direct / Through the bones of the living"; "rain hacks my head to the bone"; in the zoo, "the parrots shriek as if they were on fire" and the jaguar in his cage is "hurrying enraged . . . On a short fierce fuse." Even thrushes on a lawn are "Terrifying. . . . Nothing but bounce / and stab / And a ravening second."

Hughes was accused of morbidity and sadism, but said his work was "not about violence but vitality." His animals are "continually in a state of energy which men only have when they've gone mad. . . . Maybe my poems are about the split personality of modern man, the one behind the constructed, spoilt part." Other critics found more in Hughes's poetry than energy and power. Frederick Grubb drew attention to his very great metrical virtuosity, the subtlety and sensitivity of some of his imagery, the intelligence with which the poet struggles with nature, "arranging it in his mind."

All of these qualities are evident in one of the most quoted of his early poems, "The Thought-Fox," from *Hawk in the Rain*. It begins with the poet alone at night in his house: "I imagine this midnight moment's forest: / Something else is alive / Beside the clock's loneliness / And this blank page where my fingers move." After a while this imagined something takes shape in the poet's mind: "Cold, delicately as the dark snow, / A fox's nose touches twig, leaf; / Two eyes serve a movement. . . . // Till, with a sudden sharp hot stink of fox / It enters the dark hole of the head. / The wind is starless still; the clock ticks, / The page is printed." M. L. Rosenthal wrote: "Something like the effect in this poem of the physical realization of a meaning, quick with its own rank presence, occurs in all the best work of Hughes."

After *Lupercal*, Hughes published no new volume of adult verse for seven years. Meanwhile he wrote a great deal for radio, undertook a number of editorial chores, and published several volumes of prose and verse for tough-minded children—books which in their fantasy and extravagance recall Edward Lear (and sometimes Charles Addams).

Wodwo appeared in 1967—a collection of forty poems, five short stories or prose poems, and "The Wound," a radio play first broadcast in 1962. The volume brought Hughes the City of Florence International Poetry Prize in 1969, but disappointed most English and American critics. It takes its title from one of the beasts encountered by Sir Gawain in the fourteenth-century romance *Sir Gawain and the Green Knight*. One reviewer wrote that "Gawain, locked into a system of frozen Christian morality in a world bristling with animistic terrors, bound on a mission gratuitously inexplicable" is a highly appropriate symbol of Hughes's view of man. The collection contained fresh evidence of the poet's "gift for fierce and thrilling natural observation," but also of his relatively superficial and scornful vision of the human world. Reviewers complained moreover of "flailingly portentous verbiage," elusive rhythms, and "deep authorial evasiveness."

If, as some readers suggested, *Wodwo* was a transitional volume, the transition was accomplished in the book that followed, *Crow*. Crow (the figure was suggested to Hughes by the artist Leonard Baskin) is a scrawny carrion eater, a black-feathered feaster on death. He is also the personification of the survival instinct—a shaman of unbelief who, having no hope and no illusions, is thoroughly at home in a world which is and always has been without shape or reason or love. And he speaks for the poet, sardonically observing the predictable failures of God and man, the endless comedy of carnage, lust, and chaos which is our history and destiny.

In the beginning, God begat Nothing, "Who begat Never / Never Never Never / Who begat Crow— // Screaming for Blood / Grubs, crusts / Anything // Trembling featherless elbows in the nest's filth." Crow is with Adam and Eve in the Garden. He helpfully tries "Nailing heaven and earth together" but finds that "Man could not be man nor God God." Never mind; Crow survives. In various roles and guises Crow battles with nature, man, and God, and survives. He is present at the Crucifixion and "When God went off in despair / Crow stropped his beak and started in on the two thieves." Crow's songs are simple and ugly, repetitive and violent, "plain songs for an apocalypse."

One reviewer called the book self-indulgent, "a cozy, unperplexing wallow," and Stephen Spender thought it presented only a partial, "blankly pessimistic" view of life, but the response was in general overwhelmingly favorable. Daniel Hoffman said: "This is no mere book of verses, but a wild yet cunning wail of anguish and resilience, at once contemporary, immediate, and as atavistic as the archaic myths it resembles." Peter Porter wrote: "English poetry has found a new hero and nobody will be able to read or write verse now without the black shape of Crow falling across the page."

For Ted Hughes, poetry is "the record of just how the forces of the universe try to redress some balance disturbed by human error." He has acknowledged the debts he has contracted at various stages in his career to Dylan Thomas and D. H. Lawrence, Yeats and Donne, Chaucer and Shakespeare, but says, "Blake I connect inwardly with Beethoven, and if I could dig to the bottom of my strata maybe their names and works would be the deepest traces."

Poetry in the Making is a collection of talks delivered by Hughes on one of the BBC's programs for schools, using poems by himself and others to illustrate what he has to say about why and how poetry is written. The book is of special interest for what it reveals about Hughes's own outlook and methods. Four of his excellent plays for educational radio have been collected as *The Coming of the Kings*. His adaptation of Seneca's *Oedipus* was produced at the National Theatre in 1968. Hughes is also the author of a remarkable play, *Orghast*, which was given in 1971 at the Shiraz Festival in Iran by Peter Brook's International Center for Theatre Research. "Orghast" is also the name of the language, devised by Hughes, in which most of the play is written. According to Tom Stoppard, writing in the *Times Literary Supplement* (October 1, 1971), Orghast works on the premise "that the *sound* of the human voice, as opposed to language, is capable of projecting very complex mental states." It remains to be seen, as Stoppard says, whether the language contains "the seeds of a unique form of drama, or is just a gigantic clue to a psychoanalysis of its own author." Hughes has continued to work (in Africa and elsewhere) with the International Center for Theatre Research which is conducting, it has been said, "the most significant, radical and sustained research in the theatre today."

Ted Hughes is a tense, tall, dark man. He retains in his speech the West Yorkshire accent, which he finds "both eloquent and emphatic," and which can be heard in his poetry. He has two children by Sylvia Plath and was married in 1970 to Carol Orchard. Hughes is widely regarded as one of the two or three most distinguished English poets of his generation.

PRINCIPAL WORKS: *Poetry*—The Hawk in the Rain, 1957; Lupercal, 1960; Selected Poems of Ted Hughes and Thom Gunn, 1962; Wodwo, 1967; Crow: From the Life and Songs of the Crow, 1970; Selected Poems, 1973. *For children*—Meet My Folks!, 1961; The Earth-Owl and Other Moon-People, 1963; How the Whale Became, 1963; Nessie the Mannerless Monster, 1964; Poetry in the Making: An Anthology of Poems and Programmes from Listening and Writing, 1968 (U.S., Poetry Is, 1970); The Iron Man, 1968 (U.S., The Iron Giant); The Coming of the Kings and Other Plays, 1970. *As editor*—The Selected Poems of Keith Douglas, 1964; A Choice of Emily Dickinson's Verse, 1968; A Choice of Shakespeare's Verse, 1971. *As translator*—Seneca's Oedipus, 1969.

ABOUT: Alvarez, A. The Savage God, 1971; Finn, F. S. (ed.) Poets of our Time, 1965; Grubb, F. A. Vision of Reality, 1965; Press, J. Rule and Energy, 1963; Rosenthal, M. L. The New Poets, 1967; Who's Who, 1972; Writers on Themselves, 1964. *Periodicals*—Cambridge Quarterly Autumn 1967; Summer–Autumn 1971; Commonweal September 17, 1971; Critical Quarterly Spring 1971; Daily Telegraph Magazine September 17, 1971; Delta Winter 1961; February 1968; English Autumn 1963; Essays in Criticism January 1965; Guardian March 23, 1965; London Magazine January 1971; Newsweek April 12, 1971; Notes and Queries February 15, 1968; Poetry February 1972; Saturday Review October 2, 1971; Times Literary Supplement January 8, 1971; October 1, 1971.

HUMPHREY, WILLIAM (June 18, 1924–), American novelist, was born at Clarksville, in the Red River country of Texas which has been the scene of most of his writing. He is very reticent about his personal life. According to James W. Lee's monograph, Humphrey was quiet and withdrawn as a child, when a slight deformity obliged him to wear leg braces. In 1938 his father was killed in an automobile accident, and he and his mother moved to Dallas, where he finished high school. He completed his education at the University of Texas. In the early 1940s Humphrey went to New York, hoping to find a producer for a play about Benjamin Franklin. The play was not produced, but Humphrey remained in New York, earning

WILLIAM HUMPHREY

his living as a teacher, and soon began to sell his short stories to such magazines as the *New Yorker*, the *Sewanee Review*, and *Harper's Bazaar*. His first book, *The Last Husband and Other Stories*, was praised for its originality, sympathy, and wit, and for the powers of observation it displayed, though some reviewers noted a tendency for these stories to falter towards the end, leaving the reader with a mild sense of disappointment.

Humphrey's reputation was established by his first novel, *Home From the Hill*. It is set in the Red River country, on the border between Texas and Oklahoma. The story centers on the coming to manhood of Theron, son of the hunter and woodsman Captain Wade Hunnicutt, and his embittered wife, who destroys Theron's first love affair by revealing to him his father's reputation as a lecher. Theron rejects his father and the girl he has made pregnant. The ensuing tensions end in the death of both men and the fall of the house of Hunnicutt. Elizabeth Bowen called the book a "tragic masterpiece," and William Goyen wrote: "It displays the painstaking consideration of an artist for his tradition; it is also a story of fatal contretemps, macabre color and theatrical ingenuity. Despite its faults of over-projection, this novel, it seems to this reader, is one of the most distinguished firsts by a young writer . . . to appear in some years." Indeed the book was very widely and warmly praised, especially for its magnificent hunting scenes and sense of masculine character, and had a considerable popular success, though not all the critical admiration was unqualified. Walter Allen, for example, found the tragic situation forced and arbitrary, concluding that "what Mr. Humphrey gives us is a piece of Faulkner in which the obscurities have been clarified and the crooked made straight."

The Ordways, another Faulknerian family chronicle, though it has its share of tragedy and horror, draws more on the master's comic manner. It opens at the Ordways' grave-tending day in Clarksville, an annual family gathering, and develops into a picaresque account of the family's colorful past—what F. J. Hoffman called "a romp through history and geography." The tale is told of the epic journey of great-grandfather Thomas Ordway who, blinded and horribly mutilated at Shiloh, nevertheless brought his family by covered wagon from Tennessee to Texas. This leads into the story of Sam Ordway, born on that journey, and his own subsequent odyssey in search of his son Ned after the baby has been kidnapped by neighbors.

L. D. Rubin has pointed out that "the novel divides into two stories, the olden day events and the modern, with an unbridgeable artistic gulf between them"; and there were other complaints about the book's rambling structure. However, these considerations weighed less with most readers than Humphrey's skill as a storyteller and his "genuinely comic vision," and the book became a best seller. "*The Ordways* isn't a perfect book," wrote Elizabeth Janeway, "it's just a terribly good one, expansive, exploratory, with breathing space for its characters and their humors. . . . What's more, the way Humphrey handles the language is astonishing and individual. Funny, vivid and moving, this is a fine piece of work and a delight to read."

There was a generally enthusiastic response to the stories collected in *A Time and a Place*, all of them set in East Texas and Oklahoma during the Depression. Granville Hicks wrote: "The place at that time was a place of desperation and violence [but] the people endured and were even hopeful, hoping for oil, hoping for rain. . . . They were rough people in a rough age, but there was drama in their lives, and Humphrey knows how to reveal it to us." Humphrey's third novel, *Proud Flesh*, seemed to Christopher Lehmann-Haupt a mistake —"the Southern gothic imagination gone rococo."

Most critics are agreed that Humphrey has not so far shown himself to be an innovator; that he is content to work within a vision of life that he has inherited from other writers, notably Faulkner and Mark Twain. James W. Lee nevertheless believes that he "will prove to be the best novelist to come out of Texas. He has the potential to be one of the best writers of his generation. . . . He writes the kind of regional literature that can easily progress from the local to the universal." *The Spawning Run* is a "charming and mischievous" account of a vacation which Humphrey and his wife spent at a

Welsh fishing inn, where some of their fellow-sportsmen had declared open season not only on the Atlantic salmon but on other men's wives.

PRINCIPAL WORKS: The Last Husband and Other Stories, 1953; Home From the Hill, 1958; The Ordways, 1965; A Time and a Place (stories), 1968; The Spawning Run, illustrated by Owen Wood, 1970; Proud Flesh, 1973.
ABOUT: Hoffman, F. J. The Art of Southern Fiction, 1967; Lee, J. W. William Humphrey, 1967; Rubin, L. D. The Curious Death of the Novel, 1967; Vinson, J. (ed.) Contemporary Novelists, 1972. *Periodicals*—Book Week January 31, 1965; Chicago Sunday Tribune January 12, 1958; Commonweal February 28, 1958; Library Journal October 15, 1968; Nation February 22, 1958; New Republic February 27, 1965; New Statesman April 12, 1958; New York Herald Tribune Book Review January 12, 1958; New York Times Book Review January 12, 1958; July 19, 1964; January 31, 1965; New Yorker April 11, 1953; February 8, 1958; Saturday Review January 11, 1958; February 6, 1965; November 9, 1968; Sewanee Review LXXIII 1965; Times Literary Supplement June 17, 1965.

HUMPHREYS, EMYR (OWEN) (April 15, 1919–), Welsh novelist, writes: "At the time of writing, I am forty-six. I live with my wife and three of our four children (our eldest son is at college) in an old farmhouse on the island of Anglesey. Like most people here we are Welsh-speaking and but for an historical accident all my writing would have been in that language. I myself was born in Flintshire, the son of a schoolmaster, in an anglicised sea-side resort. As it is, my allegiance is to Welshness and I believe in all the political independence that is necessary to preserve and strengthen it. The Welsh language is as noble as the Welsh landscape and it enshrines a literature and a literary tradition that has flourished without a break from the sixth century to the present day. The Welsh community has been defined by a history that embraces both the real and the legendary Arthur; a pantheon of Celtic gods turned into characters of flesh and blood by anonymous medieval story-tellers; the fiery Owen Glyndwr and his kinsman the amorous Owen Tudor; the anglicised gentry of the Tudor and Stuart courts and the self-educated peasants that created the non-conformist theocracies of the eighteenth and nineteenth centuries.

"Small nations, like small men, can be boringly self-assertive; but I like to think that in an age of unrestricted mass communication and vast social economic change, the small nation can reinforce the sense of meaningful community that binds individuals together. The small nation can preserve a vision of the past and of the future and make it available from generation to generation as a vital tradition that enriches life and gives it meaning and colour. As a writer I feel I draw strength from this tradition. I am continuously aware of it and this creates what I imagine to be a fruitful state of tension between my individual talent and a long tradition of literary art of which I am only a small part at this point in time.

"Not all my life has been spent in Wales and not all my novels are about Wales. During and after the war I lived in Italy; for three years I was a school teacher in London; for eight years or more I worked for the BBC in radio and television; and these experiences inform part of my work. Whether they have enriched it in any way is not for me to say; but in the end I hope to be regarded as another voice added to a literary tradition of 'cyfarwydd' [storytelling] that has belonged from the beginning of recorded time to a culture that is the original joy and beauty of the island of Britain. Every man has his own image of history and this can usually be related to his view of the human condition. In our day small countries seem doomed to be absorbed by their greater neighbours and the struggle for survival seems so certain to fail that it is impossible either to sing like Negroes about overcoming some day or to serve like ex-Nazis in high positions in some glittering new order. Nevertheless the prospect of failure has its own forms of dignity. There is a sense in which the lost cause is the more accurate reflection of the human condition. In saying this I must add that I do not want to share in any of the fashionable forms of despair. To be reconciled to finitude, to accept the prospect of failure, should also imply a positive sense of progress. The future is no less of a spring-time because it is due to happen to others. To practise an art is to be on the side of the future. But much more important than this, we have to re-acquire the gift of hearing and feeling the pulse of worship that must throb under the process of living."

Two of Emyr Humphreys' novels have received major literary awards in England. *Hear and Forgive*, portraying with fine insight the petty intrigues and the jealousies in a school staff room, received the Somerset Maugham Award. *A Toy Epic*, awarded the Hawthornden Prize, records in their own words the different but subtly interrelated experiences of three Welsh boys, and was much praised for the elegance and economy of its construction. J. D. Scott noted that the characters "change and grow, revealing new aspects, new 'characters' that strike themselves and us with an echoing surprise"; and that the novel leaves behind it a "sense of the mystery of human personality."

For his skill in construction, the subtlety and compassion of his insight, and his scrupulous prose, Emyr Humphreys has been one of the most consistently and variously praised British novelists of his generation. He has all the equipment of a major

EMYR HUMPHREYS

writer except, it has been said, a certain necessary vitality, a willingness to take risks. Humphreys has also written a number of plays. *King's Daughter*, adapted from a play by Saunders Lewis, was staged in London in 1959 and produced on television the following year as *Siwan.*

He was educated at Rhyl Grammar School and at the university colleges of Aberystwyth and Bangor. From 1948 to 1950 he taught at Wimbledon Technical College, and from 1951 to 1954 at Pwllheli Grammar School in North Wales. He joined the British Broadcasting Corporation in 1955, until 1958 working in Cardiff as a radio producer, and from then until 1962 producing plays for television. From 1962 to 1965 he was a freelance writer and director, and since then he has lectured in drama at the University College of Bangor. He is a member of the Welsh Arts Council. Humphreys was married in 1946 to Elinor Myfanwy Jones and has four children. Marianglas, the isolated village in which he lives with his family, can be found only on the largest scale map. Humphreys is slim, dark, typically Welsh in features.

PRINCIPAL WORKS: The Little Kingdom, 1946; The Voice of a Stranger, 1949; A Change of Heart, 1951; Hear and Forgive, 1952; A Man's Estate, 1955; The Italian Wife, 1957; A Toy Epic, 1958; Y Tri Llais (Welsh version of A Toy Epic), 1958; Siwan (play), *in* Plays of the Year, 1959–1960; The Gift, 1963; Outside the House of Baal, 1965; Natives, 1968; Ancestor Worship: A Cycle of Eighteen Poems, 1970; (with W. S. Jones) Dinas (play in Welsh), 1970; National Winner, 1971.

ABOUT: Allen, W. The Novel Today, 1960; Contemporary Authors 7–8, 1963; Jones, G. The Dragon Has Two Tongues, 1969; Vinson, J. (ed.) Contemporary Novelists, 1972; Who's Who, 1973. *Periodicals*—Times Literary Supplement November 11, 1955; May 27, 1965.

HUNTER, EVAN (**"Ed McBain," etc., pseudonyms**) (October 15, 1926–), American author of novels, short stories, and plays, has published some of his work under the pseudonyms of Richard Marsten, Hunt Collins, and Ed McBain, as well as under his legally assumed name of Evan Hunter. He was born in New York City's "Italian Harlem" section and grew up in the Bronx, the only child of Charles F. Lombino, a postman, and Marie (Coppola) Lombino. At Evander Childs High School in the Bronx he showed much promise in art and later attended classes at the Art Students League and at Cooper Union Art School. During his two years of service in the Navy in World War II (1944–1946), he began to write stories, and when he returned home in 1946 he decided to become an author rather than an artist. He majored in English at Hunter College, graduating in 1950 with a Phi Beta Kappa key and a B.A. degree.

During the next three years, Hunter worked briefly as a teacher and as a salesman, and from 1951 to 1953 as an editor for the Scott Meredith Literary Agency. His evenings he spent writing. Hunter published about a hundred articles, stories, and juvenile books—some under pseudonyms—before reaching the best-seller list in 1954 and shocking much of the nation with *The Blackboard Jungle*, which Metro-Goldwyn-Mayer made into a film the following year. For his dramatic story of the ordeals of an inexperienced, idealistic teacher facing a classroom of juvenile delinquents, he drew on his own six-month struggle as a teacher in two New York vocational high schools and on extensive research into conditions in schools throughout the city.

A fast-paced style, realistic language, and authentic setting are among the chief merits of *The Blackboard Jungle* and most of Hunter's later work. For his novel of drug addiction, *Second Ending*, he used jazz jargon to help create a convincing musical background, probably derived in part from his own youthful experience as a pianist with a swing band. In *The Spiked Heel*, published under the name of Richard Marsten, he displayed an impressive specialized knowledge of the high-fashion shoe industry. With similar regard for clinical minutiae he detailed the mechanics of marital infidelity in his 1958 best seller, *Strangers When We Meet*, while his family chronicle *Sons* involved research into such disparate subjects as lumberjacking, Chicago (where he had never been), and the conduct of bombing missions in World War II.

Hunter also wrote the screenplay for the film *Strangers When We Meet* (1960), as well as for Alfred Hitchcock's *The Birds* (1963). One of his eight stage plays, produced in England as *The Easter Man* in 1964, reached Broadway the following year as *A Race of Hairy Men!* Another, *The*

EVAN HUNTER

Conjuror, was staged at Ann Arbor, Michigan, in 1969. His reputation, however, rests on his novels. Critical opinion has been rather sharply divided over Hunter's skill in developing fresh and fully realized characters, plots, and themes in his "straight" novels, although his competence otherwise as a craftsman has won fairly general acknowledgement. Hunter is, as Al Morgan has said, "a thoroughly professional writer: a 'pro.' His style has drive, pace, tempo and authenticity."

The best known of his detective stories are those (by "Ed McBain") featuring the 87th Precinct police detective squad, which became the basis of a weekly television program, *87th Precinct*. Both James Sandoe, formerly of the New York *Herald Tribune*, and the late Anthony Boucher, of the New York *Times*, were longtime admirers of McBain and repeatedly praised the ingenuity and vitality with which he handles his formula, his knowledge of police procedures, and his adroitness in sustaining tension. Some of the more recent 87th Precinct novels have had a strong element of often rather ghoulish humor and one of these, *Fuzz* (1968), was filmed with great success in 1972 from the author's own screenplay. Hunter nowadays also writes a great deal for television, runs his own film production company, Javelin Productions, and early in 1973 was at work on several screenplays and a stage musical, as well as novels.

Evan Hunter and Anita Melnick were married on October 17, 1949 and have three children, Ted, Mark, and Richard. In what was described in *Time* as "a wacky product of togetherness," the family produced *The Remarkable Harry* (1960) for which the children drew the pictures, the mother wrote the introduction, and the father told the story in tongue-twisting verse. Hunter, a six-footer with brown hair and blue eyes, enjoys making home movies, skiing, and snorkeling.

PRINCIPAL WORKS: *As Evan Hunter*—Find the Feathered Serpent, 1952; The Blackboard Jungle, 1954; Second Ending, 1956; Strangers When We Meet, 1958; A Matter of Conviction, 1959; The Remarkable Harry, 1960; The Last Spin and Other Stories, 1960; Mothers and Daughters, 1961; The Wonderful Button, 1961; Happy New Year, Herbie, and Other Stories, 1963; Buddwing, 1964; The Easter Man (play), 1964; The Paper Dragon, 1966; A Horse's Head, 1967; Last Summer, 1968; Sons, 1969; Nobody Knew They Were There, 1971; The Easter Man: A Play and Six Stories, 1972; Seven, 1972; Every Little Crook and Nanny, 1972; Come Winter, 1973. *As "Hunt Collins"*—Cut Me In, 1954; Tomorrow's World, 1956. *As "Ed McBain"*—Cop Hater, 1956; The Mugger, 1956; The Pusher, 1956; The Con Man, 1957; Killer's Choice, 1958; Killer's Payoff, 1958; Lady Killer, 1958; etc. *As "Richard Marsten"*—Rocket to Luna, 1953; Danger: Dinosaurs!, 1953; The Spiked Heel, 1956; Vanishing Ladies, 1961.

ABOUT: Current Biography, 1956; Vinson, J. (ed.) Contemporary Novelists, 1972; Who's Who in America, 1972–1973. *Periodicals*—New York Times Book Review August 3, 1958.

***HUSSERL, EDMUND** (April 8, 1859–April 27, 1938), German philosopher, was born at Prossnitz, Moravia. After early studies in mathematics, in which he gained a doctorate in 1881, he turned to philosophy, working in Vienna under Franz Brentano from 1884 to 1886. Until his retirement in 1929 he taught at the universities of Halle (1887–1901), Göttingen (1901–1916) and Freiburg-im-Breisgau (1916–1929). As a Jew (and in spite of his conversion to Protestantism in his youth) he was exposed in his later years to much Nazi harassment, including the removal of most of his honors and distinctions.

He was a philosopher of the utmost seriousness and dedication and his life, being passed wholly in academic surroundings, is devoid of interesting outward incident. His immensely copious writings have next to no literary interest and in their dense technicality testify to the thoroughness of his commitment to the project of developing a truly scientific philosophy. Agreeing with most philosophers since Descartes and Kant that philosophy is first and foremost a study of the mind and its workings, he began to press further Brentano's distinction between two ways in which this study could be carried out. The first, Brentano's "genetic psychology," is an empirical inquiry into the external causes and conditions of mental states, exemplified in philosophy in the work of Herbert Spencer and John Stuart Mill. The second and preferred procedure is that of Brentano's "descriptive psychology," which is concerned with mental acts and states as they appear or are given to the mind and

*hoos′ erl

EDMUND HUSSERL

not with their relations to the brain, the body, and the external world.

In Brentano's view the mind is reflexively aware of all its activities and mental acts—which, indeed, are the only things of which we can have immediate and indubitable knowledge. For him the distinguishing feature of the mental is what he called its "intentionality," that is, its property of pointing or referring to some object, whether existent or nonexistent.

In Husserl's first book, *Philosophie der Arithmetik* (1891), this technique of reflexively scrutinizing mental acts is applied to the fundamental concepts of mathematics, the idea of number, for example, being interpreted in terms of the mental activity of counting. This work elicited a penetrating criticism from the great logician and mathematical philosopher Gottlob Frege, who argued that Husserl had not succeeded in his aim of carrying out a pure or nonempirical study of the mathematical operations of the mind. To Frege, Brentano's "descriptive psychology" was still psychology, an empirical natural science.

Husserl recognized the justice of this criticism and in his *Logische Untersuchungen* (1900–1901, translated as *Logical Investigations*) worked out, as a response to it, the phenomenological method with which his name is preeminently associated. His aim was to distinguish the phenomenological study of consciousness from any sort of empirical psychology in two ways: by an account of its special method and by an account of its special objects. Its method, Husserl insists, is rendered pure, nonempirical, and thus capable of yielding indubitable results by the procedure of "bracketing" or "transcendental reduction"—in other words by a complete suspension of belief about the actual existence of the intentional objects of consciousness and by exclusive concentration on them as they are given or appear to the mind. Its proper objects are not empirical mental events, occurring at a particular time in a particular mental history, but are essences, abstract and purely conceptual entities, capable of serving as the structure of distinct mental happenings.

Phenomenology, for Husserl, is a true philosophical science. By means of its "eidetic intuition" of essences, a nonempirical awareness of nonempirical objects, it can arrive at truths which are necessary, eternal, indubitable and objective. By reason of the suspension of belief that it involves, its results are not weakened by dependence on any of the familiar conventional assumptions about matters of fact which it is the business of a true philosophy to criticize.

By 1907 Husserl was ready to make a further move away from the Brentano-like position of *Logische Untersuchungen* and, in the view of his critics, towards a position that is not fundamentally distinguishable from the more extravagant kind of German idealism in which mind is seen as constituting the world. In his *Ideen* (translated by W. R. Boyce Gibson as *Ideas*), first written in 1907 but not published until 1913, he maintains, in a way that recalls Descartes, that the primary objects revealed by the phenomenological scrutiny of the mind are a pure consciousness or transcendental ego (Descartes's *res cogitans* or thinking substance) and its dependent objects, about whose actual existence judgment is suspended. Only things which exist for and in the pure transcendental consciousness are objects of certain knowledge, an unequivocally idealistic conclusion.

In *Méditations cartésiennes* (based on lectures given in Paris in 1929 and translated by Dorion Cairns as *Cartesian Meditations*), Husserl denied that the pure consciousness which is the basic Archimedean point of his system is to be conceived in a subjective way, as the consciousness of a particular individual; Husserl's argument was thus a revival of Kant's doctrine of consciousness-in-general, which went only a little way to meet the objections of his critics.

Although Husserl was the inventor of the phenomenological method he was not perhaps its most successful user. It was to prove most fruitful in the hands of those who were unwilling to follow Husserl into the abstract idealistic speculations of his later years: most notably Max Scheler, and also Heidegger, Merleau-Ponty, and Sartre. It is ironic that the most relentlessly academic of twentieth century philosophers should have devised an instrument which underlay existentialism, the most emotionally engaged philosophical movement of the age.

PRINCIPAL WORKS IN ENGLISH TRANSLATION: Ideas: A General Introduction to Pure Phenomenology, 1931; The Phenomenology of Internal Time-Consciousness (ed. by Martin Heidegger), 1964; Phenomenology and the Crisis of Philosophy, 1965; Cartesian Meditations: An Introduction to Phenomenology, 1966; The Idea of Phenomenology, 1966; The Paris Lectures, 1966; Formal and Transcendental Logic, 1969; Logical Investigations, 1970. ABOUT: Farber, M. (ed.) Philosophical Essays in Memory of Edmund Husserl, 1940; Farber, M. The Foundation of Phenomenology, 1943; Gilson, E. H. Recent Philosophy, 1966; Laszlo, E. Beyond Scepticism and Reality, 1966; Lauer, J. Q. Triumph of Subjectivity, 1958; Mohanty, J. N. Edmund Husserl's Theory of Meaning, 1964; Osborn, A. D. Edmund Husserl and His Logical Investigations, 1949; Ryan, J. K. Twentieth-Century Thinkers, 1965; Sartre, J.-P. Transcendence of the Ego, 1957; Sokolowski, R. The Formation of Husserl's Concept of Constitution, 1964; Welch, E. P. The Philosophy of Edmund Husserl, 1965. *Periodicals*—International Philosophical Quarterly March 1967; Journal of Philosophy April 27, 1939; January 4, 1940; Review of Metaphysics July 1966; Review of Philosophy July 1938; January 1940.

MAUDE HUTCHINS

HUTCHINS, MAUDE (PHELPS McVEIGH) (1889?–), American novelist, short story writer, dramatist, and poet, whose ancestors include early New England colonists, was born in New York City, the daughter of Warren Ratcliffe and Maude (Phelps) McVeigh. She grew up on Long Island, New York, and received her secondary education at St. Margaret's School in Waterbury, Connecticut. In 1921 she married the noted educator and author Robert Maynard Hutchins. Three daughters were born of the marriage, which was dissolved in 1948.

Mrs. Hutchins received the degree of Bachelor of Fine Arts in sculpture from Yale University in 1926. She gave frequent one-man shows of painting and sculpture during the 1930s and 1940s, and has exhibited in some of America's leading art museums and galleries. Her diverse and often controversial work has also included pottery design and an illustrated edition of Shakespeare's sonnets. She caused something of a stir in Chicago art circles with the book *Diagrammatics* (1932), in which her subconscious "doodlings"—mostly sketches of nude female figures—were provided with psychological interpretations by Mortimer Adler.

When during the late 1940s her work in the visual arts ceased to satisfy her, Mrs. Hutchins turned to literature. One of her first literary works was the play *The Case of Astrolabe*, about a fictitious love child of Abelard and Heloise. It surprised no one who knew her work in other fields that the play reflected a "sublime lack of reverence for antique stuffiness"—or that the same quality has characterized the fictions which followed.

The first of these was *Georgiana*, which traces the emotional development of a sensitive girl from childhood to maturity. Its perceptions pleased a few reviewers, but most were shocked by its frankness and unimpressed by its style. *A Diary of Love* covered rather similar ground, examining in diary form the libidinal history of Noel, a girl who is raised in a sexually charged, "emancipated" household, contracts tuberculosis, and spends three years in the hectic, nightmarish atmosphere of a desert sanitarium. The book, conceived in Freudian terms, seems to take its final stand against the "exhausting freedom" of Noel's upbringing in a way more reminiscent of Mrs. Hutchins' Puritan ancestors. There was great praise for her "vivid, strange, and sometimes brilliant" evocation of life in the sanitarium, and for her portrayal of the growth of love, at first "diffuse and troubling," later localized in Noel's feeling for her cousin Dominick. *Newsweek*, reporting that the book had been banned in Chicago, said that "the narrative jerks and ricochets" and called it not a masterpiece but merely notes for one. Maxwell Geismar thought it a "beautiful little book," but some reviewers were horrified by its preoccupation with physical love. This did not prevent it from achieving considerable popularity. It was translated into a number of foreign languages—into Italian by Mrs. Hutchins—and is probably still her best-known book.

Love Is a Pie was described by Virgilia Peterson as "an uneven, unconventional collection of the imaginings of a sensitive, raw-nerved writer" (who nevertheless struck another reviewer as being "curiously aloof and unemotional"). In the novels which have followed, Mrs. Hutchins has continued to write about love in her own unclassifiable way, and to divide and often confuse her critics with what Stanley Kauffmann has called "a kind of attractive arrogance." Among the more notable of her recent books are *Honey on the Moon* and *Blood on the Doves*, both of which freely mix realism and fantasy. The first, which includes "all the frustrations and ugliness of distorted, perverted, and abnormal love," seemed to Maxwell Geismar "a curious postscript" to *Diary of Love*, "a nostalgic memory of a lost Eden" (but was read by *Commonweal's* reviewer as "pure grade 'B' melodrama"). *Blood on the Doves*, a tragic story about an Ozark family, includes among its fantasies one in which Mrs. Hutchins imagines her own rape and draws from this notion "a startling insight into killing in general and war in particular."

Mrs. Hutchins, who is an O. Henry Prize winner, has published one volume of short stories, *The Elevator* (1962). She has contributed many stories and poems to major magazines, including the *New Yorker*, *Poetry*, and *Vogue*. The mood and style of Mrs. Hutchins' work has reminded a number of critics of Colette (and one of "a lascivious Ivy Compton-Burnett"). Maxwell Geismar speaks of her as a "unique and original voice in our literature" and Virgilia Peterson wrote: "Wayward alike in innocence and precocity, cultivated, talented, erratic, bewitched, she defies analysis. She is a literary curiosity." A "tall, slim and extremely handsome woman," Maude Hutchins lives in Southport, Connecticut. She no longer flies her own airplane but still paints and sculpts when she can spare time from her writing and from the meticulous research imposed by her passion for accuracy.

PRINCIPAL WORKS: Georgiana, 1948; A Diary of Love, 1950; Love Is a Pie, 1952; My Hero, 1953; Memoirs of Maisie, 1955; Victorine, 1959; The Elevator, 1962; Honey on the Moon, 1964; Blood on the Doves, 1965; The Unbelievers Downstairs, 1967.

ABOUT: Vinson, J. (ed.) Contemporary Novelists, 1972; Who's Who in America, 1972–1973. *Periodicals*—Art Digest August 1947.

HUXLEY, ELSPETH (JOSCELINE) (July 23, 1907–), English novelist, memoirist, and authority on African affairs, was born in London, the only daughter of Major Josceline Grant and the former Eleanour Grosvenor. Her father was of a Scottish family which had helped to found both the Virginia Company and the East India Company, and which was thereafter associated with India and the Indian Civil Service. Major Grant, who had been to Africa as a young man, emigrated after his marriage to what is now Kenya, and started a coffee plantation about forty miles from Nairobi. His daughter grew up there from the age of five at a time when "Mau Mau was still a long way in the future," finding her companions mostly

ELSPETH HUXLEY

among the local Kikuyu, and riding her pony freely across the Kikuyu reserve.

She had some schooling in England during World War I, when her father was in the army. The family was reunited in Kenya in 1920 and in 1924–1925 Elspeth Grant studied for a year at a school for European children in Nairobi. In 1925 she returned to England to earn her diploma in agriculture at Reading University (1927) and then studied her subject for a further year at Cornell University in the United States.

Elspeth Grant had been "just naturally interested" in writing from an early age, and became polo correspondent of the *East African Standard* at fifteen, spending her earnings on "books of contemporary verse and conjuring tricks." In 1929 she went as assistant press officer to the Empire Marketing Board in London. She worked there until 1931, when she married Gervas Huxley, a first cousin of Julian and Aldous Huxley, and himself a writer. Her husband's work in tea sales promotion took him all over the world, and she went with him. She has continued to travel widely on her own account, particularly in Africa, which she has visited to research her books and to see her family, and on one occasion to report to the government of Kenya on the provision of reading matter for newly literate Africans.

White Man's Country, Mrs. Huxley's first book, was both a biography of Lord Delamere and a history of the making of Kenya. It was warmly praised for combining "a sense of the picturesque" with "a sound historical sense"; "lucidity and restraint" with "a sure and vivid touch." It was followed by something quite different, *Murder at*

Government House, the first of several detective stories notable for the exoticism of their African setting, and enlivened by humor and touches of satire.

Red Strangers, her first serious novel, is a long fictionalized account of the colonization of Kenya, examined through its impact on one Kikuyu family. Enthusiastically received by most critics, it was thought by some more successful as a sociological document than as a work of fiction. Similar criticisms have been voiced of some of her subsequent novels, which are often admired as documents but thought inadequate or unconvincing in character and dialogue.

Mrs. Huxley's nonfictional work, much of it devoted to Africa's contemporary problems or to the continent's history, has been less equivocally praised, except by some who resent her impatience with the quality of African political leadership. Most reviewers react warmly to her profound knowledge of Africa and Africans, her careful scholarship, "her independence of mind and the honesty and humour of her writing." She has been described as "today's best informed and most objective writer on Africa."

The most widely successful of her books were the first two volumes of her autobiography, *The Flame Trees of Thika* and *On the Edge of the Rift*, describing with a "magic strangeness," and "the innocent eye of Monet painting a haystack," her early life in Kenya. Both books were best sellers and the first was a Book Society Choice (as was her novel *The Walled City*). There was scarcely less enthusiasm for *Love Among the Daughters*, which deals with the author's return to England, and her experiences during the 1920s at Reading University and Cornell.

Elspeth Huxley, whose husband died in 1971, lives in Wiltshire. She has one son, Charles, born in 1944. Mrs. Huxley, who worked during World War II in the BBC, broadcasts on a variety of subjects and is a contributor to many periodicals. She was a member of the BBC's General Advisory Council (1952–1959) and of the Monckton Advisory Commission on Central Africa (1959) and was named a CBE in 1962. Mrs. Huxley is fair haired and blue eyed. She serves as a justice of the peace in her part of Wiltshire and is a member of the Conservative party. She says her recreation is "resting."

PRINCIPAL WORKS: White Man's Country: Lord Delamere and the Making of Kenya, 1935 (2d ed. 1953); Murder at Government House, 1937; Murder on Safari, 1938; Red Strangers, 1939; Death of an Aryan, 1939 (U.S., The African Poison Murders); Atlantic Ordeal, 1941; (with Margery Perham) Race and Politics in Kenya, 1944 (rev. ed., 1956); The Walled City, 1948; The Sorcerer's Apprentice, 1948; I Don't Mind If I Do, 1950; Four Guineas: A Journey Through West Africa, 1954; A Thing to Love, 1954; The Red Rock Wilderness, 1957; The Flame Tree of Thika: Memories of an African Childhood, 1959; A New Earth, 1960; The Mottled Lizard (U.S., On the Edge of the Rift: Memories of Kenya) 1962; The Merry Hippo, 1963 (U.S., The Incident at Merry Hippo); A Man From Nowhere, 1964; Forks and Hope (U.S., With Forks and Hope: An African Notebook), 1964; Back Street New Worlds: A Look at Immigrants in Britain, 1964; Brave New Victuals: An Enquiry into Modern Food Production, 1965; Their Shining Eldorado: A Journey Through Australia, 1967; Love Among the Daughters, 1968; The Challenge of Africa, 1971; (comp.) The Kingsleys: A Biographical Anthology, 1973.

ABOUT: Who's Who, 1973. *Periodicals*—Wilson Library Bulletin January 1961.

HYAMS, EDWARD (SOLOMON) (September 30, 1910–), English novelist, short story writer, writer on horticulture and viticulture, writes that he was: "Born in London, 1910. Educated London, France and Switzerland. I do not remember when I started to write. From 1929 to 1933 I had various jobs in offices and factories but all this time I was trying to write. I wrote my first novel in 1935 and 1936, and by then I was managing a department in a printing firm and was married. The book was published in 1938. I had done some travelling in the Old World but in that year made my first visit to America, which I was able to do as the book was also published there. At this time my hobby was flying light aeroplanes and when war broke out I joined the RAF as a volunteer. But having imperfect eyesight I was grounded, did not wish to serve in the RAF on the ground, and was allowed to leave the RAF to join the Royal Navy. During three months' gap between these services I drove an ambulance in the London blitz. Then Royal Navy as a rating in destroyers; training in radar, commissioned as radar officer RNVR and served until 1946. Went with my wife to live in the country, having a small cottage in Kent. Cultivated the three acres there and managed to live off that while resuming writing. Was given an Atlantic Award in Literature, which helped. Corner was turned when the *New Statesman*, and then the BBC Third Programme, began to accept my short stories. For the 'Third' I read these myself and most have since been republished. By 1949 I was earning enough by writing to live on it fairly comfortably, to resume travelling and to enlarge the cottage.

"The series of my post-war novels from *Blood Money* to *Into the Dream* were satirical, the most successful, both in the satisfaction it gave me and with the reading public, being *Sylvester*, which was published in eight languages. In all these books I had much the same theme; the helplessness of the individual man—usually a young man—up against human institutions; the impossibility of being 'free' in any organised society; and the absurdity of man's pretensions, under the aspect of eternity. What in-

EDWARD HYAMS

terested and interests me as a writer is that while the human condition seems to me to be essentially comic, not tragic, tragedy is real for the individual man or woman. 'The boys throw stones at the frogs in play; but the frogs die in earnest.' At the same time I am intensely interested in story-telling for its own sake; admire above all in other writers narrative power; and immensely enjoy the manipulation of language for its own sake.

"I became dissatisfied with the kind of books I had been writing to say what I wanted to say, and while sticking to a satirical tone, began to write books with more substance and a more realistic and serious story. This series begins with *Taking it Easy* (in the U.S. *The Unpossessed*) and still continues. I have not yet written a book which satisfies me.

"Meanwhile I had become interested in problems of agriculture, horticulture and, in general, the relationship between man and the soil he lives on. I wrote, chiefly for the sake of more money but not simply as potboilers, a number of books on gardening and aspects of commercial horticulture. And, finally, the historical and philosophical *Soil and Civilisation* which was very well received. I also undertook a number of translations, chiefly from the French, and have done about twenty. In 1965 I was awarded the Scott-Moncrieff prize for the best translation from the French.

"In 1960 I moved from Kent to Devon, made a large garden, entirely ornamental excepting for a small vineyard, for the wine vine had become one of my special interests: this particular interest had a conclusion in the publication of *Dionysus, a Social History of the Wine Vine*, in 1965; as my interest in the art of gardens had had its conclusion in the publication, 1964, of *The English Garden.* I have also written a good deal for radio and TV, chiefly plays. But the novel is the form which increasingly absorbs me. I still travel as much as I can afford to, write a weekly column for the *Illustrated London News* and a fortnightly one for the *New Statesman.*"

Edward Hyams, whom Ronald Bryden has described as "the most exasperatingly gifted writer in England," was educated at University College School in London, at the Lycée Jacquard in Lausanne, and at that city's university, where he received his *licence ès lettres*. He was in the RAF from 1939 to 1941, and in the Navy thereafter until the end of the war, emerging with the rank of lieutenant.

Not much need be added to his own excellent account above of his work as a novelist. In *Sylvester* (published in America as *998*), the most successful of his earlier "comedies of manners and morals," a young naval officer constructs from a perambulator and three pawnbroker's balls a mysterious instrument which he calls "998" and presents as the ultimate weapon. The situation allows Hyams scope to satirize a generous range of contemporary phenomena, including politicians, the press, and democracy. The book was greatly enjoyed, but like many of Hyams' novels was thought a little too kindly in its wit, a little too undiscriminating in its targets, to be counted a wholly successful satire.

All We Possess (*Tillotson* in America) is a much discussed example of Hyams' "more realistic and serious" novels, which illustrate man's insolent absurdity in placing the needs of his own ego above the needs of others. It is an account of the climb to power and wealth of an insignificant clerk, the failure (through greed) of his sex life, and his eventual imprisonment for fraud. It was warmly praised as a perfectly proportioned novel "on a grand scale," a contemporary morality "about a man whose god is his 'self.' " Ronald Bryden said that Hyams "writes with the lucid, populous reality of a wittier, colder, H. G. Wells" and this is a comparison frequently made and justified by Hyams' absorption in the details of commerce and technology as well as by his capacity for vigorous comic invention. Anthony Burgess however has pointed out an important difference between Wells, who blamed history for human failure, and Hyams, who "blames the human ego" and thinks it "man's duty . . . to recognize the hell of self and attempt to destroy it."

Stanley Kauffmann has made the following thoughtful assessment of Hyam's abilities as a novelist: "If his style has no extraordinary brilliance, it is astringent, wiry, precise. If there are no shattering insights into character, there is plenty of juicy observation; if no deep compelling drama, there is unflagging narrative. . . . In the most serious sense, Hyams is not a serious novelist. He writes fiction because, presumably, it is convenient to spin out his observations, ideas, reactions, in the form of a tale. . . . But his several attractive qualities and abilities make him the next best thing to a good serious novelist: a good companion."

Hyams has written many practical works on flower, fruit, and wine growing, and some more considerable studies. *Soil and Civilisation*, about the influence of soil fertility (and sterility) on human history, was found better in its anthropological than in its historical aspects. *The English Garden*, splendidly illustrated with photographs by Edwin Smith, and *Dionysus*, his social history of the wine vine, were both full of "curious learning and shrewd observations" and the latter, if a little under-researched, would it was agreed be "the standard work on the subject for some time to come." He has interested himself in a number of other subjects as well—most recently in assassination, which he is inclined to advocate as an economical form of warfare, and has discussed both in his history of assassination, *Killing No Murder*, and in his novel *The Mischief Makers*.

Edward Hyams was married in 1933 to Hilda Aylett. He lives in Devon, but frequently broadcasts from London. He is a scholarly looking man, slender, graying, and bearded.

PRINCIPAL WORKS: *Novels*—The Wings of the Morning, 1939; A Time to Cast Away, 1939; To Sea in a Bowl, 1941; William Medium, 1948; Blood Money, 1948; Not in Our Stars, 1949; The Astrologer, 1950; Sylvester, 1951 (U.S., 998); Gentian Violet, 1953; Stories and Cream, 1954; The Slaughterhouse Informer, 1955; Into the Dream, 1957; Taking it Easy, 1958 (U.S., The Unpossessed); All We Possess (U.S., Tillotson), 1961; A Perfect Stranger, 1964; The Last Poor Man, 1966; Cross Purposes: Four Stories of Love, 1967; The Mischief Makers, 1968; The Death Lottery, 1971; The Final Agenda, 1973. *Nonfiction*—The Grape Vine in England, 1949; Soil and Civilisation, 1952; (ed.) Vineyards in England: A Practical Handbook for the Restoration of Vine Cultivation and Wine Making to Southern Britain, 1953; Vin: The Wine Country of France, 1959 (U.S., The Wine Country of France); The New Statesman: The History of the First Fifty Years, 1963; The English Garden (with photographs by Edwin Smith), 1964; Dionysus: A Social History of the Wine Vine, 1965; Ornamental Shrubs for Temperate Zone Gardens (6 vols.), 1965–1967; Killing No Murder, 1969; Great Botanical Gardens of the World, 1969; English Cottage Gardens (with photographs by Edwin Smith), 1970; A History of Gardens and Gardening, 1971; Capability Brown and Humphry Repton, 1971; Plants in the Service of Man, 1971; Animals in the Service of Man, 1972; A Dictionary of Modern Revolution, 1973.

ABOUT: Burgess, A. The Novel Now, 1967; Contemporary Authors 5–6, 1963. *Periodicals*—Publishers' Weekly May 30, 1966; Vogue September 1, 1954.

HYMAN, STANLEY EDGAR (June 11, 1919–July 29, 1970), American literary critic, wrote: "I

STANLEY EDGAR HYMAN

was born in New York City, and grew up in Brooklyn. My parents, Moe and Lulu Marshak Hyman, were the children of immigrant Jews from Russian Poland, and I was raised in Orthodox Judaism. My father was a partner in a small family firm of paper merchants. The school I attended, P.S. 99, was full of savage little children or grandchildren of immigrant Jews, like myself, fiercely competing to get ahead in the world through education, to become dentists or accountants or pharmacists or whatever. I am sure that it was a dreadful educational environment, but I rather liked it, competed with great success, and think that it effectively armored me for later life. Afternoons I was forced to attend Hebrew school, which I hated and resisted because of its archaic rote instruction and brutal corporal punishment, as a result of which I began anew at a different Hebrew school each fall, and never learned the language, to my present regret. I was a bookish boy, although I participated to some extent in street games and sports, even street gang fighting. I spent childhood summers with my mother and my younger brother in Binghamton, New York, where her parents lived; later ones at a boys' camp.

"At Erasmus Hall High School I became a member of an intellectual coterie, lost my faith (I have been a militant atheist ever since), and was active in journalism and dramatics. I determined to become a drama critic, and with a loony logic (I was entirely unadvised, since I scarcely knew anyone who had been to college) I decided that the proper preparation for drama criticism was an undergraduate school of journalism followed by a graduate school of drama. In accord with that plan, I matriculated at Syracuse University, one of the few colleges then with an undergraduate school of journalism, in the fall of 1936. I found the study of journalism to be less than compelling, and would have departed, except for three discoveries in my sophomore year that have entirely shaped my life. I encountered an outstanding English teacher, Leonard Brown, who taught me what little I know, turned my interests in the direction of literature and literary criticism, and introduced me to the second, Kenneth Burke. The third discovery that persuaded me to stay was a fellow sophomore and fellow student of Brown's named Shirley Jackson. We became inseparable, scandalized Syracuse University in a variety of fashions, and were both awarded the A.B. degree in 1940, with public laudations and private sighs of relief.

"As winner of the *New Republic*'s college essay contest, I had a summer job on the magazine as editorial assistant. On the strength of that we got married, on August 13, 1940. That winter, after some success in submitting editorial paragraphs to the *New Yorker* for the 'Notes and Comment' page of 'Talk of the Town,' I was made a staff writer; I still am, although I contribute little to the magazine these days except unsigned nonfiction book notes. In 1941 we moved to a shack in the woods in New Hampshire, and in 1942 we moved back to New York City, where our first child, Laurence Jackson, was born. I began publishing reviews and critical articles in a great many periodicals; about the same time my wife's stories began to sell. In 1945, while we were both at work on books, Kenneth Burke, now retired but then a member of the literature faculty at Bennington College, proposed me for a vacancy on that faculty. I was hired, but resigned in 1946, after a year and a half, to get back to my book. We continued to live in North Bennington, Vermont, where our next two children were born, Joanne Leslie in 1945 and Sarah Geraldine in 1948, and have lived there since, except for two years in Connecticut, where our last child, Barry Edgar, was born in 1951. In 1953 I went back to teaching at Bennington College, and I do so to this day. During the girls' winter work term, when the college is not in session, I work on articles and books; summers I travel and lecture. I have been a loud-mouthed sports fan, particularly of the former Brooklyn Dodgers, and a fanatic bridge and poker player; my quieter present hobby is numismatics, principally Ancient Greek. In 1959 I was awarded a fellowship by the American Council of Learned Societies. From 1961 to 1965 I was regular lead reviewer for the *New Leader*, but three jobs proved to be one too many. Shirley Jackson died on August 8, 1965, five days short of our twenty-fifth anniversary."

Hyman's first book, *The Armed Vision*, summarized the work and analyzed the methods of a dozen contemporary critics, American and British. Reviewers noted then, as they have since, Hyman's exceptional talent as a popularizer, excelling in "concise abstraction and summary . . . from voluminous sources." But many readers were less flattering about his powers of judgment, finding him "adulatory" about such critics as R. P. Blackmur, I. A. Richards, and Kenneth Burke, but "venomous" about Edmund Wilson, among others. The *New Yorker* said "his writing is uncomplicated and often witty, but unfortunately his conclusions are sometimes marked by an almost breathless irresponsibility."

Hyman, who acknowledged that his talents were "mainly of a destructive order," moderated his opinions (or the expression of them) over the years, but as Frank Kermode says continued to enjoy "potting books and especially big miscellaneous books, where he can seek generalizations in diverse material." *Poetry and Criticism*, showing how each of four great works of literature had shattered current critical dogmas, seemed to Josephine Jacobsen "a model of combined modesty and authority, and of good sense." *The Tangled Bank* studied the work of Darwin, Marx, Frazer, and Freud, arguing that their influence derived partly from their ability as imaginative writers, and seeking the "organizing metaphors and key images" of their thought. It aroused great critical interest without winning general critical assent to its ideas, but was notably successful, Harold Rosenberg thought, in "making the minds of these innovators present to us." Two collections of Hyman's essays and reviews, *The Promised End* and *Standards* (a selection of his *New Leader* reviews 1961–1965), were both received with some specific reservations but general enthusiasm. His posthumously published *Iago* is a stimulating study of its subject "as stage villain, as Satan, as Artist, as latent homosexual and as Machiavel."

Frank MacShane, discussing Hyman's work in *Book Week*, noted his debt to Blackmur, Empson, Richards, and above all to Kenneth Burke. "Though more personal and less schematic, Hyman's position derives from Burke's attempt to create a synthesis of all methods, a 'socio-psychological integration' that makes criticism a form of action rather than a mere reaction." Hyman himself spoke of his preoccupation with certain themes: "the ritual origins of myth; the importance of a true folk tradition for art; the tragic vision; literature as secular salvation and redemption; the painful difficulty of being a writer in America." MacShane thought him "primarily an intellectual with social concerns," drawn less to poetry than to the novel, in which he valued above all (he said) "intellectual complexity, ornate and figurative language, and intense moral seriousness." For one reason or another—and a number of explanations have been offered by his admirers—Hyman never quite achieved the influence that his abilities seemed to promise but he was, as J. W. Aldridge said, "one of the most intelligent and humane critics" of his day.

Hyman was married again in 1966, to Phoebe Pettingell. In 1967 he received a grant from the National Institute of Arts and Letters. He died suddenly at the age of fifty-one, apparently of a heart attack.

PRINCIPAL WORKS: The Armed Vision: A Study in the Methods of Modern Literary Criticism, 1948 (rev., 1955); Poetry and Criticism: Four Revolutions in Literary Taste, 1961; The Tangled Bank: Darwin, Marx, Frazer and Freud as Imaginative Writers, 1962; The Promised End: Essays and Reviews, 1942–1962, 1963; Standards: A Chronicle of Books for Our Time, 1966; Iago: Some Approaches to the Illusion of His Motivation, 1970.

ABOUT: Ellison, R. Shadow and Act, 1964; Nemerov, H. Poetry and Fiction, 1963; Who's Who in America, 1970–1971. *Periodicals*—Book Week September 4, 1966; Commentary January 1964; July 1966.

IGNATOW, DAVID (February 7, 1914–), American poet, writes: "I was born in Brooklyn in that immigrant section known as Borough Park. My father was from Kiev, Russia; my mother from Galicia, Austro-Hungary. Borough Park then was a fairly recent development of two-story cold water buildings to which Jews, Italians and a sprinkling of Russians and Poles came, out of crowded, noisy Lower East Side, Manhattan, seeking more and quieter living space. In this mixed community I spent virtually my entire childhood. I was about twelve when my father's growing prosperity permitted us to move into a brand-new steam-heated two-family brick house opposite a farm in the Maplewood section of Brooklyn. I remember I was disappointed with its appearance as we drove up to it in the moving van. It had no gable roof with attic room under eaves. I had dreamt that that was to be my hideaway, where I could be alone with my treasures and my secret thoughts, just as it happened in the boys' books I was reading then. In these stories, all Americans lived in one- or two-family houses at most that had attic rooms for boys to play in and to use for their very own. I had thought our family would soon be joining that great, idyllic majority. However, I did eventually reconcile myself to this red, raw-looking building. The street it stood on was much wider, cleaner, and quieter than the one from which we were moving. There were no gangs of boys here through which it was a peril for me to walk with library books in my hand. In disgust and fright with these violent, reckless boys, I had gradually

DAVID IGNATOW

withdrawn from their company to concentrate on reading at my bedroom window. I did finally get to see that our new house had a peak to it. That was merely a facade to a flat roof, in imitation of a gable house, but it was better than none at all, I thought. Here I lived until the age of nineteen, when it became imperative that I leave, if I was to maintain my newly discovered identity as a writer.

"We were then in midst of the Great Depression and I was under severe pressure to join my father in his pamphlet bindery to help save it from collapse. The time was 1932; I had just graduated high school. Ironically, it was my father who first awoke in me an ambition to become a writer. During my early adolescence, just before the Crash, he would sit relaxed in his soft chair under a floor lamp and reminisce of his readings in Tolstoy, Turgenev and Chekhov in their original language. The reverence with which he spoke of them as men and writers impressed itself upon me indelibly. At nineteen, I had read all of the Russian classics in translation, including American, French, Spanish and English. I was living completely absorbed in the imaginative powers of these books and had been writing steadily for the last year, dividing my efforts between the short story and poetry. I could be found in a library or in my bedroom hunched over my sewing machine desk pounding away on an old upright typewriter. These were days when I was supposed to have been at the bindery, working to save a salary that otherwise would go to a hired man. My father was under dire necessity of keeping his shop going to protect his investment in it and to pay the mortgage on our house. Fortunately for me, in

1934, after the publication of my first story in 1933, which then was listed on the Honor Roll of the O'Brien collection of *Best Short Stories* of the year, I was accepted on the then newly formed WPA Writers Project. Within a year I moved into a furnished apartment of my own in Manhattan.

"During the next six years on WPA, my writing turned more and more to poetry as the way to handle immediately the tension, sharpness, and emotional upheaval to which I was daily subject. My father still was at me to join him in his shop. In the meanwhile, in 1937 I had married Rose Graubart, artist and writer. Several times we found ourselves on Relief during the annual budget slashing in Congress. With no experience in any of the ordinary mechanical or clerical jobs on the outside and with no love either for their long, exhausting hours, I had to persevere in my condition. I was determined above all to succeed first in becoming a recognized poet.

"From WPA, which began to expire by 1939, I went to Civil Service, then to shipyard work as handyman as we entered the War, then to employment as a hospital admitting clerk. I returned to my father's bindery for several years, but left again for a job in public relations writing; returned once more to the bindery to become eventually an officer in the firm, but liquidated it in 1961, a little more than a year after my father's death. I then tried representing a fine paper merchant to printers but was unhappy with that too and turned to teaching. Through this hectic hegira I had felt myself seeking to recover the ease and stability I had enjoyed as a child, but today, as my poetry has sought to express, I realize that it is just this insecurity that has affirmed my life's course, my search for freedom.

"In 1964 I received a grant from The National Institute of Arts and Letters and in 1965 a Guggenheim Fellowship in Creative Writing. I taught a Poetry Workshop at the New School for Social Research 1964–1965 and as of this writing am on a Visiting Lectureship at the University of Kentucky.

"We have two children, David and Yaedi. We live in Manhattan."

Most of David Ignatow's poems are about the ordinary drudgeries, dangers, and occasional compensations of urban life, all described and pondered with great particularity. He favors extremely short, unrhymed poems, "using the abrupt cadences and very largely the language of ordinary speech," pursuing "a rock-bottom, uncompromising truth which allows for no ornamentation or embellishment." Some of his poems have suggested comparisons with the stories of Bernard Malamud.

William Carlos Williams, the modern poet who has most influenced Ignatow's work, said of his first book that it should be sold at Woolworth's for a dime a copy: "For these are poems for the millions, in the cities and out of them, those who would read, and read poems too, poems such as these, if only they could get to them; manna in the wilderness."

In *The Gentle Weight Lifter* and *Say Pardon*, Ignatow continued to make poetry "from the apparently dull and prosaic, the commonest emotions, the obvious vices and pieties," extending his range at times to draw upon myth and history, dream and fantasy. Denise Levertov wrote of *Say Pardon*: "David Ignatow has for years been refining and strengthening his modest, muted style until one is not aware of it as technique—it is a transparent medium"; and another critic agreed that in his best poems "we respond as if to experience, forgetting the poet." But others observed that the scrupulous objectivity of Ignatow's early work was giving way to a harsher tone, "tight-lipped and dour."

Figures of the Human includes a number of poems reprinted from earlier volumes (but not the gentlest of them) as well as new work, and is altogether darker in mood than its predecessors. Richard Howard noted that "seventeen of the twenty-nine pieces are concerned with violence, generally an attack from behind, in the shadows, by Someone with a Knife." It seemed to Howard that Ignatow's "habitual nightmare of unprovoked and lethal assault" is presented to some extent as an expression of the poet's sense of personal chaos and guilt. Hayden Carruth found these short, bitter poems about "the cruelty, filth, and insanity of city life" shocking in their deep sincerity and said of Ignatow: "I have no question about his ability, but only about his future; how long can a creative instinct survive on these miniature emblems of disgust?"

But, as Ignatow has explained elsewhere, "after having written some of the most bitter, terrifying dead end poems, with no place else to go from there, I conceive of the necessity for re-establishing relationships with myself and with the world on still another level, while life goes on." *Rescue the Dead* includes some poems which confront in almost surreal terms the themes of evil and unreason, others which deal in extremely intimate terms with the problems of marriage. But beyond the pain and malice countenanced in these poems Ignatow, as one critic wrote, "achieves something of that redemptive vision he has been looking for." When Ignatow's *Poems 1934–1969* appeared in 1970, William Meredith wrote: "The beautiful attention with which he has recorded the lyric experience of thirty-five years has accumulated here to an extraordinary autobiography."

David Ignatow is the son of Max and Yetta (Reinbach) Ignatow. He has taught as a visiting lecturer at the universities of Kentucky and Kansas and at Vassar, and in 1967–1968 was an adjunct professor at Southampton College, Long Island University. He was poet in residence at York College in 1969, and the same year joined the Columbia faculty. He was associate editor of the magazine *American Scene* from 1935 to 1937, editor of the *Beloit Poetry Journal* from 1949 to 1959, and poetry editor of *The Nation* from 1962 to 1963. Since 1968 he has served as co-editor of *Chelsea*, a semi-annual literary magazine. In 1966 the Poetry Society of America gave him its Shelley Memorial Award.

PRINCIPAL WORKS: *Poems*—Poems, 1948; The Gentle Weight Lifter, 1955; Say Pardon, 1961; Figures of the Human, 1964; Earth Hard (selected poems; published in England), 1968; Rescue the Dead, 1968; Poems, 1934–1969, 1970; The Notebooks of David Ignatow (ed. by Ralph J. Mills, Jr.), 1973.

ABOUT: Contemporary Authors 9–10, 1964; Murphy, R. (ed.) Contemporary Poets of the English Language, 1970; Who's Who in America, 1970–1971. *Periodicals*—Chelsea September 1962; Hudson Review Winter 1965; Nation May 13, 1961; New Leader May 22, 1968; New Mexico Quarterly Spring 1951; New York Herald Tribune Books September 3, 1961; New York Review of Books December 30, 1971; Poetry July 1961; July 1965; Prairie Schooner Spring 1965; Saturday Review February 13, 1965; Shenandoah Summer 1965; Sixties Summer 1968; University Review (Kansas) Spring 1968.

***ILLYÉS, GYULA** (November 2, 1902–), Hungarian poet, dramatist, novelist, and essayist, writes: "I was born at Rácegres, on a small *puszta* far from any village on the gently sloping downs that stretch between the Danube and Lake Balaton. The day of my birth was All Souls' Day, so, still with tears in the corners of our eyes after lighting our candles in the graveyard that happened to be just behind our home, we would settle around the family table for a merry birthday party with mutton and wines, my grandfather being a shepherd and the whole family great vine-growers. Contrasts like this have formed my personality and encouraged my writing throughout my life. I wanted to remain among these familiar surroundings but I at last went in for study abroad instead. Though I became a lyric poet I have always reached for and clutched stubbornly to contemporary reality. As an advocate of internationalism and social revolution I had at last to fight for the truths of separate nations, among them for that of the Hungarians—a nation which has one third of her population, five millions, living outside her borders, mainly in the surrounding countries; a nation which, according to world statistics, produces almost the highest percentage of suicides and the lowest one of births. To be the signaller aboard a ship caught in danger, a signaller who at the same time sees the coasts of Eden where the ship ought to have landed—I believe this metaphor can best suggest the common feature that underlies the variety of my writings.

* il' yesh

GYULA ILLYÉS

"Originally I wanted to write in French, when at the age of eighteen I was a student in Paris, but I started my actual career with poems published in Budapest in 1928. They were a kind of surrealist poetry 'smelling' of earth in a way much like the new Spanish poetry of those years. There is nothing to wonder at in this similarity, even though the geographical distance between the two countries is significant. There are a few countries in Europe which seem to have been destined, like sensitive instruments, to measure the depths and peaks of humanity by the amount of suffering they endure. Hungary is one of these.

"Back to my youth. For a long time, I stayed abroad. I earned my living by physical labor for a while; I worked in a mine, at road construction, in a foundry, and then I learned bookbinding. In Paris I attended university and there I got acquainted and made friends with the young writers of those days: Éluard, Aragon, Tzara, Breton, and others. I returned to Hungary in 1926. In order to maintain the independence of my views I decided not to live by writing and went to work as a clerk.

"I wrote poems, novels, plays, essays, literary sociography, and travel journals; my published books amount to some thirty-five to forty volumes in Hungarian. I was on the staff of several literary journals and then edited *Nyugat* (The West), the main organ of modern Hungarian literature in the first four decades of our century; its successor *Magyar Csillag* (Hungarian Star) until 1944; and *Válasz* (The Answer) between 1945 and 1948. I also translated a great deal—novels and especially poetry—from French for the most part. I was twice awarded the Kossuth Prize and in 1965 won the Grand Prix of the International Biennale of Poetry.

"I am married; my wife is a lecturer on the psychology of handicapped children. Our daughter studies at university."

"There are only three or four living poets in the world who could gradually absorb the spirit of the century in the widest sense of the word," wrote the French critic Alain Bosquet. "In . . . Gyula Illyés their genius is present." The rifts and contradictions of the age are united in Illyés by his individual and artistic integrity: he has always served truth as he saw it rather than any political system or ideology.

Illyés grew up on a *puszta*, a range of buildings housing estate servants—a class which was paid mostly in kind, and monstrously exploited and ill-treated. His family fared better than most, and his extraordinary self-taught grandmother saw to it that the boy had an education far above his "station," including French lessons from the manor house governess. Because his family had friends in the nearby town he was able to go to school there, proved a gifted student, and went on to the University of Budapest. He took part in the Communist Revolution of 1919 as a boy soldier in the Hungarian Red Army. When the revolution failed he went to Paris, where he studied and made friends among the Dadaists and Surrealists (whose influence on his work was short-lived). He also wrote a novel in French, *Les Huns à Paris*.

When he returned to Budapest, Illyés found a mentor in the influential poet and scholar Mihály Babits, his predecessor as editor of *Nyugat*. In the early 1930s, following the example of Bartók and Kodály, Illyés called upon writers to "explore the village"—to study and take inspiration from their peasant origins. The misery and degradation they found and reported made their populist movement a political as well as a cultural movement of the first importance. Illyés' largely autobiographical study of his own class, *Puszták népe* (1936, translated as *People of the Puszta*), has something of the emotional impact of James Agee's *Let Us Now Praise Famous Men*, and has become a classic. Together with Illyés' lyric and epic poems of the same period, all advocating radical change in the countryside, it earned him a foremost place among the populist writers.

In 1939, Illyés took part in the formation of the National Peasant party. He was one of the first Hungarian intellectuals to recognize the threat to his country represented by Hitler's Germany. When *Nyugat* failed, he launched *Magyar Csillag*, and made it the last stronghold of free speech in Hungary. In 1944, when the German occupation began, the magazine was suppressed and Illyés went underground but continued to write, notably the poem "Nem volt elég" ("It Was Not Enough"), his famous indictment of the Hungarian intellectuals and bourgeoisie who had failed to prevent the catastrophe.

The Soviet-sponsored land reforms of 1945 were greeted exultantly by Illyés in a flood of lyrical poems, but disillusionment followed. In 1948 the National Peasant party lost its identity and the magazine *Válasz* was suppressed. Illyés contrived to retain his equilibrium, neither denouncing the regime nor embracing it, at times criticizing it with "measured boldness." The Party treated him with a mixture of suspicion and deference, and grudgingly allowed him to go on writing his "escapist" historical plays. It was during this period that Illyés wrote "for the drawer" the poem "Egy mondat, a zsarnokságról" (One Sentence on Tyranny), an indictment of the Rákosi dictatorship and of all tyranny which some have placed among the great political poems. It was published during the 1956 Revolution, but Illyés was spared the fresh persecutions which soon followed. In 1957 he led his fellow writers into a period of self-imposed silence which did not end until April 1960, when Tibor Déry and others were released from prison.

Illyés' dedication to national and individual freedom links him with the nineteenth-century poet Sándor Petőfi, in whose tradition he writes (and of whom he wrote an admirable biography). Illyés believes that a poet should seek to utter "a truth which has never been put into words before"; he has always chosen his words from "the daily language of simple folk," making exuberant use of the wealth, color, and plasticity of the Hungarian language, favoring bold images and strong rhythms. He is, as he says, a lyric poet (when he is not obliged to be a social one) and has written some extremely beautiful love poems. Illyés is regarded generally as "the leading personality in modern Hungarian literature." He has been widely translated into the languages of East-Central Europe and into German, Italian, and, especially, French. Illyés lives now at Tihany on Lake Balaton. In 1970 he became vice-president of P.E.N. International. His lean hawk-nosed face with its high cheekbones, keen eyes under heavy brows, and firm humorous mouth make him look much younger than he is.

PRINCIPAL WORKS IN ENGLISH TRANSLATION: Once Upon a Time (Hungarian Folktales), 1964; Tradition and Innovation in Poetry, *in* The New Hungarian Quarterly 17 1965; People of the Puszta, 1967. *Poems in* Duczyńska, I. and Polanyi, K. (eds.) The Plough and the Pen, 1963; The Literary Review Spring 1966; The New Hungarian Quarterly 11, 1963, 12 and 13, 1964.

ABOUT: Gara, L. Hommage à Gyula Illyés, 1963; Reményi, J. Hungarian Writers and Literature, 1964; Gömöri,

G. Polish and Hungarian Poetry, 1966; International Who's Who, 1971–1972; Reményi, J., Hungarian Writers and Literature, 1964. *Periodicals*—New York Times Book Review September 25, 1966; Soviet Survey July–September 1958: Hefte für Literatur und Kritik 2 1960; Combat December 19, 1963; Books Abroad Winter 1963, Spring 1964, Spring 1966; L'Express January 9, 1964; Journal des Poètes 1965.

"INNES, HAMMOND" (pen name of Ralph Hammond Innes) (July 15, 1913–), British novelist, writes: "England was my birthplace, but by nature and instinct I am Highland Scots. The original home of the Innes clan was an area about nine miles by three near Culloden which explains why most of them left Scotland. There was some sort of an artistic streak on my mother's side, but not sufficient to explain why I should start writing stories at the age of twelve. At considerable personal sacrifice my family gave me a preparatory and public school education, but when I left school in 1931 it was the worst period of the great depression. I could have gone into banking, which was my father's profession; instead I insisted upon journalism. Newspapers at that time were sacking staff, not taking them on. I was at a loose end for a year, filling in time teaching and articled to a near-bankrupt publisher. It was during this period that I met my wife, an actress and a kinswoman of Sir Walter Scott and Andrew Lang. I also wrote my first book. A lucky break then—I got a job with Brendan Bracken's *Financial News*; a lucky break because the paper, though small and specialised, was a national daily. In the next four years I covered every facet of newspaper work—reporting, leaders, feature articles, even the sub-editor's desk. It taught me economy of words. It taught me to edit my own work, to cut ruthlessly.

"During these four years I wrote four books. Married in 1937, I continued to write in the mornings before going to the newspaper and in the late evenings after I returned home. Why, God only knows! The books only earned me thirty pounds apiece, but I had to go on. I was intrigued by the technique, by the scope a book gives to the writer. It wasn't just an escape from the City; it was something compulsive, entirely instinctive. Story and words fascinated me. War broke out. I volunteered for the Navy, but their Lordships wanted me to sign on for seven years. Fortunately I refused. I now had an agent and filled with the historic sense of the times I wrote a book called *Wreckers Must Breathe*. Collins published it and it was the beginning of a lasting association with this great Scots publishing house. I volunteered for the Army, saw the Battle of Britain from a gun site at Kenley and with it all fresh in my mind 'scribbled' through the winter months, setting it down within the framework of a story. America's *Saturday Evening Post* bought it,

HAMMOND INNES

astounding a Cockney air sentry with the dollar value of the scribbling which had seemed such a strange occupation to my fellow gunners. This was the first of a whole string of my books that *Post* were to serialise.

"The Mediterranean then, travel at His Majesty's expense, which encouraged, not so much a wanderlust, but an intense curiosity about the world at large. I hadn't been outside of England before the war. It was all new to me and wonderfully exciting. Looking back now I can see that the pattern of my life has been remarkably consistent, a steady drive towards an objective. When the air war died down I moved from guns to Army newspapers—running a syndication service to the half-dozen editions, writing articles, editing, finally organising the administration of the whole complex set-up. And then with demobilisation imminent, back to writing—a not very good book, but on the strength of it the decision to strike out on my own as a full-time author.

"The first postwar book was a success and from then on I ploughed my earnings back into travel—the oil boom Canadian West, Africa, Arabia, etc., always the out-back, a new setting for each novel. Six months travelling, six months writing—that became the pattern of my working years. The sea had always attracted me, it has infiltrated into most of my books. I bought a boat of my own, took to ocean racing, explored the coasts of Europe from the Baltic to the Bay of Biscay, meeting the men of the world's seaways, absorbing a salt water atmosphere. Then a new boat, designed for my own individual requirements, and down the Atlantic coast of Europe into the Mediterranean to explore the Aegean and Ionian islands of Greece. Meantime, more travel—Labrador, the Arctic North of Canada, Yugoslavia, Tunis, the Maldives. The sea and strange lands, all sort of people, and between travelling intensive months of writing in my XIVth century Suffolk home. Films and publication in a dozen different languages; it was life lived at a great pace—hard, exciting, and enormously satisfying. Each journey was the subject of a travel piece, many of them appearing in the American magazine *Holiday*. A collection of them was published under the title *Harvest of Journeys* in 1960 and a further collection to be called *Sea and Islands* is now in course of preparation. These pieces enabled me to get the travel itself out of my system, to communicate the excitement I had felt, the vivid impact each area of the world had made on my imagination. It is this excitement, this desire to communicate that is the essential quality shared by all writers. It gives point to everything one does and because of that I regard myself as infinitely fortunate in being possessed of such a gift."

Hammond Innes's heroes are neither paragons nor supermen but human beings who find themselves in conflict as much with their environments —the sea, the Arctic, the desert—as with other men. Sometimes both his characterization and his decent prose have been thought a little conventional, but the authenticity of his settings is unchallengeable and his narrative power unsurpassed. One of the best of his books is *The Strode Venturer*, about an English adventurer who seeks to help a primitive people in the Maldives establish their rights to a volcanic island which is rich in manganese. A reviewer of the novel in the *Times Literary Supplement*, commenting upon the decline of the adventure story, wrote: "There are few practitioners nowadays, and even fewer who could hope to stay long in the same company with Haggard, Buchan, Stevenson or, say, Erskine Childers. One of these few is Mr. Hammond Innes."

Seven of Innes's books have been chosen by major book clubs in England, and three by the Literary Guild in the United States. Slim, dark, brown-eyed and wiry, Innes lives in the Suffolk village of Kersey, and sails with the Royal Cruising and the Royal Ocean Racing Clubs. His wife Dorothy has written her own account of some of their travels in *Occasions* (1972).

PRINCIPAL WORKS: *Novels*—The Doppelganger, 1937; Air Disaster, 1937; Sabotage Broadcast, 1938; All Roads Lead to Friday, 1939; Wreckers Must Breathe (U.S., Trapped), 1940; The Trojan Horse, 1940; Attack Alarm, 1941; Dead and Alive, 1946; The Lonely Skier (U.S., Fire in the Snow), 1947; The Killer Mine, 1947; Maddon's Rock (U.S., Gale Warning), 1948; The Blue Ice, 1948; The White South (U.S., The Survivors), 1949; The Angry Mountain, 1950; Air Bridge, 1951; Campbell's Kingdom, 1952; The Strange Land (U.S., The Naked Land), 1954; The Mary Deare (U.S., The Wreck of the Mary Deare), 1956; The Land God Gave to Cain, 1958; The Doomed Oasis, 1960; Atlantic Fury, 1962; The Strode Venturer, 1965; Levkas Man, 1971; Golden Soak, 1973. *Children's Stories* (as "Ralph Hammond")—Cocos Gold, 1950; Isle of Strangers, 1951 (U.S., Island of Peril); Saracen's Tower, 1952 (U.S., Cruise of Danger); Black Gold on the Double Diamond, 1953. *Nonfiction*—Harvest of Journeys, 1960; Sea and Islands, 1967; The Conquistadors, 1969.

ABOUT: Contemporary Authors 5–6, 1963; Current Biography, 1954; Innes, H. Harvest of Journeys, 1960; Vinson, J. (ed.) Contemporary Novelists, 1972; Who's Who, 1973. *Periodicals*—Books and Bookmen September 1965; New York Herald Tribune November 25, 1956; New York Times November 25, 1956; Time and Tide September 13, 1962.

***IONESCO, EUGÈNE** (November 26, 1912–), French dramatist, was born at Slatina in Rumania of a Rumanian father and a French mother. He was taken to Paris by his parents when he was one year old. His first theatrical experiences were of the Punch and Judy show in the Luxembourg Gardens, which fascinated him as "the spectacle of the world itself, which, unusual, improbable, but truer than truth, presented itself to me in an infinitely simplified and caricatured form, as if to underline its grotesque and brutal truth."

After a few years of elementary school in Paris, Ionesco developed anemia and at the age of eight was sent with his younger sister to live in the country, boarding with a farming family at La Chapelle-Anthenaise. In 1925 the Ionesco family returned to Rumania, where the boy received his secondary education (and learned his native language). He went on to the University of Bucharest as a student of French, and wrote his first poems and literary criticism. A characteristic exercise was his savage attack on Rumania's leading literary triumvirate of the time, which he followed a few days later with an adulatory essay on the same three writers—early evidence of his awareness of the relativity of truth.

In 1936 Ionesco graduated from the university and married Rodika Burileano. He began his career as a French teacher at a Bucharest *lycée*, but after two years returned to France with a government grant to prepare a doctoral thesis on the themes of sin and death in French poetry since Baudelaire. This ambitious project was never seriously begun; instead Ionesco devoted himself to "writing, writing, writing." He had no great success and, soon after the beginning of World War II, went to work as a proofreader in a Paris publishing house. His daughter Marie-France was born in 1944.

At this time Ionesco disliked the theatre, finding that "the presence on the stage of flesh-and-blood people" embarrassed him—their "impoverished,"

* yō nes' kō

concrete reality conflicting with the imaginative reality they sought to represent. His own first play was almost an accident. In 1948 he decided to learn English, and bought a primer featuring incredibly banal conversations between a middle-class English couple, Mr. and Mrs. Smith, and their friends the Martins. The absurd truisms and clichés which these characters exchanged so eagerly delighted Ionesco as a kind of parody of the meaninglessness of the contemporary theatre and, beyond that, of all human attempts at communication. By broadening this effect, he created his one-act "anti-play" *La Cantatrice chauve* (translated as *The Bald Soprano* in the United States, *The Bald Prima Donna* in England).

The play's setting is a conventional drawing room where Mr. and Mrs. Smith discuss their friends Bobby Watson (an entire family whose every member bears the same name). Two guests arrive and seem to recognize each other; they try to discover by what extraordinary coincidence they seem to be living in the same street, in the same house, on the same floor—to be sharing the same room and the same bed—and by pure logic arrive at the conclusion that they are husband and wife. A fireman enters and a series of increasingly confusing and pointless anecdotes are exchanged until the conversation lurches off into fragments of gibberish. It is a caricature of the "universal petty-bourgeoisie," a society without passion or ideas, made up of anonymous and interchangeable automata whose language has decayed into a meaningless social ritual.

La Cantatrice chauve opened at the Théâtre des Noctambules in May 1950. It was praised by Jacques Lemarchand and Armand Salacrou but otherwise vilified or ignored, and it closed after six weeks. But Ionesco was fascinated—partly because audiences had laughed at his "tragedy of language," but more because he had seen "characters move on the stage who had come out of myself. I was frightened. By what right had I been able to do this? Was this allowed?" The conventional theatre, he realized, had embarrassed him because it was "an unacceptable mixture of the true and the false." He decided that "what was needed was not to disguise the strings that moved the puppets but to make them more visible, deliberately apparent, to go right down to the very basis of the grotesque, the realms of caricature, to transcend the pale irony of witty drawing-room comedies . . . to push everything to paroxysm, to the point where the sources of tragedy lie. To create a theatre of violence—violently comic, violently dramatic."

Ionesco now ventured upon the stage himself, appearing early in 1951 as Stepan Trofimovich in a dramatization of Dostoevsky's *The Possessed.* At about the same time his second play was produced at the tiny Théâtre de Poche. This was the "comic drama" *La Leçon* (translated as *The Lesson*), in the course of which a timid professor tutors a young woman in various subjects, especially language. As he instructs her, defining the world for her in his own fatuous terms, he becomes increasingly a dominating figure, then a violent one. At the end of the lesson, he rapes and murders the girl—his fortieth such act of the day. Soon after, his maid ushers in victim number forty-one. *La Leçon* has been interpreted in various political and Freudian terms; certainly, as Martin Esslin says, it "hinges on the sexual nature of all power and the relationship between language and power as the basis of all human ties."

EUGÈNE IONESCO

Jacques, ou la soumission (translated as *Jack, or the Submission*) is about a young man who at first refuses to accept the absurd values of his family (who are all called Jacques) but is eventually seduced into conformity and marriage by the three-nosed Roberte II (the second only daughter of the Robert family). The play is full of exuberantly funny and nonsensical linguistic invention, culminating in a scene in which the two lovers, having played a childish game involving words beginning with "*chat*" (cat) or its assonants, agree that in future they will use that delightful word only, making it stand for every object and concept, and thus vastly simplifying the business of conversation. *Jacques,* written like its two predecessors in 1950, has a sequel, *L'Avenir est dans les œufs* (1951, translated as *The Future Is in Eggs*), in which society now demands reproduction, and the couple fill the stage with mountains of eggs while their families prance about the stage yelling "Long live production! Long live the white race!"

The gross and sometimes threatening proliferation of objects on the stage is a characteristic Ionesco image. It recurs in *Les Chaises* (1951, translated as *The Chairs*), the best of his early one-act plays. The setting is a tower on a lonely island, where an old man, anxious to pass on the wisdom of a lifetime, has invited a distinguished audience, including the near-mythical emperor himself, to receive his last message. Since public speaking is beyond him, he has engaged a professional orator to do the job for him. The guests begin to arrive, are announced and seated by the old man and his devoted wife, but remain invisible; the stage fills with empty chairs. The only real arrival is the orator. The old people, their work done, jump into the sea. The orator rises to address the chairs, and utters a strangled grunt; he is deaf and dumb, and the message he proceeds to write on the blackboard is nonsense.

This "tragic farce," more seriously and successfully than its predecessors, presents a powerfully suggestive image reflecting the meaninglessness of man's absurd pretentions, his inability to communicate his experience to others, his awful loneliness and isolation. Like so many of his plays, this one has the dense, unshakable logic of dreams, a form of thought that for Ionesco is "more lucid than any one has when awake, a thought expressed in images." Thus, he says, "the subject of the play is not the [old man's] message, nor the failures of life, nor the moral disorders of the two old people, but the chairs themselves; that is to say, the absence of people, the absence of the emperor, the absence of God, the absence of matter, the unreality of the world, metaphysical emptiness. The theme of the play is *nothingness*."

Another one-act piece, *Victimes du devoir* (translated as *Victims of Duty*), was staged in February 1953, and followed the same year by a program of very short and relatively lighthearted sketches. Ionesco's first full-length play, written in 1953 and first produced in April 1954, was *Amédée, ou comment s'en débarrasser* (translated as *Amédée, or How to Get Rid of It*). The romantic idealist Amédée is married to the shrewish and unloving Madeleine, and their *ménage* is haunted by the presence of a mysterious corpse which grows and grows until it threatens to fill the entire apartment. It is the corpse of their dead marriage. In the end, Amédée leaves the house, somehow dragging the huge carcass with him; outside the body ceases to be a dead weight and rises like a balloon, on which Amédée floats euphorically away into the sky. His marriage had been a disaster, but he has freed himself and can begin life again.

Although Ionesco's early plays were all financial failures, each had had its influential admirers. Gallimard published the first volume of his plays in 1954, and in 1956 a revival of *Les Chaises* gave him his first real success. Jean Anouilh, a former opponent, called the play a masterpiece, "better than Strindberg." Ionesco continued to draw attacks, however, both from conservative critics and from proponents of a politically committed theatre in the style of Brecht (Ionesco's *bête-noire*) and Sartre. Many of Ionesco's plays contain direct or indirect attacks on this kind of didactic literature, and in *L'Impromptu de l'Alma* (1955, translated as *Improvisation*) the author puts both himself and his critics on stage. He says: "It is neither from the wretchedness of the poor nor the unhappiness of the rich that I draw the substance of my drama. For me, the theatre is the projection on the stage of the world within—it is in my dreams, my anguish, my dark desires, my inner contradictions that I reserve the right to find the stuff of my plays. As I am not alone in the world, as each one of us, in the depths of his being, is at the same time everyone else—my dreams and desires, my anguish and my obsessions do not belong to myself alone; they are part of the heritage of my ancestors, a very ancient deposit to which all mankind may lay claim."

All the same, some of Ionesco's later plays have seemed more directly polemical, less personal and "absurd" in their symbolism, than his early work. *Tueur sans gages* (1957, translated as *The Killer*), regarded by some critics as Ionesco's masterpiece, was the first of four long plays centered on Bérenger, a Chaplinesque little Everyman who is to some extent a projection of the author himself. In *Tueur sans gages* Bérenger visits a beautiful new garden suburb, a "radiant city" which seems to promise happiness and the good life for all. But this utopia is half empty and ruled by fear; a mad killer haunts the lovely streets, and no one's life is safe. Bérenger tracks down and confronts the murderer, a mute degenerate dwarf, and uses every conceivable argument in a long, passionate attempt to reform him. It is useless, and in the end Bérenger himself submits helplessly to the giggling maniac's knife; the dwarf is death itself, which kills without reason, quite at random, making an absurd mockery of all man's plans and dreams.

Bérenger is resurrected in *Rhinocéros* (1958), in which one or two people catch a mysterious disease, rhinoceritis, and spread the infection to others, until everyone has turned into a rhinoceros except Bérenger, who obstinately clings to his humanity. The various stages of the epidemic correspond very pointedly to the contagious spread of a totalitarian ideology—most obviously Nazism—and the play is regarded as Ionesco's most readily comprehensible parable. It has been performed with great success all over the world and was the work that established Ionesco's international reputation.

The author has explained that "two fundamental

states of consciousness are at the root of all my plays. . . . These two basic feelings are those of evanescence on the one hand, and heaviness on the other; of emptiness and of an overabundance of presence; of the unreal transparency of the world, and of its opaqueness. . . . The sensation of evanescence results in a feeling of anguish, a sort of dizziness. But all of this can just as well become euphoric; anguish is suddenly transformed into liberty." This is the mood that Amédée experiences when he leaves his home and marriage, and that possesses Bérenger at the beginning of *Le Piéton de l'air* (1962, translated as *A Stroll in the Air*), when he learns to fly like a bird. But Bérenger's new accomplishment brings with it a broadened perspective of the world, and such an apocalyptic overview of the human condition that he returns appalled to earth.

Indeed, the almost mystical euphoria of which Ionesco speaks is a rare state of mind for him: "I am most often under the dominion of the opposite feeling: lightness changes to heaviness, transparency to thickness; the world weighs heavily; the universe crushes me. A curtain, an insuperable wall, comes between me and the world, between me and myself. Matter fills everything, takes up all space, annihilates all liberty under its weight. . . . Speech crumbles."

In *Le Roi se meurt* (1962, translated as *Exit the King*), Bérenger is the dying ruler of a kingdom which shrinks, as his power declines, until all that is left is his throne, suspended in the void. And in the end, that too vanishes. Ionesco has always written out of deep personal obsessions, but never so openly as in the last two Bérenger plays, which are unmistakable projections of the author's own preoccupation with his ultimate extinction. John Weightman has described Ionesco as "an extreme example of that common modern type, the religious temperament divorced from any religious conviction." The truth of this has become increasingly evident, notably in *La Soif et la faim* (1965, translated as *Hunger and Thirst*), an allegorical account of its Bérenger-like hero's abortive quest for faith. This not very successful play was the first of Ionesco's works to be performed at the Comédie Française, the traditional home of French classic drama. The most widely performed of his recent plays was *Macbett* (1972), a reworking of Shakespeare's *Macbeth* which demonstrates in blackly comic terms how absolutely power corrupts.

Many of Ionesco's later plays were originally written as short stories, which have themselves been published in the collection *La Photo du colonel* (1962, translated as *The Colonel's Photograph*). His other prose works include a novel, *Le Solitaire* (1973), and the volume of autobiographical, theoretical and polemical articles called *Notes et contre-notes* (1962, translated as *Notes and Counter-Notes*), which show him to be one of the most introspective and articulate of dramatists. His first film, *La Vase* (The Mire, 1973), which he wrote, directed, and performed, is a savagely destructive portrait of the artist ending, miraculously, with a vigorously defiant affirmation of life.

Two volumes of Ionesco's journal have been published, *Journal en miettes* (1967, translated as *Fragments of a Journal*) and *Présent passé passé présent* (1968, translated as *Present Past, Past Present*). His anguished obsession with death and the consequent meaninglessness of life is a recurrent theme; another is his childhood which, apart from a brief interlude of blissful happiness, seems to have been characterized by a sense of alienation from his family, and particularly from his dominating lawyer father. Since then he has found relief from the "banality of ordinary life shot through with horror" only in his rare moments of euphoric illumination, and in alcohol. He is a chronic hypochondriac and provides unself-pitying and indeed extremely funny accounts of his experiences in a succession of clinics and nursing homes. Apart from these autobiographical passages, the journals include polemical notes, rejected dialogue from plays, and records of dreams. The second volume contains a series of dark fairy tales in which it is always the child who suffers at the hands of his oafish parents. Ionesco has also produced several books for children, controversial mixtures of the real and the surreal, published very successfully as *Story Number 1*, *Story Number 2*, and so on.

In his illuminating chapter on Ionesco in *The Theatre of the Absurd*, Martin Esslin points out that the author is not concerned to *describe* his experience of life, "he is trying to make us experience with him *what it feels like*." He therefore relies far less than most dramatists on words, far more on powerfully suggestive *visual* images. As he says: "I have, for example, tried to exteriorize the anxiety . . . of my characters through objects; to make the stage settings speak; to translate the action into visual terms. . . . I have thus tried to extend the language of the theatre." Ionesco's methods, as well as his anguished demonstration of the absurdity of human life, have had an international influence equaled only by that of Samuel Beckett.

Ionesco's own literary antecedents are difficult to identify—he has, for example, professed an absolute dislike of the classic French dramatists of the seventeenth and eighteenth centuries. His most obvious immediate ancestor is Alfred Jarry, and Ionesco indeed holds the rank of Transcendant Satrap in that august body of dedicated anti-rationalists and Jarry disciples, the Collège de 'Pataphysique. Nevertheless, Ionesco believes that "the aim of the avant-garde should be to rediscover—not invent—in their purest state the permanent forms and forgotten ideals of the theatre." In that sense he is, he believes, a dramatist in the classical tradition of Sophocles and Aeschylus, Shakespeare and Büchner. So he may have been less astonished than most when in 1971 he received the signal honor of election to the Académie Française, the stronghold of French cultural conservatism. He is a small man, quiet and rather shy, with the "large, sad, eloquent eyes" of a circus clown. He is one of the most widely produced of all contemporary dramatists, but lives very unpretentiously with his wife in a top-floor apartment on the Boulevard du Montparnasse. He was named a Chevalier of the Légion d'Honneur in 1970, and received the Jerusalem Prize in 1973.

PRINCIPAL WORKS IN ENGLISH TRANSLATION: *Collected Plays*—Plays, Vol. I: The Chairs, The Bald Prima Donna, The Lesson, Jacques or Obedience, tr. Donald Watson, 1958; Plays, Vol. II: Amédée, The New Tenant, Victims of Duty, tr. Donald Watson, 1958; Plays, Vol. III: The Killer, Improvisation, Maid to Marry, tr. Donald Watson, 1960; Plays, Vol. IV: Rhinoceros, The Leader, The Future Is in Eggs, tr. Derek Prouse, 1960; Plays, Vol. V: Exit the King, The Motor Show, Foursome, tr. Donald Watson, 1963; Plays, Vol. VI: A Stroll in the Air, Frenzy for Two, tr. Donald Watson, 1965; Plays, Vol. VII: Hunger and Thirst, The Picture, Anger, Salutations, tr. Donald Watson, 1968; Plays, Vol. VIII: Here Comes a Chopper, The Oversight, The Foot of the Wall, tr. Donald Watson, 1971; Plays, Vol. IX: Macbett, The Mire, Learning to Walk, tr. Donald Watson, 1973. *Other Works*—Notes and Counter-Notes, tr. Donald Watson, 1964; The Colonel's Photograph and Other Stories, tr. Jean Stewart and John Russell, 1967; Fragments of a Journal, tr. Jean Stewart, 1968; Story No. 1, 1969; Story No. 2, 1970; Present Past, Past Present, tr. Helen R. Lane, 1971; Story No. 3, 1971.

ABOUT: Benmusa, S. Eugène Ionesco, 1956; Bonnefoy, C. Conversations with Eugène Ionesco, 1971; Coe, R. N. Ionesco, 1961; Esslin, M. The Theatre of the Absurd, 1968; Esslin, M. Brief Chronicle: Essays on Modern Theatre, 1970; Fowlie, W. Climate of Violence, 1967; Grossvogel, D. I. 20th Century French Drama, 1961 (originally published as The Self-Conscious Stage in Modern French Drama, 1958); Grossvogel, D. I. The Blasphemers: The Theater of Brecht, Ionesco, Beckett, Genet, 1964 (originally published as Four Playwrights and a Postscript, 1962); Guicharnaud, J. Modern French Theatre from Giraudoux to Genet, 1967; Hayman, R. Eugène Ionesco, 1972; Jacobsen, J. and Mueller, W. R., Ionesco and Genet: Playwrights of Silence, 1968; Marowitz, C. and others (eds.) The Encore Reader, 1965; Pronko, L. C. Eugène Ionesco, 1965; Senart, P. Ionesco, 1964; Sontag, S. Against Interpretation, 1966; Tynan, K. Curtains, 1961; Tynan, K. Tynan Right and Left, 1967; Wellwarth, G. E. The Theater of Protest and Paradox, 1964; Williams, R. Drama from Ibsen to Brecht, 1968. *Periodicals*—Books Abroad Winter 1968; Cahiers des Saisons October 1955, Winter 1959; Combat February 17, 1955; Educational Theatre Journal October 1961; Encore June–July 1957; French Review February 1959; French Studies January 1961; Horizon May 1961; Hudson Review Summer 1958; Modern Drama May 1961; New Statesman March 29, 1968; New York Times January 7, 1968; New York Times Magazine May 1, 1966; New Yorker December 1960; Nouvelle Revue Française February 1, 1958, February 1960; Observer (London) June 22, June 29, July 6, 1958; Proceedings of the Leeds Philosophical and Literary Society March 1962; Theatre Arts March, June, July 1958, August 1960; Thought Autumn 1965; Times Literary Supplement April 1, 1954; March 4, 1960; April 21, 1961; September 21, 1962; August 30, 1963; October 31, 1968; December 4, 1969; March 19, 1971; Tulane Drama Review October 1958, Autumn 1959, Spring 1960, Spring 1963; World Theatre Autumn 1959; Yale French Studies Summer 1959.

*IVANOV, GEORGY (VLADIMIROVICH)

(October 28, 1894–August 1958), Russian poet, was born in Petersburg into a wealthy, cultured family of Scottish ancestry. He entered a school for military cadets in Petersburg, began writing verse, and soon took his place in the literary life of the capital. He briefly considered himself a Futurist, joining Severyanin's ego-futurist group in 1911 and the following year producing his first book, *Otplytie na ostrov Tsiteru* (The Embarkation for the Island of Cythera, 1912), which however contains little that could be considered ego-futurist. The poems in it were in fact very eclectic, and its title indicates the influence of Kuzmin, a poet whose essay on "beautiful clarity" had become the manifesto of the acmeist movement. This was a neoclassical reaction against the mysticism and "otherworldliness" of symbolism, emphasizing instead clarity and concreteness; its leader Nikolai Gumilev was one of the critics who favorably reviewed Ivanov's book, and when they met soon afterwards Ivanov joined Gumilev's *Tsekh Poetov* (Poets' Guild).

During the next ten years, until he left Russia forever some years after the Revolution, Ivanov was to remain a minor acmeist poet, publishing five more collections which conveyed with fresh objectivity the charms of the physical world. Most of the poems in his second book, *Gornitsa* (The Chamber, 1914), describe objects—books, etchings, vases of flowers, or fruit—in minute detail, after the manner of a still-life painter. At the beginning of World War I Gumilev volunteered for military service, his place as poetry critic of the magazine *Apollon* being taken by the twenty-year-old Ivanov, who proved a penetrating critic. *Pamyatnik slavy* (Monument of Glory, 1915) contains his war poems, though unlike those of Gumilev they do not glorify battle but are notable for their deeply religious feeling, similar to that expressed by Gumilev's wife, Anna Akhmatova. His subsequent acmeist verse also tends to combine Gumilev's masculinity of form with the feminine sensibility of Akhmatova, as in his fourth book, *Veresk* (Heather, 1916) in which he turned from war back to his old themes.

After the Revolution Ivanov, his inherited income gone, became secretary of the Poets' Union. Leonid Strakhovsky recalled him at a meeting in

* ē vä′ nəf

1918 as "he read his poetry in a singing, swaying voice, almost resembling that of a somnambulist. Tall, thin, with his hair in bangs covering most of his forehead, with his protruding Bourbon-like lower-lip and half-closed eyes. . . ." After Gumilev's execution as a counterrevolutionary in 1921 Ivanov edited a collection of his friend's work, and shortly afterwards he emigrated, having published two more collections of his own poetry, *Sady* (Gardens, 1921), perhaps the best of his early books, and *Lampada* (The Icon-Lamp, 1922). It was the pictorial quality of these poems that impressed the critics: "A world of subdued, melancholy colors, half-deteriorated old etchings, the architectural grandeur of St. Petersburg—all of these pass before the reader's eyes in light masterfully composed verses. . . . Georgy Ivanov's inspiration has almost always as its source some work of art." Leonid Strakhovsky, quoting this from a contemporary review of *Lampada*, remarked that such words remind one of Ivanov's kinship to Osip Mandelstam, another poet concerned less with life than with its reflection in art.

It was not until after he settled in Paris in 1922 that Ivanov came to full maturity as a poet, though during his first decade in exile his only publications were two prose works. *Peterburgskie zimy* (Petersburg Winters, 1928) is a book of memoirs about the literary life of the former capital, giving colorful portraits of such writers as Innokenty Annensky, Gumilev, Akhmatova, and Mikhail Kuzmin. It was at first regarded as a document, though later critics have shown that much of it is fanciful. *Trety Rim* (The Third Rome, 1929) consists of fragments, published in two *émigré* journals, from an uncompleted historical novel about Russia on the eve of the Revolution.

In 1931 Ivanov returned to poetry with *Rozy* (Roses), a collection of poignant and superbly executed lyrics which many critics regard as his masterpiece. Always a fine craftsman, Ivanov had now mastered the mysterious connections between sound, rhythm, and meaning in poems which, far from the classical ideals of his early work, were neoromantic and introspective, closer to Blok than Gumilev. As Gleb Struve has remarked, by ceasing to seek the wonder of form in the external world, he discovered the higher miracle of music within the soul. This decisive change in manner accompanied and reflected a much darker view of life. The philosophical nihilism so characteristic of his later work is already well developed in *Rozy* and dominates his next collection, which has the same title as his first book, *Otplytie na ostrov Tsiteru* (1937). Vladimir Markov has said that "Ivanov saved himself as a poet by giving up all hope on the surface. His short diary-like poems outwardly present the spectacle of a poet for whom the loss of

GEORGY IVANOV

Russia is equivalent to the loss of everything, even poetry. . . . And yet Ivanov, seemingly unintentionally, produces beauty at every step, as if it were residing on his fingertips."

His later work becomes increasingly nihilistic, and many Russian critics have regarded him as the only true existentialist in modern Russian poetry. His third prose work, the philosophical essay or story *Raspad atoma* (The Splitting of the Atom, 1938), is an introspective and rather Joycean analysis of contemporary man which makes the point that for the Russian *émigré* the existential void is a very real and permanent condition rather than a purely philosophical one, since he actually has no home to return to; as Ivanov wrote elsewhere, he can only "tenderly circle in a dead men's waltz at an *émigré* ball." *Raspad atoma* apparently takes its title from a phrase in Henry Miller's *Tropic of Cancer* and it contains scenes that are deliberately pornographic. Such few notices as appeared in the *émigré* press sharply rebuked the author on this account, but in some cases also acknowledged that the work was important and moving. He also wrote a great deal of criticism and translated French and English poets, among them St. John Perse and Coleridge.

Critical opinion has been divided about Ivanov's postwar poetry, collected in the volumes *Portret bez skhodstva* (Portrait Without Likeness, 1950) and *Stikhi 1943–1958* (Poems, 1958). According to Renato Poggioli, who regarded *Rozy* as his masterpiece, "the late Ivanov was perhaps all too eager to heed the morbid appeal of the muses of dejection and rejection, of despair and cynicism." Other critics, however, think that these postwar years produced his best verse. One of these is Nina Berberova, who believes that Ivanov made of the poverty, illness, and alcoholism of his last years a powerful myth of self-destruction.

Berberova visited the poet in a home for the aged in Hyères where he died. She says: "Ivanov's arms and legs were covered with needle marks, cockroaches were all over his blanket and pillow, the room had not been made up for weeks (not by fault of the management), and in the view of outsiders the sick man was subject to heavy attacks of either rage or depression. Depression, however, almost never left him, it was with him all those last years, not only months—his verses of his last period are testimony of this. When he was told he had to wash, that his room had to be tidied up, that the sheets had to be changed, he merely repeated that he "wasn't scared of dirt.' Evidently he ascribed to this sentence not only a moral meaning, which I guessed, but a physical one. He had always feared death to the point of horror, of despair. It turned out to be for him a salvation come too late." He had been married twice, first to Gabrielle Evdovna Ternisien, an actress and dancer in Meyerhold's company, and second to the novelist Irina Odoevtseva.

Georgy Ivanov is, with Vladislav Khodasevich and Marina Tsvetaeva, recognized as one of the most important poets of the Russian literary emigration. But unlike Khodasevich, most of whose mature poetry was written before he left Russia, and who stopped writing poetry almost completely a few years later, Ivanov had been only a minor figure on the fringe of the acmeist movement before emigration. It was as an *émigré* in Paris that he developed into a major poet, making out of the loss of his native land a nihilistic myth which is expressed in poems of utter simplicity, brevity, and beauty.

PRINCIPAL WORKS IN ENGLISH TRANSLATION: *Poems in* Bowra, C. M. (ed.) A Second Book of Russian Verse, 1948; Markov, V. and Sparks, M. Modern Russian Poetry, 1966; Obolensky, D. The Penguin Book of Russian Verse, 1962; Slavonic Review December 1931; Russian Review January 1949; Tri-Quarterly Spring 1973.

ABOUT: Berberova, N. The Italics Are Mine: Memoirs of the Russian Literary Emigration, 1969; Brown, C. The Prose of Osip Mandelstam, 1965; Poggioli, R. The Poets of Russia, 1960. *Periodicals*—Russian Review January 1949, April 1955; Tri-Quarterly Spring 1973.

***IVANOV, VSEVOLOD VYACHESLAVOVICH** (1895–August 15, 1963), Russian short story writer, novelist, and dramatist, was born in Lebyazhye, near Semipalatinsk, a Siberian village on the border of Turkestan. His mother was half-Polish and half-Kirghiz, while his father, the illegitimate son of a governor-general of Turkestan, spoke seven Oriental languages and dreamed of a university career, but ended as a village teacher and an alcoholic. The sight of his father's misery led Ivanov to pledge himself not to drink or smoke, so that he read a great deal "out of boredom" when everybody else was drinking vodka. Like his master Gorky, Ivanov led in youth and early manhood a remarkably varied and adventurous life. At the age of fifteen he ran away from school to become a clown in a traveling circus, and later he spent his winters as a compositor in a printing shop, his summers in a fascinating variety of itinerant jobs: as the dervish and fakir Ben Ali Bey, as a traveling actor, sword-swallower, organ-grinder, acrobat, wrestler, clown, songwriter, lottery coupon salesman, barman, navvy, sorter in the emerald mines, and sailor.

* ē vä′ nəf

This adventurous existence inspired his early stories, the first of which appeared in 1915 in a local journal in the Siberian town of Petropavlovsk; in 1916 he sent one of them, "Na Irtyshe" (On the Irtysh) to Gorky, who published it, but rejected the next twenty, advising the young writer to live and read more. Ivanov, unlike Gorky, was never greatly concerned with political and social problems, but throughout the Civil War he was in the Siberian battle zone, narrowly escaping death from typhus as well as execution. He fought in Admiral Kolchak's White Army, perhaps as a conscript, was taken prisoner by the Reds and sentenced to be shot. Pardoned, he joined the Red Army and fought as a guerrilla, helping in the Red Guard's defense of Omsk against the advancing Czechs. But he also made speeches, wrote articles, and in 1919 brought out his first collection of stories, *Rogulki* (Fuses), printed and published by himself in Taiga Junction (Central Siberia).

At the beginning of 1921 he went to Petrograd, where he would have perished from cold and starvation but for Gorky, who installed him in his "House of Scholars," gave him some boots, and introduced him into the literary circle of the Serapion Brothers, one of whom, Fedin, provided him with a pair of trousers. Ivanov's long story "Partizany" (Guerrillas) came out in 1921 in the first issue of *Krasnaya nov* (Red Virgin Soil), a magazine in which many of his later stories and novels were also published. The guerrillas in "Partizany" are typical of many of Ivanov's characters in that they stumble quite accidentally into their warlike role. Ivanov, like Babel, is fascinated by the violence and brutality of war, and he presents the Revolution not in terms of ideology but as an outburst of instinctive passions in which his characters, mostly simple peasants whose lives are as primitive and cruel as their harsh Siberian countryside, are swept up. As Marc Slonim puts it: "The intoxication of blood, the fury of annihilation sweep over millions of men, and the Revolution in Asiatic Russia is like a prairie fire."

Ivanov is best known for his short novel *Bronepoezd no. 14–69* (1922, Armored Train 14–69), which is based on an actual event. A guerrilla band armed only with rifles has to capture an armored train carrying weapons to the Whites, and a Chinese partisan among them stops the train by lying on the tracks and allowing himself to be crushed by it. R. A. Maguire called the guerrilla commander Vershinin "a perfect example of the de-heroized hero," because he has drifted by pure chance into his present situation. In 1927 the novel was made into a play (translated by Gibson-Cowan and A. T. K. Grant as *Armored Train 14–69*), which was staged with immense success by Stanislavsky at the Moscow Art Theatre.

Ivanov's view of life was fundamentally nihilistic, reflecting the meaninglessness and aimlessness of life and human behavior. For example, the novel *Golubye peski* (Skyblue Sands, 1923) is about the struggle for the remote Siberian town of Ust-Mongolsk, which is forever changing hands in costly battles, though nobody knows why its capture should be important. At the end the heroes on all three sides—Reds, Whites, and Greens—are dead, and the town sinks back into the obscurity from which it had briefly emerged. These early works of Ivanov's are basically adventure stories, packed with incidents and characters from the author's own extraordinary life. What they lack in shape and control they make up in excitement, and in the vigor and vividness of their prose, which is full of fanciful and colorful metaphors: Ivanov writes of "the red-bearded angry Russian wind," or of a hut that smells "unhurriedly like loaves of bread."

In spite of the enormous popularity of his first books, Ivanov came to believe that Zamyatin, who had accused him of "writing with the nostrils," was right. Changing times also led him to move away from revolutionary romanticism, and the short novel *Vozvrashcheniye Buddy* (The Return of Buddha, 1923) begins his second period, in which his works have carefully developed plots and the gaudy colors of his prose are dimmed. *Taynoye taynykh* (Mystery of Mysteries, 1927), a collection of tales of village life, shows the same primitivist conception of human behavior as his early works, but the move away from battle scenes and towards simpler plots made his pessimism more obvious, so that Vyacheslav Polonsky said of this book: "In every story we come face to face with futility, frustrated hopes, and the triumph of destructive forces beyond man's control." In these stories Ivanov also attempts psychological analysis of his characters, the result being an unrestrained sexuality

VSEVOLOD VYACHESLAVOVICH IVANOV

which led to his being accused of "neo-bourgeois" spirit by Marxist critics.

His later work is much inferior to his tales and short novels of the Civil War, and most critics have shared Zavalishin's judgment that "the third period was a long-drawn decline, in spite of Ivanov's attempts at recapturing his old vivid manner." In common with most other Soviet writers his work evolved towards realism, and he tried to deal with the social aspects of life in the period of the Five-Year Plan and economic reconstruction in *Puteshestviye v stranu kotoroy eshche net* (Journey to a Country That Does Not Yet Exist, 1930), and *Povesti brigadira M. N. Sinitsyna* (Tales of Brigadier Sinitsyn, 1931). The most successful of these later works is *Pokhozhdeniya fakira* (1935, abridged and translated as *Adventures of a Fakir*), a picaresque semi-autobiographical novel based on his early adventures. *Parkhomenko* (1937) is a glorification of a Red Cavalry commander which makes its hero into a romantic legend, but lacks the vigor and excitement of Ivanov's early works about the Civil War. His plays, such as *Blokada* (Blockade, 1929), a chronicle of the Kronstadt Rebellion of 1921 and its suppression by the Red Army, show a similar decline. Several of the later ones are historical dramas such as *Dvennadtsat' molodtsev iz tabakerki* (Twelve Brave Fellows From a Snuff-Box, 1936), about the murder of Czar Paul 1.

During World War II Ivanov served as a war correspondent and also wrote many stories and the novel *Vzyatiye Berlina* (The Taking of Berlin, 1945), which however did not conform to official views and was condemned as ideologically harmful. In the last years of Stalin's reign Ivanov remained silent, faithful to the liberal ideals of his youth, until in 1953 he published his interesting reminiscences of Gorky. His last works include accounts of travels in Eastern Siberia and some posthumously published diaries and notebooks.

PRINCIPAL WORKS IN ENGLISH TRANSLATION: Armored Train 14–69: A Play in Eight Scenes, 1933; Adventures of a Fakir, 1935 (Canada, Patched Breeches; England, I Live a Queer Life); *Stories in* Cournos, J. Short Stories Out of Soviet Russia, 1929; Konovalov, S. Bonfire, 1934; Kunitz, J. (ed.) Azure Cities: Stories of New Russia, 1929; Slonim, M. and Reavey, G. Soviet Literature, 1933. *Periodicals*—Nation June 27, July 4, 1925; Living Age March 1935; Soviet Literature 10 1963, 1 1970.

ABOUT: Alexandrova, V. A History of Soviet Literature, 1963; Birkett, G. A. *English introduction to* The Saga of the Sergeant (in Russian), 1966; Block, A. C. Changing World in Plays and Theatre, 1939; Brown, E. J. Russian Literature Since the Revolution, 1963; Maguire, R. A. Red Virgin Soil, 1966; Slonim, M. Modern Russian Literature, 1953; Slonim, M. Russian Theater, 1963; Slonim, M. Soviet Russian Literature, 1964; Smith, H. (ed.) Columbia Dictionary of Modern European Literature, 1947; Struve, G. Twenty-five Years of Soviet Russian Literature, 1944; Zavalishin, V. Early Soviet Writers, 1958. *Periodicals*—Soviet Literature 10 1963; Times (London) August 17, 1963.

***JACOB, MAX** (July 11, 1876–March 5, 1944), French poet, was born at Quimper, in Brittany, of Jewish parents. The family owned a shop which was used for tailoring, embroidery, and the sale of antiques. His childhood was unhappy and he made several suicide attempts. Jacob was educated at the *lycée* in his native town and the École Coloniale in Paris. When he left school he settled in the metropolis. His ambition was to become a painter, but the need to earn a living drove him into a variety of casual jobs: music teacher, art critic, secretary, solicitor's clerk, tutor. He was always poor and often hungry.

Jacob was a small man, with a monocle. He was immensely charming and witty, an expert fortuneteller, and a mime whom some thought superior to Chaplin. His countless friends included most of the major writers and poets who lived in Paris between 1900 and 1921, and he was especially close to Picasso, one of his first admirers, and Apollinaire. They turned the rue Ravignan in Montmartre into the headquarters of cubism, and a permanent legend. Jacob retained his interest in painting, illustrated a number of his own books, and in 1920 had a large one-man exhibition of his gouaches and watercolors at Bernheim's.

Although his parents were nonpracticing Jews, he was a man with a naturally religious temperament (which accommodated a lifelong faith in astrology and the occult). In 1909 Jacob had a vision of Christ in his sunless flat on the rue Ravignan, and began a long, difficult, and extremely public journey into the Roman Catholic Church. There was a second vision, characteristically enough in a movie theatre, in December 1914, and the following February Jacob was baptized with Picasso (of all people) as his godfather. He used to describe a third vision. The Madonna appeared to him in the Church of the Sacred Heart in Montmartre and addressed him with the words: "What a lousy creature you are, my poor Max!" "Not as lousy as all that, Blessed Virgin," he replied, and caused a considerable disturbance by pushing his way huffily out of the crowded church.

* zha kōb'

In 1921, when he had become famous, Jacob felt obliged to withdraw from the temptations of Paris; he was homosexual, but wretchedly unresigned to this condition. He went to live near the Benedictine abbey of Saint-Benoît-sur-Loire. His unbelieving friends, unable to grasp the possibility that a Christian convert might remain a sinner—a very repentant sinner in this case—murmured the word "tartufe." Nevertheless, as Jean Rousselot says, Jacob was unable "to reinforce his exile by a vow of silence: to have an audience was his reason for being alive." He continued his dialogue with the world through thousands of letters—most of them still uncollected—that must be considered an important and integral part of his work.

He subsequently returned to Paris for what he described as "the most sinful period of my life," but then resumed his exile at Saint-Benoît, growing in charity and humility, until the war came. During the Occupation he was made to wear the yellow star, a bitter experience to which he refers in one of his last prose poems. He was arrested by the Germans on February 24, 1944, and died of bronchial pneumonia ten days later in the concentration camp at Drancy.

Jacob's first collection of verse appeared in 1912 under the title *Les Œuvres burlesques et mystiques de Frère Matorel* (The Burlesque and Mystical Works of Brother Matorel), and his most famous and influential work, a collection of prose poems called *Le Cornet à dés* (The Dice Box), five years later. These poems, written in the early 1900s, made use of a free association of images, of "words at liberty," of the disconnected debris of dream and fantasy—anticipating surrealism to an extent that has earned Jacob in some quarters the title of "father of modern poetry."

La Défense de Tartufe (Tartufe's Defense, 1919), described by Jacob as "ecstasies, remorse, visions, prayers, poems, and meditations of a converted Jew," was intended as a reply to those who questioned the sincerity of his religious convictions. *Art poétique* (Art of Poetry, 1922) is a marvelously free, intimate, and stimulating statement of his aesthetic. Some of his more important collections of poetry are *Le Laboratoire central* (The Central

Laboratory, 1921), *Visions infernales* (Visions of Hell, 1924), *Les Pénitents en maillots roses* (Penitents in Pink Tights, 1925), *Fond de l'eau* (Bottom of the Water, 1927), *Sacrifice impérial* (Imperial Sacrifice, 1929), *Rivage* (Riverbank, 1931), *Ballades* (1938), and *Derniers poèmes en vers et en prose* (Last Poems in Verse and Prose, 1945). His charming "Breton songs" were written under the pseudonym Morven Le Gaëlique.

Jacob was the author of a number of novels and short stories, immensely inventive and intelligent, describing contemporary types and especially the *bourgeoisie*, which he castigated for its "veiled stupidity, silent cruelty, rivalries, unending bickering." He also tried his hand at plays, an operetta, biography, translation, and even a children's book.

Much loved as he was, Jacob remained a mystery even to his friends, alternately generous and paranoid, a buffoon and a cruel satirist, an artist and a mystic. "A personality is but a persisting error," he said. It has been suggested that his clowning was an attempt to escape from life, but to him it was life itself, or an important part of it: "gaiety, especially when sad, is divine fire."

MAX JACOB

Jacob said that a work of art is "situated," that it forms an autonomous world of its own, and that "in questions of poetry only the poetry matters . . . [meaning] the agreement of the words, the images and their constant and mutual appeal." He also believed that poetry is an "amusement," recalling T. S. Eliot's "superior amusement." The "amusement" is apparent in his technical virtuosity, which derives from Verlaine and Jules Laforgue, and in his wit, his puns, his parody, his irony. And yet he could write moving religious verse of the utmost simplicity and startling frankness. "His poems," one critic has said, "could be described alternatively as arabesques traced by a refined sensibility and smudged over by the roughness of burlesque; or as the most heartrending cries trailing off into puns and ironic cackles." Wallace Fowlie sees him as "the type of modern mystic who reveals himself by means of a burlesqued fantasy in which he can permit himself every form of adventure, even the love of God. He is an example of the man who is embarrassed by having come upon a profound part in his own being, whose face bears the inwardly turned expression of the clown. . . . The clown's vocation is partly angelic. He causes laughter through understanding the source of joy and through enacting the innocency of man."

It is probably true enough that Jacob was the only true cubist poet, as he claimed. How much more than that he was is arguable. André Billy said he was "a great poet if poetry is first and foremost caprice, fantasy, play on words and juxtaposition of images, but when he has his pen in his hand he is not much of a musician and does not know the secret of verbal melody." Many accept this, but Wallace Fowlie among others believes that "the deeper, more total effect of his poetry is one of exceptional suppleness in verbal expression, of infinite metamorphosis. In a way, he is a poet for poets." These divided opinions are partly the result of unavoidable ignorance: three quarters of his work is said to be unpublished; there is no collected edition and no fully documented biography. A final judgment must wait until some of the gaps are filled. What is beyond doubt is that his poetry represents a parting of the ways. It looks back to the past, as we can see from his assurance that "the laws of beauty are eternal," and forward to those he influenced—Apollinaire, dada, and the surrealists, and through them their heirs.

PRINCIPAL WORKS IN ENGLISH TRANSLATION: Drawings and Poems, ed. and tr. by S. J. Collier, 1951. *Poems and stories in* Fowlie, W. (ed.) Mid-Century French Poets, 1955; Hartley, A. (ed.) Penguin Book of French Verse, Twentieth Century, 1959; Strachan, W. J. (ed.) Apollinaire to Aragon, 1948. *Periodicals*—Chicago Review 3–4 1966; Poetry May 1950.

ABOUT: Béalu, M. Dernier Visage de Max Jacob, 1946; Billy, A. Max Jacob, 1946 (new ed., 1965); Blanchet, A. La Littérature et le spirituel, I, 1959; Curley, D. N. and A. (eds.) Modern Romance Literatures (A Library of Literary Criticism), 1967; Emié, L. Dialogues avec Max Jacob, 1954; Fabureau, H. Max Jacob: Son Œuvre, 1935; Hackett, C. A. Anthology of Modern French Poetry, 1964; Kamber, G. Max Jacob and the Poetics of Cubism, 1972; Lagarde, P. Max Jacob, mystique et martyr, 1944; Rousselot, J. Max Jacob au sérieux, 1958; Salmon, A. Max Jacob, Poète, peintre, mystique et homme de qualité, 1927; Smith, H. (ed.) Columbia Dictionary of Modern European Literature, 1947. *Periodicals*—Catholic World July 1959; French Studies July 1953, April 1957; Mercure de France August 1951; Modern Language Notes May 1963; Modern Language Review October 1956; Nouvelle

Revue Française March 1927, April 1928; Poetry March 1950; Thought Summer 1967; Times Literary Supplement October 9, 1959; December 1, 1966.

JACOBSON, DAN (March 7, 1929–), South African novelist, essayist, and short story writer, writes: "I was born in Johannesburg, South Africa. My father and mother were both immigrants to the country from Eastern Europe. When I was four years old the family moved to Kimberley, and I spent my boyhood there, attending the Kimberley Boys High School. I matriculated at the age of sixteen, and then attended the University of the Witwatersrand, Johannesburg, from which I graduated three years later with a bachelor's degree. Subsequently I lived and worked in Israel and England, then returned to South Africa. I was employed as a journalist in Johannesburg for a couple of years, and also worked for a spell in the family business (cattlefeed milling) in Kimberley. I left South Africa in 1954, with the intention of settling in England, where I now live. Since that time, however, I have been back to South Africa several times on visits, and have also twice spent periods at universities in the United States. In 1956–57 I was a Fellow in Creative Writing at Stanford University, California; in 1965 I held a Visiting Professorship at Syracuse University, New York.

"Most of my fiction and much of my work in other genres (reportage, memoirs, essays) have been set in South Africa or have dealt with South African themes: I suppose this is inevitable in spite of the fact that much the greater part of my adult life has been spent outside that country. Whether or not I will continue to draw so much of my material from South Africa is something I simply do not know, and do not believe I can control. I should add, however, that I find it hard to imagine that I would have been a writer of any kind if I had stayed in South Africa, and that after my first spell abroad the ambition to become a writer was for me almost indistinguishable from the ambition to live in a country other than South Africa.

"So far as I am aware of a development in my writing since my first stories were published, it is in the direction of trying to combine a greater fullness and complexity of subject-matter (of situation, of character, of emotion) with a greater lucidity of style. My immediate intention or hope as a writer is to give to others the same sort of pleasure that I have got out of reading the work of writers I admire. Only if my work gives that pleasure can it possibly have any effect of any other kind.

"I married Margaret Pye in 1954, and have two sons and a stepson. We live in London. My hobby is gardening."

Soon after he moved to England ("a happier country than South Africa, a more gentle and hopeful country"), Dan Jacobson attracted critical attention with his first novel, *The Trap*. The setting is a farm on the African veldt, where the conflict between black and white is studied obliquely and in microcosm through its effects upon the lives of the four main characters. This short novel was warmly praised by the South African writer Peter Abrahams for its "cool, unhurried clarity" and in particular for its "re-creation of the feel and smell and mood of a Boer farm," while the *Times Literary Supplement* called its author "a writer of considerable promise, whose ability to write ironic dialogue is matched by a telling restraint in the use of descriptive prose."

DAN JACOBSON

Dance in the Sun is another *conte*—this time a tragicomic one—with a small cast and a confined setting; it was similarly commended for its simplicity and sureness, its skillful "handling through dialogue of complex problems of race and character." Another aspect of Jacobson's talent emerged in *The Price of Diamonds*, a warmhearted comedy of errors in which a meek and elderly Jewish mercant dabbles in crime in an attempt to confound his boastful partner.

Admirable and admired as they were, these early novels seemed to some readers too dependent on a single, limiting idea—not much more than expanded short stories. The "greater fullness and complexity" that Jacobson seeks were most successfully achieved in *The Evidence of Love*. It is set partly in South Africa and partly in London, where an African of mixed blood and a white South African girl reencounter each other, fall in love, variously betray one another, and eventually marry in the shadow of South Africa's Immorality Act. The novel did not escape charges of special pleading and strained construction, but most critics were enthusiastic—among them A. Alvarez, who called it "a considerable artistic achievement" by a writer with "the ability to create sensitive, intelligent people and make them act sensitively and intelligently despite the background of guilt and shock." Alvarez could "think of no other novelist with the range of compassion and insight to tackle the theme at all." When he attempted a large-scale family chronicle in *The Beginners* however, Jacobson was less successful. Agreeable and absorbing as it is, the book does not always rise above the level of soap opera.

The Rape of Tamar was a departure, a retelling of the biblical story of Tamar, raped by her half-brother Amnon, and Amnon's consequent murder by Absalom, which leads to Absalom's disastrous armed rebellion against his father, David. The story is narrated by Yonadab, a witty, treacherous, and brilliant Iago who is allowed to speak across the centuries to the modern reader in modern terms and out of a modern sensibility. Philip Toynbee found faults in the book but went on: "How little they count against Jacobson's profound wit, the subtlety of his insights and, perhaps most notable of all, his utterly convincing deployment of the particular political and psychological problems which confront men who are in a position of power. . . . *The Rape of Tamar* is both a *tour de force* and a novel of quite unusual depth and originality."

Some critics believe that Dan Jacobson is at his best in his short stories, and Robert Gutwillig, reviewing *The Zulu and the Zeide*, described the title piece as "a great story" and Jacobson as "one of the best writers of short fiction anywhere." "Few other writers," he said, "can evoke place so vividly or can describe a character so succinctly and finally." Elizabeth Dalton, discussing the stories in *Through the Wilderness*, said that "their literary qualities are finally human qualities as well: intelligence, moral insight, humor, and compassion."

In his fiction, Jacobson's approach to his theme is indirect; the reasons for his hatred of prejudice and injustice are implicit in the stories he tells. When he expresses his liberal views directly, as he does in his essays, he succeeds less well. A collection of his articles on society and literature, most of them from *Encounter* and *Commentary*, were published as *Time of Arrival*, of which Robert Taubman wrote: "He is intrusive with his moral fervor, runs too much to abstraction, fluffs many a grand sentence." His considerable and growing reputation as one of South Africa's finest writers rests on his fiction, and in this form, as Karl Miller has said, he "invariably writes a plain, harmonious prose which runs easily to strong dramatic and poetic effects. He has an excellent comic gift. He has achieved a deep charity towards the people he imagines, and he has a rare feeling for domesticity and family life and for their source in firm loyalty and in passionate love." Dan Jacobson received the John Llewelyn Rhys award for fiction in 1959 and the Somerset Maugham award in 1964.

PRINCIPAL WORKS: *Novels*—The Trap, 1955; A Dance in the Sun, 1956; The Price of Diamonds, 1957; The Evidence of Love, 1960; The Beginners, 1966; The Rape of Tamar, 1970; The Wonder-Worker, 1973. *Short stories*—Long Way from London, 1958; The Zulu and the Zeide, 1959; Beggar My Neighbour, 1964; Through the Wilderness, 1968; Inklings, 1973. *Nonfiction*—No Further West: California Revisited, 1959; Time of Arrival, and Other Essays, 1963.

ABOUT: Contemporary Authors 2, 1963; Vinson, J. (ed.) Contemporary Novelists, 1972; Who's Who in America, 1972–1973. *Periodicals*—Commentary June 1958, June 1959; New Republic April 9, 1956; August 27, 1966; New York Times Book Review May 31, 1959; Saturday Review February 11, 1961; Spectator June 3, 1960.

JEBAVÝ, VÁCLAV. *See* "BŘEZINA, OTOKAR"

JELLICOE, (PATRICIA) ANN (July 15, 1927–), English dramatist and translator, writes: "My mother's family is north country: practical, solid, Methodist, lower middle class; on my mother's side I have numbers of aunts, uncles, cousins; into this milieu I was born and spent my childhood for my mother and father separated when I was eighteen months old. My father's family comes from the south (in Britain the richer, more sophisticated half of the country) and has some aristocratic connection and a little money in an insecure kind of way; they are also rather intelligent. Between these two I oscillate: outwardly much closer to the pattern of my father's family, I feel inwardly the pull of the practical north country.

"I made my first appearance on any stage at the age of four when I played Beauty in *The Sleeping Beauty* in a school production. I can't remember a time since when I didn't want to work in the theatre. My childhood, which was rather unpleasant, was spent mostly at boarding school which, as I now realise, is a system designed to make children conform, to mould them to a standard pattern. At the time I could never understand why I was so unpopular, unhappy and out of step. I thought they were right and I was wrong, and I tried very hard to be like everyone else. To some extent I succeeded and after I left school it took me more than ten years to discover what sort of a person I really was, and what my ideas were.

"When I left school I came to London, to the Central School of Speech and Drama, to learn to be an actress. I did rather well, winning most of the prizes open to me; but I had so little self con-

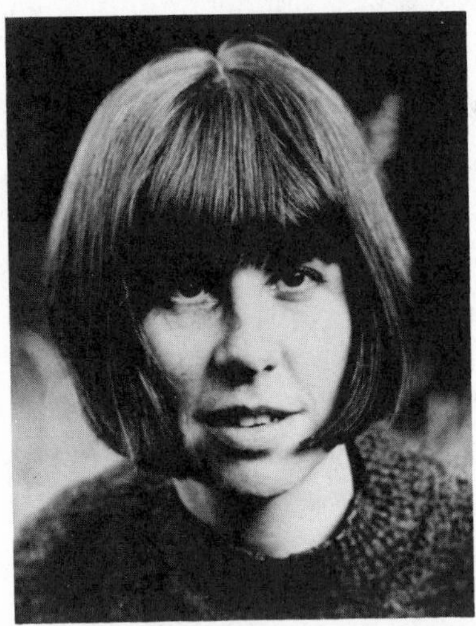

ANN JELLICOE

fidence and work was so hard to get at that time—it was just before television arrived in this country—that I didn't do a great deal of acting. Instead I began to travel; my father, who has rather pleasant Edwardian ideas, had given me an allowance as soon as I left school and this was sufficient for me to keep on a small flat in London while I roamed over Europe for months at a time. I was not in any way wild or dissipated, I was simply free. It was perhaps the first really happy time of my life and fortunately I appreciated at the time how lucky I was. I even felt rather guilty about not working but actually I was learning languages and in later years I was able to translate plays and so earn the time and independence to write my own work.

"I began to act again and to direct amateur companies. At this time I was privately commissioned to make a study of the relationship between theatre practice and theatre architecture. For the first time in my life I began to think deeply about the nature of theatre; this led to an interest in the open stage (audience on three sides) and I founded a theatre club to experiment with the form. We used professional actors but everyone worked free. Here I directed, painted the scenery, and ran the organisation. After two years the effort was too much and we closed down but we had mounted about eight plays (including a one-acter and two translations of my own) and had run at a profit, ending up with about eighteen pounds in the bank.

"I returned to the Central School to teach acting—which essentially meant directing plays—and stayed there for two years. When I left it was chiefly because you were never free to concentrate on trying to achieve an absolute work of art—if the student wasn't ready to be pushed beyond a certain point then you had to hold back. In the end this was very frustrating. About this time *The Observer* newspaper organised a playwriting competition; the conditions of entry and the names of the judges clearly showed they wanted something new and different. I had always wanted to write a play but had never been able to finish. I saw that if I didn't write a play now I never would, so I sat down and wrote *The Sport of My Mad Mother*, which won third prize and was produced at the Royal Court Theatre in 1958. So I became a playwright."

The Sport of My Mad Mother was a total failure commercially, and bewildered most critics, but impressed one or two of them as the immature work of an original and potentially exciting writer. The printed text is singularly unhelpful, since like most of Miss Jellicoe's plays this one is conceived as a total theatrical experience, in which language is only one of the stage's resources, along with gesture, lighting, and nonverbal sound.

It is about a group of teen-agers moved by their own fear and insecurity to aimless violence. They are led by Greta, who in some sense represents Kali, the Indian goddess of creation and destruction: "All creation is the sport of my mad mother Kali." The play is virtually plotless, a string of ritualistic episodes, some of them strangely powerful in their symbolism, as when the teen-agers wrap one of their victims in newspaper and dance around him in mounting frenzy until they rip the paper away. Here, as elsewhere in the work, there is little conventional dialogue, but words and cries repeated until they lose meaning and become incantations, as disturbing and abstractly menacing as accelerating drum rhythms. It is useless to ask the meaning of her plays, the author has said, "but if you allow yourself to be excited by the visual action and the gradual crescendo of noise underlining this, you may begin to appreciate what it's about."

The Girl Guides' Association, hearing perhaps of Miss Jellicoe's interest in young people, then commissioned from her a very large-scale pageant to be performed by its members. She provided them with *The Rising Generation*, a rhythmic, exuberant fable about a monstrous creature called Mother, a gross personification of the female principle, who seeks world domination and the extermination of men. This work, which might well have revolutionized the girl scout movement, was rejected by its sponsors. All the same, John Russell Taylor called it "the most interesting and imaginative work every written in the simple but spectacular form of the youth pageant," and a performance of it at the Royal Court Theatre in 1967 was very warmly received.

Ann Jellicoe had her first success with *The Knack*, which is rather more conventional than its predecessors in its theme, but uncompromising in its manner. Three young men—Tom, Tolen, and Colin—live together in Colin's house in London. Tolen has in abundance the "knack" of seducing young women; Colin has not, but wants it. The play turns on their apparently unequal contest for the favors of the apparently innocent Nancy. What happens is shown rather than described, and though there are some very witty exchanges, language is for the most part used as ritualistically as in Miss Jellicoe's first play. In one scene, where Tom and Colin gradually involve Nancy in their fantasy that a bed is actually a piano, no one says anything for three pages but "ping" or "plong."

The Knack's most remarkable quality, in the opinion of John Russell Taylor, "is the sheer drive of the action, physical and emotional, right through its three acts in one unbroken movement. . . . The spectator is carried along irresistibly by the verve and ebullience of the play, and at the end, even if he does not know what . . . it means, he certainly knows vividly what it is about." It was staged in London in 1961, in New York in 1964, and in Paris in 1967, and has been translated into a delightful film by Dick Lester. "When I write a play," Ann Jellicoe says, "I am trying to communicate with the audience. I do this by every means in my power . . . through their eyes . . . through their ears. . . . These are not loose effects; they are introduced to communicate with the audience directly through their senses, to reinforce the total effect of the play, and they are always geared to character and situation. . . . I write this way because—the image that everybody has of the rational, intellectual, and intelligent man—I don't believe it's true. I think people are driven by their emotions, and by their fears and insecurities."

In *Shelley* (1965), Miss Jellicoe tried her hand at a more orthodox play, an "almost documentary account" of the poet's life which was only moderately well received. She defended her play on television soon after it opened, giving according to one viewer an extremely photogenic and "most impressive all-round display of self-assurance." She has made some excellent translations, especially from Ibsen and Chekhov, and is a very capable director of her own work and that of others.

The Giveaway is a comedy about what happens when a family wins a ten-year supply of cornflakes in a contest. Irving Wardle found it not particularly funny, but thought it "an honest and logical effort to extend her work into popular territory."

Ann Jellicoe is the daughter of John Andrea Jellicoe and the former Frances Henderson, and was born in Middlesbrough, Yorkshire. Her awards at the Central School of Speech and Drama included the coveted Elsie Fogarty prize. Her 1950 marriage to C. E. Knight-Clarke was dissolved in 1961, and she has been married since 1962 to Roger Mayne, an actor, by whom she has a son and a daughter. Her hobbies are reading, sunbathing, music, and pictures.

PRINCIPAL PUBLISHED WORKS: The Sport of My Mad Mother, 1957; The Rising Generation *in* Ark (magazine of the Royal College of Art) 25, 1960; (tr.) Ibsen, H. Rosmersholm, 1961; The Knack, 1962 (republished with The Sport of My Mad Mother in 1964); Shelley, or, The Idealist, 1966; Some Unconscious Influences in the Theatre (lecture), 1967; The Giveaway, 1970.

ABOUT: Taylor, J. R. Anger and After, 1963; Who's Who, 1973; Who's Who in the Theatre, 1972. *Periodicals*—Granta 1964; Guardian February 25, 1972; New Theatre Magazine (Bristol University), 1957.

JENKINS, ELIZABETH. *See* JENKINS (MARGARET) ELIZABETH (HEALD)

JENKINS, (JOHN) ROBIN (September 11, 1912–), Scottish novelist, writes: "My full name is John Robin Jenkins, rather peculiar for a Scot; but then my paternal grandfather was adopted by a family called Jenkins and took its name. The true name, which I never divulge, is as Scotch as haggis, and perhaps for that reason I decided not to use it. It seems to me literary death for a Scottish writer of today to think too much of kilts, heather, and the romantic past, even if it might well mean greater financial success.

"I was born at Cambuslang, a village in Lanarkshire about six miles from Glasgow. In due course I attended Hamilton Academy and Glasgow University, taking an honours degree in English. During the war I worked at forestry, which explains the background of several of my novels. It is, to me, of melancholy interest that the most successful of my novels so far, *Dust on the Paw*, did not have in it, amongst its forty or so characters, one single Scot. I do not know if this has happened before to a novelist of any other nationality. The uniqueness was not, however, noticed by any critic; so it would appear quite proper and natural for a Scot to write about Afghans, English, and Americans, and not about his own countrymen. The consequence of all this was that while reviewing my most recent novel, *The Sardana Dancers*, my thirteenth by the way, a critic in the London *Observer* took me to task rather sternly for my feeble efforts to reproduce the Glasgow dialect, not aware, obviously, that I had lived seventeen years in Glasgow itself, and another twenty or so in its immediate vicinity, and even today can speak that dialect like any bus-driver.

"Apart from those peculiar difficulties, caused, I suppose, by our absorption by England, I am ortho-

ROBIN JENKINS

dox and traditional in my view of what the novel ought to do: that is, create credible characters, in situations that move and in some way illuminate. I find most of my fashionable contemporaries, such as Samuel Beckett, unreadable. I am naïve enough to believe that the future of literature must lie in a more hopeful view of humanity.

"I do not think it the business of a novelist to have squibs of brilliant epithet, metaphor, and allusion exploding on every page. This is showing-off, this is to attract and appease the Sunday reviewers, it is not how to write novels.

"Since my books have not been profitable enough to enable me to live by them I chose teaching rather than journalism. In recent years I have taught English in such countries as Afghanistan, Spain, and at present, 1965, in Sabah, formerly British North Borneo."

The Scottish critic Alastair Thompson, writing in the review *New Saltire*, says that Jenkins in all his novels "explores and exposes with an earnest, stern, tender intensity the many shapes of love"; that his constant theme is the need for each of us to recognize and forgive his own human frailty in order to forgive and love the humanity in others. Thus the unemployed miner in *Happy for the Child*, rejected by his family and by society, achieves a degree of peace by accepting what he has become; the idealist in *The Missionaries* becomes a whole man capable of love only when he can acknowledge human imperfection. Not all of Jenkins's characters achieve these humble victories: the liberal intellectual married to a Chinese wife in *Dust on the Paw* fears to have children but cannot forgive himself this cruelty to his wife and punishes others; the gamekeeper in *The Cone-Gatherers*, enduring without love his marriage to a deformed wife, fixes his hatred on the dwarf Calum, an unembittered "holy fool," and at length is driven to kill Calum and himself. As Jenkins himself says, his novels are conventional in shape and style; but, according to Thompson, they are seized at times with an access of perception so keen that "the scene moves with the powerful compulsion of a poem." Other critics, however, have found one novel after another marred by the author's willingness to work at times far beneath the level of his own best writing, with a perfunctory and unconvincing banality of phrase and conception.

Jenkins has nevertheless been called the best Scottish novelist to have emerged since World War II, and has been compared to the brilliant writer and historian "Lewis Grassic Gibbon" (J. L. Mitchell). In 1955 he received the Frederick Niven Award (for Scottish writing). Jenkins was married in 1937 to Mary McIntyre Wyllie, and has a son and two daughters. He left Sabah in 1968 and now lives in Scotland, at Dunoon, Argyll.

PRINCIPAL WORKS: *Novels*—So Gaily Sings the Lark, 1951; Happy for the Child, 1953; The Thistle and the Grail, 1954; The Cone-Gatherers, 1955; Guests of War, 1956; The Missionaries, 1957; The Changeling, 1958; Love Is a Fervent Fire, 1959; Some Kind of Grace, 1960; Dust on the Paw, 1961; The Tiger of Gold, 1962; A Love of Innocence, 1963; The Sardana Dancers, 1964; A Very Scotch Affair, 1968; The Holy Tree, 1969; The Expatriates, 1971; A Toast to the Lord, 1972; *Stories*—A Far Cry From Bowmore, 1973.

ABOUT: Contemporary Authors 4, 1963; Vinson, J. (ed.) Contemporary Novelists, 1972; Who's Who, 1973. *Periodicals*—New Saltire 3 Spring 1962.

JENKINS, (MARGARET) ELIZABETH (HEALD) (October 31, 1905–), English novelist and biographer, is the daughter of James Heald Jenkins, headmaster of a boys' prep school, and the former Theodora Caldicott Ingram. It was her father, she says, who taught her to find excitement in history. She was born at Hitchin, Hertfordshire, and educated there, at St. Christopher's School, Letchworth, and at Newnham College, Cambridge, where she read English and history (1924–1927). Miss Jenkins was in her own recollection a bookish young woman, who at the university spent most of her spare time in the library, and was "gauche, prim, covered with ink, and wrapped up in work." She began her career as a teacher, and from 1929 to 1939 was senior English mistress at King Alfred School, Hampstead, writing in her spare time. During World War II, she worked as a civil servant. When peace returned she withdrew to her quiet house in Hampstead, and she has devoted herself ever since to research and writing.

Virginia Water, her first novel, was published in

1930, when she was twenty-five. It tells the story of Fanny Arne, a "startled nymph" in the London drawing rooms of the fashionable intelligentsia, who falls in love with a famous and selfish historian and suffers for it. Although both the scene and the people are observed with a "poetically-misted vision," reviewers found the book interesting and full of promise.

This promise was soon redeemed by Miss Jenkins's fourth novel, *Harriet* (1934), winner of the Femina Vie Heureuse prize. It was one of her first explorations of wickedness, a story based on an actual Victorian murder case. Harriet, a woman of subnormal intelligence but considerable wealth, is murdered by her husband, his mistress, and two accomplices. The book traces with great shrewdness and delicacy the stages by which a group of ordinary people bring themselves to commit a particularly callous and hideous crime. Herbert Read was not alone in thinking the novel "an impressive work of art."

The Tortoise and the Hare by contrast is a low-keyed domestic drama about a shy, self-effacing woman who loses her barrister husband to a forceful older woman who is able to further his career. The *Times Literary Supplement* in its review called Miss Jenkins a writer "in whom the most delicate perception of shades of feeling is joined to irony and wit as well as to real gentleness and sympathy." *Brightness* is a more recent novel contrasting the behavior of two young men at Cambridge—an exploration of "the ways in which [parental] love can either fructify or blight." Margaret Parton thought it a tedious illustration of the author's belief in Christian responsibility, but to most reviewers it seemed a wise and powerful book.

The warmth, insight, and subtlety of feeling which distinguish Miss Jenkins's novels are also present in her biographies, which have if anything been even more admired than her fiction. *Lady Caroline Lamb* made skillful use of the scanty information available about that remarkable woman, so that "we have for the first time the whole woman and her spell made manifest." *Henry Fielding* was welcomed as a model of perception and of compression, and *Jane Austen* was "just about what a book of its kind should be." She has also published two admirable collections of shorter studies, *Six Criminal Women* and *Ten Fascinating Women*.

Miss Jenkins's *chef-d'œuvre* is *Elizabeth the Great*, on which she worked for three years. "I never worked so hard or became so excited about anything else," she says. "I read everything available until I seemed to develop a sort of clairvoyance that led me to make certain discoveries that other people had missed." Her reviewers agreed that, though she had relied entirely on published material, her interpretation of it was made "with great sympathy and affectionate understanding." This lively and tender book is widely regarded as the best popular biography of Elizabeth yet published. The historian Garrett Mattingly said of Miss Jenkins that "she is really not much interested in war and diplomacy, politics and finance. She is interested in people. Her speciality is the human heart. . . . We believe Elizabeth Jenkins because, by imaginative insight and instinctive sympathy, she can make the figures of a remote historical pageant as real, as living, as three-dimensional as characters in a good novel."

ELIZABETH JENKINS

The "sort of clairvoyance" involved in the writing of *Elizabeth the Great* developed in *Dr. Gully* into a much more deliberate technique. In this fictionalized but precisely detailed account of a famous Victorian scandal of adultery and poisoning, Miss Jenkins be lieves that she received, through automatic writing, the guidance of Dr. Gully himself in the reconstruction of events and their settings.

An admirer of the eighteenth century, Miss Jenkins is somewhat out of sympathy with the present one: "I think if you have an imagination it lies with you to protect it in this age of jet aeroplanes, pneumatic drills, mass production, and violent, sadistic entertainment."

PRINCIPAL WORKS: *Novels*—Virginia Water, 1930; The Winters, 1931; Portrait of an Actor, 1933; Harriet, 1934; Doubtful Joy, 1935; The Phoenix Nest, 1936; Robert and Helen, 1944; Young Enthusiasts, 1947; The Tortoise and the Hare, 1954; Brightness, 1963; Honey, 1968; Dr. Gully, 1972 (U.S., Dr. Gully's Story). *Nonfiction*—Lady Caroline Lamb, 1932; Jane Austen, 1938; Henry Fielding, 1947; Six Criminal Women, 1949; Ten Fascinating Women, 1955; Elizabeth the Great, 1958; Joseph Lister, 1960; Elizabeth and Leicester, 1961.

ABOUT: Who's Who, 1973. *Periodicals*—Guardian April

21, 1972; New Statesman June 21, 1947; December 13, 1947; New York Times Book Review January 28, 1962; Saturday Review February 28, 1959.

JENKINS, ROBIN. *See* JENKINS, (JOHN) ROBIN

JENKINS, ROY (HARRIS) (November 11, 1920–), Welsh politician, biographer, and journalist, is the only son of Arthur Jenkins and the former Hattie Harris. His father was a coal miner and trade unionist who became a member of Parliament and was parliamentary private secretary during World War II to Clement Attlee. Roy Jenkins was born in Abersychan, Wales, and went to school there. His father sent him to Balliol, reputed to be the most arrogant of the Oxford colleges, an "intellectual powerhouse." At university Jenkins became secretary of that political nursery the Oxford Union debating society, and was a cofounder and chairman of the Democratic Socialist Club. He left Oxford in 1941 with a first-class honors degree in philosophy, politics, and economics, and enlisted in the Royal Artillery as a gunner. He was subsequently commissioned as an intelligence officer, and ended the war as a captain.

Jenkins stood as Labour candidate for Solihull in the 1945 general election, which voted in Attlee's Labour government. Jenkins himself, then only twenty-five, was not elected, but his close connection with the party leadership was assured by his father's friendship with the Prime Minister, and he was a frequent visitor to 10 Downing Street. His first book was a collection of Attlee's speeches, and his second a well-written "interim biography" of the Prime Minister. From 1946 to 1948 he worked as an economist for a London finance company.

In 1948, a by-election at Southwark brought Jenkins into the House of Commons as its youngest member. He served in 1949–1950 as parliamentary private secretary to the Commonwealth Secretary, and quickly made a reputation as a cool and intellectually formidable debater. The Southwark constituency was eliminated in a rearrangement of boundaries in 1950, but Jenkins was reelected the same year as the member for Stechford, Birmingham, which he has represented ever since. The Labour government was ousted in 1951, and it was during his party's thirteen years in opposition that Jenkins made his name as a writer and as a prolific contributor to the *New Statesman*, *Encounter*, the *Economist*, the *Spectator*, and the *Observer*. Two of the books he produced during these years, *Pursuit of Progress* and *The Labour Case*, were attempts to explain the merits of past or present Labour policies. They were admired for their elegant style and common sense but had no great impact.

ROY JENKINS

Jenkins's reputation stands on his political biographies, all of them concerned with turning points in the history of the Liberal party.

"The House of Lords is not the watchdog of the Constitution," said Lloyd George, "it is Mr. Balfour's poodle." His point was that the Lords favored Tory governments and did their best to frustrate Liberal ones. In *Mr. Balfour's Poodle*, Jenkins suggests that Lloyd George's "People's Budget" of 1909 was intended from the beginning as a poodle trap. At any rate, the Lords' opposition to this popular measure so alienated public opinion that it cost them their power of veto. Jenkins's account was based more on standard biographies than on original research, but benefited greatly from his grasp of practical politics and his acute sense of history. There was much praise for the wit, clarity, and economy of his style.

Sir Charles Dilke would probably have succeeded Gladstone as prime minister if his life and career had not been wrecked in 1885 by a woman's scandalous revelations about his sexual proclivities and activities. In his biography of Dilke, Jenkins questions the truth of these revelations, inquires into Joseph Chamberlain's role in the affair, and speculates about what might have happened if Dilke had become Prime Minister. Sir Philip Magnus found it a "coolly judicious and enthralling appraisal . . . a well-written and utterly absorbing book." It was adapted for the stage by Michael Dyne as *The Right Honorable Gentleman* and produced in London and New York.

Jenkins's *Asquith*, which followed in 1964, is the most successful of his books to date. Some critics, finding it a little lacking in personal touches, and rather excessively discreet, were inclined to regard it as an interim assessment of Asquith rather than a definitive one. But there was unanimous praise for Jenkins's style and subtlety, his "almost perfect sense of proportion." D. W. Brogan described the book as "the best political biography produced in England in recent years. . . . As the inside story of British politics between 1906 and the end of 1916, this book is a masterpiece."

The Labour party returned to power in 1964. Although Jenkins's political position was well to the right of the Prime Minister's, he was given office immediately as Minister of Aviation, became a humane and progressive Home Secretary in 1965, and was Chancellor of the Exchequer from 1967 until 1970, when a Conservative government was elected. Jenkins has moved from a "cloth-cap" background, via Balliol, into a social and intellectual elite, a fact which has not endeared him to the trade union element in the Labour party. On the other hand, his proven ability, intelligence, and moral force are such that he is without doubt the most formidable threat to Harold Wilson's authority in the party, whose deputy leader Jenkins became in 1970.

Jenkins worked for the John Lewis Partnership in 1962–1964 as director of financial operations, and in 1970 became vice-president of the Institute of Fiscal Studies. He was active and prominent in the campaign which secured Britain's entry into the European Common Market, and on this account received the Charlemagne Prize and the Robert Schumann Prize in 1972. Jenkins's dedication to the ideals of the Common Market brought him in 1971 into open conflict with Harold Wilson and the majority of his colleagues in Labour's "shadow cabinet," and the following year this cost him his deputy leadership of the party. He is a former chairman of the Fabian Society (1957–1958) and has served as a governor of the British Film Institute (1955–1958) and on the committee of the Society of Authors (1956–1960). Jenkins was married in 1945 to Mary Morris and has three children. Bernard Levin has described him as the man "of the bland and carefree countenance, the erudite dome, the wagging forefinger, the courteous approach, the gentle humour . . . who carries the fastest statistic in the West." He is something of a connoisseur of food and wine.

PRINCIPAL WORKS: (ed.) Purpose and Policy: Selected Speeches of C. R. Attlee, 1947; Mr. Attlee: An Interim Biography, 1948; Pursuit of Progress: A Critical Analysis of the Achievement and Prospect of the Labour Party, 1953; Mr. Balfour's Poodle: An Account of the Struggle Between the House of Lords and the Government of Mr. Asquith, 1954; Sir Charles Dilke: A Victorian Tragedy, 1958 (U.S., Victorian Scandal); The Labour Case, 1959; Asquith: Portrait of a Man and an Era, 1964; Essays and Speeches, 1967; What Matters Now (essays and speeches), 1972; Afternoon on the Potomac: A British View of America's Changing Position in the World (Henry L. Stimson Lectures), 1972.

ABOUT: Current Biography, 1966; Who's Who, 1971. *Periodicals*—Business Weekly April 13, 1968; Encounter January 1965; New Republic February 12, 1966; New York Review of Books July 1, 1965; New York Times Magazine April 7, 1968; New Yorker December 23, 1967; April 6, 1968; Newsweek December 11, 1967; Reporter December 2, 1965; Spectator March 5, 1954; Time December 8, 1967; March 29, 1968; Times Literary Supplement July 10, 1948; November 12, 1964; U.S. News & World Report February 6, 1967.

JENNINGS, ELIZABETH (JOAN) (July 18, 1926–), English poet and critic, was born at Boston, Lincolnshire, into a Roman Catholic family. Her father, a doctor, moved the family to Oxford while she was still a small child, and she was educated at Oxford High School. "I can remember very clearly the first poem that ever really meant anything to me," she wrote in *Let's Have Some Poetry*. "I was thirteen years old and one day, in an English lesson at school, we read part of *Lepanto* by G. K. Chesterton." She found its rhythm, onomatopoeia, and alliteration vivid and exciting and shortly after made her own first attempt. "It was a very bad poem . . . I was standing alone one day waiting for a bus when the words suddenly seemed to speak themselves out of my mind. The poem . . . had a definite shape and rhythm and was written in three or four rhymed quatrains. The subject was sailors and the sea."

Her school gave her little encouragement and it was an uncle, himself a poet, who taught her to avoid "writing of experiences one has never had." He shocked her by ignoring her more ambitious efforts and admiring a simple quatrain about a dead bird: "I held it in my hand / With its little hanging head: / It was soft and light and whole, / But it was dead." This emotional honesty, clarity, and simplicity remained at the basis of her work, and her poems continued to "visit" her, as her first had done, in an almost mystical way—at their best managing "to say in a strict inevitable form something that [she] did not know before." She was influenced briefly by Auden and Eliot but has never been much affected by other poets, though she greatly admires Edwin Muir, Wallace Stevens, and, above all, Yeats.

After school Miss Jennings went on to St. Anne's College, Oxford, from which she graduated with an honors degree in English. From 1950 to 1958 she worked as an assistant at the Oxford City Library. It was during this period that her first books appeared—*Poems* (1953), which was published by Fantasy Press and won an Arts Council prize, and *A Way of Looking* (1955), which received the Somerset Maugham Award. The critics noted a certain monotony of tone and rhythm, a narrowness of range in these speculative and contemplative poems, but

ELIZABETH JENNINGS

wrote warmly of the very great purity of her verse, the uniqueness and occasional strangeness of her vision, and a sense of power held tightly in check.

In 1956 Miss Jennings was represented in Robert Conquest's *New Lines* anthology, along with Philip Larkin, Kingsley Amis, Donald Davies, Thom Gunn, and others who at that time were thought of as members of the so-called "Movement." In that company Miss Jennings, the only Catholic and the only woman, seemed (it was said) like "a school-mistress in a . . . train with a bunch of drunken marines." Since then the *New Lines* poets have moved apart in a number of different directions, and Elizabeth Jennings is one of the few whose verse has largely retained the composed, courteous, understated tone of "the Movement."

Several additional volumes appeared in the late 1950s and early 1960s, establishing her as one of the most accomplished English poets of her generation, but one particularly vulnerable to the complaints most often leveled against the Movement poets in general—of apparent emotional coldness, self-consciousness, and "gentility." Nevertheless there were always those who recognized that great emotional power spoke in some of her quietest lines. And none of those who complained of her self-consciousness was more painfully aware of it than she: "All that I love is, like the night, outside, / Good to be gazed at, looking as if it could / With a simple gesture be brought inside my head / Or in my heart, but my thoughts about it divide / Me from my object. Now deep in my bed / I turn and the world turns on the other side."

In or about 1960 Miss Jennings suffered a severe mental breakdown and attempted suicide. She recovered slowly, after analysis, and in 1966 published a volume which seemed to many a major advance over its predecessors. This was *The Mind Has Mountains*, which won the Richard Hillary prize. Many of these poems are about the time she spent in hospital. Some of them describe with great sympathy and understanding her fellow patients and their sufferings, others record her own emotional turmoil, showing a new and welcome willingness to grapple directly with strongly felt experiences.

Miss Jennings's *Collected Poems* appeared in 1967. Ian Hamilton, noting her increasing preoccupation with irrational experience, found "a kind of neutralising discrepancy . . . between the manifestly dreadful situations she's concerned with and the sensible appeasing style which is the only way she knows of giving voice to them." Most critics disagreed and, like a reviewer in the *Times Literary Supplement*, thought that the formality of her later poems "adds to, rather than diminishes, the tension felt like an unheard note behind the level cadences and the cool words." *The Animals' Arrival* and *Lucidities* were widely regarded as interim volumes —admirable but only occasionally successful attempts to mediate or to exploit this conflict between matter and manner.

From 1958 to 1960 Miss Jennings worked as a reader for Chatto & Windus, the publishers. Since then she has earned her living as an author, editor, reviewer, and translator (of Michelangelo's sonnets, among other things). *Let's Have Some Poetry* is an introduction to poetry for children. *Every Changing Shape* is a study of the relationship between mystical experience and the writing of poetry. Miss Jennings has also written a survey of contemporary British poetry, *Poetry Today*, a study of Christian poetry, and a biography of Robert Frost. She has been a Fellow of the Royal Society of Literature since 1961. She still lives in Oxfordshire, enjoys traveling, especially to Italy, does "a lot of experimental amateur painting," and goes often to the cinema and theatre. She describes herself as "shy but gregarious," likes conversation, and is unmarried.

PRINCIPAL WORKS: *Poetry*—Poems, 1953; A Way of Looking, 1955; A Sense of the World, 1958; Song for a Birth or a Death, 1961; Recoveries, 1964; The Mind Has Mountains, 1966; The Secret Brother (for children), 1966; Collected Poems, 1967; The Animals' Arrival, 1969; Lucidities, 1970; Relationships, 1972. *Prose*—Let's Have Some Poetry, 1960; Every Changing Shape, 1961; Robert Frost, 1964; Christianity and Poetry (U.S., Christian Poetry), 1965. *As editor*—The Batsford Book of Children's Verse, 1958; An Anthology of Modern Verse, 1940–1960, 1961; A Choice of Christina Rossetti's Verse, 1970. *As translator*—The Sonnets of Michelangelo, 1961.

ABOUT: Allott, K. (ed.) Penguin Book of Contemporary Verse, 1962; Jennings, E. Let's Have Some Poetry, 1960;

Jennings, E. Poetry Today, 1961; Orr, P. (ed.) The Poet Speaks, 1966; Who's Who, 1971. *Periodicals*—London Magazine February 1962, November 1964; Mademoiselle January 1955; Poetry December 1956, November 1959.

"JESSEL, JOHN." *See* WEINBAUM, STANLEY GRAUMAN

***JHABVALA, RUTH PRAWER** (May 7, 1927–), German-born novelist and short story writer, writes: "I was born in Cologne, Germany. My father was Polish-Jewish, my mother German-Jewish. I attended segregated Jewish schools, and we all went as refugees to England in April, 1939. In England I first attended Stoke Park Secondary School in Coventry, then (from 1940–1945) Hendon County School in London, and finally (1945–1951) Queen Mary College, London University, where I took an M.A. in English. In 1951 I married C. S. H. Jhabvala, an Indian architect, and went with him to Delhi, and we have lived here ever since. We have three daughters.

"I started writing as soon as I had learned the alphabet, at six. My infant writings were all religious and Jewish. When we migrated to England, I was fortunately still young enough to make the change-over from writing in German to writing in English without any difficulty at all. I think it was only a few months—and it may even have been weeks—after our arrival that I began writing stories in English, and these were no longer religious and Jewish but all about the English lower middle classes. Similarly, the moment I set foot in India I began writing about Indians. I did this quite instinctively. In any case, I seemed at that time to be in a tremendous hurry—I couldn't stop writing and didn't feel safe unless, every time I had a novel published, I had another one almost ready. If there was a gap of a few months between finishing one novel and starting another, I would cram it full of short stories. All about India and the Indians. It never struck me at that time that there was anything strange in my writing in this way about Indians as if I were an Indian. I would brush questions on the subject aside by saying rather grandly that I didn't find Europeans interesting enough to write about. However, lately I have changed. I find I still want to write about India and Indians, but now from a European viewpoint. I feel I want to write more and more about Europeans in India and have in fact already started to do so—in my last novel (*A Backward Place*), in a screenplay I wrote for a film called *Shakespeare-wallah*, and in a series of short stories I have been writing for the past year. This change of subject may reflect a change in myself. I used to feel very much at home in India, but

* jäb′ vä lä

RUTH PRAWER JHABVALA

as the years go by I feel more and more an exile and a stranger.

"Writing is the only thing I can do, and so I think it has become a substitute for many things. For instance, for my inability to cook, or play games, or get interested in politics, or take much pleasure in other people's company. Or it may be an apologia for living in a country full of poverty and sickness and misery and sitting by without once lifting a finger for anyone. Or again, it may be a substitute for that religious experience which India continually seems to promise but which I have not yet even remotely approached.

"The act of writing gets increasingly difficult but also increasingly pleasurable. I want to say rather more complicated things, but usually find I am not up to them. So I start again, and again. I am dissatisfied with everything I have ever written and regard it all only as a preparation for that one work which probably I don't have it in me to write but which I hope I can go on trying for."

Mrs. Jhabvala writes, as Whitney Balliett says, "in the tradition of the nineteenth-century comic English novel," and like her masters finds her themes and targets in "the muscular setting-up exercises of the rising middle-classes."

No social satirist could wish for a more rewarding target and laboratory than New Delhi, where a painfully acquired tradition of British rectitude conflicts with an older habit of corruption, a new social mobility conflicts with the caste system, materialism and snobbery with mysticism, intellectual enlightenment with superstition. Mrs.

Jhabvala writes of the bemused victims of these ideological collisions with a quiet humor and deft obliquity which have constantly reminded her reviewers of Jane Austen. And if she lacks the sustained brilliance of her model, she can, as one critic wrote in the *Times Literary Supplement*, "supply one ingredient quite outside Jane Austen's repertoire: an exotic, colourful background which she touches in with swift, sure strokes." She characteristically works "through the medium of many short scenes" which gradually "mount up into something impressive—lucid, controlled, eschewing commentary, unsparing in delineation of human foible and yet understanding." The same might be said of her excellent screenplays: *The Householder*, *Shakespeare-wallah*, *The Guru*, and *Bombay Talkie*.

Mrs. Jhabvala's satire is often called affectionate but is not always so. A relentless note was heard in *The Nature of Passion*, which examines the family of a rich Indian contractor, contrasting the stifling values of the older generation with the moral bankruptcy of the younger. *Esmond in India*, about two prominent Indian families and the Englishman who acts as a catalyst between them, is for all its good-humored irony not entirely free of bitterness; to one reviewer it was not clear that the author liked her characters, or her country. Nine of the stories she mentions above about Europeans in India were published in 1968 as *A Stronger Climate*, and were found reminiscent of Chekhov—often funny, often brilliant, but finally melancholy studies of men and women receiving from India something other than the love, or spiritual truth, or happiness they seek there. Mrs. Jhabvala is generally recognized as "one of the finest novelists now writing about India," and one who has so far kept, for better or worse, "unstressfully, and effectively, within her range."

PRINCIPAL WORKS: *Novels*—To Whom She Will, 1955 (U.S., Amrita); The Nature of Passion, 1956; Esmond in India, 1958; The Householder, 1960; Get Ready for Battle, 1962; A Backward Place, 1965; A New Dominion, 1973 (U.S., Travelers). *Short stories*—Like Birds, Like Fishes, 1963; A Stronger Climate, 1968; An Experience of India, 1971.

ABOUT: Contemporary Authors 4, 1963; Jhabvala, R. P. *introduction to* An Experience of India, 1971; Who's Who, 1973. *Periodicals*—Literature East and West September 1965; New Yorker June 22, 1957; Times Literary Supplement May 20, 1965.

***JIMÉNEZ (MANTECÓN), JUAN RAMÓN** (December 24, 1881–May 29, 1958), Nobel Prize winner, is widely regarded as the principal Spanish poet of his generation and perhaps of this century. He was born at Moguer, near Huelva in Andalusia. The adored son of wealthy winegrowers, he was educated in Cádiz by the Jesuits from 1891 until 1896, when he entered the University of Seville. There he studied law for a time, nourished an abiding enthusiasm for painting and music, and wrote the verses published when he was seventeen in the Madrid magazine *Vida Nueva*.

* hē me′ neth (män tā kōn′)

These attracted the attention of the modernist poets Rubén Darío and Francisco Villaespesa, who invited Jiménez to Madrid to share in the reform of Spanish poetry. In 1900 he went there and, under the influence of his modernist friends and the French symbolists, produced that year the two volumes called *Almas de violeta* (Violet Souls) and *Ninfeas* (Water Lilies). The technical unorthodoxy of these prolix verses, and their vague and morbid aestheticism, provoked savage criticism. This, following upon a business failure which had ruined his family, and coinciding with his father's death, proved too much for the young poet's always delicate health. Incapacitated by melancholia, and the conviction that his own death was imminent, he retreated to a sanatorium, subsequently spending much time in such places, and in other ways securing himself against the intrusion of the world.

Jiménez, who never became a total recluse, was involved in the publication of the modernist reviews *Helios* in 1902 and *Renacimiento* in 1906. Meanwhile, the critics were learning to hear and admire his fragile melodies, in work which at that time had something of the charm of "a Chopin nocturne played at twilight." The delicate and melancholy influence of Gustavo Bécquer, and some of his brevity and concision, was manifest in *Rimas* (Rhymes, 1902) and *Arias tristes* (Sad Airs, 1903), volumes which also reflected his continuing preoccupation with love (usually romantically unfulfilled), beauty, solitude, nature, and above all, with death. From 1905 to 1911 Jiménez was at Moguer, where he immersed himself in the Spanish classical writers. Out of this discipline developed a phase when the short measures of Jiménez's early work alternated with the alexandrines of, for example, *Elegías puras* (Pure Elegies, 1908), and a manner increasingly ornate and richly colored. Indeed, as Howard T. Young has said, "there is ample proof that from a technical point of view Jiménez could [already] do anything he liked with Spanish verse (only the sonnet remaining to be conquered a few years later)."

Returning to Madrid in 1912, Jiménez went to live at the Residencia de Estudiantes. It was during his four years in that fertile cloister that he completed *Platero y yo* (Platero and I, 1914–1917), the series of lyrical prose poems about Moguer and his wanderings there with an amiable donkey, which remains his best-known work and was established almost at once as a modern classic. At this period also he met the American-born Zenobia Camprubí Aymar, then a student in Madrid. In 1916 he followed her back to New York and married her.

This excursion was the fulcrum of his life and of his career, introducing him to the sea, which became a major symbol in his work, and to English and American poetry, and providing him with a practical and well-balanced partner who served him thereafter as nurse, secretary, and mother, as well as wife. He celebrated his marriage in *Diario de un poeta recién casado* (Diary of a Recently Married Poet, 1917), which was to have a decisive influence on the development of Spanish poetry. By then recognized as the leader of the younger generation of poets, Jiménez had been moving steadily beyond modernism, and *Diario* marked his final emancipation from the movement. In these lyrics he abandoned rhyme and fixed meter, and launched into *vers libre* (a reflection, he said later, of his first encounter with the free movement of the sea). His early verses, Jiménez wrote, had had all the charm of innocence. Then he began to dress them, to load them with jewels and secretly, he said, to detest them. After 1916 he sought only *depuración*—the purging from his verse of everything but its poetic essence: "Let my word," he wrote, "become the thing itself, newly created by my spirit."

After their marriage, Zenobia Jiménez opened a handicrafts shop in Madrid which freed her husband from financial concerns. They lived for twenty years in a quiet suburban house where Jiménez in his soundproofed room could immerse himself in his work, reviewing, writing, and endlessly revising his existing work. ("A poem," he said once, "is not finished, it is abandoned.") During this period he founded a number of short-lived but influential reviews in which he published the work of Pedro Salinas, Rafael Alberti, Jorge Guillén, and many other young poets destined for greatness. He also worked with Zenobia on their highly successful translations of the Hindu poet Rabindranath Tagore, and himself translated Blake, Synge, Eliot, and Yeats, among others.

Another aspect of his work was the "lyrical caricatures" he wrote between 1914 and 1940 and published in 1942 as *Españoles de tres mundos* (Spaniards of Three Worlds)—vivid impressionistic portraits of friends, acquaintances, and dead authors who had influenced him. There are many anecdotes illustrating Jiménez's passion for solitude at this time. One of the best known concerns Valéry's visit to Madrid in 1924. Rather than venture out to meet the great French poet, Jiménez wrote to Valéry: "Before a poet as secret, exact, and unusual as you, my greatest homage will be to forgo the pleasure of your *persona*; words, phrases, gestures: what are they but the vicious rhetoric of the body?"

The *poesía desnuda* of Jiménez's maturity is the work of a poet who fed mainly and deeply on his own resources, looking out at life only for what it could reveal to him about his own interior reality. *Eternidades* (Eternities, 1918) and *Piedra y cielo* (Stone and Sky, 1919) show a new and exalted sense of the poet's role as the namer and thus in a sense the creator and master of all things, even of death itself. There were also signs in his work at this time of an emergent mysticism, a desire (as Howard T. Young says) "to conquer death through a realization of eternity."

JUAN RAMÓN JIMÉNEZ

The poems collected in *La estación total* (All Seasons in One), published in 1946 but written between 1930 and 1936, are dominated by this theme, many of them dealing with moments of transcendent experience. In one of them, "Su sitio fiel," he writes: "The rim of the universe slowly enfolds / until everywhere in the blue hour / there is only the cloud, the tree, the wave / drawn together at the peak of splendor. / The end is in the center. Eternity / here, in its faithful site, is seated."

The developing pantheism of this volume is confirmed in *Animal de fondo* (Animal of the Depths, 1949), his last collection. It is a triumphant celebration in twenty-nine poems of a prolonged metaphysical experience which had visited Jiménez in 1948, when he was returning by sea from Buenos Aires to New York. This experience seems to have provided him with a complete fulfillment of his hunger to ascend into and partake of a divine and universal consciousness: "I am an animal of the depth of air, / with wings that do not fly in air, / that fly in the light of awareness. . . ."

In 1936 meanwhile, the Civil War had driven Jiménez into exile. He and Zenobia spent the next fourteen years traveling and teaching in Latin

America and the United States, where he lectured at the University of Miami, Duke University, Vassar, and the University of Maryland. The recluse of Madrid seems to have transformed himself very successfully into an itinerant public figure. His health continued to deteriorate, however, and in 1951 he settled down as a member of the faculty of the University of Puerto Rico. Zenobia died in Puerto Rico in October 1956, three days after Jiménez received the Nobel Prize for Literature. He survived her by only a little more than a year.

Juan Ramón, as he was always called, was short and slender, with deep-set eyes and a white beard. Poor health and hypochondria had given him a languid manner, but he was witty and "agreeably malicious" in conversation, and an indefatigable worker, the author of over thirty volumes of poetry. He lacked the mythopoeic vitality of the very greatest poets, but his acute sensibility and absolute mastery of all the resources of Spanish verse made him the dominant figure in Spanish poetry for two decades. Indeed, as Gerald Brenan has said, "The whole of contemporary Spanish poetry comes out of him."

PRINCIPAL WORKS IN ENGLISH TRANSLATION: Fifty Spanish Poems, 1950; Platero and I, 1957; Selected Writings, 1957; Three Hundred Poems, 1903–1953, 1962.

ABOUT: Brenan, G. The Literature of the Spanish People, 1951; Cohen, J. M. Poetry of This Age, 1966; Cole, L. R. The Religious Instinct in the Poetry of Juan Ramón Jiménez, 1967; Current Biography, 1957; Díaz-Plaja, G. Juan Ramón Jiménez en su poesía, 1958; Díez-Canedo, E. Juan Ramón Jiménez en su obra, 1944; Garfias, F. Juan Ramón Jiménez, 1958; Givocate, B. La Poesía de Juan Ramón Jiménez, 1959; Guerrero Ruiz, J. Juan Ramón de viva voz, 1961; Gullón, R. Conversaciones con Juan Ramón Jiménez, 1958; Gullón, R. Estudios sobre Juan Ramón Jiménez, 1960; Olson, P. R. Circle of Paradox, 1967; Pablos, B. de. El tiempo en la poesía de Juan Ramón Jiménez, 1965; Palau de Nemes, G. Vida y obra de Juan Ramón Jiménez, 1957; Penguin Companion to Literature 2, 1969; Predmore, M. P. La obra en prosa de Juan Ramón Jiménez, 1966; Sánchez Barbudo, A. La segunda época de Juan Ramón Jiménez, 1962; Young, H. T. Juan Ramón Jiménez, 1967. *Periodicals*—La Torre 19–20 1957; Poetry July 1953; Revista Hispánica Moderna 2–3, 1958.

***JOHNSON, UWE** (July 20, 1934–), German novelist, was born at Cammin in Pomerania, the son of Erich and Erna (Sträde) Johnson. As a child he lived at Recknitz, in Mecklenburg, and attended school at Güstrow. After matriculating he studied German at the University of Rostock, moving on to the University of Leipzig in 1954. He graduated in 1956 and returned to Mecklenburg, living at Güstrow till 1959. In that year Johnson's first novel was returned by an East German publishing house with demands for alterations, whereupon he moved to West Berlin. *Mutmassungen über Jakob* was published in West Germany the same year, and Johnson was immediately acclaimed as a major novelist and the first to come to grips with the implications of his country's partition. He received the West Berlin Fontane Prize in 1960.

* yōn′ sun

Mutmassungen über Jakob was translated in 1963 by Ursule Molinaro as *Speculations About Jakob.* Johnson wrote it, he says, because "I thought the partition of Germany was in certain aspects representative of the partition of the world, that the confrontation of two ways of life, of two different cultures, two different economies and kinds of government could clarify the choices with which we are faced." Jakob Abs is an East German railroad dispatcher, efficient, hardworking, and politically reliable. He falls in love with a West German girl, Gesine Cresspahl, who visits East Germany as a NATO employee. Her return to the West is mysteriously facilitated by the secret police, as is Jakob's subsequent visit to her. The reader is not told the purpose of this mission, but is made to understand that it fails. Jakob returns to East Germany, and dies under the wheels of one of his locomotives. He himself does not speak throughout the book.

Johnson presents his characters and situations from the point of view not of an all-knowing narrator, but of one who can only collate fragments of evidence and speculate about their meaning. Deductions and conclusions are left to the reader. The distinction, and some of the difficulties, of Johnson's style derive from his awareness—shared with the French "New Novelists"—of how little any individual can know of another, or indeed of himself. Some reviewers found that this method gave great solidity and actuality in characterization, but failed as a narrative technique; some lost patience altogether with such painfully exact and cautious documentation. But for others, as R. C. Raack wrote in *The Nation*, the technique "created a world of the subjunctive which captures stylistically the frustrations and incompleteness of human understanding. Out of the stuff of everyday life in the two Germanys, Johnson conveys verbally a sense of the befogging of the faculty of judgment which has resulted from the long-term juxtaposition of two opposing world systems . . . the Kafkaesque distortion of perspectives of truth and reality."

Uwe Johnson's next two novels demonstrated the same preoccupation with the division of Germany—were, as he puts it, "attempts to cross a frontier." *Das dritte Buch über Achim* (1961, translated by Ursule Molinaro as *The Third Book About Achim*) concerns a racing cyclist, a hero of the East German Republic who, we learn, has already been the subject of two official and conventional biographies. Karsch, a West German journalist who meets Achim by chance, attempts an account of the cyclist's career that will convey not the whole truth—this is not possible—but nothing other than the truth.

Throughout the book, the glamour of Achim's status in East Germany is contrasted with the activity itself, with what it feels like to train and compete, and Achim's relation to bicycles is traced back to childhood with a kind of delicacy, concentration, and thoroughness which more bourgeois writers reserve for the analysis of a love affair. In the same way, Jakob Abs's involvement in his work on the railroad had not been merely described, but woven into the very texture of the narrative of *Mutmassungen über Jakob.* Johnson's critique of Communist bureaucracy is a critique from the inside; that is its great strength. It is as though he had remained true to one aspect of Marxist doctrine at least: that which concerns the worker's relation to his work and the economic roots of alienation. But his approach to such questions is that of a novelist, not of an ideologist, and his concern is to test the quality of such ways of life as he knows in terms not of preconceived notions, but of his acute and searching sensibility. His second novel received the International Publishers' Prize at Formentor. *Karsch und andere Prosa* (1964) is a collection of shorter prose pieces whose title novella (translated by Richard and Clara Winston as *An Absence*) was an early version of the story expanded as *Das dritte Buch über Achim.*

Zwei Ansichten (1966) was translated by the Winstons as *Two Views.* It is about an East German nurse and a West German photographer whose casual affair, cut short by the building of the Berlin Wall, grows steadily in intensity precisely because of this separation—becomes a question of personal self-assertion. The story is told in alternating chapters by the man and the woman, and for the first time the reader is allowed a great deal of information about the protagonists' thoughts and even their dreams, so that we come to know them very fully. Reviewers found the book notably less intricate and ponderous than the earlier novels, and gripping in the detailed authority with which it describes the mechanism of escape from behind the Wall. The *Times Literary Supplement* called it the first of Johnson's books "to show the passion which moves him to write as he does."

It was followed in 1970 by the first volume of Johnson's most ambitious work to date, a proposed trilogy called *Jahrestage aus dem Leben von Gesine Cresspahl* (Anniversaries from the Life of Gesine Cresspahl). The heroine, the lover of Jakob Abs in *Mutmassungen über Jakob,* has left Germany and settled in New York City with Marie, her ten-year-old daughter by Jakob. The book is a kind of diary of her daily jottings and reflections between August and December 1967, but ranges widely beyond the time and place of its supposed composition. In her

UWE JOHNSON

conversations with Marie and in her thoughts, Gesine recreates life in Mecklenburg before, during, and after Hitler, providing a history of one German family over three decades. At the same time, contemporary America is evoked through the experiences of life there of the foreign Gesine and the almost completely Americanized Marie, and also through copious and generally bleakly disturbing quotations from Gesine's favorite daily reading, the New York *Times.* Yet another narrative level is occupied by Uwe Johnson himself, who intervenes from time to time, at Gesine's invitation, in the unfamiliar role of omniscient author.

The publication of *Jahrestage* was a major literary event in Germany, though critics there and elsewhere have been understandably reluctant to commit themselves to any very firm judgments on the strength of the first volume. One reviewer in the *Times Literary Supplement,* who called the book a "fascinating, infuriating, inchoate jumble," concluded all the same that "there is some hope, some chance, that with this first helping of *Jahrestage,* this beginning of a long, difficult, unpopular book, Johnson will have begun a more serious statement about his readers' lives, their immediate past and their prospects, than would have been possible had he been more conventional . . . a chance, indeed, however faint, that he might have found the best if not the only way of presenting multidimensional views of the modern world which have been seen too seldom in literature."

In Germany Uwe Johnson is regarded by many as "the most serious and original writer of his day." Unlike Günter Grass, with whom he is often associated, he finds little use for fantasy in his novels.

It is significant that in *Das dritte Buch über Achim* he chooses to look through the eyes of a journalist (not a novelist); in *Zwei Ansichten* through the eyes of a photographer (not a painter). Like the reporter and the photographer, Johnson proves his skill by the arrangement and presentation of given realities.

In 1961 Johnson visited the United States to give a series of readings, and the following year went to Italy with a Villa Massino grant. He is a member of Gruppe 47. From 1966 to 1968 he lived in New York not as a visiting celebrity but as a wage-earning employee of his American publisher, then Harcourt, Brace and World (no doubt to prepare himself for the writing of *Jahrestage*). Johnson is a tall man, rapidly losing his reddish blonde hair. He was married in 1962 to Elizabeth Schmidt. They have one daughter.

PRINCIPAL WORKS IN ENGLISH TRANSLATION: Border of the Divided World, *in* Evergreen Review 21, 1961; Speculations About Jakob, 1963; The Third Book About Achim, 1966; Two Views, 1966; An Absence, 1969.

ABOUT: Enzensberger, H. M. Einzelheiten, 1962; International Who's Who, 1973–74; Schwarz, W. J. Der Erzähler Uwe Johnson, 1970. *Periodicals*—Metamorphosis June 1963; Neue Deutsche Hefte 96 1963.

JONES, (ALFRED) ERNEST (January 1, 1879–February 11, 1958), Welsh writer on psychoanalysis and biographer of Sigmund Freud, was born in the village of Gowerton, South Wales, the eldest of three children. His father started his working life as an office boy and ended it as a coal mine proprietor, but in Ernest Jones's youth there was still very little money, and he owed his education to a series of scholarships. He entered the village school at the age of three and, conquering repeated bouts of ill health, went on to Swansea Grammar School and Llandovery Public School, entering Cardiff University at sixteen.

Jones qualified as a physician at University College, London, in 1900, and received his M.D. three years later, winning gold medals in both examinations. He became a Member of the Royal College of Physicians in 1904 and earned the Diploma of Public Health in 1905. After periods at University College Hospital and various other London hospitals, Jones was appointed a lecturer in practical neurology at the London School of Clinical Medicine. In 1908 he went to Canada, where he became Professor of Psychiatry at Toronto University and Director of the Ontario Clinic for Nervous Disorders.

His interest in psychology had developed while he was still a student, when together with his friend Wilfred Trotter he had discovered the psychoanalytic theories of Sigmund Freud. Jones became the first writer in English to contribute to the literature of psychoanalysis, his earliest articles on the subject appearing in about 1905. A few years later, at Freud's historic Clark University lectures, he met the master himself, and committed himself to his life's work, the international development of psychoanalysis. Before he left North America he became a founder and the first secretary of the American Psychoanalytic Association and a founder-member of the International Psychoanalytical Association.

In 1913, after a period of research in Europe, Jones returned to England as Freud's more or less official representative and prophet. Things were very difficult at first, but interest was stimulated by the prevalence of shell shock and the other psychological casualties of World War I. Jones's London Psychoanalytical Society was followed in 1919 by the British Psychoanalytical Society, in which he was again the prime mover. In 1920 Jones also became president of the International Psychoanalytical Association, a post he retained until 1924, and resumed from 1932 to 1949. It was in 1920 also that he founded the *International Journal of Psychoanalysis*, which he edited for twenty years.

An Institute of Psychoanalysis was set up in England in 1926 to promote understanding and acceptance of the movement. Among other things it published the influential International Psychoanalytical Library (which Jones edited) and founded the London Clinic of Psychoanalysis (which Jones directed). Hostility to psychoanalysis remained nevertheless and was exacerbated by the activities of unqualified "psychoanalysts." The movement was studied in 1928 by a special committee of the conservative British Medical Association. Jones, a born controversialist, according to one account single-handedly "fought his critics to a standstill." The committee concluded in effect that only practitioners trained by Freudian methods could call themselves "psychoanalysts," thus indirectly giving recognition and respectability to the movement.

All these developments took place in a context of close personal contact with Freud himself. Soon after World War I, Jones took the initiative in establishing "the committee," a small group of colleagues who attempted to relieve Freud of some of the administrative burdens of the expanding movement—the members were Otto Rank, Karl Abraham, Max Eitingon, Sandor Ferenczi, Hanns Sachs, Jones, and Freud himself. It was Jones who sent Freud foreign patients during Austria's postwar depression; and in 1938, when the Nazis invaded Austria, it was Jones who flew to Vienna and helped Freud and his family escape to London.

Jones's professional life was one of continuous struggle against the medical establishment and other opponents of psychoanalysis—he was not elected a Fellow of the Royal College of Physicians until 1942. And his personal life had its share of tragedy. His first wife, the gifted Welsh musician Morfydd Owen, died fifteen months after their marriage in 1915. And the first child of his second marriage died at the age of seven. Ernest Jones himself suffered throughout his life from poor health, and died of cancer at the age of seventy-nine after a long and painful illness. He was survived by his second wife, the Austrian historian Katherine Jokl, and by two sons and a daughter.

A man of wide culture and insatiable curiosity, Jones's interests extended (as his professional writings show) to sociology, mythology, literature, language, painting, and many other related and unrelated fields. He was a first-class chess player (and a collector of chess sets) and, in his youth, a fine figure skater—he was an examiner for several years in the British Figure Skating Society and the author of a textbook on the subject. During World War II Jones retired to a cottage in Sussex where he spent the last years of his life, growing roses, enjoying long country walks, and writing.

He contributed some three hundred articles to professional journals, some of them collected in three volumes of the International Psychoanalytical Library—*On the Nightmare*, and two collections of essays on applied psychoanalysis. His subjects range from the psychology of the Jewish question to the influence of Andrea del Sarto's wife on his art. One of his best-known studies sets out to prove that *Hamlet* reflects a strong element of homosexuality in Shakespeare's makeup.

Jones's magnum opus is his definitive biography of Freud, an immense, three-volume compendium which has been universally praised for its thoroughness, clarity, and scrupulous honesty—Jones never allowed his profound sympathy for his subject to blind him to Freud's faults. The book was widely recognized as one of the great biographies of the era, and a document of immense importance in contemporary intellectual history.

Edward Glover, in his obituary of Jones in the *British Journal of Psychology*, wrote: "Ernest Jones was the last survivor of this band of conquistadors [who established psychoanalysis as a firmly organized international movement]. In his time he . . . fought in every battle of offence and defence throughout the pioneering period that lasted almost twenty years (1908 to 1928); and on the death of Freud in 1939 became the acknowledged leader of psychoanalysis throughout the world. During that time he organized and expanded Freud's approaches to the cognate sciences of psychology, sociology, and anthropology, and to the territories of aesthetics, movements which were regarded as unwarranted invasions. And he left behind him a richly documented record of progress as a teacher, research scholar, writer, organizer and finally leader in the field of psychoanalysis."

PRINCIPAL WORKS: Psychoanalysis, 1929 (republished as What Is Psychoanalysis?, 1948); On the Nightmare (U.S., Nightmare, Witches and Devils), 1931; Essays in Applied Psychoanalysis, 1933; Papers on Psychoanalysis, 1938; Hamlet and Oedipus, 1949; Sigmund Freud, Life and Work: Vol. 1, 1953; Vol. 2, 1955; Vol. 3, 1957; Free Associations: Memories of a Psychoanalyst (autobiography), 1959; Sigmund Freud: Four Centenary Addresses, 1966.
ABOUT: Alexander, F. and others (eds.) Psychoanalytic Pioneers, 1966; James, N. (ed.) Wisdom, 1958; Vyvyan, J. A Case Against Jones, 1966; Who Was Who, 1951–1960. *Periodicals*—British Journal of Psychiatry August 1958; New Republic December 9, 1957; New Statesman October 5, 1957; New York Herald Tribune Book Review October 25, 1953; October 13, 1957; New York Times October 13, 1957; Saturday Review November 2, 1957; Times October 19, 1953; September 7, 1959; Times Literary Supplement November 29, 1957.

ERNEST JONES

JONES, DAVID (MICHAEL) (November 1, 1895–), Welsh poet and artist, writes: "I was born in a part of Kent which has long since become absorbed into Greater London. My father was a Welshman who had come to London twelve years before I was born; he was, by profession, a printer. His family was of farming stock but his father was a master-plasterer. My mother was English, with Italian blood on her maternal side. Her father was a master mast and block maker, and her girlhood had been by Thames-side when the Pool of London was perhaps at its busiest.

"If it was from my mother that I received the mores and traditions of the Port of London, it was from my father that I heard of his youth in the hills of Wales; and from a very early age had a sense of belonging to the Welsh nation. These mingled but separate haecceities of the Island of Britain have played a determining part in my work and thought.

"It chanced that my one obsession, as a small

DAVID JONES

child, was drawing. I was backward at lessons and managed (to my great regret since) to evade all but the minimum of formal education. A little before my fourteenth birthday in 1909, I was permitted to go to an art-school.

"I remained as an art student until the 1914–18 War. I enlisted in the Royal Welch Fusiliers and served with them on the West Front from December 1915 to February 1918. The first seven months of those two years and three months of trench warfare are the basis of *In Parenthesis* (written between 1928 and 1936). I was demobilised in December 1918 and returned to my studies as an art student.

"About 1917, while in the Forward Zone, I began to be aware of the claims of the Catholic Church. I was not formally received into the Roman Communion until 1921, but the whole sacramental principle upon which the Church rests had, in innumerable ways, been operative in my mind for many years—indeed, in some sense, all my life. For example the principle implicit in the making of a work that is essentially non-utile, a *signum* or representing of something or other; the employment of corporal, material things as a signification of something quite apart from utilitarian values—the very essence of the 'artist's' job—is clearly also the principle presupposed in the sacraments of religion.

"In 1922 I left London and apprenticed myself to a carpenter and builder who was one of a group of workmen the best-known of whom was the sculptor Eric Gill. I was hopeless as a carpenter, but the experience of using and sharpening tools and doing simple jobs was most valuable when I took to engraving.

"In the autumn of 1924 I returned to London, but in the late winter of that year went to stay at Capel-y-ffin in the mountains of south-east Wales, to which place the Gills had moved. There, and during long visits to Ynys Bŷr (Caldy Island) off the coast of Pembrokeshire, I made many water-colour drawings and various engravings. Early in 1927 I returned from Ynys Bŷr to live in London and continued to paint, mainly in water-colour, and to make wood-engravings. In 1928, while staying in a house on the sea near Brighton and painting sea-scapes, I began to write what was eventually to become *In Parenthesis*.

"I had never previously made a written work and it began in a purely experimental way and indeed as a private, personal experiment. Space forbids me saying more than that, having certain notions about and contactual experience of, the problem of the wedding of 'form' and 'content' in the visual arts, I was concerned to know in what fashion this same problem presented itself in the making of a written work.

"My chief occupation remained that of a visual artist and for about a year *In Parenthesis* was gone on with when I was not painting. Eventually I read part of what I had written to a close friend who insisted I must proceed with and complete the work.

"The period of 1926–1932 was one of development and of pretty intensive work: mainly water-colours but also engravings. Late in 1932 I became ill and for a good while little was done, which largely accounts for *In Parenthesis* not being presented to the publishers until 1937 and accounts also for the decreased output in visual works.

"Over this period I had various exhibitions, nearly all of water-colour drawings, in London galleries. Most of these were purchased by private collectors or galleries, some in Britain, some elsewhere. Apart from landscape, still life, and some drawings of people, there were a good number of water-colour drawings of animals. This has been a persistent tendency, and one of the earliest extant drawings made as a child is of a dancing bear seen in the street when I was seven.

"For various reasons I had to be in London throughout World War II, and did more writing than drawing. However, works were represented at various war-time exhibitions, at the National Gallery, etc., and immediately after the war in Paris and other European centres. I again became ill in 1945 but, after treatment in 1946 was able to recommence painting and writing.

"Between 1946 and 1952 I was, apart from making various water-colour drawings, engaged in writing *The Anathemata*, published in England in 1952. More recently it was published in the United States, as were *In Parenthesis* and *Epoch and Artist*, a selection of occasional essays, articles, etc., edited by my friend Mr. Harmon Grisewood.

"In 1954–55 the Arts Council of Great Britain organised a Retrospective Exhibition of my water-colours, engravings, etc., which was shown at Aberystwyth, Swansea and Cardiff, then in Edinburgh, and finally at the Tate Gallery in London.

"I ought to mention that inscriptions, mostly made in opaque water-colour on a Chinese-white background, have been, for me personally, an important part of the work of my later years; perhaps because they unconsciously made a link between my written and my visual work.

"I was pleased and honored in 1954 to be awarded the Russell Loines Award for poetry for *The Anathemata*, and also to receive other awards from the United States for shorter works which I hope, at a later date, to get published in one volume, along with other pieces still in preparation. *The Wall* and *The Tutelar of the Place* were both published in *Poetry*, Chicago.

"I shall have to ask the reader who wishes to do so to consult such works of reference as the English *Who's Who* and the American *Contemporary Authors* for a fuller account of dates and details of exhibitions, awards, etc. Here I have tried only to give a rough account of some of the things that have shaped my life and way of thought.

"But I wish to say that my abiding conviction is that all the things we call 'the arts' are one, and that whatever else they are, they most certainly presuppose man to be a 'sign-making' or 'sacramental' animal. Which means that, basically, the 'artist' no less than the 'priest' is, in that sense, a misfit in our present 'technological society.' But he is not a 'misfit' as a 'human being,' as that term has hitherto been understood. Man, in my view, *is* man-the-artist. Not being a prophet I hazard no guess as to how, in a positivist-materialist technological set-up which is virtually ubiquitous, 'man-the-artist' may continue to function. But that there is a basic dichotomy seems to me obvious."

David Jones was born in Brockley, Kent, the son of James Jones and Alice Ann (Bradshaw) Jones. He was at Camberwell School of Art from 1910 to 1914, but his genius for draughtsmanship had manifested itself at a very early age, as the famous drawing of a bear (mentioned above) clearly demonstrates. Jones was known as an engraver and watercolorist long before he became a writer; yet, as Bernard Bergonzi has said—in a critique of *In Parenthesis* that may be applied to all that has come after it—"it is one of the few works of literature by a native Englishman (or Anglo-Welshman) to contribute importantly to the twentieth-century Modern Movement."

In Parenthesis, which won the Hawthornden prize for 1938, is the story of Private John Ball (the name is that of a priest executed for his share in the Peasants' Revolt of 1381) from his enlistment in a Welsh regiment until his wounding in the final attack on Mametz Wood: we see him parade with his battalion for overseas embarkation, travel to Flanders, march up the line, acclimatize himself to the world of trench warfare, assemble for the Somme offensive and, finally, fight and fall wounded.

The narrative is a mixture of prose and poetry; Ball's own story is told starkly, with a sharp compactness, but against a rich and recondite tapestry of literary, mythological, and religious allusions. T. S. Eliot called it a work of genius, and W. H. Auden has referred to it as "very probably the finest long poem in English in this century." Its readers have seen it, almost the last of the war books of the 1914–1918 war, as the most evocative of them all. It has failed to achieve popularity not because it is literary, but simply because—utterly unpretentious as it is—it is too difficult, too demanding.

Nevertheless, Jones's work will undoubtedly live, and will provide inspiration to other writers. It is indeed arguable that *In Parenthesis* and its successor *The Anathemata* (1952) are the finest "public" poems of their time: public in the sense, not that they are easy to understand, but that they are primarily "incantations for the ear" rather than words on a page. *In Parenthesis* takes much of its shape from the earliest known poem in the Welsh language, *Y Gododdin*, also a battle piece. The extent to which Jones was indebted to Eliot and Joyce in this work is difficult to determine; it seems most likely that the similarities of method proceed from the fact that all three writers share a twentieth-century sensibility rather than by any direct influence.

The Anathemata, "fragments of an attempted writing," is a highly idiosyncratic vision of British history, and incorporates the allusive polyglot methods first employed in *In Parenthesis*. Again, it mixes poetry and prose. This work is David Jones's tribute to God, fashioned with as much loving care as a prayer: he sees man as *homo faber*, man the maker, creating order out of chaos to the glory of God. In *The Anathemata* he builds up many different signs, emblems, images, into single statements whose coherence is at first apparent only in their incantatory effectiveness. The work may be seen as a representation of the way order underlies apparent chaos: as David Blamires has put it: "The signs cohere; the heap is in fact a pile . . . an edifice."

Apart from *Epoch and Artist*, a collection of essays, letters, broadcasts, and other critical writings, which is important for an understanding of his creative work, David Jones has for many years now had in hand a long work in progress, some parts of which have been published. This brings together three aspects of human experience:

the pagan Roman world of the first century A.D., particularly in Britain; the development of Christianity in the same period; and (analogically) the twentieth century. The methods employed are the same as in the previous works; and there is a sense in which the author is still the soldier, viewing his century from a dugout on the Somme; this experience fixed his vision once and for all.

David Jones is essentially a sacramental writer, who is concerned with the normality—rather than the uniqueness—of the sacraments. His literary works are "made," and they are part and parcel of the whole man: water-colorist, engraver, and calligrapher as well as poet. The calm and optimism at their center does not require a Christian sensibility for its apprehension, for the spirit of Spinoza, accepting all evil as a larger good, pervades it. For Jones, everything material is a sign of the spiritual: ultimately, of God's universe.

Jones is unmarried. He has won many prizes, including the Harriet Monroe Memorial Prize (1956) for "The Wall" and the Levinson Prize for "The Tutelar of the Place" (1961). He was made a CBE in 1955. In 1960 the University of Wales honored him with a Doctorate of Literature, and at the 1964 Royal Eisteddfod of Wales he received the Gold Medal for Fine Arts. The Midsummer Prize of the Corporation of London followed in 1968. He is a Fellow of the Royal Society of Literature.

PRINCIPAL WORKS: In Parenthesis, 1937 (U.S., 1962); The Anathemata, 1952 (U.S., 1963); Epoch and Artist (criticism), 1959. Parts of a work in progress have appeared as follows: The Wall, *in* Poetry 2, 1955; The Tutelar of the Place, *in* Poetry 4, 1961; The Dream of Private Clitus, *in* Art and Literature 1, 1964 (*also in* Agenda 1–3, 1967); The Fatigue, 1965 (*also in* Agenda 1–3, 1967); The Hunt, *in* Agenda 1–3, 1967; The Tribune's Visitation, 1969.

ABOUT: Bergonzi, B. Heroes' Twilight, 1965; Blamires, D. David Jones, 1971; Contemporary Authors 9–10, 1964; Deutsch, B. Poetry in Our Time, 1952; Eliot, T. S. *introduction to* In Parenthesis (1961 ed.); Holloway, J. The Colours of Clarity, 1964; Johnstone, J. H. English Poetry of the First World War, 1964; Kermode, F. Puzzles and Epiphanies, 1962; National Book League, Catalogue of an Exhibition (Word and Image series); with an introduction by Douglas Cleverdon, 1972; Nemerov, H. Poetry and Fiction, 1963; Orr, P. (ed.) The Poet Speaks, 1966; Who's Who, 1973. *Periodicals*—Agenda (special issue) 1–3 1967; Apollo February 1963; Commonweal October 19, 1962; Encounter February 1954; Listener May 14, 1959; New Statesman November 22, 1952; New Yorker August 22, 1964; Review of English Literature April 1966; Sewanee Review Autumn 1967; Times Literary Supplement August 6, 1954; July 27, 1967; Twentieth Century July 1960.

JONES, ERNEST. *See* JONES, (ALFRED) ERNEST

JONES, (EVERETT) LEROI (IMAMU AMIRI BARAKA) (October 7, 1934–), black American poet, dramatist, novelist, jazz critic, and essayist, was born into a middle-class family in Newark, New Jersey. His father was a postal superintendent and a champion bowler, his mother a social worker. He began to write—comic strips and science fiction—when he was nine or ten. He attended integrated, largely white, schools in Newark, went on to Rutgers University for a year, then transferred to Howard University. LeRoi Jones consistently did well, even brilliantly, in his academic work, but even in high school "used to drink a lot of wine, throw bottles around, walk down the street in women's clothes, just because I couldn't find anything to do to satisfy myself." Howard University disappointed him, seeking he thought to teach "the Negro how to make out in the white society, using the agonizing overcompensation of pretending he's also white." He says that he was once "chastised severely for daring to eat a piece of watermelon on the Howard campus." At Howard, Jones abandoned his first ambition, which was to enter the church, switched to premed studies, and finally majored in English, graduating at nineteen.

From 1954 to 1957 Jones served with the Strategic Air Command as an aerial gunner and climatographer, most of the time in Puerto Rico. It was an experience which did nothing to overcome his dislike of whites. Jones was painting a great deal at this time, but also writing poetry. After his discharge, recognizing his vocation at last, he settled in New York City and soon made a name for himself in Greenwich Village as a writer connected with but not of the Beat movement, and a perceptive critic of jazz. He resumed his education, studying philosophy at Columbia University and German literature at the New School for Social Research. Jones was married in 1958 to a white woman, Hettie Cohen. Their two daughters, Kellie and Lisa, were born in 1960 and 1962. At about this time he and his wife founded *Yugen*, an influential poetry magazine, and helped to launch the American Theatre for Poets.

His first book of verse, *Preface to a Twenty Volume Suicide Note*, appeared in 1961. These were brooding, rhapsodic and personal poems, in structure often resembling jazz improvisations, and showing, according to M. L. Rosenthal, "a natural gift for quick, vivid imagery and spontaneous humor." In 1961–1962 he held a John Hay Whitney fellowship. He taught at the New School in 1963, at the University of Buffalo as a visiting professor in 1964, and then intermittently at Columbia. Meanwhile his political ideas were evolving. In 1960 he had visited Cuba, finding there an enthusiasm and sense of purpose that made life in the United States seem by comparison an "ugly void." As the confrontation between white and black America developed, and black America became increasingly aware of itself, he began to emerge as one of its most militant spokesmen.

In 1965 LeRoi Jones left Greenwich Village, his white friends and his white wife, and settled in Harlem. There, with a Federal antipoverty grant, he founded the Black Arts Repertory Theatre, and a Black Arts School to teach drama, the arts, and black nationalism. Criticism mounted in Washington and New York after an arms cache and rifle range were found on the theatre premises. In 1966 Jones moved back to Newark, where he became director of a new black theatre and community center, Spirit House. In 1968 he founded there the Black Community Development and Defense Organization. The same year he ran unsuccessfully for election to the Newark Community Council, established to oversee the city's slum rehabilitation plan. Since then, however, his power and influence in Newark have grown steadily.

"No amount of pacifism is going to break Charlie's back," Jones said once; and: "We must eliminate the white man before we will ever be able to draw a free breath on this planet." The extremity of his views has frightened and alienated many of the white liberals who once lionized him, and led him into endless conflicts with law enforcement agencies. In 1966 he was accused of assaulting the editor of the *East Side Review* for nonpayment of a fee (the case was dismissed). On another occasion he was charged with sending obscene literature through the mails (a William Burroughs burlesque on Roosevelt and one of his own plays). During the Newark riots in 1967 he was arrested, charged with the possession of two revolvers, and sentenced to two and a half years imprisonment and fine of one thousand dollars; appeal led to a retrial and acquittal. In November 1968 he received a sixty-day sentence for resisting arrest after an argument with the police.

There were some personal, lyrical, and nonaggressive poems in Jones's second collection, *The Dead Lecturer* (1964), but many that reflected in form and content the violence of his social feelings: "Come up, black dada / nihilismus. Rape the white girls. Rape / their fathers. Cut the mothers' throats." David Littlejohn calls him "the most difficult of all Negro poets," adding that "it is hard to say whether any reader can be guaranteed a just repayment for his effort." The difficulty is syntactical, even logical—most of his verse is associative and disjunctive; it hurls back in one's face any attempt to impose order on an intense and frequently inchoate emotion. At this time his work was much influenced by the experiments in "projectivist" verse of Robert Duncan and other disciples of William Carlos Williams.

Littlejohn feels that Jones is "highly suspicious of the whole nature of verbal communication," and quotes: "A compromise / would be silence. To shut up, even such risk / as the proper placement / of verbs and nouns. To freeze the split / in mid-air, as it aims itself / at some valiant intellectual's face." But elsewhere he writes: "I want to be sung. I want / all my bones and meat hummed / against the thick floating / winter sky. I want myself / as dance. . . . / And let me once create / myself. And let you, whoever / sits breathing on my words / create a self of your own. One / that will love me." An English reviewer called these poems "enactions of distress and desperate irony. The poems deliver a hard anguish, fraught with self-hatred and loathing for America, which moves towards a limited self-therapy within the bitter imagination of catastrophe." A collection of Jones's poetry from 1961 to 1967 was published in 1969 as *Black Magic*. The author presented the volume as evidence of his spiritual awakening and growth but for many reviewers it represented a decline from literature to fascistic racial propaganda, the product of "an intelligence self-maddened."

LEROI JONES

There is a strong poetic element in Jones's plays—the form in which he has made most impact. He believes in communal art and a communal revolutionary theatre: "The revolutionary theatre should force change: itself should be change. And what we show must cause the blood to rush, so that prerevolutionary temperaments will be bathed in this blood, and it will cause their deepest souls to move. . . . Basically," he adds, "I want to write plays that will make good people happy and will frighten evil people. In America, it usually turns out to be black and white . . . through no doing of my own."

His early one-act plays were almost universally condemned. Edward Margolies dismissed *The Baptism*, an attack on the prurience of American churches and American women, produced on the Writers' Stage in 1964, as "unimaginably bad," and *The Slave*, staged the same year off-Broadway at the St. Mark's Playhouse, as equally so. David Littlejohn calls the latter "a blatant, unmodulated scream of racial abuse." In it, a black power leader confronts a white couple, one of them his former wife, while a riot rages outside. He insults them, beats them, and finally shoots them in an orgy of bitterness and what Littlejohn calls "wish-fulfilment projections." *The Toilet*, staged with *The Slave*, had a slightly better reception. Black boys in a slum high school lure a homosexual white boy into the lavatory and beat him senseless. But later their leader, whom the white boy loves, returns, throws his arms around the wounded youth, and weeps. Most reviewers detested the obscene and violent language but found the pathos of the ending genuinely moving. (But Jones himself now finds that ending painfully embarrassing, a dishonest concession to the milieu he then lived in.) His only three-act play is *A Recent Killing*, a partly autobiographical work, written in 1964, about a young black airman who is determined to be a poet.

The best known of Jones's plays is *Dutchman*, which ran for a year at the Cherry Lane Theatre in Greenwich Village and received the 1964 Obie Award. It has been performed all over the world, and filmed. It is set in a subway train where a white girl accosts a young bourgeois Negro, provokes him sexually, taunts him racially, and drives him at last to reveal the black violence buttoned down under his white collar. This is her victory. She stabs him and sails coolly on to find a fresh victim. The theme is one explored by many black writers—the symbolic castration of the black man in a white society, and the implication that violence alone can restore his manhood.

Robert Brustein regards Jones's plays as "sadomasochistic racial fantasies," and Ronald Bryden called *Dutchman* "a posturing, inflammatory, deliberately dishonest work, destructive for the malicious excitement of destruction." But Bryden, like many other critics, went on to pay tribute to the "talent of its writing" and the power of Jones's rhetoric, and Norman Mailer has called it indeed "the best one-act American play."

Jones's early plays were attempts to shock white audiences into an awareness of the racial disaster towards which American society was moving. After *Dutchman* he turned his back on what he regards as a bankrupt culture, and since then has deliberately addressed himself solely to black audiences—an example which has been followed by many other black writers. Such plays as *J-E-L-L-O*, a brutal burlesque of the old Jack Benny show, *Slave Ship*, and *Experimental Death Unit #1* have a single message: Be Black. Many of them end with a genocidal attack on whites and the triumph of black. Some regard them as literary artifacts in the tradition of Artaud's "theatre of cruelty"—as "the truthful precipitates of dreams," but for most white reviewers they are of interest only as racist documents.

The System of Dante's Hell, Jones's only novel to date, is an account of the author's childhood and adolescence as a "black Job," arranged into Dantean categories—incontinence, violence, fraud, treachery, and their subdivisions. It was coolly received on the whole, and *Newsweek* called it "a diary of bad dreams" and impotent anger, in which "reality and dream are moiled beyond recognition in the jargonized gibberish of pop writing." Emile Capouya however gave it a more sympathetic reading. Its episodes, he said, "tend to be representations of states of mind and states of soul rather than sections of conventional narrative. Especially in the earlier sections, the author's method is less novelistic than lyrical—fragmentary, allusive, private." Capouya thought that in two of these "appalling" stories, "the author has ordered his materials as if man were still the master of creation, and the effect on the reader is close to exaltation." The short stories collected in *Tales* similarly announce the extremity of black frustration in a manner resembling prose poetry rather than traditional narrative. That they also had a mixed critical reaction is not surprising, since most critics are white and Jones, in his fiction as in his verse and plays, is now writing exclusively for black readers.

LeRoi Jones has also published two books of essays and two important books on black music, *Blues People* and *Black Music*, in which he examines the history of blues and jazz in America as the principal expression of the developing consciousness of blacks; *Blues People* was perhaps the most universally and unreservedly praised of all his books, and is widely regarded as the best available work in its field.

Jones and his followers at the Temple of Kawaida in Newark are "dedicated to the creation of a new value system for the Afro-American community." They wear African dress and speak Swahili as a second language. He has adopted the name Imamu Amiri Baraka. His second wife, the former Sylvia Robinson, is now known as Amini Baraka; they have two children. He is a slight, black-bearded man, whose deep brown eyes have been variously described as "wounded," "blazing," and "angry." Judging by recent essays and interviews, his old ambition to "break Charlie's back" has been replaced by a more positive concern—to help build, through his writings and political action, a strong, proud, self-aware black community, freed from contaminating involvement with the dead body and spirit of materialist-individualist white America: "Our entire thing now is love—love ourselves. Let the whites work out their own salvation."

One bitterly controversial proof of his belief in self-help for blacks is Kawaida Towers, a sixteen-story housing project sponsored by the Temple in the predominantly white north ward of Newark, where construction was delayed in 1972–1973 by white picketing and demonstrations, and the resulting violence. He also looks beyond Newark —and beyond America—seeking the establishment of a Pan-African political party serving the needs of blacks all over the world.

PRINCIPAL WORKS: *Poetry*—Preface to a Twenty Volume Suicide Note, 1961; The Dead Lecturer, 1964; Black Magic: Sabotage, Target Study, Black Art — Collected Poetry, 1961–1967, 1969; In Our Terribleness: Some Elements and Meaning in Black Style (photographs by Billy Abernathy, with poetic commentary by Jones), 1971. *Plays*—Dutchman, *and*, The Slave, 1964; The Baptism, *and*, The Toilet, 1967; Four Black Revolutionary Plays (Experimental Death Unit #1, A Black Mass, Great Goodness of Life, Madheart), 1969; The Death of Malcolm X *in* Bullins, E. (ed.) New Plays From the Black Theater, 1970. *Fiction*—The System of Dante's Hell, 1965; Tales, 1967. *Nonfiction*—Blues People, 1963; Home (essays), 1966; Black Music, 1967; Raise Race Rays Raze (essays), 1971. *As editor*—The Moderns: An Anthology of New Writing in America, 1963; (with Larry Neal) Black Fire: An Anthology of Afro-American Writing, 1968; African Congress: A Documentary of the First Modern Pan-African Congress, 1972.

ABOUT: Abramson, D. E. Negro Playwrights in the American Theatre, 1969; Allen, D. M. The New American Poetry, 1960; Contemporary Authors 21–22, 1969; Current Biography, 1970; Davis, J. P. The American Negro Reference Book, 1966; Downer, A. S. The American Theater Today, 1967; Ellison, R. Shadow and Act, 1964; Hill, H. Soon One Morning, 1963; Hill, H. (ed.) Anger and Beyond, 1966; Lewis, A. American Plays and Playwrights, 1965; Littlejohn, D. Black on White, 1966; Margolies, E. Native Sons, 1968; Ossman, D. The Sullen Art, 1963; Ricard, A. Théâtre et nationalisme, 1972; Rosenthal, M. L. The New Poets, 1967; Who's Who in America, 1972–1973. *Periodicals*—Antioch Review Fall 1967; Avant Garde September 1968; Dissent Spring 1965; Drama Review Summer 1968; Ebony August 1969; Hudson Review Autumn 1964; Kenyon Review 5 1968; Nation November 14, 1961; Negro Digest April 1966, April 1967; New Republic January 23, 1965; New York Herald Tribune October 27, 1965; New York Times November 22, 1969; June 19, 1971; March 13, 1972; December 5, 1972; March 13, 1973; New York Times Book Review November 26, 1965; May 8, 1966; February 4, 1968; March 17, 1968; June 27, 1971; New Yorker April 4, 1964; December 26, 1964; March 4, 1967; December 30, 1972; Newsday August 20, 1969; Newsweek December 4, 1972; Partisan Review Summer 1964; Poetry February 1967; Publishers Weekly September 11, 1972; Ramparts June 29, 1968; Saturday Review April 20, 1963; January 9, 1965; Society July 1972; Times Literary Supplement November 25, 1965; October 9, 1969.

JONES, GLYN (February 28, 1905–), Welsh poet, short story writer and novelist, writes: "I was born in Merthyr Tydfil, Glamorgan, Wales, and christened by my Welsh-speaking parents Morgan Glyn Dŵr. Merthyr was strategically placed. It was a coal and steel town built on the edge of a vast area of great natural beauty—rivers, woods, lakes, mountains—which began outside the walls of the Merthyr grammar school I was lucky enough to attend. The town itself has a turbulent political and industrial history, and, as well as being strongly radical and non-conformist, possessed a rich literary and musical tradition. My mother's family had long been established in the Merthyr valley, but my father's people, farmers from the agricultural west of Wales, arrived only in the last century. My father, before and after a bout of soldiering, worked in the post office. My mother was a school-teacher.

GLYN JONES

"My parents' home was politically conscious, deeply religious, intensely Welsh, and Welsh was my own first language. But my formal education was carried on entirely in English, and that is the language in which I have written all my books.

"It was my mother's wish, since I showed some promise at school as a painter, that I should become an art student, but somehow, to my regret, I found myself instead at St. Paul's College, Cheltenham. In 1925 I started to teach in Cardiff, and my education really began. Between that date and 1930 I attended classes in English literature at the local university college, and I also read widely in modern English literature. Joyce, Lawrence, Wyndham Lewis, and G. M. Hopkins were the writers who meant most to me then. The Thirties in Wales, as elsewhere, was a time of great poverty, suffering, unemployment, emigration, and despair, and living in the middle of this pervasive misery I could not but be deeply affected by it. At this time, too, I became increasingly aware of my own Welsh heritage, of the literature and the political aspirations of my own country, Wales. When I was about twenty-five I wrote my first poems, and a little later my first short stories. My first book, which reflected some of the concerns mentioned above, was published in 1937. It was a volume of short stories called *The Blue Bed*.

"Since then I have done a large amount of literary journalism, broadcasting and translating. My poems used to appear in *New Verse*, the *Adelphi*, *Twentieth Century Verse*, *Wales*, *Poetry* (Chicago), *Poetry* (London), etc., and my stories in *Life and Letters Today*, *Penguin Parade*, the *Welsh Review*, and *English Story*. My last three books have all been novels.

"I have spent my life teaching, chiefly English, in various towns in South Wales, and now, having finished with it, I am able to give a little time to painting again. I am currently engaged on a book about some of the Welshmen I have known who have, like myself, done their writing in English—Dylan Thomas, Caradoc Evans, Rhys Davies, Vernon Watkins. I myself have never written a word that was not about Wales and her people. The highest literary honour I have received was an invitation to become a member of the Academi Gymreig, the Welsh Academy of Letters.

"Although the finished product might often seem to belie this, I am a laborious writer, a dedicated note-book keeper and word collector, an endless chopper and changer and re-writer. I have no one clear theory about my own work, rather a large number of remarkably hazy ones. I am inclined to be suspicious of the too confident and explicit accounts which some writers seem to be able to give of their own work and creative processes and future projects. I find sympathetic the story of Henry Moore abandoning the reading of an analytical book about his own sculpture because it told him too clearly how he came to do it."

Peter Quennell once described Glyn Jones as "a Communist and a Welshman" with "a mystical tendency inherited from both sides." He is a tall man with a moustache, said to be a little retiring. He has been married since 1935.

Jones's earliest verse, full of a richly sensual Welsh eloquence, gave way during the 1930s to proletarian poems and then, under the influence of Gerard Manley Hopkins and Dylan Thomas, to apolitical lyrics—highly visual, strongly consonantal poems which, as he says, are "built up solid out of concrete nouns." Since 1940 he has written little verse, publishing in book form only the poem for radio *The Dream of Jake Hopkins*. Jones is bilingual and has made good unpoeticized translations from the fourteenth century bard Dafydd ap Gwilym.

Better known are his short stories, in which his "urgent prose is matched by precision of fancy and, especially in his splendid stories of working-class childhood, a surging exuberance of wit." The most recent and most admired of Jones's novels is *The Island of Apples*, set in a Welsh industrial town where a boy is led by his mysterious wandering friend into an orgy of arson and murder. One reviewer described it as a stunning mixture of "legend, fantasy, poetry, savagery, farce [and] minute Zolaesque realism," lacking in control but richly imaginative and haunting in its symbolism. The work he mentions above about Anglo-Welsh writers was published in 1968 as *The Dragon Has Two Tongues*. It was called "at once entertaining, instructive, and important"—"a lovely book."

PRINCIPAL WORKS: The Blue Bed (stories), 1937; Poems, 1939; The Water Music (stories), 1944; The Dream of Jake Hopkins (poem), 1954; (tr. with T. J. Morgan) The Saga of Llywarch the Old, 1955; The Valley, the City, the Village (novel), 1956; The Learning Lark (novel), 1960; The Island of Apples (novel), 1965; The Dragon Has Two Tongues (essays), 1968; Selected Short Stories, 1971.

ABOUT: Contemporary Authors 9–10 1964; Grigson, G. (ed.) Concise Encyclopedia of Modern World Literature, 1963; Jones, G. The Dragon Has Two Tongues, 1968; Murphy, R. (ed.) Contemporary Poets of the English Language, 1970; Norris, L. Glyn Jones, 1972; Vinson, J. (ed.) Contemporary Novelists, 1972. *Periodicals*—Times Literary Supplement April 8, 1965; November 14, 1968.

JONES, JACK (November 24, 1884–May 7, 1970), Welsh novelist and playwright, wrote: "I was born in Merthyr Tydfil in South Wales, the town which George Borrow described as the greatest coalmining place in Britain, and naturally I began work as a coal-miner in 1896. My father had been taken to work down the mine when only eight years old, so he saw nothing wrong in taking me to work down the mine with him when I was twelve years old. I considered this a privilege, not a hardship, for my father was such a skilled coal-hewer that I have always thought of him as an artist of the underworld. He could read and write a little, having had one year's schooling before he was taken down the mine to work a twelve-hour day.

"My mother was illiterate, never having had a day's schooling, but what a woman about the house! She was a dab-hand at cooking, baking, sewing, knitting, washing and ironing and keeping house as clean as possible. They had fifteen children and I was the eldest son. Six died in infancy, the other nine grew to be men and women. We children had schooling at a primary school from the age of six to the age of twelve.

"As a family we graduated from a backless hovel, without water or any convenience, by stages to a house which had a bathroom. My mother was passionately fond of going to the theatre, first the little wooden fit-up place known as 'the thrupenny 'orrible,' later the permanent Theatre Royal. My father preferred the pub to the theatre, so it was I who was for years my mother's escort.

"In 1902 I left home to join the Welch Regiment and went to South Africa at the tail-end of the Boer War. From South Africa to India, where I served three years in the Second Battalion. Transferred then to the Reserve and as such I was called up to fight in World War One. Was wounded at Ypres and sent home, a married man with three children by this time. There were five children when I was appointed to represent the miners of Blaengarw in the Garw Valley.

"The Welshman's fatal gift of eloquence drove me into politics and I stood, I am glad to say, unsuccessfully for Parliament. After this I was unemployed, off and on for some years, before I tried my hand at writing and typing on a rebuilt typewriter purchased on the instalment plan. My family thought I was wasting my time and urged me to try for a proper job of work. Got one eventually, only to throw it up to write again. Family unto the fourth generation—my daughter had two children—thought me insane. In my fiftieth year my first publication, the novel entitled *Rhondda Roundabout*, earned me the highest praise of Britain's leading reviewer, Gerald Gould of the *Observer*, who hailed me as 'a born writer.' If that were so then I was born rather late in the day.

"My family continued doubtful of my sanity until the first volume of my autobiography, *Unfinished Journey*, established me as a writer. For this had three simultaneous publications, Hamish Hamilton Ltd. in London, The Oxford Press in New York, and The Readers Union in London did an edition for its membership. Now the family conceded that perhaps I was a born writer after all.

"My writing was interrupted by the second world war, through which I was called upon to talk myself. Two longish tours of America and two to battle fronts, talking to British troops on how things were back home. All my sons, four, had gone to war; two were killed, one quickly and the other slowly with T.B. through exposure.

"Back to writing again and the *Observer* did one of its famous profiles of me, which was gratifying but no consolation for the loss of my sons. I wrote a couple of plays that were presented in the West End of London, at the Globe and the Fortune theatres. Wrote in all a score of books, of which fifteen were published. Wrote articles and scripts for radio, a screen play which starred Paul Robeson, and, eventually, found myself before the television cameras, confidently treating the medium as a friend and so getting away with it in my eighty-

JACK JONES

first year. At the moment I am writing about that wonderful mother of mine, whose name was Saran, still my unfailing inspiration after she has been dead twenty-five years. What am I saying? Such women never die."

Jack Jones became an almost legendary figure in Wales and after reading his account of his crowded life it is easy to see why. It was not always so. According to his *Observer* profile, "He must be the only man who has been an active member of the Communist, Labour, Liberal, and New Party organisations, and who also has spoken well of Baldwin." This political eclecticism made him many enemies among his fellow miners, especially when he stood as a Liberal candidate for Parliament at Neath. But Jack Jones was a "tough nineteenth century fighter," well able to deal with hecklers, and in time he weathered the storm.

More trouble followed when he began to write. *Black Parade*, his second novel, was banned in some Welsh libraries and bitterly attacked by Welshmen unwilling to believe that life in Wales could have been so ugly so recently. After the book's publication Jack Jones went back to manual labor on the roads. As he says, it was not until 1937 that *Unfinished Journey* established him as a writer.

Black Parade is a succession of grim pictures of the misery, hard labor, drunkenness, and near bestiality of the miner's life, relieved by the author's affection for his characters, written very simply but with great visual power. Some now consider it his best book, though others prefer the more directly autobiographical *Bidden to the Feast*. In fact all of Jones's books were drawn from life, and it may be that he was at his best when he made no pretense of writing fiction, in the autobiographical volumes, which have a gusto and vividness that "brings the reader right into the living presence of those he describes." Even his biography of Lloyd George is an "imaginative presentation," said to throw more light on its author than on Lloyd George. The *Times Literary Supplement* called Jack Jones "a big man breathing humanity" who "belongs to the tough school of reportage rather than to literature," and "whose personality is apt to overshadow, if not actually dwarf, the work in hand."

"All I want to do in my work," Jones said once, "is to tell people about life in the Glamorgan coalfield—one of the most remarkable societies the world has ever seen." He did that, and in the process told people about one of the most remarkable products of that remarkable society. He omitted to say above that he was mentioned in dispatches during World War I for gallantry at Ypres, and that his propagandist work during World War II brought him a CBE in 1948.

PRINCIPAL WORKS: Rhondda Roundabout (novel), 1934; Black Parade (novel), 1935; Unfinished Journey (autobiography), 1937; Land of My Fathers (play), 1937; Bidden to the Feast (novel), 1938; Rhondda Roundabout (play), 1939; The Man David: An Imaginative Presentation Based on Fact (about David Lloyd George), 1944; Me and Mine (autobiography), 1946; Transatlantic Episode (play), 1947; Off to Philadelphia in the Morning (novel), 1947; Some Trust in Chariots (novel), 1948; Give Me Back My Heart (autobiography), 1950; Lily of the Valley (novel), 1952; Lucky Lear (novel), 1952; River Out of Eden (novel), 1952; Time and the Business (novel), 1953; Choral Symphony (novel), 1955; Come, Night; End, Day! (novel), 1956.

ABOUT: Adam, G. F. Three Contemporary Anglo-Welsh Novelists, 1950; Jones, G. The Dragon Has Two Tongues, 1968; Jones, J. Unfinished Journey, and subsequent volumes of autobiography; Who's Who, 1970. *Periodicals*—Observer February 27, 1955; Times Literary Supplement October 11, 1947.

JONES, LEROI. *See* JONES, (EVERETT) LEROI

***JOUHANDEAU, MARCEL (HENRI)** (July 26, 1888–), French novelist, writes (in French): "I was born at Guéret at eight o'clock on a Thursday morning under Leo, like my father. Guéret is the principal town in the department of Creuse, which has almost the same boundaries as the old province of Marche. Being a border area this province, while retaining its own character, was very susceptible to the influence of its neighbors. My mother's family came from the region near Limousin, while my father's family lived in the area next to Bourbonnais and bore the mark of that rich province, more concerned with hygiene than the Limoges region.

* zhōō äɴ dō′

"My parents were of very humble origin, descended on both sides from peasant stock. I should perhaps mention that all the Blanchet family, to which my mother belonged, had faces of an oriental appearance, as I and my nephews still do. According to Gobineau there were in France scattered islands of Finns, by which he meant people who had come from Asia.

"My father was a butcher, and this certainly had a profound effect on my feelings and behavior. Colette once said to me: 'It is to this that your style owes its color.' Born gentle, and inclined towards tenderness, I suffered from the constant sight of knives and blood which was forced on me in my home. The church soon offered me a sort of refuge where I could at least escape from the cruel sights which horrified me at home, and my adolescence thus gradually became devoted to mysticism. Until I was seventeen I dreamed of becoming a priest; my first book gives an honest account of the incident which led me to renounce the priesthood.

"After I had brilliantly completed my secondary schooling at the *lycée* in Guéret my father agreed, on the insistence of my teachers, to send me to Paris to take a more advanced course at the Lycée Henri IV; the contacts which I made there with eminent teachers and brilliant friends have been very useful to me. I afterwards enrolled at the Sorbonne, intending to take a degree, but I was preoccupied more with literature than with preparation for my exams, and soon incurred the reproaches of my family, who cut off my allowance. After a short stay with the famous impresario Charles Baret, whose secretary I was for a few weeks and had thought to train under, I became convinced that I was not cut out to manage a troupe of actors. In December 1912 I applied for and obtained a position as a teacher at a boarding school in Passy, where I continued to teach for thirty-seven years, until 1949.

"It is certainly due to this stability of my life that I have been able to produce all my work. I led a double life. I have never written for a living, since my profession as a teacher provided me with independence and enough to live on. I wrote at night, and taught by day.

"As a result of a crisis of conscience in February 1914, when I was twenty-six years old, I completely destroyed everything I had written, a library of manuscripts.

"My health, nowadays excellent, was precarious throughout my youth. Though I was exempt from military service in the 1914 war I became an auxiliary soldier. Mobilized and made secretary to the captain-paymaster of the 78th Infantry Regiment, I drew up the reports of the Administrative Staff, which for four years signed without comment the decisions which I alone had taken, though it is true only after serious inquiries and making up an impressive dossier.

"When demobilized and back in Paris in 1919 I sent a first manuscript to my present publisher, M. Gaston Gallimard. My first published work, the stories 'Les Pincengrain' (The Pincengrain Family), appeared in the *Nouvelle Revue Française* in October 1920; and my first book, *La Jeunesse de Théophile* (The Youth of Théophile), came out in June 1921 and at once met with a sympathetic reception. Henri Bidon wrote about me in his weekly article in *Les Annales*, quoting long extracts from my work.

"My vocation as a writer is certainly unexpected, since nothing seemed to predestine me, born of an obscure family in the chief town of a neglected province, for what my life became.

"As far as I remember, however, although my parents were small shopkeepers, they were, as often happens in France, far superior to their circumstances in life. My father was a very good storyteller. He had been handsome, a sort of Don Juan, and I have seldom seen a face more witty and alive with sensuality than his. I can still hear the way he would, when he had finished eating, tell his stories with consummate skill, unconsciously inventing techniques of suspense. As for my mother, who wrote to me every day for more than twenty years, from 1908 to 1929, she wrote in a style which was as personal as her conversation was enchanting. She had a great success each time I quoted one of her letters in my classes. M. Gallimard has a copy of this correspondence, and may perhaps publish it after my death. Obviously, thanks to this daily contact with my birthplace, my umbilical cord was never quite severed.

"My work can be divided into various cycles. My principal tales, as my German publisher M. Rowohlt understood so well, make up the story of Guéret, which I called Chaminadour. But the stories called *Chaminadour* (1934–1941) are much less important for a knowledge of the milieu in which I grew up and the people who fascinated me as a child and as a young man than the stories which I published at the beginning of my career: *Les Pincengrain* (republished as a book in 1924), *Prudence Hautechaume* (1927), *Le Journal du coiffeur* (The Diary of a Hairdresser, 1931), *Le Saladier* (The Salad-Bowl, 1936), etc., which are related to *La Jeunesse de Théophile*.

"After Théophile I embodied myself in two other characters, Juste Binche and Monsieur Godeau, the latter of whom is associated with Véronique, Éliane and Prisca, the three Pincengrain sisters.

"Part of my work centers on an exceptional woman whom I called the Duchess. I have said of her that I have never known anyone who was more scornful. She appears in *Opales* (Opals, 1928) and in

MARCEL JOUHANDEAU

three travel stories: *Le Jardin de Cordoue* (The Garden of Cordova, 1938), *Don Juan*, and *Les Argonautes* (The Argonauts, 1959).

"In 1928 I met Élise, who became my wife on June 4, 1929. Under the name Caryathis she had known her hour of fame when she created [the ballet] *La Belle excentrique* for Erik Satie.

"This surprise marriage led me to write many books about our domestic strife: *Monsieur Godeau marié* (Monsieur Godeau Married, 1933), *Chroniques maritales* (Chronicles of Married Life, 1938), *L'Imposteur* (The Impostor, 1950), *Élise* (1933), *Chroniques d'une passion* (The Story of a Passion, 1944), *Ménagerie domestique* (The Domestic Menagerie, 1948), *Élise architecte* (Elise as Architect, 1951), *Ana de Madame Apremont* (1954), *L'Éternel Procès* (The Eternal Trial, 1959). Besides these books centered on a woman I must mention my animal books: *Animaux familiers* (Familiar Animals, 1947), *Animaleries* (1961); stories about my family: *Le Parricide imaginaire* (The Imaginary Parricide, 1930), *Binche-Ana* (1933), *Portraits de famille* (Family Portraits, 1951); books about teaching: *Ma Classe de sixième* (My Class of the Sixth, 1949), *Carnets du professeur* (A Teacher's Notebook); my essays about sexuality: *De l'abjection* (On Baseness, 1939), *Éloge de la volupté* (In Praise of Pleasure, 1951), *Du pur amour* (On Pure Love, 1955), *L'École des garçons* (School for Boys, 1952), *Carnets de Don Juan* (Don Juan's Diary, 1947); or about morality: *Eléments pour une éthique* (Elements of a Morality, 1955), *De la grandeur* (On Greatness, 1952), *Réflexions sur la vie et le bonheur* (Reflections on Life and Happiness, 1958), *Réflexions sur la vieillese et la mort* (Reflections on Old Age and Death, 1956).

"The six volumes of my *Mémorial* (Memorial, 1948–1958) complete my memories of childhood and youth, casting aside fictionalization.

"At seventy-eight my health is perfect, my serenity is proof against almost anything, my step brisk, and my ability to work as great as ever.

"To know me well it is necessary to read *L'École des filles* (School for Girls, 1960) and the series of *Journaliers* (Diaries, 1957—)."

Jouhandeau has published more than a hundred books, a few of them under the pseudonym "Marcel Provence." His work is almost entirely autobiographical, and in it he projects what Claude Mauriac has called a *mystique de l'enfer* (mystique of hell), a dualist approach to Christianity in which Satan and God are equally real and a vivid apprehension of evil is as necessary as a belief in immortality. His central preoccupations are his homosexuality, which he calls his "vice," the pettiness of provincial life, and the crimes, vices, and perversions which abound in Chaminadour, his fictionalized version of his native town. But in his ruthless dissection of the mean little souls of its inhabitants, and in his own pitiless and exhibitionistic introspection, he continually detects the presence of the holy, which for him is found especially in baseness and sin.

La Jeunesse de Théophile, though nominally a novel, is the closely autobiographical story of Jouhandeau's own youth, revealing his early antipathy to his father and his deep attachment to his mother and to her sister, the beginning of his involvement in tortuous relationships with a series of older women. His boyhood passion centers on Jeanne, a Carmelite nun ten years older than himself, but when he is sixteen this gives way to a mystically erotic relationship with Madame Alban, a middle-aged married woman who dabbles in theology and philosophy and has an unreciprocated taste for priests. As Martin Turnell has said, Jouhandeau gives "a striking account of the atmosphere of genuine eroticism and sham mysticism in which she succeeded in enveloping him."

Jouhandeau's most famous autobiographical projection is Marcel Godeau, who becomes the observer and chronicler of Chaminadour. Such books as *Monsieur Godeau intime* (The Innermost Monsieur Godeau, 1926) are written in the third person, but *Monsieur Godeau marié*, which begins the marriage series, is written in the first person, and in more recent volumes Jouhandeau doesn't bother to modify his surname. He had met Élise through the artist Marie Laurencin, who told him one day "I've found just the woman for you." Since their marriage he has chronicled their love-hate relationship in a series of books which are loosely constructed in diary-like episodes and scenes.

Though like Gide he married partly to escape from his homosexuality, he continually yields to temptation, as in the homosexual affair of *Chroniques d'une passion*. But even then Élise, a much stronger character than Gide's wife, remains in the center of the picture. She appears as the eternal female, strong-willed, flamboyant, and impulsive, her character a strange mixture of economy and extravagance. Completely self-centered, she on one occasion gives away all his overcoats to make room in the wardrobe for her furs. "Whatever else it has or has not achieved," said the *Times Literary Supplement*, "the marriage of Marcel and Élise has provided Jouhandeau with an endless subject of inquiry and an apparently inexhaustible source of inspiration. As such it must rank as one of the foremost literary marriages of our time." During the 1960s Élise also wrote an autobiography, presenting their relationship from her point of view.

Martin Turnell, who has translated extracts from seven of these books under the title *Marcel and Élise* (1953), regards these characters as "two of the most formidable creations in contemporary literature. The exchanges between them provide us with fresh and disturbing insights not merely into human nature, but into the human couple in marriage." Other critics, however, have been fascinated not by what is universal in the marriage but by its exotic abnormality.

Estimates of the value of Jouhandeau's work vary greatly. John Weightman considers that "the greatest part of his output is a confused psychological document, spangled with particles of literature." Jouhandeau's most notable talent, in Weightman's opinion, is his gift for cruel and erotic anecdotage, most evident in his accounts of his early life in "Chaminadour"; "he provides glimpse after glimpse of a bright morning world where lusty butcher boys discover their virility together, tough old peasants strenuously rape their granddaughters, and satanic wenches roast live rats over braziers. Compared to this direct, pagan vision, the religious questionings of the later books, and even the accounts of personal relationships, seem dim and tedious."

As Rayner Heppenstall says, Jouhandeau is something of a writer's writer. He has been highly praised by Philippe Soupault and Thornton Wilder, and by Havelock Ellis, who regarded him as the modern Cervantes. Gide called him his "spiritual brother" and said that Jouhandeau had brought him into regions and depths he had thought inaccessible. Until quite recently his work was not well known even in France outside a small circle, but after the war his books about married life suddenly achieved notoriety, and with *L'Imposteur* in 1950 he reached a wider audience than he had ever known before.

PRINCIPAL WORKS IN ENGLISH TRANSLATION: Marcel and Élise, 1953; St. Philip Neri (biography), 1960.
ABOUT: Curtis, J.-L. Haute École, 1950; Gaulmier, J. L'Univers de Marcel Jouhandeau, 1959; Heppenstall, R. The Fourfold Tradition, 1961; International Who's Who, 1973–74; Mauriac, C. Introduction à une mystique de l'enfer, 1938; Moore, H. T. Twentieth-Century French Literature to World War II, 1966; Penguin Companion to Literature 2, 1969; Turnell, M. *introduction to* Marcel and Élise, 1953; Who's Who in France, 1971–1972. *Periodicals*—Commonweal June 18, 1954, September 23, 1960; New Republic February 8, 1954; New Statesman October 29, 1955; Times Literary Supplement November 4, 1955; January 11, 1957; April 8, 1960; May 28, 1964; January 25, 1968; August 13, 1971.

***JOUVE, PIERRE JEAN** (October 11, 1887–), French poet, novelist, and critic, was born at Arras in Artois. His father, Alfred Jouve, was a businessman; his mother, the former Aimée Rosé, had been a music teacher. Jouve attended schools at Arras and Lille, and went on to the universities of Paris and Poitiers. His education seems to have been unusually wide, embracing mathematics, law, archaeology, and medicine. From his mother he inherited a taste for music, and he spent his leisure at the piano rather than in reading. "When I left the lycée about 1905," he has recalled, "I had a profound contempt for poetry. Aptitudes of a scientific nature led me to believe that it was sterile and useless. . . . It was Stéphane Mallarmé who one day and at a single blow demolished my negative attitude by his *Vers et prose*."

He was quick to learn. Two years later, in 1907, he founded with Paul Castiaux a literary magazine called *Les Bandeaux d'or* (Golden Headbands), in which his earliest poems appeared. It ran for three years and was closely associated with Jules Romains' *unanimiste* movement. Jouve published three volumes of verse between 1910 and 1913, more or less in the Parnassian tradition—rich, musical, vigorous—but already showing a characteristic tendency to juxtapose abstract philosophical speculations and sharply visual imagery.

At the outbreak of war in 1914 he volunteered for service as a hospital orderly, but was soon obliged by ill health to give the work up. He spent the next four years in Switzerland, where his pacifism was reinforced by his friendship with Romain Rolland, and was expressed in such volumes as *Vous êtes des hommes* (You Are of Mankind, 1915), *Poème contre le grand crime* (Poem Against the Great Crime, 1916), and *Danse des morts* (Dance of the Dead, 1917). He described his *Romain Rolland vivant, 1914–1919*, published in 1920, as "a poem and an act of faith." *Tragiques* (1923) collected some of the verse he had written at the end of the war and immediately after it, when he left Switzerland and traveled in other parts of Europe.

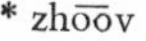
* zhōōv

PIERRE JEAN JOUVE

But what Jouve has called the "bitter maze" of his youth had left him with a personal sense of despair not to be assuaged by the optimistic humanitarianism of Romains and Rolland. While staying in Italy in 1923 he went through a spiritual upheaval and the following year returned to the Catholic Church. This was the beginning of what he has called a *vita nuova*. Although the event was reflected in two novels, *Paulina 1880* (translated under that title by Rosette Letellier and Robert Bullen) and *Le Monde désert* (The Deserted World), which appeared in 1925 and 1927, and in several small volumes of verse, it was not until 1928, when two of these volumes were republished as *Noces* (Weddings), that he made any public announcement. He then declared that his conversion did not imply a passage from unbelief to belief, but from one conception of Catholicism to another. He went on to reject everything written by him before 1925 and said that his "true" work had begun that year.

After 1925 the main intellectual influences on his writing were Catholicism and the theories of Freud. (It cannot be coincidental that in that critical year he married, as his second wife, the psychoanalyst Blanche Reverchon). In the preface to *Sueur de sang* (Sweat of Blood, 1933), he had this to say of his new allegiances: "Modern man has discovered the unconscious and its structure; he has seen in it the impulse of Eros and the impulse towards death, indissolubly linked. The face of the world of sin, which means the world of man, is definitely changed by it. It is impossible to break the bond between guilt—man's deepest feeling—and the initial connection between these two fundamental instincts. . . . Man is an unresolved conflict."

Jouve's subsequent poetry can be seen as an attempt to resolve this conflict between Christ and Eros, to find a chord expressing the connection between death and sex. In *Le Paradis perdu* (Lost Paradise, 1929), the fall of man is ascribed not to Eve's eating the apple but to her sexual intercourse with Satan. Squeamish critics have been disturbed by the mixture of religious and erotic elements in *Sueur de sang*, which, according to Margaret Callander, "reveals life as an endless, hopeless circle of lust and despair in a stifling, sin-laden climate." His poems at this time grew increasingly austere in their language, harshly simple in their style—seeking, as he said, a condition of "nakedness." Jouve pursued a similar course in his fiction, which is generally regarded as of less importance than his verse. *Hecate* (1928) and *Vagadu* (1931), which were brought together in *Aventure de Catherine Crachat* (Catherine Crachat's Adventure, 1947), are virtually studies, from Jouve's special viewpoint, in sexual pathology. "Dans les années profondes" (In the Deep Years), one of the stories in *La Scène capitale* (The Crucial Scene, 1935), includes touches which might have made even Freud raise his eyebrows a little.

Jouve's groping towards "a theology of absence, catastrophe and apocalypse"—and the poetic means to express it—entered a new phase in "Hélene" (1936), subsequently incorporated in *Matière céleste* (Celestial Matter, 1937), in which his half-formed ideas of love, death, and God are crystallized and humanized into a single symbolic figure. World War II, which he spent in exile in Geneva, brought a widening of Jouve's vision, an increased ability to relate his own problems to those of his country and the world. *La Vierge de Paris* (The Virgin of Paris, 1944), in which he collected his poems of the war years, is regarded by some critics as his best-integrated and most important work.

Others, however, disagree and speak of the years between 1925 and about 1950 as a middle period in Jouve's development, a period of search in which he argued rather than expressed his theology. They complain of the grandiose abstractions which fill these poems, of an intellectual tension so great that they seem scarcely to move at all—"word agglutinated with word," as Gabriel Bournoure put it, "in agonizing slowness." For critics who hold this opinion, Jouve has done his best work since the war, in such volumes as *Ode* (1950), *Langue* (1954), *Lyrique* (1956), *Mélodrame* (1957), *Inventions* (1958), and *Moires* (1962). Since 1950, according to C. A. Hackett, "Jouve's development has been towards less metaphysical and more musical modes of expression; and his themes which were always aspiring to universality have at last achieved it, because they have become fully personal and human."

Jouve has translated the sonnets of Shakespeare and several of the plays. His critical works include striking essays on Baudelaire and Rimbaud, to both of whom his own work is greatly indebted. The phrase he invented to describe Rimbaud—"the eye of catastrophe"—has been applied to himself. *Le Don Juan de Mozart* (1942) is notable not only for its profound insight into the composer's genius but for what it reveals about Jouve's own agonized inquiry into the theme of *Don Giovanni*, the myth of love and death.

Of Jouve's talent there is no question; it is the use to which he has put it that divides the critics. Many regard him as France's greatest living poet; others have described his work as "obsessed," "erotic," and "obscene." His influence, at any rate, has been considerable, especially on Pierre Emmanuel and Yves Bonnefoy, and on the English poet David Gascoyne. His collected poems were published in four volumes in 1964–1967.

Since 1945 Jouve has lived in Paris. In 1962 he received the Grand Prix National des Lettres, and in 1966 the Grand Prix de Poésie de l'Académie Française. *Paulina 1880* has been filmed.

PRINCIPAL WORKS IN ENGLISH TRANSLATION: Men of Europe, 1915; Mozart's Don Juan, 1957; An Idiom of Night: Poems (selected and tr. by K. Bosley), 1968; Paulina 1880, 1973. *Poems in* Gascoyne, D. Poems 1937–42, 1943; Hartley, A. Penguin Book of French Verse, Twentieth Century, 1959; Strachan, W. J. Apollinaire to Aragon, Thirty Modern French Poets, 1948. *Periodicals*—Folios of New Writing Spring 1940; London Magazine February 1955; Poetry August 1964.

ABOUT: Boisdeffre, P. de. Dictionnaire de littérature contemporaine, 1900–1962, 1962; Callander, M. The Poetry of Pierre Jean Jouve, 1965; Hackett, C. A. An Anthology of Modern French Poetry from Baudelaire to the Present Day, 1965; International Who's Who, 1971–1972; Jouve, P. J. Commentaires, 1950; Jouve, P. J. En Miroir, 1954; Micha, R. Pierre Jean Jouve, 1956; Smith, H. (ed.) Columbia Dictionary of Modern European Literature, 1947; Starobinski, J. and others. Pierre Jean Jouve, poète et romancier, 1946; Who's Who in France, 1971–1972. *Periodicals*—Books Abroad Summer 1958; Cahiers du Sud April 1936; Mercure de France February 1953; Romanic Review April–June 1933; Sewanee Review July 1933; Times Literary Supplement April 24, 1948.

***JÓZSEF, ATTILA** (April 11, 1905–December 3, 1937), Hungarian poet, was born in great poverty in Budapest, and remained poor all his life. His father, Áron, a day laborer, abandoned the family and went to America when Attila was three. His mother's income as maid and washerwoman was not enough to support the boy and his two sisters, and he was handed back and forth between home, orphanages, and a village where he worked for his keep minding geese and pigs before he was seven. A long line of subsequent jobs—newsboy, freight hustler, Danube sailor—echoes in many of his poems. József's mother died in 1919, and in his

* yō′ zhef

terrible grief he abused her as a swindler for abandoning him: "In that final hour you stole back the lot." The boy had first tried to escape his wretched life at the age of nine; now he attempted suicide again, but the train that was to kill him never came —it had run over another man a mile farther up the line. "Somebody else has died for me," József used to say afterwards.

Against all obstacles, József managed to acquire some education. While he was still at high school he published "blasphemous" and "treasonous" poems in a local paper and had his first clash with authority. Later he enrolled at the University of Szeged, where he studied Hungarian and French literature, and began to contribute to the great progressive magazine *Nyugat* (The West). His first collection of poems, *Szépség koldusa* (Beggar of Beauty, 1922), created a sensation, and a poem about Christ as a revolutionary brought fresh charges of blasphemy. József was expelled from Szeged and went on to study in Vienna and at the Sorbonne in Paris. There his thought matured under the influence of Hegel, Marx, and the French avant-garde.

Returning to Budapest in the late 1920s, József joined the underground Communist movement and wrote poems for its clandestine broadsheets, only to be expelled in 1930 for his "attachment to folklore" and to the "bourgeois," and for "militant discords within himself." József was incapable of submitting to party discipline, but remained in sympathy with the Communist movement and in 1932 was fined for a courageous protest against the execution of two Hungarian Communist leaders. In his poetry, he never ceased to pour out his protests against the squalor and misery of the proletariat, his invective against their masters. The authorities regarded him as a dangerous subversive, and hounded his every step.

Arthur Koestler thus described József at the age of twenty-seven: "He was of pure-bred Magyar, rural stock: of medium height, lean, sparse, sinewy, he carried his body like a regimental sergeant-major. He had a narrow face with a high forehead, calm brown eyes and calm, regular features, . . . [and] a trim moustache with pointed ends." He was a passionate chess player and tireless in argument. Koestler found him in spite of everything an "extremely amiable and amusing, though somewhat exhausting companion." Nevertheless, József was by that time losing a long battle against schizophrenia, a condition which fed on, and in turn nourished, his persecutions and privations, his unhappy love affairs, and the ups and downs of his troubled marriage.

The last five years of his life were for József a time of great misery and sickness, but also his richest creative period, in which he "grew into a poet of national and world importance." Much of his finest work is included in *Medvetánc* (The Bear's Dance, 1934), a collection of poems inspired by his friendship with Béla Bartók; *Nincs bocsánat* (There Is No Pardon, 1936–1937); and *Utolsó versek* (Last Poems, 1937). But the same collections contained evidence of his madness (which a course of psychoanalysis had done nothing to alleviate). In 1937 József spent a few weeks in a mental hospital, and afterwards seemed much improved. One evening late in the year he walked down to the small railroad station at Balatonszárszó, where a freight train was moving off. He thrust his right arm between the wheels, and was killed.

ATTILA JÓZSEF

József's poetry reflects his profound interest both in Marx and Freud, but even at its most complex and cerebral reads "like folk-songs and sometimes like nursery rhymes." He utilized a ballade form like that of Villon (whom he admired and translated) and interior rhythms in the manner of the Finnish folk epic *Kalevala*, and borrowed also from German expressionism, French surrealism, and Hungarian folklore, mixing all these ingredients in a purely personal style brimming with free associations and rich in "rolling four and five-syllable words." Joseph Remenyi has said that József's poetry is sometimes undisciplined in its passionate honesty and fervor, but that he could "write hexameters like a classical poet and sing like a nervous lark."

His "songs of the slums" are "pure and fresh and lyrical, even at their most terrifying"—and never more so than when he is writing about his mother, or about love. He called himself "freedom's beautiful, serious son," who strove for "order and brave words" and "who dared everything," while tragically aware of "so many monsters housed / within the caverns of my heart."

Excommunicated by the Communist party during his lifetime, little read during the Zhdanov era, József has at last come into his own, canonized by the postwar Communist regime as the greatest national poet. His "miraculous union of intellect and melody" has found many admirers in Europe, and he has been praised and translated in Poland, France, England, Germany, and elsewhere.

PRINCIPAL WORKS IN ENGLISH TRANSLATION: Poems, 1966; Selected Poems and Texts, tr. by John Bátki, ed. by George Gömöri and James Atlas, 1973. *Poems in* Duczyńska, I. and Polanyi, K. (eds.) The Plough and the Pen, 1963; Chicago Review 18, 1965; Literary Review II, 1959.

ABOUT: Duczyńska, I. and Polanyi, K. (eds.) The Plough and the Pen, 1963; Gömöri, G. Polish and Hungarian Poetry 1945–1956, 1966; Hommage à Attila József par les poètes français, 1955; Reményi, J. Hungarian Writers and Literature, 1964. *Periodicals*—Encounter May 1954.

"JUDD, CYRIL." *See* KORNBLUTH, CYRIL M. and also MERRIL, JUDITH

***JUHÁSZ, FERENC** (August 16, 1928–), Hungarian poet, was born in Bia, near Budapest, the son of a maidservant and of a mason who died early of tuberculosis. His childhood on the Transdanubian plain was poor and hard. Juhász began writing verse in his early teens and by the time he was nineteen had filled two suitcases with what he later decided were "random lines that did not link up." In 1947 Juhász was admitted to the faculty of literature of the Attila József People's College. As he entered the college—"diffidently, carrying my humble belongings"—a girl called Erzsébet Szeverényi was standing at the top of the stairs. He fell in love with her and they were married shortly afterwards. At college, Juhász burned his juvenilia and "turned into a poet."

His master at first was the great revolutionary poet Sándor Petőfi. Juhász's first published book of poems, *Szárnyas Csikó* (The Winged Colt, 1947), established his reputation before he was twenty. This collection and the two epics which soon followed were fervent in their naïve enthusiasm for the new communist regime, scrupulous in their adherence to the principles of "socialist realism" (the "winged colt" is a tractor). But the regime's impressive land redistribution program was followed by the injustices of enforced collectivization; the party's ban on literary experiment and spontaneity brought a rapid decline in the quality of Hungarian poetry. At the First Congress of Hungarian Writers in 1951, Juhász was prominent among those who attacked this "colorless and

FERENC JUHÁSZ

flavorless" representation of reality, and was rebuked by the ideologist Márton Horváth. The same year Juhász parodied his own style and satirized collective farms and farmers in *A jégvirág kakasa* (The Frost-Flower's Cockerel), a mock-epic which was generally attacked by the literary establishment.

In *Óda a repüléshez* (Ode to Flight, 1953), Juhász made a fresh start; the poem was an ode to personal freedom, ignoring party didactics. Juhász has never rejected communism but has sought a "socialism of the people" owing much to populism, the cultural-sociological movement of the 1930s which had sent Hungarian artists back to their peasant roots for inspiration. Perhaps, as some critics have said, Juhász is fundamentally an apolitical writer, concerned most urgently with poetry's abiding themes: life. love, death. During the early 1950s Juhász began a period of intense stylistic experimentation. According to George Gömöri, "in the course of two years his poetry passed through practically every stage in the development of modern Western poetry: Parnassism, symbolism, expressionism, surrealism." He emerged from this search the master of a unique neoromantic manner which makes use of all of these modes and is stuffed with fantastic and often grotesque images borrowed from technology and biology.

The massive epic poem *A tékozlo ország* (The Prodigal Country) appeared in 1954, and is regarded by Gömöri as his masterpiece, the beginning of "a new epoch in modern Hungarian poetry." In a "Dionysiac torrent of images" it tells the story of the tragic peasant revolt of 1514, and is an indictment of tyranny clearly applicable to

* yōō′ häs

Stalinism. Juhász, already a whipping boy for the party mandarins, accused of deviation and "death-sentiments," became the victim of a fresh offensive. Meetings were organized to discuss and condemn his poetry. In spite of his popularity, only five hundred copies were published of his next collection, *A virágok hatalma* (The Power of Flowers, 1955).

This volume, containing poems variously reminiscent of Apollinaire, Attila József, and Sándor Weöres, marked a further withdrawal from political preoccupations, influenced no doubt by the poet's misery and loneliness during his wife's temporary insanity. These uneven poems reflect a universe perceived, Gömöri says, as "a chaotic theatre where creation, destruction, and procreation are but links in an eternal chain," in which the poet struggles "with his own vision of prehistoric and pre-human existence." Another critic speaks of this private world as "a strange compound of nature, folk-tale and technology. . . . An expanded universe of the senses, biological visions, macrocosmic phantasy." Juhász himself writes: "things often break loose before me / their order falls apart . . . / devils rut over me dividing my wounded heart. . . ." This apocryphal vision dominates *Harc a fehér báránnyal* (Battling the White Lamb, 1957), containing the "myth-creating folk-tale poem" translated by Kenneth McRobbie as "The Boy Changed Into a Stag Cries out at the Gate of Secrets"; W. H. Auden called it "one of the greatest poems written in my time."

Juhász took no active part in the 1956 revolution; he had, indeed, already made his rebellion. After the publication of *Battling the White Lamb* he joined other Hungarian writers in their "protest of silence." He began to publish again in 1962, and his recent work, it is said, is marked by "an intense feeling of solitude." A cartoon which appeared in Hungary at this time showed Juhász crouched alone on the roof of a house, remote from the political struggle, while other writers are trapped in the crowded rooms below. It is reported that he aroused official anger in 1964 with his "Christmas Song at the Grave of Attila József," an attempt to rehumanize the image of that poet, posthumously canonized by the Communist party. However, Juhász's eighth collection of poems, *Viragzo vilagta* (The Blooming Word-Tree, 1966), was very well received. His travels to London, Vienna, and elsewhere during the 1960s as a member of Hungarian writers' delegations suggests that he now enjoys official trust. Young Hungarians regard him as the finest poet of his generation, the heir to Attila József. Juhász's poems have been translated into French, German, Russian, Polish, and other languages, as well as English. The English critic A. Alvarez has ranked him with Bartók and József as one of the geniuses of Hungarian art.

PRINCIPAL WORKS IN ENGLISH TRANSLATION: Selected Poems of Sándor Weöres and Ferenc Juhász (tr. by Edwin Morgan and David Wevill), 1970; The Boy Changed Into a Stag: Selected Poems 1949–1967 (tr. by Kenneth McRobbie and I. Duczyńska), 1970. *Poems in* Duczyńska, I. and Polanyi, K. (eds.) The Plough and the Pen, 1963; Steiner, G. (ed.) Penguin Book of Modern Verse Translation, 1966.

ABOUT: Duczyńska, I. and Polanyi, K. (eds.) The Plough and the Pen, 1963; Gömöri, G. Polish and Hungarian Poetry 1945–1956, 1966.

JUSTICE, DONALD (RODNEY) (August 12, 1925–), American poet, was born in Miami, Florida. He is the son of a carpenter, Vasco Justice, and of the former Ethel Cook. The osteomyelitis he contracted as a child debarred him from any kind of military service. Justice received his B.A. degree from the University of Miami in 1945, his M.A. from the University of North Carolina in 1947, and his Ph.D. from the State University of Iowa in 1954. In 1954–1955 he traveled in Europe on a Rockefeller poetry fellowship. After teaching English at the University of Missouri (1955–1956) and at Hamline University in Minnesota (1956–1957), he returned in 1957 to the State University of Iowa. There he remained for ten years, teaching both poetry and fiction in the Writers' Workshop, until in 1966 he went to the University of Syracuse as professor of English.

Although he began writing seriously in his mid-twenties, Justice found none of his early verse worth preserving, and did not publish his first book until 1960. This was *The Summer Anniversaries*, a Lamont Poetry Selection and winner of the Inez Boulton prize. Gene Baro found Justice largely traditional in his meters and unadventurous in his language, but nevertheless "a poet of fine skill, often moving to read, a man searching for a universal meaning in his personal experience"; Thom Gunn called him "a gentle poet," but one in whose best poems "the gentleness has its own firm clear strength." The book was indeed welcomed by most reviewers, though Dudley Fitts damned it comprehensively for following "the decorous, subdued, gray formula of our younger poets: correct shapes, correct diction . . . the correct stance, flat on the face."

Night Light, containing low-keyed, good-mannered "poems of memory and of concern for the brevity and precariousness of the human condition," seemed to one reviewer to reflect "a kind of contemporary stoicism," and was also generally liked. A critic in the *Times Literary Supplement*, who said that Justice was "witty, gentle, sophisticated, a quiet recorder of the pathetic and inconsequential," went on: "The poems . . . are undemanding notations; and if they get no louder applause than that, it is because they do not seem to expect it."

Justice is not solely a poet. Two of his short

DONALD JUSTICE

stories have received O. Henry awards, appearing in the *Prize Stories* collections for 1950 and 1954. He is also interested in the drama (he held a Ford Fellowship in theatre in 1964–1965) and in music. Several of his compositions have been performed, among them a concert piece for piano and woodwinds, and some songs. Justice was editor of *The Collected Poems of Weldon Kees*, and coeditor with Alexander Aspel of *Contemporary French Poetry*, an anthology of translations by twenty-four poets who had been associated in one way or another with the State University of Iowa. Donald Justice was married in 1947 to the short story writer Jean Ross. They have one son. The author received the Harriet Monroe Memorial Prize in 1965 and a grant from the National Council on the Arts in 1967.

PRINCIPAL WORKS: The Summer Anniversaries (poems), 1960; (ed.) The Collected Poems of Weldon Kees, 1962; (ed. with Alexander Aspel) Contemporary French Poetry, 1965; Night Light (poems), 1967; Departures (poems), 1973.

ABOUT: Contemporary Authors 7–8, 1963; Murphy, R. (ed.) Contemporary Poets of the English Language, 1970.

KACEW, ROMAIN. *See* GARY, ROMAIN

***KANIN, GARSON** (November 24, 1912–), American dramatist, short story writer, novelist, and memoirist, writes: "I was born (they tell me) in Rochester, New York. My parents were Russian-Jewish immigrants who met and were married in the United States. My childhood, shared with a brother three years my senior, and a sister seven years my junior, was jolly and peregrinating. That distant relative, the adolescent I, worries me still—rebellious, precocious, unconventional, audacious, and difficult. My patient, loving, practical parents coped somehow. A year-and-a-half of high school exhausted my patience for scholastic life and I began a vague and aimless voyage on the seas of the Depression. When my father's fortunes foundered I was made sharply aware of the dynamics of have and have not. A series of jobs began: stock clerk at Macy's, messenger for Western Union, honky tonk saxophone player, burlesque comedian, and radio actor.

"In 1932 (thank Fate!) I entered the American Academy of Dramatic Arts and upon my graduation made my Broadway debut with a role in *Little Ol' Boy*. I acted in many Broadway productions, among them *Three Men on a Horse* and *Boy Meets Girl*, which led to the great good fortune of becoming George Abbott's assistant. In 1937 I went to Hollywood as a member of Samuel Goldwyn's production staff. A year later I went to RKO where I directed Edward Ellis, Anne Shirley, and Lee Bowman in *A Man to Remember*; Lucille Ball in *Next Time I Marry*; John Barrymore in *The Great Man Votes*; Ginger Rogers and David Niven in *Bachelor Mother*; Carole Lombard and Charles Laughton in *They Knew What They Wanted*; Cary Grant and Irene Dunne in *My Favorite Wife*; Ginger Rogers, Burgess Meredith and George Murphy in *Tom, Dick and Harry*.

"Early in 1941 I was drafted under the terms of the Selective Service Act for what began as an eighteen-month training period, but resulted in a five-year army hitch. It was during this time that I began to write: short stories, journals, screenplays, plays, and half of a novel. With Carol Reed I directed General Eisenhower's official film report of the war in Europe, *The True Glory*.

"In 1942, Ruth Gordon and I were married.

"Following my discharge, I directed Spencer Tracy in Robert E. Sherwood's play *The Rugged Path*. This was followed by my own play *Born Yesterday*, which I had written during my army service, and my wife's autobiographical play, *Years Ago*. A long succession of plays and films have followed. In 1954, I published a novelette called *Do Re Mi* and in 1959 a novel, *Blow Up a Storm*. My first long work of non-fiction, *Remembering Mr. Maugham*, appeared in 1966.

"I have also published some forty-odd short stories in publications here and abroad. My wife and I own a house in Turtle Bay Gardens on Manhattan Island, but find that our work takes us away from it for increasing lengths of time.

"I have been writing for twenty-five years, and some day I hope to become a writer."

Kanin's greatest success was his satirical comedy

* kā' nin

Born Yesterday, about the downfall of a wartime profiteering junk dealer at the hands of his mistress, an ex-chorus girl who picks up moral standards along with an education from a reforming journalist. Burton Rascoe expressed the majority opinion when he called the play "ribald, adult, witty, clever" and praised its obvious but sharp characterization, its air of timeliness and melodramatic force. Gerald Weales described it as "a combination of *Pygmalion* and liberal platitudes," but admitted to an affection for the play and for the character of its heroine, "a variation on the standard dumb blonde, but one with individuality enough to get up and walk out of her play." Kanin received two Donaldson awards for *Born Yesterday*—as the author of the best first play of 1945–1946, and as its director—and the Sidney Howard Memorial (shared with Arthur Laurents). The play was later filmed and has taken its place in the modern repertory both in the United States and abroad.

None of Kanin's subsequent plays has been so successful, though they have shown spasmodically the tough-minded sense of humor and the Saroyanish affection for "little people" which distinguished *Born Yesterday*. Similar virtues have been found in Kanin's screenplays, which include such notable comedies as *Adam's Rib*, *The Marrying Kind*, and the screen version of *Born Yesterday*. Kanin has written a number of his films in collaboration with his wife Ruth Gordon, who is also well known as an actress.

Do Re Mi, a Runyonesque story about four inadequately reformed gangsters, attracted little attention when Kanin first published it as a novella and was scarcely more successful as the basis for Jule Styne's musical. Kanin's first full-length novel, *Blow Up a Storm*, had more impact. An account of race problems in the jazz world, it clearly drew on Kanin's own experiences as a saxophonist in the 1930s. Some reviewers found it nostalgic to the point of sentimentality, or uncomfortably "slick," but there was much praise for the novel's authenticity, and Edward Weeks called its "exposition of the creativity of jazz . . . the most brilliant I have read anywhere."

Kanin was a disciple and for twenty-five years a friend of Somerset Maugham. In 1966 he published *Remembering Mr. Maugham*, a record of their friendship which was enjoyed by most readers as a "haphazard and entertaining nonbook of quotes and anecdotes." One reviewer suggested that it was Kanin himself—"warm, brash, over-admiring, terribly sensitive about American callowness"—who "emerges as the more sympathetic, and perhaps even more interesting, figure." Kanin has written for television, a medium whose intimacy he likes, and also for opera. In 1950 he revised the libretto of *Die Fledermaus* and directed it in a spectacularly successful production by the Metropolitan Opera Company. His short stories have appeared in the *Atlantic*, the *Saturday Evening Post*, *Cosmopolitan*, *Esquire*, and *Playboy*, among other magazines.

GARSON KANIN

Garson Kanin is the son of David and Sadie (Levine) Kanin. He is a sharp-faced, balding man with a wide and humorous mouth, a little below average height. He is, as he says, rich and successful enough to "do now the things, and only the things, which I feel strongly about."

PRINCIPAL WORKS: *Plays*—Born Yesterday, 1946; The Smile of the World, 1949; The Rat Race, 1950; The Live Wire, 1951; A Gift of Time (adapted from Death of a Man, by Lael Tucker Wertenbaker), 1962. *Fiction*—Do Re Mi, 1955; Blow Up a Storm, 1959; A Thousand Summers, 1973. *Memoirs*—Remembering Mr. Maugham 1966; Tracy and Hepburn: An Intimate Memoir, 1971.
ABOUT: Celebrity Register, 1963; Current Biography, 1952; Weales, G. American Drama Since World War II, 1962; Who's Who in America, 1970–1971. *Periodicals*—Atlantic September 1959; Hudson Review Winter 1962–1963; New York World Telegram February 5, 1946; Saturday Review January 14, 1956; Theatre Arts December 1946.

***KÄSTNER, ERICH** (February 23, 1899–), German novelist, poet, satirist, and journalist, was born in Dresden, Saxony, the only child of Emil and Ida (Augustin) Kästner. Hard times downgraded his father, a harness maker and a fine craftsman, to a luggage factory, and the family was kept afloat by the enterprise and ingenuity of his mother, who took in boarders and worked for her neighbors as a seamstress and a hairdresser. A warm

* kest′ nər

ERICH KÄSTNER

friend to her son and a lasting influence, she never recovered from the bombing of Dresden in 1945, and died in 1951. This remarkable woman survives as the mother of Emil and Anton in Kästner's children's books, and in his warmly humorous reminiscences of childhood *Als ich ein kleiner Junge war* (1957, translated as *When I Was a Boy*).

An able and willing student, Kästner was generally head of his class at the Dresden teacher training college he attended from 1913 to 1917. Nevertheless he hated the ardent militarism of the place, which changed him from a model boy to a rebellious one. His encounter with the even harsher discipline of the Imperial Army, into which he was drafted in the summer of 1917, left him with a permanent heart ailment and strongly antimilitaristic views. After the war Kästner taught and studied for a time at the König-Georg-Gymnasium in Dresden, a happy and liberal institution where he wrote his first poems, edited the school magazine, and discovered his love for the theatre. In 1919 he entered the University of Leipzig, studying German and French literature, history, and philosophy. As an undergraduate Kästner spent his leisure time at the theatre, or writing in the Leipzig cafés, most often at the Café Merkur, where the city's intellectuals met. He lived so frugally that at the end of his first term he was able to return to his mother exactly half the money she had given him for living expenses.

During the early 1920s Kästner did some graduate work at the universities of Rostock and Berlin, and he continued his studies while working in Leipzig as, variously, a bookkeeper, publicist, drama critic, and journalist. Kästner's doctoral thesis, on Frederick the Great's *De la littérature allemande*, is evidence of his academic brilliance. One of his examiners remarked that it would be a good thing if all the professors of German among them could produce an equally able work once in five years. Kästner received his doctorate in 1925 and celebrated by taking his mother on a holiday to Italy and Switzerland, his first trip abroad.

Kästner settled in Leipzig and quickly made his name as a contributor to various liberal journals, and as drama critic and associate feuilleton editor of the *Neue Leipziger Zeitung*. That newspaper was obliged to dismiss him in 1927, when he outraged public opinion by publishing an indelicate satirical poem about Beethoven during the composer's centenary year. Kästner moved to Berlin, where he earned his living as a freelance drama critic for the *Neue Leipziger Zeitung*, the *Prager Tageblatt*, and other newspapers. He was welcomed by such liberal writers as Carl von Ossietzky, Kurt Tucholsky, Rudolf Arnheim, and Arnold Zweig, and began his literary career in earnest.

A first volume of poems, *Herz auf Taille*, appeared in 1928, and the same year Kästner published *Emil und die Detektive*, the children's book that made him famous all over the world. It is about a boy who, robbed on his first visit to the big city, enlists the aid of a gang of city children to capture the thief. A highly moral story, unobtrusively didactic, it was everywhere recognized as a landmark in the history of children's literature, a funny and exciting story about ordinary children in a contemporary city setting, told in a direct conversational style. Innumerable foreigners have learned German with Emil's adventures as their text, and the book has been translated into nearly thirty languages. It appeared in English as *Emil and the Detectives* in 1930, when one American reviewer wrote: "Not for a long time have we met in a book children so real, real as salt and bread." The story has been adapted for the stage, radio, and television, and filmed in German, Spanish, and English. Walter Trier's illustrations for this and Kästner's subsequent books are almost as well known and well liked as the stories themselves.

Three more volumes of verse followed in the late 1920s and early 1930s—brief, astringent poems which, as a critic has said, "skilfully shape conversational idiom to a fine point of wit and pathos." Kästner calls his verse "*Gebrauchslyrik*"—lyric poetry with a social purpose. At that time, as the Nazi party moved towards power, Kästner's purpose was "to sound the warning by use of criticism, accusation, ridicule, and laughter." His semiautobiographical novel *Fabian* (1931) was a more direct expression of his anguish at what was happening to Germany, "a poignant, almost an unbearable lament for a murdered beauty." It has been said that Kästner's work at this time, his children's books as much as his sardonic verse, "achieved a remarkable balance of genuine goodness and the most caustic kind of criticism"—a sense of desperation "held in check by a kind of cosmic sense of proportion."

When Hitler came to power in 1933, Kästner chose "inner emigration," and said: "A writer will and must experience how the nation to which he belongs bears its fate during troubled times." The Nazis regarded him as undesirable and politically unreliable. Kästner saw his books burned publicly, and during the next twelve years his friends were murdered, he himself lived under surveillance, and he was twice arrested by the Gestapo. At first he was allowed to publish his books abroad, mostly in Switzerland: children's books, including another story about Emil, poetry, and fiction. His novels, characterized by his verbal humor and a rather sentimental charm, were immensely popular. They included *Drei Männer im Schnee* (1934, translated as *Three Men in the Snow*), *Georg und die Zwischenfälle* (1938, translated as *A Salzburg Comedy*), and an entertaining mystery story *Die verschwundene Miniatur* (1935, translated as *The Missing Miniature*).

After 1942 Kästner was forbidden to publish altogether, and by the end of the war he was penniless. He settled in Munich and gradually began to find work—as feuilleton editor of the Munich *Neue Zeitung*, then as editor of a new children's magazine, *Pinguin*. He was one of the founders of the literary cabaret Schaubude, and of its successor Die Kleine Freiheit, named after one of his songs. Kästner's sharply funny satire about man's inability to secure peace, *Die Konferenz der Tiere*, appeared in 1949 and was translated as *The Animals' Conference*. A notable children's book, *Das doppelte Lottchen*, also published in 1949, has been filmed in three countries and translated as *Lisa and Lottie*. The play *Schule der Diktatoren*, a tragicomedy about totalitarianism on which Kästner had worked for many years, was published in 1956. Several volumes of poems, songs, and epigrams have also appeared since the war. Many of his admirers feel that Kästner has never fully recovered from the sufferings and enforced silence of the Nazi years, and that his postwar work, by and large, reflects this.

Among the many literary prizes he has received in recent years, the most important are the Büchner Prize (1957) and the Hans Christian Andersen Medal (1960). He belongs to several German literary academies, has served as president of the German P.E.N. center and vice president of the International P.E.N. Club. Kästner, a bachelor, is a small man with bushy eyebrows and a quizzical cast of countenance: "He looks like his books," Thornton Wilder said. He lives in Munich with a family of cats, and still does most of his writing in cafés. Kästner is a liberal democrat and a Protestant, but has made it clear that he has little enthusiasm for programs and ideologies, and puts more faith in the good sense of children than in their elders.

PRINCIPAL WORKS IN ENGLISH TRANSLATION: Fabian: The Story of a Moralist, 1932; Three Men in the Snow, 1935; The Missing Miniature, 1937; A Salzburg Comedy, 1950; The Animal's Conference, 1953; When I Was a Boy (autobiography), 1961 (England, When I Was a Little Boy); Let's Face It (poems), 1963. *For children*—Emil and the Detectives, 1930; Annaluise and Anton, 1932; The Flying Classroom, 1934; The 35th May, 1934; Emil and the Three Twins, 1935; Lisa and Lottie, 1951 (England, Lottie and Lisa); The Little Man, 1966; Pünktchen and Anton, 1967; The Little Man and the Little Miss, 1969. *Poems in* Hamburger, M. (ed.) Modern German Poetry, 1962; Kaufmann, W. (ed.) Twenty German Poets, 1962.

ABOUT: Bossmann, R. Erich Kästner: Werk und Sprache, 1955; Current Biography, 1964; Enderle, L. Erich Kästner in Selbtzeugnissen und Bilddokumenten, 1966; International Who's Who, 1973–74; Kästner, E. Notabene 45, 1961; Kästner, E. When I Was a Boy, 1961; Penguin Companion to Literature 2, 1969; Who's Who, 1973; Winkelman, J. The Poetic Style of Erich Kästner, 1957; Winkelman, J. Social Criticism in the Early Works of Erich Kästner, 1953. *Periodicals*—Hudson Review Winter 1957–1958; South Atlantic Quarterly April 1951; Times Literary Supplement June 19, 1959; December 1, 1966.

KAUFFMANN, STANLEY (JULES) (April 24, 1916–), American novelist, dramatist, and critic, writes: "I was born in New York City, the son of a dentist and of a mother whose father had kept a dry-goods shop on the ground floor of a small house in Bleecker Street. I went to the public schools, and two social notes about them are perhaps interesting: my last grammar school was in midtown Manhattan and, as late as 1927, I used to pass a blacksmith shop on my way to school. Second, my companions were mostly immigrants or the children of immigrants; I was extraordinary because two of my grandparents had been born in America, and I was referred to jokingly as 'the Yankee.'

"I was too quickly 'skipped' in elementary school and reached high school at eleven. There I deluded myself that I was preparing for medicine (and thereby made the first major mistake of my life—studying Latin instead of French). Other impulses prevailed in time, mostly as a result of amateur theatricals, and I went to New York University's Department of Dramatic Art at fifteen, intending to be an actor. I had already published poems and stories, and soon turned to writing plays, at which I was too quickly and superficially skilful. I wrote and published dozens of regrettable one-act plays in my college days to help pay my way through. I was also invited, early in my theatrical training days, to be a member of the Washington Square Players—not the first

STANLEY KAUFFMANN

group of that name which subsequently became the Theater Guild. This second group, directed by the head of New York University's dramatic faculty, was intended to be a permanent acting company. It was not a college company; it included undergraduates, graduates and others. All (like myself, after graduation) supported ourselves at other jobs—in the manner of the early Abbey Theatre—so that we could do the plays we wanted as we chose. The repertoire was largely Shakespeare and Shaw; but it came to include a long play of mine and a children's play, *Bobino*, which was subsequently published and produced elsewhere. We played at the university's theatres and a summer theatre we built in Cooperstown, New York. I stayed with this company for ten years, as actor, stage-manager, and prospective playwright. Its breakup, because of internal personality conflicts and the advent of the Second World War, represented a considerable loss of investment of time and hopes.

"Temporarily disaffected from the theatre, I began to write novels and took various jobs to support myself while doing so. These latter included editorial work on popular magazines and the writing and directing of radio plays. My first novel appeared in 1941; my last (in Britain only) in 1960. In 1949 I entered book-publishing as an associate editor of Bantam Books, a paperbound reprint house where I was happily allowed to specialize in the numerous good books on the list. In 1952 I became editor-in-chief of Ballantine Books, which was founded to publish books of merit in simultaneous paperbound and hardcover editions and which for a time was an enterprise of great interest to me. In 1956 I resigned to live in Europe for something more than a year. My last book-publishing job was from 1959 to 1960 at Alfred A. Knopf Inc., an experience of decidedly mixed memories.

"All through these years I had been publishing short stories and occasional book reviews as well as novels. In early 1958, through a series of coincidences, I became the film critic of the *New Republic*, an engagement that immediately made me feel as if I had been a fish flopping on land and had just fallen into the water. My eight years as their regular critic of films and occasional critic of books were the most congenial in terms of my sense of development and my reception that I had known as a writer. My work for the *New Republic* led to critical writing for numerous other journals, such as *Commentary*, the *New York Review*, the New York *Times Book Review*, *Book Week*, the *New Leader*, and to numerous lectures at colleges and universities. I contributed the twenty-thousand-word essay on literature to *The Great Ideas Today* (1964). In 1963 I was invited by WNDT, the New York educational television station, to conduct a weekly program called *The Art of Film*, consisting of illustrated talks by me and interviews by me of distinguished film workers; I also became that station's drama critic. *The Art of Film* won an award from the local chapter of the National Television Academy in 1964, in which year I was also made an Honorary Fellow of Morse College of Yale University and was given a Ford Foundation fellowship for three months' film study abroad.

"On January 1st, 1966, I became the drama critic of the New York *Times*.

"I am married to Laura Clandon (Cohen), who was a member of the Washington Square Players. We live in New York.

"I have listed below the only books of mine—so far—to which I would refer interested parties."

———

Stanley Kauffmann's first play, *The Red Handkerchief Man*, was accepted when he was seventeen; as he says, he subsequently wrote about forty potboilers, most of them one-acters, with titles like *Father Spills the Beans* (1936), *A Word from the Wise* (1937), and *Right Under Her Nose* (1938). The only one of his plays that he cares to remember is *Bobino*, a piece for children that was produced in 1944 at the Adelphi in New York.

The seven novels Kauffmann wrote between 1941 and 1960 are all in one way or another novels of ideas. *The King of Proxy Street* (1941) examines the conflicting doctrines of predestination and free will, and this theme—of the individual's freedom to choose, however painfully, a life of moral integrity and wholeness—is taken up in most of the books that followed. *The Hidden Hero* (1949) is about a woman's struggle to face up to the tragic consequences of her own act of moral cowardice. In *A Change of Climate* (1954) a young college professor goes into the business world, where he is forced to reexamine his philosophy, and *Man of the World* (1956) studies another complex moral dilemma and its successful resolution.

Kauffmann's first novels were respected for their sincerity and for his "lucid, graceful and precise" prose, but his characters were found flat and unconvincing, mere spokesmen for his own deeply felt concerns. Subsequent books, however, showed growing psychological insight and narrative skill and *Man of the World*, for example, was warmly praised as an engrossing story about "real characters whose destinies stir our concern."

As a drama critic, Kauffmann has deplored the "sterility" of the contemporary American theatre, but maintains that "every critic has an obligation to hope." As the New York *Times*' resident critic he was more receptive to avant-garde plays and intellectually more demanding than his predecessors. His tenure on the *Times* lasted only from January to September 1966 when, after being replaced by Walter Kerr, he returned to the *New Republic*. The *Times* said in effect that it was not dissatisfied with Kauffmann's work, but could not pass up the opportunity to hire Kerr, the best-known drama critic in America, whose services were then on the market because of the demise of the New York *Herald Tribune*.

The first collection of Kauffmann's film reviews, *A World on Film*, confirmed his reputation as an original and thoughtful critic of that art. His approach is literary and intellectual rather than visual and technical—an approach which some readers find unsatisfactory in a movie critic but which others have welcomed. Lawrence Goldstein has said that "Kauffmann does not merely mediate between his readers and the work of art, he allows the play of his intelligence to respond to the force of that work. His language captures the thrust of a film and tests it against its own possibilities. He is neither blinded by technique nor alienated by innovation." A second volume of film reviews, *Figures of Light*, appeared in 1971.

PRINCIPAL WORKS: *Novels*—The Tightrope, 1952; A Change of Climate, 1954; Man of the World (England, The Very Man), 1956. *Criticism*—A World on Film, 1966; Figures of Light, 1971; (ed., with Bruce Henstell) American Film Criticism, 1972. *Play*—Bobino (for children), 1941.

ABOUT: Warfel, H. R. American Novelists of Today, 1951; Who's Who in America, 1972–1973. *Periodicals*—Best Sellers June 1966; Book Week June 12, 1966; Nation March 14, 1966; New American Review 1, 1967; New Republic December 1, 1958; February 23, 1963; New Statesman July 10, 1954; Newsweek December 20, 1965; February 28, 1966; September 12, 1966; New York Review of Books October 27, 1967; New York Times December 9, 1965; New York Times Book Review September 18, 1949; July 22, 1956; May 15, 1966; Saturday Review September 24, 1949; September 11, 1954; Time February 25, 1966.

KAVANAGH, PATRICK (JOSEPH GREGORY) (1905–November 30, 1967), the most celebrated of post-Yeatsian Irish poets, was born in the townland of Mucker, near Inniskeen in Monaghan—one of the poorest of the Irish counties, but for Kavanagh a place "where the spirit of the old poets haunted the poplars." The son of a bookish cobbler who also worked a small farm, and one of "roughly eleven" children, he had a happy childhood, little formal education, and was early "addicted to versing."

His first poems were sent to newspapers while he still worked on the farm, and at length one was accepted by "AE" (George Russell) for the *Irish Statesman*. His first book, *Ploughman*, appeared in 1936, containing sentimental poems which nevertheless showed traces of a lyrical gift. (He later attributed the "armchair rurality" of this collection to the pernicious influence of the then moribund Irish literary renaissance.)

That Kavanagh had retained a real feeling for his native countryside was evident in *The Green Fool*, a nostalgic volume of autobiography written during a stay in London in 1938, then withdrawn to avoid a libel action. The book is marred by Kavanagh's irritatingly self-conscious poetic prose and Irish whimsy, but it is vigorous, colorful, and funny, and at its best shows genuine insight into the life of the Irish peasantry.

Returning from London, Kavanagh settled in Dublin, where he thereafter made his living as a journalist and broadcaster. *The Great Hunger*, his only large-scale poem, appeared in 1942. It is a modern morality about the "man who made a field his bride"—the Irish peasant whose hunger for love and sexual gratification is sacrificed to his hunger for the land. This poem, reprinted in *A Soul for Sale* (1947), in the *Collected Poems*, and elsewhere, has earned comparison with Goldsmith's *The Deserted Village*. Imperfect as it is in its structure, it has (as one critic said) none of the sentimentality which so often spoils Kavanagh's work "but a complete integrity of imagery, and a devastating integrity of vision."

Tarry Flynn, a strongly autobiographical novel, has some of the usual Kavanagh faults, in particular an excess of naïve and pompous philosophizing, but is redeemed by passages of great lyrical beauty and wry humor, and is the best of Kavanagh's prose works. It has been dramatized and successfully staged at the Abbey Theatre in Dublin. *Collected Pruse* is an expensive volume of reprinted articles and other scraps, including some embarrassingly weak aphorisms.

At one time or another Kavanagh contributed to

PATRICK KAVANAGH

Irish newspapers and magazines as a gossip columnist, reviewer of films, television, and books, sports writer, agricultural writer, and general columnist. His critical articles, poems, and short stories also appeared in English and American periodicals. In 1952 he launched his own lively and scurrilous paper, *Kavanagh's Weekly*, which, however, expired after thirteen issues. Kavanagh described Shaw as a journalist, and Whitman as "a writer who tried to bully his way to prophecy," and much of his literary criticism was at this superficial and malicious level. He was often involved in literary and journalistic quarrels, notably his famous (and unsuccessful) libel action in 1954 against the Irish weekly *The Leader*.

In 1955 Kavanagh was found to be suffering from lung cancer, and he underwent a successful operation for the removal of a lung. During his convalescence, walking beside Dublin's Grand Canal, he experienced what he called a "poetic hegira" in the light of which he rejected most of his earlier work and set out to write poetry which would be "the real thing." He succeeded in perhaps a score of the poems he wrote during his last decade, and included in *Come Dance With Kitty Stobling* and the *Collected Poems*. In these poems he managed to balance, with a unique irony couched in appropriate language, his regret at his sexual deprivation and loneliness and his compensating delight in his emotional independence: "Me I will throw away. / Me sufficient for the day / The sticky self that clings / Adhesions on the wings / To love and adventure, / To go on the grand tour / A man must be free / From self-necessity." Kavanagh also wrote a few exceedingly attractive, very simple, lyrical poems, in particular the two about his father and his mother. These, and *The Great Hunger*, are the essential parts of his small but real achievement. Louise Bogan said that his was an "astonishing talent" that "kept on renewing itself not so much by a process of orderly growth as by a continuing breaching of boundaries"; most critics thought him the most original and the best Irish poet of his day.

Kavanagh was an extramural lecturer at University College, Dublin, in 1957 and in 1965–1966 he toured the United States, lecturing and reading his poetry. He was always more likable in person than on paper—gentler, more generous, wittier and wiser—and in the later part of his life he became a Dublin institution. He was a big man, with a bespectacled equine head. He hated publicity, or pretended to, and was contemptuous of the literary life, spending most of his days earning free drinks at McDaid's or some other Dublin pub, entertaining the regulars with his "superb vocabulary of scatological abuse." As one acquaintance wrote in the *New Yorker*, Kavanagh "was a great hater of cant [and] he never lacked for targets—local, national, or over the sea. Nor did he fear to lacerate himself for however and whenever he had played the fool with his talent." He believed totally and even desperately in poetry "as a mystical thing, and a dangerous thing." He was married at last, less than a year before his death, to Katherine Moloney, a niece of the boy patriot Kevin Barry.

Robin Skelton says that Kavanagh was "his own man, a strange and wonderful phenomenon in a world sick with togetherness." Kavanagh himself wrote: "If ever you go to Dublin town / In a hundred years or so / Inquire for me in Baggot Street / And what I was like to know, / O he was a queer one, / Fol dol the di do, / He was a queer one / I tell you."

PRINCIPAL WORKS: *Poetry*—Ploughman and Other Poems, 1936; The Great Hunger, 1942; A Soul for Sale, 1947; Come Dance With Kitty Stobling, 1960; Collected Poems, 1964. *Fiction*—Tarry Flynn, 1948. *Autobiography*—The Green Fool, 1938; Self-Portrait, 1962. *Miscellaneous*—Collected Prose, 1967; November Haggard: Uncollected Prose and Verse; ed. by Peter Kavanagh, 1971.
ABOUT: Kavanagh, P. The Green Fool, 1938; Kavanagh, P. Self-Portrait, 1962; Who's Who, 1967. *Periodicals*—Guardian July 29, 1960; London Magazine February 1963; New York Times December 1, 1967; New Yorker April 10, 1955; May 4, 1968; Poetry June 1965; Publishers' Weekly December 25, 1967; Review of English Literature July 1964; Spectator July 31, 1964; Times (London) December 8, 1967; Times Literary Supplement August 12, 1960; July 9, 1964; August 27, 1964.

KAWABATA, YASUNARI (June 11, 1899–April 16, 1972), Nobel Prize-winning Japanese novelist and short story writer. The following note is based partly on printed sources, partly on a short biography provided, with Kawabata's approval, by his secretary, Miss Chika Minamimoto: He was born in Osaka, the son of a physician who died when he was two years old. His mother died the next year, followed soon after by his sister, and his maternal grandmother with whom he had been sent to live. For nine years he lived with his grandfather, whose death when he was sixteen left him entirely alone in the world. Thus he developed very early an awareness of the fragility and isolation of man's existence.

Though he had at first thought of himself as a painter, Kawabata became interested in literature around the age of twelve, when he immersed himself in Buddhist writings, and the Heian classics of the ninth to twelfth centuries. He wrote years later, "I value the Buddhist scriptures in particular, not so much as religious teachings, but as literary visions, fantasies."

When only sixteen he wrote *Jurokusai no Nikki* (Diary of a Sixteen-Year-Old, 1925), an account of the protracted and painful death of his grandfather, the old man's querulous demands and constant taunting of the boy, who is torn between irritation and compassion. It was, as Donald Keene says, an extraordinary story for a boy to have written.

From school in Osaka, Kawabata went to Tokyo First Higher School, then to Tokyo University, where he abandoned the English course to study Japanese literature. In 1921 the publication in a coterie magazine of his *Shokonsai Ikkei* (A Scene of the Memorial Service for the War Dead) caught the attention of the well-known dramatist and novelist Kan Kikuchi, who appointed him to the staff of his journal *Bungei Shunju*. He also met Riichi Yokomitsu, who, with Kawabata, was to prove one of the major Japanese novelists to emerge in the decade. They were among the founders of the literary magazine *Bungei Jidai*, organ of the avant-garde "neo-sensualism" or "neo-sensationism" movement, which rejected both the stark naturalism of the literary establishment and the proletarian literature of social protest which arose in the 1920s. The neo-sensualists experimented with cubism, dadaism, futurism, and surrealism, and Kawabata for a time was interested in stream-of-consciousness techniques. He soon reverted to a more traditional style, however, and Western influence on his subsequent work is very little apparent.

In 1926 appeared his first popular success, *Izu no Odoriko* (translated by Edward Seidensticker as "The Izu Dancer"). So much of his later work is prefigured in *Izu no Odoriko* that his reputation and popularity would almost stand by it alone. It is little more than a longish short story. A student wandering in the Izu Peninsula meets a simple family group of itinerant entertainers and is invited

YASUNARI KAWABATA

to travel in their company. Attracted by a young girl, a member of the troupe, he joins them, planning to buy the young woman's favors. Before he succeeds in making any sexual approach, he sees her bathing: "A naked female figure ran from the steamy deeps of the bathhouse and, calling something, poised, arms extended, on the very lip of the dressing place as if about to leap down to the river bank. She held no towel to shield her nakedness. It was the dancer. Gazing at that white young form and sapling legs, a cold spring seemed to well within me and, exhaling deeply, I laughed in pure joy. She was a child; who but a child would run naked into the sunlight from the sheer happiness of discovering us? I laughed on, a mist over my mind had lifted, the laughter was ceaseless. Because of the luxuriance of her hair, I had taken her for seventeen or eighteen. As she had been dressed as a young woman in the full flower of youth I had made an extraordinary mistake." Another writer might have used this revelation as a denouement. Kawabata uses it as the prelude to a delicate and unconsummated love affair.

Yukiguni (translated by Edward Seidensticker as *Snow Country*) was published in an unfinished version in 1937; it was not completed until ten years later, and it is characteristic of Kawabata to spend so long perfecting a single short novel. It is set in a mountain hot-spring resort, and explores a love affair between Shimamura, a wealthy and self-centered Tokyo dilettante, and Komako, a geisha of fading beauty. She loves; he cannot. This is implied rather than stated, through the couple's veiled and fragmentary conversations, and through the man's attraction to the clear fresh beauty of a girl he first sees reflected in the window of a train. Donald Keene has drawn attention to the brilliantly achieved scene in which Komako "staggers drunkenly into Shimamura's room murmuring almost incomprehensible phrases about a party she has left, gulps down some water, then staggers back to the party. . . . Kawabata manages to make us sense under the incoherent words the blazing intensity of Komako's feelings." C. J. Rolo called the English translation, *Snow Country*, "one of the finest short novels since the war."

During World War II Kawabata traveled in Manchuria, thus avoiding any direct involvement. But it was a painful time for him, and he declared in 1945 that henceforth he would write only elegies. He had devoted the war years to reading the Japanese classics, especially *The Tale of Genji*, in which he found "the traditional sadness of Japan" but also "consolation and salvation." The sadness of which he spoke is remote from "the Western kind of intense grief or anguish," which he said he had never experienced, but something far more delicate and controlled. It is perhaps also more profound, the product not of some naked emotional conflict but of a permanent awareness of the transience and loneliness of life.

This awareness pervades Kawabata's work. As one English critic has said, "his world is a world of loneliness and death, his assessment of the value of human relationships is cold to the point of cruelty, and his awareness of night and the void is always there behind the sensual surface of his writing." In *Sembazuru* (1949, translated by Seidensticker as *Thousand Cranes*), the brevity of human beauty and innocence is implied by contrast with the ancient rituals of the tea ceremony, which provide a background to the action of the novel. *Sembazuru* is about a young man's dealings with several worldly women and one, "the girl with the thousand-crane kerchief," who represents that ideal of youthful purity which so fascinated Kawabata. *Yama no Oto* (1954, translated by Seidensticker as *The Sound of the Mountain*), is an elegiac, unillusioned study of an aging man's recognition of his failing powers and the approach of death.

In his later novels, Kawabata seemed to share Tanizaki's interest in the erotic and grotesque, though he never dwelt obsessionally on these things as Tanizaki did. *Nemureru Bijo* (1961, translated by Seidensticker as "The House of the Sleeping Beauties") describes the experiences, recollections, and reflections of the aging Eguchi during the six nights he spends in a house of pleasure where drugged virgins are provided for the visual entertainment of old men. Donald Keene thought it "a triumph of Kawabata's virtuosity that he managed to make each of Eguchi's experiences entirely different, even though the six women do not utter a word or reveal anything about themselves but their nakedness." *Kyoto* (1962), centered upon the ancient imperial city, is an implicit attack upon the postwar Americanization of Japan. *Meijin* (translated by Seidensticker as *The Master of Go*) is a delicately fictionalized account of a 1938 Go championship match which Kawabata had reported for a Tokyo newspaper. The old Master is defeated and dies and this book, which is at times closer to a poem than a novel, is an elegy for him and for the old aristocratic traditions of Japan that he symbolizes.

Kawabata was admired above all for the delicacy, simplicity, and elegance of his prose style, and for his understanding of feminine psychology. His male characters are by comparison often mere sketches, serving as one critic says "like a ballerina's partner, mainly to enable her to dance." Edward Seidensticker, whose translations of Kawabata's work have been warmly praised, says that "his best writing is episodic and wanting in grand climaxes, a stringing together of tiny lyrical episodes. . . . The linking, the relation of episode to preceding and following episode, is more important than the over-all form."

In his *Bungakuteki Jijoden* (Literary Autobiography), Kawabata declared: "I was an orphan early in life and have depended too much on the kindness of others. Consequently, I have become a person who can never hate or grow angry at anyone. But, again, my daily existence is rendered peaceful by the naïve expectation . . . that anyone would grant me whatever I wish if I only ask for it. . . .

"I believe that the Eastern classics, particularly the sacred works of Buddhism, are the greatest literature in our world. . . . For the past fifteen years, I have thought of writing a work entitled *Toho no Uta* (Song of the East), which would be my swan song. I want to write a song of praise for the Eastern classics, in my particular fashion. I might possibly die before this is realized, but I want everyone to know that I had such a plan in mind."

Kawabata was president of the Japanese P.E.N. Club from 1948 to 1965, and became vice-president of International P.E.N. in 1959. During 1957, 1960, and 1964 he visited Europe and America under P.E.N. auspices. He was a member of the Japan Art Academy and held the Goethe Medal of the City of Frankfurt, the French Ordre des Arts et Lettres, and the Cultural Medal of the Japanese Government. He received most of Japan's major literary awards, including the Akutagawa prize. In 1968 he was awarded the Nobel Prize for Literature, the first Japanese ever to receive the award and the first Asian since Rabindranath Tagore.

A mild, frail, puckish-looking man, a connoisseur of Japanese works of art and particularly of the artifacts used in the tea ceremony, Kawabata lived in Kamakura—always very quietly until 1971, when he ventured into active politics to support the unsuccessful conservative candidate for the governorship of Tokyo. The following year, for no known reason, he committed suicide, gassing himself in his work room in the seaside town of Zushi. His health had been rather poor (though he had no serious illness) and he had been sleeping badly. He had been profoundly shaken by the spectacular ritual suicide in 1970 of his protégé Yukio Mishima, at whose funeral service he had presided. Kawabata was survived by his wife, Hideko, and a daughter.

PRINCIPAL WORKS IN ENGLISH TRANSLATION: Snow Country, 1957; Thousand Cranes, 1959; The Existence and Discovery of Beauty (essay), 1969; The Izu Dancer and Others (Tokyo), 1969; The House of the Sleeping Beauties and Other Stories, 1969; The Sound of the Mountain, 1970. *Stories in* Keene, D. Modern Japanese Literature, 1956; Morris, I. Modern Japanese Stories, 1961; Atlantic Monthly January 1955.

ABOUT: Current Biography, 1969; Grigson, G. (ed.) Concise Encyclopedia of Modern World Literature, 1963; International Who's Who, 1971–1972, Penguin Companion to Literature 4, 1969. *Periodicals*—Commonweal March 6, 1959; Guardian August 13, 1957; New York Herald Tribune Book Review March 8, 1919; New York Review of Books March 27, 1969; New York Times October 18, 1968; October 29, 1968; April 17, 1972; New York Times Book Review December 8, 1968; September 14, 1969; Saturday Review January 5, 1957; Times Literary Supplement June 5, 1959.

***KAZAKOV, YURY (PAVLOVICH)** (1927–), Russian short story writer, was born into a working-class family in Moscow. He studied the cello at Gnesin Music School in Moscow, graduating in 1951, and during the next two years played in symphony orchestras and jazz groups. His first stories began to appear at this time, and from 1953 to 1958 he studied literature at the Gorky Literary Institute in Moscow. Though he has spoken of writing a novel his work, apart from a couple of travel essays, has so far been restricted to short stories. He loves travel and hunting, and his journeys in Russia have often given him the settings for his stories: the forests and rivers of central Russia, with the old towns along them, and the shores of the White Sea in the far north, where he has spent periods living with the fishermen.

It was in the northern city of Archangel that his first book, *Manka*, a collection of eleven stories, was published in 1958. These early stories are typical of Kazakov's work in their concentration not on plot but on the inner world of personal relationships, and on the accumulation of small incidents which create a mood. The title story (translated as "Manka") beautifully evokes the miseries of adolescence. Set against a brooding northern landscape, it is about a shy orphan girl who falls in love with a young fisherman. As one critic wrote, the story fully displays Kazakov's "rare gift of entering into another person's life, penetrating it from within, grasping to the finest detail a character which has attracted his notice."

YURY KAZAKOV

Eight of these first stories and four new ones were published in Moscow the following year. The title piece, "Na polustanke" (translated variously as "At the Station" and "At the Railway Halt"), is a sad vignette about a country girl bidding farewell to her crass and spiteful boyfriend as he leaves for the city (from which he has no intention of returning to her). One of the best known of these early stories is "Arktur, gonchy pes" (translated as "Arcturus the Hunting Hound" and in a different version as "Arktur—Hunting Dog"). Arcturus is born blind and seems destined to be one of nature's victims, chased by bulls and kicked by herdsmen. Adopted out of pity by the local doctor, he becomes a famous and valuable hunting dog because his blindness is compensated for by the extraordinary keenness of his other senses. The central character in "Otshchepenets" (translated as "The Outsider" and also as "Oh, Forget It!") is the drunken, boastful Egor, who works (not very hard) as a buoy keeper on a large river. Yet, Kazakov shows, though he is a failure by any society's standards, Egor is not to be dismissed; like Arcturus, he has redeeming talents—in his case a yearning, almost religious, sense of natural beauty and a magnificent singing voice. The duets he sings with his girl beside the river are, it is implied, sufficient justification for his existence.

Egor is typical of many of Kazakov's characters,

* kaz ə kôf′

who are often solitary people separated by their work, and also by their values, from the rest of society. As George Gibian has pointed out, "Kazakov frequently creates characters engaged in emotional searches. They feel the mystery of nature, listening to voices apparently emanating from it; they look expectantly at the aurora borealis, or they live with their memories. . . . He is the creator of characters with a nostalgia for an intense, high, somehow mysterious, experience."

Thus in "Po doroge" (translated as "Along the Road"), which gave its title to Kazakov's third collection of stories (Moscow, 1961), a truck driver, made restless by the coming of spring, dreams of the mountains and raging rivers of Siberia, and sets off to go there, even though he has already been disillusioned by a previous visit. One of Kazakov's most perfectly realized stories is "Na okhote" (The Hunting Trip), in which a father takes his son duck shooting for the first time in the place where his own father had taken him years before, and with a mixture of delight and nostalgia watches the boy make the same discoveries that he had made.

"Goluboye i zelenoye" (1956, translated as "Light Blue and Green"), which in 1963 became the title story in Kazakov's fourth collection, is unusual in that it is set in Moscow. In it a young man recalls his brief love affair at the age of seventeen with a girl who soon marries someone else and passes out of his life, though she remains in his thoughts years afterwards. The opera house, cinemas, and subways of Moscow are only a background for these "unsolicited dreams" and the activities which help him to forget them.

Kazakov has never been a prolific writer, and in recent years he seems to have published very little. Such Soviet critics as Leonid Sobolev have predictably reproached Kazakov for "decadence," "pessimism," and "morbid interest in weak passive creatures." Konstantin Paustovsky, on the other hand, singled him out for special praise: "Kazakov's great literary gift and remarkable power of observation as a writer put him first among the younger Russian writers of today. His vision of people and of the world around him is clear, sharp, sometimes harsh, sometimes even ruthless. Yet he is not merciless." Many critics have pointed out that Kazakov's work illustrates the essential continuity of the Russian literary tradition, and Katherine Hunter Blair says, "It is impossible not to be reminded of Turgenev's earlier works when one reads Kazakov. He too writes in a lyrical, dignified prose, creates his characters with extraordinary delicacy, and leaves the reader with a deep, elusive sadness."

PRINCIPAL WORKS IN ENGLISH TRANSLATION: Going to Town and Other Stories, tr. by Gabriella Azrael, 1964; The Smell of Bread and Other Stories, tr. by M. Harari and A. Thomson, 1965; Arcturus the Hunting Hound and Other Stories, tr. by Anne Terry White, 1968. *Stories in* Bearne, C. G. (ed.) Modern Russian Short Stories 1, 1968; Blake, P. and Hayward, M. (eds.) Dissonant Voices in Soviet Literature, 1964; Blake, P. and Hayward, M. (eds.) Half-Way to the Moon, 1964; Field, A. (ed.) Pages from Tarusa, 1964; MacAndrew, A. R. Four Soviet Masterpieces, 1965; Whitney, T. P. The New Writing in Russia, 1964. *Periodicals*—Soviet Literature 4 1963, 4 1967, 6 1968.

ABOUT: Alexandrova, V. A History of Soviet Literature, 1963; Blair, K. H. A Review of Soviet Literature, 1966; Brown, E. J. Russian Literature Since the Revolution, 1963; Brown, E. J. (ed.) Major Soviet Writers, 1973; Gibian, G. *English introduction to* Selected Short Stories (in Russian), 1963; Hayward, M. and Crowley, E. L. (eds.) Soviet Literature in the Sixties, 1965; Hayward M. and Labedz, L. (eds.) Literature and Revolution in Soviet Russia, 1917–62, 1963; Slonim, M. Soviet Russian Literature, 1964; Whitney, T. P. The New Writing in Russia, 1964. *Periodicals*—New York Review of Books April 2, 1964; Slavic and East European Literature 8, 1965; Times Literary Supplement November 18, 1965.

KEELEY, EDMUND (LEROY) (February 5, 1928–), American novelist, critic, and translator, writes: "I was born in Damascus, Syria, of American parents. My father was a career diplomat in the United States Foreign Service, and I spent my childhood in various foreign posts (Beirut, Montreal, Salonika) before settling more or less permanently in the United States at the beginning of World War II, first in Washington, D.C., for junior and senior high school, then in Princeton, New Jersey, for college, and after a break for graduate study at Oxford, back to Princeton as a member of the faculty. My early years abroad (through the age of eleven) perhaps explain my ambivalent attitude towards the United States: I find myself ready to satirize many aspects of American life and thought, while remaining passionately interested in much that other writers might choose to satirize or dismiss (American football, American politics, the local movie theatre, juvenile delinquency). I have always felt something of an outsider in the United States, much as a prewar refugee must feel, and I continue to spend all my vacations and leaves of absence in Europe; at the same time, I cannot conceive of living very long without the intellectual stimulation and literary vitality that one finds in America as in no other country.

"Since the day in 1936 when my father landed the first trailer ever seen in Macedonia and hauled his family away over a pot-holed road for a vacation in the brigand-rich mountains west of Salonika, I have taken Greece for my native playground. My wife and I have spent each of the past fifteen summers in some part of Greece—Spetsos, Pelion, Euboea, Athens—and we now own a plot of land outside the town of Limni, Euboea, with the deepest Aegean channel below us and Parnassus in the distance. Until recently, most of my writing focused on, or derived from, my long association with Greece: a novel set in Macedonia, a novel set in Athens and Crete, and, in collaboration with Philip Sherrard and my Greek-born wife, Mary, an anthology of modern Greek poetry in translation, a translation of the *Collected Poems* of George Seferis, and a translation of the novellas of Vassilis Vassilikos. Twice I taught in Greece under the Fulbright Program, once at the American Farm School in Salonika and once at Salonika University. Lately I've been spending so much time in the Kolonaki district of Athens that I begin to see it as my village home, where the butcher, baker, pharmacist, and newspaper dealer know one by name and preference.

"But if my hedonism continues to find its largest fulfillment in Greece, my intellectual interests turn more and more to America. The central characters in my current novel are all Eastern intellectuals, and though they cross to Europe regularly in keeping with the times, their predicament is at heart strictly an American predicament. As a full-time teacher in the English Department at Princeton, most of my working and non-working hours for nine months of the year are taken up by discussion and study of American themes in literature, education, politics, civil rights, sex, and what have you—all of which I find immensely stimulating if time-consuming. I have visited and worked in all but a few of the States, including waiting on table in Mesa Verde, scrubbing a slaughterhouse in Los Angeles, controlling blister rust in Yosemite, picking hops in Oregon, instructing English at Brown University in Providence, and lecturing in the Writers Workshop at Iowa University. It is to the United States that I always turn for moral and financial support, and though my books haven't sold enough to pay for the small cabin cruiser I sometimes use to tour the Greek Islands, American foundations have been bountiful in their aid to me: two Fulbright grants, a Guggenheim Fellowship for creative writing in fiction, and a Prix de Rome from the American Academy of Arts and Letters for my first novel.

"I have no precise definition of what I want to be as a writer—except, perhaps, to be good and to be new, both lofty, treacherous ambitions. I believe in style, in verisimilitude, in tight structure—all of the ancient virtues—yet I also believe in experimentation, and the older I get the less satisfied I am with realism and its offspring. As a man constantly tempted by pleasure, I preach hard work; as a critic obsessed with craft, I preach against literary talk. I am happiest when I am writing well, and when I am, all else seems pallid. Though I myself read less than I used to, I still consider literature the most exciting business in the world."

EDMUND KEELEY

Edmund Keeley's first novel, *The Libation*, concerns a young American who returns after World War II to the scene of his childhood in Greece, and there makes a series of appalling discoveries about his parentage, and about his relationship with his boyhood sweetheart, with whom he is once more involved. This tale of incest, treachery, and madness takes its plot from the dark legendary history of the House of Atreus, and seemed to some readers the work of a born storyteller, though some found the use of flashback cumbersome. In general there was more praise for Keeley's narrative power, and his ability to evoke the mood and presence of Greece, than for his skill in characterization. *The Gold-Hatted Lover* is also set in Greece and is in a way *about* that ancient country and its influence on modern morals, centering on a young American diplomat's conflict between his conscience and his desire for his friend's wife. The novel was thought urbane and agreeably bawdy, but somewhat lacking in compassion. And there was a chilly reception for *The Imposter*, a "self-consciously intricate" highbrow thriller in which a CIA dropout pursues his identity in London and Greece.

The versions which Keeley and his wife prepared of three novellas by Vassilis Vassilikos were greatly admired. Kimon Friar said they were "beautifully translated . . . with a fine sense of nuance." There has been no less praise for the translations of Greek poets which Keeley has done in collaboration with Philip Sherrard, while their introduction to *Six Poets of Modern Greece* was variously described as "helpful," "admirably constructed," and "brilliant."

Keeley is now professor of English and the creative arts at Princeton and director of the creative writing and performing arts program. He enjoys teaching but considers writing a vocation "that has some of the joy of an avocation." The author is the son of James and Mathilde (Vossler) Keeley, and was married in 1951 to the former Mary Stathatos-Kyris. Keeley served in the United States Naval Reserve (1945–1946) and in the United States Air Force Reserve (1952–1956). He has lectured in England on the BBC and at Oxford University, which gave him his D.Phil. in 1952. He does much of his writing during the summer, while crossing on a "slow freighter" to some part of the Mediterranean, and he has listed travel and skin diving as his favorite recreations. He became president in 1969 of the Modern Greek Studies Association, and was co-editor of *Modern Greek Writers,* a collection of essays based mainly on papers delivered at the MGSA's first symposium, held at Princeton in 1969.

PRINCIPAL WORKS: *Novels*—The Libation, 1958; The Gold-Hatted Lover, 1961; The Imposter, 1970. *Translations*—(with Philip Sherrard) Six Poets of Modern Greece, 1960; (with Mary Keeley) Vassilikos, V. The Plant, the Well, The Angel, 1964; (with Philip Sherrard) Four Greek Poets, 1966; (with Philip Sherrard) Seferis, G. Collected Poems, 1924–1955, 1967; (with Philip Sherrard) Cavafy, C. P. Selected Poems, 1972; (with George Savidis) Cavafy, C. P. Passions and Ancient Days: Twenty-one New Poems, 1972. *As editor*—(with Peter Bien) Modern Greek Writers, 1972.

ABOUT: Contemporary Authors 1, 1963; Who's Who in America, 1972–1973. *Periodicals*—Library Journal February 1, 1958; May 1, 1961; Minnesota Quarterly Summer 1962; New York Herald Tribune August 3, 1958; New York Times Book Review April 13, 1958; Saturday Review May 24, 1958; Times Literary Supplement September 20, 1960.

***KEES, WELDON** (February 24, 1914–July 18, 1955?), American poet, was born at Beatrice, Nebraska, the son of John A. Kees. He was educated at the University of Nebraska, graduating in 1935. By then Kees had already published short stories in midwestern literary magazines. His first job was an editorial one with the Federal Writers' Project in Lincoln, Nebraska. Kees turned more or less conclusively from fiction to verse in 1937, when his first published poem appeared in *Signatures.* The same year he moved to Denver, where he became director of the Bibliographical Research Center for the Rocky Mountain Region. By 1943 he was in New York City, writing for *Time* magazine and working on documentary films. Kees also began to paint at about this time, in a manner which aligned him with the abstract ex-

WELDON KEES

pressionists. His work was shown at least once with paintings by such artists as Hans Hofmann and de Kooning, and he had several one-man shows at the Peridot Gallery.

In 1951 Kees moved to San Francisco, where his restless creativity found fresh outlets. He became a jazz pianist and composer, and wrote the score for an experimental movie called *The Adventures of Johnny.* He himself made several films, and he emerged also as a still photographer of exceptional ability. Hundreds of remarkable photographs by Kees illustrate *Non-Verbal Communication,* in which he and the psychiatrist Jurgen Ruesch studied the ways in which people "speak" to each other visually, for example through gestures and facial expressions.

None of these experiments brought him peace or satisfaction. He spoke to friends of suicide, and also of going away to start a new life, perhaps in Mexico. On July 18, 1955, his car was found abandoned on the approach to the Golden Gate Bridge, and after that he was never seen again. His last act of communication was thus a "non-verbal" one, symbolic, ambiguous, and ineluctable.

His first collection of poems was the pamphlet *The Last Man.* It attracted some attention as an unusually successful work in the current idiom, oblique in its references, crabbed in its diction, sharp in its satire. *The Fall of the Magicians* included some studies in the macabre and several technical exercises, among them a sestina and five villanelles, though Kees preferred to work in blank verse, usually arranged in short paragraphs. Milton Crane said that he wrote within this form "easily and fluently and with nice variety of rhythm and

* kēz

sound." There was praise for Kees's expert use of contemporary detail, "the calculated understatement, the illuminating commonplace." And there was recognition also that his harshly ironical tone was more than fashionable attitudinizing—that Kees "believes chaos is upon us" and "writes calmly in that acceptance." Crane called the book "a chapter in the history of the disintegration of our world, written by an intelligent, witty and detached mind." *Poems, 1947–1954* contained, Kenneth Rexroth thought, "just the right amount of 'irony and pity'—pathos, terror and bathos." Many of these poems feature as their alienated Everyman a Madison Avenue "communicator" named Robinson, a Crusoe shipwrecked in the shoddy chaos of modern America. Kees, who was "only distinguishable from his hero by his pity," shared Robinson's horror of this world and at last took his own way out of it.

Donald Justice's edition of *The Collected Poems of Weldon Kees* appeared in a deluxe volume in 1960 and was reprinted in 1962 in a cheap popular edition. In his preface, Justice suggests that none of Kees's poems is flawless, but speaks of "a cumulative power to the work as a whole to which even the weaker poems contribute" and which places Kees "among the three or four best [poets] of his generation." Although Kees's work includes a variety of technical experiments, his ear, Justice says, was guided by the "law of naturalness"; he preferred "natural words in a natural order" and "belongs to what might be called the Prose Tradition in poetry." Howard Nemerov speaks of the air of gaiety which survives, even in some of Kees's darkest poems, as "a courageous assault on the deep melancholy of self-doubt." His world, Nemerov goes on, is "a place where one lonely human mind, witty in its worst despair, strives to assert necessary connections among a million pieces of random information, seeking its own image in one sliver after another of the world's shattered mirror." Rexroth says that Kees left an excellent unpublished play called "The Waiting Room" which, "like his poems . . . was just a few years too early."

PRINCIPAL WORKS: The Last Man, 1943; The Fall of the Magicians, 1947; Poems, 1947–1954, 1954; The Collected Poems of Weldon Kees, 1960.

ABOUT: Justice, D. *preface to* The Collected Poems of Weldon Kees, 1960; Nemerov, H. Poetry and Fiction, 1963; Rexroth, K. Assays, 1961. *Periodicals*—Poetry June 1956.

"KELL, JOSEPH." *See* "BURGESS, ANTHONY"

KELLEY, WILLIAM MELVIN (November 1, 1937–), black American writer, writes: "I was born and raised in New York City, in a predom-

WILLIAM MELVIN KELLEY

inantly Italian-American neighborhood in the Bronx. My father, William M. Sr., was a civil servant, but during the 1920s and '30s he had been a newspaperman, at one time the editor of the *Amsterdam News*. He had come North from Chattanooga, Tennessee, in the early part of the century. My mother, Narcissa Garcia Kelley, was the great-grand-daughter of Colonel F. S. Bartow, who had the dubious distinction of being the first Confederate officer killed at the first battle of Bull Run—and the daughter of a cigar-maker from Ponce, Puerto Rico.

"My childhood was uneventful, or at least it seemed so at the time. Now I realize that I was growing up in one of the most racist countries on the face of the earth. I went to public school for two years, and then, for the next twelve, to the Fieldston School, a private school in New York, where I was a 'golden boy'—captain of the track team and president of the student council.

"From Fieldston School, I went on to Harvard College, planning to be a lawyer. But at the beginning of the spring term of my sophomore year, looking for a course without a final examination, I decided to take John Hawkes' class in prose fiction. (Hawkes is, to quote Leslie Fiedler, 'the least read novelist of substantial merit in the United States.') By the end of that term, I knew I was going to write forever. From John Hawkes' class I went on to other writing classes, most notably Archibald MacLeish's English 8.

"In February 1961, after having completed three and one-half years at Harvard, I was asked to take a one year 'leave of absence.' I had flunked everything but my writing class. I have not yet returned.

"My first novel, *A Different Drummer*, started while I was in MacLeish's class, was published in June 1962; a book of short stories, *Dancers on the Shore*, in March 1964; *A Drop of Patience* (a novel) in 1965.

"I am married to Karen Gibson of Chicago, a painter, and we have one child, a daughter, Jessica, born February 18, 1965."

Kelley was still at Harvard when in 1960 he received the Dana Reed Prize for "the best piece of writing published in an underground publication." In 1962 he was awarded fellowships to the New York Writers' Conference and the Breadloaf Conference, and in 1963 *A Different Drummer* earned him the Rosenthal Foundation Award of the National Institute of Arts and Letters. He was author in residence at the State University College, Geneseo, New York, in 1965.

In Kelley's first novel Tucker Caliban, an archetypal black sharecropper in a mythical Deep South state, listens to "a different drummer" and opts out of oppression. He salts his land, burns his house, kills his beasts, and, with his past destroyed behind him, goes north in search of a future. Seeing the rightness of this, every other black in the state pulls up his roots and joins the exodus. This bitter story, which seemed to F. H. Lyell an oversimplified and "highly improbable fantasy," impressed Archibald MacLeish as a powerful contemporary myth. And there was no disagreement about the extraordinary clarity and economy of Kelley's "low-keyed" prose style.

The short stories in *Dancers on the Shore* made no great impression, but Kelley's second novel divided the reviewers much as his first had done. *A Drop of Patience* tells the story of Ludlow Washington, who is both black and blind, and whose career—from poverty in the South to success as a musician in New York—encompasses a foreshortened history of jazz. Along the way Washington exchanges his black wife and baby for a destructive affair with a rich white girl. He is last seen seeking a truer music for himself in the storefront churches of his own people. Like Caliban in *A Different Drummer* he is a summary of the black experience of America. The novel contains scenes of great power: Washington's blank inherited fear when at the age of five he is committed by his father to a home for the blind; his breakdown at a New York concert, where he puts on blackface and tells obscene "nigger" jokes. A reviewer in *America* called the book "dull, awkward, ugly," but C. A. Hoyt, who found its conclusion unsatisfactory, said: "We must believe, however, that the great novel is coming; and it seems entirely possible that Mr. Kelley may write it."

In *dem*, the wife of a white advertising executive produces twins, one of them black, and her husband plunges into black New York, as into a different dimension, in search of the black child's father. It is not the great novel C. A. Hoyt looked for, but it is intermittently powerful in its corrosive satire and interesting in its surrealistic experiments, reminiscent of the work of John Hawkes.

Robert Bone found *dem* "alienated to the point of secession," and in 1967 indeed Kelley went to Europe. He settled in Paris, intending he said to learn French, and then to pursue his "exploration of blackness" in Africa, to which he is drawn not only by racial ties but by the existence of an oral tradition from which he hopes to learn. There is evidence of Kelley's interest in a black oral tradition in the first book he completed in Europe, *Dunfords Travels Everywheres*. The novel centers on Chig Dunford, a Harvard-educated black American tourist in Paris, and his alter ego Carlyle Bedlow, a Harlem street hustler. The book moves from naturalism into long hallucinatory scenes evoked through verbal play in the manner of *Finnegans Wake*, but derived from Harlem argot and also at times from Bantu, Pidgin English, and other black or creolized languages. It is, as one reviewer wrote, "an escape from the 'Langleash language,' a descent into a racial collectivity of blacks." Most readers found the novel absorbing, witty, and often effective, but thought the ingenious experimental idiom finally too thin and cryptic. It received the five-hundred-dollar prize for fiction of the Black Academy of Arts and Letters.

PRINCIPAL WORKS: *Novels*—A Different Drummer, 1962; A Drop of Patience, 1965; Dem, 1967; Dunfords Travels Everywheres, 1970. *Short stories*—Dancers on the Shore, 1964.

ABOUT: Vinson, J. (ed.) Contemporary Novelists, 1972; Who's Who in America, 1972–1973. *Periodicals*—Chicago Tribune Book World October 22, 1967; New York Times April 21, 1968; September 7, 1970.

"KELLOW, KATHLEEN." *See* HIBBERT, ELEANOR BURFORD

***"KEMAL, YASHAR" (pseudonym of Yasa Kemal Gökceli)** (1922–), Turkish novelist and journalist, writes: "I was born in the South Anatolian plain of Cilicia, now called the Chukurova, but my parents came from the shores of Lake Van on the eastern frontiers of Turkey, whence they had fled before the Russian advance in World War I. The story of their long trek on foot is still told among the members of my family in the form of an epic tale. My father belonged to a family of well-to-do feudal landlords, but my mother's family was renowned in all the east for its banditry. Hemite, the forty-house hamlet where I grew up, is on a hot and rocky ridge spearing out into the rich

* kə mal'

Chukurova cotton plain which stretches, vast and wonderfully flat, right up to the Mediterranean Sea.

"At the age of five, after witnessing the murder of my father, I was afflicted with a severe stutter that lasted for years and only left me when I sang. I remember very well the day when a strolling minstrel visited the village. He had a beautiful voice and played the traditional stringed 'saz.' The villagers, proud of me, though I could play no instrument, pitted me against him in a competition of improvised songs, which ended in a tie in the early hours of the morning.

"There was no school in my village. In fact, the only person who could read and write was the village Imam, and he had come from another province. But an hour's walk away was a village with a three-class school. I was nine when, without asking anyone, I decided to walk all the way over to the other village every day to attend this school. Later, I went to stay with relatives who lived in the small town of Kadirli, and there I completed primary school. Two more years at a secondary school, and that was the end of my formal education. I had to work. I took up all sorts of jobs, teaching, laboring in the cotton and rice fields, working in factories, but, having at an early age denounced the large landholding system and the misery of the people, I was branded as a Communist and hounded out of every job I took up.

"Eventually, I saved enough to buy a typewriter and set myself up as a public letter-writer. Soon after, in 1950, I was arrested for alleged Communist propaganda, but acquitted at the trial that took place a few months later. I resumed my public letter-writing, but the landowners, who had already attempted to get me killed in prison, made my life a constant nightmare by denouncing me to the police, who would search my house to tatters regularly twice a week for evidence of subversive activities. I decided to leave and, without telling anyone, I went to Istanbul, where with the help of friends I managed to obtain a job on the newspaper *Cumhuriyet*, one of the foremost Istanbul dailies, under the pseudonym of Yashar Kemal so that the police should not continue to persecute me in Istanbul as well. When they did find me out, I was already too well-known.

"Up to 1950 I had published several poems, short stories and folklore research in various magazines and had done a lot of reading in translation because I know only Turkish. Now, with my first series of reportages, I earned for myself a reputation in the newspaper world. At the same time, I published my first volume of short stories and in 1956 won the Varlik Prize for my first novel, *Ince Memed* (*Memed, My Hawk* in English), which has been translated into at least twelve languages. I have since written four other novels.

YASHAR KEMAL

I am married and my wife translates some of my books for my English publishers.

"Traditionally and temperamentally, I feel drawn to the art of Homer and Cervantes, to the light and poetry in life. My search is for the forces that bind us to life and the world we live in, and I believe this is to be found in the boundless energy and richness of the peoples of all nations, as distinct from the contemporary bourgeois class and its art which I consider a rotten bough in the tree of humanity."

Yashar Kemal, the best known of contemporary Turkish novelists, and one who has been mentioned as a possible candidate for the Nobel Prize, is a figure of considerable political as well as literary importance in Turkey. Early in his career he became a member of the Turkish Workers' party, which he hoped would continue the reforms instituted by Kemal Ataturk and destroy the autocratic powers of the rural landowners, the Aghas.

Ince Memed, the hero of his first novel, is a kind of Anatolian Robin Hood. He tries but fails to incite a rebellion against his village's tyrannical Agha, becomes a famous outlaw and, after the death of his beloved Hatche, kills the Agha and disappears into legend. In Turkey the book sold thirty-five thousand copies—an astounding accomplishment in a country with a low literacy rate and little familiarity with the novel form. It was translated by Edouard Roditi in 1961 as *Memed, My Hawk*. Frederic Prokosch wrote: "The style of the book is excessively simple; at times, it rises to an epic fervor or a lyrical delicacy, but much of the time it is rather wooden and artless. The characterization is clear but primitive, the psychology firm but shallow. . . . It is the sense of heroism, the animal tenderness, the marvelous feeling for the land, and the intuitive narrative rhythm that give the book its raw vitality and its pure immediacy." This reflects very well the mixed but generally enthusiastic reaction of most Western critics, though some of them took the book far more seriously as a political tract than Prokosch did. Indeed, its eventual translation into over thirty languages can be attributed at least in part to its passionate social indignation and revolutionary spirit, and it is said to have had a powerful political effect in Turkey.

At any rate, the success of *Ince Memed* brought fresh attacks upon Kemal from the landowners and other right-wing elements in Turkey, and he has been several times imprisoned since its appearance. He has nevertheless continued to plead the cause of the Turkish peasantry in many short stories, plays, and essays, and in several novels. One of the latter was translated into English by Kemal's wife Thilda as *The Wind from the Plain.* It is an account of the desperate efforts of an impoverished mountain family to reach the distant cotton fields in time for the harvest, reminiscent in theme if not in manner of Steinbeck's *The Grapes of Wrath.* By comparison with *Ince Memed* the book is a spare and sober social document, of relatively limited interest to Western readers. Part II of *Ince Memed* has been translated by Margaret E. Platon as *They Burn the Thistles.*

In 1966, when Kemal's political views brought him another period of imprisonment, the British Socialist Member of Parliament Lena Jeger pleaded for his release in the *Guardian.* He could, she pointed out, have found asylum in the West, but insisted that "I must stay with my roots." Certainly Kemal has never become westernized in the sense that his novels imitate European or American models. The principal influences on his work are still the Turkish folk epics and songs, and he has published a collection of these, translated by his wife, as *Anatolian Tales.* He visited Britain twice in the early 1960s to improve his English, and has read much European literature in translation, but he has never left Turkey for long, physically or spiritually.

Kemal lives with his wife and son in Istanbul. He is, according to the London *Times* correspondent, "a large man, with a bulky, humorous figure, a deep-bellied chuckle, and robust humanity." An injured eye makes him look a little like a bandit from one of his own novels, but he is, Lena Jeger says, an "immensely gentle" man. Although he writes of poverty and injustice, the tone of his books is fundamentally one of affirmation. "What good men there are in the world!" says one of his characters, speaking in the midst of violence.

PRINCIPAL WORKS IN ENGLISH TRANSLATION: Memed, My Hawk, 1961; The Wind from the Plain, 1963; Anatolian Tales, 1968; They Burn the Thistles, 1973.
ABOUT: International Who's Who, 1973–74; Twentieth-Century Writing, 1969. *Periodicals*—Guardian March 11, 1966; New York Times June 13, 1961; Saturday Review August 19, 1961; Time June 16, 1961; Times (London) July 30, 1959; Times Literary Supplement April 14, 1961.

KEMPTON, (JAMES) MURRAY (December 16, 1918–), American journalist and essayist, was born in Baltimore, Maryland, the son of James Branson and Sally (Ambler) Kempton. He attended Baltimore schools and the Johns Hopkins University, where he majored in government and history, and did a variety of summer jobs including a stint as a seaman. After graduating from Hopkins with a B.A. in 1939, he was for ten months a welfare investigator in Baltimore and then went to New York City. There he worked as an organizer for the International Ladies' Garment Workers Union and as publicity director for the American Labor Party. During this period he also wrote pamphlets for the Young People's Socialist League and the Workers' Defense League.

After serving briefly in 1942–1943 as a reporter for the New York *Post,* Kempton spent two years in the United States Army and saw combat duty in the Pacific. Upon his discharge, he worked for a year as a reporter with the Wilmington (North Carolina) *Star.* He returned to the New York *Post* in 1947, as assistant to the labor editor, Victor Riesel. From 1949, when he succeeded Riesel, until 1963, Kempton was a regular columnist with the *Post.* He soon became known for his brilliant and often controversial articles, dealing not only with labor but also with civil rights and civil liberties, as well as domestic politics and foreign affairs.

Awarded a Fulbright grant in 1958, he took a temporary leave in Italy and taught journalism at the University of Rome. In the spring of 1963 Kempton moved from New York to Washington, D.C., to join the editorial staff of the liberal news magazine *New Republic,* for which he wrote a weekly column. He returned to New York in the fall of 1964 as a columnist with the New York *World-Telegram and Sun.* When the *World-Telegram* ceased publication in the spring of 1966, Kempton resumed his old position at the New York *Post,* leaving it in 1969 to join the staff of the *New York Review of Books.* Since 1970 he has also been a commentator on CBS television.

Kempton's first book was called *Part of Our Time: Some Ruins and Monuments of the Thirties* (1955). It is a critical, though sympathetic, analysis of the American radical left of the 1930s, and an appraisal of some of the personalities of the "Red

Decade." The book covers such topics as the influence of the left in Hollywood and in the American labor movement. It discusses with "a blend of compassion and vitriol, sympathy and sarcasm," such diverse individuals as Alger Hiss, Whittaker Chambers, J. B. Matthews, Lee Pressman, Paul Robeson, Joe Curran, Elizabeth Bentley, Gardner Jackson, and Walter Reuther. In the view of a *New Yorker* critic, the book was "easily the best essay on American Communism and Communists."

America Comes of Middle Age collects one hundred and thirty-six of Kempton's New York *Post* articles, and forms a kind of survey of American social and political history between 1950 and 1962. Included are his moving dispatches on the civil rights struggle in the South, which he covered during visits to Alabama and Mississippi in the spring of 1961. In his treatment of foreign policy issues he is especially critical of the American position toward Cuba, which he likens to that of an "elephant confronted by a mouse." His colorful array of characters includes among others Nikita Khrushchev, Senator McCarthy, James Hoffa, and Billy Graham. It seemed to most reviewers an invaluable and wonderfully readable source book for future analysts of the 1950s in America. *The Briar Patch* (1973) is Kempton's account of the New York "Panther 21" trial of 1970–1972.

Although he has been a columnist for so long, Kempton has an old newsman's urge to cover an event himself before pontificating about it. *Newsweek* has called him "a master phrase-maker, with a sharp eye and a sharper pen," but another colleague says he is "a poet, and the worst political reporter in the country," while Nat Hentoff has referred to him as "a novelist *manqué*." The influence on his style of Thomas Wolfe has not always been fortunate, and his work has been found at times excessively wordy and shaky in its logic. However, according to one of his admirers in Congress, if Kempton's style is sometimes opaque, "the end effect is enormous. He's a breath of fresh air with political insights." It is Kempton's emotional involvement with his subjects which breathes life into his columns. Nat Hentoff said: "He is able to identify with an astonishing range of human subjects so that when he judges them in anger, irony or with rare but resilient hope, Kempton is persistently judging himself."

Murray Kempton is a tall, slender man with graying reddish-brown hair, a youthful appearance, and a scholarly manner, who wears glasses and smokes a pipe. From his first marriage, in 1942, to Mina Bluethenthal, which ended in divorce, he had a daughter, Sally Ambler, and three sons, James Murray, Arthur Herbert, and David Llewellyn; James Murray Kempton Jr. was killed in a traffic accident on November 26, 1971. Kempton and his second wife, the former Beverly Gary, have a son, Christopher. Kempton is a member of the American Civil Liberties Union, the Committee for Cultural Freedom, and the League for Industrial Democracy. He received the 1950 Sidney Hillman Foundation award for reporting. In February 1967 he was named winner of the George Polk Memorial Award for interpretive reporting that is "intellectually sensitive, morally responsive, and powerfully instructive." He was a delegate to the Democratic National Convention in 1968.

MURRAY KEMPTON

PRINCIPAL WORKS: Part of Our Time: Some Ruins and Monuments of the Thirties, 1955; America Comes of Middle Age: Columns 1950–1962, 1963; The Briar Patch, 1973.

ABOUT: Current Biography, 1973; Who's Who in America, 1972–1973. *Periodicals*—New York World-Telegram and Sun September 9, 1964; Newsweek June 17, 1963.

KENDRICK, BAYNARD (HARDWICK) (April 8, 1894–), American novelist, mystery writer, short story writer, biographer, and historian, writes: "I was born in Philadelphia, Pennsylvania. My father, John R. Kendrick, was a brilliant Georgian, who moved to Philadelphia from Atlanta in 1879, and founded the Trades Publishing Company. My mother was Juliana Lawton, the daughter of a wealthy, pre-Sherman, plantation owner in Allendale, South Carolina. I had two brothers and two sisters, all Georgia born. The younger of the girls was thirteen when I was born. The elder of the two boys was twenty-five. Through the Lawtons, Baynards, and Willinghams, my mother was related to everyone, white, south of the Mason and Dixon's line.

BAYNARD KENDRICK

"My father was only related to half, since his father was one of the seven sons of the Reverend Clark Kendrick, of Poultney, Vermont, a clutch of Baptist ministers and university founders (Rochester, Hamilton, and Vassar). My mother was a member of the D.A.R.'s, the U.D.C.'s and the Huguenots. My sisters made their debuts in Charleston at the St. Cecilia Ball. My father was a member of the Georgia Society and the Union League Club, of Philadelphia.

"The grandeur of this heritage was too much for one small 'damn-Yankee' boy. I could definitely sense a coldness between me and my family by the time I was five years old. I fled to the sympathetic arms of our two North of Ireland domestics, privileged characters due to their length of service. They taught me about 'banshees,' the 'wee-ones' and how to read tea leaves. They also took up cudgels in my defense when it was discovered that my three pet playmates were a Jewish, Irish Catholic, and Negro boy.

"I was precocious in reading, and found an additional sanctuary in my father's extensive library, where I played the field. I had been through everything from Grimm's, Hardy, Ingersoll, and Thomas Dixon, Jr., to Hawthorne, Dickens, Conan Doyle, and Shakespeare (more than five hundred books) before it was decided that I was a menace to organized society and the Old South. (I even had a crack at Kant, but didn't understand him, and still don't!)

"In 1904, at the mature age of ten, I was shipped off to boarding school at the Tome School, Port Deposit, Maryland, where I made editor of the school paper and captain of the debating team. I left Tome after eight years, when my mother died in 1912, and was graduated from the Episcopal Academy in Philadelphia. My father remarried. I went to Detroit to work in the automobile factories, and in two years finished up on a park bench as a bum. Canada declared war August 8, 1914. It looked like a good job with a buck a day, clothes and chow. I became the first American to enlist in World War I. After four and a half years' service overseas, I was discharged medically unfit on January 1st, 1919. My present wife and I were married in May of that year.

"Due to the fact that my closest friend (also an American) was blinded in the Canadian Army, and died, frustrated and broke, in the alcoholic ward of Bellevue Hospital in 1934, I created a fictional blind detective, Captain Duncan Maclain. In an attempt to keep Maclain's feats absolutely authentic through fifteen books, I had done so much research on the capabilities of the blind that I was asked by the United States Army to serve as Academic Consultant on rehabilitation of the blinded veterans in World War II. (One dollar a year.) Out of that experience came my book *Lights Out*, made into the movie *Bright Victory*. All of the proceeds went into the formation of the Blinded Veterans Association. I hold Honorary Life Membership Card #1 in the B.V.A.

"Another #1 Membership Card, of which I am very proud, is in the Mystery Writers of America, Inc. I was elected the first president after its organization in 1945. The slogan of the MWA is: 'Crime does not pay—enough!'

"In spite of more than a hundred short stories, none of them mysteries, four straight novels (one Literary Guild), one biography, one history, and two hundred historical columns, I am complimented that the critics detect a touch of 'mystery writer' in everything I have published. I prefer Poe to Proust, Conan Doyle to Stephen Crane, and the conscious care of any first-class mystery writer to the mad maunderings inflicted on the world by the 'way-out' school of writers today.

"Probably due to my training as an accountant, I have made a fetish of accuracy, although I am well aware that extensive research has slowed down my production. I have never been able to write anything, fictional or factual, unless I felt it would be helpful to some class of people, usually an oppressed minority. I am not, consciously, a crusader. Writing for me is arduous and I have needed the added impetus of some purpose to keep me at it day after day. My last book, just completed, is a fictionalized account of a Cuban doctor's attempt to rescue his wife from the hell of Castro's Communist Cuba."

When he returned from World War I, Kendrick

began a brief but extremely successful business career. He passed bar examinations (but never practiced), qualified as a certified public accountant, and held high executive positions in a variety of enterprises (including the Trades Publishing Company, his father's firm, of which Kendrick was president in 1928). The considerable fortune he amassed was destroyed in the 1929 stock market crash, and in 1932 he left a job as a hotel manager to become a full-time freelance writer.

Kendrick did his first writing for the pulp detective magazines. In 1934 he won a prize for his first novel, a "thrilling yarn" called *Blood on Lake Louisa.* His second book, *The Iron Spiders,* featured the lanky Florida sheriff Stan Rice, who appeared also in *Eleven of Diamonds* and *Death Behind the Go-Through.* But Kendrick's most original and memorable sleuth is the blind Captain Duncan Maclain, who was introduced in *The Last Express* (1937) and who has made an asset of his handicap in many subsequent stories. Kendrick is, as he says, a slow and careful writer who makes no arbitrary story outline but allows his often brilliantly original plots to develop logically from character.

The Duncan Maclain books attracted the attention of agencies concerned with the welfare of the blind because, it was said, Kendrick "was able to get across to the public, while entertaining it, ideas which workers for the blind have striven for years to instill." One result was Kendrick's work as an Army consultant and as an instructor of sightless veterans, which in turn inspired his first serious novel, *Lights Out.* It describes the rehabilitation of a blinded soldier, who learns how to live with his handicap and also, for the first time, how to live with his fellowmen. This probing and harrowing book was warmly praised for its "skill, accuracy, and deep feeling."

Several of Kendrick's novels have been filmed, and a number have been recorded as Talking Books, transcribed into Braille, and translated into many foreign languages. He was the first honorary chairman of the Blinded Veterans Association, and gave up writing for a year to get the organization firmly established. Kendrick, who is six feet three inches tall and heavily built, has in his time been an ardent hunter and fisherman, and a chess and bridge player of professional standing.

PRINCIPAL WORKS: Blood on Lake Louisa, 1934; Eleven of Diamonds, 1936; The Iron Spiders, 1936; The Last Express, 1937; The Whistling Hangman, 1937; Death Beyond the Go-Through, 1938; Odor of Violets, 1941 (England, Eyes in the Night); Blind Man's Bluff, 1943; Death Knell, 1945; Lights Out, 1945; Out of Control, 1945; Make Mine Maclain (contains The Silent Whistle, Melody in Death, The Murderer Who Wanted More), 1947; Flames of Time, 1948; The Tunnel, 1949; You Died Today, 1952; Blind Allies, 1954; (with Henry Trefflich) They Never Talk Back, 1954; Reservations for Death, 1957; Clear and Present Danger, 1958; Hot Red Money, 1959; Aluminum Turtle, 1960: Frankincense and Murder, 1961; The Spear Gun Murders, 1961; Florida Trails to Turnpikes, 1914–1964, 1964; Flight From a Firing Wall, 1966.

ABOUT: Contemporary Authors 4, 1963; Current Biography, 1964; Warfel, H. R. American Novelists of Today, 1951; Who's Who in America, 1972–1973.

KENNAN, GEORGE F(ROST) (February 16, 1904–), American diplomat, historian, and memoirist, was born in Milwaukee, Wisconsin, the son of Kossuth Kent Kennan and the former Florence James. The family was a prosperous and cultivated one, established in America since colonial times. George Kennan's uncle and namesake was an authority on czarist Russia and the author of a famous and influential history, *Siberia and the Exile System* (1891).

Kennan attended St. John's Military Academy in Delafield, Wisconsin, and then went east to Princeton University (to which he was attracted, he says, by Fitzgerald's account of it in *This Side of Paradise*). He remembers himself there as a youth of "false pride, self-pity and thirst for martyrdom." Kennan majored in history, receiving his B.A. in 1925.

In September 1926 he entered the United States Foreign Service, and during the next two years served in a series of vice-consular positions at Geneva, Hamburg, Berlin, and Tallinn, in Estonia. In 1929, as third secretary, he was assigned to Riga (Latvia), Kaunas (Lithuania), and again to Tallinn—three "listening posts" on the Soviet Union, where the United States had at that time no diplomatic mission.

From 1929 to 1931 Kennan was engaged in a State Department program of Russian studies in Berlin, and in 1933 he was called to the newly reopened United States Embassy in Moscow. During the next few years he served as vice-consul in Vienna (1935), second secretary in Moscow (1935–1936), second secretary and later consul in Prague (1938–1939), second and then first secretary in Berlin (1939–1941). Kennan was interned by the Nazis in December 1941, when the United States entered the war, but was repatriated in June 1942. After a brief assignment in neutral Portugal, Kennan was sent as counselor (1943–1944) with the American delegation to the European Advisory Commission in London. In 1944–1946 he was minister-counsel in Moscow.

At the end of World War II, when America was uncertain of Stalin's intentions but hoping for the best, Kennan had concluded in his Moscow station that the USSR "aimed at the achievement of maximum power with minimum responsibility." His dispatches brought him great prestige, and in the spring of 1947, after a period as foreign affairs lecturer at the National War College, Kennan was

GEORGE F. KENNAN

invited to establish and direct the State Department's policy planning staff, responsible for the long-range planning of the nation's foreign policy. His influence in that post was far-reaching and lasting; according to Joseph G. Whelan, whose article about Kennan appeared in the *Virginia Quarterly Review*, he "gave the American people and their political leaders a formal doctrine of foreign policy for the postwar era."

In the July 1947 issue of *Foreign Affairs* there appeared a now famous article, "The Sources of Soviet Conduct," by "X." After a brilliantly lucid analysis of Soviet foreign policy, it proposed that the United States should "confront the Russians with unalterable counterforce at every point where they show signs of encroaching upon the interests of a peaceful and stable world." It soon emerged that "X" was George F. Kennan. His article laid the foundation of American postwar containment policy towards the USSR. What is ironic is that "X," as he has subsequently explained, was advocating not a hawkish military containment but, as Whelan puts it, "containment in an economic, political, almost spiritual sense." Kennan played a major role in formulating the policy underlying the Marshall Plan and, in Whelan's opinion, it was this approach to containment, "unprovocative, inoffensive, and positive," that Kennan intended.

By 1949 Kennan's influence was on the wane. His donnishness and intellectual subtlety had always irritated many of his colleagues, and Dean Acheson, who became Secretary of State in 1949 and gave Kennan a new post as counselor to the Department, once accused him of taking "a rather mystical attitude" toward the realities of power relationships. A difference of opinion over the reunification of Germany, which Kennan favored and his superiors did not, brought matters to a head. In 1950 he spent a leave of absence at the Institute of Advanced Studies at Princeton. That was virtually the end of his career with the Foreign Service. In May 1952 he returned to Moscow as Ambassador, but within a year had been declared *persona non grata* by the Russians. In 1953 his differences with the new Secretary, John Foster Dulles, led to his resignation. Max Frankel called Kennan "the Herzog of recent American diplomacy . . . a brilliant but tragic failure among official men . . . an early combatant in the cold war between men of word and men of deed."

And since 1951, as a "man of word," Kennan has made himself a second reputation, less equivocal and even more distinguished than the first. *American Diplomacy, 1900–1950*, reprinting Kennan's 1951 Walgreen lectures at the University of Chicago, received the Freedom House award and earned unanimous critical enthusiasm for its lucidity and scholarship. Four Princeton lectures, collected as *Realities of American Foreign Policy*, were also praised for their wisdom, balance, and penetration.

In 1956 Kennan published the first volume in a projected series on Soviet-American relations from 1917 to 1920. *Russia Leaves the War*, concentrating on the period between November 1917 and March 1918, was described by Bertram D. Wolfe as "a specialist's study that reads like a first-rate historical novel." The truth of this judgment was reflected in the warmth of its reception by both historians and literary journalists and in the astonishing assortment of honors it carried off. It brought Kennan the Pulitzer Prize in history, the National Book Award, the Bancroft Prize, and the Francis Parkman Prize. It was called the work of "a poet as well as a philosopher," with "the feeling, the sureness, the insight and the emotional overtones" of one who knows and loves Russia. A sequel, *The Decision to Intervene*, appeared in 1958.

Kennan's BBC Reith Lectures, given in 1957 and published in 1958 as *Russia, the Atom and the West*, elucidated his views on containment and called for a policy towards the USSR of disengagement and peaceful coexistence. This eloquent book by a "compassionate, humble, contemplative man" stirred up a violent and worldwide controversy. A later work, *On Dealing with the Communist World*, seemed to one reviewer "the most persuasive plea for coexistence yet on record."

For many readers, *Russia and the West Under Lenin and Stalin* confirmed Kennan's right to be regarded as "the most distinguished living writer on Soviet affairs in any Western country." Kennan was praised by reviewers not only for his scholarship and prophetic judgments, but for his ability to "make his characters live and bring scenes and situations vividly before the reader's imagination," and for the ease and grace of his prose. But what made this "one of the most important books to have appeared in the United States since the . . . war" is the "restrained but unmistakable moral passion" which informs the writing. The inconsistencies which troubled one or two reviewers seemed to a critic in the *Times Literary Supplement* the book's most attractive feature, reflecting the tension between "Mr. Kennan the idealist and the prophet . . . and Mr. Kennan the highly trained, highly competent and hard-boiled professional diplomatist."

Kennan's *Memoirs, 1925–1950* appeared in 1967 and brought him a second Pulitzer Prize, this time in biography. The Pulitzer citation said that this book, "like Henry Adams's education . . . is also that work of rare art which, in illuminating the time and the man, reveals the complex fate it is to be an American today." The *Memoirs, 1950–1963* followed in 1972.

Kennan was a member of the Institute for Advanced Study, Princeton, in 1953–1961 and is a permanent professor in the Institute's history faculty. In 1961–1963 Kennan returned to practical diplomacy as Ambassador to Yugoslavia, and in 1967, when Stalin's daughter Svetlana Alliluyeva left the Soviet Union, it was Kennan who met her in Switzerland and played a key role in her decision to come to the United States. The author holds honorary degrees from a number of universities. He was a University Fellow of Harvard from 1965 to 1970, and became a Fellow of All Souls College, Oxford, in 1969. He held the Benjamin Franklin fellowship of the British Royal Society of Arts in 1968. In 1964–1967 he was president of the National Institute of Arts and Letters and in 1968–1972 he was president of the American Academy of Arts and Letters. A tall, slender, balding man, with blue eyes and a genial manner, Kennan was married in 1931 to Annelise Sorenson, and has three daughters and a son. He plays the piano and the guitar, and reads very widely and unfrivolously, in Russian and German as well as in English. He has confessed to some interest in writing a novel, or perhaps a play.

PRINCIPAL WORKS: American Diplomacy, 1901–1950, 1951; Realities of American Foreign Policy, 1954; Soviet-American Relations, 1917–1920: v. 1, Russia Leaves the War, 1956; v. 2, Decision to Intervene, 1958; Russia, the Atom and the West, 1958; Soviet Foreign Policy, 1917–1941, 1960; Russia and the West Under Lenin and Stalin, 1961; On Dealing with the Communist World, 1964; Memoirs, 1925–1950, 1967; (with others) Democracy and the Student Left, 1968; From Prague After Munich: Diplomatic Papers 1938–1940, 1968; The Marquis de Custine and His "Russia in 1839," 1971; Memoirs, 1950–1963, 1972.

ABOUT: Contemporary Authors 3, 1963; Crossman, R. H. S. The Charm of Politics, 1958; Current Biography, 1959; Hilsman, R. and Good, R. C. (eds.) Foreign Policy in the Sixties, 1965; Lerner, M. Actions and Passions, 1949; Who's Who in America, 1970–1971; Wilson, E. The Bit Between My Teeth, 1965. *Periodicals*—American Mercury March 1952; New York Times Magazine March 27, 1966; Virginia Quarterly Review Spring 1959; Western Political Quarterly March 1967.

KENNAWAY, JAMES (PEBLES EWING) (1928–December 21, 1968), Scottish novelist, screenwriter, and dramatist, published little information about his own life. He was brought up in Perthshire, Scotland, one of a large and presumably upper-middle-class or aristocratic family, and was educated at Glenalmond, Perth. From 1946 to 1948 he served as an officer with the Cameron Highlanders before going up to Oxford. In 1951 he joined the London publishing house of Longmans, Green, but resigned in 1957 when the success of his first novel made it possible for him to earn his living as a writer.

Tunes of Glory is about an ancient Scottish regiment, like Kennaway's own, and the peacetime conflict in it between Acting Colonel Jock Sinclair and his successor in command. Critics responded warmly to the unsentimental but moving portrait of Jock Sinclair, who is "of that species of soldier who refuses to fade away into retirement" and who "outrageously survives his more polished successor." Already visible in this book was the author's preoccupation with "the surprising reality behind facades." In 1960 Kennaway achieved an even greater success with the film version of *Tunes of Glory*, made from his own screenplay and starring Alec Guinness as Jock Sinclair.

Kennaway's second novel, *Household Ghosts*, was set in the Scottish lowlands, and probed the behavior and motives of the participants in a domestic triangle. Most reviewers found it profoundly and subtly perceptive, mixing humor and sadness in a way which reminded one of them of Chekhov. It is the wife, Mary, who is the most closely examined of the three, and her emotional dissatisfactions are traced back to childhood through her relationship with her brother, "an unforgettable portrait of failure" known as "Pink." Their intimacy is reflected in dialogue which seemed to Isabel Quigly coy, but to Francis Hope a "marvellously captured private vernacular." This relationship is also the theme of Kennaway's play *Country Dance*, staged at the Hampstead Theatre Club in 1967. Here, as in the novel, Pink seeks to align his sister with himself against the rest of their High Tory society, invoking through family jokes and passwords a contract somewhere between incest and a childhood game. Ronald Bryden found it ambiguous, interesting, and very funny, "a curiously isolated,

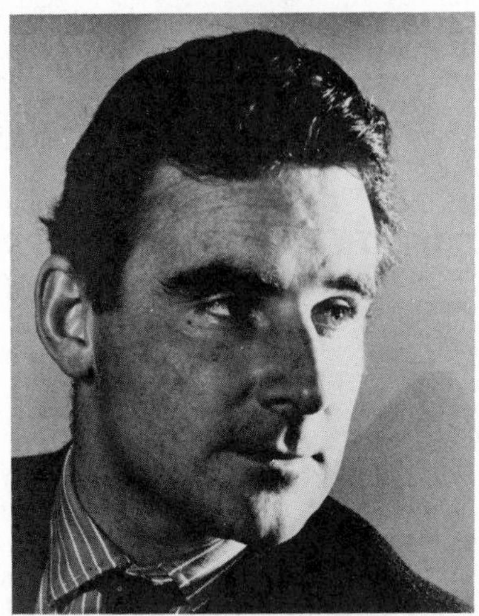

JAMES KENNAWAY

self-indulgent play, veering unevenly from genuine brilliance to a luscious over-writing which recalls Rosamond Lehmann."

The Mind Benders, adapted from the author's film scenario, is a thriller about the devastating effects of an experiment in total isolation upon the personality and beliefs of a young scientist. Another test of values is studied in *The Bells of Shoreditch*, about a young woman, happily married and a devoted socialist, who falls in love with a ruthlessly successful capitalist. These two books added to Kennaway's reputation as an extremely intelligent and versatile novelist and as an ironist concerned to attack those "self-deceptions that parade as moral strengths" and strip away "the comfortable assumptions with which we normally blunt the realities of any moral controversy." The criticism that he tended to manipulate his characters in accordance with the demands of his plot was made more than once, especially in connection with *Tunes of Glory* and with *The Mind Benders* (which however does not pretend to be much more than an intelligent entertainment).

Kennaway's technique was highly visual and indeed specifically cinematic in the way "attention shifts from one character to another, lingers, cuts sharply away." The novel *Some Gorgeous Accident* is actually laid out rather like a film script, "with italicized subheadings, leading into scraps of dialogue and comment, telescoped narrative, and miscellaneous conceits." It is, appropriately enough, about a photographer, named Link, and his friend Fiddes, who are both in love with Susie, a magazine editor in "swinging London." All three are lonely, destructive, yet searching for love. Kennaway's staccato, fragmented juxtaposition of their self-revelations and responses irritated some critics, who thought he was "trying a little too hard to be with it," but a reviewer in the *Times Literary Supplement* found the technique "very skilfully handled" and both the characters and their milieu admirably conveyed.

The author was killed in an automobile accident in December 1968 at the age of forty. His novel *The Cost of Living Like This* was published posthumously the following year—a short, intense story about an Oxford don, dying of cancer, and his last hungry grab for life, centering on a bizarre adventure in Glasgow where the don, his wife, and his teen-age working-class mistress "thrash out their contradictory wants, cross-examine one another cunningly and mercilessly, and in general submit their complaints against life." Melvin Maddocks suggested that the book was about the cost of living life as if it were a game, and concluded: "Kennaway's considerable achievement was to play out the game with courage and style. He fully accepted the blessed curse of self-awareness and gave the act of looking into the mirror all the passion, humor and terror of any first-hand experience."

Silence, another posthumous novel, was assembled from Kennaway's drafts by his friend Lynn Hughes. It explores the relationship between a white man, hiding from black militants in an American ghetto, and the black woman who saves him but will not speak to him. One reviewer called it "a strange, over-ambitious conundrum of a novel, juggling large moral issues with one hand while introducing tricky stage effects with the other."

PRINCIPAL WORKS: *Novels*—Tunes of Glory, 1956; Household Ghosts, 1961; The Mind Benders, 1963; The Bells of Shoreditch, 1964; Some Gorgeous Accident, 1967; The Cost of Living Like This, 1969; Silence, 1972. *Plays*—Country Dance, 1967.

ABOUT: Life September 5, 1969; Listener March 1, 1973; New York Times December 25, 1968; Observer (London) July 2, 1967; Times Literary Supplement September 15, 1972; Twentieth Century April 1957.

KENNEDY, X. J. (pen name of JOSEPH CHARLES KENNEDY) (August 21, 1929–), American poet, writes: "I was born, on the brink of the Depression, in the industrial town of Dover, New Jersey, where my father clerked for thirty years in a boiler factory. An erect, sprightly, innocent man, he would take me on long Sunday walks during my childhood, quoting me 'Snowbound' and other verse he loved. My mother was a former registered nurse; I was a late and only child. Both parents had Irish blood, my father being half Cornish too, and my mother half German. To this mixture I think I owe a tendency toward Celtic humor and misty-headedness, together with a Teutonic respect for order and tradition (I like verses that scan).

"People sometimes ask what the X in my name stands for. It is only a front: my legal name is Joseph Charles Kennedy. The pseudonym came about because, when a Navy whitehat serving aboard the U.S.S. Joseph P. Kennedy, Jr., I took hard ribbing from the crew, and so decided (on sending some verses to a magazine) not to be another Joseph Kennedy. The magazine that first printed me was the *New Yorker*, so I felt the X had somehow brought me luck, and determined to go on with it.

"That period in the Navy—four years during the Korean crisis—turned out unexpectedly to be valuable. Though in high school I had published a mimeographed magazine called *Vampire* and, during four years at Seton Hall College and a year at Columbia, had begun to dabble in verse, it was not until the Navy took me in that I started to write in quantity. My job was to make cruises aboard various destroyers in the Atlantic, taking photographs of crew members for release to their hometown newspapers. On a long cruise I could clean up my work in a few days, then, for the rest of the time at sea, had nothing to do but turn inward and put rhymes together.

"In 1955–1956 I attended the University of Paris on the G.I. Bill, again doing no more honest work than necessary, then became a teaching fellow in English at the University of Michigan. I never did complete the Ph.D., but Ann Arbor (and nearby Detroit) between 1956 and 1962 abounded in people who cared for poetry and who irritated one another constructively. Young bards and critics used to stay up half the night, attacking and defending new-made poetry. Among those who taught me things were Donald Hall, Bernard Waldrop, W. D. Snodgrass, Glauco Cambon, and visiting professor John Heath-Stubbs, in a production of whose play *The Talking Ass* I played the front end of the title role. The University of Michigan also brought me a Hopwood writing award for a rough draft of a first book of verse; and, better still, enabled me to meet my wife, Dorothy Mintzlaff. We have four children.

"Since Michigan, I have been teaching steadily for a living: at the University of North Carolina (Greensboro), Wellesley, and Tufts. I suppose this fact makes me an 'academic,' but so far, the campus towers have seemed brick and not ivory, and have not been far removed from the ground. In 1961 I succeeded Donald Hall as poetry editor for the *Paris Review*, but was unable to be brisk about the job, spending all my time writing apologetic letters to people, so I gave it up after two years. I have written other things besides verse, unhappily and for cash: reviews, schoolbooks, translations.

X. J. KENNEDY

"Critics, the more kindly ones, have called my work 'witty,' a dangerous label to wear, since to many it suggests 'trivial' and 'superficially felt.' I would wish to be seriously funny, and cannot understand the supposed difference between certain poems called light verse and others ranked as poetry. Right now my commitment is almost wholly to verse of an old-fashioned rhymed, metrical, stanzaic sort. I have written a few ballads and songs, and I sing them to audiences on occasion, especially when there is a drink in me. I write a lot, but like very little that I do; and my dearest joy is to keep every effort for a long time, pecking at its commas like a broody hen, perpetually fussing with it."

X. J. Kennedy's Avery Hopwood prize was for the rough draft of *Nude Descending a Staircase*, a collection of poems most of which had first appeared in the *New Yorker*, *Poetry*, *Paris Review*, and other magazines. When the book was published in 1961 it also brought him the Bess Hokin and the Lamont prizes, and almost universal praise from the critics.

The volume includes wry intimations of a Catholic boyhood, serene ones of a Catholic maturity, and this "Little Elegy, for a child who skipped rope": "Here lies resting, out of breath, / Out of turns, Elizabeth / Whose quicksilver toes not quite / Cleared the whirring edge of night, / Earth whose circles round us skim / Till they catch the lightest limb, / Shelter now Elizabeth / And for her sake trip up Death."

There are irreverent speculations on classical themes, ballads and blues, children's poems, and such thoughtful apothegms as "Ars Poetica": "The goose that laid the golden egg / Died looking up its crotch / To find out how its sphincter worked. / Would you lay well? Don't watch." And there are some sour poems about love and the death of it: "She might have stolen from his arms / Except that there was nothing left / To steal . . ." *Growing Into Love*, a subsequent collection, seemed to some reviewers similar, but rather less overtly humorous. A selection of poems from both volumes, with some new work, has been published in England as *Breaking and Entering*.

Kennedy says above that he "would wish to be seriously funny," and this, together with his formidable technical equipment, is what distinguishes his poetry. His real theme, Theodore Holmes suggests, is "the fragmentation, impersonality unto death, and the disintegration of human values." His poems work through "the peculiar disjunction in his sensibility that is the source of all wit, his mastery of vocabulary, syntax and the special quality of the American idiom, the purity of his style, the wry just off-tune harmonies of his ear." And Donald Hall says: "He does not apply wit from the outside (which is often a means of evasion); his wit is his way of understanding. No one writing is capable of the effects in which Kennedy specializes."

The poet is a big man, six feet three inches tall. He says that he is a science fiction fan, a collector of bad poems, and a drawer of cartoons. In 1971 Kennedy and his wife founded *Counter/Measures*, a magazine devoted to poetry in traditional forms. He has been teaching at Tufts University, where he is now an associate professor, since 1963. In 1967–1968 he received a grant from the National Foundation on the Arts and Humanities, and in 1970 the Shelley Memorial Award.

PRINCIPAL WORKS: Nude Descending a Staircase, 1961; An Introduction to Poetry, 1966; Growing Into Love, 1969; Breaking and Entering, 1971.

ABOUT: Contemporary Authors 2, 1963; Leary, P. and Kelley, R. (eds.) A Controversy of Poets, 1965; Murphy, R. (ed.) Contemporary Poets of the English Language, 1970; Who's Who in America, 1972–1973. *Periodicals*—Epoch Winter, 1962; Poetry August 1962; Wisconsin Studies in Contemporary Literature Winter-Spring 1965.

KENNER, (WILLIAM) HUGH (January 7, 1923–), Canadian literary critic, writes: "My work is describing how the imagination operates. Its achievements are in books, its materials include the things people assume about their lives. Although I've lived in the United States since 1948, I still draw on what I learned about those assumptions in the small Canadian city (Peterborough, Ontario) where I spent my first twenty years in the quiet time between the wars. The ice-man drove a horse, and you still, as a matter of course, learned Latin in high school. Englishmen patronized us as provincial (we didn't know what a past was), and Americans as retarded (we didn't drive fast enough), and we had a chance to learn things about both cultures that were hidden from their natives. We grew to learn that your past is what you can remember having around you. And we shared more than we would have liked to think with Anglo-Saxonry's professional outsiders, the Irish. The minds of great Americans and great Irishmen have been my professional province ever since.

"There was one public high school, and my father was its principal. He came to it as a young classics master in 1908, and when he retired fifty years later he had touched on the life of everyone in the city who got past eighth grade. The community that presented him with a grandfather clock was demonstrating that its consensus could endorse the value of such a life, and the few folk who thought he had simply stayed in a rut were still outsiders to the consensus. He was fifty-six when I was born; I was twenty-one when he died. My mother, who had taught French and German before her marriage, survived him by ten years, and was able to examine two of my books. I was their only child.

"When I was twelve a shrewd uncle gave me a ream of typing paper for Christmas. By the time I had graduated from the University of Toronto my sustaining interest—the one that was never really out of my mind, underlying the succession of themes that seemed to be holding my attention—was constructing English sentences, and testing as many as I could find in other people's books of the endless ways their structures can be combined. My first book was my master's thesis, rewritten; it gratified my desire to write a book. I was lucky enough not to have wasted time: I had sketched, as it turned out, the kind of book I was to continue writing, neither biography nor profile nor critical essay, but what a friend likes to call an X-ray Portrait. I devoted fifty thousand words to the mind of G. K. Chesterton, without touching on his corpulence, or his drollery, or his opulent wit. Those were things you could see without having a critic point them out; I thought it was more useful to locate, under the personality, a coherent set of mental habits, and portray those. My portrayal, like a radiologist's, isn't intended to remind you of the sitter, but to help you see into him.

"My mature life, like that of so many members of my generation and the one before mine, dates from my first encounter with Ezra Pound. It could not have been better timed. I was just about to commence work on my doctorate at Yale, and it was salutary to be immunized by example against the easy belief that professors, even the best performers, constituted an intellectual ultimate, or that study was more important than the relevance (here and now) of what you were studying. And he imparted, by conversation and letter, an unslakable love of the particular, of its radiance, its substantiality: the particular is not all that there is to know, but it is the only encounter through which we can know anything. The torque of a writer's mind is in sentences he gets on a page, accessible there and not in his 'philosophy.' And a place is things you can see, and a time is things you remember, or read of, or are told of: not somebody's evocation of its 'spirit.'

"I teach English at the University of California in Santa Barbara, where I have lived since 1950. I have also taught as a visitor at Michigan, Chicago, and Virginia, and have twice gone abroad on Guggenheim Fellowships. I married Mary Josephine Waite of Peterborough, Ontario, in 1947; all our five children are learning, I hope, the value of a usable past. After she died in 1964, I married Mary Anne Bittner of Maryland. We live in the foothills of the Santa Ynez mountains, in a house to which deer have been known to come. I was seventeen before I saw a Canadian deer, the woods have been pushed so far back from where anyone lived. And yet we Canadians used to suppose that our spirit drew immediate nourishment from the contiguous wilderness: so little did we know, and so little does anyone normally reflect, what actually may be."

The function of criticism for Kenner is elucidation and the "correction of taste," and its foundation is exegesis, in which he excels. He believes (Guy Davenport has said) that "literature is made from the contemplation of a created world, and, further, it is the poet, not the philosopher, who tells us how to take this world." Kenner sees, in the literary and intellectual upheaval that accompanied and followed World War I, a change of direction as fundamental as those inspired by the Augustans and the Romantics. His criticism has been devoted almost entirely to the leaders of this revolution.

The sitters for his full-length "X-ray Portraits" have included Ezra Pound, Wyndham Lewis, Joyce, Eliot, and Beckett. *Gnomen* contains essays on a number of contemporaries, especially those whose writings seem to him to need clarification. *The Stoic Comedians* considers, through an examination of works by Flaubert, Joyce, and Beckett, "the impact that printing has had on the form and purpose of the novel." *The Counterfeiters* studies the creative and parodic uses of eclecticism—the ways in which writers and others employ in their own work the words and ideas of others—and traces the development of this kind of "counterfeiting" from the seventeenth century to its full flowering in the work of (among others) Wyndham Lewis, Buster Keaton, Eliot, Beckett, and Andy Warhol.

HUGH KENNER

It is slightly easier to list the subjects of Kenner's books than to summarize the critical response to them. Most of his heroes are of the right, and so he tends to please right-wing critics more than liberal ones. Guy Davenport, for example, writing in *National Review*, said that Kenner "is performing a long, complex, heroic action, nothing less than a renovation of public taste." Steven Marcus, writing in *Partisan Review*, said that Kenner's "special genius lies in explaining more than he has understood in ways that few others will ever care to understand. . . . In his most typical essays he does nothing less than conjure up an autonomous, self-referring universe, whose terms have virtually nothing to do with experience, and which functions according to . . . rules whose unintelligibility is the safeguard of their inconsequence."

More moderate critics tend to admire Kenner's exegetical talents, but to dislike or dismiss his theories, to regret his unqualified commitment to his heroes' opinions, and to be irritated by his manner and style (or styles). Thus Dudley Fitts called *The Poetry of Ezra Pound* "as serviceable a guidebook to the Cantos as we are likely to get for a long time," but also recorded his "distaste for almost everything else the book is and stands for"; Selden Rodman similarly complained that Kenner seemed to share his subject's "pedantry and snobbism."

The Invisible Poet, Kenner's study of T. S. Eliot, is the most widely admired of his books, and has been particularly praised for its demonstration of Eliot's debt to F. H. Bradley. S. F. Morse wrote: "With an intellectual and sympathetic authority that is sometimes astonishing, sometimes illuminating, and often irritating, he presents not so much the case for Eliot but rather a kind of commentary on Eliot as something very much like scripture." The *Times Literary Supplement* found it a work of "brilliant sustained originality," and Philip Toynbee took it as confirmation of the preeminence of American criticism in the English-speaking world. Cyril Connolly, however, saw "a brilliant but maddening display of auto-intoxication" suffused with "the fatal atmosphere of the lecture-room, the subsidised incandescence which plays about with his subject and which ends by wearying us."

One critic noted that in *The Poetry of Ezra Pound* Kenner's "tone of voice approximates that of Pound himself," and Stephen Spender was struck by the fact that *Samuel Beckett* is "often written in a style which seems very close to [Beckett's own]." Spender found that the interest of the book "partly lies in its being itself a kind of serious joke. The rather cryptic preface seems at once to suggest and to disclaim the idea that the book emanated from Mr. Beckett and that Mr. Kenner is only the medium who communicates it." Kenneth Millar said of *The Invisible Poet* that Kenner sometimes "appears to be sharing a private joke with Mr. Eliot." All this implies that Kenner is himself a "counterfeiter," though to what extent and with what precise intention remains unclear. He is certainly Procrustean—confidently assigned by Maxwell Geismar to "the Formalist branch of the New Criticism," he stubbornly remains one of the most damaging and persistent attackers of the aridity and pomposity of the New Critics. "Entertaining and fearless" he seemed to Marianne Moore, who added: "he can be too fearless, but we need him."

Kenner's parents were Henry Rowe Hocking and the former Mary Williams. He now has a child by his second marriage, as well as five by his first. A gold medalist of the University of Toronto in 1945, he received his master's degree in 1946 and his doctorate, together with the Porter Prize, at Yale in 1950. He has been chairman of the English department at the University of California, Santa Barbara, since 1956, and is a contributing editor of *Poetry*. In addition to his two Guggenheim Fellowships (1956 and 1963) he has received a grant from the American Philosophical Society (1956). He is a Fellow of the (British) Royal Society of Literature. The playful spirit that has been detected in his criticism is evident in other fields, allowing him to regard politics, for example, as "primarily entertainment." He is a Roman Catholic.

PRINCIPAL WORKS: Paradox in Chesterton, 1947; The Poetry of Ezra Pound, 1951; Wyndham Lewis, 1954; Dublin's Joyce, 1956; Gnomen: Essays on Contemporary Literature, 1958; The Invisible Poet: T. S. Eliot, 1959; Samuel Beckett, a Critical Study, 1962; Flaubert, Joyce and Beckett, The Stoic Comedians, 1963; Studies in Change: A Book of the Short Story, 1965; The Counterfeiters, 1968; The Pound Era, 1972; Bucky: A Guided Tour of Buckminster Fuller, 1973; A Reader's Guide to Samuel Beckett, 1973. *As editor*—Art of Poetry, 1959; T. S. Eliot: A Collection of Critical Essays, 1962.

ABOUT: Connolly, C. V. Previous Convictions, 1965; Contemporary Authors 23–24, 1970; Marcus, S. Three Obsessed Critics, *in* Phillips, W. and Rahv, P. (eds.) The Partisan Review Anthology, 1962. *Periodicals*—Book World August 4, 1968; Commonweal April 4, 1958; National Review May 8, 1962; February 13, 1968; New Statesman August 11, 1956; New York Times Book Review July 6, 1947; August 22, 1954; March 26, 1972; Saturday Review February 22, 1958; Times Literary Supplement May 13, 1960; Yale Review December 1959.

KERMODE, (JOHN) FRANK (November 29, 1919–), English critic, writes: "I was born in Douglas, Isle of Man and went to school there. There is much to be said for the Isle of Man, which is small, often beautiful, and up to a point independent; but it is not a particularly good birthplace for a critic. Cut off from Liverpool by eighty miles of disagreeable water, it has virtually no bookshop, no theatre, and no literary society. It is provincial to the point of being suspicious of even the provincial English as too smart and free in their manners. Apart from occasional very brief excursions to Liverpool—the capital, as it seemed, of the world—I never left the Island till I was almost eighteen, and since then I have briefly visited but never lived there.

"Having won a scholarship to Liverpool University, I went there in 1937 and learned fast, coming from so far behind. In 1940 I took my final examinations, the last paper on the day Paris fell, and a few weeks later I was in the Navy. This went on till the beginning of 1946, and was in some ways less horrible than it might have been; but apart from allowing me to read Russian novels (which I always associate with a bookshop in Reykjavik which had a good supply of them) and to write a lot of poems, it afforded little that might be called literary experience. However, I saw the Atlantic, the Pacific, and the Mediterranean, lived for a while in Portland, Oregon, and left the Navy with some reluctance. Some poor years as a graduate student followed; in 1947 I began to teach, first at Newcastle and then at Reading. In 1958 I went to Manchester as Professor; in 1965 to Bristol; in 1967 to University College, London.

"For many years I lived the inelegant and surprisingly hard-working life of a provincial don; thinking of myself as interested mostly in sixteenth- and seventeenth-century literature, but without quite losing more general literary ambition. The years at Reading, which was very small and lively —for years John Wain was in the same department —were very fruitful. Broadcasts on the Third Programme, occasional reviewing, kept one in touch with a non-academic world; and in 1955 I wrote, virtually in one burst of a few weeks, *Romantic Image*. After that I contrived, and still do, to combine some scholarship in the earlier period with much writing on modern literature. I like both scholarship and high-journalism, which is why I enjoyed trying to combine the Bristol Chair with the co-editorship of *Encounter*. This slightly frantic period ended in May 1967, when I resigned from *Encounter* after much-publicised disagreements.

"I was married in 1947 to Maureen Eccles and we have twins, Mark and Deborah, born in 1956. We live in Hampstead."

Until his late thirties, Frank Kermode was known only as an academic writer on Renaissance literature, the editor of Shakespeare's *The Tempest* in the Arden edition and of an anthology of English pastoral poetry. But the appearance of *Romantic Image* in 1957 introduced him to a wider audience. This is a short, compressed, highly speculative study of the place of the image in modern poetry; among other things, it traces the connections between the symbolist assumptions of twentieth century literature and the attitudes of the major romantic poets. It contains some illuminating criticism of Yeats and is very scornful of the idea of the "dissociation of sensibility" as propounded by Eliot and enthusiastically taken up by a whole generation of English and American critics. From the beginning Kermode was as much cultural historian as critic. He brought to the writing of criticism a great deal of learning, an extremely subtle mind, an acute sense of history, and a style that was both relaxed and oblique.

Following the success of *Romantic Image*, Kermode added to his academic career a new role as a prolific literary journalist. In 1960 he published an admirable short study of Wallace Stevens, and edited a book of essays on Milton, and in 1962 he brought out a collection of articles and reviews under the title of *Puzzles and Epiphanies*. These essays showed Kermode extending, as a reviewer, the inquiry he had launched in *Romantic Image*. Most interestingly, they showed Kermode's increasingly ambiguous attitudes toward the symbolist phenomenon in literature. In *Romantic Image* he had been an interested but disapproving commentator on symbolism; he felt that symbolist criticism had no place for the long poems of the Renaissance that he admired, like *The Faerie Queene* and *Paradise Lost*. In *Puzzles and Epiphanies* Kermode could still write respectfully of an antisymbolist critic like Yvor Winters, but did not seem inclined to follow Winters' practice, and elsewhere in the collection he showed himself ready to tolerate symbolist attitudes.

FRANK KERMODE

In Kermode's next book, *The Sense of an Ending*, he turned his attention to the theory of fiction, and by this time—1967—he had become very much a critic in the symbolist tradition, more interested in questions of form and structure than in "life" or content, a bias for which Kermode was sharply attacked by John Bayley. *The Sense of an Ending* collects Kermode's Mary Flexner lectures (Bryn Mawr, 1965). It is a short but ambitious book, which investigates connections between the novel and other kinds of fiction—historical, scientific, theological—using fictions of apocalypse as a model. He points out that humanity is constantly positing its own downfall. This apocalyptic view, he believes, is not a true but a necessary one—a useful fiction enabling us to snatch an area of order and meaning from the chaotic flux of time; in the same way, the "sense of an ending" gives shape to a novel. But he distinguishes between fictions, which we know to be untrue, and myths, whose danger is that we may seek to live by them. The "inescapable relationship between art and order" is explored in many aspects and contexts in three subsequent volumes of essays, *Continuities*, *Modern Essays*, and *Shakespeare, Spenser, Donne*.

Kermode has an immensely powerful and fertile mind, though it lacks staying power. As Graham Hough pointed out in a severe review of *The Sense of an Ending*, Kermode has always been fundamentally an essayist and has never allowed himself to develop an argument at length. In his later criticism, the point of what he says can at times be blunted by an obscure and mannered style that is heavily influenced by the prose of Wallace Stevens. Many of his colleagues find his philosophical reflections hard to accept and sometimes hard to follow, but think him always fascinating and brilliant when he applies himself to a specific work of literature. At his best, as in a memorable essay on Colette, "the choice of detail flashes out a tantalizing picture, the splendid comparisons thrust a sense of [the author's] power on us, and the hesitant tone of the large explicit claims registers the true voice of delight." As a critic and literary theorist Kermode is the one Englishman of international stature to have emerged in the generation following Richards and Leavis.

The disagreements which led to his resignation from *Encounter* were, as he says, much publicized. He and his fellow editor Stephen Spender both resigned when they learned that the magazine had in the past been an indirect beneficiary of funds from the American Central Intelligence Agency, a fact of which the principal editor, Melvin Lasky, had failed to inform them, and which in ignorance they had denied. Kermode, now Lord Northcliffe Professor of Modern English Literature at University College, London, was a visiting professor at Harvard in 1961 and Warton Lecturer to the British Academy in 1962. He edits the Fontana Modern Masters series—introductions to the work of influential philosophers and writers which have been received with universal enthusiasm. He is a Fellow of the Royal Society of Literature and chairman of the Poetry Book Society, and was a member of the Arts Council from 1968 to 1971. His principal recreational interest is music. Kermode's marriage was dissolved in 1970.

PRINCIPAL WORKS: Romantic Image, 1957; Wallace Stevens, 1961; Puzzles and Epiphanies: Essays and Reviews, 1958–1961, 1962; The Sense of an Ending: Studies in the Theory of Fiction, 1967; Continuities, 1968; Shakespeare, Spenser, Donne, 1971; Modern Essays, 1971; D. H. Lawrence (Modern Masters series), 1973. *As editor*—English Pastoral Poetry: From the Beginnings to Marvell, 1953; The Tempest, 1954; The Living Milton, 1960; Discussions of John Donne, 1962; William Shakespeare: The Final Plays, 1963; Edmund Spenser: Selections from the Minor Poems, and the Faerie Queene, 1965; (with John Hollander) The Oxford Anthology of English Literature, 1973.

ABOUT: Contemporary Authors 2, 1963; Who's Who, 1973. *Periodicals*—Book Week April 30, 1967; Commentary June 1963; Critic June 1967; Listener October 5, 1967; Delta Summer 1962; Essays in Criticism October 1963, April 1968; New Statesman May 11, 1962; August 4, 1967; November 1, 1968; Observer May 14, 1967; Spectator November 11, 1960; Time and Tide May 17, 1962; Times Literary Supplement May 17, 1957; Twentieth Century November, December 1957, February 1958.

KEROUAC, JACK (pen name of JEAN-LOUIS KEROUAC) (March 12, 1922–October 21, 1969), American novelist, poet, and memoirist, wrote: "Birth in Lowell, Massachusetts, at 9 Lupine Road, third child of Leo Kerouac, printer of small weeklies, himself born at St. Hubert in the county of Temiscouata (Quebec) and a descendant of the family recorded in *Armorial Général de J. B. Rietstap Supplément par V. H. Rolland* as '*Lebris de Keroack, Canada, Originaire de Bretagne*' with accompanying scocheon and motto per *Rivista Araldica* (IV, 240), and of Gabrielle Levesque, also descendant of French pioneers in Canada, herself born at St. Pacôme in the county of Kamouraska (Quebec). My paternal grandmother a Bernier, descendant of the Indian Ocean explorer, and my maternal family included the name of the families Guy, Jean, and Pearson, the family Guy being part Indian.

"I was baptized in St. Louis de France church, received confirmation in Ste. Jeanne d'Arc, and underwent early severe education in French Canadian parochial schools up until fifth grade at St. Joseph's (O.M.I.), all in Lowell. Old sixteenth century forms of French, having been preserved in the bastion of Quebec from 1600 onwards, and now erroneously dubbed 'Canuck patois' because it is spoken on the tongue and not through the throat, was all I spoke till I began to learn English at age six but it was good training for later readings in Middle English and Modern.

"In the public schools, especially in high school where I was already a senior by sixteen due to skipping the second and sixth grades, I often played hooky in order to study alone and at my own discretion in the Lowell Public Library, studying chess problems, reading Hugo, trying to read Goethe, scanning the *Encyclopædia Britannica* eleventh edition, and finally taking notes on history out of Wells hoping to learn everything there ever was. After school, varsity football and indoor track, which together with the grades eventually won me an academic scholarship (Columbia University Club) to prep school and Columbia College. At Horace Mann School (my prep) in New York City there were the usual early literary influences but it was at Columbia that the complete reading of Thomas Wolfe (after I broke my leg in freshman football) led me to that American-Whitman vision of the U.S.A. so out of fashion now, twenty-five years later. I cut classes to write in my dormitory room at this vision. Romantic ideas of the waterfront led me to abandon Columbia for the Merchant Marine in World War II (North Atlantic campaign, when I served on the S.S. Dorchester before she was sunk), and similar ideas about the open road led to hitchhiking in forty-seven states and culminated in three years of heavily revising labor at home over the manuscript of *The Town and the City*, which, when completed and handed in to Harcourt Brace in 1949, came to one thousand one hundred and sixty-three manuscript pages. It was 'drastically cut,' my 'rough diamond' was being polished, they said. I realized I had to invent a new prose that could not be cut, or my heartfelt writing life was in danger, and I blasted off *On the Road* in three weeks. For six years Viking Press tried to decide whether to print this book or not. I went right on writing and developing my own 'vision,' meanwhile earning my living as a script synopsizer for Twentieth-Century Fox in New York, railroad brakeman on the Southern Pacific, seaman in peacetime, forest service lookout in the Northwest mountains, etc. During this time I went all out and abandoned stereotyped forms of prose and verse, adopted a credo of literature as companionship in a transcendental world-nostalgia, and under the influence of studying the writings of everybody and his uncle, even the sutras of India, I sprung loose spontaneous subconscious materials I'd heretofore considered unliterary and placed them under the discipline of narrative reasonableness."

It was in the fall of 1941 that Kerouac left Columbia. During the following year he served briefly in both the Merchant Marine and the United States Navy, but was discharged from the latter as a "schizoid personality." By October 1942 he was back at Columbia. He dropped out of the university again almost at once, but spent the winter in an apartment near the campus which became a meeting place for disaffected students. It was then, or soon afterwards, that Kerouac met Allen Ginsberg, William S. Burroughs, Clellon Holmes, Carl Solomon, Neal Cassady, and other founder-members of what became the Beat movement.

Between 1943 and 1950, Kerouac hitchhiked throughout the United States and Mexico, living on what he could earn at odd jobs and on occasional subsidies from his mother. He made two marriages during these years, in 1944 and 1950, but both ended in divorce within a year. From time to time he settled down in New York at his mother's house, working on a novel about the profoundly happy family life he had known as a child in Lowell, Massachusetts. This was published in 1950 as *The Town and the City*, and was received with marked critical enthusiasm. "He has the ability to infuse . . . grandeur into simple doings that marked Thomas Wolfe's first books," wrote a *Newsweek* reviewer, "but he is more balanced than Wolfe. He has a zest for the ordinary."

By the time his first novel was published, however, Kerouac—whose photograph appears on the dust jacket, serious and well groomed—had left such orthodoxies far behind and was seeking "to invent a new prose" in which to affirm a new vision. Some of the elements of that vision can already be seen in embryo in *The Town and the City*: do as you want, explore all the paths to self-fulfillment and self-gratification, learn to be innocent and tender and spontaneous.

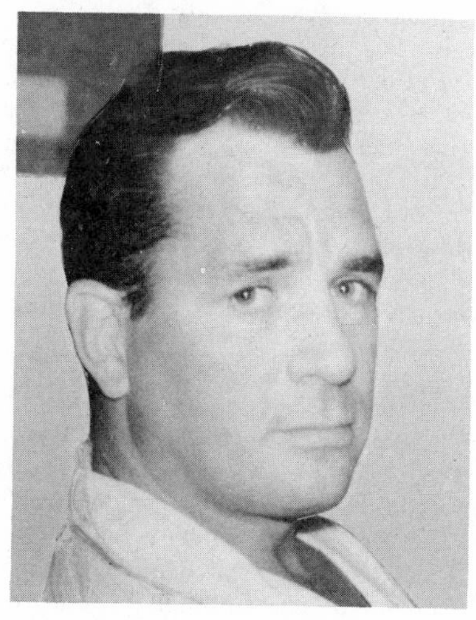

JACK KEROUAC

Kerouac adumbrated a specifically American mythology, nourished by the generous immensity and beauty of his country, and the grandeur of its history—"the great raw bulge and bulk of my American continent." The evil gods of this mythology were the captains and cohorts of industry, commerce, law and order—the armies of a mean and ugly bourgeois ethic. Kerouac's heroes were the dropouts from a betrayed and corrupted America—the mad, the poor, and the stoned; the blacks; the insulted and injured failures and the ecstatic sinners. In his search for a liturgy to celebrate his fundamentally religious vision, Kerouac was heavily influenced by Walt Whitman and by the theories and example—the "fast, mad, confessional" style—of Neal Cassady, a young wanderer from Denver with a taste for literature and theology who was Kerouac's favorite traveling companion.

In 1951, when Kerouac began his second novel, he fed one end of a long roll of paper into his typewriter, and began a spontaneous and unrevised account of the wanderings, conversations, and opinions of Sal Paradise (himself), Carlo Marx (Ginsberg), and Dean Moriarty (Neal Cassady). In the course of this random pilgrimage, Sal learns from Moriarty to shed his haunting sense of "homelessness, valuelessness, faithlessness," and to recognize "the ragged and ecstatic joy of pure being." As he says, it took Kerouac only three weeks to complete *On the Road*, his most famous novel.

The style and attitude of the book are well enough

exemplified in this description of the first meeting between Ginsberg and Cassady: " . . . they danced down the streets like dingle-dodies, and I shambled after as I've been doing all my life after people who interest me, because the only people for me are the mad ones, the ones who are mad to live, mad to talk, mad to be saved, desirous of everything at the same time, the ones who never yawn or say a commonplace thing, but burn, burn, burn like fabulous yellow roman candles exploding like spiders across the stars and in the middle you see the blue centerlight pop and everybody goes 'Awww!' "

In 1957, when *On the Road* at last appeared, it rapidly became the bible and manifesto of all those young people who, growing up under the threat of the atom bomb, were disgusted by the greed, conformity, and militarism of their elders. It ushered in the Beat Generation, which led in turn to hipsterism and all the other bohemian and apolitical manifestations of the continuing "youth revolution." Kerouac said that the word "beat" was first used by a friend to express a sense of spiritual exploitation and exhaustion, of imminent apocalypse; later, during a moment of revelation in a church in Lowell, he realized that the word had overtones for him of "beatific," and it has also been associated with the restless "bop" music rhythms of the time.

Kerouac's "instantaneous" narrative deliberately rejects form, and does so far more completely than Whitman ever did. Such unity as his work retains derives from the sensibility it reveals, and there were mixed impressions of what the result was worth in literary terms. Whereas Allen Ginsberg said that Kerouac had created a new form, "a spontaneous bop prosody," Truman Capote thought that what Kerouac was producing was not writing but typewriting.

After the publication of *On the Road*, the books Kerouac had written during his years in the wilderness began to appear in rapid succession, along with other, newer, works. They are all more or less autobiographical and picaresque, and similar in style and content to *On the Road*. Most of them show Kerouac's growing (and influential) interest in Zen Buddhism—especially *The Dharma Bums*, which culminates in a search for *dharma* (truth) in the mountains of the Pacific Northwest. *The Subterraneans*, still one of the most popular of Kerouac's books, is about his unhappy love affair with a black girl.

Subsequent works, from *Doctor Sax* (about the author's childhood) to *Desolation Angels* (about beat travels in the state of Washington, Mexico, London, and Tangier), showed no noticeable development in style or content. *Satori in Paris* was something of a departure, in that it makes no pretense to be fiction; it describes the author's short visit to France to explore his ancestry, and tries but fails to convey a moment of *satori* (illumination) experienced there.

In *Vanity of Duluoz*, the last book published during his lifetime, Kerouac comments sharply on such post-Beat phenomena as the Beatles, McLuhan, and "the expanding consciousness crap." During the 1960s indeed he felt himself less and less in sympathy with the revolution he had helped to create as it became increasingly social and political in its aims, and his own contribution to it became less significant. Most of his last years were spent in seclusion, at Lowell and elsewhere, with his invalid mother and his third wife, Stella Sampas, whom he married in 1966. He died in a Florida hospital at the age of forty-seven, following massive abdominal hemorrhaging. His wife said: "He had been drinking heavily for the past few days. He was a very lonely man."

Kerouac, in spite of his interest in oriental religions, continued to think of himself as a Catholic. It is true that he failed to mature, either as a man or a writer, but he wrote some books of great originality, freedom, and sweetness that were a necessary antidote to the bloodless academicism of the 1950s. As one critic said, he was a writer we "should have had to invent if he did not exist."

There were many signs of a revival of interest in Kerouac and his work in the early 1970s. A volume of previously uncollected poems was published in 1971 and his last novel, *Pic*, appeared the same year —a characteristically vagrant tale narrated by a ten-year-old black boy who leaves the North Carolina backwoods when his grandfather dies and goes north to Harlem with his jazz-musician brother. Ann Charters' biography of Kerouac was published in 1973, and another by Aaron Latham was promised. *Visions of Cody* (1972) is a lively assortment of mood pieces, reminiscences, and conversations with Neal Cassady. (Excerpts from this work had appeared in a limited edition in 1960, when the book as a whole was considered too gamy for publication.)

PRINCIPAL WORKS: *Fiction and fictionalized memoirs*—The Town and the City, 1950; On the Road, 1957; The Subterraneans, 1958; The Dharma Bums, 1958; Doctor Sax, 1959; Maggie Cassidy, 1959; Excerpts from Visions of Cody 1960 (Visions of Cody published in full in 1972); Tristessa, 1960; Big Sur, 1962; Visions of Gerard, 1963; Desolation Angels, 1965; Satori in Paris, 1966; Vanity of Duluoz, 1968; Pic, 1971. *Verse*—Mexico City Blues, 1959; Scattered Poems, 1971. *Travel*—Lonesome Traveler, 1960. *Miscellaneous*—The Scripture of the Golden Eternity, 1960; Book of Dreams, 1961; Pull My Daisy (text ad-libbed for the film by Robert Frank and Alfred Leslie), 1961.

ABOUT: Charters, A. Kerouac: A Biography, 1973; Current Biography, 1959; Fried, F. No Pie in the Sky, 1964; Lipton, L. The Holy Barbarians, 1959; Moore, H. T. (ed.) Contemporary American Novelists, 1965; Rigney, F. and Smith, L. D. The Real Bohemia, 1961;

Who's Who in America, 1968–1969. *Periodicals*—Atlantic July 1965; Chicago Review Spring 1956; Encounter August 1959; Harper's October 1960; Idea April 1967; Life November 30, 1959; Mainstream June 1962; Nation February 23, 1957; New World Writing 11, 1957; New York Review of Books May 20, 1965; New York Times October 22, 1969; New York Times Book Review February 18, 1968; New York Times Magazine November 16, 1952; Partisan Review Spring 1958; Tamarack Review Spring 1959; Times October 22, 1969.

KERR, (BRIDGET) JEAN (COLLINS) (July 10, 1923–), American humorist and dramatist, was born Bridget Jean Collins in Scranton, Pennsylvania. She is the daughter of Thomas J. Collins, a building contractor, and Kitty (O'Neill) Collins, a second cousin of Eugene O'Neill. Jean Collins graduated from Marywood Seminary, Scranton, in 1939 and received her B.A. in 1943 from Marywood College. In 1941, while she was working as stage manager on a college production of *Romeo and Juliet*, she met the drama critic Walter Kerr, then professor of drama at the Catholic University of America in Washington, D.C. In 1943 they were married. Two years later, Mrs. Kerr received a Master of Fine Arts degree from Catholic University, where she also taught.

JEAN KERR

One of her first plays was an adaptation of Franz Werfel's novel *The Song of Bernadette*, written in collaboration with her husband. It was intended for the amateur market and originally produced at Catholic University. Brought to Broadway in 1946, it closed after three performances but impressed some critics with its "simplicity, eloquence and dignity." Jean Kerr's comedy *Jenny Kissed Me*, which also made its way to Broadway via Catholic University, was scarcely more successful, but *Touch and Go*, a revue written with her husband and produced on Broadway by George Abbott in 1949, ran for one hundred and seventy-six performances. The 1954 comedy called *King of Hearts*, the result of a collaboration with Eleanor Brooke, ran for nine months on Broadway under Walter Kerr's direction, and in book form was a selection of the Fireside Theatre book club. *Goldilocks*, written with Walter Kerr, was described by Brooks Atkinson as "a bountiful, handsome musical comedy with an uninteresting book."

Remembering such productions as *Jenny Kissed Me*, Mrs. Kerr wrote in *Please Don't Eat the Daisies:* "I won't say that my early efforts were crowned with glory. Oh, I'd say it, all right, but could I make it stick?" She could probably make it stick if she said it of *Mary, Mary*, her 1961 hit comedy which Henry Hewes called "two almost constantly funny hours of her own brand of comic verisimilitude." Gerald Weales, agreeing that "every line is a laugh line," suggested that precisely for this reason "the play refuses to operate" and at times "seems like a production of 'The Ugly Duckling,' doctored by six of Bob Hope's writers." Whitney Bolton was also unimpressed, finding the play "thin as blown glass and just as transparent"; it was a judgment he recalled rather wryly in 1964, "three years and ten million dollars later." *Mary, Mary* was subsequently filmed from a screenplay by Richard L. Breen. *Poor Richard*, which had a considerably shorter Broadway run in 1964–1965, was about a British poet's exploits and tribulations in the United States, modeled on the American adventures of Brendan Behan. A later play, *Finishing Touches* (1973), a rather predictable situation comedy, seemed to Clive Barnes nevertheless "one of the most professional pieces of work Broadway has seen for some time—smooth, glossy and even elegant."

Mrs. Kerr's modest theatrical ambitions are "to make a lot of people laugh and to make a lot of money," and she has done so. Some critics have found her plays irritatingly pure, but not many have tried to deny that she is "one of the funniest women writers of her generation."

Millions who have seen none of Jean Kerr's plays know and delight in the autobiographical articles she contributes about the hazards of American domestic life to such magazines as *Vogue* and *Ladies' Home Journal*. The first collection of these "familiar essays" was *Please Don't Eat the Daisies*. Orville Prescott wrote of it: "Mrs. Kerr is funniest when writing about the perfectly normal frenzy that is life with four small boys. . . . 'There are four of them and only two of us,' she says, which is an entirely understandable explanation for the fact that Mrs. Kerr does most of her writing in an automobile parked several blocks away from her home." Elizabeth Janeway found it "a very funny book by a woman with a wonderful eye and ear for those moments of lunacy in which every normal life abounds." The book headed the non-fiction best-seller lists for over twenty weeks. Two similar collections, *The Snake Has All the Lines* and *Penny Candy*, were also well received.

Jean Kerr has honorary L.H.D. degrees from Northwestern and Fordham universities, and in 1971 received both the Campion award and the Laetare medal. She and her husband now have five sons and a daughter. They live in Larchmont, New York, in what was originally the stables and coach house of a large estate. Mrs. Kerr is a tall woman, and pretty, with a clear Irish complexion. She says: "The most important thing about me is that I am a Catholic. It's a superstructure within which you can work, like the sonnet. I need that."

PRINCIPAL WORKS: *Plays*—(with Walter Kerr) The Song of Bernadette (based on the novel by Franz Werfel), 1944; Our Hearts Were Young and Gay (dramatization of the book by Cornelia Otis Skinner and Emily Kimbrough), 1946; Big Help, 1947; Jenny Kissed Me, 1949; (with Eleanor Brooke) King of Hearts, 1954; (with Walter Kerr) Goldilocks, 1959; Mary, Mary, 1963; Poor Richard, 1965. *Humor*—Please Don't Eat the Daisies, 1957; The Snake Has All the Lines, 1960; Penny Candy, 1970.

ABOUT: Current Biography, 1958; Kerr, J. Please Don't Eat the Daisies, 1957; The Snake Has All the Lines, 1960; Who's Who in America, 1972–1973. *Periodicals*—Cosmopolitan August 1958; Good Housekeeping October 1959; Ladies' Home Journal November 1955; June 1964; Life April 24, 1954; February 24, 1958; Milwaukee Journal April 21, 1963; New York Herald Tribune February 19, 1958; New York Post December 6, 1964; Theatre Arts March 1961; Time April 14, 1961; World-Telegram and Sun Feature Magazine September 6, 1958; Vogue July 1954.

KERR, WALTER (FRANCIS) (July 8, 1913–), American critic and dramatist, writes: "I was born in Evanston, Illinois, and was taken to my first show (*No, No, Nanette*) by a generous aunt and to my first movie (William S. Hart, with a Chaplin trailer) by my father. I was five or six at the time and that settled it. Thereafter I badgered my mother to let me roam the town and nearby Chicago at will looking at all the movies I had dimes for, which she permitted when I was seven. At thirteen, through someone's oversight, I was allowed to print my own movie reviews in the Evanston *Review*, which I continued to do, moving to the daily Evanston *News-Index*, for ten years. During high school I was regularly employed covering sports, films, and theatre, and I caught up with all the plays of the previous twenty years in stock. Out of high school and into the Depression, I made what money I could writing and directing any sort of community entertainment that was offered me (six weeks' work for twenty-five dollars as a rule) and by publishing some minstrel formats and revue sketches I was able—with the help of a life-saving scholarship—to go back to school, the School of Speech at Northwestern to be specific. While there I drew my first taste of professional blood by writing occasional jokes for Edgar Bergen's radio show.

"Having acquired an absolute appetite for theatre, I greedily tried everything. I acted in college (badly), I wrote plays so that I would have something to direct, and when I went to the Catholic University of America as a young teacher I spent my after-hours directing four to six plays each year for eleven years. Generally I chose plays I thought I'd never see if I didn't do them myself: *The Knight of the Burning Pestle, The Ascent of F6, Life Is a Dream, The Birds, Tom Thumb the Great*, all that sort of thing.

"Meantime I'd been able to get several musicals on Broadway—*Sing Out, Sweet Land* is the one I care to remember—and in 1949 my wife Jean and I collaborated on a revue called *Touch and Go*, produced by George Abbott whom we both love to this day. While *Touch and Go* was running I took a year off from teaching to think things through. I'd noticed that if I wrote a Sunday article for the New York *Times* I generally got more mail and newspaper response than I ever did on a show, and the message came loud and clear: any abilities I might have were analytical rather than creative. So, to echo Groucho Marx, we talked it over and decided to move to New York ('where, in a little house in the Bronx, Abraham Lincoln was born, much to my father's surprise' is the way Groucho finishes the line) with the idea that I would try my hand at criticism. I began reviewing for *Commonweal* in 1950 and for the New York *Herald Tribune* a year later. In short, after many detours and much fun, I was back where I started, which is where, certain producers to the contrary, I probably belonged. I broke my resolve about not attempting creative work only once after 1949, and then I did it—a musical called *Goldilocks*—just for fun. Just for fun is no way to do a show, as I could have told myself if I'd been listening. During my years of hard work on the *Tribune*, my wife became famous. As for myself, I like reviewing, sweat over the deadline, and snatch what little time is left to work on books. I also like to collect books and films, particularly films which are vanishing. My wife and I also collect children and have six."

In 1966, when the New York *Herald Tribune* ceased publication, Walter Kerr became drama critic of the New York *Times*, surrendering that post the following year "to take a somewhat longer view" as the newspaper's Sunday drama critic. He is one of the three children of Walter

Kerr, a construction foreman, and the former Esther Daugherty. Kerr had been at De Paul University in Chicago for two years (1931–1933) when the Depression sent him out to work. He resumed his education in 1935 at Northwestern University, which gave him his B.A. in Speech in 1937 and an M.A. in 1938. The following year he went to Catholic University in Washington, D.C., as instructor in speech and drama (1938–1945) and subsequently as associate professor (1945–1949). His teaching career was spectacular: within three years, student enrollment in the drama courses had expanded from twenty-five to over two hundred. Kerr taught playwriting, acting, and direction, as well as writing and directing himself, and the university's reputation for exciting productions grew rapidly, until they were attracting the regular attention of Washington's major critics.

Many of Kerr's Catholic University productions are still remembered. His "cockeyed farce" *Christopher Over Chaos* (1939) won a Maxwell Anderson play contest. *Yankee Doodle Boy*, a musical biography of George M. Cohan which Kerr wrote with Leo Brady was another 1939 success. In 1942 the undergraduate revue *Count Me In* was transferred (albeit unsuccessfully) to Broadway, where Kerr's "musical biography of American song," *Sing Out, Sweet Land*, had a kinder welcome two years later. In 1943, meanwhile, Kerr had married Jean Collins, then a nineteen-year-old student at Marywood College, now very much better known under her married name. She collaborated with Kerr on a Catholic University revue which became his most considerable Broadway success, *Touch and Go* (1949). Brooks Atkinson found it funny, intelligent, and "the most enjoyable new show of this season." It was a sellout in New York for five months and ran for another six in London.

When Kerr resigned from Catholic University in 1949 he left behind him what has been called the finest nonprofessional theatre in the country; after 1951, when he joined the New York *Herald Tribune*, he rapidly established himself as "king of the New York critics." And with reason, for he brought to his work a very rare combination of scholarship and practical experience, and a notably urbane, witty, and exact style. According to the *Times Literary Supplement*, one of Kerr's principal strengths "is his catholicity, his ability to draw equally on Aristophanes and Buster Keaton, and to mingle academic and colloquial language without stylistic impropriety."

Kerr has never doubted that great theatre is popular theatre, and has been willing to discuss Broadway's offerings, however puerile, thoughtfully, carefully, and generously. He has also, on the whole, shown an intelligent appreciation of the

WALTER KERR

experimental theatre. But he is a basically conservative critic, committed to a vision of quality theatre for "massive audiences," and instinctively unsympathetic to the abrasiveness and difficulty of the serious contemporary drama. His lack of enthusiasm for such works as *Waiting for Godot* has infuriated his more radical colleagues, of whom the most vocal in attack has been Robert Brustein. When Kerr succeeded Stanley Kauffmann as drama critic of the New York *Times*, Brustein said: "The fact that Walter Kerr will be the only drama critic of importance and will determine the success or failure of every production dooms the theatre to twenty-five years of mediocrity." In March 1967, however, it was announced that Kerr, at his own suggestion, was to become the *Times* Sunday drama critic. Clive Barnes, who followed him as weekday reviewer, said: "The paper should become a forum rather than a one-man operation. Between Mr. Kerr and myself, we are prepared to break the power of the *Times* critic."

How Not to Write a Play, Kerr's first book, was a vigorous, thoughtful, and witty plea for the restoration of the theatre to its original popularity. *The Decline of Pleasure* contains seven essays whose concerns are more philosophical than specifically theatrical, attacking a new Benthamism that values only utility and fears pleasure. Harold Taylor called it "a genial, warm-hearted and provocative book which gains assent by the sharpness of its perceptions of human failure and the kind of view it takes of human possibility." Melvin Maddocks said that "in a special, camouflaged way it is a form of autobiography." *Comedy and Tragedy* analyzes a number of the theatre's classics in search of a definition of those forms that can usefully be applied in the theatre today. Lionel Abel, who remained unconvinced that Kerr is a theorist, found the book nevertheless "intelligent, sensitive, suggestive, containing some of the author's best writing on the theatre." There have been four collections of Kerr's reviews and articles, *Pieces at Eight* (1957), *The Theater in Spite of Itself* (1963), *Thirty Plays Hath November* (1969), and *God on the Gymnasium Floor* (1971). These volumes, which show how little his views have changed over the years, have all been warmly received by most critics.

Walter Kerr is a member of the New York Drama Critics Circle, and was its president from 1955 to 1957. He received the George Jean Nathan Award for theatre criticism in 1964, the Dineen Award in 1966, the Iona Award in 1970, the Campion Award and the Laetare Medal in 1971. He holds honorary degrees from several universities. In 1965 he served as "host" on a television series, Esso Repertory Theatre, and he has been for some years a drama consultant to the theatrical agents Saudek Associates. Asked to list some books and articles about himself and his work, Kerr wrote simply: "See Robert Brustein."

PRINCIPAL WORKS: How Not to Write a Play, 1955; Criticism and Censorship (Gabriel Richard Lecture, 1954), 1956; Pieces at Eight, 1957; The Decline of Pleasure, 1962; The Theater in Spite of Itself, 1963; Tragedy and Comedy, 1967; Thirty Plays Hath November, 1969; God on the Gymnasium Floor, 1971.

ABOUT: Contemporary Authors 7–8, 1963; Current Biography, 1953; Who's Who in America, 1970–1971; Who's Who in the Theatre, 1967.

***KESSEL, JOSEPH (ÉLIE)** (February 10, 1898–), French novelist and journalist, is the son of Samuel Kessel, a physician, and the former Raïssa Lesik. His parents were Russian Jews who had gone first to France, where Samuel Kessel completed his medical studies, and then to the *émigré* colony founded by Baron Hirsch in Argentina. Joseph Kessel was born there, in the Argentinian city of Clara, but spent his early childhood in Russia, on the edge of the Ural mountains where Europe borders Asia. When he was ten the family returned to France, which has been Kessel's home ever since. He was educated at the *lycée* in Nice and the Lycée Louis-le-Grand in Paris, and went to the University of Paris for his *licence*. Kessel stayed on at the Sorbonne to earn his advanced diploma in literature, and at the same time became a student at the Conservatory for Dramatic Art.

In 1916 he put aside his theatrical ambitions and volunteered for military service. He became an aviator, winning the Croix de Guerre (with palms) and the Médaille Militaire. In 1918 Kessel left with his squadron for the Far East, beginning a journey which, by the time he returned to France for his release in 1919, had become virtually a world tour.

* ke sel′

Kessel began his career as a journalist in 1920, when he was sent to cover the Sinn Fein uprising in Ireland. His first book appeared in 1922—a collection of short stories about the Russian Revolution and its terrors called *La Steppe rouge* (The Red Steppe). It reflected Kessel's acute consciousness of his Russian ancestry, and his fury and frustration at being excluded from Russia, as he was after World War I. At one point indeed he attempted to reenter the country of his childhood as a journalist, via Riga, and narrowly escaped being shot by the Bolsheviks. Kessel has steeped himself in Russian literature and history, and has returned to Russian subjects in *Les Rois aveugles* (1925, translated as *The Blinded Kings*), a "vivid and comprehensive historic panorama" of Russia in 1916, just before the fall of the Romanoffs, and in several other novels.

Another persistent theme in Kessel's work is war, the subject of his second book, *L'Équipage* (1923). It is about the adventures in battle and in love of the two-man crew of a fighter plane, an exciting and dramatic story which in France became a major best seller and is still regarded there as one of the finest flying novels ever written. It was translated as "Pilot and Observer" in a collection of Kessel's work called *The Pure in Heart*, but seemed to impress the English-speaking critics less than the short stories that accompanied it. There was particular praise for "Captain Sogoub's Tea," called "a little masterpiece of the life of Russian refugees in Paris." This tale was expanded into a full-length novel, *Nuits de princes*, translated as *Princes of the Night*.

In the 1920s and 1930s Kessel traveled widely, as a journalist and on his own account, and became established as a superlative writer of action and adventure stories, with a special talent for conveying the atmosphere of the exotic places in which he set his novels. Typical of his work at this time is *Fortune carrée* (1932, translated as *Crossroads*), an "always colorful and frequently exciting" novel about the adventures in Arabia of Igricheff, son of a Russian aristocrat.

For three years during World War II Kessel took an active and dangerous part in the Resistance Movement in France, again winning the Croix de Guerre with palms. Eventually he was forced to escape, via Spain, to London, where he joined de Gaulle and "did some superb reporting." He is the author, with his nephew Maurice Druon, of the words of the Resistance song "Chant des Partisans" (1942).

One of Kessel's most notable books appeared in 1944. This was *L'Armée des ombres* (1944, translated as *Army of Shadows*), a collection of true stories about the French Resistance, slightly fictionalized for security reasons, and presented as excerpts from the diary of a leader of the movement. Kessel had set out to evoke a new France, in which rebellion had become a duty, and where "in the catacombs of revolt the people are creating their own light and finding their own law." The book was very warmly reviewed, and V. S. Pritchett, praising Kessel's "gravity, intelligence and sensibility," wrote: "He makes one tremble for his people from page to page, so tenderly are they observed; their adventures excite us, but the ring of truth adds a deeper emotion to our excitement. Their sincerity is overwhelming."

After peace came, Kessel resumed his career as a novelist and journalist, and continued his travels, visiting among other places India, East Africa, Burma, Hong Kong, and Afghanistan. *Le Lion* (1958, translated and filmed as *The Lion*), regarded by some as Kessel's finest novel, is set in East Africa. A little girl, deprived of a human object for her affections, has transferred them to a lion, her pet as a cub. The narrator, a Parisian seeking in Africa an escape from his overcivilized self, finds that the child's "raw primitive need" for the beast satisfies in him "a need beyond human understanding." Some reviewers found the novel embarrassing in its attempts at philosophical profundity but it was agreed that, when he writes of animals, Kessel's "power of observation is astonishing and delightful, and the world he evokes is beautiful, innocent, and memorable."

There was less unanimity about the virtues of *Les Cavaliers* (1967, translated as *The Horsemen*). It is a novel about tribal life in contemporary Afghanistan, where the men play *buzkashi*—polo conceived as total war. Uraz, son of a famous horseman, is about to win the royal tournament when his leg is broken. Humiliated, he scorns medical aid, and sets out on an epic journey back to his distant homeland. In France the novel was a triumph for Kessel, a major best seller regarded by many reviewers as the book of the year. The English translation encountered rather less enthusiasm, but in spite of many flaws was generally welcomed as a gripping "tale of men triumphant over nature at its cruelest." The book illustrates very well "a certain savage quality" in Kessel's writing, his mastery of atmosphere, and his weakness for hyperbole.

Kessel has also written a number of travel books, an account of Alcoholics Anonymous, and biographies of the legendary French aviator Mermoz and of Felix Kersten, the brilliant manual therapist whose influence upon Himmler saved thousands of lives. Several of Kessel's novels have been filmed, including *The Horsemen* and *Belle de Jour*, his in-

JOSEPH KESSEL

teresting and quite atypical psychological study of *le diable au corps*. He has written at one time or another for most of France's best-known newspapers. Kessel was awarded the Grand Prix du Roman in 1927 for *Les Captifs*, a somber study of life in a tuberculosis sanatorium, and has also received the Prix des Ambassadeurs (1958) and the Prix Rainier III (1959). In 1962 he was elected to the French Academy. Kessel was married in 1949 to Michèle O'Brien and lives in Paris.

PRINCIPAL WORKS IN ENGLISH TRANSLATION: *Fiction*—The Blinded Kings, 1926; The Pure in Heart (short stories and a novel, Pilot and Observer), 1928; Princes of the Night, 1928; Crossroads, 1932; Sirocco, 1947; The Lion, 1959; Belle de Jour, 1962; The Medici Fountain, 1963; They Weren't All Angels (short stories), 1965; The Horsemen, 1968. *Nonfiction*—Army of Shadows, 1944; Afghanistan, 1959; Mogok, the Valley of Rubies, 1960; The Man With the Miraculous Hands (England, The Magic Touch), 1961; The Road Back: A Report on Alcoholics Anonymous 1961 (England, The Enemy in the Mouth).

ABOUT: International Who's Who, 1973–74; Liebling, A. J. (ed.) Republic of Silence, 1947; Peyre, H. French Novelists of Today, 1967; Smith, H. (ed.) Columbia Dictionary of Modern European Literature, 1947; Who's Who in France, 1973–1974. *Periodicals*—Nation July 22, 1944; New Statesman January 6, 1945; New York Herald Tribune Book Review August 26, 1928; New York Times Book Review June 21, 1959; Revue des Deux Mondes October 15, 1938; February 1, 1941; Vogue August 1, 1959.

***KEYES, SIDNEY (ARTHUR KILWORTH)** (May 27, 1922–April 30?, 1943), English poet, was the son of Captain Reginald Keyes, a director of Daren Mills, the family flour business at Dartford,

* kēz

SIDNEY KEYES

Kent. His mother was Edith (Blackburn) Keyes, daughter of a Manchester clergyman and the second of Captain Keyes's three wives. She died of peritonitis a few weeks after her son's birth at Dartford, and Keyes was raised by his paternal grandfather, founder of Daren Mills, a powerful, brilliant, violent man who was the dominant figure in the boy's life. Keyes, a frail and precocious child, was educated at home for the first half of his life. He spent most of his time alone, devouring books about history and legend, and playing with an assorted collection of animals and reptiles—from the beginning living most fully in his own imagination.

When he was nine, Keyes went to live with his father and stepmother in Sussex, and for the first time attended school—Dartford Grammar School and later Tonbridge. Books and nature remained his principal interests and he was not good at games. Accepted as an oddity at Tonbridge, he became an "amiable" recluse and a good student, particularly in history. His gift for words was recognized by his form master, the poet Tom Staveley, and with this encouragement Keyes at sixteen produced his first considerable poem, the "Elegy" for his grandfather.

Just before the outbreak of World War II, Keyes visited France, and thereafter began to perceive a new dimension in things. As he wrote later: "Everything in a vague sort of way means something else, and I want desperately to find out *what*." In October 1940, he went with a history scholarship to Queen's College, Oxford. There he met and was greatly influenced by the poet John Heath-Stubbs, and became editor of *The Cherwell* (one of the many experiences he had in common with Keith Douglas, who had dominated the Oxford literary scene immediately before him). Keyes took little part in college activities, but founded his own theatrical group and produced his morality play "Hosea." At this time, according to his friend Michael Meyer, he was a rather sallow young man, with prominent nose and cheekbones, dark brown hair, and very striking hazel eyes. He was still "amiable, pensive, impenetrable" and, though no longer shy, sought few friends.

Keyes entered the army in April 1942. His first collection of poems, *The Iron Laurel*, was published in July of that year, and in September Keyes was commissioned in his father's old regiment, the Queen's Own Royal West Kent. In March 1943 he was sent to Tunisia, and on April 29 saw action for the first time, taking part in a successful attack on a hill near Sidi Abdullah. The next morning at dawn he went out on a reconnaissance patrol from which no survivors returned. His grave was found at Massicault two months later, but the circumstances of his death remain unknown. He was nearly twenty-one.

The Cruel Solstice, his second volume of poetry, was published posthumously in 1944 and, with *The Iron Laurel*, received the Hawthornden Prize. His *Collected Poems* appeared in 1945 in Britain and two years later in the United States. His prose—plays, stories, letters, journals—appeared in 1948 under the title *Minos of Crete*.

The poets Keyes admired above all others were Yeats and Rilke, and he has been accused of sharing the death wish he recognized in Rilke's work. Michael Meyer acknowledges Keyes's "sense of guilt and of evil destiny," his preoccupation with pain and mortality, but found in his life and work not a morbid desire for death but a fearful struggle with it, ending in an acceptance which was a kind of victory. "The red rock wilderness / Shall be my dwelling place"; Keyes saw that and was ready, believing that fear could not be healed in the gardens planted by "love's gardeners." In his generation, "all who would save their life must find the desert."

The collected poems were widely praised for their originality and "intellectual passion," and for many critics Keyes was "the war poet for whom England has been waiting." Others thought the strength and astonishing maturity of these poems diminished by a certain "literariness." Michael Meyer, introducing the collection, wrote: "In articulating the dumb courage of a generation, he breathed new life into many of the traditions of English poetry: the dramatic monologue, the landscape, the macabre and, especially, blank verse. Above all, he was the first truly English poet effectively to marry Continental symbolism to the English romantic tradition. . . . He fashioned symbolism into a precision instrument." He died when he "was ready to set out."

PRINCIPAL WORKS: The Iron Laurel, 1942; The Cruel Solstice, 1944; Collected Poems, 1945; Minos of Crete, 1948.

ABOUT: Currey, R. N. Poetry of the 1939–1945 War, 1960; Guenther, J. Sidney Keyes, 1967; Meyer, M. Memoir *in* Collected Poems, 1945; Read, H. *preface to* U.S. ed. of Collected Poems, 1947. *Periodicals*—Listener November 17, 1944; Time and Tide March 25, 1944.

***KHLEBNIKOV, "VELIMIR" (pen name of Viktor Vladimirovich Khlebnikov)** (October 28, 1885?–June 18, 1922?), Russian poet, was the founder and one of the major poets of Russian futurism. Born of well-to-do parents at Tundutovo, a village in the province of Astrakhan, he was christened Viktor Vladimirovich, but for his writing used the old pagan Slavic name of Velimir, an indication of his interest in Russian mythology. There is no agreement in published literature on the exact dates of his birth and death, though the year in each case is firmly established. He went to school in Simbirsk and studied mathematics at the University of Kazan. In 1908 he moved to Petersburg and changed to biology, then Sanskrit, then Slavic studies, while writing his first poems under the influence of the symbolists. From 1908 dozens of artistic circles and groups were springing up and issuing their manifestos and Khlebnikov, first with the Burliuk brothers and later with Mayakovsky and Kruchenykh, founded and led Russian futurism, which expressed the prevailing mood of liberation and revolt of the years before the Revolution.

His first three collections of verse, all published in 1914, were *Ryav!* (Roar), *Tvoreniya, 1906-1908* (Creations), and *Izbornik stikhov* (A Selection of Poems). However, most of his work at this time—poems, prose pieces, dramas, and essays—appeared in various futurist miscellanies, anthologies, and almanacs. In 1912 Khlebnikov, with Mayakovsky, Kruchenykh, and David Burliuk, issued the futurist manifesto *Poshchechina obshchestvennomu vkusu* (A Slap in the Face of Public Taste), with an aggressively antitraditionalist program: "The past suffocates us. The Academy and Pushkin are more incomprehensible than hieroglyphics. Throw Pushkin, Dostoevsky, Tolstoy, etc., overboard from the steamship of modernity." Though Khlebnikov had no taste for the polemics or public appearances of the futurists, he was full of projects for reforming practically every aspect of human life. In ideas and feelings his work is not really futuristic, for he disliked modern life and was far more interested in Slavic mythology and in Asian languages and folklore. He published pamphlets on his linguistic and historical theories, which postulated a prehistoric paradise of primitive innocence. He believed language had originally expressed everything directly and clearly, that "one savage understood another," but that the original purity was later lost in everyday use. If it could be recovered (by a process of scientific distillation), a universal language would be possible, people would understand one another, and wars would end.

* kleb′ nyi kəf

VELIMIR KHLEBNIKOV

These theories led to two futurist ideas, the "self-oriented word" and "trans-sense language." The first meant that the word was to be exalted above its meaning, freed from outworn associations in history, culture, and everyday life, as "The word *per se*. . . ." Thus the famous poem "Zaklyatie smekhom" (Incantation by Laughter), published in 1910, consists of a series of newly invented fanciful variations on the root *smekh* (laughter), which as Roman Jakobson observed is an act of verbal witchcraft working like a charm or spell. *Zaumny yazyk* ("trans-sense" or "transrational language") depended on the idea that the sound of a word is deeply related to its meaning, so that a new poetic language could be created which, free of its associative meanings, could express ideas and emotions directly through sound.

Though Khlebnikov's work gained a reputation for obscurity, it was based on a real knowledge of philology and of mythology, so that his experiments are full of meaning, rather than arbitrary, as with some other futurists. This is so even where he uses historical references as linguistic elements, as in the short untitled poem which begins "*Usad'ba nochyu. Chingizkhan!*" (Villa by night. Genghis Khan!). This is built up from three landscape elements (the villa, the darkness of the night, the sky) combined with the names of Genghis Khan, Zarathustra, and Mozart, here treated not as nouns but as verbal roots, producing a poetic metamorphosis which is quite untranslatable into a language such as English.

In 1916 Khlebnikov was suddenly drafted into the army as a private, a life which he hated and which rapidly made him a pacifist. He welcomed the 1917 Revolution, especially as it allowed him to leave the army, and though he never became a Communist he worked for the new régime, mainly in the Caucasus, and was sent for four months to Persia in 1921 as a lecturer at the headquarters of the Revolutionary Army. But he was a utopian mystic, without any real interest in practical politics.

Shortly before the war he had been seized by what his friends called a "hunger for space," and had begun to wander across Russia like a vagrant, his only possession a pillowcase filled with poetry, mathematical formulas, and projects for reforming the world. Even during the civil war he had continued to wander, and in Kharkov he was arrested by both sides. He had been living in great poverty, suffering from chronic malnutrition, but writing constantly; most of his work in this postwar period was written in a huge bookkeeping ledger, the *Grossbuch*. He broke off his medical treatment in the hope of publishing some of his work, and by November 1921 had arrived ill and exhausted in Moscow, but met with little success. In 1922 poverty and starvation led to paralysis, and he died in agony in Korostets, a village near Novgorod. A highly impractical person, absent-minded, shy, and stammering, often losing his poems, Khlebnikov when he died had published only a small fraction of his large output.

Vladimir Markov argues in *The Longer Poems of Velimir Khlebnikov* that "Khlebnikov's overpublicized short experimental poems should probably be de-emphasized for the sake of balance in the study of his work." Besides the poetry this does in fact include prose tales, dramatic works, and a genre of Khlebnikov's own invention, the "supertale," which he probably considered the ultimate vehicle for his experimentation. This consists of pieces written at different times, often belonging to different genres, brought together into a larger whole, which may be a cycle of short poems or a mixture of poetry, prose, and dramatic fragments, like the last and most successful of them, *Zangezi*, which was produced on the stage by the painter Tatlin in 1923. Not all of Khlebnikov's short poems are experimental or difficult. His later work in particular includes some exquisite brief lyrics, wonderfully exact in diction and subtle in rhythm. His technical mastery is evident in all his verse, which includes for example one four-hundred-line poem in which every line is a palindrome.

Before Markov's study the long poems had tended to be neglected, but there are more than thirty of them covering a great variety of themes. The earlier ones are often primitivistic—sometimes savage as in *Gibel Atlantidy* (The End of Atlantis), which ends with an eschatological vision of a flood; sometimes idyllic, as in *Vila i Leshii* (The Nymph and the Wood Goblin), a sort of Slavic *L'Après midi d'un faune* with a coquettish nymph teasing a lazy old wood goblin on a hot day. Some of the late poems link the Revolution with the theme of retribution, as in the tragic *Nochnoi obysk* (A Night Search). But one of the finest of all the long poems is *Truba gul-mully* (Gul-mullah's Trumpet), a sort of poetic diary of Khlebnikov's visit to Persia, which had been the climax of his lifelong passion for the Orient.

The futurists always regarded him as a genius, but he was admired even by poets of very different tastes, such as Nikolai Gumilev. His reputation and influence were at their height in Russia during the 1920s, when much of his work was published after his death in the periodical *LEF*, but he was later attacked by the orthodox Marxists, though his reputation revived in the 1950s. Markov considers him "the greatest futurist poet of Russia and perhaps one of only two or three of the greatest avant-garde poets of the world."

PRINCIPAL WORKS IN ENGLISH TRANSLATION: *Poems in* Bowra, C. M. A Second Book of Russian Verse, 1948; Kaun, A. Soviet Poets and Poetry, 1943; Lindsay, J. Russian Poetry, 1917–1955, 1957; Markov, V. and Sparks, M. Modern Russian Poetry, 1966; Obolensky, D. (ed.) Penguin Book of Russian Verse, 1962; Reavey, G. and Slonim, M. Soviet Literature, 1934; Yarmolinsky, A. A Treasury of Russian Verse, 1949; Color and Rhyme (Hampton Bays, New York) 31, 1956; Hip Pocket Poems (Hanover, New Hampshire) 2, 1960; 4, 1961.

ABOUT: Markov, V. The Longer Poems of Velimir Khlebnikov, 1962; Markov, V. Russian Futurism, 1968; Penguin Companion to Literature 2, 1969; Poggioli, R. The Poets of Russia, 1890–1930, 1960; Slonim, M. Modern Russian Literature, 1953; Smith, H. (ed.) Columbia Dictionary of Modern European Literature, 1947; Zavalishin, V. Early Soviet Writers, 1958. *Periodicals*—Color and Rhyme 26, 1952; Russian Review October 1960; Slavic and East European Journal Spring 1958.

***KHODASEVICH, VLADISLAV (FELITSIANOVICH)** (May 29, 1886–June 14, 1939), Russian poet and critic, was born in Moscow. His father was from a family of Polish origin and his mother was Jewish. The youngest of six children, he was educated in a classical Gymnasium in Moscow and then entered Moscow University, though he did not complete his course.

He had begun to publish his poems when he was nineteen, and his first book, *Molodost* (Youth), came out in 1908. It belongs to the then almost exhausted symbolist tradition of Bely and Bryusov, as does

* kə das ye′ vich

his second book, *Schastlivy domik* (The Happy Cottage, 1914), which reflects his visit to Italy and his love for Zhenia Muratova. His major and more characteristic poetry, however, was written after the 1917 Revolution. In his third book, *Putem zerna* (The Grain's Way, 1920) and his fourth, *Tyazhelaya lira* (The Heavy Lyre, 1922), universally regarded as his best work, his poetry had become altogether more exact and prosaic—neoclassical in the manner of his master Pushkin, though unmistakably modern in its imagery and cast of thought.

Khodasevich's inspiration was metaphysical, but he learned to express it in a manner that was concrete, controlled, and ironical—one reflection of his fundamental dualism. His central concern was the tragic (and ludicrous) paradox that man's aspiring and immortal soul is trapped in a gross and transient body. Nina Berberova says, "He dreamt, as Blok had done, of finding the thread that holds all things together and, by a single pull at it, of transforming the whole cosmic order once and for all, so that in a flash the ultimate reality . . . might be revealed." And yet a similar impulse attracted him to evil, destruction, and disaster—to the notion of a "beloved storm" as another shortcut to a reality beyond the doubts and compromises of ordinary living.

Recognizing the opposing but real claims of spirit and matter, freedom and necessity, good and evil, the cosmic and the domestic, Khodasevich takes up his "heavy lyre" to reconcile them, if he can, through a poetry of irony, pathos, and condensed paradoxical imagery. Thus he speaks of the process of living as "breathing the space of time," defines hope as "a sweet memory of the future." The image of the heavy lyre occurs in one of his greatest poems, "Ballada" (Ballad), in which he writes of his own creative process. He sits in his room, contemplating "a sixteen-watt sun in a stucco sky," and musing on the stagnancy and barrenness of his life. Gradually the incantatory rhythm of his poem becomes both the vehicle and the subject of his vision: "And the room and the furniture slowly, / slowly start in a circle to sail, / and a great heavy lyre is from nowhere / handed me by a ghost through the gale." (Translated by V. Nabokov.)

In June 1922 Khodasevich left Russia with the young writer Nina Berberova, whom he had met the year before; according to her account, "if we had not met and not taken the decision then to 'be together' and 'survive,' he undoubtedly would have remained in Russia." *Tyazhelaya lira*, containing the poems which he wrote during his last two years in Russia, was published in Berlin shortly after their arrival there. For a time he worked with Gorky and Bely on the magazine *Beseda* (Table Talk, or The Colloquy) but, unable to make a

VLADISLAV KHODASEVICH

living in Berlin, he and Berberova left in November 1923, making their way through Prague and Italy to Paris, which they reached in 1924 and where Khodasevich was to live for the rest of his life.

When Khodasevich left Russia he was at the height of his poetic creativity, and for a few years he continued to write poetry. These poems written in exile make up the small collection *Evropeyskaya noch* (European Night, 1927) which was included along with his earlier verse in the volume *Sobraniye stikhov* (Collected Poems, 1927). This was his last book of poetry, and during the remaining twelve years of his life he wrote only some fifteen poems. Various explanations have been offered for this creative sterility. Vladimir Markov attributed it to "growing despair at the inability of poetry to change the state of things." Nina Berberova said that "earlier than many others, he saw the night descending on Europe. Horrified by what he had seen, he fell silent." His marital difficulties can hardly have helped, for by 1932 Berberova had finally left him. In 1934 he married Olga Borisovna Margolina, daughter of a wealthy Leningrad jeweler.

Khodasevich had published a small critical collection, *Stat'i o russkoy poezii* (Articles on Russian Poetry), in 1922, and during the 1930s he emerged as one of the most prominent *émigré* critics. His articles in the Paris daily *Vozrozhdenia* (Renaissance) were studies in depth of literature and its relation to philosophical, historical, and political problems; many of them were collected in the posthumous *Literaturniye stat'i i vospominaniya* (Literary Essays and Memoirs, 1954). One of his earliest critical books was the brilliant essay *Poeticheskoe khozyaystvo Pushkina* (Puskhin's Poetic Economy, 1929), and he had always dreamed of writing a full-scale biography of Pushkin, though he managed to complete only some literary-historical articles, including those collected in *O Pushkine* (About Pushkin, 1937). *Derzhavin* (1931) is an outstanding study of another poet in the classical tradition (and a remarkable man, who began his career as a private in the guards and ended it as Minister of Justice). Khodasevich also wrote an unfinished autobiographical sketch, *Mladenchestvo* (Infancy), which has appeared in America in *Vozdushniye puti*, Issue 4. A few months before his death he published his last important prose work, *Nekropol* (Necropolis, 1939), a book of highly subjective reminiscences about writers such as Gorky, Blok, Bryusov, and Sologub. He was thin and weak physically, in precarious health all his life; in January 1939 he became severely ill, and he died five months later, probably of cancer, the day after an unsuccessful operation in a Paris hospital.

It has become customary to regard Khodasevich as one of the three major poets of the Russian emigration, along with Georgy Ivanov and Marina Tsvetaeva, though unlike them he wrote relatively little after leaving Russia. But ever since Bely acclaimed his work in the early 1920s he has been recognized as one of the major Russian poets of the century. In 1963, forty years after his emigration, his rehabilitation in the Soviet Union began with the appearance of a selection of his poems in *Moskva*. As Poggioli pointed out, his poetry is not easy to classify: "Khodasevich began his career at the apogee, or rather at the early decline, of the symbolist movement; and while taking its achievements for granted, he felt rather detached toward its aesthetic creed. Formally and chronologically, his poetic ideal is more obviously related to that of the followers of both acmeism and clarism; yet, despite this connection, his imaginative and moral world greatly differs from Kuzmin's, Gumilev's or Akhmatova's." He had a violent aversion to futurism, and associated the "cancer" of avant-garde literature with political revolution, basing his own poetry consciously on the style of Pushkin; and yet, as Markov says, "the miracle was that he managed to create great and original poetry in this way, and poetry whose mystical content is even more poignantly apparent because of a strict classical form."

PRINCIPAL WORKS IN ENGLISH TRANSLATION: *Poems in* Bowra, C. M. (ed.) Book of Russian Verse, 1943; Bowra, C. M. (ed.) Second Book of Russian Verse, 1948; Markov, V. and Sparks, M. Modern Russian Poetry, 1966; Obolensky, D. The Penguin Book of Russian Verse, 1962; Yarmolinsky, A. (ed.) A Treasury of Russian Verse, 1949; Tri Quarterly Spring 1973.

ABOUT: Berberova, N. The Italics Are Mine: Memiors of the Russian Literary Emigration, 1949; Mirsky, D. S. Contemporary Russian Literature 1881–1925, 1926; Poggioli, R. The Poets of Russia, 1890–1930, 1960; Slonim, M. Modern Russian Literature from Chekhov to the Present, 1953. *Periodicals*—Harvard Slavonic Studies 1, 1953–54; Russian Review April 1952; Tri Quarterly Spring 1973.

KIELY, BENEDICT (August 15, 1919–), Irish novelist, short story writer, critic, historian, and journalist, writes: "County Tyrone is one of the six Irish Counties still coloured red on the map and still part of the United Kingdom, and in the west of that county, a few miles from a little village called Dromore, I was born in 1919. In the following year three young men were murdered at a crossroads near the house, in a gruesome politico-sectarian affair long remembered as the Dromore murders. For years I was foolishly optimistic enough to think that such unhappy things belonged only to the past, that stagnation in government might yield to civilisation, not collapse into horror —as it has done.

"I was reared and began my education, with the Christian Brothers, in the county town, Omagh, about ten miles from Dromore. That was a British Army garrison town, the Royal Inniskillings and the Royal Irish, where the day was punctuated by bugle calls from the barracks and where the pipes at regular intervals played the young Irishmen away to do their stint in the Indian army. Even yet when I hear the music, brass and pipes, of those regiments on a disc I feel an excitement and a melancholy; and our household was made more interesting to me because my father had been with the Leinster Regiment in South Africa and had his medals to prove it, and was also a fixed and firm Irish Republican. There are, have been and will be many Irish households of that pattern.

"The bands played the men off to India, the local farmers crowded the town once a week, two rivers met in a green valley and went on north to Londonderry and the sea, there were low brown-and-purple mountains close at hand, and the Atlantic and the Donegal Gaeltacht and the Yeats country and Ben Bulben weren't more than forty miles away. Boyhood and youth passed in that place in the usual way. A fine teacher, a man called Curry from the County Clare taught me that a taste for books and an alarming facility in writing school essays could be not ends in themselves but the beginning of a whole way of life.

"Then followed a while in a Jesuit novitiate in the soft Irish midlands—almost everybody everywhere takes a religious fit once in a while—and then eighteen months in hospital with, as they say, a spine.

"The Jesuits, to whom I forever raise my hat with respect, had nothing to do with that. It was the result of an old injury in a rugby match at school. But it did give me the opportunity for a lot of useful pre-college reading. I can imagine nothing more pleasant, if you have to lie abed, than to lie abed on a sun balcony within sight of the Dublin mountains and to read books and be surrounded by Irish nurses. The nearest I ever came to that again was to spend a year as Writer-in-Residence at Hollins College, Virginia, and to live on campus like Solomon in all his glory with one thousand American belles.

"After hospital came Dublin and college and work for a good many years on the literary side—if there be one—of newspapers. Although I write these words a long six thousand miles away and within sight of the snow on the Oregon Cascades, Dublin is the person who follows me wherever I go: the gracious gossipy old streets, the pubs, the perpetual talk, the soft air, the friends. Dublin meant history in rich layers, and St. Stephen's Green and the shades of Newman and Hopkins, and University College and the valuable advice of Roger McHugh and the friendship of such men as the novelists the late Francis MacManus and Francis Stuart and the late Brinsley MacNamara and students protesting when one obscurantist newspaper ignored the death of Joyce. It meant the company of newspaper men who are always so much more intelligent than the managerial bosses they work for. It meant the Abbey Theatre with remembered glimpses of Yeats, calm and lofty as Mount Shasta but inwardly raging against old age, before he went to France to die; and in the office of a magazine run by a famous Capuchin friar, awestruck meetings with Jack B. Yeats, Maud Gonne 'the woman Homer sung,' and John Count McCormack.

"Dublin, too, was the way to every other corner of Ireland, and to London and Paris and the Rhine, and the vast spaces of the U.S.A. Out of all which came some novels and stories and a few other books."

———

Benedict Kiely is the son of Thomas and Sara (Gormley) Kiely. Before his first birthday, the windows of their house near Dromore were blown out in a mail train raid by the Irish Republican Army, and Kiely's consciousness of Ireland's "spiritual partition" echoes in all his writing. At University College, Dublin, he read English and history. After his graduation he began his journalistic career on the *Standard*, a Dublin weekly, writing film and theatre criticism and editorials, and then for fourteen years was literary editor of the *Irish Press*. During this period he lectured at University College and Trinity College, and on radio, and began to sell the articles, stories, and books which have brought him an international reputation.

BENEDICT KIELY

His first book was *Counties of Contention*, a historical exploration of "the origins and implications of the partition of Ireland" published in Cork. *Poor Scholar* (1947) fulfilled a childhood determination to provide a study of the life and writings of the nineteenth century Tyrone novelist William Carleton. It was thought a rather unselective and excessively detailed work, but one that does evoke "the political and social background to [Carleton's] stories . . . the grim contrasts of wealth and squalor, starvation, poetry and revolution."

Kiely's novels began to appear at about the same time. *In a Harbour Green*, one of the first of them, was called a "well-written and well-mannered" story of life in a small Irish town, marred principally, one reviewer thought, by a tendency "to succumb to that sad, subdued manner, midway between whimsy and whining, to which so many Irish writers are prone." A much more swiftly paced novel with a similar setting, *Honey Seems Bitter*, was generally enjoyed but seemed to some readers a little sordid and "self-consciously earthy." *There Was an Ancient House* draws on Kiely's days as a Jesuit novice to examine the impact of the religious life on young minds.

Reviewers have noted a steady development in Kiely's work, and they particularly admired *The Captain With the Whiskers*, the story of an Ulster patriot and domestic tyrant. One critic called it a more complex and skillful treatment of the theme of *Honey Seems Bitter*—"the conflicts of sexual and romantic love and the special disabilities which both endure in Ireland," while another suggested that Captain Chesney's distorting love-hate relationship with his children symbolized Ireland's influence on its people. There was general praise for Kiely's ability to bind together comedy and tragedy in the same "haunting and remarkable novel," and for his "wonderfully conceived minor characters." A reviewer in the *Times Literary Supplement* said that Kiely "has a way of writing which, with its lyrical originality and fanciful realism, has an immediate appeal. Poetic sensuality and commonplace idiom do not, however, damage the precision of character or feeling."

Kiely's short stories, many of which first appeared in the *New Yorker*, were collected in *A Journey to the Seven Streams* and *A Ball of Malt*, and are rich in his memories of childhood and of wartime Dublin. His critical work includes some perceptive studies of contemporary Irish writers, among them an outstanding interpretation of the work of Liam O'Flaherty. Kiely says that among contemporary writers he admires in particular Joyce, Graham Greene, and Saroyan, but that Yeats is his principal source of influence, "as he should be for any Irishman." At the same time, Kiely's work shows a "detachment from the regularized pieties of Irish life" which makes it difficult to regard him as merely a regional writer.

The author was married to Maureen O'Connel in 1944 and has two sons and two daughters. In 1964–1965 he was writer in residence at Hollins College in Virginia, in 1965–1966 he taught as a visiting professor at the University of Oregon, and in 1966–1968 he was writer-in-residence at Emory University in Georgia. He has now returned to Ireland and is a visiting lecturer at University College, Dublin. He is a council member of the Irish Academy of Letters and a member of the academic committee of the American-Irish Foundation. He says that he enjoys "travel, trout fishing, studying rivers, Jameson ten-year-old whiskey, talking to a few friends in a few Dublin pubs, and singing, roaring and/or collecting ballads."

PRINCIPAL WORKS: *Fiction*—Land Without Stars, 1946; In a Harbour Green, 1949; Call for a Miracle, 1950; Honey Seems Bitter, 1952; The Cards of the Gambler: A Folktale, 1953; There Was an Ancient House, 1955; The Captain With the Whiskers, 1960; A Journey to the Seven Streams (stories), 1963; Dogs Enjoy the Morning, 1968; A Ball of Malt and Madame Butterfly (stories), 1973. *Nonfiction*—Counties of Contention: A Study of the Origins and Implications of the Partition of Ireland, 1945; Poor Scholar: A Study of the Works and Days of William Carleton, 1794–1869, 1947; Modern Irish Fiction, 1950.

ABOUT: Contemporary Authors 1–4 (first revision), 1967; Hoehn, M. (ed.) Catholic Authors, 1952; Vinson, J. (ed.) Contemporary Novelists, 1972.

***KIMBROUGH, EMILY** (October 23, 1899–), American memoirist, travel writer, and journalist, writes: "I was born in Muncie, Indiana. My family moved to Chicago when I was eleven. The school to which I had gone until our move was made up of the children of a group of friends; the total enrollment was fourteen. Our teacher was a family friend; our schoolhouse a converted children's playhouse. Since we covered a considerable range in age we could not be taught as a unit. Therefore, each child, finishing an assignment, could work outside in good weather in his garden. In Chicago I was enrolled at the Faulkner School for Girls. On the first day, finishing an arithmetic assignment, I left the classroom and the building. There was no garden and a very limited space to explore so I investigated the neighborhood. I came back to find Miss Faulkner, my mother and a policeman at the gate. This was my first awareness of a difference between small towns and cities. My second was when I heard my mother tell a salesgirl at Marshall Field's our name and where we lived. In Muncie people knew one another. I have never outgrown my awareness of these differences and my roots are deep in Indiana soil.

* kim' brō

"I went to boarding school at Miss Wright's in Bryn Mawr, Pennsylvania, and from there to Bryn Mawr College, graduating in 1921.

"The following year I had a job in a bookshop and loved it. The next year I went abroad with Cornelia Otis Skinner. (We wrote a book about this in 1942.)

"Returning to Chicago I was hired by Marshall Field and Company by means of false pretenses on my part. Learning that I had just returned from a long stay in Paris (by implication I lengthened the stay to years), the advertising manager had asked if I knew the major French dressmaking houses. Intimately, I had said. (My friend and I had gone to every sale, fought for every bargain on the racks, and worsted many a fashionable and regular customer.) Therefore, I became editor of the Marshall Field publication, *Fashions of the Hour*.

"Three years later I was living again in Bryn Mawr, Pennsylvania, and working at the Curtis Publishing Company, where I was Fashion Editor of the *Ladies' Home Journal*. In 1926 I was married and in 1927 became managing editor of the *Ladies' Home Journal*. On September 2nd, Labor Day, in 1929 I produced twin daughters. I resigned from the *Ladies' Home Journal* and shortly after I began to write. The incentive was strong though not lofty. Without having to be away from home, I was steadfast in purpose to earn enough to pay someone to wash sixty or so diapers a day, squeeze beef tea, orange juice, strain spinach *et al.*, make the formula and administer the resultant bottles. The incentive was so strong it has carried me on through the years. Looking at my daughters and their seven children, I have never regretted my choice of occupation.

"My form of writing is autobiographical. This is partly because I have not the ability nor imagination to build a plot, and partly, I think, because I share the urgency of the Ancient Mariner to tell someone what happened to me. Nothing of importance to others has happened to me; I have not lived adventurously; but I am provoked by trivia to tell about them. My memory is more vividly stirred by, and I am more susceptible to sounds than to sights. Therefore, I talk the first draft of what I am writing to a dictaphone. In order to shape the phrases, choose the words, I must say them aloud.

"I live in New York in the winter, but go on a lecture tour in the fall and early spring. I enjoy these tours. By way of them I have seen most of this country many times. I like meeting people and I love an audience. As often as I can afford it, I spend the summer in Greece."

Emily Kimbrough is the daughter of Hal Curry and Charlotte Emily (Wiles) Kimbrough. The book she wrote with Cornelia Otis Skinner about their 1922 trip to England and France was, of course, *Our Hearts Were Young and Gay*. Amy Loveman, who called it a book "compact of little nothings, made electric by the irresistible delight of youth in life and adventure," defied "anyone to read it without laughter or recall it without a smile." It was a best seller and brought its authors an invitation to Hollywood, where they worked on the screen version of the book (though their contribution to the final scenario was minimal). Miss Kimbrough's first solo book was an account of this adventure called *We Followed Our Hearts to Hollywood*. The third and last of her "Heart" books was *How Dear to My Heart*, about her childhood in Indiana. Reviewers described it variously as "mildly entertaining" and as "a period piece . . . which is going to be dear to a lot of hearts beside the author's."

Her subsequent books have been light and amusing reminiscences, many of them illustrated by Helen Hokinson. They have been about life on the lecture circuit (*It Gives Me Great Pleasure*); about Chicago (*The Innocents from Indiana*); about her years at Marshall Field's (*Through Charley's Door*); and about her travels, usually with friends, in Europe. None of her books has quite matched *Our Hearts Were Young and Gay* in popularity, but Miss Kimbrough, as she says, "attracts incident as serge attracts lint," and her unfailing good humor on this score has gained her a loyal following and a generally good press. As Anne Ross wrote of *Pleasure by the Busload*, about a holiday in Portugal, she "has a delicate skill in extracting the humorous and personal elements from such a safari. As always, most of the humor is at the expense of herself and her companions, while her attitude toward a foreign and often strange country is one of pleasant interest and sympathy." Nor are her travelogues merely entertainments; they contain much solid information of value to prospective travelers.

EMILY KIMBROUGH

Sterling North once accused Emily Kimbrough of snobbery; Cornelia Otis Skinner, who knows her better, says that she is on the contrary "that rare creature: a woman who is brilliantly witty and at the same time amazingly kind. She loves people and has the priceless gift of bringing out unsuspected qualities of humor and gaiety in the most drab individual."

PRINCIPAL WORKS: (with Cornelia Otis Skinner) Our Hearts Were Young and Gay, 1942; We Followed Our Hearts to Hollywood, 1943; How Dear to My Heart, 1944; It Gives Me Great Pleasure, 1948; The Innocents From Indiana, 1950 (England, Hand in Hand); Through Charley's Door, 1952; Forty Plus and Fancy Free, 1954; So Near and Yet So Far, 1955; Water, Water Everywhere, 1956; And a Right Good Crew, 1958 (England, Right Good Crew); Pleasure by the Busload, 1961; Forever Old, Forever New, 1964; Floating Island, 1968; Now and Then, 1972.

ABOUT: Current Biography, 1944; Who's Who in America, 1970–1971. *Periodicals*—New York Herald Tribune Book Review February 24, 1952.

KING, FRANCIS (HENRY) (March 4, 1923–), British novelist, short story writer, poet, and critic, writes: "I was born in Adelboden, Switzerland, and divided the first nine years of my life between that country—the home of my German grandmother—and India, where my father worked as a government official. I visited England for the first time when my parents sent me there to go to preparatory school. I was profoundly unhappy to exchange the permissive indulgence of life with

FRANCIS KING

my family for the discipline and austerity of life with strangers, and the darkness of that period may perhaps account for a hidden but ever-present strain of melancholy and pessimism in my character. The events of these years are described in my semi-autobiographical novel *Never Again*.

"At the age of fourteen I went to Shrewsbury School, to which I had won a scholarship in Classics. In spite of the advent of the war, the four years which followed were far happier for me. What time I did not spend on the study of Latin and Greek I devoted to helping to edit the school magazine and to writing poetry. Another scholarship in Classics took me to Balliol College, Oxford, where I started to write my first novel, *To the Dark Tower*. After two terms I had to leave Oxford, in order, as a conscientious objector, to do my national service on the land. The next five years of isolation on farms first in Essex and then in Surrey were formative for me as a writer. I have never read so much since, and have never again written so much in such a short space of time. I finished *To the Dark Tower* and produced two other novels, as well as writing reviews and a number of what I regard as my best poems.

"I returned to Oxford to take a degree in English language and literature and then began a fifteen-year period of nomadic life as a British Council officer in a variety of countries abroad: Italy, Greece, Egypt, Finland and Japan. Italy provided the setting for my novel *The Dividing Stream*, winner of the Somerset Maugham Award for 1953; Greece for three novels; Japan for a novel and a collection of short-stories, one of which, 'A Corner of a Foreign Field,' gained the Katherine Mansfield Memorial Prize, 1965. At first this life of perpetually moving from country to country stimulated my imagination and satisfied my craving, thwarted through my years on the land, for novelty, adventure and the exotic. But my work for the British Council became more and more exacting as I moved up in its hierarchy; until the strain of combining this full-time career with my other career as a writer proved so arduous that I decided to resign.

"I now live in Brighton, in a small Regency house: eking out my earnings as a writer by advising publishers, reviewing and broadcasting. Though financially less well-placed, I have never regretted leaving the British Council, even though I shall always be grateful to it for the opportunities it provided for travel, odd experiences and interesting encounters.

"As a novelist, I try to make each of my books as different as possible from its predecessors. This sometimes disconcerts and even exasperates both critics and readers, for whom familiarity tends to breed admiration. Since I am outwardly a cheerful and ebullient character, people who know me often declare that they are surprised by the savage, tragic or bitter tone of much of what I write. But my attitude to life is basically one of stoical despair. Change, I have learned, is usually change for the worse; and it is perhaps this conviction that over the years has made me inch towards the extreme right. I am a believer in liberty, but not in the equality for which liberty is the usual price."

Francis King is a cool and scrupulous writer, "deftly and quietly unblurring the secrets of unspectacular spirits." His characters, generally unsympathetic, are nevertheless "interesting, individual, and sharply alive." Most of his novels have shown a keen sense of place. *The Dividing Stream* perceptively studied the interaction of tourists and natives in postwar Florence. In *Man on the Rock* and *The Dark Glasses* King, it was suggested, used Greece as Lawrence Durrell uses Alexandria, to define the sensuality of his characters, "their moral breakdown, their gradual dissolution." Japan played a similar role in *The Custom House*, an unconventionally and (some thought) clumsily constructed novel in which a brutal murder is studied from the viewpoints of a number of different characters. *The Last of the Pleasure Gardens*, placed in England, was a painful book about the birth into a happy family of a child who is hopelessly retarded. *A Domestic Animal*, another novel with an English setting, describes the hopeless homosexual passion of a middle-aged novelist for a married Italian—"a strange romance which manages to be truthful about love and the ravages of jealousy too."

At Oxford King belonged to the set which included the poets Sidney Keyes, John Heath-Stubbs, and Drummond Allison. His own poetry is intensely personal in content, traditional in manner. He nowadays publishes very little in this form, although it was as a poet that he first attracted attention—as a protégé during the 1940s of Tambimuttu (editor of *Poetry*, London) and of J. R. Ackerley (literary editor of the *Listener*). King attaches great importance to his wartime years on the land and says that "never again has my life, increasingly troubled by the anguish and tribulations of personal relationships, achieved the same lucid, if glacial, calm." He calls himself "naturally domineering, a disciplinarian and a stickler for punctuality and efficiency," but still "a person of extreme sociability." King contributes critical articles to *Encounter*, *Cornhill*, and the *London Magazine*, reviews novels regularly for the *Sunday Telegraph*, and sometimes broadcasts on literary subjects. His nonliterary interests include oriental art and modern painting. In 1966 he received an Arts Council bursary of one thousand two hundred pounds.

PRINCIPAL WORKS: To the Dark Tower (novel), 1946; Never Again (novel), 1948; An Air That Kills (novel), 1948; The Dividing Stream (novel), 1951; The Rod of Incantation (poems), 1952; The Dark Glasses (novel), 1954; (as "Frank Cauldwell") The Firewalkers (novel), 1956; (as ed.) Introducing Greece, 1956; The Widow (novel), 1957; The Man on the Rock (novel), 1958; So Hurt and Humiliated (stories) 1959; The Custom House (novel), 1961; The Japanese Umbrella (stories), 1964; The Last of the Pleasure Gardens (novel), 1965; The Waves Behind the Boat (novel), 1967; The Brighton Belle (stories), 1968; A Domestic Animal (novel), 1970; (with Martin Hürlimann) Japan, 1970; Flights (two short novels), 1973.

ABOUT: Contemporary Authors 2, 1963; Karl, F. R. A Reader's Guide to the Contemporary English Novel, 1962; Murphy, R. (ed.) Contemporary Poets of the English Language, 1970; Vinson, J. (ed.) Contemporary Novelists, 1972; West, P. The Modern Novel, 1963; Who's Who, 1973. *Periodicals*—London Magazine July 1965.

***KINNELL, GALWAY** (February 1, 1927–), American poet, novelist, and translator, was born in Providence and raised in Pawtucket, Rhode Island. He is the son of James and Elizabeth (Mills) Kinnell. Kinnell served at the end of the war (1945–1946) in the United States Navy as a seaman first class, and then continued his interrupted education at Princeton, which gave him his B.A. in 1948, and at the University of Rochester, where he received his M.A. a year later. He taught for a while and in 1955 went to Paris to begin his translation of the poetry of François Villon, staying on in France for another year as a lecturer at the University of Grenoble.

As a traveler and a translator, Kinnell has been exposed to a wider range of influences than most

* kə nel′

GALWAY KINNELL

American poets, but so far seems to have responded most to Yeats (in his use of image and symbol) and to Whitman, with whom, it is said, he shares "an intense social consciousness and a 'oneness with all things.' " Kinnell himself has said that "in Whitman ordinary and average things are seen in a sacred light. He was the really democratic poet, who, standing among the streets, finds the sacred exists there."

The most obviously Whitmanesque poem in *What a Kingdom It Was*, Kinnell's first book, was also the poem which critics singled out for special praise. It is a long piece—four hundred and fifty lines—in which Kinnell is concerned to "find the sacred" in the ordinary lives of the average people he sees on Avenue C in New York City: "The Avenue Bearing the Initial of Christ Into the New World." S. J. Rowland called it a "loosely knit and beautifully lyrical poem" which "repeatedly transforms the rubble and slums" he writes about. Selden Rodman thought it "the freshest, most exciting, and by far most readable poem of a bleak decade."

Indeed the whole collection, as exuberantly lyrical as its title, delighted the reviewers, who, acknowledging its occasional lack of subtlety and tautness, praised its energy, its "pictorial vividness," its direct, colloquial language and general willingness to take risks. John Logan called it "the best first book of poems since James Wright's *The Greenwall* and . . . one of the finest books of the past decade." James Dickey, more cautious, welcomed it for its promise and wrote: "Kinnell's development will depend on the actual events of his life. And it is a life that I think we should watch. It is warm, generous, reflective, and friendly."

While Kinnell's book was giving such pleasure in New York, the "actual events of his life" had brought the author to Iran, where in 1960 he taught at the University of Teheran. The journey there and back took him around the world. Early in 1960, in Calcutta, he met the Indian poet Dom Moraes, who describes him as "big and powerful with a square jaw, features that seemed hewed from some pale grainy wood, and unchanging blue eyes." After another stay in France, Kinnell returned to the United States in 1962. The following summer he spent in Louisiana, working with the Congress on Racial Equality to register black voters.

Kinnell's second book appeared in 1964 and was called *Flower Herding on Mount Monadnock*. It was said to lack the concreteness and immediacy of the first collection, to be more abstract, meditative, and philosophical, but also "more various and exploratory." The poems in *Body Rags*, which followed, are darker than in Kinnell's earlier books, more preoccupied with death, violence, alienation, "the skull beneath the skin." Michael Goldman thought that the collection added to Kinnell's "growing reputation as a superior lyric poet," and that the most impressive thing about these poems "is the distance they travel inward from beginning to end. Sometimes there are vaguenesses or rhetorical flourishes . . . but the poems move deeper line by line . . . We are kept in an easy commerce with the outer world—until we discover that the inner world has spoken."

The Book of Nightmares is Kinnell's most ambitious work. It is a sequence of ten poems, each in seven sections, in which the speaker evokes in deeply ambiguous terms such events and obsessions as the birth of his children, his identification with a drunk found dead in a hotel room, the violence done by Christian man to himself and to others. These and other motifs—some grim, some tender—are subtly interwoven with each other and with an extremely complex structure of zodiacal, occult, and religious symbolism: "in March, of the year Seventy, / on my sixteen-thousandth night of war and madness, / in the hotel of Lost Light, under the freeway / which roams out into the dark / of the moon, in the absolute spell / of departure, and by the light / from the joined hemispheres of the spider's eyes." M. L. Rosenthal praised unreservedly the sequence's "moments of concrete realization, when the language exults and transfigures literal reality," but was more dubious about the "projection of some unclarified personal complex of sufferings onto the same materials," and about the "overloaded" symbolic structure. All the same, Rosenthal concluded, the sequence seems to progress, however uncertainly, from despair to affirmation; it "grapples mightily with its depressive view of reality and with essential issues of love, and it leaves us with something splendid: a true voice, a true song, memorably human."

Kinnell has also written short stories and a novel. The latter, set in Iran, is called *Black Light* and tells the ambiguous story of a quiet and simple man who one day suddenly commits a murder and, released from the morality by which he has lived, embarks upon a bizarre and perilous voyage of self-discovery. The book was praised for its austere, condensed, and persuasive style, and reminded one critic at times of Camus's *L'Étranger*. Kinnell's translation of Yves Bonnefoy's great poem *On the Motion and Immobility of Douve* won the Cecil Hemley Award in 1967. He has also received a Longview Foundation Award (1962), an award from the National Institute of Arts and Letters (1962), a Guggenheim Fellowship (1962–1963), a Rockefeller grant (1967–1968), a Brandeis University Creative Arts Award (1969), an Amy Lowell traveling scholarship (1969–1970), and the Shelley Memorial Award (1972). He was poet in residence at the University of California at Irvine in 1968–1969. He is married to Inés Delgado de Torres and has two children.

PRINCIPAL WORKS: *Poetry*—What a Kingdom It Was, 1960; Flower Herding on Mount Monadnock, 1964; Body Rags, 1968; Poems of Night (selected poems, published in England only), 1968; First Poems: 1946–1954, 1970; The Book of Nightmares, 1971. *Novel*—Black Light, 1966. *As translator*—The Poems of François Villon, 1964; Bonnefoy, Y. On the Motion and Immobility of Douve, 1968; Goll, Y. The Lackawanna Elegy (poems), 1970.

ABOUT: Cambon, G. Recent American Poetry, 1962; Contemporary Authors 11–12, 1965; Murphy, R. (ed.) Contemporary Poets of the English Language, 1970; Who's Who in America, 1972–1973. *Periodicals*—Beloit Poetry Journal, Chapbook No. 2, 1953; Princeton University Library Chronicle Autumn 1963.

***KINSELLA, THOMAS** (May 4, 1928–), Irish poet, writes: "I was born in Dublin and lived there until 1965. I was educated in a local National School and later by the Christian Brothers in St. Canice's and O'Connell Schools, Dublin. I attended University College Dublin for a time; abandoned a science scholarship in 1946 to enter the Irish Civil Service and obtained the Diploma in Public Administration in 1949; took evening lectures with a view to an Arts degree, but resigned in 1951. To my schooling with the Christian Brothers I owe my early preparation for the squalid brutalities of the world; certain experiences in UCD gave me my first encounter with those brutalities. I was lucky under both auspices, however, in meeting certain teachers and friends with whom I gratefully associate my late awakening to poetry.

"When my career in the Civil Service began, I had written nothing. I worked as a Junior Executive

* kin′ se lä

Officer in the Land Commission (Congested Districts Board) until 1950 and then, after an examination, entered the Department of Finance as an Administrative Officer, and became Assistant Principal Officer in 1960. Again, as with my schooling, the experience was of a few understanding and imaginative persons standing out from a repetitious drabness—but all finally helpless in the service of a general brutality.

"I wrote my first poems shortly before 1950, partly out of curiosity. I found that I continued to write with increasing seriousness and persistence; poetry rapidly became my only significant activity. This process was enriched and hastened by my meeting with Liam Miller who founded the Dolmen Press in Dublin in 1951 with the main aim of publishing new Irish poetry—a meaningless act, it seemed, in the Ireland of that time: without new poetry and without interest in poetry. But the Press, of which I am a director, is now a full-scale business and the centre of much new creative activity in Ireland.

"My poetry early became fused with the pursuit of the beloved. A number of love poems, which I now regard as my first of any value, were published in 1956. In December 1955 I married Eleanor Walsh of Enniscorthy, in County Wexford, through whose vitality and brilliance under suffering—a culmination, perhaps, of my earlier experiences of individual worth in brutal settings—I seem to detect a possibility of order, suggestions for a (barely) positive dream. Our children are Sara, John and Mary.

"My poetry since 1956—almost entirely lyrical—has dealt mainly with love, death and the artistic act; with persons and relationships, places and objects, seen against the world's processes of growth and fructification and extinction. I find myself more and more concerned—in longer poems—with questions of value and order. After much curious scrutiny, I think that the human function (in so far as it is not simply to survive the ignominies of existence) is to elicit order from experience, to detect the significant substance of our individual and common pasts and translate it imaginatively, scientifically, *bodily*, into an ever more coherent and capacious entity—or to try to do so until we fail.

"In 1965 I resigned from the Civil Service and was elected to the Irish Academy of Letters. I am living at present in the United States, at Southern Illinois University."

Kinsella's father, "a man of high and punishing ideals," worked in Guinness's brewery in Dublin. The poet is a Roman Catholic but not a "Catholic poet." He has written on Irish themes and has made notably good translations from Ancient Irish literature, but works as much in the English as in the Irish tradition. His real preoccupation, he says, underlying the poems about love, and death, and art, is "the passing of time."

THOMAS KINSELLA

Some critics felt that Kinsella's early work was too consciously wrought—that "the emotion seems more in the poet's feeling about the words" than in their meaning. Kenneth Allott thought that most of the poems in the first three collections "give the impression of being shaped under great pressure," which at times produces obscurity but "makes all the more admirable a coherence won against odds." *Another September* was the 1958 choice of the Poetry Book Society, and "Thinking of Mr. D.," from the same collection, received a Guinness Poetry Award.

A gnarled, oblique, but very powerful confessional note emerged in *Wormwood*, a sequence of eight short poems about a marriage in crisis, presenting an ultimately Christian view of life as an agonizing process of growth through the acceptance of suffering. M. L. Rosenthal provides an illuminating discussion of this work in *The New Poets*.

Kinsella remained at Southern Illinois University for five years, as artist-in-residence until 1967, then as professor of English until 1970; since then he has been professor of English at Temple University, Philadelphia. The first collection of his work to appear after he left Ireland was *Nightwalker and Other Poems*, which includes *Wormwood* and two other long poems. The title piece is a nocturnal reverie which (like the earlier "Country Walk") chastises the materialism and mediocrity of modern Ireland; John Montague thought it a less than successful "attempt to blend local detail with cosmic significance," but "a formidable piece of writing and typical of Kinsella's view of himself as the conscience of his society." Montague preferred "the magnificently romantic intimacies" of another long poem, "Phoenix Park," in which the poet drives beside the Liffey with his wife; it is both a farewell to Dublin and a celebration of married love. Reviewers also welcomed a more relaxed and graceful aspect of Kinsella's talent in lyrics like "Dick King" and "Chrysalides."

One of the most discussed of his recent works was *Butcher's Dozen* (1972), first published in pamphlet form. It is a satire of Swiftian savagery on British attempts to justify the Londonderry "Bloody Sunday" of January 30, 1972, when troops fired into a crowd, killing thirteen people. *Butcher's Dozen* is a public poem, utilizing the swinging rhythms and doggerel rhymes of a street ballad. Its importance is as much social as literary, in that it "gives voice to the anger, frustration and bitterness which had been inarticulate among the people." A fragmented sequence of poems, *Notes From the Land of the Dead*, takes up most of Kinsella's *New Poems 1973*. The sequence evokes a spiritual journey from despair to a painful self-renewal, and it was warmly praised for the way in which it "stays tenaciously faithful to tactile experience while boldly transmuting it into a bizarrely imaginative dream-world." Kinsella's *Selected Poems 1956–1968* appeared the same year. Many critics would agree that Kinsella is the most intellectually powerful, the most accomplished, and the most ambitious Irish poet of his generation.

In 1969 Kinsella published a translation of the early Irish epic *The Tain* that was generally well received. He received the Triennial Book Award of the Irish Arts Council in 1961, the Denis Devlin Memorial Award in 1967, and a Guggenheim Fellowship in 1968–1969.

PRINCIPAL WORKS (all poems): Poems, 1956; Another September, 1958 (new edition, 1962); Moralities, 1960; Poems and Translations, 1961; Downstream, 1962; Wormwood, 1966; Nightwalker, 1967; Nightwalker and Other Poems, 1968; Poems by Thomas Kinsella, Douglas Livingstone, and Anne Sexton, 1968; (tr.) The Tain, 1969; Notes From the Land of the Dead, 1972; Butcher's Dozen, 1972; A Selected Life, 1973; Selected Poems 1956–1968, 1973; New Poems 1973, 1973.

ABOUT: Allott, K. (ed.) Penguin Book of Contemporary Verse, 1962; Murphy, R. (ed.) Contemporary Poets of the English Language, 1970; Orr, P. (ed.) The Poet Speaks, 1966; Rosenthal, M. L. The New Poets, 1967; Skelton, R. (ed.) Six Irish Poets, 1962. *Periodicals*—Chicago Review 65–66, 1964; Dolmen Miscellany 1962; Irish Times January 24, 1966; Poetry Chicago 100, 1962; The Review August 1963; Studies (Dublin) 49 1960, 51 1962; Time March 9, 1962; Times Literary Supplement February 1, 1963.

KIRK, RUSSELL (AMOS) (October 19, 1918–), American historian, political theorist, essayist, and novelist, writes: "A connoisseur of slums and strange corners, I have dwelt in more garrets and cellars, forest cabins and island hovels, than I can recall. I have thriven upon a diet of crackers and peanut-butter during nine years of college and university; I have been content with ducks' eggs and goats' milk in the Hebrides. Conversely, I have spent dreamy months in Scottish country houses and Italian palaces.

"I was born in Plymouth, Michigan—descended from Scottish farmers on my father's side and from New England Puritans on my mother's. A tiny, romantic woman endowed with fortitude, my mother read to me Lewis Carroll and Stevenson and Scott and Grimm and the adventures of the noble company of the Table Round, so that my imagination lapped up the fabulous and chivalrous, a mighty prop to health and mind.

"From early years, I felt a strong suspicion of change, and a longing for continuity. Though bookish from the beginning, I never liked school.

"In 1940, I took my bachelor's degree in history at Michigan State College; and in 1941 wrote my master's thesis—later published as a book, *Randolph of Roanoke*—at Duke University. Conscripted in 1942, I became a sergeant in the Chemical Warfare Service, at Dugway Proving Ground, in Utah. Here it was that I commenced to move, languidly, from my early Stoicism to something more. The Great Salt Lake Desert was terrible; but awe and veneration being close allied, the fear of God is the beginning of wisdom. In the desert I began to perceive that pure reason has its frontiers.

"Mine was not an Enlightened mind, I became aware; rather, a Gothic mind, medieval in temper and structure. I hankered after variety, mystery, tradition, the venerable. I would have given any number of neo-classical pediments for one poor battered gargoyle.

"Like Sinbad transported by his roc, in 1946 I found myself discharged from the army and back in my ancestral village of Mecosta, Michigan (a place of some two hundred and fifty souls), where I live and work most of the time today. I took a post as instructor in the history of civilization at Michigan State College, but soon commenced to wander.

"Between 1948 and 1952, most of my time was spent at St. Andrews University, in Scotland, where I became the first American doctor of letters of that haunted place, and wrote a book, *St. Andrews*, about town and university.

"My tall book *The Conservative Mind* (originally my St. Andrews dissertation) was published in 1953; it was followed, the next year, by *A Program for Conservatives*. Without having intended to be anything of the sort, I found myself a leader of an intellectual movement.

"For that past decade, in consequence, I have spoken in nearly every state of the Union; and I have wandered much abroad. About two hundred of my critical essays were published in periodicals. In 1962, I began writing a daily newspaper column, which mysteriously found several million readers. By way of diversion, I published a Gothic romance (*Old House of Fear*) in 1961, and a collection of uncanny or uncomfortable tales (*The Surly Sullen Bell*) in 1962. From time to time, I have been research professor of politics, or visiting professor of American studies, or some other sort of academic creature, at universities and colleges on either coast.

"Influenced by much reading of John Henry Newman and Orestes Brownson, in 1964 I was baptized in the Catholic Church. And in the autumn of the same year, in Long Island, I was married to the young Annette Yvonne Cecile Courtemanche, known in some of my previous writings as The Conservative Beauty. Thus for the first time, at the age of forty-five, I entered upon Christian orthodoxy and holy matrimony.

"At Mecosta, I am best content when planting little trees on my family's land. To plant a tree, in our age when the expectation of change commonly seems greater than the expectation of continuity, is an act of faith. Also it is an act of historical penance, restoring the fairness of the land.

"The great task of the serious writer in our century, I believe, is the recovery of norms: the restoration of the inner order of the soul, and the outer order of society. At present, I move toward the history of letters and toward sardonic and allegorical fiction."

Kirk's parents were Russell Andrew Kirk, a railroad engineer, and the former Marjorie Pierce. Both of them in their different ways encouraged his "strong suspicion of change, and . . . longing for continuity." He was a debater and orator at Plymouth High School, but was "bored" by social activities and gave his spare time to solitary walks and much reading, especially of history and fiction. This pattern at first repeated itself at Michigan State College, where for all his instinctive toryism he felt "almost an advanced thinker" by comparison with the mindless conformity of his peers. He won prizes for speaking and for writing, and in his third year began to make friends, with faculty members as well as students, and to publish his first articles in *College English* and elsewhere. Kirk graduated in 1940 with a B.A. in history and went on to Duke University in North Carolina, which gave him his M.A. in 1941.

As he says, his M.A. thesis became his first book and his doctoral thesis his second. The latter was

RUSSELL KIRK

The Conservative Mind, a study of the heritage of conservative thought in Britain and America which was widely praised from a variety of political positions. August Heckscher called it "carefully wrought and honestly made" while G. K. Chalmers found its author "as relentless as his enemies, Karl Marx and Harold Laski [and] considerably more temperate and scholarly." In *A Program for Conservatives* Kirk turned his attention to the contemporary situation, proposing, he said, "not a neat system of positive law, but a change of heart, by which order and justice and freedom may live through these dark days, and the past may be blended with the present."

These two books established Kirk as one of the principal architects of responsible conservative thought in America. He aligns himself with those who are "resolved that all the intricate fabric of the civil social order, woven by the spirit of religion and the spirit of a gentleman, shall not be destroyed by the appetites of our present unruly generation." He is not content with the kind of greedy capitalism that often passes for conservatism, calling instead for a system embracing Christian philosophy and a sense of community: "American Conservatives ought to talk a great deal less about the laws of economics and a great deal more about the laws of justice," he has said.

When Kirk left St. Andrews he returned briefly to his teaching post at Michigan State College, but resigned in 1953, dissatisfied with "the Petrified Forest of Academe." Since then he has held a number of teaching posts but has earned his living principally as a journalist and lecturer, and with his books. His special interest in education emerges in much of his writing, notably in *Academic Freedom*, which attacks among others "the doctrinaire secularists and doctrinaire levelers in our colleges and universities," and offers his own views on the proper function of the Academy. *Beyond the Dreams of Avarice*, *Confessions of a Bohemian Tory*, and *The Intemperate Professor* are collections of essays and articles which, in spite of their violent titles and "combative zeal" have been found articulate, sensible, and fundamentally amiable, as well as highly stimulating. There was a moderately good reception in 1966 for Kirk's reassessment of Edmund Burke, who has come to have a greater influence on his thought than his earlier hero, John Randolph. *Eliot and His Age*, according to Frank Kermode, presents Eliot uncritically as "a hero of the moral imagination" through "a fat comfortable body of anecdote, chat and summary."

Kirk's gothic fictions have also been generally enjoyed, especially his "Buchanesque" thriller *Old House of Fear*. The *New Yorker* found its plot absurd but said that Kirk "sets it down in a style so majestically archaic, so rich in atmosphere and intimations of impending doom, that we follow him with dazed and delighted attention from the first muffled cry to the final midnight scream." *Time* saw in the novel a "political morality tale," haunted by the "shadow of the welfare state," but a Kirk story is in fact quite likely to be haunted by nothing more sinister than ghosts, in which he unequivocally believes.

From 1960 to 1969 Kirk was on the faculty of Long Island University, and from 1957 to 1969 he occupied a part-time post as research professor of politics at the university's C.W. Post College. He has also taught for briefer spells at the New School for Social Research in New York City, and at Los Angeles State College. In 1954 he gave the Daly lectures at the University of Detroit. He was a founder of the conservative critical quarterly *Modern Age*, and has served as editor of that publication and of the *University Bookman*. He contributes to a great variety of periodicals, learned and popular, and is a very successful lecturer. His syndicated column, "To the Point," was appearing in 1972 in over one hundred newspapers.

Kirk, who admires or admired Barry Goldwater but not Robert Welch, considers himself an "eccentric Republican." He believes that he has learned most not from his formal education but from his travels and conversations with such men as T. S. Eliot and Wyndham Lewis. Kirk holds honorary degrees from six colleges, and is a justice of the peace in Mecosta County, Michigan, where he lives. He is a small man, brown-haired and green-eyed, and enjoys walking as much as he did as a boy.

PRINCIPAL WORKS: *Nonfiction*—Randolph of Roanoke, 1951 (new ed. published as John Randolph of Roanoke, 1964); The Conservative Mind, 1953 (rev. ed., 1960); A Program for Conservatives, 1954 (rev. as Prospects for Conservatives, 1956); St. Andrews, 1954; Academic Freedom, 1955; Beyond the Dreams of Avarice: Essays of a Social Critic, 1956; The Intelligent Woman's Guide to Conservatism, 1957; Confessions of a Bohemian Tory: Episodes and Reflections of a Vagrant Career, 1963; The Intemperate Professor, and Other Cultural Splenetics, 1965; Fulminations of a Nocturnal Bookman, 1966; Edmund Burke: A Genius Reconsidered, 1966; (with James McClellan) The Political Principles of Robert A. Taft, 1967; Enemies of the Permanent Things: Observations of Abnormity in Literature and Politics, 1969; Eliot and His Age, 1971. *Fiction*—Old House of Fear, 1961; The Surly Sullen Bell (stories), 1962; A Creature of Twilight: His Memorials; Being Some Account of Episodes in the Career of His Excellency Manfred Arcane, Minister Without Portfolio to the Hereditary President of the Commonwealth of Hamnegri, and De Facto Field Commander of the Armies of That August Prince, 1966.

ABOUT: Current Biography, 1962; Kirk, R. Confessions of a Bohemian Tory, 1963; Who's Who in America, 1972–1973. *Periodicals*—Commonweal September 21, 1951; July 13, 1956; National Review March 10, 1964; April 7, 1964; September 19, 1967; New Republic August 4, 1953; April 23, 1956; May 6, 1957; Time March 28, 1955; August 13, 1956; July 7, 1961.

KIRKUP, JAMES (April 23, 1918–), British poet, prose writer, translator and dramatist, writes: "I was the only son of very poor working-class parents living at South Shields, County Durham, on the River Tyne, an area of coal mines and shipbuilding industries. Most of my youth was spent in a period of industrial depression and unemployment, and this, together with the presence of the sea and my inborn sense of deep solitude and apartness, affected my work as a writer.

"Both of my parents come from ancient Viking stock; my father, who died in 1958, was of pure Viking stock, and my mother also had Irish and Scots blood. I think the feeling for my ancestry is very strong in me and in my work.

"I remember writing my first poem when I was about seven or eight, and I was pleased with it—unfortunately, it was about fairies in gardens. It was not until about the age of sixteen that I started writing serious poetry, to the dismay of my parents but with the encouragement of one or two women teachers at South Shields Secondary School, where I was decidedly the Odd Boy Out—a pattern that has repeated itself throughout my life. I feel as if I must have been born old, for my first real poem, written in a great flush of excitement which I still remember vividly—I scribbled it at our kitchen table after I had done my French and German homework—was entitled, with amusing pretentiousness, 'Thoughts of Age on Realizing that His Days of Usefulness are passed.' It was rather long, and in blank verse, and was published in my school magazine, and signed 'Anonymous.' Needless to say, my classmates soon found out who the writer was, and this too served to estrange me from the rest of my class. I had no friends, and when I look back upon my writing career I realize that my desire to write springs always from a kind of desperation I feel in the face of loneliness; I am unable to communicate with people in real life, for I find objects much more interesting and reliable and beautiful than persons, and so I compensate by writing, which can bring me into contact with people in other and more varied ways.

"My good, kind, but rather stolid parents were puzzled by me, for we had never had a poet in the family before—which is the usual experience of poets. Indeed, originally I had no wish to be a poet at all. My first desire, felt from the earliest age I remember—three—was to be a dancer, and when I remember my earliest childhood I remember myself dancing and dancing and dancing, the steps and movements all made up by myself. When I was about seven, my mother took me to a children's ballroom dancing class, but my first lesson there so embarrassed and depressed me that I refused to go back: it was not my kind of dancing, which was a free expression of my soul. Then I persuaded my parents to let me learn the piano—we had an ancient, silk-fronted instrument with yellow keys inherited from some relative—and I made good progress for the first six months. But then we were unable to continue paying for the lessons and I had to teach myself, which led to all kinds of errors of taste and technique. But eventually I was able to play Chopin and Liszt and Scarlatti, my three favourite composers for the piano. By this time—around the age of twelve—I realized that I could never be a dancer or a pianist, so I think that my decision to be a writer (or rather, a poet) sprang from a desire to 'be something' that would not cost money or need expensive lessons. All I needed was myself, and some paper and a pencil. I could write in solitude, as I could read, without interference. That is how and why I became a writer.

"Today, I do not regret my choice. My love of dancing and music has left me. I am still interested in art and drama, but gradually I imagine I shall give those up too and give myself always to writing. I have almost stopped writing poetry and have turned to prose: I think the writing of poetry is the very best preparation for the writing of good prose. I am unmarried, with no children."

James Kirkup likes to list a different date of birth in each reference book because, he writes, "it rejoices me so when people 'find out' and tell each other 'Kirkup's trying to conceal his real age.'" He also likes "foxing literary academics, and after all a poet is beyond time." He now insists that his "correct date of birth" is "April 23 (11 p.m.), 1918."

Kirkup went on from high school to Durham

JAMES KIRKUP

University, refused military service during World War II, and instead worked in many parts of England as a lumberjack and farm laborer. He has said that "courage is a very over-rated commodity" which he nearly always distrusts, but some might suppose that the role of a conscientious objector in wartime could not be sustained without it. Kirkup held an Atlantic Award in Literature in 1950 and was the first Gregory Poetry Fellow at Leeds University (1950–52). From 1953 to 1956 he was visiting poet and head of the English Department at the Bath Academy of Art. Since then he has taught, as lecturer in or professor of English, in Sweden, Spain, Malaya, Japan, and the United States. He now divides his time between England, where he spends his summers; Japan, where he is professor of English literature at Japan Women's University and also at Nagoya University; and the United States, where he is visiting professor of English and poet-in-residence at Amherst College.

His verse is marked by a facility which, he believes, has in it an element of "automatic prompting"; at its worst it degenerates into "emotional doodling" not far from doggerel. Most critics would agree with Kenneth Allott that Kirkup "is at his best as a versatile poetic reporter absorbed in some scene or incident which he brings alive on paper with rapid verbal strokes." The best known of these poems of "direct experience," and the one that established his reputation, is "A Correct Compassion," which describes a surgical operation, making "a scientific finding shudderingly palpable." Others express Kirkup's love of stillness and the sea; or are "jokes to be seriously enjoyed," like "Tea in a Space-Ship." His verse has been increasingly influenced by Japanese and Chinese poetry, both in content and manner.

In his widely admired autobiographical books Kirkup brings his memories out, "sharp and tangible, with the shock of forgotten possessions found in the back of an old drawer." *The Only Child* was said to have "the objectivity of his best poetry, together with a modesty not always to be found there." *The Love of Others* was a "disarming" autobiographical first novel. Kirkup's travel books are never less than perceptive and charming, and sometimes more—*These Horned Islands* and *Japan Behind the Fan* confirm his assertion that he is "spiritually an Oriental," and were praised for "marvellous observation and a terrible honesty" in their evocation of the nature and spirit of life in Japan. Kirkup is an extremely sensitive, versatile, and prolific translator—of works by Camara Laye, Erich Kästner, Ibsen, and Valéry, among others. He has written plays for television and for the stage. The only recreation he lists in *Who's Who* is "standing in shafts of sunlight"; another, apparently, is mocking the earnest-minded. Kirkup received the Mildred L. Batchelder Award in 1967, and is a Fellow of the Royal Society of Literature.

PRINCIPAL WORKS: *Poetry*—The Drowned Sailor, 1947; The Submerged Village, 1951; A Correct Compassion, 1952; A Spring Journey, 1954; The Descent into the Cave, 1957; The Prodigal Son, 1959; Refusal to Conform: Last and First Poems, 1963; Paper Windows: Poems from Japan, 1967; White Shadows, Black Shadows: Poems of Peace and War, 1967; Japan Physical, 1969; The Body Servant, 1971; Broad Daylight, 1971; A Bewick Bestiary, 1971. *Prose*—The Only Child: An Autobiography of Infancy, 1957; Sorrows, Passions and Alarms: An Autobiography of Childhood, 1959; The Love of Others (novel), 1962; These Horned Islands: A Journal of Japan, 1962; Tropic Temper: A Memoir of Malaya, 1963; Japan Industrial (two vols.), 1964–1965; Tokyo, 1966; Bangkok, 1967; One Man's Russia, 1968; Filipinescas, 1968; Streets of Asia, 1969; Hong Kong and Macao, 1970; Japan Behind the Fan, 1970; Insect Summer (for children), 1971.

ABOUT: Allott, K. (ed.) Penguin Book of Contemporary Verse, 1962; Finn, F. E. S. (ed.) Poets of Our Time, 1965; Kirby, J. and Nichols, R. The Cosmic Shape, 1947; Moore, G. Poetry Today, 1958; Murphy, R. (ed.) Contemporary Poets of the English Language, 1970; Skelton, R. The Poetic Pattern, 1956; Who's Who, 1972.

***KIRST, HANS HELLMUT** (December 5, 1914–), one of the most popular of the postwar German novelists, was born in Osterode, East Prussia, the son of Johannes and Gertrud (Golldack) Kirst. His forebears were farmers and craftsmen, his father a policeman. Kirst grew up in a strongly nationalistic atmosphere in the small towns and villages of the East Prussian highlands and the Masurian lakelands—wild forest country where there were still wolves. In 1933, when he graduated from the Osterode Gymnasium, he enlisted as a professional soldier and, having, he says, "confused national socialism with Germany," joined the Nazi party. He fought during World War II in Poland, Russia, and France, won a number of decorations, and rose to the rank of Oberleutnant.

* kērst

After the war Kirst worked for a time as a farm hand and gardener, and in similar casual occupations, turning to journalism in 1947. His first novel was published when he was thirty-six and called *Wir nannten ihn Galgenstrick* (1950). A sardonic story about a young German officer who sabotages a Nazi garrison, it was warmly received at home and abroad, and translated into English as *The Lieutenant Must Be Mad.* Two more novels were published and welcomed in the next three years.

Kirst's reputation and international popularity were established by his trilogy *Null-acht fünfzehn* (1954–1955), a satire on army life translated into English by Robert Kee as *Zero Eight Fifteen.* The trilogy, which derives its title from the serial number of a German machine gun, recounts the exploits of Gunner Asch, a private soldier, in his one-man battle with the German military machine. The first volume, generally regarded as the best of the three, was *Null-acht fünfzehn in der Kaserne* (1954), translated as *The Revolt of Gunner Asch.* It was a lively satire on German garrison life just before World War II and introduced Gunner Asch who, as one critic put it, "tired of having the book thrown at him, picked it up and threw it back . . ." *Null-acht fünfzehn im Krieg* (1954, translated as *Forward, Gunner Asch*) was set on the Russian Front and in a German base during the war. *Null-acht fünfzehn bis zum Ende* (1955, translated as *The Return of Gunner Asch*) brought the story to the end of the war and the Occupation.

The 08/15 trilogy was hugely successful. It was translated into twenty-four languages, filmed, and widely praised for its wit (which in no way minimized the brutality of its subject), and for its honesty. Some critics went so far as to compare it with Hašek's great antiwar satire *The Good Soldier Schweik*, but most preferred to regard it as admirable entertainment, closer in weight to the novels of Remarque. Kirst returned to the story of Gunner Asch, but with only moderate success, in *Null-acht fünfzehn heute* (1963), translated as *What Became of Gunner Asch* by J. Maxwell Brownjohn, who is responsible for the English versions of most of Kirst's recent books.

Not all of Kirst's books have dealt with military themes. Two were novels of family life and *Keiner kommt davon* (1957) was a grim and powerful fantasy about humanity's last week on earth before a nuclear holocaust. It was translated in the United States as *The Seventh Day* and generally admired by American critics, as was *Fabrik der Offiziere*

(1960, translated as *The Officer Factory*). A study of a murder and investigation in an officers' training school, it demonstrated once more the brilliance of Kirst's narrative technique, his skillful balancing of tragedy and irony. *Die Nacht der Generale* (1962, translated as *The Night of the Generals*), was called "one of the finest detective novels . . . in recent years," and was a best seller in America. *Aufstand der Soldaten* (1965), translated as *The Soldiers' Revolt*, was a novel based on the abortive 1944 plot to assassinate Hitler.

Kirst was married in 1962 to Ruth Mueller. He lives in Switzerland. He is a heavily built man of average height, "articulate and kindly" in conversation. Kirst, a Roman Catholic, considers himself a Socialist without romanticism and a humanitarian without sentimentality. One of the few West German writers published in Eastern Europe, he has donated his Polish royalties to aid the war orphans of Warsaw, and made financial contributions to Israel. He has traveled widely in Africa and Europe, and collects African sculpture.

By 1966 Kirst's hardback sales totaled over two million in Germany and slightly more abroad. He was easily the most widely read German novelist of the 1950s, even though most of his work is an indictment of the German record and has won him the antipathy of right-wing organizations and politicians. German literary critics in general take Kirst not very seriously, dismissing him as a popular entertainer. In the United States critical reactions have been mixed—rather cool, indeed, towards his more recent books. But few reviewers have questioned his immense skill as a storyteller and literary craftsman, and none doubt the need in the new Germany for his pointed and astringent recollections of the old Reich. Unlike other German novelists who share his fear of resurgent German nationalism, Kirst confines his protests to his books. "I couldn't wave a flag for anyone now," he has said. "I've tried everything from Marx to Confucius; nothing has the exclusive answers." Instead, "I have concentrated in my novels on a mass of details, on man, humanity, a decent life, on many small battles against power and influence."

PRINCIPAL WORKS IN ENGLISH TRANSLATION: The Lieutenant Must Be Mad, 1951; The Revolt of Gunner Asch, 1955 (England, The Strange Mutiny of Gunner Asch); Forward Gunner Asch, 1956 (England, Gunner Asch Goes to War); The Return of Gunner Asch, 1957; The Seventh Day, 1959 (England, No One Will Escape); The Officer Factory, 1962; The Night of the Generals, 1963; What Became of Gunner Asch, 1964; Brothers in Arms, 1965; The Soldiers' Revolt, 1966 (England, the 20th of July); The Wolves, 1968 (England, The Fox of Maulen); Last Stop Camp 7, 1969 (England, Camp 7 Last Stop); No Fatherland, 1970 (England, Undercover Man); The Adventures of Private Faust, 1971 (England, Who's in Charge Here?); Hero in the Tower, 1972; Damned to Success, 1973 (England, A Time for Scandal).

ABOUT: International Who's Who, 1973–74; Lexicon der Weltliteratur, 1963; Wer ist Wer? 1969–1970. *Periodicals*—Sunday Times May 1, 1966; Wilson Library Bulletin September 1962.

HANS HELLMUT KIRST

KIZER, CAROLYN (ASHLEY) (December 10, 1925–), American poet and editor, was born in Spokane, Washington, and grew up in the San Fernando Valley north of Los Angeles. She is the daughter of Mabel (Ashley) Kizer and Benjamin Hamilton Kizer. Her father is a distinguished Spokane lawyer who has been a leading figure in state and regional planning in the Pacific Northwest and is himself an author. She began writing verse at the age of eight, when she was moved to address a love poem to an Episcopal bishop. For some years after that her literary activity was spasmodic, though the *New Yorker* printed one of her poems when she was seventeen. Miss Kizer graduated from Sarah Lawrence College in 1945, and was married to Stimson Bulliet the following year. In the early 1950s she attended Theodore Roethke's poetry workshop at the University of Washington, and in 1959 she was one of the founders of the quarterly *Poetry Northwest*, later becoming its sole editor.

Her first book was *The Ungrateful Garden*. Most reviewers liked the wit and intelligence of these "studied and tough-minded" poems, the "passionate impatience" which cut so sharply through softness and sentimentality. Richard Howard wrote that "the book's title and a good deal of its business . . . is an acknowledgment that we perform

* kī′ zər

CAROLYN KIZER

our functions—bodily, creative, official—in an alienated nature . . . as well as an alien one: 'a whole wild, lost, betrayed and secret life.'" The result, Howard said, owed much to Roethke, but "there is a sour or at least a wry centripetal impulse in Miss Kizer's witty emblems of womanhood . . . a bitter acceptance in her myths of identity." D. J. Enright took these poems less seriously and found them "thick with catastrophes and fortitude, bursting with bloody but unbowed puns and light-hearted quotes or misquotes."

Knock Upon Silence, published in 1965 and reprinted in 1968, contains twenty translations from the eighth century Chinese poet Tu Fu and a number of original poems, including a kind of diary of a decaying love affair, partly in prose and partly in *haiku*, which some reviewers greatly liked and some did not. Some of the original pieces were thought imitative of Tu Fu (or his translator Arthur Waley), others of Juvenal, but Richard Howard concluded "that the stomach Miss Kizer is speaking from is her own, and that all the masks are necessary to keep her pangs from drowning out her perceptions." There was something close to unanimous praise for the new and selected poems published in 1971 as *Midnight Was My Cry*.

Carolyn Kizer has traveled widely in China, Japan, and Europe. In 1964–1965, under the auspices of the State Department, she visited Pakistan, where she studied contemporary Urdu and Bengali poetry, lectured, and read her verse. She teaches occasionally at poetry workshops. In 1966 she resigned as editor of *Poetry Northwest* to become director of literary programs for the National Endowment for the Arts. Accepting the post, she promised or threatened to follow the example of Tu Fu, another poet who was a civil servant, though not of the sort most likely to succeed in contemporary America. She is now poet in residence at the University of North Carolina.

PRINCIPAL WORKS: The Ungrateful Garden, 1961; Knock Upon Silence, 1965 (reprinted 1968); Midnight Was My Cry: New and Selected Poems, 1971.

ABOUT: Rosenthal, M. L. The New Poets, 1967. *Periodicals*—Hudson Review Spring 1971; Spring 1972; New York Times January 7, 1966; Tri-Quarterly Fall 1966.

KNIGHT, DAMON (FRANCIS) (September 20, 1922–), American science fiction writer, writes: "I was born in Baker, Oregon, the only child of Frederick S. and Leola Knight. The name on my birth certificate is Damon Francis Knight. Damon was my mother's maiden name, Francis my paternal grandfather's given name; the combination was intended as a euphonious by-line, on the model of Stewart Edward White.

"I dropped the 'Francis' in horror before I was fifteen, and have never used it professionally, but librarians found it out somehow and still pencil it in on the title pages of my books.

"From hints like this, it would be easy to conclude that I was marked off to be a writer while still in the egg. So far as I know, there had never been a professional writer in my family before: my father and my mother's father showed traces of literary inclinations; otherwise, both lines were grim-jawed Midwestern farmers and preachers.

"An only child of literate parents acquires language skills early, and his loneliness drives him into fantasy worlds. I talked early and walked late, dictated a poem (not much of a poem, but it scanned and rhymed) before I could write. I got my first pair of glasses at six. I read fairy tales, Thornton W. Burgess, A. A. Milne, pirate stories, historical novels. I discovered Dumas and Dickens, and plowed through masses of close-printed text that would horrify me today.

"When I was eleven, I discovered science fiction in the form of a magazine called *Amazing Stories*, with spacesuited men and toadlike monsters on the cover. This magazine, the first of its kind, had been founded by Hugo Gernsback seven years earlier. I have often wondered what would have become of me if Gernsback had never existed.

"In my teens I wanted to be a cartoonist, and actually attended art school for a year, but lacked dedication. Anyhow, as things were, I collected science fiction magazines, corresponded with fans and eventually tried to write stories. Donald A. Wollheim, the editor of a new s.f. magazine, accepted and published one when I was eighteen.

"Later that year, I met Wollheim and other members of the Futurian Society at the World

Science Fiction Convention in Denver, and went back to New York with them. The Futurians were a fan group most of whose members, then or later, turned professional. They included Isaac Asimov, Robert W. Lowndes, John Michel, Frederik Pohl, Cyril Kornbluth, Richard Wilson; later on James Blish, Virginia Kidd, Larry Shaw and Judith Merril became members.

"In 1943 Pohl got me a job as an assistant editor at Popular Publications, Inc., and I spent about two years there, in two separate hitches, during which time I worked on about half of Popular's forty pulp magazines—Westerns, detectives, science fiction, air war, sports. I also worked for a while as a reader in the Scott Meredith Literary Agency, and got valuable training in both places.

"We now skip to the present. I have published about eighty magazine stories, four short-story collections, five novels, twelve anthologies and a book of critical essays. The Milford Science Fiction Writers' Conference, which I founded in 1956 with James Blish and Judith Merril, is now in its eleventh year. In 1965 I founded a professional organization, Science Fiction Writers of America, which has two hundred members and has sponsored an annual series of awards, an annual awards banquet and an annual anthology, published by Doubleday. After two other marriages, one of which ended in annulment and the other in divorce, I am happily and permanently married to Kate Wilhelm, herself a distinguished science fiction writer.

"My life as I now look back on it is a webwork every part of which is essential. I would not change any of it if I could. My adolescence, which lasted until I was nearly thirty, was difficult and at times unpleasant; my childhood was lonely; but maturity has repaid me a thousand times over. I have been fortunate in the friendship of writers like Cyril Kornbluth, Richard McKenna, Keith Laumer, Algis Budrys, Avram Davidson, James Blish, T. L. Sherred, Thomas M. Disch, Ted Thomas, Sonya Dorman, Carol Emshwiller and Kate Wilhelm."

Alfred Bester described Damon Knight as a "brilliant craftsman who can handle any story form with crisp finesse." In the novel *Hell's Pavement* he conjured up a utopian society terrible enough to earn comparisons with Orwell's *1984*. Kingsley Amis classed Knight's story "Four in One" as "an example of *pure* science fiction," being "the development of a novelty without any of those social or psychological implications which arguably emerge from the work of writers like Pohl and Sheckley."

Knight's book reviews and critical essays, collected in the volume *In Search of Wonder*, have established him as "probably the leading critic in

DAMON KNIGHT

the field," and as "the founder of psychological criticism of science fiction." Knight frequently employs linguistic analysis to unravel an author's attitudes and intentions. He likes his science fiction stories "strong, rich, sometimes bitter."

With his high forehead, thinning wavy hair, and serious eyes behind horn-rimmed spectacles, Knight looks like the intellectual he is. He and his wife live in Milford, Pennsylvania, where their household was described in 1966 as consisting of two "active" boys, a dog, and five cats.

"I read science fiction for fun, and am glad that it seldom takes itself too seriously," says Knight. "Nevertheless, I'm proud of science fiction for its ability to treat people as reasoning beings, for its courage in dealing with the great human questions . . . and for its unmistakable benign influence on the mental climate of our world."

PRINCIPAL WORKS: Hell's Pavement, 1955; In Search of Wonder (criticism), 1956 (2d ed., 1966); A for Anything, 1959; The Sun Saboteurs (bound with The Light of Lilith, by G. M. Wallace), 1961; Far Out, 1961; In Deep, 1963; Beyond the Barrier, 1964; Off Center, 1965; Mind Switch, 1965; The Other Foot, 1966; Turning On (stories), 1966; Three Novels (Rule Golden, Natural State, The Dying Man), 1967; Charles Fort: Prophet of the Unexplained (biography), 1970; Towards Infinity (stories), 1970. *As editor*—A Century of Science Fiction, 1962; First Flight, 1963; A Century of Great Short Science Fiction Novels, 1964; The Dark Side, 1965; Cities of Wonder, 1966; Worlds to Come, 1967; Towards Infinity, 1968; Dimension X, 1970; A Pocketful of Stars, 1971; Perchance to Dream, 1972; A Science Fiction Argosy, 1972.

ABOUT: Amis, K. New Maps of Hell, 1960; Atheling, W. The Issue at Hand, 1965; Davenport, B. (ed.) The Science Fiction Novel, 1959; Tuck, D. H. (ed.) A Handbook of Science Fiction and Fantasy, 1959.

DAVID KNOWLES

KNOWLES, DAVID (September 29, 1896–) is the name in religion of Michael Clive Knowles, who is unquestionably "the foremost living authority on monastic history." He was born in Studley, Warwickshire, the only son of Harry Knowles, a businessman, and of the former Carrie Morgan. Both parents were Roman Catholic converts, and the boy was baptized in that faith. Knowles was educated at West House School, Edgbaston, and at the Roman Catholic public school Downside. An early enthusiasm for medieval history, encouraged and fostered by his father, developed at Downside into a more specific interest in the role of the monasteries. His first article on the subject appeared in the *Downside Review* in July 1919, just before Knowles went on to Christ's College, Cambridge, where he read classics and philosophy, graduating in 1922 with a first-class honors degree. The same year he was ordained into the Roman Catholic priesthood.

After a year of theology at the Benedictine Collegio Sant' Anselmo in Rome, Dom David returned in 1923 to teach at Downside, where he served as Junior Master from 1929 to 1933. His first book was the product of a quite unmonastic amateur interest in the American Civil War. Like some of Knowles's later books, it was thought remarkably, even excessively, compressed, but eminently readable and notable for "the unusually clear way in which the author visualizes military movements." At the same time, he was becoming known to specialists as an authority on monastic history, mostly through his articles in the *Downside Review*. He was editor of that publication from 1930 to 1933, when he left Downside to work at Ealing Priory on his first major work.

This was *The Monastic Order in England*, covering the period 943–1216 and comprising a narrative history followed by a more analytic section examining the daily life, intellectual activities, and general organization of the black monks. It was universally praised for its learning, its combination of objectivity and "sympathetic insight," and for a number of admirable character studies in the first section. In 1944 Dom David became a Fellow of Peterhouse, Cambridge, and in 1946 joined the university's teaching staff as a lecturer in history. A year later he was appointed Professor of Medieval History at Cambridge, and from 1954 until his retirement in 1963 was the Regius Professor of Modern History.

The Religious Orders in England, published between 1948 and 1959 in three volumes, completed the great work begun in *The Monastic Order in England* to form what has been generally recognized as "a definitive history of the religious life in England from the tenth to the seventeenth century, written with complete understanding, sympathy and objectivity."

Knowles has written a number of other and only relatively minor books on monastic themes, and also several which reflect his profound commitment to the spiritual life. In *The English Mystical Tradition*, a radical revision of an early work called *The English Mystics*, he "shows that he can handle theological themes as lucidly and in as balanced a manner as he has long handled the most intricate historical controversies." *What Is Mysticism?*, published in the United States as *The Nature of Mysticism*, centers on (though it is not confined to) Christian approaches to the "incommunicable and inexpressible knowledge and love of God," and argues that mysticism is the culmination of the spiritual life. Another aspect of Knowles's vast knowledge of the medieval world emerges in *The Evolution of Medieval Thought*, which in the *Times Literary Supplement* was "wholeheartedly commended for its vision and power, for its serene judgement and for its lucidity and distinction of style." Dom David's lifelong interest in literature is evident in a number of informed and perceptive essays.

In 1963, when Knowles retired, a group of his friends, pupils, and colleagues prepared by way of tribute a collection of his essays published as *The Historian and Character*. The title piece, originally written as his inaugural lecture at Cambridge, expresses Knowles's belief in the importance of biography and the study of character in his kind of historiography. The collection, said K. B. McFarlane, displays to perfection "the rare qualities that have made the author not only one of the most distinguished but also one of the best-loved medievalists of his day. . . . If Dom David writes like an angel he does not often leave us in any doubt that it is the recording angel that he most resembles." He speaks as well as he writes, with "flashes of wit and humour, all the more effective for their impassive delivery," and in "a quiet, deliberate, vibrant tone" which perfectly expresses the combination in his character of "quietness and strength."

Knowles received his Litt.D. from Cambridge in 1941 and has honorary degrees from several other universities, including Oxford, where he was Ford's Lecturer in English History in 1948–1949, and Sarum Lecturer in 1964–1965. He retained his Peterhouse Fellowship until 1963, and is now an Honorary Fellow of that college and also of Christ's College, Cambridge. He is a Fellow of the British Academy and a Fellow of the Society of Antiquaries, and a member of several learned societies, including the Royal Historical Society, whose president he was in 1956–1960.

PRINCIPAL WORKS: The American Civil War: A Brief Sketch, 1926; The English Mystics, 1927; The Benedictines, 1929; The Monastic Order in England: A History of Its Development from the Times of St. Dunstan to the Fourth Lateran Council, 943–1216, 1940; The Religious Houses of Medieval England, 1940; The Religious Orders in England, vol. 1, 1948; (with R. N. Hadcock) Medieval Religious Houses: England and Wales (rev. and enlarged ed. of The Religious Houses of Medieval England, 1940), 1953; The Religious Orders in England, vol. 2: The End of the Middle Ages, 1955; The Religious Orders in England, vol. 3, 1959; The English Mystical Tradition (rev. and enlarged ed. of The English Mystics, 1927), 1960; The Evolution of Medieval Thought, 1962; Saints and Scholars: 25 Medieval Portraits, 1962; Great Historical Enterprises [and] Problems in Monastic History, 1963; The Historian and Character, and Other Essays, 1963; From Pachomius to Ignatius: A Study in the Constitutional History of the Religious Orders, 1966; The Nature of Mysticism, 1966 (England, What Is Mysticism?); Christian Monasticism, 1969; (with Dimitri Obolensky) The Middle Ages (vol. 2 of The Christian Centuries), 1969; Thomas Becket, 1970; (with C. N. L. Brooke and V. London) Heads of Religious Houses 940–1216, 1972.

ABOUT: Pantin, W. A. *introduction to* The Historian and Character, 1963; Who's Who, 1972. *Periodicals*—Contemporary Review September 1963; Dublin Review January 1941, Summer 1960; History vol. XLVII, 1962; London Quarterly Review January 1941; New Statesman August 24, 1940; July 20, 1962; August 16, 1963; Spectator December 8, 1961; Speculum April 1942, October 1948; Times Literary Supplement December 4, 1948; March 30, 1956; January 22, 1960; October 12, 1962.

KNOWLES, JOHN (September 16, 1926–), American novelist and travel writer. The following note is based in part on information supplied by the author: He was born in Fairmont, West Virginia, the son of James Myron Knowles, a vice president of the massive Consolidation Coal Company, and of the former Beatrice Shea. Knowles was educated in New England, at Phillips Exeter Academy and at Yale, where he swam for the university, was an editor of the *Yale Daily News*, and published his first stories in student magazines. During this period, he says, Thornton Wilder, who lived near New Haven, gave him "invaluable criticism and measured praise."

JOHN KNOWLES

In 1949 Knowles graduated from Yale with a B.A. in English. He spent two of the next ten years in Connecticut as a small-town reporter for the Hartford *Courant* and three more as an associate editor with *Holiday* magazine, but otherwise devoted himself to "living, traveling and writing in Europe, mainly in France, Italy and Greece." Since 1960, when he published *A Separate Peace*, he has been a full-time writer.

A Separate Peace is a moving and piercingly accurate reminiscence of adolescent life in an expensive American preparatory school. It is set during the early years of World War II, whose threat conditions the atmosphere of the novel and the behavior of its protagonists. Phineas is a born nonconformist, a daredevil and a free spirit. Gene, the narrator, is an introverted, gifted, and subtle intellectual, who in the end tricks his simpler and purer friend into maiming himself in a game of dare. Phineas's total inability to comprehend his friend's treachery is very convincingly and illuminatingly contrasted with Gene's perfect but horrified understanding of the social and psychological forces which drive him to betrayal: betrayal not only of Phineas but of what is best and most human in himself.

The critics were not slow to respond to this remarkable first novel. Edmund Fuller said it was "sensitive without being delicate, subtle without being obscure"; others praised its clean, direct, and disciplined style; and Aubrey Menen called it the "best written, best designed and most moving novel" he had read for many years: "Beginning with a tiny incident among ordinary boys, it ends by being as deep and as big as evil itself." In the sheer authority of its evocation of adolescence it has reminded some critics of Robert Musil's *Young Törless*, though it in no sense derives from that masterpiece. It received the William Faulkner Foundation Award and the Rosenthal Award of the National Institute of Arts and Letters. The critical excitement was not accompanied by any great popular success until some years after the book's publication, when it suddenly established itself, along with Salinger's *The Catcher in the Rye* and William Golding's *Lord of the Flies*, as a favorite among young people all over the United States, and a best seller.

The continuing success of *A Separate Peace* has tended to muffle the impact of Knowles's subsequent books, though all of them have been generally well received. *Morning in Antibes*, set on the French Riviera, is about a young American's struggle to salvage his foundering marriage. The style and atmosphere of a rootless cosmopolitan society is skillfully evoked, and some interesting characterizations are outlined, but the book seemed to many readers oddly perfunctory and uncommitted. *Double Vision*, which followed, is an intelligent, sometimes brilliant, but basically conventional travel book, describing a journey from the United States to England, the Lebanon, Jordan, and the Greek islands. Knowles has said that travel is an absolute necessity for him, and a kind of education which "gives you an invaluable perspective on your own country"—the "double vision" of his book.

With *Indian Summer*, Knowles returned to something resembling the form of his first novel. Whereas *A Separate Peace* was about boys haunted by the specter of a war to come, *Indian Summer* deals with a man haunted by a war that he has already fought, and from which he has now returned to his Connecticut hometown. This is Cleet Kinsolving, part Indian, and an open, physical, freewheeling personality rather like Phineas in *A Separate Peace*. His character is complemented by that of his friend Neil Reardon, a tense, self-questioning intellectual who is a millionaire. It is Cleet's dream to operate his own airline, and Neil promises to finance him if he will first serve as his secretary.

Cleet becomes entangled in the corrupt artificialities of the Reardon family and its great mansion, which has the same kind of symbolic function as the school in *A Separate Peace*. At length he realizes that he has been tricked, emasculated, and robbed of his freedom. The book ends with a rather melodramatic episode in which Cleet takes his revenge by violently seducing Neil's wife and, having thus symbolically recovered himself, leaves the great house to make his own way in the real world outside. The homosexual implications of the relationship between the two friends are subtly and unobtrusively dealt with, as they had been in Knowles's first book. Some reviewers found Cleet's betrayal of his friend alienating enough to upset the balance of the novel but, in spite of this flaw, it remains a powerful and eminently readable story. There was also a generally enthusiastic reception for *The Paragon*, set at Yale in 1953, and centering on a confused idealist—an erratically brilliant and socially alienated student named Lou Colfax. Webster Schott called it "a beautiful, funny, moving novel about a young man in trouble."

Knowles has published in *Phineas* six relatively orthodox and uncomplicated short stories, the title piece being a preliminary sketch for *A Separate Peace*. His talent is clearly for the larger structure of the novel, as shown in the brilliant achievement of his first tour de force.

PRINCIPAL WORKS: *Fiction*—A Separate Peace, 1959; Morning in Antibes, 1962; Indian Summer, 1966; Phineas (stories), 1968; The Paragon, 1970. *Nonfiction*—Double Vision, 1964.

ABOUT: Contemporary Authors 17–18, 1967; Vinson, J. (ed.) Contemporary Novelists, 1972; Who's Who in America, 1972–1973. *Periodicals*—Book Week July 24, 1966; Commonweal December 9, 1960; Guardian May 1, 1959; Harper's July 1966; Life August 5, 1966; New Statesman May 2, 1959; New York Times Book Review February 7, 1960; July 19, 1964; August 14, 1966; New Yorker April 2, 1960; Reporter November 17, 1966; Saturday Review March 5, 1960; August 13, 1966; Times Literary Supplement May 1, 1959; October 22, 1964; Wilson Library Bulletin December 1964.

***KOCH, (JAY) KENNETH** (February 27, 1925–), American poet and dramatist, was born in Cincinnati, Ohio, the son of Stuart J. Koch and the former Lillian Amy Loth. "I began writing poetry in 1930," he says, "but I don't think I wrote anything very good till 1942, when I read Dos Passos and started writing 'stream of consciousness.'" After service from 1943 to 1946 as a rifleman in the Pacific, Koch received a B.A. from Harvard University in 1948 and his M.A. in 1953 from Columbia University. Between 1953 and 1959 he taught at Rutgers University College in New Jersey, and in the latter year he earned his Ph.D. at Columbia, with a thesis, "The Reception and Influence of Modern American Poetry in France, 1918–1950." Since then he has been on the Columbia faculty, in 1971 becoming professor of English and comparative literature. From 1958 to 1966 he also directed an influential poetry workshop at the New School for Social Research where, it is said, he preached "a post-symbolist French-modern esthetic."

Koch is one of the writers associated with the "New York School" of poetry, whose other

* kōk

luminaries include John Ashbery and the late Frank O'Hara. These poets, who learned as much from the American abstract expressionist painters as from French surrealism (and each other), share an interest (as Stephen Koch says) in "experiments with shattered syntax and fragmented language, with surrealistic links between unrelated things." To some extent they seek to use language as abstractly and evocatively as the abstract expressionists used paint.

Ko, or, a Season on Earth, is a long comic epic whose multiple and interwoven plots unfold one summer evening simultaneously in Cincinnati, Tucson, Paris, Tahiti, and half a dozen other places, and involve (among many others) a Japanese baseball star, a neurotic financier seeking absolute control of the world's dogs, an English private detective, and an "action poet." Thom Gunn found the fantasy uncontrolled and the writing "slipshod," but Kenneth Rexroth enjoyed it, saying that its author, once he "achieves a more engaging form... may well be a comic writer to be reckoned with."

According to Jonathan Cott, the shorter pieces collected in *Thank You, and Other Poems* reveal Koch's debt to Ronald Firbank, William Carlos Williams, and especially to Apollinaire. Koch, Cott says, "appropriates influences, radically refocusing them, however, in order to assume an adolescent persona in many of his poems"—for example in "To You," which begins: "I love you as a sheriff searches for a walnut / That will solve a murder case unsolved for years. . . . I love you as a / Kid searches for a goat; I am crazier than shirttails / In the wind, when you're near, a wind that blows from / The big blue sea, so shiny so deep and so unlike us." Stephen Koch has called the same collection "a kind of word-playground, filled with sunlight and color, with circuses, red shimmering fish, farmyards sprinkled with yellow straw and violets, with green oceans and chugging, rusty ships. . . . Though he is sometimes insufferably silly, Koch is also a wit . . . working in the discontinuous, unexpected rhythms of the Marx Brothers." Richard Howard also liked these "anti-statements, anti-poems, tantrums against history," and the "sunny and funny" personality they exhibit. Three small volumes of poetry followed, and then another major collection, *The Pleasures of Peace.* Many of these poems were thought better disciplined than Koch's earlier work—more exact and accessible—and Hayden Carruth found in them "a depth of metaphysical concern that gives them the drive and intensity of genuinely serious experiments."

A number of Koch's brief "dadaistic farces" have been performed, among them *Little Red Riding Hood* (1953), *Bertha* (1959), *The Election* (1960), *Pericles* (1960), *The Construction of Boston* (1962), *George Washington Crossing the Delaware* (1962),

KENNETH KOCH

Guinevere (1964), and *The Love Suicides at Kaluka* (1965). A collection of Koch's plays was published in 1966 as *Bertha, and Other Plays.* The title piece is actually a series of blackout sketches about the adventures of a mad Norwegian queen. As Robert Brustein pointed out, Koch "has discovered an inexhaustible vein of dramatic material: the corpus of Western myth, historical anecdote, and fairy tale, all of which he mocks gently in the anachronistic accents of romantic verse drama."

Kenneth Koch has received Fulbright, Guggenheim, and Ingram-Merrill fellowships which have helped him to spend several years in Europe, mostly in France and Italy. From 1960 to 1962 he was a member of the editorial board of the literary magazine *Locus Solus.* He was married in 1954 to Mary Janice Elwood and has one daughter. Koch has had remarkable success in encouraging elementary school children to write poetry; he has described his methods, and given examples of the results in *Wishes, Lies and Dreams* and *Rose, Where Did You Get That Red?*

PRINCIPAL WORKS: Poems, 1953; Ko, or, a Season on Earth, 1960; Permanently (poems), 1961; Thank You and Other Poems, 1962; Bertha, and Other Plays, 1966; Poems from 1952 and 1953, 1968; When the Sun Tries to Go On, 1969; Sleeping With Women, 1969; The Pleasures of Peace and Other Poems, 1969; Wishes, Lies and Dreams: Teaching Children to Write Poetry, 1970; Rose, Where Did You Get That Red?, 1973. *Poems in* Myers, J. B. (ed.) The Poets of the New York School, 1970; Padgett, R. and Shapiro, D. (eds.) An Anthology of New York Poets, 1970.

ABOUT: Allen, D. M. (ed.) The New American Poetry, 1960; Brustein, R. Seasons of Discontent, 1965; Contemporary Authors 1–4, 1st revision, 1967; Kostelanetz, R. (ed.) The New American Arts, 1965; Murphy, R. (ed.) Contemporary Poets of the English Language, 1970;

Who's Who in America, 1972–1973. *Periodicals*—New York Review of Books October 20, 1966; New York Times Book Review February 11, 1968.

KONINGSBERGER or KONING, HANS (July 12, 1921–), Dutch-American novelist, writes: "I was born in Amsterdam, Holland, and studied at the universities of Amsterdam and Zurich, first physics, later philosophy. I saw the German armies march into Holland in May, 1940. Two years later, I and a few student friends managed to escape, and after a time in the French underground, I eventually reached England and served in the British Army until the winter of 1945. Ever since, my thinking and writing has mainly been done in English. After the war, I had a brief spell back in the university, but found I had become too restless for the academic life. I have been a writer since, and with luck—and some hardship—have managed to live on my writing from the beginning. I never tried to earn money any other way, except for a week of book selling at Doubleday's in New York one Christmas season long ago; and I do not believe in accepting funds or grants from organizations, most of whose money was made in ways I do not feel enthusiastic about.

"After a year in Indonesia, I arrived in Los Angeles in 1951 on a freighter from Singapore, and the United States has been my home ever since, with much time out for traveling. I wrote my first novel, *The Affair*, in 1953, but it took me five years to get it published (by Alfred Knopf), for no one here knew me, of course, and I resisted the advice from agents and editors to make it a more 'normal' and commercial book. It did not sell too well, but it received very good reviews, and my next novel was accepted in a day rather than in five years, which was at least an improvement.

"I have written four novels since, one 'juvenile,' that is to say a book for high school readers, two plays, two film scripts, and many articles. In my early years, much of this writing was pot-boiling, mainly done for the money, although serious enough; and it was partly to survive, but also because the original appealed to me, that I used to do considerable translating. The translation from the Dutch of Maria Dermoût's *The Ten Thousand Things*, a book I had read in Dutch in the galleys and liked so much that I went the rounds with it in New York, was the best known one, but I have also translated French and German novels. My two plays have both been done in Europe, but I have not yet managed to get them on Broadway, and will not write another one until that has been achieved. The only articles I still write are 'Reporter-at-Large' pieces for the *New Yorker*, the only magazine I know that gives me complete editorial (not stylistic!) freedom. My *Letters from China* for

HANS KONINGSBERGER

the *New Yorker* were also published in book form, and I will continue to alternate novels with such 'personal impression' books about other countries and cultures. I am particularly interested in 'new' countries and the phenomenon of revolution.

"I do not believe in the teaching of writing—although any and every studying will of course help a writer—and am wary of theorizing about the novel. A novel that needs explanation has, *ipso facto*, failed. Obviously, it is no longer interesting to write one more imitation Balzac or Jane Austen novel, and the big best sellers about some civil war soldier or a Madison Avenue executive may be highly professional entertainment, but they have no relation to literature—a statement I dare make without a touch of jealousy. I believe that a writer, like everyone else, should be 'engaged,' that is to say, work and live trying to bring about a somewhat less grim world. But I am rather pessimistic about the success of such tries. I have two daughters."

The interest aroused by Koningsberger's first novel, *The Affair*, was confirmed when he published *An American Romance*, a "sad, serious, exact and extremely readable" portrait of a marriage which had been based too exclusively on the physical. *A Walk With Love and Death* was a considerable departure, a love story set against a background of rebellion and violence in fourteenth century France. Some reviewers found the tersely contemporary first-person narration at odds with the background, but others, untroubled by any sense of anachronism, thought this spare and beautifully written tale both moving and memorable.

I Know What I'm Doing, about the American adventures of a promiscuous but emotionally frigid English girl, returns to the theme of Koningsberger's earlier novels—the relationship between love and sex. He breaks new ground again in *The Revolutionary*, the story of a young man of good family who joins the rebellion against his country's tyrannical government. Both the hero and his country are unnamed, so that the novel becomes "a parable to illustrate the trials of the revolutionary spirit"—one which implies that the roots of rebellion are personal and psychological rather than political. Written on "a cagey note of desperation and subversive gaiety," the book seemed to some critics excessively detached and abstract, to others a minor classic in the Brechtian tradition. *The Revolutionary* and *A Walk With Love and Death* have both been filmed.

There has been more unanimity about Koningsberger's "personal impression" books. *Love and Hate in China*, based on articles commissioned by the *New Yorker*, records a visit of several months made in late 1965. It was thought that Koningsberger's disapproval of the American government's policy towards China sometimes led him to overstate the Chinese case, but his book was almost universally admired for its graphic and gracefully written vignettes of city and rural life in China, its vivid evocation of the mood and atmosphere of the country. "Being in China," Koningsberger says, "is full of manic-depressive experiences for a foreigner: alternating boredom and annoyance with love and admiration." Eliot Fremont-Smith called this "sensitive and intelligent" book an example of "personal travel-writing in the grand tradition—a compact and beautiful book."

Along the Roads of the New Russia is another impressionistic account of a huge country and its people. It was written after an extended tour of European Russia undertaken in 1967 in a converted Italian army truck. Koningsberger, it was agreed, is an ideal observer, "a painter in words" who is "sophisticated, unquarrelsome and gregarious," but who is sometimes at fault when he goes beyond what he sees, to speculate about the forces at work beneath the surface of Russian life. *The Almost World* is a rather loosely organized account of his travels in many parts of the world, expressing his rage at the harm done by capitalism and colonialist exploitation. It was published as by "Hans Koning," and the author explains that he has simplified his name for the benefit of his friends in the antiwar movement (he has served on the steering committee of Resist since 1967).

The author is the son of Daniel and Elizabeth (Van Collem) Koningsberger. He has been married three times, and has a daughter from each of his first two marriages.

PRINCIPAL WORKS: *Fiction*—The Affair, 1958; An American Romance, 1960; A Walk With Love and Death, 1961; I Know What I'm Doing, 1964; The Revolutionary, 1967. *Nonfiction*—Love and Hate in China, 1966; (with the editors of Time-Life Books) The World of Vermeer, 1967; Along the Roads of the New Russia, 1968; The Future of Che Guevara, 1971; (as Hans Koning) The Almost World, 1973.

ABOUT: Who's Who in America, 1972–1973. *Periodicals*—New York Times May 18, 1966; New York Times Book Review November 17, 1968; Times Literary Supplement March 10, 1966; September 28, 1967.

***KOPIT, ARTHUR (LEE)** (May 10, 1937–), American dramatist, was born in New York City, the son of George Kopit, a business executive, and the former Maxine Dubin. He left Lawrence High School in 1955 and went on to Harvard with a scholarship to study electrical engineering. He soon lost interest in that subject, however, and after taking some creative writing courses decided that he wanted to become a playwright. He graduated *cum laude*, Phi Beta Kappa, with a B.A. degree in June 1959. It was at Harvard that his early plays were written and staged, among them *The Questioning of Nick* (1956, adapted for television by the author in 1959); *Sing to Me Through Open Windows* (1959); *On the Runway of Life You Never Know What's Coming Off Next* (1958); *Through a Labyrinth*; and *Aubade* (1959). *Oh Dad, Poor Dad, Mamma's Hung You in the Closet and I'm Feelin' So Sad* was completed after Kopit's graduation, when he was in Europe on a Shaw Traveling Fellowship, and was sent to Harvard in time to win the Adams House playwriting contest in 1959. A student production of the play in Cambridge, Massachusetts, in January 1960, caused a minor sensation and was warmly praised by the Boston critics.

Oh Dad, Poor Dad was staged in London in 1961 and had a long run off Broadway a year later, winning the Vernon Rice and Outer Circle awards. It reached Broadway itself in 1963. Subtitled "a pseudoclassical tragifarce in a bastard French tradition," it is an extravagant Oedipal burlesque. The central character is Madame Rosepettle, a predatory widow who tours the world's luxury hotels with her late husband, a cat-eating piranha fish, and not one but two carnivorous Venus's flytraps. Also in tow is her retarded son, whose sexual innocence is her most prized possession, and whose rebellion in a sultry Caribbean hotel gives the play its monstrous plot. Doors open of themselves, the piranha speaks, the Rosepettle corpse keeps falling on people, and the style might best be described as an early example of high camp.

According to Kopit himself, the play is neither allegorical nor didactic, and the action is governed more by purely musical rhythms and associations

* kōp′ ət

ARTHUR KOPIT

than by any logical structure. Moreover, he says, "I don't think there is such a thing as the Theatre of the Absurd, and if there was, my play would have nothing to do with it." None of these assertions were taken very seriously by the critics. It was evident to most of them that the play was built on the Absurdist assumption that the human condition has become too awful for anything but laughter. And it seemed almost irrelevant whether Kopit was emulating or parodying Ionesco and Beckett (as he was certainly parodying Tennessee Williams). Where the reviewers divided was in their estimate of Kopit's success. Some found the play sophomoric, more ridiculous than Absurd, its characters "comic-strip exaggerations," but to most it seemed enough that the play was genuinely and brilliantly funny. It was staged by Kopit in Paris in 1963, has been produced in many other countries, and was filmed.

Two new one-act plays were scheduled for production at the University of Minnesota in 1964, *Mhil'daiim* and *The Day the Whores Came Out to Play Tennis*. After an argument with the university authorities, Kopit withdrew his plays from rehearsal. Later the same year he resigned from the writing unit of Actors Studio on account of audience rudeness during trial performances there of the two plays. *The Day the Whores . . .*, finally produced in New York in 1965, is set in a men's club whose tennis courts have been commandeered by the eponymous whores. Reviewers were reminded once more of Tennessee Williams by the play's concern with "man-eating women," and one of them also found deliberate echoes of Chekhov's *The Cherry Orchard*. The accompanying one-acter, *Sing to Me Through Open Windows*, is an earlier piece marred, it was thought, by some rather ponderous whimsy.

Kopit has been outspoken in his criticism of the mediocrity and sterility of Broadway as compared to the European theatre, which he studied in the early 1960s on his Shaw Traveling Fellowship. In "The Vital Matter of Environment," an article published in *Theatre Arts* in April 1961, he expressed his belief that the key to theatrical vitality is a strong feeling for tradition and milieu. It was no doubt in search of that key that he wrote *Indians*. This, his second full-length play, opened like his first in London, where in 1968 it was staged by the Royal Shakespeare Company under the direction of Kopit's friend Jack Gelber.

Indians, set in Buffalo Bill's Wild West show, recounts a number of episodes in the progress of the hero from Indian scout to showman-politician. In style it is pure vaudeville, but of a most bitter kind. The President of the United States is presented as an idiot, Sitting Bull as a cynical opportunist, and Buffalo Bill himself as an unconvincing apologist for genocide against the Indians, a tinsel and sawdust idol. The play had a mixed reception in London but at least one critic, Irving Wardle of *The Times*, was strongly impressed by Kopit's successful fusion of burlesque comedy and moral debate. *Indians* seemed to Wardle "fired with moral passion . . . one of the few necessary works to have appeared from the America of the 1960s." It reached Broadway in 1969, rewritten and much tighter in its structure, and was generally acclaimed as one of the most satisfying and spectacular productions of recent years.

Kopit received a Guggenheim fellowship in 1969 and was elected to the American Academy of Arts and Letters in 1971. He was married in 1968 to Leslie Garis, a concert pianist, and has a son.

PRINCIPAL WORKS: Oh Dad, Poor Dad, Mamma's Hung You in the Closet and I'm Feelin' So Sad, 1960; The Day the Whores Came Out to Play Tennis, and Other Plays (includes Chamber Music, The Questioning of Nick, Sing to Me Through Open Windows, The Hero, The Conquest of Everest), 1965 (England, Chamber Music and Other Plays); Indians, 1968.

ABOUT: Current Biography, 1972; Lewis, A. American Plays and Playwrights of the Contemporary Theatre, 1965; Weales, G. American Drama Since World War II, 1962; Wellwarth, G. E. The Theatre of Protest and Paradox, 1964; Who's Who in America, 1972–1973. *Periodicals*—Mademoiselle August 1962; Newsweek July 29, 1968; Time July 14, 1961; Vogue August 31, 1963.

***KOPS, BERNARD** (November 28, 1926–), English dramatist, novelist, poet, and memoirist, writes: "I was born in the East End of London during the general strike. My father was unemployed and my mother had to bring up eight

* kops

children on practically nothing. This poverty persisted until the outbreak of the second world war.

"Yet, despite the poverty and the fascist pogroms, my early childhood was not unhappy. We were a tight-knit Jewish family, living within a tight-knit community that was alive and throbbing with vitality. The difficulties of the time seemed to give a sense of identity and purpose.

"There were no books in my house, no sense of art; there was just the struggle with ordinary day-to-day living. My father's love of opera was the only hint I had of something beyond our way of life.

"My schooling was elementary and did not open up my mind to any degree. I loathed my school and my teachers. I was not unlike my brothers and sisters in any way. I left school when the war began. I was thirteen years old at the time. I left London because of the bombing and saw the countryside for the first time.

"It was not until the war ended that I actually read a worthwhile book. I was almost eighteen years old when a friend gave me a copy of *The Wasteland* by T. S. Eliot. It was quite a casual gesture on his part but it changed my life. I started to devour books; I read anything and everything. The poetry of Blake and Lorca shot me into a new world. I started then to think of myself as a writer. But my work was incoherent, reflecting only the turmoil within. I felt absolutely alone, needing so much to escape from the family, who by then had started to shake their heads.

"Unlike my brothers I had learned no trade so I began to take many jobs; usually the work was menial, but it left my mind free. I was totally without direction and I saw no hope for the future. But I wrote. I loved my parents but could not follow the tribe into their dreamless existence, yet I had nothing to put in its place.

"I wandered to Soho, where I found congenial, if questionable, company. I stopped working. The head shaking grew until there was a full-scale war between me and my family. The conflict became unbearable so I started to take drugs. My mother died; the world I knew died with her. The drugs led to a total mental breakdown and in 1951 I was admitted into a psychiatric hospital.

"Whilst I was there I decided that I would finally break with the past; so that when I was discharged I found myself totally alone and suspended in nowhere. I was filled with despair and saw no glimmer of hope anywhere. I did odd washing-up jobs in order to keep myself going, but really I thought that my life was over. Yet even during this time I continued writing; it seemed to be the only thing to do. I couldn't understand what I was writing but I did manage to get a few of these poems published in little magazines. But life had no meaning and I wasn't all that interested in discovering one.

BERNARD KOPS

"Then in 1954 I met Erica. It was Christmas Eve; she came down some stairs and lit up the world. I started believing in miracles because we dovetailed so perfectly. We started a bookstall in a street off Charing Cross Road and even though no-one came to buy the books we were incredibly happy and I felt as if I had been born again. We married and she became pregnant and I started to write with white-hot speed. It was then that I wrote my first play and from that day to this I have not stopped writing.

"We have been married ten years and our son Adam is nine years old. Recently we had a daughter; her name is Hannah. We live in West Hampstead in the north of London and we have a garden.

"I am totally involved in my family and in my work; there are no other realities for me. They are inter-related. I am pessimistic about the world and optimistic about my life and work. We sing and dance and love and work within these walls, knowing they are barricades against the darkness. Yet we long for the sun and one day we are going to live in the country."

The Hamlet of Stepney Green (1956), Kops's first play, is a reworking of the Hamlet theme, placed in the context of East London Jewish life, and provided with a happy ending. It was thought naïve and clumsy, but was enjoyed nevertheless for its gaiety, freshness, and gentle sentimentality. Like many of his later plays it was episodic in structure and made use of songs and asides to the audience in a way reminiscent of Joan Littlewood's Theatre

Workshop, though Kops was never formally associated with Miss Littlewood. Appearing as it did at about the same time as the first plays of John Osborne and Arnold Wesker, it was generally labeled as an example of the "kitchen sink" drama of the day.

It soon became clear that Kops was not really a dramatist in the realist tradition, certainly not an "angry young man." If his heroes rebelled in the first act, they were usually reconciled in the last. At the end of *The Hamlet of Stepney Green*, David Levey is persuaded by his father's whimsical ghost to accept his mother's remarriage, and settles down to sell pickled herrings from his father's stall in the market. John, the escaped prisoner in Kops's second play, *Goodbye, World* (1959), works out his obsessions and gives himself up to the police. These reconciliations are voluntary and optimistic, and Kops's dreamy young heroes rebel in the first place for Oedipal rather than political reasons—cutting their emotional umbilical cords before taking their ordained place in society.

Goodbye, World and *Change for the Angel*, which followed in 1960, were failures, but interesting enough to earn Kops an Arts Council bursary and a year as resident dramatist with the Bristol Old Vic. There he wrote *The Dream of Peter Mann* (1960), a modern morality play in which a vision of a world destroyed by greed cures the young hero of his own materialistic ambitions and reconciles him to family life. It was spoiled for most critics by its philosophical pretensions and its tendency to poetic whimsy. There was much more enthusiasm for *Enter Solly Gold* (1962), a robust and extremely funny study of the rise and fall of a Jewish Tartuffe which was quite free of moral attitudinizing.

Two radio plays written in 1963 showed a much darker view of life than Kops's earlier work, and were generally welcomed by reviewers. In *Home Sweet Honeycomb* the hero, living in a nightmarish future world, assumes a succession of roles and finds each more horrible than the last. His final acceptance of ordinary domestic life is not, as in earlier plays, a triumph of good sense but an appalling defeat which reminded John Russell Taylor of Winston Smith's acceptance of Big Brother in *1984*. Taylor also found a new clarity and discipline of style and structure in the play. *The Lemmings*, an equally dark piece, pictures humanity in the grip of a mass urge to suicide. None of Kops's plays has reached the West End, London's Broadway, and in recent years he has turned to other forms.

His novels, like his plays, are often concerned with Jewish family life, and in particular with the problems of rebellion and submission. In *The Dissent of Dominick Shapiro*, Dominick's desertion of his loving middle-class family for the company of beatniks, socialists, and folksingers provides, as one critic wrote, "a wonderful inner poetry and some riotous, seamy events." In the end, Dominick learns to "dissent from dissent." Kops's intimate, colloquial verse has attracted less attention than his work in other forms.

Much of the material of Kops's books and plays is presented very directly in his autobiography, *The World Is a Wedding*. A reviewer in the *Times Literary Supplement* complained of sentimentality and clichés, but wrote that "the really valuable thing about this book, though undoubtedly it will have considerable interest for social and literary historians, not to mention psychologists, is as an extremely compulsive and luminous record of self-discovery. It is aboundingly honest—even the faked bits—and aboundingly alive."

Kops and his wife, the former Erica Gordon, now have four children.

PRINCIPAL WORKS: *Plays*—The Hamlet of Stepney Green, 1959; The Dream of Peter Mann, 1960; Enter Solly Gold *in* Satan, Socialites and Solly Gold: Three New Plays from England, 1961; Four Plays (The Hamlet of Stepney Green, Enter Solly Gold, Home Sweet Honeycomb, The Lemmings), 1964. *Fiction*—Awake for Mourning, 1958; Motorbike, 1962; Yes from No-Man's Land, 1965; The Dissent of Dominick Shapiro, 1966; By the Waters of Whitechapel, 1969; The Passionate Past of Gloria Gaye, 1971; Settle Down Simon Katz, 1973. *Poetry*—Poems, 1955; Poems and Songs, 1958; An Anemone for Antigone, 1959; Erica I Want to Read You Something, 1967; For the Record, 1971. *Autobiography*—The World Is a Wedding, 1963.

ABOUT: Murphy, R. (ed.) Contemporary Poets of the English Language, 1970; Taylor, J. R. The Angry Theatre (England, Anger and After), 1962; Wellwarth, G. The Theatre of Protest and Paradox, 1965. *Periodicals*—Best Sellers July 1, 1965; February 15, 1967; Book Week June 13, 1965; Commentary November 1963; Encounter May 1960; December 1963; Guardian September 6, 1969; Nation July 3, 1967; New York Review of Books October 28, 1965; New York Times Book Review September 8, 1963; February 5, 1967; Saturday Review August 24, 1963; June 26, 1965; February 18, 1967; Times (London) August 30, 1963; Times Literary Supplement May 24, 1963; April 1, 1965.

***KÖRMENDI, FERENC** (February 12, 1900–July 20, 1972) Hungarian-American novelist, dramatist, and story writer, wrote: "I was born into a middle-class family, and educated in the humanities, in Budapest, Hungary; I spent a happy youth in a pleasant home. Since my early adolescence I had been obsessed with literary ambitions; I was seventeen when my first poems were published and twenty-one when my first book—three novelettes—came out. But literature was an unrequited love, my juvenile efforts remained unnoticed. The post-World War I inflation left us penniless, which forced me to give up studying and writing and take up some breadwinning work to make ends meet. I married a childhood playmate

* kûr′ men di

in 1923; two years later, when my father died, it became my additional responsibility to support my mother and sister. Between 1920 and 1930 I held a great variety of jobs; the last one was washed away by the European wave of the Depression. But, at long last, I had all the time I needed to embark on writing a novel whose basic idea had haunted me for many years.

"A newspaper advertisement for an international literary competition, sponsored in London by English and American publishers, spurred me on; I concluded and sent in the manuscript in Hungarian and won the 'International Novel Prize, 1932.' In the ensuing years *Escape to Life* was published in twenty-six countries. I no longer was unknown or unappreciated. Up to the present, I have written seventeen more books (fiction, dramas, essays).

"Most of my books have been well received, and several of them topped the best-seller lists in many European countries. According to literary observers, I belonged among the novelists most widely discussed in the Continental critical literature of the thirties. My novels chronicle contemporary life in Hungary and the lot of my generation. I seem to have an inborn aversion to heroes; my interest has been focused on the life of the common man and his conflicts with an immense, hostile world. I endeavored to show how vulnerable people and institutions and ideas were; beauty and evil, how protean.

"My life took another decisive turn early in 1938. When the Nazis marched into neighboring Austria, my wife and I left Hungary. Our emigration turned out to be final. After a brief stay in Italy and Switzerland, we moved on to London, and many friendly British writers assisted us in our efforts to settle down there.

"At the outbreak of the second world war, I was invited by the BBC to join their newly-organized European Service. I worked for them until the end of the war. In London, during the blitz, I wrote a play about Hitler and, two years later, a novel on the beginnings of Nazism in Hungary.

"Early in 1946, we immigrated to the United States and became American citizens in due course. In New York and on Capitol Island, Maine, I wrote two more novels, another play, and many short stories about Hungarians living in exile in a foreign environment or under the Communist dictatorship at home. In the course of my war-time work I had grown greatly interested in political broadcasting and continued it in America. I worked for Radio Free Europe in New York for some ten years and have been with the Voice of America in Washington, D.C., since 1961.

"I wrote most of my books in Hungarian. Gradually, however, I switched to English, but even now, many years and three books later, I feel that writing in a language other than my mother tongue is like wearing an expensive tailor-made suit in place of the skin I was born into. I am a fast and rhapsodic rather than methodical worker; I rewrite a good deal. Work in progress: a volume of recollections, *Atlantis Remembered*.

FERENC KÖRMENDI

"I believe in El Greco, Beethoven, Dostoevski, Freud, Churchill, tennis, and travel."

The first half of Körmendi's life is reflected in the semiautobiographical novel *The Happy Generation* (Hungarian version 1934), a chronicle of middle-class Hungarian family life from 1900 to 1933, and of the dissolution after 1918 of a way of life. Virgilia Peterson, while finding fault with the structure and the dialogue of the book, called it "substantial social history, a navigable bridge between our world . . . and . . . Central Europe." The prize-winning *Escape to Life* had also evoked the hopelessness of Hungarian life between the wars, focusing upon the proposed visit to his native Budapest of a rich and successful expatriate, and the impact this has on his former friends.

The war and the arrival of Nazism uprooted Körmendi from his milieu and language. "Here, thanks to the war, is an intelligent playwright in our midst," was one British critic's reaction to Körmendi's debut on the London stage with *Adversary of Man* (1941) "a restrained but extremely moving" expressionist fantasy about Hitler and Hitlerism. The theme of Nazism and "hatred victorious" was further developed in the novel *Weekday in June* (1943).

The novels Körmendi wrote in America deal mainly with refugee life and the effects of exile upon character. Typical of them is *Years of the Eclipse* (1951), about a group of refugees in wartime London. The book struck some readers as melodramatic—close to caricature in its portraits of Communists—but for others it had a pace and finish which could suspend disbelief. One reviewer wrote: "Mr. Körmendi is a lively narrator. His book tumbles with incidents, his skill in dialogue is notable, his political awareness illuminating. He has a fine eye for the dramatic; he tethers life and death, comedy and tragedy, and history and prophecy with facility and flash."

This writer of "best sellers for intelligentsia," as he is called in the official literary history of contemporary Hungary, retired from his post with the Voice of America in 1969, but maintained a vigorous interest in literature and politics. He died of an occlusion of the arteries in 1972.

PRINCIPAL WORKS IN ENGLISH: Escape to Life, 1933; Via Bodenbach, 1935; Adversary of Man (play), 1941; The Happy Generation, 1945; Weekday in June, 1946; That One Mistake, 1947; Sinners, 1948; Years of the Eclipse, 1951. *As "Peter Julian"*—The Seventh Trumpet, 1953.

ABOUT: Warfel, H. R. American Novelists of Today, 1951. *Periodicals*—Christian Science Monitor February 2, 1950; Manchester Guardian December 27, 1945; New York Herald Tribune September 9, 1951; September 10, 1953; New York Times September 2, 1949; July 21, 1972; Saturday Review September 22, 1951; The World in Books June 1947.

KORNBLUTH, CYRIL M. (July 23, 1922?–March 21, 1958), American science fiction writer, was born in New York City, the son of Samuel Kornbluth, a court clerk, and the former Deborah Unger, who had been one of the founders of the Yiddish Art Theatre in London. With his brother, Louis, Kornbluth was raised in the Washington Heights section of northern Manhattan.

In the Kornbluth apocrypha there is a story about the author as an infant in his perambulator, remarking to a woman who cooed at him: "Madam, I am not the child you think me." The story was probably woven from whole cloth by Kornbluth himself, whose incorrigible and sometimes savage sense of humor delighted, and occasionally outraged, those who knew him personally.

Although the image of the articulate infant is far-fetched, Kornbluth was in fact precocious. As a student at George Washington High School in Washington Heights, he had the appearance and the vocabulary of a university graduate, and at that time wrote the short fantasy, "The Words of the Guru," which has been ranked beside works in the same genre by Lord Dunsany. He was encouraged in his writing by his English teacher, Miss Mary J. J. Wrinn, and in 1938 became a charter member of Isaac Asimov's Futurian Science Literary Society. After graduating from high school he became a

CYRIL KORNBLUTH

prolific contributor of science fiction stories under various pseudonyms to *Stirring Science*, *Cosmic*, and other magazines. He studied for a time at the City College of New York.

During World War II Kornbluth went to Europe as a United States Army infantryman and fought as a machine gunner in the battle of the Bulge, winning the Bronze Star. After returning to the United States, he worked on an Atomic Energy Commission project with Bell Telephone Laboratories and wrote and sold many detective stories. From 1949 to 1951 he was editor of the Chicago bureau of Trans-Radio Press, and during this period attended classes at the University of Chicago.

Kornbluth's first novels, *Outpost Mars* and *Gunner Cade*, both published in 1952, were written in collaboration with Judith Merril under the joint pseudonym "Cyril Judd." An even more fruitful collaboration with Frederik Pohl resulted in such novels as *Search the Sky* (1954), *Gladiator-at-Law* (1955), and *Presidential Year* (1956). The best known of the Kornbluth-Pohl novels is *The Space Merchants* (1953), first published in *Galaxy* magazine as "Gravy Planet," a social satire in which Madison Avenue techniques entirely dominate an America of the future. In a lecture given at the University of Chicago titled "The Failure of the Science Fiction Novel as Social Criticism," Kornbluth said of the book: "I see that with almost lunatic single-mindedness we made everything in our future America that could be touched, tasted, smelled, heard, seen, or talked about bear witness to the dishonesty of the concepts and methods of today's advertising." Five years after the book's publication, Kingsley Amis wrote: "*The Space Merchants* has many claims to being the best science fiction novel so far."

The first novel published under Kornbluth's name alone was *Takeoff* (1952), a story about the building of the first moon spacecraft and the conflict between scientists and bungling government bureaucrats. His best solo novel, in the opinion of some critics, was *The Syndic* (1953), a work of sociological science fiction in which Kornbluth convincingly created, on premises unique but internally plausible, a society of his own imagining. Less successful by Kornbluth's standards, but still superior science fiction, polished and craftsmanlike, was *Not This August* (1955), about a United States occupied by Communist armies. Damon Knight noted the presence in both books of qualities characteristic of Kornbluth—careful and fascinating scientific detail, tight plot construction, vivid characterization and dialogue, and skill at creating and sustaining excitement—but he also expressed disappointment with them. "If there is any serious complaint to be made to Kornbluth at this point," Knight wrote, "it must be based, oddly enough, on the very prodigality of his talent. Kornbluth's career is like that of a very bright schoolboy in a dull class; he discovered early that he could do the things the others struggled to accomplish a great deal better and with much less effort; he has been doing it ever since, with his tongue in his cheek." Referring to Kornbluth's "extensive Working Stiff and Slob vocabularies," Knight went on: "No working stiff, nor slob either, he has had deliberately to suppress the sensitive, cynical, philosophical, irreverent top slice of his mind in order to counterfeit the tribal conventions of the boobs around him."

Kornbluth's natural medium was probably the short story, in which he maintained a uniformly high quality from "Thirteen O'Clock," published in 1941, to "Gomez," written in the mid-1950s. Some of his short stories, such as "The Goodly Creatures," one of his best, were serious attempts to merge the conventional short story with science fiction. Damon Knight objected to these hybrids, on the ground that they represented "the triumph of a master technician over an inappropriate form—as if . . . Milton had written *Paradise Lost* in limericks, and made us like it." But Knight was "unable to wish that they had not been written." Kornbluth's short stories have been published in several collections, including *Mindworm* (1955) and *Mile Beyond the Moon* (1958).

At the end of his life Kornbluth was living with his wife, the former Mary G. Byers, whom he had married in 1941, and his two sons, John and David, in Levittown, Long Island. He died suddenly of a heart attack, at the age of thirty-five, on a day when he had been chopping wood and shoveling snow. At the time of his death he was consulting editor to the *Magazine of Fantasy and Science Fiction*.

PRINCIPAL WORKS: Takeoff, 1952; The Syndic, 1953; Not This August, 1955; Mindworm (short stories), 1955; Christmas Eve, 1956; Mile Beyond the Moon (short stories), 1958; Best SF Stories of C. M. Kornbluth, 1968. *Essay in* Davenport, B. (ed.) The Science Fiction Novel, 1959. *With Judith Merril as "Cyril Judd"*—Gunner Cade, 1952; Outpost Mars, 1952. *With Frederik Pohl*—The Space Merchants, 1953; Search the Sky, 1954; Gladiator-at-Law, 1955; The Town Is Drowning, 1955; Presidential Year, 1956; Wolfbane, 1961; The Wonder Effect, 1967.
ABOUT: Amis, K. New Maps of Hell; Knight, D. In Search of Wonder, 1956; Moskowitz, S. Seekers of Tomorrow, 1966. *Periodicals*—New York Times March 22, 1958; Publishers' Weekly April 14, 1958.

KORNEICHUK, NIKOLAI IVANOVICH. *See* "CHUKOVSKY, KORNEI"

***KOSINSKI, JERZY ("JOSEPH NOVAK")** (June 14, 1933–), American novelist and sociologist, writes: "I was born in Lodz, Poland, of Russian parents. They lived in Russia until 1918; after the War they settled in Poland. My father was a scholar and before the Revolution he was a university professor. In Poland he withdrew from active life to study ancient Greek and modern languages. My mother was a concert pianist.

"I received my higher education in Poland, and in 1955 I became an *aspirant* (Associate Professor) and Grantee of the Polish Academy of Sciences in Warsaw.

"I emigrated to the United States in 1957 as a private individual without any assistance. Between 1957 and 1958, when my Ford Foundation Fellowship took effect, I held a variety of jobs; scraping ships with Greek, Mexican and Puerto Rican crews (quitting only when the Greeks ganged up on me because they thought I was a Greek who refused to admit his heritage), working as a truck driver, night club photographer, bar cleaner. . . .

"Before I enrolled for my Ph.D. studies at Columbia University in New York I taught myself English, first by listening to the radio and watching television, then by translating Shakespeare and Poe into Polish and Russian and memorizing whole pages of the original texts. Finally, I would get good translations of Polish and Russian works I knew and match them, word for word, against the original.

"After I entered the graduate studies at Columbia I started writing in English—and I enjoyed it immensely. Something marvelous was happening: English, my step-mother tongue, freed me from what I had been. I was acquiring a new tradition and a new relationship not only with the external world but with my old Russian-Polish self. English

* kō sin′ skē

JERZY KOSINSKI

language regenerated in me all that was flabby and moribund, breaking down what was stiff and rigid. In English I was not afraid to be myself, to speak freely—there was no Party to police me, no censorship, no Socialist collectivity to punish me. It occurred to me that I could now do what I always wanted to do: I could write—and I could write in English. Like a polyp my imagination would expand and develop in unpredictable directions.

"I wrote my first two books (1960, 1962) in English while I was still at Columbia University and at the New School for Social Research. They were both non-fiction, giving a factual record of collective behavior, and directed to those concerned with contemporary political systems and their relationship to the individual. Both books were published in New York under the pen name of Joseph Novak to prevent my becoming involved in controversies which might have led to the interruption of my academic work.

"After completing my studies I began working on my first novel, *The Painted Bird*. I went through fifteen full drafts of it, and at least as many times through the twelve volumes of the Oxford English Dictionary 'searching for the right word.' The novel was a narrative which I felt could best be constructed outside the traditional framework of first person narratives by deliberate avoidance of any direct speech by the protagonist or by any other character. It was published in Boston in 1965 and the publishers claimed it to be the 'best reviewed work of fiction of 1966.' In April 1966 the novel was awarded in France Le Prix du Meilleur Livre Étranger.

"In 1967 I received a Guggenheim Fellowship. I immediately started working on my second novel, *Steps*. In this work I tried to convey certain impressions that do not easily lend themselves to verbal interpretations. The Joycean solution would be to stretch language into new forms, hoping that an excess of words will compensate for their inherent inadequacies. I decided to make a very different demand on the reader: he should perceive the work in a form of his own devising, automatically filling in the novel's intentionally loose construction with his own formulated experiences and fantasies.

"During my Fellowship at the Center for Advanced Studies at Wesleyan University, Connecticut, I went through twenty-seven full drafts of the novel constantly de-escalating the style. It was published in New York in 1968. In 1969 it was awarded the National Book Award in Fiction.

"Although all my books have been translated into many foreign languages, in terms of my life the fact that I could write them in English and have them published exactly as I want is of significance. Here, in the English-speaking countries, the appearance of a novel still remains spontaneous. A book is born in privacy and often strikes back at society. Its voice is heard. And it is because all of us, writers, publishers, editors, critics, and judges keep it so. Only because of this I decided to become a writer. Only because of this I am now working on my next novel."

The two books which Kosinski wrote under the pseudonym of "Joseph Novak" are *The Future Is Ours, Comrade*, and *No Third Path*. Both attempt to provide a composite picture of how the Soviet mind works, mostly by describing discussions with Russian men and women from all walks of life. Most critics found them extremely rewarding if depressing case studies.

The Painted Bird, Kosinski's first novel, is also a kind of case study, bearing witness to man's inhumanity to man. A small boy, six years old when the Germans occupy Poland, is sent by his middle-class parents to the presumed safety of a remote village. The old woman who is to care for him dies, and he begins a long flight to safety. Because his coloring is dark, he is taken for a Jew or a gypsy, an alien to be feared or despised, a "painted bird" among sparrows. He is at the mercy of an ignorant and superstitious peasantry from whom he receives every brutality and bestiality man's animal nature is capable of. This is his education, which teaches him that justice and reason will not save him; that prayer and magic are powerless; that he can survive only through and for hatred, cruelty, and indiscriminate vengeance.

Kosinski believes that "art is the using of symbols by which an otherwise unstatable subjective reality is made manifest." It is perhaps only in this symbolic sense that *The Painted Bird* is autobiographical. Certainly many incidents in the book are borrowed from folklore, and the theme itself is a dark version of the quest theme—organized, as the author has said, "in little dramas, in spurts of experience, with the links largely omitted, as is the case with memory." In his published notes on the novel, Kosinski describes his attempt to dig down to "the black roots of the fairy tale" as a Jungian device "by which the search back to the primitive is achieved" —a search for a self "with which we are either entirely unfamiliar or of which we are only faintly aware through the content of our dreams and fantasies. . . . The world depicted in *The Painted Bird* may be regarded as a world of distinctive elementary symbols, simple keys to the European culture of the mid-twentieth century." Written with the chaste directness of a fairy story, this indictment of modern man achieves something of the same universality and authority.

In *Steps*, an anonymous narrator describes or recalls a series of incidents, most of them sexual, most of them violent, perverse, or grotesque. In one a soldier found cheating in an obscene game has his genitals crushed between bricks; in another a punished child revenges himself on the world by feeding ground glass to his friends; in several others love is exploited or perverted in the pursuit of power, which is itself a tool of hatred. Here, indeed, is just such a world as might have been conceived by the emotionally crippled hero of *The Painted Bird*.

The style is once more cool, casual, and exact, and the abominations it describes are neither condoned nor condemned: "The reader is guided to an area of experience but he must digest the experience himself." The incidents of which the book is composed tell no sequential story but (as Kosinski has explained in *The Art of the Self*, his notes on the book), are designed to work directly upon the reader's perceptions, like a cinematic montage. They are selected and arranged according to a subtle pattern intended to lure the reader (the "victim") ever deeper into the toils of this predatory book until he is trapped into a state of empathy with the narrator; when the reader begins to participate vicariously in the narrator's crimes, he will be forced to confront his own.

That the author had succeeded in making this highly original mechanism work was evident from the reviews, many of which treated the book less as a work of literature than as an emotional experience. One critic, who half suspected that it was no more than a series of "leaps of self-indulgence," found nevertheless that incidents from it "return to the memory at unexpected moments, stirring up uneasy images, disturbing the reader in the very depths of his own fantasies." Stanley Kauffmann, who spoke of Kosinski's style as one "made of small, deceptively plain, exploding capsules," called the book "a very large achievement."

Being There, the novel which followed, tells the story of an illiterate and feeble-minded young gardener, an orphan significantly named Chance whose experience of the world is limited to the television he watches voraciously and indiscriminately. Expelled from his Eden by the death of the Old Man, his employer, he responds to life in the outside world in the only way he knows—as if it were a series of television dramas. And the banality and materialism of American life are such that this approach proves wholly appropriate and triumphantly successful. His trivial remarks on gardening are misunderstood by those he encounters (including the President) as metaphorical comments of great wisdom on the state of the economy; his confessions of inadequacy are taken for wry judgments on the inadequacy of his society; his bemused silences are assumed to be pregnant. He is adored by the silent majority, lusted after by women, feted by politicians and the media, and in the end is a likely candidate for the presidency.

Some reviewers complained that Kosinski's characters in this novel are cyphers, mere lay figures illustrating a theme—that he had "renounced almost all the ingredients of fiction for a few scraps from the philosopher's table." As many admired it as a neat and pointed satire, and John Aldridge went further, writing that the book "exists simultaneously on the levels of fiction and fact, fantasy and contemporary history. It is a novel ingeniously conceived and endowed with some of the magical significance of myth." There was a mixed reception also for *The Devil Tree*, another fable about power.

In 1969–1970 Kosinski spent a year at Princeton University as visiting lecturer in English prose and a senior fellow of the Council of the Humanities. In 1970–1972 he was a visiting professor of English prose at Yale Drama School, and a resident fellow of Davenport College, Yale. He received a grant from the American Academy of Arts and Letters in 1970, and the same year was awarded the John Golden Fellowship in Playwriting. Interviewers have described Kosinski as a small, slight, dapper man, fastidious and impatient. He was married in 1962 to Mary H. Weir, daughter of the steel magnate Ernest Weir. She died in 1968 and there are no children of the marriage. Before he emigrated he had built up a considerable reputation as a photographer, and his determination and self-discipline are such that he would excel in almost any field he chose. Indeed he is by no means committed to his present profession, and will write only so long as it satisfies him: "If I would stop liking it, I would try to find something else to do."

PRINCIPAL WORKS: *Fiction*—The Painted Bird, 1965; Steps, 1968; Being There, 1971; The Devil Tree, 1973. *Nonfiction (as "Joseph Novak")*—The Future Is Ours, Comrade, 1960; No Third Path, 1962.
ABOUT: Kosinski, J. Notes of the Author on The Painted Bird, 1965; Kosinski, J. The Art of the Self: Essays à propos Steps, 1968; Vinson, J. (ed.) Contemporary Novelists, 1972; Who's Who in America, 1972–1973. *Periodicals*—Harper's March 1969; Life December 6, 1968; Listener May 8, 1969; New Republic October 26, 1968; New Statesman May 9, 1969; New York Times October 20, 1968; Publishers' Weekly April 26, 1971; Saturday Review April 17, 1971; Times May 10, 1969.

***KOTT, JAN** (October 27, 1914–), Polish critic, scholar, and translator, reports that he was: "Born in Warsaw, two months after the outbreak of the First World War. Went to school and University in Warsaw, where in 1936 he graduated at the Faculty of Law. He published his first books of poetry while still a student. He was the first to translate Éluard into Polish. In 1938 he went to Paris on a French scholarship. He was connected with French surrealist poets and at the same time with the progressive Catholic movement. He passed, as he wrote later, a shortened course in surrealism and Thomism. He was a frequent guest at the house of Raïssa and Jacques Maritain and was a close friend of Tristan Tzara.

"He returned to Poland a month before the outbreak of the Second World War, was mobilised and took part in the defense of Warsaw. Afterwards lived in Lwów but came back to Warsaw where frequently he had to change addresses, names and papers. He earned his living by illegal currency transactions, took part in the Polish underground movement, edited an illegal newspaper and was a member of the Polish People's Army. At the same time he was writing his first serious book, *Mythology and Realism*, an account of tastes and literary patterns of his youth.

"After the Warsaw uprising he joined an army unit. His first postwar years he spent in Lodz, where he belonged to a radical group called 'Kuznica.' *Mythology and Realism* was one of the first books to be published after the war. In 1947 he obtained his Ph.D. at Lodz University.

"He is a founder member of the Institute of Literary Studies of the Polish Academy of Sciences; in 1949 he was appointed to the Chair of Romance Languages at the University of Wroclaw, and in 1952 to the Chair of History of Polish Literature at Warsaw University.

"Since the war he has concentrated on theatrical criticism and written regularly for various magazines. He has translated both classical (Diderot) and modern writers (Éluard, Camus, Aragon, etc.). His main interest though is in such modern dramatists as Sartre, Ionesco, Vaillant, whose plays he has translated.

* kot

JAN KOTT

"He took an active interest in the political and cultural life of postwar Poland; in 1951 and 1955 he was awarded the State Prize in Literature and Literary Studies. In 1964 he received the Herder Award in Vienna. He is an expert on the Polish Enlightment and the author of numerous essays on English and French novels of the eighteenth century. He has also published essays on Molière and on the modern European drama.

"In spring 1965 he was elected an Honorary Member of the Modern Language Association of America. He is an Advisory Board member of the *Tulane Drama Review*, New Orleans and *Dialog*, Warsaw. In September 1965 he directed two plays by Mrozek at the Royal Lyceum Theatre in Edinburgh."

Jan Kott's thought was shaped by Poland's agonizing experiences under totalitarianism. A progressive Catholic before the war, he joined the A.L. (the Communist-led resistance group) during the German occupation, finding in Marxism a faith to cling to through the Nazi nightmare. By 1950, Kott was no longer able to accept the Communist regime's cultural doctrines. He became one of the leading figures in the movement leading to the "Polish October" of 1956—so fearless and articulate an opponent of "Socialist Realism" that such heresies became known as "Kottism." He resigned from the Party in 1957, following the suppression of the planned magazine *Europa*.

His political activities apart, *Mitologia i realizm*

(Mythology and Realism, 1946) and subsequent studies had established Kott as one of the most original and influential of Polish critics. More recently, as he says, he has concentrated on the theatre, and it is in this field that he has achieved an international reputation and influence, above all as the author of *Szkice o Szekspirze* (Sketches on Shakespeare, 1961), which has been translated into a dozen languages, and into English as *Shakespeare Our Contemporary* (1964). Arguing that every age sees its own image in Shakespeare, Kott in these essays shows how the plays can seem to reflect our own agonies and grimaces: the police state, moral anarchy, nihilism, and even the concept of the Absurd. The book had an extremely controversial reception. Frank Kermode charged Kott with "rhetorical extravagance, muddled method . . . a weakness for striking but improbable historical parallels and inferences." Harold Clurman said that the book "elevates Beckett and Genet by reducing Shakespeare to our size," but conceded its brilliance. The consensus seemed to be that Kott had taken his argument too far, impoverishing Shakespeare by recognizing only the dark side of his vision, but at the same time uncovering in that region a wealth of fresh insights. These insights have illuminated a number of subsequent Shakespearian productions, notably the Royal Shakespeare Company's versions of *King Lear* and *Titus Andronicus.* Their director, Peter Brook, has said that Kott—"this quick-witted and combative man"—writes as freshly as an eyewitness at the Globe.

Kott's *Theatre Notebook* for the years between 1947 and 1967 includes a brief history of Polish drama, essays on an assortment of writers who have influenced the modern theatre, and accounts of a variety of theatrical productions in many parts of the world. The latter section is as much travel diary as dramatic criticism but, as Stanley Young wrote, Kott "seems to relate the theater to every aspect of the human condition, so that his book, which at first appears casual and even disorganized, finally assumes a masterful inner logic and form." Clurman noted that Kott "clowns a bit, plays the chameleon, flirts with too many divergent notions," but "feels theatre in his every fiber. . . . He is truly cultivated and generously informed. He possesses an alert mind, a cosmopolitan background, a canny spirit . . . [and is] one of the finest theatre critics to be read in English."

Jan Kott was married to Lidia Steinhaus in 1939 and has two children. He settled in the United States in 1966, teaching as a visiting professor at Yale (1966–1967 and 1968–1969), at San Francisco State College (1967), and at Berkeley (1967–1968). Since 1969 he has been professor of comparative drama at the State University of New York at Stony Brook. Kott is said to be "intense, dapper, and slight in stature." He has two hobbies—mountain climbing and collecting odd and ugly postcards.

PRINCIPAL WORKS IN ENGLISH TRANSLATION: Shakespeare, Our Contemporary, 1964; Theatre Notebook 1947–1967, 1968; The Eating of the Gods: An Interpretation of Greek Tragedy, 1973.

ABOUT: Contemporary Authors 13–14, 1965; Current Biography, 1969; Gömöri, G. Polish and Hungarian Poetry 1945–1956, 1966; International Who's Who, 1973–74; Who's Who in America, 1972–1973. *Periodicals*—Book Week December 4, 1964; New York Review of Books September 24, 1964; Times Literary Supplement September 27, 1963; Yale Review December 1964.

***KRAUS, KARL** (April 28, 1874–June 12, 1936), Austrian satirist, poet, and dramatist, was born in Jičin (or Gitschin), Bohemia, the son of Jacob Kraus, a wealthy Jewish paper manufacturer, and Ernestine (Kantor) Kraus. When he was two the family moved to Vienna, where Kraus was educated and where he was to spend his life. In 1895, when he graduated from the University of Vienna, he became a freelance journalist, and quickly made his mark. At the age of twenty-five he founded his own journal of literary and social criticism, *Die Fackel* (The Torch). Its early contributors included not only writers of the caliber of Strindberg, but such newcomers as Trakl, Kokoschka, and Werfel, some of whom learned much from Kraus's "despotic tutelage." In time Kraus began to write more and more of the magazine himself, and after about 1912 was its sole contributor.

Erich Heller sees in Kraus the "ethical radicalism of an Old Testament prophet"; Kraus saw in himself the embodiment and guardian of the mores and culture of Austro-Hungary. In the 922 issues of *Die Fackel* published between 1899 and his death in 1936, Kraus's corrosive satirical invective was directed against every symptom of decline from the great traditions of the past—or, as some would say, against every sign of change and progress. His targets included commercialism, noisy patriotism, galloping technology, psychoanalysis, new-fangled literary styles, corruption and hypocrisy in the church and government, and above all the shoddy opportunism, masquerading as idealism, which he called "journalism." His magazine became the "moral conscience of Vienna."

Most of Kraus's books collected matter first published in *Die Fackel*, and it was his essays that established his reputation. Explicit in many of them and implicit in all of Kraus's work was an almost mystical concern for language. His principal grievance against the liberal press was its prostitution of linguistic values, and in this, and the aborting of true communication, he saw a major cause of social

* krous

KARL KRAUS

decadence. For Kraus, therefore, literary composition was as much a moral as an aesthetic act—"My language is the universal whore whom I have to make into a virgin." In his nine volumes of verse (*Worte in Versen*, 1916–1930), traditional in subject and gentler than his prose, this scrupulous purity of form and utterance produced a certain pedestrian quality. Most critics agree that Kraus was at his best in his aphorisms, the "masterpieces of penetrating wit and precision" collected in *Sprüche und Widersprüche* (1909), *Pro Domo et Mondo* (1912), and *Nachts* (1919).

Kraus's *magnum opus* was the antiwar drama *Die letzten Tage der Menschheit* (The Last Days of Mankind, 1915–1919), for which he was three times nominated for a Nobel Prize. It would take ten evenings to perform in full, if it ever were performed, and is an immense satirical review in the German cabaret tradition of the events and personalities of World War I—of "those years," as Kraus said, "when characters from an operetta played the tragedy of mankind." It is a satire with the effect of tragedy.

In his later years Kraus enjoyed great success with his "theatre of poetry"—one-man readings and performances of plays, poems, and even of entire operettas—for which he translated Shakespeare's sonnets and a number of the plays. Personally shy, Kraus has been called a "man alone," who drew a wall around his private life and lived for his work. As a young man he was a temporary convert to Roman Catholicism, and he believed always in the possibility of salvation through the exercise of free will. He died of an embolism in Vienna at the age of sixty-two.

Kraus had his disciples, but was hated and ignored by the contemporary press, scorned by many as a spiteful and self-righteous crank, and for years little regarded by literary historians. Respect for him has grown enormously in recent years. In Germany his complete works were republished in twelve volumes between 1952 and 1964, and more recently *Die Fackel* has been reprinted *in toto*, but he has been little translated—is indeed untranslatable. As Heller says: "through him the beauty, profundity and accumulated moral experience of the German language assumed personal shape." Kraus, "one of the greatest literary personalities of his time," has also been called the "greatest German satirist of the last one hundred and fifty years."

PRINCIPAL WORKS IN ENGLISH TRANSLATION: Poems, 1930 (translated by Albert Bloch).

ABOUT: Field, F. The Last Days of Mankind: Karl Kraus and His Vienna, 1968; Grigson, G. (ed.) Concise Encyclopedia of Modern World Literature, 1963; Heller, E. The Disinherited Mind, 1952; Kohn, C. Karl Kraus, 1962; Kraft, W. Karl Kraus, 1956; Lasker-Schueler, E. Briefe an K. Kraus, 1959; Liegler, L. Karl Kraus und sein Werk, 1920; Schaukal, R. von. Kraus, 1933; Stephan, J. Satire und Sprache, 1964; Zohn, H. Karl Kraus, 1971. *Periodicals*—Books Abroad Summer, 1964; Modern Language Quarterly March 1961; New York Review of Books May 3, 1973.

***KRLEŽA, MIROSLAV** (July 7, 1893–), Yugoslav novelist, dramatist, and poet, and the dominant figure in Croatian literature, was born in Zagreb. His father, a civil servant, sent him to the Ludoviceum military academy in Budapest, which he hated. He served from 1914 to 1918 in the Austrian army, and ever since has earned his living as a professional writer.

The fall of the Austro-Hungarian Empire in 1918 ushered in a period of extreme political, religious, and cultural turbulence in the cluster of quite disparate small countries that now form Yugoslavia. On the one hand, each of these countries had a separate national heritage to be rediscovered and explored; on the other, they shared an urge to absorb the culture and ideology of the West, from which the Balkans had been separated by five hundred years of Turkish rule. "We are boring a hole from the fourteenth century to the present," Krleža once remarked.

In his own work he has looked outwards to the literature and learning of all Europe—he is a man of great erudition—and backwards into the past of his own country. But central to his writing is a political idealism which, sparked by hatred of the Hapsburg military caste, and of the reactionary Croatian bourgeoisie from which he sprang, has developed as a profound and enlightened socialism.

Krleža's early gropings towards this "radical humanism" are already evident (somewhat at odds

* kər′ le zhə

with the influence of Nietzsche and Marinetti) in his first published book, *Pjesme* (Poems, 1919). In 1919 he founded a Marxist-oriented literary review, *Plamen* (Flame) which, together with its successor, *Književna Republika* (Literary Republic), exerted a powerful influence on Krleža's contemporaries. For the young radicals of the 1920s and 1930s, Ernst Pawel wrote, Krleža was "the synthesis of poetry and revolution, of Slavic fervor and Western aesthetics, a romantic realist equally uncompromising in his literary standards and his political idealism."

With *Tri kavalira G-djice Melanije* (Three Suitors of Miss Melanie, 1920), Krleža began the long series of novels which form a vast and savage caricature of the greed and decadence of the Croatian middle class between the turn of the century and the present day. The best known of these books include *Hrvatski bog Mars* (The Croat God Mars, 1922), about the mindless squandering in the Austrian army of the lives of the peasant soldiery; *Povratak Filipa Latinovicza* (1932, translated as *The Return of Philip Latinovicz* in 1960), about an artist's struggle to regain his creativity in a world of provincial decadence; *Na Rubu Pameti* (On the Edge of Reason, 1938), about a Zagreb lawyer's revolt against his trivial and corrupt society; and *Banket u Blitvi* (Banquet in Blitva, 1938–1939), an allegorical study of dictatorship which established him as the most widely read novelist in Yugoslavia. "In the piercing light of his intelligence," wrote the Yugoslav critic Svetozar Koljevic, "the *données* of Croatian social history shape themselves into a nightmare of grotesque forms and the very flavor of his work is due to his enormous power of enacting this grotesquerie in language." Krleža's later novels have tended towards greater realism and deeper psychological analysis, but they retain "an exuberance of imagination and a narrative power comparable to those of Balzac or Victor Hugo."

Similar themes preoccupy Krleža in his plays. *Golgota* (Golgotha, 1922) is a socialist and partly expressionist drama, a triumphant experiment in mass movement set in a shipyard. Its tone has been compared to that of the early plays of Sean O'Casey. The Glembajevi trilogy (1930–1932), an "Ibsen-like vivisection of the higher middle-class," traces the degeneration of a typical capitalist family in Croatia under Austro-Hungarian rule. *Legende* (1933) uses the stories of Christ, Michelangelo, and Columbus to state a theme that recurs in Krleža's work—the close relationship between moral and artistic perception. The spiritual explorer, the artist, and the voyager are all shown engaged in man's highest endeavor, the probably hopeless but noble attempt to wring meaning from the chaos of life. One of the most admired of Krleža's works is *Petrica Kerumpuh* (1936), a satirical ballad written

MIROSLAV KRLEŽA

in the Kajkavic dialect of medieval Zagreb about the adventures of a Croatian Till Eulenspiegel.

Krleža's long struggle for socialism in Yugoslavia was recognized by the Tito government after World War II, when he became director of the Yugoslav Institute of Lexicography, vice-president of the Yugoslav Academy of Science and Art, and president of the Yugoslav Writers' Union. His collected works were published in 1953–1956. Nevertheless, Krleža's militant "radical humanism" and his outspoken criticism of every kind of political and social injustice, whether from the right or the left, have kept him at the center of a storm of controversy. Death sentences have been passed on him by Stalinists as once they were by the Croat right wing. He has ridiculed the notion of "socialist realism" in the arts, and his demands for freedom of cultural development have had great influence in Yugoslavia. Yet he has broken with the leading "revisionist" Milovan Djilas.

The author of over fifty books that include essays and criticism as well as novels, plays, stories, and poetry, Krleža is still little known in the West, except in Germany, where his work has been greatly admired, and in France, where it has earned comparison with Malraux and Céline. Only one of his major works has appeared in English—*The Return of Philip Latinovicz*. It made no great stir, and A. Alvarez wrote that it began "with a Thomas Mann-like analysis of exhausted gloom and decadence," and ended "in pure Dostoievskian excesses." There is an obvious need for much more widespread translation of this "giant of Yugoslav literature." When Ivo Andrić went to Stockholm to receive the 1961 Nobel Prize for Literature and was asked what his Swedish publisher could do for him, he replied: "Publish Krleža."

A visitor described Krleža in his seventies as "massive, blunt, yet at the same time incongruously kind, a cherubic Jupiter with an enormous head fringed by recalcitrant tufts of white hair . . . the vigor and enthusiasm of a man half his age. . . . Everything about the man conveys a lack of pretense, a spontaneous warmth which rarely appears in his work." Krleža lives in Zagreb and is editing Yugoslav's first multivolume encyclopedia—an enormous task which has not prevented him from publishing new work of his own, including a four-volume novel. In 1968, when he was seventy-five, Krleža told a writers' conference in Ljubljana: "Our mission is to open doors, to prove by our works that we have always struggled for freedom of artistic expression, for the simultaneous existence of different schools and styles, for liberty of choice and independence of moral and political convictions."

PRINCIPAL WORKS IN ENGLISH TRANSLATION: The Return of Philip Latinovicz, 1960; The Cricket Beneath the Waterfall (stories), 1973. *Stories in* Koljevic, S. (ed.) Yugoslav Short Stories, 1966; Lenski, B. (ed.) Death of a Simple Giant, and Other Modern Yugoslav Stories, 1965; Atlantic December 1962. *Poems in* Lavrin, J. (ed.) Anthology of Modern Yugoslav Poetry, 1963; Atlantic December 1962.

ABOUT: Alvarez, A. Under Pressure, 1965; Encyclopaedia Britannica, 1966; International Who's Who, 1973–74; Kolcevic, S. *introduction to* Yugoslav Short Stories, 1966; Lenski, B. *introduction to* Death of a Simple Giant, 1965; Penguin Companion to Literature 2, 1969; Smith, H. (ed.) Columbia Dictionary of Modern European Literature, 1947; Twentieth Century Writing, 1969. *Periodicals*—Books Abroad Autumn 1963; New York Times Book Review August 15, 1965, February 23, 1969; Partisan Review Fall 1957; Slavonic and East European Review January 1967; Times Literary Supplement May 6, 1960; World Theatre 4, 1955.

***KUNITZ, STANLEY (JASSPON)** (July 29, 1905–), American poet, editor, and translator, writes: "It was not an auspicious beginning. A few weeks before my birth my father, of whom I know practically nothing aside from his name, killed himself. The ostensibly prosperous dress-manufacturing business in Worcester, Massachusetts, that my parents operated was discovered to be bankrupt. My mother, then in her forties, with three children to support, opened a dry-goods shop and sewed garments in the back room. Out of pride and honor she drove herself to pay off her inheritance of debts, though she had no legal obligation to do so. She was a woman of formidable will, staunch heart, and razor-sharp intelligence, whose only school was the sweatshops of New York, to which she had come alone as a child from her native Lithuania. After a few years of widowhood she owned a substantial enterprise again, feeding her designs to a capacious loft humming with machines. She must have been one of the first women to run a large-scale business in this country.

"My mother had little time to give to her family, and my older sisters seemed somehow detached from my secret life. When I was eight, I was presented with a stepfather, Mark Dine, a gentle and scholarly man who was no help at all to my mother in her business, but who showed me the ways of tenderness and affection. His death six years later left me desolate. Both my sisters married and died young. My mother survived these onslaughts, as well as another bankruptcy—precipitated by her reluctance to discharge any of her employees in a time of depression—and lived alertly to the age of eighty-six, articulate to the last on the errors of capitalism and the tragedy of existence.

"I was educated in the Indian-haunted woods behind our house at the edge of the city; at the Majestic and Bijou nickelodeons, where I saw nearly every early movie that was made; at the public library, which I ransacked daily for treasures; and in the Worcester public schools, from whose Classical High School I was graduated as valedictorian. I studied violin with Margaret MacQuade, a favorite pupil of the Belgian virtuoso Eugène Ysaÿe, and from her acquired a precious instrument, still in my possession, that he had once played. One morning in high school my English teacher, Martin Post, tossed away his textbook and changed my life by reciting one of Robert Herrick's songs. The play of language and the subtlety of the music enthralled me. From that day forward I lost my ardor for a concert career. Immediately after Herrick the poets who shook me were Keats, Tennyson, Wordsworth, and Blake.

"At Harvard, where I was a scholarship student, I immersed myself in the poetry of the Metaphysicals and pronounced myself an advocate of the Moderns, from Hopkins down to Joyce and Eliot and Cummings. These were the writers whose techniques I chose to investigate for my Master's thesis, much to the consternation of my triumvirate of mentors, Professors Lowes and Kittredge and Babbitt. Although I had been awarded the Garrison Medal for Poetry and had been graduated *summa cum laude*, I was ultimately denied a post as teaching assistant on the ground that 'Anglo-Saxons would resent being instructed in English by a Jew.' That, of course, was in the Dark Ages of academic history, but I left Harvard in a rage and have never felt right about my *alma mater* since. The best college memories I have are of the outsiders: Ford Madox Ford, who came from England to the Yard for a short-term residence, bringing his wheeze and his fabulous tales about the literary great; Robert Gay, visiting teacher of composition, who said to

* kyōō′ nits

me, 'You are a poet—be one'; and Alfred North Whitehead, serene and beatific man, at whose feet I sat, not caring whether I understood a word, in his first and my last year at Harvard.

"For several summers I had served an apprenticeship on the Worcester *Telegram*, and now I joined the staff as reporter and feature writer. Two of my assignments left a mark on me. I was the first newspaperman to interview Robert H. Goddard, professor of physics at Clark University, scoffed at locally as 'the moon man,' after he had introduced the space age in a nearby field by firing his prototypal liquid-fuel rocket. Another Worcesterite whose path I crossed was Judge Webster Thayer, the frightened little man who sent Sacco and Vanzetti to their doom. Their case became my cause, and shortly after their executions in August 1927 I left for New York on a mission to find a publisher for Vanzetti's letters. Nobody would touch them then. Years later, when they were issued without my intervention, they were acclaimed as a noble and eloquent chapter in the American testament that is still being written.

"The early years of a writer are the decisive ones. By the time I came to New York I was already a poet, a freethinker, and a rebel. With the first money I saved from my new editorial job with The H. W. Wilson Company I departed for Europe, fully expecting to be fired; but Mr. Wilson surprised himself by giving me permission to edit the *Wilson Library Bulletin* from abroad. When I returned a year later, I moved to a one-hundred-acre farm in Connecticut (that I purchased for five hundred dollars down) and continued to perform my editorial duties *in absentia*. My place in Mansfield Center was called Wormwood Hill, which has since given its name to a poetry magazine. Through the years of Depression I tilled its stony fields with a yoke of white oxen. By then I was married and had published *Intellectual Things*, my first book of poems. The title, from Blake's phrase, 'the tear is an intellectual thing,' has generally been misconstrued as defining a cerebral type of verse, whereas in truth I meant to stress the inseparability of mind from body.

"As the thirties drew to a close, I was living in Bucks County, Pennsylvania, with my second wife. During Hitler's rise to power and the Spanish Civil War I became politically active as 'a premature anti-Fascist,' though committed to a philosophy of non-violence and consistently too much of an anti-institutionalist to identify myself with any party of the Left. After Pearl Harbor I was confronted with the necessity of reconciling my conscientious objection with my overt desire for the destruction of Hitler and everything he stood for. I tried to solve the dilemma as honestly as I could by accepting military service and at the same time refusing to

STANLEY KUNITZ

bear arms—an unorthodox and unworkable arrangement that almost wrecked me for three years in the ranks.

"After my discharge I was invited to join the faculty of Bennington College at the instigation of my friend Theodore Roethke, and there began my long love affair with teaching. Since then, as a believer in mobility, I have taught at numerous colleges, always on a year-to-year basis, without tenure, without wanting to put roots down on any campus. My present connection is with Columbia, as adjunct professor, attached to the graduate school of writing. I am also a fellow at Yale, and since 1969 have been editor of the Yale Series of Younger Poets. In Provincetown, Massachusetts, on Cape Cod, where I spend a good portion of the year with my third wife, the painter Elise Asher, I am associated with the Fine Arts Work Center, a community of young artists and writers. Our New York residence is in Greenwich Village. I have a daughter, Gretchen, by my second marriage.

"In the spring of 1967, under the aegis of the cultural exchange program jointly sponsored by the State Department and the Union of Soviet Writers, I made an extensive tour of the Soviet Union and gave an unprecedented series of lectures and readings, from Moscow to Tbilisi. Among the poets I have translated from the Russian, usually in collaboration with a linguist, are Voznesensky, Yevtushenko, and Mandelstam. In 1972 I completed and prepared for publication, with Max Hayward, a volume of translations from the poetry of Anna Akhmatova, and undertook the supervision of a collaborative project to translate the work of the contemporary Ukrainian poet Ivan Drach.

"As I look back, I can say, without apology, that I have lived a full, passionate, and productive life, of which poetry is the crystal and the flower. My loathing for bigotry and war, my feeling for plants and animals, my obsession with gardening, my zest for teaching and tennis, my pleasures of solitude no less than of companionship, my sense of mortality, my yearning for transcendence, my passion for the word . . . all seem to me of a piece. No doubt I would have written more poems over the years if I had made, in Yeats's phrase, 'a stone of the heart,' but I am not persuaded they would have been worth the cost. Each morning I still wake to the challenge of the new day. As I once wrote in an essay: 'The hard, inescapable phenomenon to be faced is that we are living and dying at once . . . my commitment is to report that dialogue.' The first demand made on me is to survive.

"I keep trying to improve my controls over language, so that I won't have to tell lies. And I keep reading the masters, because they infect me with human possibility. The vainest ambition is to want an art separated from its heritage, as though the tradition were a cistern full of toads instead of a life-giving fountain. A poet without a sense of history is a deprived child.

"Since my *Selected Poems* I have been moving toward a more open style, based on natural speech rhythms. *The Testing-Tree* (1971) embodied my search for a transparency of language and vision. Maybe age itself compels me to embrace the great simplicities, as I struggle to free myself from the knots and complications, the hang-ups, of my youth. I am no more reconciled than I ever was to the world's wrongs and the injustice of time. The poetry I admire most is innocent, luminous, and true."

Stanley Kunitz is the son of Solomon and Yetta (Jasspon) Kunitz. Because he died before Kunitz was born, his father remained an enigma, whose unrevealed and therefore "indomitable" love kept the poet for many years "in chains," and who haunts Kunitz's poetry.

As he says, Kunitz went to New York in 1927 and joined The H. W. Wilson Company, publishers of indexes and reference works. Under his editorship the *Wilson Library Bulletin* soon became something a great deal more stimulating and socially conscious than the house organ it was intended to be. The distinguished librarian Jesse Shera, looking back many years later, wrote: "To our full buoyancy of youth, the *Wilson Library Bulletin* gave a generous share of hope, and joy, and aspiration. . . . With Stanley Kunitz at its head, it was a rallying point for a group of youngsters who were in hot revolt against tradition."

Kunitz's poems began to appear in 1928 in such magazines as the *Dial*, *Poetry*, the *Nation*, and *Commonweal*. His first book, *Intellectual Things*, was published in 1930. It was received with a degree of critical attention that acknowledged the grandly ambitious scope of the poetic enterprise it represented. Many of these early lyrics, as one critic has said, are explorations of "the vast, uncharted reaches of the inner world." From these dangerous journeys the poet returns with news which, if it is sometimes personal to the point of obscurity, is often deeply revelatory of the connections between one man's sorrows and the general human tragedy, between biography and history, dream and myth.

These poems are intricate and elliptical in their conceits, traditional in their meters, musical in their language, reminding many reviewers of Donne, Marvell, and Herbert. Nevertheless they could only have been conceived by a wholly—even archetypally—modern sensibility, alienated from self, society, and religion, "whirling between two wars," aware of Freud and Jung in a way which is evident in the highly visual and often surreal imagery. Some critics were troubled by the obscurities in these poems, or by a sense that strong feeling was being handled too gingerly, with intellectual tongs. But most readers seemed aware that they were witnessing the debut of a poetic talent that might well be a major one.

During the 1930s and early 1940s Kunitz, mostly in collaboration with Howard Haycraft, edited for The H. W. Wilson Company a series of biographical reference books about authors that have become standard works. Kunitz relinquished the editorship of the *Wilson Library Bulletin* and left the Wilson Company in 1943, when World War II interrupted his career, but co-edited three subsequent volumes in the Wilson Authors Series and acted as editorial consultant in the compilation of World Authors, 1950–1970.

The dilemma which he mentions above, of how to reconcile his pacifism with his equally passionate anti-Fascism, was resolved honorably if not very happily during his three years with the Air Transport Command; he devoted himself to informational and educational duties, including the editorship of a weekly news magazine, *Ten Minute Break*, and was discharged in 1945 with the rank of staff sergeant. *Passport to the War*, a book of fifty poems, twenty-four of them from *Intellectual Things*, was published in 1944—fourteen years after the first volume. Many of the new poems were harsher than the old, full of skeletal and spiky imagery, and more overtly concerned with social and political themes, especially the spiritual pollution which the poet sees as the product of man's misuse of nature. Critics noted an increased and boldly imaginative use of scientific language and imagery, but some found poems in which the intensity of the poet's anger had marred his usually scrupulous craftsmanship. There were some fine poems, including the much quoted and discussed "Father and Son," but Horace Gregory complained of a certain shrillness, "a general lack of ease."

After the war, Kunitz went as professor of literature to Bennington College (1946–1949). Since then he has directed poetry workshops at the Potsdam Summer Workshop in the Creative Arts (1949–1953), at the New School for Social Research (1950–1957), and the Poetry Center in New York (1958–1962), and has taught as a visiting lecturer or professor at many other institutions. He has described his teaching philosophy in these terms: "Essentially what I try to do is to help each person rediscover the poet within himself. I say 'rediscover' because I am convinced that it is a universal human attribute to want to play with words, to beat out rhythms, to fashion images, to tell a story, to construct forms. . . . The key is always in his possession: what prevents him from using it is mainly inertia, the stultification of the senses as a result of our one-sided educational conditioning and the fear of being made ridiculous or ashamed by the exposure of his feelings."

It was not until 1958, after another fourteen-year silence, that Kunitz's next book appeared (and only then, he has revealed, after it had been rejected by eight publishers, three of whom had refused even to read it). This was his *Selected Poems*, a third of them new, which brought him the Pulitzer Prize in 1959. The new poems continued the history of a mind which, anguished and sometimes almost defeated in the earlier work, had now learned to "suffer the twentieth century" and survive, finding solace and order and often joy in nature and art, and in human love: "Cities shall suffer siege and some shall fall, / But man's not taken. What the deep heart means, / Its message of the big, round, childish hand, / Its wonder, its simply lonely cry, / The bloodied envelope addressed to you, / Is history, that wide and mortal pang" ("Night Letter"). Vivian Mercier wrote that "the tension in the poetry has not slackened, but much of the strain (or straining) has disappeared." It seemed to James Wright that "his book shudders with life, and flings seeds in all directions. . . . The publication of his *Selected Poems* is, I believe, an event of major importance for everyone who cares about art and human civilization in this country. The book stands on the terrible threshold of greatness."

Kunitz's Pulitzer Prize was the most important in a long list of awards including the Oscar Blumenthal Prize (1941), a Guggenheim Fellowship (1945–1946), the Amy Lowell Traveling Fellowship (1953–1954), the Levinson Prize (1956), the Harriet Monroe Award (1958), and grants from the Ford Foundation (1958–1959) and the National Institute of Arts and Letters (1959). A Brandeis University Creative Arts Award followed in 1964 and the Fellowship Award of the Academy of American Poets in 1968. In spite of these honors, and in spite of the admiration of such poets as Robert Lowell, Marianne Moore, and Theodore Roethke, Kunitz remained until recently what John Ciardi called him in 1958, "certainly the most neglected good poet of the last quarter-century." Critics seeking to explain this neglect pointed out that he writes slowly and rejects much, that his work is condensed and sometimes hermetic and sometimes painful, probing too deeply for comfort into the human psyche. Nevertheless, his reputation has grown steadily, and his enormously successful reading tour of the Soviet Union in 1967 brought him a celebrity which has been increased by similar performances in the United States, sometimes in the company of the Russian poets he has befriended and translated.

These experiences may have helped to stimulate his interest in "a more open style, based on natural speech rhythms," and therefore more suitable than his earlier work for public reading. At any rate, in his fourth book of poetry, *The Testing-Tree*, he had thrown away what Robert Lowell called "the once redoubtable armor," the hermeticism and "the passionate gnarl": "All is unencumbered and trustful. One reads from cover to cover with the ease of reading good prose fiction."

This new directness of diction and syntax is the hard-won evidence of Kunitz's victory in what he calls "my struggle to free myself from the knots and complications, the hang-ups, of my youth." The old obsessions are still there—the tyranny of time, the lost father, the death of love—but fully confronted now, their intellectual or romantic disguises put aside. But this new simplicity is far removed from the tone of astonished simple-mindedness fashionable in American poetry in the 1960s. Kunitz remains a poet in progress and his quest continues. He moves, in Stanley Moss's phrase, "from the known to the unknown to the unknowable" as he always did; the difference is that now much more is known. "The King of the River" is a poem about the last great journey upriver of the Pacific salmon, and also about a man aging: "The great clock of your life / is slowing down, / and the small clocks run wild. / For this you were born." In "River Road" the poet revisits a former home, where a marriage ended and he planted ten thousand trees: "That year of the cloud, when my marriage failed, / I paced up and down the bottom-fields, / tamping the mud-puddled nurselings in. . . . // Lord! Lord! who has lived so long? . . . / I park my car below the curve / and climbing over the tumbled stones / where the wild foxgrape perseveres, / I walk into the woods I made, / my dark and resinous, blistered land, / through the deep litter of the years."

Few reviewers were in much doubt that, with several of the poems in *The Testing-Tree*, including certainly the title piece, "River Road," and "King of the River," Kunitz had passed over "the terrible threshold of greatness." Stanley Moss, "blessed and tortured" by the book's artistry, wrote that "Kunitz, now in his mid-sixties, has found his way. His self, poetry and nature are worked with as one consubstantive stuff. This accomplishment . . . should occasion a national holiday." Robert Lowell called the volume an "awesome offering of labor and self-knowledge. . . . I don't know of another [book] in prose or verse that gives in a few pages the impression of a large autobiography."

PRINCIPAL WORKS: *Poetry*—Intellectual Things, 1930; Passport to the War, 1944; Selected Poems, 1928–1958, 1958; The Testing-Tree, 1971. *As editor*—(as "Dilly Tante") Living Authors: A Book of Biographies, 1931; (with Howard Haycraft and W. C. Hadden) Authors Today and Yesterday: A Companion Volume to Living Authors, 1933; (with Howard Haycraft) The Junior Book of Authors, 1934; (with Howard Haycraft) British Authors of the Nineteenth Century, 1936; (with Howard Haycraft) American Authors: 1600–1900, 1938; (with Howard Haycraft) Twentieth Century Authors: A Biographical Dictionary of Modern Literature, 1942; (with Howard Haycraft) British Authors Before 1800, 1952; (with Vineta Colby) Twentieth Century Authors: First Supplement, 1955; Poems of John Keats, 1964; (with Vineta Colby) European Authors: 1000–1900, 1967. *As translator*—(with others) Voznesensky, A. Antiworlds, and, The Fifth Ace, 1967; (with others) Yevtushenko, Y. Stolen Apples, 1971; (with Max Hayward) Poems of Akhmatova, 1973.

ABOUT: Current Biography, 1959; Hungerford, E. B. (ed.) Poets in Progress, 1962; International Who's Who, 1972–1973; Mills, R. J., Jr. Contemporary American Poetry, 1965; Murphy, R. (ed.) Contemporary Poets of the English Language, 1970; Nyren, D. (ed.) Modern American Literature (Library of Literary Criticism), 1960; Ostroff, A. J. (ed.) The Contemporary Poet as Artist and Critic, 1964; Who's Who in America, 1972–1973. *Periodicals*—Books July 13, 1930; College English May 1967; Commonweal April 21, 1944; February 13, 1959; Nation October 11, 1958; September 20, 1971; New York Times Book Review March 26, 1944; November 16, 1958; March 21, 1971; April 16, 1972; New York Times Magazine August 20, 1967; Newsweek April 12, 1971; Poetry July 1930; June 1944; December 1958; Wilson Library Bulletin November 1941; February, November 1943; November 1954; September 1958; September 1959; May 1960; Yale Literary Magazine May 1968.

LAMMING, GEORGE (June 8, 1927–), West Indian novelist and poet, was born of mixed African and English parentage in Barbados. He was brought up by his mother, and his autobiographical novel *In the Castle of My Skin* evokes a Tom Sawyer–like boyhood with his friends "Trumper," "Boy Blue," and "Bob." A scholarship to Combermere High School was the first in a series of steps away from his roots in the village. Suddenly, he says, the village people "had nothing to communicate since my allegiances, they thought, had been transferred to the other world."

At school Lamming's life "alternated between boyish indifference and tolerable misery"; it was at this time that he began to write. In 1946 he left Barbados to teach at a boarding school for South Americans in Trinidad: "The earth where I walked was a marvel of blackness, and I knew in a sense more deep than simple departure I had said farewell to the land." His alienation was complete when, in 1950, he left the West Indies for a writer's career in England.

At first he supported himself as a factory worker and as a freelance writer and broadcaster in the Caribbean service of the British Broadcasting Corporation. *In the Castle of My Skin*, his first book, was published in 1953 with an enthusiastic introduction by Richard Wright and was immediately recognized as the work of a major talent. As Anthony West said, it is less a novel than "a series of sharp and brilliant sketches" of a Barbados boyhood and adolescence, written "with the intensity and precision" of poetry. V. S. Pritchett found it "strange, emotional and compassionate, something between garrulous realism and pop poetry."

Part of the book is written in the first person and is confined to the narrator's experiences and observations; the rest, in the third person, gives a broader view of the village and the island, and amiably satirizes the social and racial snobberies of the islanders. The shifting point of view is a technique that has continued to interest Lamming. It is employed in *The Emigrants* to record the reactions of a mixed group of West Indians newly arrived in England. Most reviewers found this novel badly shaped, overwritten, and unconvincing, but not without passages of lyrical beauty and clear insight.

In 1955 Lamming traveled in the United States on a Guggenheim Fellowship. He subsequently returned to the Caribbean for a long stay and, as is evident in his later books, a revaluation of the people and places that had shaped him. The two novels that followed are both set on the imaginary West Indian island of San Cristobal, a composite of Jamaica, Trinidad, Barbados, and also (as is particularly evident in *voudou* sequences) Haiti.

Of Age and Innocence studies the interaction between a group of adults, most of them in one way or another damaged and disoriented by the colonial situation itself, and a group of local boys, members of an innocent secret organization, "the Society." The catalyst is San Cristobal's first election, which brings a confrontation between white colonial power and the black freedom movement. For the adults the crisis means violence, physical and emotional, and the destruction of comfortable illusions; for the boys also it means the end of innocence. Many critics think this Lamming's best book to date. Mervyn Morris, writing in *The Islands in Between*, found in it "a new and triumphant combination of the elements of Lamming's talent. In masterly language suited to his various purposes, he tells efficiently an interesting story, coherent in design yet free of incredible characters and absurd coincidence; a story which implies, and sometimes explicitly argues, a critique of West Indian society."

Season of Adventure is about the search for identity of Fola, stepdaughter of the San Cristobal police chief, who discovers that she is the daughter of a whore. Exploring her mother's background, she is drawn into the secret world of *voudou*, and eventually reaches acceptance of her situation: "I am Fola, and other than Fola, meaning bastard: other than, and other than, outside and other than." She is free to start on a "history of needs she alone would be able to distinguish: a season of adventure which no man in the republic could predict." Fola's adventure is that of her people, the tentative, tragic, and regretful transition from the secure but unacceptable colonial past to the freedom and dangers of the future. The book seemed to some readers marred by its obtrusive symbolism and rhetoric, as did the two novels that broke a twelve-year silence —*Natives of My Person*, about the strange voyage in search of Utopia of a slave ship, and *Water With Berries*, about a group of West Indian artists in London. But the author has no lack of admirers who (like Thomas Lask) relish his "highly burnished prose" and (like Jan Carew) praise him as "a chronicler of secret journeys to the innermost regions of the West Indian psyche."

Lamming received the Somerset Maugham award in 1958 and a Canada Council Fellowship in 1962. He lives in London but has traveled widely—in Europe, Africa, and North America, as well as in Britain and the Caribbean. He has continued to work as a freelance broadcaster and journalist, and as guest editor of *New World* was responsible for the Guyana and Barbados independence issues. In 1967 he spent a year as writer in residence at the University of the West Indies in Jamaica. His hatred of the system that made him "peasant by birth, colonial by education," is evident in his fiction, in his speeches and articles, and in *The Pleasures of Exile*, a long essay about the problems of the emigrant West Indian writer—the "Caliban" on "Prospero's island."

PRINCIPAL WORKS: *Fiction*—In the Castle of My Skin, 1953; The Emigrants, 1954; Of Age and Innocence, 1958; Season of Adventure, 1960; Natives of My Person, 1972; Water With Berries, 1972. *Essays*—The Pleasures of Exile, 1960.

ABOUT: International Who's Who, 1973–74; James, L. (ed.) The Islands in Between, 1968; Munro, I. and Sander, R. (eds.) Kas-kas: Interviews With Three Caribbean Writers in Texas, 1972; Press, J. (ed.) Commonwealth Literature, 1965; Vinson, J. (ed.) Contemporary Novelists, 1972. *Periodicals*—African Forum Spring 1966; Chicago Sunday Tribune November 22, 1953; New Statesman and Nation April 18, 1953; San Francisco Chronicle June 24, 1955; Time April 25, 1955; Times Literary Supplement March 27, 1953.

GEORGE LAMMING

***LAMPEDUSA, GIUSEPPE (MARIA FABRIZIO) TOMASI DI, PRINCE OF LAMPEDUSA, DUKE OF PALMA** (December 23, 1896–July 23, 1957), Italian novelist and man of letters, was born in Palermo, Sicily. He grew up there and at the family's great palace at Santa Margherita, which he remembered as "a kind of eighteenth-century Pompeii, in which everything had been miraculously preserved intact; something that is . . . almost unique in Sicily, which, on account of its indifference and poverty, is the most destructive country that exists." The *palazzo* was sold just after World War I and is now a ruin. Lampedusa's father was the head of a family traditionally descended from Tiberius I, Emperor of Byzantium. His mother came of another noble Sicilian family, and was born Princess Beatrice Filangeri di Cutò. Lampedusa was never very close to his father, an elegant man of the world, but adored his mother, a gay socialite until her life was darkened by the brutal murder of her sister by a lover in 1911.

In 1916 Lampedusa interrupted his education to go to the Austrian front as an artillery officer. He was captured near Bolzano and imprisoned at Szombathely in Hungary, but escaped on his second attempt and made his way home on foot and in disguise. He remained in the army for some years after the war, and never lost his interest in military

* lam pā dōō′ zə

GIUSEPPE DI LAMPEDUSA

matters; the works of Clausewitz were among his favorite reading. When he returned to civilian life in the early 1920s he intended to take up a diplomatic career. A nervous breakdown caused him to abandon this idea and thereafter he led a singularly quiet, uneventful, and indeed withdrawn life, spending much time abroad with his mother. He was married in 1932 (some accounts say 1934) to Baroness Alessandra (Lucy) von Wolff-Stomersee, a distinguished Freudian analyst of mixed Italian and Latvian descent.

Lampedusa was anti-Fascist and studiously avoided any public or official duties under Mussolini. In 1943 American bombs totally destroyed his Palermo town house. He himself escaped to the hills on a bicycle, carrying the family Bellini, but he was much affected by the loss of his possessions. Later he returned to Palermo and spent the rest of his life there in a house on the Via Butera. For a short time after the war he was president of the Red Cross in Sicily.

During the 1950s Lampedusa settled into a daily routine. After breakfast and a visit to his bookseller, he would install himself in a back room of the Café Mazzara or at his club, and spend much of the day reading, or in conversation with other *cognoscenti* of his own age. His great intimate was his cousin Baron Lucio Piccolo, a poet with whom he shared a subtle private world, full of literary jokes and fantasies. Lampedusa read deeply and endlessly the works of (among others) Shakespeare, Tolstoy, Dostoevsky, Montaigne, Pascal, Racine, Flaubert, Stendhal, Proust, Goethe, Mann, Dickens, Virginia Woolf, and E. M. Forster, each in his original language. In the late afternoon he would go home, where often he was visited by young writers and students who came to discuss literature. In the evening he and his wife would read to one another. At this time he was described as "quietly dressed, rather thick-set . . . his general appearance that of a retired senior officer," with gray hair, a darker moustache, and tired-looking bags under his eyes.

Over the years Lampedusa wrote a story or two and some essays on eighteenth century French writers, mostly for his own amusement. Out of his profound and appreciative knowledge of English, French, and Russian literature he had developed standards so high that he was reluctant to commit his own writings to print. It was only in 1955, when the end of his life was very near, that he began work on the novel he had been planning and discussing for years. Four chapters of *Il Gattopardo* were seen and rejected by Mondadori in 1956, and the book was then altered and expanded. It was sent to Einaudi, where it was rejected by Elio Vittorini as being *troppo saggistico*—too much like an essay. Lampedusa received the news in a hospital in Rome, just before his death of cancer. He had no children and was the last male member of his line, but had adopted a young relative, Gioacchino Lanza di Mazzarino, who succeeded him as Duke of Palma.

After his death his widow sent the manuscript to Benedetto Croce's daughter, Elena Craveri, who kept it in a drawer for a year. One day she showed it to a visitor, Giorgio Bassani, chief editor of Feltrinelli, who immediately recognized its merit. It was published in 1958 and appeared in English, splendidly translated by Archibald Colquhoun as *The Leopard*, in 1960.

Il Gattopardo is an enormous fresco of Sicilian life in the 1860s, when a virtually feudal way of life was disintegrating under the impact of Garibaldi's Risorgimento. The central figure is Prince Fabrizio, a great hereditary landowner. Fabrizio sees the paternalistic feudal aristocracy, of which he is an eminently cultured and sensitive representative, give way to a greedy bourgeoisie, and Bourbon rule replaced by Piedmontese bureaucracy. Tancredi, his favorite nephew, becomes a follower of Garibaldi and marries a girl of the new middle class. It has been suggested that Tancredi is modeled in part on Lampedusa's adopted son, and Fabrizio on other historical figures, one of them the author's great-grandfather. And it is evident that Fabrizio is Lampedusa's spokesman in the novel—that the mixture of nostalgia and irony with which the Prince observes the passing of his own way of life is Lampedusa's own. There is a sense in which he uses the recent history of Sicily to illustrate a larger theme, holding in balance a serene conviction that the essential spirit of a place and a people are immutable, untouched by social change, and a sad awareness that the individual can hope for no such permanence.

The novel is episodic in form—"a series of tableaux," as P. M. Pasinetti put it. In style it is aristocratic, urbane, and aphoristic: John Hollander heard in it "the noble voice of what seems at times to be that of Western European literature itself," and Richard Gilman called it "the kind of book that an elegant subtle mind, knowing itself about to be extinguished and not yet having revealed and immortalized itself, would write." "Compassionate and smiling, disillusioned and yet lyrical," wrote V. S. Pritchett, "he conveys his subject by catching its day-to-day life rather than its high moments." W. J. Smith praised Lampedusa's powerful visual imagination, which "gives the book its strange and haunting vitality." Max Slonim commended its compactness, brevity, and subtle modernity of spirit. It seemed to Louis Aragon one of the greatest novels of all time, and to E. M. Forster "one of the great *lonely* books."

In Italy *Il Gattopardo* was greeted with almost hysterical praise, but in 1959, when it received the most important Italian literary prize, the Strega, there was a storm of protest from other Italian writers, remembered as "il caso Lampedusa." For one thing the author was an aristocrat, not a professional writer at all. For another he had written the book to please himself, in a manner more reminiscent of Stendhal than of contemporary Italian neorealism. Lampedusa was accused of dealing unfairly with the Risorgimento, of pessimism, of a "Moslem" fatalism, of aping Federico de Roberto's novel *I Vicerè* (1894). Moravia called *Il Gattopardo* "a goodish minor novel," Carlo Levi "another sign of decadence." It was Mario Soldati who summed up the attitude of his fellow writers by saying: "He has done it, and we haven't." What Lampedusa had done, in the opinion of many Italian critics and most foreign ones, was to write one of the very few masterpieces of modern Italian literature, a work to be placed at once with Manzoni's *I Promessi Sposi* and Verga's *I Malavoglia*. It became a worldwide best seller and was filmed by Luchino Visconti.

Lampedusa's only other book was *Racconti*, published in 1961 and translated by Archibald Colquhoun as *Two Stories and a Memory*, with a preface by E. M. Forster. It contains the beginning of a sequel to *Il Gattopardo* (omitted from the translation); a memoir of childhood showing how closely the novel derived from the author's life and family history; and two short stories. The most notable of these fragments is "Lighea," translated as "The Professor and the Mermaid," a superbly constructed fantasy which more than one critic described as a masterpiece. Lampedusa, V. S. Pritchett said, "comes so marvellously close to the people and scenes he describes because he conveys, in the manner of classical artists, the hard gleam of inaccessibility that makes human beings and nature itself seem final and alone."

PRINCIPAL WORKS IN ENGLISH TRANSLATION: The Leopard, 1960; Two Stories and a Memory, 1962.

ABOUT: Curley, D. N. and Curley, A. Modern Romance Literatures (A Library of Literary Criticism), 1967; Dizionario universale della letteratura contemporanea, 1962; Essays and Reviews from the Times Literary Supplement 1963, 1964; Kermode, F. Puzzles and Epiphanies, 1962; Orlando, F. Ricordo di Lampedusa, 1963; Vitello, A. I Gattopardi di Donnafugata, 1963; Wilson, E. Europe Without Baedeker, 1966. *Periodicals*—Comparative Literature Summer 1963; Atlantic February 1963; Italian Quarterly Winter 1961–Spring 1962, Summer–Fall 1965; Modern Language Notes January 1963, January 1966; New Republic June 20, 1960; New Yorker May 28, 1966; Reporter September 17, 1959; September 14, 1961; Saturday Review April 30, 1960; Spectator May 13, 1960; Time December 7, 1962; Times Literary Supplement July 19, 1963.

LANDWIRTH, HEINZ. *See* "LIND, JAKOV"

LANE, MARGARET (June 23, 1907–), is an English novelist, biographer, and journalist whose individual works have been very warmly praised but whose total achievement has never really been assessed. She was born in Cheshire, the only daughter of H. G. Lane and the former Edith Webb, and was educated at St. Stephen's, Folkestone, and St. Hugh's College, Oxford University. She began her career as a journalist on the *Daily Express* (1928–1931). In 1931–1932 she worked in New York as a special correspondent and for the International News Service, and from 1932 to 1938 she was a member of the staff of the *Daily Mail*.

Miss Lane was married in 1934 to Bryan Wallace, the eldest son of the novelist Edgar Wallace. Her own first novel was published a year later and called *Faith, Hope, No Charity*. It skillfully interwove the stories of three very different young women, was generally admired, and received the Prix Femina-Vie Heureuse. There was an even more enthusiastic reception for *At Last the Island* (1937), a study of an egocentric novelist and his family, in flight from his creditors, which was universally praised for the excellence of its dialogue and its "exquisite" characterization. Brian Howard called it "the first English novel I have read for years in which the characters' ordinary minor reactions and idiom seem *exactly* true to contemporary life," and found "a particular kind of authenticity which makes the book as fascinating to read as the letters of some amusing, intelligent friend." Other reviewers spoke of the book's freshness and honesty, "the warmth and perspective given by a writer who is scrupulously faithful to his characters."

MARGARET LANE

What followed was not another novel but Miss Lane's first biography, a fascinating and admirably objective account of the flamboyant life and career of her father-in-law, Edgar Wallace, the newsboy and racing tipster who became one of the most prolific and successful writers in history. *Walk Into My Parlour* (1941) is a study of Emma Shardiloe, who began her famous if bogus career as a spiritualist medium in 1891 at the age of eleven. Miss Lane, who had been divorced from Bryan Wallace in 1939, was married in 1944 to the 15th Earl of Huntingdon, a writer and painter.

A third novel, *Where Helen Lies*, appeared in 1944. It is set in the upper reaches of English society just before the outbreak of World War II, and centers on the breakdown of a marriage and the husband's resumption of an old love affair. It was received with rather less excitement than Miss Lane's earlier fiction, but was generally praised for its relentlessly precise and honest observation of people and manners.

Two remarkable literary biographies followed. In *The Tale of Beatrix Potter* (1946) Miss Lane, it was agreed, had discovered a subject whose life and character were so extraordinary that any account of them would have been fascinating. Described, as they were, with consummate skill, "crisply, perspicaciously and succinctly," they formed the basis for one of the best biographies of the year. *The Brontë Story* (1953) is a reconsideration of Mrs. Gaskell's life of Charlotte Brontë, quotations from which are interwoven with Miss Lane's own interpretations, made in the light of recent scholarship. One reviewer thought that the author's "polite modern prose looks too odd beside the virtuous arrogance of Mrs. Gaskell's Victorian female style," but most critics greatly relished the book.

It is clear that Miss Lane is drawn to eccentricity and she found it in abundance in the person of the late Constantine Ionides, the eremetic collector of poisonous snakes whom she met in London and later visited in Tanganyika. Edward Weeks said of *Life with Ionides* (1963) that Margaret Lane "has caught the audacity of Ionides' mind, the peculiar rhythm of his speech, the smell of danger . . . and, strange as it may sound, the ascetism of his extraordinary career." *A Calabash of Diamonds*, which suggests that Miss Lane is not devoid of eccentricity herself, describes the search she and her husband made in 1958 for treasure reputedly buried with a Zulu chief on the border between Southern Rhodesia and Mozambique. It was an expedition in the Rider Haggard tradition, and made what Basil Davidson called a "charming and disarming book . . . filled with gentle humour, shrewd observations, fine touches of description" and "a nice play of irony between the rather squalid object of the journey and the highly civilised spirit in which it was undertaken."

Margaret Lane's versatility may explain the fact that her work as a whole has made so little impact; critics notoriously are happiest with writers whose work can be parceled up neatly in a memorable phrase and in this age of specialization it is moreover apparent that some of the people who review biographies or travel books do not read fiction. At any rate, when Miss Lane's fourth novel appeared in 1964, twenty years after her third, some of its reviewers seemed totally unfamiliar with her other work.

A Night at Sea was nevertheless very well received. The action is divided between a small yacht, containing James, his wife Molly, and two younger friends, and London, the home of James's mistress, Anthea. Only Colin Wilson thought that the book should establish its author "as the best woman writer in England at present," but other readers found it beautifully constructed, "a good, clear drama about authentic human emotions and relationships," showing a "rare gift of disciplined imagination, that creates scenes with sure, spare strokes."

Some of the characters in *A Night at Sea* reappear in *A Smell of Burning* (1965), which introduces some people who also figure in *The Day of the Feast* (1968). The last two novels, both set in Morocco, were found only moderately impressive, containing some excellent descriptive writing, interweaving their characters "on a level of complete social plausibility," but, in the opinion of Brigid Brophy, not quite compelling the reader "to the painful, ruthless curiosity imposed by works of art." *Purely for Pleasure* (1966), containing a number of literary sketches which had first appeared in magazines, was admired for its irony, wit, and sympathetic insight, and according to one reviewer deserves "a place on the same shelf as Virginia Woolf's *Common Reader*." Julian Symons commented that Miss Lane writes best and with most understanding about minor figures, and that "general ideas interest her less than individual oddity."

Margaret Lane has two daughters by her second marriage. She served as president of the Women's Press Club in 1958–1960, of the Dickens Fellowship in 1959–1961 and 1970, and of the Johnson Society in 1971.

PRINCIPAL WORKS: *Fiction*—Faith, Hope, No Charity, 1935; At Last the Island, 1937; Where Helen Lies, 1944; A Crown of Convolvulus (stories), 1954; A Night at Sea, 1964; A Smell of Burning, 1965; The Day of the Feast, 1968. *Nonfiction:* Edgar Wallace, The Biography of a Phenomenon, 1938; Walk Into My Parlour, 1941; The Tale of Beatrix Potter, 1946; The Brontë Story: A Reconsideration of Mrs. Gaskell's Life of Charlotte Brontë, 1953; A Calabash of Diamonds: An African Treasure Hunt, 1961; Life with Ionides, 1963; Purely for Pleasure, 1966; Frances Wright and the "Great Experiment," 1972. ABOUT: Who's Who, 1971; Who's Who in America, 1970–1971. *Periodicals*—Horn Book November 1946; Illustrated London News July 20, 1946; Ladies' Home Journal May 1936; Saturday Review February 7, 1942; June 20, 1953; Spectator December 9, 1938; October 1, 1954; Time November 11, 1946.

LANG, ISAAC. *See* "GOLL, YVAN"

***LANGGÄSSER, ELISABETH (MARIA)** (February 23, 1899–July 25, 1950), German poet, novelist, and short story writer, was born in Alzey, Rhenish Hesse, the daughter of Eduard Langgässer, a surveyor of works employed by the government of the grand duchy. She was half Jewish but grew up in the Roman Catholic faith (or, according to some accounts, was a convert to it). Her childhood was spent in the rural area between Mainz and Worms that was the setting of much of her early work. After her father died in 1909 the family moved to Darmstadt, where Miss Langgässer attended secondary and normal schools. For five years she earned her living as a teacher, writing in her spare time. Her first book, a volume of lyrics called *Wendekreis des Lammes*, was published in 1924.

In January 1929 Miss Langgässer moved to Berlin, where she devoted herself to writing. Her rawly realistic and often violent short stories began to appear in the Dresden literary journal *Die Kolonne*, and she quickly made a name for herself. In 1932, when she won the Literature Prize for German Women, she published two volumes of short stories and her first novel. This was *Proserpina*, a prose poem owing something to surrealism and to Freud, and more perhaps to her own spiritual

* läng′ ges ər

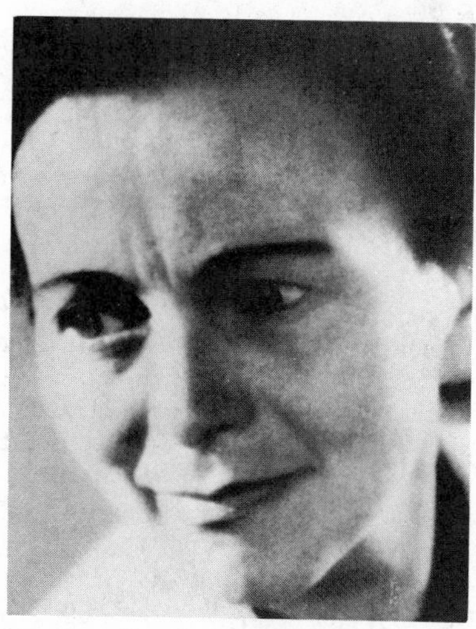

ELISABETH LANGGÄSSER

experiences, in which the forces of good and evil are shown struggling for the soul of a little girl. *Die Tierkreisgedichte* (The Zodiac Poems), a second volume of verse, appeared in 1935. Her intensely sensual and often melodious lyrics are rendered stiff and opaque at times by the intricacy of her symbolism and the obscurity of her learned allusions. Like Wilhelm Lehmann, she celebrates nature not only for its beauty but as the repository of the great myths, the symbol of eternal rebirth and of the unity of all creation.

Elisabeth Langgässer was married in 1935 to the philosopher Wilhelm Hoffmann. In 1936 she published a second novel, *Der Gang durch das Ried* (The Way Through the Marsh), and the same year, on account of her Jewish blood, the Nazis excluded her from the Reich Chamber of Literature and forbade her to publish. Later, during World War II, her eldest daughter was sent to Auschwitz, and Miss Langgässer herself was conscripted for forced labor. That nightmare ended in 1945, when the family was reunited in Berlin, albeit in great poverty and hardship.

The war over, Miss Langgässer began to publish the accumulated work of a decade. Seven books of prose and poetry appeared in quick succession, including the novel generally regarded as her major work, *Das unauslöschliche Siegel* (The Indelible Seal, 1946). Its central figure is a Jew who, in order to marry a Roman Catholic, adopts her faith. He does so casually, altering his religious and racial identity without a qualm, but in the end cannot escape the "indelible seal" of his baptism. He ends his days as an old beggar, full of joy and God's grace. The novel, which zigzags all over Europe, and back and forth across the greater part of a century, is less a coherent narrative than a collection of rhapsodic fragments, more or less related to Miss Langgässer's perennial theme: the conflict between God and the Devil. The latter's power is illustrated in obsessively detailed accounts of adultery, lesbianism, prostitution, and incest, which are contrasted with an almost equally feverish vision of the religious life. Many readers were distressed by the novel's fervent sensuality, and some thought it poorly constructed and intellectually confused; others, praising its packed symbolism and ornate descriptive passages, argued that it was a prose poem, not susceptible to the laws of fiction. Almost overnight, Miss Langgässer became one of the most discussed and debated German writers of the time.

Her other postwar publications include two notable volumes of exalted poetry, *Der Laubmann und die Rose* (The Leafman and the Rose, 1947) and *Metamorphosen* (Metamorphoses, 1949), and two collections of short stories, *Der Torso* (1947) and *Das Labyrinth* (1949). Some critics prefer her direct, laconic, and grimly realistic short stories to her novels and wish she had written more of them. In 1948, Elisabeth Langgässer moved with her husband and four daughters to Rheinzabern in the Palatinate. She died there two years later of multiple sclerosis, a week after she had traveled to Paris to deliver a lecture. Shortly before her death she had become a member of the Academy of Science and Literature in Mainz. The Büchner prize was conferred on her posthumously in the fall of 1950.

Several more books appeared after her death, including the novel *Märkische Argonautenfahrt* (1950), the only one of her works to appear in English. It is an allegorical account of a pilgrimage in search of divine grace, similar in form and tone to *Das unauslöschliche Siegel*, but rather more tightly constructed. Translated in 1953 as *The Quest*, it was received by American critics with more respect than pleasure. Several volumes of letters and essays have also been published posthumously, including a five-volume *Gesammelte Werke* (1959–1964).

Elisabeth Langgässer is an intensely controversial figure. She has been called one of the "contemporary elite of Catholic writers" and the prophet of a new Catholic world view; on the other hand certain Roman Catholic authorities detected heretical and nihilistic tendencies in her work and wanted it placed on the Index. There is a similar division in opinions of her literary merits; some find her prose style so choked with metaphor as to be impenetrable, while others admire her as a master of interior monologue and of lyrical descriptive prose, and as a technical innovator of the first importance.

PRINCIPAL WORKS IN ENGLISH TRANSLATION: The Quest, 1953. *Letters in* Commonweal October 22, 1954. *Stories in* Atlas March 1957; Commonweal June 18, 1948; Partisan Review September 1953.

ABOUT: Augsberger, E. Elisabeth Langgässer, 1962; Bithell, J. Modern German Literature, 1959; Handbuch der deutschen Gegenwartsliteratur, 1965; Waidson, H. M. The Modern German Novel, 1959. *Periodicals*—Books Abroad Winter 1951; Commentary, August 1950; Commonweal March 11, 1949; September 22, 1950; South Atlantic Quarterly April 1951.

LANHAM, EDWIN (October 11, 1904–), American novelist and mystery story writer, writes: "My full name is Edwin Moultrie Lanham and I was born in Weatherford, Texas, the son of Edwin Moultrie and Elizabeth Stephens Lanham. My two grandfathers went to Texas after the Civil War, one from Tennessee and the other, who had served in Longstreet's Corps, from South Carolina. They settled in the same town, became law partners, built adjoining houses; my maternal grandfather, I. W. Stephens, became a judge of the Texas Court of Appeals, while my paternal grandfather, S. W. T. Lanham, was Governor of Texas from 1902 to 1906. The latter became a public figure in the early 1870s after bringing to trial for murder the Kiowa chiefs Set-t'ainte (Satanta) and Ado-ette (Big Tree) because of their frequent bloody raids into Texas from their reservation in the Indian Territory; this story provided the background for my first full-length novel, *The Wind Blew West*, published in 1935.

"I attended Texas schools, the Tome School at Port Deposit, Maryland, the Polytechnic Country Day School in Brooklyn, and Williams College. I left college at the end of my junior year and lived for three years in Paris where my first book, *Sailors Don't Care*, was published by Contact Editions, an enterprise of the late Robert McAlmon which published the first work of Ernest Hemingway and several others. My book was based on my experience in working my way around the world as a seaman at the age of seventeen; it was later published in expurgated form by Cape & Smith in New York.

"I first began writing in childhood, but I was also interested in painting and originally went to France to study art. I lived in Montparnasse during the last of its good years and have missed it ever since. Returning to New York in the Depression years, I found work as a newspaperman, first on the New York *Evening Post*, then with the New York City News Association and finally on the New York *Herald Tribune*. During the fifteen years I worked on newspapers I continued to write novels, but when I was past forty I decided to live by the pen and began writing for magazines. Over the years I have published some fifty short stories and a number of serials (in *Collier's* and the *Saturday Evening Post*), which were mystery stories later published in book form. When possible I allowed myself the time to write a novel, but my freedom to work has been considerably hampered by the economics of existence. My earlier writing was much influenced by the uncertainties of the Depression, when so many writers were drawn to the Left, and I wrote a 'proletarian' novel, *The Stricklands*, about tenant farmers in Oklahoma. This book secured a Guggenheim Fellowship for me in 1940, and during that year I wrote *Thunder in the Earth*, a novel about oil which was given the annual award of the Texas Institute of Letters for 1942.

"I was married in 1929 in Paris to the former Miss Joan Boyle; we were divorced in 1936. In 1940 I married the former Miss Irene Stillman. We have lived for the past eighteen years on the shore of Long Island Sound, in Connecticut, and have one daughter, Evelyn, who is now Mrs. Kazuto Ohira of Tokyo.

"My principal works, in addition to those mentioned above, are *Another Ophelia*, *The Iron Maiden*, and *Speak Not Evil*."

EDWIN LANHAM

Lanham's good years in Paris were from 1926 to 1930. Thereafter until 1944 he worked in New York as a journalist, but made frequent trips to the Southwest to gather material for his stories and novels.

His first book, *Sailors Don't Care*, made no great impact in its expurgated American edition, but *The Wind Blew West* was an immediate success. It described the development of a Texas frontier town into a substantial community, was praised for its "simple, moving and often distinguished prose," and called "as American as the air we breathe." *Another Ophelia* is a very different kind of book, a powerful and tragic evocation of insanity in which Amy Loveman found "a kind of painful beauty."

The Stricklands, about a young man's attempts to organize white and black tenant farmers against exploiting landlords, has been called Lanham's best novel. Oliver La Farge found his use of internal monologue in Oklahoma dialect heavy going at first, "then cumulatively more and more effective." Stanley Young had no such reservations and wrote: "There is no book to lay beside it for comparison. The best elements of a labor story, of crime provoked through ignorance, of tragic love, and of family loyalty have been fused in the same book." *Thunder in the Earth*, though it was thought unsubtle in its style—"out of Hemingway by way of James M. Cain"—was enjoyed as "a brilliantly solid picture of the oil industry."

There has been less enthusiasm for Lanham's postwar novels. *The Iron Maiden* is a readable, "slickly competent," but comparatively lightweight drama about the New York newspaper world. *Speak Not Evil*, concerning the tercentenary celebrations and tribulations of a New England town, was found pretentious and weakly plotted. *The Paste-Pot Man*, which includes an account of a monstrous voyage of self-discovery through hypnoanalysis, fared rather better. Reviewers thought it raised interesting and important questions about the nature of truth and about the Freudian view of man, and Robert Granat called it a "serious, skilfully written novel" which however "remains strangely superficial as it plumbs the depths of human experience, probably because it looks with a reportorial eye on something that can be seen only by poetic vision."

The mystery stories which Lanham has produced since 1946 have been thought highly professional, but sometimes a little "tame" and "inert." One of the best of them, *Monkey on a Chain*, reflects Lanham's interest in psychoanalysis, telling the story of a girl suspected of her husband's murder who seeks help in group therapy. The group, making her problems their own, work together to establish her innocence, jointly becoming "a wholly new kind of detective." Lanham's stories, including some later published as mystery novels, have appeared in *Saturday Evening Post*, *Collier's*, *Esquire*, and many other leading magazines.

PRINCIPAL WORKS: *Fiction*—Sailors Don't Care, 1930; The Wind Blew West, 1935; Banner at Daybreak, 1937; Another Ophelia, 1938; The Stricklands, 1939; Thunder in the Earth, 1941; Slug It Slay, 1946; Politics Is Murder, 1947; It Shouldn't Happen to a Dog, 1947; One Murder Too Many, 1952; Death of a Corinthian, 1953; The Iron Maiden, 1954; Death in the Wind, 1955; Murder on My Street, 1958; Double Jeopardy, 1959; Six Black Camels, 1961; No Hiding Place, 1962; Passage to Danger, 1962; Monkey on a Chain, 1963; Speak Not Evil, 1964; The Paste-Pot Man, 1967; The Clock at 8:16, 1970.

ABOUT: Contemporary Authors 9–10, 1964; Warfel, H. R. American Novelists of Today, 1951; Who's Who in America, 1970–1971.

LARKIN, PHILIP (ARTHUR) (August 9, 1922–), English poet and novelist, writes: "My father, Sydney Larkin, was born in Lichfield in 1884, and died in 1948. My mother, Eva Emily Day, was born in Epping in 1886. They were married in 1911. At the time of my birth my father was City Treasurer of Coventry, a post he held until his retirement in 1944, and I was christened in Coventry Cathedral.

"In 1930 I went to King Henry VIII School, Coventry, a day school where I continued as a pupil until 1940, taking the School Certificate in 1938 and the High School Certificate in 1940. In that year my father agreed that I should go to Oxford at his own expense, rather than stay an extra year at school to sit for scholarships. This was because of the war. My college was St John Baptist College, and I read the Honours School of English Language and Literature. Some account of the Oxford of that time is given in the introduction to the second edition of my novel *Jill* (Faber & Faber, 1964). I had expected to be called for national service after three or four terms, but in the event was graded IV at my medical examination (presumably on grounds of poor eyesight). This meant I could stay on and take my Finals in 1943, when I gained a First Class.

"I had continued to write poems at Oxford (a habit formed about the age of sixteen), and some of these had been published in the undergraduate magazine *The Cherwell*.

"On leaving Oxford I was twice rejected by the Civil Service. In December I was appointed as Librarian of Wellington Urban District Council, in Shropshire. Here I stayed until September 1946. During this time I published a book of poems, *The North Ship* (Fortune Press, 1945), and wrote two novels. The first, *Jill*, was published by the Fortune Press in 1946. The second, *A Girl in Winter*, was published by Faber & Faber in 1947.

"In September 1946 I was appointed to the Library of the University College of Leicester (now the University) as an assistant librarian. In 1949 I was elected an Associate of the Library Association.

"In 1950 I was appointed to the Library of the Queen's University of Belfast, Northern Ireland, as a sub-librarian. In the next year I printed privately a pamphlet entitled *XX Poems*. In 1953 some of my friends began to be published in *The Spectator* and other national papers, and some of the poems I had been writing were similarly published. In 1954 the Fantasy Press published a pamphlet containing five of my poems.

"In 1955 The Marvell Press, a small publishing venture directed by George Hartley, published a collection of poems entitled *The Less Deceived*. A bibliographical account of this publication is given on the sleeve of *Philip Larkin Reads The Less Deceived*, a long-playing record produced by George Hartley's Listen Records. In the same year I became Librarian of the University of Hull, in Yorkshire.

"During the following years I did a certain amount of reviewing for the *Manchester Guardian* (now *The Guardian*), the *New Statesman* and other periodicals. In 1961 I became jazz feature writer of the *Daily Telegraph*.

"In 1964 Faber & Faber published a third collection of poems entitled *The Whitsun Weddings*. This was awarded the Queen's Gold Medal for Poetry and the Arts Council Triennial Award, 1962–5. A long-playing record *Philip Larkin Reads The Whitsun Weddings*, was issued by Listen Records. A new edition of *Jill* was published by Faber & Faber in the same year, and this firm is also planning a new edition of *The North Ship*."

Philip Larkin is regarded by many critics as the finest English poet of his generation. In the Coventry magazine *Umbrella* he has described his quiet childhood and youth in that city. Larkin was a shy boy with an acute stammer, but not without friends who shared his early and continuing enthusiasms for cricket and jazz. He found Bennett, Butler, Shaw, and Lawrence in his parents' library, and after he had discovered the public library often read a book a day. At twelve Larkin began to write funny pieces for the school magazine. In due course he abandoned his ambition to become a jazz drummer and decided on a literary career. At nineteen he sold his first poem (to *The Listener*).

Life at Oxford during the war, as Larkin describes it in his introduction to *Jill* (1964 edition), was austere and rather seedy. "At an age when self-importance would have been normal, events cut us ruthlessly down to size." Larkin seems nevertheless to have enjoyed himself. He made friends with Kingsley Amis, whom he converted to jazz, sat awestruck at the feet of the sophisticated polymath Bruce Montgomery ("Edmund Crispin"), and heard about a younger man called Wain. He was also an unimpassioned member of the University Labour Club.

Jill, which uses some of the external circumstances of Larkin's life at Oxford, is a novel about a shy working-class scholarship boy, overwhelmed at the university, who retreats into a fantasy and is nearly destroyed when this becomes confused with reality. Some critics have seen it as a forerunner of *Lucky Jim* and other studies of moving violations within the British class system. It was admired for the precision and delicacy of its observation, as was *A Girl in Winter*, which was called "as sharp and clear as an engraving . . . in its grasp of the singular beauty of the ordinary." Larkin himself, who has said that novels used to interest him more than poetry does, is almost alone in thinking these books "not very good."

Since then, at any rate, he has concentrated on poetry. His early verse suffered a little from the undigested influence of Yeats, but in the mid-1940s he found a more compatible master in Hardy. Larkin began to receive serious attention as a poet less for his first book, *The North Ship*, than for his appearances ten years later in the two "Movement" anthologies. He says he never had any sense of belonging to a literary school, but he continues to embody in his work the values associated with the Movement: the concern with clear conversational diction and formal excellence, the refusal to dip into Eliot's poetic "myth-kitty," the eschewal of rhetoric and lofty themes. Critics who see the Movement virtues as vices charge him with "genteel bellyaching," narrow provincialism, and a refusal to take risks.

Larkin's themes are loneliness, the painful stirring of dead feelings and spoiled hopes, the fear of death and the need it imposes to come to terms with oneself—the "ordinary sorrows." He has observed Herbert Read's injunction that contemporary poetry "should not raise its voice" but ranges nevertheless, as John Press says, from "colloquial ease to a sombre eloquence," from sharp irony (often self-directed) to "a plangent melancholy." For Bernard Bergonzi, "Larkin's mastery of transitions, his unrivalled ability to call unerringly home the closing lines of a poem—these are not narrowly technical skills, they are the counterpart of a deep and true feeling for human loneliness and longing." His best-known poem, "Church Going," has been called "Wordsworthian in its brooding meditation, its slow amplitude, its tentative honesty" and G. S. Fraser considers that it has claims to greatness. Larkin writes only three or four poems a year.

He is a tall, thin-faced, balding, and bespectacled man with a "slight scholarly stoop" acquired, he says, "looking for cigarette cards in Coventry gutters." He is a "mild xenophobe" and dislikes Mozart. Unmarried, he grew up "to regard sexual recreation as a socially remote thing, like baccarat or clog dancing, and nothing happened to alter this view." His favorite living poet is John Betjeman. A volume of Larkin's jazz articles from the *Daily Telegraph* was published in 1970 as *All What Jazz*. These essays and reviews, dealing mostly and most happily with traditional jazz, were found knowledgeable and entertaining, though some readers complained of the conservatism of Larkin's taste—his acknowledged distaste for "[Charlie] Parker, Pound, Picasso" as prophets of a kind of art which "helps us neither to enjoy nor endure."

PHILIP LARKIN

These attitudes naturally influenced the content of Larkin's highly individual and controversial *Oxford Book of Twentieth Century English Verse*, begun in 1965 and published in 1973. Geoffrey Grigson found it "rather peculiar and reactionary" and complained like many others of quantities of "weak, sentimental, chatty verse." A reviewer in the *Times Literary Supplement*, who found much to admire, concluded that "while not preposterous like Yeats's [*Oxford Book of Modern Verse*], it manages to be eccentric and institutional at once, and leaves the reader with a confused picture of English verse in this century."

Larkin spent a year (1970–1971) as a visiting fellow of All Souls College, Oxford, researching for his anthology. He has honorary degrees from the universities of Belfast and Leicester, and received the Cholmondeley Award for services to poetry in 1973. He dislikes literary parties and literary pronouncements, but in the anthology *Poets of the 1950's* went so far as to say: "I write poems to preserve things I have been/thought/felt . . . both for myself and for others, though I feel that my prime responsibility is to the experience itself. . . . Why I should do this I have no idea, but I think the impulse to preserve lies at the bottom of all art."

PRINCIPAL WORKS: The North Ship, 1946 (new ed., 1966); Jill, 1946 (new ed., 1964); A Girl in Winter, 1947; XX Poems, 1951; The Less Deceived, 1955; The Whitsun Weddings, 1964; All What Jazz: A Record Diary, 1961–68, 1970; (as ed.) The Oxford Book of Twentieth Century English Verse, 1973.

ABOUT: Allott, K. (ed.) Penguin Book of Contemporary Verse, 1962; Gindin, J. Postwar British Fiction, 1962; Murphy, R. (ed.) Contemporary Poets of the English Language, 1970; O'Connor, W. V. The New University Wits, 1963; Press, J. Rule & Energy, 1963; Thwaite, A.

Contemporary English Poetry, 1961; Who's Who, 1971. *Periodicals*—London Magazine November 1964; New York Review of Books January 14, 1965; Times Educational Supplement July 13, 1956; Times Literary Supplement April 13, 1973; Umbrella (Coventry) Summer 1959; Western Humanities Review Spring 1962.

"LASSANG, IWAN." *See* "GOLL, YVAN"

***LA TOUR DU PIN, PATRICE (ARTHUR ÉLIE HUMBERT) DE** (March 16, 1911–), French poet, was born in Paris, the son of Count François de la Tour du Pin and the former Brigitte O'Connor. He is descended from kings of both France and Ireland. His father was killed at the beginning of World War I, and the boy inherited the title. La Tour du Pin grew up at his family's château, Le-Bignon-Mirabeau. Although it is only seventy miles from Paris, the château commands a vast estate of meadows, forests, and swamps, and these surroundings have done much to shape the poet's work, as have an early devotion to the Bible and to the works of St. Thomas Aquinas, Dante, and Montaigne.

PATRICE DE LA TOUR DU PIN

La Tour du Pin, who received a Catholic upbringing, was educated at L'Institution Sainte-Croix at Neuilly-sur-Seine and at L'École Libre des Sciences Politiques. Intended for a legal career, he himself decided early that he would be a poet. He was only fifteen when he and a cousin brought out a volume of verse called *Lys et violettes.* Five years later, in 1931, the *Nouvelle Revue Française* published "Enfants de Septembre" (September's Children), one of his best poems, a description in the romantic manner of the migration of waterfowl over the marshes.

In 1933, when he was twenty-two, La Tour du Pin published a collection of poems called *La Quête de joie* (The Quest of Joy). These lyrics are mostly religious in their concerns, with a note of serene optimism reminiscent of Claudel, and relatively traditional in their manner, "marked by a directness and nobility of statement that has been compared to that of Dante." To conservative critics, horrified by surrealism, the book seemed to augur a classical revival, and some announced it as the greatest poetical work of its day. Some of the clarity and concreteness of these early poems was missing in the half dozen volumes which followed during the 1930s, but by the end of the decade La Tour du Pin still seemed to promise as much for French poetry as anyone of his generation. At the outbreak of World War II he was drafted into the army. Almost at once he was severely wounded and captured. He spent three years as a prisoner in Germany but was repatriated in 1942.

Une Somme de poésie (A Sum of Poetry), which had occupied La Tour du Pin throughout the war and for some years before it, appeared in 1946. It contains all of the poems which he had already published, together with prose interludes, built into a huge construction which attempts a total picture of man's spiritual life. And this massive work is only one part of what has been called the most ambitious literary project of our time, which will seek to express all human experience, physical, intellectual, and spiritual, in terms of a dramatic epic related to the Bible and the medieval mystery plays. Three further volumes in this poetical *summa* have so far appeared: *Le Second Jeu* (The Second Game, 1959), *Le Petit Théâtre crépusculaire* (The Little Twilight Theatre, 1963), and *Une Lutte pour la vie* (A Fight for Life, 1970).

The prose sections of *Une Somme de poésie* have been translated as *The Dedicated Life in Poetry*, a work which takes its title from La Tour du Pin's most important statement of his intentions, the essay called *La Vie recluse en poésie* (1938). In his introduction to *The Dedicated Life in Poetry*, Stephen Spender wrote that La Tour du Pin has "much in common with the early Yeats, above all the same curious combination of romantic, legendary qualities with a certain consciousness of purpose which the mistiness never quite obscures; the same anticipation of wider, more public responsibilities to come at a later stage in his development. . . . He represents a reintegration of the separate functions of poetry." Most critics seem to regret the poet's assumption of his "wider responsibilities," finding the vast project on which he is now engaged obscure, frequently prosaic, and lacking (in spite of recurrent themes and characters) in organic unity; they look back nostalgically to the simpler

* la tōōr dü paN

songs of *Enfants de Septembre* and *La Quête de joie*.

"Since the age of eighteen," La Tour du Pin has written, "I have tried to do but one immense work in my whole life and am remaining faithful to this task. . . . This desire of unity is not merely an artistic or architectural literary motive but a more profound desire to find, as far as possible on this earth, the unity of myself before God and in God." La Tour du Pin received the French Academy's Grand Prix de Poésie in 1961. He was married in 1943 to his cousin, Anne de Bernis-Calvière, and has three daughters and a son. A man much liked for his gaiety and spontaneity, he spends most of his time at Bignon-Mirabeau, writing, managing the estate, hunting and shooting, and entertaining the many writers and intellectuals who visit him there.

PRINCIPAL WORKS IN ENGLISH TRANSLATION: The Dedicated Life in Poetry, and, The Correspondence of Laurent de Cayeux (tr. by George Fraser, 1947). *Poems in* Strachan, W. J. Apollinaire to Aragon: Thirty Modern French Poets, 1948.

ABOUT: Boisdeffre, P. de. Une Histoire vivante de la littérature d'aujourd'hui, 1938–1958, 1958; Boisdeffre, P. de. Dictionnaire de littérature contemporaine, 1900–1962, 1962; Brereton, G. An Introduction to the French Poets, 1956; Clouard, H. and Leggewie, R. French Writers of Today, 1965; Hackett, C. A. An Anthology of Modern French Poetry, 1965; Hoehn, M. (ed.) Catholic Authors, 1952; Kushner, E. Patrice de la Tour du Pin, 1961; Rousselot, J. Panorama critique des nouveaux poètes français, 1952; Smith, H. (ed.) Columbia Dictionary of Modern European Literature, 1947; Who's Who in France, 1971–1972.

LAYE, CAMARA (January 1, 1928–   ), Guinean novelist, was born in the ancient city of Kouroussa, Upper Guinea, into a devout Muslim family which was also deeply rooted in Malinké culture. Both his father and his maternal grandfather were workers of metal, a calling that traditionally combined the role of artist with that of magician-priest. Camara Laye was educated first in the local Koranic and state primary schools, then at the École Poiret in Conakry, the capital, where he studied technical subjects, including applied mathematics and mechanical engineering. He describes himself as conscious from an early age of a fate that would drive him into a succession of exiles—spiritual exiles, from childhood and his own cultural background; and physical exiles, first from Kouroussa and later, when he was awarded a scholarship to the Central School of Automobile Engineering, near Paris, from Africa itself.

In Paris, Laye was at first overwhelmed by poverty, loneliness, and culture shock. He persevered nevertheless, and when his scholarship ran out took a variety of jobs to support himself while he completed his studies at the École Ampère, the National Conservatory of Arts and Crafts, and the Technical College for Aeronautics and Automobile Construction. It was while he was working at

CAMARA LAYE

Simca as a motor mechanic, and attending evening classes at the Technical College, that Laye translated his longing for Guinea into a lightly fictionalized autobiography, *L'Enfant noir*. It was published in 1953 and appeared the following year in English as *The Dark Child*, excellently translated, as all Laye's books have been, by James Kirkup.

L'Enfant noir retraces (and idealizes) the important events in the narrator's life: childhood, school, ritual circumcision; his discovery of the modern urban life of Conakry; and finally his departure for France. It was acclaimed by the French critics for its "limpid and unified style," and was awarded the Charles Veillon prize. Many African critics, however, condemned its apolitical nature. The Camerounian Mongo Beti asked how it was that Laye seemed never to have witnessed "the smallest imposition by the French colonial administration," and the Nigerian Chinua Achebe, though he found merit in the book, declared it "too sweet" for his taste. Certainly the book deals only by implication with the evils of colonialism and was markedly lacking in the ardent nationalism of most postwar African writing. Nevertheless, in its romantic celebration of the continent's cultural and spiritual inheritance, it proved a landmark in the development of the novel in French-speaking Africa, the prototype of the fiction of *négritude*.

Le Regard du roi (1954, translated as *The Radiance of the King*), is an altogether more ambitious book. Reversing the usual pattern of the French-African novel, it tells the sometimes funny, sometimes moving story of a penniless white man, Clarence, and his search for the king of the unnamed African territory in which he has just arrived. During his pilgrimage, Clarence gradually sheds the money-based values and the egoism of Western civilization, moving towards an African acceptance of life and human relationships, love and joy. A final act of faith and humility brings redemption, when the African king in his love calls him and receives him into his service.

The book is reminiscent of the mysterious journeys through unknown jungle that recur in African folktales, and also of the dreamlike world of Kafka, to whom Laye has acknowledged his debt. The allegory has been widely interpreted as depicting the path that the white man must take if he is to achieve spiritual wholeness, though some have read it as an account of the author's own recovery of the African values he lost in white schools and cities. Once again, there was considerable hostility from some African writers, including the literal-minded critic of *Présence Africaine*, who denounced it as a gross distortion of the real relationship between white and black. However, the South African Ezekiel Mphahlele found a "devastating irony" in Laye's image of "the white man, trembling before the African King, afraid to approach, out of a misplaced European sense of sin and shame." Because of the boldness of its conception and the subtlety of its philosophical arguments, the "alternation of narrative speed and exploratory slowness," and "the racy cryptic humor of much of the dialogue," *Le Regard du roi* is now widely recognized as one of the three or four finest African novels yet published.

Laye returned to Guinea in 1956 and, after independence in 1958, entered public life. He served in diplomatic posts in Liberia and Ghana and subsequently returned to Conakry as director of the Centre de Recherche et d'Études. There he found himself increasingly in conflict with the aims and methods of President Sekou Touré's government and at last felt obliged to go once more into exile. *Dramouss*, his third novel, was written in Senegal and translated as *A Dream of Africa*.

Dramouss begins where *L'Enfant noir* ended, forming a roughly chronological account of the author's life from his arrival in Paris to his final disillusionment in Conakry. In the mind of Fatoman, the book's narrator, Guinea has become the embodiment of the neo-colonial state, its people deluded by empty slogans, its traditional arts and culture threatened by shoddy goods and ideas imported from abroad. Laye had earlier written of the African people as "medieval" in their faith in the essential mysteries, their closeness to natural creatures and objects; now he found the future of his country in the hands of materialists and opportunists. Most of the book is perfectly realistic, but towards the end Laye introduces a nightmarish vision of Guinea as a totalitarian state, to be rescued only by the overthrow of the present leadership and a return to traditional African values (an eventuality symbolized here in a story about Fatoman-Laye's old father miraculously redeeming his chicken from the talons of a marauding hawk). *Dramouss* thus reveals the emergence of a new political commitment in Laye's work.

PRINCIPAL WORKS IN ENGLISH TRANSLATION: The Dark Child, 1954; The Radiance of the King, 1956; A Dream of Africa, 1968.

ABOUT: Brench, A. C. The Novelists' Inheritance in French Africa, 1967; Moore, G. Seven African Writers, 1962; Mphahlele, E. (ed.) African Writing Today, 1967; Penguin Companion to Literature vol. 4, 1969; Rutherfoord, P. (ed.) Darkness and Light, 1958. *Periodicals*—Afrique July 1963; Black Orpheus September 1957, May 1958, November 1959; Présence Africaine 1–11, 1955.

LAYTON, IRVING (PETER) (March 12, 1912–), Canadian poet and editor, was born in Neamtz, near Bucharest, Rumania, the son of Moses and Keine (Moscovitch) Lazarovitch. In 1913, when he was a year old, the family emigrated to Montreal, where he has lived ever since. Layton obtained his B.Sc. in agriculture at Macdonald College in 1939, served as a lieutenant in the Royal Canadian Artillery from 1942 to 1943, and received his M.A. in economics from McGill in 1946. He was a high school teacher in Montreal from 1945 to 1960, and has also lectured regularly at Montreal's Jewish Public Library (1943–1958) and since 1949 at Sir George Williams University, where in 1965 he was appointed Poet-in-Residence.

In the early 1940s Layton was prominent among the young Montreal poets centered upon the magazine *First Statement*, and in 1943 he joined John Sutherland and Louis Dudek in editing the magazine. He continued to do so when it merged with *Preview* to become *Northern Review*, but resigned in the early 1950s when Sutherland altered his editorial policy. In 1952, with Dudek and Raymond Souster, he founded the Contact Press, a cooperative publishing house established in Toronto as an outlet for Canadian poetry. Slim volumes of Layton's verse began to appear in 1945, published by First Statement, Contact, and other small Canadian presses. The first of his books to attract international attention was *The Improved Binoculars*, a selection from more than ten years of work, published in the United States by Jonathan Williams in 1956. Most of his subsequent volumes have been brought out by Williams, or by McClelland and Stewart of Toronto.

The Improved Binoculars had a very favorable reception from British and American reviewers, who were unanimous in preferring Layton's "sweet and unforced" lyrics, including his frankly sensual love poems, to those relatively diffuse and pretentious pieces in which he indulges "a weakness for philosophical speculation." Richard Eberhart found him "less formless than the most free-flowing poets," though he "eschews rhyme and fixed meters." It was the youthfulness of his poetry that pleased Eberhart: "Layton is exuberant, going off in diverse directions, laying his heart continuously on his sleeve, full of ideas about love, harking back to the Greeks, writing confessional pieces, uncensored, on contemporary subjects."

In *The Oxford Companion to Canadian History and Literature*, Layton is described as "an outstanding and original poet much of whose work expresses the concept of the poet as a man in tune with nature, oriented toward the sun as a creative force, and agonised by the blindness, pettiness, and stupidities of men whose faces are turned to waste and destruction." This "agonised" poetry predominates in *A Laughter in the Mind* and was unattractive to most reviewers, who spoke of a "myopically observant acidity," a "loud irony," a "considered nastiness." The best poems in this collection, William Meredith thought, "are those which say, in fresh but not unconventional speech, familiar things about death, poetry, love and fatherhood." Hugh Kenner, however, thought that almost all of these poems contain "some memorable feat of vigor," and it is this energy which is Layton's most impressive quality, persuading William Carlos Williams that Layton has it in him to become "one of the West's most famous poets."

In Canada Irving Layton is well known as an outspoken and controversial figure—"a ring-tailed roarer in the little zoo of Canadian letters"—and the debate over the merits of his verse has been long and vociferous. In 1966, discussing Layton's very uneven *Collected Poems* in *Canadian Literature*, George Woodcock wrote: "Layton is a poet in the old romantic sense . . . flamboyant, rowdy, angry, tortured, versatile, voluble . . . mingling personal griefs and joys with the themes and visions of human destiny. Lately a somewhat negative element seems to have entered his poems. . . . He is obviously at a point of transition." Among the many honors he has received are the Canadian Foundation Fellowship (1957), a Canadian Council award (1959), the Governor-General's Medal (for *A Red Carpet for the Sun*), and the Prix Littéraire de Québec (first prize, 1963). He has read his poetry in many Canadian and American universities, and is represented in numerous anthologies. One of his main interests is the encouragement of young writers. Layton is married to Aviva Cantor, who writes children's books. He has three children, two of them by an earlier marriage. His recreations include handball, swimming, and chess.

PRINCIPAL WORKS: *Poetry*—The Improved Binoculars: Selected Poems, 1956; A Laughter in the Mind, 1958; A Red Carpet for the Sun: Collected Poems, 1959; The Swinging Flesh (poems and stories), 1961; Balls for a One-Armed Juggler, 1963; The Laughing Rooster, 1964; Collected Poems, 1965; Periods of the Moon, 1967; The Shattered Plinths, 1968; The Whole Bloody Bird: obs, aphs & pomes (prose and poetry), 1969; Selected Poems, 1969; Collected Poems, 1971; Nail Polish, 1971. *As editor:* (with Louis Dudek) Canadian Poems, 1850–1952, 1953; Pan-ic: A Selection of Contemporary Canadian Poems, 1958; Love Where the Nights Are Long: Canadian Love Poems, 1962; Anvil: A Selection of Workshop Poems, 1966.

IRVING LAYTON

ABOUT: Canadian Who's Who, 1970–1972; Contemporary Authors 3, 1963; Oxford Companion to Canadian History and Literature, 1967. *Periodicals*—Canadian Author and Bookman Spring 1967; Canadian Literature Spring 1966; Delta October–December 1959; Macleans Magazine November 15, 1965; Nation October 11, 1958; Poetry September 1957; Tamarack Review Spring 1966.

***LÉAUTAUD, PAUL** (January 18, 1872–February 22, 1956), French diarist, novelist, and critic, was born in Paris, the illegitimate son of Firmin Léautaud, prompter at the Comédie Française, and Jeanne Forestier, a minor actress. His mother soon abandoned him and Léautaud lived with a nurse until he was eight, and thereafter, wretchedly, with his negligent and dissolute father. At fifteen he began to earn his living in a variety of jobs and proved competent and trustworthy enough to hold responsible posts in law offices for ten or twelve years. He was always penniless, since his father took most of his earnings, and he found his pleasure in the writing of verse and in the company of the prostitutes who congregated at a *crémerie* near the Folies Bergère and who made a pet of him. The Montmartre of Toulouse-Lautrec was his playground and his university.

* lā ō tō

PAUL LÉAUTAUD

Léautaud was a small man, heavily bearded in his youth. He wore steel-rimmed spectacles and his clothes were shabby, but he was far from unimpressive. He was a brilliant talker, acidly witty and cruelly frank. In 1895 he met Alfred Vallette, editor of the *Mercure de France*, who published some of his verses and encouraged him to try his hand at prose. Léautaud became a regular reviewer for Vallette, and began to move in the orbit of Verlaine and Mallarmé, Valéry and Gide, and the other great figures who appear in the diary he began in 1896.

Le Petit Ami, Léautaud's first novel, appeared in 1903. It is an ironic and very lightly fictionalized account of his early life, including an unsparingly frank record of his incestuous passion for his mother, who briefly reentered his life when he was thirty. By then Léautaud had abandoned the stately prose of the period and adopted his own concrete, terse, and vivid style, which eschews all metaphor and imagery, and uses not a single unnecessary word for the sake of grace or balance. (He valued spontaneity, and spoke of "writing well by writing badly . . . *sans recherche*.") *Le Petit Ami* was much admired and seriously considered for the Prix Goncourt, which Léautaud coveted all his life, but was rejected because of its shocking candor.

Léautaud was unable to compromise: "There are no things that one has felt, heard or seen that one doesn't intend to [write of], however sacred they may be," he said, adding characteristically: "It may be that these things were not very sacred." So his second novella was a "horrifyingly realistic" account of his father's last illness and death (*In Memoriam*, 1905), and his third and last attempt at fiction (*Amours*, 1906), was a chillingly dispassionate account of his early love affairs. These three autobiographical stories were collected in Humphrey Hare's translation as *Child of Montmartre* in 1959, and much praised. One critic wrote that "a fierce integrity, an unassailable loyalty to himself . . . makes this one of the most moving, honest, if strange self-portraits that even Paris has produced." V. S. Pritchett admired in particular Léautaud's "power of precise portraiture," his ability "to etch a small world clearly and without blobbing it with moralistic shadows."

From 1907 to 1941 Léautaud was secretary of the *Mercure de France*, and for the first seventeen of those years its drama critic as well. His reviews, written under the pseudonym "Maurice Boissard," were caustic, lively, and openly prejudiced against any kind of moral cant or literary pretension. Faced with a play he considered pompous, Léautaud would dismiss it in a couple of lines and devote his space to any subject that took his fancy. This procedure, greatly enjoyed by the *Mercure*'s readers, naturally made many enemies for the magazine and at last Vallette dismissed Léautaud, whose subsequent brief career as drama critic of the *Nouvelle Revue Française* ended similarly, when he refused to temper a harsh review of a play by Jules Romains.

Thereafter he was obliged to rely for his income on his comparatively harmless (and poorly paid) post as secretary to the *Mercure de France*. Léautaud had by then discovered that he preferred animals to people. Unable to find a home in Paris for a stray dog that had attached itself to him, he had moved to a suburb. There he settled as a semi-recluse, traveling to his office every morning, hurrying home every evening to feed as many as thirty dogs and cats, and as poor as ever.

Vallette died in 1941. His successor, Jacques Bernard, called Léautaud into his office and said without preamble: "I have decided to part with you for the pleasure of not seeing you anymore." Léautaud, then sixty-nine, survived the war somehow and at the end of it had the satisfaction of being called as a prosecution witness when this man was tried as a collaborator. (His testimony was evidently temperate, since Bernard was acquitted.) Interest in Léautaud's work revived after the war and a series of radio interviews with Robert Mallet in 1950 showed him to be, at seventy-eight, "as pig-headed and pugnacious, as vivacious, witty and prejudiced, as scornful of sentimentality, as sensible and unreasonable as he had always been." These *Entretiens* were published in 1951 and sold very well, as did Léautaud's journal when it began to appear in 1954. Thus at the end of his life he became something of a national celebrity in France. Alan Pryce-Jones visited him at that time and recalled "a bony head . . . swathed in a night-cap, on the jutting nose . . . heavy spectacles, and on the ends of the long muffler wound down to his knees . . . a pair of favorite cats. He looks grubby, cross and poverty-stricken. But his eyes have an unassailable air of mocking veracity about them." Léautaud died at the age of eighty-four, a week after he had made the last entry in his journal.

The *Journal littéraire* is Léautaud's most substantial work, a remarkable portrait of a great era in French letters, and above all of its author (who once said, with typical frankness: "I alone interest me"). Geoffrey Sainsbury's admirable translation of the early volumes was published in 1960 as *Journal of a Man of Letters*. It was said to retain all the wry charm of the original, and delighted reviewers with its many "little masterstrokes of comedy, irony, and undeceived perception."

"I have lived for no other purpose but to write," Léautaud said: "La littérature avant tout." Some of his critics believed that "his vocation was greater than his talent," but many would agree that he made of himself a true heir to the eighteenth century *petits maîtres* he so admired. "He has one string only," said Marie Dormoy, "he echoes to one note only but its quality is unique." Léautaud summed up the qualities which assure him of a place in the history of French literature, and deny him a great one, when he wrote: "Those who have known me intimately have always taken me for a man who never lies, and, what's more, who is devoid of all imagination."

PRINCIPAL WORKS IN ENGLISH TRANSLATION: Child of Montmartre, 1959; Journal of a Man of Letters, 1898–1907, 1960.

ABOUT: Connolly, C. Previous Convictions, 1963; Maugham, W. S. Points of View, 1959; Pryce-Jones, A. *introduction to* Journal of a Man of Letters, 1960; Tynan, K. Curtains, 1961. *Periodicals*—Commonweal October 2, 1959; Mercure de France February 1952; New Statesman September 1, 1956; July 18, 1959; New Yorker September 10, 1955; October 3, 1959; Times Literary Supplement June 19, 1959.

"LE CARRÉ, JOHN" (pseudonym of David John Moore Cornwell) (October 19, 1931–), English novelist, writes: "I was born in Poole in 1931 and went to school at Sherborne, where my early efforts to write were largely discouraged. I was not happy there and having tried to run away I eventually persuaded my father to let me go to school in Switzerland where I learnt German and French and how to ski. I did my military service in Austria and while I was there I resolved to return to Vienna some day. I then went up to Oxford where I read Modern Languages and took an honours degree.

"I began writing again when I was married and living in Great Missenden, where I had to spend two hours in the train every day going to London

JOHN LE CARRÉ

and used to pass the time in thinking of plots for stories. I do not think anyone has influenced me by his writing and I do not consciously model my writing on anyone else's, but the writers I enjoy most are Conrad and Graham Greene. I find it difficult to describe the process of writing because it is such a very personal business. I don't know where inspiration comes from. Tension probably. Once I begin to write I like to withdraw from life completely and live the life of my novel, but this is often difficult because one is a social being as well as a writer, a participant as well as an observer.

"It is sometimes said that my books are tortuous, involved and depressing, my heroes vacillating and hopeless, their lives meaningless and their deaths useless; I find it impossible to inject more hope into the world I have created, or rather observed, because I cannot see it in people's lives.

"After I wrote *The Spy Who Came in From the Cold* I was constantly asked whether I belonged to the Secret Service. I did not. It seems irrelevant whether the details are true or not. I find it hard to write about women; although I can understand intellectually why they act as they do, I find it difficult to imagine myself acting in that way. It distresses me when people refer to my books as 'thrillers'; I prefer Hemingway's word 'story.'

"You must by now think me a very gloomy character—this is the writing part of me, detached and therefore often lonely, shunning society at the same time as finding it impossible to live without it or outside it.

"After the success of 'The Spy' we went and lived for a time on the island of Crete and later moved to another island nearer the mainland, but their beauty was not enough. After a few months we returned to England, spending the winter in Vienna on the way."

———

John Le Carré is the son of Ronald and Olive (Glassy) Cornwell. He learned his French and German at Berne University and, when he left Lincoln College, Oxford, taught those languages at Eton College (1956–1958). He entered the British Foreign Service in 1960, serving in Bonn and Hamburg, but resigned in 1964 to devote his full time to writing.

In his first published novel, *Call for the Dead,* Le Carré introduced George Smiley of the British secret service, an agent who might have been conceived as the very antithesis of Ian Fleming's James Bond. Smiley is intellectually and morally attractive, but physically not at all so. He is miserably unsuccessful in love, and increasingly disgusted by his profession. Smiley reaches a personal and professional crisis with the apparent suicide of a Foreign Office clerk to whom he has just given security clearance, and the book is an exciting and absorbing account of his attempts to resolve his problems. *Time*'s reviewer was impressed by the book's air of "grubby realism and moral squalor, the frazzled, fatigued sensitivity of decent men obliged to betray or kill others no worse than themselves."

Smiley reappears in *A Murder of Quality,* conducting a private investigation into the death of a schoolmaster's wife at a famous public school. Anthony Boucher found this more orthodox thriller "a model of the whodunit-of-locale. . . . Puzzling and well-plotted, it is also an admirably written study in levels of snobbery and cruelty, rich in subtle explorations of character."

Le Carré's third book established him "beside Ambler and Greene in the small rank of writers who can create a novel of significance, while losing none of the excitement of the tale of sheer adventure." *The Spy Who Came in From the Cold* (in which Smiley again has a role) tells the story of a fifty-year-old British spy who has been too long in the field. Stale, tired, and bitter, he accepts one last assignment in which he is brutally deceived and spiritually destroyed by his employers. The novel is elegantly and economically written, completely convincing in its settings and characterization, brilliantly plotted, and immensely readable. It also addresses itself with a new directness and urgency to the moral problems implicit in the author's first book, raising important questions about espionage, patriotism, and more generally about ends and means; it asks, Le Carré says, "how long we can defend ourselves . . . by methods of this kind, and still remain the kind of society that is worth defending." The book, widely translated and successfully filmed, was described by Graham Greene as "the best spy story I have ever read." *The Looking-Glass War,* about an obsolescent espionage establishment and its attempt to redeem itself with a single coup, had a more mixed reception. It was followed by *A Small Town in Germany,* in which a tense and absorbing investigation into a security leak at the British Embassy in Bonn opens out into a disgusted indictment of (among other things) British diplomacy and German politics. Le Carré abandoned the thriller form altogether in his next novel, *The Naive and Sentimental Lover.* It was called "an unhappy venture into the metaphysics of love" and "a disastrous failure," and the author was begged to return at once to "what he does supremely well, writing books based in the real world which use the apparatus of the thriller, but are in their depth and subtlety excellent novels."

Le Carré has three sons by his 1954 marriage to Alison Sharp, which ended in divorce in 1971. He is a slight, fair-haired, handsome man, and an excellent lecturer. He attributes his concise and disciplined style to his training as a teacher and as a bureaucrat, and says the latter "is certainly the most rigid, the most astringent training I have had."

PRINCIPAL WORKS: Call for the Dead, 1961; A Murder of Quality, 1962; The Spy Who Came in From the Cold, 1963; The Le Carré Omnibus (U.S., The Incongruous Spy, containing Call for the Dead and A Murder of Quality), 1964; The Looking-Glass War, 1965; A Small Town in Germany, 1968; The Naive and Sentimental Lover, 1971.

ABOUT: Contemporary Authors 7–8, 1963; Vinson, J. (ed.) Contemporary Novelists, 1972; Who's Who, 1973. *Periodicals*—Encounter May 1966, November 1966; Harper's November 1965; Life February 28, 1964; Listener April 14, 1966; Mademoiselle June 1964, July 1964; New York Times Book Review May 3, 1964; Spectator November 27, 1964; Vogue July 1965.

*LE CLÉZIO, J(EAN) M(ARIE) G(USTAVE)

(April 13, 1940–), French novelist and short story writer, has provided the following chronology:

"1797—François Le Clézio, a corsair, leaves Brittany after the Revolution and settles with his family in the Île de France, in the Indian Ocean. He sinks many English ships. After the annexation of the island, which became in 1810 Mauritius, his descendants are British subjects. As a result, a strong mixture of English and French culture and habits.

After World War I, my father emigrates and becomes a medical officer in South America and Nigeria.

Mother French, from another branch of the same family; lives in Paris, then in Nice.

* lə clā zē ō

"1940—April 13; born in Nice. I have been living there ever since.
Early childhood spent in Roquebillière, a small village in the country behind Nice. There was the war. Food and toys rare.
"1945—The war is over, but I am not interested. I am interested in drawing, painting, writing.
"1947—Travel to Nigeria with my mother and my brother. I meet my father. I spend a happy year, without school, without Sunday mass, playing all the time.
First novel (unpublished): *Un long Voyage.*
Second novel (published in *Le Déluge*, twenty years later): *Oradi noir.*
"1948—Back to Nice, to school, to Sunday mass. Studving.
Total incapacity in mathematics, algebra, geometry, history, geography, Latin, Greek, gymnastics, music, social contacts. Some gifts in drawing, literature, zoology, philosophy.
I write poetry, I read comics.
"1957—Baccalauréat (literature, philosophy).
"1958—Thrown out of the Lycée, I begin studying at the University. I read, mainly American literature.
Two years spent in England, as a student in Bristol University, London University, and as a teacher in Bath.
"1960—Married in London. Wife half-French, half-Polish.
"1961—A daughter.
"1963—First published novel: *Le Procès-Verbal.* It wins the Renaudot literary prize.
Licence-ès-lettres.
"1964—Intrusion into the literary world of Paris; I feel a strong desire to keep off.
I suffer agonizing pain (tooth ache) in Yugoslavia.
"1965—My daughter is four years old.
Short stories published: *La Fièvre.*
Travel with my wife to the States: eleven thousand miles by car from coast to coast.
Travel to the volcanoes of Etna and Stromboli.
My wife prepares a thesis on Poland, I prepare a thesis on Lautréamont.
Writing, not working.
Influences: Defoe, Jules Verne, Hawthorne, Faulkner?
Not yet sure if writing is a good way of expression."

Le Clézio caused enormous excitement in France with his first novel, which, published when he was twenty-three, won the Prix Renaudot and missed the Goncourt by only one vote. *Le Procès-Verbal* (1963, translated as *The Interrogation*), with which

J. M. G. LE CLÉZIO

he made this infinitely promising debut, has no real plot and makes little attempt at characterization. It is an account of the wanderings of a young man, Adam Pollo, through the parks, cafés, and beaches of Nice. He stays for a while in an empty house, rapes (or seduces) a girl, slowly kills a white rat with billiard balls. After haranguing an apathetic crowd about brotherhood he is arrested and interrogated by psychiatrists, whose clumsy questions he answers so skillfully that he is released. Adam, who is well-educated and (like most of Le Clézio's characters) physically hypersensitive, tells his story as a monologue, which is interrupted by fragmentary conversations with the girl and by excerpts from letters to her and from his diary. He speaks of himself alternately as "I" and "he" and appears to have no aim whatever except to observe, to receive impressions. Sometimes he seems to want to identify himself with simpler forms of life, as when he follows a dog and tries to share its feelings, or when he seeks to apprehend the fear and pain of the rat he kills.

The mood of *Le Procès-Verbal* is very much that of Camus's *The Stranger* and Sartre's *Nausea*, though Le Clézio does not share their sense of social responsibility. His other masters include Beckett, Kafka, Robbe-Grillet, and the "new novelists," and perhaps the prose poet Francis Ponge, who also seeks to empathize with nonhuman things. It is not surprising that some critics found the novel a brilliant but pointless exercise in pastiche, "a dazzling tray of samples." Others, however, took it far more seriously, as did Henri Peyre: "There are . . . displays of pedantry and tricks taken over from the cinema and from detective fiction.

But the young author has an uncanny gift of psychological description and a power to move and to obsess readers which has not often been encountered since Camus's *La Chute*."

There followed the "nine tales of little madness" published as *La Fièvre* (1965, translated as *Fever*). Most of them explore the way in which physical pain, fatigue, or disease can alter the sufferer's consciousness of reality, acting like a psychedelic drug. "The Day That Beaumont Became Acquainted With His Pain," for example, is a powerfully Kafkaesque story about a man who, in the course of a long night's agony with toothache, becomes (as Page Stegner put it) "metamorphosed into that pain." The best of these stories, Stegner wrote, "achieve a complete fusion of the psychological and the physiological aspects of sensory experience. . . . Even if wearied by the repetition, we come away awed by his skill in manipulating language and dazzled by his ability to create with words vividly impressionistic paintings."

Le Déluge (1966, translated as *The Flood*) is an even darker book—an apocalyptic vision of Nice as a City of Dreadful Night. The novel begins with a brilliant passage elaborating "one of those extreme states of mind which interest M. Le Clézio more than anything else, where the brain and the world fuse in a series of hallucinations." The rest of the book records the central figure's pilgrimage through the city, which leads him to renounce his humanity and (by blinding himself) to aspire to the condition of a mineral. Some mild doubts were expressed about the integrity of Le Clézio's "fashionable flight from consciousness," but none about the brilliance of his imagination and his rhetoric. Peter Greene's translation was as much admired as Daphne Woodward's versions of the two earlier works.

There was an uncertain reception for *Terra Amata*, published in English under the same title in another notable translation, this time by Barbara Bray. It is a novel in the style of a Godard film which Dorothy Curley described as "a stylized, episodic life of a man-boy, each episode very ordinary and banal but intensified to super-realist vividness by reiteration and proliferation." In this account of one man's birth, life, and death, Le Clézio sought to sum up nothing less than the history of man on earth. It seemed to W. J. Smith "a terribly youthful work," embodying too many fashionable ideas and techniques, but deeply impressed Geoffrey Wolff as a successful and valuable experiment by "a man of very rare talent and feeling." Several similar works have since appeared—experiments which one Anglo-Saxon critic characterized rather irritably as "running commentaries on the cosmos." *Haï* (1971) was a lyrical account of life among the Indians of Central America.

Le Clézio, when he was still only twenty-seven, explained his philosophy in a rather indigestibly paradoxical essay called *L'Extase matérielle* (The Material Ecstasy, 1967). He takes up a position somewhere between McLuhan and the phenomenologists, recommending immersion in the concrete and immediate in place of value judgments, a concern with what *is* rather than with what might or should be. As one reviewer put it, one should "be oneself, know oneself, then start empathizing with one's environment, animate and inanimate."

PRINCIPAL WORKS IN ENGLISH TRANSLATION: The Interrogation, 1964; Fever, 1966; The Flood, 1967; Terra Amata, 1969; The Book of Flights: An Adventure Story, 1972; War, 1973.

ABOUT: International Who's Who, 1973–1974; Peyre, H. French Novelists of Today, 1967; Who's Who in France, 1973–1974. *Periodicals*—Atlas June, September 1963, September 1966; Cahiers du Sud 382 1965; L'Express September 26, 1963; March 15, 1965; Figaro Littéraire October 12, 1963; March 25, 1965; Guardian September 4, 1964; New York Times Book Review May 2, 1965; July 25, 1966; New Yorker September 17, 1966; Saturday Review October 31, 1964; Spectator September 4, 1964; Sunday Telegraph (London) September 6, 1964; Sunday Times (London) September 6, 1964; Times (London) October 29, 1964; Times Literary Supplement October 15, 1964; September 8, 1966; June 22, 1967.

LEDERER, WILLIAM J(ULIUS) (March 31, 1912–), American journalist, novelist, and writer on political and naval subjects, is of German ancestry. He was born in New York City and named for his father, a dentist. His mother was the former Paula Franken. Lederer grew up in Ossining, New York, and in New York City. He left DeWitt Clinton High School at sixteen and began his career as a journalist for New York newspapers, working for a time as secretary to the columnist Heywood Broun.

The Depression was not a good time for newspapermen or anyone else, and in 1930 Lederer entered the United States Navy, making his way to Annapolis a year or so later. Although he had an acute stammer, he struggled through to the presidency of the Annapolis public speaking society, and in 1936 received his B.S. degree. Shortly afterwards the Navy "booted" him out but Lederer, with characteristic determination, talked his way back in. His naval career lasted for twenty-eight years and included three years in Asia during World War II. In 1951 he was assigned to the staff of the commander-in-chief, Pacific—a post which entailed repeated visits to various part of the Far East. He retired with the rank of captain in 1958 to become Far East correspondent of the *Reader's Digest* (1958–1963).

By that time Lederer was already well known as a writer. His articles about Navy life began to appear in mass-circulation magazines after World War II and his first book was published in 1950.

The Last Cruise is an account of the sinking of a submarine, U.S.S. Cochino, during an Arctic gale—"a brief heroic tale of victory snatched from almost irremediable disaster" which Fletcher Pratt called an "almost flawless performance." *All the Ships at Sea,* also published in 1950, is a memoir, no doubt somewhat fictionalized—"a humorous, somewhat bawdy picture of life in the regular and war-time Navy." Its success encouraged Lederer to write the even taller stories assembled in *Ensign O'Toole and Me,* subsequently the basis for a popular television series.

Lederer's best-known book was written in collaboration with the late Eugene Burdick and called *The Ugly American,* a title which passed into the language. The book was an indictment in fictional terms of American policy in Asia. United States foreign aid and diplomacy was shown to be in the hands of ignorant and greedy men, totally out of touch with the Asian people. The "ugly American" of the title was not one of these venal men (as is often assumed) but an honorable exception—one of those who understood the needs of the peasants and sought to help them "solve their own problems . . . build their own defenses against encroaching tyranny from East or West and worship their own gods." What the novel lacked in literary grace it made up for in passion and readability. It was a best-selling political bombshell and led to a congressional review of American foreign aid programs.

A Nation of Sheep was Lederer's reply to the thousands of letters provoked by *The Ugly American,* asking what ordinary citizens could do to influence American foreign policy. Lederer told his readers that their first duty was to inform themselves, and he fiercely attacked "government by misinformation." Many reviewers accused him of shrillness and oversimplification, but the *Times Literary Supplement,* though it pointed out that Lederer had failed to suggest alternatives to present American policies, found his argument moving and urgent in its "almost Periclean feeling for the individual democratic basis of Western, and especially American, policy. . . . No wonder his voice at times sounds high-pitched and hysterical." *Sarkhan,* Lederer's second collaboration with Burdick, was "both a novel of suspense and a political tract flailing the American Government for its ineptitude in combating Communist subversion in the mystic East."

In *Our Own Worst Enemy* Lederer turned his attention to Vietnam, where, he said, the same kind of ineptitude, and worse, was losing the war on all its fronts, military, moral, and political. His book, which does not hesitate to name names, "has the makings of a significant exposé of American and Vietnamese corruption at the expense of the war effort," but seemed to many "so cluttered with extravagant, undocumented charges . . . that its numerous valid points are lost in the fury."

WILLIAM J. LEDERER

Robert Conquest has said that Lederer writes "in the finest tradition of the career journalist who exposes the errors which officialdom is trying to hush up. We cannot have too much of that, and the fact that he grossly overstates his points is one of the inevitable conditions of his trade." He has also produced *The Mirages of Marriage* "a provocative, mirage-crushing, and mature diagnosis of ailing marriages," written in collaboration with a psychiatrist, as well as several books for children.

Lederer held a Nieman Fellowship at Harvard University in 1950–1951, and in 1966–1967 returned to Harvard as an author in residence. He wrote the Ensign O'Toole television series and the screen version of *The Ugly American,* and is the author of a number of short stories. Lederer has three children by his first marriage in 1940 to Ethel Hackett, and four stepchildren by his second marriage in 1965 to Corinne Edwards Lewis. When he is not traveling, he lives with his family at Peacham, Vermont. His hobbies include photography, cooking, and painting.

PRINCIPAL WORKS: *Nonfiction*—The Last Cruise: The Story of the Sinking of the Submarine, U.S.S. Cochino, 1950; All the Ships at Sea, 1950; Spare-Time Article Writing for Money, 1954; Ensign O'Toole and Me, 1957; A Nation of Sheep, 1961; Our Own Worst Enemy, 1968; (with D. D. Jackson) The Mirages of Marriage, 1968. *Fiction*—(with E. L. Burdick) The Ugly American, 1958; (with E. L. Burdick) Sarkhan, 1965.

ABOUT: Contemporary Authors 1–4 1st revision, 1967; Gardiner, H. C. In All Conscience, 1959; Lederer, W. J. All the Ships at Sea, 1950; Who's Who in America, 1972–1973. *Periodicals*—Saturday Evening Post January 14, 1950; Wilson Library Bulletin April 1961.

VIOLETTE LEDUC

***LEDUC, VIOLETTE** (April 7, 1907–May 28, 1972), French novelist, was born in Arras, Pas de Calais, France. She was the "unrecognized daughter of a son of good family"—a family which had employed her intelligent but resentful and unloving mother as a maid. Her illegitimacy haunted her life and her writing: "You gave birth to a river of tears, mother, on which I set sail." After this beginning, her mother's eventual marriage seemed a betrayal, coming after years of abuse of the whole male sex. Her grandmother, who died while Violette Leduc was still a child, was the only stable influence on her early life.

Her sense of alienation from ordinary life was exacerbated by frequent illness and her consciousness of her own physical ugliness, and while she was still at boarding school she began to find emotional release in lesbian affairs, first with another girl, then with a teacher. An intellectual, "intoxicated" by literature, she also attracted a number of variously unsatisfactory men by the force of her personality and mind, and for a time was married to one of them.

The great passion of her life came during World War II. Its object was the writer Maurice Sachs. He did not reciprocate her feeling, being an egocentric and a homosexual, but allowed her to lavish on him the pent-up tenderness of a lifetime. During the Nazi occupation they lived near each other in Normandy, and Violette Leduc traveled miles to secure black-market food for him and herself, and to sell for profit. Sachs was shot by the Germans just before the end of the war, but before that she had, thanks to him, begun to write. One day, after listening in mounting exasperation to one of her endless catalogues of misfortune, Sachs lost his temper and said: "Your unhappy childhood is driving me to distraction. This afternoon you will take your basket, a pen and an exercise book . . . [and] write down all the things you tell me."

* lə dük

The result was her first book, *L'Asphyxie* (1946, translated as *In the Prison of Her Skin*). It was followed by *L'Affamée* (The Famished, 1949), about an ugly woman who sees nothing but ugliness in others until she falls in love, and *Ravages* (1955), an account of the author's first love affair at school (a theme to which she returns in *Thérèse et Isabelle*, 1966). None of her books attracted much attention until she published *La Bâtarde* (1964), an unsparing if slightly fictionalized account of her first forty years. It appeared with an enthusiastic introduction by Simone de Beauvoir, who described it as "that privileged form of communication—a work of art." In France it established its author at once as a major figure in contemporary letters.

The excellent English translation by Derek Coltman (the author's usual translator) had a more mixed reception. Some reviewers were unmoved to find that Violette Leduc "weeps, exults, and trembles with her ovaries," as Simone de Beauvoir had put it. Harold Acton complained of "pretentious mawkishness and platitude," and said: "If all that she tells us is true of her covetous greed and her torturing of those who loved her . . . one is hardly surprised that she suffered from loneliness." But a critic in the *Times Literary Supplement*, acknowledging that the author "chatters on in complete oblivion of her audience," and had failed to weld a number of fascinating anecdotes into a novel, called the book nevertheless "a brilliant essay in self-revelation." Others praised its courage, and Henri Peyre wrote enthusiastically of her "extraordinary prose, rich, sensuous, at times sumptuous with images worthy of Rimbaud, and perhaps the closest counterpart of Jean Genet at his best." A second volume of autobiography, *La Folie en tête* (1970), has been translated as *Mad in Pursuit*. It describes the beginning of her literary career, and her troubled friendships with such celebrities as Genet and Jean Cocteau.

Three novellas, published separately in France, appeared in one volume in the United States as *The Woman With the Little Fox*. All are about unhappy women, alienated in one way or another from society. In *La Vieille Fille et le mort* (The Old Maid and the Dead Man), first published in 1958, an aging spinster finds an outlet for her suppressed tenderness when she discovers a corpse in her café. *Les Boutons dorés* (The Golden Buttons) is about a girl who, denied love and understanding in real life, clings to the memory of a boy she had known for less than a day. The title story, first published in 1965, concerns an old lady who finds a dilapidated fox fur in a Paris garbage can and makes of it her lover, her child, her reason for living. At one point, to avert starvation, she tries but fails to sell it. After that she is alone with her possessions, which she loves and glorifies because they, unlike people, have not hurt her. Reading these three stories, wrote Muriel Haynes, "we waver between mystification and blood recognition; so, one imagines it must be, to witness primitive rites. . . . What can we do about Mlle. Leduc's world except open ourselves to its desperate ingenuity?"

Violette Leduc died of cancer in 1972. Later the same year appeared Helen Weaver's translation of *Le Taxi* (1971), a novella evoking entirely through dialogue the day of love between an adolescent brother and sister in a Paris taxi hired and equipped for the purpose. Paul Zweig called it "a marvellous fairy tale of incest" and a "small masterpiece."

PRINCIPAL WORKS IN ENGLISH TRANSLATION: The Golden Buttons, 1961; La Bâtarde, 1965; The Woman With the Little Fox (three novellas: The Old Maid and the Dead Man, The Golden Buttons, The Woman With the Little Fox, 1966) (England, the last title published alone as The Lady and the Little Fox Fur, 1967); Thérèse and Isabelle, 1967; In the Prison of Her Skin, 1970; Mad in Pursuit, 1971; The Taxi, 1972.

ABOUT: Contemporary Authors 13–14, 1965. *Periodicals*—Atlas February 1965; Book Week November 7, 1965; Life October 15, 1965; Nation January 23, 1967; New York Review of Books January 6, 1966; New York Times Book Review November 21, 1965; November 27, 1966; New Yorker January 23, 1965; Saturday Review October 30, 1965; November 26, 1966; Times (London) May 30, 1972; Times Literary Supplement December 9, 1965; February 23, 1967; July 11, 1968; Vogue March 15, 1965; April 1, 1966.

LEE, C. Y. (CHIN-YANG LI) (December 23, 1917–), Chinese-American novelist and journalist, writes: "I was born in 1917, two months before the Chinese New Year. In China a child is considered to be one year old at birth and becomes one year older on each New Year's Day. Therefore, at two months I was officially two years old.

"My father was a landowner and the house where I was born was about thirty miles (one day's journey by sedan chair) from Changsha, the capital of Hunan Province. Hunan is famous for rice, soldiery, and passionate women. The passions are aroused by the hot pepper which is grown in large quantities. It inflames the women and sends the men rushing off to battlefields.

"I am the youngest of eight brothers and three sisters, with one nephew and two nieces older than I. It was considered a great blessing on my parents' part, as in the old days people in China wanted a lot of children, whether they could afford them or not, and enjoyed 'five generations living under one roof.' My parents had four generations living under theirs before they passed away.

C. Y. LEE

"My early life was somewhat like that of the Mongolian nomads, constantly on the move, or seeking food or escaping enemies. When I was eleven, my father sent me to Peking to be educated in Western schools. When I attended college in Shantung, the entire institution was forced to flee southwest to Yunnan to escape the Japanese.

"I started writing when I was the secretary to the Chinese Maharaja on the China-Burma border in 1942, soon after I graduated from college. Called Sawbwa by the British, my employer was actually a big landlord owning every plot of land in his state, which was the size of Rhode Island. He was also a sort of amicable feudal lord, with a police force of twelve men, who spent all their working days sitting under a banyan tree shining their boots and picking their teeth. There was no crime. I wrote about them and it was easy to sell the stories to Chinese newspapers and magazines.

"My writing wasn't exactly professional, but my adventures appealed to the many easy chair adventurers who, as my editors told me, enjoyed the Sawbwa's demanding young Eurasian wife, his great modernization programs, his courtroom and all his hilarious headaches of the modern times. Besides being his modern secretary, I had other pleasant duties such as to keep his modern wife busy by playing cards and badminton and swimming with her. The Sawbwa just couldn't keep up with his English-Burmese redhead.

"In 1942 the Japanese landed in Burma and invaded China from the back door. I escaped to Chungking, then on to India and finally to the United States to study drama at the Yale Drama School. I received a Master of Fine Arts degree in

1947. After that I went to California where I edited a Chinese language newspaper in San Francisco, taught Mandarin at the Monterey Army Language School, and wrote for Radio Free Asia until my first novel, *The Flower Drum Song*, was made into a Broadway musical by Rodgers and Hammerstein.

"In 1963 I married and have since added gardening and raising a family to my activities in Southern California. I write every morning; in the afternoons I take long naps as I am usually not good anymore. Those naps are important, as I believe that brains function like batteries—they should be recharged."

Lee's first and best-known novel, *The Flower Drum Song*, is a slight but irresistibly charming story of San Francisco's Chinatown, where Mr. Wang, a guardian of the rigid mores of old China, comes into conflict with his Americanized son. The reviewers, sternly pointing out that it was "simple, even clumsy" in its structure and style, mostly wound up sharing Lee's affection for his "preposterous cast of characters," and delighting shamelessly in the book's revelations about life in the exotic enclave it describes, its sentimentality, and its tranquil humor. The musical based upon it was a hit, and the story was subsequently filmed.

Also well received were *Lover's Point*, drawing on Lee's experience as a teacher at the Monterey Army Language School; *Madame Goldenflower*, an exciting historical romance set in China at the time of the Boxer Rebellion; and *Cripple Mah and the New Order*, a satire on life in Communist China. Lee's virtues as a novelist include a "native talent for characterization" and for descriptive writing, a sharp ear for the nuances of speech, and a "wryly funny and compassionate" (if somewhat superficial) view of life. His novels are not well constructed, and he has a weakness for melodramatic plot devices. His characteristic manner, pleasing to most reviewers, has been variously described as "contrived naiveté" and "bare-faced innocence." *The Sawbwa and His Secretary*, Lee's account of life with the improbable ruler of Mengshih, has much in common with his novels and indeed, in the opinion of some critics, contains a generous admixture of fiction.

Lee, the son of Sun-an Lee and Lee Huang, is married to the former Joyce Lackey. He has not forgotten his drama training at Yale and still hopes to write a successful play one day. This "Chinese Saroyan," as he has been called, has no patience with the intellectual approach to literature, which seems to him an emotional business that "cannot be calculated and tabulated."

PRINCIPAL WORKS: The Flower Drum Song, 1957; Lover's Point, 1958; Madame Goldenflower, 1960; Cripple Mah and the New Order, 1961; The Sawbwa and His Secretary, 1959 (England, Corner of Heaven); The Virgin Market, 1964; The Land of the Golden Mountain, 1967.

ABOUT: Contemporary Authors 11–12, 1965; Writer's Yearbook, 1961.

LEE, HARPER. *See* LEE, (NELLE) HARPER

LEE, LAURIE (June 26, 1914–), English poet, dramatist, and memoirist, writes: "I am the youngest but one of a family of eight, and I was born in the Cotswold town of Stroud, Gloucestershire, and was not expected to survive the first day. Soon after my birth, my father skipped to London, and we moved to a village up the valley which was still semi-feudal and where I spent the first twenty years of my life. I was educated first at the village school, then later at the Stroud Central School, which taught us to make candlesticks but nothing else that I can remember. I left school at fifteen and took a job as an errand-boy in the town, and also gave lessons on the violin. My first interest was music, and I started a dance band at this time which catered exclusively for village functions. There were three of us—a cobbler-pianist, a roadmender-drummer, and myself on the violin, and we cornered the market for several years.

"The self-contained village life of my childhood and adolescence made a deep impression on me. We lived at the mercy of the seasons, saw little of the outside world, cooked on wood-fires and went to bed by candlelight. I belonged to a kind of tribal community which had lasted for a thousand years, but which has since died out, and I saw the last of it.

"Early in my teens I began to write poetry. The lush pagan valley may have had something to do with it. Otherwise I still don't quite know what started me off, and it never occurred to me to try to get any of it published. I suppose it was that living in a crowded cottage, with my brothers and sisters all round me, poetry was the only private thing I could indulge in at the time, and something which needed the minimum of space and equipment.

"Inevitably, as I grew up, the village contracted; and at the age of twenty I left home for good. Naturally, I headed for London (one hundred miles away), and, traditionally, I went on foot; but never having seen the sea, I travelled the long way round, sleeping in fields and playing the violin in the streets—a leisurely journey at the height of summer which took me a month. I worked for a year in London as a builder's labourer, and then decided to see more of the world. It was the middle-thirties, and travel was easy, so I went to Spain, and spent thirteen months wandering about the country, living off the land and playing the fiddle in the towns, and enjoying the last days of peace in Europe.

"I was still in Spain when the Civil War broke out. I came back to England, then returned to Spain briefly, crossing the Pyrenees in the winter of 1937 to find that the war was already lost. From then, till the outbreak of World War II, I travelled round the Eastern Mediterranean as an odd-job tramp, visiting Italy, Greece, the Aegean Islands, and spending a winter in Cyprus.

"It was a long, semi-idle apprenticeship; but during the war I had to start to write seriously, doing documentary film-scripts for the Crown Film Unit and other propaganda jobs. In 1940, aged twenty-six, I published my first poem (in *Horizon*), and in 1944, my first collection. Since then, I have lived almost entirely by writing, though I don't know how I managed to do it. Largely by avoiding jobs that steal the cream of one's energies, and by maintaining a moderately low standard of living. I married, rather late, a beautiful girl from Provence, the daughter of a Martigues fisherman; and we have just had, also late—after twelve years of marriage—our first child, a girl, Jesse Frances.

"Prose and poetry remain my twin obsessions; I find they are equal in their demands. I hope neither one or the other will recede from me. There is nothing else I wish to do."

Laurie Lee's "other propaganda jobs" during the war included two years (1944–1946) as publications editor at the Ministry of Information. He wrote for the Crown Park Film Unit (1946–1947) and for the Festival of Britain (1950–1951), and received an MBE in 1952.

Reviewing *The Sun My Monument*, Stephen Spender called Lee an impressionist poet, influenced by Lorca, who could produce "a sharp, sunlit impression," but whose work was "almost untouched by thought." However, *The Bloom of Candles* won Lee an Atlantic Award in 1947 and a Society of Authors' Travelling Scholarship in 1951; while *My Many-Coated Man* was the 1955 Poetry Book Society choice and received the Foyle Poetry Award. (These were very slim volumes indeed; Lee has "always been content to write lyrics of a length that never required the reader to turn over the page.") Reviewers of these books found that Laurie Lee was still an impressionist, seeking to fix intensely felt sensuous experiences in words, but an artist who had learned to employ a "disciplined intellectual effort" and a "forceful and elaborate use of image and metaphor." Geoffrey Moore, writing in 1958, said Lee had "bloomed in the fifties. . . . He used to engrave his work; now he uses a brush, but sharply, accurately still, and with a load of sensuous detail. . . ."

LAURIE LEE

Since the mid-1950s, Laurie Lee has turned increasingly and with great success to prose, notably in *The Edge of Day*, a twin choice of the Book-of-the-Month Club in America. In England, where it was called *Cider With Rosie*, it was a Book Society Choice and won the W. H. Smith £1,000 Award for Literature. It is a "rich, joyful, and poetic evocation" of his village childhood, his sexual awakening, and the development of the poetic impulse—a marvelous story, many critics thought, though for the taste of one a little "over-decorated and over-elaborated" in the telling. A sequel, *As I Walked Out One Midsummer Morning*, deals with Laurie Lee's early wanderings in London and Spain. It is, one critic wrote, "a work of art the finer for being artless," and "leaves us clamouring for more."

PRINCIPAL WORKS: The Sun My Monument (poems) 1944; The Bloom of Candles (poems), 1947; Peasants' Priest (verse play), 1947; The Voyage of Magellan (radio play), 1948; A Rose for Winter (travel) 1955; My Many-Coated Man (poems), 1955; Cider With Rosie (autobiography), 1959 (U.S., The Edge of Day); Laurie Lee (Pocket Poets series), 1960; The First Born, 1964; As I Walked Out One Midsummer Morning, 1969.

ABOUT: Allott, K. (ed.) Penguin Book of Contemporary Verse, 1962; Finn, F. E. S. (ed.) Poets of Our Time, 1965; Moore, G. Poetry Today, 1958; Murphy, R. (ed.) Contemporary Poets of the English Language, 1970; Who's Who, 1973. *Periodicals*—London Magazine February 1962; Newsweek October 24, 1960.

LEE, (NELLE) HARPER (April 28, 1926–) won the Pulitzer Prize for fiction with her first novel, *To Kill a Mockingbird* (1960), whose plot and characters were suggested by her own small-town childhood in Monroeville, Alabama. She was

HARPER LEE

born the youngest of three children to Amasa Coleman Lee and Frances (Finch) Lee—the family is kin to Robert E. Lee. Amasa Lee, the model for the novel's lawyer-hero Atticus, has a law practice in Monroeville.

Harper Lee began writing when she was seven. Her formal education took her through Monroeville's public schools, a year at Huntington College, and on to the University of Alabama in 1945, her stay there broken by a year as an exchange student at Oxford University. She left Alabama for New York City six months short of a law degree in 1950. In retrospect she felt her years in law school were "good training for a writer."

In New York Miss Lee worked as an airline reservations clerk for several years until, encouraged by an agent to whom she had submitted her work, and friends who donated financial support, she quit work to write full time. The manuscript of *To Kill a Mockingbird* was submitted to Lippincott in 1957; two and a half years later, after much rewriting, it was published.

To Kill a Mockingbird moves over three years in the childhood of "Scout" (Jean-Louise) Finch and her elder brother Jem, who live with their widowed father Atticus in the small Alabama town of Maycomb during the Depression. The novel is made up of a series of loosely connected episodes, recalled by the eight-year-old Scout, which illustrate the tone and character of small-town life in the rural South. Two of these episodes emerge as central: the children in fear and fascination bait an eccentric recluse, "Boo" Radley; and their father is called upon to defend a young black wrongfully accused of raping a white girl. Finch's determined defense of Tom Robinson is, inevitably, unpopular with most of Maycomb, and Robinson is, inevitably, convicted. In the course of the trial, however, Atticus exposes the girl and her degenerate father to the town's ridicule, and the man strikes back murderously, not at Atticus but at his children. It is Boo Radley who saves them. The children's unreasoning fear of the eccentric is obliquely compared to the community's hatred of the black. Both Robinson and Radley are symbolized by the mockingbird that it is a "sin to kill"; both are feared because unknown.

The book was an immediate and triumphant success, both popular and critical. Reviewers welcomed a novel about a southern childhood which was "refreshingly undepraved," and a plea for racial tolerance which was all the more persuasive for being implicit—brought in "casually, on the side, as it were." There was widespread praise for a warmth and humor which reminded some readers of Mark Twain, for the "easy, graceful writing," and for Miss Lee's ability to make "every person in the book in every moment alive in time and place."

Such criticism as there was centered on the relatively melodramatic climax, thought jarringly violent after the gentle realism of the earlier sections, and on the precocious maturity of Scout's account. To Richard Sullivan however, her apprehension seemed "cunningly restricted to that of a perceptive, independent child, who doesn't always understand fully what's happening, but who conveys completely, by implication, the weight and burden of the story."

The majority of critics thought it, if not a book of enduring stature, a first novel of remarkable achievement and greater promise; it was called "a welcome draught of fresh air" and the work of "a skilled, unpretentious, and totally ingenuous writer who slides unconcernedly and irresistibly back and forth between being sentimental, tough, melodramatic, acute, and funny." It became something like a fixture on the best-seller lists, was an alternate choice of the Book-of-the-Month Club, a Literary Guild selection, and a *Reader's Digest* Condensed Book. It won for Miss Lee the 1961 Pulitzer, a Brotherhood Award, and several lesser prizes; was translated into many foreign languages; and inspired an excellent film.

No second novel has appeared, but one is promised; it is also to be about southern small-town life, "the last refuge of eccentrics." Miss Lee believes "that there is something universal in this little world, something decent to be said for it, and something to lament in its passing." Her chief literary debt is to Jane Austen, "writing, cameo-like, in that little corner of the world of hers and making it universal." She herself writes so slowly and revises so much that she calls herself "more a rewriter than writer." Harper Lee is dark-eyed, with dark straight hair flecked with gray. She has been called tomboyish, "plump and pretty and unpretentious." Her main interests, she says, are "collecting memoirs of nineteenth-century clergymen, golf, crime, and music." She is a Methodist.

PRINCIPAL WORK: To Kill a Mockingbird, 1960.
ABOUT: Contemporary Authors 15–16, 1966; Current Biography, 1961; Newquist, R. (ed.) Counterpoint, 1965; Roden, D. F. and Blum, R. Harper Lee's To Kill a Mockingbird, 1966; Who's Who in America, 1972–1973.

***LE FORT, GERTRUD (PETREA) BARONESS VON,** (October 11, 1876–November 1, 1971) German poet and novelist, wrote: "I come from a Protestant family whose forefathers had lived in Cony, Piedmont (North Italy), but who in the sixteenth century had to leave their country because of religious persecution. They first settled in Geneva, where the Italian name 'li Forti' was turned into the French 'le Fort.' All members of our family are still Swiss citizens. About a hundred years later, François le Fort went to Russia where he became an admiral and a close friend of Tsar Peter I. One of his descendants came to Mecklenburg, North Germany and there acquired estates.

"I passed my childhood in different towns. My father, being an army officer, had to change residences rather often. However my favourite memories are those of the time I spent at the family estate, Boek, in Mecklenburg.

"My liking for writing little poems and short stories dates back to early childhood. As was the custom in those times, I received my early education from private tutors at home and attended school rather late. Before the first world war, university education for women was rather unheard of, so I was the only female student in all the lectures I attended. I studied philosophy, history and Protestant theology at the universities of Heidelberg, Marburg, and Berlin.

"After my father's death, my mother and I took to traveling. On various occasions, we spent considerable time in Rome, where I received my first deep impressions of the Catholic Church. My turning Catholic in 1926 decisively influenced my life and work; however it cannot be considered as a rejection of the Protestant faith but originated in a deep distress over the schism. I thus tried to bridge it.

"The Nazi regime and later the Russian invasion caused the loss of our family estates. I was happy to find a new home in the beautiful Bavarian Alps. Since 1945 I have been living at Oberstdorf."

* lə fôr′

GERTRUD VON LE FORT

Gertrud von le Fort was generally regarded as Germany's leading contemporary Roman Catholic novelist. Her father, Lothar von le Fort, a chivalrous and scrupulous man, was a colonel in the Prussian army and "a baron (Freiherr) of the old empire." It was he who first instilled in her a love of history, particularly of those large sections of European history in which the le Fort family was involved. "If he were talking about the period of the religious wars, then it was Calvin who welcomed our family in Geneva when it fled from Savoy. . . . If we turned to the French Revolution, we saw the three le Forts who, as officers of Louis XVI, had taken part in the fighting at the Tuileries." Her mother was the former Elspeth von Wedel-Pavlow, whose ardent Protestant faith was passed on to her daughter, as the latter has recalled in *Mein Elternhaus* (My Parents' House, 1941) and *Aufzeichnungen und Erinnerungen* (Sketches and Memories, 1951). This religious preoccupation was heightened at Heidelberg University, where Gertrud von le Fort studied under the Protestant theologian Ernst Troeltsch, whose *Glaubenslehre* she edited (1925).

Although she had written poems and stories all her life, and published a few of them, her first major work, the sequence of psalm-like poems *Hymnen an die Kirche* (translated by M. Chanler as *Hymns to the Church*) was not published until 1924. This was shortly before she embraced Roman Catholicism, when she was nearly fifty. For the next thirty years she wrote prolifically—novels, poems, short stories, and essays—covering an immense range of subjects and historical periods, but concentrating on the theme of Christian redemption through suffering and unselfish love. She was almost mystically drawn to the order and authority of the Holy Roman Empire, but believed that "a world so deeply and terribly destroyed as ours cannot be restored merely by negotiations and treaties. . . . Before we can make peace with man, we must make peace with God."

The novel which established her reputation, *Das Schweisstuch der Veronika* (1928, translated by C. M. R. Bonacina as *The Veil of Veronica*), is subtitled "Der römische Brunnen" (The Roman Fountain). It is set in Rome before World War I, when the adolescent Veronika, overwhelmed by the grandeur of the Church and its historic empire, becomes a convert. *Der Kranz der Engel* (The Wreath of Angels), its sequel, appeared nearly twenty years later in 1946. Veronika is now a student at Heidelberg and in love with the aggressively agnostic poet Enzio. Hoping to redeem him, she consents at the risk of excommunication to a civil marriage. This ultimate martyrdom is avoided when she falls desperately ill and Enzio regains his faith. These books are typical in several ways of Gertrud von le Fort's fiction—in their intricate symbolism, in the delicacy and classical purity of their style, in their theme, and in having as their central character a woman who has painfully achieved peace with God and become a guardian of the ultimate values.

Much of her fiction is set in the past, but her concerns were timeless and often seemed urgently contemporary. "History appears in her writings," wrote a critic in the *Times Literary Supplement*, "as a conflict between compulsion and compassion, justice and love, the sword and the heart." *Der Papst aus dem Ghetto* (1930, translated as *The Pope From the Ghetto*), a novel about papal intrigue in the twelfth century, is also a discussion of the German "Jewish problem" in the twentieth. *Die Letzte am Schafott* (1931, translated by Olga Marx as *Song at the Scaffold*), an account in letter form of the heroic martyrdom during the French Revolution of a group of Carmelites, had obvious meaning when other tyrannies were struggling for power in Germany. This novella has become her best-known work. It was adapted by Georges Bernanos as a play, *Les Dialogues des Carmélites*, and as the basis of Poulenc's opera *Les Carmélites* (1956), and has been filmed.

Other notable novels and *novellen* include *Das Reich des Kindes* (1933), *Die Magdeburgische Hochzeit* (1938), *Die Abberufung der Jungfrau von Barby* (1940), *Die Tochter Farinatas* (1950), *Gelöschte Kerzen* (1953), *Am Tor des Himmels* (1954), about Galileo's conflict with the Church, and *Die Frau des Pilatus* (1955), about the dilemma of the Christian wife of Pontius Pilate. Her fiction "stands firmly," according to H. M. Waidson, "within the limits of her conviction of preordained purpose: it has a framework of inner certainty, though it depicts people who have to wrestle hard for the retention of their sanity and faith." Her full-length novels tend to be rather shapeless and diffuse, but her *novellen* benefit from the taut structure of the medium, and are admired for their great "formal economy and burnished dignity."

The note of religious ecstasy in Gertrud von le Fort's poetry is disciplined into lucidity by the same kind of formal control that distinguishes her shorter prose. *Hymnen an Deutschland* (1932) calls for the establishment of Roman Catholicism as the state religion of Germany. *Gedichte* (1949), collecting poems written between 1933 and 1945, reflects the miseries and also the hopes of those dark years, and includes the exquisite "Deutsches Leid," a moving confession of the poet's love for her ruined country. Essays and occasional pieces are collected in *Die Krone der Frau* (1952). She believed that it is a woman's duty humbly to serve mankind, and she explained her views (which are implicit in her fiction), in *Die Ewige Frau* (1934).

Baroness von le Fort spent "the thirteen infamous Hitler years" in "utter forlornness on the very abyss of desperation." The family estates, which were in the hands of her brother, were confiscated by the Nazis and then overrun by the Russians. She received many awards and honors for her work, including the Munich Poets' Prize, the Baden State Prize, and the Gottfried Keller Prize. On her eightieth birthday she accepted an honorary doctorate in theology from the University of Munich.

PRINCIPAL WORKS IN ENGLISH TRANSLATION: *Fiction*—Veil of Veronica, 1932; The Pope from the Ghetto, 1934; Song at the Scaffold, 1937; The Judgement of the Sea, 1962. *Poetry*—Hymns to the Church, 1937. *Essays*—The Eternal Woman, 1954.

ABOUT: Bithell, J. Modern German Literature, 1959; Focke, A. Gertrud von le Fort, 1960; Heinen, N. Gertrud von le Fort, 1955; Natan, A. (ed.) German Men of Letters II, 1963; O'Boyle, I. Gertrud von le Fort, 1964; Reinhardt, K. The Theological Novel of Modern Europe, 1968; Waidson, H. M. The Modern German Novel, 1959. *Periodicals*—Germanic Review 4 1952; German Life and Letters January 1963; New York Times November 5, 1971; Studies Winter 1961.

***LEHMANN, WILHELM** (May 4, 1882–November 17, 1968), German poet, novelist, and essayist, wrote: "It may be necessary for common usage to fix a label on one's literary work. Looking back, from an octogenarian's armchair, no longer a strenuous wanderer, into my past, I should like to call what I have been living through and working at, the expression of a '*politesse envers la création*.' Born in pre-war times, I began, in 1912, to write stories and novels. As all of them are borne along

* lā′ mən

by an undercurrent of intense lyrical emotion, they may be considered as preparatory to the pure lyric poetry, arising later, on which, for most of my critics, my reputation rests. Conditions for writing solid poems are an ever wakeful imagination, standing up to the impact of sensual impressions, and, secondly, the ability to word the latter. To acquire an economy of language, a study of philology helped me much. From earliest childhood I have been feeding on what trees, leaves, plants, animals —in short all living creatures, sky, earth, water— meant and mean to me. So my life became the natural effort of the mind to describe natural things, in narrative prose as well as in singing lines—a most difficult undertaking, the average man being inclined either to embellish or to rationalise his surroundings, trusting his own fancies, not trying to get at the root of things themselves. Philosophy likes to speak of 'the infinite flatness of physical experience.' For poetry, it is pregnant with the multifariousness of life. Very often the ideas we have of things are not fair portraits, but political caricatures made in the human interest. Pseudo-poetry would address a wasp as a lady with a small waist, real poetry makes creatures speak out of their own nature, D. H. Lawrence doing this in a poem about a baby tortoise: 'Moving, and being himself, / Slow, and unquestioned, / And inordinately there, O stoic! / Wandering in the slow triumph of his own existence, / Ringing the soundless bell of his presence in chaos.' Given the singularity of the individual, viz., his limits, the result of his effort, surely, will be a limited reality, the narrowness of human conscience being forced to get at wholeness by means of getting hold of a selected something. Poets want their word portraits to be masterpieces of characterization and insight. They try hard to avoid cheap anthropomorphism, but I take as a faithful understatement George Santayana's remark: 'that something creeps in, by way of idealisation, hyperbole, myth and legend, is not an unmixed evil.'

"A paradisaic childhood—'the child is father of the man'—unruly '*wanderjahre*,' two marriages, birth of three children, friendship with Moritz Heimann, Oskar Loerke, Werner Kraft, two terrible wars, a teacher's career, have been the facts of my life.

"Born at Puerto Cabello (Venezuela), but, three years old, back to Germany; son of an iron merchant from Lübeck, Friedrich Lehmann, and the daughter of a surgeon from Hamburg, Agathe Wichmann—both his and her families originating from Mecklenburg peasants, publicans and 'Kunstpfeifern'—I grew up at Wandsbek (Schleswig-Holstein). My father, of an unstable character, left his family, leaving it to my mother to sustain, by hard work, her three lively children. I studied

WILHELM LEHMANN

philology and philosophy at the universities of Tübingen, Strasbourg, Berlin, Kiel, was promoted to a Dr. ph. Finding it impossible to live by my pen, I became a schoolmaster, teaching languages at all sorts of schools. I was a common soldier in World War I and taken a prisoner (1918) by Canadian troops. From 1923 till 1947 I held a post at an 'Oberschule' in Eckernförde. In Nazi Germany, I was considered 'undesirable.' Though awarded several official 'Kunstpreise' and some voices of unstinted appraisal apart, I have been condemned to obscurity. I live at Eckernförde. The landscape of Schleswig-Holstein has become inescapably 'die Mutter meiner Dichtung.' "

Since his earliest years, nature was for Lehmann a solace and a passion. As a boy he kept a whole menagerie of birds and animals in the attic, and all his life he spent his free time in the woods and fields where most of his poems are conceived. Lehmann's first novels, *Der Bilderstürmer* (The Iconoclast, 1917), *Die Schmetterlingspuppe* (The Butterfly Pupae, 1918), and *Weingott* (Wine God, 1921), have been called "poetic self-confessions." They reflect his misery in his first teaching post and in his early first marriage. Lehmann's wife was fifteen years older than he was, and their troubled relationship was further strained by the opposition of Lehmann's mother, and saddened by the death of their son. The heroes of these novels retreat from the torment and complexity of daily life and seek release and serenity in nature. For them there is no greater threat than what Lehmann called "*nichts*" (nothingness), by which he meant a sense of alienation from the natural world, the antithesis of that oneness with the cosmos, "the all," which he regarded as the greatest good.

"It is now a matter of literary history," wrote Jethro Bithell, "that Lehmann's first volume of verse, *Antwort des Schweigens* (Answer of Silence, 1935), resulted in the founding of a new school of poetry, 'die naturmagische Schule' (the nature-magic school)." That remarkable collection, appearing out of a long silence, recalled the nature poetry of Mörike and, together with the similar work of Lehmann's close friend Oscar Loerke, represented a quiet revolution against the political and satirical German verse of the 1930s.

Lehmann's poetry is the product of a passionate and mystical conviction that human life is a part of nature, but avoids the sentimental vagueness such a belief can induce by disciplined observation and the exact and scholarly use of language. "My poems are deeds of my eyes," he said, meaning that the poet must first of all *see* accurately—and must see the thing for what it is, not for what it may conveniently symbolize: "Abstraction and Utopia are the enemies of poetry." Nevertheless, "everything in Nature is simple and complex at the same time," and through the intense and ecstatic scrutiny of particular things the poet may hope to gain contact with what is universal: "One can only share in the whole if one takes possession of a part of it."

For Lehmann the philologist, language itself was a source of knowledge and power, and must not be used carelessly: "God and the world only appear to the summons of mysteriously definite, carefully planned syllables." Thus he was "greedy for names," and his poems are studded with recondite botanical and zoological terms that make them appear more difficult than they are, and also with words and with names from mythology and literature that carry a special meaning in his verse. Nature in Lehmann's poetry is shown in the course of perpetual renewal, an endless cycle of birth and death in which the act of procreation is central and holy, providing the closest obtainable contact with the cosmos. This cycle he found embodied in the myths, legends, and fairy tales with which his verse is charged.

The prose works which Lehmann published after the war continue and often explain the themes of his poems. They include the novel *Ruhm des Daseins* (Glory of Being), written in the 1930s but not published until 1953, and *Der Überläufer* (The Deserter), written in 1925–1927 but not published until 1962. The latter is Lehmann's most ambitious novel, the story of an unwilling soldier-poet, during and after World War I, interwoven with long discussions of Lehmann's poetic intentions and of specific poems. He also produced several volumes of short stories, literary essays, a nature diary, and *Mühe des Anfangs* (Growing Pains), a moving account of his early years. A volume of selected poems, *Meine Gedichtbücher*, appeared in 1957, and his *Sämtliche Werke* in 1962. He loved English poetry, and translated among others Marvell, Frost, and Graves. His many honors include the Kleist Prize, shared with Robert Musil in 1923, the Lessing Prize (1953), and the Schiller Award (1959).

During the Nazi years Lehmann was regarded with hostility by the authorities. His works were never proscribed, however, and his reputation grew steadily until, by the end of the war, some regarded him as a rival to Gottfried Benn as the greatest living German lyric poet. Since then West German poetry has changed violently in form and content, and today nothing could be less fashionable than rhymed nature poetry. This does not alter the fact that his work has influenced a whole generation of poets, including specifically Elisabeth Langgässer, Gunter Eich, Karl Krolow—as well as a number of their juniors—and made an indispensable contribution to the continuity of German poetry at the end of World War II. Professor Prawer has called him "a true poet of our time, whose quiet voice will still be heard when many of his contemporaries have been forgotten."

Lehmann was married in 1913 to his second wife, the former Frieda Riewerts, by whom he had three children. Until his death in 1968 he continued to write and to publish poems, many of them combining "a personal leavetaking with impersonal celebration," many of them showing undiminished delight in formal experiment.

PRINCIPAL WORKS IN ENGLISH TRANSLATION: *Poems in* Bridgwater, P. (ed.) Penguin Book of Twentieth-Century German Verse, 1963; Hamburger, M. and Middleton, C. (eds.) Modern German Poetry, 1962.

ABOUT: Bithell, J. Modern German Literature, 1959; Bruns, H. Wilhelm Lehmann, 1962; Keith-Smith, B. (ed.) Essays on Contemporary German Literature, 1966; Schug, D. Die Naturlyrik G. Brittings und Wilhelm Lehmanns, 1963; Siebert, W. Gegenwart des Lyrischen Essays zum Werk Wilhelm Lehmanns, 1967. *Periodicals*—German Life and Letters July 1962; Times Literary Supplement March 1, 1963; May 18, 1967.

***LEIRIS, MICHEL** (April 20, 1901–), French memoirist, poet, and anthropologist, was born in Paris, the son of Eugène Leiris, a stockbroker's agent, and the former Marie-Madeleine Caubet. He attended the Lycée Janson-de-Sailly, received his *licence* in literature at the Sorbonne, and a diploma from the École Pratique des Hautes Études Scientifiques et Religieuses. His early writings were surrealistic, reflecting the influence of his friends André Breton and Max Jacob. They include the poems collected in *Simulacre* (Simulacrum, 1925) and the novel *Aurora*, begun four or five years later but not published until 1946. *Aurora*, one of the

* lā rēs

most notable prose works produced by surrealism, has many of the characteristics of his later books: a horrified obsession with physical decrepitude and death and a crippling fear of life and love, expressed both in the extreme emotional coldness of the narrative and in the sadistic fantasies which end the novel "in the only satisfactory manner possible, that is in a torrent of blood."

In 1929 the fears and the self-disgust evident in *Aurora* produced a severe mental crisis and physical impotence. After extended psychiatric treatment Leiris changed his way of life completely, embarking on a new career in anthropology. He joined the Dakar-Djibouti expedition to Africa (1931–1933) and on his return joined the staff of the Musée de l'Homme in Paris. During the 1930s he wrote poems and worked on the book published in 1939 as *L'Age d'homme*. Its impact was diminished by the outbreak of World War II, but in 1946, when it was republished with an important introductory essay, it had a *succès de scandale*. It was translated in 1963 by Richard Howard as *Manhood*, with the prefatory essay, "De la littérature considerée comme une tauromachie," rendered as "The Autobiographer as Torero."

This "brilliant and repulsive" autobiography is not a history of Leiris's life and ignores his achievements, concentrating almost exclusively on his limitations: his baldness, his physical incompetence and ugliness, his meager sexual capacities, his hypochondria, his morbid fantasies, his cowardice. Susan Sontag called it "a manual of abjection-anecdotes and fantasies and verbal associations and dreams set down in the tones of a man partly anesthetized, curiously fingering his own wounds." In the book's "coolness of tone," its "great intelligence and subtlety about motives," Miss Sontag found a "very high order of literary merit," but she confessed also to impatience with its formlessness and distaste for the author's "obscene" lack of self-respect.

Miss Sontag believes that Leiris "writes to appall, and thereby to receive from his readers the gift of a strong emotion." Leiris himself has made numerous attempts to explain why he writes as he does. At the root of everything is his obsessive fear of death, his sense of being hopelessly trapped in a doomed and decaying body. He discovered his physical fear and inadequacy as a boy in the gymnasium, and ever since has been "crushed by shame, feeling his whole being corrupted by this incurable cowardice." Easily bored and craving excitement, Leiris is or was drawn to the bullfight, but shamed by its grace and courage. Easily frightened, he finds "nothing in love—or taste—for which I am ready to face death." Then what is he to live for? "There remains," wrote Claude Mauriac, "the real courage which he demonstrates above all by speaking about his cowardice." Or, as Susan Sontag puts it, "Leiris must feel, as he writes, the equivalent of the bullfighter's knowledge that he risks being gored." And "this invigorating sense of mortal danger" is possible only "by laying himself—in his own person—on the line of fire." Thus he hopes to prove "not that he is heroic, but that he is at all."

MICHEL LEIRIS

To the extent that Leiris was also attempting in *L'Age d'homme* "to liquidate a certain number of things which have oppressed him by writing about them," he evidently failed, remaining sufficiently oppressed at any rate to make (in 1958) the almost successful suicide attempt recorded in the cycle of poems called *Vivante cendres, innommées* (Living Ashes, Unnamed). He tried again "to take stock of himself in order to go beyond himself" in another autobiographical work, *La Règle du jeu* (Rule of the Game), comprising three volumes: *Biffures* (Deletions, 1948), *Fourbis* (Thingummies, 1955), and *Fibrilles* (Threads, 1967). Here again are the confessions and the self-abasements, pursued this time through a labyrinth of word associations. Many years before Leiris had written: "By dissecting words we like, without worrying about following etymology, nor accepted connotations, we discover their most hidden virtues and the secret ramifications that are propagated throughout all language, channeled by the association of sounds, forms, and ideas. Then language is transformed into an oracle and we have there a thread (tenuous though it may be) to guide us in the Babel of the mind." This is the thread Leiris follows, with much honesty and intelligence, from one emotionally charged word to another, in search of his ultimate and irreducible self.

Leiris's books, which inevitably suggest comparisons with *A la recherche du temps perdu*, have been much discussed in Freudian terms. He himself doubts that this approach "helps a great deal as far as the essential part of the problem is concerned (which remains, according to my way of thinking, related to the problem of death and to the apprehension of oblivion and so relates to metaphysics)." His writings are an attempt at "the erection of his own statue," a gesture against oblivion, an exact record and replica of Leiris that will remain when Leiris is gone. Nor is the value of his work for others solely literary; to the extent that his readers share in secret the despicable failings he confesses, his books lift a little the burden of shame and offer, as Claude Mauriac has said, "a certain comfort."

Leiris returned to Africa in 1945 and has made field trips also in the Antilles (1948–1952) and China (1955). He is attracted (Susan Sontag says) by the extreme formalism of primitive societies and fascinated (this "maniac for confession") by masks and secret languages and the ritualization of collective life. Among the best known of his anthropological studies are *L'Afrique fantôme* (Phantom Africa, 1934), *Le Sacré dans la vie quotidienne* (The Sacred in Everyday Life, 1938), and *Race et civilisation* (Race and Civilization, 1951).

Michel Leiris is married to the former Louise Godon and lives in Paris, where he directs research at the National Center for Scientific Research. He numbers among his friends most of the great names of contemporary French art and literature. He is little known by the general public, but his influence, especially on the masters of the French "new literature," is enormous.

PRINCIPAL WORKS IN ENGLISH TRANSLATION: The Prints of Joan Miró, 1947; Picasso and the Human Comedy (with 180 drawings), 1954; Manhood: A Journey from Childhood into the Fierce Order of Virility, 1963; (with Jacqueline Delange) African Art, 1968.

ABOUT: Boisdeffre, P. de. Dictionnaire de littérature contemporaine, 1900–1962, 1962; Matthews, J. H. Surrealism and the Novel, 1966; Mauriac, C. The New Literature, 1959; Nadeau, M. Michel Leiris et la quadrature du cercle, 1963, The French Novel Since the War, 1967; Pingaud, B. Écrivains d'aujourd'hui, 1940–1960, 1960; Sontag, S. Against Interpretation, 1966; Who's Who in France, 1971–1972. *Periodicals*—Times Literary Supplement June 15, 1967; Unesco Courier December 1965.

LEON, HENRY CECIL. *See* "CECIL, HENRY"

LESSING, DORIS (MAY) (October 22, 1919–), English novelist and short story writer, writes: "I was born in Persia because my father, Alfred Tayler, managed a bank there for five years. The Great War, in which he lost a limb and his health, unsettled him and he could no longer live in England. His father had been a poor country clergyman who spent his life playing the church organ; and like him my father was impractical and introspective. My mother, Emily McVeagh, was Irish and Scotch. Her mother died in childbirth. Brought up by a disciplinarian father and a stepmother, my mother was over-dutiful and inhibited, but in her was imprisoned a gay affectionate woman. I do not remember Persia much except in emotion-laden flashes; but it was a typical English middle-class family defensive against a civilisation found unsympathetic.

"In 1924 the family went to farm in Rhodesia. As this affected me, it meant a solitary childhood, for which I am now grateful, though then I was unhappy. My time was spent reading or walking through the African bush. That part of Africa had not before been farmed by white persons. Neighbours were four, seven, ten miles away: Scots lower-middle-class people, Presbyterian, hardworking, kindly. Further off were the English, mostly middle-class. All these families had left Britain to get rich. Most did. These were the white settlers of opprobrium who are, as I write this, last-ditch-fighting with Smith against the British government to preserve 'white civilisation.' Whatever their personal qualities, as a class they are stupid and unimaginative.

"Looking back now at that enormous tract of bush, dotted with lonely farms, it seems as if we all lived on brightly-lit stages where the dramas of our lives were played out to a chorus of comment and gossip. As a girl I watched these lives unfolding epically in the logic of their natures—a relentless and pitiless process it seemed then, as it still does. The storms, the winds, the silences of the bush; the sunlit or rain-whipped mountains; fields of maize miles long; sunflowers that turned their heads after the sun; cotton plants with their butterfly-like pink and white flowers—these, and the neighbours, were my education.

"At seven I went as a boarder to the Catholic Convent in Salisbury. This did me no good. I was cripplingly homesick, and the oppressive erotic-religious atmosphere of confined women, some of whom were brutal through ignorance, affected me. A year at an ordinary State school left no marks; nor did I learn anything worth knowing. I left school at fourteen, having been neurotically ill most of the time, as part of the fight against my mother who was ambitious for me. But I was refusing, as I now see, to succeed at anything on her terms. Unable to get on with my parents, I was what is now called an *au pair* girl in Salisbury for two years; then went back to the farm to write two bad novels; then was a telephone operator in Salisbury; then, at nineteen, married a civil servant. There were two children. This marriage failed and so did a second, from which I had one son whom I have brought up.

"Some of this has been described in the series of novels called Children of Violence. Which brings up the—to me—vexed question of what is autobiographical and what is not in my work. Much less than reviewers have supposed. This is important for me because if a book is read for a supposed autobiographical content, it means that what the author is trying to say in the shape of a work does not get understood. Admittedly I make trouble for myself, because I sometimes take events or phases in my life as a framework, and then add people or happenings to fit a theme.

"I was a communist for some years, from which I learned a great deal, chiefly about the nature of political power, how groups of people operate—I think according to specific but little-understood laws; and the force of self-delusion.

"I came to Britain in 1949 and have lived here since as a professional writer, at first rather poor, but now comfortable; I do not think the lives of working writers are interesting. We are all dug into protective backgrounds of one kind or another. I enjoy England, and London where I live, but like every white person brought up in Africa I long for the sun and the large empty landscapes. However I am a prohibited immigrant in Rhodesia and South Africa.

"I am still left-wing in politics, though pessimistic about the human condition; am more interested in philosophy and religion than I expected to be.

"About my writing: Yeats said that a writer must work a way inwards, into self-knowledge. I am always surprised at what I find in myself, and this to me is the most rewarding part of being a writer."

The accumulated experience of Doris Lessing's Rhodesian years was crystallized in her first two published books: *The Grass Is Singing* (1950), a novel, and *This Was the Old Chief's Country* (1951), a volume of short stories.

These were both books of great distinction and were warmly greeted by the critics as the products of a deeply original talent. Antonia White, for example, called *The Grass Is Singing* "an extremely mature psychological study. It is full of those terrifying touches of truth, seldom mentioned but instantly recognized. By any standards, this book shows remarkable powers and imagination. As a first novel by a woman barely thirty, it excites interest in her future."

The Grass Is Singing is about the gradual breakdown of an English-born farmer's wife, Mary Turner, on a remote and failing South African farm. Discontented with her arid existence, she finds her-

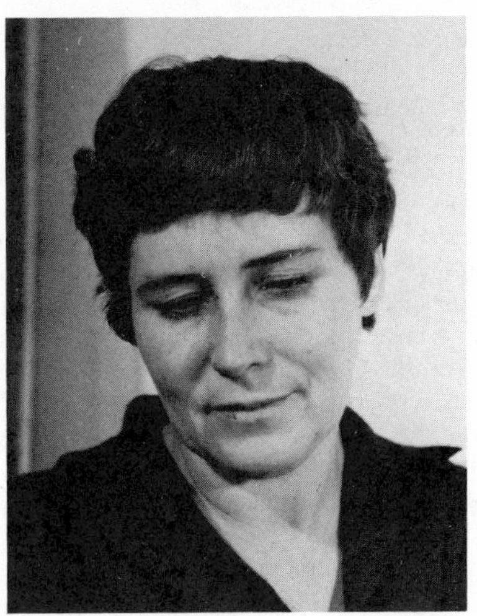

DORIS LESSING

self increasingly obsessed by her handsome, taciturn African house servant. The outcome is a sexual relationship embodying all the nightmare fantasies of white South Africans, ending with Mary Turner's death at the hands of her servant. This first novel thus introduces two of Doris Lessing's principal themes—the schizophrenic and wasteful misuse of black by white in Africa, and the equally destructive and complex conflict between men and women everywhere.

It is the former theme that inspires most of the short stories in *This Was the Old Chief's Country*, and the longer stories collected in *Five*, which received the 1953 Somerset Maugham Award. Doris Lessing's African stories have a profound sense of place, and of the way in which landscape may influence and seem to reflect human emotion, which have reminded many critics of the tales of D. H. Lawrence.

Some of the stories in *The Habit of Loving* also have racial themes and African settings, but here, and in Doris Lessing's second novel, *Retreat to Innocence*, there is a growing preoccupation with her other major theme, the situation of the modern emancipated woman. Her female characters have achieved a degree of freedom—intellectual, professional, and sexual—which goes far beyond anything dreamed of by the heroines of Ibsen or Shaw; nevertheless, they still remain a prey to their own emotions, and thus potential victims of masculine exploitation. Mrs. Lessing's work at this time showed her to be an alarmingly acute observer of human folly and pretension—particularly in their specifically masculine forms—but her manner seemed to some critics excessively slick and brittle, lacking the imaginative intensity of her earlier work.

Then in 1962 appeared what many consider her finest achievement to date, *The Golden Notebook*. This is one of the few overtly experimental novels published in England during the 1960s and it has two distinct levels of interest. Anna Wulf, the heroine, is a wholly emancipated woman in her thirties, who has published one novel and is struggling to complete another. As a sensitive account of Anna's emotional and intellectual conflicts—her relationships with men, with her daughter, with the Communist party—the novel works very effectively. Yet it is also an attempt to go beyond the conventional novel by shuffling the relations between "fiction" and "reality" in a way that recalls Gide's *The Counterfeiters*. Anna records her experiences and reflections under separate headings in four separate notebooks; the "golden notebook" is the one in which she tries, but demonstrably and inevitably fails, to integrate these four accounts into a single coherent "novel." Even those critics who found the book overambitious and overcomplicated in its structure acknowledged that it was a striking and absorbing experiment. Walter Allen thought it "impressive in its honesty and integrity, and unique . . . as an exposition of the emotional problems that face an intelligent woman who wishes to live in the kind of freedom a man may take for granted."

Meanwhile Doris Lessing had begun to publish the very long novel "The Children of Violence," which appeared in five volumes between 1952 and 1969. This is an altogether more conventionally written work, which in its technique, and in its "sober, unsentimental scrutiny of behavior, motives, and morals," prompted comparisons with George Eliot. It is an account of the life of Martha Quest and of her search for self-definition, which for her is to be achieved through total commitment to a person or a cause. We follow her from her beginnings as a wayward but intelligent child on a Rhodesian farm, through two unsuccessful marriages and active involvement in the Communist party in Salisbury during World War II. After the war Martha goes to London and becomes an increasingly disenchanted observer of London life and behavior in the 1950s; the last volume of the sequence anticipates an apocalyptic, science-fiction future, as Martha dies in a devastated, radioactive world at the end of the twentieth century.

In the past, Doris Lessing has been admired for "her readiness to use old-fashioned methods of direct attack on targets which most writers feel are too vast or too obvious for anything but allegory or indirection"; even the catastrophic view of the future which ends "The Children of Violence" is described in scrupulously naturalistic terms. In her next novel however a greatly increased use of symbolism and imagery marked an enlargement of her range which most critics found largely successful and often deeply disturbing. This was *Briefing for a Descent Into Hell*, in which two psychiatrists employ all their arts to restore an amnesiac Cambridge don to what they regard as mental health, and he regards as a fall from grace—a descent into hell. In his madness, Charles Watkins imagines (or experiences) an odyssey that is by turns horrible and intoxicatingly beautiful, so that (as one critic wrote) "a fantastic prose-poem myth struggles against and alternates with the dry formulas of a psychiatric case history." In a way that reminded many reviewers of R. D. Laing, Mrs. Lessing proposes that, in a world gone mad, madness is the true sanity. Her book is both a satire of Swiftian pessimism and savagery, and the work in which (to quote Melvin Maddocks) "Doris Lessing has finally confronted her Moby Dick. . . . The novel is a brilliant and untamed image of the possibilities that Mrs. Lessing dreams, rather than believes, may still constitute man's destiny."

In *The Summer Before the Dark*, which followed, Mrs. Lessing returned to the naturalism of earlier novels. Like *Briefing for a Descent Into Hell*, it concerns an emotional crisis experienced in middle age, this time by an ordinary suburban housewife, her children scattered for the summer, her neurologist husband away in America. No longer needed and defined as wife and mother, she sets out to discover herself, first through a summer job, then through a brief affair. She finds that she is still the eternally exploited woman, trapped and hurt in an alien environment like the wounded seal of which she obsessively dreams. It is only in illness and near-madness that she begins the radical and dangerous process of self-questioning and self-discovery that may save her. The book has its *longueurs*, and seemed to some readers too didactic a contribution to the cause of Women's Liberation, but, as one critic wrote, "for those under [the author's] spell," it has "its customary disturbing and reverberating effect." Most critics agree that Doris Lessing is one of the most gifted novelists now writing in English, even though she has sometimes sacrificed her great skill and talent to her moral and social concerns. Some consider her short stories the finest by any English writer since Lawrence.

She has also worked in a number of other fields. *Going Home* is a collection of essays about her return visit to Africa in the middle 1950s, and *In Pursuit of the English* contains her generally wry and disappointed but often extremely funny studies of English working-class life. She has written with cool and unsentimental exactness about some of her pets in *Particularly Cats*. Four of Doris Lessing's plays have been produced and two of these have been published: *Each His Own Wilderness*, which discusses the virtues and inadequacies of moral and political commitment; and *Play With a Tiger*, a dramatization of the last scene in *The Golden Notebook*.

PRINCIPAL WORKS: *Fiction*—The Grass Is Singing, 1950; This Was the Old Chief's Country (stories), 1951; Five (stories), 1953; Retreat to Innocence, 1956; The Habit of Loving (stories), 1957; The Golden Notebook, 1962; A Man and Two Women (stories), 1963; African Stories, 1964; Nine African Stories, 1968; Briefing for a Descent Into Hell, 1971; The Story of a Non-Marrying Man and Other Stories, 1972 (U.S., The Temptation of Jack Orkney); The Summer Before the Dark, 1973. *The Children of Violence:* Martha Quest, 1952; A Proper Marriage, 1954; A Ripple From the Storm, 1958; Landlocked, 1965; The Four-Gated City, 1969. *Nonfiction*—Going Home, 1957; In Pursuit of the English, 1960; Particularly Cats, 1967. *Plays*—Each His Own Wilderness, 1959; Play With a Tiger, 1962.

ABOUT: Allen, W. Tradition and Dream, 1964; Bergonzi, B. The Situation of the Novel, 1970; Brewster, D. Doris Lessing, 1965; Gindin, J. Postwar British Fiction, 1962; Ipp, C. Doris Lessing: A Bibliography, 1967; Newquist, R. Counterpoint, 1964; Shapiro, C. Contemporary British Novelists, 1965; Vinson, J. (ed.) Contemporary Novelists, 1972; Who's Who, 1973. *Periodicals*—Journal of Commonwealth Literature June 1972; New Republic December 15, 1962; April 2, 1966; New Statesman April 1, 1950; New York Times September 10, 1950; Publishers' Weekly June 2, 1969; Times Literary Supplement April 27, 1962; July 3, 1969; April 16, 1971.

LEVERTOV, DENISE (October 24, 1923–), American poet, writes: "I was born at 9 A.M., October 24, 1923, in Ilford, Essex, England, a London suburb. Astrologers may draw their own conclusions.

"My father, Paul Levertoff, was a scholar and, in the best sense of the word, an enthusiast. My mother, Beatrice Adelaide (*née* Spooner-Jones) is Welsh. I owe to her, among other things, my love of Nature and my ability to read aloud well. As I did not go to school (ever, at all) I had time and solitude to begin working in poetry at a very early age. Formal education, under my mother's tutelage, ended at about thirteen. We had a houseful of books and an excellent local public library. My sister Olga (1914–1964) introduced me to modern poetry, the Impressionists, theater (*The Dog Beneath the Skin* at the London Group Theater, dir. Rupert Doone), and many other things. After I was twelve and allowed to go about by myself in London I used to spend a good deal of time in the museums and galleries.

"During my early teens I tried to become a ballet dancer; during my later teens I thought I would be a painter; I spent several years (without finishing my training) working as a hospital nurse. Being a poet was, however, from my earliest childhood, what I never had any doubts about. Writing poems was the thing I could do and I had always done it.

DENISE LEVERTOV

There is nothing I would ever for a moment prefer to have been. This is not to say that I have not known the panic and doubts of unproductive periods.

"In the spring of 1947 I was fired from the British Hospital in Paris for refusing to form part of a guard of honor in an unveiling ceremony. I took off with a friend to hitch-hike ('faire le stop') around France. At the end of the summer we went to Switzerland to look for work and I met Mitch Goodman, a young American just beginning to write, in the Youth Hostel in Geneva. We got married soon afterwards.

"I came to the United States in 1948 and our son Nikolai was born in 1949. Although I think it was a good thing for me that I was not sent to school, we never even considered educating Nik at home, for a variety of reasons. In 1950–1951 we were in Europe on the G.I. Bill; 1957–1958 we lived in Mexico. Otherwise we have lived in New York City, with summers in New England. We now have an old farmhouse in a remote part of inland Maine. We have lived on this and that—mainly travel articles Mitch used to write. His novel *The End of It* came out in 1962 (Horizon). He is deeply engaged in writing.

"I stumbled upon my first publishers (Cresset Press) when I was a crude girl (1945). I had previously had poems published in *Poetry Quarterly* by Charles Wrey Gardiner, who was a good friend to me. My subsequent publishing history has been equally effortless, largely due to the championship of Kenneth Rexroth. He first found my poems in 1946 when he was editing the anthology *New British Poets* (New Directions, 1948). Lawrence

Ferlinghetti (City Lights) and Jonathan Williams (Jargon), who did my first two American books, both heard about me first from Rexroth, as did James Laughlin of New Directions, who became my publisher in 1959 and soon also became a dear friend.

"There are so many other poets, living and dead, whose work is important to me, and so many living ones who are also known to me as friends, that I shan't begin to list them.

"I became a citizen in 1955. By then I was already an American writer.

"I am a sketchy housekeeper but like to cook. I hardly ever sew on a button, much less mend a tear. I have given up ironing almost entirely. When I had a Guggenheim Fellowship we bought a washing machine, a dryer, a dishwasher, and a new vacuum-cleaner; they have made a great difference in my life.

"Of late my husband and I have both commenced college teaching (part-time). We are finding it demanding but enthralling. The questions raised by students stir all sorts of further questions in oneself, and the close re-reading one has to do leads to discoveries.

"My religion is, I suppose, roughly describable as tentative syncretism. In politics I am a pacifist; and I would be opposed to the present infamous war in Vietnam even if I were not a pacifist.

"I believe in living each day as fully and as well as one can, even when one feels unsure there will be a future; or as it is written (in *The Book of Delight*, by Joseph ben Meir Zabara, twelfth century, trans. by Moses Hadas in 1932): 'Prepare for the world to come as thou shouldst die tomorrow. Prepare for this world as thou shouldst live forever.'

"My hope in poetry is to attain, through true images—that is, images apprehended through Negative Capability—to Song."

Writing in *The New American Poetry*, Denise Levertov said that her mother was a descendant of the Welsh mystic (and tailor) Angel Jones. Her Jewish father, who was related to the great Hasidic Rabbi Schneour Zalman, had become a convert to Christianity as a student at Königsberg. He subsequently settled in England and joined the Anglican priesthood. An ardent advocate of the unification of Judaism and Christianity, he translated the *Zohar*, wrote a life of St. Paul in Hebrew, and filled his house with "Jewish booksellers, German theologians, Russian priests from Paris, and Viennese opera singers."

Her verse began to appear in *Poetry London* and *Poetry Quarterly* early in World War II, when she was working as a "Land Girl" on an Essex farm. "In no time at all," Kenneth Rexroth recalls, "Herbert Read, Tambimuttu, Charles Wrey Gardiner, Alex Comfort, and incidentally myself, were in excited correspondence about her. In those days she was the baby of the New Romanticism. Her poetry had about it a wistful *Schwärmerei* unlike anything in English except perhaps Matthew Arnold's 'Dover Beach.' It could be compared to the earliest poems of Rilke or some of the more melancholy songs of Brahms." Her first book, *The Double Image*, was published in England in 1946, and seems in retrospect artificial and painfully formal in its meters and rhymes.

Then, as she says, came her marriage and America, and her friendships there with Robert Creeley and others associated with Black Mountain College. She says: "My reading of William Carlos Williams and Wallace Stevens . . . of Olson's essay 'Projective Verse'; conversations and correspondence with Robert Duncan, a renewed interest through Buber in the Hasidic ideas with which I was dimly acquainted as a child; the thoughts and shared experiences of my husband; and introduction to some of the concepts of Jung; the friendship of certain painters such as Albert Kresch—have all been influential and continue to be so."

After all this, and eleven years after her first book appeared, she published *Here and Now* (1957). Richard Howard calls it "a very little book which is a kind of progress report on her affair" with the language of American poetry. By then, Howard says, she had made herself "not merely an agent but an origin of that language, a means by which poetry obtains access to reality." No one welcomed the book more warmly than Kenneth Rexroth, who said flatly that "Denise Levertov is incomparably the best poet of what is getting to be known as the new avant-garde." These were "woman poems, wife poems, mother poems," Rexroth said, "shaped and polished in the entrails of a powerful creative sensibility. . . . The *Schwärmerei* and lassitude are gone. Their place has been taken by a kind of animal grace of the word, a pulse like the footfalls of a cat or the wingbeats of a gull."

Overland to the Islands (1958) showed an increasing mastery of the loose forms, the colloquial directness and simplicity she had learned from Williams, but was not free of a certain sense of strain. M. L. Rosenthal found these transitional poems rather literary and abstract, an effect he ascribes to Black Mountain influences. For him, Miss Levertov's American apprenticeship ended with her next book, *With Eyes at the Back of Our Heads* (1959). Here she speaks clearly in her own voice—in what Thomas Parkinson called her "special tone of indolence and isolation," celebrating the world around her from "a carapace of self from which she reaches but never quite destroys." Rosenthal welcomed particularly in this book some "vivid, simple impressionist poems" which "show her able to catch the essential details of sensuous experience and to relate them so as to organize a world of insight and of emotional response with great economy and objectivity. In the same book, the poems 'Terror' and 'The Wife' introduce a confessional frankness and psychological immediacy that . . . have marked most of her best work ever since."

Richard Howard, who seems to agree, has tried to explain why in an article in *Tri-Quarterly*. He believes that her "poems of sexual fulfillment and protest" represent her most successful attempts to find images which will ritualize experience, in this way reconciling mystery and reality, spirit and flesh: "the longing for rituals . . . is the subject . . . of all her later poems." Others have spoken of her more simply as a poet in the Imagist tradition, which she has endowed "with new vigor and a compelling sensuality." Kenneth Rexroth deserves the last word; in 1961 he called her "not only the most subtly skilful poet of her generation [but] far and away the most profound, and what may be more important, the most modest and the most moving."

Denise Levertov received the Bess Hokin Prize in 1959, the Longview Award in 1961, her Guggenheim Fellowship in 1962, and an award from the American Institute of Arts and Letters in 1965. She served as poetry editor of the *Nation* in 1961 and 1963–1965. In 1964–1965 and 1965–1966 she was an associate scholar at the Radcliffe Institute for Independent Study, and she has taught as a visiting lecturer or professor at the Poetry Center in New York City, Drew University, City College of New York, Vassar College, Berkeley, and the Massachusetts Institute of Technology. Passionately opposed to the war in Vietnam, she was one of the founders of the Writers' and Artists' Protest Against the War in Vietnam in 1965, and in 1968 her husband, Mitchell Goodman, was convicted with Dr. Benjamin Spock and others of conspiring to counsel evasion of the draft. (The convictions were reversed on appeal, and the cases against Goodman and another defendant were ordered to be retried.) This crusade had its effect on her poetry. *The Sorrow Dance* (1967) and subsequent volumes include a number of poems directly concerned with the war and the resistance movement in America. These seemed to one critic to mark "a serious effort forward in her work, an encounter with more intractable material," but others regretted the development, finding in such poems a tendency to substitute preaching for poetry.

PRINCIPAL WORKS: The Double Image, 1946; Here and Now, 1957; Overland to the Islands, 1958; With Eyes at the Back of Our Heads, 1959; The Jacob's Ladder, 1961; O Taste and See, 1964; The Sorrow Dance, 1967; Penguin Modern Poets 9 (with Kenneth Rexroth and William Carlos Williams), 1967; Relearning the Alphabet, 1970; To Stay Alive, 1971; Footprints, 1972; The Poet in the World (essays and lectures), 1973.

ABOUT: Allen, D. M. (ed.) The New American Poetry, 1960; Contemporary Authors 1–4, 1st revision, 1967; Mills, R. J., Jr. Contemporary American Poetry, 1965; Ossman, D. The Sullen Art, 1963; Rexroth, K. Assays, 1961; Rosenthal, M. L. The New Poetry, 1967; Stepanchev, S. American Poetry Since 1945, 1965; Wagner, L. W. Denise Levertov, 1967; Who's Who in America, 1972–1973. *Periodicals*—Nation November 1, 1958; Poetry November 1957, November 1958, August 1960, March 1963, January 1965; Southern Review September 1972; Tri-Quarterly Fall 1966.

***LEVI, PETER (CHAD TIGAR)** (May 16, 1931–), English poet and translator, writes: "I was born in Ruislip, Middlesex, in 1931. At that time it was a greenish outer suburb of London. My father was an industrious, successful and egalitarian Jewish merchant, a physically big man with a powerful but friendly personality. My mother came from a more typical Edwardian middle-class English background; her father was an honest stockbroker who lived in Harrow. My father's family came from Constantinople (which I was never allowed to call Istanbul). When I was born, second of three, the family was already Roman Catholic. I went to school in an eighteenth-century country house with a view of Bath, run by Irish teaching Brothers, where I learnt to feel Jewish, to like solitude and have friendships, to be passionate about what is natural, confusedly to resent authority and in some way to write. Later I went to a smoother, more eccentric school by the Thames to learn Greek.

"At seventeen I joined the English Jesuits, because I liked them and for less creditable reasons; after two years' noviceship (which I found enjoyable at the time) I read mediaeval philosophers in the country, where I used to run about a lot, learnt school-teaching in London, which I came to know by walking, read Greek, Latin, a little history, and Byzantine and modern Greek in Oxford, where I began to publish a few poems and experienced the political atmosphere of the Suez crisis and the Hungarian revolution; I then taught schoolboys in Lancashire, learnt theology in Oxfordshire, published a second book, became ill, went to Greece, was ordained priest, and survived a year in the extraordinary but beautiful wilds of North Wales.

"I now teach Greek and Latin in the university of Oxford, am editing the classical traveller Pausanias with a topographical commentary, lecturing on early Greek prose, projecting translations, learned articles, long satiric poems like Pope's epistles, and prose as plain as Colonel Newcome's shirt-cuffs; actually writing rather little, but I sometimes go to London to preach.

* le′ vē

PETER LEVI

"Three volumes of poems, *The Gravel Ponds*, *Water, Rock and Sand*, and *Fresh Water, Sea Water*. Translated the Penguin *Yevtushenko* with Robin Milner-Gulland, a similar volume now in the press. Prose history of Beaumont College (social history with touches of topography). Dream-like narrative poem, *The Earthly Paradise*, and a masque *Orpheus' Head* for schoolboys, privately printed (unavailable). Straight narrative poem, *The Shearwaters*, written in 1959, later published as a pamphlet, recently printed in *Longer Contemporary Poems* (Penguin). My chief and best work (which has taken the last two years) is *Themis*, the publication of which is at present being negotiated. It is ten poems, or a long poem. I am working at present on a television film about ruined abbeys with a commentary in the metre of *Evgeny Onegin*.

"I believe that the career of a writer differs from the history of a state and the moral experience of individuals in not being open-ended; for him there can really be an absolutely right solution, though the odds are against even a great writer finding it. Of course in the end, if he does find it, the result is not a man, but a book."

Father Levi attended Prior Park School, Bath, until he was fifteen, and was at Beaumont College in 1946–1948. He went up to Campion Hall, Oxford University, in 1954. *The Gravel Ponds* contained poems mostly on pastoral themes, many of them about the purity and gentleness of animals, and was a Poetry Book Society Choice. Philip Larkin, reviewing it, thought Levi "a deft and precious writer with nothing particular to say," but Elizabeth Jennings admired his "highly coloured and firmly delineated" images, the "ease and fluidity" of his cadences.

Levi's subsequent books have earned more praise for their form and fluency than for their content. R. J. Hamilton found *Water, Rock and Sand* "thinly textured and elusive poetry," dealing "obsessively in a narrow and unvaried range of bleak landscape imagery that never quite reveals a coherent or identifiable shape." Cyril Connolly thought *Fresh Water, Sea Water* still "disembodied . . . too faintly traced," but added: "This is also part of the charm. One is conscious . . . of a distinguished mind, a warm heart, a sensuous enjoyment of nature, particularly of the Mediterranean, but some quality of inevitability is still lacking. I look on his poems like an old rake watching a finishing school trip by his window. They are not yet quite ready for me."

All the same, Levi is by no means without his admirers, who, like William Cookson, believe that at the center of his best poems is a quietude and beauty, a strangeness and solidity, which will make them endure. *Pancakes for the Queen of Babylon*, a sequence of ten poems dedicated to the Greek poet Nikos Gatsos, is perhaps the work referred to above as "Themis." Cookson wrote that "it is, like his earlier books, permeated by imagery of land and sea, but here, though still rooted in actuality, they have become part of visionary experience. This poetry is deep, but also clear like the magic and light of landscapes seen in early morning dreams."

There was an enthusiastic reception also for *The Light Garden of the Angel King*, Levi's account of his travels in Afghanistan, where among many other things he investigated the fate of Alexander's occupation forces and their descendants in the region, and pursued his passionate interest in stones and rocks, producing "a beautiful book," rich in anecdote and speculation, as well as in very skillful descriptions of scenes and places.

PRINCIPAL WORKS: The Earthly Paradise (privately published poem), 1958; The Gravel Ponds (poems), 1960; Beaumont (history), 1961; Orpheus' Head (privately published masque), 1962; Water, Rock and Sand (poems), 1962; (tr. with Robin Milner-Gulland) Yevtushenko: Selected Poems, 1962; Fresh Water, Sea Water (poems), 1966; (tr. with Robin Milner-Gulland) Yevtushenko: Poems Chosen by the Author, 1966; Pancakes for the Queen of Babylon: Ten Poems for Nikos Gatsos, 1968; Ruined Abbeys, 1968; (ed.) Pausanias: Guide to Greece (2 vols.), 1971; The Light Garden of the Angel King, 1972; Death Is a Pulpit (poems), 1972; Life Is a Platform (poems), 1972; (with John Fuller and Adrian Mitchell) Penguin Modern Poets 22, 1973.

ABOUT: Allott, K. (ed.) Penguin Book of Contemporary Verse, 1962; Contemporary Authors 7–8, 1963; Jennings, E. Poetry Today, 1961; Murphy, R. (ed.) Contemporary Poets of the English Language, 1970.

***LÉVI-STRAUSS, CLAUDE** (November 28, 1908–), French anthropologist, was born in

* lā vē strōs

Brussels. His father was an artist who in 1914 took his family to live in a house in the park at Versailles, and the boy was educated at the Lycée Janson-de-Sailly in Paris. He studied philosophy in the Faculty of Law at the Sorbonne, graduating in 1932, and for the next two years taught in provincial *lycées*. In 1935 he went to Brazil as Professor of Sociology at the University of São Paulo, where he remained for three years. During this period he made several brief ethnographic investigations in the interior of Brazil, and there was a more extensive expedition to central Brazil in 1938–1939.

Lévi-Strauss has given an account of this expedition in *Tristes tropiques* (1955, translated by J. Russell and later by John and Doreen Weightman under the same title), which Clifford Geertz has described as "surely one of the finest books ever written by an anthropologist." Although his grandfather at Versailles was a rabbi, Lévi-Strauss himself had never been religious, and he had later rebelled against the sterile "mental gymnastics" of academic philosophy. On the other hand Marxism (as a system of thought), psychoanalysis, and geology had all appealed to him because they seemed to get at fundamentals. The revelation of his true vocation came only in the 1930s when he read Robert H. Lowie's *Primitive Society*, and found in social anthropology a means to bridge the gap between philosophy and science, the possibility of a true science of man. The customs of primitive peoples seemed to him to provide "reduced models" of what is essential in all mankind, and so the journey into the Brazilian interior becomes a sort of romantic quest for an idealized noble savage. But as the title *Tristes tropiques* indicates, most of the Amerindian communities Lévi-Strauss saw were in sad decline, destroyed by the greed and cultural arrogance of the European colonizers. And when finally he confronts the Tupi-Kawahib, the uncontaminated and unstudied savages he has dreamt of, he finds that they are intellectually inaccessible and he cannot communicate with them.

But this is not the end of the quest, though in his subsequent career it takes a different direction. Throughout *Tristes tropiques* there is a sense of the decline not merely of the Amerindian societies but also of the Western monoculture which is "preparing to produce civilization in bulk as if it were sugar beet." Faced with this universal process of decline Lévi-Strauss sees his task as to "grasp the essence of what our species has been and still is," not any longer by searching for an ideal primitive society, but instead by the intellectual construction of a theoretical model: "Farewell to savages, then, farewell to journeying!"

After military service in France in 1939–1940 Lévi-Strauss went to New York in 1941 and took up a post at the New School for Social Research.

CLAUDE LÉVI-STRAUSS

One of his colleagues there was the structural linguist Roman Jakobson, and the basis of all the later work of Lévi-Strauss himself is the application of structuralist principles to human cultures and social groups. In 1946–1947 he spent a year as cultural attaché at the French Embassy in Washington, returning to France in 1947 as associate director of the Musée de l'Homme. In 1950 he became director of studies at the École Pratique des Hautes Études. Meanwhile, since before the war, Lévi-Strauss had been developing his ideas in a series of papers in learned periodicals. Seventeen key essays were later collected as *L'Anthropologie structurale* (1958, translated by C. Jacobson and B. G. Schoepf as *Structural Anthropology*), and Lévi-Strauss made a brief summary of his basic ideas in the inaugural lecture which he gave in 1960 as Professor of Social Anthropology at the Collège de France, published as *Leçon inaugurale* (translated as *The Scope of Anthropology*).

Structuralism is not a philosophy but a technique. The structural analysis of language emphasizes not individual words but their relationships, their ordering by means of a deep underlying structure which can be determined from its surface manifestations, and Lévi-Strauss applies this principle to patterns of human behavior. By studying different societies he hopes to reconstitute the deeper structures common to them all. Man confronts nature with culture, the imposition of patterns of order on it; for though the raw material of nature is itself a continuum, human thought proceeds by recognizing contrasts and polarities: human/animal, day/night, male/female, etc. Lévi-Strauss claims that all human social phenomena reflect this manner of thinking and can be reduced to such binary oppositions. In this way he tries not only to elucidate the universal patterns behind the apparent diversity of kinship relations, totemism, or mythic beliefs, but in so doing to discover the restrictive patterning inherent in the nature of thought itself.

In his early work he sought the laws of classification primarily at the unconscious level which governs the exchange of goods, language, and women among the subgroups of a society, as in his first major work, *Les Structures élémentaires de la parenté* (1949, revised edition 1967; translated as *The Elementary Structures of Kinship*), a treatment of marriage as a form of exchange. Lévi-Strauss regards the incest taboo as marking the transition between nature and culture: it is natural because it is universal, but cultural because it is a rule, and culture is the universe of rules. The dualism of tribal kinship systems results from the division of society into those who may be married and those who are forbidden in marriage, so that the exchange of women thus helps to structure the society, and the key simplification of "generalized exchange" enables Lévi-Strauss to reduce a mass of complex material to a few simple models. The book has been enormously influential and has given rise to a great deal of elaboration and of criticism, though controversy has focused more on the detailed analysis of marriage systems than on the theory as such.

In his more recent work Lévi-Strauss has been so impressed by the efforts of primitive *conscious* thought that his emphasis has shifted to this. In *Le Totémisme aujourd'hui* (1962, translated by R. Needham as *Totemism*) man stands out against a background of nature by virtue of his symbolic communication systems, and Lévi-Strauss examines totemism to discover how men categorize the world of experience and hence how verbally organized human thought develops. Most anthropologists have felt that the concern primitive people feel for natural species arises out of their biological need for them. But Lévi-Strauss argues that they are not *bonnes à manger* (goods for eating) but *bonnes à penser* (goods for thinking), that animal totemism is merely another way in which men define themselves as subgroups. It is not the specific characteristics of bear, eagle, crow, or turtle that are important but the clearly visible contrasts between them, which are put into correspondence with the sociological differences between social groups.

Thus Lévi-Strauss argues that totemism is an example of what he calls *la logique concrète*, the concrete thought of primitive men who use directly perceived realities symbolically, in contrast to the abstract conceptual thought of modern science. This is the main subject of *La Pensée sauvage* (1962, translated as *The Savage Mind*). According to Lévi-Strauss the human mind has been in full possession of its powers since the beginnings of human society. But the step from a mythical mode of thought to the analytical one has been taken "only once in human history and in one place."

Most human societies have persisted in the modes of understanding which Lévi-Strauss characterizes as *la pensée sauvage* or *la logique concrète*. Though primitive consciousness contains all the seeds of civilized consciousness it is not "progressive" because it finds in its myths a coherent cosmology and philosophy which successfully integrate social life into its physical environment, supported precisely by the desire to preserve society as it is. Lévi-Strauss attacks theories of history, especially those of Marx and Sartre, which imply progress and human perfectibility; for him Western technological civilization is certainly not superior to that of the neolithic revolution, which produced most of the skills that have provided the foundations of civilizations ever since.

In the four volumes with the collective title *Mythologiques*, Lévi-Strauss sets out to deepen and substantiate this general statement through a detailed study of certain groups of South American Indian myths. In the first volume, *Le Cru et le cuit* (1964, translated by J. and D. Weightman as *The Raw and the Cooked*), Lévi-Strauss analyzes one hundred and eighty-seven stories about the origins of fire and of cooking, which is seen as a step away from nature and towards culture. The book itself has a musical structure, for Lévi-Strauss argues that myths resemble music in having a meaning which cannot easily be put into language. They represent not analytical logic but symbolic thought, by means of which primitive man, using simple archetypal categories, is able to work out abstract ideas and consider some of the most profound issues of human life; and their analysis therefore reveals the fundamental ways in which the human mind takes hold of experience.

The argument is developed in the second volume, *Du Miel aux cendres* (1966, translated by J. and D. Weightman as *From Honey to Ashes*), which considers one hundred and sixty-five myths dealing with honey (seen as a descent toward nature) and tobacco (which follows cooking and indicates a rising towards the supernatural). From these myths Lévi-Strauss extracts a "philosophy of honey" inspired by the analogy between honey and menstrual blood, and in the third volume, *L'Origine des manières de table* (The Origin of Table Manners, 1968), analyzing myths from North as well as South America, Lévi-Strauss relates this female periodicity to the diurnal and seasonal astronomical cycles. Thus, he says, "a vast mythological system common to the two Americas becomes evident, in which the subjugation of women creates the social order. We now understand the reason for it. . . . The change from nature to culture demands the periodicity of the female system, for social and cosmic order would be jeopardized by an anarchistic rule under which the regular alternation of day and night, the phases of the moon, the female periods, the fixed duration of pregnancy and the succession of seasons would be unrelated."

The Indians of North America and their myths are his principal concern in the final volume of the series, *L'Homme nu* (The Naked Man, 1971). "If for the Indians of tropical America the passage from nature to culture is symbolized by the passage from the raw to the cooked," Lévi-Strauss told an interviewer, "it is symbolized for North American Indians by the invention of adornments, personal ornaments, and clothing, and, beyond that, by the introduction of trade."

English and American anthropologists, with their empirical approach and emphasis on fieldwork, have frequently criticized Lévi-Strauss as a visionary. But it is probably just this quality which accounts for the enormous influence Lévi-Strauss has had, for whereas anthropologists usually confine themselves to studying particular primitive societies, he is concerned with fundamental questions which promise a new insight into all forms of human intellectual experience. Edmund Leach, for whom the real subject matter of social anthropology "remains the actual social behavior of human beings," argues that Lévi-Strauss is likely to become so fascinated by the logical perfection of the "systems" he is describing that he disregards the empirical facts. But as J. O. Urmson has observed, "certainly the claims of Lévi-Strauss are hardly empirical. Perhaps the important issue is not whether these background claims are true but whether adopting structuralist technique in the social sciences brings insight." And the ideas of Lévi-Strauss, which are very relevant to creativity and aesthetics and have deeply affected literary criticism, have already had a profound influence, and occupied in the 1960s the place in French thought which those of Sartre had held a decade earlier.

Lévi-Strauss has been married three times—to Dina Dreyfus in 1932, to Rose-Marie Ullmo in 1946, and to Monique Roman in 1954. He has two sons. Lévi-Strauss holds the Gold Medal of the Centre National de la Recherche Scientifique, France's highest scientific distinction, and honorary degrees from the universities of Oxford, Brussels, Chicago, Yale, and Columbia. In 1971 he was named a Commander of the Ordre Nationale du Mérite and in 1973 he was elected a member of the Académie Française—an extraordinary distinction for a scientist.

PRINCIPAL WORKS IN ENGLISH TRANSLATION: Race and History, 1952; Tristes tropiques (England, World on the Wane), 1961 (new translation as Tristes Tropiques, 1973); Structural Anthropology, 1963; Totemism, 1963; The Savage Mind, 1966; The Scope of Anthropology, 1967; The Elementary Structures of Kinship, 1969; The Raw and the Cooked, 1970; From Honey to Ashes, 1973. ABOUT: Backès-Clement, C. Lévi-Strauss, 1970; Charbonnier, G. Conversations With Claude Lévi-Strauss, 1969; Current Biography, 1972; Douglas, M. Natural Symbols, 1970; Ehrmann, J. Structuralism, 1966; Fortes, M. Kinship and the Social Order, 1969; Fowlie, W. The French Critic 1549–1967, 1968; Gardner, H. The Quest for Mind, 1973; Gurvitch, G. and Moore, W. E. (eds.) Twentieth Century Sociology, 1945; Hayes, E. N. and Hayes, T. (eds.) Claude Lévi-Strauss: The Anthropologist as Hero, 1970; Homans, G. C. and Schneider, D. M. Marriage, Authority, and Final Causes, 1955; Hughes, H. S. The Obstructed Path, 1968; Kirk, G. S. Myth, 1970; Korn, F. Elementary Structures Reconsidered, 1973; Kroeber, A. L. (ed.) Anthropology Today, 1953; Lane, M. (ed.) Structuralism: A Reader, 1970; Leach, E. The Structural Study of Myth and Totemism, 1967; Leach, E. Lévi-Strauss, 1970; Mair, L. An Introduction to Social Anthropology, 1965; Merleau-Ponty, M. Signs, 1964; Needham, R. Structure and Sentiment, 1962; Paz, O. Claude Lévi-Strauss, 1970; Sebeok, T. A. (ed.) Myth: A Symposium, 1955; Shapiro, H. L. Man, Culture and Society, 1956; Sontag, S. Against Interpretation, 1966; Steiner, G. Language and Silence, 1967; Who's Who, 1973; Who's Who in France, 1971–1972. *Periodicals*—American Anthropologist October 1966; Book Week January 8, 1967; Commonweal June 17, 1966; Current Anthropology April 1966; Encounter April 1966, April 1967; Listener May 11, 1967; May 23, 1968; April 30, 1970; September 3, 1970; Man March 1963, June 1967, December 1967, June 1969, September 1969; Modern Language Notes December 1963, May 1966; New Blackfriars August 1966; New Left Review November–December 1965; New Society October 13, 1966; June 26, 1969; January 29, 1970; May 14, 1970; New Statesman December 9, 1966; August 1, 1969; New York Review of Books November 28, 1963; October 12, 1967; New York Times Book Review December 18, 1966; Social Research Winter 1965; Spectator March 21, 1969; August 9, 1969; July 11, 1970; Times Literary Supplement April 29, 1965; June 15, 1967; October 12, 1967; May 2, 1968; September 12, 1968; March 27, 1969; August 14, 1970; Yale French Studies 36–37 1966–1967.

LEWIS, NORMAN, English novelist, travel writer, and journalist, is the son of Richard and Louise Lewis. He was educated at Enfield Grammar School.

Neither biographical reference books nor his own works give much direct information about his life, but it is evident that he is a determined and resourceful traveler, capable of great imaginative sympathy with alien places and peoples, and nostalgic, as Dan Jacobson has said, for "the half-modern, the unsuccessful, and the violent." His first book, published in 1938, was *Sand and Sea in Arabia*, a volume of photographs whose quality varied from excellent to "magnificent." Lewis's photographs have been an important feature of his subsequent travel books.

NORMAN LEWIS

During World War II he served in Sicily and elsewhere with the Intelligence Corps. It may be that some of his own experiences are reflected in his 1950 novel *Within the Labyrinth*, about a British field security sergeant in Southern Italy at the end of the war, and his hopeless struggle against the ingrained injustice, intrigue, and corruption of the region.

It was two travel books written in the early 1950s which established Lewis's reputation. *A Dragon Apparent* describes his 1950 travels in what is now North Vietnam, and *Golden Earth* his wanderings in Burma the following year. Both countries were racked by war—the Vietminh against France in Indochina, civil war and ferocious banditry in Burma; both journeys were thought to be impossible. Lewis made them nevertheless, producing books which were urbanely understated in their accounts of the author's own brushes with dacoits and rebels, profoundly illuminating as reports on ancient cultures in violent flux. Both books were praised for the selective precision of their prose, their sharp-set portraits of individuals, and their superb photographs. Lewis has also contributed articles about an immense variety of places to the *New Yorker*, the *New Statesman*, and other magazines. V. S. Pritchett, reviewing a collection of these published as *The Changing Sky*, commended Lewis's "serious, summary and ironic eye" and went on: "In spite of an air of witty superficiality he really goes in deep like a sharp polished knife."

In Sicily at the end of World War II, Lewis had seen the Mafia at work and had access to official files on the society. Thereafter he continued his investigations and published the results, first as a series of articles in the *New Yorker*, then as a book, *The Honored Society*. There were some objections that Lewis was more concerned to tell a fascinating story than to seek out fresh information, but most reviewers were satisfied. One in the *Times Literary Supplement* defended Lewis against his critics, saying that it was "only occasionally that his anecdotes fail to make points of substance," and calling his book "vivid and absorbing . . . the most accurate assessment of the Mafia yet to have appeared in English."

Norman Lewis's novels share with his travel books an acute sense of place, exotic locales, and a preoccupation with the effects of political or economic revolution upon stable if primitive societies. Among the best and most characteristic of them—both Book Society choices in England—are *The Day of the Fox* and *The Volcanoes Above Us*. The first tells ironically, coolly, but with moments of extraordinary insight, the story of a hapless Spanish fisherman caught up and destroyed by the Civil War and its aftermath, contrasting his fate with that of an old aristocrat still powerful enough to defy history. *The Volcanoes Above Us*, set in Guatemala, is a similarly low-keyed and laconic account of conflict between an American industrialist, dictatorial local politicians, and the Indian labor force.

In their wry wit, the vividness and intelligence of their observation, and the excellence of their prose, Lewis's novels have reminded many critics of the work of Graham Greene. His principal weakness, according to a reviewer in the *Times Literary Supplement*, "is a lack of human focus, a comparative disinterest in motive on the personal rather than political level," so that the reader is left "with an image of life in certain places but not with much information about individual lives; or about Mr. Lewis."

PRINCIPAL WORKS: *Nonfiction*—Sand and Sea in Arabia (photographs), 1938; A Dragon Apparent: Travels in Indo-China, 1951; Golden Earth: Travels in Burma, 1952; The Changing Sky: Travels of a Novelist, 1959; The Honored Society, 1966. *Novels*—Samara, 1949; Within the Labyrinth, 1950; A Single Pilgrim, 1953; The Day of the Fox, 1955; The Volcanoes Above Us, 1957; Darkness Visible, 1960; The Tenth Year of the Ship, 1962; A Small War Made to Order, 1966; Every Man's Brother, 1967; Flight From a Dark Equator, 1972.

ABOUT: Who's Who, 1973. *Periodicals*—New Statesman July 11, 1959; New York Review of Books May 16, 1964; Times Literary Supplement July 10, 1959; June 18, 1964.

LEWIS, OSCAR (December 25, 1914–December 16, 1970), American anthropologist, was born in New York City and raised on a farm in upstate New York. He was educated at the City College of New York (B.S.S., 1936) and at Columbia University where, under the personal influence of

Ruth Benedict, he turned from history to anthropology, receiving his Ph.D. in that subject in 1940. His first field studies were among the Blackfoot Indians of Montana and Alberta. A year at Yale as a research associate followed (1942–1943) and then war service as a propaganda analyst in the Department of Justice (1943) and as a social scientist in the Department of Agriculture (1944–1945). Later Lewis was sent to Cuba by the State Department as a visiting professor at the University of Havana, and in 1948 he joined the faculty of the University of Illinois, where he remained professor of anthropology.

Meanwhile, as a field representative for the National Indian Institute, Lewis had gone to Mexico in 1943 to study the village of Tepoztlán, the subject in the late 1920s of a famous community study by Robert Redfield. Changes in the interim necessitated a full-scale restudy, and Lewis's funds soon ran out, but he returned in 1947 and 1948 under different auspices and completed the work, publishing his report in 1951 as *Life in a Mexican Village: Tepoztlán Restudied*, with magnificent drawings by Alberto Beltrán. The book was recognized by social scientists (including Redfield) as a first-rate piece of work, "rich in fact and provocative in ideas." During the 1950s, Lewis maintained his contact with rural families in and around Tepoztlán, tracked down some who had moved into the slums of Mexico City, and wrote *Five Families*, in which he sought "to give the reader some glimpses of daily life in five ordinary families, on five perfectly ordinary days."

Narrowing and deepening his focus, Lewis then concentrated on one of these five families, that of Jesús Sánchez, a widower living in a slum apartment with his four grown children. The life stories of these people, tape recorded in hundreds of hours of conversation, were edited down to form *The Children of Sánchez*. In Mexico the book was denounced by nationalists as "obscene and slanderous," but welcomed by reformers like Carlos Fuentes. The anthropologist E. R. Wolf thought it comparable in its impact to Frazer's *Golden Bough* and Ruth Benedict's *Patterns of Culture*. Elizabeth Hardwick wrote: "Oscar Lewis has made something brilliant and of singular significance, a work of such unique concentration and sympathy that one hardly knows how to classify it . . . The result is a moving strange tragedy . . ." The reviewers were almost unanimous in insisting that the book was to be considered not simply as a superb documentary but, by virtue of the skill and humanity with which Lewis had selected and ordered his material, as a true work of art, "very much like poetry," and a masterpiece.

There was scarcely less praise for *Pedro Martínez*, which applied the same technique to another of

OSCAR LEWIS

Lewis's "five families," this time a rural one, achieving "the first full-length picture of an intelligent, politically alert peasant and the events in his life that drive him toward a rejection of his social order."

His investigations led Lewis to the hypothesis that there exists a "culture of poverty," a psychologically demoralizing and entrapping life style, passed on from generation to generation, and much more difficult to eradicate than poverty itself. This culture moreover had cross-national similarities—"common adaptations to common problems." To test the hypothesis, Lewis undertook a study of Puerto Rican urban poor. After studying one hundred and fifty families, he settled on one consisting of five households and four generations in San Juan and New York. He recorded seven thousand pages of interviews, which he edited down to the one thousand four hundred manuscript pages of *La Vida*, centering on a former prostitute living with her sixth husband. This raw self-portrait of a family brutalized by poverty shocked middle-class American (and some Puerto Rican) sensibilities, and seemed to *Time*'s reviewer "suffocating and ugly," but Saul Maloff called it a "magnificent chronicle," and Michael Harrington said it was a "brilliant demonstration of the validity and profundity of the method Lewis has pioneered." It became a best seller and won the National Book Award in the category of science, philosophy, and religion.

A Death in the Sánchez Family studied the emotional and economic effects of the death of Aunt Guadalupe Vélez on three of the Sánchez children, and their struggle to get her a decent burial. One reviewer said that if *The Children of Sánchez* had the quality of a great novel, this book had "the power and focus of a short story." Lewis also reported on studies in Texas and in northern India. He was married in 1937 to Ruth Maslow, who assisted him in much of his field work, and had a son and a daughter. He died of a heart attack at the age of fifty-five.

In his study of Tepoztlán, Lewis initiated a new trend in independent anthropological community restudies. In his later work he introduced the voice of the poor themselves in a way unprecedented in the social sciences, and he brought to the literature of his subject a style, a humanity, and a compassion that it did not have before. "If my work has any literary merit," he said in 1967, "it is only because I have discovered a great deal of passion and poetry in the language of the poor and because their lives are not dull. . . . One of the major objectives of my work has been to bridge the communication gap between the very poor and the middle-class personnel . . . who bear the major responsibility for carrying out the anti-poverty programs."

PRINCIPAL WORKS: The Effects of White Contact Upon Blackfoot Culture, 1942; On the Edge of the Black Waxy: A Cultural Survey of Bell County, Texas, 1948; Life in a Mexican Village: Tepoztlán Restudied, 1951; (with Victor Barnouw) Village Life in Northern India, 1958; Five Families: Mexican Case Studies in the Culture of Poverty, 1959; The Children of Sánchez: Autobiography of a Mexican Family, 1961; Pedro Martínez: A Mexican Peasant and His Family, 1964; La Vida: A Puerto Rican Family in the Culture of Poverty, 1966; A Death in the Sánchez Family, 1969; Anthropological Essays, 1970.

ABOUT: Current Biography, 1968; Who's Who in America, 1970–1971. *Periodicals:* New York Post March 11, 1967; New York Times March 5, 1967; December 18, 1970.

LEWIS, R(ICHARD) W(ARRINGTON) B(ALDWIN) (November 1, 1917–), American critic and scholar, is the son of Leicester and Beatrix (Baldwin) Lewis, and a native of Chicago. From 1929 to 1930 he attended the English School in Switzerland. He went on to Phillips Exeter Academy, graduating in 1935. Lewis received his B.A. at Harvard in 1939 and his M.A. at the University of Chicago in 1941. During World War II he was assigned on "detached service" to the British Eighth Army in the Western Desert and Italy, attached primarily to the Tenth Corps. He was engaged mainly in intelligence work, and it was during two months behind the lines on an MI9 rescue mission that he gained his first knowledge of the Abruzzi and of Ignazio Silone. He was discharged from the army in 1946 with the rank of major.

After the war Lewis taught English at Bennington College (1948–1950) and spent a year as visiting

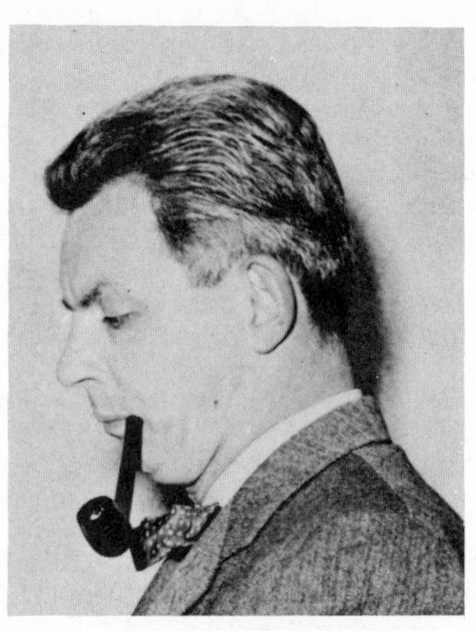

R. W. B. LEWIS

lecturer at Smith College (1951–1952). The University of Chicago gave him his Ph.D. in 1953. He was at Princeton from 1952 to 1954, first as Hodder Fellow, then as resident fellow in creative writing. From 1954 to 1959 he taught at Rutgers University, where he became professor of English. In 1959 he went to Yale as a visiting lecturer and remained to become, as he still is, professor of English and American studies. Lewis has traveled a great deal in Europe: as dean of the Salzburg Seminar in American studies (1950–1951); for six months as a Kenyon Fellow in criticism (mostly in Florence); and for a further year (1957–1958) as Fulbright lecturer at the University of Munich.

The "American Adam," who supplies the title and the theme of Lewis's first book, is the American conceived as a new kind of man in a new world. Lewis investigates this notion, postulated by Crèvecœur, as it emerges and develops in the work of a number of nineteenth century writers. This method brings him to some penetrating criticism of such major figures as Melville and Whitman, as well as new evaluations of comparatively neglected figures like the Congregationalist critic of Calvinism, Horace Bushnell, and the Swedenborgian Henry James, Sr. Some reviewers objected that Lewis's argument was developed with rather excessive neatness and glibness, and on the other hand that the book was not free of errors of fact, but it was generally welcomed for its urbanity and eloquence, and as a boldly original study of nineteenth century American thought.

The Picaresque Saint follows a similar pattern. It proposes an archetypal figure, "the logical hero of our paradoxical age," whose essential characteristic is his effort to hold in an intelligent and meaningful balance the scientific and religious impulses within himself. Having identified this personage in an introductory essay, Lewis goes on to discuss his role in the novels of Moravia, Camus, Silone, Greene, Faulkner, and (in an epilogue) Malraux. The work was recognized as a critical study of the first importance, lucid, generous, "bulging with ideas and articulate exegesis . . . a book to be grateful for." Michael Harrington called Lewis "a refreshingly discursive critic. He utilizes all the excellent analytic tools of our textual scholars, yet he also, *mirabile dictu* in this Time of the Academy, attempts to confront living ideas and even to relate them to the world around us."

A collection of Lewis's magazine articles was published in 1965 as *Trials of the Word*, and pleased most reviewers. One of them noted that these essays had as their common concern "the fertile tug-of-war between the transcendent and the concrete" in American literature, and went on: "Whether he is writing of Whitman as 'the poet of the self,' examining the intricacies of Melville's diabolical Confidence-Man, contrasting Hawthorne's and James's concept of 'the heart's sanctity,' or uncovering new depths in Edith Wharton's Lily Bart, Lewis is looking for the religious consciousness as the base of these writers' works." Lewis's admirable study of *The Poetry of Hart Crane* is "by all odds the most ambitious critical effort yet made in Crane's behalf."

R. W. B. Lewis is an important critic by any standard and is acknowledged as such. It has been said of him that "he has a wordly wisdom and maturity of mind which enable him to speak with a sometimes positively disturbing authority." His bent is as a historian of ideas and textual exegete; he is concerned far less with aesthetic values. Like all critics who attempt to organize huge areas of literature around single hypotheses, he is sometimes accused of manipulating his evidence to fit his theories, but he is never merely ingenious. Lucidity and intelligence are the recognized keynotes of his writing, and even where he most provokes he is fruitful to study. Lewis received an award in 1958 from the National Institute of Arts and Letters for "creative work in literature," and he has a Litt. D. from Wesleyan University (1961). Lewis married Nancy Lindau in 1950 and has two children. He serves as literary consultant to Universal Pictures.

PRINCIPAL WORKS: The American Adam: Innocence, Tragedy and Tradition in the 19th Century, 1955; The Picaresque Saint: Representative Figures in Contemporary Fiction, 1959; Trials of the Word: Essays in American Literature and the Humanistic Tradition, 1965; The Poetry of Hart Crane: A Critical Study, 1967. *As editor*—The Presence of Walt Whitman: Selected Papers From the English Institute, 1962; André Malraux: A Collection of Critical Essays, 1964.

ABOUT: Who's Who in America, 1972–1973. *Periodicals*—Sewanee Review Fall 1956; Times Literary Supplement May 3, 1957.

***LEYDA, JAY** (February 12, 1910–), American critic, scholar, and film maker, writes: "Born in Detroit, Michigan; through high school in Dayton, Ohio. To New York City in 1929 where first professional work was as assistant to photographer Ralph Steiner; first independent photography were portraits (later exhibitions at Julian Levy's gallery and at Moscow's Museum of Modern Western Art). When J. B. Neumann advised sale of a folk sculpture found in Dayton, 'Henry Ward Beecher,' bought film camera and enough film to make short experimental film, *A Bronx Morning*; also used camera to assist Workers' Film and Photo League. Worked as accompanist at a Bronx cinema—an opportunity to see plenty of foreign films, plenty of times. Invited to study at State Film Institute, Moscow; entered Sergei Eisenstein's direction course in September 1933. Earned extra food money as theatre correspondent for *Theatre Arts Monthly*. Married dancer Si-lan Chen. Joined crew of Eisenstein's next (unfinished) film, *Bezhin Meadow*, as apprentice director and still photographer. When smallpox forced Eisenstein to halt and revise film, he advised acceptance of invitation from New York's Museum of Modern Art to join new department, the Film Library, as assistant curator, with a grant from the Rockefeller Foundation. This job began in September 1936 and ended in 1940 when resignation was requested while editing documentary films and a quarterly journal, *Films*. Soon after Nazi invasion of Soviet Union Eisenstein cabled proposal to translate and publish the four essays that became *The Film Sense* (1942), and Eisenstein supervised the American and English editions of a later collection of essays, *Film Form*, before his death in 1948.

"War experience: assistance to Artkino, U.S. distributor of Soviet films; to Hollywood as technical advisor on Russian subjects filmed at Warner Brothers and M-G-M; basic training in tank corps at Fort Knox; honorable discharge and first research on Herman Melville as birthday surprise for Eisenstein. This grew into *The Melville Log* (1951), *The Portable Melville* (1952), and *The Complete Stories of Melville* (1952). All Melville research paid for by publishers (the *Log* financed by Reynal & Hitchcock, though published by Harcourt, Brace); the next years of research, on Emily Dickinson, supported by an extended Fellowship granted by J. S. Guggenheim Foundation: *The Years and Hours of Emily Dickinson* (1961), and help to the Harvard editions of her poems and letters.

* lī′ də

JAY LEYDA

"1957–58, at the Cinémathèque Française, Paris, with a working arrangement that made it possible to complete a book begun at the Museum of Modern Art: *Kino: A History of the Russian and Soviet Film* (1960). Before leaving America in 1957 prepared study-films (for the Museum of Modern Art) from the discarded negative of Eisenstein's unfinished Mexican film; and collaborated with Sergei Bertensson on *Sergei Rachmaninoff: A Lifetime in Music* (1956, English edition 1965); this followed their earlier collaboration, on *The Musorgsky Reader* (1947, no English edition), a translated collection of all extant documents on Musorgsky's life. Another translation, a collaboration with Ivor Montagu: Vladimir Nizhny's *Lessons With Eisenstein* (1962). Edited, with Wolfgang Klaue, for the Staatliches Filmarchiv der D.D.R., a collection of writings: *Robert Flaherty* (Berlin 1964). Latest publication, a study of compilation films: *Films Beget Films* (1964). Presently preparing a third Eisenstein collection, *Film Essays*, and working on an account of films in Asia. Now employed in the research division of the Berlin Filmarchiv.

"Other work: a poem (actually 'an essay in biography') about Emily Dickinson: *A House to Be Born In* (Northampton 1958); a libretto based on a Melville story—*Bartleby*, for an opera composed by Walter Aschaffenburg (first performance 1964, published 1966); some lectures, lately at Stockholm University; some book and film reviewing.

"Admit disadvantages in such a miscellany of subjects and jobs, but each disadvantage is balanced by unexpected, even accidental enjoyments in every new prospect that is accepted. To take everything as it comes brings more than can ever be planned."

———

Given the breadth of his interests, and his capacity for a unique kind of creative scholarship, it is easy to see how Leyda's bewilderingly varied career is in fact the logical product of his willingness to "take everything as it comes." Thus, his discovery of the Beecher sculpture coupled with his enthusiasm for photography led to his first movie; and this, together with his socialist sympathies, led to his work with the great Soviet director Eisenstein. From this association everything else follows, most obviously his influential translations of Eisenstein's theoretical writings, his own work as a film maker and archivist, and his books about the cinema. Of these the most important is *Kino*, a history of the Russian and Soviet cinema which was thought a little sketchy in its coverage of the years since World War II but otherwise a "superbly researched account" of the greatest possible importance and interest, "stuffed with marvellous anecdotes, scenario extracts, contemporary quotations and unfamiliar illustrations." It includes a description of Leyda's work with Eisenstein which, William Whitebait said, "takes us to the heart of film-making." *Films Beget Films* is a learned and avowedly left-wing account of propaganda and other films which have been compiled from footage already in film archives.

The Musorgsky Reader was not simply a collection of the composer's writings in translation: Leyda and Sergei Bertensson had so arranged their material as to form a chronological biography "in letters and documents" of their subject. When Leyda's adulation for Eisenstein turned his attention to Melville, whom the Russian director greatly admired, Leyda adopted and developed the technique of "documentary biography" introduced in the Musorgsky book. The result was the two-volume *Melville Log*. This remarkable work is composed of quotations from Melville's correspondence, from the books which influenced him, from newspaper stories about him, and from every conceivable documentary source, to form a brilliantly organized chronology of the novelist's life that was unanimously praised and welcomed as "the first work of its kind in American letters." Leyda included no comment of his own but presented the reader, as Malcolm Cowley said, with all he needed to create his own portrait of Melville.

Twenty years later the same technique produced *The Years and Hours of Emily Dickinson*, from which, according to Owen Thomas, three things emerge: "a comprehensive portrait, one of the best available, of central Massachusetts in the nineteenth century; an awareness of Emily Dickinson as a woman living in—not apart from—this complex

New England environment; and an understanding of the relation of the poet to the environment." Robert Hillyer called it "an amazing piece of scholarship indispensable to our literary history," and a critic in the *Yale Review* concluded that "few scholars have the time, patience, zeal, and uncanny skill for such undertakings. [Leyda's] is a peculiar dedication to the fact." From these two monumental feats of scholarship have flowed two tributary streams of works about, and editions and adaptations of, writings by Melville and Emily Dickinson.

PRINCIPAL WORKS: (ed. and tr.) Sergei M. Eisenstein's The Film Sense, 1942; (ed. and tr. with Sergei Bertensson) The Musorgsky Reader, 1947; (ed.) The Complete Stories of Herman Melville, 1949; (ed.) The Melville Log, 1951; (ed. with Sergei Bertensson) Sergei Rachmaninoff: A Lifetime in Music, 1956; (ed. and tr.) Sergei M. Eisenstein's Film Form, 1957; (ed.) The Portable Melville, 1959; (ed.) The Years and Hours of Emily Dickinson, 1960; Kino: A History of the Russian and Soviet Film, 1960; Films Beget Films, 1964; (ed.) Sergei Eisenstein. Film Essays and a Lecture, 1970; Dianying, Electric Shadows: An Account of Films and the Film Audience in China, 1972.

ABOUT: American Books and Authors, 1943. *Periodicals*—Film Quarterly Winter 1962–1963; Nation December 17, 1960; June 14, 1965; Times Literary Supplement August 26, 1960; November 27, 1960; June 16, 1961; November 26, 1964.

LI, CHIN-YANG. *See* LEE, C. Y.

***LIMA, JORGE (MATEUS) DE** (April 23, 1895–November 15, 1953), Brazilian poet and novelist, was a mulatto from the Northeast, descended from abolitionist plantation owners. He has been described by John Nist as "the most versatile of all modern Brazilian poets." He was born in União dos Palmares, Alagoas, the son of José de Lima and Delmina Simões. From 1903 to 1910 he was educated at the Instituto Alagoano and the Colégio Diocesano de Alagoas. He went on to study medicine at the University of Bahia for the next two years, before transferring to the University of Brazil at Rio de Janeiro, where he received his M.D. in 1916. While still a student he published his first book of poetry, *XIV Alexandrinos* (1914).

After graduation he worked as State Deputy in Alagoas from 1917 to 1921, and then as Professor of Natural History and Hygiene at the Escola Normal in Alagoas from 1922 to 1930. Becoming established as a writer, he was also appointed Professor of Literature at the Ginásio do Alagoas in 1927, holding the two positions simultaneously until he left his native town in 1930.

Although his first poems were in the dominant Parnassian mode, he abruptly abandoned that coldly sculptured style when the Modern Art Week of 1922 ushered in the modernist movement

JORGE DE LIMA

—a revolt against old forms in the name of renovation and experiment, and a nationalistic movement as well. Under this influence, Lima began to write free verse and prose poems, which drew much of their inspiration from his native region and its people, particularly the blacks. These poems made use of popular expressions and local words, and were characterized by lyric simplicity and directness.

During this early period he published *Poemas* (1925), *Banguê e Negra Fulô* (1928), and *Novos Poemas* (1929). The second of these contains his best-known poem, "Essa Negra Fulô" (That Negress Fulô), a folk-like ballad about a servant girl who is regularly whipped by her mistress until her master notices her beauty and makes himself responsible for her future punishment—to his wife's fury: "O Fulô? O Fulô? / Where, where is your master / whom our Lord gave to me? / Ah, it was you who stole him, / it was you, Negress Fulô! / That Negress Fulô!" Lima baldly records the horrors of the times: "Papa John's skin stuck to the tips of whips." But there is no overt social protest in his *negrista* poetry, which instead "celebrates the Negro as person, as individual."

In 1930 Lima left his native state and settled in Rio de Janeiro, where he was to spend the rest of his life. He continued to practice medicine and was also appointed Professor of Portuguese and Brazilian Literature in the University of Brazil in 1937. The novels of this period, *O Anjo* (The Angel, 1934) and *Calunga* (1935), still show his affinity with the Northeast in their themes, but the most notable feature of his later work is its religious motivation. In 1935 he was converted to Catholicism and in collaboration with Murilo Mendes wrote *Tempo e*

* lē′ mə

Eternidade (Time and Eternity), a free verse work depicting the constant warfare between the flesh and the spirit.

The same theme is developed in the poems collected in *A Túnica Inconsútil* (Seamless Tunic, 1938), where free verse is abandoned in favor of stately biblical forms, but a bizarre imagery is introduced, both in such religious poems as "Poema de qualquer Virgem" (Poem of Any Virgin), in which "the virgin's body is tattooed by God because she is the source of the world to be," and in those that create a strange bestiary of supernatural and monstrous creatures of the imagination.

Anunciação e Encontro de Mira-Celi (Annunciation and Encounter of Mira-Celi) is a volume of prose poems depicting the Fall as the origin of human misery. It was followed in 1949 by *Livro de Sonetos* (Book of Sonnets). Written in a style close to surrealism, and drawing heavily on subconscious impressions, the sonnets achieve a quality of timelessness and spacelessness, and leave a deep sense of religious conviction. Many of the hundred sonnets were written during a ten-day period of great mental anguish.

Lima's last work, *Invenção de Orfeu* (The Invention of Orpheus, 1952), is probably his greatest. John Nist says of it: "With more varied cadences than in the sonnets, with echoes from Camões and Dante, Jorge dissolved all logical, physical, spatial and temporal connections. . . . In an attempt to identify himself with all created things, he destroyed every barrier of individuality. What he achieved in *Invention of Orpheus* is a lucid kind of delirium, in which the metaphysical atmosphere is more Oriental than European."

Lima wrote five novels and several volumes of essays, but his prose is now principally interesting for the light it throws upon his poetry. In his person he was a simple and kindly man, interested in painting and sculpture and photography. He served for some years on the Rio city council, was married to Adila Alves and had two children. Lima received a number of literary prizes, including the first Machado de Assis prize from the Brazilian Academy of Letters.

PRINCIPAL WORKS IN ENGLISH TRANSLATION: *Poems in* Fitts, D. (ed.) Anthology of Contemporary Latin-American Poetry, 1942; Downes, L. S. (ed.) Modern Brazilian Poetry, 1954; Nist, J. A. (ed.) Modern Brazilian Poetry, 1962; Life and Letters Today July 1943; Negro History Bulletin May 1954.

ABOUT: Burnshaw, S. (ed.) The Poem Itself, 1960; Nist, J. A. The Modernist Movement in Brazil, 1967; Twentieth-Century Writing, 1969; Who's Who in Latin America: Brazil, 1947. *Periodicals*—Américas June 1951; Negro History Bulletin May 1954; Pan American February 1950.

"LINCOLN, GEOFFREY." *See* MORTIMER, JOHN (CLIFFORD)

*"**LIND, JAKOV" (pseudonym of Heinz Landwirth)** (February 10, 1927–), novelist, memoirist, and dramatist, is the son of a Polish-Jewish merchant, Simon Landwirth, and Rosa (Birnbaum) Landwirth, daughter of a Russian-Jewish cattle-dealer. He was born in Vienna, in a house a few minutes' walk from the Danube. In an autobiographical statement, Lind says: "My district was populated by clerks, tradesmen, and not a few businessmen, all of them poor. Everyone in Vienna was poor, except us—until 1929 and the crash. We moved into the new Socialist-built workers' housing estate only a few weeks before the Socialists went out of government." After the Socialists came the Austro-Fascists, and after them the Nazis, "and all Vienna became one great Swastika . . . When everyone said 'Juden raus' we couldn't afford the train fare." Lind's parents were deported and killed. In December 1938, at the age of eleven, he was sent to Holland—"a free ride on a children's refugee train."

Lind had an interlude of freedom and normality in Holland, working as a gardener and taking on a Dutch identity. "But the Germans followed us. In two years the Germans had turned 'Juden raus' into 'Juden nach Polen.' No one knew what that meant, not even the Jews." Lind avoided extermination in Holland by traveling to Germany with false identity papers, masquerading as a Nazi, and (among other things) working at the Air Ministry for a time as confidential factotum to a metallurgist engaged in the development of new weapons. A "five-year scramble for mere survival was followed by five years in a land ploughed by war—Palestine, which had just become Israel as I left it in search of education."

At twenty-three he returned to Vienna to study at the Max Reinhardt Seminar. He intended to become a theatre director, but found it was too late. He had experienced too much, done too many casual jobs, played too many roles in too many countries; all this had qualified him for only one thing, which was to write. His first book was a collection of short stories, *Eine Seele aus Holz* (1962, translated by Ralph Manheim as *Soul of Wood*). Robert Mazzocco found in it "a splendid theatrical talent, sardonic and Pinteresque, gruff and Brechtian" with "No limits to the irrational" and "no illusions." The title story is an "intricate, black, bestial" *novelle* about a German male nurse to whose care a paralytic Jewish child is entrusted and who seeks his reward for this act of charity after the war. Four others have the same idea, and the nurse Wohlbrecht is casually murdered, his torn-off wooden leg, his "soul of wood," left propped against a tree.

In this, as in his subsequent books, Lind has pre-

* lint

sented a world without moral norms, a world in which the monstrous has become the everyday. Reviewers of *Soul of Wood* stressed Lind's affinities with writers like Kafka, but wrongly described them as a debt. Lind is a natural writer utterly unconcerned with modish literary trends. If, as one critic has written, his is a vision "at once more fierce, more grotesque, and cruel than that of Günter Grass," it is because Lind's "apprenticeship" was fierce, grotesque, and cruel. Being a spontaneous writer, he does not pass judgment over his experience, but re-enacts it in his imaginative works. The years he spent during the war, living in Germany but "dreaming in Dutch," as he puts it, and half identified with the victims of Nazism, account for his remarkable capacity for imaginative self-identification both with the murderers and the murdered.

Though he has an acute eye for realistic detail, in his most successful works Lind has found strict realism inadequate, and has moved from realism to fantasy as if there were no distinction between them. His first novel, *Landschaft in Beton* (1963), was translated by Ralph Manheim as *Landscape in Concrete*. It recounts the adventures of a hugely fat Wehrmacht sergeant in search of the remnants of his regiment, shattered on the Eastern Front. Displeased by the mud in which so many of his comrades died, and by the general untidiness of nature, he is anxious to get the whole thing organized, tidied down under concrete. It is in just such a neat and empty Eden, after the holocaust, that the novel ends. Reviewing the book, Ross Wetzsteon wrote: "Reason is a parody of sanity. . . . Obeying the logic of self-preservation, we approach race suicide. In his insistence that the experience of our century is not insane but 'reasonable,' Jakov Lind is one of the handful of writers who can even begin to utter . . . the first syllables of the unspeakable."

A second novel, *Ein bessere Welt* (1966, translated by Manheim as *Ergo*), is set in Vienna, and traces the conflict between Wacholder, a customs official, and Würz, who like the sergeant in *Landschaft in Beton* sees it as man's job to tame nature. Wacholder is aided in his campaign by his lodgers Leo and Aslan, whose activities include anonymous plagiarism and the writing of threatening letters. The book was said to have "the same elliptical terseness" that distinguished Lind's earlier work, "the same delight in pushing paradox to its farthest extreme and the same penchant for grotesque horror," along with "a fractured poetry" and other signs of increasing range.

Lind's autobiography, *Counting My Steps*, warmly praised for its rueful humor and quirky humanity, was welcomed also as a key to his other work. One reviewer concluded that "what survives in Lind, despite the constant changes of scene

JAKOV LIND

and identity, the loss of idealism, love, hatred—and 'worst of all, language'—is the indestructible desire to write. . . . Many books have been and will be written to carry more of the bestiality and pathos of these years. None is more likely to affirm in so beautifully and movingly individual a way the capacity of European civilization to transcend them." Lind continued his autobiography in *Numbers*, and in *The Trip to Jerusalem* describes how in 1970 he became a "new convert to God."

Lind has written plays for radio and television, notably *Anna Laub* (1965) and *Das Sterben der Silberfüchse* (1965, translated as *The Silver Foxes Are Dead*), and also writes for the cinema. He is competent in six languages, and the play *Die Heiden* (The Pagans, 1965), published in Germany in Erich Fried's translation, was originally written in English. Since 1956 Lind has lived mainly in London. He was married in 1955 to Faith Henry, and has two children. He spent the academic year 1966–67 as writer in residence at Long Island University, New York.

PRINCIPAL WORKS IN ENGLISH TRANSLATION: Soul of Wood, 1964; Landscape in Concrete, 1966; Ergo, 1967; The Silver Foxes Are Dead (four short radio plays), 1968; Counting My Steps, 1969; Numbers, 1972; The Trip to Jerusalem, 1973.

ABOUT: Who's Who in America, 1970–1971. *Periodicals*—Book Week July 3, 1966; New York Review of Books June 17, 1965; New York Times Book Review November 2, 1969; Saturday Review June 25, 1966; December 8, 1966; May 21, 1970.

LINK, ARTHUR S(TANLEY) (August 8, 1920–), American historian, writes: "I was born in New Market, Virginia, the son of John William

ARTHUR S. LINK

and Helen (Link) Link, and grew up in parsonages in New Market and Danville, Virginia, and Mount Pleasant, North Carolina, as my father was (is) a Lutheran minister. I went to public school in Mount Pleasant, a country town, and was inspired to prepare myself for college by my parents and to become an historian by two superb teachers in a consolidated high school that was virtually in a cotton field. I went to the University of North Carolina in 1937 determined to obtain a Ph.D. in history. I was blessed with superb teachers at Chapel Hill, was elected to Phi Beta Kappa, and was graduated in 1941 with highest honors. Of course we were soon in the war, and, after being turned down for service, I taught in various army and navy programs while doing graduate study at Chapel Hill and Columbia. I received the Ph.D. from the former in 1945. In that same year, I married Margaret McDowell Douglas of Davidson, North Carolina. We have had four children—Arthur, Jr., in 1946; James Douglas, in 1950; Margaret McDowell, in 1951; and William Allen, in 1954.

"I began my professional career as an instructor in history at Princeton in June, 1945. I became an assistant professor in 1948 and, in the next year, went to Northwestern University as an associate professor, being promoted to professor in 1954. The fifties were a fairly strenuous decade for me. I was a member of the Institute for Advanced Study, 1954–55; the Albert Shaw Lecturer at the Johns Hopkins University in 1956; and Harmsworth Professor of American History at Oxford, 1958–1959. At the same time, I became increasingly active in various historical associations. I also began to lecture widely, both in the United States and in universities in Western Europe. I accepted appointment as Editor of *The Papers of Woodrow Wilson* in 1958 and returned to Princeton as Professor of History in 1960, being appointed Edwards Professor of American History in 1965.

"I wanted to be a writer while in high school, and I received rigorous training in English grammar and composition and foreign languages at Chapel Hill. Professor Fletcher M. Green of the University of North Carolina is the man who taught me what it means to be an historical writer, not just a writer. I began publishing articles while in graduate school. Intrigued by Woodrow Wilson, I began a biography of him in 1944. I have since written five volumes (all published by Princeton University Press) in what has become an increasingly large series: *Wilson: The Road to the White House* (1947); *Wilson: The New Freedom* (1956); *Wilson: The Struggle for Neutrality* (1960); *Wilson: Confusions and Crises* (1964); *Wilson: Campaigns for Progressivism and Peace, 1916–1917* (1965).

"I have, meanwhile, also edited several books and written a good many articles and other books on Wilson and twentieth century American history. Four among the latter are *Woodrow Wilson and the Progressive Era* (Harper's 1954 and 1963); *Wilson the Diplomatist* (The Johns Hopkins Press and Quadrangle Books, 1957, 1963, and 1965); *American Epoch* (Knopf, 1955 and 1963), and *Woodrow Wilson: A Brief Biography* (World Publishing Company, 1963). I was a Guggenheim Fellow, 1950–51; a Rockefeller Fellow, 1962–63; and I won Bancroft Prizes in 1957 and 1961. I have received an M.A. from Oxford and honorary doctorates from Bucknell, North Carolina, Washington College, Washington and Lee and Davidson College.

"My main literary and scholarly work now—as it will be for many years—is serving as the chief editor of the Wilson papers. We plan to put out about forty volumes, and the first appeared in 1966.

"My main avocation is study of Christian theology, my main outside activities, work in the United Presbyterian Church, which I serve as an Elder, and the ecumenical movement. I have no historical philosophy or view apart from the biblical understanding of truth and the historical process.

"I should add that my wife has made the largest contribution to my professional career, not only because she has absorbed most of the burdens of our household, but also because she is a fine editor and rigorous critic. I also owe whatever literary style I possess to a study of the masters of historical prose, particularly Winston S. Churchill."

Link's magnum opus is of course his monumental biography of Woodrow Wilson (though it already seems likely that this achievement will be matched and surpassed by his edition of the Wilson papers). He received the first of his two Bancroft prizes for *Wilson: The New Freedom*, which concentrated on his subject's development as a practical politician. The book was universally praised for the "prodigious industry" and "consummate skill' with which the author had sifted and evaluated his evidence, for his "straightforward and simple style," and his willingness to judge Wilson "by Wilsonian standards," bringing out his faults as well as his virtues.

The third volume in the series earned Link his second Bancroft prize. This was *Wilson: The Struggle for Neutrality, 1914–1915*. Reviewing the book, but referring to the series as a whole, J. M. Blum wrote: "It is a triumph in the genre of history that sets out to record how things actually were; indeed, no one need ever undertake again the task Mr. Link has executed so meticulously. The detail and integrity of this study give its restrained judgments great weight."

For a few critics, in fact, Link's restraint has seemed a little excessive; they have nothing but admiration for his ability to shape an enormous body of material into a minutely detailed but rarely tedious picture of what Wilson said and read and did; but they complain mildly that there is little attempt to reveal what the President *felt*.

His other books, most of them about Wilson, have been similarly praised for their combination of meticulous scholarship and readability. "In the debate over judgment in history," wrote Henry Steele Commager, "[Link] is on the side of continence and austerity, rather than of enthusiasm and moral righteousness. His work combines in a most impressive manner, the virtues of 'technical' history and of narrative and literary history. At a time when we are insistently required to choose between these, it is gratifying to have a demonstration that they are not antagonistic but can be married."

The historian served from 1963 to 1966 as vice president of the National Council of Churches. He enjoys music and contemporary fiction.

PRINCIPAL WORKS: *The Biography of Woodrow Wilson*—Vol 1, Wilson: The Road to the White House, 1947; Vol. 2, Wilson: The New Freedom, 1956; Vol. 3, Wilson: The Struggle for Neutrality, 1914–1915, 1960; Vol. 4, Wilson: Confusions and Crises, 1915–1916, 1964; Vol. 5, Wilson: Campaigns for Progressivism and Peace, 1916–1917, 1965. *Other Works*—Woodrow Wilson and the Progressive Era, 1910–1917, 1954; American Epoch: A History of the United States Since the 1890's, 1955; Wilson the Diplomatist, 1957; Woodrow Wilson: A Brief Biography, 1963; The Growth of American Democracy: An Interpretive History, 1968; Woodrow Wilson: A Profile, 1968; The Impact of World War I, 1969; The Higher Realism of Woodrow Wilson and Other Essays, 1971; (with Stanley Coben) The Democratic Heritage: A History of the United States, 1971. *As editor (with others)*—The Papers of Woodrow Wilson (1966–).

ABOUT: Contemporary Authors 1, 1962; Directory of American Scholars 1, 1963; National Cyclopaedia of American Biography, Current Volume J 1960–1963, 1964; Who's Who in America, 1972–1973. *Periodicals*—Theology Today April 1962.

***LINS DO RÊGO (CAVALCÂNTI), JOSÉ** (June 2, 1901–September 12, 1957), Brazilian novelist and essayist, was born on his maternal grandfather's plantation, Corredor, in the town of Pilar in Paraíba. He was the son of Dona Amélia Lins, who died a few months after his birth, and of João do Rêgo Cavalcânti, who retired grief-stricken to his plantation, leaving his son to be reared by his aunts and grandfather. His life on the plantation is the source of his major novels, the five-volume "Sugar-Cane Cycle" and the later *Fogo Morto* (Dead Fire, 1943).

Lins do Rêgo was educated at the Colégio Pio X de Paraíba, the Instituto Carneiro Leão, and the Ginásio Oswaldo Cruz in Recife, and at the age of eighteen entered the Law Faculty in the University of Recife, where he obtained his LL.B. During his student days in Recife, he met several men who, like himself, were to play an important part in Brazilian literature, and three in particular exerted great influence on him: José Américo de Almeida, Olívio Montenegro, and, in 1923, Gilberto Freyre. Lins do Rêgo considered his meeting with Freyre of fundamental importance: "From that moment . . . ," he said, "my life has been different, my thoughts have been different, my plans, my readings, my enthusiasms." He began to imitate him in all respects, even literary style, while Freyre gave him English lessons and introduced him to the works of Joyce, Pater, Browning, and others.

In 1925 Lins do Rêgo was appointed Prosecuting Attorney in Manhuassú, Minas Gerais, but returned to the Northeast in the following year as bank inspector for the federal government in Alagoas. He remained in this post until 1930, losing it with the outbreak of the revolution and subsequently becoming a tax inspector. He worked in that capacity in Alagoas in 1931–1935, Minas Gerais in 1935–1938, and Rio de Janeiro, where he lived from 1938 until his death.

His "Sugar-Cane Cycle" was published during the 1930s and most of the volumes describe his own life on the plantation and his reactions to it. This was the period of the decline of the traditional family plantation or *engenho*, and the advent of the larger and more impersonal sugar mill or *usina*. His work is the fictional counterpart of the historical and sociological studies of the same environment by Gilberto Freyre, and is remarkable for its detailed naturalism.

* lēns dō rā′ gō

JOSÉ LINS DO RÊGO

Menino de engenho (Plantation Boy, 1932), which received the Fundação Graça Aranha Prize, sees the plantation through the vivid perceptions of childhood. The narrator, Carlos de Mello, is being raised on the Santa-Rosa *engenho* by his grandfather, Colonel José Paulino. These two characters are portraits of Lins do Rêgo and his grandfather, while most of the others have their factual counterparts. The dominating figure is that of Paulino, ruling his empire with skill and harsh authority and training Carlos to take his place. But Carlos is a sickly, moody child, who prefers books and makes precocious attempts at writing. Olívio Montenegro, who knew Lins do Rêgo well, says that he was just such "a difficult child, one of those whose wishes never knew firm ground, and who seems always to be fluctuating between the earth and the moon." The novel was filmed in 1965.

Carlos's temperament earns him the nickname *Doidinho* (Daffy Boy), the title of the cycle's second volume, published in 1933. This describes his early schooling and the way his personality was shaped by the stern disciplinarian here called Maciel. In the time which elapses between this volume and the next, *Bangüê* (The Old Plantation, 1934), Carlos, like his creator, has been away at law school and has grown away from his background. When he returns to run the plantation, he proves to be neurotic, indolent, and quite incapable of following in his grandfather's footsteps. His only amusements are reading and sex—the latter a pastime to which he had been introduced, in typical plantation fashion, by the age of twelve. The death of Paulino is seen as a tragedy, for Lins do Rêgo mourns the passing of the old system, believing that its petty tyrants in fact gave their workers more freedom than the larger and more efficient *usinas*. Carlos allows himself to be tricked into agreeing to sell Santa-Rosa to a nearby *usina*, but the old plantation is saved by members of the family who buy Carlos out and form their own *usina*. These three volumes have been translated into English by Emmi Baum as *Plantation Boy* (1966).

The last two volumes were less successful. Carlos virtually disappears from the scene, and with him the first-person narrative style. *O Moleque Ricardo* (Black Boy Richard, 1935) describes the fortunes of Carlos's black playmate, who escapes to Recife but finds that city workers are even worse used than plantation laborers. He is finally jailed for participating in the general strike. *Usina* (The Sugar Refinery, 1936) describes the freedom Ricardo finds in prison and his homosexual attachment to a triple murderer. On his release he returns to Santa-Rosa, only to find that industrialization has turned it into something worse than a prison. It is finally bought up by an even bigger concern and it is this rapid expansion that forms the main theme of the book.

In his character drawing and his brilliant evocation of plantation life, Lins do Rêgo is recognized as one of the leading Brazilian writers. His prose is simple, direct, and somewhat staccato. It is generally agreed that his work suffered from the speed at which it was written—he published twenty-three books between 1932 and 1957—and from its lack of dialogue. The scope of the "Sugar-Cane Cycle" has led critics to compare him to Hardy, Dickens, Galsworthy, and Proust, but he is a less accomplished writer than any of these. Alvim Correa describes his style as a "voice without color, nostalgic, rhythmic as the beat of waves on a beach, a monotonous sound like something that comes from afar before reaching our ear, like the wind, the sound of a bell, or a ship's horn."

Lins do Rêgo went on to write several novels which reflected a growing interest in Freudian psychology, both in their themes and in their experiments with symbolism. None of these was particularly successful. The best of his later books, and his masterpiece in the opinion of some critics, was *Fogo Morto* (Dead Fire, 1943), in which he returns to the theme of the "Sugar-Cane Cycle," telling the story from a different and less personal viewpoint, and relying more on dialogue. He draws an excellent portrait of the quixotic Captain Vitorino Carneiro da Cunha, a penniless untidy figure who is generally despised but becomes the object of great admiration as his moral fortitude and courage reveal themselves. He is contrasted with the epileptic Lula de Hollanda, autocratic master of Santa-Fe, whose rise and fall is traced in the novel.

After he settled in Rio de Janeiro, Lins do Rêgo

traveled about Brazil and the world a great deal, describing his experiences in the amiable personal essays collected in *Gordos e Magros* (The Fat and the Skinny, 1942); *Homens, Sêres e Coisas* (Men, Beings and Things, 1952); *Bota de Sete Léguas* (Seven-League Boots, 1952); and *Meus Verdes Anos* (My Green Years, 1956). He contributed articles and reviews regularly to a variety of newspapers, and translated English, Spanish, and French works. He also edited several journals: *O Journal, O Globo, A Manhã*, and *Folha Carioca*.

The author was married to Filomena Masca in 1924 and they had three children. His wide-ranging interests included sport, politics, music, art, motion pictures, and science. A chronic hypochondriac, he acquired a wide knowledge of medicine. He was a typical product of the *engenho*, with the drawling, high-pitched voice and capricious syntax of the Northeasterner. An eccentric who loved to play practical jokes on his friends and to insult them elaborately in public, he was at times melancholy and introverted—much like Carlos de Mello.

PRINCIPAL WORKS IN ENGLISH TRANSLATION: Pureza, 1948; Plantation Boy, 1966.

ABOUT: Castello, J. A. José Lins do Rêgo, 1961; Ellison, F. P. Brazil's New Novel: Four Northeastern Masters, 1954; Magill, F. N. Cyclopedia of World Authors, 1958; Who's Who in Latin America: Brazil, 1947. *Periodicals*—Américas January 1958; Modern Language Journal October 1950; New York Review of Books January 26, 1967; New York Times September 13, 1957.

LIVINGS, HENRY (September 20, 1929–), English dramatist, was born at Prestwich, near Manchester. His parents, George and Dorothy (Buckley) Livings, were not wealthy but earned a comfortable living, he as a shop manager, she as a secretary. After primary school, Henry Livings went to Stand Grammar School in Prestwich. From there he won a scholarship to Liverpool University but left without taking a degree, "on the grounds that academic honours or success are useful only for academics, and I'd settled for the theatre." After university, he did his National Service in the Royal Air Force as a cook and, on returning to civilian life, drifted in and out of several jobs before starting his acting career with the Century Mobile Theatre, in Hinkley, Leicestershire. In 1956 he joined Joan Littlewood's company at the Theatre Royal, Stratford, where he played, among other roles, that of Prisoner C in Brendan Behan's *The Quare Fellow*.

The work of Joan Littlewood, with its immense zest and technical virtuosity, and its delight in mime, improvisation, and audience involvement, has influenced Livings deeply. He had already written some unproduced plays and, encouraged by Miss Littlewood, he tried again. As he says, he "chose simple stories and corny situations," and "broke down the story into 'units' of about ten

HENRY LIVINGS

minutes each—about as long, I reckoned, as you can hold a situation totally and clearly in mind. Each unit I then tried to lay against what went before and what followed, so that the audience would be fresh each time and yet carry an accumulating imaginative world along towards the . . . completion of the play."

The first result was Livings's stage play *Stop It, Whoever You Are*. It is about a downtrodden and henpecked lavatory attendant, Perkin Warbeck, whose story is told in a carefully ordered sequence of brief anecdotes. In one scene, for example, Perkin attempts to make the lavatory cistern overflow on the head of his *bête noire*, Alderman Oglethorpe, but instead drenches his esteemed employer, Captain Bootle. Perkin eventually breaks down and dies, but returns during the course of a séance to triumph at last over his horrible wife. The play caused a minor furor in London when it opened there early in 1961. Many in the audience found its humor primitive and walked out; others tried to drown the catcalls with enthusiastic applause. The reviews were equally mixed: many were scathing, but some critics recognized and welcomed the play as the prototype of a new and highly sophisticated kind of popular theatre, with the pace, skill, and broad appeal of a comic strip.

In any case, Henry Livings now found his work in considerable demand. His first play, *Jack's Horrible Luck*, a picaresque parable about a naïve sailor's night out in Liverpool, was produced on television by the BBC in 1961. The same year his highly unconventional play about Villon was staged by the Royal Shakespeare Company, and *Big Soft Nellie* was produced at the Theatre Royal, Stratford. The "nellie" is a despised and bullied mother's boy who courts the peace and security of a jail sentence. Prison eludes him, but his venture into crime establishes him as a hero among his workmates. *Big Soft Nellie* carries Livings's disregard of conventional plotting to an extreme, and its dialogue reads at times like a series of *non sequiturs*. But John Russell Taylor has pointed out that it makes perfect sense on the stage, and this accords with Livings's belief that the theatre is not a literary medium. In *Big Soft Nellie* and *Nil Carborundum* (1962), a farce about the RAF in peacetime, Livings creates a number of sharply defined portraits of human types, places them in anecdotal situations, and yet rescues them from superficiality by the variety, subtlety, and random quality of his dialogue.

Kelly's Eye, produced in 1963, surprised without greatly impressing those of Livings's critics who had failed to observe the serious social and psychological comment implicit even in his broadest farces. It is a tragic, relatively formal story, about a stupid and violent outcast and the girl he befriends and, in a sense, dies for. One reviewer found it implausible and stiffly rhetorical, "in the worst, lecturing vein of D. H. Lawrence." *Eh?*, which followed in 1964, is in the tradition of Livings's earlier plays, a comedy about a downtrodden but indestructible factory worker which was subsequently filmed.

In 1966 Livings went to the Nottingham Playhouse to write, direct, and act in *The Little Mrs. Foster Show*, a successful vaudevillian romp about emergent Africa. *Honour and Offer*, which as its title phonetically suggests is an amiable sex farce, was staged at the Cincinnati Playhouse in 1968 and was moderately successful there, but Livings has so far made no great impact in the United States. John Russell Taylor suggested that the reason for the mixed reception his work has received is that Livings is very much a British working-class dramatist—"not only does he come from the working class, but he writes principally for the working class." He uses one of the lightest and most popular forms, farce, to convey serious truths to his audience, and this confuses "the more severe playgoer, who likes to know at once where he is." For his part, Livings does not care a great deal for "the more severe playgoer" or indeed for traditional theatres—"the most important thing is to get out to your Rotary or workingmen's clubs when they ask for half an hour's worth." He has devised a suitable "highly portable event" in the form of his Pongo plays—ten-minute sketches "depicting archetypal situations via a personae of Lancashire Victorians." The fact that these interludes draw on the traditions of both the Commedia dell' Arte and Japanese Kyogen plays has done nothing to reduce their acceptance by the unsevere playgoers of Livings's part of England. His recent work includes contemporary versions, set in the English Midlands, of Gogol's *The Government Inspector* and Tolstoy's *The Power of Darkness.*

Henry Livings is of medium height, bearded, with dark hair and gray eyes. He was married in 1956 to Fanny Carter, an actress from the Theatre Royal, Stratford, and they have two children, Toby and Maria. The family live in the village of Dobcross, near Oldham in Lancashire. Livings says that he is very interested in mystical experience but has no religious convictions. He is "dedicated to beer" and enjoys "pub games, brass bands, chess, theatre, walking, swimming, fencing, crown green bowling, theatre and theatre."

PRINCIPAL PUBLISHED WORKS: Stop It, Whoever You Are, 1962; Nil Carborundum, 1963; Kelly's Eye (*containing also* Big Soft Nellie, There's No Room For You Here for a Start), 1964; Eh?, 1965; Good Grief (*containing* After the Last Lamp, You're Free, Variable Lengths, Pie-eating Contest, Does It Make Your Cheeks Ache?, The Reasons for Flying) 1968; The Little Mrs. Foster Show, 1969; Honour and Offer, 1969; Pongo Plays 1–6, 1971; The Ffinest Ffamily in the Land, 1973.

ABOUT: Contemporary Authors 15–16, 1966; Taylor, J. R. Anger and After, 1963; Who's Who in the Theatre, 1972. *Periodicals*—Guardian September 12, 1970.

LOGAN, JOHN (BURTON) (January 23, 1923–), American poet, was born in Red Oak, Iowa, and is of Irish extraction. He received his B.A. in zoology from Coe College (1943), and his M.A. in English from the State University of Iowa (1949); he has done graduate work in philosophy at Georgetown University and Notre Dame. Logan began his teaching career at St. John's College, Annapolis, Maryland (1947–1951), and from 1951 to 1963 was an associate professor in the General Program of Liberal Studies at Notre Dame. After visiting professorships at the University of Washington and San Francisco State College, he went in 1966 to the State University of New York at Buffalo. He is editor of *Choice*, the Chicago magazine of poetry and photography. Logan gives frequent lectures and poetry readings across the country and has published short stories and criticism as well as poems in a variety of literary periodicals.

Perhaps partly because he has published in *Evergreen Review*, Logan was at one time thought of by some as a "beat" poet. Glauco Cambon, discussing Logan in *Recent American Poetry*, suggests comparisons also with Thomas Merton, Galway Kinnell, and Robert Lowell. Logan's concern, Cambon says, is "with personal reality and with the possibility of the holy in an unholy world." His characteristic manner involves "sharply run-on lines, creating at times . . . a syncopating effect . . . vivid paradoxes, high pitch, and, at the same time, common speech . . . and if one looks for strength, he has it, even if sometimes at the price of form."

Wallace Fowlie called Logan's first book, *A Cycle for Mother Cabrini*, "Roman Catholic poetry" which is also "catholic in its impartiality, its sympathy, its wholeness." Cambon finds unevenness in the cycle and occasional prosiness, but also great vitality in the violent imagery and the way in which Logan "posits his own self in a dramatic confrontation with existence and with the holy." Though the religious motivation of these devotional poems is "too bristling" for some tastes, most critics were impressed.

Ghosts of the Heart is freer, less intense, but "natural, casual, and immediate." It contains a number of poems celebrating not a saint of the church but Heine, Rimbaud, Hart Crane—the poet as "secular saint . . . at loggerheads with the world." In these poems about poets, and in some directly autobiographical pieces, Cambon identified as a major and recurrent theme the early death of Logan's mother. Harvey Shapiro, one of the many reviewers who praised this "clear, unrhymed verse," wrote: "It's in the scenes out of his own life that you feel the full power of his verse."

Spring of the Thief, Logan's third book, begins with a set of monologues on biblical and mythical themes which were found powerful and moving. Other religious poems in the collection seemed to many reviewers excessively casual and breezy, "domesticating the Holy Ghost." Janet Fiscalini, writing in *Commonweal*, shared some of her colleagues' reservations but called *Spring of the Thief* Logan's best book—"if he has 'found himself,'" she said, "it is not by innovation, but by purification and development. He has dropped many easy eclectic effects, and in the long poems he has taken the space and height his talent needs. The title poem may be one of the best religious poems of this generation." The often extremely personal poems in *The Zig-Zag Walk*, which followed, were admired for a more richly sensuous note, and for a frank eroticism which at least one critic found had "qualified and deepened the piety which rings in his utterance."

John Logan was married in 1945 and has nine children.

PRINCIPAL WORKS: *Poetry*—A Cycle for Mother Cabrini, 1955; Ghosts of the Heart, 1960; Spring of the Thief: Poems 1960–1962, 1963; The Zig-Zag Walk, 1969; The Anonymous Lover: New Poems, 1973. *For children*—Tom Savage: A Boy of Early Virginia, 1962.

ABOUT: Cambon, G. Recent American Poetry, 1962; Carroll, P. The Poem in Its Skin, 1968; Dickey, J. Babel and Byzantium, 1967; Directory of American Scholars, 1964; Murphy, R. (ed.) Contemporary Poets of the English Language, 1970; Ossman, D. Sullen Art, 1963.

CHRISTOPHER LOGUE

LOGUE, CHRISTOPHER (November 23, 1926–), English poet and translator, writes: "I was born in Portsmouth where my mother had gone for her own mother's companionship. My father was a minor official in the Wages Branch of the GPO (the British postal service); a cricketer, a runner, a member of choral societies, an honest and kindly man with beautiful handwriting, who rented a small house in north London until his retirement to Portsmouth in 1933.

"I went to various schools where I was reasonably miserable. It was not that I was a particularly bad pupil, or that the schools were harsh; I didn't seem to fit in; I couldn't find my way. My attachment to my mother was intense, but hostile; in a sense, it still is. The subject which absorbed me was drawing; woodwork came second. English composition I found easy, but I never dwelt on it in private.

"Without ever thinking about it I chose the arts as my place. People in the arts struck me as being free. Nowadays, for what it is worth, I think that I would have made a better painter than a poet, but then (at twenty, say) I grasped that the one branch of the arts in which the English do consistently and exceptionally well is, God knows why, poetry. I wanted, and still want, to create something exceptionally clear and hard and truthful. So it was poetry for me.

"I went into the Army, did badly, made things worse for myself, and finished with a two-year prison sentence (served in the Middle East), and an ignominious discharge. Coming home I was completely isolated from anything saving my own dreams, though I did not realise this at the time.

"My father died and left me fifty pounds. With it I did something sensible, possibly for the first time in my life; I went to live in Paris. There I found people like myself and I became very happy. With the exception of my various love affairs I have remained happy ever since.

"I write slowly and painfully. This would be fine except for the fact that I suffer greatly from long, alternating bouts of idleness and impatience.

"Your category 'Principal Works' causes me dismay. I do not think that anything I have yet done deserves such a title. However, I know I am capable of something deserving a title rather like it. It remains to see whether or not I shall be able to get it onto paper.

"In fact, although I am deeply flattered and relieved that you have asked me to contribute to your reference work, I am not sure I should be in it at all."

Christopher Logue, "born rebel and self-appointed outcast," volunteered for the army in 1944, and after two years as a private in the Commandos was sent to the Middle East with the Black Watch. His imprisonment and discharge from the army came when he was found guilty of gun-running and other offenses in Palestine. Back in London in 1948 he worked simultaneously as a park keeper and a dentist's receptionist, and later qualified as the only registered pauper in the seaside town of Bournemouth. During these years he read all of Dryden, Milton, and Shaw. He went to Paris in 1951 and nearly starved, but in 1953 published *Wand and Quadrant* with money raised in the cafés. He became a Marxist in 1954. Logue is "short, dark, and hollow-cheeked," and dresses or used to dress entirely in black. In spite of the harshness of his work, he is said to be "the kindest of men."

In 1956 an interviewer for the *Times Educational Supplement* said that Logue, in conversation, grew "drunk with words." His early poems were similarly "often inchoate, vibrant always with passion, a treasure-house of evocative words and incantatory phrases," pouring out "like water from a hot spring." A representative selection was *Songs*, containing love sonnets, ballads, political poems, and translations from Homer and Pablo Neruda, and printed in a variety of typefaces designed by Logue.

His versions of the *Patrocleia* and *Pax* infuriated some critics with their modern slang and references, but pleased others who approached them as original English poems with a "clean and bitter quality" which was "not un-Homeric." Logue's theatrical ventures have been no less controversial. *The Lily-White Boys* was a satirical musical written with Tony Kinsey and Bill Le Sage about British low-life, which reminded some critics of Brecht and others of Gilbert and Sullivan. *Trials by Logue* consisted of a straightforward retelling of the Antigone story, followed by *Cob and Leach*, a "rough-and-ready" farcical parody of it which delighted some and irritated others. Logue collaborated with Hugo Claus in the translation of Claus's play *Vrijdag* (1969, translated as *Friday*), and wrote the screenplays for Ken Loach's film *The End of Arthur's Marriage* and Ken Russell's film *The Savage Messiah.*

Logue's experiments with poetry for jazz accompaniment and poster poems have been widely emulated. Much of his recent work has been satirical journalism like the neat Brechtian epigrams published in *ABC* and the sometimes rather tired and perfunctory attacks on capitalistic militarism and materialism in *New Numbers.* A number of Logue's poems and songs have been recorded. He is a regular contributor to the satirical weekly *Private Eye*, and in *Who's Who* reveals himself to be that "Count Palmiro Vicarion" who in 1957 published *Lust*—a pornographic novel, *A Book of Limericks*, and *A Book of Bawdy Ballads.* He has acted in several films.

Logue has been called an exhibitionist seeking to "raise the poet to the level of a pop singer." Certainly his energy and spontaneity sometimes seem factitious and strident. But Logue's translations, and some of his fables, cannot be so easily dismissed. Charles Philbrick said of his work that "more than poems or a poet, what we have here is a poetic personality—one that struts and sometimes annoys, and other times charms and compels, but never lets us forget its presence."

PRINCIPAL WORKS: Wand and Quadrant, 1953 (in Paris); Devil, Maggot and Son, 1956; (tr.) The Man Who Told His Love (based on Pablo Neruda's Los cantos d'amore), 1958; Songs, 1959; Songs from "The Lily-White Boys," 1960; (tr.) Patrocleia, 1962; The Arrival of the Poet in the City: A Treatment for a Film, 1964; Christopher Logue's ABC, 1966; True Stories, 1966; (tr.) Pax, 1967; New Numbers, 1969; The Girls, 1969.

ABOUT: Blackburn, T. The Price of an Eye, 1961; Contemporary Authors 11–12, 1965; Murphy, R. (ed.) Contemporary Poets of the English Language, 1970; Taylor, J. R. Anger and After, 1962; Thwaite, A. Contemporary English Poetry, 1961; Who's Who, 1973. *Periodicals*—Manchester Guardian May 15, 1959; Saturday Review October 29, 1960; Sunday Times December 18, 1966; Times Educational Supplement July 27, 1956; Times Literary Supplement May 8, 1959.

LOPRESTI, LUCIA LONGHI. *See* "BANTI, ANNA"

LORD, WALTER (October 8, 1917–), American historical writer, writes: "I was born in Baltimore, Maryland; uneventfully attended school there; later graduated from Princeton University and the Yale Law School.

"Law school was interrupted by World War II and four and a half years in the OSS. This was then America's intelligence agency, known as a 'cloak and dagger' outfit in the vernacular of the time, but I wore no cloak and wielded no dagger. My work, mostly in Washington and London, consisted of routine intelligence processing and administrative duties.

"After the war, I returned to law school—but only to graduate, not to practice. Instead, I went to work for the Research Institute of America in 1946. This was a business information service, where it seemed I might better combine my legal education with an interest in writing. I was not disappointed.

"For the next seven years I was Foreign Editor in the Research Institute, and later Editor-in-Chief at Business Reports, another business service. In 1953 I crossed the Great Divide into the advertising industry—first to do a series of case histories for J. Walter Thompson, later to write copy for the same agency. These postwar years all added up to experience in almost every conceivable kind of writing—newsletters, tax manuals, TV commercials, pseudo-comic strips, even popular songs—for as the result of an implausible encounter at one of those New York parties I found myself doing the lyrics for 'The Third Man Theme.'

"Through it all, history remained my favorite hobby, and the big puzzle was, of course, why so much good history was dull and so much entertaining history was poor.

"Around 1953 I found myself moonlighting in an effort to do something about this. First attempt was an editing job on *The Fremantle Diary*, a record kept by an English officer who spent three months in the Confederacy during the Civil War. Then came *A Night to Remember*, a story on the sinking of the Titanic. By 1956 I found myself so engrossed in this work that it was asking too much of even a most benevolent employer to keep me on the payroll. I left the advertising business and have been swimming upstream alone ever since."

Part historian and part journalist, Walter Lord has specialized in the detailed reconstruction of important moments in American history—usually in recent history, since much of the immediacy and vividness of his best books come from his skillful use of interviews with eyewitnesses. He introduced the technique with immense success in *A Night to Remember*, his account of the sinking of the "unsinkable" Titanic. "Using every available scrap of evidence that archive and memory can bring to the surface," says Burke Wilkinson, "he has set out to tell, simply and chronologically, the events of the night of the sinking. The result is a stunning book, incomparably the best on its subject and one of the most exciting books of this or any other year." It was filmed and televised, and was on the best-seller lists for months.

Lord has used the same technique in reconstructions of the Japanese attack on Pearl Harbor (*Day of Infamy*); of the optimistic "good years" between 1900 and 1914; of the efforts to enroll James Meredith in the University of Mississippi (*The Past That Would Not Die*); and of the Battle of Midway (*Incredible Victory*). *A Time to Stand* is a heavily researched popular history of the Battle of the Alamo, while *The Dawn's Early Light* deals with the War of 1812.

WALTER LORD

For his first book Lord interviewed forty-three survivors of the Titanic disaster, and for his second drew on firsthand accounts from no fewer than five hundred and seventy-seven of those involved in the events at Pearl Harbor on December 7, 1941. These recollections, some of them the source of important new information, many of them personal and apparently inconsequential, trace out the course of events "hour-by-hour, blow-by-blow." They form a sort of collective diary, recording every variety of human reaction to crisis, and half persuading the reader that he shares the witness's own ignorance of what is to happen next. At its best, as in *A Night to Remember*, Lord's method produces an effect of stunning realism, an almost frightening sense of participation in disaster or triumph. His books have been much praised for this quality of immediacy, and for the judgment, organizational skill, and scrupulous research he brings to them. Lord's "graphic, breathless style," relished by his innumerable readers, is a little too breezily journalistic for some critical tastes. The principal criticism made of his intrinsically objective technique is that it tells the reader all that he wants to know (and sometimes more) about *what* happened, very little about *why*.

Walter Lord is the son of John and Henrietta (Hoffman) Lord. His father died when he was three, and his only sister in 1929. He has brown hair and eyes, and is a little over six feet tall. Lord, who lives in New York City, generally works a ten-hour day in the library, but finds time to participate in civic projects and has served as vice-president of the Municipal Art Society, as a director of the Union Settlement House (chairman 1962–1964), and as a trustee of the New York Society Library, the Museum of the City of New York, and other institutions. He collects political campaign buttons and old prints and enjoys the theatre, boating, and photography. Lord is an Episcopalian and a Democrat.

PRINCIPAL WORKS: A Night to Remember, 1955; Day of Infamy, 1957; The Good Years: From 1900 to the First World War, 1960; A Time to Stand, 1961; The Past That Would Not Die, 1965; Incredible Victory, 1967; The Dawn's Early Light, 1972. *For children:* Peary to the Pole, 1963.

ABOUT: Contemporary Authors 3, 1963; Current Biography, 1972; Who's Who in America, 1972–1973. *Periodicals*—Wilson Library Bulletin October 1960.

LUCAS, F(RANK) L(AURENCE) (December 28, 1894–June 1, 1967), English critic and man of letters, wrote: "I was born at Hipperholme, near Halifax, where my father was head-master of the school said to have been attended by Laurence Sterne. In 1895 he moved to an Elizabethan grammar-school in South-east London, where I grew up to like cities far less than the countryside, and suburbs even less than cities; though Blackheath, Greenwich Park, Shooter's Hill were full of historic memories, and still kept a certain picturesque charm. Being for years an only child perhaps helped to make me an incorrigible individualist, with a sceptical distrust of groups and movements, masses and majorities, convention and conformity. In 1910 I went to Rugby School, of which my memories are Spartan, but grateful. Public schools, in this egalitarian age, are now widely regarded as wicked. But total equality seems to me attainable only in the graveyard—a fit place for it. Believing that real civilization needs individuality and variety, I find our levellers too like that ancient tyrant who demonstrated the secret of tyranny by smiting the heads off his taller poppies. Our century has had too much of uniformity and uniforms.

"We were bred mainly on Greek and Latin. Narrow? But under the modern system my children have been educated still more narrowly in science. A necessity perhaps; but an improvement? Science must deal with things rather than people: humanism implies that people are more important than things. Perhaps they are; and we may pay for forgetting it.

"In 1913 I was an undergraduate of Trinity College, Cambridge; a year later, a subaltern in the Seventh Royal West Kents; a year after that, in the Somme area of the Western Front. For a large number of my generation the only alternatives were being knocked about or being killed; so I was probably lucky to spend seventeen months, in all, in war-hospitals, where I was able to do more general reading than ever before or since. In August 1918 I was fit to go out a third time, now in Intelligence, trying with not wholly adequate school-German to pry military secrets from German prisoners-of-war. Fortunately by then most of them were ready enough to talk. January 1919 saw me a Cambridge undergraduate again; in 1920 I became a Fellow of King's; in 1921 a student, for three months, in the British School at Athens. I was sent to seek the battlefield of Pharsalus. For Caesar, content as a soldier to have won the battle, had been lamentably lax, as a historian, in indicating where it was; much to the grief of scholars, who had invented a dozen different sites, to which I duly added a thirteenth. But Greece was then still unspoilt; the tyranny of the Turk had not yet been replaced by the vulgarities of the tourist-agent. And though it was not the height of comfort to gnaw mutton-bones with Greek peasants, and be chased by their dogs about the Thessalian Plain, it was an experience.

"From 1921 till 1939, and from 1945 till retirement in 1962, I was lecturer, then Reader in English Literature at Cambridge. In the thirties, however, the horizon fast darkened with the threat from Rome and Berlin. I had no liking for politics —less than ever as Cambridge grew full of very green young men going very Red. But from 1933 it seemed clear to me that Hitler (whatever some modern historians may pretend) meant war; and that the optimistic torpor of Baldwin's England might lead to our being devoured before we were awake. So events in Ethiopia, Spain, Czechoslovakia drove me into political writing. Probably with no tangible effect—except to get my name on the Gestapo list for arrest and liquidation as soon as England was occupied. But, for me, this excursion into politics had one satisfactory result—that I was called up on the first day of the war, for confidential work, attached to the Foreign Office, somewhere in England.

"So from 1939 to 1945 that too energetic race, the Germans, having taken up four years of my earlier life, now took up six more. It was gruelling work; but interesting, exciting, and free from that sense of futility which hag-rides our age. Those were my happiest years; especially as they brought me my Swedish wife, who flew over, with what her Swedish friends thought wild recklessness, to marry me in what seemed the perhaps doomed England of 1939.

"Most of my books have been criticism—largely printed lectures. For, with no great faith in lectures, I thought they might at least become more solid, and less ephemeral, if put in print also for a larger public. In our specialized age it might have seemed more prudent to stick to this field, instead of ranging also over others—fiction, poetry, drama, essays. But how much duller! A free-running fowl has far more fun than a fatted battery-hen. A small French girl, I remember, after watching Roger Fry as he painted, remarked condescendingly: *'Tu t'amuses bien avec ta peinture!'* He did. For an artist or writer to be too much governed by success is itself one kind of failure. To amuse oneself seems to me a main reason for painting or writing. Uplift is frequently depressing. And, considering life's complex obscurity, it is a little presumptuous to go urging mankind anywhither—except in some obvious matters of staring urgency, such as the menace of Hitler, or the perhaps still grimmer menace, now, of world over-population. Enough if one does *not* (like a good deal of modern writing) influence one's readers to become more vulgar, crass, or cruel. Enough if one writes mainly for oneself and *'les âmes amies.'* "

F. L. Lucas was brought up in an academic household. He began his education at Colfe's Grammar School, where his father, F. W. Lucas, was headmaster. A brilliant academic career followed at Rugby, and at Cambridge he won the Pitt Scholarship, Porson's Prize, the Chancellor's Medal, and the Browne Medal. But Lucas was no timid scholar; his friend T. E. Lawrence spoke admiringly of his physical energy. During World War I he was mentioned in dispatches for a daring reconnaissance near Miramont, and he received an OBE for his work with the Foreign Office in World War II, when he was also an unflagging officer of the Bletchley Home Guard.

However, Frank Lucas was mainly a teacher. Although not the favorite of all of his students at Cambridge, many came to feel that they owed him a debt for his insights into the relationship between Greek and English literature. His lack of influence may in part be ascribed to the fact that his time at Cambridge coincided with the ascendancy of F. H. Leavis, with all of whose ideas he was entirely out of sympathy. "One of the arguments against a belief in the benevolent god," Leavis said on one occasion, "is the sanity of Mr. Lucas." (To which one of his pupils replied: "Now you're sounding, sir, a little like Mr. Lucas himself.") He disliked T. S. Eliot and for a time during his fellowship Eliot's works were excluded from the King's College Library.

Lucas, one of the most prolific critics of the century, tried his hand at virtually every literary form.

F. L. LUCAS

As a creative writer, he was competent in traditional forms, but lacked imagination. His best novel was probably *Dr. Dido* (1938), but he was apt, as one critic wrote, "to put his own witty conversation into the mouths of his characters . . . and add melodramatic action as though it were an afterthought." Encouraged by the successful production of two plays at the Newcastle Repertory Theatre, he wrote several more in the early 1930s, and two of them were produced without much success in London. His poetry really belonged to the nineteenth century: short lyrics and longer narrative poems, marked by archaisms and overlush descriptive phrases. His many translations from the Greek have some merit.

One of Lucas's major achievements was his four-volume edition, in 1928, of the works of John Webster. This remains a notably useful contribution to Elizabethan dramatic studies. His other important books include *Seneca and Elizabethan Tragedy* (1922); *Tragedy* (1927), a standard introduction; and *The Decline and Fall of the Romantic Ideal* (1934). As a scholar, Lucas could write attractively and urbanely in what was essentially a late nineteenth century belles-lettres tradition, and his exposition of classical theory was admirably lucid. It has been said that "the chief fault of his style . . . was a tendency to overload with irrelevant if witty allusions."

In his criticism, Lucas always remained a reactionary. In refuting the notion that literature develops or progresses, he became too fiercely entrenched in the conviction that it should not *change*. An excellent and highly scrupulous literary scholar, he lacked a good historical sense and, indeed, a healthy critical curiosity as to just what it is in literature that does change—and what does not. Thus Lucas's pronouncements frequently appear jejune and simplistic. Nevertheless, more than a dozen of his edited texts and critical works remain in print as a tribute to his usefulness as a scholar and teacher. And in such books as *The Decline and Fall of the Romantic Ideal*—his most influential work of criticism—there are many valuable observations. In Lucas a genuine mellowness and wisdom were vitiated by a sense of bitter resentment, arising mainly, perhaps, from his disappointment at not having made a more distinctive impact as a creator.

Frank Lucas was a shy man in public, probably because of his partial deafness—a relic of World War I. Among his friends, however, he was lively and charming. Romantic by temperament, he loved long walks in wild country, as is evident in his only travel book, *From Olympus to Styx*, which he wrote with his second wife. He was married three times—to the former Emily Jones, a novelist; to Prudence Wilkinson; and to Elna Kallenberg, by whom he had a son and a daughter.

PRINCIPAL WORKS: *Criticism*—Tragedy, 1927; The Decline and Fall of the Romantic Ideal, 1934; Studies French and English, 1934; Ten Victorian Poets, 1940; Literature and Psychology, 1951; Style, 1958; The Search for Good Sense, 1958; The Art of Living, 1959; Ibsen and Strindberg, 1962; The Drama of Chekhov, Synge, Yeats and Pirandello, 1963. *As editor*—The Works of John Webster, 1928. *As translator*—Greek Poetry for Everyman, 1951; Greek Drama for Everyman, 1954. *Poetry*—Ariadne, 1932; Poems, 1935, 1935; From Many Times and Lands, 1953. *Plays*—Four Plays, 1935. *Fiction*—Cécile, 1930; Dr. Dido, 1938. *Miscellaneous*—From Olympus to the Styx, 1934; Journal Under the Terror, 1939; The Greatest Problem (essays), 1960; etc.

ABOUT: Who's Who, 1967. *Periodicals*—Illustrated London News September 24, 1955; Observer February 12, 1928; New York Times August 15, 1958; March 6, 1961; June 26, 1967; Saturday Review October 11, 1958; Spectator May 7, 1954; Sunday Times September 11, 1955, February 23, 1958; Times (London) June 23, 1960; June 2, 1967; Times Literary Supplement November 6, 1937; September 16, 1955; March 14, 1958.

"LUCAS, VICTORIA." *See* PLATH, SYLVIA

LUCIE-SMITH, (JOHN) EDWARD (MC KENZIE) (February 27, 1933–), British poet and critic, writes: "I was born at Kingston, Jamaica. My father, John Dudley Lucie-Smith, was an official in the British Colonial Service. Unlike most of the colonial officials stationed in the West Indies, he came of an old local family. Tradition has it that my forebears arrived in Barbados around 1650, having been sent there as Malignants, or opponents of the Commonwealth. One ancestor on my paternal side was Euan MacLaurin, the Young Pretender's physician during the '45; another (in the 19th century) was the first to discover workable coal in India. My mother, born Mary Lushington, comes of a family which combines legal influences with literary ones. My great-great-grandfather, son of a Chairman of the East India Company, was Lady Byron's legal adviser at the time of her separation from the poet, and one of Queen Caroline of Brunswick's counsel during her trial in the House of Lords. He was a Member of Parliament and an associate of Wilberforce in the struggle against slavery. During the later nineteenth century, the Lushingtons formed part of the Pre-Raphaelite connection, and Rossetti was best man at the wedding of a great uncle.

"My childhood, an uneventful one, was spent in Jamaica. My father died in 1943, and in 1947 my mother brought me back to England. I was sent to King's School, Canterbury, where I won a scholarship open to the sons of colonial officials. It was at Canterbury that I first began to write poetry, and my first poem, an imitation of Pope, appeared in the school magazine, which I afterwards edited. It was at Canterbury that I discovered that I had a faculty for passing examinations. This led, when I was just past seventeen, to an open scholarship in Modern History at Merton College, Oxford.

"I was at Oxford from 1951–54, a period which saw a remarkable flowering of poets. I made many literary friendships there which have lasted to this day. I also wrote my earliest art-criticism for the undergraduate magazine, *Isis*. I cannot, however, say that I was altogether happy or at ease in the Oxford life of this period—partly, perhaps, because most of the undergraduates were older than I was, having done their military service before coming up. Against my own expectations, I enjoyed myself more in the two years which followed, when I was an Education Officer in the Royal Air Force.

"After leaving the R.A.F., I joined the London advertising agency for which I still work. During the past ten years I have written a great deal of journalism, mostly art-criticism and book-reviews. I have worked for *The Times*, *The Sunday Times*, *The Listener*, and *The New Statesman*, among others. I have also done a lot of broadcasting for the B.B.C. I enjoy these activities—I am forced to say this because literary journalism is so generally condemned. I have been intimately concerned, till very recently, with a group of poets who met regularly to discuss their own work. For six of the nine years that this series of meetings lasted, they took place in my house, and I acted as chairman and organiser. The discussions have had a certain amount of impact in the English literary world, though reactions have not always been favorable. An anthology of some of the poems read at these meetings has been published (*A Group Anthology*, edited by Edward Lucie-Smith and Philip Hobsbaum, Oxford University Press, 1963). Recently I founded a private publishing house (Turret Books, in partnership with

Bernard Stone) to print contemporary poetry, by authors known and unknown, in strictly limited editions. Our first publications have been well received.

"My own first separate publication was a pamphlet of poems put out by the Fantasy Press in 1954. This is now rare. I have published two full-scale books of verse, *A Tropical Childhood* (O.U.P. 1961) and *Confessions and Histories* (O.U.P. 1964). Both books were recommendations of the Poetry Book Society. *A Tropical Childhood* was joint-winner of the John Llewellyn Rhys Memorial Prize for 1961 and of the Arts Council's Triennial Award for the best first or second book of verse published in the preceding three years. My work, I think, shows a steady evolution from traditionalist and 'Movement' influences, through Browning, towards a much greater experimentalism.

"Future plans include a number of books about painting, a new selection of Browning's poetry, and another anthology for Penguin—*The Penguin Book of Elizabethan Verse*, which I edited, was published in 1965."

EDWARD LUCIE-SMITH

Edward Lucie-Smith, an acute and lucid art critic, established his literary reputation as the moving spirit, with Philip Hobsbaum, of "the Group," which began at Cambridge University as an undergraduate reaction against the cool uncommitted elegance of "the Movement," and continued in London as the kind of poetry workshop Lucie-Smith describes above. Only coffee was served at these weekly meetings, and members' work was discussed with a severity and sobriety rare in English literary circles.

The Group poets are sometimes accused of rubbing their readers' noses too vigorously in the grotesque and cruel, and the gentle elegance of Lucie-Smith's own work is unexpected—Donald Davie, indeed, once called him "the last Movement poet," and another critic finds his verse reminiscent of the novels of E. M. Forster. *A Tropical Childhood* was praised for the "just and exact" emotional tone of the poems it collected—for the "living suppleness of their response to a variety of topics, ranging from very general ones like death and punishment, more personally through early experiences of religion or school or military discipline, to very personal childhood or adult experiences, beautifully realized." *Confessions and Histories* included a set of Browningesque monologues—most of them about art and in blank verse. There were touches of "fierceness and muscularity," but these, it was said, seemed borrowed. More characteristic and original was "a directness of feeling, and a certain old-fashioned gentlemanliness of tone and diction . . . a natural kindness." There were fewer autobiographical poems in the later collection, *Towards Silence*, and a more evident interest in history and legend. Lucie-Smith's pursuit in his recent work of a more colloquial diction and freer (often syllabic) forms has been welcomed by some critics, though others have found the results sometimes rather thin and flat.

Trained as a historian, Lucie-Smith thinks of the past, he says, "as a series of exemplars demonstrating certain moral situations. . . . I think that literature and morality are entirely intertwined . . . just as I assume that writers are dependent on society." He no longer works in advertising, but is extremely active as a publisher, editor, literary journalist, and art critic. His artistic and literary interests have been combined in some of his recent work: *Towards Silence* includes a group of "emblems"—short poems inspired by old woodcuts; and his *Primer of Experimental Poetry*, planned as a three-volume work, shows how developments in poetry have accompanied related innovations in the visual arts. Lucie-Smith, who is unmarried, gives his recreations as "classical and near eastern antiquities" and "malice." He is a Fellow of the Royal Society of Literature.

PRINCIPAL WORKS: *Poetry*—A Tropical Childhood, 1961; Confessions and Histories, 1964; Penguin Modern Poets 6 (with Jack Clemo and George MacBeth), 1964; Towards Silence, 1968. *Art criticism*—What Is a Painting?, 1966; Thinking About Art, 1968; Movements in Art Since 1945, 1969 (U.S., Late Modern: The Visual Arts Since 1945); A Concise History of French Painting, 1971; Symbolist Art, 1972; Eroticism in Western Art, 1972. *As editor*—(with Philip Hobsbaum) A Group Anthology, 1963; Penguin Book of Elizabethan Verse, 1965; A Choice of Browning's Verse, 1967; The Liverpool Scene, 1967; The Penguin Book of Satirical Verse, 1968; Holding Your Eight Hands: A Book of Science Fiction Verse, 1969; British Poetry Since 1945, 1970; A Primer of Experimental Poetry: Vol. 1, 1870–1922, 1971; (with Simon

Watson Taylor) French Poetry Today: A Bilingual Anthology, 1971.
ABOUT: Contemporary Authors 15–16, 1966; Fraser, G. S. The Modern Writer and His World, 1964; Murphy, R. (ed.) Contemporary Poets of the English Language, 1970; Orr, P. (ed.) The Poet Speaks, 1966; Schmidt, M. and Lindop, G. (eds.) British Poetry Since 1960, 1972; Who's Who, 1973. *Periodicals*—London Magazine December 1964; Times Literary Supplement November 17, 1961; November 5, 1964.

***LUKÁCS, GYÖRGY** (April 13, 1885–June 4, 1971), Hungarian critic and philosopher, wrote: "I was born in Budapest. I graduated at the Budapest and Berlin universities. As a student, I established the 'Thalia-Stage,' an attempt at innovation in Hungarian theatrical life, and later was a regular contributor to the reviews *Nyugat* (The West) and *XX. század* (The Twentieth Century). I gave a course of lectures at the Budapest Free School of Social Sciences. In 1908 I was awarded the Christine Lukács Prize of the Kisfaludy Society for my *History of the Development of the Modern Drama.* Soon two collections of my essays were published entitled *The Soul and the Forms* and *Aesthetica Culture* (1911).

"After 1910, I spent most of my time in Italy and Germany. In 1912 I settled down in Heidelberg, where I formed a friendship with Max Weber. My book *The Theory of the Novel* was written in 1915.

"The experiences of the first World War turned me, a sympathizer with Socialist ideas, into a Communist. I joined the Communist party of Hungary in 1918. During the period of the Soviet Republic in Hungary I held the post of People's Commissar of Education and was the political commissar of the Fifth Red Division.

"After the fall of the Commune I emigrated to Vienna where I acted as a leading functionary of the Communist party up to 1929. In the spring of 1929 I spent three months in Budapest working in the underground movement. From 1930 to 1931 I lived in Moscow as a scientific collaborator of the Marx-Engels-Lenin Institute. During the years 1931–1933 in Berlin I did my best to organize the progressive intellectuals for the struggle against the rising fascism. I was then the deputy president in the Berlin group of the German Writers Association. After Hitler took over power, another emigration to Moscow followed, and subsequently work as a scientific researcher in the Philosophical Institute of the Academy of Sciences. At the same time I was a member of the editorial board of the journals *Internazionale Literatur—Deutsche Blätter* (International Literature—German Papers) and *Uj Hang* (New Voice).

"In 1945 I returned to Budapest as a deputy of the Provincial Hungarian Parliament and this city has remained my place of residence ever since. I was appointed Professor of Aesthetics at Budapest University. Between 1945 and 1949 my activity was concentrated upon the dissemination of Marxist theory among Hungarian intellectuals, the results of which have been collected in two books: *Literature and Democracy* and *For a New Hungarian Culture.* In 1949, when the influence of the Zhdanovian cultural policy became manifest in the countries of the people's democracy, my efforts were brought to an end by the attacks initiated by László Rudas. During the Rákosi era I dedicated almost all my energies to scientific research. These were the years in which my book against irrationalism—*Die Zerstörung der Vernunft* (The Destruction of Reason) —took shape. In a speech made in the Petőfi-circle in 1956 I demanded the renaissance of Marxism against Stalinist dogmatism. Though never a member of the Imre Nagy group, I was appointed minister of cultural affairs in the Imre Nagy cabinet in October 1956. In November of the same year I was interned in Rumania, from where I returned in April 1957. Afterwards I was pensioned off from my chair at the university. Since 1957 I have been working on my comprehensive philosophical works."

* lōō' kach

"A critic must always re-examine his work," Lukács said, "and reject what is false and outmoded; otherwise he is dishonest." Lukács repudiated his own views with a frequency and thoroughness that would have laid waste the reputation of a lesser thinker. And yet, after repeated recantations and abasements to the Communist hierarchy, his vast influence as a literary critic and philosopher remains and spreads.

He was the son of a Hungarian Jewish banker who was ennobled for his financial services to Austria-Hungary. Lukács was a brilliant and versatile university student and quickly made his mark as a critic of extraordinary range and moral authority. He was early drawn to socialism, but also—judging by his enthusiasm for Plotinus, Dostoevsky, Eckhart—to the mystic and transcendent. The influence of Hegel's phenomenology was fundamental in his fragmentary but brilliant *Die Theorie des Romans* (*Theory of the Novel*).

World War I brought Lukács into the Communist party, where he soon established himself as "the finest Marxist since Marx." This was his misfortune. Engrossed in Marx's early philosophical works, and reading them "through Hegelian spectacles," he emerged with a kind of humanism far removed from the orthodoxies of Communist materialism—a position with "subterranean links to contemporary existentialism." Lukács expounded his views in a volume of essays, *Geschichte und Klassenbewusstsein* (1923, translated by Rodney Livingstone as *History and Class Consciousness*). This seminal work, according to Morris Watnik in

Survey, was "the profession of faith of an aesthetic humanist turned Marxist, the commitment of one who had found in Marx a new analysis of the social dimension of man's self-estrangement in industrial society, in Hegel a vision of how it might be transcended in the dialectic of history, and in Lenin an élitist ethos that would work its will on men and societies to achieve that purpose."

The book wrecked Lukács's political career. Lenin attacked it and his followers began a campaign of ferocious vilification which made "Lukácsism" a term of abuse. Lukács made no reply for ten years, but in Moscow in 1934 abjectly repudiated the book and all his past work. Thenceforth, for many years, he hugged the party line, and did homage to Stalin and Stalinism. *History and Class Consciousness* remains, as a critic wrote in the *Times Literary Supplement* in 1970, "one of the turning points in the history of modern thought."

As a literary critic Lukács was a traditionalist, fundamentally opposed to modernism and the irrational spirit. He admired, understood, and illuminated above all Balzac, Tolstoy, Mann, and Gorky—the nineteenth century "critical realists" and their twentieth century heirs; as Alfred Kazin says, he was able to make the reader feel that these writers "represent a great age not only in the novel but also in man's attempt to transcend society." It was a position which suited the Communist party line when the "tamed" Lukács returned to Hungary in 1945, and he was encouraged to promulgate it as professor of aesthetics at the University of Budapest, where for three years he enjoyed considerable influence in Hungary. By 1948, the party found it expedient to replace "critical realism" with uncritical "socialist realism," but discovered to its astonishment that Lukács was unwilling to conform, insisting that propaganda values "coincide with aesthetic values only by chance." The party ideologist Rudas launched a fresh offensive against Lukács's stubborn "objectivism," carrying with him even many of the young people who had sat at Lukács's feet. In 1949–1950 Lukács recanted once more and withdrew into academic life. Six years later, at the time of the Hungarian revolution, he spoke out again, winning fresh esteem with "a gesture of intellectual integrity and outraged conscience . . . starkly in contrast to his own past record of subservience."

After that Lukács appears to have withdrawn from public life, but not to have escaped public attention. Lukács's heresies, repudiated by their author, nevertheless continued to exert a wide influence, their relative libertarianism appealing to many Communist intellectuals disenchanted with orthodox interpretations of Marxism. Fears of "neo-Lukácsism" led to fresh attacks on him in 1958. Lukács's influence spread far beyond the

GYÖRGY LUKÁCS

Communist world, moreover, and is apparent in, for example, much modern sociological thought and in French existentialism.

Lukács was the author of more than forty books. They include important studies in Russian, German, and French realist fiction of the nineteenth century: *Der historische Roman* (1955, translated by Hannah and Stanley Mitchell as *The Historical Novel*), *Thomas Mann* (1949, translated by Stanley Mitchell as *Essays on Thomas Mann*), and *Goethe und seine Zeit* (1947, translated by Robert Anchor as *Goethe and His Age*). Most Western critics esteem his early philosophical writings above the mainly critical work of his later years. Lukács wrote principally in German, the elegance of his early manner giving way in his middle years to a presumably deliberate indifference to style, which at its worst buried his insights "under a monstrous load of sociological jargon, self-conscious popularization, and polemical journalism." Nevertheless, the insights remain (and in his last years were expressed, according to George Lichtheim, in a manner by comparison "fairly detached and at times almost mellow"). Some critics assert that Lukács's commitment to realism in art disqualifies him as a commentator on all that matters most in contemporary writing; many disagree. Alfred Kazin values Lukács as "both a philosopher with great gifts of critical analysis and a critic who can marshal his points with logical rigor"; George Steiner regards him as "the only major German literary critic of our epoch . . . a radical moralist."

There has been much speculation about Lukács's many recantations and reversals. Some see in the phenomenon no more than a simple ambition to be at all costs "in the swim"; others seek a psychological explanation for Lukács's apparent attempt to cancel out all he stood for as a young man. Morris Watnik believes that Lukács's fidelity to the party line was an act of expiation prompted by the rise of nazism—a blind conviction that the kind of liberal disarray which made Hitler's success possible must never occur again. Lukács's devotion to the mimetic theory of art has been explained in similar terms, as the product of his "obsessive suspicion that beauty and, by inference, a good deal of art is a mask preventing a clear view of human evil and suffering," and his belief that "unless art can be made creatively consonant with history and human needs, it will always offer a counterworld of escape and marvelous waste."

Lukács lived in Budapest until his death at the age of eighty-six. His last major work, "Zur Ontologie des gesellschaftlichen Seins" (On the Ontology of Social Existence), his philosophical *summa*, has yet to be published, though an extract has appeared as "Hegels falsche und echte Ontologie" (Hegel's False and True Ontology). It shows Lukács returning to his early philosophical preoccupations and attempting, through Hegel, to "resume contact with the great traditions of Marxism."

The recent publication for the first time in English of many of Lukács's early philosophical works as well as of his later works of literary criticism has at last brought him into the field of consciousness of Anglo-Saxon thinkers and critics. It has already given rise to excited debate—about the fundamentals of aesthetics, and about the relationship between art and society and between the individual and history—in which George Steiner (a Lukács scholar of long standing), Alfred Kazin, Alvin W. Gouldner, and Susan Sontag have taken part, bearing witness to Lukács' surviving capacity to stimulate thinking about the bases of aesthetic and social ideas, despite the terrible cultural and political isolation of his last years.

PRINCIPAL WORKS IN ENGLISH TRANSLATION: Studies in European Realism, 1950; The Historical Novel, 1962; The Meaning of Contemporary Realism, 1963 (U.S., Realism in Our Time); Essays on Thomas Mann, 1964; The Theory of the Novel, 1964; Goethe and His Age, 1968; Writer and Critic, and Other Essays, 1970; Solzhenitsyn, 1970; Lenin: A Study on the Unity of His Thought, 1970; History and Class Consciousness: Studies in Marxist Dialectics, 1971; Political Writings 1919–1929, 1972.
ABOUT: De Man, P. Blindness and Insight, 1971; Dembo, L. S. (ed.) Criticism, 1968; Demetz, P. Marx, Engels and the Poets, 1966; Gömöri, G. Polish and Hungarian Poetry, 1945–1956, 1966; Hamburger, M. From Prophecy to Exorcism, 1965; Lichtheim, G. George Lukács, 1970; MacIntyre, A. C. (ed.) Against the Self-Images of the Age, 1971; Mészáros, I. (ed.) Aspects of History and Class Consciousness, 1971; Mészáros, I. Lukács' Concept of Dialectic, 1972; Parkinson, G. H. R. (ed.) Georg Lukács: The Man, His Work, and His Ideas, 1970; Revai, J. Lukács and Socialist Realism, 1950; Sontag, S. Against Interpretation, 1966; Steiner, G. Language and Silence, 1967; Zitta, V. György Lukács' Marxism, 1964. *Periodicals*—Commentary July 1971; Commonweal November 27, 1970; Comparative Literature Winter 1968; Contemporary Literature Summer 1968; East Europe April, May, June 1961, May 1964; Encounter May 1963, April 1965, March 1971, October 1971; International Social Science Journal 1967; Journal of Philosophy February 27, 1958; Listener November 3, 1966; Modern Language Notes December 1966; National Review June 1, 1971; New Left Review September–October 1966; March–April 1970; July–August 1971; November–December 1971; New Society September 2, 1971; New Statesman February 23, 1962; January 30, 1970, February 26, 1971; New York Times April 14, 1965; New York Times Book Review July 18, 1971; Partisan Review Spring 1964; Political Studies September 1970; Quarterly Review of Economics Winter 1971; Saturday Review May 8, 1971; Science and Society Winter 1966, Winter 1968; Times Literary Supplement April 23, 1964; June 25, 1964; July 14, 1966; September 25, 1969; April 9, 1970; June 18, 1970; June 11, 1971; Tulane Drama Review Summer 1965; Twentieth Century May 1958.

***LUNDKVIST, ARTUR (NILS)** (March 3, 1906–), Swedish poet, novelist, short story writer, travel writer, memoirist, critic, and translator, writes: "My boyhood was spent in the backward forest part of southern Sweden. Everything there was vulgarly materialistic and my passion for literature made of me an outcast almost as far back as I can remember. It seems I am a born writer, doomed by nature to be a writer. My first big city was Copenhagen in the neighboring country of Denmark. There I spent a whole winter reading in a church (where the public library was housed). When I was twenty I went to faraway Stockholm, capital of our long country, and continued my fight for self-education and for writing in a new, modernistic way. My first collection of poetry, *Glöd* (1928), has been considered a starting point for the dominant modernistic trend in modern Swedish literature.

"Since then I have written many books, about fifty I believe. Not without effort, of course, but at the same time as naturally as breathing. I have tried almost everything: poems, stories, novels, essays, criticism, travel books, reporting. And I have traveled widely. Since World War II I have spent altogether some ten years abroad, visiting all the continents but Australia. Travelling I have made into one of my 'universities' in Gorky's sense of the word.

"Politically I consider myself to be a left-wing socialist, but I have never belonged to any party. I believe in the necessity of a thorough-going revolution of the world, regardless of ideologies. I believe in culture as a means to a life really worth living. And I believe especially in books as our best companions and closest friends. People can let you down; books never.

* lund' kvist

"I think it useless to give any list of my books, as it seems impossible for me to make a selection of the principal ones. A lot of my writings have been translated into German, French, Spanish, Italian, Russian, Polish and so on, but hardly anything into English."

Artur Lundkvist was born the only son of a smallholder at Oderljunga in the northern part of the province of Skåne. He seems to have had little in common with his parents, Nils and Charlotta Lundkvist, his three elder sisters, or the peasant community in general. He has himself described his early determination to be a writer as at least partly the result of a "protest neurosis" which was also responsible for his rejection of the literary conventions of his day.

As a young writer in Stockholm, Lundkvist campaigned for modernism in Swedish literature, by which he meant a literary movement devoted to a continuous renewal of both form and content. His own early poetry, beginning with *Glöd* (Glowing Embers, 1928), represented an assault on the sterility of bourgeois culture, a vigorous if unsuccessful attempt to reconcile communism and a cult of technology with psychoanalysis and a romantic "primitivist" view of sex. His work at this time was characterized, to quote A. Gustafson, by "surging free-verse crescendos and massive accumulations of lusty, often sex-inspired images"; it showed the influence of D. H. Lawrence, Whitman, Sandburg, and the Swedish-Finnish poet Elmer Diktonius, as well as of Bergson, Marx, and Freud. Lundkvist introduced his masters and his ideas to other young Swedish poets, four of whom, including Harry Martinson, joined him in the celebrated anthology *Fem unga* (Five Young Men, 1929), which initiated the modernist movement in Sweden.

By 1932, when he published *Vit man* (White Man), Lundkvist's exuberant and aggressive assurance was somewhat subdued. His interest in French surrealism and the psychology of the unconscious produced a more introspective poetry, haunted by drifting images of loneliness and death. This fluid, reflective style dominates the poems in *Nattens Broar* (Bridges of Night, 1936) and *Korsväg* (Crossroad, 1942), a collection notable for the poet's calm meditations on his tortured relationship with his father.

For a time after the war Lundkvist seems to have rejected the discipline of logic altogether in his verse, adopting a "panic poetry: an abrupt and convulsive verse, flinging itself forward in surprising leaps, fragmentary but intensive, not least in its omissions." The profound sense of the impermanence and incoherence of human identity which inspired this "panic poetry" is reflected in

ARTUR LUNDKVIST

the title of his 1949 collection *Fotspår i vattnet* (Footprints in the Water). In time Lundkvist seems to have drawn comfort from the thought that life endures, if the individual does not. In *Vindrosor Moteld* (Wind-roses, Backfire, 1955) and subsequent collections, the tone is calmer and more measured, and some order has been imposed on the torrential imagery and the flux of sensory impressions.

Lundkvist's has been described as "the most amazing expenditure of creative energy in contemporary Swedish letters." His enormous postwar output is, he says, the product of his extensive world travels and the material and opinions they have provided him with. He has described these journeys—to Africa, India, Russia, China, South America—in a series of vivid travel books, and they are also reflected in his poetry and his fiction. The sketches in *Malinga* (1952) form "a kaleidoscope of races, customs, and prejudices." *Darunga eller Varginnans mjölk* (Darunga, or the She-Wolf's Milk, 1954), a series of studies of a Latin-American revolution, anticipates Castro's Cuba.

Some of Lundkvist's prose is comparatively realistic, as in the autobiographical novel *Vindingevals* (Vindinge Waltz, 1956) about his rebellious country childhood and youth. Usually, however, his abundant imagination carries him beyond the limits of realism, as in *Orians upplevelser* (Orian's Experiences, 1960)—stories that are experiments in life's possibilities rather than its actualities—and in *Berättelser för vilsekomna* (Stories for Lost Persons, 1961), which includes a story called "Gusty Meeting With William Blake." Blake, revolutionary and visionary, is an immensely sympathetic figure to Lundkvist, who calls his own autobiography *Självporträtt av en drömmare med öppna ögon* (Self-portrait of a Dreamer With Open Eyes, 1966).

Lundkvist's work as a critic and translator has been scarcely less influential than his poetry, and no one has done more to introduce Swedish writers and readers to new developments in foreign literatures. He remains a Marxist, but a Utopian one, with little interest in theory and dogma. He received the Lenin Prize in 1958 and became a member of the Swedish Academy ten years later. Since 1936 he has been married to the poet Maria Wine.

PRINCIPAL WORKS IN ENGLISH TRANSLATION: *Poems, short stories, essays in* Bäckström, L. and Palm, G. (eds.) Sweden Writes, 1965; Literary Review 2, 1965–1966.
ABOUT: Carlson, S. (ed.) Artur Lundkvist, 1956; Espmark, K. Livsdyrkaren Artur Lundkvist (with English summary), 1964; Gustafson, A. A History of Swedish Literature, 1961; Penguin Companion to Literature 2, 1969. *Periodicals*—Kentucky Foreign Language Quarterly 3 1955; New Mexico Quarterly 1952; Scandinavian Studies November 1965.

***LUZI, MARIO** (October 20, 1914–), Italian poet, writes (in Italian): "I was born at a point on the outskirts of Florence where, in those days, the eye could still range between the parks and the countryside, interspersed with a few scattered industrial plants; today the area is completely urbanized. There I spent the first twelve years of my life until my father, an employee of the railroad, was transferred to the vicinity of Siena. This was for three years the city of my studies and also of my first emotional contacts with life and with time and its manifestations. The simultaneous encounter with the art and the countryside of Siena made a strong and, I believe, lasting impression on my senses and my imagination. However in 1930 I was back in Florence. Here I finished my course in the *liceo* and, after considerable hesitation, enrolled in the Faculty of Letters at the University. I got my degree in 1936 with a thesis on François Mauriac. I sometimes wonder if my whole life might not be expressed in terms of these first and determinant circumstances and I am surprised when I am recalled to the chronicle of external events, which seem so scanty and insignificant compared to the internal and unnarratable ones. Yet the evidence of an existence associated with a given time in history, and modified and shaped by it, is not to be refuted.

"While I was still a student at the University of Florence I published my first small book of verses, *La barca* (The Boat, 1935), which brought me to the attention of the current literary circles. Taken together with my second volume, *Avvento notturno* (Nocturnal Advent)—published in 1940 but already well known through advance notices appearing in certain reviews, more courageous than others in matters of research and innovation—*La barca* supplied some not unimportant motifs to that vast and deep moral and aesthetic movement which has been called hermeticism. This movement was regarded as a heresy by fascism and it had a difficult life but perhaps for that very reason an intense one.

"Meanwhile in 1938 I had started off on one of the few roads open to an Italian writer who does not care for compromise: that is, a teaching career. It has taken me into various parts of Italy and finally back to Florence, where I now live. My hopes of making fruitful use of a concentrated and retiring life have been partially frustrated by the incessant literary and cultural debate that has animated and tormented these recent decades in Italy. However for our generation the central event was the second World War. Estrangement from the policies of fascism and the increasingly clear and overt rejection of its aims could not prevent the course of events from being very painful. And likewise painful were the decisions imposed by the civil struggle which followed on war and defeat. I came out of those years naked, as it were, but having gained, in compensation, an elementary understanding of existence and of the human word. My poetry, too, began to become simpler although fundamentally it could not abandon the complexity which characterizes our era. In any event it lost more and more of the adventurous characteristics which it shared with the poetry of the early twentieth century and became more sharply oriented toward a bare statement of truth—or at least that part of truth which I thought I could apprehend in modern man's condition of alienation and solitude. *Primizie del deserto* (First Fruits of the Desert, 1952), and *Onore del vero* (Honor of Truth, 1957) are the two principal books of my postwar period and they were accompanied by a number of essays later collected in the volume *L'inferno e il limbo* (Hell and Limbo, 1949). In 1960 I brought together all my books of verse in one volume entitled *Il qiusto della vita* (What Is Right in Life), published by Garzanti. Later I brought out two other small collections: *Nel magma* (In the Magma, 1963) and *Dal fondo delle campagne* (From the Bottom of the Fields, 1965). I have also made a certain number of translations of which the most important are those from Coleridge and Shakespeare's *Richard II*.

"In Italy the practice of awarding literary prizes flourishes. I have had my share of them. The most important ones were the Marzotto Prize (1957) and the Etna-Taormina Prize (1964). In spite of that I have never attained the position of 'official' poet, nor have I ever aspired to it. In Italy it would perhaps be more dangerous than elsewhere in view of the rhetorical and conformist tendencies which characterize all aspects of the public world. It

* lōō′ tsē

would be impossible to dissent from it while being a part of it; its power of corruption is enormous; even the Left, and, in general, the organized opposition, know something about it. Today too there is the additional hazard presented by the cultural industry, which creates at its pleasure fictitious fashions and values. Woe to anyone who lets himself get caught in that machinery! The trap set by facile and ephemeral cultural mythologies is always open. I try not to lose contact with the human base of communication—if I may express myself like a politician—but I keep far away from the culture of the corridors. The young men, not yet resigned to integration, who strive and torture themselves, the veterans, displaced and exiled, who put a little sauce into this stew—these are my most natural and dearest friends. For them the problem is never dormant but begins over and over again. And that's what I want."

To this account it might be added that in his early years, the late 1930s, Luzi was associated with the two so-called avant-garde reviews *Frontispizio* and *Letteratura*, the latter particularly renowned for its vigor and generous eclecticism. His teaching appointments took him to such non-Tuscan centers as Parma and Rome; neither sojourn has left much trace on his work. He was married in 1942 to Elena Monaci and teaches French literature at the University of Florence. As a critic he has written perceptively of Mallarmé and the Symbolists.

Luzi enjoys high critical esteem in his native land and his progress had been carefully and sympathetically charted. His early verses, mirroring the uncertainties of the later fascist years, have a lingering flavor of the *crepuscolari*, particularly in matters of vocabulary and imagery; and very occasionally one seems to detect an echo, quite involuntary, of certain D'Annunzian chords. The very short *Quaderno gotico* (Gothic Notebook, 1947), consisting of fourteen carefully wrought love poems, seems to indicate a withdrawal from participation in the active life and an intense concentration on inner concerns. With *Onore del vero* (1957) and the subsequent works, the poet seems more ready to recognize if not entirely to accept the world he lives in; images, often quite realistic, drawn from common and humble experience reappear in his verses.

Such at least is the conventional outline of his development. Actually one may venture the opinion that aside from a perfecting of technique and the self-confident maturity which is for any man or poet a by-product of the passing years, Luzi's poetic attitudes have not greatly changed over the decades. Whether one stresses the "social" Luzi of *Nel magma* or the "existentialist" Luzi of more recent works, his manner and his posture have been consistently and recognizably "hermetic"; like the older hermetics he follows the cult of the word as exemplified by Mallarmé, and like them too he searches tirelessly to find his own idiom and to express through highly personal imagery his particular view of life. His themes are love, the family (with the mother as nucleus), prayer, the passage of time, and what he calls "that mysterious flowing of transient beings bound one to the other by indecipherable connections."

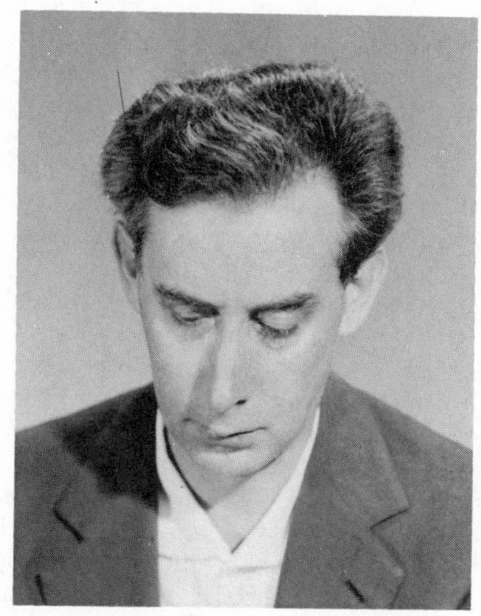

MARIO LUZI

Luzi is not everyone's poet and he is not concerned with making the approach to his work easy or comfortable. If he loves his fellow man, it does not follow that he is tolerant of his shortcomings or indeed very sympathetic to the twentieth century world that man has made. It has been remarked that his fervent and unshakable Catholicism, as well as his affinity, evident in numerous images, for the ancient hill towns with their rugged profiles and austere memories, reveal a kind of mediaevalism, and Signora Simonelli Sampoli has rightly called attention (in *Italian Quarterly*) to the echoes of Guido Cavalcanti that can be heard in some of his love poems. Furthermore Luzi's sense of mission is strong and his dedication to his art so intense that a kind of grimness in his verse gives his readers more of a challenge than a welcome.

This quality may be found to some degree in all hermetics but Luzi is *purissimo*, lacking or perhaps disdaining the warmth of Quasimodo, the mischief, even if only typographical, of Ungaretti, and the subdued irony of his master Montale. He is the most serious of the hermetics and uncompromising seriousness does not make for easy reading. Yet, at his best, there is an admirable if craggy honesty in his stance and an almost lapidary polish in his carefully wrought and hard-won imagery. He gives us indeed, as Signora Simonelli puts it, "an agonizing assertion of the existence of a reality that permits no escape." If Luzi is, as seems likely, the last of the true hermetics, he is not for that reason the least of them. One must grant him the merit of having opposed a true if bitter affirmation to the somewhat complacent abdications of some of his more musical predecessors: "The years rise over my shoulders / in swarms. It wasn't in vain; this is the work / each accomplishes alone and all together, / the living and the dead, to enter the obscure world / along plain roads and subterranean ways / dense with fleet encounters and casualties / either from love to love or in a single one / from father to son until it be clear. // And having said this, I can set out / freely in the eternal company / of all things that live and die, / I can leave off in dust or fire / If fire endures beyond its flame." (From "Nell'imminenza dei quaranta anni," translated by Charles Guenther as "On Approaching Forty.")

PRINCIPAL WORKS IN ENGLISH TRANSLATION: *Poems in* Barnstone, W. (ed.) Modern European Poetry, 1966; Golino, C. Contemporary Italian Poetry, 1962; Singh, G. Contemporary Italian Verse, 1968; Trevelyan, R. (ed.) Italian Writing Today, 1967; Italian Quarterly VI 23–24 1962.

ABOUT: Bo, C. Nuovi studi, 1946; De Robertis, G. Altro novecento, 1962; Luzi, A. La vicissitudine sospesa, 1969; Macrì, A. Caratteri e figure, 1956; Pozzi, G. La poesia italiana del novecento, 1965. *Periodicals*—Il Menabò 2, 1960; Italian Quarterly VI, 23–24, 1962.

***LYTLE, ANDREW (NELSON)** (December 26, 1902–), American short story writer, novelist, critic, and editor, writes: "Born in Murfreesboro, Tennessee, on land given by his Revolutionary ancestor to found the town, Andrew Nelson Lytle lived there and in North Alabama until at the age of thirteen he went to the Sewanee Military Academy. Afterwards he spent a year in France studying, was admitted to Exeter College, Oxford, but was called home on the death of his grandfather. He graduated from Vanderbilt in 1925. Here he met and became friends with the poets and others who showed him his true occupation, which at first he thought was the theatre. After managing a cotton farm for his father, he spent two years under George Pierce Baker in the Yale School of Drama; supported himself in New York acting, as he began the research on his first book, a Civil War biography, *Bedford Forrest and His Critter Company*.

"Returning to Tennessee, he renewed his fellowship with the Fugitive and Agrarian writers about Vanderbilt, who at the moment were taking a fresh look at their common historic inheritance. He contributed to their agrarian symposium, *I'll Take My Stand*, and at this time began writing fiction and found this, rather than the theatre, to be his proper art form. He has written stories and four novels: *The Long Night* (1936); *At the Moon's Inn* (1941); *A Name for Evil* (1947); *The Velvet Horn;* and a collection, *A Novel, Novella, and Four Stories.*

"He has taught history in Southwestern College and at the University of the South, where from 1942–1943 he edited the oldest American literary quarterly, the *Sewanee Review*. Then he tried to farm and to write at the same time, but discovered the two occupations required the same kind of energies. He went to Iowa and taught two terms in the writing program at the University in Iowa City. From 1948–1961 he was lecturer in creative writing at the University of Florida in Gainesville. In October, 1961, he again became editor of the *Sewanee Review* and Lecturer in English at the University of the South, Sewanee, Tennessee.

"He has received several literary awards, a Guggenheim Fellowship twice, and the Kenyon Fellowship for fiction. He has done certain critical essays on fiction and history. In May, 1965, Kenyon College awarded him the honorary degree, Doctor of Letters.

"He is currently living at Monteagle, Tennessee, with two of his three daughters. Mrs. Lytle, the former Edna Langdon Barker of Memphis, died in 1963."

Andrew Lytle is the son of Robert Logan Lytle, a farmer and lumberman, and Lillie Belle (Nelson) Lytle. He left the Yale School of Drama in 1929, and acted on Broadway and Long Island as a founder member of the Hampton Players.

His essay in *I'll Take My Stand* argued that there is a "war to the death between technology and the ordinary functions of living," and this and the other concerns associated with the Southern Agrarian movement have informed all of his work, fictional and factual.

As a short story writer Lytle is much admired, and it has been said that "no writer excels him in projecting through a single episode and a handful of characters the larger patterns of southern domestic life and thought."

The Long Night, a powerful regional novel set in the nineteenth century, is both a violent account of a young man's vendetta against his father's murderers and a study of the destruction of southern values by the Civil War. *At the Moon's Inn*, about De Soto's entry into America in 1539, again demonstrated Lytle's "extraordinary feeling for the sound and shape of a period." In *A Name for Evil* a man and his wife set out to restore a rundown southern mansion but are defeated by a miasmic spirit of evil which is eventually personified as the ghost of a former owner. There was a

* lī′ tl

general but not universal feeling that the novel lacked conviction as a ghost story, and some harsh comments about its "distinguished bad prose"; that the tale might be an allegory in which the haunted house represented southern society seems to have escaped most reviewers.

Lytle's fourth novel, *The Velvet Horn*, is generally regarded as his best. It is set in the Cumberland hill country where, at the end of the nineteenth century, the five orphaned Cropleigh children find and then lose sanctuary from the encroaching world. Lytle's essay in J. B. Vickery's *Myth and Literature* describes the genesis of his novel, which occupied him for eight years: he explains how he compared his chosen culture, the South of 1880–1910, to other societies; came to understand the cyclic nature of their growth and decline; and found a relevant image in the story of Adam and Eve. The "central knowledge" which emerges from the book, Brewster Ghiselin thought, "is that to place anything first except life is to fell the tree of life." A few critics, it must be said, failed to discern this or any other point to the book, which seemed to them difficult and tedious; most admired its lyrical and allusive use of language and its "carefully archaic turn of phrase," its "loving re-creation of events and places," its aspiration through myth to universality.

A Novel, a Novella, and Four Stories included three stories about the South, a story and a novella about the conquest of Mexico, and a reprint of *A Name for Evil*, which this time round earned a comparison with *The Turn of the Screw*. Jean Holzhauer observed that Lytle had here "subdued his interest in tedium, although he still writes in the leisurely pace of a man convinced that he has a subtle story to tell, and an obligation to leave no nuance unexplored." Charles Rolo, on the other hand, noting that "Lytle is working out of the same conservative tradition as Robert Penn Warren and John Crowe Ransom," concluded that "his fiction has a marked identity of its own" in which one finds "a combination of fine artistry and considerable force."

Lytle received his Guggenheim awards in 1940, 1941, and 1960; his *Kenyon Review* fellowship in 1956; and an award from the National Foundation on the Arts and Humanities in 1966–1967. Lytle has published little new work since he resumed the *Sewanee Review* editorship in 1961, but has in any case never been prolific. "My pace of writing is generally very slow," he says, "with constant cleaning up and structural revisions. Too often I will spend a day on a paragraph; a page is a good day's work."

ANDREW LYTLE

PRINCIPAL WORKS: Bedford Forrest and His Critter Company (biography), 1931; The Long Night (novel), 1936; At the Moon's Inn (novel), 1941; A Name for Evil (novel), 1947; The Velvet Horn (novel), 1957; A Novel, a Novella, and Four Stories (reprints A Name for Evil), 1958; The Hero With the Private Parts (essays), 1966; (ed.) Craft and Vision: The Best Fiction From The Sewanee Review, 1971.

ABOUT: Contemporary Authors 9–10, 1964; Cyclopedia of World Authors, 1958; Rubin, L. D. and Jacobs, R. D. (eds.) South, 1961; Vickery, J. B. (ed.) Myth and Literature, 1966; Warfel, H. R. American Novelists of Today, 1951; Vinson, J. (ed.) Contemporary Novelists, 1972; Who's Who in America, 1972–1973. *Periodicals*—Mississippi Quarterly Fall 1970; Sewanee Review LXV 1957; Southern Review Autumn 1936.

***MAASS, JOACHIM** (September 11, 1901–), American novelist, poet, dramatist, and biographer, writes: "I was born the third and youngest son of a well-to-do merchant family in Hamburg, Germany. I had a very happy childhood, disturbed only by the elementary school with its female teachers, for it went against my grain to be taught by women. I was well aware and permanently reminded of the fact that I was the son of a beautiful and proud city which was an autonomous state, a republic of long standing, and known the world over as the greatest harbor of continental Europe. The *Gymnasium* was boring with all its Latin and Greek, but much more bearable than the elementary school. I graduated from it without glory and without shame, ready to become a university student, for it was an old understanding that I should study jurisprudence and join the diplomatic service.

"Suddenly the aspect of my future changed. My two older brothers determined that in no case did they want to enter our family business, while my father insisted that one of his three sons had to become the heir of the big firm he personally had

* mäs

JOACHIM MAASS

built up. Thus one day I saw myself as a young merchant, the last thing I wished to be on earth. My good parents tried to make up for the sacrifice they had forced upon me by spoiling me with presents—money and every kind of personal kindness. This did not shake my conviction that I was not born for a life as a businessman and I reminded my father and my mother again and again that my giving in held no obligation for me and was nothing but an attempt.

"Two years later, I was sent as my father's representative to Portugal. It was a very comfortable position with good pay and little burden of work. I traveled constantly and became acquainted with almost every village and town of that country, probably the most beautiful I have ever seen. I made many friends—young men of my own age, mostly students of the ancient University of Coimbra, but also famous people, writers and artists. My main occupation, however, was a verse translation of Portuguese folk songs which, with their charming and melancholic naïveté, touched me very much. This way, so to speak, without my noticing it, the text of my first book came forth, and after I had spent a year in Portugal, I had more than ever drifted away from becoming a businessman.

"I returned to Hamburg and became what in Germany one calls a '*freier Schriftsteller*,' a free writer, which in my case meant not only free of professional obligations but especially free of any income to speak of, for having disappointed my parents badly, I could not reckon upon their help any longer. Thus my next years became rather ascetic, a long experiment in fasting and poverty. But I found that having grown up in happy and rich circumstances was a great help in this needy situation; I did not yearn for luxury. The only thing that was important for me was that I was heading in the right direction—and of this I felt all the more sure because now I had started to write verses of my own, poems partly romantic of a sweet and dreamy and partly of a rather sinister nature, some of which in serious examination I convinced myself to be beautiful beyond any reasonable doubt. (Today I am not so sure any more; but that feeling of conviction is still within me, alive and powerful, and probably the most enchanting feeling I have ever sensed, the feeling that makes artistic production an incurable addiction.)

"Finally, my financial troubles were eased. The father of a girl-friend of mine recommended me to an editor of the largest newspaper in Hamburg and I began writing short reviews of lectures, dance performances, movies and, at last, of books, which in the course of time became a kind of specialty of mine.

"But although my life seemed more or less secure now, I felt that I lacked fulfillment—that I had to do something else if I did not wish my reputation limited to that of a provincial writer.

"Thus I went to Berlin, which at that time, between 1925 and 1930, had become a European center of literary and artistic life. By a friend I was introduced to the *Vossische Zeitung*, generally known as 'Tante Voss' (Aunt Voss), which now became the base of my publications. I met many literary persons, journalistic and artistic people, and for the first time I came in intimate contact with the great political questions and conflicts of our time. I had always insisted that I was and wanted to remain a completely non-political human being, but now I fell in love with a pretty little dancer who turned out to be a Communist. This I did not consider an obstacle, but the happiness of our year together was undermined and finally broken to pieces by our political disharmony.

"I described this process autobiographically in my first novel and, programmatically, in a second one. I knew these books had started my literary career as I wished it, but already the first shadows of Nazism fell on our lives and spread and became more and more oppressing, and I recognized that living conditions, especially for my Jewish friends, would soon be desperate. Against the deluge of Nazism, I felt I had at once to formulate the ethical and spiritual values and laws without which human existence would lose all its dignity. The deeper meaning of this book had to be hidden in a seemingly harmless criminalistic plot. This was the concept of my novel, *Ein Testament*, one of the first contributions to the German secret literature during the Nazi regime. When, in November 1938, the so-called *Kristallnacht* (Crystal Night) came, the synagogues burned in Germany, Jewish stores were plundered and my Jewish friends arrested and forcibly carried away into concentration camps, I realized that this was not my country any longer and I decided to leave as soon as my friends had been set free.

"And so it happened. In May 1939 I sailed for the United States, and half a year later, assisted by Thomas Mann and the Quakers, I began to lecture at American colleges. However, writing remained my principal vocation and, together with *Ein Testament*, the books I wrote in America form the bulk of the work which I personally consider representative for my name in contemporary literature: the novels *The Magic Year* and *The Gouffé Case* and, as a byproduct of my academic work, *Kleist, Die Fackel Preussens*, a biography of Germany's greatest dramatist.

"Meanwhile, as an American citizen, I visited my native country from time to time but I never felt really at home there anymore. I do not feel at home in America either. I do not feel at home anywhere—and that I suppose is not astonishing for a man who has grown old in times such as ours."

Maass's Dutch-born father was an importer of rubber from South America; his elder brother Edgar, well known as a historical novelist, settled in the United States in the 1920s. In 1939, when Maass left Germany, he had already made his mark there as a poet and novelist. His dramatic poem *Johann Christian Günther* (1925) attracted considerable attention, and so did his novel *Bohème ohne Mimi* (Bohème Without Mimi, 1930), an account of life in Bohemian circles in Berlin. *Der Widersacher* (The Enemy, 1932) is set in the German docks during the slump, and several other works of this period deal with Maass's childhood: "Borbe," the title story in a collection published in 1934, is about his relations with a sadistic teacher; *Die Unwiederbringliche Zeit* (The Irretrievable Time, 1935) is based upon his boyhood in Hamburg; and *Ein Testament* (A Testament, 1939), which studies the problems of good and evil within a close-knit family, is an implicit indictment of the rise of Nazism in Germany.

The first of his books to appear in English was *Das Magische Jahr* (1945), translated as *The Magic Year*. In this obviously autobiographical novel, a middle-aged refugee from Nazi Germany sits alone in a small wooden hut on a New England hilltop and thinks back over a significant year in his Hamburg childhood. The city is splendidly evoked, with affection and with "Proustian exactitude." Wendell Johnson described the book as the "polished work of a sensitive, keen, poetic craftsman, verbally overwrought at times, given to occasional futile shadow-dancing with imponderables, etched at least faintly by German romanticism, but overall a literary artist of very considerable stature."

Maass's most ambitious novel, *Der Fall Gouffé* (1952), was translated by Michael Bullock as *The Gouffé Case* (1960). It is based loosely on an actual murder trial. The disappearance of Gouffé, a prosperous debt collector in Paris at the turn of the century, is investigated by the able but unpopular police chief, Goron. Gouffé's murderers are brought to trial but one of them, Gabrielle Bompard, is acquitted, and Goron is broken. In the second half of the book, Gouffé's brother-in-law Jaquemar pursues Gabrielle to America, where this beautiful and apparently innocent girl corrupts and finally kills him. Far from being a simple entertainment, *Der Fall Gouffé* is a serious investigation in Freudian terms of the "death wish" and of the problem of good and evil.

The English-language version had a mixed reception. Some critics were reminded of Thomas Mann, and Julian Maclaren-Ross thought it "surely one of the greatest German novels of this decade." Others found this very long novel too slow and portentous, and much too detailed—like the work of "a kind of Germanic Simenon." However it was generally agreed that Gabrielle, the "fin-de-siècle Lilith," is superbly alive; indeed, as Margaret Parton wrote, "she unbalances the book, overshadows philosophy, and seduces the reader almost as effectively as she does her lovers. And in the end, one gropes impatiently through the philosophic morass, hearing only Gabrielle's laughter as she mocks her creator."

Since World War II Maass has made frequent visits to Germany, where his stage and radio plays have been widely produced, and his novels generally admired. Walter Jens, for example, praised *Der Fall Gouffé* as "an exemplary synthesis of vividness and intellectualism . . . taking over the great, rich Western narrative tradition." Maass's biography of Kleist was also much praised—by Herman Hesse among others. In 1961 he was honored by the Bavarian Academy of Fine Arts. "I have come to the world as a story-teller," Maass says; "storytelling has always been my passion, sometimes my torment and frequently my salvation."

PRINCIPAL WORKS IN ENGLISH TRANSLATION: The Magic Year, 1944 (England, 1964); The Weeping and the Laughter, 1947; The Gouffé Case, 1960; Gabrielle, 1964.

ABOUT: *Periodicals*—Book Week December 24, 1944; New York Herald Tribune March 5, 1961; New York Times Book Review November 9, 1947; Saturday Review April 8, 1961; Time March 10, 1961; Times Literary Supplement October 7, 1960; October 8, 1964.

MACAULEY, ROBIE (MAYHEW) (May 31, 1919–), American novelist, short story writer, and critic, writes: "I was born in Grand Rapids and

ROBIE MACAULEY

I grew up in the flat, prosaic country of western Michigan. Its only geographical blessing is the lakes—the great one and the many smaller—so swimming and fishing are the chief pleasures of any childhood there.

"My family was not unusual in any way that I can remember—except for its considerable pride in being descended from the Macauleys of Castle Ardencaple. My father was a manufacturer (of oxygen and acetylene) with an odd interest in amateur printing. Along with this, he had a few literary interests—one of them being a lifelong friendship (largely by correspondence) with H. P. Lovecraft, the writer of weird tales.

"I got the better part of my early education in a basement room. That was where stood the foot-powered printing press and the cases of foundry type I had been given on my twelfth birthday. Through a long series of magazinelets and small books, setting every word by hand, I began to learn something about how the English language is put together—as well as a real appreciation for economy in style.

"Fairly early I decided to be a writer and I conceived the notion that the best way to that end was not through the usual university education but through a kind of apprenticeship to a writer I admired. He appeared almost by magic. In 1939, Ford Madox Ford came to teach at the little Michigan college of Olivet and I applied for admission at once. That was a piece of great good luck for me. Ford was not only a talented writer (then somewhat in eclipse) but also the greatest talker about writing I have ever known—he had talked it all his life with Conrad and James and Lawrence and H. G. Wells and Hemingway and a hundred others.

"When Ford left Olivet at the end of the year, I found another master to listen to. This was John Crowe Ransom, who had just begun teaching at Kenyon College. Ransom was entirely different from Ford—a poet with a fine critical sense in contrast to the impressionistic fiction writer and fictionizer. At Kenyon I lived in a Victorian house known as Douglass House. There were ten of us, all with ambitions to be writers, and the company was good—some of the others were Robert Lowell, Randall Jarrell, and Peter Taylor. I still think that Ford and Ransom and Douglass House, among them, offered a kind of literary education I could never have found elsewhere in America.

"Shortly after I'd graduated, I found myself in the Army (in 1942). Eventually I ended up in the Counterintelligence Corps, first in France, then Germany, and finally when the war ended in Czechoslovakia. After the German surrender, our small detachment was shipped almost at once to the Far East and I became commander of a small unit stationed in the Japanese mountain resort of Karuizawa; I was given the duty of running down and arresting various German spies and Gestapo personnel caught in Japan by the war's end. A good many of these Counterintelligence Corps experiences I later used in short stories, most of them appearing in a book called *The End of Pity*.

"When I came home again in 1946, I worked for a time in New York publishing, taught at Bard College, then went to the State University of Iowa to teach and to get my master's degree. In 1948 I married Anne Draper of Memphis, Tennessee.

"About this time, I decided to do something in justice to Ford Madox Ford, who was almost totally forgotten by then. I wrote a short book about him but I was not satisfied with the result. I decided to publish one part of it as an essay in the *Kenyon Review*. Harold Strauss at Knopf liked it and resolved to re-issue Ford's Tietgens tetralogy in one volume called *Parade's End*. It was the beginning of a gratifying Ford revival—and now there are five or six critical books on him and his best novels are back in print.

"I went on to teach at the Woman's College in Greensboro, North Carolina, and then later moved to Georgetown in Washington. In 1952 I published a novel titled *The Disguises of Love*. In 1957–1958 I had a fellowship and a year in Paris—not in a Left Bank apartment but in a pleasant bourgeois old house in Neuilly with a garden where my year-and-a-half-old son Cameron could uproot the flowers.

"I came back, at John Crowe Ransom's invitation, to become editor of the *Kenyon Review* on his retirement. Except for a Guggenheim Fellowship year in London (1964–1965) and trips to Africa, Asia, South America, Eastern Europe, and once around the world, I have been there ever since. I have written a critical book (with George Lanning) called *Technique in Fiction* and am at work on a novel. I have contributed fiction or criticism to *The Best American Short Stories*, *The O. Henry Prize Stories*, *Esquire*, the *New Republic*, *Vogue*, *Encounter*, the *Partisan Review*, the New York *Times Book Review*, the *Herald Tribune Book Week*, *The Texas Quarterly*, and a number of other periodicals. I have edited a collection of the best short stories from the *Kenyon Review* which is to be followed by a collection of criticism from its pages."

———

Robie Macauley is the son of George and Emma (Hobart) Macauley. He received his B.A. from Kenyon College in 1941, his M.F.A. from the State University of Iowa in 1950.

The Disguises of Love is a novel about a psychology professor's love affair with a student, and tells its story by interweaving three first person narratives—the professor's, his wife's and his adolescent son's. The result, which was said to resemble the later work of Virginia Woolf, seemed to some reviewers excessively and pretentiously intricate, and one thought that Macauley had "managed to disguise love very effectively indeed." But the book had its champions, who found its manner "necessary and effective," its texture "peculiarly fine and absorbing." Betty Askwith, writing in the *New Statesman*, praised Macauley's control of his multiple narrative and thought his characters solidly drawn and clearly differentiated. She agreed that the book had little narrative momentum, but concluded that "it remains a genuine and original attempt at describing human relationships."

The End of Pity contained several stories drawn from Macauley's experiences in Counterintelligence, others about family and academic life. Reviews tended to give praise with one hand and take it away with the other, commending the author as a talented and intelligent observer of the contemporary scene, but regretting that his stories "often expire in anti-climax." John F. Sullivan, reviewing the collection for *Commonweal*, found in the title story and in several others a preoccupation with the dangers of pity which reminded him of Nathanael West's *Miss Lonelyhearts*. "It remains to be said," he went on, "that these stories are solidly constructed, that they manifest a remarkable narrative talent. The style is perhaps on the plain side, but for the most part it is simply unobtrusively fitted to its task." Macauley no doubt possesses "one of the finer talents in contemporary American writing," but has so far used it so little that the real extent of his capabilities remains undefined.

Macauley received the Furioso fiction prize in 1949. In the latter part of 1966 he relinquished the editorship of the *Kenyon Review* to become senior editor of *Playboy* magazine.

PRINCIPAL WORKS: The Disguises of Love (novel), 1952; The End of Pity (stories), 1957; (with George Lanning) Technique in Fiction, 1964; (ed.) Gallery of Modern Fiction: Stories From the Kenyon Review, 1966; (as compiler, with Larzer Ziff) America and Its Discontents, 1971.
ABOUT: Contemporary Authors 3, 1963; Vinson, J. (ed.) Contemporary Novelists, 1972; Who's Who in America, 1972–1973. *Periodicals*—Commonweal August 30, 1957; Critique Fall 1962; Library Journal October 1, 1952.

"MC BAIN, ED." *See* HUNTER, EVAN

MAC BETH, GEORGE (MANN) (January 19, 1932–), Scottish poet and editor, was born in Shotts, Lanarkshire, the son of George and Amelia (Mann) MacBeth. His parents died while he was still a child, a loss which has deeply affected him and his poetry. He has not forgotten his Scottish childhood and still regards England as "abroad," though he has spent most of his life there. He was educated at the King Edward School, Sheffield, and at New College, Oxford, where he earned first class honors in classics and philosophy. In 1955 he joined the British Broadcasting Corporation as a talks producer, and he has edited and introduced many programs about poetry and the arts, including "New Comment" (1959–1964), "The Poet's Voice" (1958–1965), and "Poetry Now" (1965–).

His early verse, collected in *A Form of Words* (1954), was in the "neat, sceptical" manner of the 1950s, but towards the end of that decade it began to show the concern with modern violence and horror that characterizes the work of "the Group" poets, whose regular readings and discussions MacBeth used to attend. Like his associates in that now-defunct movement, he came to believe that "unless you think that something is more important than poetry . . . [and] you use poetry to further that, then you won't write very good poetry."

MacBeth's own work at this time, appearing in magazines, was good enough to earn him very quickly a considerable reputation, confirmed by the publication in 1963 of his second book, *The Broken Places*. It was a recommendation of the Poetry Book Society and joint winner of the Faber Memorial Award. Some of these poems were autobiographical—many of them concerned with his dead parents, and full of macabre fantasies of death and guilt. Others were about war, fascism, and the atomic bomb. The book was widely admired for its technical virtuosity and vitality, the mordant wit and savage high spirits with which the poet confronted his grisly world. M. L. Rosenthal wrote that MacBeth's "dead-serious poems, on themes involving the horror of war, the meaning of Eichmann, private suffering . . . gain in sheer intelligent

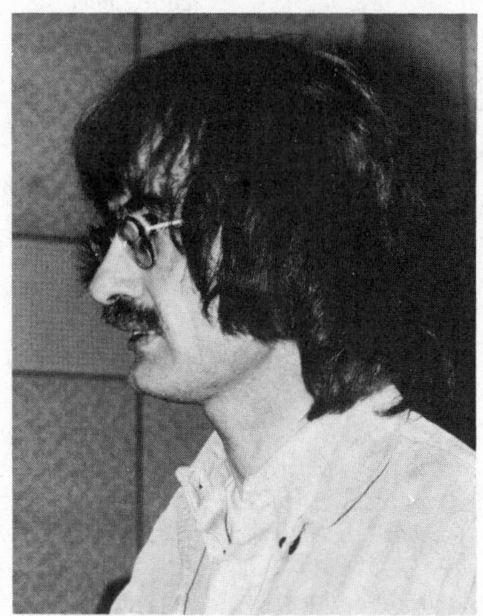

GEORGE MAC BETH

effervescence from his capacity for comic fantasy but by the same token lack a final conviction. Mind, sensibility, phrasing are pyrotechnically exploited; but the bright contriving that makes MacBeth's buffoonery so welcome also makes his more serious writing seem hollow, as though its conception was not truly his—not yet, at any rate."

This has been a persistent criticism of MacBeth's poetry. The parodies and word games in *A Doomsday Book* were enjoyed for their wit and cleverness, but it was a handful of more "ceremonially serious" poems that were most admired—like "The Return," in which the poet's father is seen beckoning him back to childhood and death, and one or two other pieces "where the personal self seems most thoroughly engaged." *The Colour of Blood*, the first of MacBeth's books to appear in the United States, convinced Ian Hamilton that his "real gift is for the bleak, nostalgically rhetorical adventure into past experience." But, as another critic wrote in his review of MacBeth's *Collected Poems*, experience is too often "held and frozen into a kind of hieratic mythology by those terse syntactical units and slow-moving rhythms, distanced by an attention to verbal 'texture' which continually runs the risk of self-absorption." Thus, while Peter Porter can speak of the author as "the most inventive poet of his generation in Britain" and say that "no poet writing today has put so much of the touchable surface of life into his poetry," another complains of "extraordinary gifts arrogantly wasted."

George MacBeth is an accomplished verse reader, as he has shown on radio and in many public readings. His own poetry lends itself very well to public performance, thanks to the regularity of his meters, the colloquial ease of much of his diction, and the immediacy of his images—like one in which he describes a bat flying "like a broken / umbrella." It may be, as he says, that working for radio has made him an aural poet, and his readings (and a taste for Victorian ballads) have increased this tendency and led him to experiment with dramatic monologues in verse. A collection of these and other pieces was assembled into a kind of revue called *A Doomsday Show*, and staged at the Establishment nightclub in London. He has also written several verse stories for children, and has edited a number of anthologies.

"If someone gave me a thousand pounds to go off and live in the wilds of Ireland for a year," he says, "I don't expect I would write a line. . . . I would come back to London and meet all my old friends and eat, drink and go to the cinema and theatre, and talk, and in the middle of the night, start writing poems as I do now." He likes his work as a BBC producer, and enjoys "the stimulus and excitement of being involved in practical concerns." He is a tall man with a moustache, and a detached, cheerful manner, who likes to shock his liberal friends with extreme right-wing views. He was married in 1955 to a scientist, Elizabeth Robson.

PRINCIPAL WORKS: A Form of Words, 1954; The Broken Places, 1963; Penguin Modern Poets 6 (with Jack Clemo and Edward Lucie-Smith), 1964; A Doomsday Book, 1965; Noah's Journey (for children), 1966; The Colour of Blood, 1967; The Night of Stones, 1968; A War Quartet, 1969; Jonah and the Lord (for children), 1969; The Burning Cone, 1970; The Dark Wind (for children), 1970; Collected Poems 1958–1970, 1971; The Orlando Poems, 1972; Lusus (lecture in verse), 1972; Shrapnel, 1973; A Poet's Year, 1973; My Scotland: Fragments of a State of Mind, 1973. *As editor*—The Penguin Book of Sick Verse, 1963; The Penguin Book of Animal Verse, 1965; Poetry, 1900 to 1965, 1967; The Penguin Book of Victorian Verse, 1969.

ABOUT: Murphy, R. (ed.) Contemporary Poets of the English Language, 1970; Orr, P. (ed.) The Poet Speaks, 1966; Rosenthal, M. L. The New Poets, 1967; Schmidt, M. and Lindop, G. (eds.) British Poetry Since 1960, 1972; Who's Who, 1973. *Periodicals*—London Magazine December 1963, October 1965; Scottish International August 1968; Times Literary Supplement July 29, 1965; December 5, 1968.

MAC CAIG, NORMAN (ALEXANDER) (November 14, 1910–), Scottish poet, writes: "Though I was born in Edinburgh and have lived nowhere else, my father was of West Highland stock and my mother a Hebridean, from Harris. This is important to me, as the Gaelic side of Scotland is the one I am closest to. The landscape, the language, the music, the people and their dying culture have always been of the deepest interest to me and I lose no chance of getting back amongst them.

"I was educated at the Royal High School in Edinburgh and read Classics at Edinburgh University. This discipline strengthened my inborn Celtic predilection for strict forms and elaborate techniques in the arts—the 'Celtic Twilight' nonsense is, of course, a myth. The music I listen to most, and I listen a lot, is that written up to Beethoven and after Bartók (including both these composers), though indeed I get a great deal of pleasure from a wide range of noises, from folksong and jazz to electronic music.

"I never found myself, as many Scottish poets do, psychologically maladjusted between the three languages spoken here—Scots, English and Gaelic. English is my spoken tongue and I feel no psychological or political urge to reject it. In fact, I am not a very political person at all, though my position, if I could be said to have one, is farther Left than Right. The only political question I'm apt to raise my voice about is the position of Scotland vis-à-vis England, which leaves much to be desired by a Scotsman. Many of my closest friends are, naturally, Scottish writers and they are Scottish Nationalists almost to a man, pushing their beliefs to a much more extreme length than I do.

"My childhood and schooldays were happy in an uneventful sort of way. Nothing traumatic happened, as seems to have happened to so many writers, so I've been able to continue to enjoy my life in a happy and uneventful way ever since, in spite of the intrusive finger of World Events. Fortunately at least for my peace of mind, amongst the handful of people that make up me you will fail to find an evangelist, so I escape the torturing frustrations of those who must mend the world. I'm not, of course, decrying them. I'm just saying I'm not a man of that sort. Thank goodness poetry can be made out of praise as well as out of suffering.

"I have been a schoolmaster all my adult life and am married, with two children, a boy and a girl—or rather, by this time, a man and a woman.

"As for public recognitions, the main ones were an Arts Council of Great Britain Award (for a collection of poems) and a Society of Authors Travelling Scholarship."

MacCaig was associated in the 1940s with the poets of the "New Apocalypse," but is most admired for his later work, that in *Riding Lights* and subsequent collections. He typically writes philosophical descriptive poems, drawing from his vividly evoked Scottish landscapes reminders of man's identity with the cosmos; or fine love poems which are also "inquiries into the essence of love." Cyril Connolly calls MacCaig "a metaphysical poet who relies on verbal key-shifts and telescoped imagery." Some critics, preferring his images to his metaphysics, wish he were content to remain a descriptive writer, leaving the "philosophizing to lesser poets."

Charles Tomlinson thinks MacCaig is "the one

NORMAN MAC CAIG

poet who survived from the New Apocalypse to write verse which, in its narrow but intense way, exhibits both a sense of philosophic comedy and a craggy integrity." The *Times Literary Supplement* has ranked him with Edwin Muir as one of the best of this century's Scottish poets writing in English. Most critics regard Donne and Wallace Stevens as the principal influences on MacCaig's poetry.

MacCaig is no longer a schoolmaster; since October 1967 he has been a Writing Fellow of Edinburgh University. He received a second Arts Council Award in 1966 and the Society of Authors Book Prize in 1967. He is a Fellow of the Royal Society of Literature. The author is the son of Robert MacCaig, a chemist. His wife is the former Isabel Munro, whom he married in 1940. He numbers among his close friends the Scottish Nationalist poets Hugh MacDiarmid and Sydney Goodsir Smith.

PRINCIPAL WORKS (all poems): Far Cry, 1943; The Inward Eye, 1947; Riding Lights, 1955; The Sinai Sort, 1957; (as ed.) Honour'd Shade: An Anthology of New Scottish Poetry, 1959; A Common Grace, 1960; A Round of Applause, 1962; Measures, 1965; Surroundings, 1966; Rings on a Tree, 1968; A Man in My Position, 1969; (as ed., with Alexander Scott) Contemporary Scottish Verse, 1959–1969, 1970; Selected Poems, 1971; The White Bird, 1973.

ABOUT: Allott, K. (ed.) The Penguin Book of Contemporary Verse, 1962; Contemporary Authors 9–10, 1964; Murphy, R. (ed.) Contemporary Poets of the English Language, 1970; Press, J. Rule & Energy, 1963.

"MC CANN, EDSON." *See* POHL, FREDERIK

HELEN MC CLOY

MC CLOY, HELEN (WORRELL CLARKSON) (June 6, 1904–), American detective story writer, writes: "I am one of the few people who can say that she was born within the city limits of the City of New York, though both my mother's and father's family came originally from Philadelphia and its environs. My mother's family were of English Quaker origin, and came to this country in the seventeenth century. My father's family were of Scottish Presbyterian origin and arrived much later, in the early 1800s. My father was for many years managing editor of the New York *Evening Sun.* Both he and my mother knew New York when the Fifth Avenue buses were drawn by horses. I can remember the hansom cabs in my childhood and the respect for the first skyscraper, the Woolworth building. I came naturally by my interest in writing for, in addition to a father who was an editor with many future writers on his staff (Algernon Blackwood, Irvin Cobb, Don Marquis to mention only three), my mother wrote short stores under her maiden name, Helen Clarkson.

"Theoretically, I received my education at the Brooklyn Friends School in New York and at the Sorbonne University in Paris (no degrees). Actually, my true education was acquired by living in London and Paris and, later, writing for English and American magazines and newspapers in Paris. I received my first check when I was fourteen from the Boston *Transcript* for a literary essay and my second check when I was fifteen from the New York *Times* for verse. My favorite market in those days was the old London *Morning Post.* It is sad to think that the *Times* is the only one of these brilliant newspapers still in existence.

"In 1953 I was lucky enough to receive an Edgar, an award in the form of a ceramic bust of Poe, from the Mystery Writers of America. I was the first woman president of that lively and enterprising organization. I am a devoted, though frequently absentee, member of the Overseas Press Club. I joined in the already far-off days when several years of consecutive service overseas was required for full membership.

"For a number of years I was married to Davis Dresser, who wrote the Michael Shayne stories under the pen-name of Brett Halliday. We have a daughter, Chloë, now eighteen years old. The nicest thing that was ever said about my writing was said by Jacques Barzun in the *American Scholar*: 'She has a superb narrative style.' That's the only thing I can think of off-hand. I am afraid that I am like Somerset Maugham: I don't read reviews, I measure them."

Miss McCloy's first novel, *Dance of Death,* was welcomed as a notably ingenious and truly exceptional mystery, full of promise. That promise has been amply realized in over a score of literate, witty, and erudite stories, a number of them featuring Miss McCloy's psychiatrist detective Basil Willing. Commenting on *Cue for Murder,* which has a show business background, Kay Irvin said it was "worked out with a beautiful efficiency and gripping interest, in all its clues and cues and happenings," and added: "Helen McCloy can not only make up a good mystery tale: she can write it as a good novel, with lively characterization, logical reasoning and satiric wit." *Cue for Murder* was included in James Sandoe's basic list of mysteries as an example of "excellent puzzling."

Having shown her mastery of the conventional detective story, Miss McCloy experimented in *She Walks Alone* and other books with tales in a more macabre and Gothic mood. Not all of her admirers welcomed this development, many of them feeling that her special talent was for plotting rather than the creation of atmosphere. Such doubts have been resolved for most reviewers by novels like *Through a Glass Darkly,* set in a girl's school, which shows all Miss McCloy's old skill in narrative and is at the same time fascinating in its paranormal lore. Anthony Boucher called it probably her best novel to date, and said she "has always resembled the best British writers of the Sayers-Blake-Allingham school in her ability to combine a warm novel of likeable people with a flawless deductive plot."

Miss McCloy was Paris correspondent of the Universal News Service in 1927–1931, and of the monthly art magazine *International Studio* in 1930–1931 (during which period she also served as London correspondent of the Sunday fine arts section of the New York *Times*). She was at one time president of Torquil and Company, a firm she founded with Davis Dresser, and for four years she was a partner in the literary agency Halliday and McCloy. The author has edited several anthologies of detective stories and has written articles about her craft. She says it is not "whodunit" that matters to her, but "How and why did he do it?"

PRINCIPAL WORKS: Dance of Death (England, Design for Dying), 1938; The Man in the Moonlight, 1940; The Deadly Truth, 1941; Who's Calling?, 1942; Cue for Murder, 1942; Do Not Disturb, 1943; The Goblin Market, 1943; Panic, 1944; The One That Got Away, 1945; She Walks Alone, 1948; Through a Glass Darkly, 1950; Alias Basil Willing, 1951; He Never Came Back, 1954; The Unfinished Crime, 1954; Long Body, 1955; Two-thirds of a Ghost, 1956; The Slayer and the Slain, 1957; Before I Die, 1963; Surprise, Surprise!, 1965; The Singing Diamonds (stories), 1965; The Further Side of Fear, 1967; Mister Splitfoot, 1968; A Question of Time, 1971; A Change of Heart, 1973.

ABOUT: Burke, W. J. and Howe, W. D. (eds.) American Authors and Books, 1962; Contemporary Authors 25–28, 1971.

HORACE MC COY

MC COY, HORACE (April 14, 1897–December 15, 1955), American novelist, was born in Pegram, Tennessee, and educated in Nashville. In adolescence he embarked on a random itinerary that took him through the South and Southwest in a variety of jobs, including door-to-door salesman, taxicab driver, and newspaper reporter. In World War I he served with the air force in France.

During the 1920s McCoy worked for the Dallas *Journal*, mostly as a baseball reporter. Periodically he took time off to journey by cattle boat to Paris where he became acquainted with many American literary expatriates, particularly F. Scott Fitzgerald and some of the writers for *Transition*. He began contributing short stories to *Hound and Horn*, *Southwest Review*, and other literary magazines. He was a talented actor and helped to found the Little Theatre in Dallas.

Lured by the money to be made in writing for motion pictures, McCoy went to Hollywood in 1931 and worked as a soda jerk, vegetable picker, and professional strikebreaker before becoming established as a writer of screenplays and adaptations.

His first and best novel was *They Shoot Horses, Don't They?* (1935). The story is recalled by a young man, Robert, as he listens to the reading of his own death sentence. Looking for work in Hollywood he had met Gloria, an embittered and corrupted girl redeemed only by her pitiless self-knowledge. Together they enter a dance marathon, the squalor and sadism of which is brilliantly realized in McCoy's flat, dispassionate account. This ordeal, and Gloria's spiritual exhaustion, destroy what remains of Robert's hope and idealism. When she asks him to help her to die, he shoots her as he might a maimed animal.

W. R. Benét thought it "a story of great power . . . as stripped-for-action as a racing car." Other American critics were reminded of the work of James M. Cain and Nathanael West. Some praised the book as an unforgettable image, recorded in "spare, unadorned prose," of human and social degradation; others thought it merely sensational. It sold well, according to its publishers, if only to "persons who enjoy hating it from the first page to the last," but made no great stir in America. In Europe, however, it became the object of real critical excitement, hailed particularly in France as a major novel by "the first American existentialist." For a time during the 1940s McCoy was ranked with Hemingway and Faulkner among the American writers most admired in France. American critics have never gone so far, but sixteen years after its publication Henry R. Warfel was able to write that the book had become "a minor American classic." In 1969 it was made into a grimly memorable film.

None of McCoy's subsequent novels matched his first. *No Pockets in a Shroud*, first published in England, with an introduction by Evelyn Waugh, was about the opposition of "respectable" elements in a small town to a journalist's crusade against crime, vice, and the Ku Klux Klan. *I Should Have Stayed Home* returned to the theme and setting of *They Shoot Horses . . .*, showing how two decent ambitious young people are corrupted by Hollywood. It was followed ten years later by *Kiss Tomorrow Good-bye*, telling the story of a well-educated man of some sensibility who becomes an amoral cold-hearted criminal; it was his most ambitious attempt to express the "lyrical quality" he found in evil and violence, but was greatly disliked by most reviewers. McCoy's last novel, *Scalpel*, has as its narrator a successful but self-doubting surgeon who finds himself through an act of heroism. Earle Walbridge thought it "vivid, readable, and not a little specious."

McCoy died at his home in Beverly Hills, California, of a heart ailment. He was survived by his wife, Helen, his sons, Horace and Peter, and his daughter, Amanda. His novels, and especially his first novel, often reprinted in hard cover, attracted renewed interest as paperbacks in the 1960s.

PRINCIPAL WORKS: *Novels*—They Shoot Horses, Don't They?, 1935; No Pockets in a Shroud, 1937 (England only; U.S. [rev. version], 1948); I Should Have Stayed Home, 1938; Kiss Tomorrow Good-bye, 1948; Scalpel, 1952; Corruption City (screen treatment, filmed as The Turning Point), 1959.

ABOUT: Adams, D. K. (ed.) The Mystery and Detection Annual, 1972; Madden, D. (ed.) Tough Guy Writers of the Thirties, 1968; Warfel, H. R. American Novelists of Today, 1951. *Periodicals*—New York Times December 17, 1955; Publishers' Weekly December 31, 1955; Wilson Library Bulletin February 1956.

"MAC CREIGH, JAMES." *See* POHL, FREDERIK

MACDONALD, DWIGHT (March 24, 1906–), American essayist and critic, was born in New York City. Both his father and his grandfather were lawyers. At Phillips Exeter Academy, Macdonald published his first short story ("Sir Harry," in the *PEA Monthly*) and launched his first magazine. This was *Masquerade*, which was noted, he says, for its "extreme preciosity." He graduated from Phillips Exeter in 1924 and went to Yale, where he majored in history, was active in college journalism, and received his B.A. in 1928. There his closest friend was Fred Dupee, who shared his enthusiasm for Proust, Joyce, Spengler, Henry James, and Irving Babbitt. Just after they left Yale, from 1930 to 1933, Macdonald, Dupee, and a few others published a small and rather dilettantish literary review, *The Miscellany*.

Meanwhile, Macdonald had begun his career as a trainee executive at Macy's. He disliked it, and in March 1929 joined the staff of Luce's new magazine *Fortune*, where he remained, as staff writer and editor, for seven years. This experience confirmed his "undergraduate suspicions" that "the men running our capitalist system were narrow, uncultivated and commonplace." After he left *Fortune* in June 1936, Macdonald moved rapidly to the left. Dupee introduced him to Philip Rahv and William Phillips, and he began to read and think his way towards a radical Marxist position.

In December 1937 Macdonald joined with Rahv, Phillips, Dupee, Mary McCarthy, and George L. K. Morris to revive the *Partisan Review*. By then Macdonald was attracted to Trotskyism; according to J. B. Gilbert's *Writers and Partisans*, Trotsky "appealed to Macdonald's half-aristocratic, half-anarchistic critique of capitalism and his highly intellectualized radicalism." In 1938 he began to write for the Trotskyist *New International* and from 1939 to 1941 was an active member of the American Trotskyist movement.

During Macdonald's years as one of the editors of the new *Partisan Review*, that magazine became established as the principal forum and voice of the American anti-Stalinist intellectual elite. In its pages, Gibson says, Macdonald developed "a new style of political journalism and a form of cultural muckraking which examined the faults and virtues of popular culture . . . and explored the presumed degeneration of mass taste." His attacks on the vulgarity of Hollywood and on the bourgeois inadequacies of the *New Yorker* are notable examples of his manner. But Macdonald, a natural anarchist, was never entirely at one with his fellow editors. In 1940 he was urging "skepticism toward all theories, governments, and social systems," and when the United States entered World War II he was appalled by those in the intellectual establishment who insisted that culture must now harness itself to the war effort. He opposed American participation in the war, broke with his *Partisan* colleagues on this and other issues, and resigned in 1943.

In February of the following year he and his first wife, the former Nancy Rodman, launched a new magazine, *Politics*. It survived until 1949 and was reprinted in 1968. Commenting at that time on the magazine's "astounding" continued relevance, Hannah Arendt credited Macdonald's "extraordinary flair for significant fact and significant thought, from which followed his flair in the choice of contributors"—they included Albert Camus, Simone Weil, James Agee, Paul Goodman, John Berryman, Mary McCarthy, and Marianne Moore. *Politics* reflected step by step Macdonald's disenchantment with Marxism, his search for a "third-camp" position, his temporary espousal of a belief that "political action must be reduced to a personal level," and his eventual loss of faith in even this kind of political action. By 1952, when he joined the staff of the *New Yorker*, he had thrown in his lot with the West. This gradual but complete *volte-face* was the painful but perhaps inevitable outcome of Macdonald's fastidious intellectual integrity, and it has not inhibited his continuing critique of Western political, moral, and cultural values.

Dwight Macdonald's progress from "buyer of

political nostrums" to his present "rather agnostic view" (as it has been called) of men and politics, is reflected in *Memoirs of a Revolutionist*, a generous selection of his political essays. Charles Rolo said that "while his reasoning strikes me as frequently fallacious, perverse, or merely a matter of hair-splitting, his writing is an unfailing delight; he is quite possibly the wittiest and liveliest polemicist on the American scene."

Against the American Grain collects Macdonald's literary and cultural essays, including "Masscult and Midcult," which elucidates the attitudes underlying all his critical writings. His unfashionable thesis is that popular culture, "manufactured for the market," is intrinsically bad because it offers distraction, not re-creation. And above the "dead sea of masscult" lies "midcult," beachcombing along the tidelines of high culture, collecting and corrupting what it can use. Macdonald's favorite targets are such classics of midcult as Hemingway's *Old Man and the Sea*, James Gould Cozzens' *By Love Possessed*, and Thornton Wilder's *Our Town*. His attacks on them are devastating, provocative, and witty; it is true to say that they have not been cogently answered. He now advocates the definition of two cultures, one for the masses and one for an intellectual (but not, emphatically not, a social or economic) elite.

This thesis is not new, but Macdonald's presentation of it is. Those he has enraged are mostly purveyors of midcult; it is from members of what he himself would recognize as the elite that he has attracted serious criticism. Conor Cruise O'Brien, while agreeing with most of his conclusions about specific writers, criticized his analysis of masscult as "confused by a tendency to run together 'the masses' and those who manipulate them." And he has remarked that Macdonald's "prose remains free to flow . . . between those fat walls of advertising [in the *New Yorker*] which symbolize the limitations of his freedom." It was O'Brien who wrote that "there was a time when Dwight Macdonald . . . might have been thought of as an American Orwell," and his charge is sympathetically made: "I do not claim that Mr. Macdonald is in any way insincere . . . but I don't think he fully realizes the coercive force of the restrictions which he has accepted." The question remains an open one, complicated by the fact that all writers, whether of midcult or of the elite, have to eat. And if Macdonald's critical mode "can be questioned at the level of premise," as Malcolm Bradbury believes, he is nevertheless a formidable critic—nonacademic, but scholarly and detailed, in a manner that is very much "in the American grain."

In addition to his essays, Macdonald has published a "highly personalized" study of Henry Wallace, an original and often very funny examination of the Ford Foundation and its work, a critique of the Warren Report on the assassination of President Kennedy, and a splendid anthology of parodies. He was awarded a Guggenheim Fellowship in 1962 to prepare his selection of the poems of Edgar Allan Poe, and was elected a fellow of the American Academy of Arts and Sciences in the same year. Apart from his work for the *New Yorker*, he was *Esquire*'s demanding (and frequently disappointed) film critic from 1960 to 1966, and has published a collection of his reviews. Since then he has contributed a political column to the same magazine, writing as what he calls a "conservative anarchist." He gave courses on movie history at the University of Texas in 1966 and at the University of California, Santa Cruz, in 1969.

DWIGHT MACDONALD

Macdonald has two sons by his first marriage, which ended in divorce. He was married again in the early 1950s to Gloria Kaufman, an art historian. His views have led him to defend "the deliberate, public and nonviolent breaking of a law because to obey it would be to betray a higher morality." In 1968 he was one of six intellectuals named as conspirators with Dr. Benjamin Spock in counseling young men to evade the draft.

PRINCIPAL WORKS: Henry Wallace: The Man and the Myth, 1948; The Root Is Man: Two Essays in Politics, 1950; The Ford Foundation: The Men and the Millions, 1956; Memoirs of a Revolutionist, 1957 (republished as Politics Past, 1970); (ed.) Parodies: An Anthology from Chaucer to Beerbohm, 1960; Against the American Grain, 1962; The Ghost of Conspiracy, 1965; (ed.) Poems of Edgar Allan Poe, 1965; Dwight Macdonald on Movies, 1969; (ed.) My Past and Thoughts: The Memoirs of Alexander Herzen, 1973.

ABOUT: Current Biography, 1969; Gilbert, J. B. Writers and Partisans, 1968; Lasch, C. The New Radicalism in

America, 1965; Macdonald, D. Memoirs of a Revisionist, 1957; Mailer, N. The Armies of the Night, 1968; Podhoretz, N. Doings and Undoings, 1964. *Periodicals*—Harper's December 1957; Nation March 15, 1958; April 29, 1961; New Republic February 24, 1958; March 17, 1958; New Society June 6, 1963; New Statesman June 28, 1963; Newsweek April 28, 1958; November 26, 1962; Reporter February 6, 1958; Saturday Review November 16, 1957; August 13, 1960; March 9, 1963; Time January 13, 1961; January 4, 1963; Times Literary Supplement June 14, 1963.

MAC DONALD, JOHN D(**ANN**) (July 24, 1916–), American detective story writer, writes: "I was born in Sharon, Pennsylvania. My father was a corporation executive, doing accounting and financial work. I have a younger sister. When I was twelve my father went with a company in Utica, New York. My mother and my married sister still live in Utica.

"I went to the public schools in Sharon and Utica, and after graduation from high school, attended the Wharton School of Finance at the University of Pennsylvania. I left abruptly after a year and a half and worked for a time in New York City at whatever I could find. I went to Syracuse University, and from there to the Harvard Graduate School of Business Administration where I received a master's degree.

"I met and married Dorothy Prentiss while at Syracuse, and our only child, Maynard John Prentiss MacDonald, was born while I was at Harvard.

"I had brief and mutually unsatisfactory encounters with several employers, and then accepted a commission as a lieutenant in the Ordnance Department of the Army in June 1940. I spent two and a half years in the China-Burma-India Theater, the latter portion with the Office of Strategic Services, and was discharged as a Lieutenant Colonel in January of 1946.

"While overseas I wrote a short story in lieu of a letter to Dorothy, hoping to amuse and entertain her. She typed it and submitted it to Whit Burnett of *Story Magazine*, who purchased it for twenty-five dollars. I did not learn of this until she met me at Fort Dix.

"Instead of seeking work I decided that I would be a writer. Our cushion was four months of terminal leave with pay. During those four months I wrote over a quarter of a million words of finished manuscript, all in short story form. I kept from thirty to forty stories in the mail at all times. I worked fourteen hours a day, seven days a week, and lost a noticeable amount of weight. I believe that, except for Dorothy, I was thought of as a readjustment problem.

"One learns only by writing. I compressed years of learning into a very few months. By the end of 1946 it became clear to us that I could support us by writing alone, and this has been our only source of income ever since. We lived in upstate New York, in Texas, in Mexico, and have lived in Florida since 1949.

"When I was a child I was continually being torn away from my books and herded out into the sunlight, into the dreary glare of reality. I required glasses quite young. In high school and in college I had the wistful feeling that I would like to write, but could not really believe that I could ever make that magic which I read so compulsively. This hesitancy kept me from making the try until I was nearly thirty.

"Now I cannot imagine being anything else or doing anything else. I feel like an impostor twice over. When my publishers and my agent tell me that over thirty-seven million copies of my sixty books have been sold all over the world, I cannot relate such an absurdity to this quite solitary adventure of trying, every time, to reach a little further, tell it more validly and simply. Learning is a constant, but it goes so slowly that impatience often becomes a kind of despair.

"The second feeling of imposture arises from my being aware of my own automatic, unconscious watchfulness. Memory and sensory perceptions provide excellent in-put and storage. The paradox is in being so attuned to reality, so anxious to write novels which create the illusion of reality, stress, randomness and man's sad and comical gallantry, that one stands a little aside from all the direct impact of life. I suspect that were I to be executed, I would watch and weigh each quantum of panic and despair, checking it for sincerity and usability.

"I work long each day, and usually have at least three books in various stages of clumsiness, letting the subconscious mind untie the knots of the ones on the shelf while I work on the one in front of me. I revise by throwing out whole chapters, sections, even whole books, and starting again—a device which seems to enhance freshness. I fight to keep from becoming too ornate, the most egocentric form of author-intrusion. I tend to neaten things up too carefully at the end. Many of my solutions are too glib.

"But the joy, of course, is in doing thirty or forty passable pages and then doing just one or two where everything works just a little bit better than you have ever been able to make it work before, and thus says more than the words themselves say. And the chance of more such pages is the carrot, forever just out of reach."

MacDonald's early sales, in the mid-1940s, were mainly to the pulp magazines—adventure, sports, mystery, western, and science fiction stories. Since his first book, *The Brass Cupcake*, appeared in 1950, he has published some sixty novels. A few of his early books, like *Wine of the Dreamers* (1951) and *Ballroom of the Skies* (1952), are readable and provocative science fiction, but the vast majority are thrillers. Fifteen of these (as of 1973) recount the exploits of Travis McGee, a hard-bitten but quixotic private detective whose home base is a Florida houseboat. These tough, sexy, and intricately plotted thrillers are written on a lower level, intellectually and stylistically, than Raymond Chandler's Philip Marlowe stories, but are in the same tradition and, since ten million McGees were in print in 1972, are evidently no less readable.

Other MacDonald stories are in a genre which Anthony Boucher once described as the author's "patented combination of the novel, the thriller, the puzzle and the social commentary." A notably successful example is *The Executioners* (1958, filmed and reprinted as *Cape Fear*). Its hero is not a detective but a successful lawyer, leading a happy suburban life with his wife and children. Many years before he had been responsible for the conviction of a GI rapist, and his security crumbles abruptly with the release of this monster, who arrives in town intent on revenge and begins a long murderous game of cat and mouse. As one reviewer said, the book "takes a deeper look than most suspense novels at the problem of private and public justice." Anne Ross called it "an exciting story which keeps you reading from start to finish. MacDonald is no practitioner of the distinguished style or the sensitive detail, but he can spin an expert yarn." There was even more critical enthusiasm for *A Flash of Green*, which studies the defeat of a group of conservationists by local businessmen who want to develop (and destroy) a beautiful bay. The result seemed to one English reviewer "an exceptionally good novel about the corruption of the human spirit."

Not all of MacDonald's books are novels. *The House Guests* (1965) is an agreeable portrait of the MacDonalds' pets, and *No Deadly Drug* is a detailed and very objective record of the 1966 trial for murder of Dr. Carl Coppolino.

It is some measure of MacDonald's popularity that Anthony Boucher in 1967 was able to report the existence of the *JDM Bibliophile*, a California magazine "which attempts to straighten out the almost infinitely complex bibliography of John D. (who doesn't know some of the answers himself)." The short list of titles below is the author's own modest selection of "the few which might properly be mentioned."

MacDonald is a big man, over six feet tall. He likes to watch pro football, hockey, and bullfighting, and himself enjoys many sports, including skiing, fishing, and sailing. He has given up bridge and golf because they take up too much of his time, but is an ardent poker player and a photographer of semiprofessional caliber. MacDonald is a former president of the Mystery Writers of America and received the MWA's Grand Master Award in 1972.

JOHN D. MAC DONALD

PRINCIPAL WORKS: *Fiction*—Cancel All Our Vows, 1953; The Executioners, 1958 (reprinted as Cape Fear); The End of the Night, 1960; A Key to the Suite, 1962; A Flash of Green, 1962; The Last One Left, 1967. *Nonfiction*—No Deadly Drug, 1968.

ABOUT: Contemporary Authors 2, 1963; Madden, D. (ed.) Tough Guy Writers of the Thirties, 1968; Moffat, L. and Moffat, J. (eds.) The JDM Master Checklist, 1969; Who's Who in America, 1972–1973. *Periodicals*—Army Times February 28, 1968; Best Sellers October 1, 1968; Chicago Daily News September 6–7, 1969; JDM Bibliophile March 1965—; National Observer September 23, 1968; New York Times Book Review March 3, 1968; September 22, 1968; New Yorker June 22, 1963; Publishers Weekly March 27, 1972; Tampa Tribune April 6, 1969; Time February 17, 1967.

"MACDONALD, ROSS." *See* MILLAR, KENNETH

MC GIVERN, WILLIAM P(ETER) (December 6, 1920–), American novelist, writes: "My point of origin was Chicago, but I grew up in Mobile, Alabama. Racial tensions weren't evident then, if memory serves. However, southern friends persisted in explaining the problems to us with such exhaustive lucidity (fearing no doubt that as northerners we were likely to confusion in this area) that it became ineluctably clear, to me at least, that they were protesting far and 'way too much. My father was invited to join the Klan, as if it were the Rotary or the Lions. He was the son and grandson of Iowa farmers, and loathed the soil and loved the city; he wore Prince Albert coats on occasion, owned three tall hats, and was a

WILLIAM P. MC GIVERN

frustrated opera singer-cum-business man; but essentially, I think, a serious person. My mother, Julia Costello, was a dress-maker and dress-designer long before ready-to-wear; her shop, Madame Julia's, was on South Michigan Boulevard, Chicago and she traveled to Paris at least twice to buy materials for her customers, and to attend the openings.

"I have an older brother, Francis M. The tone of our home was Catholic; loud with music, though not precisely musical, and discussion was encouraged. The Depression put an end to the tall hats, and threaded the discussion with frustration; inconclusive, speculative examinations of the immaterial (to which my father was addicted) suddenly were irrelevant.

"I began writing (after quitting high school) in what was at first a largely futile effort to flesh out the very small money I was paid as a laborer by the Pullman Company. (This was back once more in Chicago.) I worked in the Pennsy yards on Twelfth Street (later Roosevelt Boulevard), hauling iron from the street level to rip tracks in the yard. Elliptical springs, journal boxes, draw-bars, etc. My co-workers were Negroes, for the most part. Racial tensions were now more apparent—to me and anyone with his eyes open. This was 1937 to 1939, the three years I was in the yards.

"I read a good deal in this time. Wolfe, Hemingway, Fitzgerald, G. K. Chesterton, Robert Burns, Hawthorne. These are the writers I remember best, Thomas Wolfe in particular.

"I began selling to the pulp magazine market in 1940 (*Amazing Stories*, *Short Stories*, etc.). I served three and a half years in the United States Army, made Sergeant, was in charge of a forty-millimeter gun section, was decorated (Soldier's Medal, four campaign stars) and left the service in January, 1946, spending the last four months at the University of Birmingham in England.

"I worked for two years as police reporter for the *Philadelphia Bulletin*, and became interested in policemen and detectives, and the methodical, cut-and-dried nature of big-city corruption. I wrote three crime novels on this general subject (*The Big Heat*, *Rogue Cop* and *The Darkest Hour*) which were made into films starring, respectively, Glenn Ford, Robert Taylor and Alan Ladd.

"Since that time I have written other books, one (titled *Mention My Name in Mombasa*) in collaboration with my wife, Maureen Daly, which touched on our travels in Spain, Africa, Ireland and France, areas in which we lived, on and off, for about eight years.

"We now live (with our son and daughter, Patrick and Megan) on a non-working farm in Chester County, Pennsylvania, bought in part with the sale of *The Big Heat* to the *Saturday Evening Post* and which I was just about physically restrained from calling Crooked Copse.

"Writers tend to keep balance sheets of how much has been written, how much has been sold, etc. (See Matthew Arnold, the Goncourts). Mine would look like this: three hundred magazine pieces (*Blue Book*, *Cosmopolitan*, *Saturday Evening Post*, *Collier's*, *True*, *Show*, *Jour de France*, etc.). Twenty books, published in hard-covered editions (and pocket sizes) in the United States, France, England, Holland, Spain, Italy, Japan, Portugal, Denmark, Germany, etc.). Eleven books have been bought by various motion picture studios, but only eight made into films. Thirty TV scripts (*Kraft*, *Slattery's People*, etc. and three pilot scripts) and two screenplays.

"I talk to writing classes each year at the University of North Carolina, under the sponsorship of Jessie Rehder and Albrecht Strauss, whom I met at the University of Birmingham after the war. I have learned one thing about writing, I think; which is that unless the writer works in areas that interest him, he's in for a rough and boring time of it. An inference from this, true for me at any rate, is that it pays to look hard and intelligently for things to be interested in."

McGivern's novels are distinguished from the general ruck of crime melodramas not only by their skill, pace, and power, but also by virtues rarer in the genre. He has been praised in particular for the sensitivity of his characterization and for the wry humanity which informs his work.

These qualities were noticed in his work from the beginning, but it was *The Big Heat* and *Rogue*

Cop—both notable for their expert knowledge of police work, their "great insight and power," and both concerned with gangsters and corrupt cops—which established him. Anthony Boucher called *Rogue Cop* "a classic study in guilt, retribution and atonement." The most notable of his subsequent books have included *Odds Against Tomorrow*, admired as a novel of character (and of race) as much as for its brilliantly contrived suspense, and *Savage Streets*. The latter is set in a Long Island suburb whose model citizens, banding together against two teen-age hoodlums, exhibit qualities which raise disturbing questions about "the nature of justice and responsibility."

Dorothy Hughes has said that McGivern brought a "thoughtful, intelligent and new approach to the school of mystery inaugurated by Hammett"; that his writing is "hard but not tough . . . steel but not scrap." McGivern's combination of excitement and sardonic wit has reminded some readers of James M. Cain. He has been accused of a tendency to "liberal moralizing" and, in some of his early books, of a certain stylistic woolliness.

In some of his later work, McGivern has successfully combined high excitement and high comedy, notably in *The Caper of the Golden Bulls*, described by Anthony Boucher as "exquisitely planned, unfailingly inventive, rich in well-felt (if badly spelled) Spanish color, and more fun than a barrel of *toros*." McGivern's wife, Maureen Daly, is the author of *Seventeenth Summer* and other notable books for young people. Their joint travel memoir, *Mention My Name in Mombasa*, was greatly enjoyed and called "observant, articulate and often witty." The William P. McGivern Collection was established at the University of Boston in 1966 and will include manuscripts, notes, diaries, and other papers.

PRINCIPAL WORKS: *Novels*—But Death Runs Faster, 1948; Heaven Ran Last, 1949; Very Cold for May, 1950; Shield for Murder, 1951; Crooked Frame, 1952; The Big Heat, 1953; Margin of Terror, 1953; Rogue Cop, 1954; The Darkest Hour, 1955; The Seven File, 1956; Night Extra, 1957; Odds Against Tomorrow, 1957; Savage Streets, 1959; Seven Lies South, 1959; The Road to the Snail, 1961; A Choice of Assassins, 1963; The Caper of the Golden Bulls, 1966; Lie Down, I Want to Talk to You, 1967; Caprifoil, 1972; Reprisal, 1973. *Nonfiction*—(with Maureen Daly) Mention My Name in Mombasa, 1958.

ABOUT: Who's Who in the East, 1964–65. *Periodicals*—Philadelphia Sunday Bulletin July 10, 1960.

***MACHADO (RUIZ), ANTONIO** (July 26, 1875–February 22, 1939), Spanish poet, was born in Seville, the second son of Antonio Machado Álvarez and Ana Ruiz. Both his father and grandfather were well-known radical intellectuals and when the family moved to Madrid in 1883

* mä chä′ thō

ANTONIO MACHADO

Machado was sent to the Institución Libre de Enseñanza, a progressive school for whose teachers he later expressed "lively affection and profound gratitude." Family ties would always remain strong: Machado's mother and his brother Manuel, also a poet, were to be his constant companions. His insistence on personal relationships and his political radicalism both stem from a careful, if comfortable, upbringing.

The deaths of Machado's father (1893) and grandfather (1895) left the family in straitened circumstances. Machado could not be sent to university and for the next few years he led a somewhat bohemian life: he contributed articles to a newspaper, did a little acting, and worked for publishers in Madrid and Paris, which he visited in 1899 and 1902, meeting Oscar Wilde and Jean Moréas. Machado's early verse, published in ephemeral reviews at the turn of the century, shows the influence of Verlaine and Darío and the introverted melancholy and sensuous musicality of *modernismo*. These excesses were tempered in *Soledades* (1903), and the expanded *Soledades, galerías y otros poemas* (Soledades, Galleries and Other Poems, 1907), explorations of the "galleries" of his own mind in which Machado's mature attitudes and manner are established. This poetry is the product not of an adolescence of adventure and fulfillment but one of adult despair. His "loveless youth" was "never lived" in any real sense. Feeling a void, "the soul of the poet turns towards mystery." But the basic enigmas—time, death, God—lie beyond the comprehension of "the poor dreamer forever seeking God amidst the fog." The *Angst* and melancholy are most typically conveyed by simple, universal images—gardens and parks, above all at dusk; fountains and clocks, conveying the inexorable passage of time; roads, representing life; the sea, traditionally in Spain the symbol of death.

In 1907 Machado left the hothouse world of literary Madrid to take up an appointment as teacher of French at the State School in Soria, on the cold highlands north of Madrid. The gaunt landscape of Castile entered his poetry and his dreams, becoming, J. M. Cohen says, "a landscape of nature and the spirit together, of vision and of memory." At Soria Machado fell in love with and married Leonor, the sixteen-year-old daughter of his landlady. As his understanding of the Castilian people grew, his distress at their physical and spiritual impoverishment brought a note of radical political protest into his verse which links him with Azorín, Unamuno, and the Generation of 1898. In *Campos de Castilla* (Plains of Castile, 1912), still obsessed with time and death, the poet recognizes as their victim not only himself but Spain: "Wretched Castile, yesterday dominant, wrapped in her rags despises all she does not know."

Machado never lost his profound concern for the land and people of Spain, but his personal philosophy was to be matured in adversity. In 1911 he and Leonor visited Paris, where Machado attended Bergson's lectures. But Leonor fell ill on Bastille Day and died in Soria the following year. For Machado this was a nearly mortal blow: "Lord, Thou hast torn from me what I most loved." He moved to a teaching post at Baeza, an Andalusian backwater, and there wrote the poems of loss and absence included in the augmented 1917 edition of *Campos de Castilla*: "Silvered hills, / gray heights, dark violet rocks / where the Duero twists / a bow around Soria, somber oaks, / fierce stony ground, bald peaks, / white roads and river poplars, / Sorian afternoons, mystical and warlike, / today I feel deep sadness for you, / sadness of love . . . ."

Machado was now experiencing a still sharper sense of personal and national decline and nihilism, memorably evoking the sterility and hypocrisy of provincial life, yet hopeful of remedies, both spiritual and political: "I believe in liberty and in hope, and in a faith that is born when one seeks a God and does not come to one." From 1915 Machado was in his spare time taking a philosophy degree at Madrid University, and, in spite of his conscientious efforts to remain a "poet of the people," his use of folk song and other popular forms, his personal vision of the problems of time and death was maturing into a kind of pre-existentialism, indebted at least as much to Bergson and Heidegger as to Spanish popular wisdom. His philosophy is embedded in the epigrammatic "Proverbs and Songs" which appeared first in *Campos de Castilla* and later in *Nuevas canciones* (New Songs, 1924), his last complete book of verse.

After World War I, Machado had secured a teaching appointment in Segovia, and was once more closer to Madrid and its literary world. The years in Baeza had been vital in his development: as Tuñón de Lara emphasized, by the time he left Baeza "Machado's intellectual personality [was] complete." And by now he was a celebrity. His shabby figure, unkempt and uncaring, was recognized everywhere. In the 1920s he and his brother Manuel had a number of verse plays successfully produced and in 1927 Machado was elected to the Royal Academy, though he never took up his seat. From 1928 he was, less publicly, engaged in a passionate affair with "Guiomar," the poetess Pilar Valderrama, which brought a final flowering of Machado's poetry at its best.

He was now devoting much of his time to the essay, above all to the thoughts and observations of two imaginary philosophers, the erotic metaphysician Abel Martín and his disciple Juan de Mairena, a rhetorician who invents a poetry-writing machine. Their comments on metaphysics, poetics, and politics appeared in *Juan de Mairena* (1936). Their utterances, in H. T. Young's words "simultaneously frustrating and rewarding," are a vehicle for Machado's own views, which are of most interest when he deals with contemporary literature. Machado had often attacked the direction in which poetry seemed to be moving. Accepting Ortega's diagnosis of the dehumanization of art, he deplored the hermeticism of Guillén and the other poets of the 1927 Generation. Poetry was for Machado "the essential word in time," a kind of dialogue between the poet's "inner world" and the changing exterior reality. The Modern Movement, he thought, rejected this emotional dialogue; the contemporary lyric was full of "conceptual thought"; it suffered from "detemporalization," from "the use of images as pure intellectual games."

Machado's severe analysis did not prevent his being venerated by the younger poets, for whom he was always "Don Antonio." The advent of the Republic brought him to Madrid and his courage, Republican devotion, and lifelong socialism made him a kind of radical saint. Though rejecting Marxism, Machado and his family—apart from Manuel, who supported Franco—remained in Loyalist Spain during the Civil War and were staunch defenders of its cause. His last poems were laments—on the death of Lorca, the death of a wounded child, on the destruction and suffering of beloved cities and villages. The Republican collapse brought Machado's death. The flight from Barcelona proved too much for his constitution and he died in Collioure, just across the French border, on Ash Wednesday, 1939. His mother died three days later.

Since the Civil War Machado's reputation and influence have increased as the Spanish lyric has moved to a position of commitment and awareness of the "temporal" problems that so preoccupied him. In notes published posthumously, Machado emphasized the importance of content, of uncluttered poetic diction, and predicted a return to "objectivity on the one hand and fraternity on the other." This prophecy has proved wholly accurate. For J. M. Castellet, Machado is the indisputable master of the young poets because of his "intellectual stature, his honesty and the accuracy of his predictions regarding the future of poetry." To some extent he has become a cult figure, praised and glossed by critic and poet alike.

Jiménez said: "He always held within himself as much of death as of life, halves fused together by ingenuous artistry. . . . I have never known anyone else who so balanced these levels, equal in height or depth, as he did, and who by his living-dying overcame the gaps between these existences." Henry Gifford has written: "The eminence of Antonio Machado, a mind erect in its solitude, comes from character—his own, and that of the severe and practical language that never fails him. Beauty of tone animates his plainest verses, rectitude of design controls them, brevity and reticence are their guardians. He is the master of unobtrusive grace and of quiet finality."

PRINCIPAL WORKS IN ENGLISH TRANSLATION: Eighty Poems of Antonio Machado (tr. by W. Barnstone), 1959; Juan de Mairena: Epigrams, Maxims, Memoranda, and Memoirs of an Apocryphal Professor (tr. by Ben Belitt), 1963; Castilian Ilexes: Versions from Antonio Machado (tr. by H. G. Gifford and C. Tomlinson), 1963. *Poems in* Barnstone, W. (ed.) Modern European Poetry, 1966; Burnshaw, S. (ed.) The Poem Itself, 1960; Cohen, J. M. (ed.) Penguin Book of Spanish Verse, 1956; Flores, A. (ed.) An Anthology of Spanish Poetry, 1961; Lewis, R. (ed.) Still Waters of the Air, 1970; McVan, A. J. Antonio Machado, 1959; Trend, J. B. Antonio Machado, 1953.

ABOUT: Alonso, D. Poetas españoles contemporáneos, 1952; Burnshaw, S. (ed.) The Poem Itself, 1960; Cano, J. L. Poesía española del siglo XX, 1960; Castellet, J. M. Un cuarto de siglo de poesía española, 1966; Cohen, J. M. Poetry of This Age, 1966; Curley, D. N. and Curley, A. (eds.) Modern Romance Literatures (Library of Literary Criticism), 1967; Macrì, O. *introduction to* Poesie di Antonio Machado, 1962; McVan, A. J. Antonio Machado, 1959; Peers, E. A. Antonio Machado, 1940; Penguin Companion to Literature 2, 1969; Pérez Ferrero, M. Vida de Antonio Machado y Manuel, 1952; Sánchez Barbudo, A. Los poemas de Antonio Machado, 1968; Serrano Poncela, S. Antonio Machado, su mundo y su obra, 1954; Trend, J. B. Antonio Machado, 1953; Tuñón de Lara, M. Antonio Machado, 1967; Young, H. T. The Victorious Expression, 1964; Zubiría, R. de. La poesía de Antonio Machado, 1955. *Periodicals*—Antioch Review Fall 1958; Comparative Literature Summer 1962; Hispania March 1966; Hispanic Review July 1962; Hudson Review Summer 1962; Journal of Aesthetics Winter 1963; Modern Language Notes March 1963, March 1965; Nation April 18, 1966; PMLA March 1956, May 1964; Poetry February 1963, December 1964; Symposium Summer 1965; Times Literary Supplement January 16, 1969.

COLIN MAC INNES

MAC INNES, COLIN (August 20, 1914–), British novelist and essayist, was born in London sixteen days after the outbreak of World War I. He is the son of the distinguished Bach singer James Campbell MacInnes and of the former Angela Mackail. After his parents' divorce his mother remarried, and became famous as the novelist Angela Thirkell. Colin MacInnes is a great-grandson of Burne-Jones, and a first cousin, twice removed, of both Rudyard Kipling and Stanley Baldwin. His maternal grandfather held the Chair of Poetry at Oxford University, and his brother is the memoirist Graham McInnes. Captain Thirkell, his mother's second husband, came from Melbourne, Australia, and took his family there at the end of the war.

MacInnes grew up in Australia, and was educated at Scotch College, Melbourne. He went to England when he left school, intending to return to Australia and study law. Instead he found a job in London and settled there. In 1937 he took up painting, a career soon interrupted by World War II. MacInnes went into the army, spending a year in the infantry and five more as a sergeant in the Intelligence Corps.

It was not until 1945 that MacInnes began seriously to write, at first on the staff of the BBC, for which he produced some 1,500 radio scripts. In 1948 he completed his first novel, *To The Victors the Spoils*, an at least partly autobiographical account of the experiences of a British Field Security unit in occupied Europe at the end of World War II. MacInnes had to wait until 1950 before he found a publisher, and he has described how that came about—how he meets an "Aussie girl at the London zoo in the depths of winter, tell her my troubles, and hear from her she knew two lads called James MacGibbon and Robert Kee who were just starting up a new firm: so why didn't I give her the MS, and she'd send it to them? She did, and I was accepted within a fortnight."

Two years after this fortuitous beginning, MacInnes published *June in Her Spring*, a delicate study of adolescent love in the Australian outback. Although the author considers this his best novel, it was virtually ignored by the critics. It was his next three books, forming a kind of trilogy about London low life, which were to establish his reputation "as a sort of voice of the displaced, downtrodden, or misunderstood" and earn comparisons with Defoe and Hogarth. *City of Spades*, about London's immigrant population, was "not a sociological treatise but a first-rate novel, exciting, entertaining and often moving," and containing in the Nigerian Johnny Fortune "a truly heroic figure, . . . generous, caddish, affectionate and selfish." *Absolute Beginners*, a sympathetic account of life among teenage "drop-outs" in postwar London, convinced Keith Waterhouse that MacInnes was one of the few writers "who has any idea what these hurrying years are all about." *Mr. Love and Justice* is a carefully structured morality play about a seaman turned pimp and a zealous young policeman whose paths cross and who "come simultaneously to grief in symbolically appropriate ways." MacInnes returned to the Australian setting of *June in Her Spring* in *All Day Saturday*, a novel which was in general coolly received.

Anthony Burgess, who believes that MacInnes lacks a sharp ear for dialogue, nevertheless values his work as "psychologically accurate, very enlightening, and full of a real (and quite unsentimental) compassion." Bernard Levin thinks him "one of the most penetrating, sensible, balanced, yet deeply passionate observers of England to check in for centuries," and calls him "a highly gifted writer of romantic novels." This last comment was unexpected, since most critics had been inclined to categorize MacInnes as a "documentary" novelist; its accuracy was demonstrated in MacInnes's next novel, *Westward to Laughter*, "an eighteenth century adventure novel for a contemporary audience." It is an exciting and often brutal story of slavery and piracy in the West Indies, written in an excellent pastiche of Defoe and his contemporaries, but modern in its perception of the corrupting effect of human bondage. At least one critic however thought that the author's "formal success somewhat blurs his larger purpose; the yarn rattles too loudly for the moral." *Three Years to Play*, which followed, is another swashbuckling romance, this time about Elizabethan lowlife. Shakespeare himself appears as a character in this remarkable tale, in which a gallery of London whores, pimps, panders, and assorted rogues, gathered in Epping Forest, constitute a fanciful inspiration for the plot of *As You Like It*. One reviewer remarked that here, as in each of MacInnes's novels, "an entire section of society, unfamiliar or misunderstood, is given us in authentic and exuberant detail. . . . And into this setting he introduces a requisite range of odd, lively, essentially sketchy characters whose unlikely escapades graft fantasy onto historical or sociological fact. . . . This virtuoso display of unknown worlds is sheer romantic fiction."

Discussing his essays, Peter Porter has said that "In the mid-Fifties, Colin MacInnes emerged as the most original documentor of the English—or at any rate the London—scene since Orwell. It was exciting to read those pieces on the world we were making as they first appeared in *The Twentieth Century*." MacInnes's highly personal essays on the contemporary social scene have also appeared in *Encounter*, *The Spectator*, and regularly for a time in *New Society*, and a collection of them was published as *England, Half English*. Reviewing the book in *The Guardian*, W. L. Webb wrote: "The MacInnes prose style is an odd mixture of moderate mandarin and perky, up-to-date demotic, changing key, chameleon-like, with the subject. . . . It reflects . . . his unusual capacity for enthusiasm, concern, and love . . . its general effect is to sensitise acutely the curious mind of this unscientific but intelligent, humble, and hawk-eyed explorer of the new frontiers of society." *Sweet Saturday Night*, a history of the British music hall, appeared in 1967. *Loving Them Both* is a brief study of bisexuals and bisexuality, written "in a remarkably straightforward and unpretentious way."

Colin MacInnes is unmarried and lives in London, where his tall figure, clad in a now legendary blue anorak, is a familiar sight in some areas. He travels extensively, particularly in Africa and the British Commonwealth.

PRINCIPAL WORKS: To the Victor the Spoils (novel), 1950; June in Her Spring (novel), 1952; City of Spades (novel), 1957; Absolute Beginners (novel), 1959; Mr. Love and Justice (novel), 1960; England, Half English (essays), 1961; (with Kenneth Clark and Bryan Robertson) Sidney Nolan, 1961; London, City of Any Dream, 1962; (with the editors of Life) Australia and New Zealand, 1964; All Day Saturday (novel), 1966; Sweet Saturday Night (social history), 1967; Westward to Laughter (novel), 1969; Three Years to Play, 1970; Loving Them Both, 1973.

ABOUT: Burgess, A. The Novel Now, 1967; West, P. The Modern Novel, 1963; Who's Who, 1973. *Periodicals*—Books and Bookmen October 1962; The Listener June 8, 1967; Guardian September 17, 1957; September 1, 1961; Spectator September 1, 1963.

MACKEN, WALTER (May 3, 1915–April 22, 1967), Irish novelist, short story writer, and playwright, was born in Galway City and named for his father, a carpenter. He went to local Catholic schools and wrote his first story at the age of twelve. Five years later he joined the Galway Gaelic Theatre, eventually becoming actor-manager there. In the interim he made of himself a complete man of the theatre, proficient or better as actor, producer, director, set designer, and playwright. During the mid-1940s, Macken began to have his plays produced by the Abbey Theatre in Dublin. In 1948 he went to the Abbey and was one of its principal ornaments until 1951, acting in works by himself and others.

The first of Macken's plays to attract international attention was *Mungo's Mansion*, produced at the Abbey in 1946, and a year later (as *Galway Handicap*) in London. Both this work and *Home Is the Hero* depict life in the back streets of Galway City, and both were well received in England. The latter, Macken's best-known play (and subsequently a film), was about a drunk who returns home from a spell in jail and tries to reform his old cronies. It reached the New York stage in 1954 but, even with the author in the starring role, failed to repeat its Dublin success. This failure, it is said, did much to turn Macken away from the theatre.

Macken's career as a novelist had begun inauspiciously when *Quench the Moon* and *I Am Alone* were banned in Ireland. *Rain on the Wind*, however, was a critical and popular success on both sides of the Atlantic, and established his reputation as a novelist. It was set, like most of Macken's fiction, among the poor folk of Galway, and had as its hero a young fisherman of gigantic size and strength, humbled by a facial disfigurement. The novel traces Mico's story from early childhood to the successful conclusion of his search for a girl who will love him. It was called "a strong, beautiful book, eloquent with the humor, pathos and gallantry of life," and one critic wrote that Macken "creates characters as naturally and memorably as he does the . . . moods of the sea."

The Bogman was about a Galway youth's return to his native village; R. D. Charques wrote of it that Macken had acquitted himself "bravely and well in the vein of quasi-poetic Irish realism that stems from Synge." The author is best known in the United States for the trilogy in which he records and celebrates the continuity of the common man, and his religion, through all the vicissitudes of Irish history—from Cromwell's invasion (in *Seek the Fair Land*), through the Great Famine (in *The Silent People*), and the struggle for independence (in *The Scorching Wind*).

Macken's short stories, most of them first published in such journals as the *New Yorker*, *Atlantic Monthly*, and *Harper's*, share the virtues and defects of his other writings. That is to say, they are extremely uneven in quality—at their worst, according to Frank O'Connor, "theatrical, sentimental and imitative"—but always wholeheartedly involved in the simple lives they describe, with none of the ironic detachment which annoys some critics in the work of O'Connor himself. At their best, they have "the swift and stunning impact of the oral story told around the cottage fireside."

WALTER MACKEN

Walter Macken was married in 1937 to the former Peggy Kenny, at that time a journalist on the Connacht *Tribune*. She survives him, as do his two sons, Walter and Ultan. The success of *Rain on the Wind* had enabled Macken to buy an unpretentious country house at Oughterard in the heart of Galway. He died there of a heart attack at the age of fifty-one. Although he wrote little for the theatre in his later years, Macken never cut himself off from his first love. In 1962 he was seen in an important role in the screen version of Brendan Behan's *The Quare Fellow*, and in 1966 returned for a time to the Abbey Theatre as artistic director. He was an excellent actor—a "brilliant" one, in the opinion of Frank O'Connor. Brooks Atkinson, who relished his 1951 performance as a great shillelagh fighter in M. J. Molloy's *The King of Friday's Men*, called him "a fine figure of a man with girth and muscle, humor and humility."

PRINCIPAL WORKS: *Plays*—Mungo's Mansion, 1947; Vacant Possession, 1948; Home Is the Hero, 1954; Twilight of a Warrior, 1956. *Novels*—Quench the Moon, 1948; I Am Alone, 1949; Rain on the Wind, 1950; The Bogman, 1952; Sunset on the Window-Panes, 1954; Sullivan, 1957; Seek the Fair Land, 1959; The Silent People, 1962; The Scorching Wind, 1964; Island of the Great Yellow Ox (for children), 1966; Brown Lord of the Mountain (U.S., Lord of the Mountain), 1967. *Short*

stories—The Green Hills, 1956; God Made Sunday, 1962; The Coll Doll, 1969.
ABOUT: Contemporary Authors 13–14, 1965; Gassner, J. Theatre at the Crossroads, 1960. *Periodicals*—New York Times April 23, 1967; Saturday Review August 4, 1956; Times (London) April 24, 1967

MAC LEAN, ALISTAIR ("IAN STUART") (1922–), Scottish adventure story writer, was born in Glasgow but spent much of his youth in the remote village of Daviot, Inverness-shire, where his father was the parish minister. He was schooled at Inverness Royal Academy and, after his return to Glasgow at the age of fifteen, at Hillhead High School. His "extensive and involuntary service" in the Royal Navy began in 1941 and lasted for five years, taking him from the Arctic to the Far East and to a great many places in between. He was discharged in 1946 and entered Glasgow University, which he left in 1953 with an M.A. degree, awarded with honors.

In 1954 MacLean was teaching at a school in Rutherglen and going through "one of those periods of acute financial distress which," as he said, "chronically assail us teachers." Thus stimulated, he wrote a short story about adventure at sea called "The Dileas," and entered it in a competition in the Glasgow *Herald*. There were nine hundred entries but MacLean's story won the competition, bringing him a welcome hundred-pound prize and a suggestion from the publishing house of William Collins that he try his hand at a novel.

The result was *H.M.S. Ulysses*, which draws on MacLean's wartime experiences to tell the story of a British light cruiser and her crew shepherding a convoy from Iceland to Sweden's North Cape. The ship, swept by great seas, encased in ice and snow, bombed to near destruction, is the stage for an epic story of courage and endurance. MacLean, who had been a torpedo man, wrote from the point of view of the lower deck and, as V. P. Hass said, "with integrity, spirit, and a kind of bitterness: the British admiralty obviously is no pet of his." Taliaferro Boatwright found the novel "more a legend than a novel of real flesh and blood people," and went on: "Like most legends it is larger than life. This does not gainsay the truth of its elements . . . and despite one's foreboding of the dénouement, despite even theatrical, sometimes melodramatic touches, the Ulysses and her officers and men come to have personal meaning. The result is a moving and thrilling book."

H.M.S. Ulysses was a Book Society choice and a best seller. MacLean said cautiously that he was chary of the word "literature" but might embark on a "writing" career, and went on teaching until his second novel was finished. This swept away all doubts. It was *The Guns of Navarone*, about a small group of saboteurs on a Greek island, faced with the critical but nearly impossible task of blowing up a huge German gun emplacement. The book stamped MacLean as "a natural-born adventure story writer," was an international best seller and—like a number of MacLean's later novels—became an immensely successful movie.

ALISTAIR MAC LEAN

A succession of fast-moving and absorbing entertainments has followed, ranging for their settings from Singapore (*South of Java Head*) to Greenland (*Night Without End*), from Hungary (*The Secret Ways*) to the Florida Keys (*Fear Is the Key*). One of the most warmly praised of MacLean's stories was *Ice Station Zebra*, about a mysterious outbreak of murder, arson, and sabotage in a floating research station near the North Pole. James Sandoe confessed to finding it so overwhelmingly exciting that he had at one point to put the book down. A reviewer in the *Times Literary Supplement* wrote: "The story evolves in a succession of masterful puzzles as astonishing as they are convincing . . . there is so much swift-moving action, so much clever innuendo and such a feeling for relevant detail that one cannot help but be fascinated by the mind at work here." MacLean has also written several secret service thrillers under the pseudonym "Ian Stuart," reminding readers of Ian Fleming "with more plot and action and less sex and sadism," and excellent biographies of T. E. Lawrence and Captain Cook.

MacLean was married in 1972 to Marcelle Georgeus, and has three sons by an earlier marriage. In 1963, disillusioned with writing, MacLean bought a small chain of hotels in England; he soon found that "running hotels is a most undemanding pastime," and was glad to start work on what became *When Eight Bells Toll*. He is a small, thin, handsome man, shy and self-deprecatory, with a marked lack of interest in personal publicity. His books have been translated into many European languages, and by 1971 had sold some twenty-three million copies, making him one of the three or four highest-paid novelists in the world. Richard Schickel expressed the feeling of many critics when he wrote: "MacLean's ideas of characterization have always been primitive, his humor a trifle strained, his tendency to over-complicate somewhat distracting. But he has an uncanny compensatory gift for keeping plots boiling and the suspense building." MacLean would probably accept this judgment. He has said that his books, which take five or six weeks to write, are not novels but adventure stories: "There's no art in what I do, no mystique. It's a job like any other." He greatly admires Raymond Chandler, but says that he is more interested in science—especially physics and astronomy—than in literature.

PRINCIPAL WORKS: *As Alistair MacLean*—H.M.S. Ulysses, 1955; The Guns of Navarone, 1957; South by Java Head, 1958; The Last Frontier, 1959 (also published as The Secret Ways); Night Without End, 1960; Fear Is the Key, 1961; The Golden Rendezvous, 1962; Lawrence of Arabia (for children), 1962; Ice Station Zebra, 1963; When Eight Bells Toll, 1966; Where Eagles Dare, 1967; Force Ten from Navarone, 1968; Puppet on a Chain, 1969; Caravan to Vaccarès, 1970; Bear Island, 1971; Captain Cook, 1972; The Way to Dusty Death, 1973. *As "Ian Stuart"*—The Black Shrike, 1961; The Dark Crusading, 1961; The Snow on the Ben, 1961; The Satan Bug, 1962.

ABOUT: Who's Who, 1973. *Periodicals*—Glasgow Herald March 6, 1954; September 27, 1955.

MC LUHAN, (HERBERT) MARSHALL (July 21, 1911–), Canadian cultural critic and theoretician, writes: "The advantage of being born a Westerner is partly the unimpeded view that it provides of more densely settled areas. A Canadian enjoys somewhat the same advantage in relation to the United States, or to Europe. Canada is a kind of cultural DEW line, a kind of cultural counter-environment. A counter-environment affords opportunities of observation such as are normal to the outsider. A habit of pattern recognition and even of abstract theorizing grows in the outsider, especially if he doesn't feel any anxious need of psychological support from his contemporaries. Apart from having spent my first few years on the windy plains of Alberta, the most formative factor must have been a year of early childhood spent on the Bay of Fundy. The scent and action of the sea has permeated my being ever since. It was, therefore, a grievous shock when I discovered on the cattle boat *en route* to Great Britain that I was a very poor sailor.

"My studies at Cambridge produced many unexpected advantages; not the least of these was

MARSHALL MC LUHAN

the excitement of encountering many world figures. Seen at a great distance, famous people acquire a quite unreal and discouraging character. Seen close up, the quite human limitations and foibles of such people can be the greatest possible stimulus to self-assertion. The cult of greatness can be a very debilitating and inhibiting thing when developed in remoteness from its public. Another advantage that Cambridge conferred on me was its bland acceptance of the contemporary world as a scene to be understood and controlled.

"Cambridge has never had a predominantly commercial setting. It has never been involved in the commerce of its time. This seems to have absolved it from the need to oppose the age. A great deal of valuable energy can be expended in building up moral defences against one's time. The same energies could be more usefully spent in seeking to discover the shape and tendencies of the age. For whatever reason, Cambridge has always been rich in minds that seized upon the pattern of their period in order to foster its best possibilities. I was fortunate to encounter men like I. A. Richards and F. R. Leavis. It has been said that the job of the teacher is to save the student's time. At Cambridge there were men who knew how to do this by putting a student *in touch* with his time. Much life and energy is wasted in perceptual alienation from one's own age. The training of perception has been the aim and boast of many educators at Cambridge in this century.

"Upon leaving Cambridge in 1936 I began my first teaching job at the University of Wisconsin, an ideal spot for a Canadian to begin his acquaintance with the U.S.A. It was there at Madison that

I was received into the Catholic church in 1937.

" 'Style is a way of seeing,' said Flaubert, and since Flaubert, art and literature have consciously assumed the task of probing our new technological environments. Art and literature have revealed the characters of the new environments created by technologies, by setting up counter-environments. It has been my study of contemporary poetry and painting that has drawn me to examine the new human environments wrought by the physical extensions of our own human body. It is the artists and poets who have taught me that the 'Emperor's new clothes' are not visible without the aid of art. Men without art, to use the phrase of Wyndham Lewis, are engaged in hypnotized contemplation of the Emperor's *old* clothes.

"During the past century art has revealed that the changing environment is not perceptible to unaided human attention. Throughout all human time, men have been engaged in conscious awareness of the preceding environment, which presents itself as a nostalgic art form. The current environment creates an overload of sensation that obliterates pattern and form. My study of literature became an aid to the perception that led me to undertake the task of understanding the relation between culture and technology.

"I had begun my university studies as a student of engineering, because of my interest in structure and design. It becomes more clear each day that structure and design in all levels of human organization are becoming orchestral. Our new electric age no longer presents any specialized cultural gradient. Ours is the age of the zero-gradient in which all times and cultures are in a continuous dialogue. To be a participant in this dialogue is most satisfying.

"When I was studying the work of the Elizabethan, Thomas Nashe, at the Huntington Library, I met Corinne Lewis of Fort Worth, Texas, who was studying at the Pasadena Playhouse. We were married in 1939 and now have six children, the eldest and youngest of whom are boys. By way of participating in the dialogue of this time, I find the open perceptions of all these teenage boys and girls a very rich means of keeping in touch with our time."

Marshall McLuhan was born in Edmonton, Alberta, and the agrarian socialism of the prairie provinces has been seen as a major factor in his development. Another important influence was G. K. Chesterton, whose delight in wit and paradox is reflected in McLuhan's own style. McLuhan praised Chesterton "for seeking to re-establish agriculture and small property as the only free basis for a free culture," and eventually followed him into the Roman Catholic Church.

He is the son of Herbert McLuhan, an insurance and real estate salesman, and of the former Elsie Hall, a talented actress and monologist. He studied first engineering and then literature at Manitoba University, which gave him a B.A. in 1932 and an M.A. in 1934. He was at Cambridge University from 1934 to 1936, when he received his second B.A. His Cambridge M.A. followed in 1940, and a doctorate in 1942. McLuhan taught at the University of Wisconsin in 1936–1937 and in the latter year joined the faculty of the University of St. Louis, a Catholic institution. He remained there until 1944, when he went to the University of Toronto. He became a full professor in 1952 and in 1963 established the University's Center for Culture and Technology, to investigate the "psychic and social consequences of technologies and media." In 1967–1968 he took a leave of absence from Toronto to teach for a year at Fordham University in New York. That appointment was originally to one of New York State's five one-hundred-thousand-dollar Albert Schweitzer Chairs but, since Fordham is a Catholic university, the arrangement was abrogated as a conflict between church and state. The stipend, which supported a team of graduates investigating the mass media as well as paying McLuhan's salary, was in the end provided by Fordham itself.

The Interior Landscape, a volume of McLuhan's literary essays, includes some written during the 1940s, which show that he was then a conventional and even rather reactionary critic, for example defending the agrarian values of the antebellum American South against "northern technology," and favoring such writers as Eliot, Pound, and Wyndham Lewis—all of them painfully at odds with the democratic rationalism of their time. McLuhan knew Wyndham Lewis in Canada during World War II, and was set on his present course under the influence of Lewis's analyses of modern mass culture.

His first book, *The Mechanical Bride*, appeared in 1951. At that time McLuhan evidently shared Lewis's hostility to "the very considerable currents and pressures set up around us today by the mechanical agencies of the press, radio, movies, and advertising." The book is a series of short essays on the "folklore of industrial man," each built around some advertisement which tends to support McLuhan's theory that such things are synthetic dreams manufactured for "a somnambulist public.' The mechanical bride herself is that curious confusion of sex and technology exemplified in attitudes toward the automobile. Most reviewers endorsed McLuhan's views but deplored his presentation; one in the *New Republic* thought that "the effectiveness of the work is all but destroyed by an inflated and professorial style and by the author's predilection for positively blood-curdling puns"—a predilection that McLuhan has since elevated into an aspect of his philosophy.

From 1954 to 1959 McLuhan and his friend E. S. Carpenter, then an anthropologist at Toronto, published the journal *Explorations* as an outlet for papers by participants in their seminars in "culture and communications." In 1954 McLuhan also issued a small mimeographed pamphlet called *Counterblast*, interesting as an early example of his "mosaic" method of presentation, in which, instead of close reasoning and argument, the reader is offered a suggestive juxtaposition of comments and quotations. McLuhan's studies at this time led him to abandon his overt opposition to the mass media and their effects. Emulating (as he said) the sailor in Poe's "A Descent Into the Maelstrom," who survived by surrendering himself to the current, he plunged into the whirlpool of electronic communication and mass culture.

McLuhan's next book, *The Gutenberg Galaxy*, contains all his basic themes. He had taken up an idea propounded by the Canadian economic historian Harold A. Innis, that the main determinant of social change in any given period is the prevailing medium of communication. Extrapolating from this, McLuhan proposed that the content of any communication is unimportant. What matters is the form in which it reaches us, because it is the form that determines "the patterning of human association." In other and more famous words, "the medium is the message."

Thus, preliterate or tribal man spoke to people face to face, and communication was aural, tactile, and olfactory, as well as visual; the result was a warm, organic, closely integrated society. Man expelled himself from this Eden when he invented the phonetic alphabet. Meaning became abstract, attached to words instead of things, thought was separated from feeling, and the individual consciousness from the creative immediacy of collective response: "literacy, in translating man out of the closed world of tribal depth and resonance, gave an eye for an ear and ushered him into a visual open world of specialized and divided consciousness."

The process of decline was arrested for a while in the Catholic Middle Ages, according to McLuhan, who (A. Alvarez says) "defends the scholastic philosophers despite all their highly verbal, perverted chop-logic, on the grounds that at least their debates were oral, their learning a feat of memory, and their manuscripts were designed to illuminate God's world." The ultimate fall from grace came with Gutenberg's invention of movable type. Printing led to a linear, sequential, verbally logical method of thought and expression, and thus to every kind of evil, including individualism, indifference, inequality, mass production, nationalism, and militarism.

But print-readers are rapidly being rendered obsolete by the contemporary electronic revolution, in which information reaches us not in a linear and compartmentalized fashion, but simultaneously, from all directions. Once the tyranny of print is thrown off and sensory balance restored, man will have been redeemed by these new "audio-tactile" media and will live happily in a world which has shrunk to a "global village." Racism and war will disappear because we will all be too closely involved with one another. The prophets of this new Eden are among us: they are our children, already liberated by lifelong exposure to television, already citizens of the global village.

These theories are presented in McLuhan's mosaic style, which emulates the methods of the electronic media. The book is made up of short chapters, unnumbered to encourage random reading. It is written in an aphoristic prose stuffed with puns (to stress the associative, nonrational aspects of language) and varied by long quotations from a kaleidoscopic range of sources.

In Canada *The Gutenberg Galaxy* won the Governor-General's award for critical prose, but elsewhere it attracted surprisingly little attention. Not so McLuhan's next book, which made him famous. This was *Understanding Media: The Extensions of Man*, in which McLuhan, after Buckminster Fuller, asserts that the telephone, the computer, television, and other electronic media have extended man's central nervous system beyond his own brain and body. He goes on to apply the ideas introduced in *The Gutenberg Galaxy* to twenty-six media of communication (including such muffled forms of expression as clothes). Television, for example, is characterized as a medium low in definition, and therefore demanding a degree of audience participation; it is one of the "cool" media, which have conditioned young people towards involvement and personal discovery rather than the passive reception of instruction.

McLuhan's confident attempt to explain virtually any social, cultural, or political phenomenon in terms of media—from the rise of Hitler to the unpopularity of body odor—enraged linear-minded critics, who charged him with a ludicrous inflation of a useful but minor perception. But George Steiner hailed McLuhan as a visionary, a spiritual descendant of Blake, and the journalist Tom Wolfe called him "the most important thinker since Newton, Darwin, Freud, Einstein and Pavlov." At the very least, *Understanding Media* became, as Arnold Rockman said, "the badge of those who wished to be thought intellectually fashionable."

The Medium Is the Massage created an even bigger stir. It summarizes McLuhan's ideas with a minimum of words and a maximum of illustrations, manipulated by the designer Quentin Fiore so as to simulate electronic effects in print. The "medium is the massage" because "all media work us over completely," leaving "no part of us untouched, unaffected, unaltered." *Counterblast* is an updating, done in collaboration with Harley Parker, of the earlier work of that name. There are no pictures, but slogans like "Bless Madison Avenue for Restoring the Magical Art of the Cavemen to Suburbia" appear in a variety of typefaces, colors, and positions. *Culture Is Our Business* returns to the guided tour of "industrial folklore" begun in *The Mechanical Bride*, advertisements from various magazines being reproduced opposite McLuhan's sometimes very obscure aphorisms. A number of other books are collaborations with "people who are deeply versed in matters I know very little about." There is also a *Marshall McLuhan Newsletter*, "an early warning system for our era of instant change," containing "all the news that's not fit to print."

Most critics have a vested interest in printed books, and McLuhan is widely regarded as a renegade, an academic who has gone over to the enemy and become a traitor to the printed word, an outrageously successful "pop-cult prophet of the electronic age." He has been attacked for his much-vaunted detachment, in the name of which he has indeed allowed himself to commit grossly insensitive solecisms—for example saying that "the Negro question is a red-herring" since "black is not a color"; and "As education is war, so war is education." However, he has also been attacked for a *lack* of detachment, most often as a Catholic mystic *manqué*, seeking like Teilhard de Chardin a way back to some lost spiritual consensus. Michael Wood believes that "behind McLuhan's repeated protestations of neutrality there plainly lurks a vast, fantastic moral theology, with the Fall represented by the forbidden fruit of print, and redemption promised by electronic engineering, which will restore humanity to its lost wholeness in the new global village." Above all, perhaps, it is McLuhan's willingness to ignore facts tending to inhibit his theories that has disillusioned so many who, like Jonathan Miller, discovered his early writings with a sense of revelation.

It may be that, as Dudley Young put it, "the days of McLuhanacy are numbered." All the same, few serious critics are prepared to dismiss his theories altogether. The consensus was summed up very well by Arthur Schlesinger when he defined McLuhanism as "a chaotic combination of bland assertion, astute guesswork, fake analogy, dazzling insight, hopeless nonsense, shockmanship, showmanship, wise-cracks, and oracular mystification, all mingling cockily and indiscriminately in an endless and random monologue. It also, in my judgment, contains a deeply serious argument."

Kathleen Nott says that McLuhan "is long and lean, gives an impression of a bright sharp eye against a darkish background of complexion and clothes, and in utterance is pithy, pawky and dehydrated." He is a Fellow of the Royal Society of Canada (1964) and a Companion of the Order of Canada (1970).

PRINCIPAL WORKS: The Mechanical Bride, 1951; Report: Project on Understanding New Media, 1960; (with E. S. Carpenter) Explorations in Communications, 1960; The Gutenberg Galaxy, 1962; Understanding Media, 1964; (with Quentin Fiore) The Medium Is the Massage, 1967; (with Harley Parker) Counterblast, 1968; (with Harley Parker) Through the Vanishing Point: Space in Poetry and Painting, 1968; (with Quentin Fiore) War and Peace in the Global Village, 1968; The Interior Landscape: The Literary Criticism of Marshall McLuhan 1943–1962, 1969; (with Wilfred Watson) From Cliché to Archetype, 1970; Culture Is Our Business, 1970; (with Barrington Nevitt) Take Today: The Executive as Dropout, 1972.

ABOUT: Current Biography, 1967; Miller, J. McLuhan, 1971; Rosenthal, R. (ed.) McLuhan, Pro and Con, 1969; Stearn, G. E. (ed.) McLuhan, Hot and Cool, 1967; Theall, D. F. The Medium Is the Rear View Mirror, 1970; Who's Who in America, 1970–1971.

***MAGARSHACK, DAVID** (December 23, 1899–), English biographer, translator, critic, novelist, and journalist, was born in Riga, Latvia (then part of Russia), and educated at Riga Russian Secondary School. In 1920 he went to England, where he has remained, in 1924 receiving an honors degree in English at University College, London. For some years Magarshack was a Fleet Street journalist, and during the 1930s tried his hand with moderate success at some detective stories. Since then he has earned his living as a translator and biographer.

His first major work was the biography, now regarded as standard in the English-speaking world, of Konstantin Stanislavsky. Magarshack also translated Stanislavsky's influential lectures on the art of the stage, and provided a long preface to this volume which is still one of the best introductions to Stanislavsky's theories.

Since then Magarshack has gone on to provide biographies of most of the greatest nineteenth century Russian writers except Tolstoy. He began with a "useful factual survey" of Chekhov's life, and followed this with his "thorough, orderly" critical study, *Chekhov the Dramatist.* Biographies of Turgenev, Gogol, Dostoevsky, and Pushkin have followed, all of them making the fullest use of new material and recent scholarship, all of them rich in quotations from their subjects' works and letters, all of them solid, detailed, and well balanced.

Negative criticism has centered on Magarshack's rather "unimaginative and unenlightening" interpretation of his facts, and on the sketchiness and

* mag′ ər shak

DAVID MAGARSHACK

superficiality of his critical material. The *Times Literary Supplement*, reviewing *Pushkin*, referred to Magarshack as a "popular biographer" who had written a "racy, fluent and readable" book, but went on: "It is precisely when Mr. Magarshack departs from the straight line of biographical narrative and deviates into the undergrowth of literary criticism that he becomes entangled and loses his way—and loses his readers into the bargain. . . . His critical method is to describe the external circumstances of a work, to give a synopsis of it and to comment briefly on the contents." However, except in *Chekhov the Dramatist*, Magarshack does not claim to write critical biographies, only biographies, and it is to his accurate, informed, and readable accounts that the British or American reader with no Russian is most likely to turn.

As a translator from the Russian, Magarshack is the most prolific of his time. His grasp of idiomatic English is that of a highly literate native, and he has provided standard modern versions of Dostoevsky's great novels, of two volumes of Leskov's short stories, of Gogol's *Dead Souls*, and much else. A whole generation of readers has received their introduction to Russian literature through these responsible and skillful translations.

David Magarshack is married to the former Elsie Duella and has four children.

PRINCIPAL WORKS: *Fiction*—Big Ben Strikes Eleven: A Murder Story for Grown-up People, 1934; Death Cuts a Caper, 1935; Three Dead, 1937. *Biographies*—Stanislavsky: A Life, 1951; Chekhov: A Life, 1951; Chekhov the Dramatist, 1952; Turgenev: A Life, 1954; Gogol: A Life, 1957; Dostoevsky, 1962; Pushkin: A Biography, 1967.
ABOUT: Contemporary Authors 7–8, 1963.

MALAMUD, BERNARD (April 26, 1914–), American novelist and short story writer, writes: "I was born in Brooklyn, New York, shortly before the beginning of the First World War, the son of Max and Bertha Malamud, who had come from Russia in the early 1900s; and I lived in Brooklyn until I was married and went to live in Greenwich Village. My father, a grocer, made a marginal living. My mother, like him a kind and affectionate person, after my younger brother and I were in school, helped him in the store. During my childhood we all followed the fortunes of the store, moving from one neighborhood to another, wherever things seemed to be better. They were good for short periods but were very bad in the Depression.

"When I was nine I had pneumonia. To celebrate my recovery my father, though he could ill afford it, bought me the twenty volumes of the Book of Knowledge. And I read Merriwells and Algers in droves, and went as often as I could to the movies, particularly to see Charlie Chaplin. My mother, who had been disappointed in life, died when I was fifteen. Her family had Yiddish actors and theatre people in it and I saw plays on Second Avenue before I saw any on Broadway.

"My childhood was comparatively happy, school making up somehow for a meager family life. I played all over the neighborhood, helped build huts, cooked mickies, carried on long running games, stole tomatoes from the Italian vegetable farmers, and once in a while gypped the El to ride to Coney Island, where I spent long hours on the Midway, on rides, and watching the ocean. Some nights I rode the El the other way and wandered in Times Square. Some nights I stayed in the back room of the store, when it was closed, and tried my hand at writing stories. I had begun to write on school assignment at an early age and was encouraged by my teachers. At Erasmus Hall I became an editor of the literary magazine and acted in school plays. When my mother died I worked in the store. In 1932 I entered City College and was much excited by the possibilities of education, though I rode the subway from Brooklyn to Manhattan too many hours a day. After graduation in 1936, I worked for a short time in a factory, in stores, and as a clerk in the Census Bureau in Washington, D.C. I had written a few stories in college but after graduation began to write again. The rise of totalitarianism, the Second World War, and the situation of the Jews in Europe helped me to come to what I wanted to say as a writer. I had done part of an M.A. at Columbia and got a night school teaching job, in 1940, at Erasmus Hall. During the day, in a furnished room, I began seriously to write. I wrote in this manner for almost ten years, still teaching at night, but, after 1945,

BERNARD MALAMUD

married and living in New York. In 1949 my wife and I and our small son moved to Corvallis, Oregon. In the dozen years there—one off, on a grant, in Italy—I wrote my first four books while teaching at Oregon State College. My daughter was born in Corvallis. In 1961 we returned east and have since then lived in New England.

"I write, of course, for many reasons; one is to explain life to myself and keep me related to men."

In the 1950s and 1960s, as Ihab Hassan wrote in 1961, "the urban Jewish writer . . . emerged from the tragic underground of culture as a true spokesman of mid-century America." The leading figures in this emergence were Saul Bellow and Bernard Malamud. Malamud concerns himself with "the drama of personality fulfilling itself." Such fulfillment comes most often to Malamud's heroes when, educated by suffering, they learn to love someone more than themselves. The Jews, all-purpose contemporary symbols for what survives and transcends suffering, are thus for Malamud "absolutely the very *stuff* of drama," as well as the people he knows best.

However, his first novel, *The Natural*, has no Jewish characters, and is in other ways an uncharacteristic book. It is an often (but not fundamentally) funny account of the rise and fall of a great baseball player. Contemporary in its subject, its form closely follows that of a medieval grail-myth. The downfall of the baseball hero, Roy Hobbes, is brought about by the fact that he cannot transcend his greedy passions, professional and sexual: his failure is a failure of purity and of love. Although it contains the germ of Malamud's method in its theme, in its marriage of realism and fable, and its wit and verve, the novel was too self-consciously and puzzlingly allegorical for most tastes. It had its champions nevertheless, and Sidney Richman commended in particular the "curious poetry" of its style, in which "passages of idiomatic, terse, and slangy prose alternate with passages of lyrical intensity, and as often as not the two styles are perfectly integrated."

With his next novel, *The Assistant*, Malamud came into his own. It is set in Brooklyn during the Depression. A Young Italian-American drifter, Frankie Alpine, robs an unlucky, ailing, endlessly suffering Jewish grocer, Morris Bober. Out of reluctant guilt and pity, Alpine goes to work in Bober's dismal store. Increasingly he takes Bober's sorrows on himself and in the end, after Bober's death, he has himself circumcised. He has elected, out of love, to *become* Bober, the eternal Jew, the *schlemiel*, God's innocent. This, as Malamud presents it, is a victory, though a limited and ambiguous one.

Coming after *The Natural*, the novel seemed to some critics a work of old-fashioned realism. Others, like Sidney Richman in his monograph on Malamud, have found in it not only much buried symbolism but a resonance in the descriptions of the store and other settings which make them seem less specific places than states of mind. Richman considers the book the most successful of Malamud's attempts to unite a lyrical symbolism with the resources of the "naturalist-realist tradition. . . . Ambivalent from first to last, undercut by currents of ritual and realism, *The Assistant* seems to belong to no convention unless it be to Dostoevsky's fiercely visionary 'extra-realism.'" Theodore Solotaroff found it a revelation, partly because "it restored a sense of the dynamics of character and of the older intention of fiction to show the ways men change. Despite its small compass and thinness of social reference, *The Assistant* could thus take on some of the power and clarity of the great 19th-century novels." It brought Malamud the Daroff Memorial Award and the Rosenthal Prize, and is still regarded by some as his most perfectly realized novel.

The central figure in *A New Life* is S. Levin, a thirty-year-old failure, romantic, and former alcoholic. Pursuing his new life, he leaves New York and goes to teach at what turns out to be a wretchedly philistine and conservative "cow college" in the Pacific Northwest. Here Levin meets Gerald Gilley, a brilliantly caricatured careerist who is compiling a picture book of American literature, and falls in love with Gilley's wife, Pauline. Through this rich, frightening, often ludicrous love affair, Levin achieves redemption. In the end he leaves Cascadia College with Pauline and sets out for another new life, disgraced, penniless, jobless, and saddled with Gilley's children. "Why take that load on yourself?" Gilley asks, and Levin is able to say: "Because I can, you son of a bitch." Malamud was obviously experimenting in this book with a broader canvas and a freer form. It contains, among other pleasures, some excellent satire and one of the most likable heroines in recent American fiction. Many critics, however, found a variety of structural weaknesses and a lack of coherence in the character of Levin himself. By the standards that Malamud has set for himself, it cannot be counted a success.

The most ambitious of Malamud's novels, *The Fixer*, is based on the case of Mendel Beiliss, a Russian Jew accused of "ritual murder" in Kiev in 1913, but acquitted despite the strength of the anti-Semitic conspiracy against him. Malamud's book recounts the similar ordeal of Yokav Bok—though the result of his trial is deliberately left open. Bok is a half-starved odd-job man who leaves the ghetto and conceals his Jewishness in order to earn a living. His deception is discovered, and at about the same time a boy is murdered in Kiev. Anti-Semitic politicians are looking for a sensational incident to bolster their case, and Bok is charged with ritual murder. The rest of the book deals with the investigation and trial. Lacking evidence, the anti-Semites need a confession. And this, in spite of years of solitary confinement, torture, and every kind of degradation and humiliation, Bok will not give them. In the course of his ordeal this ignoble, ignorant, and often comic peasant becomes a philosopher, a disciple of Spinoza. He learns that "there's no such thing as an unpolitical man, especially a Jew." And symbolically he becomes a father, accepting responsibility for his wife's child by another man, much as Levin had done in *A New Life*.

No one questioned Malamud's brilliant success in sustaining Bok's limited but developing point of view, or his remarkable feat of historical reconstruction, though some found the result rather dull. One critic suggested that he had "retreated" from the problems of his own society "into someone else's history," but most thought that his fable was one of immediate and widespread relevance, political and psychological. Technically, it seemed to some readers to surpass even *The Assistant* as a fusion of symbolism and realism, in that the former grows naturally and inevitably out of the latter. Melvin Maddocks wrote: "With complete and passionate integrity, [Malamud] is denying one of the most paralyzing fears of our times: that individual goodness cannot survive the evils of history. It is as convincing and affecting an act of grace as the American novel has seen in a long time." It received the Pulitzer Prize and brought the author his second National Book Award.

The Tenants is set in a condemned tenement on Manhattan's East Side. Harry Lesser, statutory tenant, Jew, and a promising but unfulfilled novelist, lives alone on the top floor. He is struggling to find a satisfactory conclusion for the book which is to be his masterpiece and which has engaged him for ten years. Willie Spearmint, a young black writer, torn between soul and revolution, moves uninvited into the adjoining apartment to work on his own book, a clumsy but passionately sincere autobiographical novel. In spite of goodwill and mutual respect, Willie's arrival precipitates a whole gallery of tensions—territorial, racial, literary, and also sexual, since Lesser falls in love with Irene Bell, Willie's white mistress. Lesser gets Willie's girl, Willie's friends smash up Lesser's apartment and destroy his novel. At that point (as is appropriate in a novel about a novelist who cannot end his book), the reader is offered a choice of conclusions—one happy, with a double wedding, one not, with a double killing. And there is a coda in which the single word "mercy" is repeated one hundred and thirteen times. R. Z. Sheppard called it "as uncertain an affirmation as Malamud has ever written." Most critics found the book flawed. Roger Sale thought that it would have worked better as a short fable—that it had lost its "central urgency in a tangle of minor characters." Morris Dickstein called it "thin and portentously symbolic compared to the rich narrative specificity of [*The Assistant*]," but "a welcome recovery" all the same, and Malamud's "best book in years"—"a genuine effort of sympathy and tact."

Malamud's first National Book Award had been awarded in 1959 for the stories collected in *The Magic Barrel*. These are spare, densely concentrated tales, like the novels operating on several levels of meaning, dealing most often with the possibility of spiritual growth, and characterized by a conversational directness that owes a great deal to the Yiddish tradition of oral storytelling. In many of them, an old Jew, hopeless in some decaying tenement, is confronted by another man in a painful conflict of values from which the old man draws spiritual enlargement.

Thus, in the extraordinary fantasy "Angel Levine," Manischevitz's only hope of salvation from his Job-like sufferings is to believe the impossible—that his black visitor Alexander Levine is in fact a heaven-sent Jewish messenger. In "The Last Mohican," the failed painter Arthur Fidelman goes to Italy to make a new career as a critic, and is victimized into compassion by a filthy, obnoxious, thieving refugee named Shimon Susskind. "The Magic Barrel" tells the story of Leo Finkle, a gentle but unloving rabbinical student, in his dealings with the greedy marriage broker Pinye Salzman. In the end Finkle, with his innocent eyes open, chooses to marry Salzman's daughter, half-goddess, half-whore, a girl so cursed that her father weeps at the thought of her. It is a story of inexplicable beauty and power.

Idiots First, Malamud's second volume of stories, includes two more bizarre tales about Arthur Fidelman, and others which resume the themes of *The Magic Barrel*. The most remarkable and discussed of these stories is the fable called "The Jewbird." A socially ambitious Jewish family is visited by a ragged, crow-like bird who one evening flies into the kitchen. Stinking of herring and talking in dialect, the Jewbird represents everything Harry Cohen wants to forget, and Harry kills it. When his weeping son asks who was responsible for the murder, his mother tells him: "Anti-Semeets."

The three published stories about Arthur Fidelman and his hopeless but indomitable search for artistic self-expression were collected, together with three new ones, as *Pictures of Fidelman: An Exhibition*. One episode in which Fidelman, seeking to sculpt the perfect hole, descends into hell, is more markedly surrealistic than anything in Malamud's previous work. *Pictures of Fidelman* is the most zestfully comic of Malamud's books, though there are passages where comic invention deteriorates into crude farce.

Bernard Malamud received his M.A. from Columbia in 1942. Since his return from Oregon he has taught literature at Bennington College, in recent years working mostly on a quarter schedule. He was a visiting lecturer at Harvard in 1966–1968. He has received a number of fellowships and awards, one of which enabled him to spend a year in Italy in 1956–1957. Malamud was married in 1945 to Ann de Chiara, and has two children. He enjoys reading and music, walking and travel.

"The purpose of the writer," Malamud believes, "is to keep civilization from destroying itself. . . . To me writing must be true; it must have emotional depth; it must be imaginative. It must enflame, destroy, change the reader. . . . American fiction is at its weakest when we go in for journalistic case studies instead of rich character development." Sidney Richman speaks of Malamud as a writer "who seems to be defining himself anew with each work," who is constantly extending himself—even, at times, beyond the resources of his talent. "Through his portrait of a people engulfed and tortured by barbarities past and present, he has found the means to regain something of the tragic vision of the past which insists that where there is no hope man will continue to hope, where the spirit cannot endure it will continue to endure."

PRINCIPAL WORKS: The Natural, 1952; The Assistant, 1957; The Magic Barrel (stories), 1958; A New Life, 1961; Idiots First (stories), 1963; The Fixer, 1966; A Malamud Reader, ed. by Philip Rahv, 1967; Pictures of Fidelman: An Exhibition, 1969; The Tenants, 1971; Rembrandt's Hat (stories), 1973.

ABOUT: Alter, R. After the Tradition, 1969; Balakian, N. and Simmons, C. (eds.) The Creative Present, 1963; Current Biography, 1958; Fiedler, L. No! In Thunder, 1960; Field, L. A. and Field, J. W. (eds.) Bernard Malamud and the Critics, 1970; Hassan, I. Radical Innocence, 1961; Kazin, A. Contemporaries, 1962; Klein, M. After Alienation, 1964; Kosofsky, R. N. Bernard Malamud (bibliography), 1969; Moore, H. T. (ed.) Contemporary American Novelists, 1964; Richman, S. Bernard Malamud, 1967; Solotaroff, T. The Red Hot Vacuum, 1970; Vinson, J. (ed.) Contemporary Novelists, 1972; Who's Who in America, 1972–1973. *Periodicals*—Atlantic March 1967; Book Week October 13, 1963; Christian Science Monitor September 8, 1966; Commentary March 1953, October 1958, March 1962; Critique Winter–Spring 1960; English Journal July 1964; Kenyon Review Summer 1963; Massachusetts Review Summer 1964, Spring 1967; Nation October 17, 1966; New Republic December 21, 1963; September 10, 1966; New Statesman March 30, 1962; New York Review of Books September 22, 1966; New York Times Book Review September 4, 1966; May 4, 1969; October 3, 1971; Northwest Review Spring 1962; Partisan Review Fall 1958; Saturday Review May 10, 1969; Times Literary Supplement April 19, 1963; June 4, 1964; April 16, 1967; October 16, 1969; Wisconsin Studies in Contemporary Literature Fall 1962.

MALGONKAR, MANOHAR (July 12, 1913–), Indian novelist and historian, writes: "I spent my early years in a small village deep in the Kanara forests of Western India where my family have owned rice fields for over a hundred years. Even as a child, I became very fond of the jungles and took to hunting fairly early in life, certainly before I began to learn English which was at ten. After graduating (English literature and Sanskrit) I set myself up as a professional big-game hunter and, for a year or so, did some good business. But I soon became disgusted with killing wild animals for a living and decided to do something else. For the last twenty years or so I have been an ardent, if not very successful, wild-life conservationist.

"In 1937, I joined government service, and when the Second World War came, went into the army. In 1947, I married Manorama, the youngest daughter of Colonel Som-dutt of Jullunder, and the next year our daughter Sunita was born. After the war, I continued in the army and, in 1949, became a Lieutenant Colonel. But I was finding army life a little repressive, and in any case there seemed little future in the army for those of us who had joined up relatively late in life. In 1953, I left the army and returned to my village to join a younger brother in running some manganese ore mines which we had jointly acquired. The world prices of manganese ore crashed the very next year, and my business venture was a disastrous failure: I lost all my savings as well as most of the money my wife had been left by her father.

"While in the army, I had begun to supplement my income by contributing an occasional short story or an article to some magazine. Now in the jungles, with plenty of time on my hands and none of the distractions of city life, I began to write in earnest. During the next five years I wrote and published at least fifty short stories, another fifty or so articles, and about two hundred book reviews. At this stage, I also became interested in politics and, in 1957 and again in 1962, contested the elections for Parliament as an independent candidate. I lost both times, the second time by a relatively narrow margin. Politically, I follow the thinking of the Swatantra party, and I strongly believe that the economic deterioration in India since independence is due largely to the imposition of socialistic measures.

"The moderate success of one of my novels, *The Princes*, has enabled me to realize a lifelong dream: to build a comfortable house deep in the jungle. I now live in this house and normally work from seven in the morning till noon. I write very fast, using a typewriter, and finish around three thousand words in a morning's work. Naturally, this has to be revised again and again, but even so, I have so far managed a book a year since 1959. I read a lot of Indian history, have written two historical books and am working on, or at least doing research on, two more.

"I suffer from all the handicaps—and perhaps most of the complexes too—common to Indians writing in English. The things we write about and the people we write about are quite unfamiliar to most western readers who, somewhat naturally, prefer to read books about people like themselves doing the things that are familiar to them, with the result that publishers are reluctant to take us on. The language itself too is a problem for we think Indian and write English and, however carefully we revise our own writing, some flaws or peculiarities remain. I make a fairly decent living by writing stories for the Indian movies but spend much more time writing novels that make little or no money."

Malgonkar was born in Bombay, the son of Dattaray Sakharam Malgonkar and Pawati, born Walawalkar, and educated at Bombay University. It is the India of his childhood in the Kanara forests with which he identifies himself however, and which features most often in his novels. His heroes are army officers, British tea planters, and Indian princes, leading the leisured, servant-tended life of the privileged in India before and after independence. Malgonkar acknowledges the limitations of these men, but writes as one nostalgic for their self-discipline and code of honor. As a reader he admires above all the great tellers of tales in English literature, from Dickens and Kipling to Greene and Maugham. "I do strive deliberately and hard to tell a story well," he once wrote, and it is the old-

MANOHAR MALGONKAR

fashioned virtues of narration and description that are most admired in his work.

Distant Drum is about Colonel Garud, trained and shaped in the army of the British Raj, who seeks to apply the old values of discipline and devotion in the changed conditions of modern India. In spite of a rather tenuous plot line, the book was praised for the "appealing directness and sincerity of its prose."

The first of Malgonkar's novels to be widely reviewed in England and America was *The Princes*, described as an "intensely traditional and conventional novel" that would "captivate those who like their romance both exotic and authentic." It is an account of the education and coming to manhood of the young heir to an imaginary princely state, celebrating a way of life that came to an end shortly after independence with the incorporation of the princedoms into the Republic. A reviewer in the *Times Literary Supplement*, discussing the book's Victorian moral attitudes and dialogue, said, "It reads like a parody, but is the necessary documentation of a fascinating piece of social history. . . . The character of the [old Maharajah], autocratic, extravagant, maddeningly bigoted, believing that the highest good is somehow served by hunting, is vividly and boldly drawn; that of the son subtly and attractively matures; the social and political history is blended into the novel with considerable skill. And the measured, stately prose of old England proves itself to be still a wonderfully serviceable instrument."

There was also a generally favorable reception for *A Bend in the Ganges*, which centers on the conflict between two young men—one poor, and a Gandhian, the other rich and a member of the

Freedom Fighters, who chose a violent path to freedom from British rule. Another critical episode in Indian history is powerfully evoked in *The Devil's Wind*, a novel cast in the form of the autobiography of Nana Saheb, who figures in British accounts as the arch-villain of the Indian Mutiny of 1857–1858. The bloody story is told here for the first time from the Indian viewpoint, and Nana Saheb emerges as an amiable if superstitious princeling, the reluctant tool of a historical process which made him a revolutionary hero to his exploited people.

PRINCIPAL WORKS: *Fiction*—Distant Drum, 1961; Combat of Shadows, 1962; The Princes, 1963; A Bend in the Ganges, 1964; The Devil's Wind: Nana Saheb's Story, 1972. *Nonfiction*—Kanhoji Angrey, Maratha Admiral: An Account of His Life and His Battles with the English, 1959; The Puars of Dewas Senior, 1963; Chhatrapatis of Kolhapur, 1971.

ABOUT: Contemporary Authors 2, 1963; Morris, J. Eating the Indian Air, 1968; Naipaul, V. S. An Area of Darkness, 1964; Srinivasa Iyengar, K. R. Indian Writing in English, 1962; Vinson, J. (ed.) Contemporary Novelists, 1972. *Periodicals*—Book Week March 28, 1965; Chicago Daily News February 6, 1965; New York Herald Tribune February 5, 1964; New York Times Book Review November 10, 1963; November 24, 1964; February 14, 1965; New Yorker November 23, 1963; Times Literary Supplement May 12, 1961; June 21, 1963; June 4, 1964; September 24, 1964.

***MALLEA, EDUARDO** (August 14, 1903–), Argentinian novelist, was born in Bahía Blanca, a coastal town in eastern Argentina, the son of a local doctor and writer, Narciso Mallea, who was descended from one of the oldest Argentine families. Mallea was later to remember in his novels the immense influence of immigrants in the town and in his school, where he was surrounded by "silent blondes" and taught by foreign teachers before whom he felt all the inferiority of the provincial.

His mother died when he was a child, and he completed his education in an English school in Buenos Aires, where he moved in 1914. He was to study law at the university, but "was more and more inclined towards the literary life . . . trying to write myself, and already beginning to feel the isolation (almost, perhaps, the schizophrenia) of an Argentine writer—because to be an educated Argentinian then was to be Europeanized and a kind of stranger in your own country." He read voraciously—Dickens, Kierkegaard, Dostoevsky; met and formed a close friendship with Jorge Luis Borges; and in 1923 helped found a magazine, *Revista de América*. His first literary work, *Cuentos para una Inglesa desesperada* (Stories for a Desperate Englishwoman), a highly original though rather precious book, appeared in 1926.

At that point Mallea abandoned the law in favor of literature, though it was to be nine years before

* mä lyā′ ä

EDUARDO MALLEA

his next book appeared. Meanwhile he wrote for the periodicals *Revista de Occidente* and *Sur*, and in 1931 became literary editor of *La Nación*. In 1934 he was invited to lecture in Rome and Milan and made a tour of Europe, returning to Argentina in 1935. It was then that he began to publish the stream of essays, stories, novellas, and novels that quickly established him as the undisputed master of the younger generation of Argentinian novelists.

The first of his works to attract widespread attention was the novella *Fiesta en noviembre* (1938, translated by Alis de Sola as *Fiesta in November*), an account of an elegantly decadent Buenos Aires party counterpointed by a description of the arrest and execution in Spain of Federico García Lorca. The book has been found morally pretentious, and its characterization called shallow and unconvincing, too obviously at the service of its thesis. It is interesting nevertheless as an introduction of Mallea's central theme: the pursuit of a reality beyond the superficial values of materialism.

This theme owes a great deal to Sartrean existentialism, and not a little to the influence of D. H. Lawrence (evident for example in Mallea's idealization of women as the repositories of instinctive wisdom); but it is colored in his work by the deliberate attempt then being made in countries all over Latin America to discover and delineate a distinct national identity. Mallea's questing heroes are outsiders, alienated from the Europeanized societies but, like the middle-class would-be revolutionary Lintas in *Fiesta in November*, unable to realize their vague aspirations in action. Again and again in Mallea's books the authentic solitude of the soul is contrasted with the soulless greed of Argentinian social life, the "essence" of the individual with his public role, and the heroic qualities of the Argentine pioneers with the vulgarity and decadence of the mores imported from Europe.

Mallea is a philosopher who has chosen to express himself in fictional terms; the practical logic of expository prose seems to him part of the materialist ethic which must be overcome. Not infrequently, however, his thesis novels seem more thesis than novel. *Historia de una pasión argentina* (Story of an Argentine Passion, 1937), which has been called the "anguished autobiography of a nation," struck some reviewers as a work which, for all its painful intensity, is closer to an autobiographical essay than fiction.

His most successful fictional use of his theme is *Todo verdor perecerá* (1941, translated by John B. Hughes as *All Green Shall Perish*). It tells the story of Ágata Cruz, a lonely girl whose sterile marriage to an unsuccessful farmer leaves her loneliness untouched. So do the crowds of Bahía Blanca, where she goes when her husband dies, and her affair there with a lawyer; in the end her despair gives way to madness. The landscape of the novel—the parched farm and the barren town—powerfully and lyrically reflect the metaphysical anguish of the characters.

Elsewhere, as in *La bahía del silencio* (1940, translated as *The Bay of Silence*), and the trilogy *El resentimiento* (Resentment, 1966), Mallea's symbolism has seemed altogether too overt. *All Green Shall Perish* (1967) is the title of a collection which includes, in translation, the title novel, *Fiesta in November*, and several other novellas and stories, of which *Chaves* was the most admired. The volume showed Mallea's sometimes overpoetic style evolving towards a greater simplicity. One reviewer, Manuel Duran, wrote: "Mallea's characters, with their tense hopes, their mosaic of perceptions, their frustrated attempts to make out meanings and communicate, remind us of the sophisticated characters in an Antonioni film." And indeed it is not the least of Mallea's achievements to have broken away from the torrid regional novels of the 1920s and 1930s to show that Latin America is not entirely populated by sugar planters and gauchos. Few critics might now accept Lawrence Durrell's description of Mallea as "one of the two great Argentine writers of our time," but his importance as an innovator is enormous, and no one has said more about the spirit of Argentina and her people.

PRINCIPAL WORKS IN ENGLISH TRANSLATION: Fiesta in November: Stories from Latin America, 1942; The Bay of Silence, 1944; All Green Shall Perish (containing the title novel, Fiesta in November, Chaves, Anguish, The Lost Cause of Jacob Uber, The Heart's Reason, The Shoes), 1966 (In England, All Green Shall Perish, pub. alone in 1967, Fiesta in November pub. alone in 1969, remaining stories pub. as Chaves and Other Stories in 1970).

ABOUT: Anderson-Imbert, E. Spanish-American Literature, 1963; Dudgeon, P. Eduardo Mallea, 1949; Englekirk, J. E. Outline History of Spanish-American Literature, 1965; International Who's Who, 1971–72; Polt, J. H. R. The Writings of Eduardo Mallea, 1959; Torres-Rioseco, A. Aspects of Spanish-American Literature; Twentieth-Century Writing, 1969. *Periodicals*—Kenyon Review 3 1944; Saturday Review March 11, 1944; Times Literary Supplement December 28, 1967.

MALLESON, LUCY BEATRICE (February 15, 1899–), whose detective stories are written under the pseudonyms "Anthony Gilbert" and "Anne Meredith," was born in the South London suburb of Upper Norwood and was educated at St. Paul's Girls' School, Hammersmith. Her father was a stockbroker, who in 1914, at the beginning of World War I, found himself without an occupation. Miss Malleson took a course in shorthand and typing and set about earning a living. By the time she was seventeen she was writing verses which appeared in *Punch* and the literary weeklies. She became an efficient secretary and held posts with the Red Cross, the Ministry of Food, and the Coal Association.

Her first novel was rewritten a number of times but did not find a publisher. After seeing a performance of *The Cat and the Canary* she wrote a detective story which was, in her own words, "a complete flop." A second detective novel was written and rejected. By this time she felt distinctly discouraged. She continued for some time in office posts, earning a little by journalism, then in 1926 tried her hand again at detective fiction. Feeling that there was some prejudice against women as writers she used the pseudonym "Anthony Gilbert." The result was *Tragedy at Freyne* (1927) which was well reviewed and compared to *Trent's Last Case*. There was much speculation in the British press about the author's identity, which remained a secret for some years.

Since 1927, Anthony Gilbert stories have appeared regularly. Some ten books have been concerned with detective Scott Egerton, two with a French detective M. Dupuy (*The Man in Button Boots* and *Courtier to Death*). But in latter years most of the Gilbert novels have featured Arthur Crook, a brash little Cockney lawyer, unorthodox and brilliant, who defends his clients tooth and nail.

The first of the "Anne Meredith" novels, *Portrait of a Murderer*, appeared in 1934. These are "inverted" detective stories, in which the murderer or criminal is known from the beginning and finally brought to book. Many are set in Victorian times, revealing the murky passions hidden behind the façade of respectability. It was under this pseudonym that she produced her excellent autobiography *Three a Penny*.

The Gilbert novels have been praised by critics for their shrewd plotting and above all for the

LUCY BEATRICE MALLESON

warmth and vitality of their characterization. Frequently they are tales of suspense, with murder in the background. Anthony Boucher described *Black Death* as a *tour de force* of suspense writing and *A Question of Murder* as "not unworthy of Collins himself." The Meredith novels have also been commended for their stylistic precision and the authenticity of their backgrounds. Both as Gilbert and as Meredith Miss Malleson is an industrious writer; she now has over eighty books to her credit. None of them has been a best seller, but they keep up an extremely high standard of craftsmanship and ingenuity.

Under both pseudonyms Miss Malleson has had many radio plays produced by the British Broadcasting Corporation. She has been associated with John Dickson Carr in radio programs, and her story *The Woman in Red*, broadcast in America by CBS, was subsequently filmed under the title *My Name Is Julia Ross.* Her short story "You Can't Hang Twice" received a Queen's award in 1946, and others have been anthologized. She has also produced one "straight" novel, published under an unfamiliar pseudonym, but would rather it was forgotten.

Miss Malleson lives in Bayswater, London. Her interests include theatre-going, amateur dramatics, travel, and studying people. "One thing about writing for a living," she says, "is that it leaves you very little time for those mystical self communings that are so destructive of sound work. . . . I like being a writer, which is just as well, as I clearly could not be anything else. I like the thought of all the books I don't know anything about yet, that one day I shall write."

PRINCIPAL WORKS (a representative selection): *As "Anthony Gilbert"*—Tragedy at Freyne, 1927; Murder of Mrs. Davenport, 1928; The Case Against Andrew Fane, 1931; The Man in Button Boots, 1934; Murder by Experts (U.S., The Dover Train Mystery), 1937; Something Nasty in the Woodshed (U.S., Mystery in the Woodshed), 1942; Case of the Tea-Cosy's Aunt (U.S., Death in the Blackout), 1943; He Came by Night, 1944 (U.S., Death at the Door); The Scarlet Button, 1944; Don't Open the Door, 1945 (U.S., Death Lifts the Latch); A Nice Cup of Tea (U.S., Wrong Body), 1951; Miss Pinnegar Disappears (U.S., Case for Mr. Crook), 1952; Footsteps Behind Me (U.S., Black Death), 1953; Is She Dead, Too? (U.S., Question of Murder), 1955; And Death Came Too, 1956; After the Verdict, 1961; No Dust in the Attic, 1962; Knock, Knock, Who's There? 1964 (U.S., The Voice); Passenger to Nowhere, 1965; The Looking Glass Murder, 1966; Night Encounter, 1968 (U.S., Murder Anonymous); Missing from Her Home, 1969; Death Wears A Mask, 1970 (U.S., Mr. Crook Lifts the Mask); Tenant for the Tomb, 1971. *As "Anne Meredith"*—Portrait of a Murderer, 1933; The Coward, 1934; The Gambler, 1937; Three a Penny (autobiography), 1940; The Beautiful Miss Burroughes, 1945; Sisters, 1948; The Innocent Bride, 1954; A Man in the Family, 1959.

ABOUT: Meredith, A. Three a Penny, 1940.

***MALLET-JORIS, FRANÇOISE** (July 6, 1930–), French novelist and memoirist, was born in Antwerp, the daughter of a Belgian Minister of Justice and of the writer Suzanne Lilar, well known as a dramatist and a member of the Belgian Royal Academy. She was educated in Philadelphia and later at the Sorbonne, and is a French citizen by marriage. She lives and works in Paris, and has a country house in the South of France.

Although she speaks of her parents with affection, hers was an overregimented, oversupervised childhood that made her "a prisoner in a big house that ran like clock-work." Her most vivid pleasures were an occasional unaccompanied stroll, wonderfully solitary in the crowded streets; reading ("a positive disease") in her parents' large library; and writing.

A book of verse, *Poèmes du dimanche* (Sunday Poems, 1947), was published when she was only seventeen and gave her "a sudden feeling of peace to think that nothing was useless in that short imprisoned adolescence. I was athirst for solidity, usefulness, eternity. . . . The need to write was at once turned into a calling . . . at the end of each day I brought back my loot of words and impressions, and I botanized them with care. The work gave me peace for seven or eight years. Instinctively I loved order." She loved explorations as well as order, and while still in adolescence involved herself in a network of relationships that would have overpowered a less robust temperament. In later years she looked back on herself at that time: "Just eighteen, pregnant by one, in love with another, married, divorced, wonder-struck by a brand-new

* mal ā zhô rēs′

and charming baby one does not know how to handle."

Some of this emerged in her first novel, *Le Rempart des Béguines* (1951), which appeared in the United States as *The Illusionist* and in England as *Into the Labyrinth*. It is an account of a lesbian affair between the daughter of a Bruges industrialist and her father's mistress. It enjoyed a *succès de scandale*, and its sensational theme and precocious sophistication caused some reviewers to dismiss it as a cynical attempt to emulate the success of Françoise Sagan. Even then however there were those who, noting the psychological insight displayed in the book, its detachment and unaffected directness, recognized it as the impressive debut of a serious writer and were reminded not of Sagan but of Laclos.

This was the view that tended to be confirmed by the books that followed. *La Chambre rouge* (1955, translated as *The Red Room*) and *Les Mensonges* (1957, translated as *House of Lies*) both dealt with the same sort of family group as the first novel, centering on the emotional problems of the illegitimate daughter of cultured upper-middle-class parents, but showed a steadily deepening perception, and wider social range. Frances Keene found *House of Lies* "solid, interesting throughout, at times brilliant. And its strong grasp of human motivation, its understanding of the essential isolation of man . . . are truly profound . . . .Françoise Mallet-Joris is, I believe, the only young woman writing in French today who deserves the title of novelist."

The real scope and nature of her concerns, as a moralist, a social observer, and a psychologist, emerged in *L'Empire Céleste* (1958), which received the Prix Fémina. It was translated, like the majority of her novels, by Herma Briffault, and published in English as *Café Céleste*. This long novel studies some of the people who frequent a seedy café in Montmartre, passing from one consciousness to another to show how each conceals (from himself as well as others) his real motives for action. It was warmly praised for the exactness of its social observation, its touches of wit, and for its highly visual style. The comparisons now were not with Laclos, but with Balzac, Mauriac, and Zola. More than one critic thought the book rather like an Ensor painting.

Les Personnages (1961, translated as *The Favorite*) and *Marie Mancini* (1964, translated as *The Uncompromising Heart*) are both historical novels. The first is about Louise de la Fayette, a provincial innocent who was caught up in the intrigues of the court of Louis XIII, and (like the author herself) turned to religion. The second is "a marvellous portrait" of Louis XIV's first mistress. *Les Signes et les prodiges* (1966, translated as *Signs and Wonders*) returns to a contemporary setting, investigating the moral and philosophical problems raised by the Algerian war.

FRANÇOISE MALLET-JORIS

Whatever her subject or setting, the theme of Françoise Mallet-Joris's novels is the same; as M. D. Evans pointed out in *Twentieth-Century Writing*, she is fascinated by the masks people assume to conceal their nonentity—by what she calls "that damnation which consists of an intelligent man becoming voluntarily stupid, of a sensitive man in his turn becoming voluntarily hard, of a man who has been hurt becoming the one in his turn who inflicts pain, of a proud man humiliating himself to prevent himself being humiliated."

Françoise Mallet-Joris has also published a volume of short stories, *Cordélia* (1956, translated as *Cordelia*), written film scenarios, and produced in *Lettre à moi-même* (1963, *Letter to Myself*) a notable autobiography. It shows how the intensity of her moral and philosophical preoccupations is balanced by a delight in ordinary pleasures—Christmas and street parades, the countryside and children; above all the company of ordinary people—those who drink coffee around her in the early mornings in the unsmart Paris café where she goes to write. *La Maison de papier* (1970, translated as *The Paper House*) is another autobiographical volume—a collection of vignettes centering on her warm family life in a crowded Left Bank apartment—which was a best seller in France. *Les Trois Âges de la nuit* (1968, translated as *The Witches*) is something very different—fictionalized accounts of three women who were convicted of witchcraft in France between 1578 and 1620. It was generally well received, though one reviewer found it pedestrian, verbose, and "an uneasy mixture of God and melodrama."

She regards the "new novel" as an escapist form and has no patience with cultural fashions. "The theme that I dream of is Cézanne at Aix, alone with himself; Cézanne knowing that he will begin this day's work again and again until his days come to an end. . . . I prefer a modest struggle to an immense self-conscious unhappiness." She is a reader for the Grasset publishing house, and serves on the juries of the Prix Fémina and the Académie Goncourt. A recent photograph shows a tired, thoughtful, friendly face. She has been married three times and her present husband, Jacques Delfau, is a painter. She has four children.

PRINCIPAL WORKS IN ENGLISH TRANSLATION: The Illusionist, 1952 (England, Into the Labyrinth, 1953); The Red Room, 1956; House of Lies, 1959; Café Céleste, 1959; The Favorite, 1962; A Letter to Myself (autobiography), 1964; Cordelia and Other Stories, 1965; The Uncompromising Heart, 1966; Signs and Wonders, 1967; The Witches, 1969; The Paper House (autobiography), 1971.

ABOUT: Belgian Information and Documentation Institute. The Contemporary Novel in Belgium, 1966; Boisdeffre, P. de. Dictionnaire de littérature contemporaine, 1962; Curley, D. N. and Curley, A. Modern Romance Literatures (A Library of Literary Criticism), 1967; Mourgue, D. Dieu dans la littérature d'aujourd'hui, 1961; Peyre, H. French Novelists of Today, 1967; Twentieth-Century Writing, 1969; Who's Who in France, 1971–1972. *Periodicals*—Chicago Sunday Tribune December 6, 1959; Commonweal December 25, 1959; New Statesman August 27, 1965; New York Herald Tribune Book Review September 7, 1952; April 15, 1962; New York Times Book Review December 6, 1959; May 1, 1966; August 6, 1967; New Yorker September 13, 1952; July 11, 1964; Saturday Review September 20, 1952; December 19, 1959; May 23, 1964; Spectator April 13, 1962; Time July 21, 1967; Times Literary Supplement November 20, 1959; August 5, 1965; Yale French Studies 27, 1961.

MANCHESTER, WILLIAM (RAYMOND) (April 1, 1922–), American biographer, novelist, and historical writer, writes: "I was born in Attleboro, Massachusetts, and educated at the University of Massachusetts, Dartmouth College, and the University of Missouri. From 1942 to 1945 I served in the United States Marine Corps. The war was the central experience of my youth, and my postwar friendship with H. L. Mencken became the greatest formative influence upon my writing.

"Like many authors, I began early. At seven I was writing doggerel; at twelve, short stories; and my first published book—*Disturber of the Peace*—was written the year I finished college.

"There are authors who are content with small audiences, but I have never been one of them. From the outset I was determined to speak in the idiom of my own time, and in my late twenties (the late 1940s) I made a basic miscalculation. Remembering Thomas Wolfe, Farrell, and Steinbeck, I thought the novel should be my vehicle. For ten years I devoted myself to serious fiction. During that decade my work was received politely, but the great audience eluded me. I had chosen the wrong path. It was John F. Kennedy who helped me correct my error. He pointed out to me that this is an age of direction, not indirection—that men today are passionately interested in events themselves, not parables of them.

"Because of him I went to Germany, and in the autumn of 1968 I published the Krupp study which, had my gyroscope not gone wrong, I should have written long before.

"During our talks I never dreamed, of course, that the Krupp book would be preceded by an account of the President's death—that a national (and, for me, a personal) tragedy should signal my first communication to millions of my contemporaries in a language and form they would grasp. Yet the President would have understood, for he perceived both the desperate need for audible voices and the immense difficulty of making oneself heard in this baffling uproar.

"This is no place to unravel the extraordinary misunderstanding which accompanied publication of *The Death of a President*. The fact is that hours after Jacqueline Kennedy actually read the manuscript, she withdrew the suit against the book which, unwisely, she had been persuaded to file. And on June 21, 1968, upon receiving a seven-hundred-and-fifty-thousand-dollar check—royalities from the book for the John F. Kennedy Memorial Library at Harvard—she issued a statement to the New York *Times*: 'I think it is so beautiful, what Mr. Manchester did. I am glad that Senator [Robert] Kennedy knew about it before he died. All the pain of the book and now this noble gesture, of such generosity, makes the circle come around and close with healing.'

"Because I have always believed that books are important but that authors aren't, the controversy eighteen months earlier had been agony for me. Fame justly earned is one thing; notoriety is another. Therefore I was especially pleased by the recognition given to my next book, *The Arms of Krupp*. It was well received by such colleagues as Arthur Schlesinger, Jr., William L. Shirer and Allan Nevins, and remained on the New York *Times* best-seller list for over seven months.

"All of which brings me back to my novels. I believe the long years spent writing them were well spent. Though few have noted it, the decline of fiction and the rise of non-fiction has produced a new art form: narrative history. The author of narrative history (not to be confused with historical novelists, a lesser breed) deals only with facts. Whenever possible, he annotates his manuscript, and his sources are those explored by the traditional historian. However, by using fictive techniques—e.g., counterpoint, characterization—he recreates reality. Shirer, Barbara Tuchman, and Alan Moorehead are among our most brilliant narrative historians.

"I write in longhand, using a fountain pen. Mornings are spent transcribing yesterday's text on a typewriter; afternoons I write new manuscript; evenings I read. I get curiously little satisfaction from publication, and even less from prizes and awards. What counts is the completion of a manuscript, the feeling of achievement when (and if) you've done the thing right and know that perhaps a century hence a boy may take the book from a library shelf and be changed or challenged by it. That's the real thing, not what some book reviewer says now. Chekhov put it right when he said 'Critics are like horseflies. They sting, but they don't help with the plowing'."

Manchester spent a childhood largely homebound on account of ill health, and immersed in books. He served his journalistic apprenticeship as a crime reporter on the *Daily Oklahoman* after his discharge from the Marines, and later on the Baltimore *Sun*, for which he worked as foreign correspondent in Europe, the Middle East, India, and Southeast Asia between 1947 and 1954. In 1954 he was appointed confidential secretary to his "first hero," H. L. Mencken, whose influence on American letters had been the subject of his M.A. thesis and first published book, *Disturber of the Peace* (1951). Most reviewers found it a lively and entertaining account, if rather a superficial one.

In 1955 Manchester became managing editor of the Wesleyan University Press, a post he retained until 1965. He was a fellow of the Wesleyan University Center for Advanced Studies from 1959 to 1968, when he became a fellow of Wesleyan's East College. From 1968 to 1969 he lectured in English at Wesleyan University. Manchester held a Guggenheim Fellowship in 1959–1960, and was awarded a Doctorate in Humane Letters by the University of Massachusetts in 1965.

City of Anger (1953), the first of his four novels, deals with racketeering and political corruption in a northern seaport. Gene Baro commented that at its best the writing was "somewhat reminiscent of the work of Nelson Algren and John Dos Passos. Were the sensationalism and cruelty of his story somewhat tempered by the ordinary or warmed by a fuller human sympathy, he might have given us an excellent book indeed." *Shadow of the Monsoon*, a tale of manhood rediscovered on a leopard hunt, was praised by Robert Payne and others for its vivid picture of India, but dismissed in *Saturday Review* as a "thoroughly commercial undertaking, a cynical combination of sex and excitement and everything else left in the literary hydrator." There was a mixed reception also for *Beard the Lion*, about a political conspiracy centered on Cyprus, and *The Long Gainer*, in which a college president is threatened by a forgotten scandal when he runs for his state's governorship. This novel, marred by an excessively complicated plot and "feature-article prose," seemed to one reviewer "big and slick . . . moving at a catchy pace which is compensation enough for the narrative weaknesses."

WILLIAM MANCHESTER

Manchester's documentary books have been more sympathetically treated. All have been praised for the painstaking research that has gone into them, and their skill in evoking the drama of great events. However, Manchester's tendency to involve himself with his subjects leads him at times into what many reviewers feel to be too uncritical a stance—Kenneth Rexroth found in *A Rockefeller Family Portrait*, a study of the dynasty from John D. to Nelson, an "unpleasant resemblance to a campaign pamphlet"; and Tom Wicker complained that *Portrait of a President*, a profile of John F. Kennedy, could "only be described as adoring."

Two years later the Kennedy family commissioned Manchester to write an account of the murder of the President "in the interests of historical accuracy and to prevent distortion and sensationalism." The Kennedys were to give him cooperation not accorded to any other writer on the subject, and the lion's share of the profits was to go to the Kennedy Library. Manchester talked at great length with Mrs. Kennedy and nearly everyone else directly involved in the drama of November 1963. He had special access to the Warren Committee's evidence, familiarized himself with every inch of the fateful route through Dallas. The prepublication "scandal"—Mrs. Kennedy contested some of the use made of her material and finally settled out of court for the deletion of some sixteen hundred words of text—filled pages of nearly every American newspaper for weeks in 1967.

Half a million copies of *The Death of a President* were ordered before publication and a record sum was paid by *Look* magazine for the serial rights. Manchester offered his own comment on the affair: "Had the Kennedys chosen a pedestrian talent, the resulting chronicle would have been bland and flat, yet there would have been no row. My offense was that I was determined to give this generation a living history—a graphic recreation of what those November days had really been like, of what people had actually said, of what they had honestly felt. I could do this because I knew, because their diaries, memoranda, tapes and interviews with me joined in a clear, heartbreaking hymn of grief."

Given its passionately controversial theme, it is not surprising that the book, when at last it appeared, provoked even more critical dissension than Manchester's earlier work. Oscar Handlin, writing in the *Atlantic*, thought the author's emotional involvement in the tragedy a serious handicap, which had produced a book whose "contribution to the understanding of the event is negligible." Murray Kempton, writing in the same issue of the same magazine, maintained that Manchester was dealing with material "uniquely of the kind which cannot be usefully recorded in tranquillity"; the result, in Kempton's view, was a "noble and manly achievement," and a masterpiece. Elizabeth Hardwick accused Manchester of recording "some of the most ridiculous and empty dialogue ever to reach print," of "memorializing the dustbin of history." But for many other critics the sheer range and bulk of this huge accumulation of "trivia and tragedy" had its own revealing and compulsive fascination. The London *Economist* found Manchester's philosophical ruminations of less value than the facts and the quotations he supplies, but went on to praise his brilliant narrative skill and "comprehensive command of the scene." *The Death of a President* was translated within a year into sixteen foreign languages, and received the 1967 Dag Hammarskjold International Literary Prize.

The Arms of Krupp, a history of the German steel and munitions family, had a relatively cool reception. Alistair Horne complained of "the tiresomely promiscuous, visceral anti-Germanism which underlies it throughout," and Victor Lange wrote: "Absorbing and lively, macabre and grotesque though this epic of a dynasty may be, it provides, with all its abundance of picturesque incident, less the material and insights for an adequate understanding of a unique constellation of power than the scenario for a Hollywood spectacular." The book was not without its admirers nevertheless, and received the Overseas Press Club's award as the best book of the year on foreign affairs.

Manchester was married in 1948 to Julia Marshall and has three children.

PRINCIPAL WORKS: *Fiction*—The City of Anger, 1953; Shadow of the Monsoon, 1956; Beard the Lion, 1958; The Long Gainer, 1961. *Nonfiction*—Disturber of the Peace, 1951 (England, The Sage of Baltimore); A Rockefeller Family Portrait, 1959; Portrait of a President, 1962; The Death of a President, 1967; The Arms of Krupp, 1968.

ABOUT: Britannica Book of the Year, 1968; Contemporary Authors 1, 1962; Corry, J. The Manchester Affair, 1967; Current Biography, 1967; Garrett, G. (ed.) The Writer's Voice: Conversations With Contemporary Writers, 1973; Van Gelder, L. Untold Story: Why the Kennedys Lost the Book Battle, 1967; Who's Who, 1973; Who's Who in America, 1972–1973. *Periodicals*—Look April 4, 1967; National Review January 10, 1967; New Statesman December 30, 1966; New York Times April 8, 1956; January 30, 1967; New York Times Book Review September 30, 1962; April 9, 1967; November 24, 1968; Newsweek September 5, 1966; December 26, 1966; January 2, 1967; January 9, 1967; January 16, 1967; January 30, 1967; March 27, 1967; April 10, 1967; April 24, 1967; June 17, 1967; May 20, 1968; Saturday Review January 6, 1951; January 21, 1967; April 15, 1967; Time December 23, 1966; December 30, 1966; January 6, 1967; January 20, 1967; January 27, 1967; April 7, 1967.

***MANDELSTAM, OSIP (EMILIEVICH)** (January 15, 1891–December 28, 1938), Russian poet, was born in Warsaw of cultivated middle-class Jewish parents. His father was a leather merchant, and when Mandelstam was young his family moved to St. Petersburg, where he grew up and attended the Tenishev school. At sixteen he made his first trip abroad, living for a time in Paris. He was shy, awkward, and impractical, and his bourgeois parents considered his poetry sheer nonsense. But he was also oddly determined, and was not to be deterred from his absolute and almost religious dedication to poetry. When he was nineteen his mother, hoping to cure him of his obsession, took the embarrassed young poet to see the editor of the magazine *Apollon*. To her amazement some of his early poems were instead accepted and printed, launching him in the literary world of St. Petersburg. In 1910 he went to Heidelberg for a year to study Old French, then he returned to St. Petersburg University to study Greek.

Mandelstam's first poems were influenced by symbolism, which had dominated Russian poetry since the 1890s, but between 1910 and 1913 the two new poetic movements of futurism and acmeism took shape as reactions against symbolism. The acmeists rejected the mysticism and imprecision of the symbolists in favor of concern with the visible world, of concrete imagery, exact and

* man′ dəl shtam

logical diction, and the tradition of classical order. Mandelstam was both in subject matter and style an outright classicist who regarded Greek poetry as the supreme model, and he soon joined Nikolai Gumilev and Gumilev's wife, Anna Akhmatova, to become one of the three major figures in the acmeist "Guild of Poets."

The title of his first collection of poems, *Kamen* (Stone, 1913) epitomizes the architectural quality of his verse, its solid structure, impersonal and slow-moving, conveying the impression of stateliness and gravity. This desire for stability and harmony in turn led to one of his favorite themes, the empires not only of classical antiquity but also of Racine's France, and of course the Russian empire whose heart and capital was Mandelstam's beloved St. Petersburg. Other poems draw on Mandelstam's vast reading in many literatures and have their inspiration in Dickens' novels, the Homeric poems, or the plays of Racine. Mandelstam's work had indeed been criticized as a reflection of art rather than of life, and Zhirmunsky borrowed Schlegel's term "the poetry of Poetry" to describe it. Nevertheless, as Isaiah Berlin says, "His poetry, although its scope was deliberately confined, possessed a purity and perfection of form never again attained in Russia."

When the war broke out in 1914 Mandelstam was not conscripted but spent the war years in the south of Russia, mostly in the Crimea, with many other artists and writers who had moved there from the capital. After the Revolution he returned north and in 1918 was in Moscow. It was then, in a Moscow café, that Mandelstam had his famous encounter with the terrorist Blyumkin, who was drunkenly completing a pile of presigned death warrants. The shy and nervous Mandelstam, in a sudden access of quixotic heroism, snatched up the warrants, tore them to shreds, and ran out of the café. His life was saved on that occasion by the intervention of Trotsky's sister and another retreat to the Crimea. One of his autobiographical prose pieces describes his stay in Feodosia, from which he returned to Petrograd / St. Petersburg in 1920, getting himself arrested as a suspected enemy agent by the short-lived Menshevik government of Georgia on the way.

In 1922 he was married to Nadezhda Yakovlevna Khazina, and in the same year brought out in Berlin his second book of poetry, *Tristia*, which includes the poems he had written in the south. This was republished in Russia the following year as *Vtoraya kniga* (The Second Book), but the original Latin title indicates the mood of pessimism and resignation induced in him by the aftermath of the October Revolution, which was rapidly creating a world in which one of his temperament could find no place. He greeted it with an ode which

OSIP MANDELSTAM

begins "*Proslavim bratya, sumerki svobody*" ("Brothers, let us glorify the twilight of freedom") and in the desperate conditions of cold and hunger during the Civil War he recorded the crumbling of his old world and the death of his beloved city, soon to be renamed Leningrad. In *Tristia* his style also develops towards a more metaphorical use of language. Both of these volumes were reprinted, along with some later poems, in his third and final collection of poetry, *Stikhotvoreniya* (Poems, 1928).

Mandelstam had meanwhile produced his two volumes of prose, *Shum vremeni* (The Noise of Time, 1925) and *Egipetskaya marka* (*The Egyptian Stamp*, 1928). These have been translated into English by Clarence Brown with a long and very valuable introduction in which he disentangles the strange mixture of autobiography, fiction, and criticism in them. Mandelstam is always very reticent about his family and his relationships (there is only one obscure reference to his adored wife Nadia in the whole of his writings), and he himself defines his aim as "to speak not about myself but to track down the age, the noise and the germination of time." But his account of this "noise of time" is an intensely personal selection of visual impressions, fragmentary memories and episodes, brilliantly organized into a reflection of the chaotic times through which he lived. Mandelstam's prose is that of a poet, composed as Isaiah Berlin says of cascades of images "leaping out of one another, the historical, psychological, syntactical, verbal allusions, contrasts, collisions, whirling at lightning speed," but always controlled—"fused into a disturbing, often agonized but demonstrably coherent, unity."

Shum vremeni deals with Mandelstam's childhood and adolescence in *fin de siècle* St. Petersburg. *Egipetskaya marka* has been called the only true surrealist novel in the Russian language. Once again the scene is Petersburg, this time in the Kerensky summer between the February and October Revolutions, in which orderly government has collapsed and everything has gone to pieces. Through this disordered city runs a little man called Parnok who on the autobiographical level is clearly Mandelstam himself; but he is also the archetypal "little man" overwhelmed by the mob who appears in many other Petersburg stories, such as Pushkin's *Bronze Horsemen* and Gogol's *Overcoat*. The narrative covers a single day during which Parnok tries to do two things: to recover some of his clothes (including an overcoat), and to prevent the lynching of a natural victim like himself; he fails in both. But on this external narrative is hung the internal narrative of Parnok's inner thought, a dream world of memories, musings, visions, and at times of nightmare.

Mandelstam himself was soon to be overwhelmed by the mob. He was small and frail, with sloping shoulders and a large head, reminding nearly everyone who has written about him of a bird. And he had almost a genius for getting himself into danger. He was arrested in 1934 after reading aloud an anti-Stalin poem to a small group of friends, one of whom was presumably an informer. This poem, which speaks of the "cockroach moustache" and wormlike fingers of the "Kremlin mountaineer" and "peasant-slayer," was enough to earn him three years in exile. He was sent to the small town of Cherdyn, in the Ural mountains, and later to Voronezh, where he remained until his release in May 1937.

In Voronezh he suffered greatly, giving in to fits of temporary insanity, but nevertheless wrote a large number of poems in two notebooks, included by Struve and Filipoff in their collected edition of 1965. In them Mandelstam's style has developed further so that they are more directly personal, and far from being cold and polished they often contain a note of despair. This poem, written in 1935, has been translated by Robert Lowell as "The Future": "My body, all that I borrowed from the earth, / I do not want it to return here— / some flour-white butterfly. / My body, scratched and charred with thought, / I want it to become a street, a land— / it was full of vertebrae, and well aware of its length. // The dark green pine needles howling in the wind / look like funeral wreaths thrown into the water . . . ."

Mandelstam was rearrested in Moscow in May 1938 and sentenced to five years in a labor camp. There are conflicting accounts, all of them appalling, of what happened to him after this. According to George Stuckow's reconstruction he died in a transit camp near Vladivostok; he had been ill when arrested, and in his last letter to his relatives at the end of October wrote: "Health very weak, totally exhausted, terribly thin, almost unrecognizable," and asked for money and warm clothes. He did not survive the winter.

For more than thirty years Mandelstam's work was neglected in his own country, though since 1962 it has begun to be published again. His poetry —as distinct from rumors about his life and death— had also tended to be forgotten in the West until the 1950s, when the editorial work of Struve and Filipoff, and the more critical work of Clarence Brown, began to establish him ever more securely as one of the major Russian poets of the twentieth century. The rediscovery of Mandelstam received a major new impetus in 1970 with the publication in the West of his widow's magnificent memoir of their life together. It appeared in English, in a translation by Max Hayward, as *Hope Against Hope*. If most of Mandelstam's work survives, it is because Nadia Mandelstam risked everything to preserve it—much of it in her own memory. Her book is an incomparable portrait of a perfect marriage and of the diseased society that destroyed it, an important account of a great poet's creative processes, and a triumphant vindication of his values. It was everywhere recognized as a work of art in its own right, and some critics consider it as large an achievement as Mandelstam's own. A second volume of Nadia Mandelstam's memoirs, translated by Max Hayward as *Hope Abandoned*, was scheduled for publication in 1974. All of her husband's surviving work is now available in at least one English version.

PRINCIPAL WORKS IN ENGLISH TRANSLATION: The Prose of Osip Mandelstam, tr. by Clarence Brown, 1965 Selected Poems of Osip Mandelstam, tr. by Clarence Brown and W. S. Merwin, 1973; Osip Mandel′shtam: Selected Poems, tr. by David McDuff, 1973; Complete Poems of Osip Emilevich Mandelstam, tr. by Burton Raffel and Alla Burago, introduction by Sidney Monas, 1973; *Poems in* Barnstone, W. (ed.) Modern European Poetry, 1966; Bowra, M. Book of Russian Verse, 1945; Bowra, M. Second Book of Russian Verse, 1948; Lindsay, J. Modern Russian Poetry, 1960; Markov, V. and Sparks, M. Modern Russian Poetry, 1966; Obolensky, D. Penguin Book of Russian Verse, 1962; Yarmolinsky, A. and Deutsch, B. Two Centuries of Russian Verse, 1966; New York Times Book Review December 23, 1965.

ABOUT: Brown, C. *introduction to* The Prose of Osip Mandelstam, 1965; Brown, C. Mandelstam, 1973; Brown, E. J. (ed.) Major Soviet Writers, 1973; Carlisle, O. Poets on Street Corners, 1969; Mandelstam, N. Hope Against Hope, 1970; Penguin Companion to Literature 2, 1969; Poggioli, R. The Poets of Russia, 1960; Slonim, M. Modern Russian Literature, 1953; Strakhovsky, L. Craftsmen of the Word, 1949; Struve, G. P. and Filipoff, B. A. *introduction to* Sobraniye Sochinenii (Mandelstam's collected works in Russian), 1964. *Periodicals*—New York Review of Books December 23, 1965; January 27, 1972;

New Yorker December 26, 1970; New York Times Book Review October 18, 1970; Times Literary Supplement May 11, 1967.

***MANKOWITZ, (CYRIL) WOLF** (November 7, 1924–), English novelist, playwright, screenwriter, and journalist, writes: "I was born in Fashion Street in London's East End, son of Russian-Jewish parents. My father, who came to this country at the age of fifteen, was a general dealer and as soon as I could walk I was in the market. The market is a battle; a battle for your pitch, against the police, the customer, life, everything. My education came from the market, the books and antiques in which my father dealt, from Grammar School and from Downing College Cambridge, where I studied English under F. R. Leavis. My years at college were interrupted, first by conscription into the mines and then into the army. Also whilst at Cambridge I married my wife, Ann Seligmann, in 1944, and we now have four sons, Gered, Jonathan, Daniel and Benjamin.

"After graduating in 1946 (M.A. [Cantab] Eng. Trip.) and receiving an award for poetry by the Society of Authors, I worked as an extra-mural lecturer. During this period I wrote poetry, literary and theatrical criticism, and was co-editor of two literary magazines. In 1947 I started, with my sister and brother-in-law, an antique shop specialising in early Wedgwood. This has since grown into a very large business dealing in fine English modern ceramics.

"As the business flourished I was able to spend more time on writing and published three books on English ceramics. I wrote my first novel, *Make Me an Offer*, in 1952. After this was televised in the same year, my interest in the theatre grew and 1953 saw the production of my first short play, *The Bespoke Overcoat*, which won six major screen awards when it was filmed in 1955. From 1955 to 1960 I was in partnership with impresario Oscar Lewenstein and during our association we presented sixteen plays, including two of my own which I had adapted from my novels *Make Me an Offer* and *Expresso Bongo*.

"My introduction to film-writing was in 1954 when Sir Carol Reed directed *A Kid for Two Farthings*. Since then I have written some eighteen screenplays, fifteen stage and television plays, eight novels, and two or three hundred short stories."

Wolf Mankowitz, who had assembled a "reasonably good" collection of Persian pottery by the time he was twelve, and who is a world authority on Wedgwood, wrote his first novel about a London art dealer's search for a Wedgwood copy of the Portland vase. *Make Me an Offer*, called a

WOLF MANKOWITZ

"Swiftian satire" on the antique trade, was later adapted by the author both as a film and as a prize-winning musical. *A Kid for Two Farthings*, set in the London street market of Mankowitz's childhood, is a "tender fable" in which a small child's optimistic imagination translates a goat into a unicorn; it was a best seller and has been widely translated. In most of his novels, the author has very skillfully and very successfully exploited a gift for "compassionate mockery," sweetening the pill of his social satire with a coating of sentiment which only a minority of critics finds too thick. *Old Soldiers Never Die*, about a World War I veteran guarding a garbage dump in World War II, earned him wide praise for his "exuberant anarchy" and was called variously Elizabethan, Dickensian, and Runyonesque in its "rowdiness and tenderness." *Cockatrice*, attacking the British mass entertainment industry, was less kindly received by most critics, but was compared in the *Times Literary Supplement* to the Hollywood novels of Nathanael West and said to show "equal skill."

The writer's principal function, Mankowitz believes, is "continuity of productive activity," and his novels represent only a fraction of his output. His short play and film *The Bespoke Overcoat*, adapted from Gogol, was, as he says, heaped with honors. Another motion picture, *The Day the Earth Caught Fire*, was selected by the British Film Academy in 1961 as the best British screenplay of the year. Mankowitz also wrote screenplays for *The Millionairess*, *The Long and the Short and the Tall*, *The Waltz of the Toreadors*, and *Casino Royale*, among other films, and was the director as well as the scenarist of *The Hebrew Lesson* (1972). He is the

* man′ kə vich

author of a number of highly professional musicals, including *Belle*, *Pickwick*, and *Passion Flower Hotel*, as well as television plays and documentaries, short stories, and much popular journalism.

Mankowitz seems to take his work less seriously than some of his admirers do, and says he has never been much interested in "the message thing." He is six feet tall, "a hefty, broad-shouldered man" whose "pallid face, alert eyes and . . . determined chin" are familiar to a large audience from his appearances as an outspoken guest on television programs. His only listed recreation is sleeping.

PRINCIPAL WORKS: *Fiction*—Make Me an Offer, 1952 (reprinted, with Expresso Bongo and some shorter pieces, 1961); A Kid for Two Farthings, 1953; Majollika and Company (for children), 1955; Laugh Till You Cry, 1955; My Old Man's a Dustman (U.S., Old Soldiers Never Die), 1956; The Mendelman Fire (stories), 1957; Cockatrice, 1963; The Biggest Pig in Barbados, 1965; The Penguin Wolf Mankowitz, 1967; The Blue Arabian Nights (stories), 1973. *Plays*—The Bespoke Overcoat, 1954; Five One-act Plays, 1956; Expresso Bongo, 1960; The Samson Riddle: An Essay and a Play, 1972. *Nonfiction*—(with Balachandra Rajan) Sheaf: A Collection of Criticism, 1945; The Portland Vase and the Wedgwood Copies, 1952; Wedgwood, 1953; (with R. G. Haggar) Concise Encyclopaedia of English Pottery and Porcelain, 1957; Twelve Poems, 1971.

ABOUT: Contemporary Authors 7–8, 1963; Current Biography, 1956; Goldsmith, S. J. Twenty Twentieth Century Jews, 1962; Taylor, J. R. The Angry Theatre, 1962; Vinson, J. Contemporary Novelists, 1972; Who's Who, 1973; Who's Who in the Theatre, 1972. *Periodicals*—Newsweek March 28, 1960; Observer August 8, 1965; Spectator November 22, 1957; Time December 28, 1959.

MANN, LEONARD (November 15, 1895–), Australian novelist and poet, writes: "I was the eldest of three children, two boys and a girl, born in Melbourne, Australia. Both my brother (later a distinguished soldier and Chief Engineer of the army) and I won scholarships from a State School to one of the 'Public Schools.' Our parents loved us. We loved them, though as youth does, egotistically and rather selfishly. The family having fallen into financial distress I found a job as a clerk. I went to the war (of course the 1914–18 war) and served in France in the Australian infantry and engineers. As a corporal of infantry I was in and out of the line and took part in two battles, the second the terrible Passchendaele.

"It was there, at an advanced post, that I was buried by a big shell and said to myself 'I am about to die' and died. Dug out by two mates, the mud wiped off my head, I lay as the dead. Yet from a faint spark in the unconscious my life fired again. From that battle my body would recover, for I was born resilient, but the effects in the mind still linger. Chronic bronchitis, aggravated by a touch of gas, also weakened me and in London after the armistice I suffered a severe hemorrhage, saved this time by an angel in the form of a maid-of-all-work. I have always felt sure I would have made a good ordinary soldier had it not been for wear of war and had I had time to control my excessive romanticism by common sense.

"Returned to Australia I completed the law course started before the war and practised at the Bar for a few years. I loved playing football and was fairly good at it. I married. I disliked the Law and as the Depression loomed I left the Bar to serve employers' associations, as consultant and advocate in industrial jurisdictions, and industry in political affairs. A leader and authority in those fields until moved in heart and in mind I converted myself to Socialism. The second World War begun, I became the manager for the Commission and Department of Aircraft Production in all that in any way related to labour, salaried and wage-paid, and was given other assignments also, especially problems of production not entirely technical.

"The War ended, and after a few years in the Commonwealth Department of Labour I made myself a farm, thirty-six miles from Melbourne—poultry and with plans for horticulture and sheep. My son joined me. (I have two children, four grandchildren.) Alas, after some comfortable years three disasters combined to smite us. My son has revived; I have survived. Living now in the Dandenong Ranges and commuting to the city, I read for a publisher and do casual jobs of editing and organising.

"And all through this mid-century I have been writing my books, off and on. On my innate and excessive romanticism I have managed to impose the controls of realism, believing that in letters and art the thing, the event, the situation, the scene, has an inner validity of its own not to be denied but used. And like most Australian writers of my generation I felt that the time was come when the Australian people was by its own literature to be made conscious of itself, to identify, even to justify, itself, a small people of the East, in other ways than prowess in war and physical achievement. What had been inchoately done by history, war and the struggle with circumstance and the land's physique, was to be given an inner form and esprit. Our painters were to help later. But it was mainly the writers who did what had to be done, perhaps at some sacrifice of themselves."

The author is the son of Samuel Mann, who owned a men's wear and drapery store, and his wife Kate. Mann was obliged to leave Wesley College at sixteen, when the family business failed, and subsequently began his classes in law at the University of Melbourne. He is one of his country's most distinguished and original novelists, the comparative neglect of whose work is partially explained by his innate modesty and by the fact that he has produced only seven novels in almost forty years of writing. The reason for this small output is of course that he has always had to write in his spare time.

Mann's verse is interesting less on its own account than as a key to his fiction. It illustrates the perpetual conflict in him between obstinate idealism and harsh realism—the kind of dejected realism peculiar to antipodean writers. Hope, in Mann's work, remains largely unrealized; but functions nevertheless as a beneficent element in human experience: "We will not turn back to the Wasteland," he writes in *The Delectable Mountains*. The worst fault of his verse is in its diction, which at times becomes an awkward mixture of the colloquial and the ponderously rhetorical: "What won, ah what won, mate, the second race?"

In his fiction Mann is fundamentally a naturalist, but there is a poetic quality—a submerged tenderness or brooding intensity—in his treatment of the most lifelike situations. F. T. Macartney has conceded that "his narrative casualness, caught from the nature of his situations, creates admirable effects," but has said that "it results in some indifferent writing." It could be maintained on the contrary that Mann's stylistic clumsiness should be judged in the same way as Hardy's or Dreiser's, as an element in the solidity and density of his final effect rather than as a weakness to be unequivocally condemned.

Flesh in Armour (1932), Mann's first novel, tells of three members of an Australian Imperial Forces platoon as they fight in France and visit England on leave or as wounded. It focuses in particular on an ex-teacher, Frank Jeffreys, who desperately tries but finally cannot turn himself into a soldier. Defeated in love and his nerve shattered, he kills himself in the hour of the Allied victory. Jeffreys is the typical Mann victim, represented as in some ways superior to his more successful comrades. The author was originally obliged to publish this novel at his own expense. His edition of a thousand copies sold out and is now a collector's item; the book was subsequently reissued by a trade publisher. It was warmly praised for its characterization and especially for the exactness of its dialogue, and received the Gold Medal of the Australian Literary Society as the best Australian novel of 1932.

Human Drift (1935), about the Victoria goldfields in the 1850s, was followed by Mann's most successful novel, *A Murder in Sydney* (1937), set during the Depression. Barbara Hallam hates her father's mistress, kills her, but confesses when he is suspected of the crime. The incidental characters are sharply observed, and the teeming life of the city is vividly evoked; the arrogant Barbara's own redemption, through the intervention of her maimed lover Mat Dyas, is convincing. Only

LEONARD MANN

humor is lacking in this subtle and gloomy metropolitan study, a Book-of-the-Month Club selection in England. *Mountain Flat* (1939) studies the rivalry for land in a farming community, and *The Go-Getter* (1942) is an unusually optimistic account of the redemption of a political trickster in Melbourne.

Andrea Caslin appeared in 1959 after a long silence, and showed that Mann's fiction had lost none of its power (or versatility). Andrea, a woman of character and intellect, is temporarily demoralized by her father's financial ruin and suicide, but under the impetus of a successful (and adulterous) love affair enters the business world and becomes rich, only to be emotionally ruined by the death of her illegitimate son. This is a grim but persuasive study, in which Mann's sometimes obtrusive earnestness is absent, and his powers of psychological penetration at their most acute; the result is an indubitably major novel. *Venus Half-Caste* (1964) deals compassionately with problems of race in Australia, and is notable for Mann's portrait of his courageous heroine, a kind of symbol of human resilience.

Integrity is the keynote of this cautious, somber, and powerful writer's work, which has received less critical attention than it deserves. "Nothing," writes H. M. Green, "has been able to crush his ideal enthusiasm. . . . Its heat can still be felt, and it glows out sometimes."

Mann was married in 1926 to Florence Archer and has a son and a daughter. He has received the Australian Literary Society's Crouch Award (1941) and the Grace Leven Award (1957) for his poetry, and two Australian Literary Society awards for fiction.

PRINCIPAL WORKS: *Novels*—Flesh in Armour, 1932; Human Drift, 1935; A Murder in Sydney, 1937; Mountain Flat, 1939; The Go-Getter, 1942; Andrea Caslin, 1959; Venus Half-Caste, 1963. *Poetry*—The Plumed Voice, 1938; Poems From the Mask, 1941; The Delectable Mountains, 1944; Elegiac and Other Poems, 1957.
ABOUT: "Eldershaw, M. Barnard." Essays in Australian Fiction, 1938; Green, H. M. History of Australian Literature, 1960; Hadgraft, C. Australian Literature, 1960; Heddle, E. M. Australian Literature Now, 1949; Hetherington, J. (ed.) Forty-two Faces, 1963; Murphy, R. (ed.) Contemporary Poets of the English Language, 1970. *Periodicals*—Book News April 1947; Overland Winter 1970.

***MANNES, MARYA ("SEC")** (November 14, 1904–), American journalist, poet, novelist, dramatist, and social satirist, writes: "I was born in the first decade of this century in an apartment house on the West Side of New York City: daughter of musicians David Mannes and Clara Damrosch, sister of musician Leopold Mannes, granddaughter and niece of musicians; and, like them, of German, Polish and Jewish origin.

"Home was naturally filled with music, often of a very high order, and it didn't take too long for my privileged ears to realize that the family talent was not mine. A love of language took priority. I turned to words instead of notes, and rather pompously announced to my parents that I intended to do something 'silent.' Before I was ten I had started writing (and reading voraciously), and have not stopped since.

"My only formal education consisted of eleven years at a private school a block from home where a French head-mistress and an exceptional faculty put us through exacting paces in the widest range of French and English literature, gave us four years of Latin, and made us talk French in between classes. I owe to this school, long since defunct, whatever tools and disciplines I acquired as a writer, along with an abiding respect for language, native or foreign. I owe to my parents their marriage of integrity and art which made the creative life seem, to me, the only one worth living.

"I did not go to college because I could not contemplate four more years in the company of girls. Instead, I went to England alone for a year and began to learn a number of things not in books.

"Since my early twenties perhaps too great an appetite for life and a too diversified interest in forms of expression have been responsible for a very chequered professional career, which—in between and during several marriages—falls roughly into this pattern:

"1925–33: wrote poems, articles, and plays, three of which were bought by producers, one of which opened on Broadway and closed four days later.

"1933–38: joined *Vogue* magazine as a copywriter and shortly thereafter became Feature Editor and regular contributor.

"In 1936 and after a second marriage, lived in Italy and worked chiefly at sculpture, which has always been my second love. Bore a son in 1938, returned with family to United States at outbreak of war in 1939.

"From 1941 through 1945 I worked in government agencies as an intelligence analyst, the last two years for the O.S.S., here and abroad.

"After the war I was Feature Editor for *Glamour* magazine for a year, then resumed free-lance writing and in 1947 completed a novel, my first book, *Message from a Stranger*, which was published by Viking in 1948 and later in paperback by Dell and subsequently by Crowell-Collier. It was ignored by the critics but widely sold.

"Free-lanced again—mostly magazine articles and stories—until 1952, when I became staff-writer for *The Reporter* magazine. For the ensuing twelve years there I wrote television and theatre criticism, feature articles, social satire, and satiric political verse under the name of 'Sec.' Much of this material was subsequently published in book form: a collection of essays called *More in Anger* published by Lippincott in 1958; a collection of poems, illustrated by Robert Osborn, called *Subverse* and published by Braziller in 1959; *The New York I Know*, 1961, and *But Will It Sell?* 1964, both published by Lippincott.

"In between these books I have written for a great many national publications ranging from the New York *Times Magazine*, the *Herald Tribune Book Week*, *Harper's*, and the *New Republic*, to *Esquire*, *Vogue* and *TV Guide*, and appeared fairly frequently on TV and radio. In 1959 I had a television program of my own which I discontinued after thirteen weeks, convinced that it was impossible to be a TV 'personality' and remain a serious writer.

"Currently, I continue to write for various publications, make a number of speeches on a number of subjects, contribute a monthly column to *McCall's* magazine, and keep trying to write a really first-rate book.

"If I were to assess myself as a writer I would say that although I am not as good as I wish I were, I may be better than the intellectual establishment thinks I am. In the face of verbal anarchy and faddist distortion I continue to nourish a passion for clear communication, which—insofar as my readers seem to understand what I say—appears to be justified. Yet because I am equally stirred by the creative mysteries of poetry and drama, my remaining hope is to give this instinct rein in future work.

"My remaining loves include human warmth, animals, the ocean, food, drink—and music."

* man′ əs

It was Miss Veltin's School for Girls which Marya Mannes remembers so kindly. She has been married three times: to the scene designer Jo Mielziner; to the artist Richard Blow, by whom she has a son, David; and to Christopher Clarkson, a British aircraft executive, whom she married in 1948.

The critics did not really ignore her first novel, *Message from a Stranger*, though this highly original fantasy about a woman's posthumous progress to self-knowledge had a mixed reception. It was found naïve in its political and metaphysical discussions and imperfect in its structure, but intelligent, informed, and entertaining. Miss Mannes is nevertheless best known for her essays and for the satirical verse she writes as "Sec." The latter has been called dogmatic, partisan, and intensely clever. Collected in *Subverse*, it made a "devastating and destructive and alarmingly funny" book.

Her essays are habitually controversial, characterized by her "fluid, powerful, evocative prose," which is most controlled and effective in attack, and by a certain tension between the progressiveness of her social and political views and a more conservative nostalgia for things past. Her targets are most often the commercialization of American life, its softness and vulgar complacency. Harry Golden has accused Miss Mannes of negativism, of failing to understand or seek the reasons for what she deplores. She says: "To be negative is just the other side of having a very clear idea of gallantry and beauty. I would like to see the return of the hero—I mean the man who really stands up and is counted, ethically, morally and humanly, and so becomes larger than himself."

This stubborn if disappointed romanticism is very evident in *The New York I Know*, which contrasts the city of her childhood with what it has become. It is an angry but loving book, "warmed with old memories, cold with young insights," at once an obituary and a celebration. A similar, rather embittered, nostalgia is at work in Miss Mannes's late second novel, *They*, published in 1968. "They" are the young, who have inherited the earth in a near and McLuhanish future. The novel centers on the discussions and speculations of a group of sixtyish intellectuals, expelled from society on account of their age, as they wait to die in a remote beach house. Most reviewers found the book impressive in conception but disappointing in execution, its characters, according to one critic, mere spokesmen for the author's "complacent and muddled" defense of her generation's values and achievements as against the inhumanity and philistinism of the young. *Out of My Time* is a fast-paced, epigrammatic and candid record of the author's life and the development of her ideas. Miss Mannes is also the co-author of *Uncoupling*, a "guide to sane divorce."

MARYA MANNES

PRINCIPAL WORKS: Message from a Stranger (novel), 1948; More in Anger (essays), 1958; Subverse: Rhymes for Our Times (verse), 1959; The New York I Know (essays, with photographs by Herb Snitzer), 1961; But Will It Sell? (essays and verse), 1964; They (novel), 1968; Out of My Time (autobiography), 1971; (with Norman Sheresky) Uncoupling: The Art of Coming Apart, 1972.
ABOUT: Contemporary Authors 2, 1963; Current Biography, 1959; Who's Who in America, 1970–1971. *Periodicals*—Life June 12, 1964; Newsweek June 22, 1959.

MANNING, OLIVIA (March 2, 1911–), English novelist and short story writer, writes: "I was born in the naval port of Portsmouth, Hampshire. My father, who had joined the navy as a boy, had spent so much of his life abroad that he did not marry until he was nearly due to retire. He had no sooner retired than the war broke out and he was called up again.

"My first extrinsic memory is of hearing people talk about 'The War.' The war, like God, seemed to be a basic abstraction, to be accepted even if not understood, and I imagined it went on forever. It was something of a shock to learn that it had ended. On top of that my father returned home and tried to establish himself in the settled circle of my mother, my brother and me. He never really succeeded. He was good-natured, jolly and unworldly, and my mother ruled all three of us on more or less equal terms. We retaliated by laughing at her because she had no sense of humour.

"My mother was an Ulster woman who was always taking us for wet and chilly holidays in the North of Ireland. We never knew whether we were English or Irish, and I still feel the dichotomy of the half-Irish who imagines he would be more at home in the country where he is not. We were

OLIVIA MANNING

further confused by the fact that my mother's mother was an American from Missouri. My father, who was more than half a century older than his children, was born in London when it was still the London of Dickens, and served much of his life in sailing-ships. He rose to be an officer but his pension was very small. We kept up middle-class appearances on so little money that the words 'can't afford' were early engraved upon my soul.

"Like most writers, I started writing down stories as soon as I could write at all. While I was still at school, I wrote four lurid serials which I sold to an agency for twelve pounds each. With the first twelve pounds I bought my first typewriter. My parents were pleased by my ability to make money, but they were less pleased when I began to discover the major writers in the public library and became more ambitious myself. My mother was horrified to find me reading the *Times Literary Supplement* and said 'No one will ever marry you if you read papers like that.' I said it did not matter as I would prefer to write like Dostoievski. My first novel, written on Dostoievskian lines, was immensely long and I was broken by the cost of posting it to publishers. It was returned to me so quickly that I suspected no one tried to read it. One day someone typed a note on a rejection slip: 'Let me remind you of the words of a great writer: 'Look in your heart and write.' I at once started another novel about the miseries of living in a dismal provincial town where one never met any great writers. The hero escaped to Paris where he starved romantically to death. When this MS reached the publishing house of Cape, it was read by Edward Garnett who wrote an encouraging report. Cape wrote to say he would like to see my next novel and on the strength of this I decided to live and, possibly, starve in London. My parents put up the usual opposition but were sure that a few weeks of hardship would prove more than enough for me.

"I could type and managed to find the one job in London that no one else wanted. Starting work at eight A.M., I typed the delivery lists for the van-men at a big store, then spent the rest of the day tracking down the goods that had somehow never arrived. Having reached London and found a room to live in, I began to talk my way into other, more interesting jobs, but was usually soon after dismissed for incompetence. My average wage during my first year was thirty shillings a week, of which twenty-five shillings went on rent. I lived on rather less than it takes to feed a cat, but as I did not have to waste time on eating, I was able to spend all my free time writing. I completed another novel which I sent to Cape 'for the attention of Mr. Edward Garnett.' It was accepted. My advance was twenty-five pounds, which I badly needed as I had been sacked from my current job on the grounds that 'anyone who had time to write a novel could not be giving all her attention to her work.'

"Meanwhile the second war was pending. I signed on as an ambulance driver. Before anyone could discover that I could not drive, I met a young man called Reggie Smith and married him. He was home on leave from his first job, a British Council lectureship in Bucharest, and as soon as we were married, he was ordered to return to Rumania before the outbreak of war could cut him off from his employment. We reached Bucharest as the British ultimatum expired and the allies entered the war. A few days later the defeated Polish army came pouring down to Rumania. We remained a year, seeing the collapse of the country, the flight of the king and the rise of the Iron Guard. We left as the Germans marched in and reached Athens as the Italian invasion began. Six months later we left at the same time as the British troops and reached Egypt with the other refugees. A year later, my husband was sent to take charge of the Palestine Broadcasting Station and we lived for three years in Jerusalem.

"In 1945, we returned to England to find all changed. My brother had been killed in the Fleet Air Arm, my parents were retired into grief, and my hometown was in ruins.

"It was really now that my writing career began. During the war I had been able to write nothing but a few short stories. I started on a reconstruction of Stanley's rescue of Emin Pasha, doing most of the work in the British Museum reading room; but my chief interest had always been the novel form and as soon as we found somewhere to live, I settled down to write a novel that was published in 1949. This was the first book in which I dealt with reality as I had discovered it for myself. Since then I have led the necessarily unadventurous life of the creative writer. My husband is a drama producer in the BBC.

"I believe in the novel as the only true recorder of its age. I have no interest in fantasy and although I am amused by satire, I believe that those who deride their generation die with it. The novelist, if he is to fulfil his function, must portray truth as he sees it and seek to discover why we live. By doing this he maintains a spiritual territory in a world that has fallen into the hands of the scientist who can only ask: How?"

Olivia Manning was sixteen when, as "Jacob Morrow," she wrote her "lurid serials," and eighteen when she went to London, writing until midnight after her day's work, sustained principally by cups of tea. The book she produced under these conditions was *The Wind Changes* (1937), a first novel recognized as one of "unusual promise" in its "rich, yet disciplined detail, its delicate perception of fleeting moods." It was about a girl in Dublin during the Troubles, attracted in succession by three revolutionaries, and it foreshadowed the "Balkan trilogy" in that it concerned itself less with history than with the emotional problems of a few individuals caught up in great events.

Miss Manning's first book was almost her last. When she and her husband returned from Jerusalem at the end of World War II, she weighed less than ninety pounds and was desperately ill with dysentery. She recovered and settled down to learn to write all over again, beginning with *The Remarkable Expedition* (1947), her book about H. M. Stanley. A volume of tart and observant stories followed, and then *Artist Among the Missing*, which, according to G. S. Fraser, "covers the Middle-Eastern scene . . . with vivid, exact observation, with a fine sense of comedy . . . a richness of atmosphere and a patient exploration of inner distress." *School for Love*, Miss Manning's first real success, is "a study of human heartlessness and selfishness" set in wartime Jerusalem, and seen through the eyes of an awkward, engaging boy staying with a woman of "sanctimonious meanness." *A Different Face*, about a wretched schoolmaster dogged by bad luck, prompted a middle-page assessment of Miss Manning's work in the *Times Literary Supplement*, where she was called "a born writer, now elbowing her way . . . to a position in contemporary English letters she cannot be denied."

The "Balkan trilogy" has appeared since then, and most English critics would now place Miss Manning high among the country's living novelists. The trilogy is a historical tragicomedy about a British Council lecturer and his wife whose experiences during World War II parallel those of Miss Manning and her husband. Though the scenes and many of the incidents described are obviously autobiographical, Miss Manning says that the characters are fictional, but admits that friends consider her husband and Guy Pringle, the novel's quixotic hero, "much alike." The trilogy comprises: *The Great Fortune*, set in Budapest during the first year of the war; *The Spoilt City*, about the German occupation of Rumania after the fall of France; and *Friends and Heroes*, set in Athens during the Italian invasion. The trilogy was originally planned as a single novel (which would have been longer than *War and Peace*). Miss Manning says: "People want me to write a fourth (volume), and actually I could go on and on."

Discussing this work, the *Times Literary Supplement* said: "So full of intriguing minor characters is the scene, so evocative of both place and mood, and so well proportioned the incidents that provide constant narrative pleasure . . . that one might extract from the trilogy all kinds of meanings and thereby lose the overlying quality, which is simply to have covered an amazingly full and colourful canvas with people and scenes so real and so authoritatively recalled that it hardly seems like fiction." It was precisely this quality which disappointed some reviewers, particularly American ones, and Virgilia Peterson, for example, regretted that Miss Manning had chosen to fictionalize her experiences at all. Others found the Pringles rather pale creations and thought their understated marital problems swamped by history. Walter Allen, however, who had noted in earlier novels the "diminishing" effect upon character of Miss Manning's exactness of eye and style, thought the trilogy different; here, he wrote, the characters "come alive on the page, often absurd, but even so always as suffering human beings"; the drawing of Guy Pringle in particular seemed to Allen "one of the best explorations of character in contemporary fiction."

The Camperlea Girls (called *The Play Room* in England) is the history of a teen-age crush that develops between two middle-class girls in a suburb of Portsmouth—the setting at least draws on the author's own childhood—and its rather surprisingly lurid outcome. Compared to the Balkan trilogy it was thought "specifically small-scale, and reminiscent in setting and characters of earlier Manning stories." A selection of the latter, written over a period of thirty years, has been published as *A Romantic Hero*.

Miss Manning has contributed to *Horizon*, *The Spectator*, *The New Statesman*, and *Vogue*, among other magazines. Some funny and "intensely human" sketches first published in *Punch* were collected, with illustrations by Len Deighton, in *My Husband Cartwright*, which of all Miss Manning's books is the one she would most like to see reprinted. Olivia Manning lives with her husband in London, and enjoys travel and the theatre. She is addicted to Siamese cats, and has celebrated her pets in *Extraordinary Cats*. Anthony Burgess has written: "It is rarely that one finds such a variety of gifts in one contemporary woman writer—humour, poetry, the power of the exact image, the ability to be both hard and compassionate, a sense of place, all the tricks of impersonation and, finally, a historical eye."

PRINCIPAL WORKS: The Wind Changes (novel), 1937; The Remarkable Expedition (history), 1947 (U.S., The Reluctant Rescue); Growing Up (short stories), 1948; Artist Among the Missing (novel), 1949; The Dreaming Shore (travel), 1950; School for Love (novel), 1951; A Different Face (novel), 1953; The Doves of Venus (novel), 1955; My Husband Cartwright (humor), 1956; The Great Fortune (vol. 1, Balkan Trilogy), 1960; The Spoilt City (vol. 2, Balkan Trilogy), 1962; Friends and Heroes (vol. 3, Balkan Trilogy), 1965; A Romantic Hero (short stories), 1967; Extraordinary Cats, 1967; The Play Room (novel), 1969 (U.S., The Camperlea Girls).

ABOUT: Allen, W. Tradition and Dream, 1964; Burgess, A. The Novel Now, 1967; Fraser, G. S. The Modern Writer and His World, 1964; Karl, F. R. A Reader's Guide to the Contemporary English Novel, 1962; Who's Who, 1973. *Periodicals*—Books and Bookmen August 1971; Observer April 23, 1967; Times Literary Supplement September 4, 1953.

MANNING, ROSEMARY (December 9, 1911–), English novelist, writes: "I was born in a west country seaside town in England—Weymouth, Dorset, and spent the first ten years of my life there. The Mannings are a west country family, and though I left the area so young and have lived most of my life in London, it is in the south-west that I feel my roots to be. Most of my books, both for children and adults, have been set in this part of the country. I have recently built a small house there, high on the downs, where I can work in peace, when I can get the time to go there.

"My father was a doctor, and I wanted myself to follow his profession. Unfortunately he was old-fashioned in his views, and disapproved of woman doctors. I was born in 1911, ten years after the youngest of my three brothers, so that my father was well on in his forties when I was born. Discouraged from being a doctor, I had no other vocation. The one thing I knew I wanted to do, since a fairly early age, was to write.

"I was very ill-educated in a west country school, much of which went into my novel, *The Chinese Garden*. Because no one had any better ideas for me, I was sent to Royal Holloway College, London University, to read Classics, and obtained a degree in 1933. I hated my University years, found the

ROSEMARY MANNING

College like an overgrown boarding school, and disliked the fusty attitude of the professors towards Greek and Latin literature. The one professor whom I respected was a Mr. Sleeman, who introduced me to the pleasures of late Latin literature, and to the Stoic and Epicurean philosophies, which have in many ways influenced me. If I were to pick on one single book which has really had a far-reaching influence on my mind, I would select *De Rerum Natura* of Lucretius. I am a sceptic, and have been all my life. I have no religious beliefs and a profound dislike of most of the ways of the Anglican church, and of organised Christianity generally.

"On leaving the University I found myself without either a home or a job. My father had left my mother, and jobs were hard to get as we were then in the throes of an economic slump. With many of my contemporaries, I served in a shop, a large Oxford Street department store. This was an interesting experience, though I disliked it and was very ill-equipped for it. In the evenings, I taught myself shorthand and typing, and after one or two temporary jobs, became secretary to a young business tycoon, who was just building up a property development company. I stayed with him for three years, becoming increasingly disillusioned with the world of big business. I found myself perpetually involved in deals which seemed to me of dubious morality, and being extremely idealistic at the time, decided that I must quit business, and find work which was both more congenial and more worth while socially. I decided to teach.

"I was fortunate in my first school, a very small country school of a 'progressive' type. I was extremely happy there in many ways. I was there at the outbreak of war, and shortly afterwards went to another larger school. At once I realised how much I disliked the school world in its more orthodox form. I wanted to get out of teaching altogether but by that time teaching was a reserved occupation. So I went into partnership with a friend, and bought a school. In 1950, we gave this up, and moved to a large London day school, of which we are still headmistresses.

"During all this time I had been writing. In my twenties, it was mostly poetry and music, none of which I even tried to get published. Later I turned to short story writing, and was published in *Horizon* and *Cornhill* magazines. After showing these short stories to a publisher, I was encouraged to write a novel. In 1950 my first novel was published, under a *nom de plume*, and a second followed it. I then embarked on a children's book, which was published under my own name, and since then, I have published several novels for both adults and children. I write book reviews for several papers and have recently started to lecture on one of my great enthusiasms, the arts of the Middle Ages."

Critics have found it difficult to categorize the novels of Rosemary Manning, and tend instead to list a variety of other writers whom she is said to resemble. *The Shape of Innocence*, a "funny, sly, despairing book" about the destruction of a young teacher's reputation and life by self-righteous meddlers, was called a straightforward and rather melodramatic novel, removed from the ordinary by "quite startling qualities of remoteness and stylisation." One reviewer said it was "as though the strains of Miss Ivy Compton-Burnett and the late T. F. Powys had become improbably crossed." *The Chinese Garden* was narrated by a teenage inmate of Bampfield, a girl's boarding school which combines "a mortifying regime of cold water, draughts, outdoor drill and bad food" with moral corruption. The locked Chinese garden in the school park symbolizes both freedom from the regime and danger. Haskel Frankel wrote that the book conveys "something of the misty, undefined evil that pervades *The Turn of the Screw*, something of the brooding feeling of places that dominates *The Hound of the Baskervilles* and something of the controlled violence of *Wuthering Heights*." A writer compared to so many others is perhaps really comparable to none; an original. Miss Manning's stories for children share the beauty of style and some of the strangeness of her adult novels.

Rosemary Manning is devoted to music, especially to opera, and plays the viola; in her youth she set Ronsard and Baudelaire to music. Compact, fair, gray-eyed, she is an excellent speaker, forthright and sometimes controversial in her views on literature. She lives and teaches in Hampstead, London.

PRINCIPAL WORKS: *Adult novels*—(as "Mary Voyle") Remaining a Stranger, 1953; (as "Mary Voyle") Change of Direction, 1955; Look Stranger, 1960 (U.S., The Shape of Innocence); The Chinese Garden, 1962; Man on a Tower, 1965. *Children's books*—Green Smoke, 1957; Dragon in Danger, 1959; The Dragon's Quest, 1961; Arripay, 1963; Heraldry, 1966; Boney Was a Warrior, 1966; The Rocking Horse, 1970.

ABOUT: Author's and Writer's Who's Who, 1971; Contemporary Authors 3, 1963. *Periodicals*—Books and Bookmen October 1963.

***MANZINI, GIANNA** (March 24, 1896–), Italian novelist and short story writer, was born at Pistoia. Her father was Giuseppe Manzini, a socialist and atheist, by profession a journalist, who died in prison during the Fascist regime. Her mother was Leonilda Mazzoncini. The family was not well off, and Gianna Manzini's health was poor. She had a lonely and secluded childhood, scarcely seeing other children until she was nine. She says that even then she was not happy unless she had a pen in her hand.

Gianna Manzini took her degree in letters in Florence, where she lived for many years. She married a Florentine journalist, Bruno Fallaci, but is separated from him and has no children. During her years in Florence she became a regular contributor to the journals *Solario* amd *Letteratura*, and was soon established as one of the most interesting of the younger writers. Her first novel, *Tempo innamorato* (Time of Love), appeared in 1928. Since then she has published a novel or a volume of stories every two or three years. She went to Rome in 1936 and settled there permanently, though she confesses that she has never come to terms with the city.

From the beginning her work had a poetic, introspective quality which reminded some critics of the novels of Federigo Tozzi, while her vivid and rhythmical prose, full of apt and surprising analogies, suggested the influence of the essayist Emilio Cecchi. The books she published during the 1930s were received with interest and respect, but none of Italy's many literary prizes came her way until 1945, when *Lettera all'editore* (Letter to the Editor) received the Premio Costume.

A much more important award, the Viareggio, marked the publication in 1956 of *La sparviera* (The Sparrow-Hawk). It is a study of the effects upon character of chronic disease and Signorina Manzini, who says that illness lurks behind her "like a bird of prey," has acknowledged that the novel is an autobiographical one, in spite of the fact that its chief character is a man. *La sparviera* demonstrates her special skill in the evocation of physical sensations and their psychological effects, and is her best-known book.

* män zē′ nē

GIANNA MANZINI

Of her subsequent novels the most notable have been *Un'altra cosa* (Another Thing, 1961), winner of the Marzotto prize; *Il cielo addosso* (The Overwhelming Sky, 1963), an intensely dramatic novel which is at the same time sensitive and subtle in its characterization; and *Allegro con disperazione* (Gay With Despair, 1965), which received the Premio Napoli. Like so many writers of her sex in Italy, Gianna Manzini is greatly concerned with the rights of women. She nevertheless often identifies herself with the men in her books, since, she says, "it helps to make me sincere." It is this scrupulous honesty, together with her vivid and polished style, which have placed her among the four or five leading women novelists in Italy. She has read very widely, but, though her mature work is most readily comparable with that of Virginia Woolf, she remains a wholly original writer, and a very Italian one. It is no doubt for this reason that she has attracted less foreign attention than, for example, Elsa Morante, Natalia Ginzburg, or Alba de Céspedes.

Album di ritratti (Album of Portraits, 1964) was a collection of incisive studies of such figures as Virginia Woolf, Ungaretti, and Anne Frank, as well as of some "small people." For two years, 1945 and 1946, Signora Manzini edited the "international copybooks" of the journal *Prosa*. She also writes a great deal for the radio.

Gianna Manzini has said that writing for her was at first a way of escape from the real world of suffering. She is known to keep a diary, on which she draws freely for her plots. Slim, dark-eyed, pale, and still attractive, she looks and is physically frail but has a remarkable strength of mind and character. She has many friends and the constant companionship of a white Persian cat called Milordino, with whom she shares a flat so lined with books that the walls are "like tapestries."

PRINCIPAL WORK IN ENGLISH TRANSLATION: Mirrored in a Dream (story), *in* Life and Letters August 1949.

ABOUT: Contini, G. Letteratura dell'Italia unità 1861–1968, 1968; Dizionario enciclopedico della letteratura italiana, 1966; Dizionario universale della letteratura contemporanea, 1959; Robertazzi, M. Scrittori italiani contemporanei, 1942. *Periodicals*—La Fiera Letteraria 19 1950.

***MARAINI, FOSCO** (November 15, 1912–), Italian writer on travel and ethnography, one of the foremost Italian authorities on the Far East, was born in Florence. He is the son of Antonio Maraini, a sculptor whose best-known works include the bronze balustrade of the Vatican Museum's spiral staircase and the bas-reliefs on Puccini's grave. His mother was Yoi Crosse, an English novelist of Polish descent who wrote under the name Pawlowska. Maraini took his degree in natural sciences at the University of Florence. As a young man he conceived a passion for travel and went on a number of mountaineering expeditions.

In 1935 Maraini married Princess Topazia Alliata, a Sicilian artist and one of the many co-owners of the extraordinary baroque "villa of the monsters," Villa Palagonia, at Bagheria near Palermo. He paid his first visit to Tibet in 1937, in the company of the orientalist Giuseppe Tucci, and the following year went to Japan. From 1938 to 1941 he was an assistant professor at the University of Hokkaido, and from 1941 to 1943 he was reader in Italian at Kyoto University. His first book, *Dren-giong* (1939), was an account of his travels in the Himalayas. *Gli Ikuba-shui degli Ainu*, a collection of Ainu folktales from Hokkaido, followed in 1942.

When Italy left the war in 1943, Maraini and his family were still in Japan. Their anti-Fascist views cost them two years' internment at Nagoya, where they were often close to starvation. In July 1944, to prove that "Italians are not liars," Fosco Maraini chopped off one of his fingers and threw it at the white uniform of a guard. World War II ended in 1945 but Maraini stayed on in Japan until 1946, working with the United States military government in Tokyo.

Maraini and Professor Tucci returned to Tibet in 1946. The resulting book, *Segreto Tibet* (1950), established Maraini's reputation. It was a best seller and was translated into eleven languages—into English, by Eric Mosbacher, as *Secret Tibet*. It is an excellent account of the country before the Chinese occupation, showing a rare "ability to describe an alien world in solidly human terms." Maraini's photographs for the book were greatly admired.

In 1953 Maraini went back to Japan to make

* mä rä ē′ nē

documentary films. A valuable by-product of this trip was *Ore giapponesi* (1957, brilliantly translated by Eric Mosbacher as *Meeting With Japan*). This bulky collection of travel descriptions, war reminiscences, and reflections on Japanese art, history, and customs, was even more warmly admired than its predecessor. Some critics objected that it ignores Japan's sociological deficiencies, is too much a "spirituo-romantic" interpretation, but most were delighted and moved. The *Times Literary Supplement* called it "a treasure house of lively scholarly comment, interpretative description and personal reminiscence . . . a testament of love," and "one of the wisest [books] ever written by a European on Japan." Part of the book was subsequently expanded and published as *L'isola delle pescatrici* (1960), about the island of Hekura, whose economy is supported by the prowess of its young women as divers. Maraini's splendid photographs of the half-naked Hekura "mermaids" presumably contributed more to the book's success than his rather insubstantial text. A documentary film on the same theme also enjoyed exceptional popularity.

In 1958 Maraini, as chronicler and chief photographer, joined the Italian expedition to the Karakoram mountain range in north Pakistan. His account was published in 1959 as *G.IV*, and subsequently translated as *Karakoram*. The expedition's triumph was its climbing of Gasherbrum IV, a peak more than twenty-six thousand feet high, but, as A. Alvarez wrote, Maraini's "scope is wide, not just a single peak but a whole area, its people and customs." Maraini was back in Pakistan in 1959, leading another Italian party of students and mountaineers to the Saraghrar peak in the Kafiri region of the Hindu Kush. The classical writers had called this area Paropamisus, and Maraini's account of the journey was accordingly entitled *Paropàmiso* (1963). It was translated by Peter Green as *Where Four Worlds Meet*, since an important aspect of the book is the author's discussion of the interaction in the Hindu Kush of four ways of life: Oriental, Christian, Moslem, and Communist. Opinions differed about the value of Maraini's philosophical excursions, which seemed absorbing to some, naïve to others.

Maraini has published many articles about Tibet, Japan, and the Himalayas, and has made over forty documentary films. In 1960 he was elected a fellow of St. Antony's College, Oxford University, so that he could compile a study of the westernization of Japan. It was these researches, no doubt, that produced *Japan: Patterns of Continuity*, which sets out to show, in words and in hundreds of splendid photographs, that beneath the chaotic surface of modern Japan lies a "continuity that is the source of Japan's vitality."

Maraini is a handsome man of middle height.

FOSCO MARAINI

A teetotaler and nonsmoker, he is said to be very elusive and no doubt needs to be, since his extremely engaging personality makes him much sought after. He cannot be classed among Italy's leading writers in a literary sense, but his successful and widely translated books are based on careful research and detailed knowledge, even though some rival experts may consider his conclusions overcolorful. His temperament, ardent, poetic, and also thoughtful, is reflected in his "colloquial yet grandiloquent" style. Maraini has three daughters, one of whom, Dacia, has already made a name for herself as a novelist.

PRINCIPAL WORKS IN ENGLISH TRANSLATION: Secret Tibet, 1952; Meeting With Japan, 1959; Karakoram: The Ascent of Gasherbrum IV, 1961; The Island of the Fisherwomen (England, Hekura), 1962; Where Four Worlds Meet (England, Hindu Kush), 1964; Jerusalem: Rock of Ages, 1969; Japan: Patterns of Continuity, 1971.

ABOUT: International Who's Who, 1971–72. *Periodicals*—Il Giornale d'Italia January 25, 1958; Nation March 26, 1960; New Statesman September 8, 1961; New York Herald Tribune Book Review January 17, 1960.

***"MARCEAU, FÉLICIEN" (pseudonym of Louis Carette)** (September 16, 1913–), French dramatist, novelist, short story writer, and critic, was born in Cortenberg, Belgium, the son of Louis Carette, a civil servant, and Marie (Lefèvre) Carette. He attended colleges at Brussels and Louvain, and graduated in the law, but made his career in the fields of publishing and broadcasting. Marceau worked for the Belgian radio during the German occupation in World War II, was sentenced to fifteen years' hard labor as a collaborator

* mar sō′

FÉLICIEN MARCEAU

in 1946, but escaped into Italy. The New York *Times* noted in 1966 that the Israeli authorities had banned a production of one of Marceau's plays on this account, but also quoted a report that he had been cleared of the collaboration charge in 1962.

After the war, at any rate, Marceau changed his name and adopted French nationality. He made his reputation as a writer in the early 1950s, and in the theatre first attracted attention with *Caterina* (1954), an intermittently powerful but rather strained Elizabethan pastiche. It is, however, as a lucid and sometimes bitter ironist that Marceau has had his most conspicuous successes, with *L'Œuf* (1956, translated as *The Egg*), and *La Bonne Soupe* (1958, translated as *The Good Soup*). By 1961, Georges Borchardt could say that Marceau "probably is, with Jean Anouilh, the most popular playwright in France today."

The Egg is about a hopeless failure who discovers that all morality is a confidence trick, acts accordingly, and achieves success and happiness as a criminal; it captivated audiences in Paris and elsewhere but not all of its critics. Marc Beigbeder, for instance, saw it as a vulgarization of the work of Samuel Beckett, replacing the cosmic derision of *Godot* with sneers, Beckett's "metaphysical anguish" with "petit-bourgeois cynicism." All the same, he praised the play's characteristic movement—a halt and flow produced by a mixture of narrative and vaudeville techniques. In 1962, when it reached New York, most American critics denied heatedly that the world was as rotten an egg as the play insists, and the Broadway audiences apparently agreed, closing the show within a week. Robert Brustein however thought it, apart from an unsatisfactory ending, "the most consistently amusing light entertainment of the year" and admired its savage honesty.

The Good Soup, also seen in America, consists of the reminiscences which a middle-aged tart unfolds to a Monte Carlo croupier. The play advances through a series of "neat, revue-skit-sized" scenes designed to expose the woman's essential humorlessness. Her heart is mature but her head is all clichés. "I don't forgive," she says, "even the ones who have done nothing to me." The reviewers found it less disconcertingly cynical than *The Egg*, but also less witty and entertaining.

The best known of Marceau's early novels are *Bergère légère* (1953, translated as *The China Shepherdess*), and *Les Élans du cœur* (1955, translated as *Heart Flights*). The first, a euphoric fantasy, was embraced by Somerset Maugham as "a masterpiece of delight." The second, in which a young woman of good family becomes infatuated with a married antique dealer, is a macabre comedy which put one critic in mind of "Charlie Chaplin's little tramp playing the lead in a Faulkner movie." The book was said to combine a sense of pity with a sense of gaiety, and was warmly praised.

Marceau's forte, according to a critic in the *Times Literary Supplement*, is "a particular blend of fantasy and wit, of imaginative creation on the basis of acute observation of human character"; his failing has been that his characters are unparticularized, and "remain marionettes rather than human beings." This weakness is transcended, or rather deliberately exploited, in *Creezy*, winner in 1969 of the most sought-after of French literary prizes, the Goncourt. Creezy is a beautiful and internationally famous young model, her name a household word, her smiling face the emblem and promise of that spurious good life invented by the mass media. Her own life is empty and lonely until she falls in love with a rising (and married) politician, and for a time brings him into her dazzling stroboscopic world. His inevitable recognition of their absolute incompatibility costs Creezy her life. Marceau's triumph, most critics thought, was above all one of style. By brilliantly managed changes of tone and pace (well rendered in J. A. Underwood's translation) he revitalizes the clichés of which the story is compounded, and suggests "a frighteningly mechanical universe in which mankind itself has become a sort of souped-up machine."

Among Marceau's recreations are painting and Balzac, to whose work he has written a very lively, perceptive, and stimulating guidebook. He lives in Paris with his wife, the former Bianca Licenziati, whom he married in 1953.

PRINCIPAL WORKS IN ENGLISH TRANSLATION: The Flesh in the Mirror, 1953; The King's Man, 1954; By Invitation Only, 1955; The China Shepherdess, 1955; Heart Flights,

1958 (England, The Flutterings of the Heart); The Egg, 1958; Tiberius, *in* Borchardt, G. New French Writing, 1961; Balzac and His World, 1967; Creezy, 1970.
ABOUT: Beigbeder, M. Le Théâtre en France depuis la libération, 1959; Boisdeffre, P. de. Dictionnaire de littérature contemporaine, 1962; Borchardt, G. New French Writing, 1961; Bourdet, D. Pris sur le vif, 1957; Brustein, R. S. Seasons of Discontent, 1965; International Who's Who, 1972–73; Peyre, H. French Novelists of Today, 1967; Pingaud, B. Écrivains d'aujourdhui, 1960; Who's Who in France, 1971–1972.

***MARCEL, GABRIEL** (December 7, 1889–), French philosopher, dramatist, and critic, was born in Paris, the only child of Henri Marcel and Laure (Meyer) Marcel. His father was a councilor of state, a diplomat, and an administrator of the National Library. Marcel was educated at the Lycée Carnot, where he was a brilliant student, and subsequently traveled all over Europe before entering the Sorbonne to study philosophy. Between 1911 and 1941 he held various teaching posts and also worked for the publishing houses of Plon and Grasset.

Marcel had a "comparatively solitary" childhood in a nonreligious household, and says that his own religious feelings were "nurtured by the music of Bach." After years of self-exploration and metaphysical inquiry, during which he was influenced above all by Bergson, he entered the Roman Catholic Church in 1929. Marcel expresses his thought and beliefs in three distinct ways: through music, for he believes that musical improvisation involves participating in and responding to an extra-human reality; through his philosophical writings; and through the drama.

Marcel is usually described as a Christian Existentialist. He believes that faith in God and communication with other human beings are the two essential elements in personal existence. Marcel's philosophical views are expressed in (among other volumes): *Journal métaphysique* (1927, translated as *Metaphysical Journal*); *Être et avoir* (1935, translated as *Being and Having*); *Homo viator* (1945, translated under the same title); *Le Mystère de l'être* (1951, translated as *The Mystery of Being*); and *Les Hommes contre l'humain* (1951, translated as *Man Against Mass Society*).

None of these books can be said to contain a complete statement of his thought, and indeed he is averse to working out a formal metaphysical system. For him philosophy is a personal and continuing quest, a searching after truth that can never be satisfied. He says in *The Mystery of Being* that the true philosopher is not concerned with "objective truth" but is moved by the "deep sense of inner disquiet which lies at the very roots of metaphysics." His method appears at its best in *Metaphysical Journal* and *Being and Having*. They consist of jottings of everyday reflections, sometimes interconnected and sometimes random, sometimes trivial and sometimes profoundly perceptive and illuminating.

* mär sel′

GABRIEL MARCEL

Marcel is an opponent of the mechanistic philosophies, advocating a community centered on the Church, with faith forming the spiritual bond between individuals. He bases his objection to mechanistic views of the world on the grounds that these imply the technical possibility of a perfect world, which ultimately means regarding man as merely another object to be perfected, leaving out of account any recognition of the soul. For his part, Marcel considers human life in terms of "being" and "having." "Having" is the greed for possession, "the inevitable shortcoming of a fallen creature" who can nevertheless strive through prayer to achieve "being"—the state in which he focuses his life not on "he" but on "thou," the object of love. Experience of human love leads to experience of God's love and the return of the fallen creature from his lonely exile. What Marcel proposes, as his critics object and he very well recognizes, is not an intellectual process but an act of faith.

"I am convinced," Marcel says, "that it is in drama and through drama that metaphysical thought grasps and defines itself in the *concrete*." His plays he calls dramas of "the soul in exile"—of "the soul that has become a stranger to itself, that can no longer understand itself, that has lost its way. . . . But we are *not* alone, and only too often our uncertainty takes the virulent form of misunderstanding our own intentions and our own behavior to other people. Once this happens, our misunderstanding inevitably becomes contagious and tends to spread misery and bewilderment."

His plays explore the consequences of such misunderstandings, such failures of faith and love. Notable among them are *La Grâce* (1911), *La Chapelle ardente* (1925, translated as *The Funeral Pyre*, subsequently retitled *The Votive Candle*), *Un Homme de Dieu* (1925, translated as *A Man of God*), and *Le Chemin de Crète* (1936, translated as *Ariadne*). Perhaps the most effective of these contributions to what has been called a "theatre of pilgrimage" is *Un Homme de Dieu*, which was found deeply moving in its portrayal of a Protestant pastor's anguished discovery of his wife's infidelity. On the whole, Marcel's plays are more successful as vehicles for his ideas than as works of the theatre. Even a topical piece like *Rome n'est plus dans Rome* (1951), which deals with the Cold War, fails to achieve the concreteness Marcel seeks. He himself laments the absence in his plays of that "nourishing soil which has given birth to so many creations I admire" (in the work, especially, of Lorca, Chekhov, and Synge).

Marcel's Gifford Lectures at the University of Aberdeen were published in 1951 as *The Mystery of Being*. He has also visited Japan and the United States, where he delivered the William James Lectures at Harvard in 1961. These have appeared in book form as *The Existential Background of Human Dignity*. Marcel is a gifted and prolific critic of music, literature, and the theatre. His numerous awards include the Grand Prix de Littérature de l'Académie Française (1948), the Goethe Prize (1956), and the Grand Prix National des Lettres (1958). He received the Frankfurt Peace Prize in 1964 and the Erasmus Prize in 1969. Marcel is married to the former Jacqueline Boegner and has one child. He is an accomplished pianist and composer, and in recent years has become increasingly interested in parapsychology, especially telepathy.

Although some contemporary philosophers tend to dismiss Marcel's thought as illogical and fragmentary, his influence has been very considerable. Seymour Cain placed him "in the illustrious company of Martin Buber, Nicholas Berdyaev, and others who have struggled to renew and reintegrate the shattered human spirit in this terrible century." According to Rosalind Heywood, "his energy is fantastic and his activities world-wide. Like all truly wise men, he appears as unselfconscious as a child and as entranced with all the wonders around him, and, like a child's, his vision is not dimmed or distorted by a screen of *amour-propre*."

PRINCIPAL WORKS IN ENGLISH TRANSLATION: *Philosophy*—The Philosophy of Existence, 1948; Being and Having, 1949; The Mystery of Being, 1951; Homo Viator: Introduction to a Metaphysic of Hope, 1951; Metaphysical Journal, 1952; Men Against Mass Society, 1952 (England, Men Against Humanity); The Decline of Wisdom, 1954; Royce's Metaphysics, 1956; The Philosophy of Existentialism, 1961; The Existential Background of Human Dignity, 1963; Creative Fidelity, 1964; Philosophical Fragments, 1904–1914, and, The Philosopher and Peace, 1965; Searchings, 1967; Problematic Man, 1967; Presence and Immortality, 1967. *Plays*—A Man of God, Ariadne, The Funeral Pyre: Three Plays, 1952 (U.S., Three Plays).

ABOUT: Blackham, H. J. Six Existentialist Thinkers, 1952; Cain, S. Gabriel Marcel, 1963; Ewijk, T. J. M. van. Gabriel Marcel, 1965; Gallagher, K. T. The Philosophy of Gabriel Marcel, 1967; Gilson, E. H. (ed.) Recent Philosophy, 1966; Grene, M. Introduction to Existentialism, 1959; Grimsley, R. Existentialist Thought, 1955; Miceli, V. P. Ascent to Being, 1966; O'Malley, J. B. The Fellowship of Being, 1967; Ralston, Z. T. Gabriel Marcel's Paradoxical Expression of Mystery, 1961; Roberts, D. E. Existentialism and Religious Belief, 1959; Ryan, J. K. (ed.) Twentieth-Century Thinkers, 1965; Smith, H. (ed.) Columbia Dictionary of Modern European Literature, 1947; Who's Who in France, 1971–1972. *Periodicals*—Catholic World June 1953, August 1957, May 1962; Commonweal August 29, 1958; December 9, 1960; October 5, 1962; Contemporary Review February 1952; Review of Metaphysics December 1959; Review of Politics April 1959.

***MARCUSE, HERBERT** (July 19, 1898–), German-born American philosopher and sociologist, and one of the principal intellectual heroes of the international student left, was born in Berlin into a Jewish family that had been socially prominent in the capital since the eighteenth century. He is the son of Carl and Gertrud (Kreslawsky) Marcuse. From the Augusta Gymnasium in Berlin, Marcuse went on to the University of Berlin, and then to the University of Freiburg, where he received his doctorate in philosophy, *magna cum laude*, in 1922.

For the next ten years Marcuse devoted himself to research, first at Freiburg, and then, with Max Horkheimer and Theodor Adorno, at Horkheimer's Frankfurt Institute for Social Research. As an undergraduate, Marcuse had been a Social Democrat, but had been disillusioned by the murder of the Communist leader Rosa Luxembourg, allegedly the work of the Social Democratic government. His studies in the new disciplines of sociology, and the influence of the Marxist psychoanalyst Wilhelm Reich, moved him further to the left.

With Hitler's assumption of power in 1933 Marcuse fled to Geneva, Switzerland, where Horkheimer was carrying on his work, and after a year settled in the United States, continuing his collaboration with Horkheimer as a member of Columbia University's Institute for Social Research. Marcuse was at Columbia from 1934 to 1941, becoming an American citizen in 1940. After the United States entered World War II, he went to Washington, where he remained from 1942 to 1950, first as an intelligence analyst with the Office

* mər kōō′ zə

of Strategic Services, then as chief of the Central European section of the OSS's successor, the Office of Intelligence Research in the State Department.

In 1951–1952 he was a research associate and lecturer at Columbia's Russian Institute, and in 1952–1953 served in a similar capacity at the Russian Research Center at Harvard. In 1954 he went to Brandeis University as professor of politics and philosophy, and since 1965 he has been professor of philosophy at the San Diego campus of the University of California.

Marcuse's first book was a study of Hegel's philosophy and theory of history, published in German in 1932. His first work in English, *Reason and Revolution* (1941), was an attempt to demonstrate that Hegel's thought, far from lending itself to the development of Nazi ideology, was essentially revolutionary. The book provoked heated controversy but, though some scholars dismissed it as tendentious and dogmatic, many thought it an important contribution to recent intellectual history. In many universities it became required reading for students of political science and philosophy, and it has been widely reprinted and translated.

Eros and Civilization, which followed, is the principal fruit of Marcuse's work in the application of psychological concepts to the study of historical and philosophical problems, questioning in particular Freud's belief that human sexual drives must be regulated if civilization is to survive. Marcuse proposes that if this is so, civilization is at fault, as it clearly was in Nazi Germany, where sexual repression arguably produced a society in which sadism became almost a norm. He calls for an enlightened, healthy, and nonrepressive society in which man may freely gratify his instinctual needs. Criticized by some as utopian in argument and clumsy in style, the book was warmly praised by others as a profound, original, and stirring essay.

Soviet Marxism, another unorthodox study, compares Soviet practice with Marxist theory in terms which outraged extremists of both left and right, though it was enthusiastically received by others. It was followed by Marcuse's most popular book, *One-Dimensional Man*, which applies the theories advanced in *Eros and Civilization* specifically to contemporary America. By analyzing such aspects of society as art, literature, the sciences, philosophy, language, and sexual love, Marcuse sets out to show that social and political criticism in America has been absorbed into a "one-dimensional" ideology based on materialistic mass values. Like its predecessors, the work had a mixed reception, some readers finding it muddled and unremarkable, others welcoming it, like Émile Capouya, as "a turning-point in the intellectual history of our time." Marcuse's subsequent works include *Negations*, a collection of essays, *An Essay on Liberation*, which attempts to posit an alternative to the "global domination of corporate capitalism," and a collection of five lectures on psychoanalysis. *Counterrevolution and Revolt*, something of a critical reappraisal of the movement which Marcuse has helped to inspire, seemed to some readers less urgent and more mellow in tone than its predecessors. *Studies in Critical Philosophy*, translated by Joris de Beres, collects essays written over a period of nearly forty years.

HERBERT MARCUSE

Marcuse s attempt has been to show how the theories of Marx, Hegel, and Freud could be adapted to the realities of today's advanced technological cultures—a task in which he believes both East and West have failed. The utopian possibilities offered by automation and material plenty have been perverted, and the industrial nations have dedicated themselves to waste and war. Workers live unnecessarily in "exhausting, stupefying, inhuman slavery," bribed by consumer goods and "systematically moronized" by the "sewer system" of television and the other mass media, all of them preaching an anachronistic Victorian ethic, and geared to preserving the economic hierarchy.

Because his prose is scholarly, opaque, and unattractive, Marcuse's books, with the exception of the best-selling *One-Dimensional Man*, have not been widely read by the general public. Nevertheless, his radical and "permissive" views, received often at second hand by students, have been enthusiastically adopted by student revolutionaries, hippies, and the New Left. And Marcuse is a good lecturer, unimpassioned, but clear, thorough, and serene. On European lecture tours in 1967 and 1968 he was feted by young people everywhere, and consulted by such international student leaders as Rudi Dutschke in Berlin. His influence on the black militant Angela Davis has been much discussed, and his name has been associated with student rebellions in Rome, Berlin, Paris, and New York City. In his old age, this mild and scholarly man has emerged as one of the principal ideologists of the current moral, political, social, and sexual revolution.

Not everyone, naturally, shares this enthusiasm for Marcuse and his views. Attempts have been made to secure his dismissal from the University of California, and he has received anonymous threats on his life. Attacks of a different kind have come from some of Marcuse's fellow scholars who, while acknowledging his achievements as a philosopher in the 1930s, find his recent work dogmatic, inconsistent, irresponsible, and even irrational.

Marcuse's first wife died in 1951 and he was married in 1955 to Inge Werner, the widow of Franz Neumann; she died in 1973. He has a son by his first marriage and two stepsons by his second. Marcuse is a tall, white-haired man of great personal charm, a lover of music and of animals.

PRINCIPAL WORKS: Reason and Revolution: Hegel and the Rise of Social Theory, 1941; Eros and Civilization: A Philosophical Inquiry into Freud, 1955; Soviet Marxism: A Critical Analysis, 1958; One-Dimensional Man: Studies in the Ideology of Advanced Industrial Society, 1964; Negations: Essays in Critical Theory, 1968; An Essay on Liberation, 1969; Five Lectures: Psychoanalysis, Politics, and Utopia, 1970; Counterrevolution and Revolt, 1972; Studies in Critical Philosophy, 1972.

ABOUT: American Men of Science, 1962; Breines, P. (ed.) Critical Interruptions: New Left Perspectives on Herbert Marcuse, 1970; Current Biography, 1969; Habermas, J. (ed.) Antworten auf Herbert Marcuse, 1968; MacIntyre, A. Marcuse, 1970; Mattick, P. Critique of Marcuse, 1972; Vivas, E. (ed.) Contra Marcuse, 1971; Who's Who in America, 1972–1973; Woddis, J. New Theories of Revolution, 1972; Wolff, K. H. and Moore, B. (eds.) The Critical Spirit: Essays in Honor of Herbert Marcuse, 1967. *Periodicals*—New York Times Book Review March 10, 1968; New York Times Magazine October 27, 1968; Saturday Evening Post October 19, 1968; Time March 22, 1968; Times (London) September 29, 1967; Times Literary Supplement June 6, 1968; September 26, 1968; January 29, 1970.

MAREK, KURT W. ("C. W. CERAM")

(January 20, 1915–April 12, 1972), German journalist, editor, critic, and writer on history and archaeology, wrote: "I was born in Berlin and grew up there in the hectic period of good theatre and bad politics, of easy riches and mass unemployment. I despised school and teachers. At eighteen I entered a publishing house. That same year I wrote my first piece of literary criticism for the liberal *Berliner Börsenkourier*. A year later I founded in rapid succession two highly aggressive literary magazines which did not do too badly—they ran to a total of six issues. At that time I published a good many literary articles in newspapers. I was off to a remarkably good start—which came to a sudden end just as I turned twenty: criticism became *verboten* in Germany. I had an immense hunger for experience in all realms, and did a great deal of traveling during those years; but the dominant motif was an almost boundless passion for self-education. A book a day was my self-imposed stint. As a writer, I had to take shelter in the past to elude the hated censors. In this way I became a kind of specialist (in the magazines of Berlin's Ullstein Verlag) for 'cultural curiosities.' That is, I was engaged in presenting factual oddities in readable fashion. Clean facts, when put together cannily, make possible the most fascinating literary constructions. My fanatical love for facts as such was the inspiration behind my first book after the war.

KURT W. MAREK

"Although I regarded the eventual collapse as a certainty from the day the first shots were fired, it was my fate to experience that war on all the fronts; I was at Narvik, at Stalingrad, and at Monte Cassino. With the end of the war there came a period in which I was catching my breath, literarily speaking. The sudden gift of intellectual freedom led to a rage for work. From 1945 to 1948 I was simultaneously editor on the newly founded daily newspaper *Die Welt* in Hamburg, editor in chief for the famous Ernst Rowohlt Verlag, which was set up again after the war, and co-founder and editor of a magazine for young people, *Benjamin*. In addition I wrote innumerable articles and reviews for the newspapers and radio, literary prefaces and epilogues for Rowohlt Verlag. I plunged into polemics in the field of modern art.

"The painful pleasure of collecting and arranging facts retained its hold over me. I discovered a new field, the history of excavations, of archaeology. Chance put in my way the richest material on that subject that had ever been gathered in one place in Germany. For four and a half years I 'arranged,' 'constructed,' produced out of lifeless bits of mosaic a picture, a dramatic narrative (although I find writing insanely difficult). The result was *Gods, Graves and Scholars*, a book that has been translated into twenty-four languages, and that up to the present, in Germany alone, has gone into editions totaling more than 1.6 million copies.

"After two more books on the history of archaeology I wrote what I personally regard as my most important book, one which looks toward the future rather than the past: *Yestermorrow*, a collection of philosophical notes and reflections. Curiously enough, it did not arouse a strong intellectual response in America (which it was especially aimed at), but in France and Spain, where it was at once translated.

"In 1952 I married and bought a house in mountainous country in South Germany.

"In 1954 I moved to the United States, and have since lived in Woodstock, New York, in a country house surrounded by forest and fields. I have a son. I have thus fulfilled the requirements which Pythagoras supposedly set for man: Build a house, plant a tree, beget a son—and write a book."

The son of Max Marek, a carpenter and "old unionist," and the former Anna Mistol, Marek grew up, he said, in a family of independent thinkers: "It was impossible for me to be a Nazi." He attended the Lessing Hochschule and the University of Berlin. His first book, *Wir Hielten Narvik* (We Held Narvik, 1941), was an account of German army life on the Norwegian front. His only brother was killed near Leningrad. Himself wounded at the battle of Monte Cassino, Lieutenant Marek was taken prisoner by the Allies. It was in an American prisoner-of-war camp in Italy that he met some archaeologists and developed his interest in the subject.

His best-known book is *Götter, Gräber, und Gelehrte* (1949), translated by E. B. Garside as *Gods, Graves and Scholars* and published in the United States in 1951. It is a popular introduction to the discoveries made about the ancient world during the nineteenth and twentieth centuries, and to the archaeologists who made the discoveries. Although the *New Yorker* found the book "by turns cozy and popeyed, and . . . nearly always skimpy," most reviewers were enthusiastic. C. A. Robinson in *Saturday Review* said that Marek "has selected vivid episodes and related them in terms of colorful personalities. His stories are interesting and instructive, sometimes downright exciting, revealing a genuine respect for scholarship." J. H. Breasted found a few inaccuracies, but warmly recommended the book as a layman's account of what archaeology is about. It became an international best seller. There was similar enthusiasm for *The Secret of the Hittites*, about the scholarly detective work which in recent years has uncovered part of the history of an almost forgotten empire, and for *The First American*, an "eminently readable" survey of the development of North American archaeology.

These and other works on archaeology were written under the pseudonym "C. W. Ceram," as was Marek's brief account of the early history of the movies, *The Archaeology of the Cinema*. *Yestermorrow*, in which he returned to what his publisher called his "main interest as cultural historian and social observer," appeared under his own name. It is a collection of *pensées* and observations about the implications for humanity of the present technological revolution, in its total effect more often optimistic than not. Many readers found it a powerful, suggestive, and stimulating book.

Marek edited German editions of works by Ernest Hemingway, Sinclair Lewis, and Marjorie Kinnan Rawlings, among others. A series of television documentaries written and directed by him was presented as "Footsteps in the Past" on Channel 13, New York, in 1964. In 1952 he shared the Barcarella Book Award with Ernest Hemingway.

Marek was married to the former Hannelore Schipmann, a stage designer. A tall man, powerfully built, he called himself "a passionate traveler" and a lover of "good eating, drinking and cooking." He died of a coronary collapse at the age of fifty-seven.

"As a writer," Marek said, "I try to conduct myself like a Cartesian diver, moving freely up and down through the various strata of culture and opinion, lingering where it seems worthwhile to linger. This function of the writer . . . was taken for granted in the days of the Encyclopedists, and should be recaptured."

PRINCIPAL WORKS: Gods, Graves, and Scholars, 1951; The Secret of the Hittites (England, Narrow Pass, Black Mountain), 1956; Picture History of Archaeology, 1957; March of Archaeology, 1958; Yestermorrow: Notes on Man's Progress, 1961; Archaeology, 1964; Archaeology of the Cinema, 1965; (ed.) Hands on the Past, 1966 (England, The World of Archaeology); The First American: A Story of North American Archaeology, 1971.

ABOUT: Current Biography, 1957; Who's Who in America, 1972–1973. *Periodicals*—New York Times April 13, 1972.

***"MARKANDAYA," KAMALA (pseudonym of Kamala Taylor)** (1924–), Indian novelist, was born Kamala Purnaiya in southern India, into a middle-class family of "fairly orthodox"

* mär kan dā′ yə

KAMALA MARKANDAYA

Brahmins. On the distaff side the men of her family were lawyers, and her maternal grandfather was a judge. Her father, a rail transport officer, was regarded as something of a rebel by his family, which could trace its history back to the seventeenth century, and traditionally bred landowners, financiers, and government administrators. Her father's work, involving frequent transfers, meant an "intermittent and casual" education for her, but also free travel, not only in India, but in England and Europe. Miss Markandaya thinks that "the role of observer which every traveller assumes is good training for any writer. . . . It makes . . . a good starting point, and I believe it was my starting point."

At sixteen Kamala Markandaya entered Madras University, where she read history but found herself increasingly involved in writing and journalism. After three years she left without a degree to work for a short-lived weekly newspaper, and when that collapsed became an army liaison officer. When the war ended, "largely out of curiosity," she lived for a while in a village, but soon returned to freelance writing and journalism in Madras and Bombay. In 1948 she went to England, where she tried but failed to find a job on Fleet Street. She continued to write, supporting herself as a proofreader, as a secretary, and in other "dull but amiable jobs" until, in 1954, the third novel she wrote became her first published book.

Nectar in a Sieve is a study of life in a southern Indian village, drawn from the author's own experience of such a community. It tells the story of a peasant woman, Rukmani, from child marriage to widowhood. Rukmani's life with Nathan is bitterly, hopelessly hard, but as full of courage and love as of deprivation and tragedy. The novel was a dual selection of the Book-of-the-Month Club, and a notable critical success, warmly and universally praised as "unflinchingly real and moving," a "triumphant vindication of the human spirit."

Some Inner Fury sets the tragic love story of a Brahmin girl and a British official against the political tensions of the early 1940s. It was thought socially and emotionally perceptive, but a little contrived. *A Silence of Desire*, which more than one critic called a beautiful book, shows how the placid rhythms of a good marriage are shattered when the wife, thinking herself ill, turns not to a doctor but to an unscrupulous faith healer. It was followed by *Possession*, a harsh variation on the Pygmalion myth which serves as a morality about Anglo-Indian relations; *A Handful of Rice*, about a country boy who goes to the city and finds poverty there no less terrible than in the village; and *The Coffer Dams*, the author's most direct study of the conflict between East and West, old and new, in India.

Joseph Hitrec has called Kamala Markandaya "one of the crispest and most warmly personal" of Indian writers, and Margaret Parton has found in her work "a brilliance and depth outstanding even among India's current crop of highly talented novelists." She excels in the recreation of the gentle patterns and small crises of Indian social and family life, but is not merely a regional novelist; in her best work she achieves perceptions which are relevant to the whole human condition. And in *The Nowhere Man*, indeed, she switches her scene to the London suburb where Srinivas, an old Brahmin who has lived quietly there for fifty years, is overwhelmed by the rising tide of British racism. This "compassionate and disturbing novel" was slightly marred, some readers thought, by its too broadly caricatured presentation of the young thugs who give Srinivas his martyrdom.

Miss Markandaya lives in London with her English husband and her daughter, Kim. She is an extremely attractive woman who appears occasionally on English radio and television programs and who, when she has time for such things, enjoys reading, films, the theatre, and solitude. She is "anti-colonialist" and "anti-imperialist."

PRINCIPAL WORKS: *Novels*—Nectar in a Sieve, 1955; Some Inner Fury, 1955; A Silence of Desire, 1960; Possession, 1963; A Handful of Rice, 1966; The Coffer Dams, 1969; The Nowhere Man, 1972; Two Virgins, 1973.

ABOUT: Vinson, J. (ed.) Contemporary Novelists, 1972. *Periodicals*—Journal of Commonwealth Literature June 1971; Wilson Library Bulletin November 1963.

MARKFIELD, WALLACE (ARTHUR) (August 12, 1926–), American novelist, short story writer, and critic, was born in Brooklyn, the son of Max and Sophie (Monete) Markfield. He received his B.A. from Brooklyn College in 1947, and did graduate work at New York University in 1948–1950. From 1952 to 1964 Markfield worked as a publicist for philanthropic organizations, including the Anti-Defamation League. During this period he contributed critical articles and short stories to *Commentary*, *Partisan Review*, and other organs of the New York cultural pantheon. In 1954 and 1955 he was the film critic of the *New Leader*. A characteristic Markfield story is "The Country of the Crazy Horse," which portrays with humor and sadness the visit of a young Jew to the old neighborhood which he has left so conclusively behind. An excellent essay titled "The Dark Geography of W. C. Fields" throws interesting light on the sometimes rather desperate nature of Markfield's own humor as well as on his delight in popular culture.

Markfield's reputation rests, however, on his first novel, *To an Early Grave*, an irresistibly funny and sometimes moving satire on the Jewish intellectual establishment. Its story line is simple. Dead at forty-one is Leslie Braverman, an amoral, unwashed, and idiosyncratic "free spirit" who was also a writer of real talent and a literary journalist of *integrity*: "Two days he could spend over a sentence." Four of Braverman's friends spend a hot and humid Sunday driving across Brooklyn in a stuffy Volkswagen in search of his funeral, a journey recalling Leopold Bloom's ride to the funeral of Paddy Dignam in *Ulysses*. The novel describes this odyssey from the moment when Morroe Rieff learns of Braverman's death to the time, much later the same day, when he is at last able to feel his sorrow and cry.

Rieff, the most likable of the mourners, is not quite accepted by the others, since he has abandoned professional intellectualism for a career (like Markfield's) in a Jewish fund-raising agency. The Volkswagen belongs to Holly Levine, a pompous and tirelessly ambitious literary critic already pondering the best form and market for a memorial article about his dead friend. Also in the car are Barnet Weiner, poet by trade, lecher by vocation, and *der alte* Ottensteen, who writes for a Yiddish daily and is a virtuoso in the rhetoric of self-pity. The book is clearly a *roman à clef*, though the Jewish intellectuals best qualified to identify its targets were understandably reluctant to do so in their reviews.

Each of the travelers is introduced to the reader engaged in some characteristic activity, just before the telephone brings him news of Braverman's death—Levine, for example, is writing a review, and Markfield's description of this exercise is, as Stanley Edgar Hyman wrote, "enough to drive anyone of decent impulse, susceptible to shame, out of the profession." The variously inadequate

WALLACE MARKFIELD

personalities of the mourners are further explored during their long drive as they are tested and found wanting in encounters with a brutal cop and an indignant taxi driver, during a lengthy sermon at the wrong funeral, and in other frustrating situations, many of them hilarious. It emerges that the only art forms that really engage these would-be tastemakers are the popular ones of their youth, and they perform prodigies of recall when they challenge each other to name "fourteen movies wherein Bogart had been featured but not starred," or the name of the Shadow's girl friend. In the end, Morroe Rieff weeps less for Braverman than for himself. As one critic wrote, his tears "end a day of self-appraisal, commemorating the early grave of many hopes and comforting self-deceits."

To an Early Grave is, as reviewers pointed out, an uneven and lopsided book, and some found it too cruelly observant. But there was warm admiration for the richness of Markfield's comic rhetoric, his ear for Jewish speech, his marvelously economical descriptive writing. Hyman called it " a small comic triumph" and "the most interesting first novel since Thomas Pynchon's *V*." It was filmed by Sidney Lumet as *Bye, Bye, Braverman*.

Markfield's second novel, *Teitlebaum's Window*, is a Brooklyn *Bildungsroman*, the story of Simon Sloan's life in Brighton Beach from eight to eighteen. A large part of the book is made up of quotations from Simon's journal, and in this and other ways, as Thomas Lask said, "the decade between 1932 and 1942 is unrolled in a mosaic of miniature happenings, social tidbits, passing movie stars, popular radio programs, cant phrases." The novel was called "a fictional romp during which the author enjoyed himself thoroughly and the reader will too," but a number of reviewers shared Alfred Kazin's feeling that Markfield had used his gifts of mimicry "to make not believable human emotions but a warehouse of Brooklyn Jewish folklore."

Wallace Markfield was a Guggenheim Fellow in 1965 and received a ten-thousand-dollar literary award in 1966 from the National Council on the Arts. He was married in 1949 to Anna Goodman, and has a daughter, Andrea.

PRINCIPAL WORKS: To an Early Grave, 1964; Teitlebaum's Window, 1970.

ABOUT: Hyman, S. E. Standards, 1966; Who's Who in America, 1972–1973.

"MARKHAM, ROBERT." *See* AMIS, KINGSLEY

MÁRQUEZ, GABRIEL GARCÍA. *See* GARCÍA MÁRQUEZ, GABRIEL

"MARRIC, J. J." *See* CREASEY, JOHN

MARSHALL, S(AMUEL) L(YMAN) A(TWOOD) (July 18, 1900–), American military historian and critic, writes: "I learned to read and write pretty much on my own by copying epitaphs on headstones in a country churchyard at Killian, South Carolina, beginning at age five. Mother would then go over the letters in my copy. The first epitaph I did completely was: 'Here lies Eli Eisenhower, kicked by a mule which caused his death.' On Christmas morning, 1906, I was awakened by my Father's voice. He was reading about Hordle John from Doyle's *The White Company*, the volume being Mother's gift to him. I listened fascinated, forgetting Christmas, telling myself that if such wonderful stuff came from books, they were what I would go after. By age seven I was reading Doyle, Dickens, Haggard, Hocking, Alger and Henty, buying the books with money I earned selling papers and shining shoes. We were a family, poor as to money, rich as to love for one another. I mention this early influence because I think it set me on a course further fixed by the fact that Father, in particular, spoke flawless English and was an imaginative precisionist as to vocabulary. Born in Catskill, I hardly got to know my home town. We ranged all over the country. Father was a brickmaker, a genius and innovator at his trade, though he had gone only to the third grade. We moved about as he would take charge of a plant that was failing, get the business going and then shift our camp again. He did all things well but make money.

"From my eighth birthday on we lived west of the Rockies. When we started in the west, we were four brothers, two sisters. While we were still youngsters, three of the children died. This blow to the home was cushioned by the strength and loving kindness of the parents and we three who survived matured normally, without morbidity.

"As a small boy, I found I had no skill at tops, marbles, kites and other kid games, my hands being too small. By time of entry into third grade, I was therefore going for contact sports—football, baseball—and enjoying them because they were easy for me.

"Colorado west of Boulder 1908–1912 was wonderful mountain country, unfenced, full of game, with challenging peaks and mining camps still going. By age ten, I was hunting wild cats, coyotes and porcupine with a .22, being gone all day with a few companions and no objection from my parents. Alternately, we teamed in mountain climbing. I was already a horse handler. Nothing ill came of such adventuring except an increased appetite for it, though no hobby of my boyhood held over into the later years except horsemastership.

"Throughout grammar school, I either led my class or placed second. At age twelve I was chosen boy soloist of the Colorado schools after a statewide competition. Such early promise as I had of a career in music was blighted, praise the Lord, when I was gassed in World War I. Soon after we moved to California in 1912, I was chosen out of a screen test to become a juvenile in the old Western Essanay Company, and played in Broncho Billy Westerns, Snakeville Comedies, etc. My budding career as an actor was nipped when Father moved the family to El Paso, probably to save me from the studios, though I might have become a governor.

"In El Paso, then a very rugged frontier community I grew up contemporaneously with the Mexican Revolution. In high school, I was no good, and simply refused to study. I was bailed out of education when World War I came along and my parents agreed to my enlistment at age sixteen. Sophomore high school English was the last I ever had, and I failed the only two history courses I ever took.

"The Army became my University in the truest sense. To my surprise, anything military proved to be my cup of tea. I was a platoon sergeant at age seventeen, three times a company commander in the AEF before I was nineteen. From the hour of my commission, I was never sent to an Army school, or given any examination or IQ test, and how I finally became a Brigadier General remains a mystery defying regulations and custom. In the post-war army in 1922, I was suddenly given a job that required me to write and to have contact with the press. I found that I could do it, and that writing was more rewarding than soldiering. So I hopped to it. Over most of the years since, I have lived two careers running parallel, soldiering and writing. As a United States soldier I have had nineteen campaigns in which I operated with combat forces, the last ones being in Vietnam, December 1966 to February 1967, and as a correspondent or active participant, I have gone to twenty-one wars.

"My books number twenty-six, some history, others theory, others criticism. My children number four, which satisfies the only ambition I recall entertaining in my boyhood—to have a family. My son, Sam L., Jr., forty-five, an ex-pilot and highly successful business man, is by my first wife, Ruth Elstner, long since dead. My second wife, Ives Westervelt, died in 1952 after eighteen years of valiant invalidism. By my third wife, Cate Finnerty, of Sarasota, Florida, I have three daughters, Sharon, Catie and Bridget. Cate is my secretary, the one prime editor of my copy in any form before it is sent forth. We live at Birmingham, Michigan, in a home with forty-two hundred books, a professional library which I have built upward since 1920 to save myself leg work. Most of this comes of trying to work out for myself a lazy yet soul-satisfying kind of life."

S. L. A. MARSHALL

Marshall, who is probably the United States' best known combat historian, was born in Catskill, New York, the son of Caleb and Alice Medora (Beeman) Marshall. His father was of British birth and his mother came of a family established in America in Revolutionary times. Marshall first saw action in France in World War I, when he was commissioned as the youngest second lieutenant in the United States Army. After the war he began his journalistic career as a reporter on the El Paso *Herald*, where he became sports editor and then city editor. From 1927 to 1935 he worked as a foreign correspondent in Latin America for both the Detroit *News* and the North American Newspaper Alliance, and in 1936–1937 he covered the Spanish Civil War. "I qualified myself to write on military affairs not primarily as a soldier," he says, "but through independent study as a member of the working press." Marshall continued to write for the Detroit *News*, with interruptions, until 1962, at various times contributing as foreign correspondent, military critic, and chief editorial writer.

World War II brought Marshall back into uniform. In 1942 he was named Chief of Orientation in the United States Army, with the rank of major, and in 1943, as a lieutenant colonel, was transferred to the War Department's new Historical Division. Later the same year Marshall was appointed Chief Combat Historian in the Central Pacific, where he participated in the invasion of the Gilbert Islands and the Marshalls. He was sent to Europe in 1944, and in April 1945 became Chief Historian of the European Theater of Operations, taking part in the Normandy and Brittany campaigns, and subsequent actions in Holland and Germany.

Marshall's first books were written under the influence of J. F. C. Fuller, the pioneering British tactician of armored warfare (with whom, however, Marshall often disagreed radically). *Blitzkreig* (1940), according to Hanson W. Baldwin, was weakened by an "addiction to generalities" but was fundamentally sound, contained profound truths, and was a joy to read. *Men Against Fire* expressed views more characteristically Marshall's own, arguing the importance, even in "push-button" warfare, of local superiority in front-line rifle power, and making a serious attempt, "startling" in its originality, to understand "the anonymous private who actually does the fighting."

In 1950 Marshall went to Korea as an operations analyst and witnessed the Eighth Army's retreat before the Chinese Communists at the Yalu River. It was his account of this engagement in *The River and the Gauntlet* which established his reputation as a combat historian. Marshall interviewed GI's as well as generals, and filled his book with the names and deeds of private soldiers, noncommissioned officers, and junior officers. The result—inadequate as an evaluation of high policy—is a superbly vivid and detailed story which seemed to Gordon Walker among others "one of the great written epics of the Korean war, if not indeed of American military history." There was similar praise for *Pork Chop Hill*, Marshall's account of "the night war on Korea's wicked ridges." "It may be doubted," wrote Lynn Montross, "whether Stephen Crane or Ambrose Bierce have written with such sustained realism about combat." Once again, such reservations as there were centered on Marshall's abilities as a policy analyst, and one reviewer called his opinions "exasperating." Marshall was promoted to the rank of Brigadier General on August 1, 1951, and retired in 1960.

In 1966 Marshall charged in *The New Leader* that a "sedentary" American press corps was doing a poor job of reporting the military aspects of the war in Vietnam, preferring to write "off-beat yarns" calculated to "make people on the home front squirm and agonize." Angry rebuttals came from war correspondents in Vietnam, one of whom, Donald Neff, found Marshall's view of the conflict "embarrassingly romantic and distorted," and spoke of "a hoarse voice from another age, a Cyrano in fatigues and jungle boots." The General, who has made a number of visits to the Vietnam battlefront, rejected as "preposterous" suggestions that his viewpoint was "warped by a purely military bias," or that he regarded combat as the only important aspect of war. He repeated his charges in the introduction to his own book about Vietnam, *Battles in the Monsoon*, describing three engagements in which he had participated. Most reviewers found it lacking in understanding of the complexity of the conflict, and generally inferior to his books about the Korean war, but "replete with the anecdotes that convey the sense and the texture of combat."

Marshall's prose has been described by Eliot Fremont-Smith as "orderly and precise, at times courtly. The tone is gruffly sympathetic—again, the combination of the intimate and the impersonal —and by no means muffles the steady pace of suspense. It is writing that appeals primarily to the intellect; visceral reverberations are there, but . . . they are held in dignified restraint." The essence of military reporting for him is "Being With Troops." He speaks of many soldiers by name in the manner of Ernie Pyle, to whom he has often been compared. He writes a syndicated column for the Washington *Post* and Los Angeles *Times*.

Brown-eyed, short, and solid, Marshall holds the Distinguished Service Medal, The Legion of Merit, and many other decorations, American and foreign. He is a member of the American Legion and the Veterans of Foreign Wars, but has no political affiliations. He is an Episcopalian. In his earlier days he enjoyed polo and judging horse shows. Today this chronicler of countless battles, who looks as Churchillian and tenacious as he is, lists his hobbies as music and the collecting of porcelain.

PRINCIPAL WORKS: Blitzkrieg: Its History, Strategy, Economics and the Challenge to America, 1940; Armies on Wheels, 1941; Men Against Fire: The Problem of Battle Command in Future War, 1947; The River and the Gauntlet: Defeat of the Eighth Army by the Chinese Communist Forces, November 1950, 1953; Pork Chop Hill: The American Fighting Man in Action, Korea, Spring 1953, 1956; Night Drop: The American Airborne Invasion of Normandy, 1962; The Military History of the Korean War, 1963; Battle at Best, 1964; American Heritage History of World War I, 1964; Battles in the Monsoon: Campaigning in the Central Highlands Vietnam, Summer 1966, 1967; Sinai Victory, 1968; Bird: The Christmastide Battle, 1968; West to Cambodia, 1968; Ambush: The Battle of Dau Tieng . . . Operation Attleboro, and Other Deadfalls in South Vietnam, 1969; The Fields of Bamboo: Dang Tre, Trung Luong, Hoa Hoi, 1971; Crimsoned Prairie: The Wars Between the United States and the Plains Indians During the Winning of the West, 1972.

ABOUT: Current Biography, 1953; Who's Who in America, 1972–1973. *Periodicals*—Combat Forces Journal June 1951; New Leader October 10, 1966; November 21, 1966; Newsweek June 13, 1955.

"MARSTEN, RICHARD." *See* HUNTER, EVAN

***MARTINSON, HARRY (EDMUND)** (May 6, 1904–), Swedish poet, novelist, memoirist, essayist, and dramatist, was born at Jämshög in the southern Swedish province of Blekinge. His father, Martin Olofsson, a former sea captain, died when he was six, whereupon his mother abandoned him and his sisters and emigrated to California. The boy was put on offer by the parish council and entrusted to the lowest bidding foster parents. His childhood was spent in a succession of foster homes from which he became a habitual truant. At the end of World War I he made his way to Göteborg and went to sea as a cabin boy.

Martinson worked intermittently as a stoker and seaman until 1927, spending long periods ashore in various parts of the world as a casual laborer or vagrant. His early poems were inspired by Rudyard Kipling's *The Seven Seas*, and in 1929 he published his derivative first collection, *Spökskepp* (Ghost Ship). By then however he had come under the influence of the modernist poet Artur Lundkvist, and his contributions to the anthology *Fem unga* (Five Young Men, 1929) were much more daring and original.

His first mature work was *Nomad* (1931), a volume of brief lyrics in free verse, unorthodox in their language, startling in their juxtaposition of images. These poems are highly detailed miniatures, capturing delicate and fleeting impressions of the poet's childhood and youth, and dealing as scrupulously with a lump of Durham coal as with a Swedish hedge warbler. The book established Martinson's reputation at once, though some purists then and later objected to his disregard for the accepted rules of diction and syntax. Alrik Gustafson believes that Martinson's innovations and occasional obscurity "result directly from the inability of language to express the overwhelming intensity and complexity of his impressions."

* mär′ tin sôn

Martinson's early work was imbued with a rather vague "primitivism"—a belief in the goodness of nature, the artificiality of bourgeois society, the solidarity and nobility of the working class. This philosophy, and in particular the author's ideal of the carefree and unprejudiced World Nomad, totally open to experience, was expressed in *Resor utan mål* (Journeys Without a Goal, 1932) and *Kap Farväl!* (1933, translated as *Cape Farewell*). Both are collections of prose sketches of the people, places, and natural phenomena Martinson had observed during his travels. They derive from their laconic but richly resonant style a freshness and immediacy which have placed them among the most admired of all the author's writings and have reminded some critics of the work of the expressionist painters. There is a similar vividness of effect, and a remarkable absence of bitterness, in the two imaginative and irrepressible novels in which Martinson described his wretched childhood: *Nässlorna blomma* (1935, translated as *Flowering Nettle*) and *Vägen ut* (The Way Out, 1936).

During the late 1930s Martinson published three volumes of nature studies and essays, idiosyncratic in style and sometimes in content, in which he sought to defend all that was simple and natural against the values and politics of a technological and industrial age. Russia's invasion of Finland in 1939 seemed to him to symbolize all that he most abhorred, and he fought for Finland both as a writer in *Verklighet till döds* (Realism Unto Death, 1940) and as a soldier with the Swedish Volunteer Corps.

Public disasters and private unhappiness made World War II and the years immediately before it a dark time for Martinson, but he greeted the end of the war with one of his finest verse collections, *Passad* (Trade Wind, 1945). The poems and poem cycles which make up this volume deal as do those in earlier books with journeys and discoveries, but this time those of the spirit—the trade wind blows for "the uncharted islands of inner journeys." The predominant note is of meditative calm; there is a new willingness to "cultivate peace of mind and observe the views illuminated by a matter-of-fact sun."

Martinson's most important postwar works are the novel *Vägen till Klockrike* (1948, translated as *The Road*) and the verse epic *Aniara* (1956, translated under the same title). The novel is a formless anecdotal account of the life of a vagabond, Bolle, as he walks the roads of Sweden. It brought Martinson election to the Swedish Academy, an extraordinary honor for a writer almost without formal education, and was generally well received in English translation: though some reviewers found it altogether too aimless and discursive, most thought its warmth and beauty of expression and feeling outweighed its structural weaknesses.

HARRY MARTINSON

Aniara is a far darker work, a major narrative and philosophical poem about a space ship which, while taking eight thousand refugees from Earth to Mars, goes off course and carries its cargo on an endless journey into outer space. It is at the same time "a review of man in time and space"—an account of man's cultural history, and the intellectual arrogance which has alienated him from his most profound spiritual and instinctual values. Some Swedish critics consider *Aniara* to be Martinson's masterpiece, but there was a more mixed reception for the English adaptation made by Hugh MacDiarmid and Elspeth Schubert. All the same, if some reviewers of the English version thought that Martinson (or his translators) had failed to create a poetic diction out of the language of science, there was great admiration for the attempt, and one critic in the *Times Literary Supplement* concluded that "there are passages in which his conception justifies itself and the words radiate a kind of austere but delicate simplicity." An opera by Karl Birger Blomdahl based on the poem has been widely produced.

Martinson's sense of alienation from today's technological society dominates all his recent poetry, which includes *Cikada* (Cicada, 1953), *Gräsen i Thule* (The Grasses in Thule, 1958), and *Vagnen* (The Wagon, 1960). He has also written several plays, notably *Tre knivar från Wei* (Three Knives from Wei, 1964). From 1929 to 1940 he was married to the novelist Moa Martinson. His hobbies include sketching and painting.

Martinson is perhaps the most sensitive and original of the poets of his generation as well as technically one of the most sophisticated, distinguished above all by the extreme precision of his language. Alrik Gustafson has said of Martinson that his "amazing sensitivity simply *forces* him to seek out the unusual word, the fresh, frequently startling image, the flashing interplay of verbal associations which mirror the poet's wayward, lightning-like rapidity of response to sensation and idea." He was welcomed into the Swedish Academy in 1949 with the words "Life betrayed you, but you did not betray life."

PRINCIPAL WORKS IN ENGLISH TRANSLATION: Cape Farewell, 1934; Flowering Nettle, 1936; The Road, 1956; Aniara, 1963. *Poems in* Fleisher, F. (ed.) Seven Swedish Poets, 1963; Swenson, M. Half Sun Half Sleep, 1967.

ABOUT: Gustafson, A. A History of Swedish Literature, 1961; Hall, T. Vår tids stjärnsång, 1958; Holm, I. Harry Martinson, 1960; Penguin Companion to Literature 2, 1969; Smith, H. (ed.) Columbia Dictionary of Modern European Literature, 1947; Wrede, J. Sången om Aniara (with English summary), 1965. *Periodicals*—Scandinavian Studies 4 1960; Unicorn Journal 1 1968.

***MARTYNOV, LEONID (NIKOLAEVICH)** (1905–), Russian poet, was born in the Siberian city of Omsk. His father was a traveling mechanic on the Trans-Siberian Railroad, and for much of his childhood his home was his father's service compartment on a train. He left school at the age of fifteen to become a journalist, but he spent most of the 1920s wandering through Siberia, Kazakhstan, and Central Asia, taking up a remarkable assortment of jobs besides that of newspaper correspondent: collecting medicinal herbs in the Altai mountains, looking for mammoths in the Barabinsky steppes, peddling books in remote country villages; for a time he was a sailor.

He began to write verse under the influence of Mayakovsky's early poetry. His first collection, *Stikhi i poèmy* (Short Poems and Long), appeared in 1939 in Omsk, and was followed by several other collections in the early 1940s, culminating in two of his best books, *Lukomorye* (1945) and *Ertinsky les* (The Forest of Ertsin, 1945). Many of his early poems are set in the remote villages and forests of Siberia, but he was increasingly fascinated by the region's history, and he moves easily between past and present.

The most remarkable poems of this period are his strange, semiallegorical poetic myths, in which a dominant theme is the search for the fabulous lost land of *Lukomorye*. Nothing could be more remote from "socialist realism" than these poems. They were severely attacked by official critics, and Martynov was denied publication for ten years, though he continued to write. According to some reports he was arrested and spent several years in a labor camp. By the early 1950s, however, he was in Moscow, where he has lived ever since (disconcerting new acquaintances by introducing himself as "Leonid Martynov, Enemy of the People").

* mär tü' nof

LEONID MARTYNOV

Ilya Ehrenburg described Martynov's visits to him during the latter's period of silence. Sometimes, Ehrenburg said, Martynov "would pull crumpled scraps of paper out of his pocket and read them aloud to me, and each time I was struck by his poetical power: meteorology had been turned into an epic. He himself would drink tea absentmindedly and answer questions in a distracted manner. Those were the years when he attained his zenith as a poet." Ehrenburg also recalled a literary reception at the Writers' Club for Martynov's fiftieth birthday. Many younger poets recited his poems, which they said "had helped them to understand modern poetry," although Martynov's work at that time was still available only in manuscript.

From 1955 onwards his poetry began to appear again in literary magazines. In 1956 the anthology *Den' poezii* (A Day of Poetry) was published, coinciding with the tremendously successful poetry festivals of the same name that were taking place throughout the country. Together with the popular young poets who contributed to the anthology was the no longer young and still largely unknown Martynov. His own collection *Stikhi* (Poems) appeared shortly afterwards, and his reputation and influence grew rapidly. His popularity has continued to increase with later collections, which include *Lirika* (Lyrics, 1958), *Dorogi* (Roads, 1959), *Iskusstveny zver* (The Artificial Beast, 1959), *V chuzhikh beregov* (On Foreign Shores, 1959), *Stikhotvoreniya* (Poems, 1961), *Novaya Kniga* (A New Book, 1962), and *Pervorodstvo* (Primogeniture, 1965). A major two-volume selection of his short lyrics and longer poems *Stikhotvoreniya i poemy*, appeared in 1965.

In Martynov's later work Moscow and its surrounding countryside have largely replaced the earlier Siberian settings. His poems are quiet celebrations of nature, man, and the indestructibility of love—all that is free, natural, and spontaneous. These things are wryly contrasted with political authority, science, technology, and other forces which seek to control, exploit, and distort. Martynov's technical skill is greatly admired. His rhythms and language are those of everyday speech, but encompass a great range of emotional and sound effects in a way that has reminded some critics of William Carlos Williams. Many of his recent poems, and those produced during his years of silence, are unmistakably attacks on the Stalinist regime and the Stalinist mentality, like "Cold" (here translated by George Reavey): ". . . An experiment was made/To freeze all things—/To cast such grayness on everything,/So that each town/Might be chained in chill,/And each step be a risk/. . .And that even a whisper/Freeze in the throat;/So that, to its foundations,/All things might congeal: even the cooing of doves/And, in the clear sky,/The twittering of swallows . . . // Such the experiment./But this experiment—quite understandably—roused discontent . . ./And the ice was broken.//And a hungering for warmth and light/Enfolded the whole world:/The seas and the dry land,/And the human/Soul."

Martynov's earlier poetry had included many translations from Polish, Czech, and Hungarian, and more recently he has made translations of Byron, Walt Whitman, the nineteenth century Hungarian poet Sándor Petőfi, and the twentieth century Polish poet Julian Tuwim. His own deeply emotional poetry, personal rather than explicitly *engagé*, is coming to be recognized as some of the most original and important recently written in Russia.

PRINCIPAL WORKS IN ENGLISH TRANSLATION: *Poems in:* Markov, V. and Sparks, M. (eds.) Modern Russian Poetry 1966; Reavey, G. (ed.) The New Russian Poets, 1966; Kenyon Review Summer 1964; Soviet Literature, 9 1957.

ABOUT: Ehrenburg, I. Post-War Years 1945–1954: Volume VI of Men, Years—Life, 1966; Penguin Companion to Literature 2, 1969. *Periodicals*—Kenyon Review Summer 1964.

MASON, R(ONALD) A(LISON) K(ELLS) (January 10, 1905–July 13, 1971), New Zealand poet, editor, and dramatist, was born at Penrose, a suburb of Auckland. He was a New Zealander of the third generation, and was of mainly Irish and Highland Scots stock. He went to Auckland Grammar School and Auckland University, from which he graduated in classics in 1923. For the next ten years he was a teacher, primarily of literature.

R. A. K. MASON

As a precocious poet, whose first book was privately published when he was eighteen, he was powerfully influenced by classical and especially Latin verse. *In the Manner of Men* and *The Beggar*, which were scarcely noticed in New Zealand, show his predilection for strict verse forms, particularly the sonnet, his taut rhythmic sense, and a dark, often macabre imagination. Classical references came more easily to him than contemporary ones, and his early work was criticized for "poetic" phrases which sometimes seemed spurious. Two of Mason's poems appeared in Harold Monro's anthology *Twentieth Century Poetry* (1929).

No New Thing (1934), collecting poems written between 1924 and 1929, evokes, it was said, "a private hell of unfulfilled or rejected love, of strangulating parental affection, of dissolution, decay, or betrayal." Their author called them "sponges steeped in vinegar/useless to the happy-eyed/but handy for the crucified." These poems, similar in content and in their wretched self-probing mood to Mason's juvenilia, showed a new mastery of form which represented "a landmark in the history of New Zealand verse." Allen Curnow, who considers Mason to be "his country's first wholly original, unmistakably gifted poet," has written: "In sheer metrical proficiency, in the transmission of lyric energy through the syntax of his verse, he must be compared with his peers, and they are (I think) not very many in this century."

In 1933 meanwhile, Mason had become the second editor of *Phoenix*, a magazine which, though it lasted for only four issues, had a remarkable influence in New Zealand. It was not the country's first serious literary magazine but was better produced than its predecessors, with excellent typography by R. W. Lowry, more assertive about the importance of cultural values in that largely materialistic society, less deferential to English influences. Mason's political preoccupations—chiefly Marxist—turned the magazine from purely literary concerns to a passionate involvement with social issues. It is difficult to overestimate the importance of *The Phoenix* as "a symptom and a beginning" of a new national consciousness in New Zealand.

The Phoenix and *No New Thing* between them established Mason's reputation and ended his isolation. He abandoned teaching and became a company secretary (1933–1935), a public works foreman (1936–1939), editor of *In Print* (1940–1942), and then assistant secretary of the Auckland General Labourers' Union (1943–1955). He was also a founder of the People's Theatre and the New Theatre Group, which produced new plays in Auckland from 1940 to 1943. Mason became increasingly committed to Marxism, visited China, and was the first president of the New Zealand China Society.

Allen Curnow believes that "Mason's poetry draws strength from the effort to reconcile a belief in the human spirit with an obstinate will-enforced scepticism about personal immortality." The poetry Mason published after the 1930s has been less gloomy and introverted than his earlier work. *The End of Day* contains several lighthearted lyrics, and *This Dark Will Lighten* includes a fine optimistic love poem, "Flow at Full Moon," which is full of a deep sense of harmony with nature. The verses in *Collected Poems* show how his work tended away from classical forms towards a more robust, defiant, and colloquial manner. However, Mason's verse output dropped sharply after the publication of *This Dark Will Lighten* (1941), which in the opinion of some critics contains most of his best work as a poet.

Squire Speaks, Mason's first play, written for radio, was a polemical piece somewhat in the style of the Auden and Isherwood plays. *China Dances*, celebrating the achievements of the revolution in China, was no more successful than most attempts at propaganda in the theatre. Mason was a prolific contributor to left-wing political and critical journals, and active as a translator. He was a brilliant linguist, who knew all the principal languages of Europe and Asia, and was especially fluent in Chinese. After 1955 he supported himself as a landscape gardener, and as a writer and lecturer on gardening topics. In 1961 he received an award from the New Zealand State Literary Fund and in 1962 held the Robert Burns Fellowship at the University of Otago. Mason was an active sportsman in his youth and even late in his life enjoyed walking, swimming, riding, and driving. His less strenuous interests included botany, geology, and typography. Mason was married in 1962 to Dorothea Mould.

PRINCIPAL WORKS: *Poetry*—In the Manner of Men, 1923; The Beggar, 1924; No New Thing: Poems 1924–1929, 1934; End of Day, 1936; This Dark Will Lighten: Selected Poems 1923–1941, 1941; Collected Poems, 1962. *Plays*—Squire Speaks, 1938; China Dances, 1962. *History*—Frontier Forsaken: An Outline History of the Cook Islands, 1946.

ABOUT: Curnow, A. The Penguin Book of New Zealand Verse, 1960; *introduction to* Collected Poems, 1962; McCormick, E. H. New Zealand Literature, 1959; Who's Who in New Zealand, 1968.

***MATTHIESSEN, PETER** (May 22, 1927–), American novelist, short story writer, travel and nature writer, writes: "I am a New Yorker by birth, not inclination; I have never remained there very long. Many years were spent abroad, and the last five have been lived in the farm village of Sagaponack, on eastern Long Island, where I shall stay until the farms give way to summer housing.

"My formative years left me unformed; despite kind family, superior schooling, and all the orderly advantages, I remained disorderly. By the time I was sixteen, I had determined that I would write. Strange callow pieces with my byline were already appearing in the school publications, and in 1945–1946, while in the Navy at Pearl Harbor as a Ships Service Laundryman Third Class (actually, I was broken back to Seaman First Class before I got to wear the stripe of this noble office), I wrote sports articles for the Honolulu *Advertiser*; I was managing the Navy Golden Gloves team, and tried to lend class to my contenders, who lacked it in the ring. In college I wrote a hunting-and-fishing column with a confederate (we called it 'Two in the Bush'), and began to write short stories. The first of these, 'Sadie,' was an *Atlantic* 'First' in 1950, and won the *Atlantic* Prize that year. I have been trudging along towards immortality ever since.

"In 1951, I married Patsy Southgate (met two years earlier in Paris, where we both took junior years abroad); we returned to Paris, where I started (with Harold Humes) the *Paris Review*. George Plimpton, William Styron, James Baldwin, Terry Southern were among the many young writers associated with the *Review* in its first years. In Paris I wrote my first novel and outlined a second; both were distinguished chiefly by their promise. Late in 1953, we came back to the United States and went to live in the Springs, East Hampton, New York.

"From 1954 to 1956, I worked in spring and fall as a commercial fisherman, scalloping and clam-

* math′ ə sən

ming, and also on a haul-seining crew that used dories to set nets behind the surf; in the summer months I was captain of a charter fishing boat, the *Merlin*, out of Montauk Point. From November to April, I wrote steadily, and on days of bad weather as well; this was the best year-round working schedule that I ever devised.

"By 1957, I was single again, and for the next five years did the world wandering that I should have gotten out of my system before marrying people and having children (Luke and Carey). I traveled the backwoods of the Americas from Point Barrow to Tierra del Fuego, on expeditions and alone, and visited wild parts of every continent. These travels were sponsored by the *New Yorker* and other magazines, and resulted in three books of non-fiction. A third novel was also published in this period. Between trips, I bought an old place in Sagaponack (since rebuilt), and in 1961, home from an expedition to New Guinea, came here to live; except for an expedition to the Bering Sea (1964) and a stay in Ireland (1965), I have been there ever since. I am married now to Deborah Love and have two more children (Rue and Alex). In 1965, I published a fourth novel.

"I have always been a student of natural history and wild animal behavior, and the anatomy of the universe. My interest is pragmatic on the one hand —a book on the behavior of shorebirds is just completed—but I wish also to identify a sense of man's fate on earth and instill it in both fiction and non-fiction. The non-fiction is more or less spare and objective, but my fiction is realistic only in the most superficial sense; someone has called it *surreal*, in the sense of intensely or *wildly* real, and I think this is correct. At least, the idea attracts me, because in the intensity of true reality—as opposed to 'realism'—lie the greatest mysteries of all."

Peter Matthiessen's parents were Erard Matthiessen, an architect of Danish descent, and the former Elizabeth Carey. He spent most of his boyhood in Connecticut, where he attended the Hotchkiss School. Matthiessen received his B.A. in 1950 from Yale and stayed on for a year after his graduation as an assistant instructor.

The Cloud Forest is an account of his 1959 travels in some of the least accessible parts of the South American wilderness, and of his encounters there with strange birds and beasts and savage peoples. Matthiessen's chronicle, sensitive, informed, and scrupulously objective, was written in a "clean, dry, straightforward prose that is yet vivid and often aptly picturesque." It evoked much critical interest, and comparisons with the work of such travelers as Peter Fleming and H. M. Tomlinson.

In 1961 Matthiessen went with the Harvard-Peabody expedition to New Guinea to study the

PETER MATTHIESSEN

Kurelu, a small warlike tribe until then untouched by the outside world. *Under the Mountain Wall* describes the daily life of the tribe rather in the manner of the French "new novelists"—recording with great fidelity what was said and done, but refusing to pretend knowledge of what was thought and felt. Paul Pickrel, who thought the book should become "something of a classic," wrote: "It combines the scientist's precise observation with the artist's tact and grace and sympathy." His travel chronicles earned Matthiessen a grant from the American Academy of Arts and Letters in 1963.

Matthiessen's first three novels were in fact little more than novellas. *Race Rock*, about the coming of age of five young people on the New England coast, was praised for its "imaginative vigor," its "beautifully modulated and controlled" lyricism. *Partisans*, about a young American's pursuit of a deposed Communist leader in Paris, seemed by contrast "falsely portentous." It was followed by *Raditzer*, a study of man's responsibility for his fellows, in which an obscene piece of human wreckage attaches himself to a young sailor during World War II and drives him to a genuine and revelatory trial of conscience. The book's sensitivity to language and its moral seriousness reminded several critics of Conrad, but there was a general feeling that, as in *Partisans*, Matthiessen had explained too much, made his allegory too overt.

The most ambitious of Matthiessen's novels to date is *At Play in the Fields of the Lord*, which also struck reviewers as Conradian. It is concerned with the destruction by encroaching civilization of a fierce but innocent tribe of Indians in the Amazonian jungle. Civilization is represented by a group of missionaries, who seek to "save" the Niaruna; by a venal local official who wants their destruction; and by an embittered North American Indian who hopes to find himself in a reversion to their savagery. As an adventure story, and in its evocation of the beauties and terrors of the wilderness, the book is superb. Like its predecessors, however, it seemed to some critics excessively literal and explicit in its moral concerns—to fall short of that "surreal" quality which Matthiessen seeks.

Matthiessen's book on shorebirds, mentioned above, was published in 1967. His "superlative and memorable" essay was accompanied by an appendix containing more technical information, contributed by the ornithologist Ralph S. Palmer, and the fine paintings of Robert Verity Clem: the result was one of "the finest nature books ever to come off the presses in this country." *Sal Si Puedes* is a profile, generally admired, of Cesar Chavez, Gandhian head of the United Farm Workers Organizing Committee, describing his struggle to secure basic rights for the migrant laborers of California. Matthiessen has also published excellent accounts of two fascinating and successful scientific expeditions—one in 1964 to Nunivak Island in the Bering Sea to bring some specimens of the almost extinct musk ox to Alaska for breeding, the other in 1968 in search of the great white shark, the most dangerous predator on earth. *The Tree Where Man Was Born* is a tapestry of Matthiessen's impressions of East Africa, formed during several visits between 1960 and 1970, and an elegy for the ancient harmony there between man and nature—a harmony which man is racing to destroy.

Peter Matthiessen has contributed short stories and articles to many major magazines. A tall man, handsome in a craggy-featured way, he looks like Hollywood's image of an intrepid author-adventurer.

PRINCIPAL WORKS: Race Rock (novel), 1954; Partisans (novel), 1955; Wildlife in North America, 1959; Raditzer (novel), 1961; The Cloud Forest: A Chronicle of the South American Wilderness, 1961; Under the Mountain Wall: A Chronicle of Two Seasons in the Stone Age, 1962; At Play in the Fields of the Lord, 1965; The Shorebirds of North America, 1967; Oomingmak: The Expedition to the Musk Ox Island in the Bering Sea, 1967; Sal Si Puedes: Cesar Chavez and the New American Revolution, 1970; Blue Meridian: The Search for the Great White Shark, 1971; The Tree Where Man Was Born: The African Experience (with photographs by Eliot Porter), 1972.

ABOUT: Contemporary Authors 11–12, 1965; Vinson, J. (ed.) Contemporary Novelists, 1972; Who's Who in America, 1972–1973 *Periodical*—Wilson Library Bulletin March 1964.

MATTINGLY, GARRETT (May 6, 1900–December 18, 1962), American historian, was the son of Leonard Howard Mattingly, an industrialist and a civil servant, and the former Ida Roselle Garrett. He was born in Washington, D.C., and went to elementary schools there, but attended high school in Kalamazoo, Michigan, where his parents had moved. During World War I he served as a sergeant in the United States Army (1918–1919) and then entered Harvard University. As an undergraduate he received a Sheldon traveling fellowship which enabled him to study during 1922–1923 at Strasbourg and the Sorbonne, and at the University of Florence. Harvard gave him his B.A. in 1923, his M.A. in 1926, and his Ph.D. in 1935.

GARRETT MATTINGLY

In 1926 meanwhile Mattingly had begun his teaching career as an English instructor at Northwestern University. He was married in 1928 to a teacher, Gertrude McCollum. From that year until 1942 he taught both English and history at Long Island University in Brooklyn, New York, and thereafter until the end of World War II he served in the United States Navy, emerging as a lieutenant commander. After the war Mattingly resumed his teaching career, initially at Cooper Union in New York City, where from 1946 to 1948 he was professor of history and chairman of the department of social philosophy. In 1948 he went to Columbia University as professor of history, becoming William R. Shepherd Professor of European History in 1960. Mattingly spent a Fulbright Fellowship year in Italy in 1953–1954, and also received three Guggenheim Fellowships. At the time of his death he was on a leave of absence from Columbia as a visiting professor at Oxford University. He was by all accounts a fine lecturer, his deliberate manner enlivened by a sense of drama, and lightened at times by a puckish wit. It is said that he looked like Edward G. Robinson at his most suave, and sounded like Lionel Barrymore.

Mattingly's special interest was Europe in the sixteenth century, and his researches in that field produced the three books on which his literary reputation stands. The first, *Catherine of Aragon*, was a scholarly biography of the Spanish princess who had the misfortune to become Henry VIII's first wife, and an evaluation of the rights and wrongs of his treatment of her. It was a Literary Guild selection in 1942. Critics recognized at once "the strength and depth of [Mattingly's] grasp upon character," the skill with which he had recreated "in the round" the shadowy figure of the queen. The *Yale Review* said that "new material, unearthed principally in the archives of Vienna and Brussels, is largely responsible for the truth of the book; Mr. Mattingly's style accounts for its charm."

Renaissance Diplomacy, Mattingly's account of the evolution and first flowering of that art, was called "a history of Western Europe from an entirely fresh point of view," and (by J. H. Hexter) "one of the finest historical works of the past half century." The English historian J. H. Plumb wrote: "After reading this book with mounting excitement I do not think it possible to praise it too highly. Mr. Mattingly possesses so many and so varied gifts as an historian. His creative and original mind is at work in every paragraph. His prose—clear, ironic, dignified—could not be bettered; his lightly borne scholarship is as exact as it is massive (he has mastered the accumulated bibliography of five centuries and six languages); and his book is suffused with that compassionate humanity without which all historical writing becomes arid and pointless." Some critics found the book brilliantly but excessively compressed. According to one account Mattingly cut it to the bone to meet the requirements of a trade publisher, preferring even this to publication by a university press—"to him the very symbol of that withdrawal of history into the academic citadel which he deplored."

Mattingly's most successful work was *The Armada*, which received a special citation from the Pulitzer Prize committee, was a Book Society choice in England, and a selection of the Book-of-the-Month Club and the History Book Club in the United States. It is an account of Spain's attempted invasion of England in 1588, seen against its political and diplomatic background. Where previous chroniclers had told the story from the English or Spanish point of view, or both, Mattingly, "with his linguistic gifts and cultural sensibilities . . . follows all the contributory streams that ran toward the decisive events in the English Channel in that historic twelve-month." As a former naval officer he investigated the state of the tides and winds, the caliber of the guns, and the other technical factors which played their part in the long running battle. Christopher Hill said that Mattingly "writes vividly, vigorously, and wittily. His character sketches are admirable, and yet he also manages to convey a deep sense of the historical inevitability in which their actions were enmeshed." A. L. Rowse called the book "a work of art as well as of scholarship," as skillfully constructed as an accomplished novel. It was generally agreed that *The Armada* would take its place among the classics of historical literature.

PRINCIPAL WORKS: Catherine of Aragon, 1941; Renaissance Diplomacy, 1955; The Armada (England, The Defeat of the Spanish Armada), 1959.

ABOUT: Carter, C. H. (ed.) From the Renaissance to the Counter-Reformation: Essays in Honor of Garrett Mattingly, 1965; Current Biography, 1960; National Cyclopaedia of American Biography, vol. 47, 1965; Who's Who in America, 1962–1963. *Periodicals*—New York Times December 20, 1962; Political Science Quarterly September 1963; Renaissance Summer 1963.

***MAURIAC, CLAUDE** (April 25, 1914–), French novelist and critic, is the eldest son of François Mauriac, who won the Nobel Prize for Literature in 1952, and Jeanne (Lafon) Mauriac. He is a grand-nephew of Marcel Proust and also of Edmond Rostand. Born in Paris, Claude Mauriac was educated at the Lycée Janson-de-Sailly and the Faculties of Letters and of Law in Paris, where he graduated with a doctorate in law. He was employed first as private secretary to General Charles de Gaulle (1944–1949), leaving that post to found and edit the Gaullist review *Liberté de l'Esprit* (Liberty of the Spirit), which survived for four years. Mauriac reviewed films in *Le Figaro littéraire* for many years, and has been literary critic of *Le Figaro* since 1954.

He is most widely known for his tetralogy of novels, *Le Dialogue intérieur* (The Interior Dialogue), which Vivian Mercier has called "a formidable achievement, as well as a fascinating introduction to the problems and techniques of the French New Novel—indeed of the 20th-century novel in general."

The first volume, *Toutes les femmes sont fatales* (1957, translated in 1964 by Richard Howard as *All Women Are Fatal*), is more or less orthodox in structure and manner. Divided into four chapters, it introduces Mauriac's narrator-hero, Bertrand Carnéjoux, a journalist who aspires to be a novelist, and explores four episodes which reflect his attempt to forget in sexual adventure his sense of "replaceability." The next three novels become increasingly restricted in their temporal scope, and increasingly experimental in their technique (bringing to mind Dos Passos as well as Butor, Sarraute, and Beckett) and may be read as a narrative meditation on the act of writing a novel.

* mô ryak'

CLAUDE MAURIAC

Thus, *Le Dîner en ville* (1959, translated by Merloyd Lawrence as *The Dinner Party*) consists of snatches of the sophisticated conversation at a private soirée on the Île St. Louis, interspersed and contrasted with the dark unspoken thoughts of the eight participants. Carnéjoux voluptuously presides, husband of one of the women at table, lover of two of the other three (as well as of the maid)—a "slightly vulgarised, slightly larger-than-life portrait" of the stock figure of the Paris intellectual. The book dispenses with narrative and is at least a very skillful performance, in which the speakers or self-communers are never named but always identifiable. Some reviewers found it moving also, when, as Germaine Brée put it, "from time to time a gust of emotion breaks through, blending the dinner party into a whole as it releases in all the characters preoccupations common to them all: love, time in the form of age, and death."

La Marquise sortit à cinq heures (1961, translated by Richard Howard as *The Marquise Went Out at Five*) takes its title from Valéry's much-quoted complaint about the detailed verisimilitude of nineteenth century fiction. It is devoted to a single hour, between five and six P.M., as Carnéjoux, who should be thinking about the novel he means to write, ponders instead the history of and the activity at the Carrefour de Buci, a busy Paris intersection. Gilbert Highet thought that it was "like a highly intelligent film made by a mobile camera and then edited, with many flashbacks and much cross-cutting, by a poetic producer." *L'Agrandissement* (1963) purports to reproduce, in one enormous paragraph, the thoughts which pass through Carnéjoux's mind as he devotes two minutes to speculations about his novel. This novel, it soon becomes evident, is *La Marquise sortit à cinq heures*, parts of which are reproduced in not quite final form. *L'Agrandissement* is in fact an essay on writing, on literary maturation (Carnéjoux ironically recalls his first book, "Sober Pleasures," which is of course *All Women Are Fatal*), and literary fame (an American professor lectures Carnéjoux on his own work and expatiates on the "interior dialogue" that is the principle unifying the whole series).

In all four novels the same characters appear and reappear. But, as Alice Mayhew has pointed out, "they do not change, that is, they bear perpetually the same relation to each other. At the bottom of all this lies a personal obsession about the inevitability of solitude and the mystery of communion." Mauriac's fiction has not impressed everyone: J. Mitchell Morse, for example, dismissed him as "a popular imitator of Butor, nothing more." But his champions commend his "basic honesty and humanity," his patient sounding of his own capacities. "By sheer dint of writing," says Vivian Mercier, "he has worked his way out of the derivative and the slick into a personal style and an individuality whose existence he himself might paradoxically deny. . . . The career to date of Claude Mauriac seems to me all the justification that technical experiment in the novel will ever need. . . . Mauriac has learned a great deal from his experiments, not only about how to write novels, but also, I believe, about life and about himself."

Mauriac has published several collections of his essays about literature and the film, and monographs on Balzac, Malraux, Jouhandeau, and André Breton. *Conversations with André Gide* is an absorbing if immature journal of Mauriac's encounters with that master between 1937 and 1945. Perhaps the most instructive introduction to the problems Mauriac identifies as contemporary, and which he has begun to confront in his own fiction, is his spirited study *L'Alittérature contemporaine* (1958), translated in 1959 as *The New Literature*. *Un autre de Gaulle* (1971, translated by Moura Budberg and Gordon Latta as *The Other de Gaulle*), Mauriac's journal of his years of service to the General (1944–1954), was also of great interest.

The writer was married in 1951 to Marie-Claude Mante and has three children, Gérard, Nathalie, and Gilles. His study of André Breton brought him the Prix Sainte-Beuve in 1949, and ten years later he received the Prix Médicis for *Le Dîner en ville*. Mauriac is a Chevalier of the Légion d'Honneur.

PRINCIPAL WORKS IN ENGLISH TRANSLATION: *Fiction*—The Dinner Party, 1960 (England, Dinner in Town, 1964); The Marquise Went Out at Five, 1962; All Women Are Fatal, 1964 (England, Femmes Fatales, 1966). *Nonfiction*—The New Literature, 1959; Conversations with André Gide, 1965; The Other de Gaulle, 1973.

ABOUT: Boisdeffre, P. de. Dictionnaire de la littérature contemporaine, 1900–1962, 1962; Cocteau, J. The Hand of a Stranger, 1956; Curley, D. N. and Curley, A. (eds.) Modern Romance Literatures (A Library of Literary Criticism), 1967; International Who's Who, 1972–73; Who's Who in France, 1973–1974. *Periodicals*—Books Abroad Summer 1959; Horizon May 1962; Nation February 1, 1965; New York Times Book Review May 1, 1960; April 15, 1962; New Yorker May 14, 1960; Nouvelles Littéraires June 9, 1966; Vogue January 1, 1963.

***MAURRAS, CHARLES (MARIE PHOTIUS)** (April 20, 1868–November 16, 1952), French literary critic and political journalist, was born at Martigues, a small fishing village near Marseilles on the Mediterranean coast of France. His father, a tax collector who was secular, liberal, and Romantic in outlook, died when Maurras was six, and the devout royalism of his mother, coupled with the Latin tradition of Provence, thereafter dominated his upbringing. The first symptoms of the deafness that embittered his life appeared when he was fourteen, thwarting his hopes of a naval career.

In 1885, after graduating from a Roman Catholic college at Aix-en-Provence, Maurras moved to Paris and for the next five years read widely in history, philosophy, and the social sciences, supporting himself mainly by reviewing books in these subjects, but also beginning to publish fiction and poetry. This period of philosophical absorption was followed by another of similar length when he devoted himself to more purely literary questions. His criticism was neoclassicist from the beginning and directed against what he saw as a decline in French linguistic and stylistic standards. He became a disciple of Jean Moréas, and a cofounder with him of the anti-romantic École Romane.

His transition from aesthetic to political activism may be dated from 1896. In that year, covering the Olympic games in Athens for a Paris newspaper, he became passionately, almost mystically, conscious of the links between classical and French culture, and convinced that this great tradition was being progressively corrupted by foreign influences—a stream of poison leading from German romanticism to symbolism. This decadence was, he believed, social and political as much as artistic, and flourished in the mood of anarchy which sprang from the French Revolution and the teachings of its prophet, Rousseau.

Back in France, Maurras worked for a return to the pre-Revolutionary monarchic order, without Protestant, Jewish, northern European, or other "alien" dilutions. His antidemocratic zeal found its first important application in the controversy over Alfred Dreyfus, the Jewish army officer convicted of espionage chiefly on the basis of forged evidence.

* mō ra′

CHARLES MAURRAS

An article by Maurras in the *Gazette de France* in 1898 extolled the forgery as a fabrication in a good cause—the stability of the French state and army—and helped to rally nationalists of various persuasions to the Action Française, an originally pro-republican movement which Maurras helped to establish in 1899 and soon converted to his own brand of reactionary royalism. He became coeditor and a regular and influential contributor to the movement's daily newspaper *Action Française*, infamous for its systematic attacks on public figures. Maurras himself was involved in many legal actions and several duels and was more than once almost assassinated. In 1935 he was imprisoned for openly encouraging violent reprisals against members of the French assembly who favored sanctions against Italy for its invasion of Abyssinia.

Although he was himself an agnostic, Maurras regarded the Roman Catholic Church as an essential bulwark of French order, and at first succeeded in attracting a large number of Catholic clergy and lay leaders to Action Française. This changed in 1926, when the Vatican condemned the movement, along with several of Maurras's books, but Action Française survived this heavy blow and saw much of its program implemented by the Vichy government during World War II. As a leading apologist for this regime, Maurras was accused of treason after the liberation of France, and in 1945 was sentenced to life imprisonment. He was released from prison for reasons of health early in 1952, and died nine months later of uremic poisoning at Saint Symphorien, a suburb of Tours. Before his death he reportedly renounced his agnosticism and embraced the Roman Catholic faith.

Maurras's antiromanticism, which some critics have seen as an attempt to reject his own most profound attitudes, is displayed in such works as *Les Amants de Venise* (The Lovers of Venice, 1902), a psychological study of George Sand and Alfred de Musset, and *L'Avenir de l'intelligence* (The Future of the Understanding, 1905), which deals with the concept of order, and is perhaps his best known book. His views on a vast range of subjects are assembled in his five-volume *Dictionnaire politique et critique* (Political and Critical Dictionary, 1934). While in prison he wrote *Le Mont de Saturne* (Saturn's Mount, 1950), a novel that leans heavily on autobiography. Most of his other books are collections of his political and critical journalism.

His poetry, collected in *La Musique intérieure* (Interior Music, 1925), together with an excellent autobiographical essay, is on the Parnassian model, sometimes made a little obscure by extreme condensation, but felicitous in language and rhythm. His prose is marvelously lucid, vigorous, and direct, and is admired even by those to whom his political opinions are anathema. He has, according to one critic, "exerted a deep influence upon modern French thought, whether positively or negatively," and during his lifetime was recognized as "the foremost representative of the classical spirit in French literature." Apart from a few scattered excerpts, none of his work seems to have appeared in English.

ABOUT: Brogan, D. W. French Personalities and Problems, 1946; Buthman, W. C. The Rise of Integral Nationalism in France, 1939; Cazamian, L. A History of French Literature, 1959; Curtis, M. Three Against the Third Republic, 1959; Joseph, R. Le Poète Charles Maurras, 1962; Massis, H. Maurras et notre temps, 1961; Pierce, R. Contemporary French Political Thought, 1967; Rodiez, L. Maurras jusqu'à l'Action Française, 1957; Smith, H. (ed.) Columbia Dictionary of Modern European Literature, 1947; Thibaudet, A. Les Idées de Charles Maurras, 1920; Weber, E. Action Française, 1962. *Periodicals*—Encounter November 1964; Journal of the History of Ideas April 1950; Journal of Politics November 1943; New York Times November 17, 1952; Quarterly Review January 1928; Times Literary Supplement September 30, 1920; November 28, 1952; January 28, 1955.

MAVOR, OSBORNE HENRY. *See* "BRIDIE, JAMES"

MAXWELL, GAVIN (July 15, 1914–September 6, 1969), Scottish nature and travel writer, was the youngest son of Lieutenant-Colonel Aymer Maxwell, who was killed at Antwerp three months after Gavin's birth, and of Lady Mary Percy, daughter of the Duke of Northumberland and a descendant of Henry Hotspur. The Maxwells have been baronets of Monreith, in Galloway, southwest Scotland, since 1681. Gavin Maxwell was born a few miles away from the ancestral home, at Elrig, the house built by his father. He grew up there, running wild over the family lands with his sister and two brothers, surrounded by a large, ingrown, and eccentric clan of relations. His passion for birds, animals and books was fostered by his admired and remarkable uncle Sir William Percy, a barrister and explorer with a talent for intellectual stimulation, who "knew no other form of conversation than cross-examination."

GAVIN MAXWELL

At the age of ten, in accordance with the custom of his class, Gavin Maxwell was sent away to school in England, and required to conform to a rigid and hearty pattern of behavior remote from anything he had ever known and from everything he cared for. He went to a succession of preparatory schools and then to Stowe, his public school, where he was somewhat happier and less confused. At sixteen, a rare blood disease ended his public school career and almost his life, but he studied during his convalescence and duly went up to Hertford College, Oxford University. He spent most of his long vacations in the Scottish Highlands, and fell in love with them. After his graduation he began a career as a freelance journalist, accompanied an ornithological expedition to East Finnmark, and arrived home in time to join the Scots Guards in 1939 at the outbreak of World War II. In 1941 he was transferred to Special Operations Executive as a small arms instructor, and in 1944 was invalided out with the rank of major.

Maxwell bought the Hebridean island of Soay and started a shark fishery. In 1949, when that project failed, he turned his hand to portrait painting, his career for the next three years. Meanwhile, he contributed articles and poems to magazines, and after 1952 earned his living as a writer. In that year he published his first book,

Harpoon Venture, an account of his shark hunting years which Louis MacNeice called "a detailed factual record of something pregnant with symbols, and the author deeply aware of the symbolism." *Bandit* (1956), was the result of months of research in Sicily into the career of Salvatore Giuliano, the farm boy driven into outlawry who became a tragic legend. A journey with Wilfred Thesiger in Iraq produced *People of the Reeds*, an account of one of the most primitive peoples on earth and "an almost perfect book of travel," which received the Heinemann Literary Prize for 1957. *The Ten Pains of Death* (1959) constructed an appalling picture of the squalor and misery of Sicily through interviews with a cross-section of the island's population.

Meanwhile, Maxwell had bought a cottage in the remote West Highlands of Scotland. His account of his life there, and of the two otters who were his household pets, was published in 1960 as *Ring of Bright Water*. It was greeted by a chorus of praise from critics throughout the English-speaking world, and capped Maxwell's already considerable reputation. There were comparisons with Thoreau, and much admiration for Maxwell's humor, his precise and unsentimental evocation of nature, and his "serene, lucid and graceful prose." There was a film version in 1969. The story of "Camusfeàrna" and its otters was continued in *The Rocks Remain* (1963), but the book was only moderately successful.

Maxwell described his childhood and youth in *The House of Elrig* (1965). V. S. Pritchett was much taken by the "unworldliness and innocence" of the aristocratic world it described, and "by a quiet truthfulness in the writing." *Lords of the Atlas* (1966) was an account of the rise and fall of the Glaoua, a bloodthirsty Berber family which during the 1950s came close to supreme power in Morocco. *Raven Seek Thy Brother* (1969), the third volume in the Camusfeàrna trilogy, was found only spasmodically interesting. It dwells a great deal on the author's ill-health, and his mounting emotional and financial confusion, and ends with an account of the fire which gutted the cottage and killed one of the otters in 1967. Maxwell died two years later, at the age of fifty-five.

Gavin Maxwell was a Fellow of the Zoological Society, the Royal Geographical Society, the American Geographical Society, the Royal Society of Literature, and the International Institute of Arts and Letters. He was a trustee of the Danilo Dolci Committee, and active in many bodies concerned with the preservation of wildlife. He said he was "intensely interested in all forms of life and behavior, both human and animal, and correspondingly uninterested in machinery." Maxwell's 1962 marriage to Lavinia Lascelles was dissolved in 1964. He had three homes: in Chelsea; in the Kyle of Lochalsh, and the Isle of Skye. "Home is a fortress," he wrote, "behind those walls one may retire . . . to plan fresh journeys to farther horizons."

PRINCIPAL WORKS: Harpoon at a Venture, 1952 (U.S., Harpoon Venture); God Protect Me from My Friends, 1956 (U.S., Bandit); A Reed Shaken by the Wind, 1957 (U.S., People of the Reeds); The Ten Pains of Death, 1959; Ring of Bright Water, 1960; The Otter's Tale (for children), 1962; The Rocks Remain, 1963; The House of Elrig, 1965; Lords of the Atlas, 1966; Raven Seek Thy Brother, 1969.

ABOUT: Contemporary Authors 7–8, 1963; Lister-Kaye, J. The White Island, 1972; Maxwell, G. The House of Elrig, 1965 (and autobiographical material in the Camusfeàrna trilogy). *Periodicals*—Home February 1963; New York Times September 9, 1969; Times (London) September 8, 1969.

***MAYAKOVSKY, VLADIMIR (VLADIMIROVICH)** (July 7, 1893–April 14, 1930), Russian poet and dramatist, was born in the Georgian village of Bagdadi, now called Mayakovsky. His father, a forest ranger, was an impoverished member of a family of minor Russian gentry which had lived in Georgia for several generations; he died of blood poisoning while Mayakovsky was still a child. His widow took her son and two daughters to Moscow, where they knew no one and where they lived in extreme poverty on an inadequate pension, eked out by taking in lodgers and doing odd jobs.

A natural rebel, Mayakovsky became an active Bolshevik revolutionary at the age of fourteen. He was three times arrested, once for helping prisoners to escape from jail, and he himself spent eleven months in Butyrki prison—five months in solitary confinement. With only interrupted schooling, he was largely self-taught until in 1911 he entered the Moscow Institute of Painting, Sculpture, and Architecture. There he met David Burliuk, under whose influence and patronage he became a poet and joined the newly emerging futurist movement.

With Burliuk and Velimir Khlebnikov he produced the notorious futurist manifesto *Poshchechina obshchestvennomu vkusu* (A Slap in the Face of Public Taste, 1912). It demanded that Pushkin, Tolstoy, and Dostoevsky should be thrown overboard "from the steamer of modernity," and called for new poetic forms and language to express the new realities of modern life. In the winter of 1913–1914 the futurists made a tour of Russian towns, reading their works to large and sometimes hostile audiences. Mayakovsky, with his big build, huge voice, and flamboyant clothes, was himself "a slap in the face of public taste" and greatly enjoyed the role.

Meanwhile, Mayakovsky's unique style was developing rapidly. He hated "fine writing," sentimentality, and prettiness, and went to the opposite extreme in his own poetry, employing the rough talk of the streets, deliberate grammatical heresies, and all kinds of neologisms. He wrote

*mŭ yŭ kôf′ski

VLADIMIR MAYAKOVSKY

much blank verse, but also made brilliant (and quite untranslatable) use of a rich variety of rhyme schemes, assonance, and alliteration. His rhythms are powerful but irregular, based on the number of stressed syllables in a line, without regard for the unstressed syllables. In his public readings, Mayakovsky declaimed his poems with spellbinding effect in a staccato marching style which is indicated typographically by the use of very short lines, spilling down the page in a characteristic staircase shape: "Hey!/Gentlemen!/Lovers/of sacrilege,/crime,/and carnage,/have you seen/the terror of terrors—/my face/when/I/am absolutely calm?" (From "A Cloud in Trousers.")

Mayakovsky's poetry is aggressive, mocking, often fantastic or grotesque, and his imagery is violent and extreme—he speaks of himself for example as one of the lowly, "vomited by a consumptive night into the palm of Moscow." His work is dominated by his own enormous ego—the figure of Mayakovsky towers at the center of his poems, martyred by fools and knaves, betrayed by love, preposterous or tragic, abject or heroic, but always larger than life, a giant among midgets. It is typical of him that his first book, a collection of four poems published in 1913, was called *Ya* ("I"). He followed this with the "autobiographical tragedy" *Vladimir Mayakovsky*, which he wrote and performed in 1913 at the Luna Park in St. Petersburg. It portrayed the poet as a prophet in heroic conflict with the idiocies of his time and was a sensation, its two productions playing to full houses in spite of exorbitant prices. According to one account, Mayakovsky's "remarkable voice and passionate temperament carried away the audience, overcoming its initial wary skepticism." However, in 1914, when Mayakovsky tried to enlist in the army at the outbreak of war, he was rejected as politically unreliable.

Mayakovsky's work alternates between political poems and love lyrics, and the two genres are inextricably intertwined in the celebrated series of long poems which he wrote before the Revolution. The first of these was *Oblako v shtanakh* (1915, translated as "A Cloud in Trousers"—one of the poet's more colorful definitions of his own nature). It was written after he fell in love with Maria Alexandrovna in Odessa, and begins with an account of his rejection by her, full of hyperbolic but brilliant images of despair: "I stood hunched by the window, and my brow melted the glass . . ."; "The stroke of twelve fell / like a head from a block. . . ." Then the poet's suffering grows to become a paradigm of all rejection and dispossession, and his rage swells to encompass art, religion, and the entire social order, until he is threatening to bring the whole world crashing down in revenge for his failure in love. This, which remains one of his best poems, also makes it painfully clear how close to madness Mayakovsky was sometimes carried by his demonic creative energy.

Though he was attractive to women, it is always the tragic aspects of love which he emphasizes, for as Patricia Blake says, "in love, as in all things, Mayakovsky favored the impossible. He always chose women who were unavailable to him for some reason or other." The most celebrated of these hopeless romances is his triangular relationship with Lilya Brik and her husband Osip. For fifteen years he publicly lamented her coldness and inconstancy, beginning a few months after their first meeting with *Fleyta-pozvonochnik* (1915, translated as "The Backbone Flute"). Patricia Blake has called this "surely the most savage indictment of a woman and womanhood to be formulated in our time. . . . And why? Lily, the terrible, the accursed Lily has left Mayakovsky for another man."

Two other long poems of the period were *Voyna i mir* (War and the World, 1916), in which Mayakovsky expresses his hatred of the war, and *Chelovek* (Man, 1917), a parody of the life of Christ, about the liberation of man from the capitalist yoke. However, as Victor Erlich points out, "What is challenged here is not a definite social order, but the very principle of order or stasis, everything that smacks of tradition, of habit, of routine, everything that sets limits to the creator's dishevelled, colossal sensibility."

Mayakovsky welcomed the 1917 Revolution as "my" revolution, and harnessed his gigantic energy to its service. He was a skilled caricaturist, and he was soon working night and day producing hundreds of propaganda and information posters, each with a rhyming caption or slogan, as well as revolutionary poems and plays and film scripts. This "one-man factory" also founded and edited the journal *LEF* (Left Arts Front), toured the country reciting his poetry, acted, lectured, and painted in the name of the Revolution.

The verse play *Misteriya buf* (1918, translated as "Mystery-Bouffe") is "a heroic, epic, and satiric representation of our epoch." Staged by Meyerhold on the first anniversary of the October Revolution as a "vulgar circus," it is a fantastic extravaganza on the story of Noah. After a new deluge the survivors set out in a new Ark, passing through a hell full of inoffensive devils and a paradise stuffed with boring angels, until the "unclean" throw their exploiters overboard and reach the promised land on earth. In the epic poem *150,000,000* (1919–20), written during the American intervention in the Russian Civil War, the giant peasant Ivan, representing the Russian people, fights a hand-to-hand battle with Woodrow Wilson, resplendent in a top hat as high as the Eiffel Tower.

During the 1920s Mayakovsky made several trips abroad, including a long visit to America in 1925 which is reflected in several well-known poems such as "Bruklinsky most" (1925, translated as "Brooklyn Bridge"), expressing his admiration for American technology. But others of his *Amerikanskiye stikhi* (American Poems, 1926) are angry criticisms of inequality and racism in the United States and on his return to the Soviet Union he wrote the long poem *Khorosho!* (Okay!, 1927) in praise of Soviet progress. Along with all this public work and activity he still wrote many love poems, such as "Lyublyu" (1923, translated as "I Love"), whose title (and refrain) is made up of the initials of Lilya Yurevna Brik's name, and "Pro eto" (1923, translated as "About This"), a desperate lament over her infidelity.

Mayakovsky's two prose plays are caustic satires on the growing philistinism and bureaucracy of Soviet life. In the first part of *Klop* (1928, translated by Max Hayward as *The Bedbug*), the main character is the bug-ridden, guitar-strumming, vodka-soaked Prisypkin, the personification of all the vulgarity and triviality of the party members who had fallen into the debauched and drunken ways of the bourgeoisie. A fire breaks out at his wedding party and the fire brigade is called, but the jets of water from the hoses freeze and preserve the dead-drunk Prisypkin inside a block of ice. The second part takes place in the rational and utopian communist society of fifty years later, when Prisypkin is revived, along with a bedbug on his collar. Prisypkin has brought all his old qualities of ignorance, bragging, and vanity with him, and to prevent the spread of these diseases, he and his bedbug are put into a cage. At the end the people gather to stare in at him as he drinks his vodka, plays his guitar, and sings sentimental songs. But the communist millennium is portrayed as a dehumanized world where not only vodka but sex and romance no longer exist, and some critics have regarded Prisypkin, lost and frightened in a loveless society, as the real hero of the second part and the author's alter ego.

Banya (1930, translated by A. R. MacAndrew, as "The Bathhouse") attacks the ever-increasing bureaucracy of the Soviet state, with its officials who swagger and bully, take bribes, and spout socialist phrases that have become meaningless under the raging verbal inflation. As in Gogol's *Inspector General*, another comedy satirizing Russian officialdom, the officials are portrayed as grotesque buffoons whose exposure is carried out through the introduction of an outsider. In this case the catalyst is the Phosphorescent Woman, who arrives with a time machine which whisks the ordinary people into the future communist millennium, jettisoning the parasites on the way. The play naturally aroused the anger of the cultural bureaucrats and was bitterly attacked.

A month later Mayakovsky shot himself, playing Russian roulette with a single cartridge in his revolver. He had been deeply disturbed and angered by the suicide of Yesenin five years earlier, and in the poem "Sergei Eseninu" (To Sergei Yesenin, 1926) he had criticized Yesenin for taking the line of least resistance and making an easy exit from life. The reasons for his own suicide have occasioned much speculation. His disillusion at the course the Revolution had taken, the harsh attacks of his literary opponents, and especially his unhappy love for an *émigrée* Russian girl much younger than himself, may all have been factors. But this was not the first time he had played Russian roulette, and as Roman Jakobson pointed out, the theme of the poet's suicide, of gambling one's life away, had haunted Mayakovsky's poetry almost from the first. His intoxication with Bolshevism, his dramatic involvements with women, his obsession with suicide, and his poetry may all be seen as reflections of an alienated personality, alternating between bouts of depression and manic activity.

In his most important prose work, *Kak delat' stikhi* (1926, translated as *How Are Verses Made?*), he analyzes his motives and techniques in composing his poem about Yesenin's suicide. The immediate purpose of this essay was to counteract a textbook on the academic rules of literature, but it became a convincing and concise statement of the modernist, postsymbolist aesthetic. His last important poem, and one of his greatest, "Vo ves golos" (1930, translated by H. Marshall as "At the Top of My Voice"), was left unfinished at the time of his death. It is a spiritual autobiography and testament, in which he describes his inner struggle and his intentional self-sacrifice to the aspirations of the Revolution, saying that he had subdued himself, "trampling on the throat" of his song. This last poem showed him in increased control of his imagery, and in process of purging his work of its more extreme mannerisms. The following section of it was found in his pocket after he shot himself: "Past one o'clock. You must have gone to bed./ The Milky Way streams silver through the night./ I'm in no hurry; with lightning telegrams/I have no cause to wake or trouble you./And, as they say, the incident is closed./Love's boat has smashed against the daily grind./Now you and I are quits. Why bother then/to balance mutual sorrows, pains, and hurts./Behold what quiet settles on the world./ Night wraps the sky in tribute from the stars./In hours like these, one rises to address/The ages, history, and all creation."

Pasternak said of Mayakovsky, "With this man, the newness of our times was climatically and uniquely in his blood. His very strangeness was one with the strangeness of the age, an age still half unrealized." Lenin, always a conservative in the arts, called his work "hooligan communism," but Stalin rather surprisingly remarked that "Mayakovsky was, and remains, the greatest Soviet poet." This ensured that despite the promulgation of socialist realism soon after his death his work never fell from favor, and his influence on younger poets has been enormous (though even now the full implications of some of his innovations have not been fully absorbed). He remains not only a leading futurist poet, but one of the great revolutionary figures of twentieth century poetry, and the acknowledged "laureate of the Revolution."

PRINCIPAL WORKS IN ENGLISH TRANSLATION: Mayakovsky and His Poetry, tr. by H. Marshall, 1942 (enlarged Indian ed., 1955); The Bedbug and Selected Poetry, ed. by P. Blake, 1960; Mayakovsky, tr. and ed. by H. Marshall, 1965; The Complete Plays of Vladimir Mayakovsky, tr. by Guy Daniels, 1968; Timothy's Horse, il. by Flavio Constantini, tr. by Guy Daniels, 1970; How Are Verses Made?, tr. by G. M. Hyde, 1971; The Bedbug and Selected Poetry, tr. by Max Hayward and George Reavey, 1971; Wi the Haill Voice (selected poems, tr. into Scots by Edwin Morgan), 1972. *Also* The Bedbug *in* Three Soviet Plays, ed. by M. Glenny, tr. by M. Hayward, 1966; Mystery-Bouffe *in* Masterpieces of the Russian Drama, 2, ed. by G. R. Noyes, 1933; The Bathhouse *in* 20th Century Russian Drama, tr. by A. R. MacAndrew, 1963. *Poems in* Barnstone, W. (ed.) Modern European Poetry, 1966; Bowra, C. M. (ed.) A Book of Russian Verse, 1943; Bowra, C. M. (ed.) A Second Book of Russian Verse, 1948; Lindsay, J. (ed.) Russian Poetry 1917–1955, 1957; Lindsay, J. (ed.) Modern Russian Poetry, 1966; Markov, V. and Sparks, M. Modern Russian Poetry, 1966; Obolensky, D. The Penguin Book of Russian Verse, 1962; Reavey, G. and Slonim, M. Soviet Literature: An Anthology, 1933.

ABOUT: Alexandrova, V. A History of Soviet Literature, 1963; Bowra, C. M. The Creative Experiment, 1949; Braun, E. Meyerhold on Theatre, 1969; Brown, E. J. Mayakovsky: A Poet in the Revolution, 1973; Brown, E. J. (ed.) Major Soviet Writers, 1973; Bunin, I. Memories and Portraits, 1951; Burliuk, D. Vladimir Mayakovsky, 1940; Cohen, J. M. Poetry of This Age 1908–1958, 1960; Eastman, M. Artists in Uniform: A Study of Literature and Bureaucratism, 1934; Ehrenburg, I. Men, Years, Life, vol. II, 1962; Erlich, V. The Double Image: Concepts of the Poet in Slavic Literatures, 1964; Humesky, A. Mayakovskii and His Neologisms, 1964; Kataev, V. The Grass of Oblivion, 1969; Lavrin, J. From Pushkin to Mayakovsky, 1948; Lavrin, J. Russian Writers, Their Lives and Literature, 1954; Markov, V. Russian Futurism, 1968; Muchnic, H. From Gorky to Pasternak, 1961; Peterkiewicz, J. The Other Side of Silence: The Poet at the Limits of Language, 1970; Poggioli, R. The Poets of Russia, 1890–1930, 1960; Slonim, M. Modern Russian Literature, 1953; Slonim, M. Soviet Russian Literature, 1964; Slonim, M. Russian Theater from the Empire to the Soviets, 1961; Stahlberger, L. The Symbolic System of Majakovskij, 1964; Struve, G. 25 Years of Soviet Russian Literature, 1944; Triolet, E. Maiakovski, 1945; Trotsky, L. Literature and Revolution, 1960; Woroszylski, W. The Life of Mayakovsky, 1971; Yershov, P. Comedy in the Soviet Theater, 1957. Zavalishin, V. Early Soviet Writers, 1958; *Periodicals*—American Slavic Review February 1960; Encounter August 1960; New York Review of Books March 17, 1966; Partisan Review May–July 1961; Russian Review April 1958, July 1966, April 1967; Slavic Review September 1962; Yale French Studies 301 1967.

MAYER, MARTIN (PRAGER) (January 14, 1928–), American reporter, critic and novelist, writes: "I am specialized as a New Yorker: born, bred and resident. Both my parents are lawyers, representing mostly trade unions, and I was an only child. I attended a New York City public elementary school and McBurney, a YMCA high school, and entered Harvard precociously in 1943. My field was economics, and I also worked in philosophy and music, but such statements give an inaccurate impression: most of my time went to the wartime version of the Harvard *Crimson*, to tournament bridge, poker, horse racing, one or two young ladies, and totally unsupervised reading.

"My first published material goes back to fourth grade, when I and two classmates (one of them now proprietor of a suburban newspaper, the other a writer of material for musical shows) began issuing an irregular mimeographed periodical on sports. With a sound instinct, we tried to sell copies for cash money. I mucked about with mimeograph machines, school, camp and college newspapers throughout my adolescence; I literally cannot remember a time when I was not writing something essentially for my own satisfaction but also with confidence of the grace that others were going to read it.

"I worked a few months for a business newspaper, then had what now looks like the good fortune of a year's unemployment, when at the ages of nineteen and twenty I could turn out reams of unpublished (mostly unpublishable) articles and stories, one of them a novel. Thereafter, in fairly rapid succession, I was assistant editor of a scholarly magazine of the labor movement, editor of a fact-detective pulp and of a paperback house specializing in Westerns, and from 1951 to 1954 associate editor of *Esquire*.

"My major responsibility at *Esquire* was the quality of the prose (those were the days when the attitudes of Harold Ross and Frederick Lewis Allen dominated the periodicals, and heavy editing was regarded as proper procedure), but I also wrote several pieces a year for the magazine and shared the fiction-reading burden. While at *Esquire* I wrote and sold my 'first' novel, *The Experts*; and I was commissioned to write *Wall Street: Men and Money*. With the full knowledge that when I completed this book I was going to resign, Arnold Gingrich allowed me to cut down to half time (at two-thirds salary) while I wrote it. My loyalty to the magazine persists: I write for it a monthly column on music, and from two to six articles a year.

"Since 1954 I have been an independent contractor. My output includes articles for most of the nation's general-interest magazines, both the mass-circulation and the more ambitious; pamphlets on subjects ranging from sound production to advertising research; two (only two) short stories; two books and a dozen or so articles for the signature of others; a second novel, *A Voice That Fills the House*; and two large-scale reportorial books, *Madison Avenue, USA* and *The Schools.*

"From the last, there has as yet been no escape. As an 'expert' on education, I have served as a consultant to the American Council of Learned Societies (producing in the process a book called *Where, When and Why: Social Studies in American Schools*) and to the Center for Programed Instruction; I have been thrust into what might be called quasi-public life as a member of a White House Panel on Educational Research and Development and as chairman of a local school board in New York; and at this writing I hold the grandiloquent title of Research Director of a Twentieth Century Fund study in international education. I am also currently working toward a book on the lawyers and the law and (as a related matter) on a biography of the late Emory R. Buckner, commissioned by the William Nelson Cromwell Foundation, and based initially on unpublished correspondence between Buckner and the late Felix Frankfurter.

"Much of my time goes to music; in addition to the monthly column in *Esquire*, I write occasional pieces on music for the New York *Times Magazine*, *High Fidelity*, and *Opera News*; and I review concerts and opera for *Musical America.* I came late to music, and learned to read a score without ever becoming proficient as a performer (the same could be said of Wagner, of course, but he had talent).

MARTIN MAYER

My training for this part of my work has been both ambitious and spotty, an odd and sometimes worrisome combination; but experience has been filling in the holes, and constant contact with music has been the joy of my working life.

"Politically, I was brought up on the non-Communist left, and I stay there, though sometimes uneasily, having grown increasingly aware that large societal movements are the result of many individual actions rather than of central political decision. I now put much more faith in social invention than in social control—but the goals, and the likes and dislikes associated with them, have remained much the same. I am more or less committed, but certainly not engaged; the philosophy of engagement bores me.

"I have been married since 1949, to the scholar and critic Ellen Moers (author of *The Dandy* and of a forthcoming study of Theodore Dreiser). We have two boys, born in 1955 and 1958. Much of my traveling is planned in such a way that the family can go with me. We spend our summers at the end of Long Island, mostly golfing and swimming. Because I am a night worker, normally until three or four in the morning, these activities can be coupled with continuing high productivity. I am a steady rather than a fast writer; I can count on three pages a night, which makes a lot of pages over three hundred and sixty nights a year.

"Reporting is a young man's game: the concentration required to do it well is a drastic call on nervous energy. I should like to put more time into fiction, but the economic gamble is great and the work is less immediately satisfying because you never really know whether you've done it well. I haven't read either of my novels since I gave up the proofs, and my hunch is that they aren't much good. Still, a box is half-full of manuscript for a third novel, and when some time opens out I shall try again. While I share the general feeling of malaise about the novel as an art form, I also feel that ultimately there is nothing in the world but people and their perceptions, both too tricky to be stated as fact. If you work in words, then, the novel is inescapable."

Since 1966, when he wrote the statement above, Mayer has completed *The Lawyers* and *About Television*, and by now, no doubt, has his teeth fixed firmly in the hide of yet another instrument of American democracy. He has already taken care of Wall Street, Madison Avenue, and the little red schoolhouse, but city hall, the Pentagon, the churches, and the press, among other vulnerable institutions, all remain unaccounted for.

Not that Mayer's books and articles are simply old-fashioned muckraking. He possesses the racy, vivid, yet literate style of an old-time newspaperman, and an unfashionable instinct to go see for himself, but he has also mastered a number of entirely modern procedures, notably the pursuit of massively detailed accuracy. His books have been the products of "total" research, not only in the library but in the field. He is said to have talked to fifteen hundred people and visited over a hundred classrooms in five countries during the thirty months he spent on *The Schools* ("a terribly expensive book to write"), and he spent five years on *The Lawyers.*

Again, though Mayer is not above an occasional editorializing outburst, positive or negative, in his own voice, his characteristic method of presentation is to quote at length the words of the admen, teachers, or lawyers who are his subjects. It is the technique raised to a fine art by Lillian Ross of the *New Yorker*, allowing the witness to bless or damn himself out of his own mouth, allowing the reader the luxury of judgment.

Wall Street, "a work of nonfiction that crackles like a top drawer detective story," was also comprehensive and accurate enough to be used as a supplementary college text. His astonishing and frequently appalling dissection of the personalities and methods of Madison Avenue won the *New Yorker*'s comprehensive approval for Mayer's "skill in assimilating his findings, organizing his material, and presenting it, with a nice leavening of anecdote, illuminating shoptalk, and fascinating lore." *The Schools*, concentrating on primary and secondary education, and comparing American and foreign approaches, was called (even by teachers) a tour de force, balanced, readable, and brilliantly illuminating. There was less praise for Mayer's anatomy of the legal profession, which in spite of his "somewhat arrogant editorializing" was thought to lack any unifying point of view. This absence of "a sense of direction and a positive philosophy" is the most serious criticism leveled against his work; it bothers his expert critics more than it does the grateful laymen who find Mayer a marvelously knowledgeable and entertaining guide to some of their most important and mysterious institutions.

Mayer's novels have had less impact. The "brightness and bravura" of his style have been praised, and his journalist's gift for color and situation, but his generally unattractive characters, convincing as they are, are rather superficially drawn.

A tall, lean man, brown-haired and brown-eyed, Mayer is as rapid, staccato, and fertile of ideas in speech as in his books. He says: "I have been lucky enough to make a good living writing pretty much what I want to write, as I want to write it. Most things interest me, if I can get time to dig into them. For this reason I work pretty hard without feeling any pain." Rather characteristically, he is "grateful for all these blessings, but not particularly impressed by them." Mayer is a Jew and a Democrat.

PRINCIPAL WORKS: *Nonfiction*—Wall Street: Men and Money, 1955; Hi-Fi, 1956; Madison Avenue, USA, 1958; The Schools, 1961; Where, When, and Why: Social Studies in American Schools, 1963; The Lawyers, 1967; Diploma: International Schools and University Entrance, 1968; Emory Buckner, 1968; All You Know Is Facts (selected magazine articles), 1969; The Teachers' Strike: New York 1968, 1969; New Breed on Wall Street, 1969; About Television, 1972. *Novels*—The Experts (England, The Candidate), 1955; A Voice That Fills the House, 1959.

ABOUT: Contemporary Authors 5–6, 1963; Who's Who in America, 1972–1973. *Periodicals*—Commonweal April 18, 1958; July 25, 1958; Library Journal February 1, 1955; September 15, 1963; Wilson Library Bulletin October 1961.

MEGGED, AHARON (August 10, 1920–), Israeli novelist, short story writer, and dramatist, writes: "I was born in a small Polish town, Włocławek, of which I remember nothing except white snow and a stone thrown at me by a Polish boy who called me 'Żyd.' At the age of five and a half I came with my parents and smaller brother to the shore of Jaffa, Palestine, where a bulky Arab stevedore lifted me with his strong arms from the ship and dumped me into his boat.

"We settled in a very small village at that time, Ra'anana, sunk in sands, surrounded by jackals, Bedouin tents and dry weeds. My father, being the first schoolteacher there, with a flock of seven pupils under his rod, taught me, among other things, Bible, with which I fell in love, and Talmud, which I learned with tears, envying the boys playing in the street. I started writing, mostly poems à la Hebrew classics, at the age of nine or ten, first as a way to woo my little girl friend, then to irritate my rivals, then out of despair. No one saw those poems, well locked in a drawer, in our wooden hut.

"At the age of thirteen I began studying at Herzlia Gymnasium, the Eton of Tel Aviv at that time, living first with my grandmother, then in a small room on the roof by myself, homesick for the green pastures of my village.

"At seventeen, like many of my kind, members of a Zionist Socialist youth movement, I went to live in a kibbutz. There, in Sdot-Yam, I discovered the hardships of manual labor—as a stevedore in Haifa harbor, a stone-breaker in quarries or a ploughman in fields, and the profits of collective life. I had much to say about these exalting experiences, but, never a good talker, I put them on paper. My first short story, 'A Load of Oxen,' about longshoremen and animals, appeared in 1940 and was a breakthrough. Then came more stories, about fishermen, pioneers, pilgrim fathers, sons and lovers. In 1946 I was sent to the United States as a missionary to a Zionist youth movement. I spent there over two years and came back towards the end of our War of Liberation. Palestine—British cops and snobs, raids, barbed-wire, Arab biblical villages, bitter root drinks, springs hidden under stones and myrtles—suddenly became the State of Israel, free, white-washed, secretless, very dynamic.

"I left the kibbutz in 1950 for Tel Aviv. Back in the city, my eyes developed an ironic self-criticizing vision. I wrote satirical short stories, novels and plays, most of which dealt with the mental and moral effects of the crucial transition from the idealistic pioneering period, to the materialistic one. Thus were born the novels *Hedvah ve Ani* (1954), *Miqreh Haksie* (1960), *Hahai al Hamet* (1965), and comedies staged by Habimah and Ohel theaters. Israelis, lovers of self-defamation, self-irony, nostalgic for the lost heroic past, were so kind as to express their gratitude by awarding me twice the Ussishkin Prize, as well as the Brenner and Shlonsky prizes.

"I have been the editor of the literary weekly *Massa* (now a supplement of *Lamerchav* daily) for the last thirteen years, which means that I write mostly at night, after having chased away all the swarms of letters that have stung me all day long.

"I like solitude, leisure, journeys to the end of the world—all of which I have hardly achieved. Sailing on Hebrew words mostly means being drifted to ancient seas, hot deserts, gloomy diaspora lands, and, while anchoring at the Present—feeling upon the neck the yoke of 'national responsibility.' I try to bear all this with humor, hence the 'ambivalent' attitude latent in my books.

"I am married to Eda Zorit, a painter and writer, and have two sons."

AHARON MEGGED

In the year he left the kibbutz for Tel Aviv, Megged published his first book, *Ruakh Yamin* (Spirit of the Seas, 1950), a collection of the stories he had written about life and work in a small fishing kibbutz and among the stevedores of Haifa harbor. His first novel, *Hedvah ve Ani* (Hedva and I, 1954), which won the 1955 Ussishkin Prize, is a satirical story about a young couple who leave the kibbutz to return to the city. The wife is like a fish back in its own waters, but the husband hates the bureaucracy and the petit-bourgeois environment, and longs for the kibbutz. In this novel, in the stories collected in *Israel Khaverim* (Israeli Folk, 1955), and in much of Megged's later work, his principal theme, as he says above, is the conflict between the idealistic spirit of the Israeli pioneers, and the creeping materialism which followed the foundation of the Israeli state.

In *Miqreh Haksil* (1960, translated by Aubrey Hodes as *Fortunes of a Fool*) Megged's antihero, alienated from his bustling and purposeful society and from his own family, wanders among great and small events, war and office, home and friends, realities and hallucinations, seeking but not finding a resting place. Max Brod says in a foreword to the English edition that this is the only work known to him by a young Israeli writer markedly influenced by the art of Franz Kafka, and that it "tells the story of a lonely outsider, which is really the story of the human conscience. The events take place in a society which has lost its sane criterion. Like Kafka's heroes, Megged's fool has lost his spiritual links with his environment; his life is also a cry of protest against a society which is losing its faith."

Habrikha (The Escape, 1962), containing three long satirical stories, was followed by the novel *Hahai al Hamet* (1965, translated by Misha Louvish as *Living on the Dead*). It is about a young Israeli writer, Jonas Rabinowitz, who is commissioned to write the biography of Abraham Davidov, an (imaginary) national hero. The book is never written, and in the intervals of his trial for breach of contract Jonas tells the story of his failure. This quest for the facts behind the Davidov myth is also a rediscovery of the history of Israel, for ever since his immigration from Russia as a young man Davidov had been a part of the evolution of the new state, draining marshes in the Jordan valley, leading a rising against the British, organizing illegal immigration, and fighting heroically in the War of Independence. As Jonas gathers his material, his own personal life crumbles. He divorces his wife on a sudden irrational impulse and becomes involved with a group of writers, increasingly adopting not merely their bohemian habits but also their scornful rejection of the national tendency to idealize the pioneers.

Davidov's purposeful, dedicated life is contrasted with the easy but ultimately sterile and self-centered existence of Jonas and his friends. At the end of his quest Jonas finally meets the hero's wife. With her children she has had to pay for Davidov's heroism in poverty, hardship, and neglect, for his dedication to the public cause was in part a reflection of his inability to fulfill his private responsibilities (Chaim Bermant has suggested possible symbolism in the fact that his final task is to build a road to Sodom). Yet Davidov, despite his cruelty and his compulsive womanizing, was one of those who shaped Israel and its people, and Jonas's discoveries about Davidov increasingly threaten his own identity. His mental and moral paralysis grows until he "accidentally" loses the file he has built up. Stuart Hood summed it up as "a subtle book by an ironist who teases at the paradoxes in Israeli society, those contradictions at its heart which are seldom acknowledged."

Megged is a prolific dramatist, and some of his plays have been widely performed, in Israel and abroad. *Inkubator al Hassela* (Incubator on the Rock, 1950) is a comedy about a writer of the old guard who goes to a kibbutz to write a novel about its life. He has heard about "free love" there, and hopes for some of that too, but the kibbutz members make a fool of him. *Harkhek ba-Arava* (Far in the Wasteland, 1952) studies a group of five men and one woman isolated from the world while digging a well in the southern Negev. *I Like Mike* (1957), which was also made into a film, is a satire on a middle-class Tel Aviv family who try to marry off their daughter to a young American tourist, hoping to emigrate to the United States, but whose plans are upset when the boy falls in love with Israel. Some of Megged's plays have biblical settings, like *B'reshit* (Genesis, 1963), a comedy based on the first chapter of Genesis, and *Ha'ona Ha'boeret* (The High Season, 1968), in which the fate of the Jews under the Nazis, and the problems of revenge, reconciliation, and atonement, are considered in terms of the story of Job.

In 1968 Megged relinquished the editorship of *Massa* to become Cultural Counsellor in the Israeli Embassy in London, where his work has left him little time for writing. In this post he has continued to encourage interest in the new generation of Israeli writers, of whom he himself is one of the most distinguished and widely read.

PRINCIPAL WORKS IN ENGLISH TRANSLATION: Hedvad and I (play), 1957; Fortunes of a Fool, 1962; Living on the Dead, 1970. *Stories in* Blocker, J. (ed.) Israeli Stories, 1962: Kahn, S. J. (ed.) A Whole Loaf, 1957; Leftwich, J. (ed.) Yisrael, 1963; Penueli, S. Y. and Ukhmani, A. Hebrew Short Stories 2, 1965; Rabikovitz, D. (ed.) The New Israeli Writers, 1969. *Periodicals*—Atlantic November 1961; Furrows March–April 1950; Israel Argosy 6, 1958; Israel Horizons 1 November 1953; Israel Life and Letters Spring 1957; Israel Speaks March 23, 1956; Jewish Spectator December 1965; Midstream Spring 1960; New Outlook April 1958. September 1960.

ABOUT: Who's Who in Israel, 1972. *Periodicals*—Books Abroad Winter 1966; Catholic Herald August 28, 1970; Financial Times July 16, 1970; Irish Press July 29, 1970; Jewish Chronicle July 31, 1970; Jewish Echo June 26, 1970; Jewish Observer July 24, 1970; Listener July 9, 1970; Observer July 19, 1970; Oxford Times July 3, 1970; Scotsman July 4, 1970; Times (London) July 6, 1970.

***MEHDEVI, ANNE SINCLAIR** (September 12, 1922–), American memoirist, novelist, and short story writer, writes: "I was born in Manila, the Philippines, where my mother and father, both small-town Kansans, were school teachers. When I was four my parents returned to Kansas and eventually settled in Wichita, where I grew up.

"Ever since I can remember I wanted to be a writer and to travel—ambitions fostered, I suspect, by the atmosphere of my home. It was filled with memorabilia from evocative places like Zamboanga and Shanghai; and my mother used to quote Kipling, Swinburne and Shakespeare with loud and beautiful abandon as she dusted and washed dishes. In summer my father would load the family into our old Studebaker (I had three younger brothers) and off we would go to the West, the East, to mountains and deserts—every summer a different place. Wherever we went, my mother was ready with a quote and my father, a devout lover of statistics, would brief us on the history and economics.

"I began to write at fourteen—poems for myself and contributions to *True Love Magazine* and *Breezy Stories* for fame and fortune. None of my

* mā' di vē

submissions was accepted, perhaps because when the editors wrote back—and some did—asking for changes, I lost interest in the whole thing.

"After high school I dreamed of going 'East' to college, but the family finances decreed otherwise. I was enrolled at the University of Kansas when I happened to read an article in *Time* Magazine telling of 'the five largest scholarships ever offered.' Hopeful candidates were to apply to the University of Rochester. I applied and won.

"I was graduated *magna cum laude* and was elected to Phi Beta Kappa. Then, I had to go home, which seemed a terrible let-down after having written the campus musical comedy and edited the year-book and the literary magazine.

"After a year at home, during which I answered the classified ads daily with comic or negative results, I decided to seek my fortune in New York. My father had always encouraged me to save money and I had eighty dollars in a postal savings account. I withdrew the money, announced that I was going to New York, and took the train. I didn't exactly run away from home, but my father made it clear that no more money would be forthcoming. No one took me to the station.

"I was in New York one month when I landed a job as 'assistant fashion editor' of a teenage magazine. (It was wartime, perhaps that's why). From then on, for five years, I lived just like the slick magazine stories said that people in New York lived. I changed jobs, moved up, made more money, attended first nights at the theatre, lunched at '21,' had cocktails at the Stork Club, and had lots of boyfriends whose names were in the papers.

"I also wrote magazine pieces. Everyone was helpful. I was a kind of prodigy. Somewhere along about this time I began to realize that being a prodigy meant that my mentors would always keep me a pupil. I was on the staff of *Collier's* magazine at the time, and decided to send in a short story under a false name. It made a big hit, but when I confessed that I had written it, everyone began to advise again. I quit.

"Then one day I met by chance a young Persian diplomat, really a kind of office boy at the Persian Consulate. He took one look at my clippings and said: 'You don't really call this stuff writing?'

"I married him and resigned from my magazine job, lost interest in New York and made a decision which I have never regretted: to live things as they come, not to struggle to *be* anything except myself. I burned my clippings, old letters and photos—and gave up writing.

"Five years, three children and about fifty thousand miles later I was in New York again, where my husband, Mohamed Mehdevi, had become a political affairs officer with the United Nations. One day I ran into an old New York crony,

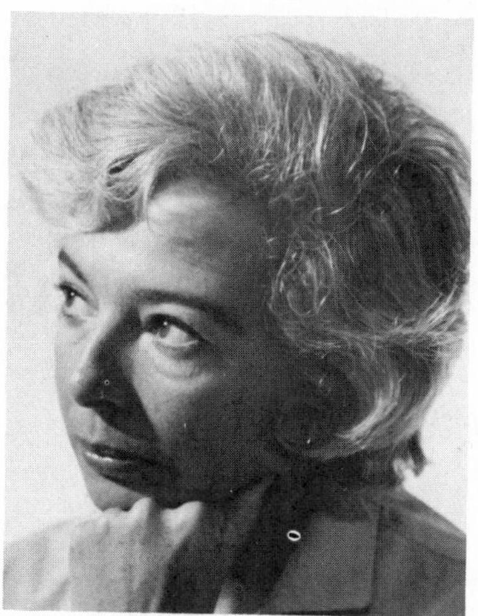

ANNE SINCLAIR MEHDEVI

Harold Strauss of Alfred A. Knopf. He said, 'You married a Persian? Why not write a book about it?'

"I did. And that is really how I became a writer —by deciding not to. My first book, *Persian Adventure*, was serialized in the *New Yorker* magazine, broadcast over the BBC, digested and translated. This unexpected good luck seemed to show me that by writing what I pleased, I wrote better. Since then, I have written six books. Each has been written in my spare time.

"On my passport I list my profession as: 'housewife.' If it wouldn't disturb the immigration officials, I would list myself as: 'wife and mother.' This is what I consider my profession.

"Writing is my hobby.

"I have three children and live in Abadan, Iran."

Mrs. Mehdevi is the daughter of Solomon Sinclair, a lawyer, and Ida (Lowry) Sinclair. She was an assistant editor of *Collier's* from 1942 to 1943, a reporter on the Dayton (Ohio) *Herald* in 1943, and a *Newsweek* researcher from 1943 to 1946. Her husband, whom she married in 1945, has become a management analyst and is also an author. They now live in Majorca.

Persian Adventure, Mrs. Mehdevi's account of her discovery of her husband's country, delighted both critics and common readers with its crisp observation, its "gay, astringent sympathy." According to a reviewer in the *Times Literary Supplement:* "To have achieved so deep and accurate a penetration into the Persian way of life and thought in so short a period is a very rare achievement. To have also recorded it in prose which is a delight to read from first to last—which is, indeed, a piece of literature in its own right—is nearly unique."

Similar qualities ensured the success of two further books of memoirs: *From Pillar to Post*, about the author's travels and endless home-making in many parts of the world with her diplomat-husband; and *Persia Revisited*, about her return to Teheran and to her father-in-law, Hajji Malek, whose remarkable houshold sheltered ninety relatives. These two "witty, graphic, and agreeable books" seemed to some reviewers rather less perceptive than the first, but both were in general very warmly received.

Mrs. Mehdevi has also written several excellent books for children, and *Don Chato*, a novel about a Spanish fishing village and its doctor which evoked as much critical enthusiasm as her memoirs. "Within its idiom of comic pathos," wrote one reviewer, "*Don Chato* is beautifully conceived and perfectly executed."

PRINCIPAL WORKS: *Memoirs*—Persian Adventure, 1953; From Pillar to Post, 1956; Persia Revisited, 1964. *Fiction*—Don Chato, 1959. *For children*—The Leather Hand, 1961; Rubies of the Red Sea, 1963; Persian Folk and Fairy Tales: Retold, 1965; Parveen, 1969.

ABOUT: Contemporary Authors 5–8, 1st revision, 1969; Mehdevi, A. S. From Pillar to Post, 1956; Mehdevi, A. S. Persia Revisited, 1964; Mehdevi, A. S. Persian Adventure, 1953.

***MEHRING, WALTER** (April 29, 1896–), expatriate German poet, novelist, dramatist, and cultural historian, was born in Berlin, where he grew up in a liberal and humanist middle-class atmosphere. His father, Sigmar Mehring, was editor of the satirical weekly *Ulk* and a translator of Villon and Whitman. His mother, the former Hedwig Löwenstein, was an opera singer born in Prague of Jewish background. Even before he entered school, Mehring had the freedom of his father's vast library, a circumstance which profoundly influenced his life and career. After completing his secondary education at the Wilhelms-Gymnasium in Berlin, Mehring studied art history at the universities of Berlin and Munich until he was drafted into the Imperial German Army in 1915.

During World War I Mehring became associated with the intellectual circle that centered around the left-wing expressionist magazine *Der Sturm*, published by Herwarth Walden. His first poems, lyrics in the expressionist manner, appeared in *Der Sturm* in 1916, and the same year he completed the drama *Die Frühe der Städte* (The Morning of the Cities, 1916). At the end of the war, Mehring became one of the founders of the Berlin outpost of dadaism, that brief but influential spasm of revulsion against the bourgeois standards of the past. In 1919, he and the artist George Grosz founded the radical journal *Pleite*.

Mehring, along with such writers as Bertolt Brecht, Kurt Tucholsky, and Erich Kästner, was one of those who developed the satirical cabaret as an art and political tool in Berlin during the Weimar Republic. From 1919 to 1921 he served as artistic director of Max Reinhardt's cabaret theatre "Schall und Rauch," and in 1920 he founded his own "Politisches Cabaret." His savage and sometimes outrageous songs and poems, written for the cabaret stage, are collected in *Das politische Cabaret* (1920), *Das Ketzerbrevier* (Breviary for Heretics, 1921), *Die Gedichte, Lieder und Chansons* (Poems, Songs and Chansons, 1929), and *Arche Noah S.O.S.* (Noah's Ark S.O.S., 1931). Mehring was among the first to apply the rhythms and syncopations of American jazz to lyrics in the German language. His harsh satirical drama *Der Kaufmann von Berlin* (The Merchant of Berlin), a crowded panoramic view of Berlin during the inflation, was staged by Erwin Piscator in 1929 and caused a furor. Jews in the audience cheered it, Nazis threw stink bombs, and the authorities quickly banned it.

During the 1920s and early 1930s Mehring divided his time between Berlin and Paris, while serving as a correspondent and art critic for such liberal German journals as Maximilian Harden's *Zukunft*, Carl von Ossietzky's *Weltbühne*, the *Literarische Welt*, and *Das Tagebuch*. His writings of this period include several topical satirical novels, among them *In Menschenhaut* (In Human Skin, 1922), *Westnordviertelwest* (West-North-One Quarter-West, 1925), and *Paris in Brand* (Paris in Flames, 1927). He also wrote a three-act review, *Europäische Nächte* (European Nights, 1924); the collection of short novels and stories *Algier* (1927); the radio play *Sahara* (1929); the film script *Das Lied vom Leben* (Song of Life, 1932); and the drama *Die höllische Komödie* (The Hellish Comedy, 1932).

With the rise of Hitler to power in Germany, Mehring was among the first authors to be condemned by the Nazi regime, and his books were among those publicly burned by the Nazis in March 1933. Soon afterwards he went into exile, and during the next few years he lived in Vienna and Paris, writing anti-Nazi poetry and novels. "I had no preparation whatsoever for a martyr's life," Mehring says, "although that was the kind of life I had to take up in order to keep my integrity as my father had taught me I must."

After the fall of France in 1940, Mehring was interned by the Vichy regime and spent some time in concentration camps. He managed to escape from Camp Saint Cyprien, and after several adventurous detours he came to the United States

* mā′ ring

in 1941 by way of Martinique. He lived in New York, and also, for a time, in Los Angeles, working as a translator and as a reviewer for the New York *Times* and other publications.

Mehring's book of poems *Kein Weg zurück* (1944) was translated into English as *No Road Back* (1944), with illustrations by his friend George Grosz. It contains "The Saga of the Giant Crab," a prophetic allegory about the consequences of Hitler's rise to power first published in 1933 by Carl von Ossietzky, and the long epic poem, or poem sequence, "Odyssey Out of Midnight," which is dedicated to Ossietzky. Mehring's is "functional" poetry, showing few signs of his association with dada. His language, Hermann Kesten said, is "at the same time . . . enraged and precious. It pours hellish loathing into delicately measured, adroitly jarring, artfully polished rhymes. It is a baroque lyricism . . . curved and vehement." In Kesten's opinion, *No Road Back* is one of the two "most important volume[s] of German verse written in exile" (the other being Werfel's *Collected Poems*). Kesten described Mehring at that time as "frail, agile in wit and gesture," and in speech provocative, "full of dark allusions and dire prophecies."

Mehring's best-known book is *Die verlorene Bibliothek* (1952), translated by Richard and Clara Winston as *The Lost Library*. This "autobiography of a culture" was originally conceived as a history of nineteenth century European literature, but evolved into something altogether more original. In exile, unpacking his father's library in a New England farmhouse, Mehring was assailed by memories and associations, and by bewilderment. From a standpoint in the midst of twentieth century catastrophe, he contemplated the humane and liberal literature of the preceding century, seeking to understand how these ideals had failed, and, if he could, "to save from the wreckage those things we can use for the future." The result is a book full of ideas, many of them "brilliant and disturbing," some of them less so. In its reminiscences of people and events it is at the same time "a veritable Who's Who of European Bohemia and literary coffeehouse society between the wars," a "beautifully conceived and beautifully executed book" by a "highly unexpendable man."

The most notable of the books Mehring has published since then are *Berlin-Dada* (1959), a chronicle based on his own recollections of the movement; *Der Zeitpuls fliegt* (The Time-Pulse Flies, 1958), a selection from published work; and the ballads and songs in *Das Neue Ketzerbrevier* (1962). He has been married since 1944 to a French painter, Marie-Paule Tessier, and lives now in Ascona, Switzerland. His hobbies are drawing and painting, and breeding dogs. A street in West

WALTER MEHRING

Berlin has been named in Mehring's honor—a permanent acknowledgment of his importance as a writer and as a guardian of the German humanist tradition.

PRINCIPAL WORKS IN ENGLISH TRANSLATION: No Road Back (poems), 1944; The Lost Library: The Autobiography of a Culture, 1951. *Essay*—Last of the Scapegoats, *in* Nation July 29, 1944.

ABOUT: Deutsche Exil-Literatur 1933–1945, 1966; Handbuch der deutschen Gegenwartsliteratur, 1965; Penguin Companion to Literature 2, 1969; Soergel, A. and Hohoff, C. Dichtung und Dichter der Zeit 2, 1963; Wer ist Wer?, 1969–1970; Who's Who in Germany, 1964; Wilpert, G. v. Deutsches Dichterlexikon, 1963. *Periodicals*—American Scholar July 1951; Books Abroad 1 1952; Commonweal August 3, 1951; Nation October 21, 1944; Saturday Review of Literature August 18, 1951.

MEHTA, VED PARKASH (March 21, 1934–), Indian memoirist, journalist, and novelist, writes: "I was born in Lahore, which is now in Pakistan. From the age of three to the age of fifteen I lived in various places in India and was in and out of hospitals and boarding schools (mostly in hospitals and out of schools). The principal memories I have of this time are connected not with games or playmates or storybooks but with official tours that my father had to make as a medical administrator in the Punjab, with charlatans of various kinds who were perpetually taking advantage of my mother's credulity, and with my sisters' and brothers' stories about their exploits at their schools. This talk in time made me, in a manner of speaking, run away from home. In 1949, I accepted an opportunity to go to Little Rock, Arkansas, where I learned English and crammed into three years the missed schooling of

VED MEHTA

many more. After getting a high-school diploma there, I spent four years at Pomona College, with a couple of summer terms at Harvard and at the University of California (Berkeley), then three years at Oxford, where I read modern history at Balliol College. A year and a half of graduate studies at Harvard followed Oxford. I got my share of honors and degrees, which in those days were very important to me, because all the time I was working toward an academic career.

"Although I set down most of my autobiography the summer I was twenty (it was published as *Face to Face* in 1957) and later contributed stories and articles to British, Indian and American publications, I had never thought of taking up writing seriously. Then, in 1959, William Shawn encouraged me to write for the *New Yorker*. I joined the staff in 1961, and he has had a strong influence on my writing.

"Besides *Face to Face* I have written *Walking the Indian Streets* (1960), a travel book about India and Nepal; *Fly and the Fly Bottle* (1963), a report on contemporary philosophers and historians in Britain; *The New Theologian* (1966), a report on contemporary Christian thinkers in the West; *Portrait of India* (1970), a study of modern India; and *John Is Easy to Please* (1971), a collection of *New Yorker* pieces on the written and spoken word—all nonfiction. I have also written a comic novel, *Delinquent Chacha* (1966).

"There is an aspect of some of my writing that has puzzled a few critics, and it may be useful to reproduce here a publisher's note that was included in the English edition of my second book (though I feel bound to say that my own final views on the subject may not be formulated for many years): 'As readers of his autobiography, *Face to Face*, will know, Ved Mehta has been totally blind since the age of three; and they may be surprised to find no reference to his blindness in this book. This is entirely deliberate. By the diligent use of four senses Mr. Mehta is able to piece together the world of five; and when he describes what he "sees" he is in fact describing what he sees through the eyes of other people. In re-creating the visual world for himself in this fashion, he finds that he is helped most by the chance and spontaneous remarks of friends and strangers.

" 'By profession Mr. Mehta is an author and journalist and he is anxious that no special allowance should be made for his work on the grounds of his disability. Indeed, he feels this so strongly that no note such as this will appear in any of his future books. It appears here only because some reviewers of the American edition seemed puzzled by the lack of any explanation.'

"I feel bound to add that it will probably take me the rest of my life to explore the private universe of a blind man, which at present is still something of a mystery to me, and that it may take me as long to formulate my own explanation of my method of writing."

Ved Mehta is one of the seven children of Amolak Ram Mehta, former deputy director general of the Indian health services, and the former Shanti Mehra. He was blinded by meningitis in infancy and endured some wretched and frustrating years in the hands of quacks and charlatans. When he was five his father enrolled him in a school for the blind in Bombay and, when he was fifteen, he went to the Arkansas State School for the Blind in Little Rock. He is the most famous alumnus of that institution, where he is remembered as a brilliant and determined student, friendly, cheerful, and much given to practical jokes. After his three years there Mehta was able to go on to Pomona College, where he was elected to Phi Beta Kappa in his junior year and received his B.A. in 1956. Oxford (B.A., 1959) and Harvard (M.A., 1961) followed. Mehta's accomplishments are by no means solely academic. He has so developed his hearing, his skin sensitivity, and his memory that he is able, for example, to ride a horse or a bicycle and play chess, and he once hitchhiked across the United States.

Mehta's immensely precise apprehension of people and places, moods and smells, is palpable in all his books, of which the first and best was *Face to Face*. It describes his education, and "deftly and somewhat ruefully explores his tangle of pride, sensitivity, gratitude, and truculence." The book was very warmly praised for its lucid and elegant prose, and its fastidious avoidance of any kind of attitudinizing. "It is extraordinary," wrote one reviewer, "when a young man of twenty-three has the material for an autobiography that deserves serious attention and still more extraordinary when a man so young can present his material in an arresting fashion."

In 1959 Mehta revisited India, accompanied for part of the time by his friend Dom Moraes; he described what he found in his native country in *Walking the Indian Streets*, a brief, impressionistic, and for the most part rather slight account, at its best in a memorable description of the author's meeting with Nehru. Most reviewers were fascinated by the book, less for what it says about India than for what it says about Ved Mehta. He "asks no quarter," wrote H. L. Matthews, and lives and writes, "in so far as it is humanly possible, as if he could see." Most of Mehta's books draw on material first published in the *New Yorker*, and nearly fifty of his essays are incorporated in *Portrait of India*, a massive companion volume to *Walking the Indian Streets*. It was found an absorbing, often illuminating, but somewhat random and uneven "collection of sights, sounds, impressions and conversations."

Fly and the Fly Bottle describes Mehta's "encounters with British intellectuals"—among them A. J. Ayer, A. J. P. Taylor, Lewis Namier, and Bertrand Russell—and "eavesdrops shamelessly, but delightfully," upon current philosophical and historical controversies. Alan Pryce-Jones praised Mehta as "a reporter who moves with elegance among abstractions," but some reviewers thought his presentation of the issues rather superficial. The same criticism was applied to *The New Theologian*, "a series of clever candid snaps" of contemporary religious thinkers written in what to many readers seemed an irritatingly condescending tone. An exception is the piece about Dietrich Bonhoeffer, whom Mehta clearly admires and who is treated with admirable care and discernment. *John Is Easy to Please* collects six essays describing an encounter with the linguist Noam Chomsky, with two Indian writers, and with others associated with "the written and spoken word." It was followed by *Daddyji*, an affectionate biography of his father.

Ved Mehta's first novel, *Delinquent Chacha*, tells the story of a middle-aged Hindu reprobate whose determination to become an English gentleman is defeated by his weakness for quite ungentlemanly kinds of behavior. Most reviewers found it only mildly amusing, and one objected to its "relentless" charm, but Anne Fremantle saw in the protagonist a "completely 'round' character . . . tragic and comic, poignant and farcical."

Mehta has never learned to write longhand, but manages very well with an ordinary typewriter and, sometimes, a tape recorder. He is one of the *New Yorker's* reporters-at-large, and lives in New York when he is not traveling. Mehta was awarded a Guggenheim Fellowship and a Ford Foundation travel and study grant in 1971, and the following year received an honorary doctorate from Pomona University.

PRINCIPAL WORKS: Face to Face, 1957; Walking the Indian Streets, 1960 (revised 1971); Fly and the Fly Bottle: Encounters with British Intellectuals, 1963; The New Theologian, 1966; Delinquent Chacha, 1966; Portrait of India, 1970; John Is Easy to Please: Encounters with the Written and Spoken Word, 1971; Daddyji, 1972.

ABOUT: Mehta, V. Daddyji, 1972; Mehta, V. Face to Face, 1957; Mehta, V. Walking the Indian Streets, 1960; Moraes, D. Gone Away, 1960; Who's Who, 1973. *Periodicals*—America September 14, 1957; Atlantic May 1959; Encounter March 1967; New York Times May 2, 1972; New Yorker January 2, 1950; May 7, 1960; Newsweek December 31, 1962; Saturday Review August 17, 1957; December 7, 1957; Time July 12, 1963.

***MEMMI, ALBERT** (December 15, 1920–), French novelist and essayist, writes (in French): "I was born in Tunis in Tunisia, North Africa, and I never went more than two or three hundred kilometers from my native city until I was twenty years old. And since the city was divided into sections which were relatively hostile, scornful, or cautiously polite towards each other, I avoided, I know, venturing much outside my own district. Each *quartier* lived for itself, by its own traditions and prejudices, its fears and hates: Arabs, Jews, French, Italians, Maltese, Greeks, etc. . . . I have described all that in my first novel *La Statue de sel* (*The Pillar of Salt*).

"But, actually, it is my second novel *Agar* (badly translated under the title *Strangers*) that contains the key to my present life. Two months after leaving Tunis and my *quartier*—now so closed to me that it appears like a dream of a former life—two months after, I had married a blonde girl with blue eyes, a Catholic, from the east of France, from the part of France which is so like Germany. Another strange dream, that I could never have imagined . . . but I have described all that in *Agar*.

"All my life was begun again, reoriented, rethought in relation to this event. I had to ask myself who I was, who I had been until then, and who I was going to be so that I could live in the new world which offered itself to me. How reconcile within myself the east and the west—that distant past, dizzily rooted in the heart of Africa; and the study of philosophy and the serene, rational humanities, undertaken in order to become, as apparently I have, the very image of a Western teacher? All this I have described in *The Pillar of Salt*. And one ought not to be sur-

* me mē′

ALBERT MEMMI

prised that in *Strangers* I describe in particular the difficulties of a mixed marriage, the shock of two cultures within a home, the discords which mount to the point of catastrophe.

"Next I wanted to understand why the disparate couple failed so often, so miserably. This caused me to write another book. (I no longer knew what to do other than write books in order to survive.) In *Portrait du colonisé* (*The Colonizer and the Colonized*) I discovered not only what I sought to understand in relation to mixed marriage and myself, but also the drama of colonization and its effects on the two parties to the colony: the colonizer and the colonized. How their whole lives, their appearance, their behavior were governed by the fundamental relation which connected them to each other in a pitiless union. At the same time I caught a glimpse of an infinitely larger and more terrifying phenomenon: the way in which power rules the relationship of so may human beings to other human beings.

"The same mechanisms, in any case, which had clarified for me my life as a colonized man were going to help me understand what a Jew was. I was also a Jew and even when the colonization ended I was still separate, a minority, often accused and attacked. It was therefore no less necessary for me to take stock of this important aspect of my life: this I did in *Le portrait d'un Juif* (*Portrait of a Jew*), which upset all my readers because in it I revealed the unhappiness of being a Jew, the constant discomfort of Jewishness, and the continual menace from others.

"I have not mentioned some works in which I sought precise, even technical verification of one point or another of this voyage of discovery, for example a sociological study on racism and an essay on psychoanalysis. Thus all my work up till now has been an inventory of my life, sometimes as fiction, sometimes as a portrait, an essay, or even a contribution towards psychosociological research."

Albert Memmi, the son of a Jew of Italian origin and a Berber woman, grew up in poverty in the Tunis ghetto. A scholarship took him to the *lycée*, where he learned to despise all that he had been and conceived the wild ambition of becoming a teacher of philosophy in France. World War II intervened, bringing the German occupation of Tunisia. The French *colons* yielded up the Jews to the Nazis and Memmi was interned in a forced labor camp. He escaped, offered his services to the French liberation forces, and was rejected.

After the war Memmi completed his philosophical studies at the University of Algiers and at the Sorbonne. In Paris he met the Roman Catholic Alsatian girl who became his wife. She returned with him to Tunis, where he began his career as a philosophy teacher, and in 1956 became director of the city's Psychology Center. In 1959 Memmi went to Paris to work at the National Center for Scientific Research and settled in the capital, where he is now a professor at the École Pratique des Hautes Études and also at the Sorbonne. Thus he has realized the improbable aspirations of his childhood—which, however, had long since ceased to be of central importance in his life. The war had shown him the extent of his deracination: he had been rejected by educated Jews because of his ghetto background, by the ghetto because of his education, by the French because of his Jewishness. He had become a paradigm of colonized man. His life and all his books are centered on the task of coming to terms with this role.

La Statue de sel (1953, translated as *The Pillar of Salt*) is a lightly fictionalized account of his childhood and youth. It is a little ungainly in its style and shape, but profoundly impressive in the urgency of the narrator's search for identity, his passionate sense of justice and clarity of vision. It is also a deeply fascinating portrayal of several unfamiliar milieus, from the magic rituals and melodramatic funerals of the ghetto to the social and militaristic rituals of the *colons*. The narrator's experience diverges from Memmi's only at the end, when he sets out for Argentina—chosen because it offers nothing of value and therefore no danger of further disillusionment.

The author's marriage, as he explains above and in his second novel, was another bewildering onslaught upon his sense of identity. Warren Preece, reviewing *Strangers*, called it "a novel easy to admire. Wiry, completely uncompromising, penetrating and intent always on the task of accurately delineating its characters at each level of development." Preece expressed a widespread critical reaction when he found the book's only major weakness in its suggestion "that a similar fate is the lot of all mixed marriages, for the overwhelming strength of Memmi's work lies in its almost perfect realization of the central characters as unique individuals."

Portrait du colonisé précédé du portrait du colonisateur (1957), was translated as *The Colonizer and the Colonized*, with a preface by Jean-Paul Sartre. This intensely personal analysis of the colonial process was a controversial book from the beginning, and has been a very influential one, admired by Léopold Sédar Senghor, the spokesman of *négritude*, and found worthy of comparison with Frantz Fanon's *The Wretched of the Earth*. Emile Capouya finds Memmi a gentler man than Fanon: "The spectacle of outrage has not tempered him to the steely hardness of the other great analyst of colonial rebellion. He is all the more convincing in his demonstration that the relation of the natives to their former and would-be masters is such that liberation, gradualism, compromise, amount to reaction."

In *Le Portrait d'un Juif* (1962, translated as *Portrait of a Jew*) Memmi sets out both to describe "the fate of a Jew as I have lived it" and "to strike a universal note," since he believes "that there exists a universal Jewish fate." Most reviewers thought that the book succeeded in its first but not in its second aim—that Memmi's rationale of what was universal in his experience could not match his "bitter plangent autobiography, written in dark colors and minor chords." There were similar feelings about the equally personal sequel, *La Libération du Juif* (1966, translated as *The Liberation of the Jew*), which sees in the state of Israel the best hope for the future of his people. A number of Memmi's essays, dealing with anti-Semitism, colonialism, and several other kinds of oppression, especially racism in America, were collected and translated in 1968 as *The Dominated Man*.

Memmi returned to the novel form in *Le Scorpion* (translated as *The Scorpion*), but with a difference. It is set in Tunis in the mid-1950s, when Tunisia, no longer a colony, is developing into an intolerantly nationalistic republic. A Jewish writer, Emile Memmi, has disappeared and his brother Marcel, a doctor, is going through his literary remains. These include fragments of a fictionalized autobiography, a journal containing some information new to Marcel (as well as entries that Marcel knows to be inaccurate or deliberately elaborated), and various aphorisms and literary reflections. Characters in the novel can be traced to the journal, and vice versa. Marcel's own comments on these products of an artistic sensibility, at first skeptical and gruffly commonsensical, come to reflect a growing sympathy with his brother's sense of alienation in his native country. This process is accelerated by a nationalistic purge at Marcel's hospital, and in the end he, like Emile, can see no solution to Tunisia's problems, and decides to return to France.

Richard Locke called the book "a richly interwoven net of autobiography, diary, commentary, aphorism, parable, *faux mémoire* and novel-within-the-novel—a complex puzzle of voices and documents, with five different typefaces used to differentiate them, and haunting photographs interspaced throughout." Locke welcomed the novel as an audacious but never precious experiment which gives Memmi scope to deploy "his one great strength—his closeness to the concrete details of personal experience. For Memmi is not a thinker so much as a sensibility. The more private he is the better he writes."

Memmi and his wife have three children. "I have," he says, "always saved for later my dreams of, let us say, a less necessary literature; I have obstinately accumulated manuscripts, and continue to believe that I have not yet produced my real work."

PRINCIPAL WORKS IN ENGLISH TRANSLATION: The Pillar of Salt, 1955; Strangers, 1958; Portrait of a Jew, 1962; The Colonizer and the Colonized, 1965; The Liberation of the Jew, 1966; The Dominated Man: Notes Towards a Portrait, 1968; The Scorpion or The Imaginary Confession, 1971.

ABOUT: Camus, A. *preface to* The Pillar of Salt, 1955; International Who's Who, 1973–74; Peyre, H. French Novelists of Today, 1967; Sartre, J.-P. *preface to* The Colonizer and the Colonized, 1965; Twentieth Century Writing, 1969; Who's Who in France, 1973–1974. *Periodicals*—America February 18, 1967; Cahiers Nord-Africains October 1957; February 1959; Commentary April 1955; November 1962; Nation December 27, 1965; May 22, 1967; New Leader January 1966; New York Herald Tribune Books October 30, 1955; September 25, 1960; June 24, 1962; New York Times May 22, 1971; New York Times Book Review September 25, 1960; June 3, 1962; March 26, 1967; Saturday Review December 11, 1965; Times Literary Supplement May 27, 1955.

MEREDITH, ANNE. *See* MALLESON, LUCY BEATRICE

MEREDITH, WILLIAM (MORRIS) (January 9, 1919–), American poet and translator, writes: "I was born in New York City and brought up in Darien, Connecticut. I liked poems, I think for rather impure and escapist reasons, almost as early as I can remember, and wrote them as much as laziness allowed from the time that I was about eight. The year after I graduated from Princeton,

WILLIAM MEREDITH

encouraged by Allen Tate and Muriel Rukeyser, and while I was working as a copy boy for a New York newspaper, I began writing more seriously. During the War, as an Army private and later as a naval aviator, I found myself relying on my writing to make sense of an experience and a world for which nothing in a protected and rather unobservant childhood had prepared me. A manuscript of poems was put together in 1943 by some friends in Princeton and submitted to the Yale Series of Younger Poets, then edited by Archibald MacLeish. I was in the Aleutian Islands at the time and the title poem of the collection was *Love Letter From an Impossible Land.*

"After the war, I taught and studied at Princeton for several years, and at the University of Hawaii. Curiously, it was two years as a carrier pilot during the Korean War that seemed to give me another start as a writer. My third book, *The Open Sea*, represents the voice and the insight that I think of as my own.

"I have tried to make my poems as public and colloquial as is honest, feeling that to accept a literary or intellectual stance was to diminish the importance of poetry. I have been aided in finding this voice by the fact that I am not very intellectual and have always read less than any writer I know. My admiration for Robert Frost, although it has better justification, may have started when I heard him commend idle and willful and desultory reading.

"Since 1955 I have taught at Connecticut College, but more and more, in readings and lectures and longer engagements, I have interested myself in public secondary education. For a number of years I was involved in programs for Negro high school students, first at Princeton, then at Connecticut College. These interests are an end in themselves but they also seem to me to come out of a search for my voice and for the real world. I would like someday to write poems honest enough to quell riots in the corridors of public high schools.

"I live on the west bank of the Thames River, in eastern Connecticut, on an old farm where I have a small nursery and tree farm. I think a good deal about trees, stars, and the sea and I wish everybody else would. These objects recur a little monotonously I'm afraid in my work. In the summer I go to Ripton, Vermont, where Frost used to live. His work and friendship were very strong influences on me. Teaching and opera are my hobbies."

Meredith is the son of William Morris Meredith and the former Nelley Keyser. He received his B.A. *magna cum laude* from Princeton in 1940 and then worked for a year on the New York *Times*, at first as a copy boy, as he says, then as a reporter. Meredith ended World War II as a Navy lieutenant; in the Korean War, during which he received two air medals, he rose a grade higher to the rank of lieutenant commander.

The early poems collected in *Love Letter From an Impossible Land* were thought not much more than cleverly imitative of fashionable models, including Auden and Spender, but, as one critic said, in those written after he became a Navy flyer, Meredith "comes to life and proves that he is an authentic poet after all." This judgment was confirmed by *The Ship and Other Figures*, a Poetry Club Selection, and *The Open Sea*. These are elegant, precise, and gracefully measured poems in the metaphysical tradition, detached but not unfeeling, the work of a renovator rather than a revolutionary, who displeased his critics only by his refusal to allow himself "the dazzling moment," the uncontrolled "flux of images and memories."

Meredith brought similar qualities—of gentle irony and speculative honesty—to his reflections on the loss at sea in 1963 of the submarine *Thresher*, a poem which, as Samuel Morse wrote, "may well stand as a model of the elegy in our time." It was the title poem of Meredith's fourth collection, in which his admiration for Robert Frost became apparent in a tone increasingly conversational and easy, though seldom slack or gauche.

The same year, 1964, Meredith published his translations of the *Alcools* of Guillaume Apollinaire. They were admired as sensitive and modest, "compromises between exactness and elegant sound, with the bias toward sound over sense." It might have been in search of a key to release his own perhaps inhibiting self-control that he chose to immerse himself in the work of an almost programmatically impulsive poet like Apollinaire; however the new poems which appeared, together with selections from previous books, in *Earth Walk*, were very much in Meredith's familiar mode. R. W. French thought that "in general, Meredith finds his poems in the small experiences of living. . . . Like Frost, he sometimes says too much, points too obviously, and lapses into easy generalizations. . . . [But] at his best, Meredith can revive the great commonplaces in subtle harmonies and make the poem appear almost a remembrance, as Keats said it should."

Meredith has also written a study of Shelley, and the libretto for Peter Whiton's opera *The Bottle Imp*, produced at Wilton, Connecticut, in 1958. He was awarded the Harriet Monroe Memorial Prize in 1944, the Oscar Blumenthal Prize in 1953, the Loines award in 1966, and the Van Wyck Brooks award in 1971. He has received grants and fellowships from the National Institute of Arts and Letters, the Rockefeller Foundation, *Hudson Review*, and the Ford Foundation. In 1955–1956 he was the *Hudson Review's* opera critic, and in 1961 he was attached to the New York City and Metropolitan Opera companies for a year to study on a Ford Foundation fellowship. He has served as a vice-president of the American Choral Foundation and chancellor of the Academy of American Poets. Since 1965 he has been professor of English at Connecticut College.

PRINCIPAL WORKS: *Poetry*—Love Letter From an Impossible Land, 1944; Ships and Other Figures, 1948; The Open Sea, 1958; (tr.) Alcools, 1964; The Wreck of the Thresher, 1964; Earth Walk: New and Selected Poems, 1970. *Nonfiction*—Shelley, 1962.

ABOUT: Contemporary Authors 9–10, 1964; MacLeish, A. *introduction to* Love Letter from an Impossible Land, 1944; Murphy, R. (ed.) Contemporary Poets of the English Language, 1970; Robson, J. (ed.) Modern Poets in Focus, vol. 2, 1973; Who's Who in America, 1972–1973. *Periodicals*—Princeton University Library Chronicle Autumn 1963.

***MERLEAU-PONTY, MAURICE** (March 14, 1908 — May 4, 1961), French philosopher and psychologist, was born in Rochefort-sur-Mer. From 1927 to 1931 he attended the École Normale Supérieure, where he met Jean-Paul Sartre, who was to become one of his closest friends. For a time their careers ran roughly parallel, both being drafted into the army after completing their *agrégation* in philosophy, though Merleau-Ponty was a second lieutenant and Sartre a private. Each taught in provincial *lycées* during the 1930s, but it was not until World War II, when in 1941 they were both members of the "Socialism and Liberty" resistance group, that the two men really came together to explore their common interest in philosophies of existence and phenomenology. They shared many assumptions, and were in revolt against the rationalism of their teachers, wishing to grasp experience as it is lived, rather than as dissected by scientific reason. But the origins of their disagreement can be traced to deep-seated differences in their ways of looking at the world which were already present in their earliest work.

* mer lō pôN ti

MAURICE MERLEAU-PONTY

Like Sartre, Merleau-Ponty was strongly influenced by the work of contemporary German thinkers, in his case especially by the later and less well-known work of Husserl; and he attempted to continue the direction in which Husserl's thought seemed to be moving. By using the existentialist view of man Merleau-Ponty hoped to escape the difficulties of traditional philosophy, but the questions with which he deals are such traditional ones as the Cartesian problem of mind and body. This is considered in his first work, *La Structure du comportement* (1942, translated by A. L. Fisher as *The Structure of Behavior*), where his intention is to "understand the relations of consciousness and nature."

How is it possible to reject the view that the world is simply "given" without being forced to conclude that it is wholly subjective, wholly made by us? Merleau-Ponty begins with a careful study and criticism of behaviorist and Gestalt psychology. He argues that behavior is neither exclusively objective nor exclusively subjective, but a dialectical interchange between man and the world. And it is out of this dialectical interchange that human meanings emerge, meanings which are neither passively assimilated from an established cosmic order, as the realists have imagined, nor constructed *de novo* by a creative mind, as the idealists have supposed. Thus man is neither a thing nor pure consciousness, but a "being-in-the-world" of which consciousness and corporeality are aspects, and it becomes possible to understand how consciousness can "make sense" of natural phenomena and yet be determined in the particular form that it takes by its natural and social environment.

This leads on to the study of perception in Merleau-Ponty's next book, for "if one understands by perception the act which makes us know existence, all the problems which we have just touched on are reducible to the problem of perception." *Phénoménologie de la perception* (1945, translated by C. Smith as *Phenomenology of Perception*) is a study of perception in this broad sense. In his introduction Merleau-Ponty speaks, as Husserl had done, of returning to things (*revenir aux choses mêmes*), of restoring "the primacy of perception." Phenomenology is for him an attempt to recapture the lived experience, to go back beyond the theories of philosophy and science to the world as we actually perceive it. For a conscious being, existence is always existence in *his* world, in his particular situation, with the particular past and body that he has. But he is free to live this situation as he chooses. "This significant life, this certain significance of nature and history which I am does not limit my access to the world but on the contrary is my means of entering into communication with it. It is by being unrestrictedly and unreservedly what I am at present that I have a chance of moving forward."

Merleau-Ponty's contention is that this lived experience has never been adequately dealt with by the two major currents in modern Western thought: empiricism (empiricist philosophy and behaviorist psychology) and "intellectualism" (idealism in philosophy and introspectionism in psychology): "Empiricism fails to see that we need to know what we are looking for, since otherwise we would not be looking for it: 'intellectualism' fails to realize that we must be ignorant of what we are looking for, or else, once more, we should not be searching." Seeking a "middle way," Merleau-Ponty begins with the notion of a body-subject involved in perception. The body-subject encounters a world which already has "meanings" incorporated in it—as a member of a particular society he perceives one substance as food and another as inedible—but he can also give new "meanings" to what he encounters; so he neither merely makes, nor merely encounters, the world he lives in, but has a dialectical relationship with it.

These first two books were regarded in France as of major philosophical importance, and brought Merleau-Ponty his appointment as professor of philosophy at the University of Lyon in 1945. He also joined with Sartre in the establishment of the existentialist review *Les Temps modernes*, acting as its political editor from its first appearance in 1945 until he resigned seven years later. Meanwhile, in 1949, he had become professor of philosophy at the Sorbonne. The war had made a profound impact on him, and it was during this period, when France faced the difficult task of political reconstruction, that his thought began to develop in the direction of a social philosophy in the important essays which he wrote on a remarkable variety of topics, from politics to the aesthetics of painting. Many of these were collected in *Humanisme et terreur* (1947, translated by J. O'Neill as *Humanism and Terror: An Essay on the Communist Problem*) and *Sens et non-sens* (1948, translated by H. L. and P. A. Dreyfus as *Sense and Non-Sense*).

Marjorie Grene has pointed out that, although history is a favorite theme of existential philosophers, "Merleau-Ponty is the first writer in this tradition to found the historical being of man in communal existence. Existentialism is known with some justice as a philosophy of the lonely, alienated individual: but for Merleau-Ponty the dimension of human togetherness . . . is a presupposition of human life." According to Albert Rabil, "the idea that the task of philosophy is to describe how men who have intentions (i.e., who are free) are related to the world (i.e., 'totality') which is always already there before them is the fundamental constant in Merleau-Ponty's philosophy. The presupposition underlying such a task is that, despite the multiplicity of perspectives which men have in the world (what Merleau-Ponty will later call the 'private world' of each man), there is a discernible human unity."

Merleau-Ponty first came to see this human unity in terms of Marxism, and the essays in *Humanisme et terreur* are part of Merleau-Ponty's attempt to find a *modus vivendi* between existentialism and Marxism, by discussing Marxist theory in relation to existing Communist governments. The central question is the meaning of violence—to what extent violence is necessary in social life. Man is faced with a dilemma, since if he uses no violence he succumbs to the powers that be, and if he uses violence he succumbs to the powers of violence; this is the contradiction Merleau-Ponty finds between the humanist ideals of early Marxism and the actuality of the Stalinist purges.

These essays provoked a storm of protest and disagreement. Sartre has indicated that they were a decisive factor in his own intellectual development towards Marxism, but Merleau-Ponty was moving towards his rejection both of Marxism and of

Sartre's existentialism in *Les Aventures de la dialectique* (1955, translated by Joseph Bien as *Adventures of the Dialectic*), in which he reflects on the vicissitudes of the dialectical approach to history. He now traces the contradictions which he found in contemporary communism back to classical Marxist theory itself, illustrating them through a consideration of two Marxists, Trotsky and Lukács, whose lives mirrored the discrepancy by which he was disturbed.

He also spells out the basic differences between Sartre's outlook and his own. They had grown steadily further apart, and their relationship had become one of mutual exasperation, needing only an act of editorial high-handedness from Sartre in 1953 to bring about Merleau-Ponty's resignation from *Les Temps modernes*. But as Merleau-Ponty pointed out, their basic disagreement was philosophical. In Sartre's thought the world of objects is totally distinct from the human consciousness that reflects it, so that consciousness has an exclusively subjective bias, tending towards solipsism. In contrast, there is a strong antidualistic tendency in Merleau-Ponty's thinking, and he posits an interaction and mutual dependence between the self and its world.

Merleau-Ponty's resignation as political editor of *Les Temps modernes* coincided with his appointment to the chair of philosophy at the Collège de France which Henri Bergson had held a generation earlier. For the remaining eight years of his life he strove to develop a social philosophy which would bring philosophy, psychology, politics, and art into one comprehensive vision of unity amidst diversity. But the collection of philosophical papers and literary essays *Signes* (1960, translated by R. C. McCleary as *Signs*) was the only work which he actually published during these last years, before his premature death in 1961.

For many years Merleau-Ponty worked on a book called "The Origin of Truth," in which he proposed to explain how objective truths could be derived from a basis merely of new "lived experiences," a question which remains a major problem in his philosophy. But he succeeded in completing only its introduction, published posthumously as *Le Visible et l'invisible* (1965, translated by A. Lingis as *The Visible and the Invisible*), in which he returns to Husserl's phenomenology and the problem of perception. If philosophy asks what the world is like before we begin to talk about it, and addresses that question to the "mixture of the world and ourselves" which preceded all reflection, the question arises how the philosopher can say *what* he finds. Whatever he tells us will inevitably be a description of the world as it is talked about, though Merleau-Ponty attempts to find a solution of this dilemma in his description of the "ambiguity" of language, through which, he argues, we can suggest more than we can explicitly say.

Another posthumous book, *La Prose du monde* (1969, edited by Claude Lefort and translated by John O'Neill as *The Prose of the World*), seems to have been written in the early 1950s, when Merleau-Ponty broke off halfway through what was to have been a two-part work on the theory of truth. The *Times Literary Supplement* welcomed it as "well worth having since . . . nothing that Merleau-Ponty wrote subsequently either repudiates or precisely repeats what he writes here. *La Prose du monde* is not philosophy in any technical sense but a serious and often suggestive essay on what is really going on when we express ourselves. . . . Merleau-Ponty has no trouble in moving continually from language as such to the consideration of painting as a language, since he sees both as participating in a wider mode of '*l'expression créatrice*.' He is careful to stipulate how, for him, all expression is creative because it can never be simply reproductive, a point briefly made by his insistence on the cultural nature of an artistic convention such as linear perspective."

Two other posthumous works were manufactured from notes taken during Merleau-Ponty's lectures. *L'Union de l'âme et du corps chez Malebranche, Biran et Bergson* (The Union of Soul and Body in the Thought of Malebranche, Biran and Bergson, 1969) considers how these philosophers dealt with the body-soul problem which preoccupied Merleau-Ponty himself. *Résumés de cours* (1969) has been translated as *Themes From the Lectures at the Collège de France, 1952–1960*. His other works include *Éloge de la philosophie* (1948, translated by J. M. Edie and J. Wild as *In Praise of Philosophy*) and a selection of his essays and lectures which appeared in translation as *The Primacy of Perception*.

For Merleau-Ponty objects are by their very nature enigmatic, so that his thought has been characterized as a "philosophy of ambiguity" because he made such widespread use of this concept, which he saw as an integral part of all human experience. One of his central claims was that his phenomenology can break the deadlock between realism and idealism and between empiricism and rationalism by making use of the best insights of Gestalt psychology in a manner which the Gestalt psychologists themselves had not been able to do, though Professor John Passmore has observed: "If one sometimes despairs of philosophy's tendency to fluctuate between absurd extremes, this fluctuation is no accident; a 'middle way,' as Merleau-Ponty's philosophy illustrates, is not easy to find or to persist in."

Professor Herbert Spiegelberg says of him: "The first impression one receives in surveying

Merleau-Ponty's writings may easily be that of a systematic spirit whose main interest is in taking up major traditional themes and fitting them into a new synthesis. There is in him little of that pioneering approach of the early phenomenologists or even of Sartre who preferred exploring the frontier to cultivating charted territory. Nor do his writings carry the provocative impact of Sartre's so much more debatable analyses. The significance of his contributions is based precisely on the fact that he resumes the more conventional themes, considers carefully the traditional solutions and particularly the scientific evidence, before attacking them directly, and integrates them into a systematic new frame based on phenomenological principles."

PRINCIPAL WORKS IN ENGLISH TRANSLATION: Phenomenology of Perception, 1962; The Structure of Behavior, 1963; In Praise of Philosophy, 1963; The Primacy of Perception and Other Essays, 1964; Sense and Non-Sense, 1964; Signs, 1964; The Visible and the Invisible, 1968; Humanism and Terror: An Essay on the Communist Problem, 1969; The Essential Writings of Merleau-Ponty, ed. by Alden L. Fisher, 1969; Themes From the Lectures at the Collège de France, 1952–1960, 1970; Adventures of the Dialectic, 1973; The Prose of the World, 1973.

ABOUT: Aron, R. Marxism and the Existentialists, 1970; Ayer, A. J. Metaphysics and Common Sense, 1969; Barral, M. R. Merleau-Ponty, 1965; Beauvoir, S. de. The Ethics of Ambiguity, 1948; Beauvoir, S. de. The Prime of Life, 1962; Delfgaauw, B. Twentieth Century Philosophy, 1969; Farber, M. The Foundation of Phenomenology, 1962; Fowlie, W. The French Critic 1549–1967, 1968; Gilson, E. W. (ed.) Recent Philosophy: Hegel to the Present, 1966; Hughes, H. S. The Obstructed Path, 1968; Kaelin, E. An Existentialist Aesthetic: The Theories of Sartre and Merleau-Ponty, 1962; Kingston, F. T. French Existentialism: A Christian Critique, 1961; Kwant, R. C. The Phenomenological Philosophy of Merleau-Ponty, 1963; Kwant, R. C. From Phenomenology to Metaphysics, 1966; Kwant, R. C. Phenomenology of Expression, 1969; Langan, T. D. Merleau-Ponty's Critique of Reason, 1966; McCleary, R. C. Ambiguity and Freedom in the Philosophy of Maurice Merleau-Ponty, 1954; O'Neill, J. J. Perception, Expression, and History, 1970; Passmore, J. A Hundred Years of Philosophy, 1957; Rabil, A. Merleau-Ponty, 1967; Sartre, J.-P. Situations, 1965; Smith, C. Contemporary French Philosophy, 1964; Spiegelberg, H. The Phenomenological Movement, 1968. *Periodicals*—America November 8, 1969; Christian Century February 2, 1966; October 23, 1968; September 17, 1969; Encounter May 1970; International Philosophical Quarterly March 1967; Journal of Philosophy January 21, 1960; New York Times May 5, 1962; Newsweek May 15, 1961; Philosophical Books May 1963; May 1965; Philosophical Quarterly October 1964; Philosophy and Phenomenological Research June 1962; December 1962; Review of Metaphysics March 1955; March, June 1966; Times Literary Supplement December 16, 1955; February 17, 1961; September 30, 1965; April 3, 1969; January 8, 1970; Yale Review December 1969.

"MERRIL, JUDITH" (pseudonym) (January 21, 1923–), American science fiction writer and editor, writes: "I was born in Manhattan, brought up in New York, Boston, and Philadelphia, moving back and forth between cities and within them often enough so that I attended thirteen public schools (that I can remember) before finishing high school. We were not so much shabby genteel as shabby intellectual; I was raised on Shakespeare, Kipling, A. A. Milne, Lewis Carroll, Chaim Nachman Bialik, Howard Pyle, and Malory, on ancient Jewish and medieval British history, on the theatre, Zionism, and a sort of soft-socialist, probably-agnostic, idealistic pacifism.

"My parents met and courted in the pre-twenties Greenwich Village days, when they were both working for the (then) new Bureau of Jewish Education. My father, Schlomo Grossman, was the American-born youngest son of a distinguished immigrant rabbi in Philadelphia; halfway through his own seminary training, he decided to become a writer instead, and associated himself with the group responsible for the beginnings of the Yiddish Art Theatre; many of his songs and plays are still in wide use in Jewish Sunday School and youth group programs. My mother, Russian-born, came to Boston at the age of five, learned to be an expert seamstress in the Beacon Street specialty shop where her father, the tailor, worked for his brother, the tailor-and-owner; also acquired a clear Harvard accent (before or) during extension courses in chemistry, philosophy, psychology, under magic names like James and Bergson.

"After my father's death, in 1930, we were poor relations for a while; then my mother worked as dietician, house-mother and social worker, in a series of settlement houses, orphan asylums and summer camps, where we lived.

"My first poem was published in a camp newspaper when I was seven, my last in a high school magazine when I was fifteen. During that time I wrote (poetry, essays, newspaper columns, plays—no fiction), and read, more or less continuously, what time I was not preparing to go to (what was then) Palestine as a *chalutzah*, or dreaming of careers as architect and lawyer. At fifteen I found my True Vocation—economist—and discovered to my horror that everyone else—teachers, mother, family, friends—thought I was going to be a writer.

"Stopped writing. (Almost: high school year book, and college paper, in my one year there.) The City College School of Business and Civic Administration turned out less compellingly fascinating than I thought it should be. Learned public speaking on soap boxes at student peace rallies (1939).

"Married a fellow-speaker when I was seventeen. *Really* stopped writing, till he was in the Pacific and I in New York with a two-year-old girl. Worked as literary assistant, research assistant, ghostwriter (to a ghostwriter, as it happened): all jobs that could be done mostly at home, while I still vowed

I would never be a writer. Somewhere in there, I met my first science-fiction people: writers and editors; got needled, coaxed, teased, into trying some fiction. By 1946, I was selling reasonably regularly to western, detective and sports pulps magazines, and still convinced I was not a writer, and *wouldn't* be. What I really wanted was to be a mathematician or physicist. Pulpwriting was to get me through a return to school. I did actually start back; lasted six weeks.

"By 1947, largely under the influence and encouragement of Theodore Sturgeon, becoming a *real* writer was the only thing that mattered. From that time on, for years afterwards, it seems to me the world conspired to accomplish this ambition, in the face of all the ambivalence, uncertainty, lack of discipline and personal confusion I could muster: Sturgeon, Fletcher Pratt, Arnold Hano, R. W. Lowndes, Frederik Pohl, Anthony Boucher, James Sandoe, Harry Maule, Mark Clifton, Robert P. Mills, Dr. Joseph Winter, Knox Burger, are perhaps the most notable among the names of those who over and over again, in the next ten years, pulled me almost forcibly along the professional path that would otherwise have terrified me even more than it fascinated.

"Although I have written, and edited, in other fields, most of my work has been in that area generally called, for want of an appropriate label, science fiction. For the past five or six years, most of it has been as editor and critic rather than writer. I am pleased to be able to say that I do not know where it will go from here; and that I am, most of the time, as dissatisfied with what I have done so far as I ever was.

"After three marriages I am still in favor of love, sex, and people.

"Some things have changed in twenty years: I am now convinced that I will continue to write, one way or another, no matter how frustrating the lag between intent and accomplishment continues to be. I am now aware that (as editor *or* writer) my field is that area of contemporary literature concerned with exploring the nature of man in relation to his many environments (natural, technological, sociological, physiological)—whether you want to call it science fiction, or 'the literature of ideas' or imaginative writing or surrealism or (as I most often do) speculative literature. My older daughter, Merril Zissman MacDonald, is married (and has produced two gratifying grandsons); my younger daughter, Ann Pohl, is away at school; at forty-three, I have finally become a fulltime writer—or editor—or both? I'm looking forward to finding out."

Miss Merril, who was born Josephine Judith Grossman, acquired her interest in science fiction

JUDITH MERRIL

suddenly and painfully. "I was eighteen," she told an interviewer, "married to a man whose favorite reading was pulp magazines. I looked down on them and never looked into them. Then one day I had a terrible toothache, followed by a bad cold, and I had nothing else to read and take my mind off my troubles, and I came under their spell."

As she says, her first sales were to the pulp magazines, and between 1945 and 1948 she wrote detective, western, and sports stories as well as science fiction, using a variety of pseudonyms, "Eric Thorstein," "Ernest Hamilton," and "Rose Sharon" among them. She established her reputation as a science fiction writer of the first rank with "That Only Mother," published in *Astounding Science Fiction* for June 1948. It is a strange and touching story about a mother who can see nothing wrong with her mutated and limbless child, and is in a way characteristic of the literally cosmic compassion which distinguishes her work and which is extended in her stories to love-starved orphans and "bug-eyed monsters" alike.

The first of Miss Merril's novels to appear in book form was *Shadow on the Hearth*, an account of what happens in one woman's family during the days following an atomic bomb attack on New York City. The action takes place entirely within the house, and the nightmare outside reaches the narrator only through the telephone and the radio. The book's point, one reviewer thought, is that "a united family is the solid base on which civilization rests." *The Shadow on the Hearth* was called "a novel of intimate immediacy and everyday urgency, quietly terrifying and deeply moving."

Outpost Mars, which Miss Merril wrote with

Cyril Kornbluth under the pseudonym "Cyril Judd," is a study of the practical and emotional problems which might face the interplanetary colonists of the future, and it also was found both thoughtful and moving. *Gunner Cade*, written with the same collaborator, is a less profound book, but still highly professional and readable. As is so often the case with writers who made their reputation in the pulps, much of Miss Merril's best work has never appeared in permanent form, although some of it survives in anthologies.

To many readers, she is probably best known as the editor of the excellent annual science fiction anthology *The Year's Best S-F*, first published as *S-F*. The anthology reflects her conviction that science fiction is gradually merging with the mainstream of literature, and has included Bernard Malamud's "The Jew-Bird" and stories from the *Atlantic* and *Paris Review*. Judith Merril lives in Port Jervis, New York. She likes good jazz, dancing, smoking, and speaking her mind.

PRINCIPAL WORKS: *As Judith Merril*—Shadow on the Hearth (novel), 1950; The Tomorrow People (novel), 1960; Out of Bounds (short stories), 1960; Daughters of Earth, 1968. *As coauthor*—The Petrified Planet (short novels), 1952; Six Great Short Science Fiction Novels, 1960. *In collaboration with C. M. Kornbluth as "Cyril Judd"*—Outpost Mars, 1952; Gunner Cade, 1952. *As editor*—Shot in the Dark, 1950; Beyond Human Ken, 1952; Human?, 1952; Beyond the Barriers of Space and Time, 1954; Galaxy of Ghouls, 1955 (reissued as Off the Beaten Orbit, 1956); S-F: The Year's Greatest Science-fiction and Fantasy, 1956–1959 (subsequently published as The Year's Best S-F); SF: The Best of the Best, 1967; England Swings SF, 1968; etc.

ABOUT: Contemporary Authors 15–16, 1966; Moskowitz, S. Seekers of Tomorrow, 1965. *Periodicals*—Middletown (N.Y.) Times Herald-Record July 1, 1965; New York Herald Tribune Book Week March 7, 1965.

MERRILL, JAMES (March 3, 1926–), American poet, novelist, and dramatist, writes: "My father, Charles Merrill, was on Wall Street; my mother, Hellen Ingram, had had a little newspaper of her own. Both were Southerners. I was born in New York City, my mother's only child, my father's third and last. We spent summers on Long Island and winters in Florida. After my parents' divorce, my mother and I moved to New York. I began going to the opera whenever possible. At Lawrenceville School I met Frederick Buechner; much precocious writing ensued. I was an Army private during the war. Afterwards, back by then at Amherst College, I wrote a thesis on metaphor in Proust, had some poems taken by *Poetry*, and played the title role in Cocteau's *Orphée*. Years later I taught at Amherst—it was the thing to do, at that time, for a poet in America. One year sufficed in my case.

"Perhaps because I do not write criticism, and suspect that I ought not to be listening when other writers begin to talk shop, I have little to say about my work in general. Others have called it elegant or mannered. Indeed, I enjoy making minor adjustments, and believe in trying to charm a reader. For myself, the finished piece represents an emotion arrived at, never entirely foreseen, complex but clarified and, with luck, ringing true. I don't get worked up over issues. I write in short spurts interrupted by hours of manual therapy in the kitchen or at the piano. There, however, I am careless, apt to leave seasonings and fingerings uncorrected.

"Since 1954 I have lived in Stonington, Connecticut, on two floors shared with my friend David Jackson. Between spells at home, we are compulsive if unadventuresome travelers, and have seen in our day many of the most looked-at places in Europe and the Orient. We now have a second residence, in Athens, which is gradually taking on the rhythms of the first—quite as if one had but a single life to lead, and led it wherever one happened to be."

Merrill's early verse, collected in *First Poems*, did indeed seem "mannered" to his reviewers, no doubt because they could locate no honest emotion behind his artfully managed imagery and impeccable technique. Louise Bogan thought these poems as "frigid and dry as diagrams." By the time Merrill published *The Country of a Thousand Years of Peace*, his readers were beginning to realize that his elaborate and urbane manner masked a fierce and "terrifying" imagination. William Meredith on the evidence of this volume called the poet "a serious philosopher, perhaps even a moralist," and said: "the verbal elegance, and the Jamesian or Proustian world he draws his people and images from, are neither frivolous nor precious. They parallel and support grave statements about human experience."

It is this view which has persisted in reviews of Merrill's later poems, though he has continued—deliberately, it seems—to elude all critical attempts to identify and label his work more exactly. Peter Davison, discussing *Water Street*, called him "an intensely visual poet," but one whose "visual sensations are as from trick mirrors, prisms, colored glass, moving pictures, all the artifices of optics."

If the critics remained uncertain about the nature of Merrill's emotional attitudes and literary intentions, they were agreed that both are growing steadily more accessible in his verse. In *Nights and Days*, which won the National Book Award for poetry in 1967, Merrill's unshakable "suavity and technical polish" were subdued, Gene Baro thought, by "a new richness and complexity of feeling . . . as if Merrill had finally built a bridge between lyrical and philosophical poetry." Richard Howard wrote: "This poet, the most decorative and glamor-clogged America has ever produced, has made himself, by a surrender to reality and its necessary illusions, a master of his experience and of his own nature."

And with *Braving the Elements*, it seemed to Helen Vendler that Merrill had "found a use, finally, for all his many talents. His surreptitious fondness for narrative . . . has now found a clear medium in his wonderfully short narrative lyrics; his almost unnaturally exquisite gift for euphony has become unobtrusive but no less exquisite, in fact more so; his ironic and wayward humor has been allowed to surface . . . ; his single best subject —love—has found a way of expressing itself masked and unmasked at once." Merrill received the 1972 Bollingen Prize.

Merrill has also had more success as a novelist than most poets achieve. *The Seraglio* was admired for its evocative imagery, its sense of mood and place, its accurate dialogue, and seemed indeed to possess every virtue except a belief in its own premises and attitudes. *The (Diblos) Notebook* attracted much more attention. In it the narrator describes a love affair or seduction undertaken by his half brother on Diblos, a Greek island, and discusses and quotes a part of his own novel about the affair, the facts of which are always shifting, uncertain, and echoing into myth. Some novelist-reviewers commented rather sourly upon Merrill's presentation of his material in the form of a rough notebook, wishing that they had themselves hit upon a device so rich in advantages usually confined to poetry. As Wilfrid Sheed wrote, "words can be crossed out, to yield alternative readings," and "tiresome exposition can be abbreviated." Sheed was one of a number of reviewers who thought it "the kind of novel it is a pleasure to take seriously, a disciplined, adventurous performance in the best tradition of fictional experiment."

Merrill's association with the Artists' Theatre produced at least two notable plays, *The Bait* (1953), a one-acter about a brother and sister dedicated to the avoidance of all emotional connection with other human beings, and *The Immortal Husband* (1955), which retells the story of Aurora and Tithonus. The latter, according to Gerald Weales, is "neatly made, the metaphors introduced and sustained, the philosophy planted and exposed periodically; and there is a kind of surface charm that, on at least one occasion . . . becomes quite effective."

PRINCIPAL WORKS: *Poetry*—First Poems, 1951; The Country of a Thousand Years of Peace, 1959; Selected Poems, 1961 (England only); Water Street, 1962; Nights and Days, 1966; The Fire Screen, 1969; Braving the Elements, 1972; Two Poems, 1972. *Plays*—The Immortal Husband, *in* Playbook, 1956; The Bait, *in* Machiz, H. (ed.) Artists' Theatre, 1960. *Novels*—The Seraglio, 1957; The (Diblos) Notebook, 1965.

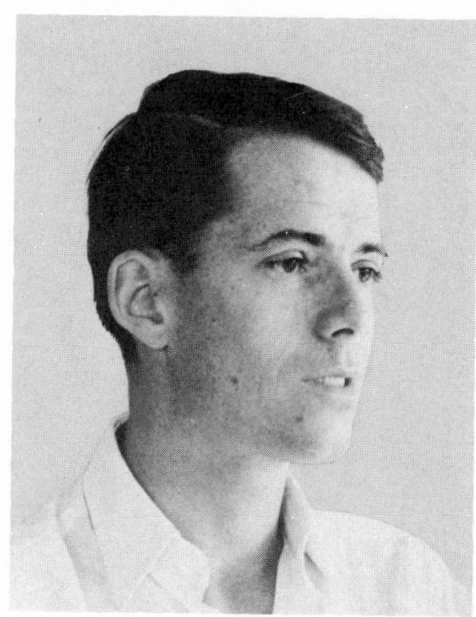

JAMES MERRILL

ABOUT: Contemporary Authors 13–14, 1965; Howard, R. Alone With America, 1969; Murphy, R. (ed.) Contemporary Poets of the English Language, 1970; Weales, G. American Drama Since World War II, 1962; Who's Who in America, 1972–1973. *Periodicals*—Contemporary Literature Winter 1968; Library Journal February 1, 1957; New York Times January 8, 1973; New York Times Book Review September 24, 1972; New Yorker March 30, 1957; Newsweek March 18, 1957; Poetry July 1951, June 1959, July 1963; South Atlantic Quarterly October 1950.

MERRITT, A(BRAHAM) (January 20, 1884–August 30, 1943), American fantasist, science fiction writer, and journalist, was born of Quaker parents in Beverley, New Jersey. He originally hoped for a legal career and took some courses at the University of Pennsylvania, but was forced to abandon this ambition for financial reasons. At the age of nineteen he joined the Philadelphia *Inquirer* as a cub reporter. One day, according to the historian of science fiction Sam Moskowitz, Merritt witnessed an event of such crucial political significance that he was encouraged to leave the country and forget what he had seen. He never revealed the nature of this mysterious happening or the identity of those who financed his extended vacation. The year Merritt spent in Mexico and Central America, studying Mayan civilization and various aspects of science, folklore, and the occult, left a permanent impression on him and his writing.

After it he returned to the Philadelphia *Inquirer*. By all accounts Merritt was a brilliant newspaperman. He had a special flair for reporting the most violent aspects of life at that time, from murders to executions and lynchings. At the same time he

A. MERRITT

possessed a degree of sensibility which drove him to harden himself against such horrors by heavy drinking. Later, Moskowitz suggests, he found another kind of escape in the fantasies he wrote. Merritt eventually became night city editor of the *Inquirer*, and in 1912 went to New York City as assistant to Morrill Goddard, editor of the Hearst chain's *Sunday Supplement*, later the *American Weekly*. Merritt worked on that publication for the rest of his life, succeeding Goddard as editor in 1937. It was one of the highest paid posts in American journalism, and enabled Merritt to maintain houses in New York and in Florida, where he also owned two experimental farms, raising avocados, mangoes, litchis, and the first olive groves in Florida, as well as a collection of exotic poisonous plants.

Merritt's first published science fiction story was a romantic fantasy called "Through the Dragon Glass," published in 1917 in *All-Story*. His reputation was established two years later when the same magazine published his short novel *The Moon Pool*, set in a strange terrain beneath the earth's surface. The story involved the traditional mixture of earth types (an Irishman, a Scandinavian, and a treacherous German), Lakla and Yolara (personifications respectively of good and evil), the Shining One (an omniscient robot who develops a lust for power), and the Silent Ones (its godlike creators and eventual destroyers).

In spite of these stock elements, Moskowitz says, "the novel holds magic for its readers," not only because of its "rich, colorful, heroic action," its inventiveness and vivid writing, but because "humanity shines from this work." Merritt's people, and especially his villains, are always "memorably, brilliantly characterized," and even his monsters are endowed with sufficient personality to involve the imaginative reader in the kind of problems faced by frog people and the dead-alive. *The Moon Pool* was published in book form in 1919 and welcomed in the New York *Times* as the debut of an extraordinary talent, whose "energy and fertility of imaginative resource never seems to lessen." Ten years later fans of the genre chose the book as the most popular science fiction story of all time.

The beautiful priestess of evil, the likable monsters, and the basic conflict between good and evil recur in most of Merritt's subsequent fantasies. These include *The Ship of Ishtar*, an overcomplicated, overwritten, but highly enjoyable story whose hero is translated back to ancient Babylon; *The Face in the Abyss*, a romance in the Rider Haggard tradition about a search for Inca treasure which ends in a mysterious valley, the haunt of dinosaurs, serpent women, and dark occult forces; and a similar story, set in Canada, called *Dwellers in the Mirage*. He also tried his hand, with immense success, at a mystery story, *Seven Footprints to Satan*—a melodrama of diabolism in New York City which reads like a cross between Hugh Walpole and Sax Rohmer—and wrote two exciting stories about witchcraft, *Burn, Witch, Burn!* (filmed as *The Devil Dolls*, with Lionel Barrymore), and *Creep, Shadow!*

Merritt wrote no more stories after 1934, though he retained his interest in science fiction. He died of a heart attack in Florida at the age of fifty-nine. Most of his novels are still in print in both hard covers and paperback, and in 1959 one of his publishers estimated that his books had at that time sold over four million copies.

PRINCIPAL WORKS: *Fiction*—The Moon Pool, 1919; The Ship of Ishtar, 1926; Seven Footprints to Satan, 1928; The Face in the Abyss, 1931; Dwellers in the Mirage, 1932; Burn, Witch, Burn!, 1933; Creep, Shadow!, 1934 (England, Creep, Shadow, Creep!); The Fox Woman (completed by Hannes Bok), 1946; Black Wheel (completed and illus. by Hannes Bok), 1948. *Nonfiction*—The Story Behind the Story, 1942.

ABOUT: Moskowitz, S. Explorers of the Infinite, 1963; Wollheim, D. A. *introduction to* Merritt, A. Dwellers in the Mirage, *and* The Face in the Abyss, 1953.

MERWIN, W(ILLIAM) S(TANLEY) (September 30, 1927–), American poet and translator, was born in New York City. He spent his early childhood in Union City, New Jersey, where his father was minister of the First Presbyterian Church. Merwin's parents were from Pennsylvania, and in the mid-1930s returned to that state, to Scranton. He was educated there and in 1944 went on with a scholarship to Princeton University.

Merwin had written hymns and poems almost as soon as he was literate, but at the university, he says, "I began to read poetry steadily and try incessantly, and with abiding desperation, to write it." He was fortunate (as he later realized) in his teachers at Princeton, learning from the example and advice of John Berryman, Herman Broch, and R. P. Blackmur. But he was not a good student, nor a respectful one, and spent much of his time reading or horseback riding, escaping expulsion only through the intercession of Blackmur. Merwin received his B.A. in 1947 and stayed at Princeton for a year of graduate study in modern languages.

Thus equipped, he became a tutor with families in France (1949) and Portugal (1950). In 1951 he went to Majorca as tutor to Robert Graves's son William, and there met the English girl who became his wife. He returned with her to England and settled in that country for some years, supporting himself mainly as a translator for the British Broadcasting Corporation's Third Programme. In 1956 he returned to the United States on a grant to write for the Poets' Theatre in Cambridge, Massachusetts, and lived for a year in Boston.

Meanwhile his first book, *A Mask for Janus*, had appeared in 1952 with a foreword by W. H. Auden and had created an immediate stir. *The Dancing Bears* followed in 1954. These books invoke the Orphic notion of the artist as magician-creator, who gives life to what he names. Glimpsing in the flux and chaos of existence "pieces of an order," the poet seeks to construct from these fragments, through the power of language, an acceptable mythology. Indeed these early poems make an almost desperate assertion of order against chaos and death, both in their closed metrical patterns and in their insistence upon the artist's duty to invent his own reality.

A preoccupation with myth and fable was very much in the air in the 1950s, and critical attention centered on the skill with which Merwin handled these fashionable elements. Along with criticism of what seemed derivative and dryly intellectual in these poems, there was much praise for their "dimmed rhyming" and "sly metrical variations," a technical facility that reminded one reviewer of the young Auden. Lawrence Ferlinghetti thought that some of these poems "outrange the utterances of all the other younger poets of America today."

A tendency to a longer line and looser forms, noticed in *The Dancing Bears*, continued in *Green With Beasts*, where, wrote Glauco Cambon, "language luxuriates in controlled abandon to sprout into heraldic animals." Here and there amid all this richness some critics encountered with approval a new "plain statement of loss," spoken in "the

W. S. MERWIN

refreshing accents of one who for the first time sets himself prosaically against his fate." This new and colloquial directness emerged as the predominant tone in *The Drunk in the Furnace*.

There is an almost Faustian defiance about the figure of the artist imagined in Merwin's early poetry, who snatches a role for himself out of the intolerable disorder of the universe, even if it is only to become "a Hades into which [he] can descend." Since then however he seems to have relinquished the attempt to impose on life the partial and solipsistic coherence which the artist can create, and to be laying himself open to the perception of a larger harmony which, he has always hoped, exists beyond language and myth. This total order is that of the world on the first morning, of Eden before the Fall: "the imagination / Before the names of things, the dicta for / The only poem."

The verse in *The Moving Target*, *The Lice*, and their successors seems almost the work of a different poet. Metrics, punctuation, and formal logic have been progressively abandoned, giving way to fragmentary sentences, cryptic images, and archetypal motifs of despair—sketches, as one critic said, "for a godless Book of Revelations." Recoiling from war, poverty, injustice, and all the works of man, the poet turns to the innocence of stones and animals: "If I were not human I would not be ashamed of anything."

There has been a mixed response to this development in Merwin's work. Some critics, like Helen Vendler, seem bored by the obsessive complaints that echo through the prose poems in *The Miner's Pale Children*, the verse in *The Carrier of Ladders:*

"one has a relentless social-worker urge to ask him to eat something, anything, to cure his anemia." Others, admitting that these poems are marred by vagueness and a long-standing tendency to sentimentality, think them nevertheless Merwin's best work, an important advance into "dangerous and uneasy areas of consciousness." Hayden Carruth notes that Merwin has been hailed as the "new American surrealist" but thinks this a misleading simplification: "In spite of their strangeness his best poems convey a sense of striking fitness and inevitability. . . . Among fellow poets and serious readers his new work is awaited with an eagerness of attention that is accorded to few other writers in America." *The Carrier of Ladders* brought Merwin the Pulitzer Prize in 1971; he found that "after years of the news from Southeast Asia and the commentary from Washington," he was "too conscious of being an American to accept public congratulation with good grace," and divided his prize money between Alan Blanchard, a painter blinded by a police weapon in California, and a draft resistance group.

Merwin's faithful and readable translations have been much admired. Several of his plays have been staged, including *Darkling Child*, which he wrote in collaboration with Dido Milroy. *Favor Island*, produced at Poets' Theatre in 1957, was broadcast by the BBC the following year, and another play, *The Gilded West*, was produced in England in 1961. Merwin received a *Kenyon Review* fellowship in 1954, a Rockefeller fellowship in 1956, an award from the American Academy of Arts and Letters in 1957, and a playwriting bursary the same year from the British Arts Council. A grant from the Rabinowitz Foundation in 1961 took Merwin and his wife to New York for nearly two years, and in 1964–1965 a Ford Foundation grant enabled him to spend a year with Roger Planchon's Théâtre de la Cité in Lyon. He also received a Chapelbrook Fellowship in 1966 and a Rockefeller grant in 1969.

PRINCIPAL WORKS: *Poetry*—A Mask for Janus, 1952; The Dancing Bears, 1954; Green With Beasts, 1956; The Drunk in the Furnace, 1960; The Moving Target, 1963; The Lice, 1967; The Carrier of Ladders, 1970; The Miner's Pale Children (prose poems, allegories, etc.), 1970; Writings to an Unfinished Accompaniment, 1973. *As translator*—Poems of the Cid, 1959; Some Spanish Ballads, 1961; The Satires of Persius, 1961; Life of Lazarillo de Tormes, 1962; The Song of Roland, 1963; Selected Translations 1948–1968, 1969; Transparence of the World: Poems of Jean Follain, 1969; Products of the Perfected Civilization: Selected Writings by Sebastian Chamfort 1969; Asian Figures, 1973.

ABOUT: Auden, W. H. *foreword to* Merwin, W. S. A Mask for Janus, 1952; Cambon, G. Recent American Poetry, 1962; Contemporary Authors 15–16, 1966; Hungerford, E. (ed.) Poets in Progress, 1962; Ossman, D. The Sullen Art, 1963; Stepanchev, S. American Poetry Since 1945, 1965; Who's Who in America, 1972–1973. *Periodicals*—Commonweal December 28, 1956; Hollins Critic June 1968; Kayak 3, 1965; Nation August 17, 1957; New Republic February 18, 1957; New York Review of Books June 3, 1971; New Yorker January 31, 1953; New York Times Book Review October 18, 1970; Princeton University Library Chronicle Autumn 1963; Saturday Review January 5, 1957.

MEYERSTEIN, E(DWARD) H(ARRY) W(ILLIAM) (August 11, 1889–September 12, 1952), English scholar, novelist, poet, dramatist, and music critic, was born in Hampstead, London, the eldest son of Sir Edward Meyerstein, a wealthy financier knighted for his philanthropies. His mother, the former Jessy Solomon, was a talented pianist. Meyerstein was educated at Harrow, where he was ostracized on account of his Jewish origins (although he was a member of the Church of England), his dislike of games, and his devotion to solitary learning. He was no happier at home, where his parents seemed to him arrogant and prying.

After this wretched childhood, Meyerstein devoted the rest of his life to an almost completly unsuccessful attempt to make a place for himself in literature or scholarship. From Harrow he went to Magdalen College, Oxford, where he worked desperately hard but failed to obtain either a First or a fellowship, achieving only a nervous breakdown. From 1913 to 1918 he worked as an assistant in the British Museum's Department of Manuscripts, with a brief interlude as a private in the Royal Dublin Fusiliers. (He had gone to Cork to volunteer, but was soon invalided out.) After the war Meyerstein took rooms in Gray's Inn, in London, where he lived the life of a literary recluse for over twenty years. He had already published a volume of poems, *The Door;* now he tried his hand, in vain, at drama. Most of his books, during this long period between the wars, were privately printed, for the one advantage he did not lack was money. His novels of this time, such as *Terence Duke*, *Séraphine*, and *Joshua Slade*, were all flawed, but did not deserve the total oblivion into which they immediately fell. Meyerstein's most solid achievement during these inter-war years, which saw the completion of thousands of poems and translations and many short stories, was his *Life of Chatterton*.

When he was bombed out of Gray's Inn early in World War II, Meyerstein went first to Cambridge and then to Oxford, where he was allowed to live in his old college, but once again was denied entrance to the Senior Common Room. Ignored by the dons, he sought his companions among the undergraduates. John Wain, who befriended Meyerstein at Oxford towards the end of the war, described him as he was then in *Encounter*, and Lionel Butler has provided a similar and more detailed portrait. Physically he was a big man, about six feet tall and thickset, with thinning gray hair, and one side of his face screwed up by Bell's palsy. His voice, hoarse when he was calm, grew high and scratchy when he was excited. He walked with "shambling gait and jerky unconscious gestures as of one arguing vehemently with an unseen Satanic interlocutor." Wain says that he "had the Greek and Latin classics more or less by heart, as well as a vast quantity of French and English literature," and Butler calls him "quite the most learned human being I have met." He was extremely mean, but littered his rooms with old books, manuscripts, and pictures, some of them very valuable. He hated women and suspected them of wanting to marry him. And yet, Wain says, "even when his crazy fits of paranoia were on him, he could be very likeable"—he had an "underlying sweetness of temperament," a "childlike simplicity that was very touching."

John Wain believes that Meyerstein's undoubted talent "produced hardly a line worth the paper it was written on," but Lionel Butler disagrees, and discusses his work at some length. *The Life of Chatterton*, he says, although it makes no concessions to readability, shows a "keen insight into the psychology of the creative mind" and a "sure sense of the English past" which lift it well above the average. And Butler is not alone in his admiration for Meyerstein's edition of Edward Coxere's *Adventures by Sea*, the reminiscences of a seventeenth century sailor which was one of the most widely circulated of his books and is yet another evidence of the diversity of his learning.

Meyerstein wrote ten novels, of which the last three had some success: *Robin Wastraw*, *Tom Tallion*, and *Phoebe Thirsk*. They were praised for their prose and their narrative skill, but their eccentric characters, often people living on the edge of the underworld, seemed the products of imagination rather than observation. L. P. Hartley, reviewing *Robin Wastraw*, a novel concerned with the influence upon human beings of nature and of inanimate objects, wrote: "Every sentence confesses its obligation to art. One never feels the untidyness of life disturbing the author's sense of style."

It was as a poet that Meyerstein most wanted to succeed, and he poured out verse endlessly, in spite of insomnia, torpor, and bursts of near insanity. He wrote his first drafts very rapidly on an ancient typewriter, and as he worked "groaned and snarled to the machine in heavy, tuneless incantation." Meyerstein published, mostly at his own expense, over five hundred and fifty poems, but they attracted little attention, and were generally disliked for their eccentricity—not least for their preoccupation with flogging, punishment,

E. H. W. MEYERSTEIN

and murder. Nevertheless, Butler says, Meyerstein was a prolific and accomplished sonneteer who left a few lyrics "to stand on their own," and whose long poem *The Visionary* seemed to Laurence Binyon as successful as any attempt at strict *terza rima* in English. Meyerstein's translation of the *Elegies* of Propertius was generally well received. He was an able music critic, who could read a score as readily as a book and was a fine pianist.

After the war he left Oxford for his old rooms in Gray's Inn, where he went on writing until his death, which followed a series of strokes. His was, as Wain says, "a perfect example of a life smashed by collision with an Establishment." By an irony that he would have appreciated but not enjoyed, Meyerstein achieved a greater measure of esteem after his death. Four publishing houses, two of them leading ones, published or reprinted one or more of his books: three novels, three books of poems, his autobiography (which some consider his best work), and a volume of letters. He has not, after all, sunk without trace.

PRINCIPAL WORKS: *Poetry*—The Door, 1911; Selected Poems, 1935; The Visionary, 1941; The Unseen Beloved, 1953; Verse Letters to Five Friends, 1954; Some Poems (ed. by M. Wollman), 1957. *Novels*—Joshua Slade, 1938; Robin Wastraw, 1951 (republished 1955); Tom Tallion, 1952 (republished 1955); Phoebe Thirsk, 1953. *Plays*—Heddon, 1921; The Monument, 1923. *Short stories*—The Pageant, 1934; Four People, 1939; Bolland, 1958. *Non-fiction*—Life of Thomas Chatterton, 1930; (ed.) Adventures by Sea, by Edward Coxere, 1945; Of My Early Life, 1889–1918 (autobiography), 1957; Some Letters (ed. by R. Watson), 1959.

ABOUT: Butler, L. E. E. H. W. Meyerstein, *in* Proceedings of the British Academy, 1955; Who Was Who, 1951–1960. *Periodicals*—Encounter August 1962; English Autumn 1959; New York Times September 13, 1959.

JAMES MICHIE

***MICHIE, JAMES** (June 24, 1927–), English poet and translator, was born into a prosperous middle-class family in Weybridge, Surrey. He is one of the three sons of J. K. Michie, a banker and businessman, and the former Marjorie Pfeiffer. The family was happy, close-knit, and intelligent, but not particularly inclined towards the arts. James Michie was educated at Marlborough from 1939 to 1945, and remembers the atmosphere of the public school as notably liberal. It was there, with the encouragement of his teachers, that he began to write verse. In 1945 Michie won a scholarship to read classics at Trinity College, Oxford. He subsequently switched to English, and graduated with a second-class honors degree in 1948.

After leaving university, he was called up for military service. By this time he had become a conscientious objector—not for religious reasons, but simply because, after Hiroshima, war seemed to him indefensible. Michie's tribunal accepted his plea for military exemption and he worked for the statutory two years, first as a hospital porter in London and later as a farm laborer. In 1951 he joined Heinemann's as an editor, rising during his ten years with that publishing house to become its chief editor. As a publisher he subscribes to no particular theory of literature, or of literature's relation to society, wanting only to publish "what [is] good as well as possible."

In his verse also Michie is an eclectic. The poems in his only collection, *Possible Laughter*, are conversational in their language, neat in their forms, sharply visual in their imagery—the robin has a "Tail like a painful splinter, / Sham blood running down his chest. . . ." Sometimes there is a note of self-admonishment, as in "Rhyme Rude to My Pride," which also shows Michie's pleasure in rhymes and off-rhymes: "O my intolerable / Pride, the rebel / Cain to my Abel, / My life-long trouble, / My hump, my double, / My Siamese growth, / You are destroying us both / By the enormity / Of your deformity."

*mi′ kē

Michie no longer writes original verse but has turned to translating the classics. He subscribes to the view that poetry can never be adequately translated, but practices the art, he claims, as a therapeutic hobby, "a form of knitting." His version of *The Odes of Horace* was warmly praised as both faithful and beautiful. It was selected by W. H. Auden as one of the outstanding books of the year in 1964, and even provoked a leader in the *Times* which showed, by a comparison of excerpts, how much more elegant, exact, and amusing Michie's reading was than earlier versions. His translations of *The Poems of Catullus* were received with no less enthusiasm. Simon Raven said that Michie had brought "a steady hand and a clear eye" to the "Alexandrian" poems, and was "sweet and deft" in his handling of the short lyrics. "But," Raven went on, "perhaps his most signal service to his poet consists in rescuing those jokes (obscene or otherwise) which don't come off. For Catullus could be as careless as the next man, and some of his squibs simply refuse to pop. When this happens, Mr. Michie can be trusted to save us embarrassment and keep the party going with a quick sally of his own which he modestly places in the mouth of his master."

James Michie left Heinemann's in 1961 and went to The Bodley Head as editorial director. Although he necessarily remains closely in touch with literary life in London, he is not much drawn to the readings and the other phenomena which in recent years have sought to make a public art of poetry. The look of words on a page is important to him, he says, and "in order to absorb anything, I have to be alone." James Michie is married to the former Sarah Courtauld and has a son.

PRINCIPAL WORKS: Possible Laughter (poems), 1959. *As translator*—The Odes of Horace, 1963; The Poems of Catullus, 1969; The Epigrams of Martial, 1973.

ABOUT: *Periodicals*—New Statesman April 4, 1959; New York Times Book Review November 17, 1963; Times (London) January 16, 1965.

MIDDLETON, CHRISTOPHER (June 10, 1926–), English poet and translator, writes: "I was born in Truro, Cornwall. My father was organist of the cathedral; his father was an Anglo-Irish carpenter, his father's father an Irish soldier. Later that year we moved to Ely and lived there in an old flint house in the cathedral precincts, with a nun's ghost (I saw her) and within earshot of the watchman who would chant at night: 'Twelve o'clock and all's well.' In 1930 we moved to Cambridge, where my father later became Senior Lecturer in Music. From the age of ten I went to boarding schools in idyllic country places. The sheltered musical and scholastic background was a pattern against which I would later violently rebel; it has also been a source for ideas of order. I took up classical studies at school and at sixteen began to write poems. On leaving school, I forgot the classical studies; and I repudiate every poem I was lucky-unlucky enough to get published (there were two books) up to 1945. On Christmas Eve 1945 I came to Hamburg as an aircraftsman-interpreter in the Royal Air Force.

"My job was to travel around with an officer asking village burgomasters if they had any old searchlights or anti-aircraft guns on their domains. In one town I thought I saw Hitler in a bath-chair. Poems I wrote then had nothing much to do with the world I was in; I wrote nothing and read nothing for over a year during a second giddy tour in Germany (1947–1948) as a sergeant-interpreter. Out of the R.A.F. in June 1948 I went to the South of France; often since then the Mediterranean has drawn me back. I went to Oxford to study German and French, again I wrote poems, but hardly any worked out. I was now reading a great deal—Russian and Chinese philosophers, Latin theologians and Ezra Pound, Rimbaud, Hölderlin, St. John Perse. People thought (I later heard) that I was a hermit, ferociously devoted to poetry and that alone. I certainly avoided the literary people, and I still do.

"In 1952 I went to Zürich to give English classes in the university there. In April 1953 I married Mary Freer. Two and a half years in Zürich resulted in about five poems that could stand. I wrote an Oxford D.Phil. thesis (on Herman Hesse) and dug myself into the environment, down to the eighteenth century thinkers Bengel and Octinger. In Robert Walser and Samuel Beckett I had found two modern stylists who, being in many ways diametrical opposites, edged me a little further along the unending mazy road of self-definition. My identification with Walser led me then and there to translate some of his stories.

"From 1955 until now I have lived in South London. With *Torse 3* I was over one hill. By 1959 I had also taken to translating modern German poems. Translating is an austere exercise in keeping one's eye on the object, perfectible only by born mediators, almost as much a matter of astonishing speech into incandescence as the writing of poems is. My present teaching-work is endurable only so long as I can resist being suffocated in the hothouse atmosphere of university culture and can indulge my curiosity in out-of-the-way research.

CHRISTOPHER MIDDLETON

"During the year 1961–1962 I taught at the University of Texas in Austin; the summer of 1962 brought us (three children and all) into the canyons and deserts of the South-West. I wish the experience of such places upon all who suffer the sedentary drabness of most life in England now. Yet I need the ancient parapets of Europe, am a 'keen student' of the societies (and their politics) which now clamber around on them or sleep and dodder in their long shadows. My conflicts declare themselves in my predilection for stark-ambiguous style in any art, for Dada, Dostoevsky and the substantial marvels of modern neurology and physics. I would not say that I felt at home in any place where men have made life automatic and the old inhuman lies keep getting told."

The early poems Christopher Middleton now repudiates were heavily influenced by Dylan Thomas, and regarded more kindly by some critics than by their author. During his long silence between the end of the war and the publication of *Torse 3* in 1962, Middleton achieved the "stark-ambiguous style" he admires. He has, as he says, "a great facility for being influenced," and very many innovators have obliged him, among them Joyce and Beckett, Eliot and Pound, the German expressionists and post-expressionists, the French surrealists and dadaists, and Americans of the school of William Carlos Williams. Not all of those who admire his attack on "contemporary platitudinous verse" believe that he has yet found his voice. He is sometimes called a *pasticheur* of modernist mannerisms, who can and deliberately does "do it all," by the same critics who commend the qualities of virtuosity and surprise which he has "coolly and unaggressively at his command." Middleton's experiments range from what he calls "the extremely abstruse, highly elaborate, mythically oriented poem" (like "Male Torso") to "a very prosy, plain, direct discourse" ("At Portscothan").

Reviewing *Nonsequences*, A. Alvarez wrote: "The half-dozen best poems have the same qualities as his best earlier work: bare, quizzical, tensely elegant. He handles his insights with great finesse, but always from a distance as though with tweezers. He uses suspended syntax and an oblique, surrealist progression which makes the things hover in the air like a mirage."

Middleton has been accused of deliberate obscurity. He believes that "poetry is one means of discourse which takes one . . . into realities beyond normally observable realities." He says his poems are most often triggered by "experiences of the strangeness of being alive, of the strangeness of living things outside oneself." His translations have been widely praised, in Germany, as well as in English-speaking countries. The author, formerly lecturer in German at King's College, University of London, has been since 1965 professor of Germanic languages and literature at the University of Texas. He received the Geoffrey Faber Memorial Prize for Poetry in 1963.

PRINCIPAL WORKS: Torse 3, Poems 1949–1961, 1962; The Metropolitans (libretto, music by Hans Vogt), 1963; Penguin Modern Poets 4 (with David Holbrook and Donald Wevill), 1963; Nonsequences/Selfpoems, 1965; Our Flowers and Nice Bones, 1969. *As translator*—The Walk and Other Stories (by Robert Walser), 1957; No Hatred and No Flag, 20th Century War Poems, 1958; (with Michael Hamburger) Modern German Poetry, 1910–1960, 1962; (with Michael Hamburger) Selected Poems by Günter Grass, 1966; George Trakl: Selected Poems, 1968; Selected Letters of Friedrich Nietzsche, 1969; Jakob von Gunten (by Robert Walser), 1970; The Quest for Christa T. (by Christa Wolf), 1970; (with Michael Hamburger) Selected Poems of Paul Celan, 1972. *As editor*—German Writing Today, 1967.

ABOUT: Murphy, R. (ed.) Contemporary Poets of the English Language, 1970; Orr, P. (ed.) The Poet Speaks, 1966. *Periodicals*—Essays in Criticism I 1963; London Magazine April 1962; November 1964; New Statesman April 6, 1962; Times Literary Supplement May 4, 1962; April 9, 1970.

***MILLAR, KENNETH ("JOHN ROSS MACDONALD," "ROSS MACDONALD")** (December 13, 1915–), American detective story writer, writes: "Fiction writers are often prepared for their calling by difficult childhoods in families which have known happier days. We grow up torn between legend and actuality, thrust back toward the former by the painfulness of the latter, and provided forever afterwards with subject matter.

"As I write now, at the age of fifty, my life has been about equally divided between Canada and the United States. I was born Kenneth Millar in Los Gatos, California, and am thus an American citizen by birth. My father John M. Millar was a Canadian newspaper editor and Scots dialect poet. His father had been a newspaper publisher in an Ontario town; seven miles away lived my mother's father, a village storekeeper descended from six generations of Pennsylvania Dutch farmers. My grandfathers' seventeen children all 'went West.'

"Some three years after I was born, my parents separated. Over the next dozen or so years I was a reluctant guest in several dozen Canadian houses, and in one boarding school, St. John's in Winnipeg. There I began, at the age of eleven, to write narrative prose and verse about Scottish and western heroes. Later, my high school ambition was to complete Coleridge's unfinished poem, *Christabel*. But my first printed story (1931) was a parody of Sherlock Holmes.

"My long dull excellent Canadian education was fortunately interrupted by a year of farm work after I left high school in 1932, and in 1936–1937 by two semesters in Western Europe. On June 2, 1938, I graduated from the University of Western Ontario, and the following day married Margaret Sturm, my fellow-student in the Kitchener (Ontario) high school, where I now taught for two years.

"In 1941 the late C. D. Thorpe got me the offer of a fellowship at the University of Michigan, where I had attended summer school. The publication of my wife's first novels made it possible for me to accept this and a later fellowship. In 1944, having completed most of the requirements for a doctorate in English, I entered the United States Naval Reserve as an Ensign and served as a Communications Officer aboard an escort carrier. The same year my first book was published—a spy novel based on a prewar sojourn in Hitler's Germany—and was well enough received to turn my life back into its main channel. I had always wished to become a professional writer living by my work.

"Released from the Navy in March, 1946, I had written two more novels before the end of the year. *Blue City* and *The Three Roads* were published by Alfred Knopf, who has remained my publisher and, without ever changing a line of it, become a paramount influence in my work. In 1951, another productive and exhausting year, I wrote *The Ivory Grin* and completed my doctoral dissertation on Coleridge. Academic habits of mind persist: I still review and edit other men's work, and teach when I can.

* mil′ ar

"The leap from Coleridge studies to the American detective novel is not so unlikely or bathetic as it first appears, if you touch the bases in order on the way. Coleridge's American disciple Poe both invented the detective story and inspired Charles Baudelaire. Baudelaire's 'Dandy,' poised in the urban inferno, is one of the prototypes of the modern detective hero from Sherlock Holmes to Sam Spade and Philip Marlowe.

"I have written twenty books, thirteen of which are novels narrated by a detective in this tradition. As I pointed out in a recent article ('The Writer as Detective Hero,' *Show*, January 1965) my detective Lew Archer is a not very impenetrable mask for the author, but this applied to some of the other characters as well. *The Galton Case* (1959) and *Black Money* (1966) are probably my most complete renderings of the themes of smothered allegiance and uncertain identity which my work inherited from my early years.

"For the past twenty years my wife and I have lived in Santa Barbara. We are active in water sports and in the conservation movement, particularly in the continuing effort to save the California condor from extinction. I have been given awards by the Crime Writers' Association of London and by Mystery Writers of America, Inc., which in 1965 elected me its president."

Millar's devotion to literature goes back to his childhood in provincial Ontario, where he used to climb the fire escape of the town library at night in order to read the authors denied to young people by day. One of them was Dashiell Hammett, master of the hard-boiled detective story, whose mantle passed to Raymond Chandler and then to Millar himself—who, his admirers maintain, has now outgrown it. Among the "great events" of his adolescence were *The Ancient Mariner*, *Oliver Twist*, and *Crime and Punishment*.

Having written for a time under his own name, Millar adopted the pseudonym "John Ross Macdonald," subsequently dropping the "John" to avoid confusion with John D. MacDonald. By the mid-1950s he was recognized as "one of the best of the hard-boiled school now practicing," and by the early 1960s as, simply, the best. Lew Archer, his "highly satisfactory private investigator," is, as he says, in the tradition of Hammett's Sam Spade and Chandler's Philip Marlowe—tough, laconically literate, ruefully moral. Each annual story evokes an equally regular chorus of critical praise. The reviewers vie in superlatives to describe the ingenuity of Millar's plotting, the solidity of his characterization, the niceness of his social observation, the excellence of his crisp, pungent, and exemplary prose.

Millar believes that the mystery story is a literary form with as great a potential as, say, the Elizabethan tragedy: "Its social and psychological range is already immense, and I believe that this convention could support a full-scale philosophic assault on the problem of evil." Many critics believe that his own novels have transcended the limitations of the genre to become serious investigations of character and of contemporary morality. Anthony Boucher noted that Millar's novels "are longer than most mysteries . . . but so rich in plot and character as still to be concise"; the same critic defined as the characteristic tone of Millar's work a fusion of "Swift's contempt for humanity with Saroyan's love."

KENNETH MILLAR

In 1969 William Goldman referred to the Archer books as "the finest series of detective novels ever written by an American." And Eudora Welty, reviewing what was widely regarded as Millar's best book so far, *The Underground Man*, wrote: "In our day it is for such a novel as [this] that the detective form exists."

The author is six feet tall, black-haired, and blue-eyed. He is a Democrat. His wife, Margaret Millar, writes mystery stories quite unlike his own, though, she says, "there has been a lot of cross-influence" in their writing.

PRINCIPAL WORKS (all novels): The Dark Tunnel, 1944; Trouble Follows Me, 1946; Blue City, 1947; The Three Roads, 1948; The Moving Target, 1949; The Drowning Pool, 1950; The Way Some People Die, 1951; The Ivory Grin, 1952; Meet Me at the Morgue, 1953 (England, Experience With Evil, 1954); Find a Victim, 1954; The Barbarous Coast, 1956; Doomsters, 1958; The Galton Case, 1959; The Ferguson Affair, 1960; The Wycherly Woman, 1961; The Zebra-Striped Hearse, 1962; The Chill, 1964; The Far Side of the Dollar, 1965; Black Money, 1966; Archer in Hollywood (contains The

Moving Target, The Way Some People Die, The Barbarous Coast), 1967; The Instant Enemy, 1968; The Goodbye Look, 1969; The Underground Man, 1971; Sleeping Beauty, 1973.

ABOUT: Adams, D. K. (ed.) The Mystery and Detection Annual, 1972; Current Biography, 1953; Warfel, H. R. American Novelists of Today, 1951; Who's Who in America, 1972–1973. *Periodicals*—Los Angeles Magazine March 1963; The New York Times Book Review July 24, 1960; November 11, 1962; January 9, 1966; June 1, 1969; February 14, 1971; Publishers' Weekly August 9, 1971; Show January 1965; Time July 26, 1954.

MILLAR, MARGARET (STURM) (February 5, 1915–), American suspense and mystery story writer, is married to Kenneth Millar ("Ross Macdonald"), who wrote the following note on her behalf: "Margaret Millar was born in Kitchener, Ontario, of German-Canadian and English stock. Her father, Henry Sturm, was a businessman who became in the nineteen-thirties Mayor of the city. Her mother, Lavinia Ferrier, was the daughter of a high school principal. Her own early years are depicted, in a humorous and somewhat idealized light, in Mrs. Millar's semi-autobiographical novel *It's All in the Family* (1948).

"Her early bent for writing had to compete with a musical education (piano) which for some years took up most of her time, and later with the study of the classics, first in high school and then as a scholarship student at the University of Toronto. On June 2, 1938, she married Kenneth Millar in London, Ontario, and the following June their daughter Linda was born.

"Mrs. Millar wrote her first book, a mystery comedy, under circumstances which she has described as follows: 'I've been an avid reader of mysteries since the age of eight. Having two older brothers with catholic literary tastes, I was practically weaned on South American arrow poisons and Lunge's reagent. I began writing when put to bed in September, 1941, for an imaginary heart ailment. After two weeks of reading three or four mysteries a day, I decided to write one and I spent the next two weeks doing just that. I rewrote it twice and it sold to Doubleday. Whereupon I rose from bed. My heart was fine; my doctor's was considerably weakened.'

"*Wall of Eyes* (1943), Mrs. Millar's fourth mystery novel and her first attempt to use the form for wholly serious purposes, was such a radical departure for her that it moved her to Random House, where she has remained with Harry E. Maule as her editor for the last twenty-three years. It was soon followed by *The Iron Gates* (1945), which is regarded as a landmark in the development of the psychological mystery novel.

"Her first six books were laid in Ontario, but now the scenes of her own life had shifted. Mrs. Millar followed her husband first to Ann Arbor, where he attended graduate school, and in 1944 after he entered the Navy, to Princeton, Boston and San Diego in rapid succession. After some months of work in Hollywood while her husband was overseas, Mrs. Millar settled in Santa Barbara, permanently, in 1945. While she has recurred more than once to Canadian settings and once to Ann Arbor (*Vanish in an Instant*, 1952) she has become a California novelist. In 1961 she was naturalized as a United States citizen.

"Not all of Mrs. Millar's books are mystery novels. *The Cannibal Heart* (1949) verges on tragedy; *Wives and Lovers* (1954) is serious comedy. But Mrs. Millar is of course best known as a mystery writer. One of her most famous books is *Beast in View* (1955; see the dialogue between Julian Symons and Edmund Crispin in the *Times Literary Supplement*, June 23, 1961) which was given an Edgar Allan Poe award by Mystery Writers of America. Like *The Fiend* (1964), it rose from her lifelong study of abnormal psychology.

"In recent years Mrs. Millar has embarked on still another study, which had its inception when she and her husband moved into a house in a wooded canyon. Fascinated by the birds which populated the canyon, she began to feed and observe them, and keep records. She has recently completed a book, her twentieth, about her personal experiences with these birds.

"Mrs. Millar is active in the Audubon Society and other conservation organizations. In 1956 she was elected president of Mystery Writers of America. In 1965 the Los Angeles *Times* gave her a 'Woman of the Year' award."

Margaret Millar began to play the piano at the age of four and was already broadcasting over local radio stations by the time she was in high school at the Kitchener Collegiate Institute. Her literary career developed rather more slowly, but she won a prize for a poem when she was nine, and published her first stories in the Kitchener literary annual, one of whose editors was her future husband. Her other activities at Kitchener included debating, acting, student government, and singing, and she also found time to develop an ardent interest in archaeology. It was this that induced her to study classics when, in 1933, she went on to University College, University of Toronto. In the end, however, she decided against a career in archaeology and left college without a degree in 1936. Two years later she married Kenneth Millar.

Her first book, *The Invisible Worm*, was an ingenious, elegant, and amusing story which introduced Dr. Paul Prye, an Ontario psychoanalyst-detective much given to "highbrow logic" and quotation from William Blake. *Wall of Eyes* and *The Iron Gates*, more serious (though frequently witty) in tone, were also set in Canada, and featured Inspector Sands, a slightly more orthodox detective. But the majority of Margaret Millar's sardonic and tough-minded psychological suspense novels center on a psychopathic personality and its victims, rather than on an idealized investigator.

As Kenneth Millar remarks above, one of the most notable of her books is *Beast in View*. Set in Hollywood, it is "a pure terror-suspense-mystery story, complete with murder, detective and surprise twist," and at the same time a completely convincing study in abnormal psychology. *How Like an Angel*, which investigates the decline and fall of a California religious cult, seemed to L. G. Offord "wonderfully plotted" and "as real as today's paper" with "as always, the sense of tragedy [underlying] suspense." *The Fiend* is a study of a man once jailed for assaulting a little girl, and his struggle against a resurgence of his obsession. Its real theme, one reviewer suggested, is "the responsibility of the strong for the weak." Anthony Boucher thought that *The Fiend* "may well be the finest example to date of the fusion of the novel of character and the puzzle of suspense," concluding that "as a superb thriller, as a model of craftsmanship, or as a deeply disturbing psychological novel . . . it is a masterwork." As one critic has remarked, Margaret Millar "never repeats herself; each of her chilling tales formulates its own kind of suspense."

Experiment in Springtime and *The Cannibal Heart* are not mystery stories but more or less straightforward psychological novels; the latter was particularly admired for the excellence of its dialogue and a prose style which is "a delight of clarity and pungency." *It's All in the Family* is quite different, a plotless but charming exercise in nostalgia about the activities over one weekend of an imaginative, precocious, and energetic little girl. It delighted most reviewers. Margaret Millar's fascinated observation of the wild life of the canyon near Santa Barbara where she and her husband live is recorded in *The Birds and the Beasts Were There*.

Margaret Millar is of average height and has green eyes. She is an ardent student of good prose, and an admirer of Scott Fitzgerald, Evelyn Waugh, Katherine Mansfield, and Rosamond Lehmann, among others. She enjoys swimming and sailing as well as ornithology.

PRINCIPAL WORKS: *Fiction*—The Invisible Worm, 1941; The Weak-Eyed Bat, 1942; The Devil Loves Me, 1942; Wall of Eyes, 1943; Fire Will Freeze, 1944; The Iron Gates, 1945; Experiment in Springtime, 1947; It's All in the Family, 1948; The Cannibal Heart, 1949; Do Evil in Return, 1950; Vanish in an Instant, 1952; Rose's Last Summer, 1952; Wives and Lovers, 1954; Beast in View, 1955; An Air That Kills, 1957; The Listening Walls, 1959; A Stranger in My Grave, 1960; How Like an Angel, 1962; The Fiend, 1964; Beyond This Point Are Monsters, 1970. *Nonfiction*—The Birds and the Beasts Were There, 1968.

MARGARET MILLAR

ABOUT: Contemporary Authors 13–14, 1965; Current Biography, 1946; Warfel, H. R. American Novelists of Today, 1951; Who's Who in America, 1972–1973.

MILLER, MERLE (May 17, 1919–), American novelist, writes: "I was born on a mortgaged eighty-acre farm near a place called Montour, Iowa, which had never been up to much (population seven hundred), and by the time I came along, it was running out altogether. When I was eight years old, my father, who has a longing for failure (a feeling I have often been accused, most often by myself, of sharing) moved to Marshalltown, Iowa, where in remarkably short succession, he failed at running a dairy farm, a candy-corn shop, a miniature golf course, and a hamburger stand called the *Wee Dug Inn*, where I worked after school and on weekends. While there I acquired, among numerous other neuroses, a lifelong aversion to chopped beef. I was an only child, which was, no doubt, fortunate, and lived in a vast run-down rooming house, just on the right side of the wrong side of the tracks. I worked hard in high school, graduating as salutatorian; the valedictorian was a nice Jewish girl who almost immediately married a doctor. In those days, I cannot remember wanting to be a writer, although I did turn out a humorous-type column for the high school weekly. The column, appropriately enough, was called *Gagline*. What I wanted at that point was anything that would get me the hell out of Marshalltown. I succeeded at the age of sixteen, making it all the way to the

MERLE MILLER

State University of Iowa in Iowa City, where I worked on the student daily and did newscasts on the university radio station. I read a great many books, none of them much good, and just before my senior year and, I think coincidentally, the beginning of the Second World War, I managed through a series of lies and various other kinds of chicanery to spend nine months in London—my mother calls it London, England—as a perfunctory student at the London School of Economics.

"I returned to Iowa City, but I never did manage to graduate, largely because I refused to take military training, which was compulsory and I fancied myself as a pacifist. Also my grades weren't very good, although I wrote a column, 'Around the Town,' which managed to rock the entire campus a couple of times each week. It was radical, disrespectful, and a great deal of fun to write.

"I left the university, came to New York, tried to get a job as a radio commentator, blessedly failed, and then took a job as a copy boy on the late Philadelphia *Record*. Again through a series of lies and chicanery, I managed after six months to become a Washington correspondent. I was by then no longer a pacifist and like to tell people I volunteered for service on December 8, 1942. Actually, my draft number came up on March 10, 1943, and after a miserable few months at a hell hole called Keesler Field, Mississippi, I managed to cajole my way onto a weekly magazine published by the United States Army called *Yank*. I spent almost a year as a *Yank* writer and editor in the Pacific, where I heard some few shots fired by the Japanese in what I presume was anger. Afterwards, I was sent to Paris where I edited the continental edition of *Yank* and through a series of stupidities and short-sightedness accidentally took some small part in the Battle of the Bulge. When I returned to the United States in July 1945, I had written the manuscript of a dreadful novel about a demonstrably fictitious military engagement in the Pacific, called *Island 49*. It was published the week The Bomb was dropped on Hiroshima and Nagasaki. The book got better notices, but The Bomb was more popular and sold better.

"I spent a few unhappy weeks as an editor of *Time* magazine, but it soon became apparent that either Henry Luce or I had to go. I went. I worked for a time, happily though not eating much, on *Harper's* Magazine, in the meantime writing a novel called *That Winter*, which a lot of reviewers, none of whom I liked much, compared to the work of Fitzgerald, Hemingway, and Dos Passos.

"I immediately quit *Harper's* and, as my mother says, often, too, haven't had any regular work since. I have written quite a few television plays, two of them respectable, two movies, both lousy, uncounted magazine articles, seven novels, two of which I like, and three books of non-fiction.

"None of the books has sold particularly well, which I attribute to their beady-eyed, even nasty view of the state of the world. At times, usually late in the evening, I conclude that the reason they haven't sold well is that they aren't all that good.

"I would rather write than almost anything else; besides, at this stage of the game, how else could I make a living? I keep telling myself—sometimes with conviction—that I now have more to say and say it better than I ever have before. Since nobody asked me to write, I don't see how anybody can tell me to stop. I live—sometimes alone—in a glass house near Brewster, New York, and as often as I can I travel in gentler climes among gentler people. I once belonged to twenty-two organizations devoted to the dubious purpose of bettering the world. Now I don't belong to any and devote what spare and sober hours there are to improving myself, an insurmountable task."

The general public as well as the reviewers welcomed *That Winter*, which studied the postwar adjustment problems of three army veterans in New York and became a best seller. *The Sure Thing*, about the Washington "witch hunts," also had many admirers, as did *Reunion*, which brought together and scrutinized a group of ex-soldiers eight years after the war. All of these novels were praised for their liberal political concerns, for their readability, and for the sardonic urban sparkle of their prose. From the beginning, however, there were those who, like John W. Aldridge, recognized in Miller "a master journalist and a sensitive observer," but deplored his "lack of seriousness, his tone of mockery and simulation, which gives to everything he writes a touch of phoniness."

None of Miller's fiction has quite escaped such charges, but they have been made less glibly since 1961, when he published *A Gay and Melancholy Sound*, which is presented as the autobiographical suicide note of a burnt-out child prodigy. Wirt Williams thought he had not "completely lost the ordinary slickness that used to be his taint—but he has gotten rid of much of it and has grown irony in its place. . . . He hasn't written a genuine tragedy . . . but he is faithful to his own vision and refuses to soften it. He has seen what he has seen."

Miller's nonfiction includes *The Judges and the Judged*, an excellent "analytical case history" of the development and effect of the "blacklist" in radio and television, and *Only You, Dick Daring!*, his account of what happened when he was persuaded to write a pilot program for a stillborn television series. Marya Mannes found that "with wit both hilarious and savage, with a good reporter's eye, and a good writer's ruthless ear, Merle Miller has set forth better than any solemn survey . . . why . . . network television entertaining is no place for the honest writer." The book was a best seller.

On January 17, 1971 Miller published in the New York *Times Magazine* an article in which—at fifty, and after forty years "in the closet"—he revealed that he was a homosexual, and showed how much of his life had been marred and wasted by attempts to conceal the fact in a society where homosexuals were despised and ill-used. A follow-up article published in the same magazine on October 10, 1971, discussed the great flood of letters, some of them savage but the majority sympathetic and grateful, written in response to the first piece, which was published in book form, with an introduction and an epilogue, as *On Being Different*. This "moving and in certain respects heroic little book" was warmly praised by most reviewers, one of whom thought it might "continue to be the most effective current statement of the homosexual's right to a respected role in society." The crippling strain placed on the homosexual by his awareness of society's hostility is the theme also of *What Happened*, a novel which (like *A Gay and Melancholy Sound*) records the rise to fame of its prodigiously talented narrator, and his gradual decline into breakdown and despair. More than one reviewer considered it Miller's best, as well as his most ambitious, novel.

A little above average height, Miller has a "sensitive, alert face, casual manner, and rich voice." He was married in 1948, hoping (like Tchaikovsky) that it would "cure" him, though he now realizes that this desperate remedy could never have succeeded. Among contemporary American writers, he admires above all Scott Fitzgerald, with whom he is often compared, and James Gould Cozzens. At one time Miller was secretary of the Authors' Guild, a member of the Writers' Board for World Government, a board member of the American Civil Liberties Union, and a member of Americans for Democratic Action. His recreations include travel, the theatre, and seeing bad movies.

PRINCIPAL WORKS: *Novels*—Island 49, 1945; That Winter, 1948; The Sure Thing, 1949; Reunion, 1954; A Secret Understanding, 1956; A Gay and Melancholy Sound, 1961; A Day in Late September, 1963; What Happened, 1972. *Nonfiction*—(with Abe Spitzer) We Dropped the A-Bomb, 1946; The Judges and the Judged (report for the American Civil Liberties Union), 1952; (with Evan Rhodes) Only You, Dick Daring! or, How to Write One Television Script and Make $50,000,000, 1964; On Being Different: What It Means to Be a Homosexual, 1971.

ABOUT: Aldridge, J. W. After the Lost Generation, 1951; Contemporary Authors 9–10, 1964; Current Biography, 1950; Warfel, H. R. American Novelists of Today, 1951; Who's Who in America, 1972–1973. *Periodicals*—New York Times Book Review October 10, 1954; Publishers' Weekly October 4, 1971; Saturday Review February 12, 1949.

MILLER, VASSAR (MORRISON) (July 19, 1924–), American poet, writes: "I am a native of Houston, Texas and received all my schooling here, including a B.S. and an M.A. from the University of Houston.

"I began to write poetry, or at least rhymes, when I was about eight. My father would lug home his office typewriter for my amusement, and I was fascinated to find I could make letters on a machine. Often I remarked that I might never have written had it not been for the typewriter, because, due to the physical handicap of cerebral palsy, I use a pen or pencil with only painful slowness. Therefore, man's inventiveness came, unknowingly, to the aid of my laziness, if not of my disability.

"Through high school and college I received prizes here and there for my poems, but not until I received my degrees did I begin being published in the little magazines. The *New Orleans Poetry Journal* brought out my first volume of verse.

"The style and content of my work has reflected and changed with the style of my life. At first I employed very strict forms, then freer ones. Yet most of my non-conventional patterns are really syllabic, instead of free, and I still like the sonnet. Form cannot be separated from content, but probably I start with an interest in content. I have something I want to say and I let the form of expression grow accordingly.

"I now keep house for myself and my dog. My interests are church, reading, friends, and, since going to Europe in the summer of 1965, travel.

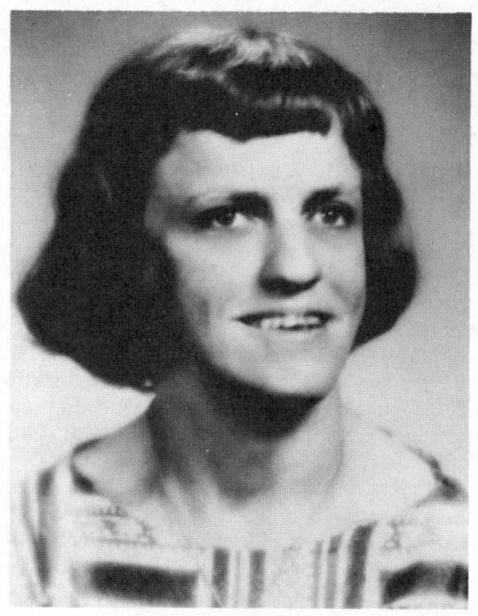

VASSAR MILLER

Presently I confer with high school students on their creative writing at St. John's School in Houston."

Religion for Vassar Miller was initially, she says, "an attempt at compensation" for the loneliness of her childhood. Her adolescent verse reflected this, "was dreadfully pious and sounded like bad hymns." By the time she got to college she had discovered the sonnet, and she worked mainly in that form for some years, liking it for the order it could impose on "inner chaos." Her first conscious influences were Edwin Arlington Robinson, whose "lonely, Spartan spirit" attracted her, and the "taut metrics" of Gerard Manley Hopkins.

The fruits of her apprenticeship were collected in her first considerable volume, *Wage War on Silence* (1960), containing brief lyrics which are sometimes religious, sometimes erotic, and sometimes both. Dudley Fitts in his review gave particular praise to "Though He Slay Me," built around the metaphor of "God's Yes" being distorted into a No "among the crevices and caves / Of the coiled ear which deep in its abyss / Resolves to music all Your negatives." The twenty lines of this poem, Fitts wrote, "sing a totality of torment and acceptance with a power that one will not soon forget; and even if one accepts as imperfectly achieved or too darkly idiosyncratic all but a handful of the other poems, what remains is enough to establish Miss Miller as a writer of extraordinary gifts. She is never going to be popular, but it seems certain that she will be read and admired by persons who are not afraid of the lyric queerness that she extracts from her self-searching." James Wright called her mastery of traditional forms "perfect"; he praised "a simplicity of diction that . . . reveals the concentration of a powerful intellect," a "grace and reserve" signifying "the modesty of a writer who possesses imaginative gifts of the rarest kind."

In recent years, as she says, Miss Miller has turned (though not exclusively) to freer forms, and this is evident in *My Bones Being Wiser* (1963). Denise Levertov thought a few of these poems weakened by sentimentality, but most of them "notably spare, taut and exact," with "a timeless sound . . . that timelessness a poetry has when it arises very directly out of a life, without being filtered through a highly charged intellectual environment. . . . The result is elegant and strong." *Onions and Roses* conveyed an "air of grieving meditation and surprise," a sense of loss which however does not disturb the quality of the verse. "Much is very fine," wrote Jane Cooper, "much is, if not large, inevitable and original."

Vassar Miller has said that "poetry, like all art, has a trinitarian function: creative, redemptive, and sanctifying. It is creative because it takes the raw materials of fact and feeling and makes them into that which is neither fact nor feeling. It is redemptive because it can transform the pain and ugliness of life into joy and beauty. It is sanctifying because it thus gives the transitory at least a relative form and meaning. Hence poetry, whether avowedly so or not, is always religious; it is akin to prayer, an act of love." More recently she wrote: "I used to say that a poem is an act of love. Now I know it is an act of hate also. At best, these two emotions are not mutually exclusive."

PRINCIPAL WORKS: *Poetry*—Adam's Footprint, 1956; Wage War on Silence, 1960; My Bones Being Wiser, 1963; Onions and Roses, 1968.

ABOUT: Contemporary Authors 11–12, 1965; Edward, M. Poets Laureate of Texas, 1932–1966, 1966; Nemerov, H. (ed.) Poets on Poetry, 1966. *Periodicals*—New York Times Book Review February 26, 1961; June 21, 1964; Poetry September 1957; December 1961.

MILLER, WARREN (August 31, 1921–April 20, 1966), American novelist, was the son of Carl and Rose Labor (Eistreicher) Miller, Russian on his father's side and "Austrian-Hungarian-Polish-Czech" on his mother's. He was born in Stowe, Pennsylvania, a mill town where "only the children spoke English," their parents being content with Polish. Miller's grandfather owned much of the town and "being his grandson was something like being the crown prince of a small barony."

When the boy was seven his family moved to nearby Pottstown. He went to local schools there and on to the University of Iowa, where his studies were interrupted by the war. After service in Britain and Normandy with the U.S. Army,

Miller returned to graduate from Iowa in 1946. He remained at the university as an assistant instructor until 1948, receiving his M.A. in 1947. Returning East, Miller was a public relations writer in New York City from 1948 to 1955, then for two years an art studio representative.

Warren Miller's literary career had begun in college, where he won the Octave Thanet Short Story Prize. Over the years he contributed stories and articles to many periodicals. His first novel, *The Sleep of Reason*, was a satire on McCarthyism. Published in England in 1956, it had to wait until 1960 to appear, largely unsung, in the United States. In 1957 and 1958 came two pseudonymous novels of considerable charm by "Amanda Vail," *Love Me Little* and *The Bright Young Things*. They described an earnest pursuit of Experience by two college girls and delighted most reviewers. Miller's second novel under his own name, *The Way We Live Now* (1958), was a study of divorce, Manhattan style. It caught a mood of "jaunty despair" and was enjoyed as much for its wit as for its considerable realism and insight. There followed three books for children.

The Cool World (1959), generally regarded as Miller's most notable novel, reflected the sense of waste he had felt when, living in East Harlem, he had watched teen-age gang fights from his window. It is the story, told in his own words, of a black boy's dedicated and resourceful efforts to fulfill an ambition. But his ambition is to own a gun which will consolidate his leadership of the "Royal Crocodiles," and success involves crime and self-prostitution. James Baldwin called this brief tour de force "one of the finest novels about Harlem that has ever come my way," and said that he could not be sure whether its author was black or white. The book was dramatized by Miller and Robert Rossen, and made into a motion picture.

Miller's several visits to Cuba resulted in a nonfiction study, *90 Miles From Home* (1961), and a novel, *Flush Times* (1962). *The Siege of Harlem* (1964) was a comic fantasy about a Harlem which had seceded from the United States. Miller's last book was *Looking for the General* (1964), a "profound and funny fable" and perhaps his most ambitious novel. It puzzled some critics but was described by one as "the most unsparing essay on the American cultural landscape" since *Lolita*.

Miller married the former Jimmy Curley in 1958 and had two daughters, Scott and Eve. Travel was the "great passion" of his life. He joined *The Nation* as literary editor in September 1965 and served there until shortly before his death, at his home in New York City, of lung cancer. He was in his forty-fifth year.

Warren Miller was a "witty and responsive man," a humane social critic, and a craftsman of

WARREN MILLER

great versatility. *Newsweek* in its obituary called him "one of that band of novelists who provide a literary period, not necessarily with its principal sources of light and power, but with its texture and density, its vitality and abundance, health and vigor. He was still growing when he died."

PRINCIPAL WORKS: The Sleep of Reason, 1956; (as "Amanda Vail") Love Me Little, 1957; (as "Amanda Vail") The Bright Young Things, 1958; The Way We Live Now, 1958; King Carlo of Capri, 1958; Pablo Paints a Picture, 1959; The Goings-on at Little Wishful, 1959; The Cool World, 1959; 90 Miles From Home, 1961; Flush Times, 1962; The Siege of Harlem, 1964; Looking for the General, 1964.

ABOUT: New York Times April 21, 1966; Newsweek May 9, 1966; Wilson Library Bulletin May 1961.

***MILOSZ, CZESLAW** (June 30, 1911–), Polish poet and essayist, writes: "I was born in Lithuania and my country of origin is important to me, but due to linguistic imbroglios in that part of Europe I was to write in Polish. Another member of our family, O. V. de L. Milosz, brought up in Paris, was a French poet.

"In my childhood I traveled much, accompanying my father, a civil engineer. My high school years in Wilno, then belonging to Poland, were marked by my rebellions, especially against compulsory religious (Roman Catholic) education. At the University of Wilno I received a diploma in law. As a university student I started to publish poems and articles. A periodical founded by my friends and myself in 1931, *Żagary*, and a literary group of that name, figure in the chronicles of modern Polish poetry as 'the catastrophist school.'

* mē′ lôsh

CZESLAW MILOSZ

We were leftists, unorthodox Marxists, and we prophesied a planetary cataclysm. In 1934-1935 I studied on a fellowship in Paris where I used to see often my 'French' relative, a major influence in my intellectual development.

"Though Warsaw under the Nazi occupation was a hardly enviable place to live, I do not regret my spending the years of World War II there. I learned many things and my writings were published by clandestine presses (including a Resistance anthology of poetry, which I edited). After the war I took an active part in the literary life of the People's Poland and combined my contributing to literary reviews with diplomatic assignments to the Polish embassies in Washington, then in Paris. Circumstances fully understandable only to those who lived through the years of Stalinism in Poland, Hungary or Czechoslovakia, made me a reluctant exile in 1951. I should add I had been a staunch opponent of 'socialist realism.' To present my position I wrote in 1951 in Paris a sociopolitical book *The Captive Mind*, though this is not my field. That book has been translated into many languages. In 1953 I received in Geneva a Prix Littéraire Européen for a novel. Royalties enabled us to live somehow in France (I am married and have two sons). I contributed to several West European magazines, mainly to the Polish language Parisian monthly, *Kultura*. In 1960 I came to the University of California at Berkeley as a visiting lecturer, was appointed the next year professor of Slavic Languages and Literatures and at this writing I live in Berkeley.

"I consider myself primarily a poet. Since poetry can be written only in the language one spoke in his childhood, I stick to Polish. Translations into Polish (I have made a considerable number of poetry translations from English, French, occasionally also from Spanish, Lithuanian and Yiddish) come next on my scale of importance. Then prose, both fiction and non-fiction, of a kind which is one way or another connected with my poetry. Then my translations of Polish poets into English. Yet I cannot entirely repudiate what is for me, subjectively, the least enticing—my scholarly essays and studies."

Milosz was born in Šateiniai, the son of Aleksander and Weronika (Kunat) Milosz. The family is an old and noble one, and his imagination was shaped by his early sense of Lithuania's history and landscape. His childhood—spent partly in Russia just before and after the Revolution—is described in a novel, *Dolina Issy* (The Valley of Issa, 1955), and in the volume of autobiography translated in 1968 as *Native Realm*, a modest book of great sociological and historical value.

As he says, Milosz began to write as an undergraduate. He quickly emerged as the leader of the "Second Avant-Garde," whose members maintained "rather chaotic" relations with Marxism, and published in *Żagary* and elsewhere apocalyptic poems reflecting their well-founded belief in the imminence of global war. Milosz was at first drawn to surrealism and other French movements of the time—partly on account of the influence of his remarkable uncle Oscar Vladislas de Lubicz Milosz, who was noted as a diplomat, scholar, philosopher, and mystic, as well as a poet. It is in his first book, *Poemat o czasie zaslygtym* (Poem of the Frozen Time, 1932), that Milosz's experiments are most obtrusive. A tendency to more classical modes was already evident in *Tzry zimy* (Three Winters, 1936). Milosz's early verse attracted much critical attention, and was especially admired for the precision of its visual images, which—thanks to a mythopoeic quality in the author's imagination—nevertheless retain great symbolic force. During the German occupation of Poland Milosz learned English, and in the years just after the war produced what some regard as his most memorable verse under the influence, most obviously, of T. S. Eliot.

Zniewolony umysl, written as he notes above to explain his reluctant defection from the People's Poland, was published in 1953 as *The Captive Mind*. It analyzes the impact of communism on four contemporary Polish writers, designated only as Alpha, Beta, Gamma, Delta. The subjects of these sharply delineated portraits are not difficult to identify. The German philosopher Karl Jaspers called the book a "significant historical document and analysis of the highest order. . . . Milosz shows what happens to men subjected simultaneously to constant threat of annihilation and to the promptings of faith in a historical necessity which exerts apparently irresistible force and achieves enormous success." E. S. Pisko found in *The Captive Mind* "a rare sincerity of self-exposure, depth of observation, and moral integrity." Stephen Spender thought that it "conveys the most intense feeling of an age" and was sure that in a hundred years' time people would still be reading "this passionate apologia."

The novel *Zdobycie Wladzy*, translated as the *Seizure of Power*, is based on Milosz's experiences in Warsaw during and after the war and is also in its way a "significant historical document." Some Western critics found it too cerebral, and one was puzzled by a "mist of political innuendo and allusion," but the novel was warmly praised by its reviewer in the *Times Literary Supplement* for its "cool, studied prose, that gives the incidents of this season of deception and treason the universality and illogical strangeness of nightmare." It was this book that brought the author the Prix Littéraire Européen.

Milosz's postwar verse includes *Swiatlo dzienne* (1953), *Traktat poetycki* (1957), and *Król Popiel.* His conception of poetry as the "consciousness of an epoch," he says, has made him as resistant to "pure art" as to "socialist realism." He seeks instead a poetry "that sometimes attains the calligraphic quality of an ideogram." However, the Polish critic Tymon Terlecki has likened him to such Italian hermeticists as Montale and Ungaretti.

Milosz has published studies of Polish writers as well as of Defoe, Balzac, Gide, Tolstoy, and William James. He has been extremely active as a translator into Polish from the English of Shakespeare, Eliot, Milton, Whitman, Jeffers, and also from French, Spanish, and Yiddish. His *Postwar Polish Poetry* contains his English versions of ninety poems by twenty-one poets, including Wat, Różewicz, Herbert, and himself. The quality of the selection and of the translations was widely praised. Milosz says that he feels equally at home in France, England, and the United States, though in the latter he misses the "feeling of history and thus the tragic sense."

PRINCIPAL WORKS IN ENGLISH TRANSLATION: The Captive Mind, 1953; The Seizure of Power (England, The Usurpers), 1955; Native Realm: A Search for Self-definition, 1968; The History of Polish Literature, 1969; Polish Post-War Poetry, 1970; Selected Poems, 1973. *Poems in* Gillon, A. and Krzyzanowski, L. (eds.) Introduction to Modern Polish Literature, 1964; Milosz, C. (ed. and tr.) Postwar Polish Poetry, 1965.

ABOUT: Gillon, A. and Krzyzanowski, L. (eds.) Introduction to Modern Polish Literature, 1964; Gömöri, G. Polish and Hungarian Poetry, 1945 to 1956, 1966; Milosz, C. Native Realm, 1968; Penguin Companion to Literature 2, 1969. *Periodicals*—Book Week May 9, 1965; New Republic May 16, 1955; New Yorker November 7, 1953; Partisan Review November 1953; Saturday Review June 6, 1953; July 11, 1953; Tri-Quarterly Spring 1967.

***"MISHIMA, YUKIO" (pseudonym of Kimitake Hiraoka)** (January 14, 1925–November 25, 1970), Japanese novelist and dramatist, was the best known and perhaps the best of his country's postwar writers. He was born in Tokyo, the son of a senior official in the Ministry of Agriculture. A bookish, precocious, and delicate child, he had a distinguished academic career at Gakushuin (the Peers' School), crowned by a citation for excellence from the Emperor.

Mishima started to write while in middle school, and his short stories began to appear when he was only sixteen in the magazine *Bungei Bunka* (Literary Culture). From the beginning he displayed the aestheticism and the "aristocratic style" that were to distinguish his later work, along with what he himself called "my heart's leaning toward Death and Night and Blood." Even as a child he was morbidly fascinated by pictures of knights dead in battle and *samurai* warriors committing ritual suicide, and particularly by Guido Reni's painting of the martyrdom of St. Sebastian, which had a specifically sexual effect on him.

During the war, while he was still at school, Mishima met the writer Yasunari Kawabata, later a Nobel Prize winner, who was to become a lifelong friend. Mishima shared with the older writer a concern for fine Japanese prose and a wide acquaintance with the Japanese classics—rare in his generation—and was also astonishingly well read in European literature, both ancient and modern.

In 1944 Mishima entered the Law Department of Tokyo University. He was conscripted in February 1945 and, though he did not see active service, said that the war had a tremendous psychological effect on him. He resumed his studies, graduating in 1947, and followed his father into the civil service, entering the Ministry of Finance. After less than a year he left to devote himself to writing.

His immensely successful first novel was *Kamen no Kokuhaku* (1949, translated by Meredith Weatherby as *Confessions of a Mask*). It is an account, largely autobiographical, of a timid and sensitive youth's struggle to come to terms with the bisexual and sado-masochistic elements in his nature. In a memorial article in the New York *Times Book Review* (January 3, 1971), to which this note is much indebted, his friend Donald Keene says that the book's title refers to the uninhibited and arrogant public mask that Mishima deliberately assumed to conceal his gentleness and vulnerability,

* mi shē mä

YUKIO MISHIMA

and which in time he made "a living part of his flesh."

Ai no Kawaki (1950, translated by Alfred H. Marks as *Thirst for Love*) was a slight, intense study of a young woman whose sexual drives, blocked by her rigid upper-class upbringing and background, are perverted into violence. In this early novel, wrote one English reviewer, there are already "most of the essential features of his later talent: delicacy of style backed by intellect, moral insight and compassion; an acute discernment of varying social attitudes in a Japan which moves into the future while falling back on the assumptions and rituals of the past; and a beautiful understanding of the plight of lonely individuals, women especially." Other books of this period, like *Sei no Jidai* (The Age of Youth, 1950), *Kinjiki* (1951, translated by Alfred Marks as *Forbidden Colors*), and *Higyo* (Secret Pleasure, 1952), explore an underworld of sodomy, destruction, and despair in a spirit of defiantly heretical aestheticism that brought comparisons with the early Gide.

Mishima's first trip abroad, which took him to Greece in 1952, showed him that his dark and literary view of life was an incomplete one and (as Keene puts it) "that he must also take cognizance of the strength of the human body displayed in sunlight." *Shiosai* (1954, translated by Weatherby as *The Sound of Waves*) is a direct result of this revelation. It is a reworking of the Daphnis and Chloë myth, set in a small island fishing village off the coast of Japan, and in spirit a much brighter work than its predecessors.

Kinkakuji (1956, translated by Ivan Morris as *The Temple of the Golden Pavilion*), which was filmed by Ishikawa as *Enjo*, is often called the finest of Mishima's early books, a compelling and intricately constructed novel narrated by Mizoguchi, a young Zen acolyte, ugly and lonely, cut off from the world by a speech impediment. Teased by the ambiguities of a corrupt friend and the complexities of his Zen master, he becomes obsessed by the beauty of a golden temple, and is seized by the idea that he can free himself from his obsession only by destroying this unattainable love object. Anthony West wrote that "with its psychological penetration and its vivid evocation of the life of Kyoto in Japan's cruelly testing years of defeat, [the book] has substantial claim to be considered one of the most interesting novels of the decade."

It was at about this time that Mishima, the physically puny and profoundly intellectual admirer of physical beauty and strength, decided to remake his body. He began to practice weight lifting with such persistence and determination that he built himself a physique of classical perfection. He went on to become very proficient as a boxer and as a practitioner of *karate* and of *kendo*, the Japanese art of sword fighting. Mishima, who as a child had been roused to such loving and fearful excitement by images of heroic martyrdom, responded very deeply to the cult of the sword and its *samurai* associations. And he strove, by sheer force of will, to perfect the public mask of which Donald Keene speaks—to subdue his natural timidity and the "excessive sweetness" he despised in his own nature. He acted in a gangster film, recorded songs, made flamboyant appearances on television and in the pages of mass circulation magazines to expound his political and cultural views, and in other ways courted and achieved national celebrity.

Moreover, even those who found Mishima's views and his antics distasteful could not deny his literary achievements. By his early thirties he had published more than a dozen novels, some thirty plays, scores of short stories and many essays and articles. He had won several important literary prizes, and was regarded by many as the spokesman of his "wounded generation." He built himself an opulent Italianate villa in Tokyo, full of valuable art objects, and sent his wife to Western-style cookery classes.

Fame, wealth, and the hero worship of the young could not assuage Mishima's "leaning toward Death and Night and Blood" or his growing distress over the arid materialism of postwar Japan. After a depressing visit to New York in 1957, he developed a philosophy he called "active nihilism," an element of which seems to have been an idealism of suicide as the ultimate existentialist gesture. This is illustrated in the novella "Patriotism" (1960), in which a ritual double suicide, performed for the honor of Japan and the Emperor, is described in almost lascivious detail. A few years later the story was filmed with Mishima himself in the bloody central role.

There is something of this also in the novel *Gogo no Eiko* (1963, translated by John Nathan as *The Sailor Who Fell from Grace with the Sea*). It is about a thirteen-year-old boy who secretly watches the coupling of his mother and a visiting sailor, whom the boy invests with all the mystery and glamour that he associates with the sea. But the man is domesticated by the woman, and leaves the sea. And for this betrayal the boy kills him.

"There is something in Mishima which yearns fiercely for the unattainable, a pinnacle of purity akin to non-existence or 'godliness,' " wrote a critic in the *Nation*. John Wain made a related (and prophetic) point when he said that this novel explores "an area of truth that is psychological and also anthropological. The king must die: it is not merely dangerous to find oneself apotheosized and turned into a sacred symbol: it is inevitably fatal, for all religions devour their gods." Mishima's stories tend to center around a single event, a moment of illumination which invests with meaning all that goes before and after—like the moment when the boy watches the sailor with his mother and a ship's siren sounds: "It was like being part of a miracle: in that instant everything packed away inside Noburo's breast since the first day of his life was released and consummated."

Mishima's plays are admired for their structural skill and sharp psychological observation, and he contributed a great deal to the enlarged range of the postwar Japanese theatre. *Sado Koshakufujin* (1965, translated by Donald Keene as *Madame de Sade*), a study of the enigmatic marquise, is a work in the Western idiom. It was praised for the quality of its rhetoric and for the author's remarkable grasp of the surface manners and mores of revolutionary France, though it was said that "real feeling only breaks through in the gloatingly detailed accounts of Sade's pleasures." Mishima also wrote for the *Kabuki* stage, and in his modern *No* plays sought to ally tradition and modernity, the theatre of poetry and that of ideas. He directed some of his own plays at the National Theatre.

Mishima's fame grew and he was often spoken of during the last part of his life as a candidate for the Nobel Prize. At the same time, according to Angus Wilson, his "vanity, boredom, fear of age" were gaining ground over his "generosity, friendliness and sensitivity." His elitist and nationalist views grew increasingly extreme and irrational, and were summed up in an essay published in 1970 and translated posthumously as *Sun and Steel*. In this muddled and poetical manifesto he attempted to explain his rejection of "words," "imagination," and "personality" in favor of "body," "action," and "group," and advocated a "philosophy of suffering" which many found repugnantly reminiscent of European rightist theories.

In 1968 Mishima had organized a kind of private army called *Tate No Kai* (the Shield Society), with a membership of one hundred young men, mostly students. It was neither rightist nor militaristic in the ordinary political sense, but an idealistic attempt to revive the tradition of *bushido*, the knightly code of chivalry of the *samurai*. On November 25, 1970, Mishima and four followers, carrying swords, entered the Eastern Self-Defense Force Headquarters in Tokyo, wounding a number of soldiers, and taking hostage the commanding general. Mishima then harangued some one thousand soldiers from a balcony, calling on them to overthrow the constitution and return to Japan's imperial traditions. The troops received his suggestion with jeering and laughter. Mishima then left the balcony and, in the presence of his followers, committed *seppuku*. Having opened his abdomen with his knife, he was beheaded by one of his companions, who died in the same way before the ceremony was ended by the arrival of riot police.

Few now believe that Mishima really expected the Eastern Self-Defense Force to join him in a coup d'état; he anticipated their scorn and wanted to die as he did—to sacrifice himself, as he wrote in his last letter to a Western friend, "for the old, beautiful tradition of Japan, which is disappearing very quickly day by day." He succeeded in embarrassing the government, which was at pains to assure the world that the tragedy did not herald a general revival of Japanese militarism but was an isolated act of madness. Some have suggested that Mishima was a victim of cultural conflict, hopelessly torn between East and West, but Donald Keene says that "he possessed both traditions and combined them brilliantly." Keene believes that his friend's death was the terrible but inevitable culmination of his life. Indeed, given his preoccupations, it is possible to see that the idea of an agonizing martyrdom in the name of Japan must always have dominated his fantasies, the ultimate challenge and the ultimate temptation. Mishima was survived by his wife Yoko and two children.

Mishima's last work, completed on the day of his death, is a tetralogy called *The Sea of Fertility* (the reference is to "the arid sea of the moon that belies its name"). Many regard it as his masterpiece, as he did himself: "I wrote everything in it, and I believe I expressed in it everything I felt and thought about through my life." The tetralogy forms a social history of twentieth-century Japan, beginning with *Haru no yuki* (translated by Michael Gallagher as *Spring Snow*). Set in 1912–1914, it is an account of an illicit, beautiful, and eventually tragic love affair between the son of one princely house and the daughter of another. "Nowhere before in Mishima's writings," wrote a reviewer in the *Times Literary Supplement*, "is the style quite so dazzling, nowhere does it recall quite so forcefully the rich and resplendent culture of Japan's Momoyama period. Nowhere has Mishima's imagination reached such powerful and complex heights."

The second volume of the tetralogy, *Homma* (translated by Gallagher as *Runaway Horses*), centers on Isao, a reincarnation of the tragic young aristocrat Kiyoaki of *Spring Snow*. Isao leads an abortive demonstration much like Mishima's own, and in the end dies as Mishima did. A further reincarnation of Kiyoaki figures in *The Temple of the Dawn*, which opens in Bangkok just before World War II and continues in India and Japan, ending in the early 1950s as Japan recovers from her defeat on a wave of gross materialism. Reviewers showed somewhat less enthusiasm for the third volume than for the first two, but a verdict on the tetralogy awaited the appearance of *The Decay of the Angel*, scheduled for publication in 1974.

Kawabata said that Mishima's was "the kind of genius that comes along perhaps once every three hundred years." Many critics who would regard that as excessive might agree with a writer in the *Times Literary Supplement* who said that "his vitality, his capacity to tell a story and to evoke atmosphere, his insight into the seamier or less rational sides of human character, and his architectonic style made him a writer of great importance not only in Japan but also in the literature of the modern world."

PRINCIPAL WORKS IN ENGLISH TRANSLATION: *Fiction*—The Sound of Waves, 1956; Confessions of a Mask, 1958; The Temple of the Golden Pavilion, 1959; After the Banquet, 1963; The Sailor Who Fell from Grace with the Sea, 1965; Death in Midsummer (stories), 1966; Forbidden Colors, 1968; Thirst for Love, 1969; Spring Snow, 1972; Runaway Horses, 1973; The Temple of the Dawn, 1973. *Plays*—Twilight Sunflower, 1958; Five Modern No Plays, 1958; Madame de Sade, 1967. *Nonfiction*—Sun and Steel, 1971; (as ed. with Geoffrey Bownas) New Writing in Japan, 1973.

ABOUT: Penguin Companion to Literature 4, 1969. *Periodicals*—Nation August 15, 1959; September 27, 1965; New Republic June 30, 1966; New York Review of Books June 17, 1971; New York Times November 26, 27, 28, 1970; December 16, 1970; January 25, 1971; New York Times Book Review January 3, 1971; New York Times Magazine August 2, 1970; New Yorker June 20, 1959; June 15, 1968; Times Literary Supplement March 12, 1971.

MITFORD, JESSICA (LUCY) (September 11, 1917–), Anglo-American memoirist, social commentator, and journalist, was born at Batsford Mansion, Gloucester, one of the six remarkable daughters of David and Sydney (Bowles) Mitford, Lord and Lady Redesdale (there was also one son). Jessica Mitford and her sisters grew up under Spartan conditions in Swinbrook, a large cold house in the Cotswolds. The girls were scantily educated at home by their mother and by a succession of ill-chosen governesses, the most popular of whom initiated the children into the art of shoplifting.

Cloistered in Swinbrook, the Mitford girls escaped during childhood into a fantasy world centered upon a secret society, the "Society of Hons," and a private language, "Boudledidge." It was the first manifestation of a rebellious streak which was later to bring them regularly into the world's headlines. Nancy Mitford described this absurd growing up in her novel *The Pursuit of Love*, and Jessica Mitford has given a more direct account of it in her memoir *Daughters and Rebels*.

Outside Swinbrook, England during the Depression was wracked by political movements of an extremity which the "Hons" found irresistible: the swastikas incised painstakingly into the windows by Unity were matched by Jessica's hammers and sickles. As the girls grew up, these games took on an ugly reality: Unity went to Nazi Germany, and Diana married Sir Oswald Mosley, leader of the British Fascists. Jessica herself made an opposite gesture. In 1936, when she was nineteen, she met Esmond Romilly, her second cousin and a nephew of Winston Churchill. Romilly was going to Spain to fight with the International Brigade, and Jessica ran away with him. They were married in Spain, against much parental opposition, in 1937.

Her first marriage was brief and hectic. She and her husband scraped a living in Spain for a while as war correspondents, then did a variety of odd jobs in France and England until they went to the United States in February 1939. There they sold stockings from door to door in Washington, D.C., ran a bar in Miami, and planned elaborate fortune-making schemes that never came to anything. When the war began, Esmond Romilly enlisted in the Royal Canadian Air Force and eventually returned to England. He was killed in action against the Luftwaffe in November 1941.

His widow, left behind in Washington, was at that time pregnant with her second child, the first having died in infancy. After her daughter Constancia was born, Jessica Mitford supported them both in a succession of jobs, including one with the Office of Price Administration (1941–1943). In June 1943 she married a Hungarian-born OPA lawyer named Robert Treuhaft, by whom she has a son, Benjamin. In 1944 she became an American citizen. The family has lived since 1947 in Oakland, California.

During the 1940s and 1950s, Jessica Mitford was "rather occupied" with the upbringing of her two children and with volunteer work for civil rights organizations. It was not until she was thirty-eight that she began to write, at first magazine articles as "Decca Treuhaft," and then her memoir *Daughters and Rebels*, which established her reputation at once. Her account of life at Swinbrook delighted most critics, though some found the second half of the book, about her life with Romilly, somewhat superficial in its approach to the personal and political tragedies of those years. The consensus was that *Daughters and Rebels* was an "objective, humorous and vividly evocative book," at times reminiscent of an early Evelyn Waugh novel, which brought a whole generation back to life.

The American Way of Death, an attack upon "the whole ghoulish paraphernalia of the death trade" in the United States, was even more successful, though it produced violent reactions from the nation's funeral directors. Miss Mitford's interest in the subject had been aroused by her lawyer-husband's anger at the depletion of small estates by grossly inflated funeral costs—the ways in which undertakers played upon grief and family feeling to sell their frequently grotesque products and services. Her book, the fruit of much research, was thought by most critics too long and repetitious, but was welcomed for its astonishing revelations and for its wit and literary grace. Like *Daughters and Rebels*, it was a best seller.

The Trial of Dr. Spock, Miss Mitford's first-hand account of the 1968 prosecution of the "Boston Five," seemed to many readers excessively biased in favor of the defendants, but was generally praised as a spirited description of the process by which Benjamin Spock and three of his co-defendants were convicted of "conspiracy to counsel, aid and abet violations of the Selective Service Act"—even though they were scarcely acquainted with each other and had never made a secret of their antiwar activities. (The convictions were subsequently overturned by a Court of Appeals). *Kind and Usual Punishment* is an intensely disturbing investigation of the United States prison system, in which, she says, the euphemistic jargon of "correctional therapeutics" masks an outrageous exploitation and psychological degradation of prisoners. In September 1973 Jessica Mitford began a new career as Distinguished Professor of Sociology at San Jose State University, California. Her appointment was opposed by some because she had been listed by the House Internal Security Committee as an "undesirable" campus speaker. A series of conflicts followed. Miss Mitford reluctantly complied with the state law requiring her to sign an oath of allegiance to the constitutions of the United States and California, but refused to be fingerprinted, and was dismissed. At the end of 1973 she was still teaching, cheerfully determined to fight in the courts for the right to serve out her contract.

JESSICA MITFORD

PRINCIPAL WORKS: Daughters and Rebels (England, Hons and Rebels), 1960; The American Way of Death, 1963; The Trial of Dr. Spock, 1969; Kind and Usual Punishment: The Prison Business, 1973.

ABOUT: Contemporary Authors 2, 1963; Newquist, R. (ed.) Counterpoint, 1965; Who's Who in America, 1972–1973; Who's Who of American Women, 1972–1973. *Periodicals*—Life July 18, 1960; National Review October 22, 1963; New York Times October 12, 1973; New Yorker July 16, 1960; Publishers Weekly October 1, 1973; Saturday Review August 31, 1963; Sunday Times July 1, 1973; Time June 20, 1960; Times (London) January 14, 1973.

MITTELHOLZER, EDGAR (AUSTIN) (December 16, 1909–May 6, 1965), who "blazed the way for the younger generation" of West Indian novelists, was born in New Amsterdam, British Guiana, the first of the four children of William and Rosamond (Leblanc) Mittelholzer. His father came of an old British Guiana family of Swiss-German origin; his mother was a Creole. Although both parents had some slave blood, they were of "European" appearance and "good family." They enjoyed middle-class status in a mongrel society which was a pathetic parody of the conventions and snobbery of Edwardian England. Mittelholzer, born a "swarthy boy," was early aware of his negrophobe father's disappointment in him. He was raised in genteel poverty, harshly disciplined and ludicrously overprotected. This disastrous childhood left him with a certain romantic intensity and a violent temper, but he was nevertheless a good student at a series of private schools and the Berbice High School.

Mittelholzer wrote his first story at the age of

EDGAR MITTELHOLZER

twelve and, five years later, when he left school, had already decided on a literary career. But, though he sold his first article at nineteen, more than twenty years were to pass before he earned his living as a writer. Meanwhile he began to pay his way as a customs officer, sales clerk, meteorological observer, and freelance journalist and in a variety of other casual occupations.

In 1941 his first novel, *Corentyne Thunder*, had its inconspicuous publication in England. The same year Mittelholzer left British Guiana to enlist in the Trinidad Royal Naval Volunteer Reserve. After the war, in 1948, he settled in England. He worked for four years in the British Council's books department, and thereafter supported himself as a full-time writer.

Mittelholzer made his name with his second novel, *Morning in Trinidad* (1950), which examined, with compassionate amusement and a wry sense of Caribbean history, the racial and sexual drives that propel the staff of a Trinidad office through the mild exigencies of a single morning.

Shadows Move Among Them (1951) confirmed Mittelholzer's reputation. It was set in a remote jungle village in British Guiana where a British "missionary" had created a kind of hedonistic utopia. The book evoked a bizarre society with an exact and formal wit which reminded some critics of Voltaire, and contained descriptive writing of great beauty. It succeeded both as a moral satire and as highly original entertainment. In 1953 it was dramatized and produced on Broadway by Moss Hart as *The Climate of Eden.*

Mittelholzer had his greatest popular success with a much inferior novel, *Children of Kaywana* (1952). This was a lewd and brutal historical romance about the days of slavery in British Guiana, built around a singularly unsavory dynasty of Dutch planters. Their story was continued in *Hubertus* (1955) and *Old Blood* (1958).

A prolific writer, Mittelholzer never lost his mesmeric powers of narration and characterization, nor his extraordinary talent for giving convincing life to a bizarre and exotic background. But he never again achieved the literary distinction of *Shadows Move Among Them.* The freshness of vision which distinguished his first books became tainted by an apparently compulsive obsession with sex and sadism, and by a growing preoccupation with the occult. His precise and lucid prose became slack and labored or, at worst, falsely poetic. Towards the end of his life, Mittelholzer sometimes had difficulty in finding a publisher.

In his last novel, *The Jilkington Drama* (1965), Mittelholzer returned to the theme of suicide which had engaged him in several earlier works. A powerful and frightening book—one of the best of his last years—it centers on Garvin Jilkington's conscious deterioration, through personal tragedy and occultism, to madness; and his suicide by fire. A month before it appeared, Mittelholzer burned himself to death in a wood near his Surrey home.

Mittelholzer was survived by his wife, the former Jacqueline Pointer. He had a son by her and four children by his earlier marriage to Roma Erica Halfhide. Mittelholzer was a talented amateur painter who liked walking, observing the weather, and listening to Wagner. In 1963 he published a first volume of autobiography and called it *A Swarthy Boy*.

According to his obituary in *The Times*, Mittelholzer "opened the pyrotechnic display of West Indian writers. . . . He himself was uniquely conscious, in the mixture of his European and African blood, through centuries of Guianese history, of being the heir of the past and the testator of the future." He was a writer of great originality.

PRINCIPAL WORKS: Corentyne Thunder, 1941; Morning in Trinidad (England, A Morning at the Office), 1950; Shadows Move Among Them, 1951; Children of Kaywana, 1952; The Weather in Middenshot, 1953; The Life and Death of Sylvia, 1954; Hubertus (England, The Harrowing of Hubertus), 1955; My Bones and My Flute, 1955; Of Trees and the Sea, 1956; A Tale of Three Places, 1957; Old Blood (England, Kaywana Blood), 1958; The Weather Family, 1958; With a Carib Eye, 1958; A Tinkling in the Twilight, 1959; Latticed Echoes, 1960; Eltonsbrody, 1960; Thunder Returning, 1961; The Piling of Clouds, 1961; The Wounded and the Worried, 1962; The Mad MacMullochs, 1963; Uncle Paul, 1963; A Swarthy Boy, 1963; The Aloneness of Mrs. Chatham, 1965; The Jilkington Drama, 1965.

ABOUT: Mittelholzer, E. A Swarthy Boy, 1963. *Periodicals*—Publishers' Weekly May 17, 1965; Times (London) May 7, 1965.

***MOBERG, (CARL ARTHUR) VILHELM** (August 20, 1898–August 8, 1973), Swedish novelist and dramatist, wrote: "I was born in a soldier's cottage as the fourth child out of seven. My father was a soldier, my grandfather had been a soldier and as long as I can remember there had been soldiers in my family. Soldiering then was socially well considered, but I soon noticed that life for farmers at that time was hard in Sweden, that the struggle for food was a struggle between life and death. With my grandmother I had a marvellous friendship: she told me over and over again stories of her childhood, her life as a soldier's wife, etc., which meant more than I can say for my future career as an author. From the age of nine I worked on the farm. But my desire to learn was great and I read everything I could find.

"Conditions in my childhood and the unjust treatment of farmers taught me what was right and what was wrong; something that has been a very important thing for me ever since. At eleven I came in contact with the labour party and joined it, hoping that their new and revolutionary ideas would bring a better world.

"During this time writing became a necessity for me. I dreamt of being an author, a dream which I thought never would become a reality. I regarded myself as a complete failure.

"After having studied for some years at a people's high school and after numerous different jobs I became a trainee-journalist on a newspaper. This was a different kind of job: here my imagination could work freely. The editor encouraged me in my writing, which meant a lot for my self-confidence. Later I became sub-editor of another newspaper and then editor, learning the newspaper business in its entirety.

"My contact with the theatre has always been important for me: I discovered more and more that it was through the drama that I could best express my political, social and psychological ideas. I started to form an imaginary stage in my mind with imaginary persons acting for me. The success of one of these plays made it possible for me to finance my first book.

"In the years before the Second World War I experienced the pressure on people, when Hitler was terrorizing the Jews and later the whole world, as a frightful nightmare. As writing has always been my way of expressing my feelings, I started the book *Ride This Night!*, with its conflict between power and right; its message to those of any century who are murdered and tortured by dictators was: 'The fiery cross is out. Ride this night!' The book was published in 1941. Of course the book's meaning was clear to the Nazi regime and accordingly it was confiscated—this I regard as the greatest reward I ever got for any book.

* mōō′ bery′

VILHELM MOBERG

"The destiny of those of my parents' relatives who had emigrated to America—a land which for me, in my childish fancy, meant '*mer rika*' [more rich]—had always fascinated me. As the years passed I had often asked myself what became of those who emigrated. I started to make investigations, in parish registers and by letters, and so the book *The Emigrants* slowly began to grow. But the investigations and the research work were time-consuming; it took me twelve years to write the book. I studied the port of departure and how life was lived on board an emigrant sailing ship. In spring 1948 I visited the United States for the first time on an emigrant's visa, in order to study and to complete the work. There I was able to collect materials about the emigrants, on tombstones, in diaries, etc., and I asked myself: How would my characters develop in their new homeland? With four years of looking for materials, I knew that I could complete the emigrant epic.

"My books have been translated into twenty languages.

"My last book, *A Time on Earth*, is a portrayal of a man's desire to live and his fear of death, his inability to grasp it but gradually increasing acceptance of it.

"I don't consider authorship as a profession but rather as a way of life which also makes it possible to protest against injustices. Without being able to write and to protest, I do not think I could exist."

Vilhelm Moberg was born in Algutsboda in the province of Småland, where according to the traditional Swedish system his father, Karl Moberg, combined soldiering with crofting. Nearly all

Moberg's work is concerned with the peasants of Småland, a stubborn race molded by a harsh way of life in a barren province: "They are *my* people!" he once declared. However, Moberg's earliest passion was for books, not farming, and he left the land to try journalism and writing.

His breakthrough came with the novel *Raskens* (The Rask Family, 1927), the story of an ambitious young farmhand who acquires a soldier's croft, marries a stalwart peasant girl, and builds up his farm and his family. While the novel is a zestful tale about particular individuals, it is at the same time a vivid piece of social history, describing the vicissitudes of peasant life in the nineteenth century. Moberg dealt with more contemporary matters in *Långt från landsvägen* (Far from the Highway, 1929) and *De knutna händerna* (The Clenched Hands, 1930), novels in which industrialization and the call of the city are shown undermining the traditional way of life of the peasant. The tragic hero of the novels, deeply rooted in the soil, refuses to yield either to his own or to his community's fate, for Moberg's highly individualistic characters are not given to compromise. Alrik Gustafson comments of these early novels that "there is honesty in Moberg's picture, and at times flashes of hauntingly sombre beauty, of genuine poetic insight. . . . But detail piles up into almost unmanageable masses, and the shadows lie so deep, so seldom relieved by light, that we tend to grow restive under the gloomy monotony of it all."

After *Man's kvinna* (Man's Woman, 1933), an attack on conventional attitudes toward sex in the form of a historical novel, Moberg returned to contemporary agricultural problems and achieved his first major success with the Knut Toring trilogy: *Sänkt sedebetyg* (Lowered Mark for Conduct, 1935), *Sömnlös* (Sleepless, 1937), and *Giv oss jorden* (Give Us the Earth, 1939). The three novels were translated by E. Björkman and published in one volume as *The Earth Is Ours*. Knut Toring, of Småland peasant origin, is a successful Stockholm journalist who comes to see the emptiness of urban civilization and returns to his native village. Life there has changed, but he involves himself with growing satisfaction in communal concerns, cooperatives, the back-to-the-soil youth movement. It is only in the final chapters that he comes to see that a confession of faith in life on the land is not enough in the face of events in Europe, and becomes a passionate advocate of resistance to Nazism.

Moberg's profound involvement in the Second World War, and his contempt for his government's neutrality, is very evident in *Rid i natt!* (1941, translated by H. Alexander as *Ride This Night!*), ostensibly about a peasants' revolt against oppressive (German) overlords in seventeenth century Småland. As noted above by Moberg, the Nazis understood the contemporary parallels, yet the historical background is convincingly portrayed. This novel marked a change in Moberg's style, which became less leisurely and sweeping, more spare and angular. "Swedish literature possesses very few historical novels with such an effective combination of documentary truth and poetic illusion," one critic wrote, and Moberg's talent for presenting social history in highly readable novel form is further illustrated by the autobiographical novel *Soldat med brutet gevär* (Soldier With Broken Rifle, 1944), the story of the growing up of a soldier's son and his experiences and political development with various left-wing groups. The book was condensed and translated by G. Lannestock as *When I Was a Child*.

Moberg's masterpiece is undoubtedly his tetralogy about American immigration: *Utvandrarna* (1949, translated by G. Lannestock as *The Emigrants*), *Invandrarna* (1952, translated by G. Lannestock as *Unto a Good Land*), and the two volumes abridged and translated together as *The Last Letter Home*, *Nybyggarna* (1956) and *Sista brevet till Sverige* (1959). It is the story of a little group of emigrants from one poor Småland parish. The characters' motives for emigrating, their experiences, their reactions, are all meant to be typical of those of a million other Swedish immigrants in the nineteenth century, yet they do not lose their individuality. The hero of this detailed and historically conscientious epic, the stubborn and unyielding Karl Oskar, is a farmer-pioneer who assumes almost mythical stature, but the author is careful to balance him with his brother Robert, a dreamer and visionary, who chooses not the farmlands of Minnesota but the adventures of the California Trail. The tetralogy has been filmed.

It has been remarked that Moberg in these novels labored too heavily the theme of American freedom versus European idealism, and idealized conditions in the United States a century ago. The balance is to some extent redressed in *Din stund på jorden* (1963, translated as *A Time on Earth*), a lyrical pendant to the tetralogy in which an old Swedish immigrant in California looks back over his life. Here, though Moberg's indignation at the narrowness, poverty, and exploitation of life in Småland is unabated, he brings an intensity of feeling to his account of that harsh land which makes the ease and comfort of California seem soft and trivial by comparison.

Moberg's novels are earthy and racy, and his style traditional and unsophisticated. His books have been best sellers in Sweden and are generally admired elsewhere, though some reviewers of the English translations have found them heavy going in their "plodding accretion of detail." He also proved to be one of the most popular of modern Swedish dramatists, with stage versions of his novels, like *Mans kvinna* (staged in 1943 and translated as *Fulfilment*); with scenes from peasant life, such as *Hustrun* (The Wife, 1928); with problem plays like *Vår ofödde son* (Our Unborn Son, 1945); and with political satires such as *Domaren* (The Judge, 1957). Moberg's political involvement was also reflected in journalism and pamphleteering against the monarchy, the secret police, and corruption in the judiciary. He collected some autobiographical sketches in *Berättelser ur min levnad* (Stories from My Life, 1968).

Moberg died shortly before his seventy-fifth birthday in a drowning accident at his summer home north of Stockholm. In the 1970s he had begun a four-volume history of the ordinary people of Sweden; two volumes were completed and have been translated by Paul Britten Austin.

PRINCIPAL WORKS IN ENGLISH TRANSLATION: The Earth Is Ours, 1940; Ride This Night!, 1943; The Emigrants, 1951; Fulfilment (play), 1953; Unto a Good Land, 1954; When I Was a Child, 1956; The Last Letter Home, 1961; A Time on Earth, 1965; A History of the Swedish People: vols. 1 and 2, 1973.

ABOUT: Gustafson, A. A History of Swedish Literature, 1961; International Who's Who, 1971–72; Mårtensson, S. Vilhelm Moberg, 1956; Moberg, V. When I Was a Child, 1956; Penguin Companion to Literature 2, 1969; Platen, M. von (ed.) Emigrationer, 1968; Smith, H. (ed.) Columbia Dictionary of Modern European Literature, 1947. *Periodicals*—American Quarterly Spring 1966; American Scandinavian Review 1942; New York Herald Tribune Book Review July 15, 1951; August 1, 1954; New York Times July 15, 1951; August 1, 1965; New Yorker July 28, 1951; July 17, 1965; Saturday Review July 28, 1951; July 31, 1954; July 10, 1965; Scandinavian Studies 3 1962, February 1966, August 1968; Times Literary Supplement August 12, 1965.

MOLINARI, RICARDO E. (March 20, 1898–), Argentinian poet, was born in Buenos Aires. His education was limited to primary and secondary school, and beyond that he is largely self-taught. His first poems appeared in the review *Inicial* (1923–1925) and he was one of the ultraist writers associated with the review *Martín Fierro*, whose contributors included Jorge Luis Borges, González Lanuza, Marechal, Norah Lange, Bernárdez, and Mastronardi. His first book, *Il imaginero* (The Religious Painter), appeared in 1927 and was warmly praised by Borges, who was at that time Molinari's principal mentor. A visit to Spain and Portugal in 1933 was profoundly important in Molinari's development, and led to his friendship with García Lorca, Vicente Aleixandre, Rafael Alberti, and other poets. He refers often to this experience in his poetry, remembering Spain as "the meadow of the days, now alas dark."

The small books of verse which Molinari published during the 1920s and 1930s reflect an assortment of influences. His earliest work was in the ultraist manner—laconic free verse, stripped of transitions and decorative adjectives, relying for its effect on a few striking metaphors. French symbolism, English and German romanticism, and the strict forms of seventeenth century Spanish verse, as well as a number of contemporary poets, have all influenced his work, which in its eclectic lyricism as well as in its metaphysical concerns is very much in the *modernista* tradition.

RICARDO E. MOLINARI

Selections from Molinari's earlier books made up the major collection published in 1943 as *Mundos de la madrugada* (Worlds of the Dawn). Here it could be seen that Molinari had developed from his experiments what J. M. Cohen called "a long and finely cadenced *vers libre*, alternating with fixed forms based on the seventeenth-century sonnet and the traditional poetry of the Spanish songbooks. These two modes of writing have gradually been pulled together to build up sequences of varying mood, similar, though on a smaller scale, to T. S. Eliot's in his *Four Quartets*."

Cohen, who places Molinari with Vallejo, Neruda, and Octavio Paz as one of the four great Spanish American poets of the century, has called him an exile in his native land. Molinari's Argentina is a vast empty landscape, unpopulated and abandoned, where the poet wanders alone, mourning his friends in Europe and a lost love: "I am living on in the stormy south; where the dust entirely covers the leaves, and salt bites the hopeless root; where the rivers bear to the sea a rough earth through which the grasses no longer push up, and only the winds sway. The abandoned South! (Where no one can take from me the perfume of a mouth that I bear adhering to my lips.)"

God as well as man is absent from this timeless land, but the poet remains, hoping against all reason that the voice he listens for will break the silence—knowing that such a voice can only be heard in such a silence. Cohen calls this poetry "a religious poetry of the dark night of the senses," but also "the history of a heart that feels itself at one with the great processes of nature."

Of all the poets of his generation in Argentina, Molinari is the one most respected by the young. In 1940 an avant-garde group of young poets protested because he had not been awarded the national poetry prize, and he received that honor in 1957 for the book *Unida noche*. According to *International Who's Who* (1972–73), he has now received every Argentinian poetry prize.

PRINCIPAL WORKS IN ENGLISH TRANSLATION: *Poems in* Caracciolo-Trejo, E. (ed.) Penguin Book of Latin-American Verse, 1971; Cohen, J. M. (ed.) Penguin Book of Spanish Verse, 1956; Cohen, J. M. Poetry of This Age, 1966; Cohen, J. M. (ed.) Latin American Writing Today, 1967.

ABOUT: Anderson-Imbert, E. Spanish-American Literature, 1963; Arístides, J. Ricardo E. Molinari o la agonía del ser en el tiempo, 1966; Cohen, J. M. Poetry of This Age, 1966; Enciclopedia universal ilustrada (Apendice), 1932; Gamo, J. M. A. Tres poetas Argentinas, 1951; Ghiano, J. C. Poesía Argentina del siglo XX, 1957; Historia de la literatura Argentina, vol. IV and VI, 1959 and 1960; International Who's Who, 1972–73.

MONTAGU, LADY ELIZABETH (July 4, 1917–), English novelist and short story writer, writes: "I was born in London. My father, George Charles Montagu, Earl of Sandwich, was an English aristocrat. My mother, Alberta Sturges, was an American whose family came from Chicago. I was the fourth and the youngest child. I was brought up in the family home, Hinchingbrooke, in Huntingdonshire, and in London where my grandmother always had a house. Until the age of twelve I was privately educated. Among the many people who tried to teach my rebellious, unconcentrated and imaginative mind, one stands out forever in my memory—Margery Strachey—sister to Lytton Strachey. To her I owe my passion for literature and my desire and curiosity for intellectual truth which has been both the whip and the carrot in my career as a writer.

"At the age of twelve I was sent to a boarding school—North Foreland Lodge—in Kent. There I stayed for four years showing no particular aptitude for anything save games. At the age of sixteen therefore, academically a dead loss, I was sent to be polished off first in Paris and later to Munich. I learnt French but loved the Germans—those whom I knew. A year later I was presented to King Edward VIII at a Royal Garden Party at Buckingham Palace and that, my parents imagined, was presumably that. I was equipped apparently. But for what?

ELIZABETH MONTAGU

"For two years I played the English Upper Class Game. I rode to hounds, attended all the right things in the right places at the right time of year. I drove fast cars fast, learned to pilot an aeroplane, danced all night.

"But unfortunately I had read too much—Dostoievsky for one—and it had become a habit. I couldn't stop. And none of the people I associated with had ever heard of Freud. I longed to be an intellectual and I couldn't make it, so I did the next best thing. I fell in love with the President of the Oxford Union and his university life became mine. It was the year of the Spanish Civil War and a great many of my men friends went to fight in it while I fretted and pottered, continued to take violent exercise, voted socialist and, privately eaten by boredom, prayed for war.

"Immediately after the Munich crisis I joined the Red Cross Society and went to work in the central office in London where I licked stamps and hid in air raid shelters until war was declared. Then I drove an ambulance until promoted to a desk where throughout the Blitz I sat beside Dame Beryl Oliver D.B.E., trying to move an infuriated Matron from one Military Hospital to another.

"I was only twenty-two and this seemed to me an undignified way of spending a war. I wanted action stations. But there was only one way out of that high powered office—to nurse. I signed on at St. Thomas's Hospital in 1941 and except for a six-month interval which I spent at Queen Charlotte's Hospital taking the first part of my C.M.B., I stayed there until 1947, when I left for family reasons.

"It was at this point that I began seriously to write.

"For five years I wrote before anything was

accepted. I wrote two novels and I cannot remember how many articles and short stories. I lived in Stratford-on-Avon in a house inherited from my grandmother and belonging (it is reputed) to Shakespeare's daughter. After I sold this I moved to London. Later there was a farm in Dorset for ten years. But always London.

"Finally in 1953 *Waiting for Camilla,* my third novel, was accepted by Heinemann on the recommendation of Graham Greene. It had a cool reception but one generous critic thought that perhaps one day I might learn to write. Encouraging. *The Small Corner* followed in 1955; *This Side of the Truth* in 1957. In 1960 I left England and have been living in the south of France ever since.

"I have been very ill for five years but I am still writing. I have one completed novel which I do not intend to publish yet as I am a perfectionist and it does not please me. I am at work at the moment on another. No book of criticism has ever, to my knowledge, appeared about my work. I have been translated into French and into Swedish. These are the bare bones.

"Apart from fiction (and poetry to amuse myself) I have never touched journalism of any kind. A book review from time to time. Now not even that. What do I do now when I am not writing? Walk about. Talk to people and think about the blank page."

Waiting for Camilla had a warmer critical reception than Elizabeth Montagu suggests. It is Camilla's dying sister and her assembled family who are waiting for her, and as they wait each of them thinks of Camilla, revealing themselves as much as her in what they remember. It was thought that "the rhythmic construction makes a definite unity of the whole story" and the novel was praised also for its detachment and searching characterization. "The small corner" of Elizabeth Montagu's second novel is the restricted world of the dangerously unhappy narrator, secretary to a successful surgeon, "who is never able to feel the truth of what she observes," and whose steady retreat from sanity is conveyed with great delicacy.

In *This Side of the Truth* the teenage narrator—a puzzled witness caught between innocence and awareness—describes "an adult drama of sexual attraction, vanity and egotism" and unwittingly precipitates the tragedy she had sought to avert. The book was recognized as a "beautifully written" *tour de force* in which "the characters grow, gradually and completely, without ever moving out of the scope of the child's-eye view." The short stories collected in *Change* were thought of mixed quality, but include at least one unqualified success in "Madame Del Vas," an example of the author's "most impressive vein: tense, terse presentation of a mood of suspended menace, waiting for the thunder to break."

Lady Elizabeth Montagu is a socialist and an agnostic. She collects furniture and modern paintings. Though she has published little she has made a place for herself among the finer English women novelists of her generation, valued in particular for her "outstanding grasp of character."

PRINCIPAL WORKS: *Novels*—Waiting for Camilla, 1953; The Small Corner, 1955; This Side of the Truth, 1957. *Short stories*—Change, 1966.
ABOUT: Contemporary Authors 11–12, 1965.

MONTAGUE, JOHN (PATRICK) (February 28, 1929–), Irish poet, story writer, and critic writes: "I was born in Brooklyn in the Depression, a suitably grim combination of time and place. Both my parents were Ulster Catholics; my father left after the Treaty which created the Six Counties and my mother joined him in 1928, with my two elder brothers. She found life terrible in the America of the period (my swift arrival did not help) and soon decided to ship the children home. My brothers returned to her mother but I was sent to my father's home, to be reared by his two spinster sisters. I have often wondered whether it was my father's wish, or my grandmother's unwillingness to harbor another young child, but that separation was crucial. Although my brothers (and later, my mother) lived eight miles away, I rarely saw them. My memories of America faded to a few jangling images: I had been transplanted into a simple rural background, a ramshackle farm without water or light, a country school, days working in the field or bog.

"But if I had been whirled backwards in time, the key to return was also given, because Garvaghey (Gaelic for The Rough Field) was a branch library and post office, as well as the remains of a large farm. A precocious bookworm, I began to move away from the valley, on a treadmill of scholarships. The first brought me to Armagh College, under the shadow of the cathedral. My aunts probably hoped I would become a Jesuit or a cardinal but five years of dawn mass, Gaelic games and benediction did not discover a firm vocation. Instead I chose the laburnum groves of Ranelagh, leading to University College, Dublin.

"My later life has extended, in ever widening circles, to bring me back to the contemporary world into which I was born. I found I liked Dublin very much, its fogs and pubs; more important still, I discovered a gift for poetry, which seemed to heal all the confusions of my background. My poems were broadcast and published while I was still at the university, and after graduation, I plunged into Dublin journalistic and literary life.

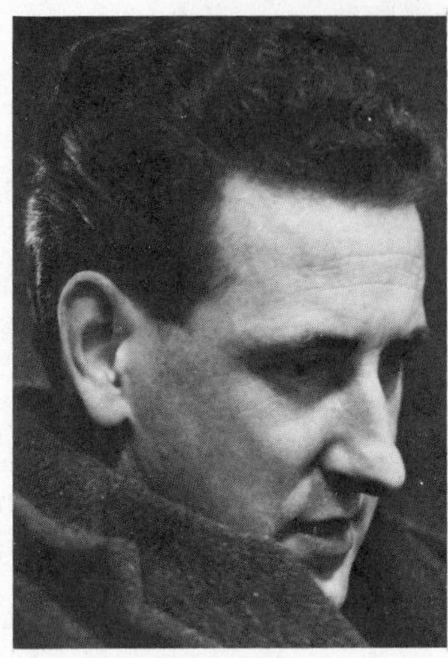

JOHN MONTAGUE

"I feel strongly that becoming a writer (like becoming a real person) is very much a matter of discovering one's own voice. There are always surface excitements and fashions, but the only struggle worth while is to uncover one's own subjects, expressed in rhythms instinctive to one's nature. For instance, although I came to poetry through Hopkins, I soon found out that my reaction to words was not as immediately sensuous: I prefer a bleaker style, like a mountain stream over gravel. A disappearing rural life, religious and political tension, the effort to love: one's subjects are not so much chosen as that they chose one, making poetry an attempt to chart the secret progress of one's life. When the experience seems too detailed, I turn to prose, which has the additional after-effect of purifying my impulse in poetry.

"Once committed (the pun seems no accident), the only relevant biography is one's work. I could say that I was surprised at how long it took me to publish my first book; I left Dublin in dismay in 1953 and only got back to writing well when I returned, three years later. My early work seems to me intensely Irish, almost a duty laid upon me by my background. But as that is whittled away, I feel less separate: now when I fly back from Paris to my aunt's funeral, I can see little difference between the road to Le Bourget and the new motorway out of Belfast. The old Ireland I knew is going: and I feel as much at home in Montparnasse, where I live, or San Francisco where I sometimes go to earn money teaching, as in Dublin. Though I still feel a kinship with the Irish writers of my generation, and an almost physical passion for what is left of the Irish countryside."

John Montague's critics have not bettered his own account of his work. His subjects—"a disappearing rural life, religious and political tension, the effort to love"—are expressed in a style as lucid and astringent as "a mountain stream over gravel"; and with a cool sympathy that reminds reviewers of Montague's principal mentor, Austin Clarke. Another comparison often made is with R. S. Thomas, who witnesses the achievements of tourism and technology in rural Wales with a bleak, intelligent regret much like that which Montague brings to the same phenomena in Ireland.

Montague calls often on Irish legend and history, as in the elegiac "A Footnote on Monasticism" and the witty "First Invasion of Ireland" in *Poisoned Lands*. He can turn as readily, in the same collection, to a sardonically sympathetic portrait of an Irish laborer swallowed up in a British industrial city ("Murphy in Manchester") or an affectionate evocation of the "marine light" of Dublin on a "rainy quiet evening."

The restraint and technical orthodoxy of these first poems has continued to characterize Montague's verse, but his subsequent work also includes experiments that show his understanding of the innovations in diction and rhythm of William Carlos Williams and the Black Mountain poets. At times moreover there rings through his later collections a new note—darker, stranger, more lyrical and sensuous—as in some powerfully moving poems of marital love, and the oddly affecting "In Dedication": "My love, while we talked/They removed the roof. Then/They started on the walls,/Panes of glass uprooting/From timber, like teeth./But you spoke calmly on,/Your example of courtesy/Compelling me to reply. . . ." Already generally recognized as one of the most accomplished of his generation of Irish poets, his most recent work shows him still developing both in technical virtuosity and emotional range.

The stories in *Death of a Chieftain* explore the strain of violence in the Irish temperament, the particular problems of the Irish intellectual, and other regional themes with the unheated compassion of the exile. "A Change of Management" satirizes big business, and "The Occasion of Sin" reminded one reviewer of Joyce's "The Dead." Montague's stories resemble his poems in their restrained elegance of style and the acuteness of the author's ear for dialect and dialogue.

In his three years of journalism between 1950 and 1953 Montague became a noted film critic for the Dublin *Standard*. He received his B.A. (1949) and his M.A. (1952) at University College, Dublin, studied at Yale as a Fulbright Scholar, and earned his M.F.A. at the State University of Iowa in 1955. From 1956 to 1961 he worked for the State Tourist Board, Dublin. Since then he has taught at Berkeley, at University College, Dublin, and at the Experimental University of Vincennes, and has served as the Paris correspondent of the *Irish Times*. Montague is a Member of the Irish Academy of Letters. His wife is the former Madelaine de Brauer.

PRINCIPAL WORKS: *Poetry*—Forms of Exile, 1958; Poisoned Lands, 1961; All Legendary Obstacles, 1966; A Chosen Light, 1967; Tides, 1970; The Rough Field, 1972. *Fiction*—Death of a Chieftain, 1964.

ABOUT: Murphy, R. (ed.) Contemporary Poets of the English Language, 1970; Rosenthal, M. L. The New Poets, 1967. *Periodicals*—Critique November 1965; Guardian October 6, 1964; Irish Times November 11, 1961; Lettres Nouvelles Spring 1966; Studies 1966; Times Literary Supplement November 9, 1967.

EUGENIO MONTALE

***MONTALE, EUGENIO** (October 12, 1896–), one of the greatest Italian poets of this century, was born and educated in Genoa. That city, and the neighboring Ligurian coast, pervade his poetry. Montale is the son of Domenico and Giuseppina (Ricci) Montale. His father, an unimaginative businessman, expected him to take over the family business, but Montale himself wanted to become an opera singer and disregarded his commercial studies to take singing lessons. His ambitions were frustrated by the outbreak of World War I, during which he served from 1915 to 1918 as an infantry officer. There are relatively few references to this experience in his verse, though he cannot have been unaffected by his involvement in the death struggle of nineteenth century optimism.

Montale had been introduced to modern poetry by his friend Camillo Sbarbaro and after the war, though he entered his father's business, he was able to give most of his time to his literary education. Genoa was not rich in intellectual circles, but Montale was lucky in his friendships. He came to know two young critics who later became famous, Giacomo Debenedetti and Sergio Solmi, and in 1922 founded with them the short-lived but distinguished review *Primo tempo*. He met Piero Gobetti, the leading anti-Fascist writer of Turin (later to die a victim of Mussolini) and contributed to his magazine *Il Baretti*.

Another friend, Roberto Bazlen, introduced Montale to the works of Italo Svevo, and at this point the family business proved helpful, since Svevo owned a similar business in Trieste. This led to a friendship, to a correspondence which is now famous, and to Montale's first important literary work, an essay on Svevo published in 1925 which did much to establish the latter's reputation in Italy. The same year, Montale's first book of poems, *Ossi di seppia* (Cuttlefish Bones), was published in Turin by his friend Gobetti.

Montale's distinctive tone and manner emerged at once in this first collection. It appeared at a time when poetry in Italy was struggling to free itself from the rhetorical tradition of Carducci, Pascoli, and D'Annunzio, when the futurists and the *crepuscolari* were both showing themselves incapable of a truly creative solution. Together with Ungaretti, Montale discovered the value of the unadorned word, and of rhythms closer to those of contemporary speech than to the traditional devices of nineteenth century poetry. What Pound and Eliot were doing at that time in English poetry, Ungaretti and Montale did in Italy.

Indeed, the similarity between Montale's poetry and Eliot's (which Montale has translated) is a critical cliché. Their common predilection for dry, desolate, cruel landscapes as a symbol of the human condition, their passion for the sea and "its hints of earlier and other creation," have been much discussed. The comparison should not be given too much weight, however, since the two poets are far apart in essentials both of sound and sense—most obviously in the contrast between Eliot's Christian faith and Montale's deep-rooted pessimism.

Montale says that "having felt, from the day of my birth, a total disharmony with surrounding reality, the matter of my inspiration could hardly be anything else if not that disharmony." At the center of his work is an anguished recognition of the distance between man's spiritual aspiration and his actual condition, bound helplessly to the wheel of life in a "delirium of immobility." Nevertheless, the prevailing images of loneliness, exhaustion, and despair—drawn most often from the harsh and barren landscape of Liguria—are fitfully relieved by mysterious moments of revelation, poignantly elusive intimations of grace. This is so in the most ambitious poem in *Ossi di seppia*, "Arsenio."

* mōn tä′ lē

D. S. Carne-Ross, in an illuminating article on Montale in *New York Review of Books* (October 20, 1966), has given this account of "Arsenio": "It is a showery late summer afternoon as Arsenio walks along the sea-front of an Italian resort. Music is heard (does it come from the smart hotels or is it inside his own head?) and this is the 'signal' for him to go down to the sea where salvation, perhaps, may be found: 'It is perhaps the long-expected moment that may save you from finishing your journey, link of a chain, motionless movement, oh too familiar delirium, Arsenio, of immobility. . . .' The storm breaks, there is a liberating downpour of rain and with a deepening sense of anguish Arsenio, 'trembling with life,' reaches out towards 'a void resonant with muffled lamentation.' But the will is too weak and he is left, paralyzed, amid the 'frozen multitude of the dead.' The moment came, but he was incapable of the 'awful daring' of surrender, and by the last line the new life struggling to birth has been 'strangled.'" This poem, which Carne-Ross speaks of as Montale's *Waste Land*, illustrates very well what Irma Brandeis regards as the outstanding quality of Montale's work, his "ability to convey the abstract through the concrete and personal without destroying the direct suggestive power of the images."

From the beginning, Montale's unique diction, combining colloquialisms with esoteric words, his echoes from other poets, his mastery of rhyme and assonance, alliteration and onomatopoeia, produced a poetry of great richness and density that was at the same time superbly light and musical in its movement. Glauco Cambon has written that "Montale transposed sound onto an inner level, varying rhyme with dissonance, shifting it into the body of the line, where it will exercise a more secret charm, and often seeking in alliteration a sound-unity for the content—a unity to be reconstructed from within, by valuing syllable and consonant to the extent of making them the vertebrae of a poetical organism." These qualities, together with his "cat-like certainty of tread" and a pessimism wholly in tune with the mood of the period, were immediately recognized, and *Ossi di seppia* established Montale as a major figure in postwar Italian poetry. The original (1925) edition of this small book was followed within a few years by two augmented editions.

In 1927 Montale settled in Florence, where the following year he became director of the celebrated Vieusseux library. The post was poorly paid, but it was agreeable to Montale, who enjoyed working in the only library in Italy adequately furnished with contemporary foreign books. Moreover, Florence was at that time a very lively center of the arts, and two of the major Italian literary magazines, *Solaria* and *Letteratura*, were edited there. Montale contributed to them some of his best critical writing, helping to make the work of Eliot, Joyce, Quasimodo, and many other Italian and foreign authors known to Italian readers. During the 1930s Montale's own work became the subject of a number of critical studies, and his reputation spread abroad. In Italy, along with Ungaretti and Quasimodo, he was categorized as a "hermetic" poet, and the Vieusseux Library became a center of that movement. Hermeticism had a marked anti-Fascist flavor which made it unpopular with Mussolini's government; in 1938, when Montale refused to join the Fascist party, he was dismissed from his post.

Le occasioni (The Occasions), his second important collection, appeared in 1939, and shows that his work had indeed become more difficult and private, more hermetic. This development was a contemptuous reaction against the noisy public rhetoric of Fascism, but not only that. Montale had become dissatisfied with the dualism in his earlier poetry between the "occasion" that produced a poem and the poem itself; he wanted to write poems that would "contain their motives without revealing them or at least without blurting them out," and this he achieved in *Le occasioni*. This volume, showing a technical mastery which some critics have compared to Mallarmé's, is full of images which, perfectly clear and often vividly sensuous in themselves, refer to an experience which is never specified. Sometimes the occasion for these brilliant clusters of imagery is a beloved woman, the unidentified "you" who recurs in many of the later poems.

Le occasioni was greeted with almost universal acclaim, which recognized not only Montale's poetic achievement but his stature in Fascist Italy as a dissenter of uncompromising integrity and dignity, a role he sustained throughout World War II and the German Occupation. After the war, in 1947, the leading Italian daily newspaper, *Il corriere della sera*, called Montale to Milan as its literary editor.

His third major collection appeared in 1956: *La bufera e altro* (The Storm and Other Poems). Montale has said that perhaps "Fascism and the war gave to my sense of isolation the alibi it needed," and *La bufera* contains some of the darkest and most despairing of his poems. And yet it also includes a great gesture of affirmation in the poem called "L'anguilla," in which the eel's epic journey from the Atlantic to the rivers and streams of Europe is made a symbol of man's unquenchable lust for life, the "spark that says everything begins when everything seems charred, the buried stump, the brief rainbow." Speaking of the group of poems called "Silvae" in this volume, Carne-Ross says: "I cannot think any sensitive reader . . . could fail to be moved by the formal splendor of these poems, the incomparable language moving in long, beautifully controlled periods; and by the gravity and courage with which the aging poet struggles to come to terms with a lifetime's experience, with his childhood and his landscapes, with his dead and his living."

A fourth volume, *Satura, 1962–1970*, includes work previously published in various limited editions. It is most notable for the "Xenia" poems, written in memory of Montale's wife Drusilla Tanzi, generally known as "La Mosca" (The Fly), who died in 1963. The colloquialism of these poems, claimed by some critics as a new style, seems to others the natural product of their intimate and domestic themes. Their touches of humor and loving irony do nothing to conceal the poet's desolate sense of loss. One English critic called the poems in *Satura* the "minor, painful works of a major poet, but how much better they are than the best efforts of most contemporary poets." Robert Lowell, who has adapted a number of Montale's poems, considers his the most distinctive voice to have emerged in Italian poetry since Leopardi.

Montale's contribution as a critic and translator who has done much to widen the provincial horizons of Italian culture is in itself of the greatest importance, comparable to Croce's achievement at the beginning of the century. Many of his essays have been collected in *Auto-da-fé* (1966), while his translations, mainly from Shakespeare, Eliot, Hopkins, Emily Dickinson, and Melville, were published as *Quaderno di traduzioni* (1948). He has also published a collection of semiautobiographical short stories and prose poems called *La farfalla di Dinard* (1956, expanded edition 1960, translated as *The Butterfly of Dinard*). Some of the articles Montale wrote as a foreign correspondent to *Corriere della sera* from England, France, Portugal, Greece, Syria, and Israel have been published as *Fuori di casa* (1969), praised by one critic for "their sharp, dry humor, psychological acumen, wit, and sarcasm—as well as the light, analytical style that is Montale's pioneering contribution to modern Italian prose." Montale's leisure interests include music, drawing, and etching. In 1967 he received an honorary degree from Cambridge University, and a permanent seat in the Italian Senate.

PRINCIPAL WORKS IN ENGLISH TRANSLATION: Poems from Eugenio Montale, tr. by Edwin Morgan, 1959; Robert Lowell: Poesie di Montale (bilingual ed. with English adaptations by Lowell), 1960; Poesie: Poems, tr. by George Kay, 1964 (republished, with English versions only, as Montale: Selected Poems, 1970); Selected Poems, bilingual ed. by various translators, ed. by Glauco Cambon, 1966; The Butterfly of Dinard, tr. by G. Singh, 1970; Provisional Conclusions (selected poems), tr. by Edith Farnsworth, 1970; Xenia, tr. by G. Singh, 1973. *Poems in* Barnstone, W. (ed.) Modern European Poetry, 1966; Fulton, R. (ed.) An Italian Quartet, 1966; Golino, C. L. (ed.) Contemporary Italian Poetry, 1962; Kay, G. R. (ed.) The Penguin Book of Italian Verse, 1965; Pacifici, S. (ed.) The Promised Land and Other Poems, 1957.

ABOUT: Burnshaw, S. (ed.) The Poem Itself, 1960; Cambon, G. Eugenio Montale, 1972; Cary, J. Three Modern Italian Poets, 1969; Cohen, J. M. Poetry of This Age, 1966; Contemporary Authors 17–18, 1968; Dizionario enciclopedico della letteratura italiana, 1967; Dizionario universale della letteratura contemporanea, 1961; Grigson, G. (ed.) Concise Encyclopedia of Modern World Literature, 1963; International Who's Who, 1971–72; Letteratura italiana: I Contemporanei, 1963; Lunardi, R. Eugenio Montale e la nuova poesia, 1948; March, R. and Tambimutto, M. J. (comps.) T. S. Eliot: A Symposium, 1949; Pacifici, S. A Guide to Contemporary Italian Literature, 1962; Pipa, A. Montale and Dante, 1968; Singh, G. Eugenio Montale: A Critical Study of His Poetry, Prose, and Criticism, 1973; Smith, H. (ed.) Columbia Dictionary of Modern European Literature, 1947. *Periodicals*—Italica December 1960, December 1962; Kenyon Review Spring 1959; Modern Language Notes January 1963; Modern Language Review October 1967; New York Review of Books October 20, 1966; June 1, 1972; PMLA December 1967; Sewanee Review Winter 1958; Studies Spring 1967; Voices May 1951.

MONTGOMERY, ROBERT BRUCE. *See* "CRISPIN, EDMUND"

MOORE, BRIAN (August 25, 1921–), Irish-born Canadian novelist, writes: "I was born in Belfast, Northern Ireland, and was educated at Catholic schools in that city. I come from a family of nine children. My father was a surgeon and both my brothers are doctors. I did not attend university but instead, when war broke out, I worked first as an A.R.P. First Aid worker and then in the National Fire Service as a fireman during the air raids on Belfast. I left Ireland to go to North Africa and Italy in 1943 as a civilian employee of the British Ministry of War Transport. After the war I spent almost two years in Poland with an U.N.R.R.A. economic mission. After that I emigrated to Canada, with the vague hope of finding a newspaper job there. During all these years I did not know what I could do with my life. I felt myself to be a failure. I wanted to write but did not believe that I would be published. I secured a job as proofreader with a Montreal newspaper and, for the first time in my life, found myself in a job for which I seemed qualified. However I realised that life on a Montreal newspaper was not the best training for anyone who wanted to become a writer and so I quit my job and tried to do freelance writing. I had some difficult times but two years later, when my first novel was published, I was already a professional writer.

"I was thirty-two when my first novel was published. From that time on, although my novels were never best sellers, I have managed to live off my writing without having to teach or do any

BRIAN MOORE

long-term hack work. I have been fortunate in that I have received a Guggenheim Foundation Fellowship, an award from the United States National Institute of Arts and Letters, a Canada Council Fellowship, a Quebec Literary Prize, the Authors' Club (Great Britain) First Novel Award and the Governor General of Canada's Award for Fiction.

"As the foregoing list shows, Canada, Britain and the United States have been kind to me. However, somewhere in my odyssey, my identity seems to have been misplaced. I was born a British subject with a Protestant name. The Catholic Irish to whom I belonged always seem to have thought of me as an Ulster Protestant. I am a Canadian citizen, but Canadians are reluctant to claim me as a Canadian author. I live in and am a permanent resident of the United States but am not thought of as an American writer. I have never been classified as belonging to any group or school of writing, either Irish, English, American or Canadian and for this reason I live in a sort of writing limbo. My work is well received in both the United States and England but no one seems able to place me. If this is the price of being a wanderer it seems a small one to pay.

"One of my novels, *The Luck of Ginger Coffey*, was made into a film, directed by Irvin Kershner. John Huston bought the film rights to *The Lonely Passion of Judith Hearne*, my first novel, and has held these rights for several years. At present I am living in New York City."

Judith Hearne, the subject of Brian Moore's first novel, is an old maid living in Belfast, who sees the destruction of her last chance for love and domesticity. Moore made of this story, an extraordinary one for a young man to attempt, "a harrowing *tour de force*." William Clancy wrote: "In its relentless pursuit of this woman's sorrow, in its refusal to sentimentalize or easily alleviate her plight, the book achieves a vision, and it is a tragic vision."

Several of Moore's novels have dealt with the failed and frail and luckless. *The Feast of Lupercal* is about a shy schoolteacher unsuccessful in his first love affair. An Irishman in Montreal, a pathetic *blagueur* at the end of his tether, is the central character in *The Luck of Ginger Coffey*, called "a breathlessly fast novel, jerky and nervous of style, always on the edge of noisy laughter or sudden tears." Brian Moore believes that "failure is a more interesting condition than success. Success changes people, it makes them something they were not and dehumanises them in a way, whereas failure leaves you with a more intense distillation of that self you are."

This opinion of success is illustrated (too schematically for some tastes) in *An Answer from Limbo*, about another Irish emigrant, a young novelist in New York. Imprisoned in domesticity, he forces his way out for long enough to finish his book, but at dreadful cost to those around him. *The Emperor of Ice-Cream*, a *bildungsroman* set in Belfast during World War II, is clearly at least partly autobiographical, and was much praised and enjoyed. One reviewer was reminded of Joyce's *Portrait of the Artist as a Young Man*, and said Moore's book showed a "similar tact" in dialogue and characterization.

A reviewer in the *Times Literary Supplement* has suggested that Brian Moore's later novels "show the vestigial religious conscience straining to give depth to North American life." Thus, in *Fergus*, a successful novelist in his late thirties, living with his young mistress in a California beach house, struggling with the latest screenplay (and with his artistic integrity), is visited by a series of apparitions from his past who confront him with all his sins of omission and commission. Most critics found the device interesting and promising, but rather inconclusive in execution. *The Revolution Script* was a complete departure, a "documentary novel" about the kidnapping by French-Canadian separatists of the British diplomat James Cross in October 1970. *Catholics*, called "a spare, concentrated fable about the destruction of religious faith," received the W. H. Smith literary award in 1973.

Some of Brian Moore's novels have been thought banal by a minority of critics; he is, rather, "a writer who accepts the challenge of banality," and one with an exceptional talent for "that exact description of common feelings which both individualizes the character and generalizes the experience." Similarly, there are a few who find his approach sentimental, and many who call it compassionate. He himself says that "a real writer wants to be terribly human and he responds emotionally, and at the same time there's this cold observer who cannot cry." Moore's characters, especially the women, are often strikingly realized. Reviewers have remarked from time to time upon the Joycean echoes in his style, which in general "steers a sure course between an ostentatious pursuit of distinction and mere documentary superfluity." Daniel Stern has called Brian Moore "one of the most accomplished novelists we have."

The author (like Fergus) has written a number of screenplays, and has published stories and travel articles in the United States, Canada, and England. He has the swarthy complexion, dark hair, and dark eyes of many Northern Irelanders. He is married to the former Jean Denney, and has a son.

PRINCIPAL WORKS: Judith Hearne, 1955 (also published as The Lonely Passion of Judith Hearne); The Feast of Lupercal, 1957 (republished as A Moment of Love, 1970); The Luck of Ginger Coffey, 1960; An Answer from Limbo, 1962; The Emperor of Ice-Cream, 1965; (with the editors of Life) Canada, 1967; I Am Mary Dunne, 1968; Fergus, 1970; The Revolution Script, 1971; Catholics, 1972.

ABOUT: Canadian Who's Who, 1967–69; Contemporary Authors 2, 1963; Dahlie, H. Brian Moore, 1969; Vinson, J. (ed.) Contemporary Novelists, 1972; Who's Who, 1973; Woodcock, G. Odysseus Ever Returning, 1970. *Periodicals*—Book Week September 19, 1965; Eire-Ireland Autumn 1968, Summer 1971; The Nation March 15, 1965; New Statesman February 18, 1966; Saturday Review October 13, 1962; Studies (Ireland) Summer 1971.

DORIS LANGLEY MOORE

MOORE, DORIS LANGLEY, English biographer, novelist, and writer on fashion, writes: "I was born in Liverpool—rather too long ago for me to enjoy announcing the date. My mother had been an actress, my father was a journalist. When I was eight, we went to South Africa, where he became editor of the *Sunday Times.* I lived in Johannesburg nearly eleven years. My elder sister returned to England married to a Yorkshireman, and I in time followed her and married his brother, Robert Sugden Moore.

"I had been reading classical languages with a tutor, and my first volume—very slim indeed—was a verse translation of twenty-nine Anacreontic odes. It was issued by a brand-new publisher, Gerald Howe, just after my wedding in 1926. My first prose book, *The Technique of the Love Affair* (1928), was brought out anonymously, as I was afraid of shocking my parents-in-law. (Nowadays it would be considered suitable for readings at the Y.W.C.A.). In England it was a best-seller; in America, not.

"After this, I wrote several books, including novels, differing so much from one another that each publication was like beginning all over again, a course very unfavourable to the building-up of a career. This I obstructed further by becoming an intensive collector, chiefly of material relating to costume history or to Byron. However, I managed to be first in the field with a biography of *E. Nesbit* (1933), published in America for the first time—with new material—in 1966.

"Early in the War, I finished a fairly substantial book, *The Vulgar Heart, An Enquiry into the Sentimental Tendencies of Public Opinion.* The incendiary bomb which destroyed Cassell's premises delayed its publication five years. By that time my marriage too was dissolved. An acute public paper shortage coincided with an acute private money shortage, so I squeezed into the film business, working sometimes on the costume side and sometimes as a script writer. I also wrote, inter alia, the scenario of a ballet, *The Quest*, which had choreography by Ashton, music by William Walton, designs by John Piper, and Fonteyn as Spenser's heroine, Una.

"In the years after the War, I did television shows on costume, using genuine specimens from my collection; and this work influenced my resolve to devise a museum of fashion, a subject either ignored or treated almost frivolously. By means of numerous exhibitions, illustrated lectures in America and elsewhere, and two books on fashion history, I was able to lay the foundations of the Museum of Costume now housed in the Assembly Rooms, Bath, where it presents what I believe to be the largest display of its kind in the world.

"Now at last I was free to settle down to the book I had always promised myself to write. By incredibly good fortune, I had made friends with

Byron's great-granddaughter, Lady Wentworth, and found the Open Sesame to her unfathomed collection of family papers. Drawing on these and other private collections, I produced *The Late Lord Byron* published in 1961 by John Murray in England and Lippincott in America. (The latter had already brought out two novels of mine, *All Done By Kindness* and *My Caravaggio Style*.) After this, I went back to films as costume designer for *Freud* with Montgomery Clift. Playing opposite him was Susannah York, and it was meditating on a part in the grand manner for her that I hit on Marie Bashkirtseff as my next subject. I went to Paris to look at the manuscript of the famous 'Journal' and found it had never been properly investigated. First I wrote a film script, *The Diary*, then a book, *Marie and the Duke of H.*, for which I used only the journals of Marie's early adolescence.

"I shall presently go back to the comparative restfulness of Byron."

Although she is an acute and indeed professional observer of manners and mores, Doris Langley Moore has never been constrained by current proprieties in her books. The *Times Literary Supplement*, which could not bring itself to review *The Technique of the Love Affair* (few respectable journals did), was pleased by Mrs. Moore's "entertaining and sensible" advice to her small daughter in *Pandora's Letter Box*, but upset again by her first novel, *A Winter's Passion*. It allowed that this account of a married woman's sexual piracy was "a clever piece of work," but found it "frankly unpleasant."

Attitudes had changed by 1945, and *The Vulgar Heart*, "a sort of anthology of . . . 'public opinion' at its worst," was generally praised for the liberal and progressive attitudes it implied in its author, and Mrs. Moore's postwar books have all been kindly received. Her entertaining novel *All Done By Kindness* made a search for lost masterpieces "as exciting as . . . a murder mystery." *My Caravaggio Style*, about what happens when a poor and lovelorn bookseller forges a transcript of Byron's burned memoirs, seemed to Carlos Baker "learned but sprightly, bristling with esoteric wit and conducted throughout at a level of literacy which puts some of our cruder naturalistic fiction to shame." Mrs. Moore's most important work of Byron scholarship, *The Late Lord Byron*, was "a reconstruction of the uproar and intrigue that followed the poet's death," forming "a kind of shadowgraph, the portrait of a man projected by the conduct of his friends, acquaintances, and enemies after his death." The book was almost unanimously praised as a work of great originality and authority.

The best known of Mrs. Moore's books on costume is *The Woman in Fashion*, a "lively, sensible, and well-written essay" illustrated by photographs of costumes drawn from her own famous collection, and modeled by such women as Margot Fonteyn, Ruth Draper, and Vivien Leigh. The author took a collection of court and ceremonial robes on a lecture tour of the United States in 1953. Described in 1967 as a "charming, dynamic woman," Mrs. Moore believes that fashion moves in cycles, and that it is set always by a privileged class (as now by the young). She sees the "caprices of fashion as the sign of a romantic spirit which triumphs over utilitarian considerations," and says: "I find the constant human endeavour to rise above its state a symptom of one of the finest things in the human spirit." She received an OBE in 1971.

PRINCIPAL WORKS: The Technique of the Love Affair, By a Gentlewoman, 1925 (rev. and enlarged, 1936); (tr.) Anacreon; Twenty-nine Odes Rendered into English Verse, 1926; Pandora's Letter Box, Being a Discourse on Fashionable Life, 1929; (with June Langley Moore) The Bride's Book, 1932 (rev. as Our Loving Duty, 1936); A Winter's Passion (novel), 1932; E. Nesbit: A Biography, 1933 (rev. 1966); The Unknown Eros, 1935; (with June Langley Moore) The Pleasure of Your Company, 1936; They Knew Her When: A Game of Snakes and Ladders, 1938 (reissued as A Game of Snakes and Ladders, 1955); The Vulgar Heart, An Enquiry into the Sentimental Tendencies of Public Opinion, 1945; Not At Home (novel), 1948; The Woman in Fashion, 1949; All Done By Kindness (novel), 1951; The Child in Fashion, 1953; Pleasure: A Discursive Guide Book, 1953; My Caravaggio Style (novel), 1959; The Late Lord Byron: Posthumous Dramas, 1961; Marie and the Duke of H.: The Daydream Love-Affair of Marie Bashkirtseff, 1966; Fashion Through Plates, 1771–1970, 1971.

ABOUT: Contemporary Authors 1, 1962; Who's Who, 1973. *Periodicals*—New York Times Book Review February 1, 1953; Times (London) June 23, 1967.

MOORE, HARRY T(HORNTON) (August 2, 1908–), American critic and biographer, writes: "I was born in Oakland, California, and have always remembered its eucalyptus and pepper trees, its outlying hills full of poppies, and its fogs blotting their way in from San Francisco Bay. My mother was also a native of that area, though her parents had come over from County Roscommon. My Scotch–Irish father was born on an Illinois farm not very far from where I now live. When I was a child he became an army officer, so that I had the scattered and rootless early life of an army brat. Revisiting Oakland I became a professional actor on my seventeenth birthday, in a stock company headed by the Ziegfield star Jack Norworth, who wrote the popular songs 'Harvest Moon' and 'Take Me Out to the Ball Game.' When I was eighteen and my father was stationed in the Canal Zone, I quit highschool there to become Caribbean-coast sports reporter for the *Panama American*. Two years later, a Citizens' Military Training Camp scholarship (awarded at Ford Sheridan, Illinois) sent me to the University of Chicago. There I resumed acting and played Hamlet, a role repeated several years later in a repertory company. At Chicago I had the privilege of studying writing with the genial and brilliant Thornton Wilder.

"In 1932, on the first of my nine trips to Europe, the sister of the late D. H. Lawrence showed me around the Lawrence country in Nottinghamshire, and elsewhere in England I also came to know some of that author's currently warring biographers, including John Middleton Murry and Catherine Carswell, as well as Lawrence's plangently vital widow, Frieda. It was as thrilling as being alive a little more than a century earlier and encountering members of the Shelley and Byron circles. I had begun reading Lawrence with enthusiasm in high-school, but now my interest in him grew, as it has continued to do.

"Before becoming a Bachelor of Philosophy in 1934 I became a husband, in those days when many universities forbade undergraduate marriages. A new marriage in the Depression meant difficulties, and for several years while living in towns near Chicago I labored on magazines and encyclopedia editorial staffs. The positive products of that time were my daughter Sharon, now married and living in Ohio, and my son Brian, who for more than a year commanded a Marine company in the Vietnam jungle.

"In the 1930s I began serious writing, turning out book reviews and what was then called reportage, chiefly for the *New Republic*, whose literary editor was the friendly and helpful Malcolm Cowley. I worked away at a novel which Maxwell Perkins liked, and in pious memory of him I hope someday to complete that book. Lewis Mumford, my favorite American writer, was also a good friend who offered encouragement. On a research trip to England in 1937 I met Herbert Read and at his suggestion wrote my first book, *The Novels of John Steinbeck* (1939), which now seems to me painfully immature. By 1940 I had decided on an academic life and in that year began teaching at the Illinois Institute of Technology while taking graduate work at Northwestern University. The next year I became an instructor at Northwestern, where I played Caliban (type casting?) at the School of Speech and completed work on my M.A. I had a reserve commission, was called up in April, 1942, and by July was overseas with the Air Corps, in the European Theatre of Operations.

"After returning to the States, I became Assistant Secretary of Air Staff, writing correspondence for General H. H. Arnold, later serving on the editorial staffs of *Impact* and *Air Force*. In off-duty hours in Washington at the end of the war I became, with Henry Miller and Selden Rodman, an associate editor of the 'intercontinental quarterly,' *Portfolio*, which the glowing Caresse Crosby launched at that time. In 1946, while stationed in Alabama, I became

HARRY T. MOORE

the founding editor of the *Air Force Quarterly Review*. In Montgomery on Columbus Day of that year, I had the extremely good fortune to marry Beatrice Walker, then a Chicago encyclopedia editor and now on the staff of Southern Illinois University Press.

"Frances Steloff of the Gotham Book Mart asked me to edit some letters Lawrence had written to Bertrand Russell in 1915–1916. These were published in 1948, the year I entered Boston University as a graduate student. In 1951 I brought out the first of my two critical biographies of Lawrence, books helped along by John Ciardi and Stanley Young respectively, as executive publishers. I have subsequently edited a good deal of Lawrence material, including his *Collected Letters* (1962). As Lionel Trilling has pointed out, commenting on contemporary literature has its perils because everyone tends to identify you with the subject matter you are merely trying to elucidate; it is continually necessary to explain to people that admiration for Lawrence as an imaginative writer does not mean complete acceptance of him as a prophet, although admittedly it is hard to disagree with him on those occasions when he utters inspired common sense. Dealing with the work of other writers has helped maintain a balance: a critical monograph on E. M. Forster, the editing of selections of Rainer Maria Rilke's letters and of Lewis Mumford's essays (the latter in collaboration with Karl W. Deutsch), as well as the putting together of an Elizabethan anthology. Lately I have been working in contemporary French literature and am preparing an edition of some unpublished letters of W. B. Yeats.

"For more than a quarter-century I have been a

fairly consistent contributor to the *Saturday Review* and also write for the New York *Times Book Review* and other journals. I am a Fellow of the Royal Society of Literature and have received two Guggenheim fellowships. I was president of the College English Association in 1961 and in 1963 was a National Book Awards judge.

"Most of my writing is connected with my teaching, which has included summer terms at Columbia University, New York University, and the University of Colorado (where I also taught for a year). Since 1957 I have been at Southern Illinois University and am now a research professor at this lively institution at the edge of the prairie, in a lake country bordered by the foothills of the Ozarks.

"As a critic and biographer I admired the achievements of the new critics in reestablishing the work of art itself as the reader's primary consideration. But some of the new critics went too far in isolating works of art from their background and treating them as if they existed in a vacuum. I belong to the newer school of biographical-social critics who admit the primacy of the work of art but who also want to study it in all its richness and complexity."

Moore is the son of Harry T. and Kathryn Moore. His father was an Army lieutenant colonel, and he himself now holds the same rank in the Air Force Reserve. Moore's first wife was Winifred Sheehan, whom he married in 1934. From 1947 until 1957, when he went to Southern Illinois University, he taught at Babson Institute, in Massachusetts, where he became chairman of the department of history and literature. He received his Ph.D. from Boston University in 1951.

It is to his work on D. H. Lawrence that Moore owes his reputation. Stephen Spender called *The Life and Works of D. H. Lawrence* the "most useful, informed and the least opinionated book I have seen on Lawrence," and there was much praise for Moore's use of biography "to illuminate the writing," his attention to language and symbolism at a time when most Lawrence students regarded their subject "as a prophet rather than a writer."

There was even more enthusiasm for Moore's second Lawrence study, *The Intelligent Heart*, which benefited from the use of many relevant memoirs and unpublished letters. Those who had found the earlier book a little pedestrian and repetitious in its manner observed that the new one was far better written, as well as more mature in its judgments, and it was agreed that all future Lawrence biographers would have to take account of it. Moore presented three Lawrences, Maxwell Geismar wrote: "the black devil, the prophet, and the artist," and "it is the artist who continually enlightens and entertains us in the solid pages of this biography." Moore has edited several collections of work by and about Lawrence, including the excellent but incomplete *Collected Letters* of 1962.

Moore's surveys of twentieth century French and German literature seemed to most but not all critics clumsily organized, poorly written, and prone to error, but useful to the extent that they assembled a very great deal of otherwise scattered information. This versatile and energetic scholar has also edited a selection of Rilke's letters and a most useful collection of essays, *Contemporary American Novelists*, among other volumes.

PRINCIPAL WORKS: The Novels of John Steinbeck: A First Critical Study, 1939; The Life and Works of D. H. Lawrence, 1951 (revised as D. H. Lawrence: His Life and Works, 1964); The Intelligent Heart: The Story of D. H. Lawrence, 1954; E. M. Forster, 1965; (with Warren Roberts) D. H. Lawrence and His World, 1966; Twentieth Century French Literature (two vols.), 1967; Twentieth Century German Literature, 1967; Age of the Modern, and Other Literary Essays, 1971. *As editor*—D. H. Lawrence: Letters to Bertrand Russell, 1948; D. H. Lawrence's Essays on Sex, Literature and Censorship, 1953; (with Frederick John Hoffman) The Achievement of D. H. Lawrence, 1953; D. H. Lawrence Miscellany 1959; Rainer Maria Rilke: Selected Letters, 1960; The World of Lawrence Durrell, 1962; The Collected Letters of D. H. Lawrence (two vols.), 1962; Contemporary American Novelists, 1964; (with Karl W. Deutsch) The Human Prospect (essays of Lewis Mumford), 1965; The Elizabethan Age, 1965; Phoenix II: Uncollected, Unpublished, and Other Prose Works by D. H. Lawrence, 1967.

ABOUT: Contemporary Authors 7–8, 1963; Directory of American Scholars II, 1964; Who's Who, 1973; Who's Who in America, 1972–1973.

MOORE, JOHN (CECIL) (November 10, 1907–July 27, 1967), English author, wrote: "I was born at Tewkesbury, Gloucestershire, where I spent a glorious country boyhood, fishing, shooting, riding horses, botanising, learning about natural history. At my country prep school in addition to learning Latin and Greek I was encouraged to continue these activities. Later I went to Malvern College where I was made to play organized games instead of hunting for flowers and birdsnests. This didn't please me so I was happy to leave at sixteen. I went into an uncle's firm at Tewkesbury and learned to be an auctioneer while secretly writing novels in the office. When my first was published (1930) I told my outraged uncle I had decided to earn my living by writing. ('But that's a hobby, my boy, not a profession!') I went to London, where I was poor and happy, writing unsuccessful novels, reviewing, and doing hack jobs which I didn't find distasteful, for all writing is fun when you're young, and you are only a hack when you think you are. Now and then I hitched lifts in tramp-steamers and found my way about the Mediterranean, which I still love and revere, feeling that all I know and believe in comes ultimately from about those shores. During the

Spanish war I was a correspondent on the Republican side; I saw it as the first skirmish of *our* war against the dictators. When that started, I joined the Royal Navy and flew as a pilot for four years; later I served on General Eisenhower's staff for the invasion of Normandy.

"During the war I married an Australian Wren, Lucile Douglas Stephens, and afterwards I brought her home to my own countryside. I had my first writing success with *Portrait of Elmbury* (called *The Fair Field* in USA) which was about my native town of Tewkesbury. Many of my subsequent tales have been set there. We live in an old mill-cum-farmhouse six miles from the town. (Domesday Book mentions a mill at this spot; the stream runs under the house, and I could catch trout from my bedroom window).

"My chief hobby is curiosity about Man and Nature, and I write about both. For the rest, I still collect butterflies, ride horses, take pleasure in birds and flowers; I like mountains and the sea, fast cars, cats, France and the French, the theatre, talking in pubs about anything from poetry to politics, reading or seeing Shakespeare. I would have liked to be born in the reign of Elizabeth I but feel the next best thing is to live in the reign of Elizabeth II.

"As a writer I work hard and variously: as well as my novels, I write short stories and books about the countryside (but the one I enjoyed writing most, *You English Words*, was about the English language). I like the cinema best of all media other than the novel for story-telling; I find TV constricting. I want a largish canvas to work on, and I think the novel has suffered recently from the limits imposed on it by kitchen-sink attitudes, a kind of self-conscious intellectualism, and minuscule themes. Two novelists whom I admire are Dickens and Hemingway; because both believed that life was a cornucopia poured out by the bountiful Gods and not something rationed on a coupon-system by the minor civil servants of a supernatural bureaucracy.

"I also think that all story-tellers are primarily entertainers (though on different levels) and that the greatest entertainer of all was William Shakespeare."

A prolific writer since 1930 of novels, stories, and topographical books, John Moore made his reputation with *The Fair Field*, a slightly fictionalized "biography" of the market town of Tewkesbury, described with "the knowledge and affection of a boyhood spent in one of its oldest houses." *Brensham Village*, using a similar technique to give a composite portrait of rural life in transition, was also widely popular. Subsequent fictional and non-fictional evocations of Gloucestershire established Moore as "an exact and vivid recorder of country scenes and pastimes" who had few equals. His last and most ambitious novel, which occupied him for over three years, was *The Waters Under the Earth*, focusing on an ancient Gloucestershire manor house and its hereditary owners to illustrate the social changes which followed World War II. Doddington Manor symbolizes England for Moore just as "Howard's End" did for E. M. Forster in his greater novel, and expresses a similar sense of the continuity of English life. Some considered the book's symbolism a little too overt, and thought Moore's anxiety to think the best of everyone robbed it of dramatic tension, but most readers found very much to admire in this "beautifully written, admirably craftsmanlike novel."

JOHN MOORE

According to one of his obituarists, John Moore "believed it to be a virtue in itself to do as many things as possible," and this virtue he practiced, in his leisure time and as a productive and versatile writer. He was the author of a number of plays for a variety of media. He wrote a history of the Fleet Air Arm, in which he served with distinction during World War II, and used the Navy's air force in two novels (*Wits End* and *Escort Carrier*). *You English Words* expressed Moore's delight in language, Bergen Evans said, "in a most contagious way." There are many among his admirers who think that Moore did his best work, not in his fiction, but in his country essays and calendars—books like *The Season of the Year; Come Rain, Come Shine;* and *The Year of the Pigeons*.

John Moore was organizer of the Tewkesbury Play Festival from 1943 to 1949 (and gave a funny and agreeable fictionalized account of such activities in *Dance and Skylark*). In 1949 he helped to inaugurate the Cheltenham Festival of Literature, and was thereafter for many years its guiding spirit. Moore served (1956–1957) as chairman of the Society of Authors. He died in Bristol after an operation at the age of sixty. "If Mr. Moore must be fitted into any category of writers on the English countryside," a reviewer once wrote, "then it is to the school of Gilbert White that he belongs"; something of White's untiring curiosity about "Man and Nature" pervades John Moore's work.

PRINCIPAL WORKS: Dixon's Cubs, 1930; Dear Lovers (U.S., Raven Rough), 1931; King Carnival (short stories), 1933; English Comedy, 1932; The Walls Are Down, 1933; The Welsh Marches, 1933; The New Forest, 1934; Country Men (biographies), 1935; Overture, Beginners, 1936; The Cotswolds, 1937; Clouds of Glory, 1938; The Countryman's England, 1939; (as editor) Life and Letters of Edward Thomas, 1939; Wits End, 1942; Fleet Air Arm (history), 1943; Escort Carrier, 1944; Portrait of Elmbury, 1945 (U.S., The Fair Field); Brensham Village, 1946; The Blue Field, 1948; Dance and Skylark, 1951; Midsummer Meadow, 1953; Tiger, Tiger (short stories), 1953; The White Sparrow, 1954; The Season of the Year, 1954; Come Rain, Come Shine, 1956; September Moon, 1957; Jungle Girl, 1958; Man and Bird and Beast, 1959; You English Words, 1961; The Year of the Pigeons, 1963; The Elizabethans (play), 1963; The White Sparrow (play), 1964; The Waters Under the Earth, 1965.

ABOUT: Contemporary Authors 7–8, 1963; Who's Who, 1967. *Periodicals*—Times (London) July 29, 1967.

MOORE, WARD (August 10, 1903–), American novelist and short story writer, writes: "Born in Madison, New Jersey, a genteel suburb on the Lackawanna, I was whisked, at five months, along with my parents to my maternal grandmother's in Montreal. I was an unpleasant child, 'trapped in a sailor suit, balefully biding his time.' Sullen, solitary, and afraid of other children, my only refuge was in books or fantasies. If childhood was unhappy, adolescence was wretched; I loathed sports (unless fishing, canoeing, or swimming be illogically so accounted), did miserably in school, except for history and geography, subjects which could be excelled in by ignoring the teachers, turning instead to reading books and looking at maps. Skinny and awkward, I was afraid of being taunted, hazed, or punched by other boys; agonizingly shy with girls, rebuff and ridicule seemed predestined. In imagination I was a victorious general, winner of hard-fought, gory battles, master of delectable, docile women, or on a slightly less surrealistic plane, the acknowledged Great Writer.

"For I had begun writing stories and poems at eleven. One expects juvenilia to be bad, or at best inept. Mine wasn't only bad and inept, it had no reason for existing: it had only the most tenuous as well as morally and aesthetically untenable connection with myself. It could not even be justified as apprentice work, for I had neither the humility nor discipline to play the sedulous ape; on the other hand I had neither the humility nor discipline not to.

"I got a job as errand boy in Joe Kling's Pagan

WARD MOORE

Bookshop, graduated to Macy's book department, Gimbels, became a sheetmetal worker and then a pattern clerk in a steelcasting foundry in Milwaukee, went on to Chicago to Marshall Field's book department and then to a bookstore of my own which went broke, then to peddling old prints in Los Angeles. Yet all the time I continued to think of myself as a writer though I was writing little or nothing; I had not learned the simple fact that a writer writes because he has stories to tell and that it is more imperative to tell them than to do anything else.

"In 1937 I wrote my first completed novel, *Breathe the Air Again*; in 1945, *Greener Than You Think*. I wrote a number of reviews, criticism, essays, and short stories. Using the device of imaginative fiction I was able to publish satire which would not have seen print otherwise. In the 1950s were published *Bring the Jubilee* and *Cloud by Day*; in 1962, *Joyleg* (in collaboration with Avram Davidson). Practically all of my published short stories, some twenty-five or more, have been anthologized and reanthologized until I have long lost count.

"Having finally learned to write better, more forcefully, and more economically, I also learned that I was without a market except for stories which could be labeled, detestably, 'science fiction.' I have at present three novels, written in the last years, *Before the Rains*, *Miss Smith*, and *On the Way I Lost It*, which editors have so far found caviar to the general. Also unpublished is an essay, *Reflections of an Old Lecher*, an attack on the morals of the mid-century. I am presently working on a novel, *Carpetbagger*, and my autobiography, *I*.

"Perhaps the autobiography should have been titled, *Monologue With Joe Gould.* Who knows?"

Breathe the Air Again is a novel about the labor struggle during the Depression, seen through the eyes of Simon Epstein, a democratic socialist who in his restlessness, driving force, and hunger for life reminded some reviewers of Thomas Wolfe's Eugene Gant. Milton Rugoff called it undisciplined and "amazingly uneven," but praised its "honest observation, realistic detail and sharp characterization," and called it a "slice-of-life as jagged as a chunk of bread hacked from a loaf."

Greener Than You Think, one of the books by Moore to be treated as science fiction, received that "detestable label" because of its subject—the production of a superfertilizer that causes grass to grow with such uncontrollable vigor that it crowds out all other crops. Its satirical element lies in the fact that a discovery promising good for all mankind is exploited for personal profit with disastrous results which science, divorced from morality, is powerless to avoid.

Bring the Jubilee was another and highly successful fantasy—not the first but perhaps the best of the many novels and stories that have speculated about what might have happened, technologically and politically, if the South had won the American Civil War. The hero finds this outcome so unattractive that he goes back in time to the Battle of Gettysburg, and swings a critical action in the North's favor. The book was found very inventive and convincing.

The critical consensus is that Moore's novels have immense vitality and originality, but represent a promise not quite fulfilled; their passionate drive has not yet found its full expression in art.

A colorful portrait of Ward Moore is recognizable in Jean Ariss's novel *The Quick Years* (1958), about an irascible and tempestuous patriarch called Joseph Baer, a city-bred Jew who (like Moore himself), has turned to farming in California in disgust with city life.

PRINCIPAL WORKS: Breathe the Air Again, 1942; Greener Than You Think, 1947; Bring the Jubilee, 1953; Cloud by Day, 1956; (with Avram Davidson) Joyleg, 1971 (*shorter version in* Fantastic, March 1962, April 1962).
ABOUT: Moskowitz, S. Seekers of Tomorrow, 1966; Warfel, H. (ed.) American Novelists of Today, 1951. *Periodicals*—Books February 8, 1942; Nation May 15, 1954; New York Times Book Review February 15, 1942; December 7, 1947; Saturday Review February 28, 1942.

***MORAES, DOM(INIQUE)** (July 19, 1938–), Indian-born poet and journalist, was born in Bombay. His family background was unique—in its racial and religious complexities, its emotional instability, and in the sheer range of contacts and

* mô rās′

DOM MORAES

experiences which it imposed on an exceptionally intelligent and sensitive child. Stephen Spender, who met him when he was very young, remembers him as "the shyest, most backing-away person I had ever seen." His father was Frank Moraes, an Indian lawyer educated at Oxford who became the editor of the *Times of India* and Nehru's biographer. His mother, the first Indian woman doctor, attended Gandhi during one of his many protest fasts against British colonial rule. A hospital has been endowed in her name in Bombay. Both his father's and his mother's families came from Goa, a part of India which had been colonized by the Portuguese; both families were Roman Catholic. However their religion did not unite the parental families but divided them, partly because Frank Moraes himself was an agnostic, partly because the families belonged to two different and rival branches of the Roman Catholic establishment in India, and often quarreled bitterly. Before Dom Moraes was ten his mother suffered the first of many mental breakdowns, during which she became violent and dangerous, neurotically jealous and possessive. Eventually she received electric shock therapy, and when this failed, was taken to an asylum.

For this reason, Dom Moraes grew up mainly in the care of his father, "who was wise enough to allow . . . complete freedom." He spent hours reading quietly in his father's office, where he met Gandhi, Nehru, and many of the leading statesmen, diplomats, and artists in the India of the time, an India undergoing a process of violent change—from British rule to independence, from a loose collection of minor kingdoms to an assertive nationalism. In spite of his Indian childhood and

Portuguese name, Dom Moraes spoke, read, and was educated in English. Gandhi reprimanded him as a child for not knowing Hindi. He was an only child, without many friends of his own age, and, apart from an unhappy period at a Catholic school, to which he was driven in solitary splendor in his father's Rolls Royce, he was largely self-taught. He passionately absorbed the English children's classics —Stevenson, Kipling, Talbot Baines Reed—and invented more stories for his heroes when the well ran dry. From the age of ten to fifteen Dom Moraes kept a diary of his life, illustrating it with little sketches and adding verses. He had already resolved to be a poet.

Frank Moraes wanted his son to go to Oxford, and after some cramming Dom Moraes obtained a place at Jesus College in October 1956. He spent some time in London before entering Oxford and met many writers and poets. In 1957 David Archer of the Parton Press published Moraes's first collection of poems, *A Beginning*. It was a critical success and a year later received the much-coveted Hawthornden Prize, which had not been awarded for fourteen years. At nineteen Dom Moraes was the youngest writer ever to win it, and the first non-English poet. As Elizabeth Jennings has said, the book was admired both for its "astonishing mastery of technique," and for Moraes's "ability to write eloquently and quite unsentimentally about very personal subjects," combining "elaborate stanzas and tough, concrete language" in a way reminiscent of Thom Gunn.

Dom Moraes lived in Oxford, as a rather unorthodox undergraduate, until 1959. His reputation as a poet and his charm of manner partly disguised the fact that he worked very little for his degree, and spent much time away from college, either abroad or with his girl friends in London. He traveled a great deal in Europe, meeting among others David Gascoyne, Allen Ginsberg, and Gregory Corso. Ginsberg and Corso he invited to Oxford where they gave a memorable poetry reading. The poets Julian Mitchell and Peter Levi were among Moraes's friends at Oxford, and he contributed to *Gemini*, the intervarsity magazine which Mitchell edited. In spite of all this, he left Oxford with an honors degree.

After graduating, Moraes went home for a brief visit and achieved something of a reconciliation with his mother, whose condition had improved. A tour of India followed with Ved Mehta, the blind Indian writer, whom he had known at Oxford. He met the Dalai Lama, Nehru, and many writers, Indian and foreign. His record of this journey, *Gone Away*, was warmly praised for its brilliant visual imagery and "a comic and ironic zest suggesting the early Evelyn Waugh," and there was much admiration for Moraes's painful and moving account of his meeting with the dying Bengali poet Devkota.

A second volume of verse, *Poems*, appeared in 1960, shortly after Moraes had returned to London, and a third, *John Nobody*, followed in 1965. A selection from all three volumes, with some new work, was published in America in 1966 as *Poems, 1955–1965*. None of these books was received with as much excitement as *A Beginning*, and there was a feeling that the poet had been a little overwhelmed by the seedy glamour of the English literary world. M. L. Rosenthal found echoes of Auden and Muir throughout Moraes's work, but said "one sees other currents running through it as well—notes of Soho romanticism, fugitive American influences and a host of others from Eliot to D. J. Enright. Little in the books is quite in Moraes's very own voice, yet a finely grained personality does emerge despite the many easy, expansive effects and the uncertainty of voice." These poems, often autobiographical, and including some "love lyrics of great tenderness and delicacy," reveal a preoccupation with death linked at times, Rosenthal suggests, "with the sharp realization of irrecoverably lost identity."

There was a rather similar response to *My Son's Father*, Moraes's autobiography, and Edward Thomas complained that the author seemed to be trying to make of the London literary world a "spiritual home, so that he need not confront a world where, like so many others, he is a wanderer between cultures." Stephen Spender, in a gentler review, wrote that the book's fascination "lies partly in its humor and affectionate warmth, but most of all in the sense of precariousness that is communicated. The precariousness of divided Indian and English loyalties; the precariousness of his life with his parents and of his rather affluent circumstances in a very poor country; the precariousness of young talent shot into the English literary world. It is a success story, but one closes it with a slight anxiety for the author in England."

Since then, in fact, Moraes has returned to Asia. He now lives in Hong Kong, where he edits the *Asia Magazine*. Long before he made this move, the *New Yorker* had recognized in Moraes "an uncommonly gifted, natural-born reporter," and he had become a highly successful journalist, writing on cricket (a lifelong passion), on the Eichmann trial in Israel, and on a great variety of other subjects, literary and otherwise. He has been married twice—in 1963 to Judith St. John, by whom he has a son, and in 1970 to Leela Naidu.

PRINCIPAL WORKS: *Poetry*—A Beginning, 1957; Poems, 1960; (tr.) The Brass Serpent (translations from the Hebrew of poems by T. Carmi), 1964; John Nobody, 1965; Poems, 1955–1965, 1966. *Prose*—Gone Away, 1960; My Son's Father, 1968; From East and West: A Collection of Essays, 1973.

ABOUT: Moraes, D. Gone Away, 1960; Moraes, D. My

Son's Father, 1968; Who's Who, 1973. *Periodicals*—London Magazine October 1965, December 1968; Newsweek October 24, 1960; New York Times Magazine May 15, 1968; February 15, 1970; New York Times Book Review August 10, 1969; Poetry March 1967.

***MORANTE, ELSA** (August 18, 1918–), Italian novelist, was born in Rome. Her father was a schoolteacher and a native of Sicily, her mother a woman from Modena. She is thus the inheritor of two very different, not to say contrasting, strains, and for that very reason a typical product of the cosmopolitan post-Risorgimento Rome, a crucible for the diverse elements of Italian provincial traditions. Elsa Morante has written that her favorite spot in the world is the Piazza Navona, in the heart of the ancient Campo Marzio of the capital. She has always regarded Rome as her home, although she has traveled widely and gives New York a high place among her favorite cities. In 1941 she married the novelist Alberto Moravia and was thus introduced into the upper reaches of Italian literary society. In 1943, like many others, she was compelled to leave Rome, then under German control, and to take refuge in the countryside near Cassino. This enforced and trying exile served to arouse in her an affectionate admiration for the South, particularly the Naples region, which is the scene of her major books.

Miss Morante never finished the conventional course of study and holds no university degree, but from her childhood she gave evidence of unusual literary precocity. Her published works however are not numerous and her reputation—which stands high among contemporary novelists—rests essentially on two long novels. They are works of marked originality which, though they differ considerably in plan and form, have certain recognizably similar ingredients. *Menzogna e Sortilegio* (1948, translated as *House of Liars*) records the attempt of a certain Elisa, living in a small unnamed city of the South, to reconstruct the story of her parents and grandparents, partly on the evidence of memories and tradition, partly through imaginative effort. The history of marriages, liaisons, intrigues, and catastrophes that emerges has the quality of a dreamy arabesque, and this impression is enhanced by the alternation of a sober, somewhat old-fashioned chronicle style with a highly charged prose of fancy and invention. One is reminded of the facade of a Counter-Reformation Church, elaborate and luxuriant yet with a firmly disciplined structure. The book earned for its author the Viareggio Prize of 1948 but also some admonishments from the critics; E. Falqui for one expressed his doubts about the integrity of the work.

In *L'isola di Arturo* (1957, translated as *Arturo's Island*), which nine years later won the Strega prize, the conflict of attitudes and manners is successfully resolved. The story has a consistent mythlike tone, even though the actual events recorded are not unlike those we find in the works of various neorealists, including Moravia. Rather as in *House of Liars*, Arturo's story is that of his own memories, related in the first person. It is the account of his childhood on his island (which is Procida in the Bay of Naples), and his upbringing by a friend of his father. His father, suggestively named Wilhelm, takes on a legendary aspect in the eyes of the boy, for the paternal visits are infrequent, irregular, and somewhat mysterious. In due course Arturo finds he has a new stepmother, only two years older than he. There follows the predictable shift from father-worship to adolescent infatuation with the stepmother, and a less predictable development in the discovery of a dark secret in Wilhelm's life. Arturo, leaving the island, also abandons the illusions of childhood.

* mō rän' tā

ELSA MORANTE

Lo scialle andaluso (The Andalusian Shawl, 1963) is another story of a child's obsessive love of a parent and subsequent disenchantment. A very different and indeed totally unexpected work is *Il mondo salvato dai ragazzini* (1968). Miss Morante has described it as "an epic-heroic-didactic poem in free verse . . . an autobiography and a document, a manifesto and a ballet, a madrigal and a color film, etcetera." Partly in verse and partly in prose poetry, the book begins with a series of ballads in classical meter, includes a contemporary Oedipus, and ends with a savage apocalyptic vision of the modern world in which only the young show themselves capable of love, honesty, and salvation. Elsa

Morante has also written a number of short stories, some of which were collected in *Il gioco segreto* (The Secret Game, 1941). She has published a volume of poems, *Alibi* (1958), and has translated Katherine Mansfield's *Scrapbook*.

Elsa Morante is no longer married to Moravia. In a note to *Il mondo salvato dai ragazzini*, she writes: "The author of this book is still alive and lives in Rome with her cat. Most of her few friends are youngsters because only the young are really interested in serious and important things. Adults are usually involved in trivial, irrelevant affairs. Since her birth, the author has been an anarchist; in other words, she considers the domination of some people over others—be it financial, ideological, military, familial or any other, of whatever origin, form or pretext—the most gloomy, hideous and shameful thing on earth."

PRINCIPAL WORKS IN ENGLISH TRANSLATION: House of Liars, 1951; Arturo's Island, 1959.

ABOUT: Cecchi, E. Di Giorno in giorno, 1954; Falqui, E. Fra Racconti e romanzi del novecento, 1950; Manacorda, G. Storia della letteratura italiana contemporanea, 1967; Pullini, S. Il romanzo italiana del dopoguerra, 1960; Pupino, A. R. Strutture e stile della narrativa di Elsa Morante, 1968. *Periodicals*—Books Abroad Winter 1959; Nation August 17, 1957; New York Herald Tribune August 16, 1959, October 25, 1959; New York Times Book Review August 2, 1952; August 15, 1959; May 18, 1969; Symposium xv 1961; Times Literary Supplement May 15, 1959.

"MORGAN, CLAIRE." *See* HIGHSMITH, PATRICIA (MARY)

***"MORI, OGAI" (pseudonym of Rintaro Mori)** (January 19, 1862–July 9, 1922), Japanese novelist, dramatist, literary critic, and translator, is regarded by many in Japan as the most influential literary figure of the Meiji and Taisho eras. As the first major Japanese writer to have lived in Europe, he became not merely a translator of European literature, but an interpreter of European thought and customs for a generation that was hungry for cultural contact with the outside world.

Mori's father, a physician of the Dutch School, was family doctor to a small feudal clan in Shimane Prefecture, South-West Honshu. But it was his mother, a strong-willed heiress of some social standing, who seems to have most influenced his career. After a precocious introduction to the Chinese Confucian classics, and the Dutch and German languages, he graduated from medical school in Tokyo at the age of nineteen, the youngest graduate in the history of the university. He then considered a political career, and it was his mother who helped to persuade him to take a post as an assistant surgeon in the army.

* mô li

In 1884 he was sent to Germany to study military hygiene, and in the four years that followed he also took the opportunity to read widely in the fields of literature and philosophy, and to attend the universities of Leipzig, Munich, and Berlin. He was particularly influenced by the idealist aesthetics of Karl von Hartmann, and attracted both by the romantic and scientific traditions he encountered in Germany. After traveling through France and England, Mori returned to Japan in 1888, to plunge at once into a dual career in medicine and literature.

In 1889, on the advice of his mother, he married Toshiko, daughter of a vice admiral. A son, Oto, was born in 1890, but the marriage was not successful, and the couple was divorced the same year. Mori was married again twelve years later, this time to Shigeko, eldest daughter of Hirotomi Araki, and by this second marriage he had three children.

Meanwhile Mori taught physiology and anatomy at the Army Medical School and Tokyo College of Art, and edited a number of medical magazines. By the age of thirty-one, he had risen to the rank of president of the Army Medical School, and from this point advanced steadily into the upper reaches of the military bureaucracy, eventually becoming chief of the Army Medical Bureau and Surgeon General in 1907.

Very soon after his return from Europe, Mori published three short novels, all obviously based on his German experiences, all exploring a similar theme—love between a young Japanese and a German girl—and all lyrical and romantic in tone, ending on a note of sadness and loss. In *Maihime* (The Dancing Girl, 1890), the first of the trilogy, the young man, homeward bound, reflects on his choice of ambition and duty over love and idealism. He finds some sort of consolation by consciously resigning himself to a life of deprivation and duty, a theme which is to recur repeatedly in Mori's work.

Perhaps even more important than the early novels, however, were Mori's elegant free translations of European prose and poetry, which set a high standard for the emerging modernist writers. In 1889 he published *Omakage* (Vestiges), a collection of translations from romantic poets, including Goethe and Heine, Shakespeare and Byron, which was to prove an important stimulus to the new Western-style poetry, *shintaishi*. And in 1892 he began what was to become a Japanese classic, *Sokkyo Shijin*, a translation of Hans Christian Andersen's little-known novel *The Improvisator*.

As a romantic, opposed to the naturalism then prevailing in Japan, Mori soon found himself engaged in heated polemics, mainly through the pages of the influential critical magazine *Shigarami Zoshi*, which he had founded in 1889. "The dirt of nature," he declared, "should be cleaned off by means of the imagination." Though the controversy reached no conclusion, it did have important effects, defining the problems of young writers, establishing more rigorous standards of criticism, and prompting Mori himself to demonstrate his theories in practice.

During the ten years around the turn of the century came first the Sino-Japanese, then the Russo-Japanese war, and Mori's military duties took him to distant battle areas. He was not entirely silenced, however, and continued to plead, in the face of the rampant nationalism inspired by the victories in China, and European references to the "Yellow Peril," for a balanced attitude toward Western learning, something between empty mimicry and chauvinist isolationism. The well-known short story "Fushinchu" (1910, translated as "Under Reconstruction") deals with this theme—the adoption and adaptation of Western customs in the reconstruction of Japan.

Returning to social and literary life, Mori became a protégé of Aritomo Yamagata, the most influential conservative statesman of the period. Mori has been criticized for this connection, and for his apparent political passivity. His defenders assert that his stand was consistently liberal, and that he made use of his position to influence and advise; that he wished to see the evolution, not the destruction, of the regime.

In any case, the years between 1909 and 1912 were years of great creativity for Ogai Mori. He wrote novels and short stories; translations of Ibsen, Hauptmann, Hofmannsthal, and Shaw which helped to lay the foundations for *shingeki*, the new-style drama; plays for the traditional *Kabuki* stage; and modernized forms of *waka* and *haiku*. He continued his critical attacks on naturalism, which he held to be mindless, mechanistic, and destructive of art. Among the writings of these years are *Ita sekusuarisu* (1909, translated as *Vita Sexualis*), which advocates self-discipline as the antidote to the naturalist's preoccupation with sex; *Chinmoku no To* (The Silent Tower, 1910), in which he voices his opposition to government censorship; *Ka no Yo Ni* (1912, translated as *As If*), which portrays the defeat of originality by tradition, and history by myth; and *Kamen* (Mask, 1909), a not very successful drama advancing a Nietzschean philosophy of stern endurance and proud independence.

In these years Mori produced his most mature and admired work. The frequent repetition of the words *asobi* (detachment), *teinen* (resignation), and *bokansha* (bystander) give some idea of the tone of his mature work, and his cool, almost clinical, attitude toward life. There is also a vein of restlessness, and in *Moso* (Delusions, 1911), one of his most pessimistic writings, he describes himself as "an eternal malcontent." This mixture of scientific

OGAI MORI

remoteness and romantic disillusion perhaps helps to explain his attraction for Japanese intellectuals even today, and is most beautifully expressed in the delicate short novel *Gan* (1911), a tragic love story which has been filmed (as *The Mistress*), and translated into English as *The Wild Geese*.

Mori retired from the army officially in 1916, and in the following year was appointed Director of the Imperial Museum, a post he held until his death. His withdrawal from literary and social life began in about 1913. Political events seem to have encouraged his introspection. The execution of the leader Shusui Kotoku, after the alleged plot of 1911 to assassinate the Emperor Meiji, the death of the Emperor in 1912, and, greatest shock of all, the self-immolation in traditional *samurai* manner of General Nogi, a personal friend, led Mori to contemplate death more closely, and reawakened his interest in the ideals of the *samurai* code. In this and other ways he greatly influenced Yukio Mishima and other contemporary writers. The last years of Mori's life were devoted to researches into obscure periods of Japanese history, and into the lives of almost forgotten minor figures like Chusai Shibue, a doctor and public servant of the late Tokugawa period, who symbolized for Mori an ideal of patient service which he felt he had been unable to achieve himself.

PRINCIPAL WORKS IN ENGLISH TRANSLATION: As If, 1925; Sansho-Dayu, 1952; The Wild Geese, 1959; Sansho-Dayu and Other Short Stories, 1970; Vita Sexualis, 1972. *Stories in* McKinnon, R. N. The Heart Is Alone: A Selection of Twentieth Century Japanese Short Stories, 1957; Miyamori, A. Representative Tales of Japan, 1914; Morris, I. Modern Japanese Stories, 1961; Taketomo, T. Seven Stories from Contemporary Japanese Writers, 1918.

ABOUT: Keene, D. Modern Japanese Literature, 1956; Kosaka, M. Japanese Thought in the Meiji Era, 1958; Nakamura, M. Japanese Fiction in the Meiji Era (in Japanese), 1966; Okazaki, Y. Japanese Literature in the Meiji Era, 1955; Shibukawa, G. Ogai Mori (in Japanese), 1964. *Periodicals*—Contemporary Japan XXIX 1966; Library Journal February 1, 1960.

***MÓRICZ, ZSIGMOND** (June 30, 1879–September 4, 1942), Hungarian novelist, short story writer, and dramatist, was born in Csécse, a small village near the River Tisza, the eldest of the six children of Calvinist parents. His father, Bálint Móricz, was a small contractor who struggled hard but successfully to provide his children with an education. Zsigmond's primary and secondary school years in and around the local town of Debrecen are graphically described in his novel *Légy jo mindhalálig* (1923, translated by L. Körösi as *Be Faithful Unto Death*). At the urging of his devout and sensitive mother, a clergyman's daughter, he began theological studies at the age of twenty, then switched to law, and finally settled upon a career in journalism.

Beginning in 1900, Móricz worked as a Budapest newspaperman and general hack for nearly ten years. Then in 1909 he was rescued from obscurity by the magazine *Nyugat* (The West), which published his moving short story "Hét krajcár" (Seven Pennies). Móricz thereupon plunged into literary work with the same zest which he showed for living, thoroughly enjoying fame and the money that accompanied it. An excellent raconteur, who could hold his listeners spellbound, he soon gathered a circle of admirers and followers (and another of those who envied and disliked him). His reformist tendencies earned him the lasting suspicion of the authorities.

Nyugat was a nursery for every kind of literary innovation; Móricz was one of dozens of major Hungarian writers who cut their teeth in its eclectic pages. For his part he was unattracted by the cosmopolitanism and formal experiments which occupied many of his contemporaries. His subject was what he knew: the Hungarian peasantry; his reaction was against the sentimental, optimistic, or picturesque accounts of rural life manufactured by the bourgeois writers of the late nineteenth century. Móricz set out to describe what was there—land hunger, lust, ignorance, pathetic snobberies, a people degraded by centuries of oppression and still in the grip of semifeudalism. His method was Zolaesque, a detailed and shocking realism, relieved only by an earthy humor.

Among Móricz's best known novels are *Sárarany* (Golden Mud, 1910), about a peasant Don Juan, and *A Fáklya* (1917, translated by A. Lengyel as *The Torch*) about a young minister trying to preach

* mō′ rits

ZSIGMOND MÓRICZ

and live Christianity in a totally corrupt village. His early work in particular brought accusations that Móricz could see only what was ugly and vicious and unjust; that he was obsessed by eroticism. Indeed there is some justice in these charges; his vision can seem almost grotesquely dark and the frenzied sensuality which possesses so many of his characters sometimes approaches the ludicrous. But no one has shown a deeper understanding of the Hungarian peasant and at its best Móricz's terse expressionist style has great power.

In his later novels, Móricz began to write also about the provincial middle classes and gentry, and to write too much. His tone mellowed, his impact diminished, and he sometimes betrayed haste in clumsy construction. Of his historical novels, the best known are those in the trilogy *Erdély* (Transylvania, 1922–1935). His short stories, collected in *Magyarok* (Hungarians, 1926), *Barbárok* (Barbarians, 1932), and other volumes, often have the force of his best novels, and a tighter structure. Móricz's plays, many of them dramatizations of his prose works, tend to be rather slow and diffuse; *Sári Biró* (Judge Biro, 1910) and *Búzakalász* (Sheaf of Wheat, 1924) have been called the best of them. His poetry is of little importance.

Móricz's first marriage ended with his wife's suicide; the second, to an actress, was happier. One of his several children, Virág, is also a writer. Móricz, who became for a time coeditor of *Nyugat*, lived for the last twenty years of his life at Leányfalu, a resort near Budapest, and died there. He wrote a rather shapeless autobiography, *Életem regénye* (The Story of My Life).

Critics have compared Móricz to Zola and to

Guy de Maupassant, to the Polish realist Wladyslaw Reymont, and to the American naturalists, especially Frank Norris and Theodore Dreiser. He has been translated into many European languages, but has made no great impact in English. Many contemporary Hungarian critics regard him as their country's greatest prose writer, and even those who think this claim excessive recognize his importance as Hungary's first modern novelist, the father of the great populist movement of the 1930s.

PRINCIPAL WORKS IN ENGLISH TRANSLATION: The Torch, 1931; Be Faithful Unto Death, (Budapest) 1962; To Eat One's Fill (story) *in* Duczyńska, I. and Polanyi, K. (eds.) The Plough and the Pen, 1963.
ABOUT: Duczyńska, I. and Polanyi, K. (eds.) The Plough and the Pen, 1963; Penguin Companion to Literature 2, 1969; Reményi, J. Hungarian Writers and Literature, 1964; Smith, H. (ed.) Columbia Dictionary of Modern European Literature, 1947; Vasvary, E. and Coleman, M. A History of Modern Drama, 1947. *Periodicals*—Books Abroad Winter 1943; New York Evening Post May 23, 1931; New York Times May 24, 1931.

MORRIS, JAMES (HUMPHRY) (October 2, 1926–), English journalist and author, writes: "I was born in Somerset, England, in 1926, the third son of a curious but altogether happy marriage between people of very different backgrounds. I come of Welsh border stock, and my paternal great-grandfather, I think it was, is said to have been the last coracle fisherman on the River Wye. My father, who was horribly gassed in the first world war, died as a result when I was a child. I was educated at Lancing, a high Anglican public school in the south of England, and at Christ Church, Oxford; between the two I had four years in the army, being commissioned into an old-school mechanized cavalry regiment which I remember with great affection and respect.

"After Oxford I spent ten years in journalism, almost all as a foreign correspondent—first with the London *Times*, then the Manchester *Guardian*. This enabled me, in a superficial but extraordinarily enjoyable way, to see almost the entire world before I was thirty-five. I covered events as varied as the first ascent of Everest, the trial of Powers in Moscow, the Algerian *coup* which brought de Gaulle back to power and the first motor crossing of the Omani desert. By 1960 I had had enough, and so I suspect had my readers. I settled down to write books, paying for the extravagances of hedonist taste by undertaking magazine and television commissions too.

"The books have been of varying quality, subject and success, ranging from a description of the World Bank and its historical significance to a long portrait of Venice. Many critics find them too ornate or whimsical; others are irritated by the style, as I sometimes am myself. Probably their defects and their merits spring from a certain easy-going amateurism that has always infused my family affairs, plus too much detachment—a physical inability to identify myself with any particular segment of any specific society. Their only modest aim, though, has been to give pleasure, and I like to think they stand in the light-hearted romantic tradition exemplified for me by Kinglake.

"I live in a large old house with a sea-trout river in a most beautiful part of North Wales, between the mountains and the sea, secluded in several layers of privacy, at the end of the bumpiest private lane in Britain. I have a wife, three sons and a daughter, and we keep a small house in Oxford as a *pied-à-terre* for the great world.

"I spend perhaps a quarter of each year travelling abroad, but I suspect that if it were not for the economics of our trade, I would stay at Trefan for ever, writing florid books of the imagination to entertain my descendants with."

In 1953, James Morris's exclusive account of the conquest of Everest in *The Times* established him at the age of twenty-seven as (to quote *The Economist*) "the leading journalist of our generation." Some of his talents are demonstrated in the graceful and apparently effortless sketch above, which gives an extraordinarily complete and objective account of his life and work, and is slightly less than five hundred words long.

But Morris's remarks about his writings should not stand without comment. As his sketch shows, his air of "easy-going amateurism" masks great professional skill and self-discipline. And while it is true that some critics think his books "too ornate or whimsical," many more would accept Alistair Cooke's appraisal of Morris as a "Flaubert in orbit." *As I Saw the U.S.A.* seemed to Denis Brogan "one of the very best travel books, one of the very best impressions of contemporary America I have ever read." The steady stream of topographical and political studies which have followed that first book have shown no dilution in quality, and have been admired most often on account of Morris's skill in conveying the "emotional tone of a place," his "irrepressible curiosity about people," and his talent for "the apt and aromatic word."

Morris received the George Polk Memorial Award for journalism in 1961 and the Heinemann Award for *The World of Venice*, his "eloquent, loving, but clear-sighted essays on that 'cheek-by-jowl, back-of-the-hand, under-the-counter, higgledy-piggledy, anecdotal city.'" *The Road to Huddersfield* was a Book-of-the-Month Club choice in the United States, where *Newsweek* called it "not merely an objective account of the [World Bank's] efforts to raise living standards around the world, but a study in the ironic disparities of modern civilization." *Pax Britannica* is an excellent if "somewhat conventionalised" account of the British Empire at its peak—during Queen Victoria's Diamond Jubilee in 1897. In *Heaven's Command* he turns back to review the sixty years of Victorian rule which led up to that apotheosis.

Morris is a Fellow of the Royal Society of Literature. He was married in 1949 to the former Elizabeth Tuckniss and they had five children, of whom one is deceased. However, Morris had long been convinced, according to one account, "that he was the victim of a genetic mixup—a woman trapped in a man's body." He underwent a sex change in 1972 and is now known as Jan Morris. *Conundrum*, the author's "sensitive and deeply moving" account of this event, and the mental and emotional changes it involved, was scheduled for publication in 1974.

PRINCIPAL WORKS: Coast to Coast (U.S., As I Saw the U.S.A.), 1956; The Market of Seleukia (U.S., Islam Inflamed, A Middle East Picture), 1957; Sultan in Oman, 1957; Coronation Everest, 1958; South African Winter, 1958; The Hashemite Kings, 1959; Venice (U.S., The World of Venice), 1960; The Upstairs Donkey, and Other Stolen Stories, 1961; Cities, 1963; The Outriders, a Liberal View of Britain, 1963; The World Bank: A Prospect (U.S., The Road to Huddersfield: A Journey to Five Continents), 1963; The Presence of Spain (with photographs by Evelyn Hofer), 1964 (repub. in 1970 as Spain); Oxford, 1965; Barcelona (Famous Cities of the World), 1967; Pax Britannica, 1968; The Great Port, 1969; Places (essays), 1972; Heaven's Command: An Imperial Progress, 1973.

ABOUT: Contemporary Authors 3, 1963; Current Biography, 1964; Who's Who, 1973. *Periodicals*—Book-of-the-Month Club News July 1963; Newsweek August 5, 1963.

"MORRIS, JOHN." *See* HEARNE, JOHN

"MORRIS, JULIAN." *See* WEST, MORRIS

MORSE, SAMUEL FRENCH (June 4, 1916–), American poet, writes: "I was born in Salem, Massachusetts, and have lived all my life in New England. I grew up in Danvers, where I went to public school; and after graduating from Dartmouth in 1936, and a year without any real job, went on to graduate school at Harvard. An assistantship there led to an appointment as a member of the English A staff. After three years in the USAAF, I held an instructorship at the University of Maine, before completing a Ph.D. at Boston University. I taught at Trinity College in Hartford from 1951 to 1958; then at Mount Holyoke. At present I am at Northeastern University. I am married. We have one son. We make our permanent residence at Hancock Point, Maine.

"Writing seemed to be the thing I did best even at high school, but I never had any illusions about making a living as a writer. Teaching I liked, too, and it was probably inevitable that I should become a teacher. The first poems I had published appeared in *College Verse*, *Poetry*, *Smoke*, and the *New Republic*. By 1943, there were enough to make a book. That Wallace Stevens should have volunteered to write an introduction for a book of mine was as flattering as it was unexpected. There have been two other books since then. The pleasure of reading poetry aloud to children has led to some trial flights with writing poems for children. The experience has been a good one; it has, I think, added a dimension to my work.

"Thoreau's observation that 'we commonly do not remember that it is, after all, always the first person that is speaking,' has provided one point of reference for my work: it has been a warning as well as a fact with which to come to terms. A clearly visible structure is useful as a means of separating what is of interest only to the first person—what is, ultimately, only private knowledge—from what may be of interest to someone else; at the same time, the structure and the raw material ought to fuse in a way that makes any separation of 'form' and 'content,' in the finished work, impossible. What I want, I suppose, is to have my cake and to eat it. As for my raw material, I remember objecting to someone's dismissal of Thoreau on the ground that 'I have traveled a good deal in Concord' was evidence of an intolerable provincialism, as if his raw material had not been metamorphosed by its context. Perhaps not, although the 'form' of *Walden* remains one of its most compelling qualities. It may be that I have traveled too much in my own province, and that my raw material remains too local. But the character of local speech, local landscape, and local attitudes is a reality I greatly respect and try to delineate with whatever skill I have and have learned. It goes without saying that it seems to me it should hardly be otherwise.

"Since I also believe that 'everything written is as good as it is dramatic,' the first person which appears more and more often in my poems—like the 'you' that sometimes appears—is meant to be an imagined person speaking or meditating in a scene. I also like the idea of dialogue in a context; and although plausible dialogue seems easy enough to write, dialogue with a real point, within the limitations imposed by pretty regular rhythmical and rhyming patterns is another matter altogether. I like to work with theme-and-variation structures: Thomas Hardy still sets a standard to emulate in his mastery of such things; the obvious flaws and awkardnesses of many of his poems do not, finally, matter very much.

"But no one is a writer all the time. Our summers in Maine mean a great deal to us. Though we are summer people at Hancock Point, we are not really 'from away' any longer. We do a lot of hiking in Acadia National Park, where the trails are not strenuous but the rewards are very satisfying; and we still have many parts of the State to explore. Gardening is another pleasure.

"In addition to poetry, I have done a fair amount of criticism and reviewing, and have edited *Opus Posthumous*, by Wallace Stevens, and a selection of his poems. I also compiled a checklist of his published writings, which the Yale University Library published in 1954, as a part of his seventy-fifth birthday celebration.

"One need not try to account for all one has done, or not done. If one is fortunate, the various things one writes accumulate, get sorted out, published in a book, and, it may be, read. A book ought to have some sort of design, I think; it ought to be more than a miscellany. Sometimes the pattern that work written over a period of years reveals is instructive: at least one sees where one has been, and may be able to learn from that where one is going. Of the judgments passed on such matters, I am not the one to speak."

Morse's subject, Wallace Stevens said in his introduction to *Time of Year*, "is the particulars of experience. He is a realist; he tries to get at New England experience, at New England past and present, at New England foxes and snow and thunderheads." Morse is indeed one of the most rewarding of the New England poets, in whose work, as John Holmes said, "the seasons come alive again."

Mark McCloskey, one of several critics who have pointed out that Morse is not, however, merely a regional poet, notes that his themes are "intensely human, stressing now the humor, now the nostalgia, at times the anguish, at others the longing in human experience. The phenomenon of childhood, the subtleties of friendship, the human relevance of geography often concern him. The imagined journeys of the spirit in search of ontological meaning are his abiding and most significant theme, in terms of which he achieves and communicates dazzling insights."

Morse's ideas are sometimes found a little conventional, his utterance too mild and bland, but by and large he is rescued from these dangers by the sharpness of his intelligence, the exactness of his language, his "blunt, vertical integrity." The "clearly visible structure" which he values is valued by others in his work: "By the use of 'forms' like the sonnet and villanelle, Mr. Morse uncovers for himself and orders for us his emotive insights, and provides the rhythmical emphasis necessary to convey them."

Wallace Stevens having introduced his first book, Morse returned the compliment by editing Stevens's *Opus Posthumous*, which rescued many good poems from oblivion, and subsequently wrote the poet's first biography. Morse is the son of Carl French

SAMUEL FRENCH MORSE

Abner Morse, a banker, and Alice (Pickering) Morse. His wife, whom he married in 1950, is the former Jane Crowell.

PRINCIPAL WORKS: Time of Year, A First Book of Poems introduced by Wallace Stevens, 1944; Wallace Stevens: A Preliminary Checklist of His Published Writings, 1898–1954, 1954; The Scattered Causes (poems), 1955; (ed.) Stevens, W. Opus Posthumous, 1957; (ed.) Stevens, W. Poems, 1959; The Changes (poems), 1964; All in a Suitcase (rhymed alphabet book for children), 1966; Wallace Stevens—Poetry as Life, 1970; Sea Sums (poems for children), 1970.

ABOUT: Contemporary Authors 9–10, 1964; Stevens, W. *introduction to* Morse, S. F. Time of Year, 1944. *Periodicals*—New York Times Book Review April 18, 1965; Poetry November 1965.

MORTIMER, JOHN (CLIFFORD) (April 21, 1923–), English dramatist, novelist, and critic, was born in Hampstead, London, the only child of Clifford and Kathleen (Smith) Mortimer. Clifford Mortimer was a barrister who continued to practice after he had gone blind, and his son as a child helped him by reading his briefs to him and entertained him by making up stories, serving a precocious apprenticeship in his two professions. John Mortimer was educated at Harrow and at Brasenose College, Oxford University, where he read law. After his graduation he worked for a time with the Crown Film Unit as an assistant director and scriptwriter, an experience which inspired his acid first novel, *Charade*. Mortimer was called to the bar in 1948 and has been a busy advocate and a prolific part-time writer ever since (aided by the fact that he needs only four hours' sleep a night).

Between 1947 and 1956 Mortimer wrote six novels, several of them with legal backgrounds, all

JOHN MORTIMER

of them more or less traditional in manner. The critical response was encouraging, and two of the novels were selected by book clubs. Reviewers found Mortimer's fiction highly readable, strong in its characterization, rather sour in its social observation. His laconic prose was much admired, but there was some feeling that he strained a little after the "curt image" in a way that reflected his admiration for Raymond Chandler. Mortimer, as "Geoffrey Lincoln," also wrote a detective novel before turning to the theatre.

His first play was the one-act *Dock Brief*, originally produced on radio by the British Broadcasting Corporation in 1957. It tells the story of Morgenhall, a totally inadequate old barrister who receives his first brief at the age of sixty-three, when he is entrusted with the hopeless defense of Fowle, a simple-minded murderer. Morgenhall dreams of a miraculous defense, an impassioned plea to the jury which will save his client against the odds and establish his own reputation. When his moment comes, words fail him and Fowle is convicted and then pardoned on the grounds that his defense was inadequate. The old lawyer's illusions are preserved when his client assumes that this happy outcome had been planned by Morgenhall from the outset.

The play was obviously the work of a dramatist with a superb ear for dialogue and a talent for drawing grotesque but believable characters. Finding that "at last, I was writing what I had wanted all my life to say," Mortimer abandoned fiction entirely. *The Dock Brief*, which won the Italia Prize as a radio play, and has been adapted also for television, the cinema, and the theatre, was first staged in 1958, with another of Mortimer's most admired one-act plays. This was *What Shall We Tell Caroline?*, in which an assistant master at a seedy prep school invents a raffish past for himself to conceal the pointlessness of his life.

Both pieces appear in *Three Plays* and illustrate Mortimer's belief, expressed in his introduction to that collection, that comedy is "the only thing worth writing in this despairing age, provided that the comedy is truly on the side of the lonely, the neglected and unsuccessful, and plays its part in the war against established rules and against the imposing of an established code of behavior upon individual and unpredictable human beings." All of John Mortimer's plays are about people who are unable to cope with ordinary life and who, for better or worse, take refuge in fantasy.

Mortimer's first full-length play was *The Wrong Side of the Park* (1960), whose heroine, Elaine, trapped it seems in a drab and miserable second marriage, pines for the happiness she had known with her first husband. It emerges that her first marriage was in fact wretched, and that her fantasies about it are a subconscious attempt to atone for the guilt she feels towards her dead husband. Where Morgenhall in *The Dock Brief* needs his illusions, having nothing else, Elaine cannot hope to live fully until she confronts the truth, as she begins to do at the end of the play. *The Wrong Side of the Park* is full of evidence of Mortimer's warmly sympathetic insight into character, and his ability to spin highly entertaining dialogue out of any situation and at almost any length. The commonest criticism of the play was that it was not really a three-act piece at all, but a one-acter skillfully padded and extended by the introduction of an irrelevant subplot.

A number of excellent one-act plays and sketches followed, several of them on television, and the conviction grew that Mortimer would be wise to confine himself to the short forms he handled so well. This view seemed justified when *Two Stars for Comfort*, his second full-length play, received mixed reviews in 1962. For a time Mortimer turned to other things, writing for the screen and, in 1965, making his very successful adaptation of Feydeau's farce *A Flea in Her Ear* (*La puce à l'oreille*) for the National Theatre.

In 1967, however, *The Judge*, in many ways Mortimer's most ambitious play, removed any doubt about his ability to sustain a full-length work. Mr. Justice Chard, a judge feared for his severity in court, chooses to conduct his last assize in the cathedral town where he was born, and which he has not visited for forty years. His presence instigates a cruel campaign against Serena, the town bohemian, who, albeit in a warmhearted and amateur way, operates above her antique shop something very like a brothel. Serena is driven from the town, but not before we learn that Chard had been her first lover. It is not Serena nor the town of his birth that he has come to judge, but himself, driven all his life by a sense of unatoned guilt. The play functions on several levels: as an extremely illuminating and often entertaining study of a community and its mores, as an investigation of character, and as an inquiry into the whole nature of crime and punishment, sin and forgiveness. Harold Hobson wrote: "The piece is written throughout with eclectic grace, and makes that remarriage between thoughtfulness and action which is a principal need of the contemporary theatre."

There was even more praise for Mortimer's next full-length play, *A Voyage Round My Father*. This undisguised family memoir, which reached the stage via radio and television, is built up from a series of short scenes, linked by a running commentary provided by a spokesman, the author-raisonneur. As the title suggests, the piece is primarily a study, witty and affectionate, of Mortimer's father, who absolutely ignores the tragedy of his blindness, and reserves all his considerable resources of anger and frustration for such domestic disasters as an undercooked egg. Mortimer Senior emerges as a frivolous man, who mocks his family, the law, and the world at large; his enigmatic heroism remains, unexplained but touching and impressive. Irving Wardle called the play "an act of love" and "formally much the most successful of Mortimer's full-length plays." There followed a translation of Carl Zuckmayer's satirical play *The Captain of Köpenick* (1971), an adaptation for the stage (1972) of Robert Graves's two novels about the Emperor Claudius, and *Collaborators* (1973), a partly autobiographical comedy about a dramatist-barrister which delighted some reviewers but seemed to one "hopelessly contrived."

At the beginning of his career as a playwright, there was a tendency for Mortimer to be thought of as one of the new wave of British dramatists who emerged with him in the mid-1950s. He himself has never had any such pretensions, though he admires the work of such writers as Pinter, Osborne, and Wesker. But neither is he, as he has been called, Terence Rattigan's likeliest heir. Though he is a careful and expert craftsman who writes almost as if the British dramatic revolution had never taken place, the attitudes illustrated by his plays are far from traditional, and he shares the humanist and anti-establishment views of his contemporaries, if not their methods. Ronald Bryden called him "the most novelistic playwright the fifties threw up," and the one with "the clearest eye for how Britain actually looked, talked and comported itself in the fifties and sixties."

John Mortimer is active as a journalist and a television debater, and was for some time the drama critic of the London *Evening Standard*. His legal career has been as active and successful as his literary career, and he was named a Queen's Counsel in 1966. Mortimer was married in 1949 to the former Penelope Fletcher, and until their divorce in 1972 their family included six children, four of them Penelope Mortimer's by her first marriage. Mrs. Mortimer is well known as a novelist and has collaborated with her husband on film scripts and on an engaging travel book called *With Love and Lizards*. John Mortimer has a daughter by his second wife, the former Penelope Gollop. He is a tall, urbane man who enjoys cooking and going to the theatre.

PRINCIPAL WORKS: *Novels*—Charade, 1947; Rumming Park, 1949; Answer Yes or No (U.S., The Silver Hook), 1950; Like Men Betrayed, 1953; The Narrowing Stream, 1954; Three Winters, 1956; (as "Geoffrey Lincoln") No Moaning of the Bar, 1957. *Plays*—Three Plays (The Dock Brief, What Shall We Tell Caroline?, and I Spy), 1958; The Wrong Side of the Park, 1960; Lunch Hour and Other Plays, 1960; Two Stars for Comfort, 1962; A Flea in Her Ear, 1965; The Judge, 1967; Five Plays (The Dock Brief, What Shall We Tell Caroline?, I Spy, Lunch Hour, Collect Your Hand Baggage), 1970; Come as You Are (four related one-act plays), 1971; A Voyage Round My Father, 1971; The Captain of Köpenick, 1971; Collaborators, 1973. *Nonfiction*—(with Penelope Mortimer) With Love and Lizards, 1957.

ABOUT: Contemporary Authors 13–14, 1965; Taylor, J. R. Anger and After, 1963; Wellwarth, G. E. The Theatre of Paradox and Protest, 1964; Who's Who, 1973; Who's Who in the Theatre, 1972.

MORTIMER, PENELOPE (RUTH) (1918–), English novelist, short story writer, screen writer, and critic, was born in Rhyl, North Wales, the daughter of the Reverend Arthur Forbes Fletcher and the former Caroline Maggs. According to a *Guardian* interviewer, her father was "a highly eccentric clergyman who discovered too late that he did not believe in God and thereupon preached about life, and took over the whole of the parish magazine to explain that the Soviet persecution of the Church was entirely right." She was educated at a succession of private schools, including one intended for daughters of the clergy, and another devoted to the tenets of anthroposophy and freedom. She left school at seventeen, spent a year at London University, and in 1937 married Charles Dimont, a journalist. That marriage ended in divorce, and in 1949 she married the writer John Mortimer. She has four children by her first marriage and two by her second.

Mrs. Mortimer has said that her first writings consisted of "poetry and short stories of immense gloom and obscurity." The gloom has persisted, but not the obscurity. She has become a sad naturalist of the "Jaguar jungle" of family life among the British professional classes; a stylist "pellucid, taut, poetic and compassionate by turns."

After a precocious first novel, *Johanna*, published

PENELOPE MORTIMER

when she was nineteen, Penelope Mortimer established her reputation with *A Villa in Summer*, which sets a sophisticated metropolitan couple down in a country cottage and observes their gradual disillusionment with the simple life and with each other, painting a "picture of the abrasions of middle-class married life" which Brendan Gill thought "just, compassionate, and dreadful." *The Bright Prison* is another tragicomedy about people disastrously released from the confining but supporting "chain of habit," and *Cave of Ice* "a terrifying, brutal, totally persuasive" revelation of the emptiness beneath the surface of an apparently happy marriage.

It has been pointed out that all of Mrs. Mortimer's heroines are women who need "corroboration" of their identities, and seek this in their men and their children. This is very evident in *The Pumpkin Eater*, in which the young narrator, after three marriages and many children, catches a "glimpse of herself, alone, afraid, and free," and has the breakdown which, described in a series of linked sketches, forms the theme of "a moving poem about a spirit in defeat." This novel, Mrs. Mortimer's best-known book, was serialized, filmed (with a script by Harold Pinter), and became a best seller.

In *My Friend Says It's Bullet-Proof*, the heroine's dreadful sense of isolation develops during her convalescence after the surgical removal of a breast. Muriel Rowbridge is a journalist who, shortly after this ordeal, is sent on assignment to the United States. There she collapses into two quite dissimilar love affairs, from one of which she retrieves some faith in herself. Critics called the book "compelling, vivid, often funny, modulating with great skill between third-person narrative and Muriel's thoughts and scribbled notes"; most of them nevertheless found it finally unconvincing, a little enigmatic. *The Home* is a partly autobiographical novel about a woman awaiting a divorce, which is to her a kind of death. One reviewer wrote: "The courage that makes her heroine sympathetic instead of self-pitying is indirectly what has enabled Mrs. Mortimer to write a novel about despair which is, nevertheless, often very funny too."

Penelope Mortimer's short stories, most of them written for the *New Yorker*, were collected in *Saturday Lunch With the Brownings*. They are, like her novels, "marvellously deft focussings-down on times of torment in the lives of almost ordinary English professional people." *With Love and Lizards* (1957) was an earlier and altogether more cheerful book—a lively account, written by Mrs. Mortimer in collaboration with her husband, of a two-month stay at Positano in southern Italy with their six children and a German nanny. John and Penelope Mortimer were divorced in 1972. Mrs. Mortimer has done some writing for the screen, but thinks the cinema "is only a very minor art—if it is an art at all." Nevertheless she served from 1967 to 1970 as film critic of the London *Observer*. The author's daughter Caroline is well known as an actress, and played the lead in Penelope Mortimer's 1973 television play *Three's One*.

PRINCIPAL WORKS: *As Penelope Dimont*—Johanna, 1947. *As Penelope Mortimer*—A Villa in Summer, 1954; The Bright Prison, 1956; (with John Mortimer) With Love and Lizards. 1957; Daddy's Gone A-Hunting, 1958 (U.S., Cave of Ice); Saturday Lunch With the Brownings (short stories), 1960; The Pumpkin Eater, 1962; My Friend Says It's Bullet-Proof, 1967; The Home, 1972.

ABOUT: Penguin Companion to Literature 1, 1971; Vinson, J. (ed.) Contemporary Novelists, 1972; Who's Who, 1973; Who's Who in America, 1972–1973. *Periodicals*—Guardian September 13, 1971; Sunday Times (London) September 12, 1971; Times Literary Supplement October 12, 1967; September 24, 1971.

"MORTON, ANTHONY." *See* CREASEY, JOHN

MORTON, FREDERIC (October 5, 1924–), American novelist, biographer, short story writer, and journalist, writes: "I was born in Vienna, the son of a manufacturer. I went to *Realgymnasium* (prep school) there, receiving A grades in Latin and Physical Education, barely surviving in all other subjects.

"After Hitler annexed Austria, my family, being Jewish, left for London in 1939. Suddenly we were penniless, and to make a living I became a baker's apprentice. I fell in love with baking, and continued going to baking school and working in bakeries in New York after transplantation there in 1943. I entered City College in New York, and studied food chemistry with the idea of becoming a baking scientist or of running a baking plant. I received a B.S. in chemistry in 1947. In the same year I wrote my first novel (*The Hound*) which won the Dodd Mead Intercollegiate Literary Prize, a fact which confused me so much that I took an M.A. in philosophy at the New School for Social Research and wrote a second novel (*The Darkness Below*) set in a bakery.

"I did not see myself as a professional writer yet and thought of an academic career laced with literary endeavors. Recipient of a Columbia University Fellowship in 1950, I became a candidate for Ph.D. in comparative literature there. But instead of completing my studies, I began to teach English on the graduate and undergraduate levels at the University of Utah, University of Southern California, Johns Hopkins University in Baltimore, New York University, and the New School for Social Research. Teaching English to Americans all over the United States was the cheapest way for a foreigner like me to see my new country.

"In the mid-fifties, though, academic life lost some of its charm for me. I decided to risk full-time freelance writing. I started to contribute to many of America's better-known magazines—like *Esquire*, the *Reporter*, the *Nation*, the *Atlantic Monthly*. Since 1954 I've been a regular contributor to *Holiday Magazine*, which financed my travels all over the world. For *Holiday* amd other magazines I've written profiles ranging from Gina Lollobrigida to Leonard Bernstein and Thomas Mann; social essays and travel articles about Europe, Africa and America.

"I also became a regular literary contributor to the New York *Herald Tribune* and the New York *Times Book Review*, reviewing books by Arthur Koestler, Evelyn Waugh, Thomas Mann, Jean-Paul Sartre, William Saroyan, Romain Gary, etc. I published two further novels (*Asphalt and Desire* and *The Witching Ship*) which were brought out in the United States as well as in England and the Continent. Though a few oddballs like Aldous Huxley, Thomas Mann, Upton Sinclair, and Dorothy Parker praised these novels, hundreds of thousands of book-buyers—did not buy them. Then I wrote a biography called *The Rothschilds*, and hundreds of thousands of people did buy that one.

"Following *The Rothschilds*, I wrote some short fiction published in *Playboy* and the *Hudson Review* and a fifth novel, *The Schatten Affair*. I think all my writing reflects in some way the increasing tension between the human personality and the progressively anti-human civilization which surrounds him.

"Looking back on my life so far, I find it a sort of fabric of contradictions. I come from a very non-literary background, from a family steeped in the bourgeois ethic of nine A.M. to five P.M. work, yet I am a writer who works late and gets up late (and, incidentally, never fails to feel guilty when waking at noon). I am middle-European by birth and early background and yet write in English (a language I've worshiped ever since my early refugee years, when I used to spend two hours a day wallowing in *Webster's Unabridged* at the public library). I am an intellectual by bent and habit and yet find my happiest release in physical exercise such as walking, tennis, skiing, and skating, and I often look back nostalgically to the strenuous years I spent as a baker's apprentice. I very much prefer fiction to nonfiction, and yet my nonfiction outsells my fiction at the ratio of about ten to one. A constant puzzlement is my feeling about where home is: when in the United States, I long for Europe with its childhood memories; when in Europe, I find myself attracted to the drive and electricity of America.

FREDERIC MORTON

"Some of these contradictions are expressed by the works-in-progress. One is a biography of the Empress Elisabeth of Austria, for which the research is completed but the writing not yet begun; another is a novel about the contemporary European scene as viewed by a naturalized American like myself; and a comedy about the pitfalls of success in this country. I am also preparing a collection of my short stories which have the most heterogeneous possible backgrounds; they are variously set in Taormina, Sicily; Kitzbuehel, Austria; New York, Vienna, Morocco, Andalusia, and London. They are, come to think of it, a pretty good mirror of my life."

Frederic Morton is the son of Frank and Rose (Ungvary) Morton. His father, a manufacturer of metal goods, after being arrested and placed in the Dachau concentration camp in 1939 was, through bribery, released. The family then proceeded to London.

Before the war, Morton says, his English vocabulary consisted of one word: "goal." He had learned a lot more by 1947, when he published *The Hound*. It is about a young Viennese aristocrat who is destroyed when World War II shatters the corrupt and artificial society in which he had flourished. *The Darkness Below* in a sense complements the first novel, showing how a refugee intellectual's work in a slum bakery reveals to him the pointlessness of his earlier life. The two novels, of which the second is at least partly autobiographical, can be read as a farewell to the old world of Morton's youth, "its sterile restrictions and refinements." Both books were regarded as promising, if a little ornate, and H. R. Warfel found in them evidence that Morton was "influenced most by the ideas of Schopenhauer and Nietzsche."

Asphalt and Desire is an unconvincing attempt to describe in her own words the experiences and feelings of a Jewish girl in New York, shortly after her graduation from Hunter College. *The Witching Ship*, about an Atlantic crossing by refugees in 1940, and *The Schatten Affair*, a "morality tale" about a public relations campaign in West Berlin, both divided the reviewers to an extraordinary extent. The first was found almost unbearably "coquettish" in its style by some readers, but seemed to a reviewer in the *Times Literary Supplement* to possess an elegance, "a delight in the unexpectedly droll," reminiscent of Nabokov. The second, dismissed as wholly without value by *Time*'s reviewer, impressed Daniel Stern as "a superbly graceful example of the story-teller's art." There was a mixed reception also for *Snow Gods*, which studies a particularly corrupt and/or foolish sample of the jet set, pursuing power and pleasure in a chic hotel in the Swiss Alps.

There was less critical conflict about the merits of *The Rothschilds*, Morton's history of a family, and no doubt at all about its popular success. Most reviewers were unequivocally delighted by the book's narrative power, its vividness, its brightly told anecdotes. A few, like W. H. Hale, thought it relatively weak in its account of the financial transactions which brought the Rothschilds to greatness. However, as Hale said, when it gets to "the visible result of all this victory, the tale grows fascinating, luxuriating in the social and human details of what happened once the Rothschild tribe had financed England, bailed out the returning French Bourbons, helped Austria intervene in Italy and lent millions to the Holy See itself." The book was subsequently translated into a warm, entertaining, and popular musical.

Morton was married in 1957 to Marcia Colman, and has a daughter.

PRINCIPAL WORKS: The Hound (novel), 1947; The Darkness Below (novel), 1949; Asphalt and Desire (novel), 1952; The Witching Ship (novel), 1960; The Rothschilds (biography), 1962; The Schatten Affair (novel), 1965; Snow Gods (novel), 1969.

ABOUT: Contemporary Authors 2, 1963; Warfel, H. R. American Novelists of Today, 1951; Who's Who in America, 1972–1973. *Periodical*—New York Times Book Review May 21, 1967.

MORTON, JOHN (CAMERON ANDRIEU) BINGHAM (MICHAEL) ("BEACHCOMBER") (June 7, 1893–), English humorist, journalist, biographer, historian, and novelist, has been described as "a foul reactionary" who "wears the accusation like a medal." At the core of his humor and of his way of life is a romantic's hatred of humbug and materialism and of "everything that's been invented since I was born" (including the typewriter; a fountain pen is the nearest he can get "to managing anything mechanical").

He was born in London, the son of Edward Morton, a journalist and dramatist, and Rosamond (Bingham) Morton. He was educated at Park House School, Southborough, and at Harrow. He also spent a year at Worcester College, Oxford, sampling a variety of courses, failing in them all, and thoroughly enjoying himself.

Morton enlisted in the Army in 1914 and fought in France, receiving his commission in 1916. He was transferred to an Intelligence department in 1917 and a year later went into the Ministry of Labour. Demobilized in 1919, he promptly began his literary career with a war novel called *The Barber of Putney*, notable chiefly as the first of about fifty books.

In 1920 Morton joined the staff of the *Sunday Express* as resident poet, "adorning the paper's leader-page with slim verses and stories about fairyland." After two years of this he moved to the newsroom of the conservative *Daily Express*, and in 1924 succeeded his friend D. B. Wyndham Lewis as "Beachcomber." His antic daily column "By the Way" has decorated the editorial page of the *Express* ever since.

According to Michael Frayn, it was Morton and D. B. Wyndham Lewis who "introduced to newspapers the superb anarchy of the English nonsense-writing tradition, the brief devastating parody, and the permanent staff of characters." As the mood takes him, Morton may subvert reality with some fantastic news item which might just be true; pillory a correspondent; recruit a few of his stock characters to illustrate some topical point; or break off to reminisce about a walking tour in France.

He has cheerfully insulted his readers for years, either directly or through Prodnose, archetypal member of the British public, who is the ponderous and imperturbable enemy of his creator's flights of fancy.

Over the years, Beachcomber has invented some thirty or forty characters to illustrate the varieties of human idiocy and knavery. Among them are Dr. Smart-Allick, headmaster of Narkover, whose greatest alumnus is the lecherous cardsharp and con man Captain Foulenough; the calamitous diva Rustiguzzi; and Dr. Strabismus (Whom God Preserve) of Utrecht, perennial inventor of the all-purpose machine. There is also Mr. Justice Cocklecarrot, with his attendant barristers Snapdriver and Gooseboote, wrestling forever with the case of Mrs. Tasker, who cannot be dissuaded from driving her twelve red-bearded dwarfs into Mrs. Renton's hallway. These and others have "outstripped the page and become members of that heterogeneous collection of public heroes who make up English mythology." In 1969 they took their places in a television comedy series.

Morton has also produced a substantial body of work under his own name as a historian, biographer, and historical novelist, drawing mostly upon a profound feeling for and knowledge of France, its history, language, countryside, and wines. He has also written an excellent biography of his master, Hilaire Belloc—a portrait "simply done, and excellently." Morton, who entered the Roman Catholic Church in 1922, met Belloc the same year and has never changed his opinion that the latter was "a great man who was also the greatest writer of his day."

J. B. Morton lives in a Georgian house in Sussex with his wife, the former Dr. Mary O'Leary. He is a small, balding man with close-cropped gray hair and an expression that is said to be by turns startled and helplessly amused. His manner is gentle, although he is a man of violent enthusiasms and equally violent antipathies. He is not given to literary theorizing but has defined a sense of humor, rather reluctantly, as "a sense of proportion." He received a CBE in 1952. In England, as Michael Frayn says, Beachcomber "is an institution, and a proper appreciation of him is a passport to the society of all right-thinking men. . . . He is a satirist whose savagery is concealed by the obviousness of his jokes . . . there is, for those with eyes to see, the perpetual challenge to the modern world which runs like some message in a simple code through all he writes."

PRINCIPAL WORKS: The Barber of Putney, 1919; Mr. Thake, 1929; By the Way, 1931; The Bastille Falls: And Other Studies of the French Revolution, 1936; By the Way, 1936; The Dauphin, Louis XVII, 1937; The New Ireland, 1938; Pyrenean, 1938; The Dancing Cabman: and Other Verses, 1938; Saint-Just, 1939; Captain Foulenough & Company, 1944; The Gascon: A Story of the French Revolution, 1946; Brumaire: The Rise of Bonaparte, 1948; The Misadventures of Dr. Strabismus, 1949; Camille Desmoulins: And Other Studies of the French Revolution, 1951; St. Thérèse of Lisieux: The Making of a Saint, 1954; Hilaire Belloc: A Memoir, 1955; Marshal Ney, 1958; Merry-Go-Round, 1959; The Best of Beachcomber, 1963.

J. B. MORTON

ABOUT: Frayn, M. *introduction to* The Best of Beachcomber, 1963; Hoehn, M. Catholic Authors, 1948; Who's Who, 1973. *Periodicals*—America October 23, 1954; Atlantic December 1958; Times Literary Supplement November 6, 1948; February 23, 1951; May 20, 1955.

MOSS, HOWARD (January 22, 1922–), American poet, critic, and dramatist, writes: "I was born in Manhattan but was brought up in Rockaway Beach—where we reportedly moved for my health—in a small suburban town called Belle Harbor. I attended the local public and high schools. I decided on the Middle West when it came time to go to college. The Middle West had the same sort of romantic aura for me that New York had for the people I met in the Middle West. I stayed at the University of Michigan for a year, transferred to the University of Wisconsin, from which I received my B.A., and somewhere in between, I spent a summer at Harvard. I did some graduate work at Columbia, but never completed it.

"I have had various jobs: a copy boy at *Time* magazine, and then a book reviewer—an embarrassing step upward, for the colleagues with whom I distributed paper clips one week distributed them to me the next—a short stint with the OWI, two years at Vassar College as an English instructor, a year as fiction editor of *Junior Bazaar*, and then the *New Yorker*, where I have been on the editorial

HOWARD MOSS

staff since 1948. Since 1950, I have been the *New Yorker's* poetry editor.

"Two facts made my early life somewhat different from most people's; my father, who had immigrated to the U.S.A. from Lithuania (at the time, Russia), once he had settled in and become 'successful,' brought his mother and father over from 'the old country,' when I was still a young child. I grew up in a middle-class community but was really under the care of my two grandparents, who were of another flavor unmistakably. Though my sister went to 'proms,' and I wore the right knickers, and my mother played bridge and mah-jongg, my grandfather made wine in the cellar and my grandmother baked her own bread. I will always be grateful to them for being there, though I sometimes had the feeling I was growing up in two places at once: Rockaway Beach and Lithuania. The other fact: because Rockaway Beach was a summer resort, yet part of New York City, my life was half sea-soaked and half citified. From the age of twelve, I was allowed to take the train to Manhattan every Saturday afternoon, and I went to the theatre once a week for years—steadily and indiscriminately. Each Saturday night, when I got back home, there was the ocean again.

"I began writing in grammar school. In high school, I wrote short stories and poems. When I was a sophomore in college, my first poem was accepted for publication by *Accent*. I have given up trying my hand at fiction—none of it is any good—but I am still trying to be a playwright. A play called *The Folding Green* was first performed by the Poets' Theatre in Cambridge, Massachusetts, in 1958, and again by the Playwrights' Unit of Theater 1965 in a workshop production in the same year. Another play, *The Oedipus Mah-Jongg Scandal*, was produced in May of 1968 by the Cooperatives Theatre Club, Inc., in New York, and a third, *The Palace at 4 a.m.*, was given a staged reading by the Playwrights Unit, also in New York.

"I have lived in the same apartment in Greenwich Village for twenty years. It has a small terrace on which I maintain a feeble garden that gives me a great deal of pleasure. I spend my summers at the sea—Easthampton or Fire Island—or in New England. I have been abroad twice, and found, to my surprise, that Ireland seems to be particularly congenial to me.

"I read a great deal and listen to music. Mozart is the composer I prefer above all others. Among writers, I admire Proust as a novelist, Chekhov as a playwright, and Donne as a poet.

"I distrust all theses and theories about writing, and dislike the idea of 'schools' of writing, both in the traditional and in the educational sense. Though I respect and sometimes envy spontaneity in writing, I revise my work a great deal."

———

Moss's first book, *The Wound and the Weather*, was published when he was twenty-four. In spite of many small successes, it was thought rather passive and static, and too full of "fashionable, half-intelligible clichés." Since then the critical response to Moss's work has warmed steadily. His excellent third book, *A Swimmer in the Air*, contained recollections of Rockaway Beach, poems about "love, memory, time passing and time very present." There were still some critics who found these lyrics too tame and facile, but as many praised Moss's "amused and amusing voice and ear," his deftness and grace. John Holmes thought him already "one of today's clearest-speaking poets."

A Winter Come, a Summer Gone was a selection of lyrics from Moss's first three books, together with new work. It confirmed his growing ability to "convey complex states of feeling"—to move as well as to delight his readers. Thom Gunn found a residue of "slickness and empty gesturing," and idiosyncrasies borrowed from Yeats, Auden, and the metaphysical poets, but concluded that Moss possessed a talent "superior to that of most of the rest of his generation."

Carol Johnson, praising the translation of Valéry's "Cimetière Marin" in *Finding Them Lost*, made the interesting suggestion that Moss "is very close to being a French poet in English, for he lacks entirely the urgent infantilism, the imperativeness of many of his contemporaries in America." This and the subsequent collection, *Second Nature*, showed him developing towards a widening range within the lyric, an increasing refinement of sensibility and delicacy of expression.

It is these qualities which were so much admired in the poet's study of *Remembrance of Things Past*, which he called *The Magic Lantern of Marcel Proust*. The book is an attempt to organize the novel's structure and content around four metaphysical concepts: gardens, windows, parties, and steeples. Opinions varied as to the over-all value of this approach, but almost all of the book's reviewers found it full of subtle perceptions and praised the vividness and lucidity of the writing. Moss's essays and reviews, collected in *Writing Against Time*, range for their subjects from Keats to Elizabeth Bowen, with an excursion into Shakespearean criticism. His dislike of "theses and theories" about writing is evident in these readable and perceptive essays, where his own critical approach varies from the detailed textual analysis of the New Criticism to purely subjective responses to Chekhov and Mann.

Moss is the son of David and Sonya (Schrag) Moss. In 1957 and 1964 he was a judge for the National Book Awards. He received *Poetry's* Janet Sewall David award in 1944, the Brandeis Creative Award in 1962, an Avery Hopwood award in 1963, and a grant from the National Institute of Arts and Letters in 1968. He was co-winner of the 1972 National Book Award in poetry, given for his *Selected Poems*.

PRINCIPAL WORKS: *Poems*—The Wound and the Weather, 1946; The Toy Fair, 1954; A Swimmer in the Air, 1957; A Winter Come, a Summer Gone: Poems, 1946–1960, 1960; Finding Them Lost, and Other Poems, 1965; Second Nature, 1968; Selected Poems, 1971. *Criticism*—The Magic Lantern of Marcel Proust, 1962; Writing Against Time, 1969. *Play*—The Folding Green, 1958. *As Editor*—Keats, 1952; The Nonsense Books of Edward Lear, 1964; The Poet's Story, 1973.

ABOUT: Contemporary Authors 2, 1963; Who's Who in America, 1972–1973. *Periodicals*—Publishers Weekly March 26, 1973.

MOWAT, FARLEY (MC GILL) (May 12, 1921–), Canadian ethnologist, nature writer, and historian, writes "I was conceived, so my father says, in a green canoe on the shores of Lake Ontario in the autumn of 1920. My father was a librarian with an itchy foot, so that I grew up in Belleville, Trenton, Toronto, Windsor, Richmond Hill, Ontario, and in Saskatoon, Saskatchewan. At the age of twelve I was reading Rabelais. At the age of fourteen I was taken to the Arctic by a great-uncle who had a passion for birds. Through my early years I too was a birdwatcher and my interest in birds, lusty living, and in the Arctic, has never left me. At one time I had thoughts of becoming a biologist. However in 1939, when Canada joined in the war against the Nazis, I enlisted in the army. During the next five years I saw action in the Hastings and Prince Edward Regiment (Infantry) in many parts of Europe and rose from Private to

FARLEY MOWAT

Captain. I may be the only soldier in history who got to be a Captain five times, and then got shoved back to a Lieutenancy. This may have been due to a chronic inability to keep my mouth shut.

"Returning from overseas in late 1945 I concluded that the society of my time was in a parlous state and I had but little respect for a world which could engender and engage in an exercise in genocide on the scale of World War II. I therefore went looking for a more civilized people, and found them in a tribe of almost unknown Eskimos in the Arctic. These people thought war was the ultimate madness; which may have had something to do with their neglect by us. After two years amongst them I came south, restored in spirit, and began my writing career with *People of the Deer*, a fierce diatribe on man's inhumanity to man and, in particular, on our inhumanity to the native peoples of this continent.

"Finding that writing was better than working for a living, I continued in this trade. I have been responsible for fourteen books. Some of them are classified (we live in a classification society) as juveniles. They may be, but I have never—and will never—insult the upcoming generations by writing 'for juveniles.' In addition to books I have written for most North American magazines, mostly on subjects of dissent, for I am a natural-born dissenter against establishments.

"I am a man of many opinions, and do not hesitate to parade them. Some samples: I am violently opposed to war in any shape or form, and resolutely refuse to allow myself to be propagandized by *either* side, in the Cold War, into a belief that armed force can ever accomplish anything of lasting merit. I have a singularly low regard for the Admass society in which we live, and confidently predict that it will lead to a social-insect type of society in the not-too-distant future, with consequent total regimentation of the individual. In this regard I see our society as being quite as much of a threat to the individual as a Communist-type society. I am appalled by the concept of *Pax Americana*, which suggests that the U.S.A. now has the right to dictate, by force when needed, the political structure and policies of other nations. In the United States–Communist confrontation I see all the ingredients for the eventual realization of George Orwell's chilling world of the future.

"In a larger sense, I believe that the world we are creating contains the seeds of our destruction as a species. We have forgotten that we are an animal, albeit a gifted one, and that no animal can long survive when it attempts to make itself completely alien in the natural environment, and when it resolutely refuses to adhere to the natural laws which govern all forms of life.

"My interests are varied in the extreme. I have written about war, about Eskimos, about Arctic voyaging, about the Atlantic salvage fleets, about the Vikings, about owls, dogs, wolves, and a wide variety of other beasts. If there is a common theme in my work it is my admiration and respect for men of adversity—that is, physical and real adversity, as opposed to the artificial and contrived adversity of our society.

"Because of this penchant, I now live in a tiny Newfoundland outport, cut off from the rest of the world except by sea. Together with some twelve hundred other men and women who have come to know themselves *as* men and women of reality, I manage to keep my sanity and to retain some perspective in a world where both sanity and perspective are becoming increasingly rare virtues. In order to prevent myself from getting 'uppity' I sail a small Newfoundland schooner in North Atlantic waters. This keeps me sufficiently terrified of the natural realities so that my opinion of myself, as a human being, remains reasonably modest.

"As a writer I have a restrained opinion of my capabilities. I consider myself a first-rate craftsman in a field where arrogant amateurs are far too numerous. I do not consider that I have a great message to deliver, nor do I believe, alas, that the pen is mightier than the sword. I have written with rage and passion directed against gross injustices, but as I grow older I am more satisfied to write with affection and delight about those things which rouse my own affections and delight me personally. In a sense I have managed to alleviate the ego-drive which is the basic motivation of most writers; but I am still, and I trust shall always be, capable of fierce diatribes against the stupidities of organizations, and of Governments in particular. If anyone cares what my politics are, I can only say that they are basically anarchistic—not because I like anarchy, but because it seems to be the natural reaction to creeping, and total, regimentation of the mind and spirit. One further point about my writing: I maintain a conviction that, as a good craftsman, it is incumbent on me to tell my tales, and state my case, in such a manner that the ordinary reader will not be frustrated by an erudite display of artistic pretensions.

"I belong to no organizations and am a member of no clubs. If, as seems likely, the day of the individual is drawing to an end, I shall at least have had the satisfaction of having lived and died as an individual—one of the last, perhaps, of that particular kind of anachronism."

Mowat is the only child of Angus McGill Mowat and Helen (Thomson) Mowat. He began his "informal education" in various libraries at the age of eight and a year later was writing a nature column for the Saskatoon *Star Phoenix*. It was in 1935, on the south edge of the Barrenlands, that he contracted the *virus arcticus*, "an obscure disease that drives its victims from the comforts of home into the frigid arms of the Arctic."

He returned home from World War II in 1945 and spent six months in the Barrens, covering some twelve hundred miles by canoe and on foot. He was married to Frances Elizabeth Thornhill in 1947, and the next spring took her to the Arctic—the first white woman ever to see the Central Barrens. Traveling officially as government biologists, they were actually historians of the Ihalmiut Eskimos. Back from the Barrens, the Mowats built themselves a log cabin near Toronto, where they raised husky dogs and grew vegetables. Mowat received his B.A. from the University of Toronto in 1949 and launched into his writing career.

His two years among the Ihalmiut moved Mowat to write *People of the Deer* (1952), a violent indictment of the Canadian government's neglect of the dying tribe. "It is not often that a writer finds himself the sole chronicler of a whole society," wrote a reviewer in the *New Yorker*, "and Mowat has done marvelously well . . . despite a stylistic looseness and a tendency to formlessness." Others applauded his "inspired" writing, his ability to combine poetic description with scientific fact, but there were also charges of inaccuracy and "fanaticism." These accusations were refuted in Mowat's well-documented sequel, *The Desperate People*, a result of his visit to the handful of Ihalmiut survivors in 1958. Most reviewers found this "tragic epic" a "profound emotional experience," as well as a "gruesome and chastening" one. The two books have contributed to improvements in the Canadian administration of Eskimo territories.

The Dog Who Wouldn't Be showed that Mowat was more than Canada's "angry young man." It is a memoir of his childhood, centering on a pet which was quite unprepared to believe that it was merely a dog, written with a warm charm and uninhibited humor that made the book a best seller. There was no less enthusiasm for *Owls in the Family*, which seemed to Hal Borland to achieve "a rare combination of simplicity, grace and distinction in the writing." *Never Cry Wolf* grew out of a trip to the Barrenlands that Mowat undertook on behalf of the Canadian Wildlife Service, which is pilloried in the book as the Canadian government was in *People of the Deer*. Gavin Maxwell found it "a fascinating and captivating book, and a tragic one, too, for it carries a bleak, dead-pan obituary of the wolf family that Mr. Mowat had learned to love and respect."

Mowat's love of the sea, and his experience of it in his Newfoundland schooner, is reflected in a number of his books, including *The Serpent's Coil*, a much-praised account of an extraordinary Atlantic salvage operation, and *Westviking*. The latter is a reconstruction of tenth century Norse exploration south and west of Greenland, based on the sagas, which Mowat interprets in the light of his own voyages in the region, and of recent archaeological evidence. Phoebe Adams called it "an unorthodox but splendidly convincing reconstruction . . . brisk, clear . . . and streaked with gingery humor." *The Boat Who Wouldn't Float* is an exuberant, funny and sometimes touching account of Mowat's long and dangerous love affair with the Happy Adventure, a schooner with suicidal tendencies.

Mowat has described his army life in *The Regiment*, published only in Canada, and is the author of several adventure stories for boys, including *Lost in the Barrens* (which received the Canadian Governor-General's Literary Award and the Hans Christian Andersen International Award among other honors), and its sequel *The Curse of the Viking Grave*. His other literary prizes include the Anisfield-Wolf Award for "outstanding work in race relations," given in 1953 for *People of the Deer*, and the Stephen Leacock medal for humor (1970).

Lean and generously bearded, Mowat is five feet eight inches tall, and says that his eyes are blue, his hair mouse-colored. He is divorced from his first wife, by whom he has two sons, and was married in 1965 to Claire Wheeler, a commercial artist. He lists his hobbies as rum drinking and "travel anywhere," and is said to be highly gregarious and "extravagantly uninhibited." The Newfoundland outport where Mowat was living when he wrote the note above was Burgeo; he has written a tribute to the Spartan (and dwindling) communities that live in such outports in *This Rock Within the Sea*, and an indictment of man's growing estrangement from nature in *A Whale for the Killing*, a moving and horrifying account of the slow murder at Burgeo in 1967 of a stranded fin whale. He and his wife now live in Port Hope, Ontario, a small town sixty miles east of Toronto.

PRINCIPAL WORKS: People of the Deer, 1952; The Regiment, 1955; Lost in the Barrens, 1956; The Dog Who Wouldn't Be, 1957; Grey Seas Under, 1958; The Desperate People, 1959; (ed.) Ordeal by Ice, 1960; Owls in the Family, 1962; The Serpent's Coil, 1962; The Black Joke, 1963; Never Cry Wolf, 1963; Westviking: The Ancient Norse in Greenland and North America, 1965; Curse of the Viking Grave, 1966; Canada North, 1967; The Polar Passion: The Quest for the North Pole, with Selections from Arctic Journals (997–1908), 1968; This Rock Within the Sea; with photographs by John de Vissier, 1968; The Boat Who Wouldn't Float, 1969; The Siberians, 1971; A Whale for the Killing, 1972.

ABOUT: Ward, M. E. and Marquardt, D. A., Authors of Books for Young People, 1964; Who's Who in America, 1972–1973; Who's Who in Canada, 1967–1969. *Periodicals* —Illustrated London News September 20, 1952; Saturday Evening Post July 29, 1950; April 13, 1957; Spectator November 21, 1952; Wilson Library Bulletin February 1961.

***MROŻEK, SLAVOMIR** (June 26, 1930–), Polish dramatist and short story writer, was born in Borzecin, Poland, the son of Antoni Mrożek, a village post-office clerk, and Zofia (Keozior) Mrożek. He received a conventional Catholic education—"very stiff, with no questioning"—but learned English at school, and thereafter devoured English and American literature. After a few semesters studying architecture, Oriental culture, and painting at the University of Cracow, he dropped out of university because he was "bored," and worked as a caricaturist on a leading humor magazine, *Przekrój*, writing in his spare time. His "inventive, subtly subversive cartoons" soon became a national institution. Mrożek is of that generation which grew up amid the terrors of the Nazi occupation and the war. He was an adolescent during the postwar period of rebuilding and recovery and tense political conflict. None of his writings were published before the "Polish October" of 1956, which ushered in, for a while, a more liberal cultural policy.

His first volume of satirical stories, *Slón* (1958, translated by K. Syrop as *The Elephant*), became a best seller in Poland and a critical success in many foreign versions. Several critics pointed out the resemblance between these very short stories and Mrożek's cartoons, and the *Times Literary Supplement*, reviewing the English-language edition, commended Mrożek's "shrewdness and toughness,

* mə rô′ zhek

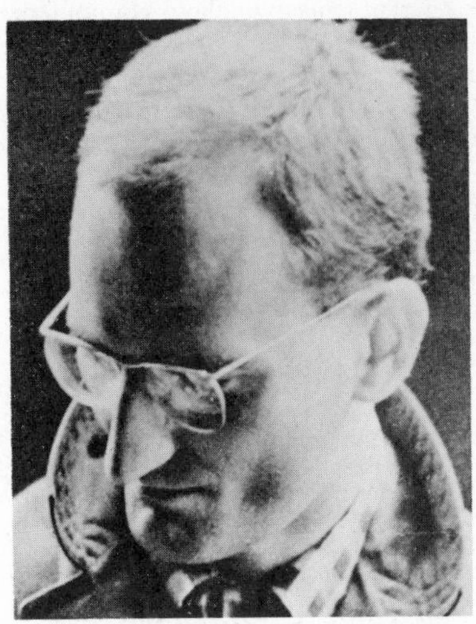

SLAVOMIR MROŻEK

his insistence on being hard-headed and open-minded," as well as "the buoyancy and delight with which he builds up his fantastic anecdotes, the feeling he gives of his imagination seeing in almost chain reaction the set of details that will make his points and yet ravish in their originality." *The Ugupu Bird*, another volume of short stories, appeared in English in 1968.

The effect of his plays, which began to appear in Warsaw in 1958, was sensational. The first impact was made by *Policja* (The Police, 1958), a short play in three acts about the dilemma of a chief of police whose only remaining political prisoner recants in favor of the government, and who is forced to persuade his loyal *agent-provocateur* to act out the role of revolutionary in order to give the penal system some reason for existing.

More short plays followed—Mrożek has written more than a dozen—most of them pointed and fairly obvious political parables. They include *Striptease* (1961), *Na Pełnym Morzu* (Out at Sea, 1961), *Czarowna Noc* (The Enchanted Night, 1962), and *Zabawa* (The Party, 1963). Mrożek has resisted efforts to interpret his plays politically, but, as A. Alvarez has pointed out, they were written at a time and place in which it was "impossible to write even about the birds and bees without someone reading into it a political metaphor or allusion," and in fact his allegorical intentions are not really in doubt. His vision is of a disjointed, alienated world, ruled by political systems that reduce laws and logic to absurdity, and people to mechanical objects.

Some of Mrożek's short plays were performed during the early 1960s in London, New York, and Paris, but it was his first full-length piece, *Tango* (1964), that led some critics to speak of him as "the outstanding dramatist east of the Elbe." Martin Esslin says that when he first saw this play in Warsaw in 1964 the tension in the atmosphere made him realize what it must have been like to attend a performance of Beaumarchais's *Le Mariage de Figaro* on the eve of the French Revolution. *Tango* was later performed in West Germany, England, and the United States and was published in two English translations in 1968—one by Ralph Manheim and Teresa Dzieduscycka, the other by Nicholas Bethell and Tom Stoppard.

The play's hero is Arthur, son of an aging bohemian liberal and a freethinking mother who has installed her brutish proletarian lover, Eddie, in the house. In revolt against so much permissiveness, seeking a return to former values, Arthur chooses to propose to his bewildered girl friend on his knees, and orders his family into formal dress for his wedding. Arthur finds this taste of power attractive: "Power, after all, is also revolt! It is revolt in the form of order." Tempted to experiment further by murdering his old uncle, he is distracted when his bride claims to have slept with Eddie. Arthur is demoralized by this and Eddie, seizing his opportunity, kills him and imposes a brutal dictatorship on the household.

Some reviewers found it difficult to grasp Mrożek's intentions in *Tango*. John Weightman, conceding that the play is an important one, crystallizing "a certain moment of Polish, perhaps European, history," found it dialectically uninstructive and dramatically uneven. To Martin Esslin, however, the play's point seemed clear enough. He saw it as a paraphrase of the Hamlet theme, about the attempt of an intellectual idealist to restore lost values. The attempt fails—idealists are never ruthless enough—and the violence he has invoked is in the end all that remains. Esslin believed that the play is as applicable to the West as to the Communist world, and found it "brilliantly constructed, full of invention and extremely funny."

According to a reviewer in the *Times Literary Supplement*, Mrożek "probably did more than any other writer to enhance that sense of a new freedom that dominated Polish life in the late 1950s." In 1959 he visited America, and found that country "still young, still open, with many possibilities, and with an elasticity that appeals very much to me." He has been living in the West, in Italy and France, since 1964. "Several of my books had already been banned, and I could see the way the situation was evolving. . . . I didn't say anything about the regime. I just took my wife Maria, to Italy."

In 1968 Mrożek made a final break with his country, when he wrote from Paris to the editors of major European newspapers denouncing the

Polish government for its part in the Warsaw Pact invasion of Czechoslovakia. His passport has since been canceled, his stories and plays banned, his books withdrawn from Polish libraries.

Mrożek was married to Maria Obremba in 1959. He is a thin, quiet man, gentle-voiced, withdrawn, and rarely smiling. He views the world sadly from behind rimless spectacles. "I do not hope for any brilliant, thundering, effective public career," he says, "but the chance remains for a less sensational but solid position, and, more important in my opinion, for continuously growing success."

PRINCIPAL WORKS IN ENGLISH TRANSLATION: The Elephant (stories), 1962; Six Plays (containing The Police, The Martyrdom of Peter Ohey, Out at Sea, Charlie, The Party, Enchanted Night), 1967; The Ugupu Bird (stories), 1968; Tango, 1968; Vatzlav, 1972; Striptease, Repeat Performance, and The Prophets: Three Plays, 1972.

ABOUT: Esslin, M. The Theatre of the Absurd, 1968; International Who's Who, 1972–73; Morgan, G. (ed.) Contemporary Theatre, 1968. *Periodicals*—Atlas July 1966; Book Week November 24, 1963; Encounter December 1965, September 1966; Newsweek January 15, 1968; New York Times January 21, 1969; Times Literary Supplement November 23, 1962; April 20, 1967; March 21, 1968; Tulane Drama Review Spring 1967.

MUGGERIDGE, MALCOLM (THOMAS) (March 24, 1903–), English journalist, critic, and novelist, was born in the London suburb of Sanderstead, near Croydon, Surrey, one of the five sons of Henry Thomas Muggeridge and the former Annie Booler. His father was a self-educated lawyer's clerk, an ardent Socialist and borough councillor (selectman), and later Member of Parliament for Romford, Essex. Muggeridge, who idolized his father, and helped him in his political work, was as he says "brought up to be an ardent believer in the religion of this age—utopianism." His well-known disenchantment with mankind and its future in this world has grown steadily more extreme since then; perhaps it began with his boyish resentment of the Fabian intellectuals who preached fraternity but in practice, he thought, patronized his working-class father.

He was educated at Selhurst Grammar School, Croydon, and at Selwyn College, Cambridge, where he read natural science and English literature, graduating in 1923. For two years he taught at a Christian college in Kerala, India, storing up comic observation on the declining years of the British raj, and from 1927 to 1930 he lectured at the Egyptian University, Cairo. In the latter year he returned to England to join the editorial staff of the Liberal newspaper the Manchester *Guardian*. He enjoyed outraging the Victorian sensibilities of Manchester, and dealt no more reverently with the sacred cows of the left wing. His first and only play *Three Flats*, for example, is said to have shocked Beatrice Webb, his aunt by marriage,

MALCOLM MUGGERIDGE

because it made light of the mystical notion of sex then in vogue in some progressive circles.

The play, staged in 1931 in London, studied the tenants of three apartments: a pair of spinster schoolteachers, a married couple, a lazy and conceited writer and his mistress. It was generally admired for its "sureness of detail and the economy of its writing." *Autumnal Face* (1931), Muggeridge's first novel, contained several thinly disguised portraits of his *Guardian* colleagues, and a later book pilloried C. P. Scott himself, denouncing the venerated editor as a "humbug"; it was rejected as libelous. *Earnest Atheist* (1936) was a study of Samuel Butler, an attempt to "debunk the debunker" which was thought brilliant but unfair.

But for all his iconoclasm, Muggeridge was apparently still a utopian. In 1932, when the Manchester *Guardian* sent him as a correspondent to Moscow, he went eagerly: "There was, as I then believed, this other paradise to go to." Stalin's campaign against the *kulaks* was at its height, and a new disillusionment awaited him, expressed in the bitterly satirical novel *Winter in Moscow* (1934). Muggeridge has often put himself in his own books, and in this one he can be recognized in the *persona* of Maxwell Wraithby, "financially embarrassed and by now even somewhat morally decayed." Frank Swinnerton called it "the work of a clever and intolerant man, ready to criticise destructively all he encounters. But it is first-hand, and is extremely entertaining."

After a period in Geneva working for the International Labour Organization, Muggeridge returned to India as assistant editor of the Calcutta *Statesman* (1934–1935), and then joined the *Evening*

Standard in London as a gossip columnist. Another *roman à clef* appeared in 1938, *In a Valley of This Restless Mind;* Mr. and Mrs. Brett in this novel, who reduce life to a series of statistics, were widely regarded as satirical portraits of Sidney and Beatrice Webb. The book has a more serious vein however, illustrated in the following passage, which seems to anticipate the author's religious conversion: "I sensed a Oneness in all this diversity around me, and this Oneness was irradiated with an inward glow of love. I saw a significance in trees budding and unfolding leaves and then shedding them, and in the gardener pushing his mowing machine up and down the lawn, and in my own shifting moods and emotions; in all the activities of Man, in the whole range of Man's being. 'Life is the good life,' I thought, and picked up a handful of earth, and crumbled it, and put it back in its place." Muggeridge's documentary account of the 1930s was widely praised, but seemed to R. H. S. Crossman better as entertainment than as a serious estimate of the period: "It is clever, hysterical and defeatist, sacrificing truth for the sake of an epigram."

During World War II Muggeridge served with the Intelligence Corps in Africa, Italy, and France, reaching the rank of major and earning the Croix de Guerre (with palm), the Médaille de la Reconnaissance Française, and membership in the Légion d'Honneur. In 1946 he joined the conservative *Daily Telegraph*, working for a while as its Washington correspondent, and serving as deputy editor in 1950-1952. Here he contrived to upset a great many people from one end of the political spectrum to the other. He dismissed the postwar years of Labour rule as a dreary example of the mob enjoying power, but also attacked the imperial myths of the Tory party, and even the Queen's accent. *Affairs of the Heart*, a novel published during this period, was enjoyed as an unusual satirical thriller.

In January 1953 Muggeridge's career took a new turn. He was appointed editor of the venerable humor magazine *Punch*—the first to be appointed from outside the magazine's own staff. A year later the *Daily Mirror* was congratulating him for injecting "new life and bite into this famous weekly magazine, for courageously publishing some of the most controversial cartoons of the year." The cover drawings in which Mr. Punch was made to respond to topical situations, the series of parodies of other journals and of the BBC, the literary pages in which celebrated names began to appear, and above all the savage political cartoons, made Muggeridge's reign at *Punch* one of the most distinguished in its history.

Since then Muggeridge has achieved even wider celebrity as a television interviewer and "personality," a form of activity which began for him in 1954, when the BBC asked him to interview Billy Graham. In 1957 he left *Punch* and joined the BBC television current affairs program "Panorama." He has met on television, as he says, "most of the eminent and the notorious figures of the day—from Bertrand Russell to Harold Wilson, from Salvador Dali to Lord Fisher of Lambeth, from Jawaharlal Nehru to Norman Mailer and six anonymous Black Muslims." He has also prepared or contributed to innumerable documentary programs, some on social or political themes, some (like *A Socialist Childhood*) about himself, and many, especially in recent years, on moral and religious questions.

In *Jesus Rediscovered* Muggeridge says that "it was while I was in the Holy Land for the purpose of making three BBC television programmes on the New Testament that a curious, almost magical, certainty seized me about Jesus' birth, ministry and Crucifixion." Much Christian dogma still seems to him "completely incredible" but he knows "without any shadow of doubt that the Christian religion is correct when it tells men and women that if they seek to satisfy themselves solely with what their flesh and the world offer they die in spirit." It is not surprising therefore that he has vigorously defended the Roman Catholic Church in its continued opposition to birth control, and in this and other ways has offended liberal churchmen as well as permissive worldlings.

Jesus Rediscovered was followed by *Something Beautiful for God*, a moving tribute to Mother Teresa of Calcutta, and by *Paul: Envoy Extraordinary*, a book derived from a BBC television series in which Muggeridge and his friend Alec Vidler talked and traveled in the steps of St. Paul. The first volume of Muggeridge's autobiography, *Chronicles of Wasted Time*, was published in 1972 as *The Green Stick*. Bernard Levin called it "the self-portrait of an honest man" but a strange one: "his picture of the vanished suburban world in which he grew up, and the even more remote world of Anglo-India, are brilliantly composed and lit; he writes with apparently effortless grace. How can this be the same man as the harsh Savonarola of the telly?"

A number of Muggeridge's recent publications have been collections of his essays, reviews, and broadcast scripts. He has mastered "a pungent, graceful and at times powerful prose," marred in the opinion of some critics by "the obsessive bitterness of the betrayed do-gooder." Certainly he lays about him with undiminished vigor, endlessly campaigning against the belief that "an orgasm a day keeps the doctor away," fulminating against modern materialism and vulgarity, cheerfully sticking pins into any reputation that seems to him inflated: "Only the greatest bores like Walter Lippmann . . ."

He is famous for biting the hand that feeds him and has not spared the BBC, through whose channels pass not only a great many Muggeridge programs but "all the rhetoric, sycophancy, cowardice and fraud of a decomposing society." John Weightman has suggested that this "Mephistopheles turned Savonarola" is both readable and important for the same reason that George Orwell was: "If a writer despises mankind in himself, you can count on him to blurt out the truth as he sees it, without fear or favour. Of course, his fidelity to the immediate impression may seem irresponsible, but it takes a certain strength of mind to turn irresponsibility into a principle. Mr. Muggeridge is a genuine anarchist, of a sort more often met with in France than in England."

Muggeridge was married in 1927 to Katherine Dobbs, niece and biographer of Beatrice Webb. They live in an Elizabethan farmhouse near Robertsbridge, in Sussex, and keep a flat in London and a villa near Monte Carlo, They have two sons and a daughter, all grown; another son was killed some years ago in an avalanche. Muggeridge, "a cadaverous, cavernous-cheeked ascetic," lives very simply, rising early, working hard, eating frugally, and walking a great deal. In the evening he listens to classical music, or plays patience while his wife reads to him. Only his continued delight in gossip shows that he has not quite outgrown the baser pleasures. He served as Rector of Edinburgh University in 1967-1968.

PRINCIPAL WORKS: *Fiction*—Autumnal Face, 1931; Winter in Moscow, 1934; In a Valley of This Restless Mind, 1938; Affairs of the Heart, 1949. *Drama*—Three Flats, 1931. *Nonfiction*—Earnest Atheist: A Study of Samuel Butler, 1936; The Thirties: 1930–1940 in Great Britain (U.S., The Sun Never Sets), 1940; Tread Softly, for You Tread on My Jokes (U.S., The Most of Malcolm Muggeridge), 1966; (with Paul Hogarth) London à la Mode, 1966; Muggeridge Through the Microphone, 1967; Jesus Rediscovered, 1969; Something Beautiful for God, 1971; (with Alec Vidler) Paul: Envoy Extraordinary, 1972; Chronicles of Wasted Time—vol. 1: The Green Stick, 1972; vol. 2: The Infernal Grove, 1973.

ABOUT: Current Biography, 1955; Muggeridge, M. Chronicles of Wasted Time, 1972—; Who's Who, 1973. *Periodicals*—Book World October 12, 1969; Chicago Daily Tribune April 21, 1934; Christian Century October 8, 1969; Christianity Today February 2, 1968; May 9, 1968; Commentary December 1966; Manchester Guardian September 4, 1936; New Republic May 5, 1937; December 17, 1966; New Statesman February 21, 1931; March 9, 1940; August 27, 1955; September 9, 1966; November 4, 1966; New York Times April 29, 1956; New York Times Book Review September 7, 1969; New Yorker January 31, 1953; May 23, 1953; Newsweek April 23, 1956; September 9, 1957; July 19, 1965; June 18, 1966; January 29, 1968; September 8, 1969; Observer October 9, 1966; October 1, 1972; Saturday Review August 30, 1969; Time September 9, 1957; January 29, 1965; January 6, 1967; January 26, 1968; Times Literary Supplement December 10, 1931; March 9, 1940.

***MUNK, KAJ** (January 13, 1898–January 4, 1944), Danish dramatist, was born Kaj Harald Leininger Petersen at Maribo, on the island of Lollard in southern Denmark, the son of a master tanner. Both parents died before he was six, and he was adopted by Peter and Marie Munk, who raised him in the traditions of popular pietism on their smallholding at Opager. Although his health was frail he was a precocious and ambitious child, and by the time he was eight he had written verses that greatly impressed his teachers. During his last year of secondary education, at the Nykøbing Cathedral school, he wrote a biblical drama, *Pilatus*, containing themes that were to recur in his work.

In 1917 Munk entered the University of Copenhagen to study theology, at the same time teaching at a local school. His religious views, shaped by his Lutheran upbringing, were much influenced at the university by Kierkegaard. Munk graduated in 1924, was ordained, and was sent to the parish of Vedersø on the west coast of Jutland, where in 1929 he married a local girl, Elise Jørgensen. At Vedersø he attracted large congregations with the vivid and disturbingly outspoken sermons that earned him his title as "Denmark's Savonarola."

Not content to preach from his pulpit, Munk soon emerged as an extremely prolific dramatist. During his lifetime he wrote some sixty plays, about a third of which have been staged. Munk's early work reflected his impatience with the "undramatic" psychological plays and drawing room comedies of the time. Devoted to Shakespeare and the Danish Romantic dramatist Adam Oehlenschläger, he sought a return to violent action and high tragedy. This, together with a youthful conservatism and tendency to hero worship, led him to build many of his plays around great, brooding, tragically flawed figures from history or the Bible. The first of his works to be produced was *En Idealist* (translated as *Herod the King*), in which Herod is conceived as a man who dares to struggle for power against God himself. The play, begun in Munk's student days, was staged at the Royal Theatre in Copenhagen in 1928 and was a fiasco. He had his first success three years later with *Cant*, a verse drama of Elizabethan gusto about Henry VIII and Anne Boleyn.

Ordet (*The Word*) was written in 1925 but not staged until 1932. It is Munk's finest play, his only direct treatment of the theme of divine grace which is an underlying preoccupation in much of his work. *Ordet* draws its characters from among the common people of Jutland, telling the story of a village Romeo and Juliet separated by their families' religious differences. In the end the simple faith of the young man is triumphantly vindicated by a

* mo͞onk

KAJ MUNK

miraculous resurrection when, in a crisis, the narrow piety of his elders proves inadequate. The pungent satire which Munk directs against religious sectarianism in *Ordet* has the fearless common sense that made his sermons so effective (and so shocking), and the play moves with a sure dramatic touch to a climax of great power. It established Munk as the most notable Scandinavian dramatist of his generation.

As a student, Munk had for a time been attracted to fascism, but during the 1930s he moved steadily toward the humane and liberal views of Bishop Grundtvig (1783–1872), the great Danish romantic poet, historian, and reformer. This was evident in *Sejren* (Victory, 1936), about Mussolini's invasion of Ethiopia, in which the dictator is presented as a corrupted idealist. *I Braendingen* (In the Breakers, 1937) is a study of Georg Brandes, while *Han sidder ved Smeltediglen* (translated as *He Sits at the Melting-Pot*) is a powerful protest against Hitler's persecution of the Jews, centering upon one of Munk's most memorable characters, a fussy academic who finds the courage to reject Nazi efforts to exploit his learning. *Egelykke* (1940) is a play about Bishop Grundtvig.

Before the German invasion of Denmark in April 1940, Munk's reputation was confined to Scandinavia; after it his fearless attacks on the Nazi regime made him known all over the world as a symbol of Danish resistance, and he came to fulfill a role much like that of Pastor Niemöller in Germany. He was several times arrested by the Gestapo and his works were banned. Nevertheless he continued to write plays and poems which were secretly printed and widely distributed. *Niels Ebbesen*, about a medieval Danish hero who had fought against German invaders, appeared in 1942 and is notable as a fine historical drama as well as an act of defiant patriotism; the one-act play *Før Cannae* (1943, *Before Cannae*) depicts Hannibal in the likeness of Hitler. On New Year's Day, 1944, Munk spoke openly in Copenhagen on behalf of the Danish resistance movement. Four days later he was found shot to death in a ditch near the German headquarters at Silkeborg. He was survived by his wife and five children.

The Elizabethan vigor and earthy wit of Munk's plays, and his use of the vernacular, did much to revitalize the insipid Danish theatre of his time, and to return it to the people. The quality of his work was uneven, but he was a master of dialogue and of unsubtle but irresistible theatrical effects, and was much imitated throughout Scandinavia, though not elsewhere. Apart from his plays, Munk published poems, including a book of children's verse, travel sketches, letters, essays, and stories. Some of his lively newspaper articles were collected in *Himmel og Jord* (Heaven and Earth, 1938). His autobiography appeared posthumously as *Foraarat saa sagte kommer* (Spring Comes So Softly, 1949).

PRINCIPAL WORKS IN ENGLISH TRANSLATION: *Plays*—Five Plays (Herod the King, The Word, Cant, He Sits at the Melting-Pot, Before Cannae), 1953; Niels Ebbesen *in* Scandinavian Plays of the Twentieth Century, Second Series, 1944; Egelykke *in* Modern Scandinavian Plays, 1954; Love *and* The Death of Ewald *in* The Norseman 1, 1949. *Sermons*—Four Sermons, 1944; By the Rivers of Babylon, 1945. *Selected works*—Keigwin, R. P. (ed.) Kaj Munk: Playwright, Priest and Patriot, 1944.

ABOUT: Blaedel, F. Kaj Munk, en Bibliografi, 1945; Geismar, O. Om Mennesket Kaj Munk, 1945; Henriques, A. Kaj Munk, 1945; Keigwin, R. P. (ed.) Kaj Munk: Playwright, Priest and Patriot, 1944; Larsen, J. K. Kaj Munk som Dramatiker, 1941; Penguin Companion to Literature 2, 1969; Smith, H. (ed.) Columbia Dictionary of Modern European Literature, 1947. *Periodicals*—American-Scandinavian Review 1939; Books Abroad Summer 1941; Scandinavian Studies 4, 1954.

MURDOCH, (JEAN) IRIS (July 15, 1919–), Anglo-Irish novelist and philosopher, was born in Dublin, the daughter of Wills Murdoch and the former Irene Richardson. She was educated in England, at the Froebel Educational Institute in London, the Badminton School in Bristol, and at Somerville College, Oxford University, where in 1942 she received her degree in classical "Greats" with first class honors. She began her career in the civil service, as an assistant principal in the Treasury (1942–1944). From 1944 to 1946 she worked as an administrative officer with the United Nations Relief and Rehabilitation Administration in London, Belgium, and Austria. In 1946 she received a scholarship to study in the United States, but as a former member of the Communist party was denied a visa. She spent the year in London, reading philosophy, and in 1947 went as Sarah Smithson Student in Philosophy to Newnham College, Cambridge, returning to Oxford in 1948 as a fellow of St. Anne's College and a tutor in philosophy.

Her first book was an essay on Sartre as a "romantic rationalist," published in 1953. It was admired as "a remarkably intelligent and penetrating introduction to and commentary upon Sartre," and is interesting for the light it throws upon her own ideas. In particular she rejects the almost solipsistic subjectivity implied for her in Sartre's existentialism. She is equally dissatisfied with logical positivism—another solipsistic school of thought in her view, and one which is by its nature incapable of formulating a serviceable moral or political position.

Rubin Rabinovitz, in his informative critical essay on Iris Murdoch, says that "she has a more objective view of the universe than the Sartrean existentialist. . . . Objectivity is also the key to Miss Murdoch's idea of love: it is in the suppression of subjectivity and through the recognition of the objective existence of other people that love begins," while "too much self-examination can end in total preoccupation with oneself. This idea recurs in Miss Murdoch's novels: moral excellence and love come with the observation of others, moral shallowness and neurosis are the result of self-attention."

After writing and discarding five novels, Iris Murdoch in 1954 published her sixth, *Under the Net*. Its hero is a raffish Irishman, Jake Donahue, a professional translator who is disenchanted with his job, with left-wing politics, and with life in general. The novel is a picaresque account of his encounters in London and Paris with an assortment of new and old friends who bring him into contact with a variety of milieus, among them the motion picture industry, philosophy, politics, and literature. In the course of the book Jake outgrows his miserable self-absorption which leads him to make endless errors (often very funny in their results) about other people's motives, achieving a degree of maturity and objectivity when he decides to settle down and write seriously.

Published at about the same time as the first novels of Kingsley Amis and John Wain, *Under the Net* was at first mistaken for a satire of similar intent. In fact its concerns are more metaphysical than social. It reflects its author's own commitment to and development beyond Sartrean existentialism, and contains many Sartrean echoes. Jake himself is admittedly modeled on Beckett's Murphy and Raymond Queneau's Pierrot. And Jake's principal teacher, the saintlike movie mogul Hugo Belfounder, has been shown to bear many resemblances to the philosopher Ludwig Wittgenstein. Hugo has come to believe that every kind of theoretical system and generalization and preconception is a snare and a delusion, a net barring us from understanding the "unutterably particular" nature of reality. Through him Jake escapes the nets of subjectivity and theory to recognize the mysterious randomness and "contingency" of life.

IRIS MURDOCH

Some reviewers complained of faults of construction and design in the novel; almost all recognized what one called its "dazzling array of virtues." A critic in the *Times Literary Supplement* wrote that it "reveals a brilliant talent. The book is an achievement in its own right and the gifts which have gone to its making promise great things. Miss Murdoch has wit, intelligence and sympathy [and] she can create character."

A lack of what Simone Weil called "attention" to others makes love for them impossible; in its place develops the destructive and corrupting desire for mastery and the equally dangerous passion for thralldom. This is the theme of *The Flight from the Enchanter*, which examines a chain or pyramid of master–slave relationships at the apex of which stands the protean magician-financier Mischa Fox, an evil Prospero who destroys those he enthralls but is himself a prisoner of his need for power. Once again the reviewers, bewildered by, as one put it, the book's "interplay of wild humor and determined, if inscrutable, purpose," found it brilliant, witty, and original.

The ease with which dominance can become a substitute for love—for "the extremely difficult realisation that something other than oneself is real"—is examined in a domestic context in *The Sandcastle*, which was felt to lack the vividness and intensity of its predecessors. This and other barriers to love—unthinking conformity, neurotic self-immersion—are illustrated in *The Bell*, which describes the failure of a lay religious community. Miss Murdoch is not herself religious in the orthodox sense, but believes that close and compassionate attention to another human being (or to a great work of art) inspires a transcendental awareness that "there is more than this." "With *The Bell*," wrote William Van O'Connor, "Miss Murdoch emerges as probably the best of the young novelists. There is the same odd assortment of characters, representing a cross section of English life, the action is bathed in an air of unreality but yet seems credible, and there are highly intelligent speculations about human freedom and the nature of the good dexterously woven into action."

A Severed Head deals with three pairs of educated and charming middle-class people, all of them more or less emotionally injured or retarded. Incapable of love, they try to make do with sex, devoting themselves to an endless adulterous game of musical chairs. Their high priest is Palmer Anderson, a psychoanalyst who, by encouraging infinite self-concern, offering endless understanding and tolerance, creates moral anarchy. The figure closest to reality in this group is the anthropologist Honor Klein, who knows that even love must be paid for—that "you cannot cheat the dark gods." Through his love for her, Mark Lynch-Gibbon, the novel's central figure and narrator, achieves a degree of maturity. F. J. Warncke called the book "a triumph of form. . . . Psychological insight, speculative complexity, and symbolic richness are abundantly present . . . but they enter into combination as a formal work, which hangs in the air like a movement of a sonata or like some witty mobile, delighting us even as it makes its comment on reality. Among so much that is trivial, so much that is only half-rendered, *A Severed Head* stands as a refreshing reminder of what the art of fiction can achieve." Dramatized by the author with J. B. Priestley, it had great success as a play, and was later filmed.

Various aspects and combinations of these same themes have been explored in Iris Murdoch's subsequent novels, which have appeared at the rate of almost one a year: *An Unofficial Rose*, *The Unicorn*, *The Italian Girl* (the basis of another successful dramatization), *The Red and the Green* (set, unexpectedly, in Ireland at the time of the 1916 Easter Rebellion), *The Time of the Angels*, *The Nice and the Good*, *Bruno's Dream*, *A Fairly Honourable Defeat*, *An Accidental Man*, and *The Black Prince*. These books have not escaped adverse criticism, many readers complaining that the philosopher in Miss Murdoch had often vanquished the novelist—that the books were increasingly motivated by philosophical ideas which were neither fully enacted nor fully revealed.

The most enjoyed of these later novels was *The Nice and the Good*, a more optimistic and entertaining work than its immediate predecessors, though it deals with an investigation into the death of a civil servant who dabbles in black magic. Its theme is a characteristic one—the importance of distinguishing between conventional niceness and the transfiguring quality, harder to achieve, of goodness. Again there was some feeling that the author had been unduly reticent about her philosophical intentions, but Elizabeth Janeway for one thought it her "best, most exciting and most successful book."

Her play *The Servants and the Snow* (1970) is a fable set in an imaginary feudal community somewhere in Eastern Europe, where a reforming young ruler finds that his peasants want, not freedom and social progress, but the brutal authority and tribal rituals of the past. Ronald Bryden, who complained that much of the dialogue was "virtually unspeakable," found it otherwise "a characteristically eerie Murdoch mixture of comedy and Gothic horror, shifting unnervingly between sophisticated modernism and myth." A later and in many ways related play, *The Three Arrows* (1972), centers on a young prince in medieval Japan, held as a political prisoner, who must choose between political action, the religious life, and love. The basis of the play, wrote Harold Hobson, "is the philosophic question what is freedom, not the melodramatic question, will the prince go free? Whether either question is unequivocally answered will be the subject of many a midnight discussion among those over whom the play casts its insidious spell."

Iris Murdoch finds the novel an essentially comic form, "something that should make one laugh. At any rate at fairly regular intervals. . . . You can't avoid being funny, because human life *is* funny." She denies that she is a philosophical novelist, but admits that her books "have a rather constricting myth-making tendency about them . . . there's a sort of *dragon* mythical power that uncurls itself within the plot and to some extent determines what the characters must do and think. And there is a danger that this dragon can take over the book"; many would agree. William Van O'Connor wrote in 1963: "It is clear by now that Miss Murdoch is a kind of twentieth-century Congreve. Her characters are interesting puppets and interesting symbols, and she can make them dance or place them erect in an eerie green light. An intellectual game is going on. There is no sweat, no anguish, and no real love-making. All of these are illusions. The real game is between Miss Murdoch and her reader, not between the reader and the characters. That is her strength and her limitation." She remains, as Walter Allen has said, possibly the only English novelist of her generation with gifts that might produce a great novel—a novel both responsibly passionate and grounded in a thorough understanding of the nature of fiction itself.

The humanistic philosophy underlying all her work receives its fullest expression in three papers, two of them first given as lectures, published together as *The Sovereignty of Good.* Philip Toynbee found it "quite impossible in a short review to do justice to the subtlety, nobility and controlled fervour" of this book, but concluded that "the least misleading summary might be to say that she has returned to the underlying Christian notions of man's nature and his good, without returning to any significant element of Christian theology." In fact, Iris Murdoch told an interviewer in 1972 that she was an "ex-Christian," attracted by the undogmatic disciplines of Zen Buddhism.

In 1963 Miss Murdoch exchanged her post at St. Anne's College for an honorary fellowship in order to devote herself to writing. She has been married since 1956 to the novelist and critic John Bayley, and they live in Steeple Aston, in Oxfordshire. Her recreations, not surprisingly somehow, include jujitsu and Japanese sword fighting. Ved Mehta, describing a meeting with her in *Fly and the Fly-Bottle*, says that she resembled his image of St. Joan—"a celestial expression cast in the rough features of a peasant, and straight, blond hair unevenly clipped." At Oxford she "has the reputation of being a saint, and she has no enemies." She is a member of the Labour party.

PRINCIPAL WORKS: *Fiction*—Under the Net, 1954; The Flight from the Enchanter, 1956; The Sandcastle, 1957; The Bell, 1958; A Severed Head, 1961; An Unofficial Rose, 1962; The Unicorn, 1963; The Italian Girl, 1964; The Red and the Green, 1965; The Time of the Angels, 1966; The Nice and the Good, 1968; Bruno's Dream, 1969; A Fairly Honourable Defeat, 1970; An Accidental Man, 1971; The Black Prince, 1973. *Nonfiction*—Sartre, 1953; (with J. B. Priestley) A Severed Head (play), 1964; (with James Saunders) The Italian Girl, 1967; The Sovereignty of Good, 1970; The Three Arrows, *and*, The Servants and the Snow (plays), 1973.

ABOUT: Allen, W. The Modern Novel, 1964; Byatt, A. S. Degrees of Freedom: The Novels of Iris Murdoch, 1965; Contemporary Authors 13–14, 1965; Current Biography, 1958; Gindin, J. Postwar British Fiction, 1961; Mehta, V. Fly and the Fly-Bottle, 1963; O'Connor, W. V. The New University Wits, 1963; Rabinovitz, R. Iris Murdoch, 1968; Shapiro, C. (ed.) Contemporary British Novelists, 1965; Stettler-Imfeld, B. The Adolescent in the Novels of Iris Murdoch, 1970; Who's Who, 1973; Wolfe, P. The Disciplined Heart: Iris Murdoch and Her Novels, 1966. *Periodicals*—Books and Bookmen September 1966; Bucknell Review May 1966; Commonweal December 4, 1964; December 3, 1965; Critical Quarterly Spring 1962; Criticism Spring 1965; Encounter January 1961; English Studies April 1962; Essays in Criticism July 1963; Guardian October 24, 1972; Massachusetts Review Spring 1967; Nation March 21, 1959; November 9, 1964; New Republic June 10, 1957; February 5, 1966; New Statesman October 22, 1965; Observer June 17, 1962; Partisan Review Spring 1963; Reporter November 3, 1966; Sunday Times March 11, 1962; October 29, 1972; Time November 6, 1964.

MURPHY, RICHARD (August 6, 1927–), Anglo-Irish poet, was born into an old Protestant family in County Galway. His mother was the former Betty Ormsby. His father, Sir William Murphy, was a distinguished civil servant and classical scholar who, after serving as mayor of Colombo (1932–1937), as colonial secretary in Bermuda (1942–1945), and as governor of the Bahamas (1945–1949), retired to farm in Southern Rhodesia. He was recalled to the diplomatic service in 1957 to act as governor-general of the short-lived Central African Federation, which disintegrated in 1963. Richard Murphy spent part of his early childhood in Ceylon with his father and part of it in Ireland. He was educated at Braymount, Dollymount, in Dublin, and in 1937 went away to the Canterbury Choir School in England, returning to Ireland in 1940.

He and a brother and sister spent the first part of World War II at the great house near Tuam, Galway, where Richard Murphy was born. There was a huge, half-wild garden, "surrounded by an Anglo-Irish wall, a great wall of pride and oppression, liberally overgrown with romantic ivy." The children took their lessons here, in the garden's "pleasure ground," with their mother as their teacher. In *Writers on Themselves*, Murphy recalls this wartime interlude as the happiest time of his life. It ended before the war did, when he entered the King's School, normally of Canterbury, at that time evacuated to Cornwall. After a brief period at another public school, Wellington, Murphy went with a scholarship to Magdalen College, Oxford. He graduated in 1951 and studied for a further year at the Sorbonne in Paris.

After a taste of the diplomatic life as his father's ADC in the Bahamas, Murphy worked for a time in an insurance office, reviewing in his spare time for the *Spectator*, then spent a year (1953–1954) as director of an English school in Crete. He revisited Paris in 1954 and then returned to Ireland. He had always been much drawn to the harsh landscape of Western Ireland and to the sea, and also to the peasants and fishermen of Galway and Connemara, people shaped by "stones, salmon-falls, rain-clouds and drownings." Murphy settled at Cleggan, on the Galway coast, and bought two Galway "hookers"—fishing boats of ancient design. These he has restored and rents to tourists for sea fishing and for trips to Inishbofin, the subject of his poem "Sailing to an Island."

Archaeology of Love, Murphy's first book of poems, was published in Dublin in 1955. It was followed in 1959 by *The Woman of the House*, a long poem about his grandmother and about the past of his

RICHARD MURPHY

family and of his country, which foreshadowed the manner of several of his later poems, autobiographical but not confessional, evocative but restrained. It was reprinted in his first important collection, *Sailing to an Island*, which also contains three poems about the seamen of Cleggan. This volume, which won the Guinness Poetry Prize, was received with universal pleasure. The sea poems in particular seemed to M. L. Rosenthal "brilliantly concrete and exciting, serving a timeless artistic purpose in the way they repossess a particular type of experience and way of life." Their quality is well illustrated in "The Cleggan Disaster" when, out of a sky that "smouldered like soot," "A storm began to march, the shrill wind piping/And thunder exploding, while the lightning flaked/In willow cascades, and the bayonets of hail/Flashed over craters and hillocks of water./All the boats were trapped." Some critics objected mildly to touches of vague rhetoric, hints of sentimentality, but for most these elegiac poems had "a fine, ringing solidity."

Partly because of the success of his three Cleggan poems, Murphy was commissioned by the British Broadcasting Corporation to write a long ballad poem for radio. While he worked on it he supplemented his income by lecturing at Reading University, and in 1965 was writer in residence at the University of Virginia. His radio poem, completed in 1967, is an account of, and meditation upon, the Battle of Aughrim (1691), which destroyed Catholic secular power in Ireland, and gave it to Protestant families like Murphy's own. It was broadcast in August 1968 with a distinguished cast of actors and poets, including Cyril Cusack, Ted Hughes, and Cecil Day Lewis. The poem is in four sections, one of them a description of the battle itself, the others containing Murphy's reflections on Ireland before and after it. P. J. Kavanagh praised "the tense, hard lines, sewn together with assonances." Ted Hughes wrote that Murphy "has the gift of epic objectivity. . . . I don't know any other contemporary poet who has so redeemed the classical manner." The principal criticism came from those who thought Murphy's objectivity extreme, to the point of flatness.

The Battle of Aughrim was published in 1968, along with "The God Who Eats Corn," Murphy's memorial poem about his father. A critic in the *Times Literary Supplement* has suggested that Murphy's talent is not really for narrative poetry at all: "A commitment to history plays an important part in his poetry, but his theme is the presence of the past. . . . His best poetry converges upon a point halfway between the moving present and the fixed past," where both "are held, for a lyric interval, at rest." In 1968 Murphy was a visiting fellow of Reading University, in 1968–1969 he was Compton Lecturer in Poetry at the University of Hull, and in 1971 he returned to the United States as O'Connor Professor of Literature at Colgate University. Since 1969 he has owned a small island off the coast of Connemara. The author was married to the former Patricia Avis, but is now divorced.

PRINCIPAL WORKS: *All poetry*—The Archaeology of Love, 1955; The Woman of the House, 1959; The Last Galway Hooker, 1961; Sailing to an Island, 1963; The Battle of Aughrim, and The God Who Eats Corn, 1968. *Poems in* Skelton, R. (ed.) Six Irish Poets, 1962; Penguin Modern Poets 7, 1965.

ABOUT: British Broadcasting Corporation. Writers on Themselves, 1964; Rosenthal, M. L. The New Poets, 1967. *Periodicals*—Guardian May 31, 1969; Reporter May 7, 1964.

***MYRDAL, (KARL) GUNNAR** (December 6, 1898–), Swedish economist, was born in Gustafa, Dalecarlia, where his father was a landowner. He studied law at Stockholm University, graduating in 1923, but soon switched to political economy, and in 1927 took a doctorate in economics. In the same year he became a lecturer in political economy at Stockholm and published a book on the theory of prices. During the academic year 1929–1930 he traveled in the United States on a Rockefeller Fellowship; in 1930–1931 he was in Switzerland as associate professor in the Post-Graduate Institute of International Studies at Geneva, and from 1933 to 1950 was professor of political economy and financial science at Stockholm University.

During the economic instability and distress of the 1930s, Myrdal concentrated his studies first on

*mür′ däl

economic analysis and then on state welfare. He was also active in public affairs as a deputy of the board of the National Bank of Sweden and from 1936 to 1938 as a Social Democratic member of the Senate. His main contribution to economic analysis at this time was *Vetenskap och politik i nationalekonomien* (1929, translated as *The Political Element in the Development of Economic Theory*), a devastating sociological analysis of traditional economic doctrine as a defense of private enterprise. This critical account of the part played by political considerations in the development of economic theory still remains, in the words of the *Times Literary Supplement*, "the classic answer to futile, but persistently recurrent, attempts to construct a non-political economic base for policy decisions."

Myrdal then turned towards broader social enquiry. He had married the sociologist Alva Reimer in 1924, and with her he wrote *Kris i befolknings frågan* (Crisis in the Population Question, 1934), which explored the problem of how to overcome the excessive decrease in the Swedish birthrate while maintaining the improved standard of living associated with it. This aroused wide public interest and directly influenced the social policies of the Scandinavian countries during the 1930s. Myrdal was appointed to the new Swedish housing and population commissions, which adopted a policy close to that of the general theories and specific suggestions in the book.

Myrdal went to Harvard University in the spring of 1938 to give the Godkin lectures on socio-economic problems, later published as *Population: A Problem for Democracy*. The Carnegie Corporation had already chosen him to direct a comprehensive study of the question of race in America "in a wholly objective and dispassionate way as a social phenomenon." Myrdal worked on this from 1938 to 1943 with a team of assistants, and eventually produced an exhaustive anthropological, cultural, social, economic, and political analysis in the massive two-volume work *An American Dilemma* (1944). The dilemma is the conflict between the American ideals of brotherhood and equality and the actual behavior of whites towards blacks which constitutes "a moral lag in the development of the nation." The sociologist Robert Lynd called it "the most penetrating and important book on our contemporary American civilization that has been written. Here we Americans are revealed . . . attempting to live along with the vast and ugly reality of what Dr. Myrdal calls our 'greatest failure,' the Negro problem." Twenty years later one of Myrdal's collaborators, Arnold Rose, published a condensation of the work under the title *The Negro in America*. It showed how brilliantly perceptive much of Myrdal's work had been, notably his prophecies that jobs and housing would

GUNNAR MYRDAL

emerge as the major racial issues in the North, voting in the South. John Torode pointed out, however, that Myrdal had been less accurate in his assumption that the white man would necessarily be the prime mover in any progress towards racial equality: "You do not need to be a separatist to see modern American Negroes more in terms of their own values and decisions and less in terms of response."

Before the book was published, Myrdal had resumed his teaching at the University of Stockholm, but in 1943–1944 he toured the United States as economic adviser to the Swedish legation, and the end of the war found him in politics. From 1945 to 1947 he was Minister of Commerce in the Swedish government, and from 1947 to 1957 Secretary of the United Nations Economic Commission for Europe. Since 1960 he has been professor of International Economy at Stockholm University, and many of his books have been concerned with the problems of underdeveloped countries.

An International Economy: Problems and Prospects is an analysis of the problem of poverty and the increasing gap between highly developed and underdeveloped areas in the world. Myrdal argues that the developed countries defeated the Marxist prophecy of growing inequality and misery by developing domestic social services, full employment, and protection for the weaker sections of the community; these same measures, he says, are now necessary on an international scale. These ideas are presented more briefly in *Rich Lands and Poor: The Road to World Prosperity*, which Eugene Staley called "one of those seminal books in which new and illuminating ways of thinking are brought to bear on a complex subject. . . . Myrdal's book . . . puts forward some concepts and hypotheses that bring us several steps nearer to a usable framework for a general theory of development and underdevelopment."

Value in Social Theory, edited by Paul Streeten, is a selection of some of Myrdal's writings on the political and philosophical aspects of economics and sociology, all of them seeking to show that "value premises are necessary in research and that no study and no book can be *wertfrei*, free from valuations." *Beyond the Welfare State* is a study of the relationship between politics and planning in developing a society, national or international, in which individuals can lead full and meaningful lives. *Challenge to Affluence* argues that America's slow and unsteady economic growth since World War II is deeply rooted in the American unwillingness to remedy through massive public expenditure the country's massive social problems. In contrast to Sweden, a welfare state which does not tolerate severe sectional poverty and has a remarkable combination of growth, prosperity and stability, "There is an ugly smell rising from the basement of the stately American mansion."

Myrdal had meanwhile been engaged in another major project which, after a decade of research with a high-powered international team of economists and sociologists, resulted in the monumental three-volume *Asian Drama: An Inquiry Into the Poverty of Nations* (1968). Its thesis is that traditional Asian societies are breaking down before Western methods and ideas have fully replaced them, while the population explosion threatens to destroy the modest gains so far made and drag South Asia below the barest subsistence level: "Behind all the complexities and dissimilarities we sense a rather clear-cut set of conflicts and a common theme as in a drama. The action in this drama is speeding towards a climax. Tension is mounting: economically, socially, and politically." Myrdal emphasizes the inappropriateness and insufficiency of Western models and concepts for the study of the economic, political, and social affairs of the South Asian countries, and the corresponding need for deep institutional and attitudinal inquiry if any sense is to be made of the area's appalling problems. Myrdal's attack on economists and economic models of development is widely agreed to be sound, as is his diagnosis of the problems. But his pessimistic conclusions and suggested remedies have aroused more skepticism. Myrdal summarized the basic research and conclusions of this book in *The Challenge of World Poverty* (1970), in which he goes on to offer his own solutions for the problems facing the Third World, emphasizing the responsibility of the rich nations to assist the poor.

From his earliest works Myrdal has opposed as fallacious the notion of a value-free social science, and he returns to this theme in *Objectivity in Social Research*. Myrdal concludes that a researcher's own values influence not only the findings and interpretation of research but the original questions asked, which often conceal biases that invalidate the claim to objectivity in the answers: "Questions must be asked before answers can be given. The questions are all expressions of our interest in the world; they are at bottom valuations."

Myrdal is considered Sweden's leading authority on American affairs, and *Time* magazine has called him "the No. 1 authority on United States Negroes." But his views have often met with deep suspicion in America, especially at the height of the Cold War; he has been bitterly attacked by Catholics for his advocacy of birth control, and by conservatives for his advocacy of planning. Despite criticisms of this sort he has long been a towering figure in the world of economic and social science, with, according to A. F. Ewing, "an excellent claim to be considered the greatest economist of his times." He holds honorary degrees from many universities in Sweden, Britain, the United States, and elsewhere. He and his wife Alva, now a Minister Without Portfolio in the Swedish Cabinet, have two daughters and a son, Jan, who has also become well known as a writer. Gunnar and Alva Myrdal were joint recipients of the West German Peace Prize in 1970.

PRINCIPAL WORKS IN ENGLISH AND ENGLISH TRANSLATION: The Cost of Living in Sweden, 1830–1930 (with the assistance of Sven Bouvin), 1933; Monetary Equilibrium, 1939; Population: A Problem for Democracy, 1940; An American Dilemma: The Negro Problem and Modern Democracy (with the assistance of Richard Sterner and Arnold Rose), 1944; The Political Element in the Development of Economic Theory, 1953; Realities and Illusions in Regard to Inter-Governmental Organizations, 1955; An International Economy: Problems and Prospects, 1956; Rich Lands and Poor: The Road to World Prosperity, 1958 (England, Economic Theory and Underdeveloped Regions), 1957; Value in Social Theory (ed. by Paul Streeten), 1958; Beyond the Welfare State: Economic Planning in the Welfare States and Its International Implications, 1958; Challenge to Affluence, 1963; The Negro in America: The Condensed Version of Gunnar Myrdal's An American Dilemma, by Arnold Rose, 1964; Asian Drama: An Inquiry into the Poverty of Nations, 1968; Objectivity in Social Research, 1970; The Challenge of World Poverty: A World Anti-Poverty Programme in Outline, 1970; Against the Stream: Critical Essays on Economics, 1973.

ABOUT: International Who's Who, 1972–73; Who's Who in America, 1972–1973. *Periodicals*—American Economic Review December 1956, September 1958; American Historical Review December 1968; American Political Science Review June 1964, December 1968; American Sociological Review August 1960; Annals of the American Academy of Political and Social Science September 1954, May 1960, November 1960, May 1964; Commentary February 1964; Commonweal February 25, 1944; October 4, 1968; Economist July 6, 1968; Encounter

July 1969; Foreign Affairs October 1956, January 1961; International Affairs October 1964, January 1969; Nation November 5, 1960; May 6, 1968; National Review July 28, 1968; New Republic March 20, 1944; May 17, 1954; July 18, 1960; May 4, 1968; July 25, 1970; New Society October 8, 1964; July 18, 1968; December 31, 1970; New York Times April 2, 1944; New York Times Book Review July 19, 1970; New Yorker April 18, 1964, February 13, 1969; Saturday Review April 22, 1944; June 15, 1968; Scientific American July 1969; Social Forces October 1944, December 1960; Spectator March 17, 1961; January 10, 1969; Springfield Republican May 14, 1944; Times Literary Supplement March 26, 1954; December 21, 1956; March 21, 1958; August 15, 1958; January 27, 1961; March 12, 1964; November 21, 1968; Virginia Quarterly Review Summer 1968; Yale Review Autumn 1956.

***NAGAI, "KAFU" (pseudonym of Sokichi Nagai)** (December 3, 1879–April 30, 1959), Japanese novelist, essayist, and critic, was born of a warrior family in the Koishikawa district of Tokyo, near the downtown quarter which he was to find so alluring. His father, a scholarly bureaucrat turned businessman, combined strong Confucian principles with Western attitudes acquired, in part, from a two-year stay in the United States. Kafu seems to have been at odds with his father for much of his life. His mother and maternal grandmother were Christians, and it was the latter who was mainly responsible for looking after him in his childhood. Although his second brother became a Protestant minister, Kafu did not adopt Christianity and religious questions scarcely figure in his writings.

His schooling was disturbed by minor illnesses during which Kafu developed his interest in literature. In 1897 he entered the department of Chinese at the School of Foreign Studies, but spent little time at the university and did not graduate. He had already started writing short stories and had found his lifetime interest—the world of the gay quarters, the geisha houses, the theatres, and the narrow streets and canal banks of the old city.

While still a schoolboy he had secretly copied out some of the lewder passages from Saikaku, the seventeenth century master, and from the erotic writers of eighteenth century Edo (as Tokyo was called then). He claimed to have made his first visit to many of the Yoshiwara pleasure houses at the age of eighteen. Kafu acquired all the accomplishments of the then almost extinct Edo dilettante: he studied the *samisen* (a stringed instrument) and *shakuhachi* (Japanese flute); took lessons in classical dancing and the tea ceremony; composed *haiku* and tried his hand at *rakugo* (comic monologue); apprenticed himself for a year to a Kabuki playwright; and then worked briefly as a gossip columnist for a daily newspaper. To finance the more expensive and clandestine of his activities he entered his short stories for prize competitions in newspapers and magazines.

* ka′ fōō nə gī′

KAFU NAGAI

Kafu's earliest work was strongly derivative, imitating the *gesaku* (popular romance) or *hisan* (pathos) novels popular at the time. In 1898, in the accepted literary manner, Kafu became the protégé of an established writer, Ryuro Hirotsu. But he quickly broke away from mimicry and cramping patronage, and in his prize-winning story "Hanakago" (Flower Basket, 1899) began to show his individuality.

By 1901 he had had his first taste of Zola—in English translation—and in that year he entered a night school to learn French. Kafu was at first attracted by naturalism. In 1902–1903 he published a successful trilogy: *Yashin* (Ambition), *Jigoku no Hana* (The Flowers of Hell), and—the most popular of the three—*Yume no Onna* (Woman of the Dream), a sad story in the style of Maupassant of a woman trapped by life. But he was soon to criticize naturalism as crude, inartistic, and dull, and to find that his own inclination was towards the veiled and elegiac rather than realistic social commentary.

His father had little faith in literature as a career, and in September 1903 sent Kafu to America with the idea of improving his English and preparing him for a commercial career. Kafu himself was quite prepared to go, welcoming a temporary escape from Japan, a chance to taste a little more of life. But most of all, America was a step nearer to his ultimate goal—Paris, the Mecca of the demimonde. During his four years in America he studied French and philosophy in Kalamazoo College; worked as a messenger in the Japanese Embassy in Washington, where he had plenty of time for reading; and was employed by the New York branch of the Yokohama Specie Bank, in his free time discovering the delights of Chinatown.

In July 1907 he secured a transfer to the Lyons branch of the bank, where he was soon asked to resign. He was at last free to go to Paris but, after only two months there, shortage of money compelled him to return home, albeit slowly. The nearer he got to Japan the more depressed he became. He felt that he was leaving a rooted and coordinated culture and returning to chaos. His early interest in Edo culture and his travels coalesced into a sense of disgust and anger at the careless way in which the Japanese past was being destroyed and replaced by the vulgar new.

Before he reached Japan in July 1908 his *Amerika Monogatari* (Tales of America) had appeared, and *Furansu Monogatari* (Tales of France) soon followed. The latter was found offensive to public morals and temporarily suppressed, but both collections, though rather literary and allusive, were well received as fresh and penetrating observations of the world outside. And there were many prepared to enjoy Kafu's attacks on Meiji culture. He soon found himself a best-selling writer and remained fairly consistently popular until his death, in spite of periods of literary inactivity and withdrawal.

In April 1910 Kafu was offered a professorship in French at Keio University and at the request of Ogai Mori and Bin Ueda began to edit a scholarly and influential anti-naturalist literary magazine called *Mita Bungaku* (Mita Literature). He found little to appeal to him in academic life and resigned in 1916. From this point he held aloof from other writers and critics and focused his attention on the oases of the Edo past lingering in the corners of modern Tokyo.

Sangoshu (The Coral Anthology, 1913), his volume of translations from French poetry, was influential and highly acclaimed, but increasingly Kafu delineated in his fiction a very narrow and essentially Japanese world peopled by geishas, actors, dancers, and musicians. A famous and characteristic novel is *Sumida Gawa* (1909, translated as *The River Sumida*), a geisha's tragic love story told with a delicate and poignant lyricism. Other well-known books of the period are *Botan no Kyaku* (1909, translated as *The Peony Garden*), *Kazagokochi* (1912, translated as *Coming Down With a Cold*), *Ude Kurabe* (1916–1917, translated as *Geisha in Rivalry*), and *Ame Shosho* (1918, translated as *Quiet Rain*). These stories are distinguished by their precision of observation and unity of mood. The characters are rather lacking in vitality and individuality (Kafu himself admitted that background often overcame personality in his books), and his work sometimes seems closer to the lyric essay than to the novel. But, by combining cynicism with poetic feeling, he conveys at his best a powerful sense of nostalgia, loneliness, and fatalism.

Kafu's longing for the past and disgust with the present silenced him almost completely during the 1920s. When he began to write again in the 1930s, the geishas of tradition were gone and his heroines were the prostitutes and bar-girls who succeeded them. Some critics have detected at least a partial return to his former naturalism in such works as *Bokuto Kidan* (1937, translated as *A Strange Tale From East of the River*), about a novelist's search for material in the Tokyo underworld. Kafu's work, full of Tokyo allusions, is not easy to translate satisfactorily.

In Japan Kafu is admired almost as much for his eccentric individuality as for his literature. He was a determined recluse, miserly and querulous. He carried on a lifelong feud with his youngest brother over the division of their inheritance, wrangled bitterly with several different publishers, and openly scorned other writers with the exception of Ogai Mori. Kafu married twice, divorcing his first wife after two years. His second wife left him after a few months of his eccentricities and returned to her geisha house. In addition he admitted to sixteen mistresses. Besides being a collector of erotica Kafu was a literary cartographer and cataloger of the various "nightless" districts and their pleasures. Until the very end of his life his tall figure was a familiar one around the strip shows and entertainment halls of Asakusa. Occasionally he appeared on stage in a skit of his own composition.

Kafu has something of a reputation as a social critic and opponent of the militarists during World War II. Certainly his work was frequently censored, perhaps as much for its aestheticism as for any direct social criticism it contained. He was always out of step with his contemporaries, looking back sadly to the past—during Meiji it was the Edo era he pined for; later the once despised Meiji seemed a golden age as the brilliant full-blown world of the geisha gradually gave way to the more tawdry world of the bar-girls. Kafu's output was tremendous, his popularity considerable. His work has been filmed and televised. In 1952 he received the National Cultural Award for his contribution to modern Japanese literature and in 1953 he was made a member of the Japanese Academy of Arts.

PRINCIPAL WORKS IN ENGLISH TRANSLATION: Geisha in Rivalry, 1963; *Selected works in* Seidensticker, E. (ed.) Kafu the Scribbler: The Life and Writings of Nagai Kafu (The River Sumida, The Peony Garden, Coming Down With a Cold, Quiet Rain, A Strange Tale From East of the River, The Decoration, The Scavengers, and excerpts from several other works), 1965; A Strange Tale From East of the River and Other Stories, 1972. *Stories in* Keene, D. Modern Japanese Literature, 1956; Matsumoto, R. Japanese Literature New and Old, 1961; Miyamori, A. Representative Tales of Japan, 1914; Morris, I. Modern Japanese Stories, 1961; Takemoto, T. Seven Stories From Contemporary Japanese Writers, 1918.

ABOUT: Grigson, G. (ed.) Concise Encyclopedia of Modern World Literature, 1963; Meiji Dictionary of Modern Japanese Literature (in Japanese), 1965; Okazaki, Y. Japanese Literature in the Meiji Era, 1955; Penguin Companion to Literature 4, 1969; Seidensticker, E. Kafu the Scribbler, 1965.

***NAIPAUL, V(IDIADHAR) S(URAJPRASAD)** (August 17, 1932–), West Indian novelist and memoirist, began his literary career by winning the John Llewelyn Rhys Memorial Prize with his first novel and subsequently received almost all of the major British literary prizes available to prose writers. He was born in Chaguanas, Trinidad, of Hindu parents, and has a brother, Shiva, who is also a writer, and five sisters. Naipaul was educated at the Queen's Royal College, Port of Spain, and at eighteen left for University College, Oxford, to read English ("a mistake," he comments, "the English course had little to do with literature"). After taking his degree, he supported himself by freelance broadcasting and for almost two years edited a weekly literary program for the BBC Colonial Service. In 1955 he married Patricia Ann Hale.

Concerning his decision to settle in England, Naipaul has said, "I knew Trinidad to be unimportant, uncreative, cynical"; "the threat of failure, the need to escape: this was the prompting of the society I knew." But in his novels he has often returned to the Caribbean he knew as a boy; it nourishes his work from a distance yet disturbs him when revisited, as his autobiographical travelbook *The Middle Passage* reveals. He has never concealed the cost of his elected exile. He recollects how, as a schoolboy, he "went to books for fantasy": the works of Jane Austen, Conrad, Dickens, George Eliot and H. G. Wells he "set in Trinidad, accepting, rejecting, adapting, and peopling in my own way . . . but it seemed impossible that the life I knew in Trinidad could ever be turned into a book." So, in one sense inhibited by his avid reading, he turned to "some local short stories" which, "never published outside Trinidad, converted what [he] saw into 'writing'" and "provided a starting-point for further observation." He began to write in earnest when almost twenty-three, but he then found, ironically, that knowing England could not make him an English writer: "the English language was mine; the tradition was not."

Ganesh Ramsummair, the Trinidad Hindu who, in *The Mystic Masseur* (1957), becomes in turn and with culpable charm schoolmaster, author, masseur, healer, and politician, is a character painted with what Lord David Cecil calls "Chekhovian delight." Advancing in his oblique, incredulous way from obscurity and failure to eminence and an OBE, he

*nī pôl′

V. S. NAIPAUL

simultaneously embodies and mocks the notion of spiritual progress; indeed, Naipaul has said, "the history of Ganesh is in a way the history of our time."

The same dry relish for the antics of modern Caribbean man characterizes the account of a riotous Trinidadian election in Naipaul's second novel, *The Suffrage of Elvira.* Wooed by Hindu and Muslim factions, the people of Elvira find life unprecedentedly exciting and then, after a democracy has been founded, bizarrely changed. The critics applauded the gentle humor; it is conducted throughout, as Kingsley Amis said, "with the utmost stylistic quietude."

For the astringent hilarities of *Miguel Street,* which won a Somerset Maugham Award, the critics were ready with allusions to Dickens and *Porgy and Bess.* A sort of Catfish Row of Trinidad, the street serves as a stage across which, according to sunstruck, euphoric rhythms all of their own, come promenading or tumbling a host of garrulous, indefatigable eccentrics created with evident relish. They have something in common with, but do not match up to the stricter mood expressed through the characters in *A House for Mr. Biswas,* generally regarded as Naipaul's most ambitious, most profound novel. Mr. Biswas is an anglicized Indian in the Creole world of Trinidad. His lifelong yearning for a house of his own movingly evokes the hunger of the culturally dispossessed for "one's portion of earth"—evidence that one will not have "lived and died as one had been born, unnecessary and unaccommodated." As Gordon Rohleht says, Biswas "is fully presented as a person whose every quirk and idiosyncrasy we know, in a world whose every sight, sound, and smell is recorded with fidelity and precision. Whatever is suggested of the numinous and universal is conveyed through a fidelity to the concrete and particular."

Naipaul's next two books were both prize-winners. *Mr. Stone and the Knights Companion*, a novella with an English cast and setting which won the Hawthornden Prize, is a suburban comedy of manners precipitated by Mr. Stone's eve-of-retirement scheme to found a club for all veterans of the firm (Excal) whose head librarian he has been. *The Mimic Men*, conceived as the memoir of a Caribbean exiled in London, studies the wan self-consciousness of an intellectual turned agitator, an islander haunted by ancestral dreams of nomadic horsemen on the endless plains of Central Asia, a man whose whole life has been attitude, posture, mimicry. Michael Ratcliffe called it "a wilful, gnomic, not always clear, but tremendously rich novel, telling of sweet defeat and gentle agony; comic still, but chastened." It received the W. H. Smith Award.

A Flag on the Island is a volume of short stories, and *In a Free State* contains the title novella, two stories, and two fragments of travel diary: the latter collection was very warmly praised, and brought Naipaul the £5,000 Booker Prize. It is, as reviewers pointed out, not a collection of occasional pieces but an entity, united by the common concern of all its variously exiled characters—the search for some dreamed-of "free state" of the heart. Nadine Gordimer, although she thought this not one of Naipaul's best books, called it "part of an achievement that I believe in the end will show him to have been a great writer."

Naipaul has painfully explored his distant heritage in *An Area of Darkness*, in which he describes a year spent traveling in India (where his grandfather was born). Throughout, as D. J. Enright observes, "his puritanical honesty, his refusal to be taken in by talk of Indian spirituality, afflicts him like an ingrowing nail." John Wain thought it a "tender, lyrical, explosive and cruel book." Naipaul himself said the journey "had broken [his] life in two." He continued his personal odyssey in a different form and context in *The Loss of El Dorado*, which Gregory Rabassa called a work of "history as literature, meticulously researched and masterfully written, as in the manner of Thucydides." It is an account of the colonization of Trinidad from 1580 to the abolition of slavery in 1834, contrasting the brilliant myths which seduced the colonizers with the sorry realities they imposed on the colonized. Naipaul was a reviewer from 1957 to 1961 for the *New Statesman*, and now contributes to many major journals in Britain and the United States. *The Overcrowded Barracoon* is a volume of his brilliant essays and articles on literature and history, on cricket and politics, and more generally on the social and human damage inflicted by the creation, and the dissolution, of the British Empire.

The *Times Literary Supplement* has called Naipaul "an important link-man, with something of the impact on the Commonwealth that Koestler has on the Anglo-European world." It is a role which has not shielded him from the hostility of some other West Indian writers, including George Lamming and John Hearne, who believe that Naipaul is "ashamed of his cultural background." His defenders point out that Naipaul's irony extends to himself; one has noted that "because he is dealing with his own personal past, his irony does not preclude sympathy but reinforces it." Alfred Kazin has called him "an exile who writes about nothing else—in the most clipped, elegant, subtle English prose. . . . No one else around today, not even Nabokov, seems able to employ prose fiction so deeply as the very voice of exile."

PRINCIPAL WORKS: *Fiction*—The Mystic Masseur, 1957; The Suffrage of Elvira, 1958; Miguel Street, 1959; A House for Mr. Biswas, 1961; Mr. Stone and the Knights Companion, 1963; The Mimic Men, 1967; A Flag on the Island (stories), 1967; In a Free State (novella, stories, etc.), 1971. *Non-fiction*—The Middle Passage, 1962; An Area of Darkness, 1964; The Loss of El Dorado, 1969; The Overcrowded Barracoon: Selected Articles 1958–1972, 1972.
ABOUT: Contemporary Authors 4, 1963; Coulthard, G. R. Caribbean Literature, 1966; Dathorne O. R. Caribbean Narrative. 1966; Howes, B. From the Green Antilles, 1966; James, L. The Islands in Between, 1967; Naipaul, V. S. The Middle Passage, 1962; Naipaul, V. S. An Area of Darkness, 1964; Ramchand, K. West Indian Narrative, 1966; Ramchand, K. The West Indian Novel, 1970; Theroux, P. V. S. Naipaul, 1972; Vinson, J. (ed.) Contemporary Novelists, 1972; Walsh, W. A Manifold Voice, 1970; Walsh, W. V. S. Naipaul, 1973; Who's Who, 1973. *Periodicals*—Caribbean Quarterly December 1962; Commentary June 1965; Encounter December 1964; Kenyon Review November 1967; London Magazine May 1967; Nation October 26, 1963; New Statesman September 29, 1961; August 3, 1962; New York Review of Books December 30, 1971; New York Times Book Review October 17, 1971; New Yorker August 27, 1960; Reporter September 9, 1965; Saturday Evening Post June 3, 1967; Southern Review Spring 1967; Times Literary Supplement June 4, 1964; September 16, 1965; December 12, 1969; July 30, 1971.

NAIRN, IAN (DOUGLAS) (August 24, 1930–), English journalist and writer on architecture, town and landscape design, and travel, was born in Bedford, the son of John and Margaret Nairn. While he was still a child the family moved to Wembley, London. Nairn went to schools in Wembley and then on to Birmingham University, ostensibly to read mathematics but primarily with the intention of joining the university air squadron there and satisfying his deeply rooted ambition to fly. When he graduated, Nairn joined the Royal Air Force with a permanent commission. He soon discovered that not even flying could compensate for the less attractive aspects of service life, and resigned.

It was at this point that Nairn turned his attention to architecture, another long-standing enthusiasm. He began to make a living, though a bare one, as a freelance journalist and book reviewer in that field, and in 1954 joined the staff of the *Architectural Review*. The quality of his work was such that within a year he was given the opportunity of editing a special issue of the *Review*, that for June 1955. "Outrage," as the issue was called, formed a report, in words and photographs, of what Nairn had seen in the course of a journey from the south of England to the north. What he found and showed to be outrageous was the performance of the country's planners. Thanks to their ignorance, insensibility, and arrogrance, "the whole land surface is being covered by the creeping mildew that already circumscribes all of our towns." Nairn found the country almost submerged under a hideous or featureless "Subtopia," and everywhere "abandoned aerodromes and fake rusticity, wire fences, traffic roundabouts, gratuitous notice boards, car parks and Things in Fields."

Nairn's "shock tactics" provoked heated discussion all over the country, and "Outrage" probably did more than any other single document in recent years to arouse public and official awareness of the subversion of the English scene. By the time it appeared in book form, a few months after its first publication, the word "Subtopia" had passed into the language and Nairn was famous. *Counter-Attack Against Subtopia*, originally the December 1956 issue of the *Architectural Review*, was a sequel to *Outrage* showing how a few planners in England and Europe had succeeded in bringing the artifacts of modern society to terms with the landscape.

Most of Nairn's subsequent publications have been guide books, but of a highly original kind. His guides are characterized by an immensely stimulating and often iconoclastic freshness of vision far removed from the sentimental reverence common in such works. He is as likely to praise a modern building as an ancient one, and will dwell as nostalgically on a derelict warehouse or Victorian factory as on a crumbling castle. His *Surrey*, for example, done in collaboration with Nikolaus Pevsner, finds more to blame than to praise in that stronghold of "stockbroker's Tudor," but relishes among Surrey's surviving treasures not only ice-age caves and medieval chapels but the thatched Village Homes for Inebriate Ladies at Duxhurst. The book was called "a sophisticated and fascinating addition to the Buildings of England series." In *Modern Buildings of London* Nairn suggests that the celebrated Shell building would be "perfectly

IAN NAIRN

acceptable somewhere else," and that "the noblest modern building in London" houses buses in Stockwell.

No one at present writing in his field can excel Nairn's ability to pin down the look and feel of a place in a single memorable phase. *Nairn's London*, which "awoke so many readers to a new vision of that peerless and preposterous city," begins with his description of St. Paul's, where "once and for all the principle of English freedom has been given spiritual form," and includes Bow Creek, "a sudden smudge of green" amid "a fag-end of railway sidings." Robert Harling, who thinks this book one of the best ever written about London, speaks of Nairn's "love-hate relationship" with British architecture, "expressed in poetic fury and fiery prose." Nikolaus Pevsner, at a loss for words to describe a particular building, once sighed for "a film or Mr. Nairn's pen."

Since then Nairn has turned his attention to foreign countries. *The American Landscape*, which in fact concentrates less on landscape than on townscapes, reaches the conclusion that "America has made the biggest hash of its environment in the history of the world." This brash and witty book is an attack on what Nairn calls "nonrelation," a plea for a new "art of environment." According to one American critic, the author "has a feel for the United States, a native's sense of its tempos, a lover's intuition for what, under 'a surface gloss of sameness,' it longs and deserves to be." Wolf Von Eckardt thought it too selective, but valuable because it can "teach us to see."

After a stint with the *Daily Telegraph*, Nairn became architectural correspondent in 1964 of the

Observer, which he left in 1968 to write on travel for the *Sunday Times*. He continues to serve the *Architectural Review*, whose townscape editor he has been since 1965, and has written and presented two series of television films on subjects and places dear to his heart. Nairn was married in 1961 to Judy Perry and, when he is not traveling, lives in London. His hobbies are flying and pubs—the only kind of building he would like to design.

PRINCIPAL WORKS: Outrage, 1955; Counter-Attack Against Subtopia, 1957; (with Nikolaus Pevsner) Surrey, 1962; Modern Buildings in London, 1964; The American Landscape: A Critical View, 1965; (with Nikolaus Pevsner) Sussex, 1965; Your England Revisited, 1965; Nairn's London, 1966; Britain's Changing Towns, 1967; Nairn's Paris, 1968.

ABOUT: Author's and Writer's Who's Who, 1971. *Periodicals*—New York Times Book Review March 7, 1965; Times Literary Supplement September 16, 1955; May 11, 1962; August 5, 1965; April 21, 1966; Twentieth Century 1967.

THOMAS NARCEJAC

***"NARCEJAC, THOMAS" (pseudonym of Pierre Ayraud)** (July 3, 1908–), French novelist and critic, writes: "My name is Pierre Ayraud and I was born in 1908 at Rochefort-sur-Mer, on the Atlantic coast, the only son in a family with a well-established sea-going tradition, which I would undoubtedly have upheld if, at the age of nine, I had not lost the sight of an eye while playing with a friend who fired an air-gun at me. So, when it was time for me to choose a career, I became a teacher of philosophy. Meanwhile I had developed an interest in the detective novel, a genre which satisfied both my personal need for scientific reasoning and my love of mystery.

"In 1918 came my first encounter with Arsène Lupin; in 1920, with Conan Doyle and Poe; then, in 1935, I discovered Simenon, another important event. Oddly enough, it didn't occur to me then to take up writing, and I remained without literary ambitions till, during a rainy summer in Brittany, I embarked, for the sheer fun of it, on a series of imitations of various well-known detective novel writers, which were published in 1945. Wishing to keep my professional activities quite distinct from my literary venture, I picked the *nom de plume* "Thomas Narcejac," in which were sentimentally united names of two hamlets where I used to go fishing as a child: "St. Thomas" and "Narcejac," on the Charente river, for the memories of my childhood have never left me.

"From 1945 onwards, I became more and more interested in the technique of detective fiction and was the author of three books on the subject. It looked like a good idea to train myself deliberately for the job, so, purely as an experiment, I wrote several novels which I threw into the waste-paper basket as fast as I produced them. A few survived, however, and were published: among them, *La Mort est du voyage*, which won the Grand Prix du Roman d'Aventures. Then came three stories. Immediately afterwards, I met Pierre Boileau. He was interested in the 'hows' and I was interested in the 'whys' of a story; moreover, I felt that the best kind of detective novel could not be written by any one person, since it involved the improbable blending, in a single individual, of two opposite personalities: the technician's and the psychologist's. That is how we eventually decided to write in collaboration. Our first joint effort became a film: *Les Diaboliques*. From then on, we have never ceased to write (although I am still teaching) and most of our books have been adapted to the screen. We also work for French television. In 1965, we were happy to be awarded the Grand Prix de l'Humour Noir for our novel: *Et mon tout est un homme*.

"I now look forward to retiring from teaching so as to devote myself entirely to writing suspense crime novels, which I believe are the modern form of the rather hackneyed, though ever respectable, 'orthodox' detective story."

The immensely successful novels that Narcejac writes with Pierre Boileau reflect Narcejac's admiration for Simenon in their compelling use of atmosphere, but have none of the scrupulous naturalism of the Maigret stories. Their stories often begin with a situation that seems fantastic or supernatural and which, once accepted, leads logically to increasingly bizarre and macabre developments. The reader, drawn deep into this

*nar sə zhak

nightmare world, is suddenly shocked awake by a violently unexpected denouement; the whole monstrous chain of events is seen to be the deliberate product of human wickedness.

This pattern emerged in their brilliant and appalling first novel, *Celle qui n'était plus* (translated as *The Woman Who Was No More*, filmed by Clouzot as *Les Diaboliques*, and released in the United States as *Diabolique*). It recurs in *D'entre les morts* (1956, translated as *The Living and the Dead*), in *À cœur perdu* (1959, translated as *Heart to Heart*), and in several other stories, In *D'entre les morts*, for example, Flavières becomes obsessed by the memory of the woman he had once loved, and whom he saw jump to her death from a church tower. Years later, she seems to be reincarnated in the mistress of an American he meets in Marseilles. So skillfully is the book written that the reader, as bemused as Flavières, is in the end half inclined to accept some supernatural explanation. And at that point comes the disclosure of a criminal plot which has exploited Flavières' fears and uncertainties as cleverly as Narcejac and Boileau have exploited those of the reader. The book was filmed by Alfred Hitchcock as *Vertigo*.

Les Louves (1955, translated as *The Prisoner*) is another variation on the theme of impersonation, which this time has ugly results for the impersonator. *Le Mauvais Œil* (1956, translated as *The Evil Eye*) is a "Gallic exercise in family nastiness" about a boy who is cured suddenly of paralysis but not of amnesia, and whose ailments seem to be mysteriously connected with his mother's death. The prizewinning *Et mon tout est un homme* (1965, translated as *Choice Cuts*) is a gruesome fantasy about what happens when portions of the body of an executed murderer are grafted onto seven people hurt in road accidents.

The novels of Narcejac and Boileau form a subgenre of their own. Their work, at least in translation, is stylistically undistinguished, but for most critics this fact is outweighed by the ingenuity of their plots and their power to involve the reader in the mood of doubt and mounting fear that they so skillfully evoke.

Narcejac was educated at the Poitiers *lycée* and the Faculté des Lettres in Paris, graduating with a degree in philosophy. He has been married twice—in 1930 to Marie-Thérèse Baret, by whom he has two married daughters, and in 1967 to Renée Swanson. Apart from his novels and critical works, Narcejac has written several plays, for the stage and for television. His hobby is fly-fishing.

PRINCIPAL WORKS IN ENGLISH TRANSLATION: *Fiction* (with Pierre Boileau)—The Woman Who Was No More, 1954 (England, The Woman Who Was); Faces in the Dark, 1955; The Living and the Dead, 1956; The Prisoner, 1957; The Evil Eye *and* The Sleeping Beauty, 1959; Heart to Heart, 1959; The Tube, 1960; Spells of Evil, 1961; Who Was Claire Jallu?, 1965; Choice Cuts, 1966; The Victims, 1967. *Nonfiction*—The Art of Simenon, 1952. ABOUT: Who's Who in France, 1971–1972.

***NATSUME, "SOSEKI" (pseudonym of Kinnosuke Natsume)** (January 5, 1867–December 9, 1916) was, together with Ogai Mori, the outstanding Japanese literary figure of the late nineteenth century Meiji period, when Japan was emerging from its ancient isolation and discovering the cultures of the West. Novelist, gifted haiku poet, and student of Chinese literature, Soseki was also one of his country's ablest critics of English literature.

He was born in Tokyo, where his father, though not quite of *samurai* status, held a responsible administrative position as *nanushi* (ward chief). At one time the family had been quite well-to-do, but during Soseki's childhood the family fortune dwindled. There was, he said, "a cold and sad shadow" over his childhood. He was the last of six children, a late and unwelcome arrival. At the age of two he was placed with a childless couple named Shiobara, and spent seven years with them in an atmosphere of squabbling and instability before they were divorced and he was returned to his parents—or "grandparents" as he had been taught to think of them. This difficult beginning was followed by the shock of discovering his identity (from a maidservant), the death of his mother when he was fifteen, and growing antagonism towards his father—factors which must all have contributed to his persistent feeling of aloneness and the nervous instability which brought him at times throughout his life to the edge of insanity.

Soseki liked to pretend that in school his specialty was idling, but he pursued his studies in Chinese and English through college and continued them at Tokyo Imperial University, which he entered in 1890. After toying with the idea of an architectural career, he had decided to become a writer. He polished his English to a remarkable level of proficiency at the university, where he also edited a philosophical magazine, working so hard that he suffered the first of several nervous breakdowns. He nevertheless graduated with distinction in 1893, and accepted a teaching post at Tokyo Normal College.

In April 1895 Soseki suddenly left Tokyo for Matsuyama in Shikoku to take up an appointment in the local middle school. Ten years later the novel *Botchan*, though he denied that it was autobiographical, caustically but humorously recorded the barbarisms and petty scheming of just such a school. Soseki was nevertheless liked and respected in Matsuyama, enjoying a higher salary than that of the headmaster. *Botchan* has been translated three

*sōō sā kē nət sōō mā

SOSEKI NATSUME

times—by Yasotaro Mori in 1918, by Umeji Sasaki in 1968, and by Alan Turney in 1972.

While in Matsuyama, Soseki became engaged to Kyoko Nakane, the eldest daughter of the then Secretary of the House of Peers. It was a fine match for an obscure young man, and the marriage was arranged in the traditional way by exchange of photographs followed by a meeting. Soseki says he was attracted by the fact that "although she had bad teeth, she made no attempt to hide them." Kyoko, for her part, was impressed by Soseki's courtesy and ability, and was prepared to put up with his eccentricities—though it is said that she later proved something of a shrew. Soseki obtained a better post at the Fifth National College, and the couple settled down in Kumamoto.

In June 1900 Soseki was offered a government scholarship to study in England. At thirty-three, married, comfortably off, and established in a good position, with a growing literary reputation, he had little incentive to uproot himself, but refusal was not proper and he left Japan in September 1900.

The two and a half years he spent in England were distressing—he was, he said, as "lonely as a stray dog amid a pack of wolves." The scholarship barely met his immediate financial needs, and no arrangements had been made for him to attend any particular university. He rejected Cambridge after seeing how sedulously wealthy young Japanese there were aping their English contemporaries: "I do not know if the gentlemen in England are so impressive as to make it worth my while to emulate them." Eventually he retired into obscurity in the London suburbs. For a few months he attended a course in literature at University College, then went for private tuition to W. J. Craig (editor of the Arden Shakespeare and an Irishman) who assured him that the English were philistines, without any sense of poetry.

Most of his time Soseki spent alone in his room reading, and working on a book on the psychological and social bases of literature in which he hoped to find common ground between oriental and occidental literature and which was later expanded into a course of lectures and published as *Bungaku ron* (Literary Studies). Loneliness and overwork exacerbated his neurosis, and it was even rumored among the Japanese in London that he had gone mad—in any case, it was an unhappy time, described in the most closely autobiographical of his later novels, *Michikusa* (1915, translated by Edwin McClelland as *Grass on the Wayside*), against a background of dreary bedsitters, aimless, hungry walks in rain-swept parks, and miserable meals in cheap cafés, with cockney chars as his only confidantes.

Painful as it was, Soseki's stay in England did much to crystallize his literary attitudes. His reading had covered the whole range of Western literature and thought, and he had been drawn especially to Swift, Sterne, Fielding, and Meredith. Deciding that it was foolish to imitate Western literature indiscriminately, but impossible to reject it out of hand, he sought to develop a kind of novel that would combine Western analytical and psychological methods with the delicate lyricism of Japan.

On his return to Tokyo in January 1903 he was appointed to a lectureship at the Imperial University, taking up the post vacated by Lafcadio Hearn. His novels began to appear in 1905, together with a spate of critical essays in various magazines. *Wagahai wa Neko de aru* (1905), is a satire on contemporary intellectual life and the new materialism as seen through the eyes of an animal. It was enormously successful and established Soseki's reputation at once. The book was translated in two volumes by Kanichi Ando as *I Am a Cat* (1906–1909), and there have been three subsequent English versions under the same title—one by Elford Eddy in 1921, one by Katsue Shibata and Motonari Kai in 1961, and another by Graeme Wilson in 1972.

In 1907 he caused something of a sensation by retiring from his university post to become literary editor of the newspaper *Asahi*. He was no doubt attracted by the added financial security for his wife and four daughters, and also perhaps by the discipline of a regular deadline. Thereafter, until his death from stomach ulcers in 1916, he wrote steadily and with deepening perception.

Two crucial themes pervade Soseki's fiction—man's isolation in a world where real communication with others is impossible, and the particular isolation of the artist in a materialistic society. In his early novels he seems to have found a temporary solution in the deliberate development of an aloof egocentricity, a conscious refusal of emotional ties. *Kusamakura* (1906) is about an artist who, in spite of his attempts at noninvolvement, is haunted by the sadness of a girl he encounters during a vacation in the mountains. In Japan it is one of the most admired of Soseki's novels, an important document in the reaction against the squalid naturalism then in vogue. Translated by Alan Turney as *The Three-Cornered World*, it seemed to Western reviewers too vague and wispy, "the merest peg for Soseki's poems and word-paintings and his observations on aesthetics and on nature."

The same theme is explored in several other novels written at about the same time, notably the trilogy comprising *Sanshiro* (1908), about a shy provincial youth who encounters disillusionment in love and friendship at the Imperial University in Tokyo (where a pond on the campus is still called Sanshiro's Lake); *Sorekara* (And Then, 1909); and *Mon* (1912, translated under the same title by Francis Mathy), in which the hero, obsessed by the feeling that he has betrayed a friend, seeks consolation in a Zen temple, is denied entry, and returns with resignation and patience to the burden of his existence. It is a moving and compassionate book, marking a transition between Soseki's early preoccupation with individuality and his later quest for a means—religious or otherwise—by which the self could be transcended.

Kokoro (1914), regarded by many critics as Soseki's masterpiece, was written in the shadow of the Emperor Meiji's death and the resulting suicide of General and Baroness Nogi; it stands as a death knell for the era with which Soseki identified himself. It is an account of the friendship between a young student and an embittered semirecluse who believes that "loneliness is the price we pay for being born in this modern age, so full of freedom, independence, and our own egotistical selves." A reviewer in the *Times Literary Supplement* of Edwin McClellan's English version wrote: "The complex web of Japanese human relationships, their inherited order, the passions and powers that underpin them, is followed in *Kokoro* with a clarity and grace that never makes anything sound easier than it is; it is a very selective naturalism that Soseki employed, so that the matter-of-fact and even banal dialogue seems suspended above something imponderable. . . . *Kokoro* has an unforgettable atmosphere of the loneliness and mysteriousness of man's relationship with man." An earlier translation of *Kokoro* by Ineko Sato appeared in 1941.

Soseki died before he could complete *Meian* (translated as *Light and Darkness*), a study of conflict within a marriage in which he seemed to be writing his way towards an ideal conception of peace through resignation. His immense popularity and influence in Japan has never waned, and he is the subject of innumerable studies.

PRINCIPAL WORKS IN ENGLISH TRANSLATION: I Am a Cat, 1906–1909 (new translations, 1921, 1961, and 1972); Botchan, 1918 (new translations, 1968 and 1972); Kusamakura, 1927 (also translated as Unhuman Tour, 1927, and as The Three-Cornered World, 1965); Within My Glass Doors, 1928; Ten Nights' Dreams *and* Our Cat's Grave, 1934; Kokoro, 1941 (new translation, 1957); The Wayfarer, 1967; Grass on the Wayside, 1969; Light and Darkness, 1971; Mon, 1972.

ABOUT: Grigson, G. (ed.) Concise Encyclopedia of Modern World Literature, 1963; Keene, D. Modern Japanese Literature, 1956; Kosaka, M. Japanese Thought in the Meiji Era, 1958; McClellan, E. Two Japanese Novelists, 1969; Meiji Dictionary of Modern Japanese Literature (in Japanese), 1965; Okazaki, Y. Japanese Literature in the Meiji Era, 1955; Penguin Companion to Literature 4, 1969; Seymour-Smith, M. Guide to Modern World Literature, 1973; Yu, B. Natsume Soseki, 1969. *Periodicals*—American Scholar Autumn 1965; Harvard Journal of Asiatic Studies vol. 22; New York Times October 20, 1957; New Yorker December 14, 1957; Saturday Review October 5, 1957; Times Literary Supplement May 27, 1965; February 1, 1968.

NEEDHAM, (NOEL) JOSEPH (TERENCE MONTGOMERY) (December 9, 1900–), English scientist, philosopher and historian of science, and Sinologist, was born in Clapham, London. His father, also Joseph Needham, was an eminent physician, a specialist in anesthesia; his mother, the former Alicia Montgomery, was an equally distinguished musician. Needham decided on a career in science as a schoolboy at Oundle. In 1918, after brief war service as a surgeon sublieutenant in the Royal Navy, he entered Cambridge University, where he studied biochemistry under Sir Frederick Gowland Hopkins, graduating in 1922. The same year he was elected a fellow of his college, Gonville and Caius, which he has served over the years as librarian, president, and, since 1966, as master. From 1928 to 1933 Needham was University Demonstrator in Biochemistry at Cambridge, and in 1933 succeeded J. B. S. Haldane as Sir William Dunn Reader in Biochemistry, retaining that influential post until 1966. He is a Ph.D. (1925) and Sc.D. (1932) of Cambridge University.

As a young biochemist, Needham devoted himself to the problems of the development of the embryo, and made his reputation in 1931 with *Chemical Embryology*, a three-volume work defining what was then virtually a new field of study but is now one of very great importance. Intensive research into the properties and functions of the morphogenetic hormones led to another valuable treatise, *Biochemistry and Morphogenesis* (1942). Needham's *History of Embryology* remains the standard work on the subject. The development of the embryo is one which lends itself readily to

JOSEPH NEEDHAM

philosophical speculations about the nature and conduct of life, and even Needham's scientific treatises express and support his philosophical views, since he sees social and political progress as a natural continuation of biological evolution. He became a Fellow of the Royal Society in 1941.

Needham has always possessed an acute sense of science's responsibility to humanity, and the depression years turned him towards a socialist view of society which he shared with such other scientists as J. D. Bernal and J. B. S. Haldane. His "quasi Marxism" is modified, however, by a belief above all in the power of love, a hope that "all under heaven shall be one community" (to quote one of his poems). He has expressed these views in a number of essays and in the lectures which he has delivered all over the world since the late 1920s. In 1935, for example, he paid his second visit to the United States to give the Terry and Carmalt lectures at Yale, the Goldwin-Smith lectures at Cornell, and the Mead-Swing lectures at Oberlin. He has subsequently lectured in Poland, France, Colombo, Singapore, Peking, Jaipur, Beirut, Jerusalem, and elsewhere; and repeatedly, before a variety of distinguished audiences, in Britain.

Many of Needham's essays and addresses have been published in book form, and reveal the astonishing breadth and depth of his learning. Thus the essays in *Sceptical Biologist* show a "penetrating and sympathetic knowledge of religious and theological thought and history," and were considered fresh, perceptive, and often funny. *Time: The Refreshing River* is "adorned with frequent and apt quotations from contemporary poets and rises on occasion to passages of considerable eloquence." C. E. M. Joad admired the book for its gaiety and vigor, and called it "the gallop of an able mind over difficult country." Needham writes, it has been said, in "a leisurely Victorian style, distinguished by its modesty and warmth."

In 1937 meanwhile, through some Chinese graduate students at Cambridge, Needham had heard something of the contributions to knowledge of the early Chinese alchemists. Excited by what they told him, he began to learn Chinese and study the scanty available literature. The outbreak of World War II did not end but encouraged these studies. In 1942 Needham was named director of the Sino-British Science Cooperation Office, and went to China as head of a British Scientific Mission. His job was to get information, equipment, and advice to his Chinese colleagues, often in remote and inaccessible regions. He and his wife, who joined him in his work in 1944, described their work in *Science Outpost* (1948). Needham's private propaganda campaign for international scientific cooperation was an important factor in the creation of UNESCO, and from 1946 to 1948 he worked as the first director of its Natural Science Division.

After 1948 Needham resumed his work at Cambridge, but at the same time laid the foundations for the great work which is now his overwhelming preoccupation. With a group of Chinese colleagues at Cambridge he is at work on a multivolume history, *Science and Civilisation in China*, which is to dispel once and for all the illusion that science is the brainchild of the West. The first volume appeared in 1954 and discusses the geographical foundations of Chinese civilization and the traffic in knowledge between China and Europe. The second volume is a history of Chinese scientific thought, and other volumes deal with mathematics, astronomy, physics, chemistry, technology, and engineering. This encyclopedic work has been called "perhaps the greatest single act of historical synthesis and intercultural communication ever attempted by one man." Arnold Toynbee wrote that "the author has set himself to interpret the Chinese mind in Western terms, and he is perhaps unique among living scholars in possessing the necessary combination of qualifications for this formidable undertaking. The practical importance of Dr. Needham's work is as great as its intellectual interest." Over the same period Needham has also published several volumes of essays and lectures and such monographs as *Heavenly Clockwork*, an account of the astronomical clocks of medieval China, which are associated with, but not a part of, the series.

Needham retired from his Cambridge Readership in 1966 to devote himself more fully to his book. His wife, Dorothy Mary Moyle Needham, who is closely involved in the project, is also a distinguished Cambridge biochemist. When she was elected to the Royal Society in 1948 they were the first husband and wife in history both to be members of that august body. Needham is a member of a number of foreign learned societies, including the National Academy of China. In 1972 he became president of the International Union of Historians of Science. His decorations include the George Sarton medal of the Society for the History of Science, the Leonardo da Vinci medal of the Society for the History of Technology, and the Chinese Order of the Brilliant Star. According to the *New Scientist*, Needham is tall and well built. "His manner, his somewhat disordered appearance, his quick, dry speech and the droop of his head are signs of his unrepentant scholarship. . . . He has been described as 'a kind of medieval polymath to whom no knowledge is unfamiliar, and none to be despised.' Equally at home expounding the theory of chemical organisers in a growing embryo, or translating a Chinese ballad into the metre of *Piers Plowman*, he is indeed a rare man."

PRINCIPAL WORKS: (ed.) Science, Religion and Reality, 1925; Man a Machine, 1927; The Sceptical Biologist, 1929; Chemical Embryology (3 vols.), 1931; The Great Amphibium, 1931; A History of Embryology, 1934; (tr.) Adventures Before Birth, by J. Rostand, 1936; Order and Life, 1936; (ed. with D. E. Green) Perspectives in Biochemistry, 1937; (ed. with W. Paget) Background to Modern Science, 1938; Biochemistry and Morphogenesis, 1942; (ed.) The Teacher of Nations, 1942; Time: The Refreshing River, 1943; Chinese Science, 1945; History Is on Our Side, 1946; (with Dorothy Needham) Science Outpost, 1948; Science and Civilisation in China (in progress), 1954– ; The Development of Iron and Steel Technology in China (Dickinson Memorial Lecture), 1958; Heavenly Clockwork: The Great Astronomical Clocks of Mediaeval China, 1960; Within the Four Seas (essays and lectures), 1969; The Grand Titration (essays and lectures), 1969; Clerks and Craftsmen in China and the West (essays and lectures), 1969; (ed.) The Chemistry of Life: Eight Lectures on the History of Biochemistry, 1970.

ABOUT: Contemporary Authors 11–12, 1965; Who's Who, 1973. *Periodicals*—Far Eastern Quarterly August 1955; Horizon Winter 1968; Journal of Asian Studies February 1957; Living Church October 4, 1930; April 23, 1932; Nation November 10, 1956; Nature April 3, 1926; March 16, 1935; New Scientist May 9, 1957; New Statesman September 11, 1954; July 20, 1962; November 4, 1966; New York Herald Tribune Book Review March 21, 1926; New York Times May 3, 1936; January 22, 1939; New York Times Book Review June 20, 1971; Nineteenth Century and After August 1943; Review of Metaphysics December 1957; Saturday Review of Literature May 31, 1930; Science August 20, 1965; Science and Society Fall 1956; Time May 25, 1953; Times Literary Supplement April 18, 1935; October 15, 1954; July 8, 1960; World Politics April 1958.

NEKRASOV, VICTOR (PLATONOVICH)

(June 17, 1911–), Russian novelist, writes (in Russian): "I was born in Kiev, in the Ukraine, but my language was at first French, since until the age

VICTOR NEKRASOV

of four I lived in Switzerland, and after that in Paris. My mother, a doctor, spent almost all her youth in Switzerland. She went to school there, and graduated from the medical faculty of Lausanne University (at that time women could not receive higher education in Russia). It was there that she married a Russian student, my father, though I do not remember him, since he died in 1917 before I was six years old.

"The First World War found us in Paris, where my mother worked in a military hospital. In 1915, by a circuitous route through England, Norway, and Sweden, we returned to Kiev, where I have since lived, with only brief interruptions, the longest of which was the war.

"My childhood passed relatively quietly, considering that Kiev changed governments fourteen times during the civil war from 1917 to 1921; Reds, Whites, Germans, Poles, and all sorts of Ukrainian nationalists. The city changed hands but we children continued to run to school, barefoot in the summer and with a bundle of firewood under each arm in the winter.

"After primary school my secondary education consisted of three years at a railway professional school; then I studied architecture for six years at the Construction Institute in Kiev. My dream was to become the Soviet Le Corbusier. But little came of my architecture, for I was attracted by the theatre. While remaining at the Institute, I enrolled in a theatrical studio, wanting to become a second Stanislavsky. (In the depths of my heart I wanted more than anything to become a well-known writer, but I had not had time to realize that dream.)

"Having finished relatively successfully at the

Institute in 1936, and then the studio, I finally gave up architecture for the theatre. I became an actor, then tried my hand as an assistant director, then designed some sets. In four years I worked in four different theatres, in Vladivostok, Kirov, Rostov-on-Don, and in a mobile theatre in Kiev. In the last we toured small towns and villages, and although we had only five actors we did everything from *Anna Karenina* to *La Tour de Nesle* by Dumas and Scribe's *Le Verre d'eau.*

"The war put an end to my theatrical career. I was drafted into the army and became an officer in the engineers. I fought in the Ukraine, then in Stalingrad (all five and a half months, from the first day to the last), then again in the Ukraine, in Moldavia, and in Poland. My part in the war ended in Lublin in the summer of 1944. I was wounded, sent to a hospital, and finally demobilized. In the hospital in Kiev I began my first book *Vokopakh Stalingrada*, which was published in the Moscow journal *Znamya* in 1946 and was awarded a Stalin prize in 1947. Since that time I have been a writer, having entirely forgotten the theatre, though not architecture; it is true I have not managed to build anything but I have always enjoyed writing on architecture in journals.

"In the twenty years I have devoted to literature I have not written a great deal: three novels, fifteen stories, three travel essays, some film scenarios, and articles on art and architecture.

"My youthful dream seems to some extent to have been realized, but one dream is still unfulfilled, that of becoming the Soviet Fellini, of making a film from my own scenario and perhaps acting in it, if only in one scene."

Nekrasov fought as a lieutenant at Stalingrad and made use of this experience in his first book, *Vokopakh Stalingrada* (1946, translated by David Floyd as *Front-Line Stalingrad*), one of the best and most popular Russian novels about World War II. The war is seen through the eyes of an engineer lieutenant whose thoughts are occupied more with digging trenches and fixing wiring circuits than with heroism or patriotism. His fellow officers are also ordinary men thrown together in a relationship which includes both comradeship and tension. During the battle for Stalingrad there is another battle, almost equally violent, between the regiment's chief of staff, Abrosimov, and the regimental commander Major Borodin. Abrosimov orders a useless frontal attack with bayonets against the German guns, and though in a later court-martial he is reduced to the ranks his order has cost many lives. Probably because of this the novel met with some official criticism, as merely the individual reportage of a "participant in a battle" who knew nothing of "the strategy of the war as a whole." Nine of Nekrasov's short stories about the war were later collected in the volume *Vasya Konakov: Rasskazy* (Vasya Konakov: Stories, 1963).

Nekrasov's second novel, *Vrodnom gorode* (Back Home, 1954), deals with the aftermath of the war. Captain Nikolai Mityasov returns partially disabled to Kiev. The homecoming of which he has dreamed is a bitter disappointment; the city is largely destroyed, and the house where he used to live with his young wife Shura has gone. He eventually traces her, but learns that she is living with another man, and leaves without seeing her. When they do meet they are able to speak only of trivialities; like almost everyone else in Kiev they are emotionally numbed. Mityasov eventually finds a girl, Valya, with whom he can communicate because she too had been at the front, and with her help begins to overcome his fear of civilian life. Orthodox Soviet critics were in general hostile because, as the novelist Aleksandr Fadeyev puts it, the central characters "are almost isolated from public life. Reality is examined by the author through the prism of their personal difficulties."

Kira Georgievna (1961, translated by Walter Vickery as *Kira Georgievna* and by Moura Budberg as *Kira*) also explores emotional indifference, this time in a woman. Kira had eloped from art school in the 1930s with Vadim, a young avant-garde poet. A year later he had been arrested, one of the innocent victims of Stalin's purges. Because she is a self-centered person who knows how "to forget quickly everything that complicates life," she soon recovers. When the story opens, twenty years later, she is a successful sculptress, married to a painter twenty years her senior, and having a love affair with her young male model. Vadim returns to Moscow, and though he also is now married they have a brief affair. Twenty years have made a difference, and they soon return to their new partners, but Vadim's indestructible integrity influences Kira even after their separation; she comes to realize that her attitude to all three of the men in her life is false and that the easy optimism of her Socialist art is equally meaningless. Though the book encountered some criticism in the USSR, American reviewers were at a loss to understand why. One called it "a touching little story told strictly within the family," and another suggested that "it might be taken for a tepid reworking of *Anna Karenina.*"

After Nekrasov's first European tour in 1957 he recorded his impressions in *Pervoe znakomstvo* (First Acquaintance, 1958). His later travels, to America in 1960 and to Italy in 1962, led to a larger work in the same genre, *Po obye storony okeana* (1962, translated by Elias Kulukundis as *Both Sides of the Ocean*). The author was accused by the Party ideologists of an unpatriotic *burzhuazny obyektivizm* (bourgeois objectivism) which had led him into "erroneous generalizations," and Khrushchev himself attacked the book. Nekrasov was threatened with expulsion both from the Party and from the Writers' Union unless he repudiated his "errors," but when he refused nothing happened, and the fuss gradually died away. Nekrasov's impressions are necessarily sketchy, but there is a sharp contrast in the book between the United States, where he met with indifference, and Italy, where he was enthusiastically welcomed. However, if he disliked some things about America, such as the advertisements, he liked the architecture, the literature, and even Coca-Cola. Paul Pickrel wrote that Nekrasov "is a heavy-handed writer and a traveler who saw only the most obvious things. The personality that comes through his book, however, is charming and open."

PRINCIPAL WORKS IN ENGLISH TRANSLATION: Front-Line Stalingrad, 1962; Kira Georgievna, 1962 (also tr. as Kira, 1963); Both Sides of the Ocean, 1964 (also excerpts *in* Blake, P. and Hayward, M. Half-way to the Moon: New Writing from Russia, 1964); The Perch *in* The Third Flare: Three War Stories, (Moscow), 1964.

ABOUT: Alexandrova, V. A History of Soviet Literature, 1963; Brown, E. J. Russian Literature Since the Revolution, 1963; Gibian, G. Interval of Freedom, 1960; Greene, M. *introduction to* Russian ed. of Kira Georgievna, 1967; Hayward, M. and Crowley, E. L. Soviet Literature in the Sixties, 1965; International Who's Who, 1972–1973; Swayze, H. Political Control of Literature in the USSR, 1946–1959, 1962. *Periodical*—Eastern Europe January–March 1959.

***NÉMETH, LÁSZLÓ** (April 18, 1901–), Hungarian novelist, essayist, dramatist, and philosopher, writes: "I was born in the first year of this century, in a small border town of Transylvania—now attached to Rumania—where my father was a schoolmaster. I attended schools in Budapest where I studied medicine and graduated as M.D. At the close of the year 1925, within a fortnight, I started my medical career, got married, and at the same time published my first writing, winning first prize for a short story as the result of a literary competition conducted by the periodical *Nyugat* (The West).

"For seventeen years I carried on medical practice, until in 1943 I gave it up and retired as a medical officer for municipal schools. In our marriage six daughters were born to us: of the six, two died in their early years, the other four are married now; two of them have gone in for chemistry, one has became a physicist, and the youngest is a medical student.

"During the first period of my literary career I wrote mainly studies and essays. Most of them dealt with the newly emergent writers of my own days or portrayed the most prominent figures of the former generation. Choosing some representative minds of our age (e.g., Proust, Pirandello, Ortega, Gide, etc.), I tried to assimilate modern European tastes and ways of thinking with Hungarian cultural trends. In order to treat topics outside the sphere of interest of our literary journals, I started *Tanu* (Witness)—an essay-periodical—in 1932. It contained solely my own studies, eventually ran into seventeen volumes, and was meant to provide orientation for contemporary youth and to serve as an encyclopedic source for intellectual collaboration. Of my entire *œuvre*, these studies have undoubtedly left the deepest impress on Hungarian intellectuals.

*ne′ met

"My first major work in fiction, a novel, appeared in 1929; it is the life story of a quack turned into a modern saint. Following it, and encouraged by my Greek studies, I wrote my first heroine-novel *Gyász* (Mourning), in which I portrayed pride locked up in the loneliness of a mourning peasant woman. In my *Utolsó kisérlet* (Last Trial)—a novel-cycle begun in the year preceding the Anschluss—I tried to set down the characteristic pattern of Hungarian life at a time when our national independence was seriously threatened by the oncoming storm of historical events. Between 1935 and 1944 I wrote the bulk of my social dramas, concerned mainly with the conflicting human emotions of the Hungarian intellectuals of those days, when ideals were doomed to crash under the weight of external circumstances.

"In 1945, in the course of the siege of Buda, our home was completely destroyed and my library lost. I managed to find a means of livelihood in a small town in the Lowlands; posted there as a schoolmaster, I started on educational experiments. The five years I spent there belonged undoubtedly to the most productive period in my creative work. I completed my novel *Iszony* (Revulsion)—a counterpart of *Gyász*; and inspired by the Chekhovian figures encountered in this town, I wrote *Égető Eszter* (Esther Égető), the most important of my novels. From this time date also several of my historical plays, regarded as the best I have produced in this genre.

"In 1950 I joined my family and until 1956 the main source of our income was provided by translations. All in all, I have translated more than ten thousand pages, the bulk of which consists of Russian literature, including *Anna Karenina* and Alexey Tolstoy's *Peter I.* I also translated some Czech and German authors, and with my numerous drama translations contributed to our recent Shakespeare, Ibsen and Lorca publications. This work left me hardly any time or energy for original creative work, except for the few plays I produced in these years. One of them, *Galilei*, first performed on the eve of the tragic events of 1956, had a run of one hundred and twenty nights.

LÁSZLÓ NÉMETH

"Since 1954 I have been in poor health, owing to a serious case of hypertonia. However, thanks to my analytic training and my rebellious protest against schematic treatment, I succeeded in getting at the root of my ailment (as I explained in my book *Letters on Hypertonia*) and I decided to take the curing of my illness into my own hands. Evidently I am justified by the results: twelve years have elapsed since the danger signals gave rise to a serious prognosis, and I am still alive, and what is more, still at work. I have been able to add a new novel, *Irgalom* (Charity) and several volumes of plays (among others *Gandhi's Death*) to my life work.

"Not until 1960 had any of my writings traversed the frontiers of Hungary; in that year however a West German publishing house made a start with publications of *Iszony*, which has been translated into eleven languages in the past years. Further German translations include *Égető Eszter*, a collection of historical plays, and a volume of selected essays."

Between the wars, outraged by the social conditions he saw as a country doctor and as a school physician in Budapest, this fierce Calvinist thundered continuously against his country's manifold failings. In his magazine *Tanu*, written entirely by himself, Németh maintained a one-man crusade against Hungarian social injustice, moral decay, and declining literary values reminiscent of that preached in Vienna by Karl Kraus. Németh was a pioneer and theoretician of the "village explorers," who sought a social and cultural revolution drawing its strength from Hungarian peasant traditions, though he was too original a thinker to be submerged in populism or any other movement. He had his disciples, who were dazzled by his extraordinary erudition, his unshakable faith in his own oracular pronouncements, and the hyperbolic brilliance of his essay style. But the authorities naturally regarded him as a dangerous subversive, and many of his fellow reformers resented his air of moral superiority, were suspicious of his preoccupation with racial purity, and bemused by his utopian theorizing about the "deep Hungarianism" which would produce a "garden Hungary."

Németh's novels and plays incorporated his views and also came under attack, but were not suppressed. They carried their author gradually into the front rank of Hungarian writers. After the war, Németh brought his energy and originality to bear on the problems of high school teaching—with such effect that the whole town came to hear his lectures. The novel *Iszony*, published at this time, and widely translated in the 1960s, is the story of a marriage, narrated as by the frigid wife. It has been called the finest postwar Hungarian novel to reach West Europe, and was praised by critics in France, Germany, the United States, and England (where the *Times Literary Supplement* commended Németh's "psychological knowledge, combined with intensity and seriousness of literary purpose," and found in the book the "often ambiguous ring of truth"). Németh's monumental *Égető Eszter*, tracing the life of its small-town heroine from childhood to middle age, was completed in 1948 but had to wait eight years for publication. It was at this time that the critic György Lukács fell from grace and Németh, who had enjoyed his protection, was thereafter permitted to publish only translations.

Németh emerged from his isolation at the time of the 1956 revolution, and since winning the Kossuth Prize in 1957 has become one of the most widely published writers in Hungary. His historical parable *Galilei*, an attack on intellectual tyranny which had been banned in 1955, was very successfully produced in 1956. A collected edition of his social and historical plays appeared in 1957. *Égető Eszter* appeared the same year and was acclaimed as his masterpiece. The whimsical autobiographical play *Utazás* (Journey, 1962), without resorting to historical camouflage, attempts a direct portrayal of contemporary Hungarian life.

As a playwright and novelist, Németh makes his effects by the slow and loving accumulation of detail. Paul Tabori has compared him to Theodore Dreiser, as a serious and humorless writer, epically inclined, lacking in subtlety, who "convinces the reader both by narrative power and his unfaltering belief in the importance of his plot and characters."

PRINCIPAL WORKS IN ENGLISH TRANSLATION: Revulsion (novel), 1965; Guilt (novel), 1966; Galileo (Act IV) *in* Duczyńska, I. and Polanyi, K. (eds.), The Plough and the Pen, 1963; The Journey *in* East Europe August 1962; Voyage (excerpt) *in* Literary Review Spring 1966; *Essays in* The New Hungarian Quarterly September 1960, April–June 1961, January–March 1962, Spring 1964.
ABOUT: Duczyńska, I. and Polanyi, K. (eds.) The Plough and the Pen, 1963; International Who's Who, 1972–73; Klaniczay, T. and others, History of Hungarian Literature, 1964; Reményi, J. Hungarian Writers and Literature, 1964. *Periodicals*—East Europe September, November 1966; The Hungarian Quarterly April–July 1962; Der Monat February 1964; The Personalist October 1950; Spectator August 27, 1965; November 11, 1966; Times Literary Supplement August 19, 1965; October 6, 1966; April 2, 1970; Tulane Drama Review Spring 1967.

"NICHOLS, PETER S." *See* YOUD, SAMUEL

"NICOLAS, F. R. E." *See* FREELING, NICOLAS

NOJIRI, KIYOHIKO. *See* "OSARAGI, JIRO"

"NORTH, ANDREW." *See* NORTON, "ANDRE"

NORTON, "ANDRE" (ALICE MARY NORTON), American science fiction writer and novelist, writes: "I was born and lived most of my life in Cleveland, Ohio; one branch of our family having settled in that state on bounty land paid for services in the Maryland Line during the Revolution. This same ancestor married an Indian to confirm his title at a later period.

"My writing began in junior high school with short efforts aimed at the school magazine. But in senior high I made a more serious and continued effort as one of the staff of the school newspaper, and a member of the Quill and Scroll, under the direction of a very competent instructor. My first book, written the year I graduated from high school, I later revised, to have it the second title of mine to be published.

"When the Depression broke off my full time college studies, I became a staff member of the Cleveland Public Library, continuing with night classes in journalism and creative writing at Cleveland College of Western Reserve University.

"In 1941 I went to Washington, D.C., where my essay at the ownership of a bookshop was brought to an end when I went into government service. Then, in 1942, I returned to the Cleveland library once again as an assistant in the Children's Department.

"My first book was published before I was twenty-one and two others were issued during this period before the war. Then I was approached by the director of the Cleveland Press World Friends Club to write a book based on correspondence between American children and Europeans. The result was *The Sword Is Drawn*, dealing with the Dutch Underground. This book, after the war, was awarded a plaque by the Netherlands Government.

ANDRE NORTON

"Out of my library work came two books based on legendary material used in special story hours: *Huon of the Horn* and *Rogue Reynard.*

"Until 1951 I had written adventure, spy and historical novels. But then, having been asked to edit a series of science-fiction anthologies, I began writing in that field. Having my material become increasingly popular, I now write mainly on that subject.

"Ill health dictated resignation from the library at this time and since that date I have given all my energy to writing alone.

"My work has earned: Honorable Mention, Ohioana Library Award; Headliner Award, Theta Sigma Phi; Invisible Little Man trophy (science-fiction award) and Boys' Clubs of America Certificate of Merit. It has been translated into Arabic, Danish, Dutch, German, Italian, French, Spanish, Portuguese and Russian.

"I have edited four anthologies, had published forty-seven books, and collaborated on an adult mystery with another author. Though most of these were written for teen-age readers, I have had three books for younger children, and a series of sword and sorcery novels for adults.

"My interest in reading has always been great since I first learned that art and it furnishes me with not-to-be-exhausted material. All of my books are the result of concentrated research in the fields of history, archaeology, natural history, folklore, and anthropology."

Andre Norton has discussed her large output in some detail in *More Junior Authors*. Her first published book, "a Graustarkian romance for teen-agers," was *The Prince Commands* (1934). Three spy thrillers with contemporary settings, beginning in 1944 with *The Sword Is Drawn*, were warmly welcomed for their breath-taking plots, the authenticity of their backgrounds, and their exceptionally convincing dialogue. The same qualities, together with scrupulous scholarship, have distinguished her historical fiction, which has included *Follow the Drum*, about the settlement of Maryland; *Scarface*, a memorably exciting pirate story; and *Stand to Horse*, a chronicle of the Apache wars.

However it is probably for her science fiction stories that Miss Norton is best known. Her work in this field has been repeatedly praised for its "taut action, hearty characters, sound motivations," and a skill in descriptive writing which involves the reader willy-nilly in the swashbuckling adventures of her teen-age heroes (and heroines). Miss Norton's science fiction is seldom "cut-and-dried star hopping" but has a strong element of fantasy. She is prolific in the creation and population of her strange worlds in space, and adept in the evocation of an appropriate sense of awe and wonder, less by what she says than by what she leaves out. Miss Norton is one of the few science fiction writers for young people whose work is taken seriously by adult fans and critics of the genre, and Sam Moskowitz believes that she is "probably the outstanding science-fiction writer currently writing in the romantic tradition."

Some of her recent books have been pure fantasies, not science fiction at all. *Octagon Magic*, in which an old doll's house transports the heroine back into another age, was described in the *Times Literary Supplement* as a "subtle and delicate story," a "marvellously controlled" fantasy reminiscent in its "careful, loving use of detail" of Lucy Boston.

Miss Norton is the daughter of Adalbert Freely Norton and the former Daisy Stemm. Her father's family came to this country from England in 1634, while her mother's combines Scots, English, Pennsylvania Dutch, Irish, and American Indian strains. Andre Norton believes that a good knowledge of history is a fine tool for a writer of science fiction, "for history repeats itself." Miss Norton, a Presbyterian and a Republican, enjoys needlework, cooking, and research, and collects antiques and old dolls. Her favorite authors, she says, include Trollope, Jane Austen, Angela Thirkell, Josephine Tey, and Georgette Heyer. She is five feet seven inches tall, brown-haired, and green-eyed.

PRINCIPAL WORKS: *Spy novels*—The Sword Is Drawn 1944; Sword in Sheath, 1949; At Swords' Points, 1954. *Historical novels*—Follow the Drum, 1942; Scarface, 1948; Yankee Privateer, 1955; Stand to Horse, 1956; Shadow Hawk, 1960. *Science fiction and fantasy*—Star Man's Son, 1952; Star Rangers, 1953; The Stars Are Ours!, 1954; Star Guard, 1955; Star Born, 1957; Storm Over Warlock, 1960; The X Factor, 1965; Octagon Magic, 1967; Operation Time Search, 1967; Dark Piper, 1968; Fur Magic, 1968; Postmarked the Stars, 1969; Moon of Three Rings, 1969; Ice Crown, 1970; Dread Companion, 1970; Exiles of the Stars, 1971. *As adapter*—Rogue Reynard, 1947; Huon of the Horn, 1951. *As editor*—Space Service, 1953; Space Pioneers, 1954; Space Police, 1956. *As "Andrew North"*—Sargasso of Space, 1955; Plague Ship, 1956 (later published as by André Norton).

ABOUT: Contemporary Authors 4, 1963; Current Biography, 1957; Fuller, M. (ed.) More Junior Authors, 1963.

NOSSACK, HANS ERICH (January 30, 1901–), German novelist, poet, dramatist, and essayist, writes (in German): "I was born in Hamburg, a port and business city. My father was an importer, and for those days was quite well off. Nevertheless, like most European intellectuals of my generation, whether of bourgeois or proletarian background, I found myself early in life on the political left. The reason for this was perhaps that as children we experienced the First World War, which signified the collapse of bourgeois society. That forced us from the beginning into opposition to a past which was no longer valid for us.

"I studied for a while in Jena, but had to give up my studies both because of inflation and because of my political activities, and made my way for years as a factory worker, a bank employee, a clerk, and such things. In 1925 I got married in Hamburg. From the business point of view things were going very badly for us—by present day standards—but that made no difference to us. Then along came Hitler, and the year 1933 with its consequences. I was not able to publish and, since I did not want to emigrate, I went into my father's firm, which I then had to direct all by myself for over twenty years. I have been living as a freelance writer only since 1956. I have tried to settle down in various cities, and at the present time live in Frankfurt. That too was to be typical of my generation, that we could no longer settle down.

"In 1943, during the air raids on Hamburg, all that I had written up to that time went up in flames. In that way I was at last rid of the past. I had to begin all over again without any past. I suppose that since that time I have written completely differently from before. It is no wonder that we European writers, who survived the hell of dictatorship and total destruction, after 1945 spoke of a season spent in the realm of the dead, which has for ever marked us. After such an experience one is skeptical about all grand words, one speaks more modestly and never again entrusts himself to anything which announces itself as certainty.

"After the war I was finally able to publish. My first books, a short novel *Nekyia* and the volume of stories, *Interview mit dem Tode*, were relatively successful. In 1947 Sartre discovered me for France. After that I was taken for an Existentialist for a couple of years, without understanding anything about that philosophy. People also called me a Surrealist and, of course, a Nihilist. That has little to do with me. What I know about myself as a writer comes from my critics, who doubtless have a better perspective than I. At the beginning of the 1950s I tried my hand at writing plays, then in 1955 the novel *Spätestens im November* was a success, I won several literary prizes, books of mine were translated into fifteen languages, and, as I have heard, doctoral dissertations are even being written about me.

"Once again, what does all that have to do with me? Every form of publicity, which is so necessary today, is deeply repugnant to me; it falsifies the picture for the sake of success. Naturally I think often enough about why I have been writing since my earliest youth and keep on writing constantly. I suppose it is because what claims to be reality is for me not real enough. I cannot possibly satisfy myself with it, and for that reason I try to get a look behind the contemporary historical facade, to see whether there is not some truer reality there. In such border crossings and when one leaves behind every cliché, one easily goes astray and seems to himself to be lost. But one can never look back—I strongly advise against that—because there is no help from behind. And one must constantly look further, because that which one finds is satisfying for a brief moment at the most. Nevertheless, and for just that reason, I consider myself a realist.

"In other words: for me writing is no goal in itself, but is a method for getting closer to my truth. It is questionable whether in that sense I can qualify as an authentic literary man, but other people must decide about that."

In November 1943, four months after he had witnessed the destruction of Hamburg by Allied bombers, Nossack wrote *Der Untergang* (The Defeat), published five years later in 1948. It is a personal report on the holocaust which swept away a city and a way of life, destroying Nossack's earlier unpublished manuscripts and diaries and thus his past. A vivid and unblinking account of human savagery, *Der Untergang* is by no means a merely nihilistic document. It proposes that the war's survivors have a chance to begin life again, free of illusions, preconceptions, ideologies, metaphors, and able at last to see things as they really are. Explicit in Nossack's essays and lectures, and implicit in all his fiction, is this conviction that the artist's duty is to discover *for himself* what is true, and to bear witness to it.

HANS ERICH NOSSACK

Time and place were two of the conventions that Nossack sought to escape, most noticeably in his early postwar writing, and it is for this reason that critics tended to label him as a Surrealist, while he sought only a truer reality. His first published novel, *Nekyia*, is a reworking in fictional terms of *Der Untergang*. It is a "report by a survivor"—one who has survived the war, the past, and death itself, and like Nossack finds in the chaos of 1945 a chance to break free of centuries of delusion and corruption. This awful but promising chaos is reflected in the novel's form, which ignores surface realities and chronology to summon up the profounder realities of a dream. A similar theme is explored in the first story in *Interview mit dem Tode* (Interview With Death, 1948, revised in 1950 as *Dorothea*), which again deals with the destruction of Hamburg, observed this time through the eyes of a visitor from space, and sees in the emergence of West Germany's postwar materialism a new ideology destructive of reality.

The first of Nossack's works to achieve any wide popularity was the novel *Spätestens im November* (In November at the Latest, 1955), a more orthodox study of postwar German society and the "economic miracle." It is narrated by the wife of a self-absorbed and wealthy industrialist. Deluded by the promise of romance, she runs off with a young writer who turns out to be equally self-centered. Lacking any real individuality of her own, her personality disintegrating, she eventually dies in her lover's Volkswagen. The danger of assuming roles belonging to others, rather than discovering one's own, is also the theme of *Der Jüngere Bruder* (The Younger Brother, 1958).

Spirale (1956) contains five stories of which the best known is "Unmögliche Beweisaufnahme" (translated by Michael Lebeck as *The Impossible Proof*). This is an account of a man's self-trial, in the course of a sleepless night, in connection with the mysterious disappearance of his wife. As Nossack says, the narrator "tries his own case, taking all the parts; accuses, defends, and asks pardon, to find rest at last. Yet, each time his spiraling thoughts seem on the verge of going under in sleep, they strike a new fragment of his life, and once again they rise up into the merciless twilight of insomnia." The narrator is a successful insurance broker whose life is revealed, in the course of the book, as an elaborate defense against "the uninsurable"—against love, children, and life itself.

Reviewers of the English version were divided, and some found it trivial and monotonous. Others reacted quite differently, however, and E. M. Potoker wrote that "notwithstanding the tissues of innuendo, nerve-wracking circumstantial evidence, and obsession with trival objects, [this] is a brilliantly sustained piece of fiction in which Nossack often successfully explains metaphysical realities with physical words." The German critic Hans Henny Jahnn was referring to the same quality when he said: "If Hans Erich Nossack has a gift then it is this, an ability to strip the strangely simple and unnoticed down to the natural and elemental. He endows bad words with good meanings, and makes inconspicuous details cry out with life."

Nossack's other major fictional works include *Nach dem letzten Aufstand* (After the Last Uprising, 1961), *Das kennt Man* (The Known Man, 1964), *Das Testament des Lucius Eurinus* (The Testament of Lucius Eurinus, 1965), *Der Fall d'Arthez* (1968, translated by Michael Lebeck as *The D'Arthez Case*), and *Dem unbekannten Sieger* (The Unknown Conqueror, 1969). He has also written poetry, rather in the manner of T. S. Eliot, and a number of plays, none of them particularly successful. Some of his essays have been collected in *Der Mensch in der heutigen Literatur* (Man in Modern Literature, 1962–1963), and *Die schwache Position der Literatur* (The Weak Position of Literature, 1966).

The small and ardent circle of admirers that has been Nossack's since he began to publish has grown considerably in recent years, and not only in Germany. Sartre's remark, that Nossack was "the most interesting contemporary German writer," did much to extend his reputation. But there is, as Walter Boehlich says, something in his work which will always restrict his general popularity: "He thinks out no stories, he gives testimony, he reports something out of a life."

Nossack is a tall, powerfully built man. He received the Georg Büchner Prize in 1961 and the Wilhelm Raabe Prize in 1963. "Now as in other critical moments in history," he told an interviewer in 1968, "intellectuals have to choose between being rebels or nothing. I made the choice in Germany before the war by joining the Communists in the fight against the Nazis. Then I had to be silent for ten years, and now I am rebelling again."

PRINCIPAL WORKS IN ENGLISH TRANSLATION: The Impossible Proof, 1968; The D'Arthez Case, 1971. *Stories in* Middleton, C. (ed.) German Writing Today, 1967; Spender, S. (ed.) Great German Short Stories, 1960.

ABOUT: Closs, A. Twentieth Century German Literature, 1969; Handbuch der Deutschen Gegenwartsliteratur, 1965; International Who's Who, 1972–73; Keith-Smith, B. Essays on Contemporary German Literature, 1966; Penguin Companion to Literature 2, 1969; Sinn und Form, 1955; Werkstattgespräche mit Schriftstellern, 1962. *Periodicals*—German Life and Letters October 1965; Library Journal March 15, 1968; New York Times March 12, 1968; Saturday Review March 30, 1968; Times Literary Supplement September 12, 1968; January 8, 1970.

NOTT, KATHLEEN, English poet, critic and novelist, writes: "I was born in London of Celtic forebears (one half Cornish, the other Irish). I never intended to write anything but poetry (but intended that from the age of six or when I began to be able to write at all). Nevertheless I have tried practically every other kind of writing and this parcelling of energies which I still somewhat deplore has not been wholly due to economic circumstances but rather to the feeling that poetic intuition ought to be extended in all directions and act like a leaven.

"After school in London and a short spell at London University I won an Open Exhibition to Oxford (Somerville College) at the latter end of the Twenties. This was for English literature—which was the easiest thing to mug up in a month's work (it was all done at very short notice)—but which I had no intention of reading. I switched as I intended to Modern Greats (Philosophy, Politics and Economics) with philosophy as my main subject. I did this in the naïve belief that philosophy would have some significant bearing on my life and problems.

"Oxford disillusioned me without curing me. I simply refused to absorb any philosophy through the academic pipe-line, read Dante, French literature and what science I could understand, instead, and made a hash of my degree. I read hard in philosophy (particularly ethics), and in psychology, as soon as I escaped from conventional guidance.

"I have always gone on writing poetry and have written a novel whenever I have had a novel to write.

"I married a scientist and technologist, deeply involved in electronics and computers; in his way a Two Culture man but with, I now believe, a premature confidence in the adaptability of technology —e.g. to the possibilities of computer-poetry.

"This marriage lasted over twenty years, superficially a happy partnership (I at least thought it was really so)—and then simply exploded almost literally over-night. It left me with only one stable conviction—that neither poetry nor emotion can be automated.

"The other trade I had learned apart from poetry and novels now came in handy. For the past twelve years I have done a great deal of literary and philosophic journalism which brings me in a small living—I provide some of my basic needs apart from this by editing a small quarterly published by PEN and UNESCO.

"I am finishing a book on the relation of ethics and literature which is partly polemic. The first half is an attack on anti-subjectivism in philosophy and psychology—it has its roots in my disappointment while at the university—and it moves towards a consideration of the Two-Culture dichotomy from the moral angle, which seems to me to be largely neglected. I enjoy doing this; at the same time I always hear Time's winged chariot and I resent not being able to devote the whole of the next twenty years to the exploration of what seems to me to be the only truthful language—poetry. I am supposed to be a Humanist. If this means one who believes we ought to become human, then and only then, I am one."

During the 1930s Miss Nott was a social worker among poor Jews in the East End of London, and out of this experience wrote her first novel, *Mile End*, which was thought to show great insight into the Jewish temperament and a sharply individual style, but which seemed a little clinical and donnish, as was her postwar satirical fantasy *The Dry Deluge*. Of her later novels, *An Elderly Retired Man* was particularly admired as a deeply satisfying and "exquisitely intelligent" study of a man who, with time to reflect, is able to discard his doubts and self-delusions, and to find what is real and solid in him.

Miss Nott's verse shows a "rich, harsh and rather masculine talent." Her thought has been said to find its own vocabulary as it goes along, with the effect that language in her poems is not "literary," but used "as it were without memory," and wrenched into order with almost "muscular" effort.

KATHLEEN NOTT

The Emperor's Clothes attacked (sometimes dogmatically) the "dogmatic orthodoxy" of such writers as Eliot, Graham Greene, and C. S. Lewis. Miss Nott's distrust of the "unified sensibility," drawing upon an ideal religious or moral order, also pervades *A Soul in the Quad*, in which she describes "in an autobiographical and intellectual-social setting what I conceive the relations of poetry and philosophy to be." She is a poet and novelist whose work is characterized by its "particularity and solidity"; a critic and reviewer who believes that culture "is about individual lives and individual insights."

Kathleen Nott is vice-president of the English Centre of PEN International and editor of the *PEN Bulletin of Selected Books.* She is a former president of the Progressive League of Great Britain. She received an Arts Council Bursary in 1968.

PRINCIPAL WORKS: Mile End (novel), 1938; The Dry Deluge (novel), 1947; Landscapes and Departures (poems), 1947; The Emperor's Clothes (criticism), 1953; Poems from the North, 1956; Creatures and Emblems (poems), 1960; Private Fires (novel), 1960; A Clean Well-Lighted Place: A Private View of Sweden, 1961; (as joint author) Objections to Humanism, 1963; An Elderly Retired Man (novel), 1963; A Soul in the Quad, 1969; Philosophy and Human Nature, 1970.

ABOUT: Holloway, J. The Colours of Clarity, 1964; Murphy, R. (ed.) Contemporary Poets of the English Language, 1970. *Periodicals*—Times Literary Supplement December 3, 1938; May 24, 1947; June 7, 1947.

"NOVAK, JOSEPH." *See* KOSINSKI, JERZY

O'BRIEN, CONOR CRUISE (**"Donat O'Donnell"**) (November 3, 1917–), Irish critic,

CONOR CRUISE O'BRIEN

historian, and essayist, was born in Dublin, the son of Francis Cruise O'Brien and the former Katherine Sheehy. His father, a literary critic and journalist, was a Catholic who became a vigorous convert to agnosticism; his mother came from a long line of political intransigents. This parentage no doubt accounts for the variety of O'Brien's own interests, and for the fact that he "is, and glories in being, a controversial figure."

He was educated in Dublin. From the age of ten he attended Sandford Park School, a non-Catholic institution. ("But everything in Ireland," he says, "including Irish agnosticism, is profoundly affected by the Catholic environment and tradition.") He went on to Trinity College, where he acquitted himself brilliantly, obtaining a B.A. (and a gold medal) in modern languages in 1940, and an honors degree in history a year later. His Ph.D. followed in 1953. Meanwhile O'Brien's knowledge of Russian, French, and Spanish played their part in shaping his career as a writer and diplomat. He entered the Irish Civil Service in 1942 and soon found his way into the Department of External Affairs. By 1955 he was counselor at the Irish Embassy in Paris. The same year Ireland was admitted to the United Nations, and in 1956 O'Brien went home to establish and direct his department's UN section. He was Ireland's UN representative in New York for the next four years, and in 1960 was promoted to the assistant secretaryship of the Department of External Affairs.

O'Brien's first book was *Maria Cross*, originally published pseudonymously as by "Donat O'Donnell," reprinted in 1963 under his own name. It seeks to distinguish and interpret the "imaginative patterns" in the work of eight contemporary Catholic writers, most of them French, and in particular to explain their preoccupation with both sacred and profane love. Most reviewers found these essays acute and even brilliant as literary criticism, but less illuminating in their psychological delvings. Frank Kermode was reminded of Edmund Wilson and said it was "a remarkable book: idiosyncratic but civilised in style, cleverly planned, learned and witty. It contains so many good jokes . . . that one begins to see how criticism could have once been a gay science."

O'Brien's next book demonstrated that he was no less accomplished as a historian. *Parnell and His Party*, the product of exhaustive and pioneering research, in fact concentrated more on the party than on Parnell, and was thought the first wholly satisfactory explanation of how he had managed to weld together "the queer lot of opposing interests and cross-purposes that constituted Irish life at that time." D. W. Brogan called it "a tragic story told with sobriety, style, and understanding."

In the spring of 1961 O'Brien's distinguished diplomatic career took a major but fatal step forward when Dag Hammarskjöld, then Secretary-General of the United Nations, brought him into the UN Secretariat. O'Brien's first and only mission as Hammarskjöld's representative was to the Congo in 1961. There he assumed a central role in the UN's attempt to prevent the secession of Katanga. He was blamed for the inconclusive and costly fighting that broke out between UN and Katangese forces in September 1961, and became "the most controversial figure in the UN Secretariat and, for a time, in international diplomacy itself." Only Dag Hammarskjöld knew the extent of O'Brien's responsibility, and the Secretary-General was killed during the fighting, on a flight to negotiate with the Katangese leader. In December 1961 O'Brien resigned from the UN Secretariat and from the Irish foreign service "in order to recover [his] freedom of speech and action."

These freedoms he employed in the writing of *To Katanga and Back*, in which he argues that his Congo mission was doomed to failure because Hammarskjöld had allowed the mission and the United Nations itself to become instruments of American foreign policy. This "frankly partisan account of highly contentious events" provoked great controversy. It was severely criticized by UN officials and by some reviewers for its use of confidential information and for "its self-admitted contradictions and second thoughts." Other readers found it a convincing and absorbing story, by an impassioned but witty participant, of history in the process of being made.

The United Nations: Sacred Drama was written to

accompany a notable series of drawings by Feliks Topolski. O'Brien proposes that the UN's activities can be seen as constituting a sometimes tragic, sometimes farcical, passion play, and that the Secretary-General's role should be that of high priest. In support of this thesis O'Brien subsequently published *Murderous Angels*, a well-constructed if crudely characterized play, often extremely funny, which suggests among other things that Hammarskjöld was a homosexual religious fanatic. In spite of O'Brien's Aristotelian assurance that "My Hammarskjöld and my Lumumba . . . are not to be thought of as the 'real' characters of that name," many were deeply offended by the play, which was produced in the 1971 Dublin Theatre Festival.

In 1962 O'Brien became vice-chancellor of the University of Ghana. He was there for three years, leaving when government encroachments on the academic freedom of the university became intolerable to him. There are essays about Ghana and about the Congo in *Writers and Politics*, a collection of articles, reviews, lectures, and other occasional pieces on a great variety of themes. Irving Kristol called it "the work of an ideological guerilla," complained of O'Brien's "virulent anti-Americanism," but ended by describing him as "a man of more natural gifts than can be found in a dozen randomly-selected historians or literary journalists." An appropriate use for at least some of these talents was found in 1965, when O'Brien became Regents Professor and holder of the Albert Schweitzer Chair in Humanities at New York University. He left that post in 1969 to become Labour Member of the Dáil (Ireland's parliament) for Dublin North-East.

As Labour's spokesman on Northern Ireland affairs, O'Brien expressed views that were often directly contrary to those of the party leadership. He questioned the sanctity of the myths that have grown up around the 1916 Easter Rising and its martyrs, attacked the murderous fanaticism of the IRA, and maintained that Irish unity is at present neither desirable nor possible. His distrust of political rhetoric and romanticism, and his advocacy of an intelligent skepticism, are what give unity to his T. S. Eliot Memorial Lectures (on Machiavelli, Burke, Nietzsche, and Yeats), delivered at the University of Kent in 1969 and later published as *The Suspecting Glance*. His views on the two Irelands are expressed with "corrosive honesty" in *States of Ireland*, a skillfully interwoven mixture of Irish history, family history, autobiography, and observation. The book provoked furious controversy in Ireland, but did not prevent O'Brien's appointment as Minister of Posts and Telegraphs in the 1973 coalition government.

He is a big man, black-haired, always elegantly dressed and immaculately groomed, with an Irish gift of the gab and a notable talent for mimicry. He has a son and two daughters by his 1939 marriage to Christine Foster, from whom he was divorced in 1962. His second wife, Máire, is the daughter of Seán MacEntee, formerly deputy prime minister of Ireland. She is well known as a Gaelic poet and translator, and is co-author with her husband of a short history of Ireland. They have two adopted children.

PRINCIPAL WORKS: (as "Donat O'Donnell") Maria Cross: Imaginative Patterns in a Group of Modern Catholic Writers, 1952 (reprinted under own name, 1963); Parnell and His Party, 1880–1890, 1957; (ed.) The Shaping of Modern Ireland (essays), 1960; To Katanga and Back: A U.N. Case History, 1962; Writers and Politics (essays), 1965; The United Nations: Sacred Drama (with drawings by Feliks Topolski), 1968; Murderous Angels (play), 1969; Conor Cruise O'Brien Introduces Ireland, 1969; Camus, ed. by Frank Kermode, 1970 (U.S., Albert Camus of Europe and Africa); The Suspecting Glance, 1972; States of Ireland, 1972; (with Máire Cruise O'Brien) A Concise History of Ireland, 1972 (U.S., The Story of Ireland).

ABOUT: Current Biography, 1967; O'Brien, C. C., To Katanga and Back, 1962; Who's Who, 1973; Who's Who in America, 1972–1973. *Periodicals*—Book Week June 20, 1964; Commentary September 1965; National Review March 26, 1963, December 15, 1965; New Statesman October 26, 1961; November 16, 1962; July 12, 1963; December 3, 1965; Newsweek October 17, 1966; Observer Magazine September 2, 1973; Spectator May 3, 1957; December 8, 1961; Times Literary Supplement November 16, 1692; July 7, 1972; November 10, 1972.

O'BRIEN, EDNA (December 15, 1932–), Irish novelist and short story writer, was born in County Clare into a Roman Catholic farming family, the daughter of Michael and Lena (Cleary) O'Brien. Although she was one of four children, and very close to her mother, she thinks of her childhood as essentially solitary, dominated by fear of her father, the splendors and miseries of her Roman Catholic upbringing, and girlish yearnings for romantic love. From her convent school she went on to the Pharmaceutical College in Dublin, where she qualified as a Licentiate of the Pharmaceutical Society of Ireland. In Dublin she met the novelist Ernest Gebler. They were married in 1952 and subsequently moved to London. It was only then that Edna O'Brien began to write.

Her first novel, *The Country Girls*, describes the childhood and adolescence of the shy and sensitive Caithleen and her volatile and malicious friend Baba. After Caithleen's mother is killed she is rescued from her drunken father by Baba's parents, who send both girls to a convent boarding school. They eventually contrive to be expelled from the convent, and set off to start a brave new life in Dublin. *The Country Girls*, which is no doubt largely autobiographical, remains Edna O'Brien's favorite among her books: "It came like a song," she says. "It was effortless." And this quality was recognized by the reviewers, who were delighted

EDNA O'BRIEN

by its "fresh comic bawdiness" and unforced charm. It received the Kingsley Amis award.

The emotional adventures of Caithleen and Baba are continued in *The Lonely Girl* (set in Dublin and filmed as *The Girl With Green Eyes*), and *Girls in Their Married Bliss*, set in London. Though the vein of comedy is still strong, city life hardens Baba and saddens Kate, and neither book has the unselfconscious gaiety of *The Country Girls*. What begins to emerge instead, wrote Paul Scott of *Girls in Their Married Bliss*, is "a sly, tentative elegance."

August is a Wicked Month tells in great detail the story of a young woman, separated from her husband, who sets out to enjoy a private sex festival on the French Riviera, and is punished by boredom, disease, and the accidental death of her son. This highly moral tale shocked many reviewers and disappointed even those who interested themselves in its literary qualities. Here, as elsewhere in Miss O'Brien's books, her male characters are treated rather superficially, and with something like resentment, as creatures sexually necessary but otherwise irrelevant.

There was a somewhat warmer reception for *Casualties of Peace*, another gloomy study of the female dilemma, this time centering on an artist, her housekeeper, and their love affairs. The book's rather contrived shape and complicated symbolism irritated some reviewers, but did not blind them to its virtues. Brigid Elson was impressed by the author's "gift for odd, vivid metaphors and singing prose lines," and went on: "Her characters . . . speak and write more precisely and more musically than we ordinarily do, yet their statements are seldom artificial or pretentious." (Very much the same thing has been said of the author herself.)

Miss O'Brien's growing technical mastery is nowhere more evident than in her short stories. "Just as one begins to suspect that the artlessness is concealing not art but merely an alert memory," wrote one reviewer, "Miss O'Brien will twist a phrase, introduce an image, or sneak in a quiet sardonic comment, and force one to recognize how considerable is the skill and care needed to make it all seem so simple." A number of her stories have been or will be filmed, and her original screenplay for the film *Zee and Co.* has been rewritten as a novel. She has also tried her hand at plays for television and the stage—most successfully, so far, with *A Pagan Place*, an adaptation for the stage of her novel of the same name. This memoir of a West of Ireland childhood impressed Irving Wardle as being "like a series of old snapshots, which gradually take shape in a composite picture full of internal ironies and cross-references. In this sense, it is fair to describe it as Chekhovian."

Miss O'Brien still thinks of Ireland as "the only place I belong to." Her books are banned there nevertheless, presumably because of their frankness about the sexual feelings and needs of women and their precise descriptions (lyrical or hilarious) of physical intercourse. Having a dread of dishonesty and superficiality, she is equally open and candid in interviews (and is therefore much interviewed). As far as her work is concerned, it is evident that she has moved beyond the easy charm that established her so effortlessly, and has set out upon the harder path of the conscious artist. So far, when her books have failed, they have seemed to do so in overall conception rather than in their page-to-page performance, and this lends some weight to Bernard Bergonzi's assertion that her work suffers most from "her feminine-primitivist rejection of intelligence; the kind of intelligence that controls and mediates the 'feminine' insights of Jane Austen or George Eliot." After a separation of some years, Edna O'Brien was divorced from Ernest Gebler in 1967. She lives with her two sons, Carlos and Sasha, in a riverside house in Putney, South London.

PRINCIPAL WORKS: The Country Girls, 1960; The Lonely Girl, 1962; A Nice Bunch of Cheap Flowers (play) *in* Plays of the Year 1962–1963, 1963; Girls in Their Married Bliss, 1964; August Is a Wicked Month, 1965; Casualties of Peace, 1966; The Love Object (short stories), 1968; A Pagan Place, 1970 (published as play, 1973); Zee and Co., 1971; Night, 1972.

ABOUT: Contemporary Authors 3, 1963; Vinson, J. (ed.) Contemporary Novelists, 1972; Who's Who, 1973. *Periodicals*—Books and Bookmen December 1964; Guardian April 23, 1969; Listener November 11, 1964; New York Times January 2, 1973; Spectator November 30, 1962; Sunday Times Magazine May 12, 1968; Vogue September 15, 1964; November 15, 1964.

"O'BRIEN, FLANN." *See* O'NOLAN, BRIAN

O'CONNOR, EDWIN (GREENE) (July 29, 1918–March 23, 1968), American novelist, belonged by birth and background to the Catholic, middle-class Irish-American community which he interpreted with such keen understanding in his novels. The son of John Vincent O'Connor, a doctor, and Mary (Greene) O'Connor, he was born in Providence, Rhode Island, and grew up just north of there in Woonsocket. He attended La Salle Academy in Providence and then the University of Notre Dame, where he majored in English literature. After graduating with the B.A. degree in 1939, he worked as a radio announcer in Providence, Palm Beach, Buffalo, and Hartford.

During his World War II service in the United States Coast Guard, O'Connor was stationed for two years in Boston, and it was at about this time that he became interested in politics. He decided to stay on in Boston, which he once described as a "crazy, shabby place, but a good one in which to work." He and his wife, the former Veniette Caswell Weil, had a home on Beacon Street. O'Connor's jobs in Boston after the war included writing and producing radio shows for the Yankee Network, writing TV columns under a pseudonym for the *Boston Herald*, and helping to edit *Treadmill to Oblivion*, a book by his friend the late Fred Allen.

O'Connor's radio work gave him a fine ear for dialogue and also the subject of his first novel, *The Oracle* (1951), a caricature of a bombastic broadcaster. *The Oracle* seemed to O'Connor, as he ruefully remarked some years later, "perhaps the most widely unread novel ever published," but critical notices had not been unfavorable, and during the next four years he devoted himself to a novel on what he called "the whole Irish-American business."

One of his objectives was to set down the characteristic humor of the people, which he felt was lacking in most fiction about Irish-Americans. He focused his story on the flamboyant last campaign of Mayor Frank Skeffington, an old-time political boss of great charm, sardonic wit, and rascality. *The Last Hurrah* (1956) was welcomed by many critics as one of the most richly entertaining and revealing socio-political novels of our time. O'Connor denied vehemently, though more or less in vain, that Skeffington was modeled on Boston's Mayor James Michael Curley.

Apart from a few reviewers who protested that the book sentimentalized corruption, it was received with universal pleasure. Clifton Fadiman was impressed above all not by "its political theme . . . nor its story . . . but [by] its talk, its spate of

EDWIN O'CONNOR

wild, outrageous, *useless* talk cascading down every page, talk indulged for its own sake." It was a Book-of-the-Month Club selection, won the $5,000 Atlantic Monthly Prize and the Golden Book Award of the Catholic Writers' Guild, and was later filmed.

The many admirers of *The Last Hurrah* had to wait six years for O'Connor's next engagement with the "Irish-American business."

More serious in tone than *The Last Hurrah*, though not much less exuberant, *The Edge of Sadness* (1961) was described as "a rich, dark novel, exclusively Roman Catholic in atmosphere but often catholic with a small 'c' in its view of human relations and aspirations." It became a best-seller and won the 1962 Pulitzer Prize for fiction—a distinction which some felt would have gone more appropriately to *The Last Hurrah*. It is an account of the life, the work, and the spiritual and practical struggles of Father Hugh Kennedy, a reformed alcoholic and rector of a run-down parish in a city that O'Connor, again, insisted was not Boston. The most striking of the Irish Catholic types seen through his eyes is the miserly patriarch Charlie Carmody, who in the Dickensian richness of his characterization was compared to Frank Skeffington. Another aged Irishman with the gift of the gab, Daniel Considine, is the central figure in a play, *I Was Dancing*, which was also published as a novel.

Resuming his chronicle of the Irish-Americans in Massachusetts politics, O'Connor turned in *All in the Family* (1966) to the new style of politics introduced by the Kennedys. There are several links with *The Last Hurrah*, including the narrator, Jack

Kinsella, who had been Skeffington's secretary. This absorbing if ultimately ambivalent novel, like much of his earlier work, was praised above all for O'Connor's mastery of dialogue.

O'Connor died suddenly of a cerebral hemorrhage at the age of forty-nine. *The Best and the Last of Edwin O'Connor*, published two years later, contained excerpts from all of his books, including two that were unfinished when he died. One of these, "The Boy," seemed to many reviewers more exact and controlled in its language than any of his previous work. O'Connor was tall and fair-haired, a man of exceptional warmth, and an excellent mimic and raconteur. His friend Arthur Schlesinger, Jr., wrote of him that "he saw life steadily, without sentimentality or illusion, and with invincible gaiety, joyousness and grace of spirit."

PRINCIPAL WORKS: The Oracle, 1951; The Last Hurrah, 1956; Benjy; A Ferocious Fairy Tale, 1957; The Edge of Sadness, 1961; I Was Dancing, 1964; All in the Family, 1966; The Best and the Last of Edwin O'Connor, ed. with an introduction by Arthur Schlesinger, Jr., 1970.

ABOUT: Celebrity Register, 1962; Current Biography, 1963; Milne, G. The American Political Novel, 1966; Schlesinger, A., Jr. (ed.) The Best and the Last of Edwin O'Connor, 1970; West, A. Principles and Persuasions, 1957; Who's Who in America, 1967–1968. *Periodicals*—Book Week October 2, 1966; New York Times March 24, 1968; New York Times Book Review February 5, 1956; May 28, 1961; Newsweek October 21, 1957; Saturday Review February 4, 1956.

O'CONNOR, (MARY) FLANNERY (March 25, 1925—August 3, 1964), American novelist and short story writer, was born in Savannah, Georgia, the only child of Roman Catholic parents, Edward O'Connor and the former Regina Cline. She briefly achieved national celebrity at the age of five as the owner of a bantam chicken that could walk backwards, and retained all her life a fondness for fowl. In 1938 her father was found to have an incurable disease, disseminated lupus, and the family moved to the Cline house in Milledgeville, Georgia. There Flannery O'Connor attended high school, in her spare time riding, making jewelry, and beginning to write. Her father died in 1941. She graduated a year later and enrolled in the Georgia State College for Women in Milledgeville, majoring in social science and English. At college she edited the literary quarterly, *The Corinthian*, tried her hand at cartoons, and in 1945 received her A.B.

On the strength of some of her *Corinthian* stories she was awarded a fellowship at the Writers' Workshop of the University of Iowa. She sold her first story to *Accent* in 1946, received her M.F.A. in 1947 and, after another year at Iowa, spent a winter reading and writing at Yaddo, the artists' colony in Saratoga Springs, New York. Her stories began to appear with some regularity and she started her first novel, *Wise Blood.*

In 1948 Flannery O'Connor moved to New York City. Four chapters of *Wise Blood* were published in magazines in 1948 and 1949. In the latter year she went to Ridgefield, Connecticut, boarding with two New York friends, Robert and Sally Fitzgerald, who had bought a house there. Late in 1950 she became very ill with what was diagnosed as lupus. New treatments arrested the disease, and in 1951 she settled down with her mother on a five-hundred-acre dairy farm belonging to the Cline family outside Milledgeville. There she began to work again, writing in the mornings, and spending the remainder of the day resting, reading, writing letters, entertaining friends or painting. She could walk, at first with a cane, later with crutches, and raised peacocks, a symbol of Christ's divinity and the Resurrection.

Wise Blood was published in 1952. It is a frequently grotesque tragicomedy about a young man, Hazel Motes, who, having lost his faith during his army service, goes to the city of Taulkinham to "preach the Church Without Christ, the church peaceful and satisfied," which puts its faith in the reality of the flesh, the "wise blood." Hazel denies Christ in order to free himself from the burden of original sin, but he cannot escape his Christian vocation. He murders one of the false prophets who abound in the novel, expresses his spiritual blindness by putting out his eyes with lime, and mortifies his flesh with increasing savagery—"to pay," as he says, though for what he will not allow himself to admit. In the end, a Christian in spite of himself, he achieves martyrdom at the hands of the police.

The novel is a pungent and often funny attack on the contemporary secularization of religion. Its blasphemy, vulgarity, and often perverted sexuality offended readers who thought these matters should not be treated in comic terms. Many were confused by the book's complex and sometimes uncontrolled symbolism and imagery, and failed to understand that it was intended as an indictment of a world without God. This became a little clearer some years later, when Flannery O'Connor, in Granville Hicks's symposium *The Living Novel*, wrote: "For I am no disbeliever in spiritual purpose and no vague believer. I see from the standpoint of Christian orthodoxy. This means that for me the meaning of life is centered in our Redemption by Christ and what I see in the world I see in its relation to that." A Roman Catholic herself, she wrote mainly of Protestant Fundamentalists (sometimes to their distress). As she said, Catholics were rare where she came from. Moreover Protestant believers, unlike their Catholic counterparts, "express their belief in diverse kinds of dramatic action which is obvious enough for me to catch."

In any case, many critics, even those who misunderstood it, recognized the importance of *Wise Blood* from the outset. J. W. Simons called it "a remarkably accomplished, remarkably precocious beginning. Written in a taut, dry, economical and objective prose, it is . . . a kind of Southern-Baptist version of *The Hound of Heaven.*"

A collection of ten short stories followed in 1955, *A Good Man Is Hard to Find.* It contains, in "The Artificial Nigger," what some consider her most perfectly accomplished story, exemplifying what Caroline Gordon called her "unerring eye in the selection of detail" and "exquisite ear . . . for the cadences of everyday speech." Mr. Head, an old man from the Georgia backwoods, takes his grandson Nelson on a visit to the city. Nelson accidentally knocks down an old woman in the street, and Mr. Head in his distress denies the boy, saying, "I never seen him before." The estrangement that follows between them, beautifully conveyed, ends when they see a plaster statue of a black eating a watermelon and exclaim simultaneously: "An artificial nigger." Stanley Edgar Hyman, on whose pamphlet about Flannery O'Connor this note draws heavily, wrote: "The artificial Negro is God's grace. . . . Mr. Head has a moment of true repentance and charity, he and the boy are united in love, and the story is over." In "The Displaced Person," the most ambitious story in the collection, the sufferings and death of a Polish refugee on a Bible Belt dairy farm becomes an analogy of the Passion of Christ; it seemed to Theodore Solotaroff to mark the turning point in its author's career, "the first full merging of natural and religious experience as well as a subtle assimilation of social meanings to anagogical ones."

Flannery O'Connor's second novel, *The Violent Bear It Away*, is like the first about a young man called, against his will, by God. Francis Tarwater is the great-nephew of a drunken prophet, and nephew of George Rayber, a fanatic of the rational and the secular. Young Tarwater is to begin his ministry by baptizing Rayber's idiot son, but in the process, possessed by the devil, he drowns him. The possession then becomes literal when the devil, appearing in the flesh, drugs Tarwater and rapes him. But Tarwater sets fire to the woods and, his sins burned away, is at last a prophet, "trudging into the distance in the bleeding stinking mad shadow of Jesus." Miss O'Connor's Dostoevskyan message, here as elsewhere, seems to be that the Kingdom of Heaven is won not through reason and good works, but through fire, madness, crime, and violence.

Lupus can be arrested but not cured; Flannery O'Connor's illness was reactivated by an abdominal operation in 1964 and she died the same year. By an effort of will she had just completed enough stories for a second collection, which was published in 1965 as *Everything That Rises Must Converge.* Theodore Solotaroff called it "a book by a major writer who in the last years of her painful and foreshortened life achieved a mastery of form and an austere strength of moral vision that enabled her to create tales that have the measured, unexpected, and inevitable effect of an electric shock." Not everyone shared this view, and some critics complained of the repetitiveness of these stories, their apocalyptic violence, their tendency to end, almost mechanically, with a death. "Caring almost nothing for secular destinies, which are altogether more various than religious ones," wrote Richard Poirier, "she propels her characters toward the cataclysms where alone they can have a tortured glimpse of the need and chance of redemption."

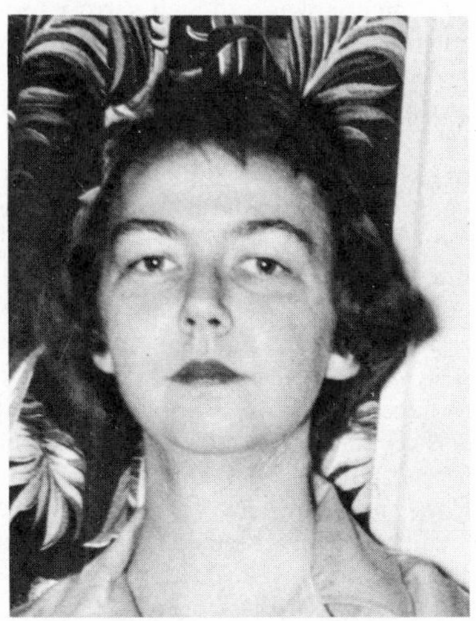

FLANNERY O'CONNOR

Certainly, as Walter Allen says, hers is a "God-intoxicated" world, where everything that is not of God is the Devil's. Hyman said that "Flannery O'Connor's meanings are not only Christian, they are Christian mainly in the mystic and ascetic tradition of St. John of the Cross. . . . As a fiction-writing theologian, she seems the most radical Christian dualist since Dostoevsky." She has often been compared with Faulkner, as a "Southern Decadent," but this is misleading; Hyman believed that she had more in common with Dostoevsky, Nathanael West and, interestingly, Mark Twain. By a familiar mechanism, her tragically early death has led to exaggerated estimates of her achievement, which it is too early to assess. Robert Drake's cautious conclusion, however, seems acceptable: "Miss O'Connor's work, though narrow in scope and limited in appeal, is unique; and it has an urgent intensity, even an ordered ferocity, that may ultimately give her a place in our fiction comparable in a minor way to that of Donne or Hopkins in English poetry." A complete collection of her short stories appeared in 1972, and received the National Book Award in Fiction.

A volume of Miss O'Connor's thoughtful and characteristically witty occasional pieces, edited by Sally and Robert Fitzgerald, was published in 1969 as *Mystery and Manners*. D. K. Mano said that he "had never read more sensible and significant reflections on the business of writing." Many of these pieces had been read by the author as addresses at colleges and elsewhere, for she was never a recluse and always accepted lecture invitations when her health allowed. In her encounters with people she had much the same kind of directness and sardonic humor as in her books. She took an ambiguous pleasure "in being photographed, grim and unsmiling, against the unpainted and dilapidated homes of [her mother's] Negro tenant farmers," and after her trip to Lourdes reported: "I had the best-looking crutches in Europe." She received a *Kenyon Review* Fellowship in 1953 and a renewal of it in 1954, a grant from the National Institute of Arts and Letters in 1957, and a Ford Foundation grant in 1960. She had honorary degrees from St. Mary's College, Notre Dame, and Smith.

PRINCIPAL WORKS: Wise Blood, 1952; A Good Man Is Hard to Find, 1955; The Violent Bear It Away, 1960; Everything That Rises Must Converge, 1965; Mystery and Manners (lectures and essays), 1969; Flannery O'Connor: The Complete Stories (ed. by Robert Giroux), 1971.

ABOUT: Baumbach, J. The Landscape of Nightmare, 1965; Contemporary Authors 1, 1962; Current Biography, 1958; Drake, R. Flannery O'Connor, 1966; Driskell, L. V. and Brittain, J. T. The Eternal Crossroads, 1971; Eggenschwiler, D. The Christian Humanism of Flannery O'Connor, 1972; Feeley, K. Flannery O'Connor: Voice of the Peacock, 1972; Fitzgerald, R. *introduction to* Everything That Rises Must Converge, 1965; Friedman, M. J. and Lawson, L. A. (eds.) The Added Dimension: The Art and Mind of Flannery O'Connor, 1966; Gossett, L. Y. Violence in Recent Southern Fiction, 1965; Hendin, J. The World of Flannery O'Connor, 1970; Hyman, S. E. Flannery O'Connor, 1966; Kazin, A. Bright Book of Life, 1973; Martin, C. W. The True Country: Themes in the Fiction of Flannery O'Connor, 1969; Muller, G. H. Nightmares and Visions: Flannery O'Connor and the Catholic Grotesque, 1972; Waldmeir, J. J. (ed.) Recent American Fiction, 1963. *Periodicals*—America May 13, 1961; American Benedictine Review June 1964; Book Week May 30, 1965; Christian Century September 30, 1964; Colorado Quarterly Spring 1962; Columns Fall 1964; Critique Fall 1958, Winter-Spring 1960; Esprit Winter 1964; The Flannery O'Connor Bulletin (annual), 1972– ; Georgia Review Summer 1958; New Leader May 10, 1965; New Statesman April 1, 1966; New York Review of Books August 8, 1964; New York Times August 4, 1964; Newsweek May 19, 1952; August 17, 1964; Saturday Review May 12, 1962; May 29, 1965; Sewanee Review Summer 1962, Autumn 1964; Shenandoah Winter 1965; Thought Autumn 1962, Winter 1966; Times Literary Supplement March 24, 1966; February 1, 1968.

O'CONNOR, PHILIP (MARIE CONSTANT BANCROFT) (September 8, 1916–), Irish memoirist and poet, writes: "My father was an Irish surgeon, known in the family as 'the cad,' who disappeared in the year of my birth and whom I have never seen; my mother was of Irish, Dutch and Burmese descent, and had spent her childhood in India; her father and many of her relatives were in the Indian Civil Service. Due to my father's passion for travel (especially in China) and his distaste for surgery (so I am told) mother lost all her money when I was three years of age; she left me in France for four years, and I returned to England at the age of seven a French and *déclassé* little boy. I was then adopted, sent to a 'private' school from which I ran away at the age of sixteen; took to a Bohemian way of living, with occasional tramping in the British Isles, had a period of prosperity, several cohabitations with girl friends, and two marriages.

"After three years of writing poetry for little magazines—*New Verse*, etc.—my writing has split into two main kinds; in the one, the surrealist influences of the Thirties are still strong, in the other I have developed a kind of sociology strictly based on the personal experiences of a 'class mongrel.' Due to these experiences in class-ridden English society, I have become convinced that the ramifications of class have a far greater effect on personal philosophy, mentation and character than is generally accepted. Politically, I am of the Left, in that I regard cooperation (which must be economical) as the only way of preserving the species and *introducing* it to civilization. I have come to regard competitive individualism as our curse.

"I began to write at the age of nine and found therein, immediately, a form of release, a mode of confiding something otherwise incommunicable which has not left me and which has made my writing the centre of my life. I think that due both to French having been my first language and to the 'class mongrelism' mentioned above I have been forced to write in a very 'personal' way, which has earned me constant accusations of obscurity. To justify my style, I would say that English as written in England has become disastrously weakened by a severance from literal meanings, by the general spread of a metaphorical attitude to life. From my reading, I think that language is better employed by certain American writers—e.g. Saul Bellow. Americans, I think—or at least certain American writers—are less afflicted with the allergy to the kind of new ideas which come from perception, as opposed to those which result from permutations of an Academic tradition. Probably a long tradition of mercantilism severed living from cultural mentation in England. My interests have made me, I think, as much of an outsider as anyone writing in England now; because I cannot even subscribe to group anti-establishment principles, or lack of them. My main ambition is to contribute (in my rather personal and perhaps eccentric manner) to an ethic of non-competitive individuality in a real community; I regard much of neurosis as the result of attempting the impossible conjunction of Christian ethics and economic rat-racing, guaranteed to induce general schizoid tendencies.

"My surrealist writing (not strictly in free-association, but employing it as a means to new perceptions and combinations of ideas) is my refuge when I am exhausted from over-abstraction, to which by nature I am not exactly fitted.

"I cannot think of a more perilous way of making a living than by writing what one likes if one hasn't the luck to be born in tune with the times; being one's own salesman anyway horribly detracts from the commodity offered. Only the *love* of art, and the incomparable excitement of allowing ideas to generate, keep one going. That has been enough to date; one would be happy to be afflicted with a best-seller. Broadcasting (mainly for the Third Programme) has kept the wolf from the door; sometimes by means of (I fear) some sheepish baa-baaing."

Philip O'Connor's verse, a volume of which appeared as *Selected Poems* in 1968, was published in many small magazines before World War II, but attracted little attention. Wholly surrealist in its intention, it was less successful in carrying over the European spirit of the surrealist movement than that of David Gascoyne; despair and anarchy are its real keynotes—it exactly reflects the kind of personality which O'Connor later described himself to be, in the book in which he discovered himself and his talents: *Memoirs of a Public Baby* (1958). *Steiner's Tour*, a surrealistic novel, may be classed with the verse as the less vital part of O'Connor's output.

Of the autobiography *Memoirs of a Public Baby*, which was an immediate critical success, Philip Toynbee said: "Mr. O'Connor has come to his partial salvation by dragging his eyes away from himself and looking with sharp-eyed compassion at the world about him"; he also spoke of O'Connor's "humour and humility combined with a proper ferocity." This almost appallingly sincere account of the author's failures through

PHILIP O'CONNOR

alcohol and violent egoism, and of his indignation at the facts of poverty and underprivilege, has been compared to the serial autobiographical work of the French anthropologist Michel Leiris. The comparison seems particularly apt when it is considered that Leiris wrote so frankly in order, as he said, to put himself into danger (from public opinion), thus creating a challenge that would set him on the sharpest possible creative edge. However, O'Connor is far more polemical than the French writer. As Stephen Spender wrote in his introduction to the book, "The physically coarse but true is held up as a criticism of inverted-commaed 'spirituality'; the vulgar, upheld against 'politeness,'" And Spender drew attention to a feature which is both a philosophical weakness and a stylistic strength in O'Connor's writing; he "never 'sees life whole.' He sees it in little bits." *Memoirs of a Public Baby* remains O'Connor's best book; the quality of its author's self-scrutiny is remarkable, and his social indignation is compelling.

The Lower View is a description of visits O'Connor made, on a bicycle, to literary and artistic personalities—such as Bertrand Russell, Alan Rawsthorne and Stephen Spender—who had interested him. The interview with the critic Sir Herbert Read is shrewd and revealing, and the offbeat style of reportage continually gives insights that would be denied to a more conventional interviewer; but as a whole the book is scrappy.

O'Connor then went to live in Croesor, a Welsh village above the Glaslyn Estuary. He described his experiences in a book, *Living in Croesor* (1962), which called forth some acid remarks from its reviewer in the *Times Literary*

Supplement. These are perhaps typical of thc reaction O'Connor evokes in readers less eccentrie than himself: "For the first time in his adult life, he found himself [in Croesor] attached to (though scarcely part of) a community. . . . He began to take interest in people other than himself. . . . He can now see at least some point in working for a living.... Croesor has obviously been good for Mr. O'Connor; whether he has been good for Croesor is perhaps for its own people to decide." The reviewer allowed that the descriptions of people, hitherto "caricatures," were now "real." The review, although probably unfairly tart, is valuable in that it draws attention to a fundamental contradiction in O'Connor: between what the reviewer not quite accurately calls the "Marxist" (by which he means the not always articulate advocate of "cooperation") and the "loner," the eccentric so brilliantly described in *Memoirs of a Public Baby*.

Meanwhile, O'Connor has distinguished himself as an amateur sociologist, interviewing vagrants and other refugees from society on the BBC Third Programme, often revealing their inner core more clearly than any professional could hope to do. When he is intuitive rather than polemic. O'Connor provides invaluable sociological data. *Vagrancy* (1963) is a study of real value.

O'Connor was born in Leighton Buzzard, Bedfordshire. He was married in 1963 to Anne Gaillard-D'Andel, and has six children. He has been a painter (but an unsuccessful one), has worked in a continental telephone exchange and a library, and has attended teachers' training college. He is interested—"hopelessly"—in a "kind of theatre." He greatly admires Brecht. In person O'Connor is gentle, friendly, and capable of sustained comic performances—particularly when "interviewing himself" on a tape recorder—that match the best of his writing.

PRINCIPAL WORKS: Memoirs of a Public Baby, 1958; The Lower View, 1960; Steiner's Tour, 1960; Living in Croesor, 1962; Vagrancy, 1963; Selected Poems, 1936–1966, 1968.

ABOUT: Contemporary Authors 11–12, 1965; Murphy, R. (ed.) Contemporary Poets of the English Language, 1970. *Periodicals*—Nation June 21, 1958; New Statesman January 11, 1958; New York Times May 25, 1958; Spectator November 25, 1960; Times Literary Supplement December 30, 1960.

"O'DONNELL, DONAT." *See* O'BRIEN, CONOR CRUISE

OGDEN, C(HARLES) K(AY) (June 1, 1889–March 20, 1957), English polymath, inventor of Basic English, and "an unconventional but deeply learned and profoundly original thinker," was notably accomplished as a semanticist, educational theorist, and philosopher, and as an enormously prolific writer and editor. He was educated at Rossall School, in Lancashire, and in 1908 went with a scholarship to Magdalene College, Cambridge. There he distinguished himself in a variety of ways, representing the university at billiards in 1909, and graduating with first class honors in the Classical Tripos in 1910. Even then, as Professor I. A. Richards later observed, "there was a central clarifying talent, a flame of curiosity and impatience, a belief in mind and the facts of mind which, even as an undergraduate, made him one of the forces of his age."

When he left the university, Ogden settled in Cambridge, where he lived (or at least had his headquarters) for the rest of his life. His friend Kingsley Martin was once a member of a Cambridge "Association for the Investigation of the Source of Ogden's Income," which never managed to discover how Ogden supported the causes he embraced or his own expensive tastes. He was a connoisseur of food and wine, always faultlessly dressed, who acquired over the years a huge collection of rare and valuable books and curious artifacts.

In 1912 and 1913 Ogden traveled widely in Europe and in India, investigating methods of language teaching, and serving as guide and philosopher to an itinerant American millionaire. At least for a time some of Ogden's income presumably came from *The Cambridge Magazine*, which he founded in 1912 and which was partly made up of material from foreign newspapers. It had a very large circulation during World War I, when it "infuriated the Blimps by regularly quoting extracts from the German press to show that not all Germans wanted to fight to the bitter end." Kingsley Martin inclines to the view that Ogden made most of his money by supplying rare books to American libraries. At one time Ogden owned at least four bookshops in Cambridge, festooning their interiors with galley proofs of his books and their exteriors with publicity for his various projects. One of his shops became a meeting place of the Heretics, a discussion group which he founded and ruled, and which included Lytton Strachey among its celebrated members. Even in such company as this, Ogden was distinguished by his "readiness to tell you more, and more important, things about more subjects than anyone else could."

The same talent is evident in his books, most but by no means all of which deal with language and education. During World War I, for example, he wrote some fierce feminist tracts, with titles like *Fecundity Versus Civilisation*, using the pseudonym "Adelyne More." In these books he would occasionally reveal details of Miss More's character and in the end he married her off, supplying "a discreetly unrevealing photograph of the occasion."

The Meaning of Meaning, written in collaboration with I. A. Richards, is the most significant and lasting product of Ogden's studies in semantics. It discusses the way in which we think, and proposes a "Science of Symbolism" by means of which we could estimate how accurately we *express* what we think. Some professional philosophers dealt harshly with the book, but in less exacting circles it was warmly received as "the first serious attempt to consider the central linguistic problem of Meaning in the light of modern psychological research," composed with "admirable clarity and a strong sense of humour."

The Meaning of Psychology, though it is now out of date, was universally welcomed in 1926 as the best available introduction to its subject, remarkable for its lucidity and completeness and for its "sanity of spirit." *Opposition* was another important and original work, in which Ogden claimed that opposition is one of the chief principles on which language works. Opposition is now becoming a key concept in methodology, according to I. A. Richards, being indispensable to the understanding of several scientific hypotheses. Ogden also wrote about the philosopher Jeremy Bentham, whose ideas influenced his own considerably.

In 1922 Ogden became editor of *Psyche*, an international journal specializing in linguistic psychology. The following year he took over financial control of the magazine, and also established Kegan Paul's famous International Library of Psychology, Philosophy, and Scientific Method, which grew over the next ten years to nearly a hundred titles. At the same time, between 1923 and 1929, his "Today and Tomorrow" series developed into a library of similar size in educational topics, and he simultaneously edited the History of Civilization series, as well as the Science for You series and the Library of Educational Psychology. During the same period he was developing his plans for Basic English and making a number of important translations from French and German, among them Hans Vaihinger's *The Philosophy of As-If* (1924), Henri Pieron's *Thought and the Brain* (1925), and August Forel's *The Social Life of the Ants* (1926).

Kingsley Martin believes that Ogden "had a fierce intellectual passion to save mankind from destruction" (though "he took care that no one should imagine he thought it worth saving"). In Ogden's view, war resulted from a failure of understanding, and his prime interest all his life was the improvement of international communication. He came to believe that an international language was an essential prerequisite if the peoples of the world were

C. K. OGDEN

ever to recognize their common humanity. Having considered and rejected Chinese for this purpose, he turned his attention to English. Between 1920 and 1930 he worked out a simplified version of the English language, adequate for most nonspecialist kinds of communication, but containing only eight hundred and fifty words. Ogden introduced his universal language in *Basic English*, and subsequently wrote many books about "debabelization." He established the Orthological Institute in Cambridge as his headquarters, and during the 1930s the experiment was taken up in about thirty different countries. Basic English achieved its greatest success during World War II, when Winston Churchill expressed keen interest in it. Ogden set up the Basic English Foundation with a government grant in 1947, but the movement seems to have lost momentum since the 1940s. It remains "one of the most interesting educational notions" of the era.

Ogden's studies in communication led him up all sorts of fascinating bypaths, among them photography, acoustics, social psychology, economics, industrial relations, and color notation. It was characteristic of him that, lacking adequate recording equipment, he invented it; finding the patent laws ridiculous, he set about reforming them. The extraordinary breadth and depth of his learning was memorably demonstrated in his famous review, published in the *Saturday Review* in 1926, of the supplementary volumes of the *Encyclopaedia Britannica*. (He was in the United States at that time studying American teaching methods and serving as science adviser to *The Forum*.)

Ogden's friends remember him as a "restless,

fanatical, lucid expositor of his ideas . . ."; "a witty, devastating and indefatigable conversationalist . . . a connoisseur of good living, and an excellent host." He had three houses, in London, Buxton, and Brighton, full of books, "singing models of birds, musical boxes as large as coffins, and strange clocks of all descriptions." He was also celebrated for his impersonations: "Had his circumstances been different he might have made a fortune as a music-hall comedian." But in spite of all his eccentricities, he aroused genuine affection and concern in the people he came in contact with. As Professor Richards says: "To many, C. K. Ogden will be the most memorable man they have known."

PRINCIPAL WORKS: (with I. A. Richards and James Wood) The Foundations of Aesthetics, 1922; (with I. A. Richards) The Meaning of Meaning, 1923; The Meaning of Psychology, 1926; Basic English: A General Introduction with Rules and Grammar, 1930; Jeremy Bentham, 1832–2032, 1932; Opposition, 1932.

ABOUT: Black, M. Language and Philosophy, 1949; Cohen, F. S. The Legal Conscience, 1960; Current Biography, 1944; Dictionary of National Biography 1951–1960, 1971; Leavis, F. R. (ed.) Determinations, 1934; Wasserstom, W. (ed.) A Dial Miscellany, 1963; Who Was Who, 1951–1960. *Periodicals*—Journal of Philosophy May 21, 1942; May 13, 1943; Life December 2, 1957; New Republic May 2, 1934; New Statesman March 30, 1957; New York Times July 1, 1923; March 23, 1957; Times (London) March 23, 1957; March 29, 1957.

NED O'GORMAN

O'GORMAN, NED (September 26, 1929–), American poet, was born in New York City and spent most of his early life in Southport, Connecticut, and Bradford, Vermont, receiving a Roman Catholic education. In 1953 he graduated from Saint Michael's College in Winooski, Vermont, going on to Columbia for his M.A. in English. For a time he studied acting at New York's Neighborhood Playhouse. The verse that began to appear in *Poetry* and elsewhere in the mid-1950s brought him a Guggenheim Fellowship in 1956, and this made it possible for him to spend sixteen months in Europe, mostly in Italy. His first book of poems, *The Night of the Hammer*, was the Lamont Poetry Selection for 1958. Although several critics complained about its "self-indulgent rhetoric," none denied its power. "The impact of any one poem is breath-taking, and there are forty-four," wrote John Holmes.

The nature of Ned O'Gorman's talent emerged more clearly with his second collection, *Adam Before His Mirror*, which aroused widespread enthusiasm. He is, his critics decided, a religious poet with a unique and very considerable lyric gift, whose weakness for "bejeweled" language, decorative forms, and baroque contesting imagery is redeemed by "the great intensity" of his responses. If his symbolism is sometimes private and obscure, Joseph Stater suggested, it is because O'Gorman (as one of his titles implies), is pursuing "a language of the ineffable." When he achieves it, Stater wrote, "he can flesh mystery in imagery and metaphor of irresistible eloquence."

The poems in *The Buzzard and the Peacock*, though their settings reflect O'Gorman's travels in Africa, Egypt, and Ireland, are all "concerned with the dichotomy of life torn between darkness and light, the spirit and flesh." Josephine Jacobsen thought that "the poetic vitality is so intense, the radius of poetic intuition so wide, that the poetry itself often suffers from a sense of congestion." There was some similar comment on O'Gorman's next collection, *The Harvesters' Vase*, in which one reviewer found a share of "sloppy Christian bombast" but of which another wrote: "The religious sensibility runs in the poetry like blood or sap or electricity—inside."

If O'Gorman has the faults of his virtues, most critics seem prepared to allow that the virtues are large ones, and many argue that his failures grow less frequent and are in any case justified by the exhilarating risks he takes. Mark Van Doren calls O'Gorman's poems "leaps into excess and out of it again back into measure . . . both wild and wise: a heady combination." The quieter and more restrained poems which predominated in *The Flag the Hawk Flies* aroused, on the whole, rather less critical enthusiasm.

O'Gorman has served on the editorial staff of *Jubilee* and has taught at Iona College in New Rochelle, New York; in the English department of Brooklyn College; and at Manhattan College, where in 1967 he gave a course called "Revolution and Prophecy." He received *Poetry*'s Inez Boulton

Prize in 1958 and a second Guggenheim in 1962. In 1966 he opened a small storefront school and library in Harlem, supported partly by Federal antipoverty funds and partly by money donated by O'Gorman and his friends; it has since moved to the basement of a Roman Catholic Church in East Harlem. In 1968 O'Gorman was invited to become poet in residence at the City College of New York but rejected the offer, feeling unable to sign a loyalty oath supporting a system which had dealt so harshly with the black people of America. At that time he told an interviewer: "I love the streets. The black people are strong. There is a genius and a grandeur in them. . . . My loyalty to this country is loyalty to the black man and his revolution." O'Gorman has written a moving account of his "community of children," *The Storefront*, and has explained his educational theories in *The Wilderness and the Laurel Tree*.

PRINCIPAL WORKS: *Poetry*—The Night of the Hammer, 1959; Adam Before His Mirror, 1961; The Buzzard and the Peacock, 1964; The Harvesters' Vase, 1968; The Flag the Hawk Flies, 1972. *Education*—The Storefront: A Community of Children on 129th Street and Madison Avenue, 1970; The Wilderness and the Laurel Tree: A Guide for Teachers and Parents on the Observation of Children, 1972. *For children*—The Blue Butterfly, 1971. *As editor*—Prophetic Voices; Ideas and Words on Revolution, 1969.
ABOUT: Who's Who in America, 1972–1973. *Periodicals*—Commonweal March 13, 1959; New York Times August 5, 1968; New Yorker December 2, 1967; Poetry February 1960, December 1964.

O'HARA, FRANK (June 27, 1926–July 25, 1966), American poet, playwright, and art critic, was born in Baltimore, Maryland, and grew up in New England. He served in the U.S. Navy from 1944 to 1946 before entering Harvard University, which gave him his A.B. in 1950. An M.A. in English and creative writing followed from the University of Michigan in 1951, when he also received the Hopwood Award for poetry. O'Hara had begun to write verse in the 1940s, but from the beginning was almost equally drawn to the visual arts, finding his friends among the Abstract Expressionists of the so-called "heroic" period, rather than among the academic poets of the immediate postwar years. In 1951, when he graduated from Michigan, he went to work at the Museum of Modern Art in New York. His first volume of poems, *A City Winter*, was published in 1952, and in 1953 he joined *Art News* as an editorial associate. He returned to the Museum of Modern Art in 1955, in 1960 becoming Assistant Curator of the Department of Painting and Sculpture Exhibitions.

In 1956, meanwhile, O'Hara had received a one-semester fellowship to work with the Poets' Theater in Cambridge, Massachusetts, and later he wrote

FRANK O'HARA

for the Living Theater and the Artists' Theater in New York. A number of his rather contrived experimental one-act plays were produced, including *Try! Try!*, about a soldier's homecoming to his wife and her new lover, and *The General Returns From One Place to Another*, described by Susan Sontag as "a set of skits involving a kind of General MacArthur type and his entourage in perpetual orbit around the Pacific." O'Hara's brilliant criticism of modern painting and sculpture appeared in *Art News*, *Evergreen Review*, *Folder*, and elsewhere. He published a monograph on Jackson Pollock, and catalogs for the exhibitions he mounted of work by Robert Motherwell and Reuben Nakian, among others.

But O'Hara thought of himself as primarily a poet: "At times when I would rather be dead," he said in *New American Poetry*, "the thought that I could never write another poem has so far stopped me." His poetry is totally subjective, a playful disorder of undigested autobiographical notes, quotations from letters, lists of food eaten or things bought, gossip, questions, conjectures. Like his master Mayakovsky, if more urbanely, he writes, according to Jonathan Cott, the poetry "of an explosive, high-pitched adolescent sensibility displaying and celebrating itself alone." Like others of the so-called New York school, he ransacks his urban world for words and images, snatching up telephone numbers, brand names, commercials, anything that glitters or pleases.

At their worst, his poems read like random jottings from a quirky and often sentimental commonplace book; at their best, his "long lines of fantastic exploding images and skittish humor," his "dissociative leaps of feeling," are handled with a precarious but absolute control and achieve a startling freedom and immediacy. His friend John Ashbery, conceding that O'Hara's verse has no program and no awareness of "even the basic etiquette of prosody," compares it to the paintings of Jackson Pollock and says: "Like Pollock, O'Hara demonstrates that the act of communication and the finished creation are the same, that art is human will-power deploying every means at its disposal to break through to a truer state than the present one."

Frank O'Hara was killed by a car on Fire Island, New York, at the age of forty. The six volumes of verse published during his lifetime had a mixed critical reception and enjoyed no great popularity with the general public. But Ashbery calls his death "the biggest secret loss to American poetry" since the similar death of John Wheelwright in 1940, and speaks of a "whole school of young poets who claim him as their chief influence." Perhaps there will be a reassessment of Frank O'Hara's poetry. At least it will be a long time before he is forgotten. The painter Larry Rivers said at his funeral: "I am one of about sixty people in New York who believed that Frank was my best friend." Six years later, in the spring of 1972, Composers' Showcase at the Whitney Museum in New York presented a remarkable memorial to O'Hara—an entire concert of his poems set to music by seven different composers—Virgil Thomson, Ned Rorem, Charles Mingus, Lester Trimble, Lukas Foss, Lucia Dlugoszewski, and Jimmy Giuffre.

PRINCIPAL WORKS: A City Winter (poems), 1952; Meditations in an Emergency (poems), 1957 (reissued 1967); Jackson Pollock, 1959; Second Avenue (poems), 1960; Try! Try! (play) *in* Machiz, H. (ed.) Artists' Theater, 1960; Odes, 1960; New Spanish Painting and Sculpture, 1960; Lunch Poems, 1964; Motherwell, 1965; Reuben Nakian, 1966.

ABOUT: Allen, D. M. (ed.) New American Poetry, 1960, Contemporary Authors 9–10, 1964; Kostelanetz, R. (ed.) The New American Arts, 1965; Leary, P. and Kelly, R. (eds.) A Controversy of Poets, 1965. *Periodicals*—Art News September 1966; Book Week September 25, 1966; Poetry June 1958, February 1966.

OLDENBOURG, ZOÉ (March 31, 1916–), Russian-born French novelist and historian, has lived in Paris since 1925, when she fled to that city from her native Petrograd (now Leningrad) with her parents, sister, and two brothers. She belongs to a family of scholars and writers: one of her grandfathers served as permanent secretary of the Petrograd Academy of Science; her father, Serge Oldenbourgh, was a journalist and historian; and her mother, the former Ada Starynkevitch, was a mathematician. Her early life, both in Russia during the civil war and as an émigrée in France, was one of deprivation. But if at times she had little food or little heat at home, she never lacked an abundance of books to enjoy.

In Paris, Zoé Oldenbourg received her *baccalauréat* from the Lycée Molière in 1934 and afterwards attended the Sorbonne, but did not take a degree. Intending to become an artist, she also studied painting at the Académie Ranson. From childhood, however, she had obeyed what she thinks of as an inborn compulsion to write, turning out plays, stories, and novels that were considerably influenced by Tolstoy. While earning her living by painting scarves in a Parisian workshop, from 1940 to 1946, she completed *Argile et cendres*, which was published in France in 1946 and two years later reached the United States as *The World Is Not Enough*. A massive historical novel set in France and the Orient in the twelfth and thirteenth centuries and dealing in part with the second and third crusades, it grew out of her fascination with the Middle Ages, to which she had devoted many years of research and reflection. "It seems to me," she once said, "that present-day writing is taking too realistic roads and stressing too much the minute and particular, at the expense of what is great and eternal in man. It seems to me that in the Middle Ages man had a more humble concept of his condition."

The Cornerstone (*La Pierre angulaire*, 1953) continued the story begun in *The World Is Not Enough* of Lady Alis and her crusading husband, Ansiau of Linnières, and their descendants. Mme. Oldenbourg's second novel, which won the Prix Fémina in France and was a Book-of-the-Month Club selection in the United States, confirmed for her the place among the world's finest historical novelists that admirers of *The World Is Not Enough* had felt she deserved. A few reviewers would have welcomed a generous cut in length, complaining of unselected details and "overpopulated" subplots, but, in general, criticism of her early work was exceedingly favorable. She achieved as a writer the color, movement, and form that she perhaps would also have sought as a painter. A critic for the *Times Literary Supplement* commented on her "vivid pictorial perception" in delineating medieval life and observed that *The Cornerstone* offered "all the pleasures of a social history, practised, as Dr. G. M. Trevelyan teaches us it should be, as a fine art."

Then in two novels with a contemporary setting —*The Awakened* (*Réveillés de la vie*, 1956) and *The Chains of Love* (*Les Irréductibles*, 1958)—Zoé Oldenbourg told of the tragic love affair of two young exiles, Stéphanie and Élie, in the émigré world of postwar Paris, of homelessness and family disintegration, of personal agonies that reflect the greater social upheaval. It was her own well-known world of the refugee but her handling of it was thought unconvincing. Her perspective had changed, Virgilia Peterson said: "Before, like a narrative painter, she brushed across her canvas an intricate pattern of objective scenes. Now, she has taken up the scalpel, and the tissue beneath which she probes is too immediate, too living, too poignantly felt and remembered for the mastery of even so stern a craftsman as, in her historical novels, Mrs. Oldenbourg proved herself to be."

The unsparing honesty and gravity with which she treats the human condition, both in the past and present, however painful to some of her readers, is the source of much of her power. Returning very soon to the Middle Ages, she devoted several books to the grim religious persecutions and terrors of the Albigensian Crusade—the bloody suppression of the Cathar heresy in the Midi, which is now part of southern France, by the combined forces of the Church of Rome and the barons of northern France. Her compassionate, openly biased stories of martyrdom are graphically and peculiarly medieval, and yet have a great deal of relevance to the present day. In reviewing *Cities of the Flesh*, 1963 (Anne Carter's translation of *Les Cités charnelles*, 1961), Neal Ascherson remarked in the *New Statesman* that the trials of Roger de Montbrun evoked "with unbearable horror the nightmares that have invaded France since 1939." No less appalling was *La Joie des pauvres* (translated as *The Heirs of the Kingdom*), her account of the first crusade.

Because of the soundness of her scholarship, Mme. Oldenbourg had sometimes been called a historian of the Middle Ages. She preferred, however, for some years to be considered only a novelist, until the publication of her history of the Albigensian Crusade, *Massacre at Montségur* (*Le Bûcher de Montségur*, 1959, translated by Peter Green). To one or two reviewers it seemed a brilliantly descriptive adventure tale rather than an impartial factual account unerring in every detail. But just as she did in her history of the first three crusades—*The Crusades* (translated by Anne Carter from *Les Croisades*, 1965)—she conveyed an understanding of the way people felt and lived centuries ago with an intensity, sympathy, and exactitude perhaps unmatched in any contemporary writing except her own novels.

As if in preparation for interpreting the behavior of men and women whose motivations are comprehensible only in the light of their overpowering spiritual convictions, Zoé Oldenbourg had been a serious student of religion in her youth, at one time, in 1938, attending a missionary college of the Society for the Propagation of the Gospel in England for instruction in theology. She was born a Greek Orthodox, but later disclaimed any church affiliation. She was married on September 18, 1948, to Heinric Idalovici (or Henri Idalie), who runs a

ZOÉ OLDENBOURG

bookshop in Paris, and has a son and a daughter. Writing is "an exhausting occupation" for a novelist and historian of vast panoramic reach and allows her little leisure. She has found time, however, to serve since 1961 as a member of the jury of Prix Fémina.

PRINCIPAL WORKS IN ENGLISH TRANSLATION: *Novels*—The World Is Not Enough, 1948; The Cornerstone, 1954; The Awakened, 1957; The Chains of Love, 1959; Destiny of Fire, 1961; Cities of the Flesh; or, The Story of Roger de Montbrun, 1963; The Heirs of the Kingdom, 1971. *History*—Massacre at Montségur: A History of the Albigensian Crusade, 1961; Catherine the Great, 1965; The Crusades, 1966.

ABOUT: Gardiner, H. C. In All Conscience, 1959; Who's Who, 1973; Who's Who in France, 1971–1972. *Periodicals*—America January 15, 1955; New York Times Book Review May 20, 1962; July 17, 1966; Publishers' Weekly July 19, 1971; Wilson Library Bulletin March 1960; Yale French Studies 27, 1961.

***OLESHA, YURI (KARLOVICH)** (1899–May 10, 1960), Russian novelist and dramatist, was born in Elisavetgrad (now Kirovograd), in southern Ukraine, the only son of middle-class parents. His mother was a Polish Catholic and his father, also of Polish origin, was a landowner who drank and gambled away his inheritance and became an excise officer in Odessa, where the family moved when the boy was three. Olesha has described how he invested the city with "all the lyrical emotions connected with one's birthplace," but all the same felt that he and his family were to some extent isolated in Odessa by their Polish background and by their gentility, impoverished though they were. His father, believing that the

*ol yô′ shə

YURI OLESHA

future would belong to the technocrats, insisted that he should train as an engineer, despite a technical incompetence so great that, as he put it, he felt his life threatened even by a pair of compasses. Hedging his bet, and convinced that his son had unlimited talent, his father obliged him to pursue a classical education as well.

Olesha welcomed the Revolution and fought in the Red Army during the Civil War. He began his career as a journalist, working mostly for the railwaymen's newspaper *Gudok* (The Whistle), for which he wrote stinging satirical poems under the pen name *Zubilo* (Chisel). Besides Mikhail Bulgakov, his fellow writers on this remarkable journal included the satirists Ilf and Petrov, and Petrov's brother Valentin Kataev, who like Olesha came from Odessa.

Olesha's first novel, *Zavist* (1927, translated in various versions as *Envy*), was an immediate and sensational success, and was at first highly praised by Soviet and émigré critics. It was later made into a play called *Zagovor chuvstv* (translated as *The Conspiracy of Feelings*). Andrei Babichev is a Soviet sausage maker, the embodiment of complacent success and energetic good health. One night he finds the drunken Kavalerov helpless in the street and takes him home, moved by sentimental memories of his adopted son Volodya, a famous football player who is temporarily absent.

Kavalerov is descended from Dostoevsky's "underground man" and from the various "superfluous men" of Russian nineteenth century literature. He is a dreamer, so remote from the Soviet world of clumsy objects, ledgers, and cheap food that he cannot even *see* these things directly, only reluctantly glimpsing them in the reflecting and distorting surfaces of mirrors, dirty windows, and metal buttons. He hungers for success in the new society, but is hopelessly at odds with a world whose laurels go to sausage makers and football players, and bitterly envious of Babichev. He joins forces with Babichev's anarchistic brother Ivan in a "conspiracy of feelings" against mechanization and collectivization. Their weapon is "Ophelia," a machine designed by Ivan to destroy machines, which unfortunately runs amuck on a football field. The football players and sausage makers inherit the earth and the conspirators end in wretched squalor, vying for the favors of their ugly old landlady and drinking themselves into insensibility and indifference.

This struggle between the old and the new, between romanticism and realism, is described in a lucid and expressive prose, rich in striking and unexpected images, which is nevertheless thoroughly ambiguous in total effect. Some early Soviet critics saw the book as a condemnation of surviving elements of the bourgeois mentality, while for others it was a defense of individualism against the collective state. Marion Jordan has shown that it can now be read as a more general attack on the utilitarian values of modern society, in which there is no room for dreams, and concludes: "If the book is to be viewed at all in extra-literary terms, its conflicts can most profitably be seen as originating in Olesha's early life rather than in his post-Revolutionary experience." R. A. Maguire, analyzing the book in Freudian terms, calls it "a classic of Oedipal literature."

Olesha never surpassed this short but richly complex book, which contains the seeds of all his later work. Several of the short stories collected in *Lyubov* (Love, 1928) and *Vishnevaya kostochka* (The Cherry Stone, 1930) pursue the conflict between reality and fancy in terms reminiscent of the theories of the critic Viktor Shklovsky, showing how profoundly our perception of the world and its contents is at the mercy of our attitudes and emotional states. Thus, in "Vishnevaya kostochka," the misery of unrequited love heightens the hero's sense of touch and alters his imaginative patterns like a drug. "Liompa," a story in *Lyubov*, contrasts a dying man, for whom things are becoming only names and abstractions, with his little grandson who, as Edward Brown says, inhabits "a world of direct sense impressions which, unnamed and as yet uncataloged, still have the freshness of surprise." Such stories as these demonstrate Olesha's great virtuosity in conveying the smell and taste and feel of everyday things. *Tri tolstyaka* (1928, translated as *The Three Fat Men*) is a fairy-story version of the

Revolution. It enjoyed enormous popularity as a children's book, was staged as a play by the Moscow Art Theatre, made into a ballet, and in 1966 into a film.

Olesha's play *Spisok blagodeyany* (1931, translated as *A List of Assets*) deals with an actress who, unable to reach her new audience, the workers, goes to Paris, only to find that in the West art is corrupted by commercialism. She is to some extent a projection of and apology for Olesha himself, who by this time was increasingly under attack for dealing with personal rather than social themes. Olesha's world, as he was at pains to show in this rather melodramatic and simplistic play, was that of the irresolute and the misfit—of Hamlet, Chaplin's "little man," Andersen's ugly duckling. Like Modest Zand in one of his later stories, he longed to create an optimistic proletarian masterpiece, but always found that, however positively he began, the old introspective misery sooner or later appeared, pushing its head or tail onto the page like a lizard.

Zand is also the hero of the film scenario *Cherny chelovek* (The Black Man, 1932). Another film script, *Strogy yunosha* (A Strict Young Man, 1934), was banned on ideological grounds after a film had actually been made of it. At the first Congress of the newly formed Writers' Union in 1934, Olesha made a speech pleading for a new humanism and confessing his inability to write about themes which did not engage his emotions. After this he was only on the periphery of the Soviet literary scene, writing plays for children's puppet theatres or adapting novels for the stage. When he died in 1960, of heart failure, Olesha was working on "a book about my life," which was published posthumously in 1965 as *Ni dnya bez strochki* (Not a Day Without a Line). As Marion Jordan has said: "Despite the liveliness of individual passages it lacks the organization to make it fully successful as a book in its own right."

Olesha's complete works would all fit into a single volume, and this is only partly the fault of his Soviet critics; in his last book he says that one of his files contained three hundred manuscript pages, each of them a draft for the first page of the novel *Zavist*, none of them actually used in the final version. Like Babel, another member of the southern school of writers, Olesha was a perfectionist whose work is small in bulk but of lasting significance. Helen Muchnic speaks of him as "the craftsman of unrest"; "he was never at home, except in his 'shop of metaphors.' . . . Olesha's essence is homelessness and a longing for a home, which he finds only in craftsmanship, in precise, metaphoric statements of unresolved questions."

PRINCIPAL WORKS IN ENGLISH TRANSLATION: Envy, tr. Anthony Wolfe, 1936; Envy (*with* V. Kaverin's The Unknown Artist) tr. P. Ross, 1947; Envy and Other Works, tr. A. R. MacAndrew, 1967 (originally published in 1960 as The Wayward Comrade and the Commissars, 1960); The Three Fat Men, tr. Fainna Glagoleva, 1964; Love and Other Stories, tr. Robert Payne, 1967. *Plays*—A List of Assets *in* MacAndrew, A. R. (ed.) Twentieth Century Russian Drama, 1963; The Conspiracy of Feelings, *in* Dukore, B. F. and Gerould, D. C. (eds.) Avant Garde Drama: Major Plays and Documents, 1970. *Stories in*—Bearne, C. G. (ed.) Modern Russian Short Stories, 1969; Montagu, I. and Marshall, H. (eds.) Soviet Short Stories, 1942; Newnham, R. (ed.) Soviet Short Stories, 1963; Slonim, M. and Reavey, G. (eds.) Soviet Literature: An Anthology, 1933; Yarmolinsky, A. (ed.) Soviet Short Stories, 1960; Russian Review January 1964; Soviet Literature 4, 1967; 3, 1969.

ABOUT: Alexandrova, V. A History of Soviet Literature 1917–1964; Beaujour, E. K. The Invisible Land: A Study of the Artistic Imagination of Iurii Olesha, 1971; Belinkov, L. Yuri Olesha, 1966; Brown, E. J. Russian Literature Since the Revolution, 1963; Jordan, M. *English introduction to* Zavist (Envy), 1969; Maguire, R. A. Red Virgin Soil, 1968; Mathewson, R. W. The Positive Hero in Russian Literature, 1958; Paustovsky, K. G. *in* Pages From Tarusa, 1964; Reeve, F. D. The Russian Novel, 1967; Simmons, E. J. (ed.) Through the Glass of Soviet Literature, 1953; Slonim, M. Modern Russian Literature, 1953; Slonim, M. Russian Theater, 1963; Slonim, M. Soviet Russian Literature, 1964; Struve, G. Twenty-five Years of Soviet Russian Literature, 1918–43, 1944; Swayze, H. Political Control of Literature in the USSR, 1946–1959, 1962; Zavalishin, V. Early Soviet Writers, 1958. *Periodicals*—New Statesman September 27, 1947; New York Review March 28, 1968; Slavic Review September 1966; Soviet Literature 12, 1966; Yale Review March 1931.

OLSON, ELDER (JAMES) (March 9, 1909–), American poet and critic, writes: "I was born in Chicago. My mother, Hilda M. Olson (née Schroeder), was of German ancestry, my father, Elder James Olson, of Norwegian. My father died when I was twenty-two months old, and my mother returned with me to her parents' home. I went to Harvey G. Wells Elementary School; subsequently to Tuley and Schurz High Schools. I attended the University of Chicago for two years, took a job with the Commonwealth Edison Company for two years, then spent two years (1931–1932) traveling (in Europe), writing and studying. I returned to the University in 1933, obtaining my Ph.B. in 1934, my M.A. in 1935, and my Ph.D. in 1938. My graduate work was done under R. S. Crane and Richard McKeon. I began teaching in 1935 at Armour Institute of Technology; in 1942 I joined the faculty of the University of Chicago, where I have remained except for visiting professorships which include a Rockefeller Professorship at Frankfurt a/M, Germany (1948), a visiting professorship at the University of Puerto Rico (1952–1953), and a succession of appointments at Indiana University: Mahlon Powell Professor of Philosophy (1955), Professor of Literary Criticism (1958–1959), Fellow of the School of Letters (1962), and Patten Lecturer (1965). During 1966–1967 I was

ELDER OLSON

Rockefeller Professor at the University of the Philippines. I married Ann Elisabeth Jones in 1937; after our divorce I married Geraldine Louise Hays (1948). Ann and Elder J. (III) are children of the first marriage, Olivia and Shelley of the second.

"I began writing poetry when I was seven, and contributed verse, fortunately under pseudonyms, to various newspaper columns. In 1926 I sent some poems to Harriet Monroe, editor of *Poetry* magazine; these she rejected, but she invited me to talk with her. To her shrewd but kind criticism I owe my first understanding of the art. I owe a similar debt to Professors Crane and McKeon, who developed my philosophical, as she did my practical, understanding of poetry as an art.

"I write poetry only when something inside me forces me to. I compose, sometimes very slowly, sometimes very swiftly, always very painfully. My profession has misled some reviewers into supposing my work 'academic,' but few poets have ever thought so. Personally, I do not care what it is called; my only ambition is to make the poems as good as possible. I am naturally aware of, but quite indifferent to, current literary fashions; I follow my own lights. I have always disliked a fixed, 'individual' style; I write as the poem demands. I became a professor and a theoretician because I had to understand my art."

Elder Olson is a prominent member of the Neo-Aristotelians, a group of critics and scholars who emerged in the 1940s at the University of Chicago in reaction to the New Criticism. They shared the New Critics' impatience with the biographical–historical approach to literary criticism, but deplored their neglect of traditional poetics. The Neo-Aristotelian manifesto was *Critics and Criticism* (1952), a collection of essays edited by the movement's leader, Ronald S. Crane. Crane urged a systematic and comprehensive approach to criticism based on Aristotle's *Poetics*. Olson, an important contributor, echoed Crane's arguments and attacked the New Critics for their preoccupation with poetic diction, irony, and ambiguity.

Olson applied his theories in *The Poetry of Dylan Thomas* in which, it was said, "he pays less attention to the puzzling verbal details of the poems than to their dramatic plotting as wholes." One critic thought the book "in many ways a triumph of structural analysis," which made sense of several previously incomprehensible poems, albeit at the cost of making Dylan Thomas "look tidier than he is."

Ashley Brown believes that Olson's own poems are also conceived in an Aristotelian spirit, "as imitations of actions." His first book of verse was *Thing of Sorrow*, containing a score of lyrics, mostly on metaphysical themes. Marion Stroebel said that they showed their author to possess "as sensitive an ear as any lyric poet writing today." W. R. Benét was even more impressed, and thought that the volume "awakens new hope for American poetry." It won a Friends of Literature Award in 1935.

The Cock of Heaven is a long poem written in a great variety of styles as a commentary on an imaginary text, "an epitome of human history." Henry Rago found "swiftness and neatness in the manipulation of plot, a competence at really distinguished parody, and an intellectual gift for sharp aphorism." Other reviewers admired the poem's rich imagery and lyric power, and its "profound erudition." A similar virtuosity was evident in *The Scarecrow Christ*, which included ballads and parables, many of them macabre or tragic treatments of traditional religious themes, and was full of echoes of old English poetry. Many readers shared Olson's delight in alliteration and assonance and complex rhythmic effects, and admired his formal skill and the precision of his diction and imagery. To some critics, however, the book seemed lacking in emotional impact; Randall Jarrell complained that Olson "seemed to know the world only through literature," and found him more successful in pastiche than in his own voice. Five short plays, four of them in verse, were collected in *Plays and Poems*, united thematically by their concern for human values in a world dominated by science. Most reviewers found them fundamentally undramatic, but lively, witty, and urbane.

Olson's *Collected Poems* (which is in fact a *selection* from his earlier books, with some new poems) called for an assessment of his work as a whole which critics found it difficult to provide. Gilbert Sorrentino said it was "a strangely uneven book, a pastiche of the academic and the contemporary," and an English critic dismissed it as "intolerably boring." It seemed to George Garrett that the "dominant quality of this book is the poet's voice. It is consistent, a voice that does not try to please and is not, in fact, a pleasing voice. But it is a true one. Serious, cerebral, self-conscious, introspective, and often anguished, it is an accurate echo of the intellectual of our times."

PRINCIPAL WORKS: *Poetry*—Thing of Sorrow, 1934; The Cock of Heaven, 1940; The Scarecrow Christ, and Other Poems, 1954; Plays & Poems, 1948–1958, 1958; Collected Poems, 1963. *Criticism*—(with R. S. Crane and others) Critics and Criticism, 1952; The Poetry of Dylan Thomas, 1954; Tragedy and the Theory of Drama, 1961; (ed.) American Lyric Poems, 1964; (ed.) Aristotle's Poetics and English Literature: A Collection of Critical Essays, 1965; The Theory of Comedy, 1969.

ABOUT: Contemporary Authors 7–8, 1963; Lucas, T. E. Elder Olson, 1972; Ransom, J. C. Poems and Essays, 1955; Sutton, W. Modern American Criticism, 1963; Who's Who in America, 1972–1973. *Periodicals*—Comparative Literature Spring 1963; Virginia Quarterly Review Spring 1964.

OMAN, CAROLA (MARY ANIMA) (LADY LENANTON) (May 11, 1897–), English biographer and novelist, writes: "I can perfectly remember the moment in which I realized that I could read. I was four years old, and seated on the ottoman in the night-nursery of our Georgian home in St. Giles's, Oxford. The book was an outsize illustrated edition of Grimm's fairy tales, and I never cared for them much, then or later, but that was one of the most wonderful moments of my life. Suddenly, I could read. Of course, I had listened to my elder sister being taught. I began to be an author at once and my mother presented me many years later with my first story. It was colourful—'Coral and the Bear.'

"I went to day-school at Oxford and saw a good many other authors who came to visit my father who was a Professor and Librarian and always writing in the study. I went to France in the First War, with the British Red Cross Society, and produced my first book—poems—when I was demobilized. Then I married, and as my husband was a very busy junior partner in a firm of timber agents and brokers I took up the profession of author seriously. I was living in a flat in London, and I had time. He was often away for six weeks together. I began with historical novels but gave them up in a rage when a reviewer wrote 'Princess Amelia is supposed to have been a young girl who lived in the eighteenth century.' I had spent months looking up facts about this most picturesque child of George III! Then a young publisher came down to my country home (for we had moved out as

CAROLA OMAN

soon as we could) and suggested I should write historical biography. *Henrietta Maria* is still selling. An historical biography takes me about five years, from start to finish, index and all. (But the best index I ever got was one Georgette Heyer made for me during the blitz.) I was just going to write my third life of a Stuart queen (*Mary of Modena*) when the Second War broke out, so I had to wait until that was over to get to Italy, and meanwhile I wrote *Nelson*. I remember coming in from night-duty one morning and finding a cable from America asking me to write that. It was a wonderful life to write, and my sailor patients used to say, 'Well so long, nurse. Go along and write the Death of Nelson.' This book was awarded the *Sunday Times* annual prize for English literature and I followed it with a life of a famous soldier *Sir John Moore* which was awarded the James Tait Black Memorial prize for biography.

"After that I had, like Shakespeare, a dark period, for my husband died very suddenly and I had to make a new life for myself. It was a great help being an author, as once you are seated at the desk you can really forget everything except your subject. I find also that a good day in the Record Office or the British Museum Reading Room or Manuscript Room is surprisingly refreshing. In the Reading Room the hours pass so fast I can tell from the colour of the sky, seen through the glass roof, that it's dark outside again, and time to go. I live in an old house in the country, not too far outside London, and go abroad about twice a year, generally once on business and once for pleasure. I enjoy listening to concerts and going to plays, and sewing and gardening and walks with the dogs.

I have no secretary and sometimes feel that I cannot find time to write books because like the Duke of Wellington, I suffer from a nervous disability to refrain from answering correspondents."

Carola Oman is the daughter of the eminent historian Sir Charles Oman. She was educated at Wychwood School in Oxford. Sir Gerald Lenanton, whom she married in 1922, died in 1952.

As she says, she began with historical novels, and wrote nine of them before World War II began in 1939. *The Road Royal*, about Mary Queen of Scots, and *Over the Water*, an account of Bonnie Prince Charlie's escape to Skye, are among those that reflect her special interest in the Stuarts. Other notable books in this mode are *Crouchback*, a novel about Anne of Warwick which contains an excellent portrait of Richard III, and *The Best of His Family*, a life of Shakespeare. The fictitious element in these impeccable historical reconstructions is often very slight indeed, and they offer in fact a particularly agreeable way of reading accurate history. Indeed the history in Miss Oman's novels is too exact, detailed, and objective to attract the mass readership commanded by romances in the Hollywood tradition; her appeal was always to a more discriminating audience, who admired her Augustan prose and quiet wit, her talent for character drawing, and her minutely detailed backgrounds.

Several of her excellent children's books have remained in print, including those about Robin Hood and King Alfred, but her adult novels with contemporary settings—agreeable books about likable people—have survived less well in an uncharitable age.

Since the late 1930s Miss Oman has concentrated principally on the historical biographies for which she is now best known. Three deal with Stuart queens: Henrietta Maria, the tragic queen of Charles I; Elizabeth of Bohemia, daughter of James I; and Mary of Modena, who wanted to enter a nunnery but was married at fifteen to James II. Unlike many of her colleagues, who seem irresistibly drawn to the colorful villains of history, Miss Oman likes to write about decent, honorable, devoted men—Nelson; the humane reforming general Sir John Moore; the self-sacrificing Eugène de Beauharnais, Napoleon's stepson. Her biographies have the virtues of her novels and some of the flaws. They are readable, thorough, and totally sound, but inclined to be excessively detailed, and dispassionate to a fault. Most biographers start out with a case to prove, or arrive at one, and select their material accordingly; Miss Oman, "searching for nothing, and with nothing to discard . . . must fill in every cranny." She provides a comprehensive, vivid, and wonderfully useful portrait of her subject, but directs the reader to no conclusion about him. "She must," wrote one critic, "be the most disinterested of all historical sleuths."

Carola Oman is a Fellow of the Royal Society of Literature, of the Society of Arts, and of the Royal Historical Society. She received a CBE in 1957.

PRINCIPAL WORKS: *Poems*—The Menin Road, 1919. *Novels*—The Road Royal, 1924; King Heart, 1926; Miss Barrett's Elopement, 1929; Crouchback, 1929; Major Grant, 1931; The Empress, 1932; The Best of his Family, 1933; Over the Water, 1935. *For children*—Ferry the Fearless, 1936; Johel, 1937; Robin Hood, the Prince of Outlaws, 1937; Alfred, King of the English, 1939; Baltic Spy, 1940. *Biographies*—Prince Charles Edward, 1935; Henrietta Maria, 1936; Elizabeth of Bohemia, 1938; Nelson, 1946; Sir John Moore, 1953; David Garrick, 1958; Mary of Modena, 1962; Ayot Rectory, 1965; Napoleon's Viceroy: Eugène de Beauharnais, 1966; The Gascoyne Heiress: Diaries of the Second Marchioness of Salisbury, 1968; The Wizard of the North, 1973.

ABOUT: Contemporary Authors 7–8, 1963; Who's Who, 1973. *Periodicals*—New York Times January 24, 1937; August 9, 1942; December 15, 1946; Times Literary Supplement October 25, 1947; December 11, 1953; August 6, 1954; January 30, 1959; May 4, 1973.

O'NOLAN, BRIAN ("Flann O'Brien," "Myles na Gopaleen") (October 5, 1912–April 1, 1966), Irish novelist and humorist, wrote: "After a run-of-the-mill education in Dublin, in 1929 I entered University College, Dublin, a non-resident foundation and in five years had progressed to take the M.A. degree. In the interval however I had gone to Cologne University on a studentship and spent many months on the Rhineland and at Bonn, drifting away from the strict pursuit of study. In later years I got to know Berlin very well, and had a deep interest in the German people.

"My writing probably began with college journalism, and proceeded to short stories published where a market was to be found. My first major book was *At Swim-Two-Birds* (Longmans, London, 1939). This was republished by another London house in 1960, and in New York. In the same year my second book *The Hard Life* was published in London and New York. Similarly published internationally in 1964 was *The Dalkey Archive*, later made into a very successful play named *When The Saints Go Cycling In*, with the collaboration of Hugh Leonard.

"Through all that time I had been contributing a column to the *Irish Times* (daily for some years) of comic, satiric comment, with always a serious streak beneath the laughs, and provoking many controversies. This was a massive *œuvre*, if only in bulk. I also contributed many short stories to major journals, had books translated into French and German, and two in paperback."

Brian O'Nolan was born in Strabane, County Tyrone, the son of a revenue commissioner. He made his mark at University College as a philologist of exceptional ability, equally at home in Latin, Greek, Irish, and German. After the university he went into the Irish Civil Service, and by the time he retired in 1953 had served as private secretary to four successive Ministers for Local Government. O'Nolan did not write professionally until the late 1930s, and then his great gifts for satire and polemics were discovered almost by accident; his performance in a literary correspondence in the *Irish Times* so impressed the editor that O'Nolan was invited to contribute a daily column. "Cruiskeen Lawn" appeared in the *Irish Times* almost without a break for twenty-five years, under the pseudonym "Myles na Gopaleen" or "Myles na gCopaleen." It quickly became famous (and feared) for its wit and admired for its casual erudition—one article was written in Irish but employed Greek script. A selection of these columns, made by the author's brother Kevin, appeared posthumously in 1968 as *The Best of Myles*. O'Nolan divided his life between his office, the pub, and his home. In this entertaining, witty, melancholy Irishman many would have recognized the incomparable columnist, few the comic genius of his fiction.

Just before the outbreak of World War II, O'Nolan (writing as "Flann O'Brien"), published his first novel, *At Swim-Two-Birds*. It was an unfortunate time for a work of genius to appear. James Joyce himself, whom John Wain has described as O'Nolan's "ultimate master," said of the novel: "That's a real writer, with the true comic spirit. A really funny book." Dylan Thomas thought it was "just the book to give to your sister, if she is a dirty, boozy girl." *At Swim-Two-Birds* gathered very few devotees at the time of its publication, but over the years these were persistent enough to persuade a publisher to reissue it in 1960, whereupon it met with instant acclaim. O'Nolan was encouraged to write two more novels in rapid succession, *The Hard Life: An Exegesis of Squalor* (1961) and *The Dalkey Archive* (1964). *The Third Policeman*, which appeared posthumously in 1967, had been written after *At Swim-Two-Birds*. Meanwhile he had written (in Irish) a satire on the Irish language movement, *An Béal Bocht*, which was published in 1941 and has since been translated by Patrick C. Power as *The Poor Mouth*.

At Swim-Two-Birds (the title is a literal translation of an Irish place-name) is O'Nolan's masterpiece. Unlike that of its successors, the highly complex structure of this novel is continuously and successfully sustained; the action, however fantastic or extravagant, always has about it a sense of inevitability, and as the reader becomes aware of the number of levels at which the book operates, he becomes excited rather than confused. The nameless narrator is writing a book about a man called

BRIAN O'NOLAN

Trellis who is writing about certain characters who are doing their best to live lives quite different from the ones their creator devises for them. One of the purposes of *At Swim-Two-Birds* is to make a comment, cast in the form of a joke but ultimately very serious, about the nature of fiction—to give an answer to the perennial question of how it can be of value when it is a sham. O'Nolan simultaneously mocks—with a powerful sense of peculiarly Irish despair—and passionately explores the art of fiction. There is much loving parody, some of it shading into inspired imitation, of early Irish literature. The immensely complex structure of the novel cannot be described in a short space; there is an excellent description of it in John Wain's memorial essay on O'Nolan (*Encounter*, July 1967), the most substantial critique of him yet made.

Most readers will be moved more by O'Nolan's farcical ingenuity and subtle inventiveness than by his humanity; *At Swim-Two-Birds* has been compared favorably to *Ulysses*, but there is a certain coldness in it, a failure to come to grips with the emotions of people. This deficiency emerges more clearly in the three succeeding novels, and may be seen in the exclusively verbal nature of the puns O'Nolan made in his *Irish Times* pieces—"the last roes of summer," "the great mines which stink alike." The sheer structural ingenuity of the later novels can become as tiresome and unprofound as the succession of bad and not always profound puns. *At Swim-Two-Birds* will always be regarded as a work of genius; but when critics get back the breath that its brilliant ingenuity took from them, it may be seen as one that is flawed by a refusal on the part of the writer to commit himself emotionally.

Nevertheless, the humor of the three last novels is a perpetual and a refreshing delight. *The Hard Life* takes up the theme of Roman Catholicism, with which O'Nolan was deeply concerned, and has a "projector" (reminiscent of Swift) as one of its heroes: he invents one fantastic money-making scheme after another, giving O'Nolan full scope for his powers of farcical invention. The book ends despairingly in the narrator's "tidal surge of vomit."

The Dalkey Archive includes among its characters a man who is in danger of turning into a bicycle, James Joyce, and a number of "serious drinkers"; the most substantial of its many threads is the one concerned with the subject of reincarnation, a notion that clearly tended to subdue O'Nolan's frivolity. It introduces a character called De Selby, who was to O'Nolan what Ubu was to Jarry: a kind of devil, and clearly a symbol both of the novelist and of O'Nolan himself, he is able to abolish time and extinguish all earthly life (he intends to carry out both projects). Joyce himself appears—as a pious Catholic barman who complains that *Ulysses*, the work of "various low, dirty-minded ruffians," has been falsely attributed to him by Sylvia Beach.

O'Nolan had in fact invented De Selby in *The Third Policeman*; here he is worried, among other things, by the water we drink. Is it too strong? Can it be diluted? Upon his instigation the narrator and another man murder a rich old farmer, who reappears three years later and directs them to a police barracks . . . This, despite occasional comic felicities, is O'Nolan's thinnest book, and is perhaps less readable than an account of its plot suggests. He also wrote two original plays, *Thirst* and *Faustus Kelly*, the latter produced at the Abbey Theatre in 1943.

PRINCIPAL WORKS: At Swim-Two-Birds, 1939 (reissued, 1960); An Béal Bocht, 1941; The Hard Life, 1961; The Dalkey Archive, 1964; The Third Policeman, 1967; The Best of Myles, 1968; The Poor Mouth, 1973.

ABOUT: O'Keeffe, T. (ed.) Myles: Portraits of Brian O'Nolan, 1973; O'Nolan, K. *introduction to* The Best of Myles, 1968. *Periodicals*—Encounter July 1967; New Statesman December 8, 1967; Spectator September 13, 1968; Times (London) April 2, 1966.

***OOKA, SHOHEI** (March 6, 1909–), Japanese novelist, writes: "My family came from Wakayama, a small city in southwestern Japan. They were small landowners, but my father decided to establish himself in a business career in the capital, so I was born in Tokyo, the eldest son in a family of three. My father was successful as a stockbroker but was completely ruined in 1931 during the Japanese war adventure in North China. I had then finished my schooling, graduating from Kyoto University's department of French Literature in 1932.

"I started my literary career writing critical essays in literary magazines on modern Japanese writers and French literature, especially the works of Stendhal. In 1938 I entered the Teikoku Sanso Corporation, a joint Japanese–French company dealing in oxygen, as a French translator. In 1944 I was drafted into the army and sent to the Philippines, where I was captured by the U.S. Army in 1945. I returned to Japan at the war's end.

"My first novel was *Furyoki* (Memories of a Prisoner of War), published in 1948. This was an account of my war experiences, partly fictional. Critics recognized in it some realistic, unemotional, lucid observation. This novel received the Yokomitsu Prize. It was translated into Italian in 1965.

"My next novel was *Musashino Fujin* (A Woman of the Musashino Plain), a story of love between an old-fashioned Japanese wife and a young ex-soldier. As adultery was a prohibited theme during the war, on publication in 1950 it had some novelty and became a bestseller.

"My third novel, *Nobi* (translated as *Fires on the Plain*), was another war novel, but entirely fictional. This was less widely read than *Musashino Fujin* but received the Yomiuri Prize in 1952. It has been translated since 1957 into English, French, Italian, etc. The story of a defeated Japanese soldier wandering in the mountains of Leyte, it is an account of the demoralization of a man driven by hunger to the point of cannibalism, but saved by the power of Christian faith. The subject attracted Western readers' interest, partly as a harrowing war story describing the conflict between the desires and the conscience of a man, and partly as the story of the conversion of a pagan to Christianity. In 1959 Ken Ichikawa made a film adaptation of *Nobi* which received international acclaim, and this contributed much to its popularity in Japan.

"Meanwhile I lectured on French literature in Meiji University from 1952 to 1957. I translated into Japanese Stendhal's *De l'amour* in 1949, and *Chartreuse de Parme* in 1951. My case is that of a Japanese intellect, schooled in the discipline of European thought, adapting the realistic and social methods of Stendhal and others to Japanese social life.

"I dealt with some of the problems affecting post-war Japan in a serial published in the *Asahi* newspaper in 1961. It is called *Wakakusa Monogatari* (A Story of Tender Shoots) treating the present changed aspect of rural life in the neighborhood of large cities, in this case specifically Yokohama, where youths, abandoning their country homes, go to the city to work in factories and are speedily corrupted. It deals with the case of a farmer's son who commits murder and is sentenced to five years' imprisonment. I had two objects in view in writing the story—one to depict the evils of juvenile crime, and the other the peculiarities of

*ōō kə

the criminal procedure of Japanese courts. *Kaei* (Under the Shadow of the Cherry Blossoms), which received the Shincho and Mainichi Prizes in 1961, is a simple story of the suicide of a prostitute.

"Of recent years my interest has turned to historical and biographical studies. In 1958 I published *Asa no Uta* (A Morning Song), a biographical study of Chuya Nakahara, a modern poet and close friend of mine who died in 1937. In 1963 I began an historical novel, still unfinished, *Tenchugumi*, a story of a royalist revolt on the eve of the Meiji Restoration.

"In 1953 I received a Rockefeller Foundation grant and traveled for a year in Europe and the United States. In 1961, on the invitation of the Writers' Union, I visited the USSR, and in 1963, Communist China. I am married with a married daughter and a son just graduated from university."

Ooka grew up in what he has described as a petit-bourgeois environment, and was educated at Aoyama Gakuin, a Methodist mission school. That he received some stimulus from the school's Christian teachings is evident in *Chichi* (Father, 1951), a semi-autobiographical account of his rebellious adolescence which includes a description of his conflict with his father over the purchase of a Bible. But his primary interests were literary, and he was much influenced during his teens by the novels and stories of Soseki Natsume and Ryunosuke Akutagawa, and deeply affected by the suicide of Akutagawa in 1927. At about this time he was introduced to Hideo Kobayashi, an eminent critic and scholar whose influence probably explains Ooka's decision to concentrate on French literature at Kyoto University.

Before World War II he published little but some translations and critical studies of Stendhal, whose interest in psychological exploration and whose prose style have become so much a part of Ooka's own manner. *Furyoki*, which established his reputation in 1948, was followed by several briefer sketches of his wartime experiences in the terrible Leyte campaign, and after it as a prisoner of war. One critic has suggested that Ooka's chief weakness as a novelist is his inability to place his characters convincingly in their social setting, and certainly his best book is about an individual outside society, the wretched narrator of *Fires on the Plain*.

The novel describes this man's lonely wanderings after his unit has abandoned him as too weak and ill to fight, his encounter with two other refugees who are kept together only by mutual distrust and fear, his discovery that the meat on which he lives is human flesh, and his eventual murder of his companions. This dreadful story is recounted with great detachment and has the authority of a fable, as well as the grim verisimilitude associated with

SHOHEI OOKA

Japanese naturalism. The *Spectator*'s reviewer found it "a more impressive novel about the war than any I have come across from England and America," and Walter Allen spoke of its "almost hallucinatory vividness," which spares the reader no horror, yet leaves a final impression "of a strange and terrible beauty."

The war's impact can be seen in Ooka's fiction even when war is not the theme—most obviously in a preoccupation with death which pervades such books as *Musashino Fujin* and *Sanso* (Oxygen, 1952). However, none of his later books has had anything like the authority and originality of *Fires on the Plain*.

PRINCIPAL WORKS IN ENGLISH TRANSLATION: Fires on the Plain, 1957.

ABOUT: Grigson, G. (ed.) Concise Encyclopedia of Modern World Literature, 1963; International Who's Who, 1972–73; Penguin Companion to Literature 4, 1969. *Periodicals*—New Statesman April 27, 1957; San Francisco Chronicle July 27, 1957; Spectator March 29, 1957; Time July 22, 1957.

***ORIGO, IRIS (CUTTING), MARCHESA** (August 15, 1902–), Anglo-Italian biographer, was born in England, at Birdlip, Gloucestershire. She is the only child of William Bayard Cutting, an American diplomat, and his wife, Lady Sybil Cuffe, younger daughter of the fifth Earl of Desart. Her father died in 1910 and she was raised by her mother and governesses at the historic Villa Medici, near Florence. Lady Sybil, who herself had a flair for writing, was a friend of Bernard Berenson and was married in 1918 to Geoffrey Scott, Berenson's secretary and the brilliant author of *The Architecture*

* ô rē′ gō

IRIS ORIGO

of Humanism and *Portrait of Zélide*. Lady Sybil made a third marriage in 1926 to another writer, Percy Lubbock.

Iris Cutting grew up in the Berenson ambience and in 1924, when she was twenty-two, married a Tuscan landowner, the Marchese Antonio Origo, by whom she has two daughters. As the Marchesa Origo she is a charming cosmopolite, fond of travel and gardening; as Iris Origo she is the author of half a dozen scrupulous and sensitive biographies, most of them about Italian figures of the Renaissance or of the nineteenth century.

Leopardi, her life of the poet, established her reputation in 1935. The book has no pretensions to being a critical study, drawing on Leopardi's work only insofar as it throws light on his character. This disappointed some reviewers but the critical reception was otherwise unanimously enthusiastic. Peter Quennell called it "a brief but vivid and remarkably readable book . . . well written, nicely balanced, [and] carefully documented." *Tribune of Rome*, which followed, is a biography of Cola di Rienzi (1313–1354), an Italian patriot who was known as "the last of the Romans." Iris Origo published nothing during the war years, but in *War in Val d'Orcia* (1947) she described the successive waves of refugee children, British prisoners of war, partisans, and German troops who laid waste the Origo estates and eventually drove the family north for the last part of the war.

The Last Attachment, about Byron's liaison with Teresa Guiccioli, makes excellent use of their letters and family papers in "a study which uncovers original materials and treats them with thorough and impeccable scholarship, and which at the same time presents a story of great human interest." *The Merchant of Prato* is in effect a social history of fourteenth century Italy, built around the life and career of a merchant, Francesco di Marco Datini. The author's skillful handling of a mass of intricate detail was warmly praised, and the book was thought "splendid proof that the best history comes from the best sources best observed."

Five shorter essays about nineteenth century figures were collected in *Measure of Love*. The volume includes Iris Origo's compassionate portrait of Byron's illegitimate daughter Allegra, first published as a monograph in 1935, and also studies of the Contessa Marina Benzon, of the Carlyles and Lady Harriet Ashburton, of Mazzini, and of Marie Lenéru, the deaf and nearly blind dramatist and diarist. *The World of San Bernardino* is a biography of the great Renaissance Franciscan preacher and scholar who was canonized only six years after his death. This "scholarly and . . . sweetly made" book draws on Bernardino's sermons and other contemporary documents "for a vivid and lively picture not only of the saint and his work, but also of the world in which he lived and the people to whom he preached."

"All one can do," Iris Origo says of the biographer's task, "is to set down, when one can, the very words written or spoken, so that each reader may call up his own ghosts." Her advice to an apprentice biographer would be "to examine [the documents], if he can, with an almost blank mind: to let them produce their own effect. Later on he will come to compare, to sift and draw conclusions; but first he should 'listen without interrupting.'" She has consistently followed her own advice, proving, as John Davenport put it, that "given patience, love, scholarship and intelligence it is possible to illuminate the darkest recesses of the human soul." The same qualities distinguish her own autobiography, *Images and Shadows*.

The Marchesa Origo has been honored for her work in three countries: she is a Fellow of the Royal Society of Literature, has honorary doctorates from two American colleges, and in 1966 received the Italian Isabella d'Este Medal. She lives now at Chianciano, in Siena.

PRINCIPAL WORKS: Allegra, 1935; Leopardi, 1935 (revised ed., 1953); Tribune of Rome, 1938; War in Val d'Orcia, 1947; The Last Attachment, 1949; Merchant of Prato, 1957; A Measure of Love, 1957; The World of San Bernardino, 1962; Images and Shadows: Part of a Life, 1970. *For children*—Giovanna and Jane, 1950. *As compiler*—The Vagabond Path (anthology), 1972.

ABOUT: Clifford, J. (ed.) Biography as an Art, 1962; Mariano, N. Forty Years With Berenson, 1966; Origo, I. War in Val d'Orcia, 1947; Origo, I. Images and Shadows, 1970; Who's Who, 1973.

***"OSARAGI, JIRO" (pseudonym of Kiyohiko Nojiri)** (October 9, 1897–April 30, 1973), Japanese novelist, was born in Yokohama, the son of a shipping company official. He was educated in Tokyo, where he entered the French Law department of the First High School (now part of Tokyo University) in 1915, and three years later went on to the politics section in the law department at the Imperial University. Appearing, he admitted, only for examinations, he devoted most of his time to reading French literature, studying European Socialist thought (including the works of Marx, Kropotkin, and Russell), writing for magazines, and running a small theatrical group.

Upon graduation in 1921 he went to live in Kamakura, a coastal town rich in historic and literary associations, not far from Tokyo, where he translated some of the work of Romain Rolland and taught for a few months in a local girls' school. He then entered the treaties bureau of the Ministry of Foreign Affairs. Partly to conceal his identity from his superiors, he began to write under the adopted name Jiro Osaragi—Osaragi means Great Buddha, suggested by the fact that he lived near the huge and famous bronze statue at Kamakura. He contributed stories and abridged translations to a number of literary magazines and newspapers, and when popular success greeted his *Kurama Tengu* stories (serialized in the magazines *Pokketo* and *Dokuritsu*), he left his post at the Ministry and devoted himself to writing.

The *Kurama Tengu* tales are examples of a genre extremely popular in Japan, the *jidai shosetsu*, or period story. Their hero is a *samurai* superman, a Robin Hood of the sword, but at the same time he is a *ronin*, an outsider, and in Osaragi's vision an intellectual with a humanist code—an independent, fair-minded protector of other people's freedom. Kyogo, the falsely condemned outcast who returns after a long exile for a glimpse of Japan and of his daughter in *Homecoming*, and the old-fashioned, gentle, and tolerant Professor Segi in *The Journey*, are modern-dress versions of this paragon, and perhaps also reflect something of Osaragi himself. Parallels might be seen between Osaragi's romantic rebel swordsmen and the Three Musketeers, but the author denied the connection, claiming that he has tried to keep his French scholarship and Japanese fiction distinct.

Encouraged by the enormous success of the *Kurama Tengu* stories, which have provided material for films, television, and stage dramas, Osaragi went on to write further historical novels, such as *Ako Roshi* (The Ronin of Ako, 1927), in which he gives a modern relevance to the tale of the forty-seven *samurai* who, in feudal loyalty, sought the death of the man who had disgraced their lord.

*ō sə ra gi

JIRO OSARAGI

He set the tale in the political context of a decaying feudal society, presenting the *samurai* leaders as idealists restless in the culturally brilliant but static Genroku period, urging on towards a new age.

Osaragi's period novels have been criticized as mere romantic entertainments, and it is true that they have enjoyed great popularity, and never lose their narrative pace and readability. But they also have considerable intellectual content, and Osaragi was clearly a cultured and politically conscious writer who was simply not prepared to limit himself to a minority audience of intellectuals.

He displayed his learning more directly in a series of historical studies. Writing about the crises facing the French Third Republic, or anarchism and terrorism in Czarist Russia, he seems to have found a means of commenting indirectly on political events in Japan. *Buranje Shogun no higeki* (The Tragedy of General Boulanger, 1935), for example, can be read as a criticism of the spread of fascism, ultranationalism, and terrorism after 1931; and *Dorefusu jiken* (The Dreyfus Case, 1930) may have been partly inspired by the mass anti-Communist witch-hunt in 1928, when more than three thousand people were arrested in Japan.

After the war appeared the two modern novels by which Osaragi was known to Western readers, *Kikyo* (1948, translated by Brewster Horwitz as *Homecoming*), and *Tabiji* (1952, translated by Ivan Morris as *The Journey*). Although they were written in the harsh postwar years, and deal with Japan in defeat and under foreign occupation, they provide rich insight into the industrialized Japan of today, comparing it unfavorably with the grace, humanity, and subtlety that for Osaragi characterized the culture of his father's and grandfather's generations.

"I'm sure that in his heart Basho had no fixed destination. He walked in order to walk. Arrival was never his objective. . . . For us poor worldlings on the other hand, the destination has become everything," he lamented in *The Journey*. But though his criticism of modern society is sharp, both novels finally express a sincere and generous optimism and an undestroyed idealism. Osaragi's protagonists are solitary individuals, but they recognize the need to tolerate and sustain others.

Osaragi's technical skill—his "tidy structure, efficient characterization, and clarity of style"—laid him open to charges of slickness and superficiality, and in the West his two translated novels have had a mixed reception. *Homecoming*, which deals with the return of a soldier to a Japan stripped of its past, was called a "fine, patient novel" by James A. Michener, and praised by the *Times Literary Supplement* for its "luminous atmosphere and its economy of style." But *The Journey* was damned by Anthony West with only the faintest praise: "*The Journey* is superior to soap opera," he wrote, "because it has the background of sensitivity and poetic reference that is hard to evade in Japan. But the sensitivity is severely limited to the minor emotions. . . . Most Japanese novels are written in haste for readers who are uncritical, sentimental, and bourgeois in the harshest sense of the word. . . . *The Journey* is a fair example of much of what they get."

Nevertheless, Osaragi received most of the honors available to literary figures in Japan. *Homecoming* was awarded the Japan Academy Prize; in 1959 he was elected to the Japan Academy of Arts, and in 1964 was awarded the National Culture Prize. He visited Europe and the United States in 1958 on a research tour which produced *Pari Moyu* (Paris in Flames, 1961), a study of the Paris Commune. He died at the National Cancer Center in Tokyo at the age of seventy-five.

PRINCIPAL WORKS IN ENGLISH TRANSLATION: Homecoming, 1955; The Journey, 1960.

ABOUT: Penguin Companion to Literature 4, 1969. *Periodicals*—New York Herald Tribune Book Review January 16, 1955; New York Times May 1, 1973; New York Times Book Review January 16, 1955; July 17, 1960; New Yorker October 1, 1960; Saturday Review January 22, 1955; Times Literary Supplement September 9, 1955.

OSBORNE, JOHN (JAMES) (December 12, 1929–), English dramatist. The first production of his play *Look Back in Anger* at the Royal Court Theatre in May 1956 was the opening broadside in the long-awaited revolution in the British theatre, its resumption of serious concerns after years of triviality. Osborne was born in Fulham, London, the son of Thomas and Nellie (Grove) Osborne. His father was a commercial artist who died of tuberculosis while Osborne was still a child. His mother worked as a barmaid in his grandparents' pub, and he speaks of this side of the family—emotional, boozy, vulgar, and indomitable—with great affection. He suffered as a child from rheumatic fever and this, as well as interfering with his formal education, encouraged in him the habit of introspection.

After attending state schools until he was twelve, Osborne was sent to a minor public school, Belmont College, in Devon, where he took part in amateur theatricals and excelled at boxing and cricket. He was expelled at the age of sixteen, reportedly for jeering at the royal family and for slapping his headmaster's face (the headmaster having initiated the exchange). Obliged to earn his living, Osborne was briefly a journalist, working on a group of trade journals, then a tutor to a party of children touring with a repertory company. From that he drifted into a not very successful career as a repertory actor, with frequent periods on the dole. This lasted for ten years and allowed him plenty of time to try his hand as a dramatist.

One of his apprentice plays, *The Devil Inside*, written in collaboration with Stella Linden, was produced in Huddersfield in 1950, and another, *Personal Enemy*, written with Anthony Creighton, had some success at Harrogate in 1955. Meanwhile, in 1951, he had made the first of his four marriages, to Pamela Lane. They were living, penniless, on a Chelsea houseboat, when *Look Back in Anger*, originally called "On the Pier at Morecambe," was accepted by the Royal Court Theatre. The time was ripe for it: the solidarity and sense of purpose of the war years had gone, the British class barriers were back in position, and the young in particular were increasingly bored and disillusioned by the bourgeois complacency of the period, and its reflections in the musicals and genteel dramas that dominated the British stage.

Look Back in Anger, as Osborne has said, is in form realistic and traditional, but it is set not in a southern drawing room but in a shabby attic in a Midland town. Here lives Jimmy Porter, who has emerged from university a bitterly dissatisfied intellectual, cut off from his proletarian roots, yet furiously contemptuous of the ruling class he has equipped himself to join. A revolutionary in the Welfare State, where there "aren't any good, brave causes left," he vents his frustration on his wife Alison, his hostage from the middle classes, and on the other member of this ménage, his docile working-class friend Cliff.

As a small and negative protest Jimmy Porter has rejected the commercial advantages of his education and makes his living by selling candy in a street market. His revolution is mostly verbal, and a large part of the play consists of his violent and often very funny tirades against the materialism and ignorance of the new generation of workers, the corruption and stupidity of their rulers, the dead-alive apathy of all England. His cruelest rhetoric is aimed at Alison, in an attempt above all to shatter her calm, to hurt her so much that she will fight back, become a lover-enemy worthy of him. She cannot be this, but her friend Helena can and, for a time, in Alison's absence, Helena and Jimmy live together fairly happily. This interlude ends when Alison returns, her self-control shattered at last by the death of her baby. She and Jimmy begin to play their old childish game about bears and squirrels, achieving in make-believe a tenderness that is impossible for them in the real world.

Alison, Helena, and Cliff are perfectly convincing three-dimensional characters, but their sole purpose is to provide Jimmy Porter with punching bags and sparring partners; he is the play. On the face of it he is a strange hero—a neurotic and futile malcontent whose rebellion is limited to bullying the defenseless. And yet that is not the impression he left on his audiences. Many reviewers were guarded, speaking of the play as exciting and promising but deeply flawed; a few were outraged. But for thousands, Jimmy Porter's impotent rage taught them their own frustrations, crystallized the dreary half-awareness that, ten years after the war, the old guard was back in the saddle, and not even the saddle was worth much any more; they heard for the first time in that outrageous iconoclasm and furious laughter the authentic voice of their generation.

The Sunday after the play opened, Kenneth Tynan wrote in the *Observer*: "I agree that *Look Back in Anger* is likely to remain a minority taste. What matters, however, is the size of the minority. I estimate it at roughly 6,733,000, which is the number of people in this country between the ages of twenty and thirty. . . . I doubt if I could love anyone who did not wish to see *Look Back in Anger*. It is the best young play of its decade." After a shaky start the play was a success. It went on to win the New York Critics' award as the best foreign play of 1957, to be filmed, to become a turning point and a monument in the history of the British theatre. Ten years later Alan Sillitoe wrote: "John Osborne didn't contribute to the British theatre: he set off a land-mine called *Look Back in Anger* and blew most of it up. The bits have settled back into place, of course, but it can never be the same again."

Laurence Olivier, who disapproved of Osborne's social doctrines, acknowledged his talent by actually asking for the lead role in *The Entertainer* (1957), which is recognized to be "one of the greatest acting parts of our age." *The Entertainer* is another play built around a complex, tormented

JOHN OSBORNE

hero-villain. Archie Rice is a fading music-hall comic (blue jokes and patriotic songs), exploiting every kind of emotional dishonesty in his struggle to finance one more seedy entertainment. Not even the news that his son has been killed at Suez can stop Archie's act: the sad degrading show must go on because it always has, and because Archie has long since surrendered his rights as a human individual. Even offstage he is a clown, burying his intelligence and despair under layers of stale jokes.

The play is interspersed with music-hall numbers which, in the Brechtian fashion, comment obliquely on the main action. From these it is clear that Osborne is using the decline of the music hall as a symbol of the decline of England: "Don't clap too loud," Archie tells his audience; "it's a very old building." Jimmy Porter's grudging admiration for Alison's father, the apotheosis of middle-class values, in *Look Back in Anger*, is echoed in *The Entertainer* by the affectionate treatment of Billy Rice, Archie's father, who had been a great star in the heyday of the music hall as a true folk art. There has been much critical discussion of this conflict in Osborne between his revolutionary principles and his reactionary nostalgia for the moral certainties and simple gusto of the good old days.

An earlier play, *Epitaph for George Dillon*, written in collaboration with Anthony Creighton, was revised and staged in 1958. Dillon is an actor-writer, part artist and part confidence trickster, part Jimmy Porter and part Archie Rice. Deeply uncertain of his own talent, he sells out, rewrites his play as a sex shocker, and settles down to a life of soulless suburbanism. The critics seemed uncertain whether Osborne's target in the play was the crassness of the commercial theatre or himself, for there is obviously an autobiographical element in the capacity for brutal self-analysis shared by all his heroes. It was followed by a disastrous attempt at a satirical musical, *The World of Paul Slickey*, and an equally unsuccessful television play, *A Subject of Scandal and Concern*, a near-documentary about George Holyoake, who in 1842 was the last man to be imprisoned for blasphemy in England.

Meanwhile Osborne had begun to publish his notorious open letters to the press which, under titles like "Letter to the Philistines," and "Damn You, England," expressed with almost breathless violence some aspects of his passionate love-hate relationship with his country and its people. This had not on the whole endeared him to his audience, and those who had always sought to dismiss him as an overarticulate ruffian were preening themselves when he achieved a third major success in *Luther* (1961).

Straightforward in its presentation of the historical material (and using Luther's own words whenever possible), it is Brechtian to the extent that a narrator sets the time and place of each scene. The psychological and physiological distress and stubborn honesty which drove the Oedipal and constipated hero to revise the history of the world is brilliantly conveyed. As Harold Hobson said, the play showed that Osborne "can use ordinary dramatic construction as skillfully as any conventional craftsman." This was not quite enough for those who had hoped for something rarer than competence but, thanks partly to Albert Finney's performance, the play was a commercial and critical hit.

There was a mixed reception for *The Blood of the Bambergs* and *Under Plain Cover*, the double bill presented in 1962 as "Plays for England," but Osborne had another triumph with *Inadmissible Evidence* (1964), which this time provided a magnificent acting part for Nicol Williamson. He played Bill Maitland, a shady, failing solicitor whose comprehensive sense of guilt is dramatized in a long nightmare in which he dreams himself in the dock, charged with professional misconduct, greedy promiscuity, and personal mediocrity. The rest of the play substantiates these charges, as Maitland is abandoned, in boredom or disgust, by friends, employees, family, and lovers, until in the end his last lifeline, the telephone, is silent; that is his punishment, to be quite alone with his hated self. Like Nathanael West's *Miss Lonelyhearts*, the play is a tragedy about a man who feels too much in an unfeeling society. In form it moves between naturalism and something close to expressionism, and there were complaints that variations in style and tone were not satisfactorily controlled and integrated, a criticism which has been applied to most of Osborne's work; many nevertheless thought *Inadmissible Evidence* his most moving and compassionate play.

A Patriot for Me (1965) is about an able young Jewish officer in the Austro-Hungarian Army, driven to suicide when the Russians discover his homosexuality. The critics seemed puzzled by it, as they were by *A Bond Honoured* (1966), Osborne's adaptation of Lope de Vega's *La fianza satisfecha*, which studies a kind of clinical experiment in evil and runs to a great deal of incest, blasphemy, and other naughtiness, presented for the most part in semidarkness.

Time Present (1968) was a departure for Osborne, in that the familiar tirades of dissatisfaction and disgust are spoken by a woman, played by Osborne's fourth wife, Jill Bennett. Pamela is a spiky out-of-work actress who cares for very little but her actor father and finds herself, to her amused disgust, punished for a meaningless act of promiscuity by pregnancy. Not much else happens and, as usual, Osborne fails to provide his central character with any opposition strong enough to turn her monologues into real dialogues. But that central character is courageous, witty, and wholly believable, and the play was generally admired.

So was *The Hotel in Amsterdam* (1968), where three couples escape for a weekend from the megalomaniac film director who employs all of the men and one of the wives. Again there is almost nothing but talk, but it is brilliant and stimulating talk, about friendship and love, success and the fear of failure, and, ultimately, about goodness. And for the first time in an Osborne play we are offered not a monologuist and his "feeds" but a real give and take, emotional and intellectual, between a group of people who are all of equal interest to the dramatist. As one critic wrote, it is, "for all its lack of real drama, a strangely hypnotic, amusing and agreeable evening." This is a long way from the walloping cultural shock Osborne administered in *Look Back in Anger*, and it is clear, from his public pronouncements as well as his plays, that the archetypal angry young man has mellowed a little.

West of Suez, which followed in 1971, seemed to most critics a considerable advance in maturity, technical and emotional, over its predecessors. It is set on a Caribbean island, where Wyatt Gillman, an elderly English writer, has exiled himself for tax reasons. His four daughters, three with husbands, the old man's secretary, and two or three others, all more or less resigned and inert, provide a sad microcosm of Western culture in decline. Their precarious dream world is threatened by blundering American tourists, by an insanely destructive young yippie, and ultimately and violently by black nationalism. Gillman himself, a skeptical, ironical, burnt-out case, is as much a symbol of his time and place as Archie Rice had been of his, and the role (brilliantly created by Sir Ralph Richardson) is no less challenging. Around this "towering portrait of spiritual exhaustion" the play is organized with a skill and sustained tension unmatched in Osborne's earlier works. Helen Dawson called it "a brave and loving play" in which the author had "dared to appear reactionary." J. W. Lambert spoke of "the vastly increased resonance with which [the play] expresses the disappointment at the heart of almost all Osborne's work."

In *A Sense of Detachment* (1972) this disappointment seemed for the moment to have extended to the theatre itself. This work has neither plot nor characters. Half-a-dozen actors distribute themselves about the stage and devote the evening to discussions, harangues, songs, and readings which express the author's distaste for the audience, the present state of the drama (with particular reference to Beckett and Pinter), and the even more disappointing state of life in general. Two more actors planted in the audience interrupt with complaints about the banality, ineptness, unpleasantness, and tiresome self-consciousness of what they are watching. Most critics thought these complaints justified.

Osborne wrote in 1957: "I want to make people feel, to give them lessons in feeling. They can think afterwards." He has done so, in a body of work which, for all its self-indulgent errors of tone and balance and shape, its several total failures, has had an emotional impact on the British people and the British consciousness unmatched by any other contemporary dramatist. As Angus Wilson wrote in 1966, "John Osborne's passion saved the British theatre from death through gentility. At a time of uncertain and hovering formal experiment, he has shown that the conventional theatre can still extend its emotional and verbal range beyond what we had any of us hoped. But above all, in an age when the conventional pay lip-service to humanism, he has challenged humanistic hypocrisies by demanding and obtaining a complex compassion for a wide range of the least lovable, least cosy and least glamorous of human beings."

Look Back in Anger and *The Entertainer* have been filmed, both more or less unsatisfactorily, and Osborne wrote the scenario of the movie *Tom Jones*, made by Woodfall Films, of which he is a director. *The Right Prospectus* (1970), his second television play, had a generally cool press but is interesting inasmuch as it is a fantasy. Based on a dream, it is about a middle-aged married couple who return to the pleasures and horrors of school. Osborne has continued to act from time to time, in the theatre, on television, and in the cinema, and he has tried his hand as a director. He was divorced from Pamela Lane in 1957 and has been married three times since then: in 1957 to the actress Mary Ure (Alison in *Look Back in Anger*), by whom he has a son; in 1966 to Penelope Gilliatt, the critic and novelist; and in 1968 to Jill Bennett. Kenneth Tynan has described Osborne as "a rather impenetrable person to meet: tall and slim, wearing his shoulders in a defensive bunch around his neck; gentle in manner, yet vocally harsh and crawing; sharp-toothed, yet a convinced vegetarian." In recent years he has, from time to time, added a moustache and/or a beard to this equipment.

PRINCIPAL PUBLISHED WORKS: Look Back in Anger, 1957; The Entertainer, 1957; Epitaph for George Dillon, 1958; The World of Paul Slickey, 1959; Luther, 1961; Plays for England (The Blood of the Bambergs, Under Plain Cover), 1963; Tom Jones (film script), 1964; Inadmissable Evidence, 1965; A Patriot for Me, 1966; A Bond Honoured, 1966; Time Present *and* The Hotel in Amsterdam, 1968; The Right Prospectus (television play), 1970; Very Like a Whale (television play), 1971; West of Suez, 1971; Hedda Gabler (adaptation), 1972; The Gift of Friendship (television play), 1972; A Subject of Scandal and Concern (television play), 1972; A Sense of Detachment, 1973; A Place Calling Itself Rome (adaptation of Shakespeare's Coriolanus), 1973; The Picture of Dorian Gray (adaptation of Wilde's novel), 1973.

ABOUT: Allsop, K. The Angry Decade, 1968; Banham, M. Osborne, 1969; Brown, J. R. Theatre Language: A Study of Arden, Osborne, Pinter and Wesker, 1972; Carter, A. John Osborne, 1969; Current Biography, 1959; Hayman, R. John Osborne, 1968; Kershaw, J. The Present Stage, 1966; Kitchin, L. Drama in the Sixties, 1966; Lumley, F. New Trends in 20th Century Drama, 1967; Maschler, T. (ed.) Declaration, 1957; Taylor, J. R. The Angry Theater, 1962; Taylor J. R. (ed.) Look Back in Anger: A Casebook, 1968; Trussler, S. The Plays of John Osborne, 1969; Wager, W. (ed.) The Playwrights Speak, 1967; Wellwarth, G. E. The Theatre of Protest and Paradox, 1964; Who's Who, 1973; Who's Who in the Theatre, 1972. *Periodicals*—Commonweal October 18, 1963; Encounter December 1957, August 1966; Guardian August 12, 1971; Hudson Review Fall 1959; London Magazine April 1957; Modern Drama September 1967; New Statesman January 19, 1957; October 12, 1957; August 4, 1961; June 17, 1966; New York Times Magazine October 27, 1957; New Yorker March 25, 1961; December 19, 1964; Newsweek February 24, 1958; Observer July 7, 1968; Partisan Review Winter 1959, Winter 1964; Saturday Review July 27, 1957; Theatre Arts December 1957; Time October 14, 1947; Tulane Drama Review Winter 1962; Twentieth Century July 1956, January 1957.

OSTROFF, ANTHONY (November 9, 1923–), American poet, short story writer, and critic, writes: "I was born in Gary, Indiana, moved to Chicago at about age two and, a year and a half later, to Aurora, Illinois, where I lived until college age. My father, short, broad, intense, was a Russian immigrant, a man of great intelligence and of violent passion and temper. He was largely self-educated, possessed of remarkable bits of

ANTHONY OSTROFF

knowledge separated by broad (but often broad-minded) gaps of ignorance. A stern disciplinarian with a dogged sense of Old World family tradition, he never really adjusted to his twentieth century New World family. He was a frustrated artist—a terrible perfectionist who gave up a promising career as a young violinist after hearing Heifetz perform, and never again took up his instrument except briefly, to woo my mother who had been a professional pianist in the Scandinavian countries before they met. He made his living as a first rate photographer.

"My mother, blonde, blue-eyed, sensitive, bewildered by the violence and frustration of the man she had married, worked more than dutifully in both studio and home, raised her children (I have a sister two years younger than I), and suffered migraine headaches. Danish by birth and a great beauty, she was loved and admired by everyone—to the despair of my father who had few friends of his own.

"I grew up between the strategies of my parents in their perpetual, desperate war—cold, wounded silence on one side, furious, wounded thunder on the other. Almost from the beginning of coherent memory, I wanted to be a writer.

"As a child, and through adolescence, I found my greatest (or at least my most consistent) pleasures in the worlds of fiction, which filled me with high romance and a fine sense of mission: I would add to them. But when my father would see anything I had written he would angrily tell me that I couldn't write about what I didn't know —I must live a long time, see life, before I could write worthily—and this always dashed my hopes for speedy success (and, not just incidentally, the freedom it would surely bring). To hasten things, I hopped freights, worked on farms, in steel factories (as soon as I was old enough), and played piano in dives. As a sixteen-year-old beginning freshman I spent weekends wandering the streets of Chicago all night, assiduously 'learning about life.' When World War II came, I enlisted at once: no writer could afford to miss it! And that was the end of childish things.

"What does one say of three years in the army?

"After the bomb had been dropped, in August of 1945, I was discharged. Then several hungry months in New York, back briefly to Northwestern University for a B.S., to New York again and various jobs, in publishing, radio, advertising. All seemed hollow. I decided the only honest living I could make would be teaching. I went to Michigan for my M.A. While there I married Miriam Border, who has been astonishingly patient and loving ever since. In the fall of '49 I took a job at the University of California at Berkeley, which has continued to the present. (Time off for good behavior: a year in France, a half year in Mexico, a visiting teaching year at Vassar, a free semester in Berkeley, another in Los Angeles.)

"What to say of the teaching years so far? Nothing, in a place like this—except that luckily (save for getting writing done) there *were* the students.

"To speak of these years as writing years is another thing. I wrote as I could steal the time to write, in the early fifties began to publish stories and poems in literary journals. But there was never time to write enough: I was a timid thief. Or perhaps, worse yet, for the purpose that matters most to me, I was not a thief at all.

"I look back on my academic career with some irony, for I thought as a boy that I might, at the advanced age of forty or so, turn to university teaching which seemed to me a fitting occupation for old men. It seems that I have reversed the order of my careers. I find that I have only now reached the point at which I have seriously begun the work I have most wished to do. Perhaps I was reluctant to try it earlier, perhaps I have been learning how to do it all this time. In any event, nothing seems more important now—which eases everything."

Reviewers of Ostroff's *Imperatives* were in broad agreement about his technical ability, finding his verse spare and epigrammatic, neatly rhymed, and orderly in its meters. Nor was there any question about the emotional balance of these "bittersweet" poems, their ease in a variety of modes and on a variety of subjects. But there unanimity broke down, each reviewer reacting according to his conception of what poetry should be. While Cecil Hemley welcomed "a fine geniality," a coherence which struck him as the product of much reading and much thought, and reminded him of Herrick, Robert Creeley was irritated by what seemed to him mere expertise, arrived at with no thought at all. *Time*'s reviewer found vision as well as precision, allowing that Ostroff appears at first merely an observer, but suggesting that "with the resolution of each poem, it becomes evident that he is above all an epistemologist, tirelessly examining the nature of understanding, endlessly checking the value of knowledge." Harvey Shapiro cannot believe that Ostroff "has yet put his full weight behind a poem or committed himself to one entirely," and this, if it is true, may explain the ragged critical response to his first book.

The poet is the son of Anthony and Anna (Nielsen) Ostroff. At Berkeley, where he is Professor of Speech, he has narrated movies for the university's film production service, and served as a panelist, lecturer, director, and performer for local radio stations. He was the editor of *The Contemporary Poet as Artist and Critic*, a kind of panel discussion in book form, in which contemporary poets apply their critical talents to the work of their colleagues. Ostroff has received Avery Hopwood awards in fiction (1948) and criticism (1949), the Borestone Mountain Poetry Award (1957) and a Robert Frost Fellowship in Poetry (1958), among other awards. In 1950–1951 he did postgraduate study at the Sorbonne and the University of Grenoble as a Fulbright Fellow. He and his wife, whom he married in 1948, have one son.

PRINCIPAL WORKS: Imperatives (poems), 1962; (ed.) The Contemporary Poet as Artist and Critic: Eight Symposia [by] Leonie Adams [and others], 1964.
ABOUT: Contemporary Authors 7–8, 1963; International Who's Who in Poetry, 1972–1973. *Periodical*—Time October 5, 1962.

***OTERO, BLAS DE** (March 15, 1916–), Spanish poet, was born in the industrial city of Bilbao, where his "defenseless, schoolboy childhood" he later remembered as a time of rain and restriction, "gray wet nightfalls. Forbidden joys." He received his secondary schooling in Madrid with the Jesuits. There the "joyful days of confused adolescence" soon turned with the Civil War to "days of hunger, scandals of hunger." He took a degree in law, and began another in the humanities, though he did not complete the course.

In a poem about the years just after the Civil War, "1939–1942," he speaks of "a slow death piercing life slowly, slowly." His struggle to

*ō tā' rō

BLAS DE OTERO

preserve his religious faith in the face of so much horror is the theme of his first book, *Cántico espiritual* (1942), whose title recalls the "Spiritual Canticle" of St. John of the Cross. Otero has chosen never to reprint these metaphysical first poems, and he published nothing after them for eight years. Meanwhile he earned his living as a teacher, mostly in Bilbao, "city full of churches and brothels. . . . Blessed city full of stigmas, infested with adulteries and indulgences."

Despite his long silence, Otero was already well known in Spanish literary circles when his next books appeared: two volumes of poems, many of them sonnets and most of them traditional in form, but jagged in their rhythms and violent in their imagery. There are despairing love poems to a God who has abandoned him to death, others which evoke a deep personal conflict between human love and eroticism, and some that reflect Otero's growing awareness of being part of "an uprooted generation. Men with no destiny but to prop up the ruins." According to J. M. Cohen, "the primary influence is . . . that of the tough and questioning Miguel de Unamuno." The first of these two collections, *Angel fieramente humano* (An Angel Fiercely Human, 1950) would almost certainly have received the 1950 Adonais Prize but for its rebellious political and religious questionings; the second, *Redoble de conciencia* (Drumbeat of Conscience, 1951), won the Boscán Prize. The two books are brilliantly fused in a later volume, *Ancia* (1958).

From the existential despair of these poems, with their sense of personal separation from both divine and human love, Otero turned deliberately in his later work to an increasingly overt social and political commitment. In *Pido la paz y la palabra* (I Ask for Peace and a Chance to Speak, 1955) Otero aligns himself with the working class in poems which Cohen has called "monotonously angry" and sometimes "fragmentary and ill-organized." The book is the first volume of a proposed quartet whose second part, *En castellano* (In Castilian, 1960) also "contains only flashes of authentic poetry"; in it Otero writes: "Formerly I was—they say—an existentialist./ I say that I am a co-existentialist." The quartet's third and so far most successful volume, *Que trata de España* (Which Treats of Spain, 1964), contains some splendid impressions of the Spanish countryside and lyrics in the popular tradition.

In these later poems Otero has deliberately addressed himself not to Jiménez's "immense minority," but to the common man. Poetry, he says, must become an instrument—hammer and scythe—in the struggle for peace and social justice. Accordingly he has exchanged the closed and sonnet forms of his early books for looser rhythms in brief lyrics which sometimes resemble folk songs. All the same, he has never succeeded in capturing the working-class audience he seeks, at any rate in Spain—presumably because his verse, threaded with dark images and irrational juxtapositions reminiscent of surrealism, is seldom as simple as he intends it to be. Moreover, for all his hopeful affirmations of faith in future generations, his own deep metaphysical distress remains: "Others will come. They will see what we have not seen. / But now I do not know, up to the elbows in shadow, / what we are living for, or why we were born."

In the 1960s Otero published two collections: *Esto no es un libro* (This Is Not a Book, 1963), which builds earlier poems referring to people and places into a new poetic structure, and *Expresión y reunión* (Expression and Reunion, 1969). The latter is a selection from his work between 1941 and 1969, and includes material from three unpublished works, two of poetry and one of prose. These new books speak of Cuba and China as well as Spain, and serve as a reminder that Otero has become a truly international figure. He has lived in Cuba and has traveled throughout the Communist world; his work is widely translated. Yet he remains deeply Spanish, obsessed, in love and horror, with his country. His poetry often draws upon the masters from Cervantes to Machado, and is full of traditional rhetorical devices. Despite his commitment to the Socialist struggle, he is seldom a merely polemical poet: he cannot disregard "the need to write, that I patiently bear as one of the many calamities of my life."

Otero, "a quiet, slow man," is married. He is well known for his readings of his own verse, especially in France and the Socialist countries. He played an important part in the ceremonies which marked the death of Antonio Machado in 1959.

PRINCIPAL WORKS IN ENGLISH TRANSLATION: Twenty Poems, tr. Hardie St. Martin, 1963; Baland, T. (compiler) Miguel Hernández and Blas de Otero: Selected Poems, 1972. *Poems in* Cohen, J. M. (ed.) Penguin Book of Spanish Verse, 1960.

ABOUT: Alarcos Llorach, E. La poesía de Blas de Otero, 1966; Alonso, D. Poetas españoles contemporáneos, 1952; Cano, J. L. Poesía española del siglo XX, 1960; Castellet, J. M. Un cuarto de siglo de poesía española, 1966; Curley, D. N. and Curley, A. Modern Romance Literatures (Library of Literary Criticism), 1967; Grigson, G. (ed.) Concise Encyclopedia of Modern World Literature, 1963; Ley, C. D. Spanish Literature Since 1939, 1962; Mantero, M. Poesía española contemporánea, 1966; Penguin Companion to Literature 2, 1969; St. Martin, H. *Introduction to* Twenty Poems, 1963. *Periodicals*—Encounter February 1959; Insula June 1968; Mercure de France April 1964; Papeles de Son Armadans August 1966; Poetry February 1966.

OWEN, ALUN (DAVIES) (November 24, 1926–), Welsh dramatist, was born at Menai, North Wales, the son of Sidney and Ruth (Davies) Owen. During his early childhood he spoke only Welsh. He began to learn English when he started school and in 1934 the family left Wales and moved to Liverpool, where he attended Oulton High School. "Liverpool and Wales," he has said: "they're the two things I really know, and yet I'm not completely at home in either." He left school at fifteen and began his career soon afterwards in Perth, Scotland. Owen, who had begun to write at thirteen or fourteen, was looking for a job in journalism. The local newspaper had nothing for him but directed him to the Perth Repertory Theatre, where he soon found himself employed as an assistant stage manager.

Thereafter, from 1942 until 1957, Owen worked in the theatre whenever he could—preferably as an actor, but sometimes as an assistant stage manager or scene painter, and for a time as straight man to the comedian Arthur Askey. In 1945 he did his war service as a "Bevin Boy" miner and when theatrical work was scarce he earned his living as a waiter in Paris, a lorry driver, or a warehouse hand. In 1952 he settled in London, where he was beginning to get roles in films and television, and discovered that his Welsh accent was an asset in the West End theatre. He was never a leading actor, but he built up a richly varied experience which stood him in good stead when he began to write seriously, and contributed a great deal to his immediate success as a dramatist.

Owen's first play, *Two Sons*, which was broadcast by the British Broadcasting Corporation's Third Programme in 1957, deals eloquently with the conflict between two brothers, both sailors, and their bullying father. It was followed by two plays written simultaneously in 1957–1958.

The Rough and Ready Lot, staged in June 1959, studies a group of British mercenaries fighting in South America shortly after the American Civil War. Their advance is blocked by a monastery commandeered by the enemy as a fortress, and the conflict turns on whether or not it should be destroyed. Morgan, the fanatical Welsh atheist, knows that it must; O'Keefe, an equally fanatical Irish Catholic, knows that it must not. The others are less simply motivated and it is one of these, the indecisive, uncommitted Kelly, who survives the action and leads his army to victory. "The battle between Catholic and Atheist is one of particular importance to me," Owen said, "and one in which I was very much involved at the time of writing the play. I wanted to work it out for myself in dramatic terms, but of course I couldn't because there's no ready-made answer, so both had to die in the end while the simple and ordinary survived." *The Rough and Ready Lot* is the most tightly plotted of all Owen's plays, and was welcomed by most critics as the work of a new dramatist of great promise.

Less successful but in many ways more characteristic of Owen's work was *Progress to the Park* (1958), which deals in very different terms with a very similar theme—the cost in human terms of absolute commitment to any set of religious or cultural values. The play is set in contemporary Liverpool and tells the simple story of two young lovers from different religious backgrounds who try but fail to transcend the prejudices of their parents. The reviewers were impressed by Owen's ear for dialogue and his talent for rhetoric, but objected that most of the action is confined to the second half of the play—that the first act is choked with almost aimless dialogue. John Russell Taylor, who has been one of Owen's most articulate champions among the British critics, concedes the point but argues that the desultory conversations in the first act effectively establish the atmosphere of Liverpool and the temper of its people. And this, he says, is the play's intention—to explain people who can only be understood when their environment is understood.

Owen, who says that he never set out to write for television, took naturally to a medium so perfectly equipped to convey the subtle and intimate interplay of character at which he excels. His first television play was *No Trams to Lime Street* (1959), which develops and extends the theme of *Two Sons. After the Funeral* and *Lena, Oh My Lena* followed in 1960, completing a trilogy of plays about working-class life in Liverpool, and bringing Owen an award as the best scriptwriter of the year. Another prize-winning

ALUN OWEN

play, *The Rose Affair* (1961), is a faintly surrealistic parable which must have puzzled those who had categorized Owen as a semidocumentary dramatist of the "kitchen sink" school. Television has become Owen's favored medium and he is firmly established as one of the best of Britain's many fine writers in that field. His television dialogue, wrote one reviewer, "is like involuntary undressing. His characters are as if mesmerised—and therefore mesmeric." That was in 1968, when no fewer than five of Owen's plays appeared on television within a month.

He has not abandoned the theatre, however, and his recent stage works include his Liverpool musical *Maggie May* (1964), with music by Lionel Bart, *A Little Winter Love* (1963), a moving and sharply observed drama about conflict in a red-brick university, and the comedy *There'll Be Some Changes Made* (1969). Owen has also written two notable films, Joseph Losey's *The Criminal* (1960), and the Beatles' movie *A Hard Day's Night* (1964).

In 1965 J. W. Lambert expressed the feeling of many British critics about Alun Owen when he said that he was "in theory one of our most interesting dramatists" but implied that his plays were weakened by "an over-riding sense of indirection." John Russell Taylor believes that such critics miss the point—that Owen regards human beings as the largely helpless products of their environment, incapable of the kind of development which shapes the well-made play. He is concerned instead to illustrate what he sees as insoluble conflicts, in order to reveal the nature of the people trapped in these dilemmas and the societies which formed them. To this task, Taylor says, Owen brings a marvelously "acute ear for English as it is really spoken," a mastery of atmosphere, and a range which "seems potentially wider than that of almost any of his contemporaries."

Owen was married in 1942 to Theodora O'Keefe, who is a stage designer, and they have two sons. His hobbies are languages and history. He lives in London but has a farm in North Wales where he writes and relaxes.

PRINCIPAL PUBLISHED WORKS: The Rough and Ready Lot, 1959; Three T.V. Plays (No Trams to Lime Street, After the Funeral, Lena, Oh My Lena), 1961; Progress to the Park, 1961; The Rose Affair, *in* Taylor, J. R. Anatomy of a Television Play, 1962; Maggie May, 1964; A Little Winter Love, 1964; George's Room, 1968; Shelter, 1968. ABOUT: Contemporary Authors 7–8, 1963; Taylor, J. R. Anger and After, 1963; Who's Who, 1973; Who's Who in the Theatre, 1972.

PACK, ROBERT (May 19, 1929–), American poet, critic, editor, and writer of children's books, was born in New York City and educated there at the Ethical Culture School. He went on to Dartmouth College (B.A., 1951) and Columbia University (M.A., 1953). Pack was on the faculty of Barnard College from 1957 to 1964, and since then has taught at Middlebury College in Vermont, where he is an assistant professor of English.

ROBERT PACK

Some of his poems were collected as "The Irony of Joy" in *Poets of Today II*, published in 1955. His first book of verse, *A Stranger's Privilege*, appeared in 1959 and received wide critical attention in the United States and, especially, in Britain. It was suggested indeed that, "in his feeling for the texture of the language, in his restrained imagery, in the construction of his poems, [Pack] is much more like an English than an American poet." A second collection, *Guarded by Women*, followed in 1963, and the volume *Selected Poems* has appeared in England.

John Engels has called Pack "a skillful poet who writes economical, direct, and highly formal poems from a painful sense of time, of loss, and of separation from the world and himself," the best of whose work "is finally successful by reason of the controlled quietness with which it proposes, and realizes, a violent theme, achieving thereby a superior kind of irony." In many of Pack's poems, the violence of which Engels speaks breaks suddenly out of a dark animalistic past into the apparent security of the poet's home and family circle. In other poems, critics have observed a certain "muzziness," a tendency to become "overly descriptive, adjectival." But, as Judson Jerome says, Pack "does not overwork this vein" and the reader "wakes up when he becomes tougher, knuckly with sound and meaning." The 1969 collection *Home From the Cemetery* included a number of comic poems and satiric fables and others which, as one critic wrote, show "a startling new inwardness in poems that speak convincingly in the persona of a weasel or a stone."

Wallace Stevens was generally welcomed as an able and instructive introductory study, though many critics objected to what was seen as an attempt "to extract a philosophy from the poetry." The book was re-published in 1968. Pack has also written several very agreeable nonsense stories in verse for children, and has served as co-editor of two anthologies of modern verse, one of them devoted to religious poetry.

Robert Pack has lectured on poetry at the YMHA in New York, at the New School for Social Research, and (on several occasions) at the Bread Loaf Writers' Conference. He spent a Fulbright fellowship year in Italy in 1956–1957, and has also received an award from the National Institute of Arts and Letters for creative work in literature (1957), and a Borestone Mountain Poetry Award, first prize (1964). He serves as poetry editor of the magazine *Discovery*. Pack has been married twice, in 1950 to Isabelle Miller and in 1961 to Patricia Powell. He has one son. His great interest in music, and especially in opera, is reflected in *Mozart's Librettos* (1961), a trilingual text prepared in collaboration with Marjorie Lelash.

PRINCIPAL WORKS: *Poetry*—The Irony of Joy *in* Poets of Today, II, 1955; A Stranger's Privilege, 1959; Guarded by Women, 1963; Selected Poems (England only), 1965; Home From the Cemetery, 1969; Nothing But Light, 1972. *Criticism*—Wallace Stevens: An Approach to His Poetry and Thought, 1958. *As translator*—(with Marjorie Lelash) Mozart's Librettos, 1961. *As editor*—(with Donald Hall and Louis Simpson) New Poets of England and America, 1957; (with Donald Hall) New Poets of England and America, Second Selection, 1962; (with Tom Driver)

Poems of Doubt and Belief: An Anthology of Modern Religious Poetry, 1964; (with Marcus Klein) Short Stories, 1967. *For children*—The Forgotten Secret, 1959; Then What Did You Do, 1961; How to Catch a Crocodile, 1964.

ABOUT: Contemporary Authors 1–4, 1st rev., 1967; Leary, P. and Kelly R. (eds.) A Controversy of Poets, 1965; Ward, M. E. and Marquardt, D. A. Authors of Books for Young People, 1967.

PACKARD, VANCE (OAKLEY) (May 22, 1914–), American sociological writer and journalist, was born in Granville Summit, Pennsylvania, one of the three children of Philip Joseph and Mabel (Case) Packard. His father was farm supervisor at Pennsylvania State College, and Vance Packard grew up in the town of State College, attending both high school and college there. As a student majoring in English, he spent much of his free time writing for and editing school publications. After taking his B.A. degree in 1936, he held a job briefly as a reporter for a local paper and the following year earned his master's degree at Columbia University's Graduate School of Journalism.

Packard's career in newspaper work included four years, from 1938 to 1942, as a feature writer with the Associated Press in New York City, where he was mainly occupied with "pulling together trends." Then joining the Crowell-Collier Publishing Company, he served for more than a decade as staff writer for the *American Magazine*. During this time Packard, who had earlier lectured at the Columbia School of Journalism, conducted classes in magazine writing at New York University. He also wrote two books. For the first, *How to Pick a Mate*, published in 1946, he collaborated with Clifford Rose Adams, a specialist in marriage counseling. His second book, *Animal IQ: The Human Side of Animals* (1950), gave a popular account of tests and experiments in animal psychology.

The latter book exemplifies the qualities that brought Packard notable success as a magazine writer—an engaging style, an eye for a vivid anecdote, and a knack for making factual information entertaining. By the time of the publication of his first major book, *The Hidden Persuaders* (1957), he had sold more than one hundred and fifty articles to national magazines—handling a massive variety of topical subjects, but gradually acquiring, as he has said, "the specialty of social sciences and human behavior."

In *The Hidden Persuaders* he examined the application in advertising and public relations of socio-psychological techniques—devices like "subliminal projection," developed by motivational research groups. It was the first in a series of best-selling books whose general purpose was to make his readers aware of the effect on their lives of new and often pernicious social pressures. This intention was

VANCE PACKARD

explicit in the title of his ambitious 1959 study of class stratification in the United States, *The Status Seekers: An Exploration of Class Behavior in America and the Hidden Barriers That Affect You, Your Community, Your Future.*

Packard proceeded to an indictment of American marketing and production methods as promoting consumption for the sake of consumption in *The Waste Makers* (1960), and then surveyed the big-business rat race in *The Pyramid Climbers* (1962). *The Naked Society* (1964) is an exposure of the methods used to invade privacy by prying government and business interests, *The Sexual Wilderness* (1968) is a hostile assessment of the "permissive" society, and *A Nation of Strangers* (1972) studies the implications of the extreme mobility and rootlessness of contemporary American society.

If Packard were pressed to accept any one label, he would probably prefer that of social critic. Quite often opinionated and indignant, and sometimes bemused, he has stepped on many professional toes. The very persons he is said to offend—such as experts in the communications industry and marketing, big businessmen, and investigators—have bought his books no less eagerly than the laymen whom he particularly addresses. Reviews of his work in sociological journals tend to be resentful of a crusading journalist who so profitably harvests the fruits of scholarly research, and he has sometimes been accused of using his sources selectively to strengthen his case.

His clip-and-file or scissors-and-paste reportage, however, has been defended about as often as it has been ridiculed. Comments on *The Status Seekers* in *Social Education* (October 1959), for example, included the observation that while Packard "does not attempt to burrow through esoteric intellectual tunnels, . . . he has made a real contribution to society by familiarizing thousands of readers with the important findings" of many highly reputable scholars. "His real value," William Barrett remarked in the *Atlantic Monthly* (April 1964), "has not been as a scientist, but as a publicist alerting the public conscience to some of our worst social habits."

Packard is a man of medium build, with blue-gray eyes and brown hair. His home in New Canaan, Connecticut and his property on an island near Martha's Vineyard provide plenty of opportunities for do-it-yourself work—one of his few hobbies. His wife, the former Mamie Virginia Mathews, whom he married in 1938, has taught art in a Connecticut school. They have three children, Vance Philip, Randall Mathews, and Cynthia Ann. Packard belongs to the Congregational Church and serves on the publicity committee for Christian Social Action of the National Council of Churches.

PRINCIPAL WORKS: (with C. R. Adams) How to Pick a Mate, 1946; Animal IQ: The Human Side of Animals, 1950; The Hidden Persuaders, 1957; The Status Seekers: An Exploration of Class Behavior in America and the Hidden Barriers That Affect You, Your Community, Your Future, 1959; The Waste Makers, 1960; The Pyramid Climbers, 1962; The Naked Society, 1964; The Sexual Wilderness, 1968; A Nation of Strangers, 1972.

ABOUT: Celebrity Register, 1963; Contemporary Authors 11–12, 1965; Current Biography, 1958; Who's Who, 1973; Who's Who in America, 1972–1973. *Periodicals*—Nation January 28, 1961; New York Times Book Review May 3, 1959; March 15, 1964; Newsweek October 3, 1960.

***PAGNOL, MARCEL (PAUL)** (February 25, 1895–), French dramatist, film maker, and memoirist, was born in a suburb of Marseilles, Aubagne, where his father, Joseph Pagnol, was the school superintendent. The family is descended from Spanish swordsmiths who fled from Toledo during the Inquisition. Pagnol, who was supposed to follow his father's career, studied at the Lycée Thiers in Marseilles and received his teaching diploma from the faculty of letters at the University of Montpellier.

At sixteen, while he was still at the *lycée*, Pagnol and some of his friends launched a literary magazine called *Fortunio*, which survived as *Les Cahiers du Sud*. It published Pagnol's early poetry, a novel called *La Petite Fille aux yeux sombres* (The Little Girl With Sad Eyes), and a four-act verse play, *Catulle*, which he had audaciously but unsuccessfully submitted to the renowned Théâtre Français.

Pagnol began his career in 1915 at a school in Tarascon, but was drafted almost at once into the army, and served with the infantry until 1917. He returned to Provence and during the next five years taught at Pamiers, Aix-en-Provence, and Marseilles, writing in his spare time. A play, *Tonton*, was staged in Marseilles but attracted little attention; no more did his novel *Pirouettes*, published in 1922. In that year, hoping to fare better in the capital, Pagnol secured a post as teacher of English at the Lycée Condorcet in Paris. Two plays written in collaboration with Paul Nivoix received some critical approval in 1925 and 1926, but closed rapidly. Pagnol persisted, however, and had a minor success with his own play, *Jazz*, produced at the end of 1926.

* pa nyôl′

It was his next play which established him. *Topaze* is a farcical comedy about a scrupulous schoolteacher whose honesty costs him his job. Employed by a corrupt businessman, thoroughly disillusioned, *Topaze* abandons morality and ends as a more ruthless and successful tycoon than his employer. The play, which demonstrates the mastery of stage technique that Pagnol had acquired during his long apprenticeship, has some interest as a comment on the breakdown of values after World War I, and, such considerations apart, is superb entertainment. It opened in Paris in October 1928, ran there for two years, was adapted for Broadway (1930), and was filmed several times.

Marius, written in 1928 and produced in 1929, introduced the characters and the setting which have made Pagnol famous. It tells the story of Fanny, a Marseilles fishmonger; Marius, who loves her but also the sea; and his father César, who operates a Saroyanish café on the Marseilles waterfront. *Marius* was an immediate and triumphant success, and gave Pagnol the confidence to abandon teaching and devote himself to writing. *Fanny*, a sequel, was presented in 1931, and *César*, originally written as a film, followed in 1936. This trilogy, full of the sounds and sights of the Marseilles waterfront, of the ordinary problems and extraordinary talk of the people who live there, has carried Pagnol's name all over the world, and has been adapted and re-adapted into every conceivable medium. "*Topaze* satisfies our sense of justice and amuses us," wrote Marcel Achard, but the characters in the Fanny trilogy are "our friends for life."

In 1930 Pagnol had seen his first talking picture; it was a revelation from which he never recovered. "What we see on the stage today," he declared, "are relics of another age." He was equally contemptuous of the silent cinema, and of those connoisseurs who continue to maintain that the film is a purely visual medium. In 1931 he launched his magazine *Cahiers du Film* to preach a revolution, calling for a theatrical cinema relying not on elaborate sets and camera work, but on straightforward action and strong dialogue delivered by great actors.

What he proposed, in effect, was an adaptation of the traditions of French classical theatre to the freedom offered by the movie camera.

Pagnol set about learning his new craft with characteristic thoroughness, studying direction, camera technique, laboratory processes, publicity, and distribution. In 1931 he wrote for Alexander Korda a film version of *Marius* (which was also filmed in Hollywood, Sweden, and Germany), and in 1932 turned *Fanny* into a screenplay for Marc Allégret. *Topaze* was screened the same year, with Louis Jouvet in the title role. All three movies are still frequently revived.

By 1933 Pagnol was no longer content simply to write films. He opened his own studios near Marseilles and made a series of adaptations of stage plays, with himself as writer, director, and producer, with cameramen trained according to his theories, and actors recruited from the Comédie Française. Critics and public alike found the results too static and Pagnol was forced to realize that the stage could not supply him with the stories he needed. In 1934 he began his fruitful collaboration with the Provençal novelist Jean Giono and, dealing once more with the southern scenes and people he understands so well, created a number of films now recognized as classics: *César* (1936), starring Raimu, Pierre Fresnay, Charpin, and Orane Demazis; *Regain* (*Harvest*, 1937), which starred Fernandel and Orane Demazis and received the New York Film Critics' award as the best foreign film of 1939; *La Femme du boulanger* (*The Baker's Wife*, 1938), starring Raimu; and *La Fille du puisatier* (*The Well-Digger's Daughter*, 1940), with Raimu and Fernandel.

Pagnol fought during World War II alongside some of his leading actors. His first film after the war was *Naïs* (1945), adapted from Zola's novel about a hunchback's hopeless love for a beautiful young girl. Archer Winston said that "Pagnol, in that quiet bucolic manner of his, is again exploring the heartaches that can torture unattractive, simple people. He persistently widens the areas of sympathy and human understanding." Among the other notable films Pagnol has made since the war at his superb modern studios near Marseilles are *La Belle Meunière* (1948), based on the life of Franz Schubert and shown in the United States as *The Miller's Daughter*; another version of *Topaze* (1950); and his adaptation of Daudet's *Lettres de mon moulin* (1954). His play *Judas*, staged in 1955, was an idiosyncratic version of the biblical story which was not much liked.

In 1946 Pagnol was elected to the French Academy, a unique honor for a film maker, all the more remarkable in that his delight in slang and dialect might be supposed unwelcome to an institution dedicated to preserving the purity of the French

MARCEL PAGNOL

language. Pagnol has written extensively on the art of the cinema and has translated *Hamlet*, *A Midsummer Night's Dream*, and the *Bucolics* of Virgil. His *Souvenirs d'enfance*, a nostalgic account of his childhood in Provence, was received with great enthusiasm by the critics and the public. The first two volumes, *La Gloire de mon père* and *Le Château de ma mère*, appeared in 1957 and have been translated in one volume as *The Days Were Too Short*; the third volume, *Le Temps des secrets* (1960) was translated as *The Time of Secrets*.

Pagnol has two sons and a daughter by his 1916 marriage to Simone Collin, and two sons by his second wife, the actress Jacqueline Bouvier, whom he married in 1945. The writer, still ruggedly handsome, is a man of much geniality and charm. He likes to read and translate the classics, to play *boule*, and to hunt rabbits. He shares Daudet's delight in windmills and owns several.

PRINCIPAL WORKS IN ENGLISH TRANSLATION: Fanny (text of the musical by S. N. Behrman and Joshua Logan), 1955; Topaze, tr. by Renée Waldinger, 1958 (also tr. by Anthony Rossi in 1962, by Tom Van Dycke in 1966); The Days Were Too Short (autobiography), 1960; The Time of Secrets (autobiography), 1962.

ABOUT: Current Biography, 1956; International Who's Who, 1973–1974; Knowles, D. French Drama of the Inter-War Years, 1967; Smith, H. (ed.) Columbia Dictionary of Modern European Literature, 1947; Who's Who, 1973; Who's Who in America, 1972–1973; Who's Who in France, 1973–1974. *Periodical*—Livres de France March 1964.

PAINTER, GEORGE D(UNCAN) (June 5, 1914–), English biographer, writes: "I was born in Birmingham, an unreal city in the English Midlands, ugly and black to outsiders, but to natives

GEORGE D. PAINTER

and exiles beautiful and haunting, navel of the labyrinth of place and time. Wandering alone in a public park there at the age of six towards a dead tree which I never reached, I had a moment of vision, a sense of personal identity and the reality beyond appearances, that marked me for life. I am still walking towards that dead tree. My father was a musician and singer (Rutland Boughton wrote the part of Eochaidh in *The Immortal Hour* for him), and became a schoolteacher of English; my young mother was an artist, and became a housewife. They gave me, and my sister Lorna and brother Allan, holidays in tents in Devon and Cornwall, reading, and solitude. I was taught to teach myself at King Edward's School, Birmingham, and at Trinity College, Cambridge, where I studied classical Greek and Latin literature, supporting myself with scholarships. In 1938 I joined the staff of the Department of Printed Books at the British Museum, London, where since 1954 I have been in charge of books printed in the fifteenth century. The Museum has more than ten thousand of these incunabula, the largest and finest collection in the world. In 1942 I married my cousin Joan, a stepdaughter of my father's brother. We have two daughters, Charlotte and Louise.

"In the fatal years 1937 to 1942—fatal for everyone in the world as well as for me—I read English, French and American romantics, and tried to write poems, some of which were later published as *The Road to Sinodun*, in plain English that rhymed and scanned. At this time, but never since, I thought (or rather, it really happened) that I was haunted by a *doppelgänger*, a wraith of myself, sometimes friendly, sometimes violently hostile; or I had momentary glimpses of eternity, truth, God. I don't know what these things are, but I still dimly remember what they feel like. These experiences, the deepest of my life excepting marriage, had the unexpected effect of making me a biographer, instead of the novelist or poet I had thought I wanted to be. The creations, minds, and lives of my favourite writers were, I now saw, far more interesting to me than my own; and most interesting of all was the mysterious relationship between these creations and these minds and lives.

"During a bout of influenza in 1947 I first read a volume of Proust's letters, and found in them the very people and situations in his actual life that reappear transformed to the level of high art in *À la recherche du temps perdu*, which I have read incessantly since the age of fourteen. I resolved to write his biography in order to explain him to myself, little knowing that the task would demand eighteen years: six years of preliminary research and thinking, and twelve of writing. I am now engaged in a life of Chateaubriand—another great writer whose work is a symbolic autobiography—which will perhaps take as long; shall I live to write another? But I feel that literary biography, to be worthwhile, should be on this scale, and take as long as this to complete. Ellman's *Joyce*, Marchand's *Byron*, Newman White's *Shelley*, are biographies of the kind that I have tried to write.

"It is true of every great writer that his works are formed by the same inner tensions that underlie his life; his books are complex living acts, his life is a work of art that includes his books. If the great writers of the past were human beings communicating with living words, not semantic computers emitting verbal algebra, then biography is an essential preliminary and part of criticism. 'A man's life of any true worth is a continual allegory,' said Keats, who believed in what it is temporarily fashionable, in our age of sterile anti-criticism, to call the biographical heresy. In this faith will I live and die."

In the course of his brilliant academic career at Cambridge, Painter carried off three scholarships, including the Porson and the Waddington, and was Bell Exhibitioner, Craven Student, and a classical medalist. He graduated with first class honors in both parts of the Classical Tripos, and taught Latin for a year at Liverpool University before he went to the British Museum.

It is interesting that his "heretical" faith in biography as a tool of criticism was expressed, in terms very like those he uses above, in his first book. This was his study of André Gide, which most critics found a well-written and extremely useful introduction, rather more successful as biography than as criticism. The new edition published in 1968 contained important additional material. His book of poems was published in 1951, without attracting much attention.

Painter's reputation stands on his biography of Marcel Proust. The first volume appeared in 1959, dealing with Proust's life up to the death of his father in 1903; the second and last volume followed in 1965. Painter believes that *À la recherche du temps perdu* is not a work of fiction but "a creative autobiography." Using the letters of Proust and his friends, memoirs of the period, and every available scrap of primary material, he builds up a minutely detailed account of the novelist's life, and a Freudian interpretation of it based on Proust's powerful but ambivalent feelings for his mother. Painter goes on to show—event by event, person by person—how that life was transformed into a great novel, which in turn provided the author with a sense of fulfillment life at first hand never gave him.

The book naturally provoked the New Critics, one of whom in the *Times Literary Supplement* denied "that the discovery of the originals of the characters can have any bearing on our valuation of the novel." There were others who felt that, though the book recorded everything known and almost everything knowable about Proust, it nevertheless failed to bring the man alive. It remains for many people one of the finest of contemporary literary biographies, the magnificent product of great erudition and of "imaginative sympathy, love and cool-thinking." Raymond Mortimer said that "no biography has ever before thrown so much light on the making of a masterpiece." It received the Duff Cooper Memorial Prize. Painter has also published a number of translations of modern French writers, including Gide and Proust.

George D. Painter was married in 1942 to Joan Britton. He enjoys family life, walking, gardening, travel, and music, and is interested in medieval art. He has been a Fellow of the Royal Society of Literature since 1965.

PRINCIPAL WORKS: André Gide: A Critical and Biographical Study, 1951 (rev. 1968); The Road to Sinodun (poems), 1951; Marcel Proust (U.S., Proust), two vols., 1959 and 1965; (with R. A. Skelton and T. E. Marston) The Vinland Map and the Tartar Relation, 1965.

ABOUT: Who's Who, 1973. *Periodicals*—Encounter October 1965, February 1966; Nation October 3, 1959; New Statesman September 19, 1959; July 9, 1965; New York Review of Books November 25, 1965; New York Times Book Review November 7, 1965; June 23, 1968; Observer July 11, December 19, 1965; Réalités August 1966; Times Literary Supplement November 13, 1959; August 5, 1965; Washington Post November 7, 1965; Year's Work in French Studies 1965.

***PALAMAS, KOSTES** (January 13, 1859–February 27, 1943), Greek poet, dramatist, and critic, was born in Patras, the son of a magistrate. Orphaned

* pa′ lə məs

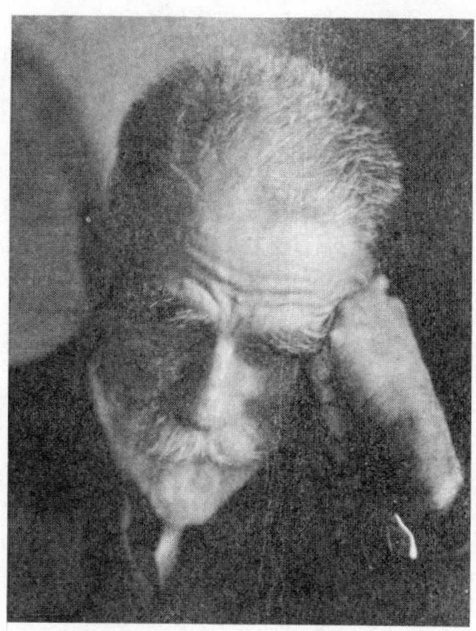

KOSTES PALAMAS

at the age of seven, he was brought up by an uncle in Missolonghi, center of Greece's nineteenth century struggle for independence from Turkish rule, in which his family had played a prominent role. In 1875 Palamas went to Athens to study law, but left the university without a degree to embark upon a career as a journalist, critic, and writer.

His long lifetime spans the period of a modern renaissance in Greek literature. One of the greatest poets of this renaissance, Palamas was also one of its pioneers and leaders. When he first arrived in Athens, he found himself involved in the fierce and sometimes physically violent controversy between the classicists, who strove to write "in the style of Xenophon," the written language of the educated classes that had survived for fifteen centuries, and those who championed the cause of the demotic tongue, the living language of the people. Palamas threw in his lot with the latter, saying: "To write as we speak: a light-hearted, thoughtless beginning, source of evils. To write the spoken language as it should be written: here is the beginning of the correct way." He became the most influential figure in the movement, which eventually triumphed when the government decided to introduce demotic textbooks into the schools.

Meanwhile, Palamas had quickly established a reputation as an original and sympathetic critic, able to bring to the discussion of Greek writing an extraordinarily broad knowledge of European literary, philosophical, and scientific ideas. The influence of French Parnassian and Symbolist trends was evident in his own first volume of poems, *Tragoudia tes patridos mou* (Songs of My Country, 1886), a collection of lyrics evoking the poet's youth in

Missolonghi. The following year he married Maria Valvi, by whom he had three children. It was the death of his youngest child, Alki, which inspired *O Tafos* (1898, translated by D. A. Michalaros as *The Grave*), one of the finest of his early works. It is a cycle of poems in which imagery evoking a child's vision of life is movingly contrasted with the bereaved parent's bewilderment and sense of loss.

In 1897 Palamas was appointed secretary-general of the University of Athens, a post which he retained until his retirement thirty years later. His next major collection was *I Asalefti Zoi* (1904, translated by Aristides Phoutrides as *Life Immovable*), a wide-ranging volume which illustrates the great variety of his interests and technical resources.

This was followed by what many regarded as his masterpiece, *O Dodecalogos tou Gyftou* (1907, translated by Frederic Will as *The Twelve Words of the Gypsy* and by George Thomson as *The Twelve Lays of the Gypsy*). In twelve cantos it tells the Orphic story of a gypsy who comes to decadent Constantinople shortly before the fall of Byzantium. After all kinds of failures, degradations, and false starts, he learns to see beyond the self, beyond the life-denying attitudes of his time, until in the end he is able to accept, and affirm as an Artist, the true nature of life. The philosophy which Palamas advances in this work (and elsewhere) is an odd mixture of Nietzschean ideas and fatalism, involving a cyclic view of life in which man participates in an endless ritual—physical and metaphysical—of birth, death, and rebirth. But the work itself is a virtuoso achievement of headlong lyricism, Byzantine rhetoric, and incomparably bold and dazzling imagery.

Palamas was deeply interested in the demotic traditions of the past—folk poetry and the medieval Byzantine epics, particularly that of *Digenis Akritas*, discovered in 1868. He draws on this and similar works in *I Floghera tou Vasilia* (1910, translated by Frederic Will as *The King's Flute*), an epic about the exploits of the Emperor Basil II, his journey to the Parthenon to worship the Virgin Mary there and to slay numberless Bulgars en route. Here, as in *The Twelve Lays of the Gypsy*, language fuses with the narrative, lending it a powerful irregularity. The epic quality of the work is authentic and deeply embedded, linguistically, emotionally, and philosophically, in the Greek Byzantine past.

The achievement of these two epics was in itself vast, and moreover imparted a new authority and confidence to modern Greek poetry. The richness of post-classical Greek verse was illustrated in them, as were the resources of the language itself. Palamas' later works, including a treatise on poetics and an intellectual autobiography, had great influence in Greece but attracted less international attention. He died in the darkest winter of the German occupation, when public meetings were banned, but news of his death spread from mouth to mouth, and hundreds of thousands gathered for his funeral, encircling the Nazi guns. It is possible to imagine the effect, in such a setting, of Sikelianos' impromptu valediction, which ended: "Let songs of triumph arise, and let fearful banners / Float high and free on the breeze of liberty."

PRINCIPAL WORKS IN ENGLISH TRANSLATION: *Poetry*—Life Immovable, 1919; The Grave, 1930; The Twelve Words of the Gypsy, 1964 (published in another translation as The Twelve Lays of the Gypsy, 1969); The King's Flute, 1966; Three Poems, 1969. *Drama*—Royal Blossom, 1923.

ABOUT: Chalas, A. P. Ta Satyrika Gymnasmata tou Kosta Palama, 1933; Courmouziou, A. O Palamas kai e Epoche tou, 1944; Demaras, K. T. Kostes Palamas, 1947; Jenkins, R. J. H. Palamas, 1947; Karantonis, A. Gyro ston Palama, 1958; Keeley, E. and Bien, P. (eds). Modern Greek Writers, 1972; Palamas, L. K. A Study on the Palm-Tree of Kostes Palamas, 1931; Panagiotopoulos, I. M. Ta Prosopa kai ta Keimena, Kostes Palamas, 1944; Penguin Companion to Literature 2, 1969; Politis, L. A History of Modern Greek Literature, 1973; Sherrard, P. The Marble Threshing Floor, 1956; Smith, H. (ed.) Columbia Dictionary of Modern European Literature, 1947; Thomson, G. *introduction to* The Twelve Lays of the Gypsy, 1969; Tsatsos, K. Palamas, 1936.

***PANOVA, VERA (FEDEROVNA)** (March 20, 1905–March 4, 1973), Soviet novelist, short story writer, and dramatist, was a naturalistic writer in whose work the feminine viewpoint is often prominent. She was born at Rostov-on-the Don. Her father, a bank clerk and a man of some culture, drowned in a boating accident when she was only five, leaving his family in difficult financial circumstances. Panova was forced to go to work in a laundry while still a child, and had little formal education. She nevertheless read whatever she could find and began to write poetry at an early age.

In 1922, when she was seventeen, a relation secured a post for her on a Rostov newspaper. Her early experiences in journalism were utilized many years later in her novel *Sentimentalny roman* (1958), in which she describes the cramped and difficult working conditions of those times, and her complete inexperience. She learned as she went along, serving in turn as an apprentice, a reporter, and (under the pseudonym of "Vera Veltman") a writer of humorous *feuilletons* and sketches. Her work took her all over the Northern Caucasus.

Panova's emergence as a writer was slow. Her first plays, produced during the early 1930s and subsequently published, were rather in the manner of Gorky. These brought her several literary prizes but attracted little general attention. There was more interest in *Devochki* (Girls, 1945), an altogether more individual play about two motherless sisters, evacuated to the Urals and awaiting their father's return from the war. It won a Committee

* pä′ nə və

on the Arts award as the best play for young people on a contemporary theme.

At about this time, finding the dramatic form excessively confining, Panova turned her attention to prose fiction. During the war she had been assigned to an ambulance train to write dispatches and essays about the deeds of wounded Soviet soldiers. Out of this experience she wrote *Sputniki* (1946, translated by Eve Manning as *The Train*). This virtually plotless novel consists of a series of character sketches of the train's personnel—the circumstances that brought them to the work, and the ways in which it affects their lives. These people, drawn with much affection, humor, and insight, are moved by the perennial concerns of humanity: birth, love, and death, the ordinary pleasures and sorrows. Though the novel does no violence to the Soviet orthodoxies (and on this account annoyed some Western reviewers), the "New Soviet Man" is nowhere to be found on Panova's train. The book was published in 1946, received the Stalin prize, and had an immediate and enormous success. The same year Panova was admitted to the Soviet Writers Union.

Thereafter her novels and short stories appeared in fairly rapid succession. *Kruzhilika* (1947, translated by Moura Budberg as *The Factory*) is set in a factory town (probably Molotov in the Urals, where Panova worked as a radio and newspaper journalist in 1944). It is again a series of character sketches, showing how the factory eats into the lives of its director and its workers, or is used by them as an escape from their personal problems. In Russia it was criticized for failing to distinguish neatly enough between "good" people and "bad"; in fact Panova has the ability (possessed by very few writers) to engage the reader's interest in the behavior of ordinary nice people.

Vremena Goda (1953, translated by Vera Traill as *Span of the Year*) implies a parallel between a rebellious young criminal and a corrupt Soviet official. It was sharply attacked by some Russian critics for suggesting that such outrages could go unpunished, or even exist, under the Soviet system, but in England and America it was generally well received, and praised for its skillful characterization and well-observed background. *Vremena Goda* has a moral (that power corrupts) and a relatively dramatic plot. More characteristic of Panova's quiet, compassionate, and gently humorous tone of voice is *Seryozha* (1955, translated as *Time Walked*), a series of stories describing incidents in the life of a little boy. "Within its carefully limited scope," wrote one British reviewer, "this book is a work of art, and profoundly humane." The title story, which poignantly and tenderly conveys the boy's distress when he is uprooted from his home, and his gradual adjustment, was memorably filmed as *A Summer to Remember*.

VERA PANOVA

In *Sentimentalny roman* (Sentimental Story, 1958), the journalist Sevastyanov returns after more than thirty years to his native town in southern Russia, and remembers his defiant and hungry youth, his love affair with a girl incapable of fidelity, and his painful apprenticeship as a newspaperman. A German critic has suggested that the novel is to some extent an "answer" to *Dr. Zhivago* and indeed, though it contains much autobiographical material, it does have parallels with Pasternak's much greater novel.

Panova did not abandon the theatre, and a number of plays written during the 1960s were collected in *Pogovorim o stranostyakh lyubvi* (1969). A reviewer in the *Times Literary Supplement* noted that "her characters inevitably come round to the right [ideological] conclusions" but said that there was more to her work than social optimism: "her great strength [is] a sense of the poetry and glamour of quite ordinary lives at certain moments."

PRINCIPAL WORKS IN ENGLISH TRANSLATION: The Train, 1948; The Factory, 1950; Span of the Year, 1957; Time Walked, 1957 (reissued in 1962 as A Summer to Remember); Yevdokia, 1964; Looking Ahead, 1964; On Faraway Street, 1968.

ABOUT: Alexandrova, V. A History of Soviet Literature, 1963; International Who's Who, 1971–72; Plotkin, L. A. Tvorchestvo Vera Panova, 1962; Who's Who in the USSR, 1965–66. *Periodicals*—New Statesman July 31, 1954; New York Times March 6, 1973; Saturday Review April 30, 1949; Times Literary Supplement June 3, 1969; World Today July 1955.

***PARGETER, EDITH (MARY) ("Ellis Peters")** (September 28, 1913–), English novel-

* pär′ jə tər

EDITH PARGETER

ist, writes: "I was born at Horsehay, Shropshire, the youngest of three children, with no particular literary background to account for me, though I think my mother was a writer lost for want of opportunity. Possibly this Shropshire countryside, set between the Welsh marches and the ancient industrialisation of the Coalbrookdale coalfield, where the Industrial Revolution and the modern world began together, helped to turn my imagination first towards the past, and then by reflection back upon the people round me, the heirs of the past, and helped to determine that story-telling should become my life. This region is teeming with novels waiting to be written.

"I was educated at the local church school and Coalbrookdale County High School, and began to write as soon as I learned how. On leaving school at eighteen I worked at whatever came handiest until I could work full-time at writing. For about five years I was assistant and dispenser in a chemist's shop, and during that time I began to publish both novels and short stories. After the outbreak of the Second World War I wanted to enter one of the women's services, but found that as a dispenser I was in a reserved occupation, so that they could not accept me. I therefore left my job in order to be able truthfully to describe myself as a novelist; and novelists being expendable, I was able to join the Women's Royal Naval Service. Nothing then seemed worth doing that was not directly connected with the war against Nazism. I served in the Signals Department of Commander in Chief, Western Approaches, for five years, ending as a Petty Officer, and in 1944 was awarded the B.E.M. The novels written during my service years, not opportunist works but forced out of me by the pressure of events, had reached a wide public, and after demobilisation at the end of the war I was able to devote all my time to writing.

"I am unmarried, and share a house at Madeley, in Shropshire, with my brother. Shortly after the end of the war I visited Czechoslovakia for the first time, and found country and people so congenial that it has become my second home, and I spend some time there every year. I learned Czech for pleasure, and have published several translations of both prose and poetry from that language, though I still speak it badly. I have travelled in most parts of Europe, and in India, where I have many friends.

"During the last few years I have also been writing crime novels under the name of Ellis Peters. The third of these, *Death and the Joyful Woman*, was awarded the 'Edgar' of the Mystery Writers of America as the best crime novel of 1962. Most of my books under my own name are concerned with contemporary life, and the problems and urgencies of war and peace, and critics have described me, among other things, as 'a forensic novelist of great sincerity and integrity'; but another work is a trilogy set in my own Welsh border country in the thirteenth century. I have also published one volume of short stories, and occasionally broadcast stories or talks in BBC programmes, and readings of translated poetry from Prague Radio in their English service. In 1961 I was elected a Fellow of the International Institute of Arts and Letters, and in 1965 awarded the Gold Medal of the Czechoslovak Society for International Relations, as an acknowledgement of my work in translating from the Czech.

"I wrote with extreme facility when I was younger; I write with increasing labour and pain now. I think this is as it should be. I re-write more and more, discarding whatever cannot be read aloud with pleasure and conviction. Music, which I love, strongly inflects my use of words and the balance of my sentences, and even infiltrates into my plots very frequently. I do not think I have been much influenced by any other writer, nor have I ever wished to discuss, dissect or speculate about the novel, only to read it and write it. I am essentially a professional writer: I profess writing as my calling, I take a pride in it, and I accept the living it returns me, good or bad. I wouldn't have it any other way."

Edith Pargeter is a storyteller of unusual accomplishment, perception, and range. She first attracted attention in 1939 with *The City Lies Foursquare*, a most curious ghost story about an earthbound spirit who discovers, with the long-awaited death of his beloved, that she has "no soul . . . at all." This was followed by *People of My Own*, the story of an ordinary English family between the wars. Margaret Wallace said of it that it was not a major novel "only because Miss Pargeter had no such lofty intention when she set out to write it. We rarely come across a book, particularly from the pen of a writer still in her twenties, which gives us so completely an assurance that the material has been mastered, the precise effect aimed for achieved, the exactly desired shade of emotional response elicited." *The Eighth Champion of Christendom*, Miss Pargeter's trilogy about World War II, has been compared in its scope with the World War I novels of R. H. Mottram and Henry Williamson. A reviewer in the *Times Literary Supplement* wrote of the first volume: "In its genuinely popular style . . . this is a sound and thoughtful piece of story-telling about the so-called ordinary man . . . in England at war."

Miss Pargeter has also written such "forensic" novels as *Soldier at the Door*, probing the feelings of a woman whose son is killed in Korea, and *A Means of Grace*, an attempt to show that life can be lived happily on both sides of the Iron Curtain. Recently, as she says, she has returned to the historical themes which occupied her in her first writings. *The Heaven Tree* trilogy was called "dramatic and intense" and generally praised for its convincing historical detail, although some readers thought the characters were drawn considerably larger than life. As "Ellis Peters," Miss Pargeter achieves a "special atmosphere of freshness and sympathy," an authenticity of background, and a richness of characterization which have earned her comparison with Dorothy Sayers and Marjorie Allingham.

Edith Pargeter reads "anything and everything," likes going to the theatre, and collects phonograph records, particularly of the voice. She lives in rural Shropshire, where her favorite recreation is "walking, preferably with canine as well as human companions."

PRINCIPAL WORKS: Iron-Bound, 1936; Hortensius, 1937; The City Lies Foursquare, 1939; Ordinary People, 1941 (U.S., People of My Own); She Goes to War, 1942; The Eighth Champion of Christendom: The Lame Crusade, 1945; Reluctant Odyssey (vol. 2 of The Eighth Champion . . .), 1946; Warfare Accomplished (vol. 3 of The Eighth Champion . . .), 1947; By Firelight (U.S., By This Strange Fire), 1948; The Fair Young Phoenix, 1948; The Coast of Bohemia, 1950; Lost Children, 1951; Fallen Into the Pit, 1951; Holiday With Violence, 1952; This Rough Magic, 1953; Most Loving Mere Folly, 1953; The Soldier at the Door, 1954; A Means of Grace, 1956; The Assize of the Dying (published in England with Aunt Helen *and* Seven Days of Monte Cervio, in the U.S., with Aunt Helen only), 1958; The Heaven Tree, 1960; The Green Branch (vol. 2 of The Heaven Tree trilogy), 1962; The Scarlet Seed (vol. 3 of the Heaven Tree trilogy), 1963; The Lily Hand and Other Stories, 1965; A Bloody Field by Shrewsbury, 1972. *As "Ellis Peters"*—Death Mask, 1959; The Will and the Deed (U.S., Where There's a Will), 1960; Death and the Joyful Woman, 1961; Funeral of Figaro, 1962; Flight of a Witch, 1964; A Nice Derangement of Epitaphs, 1965; Who Lies Here?, 1965; The Piper on the Mountain, 1966; Black Is the Colour of My True-Love's Heart, 1967; The Grass-Widow's Tale, 1968; The House of Green Turf, 1969; Mourning Raga, 1969; The Knocker on Death's Door, 1970; Death to the Landlords, 1972; City of Gold and Shadows, 1973.

ABOUT: Contemporary Authors 4, 1963; Who's Who, 1973.

"PARKES, LUCAS." *See* "WYNDHAM, JOHN"

PARKINSON, CYRIL NORTHCOTE (July 30, 1909–   ), British historian, satirist, biographer, and novelist, writes: "I was born at Barnard Castle, County Durham, the younger son of an artist who had married a musician. The family moved to York just before World War I, both sons being sent to St. Peter's School. Such talent as I then displayed was in drawing and painting and it was assumed at first that I would follow my father's profession, probably as a marine artist. While at school, however, I turned to history, a change of direction which was confirmed by my father's death in 1927. Two years later I entered Emmanuel College, Cambridge, where I graduated in 1932. My special field of study was naval history, for which the University did not provide. I went on, therefore, to the Royal Naval College, Greenwich, where I assisted for three years in the formation of the National Maritime Museum, simultaneously working for my doctorate in the University of London. In 1934 I published my first book, a biography of Edward Pellew, Viscount Exmouth, Nelson's contemporary and a distinguished Admiral of that period. In 1936 I achieved my Ph.D., the Julian Corbett Prize and a Fellowship at my own College. Back at Cambridge, I specialised in Maritime History, publishing *Trade in the Eastern Seas, 1793–1813* in 1937. At the same period I commanded the infantry unit in Cambridge University Officers Training Corps. By the time of the outbreak of war in 1939 I was teaching at the Royal Naval College, Dartmouth, and could claim to be an authority on the naval side of the Napoleonic Wars. That being so, it might seem odd that my war service should be in the Army, and indeed for some time with the RAF. So it was, however, and by 1945 I was a Major in the Queen's Royal Regiment and appointed G.S.O.II on the General Staff. I was married by that time with two children and had become the owner of Elham Manor in Kent. When the war ended I was chosen as Lecturer in Naval and Maritime History at the University of Liverpool and held that post until 1949.

"Had my first marriage been more successful and had any British University offered me a Professorship in Naval History, I might have devoted the rest of my life to historical work. But frustration

CYRIL NORTHCOTE PARKINSON

and divorce ended that phase of my career. I accepted the Raffles Chair of History at the newly-formed University of Malaya and sailed for Singapore in March, 1950. I thus began what was almost a new life as orientalist and university administrator, the change in direction being coincident with my marriage in 1952 to Ann Fry, journalist, authoress, and descendant of Elizabeth Fry (the Quaker heroine and prison reformer), related also on her mother's side to Anthony Trollope, the Victorian novelist. We lived in Singapore until 1958 and I expected at that time to teach and write history until the age of retirement. Fate decreed otherwise, however, for the politics of Singapore and Malaya made the post untenable. Simultaneously I had published, in 1955, an essay called 'Parkinson's Law.' This turned into a book (1957) which became a best-seller in Britain and U.S.A. After a period as Visiting Professor in the American Universities of Harvard, Illinois and California, I found that my academic career had finished. I had become an author and lecturer, familiar with television and radio and widely known through the translation of my works into some sixteen other languages. I have since lectured throughout U.S.A., and Canada, as also in Germany, Scandinavia, Holland, Austria, and France.

"In 1960 we settled, my wife and I, in the Island of Guernsey, one of the Channel Islands; a group owning British allegiance but within sight of the coast of Normandy. Les Câches House, which we acquired in 1959, dates in part from 1498 and 1595 and the rest from 1720. Almost derelict when we came to live there, Les Câches has been at once restored and modernised, its added features including a small theatre. We have three children, the first two born in Singapore, the last (1960) in Guernsey. We are both active in the affairs of the island and the children divide their energies between ponies and boats. Something of the island life is reflected in *Ponies' Plot* (1965), the first book I have written for children. But while islands are good places in which to live, they are bad places in which to vegetate. We travel, therefore, and are likely to go farther afield after the children have come to depend upon us less. Our wanderings have taken us to Jamaica and Finland, to Malta and Poland, but we hope eventually to see South America, Mexico, Turkey, and Spain. We have nowadays, nevertheless, a base to which we can return.

"Although my works have had a considerable circulation I am no favorite with the critics. I have always, for one thing, been difficult to classify. My career has included too many different phases as journalist and painter, scholar and soldier. My writings vary as widely between history and drama, satire and politics, biography and business, humor and art. Even my historical works swing from economic history to political theory, from the military to the naval, from the West to the East. Were I left a fortune, gaining the freedom to do as I please, I should probably turn once more to painting; a first trade which may yet prove to be my last."

It was his "first trade" as a schoolboy marine artist that turned Parkinson to maritime and naval history, the teaching and writing of which occupied him for so long. By the time he went to Singapore he had already made one reputation as a world authority on naval warfare in the late eighteenth and early nineteenth centuries. In Singapore Parkinson found a new subject when he discovered the paucity of Malayan historiography, and set out to remedy this deficiency.

Parkinson was always confident that he would "succeed in some capacity," and so he did. It has been called ironical that this success should come not to reward his twenty-five years as a historian but as the result of an essay written during a five-day vacation near Bangkok. But that essay had its origin in World War II, when Parkinson was engaged on a secret project manned by an admiral, a colonel, a major, and himself. Captain Parkinson (as he was then) noticed that in his superiors' absence he could handle the project's entire daily work load single-handed in a matter of an hour. This simple observation, pondered over the years, at length achieved the majestic universality of Parkinson's Law: "That work expands so as to fill the time available for its completion." It passed into the English language in 1955, when it appeared in Parkinson's essay in *The Economist*, and into many more languages after 1957, when it was published in book form, accompanied by other salutary observations on bureaucracy. *Parkinson's Law* was called "a series of shockingly improbable assertions which are improbably backed up by incontrovertible evidence. The tone varies from savage glee to coldly amused brutality. The style is faultless, arrogant, didactic."

As Parkinson says, "A sane and logical argument can be disguised as a joke and so become twice as effective." He has used this approach in *The Law and the Profits* (on the theme that, for bureaucrats, expenditure rises to meet income), in *In-laws and Outlaws*, assorted skirmishes against the Organization Men, and in other books; none of them, however, has quite recaptured the unstrained wit and economy of *Parkinson's Law*, and some of them have seemed to some reviewers reactionary, humorless, and even bigoted. The author's views on political and historical cycles are set down in more serious terms in *The Evolution of Political Thought* and *East and West*, which also had mixed reviews—the latter striking some critics as stimulating, others as eccentric and at times inaccurate. Much more enthusiastically received was *A Law Unto Themselves*, containing portraits of eleven people who had influenced Parkinson's life and thought, among them his father, Eric Gill, and Arthur Bryant. G. K. Chesterton, who is not discussed in the book, was also a major influence on Parkinson's ideas and on his colorful and witty literary style. *The Life and Times of Horatio Hornblower* is a long, detailed, and splendidly convincing "biography" of the fictitious naval hero created by the novelist C. S. Forester. *Devil to Pay*, set in the same period, is an entertaining novel about the adventures of a young naval lieutenant.

Parkinson has contributed to *Fortune*, *The Saturday Evening Post*, *The Guardian*, and *The Economist*, as well as to more scholarly journals. He is a member of the French Académie de Marine, the U.S. Naval Institute, and the Archives Commission of the Government of India. On Guernsey he owns the title of Seigneur of Anneville, Mauxmarquis, and Beauvoir. Shepherd Mead, who described a visit to Les Câches House in the New York *Times Book Review* (November 13, 1966), says the author is "heavy-set, of military bearing, but with an unmilitary twinkle of the eye." Parkinson is a member of the Church of England and of the Liberal party, though his economic theories, as expressed in *The Law and the Profits*, seem to place him well to the right of his party. His recreations include oil painting, sailing, badminton, and travel, and he is the author of two plays. Parkinson believes that his sense of humor "must have been innate" but that "ability, though hereditary, is improved by an early measure of adversity, and improved again by a later measure of success." Shepherd Mead calls him "one of the great individualists of our age."

PRINCIPAL WORKS: Edward Pellew, Viscount Exmouth, Admiral of the Red, 1934; Trade in the Eastern Seas, 1793–1813, 1937; Portsmouth Point: The British Navy in Fiction, 1793–1815, 1948; (ed.) Trade Winds, a study of British Overseas Trade During the French Wars, 1793–1815, 1948; (ed.) Samuel Walters, Lieutenant R.N., His Memoirs, edited with an introduction and notes, 1949; Always a Fusilier: The War History of the Royal Fusiliers (City of London Regiment), 1949; The Rise of the Port of Liverpool, 1952; War in the Eastern Seas, 1793–1815, 1954; A Short History of Malaya, 1954; Templar in Malaya, 1954; Marxism for Malayans, 1956; (with Ann Parkinson) Heroes of Malaya, 1956; Parkinson's Law, or The Pursuit of Progress, illustrated by Osbert Lancaster (U.S., Parkinson's Law and Other Studies in Administration, illustrated by R. C. Osborn), 1957; The Evolution of Political Thought, 1958; The Law and the Profits, illustrated by Osbert Lancaster (U.S., illustrated by R. C. Osborn), 1960; British Intervention in Malaya, 1867–1877, 1960; In-Laws and Outlaws, illustrated by Osbert Lancaster (U.S., illustrated by R. C. Osborn), 1962; East and West, 1964; Ponies' Plot (for children), 1965; A Law Unto Themselves, Twelve Portraits, 1966; Left Luggage, 1967; Mrs. Parkinson's Law, illustrated by R. C. Osborn, 1968; The Law of Delay, illustrated by Osbert Lancaster, 1970; The Life and Times of Horatio Hornblower, 1970; The Fur-Lined Mousetrap, illustrated by Michael ffolkes, 1972; Devil to Pay (novel), 1973.

ABOUT: Contemporary Authors 7–8, 1963; Current Biography, 1960; International Who's Who, 1972–73; Parkinson, C. N. A Law Unto Themselves, 1966; Who's Who, 1973; Who's Who in America, 1972–1973. *Periodicals*—New York Herald Tribune Book Review July 6, 1958; New York Times Book Review July 13, 1958; November 13, 1966; New Yorker January 20, 1962; Sunday Times June 8, 1958; Time October 28, 1957; February 29, 1960; August 24, 1962.

***PASOLINI, PIER PAOLO** (March 5, 1922–), Italian poet, novelist, essayist, philologist, translator, and film maker, writes (in Italian): "I was born at Bologna on March 5th, 1922. My father, however, was from Ravenna and my mother from the province of Friuli. So I am one of the many *pastiches* of Italian unity (as for my grandmothers, one of them was a Sicilian and the other was Polish). An uncle, who was called Pier Paolo and who wrote poetry, died at sea at the age of twenty. My mother too wrote poetry as a girl. I began to write at the age of seven—it was a poem dedicated to my mother. I say all these things (which would seem suitable material for a poem by Olson) because the one important thing in my life is to write; nothing else has happened to me or is happening to me. By 'to write' I mean, according to the terminology of the linguists of the school of Saussure, 'to connote.' When I was a youth I 'connoted' through the sign system of painting and now I do so through the sign system of the cinema. What do I connote? My life—which has always been anomalous and filled with vexations (even though I have taken part in sport and dancing). At the age of twenty I was involved in the war around me, and for a year or two ran the risk of ending up 'swas-

* pä sō lē′ nē

PIER PAOLO PASOLINI

tikaed' or hanged or sent to a concentration camp. As soon as the war ended, in the time of flags and euphoria, news reached me of the death of my brother, a partisan. In 1959 my father died, after his return, ill, from a long imprisonment in Kenya. Then for ten, for fifteen, years I endured the wretchedness, which I find it charitable not to dwell upon, of petty bourgeois Italy, of everyday morality. I have paid dearly for my courage (an easy matter for a writer) in 'describing' the lives of the humblest and poorest members of society—and the courage (rather less easy) of criticizing in prose and rhyme the high religious and political authorities of my country. But nothing has ever really been able to sour for me the joy of 'connoting.' There you are; that has been, and is, more or less, my life."

Pasolini, whom some regard as the most notable poet to have emerged in Italy since the war, is an extraordinarily versatile artist and a very controversial one. Educated at the Bologna *liceo*, he began to write verse and illustrate it as a small child. His father was an officer in the regular army, and for much of his early life he lived a rootless existence as the family moved from one army post to another in northern Italy. In the process Pasolini was able to study the many dialects of the region, and developed his passionate sympathy for the poor. At seventeen, impatient with the refined and private language of the dominant hermetic school of poetry, he began to write in Friulan, the language of the north Italian peasants from whom his mother came. His first small book of verse, *Poesie a Casarsa*, appeared in 1942 when he was twenty. By then he had returned to Bologna to study first art, then literature, at the university. He was conscripted into the army at the end of August 1943, only a week before the Italian surrender.

Moving to Friuli, Pasolini became an active Communist, working on behalf of the *braccianti* (day laborers) against their exploiters, the landlords. He was actually a member of the Communist party for only a year (1947–1948), but he was permanently influenced by the Marxist texts he read, and especially by the works of Antonio Gramsci, the leading theoretician of Italian communism. He shares with Gramsci, among other things, a conviction that the socialist artist has a reforming and educational duty, rather than a purely aesthetic one, and must therefore address himself to the masses in their own language.

In 1950 Pasolini went to Rome. After a year of poverty, he became a teacher at a school in Ciampino and lived in Ponte Mammolo, a slum on the outskirts of Rome. It was here that he encountered the Roman *borgate* (subproletariat), whose wretched lives became his principal subject: "Waste paper and dust / the blind breeze dragged here and there; / Impoverished, echoeless voices // of womenfolk come from the Sabine / Mountains or the Adriatic / to camp here with swarms // of worn-out, tough, strident kids / in ragged undershirts / and grey threadbare trousers; // African suns and agitated rains / that turned streets to muddy torrents, / buses sunken in corners // at the end-of-the-line, between / the last stripe of white grass / and some acid, ardent trash heap— // this was the center of the world / just as the center of my story / is the love I bore it." (Translated by Lynne Lawner.)

His first novel, *Il ferrobedò*, appeared in 1951, but it was his second that made his name. *Ragazzi di vita* (1955, translated as *The Ragazzi*), is a record of life in the Roman slums, centering on a group of youths as they grow up between the war and 1950. They have been reduced by poverty and indifference to a condition less than human. They are pitiless, vicious, and voracious, caring for nothing but drink, gambling, and sex (heterosexual or homosexual), and living by crime until they meet their violent and arbitrary deaths. A series of loosely connected sketches, with the detached and matter-of-fact realism of a news report, the book made no concessions to Italian complacency. The life of the *ragazzi* is shown to be hopeless and meaningless, and their vile dialect is freely reported. Émile Capouya's translation, appearing in the United States thirteen years later, attracted little attention, but in Italy in 1955 the book caused a national furor and led to Pasolini's prosecution for obscenity. A similar kind of public uproar has greeted many of his subsequent works.

Una vita violenta (1959, translated by William F. Weaver as *A Violent Life*) is a more coherent study of another slum boy, Tommaso, who in the end is able to transcend his environment through his faith in communism. The novel is by no means merely a political tract, however, and the English version was widely praised for its powerful realism and subtle characterization. Here, as in *The Ragazzi*, Pasolini makes no direct authorial comment, but indirectly emphasizes the impermanence and arbitrariness of the lives he describes by drawing attention to the permanence of the city itself. "His achievement is to invest Tommaso with some dignity," wrote one critic, "without glossing over his stupidity and violence."

Meanwhile Pasolini had published four more volumes of verse, including his best-known collection, *Le ceneri di Gramsci* (The Ashes of Gramsci, 1957). This work (from which the quotation above was taken), received the Viareggio Prize. Believing as he does that the artist's first duty is communication with the masses, Pasolini, even when he is not writing in dialect, favors a diction with some of the qualities of prose—a "rational and historical language" that can support a rational and often a Marxist argument, expressed however with passionate force and in hauntingly evocative imagery. Raleigh Trevelyan says, "there is something omnivorous in the way his poems cover such various and contrasting fields of experience and comprehension. None of the younger poets in Italy can match him in content or technique." Elena Croce agrees that Pasolini "has attempted stylistic and metrical innovations of far greater interest than anything we have seen lately in the field of Italian verse," but finds his social indignation vitiated by sentimentality and what she calls "aesthetic acrobatics."

From 1955 to 1958 Pasolini edited the influential avant-garde magazine *Officina*. It was obliged to cease publication as a result of the outrage caused by Pasolini's poem to the dying Pope Pius XII, in which he said: "How much good you could have done! And you / didn't do it: / there was no greater sinner than you." Meanwhile, Pasolini was making a new reputation as a film scenarist, and a few years later, in 1961, he began to write and direct his own films.

His early films, *Accattone* (1961) and *Mama Roma* (1962), were, like his novels, socialist studies of the Roman slums. By 1964, when he made *The Gospel According to St. Matthew*, Marxism (though he has not rejected that ideology) had ceased to be sufficient: "My film is a reaction against the conformity of Marxism. The mystery of life and of death and of suffering—and particularly of religion—is something which Marxists do not want to consider." The film is a wonderfully simple and direct translation to the screen of the Gospel, acted mostly by peasants in the desolate landscape of southern Italy. At the Venice Film Festival, where it received several awards, Pasolini was mobbed and physically attacked before the film began, but cheered at the end of it. Cardinal Feltin has said that "no other religious film resembles this one—in which Christ is restored in all his humanity, in all his divinity."

Another film of great importance in Pasolini's development as an individual and artist was *Edipo Re* (1967), said to be a working-through of his own Oedipal relationship with his parents. At about the same time he wrote several verse plays, one of which, *Affabulazione*, is also largely autobiographical. He has expressed his views on the drama in *Manifesto for a New Theatre*. Pasolini regards his film scenarios as an important part of his literary output, and all of them have been published.

His recent poetry, collected in *Poesia in forma di rosa* (Poetry in the Form of a Rose, 1964), *Poesie* (1970), and elsewhere, tends to be less violent and indignant than his earlier work, more personal and reflective. Pasolini published four more novels during the 1960s, *Donne di Roma* (1960), *Il sogno di una cosa* (1962), *Ali dagli occhi* (1965), and *Teorema* (1968). He is extremely interested in philology and semiology (the science of signs and symbols), and applies these techniques to the study and criticism of the theatre, the cinema, and the other arts. His literary essays have been collected in *Passione e ideologia* (1960), *La poesia popolare Italiana* (1960), and *Empirismo eretico* (1972), and he has edited two anthologies of Italian popular verse. He also finds time to write a weekly column—on politics, the arts, or anything else that interests him—for *Tempo Illustrato*.

"Pasolini has two souls," Pietro Bianchi says, "one mad, damned, riotous, malicious; the other mild, tranquil, charitable, full of compassion for his fellow man. But it's his first that puts him in the limelight . . . agitates polemics, motivates his incredible, inexhaustible vocation for scandal." Pasolini's "vocation for scandal" (if that is what it is) is not limited to his writings. He has, for example, been accused of helping a gangster to escape arrest and of an attempted gas station hold-up. Pasolini is a lean dark man with an air of nervous intensity. He is deeply attached to his mother, who has appeared in some of his films, notably as the mother of the adult Christ in *The Gospel According to St. Matthew*.

PRINCIPAL WORKS IN ENGLISH TRANSLATION: A Violent Life, 1968; The Ragazzi, 1968; Oedipus Rex: A Film, 1971. *Poems in* Barnstone, W. (ed.) Modern European Poetry, 1966; Golino, C. (ed.) Contemporary Italian Poetry, 1962; Trevelyan, R. (ed.) Italian Writing Today, 1967.

ABOUT: Anzoino, T. Pasolini, 1973; Current Biography, 1970; Dizionario enciclopedico della letteratura italiana, 1967; Dizionario universalle della letteratura contemporanea, 1961; Ferretti, G. Letteratura e ideologia, 1964; International Who's Who, 1972–73; Mariana, G. La giovane narrativa italiana tra documento e poesia, 1962; Penguin Companion to Literature 2, 1969; Pullini, S. Il romanzo italiano del dopoguerra, 1960; Stack, O. Pasolini on Pasolini, 1969; Who's Who, 1973; Who's Who in America, 1972–1973. *Periodicals*—Corriere del Ticino April 24, 1943; Guardian March 6, 1969; New York Times April 10, 1966; Screen May–June 1969.

"PATRICK, Q." *See* WHEELER, HUGH CALLINGHAM

***PAULHAN, JEAN** (December 2, 1884–September 10, 1968), French critic, essayist, and story writer, wrote (in French): "I am now more than eighty years old. This is perhaps more than I deserve. But I am surprised to see how delightful it is to grow old: delightful and even interesting. A host of feelings come to you which until then seemed the pure invention of writers, falsehoods. I could do nothing better than recommend old age first to all literary critics, and then to all men for whom I feel sympathy, friendship, affection; and finally to *all* men, with four or five exceptions (if I had no hatreds, there would be something wrong, I suppose, with my loves).

"Having passed through various examinations and competitions (*licence*, etc.) that bored me greatly, I decided in 1907 to go and live in China. Chinese, which I studied for four years, seemed to me to be a valuable language, inasmuch as it combines drawing, literature, calculation, history, and other disciplines (like arithmetic or philosophy) which it is discouraging to study. But China, in the long run, didn't want me, whereas Madagascar offered me a position as teacher (and even as headmaster, deputy headmaster, and bursar) of the *lycée* at Tananarive, which had yet to be created.

"I therefore created this *lycée* and taught there for three years, and then looked for gold in the Ikopa. Unfortunately, this experience made me realize that I was not cut out for teaching, or for gold prospecting. But I collected some very curious popular poems (more logical than sentimental), based on frameworks of proverbs, which led to my being called back to Paris to teach Malagasy at the School of Oriental Languages.

"Then came the 1914 war. Well, I didn't show any great talent for war, which I spent first as a sergeant in a Zouave regiment (wounded on the Marne), then as an airplane spotter, and finally as a driver of military cars. Without great success.

"Why all the deceptions? It always seemed to me that a teacher—for instance—must say a little more than he knows; and even that, things being as they are, no one acts or speaks without some sort of falsehood.

"In 1925 I became editor of the *Nouvelle Revue Française* and remained there until 1940. I wrote quite a few books, each of which had between seven hundred and two thousand readers. This appears to me to be quite a respectable number, although my publishers have not always been of this opinion. (But it is true, as the Chinese hold, that the publisher is some sort of saint, who sacrifices himself in order to bring some truths into men's understanding, and then dies ruined.)

"Of these books, some are simple tales, rather sad, like *La Guérison sévère*, *Aytré qui perd l'habitude*, *La Métromanie ou les dessous de la capitale*, *Les Causes célèbres*. The others, in which I outline a new logic based on the chatter in the streets and electoral proclamations, are called: *Entretiens sur des faits-divers*, *Les Hain-tenys malgaches, poésie obscure*, *Les Fleurs de Tarbes*, and *La Conscience à midi* (where I think I was able to educe the reason and at the same time the remedy for my literary problems). The disappointments of writing sent me back to painting and drawing: I wrote some brief essays on painters I admire: *Braque le Patron*, *L'Art informel* (Klee, Wols, Michaux), *La Peinture cubiste*, *Fautrier l'enragé*. I also contributed to various journals, and founded three or four myself: *Le Spectateur* (1909), *Les Lettres Françaises* (a clandestine journal, 1942), *Les Cahiers de la Pléiade* (1948). As for the short stories and essays mentioned above, they are not at all as boring as one might imagine from this summary."

* pō lăɴ

Jean Paulhan was the son of Frédéric Paulhan, a philosopher, and the former Jeanne Thérond. He was born and educated at Nîmes, and went on to the Lycée Louis-le-Grand and the Faculty of Arts in Paris, where he received his *licence*. It was in 1912 that he returned from his adventurous years in China and Madagascar to teach at the National School of Living Oriental Languages in Paris. His first book was his collection of Malagasy popular poems *Les Hain-Tenys Merinas* (1913). (The Hain-Tenys collection mentioned above is another, later, volume.)

This early book showed that Paulhan already possessed the interest in language and meaning which characterized all his work. Another abiding interest, in psychology and especially abnormal psychology, was evident in the short novels he began to publish during World War I, among them *Le Guerrier appliqué* (The Dedicated Warrior, 1915), *Le Pont traversé* (The Crossed Bridge, 1921), *La Guérison sévère* (The Cruel Cure, 1925).

After the war, in which Paulhan earned the Croix de Guerre, he joined the staff of the *Nouvelle Revue Française* and in 1925 he succeeded Jacques Rivière as editor of that journal, for many years the most important in France. Here, and as chief literary adviser to the great publishing house of Gallimard, his influence was enormous. He abominated banality of thought and expression and was a leader and champion of the avant-garde, numbering among his friends Jarry, Apollinaire, Claudel, Gide, Artaud, Valéry, Michaux, and innumerable other makers and breakers of literary tradition.

After the mid-1920s Paulhan turned increasingly but not exclusively to criticism, first literary, then artistic. As his note above suggests, he did not consider himself a successful writer, and for many years he was esteemed as the *éminence grise* of modern French literature rather than as an author in his own right. His best-known book is *Les Fleurs de Tarbes* (The Flowers of Tarbes, 1941), in which he worked out his views on the relationship between language and thought, and attacked the theory that a writer is the prisoner of his language. Discussing it in the *Partisan Review*, one critic said that his manner was "somewhat pixyish; he circles around his problems, delicately sticking pins into other people's balloons but hardly doing much else." *Clef de la poésie* (Key to Poetry, 1944) is another study of the philosophy of language.

In World War II Paulhan joined the Resistance movement. On one occasion he was arrested by the Gestapo, and he earned the Médaille de la Résistance for his work on *Les Lettres Françaises*, the clandestine review he founded with Jacques Decour, and in other capacities. In 1945 he received the Grand Prix de Littérature of the Académie Française and in 1951 the Grand Prix of the City of Paris. With Marcel Arland he revived the NRF in 1953, but it never regained its former authority. However, an issue of *Cahiers des Saisons* in 1957 devoted several articles to his work and showed that his entire achievement, as a writer as well as an editor, was earning recognition as "one of the richest and most original of our time." In 1963 he was elected to the Académie Française, and at about the same time the publication of his collected works began. In March 1968, not long before his death, Marc Slonim wrote that "one of the most curious events of French literary life in the last months has been the growing fame of Jean Paulhan as a writer."

Slonim says that Paulhan's novels and stories, "whether psychological, or symbolic, or philosophical, are always written in an elegant, subtle prose; and the author insists on an absolute unity of words, ideas, and acts. Most often they are strongly erotic." Paulhan wrote a serious study of the Marquis de Sade, and on one occasion half acknowledged authorship of the grave sadomasochistic sadistic fantasy *The Story of O*. With this possible exception none of his books has yet been translated into English. Paulhan was revered, Slonim says, "as a man of rare intelligence, erudition, talent and taste, as a smasher of idols, a merciless critic of clichés, and an enemy of mediocrity." He was married twice: to Saloméa Prussak in 1911 and to Germaine Dauptain in 1933. He had two sons by his first marriage. He disliked publicity, and once told Marcel Proust that the height of misery for him was "to be in evidence."

JEAN PAULHAN

PRINCIPAL WORKS IN ENGLISH TRANSLATION: *Essays and excerpts in* Liebling, A. J. Republic of Silence, 1947; O'Brien, J. An Image of the Twentieth Century (from Nouvelle Revue Française), 1958; Sewanee Review April 1945.

ABOUT: Boisdeffre, P. de. Une Histoire vivante de la littérature d'aujourd'hui, 1958; Judrin, R. La Vocation transparente de Jean Paulhan, 1961; Lefebvre, M.-J. Jean Paulhan: Une Philosophie et une pratique de l'expression et de la réflexion, 1949; Penguin Companion to Literature 2, 1969; Toesca, M. Jean Paulhan, 1948; Who's Who in France, 1967–1968. *Periodicals*—Cahiers des Saisons April–May 1957; French Review April 1958; New York Times October 11, 1968; New York Times Book Review March 24, 1968; Partisan Review July 1951.

***PAUSTOVSKY, KONSTANTIN (GEORGIEVICH)** (May 10, 1892–July 14, 1968), Russian memoirist, short story writer, novelist, and dramatist, was born in Moscow. His most remarkable work is his six-volume autobiography, *Povest o zhizni* (The Story of a Life, 1946–1964), which traces, on a broad epic canvas swarming with incidents and characters, the great events through which he lived from the turn of the century to the early 1930s. In its first volume, *Dalekiye gody* (1946, translated by Manya Harari and Michael Duncan as *Story of a Life: Childhood and Schooldays*) his early life emerges through a series of sketches and stories about his extensive family.

He grew up in Kiev, where his paternal grandfather, a Ukrainian oxcart driver descended from

* pōō stof′ skē

KONSTANTIN PAUSTOVSKY

the legendary Zaporozhian Cossacks, told him tales among the yellow pumpkin blossoms and the beehives, at a safe distance from the house and his termagant of a Turkish wife, who smoked, in her short clay pipe, more than a pound of strong black tobacco a day. His other grandmother, a tall old Polish woman, always wore black in permanent mourning for the suppression of the 1863 Polish revolt.

Paustovsky's father, despite his sober job as a railway statistician, is presented as an incorrigible dissenter and dreamer who encouraged his son to write. After throwing up his job and getting heavily into debt, he left his now impoverished wife and children for a young girl, and finally, after much wandering, died of cancer on an island in a flooded river. His dramatic death forms the first chapter of the book, whose structure is an artistic, not a chronological, one. Paustovsky's mother, "a domineering and severe woman," moved back to Moscow with her two elder sons and her daughter, and ended broken by her husband's desertion and her daughter's blindness. Paustovsky stayed behind in Kiev to complete his high school course, paying his way by coaching the children of wealthy families. He began writing while still at school, and his first story was published in 1911.

The second part of Paustovsky's autobiography, *Bespokoynaya yunost* (1955, translated by Harari and Duncan as *Slow Approach of Thunder*), deals with the period of World War I. The Russian title actually means "Restless Youth," and it was with the outbreak of the war that Paustovsky began his long years of wandering. Too nearsighted to join the army, he nevertheless left Kiev University and for the next fifteen years moved from one job to another and from one end of Russia to another in an unceasing quest for new and varied experience. He was a tram driver in Moscow, then a medical orderly on a hospital train and later with a field unit. With the army in disorderly retreat there were epidemics, chaos, and starvation. The nurse whom Paustovsky loved died of smallpox in the mud, filth, and horror of a disease-stricken Byelorussian village; he himself, lying wounded in a hospital, read, on a grease-stained sheet of newspaper which had been wrapped round a piece of cheese, that both his brothers had been killed on the same day.

Paustovsky was dismissed from the hospital service for writing a humorous letter about the Czar's visit to the front. He became a factory worker in the Donbas, a fisherman in Taganrog on the Sea of Azov, and then a journalist in Moscow. On an assignment to a Central Russian village he heard of the outbreak of the February Revolution and saw the joy of the country people, desperately war-weary and hoping that a miracle would now happen.

But as he says at the beginning of the third volume, *Nachalo nevedomogo veka* (1956, translated by Harari and Duncan as *In That Dawn*), the Kerensky government failed to provide that miracle, the war dragged on, and the idyllic mood of the first days of the revolution soon passed. Narrowly escaping execution by the Bolsheviks, who mistook him for a sniper, Paustovsky heard Lenin addressing mutinous soldiers and witnessed the crushing of the revolt of the Left Socialist Revolutionaries. Most of the large private houses in Moscow were taken over by the anarchists, and Paustovsky was imprisoned in one as a Bolshevik spy; but when the Bolsheviks stormed the house he was arrested as an anarchist. He made his way to Kiev to join his mother and sister and was caught up in the struggle of the Whites, nationalists, anarchists, and Reds for the Ukraine, being conscripted first by the nationalists and later by the Bolsheviks. Finally he reached Odessa and witnessed the evacuation of Denikin's defeated Whites. A different translation by Joseph Barnes of these first three books was published in a single volume in 1964 as *The Story of a Life*.

The fourth volume, *Vremya bolshikh ozhidanii* (1959, translated by Harari and Andrew Thomson as *Years of Hope*) is about Odessa in 1921, during the first days of Soviet rule with the Allied blockade of the city still in force. It contains some of Paustovsky's most brilliant writing, jaunty and flippant in the style of Babel or Ilya Ilf—Odessa writers with whom Paustovsky became close friends. Amidst the destitution and anarchy, the unreconstructed individualists of this most cosmopolitan of Russian cities devised all sorts of colorful stratagems for survival, rather like Ilf and Petrov's famous picaresque hero, Ostap Bender. The author himself avoided starvation with the help of an enterprising friend who provided his journalist companions with jobs and ration cards by installing them in one of the newly opened government offices, where they masqueraded as civil servants. Paustovsky helped to revive a periodical called *Moryak* (The Seaman) which was printed on old tea-chest wrappers, since no other paper was available, and which quickly developed into a vehicle for the Odessa school of writers and poets, with Babel as their greatest contributor. Paustovsky finally left on a Black Sea voyage on a leaky old tramp steamer, in search of copy.

Brosok na yug (1960, translated by K. Fitzlyon as *Southern Adventure*) is an account of the time that he spent in the Caucasus during the early 1920s. The book captures in vivid sketches all the color and exoticism of the region, with its startling discrepancies between the old patriarchal way of life with its traditional blood feuds and the new Soviet bureaucracy. In Tbilisi, the capital of Georgia, he fell romantically and hopelessly in love with a Polish girl, but she did not return his affection and finally left him. After this Caucasian intermezzo Paustovsky returned to his travels in Russia in *Kniga skitanii* (The Book of Wanderings, 1946), working as a journalist first on ROSTA and later on the railway workers' newspaper *Gudok* (The Whistle).

During the 1920s Paustovsky increasingly turned from journalism to writing on his own account. His first published book, *Morskiye nabroski* (Sea Sketches, 1925), is a collection of impressions of Odessa and other places along the shores of the Black Sea. His numerous early stories, and the novels *Romantiki* (The Romantics, 1935), begun in 1916 and finished in 1923, and *Blistayushchiye oblaka* (Shining Clouds, 1929) are in a strongly romantic vein, full of extravagant colors, melodious sounds, and startling metaphors. He writes about exotic lands far away beyond the sea, inhabited by romantic idealists—sea captains who refuse to accept the drabness of reality, writers and artists guarding their ideal inner worlds, lovely unhappy women, and beautiful girls with strange destinies.

These stories, in which harsh reality is contrasted with the infinitely varied worlds of man's imagination, have remained very popular with children. However, Paustovsky has described how in 1929, after a visit to a planetarium, he experienced a feeling of revulsion against his own early work: "We left the planetarium in the early evening. It was a dry October; there was a smell of fallen leaves on the street. And suddenly, as if for the first time, I saw above me the enormous, *living* sky ablaze with stars. . . . It was as if the black autumn air intensified the blazing of the firmament. And I felt that almost everything I had written before that evening was as artificial as the sky in the planetarium with its fake constellations. . . . After that evening I burnt some of my more extravagant and pretentious stories."

Paustovsky did not completely abandon the lyrical tone of his early work; instead he gave his romantic impulse a new direction and sought "the extraordinary in the ordinary," in the challenge of contemporary life. He found the proper form for his subsequent work in a unique kind of long tale, constructed as Vera Alexandrova says "of a series of seemingly independent and almost complete fragments, which are unified by a common theme and by the unexpectedly revealed connection, across decades, between the characters." Thus the past re-echoes in the present, creating a sense of continuity from generation to generation.

The first of his works in this form was *Kara-Bugaz* (1932, translated as *The Black Gulf*), the violent history of a gulf and desert island east of the Caspian Sea rich in the important mineral Glauber's salt. *Sud'ba Sharlya Lonsevilya* (The Fate of Charles Lonceville, 1933) combines the history of one of Russia's oldest steelworks with the romanticized biography of a young French officer who had become stranded in Russia after Napoleon's invasion. *Kolkhida* (Colchis, 1934) is an account of the reclamation of subtropical swamplands, and *Chernoye more* (The Black Sea, 1936) was envisaged as an "artistic encyclopedia" of the Black Sea coast, from the ancient Greeks to the mutiny on the battleship Potemkin.

Povest o lesakh (Tale of the Woods, 1948) opens with Tchaikovsky living in a remote forest and working on a new symphony, while a young girl sits listening on the step outside, and it ends with her daughter more than half a century later. Another dominant theme in this story is that of nature; in the 1930s Paustovsky settled in Central Russia, a region that provided the setting for most of his mature work, which includes nature descriptions unsurpassed in Soviet literature, and in which the style is simple, with the words pruned to an irreducible minimum after the example of Babel. He has also written historical and biographical stories and plays, about writers such as Pushkin and Lermontov.

During World War II Paustovsky was a war correspondent at the southern front, and some of his stories have the war as a background, though their tone does not otherwise differ from that of his other writing. One work which stands rather apart from the rest of his output is *Zolotaya roza* (1955, translated as *The Golden Rose*), a semi-autobiographical book about the making of literature. It opens with a story of a man who earns a living by sweeping Paris shops and who over several years sifts enough gold from the dust of a goldsmith's shop to make a precious rose for the girl he loves.

This "golden rose" becomes for Paustovsky the symbol of the work of the writer, who accumulates in his memory a multitude of minute impressions which are transmuted into the finished work of art.

But Paustovsky's major postwar work was his autobiography. In writing this vast memoir Paustovsky had not really abandoned his short-story technique, for each episode or portrait is complete and self-sufficient. The whole work is, however, unified by the personality of the author, and by a single underlying theme—the gradual breakup of his family and his increasing loneliness as he enters a world of portentous and continuous change. As Marc Slonim has said, Paustovsky "constantly and intentionally opposes two worlds: that of war, destruction, fear, and violence, with that of joy and happiness, creativeness, enrichment and love." Several critics have pointed out that (as one wrote in the *Times Literary Supplement*) "his narrative has something of that human warmth and that blend of sympathy, understanding, gentle humor and an occasional touch of angry satire which one associates with some of the best pre-revolutionary writing." For younger writers, Paustovsky's masterpiece stands as a great bridge across the gulf torn in Russian literature by the Stalinist era.

Paustovsky was married twice but had no children of his own, only a stepdaughter by his second marriage. For over ten years he ran a seminar for young writers, and his anthology *Tarusskiye stranitsy* (1961, translated as *Pages From Tarusa*) includes stories and poems mostly by young writers who, like himself, had country homes in the small town of Tarusa, an artists' and writers' colony on the Oka river south of Moscow. The liberalism of this collection, and its championship of classic Russian literary values, made it one of the cultural sensations of the Khrushchev era. Paustovsky invariably supported liberal views and opposed bureaucratic philistinism, successively supporting Dudintsev, Daniel and Sinyavsky, Solzhenitsyn, and Yuri Galanskov when they were under attack. Before his death he was one of the most revered figures in Soviet literature, and his works remain enormously popular. He received the Order of Lenin in 1967. He was virtually unknown abroad until his memoirs began to appear in translation in the 1950s and 1960s, but these rapidly won him wide international acclaim, and led to the publication of his stories in many foreign periodicals and collections.

PRINCIPAL WORKS IN ENGLISH TRANSLATION: The Black Gulf, 1946; Selected Stories, 1949; The Flight of Time (stories), 1955 (Moscow); The Golden Rose, 1961; The Story of a Life (tr. Joseph Barnes), 1964; Story of a Life (tr. Manya Harari and others), Vol. 1: Childhood and Schooldays, 1964; Vol. 2: Slow Approach of Thunder, 1964; Vol. 3: In That Dawn, 1967; Vol. 4: Years of Hope, 1968; Vol. 5: Southern Adventure, 1969. *Miscellaneous*—Reminiscences of Babel *in* Blake, P. and Hayward, M. Dissonant Voices in Soviet Literature, 1962; A Few Words about Babel *in* Babel, I. You Must Know Everything: Stories 1915–1937, 1970; *excerpts from* The Golden Rose *in* Field, A. (ed.) Pages From Tarusa, 1963.

ABOUT: Alexandrova, V. A History of Soviet Literature, 1963; Henry, P. *English introduction to* Selected Stories (in Russian), 1967; Kazin, A. Contemporaries, 1963; Penguin Companion to Literature 2, 1969; Simmonds, G. W. (ed.) Soviet Leaders, 1967; Slonim, M. Soviet Russia Literature, 1964. *Periodicals*—Nation May 11, 1964; New York Review of Books August 20, 1964; New York Times July 15, 1968; New Yorker January 2, 1965; Times (London) July 16, 1968.

***PAZ, OCTAVIO** (March 31, 1914–), Mexican poet, critic, and essayist, was born and grew up in a big crumbling house in a wooded garden on the outskirts of Mexico City. The profusion of mirrors indoors and the overgrown and fantastic trees outside recur as images throughout his poetry. And among the twelve thousand books of his grandfather's library he began an endless intellectual pilgrimage.

The family was of mainly Spanish but partly Indian descent. The grandfather was a writer and journalist, a defender of the rights of the Indian peasantry and the author of one of the first novels to deal with their brutal exploitation. Paz's own father, a lawyer and an influential pioneer of agrarian reform, had joined Emiliano Zapata during the revolution of 1910 and represented him in the United States. His mother he remembers as a woman "good as bread." An aunt taught him French and introduced him to the work of Victor Hugo, Michelet, and Rousseau.

In his teens Paz was already familiar with modern Spanish and Spanish-American literature, with Novalis, Nietzsche, and Marx. Three poems affected him profoundly: Eliot's *The Waste Land*, Saint-John Perse's *Anabase*, and André Breton's *L'Amour fou*. In 1931, barely seventeen, he founded the avant-garde review *Barandal*. At nineteen he published his first volume of poems, *Luna silvestre* (Forest Moon).

Paz studied literature at the university, refused to take his degree, and set off suddenly for Yucatán to found a secondary school and to discover for himself something of the Mexican past. At the outbreak of the Spanish Civil War he identified himself immediately with the Republican cause and left for Spain as soon as he could, in 1937. In the words of Ramón Xirau, "Paz seems to have set out in search of the most desperate experience in order to emerge from it with at least a grain of hope."

The surrealism Paz had learned from Breton is already very evident in his second book, *Raíz del hombre* (Root of Man, 1937), in which he writes of "stones cold with anger / houses high on the lips of

* päs

saltpeter, / houses rotted in the bag of winter / night / breasts uncountable." This dark disjointed vision was intensified during his year in Spain by what he saw of the horrors of war and by the example of such comrades as Pablo Neruda and Vicente Aleixandre. Paz also shared his friends' politics, though his socialism was never as unquestioning as that of Neruda, with whom he broke in 1940 on the issue of Stalinism. His sympathies have remained with the left, but he has come to believe that "today's police states have their roots in the past of the parties who yesterday were revolutionary."

For several years after his return from Spain, Paz lived in Mexico City, where he helped to found the literary reviews *Taller* and *El Hijo Pródigo*, and contributed to these and other magazines many translations from French, German, and English, as well as original work. In 1943 a Guggenheim Fellowship took him to the United States, and in 1945 he entered Mexico's diplomatic service. His first posting was to Paris (1946–1951), where he met Breton, Superveille, Camus, Sartre, and many others. It was at this time that Paz wrote *Aguila o sol?* (1951), a haunting sequence of prose poems presenting an incandescent vision of Mexico's past, present, and future. The volume has had great influence, and has been translated by Eliot Weinberger as *Eagle or Sun?*

In the early 1950s Paz's duties took him to Japan and India, where he immersed himself in oriental poetry, painting, and architecture, and in the Buddhist and Taoist classics. "More than two thousand years away," he wrote, "Western poetry is discovering what is essential in Buddhist teaching: that the self is an illusion, a sum of sensations, thoughts and desires."

It is this belief, "that the self is an illusion," which lies at the root of Paz's poetry. It is what prevented him, for all his sense of social justice, from being anything so simple as a Socialist poet. As J. M. Cohen points out, he is a mystic. The violence and pessimism of his early surrealist verse reflect his shocked awareness of time, mortality, nothingness —a despair as large as Eliot's in *The Waste Land*. And like Eliot, but with less success, he has sought to involve himself with some absolute beyond the power of time—with love, art, humanity, Mexico, God.

In every case the vision of certainty has sooner or later wavered and dissolved. Even words fail: "A second ago it would have been easy to grasp a word and repeat it once and then again, / any one of those phrases one utters alone in a room without mirrors / to prove to oneself that it's not certain, that we are still alive after all, / but now with weightless hands night is lulling the furious tide, and one by one images recede, one by one words cover their faces."

What remains, when the vision turns its back

OCTAVIO PAZ

and words die, are the verses that have been written, each an affirmation, an act of faith beyond reason. It is not surprising that most of Paz's poems are short. The most sustained of them, and the most famous, is *Piedra de sol* (Sunstone, 1957), of which there are at least four English versions. It is a poem to the planet Venus, whose 584-day cycle is represented by the poem's 584 lines. Venus is addressed as both the morning and the evening star and, as in Náhuatl mythology, as the symbol of sun and of water.

It is thus a poem of reconciliation—between night and day, love and war, life and death, dream and memory, silence and speech. In one much-quoted passage it characteristically recalls an act of love undertaken in the midst of an air raid in Madrid in 1937: "We took our clothes off and made love / to defend with our lives our eternal portion, / our rationing of time and of paradise." Cohen calls *Piedra de sol* "one of the last important poems to be published in the Western world," and many would accept this, as they would agree that Paz is one of the two or three greatest living poets of Spanish America.

His prose is of comparable value. *El laberinto de la soledad* (1950, translated by Lysander Kemp as *The Labyrinth of Solitude*) was greeted as a work of genius, the first book successfully to illuminate the divided consciousness which modern Mexico has inherited from "the raping conquistador" and "the violated Indian mother." The result, Andrew Sinclair wrote, has been "a terrible sense of . . . solitude," which the Mexican "has to defend by untruths and to forget by fireworks." The book has become dated where it is most tendentious, especially in the comparisons drawn between the two Americas.

Something of Paz's poetics is expressed in *El arco y la lira* (The Bow and the Lyre, 1956) and in the first section of *Alternating Current*, an important collection of his essays on art, ethics, Oriental thought, McLuhanism, drugs, third world politics, and much else. "Everything tempts Paz," wrote Irving Howe, "as if the world of modern culture were still young, still fresh." Howe finds in Paz's critical writing "an epigrammatic philosophical dramatism, with a high quotient of generality and not much effort at textual detail or expository sequence. At its best, this can be strikingly effective. . . . But sometimes Paz's criticism becomes a relentless hammering of displayed brilliance, a little wearying in its emission of insights and formulas."

Paz remained in the Mexican diplomatic service until 1968, when he resigned in protest at his government's brutal suppression of internal opposition at the time of the Olympic Games, discussed in his long essay *Posdata* (1970, translated by Lysander Kemp as *The Other Mexico*). The post that he left was that of Mexican Ambassador to India and his experience of India, Afghanistan, and Ceylon is recorded in *Ladera este* (Eastern Slope, 1969), containing poems written between 1962 and 1968. After teaching for a time at the University of Texas Paz spent a year in England as Simón Bolívar Professor of Latin American Studies at Cambridge University, and in 1971–1972 was Charles Eliot Norton Professor of Poetry at Harvard. He then returned to Mexico City, where he edits the literary and political magazine *Plural*.

In his most recent work he has taken a new direction. The spatial poems of *Topoemas* (1968) resemble concrete poetry; *Blanco* (1967) is a long poem printed as a folding scroll in such a way as to allow a number of alternative readings. *Renga* (1969) is a cumulating chain of linked sonnets in four languages by four poets—Paz, Jacques Roubaud, Edoardo Sanguinetti, and Charles Tomlinson—an interesting and perhaps important attempt to put an ancient Japanese form to contemporary use. According to a reviewer in the *Times Literary Supplement*, Paz in these experimental works is as preoccupied as ever with "the moment of pure apprehension and creation . . . in which darkness and light are transcended and the act of seeing is forgotten in the immediacy of the vision." Paz's work is now being widely translated, notably in *Configurations*, a major bi-lingual collection drawing on fifteen years' work, with English versions by a distinguished team of poets and scholars. In 1963 Paz received the International Grand Prix for Poetry. He is married to the former Marie José Tramini, and has a daughter.

PRINCIPAL WORKS IN ENGLISH TRANSLATION: The Labyrinth of Solitude, 1961; Selected Poems, 1963 (revised as Early Poems 1935–1955, 1973); Sun Stone, 1963; Marcel Duchamp or The Castle of Purity, 1970; Claude Lévi-Strauss: An Introduction, 1970; Configurations, 1971; Aguila o sol? Eagle or Sun?, 1972; The Other Mexico: Critique of the Pyramid, 1972; (with others) Renga: A Chain of Poems, 1972; Alternating Current (essays), 1973. *Poems in* Barnstone, W. (ed.) Modern European Poetry, 1966. *As editor*—Anthology of Mexican Poetry (tr. Samuel Beckett), 1965. *As compiler*—(with others) New Poetry of Mexico, 1970.

ABOUT: Bosquet, A. Verbe et vertige, 1961; Céa, C. Octavio Paz, 1965; Cohen, J. M. Poetry of This Age, 1966; International Who's Who, 1972–73; Who's Who, 1973; Xirau, R. Octavio Paz: el sentido de la palabra, 1972; Xirau, R. Tres poetas de la soledad, 1955. *Periodicals*—Modern Language Journal March 1964; Nation February 24, 1964; New York Times Book Review January 26, 1964; Poetry September 1964; Saturday Review April 7, 1962; Times Literary Supplement December 26, 1963; September 7, 1967; October 17, 1968; November 14, 1968.

PEAKE, MERVYN (LAURENCE) (July 9, 1911–November 17, 1968), English novelist, poet, dramatist, and artist. The following note was prepared on his behalf by his wife during his long last illness: "I was born in Kuling, in Central China in 1911. My father was a medical missionary, and the first and most formative eleven years of my life were spent in China, going to the Tientsien Grammar School by way of education. My parents returned to England after the revolution. I went to a school for the sons of missionaries at Eltham in Kent. From the earliest moment that I can remember I have always written and drawn and painted, and have turned to whichever medium seemed most appropriate for what I wished to express.

"I went to the Academy Schools in London for three or four years, and on leaving there I went to Sark, the smallest of the Channel Islands, where a gallery had been opened, and a group of artists had decided to live, work and exhibit. But economic survival was difficult, and when I was offered a job teaching life drawing at the Westminster School of Art, I decided to accept, and went back to London. In the sculpture class I met Maeve Gilmore, whom I married not long after.

"All this time, apart from teaching, I was writing, mainly poetry, and I published many poems in *The Listener*, and the *New English Weekly* (now defunct). I also did many drawings of literary figures for the also defunct *London Mercury*.

"I was called up to the army at the beginning of 1940. Just before being called up, I had begun the first part of the Titus Groan trilogy. Most of it was written in billets and during training. It was written longhand in publishers' dummy books—interspersed with drawings, and sent back to my wife for safe keeping. During one leave, at the Café Royal, I told Graham Greene about the book *Titus Groan* that I was writing, and then thought no more about it. I hadn't thought about the publication of it, but one day, after the war, I had a telegram from him asking me to send him a copy. He was at the time with Eyre and Spottiswoode. I sent it to him and heard a little time later that it had been accepted. This was very big news.

"My wife and two sons went back to live in Sark after the war and there I wrote the second part of the trilogy, *Gormenghast.* For economic reasons I illustrated many books, including *Treasure Island, Alice in Wonderland, Hunting of the Snark*, etc., as well as having two volumes of poetry published: *Shapes and Sounds* and *The Glassblowers.* Also some of my own nonsense verse and drawings—called *Rhymes Without Reason*—and a children's book, *Letters from a Lost Uncle*, which was subsequently animated and televised.

"Once more I found that, for economic reasons, with a wife and three young children, living on an island, however idyllic, was extremely difficult. We returned to England where I taught drawing at the Central School of Art in Holborn. I began to write the third part of the trilogy, which was subsequently called *Titus Alone.* In between the last two parts I had written a book called *Mr. Pye* which had as its setting the island of Sark. This was later turned into a play for radio. The first two volumes of *Titus Groan* were also adapted for radio. In 1957 a play called *The Wit to Woo* was produced at the Arts Theatre in London, and has also been produced in repertory theatres since, including the Cambridge Arts and the Oxford Playhouse. A ballad poem called *The Rhyme of the Flying Bomb* was produced on radio in August 1964. *Gormenghast* and *The Glassblowers* were awarded the Heinemann Award for Literature in 1950."

It was in 1934 that Peake left the Academy Schools and went to Sark, exhibiting there the work that earned him his teaching post at the Westminster School of Art in 1936. More showings followed in London and quickly established his reputation as a draftsman. Peake's three years in the army ended in a nervous breakdown in 1943, and he finished out the war with the Ministry of Information, working on *Titus Groan* in his spare time. He had a major exhibition of paintings and drawings at a big London store in 1944, and after the defeat of Germany was sent by the Ministry to sketch the survivors of Belsen. According to the *New York Times*, "the work he produced, sensitive yet terrifying, has been described as among the most poignant illustrations of the war."

Titus Groan was published in 1946. It is a Gothic fantasy, undertaken perhaps as an escape from the bleak realities of war—if indeed it was not one of those cumulative daydreams that have their beginnings in childhood. The story begins with the birth of Titus, heir to the earldom of Groan, and ends with his installation as seventy-seventh earl at the age of two, along the way introducing the readers to his vast castle, its bizarre and ancient rituals, and its grotesque inhabitants. *Gormenghast* describes Titus's youth and education, and *Titus Alone* leaves him prepared at last to face the outside world, the castle and its rituals outgrown. Notable among the trilogy's gallery of portraits are those of Titus's mother, a lioness in defense of the Groan family fortunes, gliding about the castle with her red hair streaming like a flame above the "furlong of white cats" that accompany her everywhere; and Steerpike, the sinister kitchen boy, whose pursuit of power provides much of the story's impetus.

MERVYN PEAKE

The trilogy, which is illustrated by the author, is very much a matter of taste. Many critics thought it uninventive, obscure, shapeless, heavily facetious, and far too long. As many were delighted, finding it, as R. G. Davis did, a work "of such freshness, variety and visionary power that in his own modest, special way Mervyn Peake liberates and elevates as well as charms." Henry Tube saw the influence of Robert Louis Stevenson, Dickens, and Lewis Carroll, and others were reminded of the dark visions of Hieronymus Bosch. A critic in the *Times Literary Supplement* wrote: "He has a magnificently haunted imagination, and his writing, in certain passages, rises to an astonishing pitch of intensity. His weakness lies in the structure of the work as a whole, which is too diffuse and episodic . . . what stay in the memory are isolated scenes, perceived with the terrifying vividness of nightmare, and the descriptive details which go to make up Mr. Peake's strangely convincing world."

That the trilogy might be something more than a uniquely fanciful entertainment occurred to several readers, and seemed clear to B. A. Beatie, whose notice in *Saturday Review* is worth quoting at some length. Beatie believes that the trilogy's theme is "the contemporary and indissoluble tensions between 'tradition and the individual talent,' between apparent illusion and inner reality. . . . [Various] plots are interwoven in a pattern as complex as a baroque fugue, and, like counterpoint, they reflect upon and illuminate one another. . . . The result is a novelistic structure initially confusing but ultimately revealing, an ironic inversion of the romantic quest. . . . Peake's affinities are not Lewis Carroll, E. R. Eddison, or J. R. R. Tolkien, but rather Joyce, William Golding, Max Frisch, and Samuel Beckett. [This trilogy] is a *nouveau roman* using fantasy as one of many devices, an experimental confluence of several novelistic conventions."

Peake's poetry draws its tension from the contrast between the extravagance of its imagery, and the strictness and propriety of its forms. One reviewer of *The Glassblowers* called it "unique chiefly in the weirdness and vitality of the poet's fancy," and said that in its best moments "one feels that a new fire of language and vision has been kindled"—that, to use a phrase of the poet's, "the air is full of gestures suddenly lit."

The most notable of Peake's other books is *Mr. Pye*, an entertaining fantasy about an evangelist who carries the gospel of love to the unlovely inhabitants of a larger-than-life Sark, and then to his horror sprouts wings. Mr. Pye is driven to the desperate conclusion that, if wings are produced by excessive goodness, they must be removed by its opposite. *The Wit to Woo* is another exercise in Gothic fantasy, "a blank-verse comedy" which reminded reviewers of the work of Christopher Fry. *The Rhyme of the Flying Bomb* is a ballad about a sailor in World War II who unexpectedly finds and adopts a baby—an act of tenderness amid the brutality of war intended as an illustration of "man's continuing hopefulness in adversity."

Peake's work, as an artist and as a writer, is considered as a whole by Henry Tube in the *Spectator* (July 15, 1966). Tube believes that Peake's "peculiar vision is entirely consistent: the novels could not have been written by anyone but an artist, while the drawings are those of a man soaked in the text he is illustrating. This cross-fertilization accounts at least partly for the unique quality of his best work in both fields." Peake and his wife were members of the bohemian set that flourished in Chelsea long before the King's Road became the center and symbol of "swinging London." The first signs of his fatal brain disease appeared shortly after the publication of *Gormenghast* in 1950, making writing and painting increasingly difficult. By 1964 he could do neither, and he was probably unaware of the republication of the Gormenghast trilogy. He died in 1968 at Burcot, Oxfordshire. His wife's moving memoir of their life together, *A World Away*, appeared in 1970. Since his death, Peake, Gormenghast, and Titus Groan have become a cult in Britain. The National Book League's Peake exhibition in 1972 had a success, especially with young people, far beyond the expectations of the organizers. *Selected Poems* was published the same year, as was *A Book of Nonsense*, a miscellany of humorous writings and drawings.

PRINCIPAL WORKS: Shapes and Sounds (poems), 1941; Titus Groan, 1946; Gormenghast, 1950; Titus Alone, 1959 (all three republished as The Gormenghast Trilogy, U.S., 1967; Titus Groan and Gormenghast republished separately, England, 1968; longer version of Titus Alone, 1970); The Craft of the Lead Pencil, 1946; Drawings, 1950; The Glassblowers, and Other Poems, 1950; Mr. Pye, 1953; Boy in Darkness (in Sometime Never: Three Tales of Imagination), 1956; The Wit to Woo (play), 1957; The Rhyme of the Flying Bomb, 1962; A Reverie of Bone, and Other Poems, 1967; Selected Poems, 1972; A Book of Nonsense, 1972. *For children*—Captain Slaughterboard Drops Anchor, 1939; Rhymes Without Reason, 1944; Letters from a Lost Uncle, 1948.

ABOUT: Contemporary Authors 7–8, 1963; Gilmore, M. A World Away, 1970; Lynd, R. Essays on Life and Literature, 1951; Miller, B. E. and others. Illustrators of Children's Books, 1946–1956, 1958; Newton, E. In My View, 1950; Who's Who, 1969; Who's Who of Children's Literature, 1968. *Periodicals*—American Artist February 1955; Chicago Review Autumn–Winter 1960; New York Times November 10, 1946; November 19, 1968; Saturday Review December 16, 1967; Spectator July 15, 1966; Studio September 1946; Times (London) November 19, 1968; Times Literary Supplement June 25, 1970; February 11, 1972.

PERCY, WALKER (May 28, 1916–), American novelist, writes: "I was born in Birmingham, Alabama. My father was a lawyer from a family of lawyers traceable to an English army officer who settled in Spanish West Florida shortly after the Revolutionary War. My mother was a Phinizy from Georgia. My parents died before I was sixteen. With my two brothers I was adopted by my father's first cousin, William Alexander Percy of Greenville, Mississippi, author of *Lanterns on the Levee*. Will Percy, soldier, poet, planter, lawyer, was an extraordinary man. His influence, which accounts at least in part for the fact that Greenville is presently unlike the rest of Mississippi, was all the greater on a member of his household, a shy, callow, solitary, but watchful youth.

"My adoptive father, alumnus of Sewanee and Harvard, sent me to the University of North Carolina because he thought it was the best university in the South and he preferred the democratic atmosphere of a state school. At Carolina I spent a great deal of time in laboratories as a consequence of my conviction at the time that scientific truth was the only truth worth pursuing. The rest of the time I spent pleasantly in the company of some very good fellows in the Sigma Alpha Epsilon fraternity house.

"I chose medicine as a profession mainly because I didn't want to go into law. Until recently in the South, like medieval Europe, one felt limited in the choice of professions. I chose Columbia University's College of Physicians & Surgeons because it was a good medical school and it was in New York where, presumably, one could get the best of music, art, theatre, etc. As it turned out I frequented, instead of Carnegie Hall, Loew's and RKO Orpheum movie palaces in Washington Heights. Upon graduation I began my internship at Bellevue Hospital where I performed some seventy-five autopsies on derelicts who had died of chronic diseases and in doing so, contracted pulmonary tuberculosis myself and retired to Trudeau Sanitarium in the Adirondacks for two years. During this time I read a good deal, met divers fellow patients from the Northeastern states, and listened to the radio from Montreal.

"My tuberculosis arrested, I might have continued my medical career, but instead I took my illness as the occasion, or perhaps the excuse, to do thereafter what I had wanted to do for some time. This was to think about the curiousness of man's condition and perhaps even to write about it. In 1954 I wrote an article about Suzanne Langer's *Philosophy in a New Key*, a book which both excited and irritated me. I decided to submit it for publication. It was published in *Thought* quarterly.

"Meanwhile I married Bernice Townsend, a Mississippi girl, and moved to New Orleans, one of the few inhabitable cities in the United States. There I entered the Catholic Church. In the next few years I wrote a good many articles for philosophical, literary and psychiatric quarterlies. One day I decided to write a novel about a young man who has all the advantages of a cultivated old-line Southern family, a feel for science and art, a liking for girls, sport cars and the ordinary things of the culture, but who nevertheless feels himself quite alienated from both worlds, the old South and the new America. This novel became *The Moviegoer* and won the National Book Award for 1962.

"With my wife and two daughters I presently live on a bayou in Covington, Louisiana, a pleasant town in the piney woods."

Walker Percy is one of the most original and unusual of modern American novelists; as he has himself said, writing in *Book Week* about his comparatively late development from doctor to writer, "a serious writer . . . is a peculiar bird who has to find his own way in his own time and who had better be left alone to do so." The importance of Percy's early scientific training can hardly be overestimated, as the following quotation from the same article makes clear: "If the first great intellectual discovery of my life was the beauty of the scientific method, surely the second was the discovery of the singular predicament of man in the very world which has been transformed by this science. An extraordinary paradox became clear: that the more science progressed and even as it benefited man, the less it said about what it is like to be a man living in the world." Walker Percy's fiction may be said to be a search for an intelligent and positive resolution of this paradox. At the very back of it lies the influence of his self-discovered Roman Catholicism. More obvious influences, and familiar ones today, are the existentialist philosophers, Jaspers, Camus, Heidegger, Kierkegaard—and, above all perhaps, Gabriel Marcel.

WALKER PERCY

Percy's apprenticeship to fiction, in his thirties, was painful: his first two novels were rejected out of hand—and he now seems to agree with the publishers' judgment. He was poor and in ill health, and only selling a few articles on philosophical and religious subjects. At one point, he wryly recalls, "I even wrote a book about the philosophy of language which the publisher didn't even bother to return and I didn't bother to ask for." Then some complex emotional mechanism—which Percy himself does not presume to try to explain—released the springs of his talent. *The Moviegoer*, written in a little over a year, was published in 1961, won the National Book Award, and became a best seller. Its popular success was interesting to the extent that it confirmed the National Book Award jury in its controversial choice, as the year's most distinguished novel, of an offbeat first book by an unknown writer.

The Moviegoer is about "Binx" Bolling, a successful and handsome young Louisiana stockbroker who suffers chronically and sometimes acutely from a sense that he lacks identity or even reality, and who is fondly preoccupied with death. The activities that alleviate his "invincible apathy" are "working, making money, going to movies and seeking the company of women." Bolling is in despair, and is ignorant of his condition only because, in the words of the book's epigraph (from Kierkegaard), "the specific character of despair is precisely this, it is unaware of being despair."

Bolling goes to the movies ritually, the quality of the experience depending to an important degree on its physical circumstances—theatre, seat, company if any, occasions on which he has seen the same or a related film before, where, and with whom. The movies are for Bolling a version of reality which is reassuringly finite and controllable, and from them he begins to learn to focus on other people, to give them that "attention" recommended by Simone Weil.

The central action of the book, which is set mostly in New Orleans during Mardi Gras, concerns Bolling's relations with another neurotic, his cousin Kate, whose misery is more dangerously acute than his own. These two, perceiving each other's suffering, find the generosity and courage to share their despair and, in fear and trembling, make love. With this act of faith they break through to a relationship which may save them both.

Percy's style, occasionally mannered and mandarin, is for the most part direct and laconic. His ear for Southern speech was widely praised and so was his talent for characterization, some of it gently but brilliantly comic, as in the portraits of Bolling's beautiful but terrifying secretary and his bluestocking Aunt Emily. Stanley Edgar Hyman went so far as to call *The Moviegoer* "a better novel than the work it brings most readily to mind, Albert Camus's *The Stranger*."

The central figure in Percy's second novel, *The Last Gentleman*, is Williston Bibb Barrett, a courteous young Southerner given to bouts of amnesia that leave him unable to remember who (or when) he is—a failing which suggested to some reviewers that he is a symbol for the South itself in its postbellum loss of identity. The book begins in New York where Barrett, scrutinizing Central Park through his telescope, falls in love at first sight and at some considerable distance with Kitty Vaught. Coincidence then allows Barrett to be hired by the Vaught family (of Alabama) as tutor-companion to Kitty's dying brother Jamie. He returns with them to the South, to search for himself among his roots.

The novel is a complex and ambitious existentialist investigation into the nature of perception, of morality, and of being, as well as an analysis of the South. There are parodies of a number of contemporary literary *genres*, excerpts from the commonplace book of Kitty's older brother Sutter, "a kind of holy lecher," and, again, a large gallery of superbly drawn characters. This time however there was a widespread (but not universal) feeling that the novel was less than the sum of its parts. John Wain, for example, objected that "everything is prismatic, discrete, a matter of half-conveyed hints." But at the same time Wain conceded that Percy "is a breathtakingly brilliant writer," and Wilfrid Sheed said that "page-for-page and line-for-line, this is certainly one of the best-written books in recent memory. . . . As a Southern Catholic and as a comparatively late-blooming novelist, [Percy] sees everything his own way. . . . By a constant play of metaphor and acute literalness—seeing the thing as something else, seeing it as precisely itself, a whipsaw arrangement—he recreates the world, and gives the reader the run of a brand-new sensibility."

Love in the Ruins, which followed, is a satirical fantasy set in the United States in the near future, with the country on the edge of total collapse, destroyed by soulless pragmatism. Dr. Thomas More, a Catholic scientist, awaits the apocalypse in a derelict motel. His satyriasis, alcoholism, and other failings not withstanding, he is the nation's only hope. He has invented the lapsometer, a device which could help to restore the country to grace, and which precipitates countermeasures by the devil himself. Most critics found much to enjoy and admire in the book, but most had reservations about its plot and characterization. V. S. Pritchett, in his review, called Percy "a spirited and inventive writer" with "a charred hell-fire edge to his observation" but concluded that "in the eye of this hurricane of laughing anger, there is a sentimentalist." The novel received the 1971 National Catholic Book Award for fiction.

PRINCIPAL WORKS: The Moviegoer, 1961; The Last Gentleman, 1966; Love in the Ruins, 1971.

ABOUT: Contemporary Authors 3, 1963; Hyman, S. E. Standards, 1966; Kazin, A. Bright Book of Life, 1973; Who's Who in America, 1972–1973. *Periodicals*—Book Week December 25, 1966; Harper's June 1971; New York Review of Books July 28, 1966; July 1, 1971; New York Times Book Review July 4, 1971; Sewanee Review Autumn 1961; Shenandoah Spring 1967; Southwest Review Autumn 1964; Times Literary Supplement December 21, 1967.

"PETERS, ELLIS." *See* PARGETER, EDITH

PETERSON, VIRGILIA (May 16, 1904–December 24, 1966), American journalist and memoirist, was born in New York City to Dr. Frederick Peterson, a prominent alienist, and Antoinette (Rotan) Peterson. Her childhood was spent in the comfortable and genteel surroundings of upper middle-class New York society—a brownstone house off Fifth Avenue, with servants, a governess, elocution lessons, and formal education at fashionable private schools—Charlton, Brearley, MacIver's, and the Westover School in Connecticut. At Vassar, where she studied from 1921 to 1923, she majored in modern languages, and she continued her studies in French at the University of Grenoble in 1924.

At that time she met and became engaged to a young Polish prince, Paul Sapieha, but the objections of their families prevented their marriage. Returning to the United States, Miss Peterson began contributing short stories to magazines like *Scribner's* and *Harper's* and reviewing books for the New York *Herald Tribune*. Her first marriage, to Malcolm Ross, ended in divorce. In 1932 she was back in Europe, this time settling in Vienna to write a novel. The following year, in London, she was married to her former fiancé, Prince Paul Sapieha.

The first years of Princess Sapieha's life on her husband's estate in Poland are described in her book *Polish Profile* (1940). The Sapiehas were an old and influential family, and her picture of aristocratic European life in the ominous days before the outbreak of World War II caught the attention and imagination of American readers. With her two young children, Christine and Nicholas, Princess Sapieha fled from Poland in September 1939 just ahead of the Nazi invasion of that country. Back in America, she wrote a series of articles about Poland for the *New Yorker* and after the United States entered the war took a writing job with the Office of War Information. In 1942 she published a novel, *Beyond This Shore*, retracing in fictional form ground similar to that covered in her first book. Her own uncompromising opinion of the novel was that "it stinks."

Resuming her maiden name, Virgilia Peterson worked as publicity director for Appleton-Century-Crofts in 1947 and 1948, and from 1949 to 1951 was assistant to the director of special events for Radio Free Europe. She continued her freelance writing as well, publishing magazine articles, book reviews, and translations from the French, and established a considerable reputation as a lecturer and television personality. Poised and attractive, with a beautifully modulated speaking voice, and the advantage, she insisted, of an appropriate "severity of appearance," she appeared on many radio and television panel discussions, most notably "The Author Meets the Critics," which she moderated from 1952 to 1955. In 1956 she received a Peabody award for her radio program "Books in Profile."

Miss Peterson was divorced from Prince Sapieha

VIRGILIA PETERSON

in 1950 and in the same year married C. Gouverneur Paulding, an editor of the *Reporter* magazine. In 1961 she published her autobiography, *A Matter of Life and Death*, an extraordinarily candid and subjective book written in the form of a long, accusing letter to her late mother. In her foreword she said of the writing: "I was driven by an irrepressible need, a high wind of compulsion. . . . I often wakened at night to wonder why it should be of such overwhelming moment to me to expose and explain myself. I do not know. I can only say it was." The book is painful in the intensity of its self-recriminations. Written in a rich, eloquent style (which at least one reviewer characterized as "Proustian"), it becomes a work of diminishing returns. Sybille Bedford observed of it: "The high tone, the triple reference, the grand style, by the very intensity of their effect can remain effective only for a given time; beyond, reading becomes like listening to a symphony composed entirely in andante movements."

Her husband died in 1965 and she a year later, at the age of sixty-two.

PRINCIPAL WORKS: Polish Profile, 1940; Beyond This Shore, 1942; A Matter of Life and Death, 1961.

ABOUT: Current Biography, 1953; Peterson, V. A Matter of Life and Death, 1961; Who's Who in America, 1966–1967. *Periodicals*—New York Times December 27, 1966.

***PETRONI, GUGLIELMO** (October 30, 1911–), Italian novelist and poet, short story writer and essayist, writes (in Italian): "I was born at Lucca in Tuscany where my family ran a small business. Even today, in that city, my brother man-

* pā trō′ nē

GUGLIELMO PETRONI

ages a shoe shop in which, from the age of thirteen until about twenty, I too worked, alternating the drudgery of toil with the studies intended to assist me in fulfilling my artistic aspirations.

"By about the age of twenty I was a painter of some reputation among the masters of that time, but I soon gave up painting for literature. In 1930 one of my poems won a prize, almost the only one awarded at that time, for which the judges were, amongst others, F. T. Marinetti, Giuseppe Ungaretti, Ugo Betti and Massimo Bontempelli.

"After 1935 I gave up all activity in my family business and moved to Rome where I joined the editorial staff of the review *Perspettive*, whose editor was Curzio Malaparte. Before the outbreak of war I published a book of poetry, *Versi e memoria*, and one of short stories, *Personaggi d'elezione*, as well as various articles and essays in the more important reviews of that time.

"During the last war I felt that I had to abandon all literary activity and, in 1942, I became a member of groups engaged in anti-Fascist and anti-Nazi activities in Rome and for that matter in all other parts of Italy. In 1943 I was arrested by the Fascists and was handed over by them to the German armed forces who incarcerated me in the notorious Nazi prison in the Via Tasso in Rome. I was brought before the Nazi military court at Rome, and was sentenced, but before the sentence could be carried out I was freed by the Allied armies in our capital.

"After the Liberation I resumed my literary activities. In 1948 I published *Il mondo è una prigione*, which tells the story of the generation which had grown up under fascism and was led to take part in the Resistance and to nourish hopes of democracy in spite of a far from easy experience of life; it is widely read by the more recent generations and has been adopted by many schools. In 1965, almost twenty years later, this book was awarded a prize for the best literary writing on the Italian Resistance.

"Since the war and up to the present day I have alternated poetry and essays with narrative works. In reviews and newspapers I have fought particularly for the independence of creative work from every interference, direct or indirect, through political activity and also through the overwhelming influence of industrial culture, thus arousing the hostility of all those who prefer political or financial interests to freedom of expression in art and in poetry.

"My books have always met with the approval of the most authoritative Italian and foreign critics; in Italy my readers are mainly those few thousands who still seek unadulterated commitment and moral purpose, those who wish to condemn—and to free themselves from—any form of violence expressed in the society of today."

The son of Bruno Petroni and the former Giuditta Santini, Petroni grew up in a close and united family atmosphere. In the 1930s he became a Communist and suffered considerable privation because he refused to work for the Fascist government during the war. At the same time, in order to protect his comrades in the Resistance, he developed the habit of silence and reserve. By 1943, when the Nazis incarcerated him in the infamous Regina Coeli prison in Rome, he found himself unable to communicate at all, even with his fellow prisoners. "Even now," he said years later, "I am nothing but a literary man."

After the Liberation, out of tune with the national mood of celebration, he felt himself a stranger in his own home at Lucca, and in Rome broke with the Communists who had been his comrades during the years of persecution, in his loneliness experiencing something like nostalgia for the prison where he had lived like an animal among animals. "It struck me," he has said, "that life is a prison, or our prison may be other people, in which case we may come to love them as I loved Regina Coeli."

This is the theme of the work which established Petroni's reputation, *Il mondo è una prigione* (The World Is a Prison). It appeared first in *Botteghe Oscure* in 1948 and was published in book form the following year. An account of his imprisonment, sensitive, reflective, and astonishingly unvindictive, it has reminded many readers of *Le mie prigioni* (My Prisons), by the nineteenth century Risorgimento hero Silvio Pellico. Petroni's book indeed is far more than a memoir; it is a powerful and moving statement of the belief that is central to his work—

that for the artist, or at any rate for Petroni, the way to understanding is through the lonely and dedicated pursuit of self-knowledge. In Regina Coeli he learned "that the immense whirling of wars, social tragedy, were not merely around us but within the most secret part of our lives . . . that the first steps toward life cannot be taken unless one starts from the depth of one's own soul . . . by discovering within ourselves the meaning of things that arise around us."

This theme is illustrated in Petroni's first novel, *La casa si muove* (The House Is Moving, 1950). It describes the life and death of a hermitic country gentleman, Ugo Gattegna, who has cut himself off from all communication with others and who spends his time in reading and meditation. Towards the end of the war he shelters a political refugee but establishes no real relationship with him. When the retreating German army reaches his farm he refuses to leave and is shot. Throughout the story he maintains an entirely private conversation with himself, scribbling cryptic messages on scraps of paper, and calmly awaiting death: "It will come, it will not come, what difference does it make? Certainly, everyone, come, comes, will come, will come without doubt." This eccentric and enigmatic man, through the sheer tenacity with which he guards his personal integrity, earns the involuntary respect of those around him, and of the reader.

Noi dobbiamo parlare (We Must Speak, 1955), on the other hand, can be read as a parable about the dangers of too much involvement (however well-intentioned) in the lives of others—of too much "communication." It tells the story of Natalia's heroic struggle to convince her wealthy and callous uncle Venturino that he must support his impoverished parents. At first she is beaten and abused for her pains, but she will not give up and in the end Venturino responds, becoming a warmer and better and more generous man. But the struggle has exhausted Natalia and, emotionally drained, she rejects her devoted suitor. Venturino has been in a sense saved, but at the cost of two lives ruined. This novel gains great narrative fascination from the remorseless conflict between Natalia and Venturino, and has been called a "tragic masterpiece."

Il colore della terra (The Color of the Earth, 1964) again calls on memories of the Liberation, and presents the same kind of enigmatic protagonist as the earlier novels. Petroni's verse (collected in *Poesie*, 1959), hardly noteworthy as compared to his prose writings, is characterized by a simplicity of theme and language. He has also expressed his belief in "participation" through "isolation" in many short stories and essays. Petroni was married in 1945 to Carla Luisa de Vecchi, lives in Rome, and has served as secretary of the Associazione Italiana per la Libertá della Cultura.

PRINCIPAL WORKS IN ENGLISH TRANSLATION: *Excerpts from novels in* Caetani, M. (ed.) New Italian Writers, 1951; World Review September and November 1951.
ABOUT: De Robertis, G. Altro Novecento, 1962; Pacifici, S. A Guide to Contemporary Italian Literature, 1962; Pancrazi, P. Scrittori d'Oggi, 1950. *Periodicals*—Fiera Letteraria January 16, 1955; World Review September 1951.

PEVSNER, SIR NIKOLAUS (BERNHARD LEON) (January 30, 1902–), German-born historian of art and architecture, writes: "I was born at Leipzig in Germany and brought up in that country. My father was a merchant, quite wealthy, and my mother was keenly interested after the First World War in the most up-to-date arts. I have an Archipenko drawing from her, and from my father-in-law water colors and drawings by Nolde and Barlach. I went to grammar school and had decided to read history of art even before I left school. I attended university lectures while in sixth form and then completed my studies in three years. My thesis was on baroque architecture at Leipzig. I married my wife before I got my degree and we had indeed already a baby when I took my exams. A happy married life followed for forty years. We had three children and, when my wife suddenly died, seven grandchildren. After my exams I at once got onto the staff of the Dresden Gallery, worked on the catalogue and privately on Italian mannerist painting. For one year I was also assistant to the director of the Dresden International Art Exhibition of 1925. It was a most interesting experience. I was commissioned when twenty-four or twenty-five to write the volume of the German *Handbuch der Kunstwissenschaft* on Italian painting of mannerism and baroque. In 1928 I was made a lecturer at Göttingen University. There ensued a gradual change of interests to the social history of art (the result was a history of academies of art), to nineteenth century architecture (especially the history of building types) and also to English art and architecture. I traveled extensively in England in 1930.

"So, when the Nazis came into power, it was England I went to, especially as I had become more and more fascinated by English architecture and the psychology of this strange race. On the strength of my interest in the social history of art and current affairs, I was offered a studentship at Birmingham University, the result of which was published in 1937 as *An Enquiry into Industrial Art in England*, a factual investigation of a kind not tried anywhere before. In order not to lose touch with historical research I also worked on a history of architecture and design from the late nineteenth to the early twentieth century, and this came out in 1936. However, my studentship came to an end and I had to see how I could get my family over who still lived

NIKOLAUS PEVSNER

in Germany and how I could set up house. So I joined Gordon Russell's, the best furniture and furnishing firm in England, as their buyer and held this job from 1936 to 1940. It was a very welcome and wholesome experience for an academic.

"Then the war came, and cultural jobs shriveled up. I did odd things for a year or eighteen months, debris-clearing and full-time fire-watching. In 1941, when people had settled down to the idea of a long war, prospects improved for me. I was offered several jobs at the same time and chose two: the editing of the *Architectural Review* and of King Penguin Books. Both connections go on to the present day. I am now one of four editors of the *Review* and I edit for Penguin Books the Pelican History of Art. I also write for them The Buildings of England. Both are series of many volumes. Work on both started after the war. But already during the war I had returned to university teaching at Birkbeck College. It was during the long fire-watch nights there that I wrote the *Outline of European Architecture*, the only best seller I have succeeded in producing.

"Since 1949 there have been no changes in my programme, except that in that year I also started a weekly lecture at Cambridge. Of the P.H.A. about twenty-five volumes are out now, and there would be more, if authors were not so unreliable. Of The Buildings of England, thirty is the total up-to-date. More than fifteen more must be produced, and as until 1963 they were done in very close companionship with my wife, they can now and in future not be any longer what they were."

Nikolaus Pevsner, the son of Hugo and Anna Pevsner, was educated at St. Thomas's in Leipzig, and at the universities of Leipzig, Munich, Berlin, and Frankfurt. His thesis, *Leipziger Barock*, brought him his doctorate in 1924. It was published in 1925 and was followed by his study of Italian mannerist and baroque painting. Pevsner was an assistant keeper at the Dresden Gallery from 1924 to 1928, and thereafter until 1933 lectured at Göttingen on the history of art and architecture.

The first of his books to appear in English was *Pioneers of the Modern Movement* (1936, revised as *Pioneers of Modern Design*), a clear, alert, and notably sensible study of the Modern Movement in architecture and design from William Morris to Walter Gropius. *An Inquiry into Industrial Art in England* was based on much thorough and objective research into "the conditions and artistic value of design" in a wide variety of British industries. It was thought the most valuable contribution to its subject yet produced, especially interesting on the relationship between design and public demand. Pevsner's *Academies of Art* was also much admired, though there was some feeling then (as there has been since) that his very virtues as a historian—his thoroughness and scrupulous objectivity—"make heavy demands upon the attention" of the reader.

An Outline of European Architecture studies the development of architectural styles as an expression of "the changing spirit of changing ages." It is a work so packed with information that the thread of Pevsner's argument is at times almost broken by the weight of illustrative detail, but to most critics it seemed nevertheless "a brilliant summary of the rise and progress of modern architecture." It has gone through many editions, has been much translated, and has had great influence.

Pevsner's survey of the buildings of Cornwall was published by Penguin in 1951, launching his monumental series, The Buildings of England. Several new volumes have been added to the thirty already completed when he wrote the note above. According to Geoffrey Grigson, "The principle on which these guides to the architecture of all England are being compiled is critical. It is not one of quaintness, oldness or association, the three dictatorial qualities of our guidebook trade. Art is art, excellence is excellence and the counties are being combed for all that is architecturally noble." In this series, Grigson went on, we have "the rare application to our local buildings of a European scholarship," and Rayner Banham has pointed out the "sometimes shattering disparity between what is recorded by [Pevsner's] exploring but dispassionate eye and the valuations that local sentiment puts upon the same structures." The series has been warmly and unanimously praised for "its devotion to England, the splendidly catholic taste that informs it, the unrivalled knowledge within and behind, the infectious enthusiasm for each new venture."

The Pelican History of Art, planned and edited by Pevsner, is expected to comprise about fifty volumes, while the King Penguin series ran to seventy-six volumes before it ceased publication in 1957. However, in spite of the magnitude of his responsibilities to Penguin, Pevsner has never entirely abandoned his other interests, as was evident when in 1968 he published *The Sources of Modern Architecture and Design*. The volume supplements *Pioneers of Modern Design*, examining the new designs and techniques that appeared in the later nineteenth century in architecture, textiles, furniture, and many other fields. "No one but Dr. Pevsner could have packed so much information into so compact a work or illustrated it more effectively," wrote one reviewer in the *Times Literary Supplement*, adding that the book was well provided with the two "most comforting" characteristics of the Pevsner manner, "his clarity of expression and his firmness of opinion." *Studies in Art, Architecture and Design*, a two-volume collection of essays, appeared in 1968, and Pevsner's Neurath lecture on Ruskin and Viollet-le-Duc in 1971.

Pevsner was Professor of the History of Art at Birkbeck College from 1945 to 1969, when he became Emeritus Professor. He was Slade Professor of Fine Art at Cambridge (1949–1955), and at Oxford (1968–1969). His 1955 BBC Reith lectures were published as *The Englishness of English Art* and admired as a "sympathetic analysis of the abiding characteristics of English art," while the Oxford Slade Lectures have appeared in greatly extended form as *Some Architectural Writers of the Nineteenth Century*. Pevsner received a CBE in 1953 and a knighthood in 1969. He holds many honorary degrees and is an honorary fellow of the Royal Institute of British Architects and also a fellow of the British Academy and of several foreign ones. Yale University awarded him its Howland Prize in 1963. Pevsner has served on the Royal Fine Art Commission, the Historic Buildings Council, and the Royal Commission on Historical Monuments, among other such bodies. He is chairman of the Victoria Society, and is associated with a number of other organizations. Pevsner's wife was the former Karola Kurlbaum. A genial and friendly man, he was publicly saluted by Penguin Books in 1967 as "a tireless worker, a good friend, and a great scholar."

PRINCIPAL WORKS: Pioneers of the Modern Movement, from William Morris to Walter Gropius, 1936 (rev. in 1949 as Pioneers of Modern Design); An Enquiry into Industrial Art in England, 1937; Academies of Art, Past and Present, 1940; An Outline of European Architecture, 1943; High Victorian Design, 1951; The Englishness of English Art (lectures), 1956; The Sources of Modern Architecture and Design, 1968; Concerning Architecture, 1968; Studies in Art, Architecture, and Design (2 vols.), 1968; Ruskin and Viollet-le-Duc, 1971; Some Architectural Writers of the Nineteenth Century, 1972. The Buildings of England—Cornwall, 1951; Nottingham, 1951; Middlesex, 1952.

ABOUT: Contemporary Authors 9–10, 1964; Hutchinson, G. E. Itinerant Ivory Tower, 1953; International Who's Who, 1972–73; Who's Who, 1973. *Periodicals*—Architectural Review August 1967; Bookseller January 28, 1967; Design June 1967; Guardian April 21, 1960; October 10, 1970; New Statesman September 15, 1951; January 20, 1961; September 28, 1962; Royal Institute of British Architects Journal August 1967; Sunday Times October 27, 1968; Times (London) January 4, 1967; Times Literary Supplement January 26, 1967; Twentieth Century January 1960.

***PEYREFITTE, (PIERRE-) ROGER** (August 17, 1907–), French novelist, was born at Castres, Tarn, in southern France, to Jean Peyrefitte, a landowner, and Eugénie Jamme Peyrefitte. He attended Catholic boarding schools at Saint-Pons and Toulouse, received his Bachelier ès Lettres degree, and did graduate work in French literature at the University of Toulouse before entering the École Libre des Sciences Politiques in Paris.

In 1931 Peyrefitte joined the diplomatic service, and two years later was assigned as secretary to the French Embassy in Athens, a post he filled until 1938. In 1938–1940 he was attached to the Ministry of Foreign Affairs in Paris, and he returned to a post there in 1943–1945, during the German occupation. This brought his dismissal from the government in 1945, but his discharge was revoked some fifteen years later and he was reinstated by judgment of the Council of State in 1962.

At the end of the war, Peyrefitte was already better known as a writer than as a diplomat. *Les Amitiés particulières*, published in 1945, soon sold more than a hundred thousand copies in France. This tragic story about the clandestine relationship between two boys in a Catholic boarding school aroused less enthusiasm in the United States, where it appeared in 1950 as *Special Friendships*. (It was reissued in 1958 in a new version by Edward Hyams, who has been Peyrefitte's chief English translator.) Some British and American reviewers complained that the novelist had wasted his talent on a fundamentally trivial subject, but there was no question that the talent existed. There is, one critic noted, "a smoothness to the prose . . . a skill in building up situations, an exploratory thoroughness that will not be hurried yet gives no sense of delay, that marks the author as a first-class craftsman." In 1964 François Mauriac's objections to the filming of the book led to a vitriolic dispute that divided the Paris literary world.

By that time Peyrefitte had written two plays and about a dozen novels, and had acquired his

* pā rə fēt′

ROGER PEYREFITTE

reputation as an outrageous satirist, a professional exposer of real or imaginary scandals in the highest circles of the church and state. Thus *Les Ambassades* (1951, translated as *Diplomatic Diversions*) draws a "perverse and ignoble" but irresistibly funny account of the rivalries, intrigues, and erotic adventures which, according to Peyrefitte, occupied the Athens diplomatic community between the wars.

Peyrefitte writes somewhat in the anticlerical tradition of Voltaire, and the Roman Catholic hierarchy is a favorite target. His 1955 novel *Les Clés de Saint Pierre* (*The Keys of St. Peter*, 1957) tells the story of the "education" of a French seminarist in Rome, in the process charging Vatican officials (many of them named) with every kind of duplicity, greed, cynicism, and superstition. The Vatican protested violently that the novel was "lewdly libelous," whereupon its sales rose in France and Italy to over half a million copies. There is a note of genuine indignation in Peyrefitte's conscientious blasphemies which has made some critics wonder if he really is as antireligious or even as anti-Catholic as he seems.

In 1958 the Italian government began a criminal suit against Peyrefitte on charges that his article in a Rome newspaper ridiculed Pope Pius XII, but proceedings were dropped in 1960 when the author accepted amnesty. The publication in 1965 of *Les Juifs* (*The Jews*) involved the writer in another legal fight. This "novel," which to many seemed anti-Semitic, had according to its author quite opposite intentions. It attempts among other things to establish the Jewish lineage of Presidents Johnson and Kennedy, Charles de Gaulle, Queen Elizabeth II, and many other august personages—to prove indeed that the Jews are not a minority but a majority and thus (says Peyrefitte innocently) to end the Jewish problem. Unmoved by this argument, three members of the Rothschild family found the book so offensive that they brought suit to bar its sales. A French court found largely in Peyrefitte's favor, stipulating only that a few lines be changed in subsequent printings.

Against all the claims that Peyrefitte is a mere scandalmonger and sly pornographer, some critics maintain that he is an artist. Reviewing *La Nature du prince* (1963), another of his scabrous attacks on the Roman Catholic Church, translated as *The Prince's Person*, Laurent LeSage pointed out that "to tell a tale so bawdy Peyrefitte deploys all the graces of his style. Nuance, delicate thrust, allusion, humorous understatement, and the strictest propriety of language keep the story from floundering in its offensiveness. . . . As with every work of this specialist in scandal, we may regret that such art is not put to nobler purposes." Cecily Mackworth has characterized Peyrefitte as a writer who "takes a sadistic pleasure in demolishing and destroying, with great wit and a perfect style, everything he touches," but who is quite incapable of drawing an admirable character. There are indeed few traces in his later work of the compassion and understanding which distinguished *Les Amitiés particulières*. Peyrefitte succeeds, Miss Mackworth says, "only when he paints in exquisitely perfumed mud and vitriol and these materials are limiting in the search for truth."

The author lives in Paris and is unmarried. His recreations are traveling, taking long walks, and collecting antiques.

PRINCIPAL WORKS IN ENGLISH TRANSLATION: Special Friendships, 1950 (new tr. 1958); Diplomatic Diversions, 1953; Diplomatic Conclusions, 1954; South from Naples, 1954; The Keys of St. Peter, 1957; Knights of Malta, 1959; The Exile of Capri, 1961; The Prince's Person, 1964; The Jews, 1967; Manouche, 1973.

ABOUT: Boisdeffre, P. de. Dictionnaire de littérature contemporaine, 1962; Boisdeffre, P. de. Une Histoire vivante de la littérature d'aujourd'hui, 1958; International Who's Who, 1972–73; Jouhandeau, M. Riposte à Roger Perfide, 1965; Pingaud, B. Écrivains d'aujourd'hui, 1960; Who's Who, 1973; Who's Who in France, 1973–1974. *Periodicals*—Jewish Social Studies January 1967; Kenyon Review Summer 1962; New York Times June 5, 1964; New York Times Book Review October 14 1965; Newsweek July 19, 1965; Time July 16, 1965; Twentieth Century October 1955.

***PICHETTE, HENRI** (January 26, 1924–), French poet and dramatist, was born at Châteauroux, near Tours, to a French-Canadian father (who became an American citizen) and a French mother. He spent some time in the youth camps operated by the Vichy government during the German occupation until he was old enough to join the First French

* pē shet′

Army. He subsequently served as a war correspondent in Germany and Austria. One of the key events of his life came in 1945 when he met Antonin Artaud, whose ideas he has sought to realize in his plays, and with whom he collaborated in writing the pamphlet *Xylophonie pour la grande presse et son petit public* (Xylophony for the Big Press and Its Little Public, 1946).

Pichette's first volume of verse, *Apoèmes*, and his first play, *Les Épiphanies*, established his reputation when he was twenty-three. The latter was first performed on December 3, 1947, at the minute Théâtre des Noctambules in Paris, under the direction of Georges Vitaly and with a cast including Gérard Philipe, Roger Blin, and Maria Casarès. The work is intended to represent the struggle between love and death, between betrayed youth and the corrupt old world, between the Poet and War. In fact, the conflict which would have given it dramatic life never quite reaches the stage, and what emerges is a kind of monologue by one character, the Poet, with interruptions by the others—a marvelously sustained firework display of violent language and dazzlingly inventive rhythms, which its cast turned into "a brilliant poetic recital." At the end of the first performance, Pichette was congratulated backstage by André Gide. By the next morning, he was famous.

A second play by Pichette, *Nucléa*, was staged by Gérard Philipe in 1952, with sets by Alexander Calder. It is another, more explicit, demand that the world should make love, not war. The first half is a tableau employing the devices of Artaud's "total theatre" to involve the spectator in the experience of modern war: diving bombers, machine-gun fire, shocking visual images, screams, and intolerable discords. This section, written in frenzied poetic prose and wholly concerned with war, suppression, and death, comes as close as any theatrical work has to achieving the sense-shattering impact Artaud demanded. Unfortunately the second half of the play, lyrically evoking the triumph of human love in rhymed alexandrines, exemplifies the kind of "literary" theatre that Artaud abominated.

Pichette's verse and prose poetry resembles his plays not only in its verbal shock tactics and packed imagery, reminiscent of Artaud and the surrealists, but also in its themes and in its tendency to hortatory monologue. Like Artaud, and even more like Rimbaud, Pichette is a natural revolutionary who speaks now in the prophetic tones of the seer, now with a desperate awareness of the inadequacy of words in the face of human misery. Both his poetry and his published plays have made use of visual devices—pages of dots, mixed type faces, bellowing capitals—in an attempt to smash the barriers between man and language, to "achieve the levitation of the poetic body."

HENRI PICHETTE

A militant Socialist, Pichette sees it as the poet's duty to denounce injustice and invoke revolution through an art as public and involving as a football match, as simple and brutal as a news report. But his talent is verbal and imagistic rather than dramatic. Like the English Socialist poet Christopher Logue, whom he resembles in many ways, Pichette has tended increasingly to sacrifice a natural lyricism on the altar of political rhetoric. At the same time, his poetry has gained in verbal skill and control since his delighted discovery of James Joyce in the late 1940s. It remains to be seen how he will develop. Some critics have been intrigued by a recurrence of Christian symbolism in his work, and what they see as hints of a "Christian solution."

Pichette has published several volumes of essays, most of them written in "impassioned appreciation" of Michaux, Artaud, Joyce, Gérard Philipe, Chaplin, and other artists he admires. The standard indexes list no English translations of his work, apart from a short prose poem in *French Writing Today* (Penguin, 1968), but others may well have appeared in unindexed publications.

ABOUT: Boisdeffre, P. de. Dictionnaire de littérature contemporaine, 1962; Boisdeffre, P. de. Une Histoire vivante de la littérature d'aujourd'hui, 1958; Guicharnaud, J. Modern French Theatre, 1961; Pingaud, B. Écrivains d'aujourd'hui, 1960; Pronko, L. C. Avant-Garde, 1962; Rousselot, J. Panorama Critique des nouveaux poètes français, 1952; Taylor, S. W. (ed.) French Writing Today, 1968. *Periodical:* French Review December 1958.

***PINGET, ROBERT** (July 19, 1919–), French novelist and dramatist, was born in Geneva. He at first read law, but after the war, in 1946, entered the

* paN zhā'

ROBERT PINGET

École des Beaux-Arts in Paris to study painting. He taught French and drawing in England for a while and has also worked as a journalist. There was an exhibition of his nonfigurative paintings in 1951. The same year he began seriously to write. His first novel, *Mahu ou le matériau* (1952, translated as *Mahu or the Material*), was very much in the manner of the French "new novelists" and was enthusiastically welcomed by Alain Robbe-Grillet. The other major influence on Pinget's work is that of his friend Samuel Beckett, who has translated Pinget's radio play *La Manivelle*.

Pinget's theme is himself or, more generally, the dilemma of the artist in a self-conscious age. The self-conscious writer cannot sustain the author's traditional pretense of omniscience; he knows no more of the truth than the reader does. He must therefore be silent, or content himself with a strictly limited creative role, scrupulously passing on, with a minimum of interference, the fragments of information that his own senses record or his own imagination suggests. Some writers, like Pinget, see even this as an ultimately impossible task. The act of writing down a sensory or emotional experience inevitably distorts it, changing it from a subjective to an objective happening, and exposing it to the action of language—an entity with a powerful emotional and intellectual life of its own.

All of Pinget's novels are therefore "antinovels," *intended* to fail, as illustrations of his thesis. Given that thesis, they are also acts of faith and of the will, things said when silence would be easier. The characters and events in these novels are unimportant; they are dredged up out of Pinget's mind by something like free association, and might as well tell one story as another. He says that "only the manner of speaking interests me," and the reader is supposed to interest himself not in "anecdotage," but in the drama of Pinget's style, the ways in which he makes words dance, stumble, gossip about each other, go mad, die.

Mahu ou le matériau is in its conception similar to Flann O'Brien's *At Swim-Two-Birds*. Mahu is writing a book about Latirail, himself a writer, some of whose characters from time to time spawn other personages. And all of these people interact not only with each other but with Pinget, of whom they are all reflections (since they came out of his mind). Mahu abandons his disorderly novel halfway through and the rest of Pinget's book is a sort of montage of incidents and quotations showing that fact is no more coherent and plausible than fiction. Other demonstrations of the relativity of truth, the impossibility of self-knowledge, occur in *Graal Flibuste* (1957), *Baga* (1958, translated under the same title), and *Le Fiston* (1959, translated in America as *Monsieur Levert*, in England as *No Answer*).

Pinget's most important book is *L'Inquisitoire* (1962, translated by Donald Watson as *The Inquisitory*). It records the questioning of a retired servant by an interrogator anxious to establish that the old man's former masters are perverts and criminals. The interrogator (like the reader) wants an indictment, a coherent pattern, a story. For the old servant (as for the artist), it is sufficiently difficult to express accurately in words what he knows. As the interrogation proceeds, he realizes that "the truth lies to one side, in what I don't know anymore or what I don't know yet or what you forgot to ask me."

Many French critics were charmed by the style of *L'Inquisitoire*, by "this humor in words, this disconnectedness, this intentional stuttering." Hubert Juin wrote: "As one frees oneself from the anecdotage, interest grows for the fascinating object that this book is. . . . It was in my hands, while I was reading, like a piece of *another being* into whom I was probing." Samuel Beckett called the book "one of the most important novels of the last ten years," and it received the Prix des Critiques. British and American critics, unaccustomed to freeing themselves from the anecdotage, were for the most part less warm. Although Vivian Mercier found in the old servant "a character fit to rank with Joyce's Bloom," most reviewers of the translation seemed to agree with Nigel Dennis, who called it "generally unreadable and appallingly boring."

All or most of Pinget's novels are set in a vague geographical area which has become recognized as "Pinget country." It is, as one reviewer put it, "a territory delineated essentially by names: of people, small towns, rivers, institutions, events." This territory receives its most detailed and coherent description in *L'Inquisitoire*, where, Pinget says, "I forced my imagination to descend into the real, to go toward a form which would give me a larger audience." It follows that his subsequent novels are even less accessible to the common reader. They include *Quelqu'un* (1965, translated as *Someone*), which received the Prix Fémina and turns, if that is the word, on a botanist's hopeless search for a document essential to his thesis; *Le Libera* (1968, translated as *The Libera Me Domine*), in which a chorus of village gossip is shaped into a dreamlike montage; and *Passacaille* (1969).

Pinget is also the author of a number of plays. *Lettre morte*, based on *Le Fiston*, was staged in Paris in 1960 and translated in 1963 as *Dead Letter*. *Baga* has been dramatized in part as *Architruc*, and translated under that title. *Ici ou ailleurs*, a stage version of the novel *Clope au dossier* (1961), has been translated as *Clope*. *La Manivelle* (translated by Samuel Beckett as *The Old Tune* and broadcast in England in 1960) is a play about two old men, an organ-grinder and his friend, whose recollections of the past totally contradict and cancel each other. Martin Esslin said that "this short radio play, brilliantly translated by Beckett into an Irish idiom, creates, out of fragments that in their strict naturalness are incoherent to the point of imbecility, a strange texture of nostalgic associations and lyrical beauty." Pinget has made French versions of Beckett's *All That Fall* (*Tous ceux qui tombent*, 1957) and *Krapp's Last Tape* (*La Dernière Bande*, 1959).

PRINCIPAL WORKS IN ENGLISH TRANSLATION: *Fiction*—Monsieur Levert (England, No Answer), 1961; The Inquisitory, 1966; Mahu or the Material, 1967; Baga, 1967; The Libera Me Domine, 1972. *Plays*—Plays, vol. I (The Old Tune, Clope, Dead Letter), 1963 (U.S., Three Plays); Plays, vol. II (Architruc, About Mortin, The Hypothesis), 1967 (U.S., Three Plays, vol. II, 1969).

ABOUT: Esslin, M. The Theatre of the Absurd, 1962; International Who's Who, 1972–73; Le Sage, L. The French New Novel, 1962; Peyre, H. French Novelists of Today, 1967; Ricardou, J. and Van Rossum-Guyon, F. (eds.) Nouveau Roman, 1972; Robbe-Grillet, A. For a New Novel, 1966; Who's Who in France, 1973–1974. *Periodicals*—Books Abroad Summer 1966; London Magazine October 1964; New York Review of Books March 23, 1967; New Yorker April 1, 1961; November 4, 1967; Saturday Review February 11, 1967; Times Literary Supplement March 26, 1964; December 16, 1965; January 6, 1966; July 27, 1967; April 18, 1968; August 14, 1969.

PINTER, HAROLD (October 10, 1930–), English dramatist, writes: "Was born and went to school in London. At about eighteen went to Dramatic School for a short time and was a conscientious objector to military service. Went to Ireland with Anew McMaster and played in Shakespeare fit-up for a couple of years. Wrote many poems and prose pieces. Acted all over England during the 1950s in rep. Wrote first play *The Room*

HAROLD PINTER

in 1957. Just before this married Vivien Merchant. Son born in 1958. Have written about twelve plays and a number of filmscripts. Very fond of cricket."

Pinter is the only child of Hyman Pinter, a tailor, and the former Frances Mann. The family is descended from Portuguese Jews named da Pinta. He was born and grew up in Hackney, on the impoverished eastern edge of London. British Fascists, driven underground by World War II, held revivalist meetings near a Jewish club which Pinter used to visit, and anti-Semitic brawls were common. The memory of this violence—arbitrary and, particularly to a child, irrational—helps to explain the latent violence in his plays.

From local primary schools, Pinter went on to Hackney Downs Grammar School, where an enthusiastic drama teacher, and his own success as an actor in school plays, directed him towards a stage career. In 1948 he entered the Royal Academy of Dramatic Art but, finding "a terrible atmosphere of affectation and unreality, ankle bands and golden hair," he soon left. In 1949, as he says, he went to Ireland with the venerable and eccentric Shakespearian actor Anew McMaster (of whom he has written an affectionate memoir, *Mac*). After this colorful beginning, and another period of study at the Central School of Speech and Drama, he worked (as David Baron) with a number of more orthodox British repertories. Between engagements he was a doorman, salesman, waiter, dishwasher; in his spare time he wrote poems and short stories and tinkered with a novel, *The Dwarfs*.

In 1956, at a party, Pinter came upon two people in a small room: a big man wearing a cap, seated, and a small man with bare feet, standing. The big man was silent but the little man was chattering on brightly, and feeding the other as if he were a child. This ludicrous but somehow disturbing scene impressed Pinter. He described it to a friend who taught drama at Bristol University, was asked to work it up into a play for student production, and in four days wrote *The Room*. It is set, like most of Pinter's early plays, in a single room which represents a limited and threatened security, a refuge from unknown horrors outside. The characters are Rose, a talkative woman; her husband, Bert, whom she mothers; and a succession of visitors who in various ways threaten their sanctuary. Of these the most mysterious is a blind black man who insists that he has claims on Rose (who insists that she doesn't know him).

Immature and imperfect as it is, this play contains most of the elements that identify Pinter's early "comedies of menace"—the marvelously exact and funny reproduction of the stupidities, irrelevancies, and evasions of ordinary speech, the convincingly circumstantial statements which are then contradicted, the anxiety-inducing sense that nothing is certain, that unfamiliar rules are operating—or none. (In the end Bert turns on the blind man and beats him cruelly. We wait for Bert to be punished, but what happens is that his wife goes blind.)

Pinter's sense of life's uncertainty is his own, like his ear for the poetic and the dramatic possibilities of banal conversations; but he has acknowledged the influence on his work of Kafka, American gangster films and, above all, of Samuel Beckett. He saw *Waiting for Godot* in London in 1956 and responded profoundly to the quality of the relationships it illustrated and the general atmosphere of ambiguity and despair. He differs from Beckett most obviously in that his plays, however "Absurd" or arbitrary in their motivation and development, are usually impeccably naturalistic on the surface.

In *The Dumb Waiter* (1957), two professional killers are uneasily awaiting their orders in a squalid basement room in an otherwise empty house; there is going to be a murder but they don't know yet who the victim will be. They talk, read the newspaper, argue about football and grammar, eat biscuits. Suddenly a dumb waiter in the wall clatters down, bearing a demand for "Two braised steaks and chips. Two sago puddings. Two teas without sugar." This order, so unlike the one they had expected, is followed by others for increasingly exotic foreign dishes. Bewildered, anxious, afraid of discovery, the two men send up their pathetically inadequate provisions until nothing is left. Another order comes down and after that one of the killers is waiting for the other, his gun drawn.

Pinter's first full-length play, also written in 1957, was *The Birthday Party*. Once again the setting is wholly naturalistic—a shabby seaside boarding house modeled on those that Pinter knew as an actor. Here lives Stanley, an indolent, self-indulgent man who claims without conviction that he was once a concert pianist of promise, whose career had been ruined by jealous enemies. Now he does nothing at all, but lives by exploiting the generosity of his sluttish but motherly old landlady, Meg. This cozy idyll is ended by the arrival of two mysterious strangers, Goldberg and McCann, who, in a manner reminiscent both of Kafka's *The Trial* and *Alice in Wonderland*, begin to cross-examine Stanley. Between them they accuse him of every kind of evil—of betraying the "organization" and religious heresy, of embezzlement and murder, of unspecified crimes against Ireland, cricket, big business, and the Blessed Oliver Plunkett. This is followed by a kind of ritual humiliation of Stanley at his birthday party. Stanley, who insists that it is not his birthday anyway, finally collapses into numb silence. Next morning, clean, bowler-hatted, anonymous, he is led away to a waiting car and an unknown fate.

Critics have interpreted the play as an allegory variously of death, or of society's hostility to the artist, or of a young man's painful and unwilling rite of passage into conformity. Martin Esslin would rather view it as an exploration of "a situation which, in itself, is a valid poetic image that is immediately seen as relevant and true. It speaks plainly of the individual's pathetic search for security; of secret dreads and anxieties, of the terrorism of our world . . . of the tragedy that arises from lack of understanding between people on different levels of awareness." This is much closer to Pinter's own view of his work than any attempt to read it as illustrating some abstract theme or idea; he says: "I start writing a play from an image of a situation and a couple of characters involved, and these people always remain for me quite real."

Most of the scholarly and ingenious speculations about *The Birthday Party* came long after its first production in 1958. Then, after a promising beginning in the provinces, it closed within a week of its London opening, savaged by critics who called it "a bad farce alternating with stale misery" and "a masterpiece of meaningless significance." Out of work, with a wife and young baby to support, and bitterly discouraged, Pinter went on writing only because the BBC came to his rescue, commissioning what became *A Slight Ache*, broadcast in 1959 and later staged.

A Slight Ache is concerned with a middle-aged couple, Edward and Flora, who become obsessed with an old match-seller outside their house and invite him in. Indoors, he cannot be persuaded to say or do anything whatever. The weak and talkative Edward, increasingly worried and suspicious, batters himself into breakdown against this monumental (but really quite vacant) silence. Flora, on the other hand, warms to this old derelict, who so obviously needs her womanly attentions. In the end, under Flora's guidance, tramp and husband exchange roles.

Edward's mistake is that he reveals himself too completely—literally gives himself away. Pinter believes that the usual aim of conversation is not self-revelation but its opposite: "I think that we communicate only too well, in our silence, in what is unsaid, and that what takes place [in conversation] is continual evasion, desperate rear-guard attempts to keep ourselves to ourselves. Communication is too alarming. To enter into someone's life is too frightening. To disclose to others the poverty within us is too fearsome a possibility." Instead "there is a continual cross-talking" between people, "a continual talking about other things rather than what is at the root of their relationship." This perception is illustrated in all of Pinter's work. The early "comedies of menace" derive additional suspense from the threat of some unknown horror outside, but the later plays, after *A Slight Ache*, relinquish this device to concentrate without distraction on the study of relationships, drawing tension from what John Russell Taylor calls their "endless skirmishing on the threshold of communication, with each character determined to find out more than he tells."

By 1959 Pinter was beginning to win some recognition from a perceptive minority, and he achieved his first popular success with the sketches he contributed in that year to the revues *One to Another* and *Pieces of Eight*. But his real arrival as a major figure in the British theatre came in 1960, when his second full-length play, *The Caretaker*, opened in London. The setting is familiar—a junk-filled attic in a derelict London house—but this room is in no way threatened from the outside. The "menace" that can be felt in *The Caretaker* is intrinsic, arising from the frightening sense of man's isolation that the play evokes, for each of the three characters is tragically, but also comically, sealed within his own mind and personality.

Aston, the kindly, simple man who lives in the attic has, we learn, received electric shock treatment after a mental breakdown and is permanently dulled and diminished. Davies, the blustering, cringing old vagabond to whom Aston offers a bed, is so afraid of communication that he won't even acknowledge his place of birth. Aston's younger brother Mick is an elusive and volatile player of roles; he alternately torments and flatters Davies, offers him a job as caretaker of the house, encourages him to insult Aston, and finally uses the insult as an excuse to throw him out (presumably his intention all along).

The Caretaker was acclaimed by the British critics and won the London *Evening Standard*'s award as the best play of 1960; it was equally successful the following year in New York and has since been staged all over the world and filmed from the author's own scenario. It has been the most discussed and "interpreted" of all of Pinter's plays, construed as a political and as a religious fable, or simply as a vision of man in his animal nature, endlessly struggling to protect his territorial rights and to dominate his fellows. Pinter will say only that he feels "very strongly about the particular, not about symbolism," and that the play is about "three men in a room." Even at this level, as a study in character and relationships, motives and actions are often deeply ambiguous, and open to a variety of readings.

A Night Out, written at about the same time as *The Caretaker*, and produced on radio and television before it reached the stage, is the most conventional and approachable of Pinter's plays. It is a more or less comic account of a young man's attempt to throw off the domination of his possessive mother by visiting a prostitute. All that happens is that he acts out his need for rebellion by bullying the unfortunate girl, accusing her of his mother's faults, before returning meekly to the status quo. Another genteel prostitute appears in the television play *Night School*, which Pinter once called the worst thing he has written.

This was followed by *The Dwarfs*, a radio play derived from Pinter's unpublished and partly autobiographical novel (and subsequently expanded and adapted for the stage). It is of considerable interest because for the first time in a Pinter play we are offered interior monologue, and consequently direct insight into a character's thought processes. This character is Len, whose relationships with two friends and with himself provide the theme of this very difficult play. Its conclusion (clouded by the fact that Len is obviously very close to a mental breakdown) seems to be that there is no such thing as an absolute truth or a unique, consistent, human identity; we are each simply the sum of the roles we play.

This theme is pursued in two subsequent television plays: *The Collection* (1961) and *The Lover* (1963). The first is a complicated social comedy turning on the question of whether Bill, a clothes designer, slept with Stella, a married colleague, at a fashion show in Leeds; each concedes and then—at a different time or to a different auditor—denies that this has happened. The audience is left not knowing whether the accusation is morally or actually true or wholly false, or what kind of people it has been watching. *The Lover* is about a happily married couple—though, we learn, the wife has a lover. It emerges that the lover is her husband, who visits her in the afternoons, taking on a different name and an appropriate persona in which to fulfill their mutual need for fantasy and excitement.

John Russell Taylor has suggested that the exploration of the ambiguity of character brought Pinter at this point to a logical and emotional impasse. For about two years he produced no new play but instead wrote scenarios for four films based on the work of other writers: *The Pumpkin Eater*, *The Quiller Memorandum*, and two films by Joseph Losey, *The Servant* and *Accident*. There was another television play, *Tea Party*, in 1965—a study in paranoia, and hence in suspicion, the subjective interpretation of evidence, the questionable nature of reality.

Pinter's third full-length stage play, *The Homecoming*, opened the same year. Teddy, the long-absent son of an East End Jewish family, comes home on a visit from America, where he has made good as a scholar and critic. All his life he has been contemptuously dominated by his villainous old father and his brothers; now, successful, equipped with a beautiful wife, he expects to receive the respect and admiration he deserves. On the contrary, his claims (always slightly suspect) and he himself are dismissed as scornfully as ever. His family are more impressed by Ruth, his enigmatic wife. They suggest that she should abandon her husband and children, and stay with them as their communal mistress, earning her keep as a whore. This proposition she considers and graciously accepts, and Teddy returns alone to America.

The play had great success in London and later in New York, where it received the New York Drama Critics' Circle Award and the Antoinette Perry Award. Critics saw parallels with (or ironic inversions of) the biblical stories of Ruth and of the prodigal son, and Hugh Nelson has pointed out some interesting similarities to Shakespeare's *Troilus and Cressida*. Some regard Ruth's process of self-discovery as the central movement of the play and it has of course been given a variety of Freudian interpretations. Technically, it is one of the most accomplished of Pinter's plays—Hugh Nelson has called it an Ibsenite well-made play in which "exposition, development, and resolution have been driven underground through a healthy distrust of language" and a refusal "to compel any character to say more than he wants to say or can say at a given moment." The characters are revealed in spite of themselves, through their lies, evasions, hesitations, and silences. *The Homecoming*, wrote John Russell Taylor, "may haunt the spectator, or it may say nothing to him at all. It is, either way, impregnable in its monumental detachment from what he thinks: a monolithic statement of its own right to exist."

Another television play, *The Basement* (1967), derives from a very early sketch called "Kullus," which dates back to 1949. It is an unusually abstract study, with some of the quality of a writer's exercise, centering on the struggle between two men for the ownership of a girl and a room. In 1970 Pinter returned to the stage with three short plays connected by a preoccupation with memory. In *Landscape* an old couple seem to be exchanging reminiscences, but are actually pursuing private monologues. A married couple, remembering their first meeting and early happiness in *Night*, are so far from connecting that they might be talking about quite different people. In *Silence*, two men and a woman muse, mostly privately but sometimes in conversation, about their relationship with each other, and the almost forgotten past. Pinter's debt to Beckett is nowhere more evident than in these three plays, and especially the last, which, moreover, in the near absence of interaction or even contact between the speakers, and its incantatory use of rhythm, refrain, and counterpoint, seems closer to a choral poem than to the drama.

No such criticism was or could be made of Pinter's next full-length play, *Old Times*, which also explores the uncertainty (or the autonomy) of memory. A married couple, Deeley and Kate, live in the country in a converted farmhouse. They await the arrival of Kate's friend Anna, whom Kate has not seen since as young secretaries they shared a flat in London. Anna arrives (or rather her presence on stage is revealed). At that point the high-comedy banter of the opening scene gives way to a subtle but increasingly ferocious contest of memory between Deeley and Anna—about the words of some popular songs of the 1940s, about how Deeley picked up Kate in a movie theatre showing the film *Odd Man Out* (if he did), about the man (was it Deeley?) whom Anna remembers crying on Kate's bed. The prize for whom they fight is Kate. Is she the Kate who was a part of Anna's youth, or the Kate who is an essential element in Deeley's image of himself? It becomes clear that she is neither. And when Anna is exhausted and Deeley is broken by the struggle, it is Kate, by her indifference, her languid nonparticipation, who has won. The stage darkens except for a single light on Kate; she remains, J. W. Lambert wrote, "expressionless at the centre of perhaps the most piercing stage picture I have ever seen, creator and destroyer in one."

The members of the audience, who have been led unsuspectingly through the play, chuckling and guffawing at the good jokes, smiling fondly at the nostalgia, know in the end that they have been watching not a comedy but a tragedy, and one in which they share. Deeley and Anna have constructed their lives by selecting what is bearable from among their memories and inventing the rest. So do we all; the revelation is inescapable. Lambert thought that *Old Times* was Pinter's "finest play so far, constructed with a sure formal beauty, embracing a humane imaginative scope far beyond anything Pinter has previously attempted." Harold Hobson (who maintains quite plausibly that the entire play is composed of Deeley's jealous speculations *before* Anna actually arrives) called it "one of the finest plays, one of the most mind-startling, one of the most immaculately written, of its generation."

Vivien Merchant, Pinter's wife, is among the most respected of English actresses, not least for her performances in her husband's plays. Pinter himself still acts occasionally, and has also made a new reputation as a director—of a revival of *The Birthday Party* in 1964, of Robert Shaw's *The Man in the Glass Booth* (1967), of Joyce's play *The Exiles* (1970), and of Simon Gray's comedy *Butley* (1971). In 1973, when Peter Hall succeeded Laurence Olivier as director of the National Theatre in London, Pinter joined the company as one of four associate directors. His recent film scenarios include adaptations of *The Birthday Party* (1968), L. P. Hartley's *The Go-Between* (1969), and Aidan Higgins' *Langrishe, Go Down* (1970).

Pinter is a little under six feet tall, cool and temperate of speech, and in conversation scrupulously honest and precise. He was once voted one of the ten best-dressed men in England. He received a CBE in 1966.

Pinter has been criticized for the lack of any political or social commitment in his plays, and called an "anti-humanist" who sees life as "inconsequent to the point of insanity." In fact, though he dislikes politics and distrusts all ideological statements, he is by no means indifferent to the state of the world (as is evident from his determined and eventually successful refusal of military service as a young man). After *The Caretaker* he wrote a full-length play called *The Hothouse*, an anti-establishment satire which he thought "quite useless" and discarded: "I never began to like any of the characters, they really didn't live at all."

Walter Kerr regards Pinter as an existentialist who manages to write as if "existence" does indeed "precede essence." Martin Esslin claims him as an exponent of the Theatre of the Absurd (but Pinter says, "Sometimes I feel absurd, sometimes I don't"). John Russell Taylor believes that Pinter's plays are "the true poetic drama of our time, for he alone has fully understood that poetry in the theatre is not achieved merely by couching ordinary sentiments in an elaborately artificial poetic diction. . . . Instead he has looked at life so closely that, seeing it through his eyes, we discover the strange sublunary poetry which lies in the most ordinary object at the other end of a microscope." He is generally regarded as the most important English dramatist to emerge since World War II.

PRINCIPAL WORKS: *Plays*—The Birthday Party and Other Plays (with The Room, The Dumb Waiter), 1960; The Caretaker, 1960; A Slight Ache and Other Plays (with A Night Out, The Dwarfs, some revue sketches), 1961; The Collection, and, The Lover, 1963; The Homecoming, 1965; Tea Party and Other Plays (with The Basement, Night School), 1967; Landscape, 1968; Landscape and Silence (with Night), 1969; Five Screenplays (The Pumpkin Eater, The Quiller Memorandum, The Servant, Accident, The Go-Between), 1971; Old Times, 1971. *Miscellaneous*—Mac, 1968; Poems, 1968.

ABOUT: Brown, J. R. Modern British Dramatists, 1968; Brown, J. R. Theatre Language: A Study of Arden, Osborne, Pinter and Wesker, 1972; Burkman, K. H. The Dramatic World of Harold Pinter, 1971; Current Biography, 1963; Esslin, M. The Peopled Wound: The Work of Harold Pinter, 1970 (revised as Pinter: A Study of His Plays, 1973); Esslin, M. The Theatre of the Absurd, 1968; Ganz, A. (ed.) Pinter: A Collection of Critical Essays, 1972; Gilman, R. Common and Uncommon Masks, 1971; Hayman, R. Harold Pinter, 1968; Hinchliffe, A. P. Harold Pinter, 1967; Hollis, J. R. Harold Pinter, 1970; Kerr, W. Harold Pinter, 1967; Kitchin, L. Drama in the Sixties, 1966; Lahr, J. (ed.) The Homecoming: A Casebook, 1969; Lewis, O. Anthropological Essays, 1970; McCrindle, J. F. (ed.) Behind the Scenes, 1971; Schroll, H. T. Harold Pinter: A Study of His Reputation (1958–1969), 1971; Sheed, W. The Morning After, 1971; Sykes, A. Harold Pinter, 1970; Taylor, J. R. Anger and After, 1962 (U.S., The Angry Theatre); Trussler, S. The Plays of Harold Pinter, 1973; Wager, W. (ed.) The Playwrights Speak, 1967; Wellwarth, G. E. The Theatre of Protest and Paradox, 1964; Who's Who, 1973. *Periodicals*—Catholic World April 19, 1971; Drama Review Winter 1968; Drama Survey Spring 1967, Spring 1968; Encounter March 1968; Life September 17, 1971; Massachusetts Review Autumn 1967; Modern Drama June 1964, September 1965, September 1966, September 1967, September 1968, December 1968; Nation June 7, 1971; New Statesman June 26, 1964; June 11, 1965; New York Times January 1, 1967; October 1, 1967; October 27, 1967; New York Times Magazine December 5, 1971; New Yorker February 25, 1967; Observer February 19, 1967; Paris Review Fall 1966, Spring 1967; Spectator June 29, 1962; September 27, 1963; Time November 10, 1961; Times (London) March 14, 1973; May 11, 1973; Tulane Drama Review Spring 1962, Winter 1966, Winter 1967; Twentieth Century September 1960, February 1961.

***PIOVENE, GUIDO, COUNT** (July 27, 1907–), Italian novelist, journalist, and critic, was born at Vicenza in that part of northern Italy called the Veneto. He is the son of Count Francesco Piovene, whose title he has inherited, and a descendant of Antonio Pigafetta, who sailed with Magellan. Piovene grew up on his father's estate at Vicenza and in various family houses in the Po Valley. He was educated in a Barnabite college at Lodi, near Milan, and at Milan University, where he obtained a degree in philosophy. In 1930 he went to Germany as correspondent for the journal *Ambrosiano*, and later was its literary critic. In 1933 he joined the editorial staff of the short-lived Florentine review *Pan*, and in 1935 moved to *Il Corriere della Sera*. As a young man Piovene was an ardent Fascist, and

* pyō vā′ nā

GUIDO PIOVENE

defended Mussolini and his military ambitions in his articles. Later, disillusioned, he turned to communism.

His first book was *La vedova allegra* (The Merry Widow, 1931), a collection of short stories of which he is no longer proud. Ten years passed before his next book appeared, the novel *Lettere di una novizia* (1941, translated as *Confession of a Novice*). It is about a girl who is forced against her will into a convent from which she eventually escapes. The story is told in the form of letters which gradually reveal her waywardness of mind and the deficiencies of her character, unfolding her personality with a skill which reminded some critics of Laclos. The book was filmed in 1960, and is the most admired of Piovene's novels.

A second novel, written at about the same time as the first, was published in 1943 as *La gazzetta nera* (The Black Gazette). Set in a newspaper office, it is a series of biographical sketches which center around and finally elucidate a crime. Though it was received with rather less enthusiasm than its predecessor, one episode, "Il monaco spagnuolo" (The Spanish Monk), was singled out for praise by the critics.

In all of Piovene's novels the faults and virtues of the protagonists are presented as very much the products not of free will but of their noble heredity and wealthy environment. They "move aimlessly in a sheltered bourgeois world, unable to face the truth about themselves," but "titillating their conscience" with "ambiguous self-confessions of real or imagined crimes." And always it is the step-by-step revelation of character which concerns him, sometimes to the detriment of plot and structure. His novels, it has been said, are full "of flashbacks, digressions, narrations within the narration," like Chinese boxes; or they are like jigsaw puzzles in which the picture cannot be understood until the last piece is inserted. Piovene's overwhelming concern for character, his interest in people torn by religious conflict, and his great feeling for the architecture, climate, and landscape of his native Po Valley, have led to his being described as "the last and most dyed-in-the-wool" disciple of another novelist of the Veneto, Antonio Fogazzaro. One of Piovene's best-known and most valuable critical essays is a study of Fogazzaro, published in 1942 in *La letteratura.*

Two more novels followed in 1946 and 1949, *Pietà contro pietà* (Piety Against Piety) and *I falsi redentori* (The False Redeemers). At that point Piovene temporarily abandoned fiction and for a long time concentrated on journalism. Between 1935 and 1953 he served *Il Corriere della Sera* as its special correspondent in London and Paris, and for a time as its film critic. In 1953 he moved to *La Stampa.* He became famous and greatly esteemed as a foreign correspondent, especially for his brilliant and voluminous reporting from France, Poland, Bulgaria, the Soviet Union, and America. In his journalism, as in his fiction, he is a polished stylist who goes to immense pains to get to the heart of the facts.

Piovene's impressions of the United States, *De America* (On America), were published in 1953. The book is now regarded as the most important study of American life and culture written by an Italian. *Viaggio in Italia* (Travels in Italy, 1957) was also very successful. *La coda di paglia* (The Tail of Straw, 1962) is a collection of his essays in which he discusses, among other things, his former connection with fascism, pointing out how difficult objectivity had been in the climate of the 1930s.

But Piovene's youthful admiration for Mussolini has not been forgiven, and according to some accounts cost him the Viareggio prize when at last his next novel appeared. This was *Le furie* (The Furies, 1963), a long book, far more ambitious than its predecessors, but set like them in Vicenza. It is a "visionary novel," a sort of journey of the mind which draws on dreams as well as reality, and which puzzled many critics and irritated some. They found its intention unclear, its references too subjective and private, even when they recognized that the book had been a cathartic necessity for Piovene. It is no doubt an attempt, and an interesting and courageous one, to submit himself to the kind of "moral inquest" which he had conducted on fictional characters in earlier novels.

Piovene has served as director of UNESCO's Art and Letters Division, and on the executive council of the Congress for Cultural Freedom. He is a member of the Accademia Olimpica of Vicenza. A stocky, distinguished-looking man with a military moustache, Piovene says that his hobby is the appreciation of objets d'art and that his favorite sport is mountaineering. When he is not traveling, he lives either in Milan or at his wife's house in the Veneto. Although Piovene's flirtation with communism has earned him the nickname of "Il Conte Rosso" (The Red Count), his "aristocratic approach" to the writing of novels has often been commented upon, and indeed his present way of life might be considered very far from socialistic.

PRINCIPAL WORKS IN ENGLISH TRANSLATION: Confession of a Novice, 1950; Italy, 1955. *Extract from* Pietà contro pietà *in* New World Writing, Seventh Mentor Selection, 1955. *Articles in English in* Burnham, J. (ed.) What Europe Thinks of America, 1953; Hutchins, R. M. and Adler, M. J. (eds.) The Great Ideas Today, 1964; Atlantic December 1958; Italian Quarterly 4, 1958.

ABOUT: Dizionario enciclopedico della letteratura italiana, 1966; Dizionario universale della letteratura contemporanea, 1959; Heiney, D. W. America in Modern Italian Literature, 1965; International Who's Who, 1972–73; The Penguin Companion to Literature 2, 1969.

"PITCAIRN, FRANK." *See* COCKBURN, (FRANCIS) CLAUD

"PLAIDY, JEAN." *See* HIBBERT, ELEANOR BURFORD

PLATH, SYLVIA (October 27, 1932–February 11, 1963), American poet, was born in Boston, Massachusetts. Her mother, the former Aurelia Schober, was of Austrian descent. Her father, Otto, who came from Grabow in the Polish corridor, was a professor of biology at Boston University and an authority on bees. Sylvia Plath and her younger brother grew up beside the sea at Winthrop, Massachusetts. Her father died in 1940 and the family moved inland to Wellesley, Massachusetts, where Mrs. Plath worked as a teacher. Sylvia Plath felt her father's death as a betrayal, a desertion, and nothing in her life ever quite made up for this double loss, of her father and the sea.

She began to write verses when she was about eight, winning occasional newspaper contests and other encouraging marks of recognition. She went on to write short stories and to develop a talent for sketching and painting. The first of many sales to *Seventeen* came in 1950. At high school in Wellesley she gave a convincing performance as an "outgoing All-Round student" without, apparently, convincing herself: her stories and poems usually ended on a wry note of withdrawal. But the performance continued at Smith College where, after a difficult first year, she emerged as a socially successful Phi Beta Kappa student, "remorselessly winning all the prizes" but still troubled by self-doubts.

In 1952 Sylvia Plath was one of the two winners

SYLVIA PLATH

of the *Mademoiselle* fiction contest. The following summer she spent a hectic month as a guest editor of the magazine's annual college issue, and sold three poems to *Harper's* for a hundred dollars. "All in all," she wrote, "I felt upborne on a wave of creative, social and financial success." Back home in Wellesley however she plunged into a disabling state of depression and made several suicide attempts, one of them nearly successful. Hospitalization, psychiatric treatment, and electric shock therapy returned her to Smith by the winter of 1953–1954, apparently as good as new. She graduated in 1955, *summa cum laude*.

Later that year Sylvia Plath went to England on a Fulbright Fellowship to study at Newnham College, Cambridge. She met the English poet Ted Hughes, and married him in June 1956. In 1957 they went to the United States, where for a year she was a notably successful and popular English instructor at Smith. She spent another year in Boston, writing, attending Robert Lowell's classes at Boston University, and meeting George Starbuck, Anne Sexton, and other poets. In 1959 she and her husband made a camping tour of the United States, and in December, after two months at Yaddo, the artists' colony in Saratoga Springs, New York, returned to England for good.

Their first child, Frieda, was born in London in April 1960, and Sylvia Plath's first book, *The Colossus*, was published later the same year. A few years later she found that she was bored by these civilized, accomplished, sometimes rather ornate poems. Nevertheless, the best of them foreshadow the lucidity, the passion, and the intense awareness of metaphysical danger that was to come: "Droll, vegetarian, the water rat / Saws down a reed and swims for his limber grove, / While the students stroll or sit, / Hands laced, in a moony indolence of love— / Black-gowned, but unaware / How in such mild air / The owl shall stoop from his turret, the rat cry out." ("Watercolor of Grantchester Meadows.")

Sylvia Plath was a tall, rawboned woman with high coloring and long sandy hair which she sometimes wore in a bun. Her social manner has been described by A. Alvarez as one of "anxious pleasantness." Her husband says that she had strong psychic gifts. She was ambitious for praise and acceptance, and taught herself to be an efficient wife and mother as she had taught herself to be a good student and poet. In 1961 the couple bought a thatched house in Devon. She threw herself enthusiastically into country life, working hard to make the house comfortable, keeping bees and collecting honey, learning to ride.

By then, Sylvia Plath's poetry had undergone a decisive change. She had been guided by Robert Lowell's *Life Studies* (1959)—"this intense breakthrough into very serious, very personal, emotional experience which I feel has been partly taboo." Moreover, according to Ted Hughes, "with the birth of her first child she received herself, and was able to turn to her advantage all the forces of a highly disciplined, highly intellectual style of education which had, up to this point, worked mainly against her, but without which she could hardly have gone so coolly into the regions she now entered. The birth of her second child [Nicholas], in January of 1962, completed the preparation."

The poems in *The Colossus* were written slowly and laboriously, with a careful regard for the laws of prosody, and her father's thesaurus in hand; her new poems were written at great and increasing speed. During 1962 she was repeatedly ill, with flu and fevers. At the end of the year she and her husband separated, and she moved with her children to London, where she was doing some work for the British Broadcasting Corporation. She was writing now between four in the morning and about seven, when the children woke up, sometimes producing two or three poems in a day in "one of the most astonishing creative outbursts of our generation."

Her novel *The Bell Jar* appeared in January 1963 under the pseudonym Victoria Lucas. It is based on her experiences during the summer of 1953—the month with *Mademoiselle*, breakdown, attempted suicide, and eventual escape from the "bell jar," the private vacuum, in which her madness had confined her. It is a vivid and very readable novel, wryly funny, and of extreme importance to the understanding of her poetry. Thus, for example, she describes the moment when her heroine, poised at the top of the Mount Pisgah ski slope, first realizes that she might kill herself. She launches herself straight down, feeling, as she gathers speed: "This is what it is to be happy. . . . I plummeted down past the zigzaggers, the students, the experts, through year after year of doubleness and smiles and compromise, into my own past." Sylvia Plath was unhappy about the novel and its reception, though in fact it has been greatly admired. Less than a month after its publication, following a uniquely fruitful spasm of creativity, she gassed herself.

Ariel, made up mostly of poems written during the last months of her life, appeared in England in 1965. George Steiner wrote: "It is fair to say that no group of poems since Dylan Thomas's *Deaths and Entrances* has had as vivid an impact on English critics and readers." In these poems Sylvia Plath was no longer composing by finger-count but by ear-count, speaking them out loud as they came in the urgent and accelerating rhythms of her own voice. Many of them are furiously and destructively intimate revelations of her feelings about herself, her friends, father, husband, and children, about life and, often, death. The most powerful of them is about what she herself called her "Electra Complex": "You stand at the blackboard, daddy, / In the picture I have of you, / A cleft in your chin instead of your foot / But no less a devil for that, no not / Any less the black man who // Bit my pretty red heart in two. / I was ten when they buried you. / At twenty I tried to die / And get back, back, back, to you. / I thought even the bones would do // . . . . I made a model of you / A man in black with a Meinkampf look // And a love of the rack and the screw. / And I said I do, I do. / So daddy, I'm finally through. / The black telephone's off at the root, / The voices just can't worm through. // . . . . There's a stake in your fat black heart / And the villagers never liked you. / They are dancing and stomping on you. / They always *knew* it was you. / Daddy, daddy, you bastard, I'm through." ("Daddy," 1963.)

What is most remarkable about these violently personal utterances is that they never escape the control of wit and art. This jaunty control, maintained at unimaginable cost, elevates what could have been neurotic confessions of a now fashionable sort into authentic statements of a specifically contemporary era of suffering. The poet in her despair puts on the *persona* of the Japanese at Hiroshima, the Jew at Dachau. In "Lady Lazarus" (1963) she says to her father: "I am your opus, / I am your valuable, / The pure gold baby // That melts to a shriek, / I turn and burn. / Do not think I underestimate your great concern. // Ash, ash— / You poke and stir. / Flesh, bone, there is nothing there — / A cake of soap, / A wedding ring, / A gold filling . . ."

The prevailing view of Sylvia Plath is still that advanced by her friend, the critic A. Alvarez. He regards her as one of art's martyrs, an "Extremist" poet who achieved the authority and intensity of her last poems by driving herself down through her own despair to its roots. He believes that she deliberately gambled with madness and death, and lost. George Steiner on the other hand believes that her suicide was inevitable—that from the country of her last poems there could be no return. Steiner calls her "a minor poet of great intensity," whose work culminated "in an act of identification, of total communion with those tortured and massacred." Charles Newman makes larger claims; he says that she "rewedded imagist technique to the narrative line" and "showed us that a poet can still deal with the most mystical elements of existence without sacrificing any precision of craftsmanship. One is reminded of Beethoven's atonal explosions in the last quartets, of Turner's last seascapes as they became abstractionist holocausts. In the last poems there is not the slightest gap between theory and realization, between myth and the concrete particular—they utterly escape the self-consciousness of craft."

Although it was the rage and despair in her work that caught the public imagination, an opposing quality of generous affirmation persisted alongside it, and should not be overlooked. As her husband says, "Her elements were extreme; a violent, almost demonic spirit in her, opposed a tenderness and capacity to suffer and love things infinitely, which was just as great and far more in evidence. Her stormy, luminous senses assaulted a downright, practical intelligence. . . . Her vision of death, her muse of death in life and life in death, with its oppressive evidence, fought in her against a joy in life, and in every smallest pleasure, for which her favorite word 'ecstasy' was simply accurate, as her poems prove."

Since her death, predictably, Sylvia Plath has become the object of a cult. Much has been and is being written about her. *The Bell Jar*, when at last her family allowed its publication in the United States, at once became a best seller. Her uncollected poems, of which there are said to be a great many, are being published (presumably for financial reasons) in dribs and drabs—apart from various limited editions, there were thirty-four "transitional" poems in *Crossing the Water*, a mere eighteen from the last great "blood jet" (as she called it) in *Winter Trees*.

PRINCIPAL WORKS: The Colossus, 1960; The Bell Jar (novel) (published as by "Victoria Lucas," 1963; republished under her own name, 1966); Ariel, 1965; Three Women (radio play), 1968; Crossing the Water, 1971; Winter Trees (with the play Three Women), 1971.
ABOUT: Aird, E. Sylvia Plath, 1973; Allott, K. Penguin Book of Contemporary Verse, 1962; Alvarez, A. Beyond All This Fiddle, 1968; Alvarez, A. The Savage God, 1971; British Broadcasting Corporation, Writers on Themselves, 1964; Contemporary Authors 19–20, 1968; Newman, C. (ed.) The Art of Sylvia Plath, 1970; Orr, P. (ed.) The Poet Speaks, 1966; Steiner, G. Language and Silence, 1969; Steiner, N. H. A Closer Look at Ariel: A Memory of Sylvia Plath, 1973. *Periodicals*—Atlantic August 1966; Cambridge Review February 7, 1969; Chicago Review 1 1968; Critical Quarterly Spring 1965; Encounter August 1968; London Magazine February 1962; Ms. September 1972; New Republic June 18, 1966; New Society July 11, 1968; New York Review of Books August 12, 1971; New York Times June 8, 1966; New York Times Book Review October 10, 1971; Newsweek June 20, 1966; Partisan Review Winter 1967; Poetry October 7, 1965; The Review 9 1963; Spectator January 17, 1970; Time June 10, 1966; Times Literary Supplement November 24, 1965; January 12, 1970; Triquarterly (special issue) Fall 1966.

PLUMB, J(OHN) H(AROLD) (August 20, 1911–), English historian and biographer, was born in Leicester, the third son of James and Sarah (Timpson) Plumb. He was educated in Leicester at Alderman Newton's School and University College, Leicester, where he took a first class honors degree in history in 1933. Plumb went on to Christ's College, Cambridge, where his researches in the social structure of the House of Commons under William III were supervised by the great social historian G. M. Trevelyan. He received his Ph.D. in 1936 and stayed on at Cambridge, in 1939 becoming Ehrman Research Fellow at King's College.

During World War II Plumb worked from 1940 to 1945 in the intelligence division of the Foreign Office, but retained his Ehrman fellowship until 1946. Since then he has taught at Cambridge as a university lecturer in history (1946–1962), reader (1962–1965), and professor of modern English history (1966–). He is a fellow of Christ's College, and has served his college as steward (1948–1950), tutor (1950–1959), and vice-master (1964–1968).

Plumb's specialty is England in the eighteenth century, and this was the title of his first book, published in 1950 and tracing the development of English society during the days of Walpole and the two William Pitts. A biography followed of Pitt the Elder, first Earl of Chatham. It was a stimulating contribution to the Brief Lives series, developing the controversial theory that Chatham's frequently outrageous behavior was a symptom of manic-depression. The critics found it historically sound and "a vivacious and thoroughly enjoyable" treatment of a rather stale subject, in which "personalities and policies are drawn with a firm hand."

It was the two published volumes of Plumb's biography of Robert Walpole that established him as a historian of the first rank. Walpole is scarcely an attractive figure—a master technician of politics "without principles, convictions, or solutions," greedy and treacherous, but at the same time an enlightened patron of the arts, a complex and full-

J. H. PLUMB

blooded personality. "The more I have come to know this great man," Plumb writes, "the stronger has my admiration grown."

Yet his biography is notably objective, eschewing conjecture and even the kind of anecdotage usually thought essential to "readability," and based meticulously on firsthand sources. Plumb has written amusingly in the New York *Times Book Review* (March 13, 1966) about his researches in the documents rooms of some of the noblest and most Spartan houses in England. This patient and scrupulous approach to a boorish individual, involving as it does "many dull details of eighteenth century diplomacy," produces not a dull book but a superlatively good one. The reason, as John Brooke wrote, is that Plumb brings to bear on his material "some of the highest qualities of the historian's art: imagination, insight into character, and a lively and almost rollicking style. It might be Macaulay with a dash of Freud."

In *The First Four Georges*, Plumb applies his infectious enthusiasm, his exceptional skill in depicting character and conduct, to a portrayal of four monarchs who have been in general little regarded by other historians. Viewing them as "human beings caught in exceptional circumstances," he does much to rehabilitate them, and provides at the same time an excellent picture of eighteenth century England. *Men and Places*, published in America as *Men and Centuries*, is a collection of articles about "those splendid extravagant days when Britain lost one Empire, conquered a second, and in Africa began to prospect a third."

The Ford Lectures which Plumb gave at Oxford in 1965–1966 were published as *The Growth of Political Stability in England, 1675–1725*. They are, according to one critic, "not merely a powerful and original contribution to the study of the political history of this particular half-century; they are designed as a case history intended to draw attention to the general problem of political stability." Plumb had set out "to clear up some of the confusion that has been growing in the political history of late seventeenth-century England." Specifically, as J. P. Kenyon has explained, "Plumb interprets the tortured and complex history of these years in terms of a modified two-party system, Whig *versus* Tory, which has been too lightly dismissed as sentimental and teleological by apprentice pupils of Sir Lewis Namier"—"lesser men who have lately usurped a position of authority in this field." This being so, there were naturally some critics who questioned Plumb's basic premises, though none doubted the book's importance. Lawrence Stone called it "a landmark in English historiography." In his Saposnekow Lectures, given at the City College of New York in 1968, and published as *The Death of the Past*, Plumb discusses the contemporary loss of faith in tradition as a means of justifying national confidence, or class supremacy, or any set of moral attitudes. History, he believes, must use the past to sanctify not authority or morality, but reason.

Plumb has served since 1959 as European advisory editor to *Horizon*, and provided the main text for the sumptuously illustrated *Horizon Book of the Renaissance*. He is Penguin's advisory editor for history, and in addition supervises Knopf's thirty-volume History of Human Society series. Plumb is a trustee of the National Portrait Gallery and of the Fitzwilliam Museum in Cambridge. He is an excellent public speaker whose lectures at Cambridge command "huge undergraduate audiences." Plumb is a Fellow of the British Academy and of several learned societies. He has taught as a visiting lecturer or professor at Columbia, the City College of New York, the University of Minnesota, and Brooklyn College. A scholarly looking man, with thin-rimmed spectacles and receding dark hair, the author is a connoisseur of wine and of French china, and enjoys sailing. He believes that history should be part of the literary culture of Britain and America, and few contemporary historians have done more to make it so.

PRINCIPAL WORKS: England in the Eighteenth Century: The Development of English Society during the Age of Walpole, Chatham and Pitt, 1950; Chatham, 1953; (ed.) Studies in Social History: A Tribute to G. M. Trevelyan, 1955; The First Four Georges, 1956; Sir Robert Walpole: vol. 1, The Making of a Statesman, 1956; vol. 2, The King's Minister, 1961; (with the editors of Horizon) The Horizon Book of the Renaissance, 1961 (published as The

Penguin Book of the Renaissance, 1964, and adapted for young readers by Irwin Shapiro as The Golden Book of the Renaissance, 1962; also published as The Italian Renaissance, 1965, and Renaissance Profiles, 1965; Men and Places (U.S., Men and Centuries), 1963; (ed.) Crisis in the Humanities, 1964; The Growth of Political Stability in England, 1675–1725 (U.S., The Origins of Political Stability: England 1675–1725), 1967; The Death of the Past, 1969; In the Light of History (essays), 1972.

ABOUT: Who's Who, 1973. *Periodicals*—Illustrated London News April 14, 1956; New York Review of Books September 28, 1967; New York Times Book Review March 13, 1966; Observer February 5, 1967; Spectator April 6, 1956; January 20, 1961; Times Literary Supplement April 6, 1956.

***PODHORETZ, NORMAN** (January 16, 1930–), American critic and editor, writes: "I was born in Brooklyn, New York, of East-European Jewish parents (both my mother and father came to the United States from what was then Austria-Hungary, and what is now Poland). I was educated in local public schools and then at Boys High School. Encouraged by various teachers there, especially English teachers, I applied for a Pulitzer Scholarship and was awarded one, which made it possible for me to go to Columbia—a college to which my parents could certainly not have afforded to send me. Simultaneously, evenings and Sundays, I attended the Seminary College of Jewish Studies, which is the equivalent of the Liberal Arts division of the Jewish Theological Seminary. Eventually, I earned the degree of Bachelor of Hebrew Literature.

"At Columbia, with the help of Mark Van Doren and Lionel Trilling, I discovered that I was not a very good poet (as far back as I can remember I had been writing poetry), and I began to fancy myself a critic instead. Criticism was all the rage in the late forties; if I remember rightly, most of the young literati at Columbia were eager to become critics and to publish in the quarterlies. By the time of my graduation in 1950, I had decided to pursue an academic career and to write books and essays on literary subjects (Lionel Trilling was my hero).

"I spent the next three years (thanks to a Kellett Fellowship and a Fulbright Scholarship) at Clare College, Cambridge, during which time I fell under the influence of F. R. Leavis, studied intensely for the English tripos, and read a great deal of political philosophy. In 1951, I published my first piece, an article about Trilling in Leavis' magazine, *Scrutiny*. From that point on, I have been contributing sporadically to various American magazines (*Commentary*, *Partisan Review*, the *New Yorker*, etc.).

"My third year at Cambridge was devoted to research which was supposed to lead to a Ph.D. Before I could finish, however, I was drafted and spent two years in the army—an experience which, among other things, convinced me that it would be

* pod hor′ ets

NORMAN PODHORETZ

pointless to return to graduate school. Upon discharge from the army, I went to work as an assistant editor at *Commentary*; my writing was done evenings and weekends. I left *Commentary* after a couple of years to try my hand at full-time freelance writing, but having acquired a family, I found it exceedingly difficult to make ends meet. In 1960, I returned to *Commentary*, this time as editor-in-chief, a position I still occupy.

"In recent years, I have found myself becoming less a literary critic than a general commentator on American culture. Literature remains my primary point of departure, but I no longer have as strong an inclination as I once did to pronounce judgment on all the novels pouring off the presses. My first book—a collection of essays—was largely, though not exclusively, devoted to post-war American fiction. My next book was a semi-confessional, semi-analytic study of the problem of success in America.

"I live in New York City with my wife Midge (who also writes), my two teenage stepdaughters, my eight-year-old daughter, and my four-year-old son. It is a crowded and noisy household in which to write, but writing is an agony anywhere."

Norman Podhoretz is the son of Julius Podhoretz, a milkman, and the former Helen Woliner. As his account suggests, he was a brilliant student and a fiercely ambitious one. At Columbia, seeking to overcome through academic success a sense of social inferiority, he worked furiously, aided he says by "something like total recall and a great gift for intellectual mimicry"; at Cambridge he earned his second B.A. with first class honors. And in 1953 he returned to New York, intent on becoming nothing less than "a famous critic." He took his first step in that direction the same year, when his shrewd attack on Saul Bellow's much-praised *The Adventures of Augie March* provoked a notable literary squabble.

Between 1958 and 1960, as he says, Podhoretz worked as a freelance, and for a time was associated with Jason Epstein in the paperback publishing field. *Commentary*, to which he returned as editor in 1960, was founded by the American Jewish Committee as "a journal of significant thought and opinion on Jewish affairs and contemporary issues." Under Podhoretz's editorship it has concentrated less on Jewish affairs, more on American culture in general, and has moved to the left in its political attitudes. Its circulation has increased dramatically and it is generally admired as one of the most important and exciting house organs of what Podhoretz calls "the family"—the New York intellectual establishment.

One of the mostly hotly discussed articles ever to appear in *Commentary* was Podhoretz's own essay "My Negro Problem—and Ours" (1963). In it, as an astringent antidote to the sentimental optimism which then suffused liberal discussion of the race problem, he discussed his "integrated" childhood in Brownsville, "where it was the Negroes who persecuted the whites." This often moving and beautifully written piece provoked a national controversy, and was unfairly denounced as racist as often as it was praised for its honesty.

That famous essay appeared with other articles and critical pieces in *Doings and Undoings: The Fifties and After in American Writing*. Podhoretz takes the Leavisite view that literature is "not an end in itself" but "a mode of public discourse that either illuminates or fails to illuminate the common ground on which we live." If his reviews seem to many of his colleagues gratuitously destructive and negative, it is because his standards are extremely high. Some of the longer essays in *Doings and Undoings* show real critical distinction, and even the shorter ones are models of literary journalism, lucid, intelligent, and absorbingly interesting. All the same, the collection is far short of the systematic study of modern American literature which Podhoretz had originally planned to write but was unable to finish.

The "study of the problem of success in America" that he speaks of above was published in 1968 as *Making It*. Podhoretz believes that personal ambition has replaced sex as "the dirty little secret" of our time, and *Making It* is offered as a crusading attempt to exorcise this last remaining literary taboo. And so he describes with impersonal frankness the tactics by which he fought his way to the *Commentary* editorship, and his triumphant progress from his "first party at Lillian Hellman's" to his "first summons to the Park Avenue salon of Mr. and Mrs. Kirk Askew." It is partly for these rewards, he concludes, that he has driven himself to write.

This exercise in what Saul Maloff called "sociological pornography for our time" seemed offensively tasteless to many, and to others a morbid act of self-denigration by a man with more integrity than he pretended. There were complaints also that Podhoretz provided no more than "tantalizing glimpses" of the literary celebrities he had encountered on the way up. "As a life story—or even as a confession," wrote the author of an excellent review in the *Times Literary Supplement*, "it is less than full. It is inexhaustibly intelligent. . . . But Mr. Podhoretz is not by instinct either a narrator or an observer. Only when events fit a thesis, or when telling them is itself a moral posture . . . does his prose catch fire." Eliot Fremont-Smith in the New York *Times* reached a similar conclusion—that Podhoretz's "analytical forays into the intellectual history of the period" are what make this "a book that will be thought about long after the amused and envious chattering dies."

PRINCIPAL WORKS: Doings and Undoings: The Fifties and After in American Writing, 1964; Making It, 1968; (ed.) The Commentary Reader, 1966.

ABOUT: Current Biography, 1968; Podhoretz, N. Making It, 1968; Who's Who in America, 1972–1973. *Periodicals*—Esquire April 1968; New York Review of Books February 1, 1968; New York Times Book Review January 5, 1968; Newsweek March 16, 1964; Times Literary Supplement August 29, 1968.

***POGGIOLI, RENATO** (April 16, 1907–May 3, 1963), American scholar, critic, and translator, was born in Florence, the son of Gino and Amina (Buoninsegni) Poggioli. He specialized in Slavic studies at the University of Florence and received his doctorate in 1929. A period of further study followed in Czechoslovakia, and then Poggioli taught for a time in Poland. He had an intimate working knowledge of ten languages. Mussolini's Italy, when he returned there, became increasingly unacceptable to him—as a social democrat and an intellectual—and the suicide of a friend, a Jewish literary editor, brought matters to a head. In 1938, very reluctantly, he left Italy and went to the United States, becoming a citizen in 1950.

After a visiting professorship at Smith College (1938–1939), Poggioli became an assistant professor at Brown University, where he remained from 1939 to 1947, apart from two years (1943–1945) in the United States Army. The rest of his career was spent at Harvard University where he went as associate professor in 1948, becoming a full professor in

* pôd jō′ lē

1950 and Curt Hugo Reisinger Professor of Slavic and Comparative Literature in 1960. After the war Poggioli maintained close contact with European cultural affairs as foreign editor of *Inventario*, an international cultural quarterly edited by his friend Luigi Berti, and through visiting professorships at the University of Rome and at the Sorbonne. He died in a road accident in California, near the Oregon border, and was survived by his wife, the former Renata Nordio (whom he married in 1935), and his daughter Silvia. A much loved and respected man and an inspiring teacher, he was, Harry Levin says, one of a handful of émigrés who "shifted the center of gravity in the field of Comparative Literature."

Apart from *Il fiore del verso russo* (1949), Poggioli's first books were in English, which he wrote, one critic said, "with a nervous delicacy that many [natives] might envy." *The Phoenix and the Spider* (1957) is a collection of essays about Russian prose writers, setting out to convey "the Russian view of the psyche." It was welcomed as a highly intelligent and learned guide, especially to the work of Tolstoy and the aphorist Vasili Rozanov, from whom the title derives. *The Poets of Russia, 1890–1930* has become a standard work. This notably thorough, sympathetic, and well-constructed study focuses mainly on the years between 1890 and 1910, when symbolism, futurism, acmeism, and the other movements of the period transformed the Russian cultural tradition.

Teoria dell'arte d'avanguardia, on which Poggioli worked intermittently for sixteen years, was published in 1962 and translated by Gerald Fitzgerald in 1968 as *The Theory of the Avant-Garde*. It studies avant-garde art "as a historical concept, a center of tendencies and ideas," examining its influence on modern culture and society and seeking to discover its "common psychological condition." Poggioli concluded that "avant-garde art seems destined to oscillate perpetually among the various forms of alienation—psychological and social, economic and historical, aesthetic and stylistic." It is a difficult and immensely learned work, as much a sociological treatise as a literary one. Many critics found too much abstract theorizing, insufficiently supported by specific examples.

Poggioli translated Wallace Stevens, Novalis, and a number of Russian poets into Italian, and inspired many other translators. His mature thoughts about the art of translation may be found in his posthumous *The Spirit of the Letter*, which also contains, among others, essays on Kafka, on Poggioli's compatriots Svevo and Pirandello (whose guide he once was, on a visit the older writer made to Prague), on the relation of poetic technique to poetry itself, and on the Paolo and Francesca episode in Dante's *Inferno*—an essay that has led more

RENATO POGGIOLI

than one scholar to regret that he did not write more on Dante. None of Poggioli's books more brilliantly demonstrates his learning and versatility.

In 1962 Poggioli became a member of the councils of the Dante Society and of the American Academy of Arts and Sciences. He was essentially a theorist, but one of the most remarkable of his time in that he always passionately related his theses to experience—particularly to political experience. His mastery, Harry Levin wrote, lay in his capacity to extract "the universal from the technical, the history of ideas at many periods from the *explication des textes* in many languages."

PRINCIPAL WORKS IN ENGLISH: The Phoenix and the Spider, 1957; The Poets of Russia, 1890–1930, 1960; Rozanov, 1962; The Spirit of the Letter: Essays in European Literature, 1965; The Theory of the Avant-Garde, 1968. ABOUT: Contemporary Authors 1, 1962; Levin, H. *preface to* The Spirit of the Letter, 1965; Who's Who in America, 1964–1965. *Periodicals*—New York Times December 2, 1957; May 4, 1963; New York Times Book Review May 29, 1960; Saturday Review December 25, 1965; Spectator October 18, 1968; Times Literary Supplement June 23, 1966; Yale Review Spring 1966.

POHL, FREDERIK (November 26, 1919–), who has been described by the New York *Times* as one of America's "four or five most successful science fiction writers," is equally well known in his special field as an editor and literary agent. He was born in New York City, the son of Fred and Anna (Mason) Pohl. Biographical information about his early life is hard to come by, but it is known that in 1938 he was a charter member, with Cyril Kornbluth and others, of Isaac Asimov's Futurian Literary Society, which was founded in

FREDERIK POHL

Brooklyn. Soon afterwards, when he was scarcely into his twenties, he became the first editor of *Astounding Stories* and *Super Science Stories*, low-budget science fiction magazines launched by Popular Publications in 1939. Pohl contributed many stories to these and other magazines, writing as "James MacCreigh" and, with Kornbluth, as "S. D. Gottesman." He left Popular Publications in 1943 to serve for two years with the USAAF. In 1946, after a brief stint as an advertising copy-writer, he joined the staff of the Popular Science Publication Company, where he remained for three years. From 1949 to 1953 Pohl worked as a literary agent, acting for many of the leading science fiction writers of the period. *Star Science Fiction Stories*, a series of collections of original stories which he prepared at this time for Ballantine Books, made his reputation as an editor of outstanding ability. In 1953 he abandoned his agency work to become a full-time writer.

Pohl's best-known book is *The Space Merchants* (1953), the result of a collaboration with Cyril Kornbluth which originally appeared in *Galaxy Science Fiction* as "Gravy Planet." It is a pungent social satire, extrapolated from contemporary trends, envisaging a world in which "hidden persuasion" has given way to overt domination by the advertising tycoons. Welcomed both as entertainment and "sharp social criticism," it seemed to many critics "a novel of the future that the present must inevitably rank as a classic."

Subsequent collaborations with Kornbluth were in general well received but less spectacularly successful. Pohl has also worked on a number of solid and workmanlike novels with Jack Williamson, and, as "Edson McCann," collaborated with Lester del Rey to produce *Preferred Risk*. This appeared in 1955 after serialization in *Galaxy Science Fiction*, and in outline resembled *The Space Merchants*, prophesying a dictatorship imposed by the great insurance companies. It was coolly received, and few reviewers managed to identify "Edson McCann," though one called it "a slavish but lifeless imitation of the successful Pohl-Kornbluth serials in *Galaxy*."

The solo novels and stories which Pohl has published under his own name have established him as one of the most consistently able of contemporary science fiction writers—inventive and highly professional as a plot carpenter, though unremarkable as a stylist. In 1961 Pohl succeeded H. L. Gold as editor of *Galaxy Science Fiction* and of its companion publications, *If*, *World of Tomorrow*, and *Magabook*. He left *Galaxy* in 1969, and in recent years has been much in demand as a "blue skyer," addressing business conventions on what the future may be supposed to hold for them. Pohl himself has been called an "effective businessman." He is a tall, spare, urbane man, dark-haired and with "John L. Lewis eyebrows." Married, with four children, Pohl lives at Red Bank, New Jersey. He is a Unitarian and a Democrat, an executive board member of the Monmouth County Civil Liberties Union, and a director of Opera Theatre, New York. He ran (and lost) in a local primary as a Democratic delegate pledged to Eugene McCarthy in the 1968 convention, and in *Practical Politics 1972* provides a lively and lucid guide for the amateur politician.

PRINCIPAL WORKS: Alternating Currents, 1956; Edge of the City, 1957; The Case Against Tomorrow, 1957; Slave Ship, 1957; Tomorrow Times Seven, 1959; The Man Who Ate the World, 1960; Drunkard's Walk, 1960; Turn Left at Thursday, 1961; The Abominable Earthman, 1963; A Plague of Pythons, 1963; The Frederik Pohl Omnibus, 1966; Digits and Dastards, 1968; The Age of the Pussyfoot, 1969; Day Million, 1970; The Gold at the Starbow's End, 1972; Practical Politics 1972, 1972; Like to the Lark: The Early Years of Shakespeare, 1972. *With C. M. Kornbluth*—The Space Merchants, 1953; Search the Sky, 1954; Gladiator-at-Law, 1955; A Town Is Drowning, 1955; Presidential Year, 1956; Wolfbane, 1959; The Wonder Effect, 1962. *With Jack Williamson*—Undersea Quest, 1954; Undersea Fleet, 1956; Undersea City, 1958; The Reefs of Space, 1964; Starchild, 1965; Rogue Star, 1969. *With Lester del Rey as "Edson McCann"*—Preferred Risk, 1955. *As editor*—Beyond the End of Time, 1952; Star Science Fiction Stories (3 vols), 1953–1954; Assignment in Tomorrow, 1954; Star Short Novels, 1954; Star of Stars, 1960; The Expert Dreamers, 1962; Time Waits for Winthrop, 1962; The Seventh Galaxy Reader, 1964 (and later volumes); Star Fourteen, 1966; The If Reader of Science Fiction, 1966 (and later volumes); Nightmare Age, 1970.

ABOUT: Moskowitz, S. Seekers of Tomorrow, 1966; Vinson, J. (ed.) Contemporary Novelists, 1972; Who's Who in America, 1972–1973.

POLANYI, MICHAEL (March 11, 1891-), British scientist, social scientist, and philosopher, writes; "I was born in Budapest, into a family which for some time had achieved prosperity as manufacturers, mill owners, and the like. In my father's generation they entered the professions and when I was born, a beginning had been made of a home of some intellectual ambitions. When I was eight years old, my father, who as a civil engineer had been constructing railways in Hungary and financing them, lost his considerable fortune. My older brothers and sisters, whose education until then had been in the hands of tutors and governesses, were sent to schools and I myself, the fifth child, entered school too. My father died when I was fourteen and we were left in straitened circumstances, which obliged me to earn my living henceforth by tutoring rich schoolboys. At the same time, my mother, a woman of great intellectual charm, became the centre of friends comprising young painters, poets, novelists and scholars of the new generation in Hungary.

"I grew up in this circle, dreaming of great things. At school I started to produce scientific theories and literary essays, on subjects of which I knew nothing. I was about eighteen when George Polya, a fellow-student a few years my senior, who was to become a great mathematician, warned mother: 'Michael walks alone, he will need a strong voice to make himself heard.' Today my voice has not yet carried far; I shall die an old man as an infant prodigy.

"While a student of medicine (as which I had entered the University of Budapest at seventeen) I published a few scientific papers of negligible importance; my real entry to a scientific career occurred in my fifth academic year. In the summer of 1912 I had spent a few weeks at the Technische Hochschule in Karlsruhe (Baden), where I made an impression on Professor Bredig by my familiarity with the Third Law of Thermodynamics, which at that time was still regarded as a novelty. I had an idea, that the Third Law—which applies to the absolute zero of temperature—would also hold at extreme pressures. Back in Budapest, I set aside my medical studies and worked frantically for six months in developing this theory. The product was sent to Professor Bredig in Karlsruhe for approval. Not feeling competent to judge my paper, Bredig forwarded it to Einstein. The manuscript came back with the words 'I like the paper of your Mr. Polanyi very much.'

"Bang, I was created a scientist. The paper was published at full length in the principal German journal of physical chemistry in Leipzig. I expected to hear from all sides about my discovery of a new law of thermodynamics; but nobody paid attention to it. I was unknown, my ideas were above the

MICHAEL POLANYI

heads of many and seemed unexciting to those who understood them. The paper was really not important and since I did not pursue it further, it was soon forgotten.

"The following year, having concluded my medical course, I went back to Karlsruhe as a student of chemistry. By the end of the academic year I had produced and published a number of theoretical papers, among them one on adsorption, which is the condensation of gases on the surface of solids. In August 1914 the war broke out and I joined up as a medical officer. But in 1916, during an illness in hospital and while recuperating afterwards, I finished my theory of adsorption and presented it to the University of Budapest as a thesis for the Ph.D.

"The professor of mathematical physics, to whom my paper was assigned, had never heard of my subject matter. He studied my work bit by bit and then asked me to explain a curious point: my result seemed correct, but its derivation faulty. Admitting my mistake I said that surely one first draws one's conclusions and then puts their derivation right. The professor just stared at me.

"However, this way of following my nose without proper guidance was to have peculiar results. My theory was acclaimed at first, but soon after declared unscientific, impossible. I had conceived it in ignorance of the discoveries made two years earlier by Debye and Bohr, which apparently excluded the possibility of the lines I had adopted. Acclaim had come from people as ignorant as myself of the new discoveries. Then, after ten to fifteen years, it turned out that I had been right. But my theory had been discredited too long, and though it is now well established, the whole subject matter is still darkened by long-standing error. I have told this story in *Science* in September 1963 (Vol. 141, p. 1010–1013).

"I shall skip my main scientific work between 1918 and 1948. My notes, if published, will show how this work continued to benefit and also to suffer from my defective schooling and excessive speculations. Icarus-like I flew so near the sun that my wings were ever in danger of melting away. I shall skip also my work on Soviet economics (1935) and my *Full Employment and Free Trade* (1945), which first derived from the Keynesian theory of the policy of deficit financing as the bulwark of capitalism.

"I believe that I came into my true vocation in 1946 when I set out on the pursuit of a new philosophy to meet the need of our age. My way of starting with little or no schooling was wholly beneficial here. For a sound knowledge of philosophy makes the necessary radical advances extremely difficult; one must shoot here first and ask questions afterwards, as I have always done—for better or worse."

Michael Polanyi, the son of Michael Pollacsek and the former Cecilia Wohl, began his career in 1923 at the Technische Hochschule in Berlin, at the same time becoming a member of the Kaiser Wilhelm Institute for Physical Chemistry. He left Germany in 1933 and went to England as Professor of Physical Chemistry at Victoria University, Manchester. As a scientist Polanyi has interested himself in a great variety of subjects—among them X-ray crystallography, plasticity, adsorption, chemical reaction kinetics, bond energies, and polymerization. The quality and importance of his work was such that in 1944 he received the immense distinction of election as a Fellow of the Royal Society.

Meanwhile Polanyi's willingness to "follow his nose" had led him into an assortment of fields far removed from physical chemistry. Thus the pamphlet *U.S.S.R. Economics* (1936) was followed by *The Contempt of Freedom*, in which he argued that liberty, which survives only if it can develop, was impossible under the Soviet system. The restrictiveness of Marxist doctrine is also discussed in *Science, Faith and Society*, while *Full Employment and Free Trade* reflects Polanyi's adherence to Keynes's economic theories and his disapproval of the ways in which these theories have been applied.

Polanyi's growing interest in the social sciences was confirmed when in 1948 he exchanged his chair in physical chemistry at Victoria University for one in social studies. His work on liberty, best approached perhaps through the essays collected in *The Logic of Liberty*, led to his principal achievement as a philosopher, the doctrine of tacit knowing. Polanyi has always believed (as he says above) that "one first draws one's conclusions and then puts their derivation right." The doctrine of tacit knowing develops from this attitude, stating that we know far more than we can express, far more than science has yet confirmed. Polanyi believes that this tacit dimension of knowledge is the source of man's infinite potential, and for this reason opposes any political or intellectual system which tends to limit freedom of thought. The notion that belief precedes understanding is developed in *Personal Knowledge* and *The Tacit Dimension* into "a sweeping humanist epistemology in which science, the arts and humanities are seen as unified."

Many academic philosophers tend to dismiss Polanyi's philosophical writings as no more than "a lively discussion of the personal element in the work of thought," but this view is by no means universally accepted, as Fay Sawyer's comments in *Ethics* (October 1960) suggest: "Almost any reader of Polanyi's works can ferret out alleged facts to dispute. A restrained Anglo-Saxon critic is likely to react with distaste to many of the impassioned, not to say overblown passages. More disturbing is the number of undefined terms and improbable usages. . . . Polanyi is no philosopher's philosopher. He was an outstanding scientist and is now struggling—not altogether successfully—to make systematic and coherent a large view. . . . He has constructed an interpretation of all knowledge which is both illuminating and consistent. Apart from the relatively picayune objections noted earlier, the residuum of incoherence may be due to the absence of any rigorous metaphysics, which might rationally . . . have related the various parts of Polanyi's philosophy."

Michael Polanyi was married to Magda Kemeny in 1920 and has two sons. He retired in 1958 from Victoria University, where he is now professor emeritus. Polanyi has taught as a visiting lecturer or professor at a number of British universities, and in the United States at Chicago, Virginia, Berkeley, Yale, and Duke. He was a senior research fellow at Merton College, Oxford, in 1959–1961; distinguished research fellow at the University of Virginia in 1961; fellow of the Center for Advanced Study in the Behavioral Sciences at Stanford in 1962–1963; senior fellow at the Center of Advanced Studies, Wesleyan University, in 1965. He holds honorary degrees from nine English and American universities.

PRINCIPAL WORKS: Atomic Reactions, 1932; U.S.S.R. Economics, 1936; The Contempt of Freedom, 1940; Full Employment and Free Trade, 1945; Science, Faith and Society, 1946; The Logic of Liberty (essays), 1951; Personal Knowledge, 1958; The Study of Man (lectures), 1959; Beyond Nihilism, 1960; The Tacit Dimension, 1966; Knowing and Being (essays), 1969.

ABOUT: Jelenski, K. A. (ed.) Congress for Cultural Freedom, Berlin, 1960: History and Hope, 1962; The Logic of Personal Knowledge: Essays Presented to Michael Polanyi, 1961; Who's Who, 1973. *Periodicals*—American Anthropologist October 1960; Christian Scholar March 1960; Ethics July 1967, April 1969; Journal of Religion January 1966, April 1968; Nature January 3, 1948; Religion in Life Spring 1965; Review of Metaphysics June 1960; Science September 1963.

POLI, UMBERTO. *See* "SABA," UMBERTO

***PONGE, FRANCIS** (March 27, 1899–), French poet and critic, was born in Montpellier, the son of Armand Ponge, a bank director, and the former Juliette Saurel. He attended schools in Avignon and Caen, and the Lycée Louis-le-Grand in Paris, and served briefly in the army. Further studies in literature and law qualified him to enter the École Normale Supérieure, but at that point he decided to devote himself to writing. His first poems appeared in *La Nouvelle Revue Française* in 1923. For a time he worked in the publishing houses of Gallimard and Hachette and was also editor of the Lyon newspaper *Progrès*. During World War II he joined the Resistance under the pseudonym Roland Mars. He was an active member of the Communist party from 1937 to 1947.

Ponge's work was not widely noticed until the publication of his slim but hotly discussed volume of prose poems *Le Parti pris des choses* (Taking the Part of Things, 1942). Each of these poems is devoted to a single object—a plant, a shell, a cigarette—which is scrutinized so intensely that it becomes a strange and richly complex world in itself. In his geography of these microcosms, Ponge employed allegory, metaphor, and a great variety of rhetorical devices, especially puns, seeking, he said, "to assist man to see things and to see himself through things."

One of the many writers who admired and learned from these prose poems was Sartre, who discussed them in *Situations 1* (1947), welcoming Ponge's determination to limit himself to "things," and to lay the foundations of a "phenomenology of nature." Ponge, however, has denied that he is a phenomenologist, though he starts from the same point of view: that we are prevented from gaining a full knowledge of the world by the stereotyped modes of thinking and seeing that we impose upon it—our tendency to assign things to neat categories, ignoring those potentialities that do not fit.

In *Le Grand Recueil* (The Great Anthology, 1961) he explains what he is trying to do. This collection of essays and poems is in three volumes: in *Lyres* he writes of art and artists, love and death, emphasizing the need for a new definition of things; in *Méthodes* he shows how this definition is to be reached; and in *Pièces* he gives some examples of

* pôNzh

FRANCIS PONGE

the practical application of his method. He says that a single object contains so much richness that he cannot imagine attempting to write about any but the simplest things: stone, grass, fire, etc. The truth of a thing's existence can be expressed only when the poet breaks through the abstractions that have grown up around it, and sees it concretely. The man who has direct contact with the sensual world is not the one who thinks in clichés like "hard as a stone" and orders experience in terms of received ideas, but the man who accepts things as his equal.

Most of Ponge's poetry since *Le Parti pris des choses* is scattered in periodicals and limited editions, and is characteristically tentative and reiterative—speculations about the nature of language as well as of things, "notebooks on the making of poems" rather than fully realized works of art. This is exemplified in *Le Savon* (1967, translated as *Soap*), which assembles his reflections on that humble commodity over a period of twenty-five years. As one critic wrote in the *Times Literary Supplement*, Ponge "began tackling his soap in 1942 . . . [and] continued to turn it this way and that in jets of language until 1967, by which time he had exhausted it to the point of non-existence. . . . The critic has to ask himself whether *Le Savon* amounts to a genuine prose poem, or whether it remains just a quaint collection of notes and doodles. The answer is, perhaps, that like so much of M. Ponge's writings it is a failed poem with a special interest for poets and linguists." It would be possible to apply this judgment to *Pour un Malherbe* (1965), which contains the notes Ponge wrote between 1951 and 1957 for a critical work on François de Malherbe (1555–1628), a poet and critic with whom he identifies himself closely. The result is "as much Ponge in the light of Malherbe as it is Malherbe in the light of Ponge." Similar pieces, and some more orthodox critical essays, appear in *La Rage de l'expression* (1952) and *Nouveau Recueil* (1968).

According to David Plank in *Modern Language Quarterly*, "Ponge's poetry assumes its full meaning and beauty only after the reader has reconstructed a totally materialistic universe where man assumes a new and unique position in relation to his surroundings." The reconstruction, Ponge says, is less a question of knowledge than of being reborn: it is an experience following from the "sleep" of the ego. He believes that artistic creation is a process that demands withdrawal from the world of human experience; the artist must find his law and his god within himself: "Le Verbe est Dieu! . . . Je suis le Verbe!" (The Word is God! . . . I am the Word!)

Ponge has been seen by some critics as a forerunner of the *nouveau roman*, and he has greatly influenced the writers associated with the magazine *Tel Quel*, whose spokesman, Philippe Sollers, has written a book about Ponge. English-language critics have given his work a more mixed reception. One of them in the *Times Literary Supplement*, thinks him "almost by vocation a minor poet," whose method at its best "produces animal pieces that remind one irresistibly of the finest Lawrence. They have the same extraordinary gift of catching a gesture as if it were an essential attitude, of casting a mood. The almost fetichist excitement which Ponge clearly feels in the precise delineation of scenes and things seems to be his essential gift." For David Plank, Ponge is the prophet of the greatness of man—"of a new man, the man of the future with all the power of his mind . . . freed from the impedimenta of communication. This is the true transformation Ponge makes; he gives back to man those powers he lost in the Fall."

Ponge spent two years in Algeria after the war. From 1952 until his retirement in 1965 he taught at the Alliance Française in Paris, and he has made many lecture tours in France and abroad. In 1966–1967 he taught as a visiting professor at Barnard College and Columbia University in New York. He was married in 1931 to Odette Chabanel and has one child, Armande. He says that his principal leisure interest is "listening to and reading about the universal lot." Ponge divides his time between Paris and a house in the Maritime Alps. He is an officer of the Légion d'Honneur, and received the International Poetry Prize in 1959.

PRINCIPAL WORKS IN ENGLISH TRANSLATION: Soap (tr. by Lane Dunlop), 1969; Things (tr. by Cid Corman), 1971; The Voice of Things (tr. by Beth Archer Brombert), 1972. *Poems in* Gavronsky, S. Poems and Texts (translations and interviews with Ponge and others), 1969; Laughlin, J. (ed.) New Directions in Prose and Poetry 17, 1961; Marks, E. (ed.) French Poetry From Baudelaire to the Present, 1962; Strachan, W. J. Apollinaire to Aragon: Thirty Modern French Poets, 1948; Taylor, S. W. (ed.) French Writing Today, 1968; Poetry September 1952; Yale French Studies 21 1958.

ABOUT: Boisdeffre, P. de. Une Histoire vivante de la littérature d'aujourd'hui, 1938–1958, 1958; Clouard, H. and Leggewie, R. French Writers of Today, 1965; International Who's Who, 1972–73; Ponge, F. Entretiens avec Philippe Sollers, 1970; Rousselot, J. Panorama critique des nouveaux poètes français, 1952; Sartre, J.-P. Situations 1, 1947; Sollers, P. Francis Ponge, 1963; Thibaudeau, J. Ponge, 1967; Who's Who in France, 1973–1974. *Periodicals*—Comparative Literature Fall 1965; French Studies January 1959; Horizon September 1947; Hudson Review Spring 1973; Mercure de France June 1949; Modern Language Quarterly June 1965; New York Review of Books November 30, 1972; Poetry September 1952; Times Literary Supplement May 4, 1962; September 30, 1965.

POPE, DUDLEY (BERNARD EGERTON) (December 29, 1925–), English naval historian and novelist, writes: "I come from an old Cornish family, but arrived on the scene too late to benefit from the land and a couple of abbeys which Henry VIII gave to my seventh great-grandfather in return for some unspecified services connected with the Dissolution of the Monasteries. We later lost half the land to the Roundheads because Cromwell accused the Popes of being Royalists, and the other half to the Royalists who accused us of collaborating with the Roundheads. This must have taught my forebears a lesson, since the family motto became—and still is—'Neither to the right nor the left.'

"The Second World War arrived to find me a schoolboy, but I was able to get to sea in the Merchant Navy as a midshipman. This was a brief and inglorious interlude: my ship was torpedoed in the Battle of the Atlantic, with a heavy loss of life, and I was lucky to escape with a few wounds which led to me being given a pension and returned to civilian life. Since I had left school to go to sea I had no training—a fascination for history in general, and sea life and warfare in Nelson's day in particular, would hardly have gladdened the heart of a prospective employer. However, someone suggested that as I wrote interesting letters, I ought to become a journalist.

"So I joined the local newspaper, the *Kentish Express*, and three months later bluffed my way into getting a job in Fleet Street. From 1943 until 1959 I was a journalist, the last fifteen years being spent with the *Evening News* as naval correspondent and latterly deputy foreign editor. In 1953, just about the time the editor's secretary and I realised we had more than an interest in newspapers in common, a publisher commissioned me to write a book on the work of the Royal Navy's motor torpedo boats (PT boats) in the Mediterranean during the Second World War. The Admiralty gave me access to hitherto secret records, and the book, *Flag 4*, was finally published with a Foreword by the then First Sea Lord.

"In the meantime I had taken up sailing and was living on board my yacht. I married the editor's secretary, who was undeterred by a courtship spent helping me do research at the Admiralty. There were two more books I wanted to write about the Second World War before going on to my real love, Nelson's Day. These were the Battle of the River Plate (the book, *Graf Spee: The Life and Death of a Raider*, was a best-seller in the USA), and the Battle of the Barents Sea, which was also highly successful in the United States under the title *73 North*.

"By this time I was getting the reputation of being a naval historian who did 'research in depth.' This was due to a fascination for the subject and a contempt for many of my colleagues who rarely seemed to go farther than a library to do their research. Both my British and American publishers let me choose my subjects, so to begin the Nelson period I dived in the deep end with a book on Trafalgar. My wife and I traced every living descendant of Nelson's captains and to everyone's surprise, produced a book in which about thirty per cent of the material had never before been published. Far more important, though, was the fact I was able to solve most of the so-called 'mysteries' about the battle. The previous classic on the subject, written by an historian who received a knighthood for his work, contained such phrases as 'The role of the third in command at Trafalgar is shadowy.' There was little excuse for this sort of thing, since the family had all his papers, and the success of the book, *Decision at Trafalgar*, was partly due, I think, to the fact we really did do the necessary research.

"This book was sufficiently successful to allow me to resign from my job, and we went to live in Italy for the next four years. We visited most capital cities and naval ports in Europe during that time doing research, and the two books which appear to have made the greatest impression in the academic world, *At Twelve Mr. Byng Was Shot*, and *The Black Ship*, were written while we were in Italy.

"We lived in a house on the side of a mountain above the Tuscan fishing port of Porto Santo Stefano, and my yacht, a fifteen-ton ketch, was kept there. My wife and I did a great deal of sailing round those waters, and about this time two things happened which led to me becoming a novelist as well as a naval historian. In the course of years of research into all the things that went up to make life in Nelson's Navy, I was accumulating a great deal of material about the ships and the men that I could not use in my naval histories but which I wanted to get into print so that the knowledge should not be lost for future generations. At the

DUDLEY POPE

same time my publishers wanted me to turn this knowledge to good use with novels, since C. S. Forester was obviously not going to write many more of his splendid Hornblower books. (Forester and I were in frequent correspondence, incidentally.)

"Finally I wrote the first chapter of a novel, setting it round Porto Santo Stefano just to see if I could write fiction, and both publishers promptly commissioned the first four novels in a series written round the same hero, 'Nicholas Ramage.' Round about this time my wife and I decided that after four years in Italy we wanted to live in England again for a spell, and to live afloat. We went back and bought a twenty-one-ton sailing cutter, Golden Dragon. The novel was finished, and I went on to write a large, illustrated history of guns. By the time our first infant, Jane, was born, the novel, *Ramage*, had been published, made a Book Society Choice, and hailed in the United States as the successor to Hornblower.

"As I wanted to set the second novel off Cape Trafalgar, in Spain, and the third and fourth in the Caribbean, we decided to sail to these places in the Golden Dragon. Thus in the autumn of 1965 we sailed five thousand, eight hundred miles from Plymouth, England (where, in Nelson's day, my great-grandfather had been a shipowner) to Barbados, arriving there when Jane was nine months old and one of the youngest ever to have sailed the Atlantic.

"Reviewers have been kind enough to say that anyone reading my books gets the impression he is taking part in the activities involved. This is almost entirely due, I think, to the fact that almost alone among naval historians, I am primarily a sailor. The problems of seamanship facing Nicholas Ramage in the novels are the ones that face me and anyone else in a sailing ship.

"As I write, the thing that has surprised me is that in this highly sophisticated age where what is science fiction one moment becomes a reality the next, a novel about the adventures of a young lieutenant at sea in Nelson's day can get to number two on the best-seller list within a few days of publication and stay there. Since *Ramage* is not riddled with characters who are moral or sexual perverts, contains no pornography, isn't crusading for or against anything, and only tries to portray men and women as they really behave in times of stress, I can only think that perhaps there is still a chance for writers who just want to tell a tale in the tradition of Conrad, Maugham, Forester and, more recently, Fleming."

Dudley Pope is one of England's best-known naval historians. From the beginning, his work has been praised for the depth and soundness of his scholarship and the vigor of his style. *At Twelve Mr. Byng Was Shot* is "a model history" of the scandalous execution in 1757 of Admiral John Byng, falsely accused of treason, in fact a government scapegoat for the loss of Minorca. The bloody mutiny on the naval frigate Hermione is the subject of *The Black Ship*. Pope's account, reconstructed from contemporary documents, is "tremendously detailed and tremendously accurate—even the conversations are exact." The appalling story, from its origins in the sadism of the Hermione's young commander, who killed men in the name of smartness, to the yardarm hangings of more than a score of the mutineers, was pieced together with a narrative power which made the book as readable as a novel.

It was not surprising therefore that, when Pope turned to the novel form, his first attempt was notably popular and successful. Set during the Napoleonic Wars, with a dashing romantic hero in the Hornblower tradition, *Ramage* was found stylistically but not otherwise inferior to the C. S. Forester novels—and, as one reviewer said, "the panoramic sweep of his battle scenes is tempting enough for the sickliest of landlubbers." Later Ramage novels have received similar notices, all of them earning high praise for their authoritative and exciting accounts of action, but none of them escaping criticism for purple passages of descriptive writing and stilted dialogue.

PRINCIPAL WORKS: Flag Four: The Battle of the Coastal Forces in the Mediterranean, 1954; Battle of the River Plate, 1956 (U.S., Graf Spee, 1957); 73 North: The Battle of the Barents Sea (U.S., 73 North: The Defeat of Hitler's Navy), 1958; England Expects, 1959 (U.S., Decision at Trafalgar); At Twelve Mr. Byng Was Shot, 1962; The Black Ship, 1963; Guns, 1965; The Great Gamble: Nelson at Copenhagen, 1972. *Novels*—Ramage, 1965; Ramage and the Drum Beat, 1967 (U.S., Drumbeat); Ramage and the Freebooters, 1969; The Triton Brig, 1969; Governor Ramage, R.N., 1973.

ABOUT: Contemporary Authors 7–8, 1963; Who's Who, 1973; Who's Who in America, 1972–1973. *Periodical*—Books and Bookmen July 1965.

POPE-HENNESSY, JAMES (November 20, 1916–), English biographer, historian, and travel writer, was born in London, the son of Major-General L. H. R. Pope-Hennessy and the writer Dame Una Pope-Hennessy. It was his mother, he once said, who through her constant influence equipped him "with those things that are essential if one is to try to write a book at all." His elder brother John, under that same influence, became a distinguished art critic and director of the Victoria and Albert Museum.

The family is a Roman Catholic one, and James Pope-Hennessy was educated at the famous Catholic public school Downside, except for three years at St. Albans Cathedral School in Washington, D.C., when his father was military attaché at the British Embassy there. On his return to England, Pope-Hennessy entered Balliol College, Oxford, which he left after two years without a degree. A year with the Roman Catholic publishing house of Sheed and Ward (1937–1938) was followed by a wretched interlude, of great significance in his life and writings, as private secretary to the governor of Trinidad and Tobago. He later referred to Trinidad as "a place in which some of the most miserable weeks of my existence had been spent." With the outbreak of World War II in 1939, Pope-Hennessy joined the Royal Artillery as a gunner. He was commissioned in the Intelligence Corps in 1940, spent most of the next four years in the War Office, and returned to Washington to serve on the Army General Staff in 1944–1945.

His literary career began auspiciously in 1939, when he won the Hawthornden Prize with his first book, *London Fabric*. It was "an attempt to recall a few of the associations dormant in some London buildings" before the impending war destroyed them forever. His conversations with Perdita, a female sounding board for his opinions as they tour London, were thought stilted and contrived, but there was nothing but praise for the eloquence and sensitivity of his descriptive prose.

West Indian Summer, also published during the war, was Pope-Hennessy's first attempt to digest his encounter with Trinidad. Instead of recording his impressions directly, Pope-Hennessy uses an *alter ego*, Cashel, a member of the Governor's staff, to recall the history of the island, and to contrast its natural beauty with the miseries and stupidities imposed by white administrators. Sir Walter Raleigh, Trollope, Froude, and others are invoked to describe the West Indies they had known. Pope-Hennessy returned to the West Indies in 1952, "rummaging among old and odious memories." In *The Baths of Absalom* he compares the beauty of French Martinique with the ugliness and squalor of the British West Indies, where, he suggested, conditions had in some places deteriorated since 1886, when they had provoked Froude's outraged criticisms. The author's other travel books include *America Is an Atmosphere*, which warmly recalls "the friendliness, the openness, the candour" he found in the United States at the end of the war, *Aspects of Provence*, and his Hong Kong notebook *Half-Crown Colony*. As Alan Ross said of the latter book, Pope-Hennessy in his travel writing "never seems to strain after effects, but quietly achieves them."

It is however Pope-Hennessy's biographies which have been the most admired of his works. His first subject was Richard Monckton Milnes, Lord Houghton, known as "the Bird of Paradox," who never fulfilled either his literary or his political ambitions, but who was an exuberant and fascinating character and a talented literary and social impresario. The book, published in two volumes, was universally welcomed as a vivid portrait of the man and of his age. Pope-Hennessy, wrote one critic, "has shaped an enormous mass of material into a scholarly, and well-documented, yet clear and entertaining narrative."

There was an even warmer reception for the author's best-selling official biography of Queen Mary, wife of George V, which "reconstructs a vast British, foreign, and historical background," and fills it with "many brilliant literary sketches of individual men and women." A. L. Rowse said it was "the most human of such biographies, as skilful and accomplished as it is thoro and conscientious, beautifully written, entertaining, and with a sense of humor that plays over the vast, rich canvas like the light of spring."

Pope-Hennessy's dislike of the British colonial system echoes that of his grandfather, Sir John Pope-Hennessy, an ambitious, talented Irishman who became known as "the stormy petrel of the Colonial Service," and is thought to be the original of Trollope's Phineas Finn. James Pope-Hennessy, who visited each of his grandfather's far-flung territories in turn, wrote in *Verandah* not only a detached and thorough biography of this remarkable man but an absorbing portrait of the British Empire as "a kaleidoscope of inter-related factors, not the least of which was the human."

What Pope-Hennessy had learned of man's inhumanity to man, in the British Empire and elsewhere, impelled him to write *Sins of the Fathers*, "a study of the Atlantic slave traders, 1441–1807," based on contemporary accounts by traders, seamen, slave owners, and the slaves themselves. J. H.

JAMES POPE-HENNESSY

Plumb found it "alive with pain, heavy with human misery," but doubted the value of a history which added nothing to previous accounts. However, another reviewer, in the *Times Literary Supplement*, thought it more than a history—a vivid and harrowing account of "how exposure to the history of the trade affected the author."

James Pope-Hennessy served as literary editor of *The Spectator* from 1947 to 1949. He became a citizen of the Irish Republic in 1970, and has a residence in County Offaly as well as one in London. He gives his principal recreation as travel. He was named a Commander of the Royal Victorian Order in 1960.

PRINCIPAL WORKS: London Fabric, 1939; West Indian Summer: A Retrospect, 1943; America Is an Atmosphere, 1947; Monckton Milnes, vol. 1, The Years of Promise, 1809–51, 1950; vol. 2, The Flight of Youth, 1851–85, 1952; Aspects of Provence, 1952; The Baths of Absalom: A Footnote to Froude, 1954; Lord Crewe, 1858–1945: The Likeness of a Liberal, 1955; Queen Mary, 1867–1953, 1959; (as ed.) Queen Victoria at Windsor and Balmoral: Letters from Her Grand-daughter, June 1889, 1959; Verandah: Some Episodes in the Crown Colonies, 1867–89, 1964; Sins of the Fathers: A Study of the Atlantic Slave Traders, 1441–1807, 1967; Half-Crown Colony: A Hong-Kong Notebook, 1969; Anthony Trollope, 1971.

ABOUT: West, A. Principles and Persuasions, 1957; Who's Who, 1973. *Periodicals*—Illustrated London News October 24, 1959; New Statesman February 18, 1950; October 17, 1959; New Yorker December 31, 1955; May 21, 1960; Times Literary Supplement July 5, 1941; October 9, 1943; February 17, 1950; January 25, 1952; January 30, 1964; November 30, 1967.

POWELL, LAWRENCE CLARK (September 3, 1906—), American librarian and essayist, writes: "I was born in Washington, D.C. of Quaker parents. My father was in the Department of Agri-

LAWRENCE CLARK POWELL

culture, and his research in citrus took the family to California and back every winter until I was four. Thereafter we lived in Pasadena, and as a boy I roamed the orange groves eastward to the San Marino estate of Henry E. Huntington. An abiding love of travel, nature, people, and reading came both from environment and heredity.

"The desire to write just came, beginning in grammar school when my lifelong friend Ward Ritchie (later to become the noted printer-publisher) founded the *Marengo Literary Leader*, to which I contributed a Fu-Manchuesque thriller called 'The Purple Dragon.'

"At Occidental College in Los Angeles I was too busy being an activities man to write much. During my sophomore year, I worked as musician on the round-the-world Dollar Steamship Line. Back at college I was influenced by two professors, B. F. Stelter and C. F. MacIntyre, to go abroad for post-graduate study, my ultimate intention being to teach English.

"First however I was diverted by Ward Ritchie to join him as an employee of Vroman's Bookstore in Pasadena. He had been elevated from shipping clerk to sales clerk and I took his place in the cellar. This is known as starting at the bottom. Added inducement was the employees' discount on book purchases. A bent toward reading and collecting, begun by my parents and encouraged by Mrs. Nellie Keith, librarian of the South Pasadena Public Library, was refined by my college professors and Ritchie.

"In France for three and a half years I completed a doctorate at the University of Dijon in Burgundy, writing my dissertation on Robinson Jeffers. I also wrote several drafts of a jazz novel, none of them any good.

"Back in Los Angeles in 1934 I married my college sweetheart, Fay Ellen Shoemaker, and we eventually raised two sons, Norman and Wilkie. The Depression diverted me from teaching back into the book trade, and I worked for a couple of years as biblio-factotum in Jake Zeitlin's bookshop, adding lasting things to my education, until Althea Warren, head of the Los Angeles Public Library, persuaded me to become a librarian.

"And so it was library school in Berkeley and a beginning job under Miss Warren, after which I settled in at UCLA in 1938 and made my career there until, in 1966, I retired at sixty. I had served variously as junior assistant in acquisitions, director of the William Andrews Clark Memorial Library, university librarian, and finally as founding dean of the graduate School of Library Service. Throughout these years and in all weathers, my wife proved both sail and anchor.

"I found that my margin of energy after the day's work as librarian best allowed writing in the shorter essay form, and so I came to write about reading and writing and collecting, finding a responsive audience among librarians and readers throughout the world. I became a columnist and reviewer of Californiana and Southwestern Americana, happily combining reading, traveling, and writing.

"Gradually my publishing outlets widened, as I wrote for *Westways*, *Arizona Highways*, *Southwest Review*, and the New York *Times Book Review;* and thanks to William Targ my books received national publication and distribution.

"In 1955 we moved to the Malibu coast, thirty miles northwest of UCLA, where I have been a back-up gardener for my wife, a gleaner of driftwood, and the head of a mixed family of cats and dogs.

"I am a writer made not born and the making is endless. I believe that most of what I have written thus far has been practice and learning, and that with freedom from academic and professional demands, my best work can now be written. I am also confident that its form and content will be revealed when I sit down with my Scripto pencil and pad of yellow paper."

Powell's career has been to an unusual extent a product of his enthusiasms. That these are passionate and varied became evident at Occidental College (1924–1929), where he was "yell leader, actor, sports editor, jazz pianist, saxophonist, and fraternity president." Later it was his delight in books that first "diverted" him from his intended career as an English teacher, and led him eventually into his proper sphere as a librarian and bookman. Six years after he received his library degree he was librarian of UCLA and director of the William Andrews Clark Memorial Library there, which specializes in works on English civilization of the seventeenth and early eighteenth centuries. Powell's travels in pursuit of books took him all over the United States and regularly to London, where his nose for bibliographical treasure, and his vast spending power, earned him the rueful respect of his British colleagues. The UCLA book collections are an enduring monument to Powell's bibliographical passion and knowledge. The library school he founded there is called a School of Library Service, not of "library science," and is dedicated to the unfashionable notion that books and people, not administration and technology, are a librarian's first concern.

More often than not, Powell's writings also are a product of his wide-ranging enthusiasms—a generous and often lyrical attempt to infect others with his pleasure in some book or person, place or idea. His first book was his doctoral dissertation for the University of Dijon on Robinson Jeffers, published in France in 1932 and in the United States two years later. W. R. Benét thought it a "strikingly complete" and "unusually intelligent" study. Most of Powell's subsequent books have been collections of occasional pieces—reviews, essays, lectures, prefaces, and the like—dealing with the author's travels and discoveries as a book collector, the history of the American Southwest, libraries and librarianship.

The most admired of these volumes was *A Passion for Books*. E. F. Walbridge called it "far and away the best book LCP has yet published. The style is evocative, but hard-hitting when necessary; there is little of the 'precious polemics' which . . . have been imputed to him." *Bookman's Progress*, containing a selection from Powell's work over the years, had a mixed but generally very favorable reception. George Piternick, reviewing the book in *Library Journal*, commended the author's "profound and catholic" sensitivity to literature and landscape, but thought his style marred by overenthusiasm and "gush." Another reviewer, in the *Times Literary Supplement*, had no such reservations, and welcomed the essays as "zestful, companionable, redolent of . . . their author's 'lifelong love affair with books and bookmen.' " There was little but praise for *Fortune and Friendship*, Powell's "honest, sometimes tough-minded, often moving" autobiography.

Powell spent a year in England in 1950–1951 on a Guggenheim Fellowship, and gave the Library Association's annual lecture there in 1957. He has lectured at many universities, and has collected a number of honorary doctorates. In 1960 he received the Clarence Day award, given by the American Textbook Publishers Institute for "outstanding work in encouraging the love of books and reading" and in 1968, when he was a fellow of the Center for Advanced Studies at Wesleyan University, Drexel Institute gave him its Distinguished Achievement award. Powell is physically a small man, five feet six inches tall and slight in build. A Quaker and a Democrat, he enjoys beachcombing, gardening, and music, as well as reading and book collecting.

PRINCIPAL WORKS: Robinson Jeffers: The Man and His Work, 1934; Philosopher Pickett, 1942; Island of Books, 1951; Land of Fiction, 1952; The Alchemy of Books, and Other Essays and Addresses on Books and Writers, 1954; Books: West Southwest: Essays on Writers, Their Books, and Their Land, 1957; A Passion for Books, 1959; Books in My Baggage: Adventures in Reading and Collecting, 1960; Southwestern Book Trails, 1963; The Little Package, 1964; Bookman's Progress, 1968; Fortune and Friendship: An Autobiography, 1968; California Classics, 1971.

ABOUT: Current Biography, 1960; Powell, G. C. The Quiet Side of Europe, 1959; Rosenberg, B. Checklist of the Published Writings of Lawrence Clark Powell, 1966; Who's Who in America, 1972–1973. *Periodicals*—American Library Association Bulletin November 1954; Bulletin of Bibliography January-April 1953; Library Journal December 15, 1958; June 1, 1960; December 15, 1961; October 1, 1962; December 15, 1965; Library Quarterly April 1950.

POWELL, RICHARD (PITTS) (November 28, 1908—), American novelist and detective story writer, writes: "It always makes me feel humble and unworthy when I read autobiographical notes by other authors. Reading their well-groomed words, one realizes how laudable were the motivations that led them into writing careers. My motivation is, alas, not laudable. Critics sneer at it, and other authors do not confess to it. My motivation is money.

"Apparently this urge seized on me not many years after my birth on November 28, 1908, in Philadelphia. My first attempt at authorship, at the age of three, was a dunning letter to Santa Claus. When I was about eight my father, trying to bribe me to read more slowly, offered me ten cents for a synopsis of each book I read. This did not have the desired effect; I doubled my reading and wrote countless synopses.

"At college one of my history professors coaxed me to enter a contest, held by the Society of Colonial Wars of New Jersey, for the best essay on 'Travel and Transportation in Colonial New Jersey.' He pointed out the honor involved if I won the contest. The first prize of fifty dollars tempted me more, and I won it.

"I was graduated from Princeton University in 1930 and found myself in a world that was learning the meaning of a strange new term: The Depression. I began work on the Philadelphia *Evening Ledger* as a reporter at twenty dollars a week. Four years

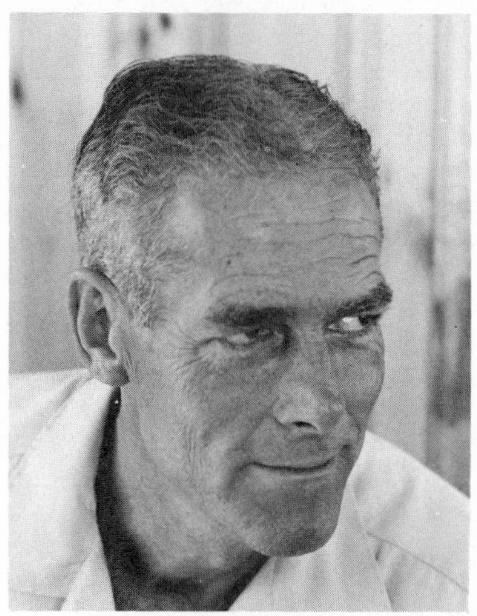

RICHARD POWELL

later, after three promotions, my pay was eighteen dollars a week, due to a general ten percent pay cut and a policy of no raises. During this period I wrote furiously in my spare time: short stories, novels, plays. I feared that, with a few more promotions, I might end up paying tuition to the *Ledger*, and outside writing seemed to offer the only hope of feeding a lovely but hungry wife who took the bad gamble of marrying me in 1932.

"My short stories began selling to leading magazines in 1936. As soon as my byline started appearing in magazines, the *Ledger* decided that I was a star reporter, and began to raise my salary. But it was too late; I have a weak character, and the urge to make money was now firmly fixed in it.

"I wish I could report how selflessly I served my country in World War II. I did spend four years in the Army, ending the war as Chief News Censor for General MacArthur. But I must confess that, in moments snatched from military duty, I managed to write and sell four serials to leading magazines. I finished one serial while on a ten-day voyage in a Landing Craft, Infantry, from Morotai to Borneo, where we were to make an assault landing at Brunei Bay. I am sure there are more heroic things a man can do aboard an invasion convoy, but I seemed to have overlooked them.

"After the war I kept on writing for magazines while becoming a vice president of N. W. Ayer & Son, in Philadelphia, the country's oldest advertising agency and one of the largest. These activities paid distressingly well. In 1955, however, I tried to reform. I told my wife (the same one, by the way; it is expensive to change wives, so I don't do it) that we had enough money and that I was going to give up my money-grabbing habits and write a serious novel that would be a masterpiece and would earn us two dollars and fifty-two cents, before returns.

"My intentions were good, but apparently it was too late to change. My serious novel was published in 1957. It was titled *The Philadelphian*, and it skylarked on the best-seller lists for months and sold to a book club and the movies.

"If my attempt at reform had not been sincere, I would have followed up this gold strike by writing 'The Son of the Philadelphian' or 'The Philadelphian Strikes Back.' Instead, I made another effort to go straight. I wrote a completely different novel called *Pioneer, Go Home!* It was a satire and, as they say in the Broadway theatre, satire is what closes Tuesday night. But obviously I can't write satire. Hollywood began scrambling for film rights before the book was even in galley proofs, and there we went again down the book club-best seller road to hell. For my third serious novel I wrote a story of World War II, *The Soldier*. This was in 1960 and nobody was interested in World War II. For once, I was going to succeed in being non-commercial. I was, that is, until the *Saturday Evening Post* bought it for serialization.

"Since then I have published two more novels and have a couple more underway, and I have given up hope of becoming non-commercial. I am not even sure I should be listed under the honorable title of 'author.' Probably I am just a plain writer."

Powell's first published novel, the thriller *Don't Catch Me*, introduced as its unorthodox amateur detective the cautious young antique dealer Andy Blake, who, much against his will, is involved by his high-spirited wife in the investigation of a particularly nasty crime. Readers liked its mixture of thrills, humor, and romance, and the story was serialized in *American Magazine*, and produced by Orson Welles on network radio, with Rita Hayworth playing Arab Blake. It was the first in a series of scrupulously researched Andy and Arab stories about skullduggery in the antique trade. Powell has also written a number of other detective stories, some of them set in his adopted state, Florida, and all of them "deft, light suspense entertainment, excitingly plotted, lively . . . in portrayal of the battle of the sexes, and rich in some of the most amusing dialogue to be found in any field."

Similar qualities have been recognized in what Powell calls his "serious" novels. *The Philadelphian*, though it was said to contain "faint echoes of John Marquand, Edwin O'Connor, and John O'Hara" was in general most praised for its entertainment value. It is an engrossing account of the rise of a Philadelphia family to wealth, power, and a sense of social responsibility.

Powell has since demonstrated his great skill as a

storyteller in a variety of novelistic genres. *Pioneer, Go Home!* mixes farce and satire in the story of one family's triumphant guerrilla campaign against Florida officialdom. *The Soldier*, set in the South Pacific during World War II, is "an immensely readable novel, solidly researched, tastefully and competently written." *I Take This Land*, an account of the conquest and development of southwest Florida from 1895 to the present, was called a "red-blooded, full-bosomed" historical melodrama. Powell drew on his newspaper experience for *Daily and Sunday*; on his knowledge of the Caribbean for *Don Quixote, U.S.A.*, about the Peace Corps adventures of a contemporary Candide; and on his passion for tournament bridge in *Tickets to the Devil*.

The novelist is the son of Richard Percival Powell, a seventh-generation Philadelphian who dealt in real estate, and Lida (Pitts) Powell. He was married in 1932 to Marian Roberts, and has a son and a daughter. Tall, brown-eyed, and gray-haired, he is an Episcopalian of "variable" political affiliation. He enjoys sailboat racing, fishing, bridge, gardening, and "writing, writing, writing, writing."

PRINCIPAL WORKS: *All fiction*—Don't Catch Me, 1942; All Over But the Shooting, 1944; Lay That Pistol Down, 1945; Shoot If You Must, 1946; And Hope to Die, 1947; Shark River, 1950; The Shell Game, 1950; A Shot in the Dark, 1952; Leave Murder to Me, 1952; Say It With Bullets, 1953; False Colors, 1955; The Philadelphian, 1956; Pioneer, Go Home!, 1959; The Soldier, 1960; I Take This Land, 1963; Daily and Sunday, 1965; Don Quixote, U.S.A., 1966; Tickets to the Devil, 1968; Whom the Gods Would Destroy, 1970.

ABOUT: Who's Who in America, 1972–1973. *Periodicals*—Wilson Library Bulletin September 1962.

PRESS, JOHN (BRYANT) (January 11, 1920–), English poet and critic, writes: "I was born in Norwich, and was educated at King Edward VI School. My schooldays were extremely happy. I was taught by intelligent, cultivated, generous masters and was given an excellent grounding in the subjects which really interested me—history, English, French and Latin. I enjoyed playing games, for which I had some talent, and recall with affection the playing-fields at the end of the Close between the Cathedral and the river Wensum, on which barges went to and fro. Norwich, though a provincial city of only about one hundred and thirty thousand inhabitants, was a lively place, with a fine amateur theatre, the Maddermarket, run by a remarkable professional director, Nugent Monck, a Philharmonic Orchestra, and a tradition of local culture going back to the late eighteenth century. It was a city of enormous churches and dignified houses, as well as of disgusting slums; the sea was twenty miles away; and on Saturday afternoons, when I was not playing games, I watched the local

JOHN PRESS

football team, resplendent in their yellow-and-green. Then, as now, I was a fervent supporter of the Canaries.

"I began to write poems when I was eighteen, and have continued to do so ever since. There have been weeks, even months, of silence; but so far, unpredictably, even involuntarily, I have always experienced the recrudescence of the familiar need to find the appropriate form for the complex of thoughts and emotions which is troubling me. I write poems at all times and seasons, in sickness and in health, on ships, in railway trains, in hotels, even on double-decker buses, as well as in my home.

"From 1938 to 1940 and again from 1945 to 1946 I completed my formal education by reading history at Corpus Christi College, Cambridge. Service in the Royal Artillery in the intervening years supplied the gaps in the university curriculum. I served in the ranks for fifteen months, joined the raiding-party that stole coke to warm a freezing Nissen Hut, learned that the underprivileged were usually morally superior to their masters. From 1942 to 1945 I enjoyed the pleasures of privilege as an officer in East Africa. I was entertained in the superb Highlands and sampled the delights of swimming in the Indian Ocean and picnicking on the hard, white, moonlit beaches from Mombasa to Malindi. I travelled to the borders of the Congo and visited Dar-es-Salaam, Zanzibar, Madagascar and the Seychelles. Parties, sport, military routine, inspection of prisons, responsibility for the education of African troops, hours of reading on lonely gun-sites, music in an enchanting house at the foot of the Ngong Hills where Karen Blixen had once lived—such was my life in these formative years.

"For the past twenty years I have worked very happily for the British Council in Greece, that most tragic and beautiful of all lands, in India, Ceylon and England. My childhood was calm and full of delights; I have had a felicitous domestic life of my own since 1947, with a son and a daughter to complete my family.

"Although I had been writing poetry from 1938 onwards and sporadically trying to get them printed, the first of my poems to be accepted for publication appeared in the PEN anthology, *New Poems 1954*. In 1955 my first attempt at writing prose was published. This was *The Fire and the Fountain*, a study of the way in which a poem comes into being. From that time onwards my poems began to acquire merits in the eyes of editors. I have destroyed or suppressed most of the verse written before 1945, but a few poems of this period were printed in *Uncertainties* (1956) and *Guy Fawkes Night* (1959).

"In 1963 Michael Powell commissioned me to write a new libretto for his colour television-film version of Bartók's opera, *Bluebeard's Castle*. My ambition is to write original libretti for operas or for musicals. The technical problems fascinate me, and I believe that poetry should have a social function, by which I do not mean that poets should versify the sociological opinions of left-wing progressives."

The Chequer'd Shade, which received the RSL Heinemann Award, discussed obscurity in poetry, showing by copious quotation that the phenomenon is far from new. *Rule and Energy*, based on Press's 1962 Elliston Lectures at the University of Cincinnati, examined trends in British verse since World War II. Both of these critical works, and the earlier *The Fire and the Fountain*, were generally praised as scholarly, sensitive, agreeably written introductory studies, of great reference value. All the same there are some critics who wish that Press's work were motivated more urgently (as one put it) "by fervour, distress [or] the curiosity that insists on an explanation." *A Map of Modern English Verse* is primarily a source book, dealing with major poets and poetical movements from Yeats to the 1950s, and providing for each a brief critical introduction, a selection of critical comment by others, some relevant poems, and a select bibliography. *The Lengthening Shadows* is a useful history of "forces hostile to poets and to poetry" from Plato to the Nazis.

Press's verse has been reviewed in much the same terms as his criticism. As a poet, his preoccupations are said to be personal rather than social (which does not contradict his own comment above), with a "spirited lyrical quality" reminiscent of the Georgian poets. D. J. Enright, reviewing *Guy Fawkes Night*, called Press a "decent, gregarious, cultivated" poet, but thought he would do well to "lash out now and again." From 1966 to 1971 Press served in Paris both as the British Council's deputy representative, and as assistant cultural attaché at the British Embassy, and since 1972 he has been the British Council's area officer for Oxford.

PRINCIPAL WORKS: The Fire and the Fountain, 1955 (2nd ed. 1966); Uncertainties, 1956; (ed.) Poetic Heritage, 1957; The Chequer'd Shade, 1958; Guy Fawkes Night, 1959; Rule and Energy, 1963; (ed.) *fifth book of* Palgrave's Golden Treasury, 1964; A Map of Modern English Verse, 1969; The Lengthening Shadows, 1971.

ABOUT: Orr, P. (ed.) The Poet Speaks, 1966; Who's Who, 1973. *Periodicals*—Christian Science Monitor July 25, 1963; Critical Quarterly Summer 1963; London Magazine November 1955; Times Literary Supplement September 23, 1955; January 16, 1959.

***PREVELAKIS, PANDELIS** (February 18, 1909–), Greek poet, novelist, playwright, art critic, and translator, writes: "I was born in Rethymnon, Island of Crete, Greece. My father was George Prevelakis and my mother formerly Miss Irene Frangiadaki. A village (Preveliana) and a monastery (Preveli) in Crete bear the name of my ancestors, among them many men of devotion and self-sacrifice: priests, monks, painters of icons, warriors and scholars. I received my early education in my native town, and then studied literature and art in the universities of Athens and Paris (Licence ès Lettres of the University of Paris; Diploma of the Institute of Art and Archaeology, Paris; Ph.D., University of Salonika). I have been Director of Fine Arts in the Greek Ministry of Education (1937–1941) and since 1939 I have been teaching history of art as professor in the National Academy of Fine Arts, Athens.

"In spite of a long career in the civil service I never considered myself either a professional teacher or a writer; my double activity only helped me become conscious of myself and give testimony of some problems of my time. Part of my work (some of the novels) is inspired by my native land and its struggles to reconquer its independence from Turkish domination. Another part is focussed on myself (the recent novels, the poetry and the drama). I wrote long essays on El Greco and Kazantzakis, my fellow-countrymen. Through their life and work I tried to understand my own roots and inclination. I knew Kazantzakis intimately and receive some four hundred letters from him during the thirty-one years of our friendship. I have traveled through Europe (France, Italy, Spain, Great Britain, etc.) and translated some twenty works of European literature. In my own work I am less interested in social problems than

* pre ve lä′ kis

human fate: I could characterize my attitude as that of an Outsider who longs for the harmonious life experienced by his ancestors. My novel *The Sun of Death*, reflects some of my principal concerns."

Apart from his excellent modern Greek version of Euripides' *Medea*, Prevelakis has mainly translated from Romance languages, including works by Molière, Claudel, Valéry, and Benavente, Luis Cernuda's elegy on Lorca's death, Calderón's *La vida es sueño*, and Cassío's monumental study of El Greco. In his numerous essays on art and literature his scholarly appreciation of the artists of his native Crete has a special place, and is closely bound up with his own imaginative work. His studies of the Cretan painter El Greco include *Domenikos Theotokopulos* (1930), *Theotokopulos. Ta biografika* (The Biography of Theotokopulos, 1942), and *Greco in Roma* (1941). His long friendship with the Cretan poet Nikos Kazantzakis led to several studies which culminated in a major critical work, *O poiitis kai to poiima tis odysseias* (The Poet and the Poem of the Odyssey, 1958); in this Prevelakis interprets Kazantzakis' 33,333-line poem and in so doing explains the development of the poet's life work and the various influences on it at different stages of his life.

Prevelakis' own creative career began with the lyrical epic *Stratiotes* (Soldiers, 1928), and he subsequently produced two slender volumes of lyric poems *I gymni poiisi* (Naked Poetry), and *I pio gymni poiisi* (Most Naked Poetry, 1941). He has also written plays, including *To iero sfagio* (The Sacrificial Victim, 1952), *O Lazaros* (Lazarus, 1954), *Ta kheria tou zontanu Theou* (The Hands of the Living God, 1955), and *To ifaisteio* (The Volcano, 1962).

But Prevelakis is best known for his novels, which began with *To chroniko mias politeias* (The Story of a Town, 1938), a fresh and attractive portrait of life in his native town of Rethymnon. After World War II he wrote a series of books dealing with the struggle for Cretan independence, of which the first, *Pandermi Kriti* (Desolate Crete, 1945), is a chronicle of the Cretan rising of 1866. *I trilogia tou Kritikou* (The Trilogy of 'The Cretan,' 1948–1950)—made up of the novels *To dendro* (The Tree, 1948), *I proti eleutheria* (The First Freedom, 1949), and *I politeia* (The City, 1950), in which the characters are types who embody the Cretan ideals of heroism and honor—follows the destiny of Konstantinos Marcantonios from his childhood after his father has been assassinated.

His next three novels again make up a trilogy, though this time one which is to a large extent autobiographical. *O Ilios tou thanatou* (1960, translated as *The Sun of Death*) was the 1962 selection of the International Peace Library in Oslo. Set in Crete during World War I, it is the story of how the boy Yorgaki attains manhood and discovers his vocation as a writer. His world falls apart at the age of thirteen when his father's ship is torpedoed and his mother flings herself from a cliff. Aunt Roussaki, a simple and pious woman who is the embodiment of the Cretan folk virtues and whose speech is a continuous and sometimes tedious flow of peasant wisdom, takes him to live with her in her village beneath Mount Ida which, however, has been transformed by the war. Sons and husbands are away fighting on the mainland, food is scarce, and the Bulgarian prisoners of war who are making a road on the mountain are starving to death.

PANDELIS PREVELAKIS

Death continues to follow Yorgaki, who becomes involved in a senseless blood feud which is a microcosm of the war itself. Through him the girl he loves is killed in an accident, and his dreams are haunted by violence. But his sexual experiments, his experience of death, the beauty of nature, and the example of Aunt Roussaki all help to bring him to maturity, while another mentor, Loizos Damolinos, opens Yorgaki's eyes to the world of philosophy and of art.

Critics especially praised the novel's visual beauty, what the *Times Literary Supplement* called "small individual pictures, Cretan scenes of vivid colour and freshness. He shows, like figures in a frieze, the white stallion led by a child along the cobbled street to drink at the trough, the village girls singing at the olive harvest, the mothers, still as stone in their anxiety and grief, waiting for news from the front." Robert Payne thought it "a good novel," in which "the characters come alive and move about in a recognizable air, but there is always the sense of *déjà vu*. An ancient tragedy is played out in a modern setting. . . . What could have been a simple and utterly charming evocation of childhood is spoiled by the insistent demands of the tragedian, who must paint his brooding cloud over the stage."

The trilogy's other two novels follow Yorgaki, now a poet and novelist, into self-exile. In *I kefali tis Medousas* (The Head of the Medusa, 1963) he completes his education in Athens and spends the years up to World War II there. The Medusa head which he has to learn to face is the madness of the modern world, with its rapid changes and its competing ideologies. His search for himself ends after twenty years with the feeling that he belongs to his native Crete, and in *O artos ton angelon* (The Bread of the Angels, 1965) he hopefully returns. But World War II, the civil war which followed, and the era of the atomic bomb have brought change here too, and his people seem to him to have become corrupt, to have lost their individuality, their tradition, and the meaning and harmony of their lives. Ideals can remain ideals only at a distance, and Yorgaki departs once more.

Andonis Decavalles has observed that the imaginative chronicle is Prevelakis' favorite genre, and that just as the earlier trilogy is a testimony of Cretan nineteenth century history so this later trilogy is a "testimony of my age" by its author who, through his account of the development of a poet and of the struggle between the inner and the outer world, builds "a faithful, sincere and inspired picture of our modern agony and our isolation."

PRINCIPAL WORKS IN ENGLISH TRANSLATION: The Sun of Death, tr. by Abbott Rick, 1964 (also tr. under the same title by Philip Sherrard, 1965).

ABOUT: Penguin Companion to Literature 2, 1969. *Periodicals*—Book Week December 27, 1964; Books Abroad Summer 1968; New York Times Book Review November 29, 1964; Odyssey Review June 1962; Times Literary Supplement April 8, 1965.

***PRÉVERT, JACQUES** (February 4, 1900–), French poet, screen writer, and dramatist, was born at Neuilly-sur-Seine, Paris, the son of André Prévert, a clerk from Brittany, and Suzanne (Catusse) Prévert. He went to the École Communale in Paris and supported himself as a young man in a variety of jobs. Prévert was a member of the surrealist movement from 1926 to 1929, but remained unknown until 1931, when the review *Commerce* published his long story-poem *Tentative de description d'un dîner de têtes à Paris-France* (Attempt to Describe a Dinner of Important People in Paris). This savage surrealistic poem made Prévert's reputation overnight and is considered by some critics his best work. In it he bitterly satirizes the "bosses" of the world—the rulers, the industrialists,

*prā vâr'

JACQUES PRÉVERT

the warmongers, the academicians—and speaks in defense of the poor, the innocent, the exploited. It sets the theme of all his work, not only in his books but in his films and theatrical pieces.

Prévert's first film was *L'Affaire est dans le sac* (It's in the Bag), which he made with his brother Pierre in 1932. It is a sardonic fantasy about capitalism, featuring for example a millionaire who weeps constantly from sheer boredom. In his later films Prévert achieved a kind of melancholy poetic realism. It is this quality which characterizes the scenarios he wrote for the director Marcel Carné, including several of the permanent triumphs of the French cinema's great age of romanticism: *Quai des brumes* (*Port of Shadows*, 1938), *Le Jour se lève* (*Daybreak*, 1939), and *Les Enfants du paradis* (*Children of Paradise*, 1945).

Hazel Hackett has described Prévert in *Sight and Sound* as "the most poetical of script-writers," and also as "the most unliterary of poets." In fact his first volume of poetry, *Paroles* (Words), did not appear until 1946, and even then owed its existence to the devotion of its editor, René Bertelé; some of these poems had appeared in forgotten reviews and old newspapers, some had been sung in cabarets, others had been scribbled for friends on backs of envelopes or on the paper tablecloths of Paris cafés. Once collected, however, *Paroles* achieved and maintained a phenomenal popularity, establishing Prévert, in the words of Patricia Terry, as "the one great success" among the "numerous poets who under the double influence of surrealism and Marxism intended to write a truly accessible, popular poetry."

There is in fact none of the obscurity of surrealism

in Prévert's work, no tapping of the unconscious, no metaphysics. What he does take from surrealism (and/or from the cinema) is a penchant for long sequences of "verbal snapshots" in ironic or startling juxtaposition. In the opinion of some critics, he wins clarity at the expense of profundity. C. A. Hackett calls Prévert's feelings, though sincere, "instinctive, crude reactions to the complexity of experience; his 'realism' an escape from, not an acceptance of life," and his language lacking in "the simple, memorable intensity of great poetry." All this is no doubt true, and there has been no sign of development in the collections which have followed *Paroles* and which have included *Spectacle* (1951), *Charmes de Londres* (The Charms of London, 1952), *La Pluie et le beau temps* (Rain and Fine Weather, 1955), and *Choses et autres* (Things and Others, 1972).

Prévert writes in the tradition and often in the rhythms of the French *chansonniers*, and his work is direct because it is designed to be heard rather than read. Many of the poems in *Paroles* comment on the German occupation, but in all his verse Prévert is the enemy of interfering officialdom, the champion of the ordinary people of Paris. And the ordinary people know this and buy his books, whatever the academy may say, grateful to find themselves a little romanticized, a little idealized, and delighting in Prévert's puns, his "bawdy anticlericalism," his "spontaneous disrespect for the rhetoric of authority," and a voice which is "the voice of the wise street-urchin—precocious, mocking, bitter, dupe of nothing and no one."

Many of Prévert's farces, pantomimes, ballets, and skits have been performed, mostly in avant-garde theatres in Paris. One of the best-known of his pieces is the mime play *Baptiste*, which was in the repertory of Jean-Louis Barrault during the 1940s and was introduced in part into *Les Enfants du paradis*. Discussing one of Prévert's farces, *La Famille tuyau de poêle* (Top-hat Family, 1935), Eric Bentley wrote: "Prévert does not belong in the world of Labiche, Courteline and Feydeau; but he makes a comment on it with something of their intelligence and their imaginative extravagance."

Prévert has been married twice: in 1925 to Simone Dienne and in 1947 to Janine Tricotet. His hobbies are sketching, photography, and making collages. "Two men coexist in Prévert," writes Pierre de Boisdeffre. "One is a lay Savonarola, who rises against the follies and atrocities of the time, who sometimes recovers the inspired tone of Daumier . . . and sometimes trips into near-offense and bad taste. The other Prévert is a tender and delicate friend of lovers, the poor, the humiliated ones, the poet of benches and public parks, of a melancholy and smiling humanity."

PRINCIPAL WORKS IN ENGLISH TRANSLATION: Selections from Paroles (tr. Lawrence Ferlinghetti), 1958; Prévert II (tr. by Teo Savory), 1967. *Plays in* Bentley, E. R. (ed.) Let's Get a Divorce, 1958. *Poems and stories in* Barnstone, W. (ed.) Modern European Poetry, 1966; Canfield, K. F. (ed.) Selections from French Poetry, 1965; Marks, E. (ed.) French Poetry From Baudelaire to the Present, 1962; Strachan, W. J. Apollinaire to Aragon: Thirty Modern French Poets, 1948; Coronet January 1956, February 1959; Harper's Magazine November 1964; Kenyon Review Spring 1949; Life and Letters December 1947; Nation November 16, 1957; December 7, 1957; November 14, 1959; Poetry June 1949; Spectator February 6, 1953; Yale French Studies No. 21, 1958.

ABOUT: Baker, W. E. Jacques Prévert, 1967; Boisdeffre, P. de. Dictionnaire de littérature contemporaine, 1900–1962, 1962; Greet, A. H. Jacques Prévert's Word Games, 1968; Grigson, G. (ed.) The Concise Encyclopedia of Modern World Literature, 1963; Hackett, C. A. An Anthology of Modern French Poetry From Baudelaire to the Present Day, 1965; Rousselot, J. Panorama critique des nouveaux poètes français, 1952; Who's Who in France, 1971–1972. *Periodicals*—Guardian March 7, 1961; Mercure de France June 1949, November 1949, April 1951, March 1953; Sight and Sound 60 1946–1947; Wisconsin Studies in Contemporary Literature Summer 1966.

PRICE, REYNOLDS (February 1, 1933–), American novelist and short story writer, writes: "I was born in Macon, North Carolina (a town of two hundred and twenty-seven cotton and tobacco farmers nailed to the flat red land at the pit of the Great Depression) on February 1, 1933—a month before Franklin Roosevelt's first inauguration and in the week that Hitler demanded dictatorial powers from the Reichstag. I was reared in several small Carolina towns where my father (William Solomon Price) sold first insurance and then electrical appliances; and my clear memories of those years at the weak-bottomed end of the Depression, the start of the war, are our small family (my burdened hilarious father, Elizabeth Rodwell my vivid mother, and Will my buoyant young brother), the terror of financial ruin (losing the only house we ever built, continuing from one small loan to another), hundreds of solitary days with books or in woods up trees suspecting I was miserable—though I was not nor I think were my parents. I knew as a child—from the endless nostalgia of my father and mother, long before I discovered Proust—that it is most necessary to arrange to have had a happy past. On the whole, we had one. I attended small public schools and received the encouragement of my parents and many of my teachers and the bafflement of almost all my contemporaries at my early and passionate interests—painting and drawing. Only in late adolescence, when I had seen that my drawings were merely copies and thus no means of exploring the genuine mysteries and fears that had by now begun to rise in full strength and size, did I begin to write—my first pieces, a Christmas pageant and a play about Columbus (*The Jewels of Isabella*) and then a stream of love poems full of Pearls, Opals, Beryls. But again throughout

REYNOLDS PRICE

high school in Raleigh (where we settled finally in 1947) and at Duke University, I was encouraged by my elders and now by a few of my trapped fellows and—most crucially, in my senior year, by Eudora Welty—so that when I left for Merton College, Oxford, in September 1955, I had finally seen that my only way of earning what some had freely given (confidence, fidelity) lay through the writing of prose fiction. I spent those three years dangerously dividing my time among duty (a thesis on the chorus in *Samson Agonistes* supervised by Helen Gardner and Lord David Cecil—I still seem to be the only person, Milton perhaps included, who has understood its use in the drama), compulsion (the writing of a number of stories, none of which any American magazine published but which Stephen Spender began to use in *Encounter* in 1958) and pleasure (lunging around Europe, Norway to Italy, looking; and lazing in England with the kinds of friends—meticulous, total—one only has in England). In 1958 I returned to North Carolina to teach English literature at Duke (where I still teach half the year) and began to write, in the exhausted hours left from teaching Freshmen Composition, what I thought would be a story but what ended two years later as a novel—*A Long and Happy Life*. That was published in 1962 when I was again in Oxford for a year, completing *The Names and Faces of Heroes*, stories which followed in 1963. Both were met in ways that confirmed me perhaps for life in my earlier choice and clarified the size of the attempt—comprehension, control and celebration of the urgent mysteries (the people I love, those I hate, myself, things, God) through the making of stories which transmute the lethal disorder of experience into well-formed but honest and useful public objects—mirrors, microscopes, telescopes but also shields."

A Long and Happy Life, set in and around a small town in North Carolina, was unusual for a first novel in that it dwells chiefly upon hope rather than despair. Not that its heroine, Rosacoke Mustian, does not encounter despair, anger, and misery in her love for the remote and careless Wesley Beavers; but through it she grows up, she changes and her love changes. The whole episode is told in a language which is exact, often wryly funny, and wholly appropriate to its passion and its locale. Rosacoke's sudden awareness, at the end of the book, of the nature of her love for Wesley and for all her other neighbors, as she takes the part of Christ's mother in the Christmas pageant, is a fine example of successful symbolist writing: the performance by these now familiar people of the Christian story is fully satisfactory both in mythic terms and in terms of what we know of the individuals concerned. The description of Rosacoke's transformation from a merely sweet to a lovely and generous young woman is deeply moving and was almost universally acclaimed as such. "To have created Rosacoke Mustian is an achievement that the most mature novelist might envy," wrote Granville Hicks, and only the *New Yorker* dismissed the book as imitation Faulkner.

There is a similar lyric grace in the seven North Carolina stories collected as *The Names and Faces of Heroes*—a kind of innocence recaptured by extreme sophistication in the process of transcending itself. Only occasionally does this quality degenerate into a self-conscious false naïveté.

A Generous Man centers on an earlier episode in the history of the Mustian family, and particularly on Rosacoke's beloved elder brother Milo, who is fifteen at the time of the story, and in search of his manhood. It is at one level a comic novel, dealing with a wild chase through the woods in search of Milo's lost small brother, the boy's supposedly rabid dog, and a twenty-foot python named Death. Milo's adventures in the course of the chase include a sexual encounter with the wife of an impotent sheriff, in which he proves his virility, and his achievement of a mature and loving relationship with the mysterious girl he meets at a fairground. At the same time another, older story is being worked out and Milo's intervention in the past and in supernatural events seems to imply a mythic and universal significance.

Most reviewers, whether they attempted a symbolic or a realistic reading of the novel, seemed in the end puzzled and dissatisfied, and there were complaints once more that the book owed too much too obviously to Faulkner. Price, defending it in *Afterwords*, says that he was not borrowing from but parodying "the sacred solemnities of Southern fiction," and suggested that his novel was closer to "Japanese *No* drama or to *The Magic Flute* . . . than to most twentieth-century fiction"; its meaning, he insists, "is itself, its physical shape."

In *Love and Work*, Price tackles the subject that so many serious novelists seem impelled to explore: the writer-as-character. The book seems to refute what Price says above about the purpose of his stories. Thomas Eborn, the teacher-novelist in *Love and Work*, also seeks to make stories which will control "the lethal disorder of experience," but this is his weakness as a writer. The effort to shield himself from the pain of raw experience is also destroying his marriage, and his personal and creative difficulties come to a crisis with the death of his mother. It is then, browsing through her papers and letters, that he at last confronts the nature and meaning of his parents' life together, and through them of his own life. He begins a novel which will perhaps succeed in joining his life and his work. Some critics thought *Love and Work* less well-wrought than its predecessors, but Peter Wolfe wrote that it "makes you feel that you are living through an experience, not reading a book." There is in any case no doubt that Reynolds Price is one of the most gifted and original novelists of his generation.

The novella, stories, and other prose pieces collected in *Permanent Errors* are all part of an attempt "to isolate in a number of lives the central error of act, will, understanding, which, once made, has been permanent, incurable, but whose diagnosis and palliation are the hopes of continuance." The book was found "impressive, oppressive and disturbing," though to some reviewers the style seemed at times altogether too self-conscious. *Things Themselves* is a volume of Price's criticism, personal essays, and comments on poems, novels, and paintings. The author, now an associate professor at Duke University, was writer in residence at the University of North Carolina in 1965, at the University of Kansas in 1967 and 1969, and at the University of North Carolina in 1971, when he was also Glasgow Professor at Washington and Lee University in Lexington, Virginia. *A Long and Happy Life* brought him the 1962 Faulkner Foundation award for a notable first novel. Price is an advisory editor of *Shenandoah*.

PRINCIPAL WORKS: A Long and Happy Life, 1962; The Names and Faces of Heroes (stories), 1963; A Generous Man, 1966; Love and Work, 1968; Permanent Errors (stories), 1970; Things Themselves: Essays and Scenes, 1972.

ABOUT: Contemporary Authors 2, 1963; McCormack, T. (ed.) Afterwords: Novelists on Their Novels, 1968; Vinson, J. (ed.) Contemporary Novelists, 1972; Who's Who in America, 1972–1973. *Periodicals*—Atlantic Monthly April 1962; Harper's August 1963; Hudson Review Autumn 1962; New York Herald Tribune Books June 23, 1963; New York Times Book Review June 30, 1963; March 27, 1966; June 30, 1968; October 11, 1970; New Yorker April 7, 1962; Saturday Review March 10, 1962; March 26, 1966; May 25, 1968; September 26, 1970; Shenandoah Summer 1966; Times Literary Supplement March 23, 1962; September 21, 1963.

PRICHARD, KATHARINE SUSANNAH (December 4, 1883–October 2, 1969), Australian novelist, short story writer, and dramatist, wrote: "My father, Tom Henry Prichard, was editor of the *Fiji Times* when I was born at Levuka, in a hurricane, on December 4th, 1883. His parents were free settlers who came to Australia, when father was four years old. The family were passengers on the Eldorado and came from Monmouth in Wales in 1852. Mother, Edith Isobel Fraser, was born in Australia. Her parents, Simon Lovat Fraser and Susan Rochead, were also passengers on the Eldorado, so the infant Katharine Susannah represented a fusing of English, Welsh, Scottish and Irish ancestry in an Australian environment. When I was three years old father returned to Australia and edited a Melbourne journal. My education at South Melbourne College owes a great deal to J. B. O'Hara who was a teacher and poet beloved of the youth of my day. Later while teaching and writing short stories for Australian magazines, I attended night lectures to study English and philology at the University of Melbourne.

"After a visit to London, reporting the Franco-British Exhibition for the Melbourne *Herald*, I joined the staff of the *Herald* in charge of women's work and interests; paid a brief visit to the U.S.A.; and in 1912 worked as a journalist in London, contributing to several leading newspapers and continental reviews, for three years before the first world war. I returned to Australia after winning the Hodder and Stoughton prize for a novel with *The Pioneers*.

"Although there were more opportunities for a writer in London at that time, I wanted to write about Australia and the Australian people—and have never regretted devoting my life to them and interpreting them to the people of other countries. Now as the author of twelve novels and three volumes of short stories, most of which have been published in London, I have been fortunate in being able to do this. The novels and short stories have been translated into nineteen different foreign languages: three novels have had editions in the U.S.A.

"In 1919, with my husband, Hugo V. H. Throssell, V.C., I came to live in Western Australia. Here at Greenmount our only son, Ric Prichard Throssell, was born, and many happy years were spent. It was in this setting I wrote 'The Grey

KATHARINE SUSANNAH PRICHARD

Horse' which won the Art in Australia prize for a short story. Two or three years later *Brumby Innes* was awarded the prize for a three-act play, and the following year *Coonardoo* won the prize for a novel.

"Always an avid reader of French, German and Russian literature, at the same time I studied the works of great thinkers in philosophy and political economy. The theories of Marx and Engels made a profound impression on my mind. A visit to the U.S.S.R. later confirmed an impression that scientific socialism in practice could solve many of the problems troubling nations nowadays. As a member of the World Peace Council, I have been concerned for many years to promote organisations for international cooperation so that we may bequeath a way of life, without war, to future generations of the earth's people."

Katharine Susannah Prichard was certainly, as H. M. Green has said, her country's most representative novelist, and her fiction is deeply rooted in Australian life. She was a founder-member of the Australian Communist party, and her work stems from the tradition of the Australian Left. In a more cosmopolitan sense, Miss Prichard continued the European and American tradition of naturalism, like Zola and Dreiser working hard to achieve a densely authentic background, but replacing their pessimism with Marxist optimism. Whether this concern for realism was natural or acquired is a matter of opinion, and Cecil Hadgraft is one of a number of critics who consider that her best work showed her to be "by talent a fabulist, a writer of a sort of pastoral, serious and tender. The change in her work [was] from idyll to ideology."

She began her career as a teacher in outback schools in Victoria and New South Wales, and had begun to publish short stories in Australian magazines before she went to London as a journalist. Her first published novel, *The Pioneers* (1915), is a melodramatic tale of self-sacrifice; it is crude and immature, but conveys her powerful feeling for the Australian bush, and was later filmed and dramatized. *Windlestraws*, published in 1916, was actually written earlier, also in London, where it is set. It is equally immature, but full of a characteristic concern for the poor and underprivileged.

Returning early in World War I to Australia, she established her reputation with *Black Opal* (1921), a study of workers in the Fallen Star Ridge opal fields. The savagely exploited miners are the heroes; the capitalist Armytage is the villain, but a complex one—"bad" only because he is corrupted by capitalist ideas. Marjorie Barnard and Florence Eldershaw, the critics who wrote in collaboration as "M. Barnard Eldershaw" commented: "It is a little naïve, and as an artist Prichard has traveled a long way since, but the same ideas, modified and matured, underlie all her books."

Working Bullocks (1926) has often been called Miss Prichard's best book, though some have preferred *Coonardoo* (1929), and a minority *Haxby's Circus* (1930). The first deals with a community of lumberjacks in the great forests of Western Australia, and the impact upon it of a Communist agitator. This is an intensely naturalistic book, both in its determinism and its brutality (several characters are killed at their work); but although fate triumphs, human vitality is eventually shown to be the hero. *Coonardoo* is an account (based on fact) of the tragic romance between a black Australian woman and a white man. The portrait of Coonardoo herself is "a revelation of strange modes of being," wrote E. A. Baker. Set in the arid northwest, the book is sordid and melodramatic, but beautifully written and psychologically convincing. *Haxby's Circus*, for which the author spent months traveling with Wirth's Circus, is another excellent piece of realistic writing. It describes the gallantries and crudities of circus life, with more humor than in any of Miss Prichard's other novels. *The Wild Oats of Han*, which draws on the author's own childhood, has been called a kind of Australian *Huckleberry Finn*.

Miss Prichard was also a notable short story writer. In this form she was more meticulous as a stylist and (sometimes) more experimental than in her novels, and most impressively fused poetry with stark realism. The fact that she was a keen reader of Jung as well as of Marx and Lenin is significant in this respect.

It is almost universally acknowledged that in Miss Prichard's later novels "her social sympathies

. . . finally override the artist in her" (H. M. Green). The change began in *Intimate Strangers* (1937), a new departure for the author since it dealt in part with Australian suburban life, and was confirmed in the trilogy *The Roaring Nineties*, *Golden Miles*, and *Winged Seeds*, which very thoroughly chronicled the discovery and development of the Western Australian goldfields. As F. T. B. Macartney has written, the trilogy "is rather overweighed with tendentious political matter." This is to criticize it only as fiction, however: as documentary it will certainly be revived, enjoyed, and valued. *Moon of Desire* was a thriller.

Miss Prichard published a volume of verse, and two plays. *Brumby Innes* (written 1927, published 1940), which brings an aborigine festival on to the stage, is a study of a bully; it had its admirers, won a prize (from *Triad*), but is somewhat overwritten, has some contrived scenes, and is not reckoned to be successful theatre; her one-act play *The Pioneers* (1937) improves on her novel of the same name, and is an impressive and concise piece of stagecraft.

In spite of her unquestioned place in Australian letters, and her respected old age in her home near Perth, tributes to Katharine Prichard since her death have described her as an essentially tragic figure. She never fully recovered from her husband's suicide in 1933: "The end of our lives together is still inexplicable to me," she wrote in her autobiography, *Child of the Hurricane*, nearly thirty years later. And to her friend Dorothy Hewett, it seemed that she had "willed her own creative death." The sensuous imagery in her writing seemed to have dried up, the emotional and sexual power to have gone out of it.

Dorothy Hewett, like Cecil Hadgraft, sees her in fact as less a realist than a romantic writer: "the landscapes she saw, the idealised Rousseau-like Australian proletariat who are her heroes, are not 'real,' but are created landscapes of the mind." Her finest works attempt "the poetic dissolving of landscape and character into one indivisible person (Red Burke, the working bullock, or Coonardoo, the spirit of place)." Her artistic tragedy arose from the fact that, in her lifetime, she "could not hope to gain real sustenance for her peculiar metaphysical vision of earth and man . . . her roots died for lack of sap." Her political convictions (she remained a loyal though anguished member of the Communist party up to her death) insured that her critics frequently overpraised or dismissed her for ideological rather than artistic reasons; while her insistence that she wrote for the "common man" rather than for her peers, seemed to Dorothy Hewett "crippling and divisive. . . . She seemed to have no real inbuilt critical sense."

Katharine Prichard's personality was both reserved ("No-one will ever see me in my petticoat"), and courageous—she has been described "frail amongst epithets and flying bottles" while campaigning for her party in the 1949 elections. And she is acknowledged to have played a unique part in laying the foundation for a new Australian literature. She was "a pathblazer," wrote Tom Hungerford, "who showed Australian writers how to free themselves from the dominating idea that Britain was the arbiter of taste. She called a gully a gully and not a dell . . . she was one of the great Australian writers."

PRINCIPAL WORKS: *Fiction*—The Pioneers, 1915; Windlestraws, 1916; Black Opal, 1921; The Grey Horse (short stories), 1924; Working Bullocks, 1926; The Wild Oats of Han (for children), 1928; Coonardoo, 1929; Haxby's Circus, 1930; Kiss on the Lips (short stories), 1932; Intimate Strangers, 1937; Moon of Desire, 1941; Potch and Colour (short stories), 1944; The Roaring Nineties, 1946; Golden Miles, 1948; Winged Seeds, 1950; N'Goola (short stories), 1959; On Strenuous Wings (selected works), 1965; Subtle Flame, 1968. *Plays*—Brumby Innes, 1940. *Poetry*—Earth Lover, 1930. *Autobiography*—Child of the Hurricane, 1963. *Travel*—The Real Russia, 1934.

ABOUT: Baker, E. A. A Guide to the Best Fiction, 1930; Beasley, J. The Rage for Life: The Work of Katharine Susannah Prichard, 1964; Cassell's Encyclopedia of Literature, 1953; Drake-Brockman, H. Katharine Susannah Prichard, 1967; "Eldershaw, M. Barnard" Essays in Australian Fiction, 1938; Green, H. M. A History of Australian Literature, 1960; Hadgraft, C. Australian Literature Now, 1949; Hetherington, J. Forty-two Faces, 1963; Prichard, K. S. Child of the Hurricane, 1963. *Periodicals*—Australian Author July 1970; Australian Literary Studies June 1, 1963; Meanjin Spring 1951; Overland Summer 1969–70; Southerly 4 1953; Sydney Morning Herald October 4, 1969; Westerly 3 1961.

PRINCE, F(RANK) T(EMPLETON) (September 13, 1912–), South African-born English poet and scholar, writes: "I was born in Kimberley, Cape Province, South Africa, the second son in a family of three children; my mother had come to South Africa from Scotland, my father from England. I was educated at the Christian Brothers' College, Kimberley, though my schooling was interrupted more than once by visits to England. After leaving school I spent a year at the University of the Witwatersrand, in Johannesburg, my family having come there from Kimberley in 1930.

"In 1931 I entered Balliol College, Oxford, and read English Literature, taking my degree in 1934. In 1935–1936 I was a Visiting Fellow at the Graduate College, Princeton University, New Jersey. But on returning to England I gave up the study of English for a time, taking a post in 1937 in the Study Groups Department of the Institute of International Affairs in London (Chatham House); I remained a member of the Department until the summer of 1940, when I went into the Army. I was commissioned in the Intelligence Corps in 1940, and served until 1946. In 1946 I returned to academic life as a lecturer in the English Department of

F. T. PRINCE

the University of Southampton (then a University College). In 1957 I became Head of the Department.

"In 1943 I married Pauline Elizabeth Bush, and have two daughters, the elder born in 1945, the younger in 1948. I became a Roman Catholic in 1938.

"At about the age of fifteen I began to write poetry, and published my first volume in 1938 (Faber and Faber); the second came out in 1954. The best poems in the two earlier books were reprinted, together with some new poems, in *The Doors of Stone* (Rupert Hart-Davis, London 1963).

"My best known scholarly book is *The Italian Element in Milton's Verse* (1954). I have also edited Shakespeare's narrative poems for the New Arden edition (1960).

"As a boy in South Africa I was influenced by the poetry of Roy Campbell, though I did not meet him until many years later; through his work I was led to the poetry of Rimbaud, Baudelaire and Valéry. An early friend was John Niemeyer Findlay, then a lecturer in Philosophy at Pretoria University, now Professor at King's College, London. He introduced me to new authors, who included Proust, Henry James and T. S. Eliot. The formative influences on my poetry were those of Ezra Pound, Eliot and Yeats. While I was at Oxford I learnt Italian, and Italian culture has meant much to me ever since those days. I have always been interested in painting and sculpture, and enjoy music; I am sure that these other arts have had a considerable effect on my verse."

The Italian Element in Milton's Verse is a work of scholarly criticism which was "highly and deservedly praised," according to Kenneth Allott. Professor Prince's reputation as a poet rested until recently almost entirely upon a single poem, "Soldiers Bathing." A group of British soldiers, "worn by the trade of war," are swimming and shouting on a beach. The poet is reminded of the savagery of older wars as it was seen by other artists, and then by contrast of the Crucifixion. He thinks, gratefully, "That some great love is over what we do, / And that is what has driven us to this fury, for so few / Can suffer all the terror of that love." This work, in its "unfaltering grandeur and profound compassion," is widely regarded as one of the finest English poems of World War II, and by some as one of the major poems of our time.

The Doors of Stone, collecting poems Prince had written between 1938 and 1962, reminded critics that "Soldiers Bathing" was not an isolated phenomenon, but the masterpiece among a body of strong, intricate, fastidious poems. A reviewer in the *Times Literary Supplement* called Prince "one of the best love poets of the age, a lyricist of great charm and tenderness of emotion, counterbalanced by a subtlety of thought and metaphor which often remind one of Donne, and he frequently succeeds in creating at least glimpses of the relationship of human love to the divine." In 1968–1969 Prince held a visiting fellowship at All Souls College and wrote the long autobiographical poem *Memoirs in Oxford*.

PRINCIPAL WORKS: Poems, 1938; Soldiers Bathing, 1954; The Italian Element in Milton's Verse (criticism), 1954; The Doors of Stone, Poems, 1938–1962, 1963; Memoirs in Oxford, 1970.

ABOUT: Allott, K. (ed.) Penguin Book of Contemporary Verse, 1962; Murphy, R. (ed.) Contemporary Poets of the English Language, 1970; Press, J. Rule and Energy, 1963; Thwaite, A. Contemporary English Poetry, 1961; Who's Who, 1973. *Periodical*—Times Literary Supplement July 26, 1963.

***PUDNEY, JOHN (SLEIGH)** (January 19, 1909–), English poet, fiction writer, and journalist, writes: "I was born at Langley, Bucks, about twenty miles from Piccadilly Circus, when Langley was a village with dusty roads. My father farmed, not very actively. At the time when I was born he enjoyed fox-hunting two days a week. My mother was a Sleigh, brought up in Australia, where the Sleighs now flourish, and trained before her marriage as a nurse. I went to a prep school near Westerham where I was brilliant, particularly at writing Latin poetry and looking after the horses owned by one of the masters. I then failed a scholarship for Gresham's School, Holt, Norfolk, but owing to an unexpected vacancy was admitted to that school where my brilliance totally deserted me. I had the great advantage, however, of the com-

*pud′ nē

panionship of W. H. Auden, a slightly senior boy who loathed the poetry I was then beginning to write, threw my volumes of Swinburne out of the window and gave me a severe grounding in the writing of verse.

"I was incapable of passing any sort of exam and left Gresham's at an early age to become apprenticed to a famous firm of estate agents in the West End of London. In the mistaken belief that it was a simple and innocent job they put me on to rent-collecting in Soho. This contributed greatly to my adult education, and provided me with a fund of literary material. In spite of such distractions I then passed all the necessary exams and became qualified. Having achieved this I left the profession for ever. And without any qualifications whatever entered the BBC, where I began doing the most inefficient job of my life making up a picture page on the *Listener*. I was quickly moved away from this to become writer-producer in the then infant overseas services, and ended up in the Features Department.

"Meanwhile I published books of verse, short stories, and a novel. Some instinct told me that five years in the BBC was enough—though in those days it was not done to resign from the BBC. I went to the *News Chronicle* as columnist and feature writer and stayed there till the war when I joined the RAF. I wrote a good deal of verse about the RAF during my service which was somewhat restless as it took me to about forty-five different countries, ending rather absurdly with a lecture tour in neutral Sweden.

"After the war I became a freelance writer—books, films, radio, and television. I also went into publishing, first as director of Evans Bros., then for ten years I was a director of Putnam's. I enjoyed office routines and my years in publishing were stimulating. I am now back in my late fifties working as a freelance. Being country-bred I have usually managed to live in the country. Currently I divide my time between a cottage in Ashdown Forest where I grow my own produce (and even sell the surplus) and a fifth floor modern flat on Sydenham Hill with a view over London. I write a great many children's books which are rewarding not only because they are fun, but because they stay in print and prosper. I specialise to some extent in aviation subjects in adult books. But I also continue to write fiction and verse. My teeth tend to drop out: I am likely to be a grandfather: I sometimes wish I had stuck to real estate. But on the whole I am a happy if somewhat overworked man."

John Pudney was an only child whose mother died when he was fourteen and whose father was a cool and remote man. Pudney went to work on his seventeenth birthday. He was married at twenty-

JOHN PUDNEY

five to Sir Alan Herbert's daughter Crystal, and has a son and two daughters by that marriage, which was dissolved in 1955. The same year he married Monica Curtis. In 1945, Pudney was an unsuccessful Labour party candidate for Parliament. His postwar career has included a year as book critic of the London *Daily Express* (1947–1948) and two years as literary editor of *News Review* (1948–1950). His recreation, he says, is bonfires.

Pudney began to make his reputation in the mid-1930s with his short stories and with *Jacobson's Ladder* (1938), a vivid and racy first novel about Soho. During World War II, Pudney became very widely known as a poet when some of his lyrics were used in *The Way to the Stars*, a film about the Battle of Britain.

The short stories collected after the war in *It Breathed Down My Neck*, many of them satirical fantasies directed against lower middle-class gentility, earned Pudney comparisons with Saki. The novels that he has published since then share some of the same characteristics—a penchant for fantasy and social comedy, a graceful and witty style. Pudney's poems evoke a personality "masculine, honest, agreeable, unpretentious." He has been called "an occasional poet who writes verses as others keep a diary," and whose "deservedly renowned" war poems remain his best work in this form. From 1949 to 1963 Pudney edited the annual anthology *The Pick of Today's Short Stories*. His "cheerful fantasies" for children are much admired.

Pudney has described how, in the early 1960s, after he left Putnam's, he went through a very dark period. He became an alcoholic, but received psychotherapy and by 1967 had conquered the disease. (He is now a total but by no means evangelical abstainer.) During the same period he was seriously injured and almost killed in a car accident. These experiences have left him with an exuberant commitment to "the wonder of being alive," expressed partly in a continuing burst of intense creativity. He has published several books of poetry since then, and one of the most admired of his novels. He is much in demand at university poetry readings and pop festivals, and says with satisfaction that some of his poems "are read a lot by people under thirty." The musical *The Little Giant*, about the Victorian engineer I. K. Brunel, with Pudney's book and lyrics, was produced at the Greenwich Theatre in 1972.

PRINCIPAL WORKS: *Poetry*—Ten Summers, 1944; Selected Poems, 1946; Sixpenny Songs, 1953; Collected Poems, 1957; The Trampoline, 1959; Spill Out, 1967; Spandrels, 1969; Take This Orange, 1971; Selected Poems 1967–1973, 1973. *Short Stories*—And Lastly the Fireworks, 1935; Uncle Arthur, 1939; It Breathed Down My Neck (U.S., Edna's Fruit Hat), 1946; The Europeans, 1948. *Novels*—Jacobson's Ladder, 1938; Estuary, 1948; Shuffley Wanderers, 1949; The Accomplice, 1950; Hero of a Summer's Day, 1951; The Net, 1952; A Ring for Luck, 1953; Trespass in the Sun, 1957; Thin Air, 1961; The Long Time Growing Up, 1971. *Adult nonfiction*—The Green Grass Grew All Round, 1942; Who Only England Know, 1943; World Still There, 1945; The Smallest Room, 1954; The Seven Skies, 1959; Home and Away (autobiography) 1960; A Pride of Unicorns, 1960; Bristol Fashion, 1960; The Camel Fighter, 1964; The Golden Age of Steam, 1967; Suez: De Lesseps' Canal, 1968; A Draught of Contentment: The Story of the Courage Group, 1972; Crossing London's River, 1972.

ABOUT: Pudney, J. Home and Away, 1960; Vinson, J. (ed.) Contemporary Novelists, 1972; Who's Who, 1973. *Periodicals*—Guardian April 6, 1972; Times Literary Supplement May 3, 1957; July 8, 1960.

PURDY, JAMES (July 14, 1923–), American novelist and short story writer, writes: "I grew up between the first and second World Wars, in small-town and rural Ohio, of a broken family, in rather severe circumstances. Both my father and mother were of Scotch-English Presbyterian ancestry, though my great-grandmother, on my mother's side, was said to be part Indian. My paternal grandmother was from New York state, and her brothers were tug-boat operators in Brooklyn, where I now live.

"I never enjoyed school, but a few good teachers made it almost bearable, and one of my English teachers encouraged me to be a writer. At a fairly early age I went to Chicago and from there to Mexico, where I attended school, and learned Spanish. After Mexico, I went to Havana, Cuba, where I taught English for a year or so in a private boys' school.

"Since I had wanted to be a writer from earliest memory, I never found the many different kinds of jobs I landed anything but onerous and an interruption of my real life. I had been writing since childhood, and seriously composing fiction since I was twenty, and over the years had collected a group of stories which I thought were good, although editors and publishers in New York, as well as small magazines, had rejected them with astringent comments. The *New Yorker* magazine assured me I had no talent whatsoever.

"In 1955, Mr. Osborn Andreas, an American businessman who had written a book on Henry James, read my stories and felt they deserved to be privately printed, since formal publication seemed impossible. In the same year, a young professor of inorganic chemistry, Dr. J. J. Sjoblom, borrowed money to publish privately my short novel *63: Dream Palace*. Once the stories and the novels were 'printed,' there was the embarrassing problem of what to do with the thousand or so copies. Mr. Andreas suggested that I send them to writers whom I admired. Owing perhaps to some strange hunch, I first sent the book of stories to Dame Edith Sitwell, although I did not know her. To my stunned surprise Dame Edith, unlike the army of New York editors, was deeply moved by my work and talent, and began writing me the wonderful letters of encouragement which never stopped until her death in 1964. When I sent her *63: Dream Palace*, she went out of her way to persuade Victor Gollancz to publish me in England.

"After British publication in 1957, a small American publisher decided to take the great risk of introducing me to the United States—the same American publisher, by the way, which had been rejecting my work with clock-like regularity for over ten years—and *Color of Darkness* made its appearance here in New York.

"An American man of letters, Carl Van Vechten, was one of the first in this country to be impressed by my work, and he urged me to come from a small town in Pennsylvania, where I was living, to meet him in New York. In 1957, he made arrangements for Yale University to be custodian of all my papers.

"Since 1957 I have lived precariously off the meager earnings of my writing, and from the generosity of friends and sometimes foundations, for the literary establishment in New York, as arbitary in its rejections of anyone it has not 'elected' as, I suppose, my Calvinist ancestors, has ever voted oblivion for my literary career from the beginning, and though it now grudgingly admits I exist, it has never forgiven me—in the words of a writer for *Harper's Bazaar*—for 'having discovered myself.' I very much doubt that I would ever have been heard of had not Dame Edith Sitwell championed me and secured me English publication, and I would have died unknown.

"Those interested in my work have often asked

why my stories and novels have aroused such ferocious resistance in publishers, reviewers, and general public. The answer seems to me simple: publishers, reviewers, and general public have seldom been interested in writing or the truth. I can describe my books as I see them as American, imaginative, symbolic. My literary ancestors are two other Calvinists, Hawthorne and Melville.

"The best appraisal of my work is still Dame Edith Sitwell's essays on me, and in addition David Daiches's essays on *Malcolm*, William Weatherby's 'The Choler of Despair' in the (London) *Times Literary Supplement*, June 10, 1965, and Edward Albee's piece in the New York Sunday *Times* drama section, January 9, 1966.

"My books are translated into over fifteen languages, including Chinese and Japanese, and besides the stories collected in *Color of Darkness* and *Children Is All* include the novels *Malcolm*, *The Nephew*, *Cabot Wright Begins*, and *Eustace Chisholm and the Works*."

"Each human being should be treated as a human being," Purdy said once, "and that has never happened, as far as I know." What happens instead, and this is his theme, is that we *use* each other. Doubting our own humanity, our own reality, we deny the humanity and reality of others, and see in them not what they need but what we need: "We none of us, I'm afraid, know anybody or know one another." The only hope for us is love and, with so much greed and egotism and fear in the world, love is hard to feel and almost impossible to share.

The critics' argument about Purdy's work began in 1956, when he published his volume of stories *Color of Darkness*. The chorus of praise which greeted the book was so high-pitched that a reaction was inevitable: James T. Farrell, Winfield Townley Scott, Katherine Anne Porter, Horace Gregory, Dorothy Parker, and Kenneth Rexroth, among others, wrote with the greatest possible enthusiasm of Purdy's talent and skill, his originality, subtlety, and compassion; Edith Sitwell called the tragic novella *63: Dream Palace* a masterpiece, and placed Purdy "in the very highest rank of contemporary American writers"; John Cowper Powys called him "the best kind of original genius of our day."

There was almost as much excitement about Purdy's first novel, *Malcolm*, which is a very direct treatment, albeit in grotesquely comic terms, of his principal theme. Malcolm is a fifteen-year-old innocent, a young Candide in a dirty world, who is searching for his enigmatic father (or God, as some thought) and for his identity: "I am, well, as they say, a cypher and a blank." Malcolm's search takes him to a succession of bizarre *ménages*. In each he is monstrously exploited and ill-used; in each, as Gerald Weales said, "he becomes what another

JAMES PURDY

person, in a scramble to avoid his own facelessness, wants him to be." In the end, married to a pop singer, destroyed by sex and drink, he dies, believing that "maybe my father never existed." His wife provides an epitaph: "What did I buy you for, kiddy?"

This time Dorothy Parker, David Daiches, and R. W. B. Lewis were among the cheerleaders, the first calling it "the most prodigiously funny book to streak across these heavy-hanging times," the last comparing Purdy with Saul Bellow, Ralph Ellison, and Melville. Others however complained of a "smug effeteness" in the writing and suggested that Purdy himself subscribed to the statement of one of his characters: "Texture is all, substance nothing." The novel was adapted for the stage by Edward Albee, but failed on Broadway in 1966.

The Nephew is, superficially at least, a more naturalistic treatment of Purdy's theme. Set in a small town in the Midwest, it describes how Alma Mason, spinster and retired schoolteacher, attempts to compile a memorial account of her beloved nephew Cliff, missing in action in Korea. The trouble is that everyone she consults has a different impression of Cliff, who thus slips further and further out of focus as the story proceeds. In the end Alma's record book is empty and, when Cliff's death is confirmed, the reader is not surprised to learn that "there wasn't even enough left of him to ship home in his casket. There was nothing of our Cliff left." Indeed, "our" Cliff never existed: only Cliff's Cliff did that, and no one knew him. What is left for the reader is a very gentle and compassionate portrait of Alma Mason and of her widower brother Boyd.

The central figure in *Cabot Wright Begins* is a Yale graduate and Wall Street broker who, his libido released by a miracle of psychiatry, becomes a highly successful mass rapist. The novel is concerned with the efforts of assorted predatory writers, editors, and publishers to make a best-selling book from his experiences—to use Cabot Wright and, presumably, their readers, just as Wright has used his victims. The result is an elaborate structure of narratives within narratives, commenting on life, on literature, and on the present relationship between the two.

Theodore Solotaroff found the first part of the book "a rich, resonant, and deadly accurate satire on American values, as good as anything we have had since the work of Nathanael West," but he and most other critics thought it deteriorated into a mannered and petulant whine of despair about the American way of life. This may be a hasty judgment; Charles Newman in *Tri-Quarterly* has shown to what extent this remarkable novel is parody as well as satire. Purdy's point, Newman suggests, is that human behavior is not to be "explained" in psychological, journalistic, or conventional literary terms; he uses the inflated jargon of these disciplines only in order to discredit them—to show how they reduce Cabot Wright to mere words. The novel's conclusion, spoken by Wright's "ghost writer," is one shared in some sense and to some degree by Beckett, Nabokov, the French "New Novelists," and Purdy himself: "I won't be a writer in a place and time like the present."

This argument is continued in *Eustace Chisholm and the Works*, which is set during the Depression in Chicago. Chisholm writes his poetic epic ("the Works") in charcoal on old copies of the Chicago *Tribune*, only to destroy them in the end, confessing the failure of Literature and turning instead to Life. The events which drive him to this pass, and which provide the book's central action, concern the mutual but undeclared love of the beautiful youth Amos and the tough ex-miner Daniel. This generous and tender passion, uncommunicated and unused, is diverted into disastrous channels: Amos sells himself unlovingly and dies; Daniel, escaping into the army, is tortured to death by an insane homosexual sadist.

The first part of the novel is told in the "mannered, mock-pompous language" which had irritated some critics and delighted others in Purdy's earlier work. "But slowly," according to Wilfrid Sheed, "and one might guess diffidently, the book becomes a little more serious. . . . The whole last section is a purple feast of sadomasochism. It is also a risky and serious piece of writing, which waives the extenuations of humor, and is possibly the best writing Purdy has done." Ross Wetzsteon arrives by a different route at a similar conclusion, saying that here Purdy "at last finds his theme, confronts despair, and surrenders to emotion, finding the proper balance between control and rage by giving up both, replacing the release of laughter with the release of compassion, and creating for the first time 'that rare thing; the authentic, naked, unconcealed voice of love.' Through an extraordinary act of courage and insight, Purdy seems to have achieved a kind of self-liberation—and has written what I consider far and away his finest novel."

At that point Purdy embarked on his most ambitious work to date, a projected trilogy of novels, set in a small midwestern town, called Sleepers in Moon-Crowned Valleys. The first volume, *Jeremy's Version*, is set in about the 1920s. It centers on Elvira, who runs a boarding house and is a whore, her three sons, and her dissolute absentee husband Wilders Fergus. This violent, even gothic, story is passed on many years later by one of Elvira's sons to his "amanuensis," the fifteen-year-old Jeremy, who is the novel's narrator. Reviewers found this device unsatisfactory, the plot melodramatic, the characters larger than life—monstrous figures performing mostly primal acts for primary motives. At the same time, as one critic said, "there is a way to see it all as the working of American legends, which have attained mythical weight, and American history of a sort which has attained common literary currency, into a grand tragi-comedy." And there was a general feeling that the novel teases the reader "into the primitive circle a compelling story-teller draws about him."

I Am Elijah Thrush, which followed, is not a part of the trilogy but another American parable (and American *Satyricon*, one reviewer thought) about the struggle between the millionaire bitch-goddess Millicent de Frayne and her lover Elijah Thrush, ancient Narcissus and all-round artist and prophet, who is himself in love with his mute great-grandson, known as the Bird of Heaven. The result, too rich a "mixed curry" for the taste of one critic, was enjoyed by others as a "Firbankian romp" and a pungent satire.

Stanley Edgar Hyman thought Purdy a social satirist rather than a novelist, and pointed out how often his prose is clumsy and even ungrammatical; Edith Sitwell, reviewing the stories and short plays collected in *Children Is All*, had no doubt that Purdy would "come to be recognized as one of the greatest living writers of fiction in our language." It is still not clear which opinion is correct, though the odds seem to be on Dame Edith. Purdy has still not perfectly matched his tragic vision to his means, but it is evident that both his vision and his resources are growing, and that both are large enough to allow him the masterpiece which he has not yet quite achieved.

According to Dick Schaap, Purdy is "a soft-spoken man, gentle and shy and immediately likable, with light thinning hair and a pleasing smile." He studied at the University of Pueblo in Mexico from 1944 to 1945, at the University of Chicago in 1945–1946, and at the University of Madrid in Spain in 1947. From 1949 to 1953 he taught at Lawrence College, Appleton, Wisconsin. He lives alone in Brooklyn Heights.

PRINCIPAL WORKS: Don't Call Me By My Right Name (stories, privately printed), 1956; 63: Dream Palace (novella, privately printed), 1956; Color of Darkness (containing stories and 63: Dream Palace), 1957 (similar collection published as 63: Dream Palace, England, 1957); Malcolm, 1959; The Nephew, 1960; Children Is All (stories and plays), 1962; Cabot Wright Begins, 1964; Eustace Chisholm and the Works, 1968; Jeremy's Version: Part One of Sleepers in Moon-Crowned Valleys, 1970; The Running Sun (poems), 1971; I Am Elijah Thrush, 1972.

ABOUT: Daiches, D. More Literary Essays, 1962; Hyman, S. E. Standards: A Chronicle of Books for Our Time, 1967; Kostelanetz, R. On Contemporary Literature, 1965; Moore, H. T. Contemporary American Novelists, 1965; Schwarzschild, B. The Not-Right House: Essays on James Purdy, 1969; Vinson, J. (ed.) Contemporary Novelists, 1972; Waldmeir, J. J. (ed.) Recent American Fiction: Some Critical Views, 1963; Who's Who in America, 1972–1973. *Periodicals*—Book Week May 9, 1965; May 28, 1967; Chicago Review Autumn 1960; Critique Spring 1963; Encounter August 1961; New York Times January 9, 1966; New York Times Book Review October 6, 1957; May 21, 1967; June 22, 1968; Texas Quarterly Spring 1967; Times Literary Supplement June 10, 1965; March 28, 1968; June 4, 1971; Tri-Quarterly Fall 1967; Wilson Library Bulletin March 1964; Wisconsin Studies in Contemporary Literature Summer 1965.

PYNCHON, THOMAS (May 8, 1937–), American novelist, was born in Glen Cove, Long Island, New York, the son of Thomas R. Pynchon, an industrial surveyor. He attended New York schools and, after a brief spell in the United States Navy, completed his education at Cornell University. Graduating in 1958, Pynchon lived for a time in Greenwich Village, and then went to Seattle, working from 1960 to 1962 as a technical writer for the Boeing Aircraft Corporation. Finding the business world increasingly unattractive, he left his job and spent a year in Mexico, where he completed his first novel.

This was *V.*, which impressed most critics and disgusted some. It interweaves two distinct plots. One concerns Benny Profane, an Italian-Jewish drifter, and the Whole Sick Crew, his friends. Benny, on the loose in New York after a hitch in the Navy, is concerned to perfect his performance in his chosen role as *schlemiel*, or victim. He works as (among other things) an alligator hunter in the New York sewers, and is irresistibly attractive to women (but is repeatedly prevented, by some chance intrusion, or his own talent for failure, from taking advantage of this attribute).

The novel's other, and dominant, story is about Herbert Stencil's attempt to unravel the secret history of "V.," an international spy and adventuress who appears and reappears in an incredible variety of forms and disguises over a period of sixty years in such diverse places as New York, Paris, Malta, Alexandria, Florence, and Africa. She also represents Venus, the Virgin, and the female principle in general, as well as a great many other quest objects, including ultimately the Void, Mother Night.

The preposterous adventures of "V." comprise an anthology of parodies—of E. Phillips Oppenheim, Lawrence Durrell, and the French "New Wave" writers among others. The chapters dealing with Benny Profane suggest a sensibility rather like that exhibited by Joseph Heller in *Catch-22*. There are also passages of sheer (and apparently irrelevant) horror, like the chapter which describes atrocities committed by the Germans in South-West Africa early in this century.

The Times Literary Supplement was distressed by the book's "nauseous themes," another reviewer called it "verbal garbage," and many were puzzled. However Stanley Edgar Hyman, admitting that it flagged at times into boring whimsy, called it "powerful, ambitious, full of gusto, and overflowing with rich comic invention." He pointed out how subtly the novel's two themes complement and enlarge each other, concluding that Pynchon, offering "the slogans of revisionist psychoanalysis—kindness, unselfishness, 'moderate adjustment'—has the imagination to realize that there is something more: the eternal, mythopoeic, passion of 'V.'" Arthur Gold has carried the discussion a little further, implying that the book is a history of the gradual numbing and stifling of the life force, the contemporary engulfment of the human by the inanimate and unloving forces of technology. Richard Poirier thought it no less than "the most masterful first novel in the history of literature, the only one in its decade with the proportions and stylistic resources of a classic." It received the William Faulkner Award, and has found its way onto college reading lists as, at the very least, an important manifestation of the black humor of the 1960s.

The Crying of Lot 49, which carried off the Rosenthal Foundation Award for 1967, is a briefer but similar fable. Oedipa Maas, a California housewife, is made the executor of the estate of her late lover, the entrepreneur Pierce Inverarity. Unraveling his tangled and mysterious dealings (and encountering in the process a large gallery of more or less bizarre people), she stumbles upon the Tristero System, which may be an ancient, anarchic, and worldwide courier system, or a plot to make her believe in such a conspiracy, or her own paranoiac fantasy. It has been suggested that the Tristero

System, like the network of sewers in *V.*, is a metaphor for those shifting patterns of experience and coincidence which sometimes seem to hint that there is, almost within our grasp, a total order in things—some all-embracing plan (or plot) which would make sense of history, and show us how to live.

The fascinations, and the dangers, of this kind of abstract determinism, also provide the theme of *Gravity's Rainbow*, the massive and perhaps major novel that Pynchon published in 1973, after a total silence of seven years. The book is set in England, France, and Occupied Germany in 1944 and 1945, though there are many references and flashbacks to earlier events, and to characters from Pynchon's earlier novels. One such is the German Lieutenant Weissmann, who had been V.'s sado-masochistic lover in Africa in 1922, and who reappears here under the SS code name "Captain Blicero." Blicero is now committed to the perfection of the V-2 rocket, and at the end of the war fires the secret missile 00000 towards the North Pole. Embedded in the rocket is the blond Aryan boy who is the present object of Blicero's love and sadism. Meanwhile, an earlier lover, the African Enzian, has become the leader of a group of black nationalists who seek Blicero's rocket in order to copy it. The quest for 00000 (nullity) provides the novel's central narrative line, and introduces along the way the suggestion that the whole of modern history is the result of a conspiracy of rocket manufacturers. This and similar paranoid theories are compromised by the activities of the comic strip Ishmael and eventual drop-out Tyrone Slothrop, and the romantic statistician Roger Mexico, who rejects determinism and holds, with Wittgenstein, that "the world is all that is the case." Beyond these are innumerable other sub-plots, counterplots, set-pieces, songs, and dissertations, which balance and counterpoint and enrich each other with the utmost brilliance—thus providing in the very fabric of the novel a uniquely elaborate example of the compulsive pattern-making which is its theme. Everything clusters around the image of the rocket's flight, whose "great airless arc" is Gravity's Rainbow, and "a clear allusion to certain secret lusts that drive the planet . . . over its peak and down, plunging, burning, toward a terminal orgasm."

Richard Locke believes that Pynchon has "brilliantly combined German political and cultural history with the mechanisms of paranoia to create an exceedingly complex work of art." He compares the book to *Moby Dick*, finding "the same appetite for technical data, the deliberate bookishness, the dense exalted prose. It, too, is a voyage into space, time and human consciousness, an exploration of the Faustian impulses that drive men's souls." However, Locke suggests, Pynchon invokes a world where "there is almost no trust, no human nurture, no mutual support, no family life. . . . Pynchon's sensibility and achievement here are limited by the very paranoid traits that he is ostensibly criticizing. . . . His imagination—for all its glorious power and intelligence—is as limited in its way as Céline's or Jonathan Swift's."

Richard Poirier expressed no such doubts and declared that "at thirty-six, Pynchon has established himself as a novelist of major historical importance. More than any other living writer . . . he has caught the inward movements of our time in outward manifestations of art and technology." . . . The book is . . . a profound (and profoundly funny) historical meditation on the humanity sacrificed to a grotesque delusion—the Faustian illusion of the inequality of lives and the inequality of the nature of signs."

PRINCIPAL WORKS: V., 1963; The Crying of Lot 49, 1966; Gravity's Rainbow, 1973.

ABOUT: Contemporary Authors 19–20, 1968; Hyman, S. E. Standards, 1966; Vinson, J. (ed.) Contemporary Novelists, 1972. *Periodicals*—Commentary September 1963; Commonweal July 8, 1966; Critique Winter 1963, Winter 1964, Winter 1967; Nation September 25, 1967; New Leader May 23, 1966; New Statesman October 11, 1963; New York Herald Tribune Book Review April 21, 1963; New York Review of Books June 23, 1966; March 23, 1973; New York Times Book Review April 21, 1963; April 28, 1963; May 1, 1966; March 11, 1973; Newsweek April 1, 1963; May 2, 1966; Partisan Review Summer 1966; Punch April 26, 1966; Saturday Review April 30, 1966; Saturday Review of the Arts March 1973; Times Literary Supplement October 11, 1963; April 27, 1967; Tri-Quarterly Winter 1967.

***QUASIMODO, SALVATORE** (August 20, 1901–June 14, 1968), Italian poet, translator, and critic, received the Nobel Prize for Literature in 1959. The award, as it often does, provoked much controversy. Some critics thought that the better-known Italian poets Ungaretti and Montale had been unfairly passed over; others maintained that the award was justified, but thought it should have been given for Quasimodo's early "hermetic" poetry, not (as it was) for the more engaged and accessible verse of his later years.

Quasimodo was born in Modica, Sicily, of Sicilian-Greek parents, Gaetano and Clotilde (Ragusa) Quasimodo. His father's work as an employee of the state railroad took the family from Gela, where the boy had begun his education, to Messina, where the family arrived two days after the great earthquake of 1908. The dreadful spectacles Quasimodo saw then, as a child of seven, made a deep and lasting impression on him.

Although he had learned to read and write at an exceptionally early age, and had shown a precocious interest in poetry, Quasimodo was at first

*kwä sē mō' dō

more drawn to mathematics. With his mother's encouragement, he decided on a career in engineering, attended the Palermo technical college, and in 1918 went to Rome, where he studied for two years at the Polytechnic. Finding that he lacked sufficient funds to complete an engineering degree, he qualified as a surveyor instead. It was at this time that he met Monsignor Rampolla del Tindaro, a Sicilian priest at whose urging he began to learn Greek and embarked on an intensive program of reading, not only of the Greek and Roman classics, but of ancient and modern philosophy.

As his passion for the classics developed, Quasimodo's interest in surveying waned. He was obliged to earn his living nevertheless, and in 1920 he became a technical designer for a construction firm. In 1924 he exchanged this job for one in a hardware store, and in 1926 he joined the state department of civil engineering.

Quasimodo's new post took him to many different parts of Italy—initially to Reggio Calabria in the south, where he was able to renew his contacts with his friends in Messina. He had been writing verse intermittently since his teens, but now, encouraged by the admiration of his circle, he began work in earnest. At the invitation of his brother-in-law Elio Vittorini, Quasimodo sent some of his poems to the Florence review *Solaria.* He was quickly established as a member of the *Solaria* group, which included Manzini, Montale, Loria, and Bonsanti, and which in 1930 published his first book, *Acque e terre* (Waters and Lands).

Soon after this, Quasimodo's work enabled him to leave the south. In 1938, after brief terms of residence in various northern towns, he settled permanently in Milan, at the same time resigning his government post. From 1938 to 1940 he worked as assistant editor and drama critic of *Il Tempo*, and in 1941 he was appointed professor of Italian literature at the Milan Conservatory of Music, where he was to remain until 1964.

Critics concur, more or less, in identifying three stages in the development of Quasimodo's verse, beginning with the hermetic poetry of the 1930s. Italian hermetic poetry, which derives from French symbolism, attempts a renewal of language in which each word is returned to its former sovereignty, given its full value of meaning and sound and association, purged of all merely decorative effects. The hermetic poet turns his back on his society and looks inside, exploring his own interior landscape, and recording his findings in his "new language" and with an often deeply private imagery.

Ungaretti's work in the hermetic mode was already well known when Quasimodo published his first book, but Quasimodo always regarded Ungaretti as a developer of the French tradition,

SALVATORE QUASIMODO

himself as the first truly Italian hermetic. This is a vexed question, since Quasimodo obviously learned from Ungaretti. Both inherit and proclaim the cult of the word (Quasimodo somewhat more overtly). Both have a fondness for sharply chiseled images, short lines, and strained syntax. In both poets the brevity of their compositions suggests the fragmentary.

Nevertheless Quasimodo's voice is very much his own, most obviously in the tension between his acquired austerity of diction and melody, and a more instinctive sensuality and lyricism. He writes of the fragility of man's world, the bittersweet consolations of memory, and the persistent presence of death in an elliptical language of metaphors which matches the cryptic but richly evocative shorthand of his language: "The desire of your hands transparent / in the penumbra of the flame: / they smelled of oak and of roses; / of death. An ancient winter." He may fairly be claimed as the most extreme, if not the first, Italian exponent of hermetic poetry.

In Geoffrey Grigson's *Concise Encyclopedia of Modern World Literature* there is a brief but very illuminating account of Quasimodo's character as a poet, "his constant searching for a poem which grows from the moment, and is at the same time as pure as remote music. Each poem is an attempt at this immediate-ultimate, and though Quasimodo's image of perfection changes, his poems of any one period are as interrelated as musical variations." The "image of perfection" in Quasimodo's early poems is most often the Sicily of his childhood, glimpsed through a cloud of introspective anguish: "Tindari, I know you gentle / in broad hills hung over waters / of the gods' sweet isles; / today you assail me / and lean into my heart."

Acque e terre was followed by *Oboe sommerso* (The Submerged Oboe, 1932), in which Grigson sees a new fineness of imagery: " . . . the heart migrates / and I am untilled / and the day a heap of rubble." The other books of Quasimodo's hermetic period are *Odore di eucaliptus* (Scent of Eucalyptus, 1933), *Erato e Apollion* (Erato and Apollyon, 1936), *Poesie* (Poems, 1938), and *Ed è subito sera* (And It Is Suddenly Evening, 1942). The development in these collections is towards a recognition that the poet's poignant sense of personal loneliness and exile represents a universal human condition; the bare landscapes which in the first poems "had offered only a few elements standing in their own light" become a little less deserted.

In Italy Quasimodo's exquisite verbal and rhythmic sensitivity was admired from the beginning by Macrì, Bo, Contini, Montale, and some other critics and poets, but widespread recognition came only with the publication in 1940 of his magnificent translations of the Greek lyricists, *Lirici greci*. His greatness as a translator was confirmed by his subsequent versions of Homer, Vergil, Ovid, Catullus, Aeschylus, Sophocles, and also Molière, Shakespeare, and Neruda. One critic has described Quasimodo's classical translations as "masterful re-creations imbued with a personal fire that, despite the antiquity of the original texts, makes them particularly meaningful to the modern reader." There is no doubt that his close absorption in these texts contributed to the development of his own work.

With *Poesie nuove* (New Poems, 1942), including poems written as early as 1936, a perceptible change of mood and manner emerged. The verbal and grammatical tensions have become less evident, partially replaced by a kind of expansive languor. The vision is still very personal and often veiled but the exposition is more open; we remark, as Gianni Pozzi says, "a melodic and discursive unfolding." Quasimodo's characteristic work of this middle period, if it has lost the enigmatic glitter of his earlier poems, has a new warmth and richness of color and shows a greater readiness to communicate. It is a progression which leads the way to Quasimodo's third period, in which he casts aside the hermetic cloak and speaks out as a poet of social engagement.

During World War II Quasimodo worked and wrote for the Italian Resistance, and as a result was imprisoned for a time at Bergamo. It was the war, and what it showed him of human lunacy and agony, which convinced Quasimodo that the poet has a duty to "remake" man—at the social level, presumably; he saw that "the poet cannot console anyone, cannot accustom man to the idea of death, decrease his physical suffering, cannot promise an Eden, nor a milder hell."

After about 1943, Quasimodo's poetry, as he said, "aspires to dialogue rather than monologue." He writes of partisans, the Korean war, the atom bomb, in classical forms and a charged but everyday vocabulary full of sirens, rifle shots, iron, dust, and blood—these fearful images often plangently counterpointed against his memories of Sicily: "I call to your memory that flaming geranium / on a wall riddled with machine-gun bullets."

It was in this strain, with an intense awareness of contemporary history, but by no means without hope for the future, that Quasimodo continued to write until his death. His postwar publications include *Giorno dopo giorno* (Day After Day, 1947), *La vita non è sogno* (Life Is Not a Dream, 1949), *Il falso e vero verde* (The False and the True Green, 1956), and *La terra impareggiabile* (The Incomparable Land, 1958). A much quoted example of his later manner is "Man of My Time": "You are still the one with the stone and the sling, / man of my time. You were in the cockpit, / with the malign wings, the sundials of death, / —I have seen you—in the chariot of fire, at the gallows, / at the wheels of torture. I have seen you. . . . / And this blood smells as on the day / one brother told the other brother: 'Let us / go into the fields.' And that echo, chill, tenacious, / has reached down to you, within your day. / Forget, O sons, the clouds of blood / risen from the earth, forget the fathers: / their tombs sink down in ashes, / black birds, the wind, cover their heart." (Translated by Allen Mandelbaum.)

Some critics believe that the war renewed and fulfilled Quasimodo. Sir Maurice Bowra wrote in 1960: "More than any living poet he speaks for the whole of Europe, and is not afraid of attempting themes of profound and common concern." Others, like Filippo Donini, held that "where the new Quasimodo is the most *engagé*, he is at times absurdly far from poetry: it is not enough for him to choose dutiful themes . . . he actually adopts dutiful language, and employs the slogans of poor journalists, confirming the saying that the translator of the Greeks and Shakespeare is now translating from *Pravda*." It was, however, for his last books, beginning with *Ed è subito sera*, that the Nobel jury made its award.

Some have seen in Quasimodo's early verse a typically Sicilian reaction, of sullen withdrawal or ironic mockery, bred of centuries of continental indifference. This may well be true so far as it goes, and certainly the roots of his poetic lie in an almost morbid sensitivity. But Quasimodo, even in his most hermetic period, was never merely an arid intellectual, and in his warm and tender music it is possible to detect a deeply religious temperament which is neither Sicilian nor continental, but gives him a kinship with such great forerunners as Petrarch, Tasso, and Leopardi.

In addition to his poetry and his translations, Quasimodo wrote a number of essays, collected in *Il poeta e il politico* (1960, translated as *The Poet and the Politician*), and containing somewhat gnomic pronouncements on the role of the poet in society and the nature of contemporary Italian verse, and criticism of Dante, Petrarch, and other figures. He also published a volume of drama reviews.

Quasimodo died in Naples. He was small and slight, balding, with a dark moustache, quiet, shy, and apparently lonely. He was separated from his wife, Maria Cumani, a dancer, whom he married in 1948, and had a son and a daughter. Just after World War II he was for a few disillusioning months a member of the Communist party, and this fact, together with his unorthodox religious views, brought unfounded charges that he was an atheist. The controversy over his Nobel Prize also caused him much distress, and he said once that "when you achieve something here, there are far too many who would like to stab you right in the back." He also received the Premio Viareggio in 1958, and shared the Taormina Prize with Dylan Thomas in 1953.

PRINCIPAL WORKS IN ENGLISH TRANSLATION: The Selected Writing of Salvatore Quasimodo (ed. and tr. by Allen Mandelbaum), 1960; The Poet and the Politician (tr. by Thomas G. Bergin and Sergio Pacifici), 1964; Quasimodo: Selected Poems (tr. by Jack Bevan), 1965; To Give and to Have (tr. by Edith Farnsworth), 1969; Debit and Credit (tr. by Jack Bevan), 1972. *Poems in* Barnstone, W. (ed.) Modern European Poetry, 1966; Fulton, R. An Italian Quartet, 1966; Golini, C. L. (ed.) Contemporary Italian Poetry, 1962; Kay, G. R. (ed.) Penguin Book of Italian Verse, 1965; Pacifici, S. (ed.) The Promised Land, 1957.

ABOUT: Angioletti, A. E fu subito sera, 1968; Burnshaw, S. (ed.) The Poem Itself, 1960; Ciardi, J. Dialogue with an Audience, 1963; Cohen, J. M. Poetry of This Age, 1966; Contemporary Authors 15–16, 1966; Curley, D. N. and Curley, A. Modern Romance Literatures (Library of Literary Criticism), 1967; Current Biography, 1960; Dizionario enciclopedico della letteratura italiana, 1967; Dizionario universale della letteratura contemporanea, 1961; Finzi, G. (ed.) Quasimodo e la critica, 1969; Letteratura italiana: I contemporanei, 1963; Pacifici, S. A Guide to Contemporary Italian Literature, 1962; Stefanile, M. Quasimodo, 1943; Tedesco, N. Salvatore Quasimodo, 1959; Zagarrio, G. Quasimodo, 1969. *Periodicals*—Books Abroad Winter 1960, Winter 1967; Chicago Review Spring 1960; Horizon December 1947; Italian Quarterly Fall 1959; Italica March 1948; London Magazine December 1960, September 1968; Meanjin Quarterly September 1961; New York Times Book Review July 3, 1960; Reporter December 10, 1959; Saturday Review November 7, 1959; June 11, 1960; Twentieth Century December 1959.

"QUENTIN, PATRICK." *See* WHEELER, HUGH CALLINGHAM

QUINE, WILLARD V(AN ORMAN) (June 25, 1908–), American philosopher, writes: "My

WILLARD V. QUINE

father was born in Akron of immigrant parents, Palatinate and Manx. He made his way to prosperity in heavy industry. My mother, née Van Orman, came from a nearby village. I was born and raised in Akron and went to the public schools. From early childhood I admired maps and longed to travel. I would pore over Africa, Europe, and America, but skipped the Asia page because the word connoted nothing. Then one great day I looked at it and found China, India, Persia, Japan, Arabia, Jerusalem—places I had vaguely supposed lost or fictitious.

"Intermittently I attended Sunday school. My philosophical activity began with questioning all that and trying to unsave my schoolmates. My first quasi-philosophical reading came at fifteen, in Poe's 'Eureka.' Add two philosophy texts (Otto and James) that my brother brought from college, and you have my philosophical background on entering Oberlin in 1926.

"Besides the philosophical interest I had a taste for mathematics and for the history of language. When I was pondering the choice of a major, a senior in English told me of Bertrand Russell's 'mathematical philosophy.' This seemed to combine two of my leanings, so I majored in mathematics and did honors reading in Russell's domain. The topic was not in Oberlin's curriculum, but my professor inquired around and assembled a reading list, culminating in Whitehead and Russell's *Principia Mathematica.*

"My admiration for *Principia* led me to Russell's more philosophical work, and this nourished my general interest in philosophy. The same admiration led me to apply for a scholarship at Harvard, where

Whitehead taught philosophy. In 1930 I graduated from Oberlin *summa cum laude* in mathematics, married Naomi Clayton of Oberlin, and entered Harvard in philosophy. Impatient to earn a living, I took my Ph.D. in two years, thereby maximizing the ratio of drudgery to reflection. Whitehead sponsored my dissertation, which was in logic.

"My enthusiasm for geography was unacademic but unabating. One summer during college I roamed the West with friends by jaloppy, freight trains, and hitch-hiking. The next summer my father paid my way to Europe, which, with its old streets and Romance languages, was a dream come true. In 1932, on getting my Ph.D., I won a traveling fellowship that took me back to Europe with my wife. Between academic sojourns at Vienna, Prague, and Warsaw that year we made our frugal way to twenty-seven countries.

"At Prague my man was Carnap. I read his *Logische Syntax* in manuscript and talked much with him, receiving his philosophy with enthusiasm. Though his views and mine have since diverged, his impact on my philosophical thought has been the greatest of anyone's. In Warsaw I came abreast of the current phase of mathematical logic, and my greatest debt was to Tarski.

"Whitehead wired me in Prague that I was elected to Harvard's new Society of Fellows. This meant three years in bright company with no duties. The leisure for reflection that I forwent in rushing my Ph.D. was richly restored. The measurable yield of those happy years was a book and a dozen articles.

"Since 1936 I have been in the Harvard philosophy department. But there were leaves of absence. In 1938–1939 I settled with wife and two babies in the Azores to work at my *Mathematical Logic*. The Portuguese that I learned helped me in 1942, when I lectured on logic in Brazil. The Brazilians adjusted my Portuguese and made a book of my lectures.

"After Brazil I served the Navy in Washington, becoming lieutenant commander. In 1946 I returned to Harvard. My marriage ended, and in 1948 I married Marjorie Boynton. We moved to Oxford with our small son in 1953 for my year as Eastman Visiting Professor. Our daughter was born there. In three subsequent years I have enjoyed luxurious freedom for thought in the best retreats—the Institute for Advanced Study in Princeton, the Center in Stanford, and the Center at Wesleyan. I was visiting professor at Tokyo and lecturer in South Australia. And I have had other trips to oblique continents, some for business, all for pleasure. Of one hundred and sixty-eight countries that perhaps exist today (the concept is hazy), I have been in eighty-one. In this I am sensible of a certain fulfillment.

"Still my main line is thinking and writing and, in third place, teaching. My teaching has been partly logic, including a graduate course most years in the mathematics department, and partly philosophy with stress on language. My disparate college interests—philosophy, mathematics, language—have thus come to terms."

Willard V. Quine is the leading logician-philosopher of the present day, much as Rudolf Carnap was in the 1930s and Bertrand Russell in the period before that. Neither a logician who makes occasional forays into philosophy nor a philosopher influenced by developments in formal logic, he has made substantial contributions in both fields. This has been an increasingly rare accomplishment since the 1930s when the two disciplines, so fruitfully associated by Russell, began to diverge. Formal logic is more and more a mathematical specialty. Philosophers have been led by the later Wittgenstein to reject the mechanical rigor of formal logic as inadequate to the complexity and variety of our established processes of rational thinking.

Quine's first book of 1934 was a straightforwardly formal treatise on logic, but a year later he wrote an important essay, "Truth by Convention," which was the first shot in his long, often lonely, and still continuing campaign against the view of logical and mathematical truth most widely accepted by philosophers of the dominant analytic persuasion. The usual view was and is that the propositions of logic and mathematics have a special kind of truth, quite distinct from that of factual beliefs. Where the latter depend for truth on correspondence with the extralinguistic world, the former, it is held, owe their truth, in the end, to linguistic convention. The most sophisticated mathematical theorem, as much as a verbal truism like "all bachelors are unmarried," is true, despite appearances, solely in virtue of the conventionally established meanings of the terms it contains. Quine has fought against this dualism of the analytic and synthetic with unceasing ingenuity and resource. If he has not made many complete converts he has wholly changed the terms in which the topic is discussed.

Another persistent interest has been ontology, the theory of what main kinds of things exist. Although sympathetic to the nominalist idea that concrete things alone exist, he has concluded that the acceptance of mathematics as true implies the existence of classes, which are abstract entities. This, together with his rejection of the usual positivist criterion of empirical significance, undermines the attempt to find a hard-and-fast line of demarcation between meaningful science and empty metaphysics.

Quine is very much a stylist; he is witty, elegant, and brilliantly concise. He handles topics of the greatest possible abstract desiccation with the lightest of touches. These are qualities that show to particular advantage in his series of textbooks on logic, which are marked by notable felicities of arrangement and notation, a remarkable talent for exploiting "the submerged associations and resonances of technical terms." Anthony Quinton, writing in the *New York Review of Books*, says that Quine is "probably the contemporary American philosopher most admired in the profession. . . . [His] philosophical innovations add up to a coherent theory of knowledge of great boldness and originality which he has for the most part constructed single-handed"; its final importance "is an assertion of the essential unity of science and, even more, of the ultimate identity of science with all rational thought."

As he says, Quine has been since 1936 on the faculty of the Harvard philosophy department—since 1956 as Edgar Pierce Professor of Philosophy. He has lectured, or taught as a visiting professor, at the universities of Oxford and Tokyo, at Rockefeller University, at the Collège de France, and at the universities of London and Adelaide. He was John Dewey Lecturer at Columbia in 1968, Paul Carus Lecturer before the American Philosophical Association in 1971, and Hägerström Lecturer at Uppsala in 1973. In 1973–1974 he was Sir Henry Saville Fellow at Merton College, Oxford. He has served as consulting editor of the *Journal of Symbolic Logic* (1936–1952), president of the Association for Symbolic Logic (1953–1955), and president of the eastern division of the American Philosophical Association (1957). He is a Fellow of the American Association for the Advancement of Science, and a member of several national and international societies devoted to philosophy and science.

PRINCIPAL WORKS: A System of Logistic, 1934; Mathematical Logic, 1940; Elementary Logic, 1941; O Sentido da Nova Lógica, 1944; Methods of Logic, 1950; From a Logical Point of View, 1953; Word and Object: Studies in Communication, 1960; Set Theory and Its Logic, 1963; The Ways of Paradox and Other Essays, 1966; Selected Logic Papers, 1966; Ontological Relativity and Other Essays, 1969; Philosophy of Logic, 1970; (with J. S. Ullian) The Web of Belief, 1970.

ABOUT: Contemporary Authors 4, 1963; Hill, T. E. Contemporary Theories of Knowledge, 1961; Passmore, J. A. A Hundred Years of Philosophy, 1966; Who's Who, 1971; Who's Who in America, 1972–1973. *Periodicals*—Journal of Philosophy July 8, 1954; July 20, 1961; February 2, 1967; January 25, 1968; National Observer July 20 1964; New York Review of Books January 12, 1967; Partisan Review Spring 1967; Philosophical Review January 1951, April 1956; Review of Metaphysics June 1961, September-December 1967; Rivista di Filosofia October 1956; Science May 12, 1967; Synthese 1968; Times Literary Supplement October 9, 1970.

QUOIREZ, FRANÇOISE. *See* "SAGAN, FRANÇOISE"

EDWARD D. RADIN

RADIN, EDWARD D(AVID) (April 28, 1909–March 28, 1966), American crime writer, editor, and journalist, was born in New York City, the son of Philip and Ida Radin. Graduating from New York University in 1932 with a B.S. degree, he became a reporter on the *Long Island Press*, came to specialize in crime reporting, and covered many murder trials.

In 1936 Radin began to sell freelance articles on crime, and by 1941 was able to leave newspaper work and devote himself to magazine writing. His articles appeared in many major magazines, including *Collier's*, *Cosmopolitan*, the *Saturday Evening Post*, and *Esquire*. His work from the beginning was distinguished by its literacy and restraint, and by its scrupulous reliance on official records, and was said to represent "the highest level of the straightforward, no-frills-about-it writing of the better detective magazines." For a time he was in fact editor of the true crime story magazine *Detective*.

Radin's first book was *Twelve Against the Law*, accounts of cases chosen not for their sensationalism but because of the excellence of the detective work involved. It was universally praised and brought Radin the first Edgar Allan Poe award of the Mystery Writers of America. He received a second Edgar for *Twelve Against Crime*, which deals with such unpublicized heroes of modern detection as toxicologists and psychiatrists. These and his subsequent books established him as "the soundest crime expert of our generation."

The best-known and most successful of Radin's books was *Lizzie Borden: The Untold Story*. Although Lizzie was found not guilty at her trial, it had been widely supposed that she did in fact murder her father and stepmother. This belief stemmed mostly from the writings of Edmund Pearson, whose views Radin at first accepted. Two years of research convinced him, however, that Pearson had ignored or minimized much evidence pointing to Lizzie's innocence. His own book sought to set the record straight and offered a new suspect—the Bordens' servant Bridget.

Few reviewers thought that Radin had made a watertight case against Bridget, and some suggested that his arguments for Lizzie's innocence were nearly as partial and selective as Pearson's for her guilt. But, as E. F. Walbridge wrote, "one need not accept Mr. Radin's thesis to enjoy the fruits of his labors." The book was widely praised as a completely absorbing tour de force, equally remarkable for its humanity and its "powerful reasoning." A reviewer in the *Times Literary Supplement* wrote: "It contains some first-class detective work on his part and some sound scholarly research and he has excellently reconstructed the life of the Borden family in its Fall River environment, building up a picture of individuals and a society as well as of a crime. . . . Mr. Radin's book is one of the most interesting and valuable reconstructions of a celebrated crime to have appeared for many years." Radin received an Edgar Scroll for *Lizzie Borden.*

Radin's work has been translated into a number of European languages and even into two Indian dialects. He was married in 1938 to Beatrice Hollander and had two daughters. Radin died of cancer at his home in Glen Cove, New York, at the age of fifty-six. After his death, an Edward D. Radin Award for outstanding fact-crime writing was established by the Mystery Writers of America, of which Radin had been a founder and a former president.

PRINCIPAL WORKS: Twelve Against the Law, 1946; Twelve Against Crime, 1950; Headline Crimes of the Year, 1952; Crimes of Passion, 1953; Lizzie Borden: The Untold Story, 1961; (with George P. Lebrun) It's Time to Tell, 1962; (with George W. Herald) The Big Wheel: Monte Carlo's Opulent Story, 1963; The Innocents, 1964; *As editor*—Masters of Mayhem: The Mystery Writers of America Anthology, 1965.

ABOUT: Who's Who in America, 1966–1967. *Periodicals*—Publishers' Weekly April 25, 1966; New York Times March 29, 1966.

RAGO, HENRY (ANTHONY) (October 5, 1915–May 26, 1969), American poet and editor, wrote: "I have been writing poetry since the age of seven. When I was about thirteen, Harriet Monroe, the Editor of *Poetry*, took an interest in my development, suggesting poets for me to read and scribbling criticisms on the juvenilia I would send her from month to month. When I was fifteen, she accepted one of my poems for publication in her magazine. It was called 'I Live,' and it appeared in the December 1931 issue.

"Despite that early start, I've taken a slow and long way toward what has seemed the only honest fulfillment of a gift primarily lyrical, personal, and affirmative. For me the hope of that fulfillment has been in a simplicity on the far side of complexity. My education was a long process—through law, religion, and philosophy. The poetry had to go through it with me. And so through all my early twenties, the poetry I wrote went chiefly into what we have come to call the modern 'long poem,' struggling with large philosophical and religious concerns. I would say now that in general the poetry could not carry the load. Whatever compliments were paid these poems I now feel they owed only to the undeniable if inarticulate energy that drove them. But this line of development was soon interrupted: for slightly more than three years, when my whole personal life was immersed in the war, I could write nothing at all.

"When I came back to America, it was almost another beginning. I wrote a long stretch of almost weekly reviews for *The Commonweal* and a considerable range of other things just to get my hand moving again. It was three years before I felt ready to publish a book. This was *The Travelers*, which came out in 1949, and I ventured it only in the modest size of a chapbook. It represented the burning away of a great mass of poetry; and even as it was being printed I felt that it was only tentative and that in turn it would need a whole new range of poetry before its experience could rest in a definitive scale.

"The trilogy that opens *A Sky of Late Summer* seemed to perform this function for me. It came out first as a small book of its own, *Conoscenza della Luce*, in a bilingual edition published in Italy by Palmaverde (Bologna), with translations into the Italian by Alfredo Rizzardi. Small as it was, it seemed and still seems to me my first really complete book; an end; and a vantage-point from which to see new country.

"I hope that *A Sky of Late Summer* suggests that new country, moves from the darker, more entangled poetry to a reclaiming of what I have already called the lyrical, the personal, the affirmative. I would be happy if the reader saw in a new simplicity those philosophical and religious themes which have been my own since I was nineteen or twenty, which I stammered with (or argued with) in those earlier long poems, and which have been implicit in almost everything I have ever published in my adult life. *The Travelers* implies them negatively, but *A Sky of Late Summer* begins to *sing* them, no matter how modestly. It is in this *song* that I recognize these themes now; as the breath of my poetry rather than its burden; as its understanding rather than that which it struggles to understand; as the depth of its light rather than the depth of its obscurity.

"I have been the Editor of *Poetry* since 1955. It seems a natural place to be, for reasons of an old piety; and paradoxically, the ideal place in which to feel absolutely alone with one's own poetry; all else that engages me in the work of other poets only leaves in clearer relief than ever the poetry that I alone must write."

Henry Rago was born in Chicago, of parents who had migrated from Potenza, Basilicata, in southern Italy. He was the son of Louis Rago, who became a very successful and well-known funeral director in Chicago, and of the former Theresa Argenzio. Rago received an LL.B. degree from De Paul University in Chicago (1937) and an M.A. in religion from Notre Dame University (1939), which also gave him his doctorate in philosophy (1941). In 1942, after a year's teaching, he went into the Army, emerging in 1946 with a Bronze Star and the rank of first lieutenant. Thereafter, until he joined *Poetry* magazine, he taught at the University of Chicago (1947–1954) and at Saint Xavier College for Women, where he occupied a chair in the humanities (1954–1956).

The Travelers was no more than a pamphlet, though an attractive one. It contained only a handful of poems, according to Dudley Fitts, who wished there were "twice as many," and praised their "striking" unobtrusiveness, their calm balance and authority. *In Praise of Comedy* was a Phi Beta Kappa Poem (1962), read at William and Mary College.

That Rago had worked his way through to "a new country" in *A Sky of Late Summer* was widely recognized. The collection, which is arranged in four sections, contains a number of epigrams and occasional pieces and four longer poems of larger importance: the title poem, "The Knowledge of Light," "The Attending," and "The Promising." These are religious poems in the sense that they seek and celebrate the light, natural and spiritual. They are also, as Rago said, personal and affirmative—indeed too affirmative for Denise Levertov, who admired them but believes a poem should not be free of the anguish that is a part of life. Other readers found them too abstract or too simple. But to many critics their simplicity seemed of a rare and astonishing kind, won with great difficulty from profundity and complexity. Stanley Kunitz spoke of "*claritas*, the splendor of the true." Mark Van Doren said that Rago had performed "the miracle of distilling experience without making it disappear," and others called these poems "weightless" or "peculiarly wordless."

To Hayden Carruth it seemed that Rago, "who

HENRY RAGO

began with a surpassing lyrical talent and a mind as quick as a fish, has stood off the blandishments of his own abilities . . . without one surrender to the siren of virtuosity. . . . In these splendid, almost unbelievable poems, Rago brings back the crystalline, Arielesque quality that poets forty years ago considered indispensable—compression without density, harmony without artifice."

Rago received a Rockefeller Foundation grant in 1960–1961 to study contemporary European literature and to write poetry, and had an honorary doctorate from De Paul University. In 1965 he returned to the University of Chicago as professor of theology and literature in the divinity school. Four years later he announced his resignation as editor of *Poetry*, intending to devote himself exclusively to teaching, but died before his resignation became effective. Rago was survived by his wife, the former Juliet Maggio, and four children.

PRINCIPAL WORKS: The Philosophy of Esthetic Individualism, 1941; The Travelers, 1949; In Praise of Comedy: A Discourse, 1963; A Sky of Late Summer, Poems, 1963.

ABOUT: Peragallo, O. Italian-American Authors and Their Contribution to American Literature, 1949; Who's Who in America, 1966–1967. *Periodicals*—New York Times May 28, 1969; Poetry August 1969, December 1969.

***RAJA RAO** (November 21, 1909–), Indian novelist and short story writer, was born of a distinguished Brahmin family in Mysore, South India, and educated at Madras University, where he gained a degree in English and history. At the age of nineteen he left India for Europe, where he pursued

* rä′ jə rō

RAJA RAO

postgraduate studies at the University of Montpellier and later at the Sorbonne under Professor Louis Cazamian. But he soon abandoned literary research for writing, and his first stories, published in French and English, were warmly praised by, among others, Romain Rolland and Stefan Zweig.

After a decade in Europe Raja Rao returned to India, where he spent the war years in a quest for his spiritual heritage, traveling from the Himalayas to Cape Comorin in the extreme south. The result of this quest was his most celebrated novel, *The Serpent and the Rope*, published in 1960. During the war, Raja Rao edited an international literary journal, *Tomorrow*. Raja Rao, together with Mulk Raj Anand and R. K. Narayan, is one of India's three outstanding English-language novelists, all of them products in one way or another of the Gandhian social rebellion of the 1930s.

His first book, *Kanthapura*, was published in 1938 and elicited high praise from E. M. Forster. Santha Rama Rau, writing more recently, referred to its "elegant style verging on poetry; it has all the content of an ancient Indian classic, combined with a sharp, satirical wit and a clear understanding of the present." It is an account of the impact of Gandhism on a South Indian village, told in the racy, parenthetical, anecdotal style of the old woman who is the narrator. It is 1930, the year of Gandhi's march across India to defy the salt laws, and passive resistance sweeps the country, engulfing even the obscure village of Kanthapura in conflict. And looking back, the old woman, in the way of village storytellers, merges history with myth. As Srinivasa Iyengar writes, "Gandhi is [the god] Rama; the red foreigner or the brown inspector of police who flourishes a *lathi* is ten-headed Ravana's army of occupation. . . . The political revolution is thus transcended and assimilated into the racial heritage as myth and legend."

Raja Rao explains in an introduction to the book his efforts to evolve a style, in English, to express the consciousness of an Indian villager: "The tempo of Indian life must be infused into our English expression, even as the tempo of American or Irish life has gone into the making of theirs. We, in India, think quickly, we talk quickly, and when we move we move quickly. . . . We have neither punctuation nor the treacherous 'ats' and 'ons' to bother us—we tell one interminable tale." Critics are divided on the degree of his success—Robert J. Ray, for instance, finds the effect of this breathless and undifferentiating style "not speed . . . but monotony."

There is no such disagreement about Raja Rao's short stories, which have been universally praised. They were first published in book form as *The Cow of the Barricades* in 1947, though many of them in fact predate *Kanthapura*. Nearly all of them, like that novel, are set in rural South India during the 1930s and reflect the impact of Gandhi's passive resistance campaigns, though the best of them are far more than merely regional or topical tales. They evoke a society governed by religion, superstition, and caste, by poverty and self-denial. There are village matchmakers and moneylenders, feudalistic elders and subversive young men educated in the city, learned Brahmins and ignorant shepherd boys, domineering mothers-in-law and wretched widows unwanted by anyone except as drudges.

All are brought vividly to life in a language rich in native idioms and sharp, sensuous imagery. The title story illustrates Raja Rao's method very well. It is about Gauri, the saintlike village cow, who will take food only from the village holy man. In a desperate confrontation between the peasants and the soldiers of the British Raj, she mounts the barricades and is shot, but in dying she dissipates the murderous tension and saves the village. M. K. Naik, acknowledging that Raja Rao lacks the range and variety of Anand, Narayan, or Tagore, says that none of these "has felt the pulse of village India with a surer touch, has seen the traditional, the transitional and the universal in it more clearly than Raja Rao. . . . This is perhaps the reason why he has the most distinctive style of all the Indo-Anglians."

His second novel, *The Serpent and the Rope*, appearing in 1960, more than twenty years after his first, is a very different kind of work, an ambitious study of the interpenetration of Indian and Western culture, in a semi-autobiographical framework. It centers on Rama, a South Indian Brahmin, who goes to Europe to study the Albigensian heresy and its roots in Asian philosophy. His marriage to a French girl, the death of their two children, his affair with an Indian girl in England, place him at the crossroads between two cultures, two methods of perception. Martin Tucker found it "impossible to state the meaning of the novel, for to catch and hold onto the main thread one must tear the fabric. Where one ordinary stitch would do, Rao has woven thousands, but what an extraordinary feat he has accomplished in the multiplicity of his pattern and the vision within the eye of the needle. . . . Yet the symbolism is easily apparent. Either one believes in the serpent or one believes in the rope. The serpent is the imagination; the rope is reality. Either the world is real and each man a part of it; or each man creates the world in his own image."

This dualism is expressed directly in the novel's style, which represents a remarkable attempt to accommodate the rhythms of Sanskrit to English prose. The London *Times* reviewer thought the writing "utterly beautiful," but some Western critics found this long novel weakened by often obscure philosophical passages, and most thought it fell short of greatness. Nevertheless Srinivasa Iyengar considers it perhaps "the most impressive novel yet written by an Indian in English," and says that "never has the subtle and tortuous mind of the cultivated Indian . . . caught in the narrows of the ambiguous agonizing present . . . been presented so engagingly and excitingly in a work of fiction."

The Cat and Shakespeare, which followed, is a slighter book but still a demanding one, which blends the naturalism of the short stories with the philosophical concerns of *The Serpent and the Rope*. This gentle and amusing allegory, set in a South Indian town during World War II, deals once more with illusion and reality, and the dangerous wall between them that can be walked so easily by kittens and other solipsistic creatures.

Raja Rao has spent half his life in France, and has traveled in most parts of the world. He now divides his time between India and the West. Since 1965 he has been professor of philosophy at the University of Texas, teaching one semester a year. He has been married twice—to Camille Mouly in 1931, and to Katherine Jones in 1965. He has one son. Raja Rao was awarded the Indian Literary Academy Award in 1965 for *The Serpent and the Rope*.

PRINCIPAL WORKS: *Fiction*—Kanthapura, 1938; The Cow of the Barricades and Other Stories, 1947; The Serpent and the Rope, 1960; The Cat and Shakespeare, 1965. *As editor (with Iqbal Singh)*—Changing India, 1939; Whither India?, 1948.

ABOUT: International Who's Who, 1972–73; Naik, M. S. Raja Rao, 1972; Srinivasa Iyengar, K. R. Indian Writing in English, 1962; Vinson, J. (ed.) Contemporary Novelists, 1972. *Periodicals*—Best Sellers February 15, 1963; Books Abroad Autumn 1966; Book Week January 31, 1965; Commonweal January 25, 1963; Journal of Commonwealth Literature July 1968; New York Times Book Review January 5, 1964; November 29, 1964; Saturday Review January 16, 1965.

***RAJAN, BALACHANDRA** (1920–), Indian novelist and critic, writes: "I was born in Burma and educated at Madras to what is now the A level. At Cambridge I did economics to please my father and English to please myself. It was then 1942, the Suez Canal was closed to passenger traffic, passages home were unavailable and in any event, I had disqualified myself for the Indian Civil Service by my mild indulgence in nationalist activities. I had therefore a plausible excuse for research. I became a Fellow of Trinity College and taught at Cambridge for four years. When India achieved independence I joined its foreign service. I was a member of the Permanent Mission of India to the United Nations for several years and became Chairman of the Executive Board of the United Nations Children's Fund. Then, because of my total ignorance of physics, I represented India for two years at the International Atomic Energy Agency. I left the Foreign Service in 1961 and was Head of the Department of English at Delhi University until 1964. I then joined the Institute for Research in the Humanities of the University of Wisconsin as a visiting professor. At present I'm a Senior Professor of English at the University of Western Ontario. This is a professional career which sounds nomadic in the retelling but I believe the things in my head have remained relatively constant.

"After my first novel had been accepted in the United States the publisher asked me if it was complete in my mind before I put pen to paper. I did not tell him the whole truth since the question implied that he would not have understood it. I do not start with a blueprint but with a limited sense of what meaning might be found if I could find the right people, the right situations and above all the right words. In the effort to break through to a meaning the meaning alters and if it did not I would be suspicious of what I was writing. In writing a book one always hopes to reach that stage in its evolution when the book will acquire its own life. Creative satisfaction is least delusive when the writer can follow with skill the logic that he has liberated. This does not always happen and there is usually far more engineering in a book than one wants; but a good book ought to convey the dominant impression of loyalty to itself.

"During the forties I edited five issues of *Focus*, a miscellany in book form on various aspects of contemporary writing. I also published poetry in several English and American magazines before my interest in the novel became dominant. I want my work to have more than one side to it because I'd

* rä′ jən

BALACHANDRA RAJAN

like to avoid the specialized sensibility. But whether I am writing a poem, a novel, or a work of scholarship, I am trying to move forward, I think, along the same proposition; if I could find the right words I could find what makes the words right. In criticism I am continually surprised at how long you can live with a poem before you can see what is overwhelmingly obvious once you've seen it. If this were not so criticism might be an unacceptable activity.

"The primary business of a writer seems to me to write literature rather than to contribute to a national myth, image, or idiom. He can achieve these lesser objectives in finding himself as a writer or even find himself as a writer in achieving them. But literature which fails to meet certain collective specifications is not, for that reason, any the worse as literature. The criteria for judging it must remain aesthetic rather than pseudo-political. We live in one world and literary nationalism may only be a prestigious provinciality."

Rajan made his international reputation with *The Dark Dancer*, a novel centering on the dilemma of Krishnan, returning to India in 1947 (like the author himself) after ten years at an English university. He submits to an arranged marriage and a secure job in government service, and then is challenged by the arrival of Cynthia, an articulate and independent girl whom he had known at Cambridge. Krishnan leaves his wife, Kamala, for what he conceives of as a free relationship between individuals—only to learn that freedom for him means acceptance of the "Indianness" he shares with Kamala. The climax of the novel comes during the communal riots that followed Partition, when he and Kamala find their destiny, and a measure of peace, in tending the riot victims. The book was much admired for its intelligence and some fine lyrical passages, but thought a little overloaded with "philosophic brooding" and "well-turned abstractions."

Too Long in the West, by contrast, is a comedy. This time it is a young woman, Nalini, who has returned from a foreign education (at Columbia University) to the social necessity of an arranged marriage; this time the place is the remote and impoverished feudal village of Mudalur. Nalini's eventual choice from an assortment of unlikely suitors, each with a different wild scheme for the salvation of Mudalur/India, is a symbolic marriage of tradition and rebellion which brings miraculous prosperity to the whole village. There was some feeling that the book's humor derives too much from fantasy—is used "not for its classical function to purge error, but rather to exorcise harsh reality." The *Times Literary Supplement* on the other hand called the book "a comedy of the purest kind, for all its effects arise from the way in which the subject is seen." Most critics shared this view, and had nothing but praise for Rajan's acute insight and his skill in evoking the atmosphere of a particular time and place.

Rajan has published studies of Milton and Eliot, and a "compact, lucid, and balanced introductory survey" of Yeats which was warmly praised as "the fruit of long years of loving and intelligent reading."

PRINCIPAL WORKS: *Fiction*—The Dark Dancer, 1958; Too Long in the West, 1961. *Nonfiction*—Paradise Lost and the Seventeenth Century Reader, 1947; W. B. Yeats, A Critical Introduction, 1965; The Lofty Rhyme: A Study of Milton's Major Poetry, 1970. *As editor*—T. S. Eliot: A Study of His Writings by Several Hands, 1966; The Prison and the Pinnacle: Papers to Commemorate the Tercentenary of "Paradise Regained" and "Samson Agonistes," 1973.

ABOUT: Burgess, A. The Novel Now, 1967. *Periodicals*—New York Times June 29, 1958; New York Times Book Review March 4, 1962; Thought (New Delhi) May 19, 1962; Times Literary Supplement May 19, 1961; Yale Review September 1958.

***RAMA RAU, SANTHA** (January 24, 1923–), is an Indian memoirist, travel writer, and novelist whose work has established her as an uncommonly sophisticated and perceptive interpreter to Western audiences of Eastern ways and peoples. Of high Brahman lineage, she was born in Madras, one of the two daughters of the distinguished diplomat Sir Benegal Rama Rau. Her mother, Dhanvanthi, is a social reformer who has been called "the Margaret Sanger of India." At the age of six, Santha Rama Rau was sent to school in England.

*rä′ mä rou

She graduated in 1939 from St. Paul's School for Girls in London, and two years later entered Wellesley College in Massachusetts, where as a member of Phi Beta Kappa she took her B.A. degree with honors in English in 1944. Her first book appeared the same year.

Home to India describes Santha Rama Rau's return to her native country in 1939, after ten formative years in England. She had made a long journey of rediscovery, seeing India and Indians from a point of view "partly that of a tourist and partly that of an initiate." The grace, honesty, and humor of her account made it a best seller both in England, where it was a Left Book Club Choice, and in the United States, where it was a Harper Book Find. The book's youthful charm and gaiety did not disguise its author's total commitment to the cause of Indian nationalism.

After her graduation from Wellesley, Miss Rama Rau worked for a time in Bombay as editor of *Trend* magazine. In 1947, when her father became India's first ambassador to Japan, she accompanied him to Tokyo as his hostess. There she met Faubion Bowers, American censor of the Japanese theatre during the postwar occupation. With Bowers and other friends she made a tour in 1948 of China and several Southeast Asian countries. Her description of that journey and of her stay in Japan in *East of Home* (1950)—largely a recollection of impressions and conversations—particularly fascinated some of her American readers as a revelation of her growing awareness of herself as an Asian. For one reviewer however, its value was not primarily that of an Asian writing about Asia: "What makes *East of Home* so singular and so pleasing is the youth of it, its serious view of life as something precious to be adorned with friendship and sociability and the study and practice of art."

In 1952 Santha Rama Rau and Faubion Bowers were married. They made their home in New York City, but they continued to travel and later took their son, Jai Peter, along on some of their trips. Because of their command of several languages, they often had more independence than most tourists and came into closer contact with the people in foreign countries. Miss Rama Rau related her experiences in articles for *Holiday* magazine that were later incorporated into *View to the Southeast* (1957) and *My Russian Journey* (1958). Some of the episodes of her wide travels were included in the personal essays that she contributed to the *New Yorker* and other magazines and then collected in *Gifts of Passage* (1961).

Reviewing *Gifts of Passage*, Rumer Godden wrote: "Charm and power make a rare combination . . . but these two qualities have always been combined in the books by Santha Rama Rau. . . . Her stories give only glimpses but they should be called flashes, because they illuminate far more than they tell . . . one is grateful, refreshed and filled with respect."

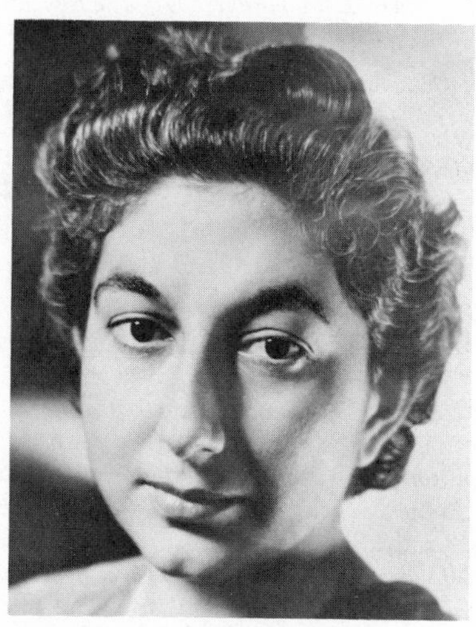

SANTHA RAMA RAU

The same qualities led several critics to insist upon the word "brilliant" in appraising her first novel, *Remember the House*. It evoked the author's own Bombay social set with a "documentary" vividness and authority which, some readers thought, rather overshadowed the book's narrative interest. In its style and calm humanity, the novel reminded several reviewers of E. M. Forster's *A Passage to India*, which Santha Rama Rau dramatized some years later. The play was produced in London in 1960 and in New York in 1961–1962. A second novel, *The Adventuress*, is a picaresque tale, set in the years just after World War II in Tokyo, Manila, and Shanghai. Its central character is Kay, a Eurasian girl living by her excellent wits, "a mercenary angel of mercy" aware of no fate worse than death. Most reviewers thought it a slight book but a highly entertaining one.

During the 1960s Miss Rama Rau made a number of lecture tours in the United States and was presented on radio and television programs. She also emerged in a new and unexpected role as the author of a monthly horoscope feature, prepared in accordance with an Indian system of astrology and published in the magazine *Family Circle*. She was divorced from Faubion Bowers in 1966 and in 1970 made a second marriage to Gurdon W. Wattles, an American international lawyer with the United Nations.

PRINCIPAL WORKS: Home to India, 1944; East of Home, 1950; This Is India, 1954; Remember the House (novel), 1955; View to the Southeast, 1957; My Russian Journey,

1959; Gifts of Passage, 1961; A Passage to India: A Play from the Novel by E. M. Forster, 1961; The Adventuress (novel), 1970; (with the editors of Time-Life Books) The Cooking of India, 1970.

ABOUT: Contemporary Authors 1, 1962; Current Biography, 1959; International Who's Who, 1972–73; Who's Who, 1973; Who's Who in America, 1972–1973. *Periodicals*—Christian Science Monitor May 11, 1961; New York Times October 9, 1970; Time April 16, 1956.

RAO, RAJA. *See* RAJA RAO

RAPHAEL, FREDERIC (MICHAEL) (August 14, 1931–), English novelist and scenarist, writes: "I was born in Chicago, Illinois, of an American mother and a British father. I am an only child of only children. We lived in the States, largely in New York, until I was seven. My father worked for the Shell Oil Company, first as a salesman and later in executive positions; we were never well off, but I never had any sense of even possible privation. My only feeling of insecurity derived from our being Jewish; I had no clear idea what danger threatened, but I knew an obscure fear. I did not have a religious upbringing. My parents had no positive faith; their attitudes were liberal and non-political. In 1938, we came to England, where my father had a new job. We lived in a flat in Putney, in South West London, where my parents still live. I soon lost my American accent and became English.

"I went to a typical middle-class preparatory school, where I was fairly happy, and then, by a fluke, to Charterhouse, where I was unhappy. I found one excellent master, however, Ivor Gibson, who taught me Classics. Thanks mainly to him, I gained a Major Scholarship at St. John's College, Cambridge. I read first Classics and then Moral Sciences. I missed being taught by Wittgenstein by a year or so, but was much influenced by the philosophy of his great disciple John Wisdom.

"I think it was Malraux who said that artists become involved in art not through their experience of life, but through their experience of art. I did not find it so. Though I am now greatly interested in criticism (and contribute regularly to the London *Sunday Times*), I began to write as a response to despair. I have always imagined myself more alone than perhaps I really am. A bout of schoolboy anti-Semitism at Charterhouse (where such outbreaks were encouraged) made me believe in my utter isolation. I started writing to find some connection with the world. If the habit of Latin and Greek composition made me servile to inappropriate models, I still find it difficult to enjoy writers who flout grammar. Though I am conscious of my own awkwardness, I cannot enjoy any prose which blatantly lacks a sense of form, unless it clearly earns its licence. Yet the rigidities of much English writing are uncongenial to me. I admire the freedom of American writers of whom, in some ways, I like to count myself one.

"I married in 1955. My wife, whom I call Beetle, is, to say the least, very important to me. We have two children, Paul and Sarah. We have lived a good deal abroad and have never had many social commitments. In consequence, though I would call myself a Socialist, I have never been a member of any groups of either a political or a literary nature.

"I have always been an amateur painter and my urge to visualise led me to film. I did some hack work in my twenties and then abandoned film altogether; I came back to it in 1963, when I wrote *Nothing But the Best*, which won a Screenwriters' Guild Award for 1964. I then wrote *Darling*, which John Schlesinger directed, and for which I won another Screenwriters' Guild Award, the British Film Academy Award for the best screenplay, and the American Academy Award (the Oscar) for 1965. Two of my screenplays are being filmed in 1966: the first, an original screenplay entitled *Two for the Road*, is being directed by Stanley Donen, with Audrey Hepburn and Albert Finney in the main parts; the other, an adaptation of Thomas Hardy's *Far From the Madding Crowd*, will be directed by John Schlesinger, with Julie Christie in the main part.

"I may confess to being at a decisive stage in my relationship with film and I think it likely that I shall proceed to directing, not so much because I believe that I can do it better than other people (certainly I shall do it much worse than some) but because, ultimately, a writer like myself cannot find congenial the notion that someone else should be the final arbiter of the interpretation of his work.

"I do not take the view that screen writing is a form of prostitution and I think it honest to say that I would regard the writing only of fiction as an unhappy limitation of my creative opportunities.

"I always intended to be a playwright (my first written work, at the age of twelve, was an adaptation of *Rupert of Hentzau* by Anthony Hope, which was ultimately banned because my headmaster refused to allow us to use uncorked swords) but I now find the theatre slow-moving and too limited in its audience. I would like to write a play but the electric possibilities of the cinema are too seductive for me. Nevertheless, I do believe that it is in fiction that one expresses oneself best and I am deeply involved in a new novel, *Orchestra and Beginners*, which I hope will be the first of a cycle.

"My life is now lived largely in England, where we have a house in the country, near Colchester, with the kind of garden in which life seems worth living. We are obliged to spend a good deal of time in London, but it is only at The Wick [his house in England] and around the Mediterranean that I have found contentment.

"We have a small shack on an island in the Aegean, which shall be nameless, but on which I am happy to advertise the presence of huge, poisonous snakes, which I trust will deter all but the happy few. From there life looks simple and I wish only that I could spend all my time writing on the terrace overlooking the huge, empty beach and the blue bay and the pale shapes of the islands. If I am a cynic in England, I am a romantic in Greece."

It was Frederic Raphael's "springy, inventive, and alert" script for *Darling*, a "mercilessly observant" exposure of the "barrenness and triviality of a certain contemporary way of life," which brought him into the front rank of screenwriters. His scenario *Two for the Road*, examining twelve years in the history of an ultimately happy marriage, received the unusual accolade of book publication in 1967, appearing with an introduction in which Raphael discusses the nature and problems of "visual writing." His screenplays for *The Best of Everything* and *Far From the Madding Crowd* were also greatly admired, and he has since written screen versions of Iris Murdoch's *A Severed Head* and Muriel Spark's *The Driver's Seat.*

Although Raphael's films are better known than his books, he is highly regarded among the English novelists of his generation. Not surprisingly, his fiction has been most praised for qualities which hindsight classifies as cinematic. In particular his "uncanny" ability to reveal character through dialogue has been evident and noticed from the first: in *Obbligato*, a not very successful satirical account of the rise of a jazz trumpeter; in *The Earlsdon Way*, about the horrors of suburbia; in *The Limits of Love*, a vigorous but rather clumsy book about young Jews in postwar London, drifting away from orthodoxy. *A Wild Surmise*, the first of Raphael's novels to receive widespread critical approval, made expert use of a number of film techniques. Set in a South American dictatorship, where a young Englishman is forced to abandon his determined noncommitment, it achieves its tension and interest, as J. D. Scott said, "by staccato cutting from one scene to another, by terse, effective dialogue and by the hard, lurid brilliance of [its] local colour."

The pseudo-eponymous central figure in *Lindmann* is presented as an Austrian-Jewish refugee, withdrawn and enigmatic, living in a London boardinghouse. According to a film script which is based on his life, Lindmann is the sole survivor of an illegal immigrant ship, lost on the way to Israel through political indifference. He is driven at last to reveal himself as something quite different, an English civil servant tormented by his contribution to the tragedy. The novel's large intentions, it was

FREDERIC RAPHAEL

thought, were not completely realized; but few denied its force. Walter Allen, for whom the film script was the high point of the novel, found in this and other sections "a sustained brilliance that can scarcely be questioned."

Orchestra and Beginners, set during World War II, studies the marriage between an American woman and her Anglo-Jewish husband whose young son finds in microcosm at his English boarding school the same mixture of fear, sadism, and misplaced idealism which had made the war possible. Most critics thought this presumably autobiographical book too long, uneven, and self-indulgent. One, in the *Times Literary Supplement*, wrote: "It is by no means a first-rate novel; but it is stiff with instructive thought and strong feeling, struggling beneath an ornate and over-sophisticated prose style." *Like Men Betrayed* is a rather excessively cerebral account of a young Greek's search for an ideology in the midst of oppression and chaos during and just after World War II. *Who Were You With Last Night?*, about an average sensual man whose average sensuality gets him into extraordinarily serious trouble, was called "a clever exercise in first-person narration, which becomes endearing without ever being lovable."

Raphael's stage play *A Man on the Bridge* was produced in England in 1961 with a special Arts Council grant. He has written other plays for radio and television. His interests include philosophy and bridge. John Coleman has called Raphael "probably the most gifted author of bad novels we now have." Anthony Burgess says that, in spite of his rapid output, he maintains "one of the highest levels of craftsmanship that the contemporary

British novel has seen." He and his wife, the former Sylvia Glatt, now have three children.

PRINCIPAL WORKS: Obbligato (novel), 1956; The Earlsdon Way (novel), 1958; The Limits of Love (novel), 1960; (with Tom Maschler, under joint pseudonym "Mark Caine") The S-Man, a Grammar of Success, 1960; A Wild Surmise (novel), 1961; The Graduate Wife (novel), 1962; The Trouble With England (novel), 1962; Lindmann (novel), 1963; The Day Franco Came (novella) *in* New World Writing, 1964; Two for the Road (film script), 1967; Orchestra and Beginners (novel), 1967; Like Men Betrayed (novel), 1970; Who Were You With Last Night? (novel), 1971; April, June and November (novel), 1972; Richard's Things (novel), 1973.

ABOUT: Burgess, A. The Novel Now, 1967; Contemporary Authors 4, 1963; Vinson, J. (ed.) Contemporary Novelists, 1972; Who's Who in America, 1972–1973. *Periodicals*—Critique Fall 1965; Times Literary Supplement October 19, 1967.

RATTIGAN, SIR TERENCE (MERVYN)

(June 10, 1911–), English dramatist, writes: "I was born, for a modern writer unfashionably, in a large house in a solidly bourgeois district of London, South Kensington. My father was a career diplomat of great good looks and charm and my mother, born Vera Houston in Dublin, and daughter of an Irish Q.C., was one of the most beautiful women of her day. When I was three I was taken to Berlin, where my father was First Secretary at the British Embassy, and I can still conjure vague memories of being given an immense bottle of brightly-coloured sweets by Crown Prince Wilhelm, embraced by him and consoled for not in the least resembling either of my beautiful parents. My mother tells me the story is apocryphal, but the Crown Prince had by then become a great friend of theirs. I don't, unhappily, look much like either of them, and someone did give me those sweets. I still think it was the Crown Prince.

"Despite this unpromising beginning, I somehow managed to carry into my early teens, and through the later ones, a fierce determination one day to break my father's heart by becoming a professional dramatist, and not a diplomat.

"Why dramatist? I don't know. An eleven-year-old's work (Self-Sacrifice, an enthralling Novelette by the famous Author and Playwrite [sic] T. M. Rattigan) seems to show signs of another literary ambition; but it appears to have been abandoned on page three, both novelette and ambition, for thereafter there are no indications among my fairly extensive juvenilia of anything but the dialogue form.

"It may have been because I lived in London and was able to spend my pocket money by queuing up for theatre galleries, at a shilling a time, to see Gerald du Maurier and Tallulah Bankhead. (Once, in *The Dancers*, notably together.) As I invariably suffered acute guilt about such jaunts, feeling that any pleasure so intensely felt must be somehow immoral, I would lie to my parents with, apparently, some early signs of creative invention, anyway with invariable success, to explain why my pocket money had so quickly disappeared and why I needed another shilling to indulge myself in the more conventional pleasures of childhood. My parents must have thought me a very greedy, careless and over-generous little boy (my three main excuses) but they never caught me in Shaftesbury Avenue.

"I went to Harrow in 1925, where, even in my first term, I seem to have risked punishment by deciding to write a play about the Borgias in hours in which I should have been learning about Homer. And, in that first term too, I discovered that in the school library they had the collected plays of Galsworthy, Barrie and Shaw and that, if one made a friend of the librarian (not too difficult) one could get that copy of *Plays Unpleasant* which was not supposed to be shown to boys under seventeen, and was kept under lock and key.

"The pleasure of seeing plays may have been great, but the pleasure of reading them, I found, was even greater. One could make one's own Gerald du Maurier and one's own Tallulah Bankhead, in, of course, the rough image of the famous author and playwrite, now scholar of Harrow, and rising thirteen-year-old author and playwright. (At Harrow they did at least teach you how to spell. Quite a lot of other things too, things which I absorbed or disregarded as they suited or didn't suit my ambitions. As a scholarship boy I was forced scholastically to progress rather faster than Sir Winston Churchill, who succeeded in spending at the same school 'three happy years as the very lowest boy in the very lowest class.' But our ideas about the uselessness of a classical education seem to have been identical.)

"On my paternally-planned course towards the British Embassy in Washington, or Paris, which was then thought slightly superior, I was made in 1930 to sit for a history scholarship at Trinity College Oxford and, to my parents' surprise and my own stupefaction, got one. To this day I don't know how. My idea had been, obviously, to fail, as the first move in the long battle to persuade my father that I would make a highly unsuitable diplomat, a moron fit only for the hazards of artistic creation. But I failed to fail—possibly because they confused my papers with a boy called Rattray who sat next to me and, judging from what I could read, had scholarship material stamped all over him. Or possibly because, as I had shed all inhibitions, I may—I don't remember now—have attacked Wellington's generalship, or asserted the claims of Philip of Spain against Elizabeth of England, or even risked a bash at Magna Carta; thereby, no doubt, gaining from the examiners a reputation for brilliant heterodoxy which I have not, unhappily, subsequently sustained.

"At Oxford I didn't fail to fail. I didn't need to. Having spent three years indulging in extra-curricular and almost exclusively theatrical activities, a play which I had written with a fellow undergraduate was accepted by an obscure London management and, after vicissitudes, achieved a West End production. This seemed sufficient excuse to come down from Oxford without a degree (I am still technically an undergraduate of Trinity College), issue a defiant manifesto to my father, and rent a studio flat in London to pursue my now determinate career.

"It wasn't sufficient excuse. The play was a flop and within three weeks I was back under the parental roof, penniless though not entirely penitent.

"My father bowed to fate. I was allowed a room to write in and two years probation before the threat of a 'proper occupation' need be realised. In this I was lucky. Most writers, I know, have perforce to begin part-time. I began whole-time and as the end of the probationary period drew near, much more than whole time. I was rescued by a hair's breadth from a fate worse than diplomacy by a comedy called *French Without Tears*.

"I am often described by critics as a playwright of the thirties. If they mean that in point of time they are wrong. *French Without Tears* was the only solo work of mine to be performed in the thirties. But if they mean it in point of style and approach they have, I suppose, a case. Professionalism is not now considered a virtue. It has become in drama synonymous with insincerity of aim (only in drama, it seems. The same criterion isn't yet applied to such self-avowed professional novelists as Graham Greene or Angus Wilson. But let that pass).

"So if I have to defend myself against the charge of professionalism, and I quite often do, I can only repeat that, although I didn't do much writing in the thirties, the thirties did inevitably condition my writing. It was a time of slump, jobs of all kinds were hard to come by and I had to make a career. We had no Royal Court Theatre, and no off-Broadway. No playwright then could make a name for himself by writing a series of distinguished failures at small outlying theatres, and capitalising that name profitably thereafter in other media. We had no television and films were made only in Hollywood, which wasn't in those days very interested in giving employment to distinguished failures.

"In the thirties a playwright without means, and I was emphatically that, had to please an audience or starve. (Or, worse still, get a job in a bank, if he could find one.) The choice was as marked as that.

TERENCE RATTIGAN

Small wonder that we who learnt our craft in that era abjured the perils of audience-baiting so blithely seized upon today by the Absurdists, the Alienators, the Anti-theatrists, the Artaudists, and others. We just weren't brave enough. But then we didn't have a Welfare State to look after us, either.

"So I plead guilty to the crime, several times committed and many more times attempted over the last thirty years, of barefaced audience-pleasing. But I plead on the whole not guilty to the charge of audience-wooing which, in my calendar, is worse than a crime. A blunder.

"As for audience-pleasing—well, audiences are, after all, pleased by many different kinds of plays. It has always been my hope to please them with the best that I am capable of, and it remains my hope."

As he says, Terence Rattigan began his theatrical career as an undergraduate, when he joined the Oxford University Dramatic Society, played a small part in John Gielgud's production of *Romeo and Juliet*, and saw his first play staged in both London and New York. This was *First Episode* (1933), "a loitering little piece of autobiographical hilarity about undergraduate life," written in collaboration with Philip Heimann. Over the next two years Rattigan wrote half a dozen plays that remained unproduced but taught him a great deal. In 1936 he found a suitable vehicle for his growing technical skill—the summer he had spent on a residential course in the South of France, learning the language in unwilling preparation for a diplomatic career. The result was *French Without Tears*, a sunny farce-comedy which derives much humor from national peculiarities, French and English, and turns on the machinations of a flirtatious female student who litters the Villa Maingot with youthful broken hearts until her victims conspire to teach her a lesson. It was an immediate and triumphant success, running for over one thousand performances in London, and subsequently playing in New York and all over Europe. It is still revived, as is the author's excellent movie version of the play.

In 1940, after a brief stint in the Foreign Office, Rattigan joined the Royal Air Force, in which he served as an air gunner on Atlantic U-boat patrols, rising to the rank of flight lieutenant before his release in 1945. He drew on his RAF experience in *Flare Path* (1942), a romantic drama which enjoyed a long run in London. It was followed by an even bigger success, the light comedy *While the Sun Shines* (1943), the second of Rattigan's plays to run for over a thousand performances. *Love in Idleness* (1944), starring Alfred Lunt and Lynn Fontanne, was another popular success in England and Europe, and also in New York, where it was staged as *O Mistress Mine*.

Although Rattigan was by this time solidly established in England as a master of the neatly constructed and good-mannered entertainments which then dominated the London stage, he had been rather coolly received by the American critics, who in general found his work "about as real—and as valuable—as stage money." They took a different view of *The Winslow Boy*, based on fact, about a father's long struggle, just before World War I, to clear his son of an accusation of petty theft. The play was welcomed as an intelligent, absorbing, and richly dramatic treatment of a serious and important theme. The London critics gave it the Ellen Terry award as the best play of 1946, while their New York colleagues found it the best foreign play of 1947; Howard Barnes called it "a work of stirring dimensions." *The Browning Version*, which brought Rattigan a second Ellen Terry award in 1948, was another popular and critical success. It is an extremely original, perceptive, and exact portrait of a failure—a schoolmaster cheated by his wife and generally despised, who nevertheless retains his own pedantic but scrupulous standards.

After *Adventure Story* (1949), a play about Alexander the Great, and the comedy *Who Is Sylvia?* (1950), Rattigan returned to a more serious theme with *The Deep Blue Sea* (1952), in which a woman is destroyed by her obsessive love for a drunken philanderer. Warmly praised in England, it seemed to most American reviewers no more than an excursion into "slick paper magazine fiction." *The Sleeping Prince*, a fanciful romance which starred Laurence Olivier and Vivien Leigh, was followed by *Separate Tables* (1955), two short plays connected by their setting—the dining room of a residential hotel. Both deal with the loneliness and frustration caused by the pressure of social conventions. *Separate Tables* was a major hit in London and was also well received in New York. "What makes these plays so engrossing," wrote Marya Mannes, "is Rattigan's complete command over his characters. . . . You care for Rattigan's lovers; it matters greatly from moment to moment what happens to them. This is, of course, the secret of good theatre."

Ross (1960), about Lawrence of Arabia, and *A Bequest to the Nation* (1970), a compassionate and powerful study of Nelson's infatuation with Emma Hamilton, were the most admired of Rattigan's later plays. He has written highly successful screen versions of many of his plays and a number of original scenarios, among them *The Way to the Stars*, *The Yellow Rolls-Royce*, and *The V.I.P*'s. He has also written several plays for television.

Rattigan believes that "from Aeschylus to Tennessee Williams, the only theatre that has ever mattered is the theatre of character and narrative." A statement along these lines, published in the *New Statesman* in 1950, drew a scathing reply from George Bernard Shaw, who defended the play of ideas and called Rattigan, amongst other things, "an irrational genius." In 1956, unrepentant, Rattigan reiterated his views in the New York *Herald Tribune*, welcoming "the death of the cult of the play of ideas and the re-emergence since the war, in Europe as in America, of the play that unashamedly says nothing—except possibly that human beings are strange creatures, and worth putting on the stage where they can be laughed at or cried over, as our pleasure takes us." Rattigan's rejoicing was premature; the same year John Osborne's *Look Back in Anger* ushered in a continuing revolution in the English theatre which has called into question not only the "well-made" play but the moral and intellectual assumptions it expresses. Many of Rattigan's plays have passed into the British repertoire, amateur and professional, but they remain there without the blessing of serious students of the contemporary theatre. Even his most substantial plays now seem to many critics bourgeois, complacent, and superficial. Rattigan replies that he does not write to please the critics, but for the "Aunt Ednas" in the audience. He remains an immensely accomplished craftsman, an exact if unprofound observer of character, and an absolute master of eminently speakable and agreeably witty dialogue; it seems unlikely that the present eclipse in his reputation will be permanent.

Terence Rattigan, a handsome and urbane bachelor, received the CBE in 1958 and a knighthood in 1971. He enjoys golf and watching cricket.

PRINCIPAL PUBLISHED WORKS: French Without Tears, 1937; Flare Path, 1942; While the Sun Shines, 1944; The Winslow Boy, 1946; Playbill (containing The Browning Version and Harlequinade), 1949; Adventure Story, 1950; Who Is Sylvia?, 1951; The Deep Blue Sea, 1952; The Sleeping Prince, 1954; Separate Tables, 1955; Variations on a Theme, 1958; Ross, 1962; Man and Boy, 1964; A Bequest to the Nation, 1971. Also Collected Plays, vols. 1 and 2, 1953; vol. 3, 1964.
ABOUT: Current Biography, 1956; Taylor, J. R. The Rise and Fall of the Well-Made Play, 1963; Who's Who, 1973; Who's Who in the Theatre, 1972. *Periodicals*—Commonweal November 30, 1956; Newsweek May 30, 1960; Theatre Arts August 1950, November 1956, April 1962; Time June 17, 1946.

RAVEN, SIMON (ARTHUR NOËL) (December 28, 1927–), English novelist and dramatist, writes: "Born in London of wealthy middle-class parents, I was educated at Charterhouse and King's College, Cambridge, in the Greek and Latin Classics. It was my early ambition to become a don (if only because my college was such a pleasant place to live in), and indeed in 1951, when I graduated Bachelor of Arts, I was awarded a Studentship to enable me to write a thesis in competition for a prize Fellowship. But although the subject which I had chosen was of interest (upper-class education in nineteenth century England), I neglected it in favour of a fatuous and newly found pretension to be a 'creative' writer, a pretension which was inflated by the publication, over my name, of several reviews in *The New Statesman* and *The Listener*.

"Since I had nothing to show after a year of 'research' except two unpublishable novels, I resigned my Studentship before I could be removed from it and then, in search of livelihood and change of air, joined the King's Shropshire Light Infantry with a Regular Commission, a proceeding which was easy enough on the strength of my degree and an Emergency Commission which I had held some years previously. There followed four or five amusing and informative years in Germany and Kenya; but I was soon compelled to resign my commission because of unpaid gambling debts which, had I continued in the service of Her Majesty, must have led to my Court Martial on charges of conduct unbecoming the character of an Officer and a Gentleman.

"Deprived of my military stipend and having no private means (for my wealthy middle-class parents were of economical disposition), I at first contrived some sort of living from work given me by kind-hearted literary editors who remembered the reviews which I had written while still at Cambridge. Then, early in 1958, I met an old acquaintance turned publisher who had the generosity and, as I like to think, the foresight to pay me ten pounds a week while I wrote a novel. The result was *The Feathers of Death*, a story of homosexual romance

SIMON RAVEN

in the Army, which was published early in 1959, winning me a certain notoriety, a substantial sum of money, invitations to contribute to journals of repute, and some valuable commissions from the BBC. Since then I have written a number of novels, plays and essays both long and short, most of which have been as well received as they deserve and probably rather better. Quite recently (1964) I embarked on a series of ten novels which are to describe the English upper-middle class in its frustration and decline from 1945 to the present day.

"I consider myself to be a professional writer, which is to say that I write for money. I enjoy my work, am at times absorbed by it, and I take a lot of trouble; but my essential aim is to do what I have been asked to do within the stipulated time, and to receive in return punctual payment in full. If no great book was ever written in this attitude of mind, it has nevertheless accounted for many excellent productions of the second class; and I am well aware that I do not belong in the first.

"I have been married and divorced, have fathered a son, have otherwise enjoyed a variety of sexual amusement, but now prefer the pleasures of the table to those of the bed. My other pleasures are reading (mainly history and philosophy), travel (mainly Mediterranean), and watching cricket. I believe in a first cause but not in a personal god. I mistrust all forms of technical progress or social change. I regard the 'equality of man' as a myth invented by those who, deficient whether in intelligence, money, or charm, understandably want compensation. I consider the system of Christian morality an insult to the intellect. I detest noise and set high value on good manners. I am unimpressed by virtue or enthusiasm. On balance, I find the world an entertaining place but shall be well content to leave it, holding with Horace that it is unseemly in the old and feeble to linger at the banquet, where they merely spoil the pleasure of other people."

Simon Raven is a romantic writer whose books celebrate the idea of honor, or lament its passing with an often perverse and outrageous savagery. The moral obligations once attached to privilege, now dissolved away in his opinion by egalitarianism, are discussed and colorfully illustrated in *The Decline of the Gentleman* and—scarcely less explicitly—in his novels and plays. Under the guise of an espionage thriller, *Brother Cain* "presents an elaborate dream sequence, a lament for the man of honor in a neo-Fascist world, and a homosexual guilt fantasy"; it was thought "an unwholesome, caddish, talented book" with "echoes of Daisy Ashford and Ian Fleming in the chilly, jolly tone." *Doctors Wear Scarlet*, which seemed to one critic "a shrill, sentimental, and ignorant salute to homosexuality and the cult of the vampire," struck Norman Shrapnel as a deliberately preposterous "allegory . . . about a man's soul" with "an uncommon devotion to traditional concerns like form and structure, amplitude of statement, precision of tone, and development of character."

Raven's social attitudes no doubt account for the hostility to his work of some members of the English literary establishment, one of whom suggested that he was unqualified because of "his attitude to people and writing talents" to attempt the ten-volume "Alms for Oblivion" sequence, planned as a record of the English upper-middle-class scene since the war. The accuracy of this judgment depends on the caliber of Raven's intentions—the sequence has never been less than entertaining. *Places Where They Sing*—to take one volume (the sixth) as an example—is about a student revolt at a Cambridge college. Its reviewer in the *Times Literary Supplement* said that it was "conceived partly as well-educated nonsense, in the Dorothy Sayers tradition, partly as a political fable. As usual, the right-wing elements (with whom the author's real sympathies lie) show up rather badly: most of them are shown to be effete and futile. Constable and Llewellyn, those engagingly arrogant Labour Party stalwarts, once again take responsibility for holding the fort against the ever-present menace of the Mob. . . . The pattern is well wrought . . . but only as a collage of odd juxtapositions which jar and startle."

The radio and television plays collected in *Royal Foundation* were called by John Mortimer exercises in "right-wing romance," of which the essence "is the belief that some organisation—the Club or the Regiment or the School or the Game—has a mystic importance greater than those who make use of it." Mortimer conceded that the plays were worked out with "Galsworthy-like precision" and had all the compulsion of good school stories. Raven has also made adaptations for television of Huxley's *Point Counter Point* and Trollope's Palliser novels and *The Way We Live Now*, and wrote the film *Unman, Wittering, and Zigo* (1971).

PRINCIPAL WORKS: *Novels*—The Feathers of Death, 1959; Brother Cain, 1959; Doctors Wear Scarlet, 1960; Close of Play, 1962. *Novels in the "Alms for Oblivion" sequence:* The Rich Pay Late, 1964; Friends in Low Places, 1965; The Sabre Squadron, 1966; Fielding Gray, 1967; The Judas Boy, 1968; Places Where They Sing, 1970; Sound the Retreat, 1971; Come Like Shadows, 1972. *Nonfiction*—The English Gentleman, 1961 (U.S., The Decline of the Gentleman); Boys Will Be Boys, 1963. *Plays*—Royal Foundation and Other Plays, 1966. *As editor*—The Best of Gerald Kersh, 1960.

ABOUT: Vinson, J. (ed.) Contemporary Novelists, 1972; Who's Who, 1973. *Periodicals*—Guardian November 11, 1960; April 19, 1972; New York Herald Tribune Book Review October 2, 1960; Observer May 8, 1966.

RAYMOND, ERNEST (December 31, 1888–), English novelist, has written over fifty books since *Tell England* appeared when he was thirty-four. The earlier part of his life is described in *The Story of My Days* (1968), a fascinating portrait of Victorian and Edwardian London which reads a great deal like one of his novels. Officially registered as the son of William and Florence Bell Raymond, he grew up in an oddly assorted London household which included Miss Emily Calder (known as "Auntie"), Major-General George Frederick Blake ("Dum"), and Dorothy Makepeace ("Dots"). Under the shadow of Auntie's frequent beatings, Raymond as a child became "more and more a shy and dreaming solitary." Gradually, his suspicions about his birth were confirmed by devious and secretive detective work, which established that both he and Dots were the General's children, conceived the same year by different mothers. Dots' mother was Auntie Emily Calder; his own mother was Emily's sister, Ida.

It emerged that Raymond had been born in Switzerland and brought to England about 1891. His mother settled in London near the General's household, and Raymond visited her frequently, though he was never greatly attached to her. She admitted their relationship on her deathbed; his father never did. Raymond was nevertheless devoted to the General, who figures under various guises in a number of his novels. Dum is most fully and faithfully drawn as Sir Edmund Earlwin in *Newtimber Lane* (1933), which also reconstructs his meeting with the Calder family in Boulogne and his subsequent dealings with them.

Raymond was educated at Colet Court and

went on at twelve to St. Paul's, a famous London public school. Many of his books draw on his years there, and *Mr. Olim* (1961) is a notable portrait of his brilliant and cantankerous headmaster. A sensitive and lonely boy, Raymond read widely but desultorily until, in 1901, he discovered *The Pickwick Papers* and was seized by an ambition to write similar books. It was an ambition, he says, in which an important ingredient was "a longing to win the applause of the world, and of posterity." That applause was still twenty years away.

In 1904 meanwhile, the General died and Raymond was forced to leave St. Paul's for a cheaper school. A year later, at seventeen, he went to work, first as a clerk in the Army and Navy Stores, then as a prep school teacher in Eastbourne (1908–1911) and Bath (1911–1912). At Bath he caught "the splendid fever of Anglo-Catholicity" and decided on the priesthood. He had been an indifferent student at St. Paul's but emerged as a brilliant one at Chichester Theological College, aided by a photographic memory, and spurred on by "a need to flatten out" the scornful Calder sisters. He passed first in his class, and, entering the priesthood in 1915, immediately volunteered for Gallipoli as an army chaplain, arriving there in August 1915. He subsequently served in Egypt, France, Mesopotamia, Persia, and Russia.

Raymond's experiences at St. Paul's and in the war provided the theme of his first novel, *Tell England* (1922), about three boys from an English public school, all of whom are eventually killed in action. The section about their schooldays, begun when Raymond was eighteen, is extremely shapeless and sentimental; the later part is much stronger and rich in movement and vivid description, though the sentimentality still predominates. The critics were divided, some calling the novel grossly unrealistic, "the most nauseating book to have come out of the war," others praising it as a work of great beauty, charm, and nobility. The author himself came to side with his hostile critics, saying that he could "almost cry aloud in distress" at its naïveté, piety, and facility, and "the indubitable but wholly unconscious homosexuality in it." Whatever its failings, *Tell England* was immensely successful and popular, and is by no means forgotten. In 1965 it reached its fortieth printing.

After the war, Raymond became a curate at Brighton Parish Church, but found it increasingly difficult to accept the miraculous aspects of Christianity. In 1923 he made the painful decision to leave holy orders. Such a crisis of conscience is the subject of *Wonderlight* (1924), and a number of Raymond's other novels center on clergymen, like the hypocritical canon who redeems himself by lying to save his protégée from a murder charge in *The Witness of Canon Welcome* (1950); and the devoted Anglo-Catholic priest Father Dawbeny, whose dedicated life in the London slums is the subject of *The Chalice and the Sword* (1952).

ERNEST RAYMOND

Sixteen of Raymond's novels comprise "A London Gallery," depicting half a century of London life. The most notable of these is the second volume in the series, *We the Accused* (1935). It is "a delicate, profound and convincing study" of a totally unremarkable man—his unhappy childhood, his unsuccessful career as a teacher, his unsatisfactory marriage, and then the late love affair which step by step turns this kindly, ineffectual man into a murderer. The manhunt and the trial which follow were less successfully managed than the earlier sections, but Frank Swinnerton called the novel "emotional, powerful, and highly dramatic," and most critics found it free of the sentimentality and facetiousness which so often mar Raymond's books. Several readers were reminded of Dreiser's *An American Tragedy*. It received the Book Guild's gold medal and is undoubtedly Raymond's best book.

Many of Ernest Raymond's other novels are chronicles of family life, often centering on one character whose life story is traced from birth to death. He retains a large following among readers who relish the skill and abundance of his character drawing, the vividness of his descriptive writing, and his strong plots. Indeed, when his novels began to appear in the United States in the early 1970s, after an absence from American publishing lists of some thirty years, these qualities (combined with the prevalent nostalgia for lost innocence) brought this "veteran spellbinder" at once onto the bestseller lists.

Raymond has written two plays, *The Berg*, produced in London's West End in 1929, and *The Multabello Road* (1933). His own life story, begun in *The Story of My Days*, is continued in *Please You, Draw Near*, covering the years from 1922 to 1968, and *Good Morning, Good People*. The latter, "more a series of spiritual reflections than formal autobiography, describes his return to the Church of England as what he calls "a learning layman." He is also the author of biographies of Keats and Shelley, the Brontës, and St. Francis, and of two volumes of essays. Raymond has been married twice: to Zoe Doucett, by whom he had two children before the marriage was dissolved, and to Diana Young, who now writes under the name of Diana Raymond. They have one son and live in Hampstead, London. Raymond lists his recreations as climbing, traveling, and watching cricket. He became president of the Dickens Fellowship in 1971 and received an OBE in 1972.

PRINCIPAL WORKS: *Novels in "A London Gallery"*: Child of Norman's End, 1934; We, the Accused, 1935; The Marsh, 1937; A Song of the Tide, 1940; Was There Love Once?, 1942; The Corporal of the Guard, 1943; For Them That Trespass, 1944; The Kilburn Tale, 1947; Gentle Greaves, 1949; The Witness of Canon Welcome, 1950; A Chorus Ending, 1951; The Chalice and the Sword, 1952; To the Wood No More, 1954; The Lord of Wensley, 1956; The Old June Weather, 1957; The City and the Dream, 1958. *Other novels*—Tell England, 1922; Once in England (*trilogy comprising* A Family that Was, The Jesting Army, *and* Mary Leith) 1932. *Travel and biography* — In the Steps of St. Francis, 1938; In the Steps of the Brontës, 1948; Two Gentlemen of Rome, the Story of Keats and Shelley, 1952; Paris, City of Enchantment, 1961. *Essays, etc.*—The Shout of the King, 1924; Through Literature to Life, 1928; (with Patrick Raymond) Back to Humanity, 1945. *Plays*—The Berg, 1929; The Multabello Road, 1933. *Autobiography*—The Story of My Days: An Autobiography, 1888–1922, 1968; Please You, Draw Near: Autobiography, 1922–1969; Good Morning, Good People, 1970.

ABOUT: Raymond, E. The Story of my Days, 1968 (and subsequent volumes of autobiography); Vinson, J. (ed.) Contemporary Novelists, 1972; Who's Who, 1973.

"MISS READ" (pseudonym of Dora Jessie Saint) (April 17, 1913–), English novelist, was born in the London suburb of Norwood, the daughter of Arthur and Grace (Read) Shafe. She attended a country school in Kent at the age of seven and has, she says, been "besotted with village schools" ever since. Thus indoctrinated, her choice of teaching as a career came naturally. She went to a secondary school in Bromley, Kent, and on to a teacher training college in Cambridge, graduating in 1933. Thereafter she taught in infant and junior schools in Middlesex until 1940, when she married a schoolmaster, D. E. J. Saint, who took her to Berkshire. She taught there also, from time to time, in a substitute capacity.

MISS READ

Mrs. Saint began to write after World War II, and for four years was a regular contributor under her own name to *Punch*—a "wonderful" phase, she says, "and very good discipline." She also wrote for the BBC—scripts for school broadcasts and play adaptations—and did other journalistic chores. "Miss Read" owes her existence to an article by Mrs. Saint in the London *Observer*, which attracted the attention of a publisher, who suggested a book.

The result was *Village School*, an affectionately ironic account of a year of "outings, festivals, quarrels, and friendships" in a village in southern England, as seen by "Miss Read," headmistress of Fairacre's two-room school. Fairacre, according to Mrs. Saint, is so "purely imaginary" that she had to write the book with a sketch map in front of her. She produced in this way a portrait of rural education so accurate and universal that an American reader said "her account would need but slight change" to fit the school at which he had once taught on the other side of the Atlantic. Almost all of the book's reviewers on both sides of the Atlantic praised its unsentimental charm and grace, its "seemingly effortless literary skill." The *New Yorker*'s reviewer complained about "short, lumpy tracts on rural education," and "a leafy placidity that embraces death and sack races with identical fervor," conceding nevertheless that Miss Read possessed "unerring intuition about human frailty, a healthy irony, and, surprisingly, an almost beery sense of humor." An equally anonymous but less cantankerous writer in the *Times Literary Supplement* called her portraits of Fairacre "delightful" and said: "They emerge gradually like things seen on a slow walk when children, lagging behind, force the adult to pause before what might otherwise have had only a cursory glance." Several critics thought the book had the makings of a minor classic.

Two sequels followed—*Village Diary* and *Storm in the Village*—which had scarcely less success than *Village School.* Mrs. Saint's other adult books, some of them set in Fairacre, others in Thrush Green (another fictional village), or elsewhere, are for the most part more conventionally novelistic in form. Critics have tended on the whole to find them less pleasing than the first trilogy—more unabashedly romantic, less carefully written. For some admirers of "Miss Read" however, "even at her second best she has much to offer." The author has also written several children's books.

Mrs. Saint lives near Newbury, in Berkshire, where she is a justice of the peace. She has a daughter, now grown up. Her interests include the theatre, music, reading, and wildlife.

PRINCIPAL WORKS: *Fiction*—Village School, 1955; Village Diary, 1957; Storm in the Village, 1958; Thrush Green, 1959; Fresh from the Country, 1960; Winter in Thrush Green, 1961; Miss Clare Remembers, 1962; Over the Gate, 1964; The Market Square, 1966; Village Christmas, 1966; The Howards of Caxley, 1967; Fairacre Festival, 1968; News from Thrush Green, 1970; Emily Davis, 1971; Tyler's Row, 1972; The Christmas Mouse, 1973. *Nonfiction*—Miss Read's Country Cooking, 1969.
ABOUT: Contemporary Authors 13–14, 1965.

REDGROVE, PETER (WILLIAM) (January 2, 1932–), English poet, was born at Kingston-on-Thames, Surrey. He was educated at Taunton School, Somerset, and at Queens College, Cambridge University. At university he read Natural Science, and this is important in his poetry which, he says, is "like crystallography in a way, giving shape to experience." It was as an undergraduate that Redgrove began to write, since, as he puts it, "it wasn't until I started falling in love that I realised that crystallography just wasn't enough to express the sum of human experience." Though "a clumsy scientist . . . cut off from any poetic or literary set at Cambridge," he started the poetry magazine *Delta* and became closely associated with "the Group." This was launched in 1955 by Philip Hobsbaum as a reaction against the so-called "Movement," and continued in London as a forum where poems were analyzed and discussed. Other prominent members included the poets Edward Lucie-Smith and George MacBeth.

When Redgrove came down from Cambridge he worked variously as a research chemist, as a teacher, as a journalist, as a reader for the BBC, and in advertising, writing brochures about scientific products. In 1961 he won a Fulbright award and went to the United States as visiting poet at Buffalo University, New York. He returned to England the following year, and from 1962 to 1965

PETER REDGROVE

was Gregory Fellow in Poetry at Leeds University. There he instituted a writing seminar modeled on certain of his courses at Buffalo and on the procedures of the Group. He has read his poetry and lectured widely in England and the United States. Since 1966 he has been a lecturer in complementary studies at Falmouth School of Art in Cornwall.

Redgrove's verse, like that of many of the Group poets, is characterized by a brutality of both matter and manner; as one critic says, it is always "sweating, guzzling, peering, prodding, holding an enormous magnifying glass up to nature." He dwells on the grotesque and ugly—squashed insects, insane decaying trees, mud and death and ghosts. His poem "The Collector" could well refer in some respects to himself: ". . . with reasonable curiosity he saw / Crows fall from the sky, lilac tongues / Of death in the square-cut hedge: such omens / were full of interest. . . ." Though critics have discovered affinities with Wallace Stevens, Rimbaud, and Hopkins (among others), Redgrove's voice is his own. His most distinctive attribute is an immensely wide-ranging, fecund, and violent vocabulary, which has led some critics to praise his mastery in forcing tactile and kinetic effects from the language, and others to accuse him of "rhetorical over-kill" and the whipping up of factitious excitement. It is also said that Redgrove's sense of rhythm is uncertain, that his themes are limited and repetitious, and that only a minority of his poems succeed as structurally convincing wholes.

M. L. Rosenthal thinks that "the final referent of all of Redgrove's quick, tormented concreteness is probably the sense of private humiliation at the nastiness of physical existence." But John Barnard has suggested that Redgrove's choice of themes reflects a central concern with the "metamorphic economy" of nature—its constant transformations and renewals of matter and energy, and that his prodigal and sometimes confusing use of synesthetic effects reflects this premise. This view goes a long way towards answering those critics who demand more exactness and self-discipline of Redgrove, and supports those who, like John Fuller, believe that "no other poet shows life so intensely in terms of its basic forces, or in the context of a scientific education has discovered poetry so consumingly as a 'new sense' or 'a textbook of the soul.'"

Redgrove's first work of fiction, *In the Country of the Skin*, is not a conventional novel but a kind of extended prose poem in which the author explores his own psychological and sexual compulsions and confusions, seeking to discover and come to terms with his true nature. Much of the book's surreal imagery derives from a period in Redgrove's life when, suffering from what was diagnosed as "incipient schizophrenia," he experienced fifty insulin coma shocks, "fifty deaths." A reviewer in the *Times Literary Supplement*, praising the courage with which Redgrove confronts the darkest regions of his own personality, concluded: "His imagery is often surprising and beautiful; it is often obscure too, and sometimes impenetrably so. In any case, it has a brilliance and intensity one cannot but recommend." The book received the *Guardian* Fiction Prize.

A large squarish man, Peter Redgrove is very conscious of growing older and larger, and seeks redemption in judo classes. In conversation he is said to be easy and unpretentious but to dislike talking about his poetry. He is married to the sculptor Barbara Redgrove, and has three children.

PRINCIPAL WORKS: *Poetry*—The Collector, 1960; The Nature of Cold Weather, 1961; At the White Monument, 1963; The Force, 1966; Work in Progress, 1969; Dr. Faust's Sea-Spiral Spirit, 1972; Three Pieces for Voices, 1972; (with Penelope Shuttle) The Hermaphrodite Album, 1973. *Fiction*—In the Country of the Skin, 1973.

ABOUT: Contemporary Authors 4, 1963; Murphy, R. (ed.) Contemporary Poets of the English Language, 1970; Rosenthal, M. L. The New Poets, 1967; Schmidt, M. and Lindop, G. (eds.) British Poetry Since 1960, 1972; Thomas, D. M. *introduction to* Work in Progress, 1969. *Periodicals*—Books and Bookmen March 1967; The Guardian December 16, 1966; London Magazine April 1962, December 1963, March 1967; The Review April 1967; Times Literary Supplement December 12, 1963; February 23, 1967; August 11, 1972; March 23, 1973.

REED, HENRY (February 22, 1914–), English poet, translator, and radio dramatist, was born in Birmingham, the son of Henry and Mary Ann (Bell) Reed. He was educated at King Edward VI School in Birmingham, and at Birmingham University, where he became one of a circle of writers and artists that included W. H. Auden, Louis MacNeice, and Walter Allen, the painter John Melville, and the sculptor Gordon Herrick.

Reed had begun to write at school, and when he left the university in 1937 he began his career as a freelance writer and journalist, eking out his income with a little teaching. His early poetry, like that of his friends, was deeply involved with the political events of the time, the war in Spain, the refugees and freedom fighters. Simple and conversational in diction, gentle in tone, it achieved an elegiac quality by the use of murmured refrains and subtly controlled vowel sounds. The effect can be very moving, as in "Hiding Beneath the Furze," where the refrain "And this can never happen, ever again," referring to the horrors of war, takes its sad irony from the fact that the poem was written in the autumn of 1939, as World War II began.

In 1942, after a year in the army, Reed was released to work in the Foreign Office. This period of intense emotional strain produced some of his best verse, collected in his only volume of poetry, *A Map of Verona*. The book demonstrates Reed's skill in a great variety of modes, from the stately formality of "Philoctetes" and "Tintagel" to "Chard Whitlow," which Kenneth Allott described as "the wickedest and funniest parody of Mr. Eliot known to me." Reed will no doubt be best remembered for "Naming of Parts," "Judging Distances," and the other poems which make up "The Lessons of War."

The sequence is based on Reed's army training as an officer cadet in the spring and summer of 1941. The tragic absurdity of training for war and death in the midst of the beauty and fecundity of an English pastoral scene is brilliantly pointed in these poems, with an effect that is sometimes ruefully funny, sometimes sharply poignant, and sometimes both together. In "Judging Distances" the dehumanized instructor, completing his lecture, addresses his cadets: "I am sure that's quite clear; and suppose, for the sake of example, / The one at the end, asleep, endeavours to tell us / What he sees over there to the west, and how far away, / After first having come to attention. There to the west, / On the fields of summer the sun and the shadows bestow / Vestments of purple and gold. // The still white dwellings are like a mirage in the heat, / And under the swaying elms a man and a woman / Lie gently together. / Which is, perhaps, only to say / That there is a row of houses to the left of arc, / And that under some poplars a pair of what appear to be humans / Appear to be loving." Kenneth Allott thought these "among the best and most intelligent poems produced during the war."

Since the war Henry Reed has devoted himself

principally to radio writing. His much-admired adaptation of *Moby Dick*, broadcast by the BBC in 1946 and published in 1947, compresses the story line but retains the emotional and philosophical range of the story, as well as Melville's naturally dramatic rhetoric. It was Reed also who introduced to English-speaking theatre and radio audiences the work of the Italian dramatist Ugo Betti.

Reed's original work for radio includes such notable verse plays as the autobiographical *Return to Naples* and the impressionistic *Streets of Pompeii*. His "Hilda Tablet" series, produced by Douglas Cleverdon for the BBC's Third Programme, affectionately satirizes English upper-class and intellectual life between the wars—the earnest Socialists, the Blimpish soldiers, Herbert Read, Virginia Woolf, and Edith Sitwell, and all the eccentrics and dilettantes in which the 1930s were so rich. These amiable parodies sustained a level of real wit and knowledge seldom equaled in the more abrasive satires that were such a feature of British broadcasting in the 1960s.

Henry Reed has also been active as a reviewer, though none of his criticism has appeared in book form except his useful British Council pamphlet *The Novel Since 1939*. He has published a number of prose translations, notably of Flaubert.

PRINCIPAL WORKS: A Map of Verona, 1946; Moby Dick: A Radio Play, 1947; The Novel Since 1939, 1947; The Streets of Pompeii (six plays set in Italy), 1971; Hilda Tablet and Others (four plays), 1971.

ABOUT: Allott, K. (ed.) Penguin Book of Contemporary Verse, 1960; Taylor, J. R. Anger and After, 1962; Who's Who, 1973. *Periodicals*—Commonweal January 16, 1948; New York Times December 28, 1947; Times Literary Supplement May 11, 1946; November 1, 1947; December 6, 1947.

JAMES REEVES

REEVES, JAMES (July 1, 1909–), English poet, critic, anthologist, and editor, writes: "I was born in North London. My father, a conscientious company secretary, and my mother, an ex-teacher, were active Nonconformists: among the influences which were formative in my early years were plain living and high thinking, Ruskin and Browning, total abstention and the Hampstead Garden Suburb, where my education began at an excellent Montessori School. Except one, all my schools were good. I underwent all the disadvantages which a potential creative writer can get from almost complete educational happiness. I went to Stowe and Cambridge on open scholarships. I am married and have two daughters and one son.

"School teaching and, later, teacher training occupied the greater part of my time until I was forty-three. Then deteriorating eyesight and the discovery that I had only one life caused me to break out as a full-time professional author. The comparative tardiness of this decision may have been due to a basic lack of self-confidence. I have never been affected by a burning desire to tell the world anything. On the other hand, an early compulsive obsession with poetry was connected with the need to work out problems of personal emotion and introspection by writing poems. Towards this activity most of my writing in other fields has been directed. In editorial work and in writing for children, it is the poetic in literature and life which has attracted my attention. Under the heading 'poetic' I include all those apparently chance manifestations of grace, beauty, pathos, humour and delight which arise from things natural or made, from human behaviour and personality, thought and feeling. Of these manifestations poems are the realisation as language. Form in poetry is the means by which this realisation is given permanence. According to this view poems are not contrived artifacts, but rather the accidents of fusion between language and circumstance occurring unpredictably in a context of poetic activity. Writing for children and writing about literature demand a continuous exercise of the imagination, a scrupulous insistence on truth of feeling and propriety of language.

"My conviction that truth of feeling and propriety of language are crucial for a writer of poems in English drew my attention towards the traditional verse of the so-called folk songs. It is the comparative honesty of this material, as contrasted with the comparative dishonesty with which it has been presented to a sophisticated public, that gave this editorial work its relevance to what I found I was trying to do as a poet. Authenticity of feeling, warmth without sentimentality, freshness of expression without idiosyncrasy—these are what I would look for in a poem, whether by me or by anyone else. Such a search is not easy in a context of shrill public utterance and competitive exhibitionism; so that what is to me the authentic voice of poetry today is apt to be called, if it is noticed at all, 'quiet,' 'haunted,' or even 'naïve.' "

The Natural Need, Reeves's first book of poems, was published by Robert Graves's Seizin Press in Majorca. According to Graves, Yeats excluded Reeves from *The Oxford Book of Modern Verse* because he was "too reasonable, too truthful" (the Muse preferring "gay, warty lads"). Kenneth Allott, who told this story with indignation, conceded that James Reeves is "a quiet poet, not much given to self-assertion." Reeves, who has written much "delicious" verse for children, has been called in the *Times Literary Supplement* "essentially a lyric poet, in whom the ironies reverberate through a refinement of private perception rather than through a sense of social discrepancies . . . he has survived fashions by an insistent commonsense control and modulation of rhetoric; his diction always gives the *impression* of natural speech and his structures appear tough without flaunting density or knotty argument." Most of Reeves's poems are rooted, as he himself says, "in the particular and the immediate," and short, though he has tried his hand at verse plays. He has acknowledged the influence of Graves, among other poets, and also, in some way, of music (which provides his principal recreation).

Reeves is one of England's best and most prolific editors and anthologists; only a selection of his work in these fields is listed below. As general editor of the Heinemann "Poetry Bookshelf" series, he himself made the selections from D. H. Lawrence, Donne, Hopkins, Clare, Browning, Emily Dickinson, and Coleridge. His *Understanding Poetry* was called "a beautifully clear and concise book" which "stands worthily beside" such predecessors as C. Day Lewis's *Poetry for You.*

PRINCIPAL WORKS: *Poetry*—The Natural Need, 1936; The Imprisoned Sea, 1949; The Wandering Moon (for children), 1950; The Password, 1952; The Blackbird in the Lilac (for children), 1952; (with Edward Ardizzone) Prefabulous Animiles (for children), 1957; The Talking Skull, 1958; The Idiom of the People: English Traditional Verse from the Mss. of Cecil Sharp, 1959; The Everlasting Circle: English Traditional Verse from the Mss. of S. Baring-Gould, H. E. D. Hammond and G. B. Gardiner, 1960; Collected Poems 1929–1959, 1960; The Questioning Tiger, 1964; Selected Poems, 1967; Subsong, 1969; Poems and Paraphrases, 1972; Complete Poems for Children, 1973. *Prose for Children*—English Fables and Fairy Stories, 1954; Pigeons and Princesses, 1956; Mulbridge Manor, 1958; (as ed.) A Golden Land, 1958; Exploits of Don Quixote, 1959; Fables from Aesop, 1961; Sailor Rumbelow and Britannia, 1962; The Strange Light, 1964 Heroes and Monsters: Greek Myths for Children, 1969; The Angel and the Donkey, 1969; Mr. Horrox and the Grath, 1969; The Cold Flame, 1970; Maildun the Voyager, 1971; How the Moon Began, 1972; The Path of Gold, 1972; The Voyage of Odysseus, 1973. *Criticism*—The Critical Sense, 1956; Teaching Poetry, 1958; A Short History of English Poetry, 1961; Understanding Poetry, 1965; Commitment to Poetry (essays), 1969; (with Martin Seymour-Smith) Inside Poetry, 1970; How to Write Poems for Children, 1971.

ABOUT: Allott, K. (ed.) Penguin Book of Contemporary Verse, 1962; Murphy, R. (ed.) Contemporary Poets of the English Language, 1970; Orr, P. (ed.) The Poet Speaks, 1966; Who's Who, 1973. *Periodicals*—Guardian July 14, 1969; Times Literary Supplement November 19, 1964.

REID, ALASTAIR (March 22, 1926–), Scottish poet, essayist, and translator, was born in Whithorn, Scotland, one of the four children of William Arnold Reid, a clergyman, and Marion (Wilson) Reid. He spent most of his childhood on the Isle of Arran, off the west coast of Scotland, where his father became the minister. In *Passwords*, Reid says that the family was not "particularly religious—instead we were a fairly standard mixture of good and bad, wild and warm, lucky and terrified, like all children. God we knew as a friend of *our* father, his Boss in some incalculable way; and though a goodly company of angels and prophets ran through our dreams, they seemed no more real or awesome than Hamlet or the Bad Brownies."

After studies at home and in the local school, Reid went to the University of St. Andrews, near Dundee, from which he graduated with an honors degree in philosophy. As an undergraduate, he published his first poems in Scottish literary magazines. During World War II, he served from 1943 to 1946 with the Royal Navy and left Scotland for the first time: "A spell at sea in the East gave me my first taste of strangeness and anonymity." After the war, he visited the United States "out of curiosity," and has since lived there "off and on," although he later acquired a longing for Europe, and for Spain in particular. He now has a house in Barcelona where he lives for about six months of the year.

Reid taught at Sarah Lawrence College in Bronxville, New York, from 1951 to 1955. His essays and short articles soon began to appear in such magazines as the *New Yorker*, the *Atlantic Monthly*, and *Encounter*, and in 1953 he published his first book of poetry, *To Lighten My House*. Another volume of verse, *Oddments, Inklings, Omens, Moments*, appeared in 1959. Reid's poetry is characterized by his delight in language, and above all in the sounds of words—in rhyme, alliteration, and onomatopoeia. A line like "grudges long hidden in their old throats" in "Frog Dream" perfectly evokes the sound of frogs croaking, and the same poem illustrates Reid's skill in off-rhymes: "Nightlong, frogs in the pool / croak out calamity till, wakeful, / I interpret each crooked syllable."

ALASTAIR REID

John Thompson has spoken of Reid's poetry as "modest, cheerful, and trivial," but Thom Gunn, conceding that Reid writes light verse, adds that "it is excellent light verse."

Of Reid's several books for children, the best known is *Ounce, Dice, Trice*. Illustrated by Ben Shahn, it was designed as an introduction to the attractions of language for young people, but has delighted many adults as well. These little essays range from whimsical musings about the personalities of the letters of the alphabet to a collection of unusual and marvelously apt words like "gnurr," which means the fluff that accumulates in pockets. And the book includes this preposterously long palindrome: "T. Eliot, top bard, notes putrid tang emanating, is sad. I'd assign it a name: 'Gnat dirt upset on drab pot toilet.' "

Reid's essays—mostly from the *New Yorker*—about the joys and hazards of being a foreigner in such places as Madrid, Gibraltar, and Barcelona, are collected in *Passwords*, along with a number of poems. Godfrey John, reviewing the book in the *Christian Science Monitor*, said: "Reid writes with the detachment of the historian and the intimacy of the diarist. His desire above all things is to preserve a clear eye. We find a kind of higher journalism in which objectivity is enriched by a ready sympathy with people and with language. Nothing ever remains at the level of mere observation."

In view of this "sympathy with people and with language," it is not surprising that Reid is greatly admired as a translator. He received Guggenheim Fellowships in 1956–1957 and 1957–1958, and is a *New Yorker* staff writer. Reid is married and has one son. He considers himself a "foreigner"—a professional traveler whose passport description as "a writer" serves as "a useful cloak for [his] curiosity." For Reid, poems are "the consequences of the odd epiphanies which from time to time miraculously happen; prose I keep for a calmer, more reflective everyday attention to the world."

PRINCIPAL WORKS: *Poetry*—To Lighten My House, 1953; Oddments, Inklings, Omens, Moments, 1959. *Essays*—Passwords: Places, Poems, Preoccupations, 1963. *For children*—I Will Tell You of a Town, 1956; Fairwater, 1957; Allth, 1958; Ounce, Dice, Trice, 1958; Supposing, 1960; Uncle Timothy's Traviata, 1967; A Balloon for a Blunderbuss, 1961. *As translator*—We Are Many: Poems by Pablo Neruda, 1967.

ABOUT: Contemporary Authors 7–8, 1963; Reid, A. Passwords, 1963; Ward, M. E. and Marquardt, D. A. Authors of Books for Young People, 1967. *Periodicals*—Christian Science Monitor December 5, 1963; Mademoiselle August 1953; Poetry November 1959; Times Literary Supplement December 4, 1959; May 20, 1960; Yale Review June 1959.

"RENAULT, MARY" (pseudonym of Mary Challans) (September 4, 1905–), English novelist living in South Africa, writes: "I was born in London, where my father, a doctor, had a busy practice on the margin of the East End and the outer suburbs. My two earliest ambitions were to write, and to live outside a city. My first novel, a Western, was begun at eight years old. Having packed all the action into Chapter I, I left it unfinished. It never occurred to me to wind it up as a short story. I must have known the novel was my length.

"My first school, a homely local prep., was coeducational. Though my relationship with the boys was strictly that of an honorary boy, I missed it greatly when transferred to a conventional girls' boarding school. Later, the exploration of a well-stocked school library kept me happy. I discovered for myself first Malory, then a good translation of Plato, and read—for the story—the whole of Spenser's *Faerie Queene*. Innocent of its barbarities, for some time I regarded the mediaeval period as a golden age. With a little more maturity, I turned to the Greeks.

"I read English at Oxford. Most women graduates then went into teaching, but I distrusted it (and still do) as a writer's bread and butter; it digs too deep into the sources of creation. I took a placid clerical job, and produced a naive and earnest novel, beaming with ignorance, which happily no one did me the disservice of publishing. I decided to write nothing more for three years and train as a hospital nurse. This was one of the most valuable experiences of my life. After it I took another quiet job and wrote my first published novel, *Promise of Love*.

"This brought me in enough to live and write on; but then came the war, and I was back in nursing for the duration. The two books I managed

MARY RENAULT

to turn out during those years suffered from interruption and fatigue, and show no advance on the first. One, however, sold film rights and gave me independence. The Mediterranean being closed by currency restrictions, I went with a friend to see South Africa (then governed by the English, not the Afrikaner group) and have lived there ever since.

"There is here no room to explain how the short but complex story of South Africa illuminates world history in so many of its phases. At all events, when re-reading the story of the Peloponnesian War I no longer felt that insulation from the past which is imposed by today's megalopolitan societies. I now find it one of the most alarming facts of our time that so much power lies in the hands of men thus insulated, who are scarcely aware how great a majority of mankind still lives outside the capsule.

"One of the first results of leaving it is the knowledge that every phase of man's development, from the neolithic up, exists in the present, defying formulae; the only bridge is goodwill. The lesson of Africa, as of all past life if we could return to share it, is that the typical is a fiction, that generalisations are dangerous lies, that the universals of human nature are perennial, but the moulds into which it is poured constantly changing; in the words of Herakleitos, 'You cannot step twice into the same river.'

"As a historical novelist I have a powerful horror of exploiting the dead; either for sensationalism, or to force false parallels from their lives in the service of some end preferred to truth—the real meaning of 'commital.' Full knowledge of them is impossible; but I don't think this exempts the novelist at all from the duty to respect what truth he knows; truth is a continuum and is never without relevance. I have tried to fill in the gaps, but never knowingly falsified; my imaginary characters have invented names. I would rather approach the graves of our forebears upon earth as a guardian and servant, than as a tomb-robber.

"I have always tried to avoid appearing anywhere as a literary personality, probably the most insidious way in which a writer can waste his time and dissipate his creative energies. Interest in the worker takes meaning only from the quality of the work, which a lifetime is too short to learn. Vanity and idle curiosity are corruptions which feed on one another; I believe every artist will do better to resist them."

Mary Renault is of Huguenot stock through her father, and a descendant on her mother's side of the seventeenth century Nonconformist scholar and divine Richard Baxter. She was educated at Clifton High School, Bristol, and at St. Hugh's College, Oxford (where she produced quantities of verse), and did her nursing training at Radcliffe Infirmary in Oxford.

Promise of Love, like generations of slighter fictions, describes the progress of a love affair between a trainee nurse and a young doctor in an English provincial hospital. The result, in Miss Renault's hands, is not a romantic entertainment but a shrewd and often moving study of character, and of the tensions created when a private and anarchic emotion develops in a public and tightly ordered institution. There is, as one reviewer wrote, "a fusion between background and personal drama, between inner and outer reality, which enriches and dignifies both." The assurance and flexibility of Miss Renault's style were warmly commended, and Lewis Gannett found a "shining, breathless intensity" in this first book which made it "one of the distinguished novels of 1939."

Similar qualities marked *Kind Are Her Answers*, another love story with a medical background. Miss Renault herself believes that this book "suffered from interruption and fatigue," and indeed some readers thought it shallower and less original than her first novel. It had its admirers nevertheless, and Rosamond Lehmann found "an un-English physical directness" in its treatment of love, "a tremendous feminine vitality" in its style. Four more contemporary novels followed, all concerned with one aspect or another of love. One of these, *Return to Night*, won a Metro-Goldwyn-Mayer contest at the end of the war and, though it was never filmed, brought its author a prize of one hundred and fifty thousand dollars and financial independence. *The Charioteer* (1953), a sharply realized portrait of a young British soldier and his attempt to reconcile his homosexuality with his moral standards, was the last of Miss Renault's six contemporary novels. They established her as an extremely attractive and likable writer, of great ability and greater promise.

This promise was fully redeemed only when she turned away from her own direct observation of life to begin, on a much larger canvas, her brilliant and tough-minded reconstructions of life in ancient Greece. *The Last of the Wine* is set during the Third Peloponnesian War. It is narrated by a fictional character, Alexias, and describes his daily life in Athens, his views of his master Socrates and of such other figures as Alcibiades and Phaedo, his love affair with his friend Lysis, and his later experience of war against Sparta. The critical excitement that greeted this book was succinctly expressed by a reviewer in the *Times Literary Supplement*, who called it "a superb historical novel" and went on: "The writing is Attic in quality, unforced, clear, delicate. The characterization is uniformly successful and, most difficult of all, the atmosphere of Athens is realized in masterly fashion."

The King Must Die, which followed, is regarded by many as the most brilliantly imagined and perfectly achieved of Miss Renault's novels. It is a retelling of the Theseus legends, up to his slaying of the Minotaur, narrated as by Theseus himself. The hero is demythologized into a shrewd but unsophisticated Bronze Age warrior, "touchy, quick, tough, and highly sexed." Anthony Burgess suggests that Miss Renault's aim is "to find a core of anthropological plausibility" in the legends, and most critics thought that she had succeeded superbly in telling a story, rich in excitement, and wholly of its time and place, which is yet perfectly accessible to the modern reader.

The story of Theseus is continued in *The Bull From the Sea*, a somewhat less satisfactory book, by its nature less exciting and (some thought) more loosely integrated. *The Lion in the Gateway* is an excellent book for children about the wars between the Greeks and the Persians, and *The Mask of Apollo*, set in Syracuse and Athens in the fourth century B.C., and narrated by the actor Nikeratos, interweaves an account of Dion's struggle against the tyrant Dionysios the Younger with disquisitions on the nature of power, on art, and in particular on classical drama and the actor's art. This was followed by *Fire From Heaven*, a novel about the boyhood and youth of Alexander the Great, and its sequel *The Persian Boy*.

The author is a member of the Progressive Party of South Africa, has served as president of the PEN Club of South Africa, and is a Fellow of the (British) Royal Society of Literature. She lists her recreations as "conversation and dogs."

PRINCIPAL WORKS: Purposes of Love (U.S., Promise of Love), 1939; Kind Are Her Answers, 1940; The Friendly Young Ladies, 1944 (U.S., Middle Mist, 1945); Return to Night, 1947; North Face, 1948; The Charioteer, 1953; The Last of the Wine, 1956; The King Must Die, 1958; The Bull From the Sea, 1962; The Lion in the Gateway (for children), 1964; The Mask of Apollo, 1966; Fire From Heaven, 1969; The Persian Boy, 1972.

ABOUT: Current Biography, 1959; International Who's Who, 1972–73; McCormack, T. (ed.) Afterwords: Novelists on Their Novels, 1969; Vinson, J. (ed.) Contemporary Novelists, 1972. Who's Who, 1973. *Periodicals* —Critique Winter 1963–1964; New Republic November 19, 1966; Publishers' Weekly September 7, 1946; Saturday Review July 12, 1958; February 17, 1962; Times Literary Supplement September 19, 1958; Wilson Library Bulletin December 1963.

***REVERDY, PIERRE** (September 11, 1889–June 17, 1960), French poet, was born at Narbonne in the south of France, and educated there and at Toulouse. His family, a very old one, had produced many painters and sculptors, a number of them drawn particularly to religious art. Though he chose a literary career, Reverdy had some talent in drawing and retained an interest in painting throughout his life.

His father, a highly literate wine merchant, encouraged the boy in his poetic ambitions, and in October 1910 Reverdy settled in Paris. A year later his father died and Reverdy, physically delicate, dreamy, and sensitive, began a struggle for survival which marked him permanently. He earned a meager living as a proofreader and lived in Montmartre, where his friends included Max Jacob and Apollinaire, and the cubist painters Picasso, Braque, and, particularly, Juan Gris. At the deepest level Reverdy remained alone and lonely, sealed off in the world of his imagination, escaping whenever he could to a farm in the country where his dreams had free rein.

The war scattered his circle and left him more than ever isolated; he had volunteered for the army but was rejected. His first book of verse, *Poèmes en prose*, appeared in 1915. Five more short volumes appeared during the next four years, including *La Lucarne ovale* (The Attic Window, 1916) and *La Guitare endormie* (The Sleeping Guitar, 1919). These poems showed a fresh vision owing much to cubist painting, but made little impact in the brouhaha of the war.

In March 1917, Reverdy and his friends launched *Nord-Sud*, a small monthly review which published his own work and that of Apollinaire, Jacob, Aragon, Breton, and Soupault, among others. Poorly produced under wartime conditions, it expired after sixteen issues in October 1918, but served as a rallying point for the cubist writers and for literary innovators of all kinds.

Reverdy, who had so far won scant recognition, found a much larger if still limited audience when

* rə ver dē′

PIERRE REVERDY

he collected his early poems in *Les Épaves du ciel* (The Flotsam of Heaven, 1924). Anna Balakian said of these poems that they give the impression of "walls pushing back, doors and windows opening wide only to be confronted with things and beings that immobilize themselves in the face of [this freedom]. Objects seem to force nature to act in contradiction to its expected movements." Shortly after the book's publication, the surrealists hailed Reverdy as the greatest living poet.

Reverdy had not received a religious education but, in the early 1920s, he became an ardent convert to Roman Catholicism. In May 1926 he turned his back on the intellectual life of the capital and made his home at Solesmes, close to the celebrated Benedictine abbey. Two years later he experienced a spiritual crisis, and never entirely regained his faith. Thereafter, nevertheless, he left Solesmes only to make occasional visits to Paris and to travel for short periods abroad. He became something of a recluse, gardening a little, spending much time in study and contemplation.

The poems he published from Solesmes included *Flaques de verre* (Pools of Glass, 1929); *Sources du vent* (Sources of the Wind, 1929); *Pierres blanches* (White Stones, 1930); *Ferraille* (Scrap Iron, 1937); *Plein Verre* (Full Glass, 1940); and *Chant des morts* (Song of the Dead, 1948). Reverdy's poetry was collected in *Main d'œuvre* in 1949. He also published several volumes of *contes*, a poetic novel, and four critical and theoretical works.

Reverdy has been called one of the half dozen leading cubist writers, and one of the most successful surrealists. The scattered, jerky appearance of his poems on the page and such titles as *La Guitare endormie* do suggest affinities with cubist painting, while Reverdy's intuitive apprehension of an a-logical spiritual reality pleased the surrealists. But most critics now agree that, guided though he was by cubism, and much as he influenced both movements, his intentions were different and unique.

In *Le Gant de crin* (The Hair Glove, 1927), Reverdy wrote of his introspective search for "the absolute and the real." Obscured in the "purely imaginary" world of everyday, they can be perceived only fleetingly, through dream or contemplation or, intuitively, at the heart of the most commonplace scenes. Reverdy called his poems "crystals deposited after the effervescent contact of the spirit" with this ultimate reality. They have the purity and delicacy of crystals, and if at first sight they seem spasmodic and difficult, it is because they have been distilled to the essence, purged of every excess word and even of connecting thoughts, in a manner reminiscent of the work of the Spanish poet Juan Ramón Jiménez. There is bitterness in this crystalline poetry, and great loneliness, but also an anxious tenderness for all who are frail and defeated. For Aragon, Reverdy was the poet of fear and silence, the poet of the night.

John Ashbery writes that, while few American poets have been influenced by Reverdy, there are some to whom his name is full of magic. In France he has been an important and increasingly influential force for many years. He has been accused of monotony, both in theme and style, but even his detractors concede that "the style is superb." Soupault said of him that, "with Paul Éluard, he is the purest of the writers of his time."

PRINCIPAL WORKS IN ENGLISH TRANSLATION: Poems, tr. by Anne Hyde Greet, 1968; Selected Poems, tr. by Kenneth Rexroth, 1969. *Poems in* Aspel, A. and Justice, D. (eds.) Contemporary French Poetry, 1965; Barnstone, W. (ed.) Modern European Poetry, 1966; New World Writing, tr. by Kenneth Rexroth; Evergreen Review, tr. by John Ashbery; Wake, tr. by Daisy Aldan. *Part of text of* The Last Works of Henri Matisse, 1958.

ABOUT: Balakian, A. Literary Origins of Surrealism, 1947; Cornell, W. K. The Case for Pierre Reverdy, *in* Peyre, H. M. (ed.) Essays in Honor of Albert Feuillerat, 1943; Greene, R. W. The Poetic Theory of Pierre Reverdy, 1967; Guiney, M. La Poésie de Pierre Reverdy, 1967; Hackett, C. A. Anthology of Modern French Poetry, 1952; Hommage à Pierre Reverdy (Entretiens sur les lettres et les arts), 1961; Kamber, G. Max Jacob and the Poetics of Cubism, 1971; Lemaître, G. E. From Cubism to Surrealism, 1947; Rizzuto, A. Style and Theme in Reverdy's *Les Ardoises du toit*, 1971; Rousselot, J. Pierre Reverdy, 1951; Smith, H. (ed.) Columbia Dictionary of Modern European Literature, 1947. *Periodicals*—Mercure de France January–April 1962.

***REYES, ALFONSO** (May 17, 1889–December 12, 1959), Mexican poet, critic, and essayist, was born in Monterrey. His father, General Bernal de

* rā′ yās

Reyes, was a distinguished soldier who became an efficient and enlightened governor of Nuevo León, the state of which Monterrey is the capital. Reyes entered the Escuela Nacional Preparatoria in Mexico City in 1905, went on to the Escuela Nacional de Altos Estudios, and received a law degree from the University of Mexico in 1913.

At the university his extracurricular activities were more important to him than his law studies. He learned Greek and Latin, beginning the classical studies which so influenced him, and made friends among his professors and the young intellectuals of Mexico City. He became the youngest member of the "Generation of the Centenary," the group of essayists and philosophers who in 1909 founded the Ateneo de la Juventud, an institution that flourished until 1940 and played an important part in the approaching Mexican renaissance.

Reyes began his career in 1913 as a teacher, and then entered Mexico's diplomatic service. At this time, during the Huerta dictatorship, there was a brief respite from internal strife in Mexico. By the time the civil war broke out again, Reyes was in Paris as second secretary to the Mexican legation. This was disbanded at the beginning of World War I, and Reyes went to Madrid, where he and his wife and their small baby at first lived in great poverty. Eventually he found work, at first as a translator, then as secretary of the Madrid Ateneo, and finally in the research group known as the Centro de Estudios Históricos. He returned to the diplomatic service in 1920 and in 1924 became head of the Paris legation.

The years in Madrid were the most productive of Reyes' life, and it was then that he wrote many of the poems and essays for which he is best known. His first book of verse, collecting work done between 1906 and 1919, appeared in 1923 as *Huellas* (Marks). The early poems here shared with other Latin American verse of the time a strong French and specifically "Parnassian" influence. But many already bore the distinctive but indefinable mark of Reyes' own style—indefinable because of his extraordinary versatility. He strayed from subject to subject and mood to mood, combining great learning with a certain naïve charm and sampling all the literary styles available to him. Some of Reyes' poems record his impressions of Mexico with concise realism; others, like *Golfo de Mexico* (Gulf of Mexico, 1934), experiment with surrealism. He could be autobiographical, chatty about friends and loves, anxious about death, or simply frivolous.

Reyes' poetry has been thought to lack a sufficient seriousness or intensity, though some critics believe it has been underrated. His fame, however, rests quite properly on his essays. He was an absolute master of this most Latin American of forms, which seems to serve a characteristic eclecticism in the continental temperament. A typical example is the series called *Simpatías y diferencias* (Sympathies and Differences), published between 1921 and 1926. They are, as one critic said, a medley of "impressionistic sentences, fantasies, elegances, narrative flights of fancy, biographical sketches, notes and reflections."

ALFONSO REYES

Much of Reyes' work as a critic came out of his researches with the Madrid Centro de Estudios Históricos. He contributed to the *Revista de Filología Española* (Journal of Spanish Philology), under the distinguished Spanish scholar Menéndez Pidal, and wrote important studies of Spanish literature, among them *Capítulos de literatura española* (Chapters on Spanish Literature, 1939); *Cuestiones gongorinas* (Gongorist Topics, 1927); *El deslinde; prolegómenos a la teoría literaria* (The Frontier; Prolegomena for a Theory of Literature, 1944). When Reyes began his work on the great seventeenth century Cordovan poet Luis de Góngora, the latter's reputation was in eclipse. Reyes' pioneering and ultimately successful efforts to rehabilitate him have had an impact on Spanish literature comparable to that of the rediscovery of John Donne on English literature.

Reyes' criticism was never narrowly academic. "The art of expression, it seemed to me," he once wrote, "was no mere rhetorical exercise, divorced from conduct, but rather the richest means of expressing human feeling. . . . For a man—so far as he is a man—to exist fully is to transform that other thing, that basic sustenance, into feeling and thought, and the 'catharsis' for this is the word. . . . Do I make it clear what the practice of letters has meant to me? Double redemption by the word:

first through the concord of bloods; second through the shaping of the personality, in its relation to others as well as in its inner growth."

One of his principal concerns was to establish Latin American culture as a part of the same Latin civilization that stretches over half of Europe, and to bring about some cultural reconciliation between Spain and her former colonies. His own literary consciousness was firmly rooted in a profound knowledge of the Greek and Roman classics, and a particular sympathy for Vergil and the Aeneid. He once drew a comparison between the meetings of Aeneas and Latinus, Cortés and Montezuma. But he was also deeply sympathetic to modern literature and a prolific and sensitive translator of, among others, Chesterton, Sterne, Mallarmé, and Stevenson.

Reyes remained in the diplomatic service, and from 1924 to 1939 represented his country in France, Argentina, and Brazil (where he was particularly happy). During the last twenty years of his life Reyes devoted himself to writing and teaching, and to the Colegio de México, which he founded.

PRINCIPAL WORKS IN ENGLISH TRANSLATION: The Position of America (essays), 1950; Criticism and the Roman Mind, 1963; Mexico in a Nutshell and Other Essays, 1964. *Poems in* Fitts, D. (ed.) Anthology of Contemporary Latin American Poetry, 1942; Paz, O. (ed.) An Anthology of Mexican Poetry, 1958.

ABOUT: Anderson-Imbert, E. Spanish-American Literature, 1963; Cohen, J. M. Poetry of This Age, 1966; Englekirk, J. E. An Outline History of Spanish-American Literature, 1965; Trend, J. B. Alfonso Reyes, 1952; Twentieth Century Writing, 1969. *Periodicals*—Books Abroad 19, 1945; Hispania 32 1949, 34 1951, March 1966.

***RHYS, JEAN** (August 24, 1894–), British novelist and short story writer, was born at Roseau, on the island of Dominica in the West Indies, one of the five children of a Welsh doctor and his Creole wife. She still remembers with longing the lush warmth of the place: "I think it does something to one to be brought up in such a beautiful place, to know nothing but that." She was very lonely as a child, and began to write poetry, which she showed to no one, and plays. "At that early age," she remembers, "I learned that you can write-out a sadness, and then it isn't so bad. It is the only lucky thing about being a writer. Since then, I have had glimpses of happiness and wealth in my life, but during those periods, I never wanted to write."

After a convent education, Jean Rhys was sent to England at the age of sixteen to live with an aunt in Cambridge. She went to the Royal Academy of Dramatic Art for a while, which she enjoyed, but when her father died she had to scrape a living in the chorus of touring companies performing musical comedies and operettas such as *Maid of the Mountains* and *The Count of Luxembourg*. Later she worked as a mannequin, as a ghost writer (of a book on furniture), and in a variety of other casual jobs. She was unhappy in London, and after World War I married a Dutch poet, journalist, and *chansonnier*, and lived with him in Vienna, Paris, and Budapest. Some of her husband's activities were distinctly shady, and they lived a highly bohemian life on the fringes of the underworld. They had a daughter, Maryvonne, now married and living in Holland.

This interlude ended when her husband abandoned her suddenly. It was then that her professional writing career began. Ford Madox Ford began to publish her stories and to introduce her to the Paris of Gertrude Stein and Ernest Hemingway—an association which, as Francis Hope has remarked, has left its mark on her "spare, edgy" style.

Her first book, *The Left Bank* (1927), consisted of sketches and short stories set in the Montparnasse of the 1920s, and, enthusiastically introduced by Ford Madox Ford, served to establish her on the literary scene. *Quartet* (1929), her first novel, introduces Marya Zelli, the initial incarnation of the Rhys heroine—always, whatever her name, the same "quintessentially supine" woman. Marya Zelli, ex-chorus girl living in Paris with her charming, irresponsible husband, loses him suddenly to prison and, in turn, is herself taken over and drawn into a *ménage à trois* by a middle-aged couple who befriend her. She falls in love with the man with the typical infatuated terror of the Rhys victim—here expressed, as one critic put it, with "a rare combination of quivering immediacy and glassy objectivity."

After Leaving Mr. MacKenzie (1930), also set in Paris, is even more desolate. Jilted and almost penniless, Julia Martin sets off for London to look up her former lovers; but, snubbed by all, she returns to Paris, her looks going, hope gone. The novel has a more alert, less passive quality than its successor, *Voyage in the Dark* (1934), in which the helpless, pretty Anna Morgan, longing for love, shrinks from it when at last she finds it and, finally, is dropped. She becomes a prostitute and the novel ends with her recovering from an abortion, "ready to start all over again."

In *Good Morning, Midnight* (1939), the heroine, now over forty, is revisiting Paris in 1937. Sasha Jensen is complex and aggressive, both fatalistic and firm of will. "Her self-knowledge is exact, her observation of others comical and freezing," it was said, "but she is not malicious. . . . This is not only a study of a lonely, aging woman, who has been deserted by husbands and lovers and has taken to drink; it is the tragedy of a distinguished mind and generous nature that have gone unappreciated in a conventional, unimaginative world."

* rēs

According to Gerald Kersh, Jean Rhys, "who had been fighting oblivion since the middle 1920s . . . was barely ahead by a point or two when *Good Morning, Midnight* . . . came out precisely at the moment [1939] when it was most likely to be ignored." Jean Rhys fell out of sight. After World War II the death of her second husband, a publisher's reader, left her desperately lonely once more. She married his cousin, Max Hamer, a poet and retired naval officer, and settled with him in Bude, Cornwall. There she was traced, through a press advertisement, by a BBC producer planning a dramatization of *Good Morning, Midnight*, successfully broadcast in 1958.

Jean Rhys had almost ceased to write but, thus encouraged, began work on the novel published in 1966 as *Wide Sargasso Sea*. It was inspired by the glimpse that is all that Charlotte Brontë affords us of Bertha Mason, Rochester's mad Creole first wife in *Jane Eyre*. This haunted and shadowy character becomes Jean Rhys's Antoinette, the child of slave owners brought low by emancipation in the early nineteenth century. As much a helpless pawn in a man's world as Marya Zelli or Anna Morgan, she is married off to Rochester, wrenched from her West Indian home, and cloistered, cold and loveless, at Thornfield.

Walter Allen called the book "a triumph of atmosphere—of what one is tempted to call Caribbean Gothic atmosphere. . . . It has an almost hallucinatory quality." It brought its author an Arts Council Bursary, the thousand-pound W. H. Smith Literary Award, and the Heinemann Award of the Royal Society of Literature, and began something like a Jean Rhys cult. Thirty years after Ford had recognized her passion, insight, and acid elegance, she was discovered again. *Tigers Are Better-Looking*, containing sketches from *The Left Bank* together with some more recent stories, appeared in 1968, and Jean Rhys's early novels have been republished.

The reassessment of her work continues. Francis Wyndham, in his introduction to *Wide Sargasso Sea*, suggests that her prewar novels were never properly appreciated because "they were ahead of their time, both in spirit and in style." Not everyone accepts this, Walter Allen for example enjoying them primarily as products of their period, and Mary Conroy finding them sentimental in their "double plea for admiration and condolence," their insistence that "sin is glamorous and sadness rather fine." For W. L. Webb, "what stamps her work indelibly in the mind, what gives it a disturbing coherence is the sheer personality of its creator. This girl, these women are particular, not to be avoided or set aside: what they look at one sees; what they say, one must hear."

Jean Rhys, once more a widow, lives alone in a bungalow in a small Devon village, without a telephone or television. She is a small, frail woman, not completely recovered from a serious heart attack.

JEAN RHYS

PRINCIPAL WORKS: The Left Bank, 1927; Quartet (England, Postures), 1929; After Leaving Mr. MacKenzie, 1931; Voyage in the Dark, 1934; Good Morning, Midnight, 1939; Wide Sargasso Sea, 1966; Tigers Are Better-Looking, 1968.

ABOUT: Current Biography, 1972; Ford, F. M. *introduction to* The Left Bank, 1927; Grigson, G. (ed.) Concise Encyclopedia of Modern World Literature, 1963. Vinson, J. (ed.) Contemporary Novelists, 1972; Who's Who, 1973; Wyndham, F. *introduction to* Wide Sargasso Sea, 1966. *Periodicals*—Books and Bookmen December 1966; Guardian December 14, 1967; August 8, 1968; January 10, 1972; Library Journal May 15, 1967; London Magazine January 1960, October 1962; Nation October 2, 1967; New Statesman October 28, 1966; New York Times February 10, 1929; June 18, 1967; New York Times Book Review March 17, 1935; Observer June 1, 1969; Saturday Review July 25, 1931; July 1, 1967; Times Literary Supplement October 4, 1928; November 17, 1966; July 20, 1967; May 2, 1968.

RICH, ADRIENNE CECILE (May 16, 1929—), American poet, was born in Baltimore, Maryland, the daughter of Arnold Rich, a physician, and Helen (Jones) Rich. She attended the Roland Park Country School in Baltimore (1938–1947) and Radcliffe College, where she became a member of Phi Beta Kappa and received her B.A. *cum laude* in 1951. In 1953 she married Arnold Haskell Conrad, an economist, by whom she has three sons. She lives in New York City.

A Change of World, her first volume of poems, was published in the Yale Series of Younger Poets while she was still a Radcliffe senior. Alfred Kreymborg identified her on this evidence as "the

ADRIENNE CECILE RICH

kind of neoclassic poet who relies on true form," and there was very nearly universal praise for the proportion, humor, and variety of her poems and the excellence of her technique. W. H. Auden said: "These poems are neatly and modestly dressed, speak quietly but do not mumble, respect their elders but are not cowed by them, and do not tell fibs: that, for a first volume, is a good deal." A second collection, *The Diamond Cutters*, displayed her growing ease in the use of colloquial language and larger forms, reminiscent but hardly imitative of Frost, and a kind of Wordsworthian philosophical bent. In her youth and gravity and clarity she seemed to Randall Jarrell at that time "an enchanting poet . . . a sort of princess in a fairy tale."

Snapshots of a Daughter-in-Law broke the spell. Many of the poems in this third collection forfeited the easy technical perfection of her early work for a new recklessness. These were poems, Adrienne Rich said, "concerned with knowing and being known; with the undertow and backlash of love and self-love; with the physical world as mime for the inward one." Robert Lowell, who had felt from the beginning in Miss Rich's work "tremors of discontent," welcomed what was "gnarled, sketchy and obscure" in the book as evidence of a painful metamorphosis, a "tortuous and sometimes tortured" advance.

And in *Necessities of Life* Lowell announced "an arrival, a poised and intact completion." The whole book, he wrote, "gives an impression of having the continuity and force of a single stream of contemplation. . . . One feels the leisure, rest and elbow-room, and trusts every cadence, image and reflection. Nothing has been put in to startle, nothing has been left out because of caution. The only limits are the necessary, inevitable limits of a trained mind." Another critic, noting that Miss Rich had virtually abandoned formal structures, praised "her mastery of her own irregular, emphatic verse lines, her wholly internal modulations and cadence."

Selected Poems, which seemed to some excessively selective, was published in England in 1967, and was followed by *Leaflets* (1969) and *The Will to Change* (1971)—volumes which reflect in form as well as content Adrienne Rich's new commitment to radical politics. "She writes now," says Hayden Carruth, "with explosive force, with short lines, hard images, in poems of restless energy. . . . Many poets, probably most poets in America today are writing *about* revolution. The poetry of Adrienne Rich *is* revolution. In its actual methodological progress it denies the older humanist concept of the world of imagination as separate from or contrary to ordinary reality; it shows the poem at work not only as a part of reality but as a creating and transforming part. Thus her poetry makes and at the same time exemplifies a new aesthetic. It has nothing to do with discredited social realism, but a great deal to do with the existential notion of the artist as self-creator, extended to a social plane. . . . It is one of the most important continuing experiments in American literature." David Kalstone, reviewing *The Will to Change*, wrote that it is "about departures, about the pain of breaking away from lovers and from an old sense of self." Another and associated theme is the problem of expressing new and liberated ideas in an old "oppressor's language": "Our whole life a translation / the permissible fibs / and now a knot of lies / eating at itself to get undone / Words bitten thru words / meanings burnt-off like paint / under the blowtorch."

Adrienne Rich lived in the Netherlands in 1961–1962. She was a lecturer in English at Swarthmore College in 1966–1968 and adjunct professor of writing at Columbia's Graduate School of the Arts in 1967–1969. She has taught English in the SEEK program of the City College of New York, and in 1972–1973 was Fannie Hurst Professor of Creative Literature at Brandeis University. She received Guggenheim Fellowships in 1952 and 1961, and in 1962 a Bollingen Foundation grant and an Amy Lowell Traveling Fellowship for her translations of Dutch poets. The National Institute of Arts and Letters gave her an award in 1961, and *Poetry* awarded her the Bess Hokin Prize in 1963.

PRINCIPAL WORKS: *All poetry*—A Change of World, 1951; The Diamond Cutters, 1955; Snapshots of a Daughter-in-Law, 1963; Necessities of Life, 1962–1965, 1966; Selected Poems (London), 1967; Leaflets, 1969; The Will to Change, 1971; Diving Into the Wreck: Poems 1971–1972, 1973.

ABOUT: Contemporary Authors 11–12, 1965; Howard, R. Alone With America, 1969; Leary, P. and Kelly, R. (eds.) A Controversy of Poets, 1965; Murphy, R. (ed.) Contemporary Poets of the English Language, 1970. *Periodicals*—New York Times Book Review July 17, 1966; New Yorker November 3, 1951; Times Literary Supplement November 23, 1967; Yale Review Autumn 1956.

RICHARDSON, JACK (CARTER) (February 18, 1935–), American dramatist and novelist, was born in New York City, the son of Arthur and Marjorie Richardson. His father was a professional pianist. His mother died when he was young, and after his father remarried Richardson lived with his grandmother. He graduated from Collegiate School, a New York preparatory school, in 1951. That summer he did a little summer stock acting at the Grist Mill Playhouse in Andover, New Jersey, and then studied acting for a few months at the American Theater Wing in New York City.

In 1952, at seventeen, Richardson enlisted in the Army, for the sake of "a place to stay for awhile." He spent the time in Frankfurt and Paris in public relations, writing biographical news releases about United States officers stationed in Europe. In his spare time he studied fine arts and philosophy at the University of Paris. Discharged from the army in 1954, he returned to the United States and entered Columbia University, graduating *summa cum laude* with a B.A. degree in 1957; he also won the Adenauer Fellowship for Germanic Studies, which took him to the University of Munich. There he studied German philosophy and lectured in German on American philosophers, principally William James and John Dewey. It was at the University of Munich that he met and married, in 1957, Anne Gail Roth, the daughter of a New York corporation lawyer. "Mr. Roth put some money into *The Prodigal*," Richardson has said. "He's also a very intelligent man and this is a great help."

The Prodigal was written during Richardson's stay in Germany. In 1958 he returned to America, and the play—a version of the Orestes legend—was produced off-Broadway in 1960. Richardson's Orestes is an entirely contemporary figure—an "outsider" who wants nothing so much as to dissociate himself from a society which seems to him insane, but who is in the long run unable to resist the octopus embrace of that society. *Time* acclaimed "the season's best new playwright"; Walter Kerr called *The Prodigal* "a permanent contribution to the contemporary theatre"; George E. Wellwarth thinks it "not merely a solid, well-written play, as sophisticated in content as it is precisely constructed in form: it is undoubtedly the most brilliantly written new American play to come out since the end of World War II." Gerald Weales disagreed, finding Richardson's argument interesting but his

JACK RICHARDSON

execution inadequate, especially in its characterization. But there were few such demurrers, the play had a moderately good run at the off-Broadway Downtown Theatre, and it received both the Vernon Rice and the Obie awards. It has since been revived in summer stock and in college theatres.

Gallows Humor, produced off-Broadway in 1961, is in fact two short plays joined by a common theme. In the first a condemned man, comfortably adjusted to death, tries but fails to resist the favors of a state-supplied whore; in the second his executioner, desperately bored with his way of life, tries but fails to escape from it: there is, these days, not much to choose between life and death. Jerry Talmer pointed out that *Gallows Humor*, like its predecessor, was concerned with "the balance we find, or fail to find, between a super-imposed order and our personal freedom." The play failed to win either popular or critical support, and there was some feeling that Richardson had labored an excellent idea to death.

There was a mixed reception for *Lorenzo*, Richardson's first play on Broadway. A story about strolling players in Renaissance Italy, it seems to argue the superiority of illusion to reality. Some reviewers found themselves greatly moved and excited, but more thought it rambling and melodramatic, and the play closed after four performances. Another Broadway play, a comedy called *Xmas in Las Vegas*, also failed.

George E. Wellwarth, one of Richardson's most ardent champions, considered him "America's best young playwright," with a better mind and greater integrity than Edward Albee. Wellwarth sees Richardson as a dramatist in the same tradition as

Shaw, Dürrenmatt, and Frisch, with "the same sardonic view of the world, the same precision of technique, the same effect of intellectual stimulation." Others have called him a writer of great promise, who possesses intelligence and an excellent theatrical sense, but who has not yet transcended the French and German influences in his work and found his own voice.

Richardson's first novel, *The Prison Life of Harris Filmore*, was published in England, Germany, and France before it appeared in the United States in 1963. It is a satire about an embezzling Westchester banker who finds happiness in the orderly rhythms of prison life, and makes a point rather similar to that of *Gallows Humor*. Some American critics thought it pretentious, but others were amused and the London *Times Literary Supplement* called it "an extremely funny book, in which the background is sufficiently well described to be convincing and the characters of the satire express their views with fluency and freedom."

Richardson has written about the theatre in such periodicals as *Show* and *Theatre Arts*, and he has contributed work to *Botteghe Oscure*, *New World Writing*, *Transatlantic Review*, and *Esquire*. In 1963–1964 he received Guggenheim and Brandeis University fellowships.

Describing Richardson in the New York *Herald Tribune* in 1960, Don Ross wrote: "He is a tall (six foot one inch), slim, rather stooped man with a long bony face and longish hair that falls over his forehead like a fringe. . . . He speaks with the broad 'a' and the rolling 'r' of Sir John Gielgud. This is not an accident. When he first saw Sir John in a play (it was *The Lady's Not for Burning* in 1951) Mr. Richardson said to himself: 'I love this way of speaking. This is the way one should speak the language.'" He and his wife have a daughter and live in New York City.

PRINCIPAL WORKS: The Prodigal (play), 1960; Gallows Humor (play), 1961; The Prison Life of Harris Filmore (novel), 1961; Xmas in Las Vegas *in* Stasio, M. (ed.) Broadway's Beautiful Losers, 1972.

ABOUT: Biographical Encyclopedia & Who's Who of the American Theatre, 1966; Weales, G. American Drama Since World War II, 1962; Wellwarth, G. E. The Theater of Protest and Paradox, 1964; Who's Who in America, 1970–1971. *Periodicals*—Boston Herald January 30, 1963; New York Herald Tribune February 28, 1960; August 14, 1960; April 16, 1961; New York Post March 21, 1960; May 3, 1961; September 5, 1965; Show February 1962; Theatre May 1960; Theatre Arts March 1962.

RICHLER, MORDECAI (January 27, 1931–), Canadian novelist, writes: "Born in Montreal of immigrant Polish Jewish parents and as a child was embarrassed by their accents. Now I live in London with my Canadian wife where our children, British-born, are occasionally embarrassed by *our* foreign accents, which only serves us right. I have three children and a step-son by my wife's first marriage. My father was—and still is—a junk dealer, but the Montreal ghetto I still cherish as home has long since disintegrated. My maternal grandfather was a Hasidic rabbi and a Zaddik (a righteous sage) and I had a traditional orthodox Jewish education. Went to Sir George Williams University but quit, disheartened, after two years in 1951 and went to Europe to write and travel widely in France, Germany, and Spain. Paris in the fifties was a rare and lively place to be, and I first published there in an obscure magazine called *Points*. Published my first raw and, alas, derivative novel, *The Acrobats*, in 1954, and have brought out four more novels since then.

"In retrospect, often regret I began to write so early and so suffered no sequence of boring jobs first. As a result, I know pathetically little first-hand about office or factory life.

"After a TV drama apprenticeship, got my start in films by working with Jack Clayton on the final draft of the screenplay for *Room at the Top*, and have written several films since, including *Life at the Top* and *The Looking Glass War*. Truth is I count on films for economic survival and do a script about once every eighteen months.

"Contribute on and off to *Encounter*, *Commentary*, *Spectator*, *New Statesman*, *New York Review of Books*, *Observer*, *Sunday Times*, and so forth. A story I published in *Kenyon Review* in 1962 was reprinted in Martha Foley's *Best American Short Stories* 1963.

"I've been lucky with writing grants. In 1960 I was awarded a Canada Council Junior Arts Fellowship which was renewed the following year. In 1962 I won a Guggenheim Fellowship for Creative Writing. At the moment I hold another Canada Council grant, a Senior Arts Fellowship, which is an enormous help while I work on a new long novel, *St. Urbain's Horseman*, an attempt to fuse Canadian and European experience."

Since he wrote the note above, Richler has published *St. Urbain's Horseman*, universally regarded as his best book to date. He and his wife, the former Florence Wood, now have five children, and live in a rambling house at Kingston Hill, Surrey. The author returned to Canada in 1968–1969 as writer-in-residence at Sir George Williams University, and in 1972–1974 held a visiting professorship at Carleton University, Ottawa.

Encounter has published an amusing account by Richler of his adolescent aesthetic posturings, his growing despair in the "cultural desert" of Montreal, his escape at twenty to England, the intellectual Mecca. England proved drab and disappointing (though it later drew him back), and he moved on to more colorful parts, including Valencia, the setting of his precocious first novel. *The Acrobats*, "an impressionistic parade of polyglots" in search of something to believe in, is pretentious and, as Richler says, derivative (of Hemingway, Dos Passos, and Henry Miller, among others). But it also has "a fire and a frenzy of its own" and characters with life in them. John Metcalf called it "the work of a worried, whirling, over-read young man of twenty-two who's prepared to face up to *not* seeing the way out." *Son of a Smaller Hero* focuses with a similar angry intensity and some nostalgia on the Montreal ghetto, and, overwritten as it is, is about "real people, honestly seen and described." This honesty angered some Canadian Jewish readers but meant a great deal to others, like the novelist Marian Engel, who calls Richler "our angry young man" who "first told us how it was to be a Jew here."

By the time Richler wrote *The Apprenticeship of Duddy Kravitz*, he had come to expect less of life. The novel was called a "Canadian *What Makes Sammy Run?*" It tells, with deep cynicism but irresistible gusto, the picaresque story of a young Montreal Jew who sets out to beat society at its own materialistic game. The "rasping humor" evident in the earlier books had come to the fore, and the trend continued in *Stick Your Neck Out*, an outrageous account of the exploitation and corruption of an Eskimo poet in Toronto, and *Cocksure*, set in London, both of them savage and fantastic satires aiming at any target that comes within range, but in particular at the fashionable "media," their exploiters and votaries, and at every kind of cultural, racial, and moral exhibitionism. *Cocksure*, excerpts from which had won the *Paris Review*'s award for humor, also carried off the Governor-General's Award for fiction.

At this point in his career, it was said that Richler had the wild imagination, sharp perceptions, and deliberate "bad taste" of "a literary Lenny Bruce." His critics complained that his satires were shapeless and deteriorated too readily into farce—that in general his "prodigious talent" had not been brought firmly under control.

This control was achieved, most readers thought, in *St. Urbain's Horseman*, the most ambitious of Richler's novels to date, and his first major success. The title refers to St. Urbain Street in Montreal, where the novel's hero (like the novelist) was born. Jake Hersh escapes from the ghetto to London, where his happy mixed marriage, profitable (if mediocre) career as a film and television director, and "inert Hampstead liberalism" are troubled by an acute sense of guilt. These guilt feelings engender Jake's obsession with his Cousin Joey, a probably villainous but mysterious adventurer translated by Jake's self-despising imagination into a symbol of dedicated, resourceful, meaningful Jewishness. An attempt to help one of the many

MORDECAI RICHLER

people Joey has wronged ends in disaster, with Jake convicted of rape. Disgraced and defeated as he is, and with Joey reportedly dead, Jake clings all the same to his shining, spurious image of his cousin as St. Urbain's Horseman, "the Jewish Batman."

The novel is long, bawdy, and often very funny, with a huge cast of characters (including Duddy Kravitz rampant). It is both more naturalistic and more compassionate than its immediate predecessors. At its worst it too much resembles all the other contemporary accounts of the splendors and miseries of Jewishness, but at its best it is a serious and valuable defense of the maligned tradition of well-meaning liberalism. It was received with a great deal of admiration and affection, as was *The Street*, a subsequent collection of more or less autobiographical stories and sketches.

PRINCIPAL WORKS: The Acrobats, 1954; Son of a Smaller Hero, 1955 (republished 1966); A Choice of Enemies, 1957; The Apprenticeship of Duddy Kravitz, 1959; Stick Your Neck Out (England, The Incomparable Atuk), 1963; Cocksure, 1968; Hunting Tigers Under Glass (essays), 1969; (as ed.) Canadian Writing Today, 1970; St. Urbain's Horseman, 1971; The Street (stories and sketches), 1972; Shovelling Trouble (essays), 1972.

ABOUT: Herzberg, M. J. (ed.) The Reader's Encyclopedia of American Literature, 1962; International Who's Who, 1972–73; Oxford Companion to Canadian History and Literature, 1964; Penguin Companion to Literature 1, 1971; Sheps, G. D. Mordecai Richler, 1971; Who's Who, 1973; Woodcock, G. Mordecai Richler, 1970. *Periodicals*—Books and Bookmen April 1957, October 1963; Canadian Literature Autumn 1960, Spring 1965; Encounter July 1962; Guardian September 15, 1971; Holiday April 1964; Journal of Commonwealth Literature June 1972; New York Times Book Review May 5, 1968; Publishers' Weekly June 28, 1971; Tamarack Review Winter 1957, Summer 1958.

EDGELL RICKWORD

***RICKWORD, (JOHN) EDGELL** (October 22, 1898–), English poet and editor, writes: "I was born in Colchester, Essex. About the same time, my father became Borough Librarian, the first to hold the position, as Borough Councils had only recently been empowered to set up free Public Libraries to meet the needs of the literate masses created by the Education Act of 1870. Undoubtedly the proximity of my cradle to a bookstack helped to decide my destiny.

"I was the last of five children, and before long realized that it was something of a struggle for my parents to keep up their middle-class status on what was then only a skilled workman's wage. But we were a harmonious family and I cannot blame later vagaries onto home influences.

"Till the age of ten I was taught at a Dame's school, where we used slates and learnt a lot of Scripture. I won a Foundation scholarship to the Grammar School. We boys were very snobbishly distinguished from boys with scholarships from the Elementary Schools; we had to wear Tudor gowns and square caps at Prayers and civic functions. I wasn't very good at school. I was lazy, but scraped through the Cambridge Senior exam. I might have had one of the school's university exhibitions but the war intervened and I joined up in the Artists' Rifles, a City of London Territorial Regiment, in October 1916. My basic training was at Hare Hall Camp, just outside London. The poet Edward Thomas had passed that way not long before. But I was to meet a poet there, W. J. Turner, nine years my senior, who helped my development enormously. At this time I was struggling, between drill and duties, with imitative prose fantasies, heavy with Paterian ecstasies.

"I moved on to a tough Officers' Training Battalion and was commissioned in October 1917, in the Royal Berkshire Regiment, and soon posted to the Fifth Battalion in France, near Armentières. It was a quiet sector then; war wasn't so bad, we thought, though very cold and uncomfortable. But in the Spring we were digging trenches to meet the great German offensive known to be imminent; indeed, their artillery was already ranging on our new defences. One shell exploded near enough for a splinter to wound me slightly. So when the storm burst, I was not there. But I was soon back with the battalion, and we moved down to the Somme, where the big German offensive threatened a break-through. After some weeks of heavy fighting I was slightly wounded during a trench raid, and this time was sent back to England. I spent a very pleasant summer, reading quantities of books and beginning to scribble lots of verse—much easier than prose. Then back to duty, to Dublin, where my reserve battalion was stationed. I had read an exciting review of James Joyce's *Portrait of the Artist as a Young Man*, and bought a copy literally from under the counter in a Grafton Street bookshop. I was back in France in September, having picked up Siegfried Sassoon's *Counter-Attack and Other Poems*, on my way through London. A revelation as to how the hell of modern war could be communicated in everyday words!

"Not many of the same men were there when I got back to my company, on the outskirts of the formidable Hindenberg Line. The Germans were retiring, fighting back fiercely; but the end came on November 11th. After the Armistice I was invalided to England, demobilised and went up to Oxford on a Service scholarship, in October, to Pembroke College. Here I read savagely, but mainly outside the academic curriculum. I was fortunate to meet many young men who were passionately involved in the creative arts, many of whom became my friends. Particularly Edmund Blunden, Louis Golding, T. W. Earp, Robert Graves, Vivian de Sola Pinto.

"At the end of my first year I got married, and soon after became a parent; economic pressures compelled me to leave Oxford without a degree. I had a quite unrealistic sense of the possibility of living by free-lancing but was lucky to make some needed contacts through W. J. Turner, music critic of the *New Statesman*; and Desmond MacCarthy, its literary editor, gave me an introduction to Bruce Richmond, who edited the *Times Literary Supplement*. There was quite a flock of people of my own age drifting about looking for the same kind of work. We used to visit such papers as the *Spectator*, whose proprietor's daughter was its

* rik' wərd

generous-minded literary editor; and the *Daily News*, where the essayist Robert Lynd was sometimes able to squeeze in a review by an unknown. So somehow I kept afloat and in 1921 published a small collection of poems through Sidgwick & Jackson, a small firm not unsympathetic to the avant-garde. Though the book had as many favourable reviews as it deserved, its influence on my financial position was negligible.

"By that time I was father of two. I can't remember how I managed to collect material for and write a study of Rimbaud, then almost unknown in England. This brought in some congratulatory reviews and twenty-five pounds, less seven pounds for cost of excessive proof corrections.

"In the twenties my closest friends were Bertram Higgins, an Australian I had met at Oxford, and Douglas Garman, at a loose end from Cambridge, both of whom wrote poetry. I suppose what we had in common was a sense of the inadequacy of contemporary writing to reflect the deeply changed conditions of our world after the cataclysm of the War and the Russian Revolution. There was a very specific demarcation in those days, very hard to define. There were those who were aware that the elder generation, not only Gosse and Bridges, but Masefield and Wells and Galsworthy and Shaw, let alone Sir James Barrie, had not a thing to say for our generation; and there were those who went on as if nothing much had changed. We thought there were enough of the first sort to make a public of their own.

"So when a friend offered to finance a literary magazine, we started the *Calendar of Modern Letters*, which came out as a monthly in 1925–1926, until lack of funds reduced it to a quarterly, and finally overcame it. The following years were rather difficult. I found jobs hard to come by. There was some sporadic reviewing, but basically what kept me going was my work for Wishart's, the publishing firm set up by the sponsor of the *Calendar*. We aimed to choose books of minority appeal which bigger firms would often fight shy of publishing, and over the years we discovered a number of writers who later made names for themselves—among them Mary Butts, Mulk Raj Anand, Gerald Kersh. But as the economic depression became more acute, we began to feel the need for a more radical programme, and turned to books more directly dealing with public affairs, though never failing to publish anything coming our way that struck us as having literary originality. Finally the directors decided to amalgamate with Martin Lawrence Ltd., a firm committed to the publication of the basic works of Marx and Engels, and the new company was Lawrence and Wishart.

"It was the patently and obviously threatening international situation—the reactionary nature of the Nazi movement rising to power in Germany—that fused together the literary and political motivation of our work, and it was natural to wish for a periodical that should publicise the defensive views beginning to take shape among many individuals, and in many countries. Thus in 1934 we launched the *Left Review*. The first years of the publishing firm had been quite prolific in creative and cultural work, and this was reflected in the contents of the *Left Review*—during an upsurge of activity, particularly among the younger generation, as the significance of the Spanish Civil War entered their consciousness. But once again financial stringency brought the magazine to an end, in 1938.

"I wrote very little poetry after 1930; people are puzzled about this, but I don't think it should be puzzling. Lots of poets have written for about ten years, and then stopped. Most of the writing of the time was occasional, historical or literary-historical. Mine was philosophical, intellectual. One would like to write poetry for the historical moment: it's not impossible, lots of poetry is written out of the actual social struggle, but I found *too much* emotional stimulus in it. And partly I suppose I got isolated, and went into bookselling. And the world of booksellers is very far from the world of political action and thought.

"My poetry has been influenced, I suppose, mainly by Donne, and by Baudelaire. It is about my attitude to society, to love and to war. But that attitude is generally oblique, I haven't often written pro or anti this or that. Yet I still look forward to writing something more comprehensive than I've done so far, a philosophical jest-book or an heroic farce, perhaps. I cannot imagine there would be anything more to live for after completing a *Samson Agonistes* or *Rape of the Lock*."

Edgell Rickword is one of the most distinguished but also one of the least known of living English poets, whose work, according to Roy Fuller, "no proper account or anthology of the century's poetry—possibly English poetry—could afford to omit." Though his literary life has been long, his poetic output, as he says, was concentrated into a mere ten or twelve years after World War I, and, though appreciated in avant-garde literary circles of his own generation, he had to wait until the 1960s for formal public recognition: in 1966 he received one of three special Arts Council grants to writers whose work had been long unrecognized (the others went to Rayner Heppenstall and James Stern).

Rickword has said that he "felt himself a socialist since about 1911," when he was deeply shocked by the human consequences of a lockout of engineers in his home town; and politics have been central to his life as man and poet. "I am convinced," he said in an interview, "of the political responsibilities of the writer. But I would interpret 'political' in the widest sense, as being a concern with the fate of human beings, in general and in particular." One of his earliest verses was a rebuke to the British Government for executing the leaders of the 1916 Easter Rising.

His early work, however (published in *Behind the Eyes*, 1921) was more personal, much of it love poetry, which had, in Fuller's words, "a sophisticated simplicity quite new in English verse—at least, it had scarcely been heard since the Seventeenth Century." Already he was fundamentally a metaphysical poet, inspired particularly by the works of John Donne. And with *Invocations to Angels* (1928), which contains many of the war poems for which he is best known, the metaphysical style had been made his own. Even more satirically concentrated than the poems of the more famous Siegfried Sassoon, Rickword's war poetry is a startling fusion of emotion and wit: "The Soldier Addresses His Body," "Winter Warfare," and above all the beautiful and terrifying "Trench Poets": "I knew a man, he was my chum, / but he grew darker day by day, / and would not brush the flies away, / nor blanch however fierce the hum / of passing shells. I used to read / to rouse him, random things from Donne— / like 'Get with child a mandrake-root.' / But you can tell he was far gone, / for he lay gaping, mackerel-eyed, / and stiff and senseless as a post / even when that old poet cried / 'I long to talk with some old lover's ghost.'"

Rickword's other large contribution to the century's literature has been as an editor. The *Calendar of Modern Letters* published D. H. Lawrence, Hart Crane, Robert Graves, Aldous Huxley, and helped to make known emerging figures such as T. S. Eliot. It was an essential and acknowledged precursor of F. R. Leavis's widely influential *Scrutiny*. When it was republished in 1966, one reviewer praised it for maintaining "in detail, and with passion, intelligence and scorn, the kinds of standards that the pundits have no time for"; it had, he went on, "precisely the qualities that one looks for, unsuccessfully, in current publications." The Communist *Left Review*, child of the years of unemployment, the rise of Nazism and the growing crisis in Spain, reflected a new political commitment, and a conscious effort to deal with the alienation of the working people from a culture traditionally middle class. Julian Symons has accused Rickword and his colleagues (among them Montagu Slater, Ralph Fox, Randall Swingler) of "editing down" to their less educated readers, and doing them no service by publishing undistinguished work. But Rickword's standards were nevertheless high, and he defended his policy on the *Review*: "The real triumph [of the period] was the drawing into the cultural ambit of a significant number of men and women who were barricaded out from participation in what was regarded as a middle-class preserve." *Left Review* was reprinted in 1968 and *Our Time*, which Rickword edited from 1944 to 1947, in 1966.

Perhaps partly because his own poetic style—ironic, dense, ambiguous—was so little suited to the popular readership he sought, Rickword has written little verse since 1930, except for a long and not altogether successful satire inspired by the Spanish Civil War, "To the Wife of a Non-Interventionist Statesman." His book on Rimbaud, however, remains of real value; he wrote a study on Milton as revolutionary (1940); compiled a collection of Wordsworth criticism in 1950; and in 1971 published a volume of eighteenth-century political pamphlets, lampoons, and cartoons, *Radical Squibs and Loyal Ripostes.*

Rickword remains an isolated figure, shockingly neglected for a writer whom a *Times Literary Supplement* critic rated "the best English poet between Eliot and Empson." In fact his *Collected Verse* was so much ignored when published in 1947 that the author bought back the entire edition, which he republished in 1967. Then the *Times Literary Supplement* wrote that "Rickword is superbly intelligent and musical, and echoes bow before him, not accuse. . . . Mr. Rickword should be read. Now."

PRINCIPAL WORKS: *Poetry*—Behind the Eyes, 1921; Invocations to Angels, 1928; The Twittingpan and Some Others, 1931; Collected Poems, 1947; Fifty Poems, a Selection, 1970. *Tales*—Love One Another, 1929; *Criticism*—Rimbaud, the Boy and the Poet, 1924; Milton, the Revolutionary Intellectual, 1940. *As translator*—Poet Under Saturn: The Tragedy of Verlaine, by Marcel Coulon, 1932. *As editor*—William Wordsworth 1770–1850, 1950; Radical Squibs and Loyal Ripostes, 1971.

ABOUT: Bergonzi, B. Heroes' Twilight, 1965; Ford, H. D. A Poets' War: British Poets and the Spanish Civil War, 1965; Fuller, R. *introduction to* Rickword's Fifty Poems, 1970; Murphy, R. (ed.) Contemporary Poets of the English Language, 1970; Sisson, C. H. English Poetry, 1900–1950, 1971; Symons, J. The Thirties, 1960. *Periodicals*—Essays in Criticism July 1962; Life and Letters June–August 1940, February 1949; The Review 11–12 1964; Times Literary Supplement July 21, 1966; November 9, 1967; February 19, 1971.

RIDLER, ANNE (BARBARA) (July 30, 1912–), English poet, dramatist, and scholar, was born in Rugby, Warwickshire, the only daughter of Henry Christopher Bradby, a housemaster at Rugby School, and of Violet (Milford) Bradby. She was educated at Downe House School, in Florence and Rome, and at King's College in the University of London, where she received a diploma in journalism in 1932. From 1935 to 1940 she worked as a secretary and reader for the publishing house of Faber & Faber. She was married in

1938 to Vivian Ridler, later printer to the University of Oxford.

Hers is a poetry of "piety and acceptance, of Anglicanism, domesticity, and a feeling for traditional ways and scenes." In *The Nine Bright Shiners* she wrote as a mother-to-be; *The Golden Bird* includes poems written during World War II, some of them to her absent husband; *A Matter of Life and Death* evokes the emotional struggle of a mother watching her child grow up and away from her, feeling the pain of that separation, but recognizing "some more difficult good / That draws us on its beam—the ineluctable love of God." In these and other collections her theme is most often some form of human love, expressed with great understanding and delicacy, and interpreted as a mode of the "quickening good" of divine love. K. E. Morgan says that Anne Ridler "writes as one who has experienced the happiest of human relationships, as daughter, wife and mother, and her life within that of the family is related to the larger life of the individual as child of God."

Mrs. Ridler has said that "it was Eliot who first made me despair of becoming a poet; Auden . . . who first made me think I saw how to become one." Traces of Donne and of Herbert and Patmore have also been noted in her work. Desmond Hawkins, reviewing her first collection in 1939, admired the freshness and precision of her language, but thought her style crabbed and strained, overloaded in its imagery and awkward in its syntax. A few years later Kathleen Raine found in *The Golden Bird* a tendency for her "to embark upon themes too large for her talent" as well as some poems written with "exquisite delicacy of feeling, rich, true." In her subsequent work the poet has evidently found her level, and Norman Nicholson credited her with "the art of stating the occasion quite quietly, and leaving the emotion to rise by sympathy in the reader's mind, instead of emphasizing it and trying to play on the reader's feelings." Mrs. Ridler, who can write occasional poems to her headmistress and to her parents on their golden wedding anniversary, is rescued from sentimentality by her honesty and intelligence, and by a verbal wit expressing itself, as Kenneth Allott says, "with the utmost neatness rythmically." Her imagery is visual and sometimes strikingly original: "The muddy sea-mouse, hiding a sunset / In his hairs." Her images are drawn most often from the sea and rivers, flowers and fruit: the growth of a mother's love for her child is compared to the unfurling of an iris.

The best of Mrs. Ridler's several verse plays is *The Trial of Thomas Cranmer*, a "dignified and moving play," modest in tone and convincing in its characterization, which gives "a clear and sympathetic picture of a scholarly mind trapped in the prison of its own logic and of an imagination which could not bear to contemplate physical torment." Even so, one critic found the play "oddly thin," and it seems to be generally recognized that Mrs. Ridler writes better poems than plays.

ANNE RIDLER

Anne Ridler contributes verse to the *New Yorker* and *Poetry*, among other magazines, and reviews to the *Guardian*. She has two sons and two daughters and lives with her family in Oxford. Her interests include the theatre, the cinema, and music.

PRINCIPAL WORKS: *Poetry*—Poems, 1939; A Dream Observed and Other Poems, 1941; The Nine Bright Shiners, 1943; The Golden Bird, 1951; A Matter of Life and Death, 1959; Selected Poems, 1961; Some Time After, 1972. *Plays*—Cain, 1943; The Shadow Factory, 1946; Henry Bly and Other Plays, 1950; The Trial of Thomas Cranmer, 1956; Who Is My Neighbour? and, How Bitter the Bread, 1963; The Jesse Tree: A Masque in Verse, 1973. *As editor*—Shakespeare Criticism 1919–1935, 1936; A Little Book of Modern Verse, 1941; Best Ghost Stories, 1945; Supplement to Faber Book of Modern Verse, 1960; Shakespeare Criticism 1935–1960, 1963; James Thomson: Poems and Some Letters, 1963; Thomas Traherne: Poems, Centuries, and Three Thanksgivings, 1966; (with Christopher Bradby) Best Stories of Church and Clergy, 1966.

ABOUT: Allott, K. (ed.) Penguin Book of Contemporary Verse, 1962; Contemporary Authors 5–6, 1963; Jennings, E. Poetry Today, 1961; Morgan, K. E. Christian Themes in Contemporary Poets, 1964; Thwaite, A. Contemporary English Poetry, 1961; Who's Who, 1973. *Periodicals*—Drama Fall 1956; New Statesman November 24, 1951; Poetry March 1963; Times Literary Supplement June 10, 1939; November 6, 1959.

RITCHIE-CALDER, BARON, OF BALMASHANNAR (July 1, 1906–), Scottish science writer and journalist, received a life peerage in 1966. He was born Peter Ritchie Calder in Forfar, Scotland, one of the four children of David

RITCHIE-CALDER

Calder, a jute worker who became a factory manager, and Georgina (Ritchie) Calder. He had his first byline at the age of twelve, when an essay of his was published in the *Forfar Dispatch*. Ritchie-Calder was educated at the Forfar Academy. At fifteen he left school, taught himself shorthand, and joined the *Dundee Courier* as a police court reporter. He gained varied journalistic experience with the D. C. Thompson Press in Glasgow and London (1924–1926), spent four years with the London *Daily News*, and in 1930, after a brief stint with the *Daily Chronicle*, joined the staff of the *Daily Herald*.

Ritchie-Calder worked on the *Daily Herald* for eleven years, and it was during this period that he discovered his interest in science and became conscious of the gulf between scientists and laymen—a gulf even wider then, before the advent of science journalism, than it is now. Ritchie-Calder began to write regularly on science for the *Daily Herald*, learning his subject as he went along. He was soon recognized by scientists as a responsible and accurate reporter, and by lay people as a lively and readable one—a kind of foreign correspondent from an unfamiliar but fascinating world.

His first book was *The Birth of the Future* (1934), in which an account of contemporary developments in science, gleaned from visits to British research establishments, leads into hopeful speculations about the future. *The Conquest of Suffering*, also published in 1934, discussed the problems currently engaging physiologists and physicians. It was followed a year later by *Roving Commission*, a lighter and more personal book about Ritchie-Calder's work for the *Daily Herald*.

During World War II Ritchie-Calder put aside his specialty to cover the Battle of Britain and the London blitz for his newspaper. Three books published in 1941 all dealt with the war. Two of them, *The Lesson of London* and *Carry On, London*, described the bombing and the cheerful courage with which it was borne, and severely criticized the inadequate preparations made for these long-anticipated attacks. *Start Planning Britain Now*, with characteristic optimism, put forward the author's views on how the postwar reconstruction of the country should be tackled.

It is said that Ritchie-Calder's criticisms of London's defense arrangements nearly led to a jail sentence, but in the end some of his suggestions were adopted and his forthright common sense was recognized in high places. In 1941 he left the *Daily Herald* to become director of plans in the political warfare executive of the Foreign Office. In 1944 both his house and his office were wrecked by bombs, and later the same year he collapsed in the street with a brain hemorrhage. He recovered to join General Eisenhower's Supreme Headquarters as a special adviser, and in 1945 received a CBE for his wartime services. Ritchie-Calder returned to journalism as science editor of the *News Chronicle* (1945–1956), at the same time joining the editorial board of the *New Statesman* (1945–1958).

But since the war journalism has claimed only a fraction of Ritchie-Calder's prodigious energy. In 1946 he began his work for the United Nations as a member of the British delegation to the UNESCO general conference in Paris, and as a special adviser to the Famine Conference called in Washington by the Food and Agriculture Organization. He has played an important part in UN affairs ever since, and has written several books about the organization and its agencies.

In 1949 Ritchie-Calder went to the Middle East on a special UN mission to study the manifold problems of the arid zones. He gave a nontechnical account of his findings in *Men Against the Desert*, describing the varied activities of the UN technical assistance programs in the region and suggesting improvements. Subsequent UN missions were dealt with in *Men Against the Jungle* (1954), studying conditions in Southeast Asia, and *Men Against the Frozen North* (1957), about a forty-thousand-mile journey in the Arctic. These books, quite apart from the important information and ideas they contained, established Ritchie-Calder as "a superb writer of travelogues, with an eye for significant detail in exotic settings, and a special gift for vivid characterization in a few words." In 1960 he visited the Congo and wrote a shocked and angry account of what he had seen, highly critical of the Belgians for their contribution to the country's misery. He made a return visit to Southeast Asia in 1962.

Ritchie-Calder's travels in the wretched parts of the world and his faith in science combined to produce his most ambitious book, *The Inheritors,* published in the United States as *After the Seventh Day*. It traces man's gradual mastery of his environment from the first tools to the present nuclear age, in which the race's ability to survive paradoxically threatens its existence as population growth outruns food supplies. For Ritchie-Calder, the solution lies in global cooperation to exploit all the resources of science. The world community he hopes for would, he believes, ensure not merely continued existence for mankind, but utopia. It is a disjointed book, but a passionate, provocative, and exciting one.

Over the years Ritchie-Calder has also produced many less polemical works, excellent popular accounts of scientific and technological history, of important new discoveries and various aspects of medicine. He has been called "Wellsian in his gift for expounding facts and theories with lucidity and liveliness." In 1961 he received the Kalinga Prize for his work in "promoting the common understanding of science." Ritchie-Calder's books have been translated into a score of languages, his articles have appeared in over a thousand publications throughout the world, and he broadcasts frequently on radio and television. He is a humanist and a member of the Labour party and has been active in the Workers Educational Association, the Fabian Society, the Campaign for Nuclear Disarmament, the National Peace Council, and various scientific societies. In 1961 Ritchie-Calder, who had left school at fifteen, was appointed to the Montague Burton Chair of International Relations at the University of Edinburgh, where he remained until 1967. He had been Charles Beard Lecturer at Ruskin College, Oxford, in 1957, and has also lectured in the United States. In 1966 he found a new forum for his opinions when he entered the House of Lords as a life peer, taking the title Baron Ritchie-Calder of Balmashannar. He was chairman of Britain's Metrication Board from 1969 to 1972, when he took up a senior fellowship at the Center for the Study of Democratic Institutions at Santa Barbara in California. He received the Victor Gollancz Award for service to humanity in 1969.

Ritchie-Calder was married to Mabel McKail in 1927 and has three sons and two daughters (the eldest son, Nigel, is also a noted science writer). He is "a strongly built dynamic man . . . with a strong voice, a quick wit and a versatile platform approach." His recreations are travel, golf, and carpentry. The *New Scientist* called him a "common-law scientist who has lived with science so long that he is married to it by habit and repute . . . he has made an immense contribution to demolishing the ivory towers, and to giving contemporary science a sense of direction and social purpose."

PRINCIPAL WORKS: The Birth of the Future, 1934; Conquest of Suffering, 1934; Roving Commission, 1935; The Lesson of London, 1941; Carry On, London, 1941; Start Planning Britain Now, 1941; Profile of Science, 1951; Men Against the Desert, 1951; The Lamp Is Lit, 1951; Men Against Ignorance, 1953; Men Against the Jungle, 1954; Science Makes Sense (U.S., Science in Our Lives), 1955; Men Against the Frozen North, 1957; From Magic to Medicine, 1957; Medicine and Man, 1958; The Wonderful World of Medicine, 1958; Ten Steps Forward, 1958; The Hand of Life: The Story of the Weizmann Institute, 1959; The Inheritors (U.S., After the Seventh Day), 1961; Agony of the Congo, 1961; The Life Savers, 1961; Living With the Atom, 1962; Commonsense About a Starving World, 1962; Two-Way Passage, 1964; Man and the Cosmos, 1968; The Evolution of the Machine, 1968; Leonardo and the Age of the Eye, 1970.

ABOUT: Contemporary Authors 1, 1962; Current Biography, 1963; Who's Who, 1973. *Periodicals*—New Scientist January 5, 1961; New York Herald Tribune Book Review August 13, 1961; Saturday Review September 9, 1961; July 14, 1962; Times Literary Supplement March 12, 1954; May 13, 1955.

***RIVIÈRE, JACQUES** (July 15, 1886–February 14, 1925), French critic and novelist, was born at Bordeaux. He was the son of Dr. Maurice Rivière, Professor of Medicine at the University of Bordeaux, and the eldest of four children. His childhood was unhappy. His mother died when he was ten and his father remarried when he was fifteen. He disliked his stepmother, who was extremely jealous of the first wife and removed from the home everything which recalled her.

Rivière was educated at the *lycée* of Bordeaux until 1903 and returned there to take his *licence ès lettres* during his military service in 1907. Meanwhile he studied for a time at the Lycée Lakanal in Paris. At Lakanal in 1903 he met Henri Fournier (better known as Alain-Fournier), the future author of *Le Grand Meaulnes*. It was the beginning of a friendship which ended only with Fournier's death in action in World War I and which produced one of the most delightful of literary correspondences (*Correspondance 1905–1914*, 1926–28). In 1909 Rivière married Fournier's sister Isabelle. There were two children: Jacqueline who was born in 1911 and died in 1944, and Alain who was born in 1920. Both became Benedictines at sister houses in Dourgna (Tarn).

Rivière was intended for an academic career. Between 1907 and 1909 he studied philosophy at the Sorbonne, and from 1909 to 1911 he taught at the École Saint-Joseph des Tuileries and the Collège Stanislas in Paris. Then, after failing the *agrégation* for the second time, he gave up the idea of teaching and became secretary of the recently founded *Nouvelle Revue Française*. He was called up as a sergeant in the 220th Infantry Regiment on the outbreak of war and was taken prisoner on August 24, 1914. He spent two years as a prisoner of war

* rē vyâr′

JACQUES RIVIÈRE

in Germany, and the rest of the war interned in Switzerland. Rivière had already begun to make a name for himself as a critic, and his work matured greatly during his imprisonment, when he wrote most of his first novel, *Aimée* (published in 1922); a brilliant critique of the German character, *L'Allemand* (1918); and a work of Christian apologetic published posthumously as *À la trace de Dieu* (1925).

Rivière was repatriated in 1918 and was appointed editor of the *Nouvelle Revue Française* when it resumed publication in 1919. He retained the post until his death from typhoid fever six years later, fostering the NRF's reputation for publishing the best of the new writers, and preserving in its pages the work of many who had died in the war. He ranks as one of the great literary editors of our time.

In Rivière's own writing, the main formative influences—never wholly reconciled—were those of Gide and Claudel. He had been brought up as a Catholic, but like many young men of his generation surrendered his faith almost unconsciously. A turning point came with his discovery of the plays of Claudel in 1907. In that year Rivière published a long appreciation of Claudel in the *Occident* (reprinted in *Études*, 1912). This led to a long exchange of letters with the poet (*Correspondance 1907–1914*, 1926, translated as *Letters to a Doubter*) and to Rivière's return to the Church in 1913. Another work of apologetic, *De la foi*, appeared posthumously. Rivière's religious writings are those of a literary critic rather than a theologian, but are important for an understanding of the man. They belong clearly to the pragmatic psychological apologetic which had its roots in Montaigne, Pascal, and Descartes.

A second and unfinished novel, *Florence*, was published in 1935. In spite of denials by the family it is, like *Aimée*, largely autobiographical. Whereas the earlier novel had dealt with a crisis in the emotional life of a young married man, *Florence* is concerned with the marital crisis of a man of mature years. Rivière's study of the French mind, *Le Français* (1928), was a companion work to *L'Allemand*, but was too accurate a revelation of the shortcomings of his compatriots ever to be popular in his own country.

It is, however, as one of the most brilliant and penetrating literary critics of the century that Rivière deserves primarily to be remembered. "My masters are Descartes, Racine, Marivaux, Ingres, that is to say, those who refuse the shadow," he once wrote. But this strong sense of tradition was combined with a sensitive appreciation of what was valuable in contemporary writing. As early as 1914, in a brilliant study of the Symbolists called "Le Roman d'aventure" (The Adventure Story), he had called for a new kind of psychological realism, and this became a dominant theme in his criticism, along with a disinterest in "messages," a dislike of what he called "*moralisme*." In 1919, in a kind of manifesto in the NRF, he wrote: "A work of art is beautiful for reasons which are absolutely intrinsic and which can only be unraveled by direct study and by a sort of *corps à corps* with the work itself." It was his un-Gallic willingness and ability to come to grips with the book before him, rather than trying to fit it into some personal philosophical system, which distinguished his criticism. T. S. Eliot, a very different kind of critic, recognized this and praised the combination of "a precision which is free from rigidity with intellectual suppleness and finesse."

Rivière found the kind of realism he sought in Proust's *À la recherche du temps perdu*, parts of which were first published in the *Nouvelle Revue Française*. In this way, and with such studies as "Marcel Proust and the Classical Tradition," Rivière played a considerable role in securing recognition for that master. Other highlights of his criticism are his monograph on Rimbaud (1930), the pages on Racine in *Moralisme et littérature* (1932), and the essays on surrealism. Much of his best critical work can be found in an excellent selection translated by Blanche A. Price as *The Ideal Reader* (1960).

PRINCIPAL WORKS IN ENGLISH TRANSLATION: Letters to a Doubter, tr. by H. L. Stuart, 1927; The Ideal Reader (selected essays), ed., tr., and introd. by Blanche A. Price, 1960.

ABOUT: Beaulieu, P. Jacques Rivière, 1956; Cook, B. Jacques Rivière: A Life of the Spirit, 1958; Naughton, H. T. Jacques Rivière: The Development of a Man and a Creed, 1966; Smith, H. (ed.) Columbia Dictionary of Modern European Literature, 1947; Turnell, M. Jacques Rivière, 1953. *Periodicals*—Commonweal August 24, 1951; Correspondent September 25, 1925; Dublin Review

October 1936; Fortnightly Review June 1926; Living Age June 16, 1923; Mercure de France November 1, 1923; March 1, 1925; Modern Language Quarterly June 1964; Modern Language Review October 1940; Nouvelle Revue Française April 1925, March 1927; Partisan Review March 1953; Theology May 1933.

***ROBBE-GRILLET, ALAIN** (August 18, 1922–), French novelist, screenwriter, essayist, and theoretician of the "new novel," was born in Brest, Finistère, of parents who had migrated there from the Jura. He is the son of Gaston Robbe-Grillet, an engineer, and Yvonne (Canu) Robbe-Grillet. His fascinated scrutiny of the plant and animal life of the Breton seacoast is no doubt one source of his preoccupation as a writer with the surface appearance of things, as well as of his choice of a career in agricultural engineering. He studied at the Lycée Buffon, the Lycée de Brest, and the Lycée St. Louis, eventually receiving his diploma at the French National Institute of Agronomy.

During World War II Robbe-Grillet was deported to Germany to work in a tank factory at Nuremberg. It was there that he began to form his literary attitudes in conversations with another French writer, Claude Ollier. After the war, from 1945 to 1948, Robbe-Grillet worked in Paris at the National Institute of Statistics, and for the next three years served the Institute of Colonial Fruits and Crops in Morocco, French Guinea, Martinique, and Guadeloupe. Since 1955 he has been literary director of Jérôme Lindon's publishing house Les Éditions de Minuit, which publishes his own books as well as those of Samuel Beckett, Claude Simon, Michel Butor, Nathalie Sarraute, Ollier, and others associated with the *nouveau roman*.

Robbe-Grillet has explained his views in the essays collected in *Pour un nouveau roman* (1963, translated like many of his books by Richard Howard and published in English as *For a New Novel*). The "new novel" is what is left when the writer has swept away all the delusions and dishonesties which encumber the traditional novel. It is first of all nonsense, Robbe-Grillet says, to try to interpret the natural world in human terms. A mountain is not "majestic"; it is not a challenge to the aspirations of mountaineers; it is not a symbol of God's finger pointing to heaven: "The world is neither significant nor absurd. It just is." Equally misguided is the writer who fabricates a neat plot and presents this as an accurate account of reality, or who pretends that he can explain the motives or the psychological processes of another person or creature.

With the rejection of the "pathetic fallacy," the tragic sense evaporates, leaving a literature of scrupulous and dispassionate report. The reader is presented with an account which is, ideally, totally complete and accurate, and which he will interpret for himself in the light of his own experience, intelligence, and sensibility. There is to be no preconceived "story" or "characters" as a starting point, only a structure. Bruce Morrissette believes that "to Robbe-Grillet, a literary work can only acquire its meaning, and hence its value, through form."

* rôb grē ā′

ALAIN ROBBE-GRILLET

Trying to interpret the evidence provided by the senses, says Robbe-Grillet, the mind cheats itself. Much of his work illustrates the discrepancy between objective and subjective reality. In his first novel, *Les Gommes* (1953, translated as *The Erasers*), Wallas, a secret agent, is assigned to investigate the murder of Dupont, a recluse who has been a power in international politics. For twenty-four hours Wallas "enacts the odyssey of a precise-minded man at the mercy of a kaleidoscope created by false clues, mistaken identities, and the fanciful ruminations induced by fatigue." His investigations lead him back to the scene of the crime, where he kills a man whom he assumes to be Dupont's murderer; in fact it is Dupont himself, who has been not dead but in hiding. Thus an imaginary crime becomes reality, accomplished by the man who was to have solved it.

There are hints that Dupont may have been Wallas's father, and in many respects *Les Gommes* may be read as an ingenious transposition of the Oedipus myth into the framework of a modern detective story—a device which suggests an uncharacteristic concern with plot. But in many other respects the book is a prototype for Robbe-Grillet's later novels, marked as Morrissette says by "circular structure, use of nonlinear chronology, 'false' or imagined scenes, interior duplications of characters and events, concealed correspondences, serial objects, *chosiste* descriptions, 'troubling' or neosymbolic objects (such as the eraser that the protagonist vainly seeks throughout the novel), metamorphoses . . . , psychopathology, a labyrinthine, almost surrealist décor, repetitions, 'frozen' scenes, echoes, verbal enigmas, and mythic allusions. All these are incorporated in a plot which, through the use of ellipse and implication, remains open-ended and ambiguous."

Critical attention focused in particular on Robbe-Grillet's obsessively detailed and mathematically precise descriptions of *things*, which Roland Barthes describes as *chosisme*, and Morrissette associates with the existentialist notion that the human consciousness can define itself only in relation to objects. A famous example of this kind of writing is the account of one of the objects Wallas finds on his plate in an automat: "A quarter section of tomato quite perfect and without defect, sliced by machine from an absolutely symmetrical fruit. The peripheral flesh, compact and homogeneous, of a fine chemical redness, is uniformly thick between a band of shiny skin and the semicircular area where the seeds are arranged, yellow, of uniform caliber, held in place by a thin layer of greenish jelly. . . . At the top, a scarcely visible accident has occurred: a corner of the skin, detached from the flesh over the space of one or two millimeters, sticks up imperceptibly."

Many of these devices recur in *Le Voyeur* (1955, translated as *The Voyeur*), which also illustrates the preoccupation with psychosadism that is another characteristic of Robbe-Grillet's work. Either Mathias, an apparently schizoid young salesman, or Julien, a young fisherman, has tortured and murdered a girl while the other watched. But who did which is not to be established from the novel itself, which includes no objective account of the crime.

In *La Jalousie* (1957, translated as *Jealousy*), chronology and conventional plot are abandoned. The book deals instead with the reflections, recollections, fantasies, and observations of a banana planter whose wife has gone on a shopping trip to the coast with a man who may be her lover. Time is irrelevant, because the mind of the "narrator" moves freely backwards and forwards in time, compulsively rehearsing and reinterpreting a few events that he regards as crucial. And the book is shaped not by actions but by the growing intensity of the planter's jealous imaginings, which dissolve as soon as the couple return, clearly unenamored of each other. Since the husband in his musings never specifically identifies himself, the reader ideally "becomes" the narrator, and is intensely involved in his feelings—an effect which has been compared to those "subjective camera" films which are photographed from the point of view of the protagonist.

Dans le labyrinthe (1959, translated as *In the Labyrinth*) is even closer to the "pure novel" advocated by Flaubert. It is an account of a soldier's wanderings through a maze of unfamiliar streets, carrying a box that he must deliver to an unknown person at an address he has forgotten. This story is being invented as it occurs by a writer whose room contains its elements—the mysterious box, an engraving of the soldier, etc. There have been many attempts to explain this novel in allegorical terms, though Robbe-Grillet himself had intended "a strictly material reality, which is to say a reality without allegorical force." Some found in the book an odd lyricism and pathos; others, like Henri Peyre, thought it "too puritanical in its fulfillment of Flaubert's dream: a novel made of and with nothing, a Mallarméan work of absence by an anti-poet."

Robbe-Grillet's interest in the aesthetics of sexual aberration, especially sadism, dominates *La Maison de rendez-vous* (1965, translated under the same title), which features a Hong Kong brothel where "highly bred and delicate dogs" strip the clothing from tethered ladies. Similar themes are explored in some of the short sketches collected in *Instantanés* (1961, translated as *Snapshots*), and the novel *Projet pour une révolution à New York* (1970, translated as *Project for a Revolution in New York*). Robbe-Grillet's New York is an imaginary city—an agglomeration of myths from a thousand B-pictures, a city of fearful dreams, wholly given over to muggings, sirens, torture, and rape. The deliberate fracturing in this book of chronology and psychological coherence was enjoyed by one critic as an "ontological romp," and dismissed by others as self-indulgent doodling. Robbe-Grillet's technique, which owes so much to the cinema, may also be studied in his profoundly influential (and controversial) scenarios for *L'Année dernière à Marienbad* (1961, *Last Year at Marienbad*), *L'Immortelle* (1963, *The Immortal One*), and other films. The author visited New York in 1972, teaching at New York University and Columbia.

The author was married in 1957 to Catherine Rstakian. He received the Prix des Critiques in 1955 and the Prix Louis Delluc in 1963.

PRINCIPAL WORKS IN ENGLISH TRANSLATION: The Voyeur, tr. by Richard Howard, 1958; Jealousy, tr. by Richard Howard, 1959; In the Labyrinth, tr. by Richard Howard, 1960 (also tr. by Christine Brooke-Rose, 1968); Last Year at Marienbad (scenario for the film by Alain Resnais, tr. by Richard Howard), 1962; The Erasers, tr. by Richard Howard, 1964; For a New Novel, tr. by Richard Howard, 1965 (also tr. by Barbara Wright as Towards a New Novel, *published with* Snapshots, 1966);

La Maison de Rendez-vous, tr. by Richard Howard, 1966; Snapshots, tr. by Bruce Morrissette, 1968; The Immortal One (film scenario, tr. by A. M. Sheridan Smith), 1971; Dreams of Young Girls (photographs by David Hamilton, captions by Robbe-Grillet), 1972; Project for a Revolution in New York, 1972.

ABOUT: Alter, J. La Vision du monde d'Alain Robbe-Grillet, 1966; Bernal, O. Alain Robbe-Grillet: le roman de l'absence, 1964; Contemporary Authors 9–10, 1964; Cruickshank, J. (ed.) The Novelist as Philosopher, 1962; Gardies, A. Alain Robbe-Grillet, 1972; Greshoff, C. J. Seven Studies in the French Novel, 1964; International Who's Who, 1972–73; Jaffé-Freem, E. Alain Robbe-Grillet et la peinture cubiste, 1966; Kostelanetz, R. On Contemporary Literature, 1964; Le Sage, L. The French New Novel, 1962; Mauriac, C. The New Literature, 1959; Mercier, V. The New Novel, 1970; Miesch, J. Robbe-Grillet, 1965; Morgan, H. W. (ed.) The Gilded Age: A Reappraisal, 1963; Morrissette, B. Les Romans de Robbe-Grillet, 1963; Morrissette, B. Alain Robbe-Grillet, 1965; Nadeau, M. The French Novel Since the War, 1967; Peyre, H. French Novelists of Today, 1967; Ricardou, J. and van Rossum-Guyon, F. (eds.) Nouveau roman, 1972; Standford, D. (ed.) Nine Essays in Modern Literature, 1965; Stoltzfus, B. F. Alain Robbe-Grillet and the New French Novel, 1964; Who's Who, 1973; Who's Who in France, 1973–1974; Will, F. (ed.) Hereditas: Seven Essays on the Modern Experience of the Classical, 1964. *Periodicals*—Books Abroad Winter 1966; Book Week November 20, 1966; Encounter March 1962; Film Quarterly Fall 1963; Hudson Review Autumn 1963, Summer 1967; Modern Fiction Studies Winter 1965–66; Modern Language Notes May 1962, May 1963; Modern Language Quarterly Summer 1962; Modern Languages Review July 1967; New York Review of Books June 1, 1972; New York Times Book Review May 28, 1972; PMLA September 1962; Publishers Weekly March 13, 1972; University Review March 1964; Wisconsin Studies in Contemporary Literature Summer 1967; Yale French Studies Summer 1959.

***ROCHEFORT, CHRISTIANE** (1917–), French novelist and journalist, was born in Paris and has lived there all her life. Very little biographical information has been published about her, except that she is a sculptor as well as a writer and that she worked as a reporter and scriptwriter until the publication of her first novel.

This was *Le Repos du guerrier* (1958), narrated by a "nice" young Parisienne who accidentally thwarts a suicide attempt by Renaud, an alcoholic former soldier, and then feels responsible for him. Renaud, far from grateful, exploits her, beats her, and separates her from her bourgeois family and friends. But he also makes love to her, and so satisfactorily that she marries him before depositing him, at last, in a home for incurable alcoholics.

The novel's immense success obviously owes much to its revelations of female sexuality. It was a best seller in France and became a movie vehicle for Brigitte Bardot. It also received the much-publicized Prix de la Nouvelle Vague and more serious attention than perhaps it deserved from literary and social critics. Nevertheless it is a most

* rōsh fôr′

CHRISTIANE ROCHEFORT

expert piece of work, told in a restrained and elegant style, and often extremely amusing in its social observation. Translated in 1959 as *Warrior's Rest*, it seemed to Alfred Kazin "a brilliant novel rather than an important one; it is brilliant in the testimony given to Renaud, whose speeches denouncing contemporary life run away with the book, and brilliant in the rhythm and pace of the narrative."

Le Repos du guerrier established a pattern which Christiane Rochefort has so far followed in her subsequent novels, all of them satirical comments upon the conformity, hypocrisy, and gross materialism of life in welfare state France, focusing on an individual of some originality or creativity who struggles for personal and sexual freedom and, usually, loses.

Les Petits Enfants du siècle (1961, translated by Linda Asher as *Children of Heaven* and by Edward Hyams as *Josyane and the Welfare*) has as its narrator and heroine Josyane, a working-class girl in whose milieu children are conceived not from love but because they bring a state subsidy, rapidly translatable into a new television set or refrigerator. Josyane attempts through promiscuity to escape from this shabby materialism but is soon trapped. Her condensed, slangy, and often witty narrative reminded some reviewers of Raymond Queneau's *Zazie*, though it lacks Queneau's subtlety. Like its predecessor, *Les Petits Enfants* was a best seller and a prizewinner, receiving the Prix du Roman Populiste. Edmund Wilson praised it for "trying to escape from the literary fashions of French fiction and to show us what life in modern Paris is really like for the ordinary people submerged in it." Christiane Rochefort returned to a similar theme in

Une Rose pour Morrison (A Rose for Morrison, 1966).

In *Les Stances à Sophie* (1963), the narrator is Céline, a natural bohemian who surrenders her freedom in a bourgeois marriage, finds this intolerable, and escapes happily into a more rewarding life as an idea girl in a strip club. She is the first of the author's heroines to win her struggle against society, and her language is a suitably colorful mixture of five-letter words, Paris argot, and hipster jargon—a challenge admirably met by her translator, Helen Eustis, in the English-language version. This appeared as *Cats Don't Care for Money*; the French title actually refers to an obscene song about a disgustingly depraved woman. It was yet another best seller for Christiane Rochefort in France, and was well received abroad. Edmund Wilson found it her best book to date and called her a writer of "a certain importance," whose novels are "not only amusing but also to be taken seriously as studies of contemporary France." Other critics have objected that her characters are more important as symbols of social malaise than as people, but agree that they are presented "with a cool sympathy and a sophisticated *élan* that keeps the reader's interest engaged till the end, if not beyond the end," of their adventures.

PRINCIPAL WORKS IN ENGLISH TRANSLATION: Warrior's Rest, 1959; Children of Heaven, 1962 (England, Josyane and the Welfare); Cats Don't Care for Money, 1965.

ABOUT: Boisdeffre, P. de. Dictionnaire de littérature contemporaine, 1962; Kazin, A. Contemporaries, 1963; Peyre, H. French Novelists of Today, 1967; Wilson, E. Europe Without Baedeker, 1966. *Periodicals*—Atlas August 1966; New Yorker May 21, 1966; Yale French Studies no. 27 1961.

ROLO, CHARLES J(AMES) (October 16, 1916–), English-born journalist, literary critic, writer on financial subjects, writes: "I was born in Alexandria, Egypt, a philistine city which—romanticized and mythologized—was projected onto the map of contemporary literature in the 1950s by Lawrence Durrell's famous Alexandria 'quartet.' At the age of eleven, I was taken to see a performance of a revue, composed by a local French *boulevardier*, which poked fun at the doings of the foreign colony. Instantly stagestruck, I decided to confect a similar entertainment about the small fry—and did so forthwith. For reasons which elude me today, I chose to write the skit in French—indeed in rhymed Alexandrines—and a grown-up cousin set it to music. It received two performances (in which I played the lead) and was, as I recall, a huge success. My subsequent ventures into show business proved far less fortunate. In the late 1940s I rewrote an English murder mystery for a Broadway producer, and a film script of the life of Anton Dvorák, both of which failed to reach production.

"My father being British, I was sent to school in England. Having grown up in Egypt in considerable luxury, I loathed the Spartan regime—cold classrooms, freezing dormitories, unspeakable plumbing, and inedible food—which was supposed to build the character of young English gentlemen. This experience had the opposite of the intended effect: it left me with a resolute dedication to modern comforts, and a vulgar attachment, whether at home or abroad, to the most luxurious surroundings and means of transportation I can possibly afford.

"After the rigors of my schooldays at Charterhouse, Oxford was paradise. The life of an undergraduate with some means had not changed much from that described by Evelyn Waugh in *Brideshead Revisited*. One had a servant; gave small, elegant luncheon parties with cold lobster and Rhine wine; and ran up charge accounts at the tailor, the bootmaker, and the wine merchant. I did some writing for the undergraduate magazine, *The Isis*, and formed a vague idea of earning my living by journalism, but didn't know how to begin. When I graduated (with an Honors degree in Politics, Philosophy, and Economics) the editor of *The Isis*, an American, suggested I enroll in the Columbia School of Journalism in New York. It seemed an alluring idea, and in the fall of 1938 I found myself at Columbia.

"A year later, I had a master's degree in journalism and a job as translator of French, German and Italian at the Princeton Listening Center, a Rockefeller Foundation project formed to study shortwave radio propaganda. The job gave me what most beginning writers of nonfiction lack—a timely subject and source material to which very few people had access. I started to publish magazine articles—the first appeared in *Harper's*—and later expanded them into a book, *Radio Goes to War*.

"When the war in Europe broke out, I had called the British Consulate and had been told to stay put. In due course, I went to work for the British Ministry of Information in New York, where I did a great deal of writing for U.S. magazines about the British war effort. One of these articles grew into a book, *Wingate's Raiders*, the story of Major-General Orde Wingate's campaigns behind the Japanese lines in Burma.

"I spent the last year of the war as a war correspondent for the *Atlantic Monthly* in the Middle East and Europe, and later became the *Atlantic*'s literary critic and travel editor, a position I held until 1960. During these years, I also taught (at the Columbia School of General Studies); lectured; and did a great deal of writing—literary essays, travel, and political and economic reportage. (All told, I must have published to date more than a hundred articles in magazines ranging from the *Saturday Evening Post* and *Reader's Digest* to the

[London] *Spectator* and *Barron's Financial Weekly*.) I served on the fiction and nonfiction juries of the National Book Awards in 1952, 1960, and 1963; was on the Executive Board of the P.E.N. from 1952 to 1962 and vice-president of the P.E.N. in 1955 and 1956.

"By 1960 I had been writing a monthly book review column more or less continuously for twelve years—and I felt thoroughly stale. At this point an opportunity presented itself to strike out in an altogether new direction. I had been active for some fifteen years in the stock market with gratifying results, and, unlikely though it may seem, I was offered—and accepted—a job as security analyst and research editor in a large New York brokerage house. I have been working in Wall Street ever since then and have not lost my fascination with the marketplace.

"I continue to do a good deal of writing, mostly on financial and economic subjects. My work in progress is a symposium on investments, and, like most writers of nonfiction, I keep toying with the idea of a novel—something in an extravagant and farcical vein. I live in Manhattan, close to two great museums, with a wife, a son of eight, a large library, and a modest collection of pictures."

Not much needs to be added to Rolo's characteristically lively account of his varied career. *Radio Goes to War* was an absorbing and carefully written study of Allied and Axis broadcast propaganda in the early years of World War II, while *Wingate's Raiders* was enjoyed not only on account of its fascinating subject but for the author's "splendid gift for narrative," his avoidance of "tedious heroics." Not content with official records of the campaign, Rolo had interviewed men who had served under the brilliant and idiosyncratic Wingate, and wrote as if he himself had taken part in the jungle fighting. As one reviewer wrote, "he picked up the human details that make the story live and wove them together with the skill of a dramatist."

The same brisk, buoyant, and highly readable manner distinguished Rolo's reviews for the *Atlantic*, where he established himself as one of the most perceptive, balanced, and entertaining literary journalists of the day. These years of wide reading have left their mark on his financial writing, in which he is liable (for example) to quote Oscar Wilde in a discussion of bull markets, and which shares with his literary criticism a rare and welcome ability to expound abstract ideas in solidly human terms. Rolo has edited Waugh, Huxley, and Moravia, and also a symposium, *Psychiatry in American Life*.

PRINCIPAL WORKS: Radio Goes to War: The "Fourth Front," 1942; Wingate's Raiders: An Account of the Fabulous Adventure That Raised the Curtain on the Battle for Burma, 1944; (ed.) Psychiatry in American Life, 1963.

CHARLES J. ROLO

ABOUT: *Periodicals*—Atlantic June 1944; Nation February 19, 1944; New York Times February 12, 1944; April 12, 1958; New York Times Book Review January 25, 1942; February 13, 1944; Saturday Review January 24, 1942; February 12, 1944.

ROOKE, DAPHNE (MARIE) (March 6, 1914–), South African novelist, is the daughter of Robert and Marie (Knevitt) Pizzey. She was born at Boksburg, in the Transvaal, and educated at Durban Girls' High School. In 1937 she was married to Irvin Rooke. She left South Africa in 1946 and went to live in New South Wales, Australia. The same year her first novel, *The Sea Hath Bounds*, won first prize in a South African literary competition. It was published the same year in South Africa, and appeared in the United States four years later as *A Grove of Fever Trees*. Aptly named, it was a hectic evocation of life in an isolated white farming community in Zululand, narrated as by a man, virtually deranged, who retraces with total recall the family jealousies leading to the sinister "accident" which has confined him to a wheelchair.

The novel, with its sensuous imagery, its dark Conradian undertones contrasting strangely with the flamboyant brilliance of the setting, made an immediate impact. Mrs. Rooke continued in the same vein in *Mittee*, a violent chronicle of Transvaal life in the 1890s, when a Boer community's attempts to survive and prosper are overwhelmed by crime, incest, miscegenation, and every kind of tragedy. The narrator this time is Selina, devoted African servant of Mittee, the childlike wife of a

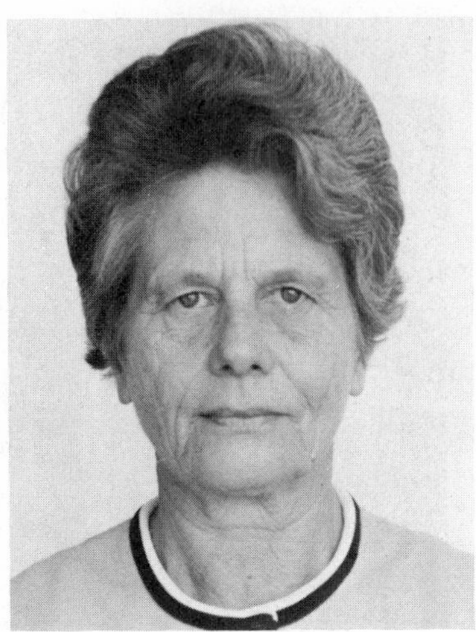

DAPHNE ROOKE

brutal Boer farmer. The book was called "melodramatic, savage, vivid," a lurid story which owes its air of authenticity to the author's wholehearted belief in her characters, "the fervent feeling that lies just behind her vigorous, graceless style." *Ratoons*, reviewed in similar terms, is a saga of fifty years in the progress of another farming family on the stormy coast of Natal, where the Hindu population arouses the antagonism of both whites and blacks.

Mrs. Rooke has continued her assault on her readers' nerves and emotions with a succession of rasping romances. *Wizards' Country* was a tour de force reconstruction of the Zulu wars, a racial tragedy seen through the eyes of Benge, a hunchback feared for his supposed magical powers. In *Beti*, a mixture of charming fantasy and grim truth, set in India, she creates "simply by excellent dialogue and brief, brilliantly cut narrative, a whole world of reality." In *A Lover for Estelle*, about the fatal interaction of two quite different families in Zululand in 1920, the artful simplicity of her style "gives a grandeur and dignity to a story that in any other hands could be . . . melodramatic and sentimental." *The Greyling*, which centers on the murder of a half-caste girl by an Afrikaner, is for Mrs. Rooke an unusually direct and contemporary approach to the South African tragedy, and had a mixed reception. *Diamond Jo* is an energetic epic of frontier life in the Transvaal during the diamond rush of the 1860s.

Mrs. Rooke has repeatedly demonstrated that she is not only a first-class romantic entertainer, but, as the *Times Literary Supplement* has said, "an outstandingly accomplished writer of English prose. She has a lyrical quality, an extreme felicity in the construction of her sentences, a choice of words and images that make many of today's novelists seem like stumbling drunks." She has written several books for children. Mrs. Rooke has one daughter. Her hobby is the breeding of boxer dogs.

PRINCIPAL WORKS: *All novels*—A Grove of Fever Trees, 1950; Mittee, 1951; Ratoons, 1953; Wizards' Country, 1957; Beti, 1959; A Lover for Estelle, 1961; The Greyling, 1962; Diamond Jo, 1965; Boy on the Mountain, 1969.

ABOUT: Vinson, J. (ed.) Contemporary Novelists, 1972; Ward, M. and Marquardt, D. A. Authors of Books for Young People, 1964; Who's Who, 1973. *Periodicals*—New York Herald Tribune Book Review February 17, 1952; December 20, 1953; New York Times March 1, 1950; Saturday Review March 7, 1959.

ROSA, JOÃO GUIMARÃES (June 3, 1908–November 19, 1967), Brazil's greatest contemporary novelist, was born in Cordisburgo, in the backwoods state of Minas Gerais. The son of wealthy patrician parents, he earned a medical degree and worked for some years as a doctor in Minas Gerais, thus coming into intimate contact with the landscape and people which his fiction was later to celebrate. Rosa took part as a doctor in the Brazilian revolution and civil war of 1930–1932 and then entered his country's diplomatic corps, serving in Hamburg just before World War II, in Bogotá from 1942 to 1944, and in Paris from 1948 to 1951. He ended his career as director of the Frontiers Service of the Ministry of Foreign Affairs in Rio de Janeiro.

A modest and introspective man, Rosa published nothing until the appearance of *Sagarana*, a volume of short stories, in 1946. His sparse output also includes a two-volume collection of novellas, *Corpo de baile* (1956), another book of short stories, *Primeiras Estórias* (1962), and his great novel *Grande Sertão-Veredas* (1956).

Sagarana (translated under the same title by Harriet de Onís), contains nine subtly related parables of the *sertão*, the Brazilian wilderness, all of them full of human and natural violence, of brutality and magic, and told with wit, vitality, and a poet's exactness of observation and image. Animals play an important part in these stories, often behaving with more intelligence and goodwill than the human beings (as in one tale in which a donkey with mystical leanings rescues his drunken and brutish master during a flood). The title of the collection is an invented word, combining the Norse *saga* with the Tupi suffix *rana* (signifying "in the manner of"). It is a device typical of Rosa's synthetic method, which seeks to free Brazilian Portuguese from its exclusively European orientation. *Sagarana*, according to Alexander Coleman, "marks the beginning of a new direction for

Brazilian letters." In it, Rosa "began the forging of a new language through prodigious linguistic play and the creation of new words. In his work, oral, literary, archaic and slang languages are fused into a highly personal instrument which can only be called Brazilian."

This extraordinary instrument is employed to its fullest effect in Rosa's novel *Grande Sertão-Veredas* (translated by J. L. Taylor and Harriet de Onís as *The Devil to Pay in the Backlands*). Like many contemporary Latin American novels, it displays the effects of influences that are so heterogenous—Joyce, Proust, and Faulkner being the most notable—that they result in a highly original eclecticism.

The novel is written in the form of a monologue delivered by Riobaldo, a former bandit of the *sertão*, to a listener of Conradian forbearance. The events he recalls with such nostalgia take place at the end of the nineteenth century. Riobaldo tells of his campaign to revenge the death of a comrade and his relationship with his remarkable friend Diadorim. The story develops, in fact, as a progressively less reticent confession, which includes the narrator's firm conviction that he has been in league with Satan, in contrast to whom the beautiful Diadorim is cast as a rather ambiguous angel.

The book tells a story that is enthralling in itself. The brutal landscape and the violence it inspires in its inhabitants provide powerful reading. Rosa, moreover, skillfully lets his story slip from reality to fantasy, and from fantasy to myth—he does the same in many of his short stories and has been called "the first expressionist writer in Brazilian, and a myth maker of the first order." The brilliance of the novel's structure survived translation, it was thought, but the power of the language inevitably suffered. Nevertheless, Thomas G. Bergin, in his review of the English version, called it "an epic . . . somewhat on the lines of *Moby Dick*, less subtle, less profound but not unworthy at least of the comparison."

The abrupt change of manner in *Primeiras Estórias*, published in 1962, has been attributed to the nearly fatal heart attack which Rosa suffered in 1958. This volume of brief, richly suggestive stories, sympathetically translated by Barbara Shelby as *The Third Bank of the River*, showed, Alexander Coleman wrote, "a newly attained distance from local realities; the stories are much closer to the self, so much more 'essential.' There is in them a sense of leave-taking, elegiac in tone, along with an even more scrupulous reading of Nature's signs. Guimarães Rosa was always something of a contemplative Taoist, but here he wrenches the last possible significance out of every pebble."

Rosa died in 1967 at his home in Copacabana only three days after he had been received with great acclaim into the Brazilian Academy of Letters. He had been elected in 1963, but postponed the investiture because, he said, he feared "the emotion of the moment." Emir Rodriguez Monegal says that he was "tall, with a faintly ironic smile, heavily built but still agile . . . a man elusive as his prose."

JOÃO GUIMARÃES ROSA

PRINCIPAL WORKS IN ENGLISH TRANSLATION: The Devil to Pay in the Backlands, 1963; Sagarana, 1966; The Third Bank of the River and Other Stories, 1968.

ABOUT: Penguin Companion to Literature 3, 1971. *Periodicals*—Christian Science Monitor October 7, 1968; Encounter September 1965; Nation July 11, 1966; New York Times May 21, 1966; November 21, 1967; New York Times Book Review April 17, 1966; September 29, 1968; Saturday Review April 16, 1966; October 19, 1968; Time October 4, 1968; Times Literary Supplement October 23, 1969.

ROSENBERG, HAROLD (February 2, 1906–), American art critic, was born in Williamsburg, Brooklyn, "next door to the world's first movie house." ("Since then," he says, "I have loved the movies but detest film and cinema and particularly film criticism.") He is the son of Abraham and Fanny (Edelman) Rosenberg and was educated at the City College of New York and at St. Lawrence University, where he took a law degree in 1927. Rosenberg married Maynatalie Tabak in 1932. They have a daughter and live in East Hampton, New York.

Rosenberg belongs to that generation of socially conscious Greenwich Village intellectuals whose ideas were shaped most conspicuously by Marx and the Depression. His interests were at first primarily literary, and his poems—Imagist in style but political in their preoccupations—began to appear

HAROLD ROSENBERG

during the 1930s in such magazines as *transition* and *Poetry* (Chicago). His verse was well received on the whole, but thought rather uneven in technical accomplishment and excessively intellectual. Rosenberg served from 1938 to 1942 as national art editor for the WPA American Guides series, and from 1944 to 1945 was deputy director for domestic radio services in the Office of War Information. A volume of verse called *Trance Above the Streets* appeared in 1943; by then he had become deeply involved in the New York art world, and this first book of poetry was also his last.

During the 1930s, left-wing artists and writers were struggling to evolve forms whereby their work could directly serve their political convictions—to break from tradition towards a popular and revolutionary art. His study of avant-garde literature and painting had convinced Rosenberg that the social realists were on the wrong track. Hence the apolitical nature of *Possibilities*, the short-lived but interesting art magazine founded by Rosenberg and Robert Motherwell in 1947. Rosenberg has come to believe that revolution for the artist is in the act of painting itself. "It was necessary [after the 1930s] for each individual artist to break with what he had perhaps considered to be a philosophy of life in order to make painting itself a philosophy of life." In the future, "self-development shall be the motive of all work."

The Tradition of the New is a collection of essays about modern painting and painters in New York, where one trend has followed another in such a rapid and accelerating sequence that the "new" has itself become a tradition, forcing the painter constantly beyond his resources. For this state of affairs, in which one wave is submerged by the next before its impact can be properly absorbed, Rosenberg blames not the artist but the artistic establishment of dealers, museum directors, publishers, and critics. He is, as Wylie Sypher says, "a critic passionately devoted to the contemporary who is also dissatisfied with the contemporary . . . he repudiates the vanguard audience and vanguard critics in order to defend the vanguard painter."

The logical outcome of the situation Rosenberg describes is what he called "action painting," in which the painter accepts as valid only what he is at any given moment *in process* of creating. This was the theme of the most discussed essay in *The Tradition of the New*, in which Rosenberg writes: "At a certain moment the canvas began to appear to one American painter after another as an arena in which to act—rather than as a space in which to reproduce, re-design, analyze or 'express' an object, actual or imagined. What was to go on the canvas was not a picture but an event." Rosenberg's essays are, as Dudley Fitts has said, "sharp, controlled, witty, and, at their best, urgently illuminating," though his prose is on occasion so densely concentrated as to seem opaque, and may be rendered even more difficult by "sudden plunges into metaphysical speculation."

Rosenberg's views on the apolitical function of art are further illustrated in his admirable short book on Arshile Gorky, the Armenian painter who arrived in the United States in 1920 and committed suicide in Greenwich Village in 1948. Gorky had at first attempted to harness his art to his political beliefs (as in his murals at LaGuardia Airport), and then had turned inwards to produce out of his own wretched experience of life his prototypical action paintings.

Another collection of essays, most of them first published in the *New Yorker*, appeared in 1964 as *The Anxious Object*, continuing the line of argument laid down in *The Tradition of the New*. Rosenberg's "anxious object" is the painting produced as part of the incessant search for novelty, in which every fresh development increases the artist's feeling that "everything has been done," and forces him to take ever bigger risks in the pursuit of innovation. Rosenberg argues that we must not be cozened into looking at pictures as examples of this or that school or trend, but must find the reality of art in "the particular work." Deploring the academicism or mere showmanship of much modern painting, he nevertheless believes that "new art is valuable for the novel state it induces in the spectator and for what it reveals to him about himself, the physical world, or simply his way of reacting to paintings."

Wylie Sypher thought the book "an indispensable examination of the conditions under which the New York painter paints, though Rosenberg does not—perhaps cannot—confirm the esthetic values in the paintings themselves, much as he may wish to do so." Most other critics shared Sypher's high estimate of the book's value, and *Newsweek*'s admiration for its "swift, crackling prose." Another volume of *New Yorker* essays appeared in 1969 as *Artworks and Packages*, and this was followed by his gloomiest report so far on the state of art, *The De-definition of Art*. Here he argues that such a ridiculous assortment of objects and activities are now being offered to the public as "art" that the term has ceased to have any real meaning, so that we live in effect in a "Post-Art" period.

Rosenberg's "incomparable acquaintance with what is happening, how, and to whom, in the New York School" is regularly demonstrated in the *New Yorker*, whose art critic he has been since 1967. He is also much in demand as a visiting lecturer, teaches at the University of Chicago, is a consultant to the Advertising Council, and program director for the Longview Foundation. "Being born in Williamsburg," he says, "gave me the same accent as Henry Miller but a different set of ideas. I once heard him on the radio, mistook him for me, and was about to repudiate myself when the announcer told us who he was."

PRINCIPAL WORKS: *Poetry*—Trance Above the Streets, 1943. *Criticism*—The Tradition of the New, 1959; Arshile Gorky: The Man, the Times, the Idea, 1962; The Anxious Object: Art Today and Its Audience, 1964; Artworks and Packages, 1969; The De-definition of Art: Action Art to Pop to Earthworks, 1972; Discovering the Present: Three Decades in Art, Culture, and Politics (selected essays), 1973.

ABOUT: Ashton, D. The Unknown Shore, 1962; Who's Who in America, 1972–1973; Who's Who in American Art, 1970. *Periodicals*—Hi Fi January 4, 1962; Library Journal April 1, 1959; New Republic February 22, 1960; February 20, 1965; New Statesman August 3, 1962; New York Review of Books December 17, 1964; New York Times Book Review January 17, 1965; Newsweek December 14, 1964; Partisan Review Summer 1962, Fall 1962, Spring 1964; Saturday Review January 23, 1965.

ISAAC ROSENFELD

ROSENFELD, ISAAC (March 10, 1918–July 14, 1956), American critic, essayist, novelist, and short story writer, was born in Chicago to immigrant parents, Sam and Miriam (Dubin) Rosenfeld. With his two sisters he grew up in a Yiddish-speaking lower-middle-class milieu on the West Side. The death of his mother while he was still a child left him with a permanent sense of loss and longing for affection.

Saul Bellow, a lifelong friend, remembers him, still in short pants, reading an essay on Schopenhauer before their high school debating club. Rosenfeld went on to major in philosophy at the University of Chicago, where he studied under Eliseo Vivas and Rudolf Carnap and was immersed in the radical atmosphere of the late 1930s, when "politics was form and substance, accident and modification, the metaphor of all things."

In 1941 Rosenfeld received his M.A. at Chicago and began doctoral studies at New York University. The same year he married Vasiliki Sarantakis and published his first story in *New Republic*. He left the university and became a regular contributor to that magazine, which in 1943 made him an assistant editor. A few months later Rosenfeld lunged off in quite a different direction, spending the rest of the war as the operator of a barge on the East River.

After the war Rosenfeld settled in Greenwich Village, whose bohemianism attracted him. By then he had two children, Eleni and George, and to support his family he taught part-time at New York University and contributed essays and stories to a score of reviews, among them *Commentary*, *Jewish Frontier*, *Nation*, *New Republic*, *Kenyon Review* and *Partisan Review*. He remained in New York for ten years, earning a reputation as a "Greenwich Village sage," an institution in the Waldorf Cafeteria on Sixth Avenue, where he would talk and argue for hours. He subsequently taught for a while at the University of Minnesota, where he was followed everywhere by a group of freshman disciples to whom, it is said, he would distribute A's as marks of affection. Rosenfeld finally returned to the University of Chicago as an instructor in literature. He was on the verge of resigning when he died suddenly, at thirty-eight, of a heart attack. At least as much as for his writings, many of which have been published in book form only since his death, he is remembered as a legendary figure, whose life and personality symbolize for his time and place the alienation and despair felt by many but lived out only by a few.

For Rosenfeld, an assigned review was often only the point of departure for a literary essay. "What is surprising—indeed astonishing," wrote Theodore Solotaroff, "is the quality of almost every performance, the calm, confident strength of the writing, the intellectual grasp of his ideas, the richness and concentration that he brought to the traditional methods of serious literary journalism." He gave to the most routine tasks a sensitivity, independence of judgment, and a trained talent for philosophical analysis that exposed pretension and, as Bellow says, "consistently antagonized 'intelligent opinion.'" Although dialectic and intellectualism for their own sakes tempted him, he saw abstraction as a threat to feeling, and indeed the force of his criticism proceeds partly, as Theodore Solotaroff puts it, "from his ability . . . to make one care." He affected people, in another critic's words, "in a direct and troubling way."

He followed no precise methodology or aesthetic credo, but he had a talent for grasping the essence of the book under discussion, and he concerned himself, as he said, with restoring "confidence in our ability, within our right, to take a simply human measure of literature." He was interested in the interaction of man and writer, united through the imagination, in what he called "character"; in the contribution of a work of literature to our understanding of ourselves, as feeling beings in a society. John O'Hara, Henry Miller, and Anaïs Nin, for example, are all criticized for their failure to "make an imaginative synthesis of what society has dismembered," a synthesis of the human and animal in man, or, as he wrote of Anaïs Nin, to close "the gap between personification and personality . . . which no amount of psychoanalysis, or sensitive writing . . . can fill."

His basic concerns were with the existential problems of alienation and freedom, and he was much influenced by Wilhelm Reich's theories of orgasmic fulfillment as the means towards individual liberation and social connection. At the same time he admired Kafka and his struggle for a "purely human freedom," and Tolstoy for his ability to fuse nature and morality—an ability which, Rosenfeld thought, derived from a strong sexual drive and an equally potent religious drive, enabling Tolstoy to bypass the struggles of the ego and give himself up to greater themes.

Rosenfeld's fiction, less accomplished than his criticism, was also full of promise. In 1945 he won the Dial Press-*Partisan Review* novelette contest with *The Colony*, and the following year brought out his only published novel, *Passage From Home*. It is the largely autobiographical story of a boy philosopher, "sensitive as a burn," growing up in an enclosed petit-bourgeois family on the Chicago West Side. In search of freedom, Bernard runs away to live with his bohemian Aunt Minnie but finds with her only bitterness and waste. He goes home, aware now that his real longing "looked neither to home nor exile, but to a life foreign to both in which some beauty and freedom prevailed." The novel was moderately praised for its craftsmanship and sensitivity.

His stories also deal with isolation, nostalgia, and the joy that comes at rare moments of human contact and revelation. There is little incident in these stories, and the narrative depends in nearly every case on the personal development of its hero. Rosenfeld became a master of the technique of revealing character in depth, often obliquely, and in few words. Robert Alter has written of Rosenfeld's remarkable ability to convey a sense of the preciousness of life "from a viewpoint that is absolutely unillusioned, and through the very form of his fiction to elicit in his readers the movements of the mind that involve them, too, in the difficulty of holding to life"; Rosenfeld, Alter concluded, was "one of the very few American writers in the past two decades to realize something like an authentic personal vision in his work."

One of the most admired of Rosenfeld's stories presents King Solomon as an aging East Side Jew, to whom come mysteriously, year after year, a procession of young girls who lay themselves beside him. Eventually he is visited by the Queen of Sheba, who also offers herself to him; past her youth, she is rejected. Before she leaves she says: "Yours is the wisdom of love, which is the highest . . . [but] your power rests on despair. Yours is the power of drawing love, the like of which has not been seen. But you despair of loving with your own heart." And Solomon dies alone. This story was written towards the end of Rosenfeld's life, and, it has been suggested, reflects his struggle to liberate and enlarge his own capacity to love.

During the late 1940s Rosenfeld began work on another novel, *The Enemy*, of which a few chapters appeared in magazines, but which was rejected when it was completed in 1951. Rosenfeld was profoundly affected by this rebuff and wrote less and less in his last years, assailed according to Saul Bellow by "boredom and deadness, despair, even madness" in his effort to keep alive his faith in the natural, in love and joy, during a period with which he had little sympathy. All the same, Bellow believes, "He won. He changed himself. He enlarged his power to love. Many loved him. He was an extraordinary and significant man."

Rosenfeld had been divorced from his wife and, though he had many friends, he died alone in a seedy furnished room that was infested with cockroaches which he refused to kill. He was a round-faced, heavyset man who loved to clown and mimic. Norman Podhoretz called him "possibly the most gifted writer to appear in America in the last few decades," but few other critics would go so far. In the words of Theodore Solotaroff, "the figure that survives is less of an immensely gifted writer than of a man whose life and character have come to seem more remarkable than anything he wrote—or could have written."

PRINCIPAL WORKS: *Fiction*— Passage From Home, 1946; Alpha and Omega (stories), 1966. *Criticism*—An Age of Enormity: Life and Writing in the Forties and Fifties, 1962.

ABOUT: Bellow, S. *foreword to* and Solotaroff, T. *introduction to* An Age of Enormity, 1962. *Periodicals*—Commentary June 1957, May 1962, October 1962, November 1966; New Republic September 3, 1956; October 15, 1956; December 31, 1956; New York Times July 16, 1956; Partisan Review Fall 1956; Wilson Library Bulletin September 1956.

ROSENFELD, SAMUEL. *See* "TZARA, TRISTAN"

ROSENTHAL, M(ACHA) L(OUIS) (March 14, 1917–), American poet, critic, and editor, writes: "I was born in Washington, D.C., in 1917. My immigrant parents and their friends were intense, idealistic, highspirited people. We lived in many working-class neighborhoods and I went to many schools. My father, a music lover with a fine though untrained voice, worked at every sort of job from railroading to paper-hanging, had a hard time in the Depression but came through it on his feet. My mother, an ardent young Zionist, was a friend of several people who were later to be leaders in the state of Israel. Her capacity for friendship and her psychological insight have always been remarkable.

"In 1932–1933, I attended Boys' Public Latin School in Boston. It was the year of adolescent awakening in any case, but the school played a special role that I have always appreciated. We moved to Cleveland the next year, and from there I won a scholarship to the University of Chicago. There I benefited greatly, and with joy, from the clash of philosophies, ideologies, and political movements and from the rigorous, imaginative course of studies. I earned my B.A. and M.A. degrees there, and studied toward the doctorate for another year while working for the Federal Writers' Project. In 1939 I accepted an instructorship at Michigan State University, where during the war I was to be involved with the Army Air Force and Army Specialized Training Programs. In 1945 I decided to specialize in modern literature and was encouraged to complete the doctorate at

M. L. ROSENTHAL

New York University under the direction of Professor Oscar Cargill. I had by then published some of my poetry and criticism; and after a while I was invited to teach at New York University, where I am now Professor of English.

"The academic life has its particular joys and sufferings, needs and relationships. It is hard to generalize at all about its effect on the character of a writer, or of anyone else. It does not change the quality of the rest of one's life, though it must be deeply experienced to be rightly felt. I have practiced it in the midst of everything else that goes to make up my life, side by side with my critical and editorial work and my poetry—all these are in some mysterious way aspects of one another. I like teaching, both the relationship with students and the kind of thinking and feeling that I do when engaged in it. It takes me far along the road that I have given myself to, of a certain exploration of creative sensibility, partly through the study of literature and of critical theory and partly through what I discover in myself and in others with whatever empathy I possess.

"Among my more interesting editorial experiences I count my poetry editorship of the *Nation* from 1956 to 1961 and my service as advisor to the Macmillan Company during the period of their Paperback Poets series (roughly, 1957–1962). My own poems, essays, and reviews have appeared in a wide variety of publications, and I have contributed more or less regularly to a number of them—most recently to the *Spectator* (London). As a critic and editor, I have helped young or neglected people to publish and have sought as well to refocus attention in the contemporary context on older figures of this age by pressing, for instance, for the publication of Hugh MacDiarmid in the United States and of William Carlos Williams in England. Though recognizing the limits of critical 'influence' and the presumptuousness the very thought of it can invite, I have tried to encourage a poetry true at once to the poet's own voice, to the demands of a serious and spirited sensibility, and to the more advanced artistic positions of the century. I am for both an art that explodes and a rigorous, exquisite, and sophisticated craftsmanship, and have tried to gain sympathy with the inward vision or 'magic' of individual poets as much as possible. In my own poetry, so far as I can help it, I do not repeat myself or the effects of others but try to be true to my own sense of the pity and the ludicrousness and the superb reality of things.

"I am an ACLS Fellow (1942; 1950–1951) and a Guggenheim Fellow (1960–1961; 1964–1965), and my family and I have twice recently lived for a year in London, and these sojourns have been meaningful to us in many ways."

M. L. Rosenthal is one of those rare and courageous critics who are not content to mull over the poetic wars and heroes of the past, but plunge into the thick of today's action to bring back, as he puts it, the "news from the front." He is, according to Thomas Lask, "allied to no school and is a spokesman for no manifesto." He is in his criticism "concerned only with the matter at hand—the poem."

The Modern Poets was intended as an attack on "the formidable but quite unnecessary barriers between poetry and the general reader," and if it failed to destroy those barriers it at least knocked some illuminating gaps in them. The *Times Literary Supplement* praised in particular Rosenthal's "brilliant popular essays" on Yeats, Pound, and Eliot, but thought the book deteriorated when it turned to the poets of the 1940s and 1950s. There was some feeling that the book was excessively emotional in its language and "all but unrelievedly solemn," but general praise for its insights, "its grasp of the range of modern poetry," and the consistency of its author's critical standards.

The New Poets concentrates on American and British poetry since World War II, finding in the work of Robert Lowell and the "confessional" poets the mode most characteristic of the period, without overlooking its antecedents or its dangers. R. D. Spector wrote that Rosenthal's "patient analysis of individual poems, his ability to place them within a larger pattern, and his respect for the artist and his problems—all gracefully and authoritatively expressed—set [him] in the first rank of American critics." *The New Modern Poetry*, including selections from the work of one hundred and four poets, complements *The New Poets*, so that the two books provide, as Robie Macauley said, "the first broad view of the new poetry and at the same time the first study that distinguishes and examines the major trends in a satisfactory way."

A reviewer in the *Times Literary Supplement* of *Blue Boy on Skates*, a collection of Rosenthal's own poems, identified its theme as "love's long waste" and went on: "When he concentrates on situations from his Jewish childhood he comes near to making an individual impact; unfortunately, even here he is reluctant to project his memories in very specific terms and is all too ready to fall back on the generalized lament." There was a general feeling that Rosenthal, like so many critic-poets, was inclined to pastiche and "excessively literary allusiveness." *Beyond Power*, a later collection, also evoked (as one critic wrote) no more than "a murmur of polite appreciation."

M. L. Rosenthal is the son of Jacob and Ethel (Brown) Rosenthal. He was married in 1939 to Victoria Himmelstein and they have three children. He exerted much influence as poetry editor of the *Nation*, not least because of his willingness "to annoy poets by pointing to weak passages, requesting their improvement." No doubt he has followed the same procedure as poetry editor, since 1970, of *The Humanist*, the journal published jointly by the American Humanist Association and the American Ethical Union.

PRINCIPAL WORKS: *Criticism*—(with A. J. M. Smith) Exploring Poetry, 1955; A Primer of Ezra Pound, 1960; The Modern Poets: A Critical Introduction, 1960; The New Poets: American and British Poetry Since World War II, 1967; Randall Jarrell, 1972. *Poetry*—Blue Boy on Skates, 1964; Beyond Power, 1969; The View From the Peacock's Tail, 1973. *As editor*—(with T. H. Jameson) A Selection of Verse, Lyric and Contemplative, Since the Fourteenth Century, 1952; (with G. D. Sanders and J. H. Nelson) Chief Modern Poets of England and America (5th ed.), 1970; William Butler Yeats, Selected Poems, 1962; The William Carlos Williams Reader, 1966; The New Modern Poetry: British and American Poetry Since World War II, 1967; One Hundred Postwar Poems, 1968.
ABOUT: Contemporary Authors 4, 1963; Directory of American Scholars, 1964; Who's Who in America, 1972–1973. *Periodical*—Nation September 20, 1965 (100th Anniversary Issue.)

ROSS, LILLIAN (June 8, 1927–), American journalist and short story writer, was born to Louis and Edna (Rosenson) Ross in the upstate New York city of Syracuse. Little is generally known of her private life, and she is said to regret having revealed even her place of birth. According to the few details that have been published, she comes from a middle-class Jewish background and has a son, Erik. In 1948, after attending Hunter College in New York City, she began working for the *New Yorker*. At that time it was still under the editorship of its founder, Harold Ross (who was not related).

In 1949 she became a staff writer of the *New Yorker*, and virtually all of her work published in book form first appeared in that magazine.

"El Único Matador," Lillian Ross's study of the Brooklyn boy, Sidney Franklin, who became one of Spain's top-ranking bullfighters, appeared in 1949 as her first *New Yorker* profile. In the course of her research during 1947 on Franklin and on bullfighting, she met Ernest Hemingway, who helped her generously. When Hemingway and his wife visited New York City in late 1949, she accompanied them around town, recording everything she saw and heard during their two-day stay. Her 1950 *New Yorker* profile of the novelist delighted many of his admirers, but enraged others who thought that she was ridiculing him. Hemingway himself assured her that her article was "funny and good." The controversy flared up again when the piece was published as a hardcover book in 1961 as *Portrait of Hemingway*.

Miss Ross has suggested that those who found the Hemingway profile malicious were attributing to her "their own pious disapproval" of the novelist. This is a possible reaction to a Lillian Ross profile because her own opinion of her subject (or victim) is never stated. Instead the reader is offered a beautifully observed description of a person's appearance and manner as he goes about his affairs, and a transcription of what he says (and the way he says it) that could stand as a model of the revelation of character through dialogue. Thus the reader is obliged to form his own opinion of the person in whose company he seems to find himself. It has been said that Lillian Ross creates "the illusion that the reporter has vanished altogether"; an illusion is what it is, however, since the reporter's hand is evident in what she chooses to record and in what she leaves out: "without statement," as one critic says, "her affections come through as clearly as her skepticisms."

Character drawing through the telling detail, the revealing quotation, is of course the technique of the short story writer, imported into factual journalism by Miss Ross with great originality and skill, and subsequently much emulated. In *Picture* she carries the technique a stage further. The book is a narrative of the making of John Huston's screen version of Stephen Crane's *The Red Badge of Courage*, describing the studio conferences, conflicts, and compromises, the shooting, cutting, and ballyhoo, and above all the personalities of the technicians, artists, and administrators involved in the project. The result is a fundamentally depressing but often brilliantly funny revelation of the conflict between commerce and art in the American motion picture industry, and remains for many people "the best study of Hollywood ever done." In its development, and in its handling of "the dramatic interplay of a large group of characters," it justifies its designation as "the first reportorial piece ever to be written in the form of a novel"—the prototype of such "nonfiction novels" as Truman Capote's *In Cold Blood*.

LILLIAN ROSS

The Player assembles fifty-five "self-portraits" of leading actors and actresses. These are the products of interviews conducted by Lillian Ross and her sister Helen over a period of four years (1958–1962), with the skillful questions which elicited these revealing statements removed. "What we try to do," according to Lillian Ross, "is to give the actor or actress to the reader, as though he were on the stage, presenting himself to the audience." Miss Ross also took the photographs which illustrate the book, wanting not publicity pictures but natural ones matching the spirit of the pieces.

If Lillian Ross applies the techniques of fiction in her journalism, she may also be said to have applied the techniques of journalism to *Vertical and Horizontal*, a collection of stories in which she exercises "her gifts of observation on characters she presumably made up herself"—notably a New York bachelor physician and his bogus Viennese psychoanalyst. The book was generally well received and seemed to Granville Hicks "as touching as it is brilliant."

A number of Miss Ross's *New Yorker* pieces were reprinted in *Reporting*, which contains among other items "El Único Matador," *Portrait of Hemingway*, and *Picture*, while sixty of her "casuals" from "Talk of the Town" were brought together in *Talk Stories*. Reviewing the latter, Irving Wallace called Lillian Ross "one of the most creative innocent bystanders of our time," and Murrah Gattis wrote: "Her style is always modest, elliptical, precise. . . . Her eye and ear are perfect." She is said to be a quiet, friendly woman, a master of the art of listening.

PRINCIPAL WORKS: *Nonfiction*—Picture, 1952; Portrait of Hemingway, 1961; (with Helen Ross) The Player: A Profile of an Art, 1962; Reporting, 1964; Adlai Stevenson, 1966; Talk Stories, 1966. *Fiction*—Vertical and Horizontal, 1963.

ABOUT: Contemporary Authors 11–12, 1965; Newquist, R. (ed.) Counterpoint, 1965; Who's Who in America, 1972–1973. *Periodicals*—Newsweek December 18, 1961; Partisan Review September–October 1951; Reporter May 19, 1966; Saturday Review March 14, 1964; Time May 1, 1964.

ROTH, HENRY (February 8, 1906–   ), American novelist and short story writer, was born in Tysmienica in Austria-Hungary (now in the Ukrainian SSR) and brought to the United States a little over a year later. He is the son of Herman and Leah (Farb) Roth. The family settled first in Brownsville, Brooklyn, then moved over to Manhattan's Lower East Side, where Henry Roth began his education. In 1914, when he was eight, the family moved again, to East 119th Street in Harlem, where Roth grew up. He graduated from De Witt Clinton High School in 1924 and received his B.S. in English at the City College of New York in 1928.

It was at City College that Roth began to write, encouraged by his English professor, Eda Lou Walton. She was so confident of his talent that she herself helped to support him during the four years, from 1929 to 1933, which he devoted to his novel *Call It Sleep*. The book was published by Robert Ballou in 1934, with the financial backing of David Mandel, a friend of Professor Walton. Some critics recognized its quality, but others seemed puzzled by a proletarian novel that was neither behavioristic nor revolutionary, and a few obviously regarded it as an offense against the radical spirit of the time. It made no great impact on the general public and was soon forgotten by all but a small band of loyal admirers.

In 1936, with an advance from Maxwell Perkins of Scribner's, Roth began work on a second book, a novel about a worker who loses an arm in industry and becomes a Communist organizer. Researching this book, Roth spent much time with the Italian longshoremen of the New York waterfront. "One day," according to David Mandel, "he was set upon by a squad of union goons and was beaten. He destroyed his manuscript, which was virtually finished at that time. He told me that no one could describe the American scene with detached imagination, and he did not think that any writers of first rank could appear in what he termed an abominable society."

HENRY ROTH

In 1939 Roth married Muriel Parker, a composer whom he had met at the Yaddo artists' colony, and for the next two years he taught at Theodore Roosevelt night High School in the Bronx. At this time he was concentrating on short stories, two of which, "Broker" and "Somebody Always Grabs the Purple," were published in the *New Yorker* in 1939. Throughout the war years, from 1941 to 1946, Roth was a precision tool grinder, working in New York, Providence, and Boston. His sons Jeremy and Hugh were born in 1941 and 1943.

After the war, impelled by a "longing for the tranquil rural life," Roth and his family settled in Maine. They lived at first near Center Montville (1946–1949), where Roth taught in a one-room school, fought forest fires, and did a variety of odd jobs. In 1949 they moved to a three-acre farm on the outskirts of Augusta, Maine. Roth worked from 1949 to 1953 as an attendant at Maine State Hospital, and then for the next ten years made a living raising ducks and geese, eking out his income with some private tutoring in mathematics and Latin. His wife also became a teacher, principal of a local elementary school. Roth had by then virtually abandoned his writing career, but a short story, "Petey and Yotsee and Mario," appeared in the *New Yorker* in 1956, and two autobiographical "parables" were published in *Commentary* in 1959 and 1960.

In 1956, meanwhile, *Call It Sleep* received some critical attention in W. B. Rideout's *The Radical Novel in the United States*, and the same year was named by both Alfred Kazin and Leslie Fiedler in an *American Scholar* symposium, "The Most Neglected Books of the Past Twenty-five Years."

During the next few years there were further signs of reviving interest in the novel, and in 1960 it was reissued by a small press, Pageant Books, Inc., now Cooper Square Publishers. It caused a mild critical stir then, and in 1964 it reappeared as an Avon paperback and was an immediate success.

Call It Sleep is an account of the inner life, between the ages of six and nine, of David Schearl, a Jewish immigrant boy in the New York ghetto just before World War I. His father, Albert, a printer, is a man half mad with pride and bitterness. His paranoid behavior costs him one job after another, and he turns increasingly against David, convincing himself that the child is not his son. David's bulwark against his father and all the terrors of the New York slums is his mother, Genya. Isolated in America by her ignorance of the language, she lavishes on the boy all of her abundant capacity for love.

It is, as many critics have pointed out, a classical Oedipal situation. It produces in David intense emotional confusion, an overheated imagination, and above all fear—fear of his father, of the slum streets, of the dark cellar downstairs, of the sexually aggressive lame girl upstairs, of the irascible Rabbi Pankower. What happens is seen almost entirely through the eyes of the little boy, so that the reader is drawn deep into his nightmare. As Irving Howe says, "We are locked into the experience of a child, but are not limited to his grasp of it."

At last the cacophony of fears and guilts reaches a crescendo, and David runs away. His brilliantly rendered flight from his father and from himself ends when, seeking a kind of purification by fire, he thrusts a metal tool onto the live rail of a streetcar track. Shocked almost to death, he receives a vision in which the disparity between the real world and his imagined one is burned away, and he achieves a kind of acceptance of his life.

Walter Allen, in his afterword to the Avon edition, said that "Roth seems to me to plunge us into a child's mind more deeply and more intransigently than any other novelist has done. We experience the child's instantaneous apprehension of his world . . . [which is] not that of simple fantasy or make-believe but one he creates with the desperate, compulsive imagination of the poet. . . . Roth shows himself a master of the novelist's art, a master of sympathy, humor, detachment and deep poetic insight into the immigrant's lot and into the mind of childhood. Place, time and people are alike uniquely and unforgettably evoked, so that to read *Call It Sleep* is to live it." Kenneth Ledbetter wrote that "the agony—and the hope—of the proletariat have never been more powerfully portrayed in an American novel."

The novel was widely reviewed in similar terms, was adopted by several colleges for literature courses, and became a major best seller. In 1965 Roth received a grant from the National Institute of Arts and Letters, and went first to Mexico, then to Spain, to begin research on a new novel. In 1968 he held a D. H. Lawrence Fellowship at the University of New Mexico. He has said that his "avocations were formerly gardening, puttering about the farm, problem solving in math. All these are in abeyance now with the resurgence of the desire to write."

PRINCIPAL WORKS: Call It Sleep, 1934 (republished in 1960 and 1964).

ABOUT: Allen, W. *afterword to* Call It Sleep, 1964; Fiedler, L. Love and Death in the American Novel, 1960; Rideout, W. B. The Radical Novel in the United States, 1956; Who's Who in America, 1972–1973. *Periodicals*—Commentary August 1960; Jewish Social Studies July 1966; Life January 8, 1965; Modern Fiction Studies Winter 1965–1966; New York Times Book Review October 25, 1964; December 13, 1964; Twentieth Century Literature October 1966.

ROTH, PHILIP (MILTON) (March 19, 1933–), American novelist and short story writer, writes: "I was born in Newark, New Jersey. After attending the public schools there, I studied for a year (1950–1951) at the Newark college of Rutgers University, and then transferred to Bucknell University in Lewisburg, Pennsylvania, where I received my B.A. (in English literature) in 1954. In 1955 I received an M.A. in Literature from the University of Chicago. I then spent a year in the Army and returned to the University of Chicago as an Instructor in English in the College (1956–1958). I also began publishing stories at this time, in the little magazines—*Epoch*, *Chicago Review*, *Paris Review*—and in the *New Yorker*, *Commentary*, *Esquire* and *Harper's*. When my first book, a novella and five short stories, was accepted for publication in the summer of 1958 by Houghton Mifflin, I decided to give up teaching and devote my time entirely to writing. I lived for a few months in New York City, and when in 1959, following the publication of *Goodbye, Columbus*, I received a Guggenheim Fellowship and an award from the National Institute of Arts and Letters, I used the money to travel abroad for a year, living mostly in Rome, where I began work on *Letting Go*. In 1960, *Goodbye, Columbus* received the National Book Award for Fiction and the Daroff Award of the Jewish Book Council of America. I returned to America in September 1960 to teach for two years in the Writers' Workshop of the State University of Iowa. In Iowa I finished *Letting Go*, and subsequently came east to Princeton University, where I was writer-in-residence from September 1962–June 1964. I then moved to New York, where I have lived ever since, though in recent years I have spent at least half of my time in

PHILIP ROTH

the country, in Ulster County, New York. Over the years I have received grants from the Rockefeller and Ford Foundations, and I have also continued intermittently to teach, as a visiting writer, at the State University of New York at Stony Brook and the University of Pennsylvania, in Philadelphia. My novel *Letting Go* appeared in 1962, *When She Was Good* in 1967, and *Portnoy's Complaint* in 1969, all of them published by Random House. Between novels I continue to write and publish some short fiction (*New American Review*, *Modern Occasions*, *Esquire*, *New Yorker*), and several stories have been included in O. *Henry Prize Story* collections and Martha Foley's *Best American Short Story* annuals. My books have been published in England, France, Germany, Italy, elsewhere in Europe, and in South America and Japan."

Philip Roth began his career with an immensely successful book of short stories, and followed this with two ambitious novels which established him as one of the most promising recruits to the "Jewish Renaissance" of the 1950s and 1960s in American letters. His years of mere promise ended in 1969, when his third novel, *Portnoy's Complaint*, was a critical triumph and a scandalous best seller.

He is the younger son of Herman Roth, an insurance salesman whose parents had emigrated from Austria-Hungary, and of the former Bess Finkel. Roth grew up in a Jewish neighborhood in Newark. He worked on the school newspaper at Weequahic High School, where he was known to his teachers as a quiet and bookish boy, and to his friends as a comedian and mimic. At Bucknell University he edited the literary magazine, published his first short stories, received his Phi Beta Kappa key, and graduated in 1954 *magna cum laude*. As he says above, he went on to the University of Chicago for his M.A., and after his army year returned there as an English instructor.

The title piece in Roth's first book, *Goodbye, Columbus*, is a sardonic, touching, and brilliantly observed novella (later filmed), about the brief love affair between a poor Jewish boy and a rich Jewish girl. The five short stories in the collection are also fiercely ironic studies of the materialism of middle-class life in postwar America, focusing usually on Jewish communities where greed and social ambition are shown to be destroying the traditional values of Jewish life. "Eli, the Fanatic," for example, explores the reactions of prosperous suburban Jews to the establishment in their exclusive neighborhood of an orphanage for refugees from Central Europe, while "Defender of the Faith" deals with a Jewish GI's ingenious exploitation of his religion to win special favors.

Goodbye, Columbus, published when Roth was only twenty-six, was greeted with something like adulation. "What most writers spend a lifetime searching for—a unique voice, a secure rhythm, a distinctive subject—seem to have come to Philip Roth totally and immediately," wrote Irving Howe. Saul Bellow called him a virtuoso and Alfred Kazin found his "lampoonings of our swollen and unreal American prosperity . . . as observant and charming as Fitzgerald's." Roth's ear for dialogue, the range and subtlety of his humor, his ability to mix compassion and satire, were recognized as the equipment of a "born writer." Some structural weaknesses, most obvious in the novella, and a certain glibness and over-facility, were the only evidence of the author's inexperience and youth.

This first book, proclaimed by its National Book Award "the most distinguished work of fiction published in 1959," was followed three years later by Roth's sprawling first novel. *Letting Go* is about Gabe Wallach, an indecisive and vaguely guilt-ridden young university teacher in the Midwest, his splendidly bawdy, funny, and honest mistress Martha, and his disaster-prone friends Paul and Libby Herz. Gabe, a nonreligious Jew, tries to "do good without attachment," as Lord Krishna enjoins, and fails; Roth's message seems to be that attachment is all—that (as Arthur Mizener put it) "only the life committed to the demands of the private sentiments, unrestrained by any other considerations, is worth anything."

In the opinion of Stanley Edgar Hyman, Gabe's moral struggles, and the material and psychological problems of Paul and Libby, form two complementary narratives which never really cohere into a novel. The same critic complained of passages of flat-footed prose and of undergraduate Freudian analysis. But, Hyman went on, Roth "has the finest eye for the details of American life since Sinclair Lewis," and an equally remarkable ear for every kind of American speech. He can indicate character in a phrase (like the dentist who, ice-skating, makes only "little figures of eight, and all the time, smiling"). And some of his vignettes and set pieces, "at once awful and uproarious," convinced Hyman that Roth was a novelist of great promise.

If Roth's next book did not wholly redeem that promise, it was nevertheless an excellent and ambitious novel. In *When She Was Good* Roth, eschewing the Jewish characters he knows so well, produced a portrait of a puritanical midwestern housewife, Lucy Nelson. When we first meet her she is a steadfast and courageous adolescent, saddled with an alcoholic father, struggling upstream towards a college education. Transferring her trust to another man, she finds herself pregnant by and then married to a boyish poseur as weak as her father. She tries to shape him into the strong man she needs and when this fails becomes in her despair a morally arrogant reformer (and emotional castrator) of men who, in her feverish crusade, destroys her father, her husband, and herself. There was nothing but praise for Roth's account of small-town life and people, but some thought he had drawn Lucy herself too harshly—having made her a symbol of all that is ugly in modern provincial life, he was unable to muster sympathy for the result. Whether or not this is so (and not all critics agreed that it is), this venomous woman is more than a symbol: her vitality is memorably and tragically communicated.

Looking back at *When She Was Good*, Roth spoke of the "arduous" years he had spent agonizing over "its un-fiery prose, its puritanical, haunted heroine, its unrelenting concern with banality." When he had finished it, he said, he was "looking for a way to get in touch with another side of my talent. . . . I was aching to write something extravagant and funny. . . . But not until I had got hold of guilt, you see, as a *comic idea*, did I begin to feel myself lifting free and clear of my last book and my old concerns." The result was *Portnoy's Complaint*, a savage and ribald apologia delivered from his psychoanalyst's couch by Alexander Portnoy, liberal and idealistic assistant to Mayor Lindsay of New York. Portnoy is the "tight-assed" son of a man-eating Jewish mother, struggling to throw off racial and family prohibitions and guilts, "to be bad and enjoy it," to "put the id back into Yid." But forbidden affairs with *shiksas* bring only shame and lead to a traumatic nonclimax in the land of his fathers. Sections of the novel published in magazines from 1967 onwards generated such eager anticipation that Roth had earned almost a million dollars in book and film rights before it was even published.

This obscenely explicit sexual portrait, heavily auto-erotic and oral, outraged some readers but delighted most of its reviewers (though some found Roth's scenes from Jewish life too grossly caricatured). Described as a "masturbation novel," it is in fact an antimasturbation novel, for auto-eroticism is used in it not only as a vehicle for comic realism but also as a symbol of the hero's self-regarding solipsism. Portnoy feels imprisoned because, with the best will in the world, he cannot accept the reality of other people, who have been presented to him always not as individuals but as types—most obviously and persistently as Jews or *goyim*. He is so violently obscene, Roth says, "because he wants to be saved . . . [from] taboos which, rightly or wrongly, he experiences as diminishing or unmanning." It seemed to Raymond A. Sokolov that Roth had found a way of speaking about previously forbidden subjects, "a voice that echoes the way people have really been talking since sometime in the 1940s." And Geoffrey Wolff perhaps meant something similar when he wrote that "Roth has composed what for me is the most important book of my generation."

In a speech, President Nixon expressed his distaste for unrestricted abortion, which he could not square with his "personal belief in the sanctity of human life—including the life of the yet unborn." This statement inspired Roth's next book, *Our Gang*, a venomous satirical attack on President "Trick E. Dixon" and all such politicians, in which Tricky develops his stand for the unborn into a major electioneering plank. The book contains much clever and pointed parody, and some splendidly funny scenes, though most reviewers thought that the joke went on too long and finally failed.

The Breast, which followed, is a novella about what happens when a stalwart professor of literature at New York State University undergoes a Kafkaesque metamorphosis—"a massive hormonal influx" which transforms him overnight into a spongy, sightless, six-foot mammary gland. A reviewer in *Library Journal* found the book "intermittently funny, and even moving, because Roth is a marvelous writer, with limitless verbal resources. But it's still only a half-formed sketch for a novel, a tissue of unconnected and undeveloped ideas."

Nor was there anything like unqualified enthusiasm for *The Great American Novel*, which follows the miserable fortunes of the worst team in the history of baseball, the homeless Mundys of Port Ruppert, New Jersey, during their 1943 season of shame. The novel attacks an assortment of American myths—the American cult of success, for example, and the myth suggested by the title (the book contains a great deal of literary parody and jokery). It also makes rather gentler and more elegiac fun of the innocent and heroic myth of baseball itself. The result, in spite of Roth's "talent for cruel and shameless comic extravagance," disappointed most reviewers. As Thomas R. Edwards put it, "the book is too long for its own energies to sustain, too committed to a kind of 'black humor' whose charm has seen its day, too easy in its confidence that inventiveness can do the work of design."

Philip Roth was married in 1959 to Margaret Martinson, who separated from him in 1963 and died in 1968. They had no children.

PRINCIPAL WORKS: Goodbye, Columbus, 1959; Letting Go, 1962; When She Was Good, 1967; Portnoy's Complaint, 1969; Our Gang, 1971; The Breast, 1972; The Great American Novel, 1973.

ABOUT: Contemporary Authors 2, 1963; Current Biography, 1970; Hyman, S. E. Standards, 1966; Meeter, G. Bernard Malamud and Philip Roth: A Critical Essay, 1968; Solotaroff, T. The Red Hot Vacuum, 1970; Vinson, J. (ed.) Contemporary Novelists, 1972; Who's Who in America, 1972–1973. *Periodicals*—Commentary July 1959, November 1967; Life February 7, 1969; Nation July 17, 1967; New Republic June 15, 1959; New York Review of Books October 19, 1972; New York Times January 11, 1969; February 28, 1969; New York Times Book Review February 23, 1969; May 6, 1973; Partisan Review Fall 1960; Reporter May 28, 1959; Saturday Review May 16, 1959; April 11, 1969; Time June 9, 1967; February 21, 1969; Times Literary Supplement November 23, 1962; June 8, 1967; December 21, 1967; April 17, 1969; Yale Review October 1967.

***ROUSSEL, RAYMOND** (January 20, 1877–July 14, 1933), French novelist, dramatist, and poet, was born in Paris. His father was a stockbroker who made a large fortune but died young. Roussel described his fatherless childhood, with his devoted sister Germaine and their somewhat idiosyncratic mother, as a blissfully happy one. At the age of thirteen he left school and went to the Conservatoire, where he studied the piano, winning second place in the examinations. At sixteen he tried writing songs to words of his own, but soon decided that he lacked any serious gift for musical compositions, and started writing verse instead.

Three years later Roussel wrote his first major work, *La Doublure* (The Understudy, 1897), a novel in verse which begins with the unsuccessful actor Gaspard alone on stage after yet another failure as an understudy, and ends with him miserably made up as Mephistopheles in a fair booth at Neuilly, a step further downhill. The long central section, evoking an afternoon spent by Gaspard and his girl wandering through the crowds at a Nice carnival, has been much admired for its naïve charm.

* rōō sel′

Roussel was convinced that he was a genius, the equal of Dante and Shakespeare, and he later described the state of creative ecstasy in which he wrote *La Doublure* to the psychologist Pierre Janet, whose patient he became. He worked with the curtains drawn because of the glorious rays of light which his work seemed to him to give off, and for five or six months could hardly bear to interrupt his work to eat. When he published it the following year at his own expense he expected immediate fame. It received very little attention, however, and Roussel plunged into the deepest depression, actually breaking out in a rash which was at first diagnosed as measles.

Roussel's second book, *La Vue* (The View, 1904), contains three long poems each of which describes a miniature scene in enormous detail. In the title piece the poet is studying an engraving, in the handle of a pen, of a seaside resort where he once spent a holiday. In "Le Concert" (The Concert) he is reading a letter, and describes the view printed at the top of the hotel writing paper, showing the hotel, a lake, a public park, and a bandstand. In "La Source" (The Spring) he is lunching at a restaurant, and the scene presented is that on the label of a bottle of mineral water. It is in part this element of fanatically detailed scrutiny in Roussel's work which has established him as a precursor of Robbe-Grillet and other writers of the *nouveau roman*. Robbe-Grillet, in his own essay on Roussel, says that "*sight*, Roussel's favorite sense, very soon achieves a demented acuity, tending towards the infinite. This characteristic is probably made even more provocative in that it is a question of a reproduction. Roussel is fond of describing . . . a universe which he doesn't represent as real, but as already having been depicted. He likes to place an artist between himself and the world of man as an intermediary. The text we are offered is an account of a double."

In fact, Roussel disliked reality and used his great wealth to keep the real world at arm's length, with such efficiency that comparatively little is known about him, most of the available biographical information coming from Michel Leiris, whose father was a close friend of Roussel. Roussel, a homosexual, was eccentric to the point of insanity, and indeed had to be treated periodically for mental disorder. He was a small, handsome man, always impeccably dressed, and at one period his fastidiousness became so extreme that he would not wear anything that had been washed even once, but continually bought new clothes. He became a crack pistol shot, winning forty-five medals. Through his sister's marriage into the Ney family, by which she became Duchess of Elchingen and later Princess of Moscow, he was connected with all the families of the First Empire aristocracy.

Roussel's retreat from reality is very evident in his two prose novels. He made two world tours, but he rarely left his hotel or his cabin and commented: "Well, from all this journeying I have never derived anything for my books. It seemed to me that this deserved to be pointed out because it shows so clearly that in my work imagination is everything." He was a great admirer of Jules Verne, and all his works are fantasies, but he tried to develop methods of writing which would be impersonal, primarily by a deliberate exploitation of the punning possibilities of language. After the publication of *La Vue* he wrote seventeen stories in which he experimented with the first of his special procedures. Each of them ends with a variant of its opening phrase, in which one word is different, usually by only one consonant, but in which the sense is totally altered. Thus the story of a murder, in which a jealous Spaniard poisons his faithless love, begins with the pricking of the greenish skin of an over-ripe plum ("la peau verdâtre de la prune un peu mûre") for the insertion of the poison, and ends with the moon shining through the window onto the greenish face of the aging Spanish beauty ("la peau verdâtre de la brune un peu mûre") who has just been poisoned.

In these early stories it is mere ingenuity which predominates, but one of them, "Parmi les noirs" (Among the Blacks), contains the germ of the novel *Impressions d'Afrique* (1910, translated by L. Foord and R. Heppenstall as *Impressions of Africa*), in which he adopted related but more varied and complex procedures. He was revolting against the strict form of the classical realistic novel, but having rejected realism he was faced, like other twentieth century writers, with the need to find some new kind of structural underpinning. His main technique was phonic distortion: he took lines of poetry from Victor Hugo (a poet with whom he strongly identified), from nursery songs, or from other sources, and punned them into a jumble of words, which he then separated into other words with totally different meanings. This and other devices provided frameworks within which he could exercise total freedom of imagination. The result has been described by John Weightman as "a narrative like a succession of dream-sequences, in which all the details are set down as if they were realistic, but where everything is taking place in an imaginary world."

In *Impressions d'Afrique*, a ship is wrecked off the coast of Africa, and its passengers are held for ransom in the capital of the black emperor Talou VII. Besides bankers, manufacturers, artists, and scientists they include a great variety of *artistes*, ranging from circus freaks to a transvestite male soprano, and during their imprisonment they plan and produce a remarkable gala performance in

RAYMOND ROUSSEL

which their captors also participate. This carnival forms the first half of the book, presenting a puzzle which is explained when the earlier events are narrated in the second half. This pattern, the posing of some mystery and its ultimate clarification, occurs repeatedly in Roussel's work. However, the narrative framework of his other prose novel, *Locus solus* (1914, translated under the same title by R. Copeland-Cuningham), is very simple. A group of visitors is shown round the estate just outside Paris of Martial Canterel, a rich scientist, magician, and illusionist. The whole thing is really another fantastic vaudeville performance conducted by Canterel—a series of magical "happenings" mixing the gay and the grotesque with childlike exuberance.

Roussel served in the ranks as a driver during the 1914 war, coming under fire at Châlons, probably during the second battle of the Marne. In 1920–1921 he traveled round the world by way of India, Australia, New Zealand, the Pacific Islands, China, Japan, and America. He enjoyed traveling, and for his tours in Europe he built a luxurious house on wheels, with bedroom, bathroom, dining room, and servants' quarters.

The dominant images in Roussel's work concern some kind of theatrical or other doubling of reality by appearance, and it was therefore natural for him to turn to the theatre. He staged lavish productions at his own expense of stage versions of both his prose novels. Roussel made the adaptation of *Impressions d'Afrique* himself, but its performances in 1911–1912 were greeted with noisy derision and hostility, and the author was called a madman. He paid Pierre Frondaie, a popular playwright and novelist, to dramatize *Locus solus*, which was put in December 1922. The hostility was even greater, but there was some avant-garde applause, and the surrealists expressed their admiration and support. Their interest was not reciprocated by Roussel, however, and he never participated in the literary life of Paris.

His other two theatrical ventures were written for the stage in the first place. The first, *L'Étoile au front* (The Star on the Forehead, 1924), is hopelessly undramatic, consisting mainly of episodes in which the characters tell each other complicated and fantastic stories in highly stilted language. *La Poussière de soleils* (Star Dust, 1926), about a hunt for hidden treasure, was greeted with somewhat less tumultuous hostility, in spite of the fact that the audience had to sit through most of the seventeen scene changes (while an orchestra played music by Marius-François Galliard).

Roussel had begun *Nouvelles Impressions d'Afrique* (Further Impressions of Africa) in 1915, but it was completed and published only in 1932. It is a poem in four cantos which has nothing to do with even an imaginary Africa, except that each canto is given the title of a tourist attraction in Egypt. Each canto gradually builds up a series of parentheses within parentheses until it comes to resemble a series of Chinese boxes. A key to the work has been provided by Jean Ferry, who has devoted more years of his life to taking the poem to pieces than Roussel spent in putting them together.

This complex work cost Roussel immense effort, and he told Janet "I bleed over every phrase." Janet had published his study of the creative-ecstatic aspect of Roussel's psychological case history in *De l'angoisse à l'extase* (From Anguish to Ecstasy, 1926) and despite his lack of success Roussel remained convinced of his genius. He took up chess, then turned to drink, and later to barbiturate drugs. He moved into a hotel used by drug addicts and homosexuals, but though homosexual practices were his exclusive taste (according to Michel Leiris) his only true intimate was a woman, Charlotte Dufrène, at whose house he received visitors. In 1933 they went to Sicily together, taking adjacent rooms in the hotel in Palermo where Wagner, whom Roussel greatly admired, had written much of *Parsifal*. Under the influence of drugs he slashed his wrists and was found bleeding in his bath and laughing wildly. He finally killed himself with a heavy overdose of barbiturates.

Just before his death he had prepared the miscellany *Comment j'ai écrit certains de mes livres* (How I Wrote Certain of My Books, 1935), which was published two years after his death. Besides the title piece explaining some of his creative methods, the book includes the early stories and six out of a projected thirty "Documents pour servir de canevas," groups of stories within stories which were intended to serve as so many sketches towards a work in progress.

After this Roussel fell into almost total obscurity, and for thirty years virtually all his works were out of print, though during the 1950s several important French critics published articles or books on his work. Some of these were by survivors from the surrealist period, and, as noted above, he has also been hailed as a precursor by the theorists of the *nouveau roman*.

Roussel's aim was to define beyond argument the proper nature of fiction, or, as a reviewer in the *Times Literary Supplement* said of one of his works: "The lesson of *Locus solus* is above all that the exercise of human freedom demands a literature, or some other art form. It is when we reassemble the contents of our minds and create our own patterns with them that we are most free, not when we invest our attention wholly in the world about us." Rayner Heppenstall regards *Impressions d'Afrique* not merely as Roussel's masterpiece but as "quite simply, a masterpiece." Other critics have disagreed, George Steiner even claiming that he "belongs, primarily, to the pathology of letters." There is in any case no doubt that Roussel has entered the modern pantheon, along with Alfred Jarry and Antonin Artaud. And even some of those who take his work less seriously can relish the charm of his invention and the direct and unsophisticated precision of his descriptive writing, which has reminded several critics of the paintings of the Douanier Rousseau.

PRINCIPAL WORKS IN ENGLISH TRANSLATION: Impressions of Africa, 1966; Locus Solus, 1971.

ABOUT: Caradec, F. Vie de Raymond Roussel, 1972; Ferry, J. Une Étude sur Raymond Roussel, 1953; Foucault, M. Raymond Roussel, 1963; Heppenstall, R. Raymond Roussel: A Critical Guide, 1966; Matthews, J. H. Surrealism and the Novel, 1966; Penguin Companion to Literature 2, 1969; Robbe-Grillet, A. Snapshots, and, Towards a New Novel, 1965; Sturrock, J. The French New Novel, 1969. *Periodicals*—London Magazine August 1963; New Yorker October 28, 1967; Observer December 11, 1966; Times Literary Supplement July 12, 1963; January 9, 1964; October 29, 1964; December 9, 1965; November 24, 1966.

***ROUSSIN, ANDRÉ (JEAN PAUL)** (January 22, 1911–), French dramatist, was born at Marseilles to Honoré Roussin, an insurance underwriter, and the former Suzanne Gardair. His first ambition was to be a violinist, but he began to write plays at the age of fifteen, when he was a student at the Institution Mélizan in Marseilles, and as a young man completed many which, however, remained unproduced. Having completed his

* rōō saN'

baccalauréat, Roussin moved in 1931 to Paris and worked for a time in underwriting and journalism, but by then the theatre was in his blood. He returned to Marseilles, where he found work as an actor, and went on writing.

Roussin began to attract attention, both as an actor and as a playwright, during the German occupation. His first success, the comedy *Am Stram Gram*, was written in 1934 and rejected by nine producers before it was finally produced in 1943. Since the war, Roussin has written a string of hit comedies which have made him one of the most successful of living French dramatists.

The first of these, and still one of the best known, was *La Petite Hutte* (1947), in which a man, his wife, and her lover are marooned on a desert island. The husband, adapting very reasonably to this difficult social situation, agrees that his wife must be shared, and to his surprise discovers that the arrangement suits him perfectly—it is the other man who finds the scheme distasteful. This airy and extremely witty piece was a triumph in Paris and ran for three years in London, admirably translated by Nancy Mitford as *The Little Hut*. It reached Broadway in 1953 and promptly floundered—flattened, according to Eric Bentley, by poor direction, "pompous" sets, and a "massive production."

Most of Roussin's farces are variations on the triangle theme. Nina, in the play of that name, is a fading beauty who successfully plays husband and lover off against each other—until they join forces and try to poison her. Lightly played in a small and intimate theatre, it was acclaimed by both public and critics in Paris, but on Broadway flopped as miserably as *The Little Hut*. Of Roussin's other plays, the best-known are *Bobosse* (1950), "a lighthearted mixture of fantasy and nonsense on the Pagliacci theme," translated as *Figure of Fun*, and *Les Œufs de l'autruche* (1948), which Robert Morley adapted as a vehicle for himself and called *Hippo Dancing*.

Roussin has complained bitterly about the way some of his plays have been "massacred" in foreign —especially American—adaptations, "the way we are cooked in foreign sauces." *The Little Hut*, he says, was so completely altered in its screen version that "nobody laughed," and *Un Amour qui ne finit pas* (1963), which French critics esteemed above all his plays, reached Broadway as a "vulgar and humorless" farce that survived only six performances. On the art of translation, Roussin speaks as something of an expert. He has gallicized many foreign plays, including Vitaliano Brancati's *Il bell' Antonio* and Neil Simon's *Barefoot in the Park*. He has also written a number of movie scripts, among them some based on his own plays.

The French critics class Roussin with Marcel Achard as a reigning master of the boulevard theatre, but think him a better technician than Achard. Pierre de Boisdeffre, acknowledging that Roussin's eternally triangular theme is scarcely original, submits that the playwright successfully disguises this fact with his "dazzling dialogue," offering his public "the dishes it likes, prepared according to recipes which hardly differ from those of Eugène Scribe or Alfred Savoir." Harold Hobson compares him with Terence Rattigan, an almost exact contemporary, finding in his work less emotional power than Rattigan commands, but "more poetry."

ANDRÉ ROUSSIN

Roussin's reminiscences and views on the theatre are given in *Patience et impatiences* (1953) and *Un Contentemente raisonnable* (1965). In the latter, defending his work against charges of triviality, he writes: "Whether these plays are good or bad, no one can really say. And I less than anybody else. I only know that they have produced that 'proper satisfaction' which, for Chapelain of the Academy in the seventeenth century, was the sole criterion to observe in matters of dramatic art." There is evidence to support this claim in the fact that all but one of Roussin's comedies have been performed between four hundred and two thousand times. A member of the French Radio-TV Council, and a Chevalier of the Légion d'Honneur, Roussin was married in 1947 to Lucienne Deluy and has a son, Jean-Marie.

PRINCIPAL WORKS IN ENGLISH TRANSLATION: The Little Hut, 1951; Figure of Fun, 1953; Hippo Dancing, 1956; The School for Dupes (one-act play), 1964. *Article in* World Theatre January 1965.

ABOUT: Hobson, H. The French Theatre To-Day, 1953; International Who's Who, 1972–73; Who's Who in France, 1973–1974. *Periodicals*—Life October 1, 1951;

New York Herald Tribune October 8, 1953; New York Times October 8, 1953; New Yorker December 15, 1951; October 17, 1953; Theatre Arts September 1951, December 1953; Time October 19, 1953.

"ROWANS, VIRGINIA." *See* TANNER, EDWARD EVERETT

***ROY, JULES (DÉSIRÉ)** (October 22, 1907–), French novelist and journalist, writes (in French): "I was born into a peasant family in Rovigo (Algeria), and educated at a seminary there. Algeria where I lived through most of my adolescence was an important influence on me. I entered the military school at Saint-Maixent. Aviation interesting me more than the infantry, I earned my licenses as observer and pilot, and chose the air force. The war took me to North Africa from 1940 to 1942, then to England in 1943. Flight commander of a heavy bomber in the RAF, I flew thirty-seven missions over Germany. Back in France in 1945, I managed the information service of the air ministry. I was choking with things to say: I began to write.

"After a stay in Indochina as an observer, believing that the war we were waging there served no just cause, I left the army in 1953.

"Since then I have dedicated myself to literature. In my work as a reporter as well as in my books, I have tried to be a witness, often a passionate and anguished one, but faithful to my view of what man is. That is how it happened that, during the Algerian war, I was obliged, this time, to take a position contrary to that of my old comrades in arms.

"I have traveled much throughout the world, bringing back from my journeys unexpected impressions which usually offend my contemporaries. Labeled a man of the left, I happen to have the mentality of a man of the right and thus arouse hostility on all sides. Perhaps that is how I have gained the public's approval. Without preconceived ideas and not fearing to disappoint those who hope that I will support their politics, I refuse obstinately to listen to anything other than the voice of what I believe to be the truth. Unable to breathe without being possessed by a great theme, I work furiously like a painter in his attic, whether in the city or the country, eight hours a day without quitting. A woman shares my life. Few friends will put up with me. I hope before my death to be able to create a great nonconformist work, and, when I have finished the romanesque fresco which I am now going to tackle, to write all the plays which a lack of time has kept me up till now from letting loose. Experience has taught me that a playwright must run the risk of seeing his plays performed only after long delays or without success, while a writer sees his books published as soon as he finishes them.

"Albert Camus was my friend and he remains an example to me. May he, wherever he is, not be ashamed of me."

Jules Roy is the son of Louis Roy, a policeman, and of the former Mathilde Paris. He received a primary education at Staoel's and at Ain-Taya before entering the Lazarist seminary school in Algeria at the age of eleven. This choice hinged more on the quality of schooling there than on any serious intention of becoming a priest. His vocation, nourished on the works of Caesar, Tolstoy, Montluc, and Psichari, was for war. When he left the seminary he entered the military school at Saint-Maixent and he went into the army at the age of twenty. Roy committed himself completely to army life, his "proper element," and rose swiftly to the rank of second lieutenant in the infantry. But he began to weary of peacetime soldiering, and in 1935 he joined the air corps as an antidote to "the dull brew of peace," becoming a captain in 1939. When World War II broke out he was in France but, after serving briefly in Nîmes and Perpignan, he was posted to North Africa.

Here, on his home ground, his literary career began. He became friendly with writers like Armand Guibert and Jean Amrouche, and soon was a regular contributor to the literary section of *La Tunisie française*. During the summer of 1940 Roy wrote some poems that he later used to make the acquaintance of his hero, Saint-Exupéry. They were published in 1943 as *Chants et prières pour des pilotes* (Songs and Prayers for Some Pilots). These rhetorical poems, written in a free verse that is almost prose, reflect his deep emotional involvement with his chosen life, praising the courage of his fellow pilots, appealing to God to protect them, and swearing vengeance for dead comrades.

Roy's two years in Algeria, where he commanded a reconnaissance squadron at Sétif for Pétain's Vichy government, have caused him much soul-searching. The struggle between his stern personal morality and an almost religious sense of military duty, which ended when he forsook Vichy to fight with the Allies, is described in *Le Métier des armes* (The Profession of Arms, 1948), an essay reminiscent of Vigny's *Servitude et grandeur militaires*. He has returned to this theme in *Le Grand Naufrage* (1964, translated as *The Trial of Marshal Pétain*) in which, unlike the jury in that trial, Roy acquits Pétain of treason but convicts him of sacrificing the pride and honor of France: "We were hungry for danger, glory and love. You gave us gall and wormwood."

In September 1944, after retraining with the

* rwä

Royal Air Force, Roy began the bombing missions over the Ruhr Valley and elsewhere which he describes in lightly fictionalized form in *La Vallée heureuse* (1946, translated as *The Happy Valley*). This *récit*, which won the Prix Renaudot, is one of the best flying books of World War II, notable for its spare and elegant style and for its insight into the pyschology of men in action. The RAF briefing officers sent the bombers into "the happy valley," Roy says, like miners into a pit, with instructions that left no room for heroic initiative or for anything else but fear. War in practice was far removed from Roy's dream of it. Nevertheless he earned six military decorations during the war, including the French Croix de Guerre and the British Distinguished Flying Cross.

Introspection, disillusionment, and a stoic sense of duty make up the prevailing tone of Roy's early books. His prose is classical and restrained, the emotion is understated, but the effect is nevertheless powerfully evocative and dramatic. The best of his early novels is *Le Navigateur* (1954, translated as *The Navigator*), a study in cowardice, heroism, and duty strongly reminiscent of Saint-Exupéry's *Night Flight*.

In the early 1950s Roy, by then a colonel, was sent to appraise the conduct of the war in Indochina. *La Bataille dans la Rizière* (The Battle in the Rice Fields) was full of praise for the French forces, but reflected the disillusionment with French foreign policy that led to Roy's resignation from the army in 1953, when the book was published. He felt even more strongly about his country's role in Algeria when he went there in 1960, and this time felt obliged to condemn the behavior of the French military. His articles in *Le Monde* aroused strong disapproval, official and otherwise, and his book, *La Guerre d'Algérie* (1960), was set by Julliard's printers in the presence of the police. It is, in fact, an extremely valuable, thorough, and unsensational account of that brutal war, as well as a characteristically scrupulous record of the author's own feelings.

Roy's anguished indictment of French atrocities in Algeria earned him the enmity of the military authorities, who consequently did their best to obstruct his subsequent researches into what happened at Dienbienphu, the battle that ended French rule in Indochina. As a result, in the opinion of Bernard Fall, Roy's account of the battle is seriously imbalanced. It remains, as Fall acknowledged, "a remarkable human document, illuminated with hundreds of incisive vignettes." *Le Voyage en Chine* (1965, translated as *Journey Through China*) is a record of Roy's abortive visit to China in the fall of 1965, which was continually frustrated by official evasions and interference, and eventually abandoned.

JULES ROY

The best known of Roy's plays is *Les Cyclones* (1954), an air force drama in which he himself played the leading role in the Paris production. The theatre seems not to be his forte, however, and his reputation rests most firmly on *La Vallée heureuse* and on his later works of reportage. He feels a profound spiritual affinity with Saint-Exupéry, of whom he has written a biography and of whom he is regarded as a worthy heir. But, Henri Peyre says, "Roy is no imitator. His style is less dazzling and less precious than Saint-Exupéry, his message of heroism is more restrainedly expressed or rather remains discreetly implied." He has received the Grand Prix de Littérature de l'Académie Française, the Grand Prix National des Lettres, and the Grand Prix Littéraire de Monaco, and is a Commander of the Légion d'Honneur. Roy was married in 1965 to Sonia Lescaut, and has two children by an earlier marriage.

PRINCIPAL WORKS IN ENGLISH TRANSLATION: The Happy Valley, 1952; Return from Hell, 1954; The Navigator, 1955; The Unfaithful Wife, 1956; The War in Algeria, 1961; The Battle of Dienbienphu, 1965; Journey Through China, 1967; The Trial of Marshal Pétain, 1968.

ABOUT: Boisdeffre, P. de. Dictionnaire de littérature contemporaine, 1962; Boisdeffre, P. de. Une Histoire vivante de la littérature d'aujourd'hui, 1958; Peyre, H. French Novelists of Today, 1967; Who's Who in France, 1971–1972. *Periodicals*—Book World February 25, 1968; Commonweal April 16, 1965; French Review December 1954; Nation November 5, 1960; May 17, 1965; New Republic May 20, 1967; New York Times Book Review July 31, 1955; March 7, 1965; August 6, 1967; Reporter April 8, 1965; Saturday Review July 30, 1955; September 15, 1956; Times Literary Supplement July 7, 1961; June 3, 1965.

STEVEN RUNCIMAN

RUNCIMAN, SIR STEVEN (JAMES COCHRAN STEVENSON) (July 7, 1903–), is an English historian who owes his eminence in Byzantine studies less to the originality of his approach than to his ability to wring, from the crowded disorder of his subject, narratives that are as lucid and coherent as they are readable and vivid. He believes that "the supreme duty of the historian is to write history, that is to say, to attempt to record in one sweeping sequence the greater events and movements that have swayed the destinies of man."

He was born in Northumberland, the second son of Walter, the first Viscount Runciman of Doxford, and of the former Hilda Stevenson. Like his elder brother, the second viscount, he was King's Scholar at Eton and a scholar of Trinity College, Cambridge University. The first part of Runciman's career was spent at Cambridge, as a fellow of Trinity (1927–1938) and university lecturer (1932–1938). His first three books were published during this period. Two of them were detailed accounts, both well received, of meagerly documented periods in Byzantine history. The third, *Byzantine Civilisation*, attempted a general conspectus of "that Orientalised Graeco-Roman civilisation," its institutions, culture, and habits, from its beginning in A.D. 330 to its fall in 1453.

After he left Cambridge, Runciman was able to spend some years in what had been the Byzantine Empire. At the beginning of World War II (1940–1941), he was press attaché to the British Legation in Sofia. From 1942 to 1945, after an interlude with the British Embassy in Cairo, he was professor of Byzantine art and history in the University of Istanbul, and for two more years represented the British Council in Greece. *The Medieval Manichee*, published in 1947, is both a history of a religious movement, the Albigensian heresy, and a study of a pattern of thought, dualism. It is a work of enormous erudition, displaying Runciman's familiarity with Byzantine Greek, Russian, Bulgarian, Serbian, and Armenian, "finely urbane" in its diction and point of view; it was everywhere recognized as "a formidable contribution to knowledge."

The next few years were devoted to research on what is unquestionably Runciman's principal work, the three-volume *History of the Crusades*. He regards the Crusades as the inceptive force in modern history, which shifted the center of civilization from Byzantium to Western Europe. Although his emphasis is military, he examines also the circumstances in the West that gave rise to the Crusades and the circumstances in the East that permitted, encouraged, and finally ended them. His account is generally accepted as the definitive one, "far more interesting and readable than is the work of Röhricht and Stevenson, and less romantic and unreliable than that of Grousset." There was universal praise for the noble proportions of his survey, for the depth and breadth of his learning, and for the ease, clarity, and vividness of his presentation. Reviewers seemed especially grateful for Runciman's talent for characterization, and his touches of wit and irony. Rose Macaulay wrote: "It sets before us one of the formidable moral and romantic epics of time, with imagination and scholarship worthy of it."

In his next major work Runciman set out "to tell the whole story of the Mediterranean world in the second half of the thirteenth century" in such a way as to demonstrate the tremendous significance of the Sicilian Vespers. Sir Steven believes that the massacre of the French at Palermo in 1282 was "one of those events in history which altered the fate of nations and of world-wide institutions." Not everyone was convinced by this argument, and the book provided some critics with further evidence that Runciman is less happy when he is generalizing than when "dealing with actual written evidence." But it was felt that, if the book "misses that extra dimension of understanding which would make it truly great," it is nevertheless an excellent and exciting story told with rare grace and great clarity. Kenneth Rexroth in his review called Runciman "an indisputably good writer, clear, perspicuous, able to marshal immense detail and vast casts of characters; able, again, to communicate that feeling of the very time and place which is perhaps the first virtue of good historical writing."

The critics were less kind to Runciman when he temporarily relinquished his specialty to write

The White Rajahs, an official history of Sarawak. He returned to Byzantium only to chronicle its end in *The Fall of Constantinople. The Economist* had mixed feelings about the book, a masterful "task of condensation" so perfectly controlled that "we seem to be reading a report, as it might be, by a royal commission, which carefully preserves the decencies which the events themselves so outrageously ignore." Most critics however were unequivocally grateful for this "short and exquisite depiction of [an] epochal moment in history." *The Great Church in Captivity* is a kind of sequel to Runciman's Byzantine studies, exploring the history of the Greek Orthodox Church during the four centuries beginning in 1453, when Constantinople fell. Hugh Trevor-Roper called it "a model of wide learning and perfect scholarship, lightly carried and elegantly expressed."

Sir Steven was Waynflete Lecturer at Magdalen College, Oxford, in 1953–1954, Gifford Lecturer at St. Andrews in 1960–1962, Alexander White Professor at the University of Chicago in 1963, Birkbeck Lecturer at Trinity College, Cambridge, in 1966, Wiles Lecturer at Queen's University, Belfast, in 1968, Robb Lecturer at the University of Auckland in 1970, and Regents' Lecturer at the University of California (Los Angeles) in 1971. He was chairman of the Anglo-Hellenic League from 1951 to 1967 and a Trustee of the British Museum from 1960 to 1967. He has been a fellow of the British Academy since 1957 and was knighted in 1958. Sir Steven holds a number of honorary degrees and is an honorary fellow of Trinity. He has houses in Lockerbie, Scotland, and in London.

PRINCIPAL WORKS: Emperor Romanus Lecapenus and His Reign: A Study of Tenth-century Byzantium, 1929; History of the First Bulgarian Empire, 1930; Byzantine Civilisation, 1933; The Medieval Manichee: A Study of the Christian Dualist Heresy, 1947; A History of the Crusades: vol. 1, The First Crusade and the Foundation of the Kingdom of Jerusalem, 1951; vol. 2, The Kingdom of Jerusalem and the Frankish East, 1100–1187, 1952; vol. 3, The Kingdom of Acre and the Later Crusades, 1954; The Eastern Schism: A Study of the Papacy and the Eastern Churches During the XIth and XIIth Centuries, 1955; Sicilian Vespers: A History of the Mediterranean World in the Later 13th Century, 1958; The White Rajahs: A History of Sarawak From 1841 to 1946, 1960; The Fall of Constantinople, 1453, 1965; The Great Church in Captivity, 1968; The Last Byzantine Renaissance (Wiles Lectures), 1970; The Orthodox Churches and the Secular State (Robb Lectures), 1971.

ABOUT: Contemporary Authors 3, 1963; Rexroth, K. Assays, 1962; Who's Who, 1973. *Periodicals*—Church Quarterly Review July 1947; New Statesman July 5, 1947; June 25, 1965; Reporter October 7, 1965; South Atlantic Quarterly January 1956; Spectator September 30, 1960; Times Literary Supplement March 2, 1951; October 29, 1954; April 11, 1958; October 7, 1960.

"RYE, ANTHONY." *See* YOUD, SAMUEL

GILBERT RYLE

***RYLE, GILBERT** (August 19, 1900–), English philosopher, was born in Brighton, the son of Reginald John Ryle, a physician, and the former Catherine Scott. His younger brother, George, is a forestry expert. Ryle went to Brighton College and then, with a classical scholarship, to Queen's College, Oxford. There he became captain of the college boat club and had an extraordinarily brilliant academic career. He at first read classics, receiving first class honors in the first part of that examination, and going on to graduate, also with first class honors, in both *literae humaniores* (philosophy and ancient history) and "Modern Greats" (philosophy, politics, and economics). Ryle remained at Oxford after his graduation, becoming a philosophy lecturer at Christ Church in 1924 and a student and tutor of that college in 1925, a post he retained until the outbreak of World War II. Ryle served with the Welsh Guards from 1939 to 1945, ending the war with the rank of major. He returned to Oxford as Waynflete Professor of Metaphysical Philosophy. During his tenure of the chair (1945–1968), the graduate school of philosophy in Oxford became the largest and most influential in the English-speaking world. Ryle is a leading figure, if not the exclusively dominant one, in the school of philosophy concerned with "linguistic analysis" or "ordinary language philosophy." In 1947 he succeeded G. E. Moore as editor of the senior British philosophical review *Mind*, retaining this influential post until 1971.

Ryle writes in a very characteristic and recognizable style: conversationally direct, forceful, and

* ril

persistently epigrammatic. Though disdainful of the familiar technical terms of philosophy he is a productive coiner of new technicalities of his own. These often hyphenated innovations, such as "category-mistake" and "mongrel-categorical," are indissolubly associated with him, although several have passed into general circulation among philosophers. The attractive idiosyncrasy of his style, together with his indifference to the usual more or less scholarly apparatus of philosophical writing (there are no footnotes or page references to the works of other philosophers in the three hundred and thirty pages of *The Concept of Mind*) make it a little difficult to discern the main intellectual influences on him. In his twenties he was attracted by the phenomenology of Husserl, and from 1930 on the main influences upon him seem to have been first Bertrand Russell and then Ludwig Wittgenstein. Indeed Wittgenstein's later ideas, developed in Cambridge from 1929 onwards, all appear, interestingly transformed by their Rylean expression, in *The Concept of Mind*.

In the years before World War II, Ryle published some sixteen articles. Two of them, "Systematically Misleading Expressions" (1931) and "Categories" (1937), were very influential. Together with his penetrating study of Plato's *Parmenides* (in *Mind*, 1939), they foreshadowed the main outlines of his later work. In common with many other analytic philosophers of the 1930s, Ryle was at that time much concerned with establishing the right method of practicing philosophy. At the end of "Systematically Misleading Expressions" he wrote: "I would rather allot to philosophy a sublimer task than the detection of the sources in linguistic idioms of recurrent misconstructions and absurd theories." By the end of the decade and thereafter he was to hold this view without any of the ruefulness of its first expression.

Ryle's starting point, then, is a view of philosophy as the examination of the actual logical properties of words, as exhibited in their everyday use, uncorrupted by special philosophical definitions. Verbal likenesses suggest nonexistent logical similarities. For example, a person can fear ghosts although there are none; but he cannot feed goats unless there are some. "Fear" and "feed," Ryle would say, are words of different categories. And most philosophical theories are the outcome of category mistakes.

The two main applications of this central idea are in the theory of meaning (see Ryle's chapter in C. A. Mace's *British Philosophy in the Mid-Century*, 1957), and in the philosophy of mind (see *The Concept of Mind*, Ryle's first book, published in 1949). Words have meanings, but not as men have bicycles or other articles of property; the meaning of a word is not a substantive thing for which the word stands or to which it refers. For a word to have meaning is for a set of people to make a practice of using it on the same sort of occasion and in accordance with a common set of rules. Likewise men have thoughts and feelings, but these are not inner, private events. To say that a man wants a drink is not to refer to some inward perturbation of which he alone is conscious, but is to ascribe to him a disposition or tendency to seek a drink, to accept one eagerly if it is offered, and so forth; Ryle rejects the Cartesian dualism that would regard this behavior as the outward effect of an inner cause.

Behind Ryle's attack on dualism lies a concern with the problem it poses of how, if mental states are directly accessible only to those who have them, one person can ever know what is going on in the mind of another. An almost equally surprising consequence of his own position is that there is no such problem. It is a consequence that he cheerfully accepts: other people, he says, "are relatively tractable and relatively easy to understand," and again: "I know about myself in much the same way that I know about others."

In his second book, *Dilemmas*, Ryle applies his mind to a somewhat miscellaneous array of problems (about fatalism, infinity, pleasure, science, and perception). What these problems have in common, he claims, is that all of them arise from the apparently contradictory conclusions of two different ways of considering the same subject. *Plato's Progress* is an ingenious but highly speculative reinterpretation of the philosophy of Plato, its aims, development, and circumstances of composition, and its temporal and intellectual relation to the philosophy of Aristotle.

According to Ved Mehta in *Fly and the Fly Bottle*, Ryle "came from a family of clerical dignitaries, and this probably explained his anticlericalism. . . . The Senior Common Room atmosphere—any Common Room would do—fitted him like a glove. He essentially liked drinking beer with his fellow-men. He pretended to dislike intellectual matters and publicized his distaste for reading, but he had been known to reveal encyclopaedic knowledge of Fielding and Jane Austen. He loved gardening, and he also loved going to philosophical conventions, where his charm overwhelmed everyone. Young philosophers swarmed round him and he was too kind to them. He was a perfect Victorian gentleman." Gilbert Ryle is an honorary fellow of three Oxford colleges, Queen's, Christ Church, and Magdalen, and he has honorary doctorates from the universities of Birmingham, Warwick, Hull, and Sussex. He is unmarried.

PRINCIPAL WORKS: The Concept of Mind, 1949; Dilemmas, 1954; Plato's Progress, 1966; Collected Papers: vol. 1,

Critical Essays, 1971; vol. 2, Collected Essays, 1929–1968, 1971.

ABOUT: Addis, L. O. and Lewis, D. E. Moore and Ryle: Two Ontologists, 1965; Hannay, A. Mental Images, 1972; Mehta, V. Fly and the Fly Bottle, 1963; Passmore, J. A Hundred Years of Philosophy, 1966; Rorty, R. (ed.) The Linguistic Turn, 1967; Who's Who, 1973; Wood, O. P. and Pitcher, G. (eds.) Ryle: A Collection of Critical Essays, 1970. *Periodicals*—Journal of Philosophy April 26, 1951; Mind April 1950; Philosophical Review January 1951, October 1958.

"SABA," UMBERTO (pseudonym of Umberto Poli) (March 9, 1883–August 25, 1957), Italian poet, was born in Trieste, the son of a Jewish mother and a Christian father whom he was not to meet until he was twenty. His father's desertion had a profound effect on Saba's childhood, and he referred to him as "the murderer," though he later forgave him, recognizing in him the source of his poetic gifts. He writes of his father as "gay and light," while his mother "felt all the burden of life. / He escaped from her hand like a balloon." Throughout his tormented adolescence, Saba felt both natures at war in his own mixed blood.

As his mother had to earn the family's living, Saba was put in the care of a peasant woman and thus grew up with two mothers, both of whom he loved dearly and brought vividly to life in his poetry. He had only a few years of schooling and no intellectual pretensions. His first ambition was to repay his mother's devotion by becoming a "good, honest and reputable businessman." He entered the Commercial and Nautical Academy in Trieste, and, according to some sources, subsequently spent some time at sea on a merchant ship, before returning to his native city. It was then that he began the intensive reading of the classics—especially Petrarch, Leopardi, and Tasso—which so influenced his own work.

Saba often said that to be born in 1883 in Trieste (then in Austrian hands) was in cultural terms like being born elsewhere in Italy a generation earlier. Like other Triestine artists he was devotedly Italian in language and sentiment, but quite cut off from the ferment and experiment that characterized Italian intellectual life at that time. All his life he felt himself a poorly educated provincial, and it may have been his desire to link himself with an established cultural tradition that led him to the classics.

Saba was a classicist in the restraint and economy of his forms, but a lyricist in feeling. He was the most personal and human of poets, the loving celebrant of the details and objects of everyday life, the ordinary people, the animals, streets, and cafés of Trieste. He wanted nothing but "to live the life of everybody / to be like all, the men of everyday." His poems began to appear when he was about

UMBERTO SABA

seventeen and *Il mio primo libro di poesie* (My First Book of Poems) was privately printed in 1903 (and republished as *Poesie* in 1911). These, the melancholy poems of his adolescence, were followed by those written during a year of military service (1907–1908) with the Italian army. *Coi miei occhi* (With My Own Eyes, 1912) reflect, according to Sylvia Sprigge, "all the tediousness of drill, long marches, punishments, gunfire practice and lusty talk about women, common to all men in uniform."

In 1908, meanwhile, Saba had married and was working in Trieste. His work at that time was full of "varied, tender, [gently] imperative" love poems, like the famous "A mia moglie" (To My Wife), but grew increasingly sad and elegiac as World War I approached. Saba spent the war in the army, writing little. After it he returned to Trieste, now an Italian city, and became the manager and then the owner of a bookshop on the via Dante Alighieri.

This was at first a happy and busy period in Saba's life. He traveled to Rome, Florence, and Milan, and built his shop into a local and a national institution, both as a first-rate bookshop and as a meeting place for the many artists and writers who visited him there, and drank wine with him in the glass-partitioned office in the center of the store. In 1921 his reputation as a poet was firmly established with the publication of his collected poems, called *Il canzoniere* (The Song Book) after Petrarch. Saba was increasingly drawn to the theories of Freud and underwent psychoanalysis, which helped him to resolve the conflicts within his personality.

But the several volumes of verse which Saba published at this time reflected the growing anti-

Semitism of Mussolini's Italy. He himself was imprisoned for a time, and in 1935 he wrote: "There was a time / When my life was easy. The soil / yielded flowers and fruit abundantly. / Now I work a dry and hard ground." Shortly before World War II he went to live in Paris, but returned to spend the war in hiding in Rome and then in Florence. There he learned that the Fascists had wrecked the Jewish cemetery in Trieste, destroying his mother's grave. The poem "Avevo" (I Once Had) lists all that "the base Fascist and the greedy German" had taken from him—his city, his shop, his wife, his daughter.

In 1945, by then in his sixties, Saba returned to his old life in Trieste. The same year he published the first of several expanded editions of *Il canzoniere*, which had become "the story of a life relatively poor in external events, rich in times of torture, of feelings and internal echoes, and of people." He produced several more volumes of verse during the next twelve years and was also the author of some short stories and an autobiography. He died in a clinic in Gorizia, which he entered only a few days before the death of his wife, when he could no longer bear to witness her lingering illness.

In 1951 Oliver Evans called Saba the poet above all of nostalgia: "The older he grows, the more he is inclined to celebrate (in what is perhaps the most exquisite lyrical verse to come out of Italy in half a century) the phenomenon of youth. He has ceased to believe in anything except the fact of life, which for him is a constant falling away from original perfection, a gradual decay and disillusionment. It is almost a Wordsworthian conception, but with a full acceptance of the implications and consequences. . . . His poems are direct, deceptively simple, frequently dramatic, and always intensely personal. He reminds one somewhat of Housman, but his ear is more sophisticated." Carlo Golino regards him as one of the most influential of contemporary Italian poets, a bridge between the nineteenth century and "the hermetics' closed, personal world." Nora Baldi said: "The truth of his poetry was love, and the truth of his life was death."

PRINCIPAL WORKS IN ENGLISH TRANSLATION: *Poems in* Barnstone, W. (ed.) Modern European Poetry, 1966; Fulton, R. (ed.) An Italian Quartet: Versions After Saba, Ungaretti, Montale and Quasimodo, 1966; Golino, C. L. (ed.) Contemporary Italian Poetry, 1962; Pacifici, S. (ed.) The Promised Land and Other Poems, 1957; Atlantic December 1958; Italian Quarterly Fall 1957; Partisan Review Summer 1963; Times Literary Supplement January 27, 1966.

ABOUT: Baldi, N. Il paradiso di Saba, 1958; Barnstone, W. (ed.) Modern European Poetry, 1966; Burnshaw, S. (ed.) The Poem Itself, 1960; Dizionario universale della letteratura contemporanea, 1962; Letteratura Italiana: I Contemporanei, 1963; Pacifici, S. (ed.) The Promised Land and Other Poems, 1957; Pacifici, S. A Guide to Contemporary Italian Literature: From Futurism to Neorealism, 1962; Polato, L. Aspetti e tendenze della lingua poetica di Saba, 1966; Portinari, F. Umberto Saba, 1963; Squarotti, B. Astrazione e Realtà, 1960. *Periodicals*—Books Abroad Spring 1947; Italian Quarterly Fall 1957; London Magazine April 1958; Poetry January 1952; Times Literary Supplement March 31, 1950; Voices May–August 1951.

***SACHS, NELLY** (December 10, 1891–May 12, 1970), German-born poet and dramatist, received the Nobel Prize in Literature in 1966. In a sense she lived two lives—the first in Germany, from which she escaped in 1940; the second in Sweden, where she spent the rest of her life and wrote her mature poetry. In another sense, though, her whole life was one: a steady deepening of its distinctive Hebraism, a preparation for the time when she could speak in universal terms on behalf of her own people. In this sense, as J. P. Bauke says, "all her work is one great poem, a grandiose epitaph for her dead brothers and sisters."

Nelly Sachs was born in Berlin, the only child of William Sachs, a prosperous Jewish industrialist, and the former Margarethe Karger. The family was religiously liberal and cultured, and she was sensitively trained in dance, music, and literature, at first at home and later at the Höhere Töchterschule in Berlin. At fifteen she read Selma Lagerlöf's novel *Gösta Berling* and was greatly impressed, beginning a correspondence with the Swedish author that lasted for many years, and later saved her life.

When she was about seventeen she began to write, producing puppet plays and romantic sonnets of no particular distinction, all of them quite untouched by the expressionist experiments that were sweeping through German literature at the time. Her first book was *Legenden und Erzählungen* (Legends and Tales, 1921), a volume of stories many of which were set in the Middle Ages. It made no great impression; nor did the few poems she published between 1929 and 1933 in such newspapers as the *Berliner Tageblatt.* There was no need for her to earn a living, and she lived quietly with her parents, and continued to write.

After the Nazis came to power in 1933 Miss Sachs's withdrawn life became even more hermetic. The man she loved was arrested and later died in a concentration camp. She began to read the works of the Jewish and Christian mystics—the Old Testament, the Cabala, the Hasidic writers, and Jakob Böhme—studies that were reflected in the few poems she published in Jewish publications before 1938. Meanwhile, as the plight of the German Jews grew more desperate, Selma Lagerlöf interceded directly with the Swedish royal family on behalf of Nelly Sachs. In March 1940 Selma Lagerlöf died, but, two months later, thanks to her efforts, Nelly Sachs and her mother were able to

* zäks

escape to Sweden. It is known that they avoided arrest and the forced labor camp by only the narrowest margin.

Frau Sachs's health was poor and for ten years, until her death in 1950, they lived in great distress and poverty in a one-room apartment in Stockholm. Slowly Nelly Sachs began to earn a modest income as a translator—over the years she made Ekelöf, Vennberg, Lindegren and many other major Swedish poets accessible to German readers. At the same time her own poetry gained the sense of purpose it had lacked. Miraculously chosen for survival when so many of her people had died, she set herself to build a great temple of lamentation for the Jewish people, and ultimately for all mankind.

Her first postwar collections, *In den Wohnungen des Todes* (In the Dwellings of Death, 1947) and *Sternverdunkelung* (Eclipse of the Stars, 1949) showed that the girl who had written ecstatic lyrics about the beauties of nature was dead. Her careful adherence to traditional forms was abandoned and these new poems were unrhymed and irregular, propelled by psalm-like rhythms and expressing in dark visions of horror and death the poet's bitterness.

This almost Gothic obsession with the hideous details of the Jewish martyrdom gave place gradually in subsequent volumes to a calmer, deeper, more universal view. In *Und niemand weiss weiter* (And No One Knows Where to Turn, 1957) and *Flucht und Verwandlung* (Flight and Change, 1958) the Jewish tragedy began to take its place as a chapter in the long story of human suffering: "sleep and dying are without characteristics." And suffering itself began to be seen in religious terms as a purifying experience, a stage in man's pilgrimage towards reconciliation with God. Until then Nelly Sachs's work had attracted little attention, but in 1958, after the publication of *Flucht und Verwandlung*, Hans Magnus Enzensberger noted that her verses "have at last aroused German literary criticism from its miserable sleep."

More widespread recognition followed the appearance of her collected poems, *Fahrt ins Staublose* (Journey Beyond the Dust, 1961) and her reputation grew steadily with the publication of a selection from her work (*Ausgewählte Gedichte*, 1963) and *Späte Gedichte* (Later Poems, 1965). Nelly Sachs also wrote a number of plays and short dramatic scenes, of which the best known is *Eli*, "a mystery play of the sufferings of Israel." This story about the murder by a Nazi soldier of a Jewish shepherd boy in Poland was written in 1943 but not published until 1951. Since then it has been broadcast and staged in Germany and made the basis of an opera by the Swedish composer Moses Pergament. It appears, with other plays and scenes

NELLY SACHS

by Miss Sachs, in *Zeichen im Sand* (Signs in the Sand, 1962).

Nelly Sachs's poetry, Enzensberger says, is "inconceivable as a series of individual artifacts." All of her mature work forms one great cycle, even one poem, which is modeled, according to Beda Alleman, on the Cabala. Kurt Pinthus has called her poetry "the presumably final expression in the German language of the ancestral sequence of 3,000 years which began with the psalmists and other prophets."

O the Chimneys, a volume of her poetry (including the play *Eli*) appeared in the United States in 1967 and in England (as *Selected Poems*) a year later, in translations by Michael Hamburger and others. A reviewer in the *Times Literary Supplement* spoke of the difficulty of translating these "highly volatile and precarious poems," which rely a great deal on abstract metaphors, and "in which the German words may carry seven shades of meaning to every three carried by their English counterparts." He goes on: "The grand cosmic themes—love, life, death, transformation—are ventured with a single-mindedness that takes the breath away. . . . Yet her work is haunted by a paradisal levity; seldom do the drifting skeins of metaphors catch the actual scream, the phenomenon itself happening in the instant of articulation. The poem becomes an image of total relativity, supernalizing everything it touches, even the most horrific banal evils of humankind: 'I do not know the room / where exiled love / lays down its victory / and the growing into the reality / of visions begins / nor where the smile of the child who was thrown as in play / into the playing flames is preserved / but I know that this is the food / from which earth with beating heart / ignites the music of her stars—'" A posthumous collection, *The Seeker*, translated by Ruth Mead and Michael Hamburger, completed the publication of Nelly Sachs's poems in English.

In 1960 the author visited Germany for the first time in twenty years to receive the Droste-Hülshoff prize for poetry. A year later the city of Dortmund honored her on her seventieth birthday with a lifetime pension and the establishment of a Nelly Sachs prize for literature. In 1965 she was awarded the Peace Prize of the German book trade and in 1966 she and the Hebrew writer S. Y. Agnon shared the $60,000 Nobel Prize in Literature. She died in 1970. Nelly Sachs, a very small, slight, gray-haired woman, was a Swedish subject. She carried on an extensive correspondence with writers all over the world, and was often visited by them in her Stockholm apartment.

PRINCIPAL WORKS IN ENGLISH TRANSLATION: O the Chimneys, 1967 (England, Selected Poems); The Seeker and Other Poems, 1970.

ABOUT: Berendsohn, W. A. (ed.) Nelly Sachs, 1963; Current Biography, 1967; Nelly Sachs zu Ehren, 1961. *Periodicals*—Book Week July 9, 1967; New York Times November 11, 1966; May 13, 1970; New York Times Book Review November 6, 1966; Saturday Review December 10, 1966; Times (London) October 21, 1966; Times Literary Supplement November 21, 1968.

***"SAGAN, FRANÇOISE" (pseudonym of Françoise Quoirez)** (June 21, 1935–), French novelist and dramatist, was born at Cajarc, in the southwest of France, the third child of Pierre Quoirez, a prosperous industrialist of Spanish extraction, and Marie (Laubard) Quoirez. She grew up in Lyons, on a country estate at Vercors, and during part of World War II in Switzerland. It seems to have been a fairly sheltered, bourgeois upbringing, and she was educated at good convent schools in Paris, where she later discovered the company and the conversation of the Latin Quarter cafés, and attended the Sorbonne.

She had begun to write poetry and short stories in her early teens and when, in 1953, she failed her second-year university examinations, she filled in a hiatus by writing her first novel. This was *Bonjour tristesse*, published when she was nineteen, awarded the Prix des Critiques, a phenomenal best seller in twenty languages. It is a precocious adolescent's account of her tragically successful attempt to prevent her father's remarriage—a wistful story about the messy lives of aimless people, told in an unornamented classical French style of great purity.

All of Mlle. Sagan's novels have been variations on the same formula. The essence of them is contained, as Godfrey Smith has pointed out, in the opening of *Un Certain Sourire* (1956, translated as *A Certain Smile*), about a young student's affair with a weary middle-aged father figure. The first paragraph reads: "We had spent the afternoon in a café in the Rue St. Jacques, a spring afternoon like any other. I was slightly bored, and walked up and down between the jukebox and the window, while Bertrand talked about Spire's lecture. I was leaning on the machine watching the record rising slowly, almost gently, like a proffered cheek, to its slanting position against the sapphire, when, for no apparent reason, I was overcome by a feeling of intense happiness, a sudden realization that some day I would die, that my hand would no longer touch that chromium rim, nor would the sun shine in my eyes."

* sa gäN′

Françoise Sagan says that for her "writing is a question of finding a certain rhythm. . . . Much of the time life is a sort of rhythmic progression of three characters." There are nine characters in *Dans un mois, dans un an* (1957, translated as *Those Without Shadows*), and the permutations of their restless love affairs are traced rather tenuously, but she is on surer ground when she returns to the triangle situation in *Aimez-vous Brahms?*, in which a young man falls in love with the middle-aged mistress of a businessman, and in which the attractions (for the young) of maturity are again important. (Godfrey Smith calls her "patron saint to all men of forty.") *Les Merveilleux Nuages* (1961, translated as *The Wonderful Clouds*) is about a modern marriage: Josée extricates herself from her marriage to a morbidly jealous husband and finds, of course, that her freedom is emptiness. *La Chamade* (1966), one of the most admired of the recent novels, is another triangle story, this time an extramarital one. An element of something like black comedy distinguishes *Le Garde du cœur* (1968, translated as *The Heart-Keeper*), in which the middle-aged heroine has to choose between her mature lover and a young drop-out—the latter so devoted to her that he nonchalantly murders four people who, in his opinion, distress or annoy her.

In fact the plots of Mlle. Sagan's novels are in general much alike and not very important. The same might be said of her characters. They are strikingly people of the mid-twentieth century but also, rootless as they are and suspended in the moment, curiously timeless. They spend their days without obvious occupation, with no past and not much of a future, in a vacuum of inertia and lassitude. They know that their absurdity and loneliness can be transcended only through love, but also that love must die, "in a month, in a year." Mlle. Sagan offers no moral judgment: "The only morality for a novelist is the morality of his *esthétique*."

Her *esthétique* is indeed extremely moral; she finds it "not absolutely a joke to write—it is intimate, difficult, humbling, and even humiliating." The struggle seems worthwhile. Although she is a worldwide best seller she may still be undervalued —Brigid Brophy, in a brilliant essay, calls her "the most under-estimated presence in postwar French writing." Her austere epigrammatic novels, which adumbrate rather than delineate, seeking "to take reality by surprise," are marvels of elliptical lucidity in the tradition of Racine, *La Princesse de Clèves*, Benjamin Constant's *Adolphe*. Robert Parris says that "Sagan's handling of literary French is classic and formal, and for a Frenchman the conventions of tense and syntax used in a perfect academic fashion have an expressiveness and charm quite apart from the ideas they help to convey."

During the 1960s Françoise Sagan began to establish a second reputation as a dramatist. Her plays are a great deal like her novels and a number of them have been produced, including *Château en Suède* (Castle in Sweden, 1960), *Les Violons, parfois* (Violins Sometimes, 1961). *La Robe mauve de Valentine* (Valentine's Mauve Dress, 1963), *Le Cheval évanoui* (The Vanishing Horse, 1966), and *Un Piano dans l'herbe* (A Piano in the Grass, 1970). Most of them have been well received by the critics and the public, and Janet Flanner wrote of the first that for Françoise Sagan "love is the fine flower of life—the most important gift you get or give—and it fades. As a modern intelligence, she perceives that between lovers the practice of ideas usually destroys emotions, that personal liberty is a dangerous necessity, that most human beings suffer from and give off ennui, and that fantasy is a final refuge from reality, especially for the French. This inventory she used in such perfect proportion in her *Château en Suède* that the play will likely be regarded for its delights as a personal period piece, and will be revived . . . like a minor theatre classic." Several of Mlle. Sagan's novels have been adapted for the screen, and she has herself written screenplays, stories, songs, and a ballet.

Even in the middle of the twentieth century, few people of Mlle. Sagan's age have been so remorselessly analyzed and publicized, and few have survived the experience with such dignity. Her fondness for jazz, dancing, and fast cars has been much discussed, and in 1957, when one of her cars almost killed her, the accident was confidently interpreted as symptomatic of modern youth's prodigal "death-wish." Indeed from the beginning she has been confused with her characters and regarded as a symbol of a bored and amoral generation. Her novels are no doubt partially autobiographical—especially, as Brigid Brophy says, in mood. But Mlle. Sagan is a political idealist and a committed artist, and in these fundamental ways is different from the aimless people she writes about. She has been married twice, in 1958 to Guy

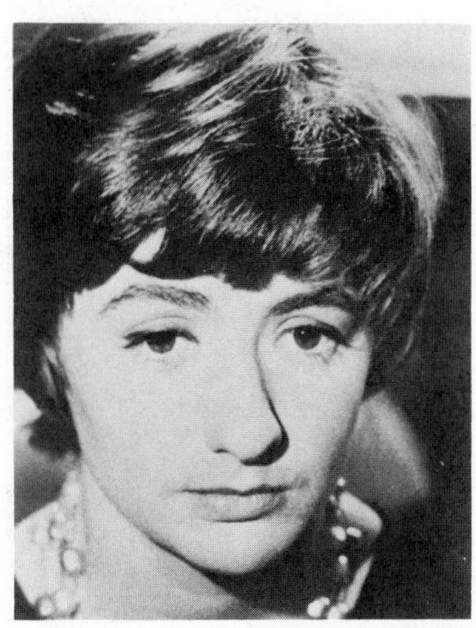

FRANÇOISE SAGAN

Schoëller, a publisher, and in 1962 to the American ceramics designer Robert Westhoff, by whom she has a son. Both marriages ended in divorce. Her pseudonym is borrowed from Proust, who gave it originally to a princess. Mlle. Sagan has a house in Normandy and an apartment in Paris, but in 1973 announced her intention of settling in Ireland. "The Irish are very noble people and they protect their women," she said. "I go to them desolate and with a broken heart. I will come back to France but as an Irish woman."

PRINCIPAL WORKS IN ENGLISH TRANSLATION: Bonjour Tristesse, 1955; A Certain Smile, 1956; Those Without Shadows, 1957; Aimez-vous Brahms?, 1960; The Wonderful Clouds, 1962; Toxique: Drawings and Calligraphy by Bernard Buffet, 1964; La Chamade, 1966; The Heart-Keeper, 1968; A Few Hours of Sunlight, 1971 (In England, Sunlight on Cold Water).

ABOUT: Boisdeffre, P. de. Dictionnaire de littérature contemporaine, 1962; Brophy, B. Don't Never Forget, 1967; Cowley, M. (ed.) Writers at Work: The Paris Review Interviews, 1958; Curley, D. N. and Curley, A. (eds.) Modern Romance Literatures (Library of Literary Criticism), 1967; Hourdin, G. Le Cas Françoise Sagan, 1958; International Who's Who, 1973–74; Mourge, G. Françoise Sagan, 1959; Pingaud, B. Écrivains d'aujourd'hui, 1960; Who's Who, 1973; Who's Who in America, 1972–1973; Who's Who in France, 1973–1974. *Periodicals* —Catholic World July 1957; Cosmopolitan August 1958; Current Biography September 1960; Guardian June 22, 1972; Ladies' Home Journal January 1965; New York Times Magazine October 27, 1957; March 30, 1958; Partisan Review Winter 1957; Saturday Review August 18, 1956; Yale French Studies No. 24 1959.

SAINT, DORA JESSIE. *See* "MISS READ"

"ST. JAMES, ANDREW." *See* STERN, JAMES

ARMAND SALACROU

***SALACROU, ARMAND** (August 9, 1899–), French dramatist, writes (in French): "I was born at Rouen, on the third floor of an attractive house facing the Cathedral, a house which was completely destroyed by war action in 1940. I spent my childhood and early youth with my parents at Le Havre, in a house which was also destroyed in the war, in 1944.

"In 1914 I saw the first British soldiers arriving, then the Belgian Government, who turned one of the quarters of my town into their capital, while our *lycée* had become a hospital.

"I began to study medicine in Paris, but as I was afraid I would make a poor doctor, I quit, preferring to run the risk of being a poor teacher. I therefore took a *licence* in philosophy after taking my *licence* in science. But having in 1922 founded a family, I decided it would be more useful to be a lawyer, and so I took a *licence* in law. Immediately after this I went into movie-making, and it was at this point, in 1925, that Lugné-Poe put on my first stage play, *Tour à terre* (The Fallen Tower), at the Théâtre de l'Œuvre. It was a total disaster, but is not yet forgotten. Then I met the admirable Charles Dullin who, by giving me a small monthly allowance—for I was short of money (and so was he)—unwittingly started me off in business. It seems that for a few years I was a tycoon, and I suppose I was, as my business venture made it possible for me to live opposite the Arc de Triomphe in Paris, and to go on living there to this day.

"Nevertheless, every day I wrote fragments of plays, and once these had been strung together they were put on, sometimes with considerable success. *L'Inconnue d'Arras* (The Unknown Woman from Arras), for example, written in 1930, was the first play in which the author (myself, that is) used the device of going back in time which has since been known as the 'flash-back.' Just before 1939 I wrote *Histoire de Rire* (A Laughing Matter), which is still being played in France at the present day. I was not very happy during the German Occupation, as I do not take kindly to people who move in on me without being invited. And now I am even less happy, much less, because old age is moving in on me, and the only thing which will put a stop to that is the very thing we had at least some hope of avoiding during the Occupation.

"In the meantime, I have been elected President of the International Institute of the Theatre (UNESCO), and I am still, at the time of writing, President of the famous 'Société des Auteurs Dramatiques,' founded by Beaumarchais in the eighteenth century.

"I am also one of the ten members of the Goncourt Academy, who meet and decide each year in Paris which will be the most widely read book in France.

"For details on my whole life, I recommend a book by Paul-Louis Mignon, illustrated with fine photographs, published by Éditions Gallimard in the series La Bibliothèque Idéale. My plays and the various texts, prefaces and postfaces which accompany them, can also be read, and are also published by Gallimard."

Salacrou is the son of Camille Salacrou, a pharmacist, and the former Gabrielle Pestel. Perhaps the most important thing to be said about him is that he was raised a Roman Catholic but lost his faith as a child. Since then he has tried to accept other systems of belief. He was a founder of the Jeunesses Socialistes (Young Socialists) and a member for a time of the Communist party, but came to regard his political activism as something which gave no more than a temporary usefulness to his life, "which has no meaning." Persuaded (before the existentialists adopted the term), of the "absurdity" of existence, he was also drawn to surrealism but never joined that authoritarian movement. And Salacrou has also flirted very profitably (but no doubt insincerely) with capitalism; in 1930, to eke out the patronage he received from the actor-manager Charles Dullin, he launched an advertising agency and nonchalantly made a fortune.

Salacrou's despairing pessimism seemed no more than cynicism to the bewildered Boulevard critics who were confronted in the mid-1920s with his early plays, *Tour à terre* and *Le Pont de l'Europe* (The Bridge of Europe). These works, Pirandellian in their concern with identity, surrealist in their

* sä lä cro͞o

nightmare logic and startling imagery, were by no means merely derivative. The latter already showed a typical Salacrian preoccupation with the irredeemability of time past, which is a corollary of his obsession with the outrageous finality of death. It must be said that Salacrou's first plays, ramshackle in their construction, verbose and "literary" in their interminable discussions, deserved the harsh press they received. But they caused a great stir and had an originality which impressed others as well as Dullin, and led Louis Jouvet to commission two plays from the young writer.

Salacrou produced two relatively naturalistic pieces, which were relatively well received by the critics: *Atlas Hôtel* (1931) and *Les Frénétiques* (The Frenzied, staged in 1934). This discipline taught Salacrou his craft, but also convinced him that the naturalistic theatre was not for him. His work, as he says, is not about society but about his own metaphysical drama—a protest against his own absurdity, an appeal for a miracle of faith, "a means of coming unobserved upon God"—in which the characters are "reflections of his own metaphysical distress."

With *Une Femme libre* (A Free Woman, 1934), Salacrou put his new-found mastery of technique at the service of his own ideas, and achieved a major success. It is about a girl who rejects her fiancé not because she does not love him but because she dare not abandon her potential, the possibility of a "miracle," for the deathlike certainties of a bourgeois marriage. It was followed by a string of critical and commercial successes which confirmed Salacrou's position as a dramatist of the first order. *L'Inconnue d'Arras* (The Unknown Woman of Arras, 1935) is a brilliantly managed expressionist investigation of a suicide's life, whose value is revealed to him, too late, in the split second between his pulling the trigger and the arrival of the bullet in his brain. *La Terre est ronde* (The World is Round, 1938), a tragedy about Savonarola, is a comment on the pointless repetitiveness of things, and was also regarded by many as an attack on the fascism then rampant throughout Europe. *Histoire de rire* (1939, translated as *When the Music Stops*) is a savage meditation on moral squalor, masquerading as a Feydeau farce about adultery; it was staged in London in 1957 and called a "glittering" tour de force, whose "theme and its inversion are as satisfying as any fugue."

In the English-speaking world, Salacrou's best-known play is *Les Nuits de la colère* (Nights of Wrath, 1946), a tragedy about the French Resistance under the German occupation. It is an experimental work in the sense that time is set aside, the living and the dead converse, but it is also Salacrou's only positive play, and this fact, and its topicality, made it a major success in postwar France. It was given a workshop production by Erwin Piscator in New York in 1948, and has also been performed in London and toured all over the world by Jean-Louis Barrault. The exultant humanism which the Resistance and the Liberation inspired in Salacrou has faded, and the shadow of "universal determinism" has lengthened over his later plays, which show an ever-increasing ability to advance his ideas in popular forms. They include *Boulevard Durand* (1960), a play about class warfare which showed that Salacrou retains his sense of solidarity with the working class; *L'Archipel Lenoir* (1947), a "shapely" black comedy which was given a rather feeble performance in London in 1966 as *Never Say Die*; and *Sens interdit* (Time Confounded, 1953), in which time is reversed and people eagerly look forward to their youth, their innocence, and their illusions.

Salacrou was married in 1922 to Jeanne Jeandet and has two children. He lives in an elegant apartment on the Avenue Foch, decorated with an impressive collection of paintings by Picasso, Modigliani, Braque, and Dufy, among others. Harold Hobson says that this "dramatist of dread" is a "remarkably merry and animated companion," a modest man, sharp-eyed, eager, and energetic, with a "bright and almost transparently clear complexion." Salacrou, who resigned from the Goncourt Academy in 1971, is a Commander of the Légion d'Honneur.

PRINCIPAL WORKS IN ENGLISH TRANSLATION: Three Plays (The World Is Round, When the Music Stops, Marguerite), 1967; A Circus Story *in* Benedikt, M. and Wellwarth, G. E. (eds.) Modern French Theatre, 1964.

ABOUT: Boisdeffre, P. de. Dictionnaire de littérature contemporaine, 1962; Esch, J. van den. Armand Salacrou, 1947; Guicharnaud, J. Modern French Theatre, 1961; Hobson, H. The French Theatre Today, 1955; International Who's Who, 1973–74; Knowles, D. French Drama of the Inter-War Years, 1967; Lumley, F. Trends in Twentieth Century Drama, 1956; Mignon, P. L. Salacrou, 1960; Moore, H. T. Twentieth-Century French Literature Since World War II, 1966; Smith, H. (ed.) Columbia Dictionary of Modern European Literature, 1947; Who's Who in France, 1971–1972. *Periodicals*—Revue des Deux Mondes December 1, 1938; Spectator February 1, 1957; Symposium Spring 1966; Theatre Arts May 1947, February 1948, April 1957; World Theatre 3, 1956; Yale French Studies 14 1954–1955.

SALISBURY, HARRISON E(VANS) (November 14, 1908–), American journalist, authority on Soviet affairs, writes: "I am a product of Minnesota. I was born and raised in Minneapolis, and there I went to school and completed my education at the University of Minnesota.

"I suppose that this is the most important circumstance of my life, since I like to think that it is the background of those Minnesota years and the atmosphere of dissent and iconoclasm nourished

HARRISON E. SALISBURY

by the Minnesota soil which have given my life its general direction and meaning.

"When I was growing up in Minnesota it was almost convention to be an 'aginner.' Protest was borne in the very air we breathed. This was the time of the La Follettes in Wisconsin, the Farmer-Laborites in Minnesota, and the Nonpartisan League in North Dakota. It was a time of economic hardship—indeed, in that agrarian milieu it is difficult to remember a time when economic want did not stalk the land.

"The second important influence on my life and career was the accidental circumstance of getting into Russia during World War II. This set in train a succession of events which has seemed to bring me back there again and again.

"No one can spend long years in Russia, particularly in a Russia dominated as it was for so many years by the harsh iron of the Stalin regime, without being profoundly influenced. It is a pervasive influence, stemming from Russia itself—the broad sweep of the Russian landscape, the broad scope of Russian history, the breadth of the Russian horizon and, one might say, the breadth and depth of the Russian ethos.

"Perhaps the most valuable gift of my Russian years has been the insight and excitement which it has given to my renewed encounter with my own country. It is not only that America looks bandbox fresh and magically sophisticated after a time spent wandering across the broad Russian lands. It is also the sensation of rediscovery, the seeing of old things new and for the first time.

"And I should not minimize the new sense of values which one acquires after prolonged exposure to an existence which is elemental, dramatic in its catastrophes, almost apocalyptic in its visions.

"Professionally, the great influence in my life has been the New York *Times*. I cannot imagine an atmosphere more conducive to the broadest development of the faculties of observation and writing."

Harrison E. Salisbury is the son of Percy and Georgina (Evans) Salisbury. His career as a newspaperman began at the University of Minnesota, where he edited the college newspaper and also worked part time as a reporter and rewrite man for the United Press in St. Paul and the Minneapolis *Journal*. Graduating with a B.A. in 1930, he joined the United Press, working in Chicago, Washington, and New York City, and in 1943 became the news agency's London manager. Salisbury made his first visit to Russia in 1944—a "quick survey" that grew into an eight-month tour. A series of articles about what he saw there was expanded into his first book, *Russia on the Way* (1946). It was warmly received as a "lucid, unpretentious, thought-provoking" book, and a very readable one.

From 1944 to 1948 Salisbury was the United Press's foreign news editor, and in 1949 he joined the New York *Times* as Moscow correspondent, a post he retained for five years. His predecessor there, Drew Middleton, had been excluded from the Soviet Union because of the frankness of his dispatches; Salisbury, seeking to avoid the same fate, was more cautious. This earned him harsh criticism in some quarters in the United States, where he was accused of "glorifying" the Soviet regime. Other commentators, however, praised the "objectivity" of Salisbury's dispatches, and this, and his excellence as "a reporter of scenes, moods, and atmosphere," brought him in 1955 the Pulitzer Prize for international reporting.

American in Russia, published after his return, painted a considerably less cheerful picture of conditions in the Soviet Union than his dispatches had done, but nevertheless advocated patience and "Yankee common sense" in United States–Soviet relations, since both countries "must go on living under the same roof or perish." It was not until 1961 that Salisbury felt able to publish *Moscow Journal*, which includes dispatches written between 1949 and 1954 but "killed" in whole or in part by the Soviet censors. Robert Conquest praised Salisbury's "eye for the significant and his general grasp of the political situation," and other critics were equally enthusiastic about "his gift for vivid reporting of sights and smells, his quick sympathy for all Russians except the most repulsive bureaucrats."

Meanwhile, Salisbury had returned to the United

States in 1954 and joined his newspaper's New York staff. One product of his years as a reporter of the American scene was *The Shook-up Generation*, a vivid study of juvenile street gangs. *To Moscow—and Beyond* and *A New Russia?* are both products of return visits to the Soviet Union, particularly valuable and interesting for their comments on the slow process of change that followed Stalin's death.

They were followed by the journalist's first novel, *The Northern Palmyra Affair*. This story, set in postwar Leningrad, was found profoundly revealing in its depiction of the political situation and of the Russian character, an exciting and "an astoundingly good novel in every sense." Two books, both published late in 1965, and both intended primarily for young people, were rather confusingly given the same title: *Russia*. One, published by Macmillan, is a brief introductory history of the country; the other, a "New York Times Byline Book," published by Atheneum, is "a tough, perceptive analysis of present-day Russia, its dissatisfactions, power struggles, political maneuverings."

In 1966 Salisbury made a thirty-thousand-mile tour of Hong Kong, Cambodia, Laos, Burma, India, Mongolia, Russia, Japan, and other countries; his report, *Orbit of China*, written with a "journalist's eye for detail and a humanitarian concern for Asian misery," nevertheless seemed to some reviewers occasionally dull and not always consistent in its conclusions. Late in 1966 Salisbury visited North Vietnam. His New York *Times* dispatches, suggesting that Hanoi was willing to negotiate an end to the Vietnam war, caused a furor, and this flared up again when Salisbury offered similar conclusions in his book *Behind the Lines*. John Mecklin, agreeing with the many critics who charged the author with "a deplorable lack of professional journalistic scepticism," added that he had "revealed so much new information on the situation in the North as to add a new dimension to the debate. . . . It is no less than a journalistic breakthrough."

Salisbury's history of the siege of Leningrad in World War II, *The 900 Days*, seemed to C. P. Snow "something like a nonfiction masterpiece, at the same time realistic, brotherly and admiring." It was followed by another controversial study, *War Between Russia and China*. *The Many Americas Shall Be One*, a plea for national reconciliation, seemed to most reviewers more well-meaning than effective in its arguments. *To Peking—and Beyond* describes what Salisbury observed during his 1972 visit to Korea and China.

Harrison Salisbury, who has twice received the George Polk Memorial Award for foreign reporting, and has several honorary doctorates, was assistant managing editor of the New York *Times* from 1964 until 1972, when he was named associate editor. He has two sons by his 1933 marriage to Mary Hollis, which ended in divorce. He was married again in 1964, to Charlotte Young Rand.

PRINCIPAL WORKS: *Nonfiction*—Russia on the Way, 1946; American in Russia, 1955; The Shook-up Generation, 1958; To Moscow—and Beyond, 1960; Moscow Journal, 1961; A New Russia?, 1962; The Key to Moscow (for children), 1963; Russia, 1965; Russia: A New York Times Byline Book, 1965; Orbit of China, 1967; Behind the Lines, 1967; The 900 Days, 1969; War Between Russia and China, 1969 (England, The Coming War Between Russia and China); The Many Americas Shall Be One, 1971; (ed.) The Eloquence of Protest: Voices of the Seventies, 1972; To Peking—and Beyond: A Report on the New Asia, 1973; (ed.) The Indignant Years: Art and Articles From the Op-Ed Pages of the New York Times, 1973. *Fiction*—The Northern Palmyra Affair, 1962.

ABOUT: Current Biography, 1955; Richards, C. (ed.) Minnesota Writers, 1961; Salisbury, C. Y. China Diary, 1973; Who's Who, 1973; Who's Who in America, 1972–1973. *Periodicals*—American Mercury January 1955; Commentary March 1955; Newsweek April 7, 1958; April 25, 1960; Saturday Review May 6, 1967.

SAMPSON, ANTHONY (TERRELL SEWARD) (August 3, 1926–), English journalist, writes: "I was born in Billingham, Durham, in the North of England, but this was by chance. My father was a research chemist with Imperial Chemical Industries and he was based in this big chemical town. I was brought up in Hampstead, London, and spent all my childhood there. My parents were both basically of academic background. My father came of a scholarly family (his father was the first serious editor of William Blake, and compiled a dictionary of the Romany language). My mother's father was a Professor of Geology at Cambridge, and so my up-bringing had a definite academic background, and one of my first ambitions was to be a don. My father never seemed really at home in the world of business: he was remote from his colleagues and rather alarmed by money problems, as I am.

"My education was fairly conventional. I went to an English public school, Westminster, whose conventionality was, however, rather modified by evacuation during the war, which gave a sense both of security and of stimulus to many of the schoolboys: the top hats which were part of the pre-war uniform were discarded in favour of open necked shirts. I had a scholarship to Westminster, and was part of a special scholars house, with an intellectual hot-bed atmosphere; but my brain became less efficient as my adolescence progressed and my academic career at Oxford (reading English) was quite undistinguished. I disliked Oxford: I was at Christ Church, the most arrogant and wealthy of the colleges, which presented a rather nasty view of the English establishment in its youth.

ANTHONY SAMPSON

"Between Westminster and Oxford I was in the Navy for the tail-end of the war. It was rather a depressing time and the Navy was slowly running down. I spent a short time in Germany watching the seedy life of the officers buying cameras and girls for cigarettes. I was also in bad health for part of the time and I was very relieved to be out of uniform, though I still have a lingering nostalgia for Naval glories.

"When I went down from Oxford at the age of twenty-five I had no idea what to do, and had a dismal time trying to come to terms with the world of business corporations, being endlessly interviewed without success. I vaguely wanted to be a publisher, and with this in mind I eventually took a job with a printing firm, which offered very little scope. After I had been there a few months I had a telegram from an old Oxford friend, which said simply: 'Can you join new Negro periodical in Capetown fly out say yes.' The periodical had been started by Jim Bailey, the son of a South African millionaire who had become interested in the African part of South Africa. I said yes and went out soon after. After four months in South Africa I found myself editing the magazine, which was called *Drum*. I stayed there for nearly four years. It was by far the most exciting experience of my life, and gave me both an opportunity to escape from the inhibitions and frustrations of England, and also a very astonishing open-sesame to the world of African writers and politicians in South Africa—which was then undergoing a period of tremendous ferment and conflict before the machinery of the Police State was finally devised.

"When I left South Africa in 1955, I assumed that this was a chapter of my life which was quite closed. But in fact it has been a constant part of my life ever since. I have been back to Africa several times, and the African friends I have made there have popped up in different parts of the world. I didn't realise at the time my extraordinary good fortune in finding myself in this creative and thrilling situation.

"Back in London I wrote a book about my experiences called *Drum*. I was offered a job on *The Observer* as assistant to the Editor, partly, no doubt, on the strength of my African connection, for *The Observer* was passionately interested in Africa. I spent a year or so in this semi-administrative job and then took over a weekly column called 'Table Talk,' which I did for about four years. This too was a very formative experience for me, because it gave me access to anybody or anything I wanted to see, and I got to know the world of politics and business in a very agreeable way. I followed round the then Prime Minister, Harold Macmillan, through Asia, Australia, Russia and Africa, and acquired an interest in the workings of power and the people who are behind it. In the meantime, too, I wrote two other books about Africa, one about the South African treason trials, called *The Treason Cage*, and the other a short guide called *Common Sense About Africa*.

"After four years of 'Table Talk,' I felt a desire to try and put my bits of gleanings together, to write a book about the machinery of power, so I took a year off from *The Observer* and wrote a book called *The Anatomy of Britain*. It was tremendously hard work and by the time I was half way through I was in an isolated and rather obsessive state: it involved writing a thousand words a day for a year, together with a great deal of research and interviewing. I just managed to get it done in time, and it proved in the end to be worth it. It had a big sale in England and also sold well in America and Europe. But it took me some time to recover from the strain and singlemindedness and to relax back into a more casual way of life. I returned to *The Observer*, writing a weekly column and travelling whenever I could. I produced a revised edition of 'Anatomy' three years later and I'll probably go on doing this at three year intervals.

"In May of 1965 my life very suddenly changed in two ways. In the first place at the age of thirty-eight I got married. In the second place I became editor of *The Observer* magazine—a colour supplement which had been started less than a year before. These two changes have obviously made a great difference to me, but it's too early to say what."

Anthony Sampson is the son of Michael and Phyllis (Seward) Sampson. He was at Westminster school from 1939 to 1944, and served in the Royal Navy from 1944 to 1947.

Drum, Sampson's account of his editorship of "the newspaper that won the heart of Africa," itself won the hearts of his readers in England and America. It is a modest and unsentimental book, not a history of the paper or a spiritual autobiography, but "a series of jaunty, almost novelistic episodes" in the running war between *Drum* and the South African authorities. What delighted its readers was Sampson's consummate reporting of the adventures of his African staff, some of whom are now internationally famous as journalists or writers. Their courage and "tough Cockney gaiety," their "rapid, racy, humorous idiom" made a splendid book. *Common Sense About Africa* added to Sampson's reputation as "a sympathetic, yet hard-eyed observer of the African scene," able to render down an immense amount of information without making it indigestible, and willing to "lean backwards to be objective and restrained."

What Sampson saw of the British elite at Oxford and during his years on *The Observer*'s superior gossip column "Table Talk" worried him a great deal. He came to believe, according to *Time*, "that the Establishment was to blame for his country's slow, erratic reactions to its new place in the postwar world." *Anatomy of Britain* is a survey of the people and institutions that make up the British Establishment. It seemed to Geoffrey Godsell "the most fascinating collection of facts and verbal snapshots" of his native country that he had ever read, and to J. H. Plumb "one of the most cunning pieces of journalism that has appeared for a generation"—a book beside which John Gunther's famous surveys "look uninformed and dull." The *Times Literary Supplement*, which thought "our troubles deeper than Mr. Sampson gives himself time to realize," nevertheless welcomed the work as "one of the most brilliant and concentrated feats of reporting in our time."

Sampson was editor of *The Observer*'s color supplement in 1965–1966, launching it as an important section of a newspaper which, with its competitor the *Sunday Times*, possibly does more to shape middle-class tastes and values than any other institution in Britain. In 1967 he published his "short, deft study" of Harold Macmillan. The same year, with his wife, the former Sally Bentlif, and their small daughter, Sampson began the tour of Europe which resulted in *The New Europeans*. It is a massive report on the mood, trends, and problems of Western Europe, discussing among other things continental attempts at unity, the impact of technology, and the relationship between Europe and the United States—a relationship which is seen as of the first importance at a time when "the common threads of European unity . . . all seem to lead off the map, westwards."

Max Beloff, discussing the book in *The Observer*, suggested that Sampson is less good at handling ideas than facts, and is "no historian," but all the same found it "more exciting reading than the celebrated *Anatomy of Britain*." A reviewer in the *Times Literary Supplement* had no such reservations, and praised it for "a breadth and completeness which it is almost impossible to fault." He attributed Sampson's success to his "absolute mastery of the full range of journalistic skills," noting in particular his talent as "a verbal cartoonist," his "ability to produce relaxed and readable accounts of the most complex international problems," and above all "his ability to sense and formulate the deep-rooted preoccupations of the new Europeans." *The Sovereign State of ITT*, which followed, is a history and an exposé of the corporation in which Sampson argues that such huge multinational conglomerates have placed themselves in effect beyond the law.

Sampson is a slim, volatile man. When they are not traveling, he and his family (he now has two children) divide their time between a house in West London and another in Suffolk. In 1968–1970 Sampson taught as an associate professor at the University of Vincennes, Paris.

PRINCIPAL WORKS: Drum, 1956; The Treason Cage: The Opposition on Trial in South Africa, 1958; Common Sense About Africa, 1960; Anatomy of Britain, 1962 (rev. as Anatomy of Britain Today, 1965, The New Anatomy of Britain, 1971); Macmillan: A Study in Ambiguity, 1967; The New Europeans, 1968; The Sovereign State of ITT, 1973.

ABOUT: Contemporary Authors 1, 1962; Who's Who, 1973. *Periodical*—Books and Bookmen April 1963.

SAMUELS, ERNEST (May 19, 1903–), American biographer, writes: "My earliest recollections can be matched, I am sure, by the children of many other Jewish immigrants of the early nineties. Life was from the outset a babel of tongues, Yiddish, Polish, German gutturals and Irish brogue. Perhaps because English lived a precarious existence on the neighborhood streets and had to fight against heavy odds, I early became a kind of defender of the faith, a quixotic purist and a haunter of the story hours at the public library.

"I was born in a flat which looked out upon the fortress-like Citizen's Brewery at the corner of Throop Street and Archer Avenue in Chicago. Belowstairs was an Irishman's saloon and beside it my father's first grocery store. Mine was a typical city boyhood in a working-class neighborhood. The playground was the broad cement sidewalk in front of the shops. Adventure was a half-mile hike to the mysterious lumber docks along the river. There were to be several removals before I entered the University of Chicago in 1919, each bringing new struggles to belong in alien neighborhoods, new efforts to understand the contradictions of the

ERNEST SAMUELS

promised land which had drawn my parents from obscure villages in Galicia and Russian Poland. Fortunately, in the democracy of the public school the tyranny of the rival religions vanished and all my mother's humane ideas and ambitions seemed realizable.

"At the University of Chicago I aimed at a career as novelist of the city streets I had known. Prudent family councils prevailed, however, and I wound up in the law school. Then a chance illness intervened which was ultimately decisive of a career. Shortly after my law degree I suffered a relapse and was shipped out to Albuquerque. Years of quiet reading while taking the 'cure' for tuberculosis confirmed my bent toward literature. For two years I practiced law in El Paso, Texas, acted in the Little Theatre, and wrote reams of publicity for it.

"As the Great Depression deepened in 1930 I was obliged to return to Chicago. My elder brother offered refuge in his law office, but the inactivity was oppressive. I re-entered the university for an M.A. in American literature and determined to become a teacher. For the next several years I tried to join teaching in a business college with the practice of law as a specialist in corporate reorganizations. The rival pressures became too great and in 1937 I left the law and went out to the State College of Washington to teach English for two years. There I met Jayne Porter Newcomer, a teaching assistant in the department, and we were married in 1938. In the following year I returned again to the University of Chicago, obtaining the Ph.D. degree in 1942. Since then I have taught continuously at Northwestern University, except for a year as a Fulbright professor to Belgium (1958–59) and a year as the Leo S. Bing Visiting Professor at the University of Southern California. In 1955–1956 I received a Guggenheim Fellowship.

"My main work as a writer has been a three-volume critical biography of Henry Adams, a project on which I was engaged for more than twenty years. To a significant degree the work became an effort to understand what I only dimly glimpsed as a child, what Adams called, in the *Education*, the 'two thousand year failure of Christianity.' I have now turned to the study of Bernard Berenson.

"As a biographer I have made little direct use of theory, though I must have absorbed a variety of principles from my reading of Plutarch, Boswell, Carlyle, Strachey, Maurois, Ludwig, and the scores of biographies which are the staple of graduate study in English and American literature. The study and practice of law gave me a realistic view of human motives and trained me in the patient pursuit of evidence. I have found Freudian psychology of real though limited value, for the evidence trails off too often into dubious speculation. From the beginning I worked on the assumption that the importance of an intellectual writer as a subject is primarily in his writing and the interest of his life is in the way his experience is transformed into thought and art. The drama of such a life is largely internal. I find myself drawn to introspective and self-aware consciousness in the figures of biography. Such minds best illuminate the ironies of life.

"The first volume, *The Young Henry Adams*, appeared in 1948. The second, *Henry Adams: The Middle Years*, came out in 1958 and was awarded the Bancroft prize and the Parkman prize. The concluding volume, *Henry Adams: The Major Phase*, was published in 1964 and received the Pulitzer prize."

The special virtue of the Adams biography was identified by F. O. Matthiessen in his review of the first volume. Professor Samuels, Matthiessen wrote, "has fully realized that the character presented in *The Education of Henry Adams* is one of its author's most subtle creations. He has consequently turned his back upon the old man's ironic evocation of his young self, and has made a fresh start. Out of the abundant record of Adams' early essays and the unceasing flow of his correspondence Samuels has revealed a quite different likeness." When the third and last volume was finished, K. S. Lynn wrote: "We can at last see Henry Adams as he was."

A few critics have objected mildly to the book's leisurely pace, but the principal reaction has been one of gratitude for its solidity and rich detail. It was generally recognized as a brilliant and definitive study and was described in the *Times Literary*

Supplement as "one of the most important American biographies." Leo Marx, pointing out that "definitive" can be a euphemism for a flat and lifeless academic endurance test, said that "the astonishing result" of Samuels' twenty-two years of research was "an engrossing book, with the man in it: cold, arrogant, tough, irascible, egocentric, sentimental, brilliant Henry Adams."

Professor Samuels is the son of Albert and Mary (Kaplan) Samuels. He was Franklyn Bliss Snyder Professor of English at Northwestern from 1942 until 1971, when he retired, and is a member of the advisory committee for the publication of the Adams papers. The Samuels have had three children, and enjoy camping and skiing.

PRINCIPAL WORKS: The Young Henry Adams, 1948; Henry Adams: The Middle Years, 1958; Henry Adams: The Major Phase, 1964.

ABOUT: Contemporary Authors 11–12, 1965; Who's Who in America, 1972–1973.

FRANK SARGESON

SARGESON, FRANK (March 23, 1903–), New Zealand novelist, short story writer, and dramatist, writes: "I was born in the Waikato dairy-farming district of the North Island, New Zealand. My father was a storekeeper who afterwards became a town clerk, and I was second in the family to my brother: there were two sisters younger than myself. My grandparents were immigrants from Ireland (Belfast), and England (London), of the 1870s.

"For five years after I left secondary school at the age of seventeen, while I worked in lawyers' offices, it seemed that nearly all the pleasure I had anticipated from adulthood must remain in cold storage until I had completed my law studies. But I was no sooner admitted as a Solicitor of the Supreme Court than I felt such a sense of suffocation, there seemed nothing else to do except buy a third class ticket for England after I had sold for about three hundred pounds a small section of land given to me by my parents as a twenty-first birthday present (hoping that I would be 'sensible' enough to marry and settle down like my brother). I walked solitarily first in Devon and Cornwall; then from Paris to Alsace, and through Switzerland to Milan. It was during this short time in Europe that I for the first time in my life felt fully confident that many of the rules taken for granted in my home town were not necessarily to be taken for granted by me. I lived in Bloomsbury, read in the British Museum Library, and bought the cheapest tickets for theatre and concerts. I tried to write a novel and was much too busy to look for a job. When my funds were exhausted I unwillingly returned to New Zealand, where I immediately began again to think of myself as stifled and unhappy. I tried working in a Government Department, but fortunately involved myself in a breakdown from which I recovered during eighteen months spent with my uncle on his sheep farm. I was greatly invigorated by my admiration for my uncle's labours in creating his farm out of heavy bush country. I made a further attempt to write, but with no idea at all that satisfying results would come only after a strenuous five-years' apprenticeship.

"My stories began to be published in the mid-thirties—first in New Zealand's *Tomorrow*; but they were soon reprinted in England by John Lehmann in his *New Writing*; and in America by James Laughlin in *New Directions*. My first short novel, *That Summer*, was not completed until I was in my thirty-ninth year, and first appeared in *Penguin New Writing*.

"I have never been a prolific writer; nor a fluent one despite what may seem evidence to the contrary in much of my published work. The difficulties of my financial insecurity have at times been exceptionally severe; but it has been my great good fortune to have always a roof over my head, and a piece of land which I cultivate for vegetables and fruit. Also, I am perennially humbled to think of the generous help and encouragement I have received. Mostly I have written of outsiders and social rejects, I expect because I see in these people a reflection of my own situation as a literary artist—I mean in a community where the artist is accepted at somewhere round about the value he may put on himself only if he is of the executant kind. What mainly attracts me about writing is its difficulty. Everything I write must be quite different from anything I have written previously: hence I like to write in the first person, each time wearing a different mask. I try for comedy and tragedy: I like writing stories best because of the strict discipline, but the difficulties of sustaining a novel also attract me: occasionally I like writing a play—because that form demands there should be absolutely nothing at all in the way of 'padding.'"

Frank Sargeson, although legendarily modest, is New Zealand's one undisputed living literary master. As Dan Davin has written, "The most distinguished of New Zealand writers, he has probably had the greatest influence on others." E. M. Forster has said of him: "He writes well, he knows heaps about New Zealand, including its Maoris . . . he believes in the unsmart, the unregulated and the affectionate, and can believe in them without advertising them"; he has the power, continued Forster, to whose liberal-humanist tradition Sargeson belongs, "to combine delicacy with frankness."

Sargeson began, as many New Zealand writers have done, as a satirist—stung to expression by the apparently peculiarly repellent complacency of the native bourgeois. But there was already, in his first pamphlet of stories, *Conversation With My Uncle* (1936), more than left-wing orthodoxy and satire of suburban life. Sargeson has gone on to make the emancipation—and, in a subtler sense (he is a subtle writer), the spiritual redemption—of young men his chief theme. In the early stories issues were simplified, and the values of capitalism were contrasted, to their detriment, with those of the working classes. But Sargeson is a literary artist, not a docile leftist: while he has remained a radical, his interest in and feeling for people have become increasingly a stronger element in his fiction than his involvement with political theory in any form.

As he explains above, Sargeson often writes in the first person, "each time wearing a different mask." The two undisputed strengths of his fiction are his magnificent ear for local dialogue—unequaled in New Zealand, and unsurpassed by any living writer—and his virtuosity. He has dealt with homosexual themes more successfully than E. M. Forster, and it is only in depth that his men are more convincing than his women. In the last analysis, however, and granting that he is a major writer, Sargeson's women are usually observed (often brilliantly) rather than fully understood.

Sargeson's second collection of stories and sketches, *A Man and His Wife* (1940), moved from the explicitly political to the social, and clearly revealed, particularly in the long title story, a potentially major writer. But it was in the novella, *That Summer* (1946), that Sargeson's genius first fully emerged. Some critics still think of it as his most satisfying, if not profoundest, work. Here the laconic crypticism of most of the early stories is replaced by a more leisurely narration. The skill with which Sargeson makes the characters emerge so vividly—one critic has spoken of "a Defoe-like actuality"—through the eyes of his narrator has been justly applauded. E. H. McCormick has described the homosexual subplot as "clumsily devised," the dialogue as occasionally "opaque with esoteric slang," but nevertheless refers to the book as one in which "skill is . . . triumphantly united with understanding."

I Saw in My Dream (1949) takes up and develops an early theme: the revolt of Henry-Dave against the values of his bourgeois, churchgoing parents is traced from childhood through youth to eventual victory. This work, which is set in the early years of the century, is rich in social history and has been universally praised in this respect. Opinions about the character of the hero differ, some finding him "too negative a figure to excite interest," others applauding a feat of realism; possibly *dislike* of the hero—a tribute, in fact, to Sargeson's skill—has something to do with the former judgment. *I For One* (1954), a novella in the form of letters, is more overtly satirical, a study-in-depth of suburban reality—but it demonstrates how much Sargeson's art had developed over two decades when compared with his first pamphlet, whose raw material is similar.

Sargeson's first full-length novel, *Memoirs of a Peon*, did not appear until 1965. Characteristically, this was a new departure. Once again, the narration is in the first person; but now the narrator (John Newhouse, whose name is an anglicization of Casanova) is intelligent and articulate, and his account of his rakish progress against the background of New Zealand in the Depression achieves a genuinely picaresque quality for the first time in antipodean literature.

The Hangover (1967) again breaks entirely new ground; "if he has written as well, he has never written better," wrote one English critic. This novel treats the pressures that build up during male adolescence in a strikingly original manner, and is particularly memorable for its detached and yet sympathetic probing of the motives behind "juvenile delinquency." *Joy of the Worm* (1969), a comedy with tragic undertones, studies the way in which another young man, critical of his domineering clergyman father, nevertheless becomes a carbon copy of the old egotist. Here, writes H. Winston Rhodes, "it is by a controlled and complex use of illusion and reality, by irony, patterned loquacity and suggestion, and above all by language that he gains his effects and achieves significance." Since he has come to the form of the longer novel, Sargeson seems to go from strength to strength.

Wrestling With the Angel (1964) contained two plays, *A Time for Sowing*, a study of the missionary who wrote the first primer of the Maori language, and *The Cradle and the Egg*. *Up Onto the Roof and Down Again*, which was serialized in *Landfall*, is experimental autobiography of a high quality.

PRINCIPAL WORKS: *Fiction*—Conversation With My Uncle, 1936; A Man and His Wife, 1940; When the Wind Blows, 1945; That Summer, and Other Stories, 1946; I Saw in My Dream, 1949; I for One, 1954; Collected Stories, 1935–1963, 1965; Memoirs of a Peon, 1965; The Hangover, 1967; Joy of the Worm, 1969; Man of England Now (*with* A Game of Hide and Seek and I for One), 1972. *Plays*—Wrestling With the Angel, 1964. *Autobiography*—Up Onto the Roof and Down Again *in* Landfall December 1950–December 1951; Once Is Enough: A Memoir, 1973.

ABOUT: Cassell's Encyclopedia of Literature, 1954; McCormick, E. H. New Zealand Literature, 1959; Penguin Companion to Literature 1, 1971. Rhodes, H. W. Frank Sargeson, 1969; Shaw, H. (ed.) The Puritan and the Waif: A Symposium of Critical Essays on the Work of Frank Sargeson, 1955; Vinson, J. (ed.) Contemporary Novelists, 1972. *Periodicals*—Landfall December 1950–December 1951 (autobiography), March 1955; Scotsman September 16, 1967; Times Literary Supplement June 17, 1965; September 16, 1965.

***SARRAUTE, NATHALIE** (July 18, 1902–), French novelist and critic, writes (in French): "I was born in Russia, at Ivanovo, to the northeast of Moscow in the Vladimir district.

"When I was two years old, my parents were divorced and my mother took me to Geneva where she, like my father, had studied, then to Paris.

"My first language was French and I went when very young to the nursery school on the rue des Feuillantines.

"However, I spent some of my time with my father in Russia. This life divided between France and Russia lasted until I was six, when my mother, remarried to a Russian historian, took me to live with her in St. Petersburg and my father left Russia for political reasons and settled in Paris. When I was eight, my mother sent me to my father in Paris where I remained thereafter.

"I went to the local school and to the Lycée Fénelon. Then to the Sorbonne where I got an English degree and to the law school where I received a law degree. Meanwhile I had spent an academic year at Oxford reading history and a winter in Berlin where I took courses in history and sociology at the university.

"Immediately after receiving my law degree in 1925, I was married and was called to the Paris bar, as was my husband, who had been studying law at the same time as I. I remained at the bar until the war, but after 1932, when I began to write, I was interested principally in literature, turning more and more from the law which attracted me less and less.

* sa rôt′

NATHALIE SARRAUTE

"Since my childhood I had always wanted to write and I took great pleasure in my French studies. But I didn't dare to make a start. I wrote my first piece, a fragment of prose, in 1932. I tried, in this first essay, to convey in condensed form, by sentence rhythms, a very rapid interior movement which slips beyond the limits of consciousness, something which has no name but which nevertheless occurs all the time in all of us.

"All the prose pieces which I wrote in this manner between 1932 and 1937, and which became parts of my first book, described similar interior movements. I called them 'Tropisms' by analogy with the movements made by certain organisms in response to external stimulation. I wished to indicate thus their irresistible and instinctive nature. I endeavored to isolate these movements. They constituted little dramas sufficient in themselves, their anonymous characters serving as props only.

"This first book was the point of departure, the nucleus, of all my novels. I finished it in 1937, but it was rejected by all the publishers to whom I sent it, except Robert Denoël, who published it in February 1939. In 1946 I finished my first novel, *Portrait d'un inconnu*. It had no more luck than *Tropismes*, in spite of a preface by Sartre, and, rejected everywhere, did not appear until Robert Marin published it in 1948. *Martereau*, published in 1953 by Gallimard, had a better critical reception. But it was the articles I wrote between 1947 and 1956 for the *Temps Modernes* and the *Nouvelle Revue Française*, which, published in book form in 1956 under the title *L'Ère du soupçon*, aroused the interest of the critics.

"In these articles, especially in the title article,

I tried to show that, contrary to what critics and the public seemed to believe, the novel, like all art forms, was and must be in a constant state of evolution. It did not follow that there would be progress, but there was a constant transformation of the substance and form of the novel, old worn-out conventions giving way to other conventions which become necessary. In particular, the conception of character in the novel, of its role, of its place and attributes, has greatly changed since the period of its apogee, in the Balzacian novel. That was also the time of romanticism, of plot, of dialogue. This book of criticism formed one of the bases of the movement which has been called the 'New Novel.'

"As for me, I have always continued to follow my original path, a very different one from that followed, each in his own way, by the authors who are considered to be part of the same group.

"I have made lecture tours in most of the countries of Europe and in the United States.

"I have three daughters each of whom follows a profession (journalist, film editor, commercial artist)."

Nathalie Sarraute is the daughter of Élie Tcherniak, a chemist, and of the former Pauline Chatovnowski, a writer of popular novels. Her husband, Raymond Sarraute, is a prominent Parisian barrister. She is a small, thin woman, her clothes, speech, and gestures exact, quiet, monochrome. She excludes melodrama from her behavior as from her books. The effort is towards intelligence, towards precision.

Tropismes, the title of her first book, is as she indicates above a biological term for those involuntary movements made by organisms in response to external stimuli, like the heliotropism which turns plants towards the sun. It is the much more complex inner dramas of human beings that is the subject of *Tropismes*, their deep subconscious responses to each other, felt but not acknowledged or recorded, and often prompted by unreasoning fear of social isolation.

The book is not a novel but a collection of twenty-four separate sketches. In one of them, for example, an apparently unforceful woman has maneuvered her family, through an instinctive manipulation of their feelings of guilt and insecurity, into behavior patterns which she considers socially desirable; yet "at times, in spite of all these precautions, all their effort, when they saw her sitting silent in the lamp-light, looking like some frail, gentle under-seas plant, entirely lined with mobile suckers, they felt themselves slip and fall with all their weight, crushing everything beneath them: then there issued from them stupid jokes, sneers, frightful stories of cannibals, all this issued from them and burst out without their being able to check it."

These small parables have been called prose poems, and indeed they employ sound, rhythm, and imagery to convey with the economy of poetry "the impression, the feeling of these tropisms produced in the character without his knowing clearly what they really were."

During the German occupation Mme. Sarraute lived outside Paris under an assumed name, masquerading as the governess of her own children. It was at this time that she wrote *Portrait d'un inconnu* (translated as *Portrait of a Man Unknown*), published in 1948 but at that time virtually ignored, as *Tropismes* had been. It is a study of an old miser and his spinster daughter, and indirectly of the narrator, a man who is obsessed by and enters deeply and imaginatively into the inner drama, the tropisms, which underlie such apparently unremarkable lives. As Ruth Z. Temple points out in her study of Nathalie Sarraute, the unidentified narrator is to some extent the spokesman for the author herself, just as the book is to some extent an account of its own creation.

In his introduction to this work in which "nothing ever happens," and which ignores all the usual machinery of plot and character development, Sartre called it an "anti-novel," a term which was also applied to the work of other writers who, emerging a few years later, used similar methods for somewhat different reasons. These writers, and Nathalie Sarraute herself, are nowadays most often called the "New Novelists."

Portrait d'un inconnu introduced the novel whose substance is the interior monologue of a hypersensitive narrator, and this is developed in *Martereau* (1953), translated like all of Mme. Sarraute's work by Maria Jolas, and published in English under the same title. The author has acknowledged her literary debts, the largest of which appear to be to Proust and Dostoevsky (the latter because of his interest in those subconscious attractions and repulsions which "never appear in broad daylight and nevertheless exist in everyone"). *Martereau* is her most Proustian novel and it has a Proustian narrator. He is a tubercular young man of the middle class, a devoted collector of tropisms; his subjects are his family and, especially, Martereau, an associate of the narrator's uncle who may or may not be the simple and practical man he appears to be.

There is a larger cast of characters in *Le Planétarium* (1959, translated as *The Planetarium*), which centers on the efforts of an ambitious young intellectual to dispossess his aunt of the apartment he covets. As Ruth Z. Temple has shown, the book has many of the attributes of the conventional novel—"comedy and melodrama, variety in scene and character, satire of the middle-class family and of literary cliques." For this reason, and because it appeared at a time when the New Novel was at the center of fashionable debate, it established Mme. Sarraute at last as a novelist to be read as well as admired.

Humor and satire predominate in *Les Fruits d'or* (1963, translated as *The Golden Fruits*); it follows, through the conversations and "subconversations" of literary society, the rise and fall of the reputation of an imaginary book of the same title. "The theme," says Miss Temple, "is, as always in Nathalie Sarraute, the fear and compensating aggression of human beings, their bitter need to belong to a group, their terror of rejection, their abject determination to conform." The book received the 1964 International Literary Prize. *Entre la vie et la mort* (1968, translated as *Between Life and Death*), forms a companion work to its two predecessors, viewing literary life in Paris this time from the point of view of a writer. He is studied in relation to his family, his critics, his public, and above all his language; it is an intimate exploration of the splendors and miseries of literary creation which has been called "a dramatic prose poem about words." In *Vous les entendez?* (1972, translated as *Do You Hear Them?*), it is the art connoisseur who is under attack, in the shape of a collector whose security is undermined by the iconoclasm of his children towards his possessions.

Nathalie Sarraute's method is in many respects ideally suited to radio drama, a field in which she has achieved notable success, especially in West Germany. Some of her radio plays have also been staged, including *Le Silence* (translated as *The Silence*, which observes the effect on an ordinary social group of the mysterious silence of one member), and *Le Mensonge* (translated as *The Lie*). Her literary theories are explained in the essays collected in *L'Ère du soupçon* (1956, translated as *The Age of Suspicion*).

Her domain, says Germaine Brée, is "the hidden, emotional life of the depths in constant flux, with its subtle interchanges, its infinitesimal variations in pressure, which reveal, way beneath the rational social patterns of behavior, the watchful, hunted human hunter, peering like some small ferocious shell-fish fearfully out of his shell. What is most curious perhaps . . . is that she manages so intensely to suggest not the modes of a solitary individual life, but patterns emerging from a common human substance, that of the 'species,' organically a whole, our ultimate reality."

PRINCIPAL WORKS IN ENGLISH TRANSLATION: Portrait of a Man Unknown, 1958; Martereau, 1959; The Planetarium, 1960; The Age of Suspicion: Essays on the Novel, 1963; The Golden Fruits, 1964; Tropisms and The Age of Suspicion, 1964; Between Life and Death, 1969; Silence, and The Lie (plays), 1970; Do You Hear Them?, 1973.
ABOUT: Boisdeffre, P. de. Dictionnaire de littérature contemporaine, 1962; Contemporary Authors 9–10, 1964; Current Biography, 1966; Greshoff, C. J. Seven Studies in the French Novel, 1964; Kostelanetz, R. (ed.) On Contemporary Literature, 1964; Kranaki, M. and Belaval, Y. Nathalie Sarraute, 1965; Le Sage, L. The French New Novel, 1962; Mauriac, C. The New Literature, 1959; Micha, R. Nathalie Sarraute, 1965; Nadeau, M. The French Novel Since the War, 1967; Peyre, H. French Novelists of Today, 1967; Pingaud, B. Écrivains d'aujourd'hui, 1960; Sartre, J.-P. *Preface to* Portrait of a Man Unknown, 1958 (*reprinted in* Situations, 1965); Sontag, S. Against Interpretation, 1965; Temple, R. Z. Nathalie Sarraute, 1968; Who's Who, 1973; Who's Who in America, 1972–1973; Who's Who in France, 1971–1972. *Periodicals*—American Scholar Summer 1963; Encounter June 1964; Guardian March 8, 1962; Listener March 9, 1961; Mercure de France August 1962; Modern Language Notes May 1963; Nation April 25, 1959; March 2, 1964; New York Review of Books March 5, 1964; New York Times November 1, 1959; July 24, 1970; New York Times Book Review February 9, 1964; April 24, 1966; Partisan Review Spring 1966; Saturday Review June 11, 1960; May 6, 1967; Times Literary Supplement January 1, 1960; Yale French Studies 16, 1955–56; 24, Summer 1959; 27, Spring 1961.

***SCHARY, DORE** (August 31, 1905–), American memoirist, screenwriter, and dramatist, writes: "I was born in Newark, New Jersey. My parents had migrated from different parts of Russia in the early 1890s. My father's name was Herman Hugo Schary. My mother's maiden name was Belle Drachler. They and both my sisters, Lillian and Frances, and my brother, Samuel, have all died.

"My wife's maiden name is Miriam Svet, with which she signs her paintings. My older daughter, Jill Zimmer, is twenty-nine, and has two children; Jeremy, seven, and Johanna, five. My younger daughter, Joy Stashower, twenty-seven, has three children; Keren, six, Saul, four, and David, three months young. Our son Jeb, twenty-five, has one daughter, Gabrielle, a year and a half old, and another child is on the way.

"To conclude my vital statistics: I am six feet one inch tall, weigh one hundred and eighty-two pounds, have blue eyes, hair that is half grey and dark brown and I have the normal complement of ailments due a man of my age; I am American by birth and a Democrat by inclination, a Jew by birth and conviction and my politics seem to grow more radical as time goes by.

"My formal education was brief and unsatisfactory. However, I always liked to read (particularly history and biography) and this interest has made me a student, but hardly a scholar.

"I started trying to frame short stories when I was thirteen and saved everything I wrote. Fortunately, all these early efforts were destroyed in a fire in a hotel, which my family owned in 1928.

"Committed by then to a career in writing and show business, I turned out a number of plays

* shâ' rē

DORE SCHARY

which were optioned. Unfortunately, none of those ever burned, but again fortunately, they were not produced.

"I followed the normal channels a young man pursues in shaping a career. I acted, directed plays in camps and community centers, gave lectures on makeup (illustrating as I talked and aging in front of the audience's eyes), worked in the Borscht Circuit and finally in 1932, just before Christmas, landed in Hollywood as a 'junior writer' for Columbia Pictures.

"During the next eight years, I wrote some forty screenplays ranging in quality from abysmal to zestful.

"Then I became an executive, not by design, but by pure accident. From 1940 to 1957, I worked as a producer or as an executive for, successively, MGM, David O. Selznick, RKO (as head of production) then back to MGM in 1948 as head of production and then studio head until a company explosion in 1957. During the Hollywood years, some three hundred and fifty films went through my fingers in one way or another and *their* quality ranged from banal to brilliant.

"Then I returned to New York to work in the theatre. My first play, *Sunrise at Campobello*, spurred me to stay on. I have since then worked on eight other shows either as writer or director or producer—sometimes in two capacities and in three instances, as all three.

"I've written two books: *Case History of a Movie* and *For Special Occasions*.

"I have no real hobbies, but like to play games (any kind) and my competitive spirit in Scrabble, Bridge, Bali and Categories is quite irritating. Beyond the demands of my work and play, I find time to lecture and work for those rather numerous political, communal and charitable organizations with which I am identified.

"While I may look like sixty, I truly don't feel like it, thank God."

Schary's boyhood and adolescence in Newark, where his colorful and close-knit family operated a kosher-catering establishment, are evoked in his "delightful, sentimental, sometimes poignant" autobiography *For Special Occasions*, which also touches briefly on his introduction to show business in the "borscht belt." *Case History of a Movie*, a detailed account of the production of Schary's film *The Next Voice You Hear*, provides at the same time a sharp impression of his own life and times in Hollywood and a fascinating and "singularly candid" description of how the movie empire went about its business. His daughter Jill has given her own impression of the family's Hollywood years in her amusing and perceptive memoir *With a Cast of Thousands*.

Schary never shared Hollywood's exclusive dedication to the box office; he had, as one wit said, "sold his soul for a pot of message." In the end he left Metro-Goldwyn-Mayer, making his Broadway debut as a dramatist in January 1958 with *Sunrise at Campobello*, his famous and immensely successful play about Franklin Delano Roosevelt's agony and triumph from 1921 to 1924. Arthur Schlesinger, Jr. expressed the majority opinion when he called the play "modest and self-effacing, austerely simple in design, convincing in dialogue and characterization and admirably effective." It was later filmed. Not all who saw the play could share in the general enthusiasm for it, however. Gerald Weales was one of those who thought that it lacked dramatic force, and was "much less a moving play than a frame of reference to which each member of the audience might bring his own feelings about FDR."

Similar doubts were expressed more generally about *The Highest Tree*, Schary's second play—an attack on nuclear bomb experiments marred by didacticism and technical weaknesses. Schary's dramatization of *The Devil's Advocate*, a novel by Morris L. West, was produced on Broadway in 1961 with "middling success," but *Brightower* (1970), an original play about a Hemingway-like writer who commits suicide, closed after one performance. *Storm in the West*, published in 1964, is something of a literary curiosity—a screenplay by Schary and Sinclair Lewis written for but rejected by MGM in 1943. It is an allegorical account of World War II, told in the form of a western.

Schary's activities in behalf of such organizations as B'nai B'rith and the United World Federalists have earned him over a hundred awards. In 1970 he became New York City's first Commissioner of Cultural Affairs.

PRINCIPAL WORKS: Case History of a Movie, 1950; Sunrise at Campobello (play), 1958; The Highest Tree (play), 1960; For Special Occasions (autobiography), 1962; (with Sinclair Lewis) Storm in the West (film scenario), 1964; The Devil's Advocate (play), 1965.

ABOUT: Current Biography, 1948; Schary, D. For Special Occasions, 1962; Weales, G. American Drama Since World War II, 1962; Who's Who in America, 1972–1973; Zimmer, J. With a Cast of Thousands, 1963. *Periodicals*—Life March 9, 1959; New Republic February 10, 1958; New York Herald Tribune November 5, 1959; New York Herald Tribune Book Review March 18, 1951; October 21, 1962; New York Times January 31, 1958; February 25, 1970; New York Times Book Review October 21, 1962.

***SCHEHADÉ, GEORGES** (November 2, 1910–), Lebanese dramatist and poet who writes in French, was born in Alexandria, Egypt. He comes of an old Lebanese family of French culture, and one of his sisters has published poems in French. Schehadé received most of his secondary education in Paris, where he also gained his *licence* in law. He divides his time between Paris and Lebanon, where he is secretary general of the École Supérieure des Lettres in Beirut.

Under the influence of Éluard, St.-John Perse, and, especially, André Breton, whose "legitimate heir" he has been called, Schehadé at first wrote poetry in a neosurrealist manner, though his later work in this form has been found increasingly lyrical. The French-Lebanese critic Robert Abirached finds in Schehadé's verse "no intoxication, no excess: in each poem, an image boxed up, a brief metamorphosis, an immemorial word found again through innocence."

Schehadé is better known for his plays than his verse, and in these also he seeks a metamorphosis, a poetic transfiguration of reality. Like most poets who write for the theatre, he relies a great deal on language and metaphor, but he is a true dramatist, who creates strange, comical, and memorable characters and effective conflict—conflict, most often, between innocence and experience, integrity and compromise. His episodic, loosely structured plays are quests or journeys in which his heroes and his audiences are led from realistic, everyday beginnings into a world increasingly metaphorical, obscure, magical.

The first of his plays to be performed was *Monsieur Bob'le*, staged by Georges Vitaly in 1951. Bob'le is his village's gentle, unofficial sage and resident saint—a personification of the poetic impulse—loved and trusted although he is constantly denying his virtues and claiming the crassest motives for his actions. He leaves the village, ostensibly in pursuit of personal gain. The villagers, lost

* shə a dā′

GEORGES SCHEHADÉ

without the mysterious sense of security and comfort he imparts, beg him to return. He starts back, but dies on the way home. This fable was received with great hostility by the Paris theatre critics, but was defended with equal vehemence by a number of poets, among them André Breton and René Char. The "bataille de Monsieur Bob'le" is long since over but, Wallace Fowlie has said, Bob'le himself is not forgotten: "What has happened is one of the mysteries of the theatre. Bob'le has become a real personage, a character of the theatre."

Jean-Louis Barrault's production of *La Soirée des proverbes* (The Soirée of the Proverbs) followed in 1954. It tells the story of a young officer who, in pursuit of knowledge, attends the mysterious soirée of the title, finds only a group of old men mourning their lost youth and idealism, and chooses death in preference to age and the end of innocence. Once again, opinions were divided, some critics finding it foolishly opaque, others praising its mysterious poetry.

The most violent storm of all was aroused by Schehadé's third play, *L'Histoire de Vasco* (1956), about a barber of great simplicity and timidity who achieves a hero's death in a ridiculous war. Many theatre critics dismissed it as a bore, and this time René Char also attacked it, finding its poetry "mediocre." But Jules Supervielle and St.-John Perse praised it, and Jean Dutourd found grounds for comparing Schehadé with Homer and Tolstoy. The play became a political issue as well as an aesthetic one, since its antimilitarism infuriated supporters of France's war in Algeria, and there were demands for censorship. The English critic Alan Brien, who saw *Vasco* at the Edinburgh Festival in 1960, found it "full of good jokes, both verbal and visual," but basically "a serious and uncompromising drama which . . . is genuinely moving." It provided the basis for an opera, *The Story of Vasco*, by the British composer Gordon Crosse.

Schehadé's later plays, *Les Violettes* (The Violets, 1960), *Le Voyage* (The Journey, 1961), and *L'Émigré de Brisbane* (1968), have explored similar themes but caused less controversy. "The world of Schehadé," writes L. C. Pronko, "a world of wonder, of innocence, of poetry and fairy tale, contrasts the pure and young in spirit with the old and corrupt who have lost touch with the poetic truth of childhood. . . . Schehadé's calm heroes are almost [always] overtaken by death. Or rather, their search for purity is a search for death, but the hero is unaware of this until death is imminent. . . . The plays of Schehadé cannot be seized in their entirety by the rational faculties. Their chief appeal is to that part of the personality to which myths speak their universal language." Serious as they are in their intentions, Schehadé's plays are extremely funny, in their language and in their characterization—Jean-Louis Barrault, indeed, finds them at one level reminiscent of the work of Chaplin, or even at times of the Marx Brothers, and hopes to see the writer "become a sort of Aristophanes for our time."

Jacques Guicharnaud, one of a number of critics who have emphasized Schehadé's Eastern origins, finds his poetry "very close to that of Persian tales, to their enigmas and their charms. And he is about the only poet of the post-war period whose works are almost entirely free of bitterness or anger."

PRINCIPAL WORKS IN ENGLISH TRANSLATION: Vasco *in* Corrigan, R. W. The New Theatre of Europe 2, 1964 *and in* Baldick, R. (ed. and tr.) Theatre of War, 1967. ABOUT: Boisdeffre, P. de. Dictionnaire de littérature contemporaine, 1962; Fowlie, W. Dionysus in Paris, 1960; Guicharnaud, J. Modern French Theatre, 1961; Pingaud, B. Écrivains d'aujourd'hui, 1960; Pronko, L. C. Avant-garde, 1962. *Periodicals*—Gambit No. 1, 1963; Mercure de France May 1951; Yale French Studies 29, 1962.

***SCHEVILL, JAMES (ERWIN)** (June 10, 1920–), American poet, dramatist, and biographer, writes: "I was born at Berkeley, California, when it was still a small town remembering the frontier. My father, Rudolph Schevill, was a Professor of Spanish at the University of California and the biographer and editor of the complete works of Cervantes. My mother, Margaret Erwin, was a painter, poet, and the author of two books on the Navajo Indians. Despite my parents, or perhaps because of them, my early life was anti-literary, devoted to the usual restless activities of a boy, sports and fantasies of adventures in the caves, hills, quarries, and woods that extended around our house. I became aware of space and nature, two rapidly disappearing factors in western cities. In my teens I was seized by the ambition to become an opera singer, the beginning of my passion for the stage. I studied singing, a primary influence on my work, and hung around backstage whenever weary, moth-eaten, operatic troupes appeared to plod through their performances. Above all I remember the smell of whiskey and sweat in the traveling trunks.

"My parents, and my uncle, the historian Ferdinand Schevill, were powerful influences on the wide variety of my interests. They were middle-aged, traveled, experienced people when I was born. They came from European immigrant backgrounds and belonged to a time when scholarship was still a romantic occupation, closely connected with creativity and life. Their friends came from many fields. The technological age of specialization had not yet begun.

"The turning point in my life came in 1938 when my parents were divorced and I went to Switzerland to study music. I traveled in Austria and Germany and saw with traumatic horror the Jewish persecution by the Nazis. These experiences were such a shock that I turned from music to writing poetry. Poetry, with its powers of compressing imagery and rhythm, seemed to me suddenly a way to struggle with the overwhelming world. However, as I turned to literature for the first time, I thought that much poetry was losing the ability to write about people and events and was becoming too abstract. Why should prose take over all the interesting subject matter? Slowly and desperately I struggled with the relationship between subject matter and form, trying to unite my desire for significant, unconventional subject matter with forms that would use the new rhythms and images of colloquial speech.

"On the eve of World War II, after returning to the United States in 1939, I went to Harvard. Although I was writing extensively (I remember one drunken afternoon of competition with a friend when I wrote fourteen poems), I majored in music. The major part of my education, however, came from extra-curricular activities, particularly the Harvard Glee Club. My interest in the theatre also increased at Harvard when I began to write plays and participate in various productions.

"After graduating in 1942, I was drafted immediately into the Army, where I spent four years working mainly in German and Italian prisoner of war camps in the United States and finally in a secret 're-education program' for German prisoners of war. All of my experiences with the Germans culminated in my long dramatic poem, *The Stalingrad Elegies*, published by Alan Swallow in 1964.

* shə vil′

"I was married in 1942 to Helen Shaner from Walpole, Massachusetts. We have two daughters, Deborah and Susanna. We separated in 1964.

"After my discharge from the Army in 1946, I began to write full-time, pouring out plays, poems, stories, and novels in a frantic attempt to learn the craft. My true direction in poetry and playwriting began to appear in 1951 with the first production of a one-act play, *Everyman's History of Love*, that I wrote for Roger Altenberg and the Drama Workshop of the California College of Arts and Crafts in Oakland, an art school where I taught English and did administrative work during the 1950s. In 1959 I joined the faculty of San Francisco State College where I teach in the English Department and direct the Poetry Center.

"As my poetry has developed, I try more and more to project a sense of narrative and dramatic power, to infuse the poem with the dramatic problems of people rather than restrict the poem mainly to subjective, aesthetic experience. I have tried to write many poems based on key events in the lives of famous and infamous people. Particularly I want to revive some of the relationship between poetry and biography, to create characters with weight and depth. For several of these poems I invented forms that I called 'poem-biographies.' The lyrical side of my work has come out increasingly in songs for my plays, love poems, and the kind of quickening experience that is best expressed in a short, colloquial, song-like measure.

"As for playwriting, I continue to work for a theatre transcending the pedestrian naturalism that has dominated the American stage. Consequently, I have written opera librettos for Leon Kirchner and Paul McIntyre, and musical plays such as *The Black President* which I wrote for Joan Littlewood after working in her London Theatre Workshop on a Ford Foundation grant in 1961. I want larger than life characters who will give the stage a scale of grandeur again. I want a theatre that will be truly theatrical, invoking an exciting use of all the arts, uniting the inner world of modern psychological discovery with the external world of social reality and racial conflict."

James Schevill's first book of poems, *Tensions*, was called serious and thoughtful, ignoring the romantic aspects of his San Francisco surroundings, contemptuous of "the lyric ideal." He has continued to report in his unified, tranquil verse on "the dramatic problems of people," using for the most part, as he says, the rhythms and diction of colloquial speech, and saving his songs for his plays. M. L. Rosenthal speaks of his "keenly active intelligence that broods over an unusually wide range of observations—from reading, travel, personal experience, and the contemplation of art

JAMES SCHEVILL

and philosophy," but adds that he can "move freely into realms of meditation, reverie, and pure poetic discovery." Though his verse sometimes deteriorates into journalistic or editorial comment on current events, at his best, Rosenthal says, he "combines the scholar's instinct for meaningful detail with the poet's subjective insight."

Four of Schevill's verse plays were published by Alan Swallow in 1965 as *The Black President, and Other Plays*. In the title piece, an American Negro sails the replica of a slave ship up the Thames to the House of Commons, and carries off prisoners, just as his ancestors had been carried off. The play, which makes use of songs, film clips, and dancers, was labeled contrived and chaotic, but there was rather more approval for the plot, characterization, and language of other pieces in the collection: *The Bloody Tenet*, about the trial in 1635 of Roger Williams for rebellion against the authority of the Massachusetts Bay Colony; and two satires, *The Space Fan* and *The Master*.

Schevill's biography of Sherwood Anderson was thought lucid and illuminating, a generally successful attempt to extract the man from the legend. *The Stalingrad Elegies* is a mixture of prose and poetry based on the undelivered letters and other documents left by German soldiers trapped at Stalingrad in 1943. There was some feeling that Schevill's verse lacked the intensity to match its appalling occasion, but most reviewers agreed the book achieved a total impact greater than the sum of its parts. Robert Pack was grateful for it, believing that "the spread of chaos, the violence we have almost grown accustomed to, requires the poet's careful reporting as well as his powers of expression."

The author left San Francisco State College in 1969 and went east to Brown University, Rhode Island, as professor of English. Schevill was married in 1966 to Margot Blum.

PRINCIPAL WORKS: *Poems*—Tensions, 1947; The American Fantasies, 1951; The Right to Greet, 1956; Selected Poems, 1945–1959, 1959; Private Dooms and Public Destinations: Poems 1945–1962, 1962; The Stalingrad Elegies, 1964; Violence and Glory: Poems 1962–1968, 1969; The Buddhist Car, 1971. *Plays*—High Sinners, Low Angels, 1954; The Bloody Tenet, 1957; Voices of Mass & Capital A, 1963; The Black President, and Other Plays, 1965; Lovecraft's Follies, 1971. *Nonfiction*—Sherwood Anderson: His Life and Work, 1951; The Roaring Market and the Silent Tomb, 1956; Breakout: In Search of New Theatrical Environments, 1973.
ABOUT: Contemporary Authors 7–8, 1963; Murphy, R. (ed.) Contemporary Poets of the English Language, 1970; Rosenthal, M. L. The New Poets, 1967; Who's Who in America, 1972–1973.

***SCHISGAL, MURRAY (JOSEPH)** (November 25, 1926–), American dramatist, was born and raised in the East New York section of Brooklyn, where his family occupied two houses at the corner of Georgia and Atlantic avenues. He is the son of Abraham Schisgal, "a scholar and a steampresser" from Lithuania, and of the former Irene Sperling. At seventeen Schisgal left Thomas Jefferson High School and joined the Navy, serving during World War II in both the Atlantic and Pacific theatres as a radioman.

After the war Schisgal began to write, concentrating at first on fiction. He supported himself in a variety of odd jobs and as saxophonist-clarinetist in "a jazz band of second cousins," meanwhile continuing his education at evening classes. Schisgal earned his high school diploma, took classes at Long Island University, and went on to Brooklyn Law School, receiving his LL.B. in 1953. For the next two years he practiced law on New York's Lower East Side, and then decided that teaching would allow him more time to write. He entered the New York City public school system as an English teacher, and studied for his B.A. at the New School for Social Research. By 1959, when he graduated, he had written sixty short stories and three novels, all of them unpublished and "quite bad." He decided to try another medium.

In 1960, with five one-act plays completed, Schisgal left his job and went to Spain to write. En route he stopped in London and, at the suggestion of a friend, showed his plays to the British Drama League. Four of them were produced the same year under the League's auspices as *Shrecks* ("an evening of hysteria"); two of these, *The Typists* and *The Tiger* (originally called *The Postman*), were subsequently presented in many foreign cities and, in 1963, at the Orpheum Theatre, New York City.

* shis′ gəl

MURRAY SCHISGAL

With Eli Wallach and Anne Jackson starring in both plays, the Orpheum production ran for two hundred performances, and won for Schisgal the Vernon Rice Award for outstanding achievement in the off-Broadway theatre, the Outer Circle award as best new playwright of the year, and the *Saturday Review* poll. *The Typists* has also been seen on television in London and Canada.

These two short plays, which established Schisgal's reputation, are each written for only two characters. In *The Typists*, an hour's conversation between two office workers reveals the whole shape of their lives, capturing in what they say and do not say "the pathos of these little machine people who know only too well that they are human." An English critic called the play "a sad, artful scherzo, like a slice of Arthur Miller adapted by Ionesco." In *The Tiger*, an intellectual letter carrier who aspires to be a sex maniac kidnaps a suburban housewife and finds that he has acquired not a victim but a soulmate.

Ducks and Lovers, a full-length satire on (among other things) romantic theories about gypsy life, was produced at the Arts Theatre in London in 1961, and struck one reviewer as "a rich agglomeration of high spirits and wide-ranging satire." The American critics were not much impressed by its successor, *Knit One, Purl Two*, another bizarre comedy, this time about circus people, which was staged in Boston early in 1963.

Schisgal's best known play is *Luv*, unsuccessful at the Arts Theatre in London (1963), but a triumph under Mike Nichols' direction on Broadway in 1964, where its three characters were played by Wallach, Miss Jackson, and Alan Arkin. The author has described the play as "a comedy of the zany gymnastics of love. How we manage to love and not love, in a loving manner." M. J. Arlen called it "funny, truly very funny, fresh, alive, intelligent and filled with a kind of human warmth one rarely sees in plays, or in anything else for that matter." Ira Peck thought that "sometimes it suggests Luigi Pirandello, sometimes James Thurber; it has moments when it is pure Marx Brothers." (But John Simon found it only "occasionally funny and largely insipid," and spoke of "Ionesco on a bagel with lox.") *Luv* ran for nine hundred performances on Broadway, has had two national tours, and at last count had been translated into nineteen languages.

Three short plays by Schisgal were produced at the 1966 Berkshire Theatre Festival and two of them, *The Basement* (originally called *Reverberations*) and *Fragments*, were staged with little success the following year at the Cherry Lane Theatre in Greenwich Village. In 1966 ABC produced his original television play *The Love Song of Barney Kempinski*. Schisgal was co-author of a screen adaptation of *Ducks and Lovers* (1962), and wrote *The Tiger Makes Out* (1967), an expanded movie version of *The Tiger* which stars Wallach and Miss Jackson and has delighted most critics. *Luv* was adapted for the screen by Elliott Baker in 1967. *Jimmy Shine*, an ambitious and relatively complex play about the difficult passage to maturity of a young artist, had a short run on Broadway in 1968.

Schisgal's plays are regularly labeled as examples of the "theatre of the absurd," a movement whose characteristics, as he says, include "language used in other than its literal sense, the fantastic made commonplace, and the focus on man as an isolated, unredeemed individual confronting his own destiny in a pitiless world." Schisgal believes that what the modern painter "has done with perceived subject matter, either obliterating it completely or distorting it to its bare essence, the playwright attempts to do with plot and theme." Roger Gellert has said that Schisgal puts "the compulsive haverings of Ionesco to more pointedly satirical use, and his fantasy is more purposeful than [N. F.] Simpson's. But no clear personality of his own seems to have emerged as yet."

In 1958 Schisgal was married to Reene Schapiro, a former teacher. They have a son and a daughter. M. J. Arlen has described Schisgal as a "stout, affable, intelligent, hard-working, unaffected, somewhat rumpled figure who regards his recent speedy escalation . . . with the sober wariness of a man who discovers that his bank has just made a sizable bookkeeping error in his favor. . . . Schisgal has a whitish face . . . and what with the beard, the dark eyebrows, and the vaguely sad look . . . the effect is powerfully rabbinical."

PRINCIPAL WORKS: *All plays*—The Typists, and The Tiger, 1963; Luv, 1965; Fragments, Windows and Other Plays, 1965; Jax, Max, Baxter and Max (two one-act plays), 1966; Five One-Act Plays, 1968; Jimmy Shine, 1969; The Chinese, and, Dr. Fish, 1970; Ducks and Lovers, 1972.

ABOUT: Arlen, M. J. *introduction to* Schisgal, M. Fragments, Windows and Other Plays, 1965; Current Biography, 1968; Pack, I. *interview with the author in* Schisgal, M. Luv, 1965; Schisgal, M. *introduction to* The Typists, and The Tiger, 1963; Who's Who in America, 1972–1973. *Periodicals*—New York Herald Tribune January 19, 1965; New York Times November 22, 1964; Observer (London) April 7, 1963; Show April 1965.

SCHWARZ-BART, ANDRÉ (1928–), French novelist, was born in Metz. He is the son of Polish Jews who had emigrated to France in 1924. In 1941, when he was thirteen, his parents were taken by the Nazis and deported to an extermination camp. Schwarz-Bart joined the French Resistance at the age of fifteen. He was arrested in Limoges, escaped, and rejoined the Maquis. After the war he worked as a mechanic, salesman, foundry laborer, miner, and librarian. At the library he developed a passion for books—*Don Quixote*, *War and Peace*, Thomas Mann, Stendhal, Georges Bernanos, Dostoevsky, and above all the Old Testament. He entered the Sorbonne and began to work on his first novel, which was published in 1959 as *Le Dernier des justes*.

The book forms a history of the persecution of the Jews, beginning with a massacre in York in 1185 and ending in the Auschwitz gas chambers some seven hundred and sixty years later. In between are pogroms and bigotry in France and Spain, Poland and Russia. This catalogue of inhumanity is given unity and meaning through the Jewish legend of the *Lamed-vaf*—the "thirty-six just men" who emerge, one in each generation, as the unknown whipping boys of history, who receive unto themselves the world's grief. The last of the just men is Ernie Levy, the novel's central figure, who in the end goes voluntarily to the gas chamber, and so brings full circle the wheel of spiritual fulfillment and ethnic destiny.

Le Dernier des justes had a phenomenal success. In France it won the Prix Goncourt and sold almost half a million copies in the original hardback edition. It was translated into fourteen languages—into English, with great skill and sensitivity, by Stephen Becker as *The Last of the Just*. The author—guided by instinct rather than experience—had told his hideous story with a mixture of passion and irony, humor and tenderness, that made what might have been an inarticulate cry of pain into an epic. In spite of moments of diffuseness and passages of overwriting, it was almost universally recognized as a noble monument to the Jewish dead. John Mander called it "very nearly adequate —there is no higher praise—to its dreadful theme."

ANDRÉ SCHWARZ-BART

After this triumph, Schwarz-Bart was not heard from again until 1967, when he published *Un Plat de porc aux bananes vertes,* written in conjunction with Simone, his wife, who was born in Guadeloupe in 1939. It opens a planned cycle of seven novels whose theme is to be the social and racial implications of *négritude* and Jewishness. The two will come together through a marriage, and the cycle will be linked with *The Last of the Just* through a concluding volume on the death camps. The overall title, *La Mulâtresse Solitude* (The Mulatto Solitude), affirms the Schwarz-Barts' intention to depict, through the lives of several generations of Martinique women, the secret and desperate struggle of most black women in Europe and the Americas in the present day.

The title, "A Plate of Pork With Green Bananas," alludes to a Caribbean dish recalled and longed for by Marie Monde, an old woman from Martinique who is living out her days in a baneful Parisian *hospice*—a nursing home with many of the attributes of a death camp. Surrounded by the indigent aged of Paris itself—"tossed away over high walls to feud and dribble their way to the grave"—she voices the full allegorical power of her name (Mary World) by saltily contrasting the antics of their decline with the last days of her own grandmother, who conducted her dying with responsible, familial propriety. The book received the Jerusalem Prize.

"On the strength of *Un Plat de porc aux bananes vertes,*" said the *Times Literary Supplement,* "M. Schwarz-Bart's novel cycle promises to be both dignified and readable. If he is to be criticised here it can only be for having chosen to write the book in the first person, for Marie Monde's mind soars so fluently and richly that it is hard when we are asked every now and then to replace it in her derelict body."

This novel, called a prelude, was followed in 1972 by the volume which provides the title of the entire cycle, *La Mulâtresse Solitude* (translated by Ralph Manheim as *A Woman Named Solitude*). It deals with the beginning of the African slave trade, centering on the life in Guadeloupe of the half-caste slave girl Solitude, who was executed for her leadership of a black insurrection. One reviewer spoke of the story's profound humanity, and also of a dreamlike quality in the way its horrors are presented: "Solitude is seen as if from far away, through grief and pity, but by way of episodic images which strike us as vividly as the images of dreams." There was all the same some feeling that the novel, the product of a Western mind, did not (and could not) convey fully an essentially African experience.

PRINCIPAL WORKS IN ENGLISH TRANSLATION: The Last of the Just, 1960; A Woman Named Solitude, 1973.
ABOUT: International Who's Who, 1972–73; Twentieth Century Writing, 1969. *Periodicals*—Commonweal December 23, 1960; Nation January 7, 1961; New Statesman February 10, 1961; New York Times February 19, 1967; New York Times Book Review December 20, 1959; October 23, 1960; Saturday Review October 22, 1960; Time October 24, 1960; Times Literary Supplement April 13, 1967; June 2, 1972.

SCOTT, GEOFFREY (June 11, 1884–August 14, 1929), English art historian, biographer, and editor, was born in Hampstead, London, into a cultured and wealthy middle-class family. He was the son of Russell Scott, a flooring manufacturer, and the nephew of C. P. Scott, the great editor of the *Manchester Guardian.* He was educated at Rugby, and in 1903 went up to New College, Oxford, where he won the Newdigate Poetry Prize and also the Chancellor's Prize for his essay "The National Character of English Architecture."

Scott had little formal training in architecture but, like Ruskin before him, he profoundly loved what he regarded as the most fundamental art, and he brought to this passion a mind well trained in literary and historical scholarship. In 1907, when he left Oxford, he joined his friend Cecil Pinsent in Florence, where they planned to work together as architects and landscape gardeners. The same year Scott became librarian and secretary to the art expert Bernard Berenson, joining a household in which, as one observer wrote, "all the beauty and wit [of Anglo-American society in prewar Florence] seemed to be gathered together."

Apart from his work for Berenson, Scott collaborated with Pinsent in designing the library and gardens of Berenson's villa, I Tatti, and on one or two other modest commissions, and began his book *The Architecture of Humanism*. Nicky Mariano, who was to become Berenson's lifelong companion and factotum, met Scott in 1913 and was soon one of his closest friends. She says that he was then a tall, thin young man, wearing a pince-nez over very shortsighted eyes. She found him physically rather unattractive, but wrote: "His voice, his laughter, his sense of fun, his whimsical expression, his choice of words, all appealed to me." Scott became a special protégé of Berenson's wife Mary, who helped him with his book and did her best to marry him off to Nicky Mariano, a project which may have been closer to Scott's heart than to Miss Mariano's.

The Architecture of Humanism was published in 1914. It is "a study in the history of taste," analyzing the theories underlying nineteenth century architecture, and seeking to demonstrate their inferiority to the classical tradition as it appears in the Renaissance and baroque architecture of Italy. Scott held that modern architecture had been weakened by an assortment of fallacious dogmas—among them the cult of originality for its own sake; the belief, on the other hand, that form must invariably follow function; and the "ethical fallacy" that ornament is dishonest because it conceals the true nature of a building.

Architecture cannot be reduced to any single formula, Scott maintained; it is "a humanised pattern of the world, a scheme of forms on which our life reflects its clarified image: this is its true aesthetic." Again, "Architecture, simply and immediately perceived, is a combination, revealed through light and shade, of spaces, of masses, and of lines. . . . And these appearances are related to human functions. Through these spaces we can conceive ourselves to move; these masses are capable, like ourselves, of pressure and resistance; these lines, should we follow or describe them, might be our path and our gesture. . . . *We transcribe architecture into terms of ourselves*. This is the humanism of architecture. The tendency to project the image of our functions into concrete forms is the basis, for architecture, of creative design. The tendency to recognise, in concrete forms, the image of those functions is the true basis, in its turn, of critical appreciation." It was this humanism that Scott so admired in the architecture of the classical tradition.

These views were revolutionary in 1914, and accordingly the book was harshly condemned by some, and praised by others as the most important work of its kind since Ruskin's *The Stones of Venice*. It is the latter view that has prevailed. The book has had immense influence on architectural ideas and more generally on the development of taste, and has been many times reprinted. In the

GEOFFREY SCOTT

balance and lucidity of its prose and the elegance of its organization, it is itself a tribute to the classical tradition; Edith Wharton called Scott's style "perfect."

Scott spoke of a sequel to the *Architecture of Humanism*, and of a study of Bernini, but in fact he wrote no more books on architecture. During World War I he remained in Italy, attached to the British Embassy in Rome. In 1918 he married Lady Sybil Cuffe, younger daughter of the fifth Earl of Desart and widow of the American diplomat William Bayard Cutting. The marriage, which Mary Berenson opposed, ended Scott's connection with I Tatti, though he continued to live nearby at his wife's house, the Villa Medici. This proximity to his old friends became painful after 1919, when Nicky Mariano returned to I Tatti as librarian, and Scott's emotional confusion induced a highly neurotic condition. He spoke of suicide and spent some time at a Swiss clinic. In 1920 he went to Rome to take up a post as press attaché at the British Embassy and in 1922 he returned for a time to England. The following year he published *A Box of Paints*, a volume (according to a contemporary review) of "light imaginings," of "fancies set forth in comfortable verse." Even then Scott's poems seemed old-fashioned and irrelevant.

There was a very different response to his next book, *The Portrait of Zélide*. It is a biographical study of Isabella van Tuyll, the rich, clever, and strikingly attractive daughter of a great Dutch family. She had many distinguished suitors (among them James Boswell), overawed most of them with her tempestuous brilliance, and ended as the wife of her brother's phlegmatic Swiss tutor, St.

Hyacinthe de Charrière. The book concentrates on an episode in her middle life: her friendship with the young Benjamin Constant, whom she helped and encouraged but who eventually deserted her for Madame de Staël.

In the rivalry of these two remarkable women Scott saw a conflict between eighteenth and nineteenth century values: Constant chose "the false mysticism of Germany"; Madame de Charrière had for Madame de Staël "the contempt of the thinker for the rhetorician." The book was described in the *Times Literary Supplement* as "an analytical biography, as acute, brilliant and witty as any that has appeared in recent years"; it is cherished by many as a small masterpiece.

Nigel Nicolson's *Portrait of a Marriage* gives an account of Scott's passionate attachment to Vita Sackville-West. This was one of a series of affairs which led to Scott's divorce in 1927. The same year, by now settled in England, Scott was at work on a biography of Boswell when he was invited by the American collector Colonel Ralph H. Isham to edit the Malahide Papers—a great cache of Boswell's letters, diaries, and manuscripts which Isham had bought a year earlier. Recalling his first meeting with Geoffrey Scott, Isham said that he was much impressed by "his erudition, his vivid conversation, and by his romantic appearance. He was of great height and heavy build. His head was large and fine, his face sensitive—at times beautiful in expression. His black hair, which he wore long, was vigorous and untidy."

In October 1927 Scott went to Isham's estate at Glen Cove, Long Island. He absorbed himself in his work (being "charmingly absentminded about everything else"). During the next twenty-one months he established the entire text of the Boswell papers, prepared for publication the first six volumes (which were welcomed as "a model of literary scholarship"), and planned the rest. At that point Scott interrupted his work and left Long Island for a two-month vacation—according to some reports irked because Isham had proved very much more generous as a host than as an employer. At any rate, Scott returned to Glen Cove on August 4, 1929. Three days later he fell ill, and he died of pneumonia on August 14, at the age of forty-five.

By all accounts Geoffrey Scott was a notable conversationalist, "humorous and witty, polished and profound, learned and inspired, critical and affectionate." His obituaries spoke of his perfect tact, his gentle and sympathetic manner, and "his great capacity for intimate friendship." A critic in the *Times Literary Supplement* once referred to Scott as "a dandy of letters up-to-date," but this seems an ungenerous view of the author of *The Architecture of Humanism* and *A Portrait of Zélide*, and a foolish one of the editor of the Boswell papers. Isham indeed testified that Scott "wrote with labor; in part because he set a high standard for himself, in part because he was sensitive to sound, in part because he allowed himself the least number of words. He was always striving for perfection." All the same, as his friend Edith Wharton said, there was something in him "dispersed and tentative, as though the balance between his creative and critical faculties had not yet been struck."

PRINCIPAL WORKS: The Architecture of Humanism, 1914; A Box of Paints (poems), 1923; The Portrait of Zélide, 1925; Poems, 1931; (ed.) Boswell, J. Private Papers from Malahide Castle (vols. 1–6), 1928–1932.

ABOUT: Gosse, E. W. Silhouettes, 1925; Johnson, P. Architecture, 1949–1965, 1966; Mariano, N. Forty Years With Berenson, 1966; Nicolson, N. Portrait of a Marriage, 1973; Reed, H. H. *introduction to* The Architecture of Humanism (1969 edition); Sprigge, S. Berenson, 1960; Wharton, E. A Backward Glance, 1934. *Periodicals* —Century October 1929; London Mercury September 1929; New York Times August 15, 1929; Publishers' Weekly August 17, 1929; Saturday Review of Literature August 24, 1929; Times (London) August 15, 1929; Times Literary Supplement November 8, 1923; January 1, 1925; March 12, 1925.

SCOTT, PAUL (MARK) (March 25, 1920–), English novelist, writes: "I was born in a place called Palmers Green, which is a suburb of London. This was in 1920. I spent my childhood and youth there, and in the neighbouring district of Southgate. I went to one of those private schools that used to be described as for the sons of gentlemen. My father was a gentle man, by which I mean he seldom raised his voice in anger. He was also a commercial artist. There were several of them in the family, as well as an uncle who painted horses and harboured uncharitable thoughts about Sir Alfred Munnings. They claimed a connexion with the naturalist and engraver, Thomas Bewick; but I never checked up on that. The closest I ever got to being a naturalist myself was reading Fabre's *Book of Insects* and starting a collection of butterflies which were destroyed by the dog of my aunt.

"My mother used to model the lavish fur coats which father painted so well for the catalogues of wholesale furriers but couldn't afford to buy her. Before her marriage she used to hide in a cupboard and write novels. On the night before her wedding (in 1916) she destroyed her manuscripts but always remembered the title of her favourite: *The Keepsake.* I have often wondered whether it was any good; or whether it ever actually existed. She had a vivid imagination. This I inherited. She imagined me as an accountant, although I was bad at mathematics. I was set to work with a member of that profession, and learned to be practical, because my own imagination was colourful enough to enable me to believe that I was.

"I have been (in this order) then, a trainee accountant, a soldier, a married man, an accountant and secretary to a group of post-war publishers now defunct, a father, out of work, an employee and then a director of a firm of authors' agents. I am still a married man and a father but am now what is euphemistically described as a full-time writer which, in spite of the butterflies, father's studio, clients' ledgers and other writers' contracts, I had always, obviously, intended. I began with poetry, went on to plays and graduated to novels, the most exacting form of literary composition there is.

"But I do not have any theory about it (The Novel), only a problem which is resolved in a theory about each novel as I come to write it. It is a question of attempting always to bite off more than you have yet proved to yourself you can chew; and a question of making the problems of each book, and their solutions, continuously interesting to yourself. I see no other way of feeding creative vitality. Some critics have said that I seldom repeat myself and that it is therefore difficult to define my commitment. This strikes me as a narrow view. Commitment is for the old and serene. I am not yet either. For myself, the act of writing a novel is an act of asking questions, not answering them. My curiosity is more valuable to me than are my transient assumptions.

"For a novel I prefer a broad canvas, which may be why I have never published a short story. I also tend to write about people in relation to their work, which strikes me as a subject no less important than that of their private lives because their work is so often affected by their sense of personal deprivation. My interest in the closing years of the British power in India is probably due to my feeling that, in India, the British as a nation came to the end of themselves as they were and have not yet emerged from the shock of their own liberation.

"The manuscripts and working notes of several of my novels are in the keeping of the University of Texas. Anyone interested in my own particular and painful method of suiting form to idea could study it there."

Paul Scott did his soldiering in India, an experience of central importance to his work. After the war he worked from 1946 to 1950 as secretary of the Falcon Press, and during the next decade he became well known and well liked by both publishers and authors as a director of the literary agency David Higham Associates. He is married to Elizabeth Avery and they have two daughters.

His first novel, *Johnnie Sahib*, was about an Indian regiment with British officers during World War II. In the excellence of its dialogue and the clarity and directness of its style, as well as in its

PAUL SCOTT

setting, it reminded some reviewers of the Far Eastern stories of Somerset Maugham.

The comparison was repeated in reviews of the other novels Scott published during the 1950s, all of them investigations of subtle psychological problems, often in exotic settings. The best of these is *The Mark of the Warrior*, an extremely perceptive study of an army officer whose growing sense of guilt for the death of two men that he has trained is extended "into a comparison of the man of peace and the man of war." As Walter Allen wrote, Scott's theme is "the mystique of the soldier and the mystique of leadership, and admirably he executes it."

Since then Scott's novels have grown increasingly exact in their perceptions and have shown a greatly extended range. One of the most widely admired of them is *Birds of Paradise*. William Conway had spent a lonely but magical childhood in a princely Indian state under the British Raj. Now, in middle age, his almost Oedipal dream of service to Mother India ruined by Independence, Conway is numbed into reactionary conservatism. This humane and powerfully evocative study recalls a life that never again matched the beauty and freedom of its beginning—a freedom enjoyed at the cost of the subjection of a great nation. The birds of paradise that recur throughout the book state its theme; they are creatures that die in captivity.

The Bender, "pictures from an exhibition of middle-class portraits," is a totally different kind of book, a picaresque set in contemporary London. The need for two hundred pounds to hush up an unwanted pregnancy upsets the financial balance of George Lisle-Spruce in a way that affects a rich variety of other lives, allowing the author to compress within the space of twenty-four hours an illumination of "the frustrations of three generations." The book topples at times into facetiousness, perhaps when the author attempts characters outside his range, but is in general, as one reviewer said, "a subtle, unemphatic novel, beautifully composed in a minor key."

Another departure from Scott's earlier concerns followed in *The Corrida at San Feliu*, employing the time-honored device of *Rahmenerzählung*, "the novel within a novel." The narrator, a publisher's reader, describes the life and death of a sixty-year-old writer, Edward Thornhill, who has died in a car crash with his beautiful (and much younger) wife. He also supplies five fragments from a novel by Thornhill, drawn from his own life but incorporating certain fictions. The book is an examination both of the creative process and of "the incapacity of men and women to love selflessly." It is an absorbing, able, and sometimes genuinely tragic story which (like *Birds of Paradise*) uses recurrent motifs and symbols and a deliberately broken narrative line to give an impression of great density.

The critical response was rather cooler when Scott resumed his earlier theme in a trilogy—*The Jewel in the Crown*, *The Day of the Scorpion*, and *The Towers of Silence*—about the end of British rule in India. But Anthony Burgess is no doubt right when he says that "Scott can best realize the tragic divisions of human beings in a foreign setting, bringing these out through symbols taken from an exotic scene, sharpening them through the strangeness of the background." Many readers continue to expect from him the major novel that he has repeatedly so nearly achieved.

PRINCIPAL WORKS (all novels): Johnnie Sahib, 1952; The Alien Sky, 1953; A Male Child, 1956; The Mark of the Warrior, 1958; The Chinese Love Pavilion (U.S., The Love Pavilion), 1960; The Birds of Paradise, 1962; The Bender, 1963; The Corrida at San Feliu, 1964; The Jewel in the Crown, 1966; The Day of the Scorpion, 1968; The Towers of Silence, 1971.

ABOUT: Burgess, A. The Novel Now, 1967; Vinson, J. (ed.) Contemporary Novelists, 1972. *Periodicals*—New Statesman October 8, 1960; April 13, 1962; April 12, 1963; New Yorker July 2, 1966; Times Literary Supplement April 12, 1963; August 27, 1964.

"SEC." *See* MANNES, MARYA

***"SEFERIS, GEORGE" (pseudonym of Georgios Stylianou Seferiadis),** (February 29, 1900–September 20, 1971), Greek poet and critic, was born in the city of Smyrna (now Izmir) on the Asia Minor coast of Turkey. His father, Stelios Seferiadis, was a distinguished member of the Greek community in that city, a lawyer and man of letters who eventually became professor of international law at Athens University. Though Seferis moved to Athens at the outbreak of World War I to complete his secondary and high school education, he always regarded Smyrna as his home; the burning of the city and the displacement of its Greek community after the disastrous war with Turkey in 1922 remained for him a personal loss that contributed, perhaps more than any other event in contemporary Greek history, to the tragic sense of life that dominated his poetry.

* se fe′ ris

From 1918 to 1924 Seferis lived in Paris with his family while studying law and literature at the Sorbonne, years that proved highly significant in determining the particular direction that his early poetry took. His first collection, *Strophe* (Turning Point, 1931), and the long rhymed poem *I Sterna* (The Cistern, 1932), though for the most part traditional in form, revealed a growing interest in the tonal and stylistic experiments of his French contemporaries and, sometimes, a kind of "pure" poetry in the manner of Valéry. These early volumes also demonstrate the poet's acute awareness of his own tradition; in his "Erotikos Logos," for example, he successfully adapts the principal meter of Greek folk poetry (the *dekapentasyllavos*) to the expression of a contemporary *symboliste* sensibility, and many of his early poems exploit in a sophisticated way some of the forms, themes, and diction that he inherited from demotic Greek literature—a literature that is the subject of most of his critical essays in *Dokimes* (1944, second edition 1962), which is generally regarded as the best volume of literary criticism in the modern Greek tradition.

After receiving his degree in law in 1924, Seferis traveled to London to perfect his English in anticipation of entering the Greek diplomatic service two years later, thus beginning a long and fruitful association with England. In his "Letter to a Foreign Friend," Seferis speaks of experiencing "the bitter taste of death in the fog" during his second visit to London in 1931, while Greek Vice-Consul, an assignment that gave him his first deep sense of nostalgia for the Mediterranean and perhaps his sharpest intimations of the "exile" theme that was to become one of the major themes of his mature poetry; but it also introduced him to a mode of expression—that of Ezra Pound and especially of T. S. Eliot—which was to serve crucially in helping him to shape the voice that we hear throughout his later verse, from *Mythistorema* (1935, translated by Rex Warner in *Poems* under the same title) through *Imerologio Katastromatos A* (1940, translated by Rex Warner in *Poems* as *Log Book I*) and *Imerologio Katastromatos B* (1945, translated by Rex Warner in *Poems* as *Log Book II*). Seferis tells us that he found in Eliot, besides a congenial style and technique, "something that is inevitably moving to a Greek: the elements of tragedy." In 1936 he published a brilliant translation of *The Waste Land*. His association with Eliot became personal as well as literary during his subsequent tours of duty in England, first in 1950–1952 while he was Counselor of Embassy and later as Ambassador (1957–1962). Upon Eliot's death in 1965, Seferis published a short commemorative diary of their relationship.

Seferis's sympathetic reading of Eliot is apparent in the distinct change of style that is found in *Mythistorema*, a change that was however at least partly the consequence of a personal stylistic catharsis that had begun to appear in *The Cistern*. The development is quite away from the more or less formal manner of the earlier volumes, towards what Edmund Keeley and Philip Sherrard in their foreword to the *Collected Poems* call "the much freer and more natural mode that is characteristic of all his mature poetry, where we inevitably find a precisely controlled style, undecorated by embellishment, the coloring always primary and the imagery sparse. In his mature poetry Seferis combines the modes of everyday speech with the forms and rhythms of traditional usage in a way that creates the effect of both density and economy."

Mythistorema is a sequence of twenty-four short poems which make up what has been described in the *Times Literary Supplement* as "a condensed epic," concerned with a quest for the sources of life, and contrasting a tragic but heroic past with a present in which man has become divorced from the values which once gave meaning to his life: "What do they seek our souls as they travel / From harbor to harbor / On ships with rotting timbers? // Shifting broken stones, inhaling / More painfully every day the coolness of the pines, // Swimming in the waters here of this sea / And there of that sea, / Without the sense of touch, / Without men, / In a country which is no longer ours / No longer yours. // We knew that the islands were beautiful / Somewhere around where we are groping / A little higher or a little lower / A tiny distance."

Seferis's career in the diplomatic service obliged him to live outside Greece for many of the years before his retirement in 1962; besides his three tours in England, he was Consul in Koritsa, Albania, from 1936 to 1938; he served with the Greek government-in-exile in Egypt, South Africa, and Italy during much of World War II; he was Counselor of Embassy in Ankara, Turkey, from 1948 to 1950; and he spent 1953 to 1956 in Beirut, Lebanon, as Ambassador to Lebanon, Syria, and Jordan.

These travels acquired a much more than private significance in Seferis's verse, which made constant use of a *persona* who is a kind of modern Odysseus, an emblem of contemporary man, tormented by a

GEORGE SEFERIS

sense of alienation and loss, and perpetually voyaging in search of the "other world," the lost paradise. In the same way, Seferis found universal metaphors in recent history. For example *Kichli* (1947, translated by Keeley and Sherrard as *The Thrush*), begins as a poem about a small ship sunk during World War II but still visible, refracted and transmuted, in the clear water off Poros. This image leads the poet to contemplate another kind of revelation, when man's tyrannical self loosens its grasp on corporeal things: "And now you are / In a great house with many windows open / And you run from room to room not knowing from where to look out first / For the pine trees will vanish and the mirrored mountains, / And the chirruping of birds / The sea will empty, shattered glass from north to south / Your eyes will empty of the light of day / As suddenly, all together, the cicadas fall silent."

Seferis's role as spokesman for his nation became crucial in the negotiations that led to the Cyprus agreements, to which he contributed both as a member of the Greek delegation to the United Nations during the 1957 debate and subsequently as Ambassador in London. *Imerologio Katastromatos C* (1955, translated by Rex Warner as *Log Book III*) suggests that his involvement in the Cyprus issue was as privately inspiring as it proved to be publicly practical: though the volume is specifically dedicated to the people of Cyprus, the poems in it—for example, "Helen" and "Salamis in Cyprus"—reveal a voice made wise and simple by the kind of vision that sees beyond the level of mere political comment or propaganda to those tragic truths regarding war that give a universal meaning to our times. In recognition of his "unique thought and style," the Swedish Academy of Letters awarded him the Nobel Prize for Literature in 1963, making him the first Greek man of letters to be so honored, and in recognition of his work both as statesman and poet he received honorary degrees from Cambridge (1960), Oxford (1964), Salonika (1964), and Princeton (1965). In 1966 he was elected an honorary member of the American Academy of Arts and Sciences, and in the same year, he was appointed an honorary fellow of the Modern Language Association.

Apart from the intensely concentrated and condensed triptych *Tria Kryfá Poiemata* (1966, translated as *Three Secret Poems*), Seferis published little in the last part of his life. In March 1969 he issued a public statement in which he attacked the Greek military regime, speaking of the tragic ending which awaits all dictatorships. One of his last and greatest poems, "The Cats of St. Nicholas," was contributed to *Eighteen Texts*, an anthology of antidictatorial prose and verse published in Greek in 1970. Seferis died the following year of complications following an operation for a duodenal ulcer.

Seferis lived in Athens with his wife, Maria Zannou, whom he married in 1941. He was a heavy, slow-moving man, bald, with a slight stoop. In speech he was quiet and courteous, but he disliked pretension and was capable of a deflating irony. A critic in the *Times Literary Supplement*, summing up his achievement, wrote: "More than any other of his contemporaries or successors Seferis has extended the frontiers of Greek literature and created for it a poetry which is attuned to the poetic idiom of the contemporary western world. He has introduced new harmonies and discords into poetic diction and subtilized the use of figurative language, and in doing all this he has employed the 'demotic' tongue and vindicated his lifelong conviction that the poetry of his country can and must be written in the language of everyday speech." When he died, the same journal spoke of him as "the greatest poet of his generation in Europe. . . . If there were never any other children of Homer, and Seferis were the last, it would not be a bad ending."

PRINCIPAL WORKS IN ENGLISH TRANSLATION: *Poetry*—The King of Asine and Other Poems, 1948; Poems, 1960; Collected Poems, 1924–1955, 1967; Three Secret Poems, 1969. *Poems in* Barnstone, W. (ed.) Modern European Poetry, 1966; Barnstone, W. (ed.) Eighteen Texts, 1972; Friar, K. (ed.) Modern Greek Poetry, 1973; Keeley, E. and Sherrard, P. Six Poets of Modern Greece, 1961; Agenda 1969. *Essays*—On the Greek Style: Selected Essays in Poetry and Hellenism, 1966.

ABOUT: Current Biography, 1964; Grigson, G. Concise Encyclopedia of Modern World Literature, 1963; International Who's Who, 1973–74; Keeley, E. and Bien, P. (eds.) Modern Greek Writers, 1972; Penguin Companion to Literature 2, 1969; Politis, L. A History of Modern Greek Literature, 1972; Sherrard, P. The Marble Threshing Floor, 1956; Stanford, W. B. The Ulysses Theme, 1955; Who's Who, 1971; Who's Who in America, 1972–1973. *Periodicals*—Accent Summer 1956; Comparative Literature Summer 1956; Kenyon Review June 1966; Life January 17, 1964; Nation September 16, 1968; New York Times September 21, 1971; Poetry January 1963, October 1964; Saturday Review November 20, 1963; Texas Quarterly Summer 1964; Times Literary Supplement September 12, 1968; Virginia Quarterly Summer 1968.

*__SEIDEL, INA__ (September 15, 1885–), German novelist, poet, memoirist, and essayist, writes: "I was born at Halle on Saale, where my father worked as a physician during the first years of his marriage. He was a son of Heinrich Alexander Seidel, parson and hymn writer and a younger brother of Heinrich Seidel (1842–1906), well-known author of poetry and humorous, fantastical prose. The family was of Mecklenburgian origin. My mother came from Riga, but had lived since early childhood in Germany. Her stepfather and the only grandfather I remember was Georg Ebers, Egyptologist and author of a series of historical novels. My parents moved to Braunschweig before I was half a year old. There my brother Willy was born and together we had a cloudless childhood in this town of medieval buildings, surrounded by a belt of dreamy gardens. Since our father was not only a successful surgeon and orthopedist but a student of nature, he couldn't be without a little private zoo; he was also a passionate amateur of the fine arts and a collector of paintings and graphics. Both our parents were young and vivacious. My mother encouraged us to sing and learn poems by heart as soon as we were able to speak. Every summer she spent weeks with us in the beautiful landscape of Oberbayern, where her parents had a country house on the Lake of Starnberg near Munich. All this ended with the tragic death of our father in 1895, when at the age of forty, overworked, and unable to withstand the calumniatory attacks of envious colleagues, he died by his own hand. The proceedings the family took against his defamers restored his professional honor completely, but that couldn't eradicate the profound change that had overcome the life of his wife and his children. My brother and our little sister were young enough not to feel the full strength of this blow. But the shock I had received from the loss of my dearly beloved father, and the turmoils that followed, were like an earthquake, ending my childhood and establishing my cast of mind forever.

"We left Braunschweig, first for Marburg on Lahn, and in 1897 for Munich, where my mother's parents lived. So Munich became the town of my

* sī del

early youth and much I owe to this town, whose atmosphere was a stimulus for any germ of talent. At the beginning of our century, Munich was the town of Stefan George, and Ricarda Huch, of the rising Thomas Mann, of artists like Franz Lenbach, F. A. Kaulbach, and countless others, of great actors and musicians—a town vibrant with spontaneity, gaiety, festivals. My brother had very early begun to write poetry and stories and so had I. But his writings being much more accomplished than my own, I preferred to regard my scribblings as some private airing of the mind after occasional fits of nostalgia and depression. By the time he published his first writings in 1908, I had married our cousin, Heinrich Wolfgang Seidel, lived with him in Berlin, had a little daughter, and was slowly recovering from a severe illness. During these years of distress the writing of poetry and prose became an occupation of the greatest importance to me and developed as a discipline as well as a passion which has never left me. My husband was a clergyman and himself a distinguished writer. We lived for seven years in Berlin North; then, during World War I and the bleak years till 1923, in a provincial town near the city, but surrounded by fir woods; and at last for eleven years again in the center of Berlin: these twenty-seven years, sometimes interrupted by 'tramps abroad,' were the best and most productive time of my life. In 1934 we withdrew to a little house of our own in Starnberg, where, still trying to work, I have remained since my husband died in the bitter autumn of 1945.

"About my work—several of my novels have a historical background, but I dare to say that their leading characters, their problems and conflicts, have a timeless, psychological, and purely human theme. While I am writing I live in the world I am inventing and concern myself only with the fates of my characters, sorry to leave them when the work is done as if a door has shut behind me. I feel closest to my poems and to some tales with an undercurrent of transcendental and lyrical elements."

Ina Seidel is the daughter of Hermann Seidel and the former Emmy Loesevitz, and a member (as her note above shows) of an extremely literary family. Her brother Willy achieved some fame as "the German Rudyard Kipling." She was married in 1907. As she says, it was in 1908, when she hovered between life and death after the birth of her first child, that she began seriously to write. Her first verse collections did not appear until World War I: *Gedichte* (Poems, 1914); *Neben der Trommel her* (By the Drum, 1915); and *Weltinnigkeit* (World Oneness, 1918). They showed a good technical command of language and meter, but were thought

INA SEIDEL

somewhat imitative. By 1927, when *Neue Gedichte* (New Poems) was published, there was a new urgency to her style, a new concreteness in her imagery and descriptive passages, particularly those concerning nature. Her selected poems, *Gedichte* (1955), showed considerable technical skill and a remarkable range, including war ballads, long didactic pieces, lyrical nature descriptions, and poems of human emotions and relationships.

Her short stories and novels also began to appear during the war. *Das Haus zum Monde* (The House on the Moon, 1917) and its sequel *Sterne der Heimkehr* (Stars Leading Home, 1923), are novels of family life, and *Brömseshof* and *Renée und Rainer*, both published in 1928, deal particularly with brother and sister relationships. Much of her work from this period has an autobiographical ring, and in 1935 she published a collection of autobiographical sketches, *Meine Kindheit und Jugend* (My Childhood and Youth).

Ina Seidel's first major work was *Das Labyrinth* (1922). It is a biographical novel about Georg Forster, an eighteenth century German scientist and poet. Forster went with his father on Captain Cook's journey to the Antipodes, and later became involved in the promiscuous literary-social world of the period, where he encountered such notables as Schiller, Schelling, and August Wilhelm Schlegel. She presents Forster as an idealistic young man who is drawn into the labyrinth of worldly affairs, eventually meeting the Minotaur, Death, in Paris. The portrait of Georg Forster—intellectually excitable, sexually erratic—is an interesting one, but Ina Seidel's analysis was described by one critic as "painfully Freudian." Jethro Bithell found the novel's general effect "somewhat televisionary: there is too much grouping of [familiar] figures . . . these figures are vividly portrayed, but too much in the ideal light of literary history." Other critics objected to the style, which they found cumbersome, rhetorical, and humorless.

Das Wunschkind, Ina Seidel's most successful novel, was published in 1930 and has been translated as *The Wish Child*. The central character is a widow who loses her only son, as she had lost his father, in the Prussian Wars of Liberation. The "insistent burden of the tale," wrote one critic, "is the absolute and the statesmanlike necessity of the Prussian military machine, and its essential humanity. . . . This doctrine of the categorical imperative is developed at immense length and with insinuating simplicity." Bayard Q. Morgan, writing in *The Columbia Dictionary of Modern European Literature*, called the novel "one of the great books of its generation . . . a story which only a woman could have written, but one which some woman had to write." *Lennacker* (1938), the last of the three major novels on which Ina Seidel's reputation principally rests, is about a professional soldier who has to adapt himself to peace; it is also a history of a parsonage and its incumbents—in a way, of the Church itself.

Order in society, and particularly religious order, is a central preoccupation in Ina Seidel's books. The stability of the home, the continuity of the Church, and the just authority of the state are recurrent themes in her novels and short stories. She is a member of the Prussian Academy of Arts and in 1958 received the Great Art Prize of Nordrhein-Westfalen.

PRINCIPAL WORKS IN ENGLISH TRANSLATION: The Labyrinth, 1932; The Wish Child, 1935.

ABOUT: Bithell, J. Modern German Literature, 1959; Horst, K. A. Ina Seidel, 1956; Smith, H. (ed.) Columbia Dictionary of Modern European Literature, 1947. *Periodicals*—Commonweal October 4, 1935; New York Times August 21, 1932; Times Literary Supplement May 12, 1932; May 23, 1935.

SELVON, SAMUEL (DICKSON) (May 20, 1923–), West Indian novelist and short story writer, writes: "I was born in 1923 in Trinidad; my father's family had come from India and my mother was half-Scots. Halfway through college I had to quit schooling and go to work. I was attracted to the sea and when war broke out I joined a local branch of the Royal Navy and worked on minesweepers and torpedo boats as a wireless operator, patrolling the Caribbean.

"Some time during those years I started to write poetry, feeling my way for some sort of expression which was very personal, and had nothing to do with the facts of war. I was vague and puzzled about things, and never thought about what I was going to do when the war was over. As it turned out, I only started to work on a newspaper because I was absent when a ship came in that needed a wireless operator.

"The BBC in London paid me for a poem and I wanted to frame the cheque; it was the first solid encouragement I ever got, and for the first time I began to have ideas about writing for a living. I helped to edit a weekly magazine the newspaper brought out, and wrote short stories and poems which I sold to the BBC. It was easy to be complacent and form premature judgements. I married a girl from British Guiana and thought I would settle down. But I was too young, and frightened of falling into a rut I chucked up everything and came to England in 1950, with nothing but a cheque for fifteen guineas which I had asked the BBC to hold until my arrival.

"I worked as a clerk with the Indian Embassy in London for two years. I had brought a few short stories with me, and thought I could develop one of these into a longer work. I wrote during my spare time, and three weeks after it was finished it was accepted for publication. The critical reception in England and America was most encouraging, but I still wasn't sure I could earn my living by writing.

"I fell ill with tuberculosis while working on my second novel and stayed in hospital for fifteen months. When I came out and resumed my job with the Indian Embassy, a Canadian magazine offered me three hundred dollars for any story I cared to write. My illness had given me a period to assess my ambitions: if I could write half a dozen stories a year, I needn't work at a regular job. So I packed up on speculation, deciding that if I wanted to be a writer there was only one way to do it.

"Luckily I was awarded a Guggenheim Fellowship shortly after. I went to America, where I was a guest at the MacDowell Colony in New Hampshire, and I also visited Canada.

"Since that time I went back to America briefly, and I visited France and Spain on the strength of a travelling award from the Society of Authors in London. In 1963 I returned to Trinidad for six months on a Government scholarship.

"Throughout these years of writing I have remained, basically, the same person I always was. The mantle of writer fits uneasily on my shoulders; in an honest appraisal of my life, I think of other things I would be much happier doing. I've never been able to divorce myself from need and want and ordinary human beings who catch early trains and dash off for various jobs which might mean the difference between having roast beef for lunch or pot-luck from last night's remains. Sometimes I actually resent the fact that I'm an author because what the hell am I going to do if I'm casually eating a bag of fish and chips in the street and I turn a corner and come across my publisher parking his car, or some impresario on his way to lunch at the Savoy? There is no discipline whatsoever when I'm working. If someone suggests a quick drink I'm off quickly, because I suppose that's what that means.

"I like good food, in the sense that what I like is good; I like to play tennis, and cards; I like ordinary human conversation, and hate literary gatherings and talk about books and authors. I've never studied the techniques of writing and haven't the faintest idea of the difference between a short story and a novel except that one is short and the other long. I have two children, Shelley Sarojini, by my first marriage, and Michael Dickson, by my second. I should have been a philosopher, though who's a philosopher these days?"

Samuel Selvon is one of a galaxy of talented West Indian writers who surprised the English-reading world in the 1950s with their comic, ribald, sometimes bitter, and always passionate pictures of Caribbean life. Selvon's is perhaps the sunniest temperament of them all, presenting his irresponsible, free-wheeling picaroons with affection, even when he is most wearily critical of the messes they make of their own and other people's lives; and he is immensely funny. His short stories, and the episodes that make up a large part of his novels, are extensions of the funny and/or lubricous anecdotes that Trinidadians call "ballads." His most serious concern is with the interaction of the various racial groups in Trinidad, their ethnocentricity, and his hopes for multiracial harmony. Selvon received a second Guggenheim Fellowship in 1968, and Trinidad's Humming Bird Medal in 1969. He now has two children by his second (1963) marriage to Althea Nesta Daroux, as well as one by his first marriage.

His first novel, *A Brighter Sun* (1952), deals with East Indians and Creoles in Trinidad—their absurd prejudices and mutual distrust—as they affect a young "East Indian," Tiger. Anthony West called this a "delightful first novel," and *Time* magazine praised a "freshness of speech and locale that is as welcome as its direct, unsurprised look at life." C. J. Rolo felt however that the novel "does not, in the final analysis, quite match up to its original promise, and its tone tends to soften the harsh realities of Tiger's life. But it is a touching story, full of charm. It blazes with local color."

An Island Is a World, which followed, is a slightly more serious work, its characters engaging in passages of philosophizing about life and art that reviewers found rather tedious. But *Lonely Londoners*, about West Indian emigrants living by their wits in the bewildering city, was greeted by the *New Yorker* as "a nearly perfect work of its kind," that is, "one of the most difficult of literary

SAMUEL SELVON

forms—the pure dialect novel." Selvon's mastery of dialogue, his ability to convey the flavor of Trinidadian speech, and the aimlessness and pathos that underlie the "kiff-kaff laughter, the ballad, the episode, the what-happening," had already reached maturity; though he had not yet achieved the economy of style which was to distinguish his later London novel, *The Housing Lark*. This is an account of the efforts of a feckless group of Trinidadians to put aside their pleasures and save for a house of their own, secure from exploitation or eviction by white landlords (whose greed and prejudice are acknowledged as an accepted fact of life, rather like the English weather). Such a plan, devised by such Runyonesque idlers, dreamers, and golden-hearted prostitutes, seems "doom to turn old mask from the very beginning." Its almost accidental fruition is described with a "leisurely showmanship" that was warmly praised.

Though nineteen short stories about Trinidad and London, published in 1958 as *Ways of Sunlight*, found a ready welcome (Claud Cockburn said that they were "all memorable, and some truly wonderful"), Selvon's subsequent novels have had a mixed critical reception. *Turn Again Tiger*, a sequel to *A Brighter Sun*, was followed by *I Hear Thunder*, also set in Trinidad and dealing with two friends, one of whom has come home with an English wife. The *Times Literary Supplement* complained of clichés in the writing of *I Hear Thunder*, and *Bookweek* of Selvon's "honeysuckle prose." *The Plains of Caroni* centers on the conflict between Luddite workers and "The Company," which is intent on mechanizing the sugar cane industry in Trinidad. It was much admired as a portrait of a society in transition, characterized by a "heady mixture of excitement and apathy." *Those Who Eat the Cascadura*, a Trinidad love story, seemed by comparison disappointingly cliché-ridden. Perhaps the aptest comment on Selvon's work is that of his fellow West Indian novelist V. S. Naipaul: "Mr. Selvon is a natural writer, at times careless, at times awkward, but never dull. In lyrical mood he is unique. . . . Mr. Selvon's gifts may not be important, but they are precious."

PRINCIPAL WORKS: A Brighter Sun, 1952; An Island Is a World, 1955; The Lonely Londoners, 1956; Ways of Sunlight, 1958; Turn Again Tiger, 1958; I Hear Thunder, 1963; The Housing Lark, 1965; The Plains of Caroni, 1970; Those Who Eat the Cascadura, 1972.

ABOUT: James, L. (ed.) The Islands in Between, 1968; Vinson, J. (ed.) Contemporary Novelists, 1973; Who's Who, 1973. *Periodicals*—Atlantic March 1953; Book Week September 29, 1963; New Statesman March 15, 1958; December 6, 1958; New Yorker February 14, 1953; January 18, 1958; Spectator December 14, 1956; Time January 19, 1953; Times Literary Supplement April 26, 1963; April 1, 1965; February 11, 1972.

SENGHOR, LÉOPOLD SÉDAR (October 9, 1906–), poet, essayist, and President of Senegal, was born of the Serere people in Joal, on the Atlantic coast of Senegal, then a French possession. His father, a successful planter and exporter of ground nuts, supported a family of some twenty children. Senghor, educated at a Roman Catholic mission school in Joal, is a devout Catholic and at first intended to enter the priesthood. He studied for four years at a seminary in Dakar, but was advised that he lacked a religious vocation. He became a brilliant pupil at the *lycée* in Dakar, and in 1928 went with a scholarship to continue his studies in Paris, at the Lycée Louis-le-Grand and then at the École Normale Supérieure of the University of Paris, where he read French literature, classics, and grammar, and was soon recognized as one of the ablest students of his day. Senghor received his *agrégation* in 1934, and was the first West African to do so. In 1935 he joined the faculty of the *lycée* at Tours.

During his years in Paris, meanwhile, Senghor had met many African and West Indian artists and writers, notably the Martinique poet Aimé Césaire and the Guiana poet Léon Damas. With them he had launched the influential review *L'Étudiant noir* to express the concept of *négritude*, of which Senghor was the principal theoretician and spokesman.

At that time the anthropologists were rediscovering the ancient cultural richness of Africa. Inspired by these discoveries, by the Caribbean *negrismo* movement, and by their own nostalgia for home, the founders of *négritude* proclaimed the *Weltanschauung* of Blackness. Where earlier African intellectuals had denounced as bigotry suggestions that there was any fundamental difference between black men and white, Senghor and his friends insisted on such a difference and exalted it.

The black man, Senghor said, apprehended the universe not intellectually but intuitively, emotionally, naturally. He was a "pure sensorial field," at one with the vital forces of the universe—unlike the white man, a sterile, alien creature, forced to rely on intellect because he lacked understanding. Senghor suggested that all natural rhythms, from the beating of the heart to the turning of the seasons, are part of a great cosmic harmony to which the black man is instinctively attuned.

At the beginning of World War II Senghor served in a French infantry battalion made up of troops from the colonies. With the French surrender in 1940 he was interned by the Germans in a succession of prison camps, but released in 1942 to resume his teaching career at the Lycée Marcelin-Berthelot near Paris. Thereafter he took an active part in the French Resistance.

Senghor had begun to write verse in 1938, but it was not until 1945 that he was able to publish his first book, *Chants d'ombre* (Songs of Shadow). His themes were those of *négritude*: nostalgia for Africa and idealization of the African past, the guiding presence of the dead, the destruction of African culture and the black man's suffering under colonialism, the beauty and dignity of the peoples of Africa: "Mother, in this study lined with Latin and Greek, breathe the fumes of the evening victims of my heart. / May the protecting spirits save my blood from slackening like that of the assimilated and the civilized! / Though I come late, I stand upright before the Ancestors and offer one chicken without stain, so that before the milk and millet beer / May spurt upon me and my fleshy lips the warm salt blood of a bull in the prime of life, in the splendor of his fatness!"

"From the outset," says Gerald Moore, "Senghor created his own distinctive music in French poetry." Critics have found in this music the majestic lyricism of Pindar, and a Gallic concern for balance and harmony, infused with the intimacy of an African folksong. Its aristocratic tone has reminded some readers of St.-John Perse, and Lilyan Kesteloot traces to the influence of the Bible and of Claudel what she calls Senghor's "processional style." Although he shares with the other poets of *négritude* an insistence on strong verbal rhythms, his rhythms are musical rather than staccato. Moore says that "almost at once we find him creating, through use of the long line, that rolling, deep-breathed sound which distinguishes all his verse."

Paris was delighted by the intellectual subtlety of *Chants d'ombre*, its surrealist flights of imagery, and its deliberate and sometimes pedantic creation of neologisms, fusing classical etymologies with

Serere or Wolof words. The book established Senghor at once both as a poet and as a spokesman for the aspirations of his people. He was a member of the French Constituent Assemblies of 1945 and 1946 as a Deputy for Senegal, and in 1946 was elected to both the French National Assembly and the General Council of Senegal. He has also served the French government as a grammarian and linguistic expert. In 1948 Senghor accepted a professorship at the École Nationale de la France d'Outre Mer in Paris. The same year he published his second book, *Hosties noires* (Black Sacrifices), and his extremely important and influential anthology *Anthologie de la nouvelle poésie nègre et malgache*.

Senghor, who calls himself a "cultural mulatto," has always been torn between his devotion to Africa and his love for Western culture. This became increasingly apparent in the poems collected in *Chants pour Naëtt* (Songs for Naëtt, 1949) and *Éthiopiques* (1956), in which, as Moore says, he swings violently "between the poles of *négritude* and assimilation," or seeks a reconciliation between the two. These two books show an extraordinary versatility, ranging from the powerful hymn to Harlem in "New York" to an epic about the Zulu king Chaka, from the driving lyricism of the love poems to the wistful sweetness of the "Princesse de Belfort": "I don't know when it was, I always confuse childhood with Eden / As I mix up Death and Life—a bridge of kindness joins them. . . ."

In 1955–1956 Senghor served in the French government, and over the next few years he led Senegal peacefully to independence. He was a principal architect of the short-lived Mali Federation in 1960, and the same year became the first president of the Republic of Senegal. His insistence on maintaining close ties with France has not pleased more nationalistic African leaders in Senegal and elsewhere. In 1968 there was student unrest at the University of Dakar, which Senghor had done so much to establish, and later the same year he was the subject of hostile demonstrations in Frankfurt, where he went to receive the 1968 Peace Prize of the German Book Trade.

Chaka in Senghor's poem accepts power for the sake of his people, sacrificing his own capacity for personal creativity. Something of the same sort has happened to Senghor, who has published only one unexceptional volume of poetry, *Nocturnes* (1961), since he became president. Instead, in essays on African culture, African socialism, and African metaphysics, he has attempted to clarify his views on *négritude*. He has modified the extreme and mystical attitudes of earlier days, and adopted a more intellectual position, based on historical and cultural arguments. Senghor has come to regard *négritude* as meaning something like "the sum total of all the cultural values of Africa" and to see in it a yeast which will reactivate the exhausted cultural values of Europe, just as Africa must assimilate "the fecundating elements of the modern way of life." In fact there are signs that *négritude* as a literary movement is dead, though its contribution to the dialectics of the Black Power movement is obvious.

LÉOPOLD SÉDAR SENGHOR

Senghor has two sons by his first marriage to the daughter of Félix Eboué, the famous black governor of French Equatorial Africa, and a son by his 1957 marriage to Colette Hubert, who had been his first wife's secretary. Gerald Moore says that younger black writers "may still stick the label 'Frenchified' across the works of this African who loves Paris, who has let the heritage of France flood his being, who has taken a French wife and embraced the Catholic faith," but Senghor "has left a monument" to the problems of his own generation of African writers "which cannot be ignored. . . . He has created a new music and expressed within it a new dilemma, a whole life."

PRINCIPAL WORKS IN ENGLISH TRANSLATION: Nationhood and the African Road to Socialism (essays), 1961; On African Socialism (essays), 1964; Selected Poems (ed. by J. Reed and C. Wake), 1964; Prose and Poetry (ed. by J. Reed and C. Wake), 1965; Nocturnes (tr. by J. Reed and C. Wake), 1972. *Poems in* Beier, U. and Moore, G. (eds.) Modern Poetry from Africa, 1963. *Prose selections in* Dathorne, O. R. and Feuser, W. (eds.) Africa in Prose, 1969.

ABOUT: Beier, U. (ed.) Introduction to African Literature, 1967; Current Biography, 1962; Guibert, A. Léopold Sédar Senghor, 1962; Hymans, J. L. Léopold Sédar Senghor: An Intellectual Biography, 1972; International Who's Who, 1973–74; Italiaander, R. New Leaders of Africa, 1961; Kesteloot, L. Les Écrivains noirs de langue française, 1963; Markovitz, I. L. Léopold Sédar Senghor and the Politics of Négritude, 1969; Melady, T. P. Profiles of African Leaders, 1961; Melone, T. De la négritude dans la littérature négro-africaine, 1962; Mezu, S. O. The Poetry of L. S. Senghor, 1973; Moore, G. Seven African Writers, 1962; Reed, J. and Wake, C. *introduction to* Selected Poems, 1964; Sartre, J.-P. Black Orpheus, 1963; Segal, R. Political Africa, 1961; Van Niekerk, B. van D. The African Image (Négritude) in the Work of Léopold Sédar Senghor, 1970; Wauthier, C. The Literature and Thought of Modern Africa, 1966; Who's Who in America, 1972–1973; Who's Who in France, 1973–1974. *Periodicals*—Comparative Literature Studies Fall 1963; Guardian July 8, 1972.

SEPHERIADES, GEORGIOS STYLIANOU. *See* "SEFERIS, GEORGE"

SETON-WATSON, (GEORGE) HUGH (NICHOLAS) (February 15, 1916–), English historian, has taken up and extended the task begun by his late father, Professor Robert Seton-Watson, who pioneered central European and Balkan studies in Britain. Because of this connection, his concern for and familiarity with the peoples of Eastern Europe go back to his childhood, and his travels in their countries, together with his formal studies at Winchester and New College, Oxford, have given him an unexcelled understanding of the region's culture and politics, and proficiency in at least a dozen of its languages. "My greatest debt is to my father," he says, "and it cannot be adequately expressed."

In 1940–1941, after he left Oxford, Seton-Watson was attached to the British legations in Rumania and Yugoslavia. He spent the rest of the war with GHQ Special Forces in the Middle East. In 1946 he was appointed fellow and praelector in politics at University College, Oxford. There he remained until 1951, when he went to his present post as professor of Russian History at London University's School of Slavonic and East European Studies.

His first book, which appeared in 1945, was *Eastern Europe Between the Wars, 1918–1941.* Seton-Watson here treats the six countries of East Europe as a single complex, defined by its poverty and its predominantly peasant population, by the instability and violence of its politics, and by the struggle of the great powers to possess it. His account of political developments during the twenty years of independence and his discussion of the peasant problem were particularly admired, and called "really new and . . . of great importance." The *Times Literary Supplement* commended the book for its breadth, freshness, insight, and especially for its courage: "the author speaks without fear or favour, and does not mince words." A. J. P. Taylor praised it in almost exactly the same terms, saying that Hugh Seton-Watson had "the virtues of his father" but also "the Seton-Watson failings—a somewhat pedestrian style, an accumulation of details, and, especially, a desire to cover every aspect of the subject." *The East European Revolution,* which followed, is a description and analysis of the sovietization of East Europe which for many critics established the author as the outstanding authority on the satellite countries.

HUGH SETON-WATSON

From the beginning, Seton-Watson had naturally taken account of Russia as the most powerful force in the recent history of his subject. In time he came to find the country intensely interesting for its own sake, and for what it could reveal about "the impact of western ideas and western economy on a backward social and political structure." This is evident in a number of books of which the first, published in 1952, was *The Decline of Imperial Russia, 1855–1914.* It contains "a wealth of authentic data, painstakingly collected and lucidly presented," though some critics thought it suffered from the author's inevitable lack of contact with Russia, and was "informative rather than illuminating."

The Pattern of Communist Revolution, the major work which followed in 1953, was published in America as *From Lenin to Malenkov,* revised in 1960 as *From Lenin to Khrushchev,* and judiciously abridged and popularized in 1961 as *The New Imperialism.* It is a history of the Communist movement as it has manifested itself in Europe, Asia, the Orient, Africa, Latin America, and indeed in almost every part of the world. Bertram D. Wolfe called it "a work of the first rank on the history of our time, useful to the statesman, illuminating to the specialist, informative to the general reader and a pleasure to review." Other reviewers characterized it as "a fascinating and exhausting roller-coaster ride," and as "a dizzying bird's-eye view of communist history." There was universal admiration for Seton-Watson's wide-ranging curiosity, his powers of absorption, talent for condensation, and rare industry. Even his prose style, which in the past had seemed merely serviceable, was by now earning praise for its ease and fluency. Only a certain lack of vision prevented this indispensable book from being a great one.

Rather similar reactions have greeted Seton-Watson's subsequent books, of which the most important are *Neither War nor Peace*, "an enormously useful survey" of world politics since the end of World War II, which was thought "likely to be accepted as the standard introduction to contemporary history," and *The Russian Empire, 1801–1917*, a volume in the Oxford History of Europe which was described as "the most complete, up-to-date, and authoritative history of the last century of Imperial Russia." This "paragon of a textbook" nevertheless dismayed some readers because it stopped short of what they regarded as its natural climax, the 1917 Bolshevik Revolution. As a result, wrote one critic, "what should have been a work of historical imagination" ends as "an encyclopedic compilation of knowledge."

It is this persistent shortage of vision and imagination, this failure to distinguish "the pattern, the general shape underlying [the] cornucopia of events," which disappoints those critics who believe that Seton-Watson has "the makings of a great scholar." Many others are content with the cornucopia, and grateful that he has brought the talents of "a modern Encyclopaedist" to a field which so greatly needs them.

Seton-Watson, who lives in Wimbledon, London, is married to the former Mary Hope Rokeling, and has three daughters. He is a Fellow of the British Academy. He taught at Columbia University in 1957–1958, was a visiting fellow of the Center for Advanced Study in the Behavioral Sciences at Stanford, California, in 1963–1964, and a visiting fellow at the Australian National University in 1964. Apart from travel, his main hobby is ornithology.

PRINCIPAL WORKS: Eastern Europe Between the Wars, 1918–1941, 1945; East European Revolution, 1950; The Decline of Imperial Russia, 1855–1914, 1952; The Pattern of Communist Revolution: A Historical Analysis, 1953 (U.S., From Lenin to Malenkov; revised as From Lenin to Khrushchev, 1960; Neither War nor Peace: The Struggle for Power in the Postwar World, 1960; The New Imperialism, 1961; Nationalism and Communism: Essays, 1946–1963, 1964; The Russian Empire, 1801–1917, 1967.

ABOUT: Namier, L. B. Facing East, 1948; Who's Who, 1973. *Periodicals*—Spectator April 29, 1960; Times Literary Supplement July 21, 1945; May 20, 1960; July 13, 1967; U.S. News October 24, 1960; October 30, 1961.

MARY LEE SETTLE

SETTLE, MARY LEE (July 29, 1918–), American novelist and memoirist, was born in Charleston, West Virginia, the daughter of Joseph Edward Settle, a civil engineer, and Rachel Tompkins Settle. She is of English and Scottish descent on both sides of her family. Miss Settle grew up in West Virginia and in Kentucky, and was educated at Charleston High School and Sweet Briar College. She left Sweet Briar without a degree but convinced, rather against her will, that she must write.

In 1942, this shy and idealistic young woman crossed the Atlantic to England at the height of the U-boat war and enlisted in the Women's Auxiliary Air Force. She endured xenophobia, abominable food, lesbian officers, sadistic sergeants, and every kind of humiliation to become a radio operator, and was eventually invalided out with "signals shock." Thereafter she made a contribution to the war effort of a different kind, writing articles for the Office of War Information.

After the war, Miss Settle chose to remain in England, which was her home for a total of fourteen years. She married Douglas Newton, an English poet and journalist, did editorial work for *Harper's Bazaar*, became British correspondent to *Flair*, wrote a film script, and in 1954 published her first novel, *The Love Eaters*. It investigates the emotional and professional tensions set up when a crippled and embittered professional director is hired to train an amateur theatrical group in an Allegheny coal town. Reviewers found in it a "raw and searching" talent for social analysis which reminded one of them of Rosamund Lehmann, another of John O'Hara; the book was praised for its sense of life, its "wholesome acids," and its underlying compassion. Her second novel, *The Kiss of Kin*, was no less well received; Walter Allen was one of those impressed by "the sharpness of her focus, her economy of means, her precision of language."

The three novels which followed form a trilogy about the settlement of West Virginia, and illustrate Miss Settle's conviction that "it is not . . . what actually happens in any given period, but what the people believe at the time it is happening, which influences the future as handed down opinions, colorings, prejudices, and habits." The trilogy began with *O Beulah Land*, the product of three years' research at the British Museum. It tells the story of Jonathan Lacey's expedition to claim and clear his bounty land and in this way reveals the social, political, and economic background of the settlers' struggle between 1754 and 1774. Reviewers were sharply divided: some thought it sugarcoated popular history, superficial in its characterization; others called it a work of art and of scholarship. Carl Carmer ranked it "far above the formula-ridden and sensational historical novels that have misinterpreted American history in recent years." Isabel Quigly found herself impressed less by the book than by its author: "one of those writers one comes across once in a very long while whose quality of mind strikes one with quite disconcerting force."

Know Nothing, focusing on West Virginia just before the Civil War, had a generally friendly reception, and Olivia Manning wrote that it conveys "with economy and subtlety the politics, fears, snobberies and scandals of daily life. An era is revealed to us." The Beulah trilogy was completed by *Fight Night on a Sweet Saturday*. It seeks, some reviewers felt, to show how West Virginia's past impinges on its present, but fails, retracing "too many well-trod paths of the Southern novel."

All the Brave Promises, Miss Settle's account of her experiences in the WAAF, appeared in 1967 and was richly praised. One English reviewer called her "a writer of powerful sensitivity," some of whose "traumatic passages read like Dostoevsky's *The House of the Dead*"; another, praising her "insight and compassion," her "taut, poetic prose style," was reminded of T. E. Lawrence's *The Mint*, and went on: "It is little or no exaggeration to place her recollections of service life on the same level as Lawrence's." There was a favorable critical response also for *The Clam Shell*, in which four alumnae of a smart East Coast college meet thirty years after graduation for a rather tense reunion, and the narrator recalls her painful first year at college. *Prisons*, a novel dealing with the long struggle for freedom of conscience and speech, is set in Cromwell's England but was found highly relevant to Nixon's America.

Mary Lee Settle is five feet eight inches tall, and has brown hair and eyes. She is a Democrat and Episcopalian. She and her husband are divorced, and in recent years she has lived in the United States. In 1957 she received a Guggenheim Fellowship. She enjoys hunting, historical research, and hymn singing.

PRINCIPAL WORKS: The Love Eaters, 1954; The Kiss of Kin, 1955; O Beulah Land, 1956; Know Nothing, 1960; Fight Night on a Sweet Saturday, 1964; All the Brave Promises: Memories of Aircraft Woman 2d Class 2146391, 1967; The Clam Shell, 1971; Prisons, 1973.
ABOUT: Current Biography 1959; Settle, M. L. All the Brave Promises, 1967. *Periodicals*—Mademoiselle January 1955.

SEWELL, (MARGARET) ELIZABETH (March 9, 1919–), English poet, critic, and novelist, writes: "I was born in India, and in those days of tottery but still extant empire, that was just part of the sheer Englishness of my background. My family on both sides, professional, middle-class, have been rooted in the southern counties for generations, and though I have exchanged their traditional conservative politics for something much more left wing, their seemly adherence to Anglicanism for what they would have called 'Rome,' and mean shortly to exchange my citizenship for American, I see this as a kind of inverted tribute to the solidity and confidence they knew how to pass on. Like all such families we moved all the time, and were continually split up, father in India, two children (I have one older sister) at school in England, mother dividing her years between the two. The disadvantages are obvious. The advantages were that one gained from the start a sense of the world, and knowledge of and real affection for people very unlike oneself.

"Words, as soon as I apprehended them at all, I recognized as mysterious friends, to be treasured and added to wherever possible. Poems produced the same effect if they were of the right kind, no children's verses so-called but the strong full-imaged ones, 'Tyger, tyger' or 'The Golden Road to Samarkand.' I began writing poetry when I was six, with the placid conviction that this was clearly My Job. I was no Minou Drouet—the productions, which my mother touchingly preserved, are very childish and very funny. I tried my hand at stories too. All through my schooldays in England, which were clouded by ill health on my part, my mother's early death, and constant changes of school, I went on obstinately writing. I began an autobiography at fourteen, and was chagrined to find my material ran out after two chapters; wrote a long poem on a mythological subject at sixteen, remarkable only because I completed it; started my first novel at eighteen, which also, did not get far. All my elders counselled, on grounds of prudence, against any thoughts of becoming a professional writer, so I drifted towards an academic career and went up to Cambridge, Newnham College, to read Modern Languages, French and German, just as the war began.

"Here bit by bit I abandoned any imaginative writing, under the pressure of a high-powered educational system concerned solely with the analytical and critical. It took the three subsequent years, which I spent on 'National Service' in London as a very junior Civil Servant in the Ministry of Education, to thaw me out again, and by the time I returned to Cambridge in 1945 to start work on a Ph.D. I had already begun my first published novel, *The Dividing of Time*, which as if to make up for lost time is very imaginative, not to say fantastical, indeed. During this renewed sojourn at the university I discovered the type of academic work I wanted to do, speculative and imagining rather than severely scholarly; discovered simultaneously that such work was not admissible in that intellectual atmosphere. So I decided to go to the United States for a year, in the hope that universities there might offer more scope and freedom. (They did.)

"Since then, 1949, my life has taken on the pattern of one year spent in America, teaching English, then one year in England, writing. My second and third novels and three of my critical books, which are essentially about poetry as is everything I do, were written in this way. I am changing the pattern this year, 1966, when I move permanently to America, though I anticipate going to and fro across the Atlantic as frequently as ever. By now my life—which is enormously enriched by the extraordinary variety of teaching jobs available across a whole continent—and my writings—which for the last few years I find American publishers will bring out and English publishers won't—are gloriously and organically entangled. This makes the shape of both, in the future, pretty unpredictable, and I like it that way."

The narrator in Miss Sewell's first book, *The Dividing of Time*, is a young woman who lives virtually in two dimensions—in one performing her drab duties as a junior civil servant, in the other pursuing love and beauty. The novel was welcomed as the work of a promising and highly original writer "who has the gift of many children of mixing dreams with reality . . . and of giving an aura of wonder, magic and mystery to everyday experiences."

The Structure of Poetry, which followed, was Miss Sewell's Ph.D. thesis. Her "inquiry," based on certain of the works of Rimbaud, Mallarmé, and Valéry (of whom she published a standard study in 1952), attempted to answer the question:

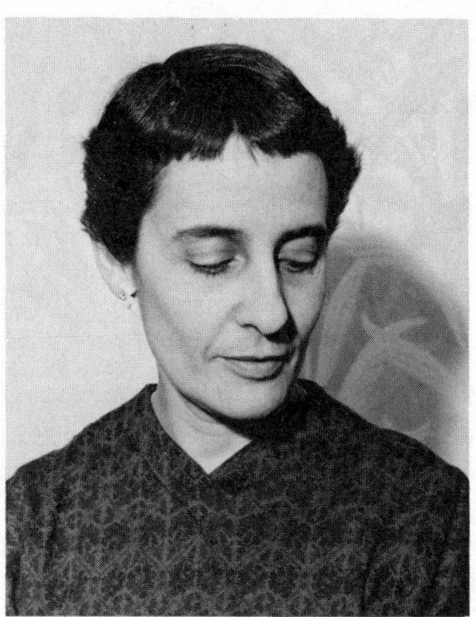

ELIZABETH SEWELL

"What makes language into poetry?" Her conclusion was that poetry's "fair and proper place" is "down the middle line of language and experience": poets try in their poems to achieve equilibrium by opposing extremes—chiefly number and dream, laughter and religion. This learned book in certain ways anticipated the concerns of French critics of the 1960s such as Roland Barthes; Miss Sewell's special concern with nonsense worlds, however, has remained her own province.

This province is surveyed in the best known of her books, *The Field of Nonsense*, whose theme is summed up in the poem she wrote as its preface: "For in my pocket I have that ancient pack, / (Father and Emperor and Pope) / And dance for ever on Babylon's plain, / In tight star-figures, shuffling the cards of speech / In a mountebank brain, / Fearing demoniac powers, / But in celestial hope / To wind God back into the dance again." In these lines we find that fascinating combination of Roman Catholic piety, obsession with mathematics and nonsense, and sheer whimsicality which characterizes Miss Sewell's work. "Nonsense," she writes, "is not merely the denial of sense, a random reversal of ordinary experience and an escape from the limitations of everyday life into a haphazard infinity, but is on the contrary a carefully limited world, controlled and dictated by reason, a construction subject to its own laws." She finds support for her argument in the work of Lewis Carroll, Eliot, Chesterton, and Ludwig Wittgenstein, and, like Chesterton, thinks of nonsense as essentially a good gift of God's, to help to bring His people nearer to Him. There was some feeling that her treatment of nonsense verse was too selective but her "thoughtful and stimulating" book remains in print and in demand.

Miss Sewell believes that "for the last four hundred years . . . poetry has been struggling to evolve and perfect the inclusive mythology on which language works and all thought in words is carried on." She argues that "this type of thinking is the only adequate instrument for thinking about change, process, organisms, and life." *The Orphic Voice* then is "an exploration of the biological function of poetry in the natural history of mankind as symbolized by the myth of Orpheus." Some of the author's poems, related to this theme, are appended. In the opinion of many critics, this difficult and very uneven work "never gets to grips with just what use science is supposed to make of poetry," but for some the book transcends its flaws. Raymond Williams called it "an extraordinary risk" but a valuable one. George Steiner found its erudition "pixyish" as well as formidable, and conceded that "on the rim of [its] argument flash the unsteady marsh lights of mysticism." But, "as one lays down the book, the intricate argument and the evidence offered by Miss Sewell's own poems, begin resounding inside one like remembered music. It is a great work."

For the most part, Miss Sewell's poems and novels have so far been most valuable as illustrations of her theories; but there is always present the promise of powerful and startling revelations to come. In certain passages imagination suddenly usurps invention altogether, and these passages are memorable.

PRINCIPAL WORKS: *Criticism*—The Structure of Poetry 1951; The Field of Nonsense, 1952; Paul Valéry, 1952; The Orphic Voice, 1960; The Human Metaphor, 1964. *Poetry*—Poems, 1947-1961, 1962; Signs and Cities, 1968. *Fiction*—The Dividing of Time, 1951; The Singular Hope, 1955; Now Bless Thyself, 1962.

ABOUT: *Periodicals*—Guardian February 10, 1961; Nation February 4, 1961; Times Literary Supplement October 17, 1952; April 29, 1955; Yale Review March 1961.

SEXTON, ANNE (November 9, 1928–), American poet, writes: "I was born in Newton, Massachusetts, and have spent most of my life on the coast of Maine in the summer or wintering in Wellesley, Newton and Weston—all suburban towns west of Boston. My ancestor, William Brewster, came to America on the Mayflower and sounds like a decent sort of man from what I read of him. My family tree goes back, I have lately found, to assortments of royalty such as William the Conqueror, King Edward III, II, I, King Philip IV of France, King Ferdinand of Spain, etc. The list amuses me most when I find such notes in the family genealogy as: *Edward III, founded the Knights of the Garter. Married Philippa of Hainault, his mistress, age fifteen.* Mistress of fifteen! Ah, those were the days! Such wisps of information about my lineage make me smile in light of my own puritanical and stifled upbringing.

"I was the third and last daughter. As a young child I was locked in my room until the age of five. After that, at school, I did not understand the people who were my size or even the larger ones. At home, or away from it, people seemed out of reach. Thus I hid in fairy tales and read them daily like a prayerbook. Any book was closer than a person. I did not even like my dolls for they resembled people. I stepped on their faces because they resembled me. I think I would have preferred to exist only in a fairy tale where people could change reality the way an actor changes his costume. In total, I can say that I learned nothing in any school that I attended and see no point in mentioning places where my body sat at a desk and my soul was elsewhere. I wrote some poems in high school but stopped when my mother suggested that I had plagiarized them. My mother was brilliant and vital. Her friends thought of her as a writer although it was only her father, A. G. Staples, who was a small town Maine newspaper editor. Nevertheless, my mother was considered to be a genius. One thought, in meeting her, that she had written all the first editions in her own library. Of course, I was unbearable, unhappy and unreachable, and as soon as possible, I became boy-crazy. In fact, I eloped at nineteen with Alfred M. Sexton. As a matter of interest I am still married to him. I have found this somewhat unusual among writers in general. Fairy tales we all have in common—but one marriage, seldom.

"After I was married I worked as a salesgirl, a fashion model, and a librarian. We lived on a farm in upstate New York, an apartment in Cochituate, Massachusetts (between a pig farm and a chicken farm). Later, when my husband went into the Navy (Korean conflict) we lived in Baltimore and San Francisco. In 1954 he got out of the Navy and we settled in our first home in Newton and had our first child, Linda, and two years later a second, Joy. A few months after Joy's birth I had a severe nervous breakdown (as they are called) and as I came out of it (and if I ever really came out of it) I started to write poems.

"In 1958 I started to write constantly and then to publish in such magazines as *Harper's*, the *New Yorker*, the *Hudson Review*, *Partisan Review*, etc. I was often told that my poetry was too personal, too private. But the art, though it be suicide or murder, chooses you. I let it do this and then I let it continue its path, deeper and deeper. One might call that *style*. I think of it as a no-other-choice project. I can't give my poems someone's face-lifting job. Further, I won't. I've even stopped trying. The critics be damned. I just let the poems alone. No. Not that I don't rework. Some poems take years and hundreds of rewrites before they have their own sound, own face. I remember the long days, years, of learning to write and that the thing I had to fight most for was this certain style. For praise or damnation, the poem must be itself. At best, one hopes to make something new, a kind of original product. Otherwise, why bother to hope, to make? And my newest poems are even more personal. They usually come from a part of me that I don't know, haven't met and won't understand for a couple of years. They know things I don't know myself.

"After publication of my first book of poems I was appointed a Scholar at the Radcliffe Institute for Independent Study for 1961–1963. This brought me in touch with other artists and scholars as well as an informal class of poetry that I taught to Radcliffe and Harvard students. My second book of poems was published soon after this period. Some of the painters and sculptors that I met at Radcliffe have influenced my work in hidden ways. After that time I was awarded the first Traveling Fellowship of the American Academy of Arts and Letters —1963–1964. This opened me up even more. I am something of a tin can—being opened up all the time. I drove and walked throughout Europe and fell in love with Italy, particularly its coastal fishing villages. In 1964–1965 I was awarded a grant from the Ford Foundation to be in residence with a theatre in Boston. Of course I wrote a play and learned lots about the theatre and about loving actors and was, again, opened up—tin can me!

"In 1965 Oxford University Press in London brought out my *Selected Poems* in the UK and I was, at that time, elected a Fellow of the Royal Society of Literature in London. So maybe I've come some sort of circle, back again to something a little royal like my Edward III and his mistress (age fifteen!) But perhaps it's all a fairy tale and I'm still locked in my room. I can only speak, from my room, my typewriter, to say I am just completing a third book of poems, waiting for someone to produce my play, to either kill it or bring it forth, and am trying myself on a little prose. But poetry is my love, my postmark, my hands, my kitchen, my face."

Richard Howard has written of Anne Sexton that "she has reported more than anyone else—anyone else who has set out to write poems—has ever cared or dared, and thereby she has gained, perhaps at the expense of her poetry, a kind of sacerdotal stature, the elevation of a priestess celebrating mysteries which are no less mysterious for having been conducted in all the hard glare of the marketplace and with all the explicitness mere print can afford." As a poet of intimate personal experience, she is the heir of Robert Lowell and of

ANNE SEXTON

W. D. Snodgrass, to whom she acknowledges a specific debt. "If anything influenced me," she told an interviewer in 1965, "it was W. D. Snodgrass' 'Heart's Needle.' I had written about half of my first book when I read the poem and it moved me to such an extent—it's about a child, and he has to give up his child which seems to be one of my themes, and I didn't have my own daughter at the time—that I ran up to my mother-in-law's where she was living and got her back. . . . At the time everyone said 'You can't write this way. It's too personal; it's confessional; you can't write this, Anne,' and everyone was discouraging me. But then I saw Snodgrass doing what I was doing, and it kind of gave me permission."

To Bedlam and Part Way Back (1960), her first book, "threw a startling light over the poetic horizon." It is the record of her recovery from a nervous breakdown. The poems, says Howard, "begin right there in Bedlam, unacclimated, unexplained, and take shape, apparently, as a therapeutic project. . . . Only gradually are we given a hint of the circumstances that brought her there, circumstances it will be Sexton's life work to adumbrate." These circumstances include her relationship with her mother, her own attempts at suicide, her estrangement from her daughter: "I, who was never quite sure / about being a girl, needed another / life, another image to remind me./ And this was my worst guilt; you could not cure / nor soothe it. I made you to find me." Melvin Maddocks found in this book "the personal urgency of a first novel. It is full of the exact flavors of places and people remembered, familiar patterns of life recalled and painstakingly puzzled over. . . . A reader finally judges Mrs. Sexton's success by the extraordinary sense of first-hand experience he too has been enabled to feel."

Anne Sexton has said that, for her, poetry "should be a shock to the sense. It should almost hurt"; and an epigraph to her second collection, *All My Pretty Ones* (1962), quotes a line from one of Kafka's letters: "A book should serve as the ax for the frozen sea within us." So she spares herself, and her reader, nothing: she writes of abortion, surgery ("The Operation"), of "Menstruation at Forty," of "Wanting to Die." For some critics, the shock has proved too much, and James Dickey dismissed *All My Pretty Ones* as "terribly serious and determinedly outspoken soap-opera." Others praised "a greater breadth of style and mood, a diversity of imagination, which in the end gives [the book] a stronger unity" than its predecessor.

Her next collection, *Live or Die* (1966), brought her the Pulitzer Prize in 1967 and a secure position "as one of the fine voices of the new candor." However it seemed to some critics that many of the frank lyrics in *Love Poems*, which followed in 1969, were less love poems than sex poems—"The trouble is," wrote Victor Howes, "that it isn't possible to develop much interest in lovers for whom love is only skin deep."

Anne Sexton is less explicitly concerned with social criticism than Lowell or Sylvia Plath, the contemporary poet whom she most resembles in her mixture of savage mockery and childlike vulnerability. As M. L. Rosenthal says, the high points of her poems "are not the magnificent fusion of private and universal motifs, but piercing, isolated strains of music and finely compassionate impressions of pitiful life." Nor is her work anything like as formal as Lowell's; as C. B. Cox and A. R. Jones noted in *Critical Quarterly*, "She tries to break down the distance between herself and her reader by working in something like a lyric form. In her most powerful poems the romantic *cri du cœur* becomes an hysterical scream. In her later, calmer poems, she achieves a precarious kind of tranquillity in the face of overwhelming conflict and torment." A recurring criticism is that her collections include too much inferior work, and she freely concedes that "there is some very bad writing in some of my best poems, and yet those flaws seem to me to make them even better. A little more honest in their own kind of silly way." Thus Richard Howard sees her career as an artist as "an excruciating trajectory of self-destruction, so that it is by her failures in her own enterprises that she succeeds, and by her own successes as an artist that she fails herself."

Transformations (1971) is something rather different—a volume of poems retelling, in terms of the blackest and most unillusioned post-Freudian comedy, seventeen of the familiar fairy tales of the Brothers Grimm (including the story of "Snow White, the dumb bunny," and the one about Cinderella and her Prince, who live for ever after "like two dolls in a museum case / . . . their darling smiles pasted on for eternity. / Regular Bobbsey Twins."

The play she mentions above, written in 1964, was staged five years later at the American Place Theatre as *Mercy Street*. It is about a young woman who has been separated from her baby while she is in a mental hospital (as Anne Sexton was). She goes to Holy Communion, hoping for absolution and peace, but is tormented by memories and fantasies and in the end is scrabbling for the overdose of sleeping pills she has sewn into her coat. The play was respectfully received by most critics and praised by Walter Kerr for its "intensely graphic" imagery, but was generally felt to be a series of striking fragments that failed to come together into a dramatic whole. Mrs. Sexton has also written several children's books in collaboration with the poet Maxine Kumin.

Anne Sexton is the daughter of Ralph Churchill Harvey, a salesman, and the former Mary Gray Staples. Her husband is an executive of a wool company. She taught at Boston University in 1970–1971, and was Crawshaw Professor of Literature at Colgate University in 1972. She holds several honorary degrees.

PRINCIPAL WORKS: *Poetry*—To Bedlam and Part Way Back, 1960; All My Pretty Ones, 1962; Selected Poems, 1964; Live or Die, 1966; Poems by Thomas Kinsella, Douglas Livingstone and Anne Sexton, 1968; Love Poems, 1969; Transformations, 1971; The Book of Folly, 1972.
ABOUT: Contemporary Authors 4, 1963 (revised 1967); Howard, R. Alone With America, 1969; Newman, C. H. The Art of Sylvia Plath, 1970; Rosenthal, M. L. The New Poets, 1967; Who's Who in America, 1972–1973. *Periodicals*—America May 13, 1967; December 20, 1969; Atlantic November 1962; Christian Science Monitor September 1, 1960; Critical Quarterly Summer 1964, Spring 1965; Epoch Fall 1960, Fall 1962; Harper's September 1963; Hudson Review Winter 1965–1966; London Magazine March 1964; Nation February 23, 1963; New Republic May 13, 1967; November 22, 1969; December 20, 1969; New York Herald Tribune Book Review April 28, 1963; New York Herald Tribune Lively Arts December 11, 1960; New Yorker April 27, 1963; Poetry February 1961, March 1963, May 1967, March 1970; Reporter January 3, 1963; Saturday Review December 31, 1966; Sewanee Review Summer 1963; Times (London) March 11, 1965.

SHADBOLT, MAURICE (FRANCIS RICHARD) (June 4, 1932–), New Zealand novelist and short story writer, writes: "I was born in Auckland, New Zealand, not long after the rioting unemployed of the depression had half-wrecked the heart of that city. On my father's side my family goes back to the pioneering 1840s of New Zealand, and on my mother's side to at least the 1850s; the latest of my ancestors to arrive in this country was an Irish first mate who left his ship here at the beginning of this century. As a result, I possibly take my country much more for granted than other New Zealanders—an unsettled, restless and rather wandering tribe—and it has never struck me that I could comfortably make my home elsewhere in the world. But the pioneer fire and fervour of my family had almost burnt out by the time I was born. My parents were briefly involved in the political agitation of the 1930s, before and after the Labour Government of 1935 made this country a welfare state, and my early childhood resembled something out of Steinbeck's *Grapes of Wrath*.

"Later we settled in the central North Island, in a muddy and dusty small town, where my most formative years were spent. In mid-adolescence I was taken back to the city—to Auckland—where I finished high school and attempted university. Illness and lack of money ended my education, plus a certain discontent: among other things I felt obliged to make some kind of sense of the political inheritance received from my now apathetic father. The fever for direct political involvement had passed out of my system by the time I was twenty. But the experience was not entirely unrewarding. There were other fevers and discontents, sexual and social, but of a more predictable kind. After a short stint as a journalist on a provincial newspaper, I married at twenty-one, and began scripting and directing documentary films. Though there were a few desultory early sketches, I didn't really begin writing until I was twenty-three—from which age I started publishing, largely in New Zealand magazines and literary journals. At that time I knew no other writers and—apart from Katherine Mansfield—was not even familiar with other New Zealand writing. When I came to read it finally it seemed to me, a certain amount of verse aside, to tell me almost nothing about the New Zealand I knew, the country and society within which I had grown up. At that time the characteristic New Zealand short story was told in a flat and bedraggled Hemingwayesque vernacular; and usually concerned inarticulate blokes named Jack and Jim and Bill. I imagine I began to write, to some degree, in antagonistic reaction. My most rewarding literary friendship was with the New Zealand poet James K. Baxter, who very gently steered me when I most needed help.

"After quitting film work and writing myself half-way round the world to London—via China, Russia, and Eastern and Western Europe as a freelance journalist—the second providential illness in my life, along with a small and unexpected grant of money, gave me time to finish my first collection of short stories. Rather arrogantly called *The New Zealanders*, it was published in England when I was

MAURICE SHADBOLT

twenty-seven, and in the USA and other countries later. A few days after London publication I returned to New Zealand with my wife. And despite certain early ambitions as a film-maker, I seem to have become more steadily committed to literature ever since. Three years away possibly gave me a degree of objectivity about my own small country, which once naturally seemed the centre of the world. Since arriving home in 1960 I have lived in three of its four major cities and in the countryside. Survival as a full-time writer in New Zealand is often ferociously difficult—I have turned to all kinds of hack work and book reviewing, and have worked in a bakehouse to pay off debts. This should not be taken to mean that I feel neglected as a writer and ignored by my fellow countrymen: it is just to say the country is small. My work is read here, as well as outside; and I have received various grants and awards, including one from the New Zealand State Literary Fund and a year on lecturer's salary as Robert Burns Fellow at Otago University.

"I would define myself as a churchless Christian and partyless liberal. In religion I find myself close to the Christian agnosticism of Boris Pasternak, and in politics closest to George Orwell of the essays. As I move toward middle age I find I have less and less patience with other writers and literary theorists; the act of creation becomes more and not less marvellous and mysterious. I now live with my wife and four children by the sea on the bush-clad outskirts of western Auckland city. Though I travel now and then, I have no desire to shift again: an Indian girl I knew in London once read my palm and told me I would die outside my own country. She was probably right, at least metaphorically.

"For as a writer I imagine my fascination with this country—a last frontier for the human race, and a paradise lost—will never cease. By my larger intentions? No more than trying to tell, obliquely or directly, the truth about human beings in a particular time, in a particular place. To bear witness, that is, and perhaps bring some news of reality. If I differ from other writers in emphasis on place, it is very likely because I share some of the uncertainty of New Zealanders as a people, still not quite at home here; and because it seems to me that the brooding and cooling volcanic shapes of these South Pacific islands tend to invest all human endeavour with a certain tragic dignity."

The short stories in *The New Zealanders* and *Summer Fires and Winter Country* successfully and sometimes brilliantly explore the conflict in New Zealand between the primitive and rural, and the urban—between the part of Shadbolt that loves and understands the Maoris, the islands' natural inheritors, and the part of him that reaches out towards Western sophistication. His writing in these stories is vigorous and demonstrates his wide knowledge of New Zealand life, but is not always controlled or careful enough in its avoidance of cliché.

Shadbolt's first novel, *Among the Cinders*, did for the much less sophisticated society of New Zealand what Salinger had done for America in *The Catcher in the Rye*. Nick Flinders, an inarticulate but intelligent teen-ager, is shattered by his part in the accidental death of his Maori friend, Sam. Nick's cantankerous but warmhearted grandfather persuades him to leave home, and their trek through the New Zealand hinterland becomes a journey back into the country's pioneer past which heals Nick's sense of guilt. The style is sometimes brash and careless, but full of zest and vigor, and the story is told with the skill and pace of a natural master of narrative. The novel is remarkable for its evocation of the New Zealand landscape and for the rich and memorable characterization of Grandfather Hubert. It is also interesting as a reflection of the author's attitude towards the intellectual, urban, and contrived aspects of New Zealand life—he satirizes and rejects them, but at the same time feels himself a part of them. One could read this book, taking hints from some of the earlier stories, as well as from Shadbolt's next book, as an allegory of how a bourgeois society stifles the creative imagination—stifles its own vitality.

The Presence of Music collects three short novels, each of which has as its principal character an artist. Shadbolt presents each of these characters from the outside, through a retrospective first-person narration by someone involved with them. In each case, as one critic wrote, the point seems to be "that the artist and the non-artist need each other, if either is to fulfil himself." Most critics praised the freshness and vividness of the writing, but there was a feeling that the threefold repetition of theme and method, and the similarity of the three narrators—all of them identifiable with the author himself—weakened the book's total effect.

With *This Summer's Dolphin* (1969), Shadbolt adopted a symbolist method that reminded many reviewers of the novels of Patrick White. The story is about the mysterious comings and goings, and the eventual murder, of a friendly dolphin. Motu, the dolphin, stands for the powers of good, and is handled just as we might expect such a symbol to be handled by a "churchless Christian." It brings out in the people of the island it visits whatever capacities they have for love, but also activates far less desirable qualities: it is used for commercial and even aggressive purposes. In this pessimistic but lyrical novel Shadbolt certainly comes nearer to producing a more fully realized work than he has before; but the structure is sometimes obtrusive and, as one critic noted, the "style at times echoes White's to the point of unconscious parody."

It was followed by *An Ear of the Dragon*, a novel about an Italian author who spends the last part of his life in New Zealand, and about the New Zealand writer who acts as his literary executor and consoles his widow. The novel draws freely upon *The Full Circle of the Travelling Cuckoo*, a collection of short stories by the late Renato Amato which Shadbolt had edited. Whether the result was to be regarded as fiction, autobiography, or collage greatly exercised its reviewers, and one critic at least refused to review it, finding it "impossible to adopt an ordinary detachment in my critical approach to it."

Strangers and Journeys is another departure from Shadbolt's earlier manner, this time a massive chronicle of New Zealand life from the end of World War I to the present, examined through the interwoven experiences and self-searchings of two men and their sons. It was felt that the influence of Patrick White had still not been entirely assimilated, and the structure was found confusing. "The virtue of the book," wrote one critic, "lies in its portrayal of life in a hard land and its oblique but faithful picture of the land itself. It is an attempt at something big. Even if its reach escapes its grasp, the bigness remains. This is easily Mr. Shadbolt's most considerable work so far."

PRINCIPAL WORKS: *Fiction*—The New Zealanders (short stories), 1959; Summer Fires and Winter Country (short stories), 1963; Among the Cinders, 1965; The Presence of Music, 1967; This Summer's Dolphin, 1969; An Ear of the Dragon, 1971; Strangers and Journeys, 1972. *Non-fiction*—(with Brian Brake) New Zealand: Gift of the

Sea, 1963; (with Olaf Ruhen) Isles of the South Pacific, 1968; The Shell Guide to New Zealand, 1968. *As editor*—The Full Circle of the Travelling Cuckoo (stories by Renato Amato), 1967.

ABOUT: Vinson, J. (ed.) Contemporary Novelists, 1972. *Periodicals*—The Bookman November 1959; The Dominion April 1962; The Otago Daily Times April 13, 1963; The Sunday News (NZ) May 16, 1963; Times Literary Supplement March 23, 1967; June 19, 1969.

***SHAFFER, PETER (LEVIN)** (May 15, 1926–), English dramatist, was born in Liverpool, the son of Jack and Reka (Fredman) Shaffer, Orthodox Jews of the comfortable middle class. In 1935 the family moved to London, where Peter Shaffer and his twin brother Anthony were educated at St. Paul's school. In 1944 they were conscripted for nonmilitary service, spending three years in the coal mines of Kent and Yorkshire. Shaffer resumed his education in 1948 at Cambridge University, to which he had won a scholarship. He did his first writing there, as editor of a university magazine. After his graduation he spent two years in the United States, most of the time in the acquisitions department of the New York Public Library. It was then that he wrote *The Salt Land*, a play that conceived of the birth of modern Israel in terms of classical tragedy.

Returning to England in 1954, Shaffer worked for a time in London, in the publicity department of the music publishers Boosey and Hawkes. He was good at the work but left it in 1955 to write full time, encouraged by the production of *The Salt Land* on television and of another play, *The Prodigal Father*, on the radio. Shaffer had already written two mystery novels in collaboration with his twin (who later wrote the prizewinning play *Sleuth*), and a solo spy thriller, *Balance of Terror*, was produced by BBC television in 1957. In 1956–1957 he worked as literary critic of the magazine *Truth*.

Shaffer's first major success came in 1958, with the production of *Five Finger Exercise*. It is an account of a weekend at the Suffolk country house of a *nouveau riche* family—the husband a smugly stolid self-made man, the wife a culture snob who despises him. Their son's enigmatic German tutor serves as a catalyst, precipitating into the open the family's muffled hatreds and tensions in a way that is totally and even ruthlessly revealing. The play was received with great critical excitement, and praised as much for its precocious mastery of the mechanics of play construction as for its psychological perception. There were comparisons with Rattigan and Pinero, and widespread recognition that a major new dramatist had made his memorable debut. In England *Five Finger Exercise* received the *Evening Standard* award as the best play of 1958,

* shaf′ ər

PETER SHAFFER

and in America, where it ran for more than three hundred performances on Broadway, the New York Drama Critics Circle voted it the best foreign play of the 1959–1960 season.

There was scarcely less enthusiasm for the relatively lightweight one-act comedies staged in 1962 as *The Private Ear* and *The Public Eye*. The first shows how a shy young man's illusions about his dim-witted beloved are shattered when he seeks guidance in his wooing from a sophisticated friend, and sees her through the friend's eyes; the second is a cheerful fantasy (which reminded one critic of Giraudoux) about an exotically improbable detective and his relations with the young wife he is hired to investigate. Another undemanding entertainment, a musical modernization of the Cinderella story, was produced by Joan Littlewood and her company at Christmas 1963 as *The Merry Rooster's Panto*.

All along there had been a few critics who had compared Shaffer's work unfavorably with that of Osborne, Pinter, and Wesker, and accused him of wasting his undoubted talent on bourgeois trivialities composed according to the outworn conventions of the "well-made play." In an article in *Theatre Arts* (February 1960) he had responded to such attacks by saying that "the big emotional crises in most city people's lives take place in living rooms, and it is the height of confused snobbery to admit this as a legitimate setting only when the room happens to be the front parlor of a 'working-class' house." He went on to reject all labels: "Uncertainty within myself is something I prize. I do not want to classify or be classified by others."

Shaffer's most effective answer to his critics came

in a play which he wrote immediately after *Five Finger Exercise*, though it could not be produced until 1964. *The Royal Hunt of the Sun* could scarcely be less like Shaffer's other plays, or more remote indeed from anything else then appearing on the British stage. It is an epic of the conquest of Peru and Pizarro's friendship with and eventual destruction of the Inca leader Atahualpa: "an encounter between European hope and Indian hopelessness, between Indian faith and European faithlessness." As Robert Brustein has pointed out, the play is similar in theme and conception to *The Conquest of Mexico*, a series of tableaux devised by Antonin Artaud for his "Theatre of Cruelty." Like Artaud, Shaffer wanted to create a "total" theatre that would involve "not only words, but rites, mimes, masks and magic."

As Shaffer said, "The text cries for illustration. It is a director's piece, a pantomimist's piece, a musician's piece, a designer's piece, and, of course, an actor's piece, almost as much as it is an author's." It requires a cast of eighty, and the Royal Shakespeare Company, for which it was originally written, could not afford it. Eventually, Laurence Olivier bought it for the National Theatre at Chichester, where it opened under John Dexter's direction in 1964, transferring later the same year to the Old Vic. This huge enterprise emerged as a brilliant synthesis of all the theatre arts, and was almost universally acclaimed. Bernard Levin said: "I do not think the English stage has been so graced nor English audiences so privileged since Shaw was in his heyday." When it reached Broadway in 1965, Norman Nadel wrote that, even apart from its pageantry, "the musical grandeur of its noble speech and shining strength of its wisdom" made it a work that "might well be a masterpiece."

Black Comedy is further evidence of Shaffer's versatility—a one-act comedy that draws on two dramatic traditions as remote from each other as French farce and the ancient Chinese theatre. A young man, anxious to impress his girl friend's father, borrows expensive furniture from a neighbor without permission. A fuse is blown, the neighbor unexpectedly returns, and the young man has to try to replace the furniture without either the neighbor or his future father-in-law guessing what he is doing. The play derives immense visual humor from the spectacle of actors' groping their way about a well-lit stage as if they were in a completely darkened room. *The Battle of Shrivings*, an ambitious full-length play, presents a confrontation between a pacifist philosopher and an atheist poet. It had a very harsh critical reception in London in 1970—by far the worst of Shaffer's career. He said afterwards that "it was like driving into a brick wall at a hundred miles an hour. I felt physically punished, debilitated. I actually lost courage, and you live with that feeling for a long time."

Equus, which followed in 1973, restored his reputation. The play centers on a youth whose spiritual appetites, stifled by his socialist-rationalist father, are translated into a kind of religious devotion to horses. He finds work as a stable boy, and then puts out the eyes of six of his idols. The reasons for this horrible and apparently inexplicable crime are followed from clue to clue, and eventually unraveled, by the boy's psychiatrist. The latter is however losing faith in the value of his work, and in the end believes that, in purging his patient of the Dionysiac religious impulse, he has blinded him spiritually—a crime worse than the blinding of the horses. Some critics thought that the play explained and expounded too much, in the end destroying belief. Nevertheless (to quote Robert Cushman), "theatrically it is a triumph. . . . Mr. Shaffer writes fair to indifferent prose, but he imagines magnificent scenes." Harold Hobson found the play noble, moving, and stunningly powerful.

Peter Shaffer, "a large-boned, square-jawed, bespectacled, bubbling bachelor," lives in Kensington, London, which he calls a "playwright's city." He is passionately fond of music, was music critic of *Time and Tide* in 1961–1962, and is an excellent pianist. Politics bore him, and he has said that "the greatest tragic factor in history is man's apparent need to mark the intensity of his reaction to life by joining a band; for a band, to give itself definition, must find a rival, or an enemy." His hobbies are architecture, walking, and simply "peering about." *Five Finger Exercise*, *The Royal Hunt of the Sun*, *The Private Ear*, and *The Public Eye* have all been filmed—the last two as, respectively, *The Pad* and *Follow Me!*

PRINCIPAL PUBLISHED WORKS: *Plays*—Five Finger Exercise, 1958; The Private Ear [and] The Public Eye, 1962; The Royal Hunt of the Sun, 1965; Black Comedy (published with another one-act play, White Lies [England, The White Liars]), 1967; Equus, 1973. *Fiction (with Anthony Shaffer)*—How Doth the Little Crocodile?, 1952; Withered Murder, 1955.

ABOUT: Current Biography, 1967; Lumley, F. New Trends in Twentieth Century Drama, 1956; Taylor, J. R. The Angry Theatre, 1962; Who's Who, 1973; Who's Who in America, 1972–1973; Who's Who in the Theatre, 1972. *Periodicals*—Life March 21, 1960: Sunday Times July 29, 1973; Vogue September 15, 1959.

SHATTUCK, ROGER (WHITNEY) (August 20, 1923–), American scholar, critic, poet, and translator, writes: "My first and forever clearest recollection is the rumble of the Third Avenue 'el' in New York City. If asked, I might well say that I was born in an East Side brownstone—not strictly but symbolically true. The majestic 'high stoop' out front had something to do with my becoming a writer. I learned about oxymorons only years later; at the time it was strictly a matter of ear crossing eye.

"My father was a hard-working, successful physician. I walked four blocks through the eye of the Depression with a B embroidered on my cap to a private school. If I took Third Avenue instead of Lexington coming home, the local toughs on roller skates beat me up. The cook had a supply of meal tickets at the basement door to offer the panhandling unemployed instead of money. We spent summers in Wilton, Connecticut, only sixty miles away but still country for blueberrying and woodchuck hunting and roaming. It's all poison ivy now. There was a country club too, and tennis, and dances.

"At thirteen I went off to St. Paul's, an Episcopal prep school in Concord, New Hampshire. In five years of beautiful countryside, I picked up a rudimentary education, not too many wrong ideas, and my best friends. I see none of those friends now—dead in the war or earning their pile in levels of living I scarcely know. I was a good student and a shrimp for a long time. Sports defined the seasons and the vigorous flow of life: football, hockey played on black ice shaved by horse-drawn cutters, spring rowing in eights on a reservoir in the wilderness. I wrote poems and essays for the literary magazine and dreamed about those New York girls. On Last Night we were close to tears and far from the world. It was 1941, and I remember listening through a master's window to the sound of soldiers marching on the radio. I was also in love with Billie Holiday.

"At Yale I floundered about for two years in a pre-med program, torn between politics, literature, and an underclassman's high living. The war was aimed at our generation, at our class it seemed. I chose flying. The Air Force sticks in my mind as a long, garish dream full of waiting, strange instruments, and a proud new vision of the earth from on high. There were close shaves and bitter losses in New Guinea, then the Philippines. After the Bomb came two months in Korea, and home.

"I finished Yale, editing the *Lit* instead of continuing in pre-med. Saved flying pay provided me the fare to Paris; I had wanted to be sent there in the first place. When funds ran low, I landed a job in the film section of Unesco. By this time I was working on fiction, translating Apollinaire, and writing more poetry. A few poems and odd pieces came out in magazines. I left Unesco and hung on in Paris for a year with odd jobs, mostly ghosting for foreign correspondents. There was an unforgettable month in Corsica. I returned to New York in 1949 to marry Nora White, a dancer from the Ballets Russes, and take an editorial job with Harcourt Brace. A year later I accepted an appointment as a Junior Fellow in the Society of Fellows at Harvard. For three unfettered years, my reading and writing moved in all directions at once. I wrote the bulk of *The Banquet Years*, plus a handful of stories and poems. I stayed on three more years at Harvard as an instructor of French, and worked with my wife at the Poets' Theatre. After some painful months at the start, teaching began to suit me fine.

ROGER SHATTUCK

"Since our move to Austin and the University of Texas in 1956, the writing goes on. *Proust's Binoculars* grew out of teaching. I have done a good deal of editing and translating and reviewing, and finished a play in 1963 about a flagpole sitter. It hasn't scratched yet. I continue to tell myself the big book lies ahead. That novel perhaps, or a study of surrealism or of Stendhal's 'second education' at twenty. The volume that means most to me so far is *Half Tame*, a collection of poems published in 1965.

"Meanwhile the real thing has grown up around us in the form of four children. Without them, I doubt if I'd still play tennis and chess any longer. They are directly present in half the poetry I write. We sometimes wonder why we stay in Texas. I think I understand. At last there begins to be a tiny group of friends to see and know the way I knew the first set now gone. We spend summers in Lincoln, Vermont. Every few months my conscience twinges because I have not held out as a free-lance writer. Why do I spend so many hours composing soul and mind to teach French literature in central Texas? Every moment seems to come out of time I could spend writing. Yet I'm forty-two and convinced the best years are ahead, for writing, teaching, and living."

Shattuck's postwar years in Paris, editing and translating Apollinaire and generally imbibing the ambience, his interest in painting and in music (which he studied with Nadia Boulanger), came together to produce *The Banquet Years*, welcomed as "a fresh approach to the founding of twentieth century art." Shattuck concentrates on the years between the death of Victor Hugo in 1885 and the end of World War I. He seeks to analyze the significance of the era through biography rather than history, concentrating on four innovators: the writers Alfred Jarry and Guillaume Apollinaire, the composer Erik Satie, and the painter Henri Rousseau. The book was praised by Marvin Lowenthal as a "brilliant study of the beginnings of 'modernism' in the arts . . . thorough, perceptive, generally sound, and altogether stimulating." Other reviewers agreed that Shattuck's four protagonists had received the "most intensive" treatment yet accorded them in English, and praised the author's versatility of mind and breadth of knowledge, without being persuaded that such eccentric figures could usefully be made to speak for an entire age.

Proust's Binoculars concerns itself with that novelist's belief that an event, originally fleeting and meaningless, may later by some reflex be recalled and seen, this time, in true focus, as with binoculars. Struck by this image, Shattuck devotes much of his study of *A la recherche du temps perdu* to an investigation into Proust's remarkably extensive use of optical metaphor. Germaine Brée praised his avoidance of "the pseudo-symbolic interpretations that mar so much analysis based on a study of a writer's use of imagery," and welcomed his "sensitive and vigorous essay." The critic's first volume of verse, *Half Tame*, was liked rather than admired, seeming to its reviewers prolix and sometimes amateurish, but at its "relaxed and confessional" best, "pleasant light verse which resembles good chat."

Shattuck is the son of Howard and Elizabeth (Colt) Shattuck. He left the U.S. Army Air Force in 1945 with the rank of captain. He joined the faculty of the University of Texas in 1956, as he says, in 1968 becoming chairman of the department of French and Italian there. He was one of a number of scholars who resigned from the university in 1971 as the result of an acrimonious dispute between the regents on the one hand, students and faculty on the other. Feeling that the university had lost its sense of purpose, Shattuck said that he was "going off to meditate and write for a while."

PRINCIPAL WORKS: (ed. and tr.) Selected Writings of Guillaume Apollinaire, 1950; The Banquet Years: The Arts in France, 1885–1918, 1958; (ed. with William Arrowsmith) The Craft and Context of Translation: A Symposium, 1961; Proust's Binoculars, 1963; Half Tame (poems), 1964; (ed. with Simon Watson Taylor) Selected Works of Alfred Jarry, 1965; (tr. with Frederick Brown) Valéry, P. Occasions, 1970.

ABOUT: Contemporary Authors 7–8, 1963; Who's Who in America, 1972–1973. *Periodical*—New York Times May 21, 1971.

SHAW, ROBERT (August 9, 1927–   ), English novelist and dramatist, is the eldest of five children of Thomas Shaw, a physician who in his youth was a noted amateur athlete, and of Doreen (Avery) Shaw, formerly a nurse. Robert Shaw was born in the north of England, at Westhoughton, Lancashire, but spent his infancy in Cornwall. When he was six the family moved north again, to Stromness, in the Orkney Islands. The four years they spent there were shadowed by Dr. Shaw's alcoholism, and in the end Mrs. Shaw returned with the children to Cornwall. Her husband followed and there was a reconciliation, but a year or two later Dr. Shaw committed suicide.

Robert Shaw was twelve at that time, and a boarder at the Truro School. He had a brilliant career there—academically, on the sports field, and in school theatricals—leaving at eighteen with a scholarship to Cambridge University. While he was waiting to take up his scholarship he taught for a while at a school in Yorkshire, where he began to write verse, and found the prospect of going on to Cambridge increasingly unattractive. Instead, against the advice of his friends, he applied for a place at the Royal Academy of Dramatic Art, was rather unenthusiastically accepted, and spent the next three years there, paying his own tuition out of a legacy.

Graduating at the end of the 1940s, Shaw played in Shakespeare with the Shakespeare Memorial Theatre and the Old Vic for several seasons, and then found minor roles in the London theatre, in films, and on television. In 1952 he married the actress Jennifer Bourke. His first major success came in 1957, when he achieved international popularity (if not personal satisfaction) as Captain Dan Tempest in the television series *The Buccaneers*. Meanwhile Shaw had begun to write plays. One of them, *Off the Mainland*, had been produced in 1956 with the author in a leading role, but was unsuccessful. When *The Buccaneers* ended, Shaw retired to the country and lived off his savings while he launched into a new medium of self-expression. His first novel, *The Hiding Place*, appeared in 1959 and was welcomed by critics on both sides of the Atlantic as an "odd, off-beat, queerly haunting" story which also raises important philosophical questions. Richard McLaughlin called it "a thriller which has tenderness and moments of poetic intensity which lead one to regard [it] with mingled awe and gratitude."

The publication of *The Hiding Place* marked a

turning point in Shaw's career. The novel sold well, was televised both in England (where the author himself made the adaptation) and in the United States, and filmed as *Situation Hopeless—But Not Serious.* At the same time Shaw began to come into his own as an actor, attracting much praise and attention for his performances in John Arden's *Live Like Pigs* (1958) and Willis Hall's *The Long and the Short and the Tall* (1959).

The Sun Doctor, his second novel, was published in 1961 and received the Hawthornden Prize. It is about a physician who has returned to England after years of devoted work in West Africa. Honored by others, he is full of self-loathing for his disastrous intervention in a remote African community where the diseased rule the healthy. The book records his gradual victory over despair, and his eventual return to his work, in a manner which reminded reviewers variously of Graham Greene, Conrad, and even of Dostoevsky. The novel was widely admired for its virility and compassion, the "harsh poetry" of its scenic descriptions, and for the "special sort of strength that is the writer's reward for daring to be awake and emotionally aware."

The Flag is a complex, argumentative, brilliantly organized novel based on the career of the Reverend Conrad Noel, the "Red" Vicar of Thaxted, in Essex. It was announced as the first in a trilogy to be called "Cure of Souls," but no sequel has yet appeared. Shaw followed it instead with another extraordinary thesis novel, *The Man in the Glass Booth.* It centers on Goldman, a rich New York Jew who pretends that he was once a Nazi war criminal. Brought like Eichmann to trial in Israel, he boasts exultantly of the thousands of Jews he has killed and proclaims his devotion to Hitler. The reviewers were puzzled but impressed. Melvin Maddocks called the book "a pop-art novel of the absurd that ranges with astonishing vitality from braying comic vulgarities to subtly and scrupulously weighing political guilt and atonement." A reviewer in the *Times Literary Supplement* suggested that the novel was a by-product of Shaw's "talent for mimicry and self-dramatization" and that "what is surprising is that his bold, brutal strokes have created something so fairminded and sensitive." Goldman, with his "witty, painful ranting and sick wisecracks" is brilliantly drawn, but whether he is "a great Jew" or a vainglorious fool, no one seemed certain.

The story's intentions seemed clearer, at least to some reviewers, when Shaw turned his book into a successful play, directed by his friend Harold Pinter and starring Donald Pleasance. Harold Hobson thought that Goldman had taken on himself the sins of the Nazis, "not so that they may be washed clean, but in order that the men who committed them may be rendered eternally hateful." Shaw himself, Hobson says, expresses no opinion. "He shows us tremendous passions; and if they shake us, if they frighten, if they destroy the glibness of facile optimism, that is as it should be."

ROBERT SHAW

His next novel, *A Card from Morocco*, is largely a duologue recording the growth (and eventual failure) of a friendship between two men, a retired British army officer and an American painter, who drink and talk together in a Madrid bar. The gradual revelation of their natures and their more or less bizarre fantasies bored some reviewers, who thought the book pretentious and confusing, but fascinated others. Shaw's play *Cato Street* (1971) is a dramatized account of the Cato Street conspiracy of 1820, when a revolutionary group of radicals planned (but failed) to assassinate the entire British government and set fire to London in the name of liberty. Shaw himself took some liberties with the historical facts, but most reviewers found the dramatization skillful and pointed, though lacking in poetry.

Shaw has appeared on Broadway in Harold Pinter's *The Caretaker* and *Old Times* and in Friedrich Dürrenmatt's *The Physicists*, and is also well known to American audiences for his performances in a number of films—notably as Henry VIII in Robert Bolt's *A Man for All Seasons*, in screen versions of Pinter's *The Caretaker* and *The Birthday Party*, and in *The Luck of Ginger Coffey*, *Custer of the West*, *Royal Hunt of the Sun*, and *Young Winston*. He also appears frequently on British television, not only as an actor but as a flamboyant and aggressive contributor to panel games and discussion programs. He is a Socialist who nevertheless makes no secret of the pleasure he derives from his large income and the power and privileges it brings him. Shaw has four children by his first marriage, which ended in divorce, and four by his 1963 marriage to the actress Mary Ure, his co-star in *Old Times*. He is a tall man, with reddish brown hair and blue eyes, and much of his father's ability as an athlete. He excels at squash, riding, tennis, and golf. "If there is a Renaissance man left in this world," wrote one interviewer, "he must be Robert Shaw."

PRINCIPAL WORKS: The Hiding Place (novel), 1959; The Sun Doctor (novel), 1961; The Flag (vol. 1 of the Cure of Souls trilogy), 1965; The Man in the Glass Booth (novel, 1967; play, 1968); A Card from Morocco (novel), 1969; Cato Street (play), 1972; Causes (poems), 1973. *As editor*—Flash Point: An Anthology of Modern Poetry, 1964. ABOUT: Current Biography, 1968; Ross, L. and H. The Player, 1962; Vinson, J. (ed.) Contemporary Novelists, 1972; Who's Who, 1973; Who's Who in America, 1972–1973; Who's Who in the Theatre, 1972; Wood, C. TV Personalities (2 vols.), 1956–1957. *Periodicals*—Guardian July 16, 1971; Life November 3, 1967; Newsweek December 7, 1964.

SHEED, WILFRID (JOHN JOSEPH) (December 27, 1930–), English novelist, short story writer, and journalist, writes: "I was born in London. Both my parents were writers and publishers (Sheed and Ward) and on my mother's side of the family some kind of writing has been going on for four generations now—a chain I once wished strongly to break but in which I now take a sort of very pale pleasure. My father's family were non-literary Australians, his father a draftsman, and his grandfather a parsimonious Scotch sea-captain—shadowy characters of whom I have never even seen pictures. His mother was Irish and lived with us and wielded a prodigious influence on everyone in sight.

"My upbringing was transatlantic and hard to disentangle school by school or even year by year. The chief thing about it was that it made a chronic foreigner out of me from the age of nine to the present and this has probably colored my writing as much as anything else. At age fourteen an attack of polio cut short an unpromising athletic career and gave a bookish tilt to my interests (before that I had read books under protest). I formed a taste for English prose and began consciously talking it to myself—a curious transatlantic brew of my own which I am still working on. (Since the first phase of my prose infatuation coincided with a spasm of dislike for postwar England, I tended to look to America for the basic sound. And although I have since admired, and scavenged, various English mandarins, I believe the undercoat is still American.)

"Such teen-age writing as I did outside of my head was mainly comic—a couple of scabrous and unplayable plays, some parodies, light verse, etc., festooned with cartoons of men with enormous heads. I wrote nothing at all at college (Oxford), for reasons which seemed clear enough at the time, but set to work on a novel shortly after leaving, scrapped this one half way through, lit another one off the end of it, scrapped that, and then finally went all the way with the third. I was living in Australia for the first part of this, working at a rather leisurely job, and failing to crack the inert Australian press with reviews, articles, stories—a low pressure apprenticeship.

"I was luckier on returning to this country and managed to place random bits and pieces in magazines, finger-exercises for the most part, carefully phrased and rather pointless. Finding something to say was the last step instead of the first: i.e., finding the point of view implicit in the style and then finding the subject matter implicit in the point of view. I do not consider myself a humorous writer. My usual method is to take a straight story and inflate and slightly distort it with humour. The story itself is never wild. Much of the humor comes by way of a modified stream of consciousness which I am constantly varying. My novels so far have formed a kind of mosaic and should be read that way and not in isolation (in other words buy the complete set, please). Writing is a life-long vocation and I don't believe in giving the game away in a single book.

"Circumstances have obliged me to do a good deal of reviewing (the last refuge of the light essayist): books, plays, etc. I find this work painful, but it serves a couple of selfish purposes. It enables me to work out various aesthetic ideas, while unloading my little burden of didacticism in a safe place; and it gives me a certain thin-lipped benignity towards my own critics, when they turn the cannon round and aim it in my direction. Unsympathetic criticism stings like hell for twenty-four hours, but you are less likely to feel a personal animus about it if you have stung a few victims yourself. (Incidentally, I use the word sting because I am convinced that criticism is carried about in the tail.)

"Meanwhile, I have temporarily lost interest in traveling and live stolidly in New Jersey with my wife and three children, waiting like everyone else for the world to come to its senses, or at least for my pool-game to improve."

F. J. Sheed and Maisie Ward, the novelist's parents, established their famous Roman Catholic publishing house in London in 1926, a few months after they were married. An American branch was opened in New York in 1933—hence Sheed's transatlantic upbringing. His highly diversified education included longish spells at schools in Torresdale, Pennsylvania (during the war years) and at Downside, the famous Benedictine school in England. Sheed went on to Lincoln College, Oxford, which gave him his degree in 1954. His first novel was begun, as he says, in Australia, during a year's stay with his father's family. The book was completed in America, where he was earning his living as a freelance journalist and a staff member of the Catholic magazine *Jubilee*.

A Middle Class Education is a satirical novel about the progress through Oxford and a scholarship year in America of John Chote, a kind of dispirited "Lucky Jim." Chote masquerades as a gentlemanly lecher and drunkard, but secretly swots for his scholarship; he would rather like love or Oxford to make a new man of him, but nothing of this sort seems to be happening and meanwhile he keeps his eye on whatever looks like the main chance. Reviewers complained that the book was shapeless and much too long, and said they didn't know whether the satire was aimed at an educational system or a whole loveless, self-absorbed, and "morally desiccated" generation. Nevertheless, as Bernard Bergonzi wrote, this "untidy, sprawling novel . . . is full of life, often very funny, and contains innumerable neat observations of the raddled face of contemporary Oxford." There was a general sense that a novelist had made his debut who possessed "comic gifts of a high order."

The Hack records the breakdown (on Christmas Eve) of a writer of inspirational stories and verse for the Catholic press. *Commonweal*'s reviewer recognized it as an attack on "popular American Catholicism at its dead-level commonest." This book, like Sheed's first, was thought blurred in some of its effects but also extremely funny and, in the end, moving. *Square's Progress*, which compares American suburban living not unfavorably with some of its alternatives, also had a rather equivocal reception from reviewers who obviously liked what Sheed had to say, admired his style and flashes of wit, but found the work as a whole oddly static and subdued.

Sheed was an associate editor of *Jubilee* from 1959 to 1966 and its film critic from 1959 to 1961. In 1964–1967 he was *Commonweal*'s drama critic and book review editor, and in 1967–1969 he was *Esquire*'s movie critic. Since 1971 he has contributed regularly to the New York *Times Book Review*. He drew on his experience of the magazine world for *Office Politics*, which describes the struggle for control of an influential American journal of opinion when its famous English editor retires. Most reviewers seemed to agree that this novel marked the end of Sheed's apprenticeship, and it was nominated for a National Book Award. "Classical in structure and style," wrote P. A. Duhamel, "this, his best work, realizes its comic intention with grace and clarity." Julian Gloag,

WILFRID SHEED

pointing out that Sheed "is one of the few writers who can handle American and English characters with equal expertise," said, "The book is a fable . . . a moral tale. Perhaps only a moral tale could be so easily humorous, so notably non-vicious, so gently penetrating in its satire, so marvelously ludicrous without being grotesque."

The Blacking Factory, a novella, and *Pennsylvania Gothic*, a long story, two somber studies of adolescence published in one volume, were also admired as examples of "pure Sheed of the finest quality," written in "prose [as] clear as a cat's eye and direct as a rifle shot." *Max Jamison*, which followed, is about life in an age of criticism, exemplified by a New York theatre reviewer whose rigorous analytical faculties, turned inwards upon himself and his relationships, almost destroy him. Richard Freedman thought that the "larger insight of this triumphantly intelligent novel is that criticism is not a mask or a pose, a way for egomaniacs to vent their hostilities or for failed artists to make a buck. It is a deep-dyed view of life, a creatively aggressive attitude to the world rather than the usual mindlessly passive one."

In the first section of *People Will Always Be Kind*, Brian Casey, an athletic young Irish-Catholic New Yorker, is crippled by polio. He experiments with an assortment of compensations, and finds his *métier* in campus politics. The second—and, most reviewers thought, more successful—part of the novel moves forward twenty years. It describes Senator Casey's campaign for the Democratic party's presidential nomination through the eyes of his speechwriter Sam Perkins, one of Casey's army of devoted young radicals. Casey is an extremely complex character, part Eugene McCarthy (for whom Sheed campaigned in 1968), part FDR, part Kennedy, all politician—a shrewd and arrogant "professional idealist" who is yet not wholly without integrity, a man with a "closetful of minds" who no longer knows which is truly his. Perkins eventually drops out of the campaign, less disillusioned than bewildered. Thomas R. Edwards wrote: "There are no lurid conspiracies, no shocking scandals, no patriotic sermons to tie it all together. The hectic, duplicitous, improvisational hubbub of real political business is theater enough for a novelist like Sheed, part *farceur* and part theologian—like Brian Casey himself."

The Morning After, a collection of Sheed's essays and reviews, brought generous encomiums from Sheed's colleagues and recognition to the author as a Christian moralist whose seriousness is concealed by "that bright, self-debunking style," and as "the best professional reviewer in the business." In 1970–1971 Sheed was a visiting lecturer in creative arts at Princeton, and in 1972 he joined the Book-of-the-Month Club's board of judges.

PRINCIPAL WORKS: Joseph (Patron Saint series), 1958; (ed.) G. K. Chesterton's Essays and Poems, 1958; A Middle Class Education, 1960; The Hack, 1963; Square's Progress, 1965; Office Politics, 1966; The Blacking Factory, & Pennsylvania Gothic: A Short Novel and a Long Story, 1968; Max Jamison, 1970 (In England, The Critic); The Morning After: Selected Essays and Reviews, 1971; People Will Always Be Kind, 1973.

ABOUT: Vinson, J. (ed.) Contemporary Novelists, 1973; Who's Who in America, 1972–1973. *Periodicals*—Time September 20, 1968.

NAOYA SHIGA

***SHIGA, NAOYA** (February 20, 1883–October 21, 1971), Japanese short story writer and novelist, and one of the molders of modern Japanese literature, was born into a wealthy family, and spent most of his childhood and youth in his grandparents' Tokyo home. When he was twelve years old his mother died in early pregnancy, and his father married again, within the year, a woman only eleven years older than Naoya.

He said that the two people who had the greatest influence over him, apart from his grandfather, were the Christian thinker Kanzo Ochimura, and the novelist and dramatist Saneatsu Mushakoji. He met both Ochimura and Mushakoji while he was still at Gakushuin (the Peers' School), and under the influence of the former became an enthusiastic though temporary Christian. But it was Mushakoji who became Shiga's closest friend and most important teacher, inspiring him with his faith in the individual and his confident humanism (Mushakoji made two attempts to set up ideal communities).

In April 1910 Mushakoji, Shiga, and some other wealthy and high-born young men started a literary magazine, *Shirakaba* (White Birch). Inspired by the ideas of Ogai Mori, Tolstoy, and Maeterlinck, *Shirakaba* opposed its optimistic utopianism to the pessimism of the prevailing naturalist aesthetic, and won considerable respect in the ten years that followed. The main spirit behind the venture was the enthusiastic Mushakoji —however sympathetic, Shiga was too much aware of the weak and selfish in human nature wholeheartedly to share his friend's idealism.

* shē′ gə

In 1906, after graduating from Gakushuin, he entered the English literature department of Tokyo Imperial University. He had by this time decided on writing as a career. In 1908 he transferred from the English to the Japanese literature department, then, losing interest, withdrew without finishing the course.

Among his early stories were "Kamisori" (The Razor, 1910), in which a barber kills an obnoxious customer; "Kurodiasu no Nikki" (The Diary of Claudius, 1912), the story of Hamlet told from his uncle's point of view; and "Han no Hanzai" (1913, translated by Ivan Morris as "Han's Crime"), about a Chinese knife thrower who one night, in the course of his act, severs his unfaithful wife's carotid artery. All demonstrate Shiga's interest in the intricacies of human psychology, and in the nature of justice—was Han's act an accident, or deliberate? Is he guilty of murdering his wife? Even Han does not know.

Shiga's intense individualism, however, set him profoundly at odds with his feudalist father, who found inexplicable his son's choice of a literary career and his irreverent attitude to tradition— when General Nogi killed himself out of feudal loyalty, Shiga is reported to have commented: "Idiot." The writer's growing popularity, and his sudden marriage in 1913 to Sada, a cousin of Mushakoji, did nothing to placate the older man. But the conflict, while providing the subject matter for many of Shiga's earlier works, also had a deeply disturbing effect on him, so that for four years, between 1913 and 1917, he produced nothing, moving restlessly about the country, until the final reconciliation described in "Wakai" (Reconciliation, 1917). The story "Kinosaki Nite" (translated as "At Kinosaki"), published in the same year, reflects a similar mood of resignation, a meditation on life and death. In 1922 he published the first part of a long novel, *Anya Koro* (Long Journey Into Night), which is a rather gloomy spiritual autobiography, a series of sketches rather than a coherent unity, but widely regarded as the masterpiece of the Taisho era.

From 1923 to 1938, Shiga lived mainly in Kyoto and Nara, pursuing the interest in ancient oriental art which had been stimulated by Mushakoji (who was also a painter). During these years he published a few short stories, his *Yamashina no Kioku* (Recollections of Yamashina, 1926), and a handbook on ancient eastern art based on his own fine collection. He also worked on the second part of *Anya Koro*, which was published in 1937. But his creative powers were slackening, and he felt more and more out of step with the proletarian literature of the 1920s and 1930s.

In 1938 Shiga returned to Tokyo. He continued to write, though sparingly, during the war and afterwards: *Haiiro no Tsuki* (Gray Moon, 1945), *Mushibamareta Yujo* (Worm-Eaten Friendship, 1947), *Itazura* (Mischief), and other volumes of short stories. From first to last, his work presents a remarkable unity, his later stories being distinguished only by their greater serenity.

Shiga has been compared with Soseki Natsume—for his humor, his apparently simple but really very complex style, his penetrating psychology, and independence of literary schools. "My feelings of like and dislike have been the criteria of judging whether things are 'good' or 'bad,'" he wrote, "and I have rarely been mistaken in these judgments"—a statement which sums up his highly individualistic, dogmatic, and fundamentally intuitive approach to life and literature. In 1949 Shiga received the National Cultural Award for Literature.

His works, writes Donald Keene, "probably more than those of any other modern author, have exercised a commanding influence over the Japanese literature of today. He did not invent the 'I-novel' . . . but his success with this genre led many other writers to seek to salvage bits worthy of preservation from the incidents of their lives." Above all, he shaped and perfected the short story, setting a standard for fine, concentrated style and precise observation.

PRINCIPAL WORKS IN ENGLISH TRANSLATION: *Stories in* Brickley, S. G. The Writing of Idiomatic English, 1951; Keene, D. Modern Japanese Literature, 1956; McKinnon, R. N. The Heart Is Alone: A Selection of Twentieth-Century Japanese Short Stories, 1957; Morris, I. Modern Japanese Stories, 1961; Sadler, A. L. Selections from Modern Japanese Writers, 1943. *Periodicals*—Far East, vols. XX, XXIV.

ABOUT: Keene, D. Modern Japanese Literature, 1956; Meiji Dictionary of Japanese Literature (in Japanese), 1965; Penguin Companion to Literature 4, 1969. *Periodicals*—Japan Quarterly October-December 1955.

***SHNEOUR, ZALMAN** (February 11, 1887–February 20, 1959), Hebrew and Yiddish poet, novelist, short story writer, and essayist, whose given name was originally Zalkind, was born in Shklov, in White Russia, a member of a noted Hasidic family. He was the fourth of the seven children of Isaac Shneour, a dealer in jewelry and works of art, and of Feige (Sussman) Shneour, and a lineal descendant of Rabbi Shneour Zalman of Ladi (1748–1813), the founder of the Habad Hasidim. Influenced by his older brothers, Shneour left home at thirteen, after completing his early schooling at the traditional *heder*, and went to Odessa, then the center of a renaissance of Hebrew culture. There he met such illustrious men of letters as the novelist Mendele Mokher Seforim and the poet H. N. Bialik who, after seeing some examples of his early verse, predicted a brilliant literary career for him.

Shneour failed to find a publisher in Odessa, and after a year went home. In 1902 he settled in Warsaw, taking courses at the university there and working in a publishing house, on the Hebrew weekly *Hador*, and then as secretary to the Yiddish author Isaac Loeb Peretz. It was at this time that he met David Frischman, who later became his literary adviser and lifelong friend. Shneour's verse and prose soon began to appear in the Warsaw newspapers and journals, and his first volume of poems, *Im Shekiat ha-hama* (At Sunset), appeared in 1906.

Continuing his university studies at Vilna, Shneour came into contact with leading Yiddish writers and began to make his mark as a bilingual author, writing with equal facility in Hebrew and Yiddish. Some of his early Yiddish poetry and prose were published in his *Gezamelte Shriften* (Collected Works, 1908). After leaving Vilna, Shneour traveled through Europe and the Near East. For a time he studied at the University of Geneva, and in 1912 he took up the study of medicine in Paris. During World War I he was in Germany, where he was interned as an enemy alien.

* shnā o͞or′

ZALMAN SHNEOUR

From 1924 to 1940 he lived in Paris, making occasional visits to Palestine. When the Nazis invaded France, he went into hiding, and emigrated to the United States in 1940.

Bialik, when he first met him, saw Shneour as "a young Samson," newly come from the wilderness to shake the pillars of the Temple. And Ribalow calls him "a poet-revolutionary. He rebels against everything: against society and its injustice, against sanctimonious virtues, against that pretentious humaneness which is inevitably cruel towards the weak. He rebels against Gentile brutality towards the Jew, at the same time aiming a blow at what he terms the fossilized institutions and moth-eaten sanctities of ancient Judaism. He assails the very universe." And indeed, whether in poetry or prose, passion and rebellion are in everything he writes. His early poems in particular celebrate the joys and pains of sexual love and the splendors of nature—both unaccustomed themes in Hebrew poetry. Himself a product of an urban environment, he rails against the devitalizing effects of civilized living, cut off from the creative forces of nature: "Blessed be thou unto me, O free Savagery / Of a period of deserts and forests! / Then would a daughter of Eve, unclad, sun-burned, / Seek her lover in the mountains."

According to Ruth Finer Mintz, Shneour "brought to modern Hebrew poetry a new dimension of sensual vitality. His ability to evoke color, texture, and motion in poetry was sharpened by the imagistic and impressionistic influences of Russian and French poetry." His uninhibited erotic imagery, however, made him a controversial figure from the start, as did his restless obsession with struggle and conflict: the conflict between man and woman—"There is neither end nor limit, O woman, to the enslavement of the man who loves you, and there is no end to his lust for domination"; between the individual and society, innovation and tradition, nature and civilization. Man, says Shneour, must insist on his own dignity, he must stand up and resist—and conflict is inevitable.

Accordingly, like Bialik before him, though in far more violent terms, Shneour condemns the humble ghetto mentality of the Diaspora Jew in such poems as *Yemath Hamashiah* (Millenium), and *Bechorah* (Birthright). He ridicules the ideas of a coming millenium of universal brotherhood in his parody of Isaiah, *Vehayah Beaharith Hayamim* (It Shall Come to Pass in the End of Days). His ideal is not the traditional meek and gentle hero of Judaism in exile, but the vigorous rebel Judah the Maccabee, who in *Belel Hanukka* (On Hanukka Night) slays the old woman, the martyr Exile Mother, crying "I am the Murderer and the Redeemer." Some of his darkest poems are poems of prophecy: in *Aharon* (The Lost Man) he predicts the downfall of Western civilization; in the famous *Yeme Habenayim Mithkarebim* (The Middle Ages Are Approaching) he foretells the coming massacre of the Jews, and calls upon them to resist, and die heroically.

Though he wrote some Hebrew prose, including two novels (*Anshe Shklov*, 1944, and *Pandre ha-Gibor*, 1945), the bulk of Shneour's prose works were written in Yiddish. Between *A Toit* (A Death, 1909), and *Downfall* (1944) appeared some dozen volumes of fiction, which have been variously compared with the work of Sholem Asch and Charles Dickens for what Moshe Spiegel calls Shneour's "vivid imagery, his sweeping range, his lively imagination, and his ability to breathe life into a multitude of characters portrayed with compassionate understanding."

Among the best-known are *Noah Pandre* and *Noah Pandre's Village*, set in a Russian-Jewish village in the early 1900s, which are clearly intended to counter the stereotype of the servile ghetto Jew. Noah Pandre is the butcher's son, a spirited and audacious youth of great physical strength, constantly in trouble, who matures into his people's champion against injustice, and at last goes off to America in search of a better life. L. S. Munn found in these stories something of the quality of folktales, and said Shneour recreates the village "with an abundance of small detail, in chuckling appreciation of the oddities and foibles of his characters, in searching knowledge of their strengths and weaknesses."

During the last decade of his life, Shneour spent several years in Israel. Yet, despite his disdain for the Diaspora, he never settled in the Jewish homeland. He died of a heart ailment at the age of seventy-two in New York City, survived by his wife, the former Salomea Landa, and two children. An acquaintance has recalled him as an imposing, bearded figure, a man of great pride, who did not always get along well with people, but who was a brilliant conversationalist and a lover of the good things of life. Among the honors accorded him are the Bialik prize, the Louis LaMed prize, an honorary D.H.L. degree from the Stephen Wise Institute in New York, and honorary membership in the Mark Twain Society. He is widely regarded as "one of the three master builders of modern Hebrew poetry," along with H. N. Bialik and Saul Tchernichovski.

PRINCIPAL WORKS IN ENGLISH TRANSLATION: Noah Pandre, 1936; Noah Pandre's Village, 1938; Downfall, 1944; Song of the Dnieper (collecting the two Noah Pandre books), 1945; Restless Spirit (selected works), 1963. *Poems in* Fein, H. H. Harvest of Hebrew Verse, 1945; Mintz, R. F. Modern Hebrew Poetry, 1966; Penueli, S. Y. and Ukhmani, A. Anthology of Modern Hebrew Poetry, 1966; Ribalow, M. The Flowering of Modern Hebrew Literature, 1959.

ABOUT: Goldsmith, S. J. Twenty Twentieth Century Jews, 1962; Mintz, R. F. Modern Hebrew Poetry, 1966; Penueli, S. Y. and Ukhmani, A. Anthology of Modern Hebrew Poetry, 1966; Ribalow, M. The Flowering of Modern Hebrew Literature, 1959; Wallenrod, R. The Literature of Modern Israel, 1956; Waxman, M. A History of Jewish Literature, 1960.

***SIGAL, CLANCY** (September 6, 1926–), American novelist and journalist, writes: "I was born in Chicago. I grew up in various neighborhoods. I read Wilde and Shaw. I was also a member of the Rockets Athletic Club of Albany Park. The crisis of my life occurred when the school moron pushed me up to the ceiling in a pair of ringers in the gym. Later, I went into the Army. After the war I went to Detroit to work. When the hiatus began, if one can so put it, I filled in the time with conventional activities until I came to England. Then I began to write.

"I have published two books, appearing both in England and America: *Weekend in Dinlock* (Secker & Warburg, Houghton-Mifflin) and *Going Away* (Jonathan Cape, Houghton Mifflin) and numerous bits of occasional journalism, mainly in British periodicals and newspapers."

Sigal's life closely resembles that of the protagonist of his second novel, *Going Away* (1962). He is the son of immigrant trade unionists, Leo and Jenny (Persily) Sigal. His education was interrupted by World War II, during which he served (1944–1946) in the U.S. Army, emerging as a staff sergeant. In 1946–1947 he worked for the UAW-CIO in Detroit. Sigal received his B.A. from the University of California in 1950. From 1952 to

* sē′ gəl

CLANCY SIGAL

1956 he worked in Hollywood, first as a story analyst for the Columbia Pictures Corporation, then with the Jeffe Agency. In 1957, after a period as a free-lance writer and journalist, he settled in England.

Going Away is not only a fictionalized memoir but also a chronicle of the American Left since the late 1930s. The narrator, raised in the Communist party and the Labor movement, leaves his job as a Hollywood agent in 1956 and drives across the continent to New York, on the way visiting friends and enemies from his radical past. This picaresque story, punctuated with flashbacks, evolves into an impassioned critique of the tameness and torpor of contemporary America, counterpointed by an account of the revolution which was taking place simultaneously in Hungary. The revolution is crushed; the journey ends; the narrator prepares to leave for Europe.

Although *Going Away* was the second of Sigal's books to appear, reviewers found in it some of the preoccupations and excesses often associated with first novels. It was nevertheless generally admired for its ambitious scope, for its moving and reckless honesty, and for a "linguistic energy" which reminded some readers of Thomas Wolfe. Nelson Algren called it "a first-hand novel by a first-rate writer driven by the discovery that he is a man fully equipped to live his life, but with no place to live it." Whitney Balliett thought it too long and encyclopedic, but attributed to Sigal "the natural writer's easy mixture of simplicity, rhythm, colloquialism, and reluctant but precise use of metaphor."

Weekend in Dinlock (1960) is set in a fictional

Yorkshire mining town, where a young collier tries but fails to escape from the pits to become a a painter. Sigal had lived in such a town, as the guest of such a man, and the book is fundamentally a compassionate but marvelously exact documentary record of what Angus Wilson called "a complete petrified seam of English life." The poet Ted Hughes, who grew up in the Yorkshire mining country, was one of many critics who praised the book's authenticity—its eschewal of either condescension or romantic glorification, the rightness of its dialect speech. The critical consensus was summed up by a writer in the *Christian Science Monitor*, who said it was "by far the most powerful insight into the harsh, monochromatic, profane but strangely vibrant life of these isolated mining communities since Orwell's . . . *The Road to Wigan Pier*."

Sigal lives in England and contributes "lively, sympathetic, informative" articles and stories to major American and English magazines. "I had learned," he wrote in *Going Away*, "that the deepest evil consisted not of corrupting a vision of life but failing to understand."

PRINCIPAL WORKS: Weekend in Dinlock, 1960; Going Away: A Report, a Memoir, 1962.
ABOUT: Contemporary Authors 3, 1963; Who's Who in America, 1972–1973. *Periodicals*—Nation July 2, 1960; New York Herald Tribune Book Review February 11, 1962; New Yorker March 17, 1962; San Francisco Chronicle June 28, 1960; Spectator January 29, 1960; Times Literary Supplement January 22, 1960.

SIKELIANOS, ANGELOS (March 28, 1884–June 6, 1951), Greek poet, was born on the Ionian island of Lefkas, the son of John and Heraklia Sikelianos. He was educated mainly at home by his grandfather, who was a scholar, and his father, a man of wide culture who spoke English, French, and Italian. Later Sikelianos studied law for a time at the University of Athens.

His poetry began to appear in little magazines when he was sixteen, and his first collection, *Alaphroiskiotos* (1909), established him immediately as a powerful lyric poet comparable, in the opinion of many critics, only with Palamas—whom he profoundly admired—in his command of language.

His first important poem, *The Visionary*, is autobiographical, describing his youth and early manhood on his native island. It already reflects one of the major themes of Sikelianos' mature work: the organic unity of man and nature, body and soul, intellect and instinct. And implicit in it also is the mythological vision of life that was to dominate all his later work. Philip Sherrard traces these attitudes to their roots in an ancient popular culture, still alive in the traditions of illiterate Greek peasants. "The problem was then for me," the poet wrote, "by what way and with what means could I

ANGELOS SIKELIANOS

achieve essential contact with and understanding of this tradition?" And in a sense, the rest of his life was absorbed in that quest.

It was a personal spiritual pilgrimage, as well as a historical one, and it brought him to the pre-Socratic traditions, Orphism, the teachings of Pythagoras and the Eleusinian Mysteries, and beyond them to "the venerable Asia, that beneath the obscure masks of her numberless civilizations seems to have preserved not only her own secret but also the secret of a brotherly relationship between us within a more ancient civilization which has vanished."

Between 1915 and 1917 appeared the fruit of these researches, the long rhapsodic poem *Prologue to Life*, which embodies an Orphic vision of poetry as an inspired expression of the divine mysteries. In such lines as the following, the *Prologue* celebrates the surrender of the self to the Dionysiac powers of nature, as a necessary stage in man's journey towards unity with the divine: "From the pitch-blind night, / held lightly beneath the armpits, / leaving my weight in I know not what hands, / placing the foot dancingly forward, / I first entered, my earth, into your mature orgies."

Sikelianos attached great importance to the ancient cult sites of Greece, especially Eleusis and Delphi, where he believed that man had once achieved that reconciliation of the earthly and the divine which he sought. With his first wife, an American, he worked for years towards a reincarnation of this vision at Delphi. There was to be a series of festivals of ancient Greek dance, music, and theatre, and a university; through learning and the arts would come a cosmic sense of brotherhood, a new golden age. In the end the Greek government proved unwilling to support the proposed university and, though two very successful festivals were held, in 1927 and 1930, the "Delphic idea" was never realized.

It survives nevertheless in Sikelianos' later poems and verse dramas: *The Dithyramb of the Rose*, *The Sybil*, *Daedalus in Crete*, *Christ at Rome*, *The Death of Iphigenia*, and the unpublished "Asclepius"—works in which he achieved a growing control, restraint, and profundity, though his plays were always distinguished more for their poetry than their dramatic sense. Sikelianos was increasingly obsessed by a notion of the divine which would gain universal acceptance and lead to universal understanding. Many of his later works represent, in their imagery and argument, attempts at a synthesis of Greek and Christian mysticism, of Dionysus and Christ. His poetry was collected in the three-volume *Lyric Life* in 1946–1947, and his plays in *Thymeli* (two volumes, 1950).

Sikelianos is described in *Modern European Poetry* as "a poet in the grand tradition, a Yeats-like figure, a prophet and a seer, a man of high visions and noble actions, one who had assimilated the cultural traditions of his own nation and those of the modern world, a revolutionary democrat and mystic who acted beyond the particular political creeds and religious faiths of the world."

PRINCIPAL WORKS IN ENGLISH TRANSLATION: The Delphic Word, 1928; The Dithyramb of the Rose, 1939; Akritan Songs, 1944; Six Poems from the Greek of Sikelianos and Seferis, 1946. *Poems in* Barnstone, W. (ed.) Modern European Poetry, 1966; Friar, K. (ed.) Modern Greek Poetry, 1973; Keeley, E. and Sherrard, P. Six Poets of Modern Greece, 1960; Sherrard, P. The Marble Threshing Floor, 1956; Trypanis, C. Penguin Book of Greek Verse, 1971.

ABOUT: Katsimbalis, G. Bibliografia Angelos Sikelianos, 1946; Penguin Companion to Literature 2, 1969; Seferis, G. On the Greek Style, 1966; Sherrard, P. The Marble Threshing Floor, 1956.

SILKIN, JON (December 2, 1930–), English poet, writes: "I was born in London in 1930 (my grandparents were Russian Jewish immigrants) and I lived there until the war started (I was eight), and then evacuated to Kent, and to Wales (Swansea, Pumpsaint, Lampeter). In 1945 I returned to London. I think of my experience in Wales as important to me, although every attempt to define, or even describe, it has failed. My three years in London, before being conscripted, were rather emotionally and intellectually arid, and although it was there, when I was fifteen, that I started to write poetry, I knew hardly anyone of my age, or older, to whom I could show my work and receive criticism. I don't imagine this to be a rare experience, but I think it is worth mentioning. In the army I taught people to read and write (among other

JON SILKIN

things) and when I came out in 1950, after a little hesitating, I decided not to go in for the law (my father's work). I had no idea what kind of work I could keep myself with, but I knew, if only from the army, that my middle-class upbringing, anxiously watched over by my parents, had almost successfully insulated me from wide and deep experience with human beings, including 'creative' people. Further, I felt, even arrogantly, that I knew nothing of how working class people lived. Moreover, I wanted a job that demanded little of my mind, which I determined to keep for my writing. Lastly, I wanted to live using both my mind and body—so that partly for these reasons, and partly because I was unequipped to do anything else, I took a labouring job. I worked with my hands until 1956 (six years), as a janitor, in a cemetery, as a brick-layer's labourer, and in factories. When I couldn't stand it any longer, and had got sacked from a job I'd had for nine months, I was in despair as to what I could do, since clearly, as a poet, I wouldn't manage to live by my writing. If that desire seems naïve, and in conjunction with my earlier statements, contradictory, I do say that during those six years I learnt not only what it was to be poor (to the point of starvation—initially, and for a brief period). I learnt also that to support oneself on that activity central to oneself is to avoid being tormented by the sense of wasting one's power. I think this seems arrogant, but I can only say what I feel, and anybody who has experienced this particular kind of frustration, desperately wanting his work to be wanted, by however few but needing to feel that his work is necessary to society, will understand this kind of misery well. Use and useful are vague words but they depend not only upon what you may think society needs but what you are best suited to. Each man has his 'value' to society and his value lies in how he can realize his potential in making society fruitful. This means, of course, that despite, or even because I have seen power manipulated by unscrupulous people, I cannot see how a labourer is of less use than a politician, or a priest. Since I think poetry is useful to society, and in spite of my vanity, I desire it to be useful there, my inability to earn my keep by my writing hurt.

"From 1956 to 1958 I taught English to 'foreign' students, and it was then that I was offered the Gregory Fellowship in Poetry at Leeds University. This Fellowship is non-academic and given to a practising poet. His obligations are to live in Leeds and to mix, as he will, with the students. It is designed to help the poet in the second, often the most difficult, stage of his development. I consider my stay in Leeds as crucial to my development as a poet. It gave me time to start working out my poetics; it brought me into contact with people accustomed (particularly at Leeds it seems) to examining poems without arid and destructive insistence. And since I had never gone to University I stayed in Leeds to take a degree in English, and am now finishing my thesis on the poets of the first world war (although I now live in Newcastle-on-Tyne). It was at Leeds that I revived *Stand*, a literary quarterly, originally begun in London in 1952, which I now co-edit with the poet Ken Smith."

The poems in Silkin's first book, *The Peaceable Kingdom*, were said to have some of the naïve power and compassion of the painting which supplied the book's title. A critic in the *Times Literary Supplement* thought these poems were also "groping towards a definition of the obscurer components of deep personal emotion, and searching for a style." This dual quest was continued in Silkin's two subsequent books, which affirmed "involvement and tenderness against violence and guilt," which were painfully and movingly honest, but which seemed sometimes too "clogged" and abstract. *Nature With Man*, which received the Faber Memorial Prize, marked an important technical advance, in which "a more sensuous vigour and ease" was added to Silkin's "very personal, slow, grave speech."

The rhythms of the Bible were an important influence on Silkin's early work, and he says that technically he "may have got something from Marianne Moore." His admirers believe that Jon Silkin, because of his disregard for British literary fashions, has been seriously underestimated, and is only beginning to receive the recognition he deserves.

Jon Silkin is a handsome, bearded man. He is the son of Joseph Silkin, a solicitor, and Dora Silkin. He was educated at Wycliffe College and Dulwich College, and received his B.A. with first class honors from the University of Leeds in 1962. He had worked for a year as a journalist before he was drafted in 1949. In his politics and often in his poems he is a socialist. Silkin still indefatigably sustains his excellent magazine *Stand*, organizes poetry festivals and readings, and in 1964 began to publish such poets as Ted Walker, Geoffrey Hill, and Michael Hamburger in a series called the Northern House Pamphlet Poets. The "Flower Poems" from *Nature With Man*, minutely detailed anthropomorphic scrutinies of flowers, have appeared as a Northern House pamphlet. Some critics think them his best work to date. Silkin's principal recreation is travel. He has made several poetry-reading tours of the United States, and has also taught there, at Denison University, Ohio, and at the University of Iowa's Writers' Workshop.

PRINCIPAL WORKS: *Poetry*—The Peaceable Kingdom, 1954; The Two Freedoms, 1958; The Re-ordering of the Stones, 1961; Nature With Man, 1965; Poems New and Selected, 1966; Amana Grass, 1971. *Criticism*—Out of Battle: The Poetry of the Great War, 1972. *As editor*—Living Voices, 1960; Poetry of the Committed Individual: A *Stand* Anthology of Poetry, 1973.

ABOUT: Allott, K. (ed.) Penguin Book of Contemporary Verse, 1962; Braun, M. E. *introduction to* The Peaceable Kingdom (2nd ed., 1969); Contemporary Authors 7–8, 1963; Murphy, R. (ed.) Contemporary Poets of the English Language, 1970; Schmidt, M. and Lindop, G. (eds.) British Poetry Since 1960, 1972; Who's Who, 1973. *Periodicals*—Jerusalem Post April 16, 1962; London Magazine October 1966; Poetry and Audience 12 (Leeds) January 26, 1962; Socialist Leader June 19, 1965; Times Literary Supplement August 25, 1966.

SILLITOE, ALAN (March 4, 1928–), English novelist, short story writer, and poet, writes: "I've always found it difficult to make facts sound interesting, especially about myself. The personal life of a writer is a very slippery thing, hard to pin down from the walking mass of imagination that the writer is. Anyway, I was born in the city of Nottingham on March 4th, 1928. My mother's father (Burton) was a blacksmith, and my father's father was an upholsterer who came from Wolverhampton in Staffordshire.

"My father was one of eight children, and he was crippled by rickets to such an extent that he was not able to go to school until he was twelve. He left at thirteen to go to work, and by then he could do simple arithmetic and write his own name. Apart from that, he was never able to read or write.

"During most of my childhood he was unable to get work. My parents constantly fought. I think they would have fought if they had been rich, but fighting among parents when they are poor is somehow much worse. Still, when the 1939 war broke out my father was able to get work, and the family atmosphere much improved. There were five children in the family, and I was the second eldest. It was often my responsibility to tell them stories in order to keep them quiet or get them to sleep.

"I went to an elementary school, and did rather well most of the time, though this was not difficult since the standards weren't high. I sat for a scholarship examination twice when I was eleven, but did not pass. I left school at fourteen, and went to work in the Raleigh bicycle factory—within a hundred yards of the house. This was in 1942. There were no thoughts of me ever becoming a writer. I earned what was considered good money for one so young: my first week's wages were about thirty shillings for forty-eight hours' work. As far as I knew, I would stick at factory work (apart from a period of conscription) for the rest of my life.

"At eighteen I went into the RAF and was trained as a wireless operator. With this skill, I went to Malaya, where I stayed for nearly two years. It was there that I really started to read. Before the age of twenty I had read very little—apart from comic books and novels written for children or juveniles. I read *Sebastopol* and *The Kreutzer Sonata* by Tolstoy, and knew immediately that I had stumbled on a new sort of writing. My work was mostly in an isolated hut far off from the main camp, and I had much time for reading—and also writing. I kept a journal, and wrote what I thought were poems.

"Then the Communist guerrillas began their war against the British—and my one thought was to get out. I didn't want to help in this war. If I had found an opportunity of helping the guerrillas I would have done so. My one hope was that I would not be killed by them. A few months later I was due to go back to England.

"When I arrived there, I was given an X-ray before discharge back to civilian life. It was then found that I had tuberculosis. I stayed in the RAF a further two years—in hospital and for most of the time on my back. It was then, of course, that I started to write. My first novel was written at twenty-one, just after leaving the hospital and returning to Nottingham. It was a hundred thousand words long and took me seventeen days to write. It has since been destroyed.

"On a small pension I lived the next nine years in England, France, and Spain, writing all the time—novels, poems, and stories. It took me ten years to teach myself how to write, and to find my own voice. My first novel *Saturday Night and Sunday Morning* was published when I was thirty.

"Because it took me so long to learn how to write I do not feel that I have much to learn from critics and reviewers. I learn from myself, from people

ALAN SILLITOE

who do not know I am learning from them, and perhaps from other writers. I write at my own pace and in my own style, evolving my own ideas slowly—so slowly in fact that year by year reviewers may not see the speed of 'development' there that they are accustomed to seeing in writers who come and go as fast as they can build them up and knock them down. I do not know many writers, but I know many people. I write slowly, and do nothing else but write. My most consistent output is of poems, and it was poetry that I wrote from the very earliest days. In fact I still consider myself more a poet than a novelist—though most people do not agree with this.

"At the moment I have just finished writing a play, which I shall call *This Foreign Field.* I think every writer should live a certain proportion of his life away from his own country. He should know at least one other language apart from his own. In this way he might learn more about his own language, and preserve that air of detachment and scepticism regarding the country (or culture) he was born in.

"My base is in London, but I like to travel, I am married, and have one son. My wife is an American, a poet, who writes under the name of Ruth Fainlight. I have known her for fourteen years."

Of the writers who emerged in England in the 1950s, Alan Sillitoe is one of the very few to whom the journalistic label "Angry Young Man" might aptly be applied. If there is any single key to his work it is his raw social indignation, his unabated conviction that "revolution is the only remaining road of spiritual advance."

Sillitoe's first book, *Saturday Night and Sunday Morning*, expressed with a harsh and powerful poetry the postwar mood of the British working class, which in material terms had "never had it so good" but remained bitterly aware that "They"—the officer class, the managerial class—still had it better, and were still making the rules. Arthur Seaton, the novel's young hero, spends his working life in a Nottingham factory whose smells make him sick. He secretly rather enjoys his meaningless and repetitive job, but will not do it as well or as fast as he could because this would benefit "Them." His education has failed to provide him with the means to use his leisure creatively, and he finds his only deep satisfaction in occasional solitary fishing trips.

It is a soul-destroying life, but Seaton is not completely demoralized. Unlike many of his peers, he is his own man, a rebel and a loner, a gleeful and anarchic enemy of the system that has produced him. On Saturday nights he drinks himself sick, quarrels and brawls, and seduces the wives of his tamer workmates. When the reckoning comes—a Sunday morning hangover, a ruined suit and, in the end, a serious beating—he pays up reluctantly but without self-pity. And when at last he half surrenders to the system, it is not because his courage has failed, or his primitive sense of honor, but because he has fallen in love with a girl more conventional than himself.

The novel was praised above all for the unsentimental honesty and real knowledge with which Sillitoe had portrayed his hero, and the total authenticity of the background and the dialogue. The style was thought "homespun" rather than inspired, and critics noted serious flaws in the book's construction. Nevertheless it received an award as the best first novel of 1958, became a best seller, and was made into an excellent film by Tony Richardson. Anthony West said that Sillitoe, "even if he never writes anything more . . . has assured himself a place in the history of the English novel."

And in fact he has written a great deal more. His second book was a volume of short stories, *The Loneliness of the Long Distance Runner*. It received the Hawthornden Prize, and the title story (which has also been filmed by Richardson) is regarded by many critics as Sillitoe's masterpiece. It is an account of the struggle between independence and conformity in the mind of a Borstal (reform school) boy. The narrator-hero has been recognized by the school governor as a natural athlete who, with encouragement and training, would justify the governor's facile theories about rehabilitation. Half-seduced by his own pride in his talent and the knowledge that he stands to win the approval of a formerly hostile society, the boy trains hard for the race that is the climax of the story. In the end he comes to understand that the race is only another kind of exploitation, and deliberately loses it. The tone of the story is conveyed well enough in this brief excerpt: "The pop-eyed pot-bellied governor said to a pop-eyed pot-bellied Member of Parliament who sat next to his pop-eyed pot-bellied whore of a wife that I was his only hope for getting the Borstal Blue Ribbon Prize Cup for Long Distance Cross Country Running (All England), which I was, and it set me laughing to myself inside."

This well-shaped long story is remarkable as an account of one individual's moral coming of age and for its relentlessly accurate exposure of the corrupting effect even of well-meaning authority. G. S. Fraser spoke of its "classical and tragic view of working-class life: you can't win but you can fight." Several other stories in the collection were also admired, and Fraser concluded that "the short story is [Sillitoe's] proper length. It permits an objectivity and clarity of line which he has not so far achieved in his novels."

Sillitoe's subsequent writing suffers by comparison with his first two books. His novel *The General* (filmed in 1967 as *Counterpoint*) is an ambitious but crude and unconvincing allegory on the theme of art's superiority to power. *Key to the Door* is set mainly in Malaya, where Arthur Seaton's brother Brian is doing his national service. Anthony Burgess, who knows the country well, said that the Malayan landscape was "wonderfully rendered" but thought Sillitoe's romantic admiration for the Malayan Communists woefully ignorant and naïve.

In *The Death of William Posters*, the first novel in a projected trilogy, Frank Dawley, after twelve years in a factory, revolts against his environment. He leaves his wife and family, and his mistress and her baby, and goes to Africa, where he becomes involved as a gun-runner in the Algerian struggle for independence. The story is continued in *A Tree on Fire*, in which Dawley, liberated by rebellion and suffering, eventually returns to foment revolution in England. Here the Dawley episodes alternate with scenes from the life of his friend Albert Handley, a newly fashionable but uncorrupted revolutionary painter who lives uproariously in Lincolnshire with his large family. An important and well-drawn subsidiary character is Handley's brother John, deranged by war, who busies himself with attempts to communicate with extraterrestrial beings until he exchanges fantasy for reality, and goes to fight alongside Dawley in Algeria.

Like Arthur Seaton and the boy in *The Loneliness of the Long Distance Runner*, Dawley and Handley refuse to be seduced by the bourgeois ethic and, more, are prepared to destroy society in order to save its soul. Most critics were less impressed by Sillitoe's revolutionary theories than they had been by the more intuitive passion of his first two books. Indeed his political views were generally thought naïve, confused, and even dishonest—the product of sterile class hatred and wishful thinking rather than of observation and knowledge. Julian Symons, in his review of *A Tree on Fire*, found it weak in construction and characterization, but said of Sillitoe: "His aims are high, his energy admirable. And there remains a genuinely sweet ingenuousness, rather like that of D. H. Lawrence, behind his most violent writing." *A Start in Life*, which attempts to combine working-class autobiography with elements of the picaresque and the thriller, had a mixed reception. So did *Raw Material*, a fictionalized account of the lives of his four grandparents in which he tries "to trace the chain of events and circumstances" that led to his becoming a novelist. *Travels in Nihilon*, a political satire set in a state dedicated to chaos, seemed flat and diffuse to some critics, but was welcomed by one as "a very pleasing reminder of Mr. Sillitoe's range."

G. S. Fraser has described Sillitoe's verse as "romantic, profoundly pessimistic, and completely hostile to organised society." Sillitoe has also published three volumes of admirable short stories, a children's book and *Road to Volgograd*, an account of a visit to Russia which showed all his exceptional talent for conveying the spirit of a place. A group of Sillitoe's short stories was dramatized and performed in 1964 by the semiprofessional Contemporary Theatre, which later produced *All Citizens Are Soldiers*, translated by Sillitoe and his wife from a play by Lope de Vega. In 1970 the same group staged Sillitoe's play *This Foreign Field*, about a land-hungry Nottingham tycoon of peasant ancestry and his feud with a landowning peer. The play has moments of Brechtian power but seemed to most reviewers inadequately realized as a whole. In 1970 Sillitoe became literary adviser to the publishing house of W. H. Allen.

PRINCIPAL WORKS: *Fiction*—Saturday Night and Sunday Morning, 1958; The Loneliness of the Long Distance Runner (short stories), 1959; The General, 1960; Key to the Door, 1961; The Ragman's Daughter (short stories), 1963; The Death of William Posters, 1965; The City Adventures of Marmalade Jim (for children), 1967; A Tree on Fire, 1967; Guzman Go Home (short stories), 1968; A Start in Life, 1970; Travels in Nihilon, 1971; Raw Material, 1972; Men, Women and Children (short stories), 1973. *Poetry*—Without Beer or Bread, 1957; The Rats, 1960; A Falling Out of Love, 1964; Love in the Environs of Voronezh, 1968; Shaman, 1968. *Travel*—The Road to Volgograd, 1964.

ABOUT: Allsop, K. The Angry Decade, 1958; Burgess, A. The Novel Now, 1967; Fraser, G. S. The Modern Writer and His World, 1964; Gindin, J. Postwar British Fiction, 1963; Shapiro, C. (ed.) Contemporary British Novelists, 1965; Vinson, J. (ed.) Contemporary Novelists, 1972; Who's Who, 1973; Who's Who in America, 1972–1973. *Periodicals*—Guardian March 24, 1970.

CLIFFORD D. SIMAK

SIMAK, CLIFFORD D(ONALD) (August 3, 1904–), American science fiction writer, writes: "I was born in my Grandfather Wiseman's home in the township of Millville, Wisconsin. The farm sits on a high bluff that overlooks the confluence of the Wisconsin and Mississippi rivers. My father, John L. Simak, was born in what was then Bohemia, in a small village near Prague, and came to the United States with his family when he was a small boy. The family was minor nobility which had fallen on hard times. My mother, the former Margaret Olivia Wiseman, traced her ancestry back to the Parker family of New England. Her father was Edward Wiseman, who came to the United States from the North of Ireland and who served in the Union army, as a cavalryman, under Grant and, later, Sherman.

"Shortly after my birth, my father bought a tract of land and developed a farm. My boyhood was a happy one. The area in which the farm was located, in southwestern Wisconsin, then provided good hunting and fishing. I swam in a hole in the creek, tobogganed and skated in the winter, roamed the woods with a gun, living, in many ways, the life of a lad in pioneer days. I attended a small country school and after the eighth grade rode a horse to high school at Patch Grove, four miles distant. After graduating from high school, I worked at various jobs to earn money to continue my education. Taking a one-year teacher's training course, I taught rural school for several years, then went to the University of Wisconsin. Caught in the Depression of the early 1930s I was unable to finish university and obtained a newspaper job as reporter on the Iron River (Michigan) *Reporter*. In a couple of years I became editor. I worked at various newspapers throughout the Middle West and in 1939 joined the staff of the Minneapolis *Star* as copy reader. Within a few years I became chief of the copy desk and in 1949, news editor. In 1959 I left the news desk to develop a school-oriented science program for the *Star's* sister newspaper, the Minneapolis *Tribune*. The program, the Science Reading Series, is now used in more than thirty-five hundred classrooms in the newspaper's circulation area, and I devote the greater part of my time to it. The program, in 1966, won a Westinghouse-American Association for the Advancement of Science award. In 1967 I was given an award by the Minnesota Academy of Science in recognition of my work with the program. I also write a weekly science column for the *Star*. My wife, the former Agnes Kuchenberg, and I live in Minnetonka, Minnesota. We have two children, Scott and Shelley.

"From the time I was a small boy, I wanted to write and early in life became convinced that I wanted to be a newspaperman. But this, while satisfying in itself, did not give me the opportunity I needed to express some of the things that were running through my mind. I had early become an admirer of science fiction from reading H. G. Wells and Jules Verne. It was to science fiction that I turned in my writing effort, not only because it was a field in which I was interested, but because I felt that it was a medium of ideas. While I had scribbled, off and on, on various subjects, from the time I first started grade school, I wrote my first short story for publication in 1929. That particular story was accepted for publication, but was never published. But the second one I wrote was. Since then, except for a time in the late 1930s, I have written fairly regularly on a part-time basis. All of my writing has been science fiction except for two science books for teen-agers—*Our New Front Yard*, descriptive astronomy of the solar system, and *Trilobite, Dinosaur and Man*, a popular account of historical geology. In 1953 my book, *City*, won the International Fantasy award and in 1964 *Way Station* won the Hugo award. A novelette, *The Big Front Yard*, in 1958 also was awarded a Hugo."

Simak's science fiction stories began to appear in 1931. He left the field at the end of the following year, when *Astounding Stories* suspended publication, but began to write again in 1937, when John W. Campbell, Jr., became editor of the magazine, which had been revived several years earlier. It was Campbell who published the series of eight stories, collected into a book in 1952 as *City*, on which Simak's reputation rests.

City is a family chronicle forming an ambitious future history of mankind. Its despondent conclusion seems to be that dogs and robots are better equipped to build a viable civilization than man. Simak wrote the series, he says, as a protest against war: "It was the creation of a world I thought there ought to be. It was filled with the gentleness and the kindness and the courage that I thought were needed in the world. . . . I made the dogs and robots the kind of people I would like to live with. And the vital point is this: That they must be dogs or robots, because people were not that kind of folks."

Simak's working out of his theme and the quality of his writing impressed many reviewers, and H. H. Holmes called the book "one of the major highpoints of modern science fiction." It won the International Fantasy Award in the year of its publication, and since then has come to be recognized as a minor classic of the genre.

City embodies many of the characteristics of Simak's work—his strong moral sense, his dislike of urban life and urban values, his rapid, cinematic style, which cuts directly from one crucial scene to the next. L. Sprague de Camp, who in 1959 included Simak in his list of eighteen "leading science-fiction writers," finds his work rather similar to Isaac Asimov's: "Their clear, spare, serious, literate, fast-moving styles are somewhat alike, and both go in for cosmic subject-matter. Simak likes to deal with robots, with interplanetary travel, and with time-travel. But unlike his more cautious contemporaries, instead of confining himself to one of these subjects at a time he likes to mix all three together in a grand . . . mélange. The result is impressive but betimes confusing."

The image of Simak's happy rural childhood casts a glow over many of his pages, and his heroes are often farmers or country people. In *Ring Around the Sun* he conjures up an innocent Arcadian counterpart of earthly life which the protagonist achieves not by technological means but by a ritual invoking memories of his childhood on the farm. *City* itself is to some extent an exercise in wish fulfillment, and purists occasionally grumble that some of Simak's work is closer to fantasy than to science fiction proper. He is no escapist however, and many of his stories embody a harsh awareness of man's inhumanity to man, and are concerned to uphold the rights of the individual (even the individual robot) against the forces of authority and conformity. Kingsley Amis has called Simak "a kind of science-fiction poet laureate of the countryside" who "comes nearest, by a familiar linkage, to being science-fiction's religious writer."

Simak's nonfictional books have been well received, and his story *How-2* (*Galaxy Science Fiction*, November 1954), a sort of allegorical approach to the civil rights question, has been adapted as a musical. The author is a "dark man whose angular features give him a slightly Amerindian look." His wife assists him in his work both as his typist and a critic. "My interests," he writes, "include chess, stamp collecting, rose growing, but I'm a mediocre chess player, have virtually given up stamps through lack of time, have decided you can't grow roses in the villainous Minnesota climate. Most of my spare time is spent at reading."

PRINCIPAL WORKS: *Fiction*—Cosmic Engineers, 1950; Time and Again, 1951; City, 1952; Ring Around the Sun, 1953; Strangers in the Universe, 1956; Worlds Without End, 1956; The Worlds of Clifford Simak, 1960; Time is the Simplest Thing, 1961; The Trouble With Tycho, 1961; All the Traps of Earth, 1962; They Walked Like Men, 1962; Way Station, 1963; All Flesh Is Grass, 1965; Why Call Them Back From Heaven?, 1967; Best Science Fiction Stories of Clifford Simak, 1967; The Werewolf Principle, 1967; The Goblin Reservation, 1968; Out of Their Minds, 1970; Destiny Doll, 1971; A Choice of Gods, 1971; Cemetery World, 1973; Our Children's Children, 1973. *Nonfiction*—The Solar System: Our New Front Yard, 1962; Trilobite, Dinosaur and Man, 1966; Wonder and Glory: The Story of the Universe, 1969; Prehistoric Man, 1971.

ABOUT: Amis, K. New Maps of Hell, 1960; Asimov, I. *in* The Hugo Winners, 1962; Contemporary Authors 4, 1963; De Camp, L. S. Science-Fiction Handbook, 1953; Moskowitz, S. Seekers of Tomorrow, 1965; Tuck, D. H. (ed.) A Handbook of Science Fiction and Fantasy, 1959.

***SIMON, CLAUDE** (October 10, 1913–), writes (in French) that he was "born in Tananarive (Madagascar) of French parents. Father a career officer killed in the war in 1914. Childhood at Perpignan in the Eastern Pyrenees; then in Paris where I completed my secondary studies. Studied painting, traveled in Europe, then began to write (*Le Tricheur*) just before the beginning of World War II in which I fought in the cavalry. Prisoner in Germany, then escaped, got back to France, and then finished *Le Tricheur*, which was not published until after the end of the German occupation.

"Since then my life, like that of all writers, has mingled with my books, most of which (notably *L'Herbe*, *La Route des Flandres*, and *Le Palace*) are autobiographical.

"I live partly in Paris and partly in the Midi, at Salses, a village near Perpignan."

Claude Simon is one of the most prominent of the French "new novelists." He has arrived at that position via his training as a painter (which left him with an intense interest in the philosophy of perception) and, as he acknowledges, through the influence of Dostoevsky, Joyce, Conrad, and above all of Faulkner. Henri Peyre says that his books seek to convey not the passage of time, but its "simultaneousness"; Simon himself speaks of creating "a succession of images born from the memory of one event."

* sē môɴ′

CLAUDE SIMON

Little of this was immediately obvious in Simon's first novels, *Le Tricheur* (The Cheat, 1945), *La Corde raide* (The Taut Rope, 1948), *Gulliver* (1954), and *Le Sacre du printemps* (The Rite of Spring, 1953). Some critics found in them signs that Simon, like Camus, saw life as a fundamentally "absurd" affair, and Peyre was reminded of Jean Giono by their "rich and sensuous poetical prose," lovingly applied to natural description. Nevertheless, their lack of interest in plot and structure (which annoyed the reviewers)—their refusal to undertake the sequential narration of events—showed the direction in which Simon was to move in his mature novels.

His first book of importance was the "baroque triptych" *Le Vent* (1957). A sailor home from the sea, a confused and inarticulate Dostoevskian innocent, goes to claim the vineyards he has inherited in the Midi. Lawyers cheat him out of his property. His clumsy attempts to make friends with a gypsy woman and her daughters fail, leading to tragedy. The *mistral* of the South blows endlessly, "envying" the human characters "their possibility of forgetfulness, of peace: the privilege of dying."

The book was translated (like its successors) by Richard Howard, and published in 1959 as *The Wind*. Martin Levin wrote: "Scraps of dialogue, frequently disrupted in the middle of words, bits of interior monologue, pungent images, abrupt shifts in time and place—these bits and pieces create a bewildering collage, that is at first tantalizingly disoriented and then increasingly significant. . . . The fragmented impressions he presents eventually fuse into a total picture that is curiously haunting."

Simon's next book took its title from a poem of

Pasternak's: "No one makes history, no one sees it happen, no one sees the grass grow." *L'Herbe* (1959, translated as *The Grass*), is a lovingly, sensuously detailed account of the slow death of an old woman, and of the influence of this lengthy, almost permanent event upon the behavior of her niece, torn between husband and lover. Less happens than in *Le Vent* (though more than in many "new novels"). In fact, as several critics pointed out, what the novel is really about is the problem of writing it. Through "cascades of parentheses and interminable sentences," Simon attempts to overcome the obstinate consecutiveness of words and achieve the "presentness" of the cinema (whose way of seeing things he constantly alludes to in this book).

La Route des Flandres (1960, translated as *The Flanders Road*) and *Le Palace* (1962, translated as *The Palace*) similarly blend events with the memory of them, fantasy with actuality, in such a way that the situations recalled in these novels—the French defeat at Flanders in 1940, Barcelona revisited after the Spanish War—are scarcely relevant. Henri Peyre says of *La Route des Flandres* that "the recapturing of the past, as in Faulkner, and the reliving of ancestors' sins by descendants fascinated by them, are the felicitous elements of that chaotic and labyrinthine novel."

In a letter prefacing the brief autobiographical note above, Simon said of his own life what his books say of time's other victims, that "what has been imagined, been lived, been dreamed, the important, the unimportant, the decisive, the trivial, are for me terribly difficult to disentangle." He makes no attempt to do so in *Histoire* (Story), the most obviously autobiographical of his novels, which brought him the Prix Médicis in 1967.

Many themes and scenes from earlier novels (and the novelist's life) are resumed in *La Bataille de Pharsale* (1969, translated as *The Battle of Pharsalus*), one of the most warmly and widely reviewed of Simon's books. The narrator's recent visit to the dusty and neglected battlefield of Pharsalia in Greece evokes comparisons between the past and a negligible present, and these reflections merge with his own interior landscape, dominated by a preoccupation with death and a vividly remembered (and obsessively embellished) moment of youthful sexual jealousy. And these memories and reflections from the past are framed by the present, with the writer at his window in Paris, watching the crowds emerge from the Metro below (just as his other images emerge from his subconscious). The book was said to be "as dense, relentless and funerary as any that Simon has published"; "a marvellously rigorous novel in the way it is organized and . . . written with an astonishing and inimitable attention to physical detail."

Simon shares with the other *nouveaux romanciers* their phenomenological interests, their preoccupation with language and the creative process—and their lack of consideration for the reader. His sentences are often several pages long and devoid of punctuation, while the difficulties of keeping so many threads and characters simultaneously in mind are such that he himself is obliged to distinguish them in the writing by the use of colored pencils. He differs most radically from the other "new novelists" in what Victor Brombert calls his "opulent, sinuous prose," his "uncanny ability to make words adhere to forms and movement." Simon has discussed his methods in a remarkable illustrated essay, *Orion Aveugle* (Orion Blind, 1970).

La Séparation, a play based on *L'Herbe*, was produced in Paris in 1963 without much success. It is evident from Simon's novels that he fought on the Republican side in the Spanish Civil War, and he has spoken of his participation in the events described in *La Route des Flandres*. As he says, he now divides his time between Paris and Perpignan, where he cultivates his vineyard. He was married in 1951 to Yvonne Ducuing.

PRINCIPAL WORKS IN ENGLISH TRANSLATION: The Wind, 1959; The Grass, 1960; The Flanders Road, 1961; The Palace, 1963; Histoire, 1968; The Battle of Pharsalus, 1971.
ABOUT: Boisdeffre, P. de. Dictionnaire de littérature contemporaine, 1962; Curley, D. N. and Curley, A. Modern Romance Literatures (A Library of Literary Criticism), 1967; Frohock, W. M. Style and Temper: Studies in French Fiction, 1925–1960, 1967; International Who's Who, 1973–74; Le Sage, L. The French New Novel, 1962; Nadeau, M. The French Novel Since the War, 1967; Peyre, H. French Novelists of Today, 1967; Pingaud, B. Écrivains d'aujourd'hui, 1960; Sturrock, J. The French New Novel, 1969; Who's Who in France, 1973–1974. *Periodicals*—New York Times Book Review February 14, 1960; May 21, 1961; September 22, 1961; Saturday Review April 25, 1959; Time April 13, 1959; Times Literary Supplement June 8, 1962; Yale French Studies 24 1959; Yale Review March 1960.

SIMON, EDITH (May 18, 1917–), British novelist and historian, writes: "I was born in Berlin, Germany, prematurely and weighing three-and-a-half pounds, a fact to which I attribute an embarrassingly healthy appetite: since for the first few months of my life it apparently took much concentrated effort to make me eat. I was the first, and for nearly seven years the only child of my parents, and my greatest wish then was for a sister; I got her in the end and we have been great friends. My next-greatest early wishes were to have a minimum of seven children as soon as possible and to have lived in the past—a past part costume-museum, part fairytale—which latter developed relatively early into a romantic interest in history. With corroboration by my elders, I can remember preferring illustrated histories to any other kind of picture book, from about the age of four; reproductions of 'old' works of art came in the same category. I can only suppose it was everybody's sighing for the good old days before 1914, during that post-war period of my childhood, which started this off; though I don't know whether it would account for my strong dislike, at the time, of short dresses and short hair for women. I am still always hoping for a return of fashion to flowing skirts and hair long enough to sit on.

"Apart from this minor dream my interest in the past and representations of it in books and pictures fairly soon outgrew the purely romantic stage. I started to draw as soon as I could hold a pencil, and to write as soon as I could read—though I hasten to soften this by adding addictions to tree-climbing, bows and arrows, and other more violent pursuits: at one time it was my ambition to become a female boxer. I was lucky in the school I went to, as it encouraged those main interests which have filled my adult life.

"My family, though agnostic, were Jews. Their ancestors, regarding this as a religious not racial denomination, had been under the impression that they were Germans, for generations. However, my father, who had served with distinction throughout the 1914–1918 war, believed as early as 1931 that all the signs pointed towards Hitler's coming to power. He was an athletic, jovial, proud and anything but nervous man; as he put it, he did not want to become regarded as a second-class citizen, and emigrated to London, England, in 1932—a move which his friends and family considered very eccentric.

"After this I put up great resistance to further formal education and apart from copious reading only went to art school, where I found many stimulating friends. Although I started out as a painter and illustrator, one thing led to another until writing gained the upper hand. But we were rather poor at this time and I worked in all sorts of odd jobs. My first book, an illustrated story for children, was published in 1937, my translation of Arthur Koestler's *The Gladiators* in 1939, and my first novel in 1940; and since then I have been only a Sunday painter. In 1942 my husband, E. C. R. Reeve, and I met and married, and he has been my greatest friend and support ever since. He is a research geneticist attached to the University of Edinburgh, and we have three children (Antonia, fifteen; Simon, fourteen; Jessica, twelve).

"With my books I find it necessary to alternate between past and present, or fiction and fact; a form of coming up for air which makes it possible to carry on without any particular 'rest' between books. Each kind is a relief, and a complete technical break, from the other. The basic theme running through them all is man and his work, and the development of character under the manifold influences of time and place. I write at once fast and

EDITH SIMON

slowly: my output is large, but I have to do almost everything several times over before it comes truly right. Besides a few articles I have also written several plays and one film treatment, but these have never been performed. Literature in all its variants seems to me the essential expression of the human animal, and the foundation of everything that we call civilization."

Edith Simon's contemporary novels, many of them dealing with the intrigues of unpleasant or at least tiresome characters, have tended to disconcert the critics. *Biting the Blue Finger*, for example, about the adventures of a culturally ambitious adolescent girl in the company of an evil artist, seemed to some reviewers a disagreeable and rather labored book, lightened by touches of "acrid" humor. *The Other Passion*, an extraordinary modern picaresque, follows the fortunes of a Polish woman, a missionary in China, who becomes a revolutionary in Russia, marries an anarchist, changes her sex, and returns to China, where her daughter falls in love with her and her son plots to kill her; "few forms of intrigue and manners of death and torture are not represented," wrote one critic. Most of Miss Simon's contemporary fictions are considerably less bizarre than this, but still scarcely conventional. *The House of Strangers* centers on the polite academic warfare within a group of archaeologists digging out a prehistoric Scottish village. This sardonic story, slow-moving and full of technical detail, seemed to some readers an oddly personal book, with "an intensity of feeling and an undercurrent of suspense that make [it] an immensely gripping experience." *The Great*

Forgery, a very long novel based in part on the career of Hans van Meegeren, was enjoyed for its detailed account of the way in which an artist fakes a Holbein, and of his motives for doing so, but seemed cruel in its humor and crude and uneven in its style.

When she turns to the past, Miss Simon's standards and attitudes seem to change. The harshness and eccentricity are still there in her historical novels, but less arbitrarily so. Her characters and settings are better realized, and her prose, as it were, rises to the occasion, seeming altogether more vivid, exact, and of a piece. Her research is impeccable, and the principal criticism of her historical fictions has been that they are so scrupulously accurate, so disciplined in their eschewal of romantic speculation, that they make at times demanding reading. Her basic theme, as she says, "is man and his work," and it is often when she is describing some great technical achievement, like the building of the cathedral in *The Golden Hand*, that her books are most absorbing. The best of her novels, *The Twelve Pictures*, is a retelling of the legend of Siegfried and Brunhilde which brilliantly combines scholarship and imagination. The barbarous story is told in twelve episodes, "as stylized and colorful as medieval tapestries." Charles Rolo called the book "a superbly imagined panorama of a world that is half legendary and half real, half Christian and half Pagan. But what is specially notable about it is a psychological depth in the characterization which is rarely encountered in historical fiction."

The Piebald Standard was the first of Miss Simon's nonfiction histories, an account of the Knights Templars which introduced no original material but was thought carefully researched and notably well written. The *New Yorker* called it "an absorbing chronicle, alive with excitement and the terror of ideological metamorphosis, and it is set down with a firmness, a balance, and a polish that are altogether admirable." Subsequent biographical and historical studies have also been generally well received.

Edith Simon is the daughter of Walter and Grete (Goldberg) Simon. She began her education in Germany, and completed it at the Slade School of Art and the Central School of Arts and Crafts—a training whose effects are evident in her highly visual descriptive writing.

PRINCIPAL WORKS: *Contemporary novels*—Biting the Blue Finger, 1942; Wings Deceive, 1944; The Other Passion, 1949; Past Masters (U.S., The House of Strangers), 1953; The Sable Coat, 1958; The Great Forgery, 1961. *Historical novels*—The Chosen, 1940; The Golden Hand, 1952; The Twelve Pictures, 1955. *Nonfiction*—The Piebald Standard: A Biography of the Knights Templars, 1959; The Making of Frederick the Great, 1963; (with the editors of Time-Life Books) The Reformation, 1966; The Saints, 1968; Luther Alive: Martin Luther and the Making of the Reformation, 1968.

ABOUT: Contemporary Authors 13–14, 1965; Current Biography, 1954. *Periodicals*—Books September 8, 1963; New York Times Book Review October 25, 1959; Times Literary Supplement June 19, 1959.

SIMON, JOHN (May 12, 1925–), American critic, writes: "I was born in Yugoslavia in 1925 of mixed Yugoslav and Hungarian parentage, and still speak Serbo-Croatian and Hungarian, for whatever good it does anyone. (I periodically resolve to do some verse translations from these languages, and periodically don't get around to it.) I went to school in Yugoslavia, England, and, later, in New York, where we moved when the Second World War was two years old and I fifteen. I went to Harvard and got my B.A. in English. For a year and a half I served in the Air Forces, but never got overseas. Back at the Harvard Graduate School, I switched to comparative literature, and in due time got my M.A. I did not get my Ph.D. till undue time—1959, to be exact—having, in the meantime, taught literature and humanities at Harvard, the University of Washington, M.I.T., and Bard College, where I worked myself up to the exalted rank of assistant professor. Just as I obtained my doctorate, I got out of teaching, and I still think there is a certain poetic justice in that. My thesis on the European prose poem remains unpublished; two university presses were interested in printing it, provided I whittled it down a bit; but as I am a terrible whittler, the seven hundred and thirty-two pages continue their year-round hibernation.

"Meanwhile, I had married a student of mine, but since I was able to teach her even less at home than in class, the marriage ended in a relatively speedy and mutually beneficial divorce. My next job was as associate editor with the Mid-Century Book Society, whose house organ, *The Mid-Century*, I edited. Working under Messrs. Auden, Barzun and Trilling was stimulating, and I started publishing critical pieces—as critical, that is, as was consistent with selling the books—in *The Mid-Century*. I had previously published a little critical prose in ephemeral journals and a certain amount of verse in better magazines. But the poetic Muse forsook me, and I was left in the arms of a harsher one, if, indeed, critical prose can be said to have a Muse at all.

"In 1961, my future publisher, then vice-president of Mid-Century, fired me; but inasmuch as my book lost money for him, I consider the score evened. At this time, I did a little art criticism for the New York *Times* and *Arts* magazine, and an occasional book review here and there. Then Robert Brustein left the *Hudson Review* for the *New Republic*, and, through his recommendation, I inherited his job as drama critic of the *Hudson*. I also began publishing articles and reviews in various national magazines, and making occasional appearances on radio and television. There was little money in all this, but my parents generously subsidized me, and, over a period of several years, two gracious girls made life more appealing.

"Late in 1962 I started writing film criticism for the *New Leader*, and the following year *Acid Test*, a collection of my criticism of various arts, was published. Since then I have been doing more freelance criticism, and occasionally lecturing or participating in symposiums, my fondness for panel discussions being one of my more sordid vices. At present I am drama critic of *New York* magazine. I have also published or broadcast reviews abroad, notably in Canada and Germany. I have written for everything, from encyclopedias to record jackets, and two-thirds of a poem of mine was anthologized by Oscar Williams. The third died of shame.

"In criticism, I have three tenets. First, to write on as many different subjects as I decently can, because nothing is worse than parochialism in the arts—unless it be the staleness that comes from writing continually about one sickly art, such as theatre in New York. Secondly, to try to make a critique something written as carefully as a story or poem. This does not mean that a review will become as important as a really good poem or play, but it does mean that it will be worth reading and thinking about. Most American journalistic criticism sees itself as a subdivision of utilitarianism, instead of as an art form. Thirdly, I have endeavored to remain absolutely independent in my criticism, recognizing no call of coterie, friendship, pity, or established reputation. Need I add that I have few literary friends, restricted literary outlets, and a clear conscience."

John Simon strictly observes his three critical tenets, to the satisfaction of some of his readers and the extreme annoyance of others. Very few critics can have applied themselves to a greater variety of art forms, and he "always seems to have available the knowledge relevant to the task at hand," thus earning both praise for his erudition and blame for his intellectual exhibitionism. Similarly, his epigrammatic prose style is admired in some quarters for its wit and "verbal energy," condemned in others as phrase-mongering. As for the independence of Simon's criticism, it is beyond question. Indeed, what Émile Capouya calls his "strongly defined tastes," his "conviction that aesthetics and morality are not unconnected," and an undoubted weakness for the scornful phrase, have brought him a reputation as a gratuitously harsh critic.

In his introduction to *Acid Test*, a collection of thirty-seven of Simon's critical pieces about

JOHN SIMON

literature, the theatre, the cinema, and the visual arts, Dwight Macdonald compares Simon to H. L. Mencken and George Jean Nathan in their prime. "He is acerb and cold-eyed, as unmoved by avant-gardists' pleas to be judged indulgently because they represent Art and the Future as by the commercial entrepreneur's grumbling about his property," Macdonald writes. "But he is also a fairminded judge . . . who has all the precedents to hand and can bring them to bear on contemporary work. In a period of confusion, this combination of knowledge and uncompromising sharpness is just what is needed." Simon is extraordinarily sensitive to visual impressions, and adept at passing on to the reader exactly what it was like to see the movie, or the play, or the picture under discussion. According to *Newsweek*, Simon greatly admires the late James Agee and, like him, "*sees* very well."

Simon is extremely effective in public debate, where his adversaries have included Susan Sontag and Marshall McLuhan. His lecture platform manner has been described as "alternately acid and charmingly alkaline."

PRINCIPAL WORKS: Acid Test, 1963; Private Screenings (movie reviews), 1967; (ed. with Richard Schickel) Film 67/68, 1968; Movies Into Film: Film Criticism 1967–1970, 1971; Ingmar Bergman Directs, 1972.

ABOUT: Contemporary Authors 21–22, 1969; Macdonald, D. *introduction to* Simon, J. Acid Test, 1963. *Periodicals*—New York Times Book Review March 21, 1971; Partisan Review Winter 1964.

SIMON, (MARVIN) NEIL (July 4, 1927–), American dramatist, was born in the Bronx, New York City, the son of Irving Simon, a dress salesman, and Mamie Simon. He grew up in the Bronx

NEIL SIMON

and in Washington Heights, graduating from the De Witt Clinton High School in 1943 when he was only sixteen. Simon studied engineering at New York University under the Army Air Force Reserve training program, and in 1945–1946 was stationed at Lowry Field in Colorado, where he was sports editor of the base newspaper. In 1946 ex-Corporal Simon became a mail clerk in the New York offices of Warner Brothers Pictures, where his older brother Danny wrote publicity.

Soon after, the two brothers did a test assignment for Goodman Ace of the Columbia Broadcasting System and were hired as a comedy writing team. During the next ten years they wrote material for the Robert Q. Lewis radio show, for the Phil Silvers Arrow Show on NBC television, for Tallulah Bankhead, Jackie Gleason, and Red Buttons, their weekly income rising from $50 to $1,600. The team broke up in 1956, when Danny Simon became a television director. Neil Simon hung on until 1960, writing for Sid Caesar, Garry Moore, and other television comics, but more and more found it "degrading to try to be funny when you don't feel like it."

The escape route was provided by *Come Blow Your Horn*, a semi-autobiographical play about two brothers who exchange the confining security of Jewish family life for an elegant bachelor apartment in Manhattan. The comedy, which Simon says was "eight weeks in the writing, three years in the re-writing, and . . . had at least eight producers before I ever saw it on stage," reached Broadway in 1961. The critics found it smoothly plotted and deftly written, but some of them objected that it relied too heavily on an endless stream of gags spoken by stereotypes rather than honest observation of character. If so, its audiences seemed not to mind, and the play ran for eighty-five weeks. The following year Simon provided the book for *Little Me*, a musical based on Patrick Dennis's parody of a star's autobiography.

Barefoot in the Park, a bitter-sweet comedy about a stuffy young lawyer's adjustment to his exhaustingly uninhibited bride, opened in 1963 and ran for four years. This time the critics were as enthusiastic as the public, finding it just as funny as *Come Blow Your Horn* and considerably more original. *The Odd Couple* (1965), like its predecessor directed on Broadway by Mike Nichols, was even more pleasing to the reviewers, and received the Antoinette Perry Award in 1966. Simon says he dictated the essence of the play into a tape recorder in half a minute: "Two men . . . neither quite sure why their marriages fell apart—move in together to cut down [on expenses] and suddenly discover that they're having the same conflicts and fights that they had in their marriages." Richard Watts praised Simon's capacity to develop so many "wise, amusing, perceptive and always recognizably human variations" on his theme, while Howard Taubman spoke of his "faultless" instinct for incongruity.

Simon wrote the book for *Sweet Charity*, a 1966 musical adapted from Federico Fellini's film *Nights of Cabiria*. His own comedy, *The Star-Spangled Girl*, opened later the same year to generally good reviews. Thus, by December 1966, Simon had his name over the marquees of no less than four Broadway theatres. And a little over three years later, early in 1970, Broadway was cheering three quite different Simon plays, all of them smash hits. These were *Plaza Suite*, which had opened in 1968—a trio of short plays set in the same suite of hotel rooms, each "an eloquent marriage of situation and hilarious dialogue"; *Promises, Promises* (1969), "an absolutely marvelous musical" based on the movie *The Apartment*; and *Last of the Red Hot Lovers* (1970), reviewing three episodes in a middle-aged man's last-ditch struggle to achieve adultery.

By this time, Simon was a theatre owner (the Eugene O'Neill), had become his own principal backer, and was said to be the most financially successful dramatist of all time, with an income (according to *Variety*) of something like $45,000 a week. In March 1970 Walter Kerr tried to explain this prodigious success, achieved in a genre—the well-made popular comedy—that was supposed to be extinct. He concluded that what Simon does "has a much more serious, perceptive, *human* base to it than ordinary mechanical farce. . . . Mr. Simon is more than a gagman, he does have an eye and an ear for the crazy, cruel world about him, and yes, he remains a writer of light comedy. . . . His special victory is to have discovered the exact amount of God's truth a light comedy can properly contain." Not everyone agreed, it should be said, and Stanley Kauffmann, writing at about the same time, called Simon's work "basically sentimental and consumer-flattering" but allowed it a certain "limited gratitude" for the absolute perfection with which it met the requirements of the "Broadway mechanism."

Simon himself once said that he had no desire at all to write serious plays: "I'm a writer of human comedy. For myself, there's nothing more important." All the same, several critics noted that *Last of the Red Hot Lovers* contained at least one important speech that was entirely serious. And Simon's next play, *The Gingerbread Lady* (1970), seemed to Clive Barnes a fundamentally serious work, even though it was "as funny as ever—the customary avalanche of hilarity, and landslide of pure unbuttoned joy." It is a study of a singing star in decline, a self-destructive nymphomaniac alcoholic whose saving grace is her wryly witty self-knowledge. The role was memorably created by Maureen Stapleton. Barnes wrote: "It is not the kind of play where you laugh till it hurts—merely it hurts till you laugh. . . . This is a remarkable and moving dialogue between a great actress and a playwright who has suddenly discovered the way to express the emptiness beneath the smart remark and the shy compassion that can be smothered by a wisecrack." *The Sunshine Boys* (1972), about two faded vaudeville stars, was found equally funny and equally moving, but *The Good Doctor* (1973), Simon's stage adaptation of nine early short stories and vignettes by Chekhov, seemed to most reviewers neither good Simon nor good Chekhov.

A number of Simon's plays have been successfully adapted for the screen, some by himself, and he has also written some original screenplays. He was married in 1953 to Joan Baim, who was a dancer and counselor at Camp Tamiment in the Pocono Mountains when Simon and his brother were writing revues there. They have two daughters and live in Manhattan. Simon is a large man, shy, genial, and soft-spoken. He lists his recreations as golf, the theatre, and "rewriting." He says that his idea of "the ultimate in comedy is to make a whole audience fall onto the floor, writhing and laughing so hard that some of them pass out." It is a notion to warm the heart of Antonin Artaud, the prophet of "total theatre."

PRINCIPAL WORKS: Come Blow Your Horn, 1963; Barefoot in the Park, 1964; The Odd Couple, 1966; Sweet Charity, 1966; The Star-Spangled Girl, 1967; Plaza Suite, 1969; Promises, Promises, 1969; Last of the Red Hot Lovers, 1970; The Gingerbread Lady, 1971; The Prisoner of Second Avenue, 1972; The Sunshine Boys, 1973.

ABOUT: Current Biography, 1968; Who's Who, 1972; Who's Who in America, 1972–1973. *Periodicals*—Life April 9, 1965; New York Times November 3, 1963; New York Times Magazine March 7, 1965; March 22, 1970; Newsweek January 9, 1967; February 20, 1970; Time November 29, 1963.

SIMPSON, LOUIS (ASTON MARANTZ) (March 27, 1923–), American poet and novelist, writes: "I was born in Kingston, Jamaica, in the West Indies. My father was Jamaican, and practiced law. My mother was born in Poland, emigrated as a child to New York, became an actress in the movies, and met my father while she was on a movie-making trip in the Caribbean. Most of my schooling was at Munro, on a mountain in a remote part of the island. During the vacations I had, now that I look back on it, an interesting time—fishing, shooting, swimming, bicycle-riding around Kingston. The school was hard, but I was lucky enough to have good teachers, especially a man named Andrews, a Scotsman, who read *Macbeth* with passion. I was fairly good at games, but I was devoted to reading. And through reading I came to think that I might be able to write too. Apart from the required school essays, my first attempts at writing were stories and poems I wrote in imitation of Hardy, Shakespeare . . . and later on, modern authors such as Eliot and Lawrence. At about the age of fifteen I fell in with a group of young Jamaicans who were agitating for independence from British rule, and I wrote and published for a newspaper called *Public Opinion*. I had also won two prizes for an essay and a short story. So at that age I was launched, without any plan, on writing.

"My parents had been divorced, and my mother now lived in the States, so when my father died—I was then seventeen—I came to New York. There had been some talk of my going to Oxford, but the war was on, and as I had no wish to go back to Jamaica, I entered Columbia University. This was in 1940. I studied at Columbia until 1943, when I went into the U.S. Army. At Columbia, Mark Van Doren was the teacher who encouraged me most. I spent three years in the army, mostly in the 101st Airborne Division, and saw action in France, Holland, Belgium and Germany. After the war I had a collapse—amnesia, the works—and it took me two or three years to come out of it entirely. During this time I worked at odd jobs—for example, as a clerk and packer in an import-export firm—and studied and wrote at odd hours. In 1948 I went to France for a year, and there finished my first book of poetry, *The Arrivistes*. From 1950 to 1955 I was a reader, then editor, for the Bobbs-Merrill Publishing Company. In 1950 I married Jeanne Claire Rogers. We were divorced; there is a son by that marriage—Louis Matthew Simpson.

"In 1955 I was married again, to Dorothy

LOUIS SIMPSON

Roochvarg. We have two children, Anthony Rolf and Anne Borovoi Simpson. In 1955, also, I gave up publishing-business and studied for my Ph.D. so that I could earn a living as a teacher. I knew that I could never be the kind of writer who made money. I got the degree, and have taught at Columbia and—since 1959—at the University of California at Berkeley.

"In 1955 I published my second book: *Good News of Death and Other Poems* (Scribner's.) My other books are: *A Dream of Governors* (poems), 1959 (Wesleyan University Press); *Riverside Drive* (a novel), 1962 (Atheneum); *James Hogg, A Critical Study*, 1962 (St. Martin's Press); *At the End of the Open Road* (poems), 1963 (Wesleyan University Press); *Selected Poems*, 1965 (Harcourt, Brace and World). For *At the End of the Open Road* I was awarded the 1964 Pulitzer Prize for poetry.

"I never knew how obscure I was, until I won the prize. Suddenly people were 'discovering' me. But I had been writing, quite happily, for years, and some people had read my work. I am grateful to those people.

"I have definite ideas about writing. The thing, I believe, is to imagine and create, not merely express opinions. We are suffering from all sorts of wrong ideas nowadays, and one of them is that confession is enough. And then there are all the kinds of wish-fulfillment—on which novelists grow rich. But there are few novelists and poets, after all. It takes intelligence and hard work to create anything.

"And time. I am thinking of poems, articles and stories that I may not be able to write for years. But they won't be hurried."

Louis Simpson is one of the two sons of Aston Simpson, a second-generation Jamaican of Scottish descent, and the former Rosalind de Marantz. His father was a lawyer with a passion for facts, his mother a romantic who loved the opera and filled his head with tales of the wolves and unimaginable snow of Poland. C. B. Cox sees in this parentage one source of the "perpetual debate" in Simpson's poetry between irony and romance. Simpson's migration at seventeen to the United States, which had long attracted him, introduced new conflicts; his effort to come to terms with his adopted country no doubt accounts for what Philip Booth calls his deep knowledge, his "huge sense" of America. During his war service as a sergeant with the 101st Airborne Division Simpson earned the Bronze Star with oak leaf cluster, two Purple Hearts, and his American citizenship. At Bastogne he suffered frostbite and delayed shock, and his complete mental collapse followed. During his slow recuperation he worked in New York at a variety of odd jobs and as a freelance writer, and spent his evenings at Columbia's School of General Studies, which gave him a B.S. in 1948. *Current Biography* suggests that the subsequent year in Paris, where he studied at the Sorbonne, was decisive for him. He disliked the intellectual and social posturing he found there and returned to New York rid of illusions, determined to write, and to allow nothing to distract him from this purpose.

The development of Simpson's verse reflects his struggle to hold in balance the effects of the long succession of violent assaults to which his personality had been subjected. His early poems, collected in *The Arrivistes* and *Good News of Death* (which includes a verse play), were by and large defensively ironic and preoccupied with technique, admired for their wit, fancy, and intelligence, but lacking a distinctive voice. An increasing mastery of traditional forms was evident in the first half of *A Dream of Governors*, "dazzling with its wit and finish," but this transitional collection also contained a number of poems, many of them concerned with dream and hallucination, which were less successful but more daring in form and content. Critics were sharply divided as to the relative merits of the two modes, especially in their reaction to "The Runner," a long poem about the 101st Airborne which seemed to some readers dull and disastrous, and to others a major advance.

Simpson has refused to "talk out" his conflicts in poems of the confessional kind or on the other hand to settle for the merely decorative verse he has learned to manage so well. Believing, according to C. B. Cox, that "no single mode of apprehending reality can ever be fully satisfactory," he has struggled to contain both irony and mystery in his poetry. When he succeeds he earns great tension, vigor, and assurance. There are such victories in *At the End of the Open Road*, which laments what has become of the American Dream but concludes: "Whitman was wrong about the People, / But right about himself. The land is within. At the end of the open road we come to ourselves." This collection, which brought Simpson the Pulitzer Prize in 1964, had for Thom Gunn "a kind of vigorous restlessness, of a most exciting sort," and seemed to William Stafford to give the reader "a sense of living in a sustained pattern which works along behind the poems and makes of them a succession of glimpses into something ever larger."

Selected Poems convinced Donald Hall that Simpson "has become primarily a poet of the imagination, but for him the imagination in no way necessitates suppressing the critical intelligence or limiting the possibilities of language." His work has increasingly escaped from the "iambic norms" to a more free and colloquial manner. Hall says that "it is America which is . . . his main entry into poetry. In his early work he wrote some of the best modern love poems, and certainly he has written the best American poems about World War II," but "America was always there, bothering him." At first "the country was largely historic and geographic: increasingly . . . he has dealt with the spirit. . . . He is the Columbus of an inward continent."

Simpson has been associated with Donald Hall, Robert Bly, and others who contribute to the magazine *The Seventies*. What they have in common, Hall believes, is "a new kind of imagination. . . . This imagination is irrational yet the poem is usually quiet and the language simple. . . . This new imagination reveals through images a subjective life which is general." And he quotes Simpson's "These houses built of wood sustain / Colossal snows, / And the light above the street is sick to death." Simpson himself speaks of a new surrealism which is not content to draw static images from the subconscious but which reveals "the movements of the subconscious. The surrealist poet . . . will reveal the drama and narrative of the subconscious. The images move, with the logic of dreams. I believe there is no limit to what may be achieved in this new kind of verse."

Riverside Drive, Simpson's first novel, is about Duncan Bell, a young Jamaican who migrates to New York, falls obsessively in love, and then undergoes experiences which closely parallel Simpson's own. It had a generally favorable reception, and was admired for the "vivid and somber sections about Duncan's experiences in the Army as Germany was collapsing and later in a state mental hospital," and for the last part of the book, which turns into a "consistently witty" ironic comedy. The author's absorbing autobiography, *North of Jamaica*, appeared in 1973.

Simpson taught at Berkeley from 1959 to 1967, when he went to the State University of New York at Stony Brook, Long Island. He spent 1957–1958 in Rome with a Prix de Rome fellowship and a *Hudson Review* fellowship, and received Guggenheim fellowships in 1962 and 1970, among other awards. He is five feet six inches tall and has black hair and eyes. He is a Democrat. Simpson, who retains a slightly British accent, enjoys carpentry, fishing, swimming, walking, and rifle shooting.

PRINCIPAL WORKS: *Poetry*—The Arrivistes: Poems, 1940–1948, 1949; Good News of Death, and Other Poems (*in* Poets of Today, II), 1955; A Dream of Governors, 1959; At the End of the Open Road, 1963; Selected Poems, 1965; Adventures of the Letter I, 1971. *Novel*—Riverside Drive, 1962. *Nonfiction*—(ed. with Donald Hall and Robert Pack) New Poets of England and America, 1957; James Hogg, A Critical Study, 1962; An Introduction to Poetry, 1967; North of Jamaica, 1973 (England, Air With Armed Men).

ABOUT: Contemporary Authors 1st revision 1–4, 1967; Current Biography, 1964; Hall, D. Contemporary American Poetry, 1962; Martz, W. J. The Distinctive Voice, 1966; Rosenthal, M. L. The New Poets, 1967; Stepanchev, S. American Poetry Since 1945, 1965; Who's Who in America, 1972–1973. *Periodicals*—Book Week December 5, 1965; Critical Quarterly Spring 1966; New York Times Magazine May 2, 1965; Poetry July 1966.

SIMPSON, N(ORMAN) F(REDERICK) (January 29, 1919–), English dramatist, writes: "People are apt to divide playwrights into two kinds: those who write plays for their own sake, and those who do it as a cover for something else. This is not a distinction I would dream of making myself, even behind a gorse bush on Wimbledon Common, but it is one which has to be reckoned with. As does the cognate question of how deep the front, if indeed this is what it is, can be said to go. Is it true, for instance, that it continues right through to the back? If so, the thing obviously wants looking into. And by someone far better qualified to do it than this particular author can ever hope to be.

"More fruitful, perhaps, as a line of enquiry, is the question as to why of all things it should be plays that one has chosen to write, rather than, say, novels. The answer, I think, lies in the fact that there is one great advantage which the play, as a medium, has over the novel; and this is that there are not anything like as many words in it. And this, for a writer condemned from birth to draw upon a reservoir of energy such as would barely suffice to get a tadpole from one side of a tea-cup to the other, cannot but be decisive. Poetry admittedly has in general fewer words still, and for this reason is on the face of it an even more attractive discipline; but alas I have no gift for it, and if I had,

N. F. SIMPSON

it would be only a matter of weeks before I came up against the ineluctable truth that there is just not the money in it that there is in plays.

"As for methods of work, what I do is to husband with jealous parsimony such faint tremors of psychic energy as can be coaxed out of the permanently undercharged batteries I have been forced since birth to rely upon, and when I have what might be deemed a measurable amount, I send it coursing down the one tiny channel where with any luck it might do some good. Here it deposits its wee pile of silt, which I allow to grow, with the barely perceptible deliberation of a coral reef, to the point where one day it may recognize itself with a start of surprise as the *magnum opus* it has been all this time aspiring to.

"Out of what turmoil of the soul do such things as these come? For an answer one must, I suppose, go back to one's early childhood, and what I remember most clearly about this period of my life—partly because in this respect things can hardly be said to have changed much since—is the embarrassing presence in my make-up of well-nigh total empathy. More than anyone else I know, I have been bedevilled and beset by Ruskin's pathetic fallacy. So much so, that it is still impossible for me to knock a nail into a piece of wood without feeling sorry for both the wood *and* the nail. (And, in a way, the hammer too.) Not only is this carried to preposterous lengths, but it is coupled at the same time with a ludicrously all-embracing sense of guilt. Small wonder that I am in perpetual fear and trepidation, and walk the streets like someone who expects round the very next corner to meet his just deserts at the hands of a lynch mob seething with righteous indignation. To feel *personally* responsible not only for every crime, every atrocity, every act of inhumanity that has ever been perpetrated since the world began, but for those as well that have not as yet been even remotely contemplated, is something which only Jesus Christ and I can ever have experienced to anything like the same degree. And it goes a long way to account for the kind of things I write. For not only must one do what one can by writing plays to make amends for the perfidy of getting born; one must also, in the interests of sheer self-preservation, keep permanently incapacitated by laughter as many as possible of those who would otherwise be the bearers of a just and terrible retribution. One snatches one's reprieve quite literally laugh by laugh.

"I am sometimes asked what I write about. I write about life. Which, for me, is a man trying to get a partially inflated rubber dinghy into a suitcase slightly too small to take it. Alternatively, it is a series of incompatible improbabilities in juxtaposition. If anything of either of these views of life comes through in my plays, it is probably not by accident.

"As for the way I write, I am inclined to think it is very English. I have a sneaking regard for what is orderly, but at the heart of every Englishman's love of order is a deep and abiding respect for anarchy. What I would like one day to bring about is that perfect balance between the two which it is peculiarly in the nature of the English genius to arrive at."

N. F. Simpson is the son of George and Elizabeth (Rossiter) Simpson. He was born in London and educated at Emmanuel School (1930–1937). After two years in a bank he joined the army. He served from 1941 to 1946, first in the Royal Artillery, then as a sergeant in the Intelligence Corps. He became a teacher after the war and resumed his own education, graduating in 1954 with an honors degree from London University. Although he had experimented with nonsense writing, particularly in the form of revue sketches, his work did not attract attention until 1956, when his play *A Resounding Tinkle* won third prize in an *Observer* play competition. Simpson gave up teaching in 1963 to devote himself to writing.

A Resounding Tinkle is "a series of incompatible improbabilities in juxtaposition." It centers on a suburban family, the Paradocks, whose living room is slightly too small to take the elephant they have bought. There are visits from "the author," two comedians, and some critics, among others, and much serious discussion of important irrelevancies. These include the play itself, Bergson's theory of comedy, and religion; also reality ("an illusion caused by mescaline deficiency"), sanity ("an illusion caused by alcohol deficiency"), and illusion ("which is an illusion"). Eventually the Paradocks solve their problem by exchanging their elephant for a neighbor's python, which is disgracefully small. The play is a satire on (among other things) the bourgeois status struggle, written in the tradition of deadpan absurdity associated with Alfred Jarry and his heirs, not to mention the Marx Brothers. But there is a distinctly English flavor to Simpson's nonsense that suggests somewhat different association—with Lewis Carroll, J. B. Morton ("Beachcomber"), and that extraordinary and influential radio campaign against reason, the Goon Show.

A one-act revision of *A Resounding Tinkle* was produced at the Royal Court Theatre in December 1957, together with *The Hole*, regarded by some critics as Simpson's "most trenchantly satiric play." The hole of the title is in a suburban road, and around it gather a group of people who speculate about its purpose and meaning. It is seen as a sporting arena, as a trinitarian and as a unitarian aquarium, as a prison cell and torture chamber, and as a cathedral. What it really is is a hole containing an electricity junction box, but this prosaic function is soon rejected by the crowd, who make of it the symbol and center of a religious cult: "It is upon this cavity that we build our faith."

Simpson's greatest success was his full-length play *One Way Pendulum*, produced at the Royal Court in December 1959, and subsequently transferred to the West End and New York. It has been filmed and televised and has passed into the British repertory. Like *The Hole*, it is about a group of characters "each of whom is preoccupied with a private world of fantasy." Among them are Kirby Groomkirby, who is dedicated to teaching a choir of five hundred speak-your-weight machines to sing the Hallelujah Chorus, and often kills people because he likes to wear black; his commonsensical mother, who pays someone to eat the family's leftover food; and his father, who builds a replica of the criminal court of the Old Bailey in the living room and is tried there for his son's crimes, in a "brilliant parody of British legal procedure and language." *The Cresta Run*, a satire about international spying, was staged in 1965 and coolly received. *Was He Anyone?*, which followed after seven years in which Simpson devoted himself to television and radio work, was much more successful. It is a surrealistic satire on do-goodism and the Welfare State—on society's need for those in need—which was found as pointed and serious as it was funny.

Charles Marowitz has said that "there is about Simpson the odour of civil service levity; the kind of pun-laden high-jinks one associates with banter around the tea trolley." John Russell Taylor agrees; he finds Simpson's work based on a single principle, the *non sequitur*, and marred by "a tendency to . . . explore every possibility in a joke and run it right into the ground by over-explicitness and rigid application of logic." Taylor further objects that Simpson makes no attempt at characterization, and that his plays are plotless and shapeless series of gags. He quotes in support of this Simpson's note to *A Resounding Tinkle*: "From time to time parts of the play may seem to become detached from the main body. No attempt . . . should be made from the auditorium to nudge these back into position while the play is in motion. They will eventually drop off and are quite harmless."

George E. Wellwarth however angrily dismisses this "humorlessly obtuse" analysis, and claims Simpson as an exponent of Alfred Jarry's 'Pataphysical "science of imaginary solutions," a serious artist whose central concern is to reveal the illusory nature of religious ritual in a world where "man can know nothing, and his attempts to understand the universe . . . are nothing but convoluted cerebrations continually twisting round on themselves." And Martin Esslin, who also regards Simpson as a dramatist of the Absurd, the author of philosophical fantasies "strongly based on reality" but often relying "on free associations and a purely verbal logic," thinks of him primarily as a social satirist—"a more powerful social critic than any of the social realists." Simpson's work is rather like the hole in his second play, a mystery in which each member of the audience can find whatever it is he is looking for.

N. F. Simpson, a tall, laconic man with a serious manner, is married to the former Joyce Bartlett and has a daughter.

PRINCIPAL PUBLISHED WORKS: A Resounding Tinkle, 1958; One Way Pendulum, 1960; The Hole (*with* The Form), 1964; The Cresta Run, 1966; Some Tall Tinkles (*containing* We're Due in Eastbourne in Ten Minutes; The Best I Can Do by Way of a Gate-Leg Table Is a Hundredweight of Coal; *and* At Least It's a Precaution Against Fire), 1968; Was He Anyone?, 1973.

ABOUT: Armstrong, W. A. (ed.) Experimental Drama, 1963; Contemporary Authors 13–14, 1965; Dennis, N. Dramatic Essays, 1962; Esslin, M. The Theatre of the Absurd, 1962; International Who's Who, 1973–74; Taylor, J. R. Anger and After, 1962; Wellwarth, G. E. The Theatre of Protest and Paradox, 1964; Who's Who in the Theatre, 1972. *Periodicals*—Guardian July 7, 1972.

SINCLAIR, ANDREW (ANNANDALE) (January 21, 1935–), English novelist and historian, was born in Oxford, the son of Stanley Charles Sinclair and Hilary (Nash-Webber) Sinclair. He was educated at Eton College (1948–1953) and then, after service as a lieutenant in the Coldstream Guards, began a brilliant academic career at Trinity College, Cambridge, where he took a double first in history (B.A., 1958). After

ANDREW SINCLAIR

research at Harvard as a Harkness Fellow of the Commonwealth Fund he returned to Cambridge as director of historical studies at Churchill College (1961–1963). He received his Ph.D. in 1963 with a thesis on prohibition in the United States.

His first novel, written while he was still at Trinity, was *The Breaking of Bumbo* (1958), about a young Guards officer who gets himself suspended from his battalion for talking against British intervention in Suez (which Sinclair has elsewhere described as "the last act of imperial farce"). An honest pacifist, Bumbo has reached his noble and glamorous regiment by way of a poor middle-class home and a scholarship to Eton. Finally cashiered and on the brink of a nervous breakdown, he generously marries a witless debutante pregnant by someone else and thereafter buries his conscience in comfortable living. Praised as a "savagely sensitive, surrealist novel-parable-pastiche" and for its wit, the book was on the other hand criticized for its "overheated imagery," its "smart-aleck, sophisticated razzle-dazzle."

Since then, as J. D. Scott says, Sinclair "has been continuously and restlessly experimenting in fiction. . . . He has abandoned, in his fiction, both the milieu and the naturalism of 'Bumbo' [and has] continued in other ways to express his concerns about such notions as the common humanity of rich and poor." *My Friend Judas* tells how the pretentious but basically decent Ben Birt, a larky campaigner against class distinctions, comes to terms with himself at Cambridge. It is, for the most part, the kind of brittle, swift comedy at which Sinclair excels, but it has an underlying seriousness which critics recognized and welcomed. (But a sequel, *The Paradise Bum*, which has Birt and his wife racketing in the steps of Kerouac across America was found strained and meretriciously clever.)

The Project examines a group of scientists living at a missile site in Australia, led by one who has decided to end the world. The novel was back-handedly praised as "sick, horrid, brilliant" and a possible "textbook for madmen," but seemed to many readers overwritten. It was followed by *The Raker*, a dialogue about death between an obituarist and a nihilistic English gentleman at the death-bed of an actress who eventually recovers. Kenneth Lamott was not alone in finding it affected, slow, and too heavily burdened with symbolism—a "bad book by a good writer." The *Times Literary Supplement* called it "a fascinating, infuriating, very curious novel," and went on to point out that Sinclair's novels "were so dissimilar from one another that they seemed to come from different hands. . . . The drawback lies in the doubt that begins to arise about his intentions."

Gog, Sinclair's sixth novel, showed how little he cared for being predictable. A huge man, his memory gone, is washed ashore at the end of World War II in Scotland. He begins a long walk to London, a bizarre pilgrimage crowded with surrealistic and symbolic encounters. In the course of this journey, "Gog's" search for his own identity becomes also a search through history and mythology for the identity of England, which is threatened by the forces of "Magog"—bureaucracy, greed, and pretension.

Sinclair had himself walked the four hundred miles from Scotland to London, traveling by the ancient tracks, the "green roads," and sleeping rough. His "extravagant, footsore descriptions" of the sights and sounds and smells of England were found unforgettably real, and there was general praise for the book's humor and learned wit. But as to its meaning and value as a whole there was much disagreement. Some critics thought it derivative, synthetic, and sentimental; an equal number admired it. David Galloway, to whom in the past Sinclair's ideas had seemed better than his books, thought *Gog* "not only one of the most intelligent, but certainly one of the most entertaining English novels of recent years." Other reviewers were reminded of Joyce, Bunyan, J. C. Powys, and William Golding, among others. But, Sinclair protested in a letter to the *Times Literary Supplement*, "*Gog* is a *new* type of book, having few fathers." It "tries to use only the traditional looseness of the saga and the picaresque novel . . . in order to present at length the complex evidence of history and myth and memory that produced one Briton in one place at one time." A sequel, *Magog*, was received with rather less excitement.

Andrew Sinclair is a witty, observant, and very serious novelist, "persuasive, intelligent and compassionate." His weaknesses include some intellectual and stylistic affectation, and perhaps some uncertainty about what, of all the things he can do, to do next. As a historian on the other hand he seems to have emerged full-fledged. His doctoral thesis, *Prohibition*, is regarded by some critics as the best account of that phenomenon, "perceptive and sophisticated social history in the tradition of Brogan, Handlin, and Hofstadter." His book about President Harding was generally (but not unanimously) praised, as was *The Better Half*, a study of the emancipation of the American woman for which he received the Somerset Maugham Award in 1967. *The Last of the Best*, an ironic study of the decline and fall of European aristocracy, much enjoyed as a "lively casserole of snobbery," was followed by a short study of Che Guevara.

A frequent contributor to journals on both sides of the Atlantic, Sinclair has also written film and television scripts and has adapted Dylan Thomas's *Adventures in the Skin Trade* and his own *My Friend Judas* for the stage. From 1963 to 1964 he held a Fellowship from the American Council of Learned Societies and from 1965 to 1967 he lectured in American history at University College, London. Since 1967 he has been managing director of Lorrimer Publishing. Sinclair launched into yet another field of endeavor in 1969, when he became managing director of Timon Films, writing and directing a screen version of his novel *The Breaking of Bumbo*. This was followed by a star-studded (but only moderately successful) movie based on Dylan Thomas's *Under Milk Wood*. Sinclair has been married twice: in 1960 to Marianne Alexandre and in 1972 to Miranda Seymour. He has one child. Sinclair lives in Soho, London, and lists his recreations as vagrancy and old movies.

PRINCIPAL WORKS: The Breaking of Bumbo (novel), 1959; My Friend Judas (novel), 1960; The Project (novel), 1960; Prohibition: The Era of Excess, 1962; The Hallelujah Bum (novel) (U.S., The Paradise Bum), 1963; The Raker (novel), 1964; The Available Man: The Life Behind the Masks of Warren Gamaliel Harding, 1965; The Better Half: The Emancipation of the American Woman, 1965; A Concise History of the United States, 1967; (tr.) Selections From the Greek Anthology, 1967; Gog (novel), 1967; Adventures in the Skin Trade (play), 1968; (tr. with Carlos Hansen) Bolivian Diary of Ernesto "Che" Guevara, 1968; (tr. with Marianne Alexandre) La Grande Illusion (screenplay), 1968; The Last of the Best (history), 1969; Guevara, 1970; Magog (novel), 1972; Under Milk Wood (screenplay), 1972.

ABOUT: Contemporary Authors 9–10, 1964; Fyvels, T. R. Intellectuals Today, 1968; Gindin, J. Postwar British Fiction, 1962; Vinson, J. (ed.) Contemporary Novelists, 1972; Who's Who, 1973.

SINGER, "BURNS" (pen name of JAMES HYMAN SINGER) (August 29, 1928–September 8, 1964), American poet, translator, critic, and marine biologist, was born in New York and remained a United States citizen throughout his short life. His father, Michael Singer, was born of Polish-Jewish parents in England, and later emigrated to the United States. His mother was Bertha Burns, born in Scotland of Irish, Scottish, and Norwegian descent. Michael Singer was emotionally unstable and often ill, an unsuccessful though always optimistic salesman, and it was his wife who provided what security there was for Jimmy Singer, his older half-sister, and younger brother. (The poet was always known as "Jimmy" but adopted his mother's name and wrote as Burns Singer to distinguish himself from the poet John Singer; he later "found satisfaction in reconciling, in my own name, two persons and two families which were never otherwise reconciled.")

When Singer was four, one of his father's many failures brought the family back to Scotland, and he grew up in and near Glasgow, in much poverty and unhappiness. A precocious child, bookish and quiet, though capable of intense rages, he began to write when he was six and was from the beginning treated as something of a freak in the slum schools he attended. At the beginning of World War II in 1939 he was evacuated to a village in Aberdeenshire, but by 1943 he was back at school in Glasgow, now keeping a diary. This remarkable journal shows that already, at fifteen, he was aware of "a mad, convulsive, neurotic, melancholic, introspective" side to his character, and of his "baffled conceit." In 1945 he wrote: "I want to revolutionise the whole appearance of English poetry, to make it roll through a dozen accented syllables and skim a dozen unaccented. God! Give me patience to bear myself or courage to destroy myself."

Meanwhile, Singer had entered Glasgow University. He found the English course intolerably narrow and conservative and, after two terms, left Scotland and went to London where, at the age of seventeen, he wrote, "I found myself teaching mathematics to helpless adolescents at a dubious private school." In this way he managed to save a little money, and went to Cornwall "to further my studies in verse composition under the tutelage of W. S. Graham. I found him living in a caravan; so I bought a tent and parked it in the next field." From there Singer went to Paris, where he joined the United States Army, but "luckily they chucked me out after a fight with an anti-Semite." There followed two years in Paris, Germany, and Holland, scraping a living by teaching, interpreting, and translating: "The paternal interest of the painter Wols is all I care to remember of that miserable period."

In 1949 Singer returned to Glasgow University, and for two years he studied zoology. Once again

BURNS SINGER

he left without a degree—this time because his mother's suicide and his father's illness forced him to earn some money. He found a junior post in the government Marine Laboratory in Aberdeen, "a job I was able to stand for four years because it involved considerable periods at sea." During this period Singer wrote a great deal of poetry and contributed to many periodicals in Britain and abroad, but he was far from happy.

Slight, with a shock of blond hair and (at the time) a wispy beard, Singer was fundamentally shy and gentle, but prickly, quick to sense rejection, and very far from conventional. When depressed and/or drunk he was capable equally of sullen withdrawal or aggressive arrogance. He was totally out of place in a grayly respectable and smugly provincial city like Aberdeen, and in 1951 he resigned and went to London. There also he quickly acquired a reputation for rudeness and arrogance, making no secret of his contempt for London literary society. But he reviewed regularly for the *Times Literary Supplement*, the *Listener*, *Encounter*, and other magazines, published his poems equally widely, made broadcasts, and in general established himself very successfully as a rising young man of letters. It was during this period also that he met and married Marie Battle, a black American psychologist who brought him more happiness and security than he had ever known before.

Still and All, the only book of poems Singer published during his lifetime, appeared in 1957. These were poems direct and austere in diction, cerebral and sometimes difficult in content. A reviewer in the *Times Literary Supplement* noted "the heavy preponderance of pronouns, prepositions, conjunctions," the sparseness of adjectives and verbal color. The effect was plain, tough-minded, and stoical, and indeed Singer was much attracted to Epictetus, and included a poem to Marcus Aurelius in *Still and All*. Critics showed particular interest in the book's final section, "Sonnets for a Dying Man," a series of profound and subtle meditations on "the mingled horror and dignity of mortality." Even the most puzzled reviewers recognized the originality of this volume, which was a Poetry Society recommendation.

In the same year, 1957, Singer published *Living Silver*, an account of the Scottish fishing industry as it appears to Jan, a young Polish refugee who becomes a fisherman. This device allows Singer an almost novelistic freedom in presenting his fundamentally documentary material, which includes exact and absorbing descriptions of the plant and animal life of the seas, as well as a vivid picture of the fisherman's brutally arduous and dangerous daily life, and an indictment of the economics of the industry, which pays twice as much to those who transport the fish inland as to those who risk their lives to catch them. V. S. Pritchett wrote that Singer had "a close, simple, patient style that insinuates the unexpected verb or adjective and excites the senses of the reader. . . . The book is an object-lesson to any documentary writer." *Living Silver* was admired no less by Singer's fellow scientists, though he himself disparaged it (as he did his acute and sometimes profound reviews and essays) as the merest hack work. Singer also wrote the documentary film *Between the Tides* and was responsible, with Jerzy Peterkiewicz, for the "delicate and sensitive" translations in *Five Centuries of Polish Poetry* (1960).

Singer and his wife moved in 1960 to Cambridge, and in that relatively calm atmosphere Singer worked hard and well, though still not free of ill health and attacks of deep depression. His interest in marine biology reawakened and in 1964 he went with a Leverhulme Fellowship to carry out a research project at the Marine Laboratory in Plymouth. He died there four months later. There were rumors of suicide, and indeed Singer had tried to kill himself some years earlier, but in fact (as W. A. S. Keir has established beyond doubt) he died of a heart disease.

Singer was a very prolific writer. The poems in *Still and All* comprise not much more than a third of those selected to be preserved in the *Collected Poems*, published in 1970 with a very informative introduction by Keir the editor. The previously uncollected poems contained no real surprises and little evidence of development. There was something like general agreement with Keir's statement that Singer had been a poet who "loved simplicities" but whose "mind was continually being tempted in Coleridgean manner by all kinds of abstruse and abstract speculations." His best poems are those that deal with people he knew well or with his scientific work at sea.

PRINCIPAL WORKS: Still and All, 1957; Living Silver: An Impression of the British Fishing Industry, 1957; (ed. and tr. with Jerzy Peterkiewicz) Five Centuries of Polish Poetry, 1450–1950, 1960; The Collected Poems of Burns Singer, 1970.

ABOUT: Keir, W. A. S. *introduction to* The Collected Poems, 1970; McDiarmid, H. The Company I've Kept, 1966. *Periodicals*—Poetry October 1957; Sea Front March 1970; Times (London) September 11, 1964; September 15, 1964; Times Literary Supplement March 25, 1957; November 8, 1957; November 20, 1970; Twentieth Century September 1956.

SINGER, ISAAC BASHEVIS (July 14, 1904–), Yiddish short story writer and novelist, writes: "I was born in Radzymin, Poland. My father as well as my paternal and maternal grandfathers were rabbis. When I was about four years old, my parents moved to Warsaw. I got the usual religious education in *heder*, where I studied the Bible, the Talmud. My elder brother, I. J. Singer, who later wrote *The Brothers Ashkenazi*, began in Warsaw to paint, to write secular stories and to express doubts about the Jewish dogmas. My parents advocated religion with all their power and I listened to these discussions. In order to strengthen the cause of faith, my parents told many tales of *dybbuks*, possessions, haunted houses, wandering corpses. I was fascinated both with my brother's rationalism and with my parents' mysticism.

"In 1917 my mother took me and my younger brother Mosheh to Bilgoray where my maternal grandfather lived, and there I learned about the life of the *shtetl*. My older brother had gone to live in Kiev, which was for a while occupied by the Germans and later by the Poles, and he worked there for the Yiddish press. He also published some of his stories. My parents never returned to Warsaw, but when my older brother went back to Warsaw from Russia, I went to live with him. It was the beginning of the twenties. I got a job in the *Literarishe Bletter* as a proofreader and soon began to publish book reviews and stories in Yiddish and sometimes in Hebrew. In 1932 I became co-editor of a literary magazine, *Globus*, where I published in sections *Satan in Goray*, as well as some of my stories.

"In 1934 my brother went to live in New York and I followed him in 1935. I parted from my wife Rachel and child. She had become a Communist and went to live in Moscow, where she had relatives. She was later expelled from Soviet Russia and brought up my son Israel in a kibbutz in Palestine. He is still there. He teaches school in the kibbutz Bet Alfa and has two children.

ISAAC BASHEVIS SINGER

"In New York I began to work for the Yiddish newspaper the *Jewish Daily Forward*, and I still work for this paper. I publish there articles, book reviews, and also most of my fiction. In 1940, I married my present wife, Alma, a refugee from Germany.

"In 1944, my brother, teacher, and master, I. J. Singer, died. This was a great blow. But I continued to write. In 1950 *The Family Moskat* came out in English translation. The publisher was Knopf. This novel was a selection of the Book Find Club. In 1954, I met Cecil Hemley, who became my publisher, editor, translator and friend. He edited and published in English *Satan in Goray* (1955), *Gimpel the Fool* (1957), *The Magician of Lublin* (1959). In 1960 Noonday (Cecil Hemley's company) merged with Farrar, Straus and Cudahy—later Giroux took the place of Cudahy—and they published *The Spinoza of Market Street* (1961), *The Slave* (1962), *Short Friday* (1964). They also reprinted my other works. I published stories in *Partisan Review*, *Commentary*, *Midstream*, *Esquire*, *Saturday Evening Post*, *Harper's Magazine*, *Mademoiselle*, *Vogue*, and *Encounter*. My stories and novels have been translated into Hebrew, French, Italian, Dutch, Norwegian, Finnish, German, and other languages. My works have been published in England. In 1966 I published a book of memoirs, *In My Father's Court*, dedicated to the memory of Cecil Hemley, who was like a brother to me.

"There are still a number of works which are not yet translated or which are still in the process of being translated and edited."

Isaac Bashevis Singer is widely regarded as the

greatest living Yiddish writer, and he is certainly the most popular. He is the son of Pinchas Menachem Singer, a Hasidic rabbi, and Bathsheba (Zylberman) Singer. As he says, the family moved to Warsaw when he was four. There, in the ghetto tenement where they lived, his father established a *Beth Din*, a rabbinical court where he dispensed advice and adjudicated disputes. Singer himself studied for a time at a rabbinical seminary in Warsaw, and discovered Knut Hamsun, E. T. A. Hoffmann, and Edgar Allan Poe in the city's libraries, before the equally instructive years he spent in the Jewish village (*shtetl*) of Bilgoray, where "the traditions of hundreds of years ago still lived." Singer is and always has been fascinated by the history of his people: "I was born with the feeling that I am part of an unlikely adventure, something that couldn't have happened, but happened just the same."

He was also fascinated, as he says above, "both with my brother's rationalism and with my parents' mysticism," and this dualism has characterized his work from the beginning. It is already evident in *Satan in Goray*, first published in book form in 1935. This novella is set in Poland in the seventeenth century, after the Cossack chieftain Chmielnicki had shattered the East European Jewish community in a terrible pogrom. In their bewilderment and despair, the survivors followed the false messiah Sabbatai Zevi, who temporarily overthrew the Mosaic law and led his followers into a prolonged erotic-mystical orgy, a kind of demonic possession that seized whole communities before Sabbatai was discredited. This extraordinary manifestation Singer describes with a vividness which shocked some orthodox readers.

The first of Singer's books to appear in English was *The Family Moskat* (1950). Unlike his grotesque and haunted shorter works, it is an entirely realistic chronicle novel rather resembling the fiction of Singer's brother, to whom it is dedicated. It studies the degeneration of traditional Eastern European Jewish life in the half-century before World War II, focusing on the disintegration of one prominent Jewish family in Warsaw. This "Jewish Buddenbrooks" established Singer's reputation at once and won the Louis Lamed Prize. Another long novel, dealing in a very similar fashion with another family of Polish Jews, half a century earlier, has been translated in two volumes as *The Manor* and *The Estate*. These dark but exhilarating chronicles, packed with incident, are excellent illustrations of Singer's narrative vigor and stylistic control, and are regarded by some readers as his finest accomplishments.

For most critics, however, Singer is at his best in his novellas and in his short stories, the first collection of which appeared in English as *Gimpel the Fool* in 1957. The title story, of which a magnificent translation by Saul Bellow had appeared in *Partisan Review* in 1948, is generally regarded as Singer's masterpiece. Set in a Polish *shtetl* in the nineteenth century, it is narrated by Gimpel, the village fool, the holy innocent, who is married for twenty wretched years to a shrew who confesses only on her deathbed that none of their six children is his. Having learned in this way that "the world is entirely an imaginary world," Gimpel becomes a wanderer, looking forward only to death because "whatever may be there, it will be real, without complication, without ridicule, without deception. God be praised; there even Gimpel cannot be deceived." Many of Singer's stories have a similar setting, a similar "compelling swiftness" (to quote Robert Alter) and "hallucinated dramatic power." And they are full of matter-of-fact depictions of the magical and irrational—of pacts with the devil, religious fanaticism, visions, miracles, sexual perversion, grotesquerie.

Irving Howe, in an extremely perceptive article about Singer in *Encounter*, has spoken of the "inspired madness" of a sophisticated modern writer who has chosen to write in a dying language about a dead world—"about places like Frampol, Bilgoray, Kreshev, *as if they were still there*." What is no less strange is that Singer's work is read in contemporary America, and in many other countries besides, and Howe has tried to explain this. Singer's work, he says, "is shot through with the bravado of a performer who enjoys making his listeners gasp, weep, laugh and yearn for more. Above and beyond everything else he is a great performer, in ways that remind one of Twain, Dickens, Sholom Aleichem." Moreover, Singer "writes Yiddish prose with a verbal and rhythmic brilliance that . . . can hardly be matched. . . . Behind the prose there is always a spoken voice, tense, ironic, complex in tonalities, leaping past connectives." He has adapted the Yiddish language to the needs of a restless modern sensibility; "what is most remarkable about Singer's prose is his ability to unite rich detail with fiercely compressed rhythms."

Singer writes vividly of a vanished way of life, with a constant awareness of its roots in an even more ancient religion and folklore. But he is not Sholom Aleichem. In Singer's hands the *shtetl* world becomes a colorful and convenient illustration of the chaotic absurdity of life, an allegory of unreason. He will convey convincingly and affectionately the unquenchable piety of one of his characters but, being a modern, he knows that virtue does not always triumph, and his hero is as likely to die in despair as to win through to glory. He believes implicitly in free will and returns repeatedly in his parables to the theme of man tempted by the Devil, but he does not assume that a morally correct choice necessarily means a happy ending. "Everyone of us has free will," he once said. "The only thing is that free will is a rare gift and we get very little of it."

It is this rejection of a benevolent world order that makes Singer a modern writer. It is this same quality that puzzles and disturbs his more orthodox readers. Some of these also regard him as a sensationalist and pornographer, and Henry Goodman has quoted against him his stated interest in a neorealism which would "follow the path of the newspaper chronicle, the bizarre cases found in psychiatry, psychoanalysis, sexology, criminology, occultism."

Singer deliberately uses a wholly realistic style for his long chronicle novels, a more charged and resonant style for his tales and shorter novels. Examples of the latter form in English, apart from *Satan in Goray*, include *The Magician of Lublin*, about a debauched circus entertainer in nineteenth century Poland who ends as a penitent ascetic. Francis King wrote that "in a small, delicate way this is an extraordinary novel, the apparent tranquillity of its surface, shining with optimism and good humor, concealing an inner chasm of violence and despair." In *The Slave*, also set in Poland but two centuries earlier, a saintly young Jewish scholar, sold into slavery, falls in love with the daughter of his peasant master. Their illicit union makes them outcasts and wanderers, but through their sufferings they achieve great wisdom and holiness.

In some of the later short stories (notably "The Cafeteria" in *A Friend of Kafka*), and in the novel *Enemies*, Singer departs from precedent to enter the territory of Saul Bellow and Bernard Malamud—urban Jewish life in postwar America. Herman Broder in *Enemies* is a Polish Jew who has escaped the Nazis with the help of a peasant girl, Yadwiga. After the war, in gratitude, he marries her. He is living with her in Brooklyn, ghostwriting for a celebrity rabbi, when he discovers that his first wife, presumed dead in the gas chambers, is alive in New York. And when his passionate and neurotic mistress announces her pregnancy, he is panicked into a third marriage and catastrophe.

Herman Broder lives in an almost ludicrously complex maze of secrecy and subterfuge, compulsively following the pattern of deceit imposed upon him during his wartime years in hiding. He and all the other characters in the novel are in fact possessed—not by dybbuks, but by the horrors of Jewish history. Warmly praised as it was by many reviewers, *Enemies* seemed to Lore Dickstein "curiously clinical and removed"—not the Bosch tableau of grotesquery it sets out to be but only "a sketch, a preliminary cartoon, pale and undefined."

In My Father's Court, Singer's memoir of his father's *Beth Din* and of his own childhood, has great interest for the light it throws on the sources of his fiction and as a further illustration of his ability to convert "piety into fable," but was thought rather too anecdotal and disconnected. Singer has also made a number of translations, including a Yiddish version of Thomas Mann's *The Magic Mountain*. He is a frequent contributor to the *New Yorker*. Since 1966 he has won great popularity with his books for children, a form in which he immediately found himself at home. *A Day of Pleasure* (1969), an account for children of Singer's own boyhood in Warsaw, received the National Book Award for children's literature. "I came to the child," he says, "because I see in him a last refuge from a literature gone berserk and ready for suicide." Singer has no use for the contemporary writer's "futile desire to teach, to explain, to change society," and he refuses to interpret his own enigmatic stories.

A small man, blue-eyed and lively, Singer has been an American citizen since 1943. He has rejected Jewish orthodoxy but maintains that a "belief in God is as necessary as sex." He is a vegetarian and devoted to animals. Singer's wife, the former Alma Haimann, who has two children by a previous marriage, has worked for many years as a sales clerk in a New York department store.

PRINCIPAL WORKS IN ENGLISH TRANSLATION: *Fiction*—The Family Moskat, 1950; Satan in Goray, 1955; Gimpel the Fool (stories), 1957; The Magician of Lublin, 1960; The Spinoza of Market Street (stories), 1961; The Slave, 1962; Short Friday (stories), 1964; The Manor, 1967; The Séance (stories), 1968; The Estate, 1969; A Friend of Kafka (stories), 1970; Enemies: A Love Story, 1972; A Crown of Feathers (stories), 1973. *Memoir*—In My Father's Court, 1966. *For children*—Zlateh the Goat, 1966; Mazel and Schlimazel, or the Milk of a Lioness, 1967; The Fearsome Inn, 1967; When Schlemiel Went to Warsaw, 1968; A Day of Pleasure: Stories of a Boy Growing Up in Warsaw, 1969; Elijah the Slave, 1970; Joseph and Koza, 1970; Alone in the Wild Forest, 1971; The Topsy-Turvy Emperor of China, 1971; The Fools of Chelm and Their History, 1973.

ABOUT: Allentuck, M. (ed.) The Achievement of Isaac Bashevis Singer, 1969; Buchen, I. H. Isaac Bashevis Singer and the Eternal Past, 1968; Contemporary Authors 1, 1962; Current Biography, 1969; International Who's Who, 1973–74; Kazin, A. Contemporaries, 1962; Madison, C. A. Yiddish Literature, 1968; Malin, I. (ed.) Critical Views of Isaac Bashevis Singer, 1970; Siegel, B. Isaac Bashevis Singer, 1969; Singer, I. B. In My Father's Court, 1966; Who's Who in America, 1972–1973; Who's Who in World Jewry, 1965. *Periodicals*—Book Week October 29, 1967; Christian Science Monitor October 28, 1967; Commentary November 1963; Contemporary Literature Winter 1969; Criticism Fall 1963; Encounter March 1966; Jewish Currents November 1962; Kenyon Review Spring 1964; National Observer Summer 1968; New York Review of Books April 22, 1965; July 7, 1966; New York Times October 23, 1968; New York Times Book Review November 2, 1964; May 8, 1966; November 9, 1969; June 25, 1972; November 4, 1973; Paris Review Fall 1968; Publishers'

Weekly October 16, 1967; Reconstructionist June 15, 1962; Saturday Review June 25, 1958; June 16, 1962; Time October 20, 1967; Vogue April 1, 1966.

SINGER, JAMES HYMAN. *See* SINGER, "BURNS"

SINYAVSKY, ANDREI (DONATEVICH) ("Abram Tertz") (1925–), Russian critic, novelist, and short story writer, was born in Moscow. He fought in World War II, then studied literature at Moscow University, where after graduating he received in 1952 the higher degree of *kandidat* (equivalent to an American Ph.D.) for a dissertation on Gorky's unfinished novel *Klim Samgin.* As a lecturer and senior research fellow at the Gorky Institute of World Literature he collaborated with I. Golomshtok in a small book (1960) about Pablo Picasso and his role in the development of modern art, and with A. Menshutin he wrote a brilliant critical work, *Poeziya pervykh let revolyutsii 1917–1920* (The Poetry of the First Years of the Revolution, 1964), which was sponsored by the Soviet Academy of Sciences. The years immediately following the Revolution, like those which preceded it, produced poetry which expressed the prevailing mood of liberation and revolt. In their almost encyclopedic analysis of the major and minor poetry of this period, the authors show that creativity in poetry is a matter not simply of new content but of new artistic forms, or the revitalization of traditional forms. The work is notable for the deft way in which the authors discreetly bypass the usual political formulations to provide sound and sensitive literary comments. As a critic Sinyavsky also wrote a perceptive introduction to the 1965 Soviet edition of the poems of his friend and mentor Pasternak, as well as numerous essays and book reviews, most of them published in the liberal journal *Novy Mir*, on a variety of subjects ranging from poets such as Akhmatova, Voznesensky, and Yevtushenko to science fiction. A collection of these essays, translated by Laszlo Tikos and Murray Peppard, was published in English in 1971 as *For Freedom of Imagination.*

Sinyavsky's other career, as a fiction writer, began in 1956 in private, until in 1959 he smuggled the first of his stories to the West for publication under the pseudonym Abram Tertz, along with the essay *Chto takoye sotsialistichesky realizm* (1959, translated by G. Dennis as *On Socialist Realism*). In the latter, Sinyavsky argues that socialist realism, with its simplistic division of characters into positive and negative, its prescribed social optimism, has become so trite that it can no longer convey any revelation about the experience of living. Only a fantastic genre can really express the quality of modern life, in the Soviet Union or elsewhere: "I put my hope in a phantasmagoric art, with hypotheses instead of a Purpose, an art in which the grotesque will replace realistic descriptions of ordinary life. Such an art would correspond best to the spirit of our time. May the fantastic imagery of Hoffmann and Dostoevsky, of Goya, Chagall and Mayakovsky . . . and of many other realists and non-realists teach us how to be truthful with the aid of the absurd and the fantastic." This searching and sometimes savagely ironical work, first published in the French review *L'Esprit*, has been widely translated, discussed, and admired.

Sinyavsky's first published work of fiction was the short novel *Sud idet* (1959, translated by Max Hayward as *The Trial Begins*). It deals with the notorious "doctors' plot," a nonexistent conspiracy invented to justify a Stalinist purge of many Jewish doctors which was averted only by the dictator's timely death. Sinyavsky was completing his university education in the last years of Stalin's reign; his own father was arrested in 1951, and the atmosphere of this period permeates much of his fiction. The anti-Semitic campaign is not dealt with directly; instead Sinyavsky imagines how it might have begun, in the family life of the public prosecutor Globov, when his wife gets rid of his longed-for child through an abortion performed by the Jewish doctor Rabinovich. Globov himself is a fanatical Stalinist, but his son Seryozha is a utopian idealist who dreams of revolution but ends up digging ditches in a labor camp, along with Rabinovich and, a prophetic touch, with the writer-narrator. Harry Schwartz thought it "the most interesting piece of writing by a Soviet citizen to reach the West in many years," and Herman Singer wrote: "There can be no doubt of the literary capacity and the intellectual courage of the author. Beneath the satire, the story is profoundly moving."

In *Fantasticheskiye povesti* (1961, translated by Max Hayward and Ronald Hingley as *Fantastic Stories*, in England *The Icicle and Other Stories*), Sinyavsky fulfills his own demand for a phantasmagoric and hypothetical literature, though one rooted in realistic details of everyday Soviet life. In "Grafomany" ("Graphomaniacs") a neurotic and unsuccessful writer becomes convinced that material from his manuscripts is being stolen by more famous colleagues. The success of the story is both specific (the writer in Russia) and general (the irrational neuroses of all writers). "Ty i ya" ("You and I") is another complex and carefully executed examination of paranoia, and also of internal sexual conflict. A struggle between the homosexual and heterosexual elements in the protagonist's makeup is resolved only when one aspect of his double personality attains a sexual climax while the other commits suicide. In "Kvartiranty" ("Tenants") the inhabitants of a flat turn out to be wood demons and water sprites, driven out of the countryside by industrialization and pollution.

What many regard as Sinyavsky's finest story, "V tsirke" ("At the Circus") is set in a much more realistic narrative fabric, although all the same his realism is never far removed from his fantasy. Its protagonist is a petty thief who dreams of becoming a master criminal. He is finally sent to prison and at the story's end makes an impossible break for freedom: "The wind played so serenely on his animated face. Far away could be seen the mauve forest—eternal refuge of legendary highwaymen. . . . He was gripped by a feeling akin to inspiration, which made every vein leap and cavort, and, in its cavorting, await the onflow of that extraneous and magnanimous supernatural power that hurls one into the air in a mighty leap, the highest and easiest in your lightweight life. . . . Ever nearer and nearer. . . . Now it would hurl him up. . . . Now he would show them . . . Kostya leaped, turned over, and, performing the long-awaited somersault, fell, shot through the head, face downward on the ground." In one sense the protagonists of all Sinyavsky's stories make that same leap for an impossible freedom of one sort or another.

Most Western critics welcomed the stories as evidence that experiment was not dead in Soviet literature, but found them all the same undistinguished, disappointingly "mechanical and willed." This cannot be said of a later story, the strangely moving "Pkhentz" (1966), in which the narrator is a multi-limbed, many-eyed creature from another planet who finds humanity hideous but is compelled for safety's sake to assume human shape. Some critics have seen in such stories as this an allegorical treatment of the problems of the "outsider"—the artist or the free spirit—in Soviet society.

Sinyavsky is a writer in the tradition of Gogol through the line of such prerevolutionary and early Soviet writers as Fyodor Sologub, Andrei Bely, and Yuri Olyesha, and this is particularly evident in the short novel *Lyubimov* (1963, translated by Manya Harari as *The Makepeace Experiment*). It is a fantastic comedy about a little bicycle mechanic, Lenya Tikhomirov (Lenny Makepeace in the translation), who has stumbled upon the secret of "psychic magnetism." This enables him to perform, or seem to perform, all kinds of convenient miracles, and to win the hearts and minds of the people of Lyubimov. The town elects him as its "czar" and he declares it an independent state, rapidly turning it into a utopia of peace and love, and planning to extend his benevolent rule all over the world. Alas, people can't eat toothpaste and get drunk on water for ever; they lose faith in their messiah, and the experiment ends in disaster. In the

ANDREI SINYAVSKY

end, released from the burden of power, and glad of it, Lenny sets off for an unknown destination.

Lyubimov is Sinyavsky's best and most ambitious work of fiction, though a complex and difficult one, "wrapped in labyrinthine symbols, ironies and riddles." The fundamental message is clear, however—that dictators, however benevolent, mislead and destroy, that power always corrupts. The story is told, with many learned footnotes, by the elderly historian Proferansov, who writes (says Helen Muchnic) "in a wonderful mixture of slang, chattiness and solemn bureaucratese—a style that, in its pretense of unconscious humor, reminds one of Gogol at his comic best." Another work which reached the West just before Sinyavsky's arrest, *Mysli vrasplokh* (translated by R. Szulkin and A. Field as "Thought Unaware" and by Manya Harari as *Unguarded Thoughts*), is an intensely personal collection of philosophical and religious speculations and sketches.

Sinyavsky was arrested on September 13, 1965, and along with the writer Yuli Daniel was found guilty of "anti-Soviet propaganda" in a shameful and Kafkaesque "trial." In February 1966 Sinyavsky was sentenced to seven years' hard labor and Daniel to five, despite protests from all over the world as well as from many Soviet writers and intellectuals. A transcript of the trial has been published in various places, e.g., *Sinyavsky i Danièl na skame podsudimykh* (New York, 1966), and an English translation which also included many of the protests and other relevant material appeared as the book *On Trial* (1967). A more comprehensive collection of documents is in the *Belaya kniga* (White Book), compiled by the young poet Aleksandr

Ginzburg, who was himself eventually imprisoned for anti-Soviet activities.

One of the main points which Sinyavsky made during his trial was that "there was always a close relationship between my work as a critic and my work as a writer"—that though he was aware of the difference between the critic Andrei Sinyavsky who was published in Russia and the writer Abram Tertz who was published abroad, "I never held that this difference was fundamental, that there was a split personality. That is why I don't consider myself a double-dealer and hypocrite." He also said: "My writings are complex and strange, and I didn't regard them as intended for the mass reader. . . . This is a literature for myself and for a few others wherever they may live or in whatever age." Sinyavsky was released in June 1971, and returned to Moscow, where he earned his living in a variety of literary odd jobs. In mid-1973 it was announced that he had received permission to go abroad. He went to France with his wife and young son, taking up a professorship at the Sorbonne. It is said that, in the Moldavian labor camp where he had been imprisoned, he had been placed among a group of Old Believers, members of a very strict Russian Orthodox sect, and that he had emerged an even "more deeply religious man" than before. It is also reported that Sinyavsky, during his imprisonment, wrote a book about Pushkin "in the camp vernacular and from the point of view of labor camp inmates," and that he has since completed a study of Gogol. *Golos iz Khora* (A Voice From the Chorus), a book based on the letters Sinyavsky wrote from the labor camp to his wife, was published in the West in 1973.

Western critics have been divided on the literary merits of his work. In the opinion of Katherine Hunter Blair, "Good critics are often less good creative writers, and this is so, I think, with Sinyavsky. In his case it may be partly due to the fact that he is apparently writing for himself and an unknown 'few others,' which is an artificial situation for any writer, and especially for a writer with as deep an understanding of literature as Sinyavsky." Labedz and Hayward, however, are by no means alone in their belief that "apart from Alexander Solzhenitsyn, Tertz is undoubtedly the most outstanding talent to emerge in Russia since the pre-Stalinist twenties."

PRINCIPAL WORKS IN ENGLISH TRANSLATION: The Trial Begins, 1960; On Socialist Realism, 1960; Fantastic Stories (England, The Icicle and Other Stories), 1963; The Makepeace Experiment, 1965; Pkhentz *in* Reddaway, P. (ed.) Soviet Short Stories 2, 1968; For Freedom of Imagination, 1971; Unguarded Thoughts, 1972. *Periodicals*—Pkhentz *and* On Boris Pasternak *in* Encounter April 1966; On Evtushenko *in* Encounter April 1967; Thought Unaware *in* The New Leader July 9, 1965; The Poetry of Boris Pasternak *in* Soviet Literature 2, 1963.
ABOUT: Blair, K. H. A Review of Soviet Literature, 1966; Brown, E. J. (ed.) Major Soviet Writers, 1973; Brown, E. J. Soviet Literature Since the Revolution, 1963; Field, A. *English introduction to* Mysli vrasplokh, 1967; Hayward, M. and Crowley, E. L. (eds.) Soviet Literature in the Sixties, 1965; Labedz, L. and Hayward, M. On Trial, 1967; Mihajlov, M. Russian Themes, 1958; Penguin Companion to Literature 2, 1969; Slonim, M. Soviet Russian Literature, 1964. *Periodicals*—Encounter January 1966; The Listener August 31, 1967; New York Review of Books October 14, 1965; New York Times January 18, 1972; Times (London) June 1, 1973; Times Literary Supplement April 29, 1965; February 8, 1968.

SKELTON, ROBIN (October 12, 1925–), Anglo-Canadian poet, writes: "I was born in East Yorkshire and my childhood was spent first in a small village and then at a boarding school near York. I wrote my first poem when I was eight, and when I was eleven I decided to become a writer. The boarding school, and my later service in the RAF provided me with enough intellectual solitude and social discomfort to force me to read widely and begin a habit of internal dialogue which has never left me. While with the RAF in India in 1945–1947 I wrote radio scripts and taught myself to broadcast and to become a proficient verse-speaker. On my return to England I entered Leeds University and there I edited the student magazine, produced plays, wrote dramatic criticism, and for a brief time ran a small publishing firm devoted to the presentation of verse in pamphlet form. In 1950 I was granted a first class honours degree in English Language and Literature. A year later I received my M.A. and went to lecture at Manchester University.

"While at Manchester I wrote drama and poetry criticism for the Manchester *Guardian*, and helped to found, first the Peterloo Group of Poets and Painters, and then the Manchester Institute of Contemporary Arts. Contact with painters has always been important to me, and during 1956 I began to make collages as well as collect paintings. I found that when my poetry dried up I could keep myself imaginatively alive by working in visual media, and I still do this. At this period I developed an interest in the relationship between words and music and wrote the words for several cantatas and motets by David Freedman. My interest in education, too, led me towards other writings. I was, for a while, Chairman of Examiners in English Literature for the Northern Universities Joint Matriculation Board, and my experience there led me to write several books for schools.

"I also found that book-collecting (I have large collections of W. B. Yeats, J. M. Synge, Siegfried Sassoon, W. S. Graham and David Gascoyne) was not only fascinating in itself but led me towards more scholarly types of exploration. In 1960 and

1961 I organized book and manuscript exhibitions at Manchester, the first concerned with contemporary poetry, and the second being part of the W. B. Yeats Exhibition of that year, which I also took over to Dublin.

"In 1962 I first visited Canada, and after a brief period as visiting professor at the University of Massachusetts returned to British Columbia to become a Professor of English Literature at the University of Victoria. In 1965 I helped organize a large exhibition of books, manuscripts, and prints, called The World of W. B. Yeats, and edited with Ann Saddlemyer a symposium of the same name. On June 13, 1965 I gave a centenary lecture on Yeats in Dublin and in August I lectured at the Sligo International Summer School. This year also a selection of my collages toured Western Canada as part of a collage exhibition. The criticism of art interests me as well as its creation, and since May 1964 I have been the regular art columnist of the Victoria *Daily Times*.

"All these activities I find helpful to my central concern, which is the making of poems. Each new foray into the world of bibliomania, scholarship, or art, results in new perspectives that eventually affect my poetry. I have always held the view that a narrowly limited style is destructive of imaginative power, in that a limitation of manner must result in a limitation of viewpoint. Thus my poetry uses many "voices." The consequence is that I find it hard to see myself as allied to any one "school," and feel that my poetry is held together as a unity more by certain themes than by modes of expression. I am seriously concerned to explore the nature of poetry and the poetic process. My investigations have led me to produce several books, and to organize a course in Poetics at Victoria University which, in turn, provides me with much new data for contemplation.

"Whenever feasible I give public readings of my verse, for I have discovered that this is one way to test my poems and discover how much I am committed to them. It is not the amount of applause or even the nature of the audience's response which is most helpful, but my own sense of whether or not the poems become, or remain, part of that internal dialogue which is for me the business of living and by means of which I attempt to communicate to others my own version of the human predicament."

In his "considerable mastery of form," and in the simplicity and directness of his verse, Skelton has been compared with the American poets Winfield Townley Scott and Richard Eberhart. He has been called a regional poet, choosing such themes as "ancestors, local characters, local customs, inarticulate traditions sullenly defending themselves." His poems tend to be "solid as wholes, though not often running to sudden concentrations or heightenings or very memorable individual lines."

ROBIN SKELTON

Skelton is a busy and ubiquitous *entrepreneur* and critic of the arts. In *The Poetic Pattern*, discussing the poetic image and its functions in Jungian terms, he argued that the poet is a kind of unfallen man, with access to a "poetic truth" which is a revelation of the unity of all experience and of the nature of God. The book was thought a courageous one, raising important questions even if it did not answer them to the satisfaction of all its readers. Skelton was married in 1957 to Sylvia Jarrett and has three children. In 1967 he founded the *Malahat Review*, of which he has ever since been editor or co-editor. He is chairman of the creative writing department at the University of Victoria, as well as professor of English. In 1972 he became a director of the Pharos Press. Skelton's recreations include stone carving and making collages, as well as collecting.

PRINCIPAL WORKS: *Poems*—Patmos, 1955; Third Day Lucky, 1958; Begging the Dialect, 1960; Two Ballads of the Muse, 1960; The Dark Window, 1962; An Irish Gathering, 1964; Selected Poems, 1947–1967, 1968; Private Speech: Messages, 1962–1970, 1971 (U.S., A Different Mountain: Messages, 1962–1970: Poems and Photo-Collages); The Hunting Dark, 1971; Remembering Synge, 1971. *Criticism*—The Poetic Pattern, 1956; The Cavalier Poets, 1960; Teach Yourself Poetry, 1963; The Writings of J. M. Synge, 1971; J. M. Synge and His World, 1971; The Practice of Poetry, 1971; J. M. Synge (Irish Writers series), 1972. *As editor*—J. M. Synge: Translations, 1961; Selected Poems of Edward Thomas, 1962; Viewpoint (anthology), 1962; Collected Poems of J. M. Synge, 1962; Six Irish Poets, 1962; Poetry of the Thirties, 1964; Collected Poems of David Gascoyne, 1964; Five Poets of the Pacific Northwest, 1964; (with Ann Saddlemyer) The World of W. B. Yeats, 1965;

Poetry of the Forties, 1968; (with Alan Clodd) Collected Verse Translations of David Gascoyne, 1970; The Cavalier Poets (anthology), 1970; Two Hundred Poems From the Greek Anthology, 1971; Jack Butler Yeats: The Collected Plays, 1972.
ABOUT: Murphy, R. (ed.) Contemporary Poets of the English Language, 1970; Who's Who, 1973. *Periodicals*—Times Literary Supplement March 23, 1956; December 14, 1962.

SLESSOR, KENNETH (March 27, 1901–June 29, 1971), Australian poet, critic, and journalist, wrote: "I was born at Orange (New South Wales) on March 27, 1901. My father was Robert Slessor, an English mining engineer and metallurgist, and my mother Margaret McInnes, Australian-born of Scottish parents who migrated from the Hebrides. My grandfather, Adolph Schloesser, was professor of pianoforte at the Royal Academy, London, and my great-grandfather, Louis Schloesser, was *kappelmeister* at the court of Hesse-Darmstadt. I went to the Sydney Church of England Grammar School ('Shore') and matriculated for the university in 1919, but joined the Sydney newspaper *The Sun* as a cadet in 1920. I have worked for Australian newspapers ever since, principally as editor, special writer, book reviewer and leader writer. In January 1940 I was appointed Australian Official War Correspondent and for the next five years had the honour of accompanying Australian forces on active service in Great Britain, Egypt, Greece, Crete, Palestine, Syria, Libya and New Guinea. In 1945, after a disagreement with the Army's higher command, my resignation was accepted by the Australian War Cabinet. For 'services to Australian literature,' I was appointed an Officer of the Order of the British Empire in 1959. I have been a member of the Advisory Board of the Australian Commonwealth Literary Fund since 1954."

Kenneth Slessor's first poems appeared in the short-lived but influential magazine *Vision*, in which, during the 1920s, Norman Lindsay and his son Jack sought to turn the course of Australian poetry away from the beery matiness of the old bush ballads towards a Nietzschean enthusiasm for "Beauty" and "Life," an antimodernist and anti-intellectual paganism expressed in Victorian or Edwardian forms quite foreign to the Australian experience. Slessor was at first strongly influenced by this movement, and poems like "Earth-Visitors," in which pagan gods visit the earth for sexual sport, partake not only of the Lindsays' "vitalism" but also of the decorative excess and intellectual vulgarity of their movement. Other poems of this period are full of echoes of Arnold, R. L. Stevenson, and even Browning: "There were strange riders once, came gusting down / Cloaked in dark furs, with faces grave and sweet, / And white as air."

KENNETH SLESSOR

Slessor's desire to forget his first book, *Thief of the Moon* (1924), and his association with the Lindsays is understandable; it was a false start for him and was followed after about 1926 by an altogether more productive period of experiment when his work developed under the influence of Pound, Eliot, the Sitwells, and other innovating contemporaries. He was especially sensitive to Wilfred Owen's rhythmic experiments—he spoke of rhythm as "a deeper level of consciousness"—though not to Owen's preoccupation with social injustice.

These technical innovations Slessor applied quite consciously to Australian themes, as in "Captain Dobbin," a work which has been described as the Australian *Prufrock*, and in *Five Visions of Captain Cook*: "So, too, Cook made choice, / Over the brink, into the devil's mouth, / With four months' food, and sailors wild with dreams / Of English beer, the smoking barns of home. / So Cook made choice, so Cook sailed westabout, / So men write poems in Australia." Here Cook, as well as functioning vividly as himself, also acts as a surrogate for the Australian poet simultaneously aware of his heritage and his birthright. During the 1930s Slessor emerged—as is generally acknowledged—as one of the first two genuinely Australian poets (the other was his contemporary R. D. Fitzgerald).

Melancholy and disillusion had been occasional characteristics of Slessor's verse from the beginning; they came to inhabit the very texture of his mature poetry. *Five Bells* (1939), a dramatic and finely sustained elegy for his old newspaper colleague, Joe Lynch, is also an elegy for Slessor's early life and work. Here the many influences to which Slessor was so sensitively attuned fuse into a personal and sophisticated expression of longing and regret. It is Slessor's best-known and most important poem, and he wrote very little after it. *One Hundred Poems* (1943) represented all that he wished to preserve up to that time; *Poems* (1957), a revision of the same book with a little additional material, was further revised in 1962.

Judith Wright has suggested that Slessor, a poet of the intuition and the senses, lacked the intellectual reach to overcome a personal sense of despair: "Looking back over Slessor's poetic life, it seems as though silence was always in the background of all he has said, and has finally triumphed over his brilliant and feverish imagery. There is something about nearly all his poems that makes them seem skeletal . . . like a neon sky-advertisement against darkness. They have about them something rootless and desperate; even the increasing mastery of technique does not quite conceal their lack of content." This is harsh comment that not everyone would accept. It does not in any case alter the fact that Slessor did as much as, or more than, any other writer of his time to nourish a specifically Australian and contemporary poetry. If his ultimate message is one of romantic renunciation, his statement of it is richly eloquent. And it should be added that Slessor's genius for pictorial description, while it is often marred by rumbustiousness, is unsurpassed in contemporary English-language verse. The poet, a former editor of the important literary review *Southerly*, was married and divorced. He had one son.

PRINCIPAL WORKS: Thief of the Moon, 1924; Earth-Visitors, 1926; Surf, 1930; Trio, 1931; Cuckooz Contrey, 1932; Five Bells, 1939; One Hundred Poems, 1919–1939, 1944; Poems, 1957; Canberra (nonfiction), 1966; Bread and Wine: Selected Prose, 1970. *As coeditor*—The Penguin Book of Modern Australian Verse, 1958.

ABOUT: Buckley, V. Essays in Poetry, 1957; Green, H. M. A History of Australian Literature, 1962; Harris, M. Kenneth Slessor, 1947; Heddle, E. M. Australian Literature Now, 1949; International Who's Who, 1970–71; Murphy, R. (ed.) Contemporary Poets of the English Language, 1970; Semmler, C. Kenneth Slessor, 1966; Stewart, D. The Flesh and the Spirit, 1948; Wright, J. Preoccupations in Australian Poetry, 1965. *Periodicals*—Australian Letters April 1958; Australian Literature Studies December 1964; Opinion December 1963; Quadrant Summer 1959–1960; Southerly 4 1955.

SLONIM, MARC (L'VOVICH) (March 26, 1894–), American scholar and critic, was born in Novgorod-Seversk, Russia, the son of Leo and Indiana (Aikhenvald) Slonim. From 1915 to 1918 he studied literature and philosophy at the University of Petrograd, and in 1917–1918 was a member of the Russian Constituent Assembly. Exiled by the Revolution, he went to Italy and took his doctor's degree at the University of Florence in 1920. Slonim spent the next twenty years in Europe. For part of this period he taught at the Russian University in Prague, and from that city edited the émigré monthly *Will of Russia* (1922–1932). From 1932 to 1940 he lived as a successful writer and lecturer in Paris and other European capitals.

MARC SLONIM

This second stage of Slonim's life was brought to an end by World War II. In 1941 he migrated to the United States, becoming a citizen in 1957. Slonim taught comparative and Russian literature at Sarah Lawrence College, New York, from 1943 to 1962. Over the years he also lectured in universities in Czechoslovakia, France, Belgium, and Yugoslavia, as well as at Yale, at the universities of Chicago and Pennsylvania, and at many other American colleges. Slonim now lives in Geneva, but he remains an emeritus member of the Sarah Lawrence faculty and has served since 1962 as director of the college's foreign studies program. Besides his books in English, listed below, Slonim is the author of many others in Russian, French, and Italian. He is a frequent contributor to European and American magazines.

Slonim's first book in English was *The Epic of Russian Literature*, a "conscientious, intelligent, and impartial" survey of the literature from its origins to Tolstoy. *Modern Russian Literature* deals in a similar way with the period from Chekhov to the present. *Three Loves of Dostoevsky*, the result of three years of research, dwelt in the opinion of some reviewers "rather extensively on the pathological and sexual aspects of Dostoevsky's love life," but provided insights into the writer's work and life which, it was thought, would be of value to all subsequent biographers.

An Outline of Russian Literature was welcomed as an excellent introduction for students, and as a "sound and accurate" feat of condensation. According to the *Times Literary Supplement*, Slonim's "judgements are often lively in style (though occasional turns of phrase carry the hint of a slightly self-conscious use of a foreign tongue), but they are almost at all times impeccably orthodox." There was some feeling that the *Outline* was more successful in capturing the spirit of pre-Revolutionary Russian writing than of Soviet literature, and *Soviet Russian Literature* was perhaps intended to redress the balance. Andrew Field thought it weakened by "minor errors and major omissions," but Maurice Friedberg argued that "Mr. Slonim's weaknesses are also his strengths. By devoting comparatively slight attention to recitation of names, dates, and titles that appear to him to be of scant interest or significance, he retains polemical vigor. This approach results in a book . . . biased in the best sense of the word—uneven, impressionistic, occasionally brilliant, abounding in astute observations condensed into brief, elegant sentences."

Slonim was married in 1920 to Suzanne Campaux; they had one daughter. They were divorced in 1922, and Slonim was married again, to Tatiana Lamm, in 1951. He has traveled very widely, not only in Europe, but in Africa and Asia.

PRINCIPAL WORKS: The Epic of Russian Literature from Its Origins Through Tolstoy, 1950; Modern Russian Literature: From Chekhov to the Present, 1953; Three Loves of Dostoevsky, 1955; An Outline of Russian Literature, 1958; Russian Theatre: From the Empire to the Soviets, 1961; From Chekhov to the Revolution: Russian literature, 1900–1917, 1962; Soviet Russian Literature: Writers and Problems, 1964.
ABOUT: Who's Who in America, 1970–1971.

SMITH, DODIE (DOROTHY GLADYS), English playwright and novelist, writes: "I was born near Manchester, England. The date is becoming more uncertain every day. When I was eighteen months old my father died, and after that my mother and I lived with her family—my grandparents, three uncles and two aunts—in an old house with a garden sloping towards the Manchester Ship Canal. It was a stimulating household. Both my mother and grandmother wrote and composed. Almost everyone sang and played some musical instrument (we owned three pianos, a violin, a mandolin, a guitar and a banjo) and one uncle, an admirable amateur actor, was often to be heard rehearsing, preferably with me on hand to give him his cues. Although I had been taken to theatres long before I could read, it was this hearing of my uncle's parts which really aroused my interest in acting and in playwriting; the cues I gave got longer and longer and, by the age of nine, I had written a forty-page play. When I read this aloud to my mother she fell asleep—to awake and say apologetically, 'But, darling, it was so dull.'

"She eventually married again and we moved to London, where I went to St. Paul's Girls' School. Soon after leaving I wrote a screen play called *Schoolgirl Rebels* which I sent to a film company named Hepworth, under the pseudonym of 'Charles Henry Percy.' Hepworth made the film with their three stars—and sent Mr. Percy three pounds ten shillings. I did not earn another penny by my writing for sixteen years.

"I next went to the Royal Academy of Dramatic Art where I narrowly scraped through the entrance examination; and it was to my teachers' admitted surprise that, eventually, I got a job on the stage the first day I looked for one. Unfortunately, I lost it almost as speedily, and many others. And after seven years of talking myself into jobs and acting myself out of them I—far from philosophically—got work in a large London shop, where I shortly became a buyer of toys and prints. It was after buying toys at the Leipzig Fair that I went to the Austrian Tyrol and found the idea and local colour for my first play, *Autumn Crocus*. This was produced in 1931 and had a disastrous first night with a booing gallery. I went to bed in despair—and woke to find that all the notices were good.

"During much of the long run I sat in my new flat in my new clothes, despairing, in case I could never write another play. But at last, after scrapping three first acts, I got one finished. And by 1938 I was credited with having written six successes in a row. Actually, my fifth play only ran three months and lost some money for the management; I noticed this because I was part of the management.

"In January, 1939, I paid my fourth visit to America. With me came my manager, Alec Beesley, who had joined me in 1934. We were married soon after we landed. We remained in America for fifteen years, living in New York, California, Pennsylvania and Connecticut; and driving six times from coast to coast, accompanied by varying numbers of Dalmatian dogs. During these years I often worked for motion pictures (but never cared for it), wrote *Lovers and Friends* which, with Katharine Cornell, ran successfully on Broadway (three earlier plays of mine had also been produced there) and I spent three years on my first novel, *I Capture the Castle*. While wrestling with this I often wondered if any publisher would ever accept it. As things turned out, it sold well over a million copies and still sells. It may be noted that I always have had beginner's luck.

"In 1953 my husband (the same one; we are still unfashionably happy together) and I came back to England, where we live in a three-hundred-year-old house with a garden, orchard and paddock which we share with two donkeys, upwards of forty fantail pigeons, visiting wild ducks on the pond—and, of course, our most recent Dalmatian, Disney, named after Walt Disney who made such a brilliant cartoon film out of my book for children, *The Hundred and One Dalmatians.* I have come to enjoy writing novels better than writing plays (which is just as well, in view of the vastly changed modern theatre). I find I can live right inside a novel; while working on a play, I can merely sit in front of it. Not that I fully enjoy writing anything. I am unhappy when not working and I do, at least, enjoy planning work. But once I start, nothing I achieve seems as good as I hoped it would be. I revise and revise and revise. I consider myself a lightweight author, but God knows I approach my work with as much seriousness as if it were Holy Writ."

Dodie Smith's first successful play was, as she says, *Autumn Crocus* (1931), which irresistibly combined gaiety, heartbreak, and a romantic Tyrolean setting. *Service* drew on her experience of life in a big London department store. These two plays, and *Touch Wood,* which followed, were written pseudonymously, as by C. L. Anthony. The best remembered of her plays is *Dear Octopus,* a "comfortably sentimental, middlebrow family comedy" which was a smash hit in 1938 and made a highly successful film. Thirty years after its first production, *Dear Octopus* was revived in London's West End, where it was received with a mixture of nostalgia and surprise—nostalgia for the innocence and security of the world it portrayed, surprise that it held up so well as a witty, shapely, well-knit entertainment. Even Ronald Bryden, a critic who found much that was soft and complacent in it, was nevertheless moved: "The faint note of elegy which underlined the niceness of it all in the winter of Munich now drowns out the self-congratulation. Here, under glass, is the self-portrait of the class which took power in England in 1832 and lost it in 1945 . . . the most haunting ghost-play for years."

I Capture the Castle, Dodie Smith's first and most famous novel, owes its success to a great deal more than "beginner's luck." It is presented as the diary of Cassandra Mortmain, whose impoverished and eccentric household includes a literary father who has done no work at all for ten years and a stepmother who communes with nature clad only in her hip boots. There are also a number of young men with one of whom Cassandra falls totally and, she supposes, hopelessly in love. Her story is told with a perfectly judged mixture of humor and humility, lyricism and vivid poignancy. The result is a sort of apotheosis of the "woman's book" which was reasonably called "the gayest and sweetest of modern novels."

DODIE SMITH

Dodie Smith's subsequent entertainments, while none of them has equaled the success of her first novel, have established her as an unsurpassed technician of the "light romance," distinguished from her competitors by a mastery of dialogue and characterization, and "an instinct for the rueful, the wry, and the paradoxical." *The Hundred and One Dalmatians,* "a fantasy of delightful horrors" for children, was much enjoyed as a book and hugely successful as a Walt Disney movie. A sequel, *The Starlight Barking,* appeared in 1968. Dodie Smith lives in Finchingfield, one of the prettiest villages in Essex. Her recreations, apart from donkeys, dogs, and pigeons, include reading and music.

PRINCIPAL PUBLISHED WORKS: *Plays*—Bonnet Over the Windmill, 1937; Dear Octopus, 1938; Three Plays (Autumn Crocus, Service, Touch Wood), 1939; Lovers and Friends, 1943; Letter From Paris (adapted from Henry James's The Reverberator), 1954; I Capture the Castle (adapted from her own novel), 1955; These People, These Books, 1958. *Fiction*—I Capture the Castle, 1948; The New Moon With the Old, 1963; The Town in Bloom, 1965; It Ends With Revelations, 1967; A Tale of Two Families, 1970. *For children*—The Hundred and One Dalmatians, 1956; The Starlight Barking, 1968.

ABOUT: Chambers, P. Women and the World Today, 1954; International Who's Who, 1973–74; Who's Who, 1973; Who's Who in the Theatre, 1972.

SMITH, FLORENCE MARGARET. *See* SMITH, "STEVIE"

SMITH, ROBERT PAUL (April 16, 1915–), American novelist, memoirist, dramatist, and verse writer, was born in Brooklyn, New York, the son of Joseph Elkin Smith, a manufacturer, and the former Esther Breckstone. He attended public

ROBERT PAUL SMITH

schools in Mount Vernon, New York, where the family lived for a time, and then went on to Horace Mann School for Boys in New York City, graduating in 1932. At Columbia College Smith worked on the school paper and was coeditor of its literary quarterly, the *Columbia Review*. He graduated with a B.A. in 1936, and went to work for the Columbia Broadcasting System, writing continuity for radio. This, he says, "paid the rent while I wrote four novels which did not."

The first of these to be published was *So It Doesn't Whistle* (1941), about four young men sharing an apartment in prewar New York. The poet and novelist Louis Simpson remembered it ten years later as a novel in which a generation waiting to be drafted found "their own illusions, their own affection for a city, their own perishable sensuality." At the time it had a mixed but distinctly interested critical reception. There was admiration for its humor, its precisely recorded dialogue, its "staccato, stream of consciousness style." One reviewer found in it "about equal parts of Joyce, Saroyan, and Budd Schulberg." The commonest criticism, made by Alfred Kazin among others, was that while Smith wrote very well, and confected many "adroit and tough and gay" scenes, his themes were neither deeply felt nor directly seen, and the book was simply aimless.

There were similar reservations about Smith's subsequent novels. *Journey*, a *bildungsroman* about a young writer, seemed to Diana Trilling "full of mis- or undirected talent," while Clifton Fadiman wrote: "I feel that he doesn't yet know quite what he wants to say but that whatever he says he says in a voice that is fresh and arresting." *Because of My Love* is a love story with a totally unexpected and violent climax which seemed to one reviewer unjustified—not "worked for"—but which for another had the validity of "a dark and unresolved dream." *The Time and the Place*, about a happily married man driven by intimations of mortality into a love affair, struck E. J. Fitzgerald as "fast and entertaining reading," but left him wishing that "Smith would slow down and really grapple with some of the ideas he tosses off so briskly."

The Tender Trap, a play which Smith wrote in collaboration with Max Shulman, had more success than his novels but like them was found a little erratic. It is a skillfully contrived farce which ran for 101 performances on Broadway and was later filmed. William Hawkins said that "much of the time the play is extremely funny, but it eventually dizzies you because its point of view revolves like the lamp in a lighthouse."

Smith's most successful book to date was his memoir of childhood "*Where Did You Go?*" "*Out.*" "*What Did You Do?*" "*Nothing.*" Martin Levin called it "a nostalgic look at the dear dead days when kids wore knickerbockers and looked like kids not thugs, when the idea of parental palship was repugnant to parent and child alike, and when doing nothing was filled with magic." William Hogan read it as "one man's protest against the era of Gesell, Spock and the overly expensive summer camp." It was a best seller and was serialized in twenty-five newspapers. Several books in a similar vein have followed, including *How to Do Nothing With Nobody All Alone by Yourself*, illustrated by Smith's wife, which provides instructions for making spool tanks, bull-roarers, cigar-box guitars, and other threats to the plastic toy industry. Smith has also written a number of books which are for, rather than about, children, and some light verse which has been generally enjoyed and earned comparisons with the work of Ogden Nash.

Smith has been married since 1940 to the writer and artist Elinor Jane Goulding, author of, for example, *The Great Big Messy Book*. They have two sons. Smith is six feet tall, builds model ships for a hobby, and enjoys reading. Julius Novick, reviewing the *pensées* collected in *Crank*, found Smith "a pleasant companion: a man of both Liberal and liberal views; intelligent, cheerfully quirky, commonsensical but not unimaginative, and capable of moral indignation without smugness."

PRINCIPAL WORKS: So It Doesn't Whistle, 1941; The Journey, 1943; Because of My Love, 1946; The Time and the Place, 1952; (with Max Shulman) The Tender Trap: A Comedy in Three Acts, 1955; "Where Did You Go?" "Out." "What Did You Do?" "Nothing." 1957; Where He Went (*contains* So It Doesn't Whistle, The Journey, The Time and the Place), 1958; How to Do Nothing With Nobody All Alone by Yourself, 1958;

Translations From the English, 1958; And Another Thing, 1959; Jack Mack, 1960; Crank: A Book of Lamentations, Exhortations, Mixed Memories and Desires, All Hard or Chewy Centers, No Creams, 1962; How to Grow Up in One Piece, 1963; When I Am Big, 1965; Nothingatall, Nothingatall, Nothingatall, 1965; Got to Stop Draggin' That Little Red Wagon Around, 1969; Robert Paul Smith's Lost and Found, 1973.
ABOUT: Current Biography, 1958; Warfel, H. R. American Novelists of Today, 1951; Who's Who in America, 1972–1973.

SMITH, "STEVIE" (FLORENCE MARGARET SMITH) (1902–March 7, 1971), English novelist and poet, wrote: "Born in Hull, Yorkshire, came to London at the age of three, to a suburb which was then open country, and has lived there, in the same house, ever since. Educated at the local high school and at the North London Collegiate School for Girls. Worked in a London publishing firm and since 1953 has lived at home." She was the younger daughter of Charles Ward Smith and the former Ethel Rahel Spear, but was raised by the aunt with whom she spent her life in their Edwardian house in Palmer's Green.

STEVIE SMITH

In 1935 Miss Smith tried to get her poems published, but was told to "go away and write a novel." The result was *Novel on Yellow Paper*, refused by the publisher who had suggested it as "too much of a risk," but published in 1936 by Jonathan Cape. It is an idiosyncratic monologue, spoken by a young woman who is apparently secretary to a magazine publisher and who lives in a London suburb with her agreeable aunt, enjoying many friendships and a lover whom she is not at all prepared to marry. Its extraordinary "nonsense gabble style" is embellished with snatches of foreign and classical languages and American colloquialisms, mannerisms which reminded many readers of Gertrude Stein, digressions which reminded others of Sterne. It was thought an "amusing, provocative and very serious piece of work, but impossible to classify—an autobiography perhaps, but of the mind . . ." The book caused an immediate stir, later appeared in American and paperback editions, and remains Miss Smith's most popular work.

Over the Frontier is a second helping of the same exotic dish and *The Holiday* again features a girl who works in a London office and lives in the suburbs with her capable aunt, but for the first time tells a coherent story—a sad one about a doomed love affair. The monologue with its curious turns of speech flows on, but moves readily from trivia to the most serious religious concerns; its predominant note, it was perceived, is "not the note of a comic writer."

Meanwhile the poetry had begun to appear, beginning in 1937 with *A Good Time Was Had by All*. Miss Smith favored short verses, with irregular conversational rhythms in which, it has been said, "she mocks the complacent, sympathises with the outsider and claps her hands for the fool." Her early poems were mostly light and childlike, with some nonsense lines, but later, and particularly in and after *Not Waving But Drowning* (1957), there was an increasing preoccupation with stronger and sadder themes, and with the concepts and language of Christianity. The Thurberish line drawings which accompany and often inspire the poems have been dismissed by some critics as mere doodles, but seem to others to intensify this sense of loneliness and loss.

In 1962 *Selected Poems* was discussed at some length by Philip Larkin. Noting that her poetic method derived from her novels, and conceding that her verse was often irritatingly facetious and disingenuous, he found in it a growing sureness and confidence, a plangency "like a hand swept across strings," an ability to "see something poetic move where we do not" and to capture it. "For all the freaks and sports of her fancy . . . ," he concluded, "Miss Smith's poems speak with the authority of sadness." This is exemplified very well in the most widely quoted and anthologized of her poems, "Not Waving But Drowning": "Nobody heard him, the dead man, / But still he lay moaning; / I was much further out than you thought / And not waving but drowning. // Poor chap, he always loved larking / And now he's dead. / It must have been too cold for him his heart gave way, / They said. // Oh no no no, it was too cold always / (Still the dead one lay moaning) / I was much too far out all my life / And not waving but drowning."

Her reputation grew steadily towards the end of her life. She received the Cholmondeley Poetry

Award in 1966 and the Queen's Gold Medal for Poetry in 1969. Her aunt died in 1968 at the age of ninety-six, and Miss Smith survived her by only three years. When she died there were tributes to her from her innumerable friends, and Kay Diek published a record of some of her conversations with Stevie Smith (and with Ivy Compton-Burnett) in *Ivy and Stevie*. Stevie Smith contributed book reviews and critical and descriptive articles, as well as poems, to the more serious British newspapers. A well-read and perceptive critic, she was, unexpectedly, a devotee of Racine. She traveled a great deal in Germany, and was much praised for her "devastating analyses of German mentality." She often read her verse on the radio and at festivals, and also sang it, since many of the poems "go" to tunes invented by herself or adapted from existing ones.

In a radio interview, Miss Smith said that she really wrote for herself, and did not know what effect her verse has on others. She spoke of "the essential loneliness of everybody, which is very painful." She felt the attraction of Christianity, with its "sweetness and cruelty" very strongly, but remained an agnostic. "I think death is a tremendous friend . . . I have this idea that death will improve one's character."

PRINCIPAL WORKS: *Poetry*—A Good Time Was Had by All, 1937; Tender Only to One, 1938; Mother, What Is Man?, 1942; Harold's Leap, 1950; Not Waving But Drowning, 1957; Selected Poems, 1962; The Frog Prince, 1966; The Best Beast, 1969; Two in One (selected poems), 1971; Scorpion, 1972. *Novels*—Novel on Yellow Paper, 1936; Over the Frontier, 1938; The Holiday, 1949. *Other*—Some Are More Human Than Others (drawings), 1958; Cats in Colour, 1959. *As editor*—The Batsford Book of Children's Verse (U.S., The Poet's Garden), 1970.

ABOUT: Dick, K. Ivy and Stevie: Conversations and Reflections, 1971; Lutyens, E. A Goldfish Bowl, 1973; Murphy, R. (ed.) Contemporary Poets of the English Language, 1970; Orr, P. (ed.) The Poet Speaks, 1966; Who's Who, 1971. *Periodicals*—New Statesman September 28, 1962.

SMITH, SYDNEY GOODSIR (October 26, 1915–), Scottish poet, playwright and critic, writes: "I was born in Wellington, New Zealand, where my father was serving as a Major in the R.A.M.C., having graduated in medicine at Edinburgh University by way of serving in a chemist's shop in New Zealand to raise the fare. My mother and I left N.Z. when I was aged about two and we made our way by stages home to Edinburgh (where my mother was born) through Singapore, our ship having been torpedoed by the famous German raider, the *Emden*. In Edinburgh my sister was born and I had my first sight of clouds, snow and open fires. That memory is still vivid.

"After the war my father was appointed medical adviser to the Egyptian Government and my early years were spent in Cairo and, during the summer, Alexandria.

"When I was about seven I was sent home to a small private school in Dorset and my holidays were mostly spent in Scotland with relations of my sister's nanny in the little village of Moniaive in Dumfriesshire, where I became leader of the local gang, largely, I think, because I had a bright red, Garibaldian shirt—the colours of my school football team, for I was a great athlete in those days, though lazy as a slug now.

"At thirteen I continued my non-education at Malvern College in Worcestershire, where I was often in trouble for pinning up reproductions of 'modernist' paintings in my study, editing an unofficial and satirical magazine (called, grandly, *Prometheus Invinctus*), not getting my hair cut and other fearsome and familiar gestures of rebellion.

"Though I was writing a lot of poetry I really wanted, at this time, to be a painter. In my parents' eyes this was 'a nice hobby' but not a real profession, so when I left school at seventeen I started following in father's footsteps by doing medicine at Edinburgh University, where he now held the chair of Forensic Medicine, but I proved to have no scientific aptitude and after barely a year went south to Oriel College, Oxford, to study English Literature. I soon switched to History, feeling I would read all the literature I wanted for myself anyway and that the study of history would be a broader education. I have never regretted that change-over.

"Being unfit for military service (I have been a chronic asthmatic from babyhood), I spent the war years instructing the Polish Forces in Scotland in the mysteries of the English language. After this war I spent a year with the British Council, then in 1947 I was given a Rockefeller Atlantic Award for my poetry (I had published three books of verse—*Skail Wind* 1941, *The Wanderer and Other Poems* 1943, and *The Deevil's Waltz* 1946) and have been a free-lance or general literary hack ever since—journalism, radio and television work, art criticism for *The Scotsman*, almost anything, in fact.

"All my early poetry, up to the age of about twenty-two or twenty-three, was in English, but then I came by chance on the Scots poetry of Hugh MacDiarmid and a great light shone, I heard ancestral voices speaking and realised that this was my true medium. I joined the ranks of the so-called Scottish Renaissance movement with enthusiasm. This had been founded in the late 1920s but with my long education in the south I had never come across it either as a literary or a political movement. Its literary aims were to pick up again the real traditions of Scottish literature which two centuries of highly anglicized education in Scotland had largely obliterated, to intellectualize the Scots and Gaelic languages as a twentieth century medium for poetry and drama and fiction and thereby to act as inspirers of the political programme, which was left-wing Scottish Nationalism. These two strands are often explicit and always implicit in my work and in 1960 they came together with a bang in my five-act play in Scots verse, *The Wallace*, which was the principal dramatic event of the Edinburgh International Festival of that year. There were one or two near-riots but no arrests!

"I married Marion Elise Welsh in 1938 and have two springoffs, both grown up and one married."

Sydney Goodsir Smith is Hugh MacDiarmid's most notable disciple, but is thought a more personal poet than MacDiarmid, influenced by him only linguistically. *Under the Eildon Tree* contains his most admired poems, "an ironic set of meditations on literary and amorous life in Edinburgh," enjoyed for the "gusto, the good-humoured cynicism, the sentimental display of some classical learning, and the sudden seriousness [which] give his elegies the quality of drunkenness." *The Wallace*, according to G. S. Fraser, is "a powerful, plain chronicle play," harshly treated by English critics at the Edinburgh Festival. *Carotid Cornucopius*, a prose extravaganza about the adventures of an Edinburgh poet, is full of Joycean word play and Rabelaisian gusto. MacDiarmid called it "a tremendous breakthrough of the old wild spirit," though some critics found the extended revision too long, a little strained. Smith's translations into Scots from other languages have been praised as tours de force.

Edith Sitwell has compared Smith to William Blake and to Robert Burns. Norman MacCaig calls him a poet "of great variety, of energy, intensity, humour, and passion," any two lines of whose work are immediately recognizable as his, and whose faults of sentimentality and rhetoric "are the excesses of his virtues"; he "can write love poems of direct and outspoken passion, political poems . . . and poems about the wild boys in the bars which are made poems by the extraordinary expressiveness of the language and his equally extraordinary tact in translating speech rhythms into the rhythms of verse." Smith, MacCaig, and MacDiarmid are old and close friends and drinking companions, and the latter made Smith the subject of his presidential address to the Edinburgh University Scottish Renaissance Society in 1962. "Being trained to observe details at a glance," he explained, "the outstanding characteristics of members of the other sex who come under [Smith's] observation—as few of them can fail to do— . . . inform his verses to a much greater extent than in the work of any other Scots poet."

SYDNEY GOODSIR SMITH

PRINCIPAL WORKS: Skail Wind, 1941; The Wanderer (poems), 1943; The Deevil's Waltz (poems), 1946; Selected Poems, 1947; Carotid Cornucopius, Caird of the Cannon Gait and Voyeur of the Outlook Touer: His Splores, Cantraips, Wisdoms, Houghmagandies, Peribibulations, and All Kinna Abstrapulous Junketings and Ongoings abowt the High Toun of Edenberg, Capitule of Boney Scotland, 1947 (rev. ed., 1964); Under the Eildon Tree: A Poem in XXIV Elegies, 1948; So Late into the Night (poems), 1952; Figs and Thistles (poems), 1959; The Wallace: A Triumph in Five Acts, 1960; The Vision of the Prodigal Son (poems), 1960; Kynd Kittock's Land (poems), 1965; (ed. with James Barke) Robert Burns's Merry Muses of Caledonia, 1965; Fifteen Poems and a Play, 1969.

ABOUT: Fraser, G. S. The Modern Writer and His World, 1964; MacDiarmid, H. The Company I've Kept, 1966; MacDiarmid, H. Sydney Goodsir Smith, 1962; Murphy, R. (ed.) Contemporary Poets of the English Language, 1970; Roy, G. R. Studies in Scottish Literature, 1969; Wittig, K. The Scottish Tradition in Literature, 1958. *Periodicals*—Lines Review Summer 1956; Poetry August 1960; Saltire Review April 1954.

SMITH, WILLIAM JAY (April 22, 1918–), American poet, writes: "I was born at Winnfield, Louisiana, a descendant, on my father's side, of Samuel Smith, one of the early settlers of Georgia. About my mother's family (Campster) I know little except that its members had settled early in Arkansas and Oklahoma and had intermarried with the Cherokees. After farming briefly on our family place, next to that of the late Senator Huey P. Long, my father reenlisted in the regular Army as a musician, and was transferred to Jefferson Barracks, on the outskirts of St. Louis, Missouri. I was brought up there in the peaceful, enclosed atmosphere of an Army post of the Twenties; except for occasional visits South, I scarcely left the immediate surroundings until I went (1935) to Washington University in St. Louis.

WILLIAM JAY SMITH

"My complete isolation throughout childhood on the edge of the Mississippi, surrounded by few books except those that I discovered for myself, was undoubtedly a major influence on my development as a poet. (This isolation was accentuated by my involvement in a tragic accident, which almost cost the life of one of my childhood companions, and by real poverty.) My father never rose above the rank of Corporal, and when we lived outside the military reservation during the Depression, he supplemented our income by bootlegging (a normal undertaking, it seemed then), as my mother did by dressmaking and laundry work. My parents were not readers but talkers and story-tellers in the Southern tradition, and when I discovered poetry at an early age, it first delighted me by its aural appeal.

"Encouraged by my teachers, I had one poem published in a national magazine while still in high-school, but it was not until college, when I met Clark Mills, the poet, and Tennessee Williams, the playwright, who became my close friends, that I became aware of the directions of contemporary poetry. After taking an M.A. in French at Washington University, I served for four years in the U.S. Navy during World War II, two years of which was as liaison officer on a French ship in the Atlantic and the Pacific. After the war, I attended Columbia University (1946–47), Oxford (1947–48) as Rhodes Scholar from Missouri, and then went on to study at the University of Florence (1948–50). My first book was published before I went to Oxford, and, at the same time, I married the poet Barbara Howes of Boston. We spent three years in Europe, and then returned to Vermont; we worked in close association over a period of seventeen years and deeply influenced each other's development as poets. The marriage ended in divorce in 1964; I have two sons, David, born in 1949, and Gregory, born in 1954. In September, 1966, I married Sonja Haussmann of Paris. She is of an old Alsatian family and is related to the Baron Haussmann, the Prefect of Paris for whom the Boulevard was named. She was married previously and has a son, Marc Hoechstetter, aged sixteen, who is now a student at the Maret School of Washington.

"Although a New Englander by adoption (I served a two-year term (1960–1962) as a Democratic Member of the Vermont House of Representatives), I consider my roots to be in the South. I have done over the years every sort of literary hack work to supplement my income. From 1959 to 1967 I was Poet in Residence and Lecturer in English at Williams College, with two years off recently, first at Arena Stage in Washington on a Ford Foundation grant, and then as Writer-in-Residence at Hollins College in Virginia. In 1967 I was named Professor of English at Hollins, and am now on leave from there in Washington as Consultant in Poetry to the Library of Congress.

"While I hope that all my poetry reflects a true tragic sense, I have been drawn to light verse because of a firm belief that humor is one of America's greatest and most enduring characteristics. Children's poetry, with its wide use of stanza forms and the range of its nonsense, has been for me a liberating influence, giving me a chance to explore in miniature certain themes that I have developed and expanded in adult work. The theatre has long been one of my chief interests, and in writing for it, which I have now begun to do, I have tried to bring out dramatically some of the lyric concentration of my verse. In all my work, whether in poetry, drama, criticism, or translation, I have served, and, often at great personal expense, paid tribute to, the power of imagination, in which, above all else, I believe."

The twenty-one engaging and sometimes impressive lyrics collected in William Jay Smith's first *Poems* were extraordinarily varied—some of them realistic, some satiric, romantic, or mystical, some direct and epigrammatic, some elaborately metaphorical. What they had in common, R. L. Lowe thought, was a sense of style. Lowe said there was not a carelessly written line in the book, but many that seemed "strained, consciously contrived, and needlessly ingenious." There were similar complaints—about a lack of involvement, of convincing imaginative force—against some of the poems in *Celebration at Dark*, but there was much said also in praise of the collection. Richard Eberhart thought that Smith is "in some ways like a painter, sensuously conscious of colors, of words as plastic tones and of music in words as color."

As he explains in Howard Nemerov's *Poets on Poetry*, Smith believes that "variety in poetry . . . is everything," and subscribes to Jean Cocteau's dictum that "the artist should find out what he can do and then do something else." In the same interesting essay he discusses the mysterious genesis of poetry, and speaks of the inexplicable resonance, the "dark sounds" which great poetry gives off, and which he strives for and sometimes achieves even in his ballads and nonsense songs.

Smith's experiments have led him in recent years away from the short forms which previously contented him, towards longer poems with long lines which he thinks of "as akin to the pleats in an accordion—each intact and trim but ready to open out resonantly to its full proportion." A half-dozen of these long poems appear in *The Tin Can*, a collection in which, as usual, Smith speaks "in many voices, all of them his own." Gene Baro was impressed by his handling of "a sinewy long line" whose "long cadences and nervous rhythms respond directly to shifts and feeling," and went on: "These poems are strongly sensuous. They give us almost a bodily reaction to what is passing in them, whether it is the poet's inner unhappiness that unfolds or his response to an aspect of the physical world. . . . There is a hungering energy in this work that is fresh and moving." In the opinion of Herbert Cahoon, Smith "has written some of the most beautiful lyrics of his generation." He received the 1972 Loines Award for Poetry.

William Jay Smith was in the Navy from 1941 to 1945, and left it as a lieutenant, with a special commendation from the French Admiralty. *The Straw Market*, the comedy he wrote as poet-in-residence at the Arena Stage, was staged at Hollins College in 1966. *The Spectra Hoax* is an informative and very funny factual account of several literary spoofs, and in particular of a famous volume of entirely nonsensical free verse thrown together by Witter Bynner and A. D. Ficke, and seriously received by the literary critics in 1916 as the work of an impressive new school of poetry. The book includes the complete text of *Spectra*. Smith has participated as a staff member in writers' conferences, lectures frequently, is an editorial consultant to Grove Press, and a prolific contributor to literary periodicals. A collection of his essays and reviews was published in 1973 as *The Streaks of the Tulip*. He served for two terms as Consultant in Poetry to the Library of Congress, from 1968 to 1970. He is a Democrat and a Protestant.

PRINCIPAL WORKS: *Poetry*—Poems, 1947; Celebration at Dark: Poems, 1950; Poems 1947–1957, 1957; The Tin Can and Other Poems, 1966; New and Selected Poems, 1970. *For children*—Laughing Time, 1955; Boy Blue's Book of Beasts, 1957; Puptents and Pebbles, 1959; Typewriter Town, 1960; What Did I See?, 1962; Ho for a Hat!, 1964; If I Had a Boat, 1966; Mr. Smith and Other Nonsense, 1968. *Nonfiction*—The Spectra Hoax, 1961; The Streaks of the Tulip, 1973. *As editor*—Herrick, 1962; (with Louise Bogan) The Golden Journey: Poems for Young People, 1965; Poems From France, 1967; Poems From Italy, 1972. *As translator*—Larbaud, V., Poems of a Multimillionaire, 1955; Selected Writings of Jules Laforgue, 1956.

ABOUT: Contemporary Authors 7–8, 1963; Murphy, R. (ed.) Contemporary Poets of the English Language, 1970; Smith, W. J. A Frame for Poetry *in* Nemerov, H. (ed.) Poets on Poetry, 1966; Untermeyer, L. Modern American Poetry, 1962; Ward, M. E. and Marquardt, D. A. Authors of Books for Young People, 1967; Who's Who in America, 1972–1973. *Periodicals*—Harper's January 1964; New York Times Book Review June 26, 1966; Poetry December 1966.

SNODGRASS, W(ILLIAM) D(E WITT) (January 5, 1926–), American poet, was born in Wilkinsburg, Pennsylvania, one of the four children of Quaker parents, Bruce De Witt Snodgrass, an accountant, and Jessie Helen Murchie Snodgrass. He grew up in Beaver Falls, Pennsylvania, and went to the local high school. Snodgrass graduated in 1943, and in the year remaining before he reached military age, he attended Geneva College in Beaver Falls, intending to major in music. From 1944 to 1946 he served in the United States Navy, emerging as Yeoman Third Class. He married Lila Jean Hank in June 1946, returned for a year to Geneva College, and went on to the State University of Iowa, by then well-known for its creative writing program and its poetry workshop. At Iowa, depending on part-time jobs and the G.I. Bill to support himself, his wife, and his infant daughter Cynthia Jean, he earned his B.A. in 1949, and two master's degrees (M.A., 1951; M.F.A., 1953), submitting original poems in lieu of theses for both. Donald T. Torchiana, a contemporary at Iowa, remembers Snodgrass as "resplendent in cast-off Navy costume, great head of hair and flowing beard, and properly abstracted poet's eye." The Iowa years saw the failure of his first marriage, which ended in divorce in 1953, and his second marriage, to Mrs. Janice Ferguson Wilson, the following year.

Snodgrass turned the experiences of these unsettled, disillusioned years into poetry of an arrestingly straightforward, personal kind. In a sense he tells all: the disappointment of sailors just back from the Pacific he records in "Returned to Frisco, 1946"; "Home Town" sets down other disappointments recognizable to most returning servicemen; the fatuity of his studies towards the Ph.D. he never completed is anatomized in "April Inventory"; and in a number of compelling poems he chronicles the disintegration of his marriage. By far the most

W. D. SNODGRASS

moving of his poems of this period is "Heart's Needle," a ten-part sequence which expresses with what Robert Lowell has called "harrowing pathos" his fear that his divorce will cost him the love of his little daughter. Yet the final effect is of affirmation—of faith in the strength of the bond between himself and the child and of confidence that a man's life need not escape his control. It is this quality of affirmation which is the distinctive element in Snodgrass's confessional poetry.

"Heart's Needle" became the title poem of Snodgrass's first book, published in 1959. Stanley Kunitz wrote—and this is typical of the enthusiastic reviews which greeted the book: "W. D. Snodgrass has the gift of transforming ordinary experience, including the domestic, into a decisive act of the imagination, remarkable for its pace and clarity and controlled emotion." His poetry's essential claim, another critic suggested, is that "it is necessary to write beautifully in spite of circumstances," and Snodgrass was called a virtuoso in the elegance of his stanza patterns, his "exquisitely schooled timing," his general mastery of his craft. *Heart's Needle* won the $1,000 prize of the Ingram Merrill Foundation, and the 1960 Pulitzer Prize for Poetry. A Guinness Poetry Award from Great Britain followed in 1961.

Heart's Needle appeared in the same season as Robert Lowell's *Life Studies*, and the two books were instrumental in initiating what may be the most significant movement in the poetry of the 1960s. Archetype and myth, both books implied, must count for less in poetry than the poet's own experiences. A poet, Snodgrass said, must make his poems "more personal, and so more universal." He believes that "the only reality which a man can ever surely know is that self he cannot help being, though he will only know that self through its interactions with the world around it. If he pretties it up, if he changes its meaning, if he gives it the voice of any borrowed authority, if in short he rejects this reality, his mind will be less than alive. So will his words."

A second volume, *After Experience*, similar in content and craft, had a more mixed reception, and some critics complained of what one called "a lurking sentimentality, a kind of complacent accomplishment in his handling of distressful material." Others, however, thought it an advance over the first book, and Denis Donoghue, noting that the book includes a section of translations (from Rilke, Nerval, and others), wrote, "The old eloquence persists, but it is richer now because it listens to other voices and knows something of what silence means."

Snodgrass had left Iowa in 1955 to become an instructor in English at Cornell. In 1957 he moved to Rochester. After a year as a *Hudson Review* Fellow in Poetry, he joined the faculty of Wayne State University, Detroit, and taught there from 1959 to 1967. Since 1968 he has been professor of English and speech at Syracuse University, New York. In 1964 he received one of the Ford Foundation grants designed to encourage writing for the theatre. The Pulitzer Prize brought Snodgrass many opportunities to read his poetry on other university campuses. "There is no money in writing poetry," he has been quoted as saying. "But there *is* money in reading it." Snodgrass's second marriage brought him a foster daughter and a son; he was divorced in 1966 and made a third marriage, to Camille B. Rykowski, in 1967. He received the Miles Modern Poetry Award in 1966. No longer shaggily nautical, but "considerably clipped," Snodgrass plays tennis, and a guitar.

PRINCIPAL WORKS: Heart's Needle, 1959; (as tr. with Lore Segal) Gallows Songs, by Christian Morganstern, 1967; After Experience, 1968.

ABOUT: Carroll, P. The Poem in Its Skin, 1968; Current Biography, 1960; Murphy, R. (ed.) Contemporary Poets of the English Language, 1970; White, W. W. D. Snodgrass: A Bibliography, 1960; Who's Who in America, 1972–1973. *Periodicals*—Harper's Magazine September 1960; Nation October 24, 1959; Northwestern Tri-Quarterly Spring 1960; Saturday Evening Post June 2, 1962.

SNOW, (CHARLES) WILBERT (April 6, 1884–), American poet, writes: "I was born on Whitehead Island, off the Maine coast, where the East end of Penobscot Bay joins up with the Atlantic Ocean. This island of eighty acres had been in the possession of my family for seven generations. When I was seven years old we moved to Spruce Head where I attended the village school until I was fourteen. From fourteen to seventeen I was a lobster catcher and fisherman. At seventeen I went to Thomaston, Maine, to live with my grandmother and attend the Thomaston High School, where I did four years' work in two years and a half. I graduated from Bowdoin College in the Class of 1907, and received an M.A. degree from Columbia University in 1910. I taught English and Debating in seven American colleges and, as an interlude, I was a reindeer agent and Eskimo educator on the Seward Peninsula in Alaska for a year and a half. I finally settled in Wesleyan University in Middletown, Connecticut where I taught for over thirty years.

"As another interlude I was a volunteer in World War I and became an Artillery officer, after which I served five years as a member of the Reserve Corps. I married Jeanette Simmons of Rockland, Maine, in 1922 and became the father of five sons.

"My first book of poems, *Maine Coast*, was published by Harcourt, Brace and Company in 1923. In 1926 my second book, *Inner Harbor*, was also published by Harcourt. My third book, *Down East*, was published by Gotham House in 1932. My fourth, *Before the Wind*, with illustrations by the marine artist Gordon Grant, was published in 1938 by Gotham House. The next book, *Maine Tides*, was published in 1940 by Henry Holt. *Sonnets to Steve*, which won a $100 prize award, was published in 1957 by the Exposition Press. Finally, my *Collected Poems* were assembled and published by the Wesleyan University Press in 1963.

"Politically, I was a New Dealer twenty-five years before the word was coined; and this fact made my stay in seven colleges rather brief. I got used to the phrase: 'We shall not require your services in our college next year.' Most of these dismissals were quiet, but the one in the University of Utah, where four professors were kicked out for political activity and nineteen resigned in protest, made something of a national stir. I stumped the state of Maine in 1912 for Woodrow Wilson who was my political hero and we carried the state. I was elected Lieutenant Governor of the state of Connecticut in 1944 as a Democrat on the same day that the people elected a Republican, Raymond Baldwin, as Governor. I ran for Governor on the Democratic ticket in 1946 and was defeated by the president of my own college, James L. McConoughy. In 1951–52 I was sent abroad by the State Department to lecture on American Literature, Politics and the American Way of Life to twenty-one countries in Europe, Asia and the Near East. I was elected a member of the State Constitutional Convention in 1965, and helped to frame a Constitution which was overwhelmingly approved by the citizens in a referendum. My five honorary degrees are: an M.A. from Bowdoin, Litt.D. from Marietta, LL.D from Wesleyan University, Doctor of Fine Arts from Nasson College, Doctor of Humane Letters from the University of Maine. I have been active in education, a member of the Middletown School Board for over thirty years, and for eleven years was chairman. At present I am engaged in writing a new book of poems and my autobiography, and I occasionally give readings and lectures to schools and colleges in the East and Middle West. In 1964 I was the first recipient of the Distinguished Bowdoin Educator Award for Alumni granted by Bowdoin College. I still live in Middletown, Connecticut, in the winter and have long summer vacations at Spruce Head, Maine, where sixteen grandchildren keep me extremely busy."

WILBERT SNOW

Wilbert Snow called his first book *Maine Coast*, and could have used the same title for each of his subsequent collections. His range is considerable—"from the long story in verse to the brief lyric of a single image"—but his poetry, whether descriptive, narrative, or reflective, most often "commemorates the natural and the human scene of the hard-rock coasts of Maine." The vigor and pungency of Snow's style (which is well illustrated in his prose note above), and his sharp sense of character, have reminded one critic of the work of George Crabbe. Another reviewer, in *The Dial*, found in Snow's verse "much the quality of Sarah Orne Jewett tales, though it gives a more intimate presentation of the foibles and philosophy of an isolated community of fishermen and sailors."

John Fandel, discussing Snow's *Collected Poems*

in *Commonweal*, praised his mastery of his traditional forms and meters, and went on: "The vigor of his plain spoken awareness of life comes through directly. A seafarer, this poet's work has the rhythm of the tides, the image of gull and fleet, the peace of the sea and its rage. He has caught the New England 'ways' and 'speech' of the 'simple folk' he knows and loves." It seemed to Homer Woodbridge that Snow's best contribution to contemporary poetry was his "strong buoyant rhythms, [his] frank and huge delight in sound and color and activity."

Wilbert Snow is a member of Phi Beta Kappa and of the Modern Language Association. He is an Episcopalian.

PRINCIPAL WORKS: Maine Coast, 1923; Inner Harbor: More Maine Poems, 1926; Down East, 1932; Selected Poems, 1936; Before the Wind, 1938; Maine Tides, 1940; Sonnets to Steve and Other Poems, 1957; Spruce Head: Selections from [His] Poetry, 1959; Collected Poems, 1963.
ABOUT: Contemporary Authors 9–10, 1964. *Periodicals*—Commonweal May 8, 1964; Dial June 1923.

GARY SNYDER

SNYDER, GARY (SHERMAN) (May 8, 1930–), American poet, writes: "I was born in San Francisco in 1930. After about a year and a half, my parents moved to the country north of Seattle, and built up a little farm. I spent most of my childhood doing farm chores and absorbing the extensive forests around our place.

"The family moved to Portland, Oregon, in 1942. All through high school and college I had various educational part-time jobs: U.P., A.P., Radio KEX, *The Oregonian*. After I graduated from Reed College—anthropology plus literature—I went to work in the woods. I've worked in logging camps, and on Forest Service trail crews and lookouts, in Oregon, Washington and California. I was kicked out of the Forest Service, without explanation, as a 'security risk' in 1954.

"I entered the graduate school of the Department of Oriental Languages at Berkeley in 1953. In Chinese Philology classes with Peter Boodberg and T'ang poetry seminars with Shih-hsiang Chen, the polarities and contradictions of my poetic influences begun to resolve: Jeffers and Whitman, Lawrence and Pound. The force behind this was the magnificent T'ang poet Du Fu; and talks with Kenneth Rexroth who was doing his Chinese and Japanese translations at that time.

"In the fall of 1955 Philip Whalen, Jack Kerouac, Allen Ginsberg, Michael McClure, Philip Lamantia, and myself gave a poetry reading at the Six Gallery in San Francisco. It catalyzed the underlying creative energy of San Francisco, with its essentially anarcho-pacifist outlook—and helped bring a new generation of writers to the public eye, which became known as 'beat.'

"Since 1959 I've lived mostly in Japan. In 1957–1958 I worked as a wiper on an American tanker, making five trips to the Persian Gulf and delivering to oil ports as far apart as Pago Pago, Samoa, and Pozzuoli, near Naples. In 1961–1962 I spent four months in India visiting ashrams and temples with my then wife, the poet Joanne Kyger. During the academic year 1964–1965 I was on the staff of the English department at Berkeley, and was a participant in the Berkeley poetry conference of July 1965. At the moment [November 1966] I am back in Japan on a Bollingen Foundation grant doing a study of traditional Rinzai Zen monastic training methods.

"As a poet I hold the most archaic values on earth. They go back to the late Paleolithic: the fertility of the soil, the magic of animals, the power-vision in solitude, the terrifying initiation and rebirth, the love and ecstasy of the dance, the common work of the tribe. I try to hold both history and the wilderness in mind, that my poems may approach the true measure of things and stand against the unbalance and ignorance of our times."

Gary Snyder, who appears as the young Zen Buddhist "Japhy Ryder" in Jack Kerouac's *The Dharma Bums*, was already well known in Beat circles when his first book appeared, and his verse has come to have an importance and relevance for young people approaching that of Allen Ginsberg.

According to Snyder, the poems in *Riprap* were written "under the influence of the geology of the Sierra Nevada and the daily trail-crew work of picking up and placing granite slabs in tight cobble patterns on hard slab. . . . In part the line was influenced by the five- and seven-character line Chinese poems I'd been reading." Robert Sward found the effect generally simple, spare, and direct, with a quiet strength and a peculiar impersonality, suffering most from a sameness of tone and shape.

Myths and Texts, Snyder says, "grew between 1952 and 1956. Its several rhythms are based on long days of quiet in lookout cabins; setting chokers for the Warm Springs Lumber Co.; and the songs and dances of Great Basin Indian tribes I used to hang around." James Dickey was reminded of the *Cantos* of Ezra Pound, and praised the book, saying that its "musing, drifting series of terse, observant statements does fix Snyder's experiences and beliefs in such a manner that they become available for us to live among and learn from." Kenneth Rexroth, noting that Snyder had learned a great deal from the Far East, commended his "feeling for the new, human significance of the landscape and the primitive peoples of the mountains and forests of the Pacific Coast."

Much of Snyder's best work, including *Riprap*, *Myths and Texts*, some translations, and a section of new poems, was collected in *A Range of Poems*, published in England in 1966. A reviewer in the *Times Literary Supplement* wrote: "Gary Snyder's best poems come, as directly as language allows, from the silent experience of work: hunting, logging, trapping, any work so long as it is physical. He can make a poem from anything, bits and scraps of experience, things that other men retain without comment or throw away. . . . Work is the way this man earns the right to be a poet, his proof of Wordsworthian grace. . . The poems of hard thinking are invariably his weakest. In his best poems the relation between body and soul, labour and spirit, is tense, vivid, worth all the trouble." *Earth House Hold* is a refreshing but uneven collection of essays and journal excerpts.

Snyder is the son of Harold and Lois (Willkie) Snyder. He has been married three times, to Alison Gass (1950–1951), to Joanne Kyger (1960–1964), and in 1967 to Masa Uehara, by whom he has two children. According to a long entry for him in *Contemporary Authors*, his heroes are Mao Tse-tung, Yeats, D. H. Lawrence, and Crazy Horse. He is in favor of courage, polygamy, polyandry, rhododendrons, and sparrow-hawks, but not of New York, which he believes should be leveled and made into a buffalo pasture. Snyder is fluent in Japanese, and reads Chinese. In 1961 he met the Dalai Lama, whom he regards as his spiritual leader. He has also reported that he hopes to establish in California "a community of Western Buddhism."

PRINCIPAL WORKS: Riprap, 1959; Myths and Texts, 1960; Riprap, and Cold Mountain Poems, 1965; Six Sections From Mountains and Rivers Without End, 1965; A Range of Poems, 1966; The Back Country, 1967; Earth House Hold (essays), 1969; Regarding Wave, 1970; Manzanita, 1972.

ABOUT: Allen, D. M. (ed.) The New American Poetry, 1960; Contemporary Authors 17–18, 1967; Kherdian, D. Gary Snyder: A Bibliography and Biographical Note, 1965; Leary, P. and Kelly, R. (eds.) A Controversy of Poets, 1965; Murphy, R. (ed.) Contemporary Poets of the English Language, 1970; Rexroth, K. Assays, 1961; Who's Who in America, 1972–1973. *Periodicals*—Americas January 1964; Poetry July 1960, February 1961; Southern Review July 1968.

***SOLDATI, MARIO** (November 17, 1906–), Italian novelist, short story writer, screen writer, and journalist, was born into an aristocratic family in Turin and educated there in a Jesuit college, a fact which has powerfully influenced his writing. He grew up in Turin, where he attended the university, wrote art criticism for local reviews, and frequented the circle of the anti-Fascist writer and critic Piero Gobetti. Soldati received his degree in literature in 1927, and thereafter for a time followed courses in the history of art in Rome. In 1929 a fellowship took him to the United States, where he studied at Columbia University, traveled widely, and eked out his fellowship as a correspondent for *Il Lavoro* of Genoa. He returned to Italy in 1931 and began his career as a film scenarist.

Salmace (1929), Soldati's first book, is a volume of short stories which attracted little attention but is interesting because it introduces themes which pervade his work. It was followed by *America, primo amore* (America, First Love, 1935), a collection of impressions and vignettes of the United States. Soldati had tried to put the sins and sorrows of Italy behind him but, confronted with the violence and materialism of America, discovered that he was after all irrevocably a European. His book, fresh, candid, and often funny, established him as a writer of perspicacity and charm. He published a book about film making in 1936 and in 1938 made his debut as a film director. Since then the cinema and (more recently) television have demanded much of his time and he has been a writer only by fits and starts.

Soldati's first novel was *La verità sul caso Motta* (The Truth About the Motta Case, 1941), a psychological thriller with elements of surrealistic fantasy. *Fuga in Italia* (Flight Into Italy, 1947), Soldati's war diary, includes an account of his escape from the Germans in 1943, when he was obliged to go into hiding. This incident provided the setting for Soldati's famous story "La giacca verde" (The Green Jacket), and the basis for one of his films.

"La giacca verde," first published in *Botteghe Oscure*, is one of the three novellas collected in *A cena col commendatore* (1950, translated as *Dinner With the Commendatore*). These stories, brilliantly

* sol dä′ tē

MARIO SOLDATI

imaginative tours de force, would have been remarkable at any time and were all the more so in that they were produced when Italian literature was dominated by a passion for crude documentary realism. Charles Rolo found them reminiscent of Somerset Maugham, but more subtle: "In each of these stories a baffling mystery of character is swiftly and tantalizingly presented and unraveled with surprising twists, flashes of insight which throw out clues without disclosing the final answer, and an engrossed fascination with the complexities of human nature. At the conclusion . . . a human being has been—not analyzed but understood. This is storytelling in the great tradition."

The novel which followed, *Lettere da Capri* (1954, translated by Archibald Colquhoun as *The Capri Letters*), received the coveted Strega prize but had rather a mixed critical reception. A study of two American expatriates in Italy, it was admired by Anne Duchene for its "passionate insight into the joys and rapt evils of sex," but seemed to many readers unconvincing in its interpretation of the American psychology. There was also only limited enthusiasm for *La confessione* (1955, translated by R. Rosenthal as *The Confession*), about a Jesuit novice's crisis of conscience. But another novella, *Il vero Silvestri* (1959, translated by Colquhoun as *The Real Silvestri*), a wry Pirandellian investigation into the complexities of personality, has been placed, with "La giacca verde," among "the best long short stories in the world."

Since then Soldati has published more collections of stories, a volume of lyric poems (which also included a longer exercise in "rhythmic prose" originally written for television), a study of Sweden, and several more novels. The latter include *Le due città* (1964, translated by Gwyn Morris as *The Malacca Cane*), set in Turin and Rome, and interesting for its evocation of Soldati's youth, and *La busta arancione* (1966, translated by Bernard Wall as *The Orange Envelope*), which is also partly autobiographical. In *La busta arancione*, wrote one reviewer in the *Times Literary Supplement*, "We are back in the strange, dreamy enchantment of the early stories." It is an account of the abundant sentimental education of Carlo Felice, "born into one of those well-off stuffy families in Turin," schooled in guilt at a Jesuit *collegio*. The result, according to the same critic, "is both splendid comedy and haunting sadness . . . a Mauriac novel turned inside out . . . a succession of unforgettable baroque scenes true to life and described by a master hand."

The effect of this kind of upper-class European education is a theme which recurs throughout Soldati's fiction, and is part perhaps of a more general absorption in the ways in which people use, shape, and misshape each other. This is the theme of *L'attore* (The Actor, 1970), an expertly suspenseful story which also includes some entertaining satire directed against the Italian film and television industries; it was a best seller and received the Campiello Prize.

Soldati's perceptions are, not surprisingly, cinematic; he is "a virtuoso of the quick, telling trait, and the *coup de scène* deftly contrived." His manner of writing is in an older tradition, represented by his eloquent and graceful style, his tolerant, ironical tone, and his mastery of narrative. He has been called one of the most gifted of all living Italian story-tellers.

Soldati's craftsmanlike films, which he generally writes as well as directs, have not often been shown abroad, but are highly respected in Italy. This enormously versatile man is also an able linguist, a popular radio and television commentator, and a perceptive critic of art and literature. In 1950 he staged an opera, *Amfiparnaso*, by the sixteenth century composer Orazio Vecchi. Each month he writes two short stories for *Il Giorno*, and he contributes regularly to *Il Corriere della Sera.* Soldati travels a great deal and is a frequent visitor to Paris and London. He has been twice married, the first time to an American, and has three children.

PRINCIPAL WORKS IN ENGLISH TRANSLATION: The Commander Comes to Dine, 1952 (U.S., Dinner With the Commendatore); The Capri Letters, 1955; The Confession, 1958; The Real Silvestri, 1960; The Orange Envelope, 1969; The Malacca Cane, 1973. *Stories in* Caetani, M. (ed.) An Anthology of New Italian Writing, 1951; Trevelyan, R. (ed.) Italian Short Stories, 1965.

ABOUT: Curley, D. N. and Curley, A. (eds.) Modern Romance Literatures (Library of Literary Criticism), 1967; Current Biography, 1958; Dizionario universale della letteratura contemporanea, 1959; Heiney, D. W.

America in Modern Italian Literature, 1965; International Who's Who, 1972–73; Pacifici, S. A Guide to Contemporary Italian Literature, 1962; Trevelyan, R. (ed.) Italian Short Stories, 1965. *Periodicals*—Atlas July 1965; New Republic December 13, 1954; Saturday Review October 24, 1953; February 11, 1956; February 15, 1958; Times Literary Supplement January 12, 1967; Twentieth Century October 1958.

***SOLZHENITSYN, ALEKSANDR (ISAYEVICH)** (December 11, 1918–), Russian novelist, short story writer, poet, dramatist, and Nobel prizewinner writes (in Russian): "I was born in Kislovodsk, a health resort in the northern Caucasus, but spent only my earliest years there; from 1924 my mother and I lived in Rostov-on-Don. My father was until 1914 a philology student at Moscow University, but throughout the First World War he was an artilleryman on the German front, and he died in June 1918, six months before I was born. My mother, who had married him at the front in 1917 and had not lived with him for even a year, never married again, fearing that a stepfather might be strict with me. (When I grew up and was able to judge I felt that this sacrifice was unjustified: in my opinion strictness at an early age can sometimes be nothing but beneficial for a small boy.) My mother and I lived together, sharing the cares of the household in those difficult years. She worked as a typist and stenographer, worked very hard, and as the years passed she was more and more frequently ill. She developed tuberculosis, and died of it in 1944, while I was at the front.

"The desire to write, and the unconscious idea (unprompted by anyone) that I ought for some reason to become a writer, arose in me at a very early age, at nine or ten, when I was not even capable of understanding what it was like to be a writer or why one wrote. From that time on, throughout my youth, I wrote a great deal of nonsense in various genres. But for a long time I did not come to know either my linguistic or my natural environment. It was only just before the war, having visited Central Russia, that I discovered for myself this unique region, where I could become not just a writer in general but a *Russian* writer.

"I completed my secondary education in 1936 in Rostov-on-Don and wanted to receive a higher education in literature, but this faculty at Rostov didn't satisfy me, though I couldn't move to another city and leave my mother alone. I therefore entered the department of physics and mathematics at Rostov University, graduating with honors in 1941, and even with a Stalin scholarship which I had been awarded in the previous year. However, despite my facility in mathematics, I felt that I was devoting myself to a subject which was not the most significant or even the most interesting one to me. Nevertheless my later life showed that mathematics unfailingly came to my aid in all the difficult periods of my life, and I believe that without this specialty I would not have been able to survive until today, to be writing this autobiographical sketch. I am also continually aware of the imprint of my mathematical training on my present literary work.

* sôl zhā nē′ tsin

ALEKSANDR SOLZHENITSYN

"In 1939, still endeavoring to obtain a literary education, I continued to study in the mathematics department at Rostov University and simultaneously enrolled for a correspondence course at the Moscow Institute of Philosophy, Literature and History, but by the beginning of the war I had been able to complete only three semesters. Looking back I have few regrets at not receiving a literary education, since I don't consider it essential for a writer, and it may sometimes even be confusing. It is another factor that in my complex and highly concentrated later life, the need to keep up with work in the scientific field severely limited my opportunities for ordinary *reading*, so that my reading remains basically that which I had time for in my youth. I know Russian literature fairly well, but of foreign literature only the greatest names from earlier centuries. Western literature of the twentieth century and especially contemporary literature, with a few exceptions, I don't know at all, simply because I didn't have time to follow it.

"Before the war I had attempted to publish my writing, but without success. It is ridiculous to recall, but at that time it seemed very difficult for me to find a topic! I longed to write, but because of the poverty of my experience I did not know about *what*.

"In 1940 I married Natalia Reshetovskaya, a chemistry student at Rostov University. I began the war as a private, but in 1942, as a mathematician, I completed a crash course at artillery school and was commissioned as an officer. I became the commander of a reconnaissance battery, and was with it continuously at the front throughout 1943, 1944, and the beginning of 1945, advancing from Orel as far as Germany.

"In February 1945, at the front, in East Prussia, I was arrested because I had criticized Stalin in correspondence with an old friend. In Moscow in the summer of 1945 I was sentenced to eight years in a labor camp; I served this term in full. During these years I was a laborer, a bricklayer, and a foundry worker, but for half of my term I worked on higher mathematics, which helped me to survive. During the years of imprisonment I spent every free moment studying my native language. In 1953, after completing my sentence, I was sent 'permanently' into exile, where I had the opportunity to teach mathematics, physics and astronomy in secondary schools. This work served as my means of livelihood until 1963. In 1956, after the Twentieth Congress of the Communist Party, I was freed from exile, and in 1957 my 1945 conviction was recognized as invalid, so that I was able to fulfill my long-standing desire to return to Central Russia.

"All through the following years, while I worked as a teacher, I wrote prose and poetry, but not until 1961 did I attempt to have any of it published. The first such attempt, the story *Odin den' Ivana Denisovicha* (*One Day in the Life of Ivan Denisovich*) in *Novy Mir*, proved successful.

"I am experimenting with the attraction which I feel to larger prose forms, as a means of portraying historical movements or periods in the life of society; I am therefore working towards a rather complex form of composition, with an abundance of characters but without one central one among them. Not only do I not share the opinion that the time for such large prose works has passed, but I think that their time is only just coming."

With the publication of *Ivan Denisovich*, Solzhenitsyn sprang from obscurity as a provincial mathematics teacher to immediate fame. Publication had been ordered by Khrushchev himself as part of his anti-Stalinist campaign, and the book was a political sensation because for the first time it gave an honest account, based closely on the author's own experience, of life in a Stalinist labor camp. The story describes a single day in the life of a camp inmate, Ivan Denisovich Shukhov, from reveille at five o'clock in the morning until lights out in the evening, when he falls asleep once more with his feet tucked in the sleeves of his jacket against the bitter cold. Ivan Denisovich is a peasant who has been sentenced to ten years "corrective labor" merely because he was taken prisoner by the Germans during the war. This uneducated but shrewd narrator tells his story without philosophical or political reflection, as a factual account of the constant fight for mere survival.

Mihajlo Mihajlov has made a detailed comparison of *Ivan Denisovich* with Dostoevsky's *Memoirs From the House of the Dead*, and the similarities are striking. Leonid Rzhevsky called its language and style "a milestone in the history of Russian literature." It is written in short staccato sentences, full of labor camp slang and obscenities, and of neologisms which, as Rzhevsky says, "are so real and convincing that it is difficult to decide what the author has borrowed from life and what he has invented." And Katherine Hunter Blair comments: "When his characters use slang they do so because they could not possibly have expressed themselves in any other way. The very familiarity of his language is deceptive: the texture of his style is so closely woven, the *mot juste* so nicely placed, that his prose has a kind of music, a harmony born of the perfect marriage between assonance and meaning. . . . Solzhenitsyn implies far more than he says. His writing is stark, unvarnished, highly economical, but in all his works one feels his intense compassion." An English translation of the novel has been filmed by the Finnish-born director Casper Wrede.

The only other works by Solzhenitsyn which have appeared in the Soviet Union are four stories, all published in *Novy Mir*. In "Sluchay na stantsii Krechetovka" (1963, translated as "An Incident at Krechetovka Station"), a panicky young lieutenant in charge of a railway station at the time of the German advance on Moscow denounces a man as an enemy agent. Later he is overcome by doubt, but though the man was probably innocent he has been swallowed up by the secret police system. The first-person narrator in "Matrenin dvor" (1963, translated as "Matryona's House") becomes a schoolmaster in an isolated and backward village. Here he finds lodgings with the poor, simple, generous woman who is the subject of the story—"that righteous soul without whom, as the proverb goes, neither village or town, nor our whole land can survive." The literary conservatives had not dared to attack *Ivan Denisovich* because of Khrushchev's backing, but now there was critical murmuring about Solzhenitsyn's praise of "bourgeois virtues."

He was also criticized for "Dlya polzy dela" (1963, translated as "For the Good of the Cause"), an ironic attack on bureaucracy. The conservatives were outraged by an explicit suggestion in the story that Stalinism was still alive, though Solzhenitsyn's supporters got the best of the argument, and in

1964 he was even nominated for a Lenin Prize for literature. But with the fall of Khrushchev and the increasing insistence on ideological orthodoxy the attacks on Solzhenitsyn grew stronger, and only one more work by him was published in the Soviet Union, once again in *Novy Mir*, the story 'Zakhar-Kalita" (1966, "Zakhar the Pouch"). These stories show, as C. G. Bearne has pointed out, that "Solzhenitsyn is an intensely Russian writer in the tradition of the Slavophils rather than the Westerners. He has an almost mystic attitude to the peasant, [and] a deep feeling for the history of ancient Russia."

In May 1967 Solzhenitsyn wrote his famous letter to the Fourth National Congress of Soviet Writers, attacking "the oppression, no longer tolerable, that our literature has been enduring from censorship for decades." He ended his letter with an account of his own experience of censorship, from the publication of his first novel, achieved only through the personal intervention of Khrushchev, to the more recent period when his novels, plays, stories, and a film script had all been suppressed.

In response to this letter eighty-two leading writers petitioned the Communist party's Central Committee on Solzhenitsyn's behalf. Nevertheless, in November 1969, Solzhenitsyn was expelled from the Writers' Union. This event, and his outspoken letter of protest, received worldwide publicity. Apart from criticism of the "negative" portrayal of Soviet life in his writing one of the main charges against him was the publication of his work abroad "as an anti-Soviet weapon"; Solzhenitsyn retorted: "Answer me first, why am I not published here at home?" He himself has been one of the principal opponents of what he calls foreign piracy of his work, and in 1970 he appointed a Swiss legal representative to prevent any but authorized translations.

While in prison Solzhenitsyn had suffered from cancer of the stomach. In 1954 it was irradiated in a hospital in Tashkent, and it has not since then been malignant. This experience provides the theme of *Rakovy korpus* (1968, translated as *The Cancer Ward*), which explores the reactions of a varied group of about a dozen men in a hospital in Soviet Central Asia to the prospect of more or less imminent death from cancer. The two central characters are utterly opposed products of Soviet society, the political deportee Kostoglotov and the party man Rusanov. Rusanov is portrayed as a greedy philistine. Kostoglotov is the opponent both of materialism and of a narrowly rationalistic "scientific" view of human life, and obviously speaks for the author. The editor of *Pravda* attacked the book as "aimed at the Soviet regime, in which he finds only sores and cancerous tumors," but it is much more than a political allegory, addressing itself to the whole question of what men live by. In any case, as the *Times Literary Supplement* pointed out, the author's radical "ethical socialism" has "little to offer most of those who have sought to use Solzhenitsyn as a weapon in the Cold War." Patricia Blake was one of several Western critics who complained of a lack of stylistic control in the novel, and "a penchant for simplistic moralizing," concluding nevertheless that it "towers above the novels that glut our marketplace."

The novel *V kruge pervom* (1968, translated as *The First Circle*) is also set in an enclosed institution —this time a scientific research station operated during the Stalin years by the secret police—and is again based on personal experience, for Solzhenitsyn was employed as a mathematician in just such an establishment. The first circle in Dante's *Inferno* is a bearable place occupied by the pre-Christian philosophers, just as the scientists in the "special prison" of Mavrino are far removed from the lower depths inhabited by Ivan Denisovich. But in return for this relative comfort they are obliged to construct such abominable machines as one capable of identifying even a disguised human voice over a telephone. The development and use of this device provides the novel's central action: a young diplomat, who unwisely telephones a warning to a potential victim of Stalinist terror, is eventually trapped by the new gadget. There is also a widely praised satirical description of the dictator himself, old and ill but still ruling from the sofa in his fortress office in the Kremlin. As in the previous novels one of the characters, here the mathematician Nerzhin, has much in common with the author; his stoic philosophy is that "for those who understand, human happiness is suffering."

V. S. Pritchett wrote of this novel: "The density of Solzhenitsyn's texture owes everything to the ingenious interlocking of incidents that are really short stories. . . . In spite of its range of scenes inside and outside prison [the novel] has a serene command of space and time. It has an architectural unity, and once the uneasy opening chapters are over, it is unshakable." The book forms an unequaled portrait, loving but painfully ironic, of a great nation in the grip of a nightmare, where morality and patriotism are defined by gangsters, where brutality and greed and hypocrisy are rewarded with power and wealth, and humanity, love, and virtue are viciously punished. Edward Crankshaw called the novel "an unqualified masterpiece," and many agreed.

The four-act play *Olen' i Shalashovka* (translated as *The Love-Girl and the Innocent*) was written in 1954, shortly after Solzhenitsyn's release from the labor camp, but while he was still in exile in Kazakhstan. With a cast of over fifty characters, it is a vivid documentary panorama of the whole of camp life. It conveys the same impression as the novels, of a nation systematically destroying the best in itself, but, most critics thought, shows no special talent for the theatre. This play was accepted by the Sovremennik (Contemporary) Theatre in Moscow for production in 1962, and was actually at the dress rehearsal stage before it was banned. Another play, *Svecha na vetru* (translated as *Candle in the Wind*), written in 1960, was also accepted for production in Moscow and then rejected. It is a partly autobiographical work, set in a fictional country, about a mathematician who has been freed after nine years in a labor camp. He participates in biocybernetic experiments designed to control personality, but comes bitterly to repent of this technological interference in human lives.

Solzhenitsyn was awarded the Nobel Prize for Literature in 1970; he was cited for "the ethical force with which he has pursued the indispensable traditions of Russian literature." This great honor for a writer excoriated by the Soviet literary establishment was, predictably, condemned by the party hacks as a hostile political gesture. Solzhenitsyn decided that he could not go to Stockholm to receive the prize, fearing that he might never be permitted to return. The private presentation that was to have taken place in Moscow in the spring of 1972 was abandoned when the secretary of the Swedish Academy was refused a visa to enter Russia, presumably because the Soviet authorities had been angered by the outspoken interview Solzhenitsyn had given to American journalists in March 1972. (Solzhenitsyn had described the officially sponsored campaign of vilification against him and his family; the difficulties placed in the way of his research; how his mail was read, his living quarters bugged, and his friends shadowed "like state criminals.") His Nobel lecture bitterly attacked literary censorship in the Soviet Union, and the world's apathy in the face of growing international violence and injustice.

Meanwhile, in 1971, Solzhenitsyn had published another major novel, *Avgust chetyrnadtsatogo* (translated by Michael Glenny as *August 1914*). For many years he had contemplated a novel about the Battle of Tannenberg in August 1914, when the Czarist army was routed by German forces. He believes that this disaster, revealing the criminal incompetence of the Czarist high command, had set the scene for the Russian Revolution and all that followed. The event also has a personal significance for Solzhenitsyn; his father had fought at Tannenberg and thirty years later he himself had marched through Tannenberg when the Red Army broke into Germany. After *August 1914* had been rejected unseen by seven Soviet publishers, Solzhenitsyn, feeling himself unable to accept the indignity of censorship, authorized its publication abroad. In accordance with his wishes, its first publication (to establish copyright) was by the YMCA Press, a small émigré publisher in Paris.

August 1914 is the "first fascicle" in a projected cycle to which the author expects to devote the rest of his life. Like *The First Circle* and *Cancer Ward* it is (in the author's term) a polyphonic novel, with no one hero. Each major character dominates the scene for a time and then gives way to another. The story deals with the first eleven days of World War I, describing with great concern for historical accuracy the Russian offensive into East Prussia, which ended in the encirclement and defeat of General Samsonov's Second Army by Hindenburg and Ludendorff at Tannenberg. This basic theme permits the introduction of a great gallery of characters, both fictitious and historical, from every walk of Russian life. Woven into the narrative is much Tolstoyan philosophical discussion. If the historical content of the novel was a departure for Solzhenitsyn, so was its presentation. The book is made up of sixty-four brief chapters, supplemented rather as in Dos Passos' *USA* by montages of quotations from contemporary newspapers and from German army despatches, as well as by passages from the shooting script of an imaginary film about the battle.

The fact that the novel was banned in the Soviet Union did not, of course, avert official attacks on it there (for "insulting" Russians and "glorifying" German militarism). However, a collection of underground reviews reached the West in November 1972, and showed that for many Soviet intellectuals (who had risked imprisonment to read typescripts of the novel) it was of great importance. Even some who found it disappointing as a work of literature welcomed it as an intellectual catalyst and a liberating moral force. Reviews of the English translation were respectful but unenthusiastic. Some critics repeated a criticism sometimes made of earlier works—that Solzhenitsyn, trained as a scientist, has great powers of observation, memory and cross-reference, but, as Anna Akhmatova once suggested, lacks great imaginative vision. While Patricia Blake thought that "the novel will inevitably and quite properly enter into literary history as the modern *War and Peace*," Philip Toynbee found the comparison with Tolstoy "disastrous" for Solzhenitsyn, and wrote that, although the book "tells us a great deal about how the battle of Tannenberg was fought, it tells us nothing new either about what it feels like to fight in a war or about what war *is*, what it means."

Solzhenitsyn became the center of another international furor in December 1972, when the American writer Albert Maltz offered him the use of the "considerable royalties" that Maltz had earned in the Soviet Union. In his widely published reply, Solzhenitsyn confirmed that his financial situation was desperate. The Soviet authorities claimed that, on the contrary, he was a millionaire, living in luxury. The author's estranged first wife, Natalya Reshetovskaya, at first confirmed this, then published a retraction. In fact, the huge royalties that Solzhenitsyn's books had earned abroad remained in foreign banks. He lived an extremely austere existence, and for years made his home in the *dacha* near Moscow of his friend the cellist Mstislav Rostropovich.

Fritz Heeb, Solzhenitsyn's Swiss lawyer, spoke of a "broadly conceived campaign of defamation conducted by the Soviet authorities" against the author. This continued during the early 1970s, but was effectively countered by Solzhenitsyn's adroit and fearless use of such publicity channels as were open to him. In August 1973 he told Western journalists that he and his family had been threatened. The threats came ostensibly from individuals, but, he said, "if I am declared killed or suddenly mysteriously ill," it could be concluded that "I have been killed with the approval of the KGB or by it." He had arranged that, if he were assassinated, "the essential part" of his work would be published abroad. This was taken to be a reference to *Arkhipelag Gulag*, a massive survey of the Stalinist labor camps which Solzhenitsyn wrote between 1958 and 1968.

Solzhenitsyn was divorced from his first wife during his years in the labor camp, but remarried her in 1956 when he was freed. They were divorced a second time in March 1973, after a prolonged struggle with the Soviet authorities. Solzhenitsyn was then able to marry the young mathematician Natalya Svetlova, by whom he has three sons, Yermolai, Ignat, and Stepan.

In September 1973, the USSR (which earlier that year had signed the Universal Copyright Convention) established a copyright agency which was to be the sole official channel between Soviet writers and the West. Authors who sought foreign publication by other means would face prosecution. Three months later, Solzhenitsyn authorized publication in the West of *Arkhipelag Gulag*. The decision was influenced, he explained, by the fact that a *samizdat* copy of the book had been seized by the state security authorities—there was no longer any point in withholding it from publication in order to protect those mentioned in it.

The first volume of *Arkhipelag Gulag*, containing Parts One and Two of the seven-part work, was published by the YMCA Press in Paris in December 1973. *The Gulag Archipelago*, Thomas P. Whitney's English version of this volume, was announced for publication in the United States and Britain the following year. The book, which Solzhenitsyn considers his most important work, is a detailed factual account of the "archipelago" of Soviet prison camps between 1918 and 1956, and of those who conceived and maintained them, and of those who suffered and died in them. It is derived from printed sources, from the author's own experiences, and from his correspondence and interviews with two hundred and twenty-seven other survivors. It contains, Solzhenitsyn says, "only real facts, places and names." Michael Glenny has described its style as an "urgent, headlong, allusive vernacular, riddled with slang, cryptic idioms and esoteric jargon." George F. Kennan called it "the most heavy and relentless book of our time. . . . Part reminiscence, part history, part sociological study, part folklore, it is a leisurely and exhaustive examination of that vast 'other Russia' [which developed ultimately] into a specific culture, complete with language, customs, legends, mythology, hierarchies of authority, overt and otherwise —everything, in fact, except hope." Another reviewer, in the *Times Literary Supplement*, found it "perhaps somewhat short of being a masterpiece of the word," but thought that "because it is written in a profound conviction of man's moral duty, it will survive as one of the bravest and finest of mankind's bequests to posterity."

Arkhipelag Gulag is no less than an attempt to call the Russian people to account for the crimes the USSR has tried to forget, and thus to purge the country of the sins of forty years. Dates are given, documents quoted, cases cited. The prosecutors, torturers, and executioners are named, and the indictment is extended to all those (including the author himself) who had kept silent out of fear. Solzhenitsyn calls for the punishment of the guilty, and implies that the Soviet system of terror, modified though it is, is still in operation.

This one-man crusade against the whole apparatus of the Soviet state could not be ignored. At the same time the Soviet authorities, who at that time urgently sought a détente with the West, did not dare to use against so illustrious a rebel the police state methods of which he accused them. Instead they contented themselves, during January 1974, with a new campaign of vilification against the author and his book, which was called a "blanket slander of the Soviet people." Several young Soviet intellectuals had the courage to denounce this campaign, and Solzhenitsyn scornfully dismissed his attackers as cowards and liars. In February, the author was twice ordered to appear before the state prosecutor. He ignored the summonses because of the "complete and general illegality ruling in our country for many years." On February 13 Solzhenitsyn was arrested by the KGB and held for twenty-four hours. He was deprived of his Soviet citizenship, and flown against his will to Frankfurt in Germany.

For days Solzhenitsyn's expulsion dominated the world's news, but the storm of protest over this brutal separation of an artist from his creative roots was tempered by relief that no worse fate had befallen him. Many countries offered him sanctuary. In fact, after spending a few days with his fellow Nobel laureate, the German novelist Heinrich Böll, Solzhenitsyn moved to Zurich, Switzerland. He continued to receive more attention from the world's news media than any literary figure had ever done before, and was so dogged and besieged by journalists that on one occasion he called a pack of photographers "worse than the KGB." The furor gradually subsided. In March, Solzhenitsyn was joined by his wife and sons, his wife's son by a previous marriage, and his wife's mother. The family has a house in the Zurich suburbs and expects to settle there. Solzhenitsyn has vowed to continue his work in exile, but has not abandoned his hope that he will one day return to Russia.

Solzhenitsyn is tall and barrel-chested, with a fringe of beard. He is said to speak very rapidly in "sentences molded in mathematically precise words," and "spiced with Latin quotations." In the long letter he sent to the Soviet leadership in September 1973, proposing solutions to what he saw as the major dangers facing the Soviet people, he wrote: "I myself see Christianity today as the only living spiritual force capable of undertaking the spiritual healing of Russia."

Except in the USSR and its satellites, Solzhenitsyn is almost universally regarded both as his country's conscience and as its greatest living writer. There is a statement in *The First Circle* which is painfully relevant to his own situation: "For a country to have a great writer is like having another government. That's why no regime has ever loved great writers, only minor ones."

PRINCIPAL WORKS IN ENGLISH TRANSLATION: One Day in the Life of Ivan Denisovich, tr. by Ralph Parker, 1963 (also tr. by Max Hayward and Ronald Hingley, 1963, and by Gillon Aitken, 1971; adapted as a screenplay by Ronald Harwood, 1972); We Never Make Mistakes (*contains* An Incident at Krechetovka Station *and* Matryona's House, tr. by P. W. Blackstock), 1963; For the Good of the Cause, tr. by David Floyd and Max Hayward, 1964; The Cancer Ward, tr. by Nicholas Bethell and David Burg, 1968 (also tr. by Rebecca Frank, 1968); The First Circle, tr. by Thomas P. Whitney, 1968 (also tr. by Michael Guybon, 1968); The Love-Girl and the Innocent (play), tr. by Nicholas Bethell and David Burg, 1969; Stories and Prose Poems, tr. by Michael Glenny (*contains* the four *Novy Mir* stories and two stories and a number of prose poems unpublished in the USSR), 1971; August 1914, tr. by Michael Glenny, 1972; Nobel Lecture, tr. by F. D. Reeve, 1972 (also tr. by Thomas P. Whitney as The Nobel Lecture on Literature, and by members of the BBC Russian Service as One Word of Truth); Candle in the Wind (play, tr. by Keith Armes), 1973.

ABOUT: Alexandrova, V. A History of Soviet Literature, 1963; Björkegren, H. Aleksandr Solzhenitsyn: A Biography, 1972; Brown, E. J. Russian Literature Since the Revolution, 1963; Burg, D. and Feifer, G. Solzhenitsyn, 1972; Current Biography, 1969; Fiene, D. M. (comp.) Alexander Solzhenitsyn: An International Bibliography of Writings by and About Him, 1973; Grazzini, G. Solzhenitsyn, 1973; Labedz, L. (ed.) Solzhenitsyn: A Documentary Record, 1970; Lukács, G. Solzhenitsyn, 1970; Medvedev, Z. Ten Years After Ivan Denisovich, 1973; Mihajlov, M. Russian Themes, 1968; Moody, C. Solzhenitsyn, 1973; Muchnic, H. Russian Writers, 1971; Rothberg, A. Alexandr Solzhenitsyn: The Major Novels, 1971; Slonim, M. Soviet Russian Literature, 1969; Tyrmand, L. (ed.) Kultura Essays, 1970. *Periodicals*—American Scholar Winter 1969; Economist November 15, 1969; Encounter March 1971; Guardian October 9, 1970; Life October 23, 1970; London Magazine April–May 1971; Nation October 7, 1968; January 6, 1969; June 2, 1969; October 26, 1970; New Republic October 19, 1968; October 16, 1971; New Statesman November 15, 1968; March 17, 1969; New York Review of Books December 19, 1968; March 21, 1974; New York Times October 9, 1970; November 13, 16, and 28, 1970; December 1, 1970; June 19, 1971; July 11, 1971; August 15, 1971; March 23, 1972; April 3, 8, and 13, 1972; August 25, 1972; September 6, 1972; November 20, 1972; December 11, 18, and 21, 1972; January 8, 1973; March 9 and 28, 1973; May 15, 1973; August 24 and 29, 1973; December 31, 1973; January 3, 1974; February 14, 1974; New York Times Magazine April 12, 1970; Russian Review April 1967; January 1968; October 1969; Saturday Review March 15, 1969; November 28, 1970; December 4, 1971; Soviet Review Fall 1965; Times Literary Supplement February 1, 1963; February 8, 1965; November 21, 1968; March 13, 1969; November 20, 1969; October 15, 1971; September 22, 1972; February 22, 1974.

SOMERS, PAUL. *See* WINTERTON, PAUL

SONTAG, SUSAN (January 16, 1933–), American critic, novelist, and short story writer, writes: "I was born in New York City, brought up in Tucson, Arizona, and Los Angeles, California, and educated in public schools. I began college at the University of California at Berkeley but did most of my undergraduate work at the College of the University of Chicago, from which I received a B.A. in 1951.

"I was married during my third year at college, when I was seventeen; a son, David, was born in 1952, when I was nineteen. During most of the years of my marriage I lived in Cambridge, Massachusetts. During that period, I studied English and then Philosophy in the graduate school of Harvard University, taking an M.A. and eventually a Ph.D. in Philosophy.

"In 1957, I left my husband and lived for a year in Paris. I was divorced the following year, and settled in New York City where I have been living ever since with my son. I spend at least a third of each year—four months—in Paris, and traveling in Europe.

"During most of the 1950s and up to 1964, I

taught: a year at the University of Connecticut (English), two years at Harvard (philosophy and humanities), a year at Sarah Lawrence College (philosophy) a year at the City College of New York (philosophy), and four years at Columbia University (philosophy and the history of religion). In 1964, for a semester, I was Writer in Residence at Rutgers University. Since then, I have supported myself by writing, with the help of fellowships from the Rockefeller Foundation, the Merrill Foundation, and the Guggenheim Foundation.

"When I was a child, until the age of thirteen, I wanted passionately to be a chemist. I had been writing essays, stories, poems, and plays since I was about eight, but I had never taken my writing very seriously. I began writing in earnest, after years of involvement with a number of academic and scholarly subjects, when I was twenty-eight. One night I sat down to write something that turned into my novel, *The Benefactor*. I wrote the first draft in a couple of months; it seemed as if it had been dictated to me. Around the same time I also began writing critical essays and reviews. Though never a primary interest, I felt the need (which I feel much less now) to unload some of my intellectual concerns, to dispose of them, as it were, by writing about them.

"I find writing to be an extremely ascetic vocation. I lead a quiet life, and my close friends are not writers. Though I have had the benefit of a good education, I am also something of an auto-didact and keep up with several of the sciences and some specialized historical subjects. The art form that has engaged me most for many years is the movies. I'm also interested in both the history of and contemporary work in painting, music, and architecture. There are not many contemporary writers whom I greatly admire, but I hesitate to insist on my taste because I know my interest in writing is specialized, technical and rather private.

"I am very interested in politics, but I have not found that my political opinions—which belong to what is usually called 'the left'—play an explicit role in my work. I am frustrated when people ask me what my work means or tell me that they cannot understand it. I don't think my work means anything beyond what is said on the page; it is written in grammatical English and seems to me not hard to understand, unless one looks for something else that is not being said. I do not think of myself as having any 'messages' or 'views' as a writer, though I have plenty in private. As a writer I am engaged in the making of autonomous objects which I hope exist at a certain level of intensity or power. I do not think of an audience. I'm glad when people like my work, but not upset when they don't; it seems enough that some people take pleasure in it."

SUSAN SONTAG

Susan Sontag is the elder of two daughters of Jewish parents, a traveling salesman and a teacher, who treated her, she says with approval, "as if my life was my own affair." A brilliant student, she received her B.A. in philosophy at the University of Chicago in 1951, when she was eighteen. By then she was married to Philip Rieff, a sociologist with whom she collaborated on a study of Freud's cultural influence, *Freud: The Mind of the Moralist* (1959). During her year in Paris (1957–1958) she studied at the Sorbonne with a grant from the American Association of University Women. She worked for a while in 1959 as an editor of *Commentary*.

The Benefactor, her first novel, is narrated by Hippolyte, a dilettante of sixty who has allowed his obsessive dreams to govern his life and his relationships with others. The book's form is that of a French *récit*, and indeed Hippolyte's precise and stylized diction gives it something of the quality of a translation—one from a work by some contemporary French writer who shares the views of Beckett and Kafka about the absurdity of reality, its resemblance to the products of the imagination.

Some critics thought it merely an exercise in fashionable European techniques, while John Wain had an "impression of delighted skill applied to an end which doesn't, finally, much interest the writer." Others, however, were unequivocally impressed, and J. R. Frakes concluded that the author was "critically engaged in a modern attempt to relocate the center of sensibility, to stretch the frontiers of imagination and introspection. And she does so with grace, with firmness, economy, and irony."

In 1962 or thereabouts, Miss Sontag's essays on many manifestations of contemporary culture began to appear in *Partisan Review*, the *Nation*, the *New York Review of Books*, and a number of other magazines, including several devoted to the cinema. These were collected in 1966 in *Against Interpretation*, which included her much talked-about account of "camp" sensibility, and essays on Simone Weil, Nathalie Sarraute, and a number of French film makers. The title of the collection reflects Miss Sontag's central thesis, which is that the traditional critical concern with the content and meaning of a work of art has become irrelevant. "In most modern instances," she declares, "interpretation amounts to the philistine refusal to leave the work of art alone." She argues that the proper response to a work of art is not intellectual but sensory or nervous, a feeling of pleasure or excitement, and that since such responses are increasingly hard to earn in "a culture based on excess, on overproduction . . . [the] aim of all commentary on art now should be to make works of art—and, by analogy, our own experience—more, rather than less real to us. The function of criticism should be to show how the work of art is what it is, even that it is what it is, rather than to show what it means. In place of a hermeneutics we need an erotics of art."

Miss Sontag called her essays "case studies for . . . a theory of my own sensibility" rather than true criticism, and certainly her reactions are often intensely and even flamboyantly personal. The book provoked heated controversy. Those who disliked it did so because it consigned "content and ethical involvement to the fire," because the author herself often practices an interpretive approach, because the style seemed to them "turgid [and] pretentiously phrased," or, on the other hand, because Miss Sontag dealt so seriously and passionately with art forms that are above all "cool." But as many critics found the book forceful, erudite, and illuminating, the clearest and most generous available guide to the proliferating labyrinths of avant-garde culture. Cyril Connolly complained mildly of Miss Sontag's "mental figure-skating" and "intellectual snobbery," but warmly praised her "sense of fun, her gift of analysis, of going directly to the centre of a problem, her cleverness and eye for significant detail"; and he called her one of the few "women critics [with] . . . a grasp of philosophic abstractions."

By 1969, when she published *Styles of Radical Will*, she was well established as the *enfant terrible* of the New York intellectual establishment, and this second volume of essays also provoked a mixture of savage scorn and enthusiastic praise. The title piece refers to the willingness of many modern artists to risk reason or life itself in pursuit of an altered or extended consciousness, achieved through the use of drugs or in a variety of other ways. Another important article recommends the acceptance of pornography as a valid literary genre; a third discusses the deliberate abortion of communication in the work of such artists as Cage, Beckett, and Warhol; and there are several pieces on the cinema. *Trip to Hanoi*, published in *Esquire* and also as a paperback book, is an account of a 1968 visit to North Vietnam which suggested to some readers that Miss Sontag was reassessing her previous apolitical aestheticism.

Many of her philosophical and cultural preoccupations are evident in her second novel, *Death Kit*. Diddy Harron, its central character, is, like Hippolyte, a fragmented personality who would prefer not to accept responsibility for his life, and cannot distinguish between dream and act. A crisis comes for him during a train journey to a sales conference in upstate New York. Did he on that journey leave the train and murder a stranger, as he believes, or did he (Diddy) not? According to a fellow passenger, Hester, a blind girl whom he seduces in the lavatory, he did not. Diddy leaves his job, becomes Hester's protector, and pursues his terrible dilemma until it is ended by madness and death. In spite of Miss Sontag's injunctions against interpretation, it is not surprising that critics found the book's content more interesting than its New Wave style.

Susan Sontag received the George Polk Memorial Award in 1966. She was a member of the jury of the 1967 Venice Film Festival and helped to select films for the 1967 New York Film Festival. Later she herself tried her hand at film making, writing and directing the movies *Duet for Cannibals* (1969) and *Brother Carl* (1971). She is a popular lecturer and television panelist, but limits such appearances. She lives in New York with her son, but spends part of each year in Europe. She has been described as a "tough, cheerful forthright woman . . . a prodigious worker, a rapid-fire talker." She is tall, black haired, and heavy featured, the possessor of "an awkward beauty."

PRINCIPAL WORKS: *Fiction*—The Benefactor, 1963; Death Kit, 1967; Duet for Cannibals (screenplay), 1970. *Nonfiction*—Against Interpretation, 1966; Trip to Hanoi, 1968; Styles of Radical Will, 1969.

ABOUT: Contemporary Authors 19–20, 1968; Current Biography, 1969; Who's Who in America, 1970–1971. *Periodicals*—Atlantic September 1966; Book Week September 22, 1963; January 30, 1966; Cambridge Quarterly Winter 1966–1967; Commentary December 1963; June 1966; November 1967; Commonweal June 24, 1966; Esquire July 1969; Life January 21, 1966; Nation February 21, 1966; New Republic September 21, 1963; New Statesman March 24, 1967; New York Review of Books June 9, 1966; September 28, 1967; New York Times Book Review August 27, 1967; New York Times Magazine March 21, 1965; Newsday December 2, 1967; Spectator January 2, 1965; March 10, 1967; Time August 18, 1967; Village Voice August 31, 1967; Vogue June 1966.

***SOREL, GEORGES** (November 2, 1847–August 28, 1922), French social philosopher, was born of middle-class parents in Cherbourg, where he attended a private school. He studied briefly at the Collège Rollin in Paris and at the age of seventeen entered the École Polytechnique, graduating in 1866. Thereafter for many years Sorel worked as an engineer for the French Department of Roads and Bridges. His duties involved constant travel, but he devoted his leisure to study and reading, acquiring a remarkable though erratic breadth of learning.

In 1892, when he was forty-five, Sorel suddenly resigned from his post and began to produce the stream of articles and books on philosophy, sociology, politics, and religion that made him famous. It is said that this crucial decision owed much to the influence of Marie David, with whom Sorel lived, but who never became his wife because his family disapproved of her proletarian origins. She died, childless, in 1897. Sorel settled in the Paris suburb of Boulogne-sur-Seine and continued his work as "a philosophical monument" to her memory.

Scorning systems ("I have never asked myself if I am consistent"), Sorel in the course of his career embraced the most diverse political ideas and movements. After discovering Proudhon and Marx, he became dissatisfied with the latter's "scientific pretensions" and moved toward Bergson. From reformist syndicalism his path led, around the turn of the century, to the radical wing of the French labor movement, the anarcho-syndicalists. This intellectual journey is charted in such works as *L'Avenir socialiste des syndicats* (The Socialist Future of Trade Unions, 1898), *Introduction à l'économie moderne* (Introduction to Modern Economy, 1903), *Les Illusions du progrès* (1908, translated as *The Illusions of Progress*), and his most famous book, *Réflexions sur la violence* (1908, translated by T. E. Hulme as *Reflections on Violence*, and many times reprinted).

From the beginning Sorel had sought a new ethical principle that would regenerate society, and he believed that he had found it in the notion of "holy violence." Violence, he said, was a fundamental and permanent human characteristic; it could be bestial and oppressive, or it could be ennobled in the service of some high purpose. Revolutionary violence in a general strike could be the expression of the proletariat's instinctive "will to power"—a "very beautiful and heroic act," taking on the authority of myth in the service of civilization's "primordial interests." In *La Décomposition du marxisme* (1908, translated as *The Decomposition of Marxism*) Sorel separated himself from the rationalism and optimism of Marxist socialism, arguing that revolutionary action was

* sô rel′

GEORGES SOREL

not a considered step in a deliberate process of social change, but the product of profound, subconscious, and irrational forces, careless of consequences and totally unpredictable in its outcome.

The class struggle, Sorel thought, would benefit the bourgeoisie as much as the proletariat, awakening it from its decadent lethargy, and so purging and purifying the entire society. His behavior was thus not as inconsistent as it must have seemed when, around 1910, disenchanted with the "opportunism" of the labor movement, he allied himself for a while with the extreme right wing—the monarchists, the ultranationalists, and the Catholic revivalists. He became a contributor, along with such figures as Léon Daudet and Charles Maurras, to the magazine *Indépendance* (1911–1913). Paul Bourget's conservative play *La Barricade* was a bourgeois reading of Sorel's theories, which also provided the basis for the political philosophy of Mussolini, who said: "What I am, I owe to Sorel." Sorel, who predicted the rise of Mussolini, nevertheless disclaimed any part in his nationalism.

During World War I he discovered another hero in Lenin. Yet Sorel's last years were solitary and clouded with pessimism. He was a sturdy old man, with a ruddy complexion, bright blue eyes, and an impressive white beard, but in fact he suffered from a heart disease which reduced him to semi-invalidism. "What a sad future we have before us," he said in 1921, a year before his death.

Sorel's was an "apocalyptic outsider's view of politics," and he had little direct influence on the French political movements of his time, except in the case of the syndicalists. His books, moreover, although their style is severe and disciplined, have been criticized as biased, ambiguous, and contradictory—collections of dogmatic statements rather than coherent and systematic arguments. Some of them are marred by the "fascistic chatter" which Sartre has found so distasteful. Nevertheless Benedetto Croce placed Sorel with Marx as the only original thinkers socialism has had. His importance lies in his insight into the irrational aspects of social behavior, and the era of totalitarianism and extreme nationalism since his death has amply vindicated his views on violence and myth. More recently, his ideas have been echoed by Frantz Fanon and other prophets of black revolution. Richard Humphrey, one of Sorel's several recent biographers, ranks him with Nietzsche and Freud as one of the great prophets of the modern age.

PRINCIPAL WORKS IN ENGLISH TRANSLATION: Reflections on Violence, 1914; The Decomposition of Marxism *in* Horowitz, I. L. Radicalism and the Revolt Against Reason, 1961; The Illusions of Progress, 1969.

ABOUT: Andreu, P. Notre Maître, M. Sorel, 1953; Bowle, J. Politics and Opinions in the Nineteenth Century, 1954; Carr, E. H. Studies in Revolution, 1950; Curtis, M. Three Against the Third Republic, 1959; Goriely, G. Le Pluralisme dramatique de Georges Sorel, 1962; Horowitz, I. L. Radicalism and the Revolt Against Reason, 1961; Hughes, H. S. Consciousness and Society, 1958; Humphrey, R. Georges Sorel: Prophet Without Honor, 1951; International Encyclopedia of the Social Services, 1968; King, P. T. Fear of Power, 1967; Lancaster, L. W. (ed.) Masters of Political Thought, 1960; Meisel, J. H. The Genesis of Georges Sorel, 1951; Smith, H. (ed.) The Columbia Dictionary of Modern European Literature, 1947. *Periodicals*—Atlantic April 1950; Journal of Modern History March 1967; Journal of Politics February 1950; National Review June 4, 1968; Political Science Quarterly June 1924; March 1968; Review of Politics January 1964; Saturday Review January 5, 1952; Times Literary Supplement December 31, 1971.

"SOSEKI," NATSUME. *See* NATSUME, "SOSEKI"

***SOUPAULT, PHILIPPE** (August 2, 1897–), French poet and novelist, writes (in French): "I was born at Chaville, near Paris, where my family owned an estate; but I spent all my childhood and adolescence in Paris itself. My father was a doctor who wrote a book on diseases of the stomach which has become a classic. I was educated at the Lycée Condorcet, where Eugène Labiche, Marcel Proust and Léon Blum studied. After passing my *baccalauréat* I was drafted for military service during the first World War which broke out on my seventeenth birthday, August 2nd, 1914. The war caused me terrible suffering at the time of my adolescence, though after the upheaval of the second World War it is probably now very difficult to understand how the 1914 war seemed to adolescents to represent the bankruptcy of a civilization. Since despite my bourgeois education I was interested in literature I believed (and I was not the only one) that the writers considered until then the luminaries of French thought were imposters; after this four-year war which conjured up for all those who lived through it a tragedy full of blood and fury, and also of mud, those who were ironically called *littérateurs du territoire* expected to continue to impose their dictates and exercise their evil influence. Many of the young prewar writers had been killed, and among the survivors Guillaume Apollinaire seemed to me to be the only poet who refused to conform and wished to explore a new world; he became my friend, and exercised a great influence on me and my poet friends. I must recall that at this time the Bolshevik revolution, against which bourgeois circles had unleased a campaign of insults and calumnies, seemed to us, without knowing much about it, to announce a new era.

* sōō pō′

"It was in this climate that I became acquainted with two young medical students, Louis Aragon and André Breton, and we decided to publish a review to which we gave the ironic name *Littérature* (Literature). Through this review we made contact with a group of Rumanian and German *émigrés* who had lived since the beginning of the war in Zürich, where they organized artistic or rather anti-artistic happenings. The arrival in Paris of the Rumanian poet Tristan Tzara, who had inspired this group, started the revolt which became celebrated and scandalous under the name of the Dada Movement. The attempt at systematic demolition which was Dada did not absorb all our activity. There was one domain where we had never ceased to belong, that of poetry. André Breton and I, in the course of daily conversations, had long discussions on the essence of poetry, and analyzed Rimbaud's *Illuminations*, Lautréamont's *Chants de Maldoror*, and works by Guillaume Apollinaire and Pierre Reverdy. In the course of our researches we established that the mind, liberated from all critical pressures and academic habits, offered not logical propositions but images, and that if we accepted what the psychiatrist Pierre Janet had called "automatic writing" we could obtain texts which would describe a hitherto unexplored universe. Breton and I therefore decided to spend a fortnight writing a work in collaboration which we would publish without correcting or erasing anything, and with growing faith we read the texts obtained by this method and decided to publish them under the title *Les Champs magnétiques* (Magnetic Fields). From this book was born what we at first prudently called a method, and which we then baptized Surrealism in memory of Guillaume Apollinaire, who had used the term to describe his poem *Onirocritique*. Surrealism became for me the decisive vocation of my literary life, and thanks to it I have since that time tried to explore new regions of poetry."

While serving in the artillery during World War I, Soupault was poisoned by a typhoid serum and had to spend several months during 1917 in military hospitals. Here he began to write the poetry which made up his first collection, *Aquarium* (1917), an expression of his loathing for the bourgeois world, much influenced by Lautréamont and Rimbaud. His friendship with Apollinaire and then with Breton followed. Soupault had been called "the true soul of Dadaism," but dissatisfaction with the absolute nihilism of that movement, the desire to express more positively the search for a "superior reality," led him and Breton to their experiments with automatic writings and the beginnings of Surrealism.

Soupault, however, soon found automatic writing an inadequate instrument, and his later verse, collected in *Poésies complètes*, was much more deliberately structured. The influence of Apollinaire dominates these graceful and subtly cadenced *vers libres*, which Matthew Josephson called "deceptively simple, often gossamer light, like the smoke of his perpetual cigarettes, yet composed of sharp images and dashes of strong color. Like Apollinaire, he wrote at great speed, under the impulse of the moment, a direct, terse, unfeigned poetry. . . . His breathless rush (like his legendary 'seven mistresses,' no doubt) was the manifestation of his being '*alive*,' he explained to us."

By the mid 1920s Soupault had left the increasingly quarrelsome Surrealist movement, though he retained his allegiance to the ideas that inspired it. He turned increasingly to fiction, journalism, and political analysis, prophesying revolution in his autobiographical *Histoire d'un blanc* (Story of a White Man, 1927), and traveling extensively in Europe (1925–1928), the United States (1929), and the USSR (1930).

During the 1920s and 1930s Soupault wrote a dozen novels, beginning in 1923 with *Le Bon Apôtre* (The Good Disciple). Régis Michaud has said that it "may well be taken for the Bible of the young *révoltés*" of the postwar years. "A most classic penman, a cold-blooded and deft analyst, Soupault has left to posterity in this book the most self-revealing portrait of those restless youths who had just graduated from Rimbaud's, Lautréamont's, and Bergson's courses." Most of Soupault's novels end, like life, without a neat conclusion, and in this and other ways reflect the restlessness and uncertainty of the period. His young intellectuals, their social and moral conditioning made meaningless by the war, pursue self-discovery through dreams, drugs, vice, crime, and every sort of excess.

Les Frères Durandeau (The Brothers Durandeau,

PHILIPPE SOUPAULT

1924), usually considered his best novel, is a portrait of the bourgeois life which Soupault hated, as he hates any social system that seeks to inhibit the freedom of the human spirit. Thus, in *Le Nègre* (The Negro, 1927), Edgar Manning's course from prison in America to success in Paris and then to military adventures in Portugal is in quest of a freedom always denied by the color of his skin, and he ends seeking solitude in the heart of Africa. *Les Dernières Nuits de Paris* (1928, translated by William Carlos Williams as *Last Nights of Paris*) is an exploration of the underworld of nocturnal Paris, whose dingy hotels, cheap cafés, and narrow cobbled streets play a central role in what an American reviewer described as "one of the most enthralling and uncanny mystery stories ever written." *Les Moribonds* (The Dying, 1934), who are of course the bourgeois, is a story with many autobiographical elements about a young man's escape from his suffocating middle-class background. The last of Soupault's novels, *Les Moissonneurs* (The Harvesters), was confiscated by the Vichy police in 1940, and has never come to light.

He had continued his travels in Europe and America during the 1930s, until in 1938 he founded Radio-Tunis, which he directed until he was dismissed by the Vichy government in 1940. He was later arrested and spent six months in prison, where he composed his *Ode à Londres bombardée* (1944, translated by Norman Cameron as *Ode to Bombed London*). Soupault subsequently spent two years traveling in America for de Gaulle's provisional government, and wrote an account of his prison experiences in *Le Temps des assassins* (1945, translated by Hannah Josephson as *Age of Assassins*).

Arthur M. Schlesinger, Jr., found it "a minor but thoughtful addition to the contemporary literature of incarceration."

Soupault's many critical works are an extension of his own creative activity, for they are mainly studies of other artists whose creative work was, like his own, directed toward liberation of the imagination: *Guillaume Apollinaire* (1927); *Henri Rousseau, le douanier* (1927); *Lautréamont* (1927); *William Blake* (1928, translated by J. Lewis May); *Baudelaire* (1931); and works on Chaplin, Debussy, James Joyce, and others.

Soupault married his second wife, Meta-Erna Niemeyer, in 1936, and they have two children. He is important above all as one of the founders of the Surrealist movement, and he has continued to proclaim himself a Surrealist, remaining faithful to the principle of being always open to and curious about new experiences. He has continued to travel both physically and mentally, and since the publication of his *Poésies complètes* in 1937 he has brought out several new books of poetry which are represented in the collected *Poèmes et poésies* of 1973, and which show his continued unity of purpose and inspiration.

PRINCIPAL WORKS IN ENGLISH TRANSLATION: William Blake, 1928; Last Nights of Paris, 1929; The American Influence in France, 1930; Ode to Bombed London, 1944; Age of Assassins, 1946; (with André Breton) If You Please (play), *in* Benedikt, M. and Wellwarth, G. E. (eds.) Modern French Plays, 1964.

ABOUT: Alexandrian, S. Surrealist Art, 1970; Curley, D. N. and Curley, A. (eds.) Modern Romance Literatures (Library of Literary Criticism), 1967; Dupuy, H.-J. Philippe Soupault, 1957; Gershman, H. S. The Surrealist Revolution in France, 1969; International Who's Who, 1973–74; Josephson, M. Life Among the Surrealists, 1962; Lemaître, G. From Cubism to Surrealism, 1941; Michaud, R. Modern Thought and Literature in France, 1934; Nadeau, M. The History of Surrealism, 1968; Smith, H. (ed.) Columbia Dictionary of Modern European Literature, 1947; Waldberg, P. Surrealism, 1965; Who's Who in France, 1973–1974. *Periodicals*—Bookman October 1929; Books Abroad 1963; Nation September 29, 1928; November 27, 1929; June 29, 1946; New Republic November 20, 1929; New York Evening Post October 12, 1929; New York Herald Tribune Books March 3, 1929; New York Times October 27, 1929; April 28, 1946; New Yorker April 27, 1946; Nouvelle Revue Française November 1923; Saturday Review May 4, 1946; Spectator October 20, 1928; Times Literary Supplement September 20, 1928.

SOUTHERN, TERRY (May 1, 1924–), American novelist, short story writer, and screenwriter, was born in Alvarado, Texas, the only child of T. M. Southern, a pharmacist, and the former Helen Simonds, a dress designer. He grew up in Dallas and was fond of books and of animals—his pets included tarantulas, chickens, steers, and an armadillo. He also enjoyed hunting, as he still does. Southern began to write when he was eleven and later, according to Francis Wyndham in the New York *Herald Tribune*, rewrote stories by Hawthorne and Edgar Allan Poe because "they never seemed to me to go quite far enough. . . . I made them get *really* going." Wyndham suggests that "going too far" has been Southern's literary aim ever since.

His first ambition was to become a doctor, like his grandfather. He went to high school in Dallas and had begun premedical studies at Southern Methodist University when he was inducted into the Army. (Whether he would otherwise have completed his medical training seems uncertain: his disgust with the inhumanity and hypocrisy he finds in the profession is very evident in his books.) Southern served from 1943 to 1945 with the Army in Europe and then resumed his education, first at the University of Chicago, then at Northwestern, which gave him his B.A. in 1948.

For the next four years he lived in Paris, at first studying at the Sorbonne on the GI Bill. When that source of income was exhausted, he reports, "I had to depend on getting money from my parents and on the kindness of strangers, as they say." It was at this time that Southern's stories and articles began to appear, mostly in the *Paris Review*, the principal organ of that generation of American expatriate intellectuals. In 1952 he returned to the United States, to Greenwich Village. The same year he met and married Carol Kauffman, a nursery school teacher. He worked (and lived) for a time on a barge carrying rocks from Poughkeepsie to Jones Beach, but thereafter devoted himself to freelance writing and journalism. There were periods of considerable poverty during the next few years, which were spent partly in Geneva (where Carol Southern taught at the United Nations' nursery school) and partly in the United States. The Southerns have one son, Nile.

Southern had begun to write under the influence of Céline, Malaparte, and Kafka. He had destroyed three prentice novels when he discovered the work of Henry Green. "I had been moving, I think, towards a style like his," Southern says, "and he had taken it so far beyond what I had been doing that it suddenly gave me an insight into what I was trying to do, and I discarded what I was working on at the time and wrote *Flash and Filigree.*"

Henry Green himself helped to secure the first publication of that novel, in England in 1958. It describes how Dr. Eichner, "the world's foremost dermatologist," is driven to murder to free himself of the attentions of the transvestite Fritz. Meanwhile Babs Mintner, a nubile nurse, is less successful in her attempts to preserve her chastity against the onslaught of Ralph, a pharmacy student. These diversions apart, the book is a "black" satire against bourgeois moral values, the medical profession, the southern California way of life, and any other target that comes within range. One characteristic scene describes the television show "What's My Disease?," a game in which popular panelists strive to identify the gruesome ailments of the "mystery guests." Martin Levin wrote that "the airless, slightly torpid climate of suburban Los Angeles, and the speech of its natives, is rendered with arresting vividness." *Time* found it "strikingly inventive in short scenes," but said that the author "seems unable to plot beyond a dozen pages."

It was followed by another episodic novel, *The Magic Christian* (1960), in which Guy Grand, a surrealist billionaire who speaks in italicized banalities, devotes his limitless fortune to practical jokes designed to humiliate and confound the smug, the greedy, and the pretentious. He markets a deodorant which is really a delayed-action odorant, takes a howitzer on safari, inserts pornographic passages into wholesome movies, and invites the populace of downtown Chicago to scrabble for hundred-dollar bills in a monstrous pile of excrement.

This short book, like its predecessor, left the general public largely unmoved, but added to Southern's growing underground following. What is more it attracted the attention of the film director Stanley Kubrick, then making a screen adaptation of Peter George's novel *Red Alert*. Southern was hired to help turn this suspense story about the cold war into the nightmarish satire screened in 1963 as *Doctor Strangelove, Or How I Learned to Stop Worrying and Love the Bomb*. There has been a great deal of bickering about the size and importance of Southern's contribution to the film, but there is no doubt that his reputation profited enormously from the great success of *Doctor Strangelove*, which *Life* called "a film so original, irreverent and appalling that it practically divided the nation into two enemy camps."

During the 1950s, many expatriate writers in Paris supplemented their incomes by scribbling pornographic fiction for Maurice Girodias' Olympia Press. Southern produced one book for Girodias, the novel *Candy*, written in collaboration with another American, Mason Hoffenberg. First published in 1959 as by "Maxwell Kenton," it was at one time banned by de Gaulle's government (and promptly reissued under the title *Lollipop*). By 1964 the United States was deemed ready to receive it, and it was published amid a flurry of legal arguments about its authorship and copyright. It caused a furor which, coinciding with the controversy over *Doctor Strangelove*, made Southern famous (or, in some quarters, infamous).

Candy, borrowing its tone and title from *Candide*, tells the story of a lovely and innocent coed who is so full of Christian charity that she cannot refuse any of the increasingly rigorous and remarkable

TERRY SOUTHERN

demands made upon her by the very many men she encounters while searching for her long-lost father. Whether *Candy* is pornography or a satire on pornography is a matter of opinion. William Styron said it was "by no stretch of the imagination" obscene, and thought it "in its best scenes . . . wickedly funny to read and morally bracing as only good satire can be"; *Time*'s reviewer believed that "its most conspicuous intent is to be more outrageous in detail than what it is satirizing." It remained on the best-seller lists for a very long time.

This success ended Southern's years of poverty. He bought a farm in the Berkshires and later moved to Hollywood, where in collaboration with Christopher Isherwood and the director Tony Richardson he wrote a widely condemned screen version of Evelyn Waugh's *The Loved One* (1964), and later described the experience in his *Journal of The Loved One*. Other films which he has written or worked on include the screen version of *The Magic Christian*, *Barbarella*, *The Cincinnati Kid*, and *End of the Road*.

A collection of the stories Southern had written since 1955 was published in 1967 as *Red-Dirt Marijuana and Other Tastes*. There was a great deal of praise for two stories exploring the relationship between a Texas boy and his father's black farm hand, and for "You're Too Hip, Baby," in which a white boy fails, through trying too hard, to enter the cool world of a black jazz musician. Many reviewers commented on Southern's absolute mastery of dialogue in these stories, but complained that other pieces, including some in the vein of gruesome humor now expected of the author, seemed disappointingly slight and opportunistic. The volume also contains characteristically ambiguous interviews with Mickey Spillane and with "a faggot male nurse."

Blue Movie is a novel about a great film director who sets out to discover how obscene a film can be before it becomes aesthetically unacceptable. Like *Candy*, it manages to have its cake and satirize it too, pornographically speaking. David Dempsey wrote that Southern has "an uncanny and deadly ear for Hollywood vernacular, and an eye for the more odious Hollywood types," but, like many other reviewers, found the novel's endless round of sexual excess joyless and unfunny.

To judge by his recent writings, Southern still believes that, as he said some years ago, "the important thing in writing is the capacity to astonish." His reviewers and interviewers however tend to treat his statements of opinion very gingerly. Like Guy Grand in *The Magic Christian* he relishes a good cliché, and when, for example, he speaks enthusiastically of the "search for values to replace those that are outmoded," journalists go away wondering if they have been assigned the stooge's role in yet another Southern spoof.

PRINCIPAL WORKS: Flash and Filigree, 1958; (with Mason Hoffenberg) Candy, 1959 (U.S., 1964); The Magic Christian, 1959; The Journal of The Loved One: The Production Log of a Motion Picture, 1965; Red-Dirt Marijuana and Other Tastes, 1967; Blue Movie, 1970.

ABOUT: Contemporary Authors 1–4, 1st revision, 1967; Haste, B. and Riley, C. (eds.) Two Hundred Contemporary Authors, 1969; Moore, H. T. (ed.) Contemporary American Novelists, 1964; Scholes, R. The Fabulators, 1967; Vinson, J. (ed.) Contemporary Novelists, 1972; Who's Who in America, 1972–1973. *Periodicals*—Life August 21, 1964; Listener September 12, 1968; Nation May 18, 1964; New Statesman July 4, 1959; New York Herald Tribune November 28, 1965; New York Times Magazine January 16, 1966; Newsweek June 22, 1964; Reporter November 18, 1965; Time September 29, 1958; June 12, 1964; Views Quarterly Spring 1965.

SOUZA BANDEIRA, MANUEL CARNEIRO DE. *See* BANDEIRA, MANUEL (CARNEIRO DE SOUZA)

***SOYINKA, WOLE (pen name of Akinwande Oluwole Soyinka)** (July 13, 1934–), Nigerian dramatist, poet, and novelist, writes: "Married with four children. I was born in Western Nigeria, of Ijegba parentage, went to school in Abeokuta and Ibadan, to university in Ibadan and Leeds. After Leeds I spent about a year and a half observing and experimenting in theatre, and was attached to one—the Royal Court Theatre—as a play reader. Returned home in 1960 first as a Research Fellow in Drama at the University of Ibadan, later on to the University of Ife to lecture in English Literature. Left Ife (political reasons) and spent about two years travelling, writing and directing plays. Joined Lagos University in October 1965 as Senior Lecturer in English for two years, then transferred to Kaduna Prisons as a political detainee for another two years. At the moment I head the Drama Department of the University of Ibadan.

"I have begun to look on my writing as a successful conspiracy to draw me away from my one idyll—a life of farming with long intervals of domestic inertia in a polygamous household, grubbing in fallen shrines for antique bronze and carvings, and—honing three or four poems a year to an exquisite clarity. Because of a tyranny in my composition however—a compulsive, prodigal response to matter and event—I am caught like others, in the vice of writing.

"I tend to view my work as varying from private experience to purposed commentary, like political satire. In between are the usual works of celebration—events, persons, life, death. Fortunately the first confines itself chiefly to the form of poetry for I cannot always truthfully deny the charge of obscurity and private symbolism in such works. The only remedy is to publish little; even in journals and anthologies I feel peculiarly vulnerable. My plays however are a different matter. It is on the stage that 'all shall be made plain' and the burden of interpretation rests on the producer.

"The satires give me the greatest pleasure, not necessarily satisfaction, in the writing. I see crimes against my society as a personal attack, for they are mostly to blame for the eternal postponement of my idyllic existence. At least one may indulge in the righteous pleasure of drawing blood from criminals who frustrate the everlasting hunger of humanity for peace.

"I have one abiding religion—human liberty. It works in me as a raging, insurgent force against the inexplicable propensity of human beings towards the enslavement of others. And especially here in the new African society where the insistence on this liberty is often regarded as some strange subversive fungus, the position of the writer has begun to follow the world-weary pattern of one-sided conflicts. Conditioned to the truth that life is meaningless, insulting, without this fullest liberty, and in spite of the despairing knowledge that words alone seem unable to guarantee its possession, my writing grows more and more preoccupied with this theme of the oppressive boot, the irrelevance of the colour of the foot that wears it and the struggle for individuality.

"I work, I think, in a productive paradox. Each work has to be the last, so each work proves more exacting and mocks my forbearance by triggering off another train of ideas which prove, in the end, unbearably insistent. All this, and the accompanying 'tyranny of response,' makes it unlikely that I

* shoy ink kä′

shall ever ceremonially smash my typewriter, pick up my hoe and slide peacefully into thrifty poetry and polygamous sloth."

Wole Soyinka was born at Abeokuta, the son of Ayo Soyinka, a school inspector. He was one of the brilliant generation of students at the University College of Ibadan in the early 1950s—a generation which produced at least four of the most significant of all African writers in English: Soyinka, John Pepper Clark, Chinua Achebe, and the late Christopher Okigbo. His first poems appeared in *Black Orpheus* while he was still at the University College. Soyinka was at Leeds University from 1954 to 1957, and in the latter year his first play, *The Inventor*, was given a Sunday evening performance at the Royal Court Theatre, where he worked as a reader. *The Swamp Dwellers*, a much more important piece of work, received a student production in London in 1958. It is a brooding tragedy in verse about an impoverished community of swamp farmers, whose wretched lives are ruled by the snake god and his rapacious priests. A young man who returns penniless from the city questions the system, but he himself dies in the end, thus atoning for the defection of his more successful brother, who will never leave the city—an early indication of Soyinka's preoccupation with the themes of sacrifice, self-sacrifice, and martyrdom.

Soyinka's triumphant return to the School of Drama at Ibadan University was celebrated with productions of *The Swamp Dwellers* and *The Lion and the Jewel* which introduced his work to his own countrymen and established him at once as a figure of consequence in Nigerian literature. *The Lion and the Jewel*, like all his plays, deals with the conflict between old and new in Africa, but in quite a different way from *The Swamp Dwellers*. Far from being an indictment of pagan superstition, it is concerned to show that some of the traditional values and virtues are worth preserving, some of the new ways imported from the West inappropriate or ludicrous. And it is not a tragedy but a richly ribald comedy, in which Sidi, the virgin jewel of the village, courted by both the wily old patriarch and the progressive but spineless young school teacher, chooses polygamous servitude with the grand old reactionary. The play, written in a beautifully handled mixture of poetry and prose, opens with an equally effective scene in mime, in which the villagers act out the visit of the drunken white photographer who had put Sidi on the cover of a famous magazine. As one critic pointed out, Soyinka's message, in this as in all his works, is that "wisdom lies . . . neither in tradition nor modernism, but in the foxiness which knows what to take from both."

The Trials of Brother Jero, written at about the

WOLE SOYINKA

same time, is another comedy, this time a high-spirited satirical farce about the Bar Beach evangelists of Lagos which makes excellent comic use of the vernacular English of West Africa. These two comedies have struck the imagination of ordinary people in Nigeria to an extent quite exceptional for plays written in English. Their reliance on simple, basic situations (the exposure and triumph of the rogue Brother Jeroboam; the seduction of the proud and beautiful girl by the cunning old chief) gives them continuity with an ancient folk tradition, though in technique they are modern and extremely sophisticated.

Soyinka made a serious study of Nigerian folk drama during the year (1959–1960) he spent at Ibadan as a Rockefeller research fellow. And it was at this time that he founded his famous amateur company, the 1960 Masks. The company was established to help in the creation of a new Nigerian drama, written in English but drawing on the ancient theatrical traditions of Africa, the religious festivals which combined words and music, drama and pantomime. The Masks, most of them teachers or civil servants, worked under huge difficulties—not the least the fact that the membership was divided between Ibadan and Lagos, one hundred miles away. Rehearsals would take place in a bucking Land Rover, over the telephone, or not at all. Nevertheless it would be difficult to exaggerate the importance of the company's influence and example in the development of West Africa's thriving theatrical life; as founder and director of the Masks, as actor, producer, and chief fund raiser, Soyinka would have a permanent place in Nigerian theatrical history if he had never written a play.

In fact, the Masks' first major production was Soyinka's *A Dance of the Forests*, commissioned from him for the Nigerian independence celebrations of October 1960. Of all Soyinka's plays it is the one most obviously indebted to the folk tradition. It shows how the tribes gather for a great festival, at which the spirits of the dead are invoked. When they appear, however, the spirits are not the heroes of legend, but mean and rather destructive people like their descendants; it is clearly foolish to glorify the past at the expense of the present. Later, when the high god Forest Head holds court, and the spirits seek to destroy the half-child who symbolizes man's aspirations, it is saved by Demoke, the eternal artist. A reviewer in the *Times Literary Supplement* called it "a dramatic poem of great beauty and profundity . . . written in a mixture of charged, rather austere prose, a short-footed verse of great energy and passion, and a few beautifully modelled songs." Others have drawn attention to the superbly dramatic use in the play of dance and mime.

As he says, Soyinka went on to teach for a while at the University of Ife, an appointment which he left for political reasons in 1963, devoting the next two years to the theatre. In 1964 the Masks were disbanded when Soyinka established a professional company, the Orisun Repertory. The following year he returned to England for the production, during the Commonwealth Festival, of his play *The Road.* It returns to the theme of sacrifice as the way to truth which underlies *The Swamp Dwellers* and another powerful verse tragedy, *The Strong Breed*, but does so in complex, sometimes comic, terms.

Most of the characters in *The Road* are people who earn their living on the highway—truck drivers, passenger-touts, motor-park idlers, and professional thugs employed by politicians. Then there is the Road itself, a hungry god forever demanding blood sacrifice, perpetually in ambush for the careless traveler. And there is the god's high priest and oracle, the frock-coated Professor, who deliberately moves vital road signs so that he can seek the Word (and a profit) among the wrecked cars and corpses. Several reviewers spoke of the hallucinatory effect of the play's dances and drumming, and all paid tribute to its language, which ranges from the racy pidgin English and knockabout repartee of the Lagos slums to the biblical English of the Professor. Penelope Gilliatt wrote that "Wole Soyinka has done for our napping language what brigand dramatists from Ireland have done for centuries: booted it awake, rifled its pockets and scattered the loot into the middle of next week" (an apposite comparison, since Soyinka has himself acknowledged a debt to J. M. Synge).

A later play, *Kongi's Harvest*, is a bitter satire about one of the new breed of African political dictators. For all its wit, and the fine songs it contains, it is perhaps too topical to survive as well as some of his earlier pieces collected in *Five Plays*. A reviewer of that volume in the *Times Literary Supplement* wrote: "Drawing deeply on his knowledge of modern Nigerian life, his plays simultaneously offer new idioms of speech, of acting, of presentation and of poetic allusion. This book is not only a splendid fanfare for the African theatre of tomorrow; it is also a mine from which many eager imaginations may borrow today."

Soyinka's first novel, *The Interpreters*, was a study of young Nigerian intellectuals seeking a firm identity between the tribal past and the Westernized future, against a background of political corruption and religious complacency. It deals harshly with the concept of *négritude*, which is seen as a pseudomystical pose adopted to avoid confronting Africa's real economic, political, and artistic problems. (Soyinka says elsewhere, "I don't think a tiger has to go around proclaiming his tigritude.") In form the novel, as one might expect from Soyinka, is highly sophisticated, employing such fashionable devices as digressions from the narrative line, time dislocations, abrupt shifts of viewpoint. Some Western reviewers were somewhat mystified by the book, and would have been grateful for a rather more straightforward introduction to so unfamiliar a society. However, a critic in the *Times Literary Supplement*, discussing its complex imagery and subtle organization, has called it a work of great distinction and wide influence, "the first really modern African novel."

As a poet, Soyinka first became known for satirical pieces like the renowned "Telephone Conversation," but his work in this form has grown more somber and *Idanre*, his first major collection, excludes all of his humorous poetry. The title poem traces the creation myths of the Yoruba deity Ogun, god of metals and metal work—and hence of the road and of vehicles—craftsman and destroyer; Soyinka, who sees it as the role of the Nigerian artist to mediate between the tribal past and the industrialized future, has adopted Ogun as his alter ego. Some of the most passionate and powerful poems in the collection reflect his distress at the massacre in October 1966 of thirty thousand Ibos by members of Soyinka's own tribe, the Yoruba.

Soyinka is now perhaps the best known of all African writers. In 1965, when he was arrested in connection with a broadcast denouncing the government's election victory, literary figures from many parts of the world protested, among them Robert Lowell, Norman Mailer, and William Styron. This was not to be his last brush with authority. "I am not an idealist only in theory," he says, and in August 1967 he was arrested again, charged by the Nigerian federal authorities with aiding the rebel Biafrans. Soyinka himself said that he had visited the secessionist leader, Colonel Ojukwu, in an attempt to end the civil war. He was never brought to trial but imprisoned, most of the time in solitary confinement, for over two years. In a letter smuggled out of jail he described his solitary confinement as "an inhuman assault on the mind," and he seems at one time to have feared for his sanity (as others did for his life).

Soyinka was released in September 1969. The full effect upon him of the war was evident in his next play, *Madmen and Specialists* (1970), which is sadly different from his earlier work. It is a grotesque, difficult, intermittently powerful allegory in which variously crippled and insane characters propound the cult of "As"—the philosophy of seeing things as they are, and accepting desperation and self-disgust. "Meaninglessness is the theme of this play," wrote one reviewer; "it demonstrates failure in communication, dramatizing the solitude and despair of a playwright who was once a source of optimism." There was a cool reception for Soyinka's version of Euripides' *The Bacchae*, given by the British National Theatre in 1973.

Soyinka managed to write a good deal during his imprisonment, scribbling on any scrap of paper that he could find. His pamphlet *Poems From Prison* (1969) was followed by a fuller poetic record of his ordeal, *A Shuttle in the Crypt* (1972), and then by his "prison notes," mostly in prose, published in 1973 as *The Man Died*. The last, which describes Soyinka's arrest, interrogation, and detention, and the devices by which he contrived to retain his sanity in solitary confinement, also expresses his implacable hostility towards the regime which imprisoned him. All three books were admired as testimonies to the author's courage, but seemed to many readers as disquietingly negative and destructive as *Madmen and Specialists*. *Season of Anomy* (1973), Soyinka's second novel, was a horrifying allegory much closer in spirit to these other post-prison works than to *The Interpreters*, though some reviewers found implicit in its conclusion a hint of hope.

The author is a handsome, witty man whose manner has been described as "princely." He resigned as director of the University of Ibadan's Drama Department late in 1972, issuing at the same time an attack on a variety of university policies. Soyinka took up a fellowship at Churchill College, Cambridge, and late in 1973 announced that he would shortly go to Ghana as editor of the African cultural magazine *Transition*. The author received the Jock Campbell–New Statesman Literary Award in 1969. He has a son and three daughters.

PRINCIPAL WORKS: *Plays*—A Dance of the Forests, 1963; The Lion and the Jewel, 1963; Three Plays (The Swamp Dwellers, The Trials of Brother Jero, The Strong Breed), 1963; Five Plays (A Dance of the Forests, The Lion and the Jewel, The Swamp Dwellers, The Trials of Brother Jero, The Strong Breed), 1964; The Road, 1965; Kongi's Harvest, 1967; Madmen and Specialists, 1971; Collected Plays: Vol. 1 (A Dance of the Forests, The Swamp Dwellers, The Strong Breed, The Road), 1973; The Jero Plays (The Trials of Brother Jero and Jero's Metamorphosis), 1973; Camwood on the Leaves (radio play), 1973; The Bacchae of Euripides (adaptation), 1973. *Fiction*—The Interpreters, 1965; (tr.) The Forest of a Thousand Daemons: A Hunter's Saga (from the Yoruba novel by D. O. Fagunwa, Ogboju ode ninu igbo irunmale), 1968; Season of Anomy, 1973. *Poetry*—Idanre and Other Poems, 1967; Poems from Prison, 1969; A Shuttle in the Crypt, 1972. *Nonfiction*—The Man Died, 1972.

ABOUT: Duerden, D. and Pieterse, C. (eds.) African Writers Talking, 1972; International Who's Who, 1973–74; Jones, E. D. The Writings of Wole Soyinka, 1973; King, B. (ed.) Introduction to Nigerian Literature, 1972; Larson, C. R. The Emergence of African Fiction, 1972; Moore, G. Wole Soyinka, 1972; Penguin Companion to Literature 4, 1969; Ricard, A. Théâtre et nationalisme: Wole Soyinka et LeRoi Jones, 1972; Zell, H. and Silver, H. A Reader's Guide to African Literature, 1972. *Periodicals*—America May 11, 1968; Books Abroad Summer 1966; Guardian September 13, 1965; Modern Drama May 1968; Nation April 27, 1968; New York Times September 2, 1967; June 8, 1969; October 9, 1969; New York Times Book Review December 24, 1972; New Yorker April 27, 1968; Newsweek April 29, 1968; Observer December 18, 1966; Reporter February 8, 1968; Spectator November 6, 1959; Times (London) October 9, 1972; November 14, 1972; Times Literary Supplement April 1, 1965; June 10, 1965; January 18, 1968; March 3, 1972; Tri-Quarterly 5 1966.

SPARK, MURIEL (SARAH) (1918–), British novelist, short story writer, poet, dramatist, and critic, was born in Edinburgh, the daughter of Bernard Camberg, a Jewish engineer, and the former Sarah Uezzell of Hertfordshire, England. She was educated in Edinburgh at the James Gillespie School for Girls, and has said that "Edinburgh is the place that I, a constitutional exile, am essentially exiled from." In view of her prominence as a writer, it is remarkable how shadowy are the published details of her personal life. She went to South Africa in 1936, presumably with her parents, was married in 1937 and later divorced, and has a son, Robin. She returned to England in 1944 and spent the last part of the war in intelligence work.

Subsequently she worked as a journalist, first for a jewelry trade paper, *Argentor*, then as a press officer. In 1947 she became secretary of the Poetry Society and editor of its publication *Poetry Review*. She left there in 1949 to establish a magazine more hospitable to innovation, *Forum*. This survived only two issues, and for the next five or six years Mrs. Spark devoted herself principally to critical and scholarly tasks, publishing among other things several volumes of literary letters, studies of Mary Shelley and John Masefield, and, in collaboration with Derek Stanford, books on Wordsworth and Emily Brontë. *The Fanfarlo*, a collection of her own

MURIEL SPARK

rather literary but often enjoyable poems, was published in 1952.

None of these works attracted nearly so much attention as "The Seraph and the Zambesi," a short story which won a national competition organized in 1951 by the *Observer*, an influential Sunday newspaper. The story, set like many that followed it in South Africa, studies the effects of a supernatural event on ordinary trivial lives, a theme to which she has returned repeatedly.

Muriel Spark became a convert to Roman Catholicism in 1954. "It wasn't anything huge," she says. "I'd been reading towards it for years and one wet afternoon I did it." Karl Malkoff suggests that she was slow to enter the Church mostly because she does not much like the majority of Catholics—an antipathy evident in her novels, where her least attractive characters are often those most conspicuously Catholic. She is a "Catholic novelist," Malkoff says, only in the sense that her faith has been for her a source of order and formal control. As she herself has remarked: "Nobody can deny that I speak with my own voice as a writer now, whereas before I was never sure what I was, the ideas teemed but I couldn't sort them out, I was talking and writing with other people's voices."

This religious conversion was accompanied by a literary one, from poetry to prose. In 1954, when Macmillan's urged her to try her hand at a novel, she still thought it "an inferior way of writing," but nevertheless set to work and in 1957 published *The Comforters*. This book, written more or less as an exercise, deals with a characteristically eccentric group of characters, each of them ruled and isolated by his particular obsession. The heroine, for example, a fastidious but tough-minded Catholic convert, is troubled by voices dictating a novel in which she is a character—a situation which raises sharp questions about the distinction, if any, between delusion and reality, about individual free will, and about the field of study in which she is engaged, "form in the modern novel."

It is an extremely sophisticated work for a first novel, rich in intellectual complexities, parallels, and paradoxes, and deliberately limited by the heroine's acute self-consciousness: "I intend to stand aside and see if the novel has any real form apart from this artificial plot." Evelyn Waugh was full of praise for this "complicated, subtle and . . . intensely interesting first novel," and others shared his enthusiasm.

Robinson, which followed, is even more obviously an allegory, and a neater one, about another Catholic convert. She is deposited by a plane crash on a remote island and isolated there for several months with three men who, it has been suggested, represent aspects of her own personality—the Id, the Superego, and the Ego, or perhaps the mystical and the intellectual approaches to religious belief. The apparent murder of the repressive and authoritarian Robinson, the search for him in the island's secret caverns, and his eventual reappearance, give the story an exciting plot, while flashbacks into the heroine's past life provide psychological density. Many were able to read the book simply as an absorbing and witty entertainment.

It was, however, with her third novel, *Memento Mori*, that Mrs. Spark achieved full command of her unique talent. It concerns a group of very old men and women who each receive an anonymous and presumably supernatural four-word telephone call: "Remember you must die." The substance of the novel is the varying reactions of the characters to this warning. Some give themselves up to an unsuccessful search for the identity of the caller, or find other ways of ignoring the message itself; others are able to come to terms with death, presented here, not exclusively in religious terms, as what gives shape and meaning to life. This short book introduces and bring to life a very large cast of characters, many of them highly eccentric, but none of them mere caricatures, and shows to excellent advantage Mrs. Spark's talent for macabre wit.

As Karl Malkoff has pointed out, in an essay to which this note is greatly indebted, Muriel Spark commonly "uses a momentous, sometimes supernatural event violently to shift perspective and reveal the bizarre underpinnings of the superficially conventional." In *The Ballad of Peckham Rye*, it is Douglas Dougal, a catalyst half devil, half angel, advocate of total individual freedom, who overturns the limiting but supporting assumptions that govern life in Peckham Rye. And Dougal, who is writing a highly fictional biography of a retired actress, represents among other things the life-enhancing but dangerously disorderly force of art. Art creates "a lie that shows us things as they are—a supreme fiction" which is closely related to religious faith.

The human subspecies which preoccupies Mrs. Spark in *The Bachelors* is that composed of the "bedsitter" dwellers of London, unmarried, incomplete, seeking another human being, a cause, or an idea that will give meaning to their lives. The central character is Patrick Seton, a spiritualist medium on trial for fraud. A reviewer in the *Times Literary Supplement* wrote: "As always, Mrs. Spark is remarkably agile in her handling of a large cast, and the story reaches a superb climax. . . . Certainly there has been no funnier or more revealing picture of spiritualist circles than this."

The most perfectly achieved of Muriel Spark's novels is *The Prime of Miss Jean Brodie*. Miss Brodie is an eccentric but charismatic teacher at an Edinburgh private school for girls. Year after year she gathers around herself a small set of young disciples, chosen for their supremacy in some schoolgirl field of endeavor, who are taught to worship beauty, grace, genius, and success (including the success of fascism). These fortunate girls are to be shaped by Miss Brodie into an elite, "the *crème de la crème*."

Miss Brodie in her prime has a rich if partly imaginary sex life, and her passion for Teddy Lloyd, the school's art teacher, is vicariously fulfilled when one of her girls, Sandy Stranger, becomes Lloyd's mistress. At the same time Sandy becomes, in a sense, Miss Brodie herself, her psychological double. In this experience of life in the mold of another, Sandy discovers a definitive sense of herself. Jean Brodie, a natural Roman Catholic, has perversely chosen to act like "the God of Calvin." Sandy, when she recognizes her mentor's *hubris*, betrays her politically dangerous views to the school's headmistress, securing her dismissal. She herself embraces Catholicism, and recalls Miss Brodie's story, years later, as Sister Helena, author of an important treatise, "The Transfiguration of the Commonplace."

Nothing is clear cut in this remarkable novel. The reader, however much he may dislike Miss Brodie's political views, cannot help admiring her originality and her courage in opposing a deadening and leveling educational system. And Sandy's betrayal, however admirable her motives, remains a betrayal, and somehow despicable. The book is no less unusual in its structure, which illustrates Muriel Spark's mastery of the "time shift." It moves freely from past to future to present and back again, ignoring the usual machinery of suspense by revealing Sandy's treachery halfway through, and yet never for a moment losing its narrative fascination or clarity of line. Moreover, though Mrs. Spark preserves her ruthlessly ironic tone, her characters, free in this novel from supernatural interference, and with few allegorical burdens to bear, deeply engage the reader's sympathy. The novel was both filmed and staged with considerable success.

The "time shift" is employed also in the telling of *The Girls of Slender Means*, about another female community, a genteel London hostel for girls near the end of World War II. The story turns on a paradox, a vision of evil which converts an atheist into a Christian and, eventually, a martyr. Most critics admired the book's skill and intelligence, its freedom from religious cant, but there was some feeling that Mrs. Spark should at this stage in her career be attempting something on a larger scale.

This she provided in *The Mandelbaum Gate*, a relatively long novel set in a divided Jerusalem. It deals in particular with two "lukewarm" and sensible people who are obliged to acknowledge deeper and less rational levels in their makeup, but it also enters boldly into the consciousness of a large and mixed cast of characters, Arab, Jewish, and British. The most ambitious and technically complex of Muriel Spark's novels, it is also the most direct and earnest in tone. It received the James Tait Memorial Prize, and was thought by some her best book, though others, it must be said, found it merely turgid. It was followed by a much slighter work, *The Public Image*, "an ethical shocker" about a film star which pleased almost no one.

In *The Driver's Seat*, Lise, a neurasthenic secretary in her thirties, flies south in search of Mr. Right. She knows exactly what she wants, and will not be distracted from her quest by student riots, Middle Eastern sheiks, macrobiotic orgasm collectors, or other contemporary phenomena. In the end she gets her man, a reluctant sex maniac who, in accordance with her precise instructions, binds her hands and feet and stabs her to death. In Mrs. Spark's words, the novel is "a whydunnit in q-sharp major [a dimension beyond diatonic reality] and it has a message." The message, George Stade believes, is that people like Lise, "bachelors" and unbelievers, freemen neither of the secular world nor God's, perforce take another master; it is not Lise who sits in the driver's seat, but the Devil. Stade called the book "a kind of concise compendium of the techniques developed by the great modernist writers in the first half of this century," in particular by Kafka, Joyce, and Mann. But Stade, like other reviewers, concluded that "the novel's theme . . . sounds a bit tinnily on the inner ear and its technical dexterity often seems like no more than dexterity."

There was a generally rather cool press also for *Not to Disturb*, another diabolical tale, set this time in the servants' hall of a mansion in Geneva. Upstairs the scene is set for a spectacular multiple crime of passion; downstairs the servants await the tragedy, coolly rehearsing the techniques by which they can most profitably sell the scandalous story to the mass media. This servants' revenge is a satire of the very blackest kind, a Jacobean drama displaying a society whose gluttonous hunger for scandal and vicarious living has eaten up real feelings and real people.

Muriel Spark has also published a number of short stories, as witty and as cruelly observant as her novels but limited, some critics feel, precisely because they are not long enough to enable her to work out the complex structures at which she excels. The same has been said of her short radio plays, which she calls "ear-pieces," and which have the virtue at least of demonstrating her impeccable ear for dialogue. She is also the author of a full-length stage play, *Doctors of Philosophy*, produced without much success in 1963, and of two children's books, *The Very Fine Clock* and *The French Window*.

Mrs. Spark is very small and very pretty. She lives with three cats in an apartment in an eighteenth century *palazzo* in Rome. She became a Fellow of the Royal Society of Literature in 1963 and received the OBE in 1967. Her pleasure is music: "All sorts of music, all day." She finds intellectual life in Rome boring—"They are obsessed with Sartre"—but relishes the frantic scandalmongering of Italian high society.

Karl Malkoff, summing up her achievement to date, wrote in 1968: "Unified by recurring motifs and configurations, her apparently glib novels comprise a serious attempt to probe the dark moral heart of man. Although often in danger of overemphasizing the intellectual structure of her writing—the ever-present suggestion of allegory, the series of contrived parallels and symmetrical arrangements of character and incident, the dominant obsessions to which most of her books can be reduced—Muriel Spark, at her best, reaches beyond wit to humanity; then her imaginative extensions of reality, though analyzable, retain something of the irreducible wholeness of experience."

PRINCIPAL WORKS: *Novels*—The Comforters, 1957; Robinson, 1958; Memento Mori, 1959; The Ballad of Peckham Rye, 1960; The Bachelors, 1960; The Prime of Miss Jean Brodie, 1961; The Girls of Slender Means, 1963; The Mandelbaum Gate, 1965; The Public Image, 1968; The Driver's Seat, 1970; Not to Disturb, 1971; The Hothouse By the East River, 1973. *Stories and plays*—The Go-Away Bird and Other Stories, 1958; Voices at Play (stories and radio plays), 1961; Doctors of Philosophy, 1963; Collected Stories, vol. 1, 1967; The Interview *in* Transatlantic Review Summer 1960. *Poetry*—The Fanfarlo and Other Verse, 1952; Collected Poems, vol. 1, 1967. *Criticism*—(ed. with Derek Stanford) Tribute to Wordsworth, 1950; Child of Light: A Reassessment of Mary Wollstonecraft Shelley, 1951; (ed.) A Selection of Poems by Emily Brontë, 1952; (ed. with Derek Stanford) My Best Mary (letters of Mary Shelley), 1953; John Masefield, 1953; (with Derek Stanford) Emile Brontë: Her Life and Work, 1953; (ed.) The Brontë Letters, 1954; (ed. with Derek Stanford) Letters of J. H. Newman, 1957.

ABOUT: Contemporary Authors 7–8, 1963; Kostelanetz, R. (ed.) On Contemporary Literature, 1964; Malkoff, K. Muriel Spark, 1968; Shapiro, C. (ed.) Contemporary British Novelists, 1965; Stanford, D. Muriel Spark, 1963; Stanford, D. (ed.) Nine Essays in Modern Literature, 1965; Stubbs, P. Muriel Spark, 1973; Vinson, J. (ed.) Contemporary Novelists, 1972; Who's Who, 1973; Who's Who in America, 1972–1973. *Periodicals*—Approach Summer 1966; Atlantic October 1965; Books and Bookmen November 1961; Commonweal February 23, 1962; Critique Fall 1962, Fall 1965; Encounter December 1965; Guardian September 30, 1970; Massachusetts Review Spring 1967; New Statesman August 10, 1962; October 12, 1962; September 27, 1963; October 15, 1965; New York Times Book Review September 27, 1970; New Yorker January 18, 1958; September 30, 1961; Partisan Review Spring 1963; Renascence Spring 1965; Saturday Review January 20, 1962; Twentieth Century Autumn 1961; Wisconsin Studies in Contemporary Literature Summer 1965.

SPENCER, (CHARLES) BERNARD (November 30, 1909–September 12, 1963), English poet, was born in Madras, India, but grew up in a country house in Oxfordshire. His father, a judge, sent him to Marlborough public school. His contemporaries there included Louis MacNeice and John Betjeman, who remembers him as a "placid and approachable" boy, "wispy" like "a shy squirrel." In his later years at Marlborough, Spencer began to write poetry, influenced at first by Keats, then by Thomas Hardy, Edward Thomas, and the metaphysical poets. He went on to Corpus Christi College, Oxford, edited *Oxford Poetry* and, with the encouragement of Geoffrey Grigson, began to publish in *New Verse*, which he later helped to edit. During the 1930s Spencer earned his living as a teacher, as a writer of film scripts, and in an advertising agency. He reviewed for the London *Morning Post*, wrote a column for the *Oxford Mail*, and broadcast for the BBC on literature, painting, and sculpture.

The poetry he wrote at this time already showed a characteristic interest in landscapes and their influence on the people who lived in them; he once said that "what really I am looking for all the time [is] a dramatic situation in some landscape." The directness and intelligence of his verse, as well as his evident social awareness, showed that he was a contemporary of Spender and Auden, but he was never really a political poet. According to his friend Lawrence Durrell "he had a sort of piercing yet undogmatic irony towards people and things. . . . He pronounced upon the world . . . in small strict pronouncements which hit home."

In 1940 Spencer joined the British Council. He

was appointed first to the Institute of English Studies in Salonika, where he learned to enjoy the poetry of Elytis and Seferis, and responded delightedly to the sun and sea and people of Greece. When the German invasion forced him out of Greece, he went to Egypt. There, he and Durrell published the magazine *Personal Landscape* from 1942 until the end of the war, drawing on the work of many notable writers stranded or stationed in the Middle East.

The Mediterranean had a profound effect on Spencer's own verse. As G. S. Fraser says, it "opened up a vein of sensuous delight in his work which the austere, nervy atmosphere of the 1930s had not encouraged." Of the thirty-eight poems in his first book, *Aegean Islands* (1946), twenty-two were written between 1940 and 1942, in Greece or Egypt. Most of them celebrate, with a wistful fastidious precision, the beauty of the earth and sea, of elegant women, of food and wine and dancing. He was, Fraser says, a poet "for whom the sadness and beauty of the world is enough": "Where white stares, smokes or breaks, / Thread white, white of plaster and of foam, / Where sea like a wall falls; / Ribbed, lionish coast, / The stony islands which blow into my mind / More often than I imagine my grassy home."

After the war Spencer became the British Council's director of studies at the British Institute in Madrid, and then for several years traveled widely, lecturing in Athens, London, Turkey, and Spain. But his health was deteriorating. In 1962 he went as a lecturer to Vienna. He married a young Scottish girl and had a child, Piers. Apart from *The Twist in the Plotting*, a slim, nostalgic volume issued in a limited edition by the University of Reading, he published no new collection; indeed, as Durrell points out, he "could seldom muster more than fifteen poems at a given time—but the fifteen were all sound as a nut." He was killed in 1963 in Vienna after stepping from a train. A posthumous volume, *With Luck Lasting*, appeared the same year, and his *Collected Poems* followed in 1965.

Some reviewers have been inclined to dismiss Spencer as "a pleasant, accomplished occasional poet, hedonistically preoccupied with pleasant foreign places and feminine glamour." Since his death, however, critical admiration for his work has grown. G. S. Fraser believes that his poems "are in a sense about finding the world and losing oneself. The roots of the hedonism are in a profound existential anxiety." In its obituary the London *Times* said that "few poets have had a subtler or profounder feeling for the inward character of places and situations. His sureness of touch was as evident in quiet satire as in delicate lyricism, though his habitual restraint was such that his purely technical accomplishment never obtruded." He was a handsome man, tall and slim, and greatly liked and respected for his cool judgment, "a man impossible to harry or fluster."

PRINCIPAL WORKS: Aegean Islands, 1946; The Twist in the Plotting, 1960; With Luck Lasting, 1963; Collected Poems, 1965.

ABOUT: Allott, K. (ed.) Penguin Book of Contemporary Verse, 1950; Fraser, G. S. The Modern Writer and His World, 1964; Hamilton, I. (ed.) The Modern Poet, 1968; Orr, P. (ed.) The Poet Speaks, 1966; Press, J. Rule and Energy, 1963. *Periodicals*—London Magazine December 1963; January 1964; November 1965; Times September 13, 1963.

SPERBER, MANÈS (December 12, 1905–), European novelist and essayist, writes: "I was born in Zablotow, a little Jewish town in Eastern Galicia (then Austrian, later Polish, now Russian). There the slightest details of everyday life were determined by religion and shaped particularly by Hasidic mysticism. In 1914 began the catastrophic breakdown of this world apart; we fled many a time to escape the danger of the battles and the Russian invaders; after the fourth exodus we did not return anymore, but remained in Vienna. My childhood finished then, too early—in the sound and fury of the battles I had witnessed, in the misery of horrifying epidemics, and finally in the loss of roots. I lost my faith. It was a disaster—I knew it then as I know it today.

"In the introduction to *The Achilles Heel* I have told what it meant to be a child in the starving Vienna of the war years, and an adolescent in the constant unrest and poverty of the post-war period.

"The Bible, which I learnt to translate at the age of four years, and the First World War were the first among my decisive experiences outside my family life. After those came the Russian and the Austrian revolutions, Marxism, Nietzsche, psychoanalysis and—for several years—the most important intellectual experience: Alfred Adler's Individual Psychology. Adler 'discovered' me, made me his pupil and advised me to give up or at least to postpone my early plan to become a writer.

"The first little book I published was a psychological essay: *Alfred Adler, der Mensch und seine Lehre*. I contributed to psychological magazines and directed one myself: *Zeitschrift fuer individualpsychologische Paedagogik und Psychohygiene*. I lectured untiringly and helped to spread Adler's teaching in Vienna and in Berlin. In the political situation of 1931, my Communist activity caused a break between Adler and myself.

"After Hitler's victory and a short imprisonment, I went into exile, first to Yugoslavia, then in 1934 to France. There in 1937 I broke with communism. At the outbreak of the war I was a volunteer in a fighting unit of the French Army.

"I began to write my first novel, *The Burned*

MANÈS SPERBER

Bramble, in 1940, after the débâcle, when it was more difficult for me not to write than to write. I did not search for the time lost, but tried to revive the hopes which were no more, and to discover what might have been their true significance: 'In order to understand the living it is essential first to know who are their dead. It is also important how their hopes ended, whether they faded away or were smashed. It is more important to know the scars of renunciation than the features of the living face.'

"Neither this novel, nor the two which followed —*The Abyss* and *Journey Without End*—suggest an *answer* to the questions of our time or, in general, of man's life and destiny. In fact, these books—a trilogy—remain, in spite of their twelve hundred pages, a fragment. I don't feel that I have ever really finished a work, or that I shall ever succeed in finishing one. My writings don't propose comforting conclusions; their author has nothing more to offer his readers than questions—and perhaps a participation in his own loneliness.

"The novels, as well as *The Achilles Heel*, have been published in many languages. A definitive version of the trilogy has appeared in German as *Wie eine Träne im Ozean* (As a Tear in the Ocean); the same version will later also appear in other languages. At present I am preparing new volumes of essays and I am writing a new series of novels.

"In the trilogy, politics was a raw material but not really the theme; in my new novels psychological experience will offer the raw material, but the topic remains always the same: 'Man's duty is not to be a hero—which is making a virtue of misery—and not to be a saint—which is making a misery of virtue—but solely to become wise.' A lifetime would not be too long to find out what is wisdom; how wise it may be to live as a wise man, or how unhuman, or even how stupid."

Manès Sperber is the son of David Sperber, whom he remembers as a good and wise man, "constantly interested in ideas," and of the former Yetti Heger. He joined the anarcho-Communists in his teens. By 1933, when Hitler came to power, Sperber was professor of psychology at the University of Berlin, and held a high post in the German Communist party. In 1934 he settled in France, though he has continued to write mainly in German. His break with communism was caused mainly but not solely by the Moscow trials: "The entire complexity does not lend itself to being reduced to a simple formula."

His first novel, translated as *The Burned Bramble*, is about European Communists in the 1930s. It centers on the growing gulf between Soennecke, totally loyal to Moscow, and his two young lieutenants—equally good men who are desperately and increasingly alienated by the naked expediency of the Soviet line. A recurring theme is Sperber's hatred of all dogma: "The need for absolute certainty transforms humanity into a sewer, transforms religion into churches and ideas into police truncheons."

Many critics found the book jerky and confusing in its movement and excessively wordy. But even those who thought it technically "primitive" recognized it as a remarkable achievement, "an impassioned and profound picture of Communist experience." Arthur Koestler, another passionate ex-Communist, said that "a new voice has been added to ours, strong, pure, lucid." He called the book "a work of exceptional depth and range: it reflects, like an image in a stream with trembling and fluid contours, the most extraordinary adventure of the human spirit since the Medieval Church." In America, Upton Sinclair thought the novel comparable in importance to *Babbitt*, *An American Tragedy*, and *The Grapes of Wrath*.

The trilogy's other two volumes provoked less excitement. Sperber's refusal to "propose comforting conclusions" disappointed some critics, and his persistent failure to dramatize his material made his work, it was said, "more like a political science textbook than a novel." However, as Granville Hicks pointed out: "He has written about the anguish of Europe between 1931 and 1944, not for the sake of arousing our pity or our indignation but in the hope of making us think." And Sperber has provided his own answer to his critics: "A tale is not necessarily a novel . . . [which] may relate hundreds of actions and yet be determined by none of them. It has to relate the development not of an action but of passions and thoughts, of situations and positions, as integrated with its characters."

The Achilles Heel, translated like Sperber's trilogy by Constantine FitzGibbon, contains six essays on political ideas, psychology, history, and literature. They include the important "Essay on the Left," which seeks to defend and to redefine the ideals of revolutionary socialism, and blistering attacks on Freud and on T. E. Lawrence. Emmanuel Litvinoff welcomed the book as the work of "a truly contemporary mind absorbed in the specific problems of the century," and a reviewer in the *Times Literary Supplement* found it "somewhat disconnected" but "full of perceptive comments." The ideal of a socialist society based on human needs rather than political ideology is pursued in a later volume of essays, *Man and His Deeds*.

Sperber has been associated with the Paris publishing house of Calmann-Lévy, and has written extensively for the French radio. He has two sons, one from each of his marriages. "We are not presenting the *results* of our political experiences," he says, "but rather trying to transmit the evolution of conscience in our age. Time will show if it is transmissible."

PRINCIPAL WORKS IN ENGLISH TRANSLATION: *Fiction*—The Burned Bramble (England, The Wind and the Flame), 1951; The Abyss (England, To Dusty Death), 1952; Journey Without End, 1954; The Lost Bay, 1956. *Essays*—The Achilles Heel, 1959; Man and His Deeds, 1970.

ABOUT: Koestler, A. The Trail of the Dinosaur, 1955. *Periodicals*—Commonweal July 4, 1952; New Leader, July 23, 1951; New York Times Book Review March 18, 1951; June 3, 1951; May 23, 1954; Saturday Review May 29, 1954; Sunday Times November 11, 1959; Times Literary Supplement November 8, 1959.

SPICER, BART (1918–), American detective story writer and novelist, was born in Virginia. Not much has been published about him, but it is known that he spent his early childhood in various parts of the British Commonwealth. Spicer began his career as a journalist and has worked for the Scripps-Howard Syndicate and as a radio news writer. With the coming of World War II he enlisted as a private in the United States Army, earned three medals and five combat stars in the South Pacific, and left the Army with the rank of captain. After the war he worked for three years in public relations for Universal Military Training and one year for the World Affairs Council.

The Dark Light, Spicer's first book, won Dodd Mead's one-thousand-dollar prize, and was praised for qualities of warmth and humanity, care and discernment, unusual in "hard-boiled" mystery stories. Its successors have been similarly praised. Thus Anthony Boucher called *Black Sheep, Run* "exciting and satisfactory as a mystery, and as human and even tender as it is hard and tough. In

BART SPICER

particular, the complex relationship between a professional policeman and a private detective has rarely been so subtly or plausibly explored." The same critic has called Carney Wilde, Spicer's Philadelphia-based private investigator, "one of the most believable, intelligent and responsible operators in the business." With his wife, Betty Coe Spicer, he also writes mystery stories under the pseudonym "Jay Barbette."

Spicer's first historical novel, *The Wild Ohio*, found an unusual theme in the adventures of a group of French émigrés, fleeing from the Revolution, who seek a new home in Ohio. Some critics thought it a routine if competent entertainment, but others were more enthusiastic. Alden Whitman wrote: "The historical background is, for the most part, woven into the story with care; it does not obscure but rather lends realism to the action. Mr. Spicer stirs his mixture vigorously. Tension mounts, the suspense races to the denouement. Admirers of Mr. Spicer's detective-adventures will not be disappointed in his first attempt at historical fiction. In fact, with some adjustment for time and locale, they'll find themselves right at home," Spicer's subsequent historical novels have been generally enjoyed.

Act of Anger, a rather more serious work of fiction than its predecessors, is about the trial for murder of a young Mexican hitchhiker, accused of killing a wealthy Los Angeles homosexual in the Arizona desert. Most reviewers found the book too long, but most enjoyed it, and William Hogan, for one, thought it a better book than Robert Traver's *Anatomy of a Murder* and "in every sense above-average adult entertainment."

Spicer has traveled widely and lived in England, India, Africa, France, Spain, Mexico, and many parts of the United States.

PRINCIPAL WORKS: *As Bart Spicer*—The Dark Light, 1949; Blues for the Prince, 1950; Black Sheep, Run, 1951; The Golden Door, 1951; The Long Green, 1952 (England, Shadow of Fear); The Wild Ohio, 1953; Taming of Carney Wilde, 1954; Day of the Dead, 1955; The Tall Captains, 1957; Brother to the Enemy, 1958; Exit, Running, 1959; The Day Before Thunder, 1960; Act of Anger, 1962; The Burned Man, 1966; Kellogg Junction, 1969; Festival, 1970; The Adversary, 1973. *With Betty Coe Spicer as "Jay Barbette"*—Final Copy, 1950; Dear Dead Days, 1953; Deadly Doll, 1958; Look Behind You, 1960.

ABOUT: *Periodicals*—Library Journal February 15, 1953.

SPOTA, LUIS (July 13, 1925–), Mexican novelist and journalist, writes: "I was born in Mexico City, the only and late son of a Spanish duchess and a Calabrian emigrant who established himself in Mexico in 1888. The first ten years of my life were those of any boy belonging to a wealthy family in a Latin American country. But in 1934, a series of circumstances changed my life. My father lost his fortune and my family met with afflictions and poverty. I had to give up school and considered the possibility of becoming a sailor or, what seemed more interesting for its possibilities of adventure, wealth and glory: a bullfighter. However, I did not become the one nor the other. In 1939 I decided that my real inclination led me to journalism and I began working as an office boy for a then important weekly magazine.

"Very soon, my newspaper activity—though my career was judged later as 'brilliant and spectacular' —became too narrow for my ambition. Audaciously, with only inadequate and chaotic literary preparation, I began writing some short stories and even attempted two longer works which were never finished. In 1947—after two published books of short stories—I won a national literary contest with *El coronel fué echado al mar*, a novel that can be classified as a work of black humor. Since then, I have published another fourteen novels, of which seven have been translated into several languages: English, French, German, Danish, Serbo-Croat.

"My literary activity has from the very beginning provoked controversies among the critics in Mexico. For a great number of them, I am the most important and influential novelist of the present generation; for some others, equally numerous, I am the most disputable of the important novelists. One way or the other, it is my books that are most read and translated, and younger novelists, consciously or unconsciously, are influenced by my style and technique.

"Though it may sound immodest, my books are largely responsible for the Mexican public's growing interest in local literature. Before 1957—when *Almost Paradise* was first published—no writer had succeeded in attracting real interest in his works. This novel (the biggest best seller up to now) served as an opening key to Mexican readers. Eight years later, more than a hundred new novels are published in this country every year.

"Politically, I am inclined to the left and act accordingly. My novels dealt in the beginning with social criticism. In the later ones, the subject of individual loneliness—in a society which becomes more dehumanized and alienated all the time—is my favorite.

"Hand in hand with my tasks as a writer, in the past years I have fulfilled political functions in the Mexican government; I have given some lectures on journalism and literature in the Universidad Nacional de México and at this moment I act as director of the most important cultural review in Mexico.

"I write every day with great discipline and devotion. I am harsh with my literary work, and normally each one of my books is written and rewritten four or five times before it reaches the editor."

Like many contemporary Latin American novelists, Luis Spota came to fiction from journalism. The numerous publications to which he has regularly contributed include *Hoy*, *Excelsior*, *Novedades*, and *Política*; his literary criticism has appeared in the literary supplement *El Heraldo Cultural*, and *Espejo*.

In his first novel, *El coronel fué echado al mar* (The Colonel Was Thrown Overboard, 1947), the story is narrated by a Mexican who served during the war on a British ship where a series of mysterious events point to the possibility of cannibalism. This macabre and suspenseful story foreshadows the grotesque humor that characterizes some of Spota's later books: it is indebted perhaps both to Conrad and Jack London, as well as to crime fiction.

Spota's left-wing sympathies are evident in many of his early stories and in his second novel, *Más cornadas da el hambre* (1948, translated as *The Wounds of Hunger*). It is a picaresque story about the rise to fame of a youth who is driven by poverty and ambition to face the dangers, moral as well as physical, of a career in the bullring. When the book was translated into English, some critics felt that it lacked dramatic power, but C. R. Smart wrote that "for a tale of unusually distinct men and women in this very special milieu, I have read nothing quite so intimately informed, unflinching and variously interesting." Like several of Spota's subsequent books, it received the City of Mexico Prize.

La estrella vacía (The Empty Star) followed in 1950 and *Las grandes aquas* (The Great Waters) in

1952. A much more notable novel is *Casi el paraíso* (1956, translated as *Almost Paradise*), another picaresque piece but this time a savagely satirical one, directed against the Mexican upper classes. It traces, with a new technical assurance, the life story of the handsome and profligate "Prince" Ugo Conti from his dubious origins in Europe, through his colorful adventures in the United States, to his prosperous activities among the corrupt and degenerate *nouveaux riches* of Mexico.

La sangre enemiga (1959, translated as *The Enemy Blood*) is a brutal story about a gypsy, left impotent after a train wreck, who lives with a beautiful girl he desires but cannot satisfy until frustration and jealousy drive him to a terrible revenge. Some critics complained that the novel's structure was needlessly complex, but most, like Edmund Fuller, found it nevertheless "compelling and harrowing . . . with a somber beauty." *Las horas violentas* (The Violent Hours), also published in 1959, is an almost equally grim account of union corruption. *El tiempo de la ira* (1960, translated as *Time of Wrath*) studies the demoralizing effect of North American economic greed on the Mexican social revolution, and *La pequeña edad* (The Early Years, 1964) began Spota's proposed tetralogy about the Mexican Revolution, centering on the fortunes of one upper-class family, the Rossis.

In some of his later work, Spota has returned to the macabre and grotesque vein he explored in his first novel. *La carcajada del gato* (The Cat's Outburst of Laughter, 1964) is about a tyrannical and eccentric reformer who imprisons his family in a house without clocks, calendars, or mirrors, hoping to defeat time itself, and all the social and moral imperatives associated with it. But his human guinea pigs have already been "contaminated" by their experience of reality, and he loses his war with time. The suspense mounts steadily throughout the story, which appropriately enough takes place in the course of a single hour, and the result is a remarkable and disturbing tour de force.

Los sueños del insomnio (The Dreams of Insomnia, 1966) shows a similar technical ingenuity and economy in its handling of the series of flashbacks through which Flavio Millán reconstructs the events which have brought him to the point of suicide. In exchange for women, wealth, and fame, he has sacrificed his ideals, his integrity, and his peace of mind; at last, betrayed and abandoned, he turns to death as the only release from his fear and misery. At the same time the novel forms another indictment of the moral bankruptcy and social irresponsibility of the Mexican professional class, and Spota returns to the attack in *Lo de antes* (In Times Gone By, 1968) with a virulence that has reminded many reviewers of the work of Carlos Fuentes.

LUIS SPOTA

Spota has acknowledged the influence on his early work of Hemingway, Dos Passos, and Steinbeck. He is a prolific writer and an uneven one, who has not entirely overcome a journalistic weakness for crudely sensational effects, and whose vision is sometimes distorted in the service of his social and political views. However, he is a natural storyteller and a master of suspense, and the discipline and technical assurance of his more recent books cannot be ignored.

PRINCIPAL WORKS IN ENGLISH TRANSLATION: The Wounds of Hunger, 1957; The Enemy Blood, 1961; Time of Wrath, 1962; Almost Paradise, 1963.

ABOUT: Bohn, D. Social Criticism in the Novels of Luis Spota, 1963. *Periodicals*—New York Herald Tribune Book Review October 13, 1957; February 26, 1961; New York Times Book Review October 13, 1957; January 29, 1961; August 4, 1963; San Francisco Chronicle April 23, 1961.

STACTON, DAVID (DEREK) (April 25, 1925–January 19, 1968), American novelist, wrote: "I was born in Nevada, but spent most of my childhood and early youth in California, where I was educated, and in British Columbia, on the shores of the Juan de Fuca. I thus belong to the region of Graves, Parks, Diebenkorn, and Snelgrove, among other western painters, and was shaped by the same environment. Originally I had wished to be a painter rather than a writer. Indeed I still paint, though not well enough, in an expressionist landscape style. It is a useful way of working out those nonverbal notions which must always stand like a forest at the back of what is said. For books are only clearings in the silence.

"California in those days was a special place, not

DAVID STACTON

the overbuilt sump it is now. We had the Orient at our doorstep, we went to school with the Japanese and Chinese, the sea was in front of us and the mountains and the yellow hills behind. The culture was provincial, international, Pacific, remotely Spanish colonial, and French. We had founding families, and a few traditions and habits of our own. In the 1930s and 1940s we were taught the world view, comparative mental disciplines, and expressionist techniques which were what an influx of German refugee scholars had to offer. At least these things were available to those who wanted them. Above all we had our sensuous and then unspoilt landscape, whose loss has made my generation and sort of westerner a race of restless wanderers.

"I know certainly that in my own case, the hang of our mountains, the shimmer of our sea, the way one range would flow into another, the hovering silence, the scrub oak and the golden velvet of our hills, above all the daily uninhabited beauty of it, did more to shape my basic attitudes to life and concepts of existence, even down to matters of style, than did any book, teacher, or intellectual discipline, except insofar as our teachers were shaped and moved by such things, too. I remember the soft hard everlasting light and a feeling that the countryside was alive. We were thus open to Oriental notions of the nature of being from birth, if we wished to be. They have influenced me profoundly, if one can call anything given from birth, an influence. I doubt one can.

"All that is gone now. But it made my generation of Californian quite unlike other Americans, and totally unlike any other group in the world. People nowadays are wont to denounce that place. But they did not know it when it was less a country than an articulated landscape of belief.

"I cannot say I feel impelled to write about it, for it *is* gone. But certainly I write out of it, as it used to be. For those sensitive to it, it combined two qualities not usually combined. It was countrified and provincial, and yet oddly Oriental and international at the same time: of course I lived in the North. And I must say I have never found a moral system of such rock bottom certainty, as that I managed to soak up from the sea, and from the eastern escarpment of the Sierra Nevada, which I took to visiting again in my teens.

"In 1950 I went to Europe for the first time. It was the standard year's travel after college. I stayed on because I liked it, and because I could not get my books in print in America. Indeed, many of them have yet to be printed in my own country.

"In 1953 I published a pamphlet of verse in England, and in the next few years there, a biography and three novels designed to get and keep me in print. They were written specifically for that purpose, and are not worth reprinting.

"In 1957 I began to publish a series of novels in which history is used to explain the way we live now. I am still at work on this. Out of ten, seven have so far been published here, but not in their order, so that their pattern is to be observed only in the English edition. However each volume is designed to stand independent of the others, if need be.

"In all, to date I have published seventeen books in England, of which nine have been done here. In 1960–61 I was a Guggenheim Fellow, and in 1965–66, Glasgow Visiting Professor at the University of Washington and Lee. I continue to move between New Mexico, Denver, and North Europe.

"Though this international mode of existence grew up by accident, I am not sure it was a bad thing. I have no politics whatsoever, and am of a conservative temper, but since we live in a world age, it does no harm to take a world view of it. Besides, parochialism in our day and age can be a dangerous thing, in prose as in everything else.

"If there is one thing about lecturing that has depressed me, it is to see the absolute refusal of most young people to face the nature of the world we live in now. Of course they are assisted in this by the habit of our intellectuals, to mouth the ideologies of thirty years ago as though they still had any pertinence to our actual condition. I have turned to history, as my own way of dealing with that condition, which no doubt is why I write as I do. Though of course there is no point in trying to write seriously at all, unless one cannot help it. The artist is an involuntary creature with a very strong will. As Erich Heller says, it is idiotic to say he is influenced by one person or the other. Instead he seeks out automatically what he *needs.* Which usually turns out to be better and clearer examples of what he thought in the first place. Hence history. For that is what history contains. Of course I choose my pressure points with that in mind, on the theory that every life is a parable of something, it is necessary only to pick and choose. Those ages and persons not pertinent to our particular present, one does not write about. Time for that, when the next present comes round, which will not be soon."

The four books that Stacton wrote to get himself in print included a lively but sketchy biography of the nineteenth century traveler Victor Jacquemont and three contemporary novels. The latter found no great favor with their English reviewers, who found them "excitable" in their style, but detected signs of "a certain rude power."

Stacton's historical novels are quite different. They range in their settings from Ancient Egypt (*On a Balcony*) to eighteenth century Naples (*Sir William*), from Washington at the time of Lincoln's assassination (*The Judges of the Secret Court*) to the court of Ludwig II of Bavaria (*Remember Me*). *Segaki*, set in medieval Japan, reflects Stacton's interest in Zen Buddhism. Erudite, vivid, and often exciting reconstructions of the past, these books are also, as he said, parables for the present. For example, *A Signal Victory*, about the Spanish conquest of Mexico, is at the same time a study in the nature and morality of power and an expression of the author's stoic philosophy. *People of the Book*, which intertwines the stories of a Chancellor of Sweden and of two orphaned victims of history during the Thirty Years' War, contrasts "the unreal rationalism of the legal mind and the real irrational cruelty of human nature."

This didactic intention is not realized without cost and Stacton's characters are often two-dimensional figures, selected to illustrate a thesis, and drawn without much sympathy or understanding. By way of compensation there is his baroque and waspish style, studded with epigram, apothegm, and aphorism, "one of the most massively complex and convoluted styles of our time." In Stacton's historical novels, the most vivid presence is that of the author, "intelligent, opinionated, rather scornful." The result is unclassifiable. Reviewers, straining for comparisons, have invoked Thornton Wilder and Nabokov, eighteenth century letter writers and nineteenth century novelists; one critic (writing in *Time*) suggested that "something similar might have been the result if the Duc de la Rochefoucauld had written novels with plots suggested by Jack London."

The critical response was extremely mixed. Some reviewers found Stacton's attitude to his characters "presumptuous or condescending," his style "distressingly affected," his attitude toward himself one of self-satisfaction increasing in proportion to the density of his epigrams. Others, perhaps more willing to approach his work on its own terms, believe that he "made a small revolution in historical fiction by rejecting its most cherished conventions." In 1963 *Time* listed Stacton among the ten most promising American novelists. He died only a few years later, while staying with friends in Denmark.

As historical novels go, Stacton's are rather short; fat novels in his opinion were suitable only for "women who lie on sofas all day." He attended Stanford University (1941–1943) and received his B.A. at the University of California (Berkeley) in 1955. He was an Episcopalian.

PRINCIPAL WORKS: *Novels*—Dolores, 1954 (England only); A Fox Inside, 1955 (England only); The Self-Enchanted, 1956 (England only); Remember Me, 1957 (England only); On a Balcony, 1958; Segaki, 1958; A Signal Victory, 1960; A Dancer in Darkness, 1960; The Judges of the Secret Court, 1961; Tom Fool, 1962 (England only); Old Acquaintance, 1962; Sir William, or, a Lesson in Love, 1963; Kaliyuga: A Quarrel With the Gods, 1965 (England only); People of the Book, 1965. *Nonfiction*—A Ride on a Tiger: The Curious Travels of Victor Jacquemont, 1954 (England only); The World on the Last Day: The Sack of Constantinople by the Turks, May 29th 1453, Its Causes and Consequences, 1965 (England only); The Bonapartes, 1966.

ABOUT: Contemporary Authors 5–8, first revision, 1969; Who Was Who, 1961–1970; Who's Who in America, 1968–1969. *Periodicals*—Book Week January 31, 1965; Time February 1, 1963; February 26, 1965.

***STADLER, ERNST (MARIA RICHARD)** (August 11, 1883–October 30, 1914), German poet and scholar, was born at Colmar, upper Alsace, the son of a state attorney. He attended the Protestant Gymnasium at Strasbourg, where his father had become curator of the Kaiser Wilhelm University, and went on to study philology and comparative languages at the universities of Strasbourg and Munich. In 1902, as a student at Strasbourg, he founded, with René Schickele and others, the short-lived journal *Der Stürmer*, which sought to reconcile the French and German traditions of Alsace-Lorraine. Stadler's early poetry, published in *Der Stürmer* and elsewhere, and collected in *Präludien* (1905), was conventionally neoromantic and impressionist, influenced by Hofmannsthal and Stefan George. He withdrew the volume soon after it appeared, and abandoned poetry for some years.

In 1906, when he received his degree from Strasbourg, Stadler went to Magdalen College, Oxford University, as a Rhodes Scholar, an experience which stimulated both his internationalism and his interest in Shakespeare. He returned to the University of Strasbourg in 1908 as a lecturer in

* städ′ lər

ERNST STADLER

philology, and produced several works of Shakespeare scholarship, including an edition of C. M. Wieland's translations of the plays, and a dissertation on Shakespeare criticism in Germany which earned him an Oxford B.Litt. in 1912. In 1910, meanwhile, he had gone as a full professor to the Université Libre at Brussels, where he lectured in French on German literature, and produced German translations of Péguy, Jammes, and Balzac, as well as some important essays on such early expressionists as Heym and Gottfried Benn. Stadler was about to accept a professorship at the University of Toronto when World War I began. As a lieutenant of the reserve he was sent into action almost at once. In October 1914 he was awarded the Iron Cross for bravery, and a few days later was killed by a British grenade near the Franco-British frontier.

Stadler's reputation rests on *Der Aufbruch* (The Awakening, 1914), a collection of poems written between 1911 and 1913, recognized as an early and important contribution to the stylistic liberation which was the most productive achievement of expressionism. The much anthologized title poem seems to prophesy and welcome World War I; in fact, as K. L. Schneider has shown, the poem's warlike imagery refers to a spiritual campaign against human apathy and bigotry. Seeking to express formally his loathing for all boundaries Stadler, while retaining rhyme and dithyrambs, experimented in these poems with a "ploughing up of form" characterized by his long, impulsive, irregular line. The influences here seem to be of Whitman and Verhaeren, the mood one of hope, of exultant faith in the oneness of all mankind—the "strömendes Weltgefühl." Herman Hesse said of Stadler that he was "an early, still isolated flower of a European spirit."

Hamburger and Middleton have called Stadler "about the most literal of the foremost early expressionists" but a poet with "the true dynamic mentality of the expressionist," committed to "the immediate presentation of a complex of feelings." Typically in these poems, the "observed world is in the grip of an inner vision advancing toward a point of ecstasy. Only when it has reached this point . . . does the vision break free from the frame of sense." Stadler's "is a style which, by telescoping normally consecutive impressions and making them simultaneous in the poetic image, aims to rescue essence from time's chaotic flux."

PRINCIPAL WORKS IN ENGLISH TRANSLATION: Poems *in* Bridgwater, P. (ed.) The Penguin Book of Twentieth-Century German Verse, 1963; Hamburger, M. and Middleton, C. (eds.) Modern German Poetry 1910–1960, 1962.

ABOUT: Bithell, J. Modern German Literature, 1880–1950, 1959; Hamburger, M. Reason and Energy, 1957; Hamburger, M. and Middleton, C. (eds.) *introduction to* Modern German Poetry 1910–1960, 1962; Hestermann, H. Ernst Stadler, 1929; Schneider, K. L. Der bildhafte Ausdruck in den Dichtungen Georg Heyms, Georg Trakls und Ernst Stadlers, 1954; Smith, H. (ed.) Columbia Dictionary of Modern European Literature, 1947. *Periodicals*—Modern Language Review October 1962.

STAFFORD, WILLIAM E(DGAR) (January 17, 1914–), American poet, writes: "Our family are from Kansas, the middle of it, where I was born. We moved from one little town to another during my school years, following my father's jobs, which varied, but always provided income for our needs and books. We liked the towns and countryside, where we fished, hunted, and camped along the mild, wandering streams. Our lives were quiet, and the land was very steady. Our teachers were good. Not till I finished my B.A. degree at the University of Kansas and went on to graduate school in another state did I ever see an adult drunk or enraged or seriously menacing. Higher education and the coming of World War II supplied a new aspect of experience.

"As a pacifist I was in camps for conscientious objectors from 1940 till 1944. We fought forest fires, built trails and roads, terraced eroding land, etc. My brother was in the Air Force, and my sister married a Navy man. My service took me to Arkansas, then California, and then Illinois, where I worked finally in the headquarters of the Church of the Brethren. After the war I worked for Church World Service (a relief organization), and then by means of part-time college training got into teaching. By 1948 I had a job teaching English at Lewis and Clark College in Portland, Oregon, where I still teach. On occasion I have taught short intervals elsewhere and have even ventured on brief lecture and reading tours.

"Earlier, encouraged by teachers in high school and college, I had attempted to write pleasing things; and while in camp during the war I found myself drawn to write meandering sequences of thoughts, or spun-out patterns of words, before the stove late, or in the early morning before work and before anyone else was stirring. This daily practice I have kept up ever since, and the pattern established then prevails as my way to write:—during a quiet interval, without felt obligation to do other than find my way from impulse to impulse. I feel ready to follow even the most trivial hunch, and my notes to myself are full of beginnings, wavery hints, all kinds of inconclusive sequences sustained by nothing more than my indulgent realization that if it occurred to me it might somehow be justified. Now and then a sequence appeals to me for long enough to be teased into something like a poem, and when I feel sufficient conviction, I detach it from the accumulated leaves—my compost heap—and half-heartedly send it around to editors. I never feel sure that I have anything worthy, though I often feel affection for this product; and of all my writing only a very small portion goes forth into the world, and of that portion a large part never receives approval. I suppose at least nine out of ten pieces which I surmise to be poems come permanently home to roost.

"The poems which have met approval appear in a wide variety of periodicals in the United States and in a few publications in England; and four collections have been published. It pleases me that my wife and four children hardly know that these poems are springing into being in our house, early and late. The family will see a new book and then be reminded that we are sustained, that these poems are always being placed with care all around us."

William Stafford was born and raised in Hutchinson, Kansas, the son of Earl and Ruby (Mayher) Stafford. An autobiographical sequence in *The Rescued Year* gives an excellent account of the small-town and rural outdoors life of his childhood. Stafford earned his M.A. as well as his B.A. at the University of Kansas, his Ph.D. at the State University of Iowa in 1954. In 1960, after twelve years there, he became Professor of English at Lewis and Clark College. He received a D.Litt. from Ripon College, Wisconsin, in 1965. The poet published his first book in 1947 and another collection, *West of Your City*, in 1960. His third book, *Traveling Through the Dark*, brought him wide recognition and the 1963 National Book Award for poetry.

Most of Stafford's poems are short and lyrical,

WILLIAM STAFFORD

characterized by a calm simplicity of image and utterance, and a force which seems an organic product of the poet's own intelligence and moral strength rather than of studied technical effects. Joseph Slater has spoken of "his dry, hard diction, his perfectly colloquial syntax and phrasing," and Stafford himself regards language as a "social process": "When you make a poem you merely speak or write the language of every day, capturing as many bonuses as possible and economizing on losses; that is, you come awake to what always goes on in language, and you use it to the limit of your ability and your power of attention at the moment."

Jonathan Cott says that Stafford is a conservative —against the pretensions and lack of genuineness of most of our lives, for a contacting of the "real" world—a world of "things we did that meant something." Cott praises the "wonderfully unsentimental, rugged, often elliptical language" of Stafford's poems, and finds in them "an understanding of death, love, lust, guilt, and making the 'responsible act' that gives the lie to the suggestion that his poetry is 'naïve.' The poet lives in a world in which one has 'to stand in absolute rain / And face whatever comes from God, / or stoop to smooth the earth over little things / that went into dirt, out of the world.'"

Stafford was married in 1944 to the former Dorothy Frantz. He says he likes "training children and dogs," as well as building, gardening, and camping. He has served on the Oregon board of the pacifist Fellowship of Reconciliation and is a member of the War Resisters League. Peter Davison, reviewing *Traveling Through the Dark* together with works by Robert Creeley, Denise Levertov, and Anne Sexton, thought that "of all the poets reviewed here, William Stafford shows the greatest promise of major stature." In 1970 Stafford and his family moved to Washington, D.C., where the author, on leave from Lewis and Clark College, had received an appointment as Consultant in Poetry to the Library of Congress.

PRINCIPAL WORKS: *Poetry*—Down in My Heart, 1947; West of Your City, 1960; Traveling Through the Dark, 1962; The Rescued Year, 1966; Allegiances, 1970; Someday, Maybe, 1973. *Criticism*—The Achievement of Brother Antoninus, 1967; Friends to This Ground, 1968. ABOUT: Contemporary Authors 7–8, 1963; Kostelanetz, R. (ed.) The New American Arts, 1965; Martz, W. J. The Distinctive Voice, 1966; Murphy, R. (ed.) Contemporary Poets of the English Language, 1970; Ostroff, A. J. (ed.) The Contemporary Poet as Artist and Critic, 1964; Stafford, W. The Rescued Year, 1966; Who's Who in America, 1972–1973.

"STAGGE, JONATHAN." *See* WHEELER, HUGH CALLINGHAM

"STANLEY, MARGE." *See* WEINBAUM, STANLEY GRAUMAN

STEINER, (FRANCIS) GEORGE (April 23, 1929–), American critic and short story writer, writes: "I was born in Paris in 1929. I was educated in France, at the University of Chicago, at Harvard, and at Oxford. This somewhat excessive academic training and the fact that I am at home in three-and-a-half languages, probably made it difficult for me to become a writer in any simple, straightforward way. Almost from the start—or at least from the moment in which I found out that I could produce verse but no poetry—I wondered whether literature was as important as I had been taught to believe. And I began asking why the essentially literary, humanistic culture of western Europe had proved so ineffective a barrier to the rise of modern political barbarism. I found very few people really interested in the question or prepared to look for an answer. My own writing is an attempt, a kind of continuous inquiry into and conjecture about the relations between literature and society, between poetic value and humane conduct. This argument underlies both my critical books and essays and what fiction I have published. In so far as these books are now translated into French, German, Italian, Spanish and other languages, my concern does seem to reach others. But I imagine it will only do so gradually. Perhaps one more point is relevant: I find it less and less useful to draw a line between fiction and non-fiction, between the imaginative and the critical. A critical argument should be written as carefully, with as much force of style, as a story or novel. Today the imagination is increasingly weary of the facility of most fiction. The future lies, I think, in the kind of books produced by Kierkegaard, by Hermann Broch, by Ernst Bloch, which are neither pure allegory nor pure argument, but a kind of dramatic philosophy, poems of the mind, as are the *Essais* of Montaigne."

Steiner's parents, Dr. Frederick George and Elsie (Franzos) Steiner, were Austrian Jews who left Vienna to settle in Paris in 1924, and moved on to New York in 1940. Although he was naturalized as an American citizen in 1944, and received most of his education in the United States, he grew up feeling himself a part of the Central European Jewish culture that produced Marx, Freud, and Einstein—that created the modern consciousness and bore the brunt of what he calls "modern barbarism." All of his works reflect his obsession with the dreadful paradox that Nazism arose "from the very core and locale of humanistic civilization."

His first major book, *Tolstoy or Dostoevsky*, therefore treats its subjects not merely as two supremely great novelists who happened to be contemporaries, but as representatives of two opposed views of life: the epic against the dramatic, the progressive against the reactionary, the rationalistic against the religious. Steiner approaches them with equal regard, although in Dostoevsky, the great analyst of the extreme situation, he finds a mind that perhaps speaks most directly to those who have undergone the public terrors of the twentieth century.

The book was a vulnerable undertaking for one who knows no Russian but, though Steiner shows himself a perceptive critic of particular passages in the novels, he is clearly not primarily interested in the narrow literary analysis now fashionable. He sees himself as an embodiment of an older tradition, subscribing to the "para-Marxist" belief "that literature is centrally conditioned by historical, social, and economic forces; the conviction that ideological content and the articulate world-view of a writer are crucially engaged in the act of literary judgment; a suspicion of any aesthetic doctrine which places major stress on the irrational elements in poetic creation and on the demands of 'pure form.' " Frank Kermode wrote that Steiner "places his mountainous subjects in a vast literary and philosophical landscape. . . . He writes on the whole clearly . . . and controls a centrifugal argument with skill."

The Death of Tragedy tackles an even more ambitious theme than its predecessors: the rise and fall of tragedy in the Western tradition. It moves with easy assurance from the Greeks, via Shakespeare and Racine and German Romantic tragedy, to

Ibsen and Strindberg. The book is full of acute observations, but was thought by some to be curiously insubstantial, with too great an imbalance between high-level generalization and detailed demonstration. Some of its failures, both in argument and in statements of fact, were exposed in a review by John Simon, who charges Steiner with making too many ringing assertions about matters of which he has insufficient knowledge.

As he says, Steiner finds it "less and less useful to draw a line between . . . the imaginative and the critical." *The Death of Tragedy*, an attempt to write criticism as literature, was followed by three short stories collected in *Anno Domini*, all of them dealing with aspects of World War II. Their horrified dwelling on the details of violence and atrocity showed a central facet of Steiner's sensibility, but remained, many readers thought, at the level of untransformed sensationalism, presented in slack and overindulgent prose.

Steiner's gifts are those of a critic. A substantial collection of his periodical essays appeared in 1967 as *Language and Silence* and showed Steiner at his best. The book is given a degree of unity by the author's recurrent preoccupation with the theme implied by the title. Steiner regards language as a living organism that can be damaged by misuse (as in pornography, or the double-think of Nazi ideology), and threatened by the growth of non-verbal communication (in mathematics, science, television). Few of Steiner's critics seemed fully to accept this argument, but most were impressed by his essays on Marxism and literature, which draw illuminatingly on the thinking of Georg Lukács, Lévi-Strauss, and Lucien Goldmann.

Frank Kermode in his review called Steiner "a very distinctive commentator on the state of the world and of the humanities," one of exceptional cosmopolitan range, who "will allow himself an occasional undomesticated linguistic usage and a degree of emotionalism, of self-display, unusual in the profession." He is, Kermode says, a master of "*haute vulgarisation* . . . a man capable of seizing and expressing the relevance of what used to seem somebody else's problem—of linguistics and phenomenology, of music and anthropology." If he is what Kermode calls a "moral terrorist" in Kant's sense—one whose thought and language are colored by a belief in impending universal catastrophe—"one has to respect the motives of Steiner's terrorism, and the power of intellect with which he feeds it."

In his next collection of essays, *Extraterritorial*, Steiner pursues his speculations about "the relations between literature and society" with special reference to the findings and controversies of modern linguistics, and to the work of such "extraterritorial" talents as Joyce and Nabokov, Borges and

GEORGE STEINER

Beckett, who, working beyond the limits of a single language, appear to him as the heroes of a linguistic revolution which mirrors and perhaps subsumes the century's social and spiritual revolutions. *In Bluebeard's Castle*, containing Steiner's T. S. Eliot memorial lectures, was subtitled "Some Notes Towards the Redefinition of Culture." One reviewer called it "an apocalyptic voyage through recent history . . . patently devised as a work of literature, endeavouring to persuade the reader by a complex of metaphor and myth and a pervasive verbal rhetoric, at the same time as it is packed with reference to real events and persons and books."

Steiner's devotion to the pursuit of ideas and the confidence with which he generalizes about the state of the world partly explain the hostility with which his work is greeted by many of his more empirical colleagues. But not even his admirers would deny that his work is uneven—that his generally "clear, colorful, urgent" style is sometimes only "provokingly pretentious," or that the same essay can contain both superb insights and "elegant flummery." And there is a growing feeling that he is dissipating his great talents in "cultural sightseeing," and should now turn to the full-length study (promised in *Extraterritorial*) of those linguistic questions "which seem to me primary and ontological." Meanwhile, a critic in the *Times Literary Supplement* has described him as "the most brilliant cultural journalist at present writing in English or perhaps in any language . . . His range of intellectual reference is as astonishing as his sense of what matters in the spiritual life of modern man is vivid."

The author received the degree of Bachelier ès

Lettres at the Sorbonne in 1947, his B.A. at the University of Chicago in 1948, and his M.A. in 1950 at Harvard, where he won the Bell Prize in American Literature and studied poetry with Archibald MacLeish. Subsequently he went to Oxford as a Rhodes Scholar, winning the Chancellor's Essay Prize in 1952 for the paper published the same year as *Malice*, and receiving his doctorate in philosophy in 1955. The same year he was married to Zara Shakow, by whom he has a son and a daughter. Steiner began his career on the staff of the London *Economist* (1952–1956). He spent the next two years at the Princeton Institute for Advanced Study and in 1959–1960 was the Gauss Lecturer at Princeton University. Steiner held a Fulbright Professorship from 1958 to 1969. He was a Fellow of Churchill College, Cambridge, and director of English studies there from 1961 to 1969, and he has remained at Churchill with an Extraordinary Fellowship. In 1966–1967 he was Schweitzer Professor at New York University. A Fellow of the Royal Society of Literature since 1964, Steiner received the Jewish Chronicle Book Award in 1968, the Zabel Award of the National Institute of Arts and Letters in 1970, and a Guggenheim Fellowship in 1971–1972. He gives his recreations as music, chess, and mountain walking. His interest in chess took him to Reykjavik in 1972 for the Fischer-Spassky duel for the world championship, which he reported and reflected upon in the *New Yorker* and later in the book *The Sporting Scene: White Knights of Reykjavik.*

PRINCIPAL WORKS: Malice (essay), 1952; Poems, 1953; Tolstoy or Dostoevsky, 1959; The Death of Tragedy, 1961; Anno Domini (stories), 1964; (ed.) Penguin Book of Modern Verse Translation, 1966; Language and Silence: Essays 1958–1966 (U.S., Language and Silence: Essays on Language, Literature, and the Inhuman), 1967; Extraterritorial: Papers on Literature and the Language Revolution, 1971; In Bluebeard's Castle: Some Notes Towards the Redefinition of Culture, 1971; The Sporting Scene: White Knights of Reykjavik, 1973.

ABOUT: Burgess, A. Urgent Copy, 1968; Simon, J. The Acid Test, 1963; Who's Who, 1973; Who's Who in America, 1972–1973. *Periodicals*—Book Week November 8, 1964; March 26, 1967; Christian Science Monitor April 27, 1967; Guardian February 19, 1960; Journal of Religion October 1959; Nation June 3, 1961; July 31, 1967; New Republic May 13, 1967; New Statesman November 17, 1961; October 29, 1967; New York Review of Books November 19, 1964; October 12, 1967; New York Times Book Review April 5, 1959; May 28, 1967; August 1, 1971; Saturday Review February 21, 1959; April 15, 1961; Times Literary Supplement December 1, 1961; July 26, 1963; September 28, 1967; December 17, 1971; May 19, 1972.

STEPHAN, RUTH (January 21, 1910–), American novelist and poet, writes: "I was born, I am told, in Chicago. The first great shock of my life came when I was eight years old and discovered that everyone did not write poetry. I had composed my first 'books'—three of them—of yellow scratch paper onto which I had penciled poems. When I showed them to my father, he commented: 'Ruth, you'll never make any money writing poetry. You should write mystery stories.' Looking back, I have concluded that environment is a secondary influence, that each person's intrinsic nature is the subtle final domination, for no one else in my family had, or has, an interest in poetry and literature, while I was swept forward on its exciting current from the time I began to read at the age of four. My father was a kind, quiet, humorous, hard-working businessman, my mother a lady involved in the enthusiasms of women's clubs and her friends' lives, and my older brother a towheaded boy who teased me and who became a businessman, too, when he grew up. We lived in modest comfort in an apartment on the South Side of Chicago, and I roller-skated on the dangerous streets of a gangster-infested and politically corrupt city with fairy-tales in my head. My ambition was to read every book in the children's section of the Abraham Lincoln Public Library and to be a ballet dancer. I achieved neither ambition.

"Now that I am to put down an account of my living thus far, I find I have lived two distinct lives, a contemplative one and an active one, which gradually have become integrated. My contemplative existence began with the clap of impressions I did not understand as a child, as well as with the dreams and ghosts I encountered at night, the bewitching adventures I ceaselessly imagined by day, and the wonder at what I watched in Nature, from the flutter of a yellow butterfly and the sparkle of stars to the awesomeness of the rugged mountains and snow-capped peaks I saw on my summer visits to my grandmother in Seattle, Washington. As I grew older, my wonder at Nature increased, the infinitude of the universe was a challenge to conception, and I was quickened by the sensation of being a human being, both in the universe and in everyday problems and desires. I sought the conclusions of notable thinkers in recorded eras and countries, and I sought my own viewpoint. More and more I became curious about what I came to call not meaning so much as the possibility of meaning. I was speechless in this contemplative life except for the written utterance, the explosive happenings of poems; poems fell like drops of water left over from a heavy rain.

"In my active life I went to school, raised a family, and participated in a modicum of civic work. After six years at the Oakland Public School, I was sent to the University of Chicago Elementary and High School for another six years, graduating in 1927, then attended Northwestern University for two years, ceasing my formal education at the age of nineteen to be married. My first husband was a businessman, my second an artist. During these marriages I had the experience and eventual joy of raising three wonderful sons; I also had a considerable share of trouble, but trouble, I found, is gold in the writer's pocket. My most important civic activity was to be head of the Book Committee of the Library of International Relations when it was being established in Chicago, an interesting pioneering position of midwest isolationist years which I resigned on moving to Connecticut in 1942. In 1947 I initiated and edited *The Tiger's Eye*, an avant-garde magazine on arts and letters, my artist husband becoming my coeditor; we suspended publication in 1949, chiefly because the magazine succeeded and we did not have time for our own arts and for taking care of the children. Immediately on ceasing *The Tiger's Eye* I began work on a novel which eventually became two novels that took ten years to complete although I previously had read and accumulated information on the subject for almost twenty years. These were my Christina novels. For two years, from 1951 to 1953, I lived in Rome where I did research on this Swedish queen who abdicated her throne and on her seventeenth century, visiting and working in the libraries of the countries in which she had lived or traveled, particularly Sweden, Austria, Italy and France.

"How can the changing and expansive effects of travel be detailed? Besides various journeyings in Europe, I had six months in Peru in 1946, and, following my second divorce in 1961, I made several trips to Asia, especially to Japan, Ceylon and India. In Kyoto, Japan, I have been given the use of a house attached to an exquisite Zen Buddhist temple in Daitokuji where I may write poetry. There are no national boundaries for the human spirit.

"In America, meanwhile, I spontaneously initiated two Poetry Centers, one at the University of Arizona, the second at the University of Texas, and I have provided poetry books for the Freedom Schools in the South, coming to know persons in the Movement after I was arrested in Jackson, Mississippi in 1964 when taking a friend from India to luncheon in a segregated restaurant.

"New York City has become my home. I am happily married to a scientist, John C. Franklin, a pioneer in aviation technology, and, formerly, as head of Oak Ridge, one of the first civilian executives of the Atomic Energy Commission. He is now Vice President in charge of corporate planning at General Dynamics. My passionate curiosity about outer and inner space, as well as human individuality, continues. I write because I have found it is a natural function of my character. As I told the priest in my temple in Daitokuji, I can't swallow the universe without letting it out. 'Like sweat,' he replied."

RUTH STEPHAN

Ruth Stephan is the daughter of Charles Walgreen, the multimillionaire founder of the Walgreen drugstores, and of the former Myrtle Norton. Her first husband was Justin Dart, and her second the artist John Stephan. Her marriage to John C. Franklin took place in 1966.

"Whatever the ostensible subject," she has said, "all of my poems are about love, the great contribution to the universe of the human being, and I am fired with the frequently frustrated wish to make the invisible within us visible. . . ." Marianne Moore said of *Various Poems*, "Throughout these various revelations, poems are embedded in the words, attesting indigenous, contagious, deep-rooted poetic imagination." Ruth Stephan has edited a collection of the songs and tales of the Quechua people, *The Singing Mountaineers*, and the University of Arizona's "Spoken Anthology of American Literature."

It is, however, her two novels about Queen Christina of Sweden which have attracted most attention. Both books are presented as memoirs written by the queen herself. *The Flight* tells her story from childhood until her espousal of Roman Catholicism obliged her to abdicate, recreating, as Fanny Butcher said, "a time, a place, and a pageantry of people as the background for a woman's deep searching of her heart." *My Crown, My Love* is not precisely a sequel but an autonomous work concerned with Christina's feelings and beliefs after she has surrendered the throne, and "her dawning and gradually absorbing love."

Dorothy Moreton wrote that the book's "forceful progress is due not merely to the events in the novel but to page upon page of beautiful descriptive writing, observations in the realm of poetic philosophy, verse clothed in prose, which command rereading."

Carl Bode, discussing both volumes, found "an elegance in the phrases, unobtrusive but clear, which no one else among the biographical novelists has yet achieved." He also praised Ruth Stephan's consistent identification with her subject, as did Ben Ray Redman, who wrote: "We have been admitted to the queen's heart and mind . . . enabled to see her as she saw herself." Ruth Stephan received the Friends of Literature Award in 1957 for *The Flight* and, in 1963, an honorary D.Litt. from the University of Arizona.

PRINCIPAL WORKS: Prelude to Poetry: Poems, 1946; The Flight (novel), 1956 (England, Christina); (ed.) The Singing Mountaineers (songs and tales of the Quechua people), 1957; My Crown, My Love (novel), 1960; Various Poems (containing Songs and Exercises, Daitokuji Poems, Love's Progress), 1963.

ABOUT: Bode, C. The Half-World of American Culture, 1965; Contemporary Authors 5–6, 1963; Who's Who of American Women, 1961–1962.

STERN, JAMES (ANDREW) (December 26, 1904–), Anglo-Irish short story writer, writes: "My mother's people were fox-hunting Protestants from Londonderry and County Kildare, my father's middleclass Jews from Berlin and Vienna. Possibly on account of this mongrel origin, and a youth spent shunting back and forth between Ireland and England, I have never felt that I belong to any particular place or country, never felt drawn to any creed or party. I feel as much at home in Western Europe as in English-speaking countries. I have had but one over-riding ambition: to find someone to live with, capable of living with me.

"The eldest child of a professional soldier in the British army, I was born near Navan, in County Meath, where my parents remained until the end of the Irish civil war. Memories of this war have had, I believe, a lasting effect upon my life.

"Eight years of expensive English schools bored me at first into playing golf alone, later into gambling and petty-larceny. A year at Sandhurst convinced my father it was useless to try and make me follow in his footsteps. After some months on a Dorset pig farm, I set sail at the age of twenty for Southern Rhodesia, where I assisted a Scot in coping with a herd of Hereford cattle and acquired a hatred of colonialism and racial intolerance. After returning, on doctor's orders, to England, I became, on family orders, a bank clerk—at first in the City of London, later in Frankfurt and Berlin.

"By the end of 1928 I had become acutely aware that for two-and-a-half years I had been living the life of a sleepwalker. That I ever published a page of prose was due primarily to the dread prospect of spending the rest of my days in a bank. But it was also due to fortune: to the sudden death of my elder sister, to a chance meeting with Alan Pryce-Jones, and to the Job-like patience of the first writer I had ever met—J. C. Squire, editor of the *London Mercury*. It was here, reading manuscripts in Squire's tiny office off the Strand, that I learned how *not to write*, and that I had *something to say*.

"But I was so inhibited by the unfamiliar literary atmosphere, so scared by the sudden appearance of lions like Chesterton and Belloc, Walter de la Mare and Lord Alfred Douglas, that when a friend asked me to accompany him, all expenses paid, on a business trip to New York, I had the ingratitude to drop my unused pen and sail from England once again. I arrived in New York during the first month of the Depression. America was a revelation: no one knew me from Adam, no one called me sir. (I vowed then and there one day to return—which I did, to live there for fifteen years.) After a fortnight in New York it was my secret ambition to travel round the world, returning to England via Russia. But I got no further than Honolulu, where I fell seriously ill. Six months later I was back in the *Mercury* office.

"But now the Editor, understandably, was in a less patient mood—Did I expect to sit here reading manuscripts for the rest of my life? Was I ever going to put pen to paper?—That evening I took a deep breath, went back to my lodgings, wrote a few pages describing an African veldt fire and, in fear and trembling, handed them to Squire. 'Finish it,' he growled, 'and I'll print it!' I think it took me a month to 'finish it'—that is, to create a couple of characters and write a story around the fire. When I saw 'my story' in print, sandwiched between the work of Chesterton and Dame Ethel Smyth in the hallowed pages of the *Mercury*, the lonely lanes of Meath had never seemed so remote.

"The following year I spent alone in a small hotel in Paris, in the room where Oscar Wilde had died. Avoiding my few friends and acquaintances, I wrote all day every day. At the end of a month a story might have reached thirty thousand words. The following fortnight was spent reducing that thirty to six, five, even three thousand words. Then I sent it to the *Mercury*, which bought it, or to an agent, who sold it. It was the first happy year of my life. By the end of it I had enough African stories to make a book.

"In Montparnasse, in 1934, I met a German girl, a refugee from Hitler. After some months I thought I had at last found someone capable of living with me. That is more than thirty years ago. At the moment she is in the kitchen, cooking supper. But for her I should long ago have perished."

"The most remarkable thing about James Stern's work," according to a critic in the *Times Literary Supplement*, "is the unaffected, unself-conscious simplicity, the candour of a man who never stops to look over his shoulder and wonder what people think of him." This was evident in his first book, *The Heartless Land*, containing eight grimly powerful stories about Rhodesia, "quite unafraid of truisms, concerned to record and encourage triumphs over racialist tyranny."

There is a similar directness about the eight stories in *Something Wrong*, in several of which upper-class British boys or young men are seen struggling against tribal pressures to conform, tested in the exhilarating rigors of fox hunting or in conflict with a ferocious hard-riding matriarchy. It is to working-class girls that these young men turn for tenderness and understanding, as their counterparts in *The Heartless Land* turn to African women. William Plomer (to whom Stern has been compared) believes that these stories "speak for themselves as the work of a man who had to fight to free himself from early trammels."

Some of Stern's stories are set in Germany, New York, Hawaii, and elsewhere, but whatever their backgrounds they are concerned most often with the efforts of their characters to break through the barriers of early conditioning and to realize, in their relationships with people of a quite different background, their capacity for love, sensual delight, or happiness—in a Forsterian sense, to "connect."

Seven stories from Stern's first two collections were reprinted in *The Man Who Was Loved*, which contained only five new pieces, and there is little new work in *The Stories of James Stern* (1968). This small output, the author's eschewal of fashionable trends, and his personal modesty, have brought in recent years a decline in his once "almost fabulous" reputation. Reviewers of his last two collections have nevertheless been unanimous in their praise for the "unpretentious perfection" of Stern's "warmly felt and expertly entertaining stories." They have been called "records of experience, based on close involvement with particular societies . . . the details of most general concern boldly stressed, so that they are of universal interest." V. S. Pritchett calls Stern a reflective writer who has every resource, is at home in many manners, "and writes with the skill, speed and aplomb of a natural storyteller."

In 1945 Stern was one of a number of civilians sent to Germany by the United States Department of War to assess the results of the Allies' final bombing of German cities. In *The Hidden Damage* he records what he saw and did there, his search for old friends, his conversations. It was found a melancholy and rather uneven book, but one full of sympathetic understanding for a defeated people.

JAMES STERN

Stern is a generous reviewer and a prolific translator (of books by Hofmannsthal, Kafka, Remarque, among others). He lives quietly in Wiltshire, but has a wide circle of friends, many of them writers, in England and America, Germany and France. In 1966 he received a special award from the Arts Council. He is a tall, lean, dark-haired man, an expert horseman.

PRINCIPAL WORKS: *Stories*—The Heartless Land, 1932; Something Wrong, 1938; The Man Who Was Loved, 1951; The Stories of James Stern, 1968. *Nonfiction*—The Hidden Damage, 1947 (in England published pseudonymously as by "Andrew St. James").

ABOUT: Stern, J. The Hidden Damage, 1947; Vinson, J. (ed.) Contemporary Novelists, 1972. *Periodicals*—London Magazine April 1968; Times Literary Supplement March 7, 1968.

STERN, RICHARD (GUSTAVE) (February 25, 1928–), American novelist and story writer, writes: "My parents were the children of immigrant German Jews whose sagas had brushed by failure and, supposedly, great fortune (a grandfather who sold Morgan the rights to the tungsten filament for a thousand original shares of General Motors common stock, 'stolen by a crooked lawyer' at his death) to settle into Manhattan apartments with their English-named children, dinosaur-clawed furniture and Germanic pot roasts (served up by Finnish, then Irish and finally Negro maids). My parents were large-minded and puzzled enough to permit their hard-nosed little *wunderkind* to set up his cave of books and records amidst the aunts and roasts, suffering a temper which sent him at six under the bed for days, at twelve into occasional weeks of silence. To every-

RICHARD STERN

one's surprise, the phenomenon was refused admission to Harvard, Yale and Michigan, but was taken, all sixteen angry years of him, to Chapel Hill where he first learned that the New York system was not universal and that there was news that went unprinted in the *Times*.

"Was it such discovery that launched one into poems, stories, moronic tracts on regulated economies and free verse? Perhaps, but what fixed ambition was the context of genteel nullity in which one garnered both general contempt and the inordinate praise of fellow poets for one's battered exercises. (Many years were spent coasting on those soft slopes.)

"After Chapel Hill, I proved incompetent in three jobs, one with an Indiana department store, a second in a Florida radio station (where my fiancée's mother rode me out of town) and the third at Paramount International Films in New York. Not foreseeing the statistical inferno of 'university writers,' I quit for a year of graduate work at Harvard where I wrote a Bowdoin Essay on John Crowe Ransom. The next year I taught at the Collège Jules Ferry in Versailles, from which I shifted—no longer a bachelor—to an assistantship at the University of Heidelberg and a night job as cable clerk with the occupation army. The third European year was spent in Frankfurt teaching illiterate soldiers and trying to wangle European jobs (with Churchill—'the Prime Minister regrets that his staff is complete'—and Fiat—I'd had lunch with an Agnelli in Cambridge and, on its small strength proposed to sell Fiats to fellow-occupiers). In 1952, I returned with a diaper pail, Biedermeier desk and enough money for a doctorate at Iowa. There, the notes, drafts, botched chapters and plans of ten years began to make some sense. One day in that first hot September, my wife waited outside the quonset hut with a letter from the subject of my Bowdoin Essay accepting my first story for the *Kenyon Review*.

"For eleven years now (1965), with fifteen months out to teach in Venice and Rome, I've been at the University of Chicago, another cave, in part of which there is the necessary isolation, in the other part of which are the woes and sweetness of mid-century institutional life. My novels and stories rarely deal directly with this life or with my own. The few friends, fellow-writers, occasional readers and critics who sustain me, sometimes see in what are for me very different works certain recurrences: an absorption in great inventors and their hangers-on, the free women and the energetic, coreless men who are the source of so much disorder; the Europe-American axis; and the use and abuse of narrative conventions. I grant but cannot imagine being governed by these or other recurrences. It is enough being governed by what more and more seems the noblest of habits."

Stern's much discussed first novel, *Golk*, records the rise and fall of a television program which, in the hands of a con man of genius, strips bare the lives and characters of its victims. It was called a "modern horror-story," a satire on television and by extension on American mores reminiscent of Nathanael West's Hollywood novels. Saul Bellow found it "fantastic, funny, bitter, intelligent, without weariness." The novel was disliked by those who do not enjoy their humor black, and some thought it almost as full of clichés as television itself. But if opinions differed about the book's content, it was widely recognized as the debut of a novelist of manifest talent and skill, with much insight into character, a mastery of narrative pace, a supple and "emotive" style. Granville Hicks denied that *Golk* was satire, saying that Stern "takes it for granted that there are no standards by which the antics he describes can be judged. He is simply amused by what he sees about him, and manages to share his amusement with his readers."

In his subsequent novels Stern has been preoccupied with the Jamesian theme of Americans in the Old World, and *Europe* was the title of his second book, which investigates the interesting Nietzschean notion that each of us "has a characteristic experience which forever repeats itself." Francis Hope, who pointed out similarities between Stern's novels and those of Nigel Dennis, wrote that Stern "knocks down one illusion after another . . . with an ironical offhandedness; his humor is dry but not cold, fantastic but not formless. He has an extraordinary economy both of phrase and of incident, and . . . his intelligence gives a kind of authority to even his wildest picaresque inventions."

In Any Case is both a remarkably subtle novel of character and a "beautifully sustained" suspense story, focusing on an elderly bore whose ineffectual life, personal treachery, and pathos, are revealed in the course of his attempt to clear the name of his son, accused of treason in World War II. Another aging antihero is featured in *Stitch*, which centers around an eccentric name-dropping sculptor who lives in Venice and is modeled on Ezra Pound. While the novel was thought not entirely successful, most reviewers found much to admire along the way—precision and authority, the "grace and glitter" of Stern's prose, and the excellence of his Poundian pastiche. There was an even warmer reception for *Other Men's Daughters*, in which a middle-aged Harvard professor of medicine abandons his family for a twenty-year-old "human sunflower" from Swarthmore. Stern "masters his fragile and banal subject," wrote Michael Wood, "by means of a fierce, precise, compressing intelligence" in what another reviewer called a rich and resonant novel.

Teeth, Dying and Other Matters collected thirteen short stories, an essay describing a 1959 interview with John F. Kennedy and Richard Nixon, and "The Gamesman's Island," a satirical three-act play. The volume attracted less attention than Stern's novels, but R. D. Spector found in it the "same humorous perception and fantastic satire," the same ability "to be biting without becoming vicious." A later collection, *1968*, included seven stories and two essays.

Stern is the son of Henry and Marion (Veit) Stern. A Phi Beta Kappa student, he graduated with honors from the University of North Carolina in 1947, received his M.A. from Harvard in 1949, and a Ph.D. from the University of Iowa in 1954. At the University of Chicago he has been professor of English since 1965, in which year he held a Rockefeller fellowship. His stories earned him the Longwood Foundation Award in 1960. Stern belongs to his university's Philological Society, and contributes to *Modern Philology*. He also likes to "eat well, travel, play all sorts of games . . . and to keep up with the world as it were." He was married in 1950 to the former Gay Clark and has four children.

PRINCIPAL WORKS: *Novels*—Golk, 1960; Europe, or, Up and Down With Schreiber and Baggish, 1961 (England, Europe, or, Up and Down With Baggish and Schreiber); In Any Case, 1962; Stitch, 1965; Other Men's Daughters, 1973. *Stories*—Teeth, Dying and Other Matters, 1964; 1968: A Short Novel, an Urban Idyll, Five Stories and Two Trade Notes, 1970. *As ed.*—Honey and Wax: Pleasures and Powers of Narrative, an Anthology, 1966. *Essays*—The Books in Fred Hampton's Apartment, 1973.

ABOUT: Contemporary Authors 1, 1962; Vinson, J. (ed.) Contemporary Novelists, 1972; Who's Who in America, 1972–1973. *Periodicals*—Chicago Review 3-4 1966; Commonweal May 13, 1960; L'Espresso (Rome) August 27, 1962; Library Journal February 1, 1960; New York Review of Books December 9, 1965; Reporter April 21, 1966; Spectator April 13, 1962.

STEWART, DOUGLAS (ALEXANDER) (May 6, 1913–), Australian poet, critic, and dramatist, writes: "I was born at Eltham, New Zealand, a small town in green rolling dairy-farming country, near Mount Egmont. It had two rivers where we fished for eels and trout and, eight miles to the east, there began a wilderness of ridges covered with bracken and bush where we hunted wild pigs. My father was a lawyer there. He had been born in Australia; the family had originally come from Appin in Scotland. My mother, a FitzGerald, was Irish.

"I went to New Plymouth Boys' High School and wrote my first poem when we were ordered to do one for the school magazine. Anybody who ever reprints it will be shot. It was a good school because we weren't shut in too much but could escape to the river bordering the school farm where we lived sensibly in caves and tin huts and ate eels and sausages. I intended to go in for law, but when I went on to University at Wellington I spent most of my time during lectures making rhyme-notes for a long poem I was writing in imitation of *Don Juan* and, naturally enough, failed.

"I decided to take up journalism, which I mistook for literature, and became sole reporter for the Eltham *Argus* at ten shillings a week. I next found myself travelling New Zealand with a merry-go-round. Then, after working at odd times for various newspapers, I worked my way to England as third pantryman aboard the *Doric Star*.

"All this time I had really been hankering to get to Australia, chiefly because the Sydney *Bulletin*, which had been publishing my poems, did have some connection with literature. In 1939 I joined the *Bulletin* staff and for twenty years selected the verse and wrote book reviews. I now work for the publishing firm of Angus and Robertson. I am married to an artist, Margaret Coen.

"The country background in New Zealand would be the basis of all my writing, except for a ballad sequence, *Glencoe*, about the massacre, which I have always suspected was written for me by one of my Scottish ancestors. I began writing nature poems in New Zealand; and, after a couple of awkward years getting used to snakes and bull-dog ants, continued to write nature poems in Australia. I should think it was roaming the New Zealand rivers for trout and the hills for wild pigs that aroused my interest in explorers, navigators and travellers, about whom—from Scott in the

DOUGLAS STEWART

Antarctic to Lord Rutherford of Nelson, seen as 'the great sea-farer of science'—I have written a good deal, both in poems and verse plays. I have looked in my plays for some theme that lifts life above the commonplace, for I don't believe that even in the twentieth century the poetic drama can dispense with Aristotle's 'excellent action.'"

Although Douglas Stewart learned to write nature poems in New Zealand, the harsher world of Australia has also made its impact on him—with particularly interesting results in his verse plays, in which many critics have found his most powerful work. As H. M. Green has pointed out in his *History of Australian Literature*, "no Australian writer has possessed a more varied talent."

It is most convenient to approach his poetry through his volume of criticism, *The Flesh and the Spirit*. This is a collection of essays first published on the Sydney *Bulletin*'s "Red Page," which Stewart edited for many years and made into the most influential literary column in Australia. He is a sensitive, acute, and extremely readable critic, and a generous one, quick to perceive ability and sympathetic to experiment. But his commitment is to the conservative, nonintellectual, though fruitful tradition of Antipodean poetry, and as a critic and a publisher he favors a robust kind of Georgianism.

This is reflected in the traditional forms of his own fresh and likable poetry, as is his deep involvement in the landscapes of New Zealand and Australia, and his devotion to folk song and folk poetry. "Douglas Stewart," wrote Vincent Buckley, "cannot help being a poet whenever he writes," and this is true, especially if "poet" is taken to mean "singer." His dramatic power and lyrical strength are both evident in his well-known short poem "The Sunflowers": "Bring me a long sharp knife for we are in danger; / I see a tall man standing in the foggy corn / And his high shadowy companions."—"But that is no stranger, / That is your company of sunflowers; and at night they turn / Their dark heads crowned with gold to the earth and the dew / So that indeed at daybreak, shrouded and silent, / Filled with a quietness such as we never knew, / They look like invaders down from another planet. / And now at the touch of light from the sun they love"— / "Give me the knife. They move."

The dramatic impact of the last line is an effect that Stewart frequently attempts, though not always with success, sometimes achieving only an impression of facetiousness or easy vulgarity. Nevertheless "The Sunflowers"—a playlet in itself—shows how naturally and powerfully equipped Stewart is for verse drama.

His best play is *The Fire on the Snow*, an account of Scott's Antarctic expedition. The verse, most of it conversational in its rhythms, tightens into strict forms only when the helpless narrator comments on the gathering tragedy. The effect is bare, quiet, and profoundly moving, and the play has been broadcast many times in Australia and elsewhere. *The Golden Lover*, also a radio play, dramatizes a Maori legend. *Ned Kelly* and *Shipwreck*, both intended for the stage but adapted for radio, are more diffuse and wordy.

Stewart's short stories, many of them set in New Zealand, are often amiably satirical and generally well characterized, but it seems that his energies need the discipline of verse fully to articulate themselves. Stewart is a member of the Advisory Board of the Commonwealth Literary Fund, and has received an OBE for his services to literature. He and his wife have one daughter.

PRINCIPAL WORKS: *Poetry*—Green Lions, 1937; Sonnets to an Unknown Soldier, 1941; The Dosser in Springtime, 1946; Glencoe, 1947; Sun Orchids, 1952; The Birdsville Track, 1955; Rutherford, 1962; Collected Poems, 1931–1967, 1967; Selected Poems, 1969. *Plays*—Ned Kelly, 1943; The Fire on the Snow *and* The Golden Lover, 1944; Shipwreck, 1947; Four Plays, 1959. *Fiction*—A Girl With Red Hair, 1944; Fisher's Ghost, 1960. *Criticism*—The Flesh and the Spirit, 1948. *Miscellaneous*—The Seven Rivers (essays on fishing), 1966. *As editor*—Australian Poetry, 1941; (with Nancy Keesing) Australian Bush Ballads, 1955; (with Nancy Keesing) Old Bush Songs, 1957; Voyager Poems, 1960; Modern Australian Verse, 1965; Short Stories of Australia, 1967; (with Nancy Keesing) The Pacific Book of Bush Ballads, 1967; (with Nancy Keesing) Bush Songs, Ballads, and Other Verse, 1968; (with Beatrice Davis) Best Australian Short Stories, 1971; The Wide Brown Land: A New Selection of Australian Verse, 1971.

ABOUT: Buckley, V. Essays in Poetry, 1957; Green, H. M. A History of Australian Literature, 1960; Heddle, E. M.

Australian Literature Now, 1949; Keesing, N. Douglas Stewart, 1965; Who's Who in Australia, 1971. *Periodicals*—Observer March 18, 1956; Tasmanian Education November 1963; Times Literary Supplement August 18, 1966; March 7, 1968.

STEWART, MARY (FLORENCE ELINOR) (September 17, 1916–), English novelist, writes: "I was born in Sunderland, County Durham, England. My father was then Curate of St. Thomas's Church, Sunderland. My mother, née Mary Edith Matthews, came from a New Zealand family of pioneer missionaries who had gone over to the North Island of New Zealand in the mid-nineteenth century. She came of mixed stock, which included Polish, Danish, Irish, Welsh and German, whereas my father is pure English, from Buckinghamshire.

"The first place I remember was our small country Vicarage in Trimdon, County Durham, where my father was Vicar for some years. When I was seven we moved to Shotton Colliery, an ugly mining village. A year later, at the age of eight, I was sent away to boarding school. I shall not give the name of my first school because I was so bitterly unhappy there that I had what amounted to a breakdown at the age of ten. I was sent next to Eden Hall, near Penrith in Cumberland, and after four years there, to Skellfield School, Ripon, Yorkshire. In 1935 I went to Durham University, where I read English, and took a First Class honours B.A. in 1938. I was also President of the Women's Union. In 1939 I took a First Class Teaching Diploma. I taught for a year in Middlesbrough at the outbreak of war, then went to a boarding school in Worcestershire, then was invited back to Durham as assistant lecturer in English at the University. Later I enrolled in the Royal Observer Corps, and served part-time through the last two or three years of the war.

"In 1945 I married Frederick Henry Stewart, then a lecturer in Geology at Durham University. We have no children. After my marriage I continued as part-time lecturer in English at the University, and also at St. Hild's Teachers' Training College. In 1956 my husband was appointed Professor (Chairman of the Department) of Geology at Edinburgh University. Since December 1956 we have lived in Edinburgh, and I have done no University work, but have concentrated on writing.

"As far back as I can remember I have written poems and stories, but my professional writing life began in 1954. I started my first novel *Madam, Will You Talk?* in 1952, with no intention of publishing it, but my husband persuaded me to send it away, and it was accepted. Before this I had had literary articles and poems published, but had never thought of publishing stories."

MARY STEWART

Mary Stewart is one of the world's best-selling novelists. By 1967, *This Rough Magic* had had four million readers. Her books are regularly serialized, in magazines and on radio, and are translated into fourteen languages. Mrs. Stewart's stories combine innocent romance and high adventure; what is unique about them is the credible charm of their English narrator-heroines, the careful excellence of the style, and the detailed authenticity of their colorful settings.

Her sensible, literate, warm-hearted girls "are as far removed as you can imagine from the Idiot Heroine who disfigures . . . so much romantic fiction," one critic wrote, while Anthony Boucher said, "There are few more attractive young women in today's popular fiction." Mrs. Stewart dislikes antiheroes (and heroines), believing the age needs to be shown "some living pattern of rightness that fits our time." Her settings are important in her books, and varied—Provence, Greece, Skye, Austria—but she never keeps travel notes, relying on an exceptional visual memory. Each of her novels takes between one and two years to write, and is the product of at least three complete drafts —"and even then," she says, "I always feel I should have spent longer and done it better." She takes her critics seriously and has learned from them, for example, to write more plainly (so that she now "detests" *Thunder on the Right* for its overwriting). In Mary Stewart's stories, as one critic has said, "There is nothing cheap in the writing and nothing machine-made in the devising. . . . They do not pretend to offer anything else but delight . . . but they are genuine triumphs of a minor art." *The Crystal Cave*, a departure from her earlier work, is a highly entertaining historical romance about the magician Merlin and his part in bringing together the parents of King Arthur. The story, up to Arthur's crowning, is continued in *The Hollow Hills*.

Mary Stewart is one of the three children of the Reverend Frederick Rainbow. As an undergraduate she swam for Durham University, did much acting and producing, and was president of the Literary Society as well as of the Women's Union. When she returned to Durham to teach, she published a great deal of verse in the university's *Journal*. She lives now in an Edinburgh suburb, and calls herself "an ordinary housewife" with "a house and a husband and a garden and a cat to love and look after." Mrs. Stewart believes that there "are really only two kinds of novels, badly written and well written." The writer who means most to her is Graham Greene, but she also praises, among many others, J. D. Salinger, James Baldwin, Mary Renault, and Francis King (whose power and discipline makes her feel "about an inch high"). She is personally bored with "the 'anti' brigade, the dirt brigade, the sicks and the beats" but doesn't deplore them "because they have their value: they're trying things out, keeping literature alive and moving." Mrs. Stewart, who believes that she thinks and plots in dramatic terms, has spoken of her interest in writing for the theatre. She is a rather tall and extremely attractive woman, gray-haired and blue-eyed, charming and unassuming in manner. Her first breath of fame as a writer reduced her to frightened tears and she says she is still frightened—"The more success one has, the more there is at stake." She enjoys the theatre, music, ballet, and painting, and also riding and gardening. She used to hunt, but recalls this now with shame (though not without nostalgia).

PRINCIPAL WORKS: Madam, Will You Talk? 1955; Wildfire at Midnight, 1956; Thunder on the Right, 1957; Nine Coaches Waiting, 1958; My Brother Michael, 1960; The Ivy Tree, 1961; The Moonspinners, 1962; This Rough Magic, 1964; Airs Above the Ground, 1965; The Gabriel Hounds, 1967; The Wind off the Small Isles, 1968; The Crystal Cave, 1970; The Little Broomstick (for children), 1971; The Hollow Hills, 1973.

ABOUT: Contemporary Authors 2, 1963; Hoffman, H. R. The Reader's Adviser, 1964; Newquist, R. (ed.) Counterpoint, 1965; Who's Who, 1973; Who's Who in America, 1972–1973. *Periodicals*—Books and Bookmen February 1960; New Statesman November 5, 1965; Times (London) June 18, 1973; Wilson Library Bulletin December 1960; Writer December 1964.

STOREY, DAVID (MALCOLM) (July 13, 1933–), English novelist and dramatist, was born in Wakefield, Yorkshire, the third son of Frank Storey, a miner, and Lily (Cartwright) Storey. He left the local grammar school at seventeen, went on to the Wakefield School of Art, and from there, with a scholarship, to the Slade School of Fine Arts in London. Storey studied at the Slade from 1953 to 1956, and thereafter until 1960 taught at schools in Aldgate and Islington in London. He continued to paint and has won a number of prizes for his work, including scholarships for periods of study in Spain and Paris.

When Storey was thirty, a *Times* reporter wrote that he "mirrors at a glance the duality which is such a striking feature of his books—his broad shoulders and heavy, muscular build remind us that he has been a professional footballer, while at the same time the delicate, mobile, sensitive features remind us of the Slade School student and until recently painter who constituted the footballer's *alter ego*." In fact Storey had signed on as a professional Rugby League footballer with Leeds in 1951, and when he went to the Slade was still under contract. In a BBC talk, published in *Writers on Themselves*, he has described the meaning to him of the journey he made each winter weekend from London and art to the harsh North: "In the strangest, yet perhaps in the simplest way, the split in my own temperament was represented by a journey across England. . . . And it was in order, so it seemed, to accommodate the two extremes of this northern, physical world and its southern, spiritual counterpart, that I started making notes which [led to] *This Sporting Life*." Storey bought himself out of his Leeds contract in 1956, and became a teacher.

In his first published novel, Storey wanted to "hack out" a character "who represented all the alien, physical forces" in his divided life, "a creature produced . . . by the very physique of the North itself." This was his narrator Arthur Machin, a hard man who smashes his way out of respectable poverty to a brief bemused glory as a Rugby League star—a twentieth century gladiator in one of the world's most savage games. His white Jaguar and his tastes of local high life do not impress his decent, genteel parents. Neither his dynamo strength nor his dumb tenderness can break down the defensive working-class pessimism of his widowed landlady, whom he loves. Machin is nothing, and when he knows this, he is destroyed. The novel was a Book Society recommendation and won the Macmillan Fiction Award in the United States. It was praised above all for its "refusal to fake anything," its "toneless air of truth." It brought alive, Paul West wrote, "the whole ethos of glum northern towns, the steaming byre of the shower room, the mud savagery and the boardroom mish-mash of fees, selectors and hangers-on." Its success enabled Storey to give up teaching and become a full-time writer.

Flight Into Camden, published like *This Sporting Life* in 1960, won both the John Llewelyn Rhys

Memorial Prize and the Somerset Maugham Award. The son and daughter of a North Country miner set out, as their father wishes, to "better themselves." When the son, a university lecturer, questions the traditional virtues and Margaret, the narrator, goes to London with her married lover, their outraged father learns that education has ethical as well as social consequences. But class is not so easily disposed of after all; it is Margaret's working-class inhibitions, her lover's social rootlessness, which defeat their almost grim determination to make a life together. The book was unanimously praised, both as a study of class in England, and as a *tour de force* portrait of a woman by a man. Jeremy Brooks wrote that Storey's prose, "though never ornamental, rises on occasion to a pitch of precise beauty which I can only . . . describe as poetry."

Storey associates the North with a masculine temperament, the South with a feminine sensibility, "the intuitive, poetic and perhaps precious world to which I felt I'd escaped." His first two books explored these two elements separately and the third brought them both "into the same arena." *Radcliffe* has two central characters, representing the two irreconcilable extremes of Storey's life, who fight out "the very battle . . . I had fought myself." They are Radcliffe, sensitive, moody, the last of an ancient family, and the raw, powerful, plebeian Tolson. They form a twisted and violent attachment that ends in murder. Many critics recognized the allegorical element in the novel and most thought it too overt. There were mixed opinions of the style, which seemed powerful to some and "tumid" to others. The *Times Literary Supplement* was unequivocally impressed: "It is a little as though Dostoevsky had set his hand to rewriting *The Fall of the House of Usher.*"

All three novels, which perhaps owe their intensity to the fact that Storey has used them in working out his own emotional problems, are also novels about class. All of his principal characters seek to escape from the inhibitions imposed by their social training in order to love, but do so, if at all, only with a crippling sense of guilt. He believes that the split between people is "the split in the whole of Western society."

After the three novels, Storey turned from fiction to the theatre. *The Restoration of Arnold Middleton,* his first play, was produced in London in 1967 and won the *Evening Standard* award. Like the novels, it is about the difficulty and the necessity of loving. Arnold Middleton is a young history teacher who cuts himself off from his wife with a wall of jokes and fills his life, literally, with junk—turning his house into a museum stuffed with ancient artifacts and broken weapons. He is "restored" to true feeling by insanity, and the meaning of the play,

DAVID STOREY

Frank Marcus concluded, is that it is the absence of emotion which is the true madness.

It was Storey's third play, *The Contractor* (1970), which established him as one of the most valuable and original of English dramatists. The play simply observes the relationships among a group of workers as they erect and later dismantle a marquee for a wedding party (a feat performed with great skill on stage in Lindsay Anderson's production). Ronald Bryden called it "one of the best British plays written in the sixties, almost Chekhovian in its subtlety . . . a wonderfully controlled suggestive study of the divisions of a society: fathers from children, owners from employees, workman from workman."

Home (1970) is another exact and delicate study of the fragility of relationships, or rather of what happens when relationships fail, set in the faded elegance of a great garden which is now the property of a mental hospital. The parts of Harry and Jack, the gentle, cheerful, unbearably sad men at the center of the play, were unforgettably created by Sir John Gielgud and Sir Ralph Richardson. Nothing much happens, but the audience is shown the courteous rituals which bravely mask despair, the blank evasions of what cannot be borne, and its perceptions are gradually enlarged and enriched. The play received an *Evening Standard* award in London and a Critics' Circle award in New York.

Equally plotless, and equally absorbing and rewarding, is *The Changing Room* (1971), about the members of a Rugby League football team before, during, and after a Saturday afternoon game. "Behind the ribbing, and the swearing, and the showing off," wrote Harold Hobson, "the piece is permeated by a Wordsworthian spirit. You can, if you listen, hear through it 'the still, sad music of humanity.' " Helen Dawson said that "in extending the boundaries of dramatic shape, in paring down traditional theatrical scales, Storey communicates more deeply—and, I suspect, in a more truly 'popular' sense—than many noisier avant-garde experimenters." In the United States, *The Changing Room* was selected by the New York Critics' Circle as the best play of the 1972–1973 season.

Critics have agreed that Storey has been fortunate in Lindsay Anderson's spare, disciplined direction of each of these plays, which has preserved them from both didacticism and sentimentality. And didacticism was precisely what critics objected to in *Cromwell*, "a generalised chronicle on the futility of war" which was given a Brechtian production in 1973 by another director. *The Farm*, staged later the same year by Lindsay Anderson, is a dense-textured domestic drama about a Brontë-like (but contemporary) family in Yorkshire which seemed to some reviewers oddly static. Both plays were written nearly five years before they were produced.

Storey returned to the novel with *Pasmore*, a quite remarkably pared-down and low-keyed account of an emotional crisis which was written in 1964 as part of an uncompleted longer novel, but not published until 1972. For no reason that he can fathom, Pasmore, a London college lecturer, finds that his marriage has died and his career become meaningless. He begins an affair, loses both his wife and his mistress, and seeks but fails to find comfort in his northern home town. Then gradually, by a slow and almost chemical process which is as inexplicable as his earlier collapse, he recovers himself and is reaccepted into his home. Russell Davies wrote that "the effect is simple and appalling—appallingly underplayed if you look to novels for intellectual embellishment of life, appallingly true if you take the view that minimalist art, stripping down experience as nearly as possible to what can be said, entirely without self-dramatisation, gets closest to the reality of suffering." The book received the Faber Memorial Prize.

It was followed by *A Temporary Life*, another novel in Storey's minimalist manner, centering on a professional boxer turned art teacher. Reviewers praised the author's technical virtuosity, his understanding of social change and its effects on the individual, but some were puzzled and troubled by an allegorical element which increasingly dominates the book and which, for one critic, "muffles rather than clarifies the effect of what he wants to say."

Storey has spoken of the importance to him of Wyndham Lewis's autobiography *Rude Assignment*, with its view of the artist as "a man isolated in an alien society." Another book that means a great deal to him is *Wuthering Heights*, which he has adapted for the screen. (He also wrote the much-honored screen version of *This Sporting Life*.) Storey has made films (including one on D. H. Lawrence) for television, and has written some art criticism. Married in 1956 to Barbara Rudd Hamilton, he has two sons and two daughters and lives in London. His brother Anthony is also a novelist and dramatist.

PRINCIPAL WORKS: *Novels*—This Sporting Life, 1960; Flight Into Camden, 1960; Radcliffe, 1963; Pasmore, 1972; A Temporary Life, 1973. *Plays*—The Restoration of Arnold Middleton, 1967; In Celebration, 1969; The Contractor, 1970; Home, 1970; The Changing Room, 1972; Cromwell, 1973; The Farm, 1973.

ABOUT: B.B.C. Writers on Themselves, 1964; Current Biography, 1973; Gindin, J. Postwar British Fiction, 1962; O'Connor, W. V. The New University Wits, 1963; Taylor, J. R. The Second Wave, 1971; Vinson, J. (ed.) Contemporary Novelists, 1972; West, P. The Modern Novel, 1963; Who's Who, 1973. *Periodicals*—America January 16, 1971; April 8, 1972; Critique 3 1969; Drama Winter 1970; Encounter September 1967, December 1969; Guardian October 8, 1970; London Magazine September 1967; Nation September 21, 1970; December 7, 1970; New Republic December 12, 1970; New Society May 1, 1969; New York Times April 20, 1973; Theatre Quarterly April–June 1971; Time November 30, 1970; December 27, 1971.

STOW, (JULIAN) RANDOLPH (November 28, 1935–), Australian poet and novelist, writes: "I was born at Geraldton in Western Australia, in the district where my mother's family had been early settlers, and grew up partly in that small seaport and partly on the surrounding farms and ranches. My father was a country lawyer, from a pioneer South Australian family, and descended from an Empire Loyalist uncle of Thomas Jefferson. I think I had a happy childhood, but then so did most of the children I knew: children are physical creatures, and could hardly fail to enjoy so much sea and empty landscape. I have tried to convey that enjoyment in most of my writing.

"I was educated at local schools, and later at Guildford (an Anglican boarding school near Perth) and the University of Western Australia, from which I graduated B.A. in 1956. Soon afterwards I went north to the tropical part of Western Australia and worked among the Australian aborigines for a few months, before accepting a tutorship in a desultory way at the University of Sydney.

"In 1959 I went to New Guinea and became assistant to the Government Anthropologist. For the best part of a year I lived in the bush in the Trobriand Islands, studying the native language, but became ill eventually and returned to Australia. In 1960 I went to Europe for the first time, and have been travelling ever since, with regular returns to Western Australia.

"I have lived at various times in Suffolk, the Scottish Highlands, Malta, New Mexico, Maine and Alaska, and for mental exercise have held temporary lectureships at the universities of Leeds and Western Australia. I do not like teaching, but I think it is good for one occasionally. I do like travelling, and feel no inclination to stop. One of the nicest things that has happened to me has been the award of a Harkness Fellowship in 1964, which has seen me comfortably through forty-six of the United States.

"I find it hard to say exactly why I am a writer, or why I started being one at such an early age. Certainly I want, like all writers, to communicate enthusiasms, indignations, doubts, ideals. But the main reason, I suppose, is the hope that, when I have finished, this vast and empty Western Australia may feel a little more inhabited than it felt when I began."

RANDOLPH STOW

Randolph Stow, regarded by many as the most promising Australian writer of his generation, is descended on both sides from pioneer families. He began to write while he was still at Guildford Grammar School—poems in the romantic manner and verse plays in emulation of Christopher Fry. It was the early death of a college friend that inspired his first personal and original poems. Stow's ability was first recognized not by the Commonwealth Literary Fund, which was unimpressed by his prentice work, but by the London publishing house of Macdonald's, which brought out his first novel, *A Haunted Land*, in 1956.

It tells the violent story of a man who, unbalanced by the death of his wife, nearly kills his children in a passion of possessiveness. Powerful and evocative as it is, this morbid story does not always avoid melodrama. *The Bystander* (1957), also written while Stow was still an undergraduate, shows the same "dark, almost lowering imagination," but greater control and psychological insight. Elizabeth Bowen was reminded by Stow's "wildness" and "authority" of Emily Brontë, and spoke of his "really amazing rendering not only of persons and their passions but of the landscape and dramatic weather."

It was Stow's third novel, *To the Islands*, that established him, winning the Miles Franklin Book Award and the Melbourne Book Fair Award. The central figure is Stephen Heriot, a sixty-eight-year-old Antipodean Lear, an eccentric on a grand scale. After a lifetime in the Western Australian outback, administering a mission to the aborigines, he discovers that he no longer believes in the value of his work. His journey "to the islands"—death—with an old aborigine has reminded more than one critic of Lear's wanderings with his fool. The novel is remarkably successful in its fusion of the real with the symbolic, for the telling is on both levels: Stow's narrative is in no way fantastic, but his prose is poetic in the best sense, and his vision, which bears witness to his anthropological reading, is almost surrealistic. Maurice Richardson called it "one of the rare novels that immediately establishes itself as having an original life of its own."

Tourmaline, a fable about man's capacity for self-deception, was followed by a less overtly symbolical and altogether more notable book, *The Merry-go-round in the Sea*. It tells the story of a boy's idolization of his elder cousin, lyrically and tenderly recreating an idyllic childhood and adolescence, ended by the war. In the second half of the book, written with rather less assurance, the older boy, demoralized by his experiences in a Japanese prisoner of war camp, tries and fails to live up to his young admirer's conception of him. *Midnite* is an extremely ingenious, funny, and charming fantasy about a teen-age bushranger.

Stow's first volume of verse, *Act One*, is distinguished by a rich lyricism, Keatsian in spirit though inspired by the Australian landscape. The poems in his second collection, *Outrider*, are closer in spirit to his prose, and they are uncannily well matched by the Sidney Nolan paintings that illustrate them. A reviewer in the *Times Literary Supplement* considered them less assured than Stow's earlier verse, and said the poet "has bravely plunged into the spiritual mysteries of his country and himself, and for the time being his personal gift has been submerged." *A Counterfeit Silence* is a selection from the body of Stow's poetry between 1954 and 1966.

Randolph Stow, who is unmarried, is a slight man with blue eyes, heavy eyebrows, and hair prematurely gray. In manner he is modest and abstracted, "as if his mind had just sidled around the corner on a journey of its own." He enjoys music and plays the piano. His novels are planned carefully, in great detail, before he begins to write, and he prefers to work at night, between ten o'clock and four in the morning. Stow received the Gold Medal of the Australian Literature Society in 1957 and 1958, and the Britannica-Australia Award in 1966.

PRINCIPAL WORKS: *Fiction*—A Haunted Land, 1956; The Bystander, 1957; To the Islands, 1958; Tourmaline, 1963; The Merry-go-round in the Sea, 1965; Midnite (for children), 1967. *Poetry*—Act One, 1957; Outrider, 1962; (ed.) Australian Poetry, 1964; A Counterfeit Silence: Selected Poems, 1969.

ABOUT: Green, H. M. A History of Australian Literature, 1961; Hetherington, J. (ed.) Forty-two Faces, 1962; Murphy, R. (ed.) Contemporary Poets of the English Language, 1970; Vinson, J. (ed.) Contemporary Novelists, 1972; Who's Who, 1973. *Periodicals*—Australian Quarterly March 1965; Critique IX, 1966; Journal of Commonwealth Literature September 1, 1965; Meanjin June 1969; Southerly 2, 1964; Times Literary Supplement June 28, 1963; Westerly 1, 1959.

STREETER, EDWARD (August 1, 1891–), American humorist and novelist, was born (thanks to a "summer accident") in Chestertown, New York, a remote village in the Adirondacks. He is the son of Harvey and Frances (Chamberlain) Streeter and was brought up in Buffalo. The family had a large library which encouraged in Streeter an early passion for books. He started his first novel at the age of nine, but flagged after a few chapters. At the Pomfret School he was editor of the school paper and the class book, and at Harvard he was editor-in-chief of the *Lampoon* and wrote the Hasty Pudding show. He received his A.B. in 1914.

From 1914 to 1916 Streeter worked as a reporter on the Buffalo *Express*, continuing as the paper's correspondent while serving with the New York National Guard on the Mexican border from June 1916 to March 1917. It was then that he conceived the idea of satirizing Army life from the doughboy's point of view, through a series of letters from an imaginary soldier to his girl. Later, during the fall of 1917, he found himself in a South Carolina training camp and in charge of the comic page of its weekly newspaper. The first "Dere Mable" letters were published there and were much relished by Streeter's fellow rookies for their assaults upon the English language and their wry irreverence toward authority. A volume of them appeared in book form in 1918 as *Dere Mable: Love Letters of a Rookie*, was an immediate success, and with its sequels is still remembered as one of the few humorous classics of World War I. *That's Me All Over, Mable* and *Same Old Bill, Eh Mable!* were both published in 1919. The three volumes were collected the same year as *Love Letters of Bill to Mable*.

EDWARD STREETER

After the war Streeter was a freelance writer for a year or two, and then joined the Bankers Trust Company of New York. In 1951 he became a vice president of the Fifth Avenue Bank (now the Bank of New York), retaining this position until his retirement in 1956. He is the author of a history of the bank, *Window on America*.

Daily Except Sunday, about the perils of the commuter's life, was well received in 1938 but had no successor for ten years. In 1947 Streeter's elder daughter became engaged and the orderly fabric of his life was shattered. *Father of the Bride* is a lightly fictionalized account of what followed, and counts the enormous costs—financial, nervous, and emotional—of a stylish wedding. It also, no doubt, helped to recoup some of Streeter's losses. Most of the reviewers applauded it as a light and lively comedy, veracious in its dialogue, felicitous in its style; the novel, a Book-of-the-Month Club selection, became a successful movie.

The most notable of Streeter's recent books is *Chairman of the Bored*, which tells the story of the founding head of a vast investment counseling firm, forced by his own rule to retire to the perils of country life at the age of sixty-five. Barbara Klaw praised the novel's "wry and quiet humor" and thought that Streeter, in his "urbane and unpretentious way" is saying "that a busy executive—because of the very traits which have made him successful—can never be happy at anything except being a busy executive." S. T. Williamson, generalizing from the same book, wrote: "Edward Streeter's characters live and move in the world of John P. Marquand, but they receive happier, less relentless probing treatment and his heroes are in a state of cheerful frustration." *Skoal Scandinavia* and *Along the Ridge* are travel books.

Streeter was married in 1919 to Charlotte Warren of Buffalo. They have had four children. He has been described as a gracious, charming man with a tremendous zest for life. He lives on Sutton Place in New York City.

PRINCIPAL WORKS: Dere Mable, 1918; That's Me All Over, Mable, 1919; Same Old Bill, Eh Mable!, 1919; As You Were, Bill! 1920; Daily Except Sunday, 1938; Father of the Bride, 1949; Skoal Scandinavia (travel), 1952; Mr. Hobbs' Vacation (England, Mr. Hobbs' Holiday), 1954; Merry Christmas, Mr. Baxter, 1956; Mr. Robbins Rides Again, 1958; Chairman of the Bored, 1961; Along the Ridge: From Northwestern Spain to Southern Yugoslavia (travel), 1964; Ham Martin, Class of '17, 1969.

ABOUT: Benét, L. Famous American Humorists, 1959; Contemporary Authors 4, 1963; Fitzgibbon, R. and Heyn, E. V. (eds.) My Most Inspiring Moment, 1965; Masson, T. L. Our American Humorists, 1922; Who's Who in America, 1972–1973. *Periodicals*—Collier's January 8, 1949.

"STUART, DON A." *See* CAMPBELL, JOHN W(OOD) (JR.)

"STUART, IAN." *See* MacLEAN, ALISTAIR

STURGEON, THEODORE (HAMILTON) (February 26, 1918–), American science fiction writer, was born Edward Hamilton Waldo in St. George, Staten Island, New York. His Dutch-French father, who was in the retail paint business, came of a distinguished Episcopalian family which had included a Bishop of Quebec and an Archbishop of the West Indies. His mother, the former Christine Hamilton, was a teacher and an amateur poet and playwright of Canadian-English parentage. When the boy was nine years old, his parents were divorced, and two years later his mother married a scholarly Scotsman named Sturgeon who taught languages at the Drexel Institute. Edward Hamilton Waldo became Theodore Hamilton Sturgeon.

After four years in a private seminary on Staten Island, Sturgeon went to preparatory school and high school in Philadelphia. A thin, frail boy with golden hair, he was much hazed and distinguished himself in no way at all until he became fascinated by gymnastics. Obsessive training made him captain of the gym team and opened up dreams of a circus career. Those ended during his junior year when Sturgeon contracted rheumatic fever, which permanently damaged his heart. Never a good student, he now made no effort to satisfy his teachers or his parents. His stepfather refused to finance a college education, and the boy went to Penn State Nautical School.

THEODORE STURGEON

One term of fierce discipline was enough for Sturgeon; he quit and went to sea as an engine-room wiper. He had already written schoolboy verse, and now tried his hand at fiction, during his three years at sea selling forty short stories to McClure's Syndicate. In 1939 he turned to science fiction, quickly found a market, and left the sea. His early work was relatively conventional and light in mood, but such stories as the horrific "It," published in *Unknown* (1940) and "Microcosmic God" (*Astounding Science-Fiction*, April 1941), about a scientist who creates a race of minute but appallingly inventive beings, soon established him as a writer of extraordinary versatility. The science fiction historian Sam Moskowitz has called him a "virtuoso," with a unique ability to match his style to his matter, "possessing an absolute pitch for the cadence of words."

A brief stint as the manager of a resort hotel in the British West Indies ended with the attack on Pearl Harbor. Sturgeon worked for the Army for a time, and then operated earth-moving equipment in Puerto Rico. This prompted a story—the first for two and a half years—called "Killdozer," about a bulldozer which is taken over by a hostile intelligence. Despite the success of this story, Sturgeon found himself unable to write more. Out of work, and divorced by his first wife, Dorothy Fillingame, Sturgeon moved to New York and the friendly editors of *Astounding Science-Fiction*. For a year he struggled to make his way as a literary agent.

In 1948 Sturgeon's "Bianca's Hands" won first prize in a contest run by the British magazine *Argosy*. This story had been scribbled down compulsively eight years before, but rejected by science fiction editors as too perverse. It is a hideously convincing account of a young man's fatal obsession with the beautiful hands of an idiot girl. Encouraged by its success, Sturgeon published many horror fantasies during the next few years, especially in *Weird Tales*. During this period he was married briefly to a showgirl, Mary Mair.

In recent years Sturgeon's stories have tended to express social concerns, and he has broken a number of science fiction taboos, including the one against sexual themes in general and homosexuality in particular. Collections of his stories have appeared regularly since 1949, and his novel *More Than Human* won the coveted International Fantasy Award in 1954. Sam Moskowitz has suggested that Sturgeon has elevated love into a philosophy, and that the key to this philosophy, "as well as the most complete expression of the growth and ramification of his faith," is contained in *More Than Human*, a study of extrasensory perception conceived in terms of Gestalt psychology. A similar preoccupation underlies *Venus Plus X*, about a civilization in which sexual conflict has been eliminated and love reigns.

Sturgeon has lost none of his versatility, however. He once left his deadlines to look after themselves and spent several months writing a three-act play, without charge, for a small-town theatre. When the radio satirist Jean Shepherd was asked to produce the lusty (but unfortunately imaginary) historical romance he kept referring to on his program, it was (according to Moskowitz) Sturgeon who helped to concoct the lively spoof on *Forever Amber* published in 1956 as *I, Libertine*. He has written for *Star Trek* and other television serials, and has also contributed to *Sports Illustrated* proposals for a new (post-holocaust) national game called "quoit." He has six children by his third wife, Marion, whom he married in 1951, and one by his 1969 marriage to Wina Bonnie Golden.

In 1961 Sturgeon became a regular reviewer of science fiction for the *National Review*, where his column reflects both a generous admiration for fellow writers and something like despair for the condition of the world: "I am ashamed of my species, and afraid for it," he has written. "I would like to run to it and shout 'Look!' and point at the avalanche. It is too late—it was, I think, too late some time ago."

PRINCIPAL WORKS: Without Sorcery, 1948; The Dreaming Jewels, 1950 (republished as The Synthetic Man, 1961); More Than Human, 1953; E Pluribus Unicorn, 1953; Caviar, 1955; Way Home, 1955; Thunder and Roses, 1957; A Touch of Strange, 1958; The Cosmic Rape, 1958; Aliens Four, 1959; Beyond, 1960; Venus Plus X, 1960; Some of Your Blood, 1961; Two Complete Novels (And My Fear Is Great, and, Baby Is Three), 1965; The Joyous Invasions, 1965; Starshine, 1968; Sturgeon in Orbit, 1970; Sturgeon Is Alive and Well, 1972.

ABOUT: Moskowitz, S. Explorers of the Infinite, 1963; Moskowitz, S. Seekers of Tomorrow, 1966; Who's Who in America, 1972–1973. *Periodicals*—Magazine of Fantasy and Science Fiction September 1962; New York Times November 22, 1953.

STURT, GEORGE ("GEORGE BOURNE") (June 18, 1863–February 4, 1927), English writer about country life, diarist, and novelist, was born at Farnham, Surrey, the younger son of Francis and Ellen (Smith) Sturt. He went to Farnham Grammar School, and taught there for seven years, beginning at the age of fifteen. Largely self-educated, Sturt never felt a part of the intellectual world of his time, though he was a close friend and valued critic to Arnold Bennett, who habitually sent him his novels in manuscript. Sturt was also a chronic asthmatic, and in consequence suffered all his life from low vitality or actual ill health.

His forebears had been wheelwrights in Farnham for several generations, and in 1884, when his father died, he inherited the family business. From Thoreau, who greatly influenced him, from Ruskin and from his own background, Sturt had acquired a profound respect for traditional crafts, and he worked hard to make himself a master of his trade. He was a generous employer, often greatly troubled in his socialist conscience by the exigencies of his modestly capitalistic role. In 1900 (or a few years earlier according to some accounts) he took a partner, William Goatcher, and thereafter was able to give more time to the "maggot urge to write." He went to live with his brother and sisters in the Surrey heathland village of The Bourne (from which he took his pen name), three miles south of Farnham.

His first book, *A Year's Exile*, appeared in 1898. It was a "vapid" novel, valuable only because it helped him to realize that his talent was not for fiction. He found his proper direction with *The Bettesworth Book*, an admirable if somewhat prolix study of an old laborer, "Frederick Bettesworth," who was actually Sturt's gardener, Grover. His story is continued in *Memoirs of a Surrey Labourer* and *Lucy Bettesworth*.

Angus Wilson believes that Sturt was obsessed by "an overwhelming desire to preserve for posterity some fragment (however tangential) of himself, of the world of his childhood." This world was rapidly disappearing as Sturt grew up. Surrey was becoming part of the "commuter belt," which he, like E. M. Forster, called "the villa world." Sturt was clearsighted enough to realize that the harsh circumstances of the Surrey villagers would be improved by these changes. In *Change in the*

Village, one of his best books, he said that he "would not lift a finger, or say a word, to restore the past time." But at the same time he felt "a forlornness in country places, as if all their best significance were gone," and regretted bitterly that the "flywheel of tradition is in fragments and will not revolve again."

In *The Ascending Effort* and intermittently in his other books, Sturt tried to assemble his feelings about art, craftsmanship, and the purpose of life into a coherent philosophy. Dealing with abstractions, he invariably became "repetitious and windy"; *The Ascending Effort* infuriated Joseph Conrad. Sturt's reputation stands on his incomparably lucid, exact, and vivid accounts of the people and manners he grew up among. His books are full of the vigorous speech of his subjects, and Sturt, in his willingness to set down verbatim what he learned in his endless interviews with old craftsmen, can be seen as a forerunner of such "tape-recorder sociologists" as Oscar Lewis, as well as a master of English prose in his own right.

In 1923, laying aside his pseudonym, George Sturt published his best and best-known book, *The Wheelwright's Shop*. Ostensibly a chronicle of the family business during the thirty-five years that the author had charge of it, it in fact reveals the whole spirit, tradition, methods and aesthetics of a craft practiced by men who themselves had no words to explain what seemed to them no more than a natural process. At the same time it illustrates with inexorable clarity the destruction by technological, social, and economic change of a whole way of life. It is a masterpiece of sociology and of literature, which Angus Wilson calls "a minor classic" and which F. R. Leavis, one of its most ardent advocates, found "incomparably more intelligent and more important than the conventional classics . . . as potently evocative of what we have lost as Lawrence."

Sturt died, unmarried, at Vine Cottage, The Bourne, after many years of semiparalyzed invalidism. He was described by Arnold Bennett as "a dark man with regular features, fine benevolent eyes and an old-fashioned dark beard . . . slightly under the average height. His voice was low and effective: his demeanour modest."

There has been a continuing interest in Sturt's work, and in 1967 the journal which provided the raw material of his books was published in two volumes. A notably fine introduction by the editor, E. D. Mackerness, points out a striking affinity between the views of the reclusive Sturt and those of D. H. Lawrence, reflected for example in Sturt's vehement conviction that the cardinal sin was living (as he himself did) at second hand. Sturt said his journal was "the best book I shall ever write." Most critics disagreed, finding it uneven, but still of intense interest, "a great joy, a benefaction."

GEORGE STURT

PRINCIPAL WORKS: A Year's Exile (novel), 1898; The Bettesworth Book: Talks with a Surrey Peasant, 1901; Memoirs of a Surrey Labourer, 1907; The Ascending Effort, 1910; Change in the Village, 1912; Lucy Bettesworth, 1913; William Smith, Potter and Farmer, 1790–1858, 1920; A Farmer's Life: With a Memoir of the Farmer's Sister, 1922; The Wheelwright's Shop, 1923; A Small Boy in the Sixties, 1927; Journals, 1890–1902, edited by Geoffrey Grigson, 1941; Journals, 1890–1927: A Selection Edited and Introduced by E. D. Mackerness (two vols.), 1967.

ABOUT: Bennett, A. Books and Persons, 1917; Conrad, J. Notes on Life and Letters, 1921; Dictionary of National Biography, 1922–30, 1937; Esdaile, A. J. K. Autolycus' Pack, 1940; Grigson, G. (ed.) Concise Encyclopedia of Modern World Literature, 1963; Pound, R. Arnold Bennett, 1952. *Periodicals*—Reviews of English Literature January 1964; Times (London) February 8, 1927; Times Literary Supplement May 31, 1923; July 13, 1967.

STYRON, WILLIAM (CLARK, JR.) (June 11, 1925–) made his way into the front rank of American novelists with his first book, published when he was twenty-six. He was born in Newport News, Virginia, the only child of William Clark Styron, a shipyard engineer, and Pauline (Abraham) Styron, a Pennsylvanian whose father had been a Confederate Army officer. Styron went from Christchurch (Episcopalian) School in Middlesex County, Virginia, to Davidson College, North Carolina, but soon left Davidson to go into the Marines. As a Marine V-12 officer candidate, Styron attended Duke University, where in William Blackburn's creative writing course he was confirmed in his literary ambitions. Mobilized as a lieutenant, he reached Okinawa just as the

WILLIAM STYRON

war was ending. He returned to Duke, graduating in 1947. Styron went to New York and worked briefly for a publisher until he was fired, he says, for "slovenly appearance, not wearing hat, and reading *New York Post.*" At this time Styron joined Hiram Haydn's writing course at the New School for Social Research and, with Haydn's encouragement and his parents' financial support, wrote his first novel.

Lie Down in Darkness (1951) describes the funeral of a young woman in Virginia, a ritual which occupies less than three hours. During this time, the events leading to Peyton Loftis' suicide are recalled in concentric and overlapping flashbacks by the half-dozen people most involved in the tragedy—among them Peyton's father Milton, who loved her and whom she loved to excess, and her unloving mother Helen. The guilt shared by these three, refracted back and forth as though through a maze of shifting mirrors, is purged clean for Peyton by her suicide. Peyton's return to innocence coincides with the dropping of the Hiroshima bomb, a global fall from innocence. The guilt is general, but redemption possible; "we lie down in darkness, and have our light in ashes."

The novel, concerned at one level with the moral decay of an old Virginia tidewater family, has been placed by many critics in the "Southern tradition." Styron acknowledges the unmistakable influence of William Faulkner (as well as of Joyce, Flaubert, Blake, and Marlowe, among others), but considers the story a "domestic tragedy" which could have happened anywhere. It has been read variously as a religious novel and an existentialist one, and its debt to the Electra myth has been widely recognized. So dense is the book's symbolism that no unilinear interpretation is useful.

On one point the critics are agreed. In spite of passages of self-consciously fine writing, "the beautiful technical virtuosity" of its structure and language, the "mysterious grace and power" of its narrative, place it among the two or three best American novels of its decade. Maxwell Geismar has called it "the key psychological work of the period." It earned for Styron the Prix de Rome and the daunting, perhaps impossible task of surpassing a triumph.

At any rate, none of Styron's subsequent books has wholly matched his readers' highest expectations. *The Long March*, inspired no doubt by his brief recall to the Marines during the Korean War, first appeared in *discovery* No. 1 (1953), and was published in book form in 1956. It is set in a Carolina Marine training camp, where the reluctant rebel Captain Mannix seeks to expose military idiocy by outdoing the super-patriots at their own game, and is destroyed. The novella was thought more controlled and concentrated than *Lie Down in Darkness*, but disappointingly unambitious.

This criticism could not be leveled at *Set This House on Fire*, which appeared after a long silence in 1960, but others were. The novel, about American expatriates in Italy, examines the murder and its moral implications of an evil man by a good one. Critics objected to its rhetoric and sermonizing, and were unconvinced by its hero's regeneration, suggesting that for all its virtues of style, observation and dialogue, the book remains a romantic melodrama. *Set This House on Fire* has its champions, however, who, like Granville Hicks, believe that after this "Dostoievskyan mystery story," Styron "is no longer a young hopeful; he is one of our important novelists."

The Confessions of Nat Turner (1967) is the working out of a theme which had occupied Styron for very many years: the slave uprising that took place in 1831 in Southampton County, near the author's childhood home. Although it was quickly and brutally crushed, the rebellion cost the lives of some sixty whites and two hundred slaves, and spread panic throughout the South. Its leader was Nat Turner, an educated, highly intelligent, and charismatic slave with a sense of divine mission. Before he was hanged, Turner dictated a twenty-page confession which forms the basis of Styron's four hundred-page first-person novel—a sustained impersonation by a twentieth century white Southerner of a nineteenth century house slave.

The novel had a generally enthusiastic reception from its first reviewers, all or most of whom were white. Philip Rahv, for example, praising its empathy with its black characters, its "imaginative realism" and "dramatic coherence," called it the best American novel published for several years. For others the book failed to give a convincing account of its hero's consciousness, or was otherwise flawed as a novel, but was highly successful as history: Martin Duberman wrote that it provided "the most subtle, multifaceted view of antebellum Virginia, its institution of slavery and the effects of that institution on both slaves and masters, available in a single volume."

The Confessions of Nat Turner became a best seller, but was the object of an increasingly savage series of attacks by black readers, culminating in the publication of *William Styron's Nat Turner: Ten Black Writers Respond* (1968). These essayists furiously rejected Styron's Nat Turner (whose failings include a repressed passion for a white girl, and an inability or unwillingness to kill) and charged that Styron had exaggerated the benevolent aspects of slavery while portraying the slaves themselves as pusillanimous and incompetent "Sambos." The author himself, and others on his behalf, responded that Styron's Nat Turner is a complex and tragic human being, not an epic force immune to error or desire. The painful debate is not likely to be resolved, but did not prevent the book from receiving the Pulitzer Prize for fiction and the Howells Medal.

William Styron is a member of the National Institute of Arts and Letters and the American Academy of Arts and Sciences. He has been since 1970 a member of the editorial board of the *American Scholar*, since 1964 a fellow of Silliman College, Yale University, and since 1953 an advisory editor of *Paris Review*. He edited *Best Stories From the Paris Review* (1959) and has contributed stories and articles to that and other magazines. His first play, *In the Clap Shack*, is a weakly plotted but vigorously written comedy, set in the urological ward of a Navy hospital in the American South during World War II. Styron, who has received a number of honorary degrees, was in 1972 appointed an Honorary Consultant in American Letters to the Library of Congress. He was married in 1953 to the poet Rose Burgunder and has four children. They live in a white frame farmhouse in Roxbury, Connecticut. A Democrat and "ardent Protestant," he has listed among his favorite recreations walking, drinking, and Mozart. Robert Penn Warren has described him as a "social man," easygoing, gregarious, and happily entertaining "hordes" of friends long into the evening.

PRINCIPAL WORKS: Lie Down in Darkness, 1951; The Long March, 1956; Set This House on Fire, 1960; The Confessions of Nat Turner, 1967; In the Clap Shack (play), 1973.

ABOUT: Aldridge, J. W. In Search of Heresy, 1956; Balakian, N. and Simmons, C. The Creative Present, 1963; Baumbach, J. The Landscape of Nightmare, 1965; Clark, J. H. (ed.) William Styron's Nat Turner: Ten Black Writers Respond, 1968; Contemporary Authors 5–6, 1963; Current Biography, 1968; Detweiler, R. Four Spiritual Crises in Mid-Century American Fiction, 1964; Fossum, R. H. William Styron, 1968; Geismar, M. American Moderns, 1958; Gosset, L. Y. Violence in Recent Southern Fiction, 1965; Hassan, I. Radical Innocence, 1961; Mackin, C. R. William Styron, 1969; Paris Review, Writers at Work, 1958; Pearce, R. William Styron, 1973; Vinson, J. (ed.) Contemporary Novelists, 1972; Who's Who in America, 1972–1973. *Periodicals*—Harper's Magazine April 1965; Hudson Review Autumn 1964; Life October 13, 1967; Newsweek October 16, 1967; South Atlantic Quarterly Fall 1960, Autumn 1963, Spring 1964; Wilson Library Bulletin April 1962.

"SULLIVAN, VERNON." *See* VIAN, BORIS

***SUPERVIELLE, JULES** (January 16, 1884–May 17, 1960), French poet, was born (as were Laforgue and Lautréamont) in Montevideo, Uruguay, where his parents and uncle, Basques from Oloron-Sainte-Marie, had emigrated to make their fortunes. Both parents died during his infancy, and Supervielle was raised in Uruguay by his uncle. At the age of ten he was sent to Paris, where he studied at the Lycée Janson-de-Sailly until he was seventeen, and afterward at the Sorbonne. His unexceptional first verses were privately published in 1900, and after his graduation in 1906 he devoted himself to poetry. He returned to Montevideo, was married in 1907 to Pilar Saavedra, and fathered six children. During World War I Supervielle worked in Paris for the Ministry of War. After it he settled in Paris and frequented the literary circle around the *Nouvelle Revue Française*, whose director Jean Paulhan was his friend and literary counselor.

A comfortable private income allowed Supervielle to write without economic distraction. He began in the free tradition of Rimbaud, Whitman, and Apollinaire, but as he matured he increasingly strove to put fantasy and whimsy under the control of reason, writing of the marvelous with conscientious simplicity and coherence. The unforced lyrical flow of his verse was allowed to find its own channels of expression. At ease in any form, he "did not," he said, "like a too exaggerated originality." This modest and essentially classical restraint is remote from the surrealism with which some critics sought to label him, and whose influence he denied. It makes him one of the most accessible of contemporary French poets.

But Supervielle's themes were far from simple. *Gravitations* (1925), his first significant book and one of his best, recorded in quiet exact poems a journey into the physical and psychic interior of man. A cardiac, Supervielle sought the rhythm of

* sü pər vyel′

JULES SUPERVIELLE

the universe in the action of his heart, the movement of his blood. In later collections, notably *Le Forçat innocent* (The Innocent Convict, 1930), *Les Amis inconnus* (The Unknown Friends, 1934), and *La Fable du monde* (The Fable of the World, 1938), he ranged wider into the cosmos and deeper into man's "interior ages."

In his poetry, Supervielle constructed a mythological universe in which consciousness merges with its objects, animating the dead and lifeless, speaking for the voiceless. It is a universe in which all the works of nature—stone, tree, and beast—share an essential harmony. At the center of this universe is man, lost and ineffably lonely, but glimpsing and sometimes reentering the harmony through dreams, or love, or the always friendly offices of death. These poems are full of the immense spaces of the stars, the sea and the pampas, but also of the reassuring voices and concerns of children. A grazing horse, turning its head, sees the dawn of creation. Rilke wrote to Supervielle: "You are a great builder of bridges in space."

The same mythology also found expression in prose fables and fantasies of great charm. The best known of Supervielle's deft novels is *Le Voleur d'enfants* (1926, translated by Alan Pryce-Jones in 1950 as *The Colonel's Children*, and included in the 1967 *Selected Writings* as "The Man Who Stole Children"). Among the gently ironic *contes*, *L'Enfant de la haute mer* (1931, translated by D. Japp and N. Nicholls as *Along the Road to Bethlehem*) is the most famous. Supervielle's plays, distinguished by the beauty of their language rather than by any specifically theatrical flair, included *La Belle au bois* (The Beauty in the Wood, 1932), a fairy tale; *Bolivar* (1936), with music by Darius Milhaud; and a dramatization of *Le Voleur d'enfants*. Some childhood recollections were published as *Boire à la source* (To Drink at the Source, 1933).

In the summer of 1939, Supervielle made one of his regular visits to Uruguay and was stranded there by the war. *Les Poèmes de la France malheureuse* (1941), written during this exile, was passed secretly from hand to hand in occupied France, and were an inspiration to members of the Resistance. Supervielle returned to Paris in July 1946, serving thereafter until his death as cultural attaché at the Uruguayan Embassy. *Poèmes, 1939–1945* was published in 1946 and *Choix de poèmes* (Selected Poems) in 1947. *Oublieuse mémoire* (Forgetful Memory, 1949), Supervielle's last major collection of verse, received the Prix des Critiques. Two plays were produced the same year and some relatively minor poetry and prose followed during the 1950s. When he died, Supervielle was an officer of the Legion of Honor and France's "prince of poets."

Supervielle has been compared to Pierre Reverdy in the cosmic scope of his vision, but was gentler and more hopeful. Joseph Chiari called him a "spontaneous poet, greater than Verlaine." In an essay about his poetry, published in *Naissances* (1951), Supervielle explained how he purged from his work the "delirium" which is an element in every poetic creation, and wrote: "I have always feared attacking the monsters I feel in me. I prefer to tame them with everyday words which are the most reassuring." But Denis Saurat thinks him the only Frenchman who could "run along the terrible paths across which Blake's tiger ranges."

PRINCIPAL WORKS IN ENGLISH TRANSLATION: Along the Road to Bethlehem (England, Souls of the Soulless), 1933; The Ox and the Ass at the Manger, 1945; The Colonel's Children, 1950; The Survivor, 1951; The Night Lover, 1961; Selected Writings, 1967; Supervielle (poems), 1967. ABOUT: Blair, D. S. Supervielle, 1961; Chiari, J. Contemporary French Poetry, 1952; Dictionnaire biographique français contemporain, 1954–55; Étiemble, R. Supervielle, 1960; Fowlie, W. Mid-Century French Poets, 1955; Greene, T. W. Jules Supervielle, 1958; Grigson, G. (ed.) Concise Encyclopedia of Modern World Literature, 1963; Hackett, C. A. An Anthology of Modern French Poetry, 1952; Roy, C. Jules Supervielle, 1949; Sénéchal, C. Jules Supervielle, 1939; Smith, H. (ed.) Columbia Dictionary of Modern European Literature, 1947; Who's Who in France, 1955–56. *Periodicals*—Books Abroad Spring 1961; Encounter June 1960; Nouvelle Revue Française October 1960.

***SWADOS, HARVEY** (October 28, 1920–December 11, 1972), American novelist, short story writer, and essayist, wrote: "I was born in Buffalo, New York, to a physician and the daughter of a physician. My mother had been trained in voice and piano, and discovered relatively late in life that her real talent lay in painting,

* swā′ dos

to which she devoted herself from my college years to her death.

"There were four in our family, which was basically a happy one. My older sister Felice, for whom my daughter is named, was remarkably gifted. She published one novel and was at work on another, far richer and more mature, at the time of her tragically early death in 1945 at the age of twenty-nine; she was my dearest and most loyal friend.

"At least until the advent of the Depression, our family life was filled with games and music. We lived outdoors a good deal, and I played the piano, not as well as my sister, and the flute also. (The passion for music persists: my three children are all excellent musicians, and I often play with them.) But throughout the 1930s Buffalo seemed a gloomy, wretched, and dismal place, and I have strong memories of the lengthy evening discussions of young intellectuals dreaming and scheming of fleeing the decaying city. I went off to the University of Michigan in 1936, returned to Buffalo at nineteen with my B.A. in 1940, and took a job in an aircraft plant as a riveter.

"After a year of it I was sure that I never wanted to live in Buffalo again, and indeed I never have. But while it is hardly one of my favorite cities, it—or someplace roughly like it—seems to serve as the locale for much of my fiction. I moved to New York, worked for another year in an aircraft plant in Long Island City and, fairly well cured of whatever romantic notions I had about the industrial working class, decided to try my luck with the seafaring workers. I enlisted in the Merchant Marine in the fall of 1942, and after being trained first as a seaman and then as a radio operator, served as radio officer on a number of ships through 1945, sailing the North Atlantic, the South Pacific, the Mediterranean and the Caribbean to various ports from Australia to Yugoslavia.

"With the war's end, I lived on my savings for a year while I worked seriously at writing for the first time (earlier I had published stories and reviews here and there). I completed a novel which was rejected by twenty-odd publishers and in fact was never published, but I became confirmed in my belief that I was a writer. Since by now I was married and children began to appear, along with my stories, articles, and reviews, I commenced the endless balancing act so familiar to so many writers. Part-time jobs at this and that, periods of unemployment during which I wrote feverishly or stagnated; but fortunately with a wife who had never for a moment questioned my commitment.

"Off and on since 1956, as our children grew up, I have taught in colleges—at the Writers' Workshop of the State University of Iowa, at San Francisco State College, Columbia University, and Sarah Lawrence College—always struggling not so much for money as for time. Since 1948 our home has been in Rockland County, some twenty miles north of Manhattan, in an area which used to be semi-rural and is now becoming a commuters' suburb. But close to five of those years have been spent in other places—among them Iowa, California, and the South of France (which we regard as our second home and to which we shall no doubt return again).

HARVEY SWADOS

"Despite the honors that have come my way in the form of grants, fellowships, and awards, I have never been able to support my family solely from my writing. My books have never sold; and I am sharply aware that my work is seldom considered in critical evaluations of what is presumed best in contemporary American fiction. Nevertheless, on balance, when I consider the miseries of those of my fellow-writers who have been treated more like movie stars than creative figures, and whose work has suffered correspondingly, I incline to the belief that my position is more fortunate than theirs. As I get on slowly with the work on my longest and most ambitious novel, which will occupy me for some years, I am concerned with pleasing myself, not with gratifying that vast and shapeless public which consumes not the work of novelists, but news about them in slick magazines and gossip columns, as it does candy bars. I remain a social radical, too, at once dismayed and exhilarated by my seemingly doomed yet endlessly optimistic native land."

Harvey Swados was the son of Aaron M. Swados and the former Rebecca Bluestone, both of Russian Jewish stock. He had his first literary success at the age of eighteen, when a story published in the University of Michigan's quarterly literary review was included in *The Best Short Stories of 1938*. He was a member of the faculty of Sarah Lawrence College from 1958 to 1960 and then from 1962 to 1970, when he accepted a professorship at the University of Massachusetts in Amherst. Swados considered himself "1) a novelist, 2) a short story writer, with 3) an interest in social forces and ideas."

Out Went the Candle, his first and (some think) his best novel, drew much critical attention. Set during and just after World War II, it is an account of the rise and fall of Herman Felton, a war-profiteering Jewish Lear, wheeling and dealing in Washington for the sake of his son and daughter, who love but reject him. "So perceptively . . . has Mr. Swados imagined this man and devised means to place him fully before us," wrote one critic, "that we put the book down with something like a sense of knowledge." The novel was admired no less as an expression of social concern, and welcomed by Irving Howe as "one of the most intelligent and at times powerful efforts to look at what is distinctive and puzzling in recent American life." There was praise also for Swados' talent for the swift character sketch, his ability to catch the spirit of time and place, and the vigor of his style, though several reviewers found the book rather jerky and clumsy in its rapid transitions of mood and scene.

On the Line, which followed, examines in eight chapters, some of them interconnected, the lives and inner conflicts of eight men working on an automobile assembly line. It is a resurrection in a middle-class age of the proletarian novel of the 1930s, but now the enemy is not economic exploitation or physical coercion but the machine, and the slow, irresistibly dehumanizing effect of lifelong service to it. It has been called "one of the finest treatments of the laboring man in recent fiction."

Swados' first failure was *False Coin*, a thesis novel about the vulgarization of art in contemporary America which seemed to many readers an uneasy mixture of satire and sermon. *The Will* was found harder to define—a novel Dickensian in its energy, Gothic in its eccentricities, but sociological in its fundamental concerns. It describes the struggle among three brothers for their father's inheritance, and Charles Shapiro has shown that it can be read as a transposition to contemporary urban America of *The Brothers Karamazov*. Here, as elsewhere in his work, Swados was seeking to write private stories about private people in a way that embodied his views about the social forces at work on these people. This experiment was not totally successful, most critics thought, but the result was nevertheless a tightly plotted, swiftly paced novel of great interest.

Shapiro says that "a good deal of Swados' most effective work appears in his stories, a genre in which he takes chances and more often than not succeeds in making art out of his severe social criticism." Richard Gilman, reviewing the stories collected in *Nights in the Gardens of Brooklyn*, wrote: "Swados has a fine comic sense of our epoch's major poses and masquerades. . . . But more than that, he is concerned with the break-through into true feeling, the attainment of moral dignity and the linking up with others through compassion, and that is where his best achievement lies." Some critics found Swados' stories a little flat in their scrupulous honesty and directness—"resolutely pedestrian," according to one; but Emile Capouya disagreed: "It is a poetic gift that permits Mr. Swados to slay dragons out of season. When other writers are inventing myths [and] recounting nightmares . . . he continues to regard the detail of our real lives as the ground of poetry." The essays and articles collected in *A Radical's America*, dealing with literature, popular culture, and the present status and problems of the working class, were thought consistently well written, "never narrowed with doctrinaire simplifications," but occasionally marred by a certain ungenerous shrillness of tone.

Swados' "longest and most ambitious novel," referred to in his note above, was published in 1970 as *Standing Fast*. It follows the fortunes of a group of anti-Stalinist socialist radicals from the Hitler–Stalin pact of 1939 to the assassination of President Kennedy in 1963, ranging from Buffalo to Panama, from a village in the Philippines to a kibbutz in Israel. Hilton Kramer called it a "grim, absorbing tale . . . of courage, idealism, and ambition overtaken by the cruel realities of history and the common vulnerabilities of the human species." Most reviewers found the book flawed—mechanical in its organization, and not free of sentimentality and "vintage Warner Brothers" rhetoric. It remains an immensely readable novel and a large achievement. More than one reviewer was reminded of John Dos Passos' *USA*, and Josh Greenfield said he had "read no other novel that conveys so precisely what our recent epoch must have been like to go . . . through for the radically idealistic members of the generation that came of age during the Depression."

The author received a Hudson Review Fellowship (1957), a Sidney Hillman Award (1958), a Guggenheim Fellowship (1961), two awards from the National Institute of Arts and Letters (1965), and one from the National Endowment for the Arts (1968). Swados, who died of a brain hemorrhage at the age of fifty-two, was married in 1946 to Bette Beller and had three children.

PRINCIPAL WORKS: *Novels*—Out Went the Candle, 1955; On the Line, 1957; False Coin, 1959; The Will, 1963; Standing Fast, 1970. *Short stories*—Nights in the Gardens of Brooklyn, 1961; A Story for Teddy, and Others, 1965. *Nonfiction*—A Radical's America, 1962 (England, A Radical at Large); Standing Up for the People: The Life and Work of Estes Kefauver, 1972. *As editor*—Years of Conscience: The Muckrakers, 1962; The American Writer and the Great Depression, 1966.

ABOUT: Contemporary Authors 7–8, 1963; Dupee, F. W. "The King of the Cats," 1965; Shapiro, C. Harvey Swados, *in* Moore, H. T. (ed.) Contemporary American Novelists, 1964; Vinson, J. (ed.) Contemporary Novelists, 1972; Who's Who in America, 1972–1973. *Periodicals*—New York Times December 12, 1972; Saturday Review October 26, 1963; August 14, 1965; Wilson Library Bulletin March 1961.

SWANBERG, W(ILLIAM) A(NDREW) (November 23, 1907–), American biographer and historical writer, writes: "I was born in St. Paul, Minnesota. My father, born in Sweden, a wonderfully skilled cabinetmaker, was a free-thinking socialist who argued politics heatedly over the back fence with a Republican neighbor with whom he was otherwise friendly. My mother, born in Norway, a firm Methodist, used to tell me confidentially that my father was a little unreasonable on the subject of politics and that I would do well to forget about politics.

"One of my vivid early memories originated at the nearby state fair, where the daring aviatrix Ruth Law, flying an enlarged box kite, raced the automobilist Louis Disbrow twenty times around the dirt track and once flew so low over Disbrow that a wheel dented the hood of his racer. Another was a glimpse of Buffalo Bill, clad in fringed buckskin jacket, at the head of a parade advertising his Wild West show appearing in St. Paul. Although it did not occur to me at the time, Ruth Law was a harbinger of the future, Buffalo Bill a memorial to the past.

"I pitched for my grade school baseball team, but thereafter athletic distinction escaped me. Intending to be a newspaperman, I attended the University of Minnesota at a time when tuition was about one hundred dollars a year. Sinclair Lewis and Scott Fitzgerald were the state's literary heroes, and Ole Rølvaag was teaching at nearby St. Olaf College. Studying a mélange of English, history and journalism, I graduated in 1930—an unhappy time, surely, to leave college. The bottom had dropped out of the economy. Newspapers, far from hiring, were dismissing married men. I was permitted to review the less important books for the St. Paul *Daily News* and Minneapolis *Star*, getting the books in lieu of payment.

"For five years I subsisted on pickup jobs of varying duration—freight loader for the Great Northern Railroad, construction laborer, YMCA clerk, chainman on a survey party—writing unsaleable stuff in my spare time. I returned to the university for graduate study in English, but went broke after two semesters. For Norman Thomas, who spoke at a college convocation, I conceived a warm admiration and began to feel that perhaps my father's socialism was not entirely unreasonable.

"In 1935 I went to New York, kept afloat by hack writing, then in 1936 got an editorial job with the Dell Publishing Company. Working on pulp Western, detective and picture magazines, I discovered a whole new world of escapist publications. It was all nonsense, of course, though undoubtedly good experience in basic narration. By the time the war came along I was married, had two children, enjoyed a good salary but was unhappy about my work. Landing a job with the Office of War Information, I was sent to England, France and Scandinavia in 1944–45, producing propaganda publications distributed in occupied countries. Returning home, I became a free-lance magazine writer and later indulged a taste for writing biography.

"I have a helpless liking for personages extravagantly endowed with gifts, flaws, dedications, prejudices and unorthodoxies—hence my work on such persons as Daniel Sickles, Jim Fisk, Robert Anderson, William Randolph Hearst and Theodore Dreiser. By their very exaggerations, it seems to me, such men illuminate the issues of their times —a simple application of the magnifying-glass principle. This principle apparently lost me the Pulitzer Prize for *Citizen Hearst*, written with the aid of a Guggenheim Fellowship, which won the vote of the examining board but was rejected by the trustees, who skipped the prize that year. Joseph Pulitzer stipulated that the subject of the biography must be 'inspiring.' The trustees no doubt felt that Pulitzer, who detested Hearst not only as his chief journalistic competitor but also for his political views, would not have approved.

"I live in Newtown, Conn. Now that the socialist program has been largely achieved, I am a staid centrist. My wife, Dorothy Green Swanberg, joins me in research and we discuss our subject incessantly across the table. Right now the ghost at the table is that same Joseph Pulitzer, an exciting one indeed."

Swanberg first "indulged a taste for writing biography" with a life of Daniel Sickles, a politician who was a hero of the Civil War and also a spendthrift and lecher who once stood trial for murder. Like Swanberg's subsequent biographies, it was welcomed as an intelligent, entertaining, and notably impartial product of careful research through firsthand sources.

Swanberg's confessed weakness for extravagant personalities is borne out by his choice of subjects.

W. A. SWANBERG

His enjoyable life of Jim Fisk was followed by a large-scale biography of William Randolph Hearst. Some reviewers felt that *Citizen Hearst* ignored a number of important psychological and social questions, but called it the best account of that remarkable figure yet produced, "exciting, fast-moving, with real sense of character, and always aided by an underlying sense of American history and mores."

The author's splendid research job on Hearst had not been limited to libraries; like the reporter in Orson Welles's film *Citizen Kane* he had also talked to dozens of people who remembered Hearst, well or ill. The same approach was used on a larger scale for *Dreiser*, which was based on "a mass of new material." The result was a thorough, detailed, and unsparingly honest portrait of "a giant of a man, well worth knowing, but undoubtedly less painful to know in print than in the flesh." Most critics agreed that it would remain the standard biography of Dreiser for many years to come.

The life of Joseph Pulitzer which was occupying Swanberg when he wrote the note above was published in 1967. "Into a factual account of the man's career," wrote G. W. Johnson, "[Swanberg] has woven a fascinating excursion into psychopathology and very illuminating passages on political, sociological and economic conditions [in] 1870–1911. The defect that prevents it from being the best biography ever written of an American newspaperman is its extravagant estimate of the historical importance of the subject. . . . One possible irony remains. It would be for this biography to be awarded the Pulitzer Prize which, technically, it well deserves."

Pulitzer did not receive the Pulitzer Prize, but Swanberg's next biography did, though its critical reception was relatively cool. This was *Luce and His Empire*, a massive and generally hostile study of the founder of *Time*, *Life*, and *Fortune* which most reviewers found altogether too long and unselective. Dwight Macdonald called it "a mass of raw material that will be invaluable to some future biographer who writes the illuminating book Mr. Swanberg hasn't."

Swanberg's historical books include *First Blood*, an absorbing description of the events leading up to the attack on Fort Sumter which launched the Civil War, and *The Rector and the Rogue*, an entirely delightful anecdote about a nineteenth century practical joker and his dealings with the rector of Trinity Parish in New York City.

The author is the son of Charles and Valborg (Larsen) Swanberg. He married Dorothy Green in 1936 and has two children. Swanberg held a Guggenheim Fellowship in 1960, and has received several awards, including the Frank Luther Mott Research Award (1962) and the Van Wyck Brooks Award for non-fiction (1968).

PRINCIPAL WORKS: Sickles the Incredible, 1956; First Blood: The Story of Fort Sumter, 1958; Jim Fisk: The Career of an Improbable Rascal, 1959; Citizen Hearst: A Biography of William Randolph Hearst, 1961; Dreiser, 1965; Pulitzer, 1967; The Rector and the Rogue, 1968; Luce and His Empire, 1972.

ABOUT: Contemporary Authors 7–8, 1963; Richards, C. Minnesota Writers, 1961; Who's Who in America 1972–1973. *Periodicals*—Saturday Review July 24, 1965.

SWENSON, MAY (May 28, 1919–), American poet, writes: "I am the first of ten children born to Dan Arthur and Anna Margaret (Helberg) Swenson in Logan, a mountain town about eighty miles north of Salt Lake City in Utah. My parents, both born in Sweden, came to America and settled in the Rocky Mountain region as converts to the Mormon Church. I was brought up a Mormon, but since the age of thirteen have had the distinction of being the only blacksheep among my living four brothers and four sisters. At thirteen I noticed that 'god' is contained in the word 'good' while 'devil' is an extension of 'evil.' This was also the age at which I began to write poetry. My father was a teacher in the Mechanical Engineering Department at the Utah State Agricultural College (now Utah State University) in Logan, and it was there, naturally, that I took my Bachelor's—the only degree I have. After graduation I worked as a reporter on my hometown paper and on the Salt Lake City *Deseret News*. Some of my earliest poems appeared in the *Rocky Mountain Review*, precursor of the *Western Review* edited by Ray B. West, Jr. My first national publication did not occur until 1949, when William Rose Benét of the *Saturday*

Review of Literature accepted a poem called 'Haymaking.' By this time I was living in New York City's Greenwich Village. At the age of twenty-one I decided not to marry. I also decided to commit suicide by the age of forty to avoid old age, but it's now too late for that. My initial attempts to support myself in New York appear comical at this distance. On failing to get a job on any of the newspapers, I began answering their Want Ads under 'Author's Assistant,' and so found myself apprenticed to a series of peculiar 'writers' who expected me to execute their generally grandiose plots for novels or scenarios. They had the ideas, I was merely required to furnish the words—at a fraction of a ghost-writer's fee. I soon learned that typing correspondence in business offices, though monotonous, was better paid—and even offered opportunities (if I was careful) of pursuing my own writing on the boss's time, as well as on his stationery inserted into his typewriter. One of my few sallies into fiction called 'Mutterings of a Middlewoman' published in Vance Bourjaily's *Discovery* in 1955, grew out of these experiences.

"The most prestigious pinnacle I reached in the commercial world was as secretary to the Executive Secretary of a drug trade association, where I edited a weekly news sheet for the membership and wrote my boss's convention speeches. On this job I earned enough to open a bank account and, after six years, enough to quit for one whole year, during which I determined to do nothing but write. On publication of my first collection of poems I received a Rockefeller grant, and what with finding my way through the hospitable gates of Yaddo and the MacDowell Colony I managed to continue my career without having to return to a nine-to-five job. I sought part-time work and supplemented my income with doing reviews and like assignments and selling my poems to magazines such as *Poetry*, *The Nation*, the *New Yorker*, *Paris Review*, *Harper's*, *Hudson Review*, etc. I worked in the afternoons as a manuscript reader and editor at New Directions for several years. In 1957 I was given a Robert Frost Poetry Fellowship to Bread Loaf in Vermont, and publication of my second book shortly afterward brought me a Guggenheim Fellowship (1959). For a year beginning in 1960 I was able to go abroad for the first time with the aid of an Amy Lowell Travelling Scholarship. I took a companion along and we bought a small French car and tenting equipment with which we toured France, Spain and Italy, living outdoors most of the time. A number of poems that later appeared in my third book were written while seated on a camp stool under umbrella pines, my portable on my knees. An award from the National Institute of Arts and Letters, also in 1960, made it a very lucky year.

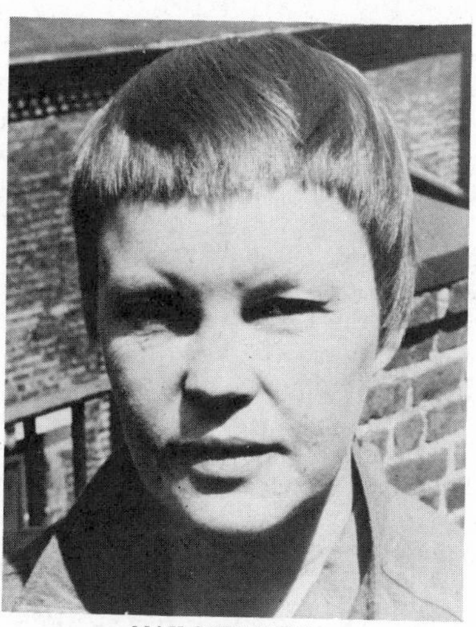

MAY SWENSON

"In recent years I have enjoyed many invitations to read to student audiences throughout the country, among them at Bennington, Bryn Mawr, Cornell, Dartmouth, Mount Holyoke, Smith, Wesleyan, the University of Arizona, the University of California, Washington University in St. Louis and New York University, as well as in my hometown at Utah State University, and I have given public readings at poetry centers and museums here and on the west coast. Among anthologies in which my work now appears are *Twentieth-Century American Poetry* edited by Conrad Aiken; *The Modern Poets* edited by Brinnin & Read; *New Poets of England and America* (Vol. 1) edited by Hall, Simpson & Pack; *A Treasury of Great American Poetry* (Revised) edited by Louis Untermeyer; *Borestone Mountain Poetry Awards Anthology*, 1958, 1962, 1968, 1969; *Erotic Poetry*, edited by William Cole; *The New Modern Poetry*, edited by M. L. Rosenthal; *Poems of Our Moment*, edited by John Hollander. A number of poems have been translated for foreign anthologies into French, Italian, German and Danish.

"During 1964–65 under a Ford Foundation grant I was affiliated with the Lincoln Center Repertory Company and the American Place Theatre as an observer of stage techniques and, in 1966, my play, *The Floor*, was produced at the American Place in New York City. For the academic year 1966–67 I was writer-in-residence at Purdue University in Lafayette, Indiana. For three years (1964–66) I served as a judge for the Lamont Book Awards, and in 1965 helped judge the National Book Award for poetry. I received an award and citation from Brandeis University in 1967, and that same year my alma mater, Utah State University, gave me a Distinguished Service Gold Medal, the first, I am sure that it has ever awarded to a poet—the other recipients were engineers and agriculturists. I held a second Rockefeller writing fellowship in 1967–68, and that year also received the Shelley Memorial Award from the Poetry Society of America, as well as being the Lucy Martin Donnelly Fellow at Bryn Mawr College. I have been most generously gifted by foundations and award committees and only hope that my own gift, and my diligent exploitation of it, makes me worthy.

"Some of my own feelings about my work and about creative writing in general are contained in an essay, 'The Experience of Poetry in a Scientific Age,' included in *Poets on Poetry* edited by Howard Nemerov, Basic Books, 1966. Under the title 'The Poet as Anti-Specialist,' the same essay may be found in the January 30, 1965, issue of the *Saturday Review*. I might say here that I cannot make a poem according to theory—my own or anyone else's. Theory and creativity are linked in quite the opposite way than one would infer from reading the literary analysts. The horse of poetry doesn't need the cart of theory to make him go—in fact, he'd better stay unhitched. The free impulse, as time goes on, may get attached to a set of techniques, methods, characteristic effects that accumulate into a theory. If so, it should be individual to the work, and it had best be left to trail *behind* the work, and not (for the sake of the readers' as well as the poet's unobstructed view) become misplaced into the foreground.

"If asked about my attitude toward politics I would say this: By the same habit of independent thought that makes me label myself a pantheist, I would call myself a 'nonpatriot' in the sense that I love the world above any nation, and look forward to pledging my allegiance to the United Nations—would that it might become, in deed, the nucleus of effective world government in my lifetime."

May Swenson's first collection of poems, "Another Animal," was published in *Poets of Today I* in 1954, and warmly praised for its verbal energy, exact observation of nature, and exceptional technical virtuosity. Richard Howard, discussing these early poems in *Tri-Quarterly* (Fall 1966), thought them incantatory rather than descriptive, spells by which the poet *became* the things—familiar or fanciful but always somehow strange—that she conjured up.

Her first book, *A Cage of Spines*, was no less admired and commended especially for its originality and experimental ingenuity, which extends to the physical shape as well as sound of her poems. W. T. Scott called her "a devilishly clever technician" whose work was full of "intensely lively, beautifully managed concentrations," and a *New Yorker* critic wrote: "She enters the world of things, animate and inanimate, without self-consciousness and with a rare sense of play."

In *To Mix With Time*, which includes many poems from the first two collections, Miss Swenson continues her runic evocation of otherness. And in the title poem she confesses the "magic notion" which Richard Howard speaks of, that "from chosen words a potion / could be wrung; pickings of them, eaten, could make you fly, walk / on water, be somebody else, do or undo anything, go back / or forward on belts of time."

To Mix With Time also includes a number of observant, expert, and often witty descriptive pieces written in Europe, and there is a larger admixture of such poems in *Half Sun Half Sleep*, along with some of the old Orphic kind. As Stephen Stepanchev says, she is now "able to make poems of ordinary public realities, offering precise images of urban life with an amazed reporter's skill—a reporter with pity—making her reader see clearly what he has merely looked at before." The experiments continue nevertheless, and Karl Shapiro said of *Half Sun Half Sleep*, "It is strange to see the once-radical *carmen figuratum*, the calligraphic poem, spatial forms, imagist and surreal forms . . . being used with such ease and unselfconsciousness." More "shaped poems," whose physical appearance on the page suggests their subject (like the spiral-shaped poem "The DNA Molecule") appear in *Iconographs*.

Babette Deutsch calls Miss Swenson "an imagist with a metaphysical approach to what she so precisely depicts. Delighting in the physical body, whether animal, vegetable or mineral, she enjoys the life of the mind, and . . . enhances both for her readers."

PRINCIPAL WORKS: Another Animal: Poems (*in* Poets of Today I), 1954; A Cage of Spines, 1958; To Mix With Time, 1963; Poems to Solve (for young readers), 1966; Half Sun Half Sleep, 1967; Iconographs, 1970; More Poems to Solve, 1971; (tr.) Windows and Stones: Selected Poems of Tomas Transtromer, 1972.

ABOUT: Contemporary Authors 7–8, 1963; Deutsch, B. Poetry in our Time, 2d ed., 1963; Murphy, R. (ed.) Contemporary Poets of the English Language, 1970; Stepanchev, S. American Poetry Since 1945, 1965; Swenson, M. *in* Nemerov, H. (ed.) Poets on Poetry, 1966; Who's Who in America, 1972–1973. *Periodicals*—Christian Science Monitor March 14, 1963; Nation August 10, 1963; New York Times Book Review February 8, 1959; May 7, 1967; Poetry December 1967; Prairie Schooner Winter 1960; Southern Review January 1969; Tri-Quarterly Fall 1966; Wilson Library Bulletin January 1962.

SYKES, CHRISTOPHER (HUGH) (November 17, 1907–), English biographer, historian, novelist, short story writer, and journalist, writes: "I was born in Yorkshire in the North of England in 1907. My father was Sir Mark Sykes, in his time well known as an Orientalist and a Conservative Member of Parliament. At the end of his life he was one of the principals in the formulation of the Balfour Declaration (1917) which ultimately led to the establishment of Israel. My mother was a daughter of Sir John Gorst who, in the years of Disraeli's Conservative party leadership, became the first modern party organiser in England. My background was therefore political, but in spite of encouragement I could not turn into a political animal. I am not keen on being any sort of animal first and foremost. This is unfashionable.

"As a Roman Catholic I was sent to school at Downside. The religious education was inferior to none in the Christian world, but the secular studies were very much open to criticism in those days, and it was a job to pass into Oxford. The education was very good in one respect, however. We were never allowed to think that school was an end in itself, and unlike most Old Etonians we almost never wear the old school tie. After Downside I spent the best part of a year as a foreign student at La Sorbonne, the University of Paris. I sat for no exams, knowing I would fail. After that came Oxford which I have loved ever since. But my incapacity in examinations proved a hindrance again and I left without a degree in 1928. In spite of this I still aimed to join the Foreign Service and only after two years of apprenticeship-study in Berlin did I give up the idea. At that time our diplomatic representative in Persia, Sir Robert Clive, needed a private secretary, so I went out to him in Teheran.

"Rather an awkward thing happened to me then. He was negotiating for an Anglo-Persian treaty and the Foreign Office concluded that he had failed, so they recalled him shortly after I had gone out to him. He allowed me to remain behind however and I started on my new career, a study of Persia. I decided to be an Orientalist, an almost extinct species now. I did not want to be a writer.

"I spent a year in Persia (1930–1931), came back to study at the School of Oriental Studies, in London, went back to Persia (1933–1934) with an Oxford friend, Robert Byron, the writer and art critic who was killed in the war. By now I recognised my fate. My first book was a novel, *Innocence and Design*, which I wrote with Robert Byron. It might be worse. Soon after I was published on my own in a book called *Wassmuss*, the biography of a German agent in Persia in the first World War. Then came some short stories, and then I toiled unsuccessfully at a novel and chucked it for a

CHRISTOPHER SYKES

history of Bonapartism, when World War II came along. I joined the Army, served in British G.H.Q. Cairo, was sent back to Persia to serve in the British Legation (happy days), and then I came back to England and got back in the army again in time to serve as a parachutist officer in the 1944 campaign of France.

"The long holiday from writing proved, I think, to have been beneficial. I went back to it with more confidence. I produced *Four Studies in Loyalty* (1946); a novel, *Answer to Question 33* (1948); *Character and Situation* (1949); *Two Studies in Virtue* (1953); two short novels: *A Song of a Shirt* (1953), and *Dates and Parties* (1955). They were all fairly well received except *Dates and Parties*, which hit a very class-conscious moment (always an English danger) and was mistaken by some class-crazed critics for a manifestation of snobbishness.

"In 1959 I produced a biography of General Orde Wingate. In 1965 I had another bash at producing a *magnum opus* in *Cross Roads to Israel*, an outline history of Zionism in Palestine from 1917 to 1949, a subject with which family connections had made me familiar. Most of my books contain autobiography which proves I suppose that like most writers I am an egotist. Apart from these possibly more durable works, I have written quite a lot of radio programmes (not T.V.) for the BBC."

Wassmuss was a German diplomat who tried with some success to raise the Persian tribes against Britain in World War I, and spent the rest of his life in a vain attempt to pay his government's debts to the tribesmen. Sykes's biography of this tragic man was his first "study in loyalty," and was very much liked for its generosity and understanding, if not for its stylistic excesses. His weakness for recondite adjectives had quite disappeared by the time Sykes published *Four Studies in Loyalty*, which established him. The subjects of these biographical essays are an earlier Christopher Sykes, who submitted in bewildered loyalty to the cruel jokes and literally ruinous extravagance of his friend Edward VII; an old Persian reprobate who paid dearly for his devotion to an idea of England; Robert Byron, killed in World War II; and the French Resistance fighters of a small town in the Vosges. These portraits were unanimously praised for their unpedantic scholarship, their "rare and delicate discrimination," and "studied, graceful prose."

Richard Sibthorp, a Victorian clergyman who vacillated endlessly between Anglicanism and Roman Catholicism, and Sykes's father, Sir Mark, were portrayed with equal skill in *Two Studies in Virtue*, which also throws much interesting light on its subjects' backgrounds, respectively the religious controversies of the nineteenth century and the formulation of the Balfour Declaration. The book confirmed Sykes's reputation as a biographer who writes with "sympathetic objectivity . . . in the urbane tradition, but not in imitation of, Lytton Strachey and Harold Nicolson."

However, his biography of the intransigent military genius Orde Wingate had an uncertain reception. Admired for its detailed thoroughness, its vivid and elegant style, it was found not free of error, too long, and oddly strained in its tone—as if, one reviewer suggested, Sykes himself was struggling to conceal mixed feelings about Wingate. *Cross Roads to Israel* was thought an excellent attempt at an almost impossible subject, "a just book . . . tempered with mercy," and the best available account of the Palestine Mandate. There was also something like unanimous enthusiasm for *Nancy: The Life of Lady Astor*, Sykes's large-scale portrait of the extraordinary woman—daughter of a Virginia entrepreneur—who married into one of Britain's richest families, became the first woman elected to the House of Commons, and remained a force in British society and politics for more than thirty years.

Each of the "brilliant, malicious" stories in *Character and Situation* studies an uncomfortably expatriated Englishman, and demonstrates Sykes's ability to sketch "scenes, character, and incident like an accomplished talker." *The Answer to Question 33*, also in its way a "study in loyalty," seemed to Walter Allen unsuccessful as a novel but "a most agreeable and civilised piece of writing." *A Song of a Shirt* was called "a first-class after-dinner story," and evoked comparisons with Evelyn Waugh, while the sociopolitical satire *Dates and Parties*, about the English upper classes in their 1938 decadence, seemed to one reviewer more reminiscent of P. G. Wodehouse. Sykes is an immaculate stylist but an indifferent architect of fictional plots, an acute and witty observer of character and reporter of "silly-clever talk," whose people nevertheless are observed from the outside and in his imaginative writing seldom quite come to life.

In 1934 Sykes was a correspondent for the London *Times* in Persia, and in 1936–1939 wrote for the *Spectator* and the *Observer*. He joined a famous Yorkshire regiment, the Green Howards, as a lieutenant in 1939 and was a staff captain at GHQ Cairo in 1940–1941. For the next two years he returned to diplomatic duties in Teheran and in 1944, as he says, joined the Special Air Service and was parachuted into France, where he earned the Croix de Guerre and was mentioned in despatches. In 1946 he was back in Persia, covering the Azerbaijan campaign for the *Daily Mail*. Thereafter, until his retirement, Sykes worked for the British Broadcasting Corporation—first as deputy controller of the Third Programme (1948), then in the features department (1949–1968). Among the many programs to which he has contributed as writer or producer are two on Evelyn Waugh, whose official biographer he is. Sykes was married in 1936 to Camilla Russell, daughter of Sir Thomas Russell Pasha. They have a son and live in Dorset.

PRINCIPAL WORKS: *Nonfiction*—Wassmuss, the German Lawrence, 1936; Four Studies in Loyalty, 1946; Two Studies in Virtue, 1953; Orde Wingate, 1959; Cross Roads to Israel, 1965; Troubled Loyalty: A Biography of Adam von Trott, 1968; Nancy: The Life of Lady Astor, 1972. *Fiction*—(with Robert Byron, as "Richard Waughburton") Innocence and Design, 1935; High Minded Murder, 1944; Answer to Question Thirty-Three, 1948; Character and Situation: Six Short Stories, with an introduction by Evelyn Waugh, 1949; A Song of a Shirt, 1953; Dates and Parties, 1955. *For children*—Albert and Emerald; or, How They Saved a Nation, illustrated by the author, 1961.

ABOUT: Hoehn, M. (ed.) Catholic Authors, 1962; Waugh, E. *introduction to* Sykes, C. Character and Situation, 1949; Who's Who, 1973.

SYPHER, (FELTUS) WYLIE (December 12, 1905–), American cultural historian, was born in Mount Kisco, New York, the son of Harry Wylie Sypher and the former Martha Berry. He graduated from Amherst College in 1927 and spent the next two years at Tufts College as a fellow in English, receiving his M.A. in 1929. Harvard gave him a second master's degree in 1932 and his doctorate in 1937. Sypher, who had joined the English faculty of Simmons College, Boston, in 1929, became professor of English there in 1945. He was chairman of the Language, Literature, and Arts Division from 1945 to 1966, when he became chairman of the English Department and Alumnae

Professor. From 1950 to 1967 he was also dean of the Graduate Division. He received Guggenheim Fellowships in 1950–1951 and 1959 for research in the theory of fine arts and literature. He has taught as a visiting lecturer at the universities of Minnesota and Wisconsin, and for many years at the Bread Loaf School of English in Vermont. Since 1968 he has also been Robert Frost professor of literature at the Bread Loaf Graduate School of English.

His first book was a study of British anti-slavery literature of the eighteenth century, *Guinea's Captive Kings*. It was followed by *Enlightened England*, an anthology of eighteenth century literature. His most influential book was his third, *Four Stages of Renaissance Style*, which examines the relationship between literature and the visual arts during the period from 1400 to 1700. It was widely praised for the detailed and illuminating way in which it investigates an assumption that is rarely tested: that there is "some recognizable unity . . . a discernible relation between all the various forms in which a given society expresses itself." W. K. Ferguson was one of those who praised the book both for its intention and its performance, commending in particular the "vividly presented detail, which saves it from the arid conceptualism that has been the curse of so much stylistic criticism." A sequel, *Rococo to Cubism in Art and Literature*, seeks and finds formal parallels between literature and the other arts in the eighteenth, nineteenth, and twentieth centuries. F. E. Faverty, who remained unconvinced that every age has its unique and pervasive style, nevertheless found the book impressive and fascinating.

Loss of the Self in Modern Literature and Art extends Sypher's premise horizontally as well as vertically. It finds a common sensibility at work not only in existential philosophy, in the "anti-novel" and the "anti-drama," and in the "brutal" painting of Dubuffet, but also in the new mathematics and physics of Goedel, Heisenberg, Boltzmann, and Bronowski. A. J. Guerard objected that Sypher's analysis tended to concentrate on ideas at the expense of "pleasure," overlooking the aesthetic effect of contemporary experimental art and fiction on its public. Nevertheless, like many of his colleagues, Guerard found this brief book brilliant and rewarding, the product of a "subtle, epigrammatic, essentially French intelligence." The argument is resumed in *Literature and Technology*, which calls for an end to the "alien vision" of much post-Renaissance art and science—their deliberate detachment and ultimately sterile preoccupation with form and technique—and a return to a more participatory and pragmatic mode.

Sypher contributes to many scholarly publications. He is a member of Phi Beta Kappa and an Episcopalian. He was married in 1929 to Lucy Johnston and has two children.

WYLIE SYPHER

PRINCIPAL WORKS: Guinea's Captive Kings: British Anti-Slavery Literature of the XVIIIth Century, 1942; (ed.) Enlightened England: An Anthology of Eighteenth Century Literature, 1947; Four Stages of Renaissance Style, 1955; Rococo to Cubism in Art and Literature, 1960; Loss of the Self in Modern Literature and Art, 1962; (ed.) Art History: An Anthology of Modern Criticism, 1963; Literature and Technology: The Alien Vision, 1968.

ABOUT: Contemporary Authors 2, 1963; Directory of American Scholars, 1964; Who's Who in America, 1972–1973.

***TAMÁSI, ARON** (September 20, 1897–May 26, 1966), Hungarian novelist, short story writer, and dramatist, wrote: "At the turn of the twentieth century I was born at Farkaslaka, in a village in Transylvania of the Szekler region. The Szeklers—or, as we call them in East Europe, the *székelyek*—have occupied the same region since the time when the nearby territory now known as Hungary was conquered by the Magyars. It is sometimes said that they were settled even before the Magyar conquest, as outposts of the advancing Hungarian tribes—that is to say, for a period of well over a thousand years. Throughout this long period in history, they have been at war, either fighting against the invaders from the East, or risen against internal oppression in the defense of liberty. Including those who have by this time migrated, their numbers amount to nearly one million.

"All my ancestors were Szeklers. My father owned a small farm. We children, eleven brothers and sisters, had to work on the farm from early childhood. We experienced much distress—the burden of taxes and the afflictions of the weather—

* tä′ mä shi

ARON TAMÁSI

but we knew freedom. I was educated at a secondary school, then at the Academy of Commerce. At the age of eighteen I had to join the Army and later on to take part in the first World War. After my graduation from the Academy, I spent three years in the United States earning a hand-to-mouth living, either by manual or by intellectual work. After this period I returned to my native country, Transylvania—now part of Rumania—for the next twenty years, until in 1944 I moved on to Budapest.

"I never intended to become a writer. The first short story I wrote in my student years was chiefly an act of bravado. However, I must surely have inherited a poetic or literary vein, for ever since my first short story I have responded to the task with all my heart and soul. Not literary ambition but this very resonance pressed me on. No doubt, once I had taken to it, I made every effort to do it properly and decently; had my job been that of a medical man or a researcher, or perhaps that of a scholar, I should have tried to do it none the worse.

"I have written short stories, novels and plays. As a writer I move in a world the savor and color of which bear all the marks of my own boyhood. As a rule, my characters also move in this world; however, their feelings and thoughts are of a kind to appeal to men and women all over the world.

"Certainly I don't follow any literary trend or movement, but maybe I'm closest to realism—not only in describing social relationships, but in trying to comprehend the life of man as a unity of science and poetry. Hardly a bed of roses for a writer! But then, if in this poor life one strives for the better, it has to be something worth striving for—one ought to be more than just an intelligent ape."

Tamási was one of the most widely read and best loved of contemporary Hungarian writers. He was of Catholic parentage and education, a descendant of freemen. His first published story appeared in 1922. Tamási enjoyed his years (1923–1925) in the United States, but went back to Transylvania because his roots and work were there, and was soon afterwards married. The nostalgic stories he had written in America were published as *Lélekindulás* (The Soul's Trek) in 1925 and enjoyed immediate success.

One of the "shipwrecked Hungarians of Transylvania" (which became part of Rumania in 1920), Tamási was a regionalist who identified himself almost mystically with the Székely people. He became active in the populist movement and was the most distinguished of those who contributed to the literary monthly the *Erdélyi Helikon* (Transylvanian Helicon) and participated in the work of the Transylvanian Artistic Guild—two institutions which sought to preserve Hungarian cultural traditions under an alien regime. His work between the wars contained much indirect social criticism, which became most explicit in his anti-feudalism novel *Címeresek* (Titled Nobility, 1931). After World War II he at first welcomed the Communists (though he was not himself one) and became a member of the legislature. He was soon disillusioned, and expressed himself so outspokenly that he was denied publication between 1949 and 1953. Tamási was one of the leaders of the rebellious Hungarian Writers' Association in 1956.

Tamási's short stories and fables have been collected in *Elvadult paradicsom* (Paradise Gone Wild, 1956) and *Világ és holdvilág* (Light and Moonlight, 1958). Duczyńska and Polanyi have called these stories the work of "a humanist and a poet. The sentences are as if carved in seasoned hardwood. . . . Tamási is a fount from which folk-myth spurts in ever new shapes and forms: the parable, unassuming anecdotes, the scurrilous tale, the pagan enchantment, the messianic heartbeat." Tamási's novels, like his stories, mix earthy realism and fantasy. The best known of them is the Abel trilogy (1932–1934), a picaresque about the adventures in the great world of a Transylvanian shepherd boy who embodies the resourcefulness, prankishness, and fortitude of the Szeklers. *Bölcső és bagoly* (Cradle and Owl, 1949) is an autobiographical novel. Tamási was at his best as a narrative writer: his plays have the flavor of dramatized social comment.

Tamási's work was flawed by oversimplification, a "stylized primitiveness," and occasional sententiousness: the weaknesses of a writer more concerned to record the spirit of a place and people than to create great art. At its best, nevertheless, his prose "captures from the spirit of the language a virginal spare beauty" and has "its own intricate hidden rhythm." Both his work and his life leave an impression of unwavering honesty and integrity, and of goodness. Joseph Reményi calls his achievement "regionalism in the best sense . . . the expression of the disinherited who, however, possess the freedom of laughter and tears."

PRINCIPAL WORKS IN ENGLISH TRANSLATION: Abel Alone (Hungary), 1966. *Short stories in* Duczyńska, I. and Polanyi, K. (eds.) The Plough and the Pen, 1963; Wolfe, L. (ed.) Hungaria, 1936; The Literary Review Spring 1966; The New Hungarian Quarterly January 1961, April–June 1962.

ABOUT: Duczyńska, I. and Polanyi, K. (eds.) The Plough and the Pen, 1963; Klaniczay, T. and others, History of Hungarian Literature, 1964; Reményi, J. Hungarian Writers and Literature, 1964. *Periodicals*—American Slavic and East European Review November 1946.

***TANIZAKI, JUNICHIRÔ** (July 24, 1886–July 30, 1965), considered one of Japan's great modern novelists, was born into the poorer branch of a wealthy Tokyo merchant family. His elder brother's early death left him heir to a family fortune that declined steadily during his childhood and youth. His father, Sogoro, who had married into the Tanizaki family and taken the family name, lacked the commercial ability of his father-in-law, Hisaemon, architect of the family fortune. There were a number of business failures and false starts. In later life Tanizaki, speaking through one of his characters, expressed mixed feelings about his Edo origins: "He had grown up in the merchants' section of Tokyo before the earthquake destroyed it, and the thought of it could fill him with the keenest nostalgia; but the very fact that he was a child of the merchants' quarter made him especially sensitive to its inadequacies, to its vulgarity and its preoccupations with the material."

At about the time Tanizaki finished his elementary schooling, his father's business failed yet again. As a result of his own entreaties, his teacher's recommendation, and the support of his relatives, the boy was permitted to enter the Tokyo Metropolitan First Middle School in April 1901. To help pay for his education he worked as a part-time private tutor. By the time he left middle school at the age of eighteen, Tanizaki had already acquired a reputation for literary brilliance.

In March 1905 Tanizaki entered the English Law Department of the First High School in Tokyo (now the College of General Education, Tokyo University). In the autumn of 1906 he changed from English law to English literature and when he entered Tokyo Imperial University in 1907 it was to study classical Japanese literature: "As I made up my mind to become a writer," he explained, "I thought the Japanese Literature Department would afford me the greatest scope for neglecting my studies."

* tə ni zä ki

JUNICHIRÔ TANIZAKI

The period between 1905 and 1915, when Tanizaki began his career as a writer, was an exceptionally fertile decade for Japanese literature. Following the Russo-Japanese war, Japan had arrived among the world powers; and the late nineteenth century translations and imitations of Western prose and poetry were beginning to bear fruit in writing freed of the strict conventions of centuries. In Tanizaki, the meeting of East and West was to be particularly apparent. Strongly attracted by Poe, Baudelaire, and Wilde, he felt little sympathy with the Japanese writers of the time, with the single exception of Kafu Nagai, whose *Amerika Monogatari* (Tales of America) he much admired. It was in 1909, a year which marked a turning point in the controversy between the established naturalist writers and their opponents (among whom Ogai, Soseki, and Kafu all produced important works during the year), that Tanizaki published his first important story, in the magazine *New Thought*, which he was editing with university friends. "Tanjo" (Birth), "Zo" (Elephant), "Shisei" (Tattoo), and "Kirin" (Giraffe) all followed in quick succession.

"Shisei" (translated as "The Victim") describes the metamorphosis of a timid young girl into a cruel beauty, under the needle of a masochistic young tattoo artist who sets out to create a force that will destroy him. The themes of beauty and power, or perhaps beauty as power, absorb Tanizaki. "All beautiful things are strong," he wrote, "ugly things weak." But the ugly things obsess him too—mutilation, blindness, morbidity, and phobia; and these intense early tales often contain sadomasochistic elements which persist and develop in some of his later work. The short novel *Shunkin Sho* (1933, translated by Roy Humpherson and Hajime Okita as *The Story of Shunkin* and by Howard Hibbett as *A Portrait of Shunkin*) is about a blind musician whose relationship with her pupil is so intense that the youth pierces his own eyes to share her blindness and suffering. Stanley Edgar Hyman called this story a masterpiece: "These awful deeds, which arouse the sort of pity and terror that the self-discovery and self-blinding of King Oedipus do, result in a love of serene beauty."

Tanizaki's concern from the beginning was to capture and preserve a concept of beauty that is specifically Japanese: "Orientals find beauty not only in the thing itself, but in the pattern of shadows, the light and the darkness, which that thing produces. . . . I would call back at least for literature this world of shadows we are losing." And in his mature work too, such as *Momoku Monogatari* (1931, translated as *A Blind Man's Tale*) and *Shunkin Sho*, he would turn to traditional or historical themes in a spirit of nostalgia.

Expelled from the university for failing to pay his fees, Tanizaki soon found himself dependent on his pen for a living. In 1911 Kafu Nagai published some of his work in the influential literary magazine *Mita Literature*. Kafu praised the depth and the mystery, the sense of physical fear so vivid in Tanizaki's work, and at the same time its urbanity and "perfect style." But though the author produced several popular collections of stories in the following six years, he was by 1920 being publicly criticized as a "satanist," and for disguising a lack of content with complexity of style.

It was only after he left Tokyo following the great earthquake of 1923, to live in Okamoto, near Osaka, that Tanizaki's art suddenly seems to have acquired the freedom to mature. His writing became more realistic and descriptive, his style less sensuous, his grasp of his theme more sure. *A Fool's Love*, serialized in 1924–1925, is a transitional work, illustrating his growing disenchantment with the West and its values.

Tade Kuu Mushi (1928, translated by Edward Seidensticker as *Some Prefer Nettles*) is set in Osaka, and concerns a marriage that is failing for lack of passion—like the writer's own. He had married Chiyoko Ishikawa in 1915, but the relationship failed, and by 1928 Tanizaki was actually encouraging an affair between his wife and a writer called Harue Sato. In 1930 the couple were divorced. (Tanizaki was to be married again, divorced, and remarried in the next five years.) In the social struggle symbolized by the psychological conflict in *Some Prefer Nettles*, with the husband drawn more and more towards the rooted and traditional and away from his smart westernized wife, Tanizaki comes down very firmly on the side of the traditional. And his next major work, a fine modern rendering of the eleventh century classic *Genji Monogatari* (The Tale of Genji), which occupied him quietly during most of the war years, was in keeping with this mood.

In 1942 he began work on *Sasame Yuki* (translated by Edward G. Seidensticker as *The Makioka Sisters*). Through the lives of four women, he depicts the heyday of opulent middle-class Osaka, in tribute to a way of life he knows to be dying. It was suppressed in 1943 by the military government, and not completed until 1948. Many have seen in its long shapely sentences the strong influence of *Genji Monogatari*. It is regarded by some critics as Tanizaki's masterpiece, but others are dissatisfied, if not bored, by its uncharacteristic realism and almost clinical detachment.

In spite of illness, Tanizaki continued writing until shortly before his death. In his seventies he returned to some of the themes he had explored in his twenties, giving new twists to the erotic and the bizarre. *Kagi* (1956, translated by Howard Hibbett as *The Key*) describes an incurably destructive sexual relationship between husband and wife; *Yume no Ukihashi* (1959, translated as *The Bridge of Dreams*) is a mysteriously beautiful tale in which a stepmother, whose image has been deliberately superimposed on that of the mother, serves as a catalyst of incestuous love; and *Futen Rojin Nikki* (1961, translated by Hibbett as *Diary of a Mad Old Man*) examines the obsessions of a wealthy seventy-year-old, and his sexual relationship with his modish young daughter-in-law who panders to his erotic fantasies in return for expensive jewelry: "Even if you're impotent, you have a kind of sex life."

All of Tanizaki's best work is characterized by an oblique elegance of style, suggesting that "pattern of shadows" he so admired, and an intricate narrative technique, which continued to develop in his last works. In *The Key*, for example, he tells his story through the diaries of husband and wife alternately, revealing only in the final pages that each has been reading the other's diary, with the knowledge of the other, so that each story is exposed as a mixture of self-revelation and disguise. In 1949 Tanizaki was awarded the Imperial Prize for Literature; and in 1964 he was elected an Honorary Member of the American Academy and the National Institute of Arts and Letters, the first Japanese so honored. When he died he was a strong candidate for the Nobel Prize.

PRINCIPAL WORKS IN ENGLISH TRANSLATION: A Spring-Time Case, 1927; Ashikari, and, The Story of Shunkin, 1936 (latter also tr. as A Portrait of Shunkin, 1965); Some Prefer Nettles, 1955; The Makioka Sisters, 1957; The Key, 1960; Seven Japanese Tales, 1964; Diary of a Mad Old Man, 1965. *Stories in* Keene, D. Modern

Japanese Literature, 1956; Morris, I. Modern Japanese Stories, 1961. *Excerpts from* In Praise of Shadows (essay), *in* Atlantic January 1955, Japan Quarterly Autumn 1954.
ABOUT: Grigson, G. (ed.) Concise Encyclopedia of Modern World Literature, 1963; Hyman, S. E. Standards, 1963; Keene, D. Modern Japanese Literature, 1956; Meiji Dictionary of Modern Japanese Literature (in Japanese), 1965; Penguin Companion to Literature 4, 1969; Seymour-Smith, M. Guide to Modern World Literature, 1973. *Periodicals*—Atlantic December 14, 1957; New Statesman August 18, 1961; New Yorker December 14, 1957; San Francisco Chronicle November 17, 1957; Saturday Review August 21, 1965; Time August 20, 1965.

EDWARD EVERETT TANNER 3D

TANNER, EDWARD EVERETT 3d (May 18, 1921–), American humorist, is better known as "Virginia Rowans," and best known as "Patrick Dennis." He was born in Chicago, the son of a stockbroker, and was sent to a succession of Illinois private schools from certain of which, it is said, he was expelled. "Patrick" Tanner, as he liked to be called, began his career as a clerk in a hardware store, and had graduated to a Chicago bookshop by the time World War II began.

During the next few years he drove an ambulance for the American Field Service in Arabia, North Africa, Italy, and France, and was attached at various times to the armed forces of seven nations, all of them fortunately friendly. By the time the war ended Tanner had been twice wounded, had suffered (or, as he says, enjoyed) a bout of amnesia, and grown a large beard. In 1945 Tanner settled in New York City, where he worked successively as an advertising account executive, as a publisher's advertising manager, and as promotion director of *Foreign Affairs* magazine. He has been a full-time writer since January 1, 1956.

Tanner's literary career began modestly enough with some ghostwriting. An idea which he had been nursing for some years crystallized in the early 1950s into a book about a character called "Auntie Mame," but no one would buy it and Tanner put it aside. His first published novel was a satire, published in 1953 as by "Virginia Rowans," called *Oh, What a Wonderful Wedding*. Some reviewers found it a little strained in its humor and malicious in its wit, but it was generally welcomed for its "fine feminine realism," its fairly comprehensive hammering of "the foibles of our competitive society." Another Rowans novel, *House Party*, appeared the following year.

It was not until 1955 that *Auntie Mame* made her debut. Based on a member of Tanner's family, she is a middle-aged *enfant terrible*, rich enough to live on Beekman Place but clever enough, in a scatter-brained way, to remain unimpressed by her social position or anyone else's. From her stronghold behind the enemy lines, Mame fights a running guerrilla campaign against phony intellectuals, racial prejudice, and every kind of snobbery. Her story, mixing broad humor and pointed satire, is narrated by her appalled but loving nephew and protégé "Patrick Dennis" in a novel which became one of the most successful events in recent publishing history. It led the best-seller lists for a hundred and twelve weeks and sold more than two million copies. It was adapted as a play, as a movie, and as a musical, and in every manifestation was a hit. Tanner's only complaint was that his carefully guarded anonymity was destroyed when, in July 1955, *Time* magazine "decided the world couldn't live another hour" without knowing his real identity.

Unmasked, Tanner has nevertheless continued to use his two pseudonyms. Virginia Rowans published *The Loving Couple* in 1956 and *Love and Mrs. Sargent* in 1961. The former describes a critical day in the crumbling marriage of a suburban couple, drawing its humor from the fact that the story is told twice, first from his point of view, then, rather differently, from hers. Mrs. Sargent, in the latter book, is an attractive young widow who writes an advice column for the lovelorn but has emotional problems of her own which provide the rather scanty meat of the story.

Patrick Dennis who is, as his creator says, more "slap-dash," less "thoughtful," than Virginia Rowans, has also been more prolific. *Guestward Ho!*, written in collaboration with Barbara Hooton, joined *The Loving Couple* and *Auntie Mame* on the best-seller lists in 1956, and *Around the World With Auntie Mame*, "as extravagantly full of gags, slapstick comedy and general hilarious confusion as its predecessor," made a lot of money in 1958. Of Dennis's subsequent books, the most enthusiastic critical reception was for *Little Me*, which tells the American success story of Belle Poitrine, a small-town girl cruelly handicapped by a total lack of talent, who nevertheless rises to Hollywood stardom. Illustrated with period photographs cleverly fabricated by Chris Alexander, this bawdy burlesque of an "as told to" biography delighted most reviewers with its "sly puns, quips, malapropisms, inside jokes and other verbal buffoonery," and was made into a musical.

Genius, also kindly received by most critics, is about a brilliant movie director, modeled perhaps on Orson Welles, and his race against time and the Internal Revenue Service to complete one more masterpiece. *First Lady* applies the *Little Me* formula to Martha Dinwiddie Butterfield, now peacefully installed in the Bosky Dell Home for the Senile and Disturbed, as she recalls her thirty accidental and disastrous days in the White House. Some reviewers found its humor rather spotty and heavy-handed, and there have also been rather mixed though generally favorable reactions to Tanner's subsequent books.

"No critic can tell Patrick Dennis how to write a bestseller," says R. D. Spector. "His books are not 'good' literature, perhaps not even literature. . . . He has little concern for credibility and less for the niceties of character delineation. But with great gusto and a genuine gift for creating the wild and boisterous scene, farcical situations, and bizarre settings, he can't miss." *Time* suggests that "he could best be ticketed as an American P. G. Wodehouse." Tanner, who writes "fast or not at all," was drama critic of the *New Republic* in 1957–1958. He is a tall man with very blue eyes and a beard. Tanner was married in 1948 to Louise Stickney and has two children. He collects antique chiming clocks.

PRINCIPAL WORKS: *As "Virginia Rowans"*—Oh, What a Wonderful Wedding, 1953; House Party, 1954; The Loving Couple, 1956; Love and Mrs. Sargent, 1961. *As "Patrick Dennis"*—Auntie Mame, 1955; (with Barbara C. Hooton) Guestward Ho!, 1956; (with Dorothy Erskine) The Pink Hotel, 1957; Around the World With Auntie Mame, 1958; Little Me, 1961; Genius, 1962; First Lady, 1964; The Joyous Season, 1965; Tony, 1966; How Firm a Foundation, 1968; Paradise, 1971; Three-D, 1972.

ABOUT: Celebrity Register, 1963; Current Biography, 1959; Who's Who in America, 1972–1973. *Periodicals*—Life December 14, 1962; Look January 20, 1959; Mademoiselle January 1957; New York Herald Tribune Book Review September 18, 1955; Saturday Review February 25, 1961; August 1, 1964; Time July 15, 1957; Vogue February 15, 1956; November 1, 1956.

TARASSOFF, LEV. *See* "TROYAT, HENRI"

***TARDIEU, JEAN** (November 1, 1903–), French dramatist and poet, was born at Saint-Germain-de-Joux, the son of Victor Tardieu, a painter, and Caroline (Luigini) Tardieu. He studied at the Lycée Condorcet and in the faculty of literature at the Sorbonne. He was a precocious playwright—one of his comedies dates from 1915—but for many years he abandoned the theatre in favor of poetry, producing lyrical verse in the manner of Mallarmé, and acquiring a reputation as a translator of Hölderlin and Goethe.

* tär dyû'

In 1944 Tardieu joined Radiodiffusion-Télévision Française, and a year or two later took charge of its experimental workshop, the *club d'essai*. It was at this time that he began to write the avant-garde plays on which his reputation rests, and his new-found interest in verbal experiment, reminiscent of Queneau, is evident also in the poetry collected in *Choix de poèmes* (1961).

Most of Tardieu's postwar plays are extremely short. They generally make no attempt at a systematic working out of a given theme, but are closer in their nature to cabaret sketches. Man in Tardieu's plays feels himself at the mercy of a hostile and incomprehensible universe, and erects for his protection a monstrous edifice of habit and convention which becomes his cage, shutting him off from human contact.

At times, as in the early plays *Qui est là?* (translated as *Who Goes There?*) and *La Politesse inutile* (translated as *Courtesy Doesn't Pay*), malign forces intrude without reason, destroying the protagonist's illusion of security at a single blow. In other plays, man is shown to be trapped in his own elaborate social constructs. An excellent example is *Le Guichet* (translated as *The Information Bureau* and also as *The Enquiry Office*), one of three plays by Tardieu produced at the Van Dam Theater in New York in 1962. In this Kafkaesque study, a man who calls at the bureau to ask the time of his train is humiliated by an arrogant official and subjected to an interrogation which reveals the whole pathetic story of his life. It emerges that the traveler hopes to learn not only when his train is leaving, but which train he should catch, where he should go, what he should do. These questions become irrelevant when the official, mellowed by the man's humility, checks his files and is able to inform him that he is about to die.

Tardieu frequently uses this method, parodying and exaggerating a familiar situation to demonstrate its inherent absurdity. The result, which is often extremely funny, sometimes cuts deep. In *La Serrure* (The Keyhole), for example, a *voyeur* watches a prostitute strip. She takes off her clothes, removes her eyes, steps out of her flesh, and is a skeleton. And to this symbol of death the watcher cries: "I'm coming to you, love of my life!"—and dies. Tardieu's plays frequently end in death but, as L. C. Pronko points out, "it is never looked upon as a restful conclusion; rather it is the last absurd silence which constantly threatens us, and finally annihilates existence, reducing it to the silence which is always its essence."

It is not surprising that Tardieu should be regarded as a pioneer of the "theatre of the absurd," but he is distinguished from others associated with the genre by an occasional glimmer of optimism in his work—a suggestion that love can overcome loneliness—and also by his preoccupation with language, meaning, and the whole problem of human communication. This has led him into increasingly extreme experiments. In *Oswald et Zénaïde*, the characters address each other entirely in polite clichés, expressing their real feelings only in asides to the audience. *Eux seuls le savent* (1952, translated as *They Alone Know*) is both a parody of the conventions of the realistic theatre and an experiment in plotless drama, in which the wretched audience is never allowed to discover what is being discussed on the stage. Elsewhere, language is used musically rather than conceptually—in *Conversation-Sinfonietta*, for example, where commonplace phrases are spoken by two basses, two contraltos, a soprano, and a tenor, and repeated in varying patterns through three "movements"; and in *Les Amants du métro* (seen in New York as *The Lovers in the Metro* and published as *The Underground Lovers*), a "comic ballet" in which word patterns replace both music and dancers. Something close to the ultimate in theatrical experiment is achieved in *Une Voix sans personne*, where the set is an empty room and the "action" is a disembodied voice recalling what has happened there in the past.

Something of Tardieu's intention is indicated by the titles of his two play collections, *Théâtre de chambre* (Chamber Theater, 1955) and *Poèmes à jouer* (Poems to Be Played, 1960). He hopes, he says, to complete a sort of "well-tempered clavichord" of the one-act drama. George E. Wellwarth considers that Tardieu has given "new life to the one-act form" and Michael Benedikt calls his plays "one-room laboratories in which many of the most advanced experiments in the avant-garde theater are taking place." At the same time, as Martin Esslin points out, "by its very awareness, its experimental consciousness, its playfulness in trying out new devices, Tardieu's work misses the obsessive compulsiveness, and thus the hypnotic power, the inevitability, of some of the masterpieces of the Theatre of the Absurd."

Tardieu retired as director of RTF's *club d'essai* in 1960, but has been administrative adviser to the company since 1964. He is a Chevalier of Art and Literature and of the Légion d'Honneur, and in 1972 received the Grand Prix de Poésie de l'Académie Française. Tardieu is married to the former Marie-Laure Blot and has one child.

JEAN TARDIEU

PRINCIPAL WORKS IN ENGLISH TRANSLATION: The Underground Lovers and Other Experimental Plays (tr. by Colin Duckworth), 1968 (includes Who Goes There?, Courtesy Doesn't Pay, The Enquiry Office, They Alone Know, Conversation-Sinfonietta, and other plays); One Way for Another (Un Geste pour un autre), *in* Benedikt, M. and Wellwarth, G. E. (eds.) Modern French Theater, 1964. *Poems in* Strachan, W. J. Apollinaire to Aragon: Thirty Modern French Poets, 1948.

ABOUT: Beigbeder, M. Le Théâtre en France depuis la libération, 1959; Esslin, M. The Theatre of the Absurd, 1961; International Who's Who, 1973–74; Pronko, L. C. Avant-Garde, 1962; Rousselot, J. Panorama Critique des nouveaux poètes français, 1952; Wellwarth, G. E. The Theater of Protest and Paradox, 1964; Who's Who in France, 1971–1972.

TARSIS, VALERY (YAKOVLEVICH) (**"Ivan Valeriy"**) (September 23, 1906–), Russian novelist, born in Kiev, writes: "I was not, as the English expression goes, born with a silver spoon in my mouth, nor in paradisiacal gardens, but in a petrol warehouse, the property of Nobel Brothers.

"And yet my childhood with the daily onion soup and patched trousers was a paradise from which I was expelled in 1917. My father, whose ancestors had come from Greece, was working at the warehouse. Mother toiled as a scullery maid at an inn; she was illiterate.

"In spite of his humble occupation and his education limited to a course at the village school, my father was an incorrigible romantic, dreaming of the revolution; he got in touch with the Bolsheviks and hid illegal pamphlets and arms in the warehouse. Mother did not sympathize with these activities. She was a God-fearing woman who loved church services and brought her children up

VALERY TARSIS

in the spirit of Christian meekness. Like all old revolutionaries my unfortunate father dragged out a miserable existence and ended his days in a concentration camp.

"I got into conflict with reality when still at school, and especially at university—I studied literature and language at the pedagogical faculty of the Rostov-on-Don University, from where I graduated in 1929. The officially sanctioned teachers impoverished and dried up the immortal, never-withering flowers of poetry and philosophy—art and life were examined under Marxist illumination by pale Incapability. In the course of a whole decade I took pains to free my mind from the Marxist rubbish it had been crammed with at school and at the university.

"From 1930 onwards I worked first as an assistant editor, then as an editor at the State Fiction Publishing House (Gosizdat Khudozhestvennoy Literatury). There I made the acquaintance of many writers, among them Mayakovsky and Boris Pilniak, whom I loved very much both as a man and as the most prominent writer of post-revolutionary Russia. Then I approached a group of young writers, 'Pereval' (Pass), and there became friends with B. Guber, Nikolay Zarudin, Ivan Kataev. All of them were arrested in 1937 and died in concentration camps.

"As a writer of fiction I first was printed in 1935, when the magazine *Novy Mir* (New World) published my first short story, 'Night in Kharachoie,' and then in 1938 my novella 'Desdemona.' I was also doing translations from various languages, but this work never quite absorbed me. My only achievement in this field I consider a book of translations of contemporary Italian poets; I translated verse by sixty-eight Italian lyric poets, but on instructions of the Soviet rulers this book was withheld from publication in Russia—it will be included in my collected works, edited abroad by the publishing house Possev.

"As time went by, and especially after World War II (I was a war correspondent), the consciousness was rooted ever more deeply in me that the Communist rulers were nothing more than a camarilla of scoundrels and murderers, oppressors of freedom, and tyrants. Right after the war I decided to write a series of novels representing the villainy of the Communist regime. I was aware that under the Communist power I would not be able to have them published in my country and so sent the manuscripts abroad. After the publication of my book *The Bluebottle* the regime had me sent to a lunatic asylum. I spent more then seven months in the psychiatric clinic of Kashchenko, and only under pressure of public opinion in the West was I released. Hundreds of papers all over the world wrote about me. Hundreds of prominent cultural personalities demanded that the Soviet Government release me. Much assistance came from abroad from my friends of the Solidarists' Union (N.T.S.), a Russian anti-Communist organization. On leaving the lunatic asylum I wrote the novella *Ward 7* that subsequently was translated into dozens of languages and was met with sympathy by the entire world.

"In February 1966 I was allowed to travel to England to lecture at some universities, and ten days after my departure I was deprived of my Soviet citizenship, which made it impossible for me to return to my fatherland. There, youth had more and more been following my example, particularly so a large group of young writers and artists known as S.M.O.G. Abroad I visited many European countries and America, unveiled the truth about the Soviet tyrants and told of the sufferings of my unfortunate Russia.

"Apart from the books mentioned above, my trilogy 'The Pleasure Factory' (Kombinat naslazhdeniy) has already been published. I am preparing another trilogy, 'The Beauty and Its Shadow,' for the press, and have just finished an anti-utopian novel *Who Likes the Impossible*. At the same time I am working on the trilogy 'The Life of Valentin Almazov,' which represents a continuation of *Ward 7* and will contain also the two novels *Not Far From Moscow* and *The Free World*.

"I have also written much lyric poetry and several long poems that make up my books of verse *The Night Divorces the Day* and *The Ladder of Enchantment*, as well as some cycles of philosophical sketches that will be published in the book *Risky Conjectures*; an historical novel on the Italian

Renascence, *The Florentine Lily*; and a comedy, *Thanks, Not for Me*. My collected works fill fourteen volumes. Thousands of articles have been written about my books and myself in all the languages of the world.

"My family life in Russia was not happy either. I was divorced from my wife. My daughter Natasha, a student, lives in Moscow. At Lucerne, Switzerland, I met my present wife, Hanna Dormann, a remarkable girl and wonderful friend, who helps me live, work, create."

After meeting Tarsis in London when he first left Russia, *Encounter*'s columnist "R" wrote: "Even the severest critic of the Soviet Union might hesitate to concur in his *simpliste* view of it as the naked and absolute embodiment of evil." This uncompromising hatred is a damaging element in his creative work, for as Katharine Hunter Blair observes: "There are passages in his works . . . which show him to be potentially a fine writer and scholar. But everything he writes is so overlaid with vituperations against the regime he hates that literature becomes as lost to polemic as it was in the Stalinist novel."

The two stories *Skazanie o sinyey mukhe* (translated as *The Bluebottle*) and *Krasnoye i chernoye* (translated as *Red and Black*) were originally published in the West under the pseudonym "Ivan Valeriy." The first tells the story of Ivan Sinebryukhov, a party philosopher who has identified communism with his own utopian vision of a society where everyone would, like himself, literally be incapable of hurting a fly. One hot summer afternoon, however, busy writing a treatise on the need for discipline in socialist societies, he chases and kills a bluebottle which has been annoying him. This experience transforms him, for if he can kill a fly, with all its zest for life, why shouldn't he kill his wife, who causes him much greater annoyance? He becomes disgusted with Communist society and then with the whole swarming fly-like mass of humanity. Society destroys spiritual values, he concludes, and he comes to see himself as the savior of mankind, "a mountain torrent to sweep away the rottenness of the world."

The hero of *Krasnoye i chernoye* is a professor of French, like Tarsis himself an authority on Stendhal, who relieves his spiritual starvation, his hunger for beauty, by idolizing his beautiful wife Rimma. The story traces his disillusionment as he discovers that she is spoiled and shallow, a typically synthetic product of our materialistic age, conditioned into a "stony indifference to human beings." On their annual holiday in Sochi, where they had met, he commits suicide by swimming out to sea.

These two stories, published together as *The Bluebottle*, were received by Western critics with almost unanimous enthusiasm. V. S. Pritchett wrote: "It is impossible to convey without long quotations the tenderness, the irony, the intense fragmentary perceptions of [*The Bluebottle*] which is a curious mixture of Stendhalian dryness and Russian poetry. . . . Tarsis is a minor writer but he is a symptom of a stirring, secret life."

Palata no. 7 (1965, translated as *Ward 7*) is in its autobiographical aspect the story of a writer whose criticisms of Soviet life are punished by incarceration in a lunatic asylum. But the choice of title and the way the novel is written suggest a deliberate parallel with Chekhov's story *Palata no. 6*, in which the doctor in charge of a hospital in a dreary provincial town finds that the only other intelligent person in the place is officially a madman. Tarsis presents the inmates of his *Ward 7* as abnormal only in their dissent from Soviet orthodoxy. The entire ward takes a "solemn oath to rouse the forces of freedom," which to them means a call for an "aristocratic, world-wide society of individuals. There needn't be many; about ten million would be enough." The masses must be destroyed, including "whole races, and with them, all the flabby humanists."

Katherine Hunter Blair wrote: "It is this sort of statement which prevents these three works of Tarsis from being the powerful indictment of the Soviet system which he obviously intended them to be. One can feel sympathy with the odd man out, and still more with the Kafkaesque victim of totalitarianism; but when he thinks of himself as the savior of mankind it is hard to take him seriously."

There have been similar reservations about the novels which make up Tarsis's "Pleasure Factory" or Black Sea trilogy: *The Pleasure Factory*, *The Gay Life*, and *A Thousand Illusions*. All three are set in a resort town, called Razdolnoye (meaning roughly *la dolce vita*), and examine the various illusions, including physical self-indulgence and social utopianism, which are all that remain to men when they lose faith in God. The same views are expressed in *Russia and the Russians*, a book of photographs with a text in which Tarsis continues his onslaught on the Soviet Union and looks forward to a future "Holy Russia"—a profession of faith reminiscent of the nineteenth century Slavophiles.

Tarsis's recent books have been criticized for their "threadbare ideological debate," their puppetlike characters, and what has been called the author's "monumental egocentricity." It may be that the undoubted interest of Tarsis's work is, as one critic puts it, 'sovietological rather than literary, its forces coming less from the author's powers of observation and description than from his extreme dislike of the Soviet system."

Tarsis is a heavily built man with thin gray hair and a massive, heavily lined face. "R," in *Encounter*, says, "It would be only too easy to see Tarsis himself as one of Dostoevsky's holy fools, an Alyosha or a Prince Myshkin, who look at society from a viewpoint so totally different from that of the established order that except in the eyes of sinners and children they are inevitably judged to be mad." According to his lights, however, "one feels convinced that he is a witness of truth, whose testimony demands the most serious consideration, particularly because one has no doubt of his own honesty, integrity, and sincerity of purpose."

PRINCIPAL WORKS IN ENGLISH TRANSLATION: The Bluebottle, tr. by Thomas Jones (published with Red and Black, tr. by David Alger), 1962; Ward 7: An Autobiographical Novel (tr. by Katya Brown), 1965; The Pleasure Factory (tr. by Michael Glenny), 1967; The Gay Life (tr. by Drive Parker), 1968; A Thousand Illusions (tr. by Michel le Masque), 1969; Russia and the Russians (tr. by Ilse Barker), 1970.

ABOUT: Blair, K. H. A Review of Soviet Literature, 1967. *Periodicals*—Encounter April 1966; New Republic September 28, 1963; New Statesman December 14, 1962; February 25, 1966; August 2, 1968; June 27, 1969; Newsweek February 21, 1966; March 14, 1966; Reporter October 21, 1965; Spectator November 16, 1962; August 16, 1968; February 28, 1970; Time May 21, 1965; March 4, 1966; Times Educational Supplement May 8, 1970; Times Literary Supplement November 9, 1962; May 20, 1965.

"TATE, ELLALICE." *See* HIBBERT, ELEANOR BURFORD

TAYLOR, A(LAN) J(OHN) P(ERCIVALE) (March 25, 1906–), English historian and journalist, was born of Quaker ancestry in Birkdale, Lancashire, the son of Percy Lees and Constance Sumner Taylor. He was educated at the Bootham School, York (1919–1924), and at Oriel College, Oxford. His graduation in 1927 was followed by a period of study in Vienna, aided by a Rockefeller Fellowship. Taylor began his career as a lecturer in history at Manchester University (1930–1938). In 1938 he returned to Oxford as fellow and tutor in modern history at Magdalen College, where he remained until 1963. From 1953 to 1963 he was also a lecturer in international history to the university as a whole. He is a superb teacher, "stimulating, often inspiring, sometimes infuriating," for whom "the paradox is his favourite method." The same qualities have made him one of the most effective and popular lecturers ever to have appeared on British television, and a highly successful journalist.

His first book was *The Italian Problem in European Diplomacy, 1847–1849* (1934). In it he wrote: "The course of national policy is based upon a series of assumptions, with which statesmen have lived since their earliest years and which they regard as so axiomatic as hardly to be worth stating." Taylor argued that the history of Europe could be seen as a series of conflicts between such assumptions, and that "it is the historian's duty to make the contradictions and the misunderstandings plain." The book contains ample evidence of Taylor's immensely wide reading and exceptional insight and, though it is a sober work by his later standards, is not devoid of his dogmatism and wit.

Germany's First Bid for Colonies and *The Habsburg Monarchy* were followed by a pungent and provocative survey of German history from 1815 to the end of World War II, *The Course of German History*. "I am not an impartial historian; I prefer the truth," Taylor wrote in his preface to this book, and indeed many reviewers complained that it was more an indictment of Germany than a history. Taylor replied that the Germans had indicted themselves: "No civilized nation has such a record of atrocity." *The Struggle for Mastery in Europe, 1848–1918*, a diplomatic history, was also characteristically full of generalizations, some of them thought overstated or prejudiced, many of them brilliantly illuminating. And there was much praise for Taylor's fascinating and convincing psychological study of Bismarck, which followed. His 1955–1956 Ford Lectures had a much harsher reception when they were published as *The Trouble Makers: Dissent Over Foreign Policy, 1792–1939*: "Verification of facts seems not to matter," one critic wrote, "provided only that they would illustrate the right points if they happened to be facts." (The author, almost predictably, thinks this his best book.)

Taylor's next book, *The Origins of the Second World War*, created a furor. In it he argues that Hitler had never sought war, only a peaceful revision of the Treaty of Versailles: "The war of 1939, far from being premeditated, was a mistake, the result on both sides of diplomatic blunders." On the face of it, this seemed a complete reversal of the "Germanophobic" opinions expressed in Taylor's earlier works. None of the book's reviewers denied that it was "a dazzling performance," brilliantly written and irresistibly readable; very few found it convincing, and most, sadly or furiously, noted in it many errors of fact and a selective use of evidence. Beyond that a few voices could be heard praising Taylor's "integrity and courage" in thus revising his views, while others thundered that he had made "a grotesque attempt to stand history on its head," and given comfort "to the neo-Nazis in Germany and to the forces of evil everywhere." The most savage and systematic attack came from Hugh Trevor-Roper, writing in *Encounter*. The two adversaries subsequently met on television where (most thought) Taylor stole the show without necessarily winning his case.

No comparable uproar has greeted Taylor's

subsequent books, of which the most notable is *English History, 1914–1945*, his contribution to the Oxford History of England. Covering two world wars and the Great Depression, and dealing with strategy, politics, economics, and social welfare, it is Taylor's most ambitious book and is widely regarded as the best one-volume treatment of this enormous subject in existence. He meets "the immense difficulties of such an effort sometimes idiosyncratically, always spiritedly—and, on the whole, admirably." The book did much to remind those who had forgotten them of Taylor's "quite outstanding gifts" as a historian.

He "escaped with relief" from teaching in 1963, and is now honorary director of the Beaverbrook Library in London and a research fellow of Magdalen College. *Beaverbrook*, Taylor's excellent if rather uncritical biography of his old friend, appeared in 1972. Taylor is or has been a contributor to a wide spectrum of newspapers, including the *Sunday Express*, the *Observer*, the *New Statesman*, and the *Guardian*. His television appearances have made him familiar to millions in England: "The tousled face; the quizzical smile; the light voice with the broad Lancashire vowels; the intense nervous vitality and emotional warmth; the sudden rat-trap snap of the mouth, the air of mischievous gaiety like a small boy playing truant from school." He has been twice married and has six children.

The *New Statesman* has called him "the pyrotechnician of history," whose wit and malicious insight are directed as much against the left (to which he is committed) as the right. "It is his own idiosyncratic vision of what actually happened that excites him, not some intellectual theory of history. . . . He frisks about the past, like a terrier hunting rabbits, occupied solely by the search, uninterested in what he may have discovered last time, or what system his discoveries will fit."

PRINCIPAL WORKS: The Italian Problem in European Diplomacy, 1847–1849, 1934; Germany's First Bid for Colonies, 1884–1885, 1938; The Habsburg Monarchy, 1815–1918, 1941 (rev. in 1949 as The Habsburg Monarchy, 1809–1918); The Course of German History, 1945; From Napoleon to Stalin (essays), 1950; Rumours of Wars (essays), 1952; The Struggle for Mastery in Europe, 1848–1918, 1954; Bismarck: The Man and the Statesman, 1955; Englishmen and Others (essays), 1956; The Trouble Makers: Dissent Over Foreign Policy, 1792–1939, 1957; The Russian Revolution (television scripts), 1959; The Origins of the Second World War, 1961; The First World War, 1963 (U.S., An Illustrated History of the First World War); Politics in Wartime (essays), 1964; English History, 1914–1945, 1965; From Sarajevo to Potsdam, 1966; Europe: Grandeur and Decline, 1967; War by Timetable: How the First World War Began, 1969; (ed.) Lloyd George: Twelve Essays, 1971; (ed.) Lloyd George: A Diary by Frances Stevenson, 1971; Beaverbrook, 1972.

ABOUT: Contemporary Authors 7–8, 1963; International Who's Who, 1973–74; Mehta, V. Fly and the Fly Bottle, 1962; Namier, L. B. Facing East, 1948; Who's Who, 1973; Who's Who in America, 1972–1973. *Periodicals*—Canadian Historical Review June 1962; Encounter July 1961, September 1961, January 1964; New Republic April 29, 1967; New Statesman June 8, September 28, 1957; December 31, 1965; November 25, 1966; New York Review of Books May 6, December 9, 1965; New Yorker December 8, 1962; Review of Politics October 1964; Newsweek July 31, 1961; Review of World Politics January 1962; Spectator June 7, 1963; Times Literary Supplement September 29, 1945; February 26, 1949; July 7, 1950; November 26, 1954; July 15, 1955; December 16, 1965; World Politics October 1955.

A. J. P. TAYLOR

TAYLOR, KAMALA. *See* "MARKANDAYA," KAMALA

TAYLOR, ROBERT LEWIS (September 24, 1912–), American novelist, journalist, and biographer, was born Robert Taylor in Carbondale, Illinois, the son of Roscoe and Mabel (Bowyer) Taylor. He went to Carbondale schools and to Southern Illinois University in the same city, but left the latter in 1930 after a year to complete his education at the University of Illinois. He did his first professional writing while he was still a student.

Graduating in 1933 with a B.A., Taylor spent a year abroad, making a bicycle tour of six European countries. He returned to the United States in 1934, worked for a year as editor of the Carbondale weekly newspaper, and then, seized once more by wanderlust, sailed for Tahiti. Taylor lived in various parts of Polynesia during 1935, supporting himself by writing articles for the *American Boy* magazine, and drifted home via New Zealand, Fiji, and Honolulu, where he worked briefly for the Honolulu *Advertiser*.

ROBERT LEWIS TAYLOR

In 1936, back in the United States, Taylor tried but failed to find work in New York, and for the next three years was a reporter for the St. Louis *Post-Dispatch*. In 1939 he received an award for his work from Sigma Delta Chi, the honorary journalism fraternity. The same year he was hired by the *New Yorker* as a "profile" writer. It was at this time that he added the "Lewis" to his professional name, to avoid confusion with other celebrated Taylors.

Taylor remained on the *New Yorker* staff, writing profiles and reporter-at-large articles, until 1948. Even during World War II, when Taylor spent four years in the Navy (1942–1946), he continued to write articles from notes supplied by other members of the magazine's staff. He was discharged from the Navy in 1946 with the rank of lieutenant commander.

Adrift in a Boneyard, Taylor's first novel, was an "astringent" fantasy about a handful of people who survive a world catastrophe, and was received with moderate approval. Much more successful was *Doctor, Lawyer, Merchant, Chief*—a collection of profiles, travel pieces, and short stories which had originally appeared in the *New Yorker*, *Life*, *Saturday Evening Post*, and *Redbook*. Reviewers were particularly impressed by the biographical articles, which showed a capacity for imaginative sympathy with a great variety of people and "a really eclectic intelligence."

These qualities were demonstrated during the next six years in as many books, all of them generally well received. There were biographies of W. C. Fields and of Winston Churchill, both commissioned by and originally published in the *Saturday Evening Post*; a second collection of magazine pieces published as *The Running Pianist*; and a series of *New Yorker* profiles of circus performers collected in *Center Ring*. *Professor Fodorski* and *The Bright Sands*, two novels published at this time, attracted less attention.

It was, however, a novel which brought Taylor his first major success. This was *The Travels of Jaimie McPheeters* (1958), "a hilarious and hair-raising fiction" about the California gold rush based in part on the journals of Dr. Joseph Middleton. The fourteen-year-old Jaimie and his father, a flamboyant failed doctor reminiscent of W. C. Fields, begin their wagon trek to California in the spring of 1849. On the way, Jaimie is kidnapped by Indians, sees much savagery, nearly starves, loses his father, but winds up as part owner of a California ranch to live happily ever after with the rest of his family and his Indian sweetheart. The *New Yorker*'s reviewer found the book "full of thoroughly researched *minutiae* . . . [and] delivered in a cheerful, funny, and headlong prose that makes its unabashed theatricality a total delight." Most reviewers agreed, and the novel received the Pulitzer Prize in 1959.

Taylor has since published two other novels in the same picaresque manner. *A Journey to Matecumbe* describes the flight from Kentucky to the Florida Keys of young Davey Burnie and his Uncle Jim, with the Ku Klux Klan in hot pursuit. It is set in the 1870s and is as scrupulously accurate as its predecessor in its historical and geographical detail. Some reviewers thought it borrowed a little too freely from *Huckleberry Finn*, but most praised it as "superlative entertainment," bubbling "with life and the enjoyment of it."

Two Roads to Guadalupé, another picaresque about a boy who runs away from home to fight in the Mexican War, was rather less successful. One critic however was impressed by Taylor's feat in "combining essentially antipathetic elements: savage, shapeless history, and jesting, shapely story." Taylor has said that the book took two years to write and that "the boy here was me, let's face it. I had a damn good time as a boy, hunting, fishing, outwitting my parents, and I can imagine I was the sort of boy in the book."

Taylor was married in 1945 to Judith Martin. They have two children and live in Sharon, Connecticut. An interviewer has said of Taylor that "he looks at the world literally with amused eyes . . . not taking himself or anything else—except the art of being funny—seriously."

PRINCIPAL WORKS: *Novels*—Adrift in a Boneyard, 1947; Professor Fodorski, 1950; The Bright Sands, 1954; The Travels of Jaimie McPheeters, 1958; A Journey to Matecumbe, 1961; Two Roads to Guadalupé, 1964. *Nonfiction*—Doctor, Lawyer, Merchant, Chief, 1948; W. C. Fields: His Follies and Fortunes, 1949; The Running Pianist, 1950; Winston Churchill: An Informal Study of

Greatness, 1952 (reissued as The Amazing Mister Churchill, 1962); Center Ring: The People of the Circus, 1956; Vessel of Wrath: The Life and Times of Carry Nation, 1966.

ABOUT: Americana Annual, 1960; Current Biography, 1959; Newquist, R. (ed.) Counterpoint, 1965; Vinson, J. (ed.) Contemporary Novelists, 1972; Who's Who in America, 1972–1973. *Periodicals*—New York Times Book Review August 30, 1964; Saturday Review February 14, 1948.

***TCHERNICHOVSKI, SAUL** (January 3, 1875–October 14, 1943), Hebrew poet, was born in the village of Mikhailovka in the Crimea, near the Ukrainian border, where he spent the first fourteen years of his life. As he recalled in one of his poems, his Orthodox Jewish family was an ancient and illustrious one. Unlike other Hebrew poets, he grew up not in the constricting atmosphere of the ghetto but in the open steppes of his native landscape, with its relics of classical antiquity and its confluence of cultures. He played with the peasant children and attended the village school. His native language was not Yiddish, but Russian, and one of the early influences in his life was his mother's love for Russian songs and literature.

When Tchernichovski began to study Hebrew at the age of seven, he was not schooled in the traditional *heder* or *yeshiva*, but was privately tutored by two Latvian teachers, who instructed him in popular Hebrew literature as well as the Talmud and the Scriptures, and stimulated his interest in Zionism. He also became acquainted at an early age with the works (in Russian) of Homer, Shakespeare, Dumas, and Jules Verne. At the age of twelve he wrote and illustrated a long poem about Uriah the Hittite.

Tchernichovski received his secondary education at commercial schools in Odessa, where he studied German, French, English, and classical languages. In 1899 he went to Heidelberg University in Germany to study medicine, and there he also took courses in Italian and the history of religions and attended the lectures in modern philosophy of Professor Kuno Fischer. After four years at Heidelberg he studied for three years at Lausanne, Switzerland, receiving his degree as doctor of medicine in 1907.

The two elements that characterized Tchernichovski's writings from the beginning were a militant Jewish nationalism and an almost pagan passion for beauty. In his first published poem, which appeared in 1892 in an American Hebrew weekly published in Baltimore, he expressed his contempt for ghetto life and called for retribution for the sufferings of the Jews. His early work also included many nature lyrics and lighthearted love poems. A young man of fine physique and much gaiety, he was as a student involved in an endless succession of affairs, many of them with non-Jewish girls. Tchernichovski's first book of poetry, *Hezyonot umanginot* (Visions and Melodies), was published in 1898, and immediately won him the admiration and friendship of the major young Hebrew literary figures of the time, Bialik, Fishman, and Klausner.

SAUL TCHERNICHOVSKI

For the first three years of his medical career, Tchernichovski practiced in the Russian provinces. In 1907 he was imprisoned for six weeks by the Czarist regime for reasons that remain obscure. Later he practiced in St. Petersburg as an assistant in the Royal Institute of Medicine. In 1914 he volunteered for service in the Russian army. He served for two years at the front and then in military hospitals, at the same time writing poems that reflected the sufferings of war. He continued to work in Russian hospitals for a few years after the Bolshevik Revolution. In 1922 he moved to Berlin, and during the next few years traveled widely in Europe, Palestine, and the United States. He settled in Palestine in 1931, becoming physician to the city schools of Tel Aviv.

Tchernichovski was active in virtually every branch of literature except the novel, but he was best known for his poems, of which he wrote some five hundred during his lifetime. They established him, along with H. N. Bialik and Zalman Shneour, as one of the "great triumvirate of modern Hebrew poetry." In his universalist outlook he differed from Bialik, who was steeped in Jewish history and tradition throughout his life. He has been described as a "strongly masculine poet," who drew strength from the elemental and primeval in nature, and whose works were colored by a passionate belief

* cher ni KOV′ skē

in humanity, a scientist's sense of realism, and an artist's eye for detail. His pantheist tendencies, which earned him the title "Hellene," or "poet of paganism," were motivated by his interest in the convergence of the Judaic and Hellenic traditions, and his belief that Judaism must free itself from the mentality of the ghetto and return to a freer, wilder, and more ancient tradition.

In his poems dealing with specifically Jewish themes, Tchernichovski pays tribute to the *chalutz*, or tiller of the soil, and describes historical and contemporary examples of Jewish martyrdom and heroism, as in the poems "Baruch Mimagenza," "Martyrs of Dortmund," "A Passover of Oppression," and "Let This Be Our Revenge," and in the cycle of sonnets "On the Blood," which dealt with the Ukrainian pogroms that took place at the end of World War I. His colorful idylls, which are among his best work, describe the joys and hardships of Jewish life in rural southern Russia. Important collections of his poetry include *Mahberet hasonnetot* (Sheaf of Sonnets, 1922); *Sefer ha idilyot* (Book of Idylls, 1922); *Hehalil* (The Flute, 1923), a volume of children's verse; *Shirim hadashim* (New Poems, 1925); *Shirim* (Poems, 1937); and *Re'i adomah* (Behold, O Earth, 1940), for which he received the Bialik prize. *Kokhvei Shamayim Rehokim* (Stars of Distant Skies), a volume of poems in which he reflects upon his life, was published posthumously in 1944.

In his prose works, which are inferior to his verse, Tchernichovski was influenced stylistically by his close friend, the Hebrew novelist Mendele Mokher Seforim. He also wrote scientific monographs, edited a Hebrew-Latin-English medical dictionary, and contributed to encyclopedias. His translations of literary classics into Hebrew are unexcelled. They include Homer's *Iliad* and *Odyssey*, the Babylonian epic *Gilgamesh*, the Finnish saga *Kalevala*, and works by Sophocles, Plato, Horace, Shakespeare, Goethe, Heine, Molière, Pushkin, and Longfellow. A ten-volume collection of his works, *Kitve*, was published in Berlin and Tel Aviv between 1929 and 1934.

Stylistically, Tchernichovski was an innovator. He wrote the first Hebrew sonnets, and drew his language and poetic forms as much from the Hebrew traditions of Spain and Italy as from the Bible and the Haggadah. He even coined his own words where he found Hebrew inadequate. "For me," Tchernichovski once wrote, "poetry is always an act of love, an act of triumph." Ruth Finer Mintz calls him "a poet at home in the world," who "accepted change as a natural law," and Eisig Silberschlag says that he "marked out a new road by his attachment to a vigorous past and by his epic insight into the healthy elements of Diaspora Jewry."

PRINCIPAL WORKS IN ENGLISH TRANSLATION: Poems *in* Birman, A. An Anthology of Modern Hebrew Poetry, 1959; Burnshaw, S. (ed.) The Modern Hebrew Poem Itself, 1965; Mintz, R. F. Modern Hebrew Poetry, 1968; Penueli, S. Y. and Ukhmani, A. Anthology of Modern Hebrew Poetry, 1966.

ABOUT: Penguin Companion to Literature 2, 1969; Ribalow, M. The Flowering of Modern Hebrew Literature, 1959; Snowman, L. Tchernichovski and His Poetry, 1929. *Periodicals*—Commentary January 1946.

***TEILHARD DE CHARDIN, (MARIE JOSEPH) PIERRE** (May 1, 1881–April 10, 1955), was a French palaeontologist and Jesuit priest whose posthumously published works on the meaning of evolution and the future of man have made him an important, though controversial, force in contemporary thought.

Teilhard was born in the village of Sarcenat, in the Auvergne district of central France. He was the fourth of the eleven children of Emmanuel Teilhard and Berthe-Adèle de Dompierre d'Hornoy, who was a collateral descendant of Voltaire; the ending "de Chardin" came from his maternal grandmother. His father was a country gentleman of means and a scholar with an interest in the history of this ancient volcanic region of the Massif Central who inculcated in the boy an abiding passion for animals and plants, and for the rocks and extinct volcanoes of the region. His "dear and sainted mother" at the same time brought him up as a deeply religious child, until in 1892 he left the shelter of the family school-room and started his formal education at the Jesuit college at Villefranche-sur-Saône. Highly intelligent and hardworking, he won many prizes, though he was nearly always bottom in religious instruction because he "didn't care for the way that they put religion across."

At the age of seventeen Teilhard decided to dedicate his life to religion and began his novitiate as a Jesuit at Aix-en-Provence in 1899. However, with anticlericalism at its height in France, the seminary was within two years evacuated to Jersey. At the age of twenty-four he was sent to Cairo to teach physics and chemistry in a Jesuit school. His *Lettres d'Égypte 1905–1908* (1963, translated by M. Ilford as *Letters from Egypt*) show his warm relationship with his parents, to whom they were addressed, and evoke his delight in searching the hills and deserts for fossils. It was at this time that he began to communicate the results of his geological expeditions in papers to learned societies.

In 1908, at the age of twenty-seven, he began the Jesuits' customary four-year study of theology, for which he was sent to Hastings, England. He also continued his scientific studies and met the amateur geologist Charles Dawson, the discoverer (and presumably the forger) of Piltdown Man. It was in

* tā yär′ də shär daN′

fact Teilhard who, visiting Piltdown with Dawson in 1913, had the "good fortune" to find "the canine tooth from the jaw of the famous Piltdown Man." He was ordained to the priesthood in 1911 and sent to Paris the following year to study natural science. His life during these years is recorded in *Lettres d'Hastings et de Paris* (1965, translated in two volumes as *Letters from Hastings, 1908–1912* and *Letters from Paris, 1912–1914*).

During World War I he enlisted as a noncombatant stretcher-bearer in the medical corps. He served throughout as a corporal, refusing a chaplain's commission, and was awarded several medals for bravery under fire, including the Croix de Guerre and the Médaille Militaire. These four years were crucial in the development both of his personality and of his ideas, which are reflected in *Genèse d'une pensée* (1961, translated by R. Hague as *The Making of a Mind: Letters from a Soldier-Priest 1914–1919*), the letters which he wrote to his cousin Marguerite Teillard-Chambon; and in the essays published as *Écrits du temps de la guerre 1916–1919* (1965, translated by R. Hague as *Writings in Time of War*). As Dr. Bernard Towers has observed, there could be no better introduction to Teilhard than these two books about his wartime experiences; "they form an indispensable stepping-stone to his more advanced works, where at times his passion for neologisms, and the dexterity with which he mingles scientific, poetical and mystical insights, become somewhat confusing."

Demobilized in 1919, Teilhard went back to the Sorbonne and finished his degree in natural sciences, then did research under Marcelin Boule for his doctorate in palaeontology, publishing his thesis in 1922. He then taught geology at the Institut Catholique, until in 1923 he accepted the invitation of a fellow-Jesuit, Father Licent, to join a palaeontological expedition to China. Between 1924 and 1926 he was back in France writing and publishing a large number of scientific papers on the work he had done in China. But some of his ideas about original sin and its relation to evolution were regarded as unorthodox by his religious superiors, who became worried by his independence of mind and the effect of his "dangerous" speculations on his students. He was instructed to concentrate on scientific work and forbidden to continue teaching or to publish during his lifetime any of his speculative philosophical and theological writings. In 1926 he was sent back to China, where he was to stay, apart from brief visits to France and the United States and excursions to Indonesia and Ethiopia, for twenty years. Many of his biographers have regarded this as virtual banishment, though the journeys of exploration he made in China resulted in his most important palaeontological work.

By the time of his first visit to the Far East the

PIERRE TEILHARD DE CHARDIN

outlines of Teilhard's thought had become clearly defined. While working as scientific adviser to the Geological Survey of China, centered at Tientsin and later at Peking, and taking part in expeditions such as the one led by Davidson Black in 1929 which discovered Peking Man, he was writing the books by which he was posthumously to become famous. What is often regarded as his greatest single work, *Le Milieu divin* (1957, translated by Bernard Wall and others as *The Divine Milieu*) was completed in 1927. In the late 1930s he wrote *Le Phénomène humain* (1955, translated by Wall as *The Phenomenon of Man*), which became an immediate best seller when it was finally published after his death.

These books, like all Teilhard's philosophical works, center on his synthesis of the scientific facts of evolution with his own Christian understanding of the history of salvation. In effect, he extends the Christian history of salvation to explain the evolution of life and the development of the universe as a whole. His central thesis is that evolution progresses in a *directed* manner, from simple atoms to the complex forms of living organisms, and so to man and consciousness. His key concept is what he called *le loi de complexité-conscience* (the law of increasing complexity-consciousness). This states that throughout time there has been a tendency for matter to become increasingly complex in its organization, and that the growing material complexity of organisms is accompanied by a corresponding development in consciousness. Science has hitherto concentrated on the opposite tendency, that of organized matter to disintegrate in accordance with the second law of thermodynamics, a form of energy which Teilhard distinguishes as "tangential energy." In contrast to this he describes the evolutionary form of natural energy as "radial energy," an energy which seeks union and is therefore a dynamic force inherent in physical structure, eventually manifesting itself as love.

Teilhard then extends this reading of the evolutionary past into the future. For although man no longer seems to be undergoing any significant physical change, evolution, Teilhard believed, has not stopped. Rather he saw it as having three stages: first a chemical process, then the organic evolution of the biosphere, and finally the development of the "noosphere"—the thinking layer of our earth represented by the mind of man. In man the evolutionary process has become self-conscious, and to some extent self-determined. But the evolutionary process is fundamentally religious in nature, since consciousness (which gives man his capacity for spiritual growth) would never have shown itself but for the indwelling spirit, operative throughout time both as alpha, the source, and omega, the end. The ultimate destiny of man is to achieve complete unity with God in what Teilhard calls the Omega point, but this is not possible by means of his mind alone. God's evolutionary purpose will be achieved by means of the Incarnation, and now that the noosphere has developed within the biosphere, it has itself started to become the Christosphere, struggling, through the process of Christogenesis which makes all things meaningful, towards the Omega point and ultimate salvation.

Two of Teilhard's scientific colleagues of the period, George Barbour and Helmut de Terra, have written books about their experiences with him, and he has left his own accounts of his expeditions to the Gobi desert, Sinkiang, and Indonesia in *Lettres de voyage 1923–1939* (1956, translated with *Nouvelles lettres de voyage 1939–1955*, 1957, by R. Hague and others, as *Letters from a Traveller*). Other collections of his letters have also been published and reveal the mental anguish he suffered because he was not allowed to publish, especially when after his return to France at the end of World War II he was also refused permission to become a candidate for the highest academic post in France, that of professor at the Collège de France. In 1951 he accepted an appointment as a research fellow with the Wenner-Gren Foundation for Anthropological Research in New York, and apart from two visits to South Africa to examine the remains of early man then being discovered there, the rest of his life was spent in the United States. He had said he hoped he might die "on the day of the Resurrection," and it was indeed on Easter Day 1955 that he died of a heart attack, without any warning, while at tea with some friends.

After his death a commission was formed to publish his work. The books which have since appeared include several collections of his essays and other occasional pieces, with titles chosen by his editors, such as *L'Avenir de l'homme* (1962, translated by N. Denny as *The Future of Man*) and *La Place de l'homme dans la nature: le groupe zoologique humain* (1956, translated by R. Hague as *Man's Place in Nature: The Human Zoological Group*). In *L'Activation de l'énergie* (1963, translated by Hague as *Activation of Energy*) Teilhard argues that human failures such as breakdown, depression, and drug taking are the consequences of human energy wrongly directed; if only our forces were channeled correctly, spiritual energy as a motor force in the universe would far outdistance technological advance.

Teilhard believed that his conclusions present man with a Grand Option, and it is this evolutionary optimism, this visionary quality in his work, which is chiefly responsible for its immense impact and popularity. However, his views are by no means universally accepted. Sir Julian Huxley wrote a preface for the English edition of *The Phenomenon of Man* welcoming Teilhard's views on human psychosocial evolution but rejecting his Christian vision. Many critics have pointed out that Teilhard's eyes were so firmly fixed on his ecstatic vision of the future that he was almost totally indifferent to the abuses of the present, as in some of his remarks about fascism. John Wren-Lewis and others have suggested that although Teilhard's writings are widely read among young people interested in mysticism, they are read as poetry rather than theology. The most scathing attack on Teilhard from the scientific point of view has come from Sir Peter Medawar, who has claimed that his work is largely antiscientific nonsense tricked out with tedious metaphysical conceits, written in an all but totally unintelligible style of tipsy, euphoric prose-poetry, by a man who "was in no serious sense a thinker. He had about him that innocence which makes it easy to understand why the forger of the Piltdown skull should have chosen Teilhard to be the discoverer of its canine tooth." Nevertheless, he has been hailed by Professor Michael Polanyi as the author of "an epic theory of evolution," and by Dr. Joseph Needham as "the cosmologist of the future." Such biologists as W. H. Thorpe, Bernard Towers, and Theodosius Dobzhansky have all regarded him as a seminal figure of great significance. Teilhard is remembered by his friends as a man of great personal charm, humor, and gaiety, but his work remains as controversial as ever.

PRINCIPAL WORKS IN ENGLISH TRANSLATION: The Phenomenon of Man, 1959; Le Milieu Divin (U.S., The Divine Milieu), 1960; Letters from a Traveller, 1962; The Future of Man, 1964; The Appearance of Man, 1965; Hymn of the Universe, 1965; The Making of a Mind: Letters from a Soldier-Priest, 1914–1919, 1965; Building the Earth, 1965; Letters from Egypt, 1905–1908, 1965;

Man's Place in Nature, 1966; The Vision of the Past, 1966; Letters from Paris 1912–1914, 1967; Teilhard de Chardin Album, ed. by J. Mortier and M. Aboux, 1967; Correspondence (with Maurice Blondel), 1967; Evolution, Marxism and Christianity, 1967; Science and Christ, 1968; Letters from Hastings, 1908–1912, 1968; Letters to Two Friends, 1926–1952, 1968; Writings in Time of War, 1968; Human Energy, 1969; Letters to Léontine Zanta, 1969; Let Me Explain, 1970; Activation of Energy, 1970; Science and Synthesis, 1971; Christianity and Evolution, 1971; On Love, 1972; On Happiness, 1973.

ABOUT: Barbour, G. B. In the Field with Teilhard de Chardin, 1965; Braybrooke, N. (ed.) Teilhard de Chardin: Pilgrim of the Future, 1964; Chauchard, P. Man and Cosmos: Scientific Phenomenology in Teilhard de Chardin, 1965; Corte, N. Pierre Teilhard de Chardin: His Life and Spirit, 1960; Cuénot, C. Teilhard de Chardin: A Biographical Study, 1965; Cuénot, C. Science and Faith in Teilhard de Chardin, 1967; Delfgaauw, B. Evolution: The Theory of Teilhard de Chardin, 1969; Dobzhansky, T. The Biology of Ultimate Concern, 1967; Gray, D. P. The One and the Many: Teilhard de Chardin's Vision of Unity, 1970; Hanson, A. (ed.) Teilhard Reassessed, 1970; Hefner, P. J. The Promise of Teilhard, 1970; Jones, D. G. Teilhard de Chardin, 1970; Keating, M. and Keating, H. R. F. Understanding Pierre Teilhard de Chardin, 1969; Klauder, F. J. Aspects of the Thought of Teilhard de Chardin, 1971; Lubac, H. de. The Faith of Teilhard de Chardin, 1965; Lubac, H. de. The Religion of Teilhard de Chardin, 1967; Macquarrie, J. Twentieth-Century Religious Thought, 1963; Medawar, P. B. The Art of the Soluble, 1967; Mooney, C. Teilhard de Chardin and the Mystery of Christ, 1966; O'Manique, J. Energy in Evolution, 1969; Rabut, O. Teilhard de Chardin, 1961; Rideau, E. The Thought of Teilhard de Chardin, 1968; Speaight, R. Teilhard de Chardin, 1967; Terra, H. de. Memories of Teilhard de Chardin, 1964; Towers, B. Teilhard de Chardin, 1965; Towers, B. and Dyson, A. O. (eds.) Evolution, Marxism and Christianity: Studies in the Teilhardian Synthesis, 1967; Tresmontant, C. Pierre Teilhard de Chardin: His Thought, 1959; Wagar, W. W. (ed.) Science, Faith, and Man; European Thought Since 1914, 1968; Wildiers, N. M. An Introduction to Teilhard de Chardin, 1968; Zaehner, R. C. Evolution in Religion: A Study in Sri Aurobindo and Pierre Teilhard de Chardin, 1971.

TENNANT, KYLIE (March 12, 1912–), Australian novelist, historian, playwright, critic, and editor, writes: "My father innocently mentions that his ancestors cultivated the oat patch next to Robert Burns. As there must have been females in the Tennant family at that time, this is an anecdote he would do better to suppress. His great-grandfather, Glenconner, swapped poems with Burns and I have seen those extant. A glen in Scotland is a gully in Australia, so out here he would be Connor of Connor's Gully. Grandfather Tennant was a Greek scholar and theologian who earned his living as a doctor. My great-grandmother was Julia Cullen, sister of an Irish Cardinal. Bespoken by a convent, Julia ran off with a Presbyterian landscape gardener. This double disgrace condemned Julia to walking three hundred miles behind a dray from Sydney to Braidwood, to take up land. The convict servants ran away to the goldfields, her husband tried his luck there, too, setting up a long family tradition by returning penniless.

KYLIE TENNANT

He beat a retreat to land closer to Sydney where he planted orange groves and a garden with a fountain, providing Julia, whom he called 'Pinky,' with a carriage with white ponies.

"Mother's relations arrived by sailing ship, probably arguing all the way. They became Christian Scientists and I inherited a metaphysical bent. My husband is High Church of England and so am I. Max Harris, the Australian critic, says I am the last of the Philistines who hold nothing sacred. Reviewing is my only blood sport. I particularly dislike books by young men whose girls have left them and who think everyone should know about it. But I do like books about people doing things and working, biographies, books about animals, weather or cookery.

"My own novels (most of which have been published in the U.S.A.) have been written very much the hard way. For *The Battlers*, I tramped or drove a cart long journeys of many hundreds of miles; for *The Joyful Condemned* I went to gaol; for *Foveaux* and *Ride on Stranger*, I lived in slums, worked in reformatories, as a barmaid, a church sister and an organizer of the unemployed. For *Lost Haven* I worked with a shipbuilder. For *The Honey Flow* I joined the migratory bee-keepers. In recent years, respectability has crept up on me. I am afraid of aeroplanes because I think the wings will fall off, but am constantly tramping aboard yet another flight to lecture somewhere or attend meetings. I have lectured at most Australian universities for the Commonwealth Literary Fund, and am the only woman member of the Advisory Board to the Fund, a government body which allocates a hundred thousand dollars a year for fellowships to writers, subsidies to publishers of books of literary merit, the literary quarterlies, and paying pensions to authors. I am also the only woman member of the Aborigines Co-operatives Board which trains promising dark-coloured youths and educates the Australian Aborigines to use their tribal system in co-operative ventures.

"Despite a willingness to cultivate an undoubted talent for doing nothing, the opportunity never presents itself. A son with a sailboat on Sydney Harbour and a daughter with a horse on a farm in the Blue Mountains make sure that these are well supported, as well as their owners, by a constant output of printed matter."

Kylie Tennant, the elder daughter of Thomas and Kathleen (Tolhurst) Tennant, was born at Manly, near Sydney. She was christened Kathleen but in childhood somehow acquired the name Kylie, an aboriginal word meaning "boomerang." She was a lonely child and like many such became an avid reader, a peculiarity which increased her isolation at Brighton College, Manly, where she says she was "a complete outsider." Leaving school at sixteen, during the Depression, she worked on a children's radio program in Sydney and as a salesgirl in Melbourne, studied psychiatry for a year at the University of Sydney, and then entered a somewhat different field as a chicken farmer. This last venture failed when she and her partner ate all the chickens. In 1932 she hitchhiked and jumped trains from Sydney to Coonabarabran in northern New South Wales, where she married Lewis Rodd, a schoolteacher.

Her first novel, *Tiburon*, is a study of a small town in New South Wales during the Depression. It was warmly received and won the S. H. Prior Memorial Prize, though Miss Tennant has come to think of it as a poor book. *Foveaux* is about the "dirty, tragic, cheery people" of the Sydney slums, and *The Battlers* about migrants, the "vagabonds, failures, and criminals" she met in the course of a long pilgrimage on foot and by horse and cart. This novel, which won the gold medal of the Australian Literary Society, was reissued in England in 1966; it seemed to a reviewer in the *Times Literary Supplement* rather shapeless in its structure and flavorless in its prose, demonstrating more affection than understanding for its characters, but undoubtedly powerful and readable. *Tell Morning This*, the unabridged version of the novel first published in expurgated form as *The Joyful Condemned*, views the "prostitutes, layabouts and toughs" of Sydney from the point of view of a young medical student whose patients they are for a time. Reviewers found it an excellent story "told with honesty, and even, despite the bumpiness of much of the writing, a degree of poetic sensitivity."

Kylie Tennant is the most notable of the Australian sociological novelists, a humorous realist, whose novels at their best are vivid and powerful portraits of certain kinds of Australian life, full of warmth and incident and colorful dialogue. Her faults are those of the Zolaesque tradition—a failure at times to shape and prune her material sufficiently, so that it seems more documentary than art, and a tendency for her reforming zeal to become too overt, turning her fictions into tracts. *Ride on Stranger*, perhaps her most successful novel, is also one of her least "improving" books. Cecil Hadgraft calls it "a sort of respectable picaresque" about a young woman who "takes the lid off" Sydney; a delightful novel in which the "characters, movements, conditions, and scenes of Sydney are hit off with satiric gusto."

Apart from her novels, Miss Tennant has written a popular history of Australia, a biography of the missionary Alfred Clint called *Speak You So Gently*, a biography of the Labour politician Herbert Vere Evatt, and a number of plays for adults and children. She is profoundly interested in the past and future of the aboriginal peoples of Australia, and tells their story in her best-known children's book, *All the Proud Tribesmen*, which won the Children's Book Award in 1960.

Miss Tennant lives with her husband at Hunters Hill, New South Wales. She is a handsome woman, gray-haired and gray-eyed, as funny in conversation as in her books, who vastly enjoys life and leaves an impression of boundless energy and enthusiasm. She says: "I have sought the society of unlettered and poor people from choice, because I took pleasure in their company and gained more from it than I did from the learned." In her writing she sets out to make what she has to say both interesting and funny: "While they laugh, they'll think."

PRINCIPAL WORKS: *Fiction*—Tiburon, 1935; Foveaux, 1939; The Battlers, 1941; Ride on Stranger, 1943; Time Enough Later, 1943; Lost Haven, 1946; The Joyful Condemned, 1953 (unabridged version pub. as Tell Morning This, 1967); The Honey Flow, 1956; Ma Jones and the Little White Cannibals (stories), 1967; The Man on the Headland, 1972. *Nonfiction*—Australia: Her Story, Notes on a Nation, 1953; Speak You So Gently (biography), 1959; Evatt: Politics and Justice (biography), 1971. *Plays*—Tether a Dragon, 1952. *For children*—John o' the Forest, and Other Plays, 1950; The Bells of the City, and Other Plays, 1955; The Bushranger's Christmas Eve, and Other Plays, 1959; All the Proud Tribesmen, 1959; Trail Blazers of the Air, 1966.

ABOUT: Contemporary Authors 5–6, 1963; Dick, M. The Novels of Kylie Tennant, 1966; Green, M. History of Australian Literature, 1961; Hadgraft, C. Australian Literature, 1960; Hetherington, J. Forty-two Faces, 1962; Moore, T. I. Social Patterns in Australian Literature, 1971; Roderick, C. A. Twenty Australian Novelists, 1947; Vinson, J. (ed.) Contemporary Novelists, 1972; Who's Who in Australia, 1971. *Periodicals*—The Listener March 23, 1943; Meanjin 4 1953; Southerly 1 1957.

"TERTZ, ABRAM." *See* SINYAVSKY, ANDREI (DONATEVICH)

THARP, LOUISE (MARSHALL) HALL (June 19, 1898–), American biographer, writes: "I was born in Oneonta, New York, the daughter of Newton Marshall Hall, a Congregational minister from New Hampshire and Louise Buffum Varney, a Maine Quaker. My mother was descended from the Southwicks of Salem, driven out of that town for their religious beliefs. My father used to tell her that his ancestors persecuted hers and he married her 'to keep up the good work.' My childhood was spent in Springfield, Massachusetts, where my father was pastor of the North Congregational Church for some twenty years. In addition to being a minister, he was a writer, his books being chiefly religious.

"During my childhood I was often cautioned not to disturb my father when he was writing. As a result, I took refuge on the third floor of our house, in space not regularly used by the family, but containing many shelves of books, such as Trollope, Scott and George Eliot, all of which I devoured. I was given a free hand in what I read, since these works had already passed my father's inspection. I remember only one restriction that he ever imposed on my reading. When I was quite young, he objected to my reading one of the popular romances that a friend had lent me. Later I read this book to see what I had missed and found nothing wrong with it except excessive sentimentality.

"In my childhood I attended The Elms, a small private school for girls, and later, I graduated from the Springfield High School. I felt that I had some aptitude for painting and decided to become an illustrator, so I studied art for two years at the School of Fine Arts, Crafts, and Decorative Design in Boston, popularly known as the Walker-Child School. We were given an assignment to design a valentine one week—our work was always displayed for criticism by C. Howard Walker when the project was due for completion. He looked upon my design with little favor, then read the lines I had written to go with it. 'H'm, not bad!' he said. But I had written much better so-called poetry and it dawned upon me that I could write better than I could paint.

"After art school, my father and I went abroad for two years, visiting museums, cathedrals and archaeological diggings. We traveled chiefly in England, France and Italy, but we also spent some months in Spain, Greece and Turkey. In Greece, we met Dr. and Mrs. Edward Robinson, he being director of the Metropolitan Museum of Art. Together, we visited the ruins at Delphi. 'Now this isn't in the history books,' Dr. Robinson would say,

LOUISE HALL THARP

as he taught me to understand and admire scientific research.

"I became interested in Girl Scouting about 1922, first on a local basis, and later, in the regional and national organization. At various times I was troop captain, camp counselor, director of plays and pageants, council member, editor of *The Trailmaker*, a magazine for Girl Scout leaders, member of the National Brownie Committee and an Accredited Speaker.

"In 1925 I was married to Carey Edwin Tharp, a Texan. At first, we moved nearly every year. Our first home was in Cambridge, Massachusetts, then we went to Rochester, Pelham, Poughkeepsie, New York, and finally, in 1932, we moved to Darien, Connecticut. We built our present house in 1936 out of stone taken from our land, the location being in the woods near Long Island Sound. Here we still live and here our two sons, Carey Edwin, Jr., and Marshall Allen Tharp, grew up, attended local schools, graduated from college, went to war and married. Now I have the daughters I always wanted—and five grandchildren, two boys and three girls.

"When my sons were small, they found that there were many things to do which interested them more than reading. The books they had bored them, so I decided to try writing a book that they would like. I received my first inspiration from a tablet on the local church which said that the minister and congregation were kidnapped by Tories during the American Revolution and taken off to Long Island. I went to the library and found a contemporary account of this raid, and from this and other materials I wrote a fictionalized story about Darien during the American Revolution, which was my first book. I soon changed to juvenile biography, and when my sons went away to college, I turned to the adult field."

———

Mrs. Tharp was already well established as a writer of fiction and biography for children when she published *The Peabody Sisters of Salem*, her first adult book. Her subjects were Elizabeth Peabody, the "grandmother" of Boston and founder of the American kindergarten; Mary Peabody, who married Horace Mann; and Sophia Peabody, the artist, who married Nathaniel Hawthorne. Mrs. Tharp's book, skillfully blending a highly readable narrative with evocative excerpts from letters and diaries, was a Book-of-the-Month Club selection and a major success. Many reviewers were delighted that so fascinating and significant a family had been rescued from oblivion, and were infected by the author's warm feeling for them. "In its scenes, in its conversation, in its detailed knowledge of the background, it is an invigorating, honestly recaptured chronicle," wrote Edward Weeks. "These people mattered largely in their day, and we enjoy that day and feel their vitality in this leisurely and attractive book."

As a biographer, Mrs. Tharp's method is "intimate and descriptive rather than objective and analytical." This was regarded by some reviewers as a disadvantage when she focused on such a figure as Horace Mann in *Until Victory*, a book which brought Mann and his wife alive as individuals but failed to convey fully his importance as an educational reformer.

Three Saints and a Sinner was another notable exercise in collective biography, dealing this time with the three Ward sisters, including Julia Ward Howe, and their brother Sam Ward. There was much praise for Mrs. Tharp's "light touch, vivid evocation, sound Boston-New York-Civil War background, [and] remarkable talent for group portraiture," and Raymond Walters called it "by all odds her best book to date." At the same time, some critics expressed mild reservations about the author's tendency to supply, as E. H. Smith put it, "the sticky stuff... the tear in the eye, the crackle of the fire on the hearth, the maidenly doubts in the bosom. They were probably all there. But Mrs. Tharp does not need such help." Her subsequent biographies have all been warmly received by most critics and praised for their careful research and excellent entertainment value.

Mrs. Tharp is a Congregationalist and a Republican, active in civic and community life in Darien. She likes swimming, motor trips, and sketching, and lists among her favorite books the novels of Marquand, the biographies of André Maurois, and Van Wyck Brooks' *The Flowering of New England*, which first aroused her curiosity about the Peabody sisters of Salem.

PRINCIPAL WORKS: *Juvenile fiction*—Tory Hole, 1940; Lords and Gentlemen, 1940; Sixpence for Luck, 1941; Champlain, Northwest Voyager, 1944. *Juvenile nonfiction*—Down to the Sea: A Young People's Life of Nathaniel Bowditch, the Great American Navigator, 1942; A Sounding Trumpet: Julia Ward Howe and the Battle Hymn of the Republic, 1944; Company of Adventurers: The Story of the Hudson's Bay Company, 1946; Louis Agassiz, Adventurous Scientist, 1961. *Adult nonfiction*—The Peabody Sisters of Salem, 1950; Until Victory: Horace Mann and Mary Peabody, 1953; Three Saints and a Sinner: Julia Ward Howe, Louisa, Annie and Sam Ward, 1956; Adventurous Alliance: The Story of the Agassiz Family of Boston, 1959; The Baroness and the General, 1962; Mrs. Jack: A Biography of Isabella Stewart Gardner, 1965; Saint-Gaudens and the Gilded Era, 1969.

ABOUT: Author's and Writer's Who's Who, 1971; Current Biography, 1955; Dictionary of International Biography, 1963; Fuller, M. (ed.) More Junior Authors, 1963; Who's Who in America, 1972–1973; Who's Who of American Women, 1972–1973. *Periodicals*—Book-of-the-Month Club News December 1949; New York Herald Tribune Book Review January 15, 1950; Saturday Review January 7, 1950; September 29, 1956.

THOMAS, EARNEST LEWYS. *See* "VAUGHAN, RICHARD"

THOMAS, GWYN (July 6, 1913–), Anglo-Welsh novelist, dramatist, and memoirist, writes: "My grandparents on the father's side deserve a mention. Grim, unbending pietists, one can still hear in the family the pop of their transmitted neuroses being uncorked. My grandfather shuttled between the building and carpentering trades and when he wanted the odd laugh he did a little undertaking. He emigrated to the States and stayed there for four years. My father and his brother turned in violent reaction against the parched Calvinism of their parents. The elder brother, on my grandfather's death, died quite young after a round of joyous excess that is still spoken of with respect by the dipsomaniacs and sensualists of this zone. My father lived on to spread the load a little more subtly. He shifted to Porth on marriage to a girl from Kenfig Hill, a lovely haunted region on the Glamorgan coast, and began one of the most erratic careers in the history of mining. He had twelve children of whom I was the youngest. I don't think he was ever sure about our names. He often called me Id and I was never certain whether he was being absentminded or Freudian. Our mother died when I was three. She made oilskin suits for the miners in a leaky draughty shed at the back of the house to try to provide some kind of stable basis for our lives. A woman of enormous creative power, whose kindliness must have embraced half the world. Our house was always full of kids even needier than we were. She died of sheer weariness of which the mortal catalyst was called rheumatic fever. Whenever in my books you come across an obsessive reference to a 'rich plangent contralto voice' I am speaking of her.

"I was born in 1913. Went to the Cymmer Elementary School, Rhondda Valley. The house was full of singing. My older brothers and sisters were ardent *eisteddfodwr* (i.e., devotees of the great Welsh music festivals) and a recurrent, still haunting experience was sitting thrilled to my infantile wick listening to the champion solo at the back of one of the local halls. A local teacher implanted in me one of the most formative cults of my life by recruiting me into a junior operatic society and I became one of the youngest monks ever to sing the 'Miserere' from *Il Trovatore*. As a family we mastered the scores of at least three operas and would drive the neighbours to madness or drink by sitting out in the garden on summer nights going through the lot. Music and talk. Around our table we were as boisterously garrulous as a treeful of baboons, if you can imagine a tree with strongly radical branches of the Workers Educational Association all over. Individually I was a boy alto with the strongest set of pipes since Titta Ruffo. I was in demand at concerts in the lower Rhondda until adolescence and a full political awareness took my mind off sheet music. My leading items were a clutch of the saddest lyrics from the hymnal of Sankey and Moody, and the warnings about drink and death I warbled from countless platforms brought me a caution from the boys from the local Library and Institute, a nest of earnest autodidacts, that I was being unduly fussy about the life-force.

"Went to the County School in 1925 and the following year, that of the great strike, furnished the thick seam of material which I have dug for things like *The Dark Philosophers*. Left the County School with a State Scholarship for Oxford. Did Modern Languages and spent some time at the University of Madrid. I still wince at some of those Oxford memories. The contrast with the Rhondda might have nourished some nerve that served me well in later years as a writer of humorous fiction, but at the time my extreme poverty and the illness that went with it provided me with all the classic impulses of bomb-throwing anarchism.

"1936–1940. Lecturer in Adult Education, operating in Welfare Halls and clubs. I added to the confusion of that strange period and learned the art of talking fast so that I could get my best points in between snooker shots.

"1940–1962. Modern Languages Master at the Cardigan and Barry Grammar Schools. You've heard of broken Spanish and broken French; I handed out most of the hammers. First novel published 1946; twelve since. I have always loved writing. It is utterly private and involves an enormous amount of sitting down. I have brought high principles to the novelist's craft. I eliminated adventure, pornography and profit. Three of my books won Book Society Recommendations. *The Keep*, which was given an *Evening Standard* playwrighting award, 1962, was my first play."

GWYN THOMAS

Gwyn Thomas did not publish his first book until he was thirty-three. It was a volume of short stories set in the mining valleys, mainly his own Rhondda, called *Where Did I Put My Pity?* Glyn Jones, the South Wales critic and editor, has called this "unquestionably one of the best collections of Anglo-Welsh short stories ever to have appeared," and cites: "First, the extraordinary vigour of the style, the brilliance, the gusto, the torrential language, the inexhaustible imagery; second, the humour, both of situation and of language, strange, fresh, fantastic, contemporary; and third, the compassion, the profound humanity," most particularly in the outstanding tale "The Teacher," describing the visit of some grammar schoolboys to a much admired master who lies mutilated and dying in a hospital.

In the following fourteen years, Thomas produced nine novels and two more volumes of short stories, nearly all of them about his own region of Wales in the 1930s. They deal with exotically named characters like Pugh the Pang, Morgan the Monologue, Erasmus John the Going Gone (the auctioneer in *The Stranger at My Side*, 1954), whose stories are told in a style ranging from wry directness to what Maurice Richardson once described as "manic flights of Cymric verbigeration." This example comes from *The World Cannot Hear You*: "After the singing, when a large group of old villagers came in, talk started and the main topic was all those voters who had been carried in funerals up the mountain and were now at rest in Troyless graveyard. We were still talking about this when we left the tavern. The night was moonlit. . . . We felt happy for them, for those people who had settled their wary, itching scores with such magic finality. We called out in a tender rhapsody the names of those graves . . . we recognised, and we had to hold back Octavius Pym, mad still with love and pity, from diving into the enclosure to caress the marbles. 'The earth has a rich and death-stuffed crust,' said Ewart Pugh."

Thomas has also tried his hand, with considerable success, at the historical novel. *The Love Man* (1958) is a splendidly comic and ironic tale about Don Juan in which, Walter Allen commented, Thomas is "more genuinely a poet than he has ever been before." *All Things Betray Thee* (1949) deals with industrial strife in South Wales, but this time the Wales of a century ago. Alan Hugh Leigh, a wandering harpist, comes to a valley town in an iron-smelting area. He is searching for his friend John Simon Adams, who he hopes will accompany him to North Wales, "the painless paradise where the sun and the stream sing to each other all day." He finds Adams leading the iron workers in a struggle against starvation wages and mass lay-offs, and becomes involved in the conflict. After a demonstration, both men are arrested; the harpist is freed but Adams is hanged. It is a book full of outrage at exploitation and hunger, sad, but also full of comedy and Thomas's characteristically colorful invective against the owners' men like the "cheese-dweller" Lemuel Stevens. Glyn Jones regards it as Thomas's best novel.

In addition to his fiction, Gwyn Thomas has written three plays, *The Keep*, *Jackie the Jumper*, and *The Loud Organs*; two books of essays, *A Welsh Eye* and *A Hatful of Humours*; and his "autobiography of sorts," *A Few Selected Exits*. *A Welsh Eye*, a book of description and travel about his native country, the *Times Literary Supplement* found delightful; "mockery is diluted with compassion, and indignation with humour." But with *A Few Selected Exits* the same paper's reviewer, like some others, complained of a certain "monotony in his sustaining the role of being Gwyn Thomas the Welsh wordspinner." Thomas, who was married in 1938, lists his recreations as opera and "staring."

PRINCIPAL WORKS: *Fiction*—Where Did I Put My Pity? (short stories, 1946); The Dark Philosophers, 1947; The Alone to the Alone, 1947 (U.S., Venus and the Voters); All Things Betray Thee, 1949 (U.S., Leaves in the Wind); The World Cannot Hear You, 1951; Now Lead Us Home, 1952; A Frost on My Frolic, 1953; The Stranger at My Side, 1954; Point of Order, 1956; Gazooka (short stories), 1957; The Love Man, 1958 (U.S., A Wolf at Dusk); Ring Delirium 123 (short stories), 1960; The Sky of Our Lives (three novellas), 1972. *Nonfiction*—A Welsh Eye, 1964; A Hatful of Humours, 1965; A Few Selected Exits, 1968; The Lust Lobby (anecdotes from Punch), 1971. *Plays*—The Keep, 1962; Jackie the Jumper, 1963; Loud Organs, 1965.

ABOUT: Jones, G. The Dragon Has Two Tongues, 1968; Who's Who, 1973. *Periodicals*—New Statesman June 21, 1958; August 20, 1960; November 27, 1964; Spectator August 19, 1960; December 1, 1961; February 15, 1963; Times Literary Supplement July 4, 1958; December 17, 1964; November 28, 1968.

THOMAS, HUGH (SWYNNERTON) (October 21, 1931–), English historian and novelist, writes: "I was born in Windsor on Trafalgar Day, 1931. The juxtaposition of these facts made me very patriotic when I was a child. My father was in the Colonial Service, in the Gold Coast (Ghana), so I did not see much of him. I was however always aware of his remote but imperial activity. No one even then had any idea that the Empire was not going to last forever. My mother also came from the Empire, being born in Simla, where my grandfather had gone in order to make his fortune painting portraits of rajahs or generals. (He failed.) I was therefore truly a child of the Empire, and, like others in similar positions, suffered by spending a certain amount of time living in my grandmother's house, in this case at Great Shelford, a Brooke village outside Cambridge.

"My childhood was nearly all spent in the country, in Cambridgeshire, Hertfordshire and Kent. During World War II I was at a private preparatory school where I peeled a lot of potatoes and where the wife of the headmaster, though brilliant, was mad. She left for an asylum shortly after I left. In 1945 I went to a traditional English public school, Sherborne, in Dorset. The special drawbacks of this school were the absence of privacy, the extraordinary autonomous powers given to the housemasters, and the equally extraordinary attention paid to Rugby football and cricket. The school was also rather philistine and conservative, though it was saved from complete lack of distinction by one or two admirable masters, among them a very good History master. In the end everything turned out quite well so far as I was concerned; I was fairly successful by schoolboy terms, and in 1950 I got a scholarship in History to Cambridge.

"History was the only subject which interested me before that time, and so I naturally read it at Cambridge. But the history I pursued in those days was exclusively political—'The Early Life of Charles James Fox' and all that—and I thought of it as a preparation for politics at that time. Most of my twenties I thought I would enter politics before long. However at Cambridge various other possibilities did open up; I started writing rather precious stories and even a play. Preciousness, partly a reaction to the war, 'austerity,' and the apparently unnecessarily gloomy Labour Government, was then the rage. Afterwards, I went to Paris for several months, nominally studying at the Sorbonne, in reality sitting in cafés, and I am glad to say that some of the gilded Cambridge parochiality began to wear off. In the middle of 1954 I started to work at the Foreign Office, and this experience, though disturbing in some ways, had a further very good effect in showing in practical terms what politics was about. The Foreign Office also had a very good effect on my prose style. I have never afterwards doubted that the essential point in writing is to make your meaning clear as simply, economically and shortly as possible. The Foreign Office had high standards in these matters and I learned from them.

"The Fifties in the age of Dulles were an unhappy time in foreign affairs and after some dramatic experiences in New York and London, chiefly at Disarmament conferences, I decided, after the terrible Suez tragedy, to try and enter politics in a straightforward way. I left the Foreign Office in early 1957, took a temporary teaching job at Sandhurst and, with surprising ease, became a Labour candidate for parliament. In the meantime I published two novels, one a romantic picture of diplomatic life, the other an unsuccessful Voltairean parable. In the summer of 1957 I began work on a study of the Spanish Civil War, inspired by a visit to Spain in late 1956. I soon found that I wanted to concentrate all my energies on this task and abandoned first the Sandhurst appointment and afterwards the parliamentary candidature. Since then I have had only one job, at the United Nations Association (for the year 1960–1961), though I have recently agreed to become Professor of Modern History at the University of Reading.

"It now seems to me that the writing of history is likely to be my main work. I approached this without general theories, only a long-standing predilection. I suppose that I increasingly see historical events as determined by economic or technical factors, though I am far from being a determinist: on the contrary, the need for specific political decisions by individuals appears to me greater than ever. I have come by accident (as it would seem on the surface) to write about Spain, now about Cuba, and the rediscovery of the real past of these countries has been my main occupation for over eight years. I don't quite know what I shall be doing next. I have a horror at the thought of being tied down to knowing more and more about less and less. I have many projects. Maybe I shall return to novels."

HUGH THOMAS

Hugh Thomas's first novel, which he speaks of above as "a romantic picture of diplomatic life," was *The World's Game* (1957). It is romantic chiefly in its rebellious disillusionment with conventional diplomacy. A young English Third Secretary, in love "with action, truth and integrity," and urgently aware that Israel and Egypt are moving towards war, is increasingly appalled by the inertia and complacency of the Foreign Office. At length, fiddling with protocol while the world burns becomes intolerable, and he decides on unilateral action. It is a young man's book, a little pompous at times, but it "catches with great skill and subtlety the ennui and unreality of this looking-glass world of government," and seemed to most reviewers a well-written, well-constructed, and generally impressive first novel. *The Oxygen Age*, a satire on international commerce and politics, was as Thomas says not wholly successful, but was admired for "some excellent scenes, full of malice and wit and special knowledge" and for its "always firm and controlled" style.

The Spanish Civil War, Thomas's first historical work, was a best seller. It is a political, diplomatic, and military history, tracing the war back to its roots in the 1920s and ending with the fall of Barcelona in 1939. Thomas, a child when the war ended, and a stranger to Spain until 1956, was as J. G. Harrison remarked "too young to be caught up in the passions aroused by that war," and had "gone into virtually every aspect of [it] with an open-minded sincerity bespoken by the fact that [he] consulted nearly a thousand books and pamphlets in Spanish, English, French, German, and Italian." The author's lack of military experience was less of an asset, and most reviewers thought the book more successful as political and diplomatic history than as an account of campaigns and battles. The most hostile review came from D. M. Friedenberg in the *New Republic*, who said that Thomas's sources included some totally inaccurate propaganda documents, complained of his weakness for sensational tidbits of gossip reminiscent of Edward Gibbon, and objected to "a certain superior Anglo-Saxon loftiness" in Thomas's approach to foreigners. The first of these reservations was also voiced by other critics, most of whom admired the book nevertheless; it was called "a model of careful, thorough, unbiased and fruitful scholarship," which "stands without rivals as the most balanced and comprehensive on the subject." R. H. S. Crossman, praising above all Thomas's "narrative skill [and] his mastery of literary stage direction," called it "a near masterpiece, an example of contemporary history ambitiously conceived and executed on the grandest scale."

An interesting history of Sandhurst, the British military academy, was followed in 1967 by *The Suez Affair*, Thomas's account of the crisis which had caused him so much frustration as a junior in the Foreign Office. This book, expanded from articles published in the London *Sunday Times* in 1966, draws on published material and also on interviews with statesmen, diplomats, soldiers, and others involved in that abortive adventure. Necessarily an interim rather than a final report, it was warmly praised as "a masterly condensation of a very complex story."

Cuba: The Pursuit of Freedom is a work on an even larger scale than *The Spanish Civil War*. It is a 1,700-page political and social history of the island from the English capture of Havana in 1762 to 1962. A large part of the book is devoted to Cuba's efforts to escape domination by the United States. One reviewer complained of Thomas's "distrust of Castro and his methods, his aversion to Marx, and his liberal-capitalist convictions"; another considered that the author lacked sympathy for the United States and had "an intense dislike of the CIA." By and large, the book was welcomed as an important study, notable for its readability, its painstaking research, and its eye for illuminating detail. *Europe: The Radical Challenge* is an optimistic survey of Britain's prospects in the European Economic Community, aimed particularly at doubters within the British Socialist movement.

Hugh Thomas is the son of Hugh and Margery (Swynnerton) Thomas. As an undergraduate he was president of the Cambridge Union debating society, the usual preliminary to a career in politics. He graduated in 1953 with first class honors in history. He has been Professor of History at Reading University since 1966, and chairman of the Graduate School of Contemporary European Studies there since 1973. Thomas received the Somerset Maugham prize in 1962, and the same year married Vanessa Jebb, daughter of the first Baron Gladwyn. It was she who compiled the outstanding index to *The Spanish Civil War*. They have two sons and a daughter.

PRINCIPAL WORKS: *Fiction*—The World's Game, 1957; The Oxygen Age, 1958. *Nonfiction*—(ed.) The Establishment: A Symposium, 1959; The Spanish Civil War, 1961; The Story of Sandhurst, 1961; (with the editors of Life) Spain, 1962; The Suez Affair (U.S., Suez), 1967; (ed.) Crisis in the Civil Service, 1968; Cuba: The Pursuit of Freedom, 1971; (ed.) The Selected Writings of José Antonio Primo de Rivera, 1972; Goya: "The Third of May 1808" (Art in Context series), 1972; Europe: The Radical Challenge, 1973; John Strachey (biography), 1973.

ABOUT: Contemporary Authors 9–10, 1964; Who's Who, 1973. *Periodicals*—New Statesman October 3, 1959; April 28, 1961; May 5, 1967; New York Review of Books August 24, 1967; Rejoinder July 1963; Spectator September 29, 1959; May 5, 1961; Times Literary Supplement April 28, 1961; April 27, 1967; January 22, 1971.

THOMAS, R(ONALD) S(TUART) (1913–), Welsh poet, was born in Cardiff, and raised at Holyhead, Anglesey. After graduating B.A. in classics at the University of Wales, he went for theological training to St. Michael's College, Llandaff, and was ordained a deacon of the Anglican Church in 1936, a priest in 1937. After two curacies, he became in 1942 Rector of Manafon, Montgomeryshire, in Central Wales.

His poems began to appear in periodicals at that time and the first collection, *The Stones of the Field*, was privately published in 1946. In his own words, "These are essentially nature poems, but they are not written in the English tradition. Their imagery is more akin to that of those early Welsh writers, whose clarity of vision was born out of an almost mystical attachment to their environment." The environment, in Thomas's case, was the harsh landscape of rural Wales in which his parishioners, mainly Welsh-speaking hill farmers, struggled to wrest a living from the meager soil. Recognizing the inadequacy of the Welsh language to express the complexities of modern life, Thomas writes in English. He is, however, sympathetic to Welsh nationalism, and seemed at first a poet with intentions comparable to those of the Scottish nationalist writers, concerned to articulate his country's identity, seeking to preserve it from the corrupting encroachment of English technology and commerce.

Song at the Year's Turning (1955) made it clear that Thomas's role could not be so simply defined. It collected the poems written since 1942 but excluded much of the specifically nationalistic and political verse of the period and showed the ambivalence of Thomas's feeling towards his principal subject, his parishioners. He was an Anglican clergyman in a largely dissenting community, a sophisticated classical scholar among hard and narrow peasants whose archetype appears for the first time in these poems as "Iago Prytherch." Thomas saw that men like Prytherch were all that was left to represent a great and ancient heritage, but also that they were ignorant and careless of that heritage. *Song at the Year's Turning* expressed both perceptions in poems reminiscent of Yeats in their philosophy, rich but tightly controlled in their imagery. The book was widely admired and received the Heinemann Award of the Royal Society of Literature.

Later collections have included *Poetry for Supper* (1958), *Tares* (1961), *The Bread of Truth* (1963), *Pietà* (1966), and *Not That He Brought Flowers* (1968). In these there has been a fundamental change in Thomas's attitude to Prytherch and his kind, a growing comprehension of the "terrible poetry" of their slow and joyless lives, coupled still with an unblinking recognition of their crudity and greed. They "come obediently as a dog / To the pound's whistle" and because of this, they and their way of life are doomed. But Thomas can say to Prytherch: "I am a man like you," and ask his forgiveness for the "thin scorn" of the early poems.

Though Thomas has so far written relatively little verse on explicitly religious themes, it can be argued that all of these later poems are Christian in their humility and compassion and in the fierce honesty of Thomas's concern for his parishioners. Recent collections have included a number of poems on the language and composition of poetry, a preoccupation reflected in the published lecture *Words and the Poet* (1963). Thomas has said that in writing a poem "one is like a fisherman playing a fish, getting the sense of it." He has edited a book of country verse, the *Penguin Book of Religious Verse* (1964), and selections from the work of three poets whom he admires—Edward Thomas, Herbert, and Wordsworth. Thomas received the Queen's Gold Medal for Poetry in 1964 and a Welsh Arts Council Award for Poetry in 1967–1968.

In 1954 Thomas left Manafon to become Vicar of St. Michael's, Eglwysfach, in Cardiganshire. Since 1967 he has been Vicar of St. Hywyn, Aberdaron, Caernarvonshire. He is married to the painter Mildred Eldridge and has one son, born in 1945. He is a handsome man, with rather gaunt Celtic features and a shock of graying hair.

R. S. Thomas is not an innovator, but critics have found in his work a "self-conscious craftsmanship as great as any shown in English verse today." His countryman R. G. Thomas has noted his habit of conversation with the reader; his ability to "freeze" a scene for us in "hard taut rhythms . . .

R. S. THOMAS

dominated by monosyllables and riveted together by short, alliterative phrases." However "local and particular" the scene we are invited to contemplate, its implications are likely to be very deep and very wide. The profundity and scrupulous honesty of his vision makes his dying Welsh village an image of general relevance and urgency.

PRINCIPAL WORKS: *Poetry*—The Stones of the Field, 1946; An Acre of Land, 1952; Song at the Year's Turning, 1955; Poetry for Supper, 1958; Tares, 1961; The Bread of Truth, 1963; Words and the Poet, 1963; Pietà, 1966; Not That He Brought Flowers, 1968; (with Roy Fuller) Pergamon Poets I, ed. by Evan Owen, 1968; Young and Old (for children), 1972; H'm: Poems, 1972. *As editor*—The Batsford Book of Country Verse, 1962; A Choice of George Herbert's Verse, 1967; A Choice of Wordsworth's Verse, 1971.

ABOUT: Cohen, J. M. Poetry of This Age, 1960; Finn, F. E. S. (ed.) Poets of Our Time, 1965; Thomas, R. G. R. S. Thomas, 1964; Who's Who, 1973. *Periodicals*—Critical Quarterly Winter 1960; English Autumn 1963; Review of English Literature III no. 4, 1962; Welsh Anvil 1949, 1952.

"THOR, JOHANNES." *See* "GOLL, YVAN"

"THOR, TRISTAN." *See* "GOLL, YVAN"

THORP, WILLARD (April 20, 1899–), American literary historian (not to be confused with the economist Willard Long Thorp), writes: "I was born in Sidney, New York, a village on the Susquehanna. My father's ancestors migrated from Greenwich, Connecticut, to Butternuts (now Gilbertville) at the end of the eighteenth century and there the Thorps stayed, working a farm which prospered well enough so that some of the sons in the

WILLARD THORP

family could go to college. My father attended Williams and then settled as a lawyer twelve miles from his birthplace. He was a disciple of Emerson and Thoreau and often neglected his clients to go fishing and huckleberrying. My mother, Harriet Willard, came from Illinois. She had studied at the New England Conservatory and she passed on to me her love of music. I think I might have become a musician or musicologist if there had been any opportunity to study when I was at college. The college I attended was naturally Hamilton because other Thorps had preceded me there. Hamilton was especially strong in the ancient and modern languages. H. C. G. Brandt, who had been among the first professors called to the Johns Hopkins, taught me German, as he had taught Ezra Pound fifteen years before. My first intention was to become a classical scholar, but I soon realized that my preparation was too limited. Two remarkable teachers steered me to English literature.

"In the fall of 1920 I went on to Harvard, chiefly to study drama with George Pierce Baker. I discovered that he had lost interest in scholarship and was spending most of his time with his students in the 47 Workshop. I became a delighted hanger-on of this group. My interest in the drama carried me through my doctoral studies at Princeton. There, in 1926, I turned out a dissertation on 'The Decline of Didacticism in Elizabethan Drama.' (It was published under another title and is fortunately now an almost undiscoverable item.) Meanwhile I had taught for three years at Smith College under the most remarkable college president of our time, William Alan Neilson. At Smith I met Margaret Farrand, who had returned to teach there. We were married in 1930.

"I joined the Princeton Faculty in 1926 and have remained at Princeton, except for eight excursions as a visiting professor at other universities, chiefly in summer sessions. The first articles I published were in the field of drama. In 1934 my two loves, music and the theater, were conjoined in *Songs from the Restoration Theater*, to which I was able to contribute some discoveries about the use of music in the theater of the Restoration wits.

"I found myself increasingly interested in American literature. When I entered the profession there was a pecking order among literary scholars, determined by your 'field.' Scholars who concerned themselves with American literature were pretty well down the line. There was a kind of snobbishness in *not* studying your native literature. I have been happy with my choice. It was rather like coming home. My first publications in the field were on Herman Melville. My Melville volume in the American Writers Series came out when there was still much to be learned about Melville's career. There was enough that was new in the book to keep it in print continuously. In 1936 I had taken on the lectures in an introductory survey course in American literature which I have offered ever since. In 1940 Lawrance Thompson and I brought the study of American literature into the graduate curriculum of the Department.

"During these years I formed pleasant associations with scholars who had pioneered in the field. Out of my friendship with Robert Spiller, Henry Canby, and Thomas H. Johnson grew plans for the cooperative *Literary History of the United States*, published in three volumes in 1948. *LHUS* has become the standard work, most evidently so from its translation into German, Serbo-Croatian, and Italian.

"Since 1941 I have had a share in the American Studies movement. In that year I helped establish Princeton's American Civilization Program and became its first chairman. This movement spread in the colleges and universities in this country and has had considerable influence abroad.

"In 1955 Alfred A. Knopf published *A Southern Reader*. The making of this book gave me more pleasure than any literary venture I have undertaken. Despite what I know, or anyone knows, about the soberer realities of Southern life, the South is to me the most exciting and dynamic region in America, and the least understood.

"Of late I have devoted considerable time to two causes: the improvement of the teaching of English in the schools and the work of the Center for Editions of American Authors, a project of the Modern Language Association of America. In academic life good causes keep coming on."

In their preface to the one-volume second edition of *Literary History of the United States*, Thorp and his fellow editors said that the work had been intended from the beginning to tell "a single and unified story" from an "organic view" of literature as "the aesthetic expression of the general culture of a people in a given time and place." The book was universally praised for its authority and unity, which did not preclude a "flavor of vigorous independent expression of [the] authors' views," remarkable in a work drawing together the contributions of over fifty scholars. It was said to be a better book "in nearly every respect" than the *Cambridge History of American Literature*, which it replaced as the standard work.

Of Thorp's other books, the most discussed was *American Writing in the Twentieth Century*, part of a Library of Congress series on American civilization. The *Times Literary Supplement* called it a readable and thorough survey in which, however, "contemporary values" had been digested so thoroughly "that the result is flat as a textbook." Perry Miller on the other hand was satisfied that the book took stock of the first half of the century "judiciously and objectively, but also with just the right amount of nostalgia." Robert E. Spiller, reviewing the book, summarized his friend's qualities in these terms: "He can be pure literary critic without losing his social and historical bearings. Such scholarship is always deceptive because the hard-earned insights and conclusions are likely to seem the simple truths that we have known all the while, once they are stated in the lucid prose of which Mr. Thorp is so fine a master."

Since 1952 Thorp has been Holmes Professor of Belles Lettres at Princeton. He is a Litt.D. of Hamilton College and an L.H.D. of Kalamazoo College. His wife, Margaret, is also a writer, the author of *America at the Movies* and *Female Persuasion* among other books, and coauthor with her husband of *Modern Writing*.

PRINCIPAL WORKS: The Triumph of Realism in Elizabethan Drama, 1558–1612, 1928; American Writing in the Twentieth Century, 1960; American Humorists, 1964. *As editor*—Songs from the Restoration Theater, 1934; Representative Selections [from Herman Melville], 1938; A Southern Reader, 1955. *As coeditor*—(with H. F. Lowry) Oxford Anthology of English Poetry, 1935; (with M. F. Thorp) Modern Writing, 1944; (with R. E. Spiller and others) Literary History of the United States, 3 vols., 1948.

ABOUT: Contemporary Authors 7–8, 1963; Directory of American Scholars II 1964; Who's Who in America, 1968–1969.

"THORSTEIN, ERIC." *See* "MERRIL, JUDITH"

TILLOTSON, GEOFFREY (June 30, 1905–October 15, 1969), English scholar and critic, wrote: "I was born in Lancashire in the small industrial nineteenth century town of Nelson, but soon migrated to Yorkshire, into the valley of the Aire, where I lived till I went up to Oxford and then to London. I was educated at the village school and at the grammar school of the local town, Keighley, and took my degree in English Language and Literature in 1927. I remained in Oxford another year starting on my B.Litt. research which I finished in 1930. Meanwhile I had been doing some teaching in Leicester and Castleford (at the school where Henry Moore was educated), but went back to Oxford to occupy the post of Sub-Librarian in the English Department Library. The salary for this was eighty pounds a year—which I supplemented by tutoring for some of the Colleges. In 1931 I was lucky enough to be appointed Assistant Lecturer in English at University College, London—university jobs were few and far between in those days—and in 1933 I married my old Oxford acquaintance, Kathleen Constable, who had become a lecturer at Bedford College about a mile away across Regent's Park. At the outbreak of war I was suspended at University College and went into that part of the Air Ministry which became the Ministry of Aircraft Production. Meanwhile I had been raised to the rank of Reader *in absentia* and then, as the war was closing, became Professor at Birkbeck College, the only college in England which is an internal college of a university teaching undergraduates and postgraduates of an evening during their spare time. Since then I have remained put, except for a visit of a semester to Harvard in 1948. I am an Honorary Foreign Member of the American Academy of

GEOFFREY TILLOTSON

Arts and Science, and the President of the Charles Lamb Society.

"We have two adopted sons.

"My writings have been mainly on Pope and nineteenth century English literature, and my critical principles, which may be gathered from my practice, were set out in the preface to my first book of collected essays, *Essays in Criticism and Research* (1942), and in the preface to my second, *Criticism and the Nineteenth Century* (1951)."

It is clear from what Tillotson wrote in *Essays in Criticism and Research*, and from his practice, that he regarded criticism as a positive and constructive function, a process of discovery and appreciation. He was a historical critic who sought to "read old authors in their own light, and the moderns in the light that he salutes as new." He therefore thought it natural to learn from biographers, textual critics, bibliographers, psychologists, social historians, and anyone else who might help him. This willingness to look beyond the text for information about it is unfashionable; not so Tillotson's belief "that the face of literature is also its spirit." To illustrate his meaning he referred to the decorative nature of Elizabethan literature, "the tell-tale fingerprint, individually whorled, sharp, left by an age voluble and also pedantically precise." Or, again, he saw Pope's "moral control" carried out and expressed in his poetry's formal control. Thus, "to study the configurations of the flesh [of literature] is . . . to study the very 'message' of the work."

This then is the purpose of criticism as Tillotson understood it, "to see the past . . . as far as possible, as it was" and then, the historical labor complete, "to describe and communicate the face, now that it can be looked at for what it was, and to assess its beauty or its particular strength." It is an approach which results not in revolutionary general conclusions about literature as a whole, but in sharp perceptions and fascinating discoveries about individual authors or groups of authors. As he said himself, Tillotson was most inclined "to write of the small trove—a village or a rich valley—in the light of the whole country tramped over."

In this way he produced two indispensable studies of Pope: *On the Poetry of Pope*, concerned mainly with the poet's methods of expression, and *Pope and Human Nature*, about the material he expresses. *Essays in Criticism and Research* contains two more extremely valuable essays on Pope, and two notable studies in eighteenth century poetic diction. In *Criticism and the Nineteenth Century*, the essays on Arnold, Pater, and Newman were particularly admired. *Thackeray the Novelist* was called "a full and deep appreciation" of a figure currently in critical disfavor.

Tillotson's recreational interests were Mozart and the arts in general. He became a Fellow of the British Academy in 1967. His wife, with whom he collaborated on several books, is a distinguished critic and scholar in her own right, specializing in Victorian literature. *Mid-Victorian Studies* collected a number of her essays, as well as thirteen by Tillotson, including his highly regarded essays on Browning and Clough. Tillotson died in his sixty-fifth year, some time after a severe operation.

PRINCIPAL WORKS: On the Poetry of Pope, 1938; Bibliography of Michael Drayton, 1941; Essays in Criticism and Research, 1942; Criticism and the Nineteenth Century, 1951; Thackeray the Novelist, 1954; Pope and Human Nature, 1958; Augustan Studies, 1961 (corrected reprint of chapters I–IV, published as Augustan Poetic Diction, 1964); (with K. M. C. Tillotson) Mid-Victorian Studies, 1965. *As editor*—The Rape of the Lock and Other Poems (vol. 2, Twickenham Edition of Pope's Poems), 1940; Prose and Poetry of J. H. Newman, 1957; (with D. Hawes) Thackeray: The Critical Heritage, 1968; (with D. Hawes) Villette, by Charlotte Brontë, 1971.

ABOUT: Contemporary Authors 13–14, 1965; Who's Who, 1969. *Periodicals*—Dublin Review Summer 1959; New Statesman January 15, 1938; March 28, 1942; Spectator November 19, 1954; Times October 16, 1969; Times Literary Supplement January 15, 1938; April 4, 1942; August 24, 1951; December 10, 1954; November 28, 1958; December 15, 1961; February 15, 1968.

TOLAND, JOHN WILLARD (June 29, 1912–), American historian, writes: "My birthplace was La Crosse, Wisconsin, a Mississippi River town, but when I was seven my father moved the family to Westport, Connecticut. He was a concert singer possessed of a remarkable baritone voice, and my early memories are of a succession of recitals in schools, theatres, and the vast studios of sculptors and artists. My sister and I would wait outside in a Model T Ford or find inconspicuous seats where we could loudly applaud. Several times I was given the uneasy honor of turning music pages for my father's accompanist, his younger brother.

"In such an atmosphere it was not at all strange that I should irrevocably vow to become a writer at the age of twelve. One day my father brought home a short, plump man with a lost face. Porter Emerson Browne had been a well-known playwright, but after his wife died he found it difficult to write. No one in our impecunious family thought it was peculiar that he had come to live with us 'until he got back on his feet.' By the end of the week Porter had replaced Babe Ruth as my hero. He had written speeches for President Teddy Roosevelt, tracked down the warlords of China and traveled with Pancho Villa. His play, *The Bad Man*, based on experiences with Villa, had a long run on Broadway. When I told him that I too wanted to be a playwright, he spent the next months teaching me the basic principles of building plays. He treated his thirteen-year-old pupil as an adult, pounding into him the theory of the well-made play: exposition, plot structure, characterization, action as dialogue, and the *scène à faire*. We used to go to the theatre in Norwalk and walk out when the movie was half over. Then we'd construct our own ending and return to see if we had bettered the film scenarist. More often than not we had. I remember how indignant Porter would get if some movie violated one of his principles. For example, a gun for the fatal killing would suddenly appear, and he would cry out in annoyance that anything on which the denouement of the play depended—be it a gun or a weakness of character—had to be planted in the first act.

"Another of his principles was patience. He hoped, he said, that the first million words I wrote would not sell. Those million words would be my apprenticeship, my character builder and antidote for eventual success. I far exceeded his hope. Twenty-nine years and two and a half million words later—after working my way through Exeter, Williams and the Yale Drama School, after riding freight trains for five summers and surviving both World War II and an unsuccessful marriage—I had completed some twenty plays, five novels and almost a hundred short stories. Not a novel or short story had been published, not a play produced. At the age of forty-two I was the Compleat Failure—except for my unquenchable determination to be a writer. That summer I went to New York, a middle-aged David Copperfield, with typewriter and fifty dollars. Within three weeks I sold a story to *American Magazine* for seven hundred and fifty dollars, more than my entire previous earnings. In the following month I wrote half a dozen better stories but never again did I sell one to a major magazine. The bottom had dropped out of the fiction market; the accent instead was on articles. A friend, Morton Hunt, gave me one of his article assignments (greater love hath no man), a piece on 'suppressed inventions' for *Cavalier* and helped me write it. In the next year I sold a dozen articles on subjects ranging from mental health to diamond smuggling. Then my agent, Rogers Terrill, got me a contract to write a book on dirigibles. A score of interviews at Lakehurst, New Jersey, convinced me that the drama and reality of the past could be found more readily by this method than in the New York Public Library, where I had done most of my previous research. *Ships in the Sky* was a critical success and portions appeared in the *Satevepost*, *Reader's Digest*, *Life* and half a dozen men's magazines.

"For the next project, *Battle: The Story of the Bulge*, I interviewed almost four hundred American and German participants in the conflict, and wandered for days over the battlefields. With each succeeding work I developed techniques in both research and writing, continually striving to be more

JOHN WILLARD TOLAND

exact and selective, while still accenting the drama that lay at the heart of history. In 1960 I made my first trip to Japan and married Toshiko Matsumura. She became my research assistant and silent collaborator. Her influence was extensive in all my subsequent books, particularly the latest, *The Rising Sun*.

"Up to this time I had regarded my histories as secondary, impatiently waiting for the time I could afford to devote my energies to plays and novels. In the spring of 1971, however, I realized what should long have been obvious: I was destined to write a new type of history and all my failures in the field of drama and the novel had only been painful but essential steps in the development of a storyteller–historian.

"Presently my wife and I are working on a biography of Adolf Hitler, and live, with our two-and-a-half-year-old daughter, Tamiko, in Danbury, Connecticut. I have two older daughters by a previous marriage—Diana and Marcia, born respectively in 1945 and 1946."

Toland's success as a writer of what he calls a "new type of history" was immediate. His *Ships in the Sky*, about the development and abandonment of airship travel in the 1920s and 1930s, was widely and enthusiastically received—a typical comment was that "many a writer of fiction might envy Mr. Toland the excitement and suspense which he has contrived to impart."

As he says, his method is based on scores, sometimes hundreds, of interviews with participants in the events he describes, and personal familiarization with the scenes of action. For *Battle: The Story of the*

Bulge, which describes the powerful but eventually unsuccessful Nazi counterattack against the advancing Allies in the last winter of World War II, he soaked himself in the recollections of survivors and in the atmosphere of the battlefields to such effect that, as one reviewer put it, "in every line Toland writes with the authority of a man who was there. . . . He tastes the bitterness of defeat of those who surrendered and writes as though he had the benefit of the eyes and ears of soldiers and generals on the other side of the line." Some critics, all the same, found Toland's "living history" approach almost overwhelming, so that the shape of the battle was at times obscured by excessive detail, too much attention to individual participants. "The book contains as much conversation as a historical novel," complained one writer in the New York *Times Book Review*, while another in the *New Yorker* expressed mistrust of "Mr. Toland's cheery national self-congratulation." In spite of (or because of) these factors, the book earned its author a national and international reputation.

There was an even warmer reception for Toland's next book, *But Not in Shame*, a "compelling and candid" history of the Pacific war against Japan in the six dark months after Pearl Harbor. S. L. A. Marshall pointed out that Toland was one of "a whole new school of historians" whose emphasis is on the human element, who compose "the big picture by weaving together hundreds of little pictures, there being no better way to reconstruct anything as chaotic and disorganized as battle. . . . Mr. Toland is a nonpareil in making [the method] work. . . . He maximizes suspense, he plumbs the depths of human emotion, he rarely overwrites, he is utterly fair-minded, there are no heroes without blemish in his book, and when he implies a judgment, the evidence presented appears to sustain his view." The book received the Foreign Affairs award of the Overseas Press Club.

Toland next applied his "terrier-like" research methods to a more domestic form of warfare. The *Dillinger Days*, drawn from police files and interviews with survivors of the gang battles of the 1930s, was generally admired and sold well, in spite of competition from another book on the same subject published at the same time. The coincidence afflicted Toland's two subsequent books as well: "I just hope mine will be the best," the author told an interviewer who asked him how it felt to produce a book with a rival "breathing on its neck."

The Last 100 Days, indeed, was a best seller and a major critical success. Toland's eye-witness technique, applied to a theme severely limited in time scale, but geographically diffused, resulted in an extraordinarily vivid and brilliantly organized panorama of the chaos, tragedy, and triumph of the last three months of the war in Europe. Telford Taylor thought that Toland had not probed very deeply beneath the events he described, but that his account had been handled with great skill: "The pace is swift but seldom frantic, the style is lucid and controlled, and sharply controversial episodes are presented with unfailing good taste."

For his next book Toland, the erstwhile "Compleat Failure," received the Pulitzer Prize for general nonfiction, and the Overseas Press Club's George Polk Memorial Award. *The Rising Sun* is subtitled *The Decline and Fall of the Japanese Empire, 1936–1945*, and is written largely from the Japanese point of view. William Craig wrote that Toland's "overall analysis is superb. . . . Nowhere in American literature has the Japanese side of the war in the jungles been so well told. . . . No longer faceless, the 'enemy' emerges from the pages of *The Rising Sun* as a flesh-and-blood foe, dying for a cause he too believed was just."

PRINCIPAL WORKS: Ships in the Sky, 1957; Battle: The Story of the Bulge, 1959; But Not in Shame, 1961; The Dillinger Days, 1963; The Flying Tigers (for children), 1963; The Battle of the Bulge (for children), 1966; The Last 100 Days, 1966; The Rising Sun: The Decline and Fall of the Japanese Empire 1936–1945, 1970.

ABOUT: Contemporary Authors 2, 1963; Who's Who in America, 1972–1973. *Periodicals*—America March 26, 1966; Atlantic March 1963; Book World January 3, 1971; Chicago Sunday Tribune October 4, 1959; Christian Science Monitor December 26, 1963; New York Herald Tribune Book Review February 10, 1957; October 4, 1959; November 5, 1961; New York Times February 17, 1957; May 4, 1971; New York Times Book Review October 4, 1959; October 29, 1961; May 12, 1963; August 27, 1966; Saturday Review January 23, 1971; Wilson Library Bulletin May 1957.

***TOLKIEN, J(OHN) R(ONALD) R(EUEL)** (January 3, 1892–September 2, 1973), English fantasist and philologist, was born in Bloemfontein in South Africa, one of the two sons of Arthur Reuel Tolkien, a bank manager, and the former Mabel Suffield. His parents were natives of Birmingham, and when his father died in 1896 his mother took her children to England, to live in a then rural village near Birmingham. This remarkable woman, his first teacher and the source of many of his permanent interests and attitudes, took him with her into the Roman Catholic Church in 1900. After her death four years later, Tolkien was brought up by Father Francis Xavier Morgan, a priest of the Congregation of the Oratory, and educated at King Edward VI School in Birmingham. The history and the countryside of the Midlands, which fascinated him from boyhood, along with Nordic folklore and literature, inspired much of his work, both as a scholar and as a writer. He studied linguistics at Exeter College, Oxford, and took his B.A. in 1915. During World War I Tolkien fought

* tol' kēn

with the Lancashire Fusiliers. He returned to civilian life in 1918 and for the next two years worked as an assistant on the *Oxford English Dictionary*.

In 1920 Tolkien began his teaching career as reader in English language at the University of Leeds. He returned permanently to Oxford five years later, first as Rawlinson and Bosworth Professor of Anglo-Saxon and a fellow of Pembroke College, and then, from 1945 until his retirement in 1959, as Merton Professor of English Language and Literature and a fellow of Merton College (to which he later returned as an emeritus fellow). It has been said that Tolkien, more than any other single man, was "responsible for closing the old rift between 'literature' and 'philosophy' in English studies at Oxford and thus giving the existing school its characteristic 'temper.' " He became well known to students of English philology and literature, not only at Leeds and Oxford but at universities throughout the world, as the compiler of *A Middle English Vocabulary* (1922), coeditor (with E. V. Gordon) of *Sir Gawain and the Green Knight* (1925), and author of *Beowulf: The Monster and the Critics* (1937), among other scholarly works.

In 1939 Tolkien gave the Andrew Lang Lecture at the University of St. Andrews in Scotland. His address, "On Fairy-Stories," explored the debatable borders of the land of Faërie, whose inhabitants are not the dainty creatures that *fairy* now denotes. Fairy stories, he pointed out, belong not exclusively or especially to literature for children. For him, "a real taste for fairy-stories was awakened by philology on the threshold of manhood, and quickened to full life by war." Fairy stories should evoke a secondary world which has its own values and logic, and which provides the reader with an opportunity for escape and recovery from the real world. Sometimes the reader will recognize an "underlying reality or truth" relevant to his own experience, but the writer must not strive for allegory.

Tolkien had married Edith Mary Bratt in 1916, and was the father of three sons and a daughter at the time that he gave his St. Andrews lecture. Some years earlier he himself had begun writing fairy tales, only partly to amuse his younger children. He had read some of them to the "Inklings," later known as the "Oxford Christians," a group of literary dons centered around C. S. Lewis. They were learned, witty, and conservative Roman or Anglo-Catholics, sharing a romantic attachment to the past and its traditions. Eventually, at the prodding of C. S. Lewis, Tolkien had sent one of his stories to a publisher—*The Hobbit, or, There and Back Again*, with illustrations by the author, appeared in 1937. Its hero, the hobbit Bilbo Baggins, is a hairy-footed, amiable, and comfort-

J. R. R. TOLKIEN

loving being about a yard high. Hobbits live in "Middle Earth," a province of the imaginary past, along with men, elves, dwarfs, and other wonders. Bilbo, involved against his will in a perilous expedition to recover treasure stolen by the dragon Smaug, discovers his heroism and comes into the possession of a magic ring forged by the evil sorcerer Sauron, Lord of Darkness and the Land of Mordor. W. H. Auden called *The Hobbit* the "best children's book written in the last fifty years" but, like the mock-heroic and amusing *Farmer Giles of Ham*, it is a children's book only in the sense that *Alice in Wonderland* is.

The story of *The Hobbit* is continued in more complex and sophisticated terms in *The Lord of the Rings*, a massive twelve-hundred-page epic trilogy comprising *The Fellowship of the Ring* (1954), *The Two Towers* (1954), and *The Return of the King* (1956). Bilbo's magic ring confers absolute power upon its wearer, and therefore represents a temptation too awful to be countenanced. It can be destroyed only in the great furnace in the mountains where it was created, and someone must take it there, preserving it meanwhile from those who would misuse it. This task falls to Bilbo's nephew, another unambitious hobbit called Frodo. Most of the trilogy is concerned with Frodo's ordeal and eventual triumph.

But this vividly imagined and sometimes terrifying narrative is only one aspect of the work's fascination. In Middle Earth Tolkien has created a complete cosmogony, with its own races, languages, songs, history, geography, and customs. The book includes about a hundred pages of glossaries, maps, genealogical charts, and similar documentation, delineating an English pastoral infused with darker elements from Celtic and Scandinavian mythology. The invented language Elvish, which shows some affinities with Finnish, was what inspired the entire work according to Tolkien, who said that "the stories were made rather to provide a world for the language than the reverse."

The Lord of the Rings has been the subject of many learned articles and theses which have attempted to decipher its symbolism in religious, political, or Freudian terms. Tolkien himself said that "it is not 'about' anything but itself. Certainly it has *no* allegorical intentions." It is, nevertheless, an account of a conflict between good and evil, and as such embodies certain assumptions about what is good and what is not. These assumptions, Christian and conservative, are very much those of the Oxford "Inklings," and they have offended some readers, who accuse Tolkien of snobbery, misogyny, and a sentimental dislike of progress.

Nor has the trilogy escaped criticism on purely literary grounds. Edmund Wilson thought it "juvenile trash," and others have attacked it less comprehensively for its thin characterization or its biblical prose. The vast majority of critics however have had nothing but praise for the vigor of Tolkien's imagination and his mastery of narrative; most are delighted by his rhetoric and fascinated by his endless verbal games and philological jokes. C. S. Lewis called it "good beyond hope," and went on: "If Ariosto rivalled it in invention (in fact, he does not), he would still lack its heroic seriousness."

The phenomenal success of *The Lord of the Rings* was not immediate. For some years it remained the property of a small but devoted coterie. Then, in the mid-1960s, for no apparent reason, it caught on, and particularly with college students. A Tolkien Society of America was established, two journals were launched to discuss his works, lapel badges appeared everywhere (in English or in Elvish) announcing that "Frodo Lives." In 1966 the trilogy headed the list of paperback best sellers, and by 1967 world sales of Tolkien's books had reached three million copies in nine languages.

The prose of *The Lord of the Rings* is interspersed from time to time with "dramatic verses" in a variety of moods and styles. Tolkien later made use of his talent for ingenious combinations of sounds in *The Adventures of Tom Bombadil and Other Verses*. A charming fairy tale, *Smith of Wootton Major*, appeared in 1967. Some of Tolkien's songs have been set to music by Donald Swann, and published, and he himself recorded some of his poems and songs for Caedmon. During his last years he was at work on *The Silmarillion*, a "prequel" to *The Lord of the Rings* which is to be completed by his son, Christopher Tolkien, and eventually published. Tolkien was W. P. Ker lecturer at Glasgow University in 1953. He received the CBE in 1972, and held a number of honorary fellowships and doctorates. He served as vice-president of the Philological Society and was a Fellow of the Royal Society of Literature. Tolkien was a slim, gray-haired, pipe-smoking man with "a square, big face." According to his *Times* obituarist, he was "the best and worst talker in Oxford"—worst for the rapidity and indistinctness of his speech, and best for the penetration, learning, and humour of what he said. He was "always best after midnight (he had a Johnsonian horror of going to bed) and in some small circle of intimates where the tone was at once Bohemian, literary, and Christian."

PRINCIPAL WORKS: A Middle English Vocabulary, 1922; (ed., with E. V. Gordon) Sir Gawain and the Green Knight, 1925; Chaucer as Philologist, 1934; Beowulf: The Monsters and the Critics (Sir Israel Gollancz Memorial Lecture), 1937; The Hobbit, or, There and Back Again, 1937; Farmer Giles of Ham, 1949; The Lord of the Rings: vol. 1, The Fellowship of the Ring, 1954; vol. 2, The Two Towers, 1954; vol. 3, The Return of the King, 1955; (ed.) Ancrene Wisse, 1962; The Adventures of Tom Bombadil and Other Verses from the Red Book, 1962; Tree and Leaf (containing On Fairy-Stories, and, Leaf by Niggle), 1964; The Tolkien Reader, 1966; Smith of Wootton Major, 1967; The Road Goes Ever On (songs), 1968.

ABOUT: Carter, L. Tolkien, 1969; Contemporary Authors 17–18, 1967; Current Biography, 1967; Davis, N. and Wrenn, C. L. (eds.) English and Medieval Studies Presented to J. R. R. Tolkien, 1962; Fuller, E. Men with Books Behind Them, 1962; Isaacs, N. D. and Zimbardo, R. A. (eds.) Tolkien and the Critics, 1968; Kocher, P. H. Master of Middle-Earth, 1973; More Junior Authors, 1963; Ready, W. The Tolkien Relation, 1968; Sale, R. Modern Heroism, 1973; Stimpson, C. R. J. R. R. Tolkien, 1969; The Tolkien Papers (Mankato Studies in English, No. 2), 1967; Vinson, J. (ed.) Contemporary Novelists, 1972; Who's Who, 1973. *Periodicals*—Atlantic March 1965; Commentary February 1967; Commonweal December 3, 1965; Critique Spring-Fall 1959; Esquire September 1966; Essays in Criticism October 1956; Guardian September 3, 1973; Hudson Review Winter 1956–1957, Summer 1964; Kenyon Review Summer 1965; Life February 24, 1967; Nation April 14, 1956; May 8, 1967; National Review April 20, 1965; New American Review No. 2 1968; New Republic January 16, 1956; New York Review of Books May 4, 1967; New York Times Book Review January 22, 1956; New York Times Magazine January 15, 1967; New Yorker January 15, 1966; Saturday Evening Post July 2, 1966; Sewanee Review Fall 1961; South Atlantic Quarterly Summer 1959; Thought Spring 1963; Time and Tide October 22, 1955; Times (London) September 3, 1973; Times Literary Supplement June 8, 1973.

TOLSON, M(ELVIN) B(EAUNORUS)

(February 6, 1900–August 28, 1966), American poet, was born in Moberly, Missouri. A year before Tolson died Karl Shapiro said of him: "A great poet has been living in our midst for decades and is almost totally unknown."

His father, A. A. Tolson, was an itinerant Methodist minister and teacher who had taught himself to read and write and gone on to master Latin, Hebrew, and Greek. His mother was Leah (Hurt) Tolson, part black and part Creek Indian—an intelligent and imaginative woman who herself wrote verse. From her Tolson learned hundreds of old poems and popular ballads to balance the love for the classics he inherited from his father. He showed precocious ability as a painter, and was framing and selling his work by the time he was ten. "I parted my hair in the middle," he said, "wore a flowing Windsor tie, and puzzled the elders with words." At twelve he gave up painting and turned to verse.

Tolson attended ward schools in Iowa and published his first poem in 1914, in an Iowa newspaper. In 1917 the family moved to Kansas City, where Tolson became senior class poet at his high school, and learned attitudes toward race which he never abandoned: "There was no race there," he said. "We were all just poor—Negroes, Germans, Jews, Irish, Italian—race made no difference." He always believed that "there is no such thing as human nature. There is only human nurture. A baby is neutral. How he is brought up means everything. . . . On this fact I base my faith in tomorrow."

Tolson went on to Fisk University, and then to Lincoln University, near Philadelphia, where he won prizes in speech, debate, drama, and the classics, and received his B.A. with honors in 1923. For a time after that Tolson was obliged to work in a Kansas City meat-packing plant, but soon found a teaching post at Wiley College, in Marshall, Texas, where he was tennis coach, football coach, boxing coach, and taught "everything under the sun." His years at Wiley were notable for the excellence of the debating teams he trained and of the Log Cabin Theatre he directed there. He also found time to complete several full-length plays and to write a quantity of verse. Tolson's first success came in 1939, when his poem "Dark Symphony" won a national contest organized as part of the Negro American Exposition in Chicago. In 1947 he went to Langston University, Langston, Oklahoma, as professor of creative literature and director of the university's Dust Bowl Theatre.

It is extraordinary that Tolson was so little known during his lifetime, since his quality was recognized, particularly by other poets, as early as 1944, when his first book was published. This was *Rendezvous With America*, in which one critic found "vigor of thought with intensity of emotion but without violence; a tragic sense of life redeemed from despair and restrained from bitterness by breadth of sympathy and an unshaken faith in democracy." Robert Hillyer noted a mild indulgence in "abstractions and preachments" but thought it otherwise an admirable collection, deft especially in the short line.

M. B. TOLSON

Tolson was elected Poet Laureate of Liberia in 1947 (riding from Texas to Washington for his state reception in a Jim Crow car), and composed for the country's centennial his *Libretto for the Republic of Liberia*. It was published in book form in 1953 with an introduction by Allen Tate, who said that it was, in effect, "an English Pindaric ode in a style derived from—but by no means merely imitative of—one of the most difficult modern poets," Hart Crane. For the first time, Tate thought, "a Negro poet has assimilated completely the full poetic language of his time and, by implication, the language of the Anglo-American poetic tradition." For John Ciardi the poem's "blend of language and vision is simply too overwhelming for first judgments. It seems a reasonable guess, however, that Tolson has established a new dimension for American poetry." Selden Rodman called it "not only by all odds the most considerable poem so far written by an American Negro, but a work of poetic synthesis in the symbolic vein altogether worthy to be discussed in the company of such poems as *The Waste Land*, *The Bridge*, and *Paterson*." In fact, in the fourth book of *Paterson*, William Carlos Williams offers his own salute "to Tolson and to his ode / and to Liberia . . ." In 1954 Tolson received from the Liberian president the Order of the Star of Africa.

He died before he had completed his most considerable work, *Harlem Gallery*, on which he had been engaged for over twenty years, and which was planned as a history of blacks in America. Only *Book I: The Curator* has so far been published. It is laid out in twenty-four sections, of which the largest is a collection of portraits of Harlem types whose voices are heard elsewhere in the poem. A reviewer in the *Times Literary Supplement* said that its literary and mythical erudition makes it a difficult work "and the linguistic complexity and use of involuted metaphors call for a reading in the line of Hart Crane. . . . In one sense the artificially created idiom is itself the poet's theme: the nature of Negro art in a white culture. . . . Gradually the analytical wit and sensuous humour move towards a final mocking, serious criticism of blackness, whiteness and the Lost Gray Cause." A reviewer in the *Hudson Review* praised the poem's "astonishing" linguistic range and the vigor and originality of its imagery, while R. D. Spector concluded that "Tolson stands apart from and above contemporary poetic accomplishment . . . as a great American poet."

In 1965 Tolson retired from his post at Langston University and went to Tuskegee Institute in Alabama as the first Avalon Professor of the Humanities. During the last year of his life, although he had already undergone operations for cancer, he lectured in many parts of the United States. He died in 1966 survived by his wife, the former Ruth Southall, three sons, and a daughter. All of his children have distinguished themselves academically: his daughter Ruth is a librarian, with a master's degree from the University of Oklahoma; Melvin B., Jr., has a doctorate in French, Arthur a doctorate in history, and Wiley a doctorate in biochemistry.

Melvin Tolson was a slender man, "with quick brown eyes and a wide smile." Convivial, unpretentious, and "a great talker," he served four terms as mayor of Langston. He was the author of several plays, including "The Moses of Beale Street" and "Southern Front," and once staged his own dramatization of Walter White's novel *Fire in the Flint* for an audience of five thousand at a national convention of the NAACP in Oklahoma City. Tolson received *Poetry*'s Bess Hokin Award in 1952. He was a Bread Loaf Fellow in Poetry and Drama and held two honorary degrees from Lincoln University.

PRINCIPAL WORKS: Rendezvous with America, 1944; Libretto for the Republic of Liberia, 1953; The Curator (Book I of Harlem Gallery), 1965.

ABOUT: Hill, H. (ed.) Soon, One Morning: New Writing by American Negroes 1940–1962, 1963; Hill, H. (ed.) Anger and Beyond, 1966; Hughes, L. and Bontemps, A. The Poetry of the Negro, 1746–1949, 1949; Ploski, H. A. and Brown, R. C. (eds.) The Negro Almanac, 1967; Shapiro, K. *introduction to* The Curator, 1965; Tate, A. *preface to* Libretto for the Republic of Liberia, 1953. *Periodicals*—Oklahoma's Orbit (Magazine of the Sunday Oklahoman) August 29, 1965; Tuskegee Institute News Bulletin December 1965.

TOMLINSON, (ALFRED) CHARLES (January 8, 1927–), English poet, critic, and translator, writes: "Four landscapes seem to contain the autobiographical essence: the English midlands, the Ligurian coast of Italy, the English and also the American southwest, particularly New Mexico and Arizona. I was born in 1927 in Stoke-on-Trent, one of Arnold Bennett's 'five towns,' a place with a dirty and homely ugliness all of its own, a skyline of bottle ovens, slag heaps and pitheads. Stoke has acquired, over the years, what one finds everywhere in the world now—a cheap commercial glitter; and a network of roads and mushrooming housing estates makes it more and more difficult to walk out of it into surrounding country. It was the once easy access between town and nature that left a chief impression behind. The rhythm which was set up then continued when, after leaving the university of Cambridge in 1948, I lived in London, but at the weekends walked and sketched in Kent, Bucks, and Essex. I was working in an elementary school in Camden Town at this time, painting at night and writing my first verse.

"A pamphlet, *Relations and Contraries*, appeared in 1951, just when the offer of a secretarial job in Northern Italy made a break with school-teaching possible. Italy saw the writing of *The Necklace* in which, in a kind of dialogue with Wallace Stevens, I moved towards my own mode of writing—a mode more interested in blackbirds than in ways of looking at them, and one confirmed by the sharp, lit *thereness* of the Mediterranean world and solidified by the practice of painting. *The Necklace* had to wait until 1955 to find a publisher.

"From this Italian setting and from that of the English southwest sprang the third and, to some degree, the fourth books, *Seeing Is Believing* (1958) and *A Peopled Landscape* (1963). By the time I was completing the first of these I was back in England where, after several years in London, I went in 1950 to live in Somerset. Here the limestone setting, the houses and walls of stone penetrated the moral texture of the poems. When *A Peopled Landscape* appeared I had also travelled in the U.S.A. for a period of six months in 1959–60 and a handful of poems here celebrate that visit. It required a second trip, spent as visiting professor to the University of New Mexico, really to write at length about my fourth landscape—the desert vastnesses of Arizona and New Mexico, a setting where, for all the differences, there is a similar unity between adobe buildings and their surroundings as between the limestone buildings of Somerset and Gloucestershire and theirs. I visited often the Indian pueblos along the Rio Grande, and also went to Mexico itself, both of which experiences seemed to deepen for me a capacity to write of the actual people in a given environment, the first real fruit of which had been 'Up at La Serra' in *A Peopled Landscape*. The result of all this travel was *American Scenes* (1966), a book whose dialectic moves between the solitudes, the misgivings of some of its opening pieces with their awareness of death—a new theme for me—and the realisation of a range of possibilities of sensuous awareness, relationship and society, coming full circle in a poem about a public square in San Francisco, 'Idyll.'

"Besides travel and landscape, foreign literature has always been a stimulant in my writing. French and German have meant a lot to me since adolescence. More recently, with the help of Professor Henry Gifford, I have translated from the Russian *Versions from Fyodor Tyutchev* (1961) and from the Spanish *Castilian Ilexes: Versions from Antonio Machado* (1963). At the moment I am working on a number of Italian poets—Gozzano, Ungaretti, Piccolo. Since 1956 I have been employed as lecturer in English at the University of Bristol."

In his "bracingly austere" criticism, Tomlinson has condemned the "self-congratulatory parochialism" of postwar English verse and called for a return to the mainstream of European culture, a working of the territory won by Yeats, Pound, and Eliot. These convictions are reflected in his fine translations from modern European writers, and in his own poetry—for example in "Antecedents," an ambitious attempt to parallel the effect of French symbolist verse.

From the time he left Cambridge Tomlinson was "haunted" by the work of a number of American poets, who seemed to him part of the modern world "as no English figure did." He learned first from Pound, Marianne Moore, and (most conspicuously) Wallace Stevens, and later employed the "three-ply" line of William Carlos Williams. It was an American critic, Hugh Kenner, who discovered Tomlinson, and in America also that his first substantial book, *Seeing Is Believing*, was originally published. Some English reviewers complain about the "tuneless austerity" of his verse, his "dogged loveless homage to a stony Nature," from which "human beings and their awkwardnesses have been squeezed out"; but others have come to admire him as a "secular contemplative poet" seeking (to quote one of his own poems) "the tranquility of consciousness / forgotten in its object." His principal champion among English critics is Donald Davie, who considers him the "most original and accomplished of all our post-war poets," and finds in his verse an "exquisitely accurate register of sense-impressions"—an exactness "controlling an exceptionally passionate and whole-hearted response to the world," and a Hopkinsonian "richness of orchestration."

Tomlinson is the son of a real estate clerk. His year in Italy was as private secretary to the writer Percy Lubbock, and was followed by a studentship at Royal Holloway College and a fellowship at Bedford College, both in London. He visited the United States again in 1967 as O'Connor Professor in Literature at Colgate University, New York, but has otherwise continued to teach at Bristol University, where he is now Reader in English Poetry. He has received the Bess Hokin Prize (1956), the Levinson Prize (1960), the Inez Boulton Prize (1964), and the Frank O'Hara Prize (1968), all from *Poetry*, Chicago, as well as a grant in 1968 from the National Translation Center at the University of Texas. Tomlinson was married in 1948 to Brenda Raybould and has two children.

CHARLES TOMLINSON

PRINCIPAL WORKS (all poems): Relations and Contraries, 1951; The Necklace, 1955 (republished 1966); Seeing Is Believing, 1958; (tr. with Henry Gifford) Versions From Tyutchev, 1961; A Peopled Landscape, 1963; (tr. with Henry Gifford) Castilian Ilexes: Versions from Antonio Machado, 1963; Poems, by Austin Clarke, Tony Connor and Charles Tomlinson, 1964; American Scenes, 1966; Penguin Modern Poets 14 (with Alan Brownjohn and Michael Hamburger), 1969; The Way of a World, 1969; Written on Water, 1972. *As editor*—Marianne Moore: A Collection of Critical Essays, 1969; William Carlos Williams: A Critical Anthology, 1972.

ABOUT: Allott, K. (ed.) Penguin Book of Contemporary Verse, 1962; Contemporary Authors 5–6, 1963; Jennings, E. Poetry Today, 1961; Murphy, R. Contemporary Poets of the English Language, 1970; Press, J. Rule and Energy, 1962. *Periodicals*—Essays in Criticism July 1967; Hudson Review 1961; Kenyon Review 1958; London Magazine November 1964; New York Times Book Review April 29, 1973; Poetry Chicago 1956, 1959.

TOOMER, JEAN (December 26, 1894–March 30, 1967), American poet and novelist, was born in Washington, D.C., where he attended public schools, later spending some time at the University of Wisconsin and the College of the City of New York but without earning a degree. During his

JEAN TOOMER

university years, Toomer began to write poetry and short stories, and in 1920 he went to Georgia, where he taught school for the better part of two years. Early in 1921 Toomer and his friend Waldo Frank traveled together throughout much of the South, a journey that Frank drew upon in his novel *Holiday*, which ends with a lynching.

In 1922 Frank introduced his friend to Gorham Munson, through whom Toomer met Hart Crane and Kenneth Burke among other literary figures, and Toomer's poems and stories began to appear in such little magazines as *Dial*, *Broom*, and *Double Dealer*. It was Frank also who prevailed upon Boni and Liveright to publish Toomer's novel *Cane* (1923). Although sections of the book had already appeared in magazines, it was received with astonishment by the critics. Here was something clearly new in American letters, a sophisticated experimental novel, making use of interior monologue and other avant-garde techniques, and written by a black author before Dos Passos or Faulkner.

Cane is in three parts. The first consists of prose sketches and stories, interspersed with poems, about black women in Georgia, emphasizing all that is instinctive, sensual, and prerational in the black peasant temperament. Part II records in similar form the development, in Washington, D.C., of a black intelligentsia which has accepted the inheritance evoked in the Georgia sketches, and freed itself from the alien and artificial values of white society. Part III is a movie-like one-act play set in Georgia, contrasting one such liberated black intellectual with one who is emotionally and spiritually crippled by his effort to reject the burden of color.

This extraordinary book is thus a celebration of blackness, which is symbolized by the "Oracular. / Redolent of fermenting syrup, / Purple of the dusk, / Deep-rooted cane." It is only when he has acknowledged and affirmed the tragedy and the beauty of his heritage, Toomer suggests, that the black can throw off the chains that history has placed upon him, and transcend himself. In style *Cane* is lyrical and metaphorical, bordering at times on the mystical, in a way which has suggested comparisons with Hart Crane and Walt Whitman. Toomer's contemporary, Arna Bontemps, has said: "Subsequent writing by Negroes in the United States, as well as in the West Indies and Africa, has continued to reflect its mood and often its method and, one feels, it has also influenced the writing about Negroes by others." Nevertheless, the novel sold barely five hundred copies and soon disappeared into obscurity.

At about this time Toomer was increasingly drawn (like a number of his contemporaries) to the teachings of George Gurdjieff, and *Cane* indeed can be read as an expression of Gurdjieff's injunction "Know thyself." Toomer spent the summer of 1924 at the Gurdjieff Institute at Fontainebleau in France, and later led Gurdjieff groups in Harlem (1925) and Chicago (1926–1933). He continued to write, in 1931 publishing *Essentials*, a slim volume of aphorisms. He was married in 1932 to Marjory Latimer, a white woman, who later died in childbirth. In 1934 he was married again to another white woman, Marjorie Content. According to Gorham Munson he hoped to establish a Gurdjieff Institute at Doylestown, Pennsylvania, with money left by his father-in-law, Harry Content, but the funds proved inadequate.

Even less information has been published about the last part of Toomer's life. It seems that sometime in the mid-1930s he settled down as a member of a Quaker community in Bucks County, Pennsylvania, spending much of his time writing religious tracts, including his "minor Quaker classic" *Friends Meeting for Worship*. For the last fifteen years of his life he was an invalid.

There were no obituaries when Toomer died in 1967, and it was only slowly that the American literary establishment realized that it had lost one of the major writers of the "Harlem Renaissance" of the 1920s. His unpublished work, now in the Fisk University library, includes several novels, philosophical works, and other full-length manuscripts. *Cane* was republished in 1967 and a paperback edition appeared in 1969; Robert Bone wrote then that "Toomer confronts the black man with the pain and the beauty of his Southern heritage. That pain, and the power to transform it into beauty, is what the younger generation means by 'soul.' It was Jean Toomer's genius to discover and to celebrate the qualities of 'soul,' and thereby to inaugurate the Negro Renaissance. For this alone he will be enshrined as a major figure in the canon of American Negro letters."

PRINCIPAL WORKS: Cane, 1923 (republished in 1967); Essentials, 1931; Balo (play) *in* Locke, A. (ed.) Plays of Negro Life, 1927; York Beach (excerpt from a novel), *in* Kreymborg, A. and others (eds.) New American Caravan, 1929.

ABOUT: Bone, R. The Negro Novel in America, 1965; Bontemps, A. (ed.) Harlem Renaissance, 1972; Munson, G. B. Destinations, 1928; Rosenfield, P. Men Seen, 1925. *Periodicals*—CLA Journal XIII 1969; New York Times Book Review January 19, 1969; February 16, 1969; Studies in Black Literature I 1970.

"TORSI, TRISTAN." *See* "GOLL, YVAN"

TRACY, HONOR (LILBUSH WINGFIELD) (December 19, 1915), British novelist and travel writer, comes of an old Anglo-Irish family, but was herself born in England, at Bury St. Edmunds, Suffolk. (Some sources give her date of birth as October 19, 1913.) She is one of the four children of a surgeon, Humphrey Earnest Wingfield Tracy, and an artist, Chrystabel (Miner) Tracy. Miss Tracy was educated at the Grove School in London, the Mädchenschochschule in Dresden, and at the Sorbonne, where she spent two years studying French civilization.

During World War II, Honor Tracy worked in the Ministry of Information. After the war, from 1946 to 1953, she was a journalist—an *Observer* correspondent in Europe and the Far East, *Sunday Times* Dublin correspondent and a special correspondent for the British Broadcasting Corporation's Third Programme. In 1946 she served as assistant editor of Sean O'Faolain's Dublin literary review *The Bell.*

Her first book was *Kakemono* (1950), the product of an eight-month tour of Japan. It was a wholehearted denunciation of General MacArthur, the American occupation, and the American way of life, received with rueful admiration by reviewers in the United States, and with unqualified enthusiasm by those in England. There was praise not only for her "Waugh-like invective," but for her sympathetic portrayal of the Japanese. One reviewer called it "the best descriptive book of post-war Japan," and another thought it a small masterpiece. There was also critical approval for her essayistic "forays in the Irish Republic," collected in *Mind You, I've Said Nothing*, a work which defines her distinctly guarded enthusiasm for Ireland and provided some of the incidents fictionalized in *The Straight and Narrow Path* (1956).

It was this novel, her second, which established her. A rational and civilized young archaeologist sees some nuns innocently engaged in what he

HONOR TRACY

recognizes as an ancient fertility rite. His account of the phenomenon involves him in a lawsuit with an Irish priest and a conflict with all the forces of Irish unreason. Isabel Quigly wrote: "Its jokes are beautifully timed to explode with serene good humour under the padded chairs of official religiosity, cant and crawthumping almost anywhere." Other readers reported that they had laughed until they could not see the page for tears, and the novel seems well on its way to apotheosis as a minor classic.

The Straight and Narrow Path set the pattern for Miss Tracy's subsequent novels, most of which, as James Gindin says, feature a well-bred and unswervingly sensible English hero in conflict with "pretentious folly and malicious delusion." In three of her novels the enemy is "a shoddily romantic and irresponsible Ireland"; in *A Number of Things* she takes on the West Indies, which she greatly dislikes. It describes the adventures of a would-be comic novelist who is mistaken for a proletarian one and sent by a "progressive" magazine to the Caribbean, where he is persecuted by arrogant natives and smug white do-gooders alike. Most reviewers appreciated its author's "demure Irish cattiness" but some laughed unwillingly, not quite approving of her choice of targets. *A Season of Mists* (1961) was more serious in its intentions, a study of an aging aesthete who, with mortality looming, is panicked into a disastrous second spring. Many readers found it "both funny and moving."

As a novelist, Miss Tracy has many devoted admirers but has won universal approval from the critics only once, with *The Straight and Narrow*

Path. James Gindin finds her novels limited, in spite of "their wit, intelligence, and clarity," and William Esty feels that they lack a strongly held viewpoint, are "merely amused." Walter Allen has said that "Miss Tracy has great gifts. She never stops being witty; she has an unerring eye for the comic situation. . . . But she lacks a sense of structure and beyond this, one suspects, sufficient respect for the novel as a form." There seem to be no such reservations about her travel books, which include, as well as *Kakemono*, two volumes about Spain much praised for their "excellent evocation of atmosphere and place" and for Miss Tracy's "affectionate, yet never indulgent understanding . . . of the Spanish national character."

Miss Tracy has contributed to *Vogue*, *Horizon*, *Mademoiselle*, and *Queen*, among other magazines. She has also written for radio, and in 1968 her radio feature *The Sorrows of Ireland* received an award from the British Writers' Guild as the best feature script of the year. The author lives in County Mayo, and lists among her pastimes music, gardening, walking, and "travelling in out of the way places in winter." She is plump and has red hair and green-gray eyes.

PRINCIPAL WORKS: *Novels*—The Deserters, 1954; The Straight and Narrow Path, 1956; The Prospects Are Pleasing, 1958; A Number of Things, 1960; A Season of Mists, 1961; The First Day of Friday, 1963; Men at Work, 1966; The Beauty of the World, 1967; Settled in Chambers, 1968; The Butterflies of the Province, 1970; The Quiet End of Evening, 1972. *Nonfiction*—Kakemono, A Sketchbook of Post-war Japan, 1950; Mind You, I've Said Nothing (essays) 1953; Silk Hats and No Breakfast, 1957; Spanish Leaves, 1964.

ABOUT: Gindin, J. Postwar British Fiction, 1962; International Who's Who, 1973–74; Vinson, J. (ed.) Contemporary Novelists, 1972; Who's Who in America, 1972–1973. *Periodicals*—Wilson Library Bulletin November 1962.

***TRAKL, GEORG** (February 3, 1887– November 3 or 4, 1914), Austrian poet, was born in Salzburg of Protestant parents and Slav descent. His father, Tobias Trakl, was a prosperous ironmonger and prominent citizen whose second wife, Maria Halik, was the poet's mother. He was one of six children but within his solidly middle-class family was understood only by his younger sister Margarete, who became a concert pianist. Trakl's relationship with her was, in fact or fantasy, incestuous. Most but not all critics assume that she is the constantly recurring sister figure in his poetry.

As a boy, Trakl shared Margarete's feeling for the piano and some of her talent. At school he was academically a failure, and toward the end of his school years began to show the psychological pattern, alternating between dark violent moods and gentle childlike ones, which thereafter characterized his poetry and personality. It was at this time that he joined a Salzburg poets' circle whose members emulated the *fin de siècle* aesthete. Trakl's literary ambitions and affectations were ridiculed by his parents. He became increasingly withdrawn, began to drink heavily, to speak of suicide, and to drug himself with chloroform, a habit which gave way to a permanent and finally fatal addiction to more extreme drugs.

* trä′kl

This addiction may have influenced his choice of career. In 1905 at any rate, when he was eighteen, Trakl left school and began a three-year apprenticeship in Salzburg as a pharmacist. Stimulated through his friendship with a Nietzsche-inspired local playwright, Gustav Streicher, Trakl wrote a one-act play, *Totentag*, apparently in the Ibsen tradition. Produced in 1906 at the Salzburg Municipal Theater it was a *succès de scandale*. Trakl began to contribute short dramatic scenes and book reviews to the local paper. Later in 1906 a second one-acter, *Fata Morgana*, was produced, but failed miserably. Trakl destroyed the manuscripts of both plays.

His apprenticeship completed, he went in October 1908 to Vienna, for further pharmaceutical training at the university. He hated the big-city atmosphere and remained lonely and depressed. During his two years in Vienna he worked on plays, one of them for puppets, and continued to write verse, some of which has survived. It is in the sensuous, exotic style of the decade, heavily influenced by Rimbaud and Baudelaire, as well as by Trakl's first master, the Austrian lyricist Nikolaus Lenau.

In 1910 Trakl began a one-year term as a pharmacist with the army medical corps and was stationed in Innsbruck and Vienna. Thereafter he lived mostly off the hospitality of friends, working occasionally in pharmacies, until 1912. In that year, when Trakl was considering emigration, he found a patron in Ludwig von Ficker, editor of the iconoclastic Innsbruck journal *Der Brenner*. The philosopher Ludwig Wittgenstein, recognizing Trakl's genius without understanding his poetry, also made a considerable amount of money available to him through Ficker. With this encouragement and support, Trakl brought his work to maturity. Most of his lasting poetry was written between 1912 and mid-1914, either at Innsbruck or Salzburg, and published first in *Der Brenner*.

By 1914 Trakl was a confirmed drug addict and alcoholic, and close to madness, though he retained his always prodigious physical strength. On one occasion at Innsbruck he slept all night in the snow after a drinking bout, continuing his journey home the next morning without ill effects. When World War I began he welcomed it as the final collapse of a social order which had rejected him and which he thought corrupt. He was called to duty as a medical corps lieutenant with the Austrian army in Galicia. After the battle of Grodek he was placed in charge of ninety wounded lying in a barn. Lacking medical supplies or training, he could do little to help, and one of the wounded shot himself in his presence. Trakl broke down and was sent for observation to the military hospital at Krakow as a possible schizophrenic. Placed in a cell with an officer suffering from delirium tremens, irrationally convinced that he was to be shot, Trakl died there intentionally or accidentally from an overdose of cocaine. One of his last two poems, written in the cell, was "Klage" (Lament), which ends: "Sister of stormy sadness, / Look a timid boat is sinking / Under the stars, / The silent face of the night."

A small collection of Trakl's poems, *Gedichte* (selected by Franz Werfel), had been published in 1913. *Sebastian im Traum* (Sebastian Dreaming) appeared posthumously in 1914. He was however little read until after World War II, when he began to receive widespread critical attention and his *Gesammelte Werke* was published (1948–1953). Since then his small body of work—about a hundred poems and prose poems excluding juvenilia—has established him among the most original and influential German-language poets of the century, and as the one closest to the expressionist ideal of the pure visionary, the "Orphic" poet. Yet Trakl learned little or nothing from the early Expressionists. He shared with them the Nietzschean view that the bourgeois materialistic world was doomed, but had none of their reforming zeal. He thought in terms more reminiscent of Dostoevsky and Kierkegaard, both of whom he had read, than of Stadler and Werfel. The world had fallen from grace and he with it. He spoke of his poetry as an "imperfect penance" for his "unabsolved guilt," and in recent years has reasonably been claimed as a prophet of Christian existentialism.

Trakl's mature poetry owes very much to Hölderlin's last poems, and a great deal to Baudelaire and Rimbaud, though his borrowings in form and imagery he made wholly his own. His language is simple and plain, his melancholy autumnal imagery obsessively limited and repetitive, full of intimations of doom and decay. This poetry has an immediate sensual appeal, and has persuaded some readers that Trakl was no more than a decadent romantic. Yet Rilke saw that Trakl's work was affirmative—that it predicated a profoundly compassionate and spiritual view of life even as it recorded the disintegration of the temporal.

The extreme ambiguity of this deceptively simple poetry derives from Trakl's use of imagery. His favorite emblems are clear enough in themselves—certain colors, for example, a garden with crumbling statues, lonely streets. But these visions are

GEORG TRAKL

not logically related in the poems, which become, as W. H. Sokel says, "a flight of images . . . resembling an incoherent dream." Heidegger maintained that all of the poems are variations on a single unwritten and unwritable poem. Trakl's recurring phrases and images are used sometimes literally and sometimes symbolically (and, if symbolically, not always with the same meaning). It has been argued that Trakl's poems are not to be read for the meaning of the words, that his images are autonomous, used as an abstract painter uses colors, for their own sakes or to complement his mood. Other critics see a parallel in Wagner's use of the leitmotiv. Much remains to be debated—notably the nature of that obscure vision of possible regeneration which persists among the guilt and dark hints that echo from poem to poem in Trakl's work.

Perhaps such questions will never be answered, since it was Trakl's purpose to hide rather than to reveal himself in his metaphors; "even a close spectator sees the poet's vision and insights as through a window-pane, and as if shut outside." But Rilke, who wrote that, said also: "In the history of the poem Trakl's books are important contributions to the liberation of the poetic image. They seem to me to have mapped out a new dimension of the spirit and to have disproved that prejudice which judges all poetry only in terms of feeling and content, as if in the direction of lament there were only lament." The chances of Trakl's work being understood were greatly increased with the publication in 1970 of *Dichtungen und Briefe*, the long-awaited historical-critical edition by Walther Killy and Hans Szklenar. This work contains some poems not previously published and an abundance of extremely illuminating variants, rough drafts, and fragments; it has been called the most inclusive edition of the work of any modern poet, demanding something like a new beginning in Trakl studies.

PRINCIPAL WORKS IN ENGLISH TRANSLATION: Decline: Twelve Poems, 1952 (tr. by Michael Hamburger); Twenty Poems of Georg Trakl, 1961 (tr. by James Wright and Robert Bly); Selected Poems (ed. by Christopher Middleton), 1968. *Poems in* Barnstone, W. (ed.) Modern European Poetry, 1966; Bridgwater, P. (ed.) Penguin Book of Twentieth Century German Verse, 1963; Forster, L. (ed.) Penguin Book of German Verse, 1957; Hamburger, M. and Middleton, C. (eds.) Modern German Poetry 1910–1960, 1962.

ABOUT: Casey, T. J. Manshape That Shone, 1964; Cohen, J. M. Poetry of This Age, 1960; Dietz, L. Die Lyrische Form Georg Trakls, 1959; Focke, A. Georg Trakl, Liebe und Tod, 1955; Goldman, H. Katabasis, 1957; Hamburger, M. Reason and Energy, 1957; Heidegger, M. Georg Trakl, 1953; Heselhaus, C. Die Elis-Gedichte von Georg Trakl, 1954; Killy, W. Über George Trakl, 1960; Killy, W. and Szklenar, H. (eds.) Trakl's Dichtungen und Briefe, 1970; Luehl-Wiese, B. George Trakl, Der Blaue Reiter, 1963; Ritzer, W. Trakl—Bibliographie, 1956; Seymour-Smith, M. Guide to Modern World Literature, 1973; Simon, K. Traum and Orpheus, 1955; Sokel, W. H. The Writer in Extremis, 1959; Spoerri, T. Georg Trakl, 1954; Weber, A. Trakl, 1957. *Periodicals*—German Life and Letters January 1949; Germanic Review February 1957; Times Literary Supplement July 9, 1970.

"TRAVER, ROBERT" (pseudonym of John Donaldson Voelker) (June 29, 1903–), American novelist and memoirist, writes: "I was born in the mining and logging town Ishpeming, Michigan, near Lake Superior, the youngest of six boys and the only one who ever got to college. My father, George Voelker, was a saloon-keeper who had married the new music teacher in the public schools, so perhaps inevitably I like to drink and listen to music. My father was the son of German immigrants who trekked across the Upper Peninsula of Michigan by ox cart to establish a brewery in the early 1840s. That canny man established his first brewery near a company of U.S. troops stationed at Fort Wilkins. When the troops vanished, he got the message and opened a new brewery in Negaunee, near the new iron mines.

"Family legend has it that my father's oldest brother Jacob was the first white boy ever born in the Peninsula (1843?), but this is unconfirmed. A girl was believed born to another family at the Sault somewhat earlier. My mother was called Annie Traver and was born in New York, raised in Detroit, and died a month after my father died in Ishpeming in 1935. Her mother was Scotch and her father was New York 'Dutch,' which I believe is really German Palatine. He was born in Rhinebeck, New York, where his ancestors settled long before the Revolution.

"I wrote my first story when I was twelve. It was entitled 'Lost Alone In a Swamp All Night With a Bear.' After that little remained to be added but 'Woof!' but despite this my mother thought it a work of genius, though when pressed she conceded the characterization was a trifle thin—a comment sometimes made by my less ecstatic critics about my later work.

"I graduated in law from the University of Michigan in 1928, in 1930 marrying Grace Taylor of Oak Park, Illinois, whom I met in my senior year at a dance. It was in the early 1930s that I began writing seriously. Since I was a newly-elected district attorney of my home county, and thought it possibly impolitic to admit making up stories on the job, I then first adopted my pen name of Robert Traver. The stratagem was really unnecessary because prior to my fourth book and first novel, *Anatomy of a Murder*, I could have accommodated my readers handily in a broom closet.

"On a Saturday in late 1956 my then publisher phoned me of their acceptance of *Anatomy*. On the following Monday the then Michigan Governor, G. Mennen Williams, phoned me of my appointment as a justice to fill a vacancy on the Michigan Supreme court. During the next three years I campaigned in two statewide elections to keep my job, wrote over a hundred court opinions, attended upon the filming of *Anatomy* in my home county, and somehow survived the indescribably awesome experience of having spawned a national best seller. In January 1960 I abruptly—and reluctantly—quit my court job, to which I had recently been re-elected for an eight-year term, at the time writing Governor Williams in part as follows: 'While other men may write my opinions they can scarcely write my books. I have learned that I can't do both so regretfully I must quit the court.' I would like to believe this was bravery on my part, but I suspect I was only doing what I had to do. And since writing books is chancier than playing the ponies, perhaps I was more foolhardy than brave.

"Primarily I am an old-fashioned storyteller. My yarns tend to have a beginning, a middle, and an end. None of my characters is alienated, or declaims out of garbage cans or open manholes, or sleeps with his sister, or indulges in similar engaging practices that occupy so many characters in much recent fiction. Nor am I unaware that in our present stage of sophistication story tellers have been firmly relegated to the critical doghouse. Nevertheless I shall probably continue to write stories, first, because I like them and, second, because I suspect it is all I can do.

"After *Anatomy* went into orbit (book club, paperback, Preminger movie, the whole bit) I began to think that writing was easy. I was wrong. My next novel *Hornstein's Boy* (1962) swiftly chased my readers back into the broom closet, from which they timidly emerged with my next book *Anatomy of a Fisherman* (1964), done with *Life* photographer, Robert W. Kelley, still remaining a little wary and gun shy with the publication of my third novel (1965) *Laughing Whitefish*, a story about Indians, iron ore and injustice. I was learning that one of the lesser rewards of bestsellerdom is that one is expected to write the same book over and over.

"Prior to *Anatomy* I had written a slender book of fishing stories called *Trout Madness* that I couldn't give away, in whole or in part. After *Anatomy* publishers and magazines were bidding for it furiously, in whole or in part. Meanwhile my wife and I had gone on a trip to Israel and other places with the Joseph N. Welches. (He and I had met and become firm friends when he came up here and played the part of the judge in the movie.) When I returned from my trip I was charmed to learn that a national magazine had paid through the nose for precisely the same fishing story it had rejected without comment prior to the publication of *Anatomy*. I hadn't changed a comma. Besides the money, this experience gave me a kind of humility. From it I think I learned that a writer should write only to please himself.

"Once upon a time . . ."

Traver's first books were lightly disguised reminiscences of his twenty-five years as district attorney of Marquette County, Michigan. Reviewers greatly enjoyed their freshness and humanity, and the "rattling good stories" they contained but, as Traver says, they found few readers.

With his first novel, the situation was reversed; the vast popular success of *Anatomy of a Murder* was by no means foreshadowed by its critical reception. The book, set in Traver's own territory, is an enormously detailed account of a murder and a trial, of what its lawyer hero "thought and did from the moment he first heard of the slaying and accepted the defense" until the verdict was brought in. When the huge manuscript reached F. Sherman Baker at St. Martin's Press, he saw, buried in a forest of verbiage, "a great American story in essential contact with humanity . . . a quality greater than mere stylistic distinction." The following year, when the book was published, prosecuting reviewers found too much of the verbiage still present, the stylistic distinction still absent, and charged "long windedness," whimsy, facetiousness, and every kind of cliché and superficiality in the drawing of character. For the defense, it was pointed out that, for all this weight of guilt, the novel somehow moved, lived and entertained, that it was compellingly readable, and an "acutely reasoned exposition of the law as social catharsis."

ROBERT TRAVER

As for the lay public, it probably never even listened to the experts. Its verdict put *Anatomy of a Murder* on the best-seller lists for sixty-three weeks.

Traver's subsequent novels have fared less well, but two fishing books, *Trout Madness* and *Anatomy of a Fisherman*, were enjoyed, and so was a civilized, stimulating, and witty collection of essays on the law, *The Jealous Mistress*. Robert Traver shares with the hero of *Anatomy of a Murder* not only a passion for trout fishing but also a liking for jazz music and "evil" Italian cigars. He is said to be shy and affable, physically "craggy," and popular with the people of Ishpeming, who "have always been proud of his independent mind." Traver retains "an abiding belief in the essential goodness and toughness of human nature," and says: "If I have not been compelled to learn that—humbly and irrevocably—then indeed I have wasted my time in an elegant course in despair." He and his wife have three children, all now grown up and married. He is a Democrat.

PRINCIPAL WORKS: *Novels*—Anatomy of a Murder, 1957; Hornstein's Boy, 1962; Laughing Whitefish, 1965. *Non-fiction*—Troubleshooter: The Story of a Northwoods Prosecutor, 1943; Danny and the Boys: Being Some Legends of Hungry Hollow, 1951; Small Town D.A., 1954; Trout Madness, 1960; Anatomy of a Fisherman, 1964; The Jealous Mistress, 1968.

ABOUT: Contemporary Authors 4, 1963; Who's Who in America, 1970–1971. *Periodicals*—Life March 31, 1958; Look June 23, 1959; Publishers' Weekly January 11, 1960.

"TREVOR, WILLIAM" (**pseudonym of William Trevor Cox**) (May 24, 1928–), Irish novelist, short story writer, and dramatist, writes: "I was born in Mitchelstown, County Cork, and

WILLIAM TREVOR

spent my childhood in Irish provincial towns of about the same size: Youghal, Skibbereen, Tipperary, Enniscorthy, Maryborough. I went to many schools, finishing at St. Columba's, Dublin, and Trinity College, Dublin. My full name is William Trevor Cox.

"I read widely as a child, and in my early teens developed an interest in the technique of the thriller and the detective story. I believed then that I would become a writer of one sort or another, but discovered a little later that I had an interest in sculpture. During my final years at school and during my University career I carved and modelled, exhibiting at the main annual exhibitions in Dublin. I taught for some years after leaving Trinity—where I had, without much success, read modern history—and in 1953 my wife and I came to England. I taught art for two further years, before moving to Somerset with the intention of earning a living as a church sculptor. I had a one-man show in Dublin in 1956 and one in Bath two years later.

"During all this time I had forgotten any notion of writing. The last writing I had done was as editor of the school magazine: a poem about hell and some editorial comments on the post-war state of Europe. But in the early fifties, with much time on my hands—for the Somerset churches apparently did not require the addition of sculpture—I wrote a novel, more for profit than anything else. This was duly published; and once again I forgot about writing.

"I began seriously to write at the age of thirty-four, in 1962. I produced some short stories and then *The Old Boys*. I was then working as an advertising copywriter, a job for which I was ill-suited and which I would prefer not to hold again. The following year I published *The Boarding-House*, and a year later *The Love Department*. By now I was managing to live by my writing. I had, since *The Old Boys*, written two television plays and a stage play called *The Elephant's Foot* which opened at Nottingham Playhouse on Easter Monday 1966 and toured the provinces.

"I come of an Irish Protestant family not of the Ascendancy class. My family had no literary interests: my father is a retired bank official; both my grandfathers were farmers. My writing is said to be particularly English; the style is remarked upon as old-fashioned. I can account for none of this. I am not much interested in myself either as a person or as a writer. I tend rather to write and to leave it at that. It has become a compulsion to invent characters, plot and dialogue. I'm fascinated by technical problems and by the way one has to use different equipment for producing a short story, a novel, a stage play, a television play, or a film script. Writing, I think, suffers from too much introspective attention.

"My life now centres about my family and my work. I meet few other writers, never discuss writing, read rather less than I used to because I have little time and because for the writer reading is not always a relaxation. I still enjoy going to the cinema probably more than any other way of spending my spare time. I began to love films when I was six, and I think that no form of entertainment has since offered me more excitement. This may possibly have something to do with being of the Irish provinces; as a child, the cinema was exotically foreign, and somehow it has remained so. Things that are strange to me interest me, which is why, perhaps, I write so much about England and the English."

A Standard of Behaviour, William Trevor's picaresque first novel, attracted little attention, but *The Old Boys* received the Hawthornden Prize and was everywhere praised and welcomed as the work of a writer whose unique view of life was expressed in an equally unusual style. It is an account of the lives and childish machinations of eight octogenarians, members of the committee of the Old Boys' Association of their public school. In particular it focuses on the efforts of Jaraby to secure his chairmanship of the committee. The book gives a beautifully observed and subtle picture, at once sad and irresistibly comic, of the shames and seedy pleasures of genteel old age. At the same time it is an oblique but very harsh comment on the emotional stunting which is a product of the English public school system. The stylized dialogue, which reminded many readers of Ivy Compton-Burnett, reduces every subject to the same level of triviality, and perfectly conveys the desiccation and unreality of extreme old age. Evelyn Waugh called the book "uncommonly well-written, gruesome, funny and original."

In *The Boarding-House*, Studdy, a failed blackmailer, and his old enemy Nurse Clock, inherit a boardinghouse and plan to fill it with exploitable old people. Like its predecessor, this novel is peopled entirely by the odd and the elderly, who here seem less a product of a particular educational or social system than of the author's "marvellous facility for macabre invention." Like *The Old Boys*, and *The Love Department*, which followed, it is set in the southwest suburbs of London, a dully respectable area which Trevor seems to approach with the delighted fascination that an anthropologist might feel for New Guinea. His wife told an interviewer that he "knows everything about this street, *everything*. . . . He spends hours just gazing out of the window."

The fruits of these researches are also evident in most of the stories collected in *The Day We Got Drunk on Cake*. Pamela Marsh, reviewing the book in the *Christian Science Monitor*, wrote that Trevor "sees his marvelously created characters from a slight angle, so that although they are thoroughly alive, they seem slightly askew, humorous portraits of serious people suffering from a terrifying isolation." *Mrs. Eckdorf in O'Neill's Hotel* is about the progress into madness of a well-meaning but intrusive photographer. It is set in Dublin, and shows that Trevor is as able a chronicler of the shabby and picturesque city of his youth as of the unromantic purlieus of Wimbledon. *Miss Gomez and the Brethren*, centering on a West Indian prostitute turned evangelist, studies another assortment of Londoners and the more or less bizarre fantasies they interpose between themselves and painful reality. A second collection of short stories was published in 1972 as *The Ballroom of Romance*. Several of these stories had already proved successful as television plays, and Trevor is also the author of a number of stage plays, including an adaptation of *The Old Boys*.

Interviewed by W. L. Webb for *The Guardian*, Trevor readily acknowledged a number of strong influences on his work: Thomas Hardy ("where all my gloom came from"), Evelyn Waugh, Anthony Powell, Mrs. Gaskell. Even judged by these standards, he is a master of his own kind of spare, sly, and subtle prose, his own ceremonious dialogue, and sad, whimsical humor. Some reviewers, however, find in his work a tendency to archness, and suggest that he is inclined to evade, through fantasy, the moral issues that so clearly underlie all his writings. It might be replied that it is not he who does so, but his characters, and that this is often what ails them. He is, he says, "very fond" of the unfortunates he writes about and, as W. L. Webb points out, "obviously admires, for example, a kind of fortitude, an innocent courage which is given to many of his people." In essence, Trevor says, "all my writing is about noncommunication —which is very sad and very funny."

PRINCIPAL WORKS: A Standard of Behaviour, 1956; The Old Boys, 1964 (published in play form, 1972); The Boarding-House, 1965; The Love Department, 1966; The Day We Got Drunk on Cake (stories), 1967; Mrs. Eckdorf in O'Neill's Hotel, 1969; Miss Gomez and the Brethren, 1971; The Ballroom of Romance (stories), 1972; Elizabeth Alone, 1973.

ABOUT: Vinson, J. (ed.) Contemporary Novelists, 1972; Who's Who, 1973. *Periodicals*—Books and Bookmen May 1965; Guardian May 1, 1965; The Scotsman March 7, 1964.

TROY, WILLIAM (July 11, 1903–May 26, 1961), American critic, was born in Chicago of Irish-descended parents and grew up in Oak Park, Illinois. He was educated at Loyola Academy, where at the age of fifteen he sold his first book reviews to a newspaper. Allen Tate says that he "was a Catholic puritan who had left the Church, but the Church never quite succeeded in leaving him." Graduating from Yale in 1925, he taught for a year at the University of New Hampshire, then at New York University, while doing graduate work at Columbia and beginning to make his reputation as a critic. In 1929–1930 he spent a year in France at the Sorbonne and the University of Grenoble, on a Field Service Fellowship, confirming a lifelong interest in the French literary and critical tradition.

He returned to New York University and taught there until 1935, when he joined the staff of Bennington College, serving as chairman of the Department of Literature and the Humanities from 1938 to 1943. And from 1945 until 1960 he lectured at the New School for Social Research, specializing in Shakespeare, and in Joyce and the modern novel. His course entitled "Three Masters of Twentieth Century Fiction: Proust, Joyce and James," was one of the best attended and most celebrated at the school. In 1955 and 1956 he returned to France as a Fulbright Professor at the universities of Bordeaux and Rennes. He retired in 1960 after an operation for throat cancer, and died the following year.

The essays and book reviews on which Troy's reputation rests appeared regularly in *The Nation* and frequently in other journals and literary quarterlies in the 1930s and 1940s—he published little in the last ten years of his life and, thanks largely to his extreme perfectionism, never managed to put his essays into final shape for book publication, though he always intended to do so. It was only after his widow, the poet Léonie Adams, had a volume of his essays published posthumously in 1967 that he was accorded the wide-

WILLIAM TROY

spread public recognition that many distinguished literary figures had long felt he deserved. The book received the National Book Award in 1968 as the work of "one of the truly original practitioners in the most active age of modern American criticism.'

Stanley Edgar Hyman called William Troy "the finest lecturer in literature that I have ever heard," as well as the most neglected of the distinguished generation of critics that included I. A. Richards, William Empson, Kenneth Burke, and Richard Blackmur. Allen Tate, in a preface to the *Selected Essays*, rated him "among the handful of the best critics of this century." And as a teacher, according to the dean of his faculty at the New School, Clara W. Mayer, he was "among those rare teachers who make a school memorable and a generation grateful."

Among Troy's subjects were Henry James, Virginia Woolf, James Joyce, Stendhal, Balzac, Thomas Mann, Valéry, Proust, Malraux, Scott Fitzgerald, Gertrude Stein, D. H. Lawrence, and Shakespeare. His approach was highly eclectic: "The problem," he wrote in "The Lawrence Myth" (1938), "is always to discover the approach that will do least violence to the object before us." But, as he said elsewhere, he believed that "of the various approaches to literature—the technical or aesthetic, the historical, the socioeconomic—the metaphysical alone has the advantage of throwing light at one and the same time on both the form and the content of the work . . . that approach which consists in showing the similarity of the problems consciously dealt with by metaphysics with those consciously or unconsciously expressed in literature." Thus he may relate the book he is discussing to the great myths; to Freudian (and later in his life Jungian) psychology; and to the permanent moral and philosophical problems of man's fate.

Hyman says that "in its range and resourcefulness, as well as in the fineness of its discriminations and evaluations, Troy's criticism is a model of excellence for our time. . . . He anticipated so much that later critics became famous for discovering." Troy was aware that other critics used his ideas without acknowledgment, and resented it. Allen Tate believes "there was a deep compulsion in him that needed neglect and failure to complete the image of himself that he must have formed early in life and that he could wrestle with but not change."

PRINCIPAL WORKS: Selected Essays, 1967. *Film reviews in* Kauffmann, S. and Henstell, B. (eds.) American Film Criticism, 1973.

ABOUT: Hyman, S. E. *introduction to* and Tate, A. *memoir in* Selected Essays, 1967. *Periodicals*—Commentary July 1967; Commonweal May 10, 1968; Kenyon Review June 1966; Nation June 12, 1967; New York Times May 27, 1961; Partisan Review February 1949; Poetry May 1968.

***"TROYAT, HENRI" (pseudonym of Lev Tarassoff)** (November 1, 1911–), French novelist and biographer, was born in Moscow, the son of Aslan Tarassoff, a wholesale merchant, and Lydia (Abessolomoff) Tarassoff. Fleeing from Russia during the Revolution, the Tarassoff family settled in Paris, where their son attended the Lycée Pasteur at Neuilly-sur-Seine. ("I spoke French just as well as I spoke Russian," he recalls, "but coming home from school I left France and plunged back into Russia.") After receiving his *licence* from the Faculty of Law in Paris, and doing military service, he began his career in 1935 as a lawyer in the Prefecture of the Seine, writing his first novels in his spare time. One of them, *L'Araigne* (The Spider), brought him the Prix Goncourt in 1938, and by 1941 he was sufficiently successful to devote himself to literature.

It is as the author of several large-scale sequences of historical novels that Troyat is best known. *Tant que la terre durera* (While the Earth Endures, 1947–1950) is a trilogy which focuses on a single family, the Arapovs, to draw a detailed picture of life in Russia before and during the Revolution. The first two volumes have been translated into English as *My Father's House* (1951) and *The Red and the White* (1957). *Les Semailles et les moissons* (The Seed and the Fruit, 1953–1958) is another family chronicle, this time in five volumes and set in France during the first half of the twentieth century. *La Lumière des justes* (The Light of the Just, 1959–1963), also in five volumes, deals with the 1825 Decembrist Revolution in St. Petersburg.

* trwa ya'

Although his historical novels are carefully researched, Troyat has generally managed to subordinate the historical framework to the vigor and variety of his characters. (He for once failed to do so in the fourth volume of The Light of the Just, *Les Dames de Sibérie*. Intent on correcting an impression that the convicted Decembrist conspirators were hideously mistreated in Siberia, he marshals and transforms into narrative a wealth of documentary evidence, and underpins his argument with some rather harshly sardonic sketches of the imperious wives who were permitted to join their husbands in exile.) Generally speaking, as one reviewer has said, Troyat's "sympathy is for the individual who suffers rather than for any abstract schemes for regenerating society." Like Tolstoy, with whom he is often compared, he seldom forgets that it is people who create the great historical movements of which he writes, and people who feel their effects; the headlines in his novels are not more important than the domestic minutiae. On the other hand, Troyat has none of Tolstoy's passion and psychological depth, and, according to Henri Peyre, "he has not convinced fastidious critics that he is more than a pleasant and often conventional spinner of overlong historical romances."

Of his shorter novels, one of the most successful was *La Neige en deuil* (1952), translated by Constantine FitzGibbon as *The Mountain*. An exciting story about a search for a plane wrecked in the Alps, it is as tautly written as a thriller, was warmly received in the United States, and was filmed. Troyat has also written biographies of Dostoevsky, Pushkin, Lermontov, Gogol, and of his master, Tolstoy. The latter, a monumental study published in America in 1967, is regarded by some critics as Troyat's masterpiece and as the definitive biography of its subject. James Lord wrote of it: "It is not a mere life that Troyat presents; it is a vast spectacle, a pageant, a panorama. It is an immense miracle play of the human situation, a tragedy, a farce, an extravaganza, a comedy of manners, a prodigious pantomime—drama from first to last. . . . That so much may be contained and conveyed by words is the measure of Troyat's talent and of Tolstoy's genius."

Henri Troyat was married in 1948 to Marguerite Saintagne, who has two children by a previous marriage. Elected to the French Academy in 1959, he is an Officier de la Légion d'Honneur, and has received a number of literary prizes. He lives in Paris and has another house in the Maritime Alps.

PRINCIPAL WORKS IN ENGLISH TRANSLATION: *Novels*—One Minus Two, tr. by James Whitall, 1938; Judith Mandrier, tr. by James Whitall, 1941; While the Earth Endures: vol. 1, My Father's House, tr. by David Hapgood, 1951; vol. 2, The Red and the White, tr. by Anthony Hinton, 1957 (England, Sackcloth and Ashes,

HENRI TROYAT

1956); The Mountain, tr. by Constantine FitzGibbon, 1953; The Seed and the Fruit; vol. 1, Amelie in Love, tr. by Lily Duplaix, 1956; vol. 2, Amelie and Pierre, tr. by Mary V. Dodge, 1957; vol. 3, Elizabeth, tr. by Nicolas Monjo, 1959; vol. 4, Tender and Violent Elizabeth, tr. by Mildred Marmur, 1960; vol. 5, The Encounter, tr. by Gerard Hopkins, 1962; Strangers on Earth, tr. by Anthony Hinton (England, Strangers in the Land), 1958; The Light of the Just: vol. 1, The Brotherhood of the Red Poppy, tr. by Elisabeth Abbott, 1961; vol. 2, The Baroness, tr. by Frances Frenaye, 1961; An Intimate Friendship, tr. by Joyce Emerson, 1968. *Biography*—The Firebrand: The Life of Dostoevsky, tr. by N. Guterman, 1946; Pushkin, tr. by R. T. Weaver, 1950; Tolstoy, tr. by Nancy Amphoux, 1967; Divided Soul: The Life of Gogol, tr. by Nancy Amphoux, 1973.

ABOUT: International Who's Who, 1973–74; Peyre, H. French Novelists of Today, 1967; Who's Who in France, 1973–1974. *Periodicals*—Annales Politiques et Littéraires October 25, 1936; November 25, 1936; November 10, 1938; Biblio July 1952; New Statesman February 3, 1951; New York Times Book Review July 23, 1961; February 25, 1962; March 17, 1962; December 17, 1967; Saturday Review August 4, 1956; July 13, 1957; December 14, 1957; Time July 20, 1953; July 15, 1957.

TSUSHIMA, SHUJI. *See* "DAZAI, OSAMU"

***TSVETAEVA, MARINA (IVANOVNA)** (September 26, 1892 [old style, i.e., October 9, 1892]-August 31, 1941), Russian poet, was born in Moscow. She was the daughter of a professor of art history, founder of the Pushkin Museum of Fine Arts in Moscow, and a Polish-German mother, a concert pianist from a wealthy Baltic family. Her permanent sense of alienation and loneliness derived no doubt from the fact that as a child she was fat, plain, clumsy, and impractical, unpopular even within her own family. She began to write

* tsve tä′ ye və

MARINA TSVETAEVA

poetry at a very early age but her mother ridiculed it, wanting for her the career as a concert pianist that she herself had relinquished. Tsvetaeva was sent to music school but spent several years traveling in Western Europe, accompanying her mother, who had contracted tuberculosis, from one sanitarium to another. Her mother's death in 1906 brought the years of enforced piano practice to an end. The year of her birth is sometimes given as 1894 because of her attempt to disguise the fact that she was slightly older than her husband, Sergei Efron, whom she married in 1912. Despite her later emotional involvements with many other men, she seems always to have retained a basic loyalty to him.

By the time of her marriage she had already published her first two books of verse, *Vecherny albom* (Evening Album, 1910) and *Volshebny fonar* (The Magic Lantern, 1911). These early poems written in her teens reveal only one side of her very complex character, an idealistic and romantic strain which led her to admire everything exceptional and heroic. Her poetry is always strongly autobiographical, and also strongly reflects her current reading, which as a girl included Rostand, Bashkirtseva, and Dumas *père*. This romantic vision lies behind poems whose subject matter is drawn from her everyday life: her childhood, her relationships with her family and friends, and her travels. A later book, *Versty* (Milestones), makes up a sort of lyrical diary of her personal and literary life in the year 1916, including Osip Mandelstam's brief infatuation with her.

She reacted strongly against the Revolution, as did her husband, who went south to fight in the civil war on the side of the Whites. Tsvetaeva was trapped in Bolshevik Moscow with their two young daughters, one of whom died of hunger in the famine of 1919. The collection of poetry she wrote at this time, *Lebediny stan* (The Swans' Camp), glorified the doomed heroism of the White armies and mourned the loss to the Reds of "white-walled Moscow." She echoes the most famous passage in the Igor epic, the complaint of Princess Yaroslavna waiting fearfully for her princely husband away fighting a lost war, as was Efron, from whom she was separated for five years. He had left Russia with the defeated Whites, and in 1922 she was allowed to join him. For the next thirteen years she lived in exile, first in Berlin and Prague and after 1925 in Paris. But her anarchic individualism made her an outcast wherever she lived, and she was no more welcome in émigré circles than she had previously been in Bolshevik Moscow. Apart from a few excerpts she never published *Lebediny stan*, and indeed it first appeared only in 1957.

She did, however, publish some of the other lyric poetry written during the desperate years in Moscow in the collections *Stikhi k Bloku* (Poems to Blok, 1922) and *Remeslo* (Craft, 1923), and it was with these, and with her last published collection of lyrics, *Posle Rossii* (After Russia, 1928), containing the short poems written in Berlin and Prague from 1922 to 1925, that she made her reputation. She was completely individual, refusing to align herself with any poetic school. Her verse is typically radically compressed, at times almost a poetic shorthand. Like Khlebnikov, Mayakovsky, and the early Pasternak, she was constantly experimenting with new rhythms, new words, and new associations of words and images; but there is an apparent dichotomy between this innovating virtuosity and the content of her poetry, which is full of romantic nostalgia for the past. Almost all of it is autobiographical, but her experience is often expressed indirectly and obscurely through historical and literary parallels and allusions.

In the 1920s Tsvetaeva also wrote twelve long poems, which fall into two groups: epic and satirical poems with plots borrowed from literary sources, and introspective lyrical poems. The first group includes *Pereulochki* (Sidestreets), a magical, incantatory poem about a sorceress, and two fairy tales in verse, *Tsar-devitsa* (The Tsar-Maiden) and *Molodets*. The long subjective poems include *Novogodnee* (New Year's Greetings), a meditation on the death of her friend the poet Rilke, and two poems about her love affair with a former White army officer whom she had met in Prague, *Poèma gory* (Poem of the Hill) and *Poèma kontsa* (Poem of the End).

During her last decade in Paris Tsvetaeva became more and more isolated as a person and neglected as a poet. Once again she was reduced to the depths of poverty and often on the brink of starvation, for her husband was too ill to work. With their surviving daughter and young son, born in 1925, they were constantly worrying about the next meal and constantly being evicted for failing to pay the rent. Nevertheless, when Mayakovsky committed suicide in 1930, she refused to join other émigré writers, such as Nabokov, in scorning him as a mere Communist versifier. Instead she wrote *Mayakovskomu* (To Mayakovsky), a magnificent cycle of seven poems lamenting the death of a great Russian poet, and expressing contempt for both his Soviet and his émigré critics. After this she found it increasingly difficult to get anything published, and her ostracism became complete when Efron's political convictions changed and he became a Soviet agent. In 1937 he was involved in the political assassinations of Ignace Reiss and of Trotsky's son, and disappeared.

Homesickness for Russia was the theme of several of her lyrics at this time. Émigré society had become intolerable to her, and she was disgusted by the rise of Hitler. She had been deeply influenced by German literature, especially Goethe, Hölderlin, and Rilke, but after Hitler's invasion of Czechoslovakia she wrote some anti-Nazi poetry which because of its savage clarity is more accessible than most of her verse. In 1939, two weeks before the outbreak of World War II, she returned in desperation to Russia. The news that her husband had preceded her there and had been executed reached Paris only a few days after her departure. In Moscow she made some translations of Georgian and Polish poetry, but otherwise seems to have written nothing. After the German invasion she and her son were evacuated in 1941 to the remote town of Elabuga in the Tatar Republic. There, unable to find work except as a kitchen maid, and once more living in desperate poverty, she hanged herself. She was forty-eight.

In the 1930s Tsvetaeva had turned increasingly to prose and, as the poet Khodasevich pointed out, she really mastered that medium only during the last decade of her life, when she wrote a series of personal memoirs, as well as three literary memoirs. Simon Karlinsky regards her best prose pieces, such as *My Pushkin*, as comparable in sheer originality of conception and execution with anything produced in Russian prose during the present century. Her dramatic works are much less important, valuable chiefly for the light they throw on her poetry.

Tsvetaeva had the unenviable distinction of being persecuted both by the Soviet government and by the anti-Soviet émigrés, and at the time of her death her poetry was almost completely neglected, though Pasternak, in some ways a very similar poet, always considered her one of the greatest Russian poets of the twentieth century, describing her verse as a "downpour of light." Her "rehabilitation" in the USSR began in 1956, when her work was represented in both the major anthologies of unorthodox writing which appeared in that year, one of them including an enthusiastic introduction to her poems by Ilya Ehrenburg. This was soon followed by a selected edition of her work, and a large edition in 1965. Her poetry has had a considerable influence on young Soviet poets like Voznesensky. From 1953 onwards her work has also been increasingly published in Russian in the United States, and Karlinsky's valuable critical study has contributed towards her revaluation in the West. But a great deal of her work has still not been published anywhere.

PRINCIPAL WORKS IN ENGLISH TRANSLATION: Selected Poems, tr. by Elaine Feinstein, 1971. *Poems in* Field, A. Pages from Tarusa, 1965; Markov, V. and Sparks, M. (eds.) Modern Russian Poetry, 1966; Milner-Gulland, R. Soviet Russian Verse, 1961; Obolensky, D. Penguin Book of Russian Verse, 1962. *Poems and prose in* Tri-Quarterly Spring 1973.

ABOUT: Carlisle, O. Poets on Street Corners, 1969; Ehrenburg, I. People and Life, 1961; Karlinsky, S. Marina Cvetaeva, 1966; Mirsky, D. J. A History of Russian Literature, 1960; Penguin Companion to Literature 2, 1969; Poggioli, R. The Poets of Russia, 1960; Slonim, M. Modern Russian Literature, 1953. *Periodicals*—New York Review of Books March 9, 1967; Times Literary Supplement May 4, 1962; February 23, 1967; Tri-Quarterly Spring 1965; Spring 1973.

***TUCCI, NICCOLÒ** (May 1, 1908–), bilingual Italian-American novelist, short story writer, dramatist, and essayist, was born in Lugano, Switzerland, and spent his early childhood there. His mother, "romantic, sheltered, unformed," came of a millionaire Russian banking family; his father was a puritanical Italian doctor of peasant stock: people "fit to have children, not to tend them." Tucci has described the contradictory demands they made on him, the demands that "came in twos and ran on the same track in opposite directions." While he was still a child the family moved to Florence, where Tucci grew up and received his strict and demanding education. He wanted to become a psychiatrist but, under his father's influence, studied the law and social sciences instead.

Educated under Mussolini, Tucci was at first an ardent Fascist and began his career in the foreign affairs branch of the Italian government. In 1936 he paid his first visit to the United States, where he worked for the Italy America Society and produced Fascist propaganda for the Italian consulate. By September 1937, when he returned to Italy, his attachment to the regime was considerably weakened. He was disgusted by the anti-Semitism imported from Nazi Germany, helped a number of

* tōō′ chē

NICCOLÒ TUCCI

refugees to escape, and resigned from his government post. Although he had not yet renounced Fascism, his position in Italy became increasingly difficult and at the end of 1938 he left the country with his wife and baby, arriving penniless in New York in 1939.

During the next year or two Tucci was gradually converted into an active and articulate opponent of Fascism, and in 1941 joined the staff of the Coordinator of Inter-American Affairs in Washington, where his task was to urge a similar change of heart upon European immigrants in Latin America. Passionately committed by then to democratic ideals, Tucci was disappointed by what he saw of their application in Washington. He left his job after three years and expressed his disillusionment in articles published in *Politics* at the end of World War II. These, and his earlier allegiance, brought a denial of his first application for naturalization in 1948. The historian Gaetano Salvemini, who has greatly influenced Tucci, drew attention to his case in *The Nation*, and Tucci became an American citizen in 1953.

Since the war Tucci has earned his living as a teacher, translator, journalist, and writer. He first attracted attention with short stories published in England, in America (mostly in the *New Yorker*), and in Italy. The novella *Il segreto*, which first appeared in *Botteghe Oscure*, became the title piece in a collection of stories published in 1956 in Italy, where it won the important Viareggio prize. *Tico-Tico*, a story for children, illustrated with photographs by Ylla and "full of sly humor," appeared in English in 1950.

The first of Tucci's adult books to be published in the United States was the lightly fictionalized family portrait *Before My Time* (1962), which is dedicated to Gaetano Salvemini. It is set at the turn of the century in Europe, where his mother, traveling as part of *her* mother's elaborate entourage, meets the provincial Italian doctor who was to become her husband. The book describes the passionate romance which sprang up between this ill-assorted pair, and the austere doctor's gradual entanglement in his wife's "insanely extravagant world of endless money and family intrigue." It is Tucci's Russian grandmother "Mamachen" who dominates the story, "a figure of tyrannical strength and intellectual power . . . both a life-giver and a life-destroyer—the matriarch of a large, wildly emotional, Russian family."

Before My Time is a unique and unclassifiable book—"an ironic satire on national traits, an analysis of . . . human emotions and actions, a series of philosophical and psychological observations—a mélange from which practically any kind of literary fare can be chosen." One of its reviewers was reminded of Proust; another of Hogarth; most thought it too long, and preferred its brilliant narrative prose to its rather stilted dialogue. Helene Cantarella called it a "paradoxical chapter of the human comedy" observed from a dual vantage point: "If [Tucci's] lucid, analytical Italian half can see and convey the magnificently grotesque humor of the tragicomic crises in which his Russian relatives thrived, his warm, generous Russian half . . . can barely conceal a good-natured contempt for the provincial, self-righteous, penny-pinching scruples of his Italian father."

Tucci's second novel, *Unfinished Funeral*, is another study of a matriarch, a "caricature of the great clichés of emotional life" in which the Duchess Ermelinda, through an endless series of faked or self-inflicted illnesses, snares her husband and children in permanent guilt. Some critics found this Freudian joke oddly moving but Carlos Fuentes, though he admired Tucci's prose, concluded that the reader is "left with a hard, brilliant central symbol, a ream of unrealized possibilities and the hurt feeling that Mr. Tucci has deprived us of a masterly novel."

Tucci's partly autobiographical play, *Posterity for Sale*, was produced off Broadway in 1967. He was one of the founders of the *Village Voice* and has written for that and for many other notable journals in the United States and Italy. In 1965–1966 he was writer-in-residence at Columbia University. Tucci is married to the former Laura Rusconi and has two children, one of them born in the United States.

PRINCIPAL WORKS: Before My Time, 1962; Unfinished Funeral, 1964. *For children*—Tico-Tico, 1950.

ABOUT: Tucci, N. Before My Time, 1962. *Periodicals*—Nation September 1948; St. Paul Pioneer July 29, 1962.

***TUCHMAN, BARBARA W(ERTHEIM)** (January 30, 1912–), American writer of narrative history, writes: "I was born in New York City, a third-generation native of that place, the daughter of Maurice Wertheim, banker, founder of Wertheim & Company, a founder of the Theatre Guild, a one-time owner and publisher of *The Nation*, art collector and sportsman. My mother was Alma Morgenthau, daughter of Henry Morgenthau, Sr., Ambassador to Constantinople under President Wilson and sister of Henry Morgenthau, Jr., Secretary of the Treasury under President Franklin Delano Roosevelt. My first experience of war, memorable through frequent family retelling rather than personal recollection, was of the Anglo-German naval battle in the Mediterranean between the Gloucester and the Goeben, in August 1914, later recounted in my book, *The Guns of August*, which we witnessed while en route to visit my grandfather in Turkey. Later influences which bent the twig toward history were chiefly literary, beginning at about the age of six, with the Lucy Fitch Perkins 'Twin' series followed by the works of G. A. Henty, Alexandre Dumas *père*, Harrison Ainsworth, Conan Doyle's *The White Company*, and Jane Porter's *Scottish Chiefs*. I attended the Walden School in New York City from which I graduated in 1929 and Radcliffe College, class of '33. I did not attend graduate school and have no earned degree other than B.A. Nor did I ever take a course in writing. At college I majored in the combined field of history and literature; in my case, of England with specialization in the nineteenth century. Although I experienced no moment of revelation that determined me to write history, I did receive impetus from great courses and great professors, among them Irving Babbitt's comparative literature and C. H. McIlwain's constitutional history. But the single most formative experience, I think, was the stacks at Widener Library where I was allowed to have as my own one of those little cubicles with a table under a window, queerly called, as I have since learned, 'carrels,' a word I never knew when I sat in one. Mine was deep in among the 940's (British History, that is) and I could roam at liberty through the rich stacks, taking whatever I wanted. The experience was marvelous, a word I use in its exact sense meaning full of marvels. It gave me a lifelong affinity for libraries, where I find happiness, refuge, not to mention the material for making books of my own. Archives like the National Archives and the Public Record Office and manuscript collections like that of the Congressional Library where one can use material in the original, are even better.

"Emerging from college in the 1930s when we all had a social conscience and felt a need for action, I

* tuk′ mən

BARBARA W. TUCHMAN

went to work in the field of international relations at the Institute of Pacific Relations, first in New York City and then for a year, 1934–1935, in Tokyo. Subsequently I worked for two years on the staff of *The Nation* as an editorial assistant and occasionally correspondent, most notably from FDR's campaign train in 1936 and from Spain during the Spanish Civil War in 1937. As for so many of us at that time, Spain absorbed my efforts for a period during which I worked in London for a year as staff writer for a bulletin, *The War In Spain*, and at the same time wrote a small historical treatise, called *The Lost British Policy; Britain and Spain Since 1700*, published in London in 1938. I came home just before Munich for what was intended to be a temporary visit to satisfy the anxieties of my family but then became caught up here with American propaganda work for the Spanish Republic. During this period I wrote a series of pieces for the *New Statesman and Nation* of London on the developments of American attitudes during the Cold War. In June 1940 I married Dr. Lester R. Tuchman, as it happened on the day that Paris fell, which then seemed to us almost more important than marriage. We spent a year at Camp Rucker in Alabama with our first daughter when my husband was attached to the Third General Hospital and after he went overseas I went to work in New York for the Office of War Information on its Far Eastern news desk, where my job was to write stories beamed to Europe, trying to acquaint our European listeners, much against their will, with the extent of America's war effort in the Far East.

"Following the end of the war and my husband's

return and the birth of two more daughters, I finally reached the point of undertaking a book whose precipitating event was the establishment, or rather recreation, of the State of Israel in 1948. This, as a unique historical event, somehow galvanized me and resulted in a book called *Bible and Sword.* Owing to maternal duties with still very young children, I could work only half a day at the most and the book took me over five years to finish and was rejected by I don't know how many publishers before its final appearance in 1956. However, the experience of writing history affected me as I suppose heroin does the addict and from then on I was caught. The other books followed, interspersed with occasional pronouncements on my craft in *Harper's*, the New York *Times* and other periodicals and even occasional lectures which surprisingly I actually enjoyed, discovering a hitherto unsuspected element of the natural ham in my make-up.

"As an historian, I belong to the How rather than the Why school; I am a seeker of the small facts not the big Explanation; a narrator not a philosopher. I find the meaning of history emerges not from what an academic practitioner has recently called the 'large organizing idea' but from the discipline of arranging one's material into narrative form. With each book I approached nearer, as I hope, to my goal of presenting history as literature. With each one, I learned more about the art and technique of achieving my object, which was composite: to captivate an audience, convey information and tell a story—and perhaps leave the reader with an idea, or view, or understanding of things he did not have before. I suspect *The Guns of August* may have accomplished this for it seems to have found readership ranging from high schools to the White House and the Pentagon. I am not sure which of these was the most important. The greatest satisfaction has been in discovering from satisfied readers that history, as I always suspected, can be written to convey to others the excitement which it has always had for me as the most fascinating subject of all—the actual, not the imagined, behavior of mankind."

Mrs. Tuchman's honors thesis at Radcliffe was called "The Moral Justification for the British Empire," and her interest in British foreign policy was also reflected in her first two books: *The Lost British Policy* and *Bible and Sword.* The latter sets out to show that the Balfour Declaration, which gave Britain's blessing to what became the State of Israel, was the fruit of religious and political attitudes shaped over centuries of intercourse between England and Palestine. There was much praise for *Bible and Sword*, and more for *The Zimmerman Telegram*, about Germany's attempt in 1917 to form an alliance with Mexico. S. F. Bemis spoke of Mrs. Tuchman's vivid writing, and said: "The value and importance of her book lies in her brilliant use of well known materials, her sureness of insight, and her competent grasp of a complicated chapter of diplomatic history."

It was, however, *The Guns of August*, Mrs. Tuchman's study of the background and the first month of World War I, which brought her real fame. There were a few complaints about errors and omissions in Mrs. Tuchman's account, and a suggestion that she was a little inflexible in her passionately held opinions, but there was otherwise very little but enthusiasm for the book's brilliant organization, its authority and dramatic force. It was said to illuminate, "practically inch by inch," the ways in which the fateful decisions were made in the world's capitals, and to "transform the drama's protagonists as well as its immense supporting cast from half-legendary . . . figures into full-dimensional, believable persons." Mrs. Tuchman's accounts of the war's first battles were called masterly. Her book, a Book-of-the-Month Club selection and a best seller, brought her the 1963 Pulitzer Prize for general nonfiction.

The Proud Tower, also a Book-of-the-Month Club selection, is an attempt to "discover the quality of the world from which the Great War came," and concentrates on social life in England, Europe, and America between 1890 and 1914. Here Mrs. Tuchman's method is impressionistic, focusing on a few key events, causes, and personalities, from aristocrats to anarchists. The result is a rich, fascinating, and often funny book which, however, it was thought, leaves many vital questions unanswered and unasked, and lacks a "ruling vision" to give it coherence. Mrs. Tuchman received a second Pulitzer Prize for *Stilwell and the American Experience in China, 1911–1945*, which was yet another Book-of-the-Month Club selection when it was published in 1971. It is both a massive biography of "Vinegar Joe" and a detailed account of the frequently misguided policies under which he labored until his headlong conflict with Chiang Kai-shek led to his recall in 1944. One reviewer commented that, even if this was not the great book that could have been written about Stilwell, it was still "a fantastic and complex story, finely told, and loaded with new information, maps and pictures." *Notes From China* is a record of a six-week visit which Mrs. Tuchman made to China in 1972.

The writer is a slight, willowy woman, five feet five inches tall, with gray eyes and silvery hair. She is an expert skier and poker player, and also enjoys swimming, canoeing, riding, and tennis. Mrs. Tuchman has a house in New York and another in Connecticut. She and her husband are divorced. In 1971 she was elected a member of the American Academy of Arts and Letters.

PRINCIPAL WORKS: The Lost British Policy: Britain and Spain Since 1700 (published only in England), 1938; Bible and Sword: England and Palestine from the Bronze Age to Balfour, 1956; The Zimmerman Telegram, 1958; The Guns of August (England, August 1914), 1962; The Proud Tower: A Portrait of the World Before the War, 1890–1914, 1966; Stilwell and the American Experience in China, 1911–1945, 1971 (England, Sand Against the Wind); Notes From China, 1973.
ABOUT: Contemporary Authors 1, 1962; Current Biography, 1963; Who's Who in America, 1972–1973; Who's Who of American Women, 1974–1975. *Periodicals*—Book-of-the-Month-Club News January 1962; The New Yorker October 6, 1962.

***TUOHY, FRANK (JOHN FRANCIS)** (May 2, 1925–), English novelist and short story writer, writes: "I was born at Uckfield, Sussex, where my father was Medical Practitioner. His family was Irish, established in Cork, connected by marriage with that of James Joyce. But in the latter part of the nineteenth century, they made the jump into the British professional class, becoming soldiers, journalists, doctors. Brought up a Catholic, my father was married outside the church. My maternal grandfather was a paper manufacturer, lowland Scottish and Presbyterian. My father and mother met early in the First War, but then my father was sent to the Middle East for some years. Both my parents were nearly forty when I was born. In a sense they had already retired, and I was constantly being told that nothing was nearly as good as it had been. From their different backgrounds, and for other reasons as well, both my parents had a strong Puritan tendency, which I suppose myself to have inherited. I was born with a congenital heart defect (cured by surgery in 1960) and spent a good deal of my childhood being ill. In spite of this I was sent to an exceedingly tough preparatory school with a Naval background, where because of my incapacity I learned a fairly lasting sense of inadequacy. Four years in the more sybaritic climate of a wartime public school did something to alleviate this. Rejected for the army, I went to Cambridge, where I did Philosophy and English, and read as much as I could. I had always thought of becoming a writer and during the next few years I wrote a number of short stories, nearly all copies of which were lost by a well-known London literary figure. I still miss them. England in the late forties was not a hopeful place, and in 1950 I went to South America, where I lived for six years. I got a very well-paid job at the University of São Paulo, and soon found myself torn between doing it properly and starting to be a writer. In the end I did both, but neither as well as I should have liked. Rio and São Paulo form the setting of my first two

* tōō′ ē

FRANK TUOHY

novels, one written before I could speak the language and the other after. My first novel was praised by C. P. Snow among others and was very well reviewed. Some critics said I was extremely detached, others thought me involved. Perhaps our present society provides no easy resting point between subjectivity and detachment. I dislike the element of narcissism prevalent in much contemporary fiction, particularly in America. In my second and third novels I tried to be very objective; the earlier of the two is too special in background, I think, to be readily comprehensible. I wrote it in Paris, thinking in Portuguese and French. *The Ice Saints*, my third novel, had the advantage of a background, contemporary Poland, about which many people feel concerned and interested. English critics liked it. For this novel I was awarded both the James Tait Black Memorial Prize and the Geoffrey Faber Memorial Prize for 1964. For my short story 'The Admiral and the Nuns' I was given the first of the Katherine Mansfield prizes in 1960."

After his six years as professor of English Language and Literature at the University of São Paulo, Brazil, Frank Tuohy taught for shorter periods at Jagiellonian University, Cracow (1958–1960), and at Waseda University, Tokyo (1964–1967). He became a Fellow of the Royal Society of Literature in 1965, and gives his recreation as "travel." The early part of Tuohy's career was something of an achievement of the will. He left Cambridge "feeling rather ill," and had in fact a hole in the heart. His work in Brazil and in Poland, and his first two novels, were managed not so much in spite of this but because of it. His life was changed by the successful heart operation of which he speaks above.

Tuohy is placed by some critics "in the front rank of current British novelists." *The Animal Game*, set as he says in Rio de Janeiro, was "a sardonic picture of men and women consumed by their own destructive passions"; *The Warm Nights of January* was similar in theme and setting, "an enormously sensitive and complex study." There followed a collection of Chekhovian short stories, *The Admiral and the Nuns*, exploring "the truths of struggle, of degradation, of compensation and redemption—among London artists, in the Poland of tyranny and agony, in the decadence of tropical Latin America." *The Times Literary Supplement* called the book brilliant, if uneven, and said that at his best Tuohy's "prose glitters [and his] camera-eye is focused to a hair's breadth."

Tuohy's somberly sympathetic but generally bleak view of humanity, his subtle and reflective manner, have so far brought him more critical than popular success. *The Ice Saints*, his third novel, was particularly admired. It is about an English girl who goes to Poland, ostensibly to visit her married sister, actually to bring news of a legacy. She finds her hosts suspicious of her news and uninterested in her, except as a counter to be used in their endless quarrels and maneuvers, and at the end returns defeated to England. The book is a deft and grim picture of modern Poland, and for most critics much more. P. N. Furbank, writing in *Encounter*, compared Tuohy to Montherlant and praised his "command of causality," calling his narrative "an immensely swift succession of little billiard-ball collisions." The book, Furbank thought, "shows a mind at a steady temperature of creation, almost embarrassed at the number of perceptions and possibilities opening up before it."

In 1967 Tuohy bought a house near Bath, and there wrote the stories, mostly with English settings, collected in *Fingers in the Door*. Once again there was warm critical praise, although one reviewer thought these stories showed no advance over Tuohy's earlier collection and found it "distressing that an author of such abundant gifts should content himself with these elegantly turned anecdotes." Tuohy resumed his travels in 1970, when he went as writer-in-residence to Purdue University. He is a Fellow of the Royal Society of Literature, and received the E. M. Forster Award of the National Institute of Arts and Letters in 1972.

PRINCIPAL WORKS: The Animal Game (novel), 1957; The Warm Nights of January (novel), 1960; The Admiral and the Nuns (stories), 1962; The Ice Saints (novel), 1964; Portugal (travel), 1970; Fingers in the Door (stories), 1970.
ABOUT: Vinson, J. (ed.) Contemporary Novelists, 1972; Who's Who, 1973; Who's Who in America, 1972–1973. *Periodicals*—London Magazine December 1964; Times Literary Supplement July 9, 1964.

***TURNELL, MARTIN** (March 23, 1908–), English critic and scholar, writes: "I was born at Birmingham in the heart of the industrial midlands. My father's family were businessmen and my mother a Welshwoman from North Wales. I was educated at Uppingham School; Corpus Christi College, Cambridge, where I read English and modern languages; and the Sorbonne where I did philosophy. I worked for two years at a London publisher's and then took up law. I was admitted a solicitor in January 1939 and two months later joined the staff of the British Broadcasting Corporation as an assistant in a department with the baroque title of Programme Contracts. In 1943–1945 I served in the Intelligence Corps in France, Belgium and Germany. I was demobilised in November 1945 and returned to the BBC. Since 1959 I have been head of my department and specialise in negotiations with the artists' trade unions.

"I have a particular dislike of people who go round saying: 'I should like to write.' Writers, whether good or bad, are born not made. A man writes because he is a writer, not because he thinks that it is 'nice' or 'smart' to write. I began by writing short stories for my preparatory school magazine when I was eight. My first paid contribution was published in a Birmingham newspaper when I was sixteen. Ancestry may have played a part in my eventual choice of French literature as my main interest. My father's family were descended from Huguenot refugees who settled in the midlands after the Revocation of the Edict of Nantes in 1685. (Our name comes from the French *tournelle* meaning 'small tower' or 'small castle.') Although I have been writing since childhood, I decided not to earn my living as a writer because I never wanted to be in a position of having to turn out a weekly article on some alien subject for money. I have been influenced by many people, but have never nailed my flag to anyone's mast. I believe I am the only person to have written for both Leavis's *Scrutiny* and Connolly's *Horizon*. As an independent operator in what is regarded as an academic preserve, I am badly looked on by dons who would like to write and can't.

"I was born under Aries, the sign of the rebel and the fire-brand: tendencies strengthened in my case by a large dose of Welsh blood. My secondary school was an extreme example of the English Protestant public school: in my time a cross between Prussian military academy and penal settlement. I went there by accident. Although I had been entered for years, there was no vacancy when the time came and plans were hastily made to send me elsewhere. Then a sudden vacancy was caused by the expulsion of a senior boy who was caught

* tur nel′

by the football master fornicating with another master's daughter. School drove me into a sort of permanent opposition. I am by nature an autocrat with a horror of every kind of authority—except one. My family were not 'religious people,' but had inherited a violent anti-Catholic prejudice from their Huguenot forebears. The first great family upheaval occurred when, at the age of twenty-three, the rebel reverted to the faith of his pre-Huguenot ancestors at a private ceremony in the chapel of the Cardinal-Archbishop of Paris. The next came four years later when I flouted convention by marrying Helen Julia Hanschell at the start of my three years' legal training. The children of Aries are said to be self-opinionated and self-righteous people who often turn out to be right in the long run. So it proved with these two youthful decisions."

Martin Turnell, except in his Lauriston Lecture, published as *Modern Literature and the Christian Faith* (1961), has been almost exclusively an expounder of French literature to his English readers. It is immediately clear from his writings, which have not been prolific, that his grasp of the language and literature of France is profound; he is, in the widest sense, a scholar. But his works, lucidly written, in an easy and unpatronizing manner, are aimed at the general reader with some knowledge of French rather than at the student. Nevertheless, most of his books remain in print, and one may reasonably suppose that it is students who keep them so. Perhaps Turnell's success as an expositor is partially explained by the fact that his early training was in English, philosophy, and other languages besides French. He is highly independent —but not dogmatic—in his critical opinions, and never allows his Roman Catholicism to influence his version of facts. Nonetheless, though not in a demonstrative manner, he is a profoundly Catholic critic.

The Classical Moment is a study of Corneille, Molière, and Racine, relating their achievements to the current of French history, literature, and thought. The book acknowledges that Corneille and Racine are virtually untranslatable into English and Turnell's achievement is to make them, particularly Racine, as accessible to English readers as they can be. There is not a great deal of original appreciation, but much exceedingly valuable exposition and painstaking explanation. The author was warmly praised for his easy familiarity with the formidable literature of the subject and "for the sensitivity with which [he] has entered the minds of his three poets."

Baudelaire, again, does not present as original a view of the poet as we obtain from Sartre's study, or even from Enid Starkie's: Turnell shares Eliot's impression of Baudelaire as an essentially Catholic poet, blaspheming against God because he believed in Him. The virtue of the book is in its sharp historical insights and its fairness to contrary views. Turnell's monograph on the critic Jacques Rivière is the standard work in English. He is particularly in sympathy with this friend of Fournier and Gide, whose combined Roman Catholicism encompassed a passionate insistence on sincerity and humanitarianism. *Jean Racine*, a long and useful study, is primarily a critical commentary on the plays with the emphasis on Racine as a psychological dramatist.

MARTIN TURNELL

The Novel in France, a more personal work than the title suggests, explores the work of seven French novelists: Madame de la Fayette, Laclos, Constant, Stendhal, Balzac, Flaubert, and Proust. Turnell, it was said, "bases his judgements on the novelist's use of language itself in mirroring the society of which he is writing," proceeding according to standards which "might justly be termed classical." The book left a final impression, one critic said, "of sincerity, decent moderation, a refusal to be hustled by mythical reputations, and a real and sometimes infectious enjoyment of good fiction." Another book conceived in a similar spirit is *The Art of French Fiction*, which deals with the work of Zola, Gide, and Mauriac, Prévost, Stendhal, Maupassant, and Proust. One reviewer, aroused by Turnell's harsh view of Gide, called the book "personal and tendentious," but most readers, even when they disagreed with Turnell's assessments, had little but praise for the work of this "sensitive and erudite conservative."

PRINCIPAL WORKS: Poetry and Crisis, 1938; The Classical Moment: Studies in Corneille, Molière, and Racine, 1947;

The Novel in France, 1950; Baudelaire, 1953; Jacques Rivière, 1953; The Art of French Fiction, 1959; Modern Literature and Christian Faith, 1961; Jean Racine: Dramatist, 1972.

ABOUT: *Periodicals*—Commonweal June 29, 1951; October 9, 1959; New Statesman April 18, 1959; New York Times Book Review May 13, 1951; New Yorker September 15, 1951; Saturday Review June 9, 1951; Times Literary Supplement August 7, 1959.

TURNER, E(RNEST) S(ACKVILLE) (1909–), English author of books on what he calls "the byways of social history," writes: "My ancestors include a Sheriff who gave the order to fire on the London mob in the Gordon Riots and a bishop who defied Charles I. I was born in Liverpool and educated at Shrewsbury and Newcastle-under-Lyme. At school it struck me that the footnotes in history books were often more interesting than the main text. During the 1930s I was variously a reporter, sub-editor, columnist and assistant leader-writer in Glasgow; my chief handicap as an evening newspaperman was probably a total and incorrigible lack of interest in sport. I free-lanced widely, writing an inordinate amount of light verse, which kept me in cars and helped to finance several visits to America, on the fourth of which, in 1937, I was married, in Brooklyn, New York, to Helen Elizabeth Martin.

"Much of World War Two I spent on anti-aircraft batteries, entirely surrounded by women; and I have a vivid recollection of the Normandy D-Day, which I spent in a mobile office near Brighton working out from recorded data what had happened to anti-aircraft rounds fired in the defence of London a couple of years before. In early 1945 I joined the staff of the British Army magazine *Soldier*, which was first produced in Brussels and later in Hamburg; and from 1946 to 1957 I edited this magazine in London for the War Office.

"I did not start writing books until I was nearing my forties, the first being *Boys Will Be Boys*, a light-hearted history of blood and thunder literature, which milked the nostalgia market most gratifyingly. At fairly frequent intervals I began to turn out histories of such subjects as advertising, courtship, doctors, courtiers, servants. The approach has been light, verging, I suppose, on irreverence, but I try where possible to dig out information of such a piquant and bizarre character that it can be left to speak for itself. The facts of life seem to me to be infinitely more entertaining than anything that can be invented. What could be funnier than the British Table of Precedence? I ransack a good many obscure sources: handbooks on the duties of housemaids, love manuals, undertakers' journals, old posters and so on. Mostly I am indebted to the long-suffering British Museum, though I try to keep any whiff of dusty bookshelves out of the text. Probably my approach could be described (indeed, it has been described) as a magpie one, but I like to think that a reasonably fair social picture emerges. My books have also been called a collection of footnotes (as I said, I am partial to footnotes); and an American reviewer has said that I rewrite history from a cockeyed angle, which is fair comment. I like a subject on which there is a mass of unfamiliar documentary information to be had, so that I can sift through it, keeping only the liveliest material. To have to scratch hard for information would not appeal to me. In two of my books I showed a perhaps unwonted restraint: *Gallant Gentlemen*, a history of British Army officers, and *All Heaven in a Rage*, an account of the campaign against cruelty to animals.

E. S. TURNER

"From about 1956 I renewed an association with *Punch*, to which I had first contributed in 1935, and wrote a great many articles using the same technique on both historical and present-day subjects (a collection of these was published in 1965 as *How to Measure a Woman*). In 1964 I was invited to join that very civilised body, the *Punch* Table. Under pseudonyms I have written two forgotten humorous novels; interest in these by film companies fortified my decision to live as a freelance writer. I also had a pseudonymous half-share in the scripting of a comedy film about the Army which reached the top ten but had no other claim to distinction."

E. S. Turner's characteristically thorough account of his life and work leaves very little to be said, except that he gives an unduly modest impression of the weight and value of his work. Beginning in 1948 with his study of the "penny dreadfuls," there has been recognition on both sides of the Atlantic of his fair and careful scholarship, his dry wit, and the moral seriousness implicit in his revelations of human stupidity, cruelty, and greed.

His method is to assemble and organize a mass of extraordinary and revealing material about his chosen subject and in the main to let it speak for itself, intruding only to underline with ironic commentary some especially salient point. *Roads to Ruin*, his "shocking history of social reform," was called an "astonishing feat" of selection, while a reviewer of *Taking the Cure* drew attention to Turner's skill in disguising "the trouble he has taken in his historical, geographical, literary and pictorial researches." Malcolm Muggeridge, discussing *What the Butler Saw*, Turner's review of domestic service since the 1700s, wrote: "I wish someone would bring out a lavishly indexed omnibus edition of his various studies—it would prove a valuable work of reference." Turner's latest novel, *Hemlock Lane*, satirizes Fleet Street and other instruments of British democracy. It was thought a little dated in its humor but was otherwise enjoyed by most reviewers.

Turner is a slim, balding man, with thick eyebrows and a quizzical expression. He lives in the London suburb of Richmond.

PRINCIPAL WORKS: Boys Will Be Boys: The Story of Sweeney Todd and Others, 1948; Roads to Ruin: The Shocking History of Social Reform, 1950; The Shocking History of Advertising, 1952; A History of Courting, 1954; Gallant Gentlemen: A Portrait of the British Officer, 1956; Call the Doctor: A Social History of the Medical Man, 1958; The Court of St. James's, 1959; The Phoney War on the Home Front, 1961 (U.S., The Phoney War, 1962); What the Butler Saw: Two Hundred and Fifty Years of the Servant Problem, 1962; All Heaven in a Rage, 1964; How to Measure a Woman, and Other Exercises, 1965; Taking the Cure, 1967; Hemlock Lane (novel), 1968; May It Please Your Lordship, 1971.

ABOUT: Author's and Writer's Who's Who, 1971. *Periodicals*—Books and Bookmen February 1959; New Statesman October 28, 1966.

***TUTUOLA, AMOS** (June 1920–), Nigerian storyteller, writes: "I was a native of Abeokuta, one of the biggest towns in Western Nigeria. Abeokuta, one of the Yoruba towns, is sixty miles from Lagos, the Federal Capital of Nigeria. I was born in the year 1920. My father, Charles Tutuola, was a farmer, who got plenty of cocoa farms in his days.

"In 1932, I started to attend the school called Anglican Central School, Abeokuta. At the end of 1932, I was promoted from Infant Class I to Standard I. A double promotion, because I was the boy who scored the highest marks in the class at the end of that year. In December 1937 I was promoted to standard six and in December 1938 my father died unexpectedly. And there my education stopped because the rest of my parents were so poor that they could not assist me to further my education. Having failed to further my education, I went to Lagos in 1939 and I started to learn smithery. In 1942, I joined the Royal Air Force as a blacksmith and I was discharged in 1945. In 1946, I joined the Department of Labour in Lagos as a civil servant. In 1952, I wrote my first book entitled *The Palm-Wine Drinkard*, which has already been translated into about eleven languages. *My Life in the Bush of Ghosts* was published in 1954, *Simbi and the Satyr of the Dark Jungle* in 1955, *The Brave African Huntress* in 1958 and *The Feather Woman of the Jungle* in 1962.

* to͞o to͞o ô′ lə

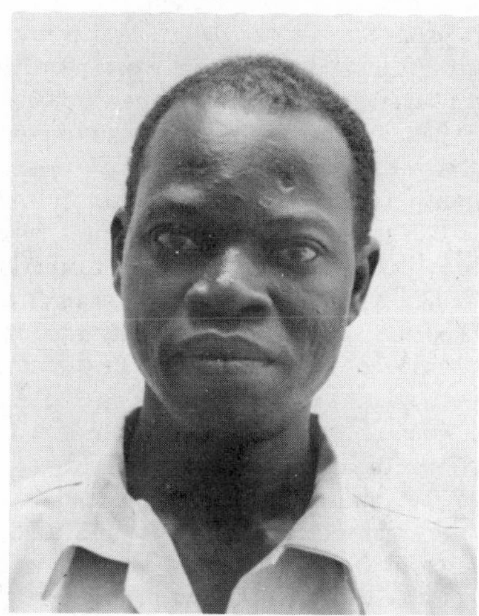

AMOS TUTUOLA

"In 1956, I joined the Nigerian Broadcasting Corporation as a storekeeper. I now live in Ibadan, Western Nigeria, with my wife named Victoria Alake whom I married in 1947. Now we have got three children, Olubunmi a girl, Oluyinka a boy and Olasunbo a girl. I am a member of the African Church and also a member of Mbari Club, the publishers and writers club in Ibadan. Many of my short stories have been published in overseas newspapers."

Thanks to the United Society for Christian Literature, the manuscript of Tutuola's first novel was sent in 1952 to Faber and Faber in London. It was published the same year as *The Palm-Wine Drinkard*, and received by the English critics with astonishment and delight. This "brief, thronged, grisly and bewitching" story, as Dylan Thomas called it, is very much in the oral tradition and wastes no time on preliminaries. The second paragraph of the book begins: "My father got eight children and I was the eldest among them, all of the rest were hard workers, but I myself was an expert palm-wine drinkard. . . . When my father noticed that I could not do any work more than to drink, he engaged an expert palm-wine tapster for me, he had no other work more than to tap palm-wine every day."

This happy state of affairs ends abruptly when the tapster falls from a tree and dies. The Drinkard is reduced to drinking water and, formerly surrounded by happy companions, soon finds himself wretched and alone. He sets out into the jungle to recover his tapster from Limbo. In the course of his journey he meets and by a ruse overcomes Death himself, rescues a lady from the terrible attractions of the "complete gentleman" (and marries her himself), slays the dreaded Red Fish and, after many other adventures and trials, finds his tapster in the Deads' Town. The tapster cannot return to the living world, but he gives the Drinkard a magic egg. Further adventures follow on the way home. The Drinkard and his wife are swallowed by the Hungry Creature, assaulted by ferocious dead babies and Mountain Creatures. Reaching home, they find the town in the grip of a terrible famine, which the Drinkard is able to relieve with his magic egg. The real cause of the famine is strife between Earth and Heaven. In the end the Drinkard, thanks to the wisdom he has acquired on his travels, is able to reestablish the cosmic harmony.

The Palm-Wine Drinkard was the first Nigerian book to achieve international fame, a fact which appalled more sophisticated West African writers, who were embarrassed by their semiliterate countryman's naïveté and his cavalier use of English. Equally misguided were the English-language critics who thought the book quaint. What is remarkable about it, as Gerald Moore has shown, is the richness and authority of the imaginative life it reveals—an imagination which seems to call directly upon the great recurrent myths: the quest, the descent into the underworld, the rite of passage, the hero's return as savior, and so many other fundamental emblems of the human adventure that some critics advanced the unlikely hypothesis that Tutuola had based his story on a careful reading of Jung. He himself acknowledges the influence of the Yoruba vernacular writer D. O. Fagunwa, and others have pointed out his affinities with Dante, Blake, and in particular Bunyan, another ill-educated visionary. These affinities are surely instinctive rather than learned, like the unique rhythms of Tutuola's private version of the English language.

His subsequent books, most of them variations on the quest theme, have had less impact, lacking the imaginative intensity of the first (though rich in splendid moments of comedy, or terror, or both). V. S. Naipaul, in his review of *Brave African Huntress*, found in it "none of the primeval nightmare fascination of the earlier books, little to attract the psychoanalyst and the anthropologist." *The Palm-Wine Drinkard* has been turned into an opera by the Yoruba composer Kola Ogunmola, and Tutuola has tried his hand with some success at the short story. He has never participated in Nigerian intellectual life, neither influencing his contemporaries nor being influenced by them. The author now has four sons and four daughters.

In the opinion of Gerald Moore, it was because "Tutuola managed to fall through the educational sieve at the first shake, with all his imperfections on his head," that he was able "to write one book of great power and beauty; it may also have prevented him from ever becoming a professional writer in the normal sense. . . . Tutuola is concerned with man alone, suffering and growing amid the images thrown forth by his own mind and by the imagination of his race. He is something much rarer and more interesting than another novelist; he is a visionary, and his books are prose epics rather than novels."

PRINCIPAL WORKS: The Palm-Wine Drinkard and His Dead Palm-Wine Tapster in the Deads' Town, 1952; My Life in the Bush of Ghosts, 1954; Simbi and the Satyr of the Dark Jungle, 1955; The Brave African Huntress, 1958; Feather Woman of the Jungle, 1962; Ajaiyi and His Inherited Poverty, 1967.

ABOUT: Collins, H. R. Amos Tutuola, 1969; International Who's Who, 1973–74; Moore, G. Seven African Writers, 1962; Penguin Companion to Literature 4, 1969 and 1, 1971. *Periodicals*—Commonweal September 25, 1953; October 8, 1954; Critique Autumn–Winter 1960–1961; Library Journal June 15, 1953; Manchester Guardian February 9, 1954; New Statesman March 6, 1954; April 5, 1958; New York Herald Tribune Book Review November 28, 1954; January 25, 1959; New York Times November 2, 1958; New Yorker December 5, 1953; Saturday Review October 17, 1953; Wilson Library Bulletin September 1963.

***TVARDOVSKY, ALEKSANDR (TRIFONOVICH)** (June 21, 1910–December 18, 1971), Russian poet and editor, was born at Zagorye, in the Smolensk region. His father, the village blacksmith, had also bought on installments a small farm of which he was very proud, though it was swampy and infertile and very hard to work. During the winter evenings the father read to the family from such Russian classics as Pushkin, Lermontov, and Gogol; and Tvardovsky began to write verse while still attending the village school, publishing some of it in local papers from the age of fourteen onwards. At eighteen he went to Smolensk, studied at the Pedagogical Institute for two years, and began his career in journalism.

His first book was the collection *Put k sotsia-*

* tvyär dôf′ ski

lizmu (The Path to Socialism, 1931), which consisted of verse tales rather than lyrics, and was favorably reviewed by the poet Eduard Bagritsky. As a newspaper correspondent in the early 1930s Tvardovsky reported the collectivization of the farms and his first major work, *Strana Muravia* (The Land of Muravia, 1936), is set against this background. It is about a peasant, Nikita Morgunok, who resists the collectivization and instead wanders all over Russia looking for the fabled land of Muravia, a legendary peasant paradise. In his wanderings he meets all kinds of people, gets involved in all kinds of adventures and, learning at last to prefer reality to dreams, goes home to create his utopia on the collective farm. Like Tvardovsky's other long poems it is full of humor and fantasy as well as peasant speech, and critics found in it the influence of folk ballads, Pushkin's verse tales, and Nikolai Nekrasov's *Komu na Rusi zhit' khorosho?* (Who Lives Well in Russia?), a long satirical poem written at another period of upheaval in the Russian countryside, that of the emancipation of the serfs.

During the 1930s Tvardovsky published many shorter poems, and was at last able to complete his education at the Moscow Institute of History, Philosophy and Literature (1936–1939). He fought in the Finnish War of 1940, and in World War II was the special correspondent of an army newspaper. At the same time he wrote the poem cycle which was to make him one of the most broadly popular of all Soviet poets—*Vasily Terkin* (Vasily Tyorkin), published in installments between 1941 and 1945. Its hero, Terkin, is a simple private soldier who is popular with his comrades because of his cheerfulness, jokes, and songs, but is otherwise presented as an average soldier, who does not like war but does his bit well, and can achieve a semblance of normal life even under the most extreme conditions. Terkin took on the stature of a national symbol because he perfectly expressed the attitudes and qualities of the Russian fighting men, who indeed sent him thousands of letters. The cycle was awarded a Stalin Prize in 1946.

Tvardovsky's other long narrative poem of the war years, *Dom u dorogi* (The House by the Roadside, 1946), deals with the fate of a husband and wife, Andrei and Anna Sivtsov, who are caught up in and separated by the war. The poem begins with Andrei happily mowing hay on a fine summer morning, when suddenly: "The ancient voice of war / Howls through the land." Andrei goes off to the army, the village is occupied by the Germans, and Anna is expatriated to Germany, where she gives birth to a son. Eventually, like Mother Courage, she trudges back to Russia pulling a homemade "house" on wheels. The poem ends with Anna still on the long road home, while

ALEKSANDR TVARDOVSKY

Andrei returns to find their house destroyed and overgrown with nettles; life must go on, and he decides to build a new house, and once more gets down to mowing.

Za dalyu dal (Distance Beyond Distance, 1953–1960), which received a Lenin Prize when it was published as a whole in 1961, is the product of Tvardovsky's journeys to Siberia and the Far East. It is a discursive commentary on Soviet Russia, held together by the personality of the poet-narrator. As he travels by rail across the vast distances of Siberia he gets to know his fellow passengers, who impartially criticize not only his own writings but Soviet literature in general. And at a small station in Siberia he meets a childhood friend returning to Moscow after seventeen years in one of Stalin's camps, and this chapter develops into a critique of the Stalin era and its cult of personality. This poem, in which Tvardovsky himself is the central character, is widely regarded as his most accomplished work.

Tvardovsky's wartime hero is resurrected in *Terkin na tom svete* (1963, translated by Leo Gruliow as *Tyorkin in the Other World*), a sharp polemic against Russia's reactionary diehards which the poet himself read aloud to Khrushchev in 1963. It is a satirical fable in which Terkin after his death finds himself in the other world, which turns out to be very like the one he knew on earth, Stalinist and full of bureaucrats, including of course a censor, and with a glimpse through a peephole at the bourgeois hell next door, with its naked girls and other such attractive capitalistic vices. The poem was later adapted into a very successful play.

Tvardovsky was at his best in these long, ballad-like *poèmas*, which tell a tale in direct and colloquial language and in which situation and character are more important than beauty of expression. A peasant and a journalist, Tvardovsky wrote simply and with great understanding of ordinary people and natural phenomena—for example, identifying late fall as the time when "in the wood the fir tree stood out clearer." Samuil Marshak in his 1961 book on Tvardovsky noted the almost complete absence of love and other personal themes in his poetry—although he wrote many short lyrics, these are mostly meditations on the landscape and history of Russia which, since his style lacks complexity and musicality, are on the whole less interesting than his epics. His devotion to his country was, however, real, deeply felt, and understated, far removed from the cheap patriotism of the party hacks. Tvardovsky's prose included autobiographical works, travel sketches, literary essays, and one well-known story, "Pechniki" (1958, translated by R. Daglish as "The Stovemakers"), an apparently pointless tale about two men rebuilding a large brick stove which, however, gives a vivid impression of Russian village life.

In his own country Tvardovsky's books have sold literally in millions, but outside the Soviet Union he was best known for his editorship of the liberal magazine *Novy Mir*, the foremost Soviet literary and intellectual review. He succeeded Konstantin Simonov as editor of *Novy Mir* in 1950, was dismissed in 1954 after publishing some articles which outraged entrenched party conservatives, but resumed the editorship in the more liberal atmosphere of 1958. During the next twelve years the magazine was responsible for publishing much of the most advanced and important Russian literature of the post-Stalin period.

Tvardovsky was also in the forefront of the always dangerous campaign for greater liberalization, shrewdly and audaciously using the jargon of "socialist realism" and party orthodoxy to urge open discussion of the defects of Soviet society. "I want to say the things I know best of all the world. And say them in my own way," he wrote in one of his poems, and he did more perhaps than anyone else to win the same freedom for other Soviet writers. Time and time again it was reported that Tvardovsky had gone too far—that he faced dismissal or worse; time and time again he miraculously survived. He was at last forced to resign from *Novy Mir* in February 1970, after the removal of his closest supporters. But on his sixtieth birthday, a few months later, many other magazines and journals published greetings, like the article in *Pravda* which hailed him as "undoubtedly one of the major and most gifted contemporary Russian Soviet poets." Tvardovsky, who had been suffering from lung cancer and the after-effects of a stroke, died in December 1971. He received the Order of Lenin shortly before his death, and after it was variously honored and praised by the Soviet establishment, but always for his poetry; his editorship of *Novy Mir* was barely mentioned.

Most Western critics regard his conventional and traditional verse as of only modest value, but many might accept Vera Alexandrova's summing up: "He will be remembered as an important poet, who was able, in his country's grim and fateful years, to retain some features of independence and to invest his great talent as a folk poet in a number of works which will remain a living part of Russian literature." Tvardovsky was survived by his wife and a daughter.

PRINCIPAL WORKS IN ENGLISH TRANSLATION: *Poems in* Johnson, P. (ed.) Khrushchev and the Arts, 1965; Lindsay, J. Russian Poetry, 1917–1955, 1957; Lindsay, J. Modern Russian Poetry, 1960; Markov, V. and Sparks, M. Modern Russian Poetry, 1966; Milner-Gulland, R. Soviet Russian Verse, 1961; Obolensky, D. Penguin Book of Russian Verse, 1962; Reavey, G. (ed.) The New Russian Poets, 1968. *Story in* Snow, C. P. and Johnson, P. H. (eds.) Winter's Tales 7, 1961. *Poems and extracts in* Atlantic June 1960; Current Digest of the Soviet Press 34, 1963; Soviet Literatuve 4, 1961; 4, 1966.

ABOUT: Alexandrova, V. A History of Soviet Literature, 1963; Current Biography, 1971; Mihajlov, M. Russian Themes, 1968; Slonim, M. Soviet Russian Literature, 1964; Turkov, A. M. Aleksandr Tvardovsky, 1960; Who's Who in America, 1972–1973. *Periodicals*—New York Times April 21, 1966; New Yorker September 11, 1965; Soviet Literature 10, 1946; 4, 1966; 6, 1970.

TYNAN, KENNETH (PEACOCK) (April 2, 1927–), English critic and journalist, was born in Birmingham, the son of Sir Peter Peacock and Letitia Tynan. His father, a wealthy store owner of working-class birth, was at one time mayor of Warrington, in Lancashire. Tynan attended the King Edward VI School in Birmingham, and in 1945 went up to Magdalen College, Oxford University. There, with his purple doeskin suit and his gold satin shirt, he quickly became a legend. The Oxford of his time will certainly be remembered as Tynan's Oxford. In spite of his sometimes acute stammer, which has never left him, Tynan made up for his youthful lack of depth by his wit, self-confidence, and energy. In addition to flamboyant undergraduate pranks he edited *The Cherwell*, wrote dramatic criticism for *The Isis*, became secretary of the Union Debating Society, served as president of the Experimental Theatre Club, acted, and produced his own adaptation of *Hamlet*, called *A Toy in Blood*.

Tynan left Oxford in 1948 with a second class honors degree in English. He began his career in 1949 as director of a provincial repertory company. The following year he directed his first London production, a successful rendering of *A Man of the World*, and later in 1950 took a production of

Othello on tour. It was in 1950 also that his first book appeared, a collection of audacious and exuberant essays on heroic drama called *He That Plays the King*. In 1951 Tynan himself played the Player King in Alec Guinness's production of *Hamlet*. At about the same time, to cap the prodigious achievements of these postgraduate years, he became drama critic of *The Spectator*.

Three years later, in early 1954, after short stints with the London *Evening Standard* and *Daily Sketch*, he reached the top of his profession as drama critic of the Sunday *Observer*. Apart from two years as guest drama critic of the *New Yorker* (1958–1960), Tynan remained with the *Observer* until he became literary manager of the National Theatre in 1963. Thereafter he served the National Theatre for ten years, until 1973, in 1969 exchanging his post as literary manager for the presumably less demanding one of literary consultant. Tynan also served as script editor for Ealing Films in the mid-1950s and edited a successful television program on the arts, *Tempo*, from 1961 to 1962. He has continued to write for major magazines and newspapers on both sides of the Atlantic—including the *Observer*, whose film critic he was from 1964 to 1966. In 1968 he became an associate editor of *Playboy*.

Tynan's books include *Persona Grata*, a coffee-table book fabricated in collaboration with the photographer Cecil Beaton; a much-reprinted study of Alec Guinness; and *Bull Fever*, which records his enthusiasm for the bullfight. *Curtains* and *Tynan Right and Left* collect his articles on plays, films, people, places, and events.

During his years with the *Observer*, Tynan became the most discussed, controversial, and influential theatre critic in Britain. He had begun by believing that the drama was an autonomous activity, "apart from life." Gradually, mainly under the influence of Bertolt Brecht, he "became aware that art, ethics, politics and economics were inseparable from each other . . . that no theatre could sanely flourish until there was an umbilical connection between what was happening on the stage and what was happening in the world." It was said of him in the end that he "not only espoused the new English realism . . . but in a way summoned it."

According to Michael Billington, Tynan is an "acute dialectical Marxist." When he was in the United States his political attitudes brought him before the Senate internal security subcommittee, and there is no doubt that his views sometimes vitiate his judgments (he reportedly has no time for Pirandello). His critical faculty is wholly subjective, and he increasingly relies upon his political convictions to provide an objective element. However, inasmuch as he is naturally liberal, humanitarian, tolerant, humorous, and shrewd, this is not, in his case, an unsuccessful procedure.

KENNETH TYNAN

Tynan writes strictly for his own times, and the oft-reiterated comparison of him with Hazlitt may for this reason prove overenthusiastic. But he nonetheless embodies some of the best qualities of his own time. The reader may disagree with some of his judgments, but must always admit that they are formed from an unusually lucid and articulate view of how the theatre should exist. A sign over his desk reads: "Be light, stinging, insolent and melancholy," and in his writings he manages to be all of these things in just about as elegant a way as is possible for an active public man in a vulgar age. Lack of interest in scholarship (he can accept the idea that Marlowe wrote Shakespeare as rational) and a too-pronounced tendency towards short-lived uncritical enthusiasms and hero worship are probably his main weaknesses.

Harold Clurman, reviewing *Curtains*, suggested that Tynan is "disposed toward the theatre in the sense that we speak of certain people being naturally musical. . . . Tynan experiences the theatre with his nerves, body, mind and spirit. He possesses in regard to the theatre something like absolute pitch." Ten years later, discussing *Tynan Right and Left*, Richard Boston said that, like Orwell, Tynan "has the ability always to pick on the important issue, and to find important issues even when briefly reviewing a film or play which is in itself of little interest. . . . Almost without exception he is readable and stimulating, whatever the subject: he is very honest and often very funny. If he is too interested in himself, there are after all a lot of people who are much less interesting."

Tynan was married in 1951 to the American writer and actress Elaine Dundy. That marriage was dissolved in 1964 and in 1967 Tynan married Kathleen Halton. He has a daughter by his first marriage, a son and a daughter by the second. Tynan is a little over six feet tall, fair-haired, and extremely thin. He is said to enjoy eating, watching bullfights, and playing word games, and he is a brilliant public speaker. An ardent and articulate opponent of censorship, Tynan finds means from time to time of annoying the middle classes. John Mortimer believes that he combines a formidable Puritan conscience with a taste for elegance—that he is a Roundhead who appears to the world dressed as a Cavalier—and that it is the Roundhead in him which drives him "to liberate the world by adding new words to the vocabulary of television."

Tynan subsequently demonstrated his passion for freedom of expression by championing Rolf Hochhuth's play *Soldiers*, which pillories Sir Winston Churchill, was refused a production at the National Theatre, and caused a furor when it was staged at the New Theatre in 1968, with Tynan as co-producer. The debate which followed helped to end the Lord Chamberlain's role as censor of the British theatre. Tynan continued his campaign in a somewhat different arena with *Oh! Calcutta!*, an "erotic revue" produced in New York in 1969 and in London in 1970. Devised and partly written by Tynan, it seemed to most reviewers fully to vindicate its claim that nudity is as legitimate a subject of theatre as of painting, but was found mechanical, flavorless, and generally unfunny in its text.

PRINCIPAL WORKS: He That Plays the King, 1950; (with Cecil Beaton) Persona Grata, 1953; Alec Guinness, 1953; Bull Fever, 1955; (with Harold Lang) The Quest for Corbett (based on a radio program), 1960; Curtains, 1961; Tynan Right and Left, 1967; Oh! Calcutta!, 1969.

ABOUT: Contemporary Authors 15–16, 1966; Current Biography, 1963; International Who's Who, 1973–74; Kazin, A. Contemporaries, 1962; Maschler, T. (ed.) Declaration, 1959; Who's Who, 1973; Who's Who in America, 1972–1973. *Periodicals*—Christian Century November 29, 1961; New Statesman October 13, 1961; New York Times November 16, 1965; New York Times Book Review March 19, 1961; New York Times Magazine January 9, 1966; Spectator October 6, 1961; Time June 7, 1954; Vogue November 1, 1958.

***"TZARA, TRISTAN" (pseudonym of Samuel Rosenfeld)** (April 4, 1896–December 24, 1963), French-Rumanian poet and founder of Dadaism, was born of well-to-do Jewish parents at Moinesti, Rumania, and educated there and at a French-speaking school in Bucharest. His earliest published poems, in Rumanian, appeared in a review in 1912 and showed the influence of the French symbolist poets. From 1914 to 1915 he studied philosophy and mathematics at Bucharest University, and in 1915 he went to continue his studies in Zurich, to which the war had driven refugees from all over Europe. Tzara immediately became involved in the city's cosmopolitan literary and artistic life, and an habitué of the Cabaret Voltaire. There, with Hugo Ball, Richard Huelsenbeck, Hans Arp, and others, he founded the Dadaist movement in 1916 and was its leader from the beginning. Thenceforth, Tzara wrote exclusively in French, his first published volume, written in Dadaist prose-poetry, being *La Première Aventure céleste de Monsieur Antipyrine* (Zurich, 1916).

* tsä'rä

Dada has been called "an extreme—an exasperated—form of romanticism." Its ancestors were such champions of unreason as Rimbaud, Laforgue, and Lautréamont, but it was World War I, demonstrating to Tzara and his generation the worthlessness of traditional values, which brought it to life. In their poems, plays, collages, and frottages, the Dadaists matched the meaninglessness of civilization with a deliberate meaninglessness of their own. Tzara reportedly took the term *dada*, a child's word for a hobbyhorse, quite at random from Larousse. In his seven Dada manifestos, he called for the abolition of history, religion, and traditional art forms—for a revolt of the individual against the whole fabric of society (including Dada itself), but for "absolute faith in every god that is the immediate product of spontaneity."

The movement spread rapidly to France, Germany, the United States, and elsewhere. After a decisive meeting with Francis Picabia in 1919, Tzara settled in Paris, where the young avant-garde writers awaited him, as André Breton said, "like the Messiah." A short, slight, graceful man, with a quick mind and a fertile imagination, Tzara was lionized by such writers as Aragon, Éluard, Soupault, and Breton himself. Dadaist demonstrations followed in Paris early in 1920 at which, among other less engaging antics, Tzara's reading of an article was drowned by the ringing of an electric bell, and Picabia made drawings only to erase them. The public turned up in its thousands to be duly outraged and to throw eggs.

Tzara's Dadaist play *Le Cœur à gaz* (1920) was translated in 1964 as *The Gas Heart* by Michael Benedikt, who thought it "a thoroughly innovative work" but less a piece of theatre than a "visual and verbal spectacle." But what Tzara called the "anarchical, unproductive revolt of Dada," dedicated to negation, has naturally enough left little permanent literature. From about 1921 the movement was increasingly threatened by internal dissension and by 1923, when Breton and Éluard exchanged blows at the first professional performance of *Le Cœur à gaz*, Dada had collapsed.

From its ruins emerged surrealism but Tzara, though he continued to write and to publish poetry, was excluded by his quarrels with Breton and others from any direct role in the early years of the new movement. Admitted into the group in 1929, he was an active member of it for five years. His most praised work, a long epic poem called *L'Homme approximatif* (1930, translated as "Approximate Man"), explored in a dynamic chaos of dislocated language and obsessively recurrent rhythms and images the "approximate man's" search for self-completion. Marcel Raymond described it as "the only poem of great sweep that can be legitimately connected with surrealism."

From 1930 onward, Tzara became increasingly involved in left-wing politics, which led to his break with the surrealists in 1935. These new preoccupations were reflected in his writings. Thus *Grains et issues* (Seeds and Outlets, 1935) argued for a "revolutionary" poetry conceived not as communication but as a free "activity of the mind," and the poems in *Midis gagnés* (Middays Won, 1939) reflected his visits to Spain during the Civil War.

Tzara spent World War II in the unoccupied southern zone of France but wrote for the clandestine Resistance magazines. He formally joined the Communist party at the end of the war, when he obtained French citizenship, but ceased to be a militant Communist after the Hungarian uprising of 1956. His dramatic poem *La Fuite* (The Flight), depicting the chaotic exodus from invaded France, was performed in Paris in 1946. In the postwar years, Tzara lectured on poetry all over Europe.

In the many collections of poems he published after 1945—*Parler seul* (Speaking Alone, 1950) is the best known of these—he retained his preoccupation with semantic experiment and free imagery but moved toward what he called a humanistic poetry. Some critics feel that what he gained in coherence and discipline he lost in fervor. Among the manuscripts unpublished at his death were his critical analyses of Villon and Rabelais, on which he had worked for many years.

Tzara wrote: "Under each stone there is a nest of words, and it is out of their rapid whirling that the substance of the world is formed." He believed all his life that poetry is "the highest activity of the human mind." In 1961 he received the Taormina International Grand Prix for Poetry. It remains questionable whether his own verse will survive but, as the moving spirit of Dada, his position in contemporary literary history is secure, if peculiar.

PRINCIPAL WORKS IN ENGLISH TRANSLATION: Approximate Man and Other Writings, tr. by Mary Ann Caws, 1973; Memoirs of Dadaism, *in* Wilson, E. Axel's Castle, 1932. *Poems and prose extracts in* Levy, J. Surrealism, 1936; Motherwell, R. The Dada Painters and Poets, 1951. *Drama*—The Gas Heart, *in* Wellwarth, G. E. and Benedikt M. Modern French Plays, 1964.

ABOUT: Balakian, A. Literary Origins of Surrealism, 1947; Barr, A. Fantastic Art, 1937; Hackett, C. A. Anthology of Modern French Poetry, 1952; Hugnet, G. L'Aventure Dada, 1957; Lemaître, G. From Cubism to Surrealism, 1947; Levy, J. Surrealism, 1936; Lindsay, J. Meetings With Poets, 1968; Peterson, E. Tristan Tzara, 1971; Raymond, M. From Baudelaire to Surrealism, 1957; Richter, H. Dada, 1965; Verkauf, F. Dada, 1957; Waldberg, P. Surrealism, 1966. *Periodicals*—Les Lettres françaises January 2, 1964; January 9, 1964; New Republic January 10, 1934.

TRISTAN TZARA

UNGARETTI, GIUSEPPE (February 10, 1888–June 1, 1970), Italian poet and one of the major European writers of his generation, was born in Alexandria, Egypt, of Italian peasant stock. His father, Antonio Ungaretti, had gone to Egypt from Lucca, in Tuscany, to work as a laborer on the construction of the Suez Canal. He died after an accident in 1900, and Ungaretti was raised by his mother, the former Maria Lunardini, who opened a small bakery in the suburbs of Alexandria, on "the edge of the desert." Many have seen in Ungaretti's birth in exile a central symbol in his work—a "poetry of absence" in which a rootless nomad, a wanderer in the wilderness, pursues "an ever-resumed journey toward an ever-changing Promised Land" which is sometimes Italy, sometimes the innocence of childhood, sometimes death itself as a point of rest from mutability. His remarkable mother, in spite of economic handicaps, sent him to the École Suisse Jacob, where he became bilingual in French and Italian, received an excellent education, and early developed a love of literature.

As a Tuscan, Ungaretti was an inheritor of the central Italian literary tradition. He became acquainted with contemporary Italian literary move-

GIUSEPPE UNGARETTI

ments and ideas through the magazine *La Voce* and through the exiled Italian socialists who congregated at his mother's house. He also devoured the works of Petrarch and Leopardi, whose influence on his own poetry increased as his style developed. Indeed, his gradual rediscovery of his roots in the Italian language and literature parallels in formal terms the spiritual quest which is so often his theme.

However, growing up in the predominantly French culture of Alexandria, Ungaretti was at first drawn primarily to French literature. He later wrote that he was acquainted with the works of Baudelaire, Mallarmé, Rimbaud, and Laforgue long before they became familiar names in Italy. It was these poets who, together with Valéry, were his first masters.

So it was natural that when he left Alexandria at the age of twenty-four Ungaretti should make his way to Paris. He studied at the Collège de France and the Sorbonne under such scholars as Bergson, Lanson, and Bédier, and seems to have met virtually all of the writers and artists who then, just before World War I, were making Paris the center of an artistic revolution. He had his introduction to cubism from Picasso and Braque, to fauvism from Matisse, to futurism from Marinetti. Apollinaire, Polish by descent but Italian by birth, became one of his closest friends. With Apollinaire and the Italian Futurists Papini and Soffici, publishers of the avant-garde review *Lacerba*, Ungaretti planned a modernist renovation of Italian poetry. It was *Lacerba* which published his own first verses, in Italian, in January 1915.

Four months later, when Italy entered World War I as one of the Allies, Ungaretti immediately enlisted in an Italian infantry regiment. He served for three years in the embattled region of the Carso, in the mountains north of Trieste, and in the spring of 1918 was sent to the Western Front in Champagne. Face to face with death in the trenches he learned, he said, to write fast and to write what was essential: that "concentration in the single instant knew no bounds. The instant contained eternity."

It was the packed and echoing instant of apprehension that Ungaretti set out to record in his war poems, trying to convey in a few charged words and images a whole world of experience, of horror and fear, comradeship and hope. And also of beauty, since, more and more, he turned to nature, comparing the brevity and precariousness of human life with earth's eternal renewal: "What is your regiment / brothers? / Trembling word / in the night / Leaf newly born."

Ungaretti's first volume of poetry was privately printed in 1916 at Udine, near the front, and was called *Il porto sepolto* (The Buried Port, a reference to the submerged seaport of Alexandria). The edition of eighty copies was subsidized by Ettore Sera and received the immediate attention of Papini and other influential critics. At the end of the war the poet returned to Paris as French correspondent to Mussolini's *Popolo d'Italia.* At this time his second book, *La guerre* (The War, 1919), was published in Paris, again in a limited edition. It was written in French, though some of the poems had been translated from Italian originals. Ungaretti lived in Paris during most of 1919 and 1920, and in June 1920 married a Frenchwoman, Anne Jeanne Dupoix.

In 1919 Vallecchi in Florence brought out *Allegria di naufragi* (Joy of Shipwrecks), containing all of Ungaretti's work up to that time, revised and rearranged. It forms a diary of his experiences and feelings during the war, each poem recording the date and place of its composition. This, his first substantial book, was the first to receive widespread attention. It established Ungaretti in the eyes of some critics as the leading Italian poet of his generation, but was savaged by many others.

Indeed, to readers unfamiliar with the experiments of Rimbaud and Mallarmé, and the mischief of Apollinaire, Ungaretti's work must have seemed gratuitously and insultingly cryptic. He had set out to purge Italian poetry of all that was vague, imprecise, ornamental—to free each word of the conventional accretions of centuries. The traditional hendecasyllable had been banished (or at any rate obscured by Ungaretti's style of line arrangement), along with virtually all punctuation. Many of his pages were almost empty, inscribed (as his English translator Allen Mandelbaum says) with only a few "indefinitely vibrating words" to "give the effect of a single moment prolonged forever."

Ungaretti said that he tried to "put into contact all that is most distant. . . . When such contacts generate light, poetry has been achieved." A celebrated example is the poem "Mattina" (Morning), which reads in its entirety: "M'illumino / d'immenso" (I am illumined / with immensity). Against the background of the wistful and loquacious *crepuscolari*, the bombast of the futurists, the pretentious offerings of the followers of D'Annunzio, this "virginal" and intensely demanding poetry, which "compelled words to their primal power," made an immense impact. Gianfranco Contini, speaking of Ungaretti's work through the publication in 1931 of *L'allegria* (a revised edition of *Allegria di naufragi*), remarked that it contains "the first formal innovations introduced into Italian verse by a true poet."

In 1921 Ungaretti had returned from Paris to Rome, where from 1922 to 1930 he was attached to the Ministry of Foreign Affairs. By 1930 he was well known as a journalist, lecturer, and poet. He seems to have had no trouble with the Fascist regime, and Mussolini himself wrote a preface to a new edition of *Il porto sepolto* in 1923. For a time Ungaretti was closely associated with *La Ronda*, a review dedicated to stimulating the cult of the Italian classics. It was at this time that he began consciously to base his poetics on Leopardi.

This development is clearly evident in *Sentimento del tempo* (The Feeling of Time, 1933), which contained among other major poems "L'Isola," "La Pietà," and "Caino." The poet's intention is no longer merely to innovate, but to connect what he had learned with the established traditions of Italian poetry. In this new and enduring phase he turned not only to Leopardi but behind him to Petrarch and ultimately to the epic of Vergil. The hendecasyllable returns, as does normal punctuation; his rhythms become less abrupt, his message more objective, more concerned with the universal mysteries of life and death, but also more abstract and difficult. As one critic has observed, the meaning of Ungaretti's poetry was henceforth to be sought "not only in the far-ranging metaphors, but even in the arrangement of the lines and the blank spaces in between." Hostile critics grew even more violently antagonistic and magazines were founded to attack his work, which was now dubbed "hermetic," in the sense that it was arcane, mysterious, sealed off from the uninitiated reader.

Between 1931 and 1935 Ungaretti traveled widely, visiting Egypt, Corsica, Holland, and several parts of Italy under the auspices of the Turin *Gazzetta del Popolo*, for which he wrote a series of travel articles. These were eventually collected as *Il deserto e dopo* (The Desert and After, 1961). According to one critic, they "transcend journalism to the point of becoming autobiographical prose of mythic range." The last part of the book contains Ungaretti's translations of the folk poetry of Brazil, where he lived from 1936 to 1942 as Professor of Italian Literature and Language at the University of São Paulo. Motivated by patriotism, Ungaretti returned in 1942 to Italy, where he was made a member of the Academy and given a chair in Italian literature at the University of Rome. He retained that post until his retirement in 1962, and was by all accounts an excellent and enthusiastic lecturer.

Many of the poems in his first postwar collection, *Il dolore* (Grief, 1947) had been written in Brazil. The title of the book seems to signify that the days of *L'allegria* (Joy) were over, and the poet writes of the Nazi occupation of Rome, of the mass deportations and, in one of his greatest poems, "Tu Ti Spezzasti" (You Shattered), of the death in Brazil of his small son Antoniello. Stylistically the volume is less difficult than its predecessor, but in emotional depth and power it transcends all of his earlier work.

La terra promessa (The Promised Land, 1950) is Ungaretti's most ambitious work, on which he had worked intermittently since about 1935. It is a version of the myth of Dido and Aeneas, used to illustrate the transitory nature of experience and the poet's own quest for his roots, and with overtones also of the Christian theme of aspiration and redemption. "Aeneas is beauty, youth, ingenuousness, ever in search of a promised land," Ungaretti says in his introduction. "Dido came to represent the experience of one who, in late autumn, is about to pass beyond it." The poem is in three sections: the Canzone, the Choruses of Dido, and the recitative of the helmsman Palinurus. Aeneas's choruses were uncompleted when the work was published. Palinurus, the man of action, and Dido, the creature of passion, are both defeated: only the poet, the contemplative, still may achieve the eternal.

As one critic has pointed out, Ungaretti set out in *La terra promessa* to "elevate his biographical experience to [the level of] ideas and myths," and the same may be said of all his poetry: he called his collected works *Vita d'un uomo* (The Life of a Man). From *Il dolore* on, the passion for revision, which had shown itself even in his earlier phase, became obsessive. The successive editions of *Vita d'un uomo* are full of such emendations, many of them made, as it were, in public, pondered intensely by critics who followed closely every second thought of a poet who had become a national institution.

Il taccuino del vecchio (Notebook of an Old Man, 1960) is an extension of the theme and form of *La terra promessa*, even including some of Aeneas's choruses. *Un grido e paessaggi* (A Cry and Landscapes, 1952) more resembles the earlier, less elaborate poetry. Ungaretti produced several volumes of verse in French, and also made a number of important translations into Italian—of Shakespeare, Racine, Mallarmé, Góngora, and others. His translation and criticism of Blake, *Visioni de William Blake*, brought him the Etna-Taormina International Prize in 1967, and he received a number of other important awards, including the Grand Prix International de Poésie in 1956 and the first ten-thousand-dollar International Prize awarded by the University of Oklahoma's publication *Books Abroad*. Ungaretti went to the United States in March 1970 to receive the latter prize. In June of the same year, shortly after his return to Italy, he died of a lung clot while on vacation in Milan. He was a short, slightly stooped man, who favored colorful and casual clothes, and whose strong, deeply lined face was capable of startlingly puckish smiles.

It is too soon for a final judgment on Ungaretti's contribution, or on that of any of the "hermetics." Comparing him to the other champions of that school, one may find his imagery less warm than Quasimodo's, his revelations somewhat less suggestive than Montale's. But he has a perfection of style and a dedication to his vision that are unmatched; he was perhaps the "purest poet" of his time. And his historical importance is beyond doubt; he suggested the idiom and indicated the path to an entire generation of Italian poets.

PRINCIPAL WORKS IN ENGLISH TRANSLATION: Life of a Man (tr. by Allen Mandelbaum), 1958. *Selections in* Barnstone, W. (ed.) Modern European Poetry, 1966; Bergin, T. G. Italian Sampler, 1964; Fulton, R. (ed.) An Italian Quartet, 1966; Golino, C. L. (ed.) Contemporary Italian Poetry, 1962; Kay, G. R. (ed.) The Penguin Book of Italian Verse, 1965; Lowell, R. Imitations, 1961; Pacifici, S. (ed.) The Promised Land and Other Poems, 1957. *Poems in* Agenda Spring 1970; Atlantic December 1958; Hudson Review Winter 1963–64; Poetry June 1956; Sewanee Review October 1951; Times Literary Supplement October 22, 1964.

ABOUT: Albe (pseudonym of R. A. L. Joostens), Giuseppe Ungaretti, 1964; Burnshaw, S. (ed.) The Poem Itself, 1960; Cambon, G. Giuseppe Ungaretti, 1967; Cary, J. Three Modern Italian Poets, 1969; Cavalli, G. Ungaretti, 1958; Contemporary Authors 19–20, 1968; Contini, G. Letteratura dell' Italia unita, 1968; Dizionario universale della letteratura contemporanea, 1962; Frattini, A. Da Tommaseo a Ungaretti, 1959; Gutia, J. Linguaggio di Ungaretti, 1959; Letteratura italiana: i contemporanei, 1963; Pacifici, S. A Guide to Contemporary Italian Literature, 1962; Petrucciani, M. La poetica dell'ermetismo Italiano, 1955; Piccioni, L. Giuseppe Ungaretti, 1970; Portinari, F. Giuseppe Ungaretti, 1967; Pozzi, G. La poesia italiana del novecento, 1965; Rebay, L. Le origini della poesia di Ungaretti, 1962; Spezzani, P. Per una storia del linguaggio di Ungaretti fino al "sentimento del tempo," 1966; Wall, B. A City and a World, 1962. *Periodicals*—Agenda Spring 1970; Italian Quarterly Winter 1961–Spring 1962; Italica December 1949; Letteratura September–December 1958; Nuova Antologia August 1, 1932; Poetry December 1951; June 1956; February 1959; Times Literary Supplement March 31, 1950; September 25, 1970; Voices Winter 1947.

UPDIKE, JOHN (HOYER), (March 18, 1932–), American novelist, short story writer and poet, writes: "I was born in Shillington, Pennsylvania, a suburb of Reading, in Berks County. The county is part of the 'Pennsylvania Dutch' region, but except for a German intonation and a certain Lutheran antinomianism in the air, the town might have been, from a boy's viewpoint, any American town small enough to traverse on a bicycle. My parents and I lived, for the first thirteen years of my life, with my mother's parents, Mr. and Mrs. John Hoyer, in a long white house, with a handsome and fertile yard, that my grandfather had bought after selling his farm ten miles to the south, in Robeson Township. My grandfather, a powerfully built, well-spoken gentleman who lived to be ninety, had taught school and achieved some prosperity through farming before the financial crash took his savings and created the interdependent, not quite impoverished household that I remember. I was an only child. My parents had met while students at Ursinus College. The Updikes were New Jersey Presbyterians derived from Friesland in the Netherlands; they arrived at Nieuw Amsterdam in the 1650s and the family tree includes the one-time owner of Coney Island, the Civil War mayor of New York, and the great Massachusetts printer and typophile. The male members of the family tend to be tall and conscientious. My father, at the time I was born, was out of work, and, though he soon acquired a job teaching algebra at the Shillington High School, my arrival in the depths of the Depression gave our relationship, perhaps, a permanent surprisingness and apologetic fervor.

"My mother, a very sensitive and witty woman whose cultural aptitude deserved a more cosmopolitan setting, wrote many short stories and several novels, all unpublished.* From her I gathered that either drawing or writing would be a noble and gay way of making a living; and I think I was very young when image-making dawned on me as a way of defying mortality. In the beginning I wanted to be an animator for Walt Disney. In my early teens my allegiance switched to the *New Yorker*, where it has remained. I read Thurber, White, Perelman, and Benchley thoroughly, and, when the time came to go to college, went to Harvard because it was the location of the Harvard *Lampoon*. In addition to cartoons for this magazine I produced light verse and, finally, fiction. Though I set out to be a humorist, my nature, or the times, have led me to attempt fiction in the broadest sense, and I am still trying to extend my scope, seeking greater precision and exhaustiveness, wanting to be true to life, being faithful to the

* Mrs. Updike's autobiographical novel *Enchantment* was published under her maiden name in 1971.

essential strangeness I feel in the mundane, avoiding as best I can the currents of propaganda and publicizing that torment the literary industry in the United States. Descended from teachers, I resolved not to teach, and think of literature as less a conveyance of ideas than a production of images, as a kind of concrete homage rendered the actual world. Among writers, I especially love Shakespeare, Melville, Proust, Henry Green, Kafka, Nabokov, and Joyce. If I have a philosophy, it is a Christian one, influenced by Kierkegaard and Karl Barth. By temperament, I am a nominalist, who suspects that all phenomena under heaven are equal, that ecstasy is spread across the surface of Creation, that most categories are unhelpful, and that all opinions are dubious. Politically I am a Democrat.

"I live in Ipswich, Massachusetts, with my wife Mary and our four children. I try to work steadily, like a bricklayer, and conduct most of my transactions with those very congenial and kind corporations, the *New Yorker* magazine and Alfred A. Knopf, Inc."

JOHN UPDIKE

John Updike is the son of Wesley Updike, a telephone cable splicer before he became a high school teacher, in whom Updike sees "the Protestant kind of goodness going down with all guns firing—antic, frantic, comic, but goodness nevertheless." His mother is the former Linda Grace Hoyer, whose genius it was, he says, "to give the people closest to her mythic immensity." The consciousness of a special destiny that Updike drew from her combined with his family's near poverty to make him both arrogant and shy. At Shillington High School he wrote, drew, and clowned frantically for the approval of his peers, becoming a specialist in the death-defying pratfall and, as he says, spending a lot of time "throwing myself over stair-railings"—an accomplishment that has not entirely left him, and which is attributed to Piet Hanema in *Couples*. These talents brought him the presidency of his class and editorship of the school newspaper, and others made him a straight A student and in 1950 earned him a full scholarship at Harvard, where he majored in English. At the end of his junior year he married Mary Pennington, daughter of a Unitarian minister, and in 1954 he graduated summa cum laude. There followed a year in England on a Knox fellowship at the Ruskin School of Drawing and Fine Art, Oxford University. In August 1955 he joined the staff of the *New Yorker* as a "Talk of the Town" reporter, and almost at once began to contribute parodies, essays, verse, and stories as well, thus in his early twenties fulfilling the fondest hopes of his adolescence.

As he says, Updike had at first thought of himself only as a humorist. He soon found that he was something more, and in March 1957 left New York and settled in Ipswich, Massachusetts, to concentrate on fiction, though he has continued to be a prolific freelance contributor of articles and poems as well as stories to the *New Yorker*. Many of his early poems, ingenious intellectual jokes or wryly elegant reflections on contemporary absurdities, were collected in his first book, *The Carpentered Hen* (1958). *The Same Door*, a volume of *New Yorker*-ish stories from the *New Yorker*, appeared the following year. Most critics were full of praise for their subtlety of perception and the exactness of their prose, though a few found them rather coldly detached, or thought the precision of their descriptive passages achieved at too great an expense of words.

Many of Updike's stories and all of his early novels derive from a continued imaginative immersion in the small-town life of his boyhood. *The Poorhouse Fair* for instance, set in a home for old people in New Jersey, is in fact based on one near Shillington. It is a surprising first novel, both in its technical skill and in its insight, remarkable in so young a writer, into the state of mind of the home's inmates and of its manager, an idealistic and ambitious homosexual struggling to systematize people who are struggling even harder to hang on to their individuality. D. J. Enright, often strongly critical of Updike's later work, called it "a perfect little cameo of old age," and it received the Rosenthal Award of the National Institute of Arts and Letters.

A very different novel followed. "Rabbit" Angstrom in *Rabbit, Run* is a former high school basketball hero, inarticulate, unreflective, almost animal in his unselfconscious physicality. As he feels marriage, fatherhood, moral responsibility closing around him, Rabbit simply runs. The book was highly praised as a "clairvoyant" character study; and as a portrait of lower-middle-class life in a small Pennsylvania town it seemed to William Van O'Connor much better than similar accounts by John O'Hara. Richard Gilman praised it both as "a grotesque allegory of American life" and as "a minor epic of the spirit thirsting for room to discover and be itself." Five years later another critic called it "Updike's best book, and possibly one of the half-dozen most powerful American novels since the war." (But it is interesting that almost every one of Updike's novels has its ardent champions who, more often than not, contemptuously dismiss the remainder of his work.)

The Centaur, in which a father sacrifices himself and his son's art is consequently liberated and enlarged, leans on the myth of Chiron, the centaur who died to atone for Prometheus's theft of fire from the gods. The Chiron of the book is George Caldwell, a fierce, self-denigrating man who teaches general science at Olinger (Shillington) High School, Pennsylvania; he is also enough of a mythical beast for his lectures on the history of the universe to bring forth living trilobites and a classroom Dionysia. The novel received the National Book Award for fiction and the French Prix du Meilleur Livre Étranger and, though most critics could have managed without the "mythological horse droppings," there was warm and general admiration for Updike's portrait of George Caldwell, which is in fact a loving and artful tribute to Wesley Updike. Stanley Edgar Hyman, praising Updike's "magical, incandescent" language, wrote that "if *The Centaur* succeeds only partly, it is a partial success in a realm inhabited only by great writers."

In *Of the Farm*, a kind of sequel by extrapolation to *The Centaur*, Joey Robinson returns for a final visit to his widowed mother's farm in Pennsylvania, bringing with him his second wife and his stepson. Beneath the quiet surface of the novel may be felt the high tension between the sensitive, possessive mother and the earthy wife, and the ambivalence of Joey himself, torn between the safe prison of the past and the dangerous freedom represented by his wife. Some thought it, in its economy and simplicity, Updike's best novel so far, a small masterpiece.

Meanwhile, Updike's other work continued to appear in the *New Yorker*, and to find its way at intervals into book form. Of his poetry Updike says that he has tried to carry over into his later "serious or lyric verse something of the strictness and liveliness" of light verse, and he has succeeded to the satisfaction and pleasure of many of his critics. His most ambitious poem, "Midpoint," is an autobiographical meditation making interesting use of photographs and typographical devices as well as words.

The majority of his short stories reflect his obsessive shuffling and reshuffling of the characters and events of his Pennsylvania beginnings. Like his novels, they are praised for their dazzling verbal brilliance and technical virtuosity, as the work of "the most gifted writer of his generation"; and condemned for "risks untaken, words too fondly tasted, and . . . a security of skill that approaches smugness." Melvin Maddocks, reviewing *Pigeon Feathers*, said that "infinite care is bestowed on infinitely small passions. When the time comes to touch the essential, the writer's grip slips, almost from embarrassment, into rhetoric, and feelings become aesthetic sensations." Updike's articles, reviews, and essays, however, collected in *Assorted Prose*, were almost universally admired—the magnificent account of Ted Williams' last game for the Red Sox as warmly as the equally perceptive tribute to T. S. Eliot, and the wickedly knowledgeable parodies.

During the second half of the 1960s there were signs that Olinger/Shillington was being gradually exorcized from Updike's imagination, and replaced as his source of inspiration by Ipswich, the Massachusetts coastal town where he has lived since 1957. A rather similar town, named Tarbox, is the setting of *Couples*, his most ambitious book to date. It studies a prosperous, attractive, and articulate set of youngish married people who for about a year form a close, boozy, gossipy Tarbox elite: "a magic circle of heads to keep the night out," a sort of church. Aware that the post-Freudian path to self-realization is through sexual love, encouraged by their corrupt high priest Freddie Thorne, bored, aggrieved, or hagridden, they drift into complex patterns of adultery. At first, the only real sufferers are the children, dumped in strange beds while their parents drink downstairs, driven home in the middle of the night. But in the end there is a real scandal, the "new morality" claims its martyrs, and the rest take up less dangerous games, their status in the community usurped by a younger set that "held play readings, and kept sex in its place, and experimented with LSD."

The novel's central character is Piet Hanema, a Tarbox housebuilder and restorer nostalgic for America's innocent past. It is no coincidence that Piet and his mistress Foxy Whitman, who spoil the Tarbox games by falling seriously in love, are also the only members of their set who go to church. The book is an elegy for the Puritan ethic that shaped America; for now, as Piet Hanema says, "America is like an unloved child smothered in candy. God doesn't love us any more. . . . We're fat and full of pimples and always whining for more candy. We've fallen from grace." So it is ironic, though not surprising, that the lyrical sexual explicitness permitted by the "new morality" made the book a best seller, brought Updike half a million dollars for the film rights alone, and put him on the cover of *Time*—symbolically a dangerously conspicuous position for a man so preoccupied with the passing of time.

John Aldridge has complained that Updike "has nothing to say"; Leslie Fiedler maintains that "he writes essentially nineteenth century novels" and is "irrelevant." *Couples* is not likely to have changed their opinions, since it is an old-fashioned realistic novel of character, with no particular message to impart. Indeed it has the qualities of all of Updike's books: an almost Proustian insight into the mechanics of human relationships, a painter's eye for colors and shapes and movements, and a Puritan craftsman's determination to express his insights and perceptions fully, every ounce, every nuance, to the uttermost limits of his poet's vocabulary (and, at times, of the admiring reader's patience). The result, whether or not it is what modern critics expect of modern literature, is an unexcelled portrait of a particular kind of American life at a particular point in history.

After this, Updike turned to something different, a novel, or story sequence, about "the silken mechanism whereby America reduces her writers to imbecility and cozenage." *Bech: A Book* recounts the adventures of Henry Bech, famous Jewish novelist (on the strength of two good books and a large-scale dud), as he makes a cultural visit behind the Iron Curtain, is guest of honor at an English publisher's party, or addresses a women's college in the Old South. Bech has a writer's block and intimations of mortality. Trapped but still struggling a little in "the silken mechanism" of the American literature industry, he bolsters his shaky ego with all the sex and all the loving praise he can lay his hands on (which is a lot), and still somehow emerges, melancholy and ironical as he is, a genuinely likable hero. Jack Richardson wrote that Updike "has written a book quite unlike any of his previous works, a book that does not have to wrest its excellence from eroded soil. Everything about *Bech* is lean, antic, and to the point, and it has a daring that is supported, rather than encumbered, by the lessons of tradition. With its intelligence and verve, *Bech* reaffirms that writing is still our most subtle way of telling things." Thomas R. Edwards thought it Updike's best and most attractive book.

The tale of Rabbit Angstrom, begun in *Rabbit, Run*, is resumed in *Rabbit Redux*. Ten years have gone by since Rabbit broke clear of his drunken wife, his drowned baby, and all the snares of maturity, and "drove South." Now he is back in the trap, stale, flabby, henpecked but trying at last to do right by his wife, his son, his job. Then his wife leaves him for another man, and Rabbit takes up with Jill, a rich teen-age addict, a middle-aged mediocrity's dream come true. But also a Pandora, who through her black messianic bad angel, Skeeter, looses around Rabbit's bemused head a whole boxful of contemporary horrors and challenges—drug addiction, racial violence, Vietnam, and the moon shot. In the end, Jill is dead and Rabbit and his wife are together again, perhaps to be happy. Christopher Ricks, in a notably clever and attentive notice in the *New York Review of Books*, complained that the book was merely clever and merely attentive, "more activity than purposefulness"—"Updike doesn't want seriously to contemplate Rabbit; so he substitutes analysis and explanation for any true curiosity." Some other critics agreed, but as many shared the view expressed by Richard Locke: "The vast social changes of the 1960's are dramatized with unprecedented subtlety and detail and with scrupulous attention to their effect on personal experience, social class, aging and individual psychology. Though there are some structural faults and blurry motivations, though characters don't always ring true, there is a dynamic balance between description and narrative energy, between symbol and event. *Rabbit Redux* is a great achievement, by far the most audacious and successful book Updike has written."

Updike writes for about three hours a day in an office above a restaurant in Ipswich, within walking distance of his seventeenth century house. In 1972 he was appointed an Honorary Consultant in American Letters to the Library of Congress. He was raised a Unitarian, but entered the Congregationalist Church in 1959. A year later he was attacked, as many are at just that age, by a persistent "sense of horror that beneath this skin of bright and exquisitely sculpted phenomena, death waits." It was at that time that Updike discovered the consolations of Karl Barth's uncompromising neo-orthodox theology.

PRINCIPAL WORKS: *Fiction*—The Poorhouse Fair, 1959; The Same Door (short stories), 1959; Rabbit, Run, 1960; Pigeon Feathers (short stories), 1962; The Centaur, 1963; Olinger Stories: A Selection, 1964; Of the Farm, 1965; The Music School (short stories), 1966; Couples, 1968; Bech: A Book, 1970; Rabbit Redux, 1971; Museums and Women (short stories), 1972. *Poetry*—The Carpentered Hen, 1958 (England, Hoping for a Hoopoe); Telephone Poles and Other Poems, 1963; A Child's Calendar, 1965; Midpoint and Other Poems, 1969; Seventy Poems, 1972. *Miscellaneous*—Assorted Prose, 1965.

ABOUT: Burchard, R. C. John Updike, 1971; Current Biography, 1966; Enright, D. J. Conspirators and Poets, 1966; Galloway, D. D. The Absurd Hero in American Fiction, 1966; Hamilton, A. and K. The Elements of John Updike, 1970; Hamilton, A. and Hamilton, K. John Updike: A Critical Essay, 1967; Harper, H. M. Desperate Faith, 1967; Kazin, A. Bright Book of Life, 1973; Levin, M. (ed.) Five Boyhoods, 1962; Moore, H. T.

(ed.) Contemporary American Novelists, 1965; Podhoretz, N. Doings and Undoings, 1964; Taylor, C. C. John Updike: A Bibliography, 1968; Updike, J. Assorted Prose, 1965; Vinson, J. (ed.) Contemporary Novelists, 1972; Who's Who, 1973; Who's Who in America, 1972–1973. *Periodicals*—Atlantic April 1968; Book Week November 21, 1965; Book World April 27, 1968; Christian Science Monitor November 4, 1965; Commentary May 1968; Commonweal February 6, 1959; September 11, 1959; October 28, 1960; March 29, 1963; December 9, 1966; April 26, 1968; Critic February 1963; December 1965; January 1966; Horizon March 1962; Life November 4, 1966; The Listener June 19, 1969; New Republic January 12, 1959; November 21, 1960; May 14, 1962; December 11, 1965; September 24, 1966; New York Herald Tribune Book Review January 11, 1959; April 7, 1963; New York Review of Books October 22, 1970; November 16, 1971; April 19, 1973; New York Times Book Review January 11, 1959; March 18, 1962; April 7, 1963; September 22, 1963; April 7, 1968; June 21, 1970; November 14, 1971; New Yorker February 7, 1959; November 5, 1960; April 13, 1963; Paris Review Winter 1968; Reporter March 14, 1963; December 16, 1965; Saturday Review August 9, 1958; August 22, 1959; November 5, 1960; February 2, 1963; November 13, 1965; April 6, 1968; Time November 7, 1960; March 16, 1962; April 26, 1968; Wilson Library Bulletin September 1961.

URIS, LEON (August 3, 1924–), American novelist and screen writer, was born in Baltimore, the son of William and Anna (Blumberg) Uris. His father, a Polish immigrant, was a paperhanger, later a storekeeper. The boy attended schools in Norfolk, Virginia, and Baltimore but did not complete high school. At seventeen, shortly after the attack on Pearl Harbor, he ran away from home to join the Marine Corps, serving in the South Pacific at Guadalcanal, Tarawa, and New Zealand. Never advancing beyond the rank of private first class himself, he met and married a woman Marine sergeant—Betty Beck—in San Francisco, where he had been sent to recuperate from malaria and dengue fever.

When the war ended, Uris found himself with no job and with a wife and a baby to support. Although he had been scribbling plays and stories since his childhood and had done some writing for Marine and war bond shows, he had no prospects of professional authorship. His introduction into journalism was oblique—a job with the San Francisco *Call-Bulletin* as a district manager for home delivery of newspapers. After collecting the inevitable mass of rejections for his writing ("It took me all my life to become an overnight success," he recalls), Uris had his first taste of success in 1950 with an article on football which *Esquire* bought for three hundred dollars. Encouraged, he began intensive work, at nights and on days off from his job, on a novel about the Marine Corps. Two years and several rejections later, the novel, *Battle Cry*, was published (1953) and sold to Hollywood. It became a best seller and launched Uris on his career as one of

LEON URIS

the most popular of contemporary fiction writers.

Literary art has never figured large in Uris's work. *Battle Cry*, a realistic and carefully detailed account of life in the Marine Corps, did not bear comparison with the major war novels like Mailer's *The Naked and the Dead* and Jones's *From Here to Eternity*. Nevertheless, it has become an enduringly popular book, notable for the warmth and sympathy of Uris's attitude toward the Marines: "Like most writers and most human beings, I hated war, but unlike most modern writers I did not hate the men who fought the war and I believed in the things I was fighting for. I respected my officers and their competence and revere the memory of the time I served as a Marine."

This combination of impassioned personal involvement with his subject and a slam-bang, adventure-romance formula proved commercially effective in the novels which followed. In *The Angry Hills* Uris drew on the actual experiences of an uncle who had fought with a volunteer Palestinian brigade in Greece. With *Exodus*, his "biggest" novel, both physically (over six hundred pages) and in scope, Uris himself lived as nearly as possible the experiences from which he drew his material. Fascinated for years by the events in the history of European Jewry which culminated in the establishment of Israel, he read voluminously on the subject, then spent many months in that country, living with the people and covering the 1956 Arab-Israeli fighting as a war correspondent. The novel has been called "one of the all-time successes in publishing history," having sold over ten million copies internationally (it has been translated into thirty-five languages). Whatever its crudities of form, style, and characterization, it has moved and entertained vast audiences.

While working on *Exodus*, Uris had read accounts of the defense of the Warsaw ghetto during World War II. He developed these in his next novel, *Mila 18*, using material in the Memorial Archives in Warsaw and interviewing survivors. The result was a melodramatic novel which most critics dismissed as a poor successor to John Hersey's *The Wall* but which had a good popular sale. *Armageddon* (1964), a story of Berlin in post–World War II days, had even harsher reviews; William Barrett in the *Atlantic* dismissed it as "not serious literature but journalism. . . . His characters are flat and one-dimensional, as if already prefabricated for the Hollywood movie in which they are bound to appear." The novel, however, was an immediate best seller and a book club selection, and was indeed bought for Hollywood. It was followed by *Topaz*, a spy thriller centering on the Cuban missile crisis of 1962, and involving a Soviet espionage network within the French government.

Film versions of Uris's novels have been box-office successes, especially *Exodus*, which Otto Preminger made into a lengthy and elaborate motion picture. Uris has had considerable experience as a screen writer. He went to Hollywood in 1953 to write the screenplay of *Battle Cry* and subsequently wrote an original screenplay western, *Gunfight at the OK Corral*. Less fortunate, however, were the motion picture versions of *The Angry Hills* ("I was fired from the screenplay," he says, ". . . because I didn't understand the characters of the novel") and of *Exodus*, where his own treatment of the screenplay was "aborted."

In 1964 Uris and the British publisher of *Exodus* were sued for libel by Dr. Wladislav Dering, who claimed that Uris had mentioned him by name as one of the German surgeons who had committed atrocities against the Jewish prisoners in Auschwitz. The trial, in London, was widely publicized. The court awarded Dering one halfpenny in damages and ordered him to pay the costs of both defendants. This incident provided the basis for Uris's 1970 novel *QB VII* (Queen's Bench Seven), "a good read" in spite of the author's weakness for clichés and some "embarrassing" dialogue.

Uris has three children by his first marriage, which ended in divorce in 1965. His second wife, Margery Edwards, whom he married in 1968, died in 1969. A year later he was married to Jill Peabody. He lives in Aspen, Colorado, partly because of his enthusiasm for skiing. He is active in many educational and philanthropical projects, especially those concerned with Israel. A hard worker, he considers that "if there are two weapons in a writer's arsenal, one is stamina, and the other is uncompromising belief in himself."

PRINCIPAL WORKS: Battle Cry, 1953; The Angry Hills, 1955; Exodus, 1958; Mila 18, 1961; Armageddon, 1964; Topaz, 1967; QB VII, 1970.

ABOUT: Author's and Writer's Who's Who, 1971; International Who's Who, 1973–74; Vinson, J. (ed.) Contemporary Novelists, 1972; Who's Who in America, 1972–1973. *Periodicals*—Wilson Library Bulletin December 1959.

***USTINOV, PETER (ALEXANDER)** (April 16, 1921–), English dramatist, screen writer, novelist, and short story writer, was born in London. He is the son of a well-known journalist, Iona Ustinov ("Klop"), and of the artist Nadia Benois. His father came from a Liberal Lutheran family which had left Russia in 1868, and Ustinov grew up in a cosmopolitan family, unusually alert to the European cultural climate. He speaks eight languages, and says: "I have Russian, French, German, Italian, Spanish, Armenian, Ethiopian—and once you have got these, why stop?—blood in my veins. Owing to the caprice of a high official in some bureau my father was transported from the Hague to London, and so, without a drop of English blood, I was born an Englishman. I am eternally indebted to England, because it gave me a language I love to use."

Even as a child, Ustinov was a brilliant mimic, his impersonations of his parents' friends and his teachers aided by his extraordinary vocal range and the mobility of his features (which, left to their own devices, suggest the petulant melancholy of a disappointed baby). At sixteen, after an undistinguished career at Westminster School, Ustinov went to the London Theatre Studio to study acting with Michel Saint-Denis. Two years later he joined the Players' Theatre Club, delighting audiences with his sketches and monologues as, for example, the Bishop of Limpopoland or a Wagnerian prima donna. His legendary versatility soon manifested itself, and in 1940, when he was nineteen, he directed Kataev's *Squaring the Circle* at the Arts Theatre and completed his first play, *House of Regrets*, staged at the Arts two years later.

In 1942 Ustinov was inducted into the army, which he hated, though he was fascinated by the eccentricities of the military life. Service in the Royal Sussex Regiment (where for a time he acted as David Niven's batman) was followed by a period with the Royal Army Ordnance Corps. His second play, *Blow Your Own Trumpet*, about the fantasies and delusions of the habitués of a London café, opened at the Old Vic in 1943, and the same year Ustinov was transferred to a unit making propaganda films. He wrote and acted in Carol Reed's memorable film *The Way Ahead* (1943) and wrote, directed, and produced *School for Secrets* (1946), about the development of radar. Meanwhile his

* yōō′ sti nov

PETER USTINOV

play *The Banbury Nose*, a perceptive study of family tradition, had been a considerable success in London in 1944, when Ustinov also played opposite John Gielgud in a dramatization of *Crime and Punishment*. He ended the war with an enviable reputation as a brilliant actor and a promising dramatist.

Ustinov produced and played the lead in his own screen adaption of F. Anstey's novel *Vice Versa* (1947), a Victorian comedy about a domineering father who magically swaps roles with his long-suffering son, and finds that school life is less idyllic than he remembers. The film was moderately successful and so was *The Indifferent Shepherd* (1948), a Chekhovian study of two clergymen with different interpretations of Christianity. In *The Love of Four Colonels* (1951), Ustinov's first real hit as a dramatist, a slight story binds together four extremely funny portraits of soldiers of different nationalities, and their varying notions of what constitutes the "ideal woman." The play seemed to some critics careless in construction and superficial in its observation of national characteristics, but it nevertheless carried off the New York Drama Critics' Award as the best foreign play of the year. It enjoyed a very long run in London and a respectable one in New York, where Richard Watts wrote: "I wish Ustinov would pull himself together and try to organize his unruly talents, but, if he did, some of that wild, free imagination might depart from him. . . . I think he deserves the audience salute he is receiving for what is fresh and delightful in his work."

Romanoff and Juliet (1956), a romantic comedy with a Cold War setting, was another major success; it was subsequently filmed, and provided the basis for the 1973 musical *R Loves J*. Ustinov's more serious plays, however, have on the whole pleased neither critics nor the general public. T. C. Worsley, reviewing *The Moment of Truth* (1951), an interpretation of the tragedy of Marshal Pétain, wrote: "It is apparently no use any longer for us to urge Mr. Ustinov to concentrate his talent and try to produce one satisfactory play instead of three or four near-misses. If he won't stop to polish and shape, and above all to cut, that is because, we must now presume, he can't." Such entertainments as *Photo-Finish* (1962), *Halfway Up a Tree* (1967), and *The Unknown Soldier and His Wife* (1968) have tended to confirm Ustinov's reputation as a dramatist who can write wonderfully funny and effective individual scenes, but lacks the self-discipline and singlemindedness to produce a wholly satisfactory play.

Ustinov has also produced two volumes of short stories and two novels, *The Loser* and *Krumnagel*. *The Loser* is about a young Junker-class Nazi officer, a stiff-necked, propaganda-stuffed young romantic seeking the glory of a hero's death. The Russian campaign knocks the romanticism out of him and leaves him a nervous wreck. Transferred to the Italian front, he takes his revenge on a group of partisans by murdering the women and children of a Tuscan village. Ironically, this proves the beginning of some sort of salvation, for contact with the feckless and irreverent Italians, the prospect of defeat, and first love with a young prostitute begin to unfreeze him, and in the end he has the grace to realize that he has been rendered unfit to live.

Like his plays, Ustinov's novels and short stories have been admired for their portrayal of national characteristics, their sometimes brilliant comic set pieces, and the enlightened and liberal views they embody, but found superficial in characterization and lacking in narrative momentum. Keith Waterhouse expressed a common view of Ustinov's literary ability when he wrote that "Mr. Ustinov, who can imitate just about anybody, has given us in *The Loser* a very skilful imitation of a novelist."

There are no such reservations about Ustinov's abilities as an actor, especially a screen actor, and he received "Oscars" for his performances in *Spartacus* (1960) and *Topkapi* (1965). In 1961 he wrote, acted in, and directed the film version of *Billy Budd*, in 1962 he produced three operas at Covent Garden, and in 1973 he both produced and designed the Edinburgh Festival's version of Mozart's *Don Giovanni*. He wrote and performed in the popular British radio series *In All Directions*, and more recently has made a fresh reputation as a superb conversationalist on television. His record, *Mock-Mozart*, in which he imitates a full orchestra and chorus, has delighted listeners in England and America. The *New Statesman* once described this outrageously versatile and talented man as Britain's "unpaid, unlicenced court jester," adding, however, that "the public will never see the cream of his great gifts of mimicry, which need the context of the small dinner party or the saloon bar."

Peter Ustinov serves or has served as rector of Dundee University, Goodwill Ambassador for UNICEF, a director of the Nottingham Playhouse, a governor of London Independent Television Producers, and a member of the Councils of the League of Dramatists and the British Film Academy. He has a daughter by his 1940 marriage to Isolde Denham, which was dissolved in 1950, and two daughters and a son by his second wife, Suzanne Cloutier, from whom he was divorced in 1971. He made a third marriage in 1972 to Hélène du Lau d'Allemans, a French press agent. He collects drawings by old masters and enjoys squash, tennis, and music.

PRINCIPAL WORKS: *Plays*—House of Regrets, 1943; Beyond, 1944; The Banbury Nose, 1945; Plays About People, 1950; The Love of Four Colonels, 1951; The Moment of Truth, 1953; Romanoff and Juliet, 1957; Photo Finish, 1962; Five Plays, 1965; The Unknown Soldier and His Wife, 1967; Halfway Up the Tree, 1968. *Fiction*—Add a Dash of Pity (stories), 1959; The Loser, 1960; The Frontiers of the Sea (stories), 1966; Krumnagel, 1971. *Miscellaneous*—We Were Only Human (cartoons), 1961; The Wit of Peter Ustinov, ed. by D. Richards, 1969.

ABOUT: Beaton, C. W. H. and Tynan, K. Persona Grata, 1954; Contemporary Authors 13–14, 1964; Current Biography, 1955; Thomas, T. Ustinov in Focus, 1972; Ustinov, N. B. Klop and the Ustinov Family, 1973; Who's Who, 1973; Who's Who in America, 1972–1973; Willans, G. Peter Ustinov, 1957. *Periodicals*—Atlantic Monthly July 1964; Drama Summer 1962; Film Quarterly September 1963; Holiday July 1958; Hudson Review Summer 1963; Life May 19, 1961; April 19, 1963; Look April 29, 1958; Nation November 27, 1967; New Statesman April 1, 1950; December 1, 1951; March 27, 1954; December 12, 1959; March 3, 1961; May 4, 1962; May 31, 1968; New York Times Book Review November 20, 1960; New York Times Magazine January 29, 1961; New Yorker July 15, 1967; November 18, 1967; Publishers' Weekly October 25, 1971; Saturday Review December 16, 1944; June 1, 1958; July 22, 1967; November 25, 1967; Spectator June 1, 1951; September 28, 1962; Time March 10, 1958; Times (London) November 4, 1972; Times Literary Supplement December 18, 1959; March 3, 1961; Vogue October 1, 1957.

"VAIL, AMANDA." *See* MILLER, WARREN

*__VAILLAND, ROGER (FRANÇOIS)__ (October 16, 1907–May 11, 1965), French novelist, journalist, essayist, and dramatist, was born at Acy-en-Multien (Oise), the son of an architect. He was educated at the Lycée in Rheims and the Lycée Louis-le-Grand in Paris, gaining his *licence* in literature and a diploma in philosophy. A natural revolutionary, Vailland was at first attracted to surrealism, but of a characteristically unorthodox

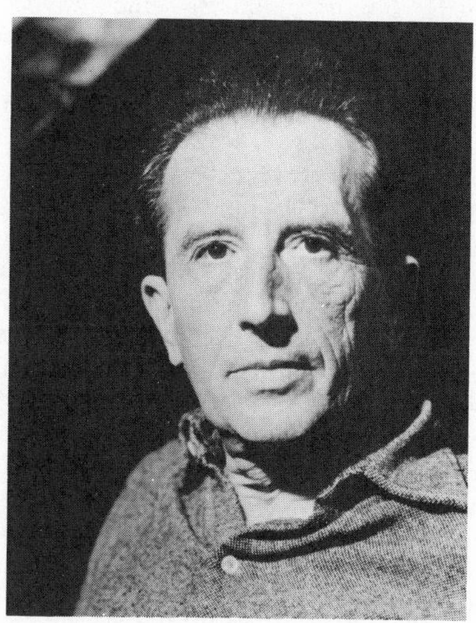

ROGER VAILLAND

kind. While they were still students, he and his friend René Daumal founded a review in which to promulgate their ideas, *Le Grand Jeu* (The Great Game). For a time it had a devoted following among the younger surrealists.

In 1930 Vailland joined the staff of *Paris-Soir*, and at various times during the next ten years served as a foreign correspondent in the Balkans, the Near East, and Ethiopia. He liked to say that he learned his lucid and economical prose style in the hard school of newspaper reporting. During this part of his life Vailland, with his first wife, became addicted to drugs, a state from which he was rescued by the German Occupation and the excitement of participation in the Resistance, where he became a specialist in the derailment of troop trains. It was then that he joined the Communist party, of which he remained a militant member until Khrushchev's revelations about Stalin at the Twentieth Party Congress in 1956.

Vailland began his first novel late in the war when, cut off from other Resistance workers, he was forced to hide in a farmhouse. It is about a small group of partisans operating in Paris during the spring of 1944. Vailland does not deny their heroism but, with his "prodigious gift for irreverence," also reveals their cynicism, greed, and selfishness. Published in 1945 as *Drôle de jeu*, it won the Prix Interallié, and has been described by Henri Peyre as "one of the earliest novels, and the best, on the French underground, a book full of destructive humor." American critics, who read it in 1948 as *Playing for Keeps*, tended to agree with the reviewer who found its "cold-blooded, critical detachment" unattractive.

* vī yäN′

After the war Vailland became a full-time writer, producing a series of novels which advocated a curious mixture of communism and sensualism. *Les Mauvais Coups* (1948, translated as *Turn of the Wheel*) illustrates the disastrous consequences of romantic love. *Bon pied, bon œil* (Good Foot, Good Eye, 1950), about an affair between a cripple and a one-eyed girl is, according to Peyre, "equally frank in its claims for a liberal and unsentimental ethics of sex, but naïve in its idealization of Communists." *Un Jeune Homme seul* (A Young Man Alone, 1951) describes a middle-class engineer's progress to Communist commitment, while *Beau Masque* (1954) and *325,000 Francs* (1955) are proletarian novels about conflicts between management and labor. These books, which mingle the ideas of Marx and Laclos, of Sade and Stendhal, are distinguished by Vailland's "great gift for crisp, economical, revealing dialogue . . . his knack of getting tension and significance out of simple, uncontrived situations." Most of them were admired in France, and *Bon pied, Bon œil* is regarded by some critics as one of Vailland's best novels, but only *Les Mauvais Coups* was translated into English, and that was not much liked in America.

Vailland owed his international reputation to *La Loi* (1957, excellently translated like most of his books by Peter Wiles, and published in the United States as *The Law*). It received the Prix Goncourt in France, was published in seventeen languages, and filmed by Jules Dassin. It is set in a small, poverty-stricken southern Italian seaport, where a tavern game is played in which the winner has the right to insult the losers, whoever they may be. The novel was warmly praised for its brilliant evocation of "a hard, tangible landscape," its great economy in characterization, its dry, exact, ironic style. Madeleine Chapsal pointed out that this short book contains all of Vailland's major themes: "the game of power, the game of love and death that only people of 'quality' can win—those people, whoever they may be and whatever their manner of life, who are free."

This special notion of freedom is also the theme of *La Fête* (1960, translated as *Fête*), in which a writer demonstrates his sovereignty over his own conduct by enjoying, with the consent of his wife, "an idyllic yet clear-eyed love affair." In his last novel, *La Truite* (1964, translated as *The Trout*), his virgin heroine Frédérique is a different kind of winner in "the game of love," whose command over herself is symbolized by her physical intactness. Neither book enjoyed the success of *La Loi*.

Vailland wrote a number of film scenarios, including one based on *Les Mauvais Coups*, and a controversial adaptation of Laclos's *Les Liaisons dangereuses*, and made a television adaptation of *325,000 Francs* in which he himself played a small role. He was also the author of several plays, among them the antireligious *Héloïse et Abélard*, which was performed in Paris in 1949 and praised for the excellence of its dialogue, though its philosophical digressions were thought overlong. Vailland's essays, highly valued in France but never translated into English, included *Esquisses pour le portrait du vrai libertin* (Sketches for the Portrait of the True Libertine, 1946); *Quelques réflexions sur la singularité d'être français* (Some Reflections on the Singularity of Being French, 1946); *Laclos par lui-même* (Laclos by Himself, 1953); and *Éloge du Cardinal de Bernis* (Eulogy of Cardinal de Bernis, 1957).

His first marriage ended with his wife's suicide. In 1954 he was married again to Elisabeth Naldi, an Italian to whom, he said, he owed much of his love and understanding of Italy and its people. When they were not traveling, the Vaillands lived at Meillonnas, near the Swiss border, where the writer found his friends among the workers and farmers of the area, and pursued his hobbies, which included botany and bird watching. His *Écrits intimes*, published posthumously, reveal that during the latter part of his life he was an alcoholic, and that his interest in sex had developed into an elaborate erotomania. Vailland was a lean, beak-nosed man, "dry as a stick, with the clear-cut definition of a sentence by one of those libertines of the eighteenth century whom he [admired] so much." He died of lung cancer, after years of illness during which he continued to write as vigorously and as prolifically as ever.

PRINCIPAL WORKS IN ENGLISH TRANSLATION: Playing for Keeps (England, Playing With Fire), 1948; The Law, 1958; The Sovereigns, 1960 (U.S., Fête); Turn of the Wheel, 1962; The Trout (England, A Young Trout), 1965.

ABOUT: Boisdeffre, P. de. Dictionnaire de littérature contemporaine, 1962; Boisdeffre, P. de. Une Histoire vivante de la littérature d'aujourd'hui, 1958; Nadeau, M. The French Novel Since the War, 1967; Peyre, H. French Novelists of Today, 1967; Pingaud, B. Écrivains d'aujourd'hui, 1960; Who's Who in America, 1970–1971. *Periodicals*—National Review December 1946; New Republic May 7, 1951; New York Times September 28, 1958; May 13, 1965; Newsweek May 24, 1965; Publishers' Weekly May 31, 1965; The Reporter November 13, 1958; November 12, 1959; Times Literary Supplement September 28, 1967.

"VALERIY, IVAN." *See* TARSIS, VALERY (YAKOVLEVICH)

***VALLEJO, CÉSAR (ABRAHAM)** (March 16, 1892–April 15, 1938), Peruvian poet, was born in Santiago de Chuco, a small town in the Andes, into a large family of mixed Indian and Spanish descent. His poetry's richest and warmest imagery derives from his memories of this peasant childhood, and

* bä ye′ hō

in particular from his love for his mother. He was educated in Santiago de Chuco and at the Colegio San Nicolás in the neighboring town of Humachuco, and went on to study science at the University of San Marcos in Lima.

Deciding that science was not for him, he transferred to the University of Trujillo, where he received a degree in literature in 1915. At Trujillo, deeply affected by the ideas of Marx, Darwin, and the Rationalists, he joined a group of intellectuals which concerned itself with the plight of the exploited Indian peasantry. For a while Vallejo taught at the Colegio Nacional in San Juan, contributing his first poems to magazines in Lima and elsewhere. He was passionately and unhappily in love and once attempted suicide at this time. In 1918 he returned to the University of San Marcos for a year of law studies, joined the avant-garde Colonida group, and published his first collection of poems, *Heraldos negros* (Black Messengers, 1918).

These early poems reflect his early preoccupations—love sacred and profane, horror at the exploitation of the peasants, nostalgia for the pre-Columbian heritage his generation had begun to discover. As one critic wrote: "These things converge at times in a sense of the pointlessness of human suffering and a conviction that God, if he exists, must himself be an imperfect, suffering being." In form they are reminiscent and sometimes derivative of such older Latin-American poets as Rubén Darío, but they express a specifically Peruvian consciousness and experience. Vallejo's friend José Carlos Mariátegui called him "the poet of a blood-line, of a race."

In 1920, visiting his mother in Santiago de Chuco, he was arrested and imprisoned for six months on an arson charge, an experience which greatly embittered him. He wrote constantly in jail, and these and other poems were collected in *Trilce* (1922), whose publication was financed with prize money he had won in a national short story contest. In these poems the rhetoric that sometimes marred his earlier work had quite disappeared, replaced by language that was stripped naked, even to the point of obscurity, and a rush of marvelously controlled images, often numerical, that conveyed his sense of time rushing towards chaos and disintegration: "I have faith in the strong / leave me crippled, wind, let me go. / I wear my zeros, my mouth a zero. / O dream give me your hardest diamond / your sense of unreality. // I have faith in the strong. / The colorless quantity / of a concave woman going by, / whose survival ends where mine begins. // . . . . I have faith in that I am, / and that I was useless. // O first of all." Pierre Lagarde said that Vallejo had "invented surrealism before the surrealists"; for another critic these poems express the poet's sense of "being orphaned in an absurd universe."

CÉSAR VALLEJO

In 1923, at any rate, desolated by the death of his mother, and hurt by the cool reception in Peru of *Trilce*, Vallejo left for France, whose poetry and thought had so much influenced his own. "I am going to Paris now to be a son," he wrote. He was to spend the rest of his life in exile, illness, and poverty.

The inheritor of two cultures—Spanish and Indian, oppressor and victim—he longed for an ideal unity but experienced only spiritual fragmentation. This is often the theme of the prose fantasies collected in *Escalas melografiadas* (1923) and in the novel *Fabla salvaje* (1923), about a man haunted by a *Doppelgänger*, "a being who aspires to unity and is condemned to duality."

Vallejo embraced communism, visited the Soviet Union in 1928, and returned there in 1929 with his young French wife Georgette, meeting Mayakovsky and other Soviet leaders and artists. Expelled for political reasons from France in 1930, he moved to Madrid. There he wrote *Rusia* (1931), an account of his Soviet travels; the novel *El Tungsteno* (Tungsten, 1931), about the exploitation of labor in Peru; and a play called *Lockout*. In Spain Vallejo met the poets and intellectuals of the brilliant "generation of 1927"—among them Rafael Alberti, Lorca, Luis Cernuda, and Pedro Salinas. His health was bad throughout all these years of exile, and his books, articles, and stories earned him scarcely enough to live on.

Life was no better when he went back to France in 1932. And with the outbreak of the Spanish Civil War he felt obliged to return to Spain as an act of solidarity with his Loyalist friends. There in 1937, out of the holocaust, he wrote the fifteen passionate poems collected posthumously as

España, aparta de mí este cáliz (Spain, Let This Cup Pass From Me, 1940). Then, desperately ill, he was rushed back to Paris, where he died the following year at the age of forty-six. The cause of his death has been given variously as tuberculosis, acute intestinal infection, and malaria. H. R. Hays suggests that "in the larger sense he was struck down by hunger and by Spain's agony."

It is believed that Vallejo left a great quantity of poetry, all of which is still unpublished except for the *España* sheaf and ninety-four poems collected in *Poemas humanos*. The latter was first published in a limited edition by Vallejo's widow in 1939, and has since appeared in half a dozen other editions. The most accurate Spanish text is no doubt the one published with Clayton Eshleman's English version, *Human Poems* (1968).

Poemas humanos stands as one of the great achievements of contemporary Spanish-American literature. These are personal poems in that they deal most often with the poet's own awareness of his dying body, his vivid sense of all that he is losing; "human poems" because a generous humility of spirit turns these wry complaints, momentary celebrations, bitter confessions, into universal statements of man's despair, endurance, courage: "I like life enormously / but, after all, / with my beloved death & my coffee / & seeing the leafy chestnuts of Paris / & saying: this is a man's eye, & that one; this / is a woman's forehead, & that one. And repeating / So much life & the tune never fails me! / So many years & always always always! // . . . I'd like to live always, even flat on my belly, / because as I was saying & I say it again / So much life and never! And so many years, / & always, much always, always always!"

These are poems of great technical variety and virtuosity, ranging from strict formality to extreme looseness, from colloquial ease to classical purity of diction. They have established Vallejo as "one of the most compassionate and verbally inventive poets of this century," and "as a major twentieth-century poet, whose continuing influence on the Spanish-speaking countries is comparable only to that of Neruda."

PRINCIPAL WORKS IN ENGLISH TRANSLATION: Twenty Poems, 1962; Human Poems, 1968; Neruda and Vallejo: Selected Poems, 1972. *Poems in* Barnstone, W. (ed.) Modern European Poetry, 1966; Bly, R. (ed.) An Anthology, 1964; Burnshaw, S. (ed.) The Poem Itself, 1960; Caracciolo-Trejo, E. (ed.) Penguin Book of Latin-American Verse, 1971; Cohen, J. M. (ed.) Penguin Book of Spanish Verse, 1956; Cohen, J. M. (ed.) Latin-American Writing Today, 1967; Fitts, D. (ed.) An Anthology of Contemporary Latin American Poetry, 1942; Hays, H. R. (ed.) Twelve Spanish American Poets, 1943.

ABOUT: Barnstone, W. (ed.) Modern European Poetry, 1966; Cohen, J. M. Poetry of This Age, 1966; Grigson, G. (ed.) Concise Encyclopedia of Modern World Literature, 1963; Monguió, L. César Vallejo, 1952; Nieto, L. C. Poetas y escritores peruanos, 1957; Seymour-Smith, M. Guide to Modern World Literature, 1973; Zilio, G. M. Stilo e poesia in César Vallejo, 1961. *Periodicals*—Nation October 28, 1968; New York Times Book Review March 23, 1969; Times Literary Supplement September 25, 1969; Tri-Quarterly Fall–Winter 1968; West Indian Review July 1939.

VAN DER POST, LAURENS (JAN) (December 13, 1906–), British novelist and writer about Africa, was born in Philippolis, South Africa. His mother, the former Maria Lubbe, came of a Boer pioneering family. His father, Christian W. H. van der Post, was born in Holland of Dutch-French parentage but became a prominent South African statesman, at one time chairman of the Orange Free State Republic Volksraad. Laurens van der Post says that as a child he faced two great problems: "One was that my people had been conquered by the British just a few years before I was born. . . . Though I liked the English people without reservation, I had inherited this bitterness. The second problem was the fact that I loved the black peoples of Africa. . . . It was a great shock to me, when I was sent away . . . [to Grey College, Bloemfontein] to find that I was being educated into something which destroyed the sense of common humanity I had shared with the black people. . . . These, I think, are the raw materials of my spirit."

When he was nineteen, with his now famous friends Roy Campbell and William Plomer, van der Post launched a magazine called *Voorslag*. It was so outspoken in its attacks on South African racial prejudices that its editors were soon forced to leave the country. Van der Post, like Plomer, went to Japan, but soon returned. His first book, *In a Province* (1934), was a novel about the corrupting effect of city life on an African youth.

Van der Post joined the British Army in 1939 as a private, and left it ten years later as a colonel, after service with the Commandos and special forces in Abyssinia, North Africa, Syria, the Dutch East Indies, and Java, where he was captured in 1943 by the Japanese while organizing guerrillas against them. He would certainly have been killed rather than imprisoned except for his knowledge of Japan and the Japanese language. From 1945 to 1947, van der Post was on the staff of the British Minister in Batavia. He received a CBE for his services in 1947. From 1948 to 1965 he farmed in South Africa, while establishing his reputation as a writer, and carrying out a number of missions in Africa for the British government and the Colonial Development Corporation.

One such mission, to investigate the agricultural potential of certain parts of Nyasaland, is the subject of his first important work, *Venture to the Interior* (1951). It is an exciting travel book, rich in superb descriptive writing, but also much more. Van der Post, in a way that owes much to Jung, believes that every human being is split between the primitive in him—"instinctive, subjective and collective," and the civilized—"objective, rational and individual." The "color problem" he sees as an attempt to externalize this internal conflict, a means by which we can suppress "the native in ourselves," or strike up "vicarious relationships with him through the black people of Africa." The author's journey from contemporary London to the ancient heart of Africa becomes in his book a venture into a different kind of interior, "the inward, nebulous, subconscious, disquieting, where Africa becomes a spiritual continent." The book received the Amy Woolf Memorial Prize and was a Book Society Choice.

The lectures van der Post delivered in 1954 to the C. J. Jung Institute and the Psychological Club of Zurich, with the discussions that followed them, formed the basis of *The Dark Eye in Africa*. It develops the thesis expressed in *Venture to the Interior*—that the white man's inhumanity to the black symbolizes his attitude to the "natural instinctive man, [the] dark brother" inside himself. The book was widely praised as the "courageous, honest, wise, and often quite beautiful" declaration of "a wonderfully mature, civilized man," though one reviewer found it "closer to poetry than to social analysis," and thought the author's personal mysticism confusing. There were similar complaints about *The Lost World of the Kalahari* and its sequel, *The Heart of the Hunter*. Together they form a record of van der Post's search in the Kalahari Desert for a dying tribe of Bushmen, one of the most ancient peoples on earth, his sojourn with them, and subsequent campaign to assure their survival. Though most reviewers were fascinated by van der Post's account of his life among the Bushmen, of their myths and culture, and their "aristocracy of spirit," many critics found the books portentous and didactic, ornate and overladen in their symbolism.

Van der Post's novels have in general been found rather weak in their characterization and marred by the psychoanalytic mysticism which some critics dislike in his nonfiction, but distinguished by brilliant descriptive writing and the generosity of spirit with which they are conceived. *The Face Beside the Fire* describes a young man's painful progress to maturity and the ability to love, and is more successful in its precise evocation of his unhappy childhood in South Africa than in the humorless "purple patches" towards the end. *Flamingo Feather* is an eloquent, often exciting, but rather long-winded African thriller with mystical undertones, a little reminiscent of Rider Haggard. *The Seed and the Sower* contains three episodes drawn from the author's war experiences in the Far East, all of them "steeped in a Tolstoyan love of one's fellow man strong enough to outlast brutality and sadism."

LAURENS VAN DER POST

The most widely admired of van der Post's fictional works to date is *The Hunter and the Whale*, a story of four summers just after World War I on a whaling ship in the area of Port Natal. The book recounts the coming to manhood of the lookout boy, Peter, and the epic struggle for power between a famous hunter of elephants and the whaler's captain, who shows the hunter even bigger game than elephants. The book was widely recognized as an allegory, but one whose meaning escaped the reviewers. "And yet," wrote one critic, "in spite of these uncertainties, [this book] stands as a work of great imaginative power, descriptively brilliant, reaching back into those rudimentary areas of the human spirit whose exploration Mr. van der Post has made peculiarly his own." Of *A Story Like the Wind*, about a boy growing up in Africa, it was said that the mystical and political overtones "do rather impinge on what is otherwise a rattlingish good yarn in a rather outworn tradition."

In 1963 *Holiday* magazine sent van der Post on a three-month tour of Russia. His account of this journey appeared in book form as *A View of All the Russias*, and was found to be full of splendid writing and illuminating perceptions. Van der Post came away convinced that the Russians, like the Africans, are in his special sense of the word a "primitive" people, struggling towards "civilized" individuality, but still fearful of losing their collective identity. In *A Portrait of All the Russias* he provided a text to accompany Burt Glinn's excellent photographs, and the same partnership subsequently produced *A Portrait of Japan*. *The Prisoner and the Bomb* is an account of the author's wartime incarceration in a succession of Japanese prison camps in Java. Not everyone shared his conviction that the destruction of Hiroshima and Nagasaki saved hundreds of thousands of lives (including his own), but it was widely recognized that, in the literature of captivity, this "brief concentrated book ranks very high."

Van der Post has been married twice, in 1928 to Marjorie Wendt, by whom he has a son and a daughter, and in 1949 to Ingaret Giffard. When he is not traveling, he divides his time among houses in Philippolis, London, and Suffolk. His interests include walking, climbing, skiing, nature study, anthropology, and cooking. In 1956 he made a fascinating documentary film about the Bushmen of the Kalahari, and two more films followed in 1971, *A Region of Shadows* and *The Story of Carl Gustav Jung*. Van der Post believes that all the arts, including his own, are breaking away from "the articulate, conscious, cerebral form of expression that existed before the war," and sees "a turn to natural imagery, a return, if you will, to symbolic thinking as if, in this natural symbolism of the human spirit, the new meaning of our lives is to be found. . . . I find this age, this transition of art, terribly exciting. I think we are on the verge of a tremendous breakthrough into rejoining the two essential poles, the two very necessary opposites in the spirit of modern man. Then we'll see something."

PRINCIPAL WORKS: *Fiction*—In a Province, 1934; The Face Beside the Fire, 1953; A Bar of Shadow, 1954; Flamingo Feather, 1955; The Seed and the Sower(includes also A Bar of Shadow *and* The Sword and the Doll), 1963; The Hunter and the Whale, 1967; A Story Like the Wind, 1972. *Nonfiction*—Venture to the Interior, 1951; The Dark Eye in Africa, 1955; The Lost World of the Kalahari, 1958; The Heart of the Hunter, 1961; Journey into Russia (U.S., A View of All the Russias), 1964; A Portrait of All the Russias, 1967; A Portrait of Japan, 1968; (with the eds. of Time-Life Books) African Cooking, 1970; The Prisoner and the Bomb, 1971 (England, The Night of the New Moon, 1970).

ABOUT: Carpenter, F. I. Laurens van der Post, 1969; Contemporary Authors 5–6, 1963; International Who's Who, 1973–74; Newquist, R. (ed.) Counterpoint, 1964; Spender, S. Destructive Element, 1936; Who's Who, 1973; Who's Who in America, 1972–1973. *Periodicals*—Holiday March 1954; Saturday Review November 10, 1951; December 17, 1955; Times Literary Supplement February 8, 1952; November 11, 1955; November 3, 1961; March 15, 1963; October 12, 1967.

VANSITTART, PETER (August 27, 1920–), British novelist, writes: "On the whole I have an easy life, though without the means or adventurousness to travel very widely, so that my work is often concerned with unease in foreign countries—France, Germany, Sweden—at the point where mere politics shade off into History. An only child, I read immoderately and reinforced my private world during very long walks in town and country, as I still do. Myths, ballads, Carlyle's *French Revolution*, biographies, and sprawling foreign novels by such writers as Merejkowski, Werfel, Feuchtwanger built up in me a sense of archaic and fantastic obsessions and possibilities surviving into our own times, particularly evident in war-time and amongst children. A feeling for melodrama, both a strength and weakness, was also provoked by eerie dormitory story-telling at my first school: war-crimes, the *Titanic*, etc. Later influences were Dickens, Mann, and the Russians, countered rather than reinforced by Proust, Virginia Woolf and such poets as Pound, Auden, Rilke.

PETER VANSITTART

"My own preoccupations and perceptions are at their most concise in *The Game and the Ground*, in which illiterate fanatic children are being rehabilitated on an ancient estate lately used as a concentration camp. For twenty years I was a teacher and my imaginative work has suffered through a didactic tendency which I have now attempted to eliminate by writing a straightforward history book, *Green Knights, Black Angels*. A critic has said that my books seem written sometimes by a poet, sometimes by a scientist and certainly at their worst they are imaginative essays rather than novels of character. Though a sense of history pervades them all, only a minority are 'Historical Novels' and these are unconcerned with the picturesque and antiquarian. *Enemies* shows the Franco-Prussian war as an image of perennial and ludricrous misunderstanding. *The Tournament*, though set in fifteenth-century Burgundy, is really about adjustment to loss of youth. 'All history,' Croce remarks, 'is contemporary.' And all such themes are pompous and platitudinous unless redeemed by language. In much modern fiction I find enviable intelligence or techniques blunted by insensitive feeling for words.

"I am now trying to unify my experiences in a novel embracing five centuries, mingling fantasy with realism, the god Loke for example eventually becoming a contemporary movie-star. The disciplines of writing verse, short stories or domestic drama escape me. Such novels as *The Overseer* and *Orders of Chivalry* deal with the interlocked tensions of a whole town or province, combining the satirical and melodramatic, the mythical, personal and comic. The set-pieces and atmospherics are usually managed better than character development. I write several novels at a time, leaving the drafts sometimes for several years before re-writing, and always with more books unpublished than published. Having bought a house when prices were low I can just afford the marvellous luxuries of solitude, daily outdoor games, plenty of music, and the freedom to write only what I care to. I have little interest in what the Novel should be doing, any more than what my neighbours should be doing. I live quietly amongst my friends and try and get on with the job, though of my sixteen published books only *The Overseer*, *The Game and the Ground* and *The Tournament* give me much encouragement. Latterly I have also begun to write for children: this is interesting in itself and a way of shedding diffuseness, flatness of characterisation, and rhetoric. Easily upset in personal life I am fortunately undismayed by critical neglect or by reviewers. As I grow older the challenges of writing become more formidable but also more stimulating, and in this too is a sort of freedom."

Peter Vansittart was born in Bedford, the son of Edward and Mignon Vansittart. He was a major scholar in modern history at Worcester College, Oxford, from 1940 to 1941. After the war he became a teacher, and directed Burgess Hill School, Hampstead, from 1947 to 1959. His first novel, published when he was twenty-two, was *I Am the World*, an ambitious if unpleasant study of the rise and fall of a dictator. The book is distinguished by "an unusual flow of words and a feeling for outward graces of style"—qualities it shares with Vansittart's subsequent novels which are otherwise remarkably different from it and from each other in theme and tone. *Broken Canes*, for example, is a "wistful comedy" about an extremely progressive private school; *A Little Madness* is a love story. Vansittart likes to write in cafés and other public places, and to think about his books on long walks. Such a walk took him once to a derelict mansion which supplied him with the theme and setting of *The Game and the Ground*, a parable reflecting the author's notions about education and also the historical sense which pervades his work. It is set in an unnamed country where on an ancient family estate two men are working to redeem children emotionally crippled by war when their brother returns to revive the pernicious hero myth which provoked the war. A "startling novel with many levels of meaning," rich with "urgent contemporary symbols," it confused some reviewers and impressed others as an allegory about Nazism (or more generally about the power of evil) comparable to William Golding's *Lord of the Flies*.

The historical novel, Vansittart believes, should be a "branch of poetry" rather than an accumulation of facts. Thus *The Tournament* was called "lapidary" in its style (though plain in its dialogue and free of "eftsoonery"), a kaleidoscope rather than a chronicle. It possessed for Edith Simon "all the bright, detailed panoramic effect of late-medieval miniatures: so that it has something of both the microscopic order and purity of the single snow crystal and the teeming abundance of a crowded tableau." Vansittart's "fondling of rhythms, names and associations," his "incrusted" style, bore some readers and deny him general popularity, but some critics consider him one of the finest living historical novelists. *Green Knights, Black Angels*, mentioned above, is a "mosaic" of English history that was warmly recommended to teen-age readers. One reviewer, who found the book maddening as well as brilliant, wrote: "Every paragraph, every sentence on some pages, is a challenge to the intellect. And some passages are pure poetry." The "novel embracing five centuries" which the author mentions above, was published in 1968 as *The Story Teller*. It escorts its central character, "S," from his childhood during the Hundred Years' War to old age in modern Sweden—a bold and interesting device which ultimately fails, some critics thought, because S himself never really emerges as a genuine individual.

A big man, tall and broad shouldered, with a bony ascetic face and thick gingery hair, Vansittart lives in Hampstead, is married to the former Jacqueline Goldsmith, and has a daughter. He likes sports and has retained his interest in education.

PRINCIPAL WORKS: *Fiction*—I Am the World, 1942; Enemies, 1948; The Overseer, 1949; Broken Canes, 1951; A Verdict of Treason, 1952; A Little Madness, 1953; The Game and the Ground, 1956; Orders of Chivalry, 1958; The Tournament, 1959; A Sort of Forgetting, 1960; Sources of Unrest, 1962; The Siege, 1962 (England, The Friends of God); The Lost Lands, 1964; The Story Teller, 1968; Pastimes of a Red Summer, 1969; Landlord, 1971. *For children*—The Dark Tower: Tales from the Past, 1965; The Shadow Land, 1967; Green Knights, Black Angels: A Mosaic of History, 1969.

ABOUT: Author's and Writer's Who's Who, 1971; Who's Who in America, 1972–1973. *Periodicals*—Books and Bookmen May 1962.

VASSILIS VASSILIKOS

***VASSILIKOS, VASSILIS** (November 18, 1933–), Greek novelist, writes: "I was born in Kavala, Greece. During the German and Bulgarian occupation we moved to Salonika, where I remained after the war, graduating from Anatolia College and the Law School of the University of Salonika. In 1956 I joined the army as an infantry reserve officer, specializing as an interpreter in French and English. Having finished my military service I went to America with a Ford Foundation Scholarship, given in 1959 to seven young European writers. In America I graduated from a television school in direction, and back in Greece in 1960 I worked for a year as an assistant director on Greek and foreign documentary films. From 1962 I was a freelance reporter for the Athenian weekly magazine *Tachydromos*, and also worked in the movies, both as a writer and as an actor. Apart from my novels I have also written a play, *In the Prison of Philippi*, broadcast on the Greek radio in 1954, and two film scenarios: *Young Aphrodites*, based on Longus' *Daphnis and Chloe*, which was directed by Nikos Koundouros and received the first prize at the 1963 Berlin festival; and *Epitaph Over Berlin*, filmed by the Czech director Jiři Sequens.

"As a Greek writer one is addressing oneself to a rather limited audience of readers, though my trilogy sold the rather astonishing number (for Greece) of ten thousand copies in four years. Nevertheless I depend on translation in order to reach a wider public. I have been called 'the angry young man of Greece,' though I think this is not true, because I have no kinship whatsoever with the 'angries' of the rest of the world, since of course Greece is not yet (unfortunately) an industrialized country. My political convictions are centre-left, and my philosophy as a writer is an advanced stage of existentialism. Writers and poets who have influenced me in my youth are Kavafy, Seferis, Gide, Eliot, Camus, Sartre, Kafka, Proust, Musil and Joyce. In 1960 I married Demetra Atsedes, painter and pianist; we have no children."

* vas i li kos′

Vassilikos was out of Greece at the time of the colonels' coup in 1967, and has since lived in exile in France, becoming best known for his political novel *Z* and the film which was based on it. His literary career began with the short tale *I diigissi tou Iasona* (The Story of Jason, 1953), which deals with the classical hero's adolescent years on Mount Pelion, where he was tutored by the centaur Chiron. *Thymata eirinis* (Victims of Peace, 1956) is a novel about a group of seven young men living in Salonika under the threat of a third world war, and their escape from the town on the pretext of stealing the Elgin marbles from London.

Vassilikos's trilogy of short novels *To fyllo—To pigadi—T'angeliasma* (1961, translated by E. and M. Keeley as *The Plant, The Well, The Angel*) received the award of the Group of Twelve for the best Greek fiction of the year. Each of the stories deals with a stage in the emotional development of a Greek adolescent, through which Vassilikos explores the meaning of love. They are written in a seemingly matter-of-fact style with a wealth of corroborative detail, and yet are exuberantly fantastic and surprising. In *To fyllo* (The Plant) a young man, Lazaros, steals a potted plant from the courtyard of a girl whose face he has never seen, nurtures it obsessively, and encourages it to grow and spread all through his apartment house, until the whole artificial place is splitting apart. When the other residents trace it and chop it down he is hiding naked in its foliage. In the end he uproots all that is left of it and wanders away, seeking that place where the sun eternally rises. *To pigadi* (The Well) describes what happens when a similar young man, Thanos, takes a servant girl to a deep well notorious for the accidental drownings it has caused. To the girl the well is only a well, but to Thanos it represents something mysterious—the womb, the chaotic, primordial element from which life springs. In *T'Angeliasma* (The Angel) the young man Angelos writes a letter from heaven to a girl on earth recalling their lyrical, sensuous love affair, which had ended unhappily before he died. He satirically describes his experiences in a training school for angels, where he is learning to fly (with wings labeled "Made in U.S.A."), but he is sustained by the belief that he will eventually become one with the light, with the dazzling, procreative, lucid stream of eternity.

Many critics saw this original and highly praised work as symbolic myth-making, allowing a wide variety of possible interpretations. Kimon Friar, who regards Vassilikos as the best young prose writer of contemporary Greece, suggested that he "has written his own Divine Comedy, that the protagonist Lazaros-Thanos-Angelos (Resurrection, Death, Eternity) wanders in the dark wood of existence seeking to find the source of light, of essence, spurred on by love that is at times narcissistic, or feared, or sublimated. This is the perennial portrait of the sensitive, poetic, romantic, idealistic, rebellious young man who expects more of life than it seems able to give him."

This was followed by *I fotografies* (1965, translated by Mike Edwards as *The Photographs*), a serious if not entirely successful investigation of the relationship between life and art, illusion and reality, pursued through the story of a young filmmaker and poet and his attempt to resurrect a lost love. *I mythologia tis Amerikis* (Mythology of America, 1964) is a travelogue, a series of personal impressions from his 1959–1960 tour of the United States. *Hors les murs* (1970, translated by Mike Edwards as *Outside the Walls*) is a collection of articles and essays on Greek social problems, published originally in the journal *Tachydromos*, together with several short stories. The *Times Literary Supplement*, which described it as "compulsively readable," said of it: "Just how repressive the last years of the Karamanlis era were is chillingly conveyed. . . . Vassilikos documents with depressing thoroughness just how many other Greeks missed out on the Karamanlis 'economic miracle.' . . . And throughout the book there broods the appalling tragedy of the murder of Lambrakis, which more than anything signified the moral bankruptcy of the Karamanlis era."

This murder is the subject of Vassilikos's best-known work, *Z* (1966, translated by Marilyn Calmann under the same title), a documentary novel with transparent aliases. Grigoris Lambrakis was a professor of medicine at Athens University, as well as a deputy who was the idol of the Greek Left. In 1963, after addressing a peace rally in Salonika, he was murdered by two men in a contrived street accident. His funeral in Athens was attended by hundreds of thousands of mourners, and the investigation into the crime uncovered evidence of the complicity of high-ranking police officers; the resulting political scandal contributed to the fall of the Karamanlis government. The letter *Z* chalked on walls at the time stands for *zei* ("he lives") and also becomes the name of the victim in Vassilikos's novel, which is an imaginative reconstruction of the murder and the investigation into it by a tenacious examining magistrate and a keen young journalist.

A common criticism was that Vassilikos had overidealized the purity of the left, while the right-wing murderers are caricatured symbols of tyranny, blustering military fools and bullying policemen. But Edwin Jahiel, for whom Vassilikos is "the best novelist of his generation," pointed out that the book was in fact intended as an indictment: "*Z* is a superbly written, angry, partisan, often immensely touching *J'accuse* of a police state where, unlike Kafka's Joseph K., Z exists in a specific historical context. It is a terrifying indictment of the political splits in a country shown as perpetuating the blackest aspects of the Nazi occupation . . . and of the Greek Civil War. Z's viscerally anti-Communist vigilantes, with Vichy-type mottoes like 'Country-Religion-Family,' lynch not only with the blessing but at the instigation of the authorities." The novel was published in Greece just before the coup by the group of colonels whose "Hellenic-Christian Civilization" was one of the slogans in the name of which Lambrakis was murdered, and after their seizure of power the book was promptly banned. The brilliant French-language film version was made by the Greek director Costa-Gavras.

PRINCIPAL WORKS IN ENGLISH TRANSLATION: *Fiction*—The Plant, The Well, The Angel: A Trilogy, 1964; Z, 1969; The Photographs, 1971; The Harpoon Gun (two novellas and thirteen stories), 1973. *Nonfiction*—Outside the Walls, 1973.

ABOUT: Who's Who in America, 1972–1973. *Periodicals*—America November 30, 1968; Atlantic August 1964; December 1968; Book Week June 14, 1964; Book World December 15, 1968; Books Abroad Summer 1968; Christian Science Monitor February 13, 1969; The Listener February 27, 1969; New Statesman February 29, 1969; New York Review of Books September 10, 1964; January 2, 1969; New York Times Book Review June 21, 1964; November 17, 1968; Saturday Review July 4, 1964; November 16, 1968; Sight and Sound Winter 1969–70; Spectator March 14, 1969; Times Literary Supplement March 13, 1969; May 7, 1970.

"VAUGHAN, RICHARD" (pseudonym of Ernest Lewys Thomas) (July 19, 1904–), Welsh novelist, writes: "I was born in the parish of Llanddeusant, under the grim shadow of the Van Rocks in the county of Carmarthenshire, South Wales. My forebears, blacksmiths on my father's side, farmers on my mother's, had lived their lives for generation after generation in this mountain-immured region. I am proud that I am a direct descendant of William Williams the great Welsh hymnwriter and of Owen Lewis who was one of the fathers of Methodism in Wales.

"Although I was born at the turn of the century, I have the feeling that my life spans the period starting back in the eighties to the present day, for night after night I listened to the tales that were recounted around our fireside. There was no end to the talk. The Welsh, like the Irish, are great talkers and dramatise every incident and situation they are

RICHARD VAUGHAN

describing. In the end I had the whole history of the parish at my fingertips. Not that the stories I heard were always wild and dramatic. Far from it. The great adversaries were usually the darkness and a road or track that was new or strange. And, step by step, I was with the story-teller wherever he went. For me, from the very beginning, the parish was peopled with giants. And horses! Such was my beginning in this parish of giants and horses. And there was something more than this, too. Wherever I went, I met the singers of the parish. It was in the chants in church and the hymns in the chapels that the parish found its voice. In those days, too—and it is still here—there was terror along the dark roads at night. We had, I suppose, lived too long under the shadow of the mountains and the Van Rocks. There was something in our blood that was attuned to the spirit of the place. We were in touch with every emanation of the soil and the air. Loneliness had begotten a sensitivity in us so that every tree and turn of the road or path had some deep significance for us. This is the reason, I think, that I am so pre-occupied with the night and darkness in my novels, and can never get away from this *locale* which is so indigenous a part of me.

"Looking back now, I see that my whole life has been subordinated to one end, namely, that I should write, and so re-create in some artistic form the impressions, wonderful and terrifying, that I assimilated in those early years. Nevertheless, it was a long road. I started off by working in a bank, then I became a journalist; served with the Forces in the last war; and then took a teaching post as an English master in a London Grammar School. Now, at last, I am back in my native parish. The tractor has displaced the horse plough, the car or van the trap and gambo; but never mind. The heart of Wales is still unchanged. There are still roads here that echo to the sound of galloping hoofs; and times, too—it could not be otherwise in Wales—great harmonies ride the wintry winds. I am home again, this time for good; and, thank Heaven, there is no rest—not as far as writing is concerned."

———

After four years in the Royal Artillery during World War II, Richard Vaughan went to a teachers' training college and thereafter for some years, as he says, both taught and wrote in London. His first novel, *Moulded in Earth*, is set in Wales during the late nineteenth century, and tells the story of a feud—and a love affair—involving two families. It is scarcely an original subject, but the setting is unusual, the characterization is strong, and most critics received the book very warmly. James Hilton praised its "picture of Welsh village life before modern civilization tamed its ferocities" and its "true poetic realism." *Son of Justin* is an unequivocally romantic sequel to the first book. In *All Through the Night*, Vaughan looked deeper into the Welsh past and produced a powerful account, dark and brooding in its atmosphere, of the fierce hard-fighting cattle drovers who in the eighteenth century took their herds from Wales to the London markets. *There Is a River* is a memoir about Vaughan's boyhood in a remote village on the River Usk, in which the river is used as a unifying symbol and sets the tempo of the narrative. The book was called "an intense, visionary sketchbook" and admired for the "exactness and vividness with which it renders sense impressions."

Vaughan has published a number of short stories, and his books have appeared in France, Holland, and Denmark. One reviewer has accused Vaughan of mixing Welsh idiom and literary English in "a kind of piebald rapture" and for another his prose "soars a little too high too often"; Vaughan continues to write his "unabashedly beautiful prose"—like the boy in *There Is a River*, proud of his heritage and satisfied that it is "no small thing to be born in a parish of giants, to have walked the fields of corn, and to have the wild poetry of the language on my tongue."

PRINCIPAL WORKS: Moulded in Earth, 1951; Who Rideth So Wild? 1952; Son of Justin, 1955; All Through the Night, 1957; There Is a River, 1961.
ABOUT: Contemporary Authors 2, 1963.

VERÍSSIMO, ÉRICO (LOPES) (December 17, 1905–), Brazilian novelist, short story writer, and essayist, writes: "I was born in a small town of southern Brazil, Cruz Alta, in the *gaucho* state of Rio Grande do Sul. My grandfathers were rich ranchers, but both went broke before I was born.

My father, who abhorred country life, had a large library and subscribed to French magazines. The pictures I used to see in *L'Illustration* plus the novels of Jules Verne that I enjoyed reading stirred my imagination, making me daydream about travels and adventures in exotic lands. Eça de Queiroz, the Portuguese novelist, fired my adolescent mind and body with his realist stories. At seventeen I had already decided to be a writer.

"Due to the financial disasters of my family, I was compelled to leave high school and go to work in a gloomy general store, where in the shadow of a sallow-faced manager with sad eyes, I secretly wrote my first tales. A little later I got a job as a clerk in a bank, where I gave more thought to the creatures of my imagination than to the clientele of the establishment. Three years later, for reasons which it would take too long to explain, I became junior partner of a pharmacy, behind the counter of which I found myself one day, at twenty-two, rather perplexed at the change, and knowing nothing about drugs. I spent most of my time reading Ibsen's and Shaw's plays, and scribbling short stories. I had no taste nor talent for commerce, and my senior partner was no better than myself. I remember how annoyed I was when someone entered our pharmacy, forcing me to leave the company of Saint Joan or Hedda Gabler just to sell him an aspirin. I was also very much interested in a good-looking, blue-eyed girl who lived in a house across the street. We became engaged exactly a month before I went broke.

"In December 1930—jobless, penniless, with no definite profession, full of debts and engaged to be married—I decided to move to Porto Alegre in search of a literary job. I found one as assistant editor of a magazine issued by a book store which was also beginning to enter the book publishing business. The company was bold enough to accept my first book. They printed fifteen hundred copies of it, sold four hundred and stored the unsold volumes in a warehouse which one day was completely destroyed by a fire. As the books were insured, I got my royalties paid as if the whole edition had been sold out.

"After such a 'flaming' success, I wrote seven books, at the rate of one per year, all of them beautiful failures as far as sales were concerned. As my salary as editor was inadequate, I had to translate books from English, French, Italian and Spanish into Portuguese, in order to make enough money to keep body and soul together. (Incidentally, in 1931 I married the blue-eyed neighbor, who has been my very patient and dedicated companion for these last thirty-four years. We have a daughter and a son, both married, and they gave us four grandchildren.)

"Not until 1938 did I have my first best seller,

ÉRICO VERÍSSIMO

Consider the Lilies of the Field, and since then I have been a professional writer.

"For a long period of time I was obsessed with the idea of writing a saga of my home state, covering two centuries, but every time I tried to start the book I felt I was not yet prepared for the task. In 1947 I decided to face the ambitious project, and after many years of hard work I got the opus ready and published as a trilogy, under the general title of *Time and the Wind*.

"In 1941 I visited the United States for the first time. In 1943–1944 I was visiting professor at the University of California, Berkeley. From 1953 to 1956 I held the position of Director of the Department of Cultural Affairs of the Pan American Union, in Washington, D.C.

"I am a quiet fellow, rather timid and vaguely lazy. I love children, music, books, paintings and travels. I detest violence, dictators, snobs, cocktail parties, gold teeth and Argentine tangos. As to religion, I am an agnostic who feels the nostalgia of a faith he never possessed. Politically, I place myself left of the center, but have the uttermost distaste for totalitarian regimes. Like most intellectuals, I am permanently ridden by a guilt complex, which has led me often to give my stories a political content as well as a tone of protest."

The son of Don Sebastião Veríssimo, a pharmacist, and Dona Abigail Lopes, the author belongs to one of the oldest Portuguese families of Rio Grande do Sul. His father was greatly attracted to things British and, until the family fortunes crashed, Veríssimo was to have been educated at the University of Edinburgh. As it was, he came to maturity in Rio Grande do Sul at a time (during the 1920s) of violent social and political unrest, storing away material and attitudes which later determined the cast of his fiction. As to early reading, the most important for him, he says, were the works of Machado de Assis, Anatole France, Swift, Wilde, Shaw, and Ibsen. In his later books critics detect the influence of modern English and American writers, especially Huxley and Faulkner.

The Porte Alegre magazine of which Veríssimo became assistant editor in 1930 was the *Revista do Globo*. He had already published a few short stories in Cruz Alta magazines as one of the circle of young writers centered around the poet Augusta Meyer, and his first rather derivative collection, *Fantoches* (Marionettes) appeared in 1932. The novel *Clarissa* (1933) was an altogether more original piece of work, and was warmly received for a quality of youthful lyricism far removed from the violence and primitive passion that dominated Brazilian literature at the time. Veríssimo's second novel was *Caminhos cruzados* (1935, translated by L. C. Kaplan as *Crossroads*). Set in Porte Alegre, it is an attempt, making use of Aldous Huxley's contrapuntal technique, to give an impression of the life of the town over a five-day period. It caused a considerable stir, was attacked by the right wing as immoral and communistic, but nevertheless received the Brazilian Academy of Letters' Graça Aranha Prize.

Clarissa and Vasco, the young people who were the central figures in Veríssimo's first novel, symbolized a new era in the social and cultural development of Southern Brazil. They reappear, together with other characters introduced in *Clarissa*, in *Música ao longe* (Music in the Distance, 1935), which was thought to show more technical assurance than its predecessor, and greater psychological perception. The story was continued in *Um lugar ao sol* (A Place in the Sun, 1936) and completed in *Saga* (1940).

Olhai os lírios do campo (1938, translated by J. N. Karnoff as *Consider the Lilies of the Field*) marked a fresh departure in Veríssimo's work. A contemporary novel with an urban setting, the message expressed in the title is illustrated in the inner conflict of the hero Eugênio, a man torn between love and selfish ambition. *O resto é silêncio* (1942, translated by L. C. Kaplan as *The Rest Is Silence*) studies the interaction of social and psychological pressures and also, since the hero is a writer, is able to include much discussion of literary style and technique, expressing Veríssimo's own preoccupation with time as a literary and a philosophical problem.

The most ambitious of Veríssimo's works is his trilogy *O tempo e o vento*, which comprises *O continente* (The Continent, 1949), *O retrato* (The Portrait, 1951), and *O arquipélago* (The Archipelago, 1962). It traces the fortunes of the Terra-Cambará family from the 1740s to the end of the nineteenth century and is in effect a history of Rio Grande do Sul over a period of radical political and social change. *Time and the Wind*, L. L. Barrett's translation of the first two volumes, appeared in 1951. Some English-language critics who enjoyed it as a colorful panorama of Brazilian history thought it unconvincing in its characterization, but Herschel Brickell called it "a full-blooded historical novel in the best traditions of the type, sound in its factual background, peopled with living men and women, well-written and well-translated, and packed with exciting reading."

Veríssimo's continued openness to experiment is evident in *Noite* (1954, translated by L. L. Barrett as *Night*), an allegory about the ordeal in a nightmarish underworld of an amnesiac known only as The Stranger. It was admired for its skillful evocation of an atmosphere of horror, even by critics who found its symbolism confusing and misplaced.

The author's impressions of his first trip to the United States in 1941 are recorded in *Gato prêto em campo de neve* (Black Cat in a Field of Snow, 1941). A similar volume followed his year at Berkeley, where he gave the lectures published (in English) as an extremely readable, informal, and amusing introduction to Brazilian literary history. *Mexico*, though it is the result of a vacation in that country, is more than a travel book, discussing also the history, society, economy, and the elusive character of Mexico. An impressionistic, effusive, and very personal book, it was welcomed as an excellent introduction. The author has also produced a biography of Joan of Arc and a number of books for children.

Veríssimo is a prolific writer and his work, uneven in quality, is generally highly readable. He is popular in Brazil both with intellectuals and the general public, and has been widely translated. Some have found his experiments with technique a little naïve and self-conscious, though his sincerity is beyond question. He received the Machado de Assis Prize of the Brazilian Academy in 1954.

PRINCIPAL WORKS IN ENGLISH TRANSLATION: *Fiction*—Crossroads, 1943; Consider the Lilies of the Field, 1945; The Rest Is Silence, 1946; Time and the Wind, 1951; Night, 1956; His Excellency, the Ambassador, 1967. *Nonfiction*—Brazilian Literature: An Outline, 1945; Mexico, 1960.

ABOUT: Coutinho, A. An Introduction to Literature in Brazil, 1969; International Who's Who, 1973–74; Twentieth-Century Writing, 1969. *Periodicals*—Christian Science Monitor December 15, 1960; O Estrado de São Paolo January 6, 1962; July 14, 1962; Hispania August 1947, February 1951; New Statesman May 7, 1960; New York Herald Tribune Book Review November 18, 1951; New York Times September 23, 1951; February 26, 1956; New York Times Book Review October 16, 1960; Publication of the Modern Languages Association September 1965; Saturday Review September 22, 1951.

***VERWEY, ALBERT** (May 15, 1865–March 8, 1937), Dutch poet, critic, and scholar, was born in Amsterdam of parents who both died while he was still very young. He left high school in 1883 and began his career in the Amsterdam offices of the Maxwell Land Grant Company. While still in his teens he became secretary to the company's vice president and accompanied him on a business trip to New Mexico. By then he had already met Willem Kloos and other members of the Tachtiger movement (the "generation of 1880"). After he returned from New Mexico he abandoned his business career and plunged into Amsterdam literary life.

From 1885 to 1899 Verwey was an editor (with Kloos) of the Tachtiger magazine *De Nieuwe Gids* (The New Guide). His own verse of this period is filled with the romantic passion for natural and ideal beauty, and the preoccupation with the poet's own moods and feelings, that characterized the Tachtigers (though even then Verwey's work was distinguished by a certain self-consciousness, an intellectual reserve). Notable products of this period include *Persephone* (1883), *Demeter* (1885), and the youthfully romantic sonnet cycle *Van de liefde die vriendschap heet* (Of the Love Called Friendship), all collected in *Verzamelde gedichten* (1889). The end of Verwey's involvement with the Tachtigers was foreshadowed in *Cor cordium* (1886), a record in intricately interwoven Shelleyan stanzas of the poet's tormented quest for his innermost self, the inscrutable core of his being.

Verwey finally broke with Kloos in 1889 and left *De Nieuwe Gids*. He was married the following year to Kitty van Vloten, a professor's daughter, and retired with her to the coastal town of Noordwijk. There he consciously prepared himself to fulfill his vocation as a poet and intellectual leader. He read history and philosophy, especially Spinoza, and was also much influenced by Shelley and by his friend Stefan George, the German idealist poet. He rejected the subjectivism of Kloos and his followers and came to regard poetry as a force that should weld together the fleeting generations of man. The poet was to be God's spokesman on earth, linking the senses, the intellect, and the soul in a cosmic harmony. In *Aarde* (1896) and subsequent volumes, Verwey abandoned personal exploration and "turned full of joy towards life."

These views were expressed not only in Verwey's poetry but throughout his voluminous writings as a critic and editor. In 1894 he and Lodewijk van Deyssel launched *Het Tweemaandelijksch Tijdschrift* (The Bi-Monthly Magazine), renamed *De Twintigste Eeuw* (The Twentieth Century) in 1902. Verwey ended his association with van Deyssel in 1905 and the same year established *De Beweging*

* fər vā′

ALBERT VERWEY

(The Movement). The authority and uncompromising honesty of the literary judgments he expressed there, and his stature as a poet, brought *De Beweging* great influence in Holland between 1905 and about 1919 and made its editor the acknowledged master of an important group of younger writers.

Like Stefan George, Verwey disliked the naturalism of Zola and his disciples, and identified himself with the traditional values of the Dutch critic E. J. Potgieter, of whom he wrote a biography. Verwey was otherwise a generous critic of wide sympathies. He wrote studies of Vondel, Hooft, Bredero, Bilderdijk, and van Maerlant; translated Dante, Shakespeare, and De Quincey; and published an influential anthology of his own translations of European poets, many of them formerly little known to Dutch readers.

Meanwhile Verwey's poetic output continued unabated. A second *Verzamelde gedichten* in three volumes appeared in 1911–1912. Other notable volumes were *Het zichtbaar geheim* (The Visible Secret, 1915), and *De figuren van de sarkofaag* (The Sarcophagus Figures, 1930). His verse became increasingly abstract and difficult, reflecting the immersion in history and philosophy that was also evident in his critical essays. In all he published some twenty volumes of poetry, while his collected prose filled another ten volumes (*Proza*, 1921–1923).

Verwey was professor of Dutch literature at Leyden University from 1925 to 1935, when he was succeeded by P. N. van Eyck, the most prominent of the *De Beweging* group. According to J. Greshoff, "Tradition meant for Verwey in the first place a respect for all life-retaining forces from the past, because he felt and understood that they had shared in the forming of his own character and thought world, and that their values would be preserved in the grand rebuilding of a unity of life he dreamed of."

PRINCIPAL WORKS IN ENGLISH TRANSLATION: *Poems in* Barnouw, A. J. Coming After, 1948; Greshoff, J. Harvest of the Lowlands, 1948; Snell, A. L. Flowers From a Foreign Garden, 1902; Steiner, G. (ed.) Penguin Book of Modern Verse Translation, 1966; Weevers, T. Poetry of the Netherlands, 1960. *Essays in* Pritchard, F. H. (ed.) Great Essays of All Nations, 1929. *Selections in* Adam July 1949; De Kim 5, 1955.

ABOUT: Baxter, B. M. Albert Verwey's Translations From Shelley's Poetical Works, 1963; Cassell's Encyclopaedia of Literature, 1966; Kamerbeeck, J. Albert Verwey en het nieuwe classicisme, 1913; Penguin Companion to Literature 2, 1969; Russell, J. D. Dutch Romantic Poetry, 1961; Smith, H. (ed.) Columbia Dictionary of Modern European Literature, 1947; Uyldert, M. Albert Verwey, 1908; Verwey, A. Mijn Verhouding tot Stephan George, 1934; Vestdijk, S. Albert Verwey en de idee, 1965; Weevers, T. Poetry of the Netherlands in its European Context, 1960; Weevers, T. Mythe en vorm in de gedichten van Albert Verwey, 1965. *Periodicals*—German Life and Letters December 1952.

***VESAAS, TARJEI** (August 20, 1897–March 15, 1970), Norwegian novelist, wrote: "I consider growing up in the country, at one with its fertile life, a great asset for the aspiring writer. And I was lucky enough to be born and brought up on an old farm in Telemark county in the south of Norway (but not in order to be a writer!). Being the oldest son, I was heir to a farm which had gone from father to son in a straight line for three hundred years—and I was naturally expected to take over when the time came. We were three brothers.

"As a boy, I worked on the farm under the supervision of my severe father. My much less severe mother, in addition to being a very efficient housewife, was particularly interested in music and song. Both had strong literary interests, but only as readers. In their leisure time they always sat with a book—and they taught their sons the value of reading.

"During the first World War I went to high school (*Folkehøyskole*). The newspaper reports from a burning Europe made an indelible impression upon me. At school I was very fond of essay writing, but never dreamt of being an author, as I was supposed to return to the old farm with its predetermined tradition. I dreamt occasionally of breaking the tradition, but only to feel free, not in order to write. The final impetus which made me a writer was very unoriginal—a girl I was fond of was snapped up by another. I was twenty-two years old. I started to 'write.' And I found dreaming and writing (even though the first two or three books were promptly refused) so enjoyable and deeply satisfying that my love loss soon became only a little veil of regret, an asset.

"My first book, published in 1923, a novel (*Menneskebonn*—Children of Man), received such favorable criticism that the twenty-six-year-old author survived and straight away started on romantic novel number two. I was still at home with my parents, but in 1925 I was awarded my first traveling scholarship. Thus began a wandering in the great cities of the continent (and England, summer of 1928) which lasted until I married in 1934. I alternated continuously between home and travel, wrote a number of books abroad, mostly in Munich, received new scholarships. It was a good and instructive time.

"In 1934 I married the Norwegian poet Halldis Moren (born 1907); the best thing I ever did. We have a son and a daughter, one grandchild and almost two. We settled in Vinje, Telemark, near my birthplace, but for diverse reasons are in constant contact with Oslo. We lived here during the second World War, wrote, and buried manuscripts in the earth until liberation came.

"Through the years there have been many books, novels, short stories, poems, plays and radio plays. Some books are translated—into English (first 1964), German, French, Italian, Dutch, Polish, Spanish, Latvian, Czechoslovakian—in addition to all the Scandinavian languages.

"My first books were very romantic, often dramatic and with a tragic ending. Today too they are often tragedies, I don't fully know why, but it is partially because the happy ending most often appears not wholly truthful—I find it difficult to go beyond a certain compromise. In a tragedy there are several planes upon which to work. I believe that man reveals himself, in a way, richer and better in his need and his tragedy than in whole and simple pleasure.

"New currents in literature interest me. I have written some novels which people say they don't understand. Be that as it may, I think one must write as one feels at the time, must personally stand by what is written, and accept the responsibility. Strong direct influence is most often to the detriment of the poetic and fictive power in a work of fiction. I at least have difficulty in combining the two. Any such things in my books come more indirectly.

"It has been a great satisfaction for me to have the support of young people, my greatest incentive and strength in the often laborious business of writing.

"Laborious? After forty years of writing I have no regrets. On thinking back I feel very grateful for having been able to do that which I most wanted to. Far too many can't."

* vā′ sus

Tarjei Vesaas was perhaps the greatest stylist among twentieth century writers in Nynorsk, the literary language derived from the host of popular dialects spoken in Norway but, before the mid-nineteenth century, never written down, the official and written language then being Danish. As Vesaas indicates above, he combined a deeply rooted attachment to a traditional way of life with an alert interest in the contemporary world—he was both a farmer and one of the most sophisticated of modern Norwegian novelists. His stories are set in the rural areas of Telemark, but it is the everyday Telemark of the twentieth century, not an idealized peasant world in national dress.

Vesaas's first novels were, as he says, very romantic and were criticized for this. He was more successful with the determinedly realistic *Dei svarte hestane* (The Black Horses, 1928) and finally established himself in the 1930s with the Klas Dyregodt tetralogy and the two volumes about Per Bufast. The first three novels *Fars reise* (Father's Journey, 1930), *Sigrid Stallbrokk* (1931), and *Dei ukjende mennene* (The Unknown Men, 1932) tell of Klas Dyregodt's close relationship with nature, but also of his lack of contact with human beings. Klas's isolation becomes increasingly serious and he considers suicide; but he is saved by a helping hand from outside and is led back to human companionship and emotional health, exemplified in the account of his marriage in the fourth volume of the series, *Hjarta høyrer sine heimlandstonar* (The Heart Hears Songs of Home, 1938).

The first of the Per Bufast novels, *Det store spelet* (1934, translated as *The Great Cycle*), describes Per's, childhood and youth on the family farm. Per dreads the prospect of a lifetime imprisoned in the traditional patterns of farm life. He rebels against his destiny, but learns in the end that true happiness for him lies in fidelity to this tradition and participation in nature's "great cycle." The eternal round of birth, life, and death is portrayed in the second volume, *Kvinnor ropar heim* (Women Calling Home, 1935), an account of Per's life as a farmer.

Up to this point, Vesaas had been refining his terse, lyrical style, cutting away all that was superfluous, developing an oblique, allusive manner that was peculiarly his. At the same time he was working to free himself of what his fellow novelist Sigrid Undset called his "narrow and closed world . . . where the people suffer hurt because they take themselves so distressingly seriously, and are inclined to see other people only as supporting characters in the drama of their own lives." It was the Bufast books, Miss Undset concludes, that mark the turning point—from here develops one of the major themes running through the rest of Vesaas's work: what James Macfarlane calls the theme of "the 'helping hand' offered, sometimes unknowingly and sometimes deliberately, to a man who has reached the very flash-point of despair."

TARJEI VESAAS

In the late 1930s Vesaas was prompted by World War II and the German occupation to return to the more neurotic and destructive impulses in men. Like other Scandinavian authors he chose to approach these traumatic historical events through symbol and allegory. In *Kimen* (1940, translated as *The Seed*) he describes a peaceful island possessed by mass insanity. The islanders' bestial instincts come to the surface as they pursue a murderer, and only the victim's father refuses to be swept away by the collective madness: "Wildness must not be tolerated," he declares, and from this seed of sanity civilization is able to grow again. *Huset i mørkret* (The House in the Dark, 1945) dispenses with realistic foundations. The dark, sealed house is a symbol of occupied Norway, and its inhabitants represent different attitudes to the occupation.

Bleikeplassen (The Bleaching Ground, 1946) is a study in individual psychology, an account of a man's growing obsession with murder, precariously restrained by his desperate longing for purity, which is symbolized by the bleached linen on the line. Once again, the helping hand of another person breaks the morbid spell and averts disaster. This highly praised novel is typical of Vesaas's mature work, both in its themes and its style. Vesaas is concerned with man's subconscious and the struggle there between good and evil, between fruitful human companionship and destructive isolation, between joy and obsessional dread. He is not interested in academic psychological analysis; the conflicts emerge from hints, from symbols—often from one central symbol—and from a thoroughly compressed language of parataxis and ellipsis. Sometimes the symbols seem uncertainly integrated with the story, sometimes they merely lead to obscurity, but in his best novels Vesaas achieves a remarkable fusion of realism and symbolism.

Vesaas also published poetry and short stories, and a collection of the latter, *Vindane* (The Winds, 1952), received an international literary prize. His radio plays were much admired, though he had less success as a writer for the stage. For many years at the end of his life he was a national figure in Norway, and he was repeatedly named as a potential candidate for the Nobel Prize.

PRINCIPAL WORKS IN ENGLISH TRANSLATION: The Seed *and* Spring Night, 1964 (The Seed, *published separately*, 1966); The Ice Palace, 1966 (U.S., Palace of Ice); The Great Cycle, 1967; The Birds, 1968; The Bridges, 1969; The Boat in the Evening, 1971; Thirty Poems, 1971; Spring Night, 1972.

ABOUT: Chapman, K. G. Tarjei Vesaas, 1970; Macfarlane, J. W. Ibsen and the Temper of Norwegian Literature, 1960; Maele, L. (ed.) Ei Bok om Tarjei Vesaas, 1964; Penguin Companion to Literature 2, 1969; Skrede, R. Tarjei Vesaas, 1947. *Periodicals*—American-Scandinavian Review 4, 1966; Library Journal July 1968; New Statesman January 14, 1966; New York Times March 10, 1969; March 16, 1970; New York Times Book Review September 22, 1968; Scandinavica November 1964; Times Literary Supplement January 13, 1966.

***VESTDIJK, SIMON** (October 17, 1898–March 23, 1971), Dutch novelist, short story writer, poet, and essayist, wrote: "I was born at Harlingen, a small seaport town in the province of Friesland, in the Netherlands. My parents were not Frisians, but came from Haarlem and Amsterdam. But then, Harlingen isn't a typically Frisian town, either.

"I was an only child, and my youth was a rather happy one, except for an unhappy love affair in my fourteenth year that has influenced me considerably ever since. I went to school at Harlingen and Leeuwarden, and beginning in 1917 studied medicine at the University of Amsterdam, where I graduated in 1927. My vocation to become a physician was not an overwhelming one, and as a student I was more interested in music, literature and philosophy. In those years I wrote poetry and tales, but with one or two exceptions I published nothing. After my final examination I worked as a *locum tenens* until 1932, and made a sea voyage as a ship's doctor to the Indies.

"In those latter years I wrote much poetry, published some, and in 1933 determined to live entirely by my pen—a rather bold resolution (the more so since my first great novel was refused by the editor!) realized not without help from journalism (literary editor of the *Nieuwe Rotterdammer Courant*, 1938–1939).

"In 1934–1935 I was one of the literary editors of the review *Forum*, the ideals of which have influenced me considerably in the direction of originality, soberness, and a matter-of-fact approach—ideals which we missed painfully in the Dutch letters of that period. My most important novels of those pre-war days are the autobiographical Anton Wachter novels (e.g. *Terug tot Ina Damman*, the history of my adolescent love affair), in later years completed in eight volumes, and some historical novels (about El Greco, Pilate). Essays. Much poetry still, but flowing less abundantly than formerly. (After 1956 I wrote no more poetry at all.)

"In the war also I wrote much, even in the hostage camp, where I was imprisoned for seven months. But here I could write only poetry. After the war I went on with journalistic work as a critic, but since about 1955 I have been able to live entirely on the royalties from my books, which is not so common in the Netherlands. I received many literary prizes, and became a Doctor *honoris causa* of the University of Groningen in 1964. For the past five or six years I have been the Dutch candidate for the Nobel Prize.

"My poetry has been influenced by Rilke, my novels by Proust, Kafka, Faulkner. With the exceptions of some fantastic novels (e.g. *De Kellner en de Levenden*, 1949), I may say that I am a psychological realist, and not particularly experimental in a modernist sense, notwithstanding my admiration for a book like James Joyce's *Ulysses*. Social, political or other extraliterary tendencies are not to be detected in my books: no 'littérature engagée.' My political convictions are seldom expressed, but they are not leftish. I have remained faithful to the historical novel, but the exacting documentation makes it difficult for me to write more than one historical novel in three or four years. For the rest it is my habit to write two novels a year (with some essays). I write rather easily, but correcting takes the most time of all. Before beginning a novel I make an outline—useful, though I deviate from it frequently.

"Among my hobbies are Alpinism (in a not too acrobatic way), astrology (formerly; but later I wrote a book about the scientific approach to astrology), and especially music. I was a music critic of the weekly *De Groene Amsterdammer* for some years, and I wrote nine books about music—aesthetics, not history. These books have been condemned nearly unanimously, but there is no point in concealing the fact that I regard the majority of the music critics in this country as bunglers.

"Since 1939 I have lived in Doorn, a small Utrecht village, with beautiful woods, and no literary acquaintances. I was married in 1965 to Mieke van der Hoeven, and we have a son."

* fest′ dik

Simon Vestdijk was rightly described as his country's "senior novelist" and, after the death of Arthur van Schendel, was its most esteemed one. He first came to the fore in the early 1930s as a leader of the *Forum* group, which had been formed in reaction to Hendrik Marsman's "vitalism"—a frenetic version of German expressionism. This *Forum* group, the leading spirit of which was the critic Menno ter Braak, opposed expressionist rhetoric, and advocated lucidity and objectivity. In most ways this reaction exactly parallels the counteractivist movement in Germany, *die neue sachlichkeit*, "the new objectivity [sobriety]." However, the sobriety of the *Forum* group, like *die neue sachlichkeit*, was as much a part of expressionism as a revolt against its excesses. It is important to bear this in mind in considering Vestdijk, who was emphatically not a traditionalist reactionary.

As well as medicine, Vestdijk studied psychology and philosophy before becoming a writer. His prolificity and virtuosity were remarkable—he wrote, it has been said, "faster than God can read," and published about forty novels, ten collections of short stories, thirty books of criticism and essays, and more than twenty books of poetry. He was also the translator of Emily Dickinson, R. L. Stevenson, and others. All his work is characterized by intellectual brilliance and psychological insight; his exploration of every aspect of life has been described as "demonic," but his refusal to draw conclusions from his analysis—this stems from his original commitment to objectivity—is frustrating to some readers. His admirers answer that Vestdijk's "diagnosis" is evident in the vitality of his writing: his message is unmistakably "love life, even while you examine it dispassionately."

One of Vestdijk's best-known and most important fictional works is the autobiographical sequence about the early life of Anton Wachter, the first volume of which, *Terug tot Ina Damman*, appeared in 1934; the eight novels were first issued together in 1950. This has been justly criticized as "overweighted with psychological analysis," but it remains a valuable and important *bildungsroman*, and its failure so far to find an English translator is to be deplored.

Vestdijk was in fact not altogether lucky in the few translations into English that his books achieved. *Rum Island*, from *Rumeiland* (1940), one of his Stevensonian historical novels, is painstakingly accurate in its re-creation of Jamaica in the eighteenth century, but there is a woodenness about the characters and even the action that makes one wonder why it was chosen to introduce a leading Dutch author to the English-speaking public.

Vastly superior is Vestdijk's one other translated novel, *De Koperen tuin* (1950), translated as *The Garden Where the Brass Band Played*. The English

SIMON VESTDIJK

version was criticized as turning Vestdijk's "simple and swift" writing into something "slow-moving and dull," but the work was nevertheless generally well received. This is a record of the destruction of beauty and trust by small-town values, and is remarkable for the psychological accuracy of its account, which quite sufficiently justifies the violent conclusion. Its method is an ironic variation of naturalism: the young lovers who are the novel's central characters are seen as dominated, not by fate, but by the absurd and trivial prejudices of provincial society at the turn of the century.

Although Vestdijk wrote historical and fantastic fiction, he was at his best in the realm of psychological realism, and especially in the short story. His fiction had a great influence between 1936 and 1950. As a poet he undoubtedly wrote too much, but a slim selection from his enormous output would establish him as a distinguished minor poet in the technically formal expressionist tradition. His writings on astrology and music would be regarded as eccentric by most readers; but they are never sentimental or unintelligent, and the latter are certainly on a level above that upon which the journalists who criticize them function. His most controversial nonfiction work was *De toekomst der religie* (1947). Vestdijk was a true original who interestingly combined the clinical detachment he aspired to from his early *Forum* days, with a perhaps more instinctive romanticism.

PRINCIPAL WORKS IN ENGLISH TRANSLATION: Rum Island, 1963; The Garden Where the Brass Band Played, 1965. *Selections in* Greshoff, J. (ed.) Harvest of the Lowlands, 1945; New Writers 2, 1963.

ABOUT: Cassell's Encyclopædia of Literature; Nord, M. and others Over S. Vestdijk, 1948; Penguin Companion to

Literature 2, 1969; Ter Braak, M. De duivelskunstenaar, 1945; Wadman, A. Handdruk en handgemeen, 1965. *Periodicals*—Times Literary Supplement November 7, 1963; July 8, 1965.

***VIAN, BORIS ("Vernon Sullivan")** (March 10, 1920–June 23, 1959), French novelist, dramatist, and poet, was born into a wealthy bourgeois family at Ville d'Avray. He studied philosophy at the Versailles *lycée*, excelled in mathematics at the Lycée Condorcet, and received a civil engineering diploma in 1942. He was employed for a time during the 1940s by the French Association for Standardization—a bizarre beginning for Vian, the high priest of spontaneity and particularity.

After the war Vian threw himself into the night world of Paris with unique versatility and zest. He played a New Orleans-style trumpet in the Left Bank *caves*, wrote several hundred songs, made a third reputation as a cabaret singer, and a fourth as a reviewer of jazz records for *Le Jazz-Hot*. He acted small parts in films and wrote film scenarios. In 1946 he created a scandal with *J'irai cracher sur vos tombes* (I'll Spit on Your Graves), a novel (written in ten days) about a black American on the run after committing a string of thefts, rapes, and murders. Mixing sex, sadism, and social protest in a brilliant pastiche of the "tough guy" American writers of the 1930s, and signed "Vernon Sullivan," the book sold 100,000 copies before it was banned as "objectionable foreign literature." Three more "Vernon Sullivans" followed in 1947 and 1948. At the same time Vian was contributing to Sartre's existentialist review *Les Temps Modernes*, and producing a stream of more or less serious novels, plays, and poems.

His first novel, *Vercoquin et le plancton* (Vercoquin and the Plankton), was written in 1943 and published in 1946. It celebrates the "surprise parties" he loved to arrange, and the dancing, jokes, and lovemaking that went with them. All this unconsidered pleasure is threatened by the dark forces of standardization, represented (predictably) by Vian's employer, the Association Française de Normalisation, but in this book at least youth and happiness triumph. *L'Automne à Pékin* (Autumn in Peking, 1947) is a more extravagant fantasy with a similar theme, set this time in the imaginary land of Exopotamia, whose future is permanently unpredictable, and which defeats all attempts to impose a railroad line on it. Vian wrote less for posterity than for his immediate friends and enemies, and both are likely to appear in his novels—Jacques Lemarchand has an avenue named for him in *L'Automne à Pékin*, and Marcel Arland appears as a foreman, referred to at all times as *ce salaud Arland*.

* vē äN′

The best known of Vian's novels, a tragic love story with surrealistic overtones, is *L'Écume des jours* (1947, translated by Stanley Chapman as *Froth on the Daydream* and also by John Sturrock as *Mood Indigo*). A rich young man named Colin falls in love with a pretty girl named Chloe and marries her. She becomes ill on their honeymoon and Colin ruins himself seeking a cure. Chloe dies and is buried in a pauper's grave. Colin's best friend Chick is also ruined, obsessively collecting the writings, fingerprints, tapes, and discarded clothing of the sage Jean-Sol Partre, author of a treatise on illuminated signs called *La Lettre et le néon*. Love and youth are inevitably destroyed by the brute facts—maturity, work, boredom, order, death. In his preface Vian says: "There are only two things: love, all sorts of love, with pretty girls, and the music of New Orleans or Duke Ellington. Everything else ought to go because everything else is ugly."

This deliberately naïve story is told in a deliberately naïve style—short sentences, simple words, childish dialogue. It is also told with a childish literalness that becomes increasingly horrifying. The young lovers are at first followed everywhere by a little pink cloud. Then cancerous water lilies invade Chloe's lungs; children are butchered in the Public Assistance Office; factory workers are torn apart by the machines they wrestle with. And when Colin feels the world closing in on him, his apartment physically shrinks until the ceiling meets the floor and "worms of inert matter sprouted out and slowly twined."

Raymond Queneau, who obviously influenced Vian's fiction, thought it "the most poignant love story of our time," but most French reviewers of the original edition were not impressed. Critics of the English version were also about evenly divided between those who found the book a flimsy undergraduate exercise in fashionable whimsy and those, like John Whitley, who thought it combined "the immediacy and beauty of love and the lurking menace of death . . . as timeless as *Le Grand Meaulnes* or even *La Princesse de Clèves*."

Two darker novels followed: *L'Herbe rouge* (1950), a time-machine story which reflects most clearly Vian's interest in science fiction, and *L'Arrache-cœur* (1953, translated by Chapman as *Heartsnatcher*), described by one critic as painting "a horrified delirium of maternal possessiveness, and the conflict between the secret, autonomous life of childhood and the tyranny of family and social life." Meanwhile Vian had published short stories (*Les Fourmis*, 1949), poems (*Cantilènes en gélée*, 1949), and a flood of translations—from Raymond Chandler, James M. Cain, and Nelson Algren, from Strindberg, Pirandello, and Behan. A short opera, *Fiesta*, written for Darius Milhaud, was performed in Berlin in 1948.

Vian's first play was *L'Équarrissage pour tous* (translated by Simon Watson Taylor as *The Knacker's ABC* and by Marc Estrin as *Knackery for All*), written in 1946 and performed in 1950. Described as "a paramilitary vaudeville in one long act," it is a blackly funny pacifist tract. Set in a Normandy knacker's yard on D-Day, it indiscriminately mocks all the variegated military personnel who invade and finally destroy the place —wartime allies, the Free French, enemies, collaborators, and resisters. Vian had already outraged French patriots with his notorious (and soon banned) cabaret song "Le Déserteur," and his play, coming so soon after the war, aroused a frenzy of protest (though Jean Cocteau welcomed it as an avant-garde landmark).

Noël Arnaud, one of Vian's innumerable friends, has described him as "brilliant, fast, inventive, always surprising, sometimes inspired by genius." He has also been called generous and gentle, a notable wit and practical joker afflicted at times with intense melancholy. Although he was not during his lifetime taken very seriously as a writer, his personal qualities, together with his prodigious energy and versatility, established him during the 1950s or before as the "prince" and guiding spirit of the jazz-hungry, post-surrealist existentialist bohemia of Saint Germain-des-Prés. He received an appropriate accolade in 1952 when he was inducted as a Transcendent Satrap of the Collège de 'Pataphysique, the august body founded to perpetuate the memory of Alfred Jarry and his "science of imaginary solutions." (Vian indeed was a natural heir of Jarry: he once calculated the height of the towers it would be necessary to erect in Paris and Marseille, and the degree of slope that would be required, so that people could *roll* from one city to the other; in 1954 he invented and patented an elastic wheel.)

A childhood illness left Vian with an enlarged heart, and his enormous exertions did nothing to improve his condition. Towards the end of his life he was obliged to give up his beloved trumpet ("each note played on it shortens my life by a day"). In June 1959 he sneaked into a private preview of the unauthorized film version of *J'irai cracher sur vos tombes*. He had a heart attack and died in the theatre, aged thirty-nine. He was survived by his second wife, the former Ursula Kübler, whom he had married in 1954; his first marriage, to Michèle Léglise, had ended in divorce in 1952.

An extraordinary revival of interest in Vian's work followed his death. It began in December 1959 at Jean Vilar's Théâtre Nationale Populaire, with a production of Vian's play *Les Bâtisseurs d'empire* (translated by Simon Watson Taylor as *The Empire Builders*). It is about a bourgeois family whose house is invaded by a mysterious but terrifying noise. They try to escape by moving upwards, every man for himself, from one floor to the next, until only the father is left, alone in a tiny attic, with the noise approaching. The noise, of course, is death. A mysterious element in this otherwise simple fable is the *schmürz*, a mute, bandaged, bleeding figure which is punched, beaten, and ignored by the family; some took this as a symbol of France's brutal and short-sighted treatment of Algeria, others as a more personal image, representing perhaps the author's ailing and ill-used body. The play was staged in England in 1962 and in New York, less successfully, in 1968.

BORIS VIAN

At some point Vian had made a translation of General Omar Bradley's *A Soldier's Story*, and this experience, a pregnant one for a pacifist and iconoclast, inspired the best known of his other plays, *Le Goûter des généreaux* (translated by Simon Watson Taylor as *The General's Tea Party*). As Ronald Bryden wrote, it presents war as a "nursery tea-party"—a chance for Vian's mother-dominated and infantile general "to escape from mummy's apron-strings and talk dirty with the other boys, a deliciously rough game of All Fall Down." A great success in Paris in 1965, it fared less well in England a year later.

During the 1960s Vian's veneration of youth and innocence, his solemn jokes and vigorous sensuality, his insolence towards the Establishment, his love of life and his early death—all these things combined to make him the patron saint and literary hero of French youth. His books, remaindered on first publication, were hurriedly reissued and became best sellers. New collections appeared of his poems, jazz reviews, short stories, plays, songs. His music was heard again in the discothèques and a Vian exhibition was mobbed. The young collected his letters and manuscripts as devotedly as Chick had collected the words of Sartre in *L'Écume des jours*. The academics joined the chase, and dozens of essays, special issues of magazines, and monographs analyzed "the parallel lives of Boris Vian." In the face of so much excitement, it is difficult to imagine how this arch-enemy of categorization will eventually be pigeonholed by the literary historians; he was probably less an important writer than an important man. Someone said once that going into his house was like going on vacation.

PRINCIPAL WORKS IN ENGLISH TRANSLATION: *Fiction*—Froth on the Daydream, 1967 (also translated as Mood Indigo, 1969); Heartsnatcher, 1968. *Plays*—The Empire Builders, 1963 (revised 1967); The General's Tea Party, 1967; The Knacker's ABC, 1968 (also translated as Knackery for All *in* Plays for a New Theater, 1966). *Story and poem in* Taylor, S. W. (ed.) French Writing Today, 1968.

ABOUT: Baudin, H. Boris Vian: La Poursuite de la vie Totale, 1966; Beauvoir, S. de. The Force of Circumstance, 1965; Clouzet, J. Boris Vian, 1966; Corvin, M. Le Théâtre nouveau en France, 1963; Esslin, M. The Theatre of the Absurd, 1968; Noakes, D. Boris Vian, 1964; Penguin Companion to Literature 2, 1969; Serreau, G. Histoire du "nouveau théâtre," 1966. *Periodicals*—Bizarre February 1966; New York Times June 24, 1959; New York Times Book Review March 12, 1967; New Yorker October 16, 1965; Partisan Review July 1950; Time July 20, 1959; Times Literary Supplement May 5, 1966.

***VIVAS, ELISEO** (July 31, 1901–), American philosopher and literary critic, writes: "I was born in Pamplona, Colombia, during my father's first political exile from Venezuela. My early years were spent in Caracas, stumbling from one bad school to another. During my father's second exile our family went to Curaçao, D.W.I., where the excellent teaching of the Christian Brothers convinced me that I was not altogether stupid. In 1915 the family moved to New York. After high school I entered Brooklyn Polytechnic Institute where, in Joseph Wood Krutch's freshman English class, I was finally born—born, of course, to the self-conscious world of the mind. I used two years in Brooklyn Polytechnic to read Nietzsche, Shaw, Mencken, Unamuno, a great deal of poetry, and whatever else came to my hands, reading voraciously with a sense that, having wasted my high school years dancing and playing chess, I had to catch up. I never did, of course. But I am no longer sure that the years before my second birth were altogether wasted.

"In June 1922, after willfully failing all my engineering subjects, I left Brooklyn Polytechnic. Since then I have put whatever time and energy I could filch from the irrelevancy of earning a living into writing. Radically opposed, on the basis of reasoned principle, to hedonism as a philosophy, I have spent my life in the pursuit of pleasure—among books and at the typewriter. As a connoisseur, I maintain that there are only two or three other pleasures that can rival those I have relentlessly pursued—and to them, too, I have given serious attention.

"In 1924 I moved to Greenwich Village where the second stage of my education began; through Sarah Cohen, who later became my wife, I was introduced to the world of art and artists. In the fall of 1926 I went to the University of Wisconsin on a Zona Gale Scholarship, began teaching in 1927, was elected to Phi Beta Kappa and received a bachelor's degree in 1928. I spent a short time in Philadelphia as Consul of Venezuela and there I attended the lectures of Albert C. Barnes at his Foundation. I went back to Wisconsin in the fall of 1929 and after stalling as much as I could (the alternative to an instructorship was a WPA job), I was forced to get my Ph.D. in 1935. I have lived the rest of my life in the University world.

"Although the life of a student is, on the surface, uneventful, its drama can be intense for one who is not able to take ideas dispassionately. Philosophical activity, which the academic careerist seals hermetically from the rest of his life, is, as I take it, a risky business in which the health of a man's soul, or of a people's, is at stake. For this reason, when forced to break with my youthful errors, I went through a most painful experience. Until the late thirties I was a naturalist in philosophy and a liberal in politics. (Naturalism is the belief that no other terms are needed to account fully for nature and man than those derived from nature itself. This turns values and God into projections of man's needs.) In the late thirties the war and the painful death of my wife from cancer after long suffering forced me to look into the adequacy of my convictions.

"At forty I was forced to make a new intellectual start. My second wife, Dorothy Gant, brought me the gift of a devotion to my work that has enabled me to dedicate all my time and energy to it.

"I have written on value, moral philosophy, aesthetics and criticism. Both in my technical writing and in such work as is addressed to the educated public, I have sought to show that values have status in being independent of and logically prior to human needs. At the heart of my mature beliefs is the conviction that our urgent need is to slow up the wreckage that our revolutionary age is inflicting on our civilization and to salvage what is still serviceable while there is still time. My life is proof that with luck and some shrewdness a rebel can get by."

———

The intense religiosity of Vivas's adolescence gave way to indifference when he was about twenty

* vē′ vas

and he was subsequently connected with the New Naturalism, which R. J. Foster calls "a modernist semipositivistic school of philosophy." His break with naturalism and political liberalism at the age of forty was painful and crucial, a step which meant giving up "old intellectual loyalties" and "losing many loved friends" who, as he says, have not forgiven his defection. In his search for a "better philosophy," Vivas was led back to Kant's moral thought, which he had grudgingly admired in younger days, and was reminded by Bernanos and St. Augustine of what constitutes "the inwardness of religious experience." Other influences in that transitional period were Kierkegaard, Dostoevsky, Berdyaev, Brand Blanshard, and Kafka. Vivas now calls himself an "axiological realist," and believes that the "moral man *discovers* the values he espouses, in the same way that the scientist or the logician discovers the laws of science." He deplores the academism of much contemporary American philosophy and its neglect of the "tragic dimension of experience."

His break with naturalism was evident in the articles he published in the 1940s and received its first full expression in *The Moral Life and the Ethical Life*, which proposes that moral values have objective existence and that "moral man becomes ethical man by recognizing the supreme value of the human person." The book displeased a number of critics, including R. J. Foster, who calls it "a various exhibition of philosophy-by-rhetoric... the rhetoric of assumption, irritably passionate assertion, and insistent repetition." But Henry Rago praised it as "something more than a treatise. It is in its own way the rehearsal of a career, a dialectic in the true sense of something really gone through." David Spitz found it "the most significant contemporary attack on naturalistic theory," and Brand Blanshard, allowing that it was more effective in attack than in construction, and in need of greater compression and incisiveness, welcomed it as "a gallant, vigorous book, with a wind of gusto in its sails."

As an aesthetician, Vivas has attacked the New Critics but holds some views similar to theirs. According to Mark Spilka, he believes "that works of art are self-contained, their meanings immanent and reflexive, yet richly relevant to life." In *Creation and Discovery*, he says that art is not merely an adornment, a source of pleasure, or therapy, but "an indispensable factor in making the animal man into a human person."

In recent years Vivas has turned increasingly to practical criticism, most notably in his study of the novels of D. H. Lawrence. It is an uneven book which had an extremely mixed reception. At its worst it was found badly written and organized, inconsistent, and self-centered, and Vivas's habit of

ELISEO VIVAS

making unsupported judgments as if they were axioms particularly annoyed his fellow critics (as it often does his fellow philosophers). Nevertheless, as Mark Spilka wrote, Vivas "proceeds with such intelligence, firmness, and authority that no Lawrence critic can ignore him."

Since 1930 Vivas has taught at the universities of Wisconsin and Chicago, at Ohio State University, and at Northwestern University, where he was John Evans Professor of Moral and Intellectual Philosophy from 1951 until his retirement as Emeritus Professor in 1969. He was advisory editor of the *Kenyon Review* from 1933 to 1942 and since 1960 has been associate editor of *Modern Age*. He has taught as a visiting professor at a number of universities. He says: "I have learned as much from direct contact with my honest teachers or with my colleagues and friends—including those of my students who have demanded the best from me—as I have from books." His students echo this statement and speak of him with warmth and admiration. Vivas has a daughter by his first marriage.

PRINCIPAL WORKS: The Moral Life and the Ethical Life, 1950; Creation and Discovery, 1955; D. H. Lawrence: The Failure and the Triumph of Art, 1960; The Artistic Transaction and Essays on the Theory of Literature, 1963; Contra Marcuse, 1971.

ABOUT: Contemporary Authors 7–8, 1963; Foster, R. J. The New Romantics, 1962; Vivas, E. *preface to* The Moral Life and the Ethical Life, 1950; Who's Who in America, 1972–1973. *Periodicals*—Commonweal September 21, 1951; August 5, 1955; Comparative Literature Winter 1956; Spring 1965; Partisan Review March–April 1951; Philosophical Quarterly October 1951; Poetry August 1956; Review of Metaphysics June 1956; Sewanee Review Autumn 1960; Yale Review September 1955; September 1960.

VOELKER, JOHN DONALDSON. *See* "TRAVER, ROBERT"

VOLPONI, PAOLO (1924–), Italian poet and novelist, writes (in Italian): "I was born in Urbino where I lived until the age of twenty-six. I attended the *liceo* during the war, between Fascist obscurantism and black-outs. I registered in the University on the 9th of September, 1943, before going into obligatory hiding. I grew up rather more on the streets, with gangs of friends, mostly orphans and sons of unwed mothers, than at home or in my various schools. These schools were, however, decent and kind, like the *ginnasio-liceo* Raffaello, which tried so hard to save me, with its bust of Pascoli—pupil of Aquilone—at the end of the stairs, and with its temporary staff permanently stunned by my insolence. My comrades didn't finish their teacher-training course and went off to the mines in Belgium, or are still working in Urbino in garages or in the fire department. If I had to say what did save us from childhood and from delinquency, its glorious sequel, I shouldn't know how to answer. Perhaps it was our football team, perhaps some chance book, some teacher more long-suffering than most, some couple or other who—scarcely aware that they were doing so—furthered our education beside the dark walls of our quarter. And certainly the movies were a great help.

"The first stories I tried to write, hopeless ones indeed, were somewhere between [Fucini's] *Le veglie di Neri*, [D'Annunzio's] *Le novelle della Pescara*, and the films of Duvivier with Louis Jouvet. Then my curiosity, my restlessness and all those avant-garde Fascist Saturday people brought me new friends and new things to read, both pretty pessimistic, until all rebellions fused in the yearning for liberty as the allied armies landed in Italy. On this psychological phase I have written perhaps the best of my poems, "La paura" ("Fear"), printed in *Le porte dell'Appennino* (The Gates of the Apennines), Feltrinelli, Milano, 1960.

"Having put aside the short stories of my youth and abandoned plans for a peasant novel—my scant schooling not having provided me with a language adequate for proper organization—I began to write poems, following the post-hermetic style that represented for me the maximum of novelty and liberty, and that enabled me to say at once what I wanted to say, as well as giving me an immediate taste for poetry. The poetry was always the same; whether it spoke of a day or a walk or a girl, it always said the same thing: the need to know everything and come to terms with everything, to live life differently and not allow myself to sink back into the indulgence of Urbino.

"My poetry is all personal, even after all those confrontations and lessons provided by the magazine *Officina*, personal in the most carnal sense: every insect, every morning or evening, every interlocutor, village, peasant, the relatives before and after, every boy or girl, protagonist or spectator, is always a part of me; they are me myself with different words or faces but always me, absolutely and entirely, and I am avid to distinguish, weigh, understand, find out how or where I stand, judge myself, and be my own companion.

"This at any rate is how my poetry seems to me today, now that I am more mature, and have written a novel, and am writing others, with the idea of finding, in that form, another rational and poetic and hence autobiographical means of portraying reality. My poems, from those of my first volume (*Il ramarro*—The Lizard, Urbino, 1948) and of *L'antica moneta* (The Old Coin, Florence, Vallecchi, 1955), right up to those published in 1960 by Feltrinelli, have come with me all the way on the road to maturity. So with what I am saying here I do not mean to repudiate them or to minimize their worth but only to place them properly in my own story, in the hope and belief that they may have some value in their own right and in the same way as I am constructing my novels today.

"With my poems I have redone (that is rethought, analyzed and resolved) my life in Urbino and, in the last ones, thanks to the enlightenment and freedom that I had won for myself, I have done the same for the whole complex of human life in Urbino and its countryside, in a way generally affirmed to be new.

"I began to write a novel, my first, *Memoriale* (*My Troubles Began*), during and immediately after those recent poems, when I felt myself in possession of an effective linguistic instrument, capable of originality and able to sustain its autonomy, unfettered by lyrical convention and traditional technique.

"I have been helped, or perhaps I should say seized, by the problems of my daily work in a great factory—the torrential, incandescent problems of a world in convulsions, as the industrial world is, striving to pursue scientific progress while carrying with it a great deal of medieval baggage. I have been in this world for ten years, conditioned to it like everyone else. Before that, on leaving Urbino in 1950, I had traveled all over the south, making inquiries on behalf of a firm dealing in public construction. I can't manage to find a less demanding job: I won't say a sinecure, but at least a consultantship or a subordinate post in government or political culture. Nor can I persuade myself that I would be able to live by my writing, getting advances or loans, or fees for collaborations, or for lectures, or for editing or appearing in anthologies, or for reviews. Nor could I write articles for the great dailies, nor attend all the parties, panels, political meetings, and publicity affairs. My days are not free and my virgin pages are sometimes spoilt by a letterhead; on this account, every time I take up my pen for my novels or my poems, it is an act of rebellion and real effort.

"This at least leads me to be careful; because to be honest—which is essential in a writer—I believe that my inspiration comes from my moral passion and my political vocation.

"I don't even dare to hope that anything I write could possibly interest a film producer. Such is the autonomy of literature that I am convinced that one day I shall write a novel based on a film."

Volponi is the director of social services of the Olivetti firm in Ivrea. That organization, famous for the elegant design of its business machinery, is equally well known as a pioneer of *neocapitalismo* (welfare industrialism), a phenomenon which Volponi studies and questions in *Memoriale*. His poems have received little attention outside Italy, though *Le porte dell'Appennino* (1960) was awarded the important Premio Viareggio.

His first novel, *Memoriale* (1962), was received with great excitement in Italy by Moravia, Italo Calvino, and others, and is still the most famous of the avant-garde novels on industrial subjects published since the war. It is about a worker, Saluggio, newly returned from a German prison camp, who finds a job in a superb modern factory and at the same time falls ill with a lung disease. Saluggio is shuttled from foreman to superintendent to company doctor to convalescent center and back again, from one paternalistic bureaucrat to another, until all this generous but soulless interference becomes a nightmare from which only the natural beauty of the countryside around his village offers any relief.

Since Saluggio tells his story in the first person, it retains a certain ambiguity: the reader is never certain whether the company management is insensitive or worse, or whether Saluggio's account is distorted by paranoia. The book can be read either as an individual case history or as a poetic parable on the alienation of the individual in a benevolent but loveless industrial bureaucracy. Admirably translated by Bélen Sevareid as *My Troubles Began*, it seemed to Anthony West "one of the most recklessly colorless and boring novels of recent years," but evoked quite a different response from most other critics, several of whom were reminded of the young Dostoevsky. M. S. Pitzele wrote: "The disciplines learned in creating poetry are clearly at work here: the images from which the reader draws his own symbols, the accretion of metaphor that builds feeling, the fugue-like progress of the tensions that mount slowly to their signaled climax, and the unity, as in a poem, of a

PAOLO VOLPONI

single voice. . . . It is with the poet's craft, and with his own personal feeling of universal guilt, that Volponi has made . . . [this] story into literature." Sergio Pacifici called it "one of the finest and most important books to have appeared in Italy over the past decade."

La macchina mondiale (translated by Bélen Sevareid as *The Worldwide Machine*) is unequivocally the diary of a madman. Its narrator, Anteo Crocioni, is a small landowner whose obsession with an idiotic scientific theory ruins his farm, his marriage, and his life. Anteo, like his namesake Antaeus, is destroyed when he loses contact with the earth (just as modern man, in the author's views, is being alienated and destroyed in an artificial society dominated by technology). The hero of this parable is far more than a lay figure; R. L. Clements calls Anteo "one of the most bewilderingly pathetic figures in contemporary Italian fiction." The book received the Premio Strega but has had rather less impact than its predecessor, seeming to most critics a confirmation of the author's great promise rather than a realization of it.

PRINCIPAL WORKS IN ENGLISH: My Troubles Began, 1964 (England, The Memorandum); The Worldwide Machine, 1967.

ABOUT: Curley, D. N. and Curley, A. (eds.) Modern Romance Literatures (A Library of Literary Criticism), 1967; Manacorda, G. Storia della letteratura italiana contemporanea, 1967; Who's Who in America, 1972–1973. *Periodicals*—Atlas October 1965; Il Contemporaneo 1962; New York Review of Books April 22, 1965; January 4, 1968; New York Times Book Review November 5, 1967; New Yorker May 8, 1965; Partisan Review Spring 1965; Saturday Review January 9, 1965; December 9, 1967.

KURT VONNEGUT

VONNEGUT, KURT (JR.) (November 11, 1922–), American short story writer, novelist, and critic writes: "I am the son and grandson of Indianapolis architects, who were also good painters, so it was natural that I should go into the arts. I am a product of the Indianapolis public schools, which were superb during the Great Depression. I was told by my father to be anything but an architect. He had been made gloomy by years and years of very little work. And, when my older brother, Bernard, began to do very well as a chemist, I was given a more or less direct order to become a chemist, too. So I kept away from the arts, which were made to seem silly and weak, and studied chemistry for three years at Cornell University. I was delighted to catch pneumonia during my third year, and, upon recovery, to forget everything I ever knew about chemistry, and to go to war.

"I was a battalion scout, and was easily captured. The most interesting thing I saw during the war, I suppose, was the destruction of Dresden, the largest single massacre in European history. I was a prisoner in a meat locker under a slaughterhouse when the worst of the firestorm was going on. After that I worked as a miner of corpses, breaking into cellars where over a hundred thousand Hansels and Gretels were baked like gingerbread men.

"After the war, I married a bright girl named Jane Cox. I had known her since kindergarten. I went to the University of Chicago, where I was allowed to be a graduate student in anthropology, though I had no degree. I stayed there for three years, also worked as a police reporter for the Chicago City News Bureau. I went broke, hired out as a flack for the Research Laboratory of the General Electric Company, where my brother was doing remarkable work with respect to cloud physics. I hated it there, but curiously made the closest friends I've ever had. At the end of my third year, I began to sell short stories to *Collier's* and the *Saturday Evening Post* and other magazines that were then very fat. I made what seemed like a lot of money, so I began a novel that mocked General Electric, quit my job, threw a party that was stopped by the police, and moved to Cape Cod.

"That was in 1951, and I've been freelancing ever since—until now. Just now I have a highly temporary appointment as a lecturer in the Writers' Workshop of the University of Iowa. It is so temporary because I have absolutely no academic background in English—am ignorant as hell.

"I paint, have an eighteen-foot piece of welded sculpture in the dining room of the Logan International Motel in Boston. It is said to represent New England's entry into the space age. On one occasion, I was the SAAB dealer for Cape Cod. On another I was the entire English Department in a school for disturbed children. I have six undisturbed children of my own. Three of them are adopted, the children of my sister, Alice, a sculptress who died six years ago.

"I miss her very much."

The novel that "mocked General Electric" was *Player Piano*, a long and rather sober book about an automated world of the future run by organization men. In the end the hero, Paul Proteus, comes to see that the machine-smashing revolution he joins will only "recreate the same old nightmare": the indictment is general. This first novel appeared in 1952. Over the next nine years Vonnegut was obliged to devote most of his energies to hacking out commercial magazine stories. Some of these "fruits of free enterprise" were collected in *Canary in a Cathouse* and again, with additions, in *Welcome to the Monkey House* which, according to one reviewer, consisted largely of "slick, slapdash prose lifted from the pages of magazines of limited distinction."

But some of these stories were speculative and/or satirical and these, together with *Player Piano*, were enough to persuade book review editors that Vonnegut was a science fiction writer. This ruling was confirmed by *The Sirens of Titan* (1959), a highly sophisticated space fantasy which suggests, for example, that the whole of human history has been arranged by the inhabitants of the planet Tralfamadore in order to provide an inter-galactic traveler with a spare part for his spaceship. Vonnegut was received into the science fiction fraternity with mixed feelings: Sam Moskowitz in *Seekers of Tomorrow* said that he had been "unfortunate enough to get started in the better magazines instead of learning his trade in the pulps. He needs discipline, practice, and considerably less smugness." Vonnegut was equally unhappy with a label that he knew would limit the reviews, audience, and market for his books, and complained that all he had done was "to notice technology."

His next novel, *Mother Night*, was unlike its predecessors both in style and content. It is about an American spy in wartime Germany who is able to stay alive and do his work because he masquerades as a Nazi and makes vile anti-Semitic broadcasts. It is a short book whose chapters, as Richard Schickel wrote, "are quick deft sketches, almost review blackouts. There is no attempt at the realistic detailing of *Player Piano*, no 'believable' plotting or 'rounded' characterization." All of Vonnegut's subsequent books have been similar in form. His message in *Mother Night* is that "we are what we pretend to be, so we must be careful about what we pretend to be." He believes that all ideologies are dangerous frauds, and contrives to satirize not only the Nazis and the American right wing, but also the left wing, and "professional" Jews and Negroes. "It is," wrote J. Michael Crichton, "an astonishing book, very gentle and funny and quiet and totally destructive."

Cat's Cradle (1963) is an apocalyptic satire set in a Caribbean island dictatorship and introducing a religion called Bokononism, which recommends living by the "*foma*" (useful lies) "that make you brave, kind, and happy." The novel began something of a Vonnegut cult, and was praised by such various writers as Conrad Aiken, Nelson Algren, Marc Connelly, Jules Feiffer, Terry Southern, and Graham Greene, who called it "one of the best novels of 1963 by one of the most able living writers." What is conceivably more important, the novel was taken up by young people, as William Golding's *Lord of the Flies* had been taken up a few years earlier. Much of the jargon of Bokononism passed into the language. What is debatable (and debated) is whether Vonnegut was himself advocating the Bokononist gospel, or satirizing it and all the myths we use to anesthetize a possibly productive desperation.

Another brief Voltairean fantasy followed. In *God Bless You, Mr. Rosewater*, Eliot Rosewater, an alcoholic young millionaire, sets out to Do Good. The result was generally well liked, though the absence of characterization or of much in the way of a plot suggested to some reviewers that the book was less a novel than a series of "random meditations." By this time Vonnegut had climbed out of the science fiction "filedrawer" only to fall into another labeled "black humor."

From the time he witnessed the bombing of Dresden, where more people died than at Hiroshima, Vonnegut felt himself under an obligation to make some kind of statement about it. He discharged this obligation in *Slaughterhouse-Five*, in which the author, lightly disguised as one "Billy Pilgrim," describes his war. From time to time, Billy is (or thinks himself) released from chronology—in one scene the bombing of Dresden is reversed, like a movie run backwards, so that the incendiaries return to the bombers, the bombers to the United States and so on, until the murderous minerals have been replaced safely in the earth. Intermittently, Billy lives on the planet Tralfamadore, or encounters Eliot Rosewater and other figures from earlier Vonnegut novels. And much of the time the author is present in his own voice—narrating, reflecting, mocking, explaining, and guiding his hero from moment to moment. The book has a double subtitle—*The Children's Crusade*, because it is an attack on all causes that demand human sacrifice, and *A Duty-Dance of Death*, because it was written as a duty and in the tradition of European gallows humor. There are no villains in it to lift the reader's sense of guilt for Dresden, "just people, doing what people usually do to each other."

Vonnegut regards *Slaughterhouse-Five* as a failure, written by someone who, like Lot's wife, looked back at a burning city and became a pillar of salt. Some critics agreed, depressed by some "easily bitter philosophizing" even when they enjoyed the book's splendid comic scenes. Others, like Robert Scholes, thought it no failure but "an extraordinary success . . . funny, compassionate and wise. The humor in Vonnegut's fiction is what enables us to contemplate the horror that he finds in contemporary existence." J. Michael Crichton wrote that "the book is written in the brief segmental manner [Vonnegut] developed in *Cat's Cradle*, organized as a collection of impressions, scattered in time and space, each told with the kind of economy one associates with poetry. It is beautifully done, fluid, smooth, and powerful."

In *Breakfast of Champions*, Vonnegut announced, he was celebrating his fiftieth birthday by flushing out of his head (and into the novel) a half-century's accumulation of foolish and incompatible ideas, and by "liberating" characters who had appeared in earlier books. There is a plot about a rich car dealer who, maddened by despair and science fiction, concludes that he is the only free and responsible man in a world where everyone else (including God) is a programmed robot. There is a great deal of literary self-consciousness (the author is almost savaged by a dog that he had tried but failed to excise from an earlier version of the novel). The rest is a scrapbook of good and bad jokes, drawings, complaints, and reflections—including the authorial reflection that "this is a very bad book you're writing." Most reviewers agreed, even one who admired it as a writer's brave attempt to "dig himself out of a hole by writing," and Martin Amis found it "flaccid, self-regarding [and] dripping with the cuteness and simper that have always threatened Vonnegut's writing." Michael Wood similarly called the book "mainly a set of distress signals: writer in trouble," even though it "winds up in a mild blaze of wit." Wood expressed his concern that Vonnegut's characteristic "dialectic between despair and its mythologies" had become mechanical and unproductive in all of the novels after *Mother Night*. Nevertheless, *Breakfast of Champions* was selected by four book clubs in the United States alone, and launched the author into a new million-dollar contract with his publisher.

Vonnegut's play *Penelope*, staged in a Cape Cod theatre in 1960, was revised and revived in New York in 1970 as *Happy Birthday, Wanda June*. It had a considerable and (most critics thought) well-deserved success. It is a contemporary version of the homecoming of Odysseus in which Harold Ryan, all-American male, returns from Hemingwayesque adventures up the Amazon and confronts his wife's suitors. One of them is a pacifist, and in the play's unexpectedly optimistic conclusion, Harold submits to the peaceful philosophy of his rival. The play was found witty, plausible, and dramatically ingenious and, as one critic wrote, "it is pleasant to find that Mr. Vonnegut now wants us to believe that there should be better answers than a resigned nihilism." The script of a 1973 television program based mainly on *Cat's Cradle* and *The Sirens of Titan* has been published as *Between Time and Timbuktu*.

Slaughterhouse-Five, which became a best seller and was filmed, made Vonnegut a literary celebrity. Several of his novels are now on university reading courses. *Cat's Cradle* has sold one hundred and fifty thousand copies and *The Sirens of Titan* two hundred thousand. He himself is much in demand as a lecturer, and in 1970 he went into the movie industry, establishing Sourdough Productions in association with Michael J. Kane and Lester M. Goldsmith. He remains a casual and unpretentious person. C. D. B. Bryan says that Vonnegut is "over six feet tall, a rumpled and shaggy . . . fourth generation German-American with a drooping moustache, a brow chevroned like a sergeant-major's sleeve and the eyes of a sacrificial altar-bound virgin caught in mid-shrug." He is the son of Kurt and Edith (Lieber) Vonnegut, and was married in 1945. He and his family live at Barnstable, Cape Cod. He says he has "worried some about why I write books when Presidents and senators and generals do not read them"; he concludes that the trick is to catch them at school, "before they become generals and senators and Presidents, and *poison their minds with humanity*." One interviewer asked Vonnegut what sort of writer he would most like to be known as, and he said, "George Orwell."

PRINCIPAL WORKS: *Fiction*—Player Piano, 1952; The Sirens of Titan, 1959; Mother Night, 1961; Canary in a Cathouse (stories), 1961; Cat's Cradle, 1963; God Bless You, Mr. Rosewater; or, Pearls Before Swine, 1965; Welcome to the Monkey House (a collection of short works), 1968; Slaughterhouse-Five, or The Children's Crusade: A Duty-Dance with Death, 1969; Breakfast of Champions or, Goodbye, Blue Monday, 1973. *Plays*—Very First Christmas Morning *in* Better Homes and Gardens December 1962; Fortitude *in* Playboy September 1968; Happy Birthday, Wanda June, 1971; Between Time and Timbuktu, 1973.

ABOUT: Current Biography, 1970; Klinkowitz, J. and Somer, J. (eds.) The Vonnegut Statement: Essays on the Life and Work of Kurt Vonnegut, Jr., 1973; Moskowitz, S. Seekers of Tomorrow, 1966; Scholes, R. The Fabulators, 1967; Vinson, J. (ed.) Contemporary Novelists, 1972; Who's Who in America, 1972–1973. *Periodicals*—Book World August 18, 1968; Commonweal September 16, 1966; Guardian November 3, 1972; Harper's May 1966; New Republic October 8, 1966; April 26, 1969; New York Review of Books May 31, 1973; New York Times March 21, 1969; New York Times Book Review September 1, 1968; April 6, 1969; September 5, 1969; August 13, 1972; February 4, 1973; Publishers' Weekly March 18, 1968; April 21, 1969; Reporter December 1, 1966; San Francisco Chronicle August 29, 1952; Saturday Review April 3, 1965; Spectator August 2, 1963; Time August 30, 1968; April 11, 1969.

"VOYLE, MARY." *See* MANNING, ROSEMARY

***VOZNESENSKY, ANDREI** (**ANDREYEVICH**) (May 12, 1933–), Russian poet, was born in Moscow. Part of his childhood was spent in Vladimir, an ancient city with magnificent cathedrals which during the twelfth and thirteenth centuries was the capital of an independent principality. During the war he was evacuated with his mother to Kurgan, in the Urals, returning to Moscow in 1944. His father was a professor of engineering and his mother a specialist in the history of Russian literature who read poetry to him from early childhood, including that of such twentieth century poets as Blok and Pasternak. He enjoyed painting and drawing and in 1951 enrolled in the Moscow Architectural Institute. Just before his graduation in 1957 the fire described in his poem "Pozhar v arkhitekturnom institute" (Fire in the Architectural Institute) occurred: during his final year Voznesensky had been designing "a spiral-shaped thing, a bit like the Guggenheim Museum," but with the other students' projects it was destroyed in the fire, and, he says, "I understood that architecture was burned out in *me*. I became a poet."

His first published poems appeared in the period-

* voz nə syen′ skē

ical *Literaturnaya gazeta* in 1958 but the long poem "Mastera" (Master Craftsmen), written in 1959, ends with his setting off to work at the Bratsk power station, and it was only with the success of this work that he finally abandoned architecture for poetry. "Mastera" deals with one of Voznesensky's major themes, that of the role of the artist in society, contrasting the creative imagination with political despotism. It makes use of the legend that Ivan the Terrible put out the eyes of the architects who had built St. Basil's Cathedral for him, so that they would be unable to build anything equally beautiful for anyone else. The poem appeared in both of Voznesensky's first two books, *Mozaika* (Mosaic), published in 1960 in Vladimir, and *Parabola*, a slightly different collection which came out in Moscow in the same year.

Some of the poems in these early collections are simple lyrics, but others already show his remarkable verbal virtuosity—the characteristic "mosaic" patterns of subtly related images and words, including slang, neologisms, scientific and technical terms. "People have had enough of rhyme," Voznesensky said. "Every sixteen-year-old schoolboy can rhyme brilliantly. In our poetry the future lies with associations." Thus, even in his early work, he made use of off-rhymes and assonances which are semantic as well as phonetic, reinforcing the whole meaning of the poem, as in an example singled out by Samuil Marshak in "Mastera" (a poem about embattled artists), where *vayateli* (sculptors) is rhymed with *voiteli* (warriors); or, as Patricia Blake and Max Hayward point out, in his later poem "Longjumeau," in which Lenin throws a stick and smashes "empires / churches, future Berias"; *imperii-berii* go together in more than sound, for the police-chief Beria had his own empire. Voznesensky's often grotesque imagery is taken from the whole range of city life and of science and technology, and he reflects the exhilaration and the dynamism of modern living in short lines and galloping rhythms.

Parabola takes its title from the much translated "Parabolicheskaya ballada," a poetic manifesto which explains another aspect of Voznesensky's art. Gauguin, he says, did not enter the Louvre by copying the old masters, but smashed his way in, via the South Seas, on a parabola: the poet likewise must not offer logical ideas and conventional truths but must sweep aside established traditions and seek the renewal of his art "in a parabolic trajectory." Another early poem, published in *Mozaika*, is perhaps the most famous of all Voznesensky's works, "Goya." The poet has recalled his father on a brief visit from the front during World War II carrying with him a volume of Goya's etchings, and the poem is Voznesensky's own vision of the horrors of war, a brilliant and haunting *tour*

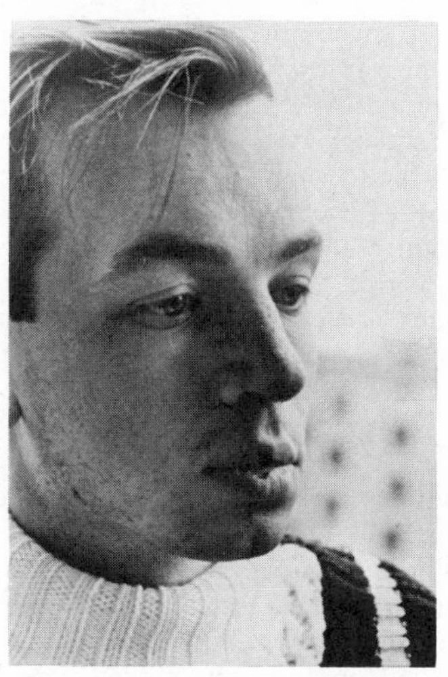

ANDREI VOZNESENSKY

de force of alliteration and assonance: *Ya Góya* (I am Goya) . . . *nagóye* (bare) . . . *ya góre* (I am grief) . . . *ya gólos* (I am the voice) . . . *góda* (years) . . . *ya gólod* (I am hunger) . . . ya górlo (I am the throat) . . . *góloi* (naked) . . . *ya Góya.*

In April 1961 Voznesensky visited the United States with his friend Yevgeny Yevtushenko and afterwards wrote *Treugolnaya grusha* (1962, translated by H. Marshall as "The Triangular Pear"), a cycle of poems inspired by this experience. He explains in his introduction that the long poem he had planned "capsized like an overburdened ship," leaving behind these "forty lyrical digressions." Indeed, as Andrei Sinyavsky has put it, Voznesensky's tonal mannerisms at times become "a key which he has made to fit too many doors," and end by becoming repetitive, mere virtuosity. Full of unexpected images and of rock and jazz rhythms, these forty poems reflect his ambivalent feelings towards the American technocracy. In one well-known poem, New York's international airport at night is a magnificent symbol of man's mastery of his environment (as Brooklyn Bridge had been for Mayakovsky), but in "Monolog bitnika" (translated as "The Beatnik's Monologue"), the free spirit runs from the enslaving machines.

The book caused a furore, coinciding as it did with a resurgence of conservativism in the USSR. The critic V. Nazarenko suggested that "the message of *Treugolnaya grusha* is that the world is immutable and that everything will remain as it always was—that man is eternal and the tragedy of the individual is eternal." One critic accused Voznesensky of "atomic catastrophism," quoting such passages as this, from another "Beatnik

Monologue": "Roaring from its rocket-sites / Sprinkling the world with atomic dust, / Time spits on me, / Just as I spit on Time . . . ."

"Longjumeau" (1963), Voznesensky's first major work after these attacks, and one of his few on an explicitly political theme, is a long poem about Lenin and the party school near Paris which he founded in 1911. The poem "Antimiry" (translated as "Antiworlds"), which first appeared in *Treugolnaya grusha*, was used in 1964 as the title poem for Voznesensky's next book. In it he borrows the concept of antimatter from physics to explore identity in terms of the dialectical dependence of all things on their apparent opposites, and to speculate about the possibility of projecting oneself into an "antiworld," just as the archetypal downtrodden little clerk Bukashkin dreams of a demon-magician Antibukashkin who governs the universe while his hands paw at Lollobrigida.

In "Akhillesovo serdtse" (1965, translated by W. H. Auden as "My Achilles Heart") the heart is the poet's Achilles heel when he or his poetry is attacked, and he tries to make it hard to locate, as a bird diverts the hunters from its nest. This poem gave its title to Voznesensky's 1966 collection. In many of these poems supreme value is placed on the inner world of feelings, and on love and personal relationships, as opposed to the computerized, cybernetic modern world in which progress means more and more uniformity.

This is the theme of his ambitious long poem "Oza" (translated by W. J. Smith and Max Hayward under the same title), which first appeared in the periodical *Molodaya gvardiya* in 1964, and was reprinted with some changes in *Akhillesovo serdtse*. Written in alternations of prose and of verse in a great variety of meters, with abrupt changes of mood ranging from lyrical to satiric, it is in the form of a diary left behind in a hotel, apparently by a young physicist from the atomic research center at Dubna. It tells the story of his ill-fated love for a girl whose ambiguous name is either Oza or Zoya, which in its Greek form means "life." (It is also the name of Voznesensky's wife, the author and literary critic Zoya Boguslavskaya.) Oza's identity is threatened; she always seems to be in danger of being transformed or distorted into a person beyond the reach of the man who loves her, either by the circumstances of her life or by modern technology in the shape of the cyclotron, which both fascinates and repels the poet. For the poet enters into a sort of dialogue with the physicist, and on this central personal thread are hung speculative passages about history and the human condition, and especially about the automation and robotization of man.

Voznesensky has made translations of Ukrainian, Armenian, and Georgian poetry, as well as of English poems. Since the mid 1960s he has been involved in a variety of theatrical projects, the first of which was an adaptation of "Antimiry" into a "poetorio," with music by Rodion Shchedrin, which was hugely successful when it was staged in Moscow in 1965. He has also collaborated with the novelist Vasily Aksenov in an opera, *Dlinnonogo* (Longlegs), with music by the avant-garde composer M. Tariverdiyev.

Voznesensky appeared on the literary scene much later than his contemporary Yevtushenko, but almost immediately achieved immense popularity in the public poetry readings which were such a feature of Russian cultural life in the early 1960s. Most critics would agree that Voznesensky is a far more deliberate and accomplished literary artist than Yevtushenko, with whom he is constantly compared, and many regard him as the finest poet of his generation in Russia. He is a small, slim man, boyish in appearance, who normally seems quiet, introverted, and rather shy. When he reads his poetry, however, he is an entirely different person, as Patricia Blake has described: "An awkward figure, slight and singularly vulnerable, he stood before the microphone with his legs stiffly apart, his Adam's apple bobbing, bearing the applause and shouts of acclaim from the audience as if they were blows. . . . He read poem after poem for perhaps an hour in a powerful, cultivated voice. His awkwardness had gone; now it was his listeners who appeared tense, straining forward to capture the flow of a language unheard-of in Russia in their lifetime. Here, clearly, was Russia's first modern poet."

Since 1961 Voznesensky has made many trips abroad, reading his poetry with great success in the United States, Britain, France, Italy, and elsewhere. In recent years he has been increasingly ready to use his reputation in the struggle against Soviet censorship. In July 1967, after he had been prevented from attending the Lincoln Center Arts Festival in New York, he wrote a fiery letter to *Pravda* which the Soviet newspaper would not print, but which appeared in several foreign journals. "I am a Soviet writer," he said, "a human being made of flesh and blood, not a puppet to be pulled on a string. It is not a question of me personally, but of the fate of Soviet literature, its honor and prestige in the outside world. How much longer will we go on dragging ourselves through the mud? . . . We are surrounded by lies, lies, lies, bad manners, and more lies." For this and other transgressions, Voznesensky was threatened with expulsion from the Writers' Union, but escaped this very serious punishment, without making the apology demanded, by leaving on a two-month tour of Siberia until things had cooled down. He was again in trouble in March 1970, however, when his play *Watch Your Faces*, an often obscure work using pantomime, music, dance, and poetry, was closed down after three performances because of "ideological defects." There were further attacks in 1973, centering on two new groups of poems, published in magazines, which satirized the shallowness, falsity, and conformity of Soviet literary life, and seemed to suggest (in a poem ostensibly about the French Revolution) that the ideals of the Bolshevist Revolution had been betrayed.

PRINCIPAL WORKS IN ENGLISH TRANSLATION: Selected Poems of Andrei Voznesensky (tr. by A. Hollo), 1964; Selected Poems (tr. by H. Marshall), 1966; Antiworlds (ed. by P. Blake and M. Hayward), 1966; Antiworlds and the Fifth Ace (ed. by P. Blake and M. Hayward), 1968; Antiworlds (tr. by Richard Wilbur) *in* Russian Literature Tri-Quarterly 5–6, 1973. *Poems in* Barnstone, W. (ed.) Modern European Poetry, 1966; Blake, P. and Hayward, M. Half-Way to the Moon, 1963; Markov, V. and Sparks, M. (eds.) Modern Russian Poetry, 1966; Obolensky, D. (ed.) Penguin Book of Russian Verse, 1965; Reavey, G. The New Russian Poets, 1966; Life April 1, 1966; Odyssey Review December 1962; Soviet Literature 7, 1960; 1, 1963; 6, 1967; Tri-Quarterly Spring 1965.
ABOUT: Brown, E. J. (ed.) Major Soviet Writers, 1973; Carlisle, O. Poets on Street Corners, 1969; Current Biography, 1967; Hayward, M. and Labedz, L. (eds.) Literature and Revolution in Soviet Russia, 1963; International Who's Who, 1973–74; Mihajlov, M. Moscow Summer, 1966; Who's Who in America, 1972–1973. *Periodicals*—Antaeus Summer 1972; Encounter July 1968; Life April 1, 1966; New York Times April 11, 1973; New York Times Book Review April 16, 1972; New Yorker September 4, 1965; Slavic Review March 1965; Survey October 1963.

WAGNER, GEOFFREY (ATHELING) (December 27, 1922–), American novelist, writes: "I was born in Malaya, then the Federated Malay States, where my grandfather was Commissioner of Police, and my father subsequently Chairman of the *Malay Mail* and other enterprises. I was sent to England for private schooling, and when war broke out went to Sandhurst (Royal Military College, Camberley) before commissioning in H.M. Brigade of Guards, with whom I served in North Africa, Sicily (as aide-de-camp to a General), and in Italy. I took undergraduate degrees in French and German at Christ Church, Oxford; on the cessation of hostilities, served for a short while as Press Officer to I.C.I. (Imperial Chemical Industries); and then went to the U.S.A., of which I am presently a citizen. I have taught at Rochester University, New York University, Columbia, and the City College of New York—generally in English and Humanities Departments, with courses in contemporary European literature. I am an associate professor in the City University of New York, a member of the Fulbright Advisory Committee, of the Executive Committee of the United Federation of College Teachers, and of the Rhodes Scholarship Trust for New York State. I have a Ph.D. from Columbia, where I was Lydig Fellow in the Faculty

GEOFFREY WAGNER

of Philosophy. I have written criticism, poetry, travel books, sociology, translations, as well as novels, and I have run my own radio program on books from New York City. My novels have been widely translated, in Italy, Germany, Holland, and France. In France, particularly, the sales have been encouraging. The late Ian Fleming selected one of my 'entertainment' novels as a 'Best' for the year in the (London) *Sunday Times*; Russell Kirk did the same for another recent novel of mine in the Sunday *Chicago Tribune*; and the late Reginald Reynolds made a similar selection of one of my fictions in the *New Statesman* before he died. I live in New York during the academic year, but also own properties in Corsica and the West Indies. My wife is the realist painter Colleen Browning. In 1957 two Wagner books were reviewed on the front page of the *Times Literary Supplement*, viz. *Wyndham Lewis: The Portrait of the Artist as the Enemy* and *Gérard de Nerval*. Apart from a variety of translations, I have been responsible for Consultantship to the new (1965) edition of S. I. Hayakawa's semantic text, *Language in Thought and Action*. I am interested in the writing of fiction, in scholarship, and in pedagogy."

Geoffrey Wagner's novels are quite unlike anyone else's. Some of them, like the shamelessly preposterous Gothic fiction *Venables*, are, as he implies above, intended simply as entertainments. Most are thesis novels, reflecting Wagner's own brand of enlightened conservatism, his penchant for satire, and his taste for melodrama. It is a highly flavored recipe, greatly relished by many but by no means all of Wagner's critics.

The Dispossessed, for example, tells the story of a British army officer who falls into the hands of the psychoanalysts when he is shell-shocked, and then is hounded by "Fraudism" to suicide. Reviewers were divided between those who commended Wagner's "remarkable talent for vitriolic satire" but found his case grotesquely overstated, and those who considered the book a small tour de force. *Rage on the Bar*, about Communism and colonialism on a Caribbean island, was praised for its exciting and well-plotted narrative and damned for its indignant "caricatures" of people and events. *The Asphalt Campus*, excoriating abysmal students and obstructive bureaucrats in a New York City college, seemed to *Library Journal* "a solid, witty satire" and to the *New Yorker* a pretentiously written "anthology of the author's complaints." In fact, few of the "hack reviewers" who are among Wagner's favorite targets have had anything but praise for his "sharp, intelligent prose," and his talent for descriptive writing has been particularly admired.

Wagner's study of Wyndham Lewis was thought most useful as an exposition of Lewis's political and aesthetic opinions, "eminently sensible, sober and thorough." There was a very mixed reception for *Parade of Pleasure*, Wagner's assault on American popular culture, which seemed to some native critics distorted and inaccurate. *On the Wisdom of Words*, however, was generally welcomed as a vigorous and amusing review of what is happening to the English language in several important fields of word use.

The son of Atheling and Helen (Eveleigh) Wagner, he married Colleen Browning in 1951. With his high forehead and patrician nose, he could be the hero of one of his own adventure stories.

PRINCIPAL WORKS: *Poetry*—Singing Blood, 1948. *Novels*—Venables, 1952; The Passionate Land, 1953; The Dispossessed, 1956; Rage on the Bar, 1957; Sophie, 1957; Summer Stranger, 1959; Season of Assassins, 1961; The Lake Lovers, 1962; The Asphalt Campus: Monotremata of the Academe, 1963; A Pride in the Desert, 1966; The Sands of Valor, 1967; The Innocent Grove (for children), 1971. *Nonfiction*—Parade of Pleasure: A Study of Popular Iconography in the USA, 1954; Wyndham Lewis: A Portrait of the Artist as the Enemy, 1957; (ed. and tr.) Selected Writings of Gérard de Nerval, 1957; Corsica, 1965; On the Wisdom of Words, 1968; Elegy for Corsica, 1968; Five for Freedom: A Study of Feminism in Fiction, 1972; Another America: In Search of Canyons, 1972.

ABOUT: Contemporary Authors 1, 1962; Kirk, R. Beyond the Dreams of Avarice, 1956; Mannin, E. Brief Voices, 1959; Viereck, P. The Unadjusted Man, 1956.

WAGONER, DAVID (RUSSELL) (June 5, 1926–), American poet and novelist, writes: "I was born in Massillon, Ohio, and grew up in Whiting, Indiana, near a group of swampy lakes that stretched inshore from Lake Michigan for miles. Many have now been filled in by Standard Oil and other industries. But they formed a landscape that has always been with me: mud, rust, marshgrass, a horizon studded with oil tanks and blast furnaces, and a sense that everything—even the mosquitoes—had to struggle to survive the bleakness. I think I may have seen the last heron on Wolf Lake in 1940.

"I began writing poems and short stories when I was ten and published my first poem—it was a ballad (the only form of poetry I knew existed) called 'Spring Cleaning'—in a highschool paper. I don't know why I wanted to write poetry: I didn't read much of it at first, but instead from as early as I can remember, I devoured all the fiction I could find: Conan Doyle, Stevenson, Dickens, Howard Spring (probably because he seemed like Dickens), E. Phillips Oppenheim, Wodehouse, and just about every pulp magazine ever printed about flying in the First World War.

"My father was an honors graduate in classical languages from Washington and Jefferson College, but in spite of several offers to teach classics and coach football, he went to work in the steel mills and was still working shift-work up to the time of his retirement (a day he spent in the hospital, with a thighbone broken on the job). I think much of what I try to do and be may be a result of what he didn't do or become.

"I began to learn to write when I stepped into the classes of Theodore Roethke during my senior year at Penn State in 1947. Everything I had done before suddenly became ridiculous to me, and the first poem I wrote under his energetic and very kind tutelage was published in *Poetry*. Along with the rest of the class, I followed his guidance in reading, in revising, and in learning how to fall out of love with one's own work. Just by being alive, he demonstrated an extraordinary truth to me: it was still possible to be a poet. I owe his example and his teaching more than I can describe.

"Other writing teachers—Edward Nichols at Penn State and Peter Taylor and Samuel Yellen at Indiana University—were generous in their help, and I later gained a great deal from the editorial suggestions of Catharine Carver and Malcolm Cowley. When I came to teach at the University of Washington in 1954, thanks to the recommendation of Theodore Roethke, I was able to renew that literary relationship in a more personal form and, I feel, benefited greatly from his advice and his example. The Guggenheim Foundation in 1956 and the Ford Foundation in 1964 gave me fellowships which enabled me to write much more than I would have otherwise.

"Here in the Northwest (just about as far as possible from where I grew up) I have found a way of living and working which seems nearly ideal for me. This has involved the discovery of a natural world still so powerful it can hold its own against the best, or worst, we can do. My wife Patt, who is a painter, and I have found in the Olympic and Cascade Mountains and on the ocean shores of the Olympic Peninsula where we frequently hike—or 'wander' might be a better word—an indescribable sense of liberation from what in the city are usually called 'daily lives.' Out of that sense I make whatever I can as a writer."

Wagoner's first book of verse, thought promising but a little contrived, was followed by *A Place to Stand*, which seemed to W. T. Scott "in its kind . . . the most brilliant work since Richard Wilbur first came on the scene," with "something of Yeats's strong management, a flavor akin to Thomas's vocabulary, and yet not imitative." These songlike poems provided reviewers with evidence of unusual technical resource, an almost flawless lyrical ear, and an alert but disciplined imagination. To Philip Booth these wide-ranging lyrics seemed fundamentally religious, "anthems to man."

The more personal poems in *The Nesting Ground*, Wagoner said, "use the objects and creatures of the natural world" to recreate the poet's own emotional and spiritual trials. W. T. Scott confirmed Wagoner's ability to transform into metaphysics the simple object or event—a bird, a picnic—"by the sheer energy of his perceptive writing," and other critics also spoke of his "enormous energy," of a strictly controlled but explosive violence. The book seemed to James Dickey most effective not when Wagoner was wholly serious but "when abandon, wild calculation and seriousness meet," and his poems take off, "drawing the reader after him like the tail on a powerful, erratic kite." There are signs of continuing development in *Staying Alive*, praised for its originality and power and wit, its "fine sense of that vague thing, the American Idiom." When Wagoner's *New and Selected Poems* appeared in 1969, one reviewer called him "the poet of the dispossessed, of the left-out," whose poems "look honestly into the coldest wind"; Wagoner, the reviewer concluded, "without fanfare, with a kind of quiet insistency . . . is becoming one of the most important American poets now producing."

Wagoner's novels share with his verse an originality of perspective and a fine ear for "the nervous . . . rhythm of American speech and thought." *The Man in the Middle* is a powerfully realistic suspense story with a splendidly realized Chicago setting; *Money Money Money* a disturbing and tragic little fable about the persecution of a halfwit. *The Escape Artist*, which attracted rather more attention than its predecessors, is a "furious comedy" about a

DAVID WAGONER

country boy whose ambition is success as a stage magician, and whose challenge to the adult world is made in the seedy setting of big city nightclub life. The novel, which reminded one reviewer of Hemingway in its treatment of personal courage, was called "solid and fascinating" in its technical detail, taut and imaginative in its language. *Baby, Come on Inside* describes the return of an aging pop star to his Midwestern home town, where he engineers much chaos. *Where Is My Wandering Boy Tonight?* is an extremely witty and entertaining Western, narrated by its hero in the vernacular, about a seventeen-year-old's abrupt coming of age in Wyoming in the 1890s.

The writer is the son of Walter and Ruth (Banyerd) Wagoner, and was married to Patricia Parrott in 1961. He served in the U.S. Navy as a midshipman from 1944 to 1946, and taught briefly at DePauw University, Indiana, and at Pennsylvania State University (1950–1954) before joining the faculty of the University of Washington, where he is now professor of English and editor of the magazine *Poetry Northwest*. In 1967 he received a grant from the National Institute of Arts and Letters, and the Morton Dauwen Zabel Prize for poetry.

PRINCIPAL WORKS: *Poems*—Dry Sun, Dry Wind, 1953; A Place to Stand, 1958; The Nesting Ground, 1963; Staying Alive, 1966; New and Selected Poems, 1969; Working Against Time, 1970; Riverbed, 1972. *Novels*—The Man in the Middle, 1954; Money Money Money, 1955; Rock, 1958; The Escape Artist, 1965; Baby, Come on Inside, 1968; Where Is My Wandering Boy Tonight?, 1970. *As editor*—Straw for the Fire: From the Notebooks of Theodore Roethke, 1943–1963, 1972.

ABOUT: Contemporary Authors 2, 1963; Murphy, R. (ed.) Contemporary Poets of the English Language, 1970;

Vinson, J. (ed.) Contemporary Novelists, 1972. *Periodicals*—Critique: Studies in Modern Fiction IX, No. 1, 1966; Library Journal June 15, 1954; Poetry October 1958, February 1964.

WAIN, JOHN (BARRINGTON) (March 14, 1925–), English novelist, poet, short story writer, and critic, says: "I was born in Stoke-on-Trent, Staffordshire, England. This city, made up of a chain of six towns lying along the valley of the Trent, had at that time virtually no suburbs; it measured some ten miles by two, and at its edges the pretty dairy-farming country of North Staffordshire began without preamble. An active boy could bicycle into unspoilt country within half an hour from any point; and we lived, as it happened, on the edge of the town. My formative environment was thus a lucky blend of intensely urban (the Potteries are Arnold Bennett's 'Five Towns') and intensely rural. I escaped suburbia, as I escaped television, by being born too early for it.

"From 1934 to 1942 I attended the High School, Newcastle-under-Lyme; long afterwards I discovered that T. E. Hulme had been at this school, but the information would have meant little to me at the time; apart from a tendency to bookishness, I was the average provincial schoolboy with no intellectual interests. My school work, which was in any case disorganized by the war which started when I was fourteen, lagged sadly, and when on leaving school I expressed a wish to go to the university, I was not considered intelligent enough even to attempt a scholarship examination; I simply walked out of school and walked into Oxford, where, at that time, even backward youths like myself could get in easily if they could pay the fees.

"I obtained a First Class degree, from which I infer that Oxford had managed to cure my backwardness to some extent, and after briefly holding a research fellowship at my college, St John's, I went to Reading University as a lecturer in English literature at a salary of four hundred pounds per annum. This was valuable, as it accustomed me to poverty, and when the desire to write instead of teach grew so strong that I had no choice but to resign my post, the small income my work brought me was no smaller than I had been used to. Since I left the profession, in 1955, university lecturers have received a large number of substantial pay increases; that I served my eight-year term in the old days of penury was, for me, another stroke of good luck. One can hardly imagine a young academic of to-day throwing up his job to scratch ten pounds a week out of free-lance writing.

"*The Observer*, which guaranteed me this income when I first became a free-lance, gave me the basic nerve necessary to abandon my security, and I should like to put on record my gratitude to this newspaper, which for ten years has allowed me to review books when I wanted to and has never once pressed me when I was busy with other things.

"As a free-lance writer with nothing to live on except what I can make by writing, I have so far resisted the usual traps into which most free-lance writers fall. I do not write detective stories, nor contribute to the mass-circulation gutter press, nor spend six months of each year lecturing at American colleges, nor compère television quiz shows, nor, as far as I am aware, disgrace my profession in any way. I live quietly in Oxford with my wife and two small sons, and spend my time writing.

"With regard to my work: I do not share the taste, so marked in many authors, including some contributors to this volume, for expounding my own work and telling people what to think of it. I will merely say that I write poetry, fiction and criticism; that I reject all labels and renounce all programmes; that I treat each work as a new beginning; that I think the writer's task is to perceive as much as he can of the truth about human life and to pass on that truth to the reader, without distortion or falsification, by whatever means he can command."

John Wain is the son of Arnold Wain, a successful dentist who was the first of his family to emerge from the working class. Wain's family was relatively bookish, and as he says affluent enough, when he was rejected for army service, to pay his way in 1943 to Oxford, where he came under the influence of C. S. Lewis, Charles Williams, and the eccentric poet and scholar E. H. W. Meyerstein. Wain's first poems were published in *Mandrake*, the spirited literary magazine he founded at Oxford. *Cherwell*, the undergraduate magazine, published his first critical work. He also acted, and had a "moment of glory" in 1944 playing Claudio to Richard Burton's Angelo in *Measure for Measure*. In spite of these distractions he earned a brilliant degree, receiving *alpha* marks in all papers.

On postgraduate visits to the university he met Kingsley Amis and Philip Larkin, who were among the young poets Wain introduced in "First Reading" (1953), a series of BBC poetry programs. Some of the "First Reading" poets formed part of the so-called "Movement," a reaction against the lush obscurities of the British poetry of the 1940s. Wain's own early poetry, influenced by Empson, struck the tough, clever, slangy note of the Movement. But *Weep Before God* (1961), published ten years after his first book of poems, was thought "boisterous, assertive verse in honour of the traditional moral virtues." And *Wildtrack* (1966), greatly admired by some critics, had none of the

Movement coolness. It was a set of variations on "the theme of human interdependence," called a "huge ragbag" of a poem, full of errors of tone, but full also of compassion and often very moving. In *Letters to Five Artists* (1969), Wain explores his friendship with the jazz musician Bill Coleman, the poets Elizabeth Jennings and Anthony Conran, the English artist Victor Neep, and the American "junk sculptor" Lee Lubbers.

Wain's fiction has followed a similar pattern of development. His first novel, *Born in Captivity*, was credited with introducing the unheroic "new hero" in Charles Lumley, whose middle-class education had totally disabled him for real life, and who experiments with an assortment of roles in what becomes a comprehensive satire on English mores. The book, published in England as *Hurry on Down* in 1953, preceded by a few months the appearance of Amis's *Lucky Jim*, and for a time, much against their will, both writers were categorized as "Angry Young Men." Wain's *Living in the Present* was another picaresque satire, about the conversion to living of a would-be suicide. Its "spectacular" failure seemed unjust to G. S. Fraser who, admitting that Wain's characters were two-dimensional, praised his almost theatrical gift for evoking violent feeling and his ability to "give us a sense of actual contemporary life."

There has been a strain of down-to-earth moralizing in Wain's subsequent novels and short stories, which have been characterized by his commitment to the individual and the personal against commercial rapacity and bureaucratic power. Thus, in *The Smaller Sky*, a successful scientist has a breakdown, drops out of the society which has wrecked him, and begins a contented vegetable existence in a London railroad station. Left to himself he might heal, but the world seeks him out and he is hounded to death by a scoop-hungry journalist. *A Winter in the Hills* is about another drop-out, an ambitious philologist who visits Wales to learn the language and finds himself caught up in a local bus owner's struggle against a criminally unscrupulous entrepreneur. Many reviewers thought it the most mature and convincing of Wain's celebrations of "minority obstinacy and individual liberty." Here as elsewhere, the author's prose style seemed (as one critic put it) "a blunt, serviceable instrument which sustains a vigorous narrative line . . . but falters at moments of high emotion."

Wain is an accomplished and prolific critic and literary journalist. He does much lecturing, editing, film and drama reviewing, radio and television work. He was Churchill Visiting Professor at the University of Bristol in 1967, visiting professor at the Vincennes University Experimental Center (Paris) in 1969, and the first recipient of a newly established fellowship in creative arts at Brasenose

JOHN WAIN

College, Oxford, in 1971–1972. In 1973 he was elected the twenty-seventh Professor of Poetry at Oxford University, succeeding Roy Fuller. Wain became a Fellow of the Royal Society of Literature in 1960 but resigned a year later. His "part of an autobiography" called *Sprightly Running* was praised for its sincerity and charm, and for its decent reticence about "the central crisis of his life," the failure of his first marriage to Marianne Urmston. (Wain was married again in 1960 to Eirian James, and has three sons.) He enjoys skiing, canoeing, walks, and nature study. William Van O'Connor thought in 1963 that much of Wain's work is "willed into existence." Certainly his rejection of the academic life has, for economic reasons, obliged him to write too much. Perhaps he has found his literary role and become, as Richard Hoggart thought he might, that "now rare person, the general man of letters." But experiments like *Wildtrack* suggest that he is still not content, still "searching for his own manner."

PRINCIPAL WORKS: *Poetry*—Mixed Feelings, 1951; A Word Carved on a Sill, 1956; Weep Before God, 1961; Wildtrack, 1966; Letters to Five Artists, 1969; The Shape of Feng, 1972. *Fiction*—Hurry on Down, 1953 (U.S., Born in Captivity); Living in the Present, 1955; The Contenders, 1958; A Travelling Woman, 1959; Nuncle and Other Stories, 1960; Strike the Father Dead, 1962; The Young Visitors, 1965; Death of the Hind Legs and Other Stories, 1966; The Smaller Sky, 1967; A Winter in the Hills, 1970; The Life Guard (stories), 1971. *Non-fiction*—Preliminary Essays, 1957; Sprightly Running (autobiography), 1962; Essays on Literature and Ideas, 1963; The Living World of Shakespeare: A Playgoer's Guide, 1964; Arnold Bennett, 1967; A House for the Truth: Critical Essays, 1972. *As editor*—Contemporary Reviews of Romantic Poetry, 1953; Interpretations: Essays on Twelve English Poems, 1955; Fanny Burney's

Diary, 1961; Anthology of Modern Poetry, 1963; Selected Shorter Poems of Thomas Hardy, 1966; The Dynasts (Thomas Hardy), 1966; Selected Stories of Thomas Hardy, 1966; Shakespeare's Macbeth: A Casebook, 1969; Shakespeare's Othello: A Casebook, 1971.

ABOUT: Allott, K. (ed.) Penguin Book of Contemporary Verse, 1962; Allsop, K. The Angry Decade, 1958; Contemporary Authors 7–8, 1963; Ford, B. (ed.) The Modern Age (Pelican Guide to English Literature), 1963; Fraser, G. S. The Modern Writer and His World, 1964; Gindin, J. Postwar British Fiction, 1962; O'Connor, W. V. The New University Wits, 1963; Vinson, J. (ed.) Contemporary Novelists, 1972; West, P. The Modern Novel, 1963; Who's Who, 1973; Who's Who in America, 1972–1973. *Periodicals*—Times Educational Supplement July 20, 1956; Times Literary Supplement July 29, 1965; Wilson Library Bulletin May 1963.

WALCOTT, DEREK (ALTON) (January 23, 1930–), West Indian poet and dramatist, was born in the Windward Islands, in St. Lucia, where the official language is English but the people speak a French Creole. He is the son of Warwick Walcott, a civil servant well known as a painter and as a designer of carnival masks and costumes. His mother, Alix Walcott, is a teacher. Walcott was educated at St. Mary's College, St. Lucia, and at the University of the West Indies in Jamaica. He at first followed his mother's profession, teaching at St. Mary's, at Boys' Secondary School in Grenada, and at Kingston College, Jamaica.

His first poems were published in Trinidad when he was only eighteen, and his poetry and plays continued to appear there and in Jamaica throughout the 1950s. In 1958 he won the Jamaica Drama Festival prize with his epic drama *Drums and Colours*. It was only then that he became at all widely known. His first major volume of poetry, *In a Green Night*, was published in London in 1962 and established him at once as the finest poet the English-speaking West Indies have produced. Many of the poems in this book also appear in his *Selected Poems*, which introduced him to American readers in 1964.

Walcott's principal subject is the extravagant natural beauty of the Caribbean, which, because of the moral "contagions" of colonialism, is for him always "a fierce background to sorrow." Beyond and a part of this is his sense of himself as the dispossessed inheritor of two cultures. He writes at times in the dialect of the eastern Caribbean, as in "Tales of the Islands": "Poopada was a fête. I mean it had / Free rum, free whisky and some fellars beating / Pan from one of them band in Trinidad." But most of his work is in a very different tradition, and critics have detected the influence of Shakespeare, Donne, Marvell, Yeats, Eliot, and Hart Crane. So Walcott sees himself as white and black, slave and master: "The gorilla wrestles with the superman. / I who am poisoned with the blood of both, / Where shall I turn, divided to the vein? / I who have cursed the / drunken officer of British rule, how choose / between this Africa and the English tongue I love? / Betray them both or give back what they give / How can I face such slaughter and be cool? / How can I turn from Africa and live?"

Robert Graves has said that Walcott "handles English with a closer understanding of its inner magic than most (if not any) of his English-born contemporaries." Others, like Robert Mazzocco, have responded more equivocally. For the latter, Walcott's "lush melancholy, that itch to be impressive," can become a bore. Yet Mazzocco recognizes his "special gifts . . . his textures are musical, he has a painter's eye, his craftsmanship is adventurous, and his moral or imaginative responses aren't shabby." *The Castaway* (1965) seemed to a reviewer in the *Times Literary Supplement* to mark a distinct advance over Walcott's earlier collections, containing poems which, if not entirely free from a tendency to "boring aphorisms" and portentousness, nevertheless showed a "fast-developing observation, and dramatic angularity of phrase."

And there was little but praise for the "packed, complex, profusely metaphysical verse" collected in *The Gulf* (1969), "held back from the edge of lushness by a deft metrical control and a terse vein of intelligence." Walcott here takes his place unequivocally as a citizen of the black world—of Harlem and the American South as well as the Caribbean. The landscape of black alienation is evoked in the long title poem with a resonance and density that reminded reviewers of Eliot's *The Waste Land* and Crane's *The Bridge*: "Yet the South felt like home. Wrought balconies / the sluggish river with its tidal drawl, / the tropic air charged with extremities / of patience, a heat heavy with oil, / canebreaks, that legendary jazz. But fear / thickened my voice, that strange, familiar soil / prickled and barbed the texture of my hair, / my status as a secondary soul." With this book, wrote Selden Rodman, "Walcott's stature in the front rank of all contemporary poets in English should be apparent."

Walcott has devoted a great deal of energy to the development of an indigenous theatre, and his own plays frequently use Creole songs, chanting, and drumming. His themes are local ones—*Henri Christophe* (1950) is about the slave who became king of Haiti (a subject which has also attracted Aimé Césaire and the Cuban Alejo Carpentier). *The Sea at Dauphin* (1954) is about the fisherfolk of the eastern Caribbean, and so is *Ione* (1954), one of the most admired of Walcott's plays. It is a tale of sexual passion and violent family feuds reminiscent of Lorca. At the end, when Ione learns that the American whose child she is carrying does not intend to return, she kills herself, disillusioned with

DEREK WALCOTT

herself, her family, her race: "I must walk the dark road to Guinea / Where the kings of our blood are drowned in dirt, / and become a white stone, as hard as a man's heart." In *The Dream on Monkey Mountain* an old man, jailed for drunkenness, remembers his past and dreams about his future so vividly that his companions become infected by his fantasies. The play, rich in comic incident, is at the same time a serious allegory about colonialism and race. It was staged in New York in 1971 and received an Obie Award. It had an excellent reception—a better reception than *Ti-Jean and His Brothers*, a folk fable with music produced by Walcott himself in New York's Central Park in 1972. Clive Barnes found the tale a little too schematic and the writing lacking in the poetic density which distinguishes *The Dream on Monkey Mountain*. Several of Walcott's plays have been produced in London.

For a time, Walcott was director of the Little Carib theatre workshop in Trinidad. He spent two years (1958–1959) in the United States on a Rockefeller fellowship, studying theatre under José Quintero at the Circle in the Square and under Stuart Vaughan at the Phoenix Theatre. Since then he has served as artistic director of the Trinidad Theatre Workshop. In 1961 he won an award from the Jamaican government for his contributions to the West Indian theatre, and in 1962 his poetry brought him a special award from the Guinness Foundation. Since then he has received the Heinemann Award for poetry (1966) and a Cholmondeley Award (1969). Walcott has worked in recent years as a journalist—as a feature writer for *Public Opinion*, organ of the People's National Party in Jamaica, and as an art critic and book reviewer for the *Trinidad Guardian*. He has been married twice—to Fay Moston, by whom he has two children, and since 1962 to Margaret Ruth Maillard.

PRINCIPAL WORKS: *Poetry*—Twenty-five Poems, 1948 (Trinidad); In a Green Night, 1962; Selected Poems, 1964; The Castaway and Other Poems, 1965; The Gulf, and Other Poems, 1969; Another Life, 1973. *Plays*—Henri Christophe, 1950 (Barbados); The Sea at Dauphin, 1954 (Jamaica); Ione, 1954 (Jamaica); Drums and Colours, 1961 (Trinidad); Malcauchon, 1966 (Jamaica); Dream on Monkey Mountain and Other Plays (The Sea at Dauphin, Ti-Jean and His Brothers, Malcochon, Dream on Monkey Mountain, and What the Twilight Says [essay]), 1970.

ABOUT: Dathorne, O. R. Caribbean Verse, 1967; James, L. (ed.) The Islands in Between, 1968; Murphy, R. (ed.) Contemporary Poets of the English Language, 1970; Penguin Companion to Literature 1, 1971. *Periodicals*—Harper's August 1964; New York Review of Books December 31, 1964; New York Times Book Review September 13, 1964; Times Literary Supplement December 12, 1969.

WALKER, DAVID (HARRY) (February 9, 1911–), Canadian novelist, was born in Dundee, Scotland, the son of Harry Giles Walker and the former Elizabeth Bewley (née Newsom). He was educated at Shrewsbury public school and the Royal Military College, Sandhurst, and in 1931 was commissioned in one of the most famous of Highland regiments, the Black Watch. In 1938, after service in India and the Sudan, he became military aide to the Governor-General of Canada, Lord Tweedsmuir (who was equally well known for the novels he wrote as John Buchan).

Walker married a Canadian woman, Willa Magee, in 1939. The same year he returned to Europe to fight in France. Captured during the British withdrawal, he spent five years in German prison camps, including Colditz, and between escape attempts began to write what he calls "indifferent verse." Imprisonment was a revelation to him: "Although we had a fairly tough active existence in India and elsewhere, I grew up with a silver spoon, and never knew what life was about until I had to face it in prison—be hungry I mean; be someone else's pawn. That shows you the other side of the tracks."

After repatriation, Walker was appointed comptroller to the Viceroy of India, Lord Wavell, but in 1947 he resigned his commission and returned to Scotland to devote himself to writing. A year later he and his wife emigrated to Canada. They settled in New Brunswick, where they and their four sons have remained.

Walker's first novel, an exciting account of a Scottish manhunt called *The Storm and the Silence*, was followed by *Geordie*, the book which established his reputation and popularity. Geordie, an undersized but determined young Highlander,

DAVID WALKER

embarks on a correspondence course in body-building with such stupendous success that he is finally induced to leave home and girl friend, and go off to America with the Olympic shot-putting team. A wide public on both sides of the Atlantic loved this book for its lightheartedness, wit, and simplicity. It won the praise of such story-tellers as A. J. Cronin, Eric Linklater, and Compton Mackenzie, and was filmed with great success.

The Pillar, based on Walker's wartime experiences, seemed to John Brooks "the most thorough and revealing and also the warmest account of military imprisonment" that he had read. It received the Governor-General's Award as the best novel of 1952 in Canada, and Walker carried off the same prize again a year later with a very different book, a lighthearted, implausible entertainment called *Digby*. A period of travel and exploration followed: by canoe up the Mackenzie River in Canada, by dogsled in the Arctic, by Land Rover across India.

Walker has said that a writer never quite stops "hunting stories and the backgrounds for them," and it is clear that *Harry Black* is to some extent a product of his return visit to India. It is a portrait of a man of action, culminating in a tiger hunt during which Harry Black is brought to a confrontation with himself as well as the beast he has undertaken to destroy. This very interesting book seemed to some critics altogether too ambitious—an allegory beyond the author's capacities. But at least one found it an august achievement and others were content to read it simply as a rather literary but splendidly realized adventure story. *Mallabec*, another exciting story with allegorical overtones, is a study of guilt and expiation set in a fishing camp on a New Brunswick river. This time (rather ironically), one critic suggested that it was "a pity that such a talented writer doesn't reach a little further beyond his easy grasp."

Walker is at any rate an extraordinarily versatile and accomplished writer, drawing on an exceptionally wide range of personal experience. He can turn from the "human comedy" of *Geordie* to international intrigue (in *CAB-Intersec*); from *Where the High Winds Blow*, a notable character study of a Canadian tycoon, to *Winter of Madness*, a "wonderfully daffy" parody of the Ian Fleming spy thrillers. Walker's short foreword to *Storms of Our Journey*, a workmanlike collection of short stories, reveals a great deal about his approach to life in a world "in which there is rather more than people." He believes that the writer should "first do the job one wanted to do as well as one could do it; and then afterwards hope for a healthy reward." He acknowledges many literary masters, and the fact that they include both Ernest Hemingway and Graham Greene—the man of action and the man of painful reflection—says much about the dichotomy in Walker's own nature which makes so many of his immensely readable books more than mere entertainments.

The author is rather below average height and has brown hair and eyes. His favorite recreations include skiing and gardening. Walker, who received an MBE in 1946, served on the Canada Council from 1957 to 1961, and is a member of the Royal Company of Archers. Since 1965 he has been Canadian commissioner of the Roosevelt Campobello International Park Commission, and he served as chairman of that body in 1970–1972. He has an honorary D.Litt. from the University of New Brunswick and is a Fellow of the Royal Society of Literature. Looking back over his work to date he concludes that "*Sandy Was a Soldier's Boy* does not stand up very well in retrospect. The rest (except perhaps *Geordie*, which was complete in its simple way) all have faults, but I wouldn't take them back. Some things I would write better now; some probably less well. You gain in skill, but your enthusiasm and vitality grow less. Simplicity is what I always seek, but these are not easy days to find a hard simplicity."

PRINCIPAL WORKS: *Fiction*—The Storm and the Silence, 1949; Geordie, 1950; The Pillar, 1952; Digby, 1953; Harry Black, 1956; Sandy Was a Soldier's Boy, 1957; Where the High Winds Blow, 1960; Storms of Our Journey (short stories), 1962; Winter of Madness, 1964; Mallabec, 1965; Come Back Geordie, 1966; CAB-Intersec (England, Devil's Plunge), 1968; The Lord's Pink Ocean, 1972. *For children*—Dragon Hill, 1962; Pirate Rock, 1969; Big Ben, 1970.

ABOUT: Author's & Writer's Who's Who, 1971; Oxford Companion to Canadian History and Literature, 1967; Vinson, J. (ed.) Contemporary Novelists, 1972; Who's

Who, 1973. *Periodicals*—Book Week February 7, 1965; Christian Science Monitor April 15, 1950; Guardian February 7, 1956; New York Times March 4, 1956; Saturday Review March 25, 1950; March 3, 1956; February 13, 1965; Times Literary Supplement February 1, 1952; Wilson Library Bulletin December 1962.

WALLANT, EDWARD LEWIS (October 19, 1926–December 5, 1962), American novelist, was born in New Haven, Connecticut, the son of Sol and Ann (Mendel) Wallant. He served in the U.S. Navy during the last two years of World War II as a gunner's mate aboard a destroyer, and in 1947 entered Pratt Institute in Brooklyn. Graduating in 1950, he worked in advertising as a graphic artist, eventually becoming art director at McCann-Erickson. He married Joyce Fromkin in 1948; had a son, Scott, and two daughters, Leslie and Kim; and lived in Norwalk, Connecticut.

Wallant began his literary career with two short stories published in *New Voices*, Nos. 2 and 3, and wrote six novels, of which the two earliest remain unpublished. The first of the novels to see print was *The Human Season* (1960), which Wallant, writing five or six nights a week, worked on for over five years. "To say I *enjoy* writing would be less a mistake of degree than of species," he said in *Library Journal*. "I sweat and ache and writhe in my chair; it is decidedly *not* in the nature of a relaxing hobby. Why do I write then? I don't know exactly, only that I must do it."

The Human Season, like its successors, was an allegory on the theme of suffering and redemption. Berman, the stricken and inarticulate immigrant plumber, cannot mourn the death of his beloved American wife; he is "a million miles underneath sad." But Berman survives his agony of bereavement, and stumbles beyond it into serenity. Admired as it was for its honesty and strength, *The Human Season* is regarded in retrospect as overambitious and imperfectly realized.

Berman is the prototype of those Jewish "warriors of suffering" who dominate Wallant's books and whose champion is Sol Nazerman in *The Pawnbroker* (1961). Nazerman, who has been called "one of the few really necessary characters in contemporary fiction," is a survivor of the Nazi camps in which his family died. Suffering and degradation have numbed him to any emotion but the fear that life will not let him go. But Nazerman is denied death and feeling returns: rage and disgust at first for those who bring to his Harlem pawnshop the flotsam of "their small dreams." It is their suffering they pawn, he comes to see, adding it to his own. The ritual of the pawnshop becomes a kind of sacrament. Nazerman the expert, haggling, reluctant, accepts the world's misery. When his assistant and disciple Jesus Ortiz dies for him, Nazerman mourns, feels love and pain, is resurrected. As Jonathan Baumbach wrote in *The Language of Nightmare*, "The novel is always on the thin edge of going wrong, of letting its allegory control its direction, of teetering into bathos. Yet it survives." It is, in his opinion, "Wallant's most powerful novel." A motion picture version appeared in 1965.

EDWARD LEWIS WALLANT

The Pawnbroker was nominated for a National Book Award in 1961 and brought Wallant a Guggenheim Fellowship. He took a leave of absence from his job and spent five months in Europe. At the end of 1962, when he was thirty-six, Wallant died of a stroke.

Wallant's last two novels were published posthumously. *The Children at the Gate* (1964), technically more accomplished than the earlier books, was set in a New England hospital, where a lapsed Catholic is rescued from despair by the ugly death of the garrulous Sammy, a Jewish "holy idiot."

The Tenants of Moonbloom (1963), published a year earlier but actually Wallant's last book, was a statement in comic terms of his faith in human redemption through the sharing of suffering. Norman Moonbloom is a thirty-three-year-old virgin and all-round failure, a man unborn. Reduced to collecting rents from his brother's slum tenements, he becomes involved in the abundant miseries of the tenants and seeks to help them by repairing, with his own hands, the decaying fabric of their dwellings. At last, purging with his pickax the obscene swelling on Bassellecci's bathroom wall, Moonbloom drunk, transfigured, drenched in excrement, can proclaim: "I'M BORN." While Wallant's other books showed the influence of Malamud and Bellow, and at times of

Dostoevsky, *The Tenants of Moonbloom* was wholly original, "an uncannily funny and discomforting book."

Wallant's strength lay in his "Chekhovian" gift for characterization and in the potency of his message—"It's so lonely not to suffer, *so lonely*." His prose, sometimes strained or hurried, "at its best, seems to brush across the nerve of our feelings." It is said that he found his true direction only in his last book and "that he never fully worked out that terminal revelation he always sought." But as a reviewer wrote in the *Times Literary Supplement*: "Few novelists have said so much by the age of thirty-six, and his four books place him among the best of the Jewish American writers. He was very much one of that family."

PRINCIPAL WORKS: The Human Season, 1960; The Pawnbroker, 1961; The Tenants of Moonbloom, 1963; The Children at the Gate, 1964.

ABOUT: Baumbach, J. The Landscape of Nightmare, 1965; Contemporary Authors 4, 1963. *Periodicals*—Library Journal June 1, 1960; New York Times December 6, 1962; Publishers' Weekly December 17, 1962; Times Literary Supplement April 15, 1965.

***WALSER, MARTIN** (March 24, 1927–), German dramatist and novelist, writes (in German): "Born in Wasserburg, on Lake Constance. My father, who had kept an inn in this village, died in 1938. In 1944 my brother became a victim of World War II. I was called up in 1944. In 1947 I began my studies: literature, philosophy and history. I completed my studies at Tübingen in 1951 with a thesis on Franz Kafka. In the years 1949–1957 I worked for radio, newspapers and television. Since 1957 I have lived in Friedrichshafen on Lake Constance, writing novels and plays. I am married, have three daughters and a dog. In 1955 I was awarded the prize of the Group 47; in 1957 I received the Hesse Prize, in 1962 the Hauptmann Prize, and in 1965 the Schiller Prize."

Walser published his first short story in 1949. Between then and 1957, when he returned as a full-time writer to the Bodensee, Walser worked as a journalist and as a radio and television writer and director. His first volume of short stories was published in 1955 as *Ein Flugzeug über dem Haus*. His first novel, *Ehen in Phillipsburg*, followed two years later and has been translated by Eva Figes as *Marriage in Phillipsburg* (in England, *The Gadarene Club*). It is a criticism of Germany's postwar "economic miracle" and the gross complacent materialism that accompanied it, focusing on Hans Beumann, a young journalist turned press agent, who step by step abandons his class, his girl friend, and his principles in order to earn membership in his town's most exclusive social club. Reviewers of the English version were reminded of John Braine's *Room at the Top*, but complained of a certain Teutonic heaviness in Walser's handling of the story.

* väl′ zər

Anselm Kristlein, the ambitious salesman in *Halbzeit* (Half-Time, 1960), is another outsider who forces his way at great cost to his integrity into a world "where efficient people grow like weeds." The resulting fragmentation of his personality is expressed in *Halbzeit* by his ability to speak in any one of three distinct voices—as detached narrator, as central character, and as the imaginary scientist (Anselm's conscience) Galileo Cleverlein. Beyond this, we are shown how skillfully Anselm can adjust his personality, and even his use of language, to the expectations of the other characters in the book—observing himself meanwhile with a mixture of admiration and disgust. The novel put critics in mind of Thomas Mann's *Confessions of Felix Krull*, and also of Proust, of whom Walser has written a valuable study. Walser shares with Proust a belief that "God exists in little details," that particularity is man's only graspable reality. This is evident both in his intensely personal use of language and in his fondness for passages of very full and precise description.

Walser's distaste for the social and cultural pretensions, the greed and hypocrisy of postwar German life, also dominates his plays. *Der Abstecher* (1961, translated by Richard Grunberger as *The Detour*), written for radio, is a grotesque "triangle" story, an attack on the immorality of the affluent male business world expressed in blackly farcical terms. *Eiche und Angora* (1962, translated by Ronald Duncan as *The Rabbit Race*) is set on a German hillside—a Nazi observation post during the war, now a popular beer garden. The central character is Alois Grübel, an excessively simple man of the people. Emasculated in medical experiments in a wartime concentration camp, he eventually goes cheerfully off to a mental asylum, obeying his "betters" in this as in everything else—including the matter of his rabbits, pointedly given Jewish names, which he is made to slaughter.

An unconvincing mixture of Brechtian satire and direct realism, overly complex in its symbolism, *Eiche und Angora* is saved by its dialogue, and by the restrained passion of the author's loathing for the worst aspects of the German character. It was performed in English at the 1963 Edinburgh Festival and impressed Roger Gellert of the *New Statesman* as a "rich, sad, funny, marvellously shaped and impressively fair-minded play." *Überlebensgrosser Herr Krott* (The Exaggerated Life of Herr Krott, 1963) deals with the inhumanity of big business in Brechtian, loosely epic scenes, and *Der schwarze Schwan* (The Black Swan, 1964) is about moral conflict between the generations in postwar Germany.

The most admired of Walser's books is the novel *Das Einhorn* (1966, translated by Barrie Ellis-Jones as *The Unicorn*). Anselm Kristlein reappears as hero and narrator, and is now a novelist, commissioned to write a book about love. In the course of his researches, he himself falls passionately in love, an experience which completes his self-estrangement, so that he returns to his wife and children literally prostrate. The unicorn of the title refers to Anselm's social alienation as well as to his erotic quest, and also no doubt to the question of his purity and integrity as a writer. All of these themes are explored in the book and shown to be closely interrelated. Moreover, since Anselm is providing the raw material of his book, as well as manufacturing it into fiction, another major theme, as one reviewer wrote, "is the discrepancy between truth and fiction, experience and memory. It is this discrepancy which defeats Kristlein," who repeatedly reformulates and revises his book, and in the end abandons it.

Walser exemplifies the writer's linguistic and structural problems through an ingenious use of interior monologues in several languages and dialects, flashbacks, digressions, and all kinds of references across the narrative line. According to a critic in the *Times Literary Supplement*, "though Herr Walser has found a distinct manner in this book, at once rich and vigorous, expressive and ironic, some of his verbalizing does tend to obscure the narrative line." Nevertheless, "*Das Einhorn* is by far the most successful of Herr Walser's works to date, because all his remarkable gifts have been applied to a structure large and intricate enough to accommodate them."

For some time after the publication of *Das Einhorn*, Walser produced no more fiction. He was one of several German writers who, as he put it in 1968, "no longer care for imitated authenticity. We no longer believe that anyone can know anything about anyone else." He had planned to write a book about the life of "Ursula Trauberg," an inmate of the prison for women at Lubeck who at the age of twenty-four had murdered her lover's wife. Instead, in accordance with his new theories, he persuaded the woman to write her own story, which he edited. It was published with great success in 1968 as *Vorleben* (Previous Life). *Fiction*, a product of this experience, is a brief and extremely abstract investigation into the relationship between art and life—an account of a sexual murder in which the fantasy-weaving murderer becomes gradually enmeshed in the web of his own fictional existence. Walser has acknowledged his debt to Kafka in *Beschreibung einer Form, Franz Kafka* (1961), and has published a volume of essays as well as a second collection of short stories.

The Kristlein trilogy was completed with *Der Sturz* (The Crash, 1973), which is distinguished from its predecessors by a pervading sense of decay and death, as Kristlein slithers down the same social slope that he had ascended in *Halbzeit*. Walser blames the capitalist system for Kristlein's demoralization, but some German reviewers thought his problems as much individual as social. However that may be, it seemed to one reviewer that "this trilogy has no equal as a portrayal of the society created by postwar prosperity in West Germany."

MARTIN WALSER

PRINCIPAL WORKS IN ENGLISH TRANSLATION: The Gadarene Club, 1960 (U.S., Marriage in Phillipsburg); The Rabbit Race, and Detour, 1963; The Unicorn, 1971. *Story in* Middleton, C. (ed.) German Writing Today, 1967.

ABOUT: Closs, A. Twentieth Century German Literature, 1969; Garten, H. F. Modern German Drama, 1964; International Who's Who, 1973–74; Penguin Companion to Literature 2, 1969; Thomas, R. H. and Van der Will, W. The German Novel and the Affluent Society, 1968; Wer Ist Wer?, 1969–1970. *Periodicals*—Atlas January 1967; New Statesman September 6, 1963; Times October 28, 1964; Times Literary Supplement October 17, 1968.

WALSH, CHAD (May 10, 1914–), American poet, theologian, dramatist, and scholar, writes: "Marion, Virginia, where I grew up, lies between the Blue Ridge and the Alleghenies. My father, an itinerant insurance agent, was home week-ends if then. My oldest brother, Ulysses, was a substitute father, and it was he who introduced me to literature, first by reading Dickens aloud, and later, when I was about ten, by suggesting that we memorize some Keats and Shakespeare. We would wander up and down a country lane declaiming, and the magic of language seized me and would not let go.

CHAD WALSH

"I was a daydreamer, frequently moody. I had fantasies of becoming a violinist (a few tentative experiments ended *that* ambition) or forester or landscape architect. Then early in high school I became ill and left school. For three years I was a Huck Finn without a Mississippi. I roamed the woods, wrote poetry (I had started at about the fourth grade), kept a diary in a top-secret cipher. I must have been the world's most contented dropout until the county nurse, with infinite tact, persuaded me that none of my vague ambitions could come true without further school. By this time I had developed an interest in foreign languages, and was reasonably sure I wanted to specialize in them. I returned to high school, eventually became editor of the student paper, took on a part-time job as linotypist and reporter with Sherwood Anderson's two country weeklies, and graduated a month beyond my twentieth birthday.

"After two years at Marion Junior College I transferred to the University of Virginia. Though I continued to write verse at a furious pace I concentrated even more on playwriting, thanks to Roger Boyle of the Virginia Players, who produced several of my one-acters.

"Receiving a fellowship at the University of Michigan, I went there to work for a master's degree in French. I met Eva Tuttle, a graduate of Middlebury College, and we were married after a courtship so brief that our four daughters—Damaris, Madeline, Sarah-Lindsay, and Alison—have always sternly told us that we mustn't urge the virtue of prudence upon them.

"By the time I received my M.A. I had decided to shift to English for the Ph.D. Meanwhile, I was taking Roy Cowden's seminar in creative writing, and turning out plays, essays, and unlimited stretches of poetry. A group of my plays won a Hopwood Award in 1939. During my time at Ann Arbor, which lasted till I became a research analyst for the War Department in early 1943, I was slowly and undramatically going through a period of transition in my religious thinking, moving toward a commitment, which led me (after coming to Beloit) to write a number of semipopular books on Christianity and to become a week-end priest of the Episcopal Church.

"Since 1945 I have been teaching English at Beloit College. There has been much debate about the merits and perils of combining teaching and writing. I never feel that academia has clipped my creative wings. The main problem is time (but most other professions offer less free time) and the fact that the satisfactions and excitements of teaching are so intense and involve so much the same kind of energy as writing, that sometimes one can go a long time without wanting to write. In certain ways, teaching is the more enjoyable experience; it has a human drama to it, and writing is pretty solitary. However, never more than a few months pass without the desire or the compulsion reviving. If I live too long away from the typewriter, there is a sense of inward drying up, of some vital ingredient missing from whatever diet feeds the spirit.

"During my stay at Beloit I have had a winter writing in Marin County (north of San Francisco), been on two Fulbrights (Finland and Rome), and taught as a visiting professor at Wellesley. To my surprise I found myself somewhere along the way chairman of the English Department at Beloit, and even discovered a certain half-sinful fascination in the minutiae of such work. As a literary jack-of-all-trades I have written almost a book a year for twenty years, including Christian apologetics, literary history (*From Utopia to Nightmare*), poetry textbooks, children's novels, a critical study of C. S. Lewis, and four books of my own verse, the last two of which won the first thousand-dollar prize given by the Council for Wisconsin Writers. A few years ago the old passion for playwriting revived (if I had lived in Elizabethan times, I'm sure I should have concentrated on poetic drama) and I wrote a long chronicle play in verse, *King Saul*, which has been much praised but neither produced nor published.

"I have often thought that I spread myself too thin in my writing; I seem incurably interested in many things, and as my British publisher told me, 'Walsh, you have a blurred image.' Now that I am on the other side of fifty, I intend for the next few years to concentrate on a few major projects. One is a long book on the relation between aesthetics and religious experience. A second is a book dealing with a number of important theological trends—existentialism, demythologizing, 'God is dead,' etc.—and attempting to establish a conceptual framework for viewing the process of theological change. The third and most vital project is my poetry; I have done about half of a fifth volume, and in the back of my mind is 'Collected Poems of——.' Whatever else I write, I always come back to poetry, as the way of saying most accurately the things I most deeply want to express. Compared to poetry, prose is (for me) an approximate and clumsy medium of thought and feeling. At the same time, I find it impossible to categorize my poetry or place myself in one of the current factions. The powerful influences I have felt at times range from Catullus to Villon, Donne, Kipling, Eliot, Frost, Vachel Lindsay, and Auden—to mention only a few of my mentors.

"My life has a yearly cycle to it. During the academic year I am a college professor, writing a little on the side. In the summer my family and I flee to our holy place, a cottage on a lake in northern Vermont. I flee still further to a tiny house (eight by twelve feet) which I built off in the woods, and there, far from telephones and committee meetings, I do most of my writing."

Chad Walsh is the son of William and Katie (Wrenn) Walsh. His "substitute father" Ulysses now works in television and has a national reputation as an authority on the history of the phonograph. Walsh received his Ph.D. at the University of Michigan in February 1943 and spent the next two years in Washington, D.C., as a research analyst with the U.S. Army Signal Corps. He went to Beloit College as an assistant professor in 1945, becoming professor of English in 1952. He was chairman of his department from 1959 until 1969, when he became writer in residence. *The Beloit Poetry Journal* was founded by Walsh and Robert Glauber in 1950.

Repelled by the "ferocious" Christianity of his childhood, Walsh had become an agnostic. The writings of Reinhold Niebuhr and of T. S. Eliot helped him to recover his faith and he entered the Episcopal Church in 1945 and was ordained a priest in 1949. He has preached as a guest in many American pulpits but is associated chiefly with St. Paul's Church in Beloit, where he serves as an assistant priest on weekends.

Walsh's first book, *Stop Looking and Listen*, was "candidly designed as a recruiting pamphlet for Christianity," and had "a crisp incisiveness and a blithe certainty" that reminded one reviewer of C. S. Lewis. Walsh has acknowledged the importance for him of Lewis's writings, and has written a "good-natured, rambling and quite personal" study of Lewis's work and ideas.

Early Christians of the 21st Century anticipates without despair the collapse of this civilization, foreseeing the rebirth of Christianity in a purer, more vigorous form. *Campus Gods on Trial*, addressed to students, discusses such contemporary substitutes for religious faith as materialism on the one hand and secular humanitarianism on the other. In *Behold the Glory* Walsh takes a more devotional and even mystical direction than in his earlier books, presenting some fresh ideas about the Christian mystery in a manner characteristically "bright, occasionally beautiful, and now and then brash."

From Utopia to Nightmare, as much critical as theological, reviews utopian literature and the work of such recent "dystopians" as Orwell and Huxley, seeing the latter "not as a signal for us to abandon utopia but to dream more intelligently and profoundly." The *Times Literary Supplement* found it on the whole "civilised, sensible and, though not very profound, illuminating." J. W. Smith, reviewing the work in *Books*, remained unconvinced by its arguments but, as Walsh's critics often do, reacted very warmly to the personality behind the ideas. *God at Large* is no doubt the book Walsh mentions above—a generously eclectic attempt "to establish a conceptual framework for viewing the process of theological change."

Walsh's verse has been found no less likable than his prose, though highly uneven in its quality—at its worst pedestrian, at its best studded with striking lines and images "like mountains rising suddenly out of a barren plain." *Eden Two-Way* was called "a warm book which portrays a poet delightful and easy to read." *The Psalm of Christ*, a sequence of forty poems on the Twenty-Second Psalm, was a selection of the Catholic Poetry Society of America and was praised for "a sharpness and freshness of imagery and a salutariness of wit all too rare in religious verse." In some of Walsh's later poems critics have found a rather excessive concern with form, which, as one reviewer wrote of *The End of Nature*, tends to "tyrannize over choice of words and syntax."

Chad Walsh is a tall, slender man, with brown hair and gray eyes. His manner is quiet and his voice pleasant and expressive. A liberal Democrat, he was a part-time unofficial assistant on Adlai Stevenson's staff in 1956. His recreations include landscape painting, photography, and playing the recorder, as well as swimming, hiking, and climbing.

PRINCIPAL WORKS: *Poetry*—The Factual Dark, 1949; Eden Two-Way, 1954; The Psalm of Christ: 40 Poems on the 22nd Psalm, 1964; The Unknowing Dance, 1964; The End of Nature, 1969. *Nonfiction*—Stop Looking and Listen: An Invitation to the Christian Life, 1947; C. S. Lewis: Apostle to the Skeptics, 1949; Early Christians of the 21st Century, 1950; Campus Gods on Trial, 1953 (rev. and enlarged, 1962); Knock and Enter, 1953; Behold the Glory, 1956; From Utopia to Nightmare, 1962; Doors Into Poetry (textbook), 1962; God at Large, 1971. *Fiction*—Nellie and Her Flying Crocodile (juvenile), 1956; The Rough Years (adult and young adult), 1960. *As editor*—Today's Poets, 1964; Garlands for Christmas, 1965; The Honey and the Gall: Poems of Married Life, 1967.

ABOUT: Bode, C. *introduction to* The Unknowing Dance, 1964; Contemporary Authors 3, 1963; Current Biography, 1962; Directory of American Scholars, vol. II, 1964; Murphy, R. (ed.) Contemporary Poets of the English Language, 1970; Pike, J. A. (ed.) Modern Canterbury Pilgrims, 1956; Soper, D. W. (ed.) These Found a Way, 1951; Walsh, C. Behold the Glory, 1956; Who's Who in America, 1972–1973. *Periodicals*—Book World October 15, 1967; Milwaukee Journal March 6, 1960.

WATERHOUSE, KEITH (SPENCER) (February 6, 1929–), English novelist and playwright, was born in Leeds, Yorkshire, the fifth child of Ernest Waterhouse, a costermonger, and Elsie Edith Waterhouse. He left Osmondthorpe Council School, Leeds, at fifteen and worked subsequently as an undertaker's and a shoemaker's assistant, newspaper boy, ice cream salesman, rent collector, and clerk before joining the RAF. After service he became a reporter for the *Yorkshire Evening Post* and, later, chief feature writer on the London *Daily Mirror*. On October 21, 1951, he married Joan Foster and in 1958 gave up journalism to devote full time to writing novels.

Waterhouse's first novel, *There Is A Happy Land*, which he wrote during a newspaper strike in 1956, rehearses some of the comic routines and sly bravura conspicuous in *Billy Liar*, whose young narrator works for Shadrack, a progressive funeral director in the small Yorkshire city of Stradhoughton. A gifted mimic and parodist, as well as a fantastic liar, Billy gets engaged to two girls while cultivating a third; he hides the stack of calendars he should have sent out for Shadrack; he spins fantasies to willing dupes about relatives, jobs, and dogs he doesn't have; and he omits to mail his mother's request-letter to a BBC disk jockey. When he is found out, he lies even harder, not just to baffle the enemy but to gratify himself anew by creating myths in which his parents become indulgent London sophisticates while he, in turn, becomes prime minister of "Ambrosia" (where he figures also as war hero, celebrated comedian at the Ambrosia State Opera, and Sancho Panza to Bertrand Russell). The novel is an account of the day of reckoning, when this monstrous fabric of deception crashes majestically down about him.

At last, though he is almost weaned away by a faint chance of working for a TV comedian in London, Billy finally decides to stay put, convinced that if Stradhoughton can perplex him and scare him into Ambrosia, the metropolis will finish him off. A "dislocated adolescent," as James Gindin calls him, he has first of all to achieve a steady identity; only then will he be able to absorb and master the bewildering multiplicity of modern life.

The critics warmed to Waterhouse's operatic inventiveness and his incisive cartoons of the English scene. Describing *Billy Liar* as "pungent, shapely, and instructive," John Updike concluded: "I would not really want this excellent book any different." The consensus was that Waterhouse is neither anti-Establishment nor anti-Welfare State, but an idiosyncratic original with a gift for creating wholesome comedy "out of a horrifying human predicament."

Jubb is gamier and harsher, the confessional monologue of a rent collector who, thanks to his activities as an inept lecher and shy pornographer, has become an outcast in Chapel Langtry New Town. A man of meticulous pomposity, Cyril Jubb was born to be excluded: his wife leaves him; no one comes to his party; the local Fascists refuse him membership even though he admires Mussolini. So he makes anonymous phone calls to a model, dreams of depravities in Hamburg, and plots revenge with matches and lighter fuel. "A glorious comic character," the *Times Literary Supplement* called him: "Mr. Waterhouse's criticism of our society is no less angry for being very funny, and he has achieved the remarkable feat of writing in the character of a man not only psychopathic, but also a repulsive bore, who nevertheless emerges as profoundly sane and even, in his own odd way, quite jolly." Other reviews, however, regretted the absence of the exuberant freshness found in *Billy Liar*. *Everything Must Go*, centering on a London antique dealer, is another portrait in professional and sexual failure; it was called "farcical but not trivial."

In the late 1950s Waterhouse in conjunction with Guy Deghy produced several humorous books and a lively account of ninety years of bohemia at the Café Royal. His collaboration with Willis Hall began in 1960 and has been referred to since as the Waterhouse and Hall "factory." They have made extremely successful adaptations for both stage and screen of *Billy Liar* and have written a number of other plays, including a musical version of Arnold Bennett's novel *The Card*, and *Who's Who*, an entertaining farce which also provides "a pure, beautifully abstract exposé of the bourgeois moral vacuum." *Saturday, Sunday, Monday*, their adaptation of Eduardo de Filippo's *Sabato, Domenica, e Lunedi*, was staged by the National Theatre in 1973. They have written for radio and television, and produced screenplays for a number of movies, including *Whistle Down the Wind* and *A Kind of Loving*. Waterhouse has also reviewed fiction for the *New Statesman*. He returned to journalism in

KEITH WATERHOUSE

1970, writing a column for the mass-circulation *Daily Mirror*, and the same year winning awards as the columnist and the descriptive writer of the year. Waterhouse, now divorced, has three children, Penelope, Sarah, and Robert. He lives in London, leaving occasionally to work in Hollywood on a screenplay.

PRINCIPAL WORKS: *Fiction*—There Is a Happy Land, 1957; Billy Liar, 1959; Jubb, 1963; The Bucket Shop, 1968 (U.S., Everything Must Go). *Plays (with Willis Hall)*—Billy Liar, 1960; Celebration, 1961; All Things Bright and Beautiful, 1963; England, Our England (revue), 1963; The Sponge Room, and, Squat Betty, 1963; Come Laughing Home, 1965; Say Who You Are (U.S., Help Stamp Out Marriage), 1966. *With Guy Deghy*—Café Royal (social history), 1955; How to Avoid Matrimony (humor), 1957. *As "Lee Gibb"*—The Joneses: How to Keep Up With Them (humor), 1959; The Higher Jones, 1961.

ABOUT: Contemporary Authors 7–8, 1963; Gindin, J. Postwar British Fiction, 1962; Vinson, J. (ed.) Contemporary Novelists, 1972; Who's Who, 1973; Who's Who in America, 1972–1973.

WATTS, ALAN (WILSON) (January 6, 1915–November 16, 1973), American writer on religion, was born in Chislehurst, England, and educated at King's School, Canterbury. He was the son of Laurence and Emily (Buchan) Watts. According to his own account he became interested in Eastern culture at the age of twelve, when he discovered the novels of Sax Rohmer. At any rate, he began his study of Eastern philosophy in adolescence, and at twenty published his first book, *The Spirit of Zen. The Legacy of Asia and Western Man* appeared a year later. In London in the 1930s he worked in the office of his father, a fund-raiser for hospitals, helped to organize the World Congress of Faiths, and edited the magazine *The Middle Way* (1934–1938). With L. Cranmer-Byng he edited the books in the series *Wisdom of the East*, published in London and New York between 1937 and 1941.

Watts immigrated to the United States in 1939, and studied for the Episcopal priesthood at Seabury-Western Theological Seminary in Evanston, Illinois. After his ordination in 1944 he served as Episcopal chaplain at Northwestern University in Evanston until 1950, when he left the church. Thenceforth he shunned affiliation with any religious sect because, as he explained, "partisanship in religion closes the mind." In an interview in 1967 he expressed his dissatisfaction with such dogmatic faiths as Christianity and Judaism: "They tell you what you ought to do, but they are not sources of power. In other words, they do not transform the way you experience your own existence or your own identity. They just talk and urge. This is one of the great lessons of history. Preaching doesn't work."

Between his arrival in the United States and his renunciation of the Anglican faith, Watts published four books: *The Meaning of Happiness*, in which he relates Eastern wisdom to the search for spiritual freedom in modern Western psychology; *Behold the Spirit*, his first personal statement on mysticism; *The Supreme Identity*, a comparative, synthesizing study of the literature of mysticism in various cultures; and *Easter: Its Story and Meaning*. In *The Wisdom of Insecurity* he emphasized the unpredictability of existence and the consequent futility of struggling for security and advocated according to one reviewer a kind of "spiritual judo . . . mastering an opposing force" by giving in to it. "The wisdom of insecurity," Philip Wheelwright has written in paraphrase of Watts, "is not a way of evasion, but of carrying on wherever we happen to be stationed, without imagining that the burden of the world or even of the next moment is ours."

In 1951 Watts joined the faculty of the American Academy of Asian Studies, a graduate school of the College of the Pacific in San Francisco, where for six years he taught comparative philosophy and psychology. From 1953 to 1956 Watts also served as dean of the school, but found time to write *Myth and Ritual in Christianity* (1954), in which he examined the contribution of Christian symbolism to Western cultural history and suggested that Christians have been misunderstanding the Christian mythos.

Watts left the College of the Pacific in 1957 and after that time devoted himself to his work as president of the Society for Comparative Philosophy and to freelance writing and lecturing. In *Nature, Man, and Woman* he contrasted the unity of spirit and nature in Eastern thought with their separation in the West, particularly in regard to sex. *The Way of Zen* is an introduction to Zen Buddhism,

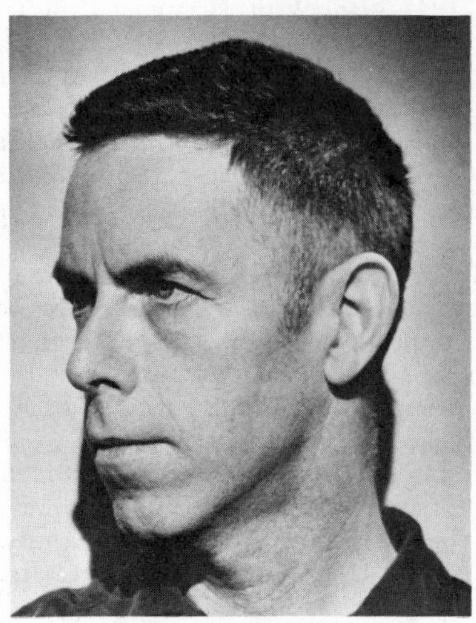

ALAN WATTS

which is the subject also of some of the essays in *This Is It*, and which he defined with maximum simplicity as meaning "No fuss."

These last two books coincided with and contributed to an extraordinary upsurge of interest in oriental religion in the United States, especially among young people. Rather against his will, Watts found himself a leader and a prophet of the Beat Generation, whose understanding of Zen he found in general inadequate. "For Zen," Watts said, "is above all the liberation of the mind from conventional thought, and that is something utterly different from rebellion against convention, on the one hand, or adopting foreign conventions, on the other."

Watts experimented with consciousness-altering drugs and described his experiences in *The Joyous Cosmology*, more a "brief poetic essay" than a textbook. *Beyond Theology* was described by its publisher as "a new kind of Divine Comedy in which the whole Christian cosmos of God and Man, Heaven and Earth, Good and Evil, is seen as a superb drama enacted by the Hidden Player who turns out to be the central and eternal Self in us all." It is in effect another attempt to temper, largely through Buddhist insights, the negativism and authoritarianism which Watts found in Western religion.

Reviewers of Watt's first books found them a little diffuse and cryptic. Clearly he learned by doing, for, after about 1950, his work was consistently praised for the tautness and lucidity of its prose, its "sense of measure and scholarly integrity." More recently Watts learned to use "colloquial speech, current slang, beat lingo, and even outrageous puns" to capture his readers' attention. Not all of his critics approved of this development, and Josh Greenfeld, reviewing *The Book* (1967), said "his pedantic arguments are always charmingly offered in the gracious manner of . . . a lecturer, with a reputation for the far out, auditioning for a woman's club tour." However N. W. Ross, discussing the same book, was satisfied that if Watts "sets out to jolt his readers, he also knows how to stretch their imagination, for no one is capable of writing on abstruse subjects with greater lucidity and cogency." There is also, and naturally, a similar division of opinion as to the value of what he had to say; he has been accused of "a distorted view of the Christian tradition" and of "doctrinally boneless preaching." It is, however, generally recognized that as an interpreter of Buddhist thought for Western laymen Watts had no equal.

Watts, who lived in Sausalito, California, became an American citizen in 1943. He was an excellent speaker and generally managed without notes. He lectured at Harvard, Cambridge (England), Columbia, Cornell, and many other universities, at the Jung Institute in Zurich, and at numerous medical schools. He was also an extremely popular broadcaster. He held Bollingen research fellowships in 1951–1953 and 1962–1964. Watts was five feet seven inches tall, had blue eyes, and wore his brown hair close-cropped. He had two children by his 1938 marriage to Eleanor Everett and five by his 1950 marriage to Dorothy DeWitt. He was married again in 1963 to Mary King. His recreations included dancing, beachcombing, cooking, and the graphic arts.

PRINCIPAL WORKS: The Spirit of Zen, 1936; The Legacy of Asia and Western Man, 1937; The Meaning of Happiness, 1940; Behold the Spirit, 1947; The Supreme Identity, 1950; Easter, 1950; The Wisdom of Insecurity, 1951; Myth and Ritual in Christianity, 1954; The Way of Zen, 1957; Nature, Man, and Woman, 1958; This Is It, 1960; Psychotherapy East and West, 1961; The Joyous Cosmology, 1962; The Two Hands of God, 1963; Beyond Theology, 1964; The Book: On the Taboo Against Knowing Who You Are, 1966; Beat Zen, Square Zen and Zen, 1967; Does It Matter? (essays and articles), 1970; Erotic Spirituality: The Vision of Konarak (with photographs by Eliot Elisofon), 1971; In My Own Way: An Autobiography 1915–1965, 1972; The Art of Contemplation, 1972; Cloud-Hidden, Whereabouts Unknown: A Mountain Journal (essays), 1973.

ABOUT: Current Biography, 1962; Watts, A. In My Own Way, 1972; Who's Who in America, 1972–1973. *Periodicals*—East Village Other May 1, 1966; Life April 21, 1961; Nation November 1, 1958; New Republic May 1, 1965; Redbook May 1966; Sewanee Review Summer 1953.

***WAŻYK, ADAM** (November 17, 1905–), Polish poet, novelist, editor, and translator, writes: "I was born in Warsaw. I was graduated in liberal arts and mathematics. Between the ages of seventeen and twenty I wrote the vanguard poems which

* vä′ zhik

were published in the two collections *Semafory* (Semaphores, 1924) and *Oczy i usta* (Eyes and Lips, 1925). I belonged to the generation whose childhood had been cut by the first world war. The day after the war broke out the world seemed to be quite different from the one I remembered; it lost the appearance of stability and at the same time it looked a little younger. Since early childhood I have been sensitive to all technical and social changes. I was interested in psychoanalysis and I believed there were a lot of things to be discovered in ordinary people. In their structure, my poems resembled what some people call poetic cubism.

"In 1935 or thereabouts I decided to write a cycle of novels about my generation, dealing either with family life and experience in love or with politics and the great social problems of that time. I had time to write only one novel, *Mity rodzinne*, before the war broke out and the German invasion of Poland began. I took shelter in the territory of the Soviet Union. There I took part in Polish radio programmes broadcast to my country, and later joined a Polish army formed in Russia. With this army I came back to Poland. The poems I had written abroad during the war, published under the title *Serce granatu* (The Heart of the Grenade), had more classical shape than my previous poetry; they were overwhelmed with nostalgia for my country, eagerness to fight the invaders, and fears for the future.

"After a year I joined the group of writers who published the weekly *Kuźnica* (The Anvil). Influenced by their war experiences, this group tried to set the world right by means of simplified literary conceptions, propagating 'humane realism.' In the process of time I came to the conclusion that poetry should be conformed to political propaganda and I expressed my opinion in this matter. However something prevented me from going on with this, for at that time I was exclusively occupied with translations. I have translated *Eugene Onegin* by Pushkin and my favorite poets like Rimbaud and Apollinaire whose work was very close to me.

"After a long break caused by sickness I was pressed by life to confront the Stalin myths. I came back to reality and in the middle of 1955 I published my *Poemat dla dorosłych* (Poem for Adults), but never supposed that this work would evoke such heated discussion in my country and abroad. One year later in autumn I got a violent lesson in history. I was in Budapest and was a witness to the tragic events there. In my poem 'Wagon' (1957) I tried to hand down the poetical reflections evoked by my generation's painful series of historical experiences and spiritual adventures, comparing them with the new generation's fresh style of life and thought.

"Since that time, in my poetical works and novels, there has appeared some obsession, some sense of the incoherence of the world in which we live, the incoherence of my own fate and own past. When writing my newest book, which I finished in 1965 as an artistic diary, *Kwestia gustu*, I saw that this obsession had its beginning in my earliest poetical works, and that it is a characteristic mark of the spiritual formation to which I belong."

ADAM WAŻYK

Ważyk's path—from French-influenced experiments to "socialist realism" and then back via the poetry of protest to individualism—is typical of many East European poets of his generation.

His early verse, much influenced by Apollinaire and Éluard (who became a close friend), earned Ważyk a considerable reputation during the early 1930s. Between 1932 and 1939 his socialist activities brought him a series of jail sentences, and during this period, as he says, he turned to the novel and also to editorial work and translating. During his wartime exile in the USSR he became confirmed in his Marxism. He also began to write poetry again, and from 1945 to 1948 devoted himself and his verse to the establishment of the Communist hierarchy in Poland. There was no trace in Ważyk's postwar work of his former irrationalism; it was propaganda poetry, as simple and direct as a poster. Ważyk became the "Poet Laureate of 'People's Poland,'" subservient to the regime and rewarded by it, and, according to George Gömöri, "one of the most feared and hated figures in literary life." From 1945 to 1950 Ważyk was coeditor of *Kuźnica*, and then was promoted to the editorship (1950–1954) of the literary monthly *Twórczość*.

But gradually Ważyk's enthusiasm for the Stalinist regime waned. For that reason perhaps, and because of his illness, he published little after 1948, concentrating on his editorial duties. In 1955 he was sent to write an article about life in a new industrial town near Cracow; he came back with the "Poem for Adults," published in *Nowa Kultura* in August 1955. The "thaw" was already under way and the braver critics of the regime had begun to find fault with the emperor's new clothes; Ważyk in his "naked poem" said loudly and savagely that the clothes were not there, that nothing covered the starved, tormented, corrupted body of Poland but lies. The people, he wrote, forced to swallow brine and pretend it was lemonade, "return quietly home / To vomit / To vomit." He demanded instead "burning reason" and "the bread of freedom."

Opinions of the poem's literary merit differ: it has been called hasty and careless in its fifteen-part structure, at times prosy; in its best passages, George Gömöri says, Ważyk "achieved a synthesis between realism and satirical symbolism, a style henceforth typical of his poetry." Of the work's political importance there is no question; having been shown the truth, the people would have nothing else. Copies passed from hand to hand all over Poland and into Hungary. Attempts to suppress it led to student riots which rocked the already shaky and divided regime; the downfall of Stalinism followed. Ważyk became a national hero.

Then Gomulka came to power, reintroduced the "hard line," and suppressed the cosmopolitan magazine *Europa* which Ważyk tried to launch in 1957. This, and the crushing of the Hungarian Revolution, destroyed whatever faith Ważyk retained in Communism. He resigned from the Party in 1957, and his subsequent attacks on Gomulka were denied publication in Poland.

Ważyk is married and has two children. He lives in Warsaw. A visitor described him in 1959 as a bespectacled, round-faced man, nervous in manner and a heavy smoker. He has been called, with much oversimplification but a little truth, "the only poet of the twentieth century to start a revolution single-handed."

PRINCIPAL WORKS IN ENGLISH TRANSLATION: A Poem for Adults *in* Stillman, E. (ed.) Bitter Harvest, 1959 *and* (with other poems) *in* Conquest, R. (ed.) Back to Life, 1958. *Poems in* Milosz, C. (ed.) Postwar Polish Poetry, 1963; East Europe April 1958; Twentieth Century December 1955, February 1957, July 1958.

ABOUT: Gillon, A. and Krzyzanowski, L. Introduction to Modern Polish Literature, 1964; Gömöri, G. Polish and Hungarian Poetry 1945–1956, 1966; Grigson, G. (ed.) Concise Encyclopedia of Modern World Literature, 1963; International Who's Who, 1973–74. *Periodicals*—New York Times Magazine August 19, 1956; Twentieth Century September 1959, November 1959.

WEBB, RICHARD WILSON. *See* WHEELER, HUGH CALLINGHAM

WEDGWOOD, DAME (CICELY) VERONICA (July 20, 1910–), English historian and biographer, writes: "My full names are Cicely Veronica but my first publisher reduced them to initials on the grounds that no serious historian could afford to be so flowery. My family have made china for generations but my father, Ralph Wedgwood, was a younger son and went into railways instead, ending a distinguished career as Chairman of the British Railways during the Second World War. My mother, Iris Pawson, came from Yorkshire where they are famous for will-power, and *her* father, a benevolent but formidable patriarch, was the principal influence on my childhood. He was immensely well-read and had travelled widely. I was quite shamelessly the favourite grand-child and acquired a considerable miscellaneous education simply from listening to him.

"Owing to my father's railway connection we travelled a lot and had adventurous holidays at the end of remote branch-lines in places like Hungary and Finland. My brother and I regarded trains as our natural home and I still find it easier to write in a train than anywhere else. When I wasn't in a train I was at a London day school. I read a fair amount, mostly poetry, wrote more than my parents thought good for me and never passed a museum without going into it. When I was about twelve my father suggested I should write history. This was an ingenious manœuvre to make me read more and write less, because you have to study history before you can write it. But it turned out to be decisive for the rest of my career.

"After learning German in Bonn and being 'finished' in Paris I went to Oxford (Lady Margaret Hall) in 1928 and left it three years later a convert to the austere academic view that any attempt to blend history with literature is fatal to historical scholarship. By 1935 when I published my first book I had been talked round by the example and influence of G. M. Trevelyan (my father's life-long friend) and A. L. Rowse who gave me much advice and encouragement in these rather difficult years.

"Since that time I have tried to combine the fruits of research with the practice of literature, though I am still intermittently troubled about the balance between the two and have tried to resolve my doubts in a number of essays and lectures some of which were reprinted in *Truth and Opinion* (1960). My first book (1935) was treated more kindly than it deserved at the time and was subsequently shown to be wrong on many points, owing to the publication of documents not available when I wrote it. This is the kind of thing the historian must be prepared for. . . . My second book *The Thirty Years War* (1938) was better; it is still quite useful to students of that squalid struggle. Since the end of the Second World

War I have been mainly concerned with English history of the seventeenth century.

"Apart from historical research, I have worked in a publisher's office, as a translator from the German, as literary editor of a weekly newspaper, as a broadcaster, and as a reviewer for American and British papers. Since 1953 I have been a member of the Institute for Advanced Study at Princeton and since 1962 I have been on the staff of University College London. I have also edited an anthology of new poetry for the English P.E.N. centre of which I was President from 1951 to 1957.

"I dislike all sports except swimming and walking. My favourite places in the world are Rome and the Central Highlands of Scotland. Outside history my interests are poetry, pictures and the drama. I live mostly in London, travel as much as I can and go to the theatre and opera more often than is good for my work."

C. V. Wedgwood was born in Stocksfield, Northumberland. Her father, Sir Ralph Wedgwood, was a lineal descendant of Josiah Wedgwood, who was the most famous of English potters and the subject of one of C. V. Wedgwood's biographies. Her mother was the author of several books on history and topography. C. V. Wedgwood wrote a play when she was nine and had produced three novels by the time she abandoned fiction for history at the age of twelve.

She is a controversial historian, for reasons that she touches on above and has discussed at greater length in her book *Truth and Opinion*, and in an interview with Ved Mehta (*Fly and the Fly Bottle*). Like her mentors G. M. Trevelyan and A. L. Rowse she is a narrative historian of the old school, interested in "*how* things happened," rather than in why they did. It is this that so upsets the analysts and interpreters among her colleagues.

In fact she is well aware that "*Why* [is] a more important question than *How*," but maintains that the former cannot be answered until the latter is established, and that for this purpose "narrative history must be written with depth and reflection, thought through stage by stage, and recorded comprehensively and with unremitting attention to chronology." She might add, as Ved Mehta has, that in any case "her natural gifts are unanalytical and literary." Since she has no choice but to write narrative history, the only useful question is how well she does it, and here the answer is clear: she is a fine scholar, a perfect storyteller, and an absolute master of English prose.

Her field is the seventeenth century. She relies almost entirely on primary sources and likes to see at first hand the terrain she is to describe, visualizing what took place there. This she did in preparation

C. V. WEDGWOOD

for her first important work, *The Thirty Years War*, published when she was twenty-eight. It was welcomed as a model of scholarship, the product of wide and thoughtful reading in all the relevant languages, written with great objectivity, clarity, and vividness—the first satisfactory book on its subject.

William the Silent, the most admired of C. V. Wedgwood's biographies, appeared in 1944. It brought her the James Tait Black Memorial Prize and has been widely translated. There was some feeling that her treatment of Philip II of Spain in this book was unfair and superficial, but there was nothing but praise for her portrait of William, for the color and action in her narrative, for "an English style that is crystal clear and a scholarship beyond reproach." She has also written excellent lives of Cromwell and Montrose. Thomas Wentworth, first Earl of Strafford, was the subject of her first book, which was revised in 1961 and called a "profound and subtle" study of a brilliant, unpleasant, and tragic figure.

A number of C. V. Wedgwood's major works center upon Charles I. In the two volumes of *The Great Rebellion* she set out, she said, not "to examine underlying causes, but rather to give full importance and value to the admitted motives and the illusions of the men of the seventeenth century. I have sought to restore their immediacy of experience." There is no doubt that she succeeds. She gives the end of the story in *The Trial of Charles I.* The historian J. H. Plumb said this was a brilliant book: "Her scholarship is comprehensive, her narrative is crisp, her style elegant and her insight into men and events profound. This is the finest account of the trial that has ever been written."

C. V. Wedgwood's other books include two volumes of essays, *Velvet Studies* and *Truth and Opinion*, the former containing some autobiographical reminiscences. She explores the literature of her period in *Seventeenth Century English Literature* and *Poetry and Politics Under the Stuarts*. Lawrence Stone has called her "by far the best narrative historian writing in the English language. She is a superb stylist . . . and she has an unrivalled capacity for catching the signs and sounds and smells of the past."

Unlike most of her colleagues, C. V. Wedgwood is not a don and says she "really can't teach," though she was a Special Lecturer at University College, London from 1962 to 1970. She depends for her income on her books, on her talks and other work for the British Broadcasting Corporation, and on reviewing and translating. For some years she was literary editor of *Time and Tide*, and she serves or has served as a trustee of the National Gallery, on the Royal Commission on Historical Monuments, on the Advisory Council of the Victoria and Albert Museum, and on the Arts Council. She was a member of the Institute of Advanced Study, Princeton, from 1953 to 1965. She was president of the English Association in 1955–1956, and became president of the Society of Authors in 1972. C. V. Wedgwood holds the Goethe Medal (1958) and a number of honorary degrees—from Oxford, Harvard, and Smith College among other institutions. In 1956 she received a CBE and in 1968 was named a Dame Commander of the Order of the British Empire. An even greater and rarer distinction followed in 1969, when she became one of the twenty-four members of the Order of Merit.

PRINCIPAL WORKS: Strafford, 1593–1641, 1935 (rev. as Thomas Wentworth, First Earl of Strafford, 1593–1641, a Revaluation, 1961); The Thirty Years War, 1938; Oliver Cromwell, 1939; William the Silent: William of Nassau, Prince of Orange, 1533–84, 1944; Velvet Studies, 1946; Richelieu and the French Monarchy, 1949; Seventeenth Century English Literature, 1950; The Last of the Radicals: Josiah Wedgwood, 1951; Montrose, 1952; The Great Rebellion: vol. 1, The King's Peace, 1637–41, 1955; vol. 2, The King's War, 1641–47, 1958; Poetry and Politics Under the Stuarts, 1960; Truth and Opinion: Historical Essays, 1960; The Trial of Charles I (U.S., A Coffin for King Charles: The Trial and Execution of Charles I) 1964; (ed.) New Poems, 1965: A P.E.N. Anthology of Contemporary Poetry, 1966; (with the editors of Time-Life Books) The World of Rubens, 1577–1640, 1967; Milton and His World (for children), 1969. *As translator*—Brandi, K. Emperor Charles V, 1939; Canetti, E. Auto-da-fé, 1946 (U.S., Tower of Babel).

ABOUT: Current Biography, 1957; Mehta, V. Fly and the Fly Bottle, 1963; Wedgwood, C. V. Velvet Studies, 1946; Who's Who, 1973. *Periodicals*—Book Week September 20, 1964; Contemporary Review August 1960, April 1962; History and Theory 1 1961; New Statesman January 29, 1955; New York Review of Books September 10, 1964; New Yorker December 15, 1962; Times Literary Supplement October 6, 1950; January 7, 1955; November 28, 1958; August 27, 1964.

WEINBAUM, STANLEY G(RAUMAN) (1902–December 14, 1935), has been ranked with Robert A. Heinlein as one of the two writers of science fiction "whose work most deserves to be considered as literature." He spent his short life in Milwaukee, Wisconsin. Weinbaum had a degree in chemical engineering but left that field in his early twenties to write fiction. He turned out a number of stories and novels on a variety of themes, including two science fiction tales which remained unpublished until after his death. More successful was a romantic novel called "The Lady Dances," syndicated as a serial by King Features in the early 1930s under the pen name "Marge Stanley," a combination of his wife's name and his own. He also wrote an operetta, "Omar the Tent Maker," with music by his sister; it has never been published or produced.

Early drawn to the work of such fantasists as Wells, Verne, Conan Doyle, and Edgar Rice Burroughs, Weinbaum had become addicted to science fiction with the first issue of *Amazing Stories* in 1926. His own first publication in the field was "A Martian Odyssey," which appeared in *Wonder Stories* for July 1934 and produced the most enthusiastic public response in the magazine's five-year history.

"A Martian Odyssey" set the pattern for most of Weinbaum's best-known stories, "almost plotless travelogues" which usually involve perilous journeys across planets inhabited by such extraordinary life forms as the silicon monster who eats sand and excretes bricks, ice ants, whiplash trees, and carnivorous plants who lure their prey by conjuring up wish-fulfillment images. Weinbaum's best-known invention is the "curiously sympathetic" ostrich-like Martian creature the "twe-er-r-rl," who appears in a number of his stories and has been called one of science fiction's "truly great characters." Sam Moskowitz believes it "was Weinbaum's creative brilliance in making strange creatures seem as real as the characters in *David Copperfield* that impressed readers most."

Some of his stories include a romantic element, an innovation in the science fiction of the period, and a number, notably "The Lotus Eaters," are works of philosophical speculation well disguised as entertainments. Weinbaum also wrote a number of stories in collaboration with "Ralph Milne Farley," who was actually Roger Sherman Hoar, a former United States Senator from Wisconsin. Of the stories he published under the pseudonym "John Jessel" (his grandfather's name) the best and best-known is "The Adaptive Ultimate," a study in fear and jealousy involving a homely and tuber-

STANLEY WEINBAUM

cular girl who is briefly gifted with total adaptability to environmental change.

All of Weinbaum's best work, whatever his theme, is distinguished by the excellence of its characterization, its humor and ingenuity, and its stylistic polish. H. P. Lovecraft wrote: "Somehow he had the imagination to envisage wholly alien situations and psychologies and entities, to devise consistent events from wholly alien motives and to refrain from the cheap dramatics in which almost all adventure-pulpists wallow. Now and then a touch of the *seemingly* trite would appear—but before long it would be obvious that the author had introduced it merely to satirize it."

Seventeen months after his first science fiction story appeared, Weinbaum died of throat cancer. A memorial volume assembled by fellow writers in Milwaukee appeared in 1936 as *The Dawn of Flame*, and other collections in book form followed. His small output, some of it posthumous, has influenced dozens of other science fiction writers, notably Eric Frank Russell, Henry Kuttner, and Philip José Farmer. "The Adaptive Ultimate," one of the most anthologized of his stories, has been repeatedly adapted for radio and television and provided the basis for the film *She-Devil*. Sam Moskowitz says that Weinbaum was "modest and unaffected, with an outgoing friendliness and a genuine interest in people."

PRINCIPAL WORKS: The Dawn of Flame, and Other Stories, 1936; The New Adam, 1939; The Black Flame, 1948; A Martian Odyssey, and Others, 1949; The Dark Other, 1950; The Red Peri, 1952.

ABOUT: Moskowitz, S. Explorers of the Infinite, 1963; Moskowitz, S. Seekers of Tomorrow, 1965.

***WEISS, PETER (ULRICH)** (November 8, 1916–), German-born dramatist and novelist, was born in Nowawes, near Berlin, the son of Eugene and Frieda (Hummel) Weiss. His father, a prosperous textile manufacturer, was a Lutheran convert of Jewish birth; his mother, who was Swiss, had been an actress. In his autobiographical novels Weiss has described the emotional tensions produced by the presence in his home of his mother's children by an earlier marriage.

After 1933 these tensions were exacerbated by the racial doctrines of National Socialism. In 1934, when Weiss was eighteen, he and his family emigrated to Britain, an escape which left him with a permanent sense of guilt. After two years in England, Weiss went to Czechoslovakia, his father's native country, where he studied painting in Prague. In 1938 he was obliged to move on again, this time to Switzerland, and in 1939 he joined his family in Sweden, where his father had acquired a textile plant near Gothenberg. Weiss left his "terribly bourgeois" home and went to Stockholm, where he found his friends in avant-garde artistic circles. He became a Swedish subject, learned Swedish, and still lives in Stockholm. He has friends in Germany, and visits there, but says, "It's not my country, and Sweden is not my country just as any other country is not my country."

Weiss turned late to literature, when he had already made a reputation during the 1940s and 1950s as a painter and as a creator of experimental and documentary films. Six early works written in Swedish and privately published have not so far been reprinted. When Weiss decided to write in German he had to master the language afresh, and did so in a number of prose works which have considerably influenced younger German writers. The first of these was *Der Schatten des Körpers des Kutschers* (1960, translated by E. B. Garside and Rosemarie Waldrop, and later by S. M. Cupitt, as *The Shadow of the Coachman's Body*), which was illustrated with Weiss's own "ingenious and sinister" collages. It is a deliberately static and grotesquely objective account of more or less trivial events in a boarding house, narrated with insane attention to detail by a young man who is trying to turn the act of seeing into an occupation.

The autobiographical narrative *Abschied von den Eltern* (1961, translated by Christopher Levenson as *Leavetaking*) is as breathlessly intense as the first book was expressionless, but no less powerful and well-sustained. It was continued in *Fluchtpunkt* (1962, translated by Levenson as *Vanishing Point*), which brought Weiss the Charles Veillon prize for literature. (The two books were later published in a different translation by Levenson, E. B. Garside,

* vīs

PETER WEISS

and Alastair Hamilton as *Exile.*) The emotional cannibalism of family life is also the theme of Weiss's early radio play *Der Turm* (written in 1948, broadcast in 1962, translated as *The Tower*), a rather strident allegory with a circus setting. *Das Gespräch der drei Gehenden* (1963, translated by Garside and Waldrop as *Conversation of the Three Wayfarers* and by Cupitt as *Conversation of the Three Walkers*) records what is said during an aimless walk by three characters (or three aspects of a single character) who interpret and arrange each other's comments in their own terms. This "three-sided" monologue impressed a critic in the *Times Literary Supplement* as the most original and remarkable of Weiss's prose works (but D. J. Enright, reviewing the translated version some years later, thought it "further testimony to the waning role of good sense in our time").

Weiss's sense of himself as an exile pervades these books. So does an even more deeply felt obsession with family life, and the need to escape its tensions and constrictions. Some critics regret that he has turned away from this theme in his plays, and believe that as a dramatist he has yet to equal the achievement of his first prose works. But Weiss is a Socialist and believes that "as long as we are not involved with the great social conflicts of the world, our work stands just isolated and fruitless." And in fact it was when he put aside his quarrel with his family and himself, and took up his quarrel with institutions and ideologies, that he achieved international recognition.

The first of his plays to be staged made no great stir. This was *Nacht mit Gästen* (Night With Guests, 1963), a ballad play in nursery-rhyme doggerel which is an allegory about greed. It was followed by *Die Verfolgung und Ermordung Jean-Paul Marats dargestellt durch die Schauspielgruppe des Hospizes zu Charenton unter Anleitung des Herrn de Sade*, translated by Geoffrey Skelton, in a verse adaptation by Adrian Mitchell, as *The Persecution and Assassination of Jean-Paul Marat as Performed by the Inmates of the Asylum of Charenton Under the Direction of the Marquis de Sade.* It had an enthusiastic reception at the Schiller Theatre in West Berlin in April 1964.

Marat/Sade is essentially an argument between aristocratic individualism and revolutionary idealism. What is remarkable about this fair-minded, subtle, but rather static discussion is its setting in the asylum where Sade did in fact devise plays for his fellow inmates. On this occasion they perform for a distinguished audience which includes the asylum's director and his bourgeois family (and also, of course, the "real" audience in the theatre auditorium—visitors from the larger madhouse outside). The wonderfully rich theatrical possibilities provided by this inspiration have been resourcefully exploited in numerous productions in Europe and elsewhere. Peter Brook's 1965 production in English was a major success both in London and in New York (where it received the Critics' Circle Award), and has been filmed.

Reviewers at the time admired Brook's production less for its ideological content than as a brilliant piece of director's theatre, and audiences tended to sympathize more with Brook's "existentialist" Sade than with his dangerous dreamer Marat, though Weiss has made it clear that his own sympathies are with the latter. Since then Weiss's text has received more serious critical attention and has been praised as an astonishingly successful attempt to combine the resources of Brecht's theatre of alienation (the songs, jingles, announcements, and other devices reminding the audience that they are watching a play) with the terrifying mimes and rituals, the visual and aural excesses, of Artaud's theatre of cruelty. Susan Sontag has defended Weiss's use of "ideas as sensory stimulants," and has described the play as "one of the great experiences of anyone's theatre-going lifetime."

Marat/Sade ends with the cry: "When will you learn to see, when will you learn to take sides?" and Weiss's subsequent plays have all asked or implied the same questions. *Die Ermittlung* (1965, translated as *The Investigation*) consists of selections from the verbatim records of the trial in 1964–1965 of Auschwitz officials accused of the systematic torture and murder of four million people. This work is in the tradition of the didactic theatre advocated by Erwin Piscator in the 1920s and revived in such pieces as Rolf Hochhuth's *Der Stellvertreter* (1963). *Die Ermittlung* was given a number of simultaneous readings in West and East

Germany in 1965, and in the West encountered great hostility, partly because of Weiss's stated (if qualified) preference for East Germany, partly because many critics thought it added no new dimension, moral or artistic, to the vile horrors it recorded. Piscator defended the "oratorio" (as Weiss calls it), arguing that the trial was a valid subject for the theatre (as Auschwitz itself was not). *The Investigation* was read in England in 1965 and in New York in 1966; one British critic concluded that it was not a good play, but "would be an obscenity if it was."

Gesang vom Lusitanischen Popanz (translated by Lee Baxandall as *The Song of the Lusitanian Bogey*) opened in Stockholm in January 1967 and reached New York a year later, in a performance by the Negro Ensemble. It is a "political musical," employing rhymed verse, discordant melodies, and ritualistic dancing, about the brutal suppression of the Angolan revolutionary movement by the Portuguese. Weiss, wrote Irving Wardle, "invents nothing and he delivers the deadliest part of his anticolonial indictment simply by aligning facts about forced labor and starvation wages with the names of the international companies with a stake in Angola." It was followed by a similar treatment of the long, tormented history of Vietnam, *Viet Nam Diskurs*, which has been translated by Geoffrey Skelton as *Discourse on the Progress of the Prolonged War of Liberation in Viet Nam and the Events Leading up to It as Illustration of the Necessity for Armed Resistance Against Oppression and on the Attempts of the U.S.A. to Destroy the Foundations of Revolution.* For the benefit of those who complain that these works resemble illustrated lectures more than plays, Weiss has explained that they are not intended for the commercial theatre, but primarily for performance in factories, schools, sports arenas, and meeting halls.

Weiss turned from the impersonal didacticism of these plays to two biographical dramas. *Trotzki im Exile* (translated by Geoffrey Skelton as *Trotsky in Exile*) is a somewhat stylized historical collage dealing with the clash of ideas among Trotsky, Lenin, and Stalin. It was written as a "contribution to the Lenin Year" of 1970 but not surprisingly was more warmly received in the West than in the Soviet Union. *Hölderlin* (1971) presents the great Swabian poet, whose early visionary idealism gave way to disappointment and madness, as one of the shapers of the modern revolutionary consciousness.

Weiss was married in 1964 to the Swedish designer and ceramist Gunilla Palmstierna. He has been deeply influenced by Kafka as well as by Brecht, and has translated Strindberg. He said in 1966: "I think audiences are ready to become concerned with the real world rather than with the private loves and hates of individuals. I want to activate them, to force them to choose positions."

PRINCIPAL WORKS IN ENGLISH TRANSLATION: *Plays*—The Persecution and Assassination of Jean-Paul Marat as Performed by the Inmates of the Asylum of Charenton Under the Direction of the Marquis de Sade, 1965; The Investigation, tr. by John Swan and Ulu Grosbard, 1966 (England, tr. by Alexander Gross); Two Plays (The Song of the Lusitanian Bogey *and* Discourse on . . . Viet Nam), 1970; Trotsky in Exile, 1972; The Tower *in* Quarterly Review of Literature 4 1968. *Fiction*—Leavetaking, 1962; Leavetaking *and* Vanishing Point, 1966 (*also published in a different tr. as* Exile, 1968); Bodies and Shadows (The Shadow of the Coachman's Body *and* Conversation of the Three Wayfarers), 1970 (*also published in a different tr. as* The Conversation of the Three Walkers *and* The Shadow of the Coachman's Body, 1972). *Nonfiction*—Notes on the Cultural Life of the Democratic Republic of Vietnam, 1970.

ABOUT: Brustein, R. S. The Third Theater, 1969; Clurman, H. The Naked Image, 1966; Current Biography, 1968; Esslin, M. Reflections, 1969; Gassner, J. Dramatic Soundings, 1968; Gilman, R. Common and Uncommon Masks, 1971; Hamburger, M. From Prophecy to Exorcism, 1965; Hampshire, S. Modern Writers, 1969; Hilton, I. Peter Weiss, 1970; Sheed, W. The Morning After, 1971; Simon, J. Movies into Film, 1971; Sontag, S. Against Interpretation, 1966; Wager, W. (ed.) The Playwrights Speak, 1967; Wer ist Wer, 1971–73; Who's Who, 1973; Who's Who in America, 1972–1973. *Periodicals*—Atlas April 1967, November 1967; Books Abroad Summer 1969; Contemporary Literature Winter 1968; Drama Summer 1971; Drama Survey Fall 1967; German Life and Letters October 1966; Life October 28, 1966; Modern Drama December 1970, May 1971; Modern Language Notes April 1971; Modern Language Review April 1968, October 1969; Nation February 21, 1966; New Left Review January–February 1968; New Republic February 8, 1968; July 6, 1968; New York Times Magazine September 1, 1966; October 2, 1966; Partisan Review Spring 1965; Saturday Review June 29, 1968; Theater Quarterly October–December 1971; Time July 5, 1968; Times Literary Supplement February 10, 1966; September 28, 1967; April 14, 1972; Tulane Drama Review Fall 1966; Vogue November 15, 1966.

WEISS, THEODORE (RUSSELL) (December 16, 1916–), American poet, critic, and editor, writes: "I was born in Reading, Pennsylvania, of an Hungarian father and an American mother. I never knew anything of my father's parents; my mother's amounted to second parents. All I remember of Reading, for we left it when I was one, is living near a fish-market and troop trains passing. Both 'memories' may have been told me later. We traveled widely and wildly in Pennsylvania, about a year going into each little town my father sought out as the likely new Eden; Allentown, however, was always magnetic center. Trying one business after another, my father finally settled on buying and selling at large—anything and everything. His restlessness seemed to find peace in animals; even in crowded towns he managed to keep some. In the back of a shoe store on Allentown's main street he bred a wallful of canaries or for hours pondered pigeons and pheasants in a barn behind his five-and-ten. Gentle as he was with these, also a man of feasts, he stuffed geese and supervised the rich recipes he taught my mother.

THEODORE WEISS

"For all our moving I have only a blurred notion of my childhood and its education. College was little better: underground years at Muhlenberg. But they were passionately studious, mostly, it now seems, submerged in Greek and gluttony for books, shared by my father who was furiously proud of my scholastic achievements. He was soon shocked awake when he learned I was for teaching, not law or medicine. Yet against his judgment he did what he could to help me. I went to Columbia, an almost stunning change from Allentown. After some fumbling in college, where I already knew I must write and, not sure what, had dabbled in the prose-poem *à la* Baudelaire and Pater, poetry now began for me with a vengeance. Turmoiled in the loneliness of New York and love for the girl back home, Renée Karol, a violinist and later a children's book writer, I lived mainly on letters, our daily ones, and my scribbling. When I was not at paper I seemed to disappear. One teacher, Mark Van Doren, by his sanity, perfect against my chaos, his unshakable devotion to great human matters embodied in literature, helped to anchor me. Important also was meeting David Schubert and his wife. A few years older, as a poet he was light years ahead. Knowing them sealed my interest in poetry. His sudden death some years later added new responsibility to my sense of vocation.

"After earning a master's degree, marrying, and studying for a year, I began teaching in the summer at the University of Maryland. Fall took us to the University of North Carolina. Here we met Warren Carrier who started the *Quarterly Review of Literature*. He asked me to join him. I was interested in appearing in, not editing, magazines, but I agreed to assist him. Shortly after when he left for the War my wife and I found ourselves total editors, something we have been now for nearly a quarter century. The magazine has been a steady, often delightful, often vexatious occupation. We came to know Stevens, Williams, Cummings and younger writers, since emerged as among our ablest. Meantime, I did what I could to keep my own writing and fulltime teaching going. After three years at North Carolina we moved to Yale. Through some of my colleagues my ties with Yale continue; I am a fellow of Ezra Stiles College. My writing by this time had begun to take shape. At John Ciardi's invitation I published my first book, *The Catch*. Though it is mainly lyrical, already my desire for larger, less confining work expressed itself in the long poem 'Shades of Caesar.' After three years at Yale, Bard College for its unusual program, its hospitality to the arts, and the beauty of its location by the Hudson appealed to me. With the exception of a teaching term at MIT, a Ford Fellowship (spent chiefly in England near Oxford), and a sabbatical in Europe, with several Russian weeks its most memorable occasion, we have been at Bard since.

"My writing has continued to be lyrical with sorties on the narrative and dramatic. For the present time's engrossment in the fragmentary and the personal I am drawn to dramatic poetry more than ever. My second volume, *Outlanders*, contains several semidramatic poems and a dramatic monologue. The third, *Gunsight*, some fifteen years making, was my first submission to print of one long poem, the only one of many I felt satisfied enough with to see through. Dramatic narrative though it is, it proceeds by devices modern poetry has developed. My recent book, *The Medium*, is a collection, again lyrical with dramatic interludes.

"Meanwhile, out of years teaching Shakespeare's plays, I am embarked on a book that tries to trace his growth, his problems and the solutions he found, as poet and playwright. Delivering lectures on him at the New York YMHA in 1965 and 1966 has sped the book's development. My latest employment, strenuous but enjoyable, is membership in the Poetry Board of the Wesleyan University Press."

Theodore Weiss is the son of Nathan and Mollie (Weinberg) Weiss. He married Renée Karol in 1941 and has been coeditor with her of the *Quarterly Review of Literature* since 1943. He went to Bard College in 1946, becoming a full professor there in 1955. In 1966–1967 he was at Princeton University as a resident fellow in creative writing and in 1968 he joined the Princeton faculty as professor of creative arts. He received the Wallace Stevens Award in 1956 and a grant from the National Foundation of Arts and Humanities in 1967–1968.

Weiss's first book, *The Catch*, attracted attention immediately, said one critic, because of the poet's technical equipment and in particular his striking handling of cadences. R. L. Lowe found evidence that Weiss had studied and learned from Hopkins and Stevens, Auden, Pound, and Eliot, while John Holmes praised "a leaping profusion of imagery and wording, a rich feeling for life."

The individual voice which some critics thought still unformed in *The Catch* emerged clearly in *Outlanders*. James Dickey said that these poems "never seem to be the products of anything but a knowable and very human mind. The mind is an exceedingly complex one which operates by building small, deeply observed details . . . into difficult and rewarding structures: poems which never give all they have to give on any one reading but withhold, always retaining something essential of themselves, something to bring the reader back and reward him again." X. J. Kennedy, similarly, relished the "rich and twisty" arguments developed by a mind that "seems to think by accretion." He noted that Weiss had edited a selection from Hopkins's notebooks, and suggested that Hopkins had inspired Weiss's fondness for condensations and coinings, some of them admirably ingenious, some of them merely difficult.

R. W. Flint found the same kind of ingenuity and "intricate circularity" in *Gunsight* and called it "the best long American poem since *Paterson*." Its central figure is a soldier wounded in World War II who is undergoing a major operation and who "becomes the theater to a flock of memories, each clamoring for his attention which has till now been denied." In this "long, beautifully joined narrative," wrote Richard Howard, "the sequence of images coincides and concentrates into one intense impression of ultimate outrage and endurance. . . . [Weiss's] lines are often harsh and yield few easy pleasures along the way. But their massive effect is one of high emotion and great exactitude." The experiments with syntactical patterns which distinguish the lyrics collected in *The Medium* were thought interesting and ambitious, but not wholly successful. Many readers welcomed the simpler and freer short poems included, along with some notable longer pieces, in *The Last Day and the First*.

M. L. Rosenthal believes Weiss to be the possessor of "a truly poetic mind . . . that seems to take naturally to a plastic sense of language and rhythm and even thought as materials for design." Weiss himself says that his concern is with "the sustained poem as against the prevailing scrappiness, coterie emphasis and coterie language, mainly personal utterance." *The Breath of Clowns and Kings* was admired as "an attractive and perceptive study of the early Shakespeare," approached in terms of its subject's developing attitude to poetic and theatrical artifice.

PRINCIPAL WORKS: (ed.) Selections From the Notebooks of G. M. Hopkins, 1945; The Catch, 1951; Outlanders, 1960; Gunsight, 1962; The Medium, 1965; The Last Day and the First, 1968; The World Before Us; Poems, 1950–1970, 1970; The Breath of Clowns and Kings: Shakespeare's Early Comedies and Histories, 1971.

ABOUT: Contemporary Authors 9–10, 1964; Howard, R. Alone with America, 1969; Leary, P. and Kelly, R. A Controversy of Poets, 1965; Murphy, R. (ed.) Contemporary Poets of the English Language, 1970; Nemerov, H. (ed.) Poets on Poetry, 1966; Rosenthal, M. L. The New Poets, 1967; Who's Who in America, 1972–1973. *Periodicals*—The Fat Abbot Summer–Fall 1961; New Republic November 16, 1963; Poetry May 1961, July 1963; Sewanee Review Spring 1961.

WELCH, (MAURICE) DENTON (March 29, 1915–December 30, 1948), English novelist, memoirist, and short story writer, was born in Shanghai, the youngest of three brothers. His father was a prosperous English merchant; his mother a Bostonian Christian Scientist who died when Welch was eleven. An aesthetic misfit in his bourgeois home, he was even more miserable at Repton, the hearty English public school to which he was consigned for his education. He ran away at sixteen and studied art for four years at Goldsmiths' College, London. In June 1935, when he was twenty, an automobile knocked him off his bicycle. He received spinal and other injuries from which he died thirteen years later.

Those years were neither wasted nor entirely unhappy. After his release from the hospital, Welch settled successively in various parts of Kent with his housekeeper Miss Evelyn Sinclair and, later, his devoted companion Eric Oliver. Welch surrounded himself with friends in whose company he ignored his implacable illness and was lighthearted. He assiduously collected antiques, made his sometimes sinister paintings, and wrote poems and articles. In 1943 he published the first of three autobiographical novels, *Maiden Voyage*, based on his last term at Repton and his subsequent visit to China. Edith Sitwell wrote in her foreword to the book that he seemed to be "that very rare being, a born writer."

In Youth Is Pleasure followed, another fragment of fictionalized autobiography remarkable, as Walter Allen has said, for the innocence "with which the central character, a boy who is plainly Welch himself, explores and translates into action a world of homosexual transvestist fantasy." A volume of short stories, *Brave and Cruel*, was published in 1948 and *A Voice Through a Cloud*, generally regarded as Welch's best novel, appeared posthumously in 1950. Told like *Maiden Voyage* in the first person, it was an account of the accident and its aftermath in the hospital. Welch had written it in great pain, a few words at a time during his last illness. It was not quite finished when he died on

DENTON WELCH

the afternoon of December 30, 1948. *A Last Sheaf*, containing stories, sketches, and poems, was published in 1951. The *Journals*, covering the period from July 1942 to August 1948, when they break off in mid-sentence, appeared in 1952. In 1963, as evidence of the continuing interest in his work, came Jocelyn Brooke's selection from Welch's published writings.

Denton Welch was a scrupulous writer who revised and rewrote endlessly to achieve his apparently rapid and easy style. In his novels, as Walter Allen has said, with their "astonishingly pure response to the sensual surface of things . . . nothing seems to come between the perception and its expression." People he described with an insight which was sometimes malicious, and beneath the pervasive tone of boyish gaiety can be felt occasionally a shocked acknowledgment of evil, an awareness of the dark.

Maurice Cranston has described Welch as "curiously ageless." "He was at once a boy and an old, old man. He was good looking. He had a tall, fine forehead, close fair curls, a wilful mouth and shy, bright eyes." It has been suggested that Welch, had he been allowed a world larger than his prettily furnished sick-room, might have been a great writer. As it is, his work is an area of order rescued with immense courage and discipline from chaos, a perfect small monument.

PRINCIPAL WORKS: Maiden Voyage, 1943; In Youth Is Pleasure, 1944; Brave and Cruel, 1948; A Voice Through a Cloud, 1950; A Last Sheaf, 1951; Journals, 1952; Denton Welch: Extracts from His Published Works, 1963.
ABOUT: Allen, W. Tradition and Dream, 1964; Brooke, J. *introduction to* Welch's Journals, 1952; Brooke, J. *introduction to* Denton Welch: Extracts from His Published Works, 1963; Connolly, C. Previous Convictions, 1964; Grigson, G. (ed.) Concise Encyclopedia of Modern World Literature, 1963. *Periodicals*—Contemporary Review December 1964; New Statesman May 17, 1963; Nineteenth Century and After October 1950; Spectator May 31, 1963.

WELLEK, RENÉ (August 22, 1903–), American literary critic and historian, writes: "I was born at Vienna, Austria. Neither of my parents was Austrian. My father, Bronislav Wellek (1872–1959), then a lawyer in government service, was born in Prague and was consciously Czech. He had written a life of Bedřich Smetana, the Czech composer, and translated Czech poetry into German. My mother, née Gabriele von Zelewsky (1881–1950), was born in Rome. Her father was a West Prussian nobleman (ultimately of Polish origin); her mother was Swiss from Schaffhausen and the Protestantism of my grandmother prevailed in our family. In 1918 with the collapse of the Empire we moved to Prague and I identified myself strongly with the new Czechoslovakia. I studied English, German and comparative literature at the Czech University from 1922–1926, with some brilliant teachers: particularly Vilém Mathesius, professor of English, the founder of the Prague Linguistic Circle, and Otokar Fischer, professor of German literature who had written well on Kleist, Nietzsche, and Heine. In June 1926 I received a Ph.D.; my thesis was 'Thomas Carlyle and Romanticism.' I had visited England in 1924, 1925 and in 1927 on my own in order to learn the language and to study in the British Museum and in September 1927 I came to Princeton Graduate School as Proctor Fellow of English. I spent a busy year attending the seminars of Thomas M. Parrott, Robert K. Root, Charles G. Osgood and Morris W. Croll. As there was no immediate opening at the University of Prague (where I wanted to become Professor of English Literature), I stayed on in this country: in 1928–1929 as instructor of German at Smith College and in 1929–1930 in the same function at Princeton University.

"I returned to Prague in 1930, after another stay in London, with the manuscript of a book *Immanuel Kant in England* which the Princeton University Press published in 1931. It served as a second thesis, *Habilitation*, which allowed me to become a *Docent* of the History of English Literature at my alma mater in 1932. That year I married Olga Brodská. During these years I joined the Prague Linguistic Circle and did translations from English (Conrad, D. H. Lawrence) and wrote many essays, articles, and reviews for Czech periodicals, largely on topics of English literature. In 1935 I accepted an offer to become Lecturer in Czech Language and Literature at the School of Slavonic Studies of the University of London and there I experienced Munich and the occupation of Prague by Hitler. I could not think of returning to Prague or staying in post-Munich appeasement England. In June 1939 I emigrated to this country for good.

"I had found a position, first as a lecturer, in the English department of the University of Iowa where Norman Foerster was the Director of the School of Letters. I spent the war years there with stimulating colleagues such as Austin Warren, with whom I eventually collaborated on a book, *Theory of Literature* (1949). From London I had brought the manuscript of *The Rise of English Literary History*, a history of English literary historiography to the end of the eighteenth century, which was published by the University of North Carolina Press in 1941. I was naturalized in May 1946. I was promoted to an associate professor in 1941 and to a full professor of English in 1944.

"In the summer of 1946 I moved to Yale, first as professor of Slavic and comparative literature. In 1952 I was named Sterling Professor of Comparative Literature, a position I hold today. From 1947 to 1959 I served as chairman of the Slavic department and since 1960 as chairman of the newly independent department of comparative literature. But I have directed the graduate program in comparative literature since 1947 which since its inception has produced some forty-five Ph.D.'s. My book *Theory of Literature* (written with Austin Warren, Harcourt Brace, New York, 1949) has made a wide impact, also in paperback editions. It has been translated into Spanish, Italian, Japanese, German, Korean, Portuguese, Danish and Serbo-Croat. Since then my main energies have gone into the writing of a large-scale *History of Modern Criticism 1750–1950*, of which four volumes were published by the Yale University Press (1750–1830 in 1955, 1830–1900 in 1965). A volume or two on the twentieth century are to follow. The books survey English, French, German, Italian, Russian and American developments in criticism. I also collected many scattered papers: *Concepts of Criticism* (1963), *Essays in Czech Literature* (1963), and *Confrontations: Studies in the Intellectual and Literary Relations Between Germany, England and the United States During the Nineteenth Century* (1965). The *History*, or rather its first two volumes, have been translated into Italian, Spanish, and German; *Concepts of Criticism* and *Confrontations* into German.

"I taught as visiting professor at Harvard in 1950 and in 1953–1954. I conducted a Gauss seminar in literary criticism at Princeton in 1950. I taught summer school at Minnesota (1947), at Columbia (1948), at the Kenyon School of Criticism (1949), at the University of Hawaii (1961), and at the University of California at Berkeley (1963). I was a Fulbright research professor at the universities of Florence and Rome in 1959–1960.

RENÉ WELLEK

"I have done much editorial work: as member of the editorial boards of *Comparative Literature*, *Philological Quarterly*, *Publications of the Modern Language Association*, *Studies in English Literature*, the *Slavic Review*; and I have taken part in the organizational life of the profession. I was president of the International Comparative Literature Association (1962–1965) and have held several functions in the Modern Language Association (I was Vice-President in 1964). I have been president of the Czechoslovak Society of Arts and Sciences in America since 1962.

"I received Guggenheim Fellowships in 1951, 1957 and 1966. In 1959 I received the American Council of Learned Societies Prize for Distinguished Scholarship in the Humanities. In 1958 I received an honorary D.L.H. from Lawrence College, Appleton, Wisconsin and in 1960 honorary D. Litt.'s from Oxford and Harvard University and the same degree in 1961 from the University of Rome and in 1964 from the University of Maryland. I have been elected member of several academies: the Connecticut Academy, the American Academy of Arts and Sciences, the Royal Dutch Academy, the Bavarian Academy of Sciences, the Accademia Nazionale dei Lincei in Rome. I have been a fellow of Silliman College since 1948.

"My views and aspirations are best expounded in my books. There is a bibliography in my *Concepts of Criticism* (1963)."

Coming from a "small nation at the crossroads of Europe," Wellek is able, as he says, to consider the great literatures "with some detachment." Immigration to the United States has only strengthened his sense "of seeing Europe as a whole, from the other shore" and convinced him of "a particular need of theoretical awareness, conceptual clarity and systematic methodology in the English-speaking countries, dominated as they are by the tradition of empiricism."

Wellek's first major attempt to meet this need was the *Theory of Literature* (1945), which he wrote with Austin Warren. It discusses but finds largely irrelevant the use in literary criticism of biography, psychology, sociology, and the history of ideas. Instead it supports and to some extent crystallizes the "intrinsic" approach of the "New Critics." According to this view, literary criticism (as Wellek has said elsewhere) should concern itself with "an analysis of the work of art itself as a linguistic structure, as a system of meaningful signs." Art, Wellek says (with Kant), does not mirror life but is an autonomous "illusion." Even those who held different opinions, or considered that the *Theory of Literature* raised more questions than it answered, found the questions important and valuable ones, and admired the book's "attempt to clarify and guide the usage of literary terminology." It has had a great deal of influence on analytical criticism at the professional level.

It should not be supposed, however, that Wellek is now (if he ever was) a rigidly doctrinaire "New Critic." Writing in the *Times Literary Supplement* (July 26, 1963), he has defended himself against charges of aestheticism and formalism and acknowledged that literary study cannot be reduced to stylistics, that criticism must go beyond language to the world of the poet. What he rejects, he says, is the facile determinism that reduces a work of art to a mere product of social or historical forces.

In any case, Wellek owes his unique place in the literary establishment not to his role in literary controversy but on the contrary to his work as a "universal umpire of literary criticism, a sort of tireless UN man who goes around ascertaining all points of view in order to do them all the justice they deserve." Willard Thorp calls him the "firm but kindly traffic policeman . . . the critic of critics, the fileleader of the literary historians and theorists." It is Wellek's *History of Modern Criticism* that has earned him these encomiums. The book has been widely praised for its "erudition, intelligence, concern" and its "great structural power." Some have thought Wellek, in his "dutiful effort to cover everything," more an encyclopedist than a historian and have called his work dull. Denis Donoghue, who found much to praise, was somewhat concerned by Wellek's emphasis on theoretical criticism, his disapproval of the inspired but nonacademic amateur. But the majority opinion is with David Daiches, who wrote: "There is no other history of criticism like it, none which combines its scope with its sense of contemporary relevance."

In some of the articles collected in *Concepts of Criticism* and *Discriminations*, Wellek applies himself to the historical development of such ideas as romanticism, classicism, and (in a "marvelously knowledgeable" essay) baroque. A recurring theme in these essays is the need for "an investigation of the unity of literature" without regard to linguistic barriers. David Daiches has pointed out that Wellek himself "is at home in the whole European literary scene in a way that few contemporary English or American scholars can claim to be."

Wellek's first wife died in 1967, and he was married again in 1968 to Nonna Shaw. He has one son. Since he wrote the note above he has garnered several more honorary degrees and fellowships. In 1969 he visited Germany as a Fulbright Distinguished Lecturer.

PRINCIPAL WORKS: Immanuel Kant in England, 1793–1838, 1931; The Rise of English Literary History, 1941; (with Austin Warren) Theory of Literature, 1949; A History of Modern Criticism, 1750–1950: vol. 1, Later Eighteenth Century, 1955; vol. 2, Romantic Age, 1955; vol. 3, The Age of Transition, 1965; vol. 4, The Later Nineteenth Century, 1965; Concepts of Criticism, 1963; Essays on Czech Literature, 1963; Confrontations, 1965; The Disciplines of Criticism, 1968; Discriminations: Further Concepts of Criticism, 1970.

ABOUT: Contemporary Authors 7–8, 1963; Demetz, P. *introduction to* Wellek's Essays on Czech Literature, 1963; Holthusen, H. E. Kritisches Verstehen, 1961; Leavis, F. R. The Common Pursuit, 1952; Sutton, W. Modern American Criticism, 1963; Who's Who in America, 1972–1973. *Periodicals*—Encounter June 1967; Times Literary Supplement July 26, 1963; September 27, 1963; February 12, 1971; Yale Review Autumn 1949; Yearbook of Comparative and General Literature VI 1957.

WESKER, ARNOLD (May 24, 1932–), English dramatist, writes: "I was born in Stepney, London's East End. My father, Joseph Wesker, was a Russian-Jewish tailor and my Hungarian-born mother, Leah, frequently supported the family by working in kitchens. During the war I was evacuated to various parts of England and Wales, but always missed London and returned whenever I had nagged my parents sufficiently to bring me home. Left school at sixteen and worked at a variety of odd jobs, among them a carpenter's mate and a bookseller's assistant. In 1945, while still at school, I was attracted to the stage and joined an amateur acting group. In 1950 I completed two years conscription in the Royal Air Force; twelve years later I wrote a play based on that experience (*Chips With Everything*). When I left the RAF I took whatever work I could find; a plumber's mate, a farm labourer, a seed sorter and a kitchen porter before I found a profession as a pastry cook which I followed for two years in London and nine months in Paris, during which time I saved enough money to enter the London School of Film Technique. I'd been writing since I was twelve and felt I'd write whatever else happened.

"One evening in 1956 I met Lindsay Anderson, theatre producer and film director, and asked him to read a short story called 'Pools' which I hoped could be made into a film. He tried to help me but nothing came of it. Then Anderson read two of my plays, *The Kitchen*, which I had written for a newspaper competition, and *Chicken Soup With Barley*. *Chicken Soup* was a desperate attempt to rise above the despair which grew out of a sense of betrayal by the world's politicians in general, and the Labour Government and the Soviet Union in particular. Anderson brought the plays to the notice of George Devine of the Royal Court Theatre in London and in 1958 the Arts Council of Great Britain, under a scheme for assisting promising new playwrights, awarded me three hundred pounds. *Chicken Soup With Barley* was produced that year by John Dexter at the Belgrade Theatre, Coventry. Later that year I shared the first prize with John Arden in the Encyclopaedia Britannica play competition for the same play.

"The Royal Court then bought the first option on a new play I was in the middle of—*Roots*. When completed they turned it down but it was picked up by Brian Bailey at the Belgrade Theatre. After its successful opening at the Belgrade the Royal Court brought it to London. By then I was in the middle of *I'm Talking About Jerusalem* and the Court made the brave and exciting decision to present all three plays of the trilogy in a special season. Meanwhile, following on the success of *Roots*, the Court was persuaded by John Dexter—who'd directed all the plays—to let him mount *The Kitchen*, with its thirty-two characters, for a Sunday night 'production without decor.'

"Despite the enthusiastic acclaim the plays received, it was only *Chips With Everything*, produced in 1962, that became the first West End success. The play opened in Sheffield and Glasgow a few days after the London opening, thereby setting a precedent which it was hoped other writers would follow of letting their new plays open in the provinces instead of having to wait years for the run to finish in the metropolis. It later transferred to Broadway.

"Between 1960 and 1966 almost my entire energies were devoted to a cultural organisation called Centre 42. Rather than struggle to find new words to explain Fortytwo, let me quote from one of our documents: '. . . so that the pursuit of the extraordinary experience of art becomes an un-extraordinary pursuit. The Centre will establish under one roof permanent professional groups of the highest artistic standards, including a drama

ARNOLD WESKER

company, an orchestra, a jazz band, and a visual arts department. The centre will provide such facilities as a theatre, a small cinema, an exhibition gallery; also committee rooms for use by local organisations, conference facilities, a dance hall, and a restaurant, bars and buffets. The various groups will present continuously changing repertoires of work at the centre BUT complete repertoires or parts of them will be available to local communities all over the country who wish to present festivals, concerts, exhibitions, and so on. The centre will offer a service to the arts equivalent to the services to education provided by the Workers Education Association.'

"Battling for the arts in this country is one of the most frustrating experiences. For me the free and natural access to the entire canvas of literature, music and the visual arts meant access to a field of experiences which could deepen man's inherent sense of justice, sharpen his sense of compassion and reassure him in the loneliness of living. Great art seemed to me to teach a denial of man's right to impose on his neighbour. But in Great Britain the wish to see the community share in this experience was itself interpreted as an imposition. It was a bitter and ironical confrontation, which to all intents and purposes I've lost. At the time of writing this piece the history of Centre 42 is dying to an end and a fuller story is contained in a collection of my lectures called *Fears of Fragmentation*.

"*The Four Seasons*, a love story for two characters, was written in 1964 and opened at the Belgrade, Coventry, in 1965. Later it transferred to the West End. The majority of critics hammered it. I had previously been accused of social sermonising and now, having produced something quite different, they accused me of not sticking to my old style! *Their Very Own and Golden City*—a story of compromise—which in contrast to *The Four Seasons* has some twenty characters, won the Italian Premio Marzotto Drama Award in 1964. The world premiere was at the Belgium National Theatre and was well received. It opened to mixed reviews at the Royal Court in 1966. A television play, *Menace*, was shown on BBC on December 8, 1963 and a film of *The Kitchen* was released in 1961. The TV play was generally hated and the film was tepidly received.

"1968 brought an invitation to visit Cuba for a second time in order to attend an international conference of artists and intellectuals. While there I decided to stay for three months and direct, for the first time, *The Four Seasons*, which had been dedicated to Cuba. From that moment I felt I wanted to direct all future plays I wrote.

"In 1969, *The Friends* was finished and offered to the Royal Court and the Royal Shakespeare Company. Both were interested but refused to consider me as director. Some West End managements were interested and would have allowed me to direct but I was not anxious to be performed in the West End. So the play was stubbornly withdrawn until Vivica Bandler, the Finnish director of Stockholm's Stadsteatern, 'phoned to invite me to direct it there. We opened in January, 1970, and received rave reviews which encouraged a new producer in England, Eddie Kulukundis, to finance my production of the play in the Round House on May 19, 1970. The critics were sharply divided. The most influential ones attacked it vigorously—both in right and left wing journals. Between the hostility aroused by Centre Fortytwo and the latter plays I feel very numbed and an alien writer in this country.

"Marriage, three children, a house in Hornsey are precarious joys. I should like to write a novel, some political profiles, another play. The Tory Party has just won the general election; Enoch Powell has increased his majority. It's not a happy time for this country."

The Kitchen, Wesker's first play in order of writing, takes place in the course of a single day in the kitchen of a large London restaurant. We see the day's work begin, build up to the lunch-time rush, slow down, then rise to a fresh crescendo. For the kitchen's thirty employees the work is hard, thankless, and unsatisfying; pressure and frustration breed not comradeship but petty snobberies, quarrels, and explosions of violence. The day ends in disaster when Peter, the idealistic young German cook, rejected by his mistress, runs amok smashing everything he can. The play offers a microcosm of a world in which capitalism, however enlightened, continues to exhaust and demean the human spirit in unrewarding labor.

This view is reflected in the construction of the play; human contacts are fragmentary—brief interludes snatched from the feverish work routine, denied development or consequence. Wesker at that time knew little of the conventions of his craft, and could not have written a "well-made" play even if he had wanted to. *The Kitchen* was condemned for this, for its lack of character development, and its failure to offer a solution to the social problems it poses; some middle-class critics, conditioned to the middle-class entertainments that then dominated the British theatre, contemptuously dismissed it, along with other working-class plays, as "kitchen sink" drama. But others have maintained that its unorthodox structure is wholly appropriate to its purposes, and a reviewer in the *Times* wrote: "The rhythm, depth of feeling, action, and characterisation, controlled in the service of a meaningful statement about the human condition, with the whole compressed into just over one hour, incline one . . . to regard this as a major drama."

What established Wesker as a major figure in the postwar British theatrical renaissance was the trilogy of plays in which, as John Russell Taylor said, he attempted nothing less than "to sum up the situation of the working classes today." The first of them, *Chicken Soup With Barley* (1958), introduces a Jewish family in the East End of London, Sarah and Harry Kahn, and their children, Ada and Ronnie. This family, tight-knit and politically conscious, is studied over a period of twenty years, through the Spanish Civil War, World War II, and the materialism of the postwar years. The dominant figure is Sarah, a woman of great vitality and warmth. She never loses her faith in people or in socialism, but Harry becomes a prematurely senile failure, Ada tries to build a private utopia in the country, and Ronnie (who generally speaks for Wesker himself) is in the end politically disillusioned and uncertain. The Kahns do not appear in *Roots* (1959), which centers on Ronnie's girl friend, Beatie Bryant. The trilogy's third play, *I'm Talking About Jerusalem* (1960), tells the story of Ada Kahn and her husband Dave, who try to escape from a dehumanized society and live a life of William Morris simplicity in the country, dedicated to art, craftsmanship, and the family.

The most eloquent and admired of these plays is *Roots*, in which Beatie Bryant, who has become engaged to Ronnie Kahn in London, rejoins her family, farm laborers in Norfolk, where Ronnie is to join her. During the period of waiting, Beatie tries to communicate to her family some of the intellectual excitement, the delight in music and art, that Ronnie has given her, but cannot break through their ignorance and apathy. In the end a letter comes from Ronnie, breaking off the engagement and denigrating his own ideas as "useless and romantic." Hurt and humiliated, Beatie begins the magnificent and much-quoted speech in the course of which, no longer Ronnie's mouthpiece, she begins for the first time to think for herself. "God in heaven, Ronnie!" she cries, as the curtain falls. "It does work, it's happening to me, I can feel it's happened. I'm beginning, on my own two feet, I'm beginning."

Roots did not escape criticism—the first act is slow and dull, Ronnie's ideas as Beatie represents them seem vague and naïve, and the characterization of Beatie herself is difficult to separate from Joan Plowright's unforgettable performance in the role. But, as Richard Findlater wrote, the play, treating members of the rural working class not as caricatures but as human beings, "may be considered as a milestone in the modern English drama, on linguistic and sociological grounds alone. What is more important, however . . . is Wesker's attitude towards his characters. . . . This author labours to show the love between people, especially people in a family; to affirm their essential individual value, as members of mankind, and to remind the audience that they belong to it, too."

Wesker's early plays made him an important and controversial figure—attacked for his disregard of theatrical conventions, his didacticism, and his intellectual limitations; admired for his honesty, compassion, and eloquence, and a remarkable ability to create memorable visual images on the stage. Wesker is the least literary of dramatists; his plays, like Eugene O'Neill's, do not read well but, at their best, come brilliantly to life in the theatre—a place where, as he says, "one wants to *see* things happening."

This is particularly true of his only commercially successful play, *Chips With Everything* (1962). It is an account of life in the Royal Air Force, which is portrayed as a class-bound instrument of the establishment, dedicated to crushing individuality and maintaining the status quo. The rebellious central figure is Pip Thompson, an upper-class conscript who, out of a feeling of solidarity with the working class, refuses a commission. Treated with equal suspicion by officers and conscripts, he eventually yields and accepts his ordained place in the hierarchy. The play is far less verbose than its predecessors, and some brilliantly effective scenes, like the famous raid which Pip organizes on the post's fuel dump, have no dialogue whatever.

Many critics, whatever their political persuasions, found Wesker's social attitudes in the play unacceptably naïve and anachronistic, but several thought this irrelevant, suggesting that it was not the naturalistic work it appeared to be. John Russell Taylor called it a "political cartoon," in which Wesker had set out to close the gap that existed in his earlier plays "between his style—a detailed and elaborate naturalism—and what he had to say, which was often extravagantly over-simplified and schematic." The play was a major success in London, and a moderate one in New York.

In some of his later plays Wesker continued his "retreat from realism," moving towards a poetic vagueness which seems to have impressed European audiences more than English ones. *The Four Seasons* is an apolitical two-character drama about the slow death of a love affair, while both *Their Very Own and Golden City* and *The Friends* turn on the betrayal of utopian ideas through human greed, apathy, and weakness. *The Old Ones*, in which Wesker returned to the London Jewish milieu of his earliest plays, is something rather different. It is a comedy and, though for most of its length it is an extremely despairing one, it ends on a note of optimism and affirmation, working (as one critic wrote) "a singular magic through its author's stubborn, glowing belief that his bruised people, undefeated in defeat, are worthy of respect."

Wesker has attributed his mood of disillusionment partly to the cool response of British critics to his recent plays, partly to the failure of British socialism to support Centre 42, a generous vision of an arts and cultural movement for the masses which, after almost a decade of devoted effort, was formally abandoned in December 1970. Wesker has told the story of his struggle for Centre 42 in the essays and lectures collected in *Fears of Fragmentation*, and it is reflected also in his plays, most obviously in *Their Very Own and Golden City*. In the summer of 1971 Wesker spent eight weeks in the offices of the London *Sunday Times*, gathering material for a play, *The Journalists*. He also wrote an account of what he saw of the newspaper and its staff that was to have been published in book form as *Journey Into Journalism*. This was withdrawn because some of those who figured in the book were offended by it. Hugh Hebert, who read the manuscript and discussed it in the *Guardian* (March 12, 1974) found it entertaining and illuminating, and thought it a pity that the objections of "a very small number of journalists should in effect veto its publication."

Wesker's immense contribution to the postwar broadening of the social range and social concerns of the British theatre is beyond dispute, but it is too soon to assess the permanent importance of his work, passionately sincere, often deeply moving, but almost always flawed.

PRINCIPAL PUBLISHED WORKS: The Wesker Trilogy (Chicken Soup With Barley, Roots, I'm Talking About Jerusalem), 1960; The Kitchen, 1961; Chips With Everything, 1962; Their Very Own and Golden City, 1966; The Four Seasons, 1966; The Friends, 1970; Fears of Fragmentation (lectures and essays), 1970; Six Sundays in January (collected stories and short plays), 1971; The Old Ones, 1973.

ABOUT: Armstrong, W. A. (ed.) Experimental Drama, 1963; Brown, J. R. Modern British Dramatists, 1968; Brown, J. R. Theatre Language, 1972; Contemporary Authors 4, 1963; Current Biography, 1962; Gindin, J. J. Postwar British Fiction, 1962; Hayman, R. Arnold Wesker, 1970; Kitchin, L. Midcentury Drama, 1960; Leeming, G. and Trussler, S. The Plays of Arnold Wesker, 1971; Mander, J. The Writer and Commitment, 1962; Ribalow, H. Arnold Wesker, 1965; Taylor, J. R. The Angry Theater, 1962; Times Education Services, Arnold Wesker (The Times Authors), 1970; Wager, W. (ed.) The Playwrights Speak, 1967; Wellwarth, G. E. The Theatre of Protest and Paradox, 1964; Who's Who, 1973; Who's Who in the Theatre, 1972. *Periodicals*—Encounter March 1962, August 1966; Guardian January 18, 1960; Nation November 19, 1960; New York Times Magazine October 13, 1963; Nova May 1965; Plays and Players April 1962; Queen May 15, 1962; Tatler August 1965; Theatre Arts October 1961, October 1963; Twentieth Century September 1960.

MORRIS L. WEST

WEST, MORRIS L(ANGLO) (April 26, 1916–), Australian novelist, is the son of Charles Langlo West and Florence (Hanlon) West. He was born in the Melbourne suburb of St. Kilda, and educated there in a school operated by the Christian Brothers. He joined that order at the age of fourteen, finding in it a refuge from an imperfect home life, and taught in Christian Brothers schools from 1933 to 1939, receiving his B.A. from the University of Melbourne in 1937. At the outbreak of World War II West joined the Australian Imperial Forces. He left the Christian Brothers without taking his final vows, and expressed some of his disillusionment with monastic life in his first novel, *Moon in My Pocket*, published pseudonymously as by "Julian Morris" in 1945. In 1943 meanwhile, Lieutenant West had been released from his work as an army cipher officer to serve briefly as private secretary to W. M. Hughes, a former prime minister of Australia. He worked for a year after that as a radio publicist, and then went into business as an independent producer and writer of radio plays and serials. After ten exhausting but very successful years, West earned the title of "wonder boy of radio," and a nervous breakdown. He emerged from a year's thoughtful convalescence determined to make a place for himself as an author, and sold his business.

West began his new life in 1954 with *The Illusionist*, a play in blank verse which was successfully produced on Australian radio. It was followed by two slight novels which earned him enough to travel with his family to Europe. In Italy he was attracted by what he heard of the work of Father Mario Borelli, priest of the street urchins of Naples. West spent some time in the Naples slums, posing as a fugitive British sailor, and out of this experience wrote his first nonfictional book, *Children of the Shadows* (1957), which made his name. The book had great success, particularly in England, and enlisted the world's practical sympathy for Father Borelli and his mission.

Some potboilers followed, eked out with periods of work in publicity and journalism, including one as Vatican correspondent of the London *Daily Mail*. *The Devil's Advocate* was published in 1959. It concerns the investigation by a dying priest of the claims to sainthood of a British Army deserter, whose memory has grown into a legend in a remote Italian province. It became an international best seller and was selected by book clubs, condensed, dramatized, and sold to the movies for a quarter of a million dollars. Some readers were shocked by the novel's "irreverence" and sexual frankness; others, more disturbed by its "slickness," called it a "religious thriller." But a number of reviewers accepted and praised it as a serious work of literature, and several compared it to the novels of Graham Greene. It received a number of literary awards, including the James Tait Black Memorial Award and the Royal Society of Literature's Heinemann Award.

The Devil's Advocate established a formula which West has followed in most of his subsequent novels—that is, to use all the techniques of popular fiction in order to focus the attention of his large readership on some moral or social problem which he considers important. Thus, *Daughter of Silence* (1961) raises ethical and psychological questions in the context of a sensational Italian court case. It was dramatized the same year by West, but failed in

New York. In *The Shoes of the Fisherman* (1963), later filmed, West considers the election of the first Russian Pope and its implications, seriously disturbing many Roman Catholic critics, who thought it "impertinent" and "crudely conceived." *The Ambassador* (1965), reflecting West's interest in Buddhism and his travels in the Far East, is set in contemporary Vietnam and studies both religious and political dilemmas. None of these novels quite equaled the popular success of *The Devil's Advocate* and critics, though far from unanimous, tended to praise them more for their readability and good intentions than for their literary merit. There was a generally warmer reception for *The Tower of Babel* (1968), a Middle East spy thriller which examines the tensions and hatreds leading up to the Six-Day War of 1967; the book was selected by two book clubs and bought for filming and serialization before it was even published. *Summer of the Red Wolf* (1971), another success, is a straightforward adventure tale—an expert piece of escapism set in the Outer Hebrides.

Morris West was married in 1952 to Joyce Lawford; they have four children. He is the joint author with Robert Francis of *Scandal in the Assembly*, "a bill of complaints and a proposal for reform in the matrimonial laws and tribunals of the Roman Catholic Church." West is a tall man, broad-shouldered and robust, with hazel eyes and brown hair. He is a stimulating speaker and popular as a lecturer in the United States and elsewhere. His recreations include sailing and reading. West is a good and scrupulous craftsman whose first concern is to produce novels that will be enjoyed. At the same time, he believes it to be the duty of a Catholic writer to affirm constantly "man's right to the minimal dignity, the minimal possession, the minimal care without which he cannot function as a responsible human being." This belief is explicit or implicit in all his books, and is asserted very directly in *The Heretic*, a play in blank verse about the sixteenth-century heretic Giordano Bruno.

PRINCIPAL WORKS: (as "Julian Morris") Moon in My Pocket, 1945; Gallows on the Sand, 1955; Kundu, 1956; Children of the Shadows (England, Children of the Sun), 1957; The Crooked Road (England, The Big Story), 1957; Backlash (England, Second Victory), 1958; (as "Michael East") McCreary Moves In, 1958; The Devil's Advocate, 1959; (as "Michael East") The Naked Country, 1960; Daughter of Silence, 1961; Shoes of the Fisherman, 1963; The Ambassador, 1965; The Tower of Babel, 1968; (with Robert Francis) Scandal in the Assembly, 1970; The Heretic (play), 1970; Summer of the Red Wolf, 1971; The Salamander, 1973.

ABOUT: Contemporary Authors 5–6, 1963; Current Biography, 1966; Hetherington, J. Forty-two Faces, 1963; Who's Who, 1973; Who's Who in America, 1972–1973; Who's Who in Australia, 1971.

PAUL WEST

WEST, PAUL (February 23, 1930–), English novelist, memoirist, and critic, writes: "I was born in a Derbyshire mining village and educated at the local elementary and grammar schools, where excellent spinsters taught me English, Latin, Greek and French in spite of my own laziness (which I still have and regard as a natural gift of sorts). It was they who persuaded me that I ought to go in for languages, or something similar, instead of becoming what I dreamed of being: an aeronautical engineer. So off I went to Birmingham University, where I managed to graduate with first-class honours in English and a scholarship to Lincoln College, Oxford, still plane-struck but now certain that writing was the mode of designing for me. At that time I wanted to be a poet more than I wanted to be anything, and I went around telling people that poems ought to electrify and change us—and I still feel the same way about literature as a whole.

"In 1952 I very luckily won a fellowship to Columbia University, New York, where I attended hardly any classes and wrote a sombre, apocalyptic first novel I finally destroyed. Manhattan was a miracle, like the Black Hole of Calcutta topped by undreaming obelisks, and I felt at home there—still do—more than anywhere else. In fact I wanted to stay on in that mouse-infested apartment next to Harlem, but the Royal Air Force fetched me back to England to do my military service, which I'd eluded doing for seven years, and so I crossed the Irish Sea to the Isle of Man for induction at the Officer Cadet Training Unit there and, in fact—a preposterous thing for me—stayed on as a member of the staff, lecturing on American foreign policy (about which I knew next to nothing) and hitching occasional flights to London in the one aircraft the station had. During this period I wrote another novel, which was eventually published, and began writing for the *New Statesman* and the *Sunday Times*. I had also begun to write critical essays, but I was a long way from being in full spate as a writer, even though my head was full of things to say.

"After the Air Force I went to the Memorial University of Newfoundland to teach English literature, attracted by an island in mid-Atlantic and a salary I thought enormous until I discovered just how far a dollar went. There in the fogs I began a new novel, did a good deal of broadcasting, and put together a book of poems which was published in Toronto. In 1960 I returned to England on a Canada Council Fellowship, finished the novel and wrote a book on Byron, returned to Canada and then, in 1962, was awarded a Guggenheim Fellowship to the United States. Since then, I have been on the faculty of the Pennsylvania State University and writing for about three-quarters of each year. I still maintain ties with England and in fact have crossed the Atlantic more times than I can count, but I feel more comfortable in America where, trite as it may sound, the increasingly far-out things I'm now writing win a readier, less hidebound response.

"Looking back, I see myself as a late starter who, between thirty and forty, in a sustained and intensive spell of application, set down half a lifetime's pondering and moved from a restless contentment with criticism and fairly orthodox fiction to an almost Fellini-like point of view. Imagination, as I see it, is an alembic in limbo: it invents, and what it invents has to be added to the sum of Creation. In other words, I think the realistic novel has served its turn and that fiction has to reclaim some of its ancient privileges, which writers like Lucian and Nashe and Rabelais and Grimmelshausen exploited to the full. I think that only the plasticity of a free-ranging imagination can do justice to late-twentieth-century man who, as incomplete as man ever was, keeps on arming himself with increasing amounts of data which, as ever, mean nothing at all. My own fiction I have come to see as, want to be, a kind of linear mosaic, which is what my second novel, *Tenement of Clay*, was in a rudimentary form and which my two most recent ones—*Caliban's Filibuster* and *Colonel Mint*—are in a much more advanced and demanding way. Actually, since both vocabulary and syntax are themselves fictive I don't regard my autobiographical writing as different from my fiction; they're both part of the mosaic I invent. What matters to me most of all is to write, and live, without preconceptions, which is something any handicapped child—such as Mandy, my deaf girl, for whom I wrote a book—can teach us. Elasticity, diversity, openness, these are the things that matter to me, in teaching as well as writing.

"Son of a pianist mother and an engineer father, I can still find two disciplines warring inside of me to my (I think) constant benefit. One day soon I shall write the short third volume of the Alley Jaggers trilogy which commemorates the village I was born in and from which I have wandered so far. It was Alley's mad imaginativeness, crude as it is, that spawned my filibustering Caliban, Colonel Mint the astronaut who said he'd seen an angel, and the secret sharer who talks his way through *Words for a Deaf Daughter*. There's a peasant in each of those itchy visionaries."

Paul West is a gifted, versatile, and prolific writer whose work as a whole, although his individual books have attracted much praise, has not yet gained the attention it increasingly deserves. His contemporaries at Oxford remember him as an enthusiast of cricket and modern living, whose poetry had a tremendous potential which his only collection, *The Snow Leopard*, disappointingly does not quite fulfill. To understand West one must recognize his energy and eclecticism, the extraordinary openness to experience of which he speaks above. This is evident in his memoir *I, Said the Sparrow*. Although his background is working-class, there is no sense of a social struggle having taken place. Rather we are given one raw, warm, and vivid impression after another of a way of life, with the author more or less in the background except as a recorder with an exceptional gift for language.

In *Byron and the Spoiler's Art*, Byron is presented as one who assumed the tragicomic pose of a Pierrot to mask his failure to come to terms with life or with himself. The *Times Literary Supplement* found it "immensely stimulating, as a modern interpretation by a critic possessed of imaginative power, dexterity and wit." G. S. Fraser wrote: "One would like to greet very warmly indeed this most promising first essay in criticism by a young writer already well known as a clever reviewer. . . . I found myself so often admiring and underlining individual sentences that I often lost track of the drift of a paragraph. . . . I found also Mr. West's method of historical comparison a little bewildering. . . . But it is fun to watch a young man unpack his bags, even if some of the items were not really wanted on voyage. Mr. West has gaiety, learning, and self-confidence; one looks forward to his further adventures as a critic."

There was a chillier reception for West's two-volume study *The Modern Novel*, which deals in some detail with American and English fiction, more briefly with the novel in Russia, Germany,

France, Italy, and Spain. Such comprehensiveness offended some reviewers, who accused West of having "skimmed the surface while appearing to have penetrated in depth." It is, in fact, an idiosyncratic compendium which abounds in valuable insights, colorfully expressed. The interesting but uneven essays in *The Wine of Absurdity* deal with such diverse figures as Yeats, Lawrence, Sartre, Eliot, Greene, and Santayana—all writers who, in West's opinion, had been forced to come to terms in one way or another with a conviction that life is without meaning. That West himself is another such "Absurdist" is evident in this book and also in the thread of unreason which runs through all his fiction.

West's first published novel, *A Quality of Mercy*, a *conte noir* set in Connecticut, was found lacking in craftsmanship but was noticed for its "wit and a rather perverse intelligence." His second, *Tenement of Clay*, begins with the discovery on a city doorstep of a helpless, hardly human, being who cannot speak and cannot bear noise or daylight. This Caliban is taken in by a self-appointed savior of the destitute, Papa Nick, and his protégé Pee Wee Lazarus, a malevolent midget wrestler. Their act of charity has unexpected results. Lazarus mischievously provides the dumb primitive, dubbed "Lacland," with the basic tools of modern living—a radio, a pinup girl, a knife, a book of poetry. The violence of Lacland's response to these things turns his benefactor into his jailer. When he eventually bursts out of his prison, it is to corrupt and destroy. Lacland ends in remorse and a new kind of dumbness, no longer innocence but a kind of madness.

This is a cruel but also extremely funny novel. Marred though it is by verbal self-indulgence, it raises important questions about the nature of innocence, civilization, and madness, and about man's duty to his fellows. The tale is told in the first person by Papa Nick and Lazarus alternately, in a curious interior monologue which shifts without warning between action, fantasy, and dreams of the past.

Alley Jaggers, in West's trilogy, is a plasterer in a squalid Midlands town, outwardly entirely brutalized by his environment and his ignorance, inwardly a spoiled artist. In the macabre final scenes of *Alley Jaggers* this conflict makes a murderer of him. Alley himself is a triumph of vitality—less a social case history than a feat of the creative imagination, the hero of a Rabelaisian epic which in its delighted accumulation of bizarre, violent, and scatological imagery approaches surrealism. Roderick Cook, who like other critics found the novel sometimes strained in its effects, nevertheless thought it a tour de force of humor, pity, and horror. The second novel, *I'm Expecting to Live Quite Soon*, centers on Alley's wife Dot, another victim of their milieu—a creature of subhuman triviality who, in Alley's absence, begins to discover herself through a series of sensual experiments which, far from degrading her, bring about her spiritual and emotional enlargement. *Bela Lugosi's White Christmas*, which completes the trilogy, describes Alley's activities in a hospital for the criminally insane (where "his runes and enigmas and impromptu koans" are his psychiatrists' delight), and during a brief period of liberty when he asserts "something of himself on an almost mytho-maniacal level."

In *Caliban's Filibuster* a scriptwriter, flying to Tokyo with his producer and an actor, fantasizes three interwoven psychodramas. Frederick Busch called it "a fiction about language, and madness, and the world of dreams we make to hide away in," and "something like a master craftsman's masterpiece." *Colonel Mint* is another mythopoeic fantasy, in which an astronaut, going about his cosmic business, encounters what might be an angel.

In the face of chaos and despair, West celebrates the autonomy of the human imagination, the human senses; and he does so nowhere more convincingly or movingly than in the book he wrote for his daughter Mandy, *Words for a Deaf Daughter*. Mandy was born not only deaf but with other defects yet to be diagnosed. This account of how her parents passionately defer to her, share her richly sensuous world, and thus enrich their own, is one of the most exuberant statements of faith in human potentiality to appear in its decade.

Paul West still teaches at Pennsylvania State University, where he is now Professor of English and Comparative Literature, and a senior fellow of the Institute for the Arts and Humanistic Studies. In 1972 he was Crashaw Professor of Literature at Colgate University, Hamilton, New York. He is a regular contributor to the New York *Times Book Review*.

PRINCIPAL WORKS: *Fiction*—A Quality of Mercy, 1961; Tenement of Clay, 1965; Alley Jaggers, 1966; I'm Expecting to Live Quite Soon, 1969; Caliban's Filibuster, 1970; Colonel Mint, 1972; Bela Lugosi's White Christmas, 1972. *Poetry*—Fantasy Poets No. 13, 1953; The Snow Leopard, 1964. *Criticism*—The Fossils of Piety: Literary Humanism in Decline (essay), 1959; The Growth of the Novel (radio talks), 1959; Byron and the Spoiler's Art, 1960; (ed.) Byron: A Collection of Critical Essays, 1963; The Modern Novel, 1963; The Wine of Absurdity, 1966. *Miscellaneous*—I, Said the Sparrow (autobiography), 1963; Words for a Deaf Daughter, 1969.

ABOUT: Contemporary Authors 15–16, 1966; Vinson, J. (ed.) Contemporary Novelists, 1972. *Periodicals*—Books and Bookmen March 1963; Book World August 28, 1966; November 20, 1966; Commonweal September 30, 1966; November 17, 1967; Guardian February 8, 1963; Kenyon Review September 1966; New American Review April 1968; August 1970; New Statesman November 12, 1960; New York Times June 12, 1966; New York Times Book Review June 20, 1971; Newsweek August 31, 1970; Observer September 21, 1969;

Southern Review Winter 1969; Time September 7, 1970; Times Literary Supplement November 14, 1963; January 21, 1965; April 29, 1965; May 13, 1965; May 12, 1966; September 15, 1966.

"WEST, WARD". *See* BORLAND, HAL

WHEELER, HUGH (CALLINGHAM) ("Q. PATRICK," "PATRICK QUENTIN," "JONATHAN STAGGE") (March 19, 1912–), British-born American detective story writer and dramatist, writes: "I was born in Northwood, Middlesex, a suburb of London which at that time still had one foot in the country. My father, Harold Wheeler, was a Civil Servant in the office of the Public Trustee, my mother, Florence Scammell, the daughter of a truck manufacturer. I had a completely standardized middle-class upbringing—prep school, public school (minor) and London University where I took an honors degree in English. Even my childish private pleasures, 'Nature,' idyllic summers in the Isle of Wight and later, Normandy to learn the language, Berlin to learn the language, D. H. Lawrence, Stravinsky, Eisenstein and Tallulah Bankhead were the accepted pleasures of the 'artistic' youths of the period. Equally predictable, I suppose, were the novels, plays, poems indiscriminately written from the age of seven on, the adolescent rebellion from affectionate and understanding parents and a tremendously smug sense of superiority to and revolt against the complacent, 'bourgeois' Britannia-Rules-the-Waves imperialism which was still in those days paramount in the British world I knew. Where others, less trivially minded than I, were falling in love with Stalin, outlawing Hitler and gesticulating around the edges of the Workers' War in Spain, I was merely thinking to myself: 'I've had enough of this.'

"The United States, which in my mind at that time seemed a fascinating never-never land of Sinclair Lewis, Lizzie Borden, iced-water and Ruby Keeler, had always fascinated me. A chance meeting with Richard Wilson Webb, an English-born American businessman and part-time mystery story writer who was looking for a replacement collaborator to work with him in the States, seemed to provide a good opportunity to 'try something else.' In 1933, I moved to Philadelphia, where Webb was working in a pharmaceutical firm, and took over the collaborator role left vacant by a Main Line girl called Patsy Kelley who, with Webb, had written four detective novels under the pseudonym Q. Patrick and who had recently bowed out to get married. There followed fifteen years of collaboration with Webb first under the pseudonym Q. Patrick alone and then, as the output grew, also under the names Jonathan Stagge and Patrick Quentin. Since my own literary tastes were far closer to Proust than to S. S. Van Dine, I had entered on this venture purely as an apprenticeship in learning the craft. However, when I learned enough to realize how terribly difficult it is to do anything well, the stylization and restrictions involved in writing this particular, and I suppose minor, form of literature began to fascinate me. And, as the collaboration gradually lessened, to end with Webb's retirement from ill health, I obsessedly continued, shedding Q. Patrick and Jonathan Stagge in my wake, to try through Patrick Quentin to write at least one satisfactory novel in this medium. Needless to say, I have been only partially successful.

"Many writers have colorful periods of economic distress in their early writing life where they 'enriched' their experience working as Argentine gauchos or street cleaners or radio comics' gag men. For better or worse (probably worse) this never happened to me so that, in terms of employment, my life other than for writing has been a blank (unless a near-comical year in the Medical Corps of the U.S. Army at Fort Dix, New Jersey, during World War II, brought compensations). However, I have managed to enjoy the advantages of a writing career as well as to have endured its many, many hours of agony, despair, and sterility. I have lived in different countries—Italy, France, North Africa, Brazil, Mexico, the West Indies and in Monterey, Massachusetts, where I have kept my most private place of residence since 1944. I have been able to follow my not very startling enthusiasms for music, gardening, obsessive reading, the theatre, etcetera and, with a temperament for which friends are important, have been able to make as many close friends as I could ever have wished for.

"An uneventful life except, perhaps, for a major change which took place in 1960. It was then that my pursuit of limited excellence through Patrick Quentin seemed to be reaching its limit and the repressed longing for a wider effort took over. With no particular objective in mind, I wrote under my own name a play, *Big Fish, Little Fish.* To my surprised delight, this and my following play, *Look, We've Come Through*, were both produced on Broadway with a response from the people whose opinion I respect in the theatre that was encouraging. To my middle-aged astonishment, I had discovered a new world in which I felt I belonged. To write a play one thinks is good and somehow to get it onto the stage without total disfigurement in the commercialized, gambling, 'success-slanted' world of Broadway is a terrifying but exhilarating challenge—identical with the almost impossible challenge of writing a 'perfect' detective story but on a level where the disasters and triumphs are tremendously heightened."

As Q. Patrick, Jonathan Stagge, and Patrick Quentin, Wheeler has produced over thirty novels, of which only a small representative selection is listed below. All of the early books were written in collaboration with Richard Wilson Webb but, as Wheeler says, Webb's contribution gradually diminished, and seems virtually to have ended early in the 1950s.

The partnership was a success from the beginning. In *Murder by Prescription*, for example, published in 1937, the circumstances surrounding the book's three murders were so vividly realized that "foreknowledge of the conclusion did not ruin the story—a rare feat in detective writing." And it was said that the excellence of *Dogs Do Bark*, which appeared the same year, "lies not only in the clever unfolding of the mystery, but perhaps even more in the graphic description of the characters that play their part in the drama."

The settings of the Wheeler-Webb novels, economically and knowledgeably evoked, range from Manhattan to Capri, from Cambridge to Mexico. The complex plots turn on wills, sexual jealousies, blackmail, and genteel forms of murder. They encompass neither the gang warfare nor political intrigue of the documentary school, nor the profound psychological delvings of a Simenon. The heroes of these stories are ordinary likable people of the professional class; the minor characters are sharply and often humorously delineated. The style is unremarkable, but direct and efficient; and the result is entertainment of the first quality.

If he has not extended the boundaries of the traditional detective story, Wheeler has persistently struggled to exploit its possibilities to the full, enlivening his stories with ingenious and inventive plots, original characters, and humor. *The Yellow Taxi* (1942), for example, was welcomed as a story "made utterly delightful by one of the most enchanting children in fiction, Dr. Westlake's daughter Dawn, who has the clue to the mystery from the start"; and *Puzzle for Pilgrims* (1947), according to Anthony Boucher, involved "one of the most tangled emotional situations on record, fused with an adroit puzzle plot and a vivid Mexican background." *Suspicious Circumstances* (1957) seemed to L. G. Offord not only "a notable Quentin," but "wildly funny."

The only one of Wheeler's fictions to appear under his own name was *The Crippled Muse* (1951). An American academic visits Capri, hoping to meet a famous poet, Merape Sloane, who is the subject of his thesis. He wants to find out why she has published nothing for thirty years—is it because she is now wealthy, cured of her tuberculosis, or has she outgrown the impulse to create? But the real answer is more sinister, and people fall over cliffs when they seem likely to find out. "Mr. Wheeler," said a critic in the *Times Literary Supplement*, "writes very well, and his insight into the English and American characters is such that it is impossible to guess his nationality."

HUGH WHEELER

His first play, *Big Fish, Little Fish*, opened on Broadway in March 1961. It is a study of a middle-aged bachelor, living in Manhattan, who has acquired a circle of friends, a mistress, and a rather dull though worthy job in a publishing house. The offer of a more exciting way of life forces him to assess the rut he is in and the people who share it with him. Are his friends parasites, is he emotionally dependent on them, or is he in fact quite normally fond of and loyal to them? He eventually rejects the idea of change. Some critics found the conclusion sentimental, but the play had a fair success in New York and London.

In *Look, We've Come Through* (1963), an intellectual girl and a young man suspected by his associates of homosexuality help each other to overcome their crippling shyness. Wheeler also adapted for the stage Shirley Jackson's *We Have Always Lived in the Castle*, and with Peter Viertel wrote the screenplay for the film *Five Miles to Midnight* (1962). He is also the author of *A Little Night Music*, a musical based on Ingmar Bergman's film *Smiles of a Summer Night*. Wheeler is a member of the Dramatists' Guild and in 1961 won the Edgar Allan Poe Award. He has been an American citizen since 1942.

PRINCIPAL WORKS: *As* "*Q. Patrick*"—The Grindle Nightmare, 1935; Death and the Maiden, 1939; etc.

As "Jonathan Stagge"—The Yellow Taxi, 1942; Death, My Darling Daughters, 1945. *As "Patrick Quentin"*—A Puzzle for Fools, 1936; A Puzzle for Fiends, 1946; A Puzzle for Pilgrims, 1947; Black Widow, 1952; The Man in the Net, 1956; Suspicious Circumstances, 1957; The Ordeal of Mrs. Snow and Other Stories, 1961; Family Skeletons, 1965. *As Hugh Wheeler*—The Crippled Muse (novel) 1951; Big Fish, Little Fish (play), 1961; We Have Always Lived in the Castle (play), 1966; Look, We've Come Through *in* Stasio, M. (ed.) Broadway's Beautiful Losers, 1972.

ABOUT: Who's Who in America, 1972–1973. *Periodicals*—Book Week December 11, 1938; New Statesman and Nation August 7, 1937; November 6, 1937; New York Herald Tribune Book Review May 11, 1947; New York Times January 10, 1937; New Yorker May 30, 1942; San Francisco Chronicle May 18, 1947; January 19, 1958; Saturday Review October 29, 1938; Times Literary Supplement November 24, 1950; November 2, 1951; September 8, 1961.

JOHN WHEELWRIGHT

WHEELWRIGHT, JOHN (BROOKS) (September 9, 1897–September 15, 1940), American poet, was born in Milton, Massachusetts, the son of Edmund March Wheelwright, the last city architect of Boston, and Elizabeth Boott Wheelwright. He was descended on both sides from wealthy and very old New England families. Wheelwright was educated at the Fay School at Southboro, St. George's at Newport, and Harvard, class of 1920. He did not graduate, but went off instead for a year and a half to Florence, where he pursued an inherited interest in architecture. More formal studies followed at the Massachusetts Institute of Technology and, though he never bothered to qualify as an architect, Wheelwright worked for many years on a critical history of American architecture which was still incomplete when he died.

Wheelwright lived for most of his life with his mother on Beacon Street, Boston. Kenneth Rexroth calls him "a perfect descendant of the revolutionary [Boston] humanists and eccentrics of the 1840's . . . an impassioned Trotskyite, Anglocatholic, and several other kinds of violent and peculiar exceptionalist." There are many anecdotes to bear this out—Wheelwright preaching socialism from a soapbox on Boston Common, a scarlet carnation in the buttonhole of his dinner jacket; Wheelwright marching up and down Beacon Street with signs slung across his shoulders demanding the release of Trotsky; Wheelwright interrupting Amy Lowell in the middle of her lecture on *vers libre* to ask: "Miss Lowell, how do you write poetry if you haven't got anything to say?" (Though he later explained that he really meant, "How does *one*?") He was killed at the age of forty-three, run down one night by a drunken driver near the bridge his father had built across the Charles.

His first collection of verse, *Rock and Shell*, has been described as a "spiritual-intellectual autobiography." The poems it contains seemed to most reviewers erudite, expert, and precise, but very difficult, full of private and abstract imagery drawn from religion and philosophy. Eda Lou Walton called them "intellectual arguments" by a poet whose "mental and emotional world is furnished almost entirely with books," and noted that most of these poems have footnotes, and need them.

Mirrors of Venus was subtitled "a novel in sonnets." Its thirty-five sonnets are unorthodox variants of the form, and the book is a novel only to the extent that it tells the story of a brief, uneventful, and not very rewarding friendship as a paradigm of "the entire problem of human relationships in their most subtle form." Those who admired these poems did so for their absolute honesty and originality, their concentrated, sometimes cryptic, intellectual toughness. *Political Self-Portrait* is addressed to and about a number of political figures, among them Harold Laski and Trotsky.

After Wheelwright's death a volume of short poems, half of them new, was published as *Selected Poems*. R. P. Blackmur in his preface warned that "you need to read a good deal of Wheelwright before you catch on to what he was trying to do with his meters and how he went about doing it." Others were ready to defend him against charges that he had no ear by suggesting that he sought harmony rather than melody. And what some saw as misleading or captious in his work seemed to Clement Greenberg evidence of an inability or unwillingness "to practice the necessary insincerities of communication." Blackmur, more successful than most of those who have tried to describe Wheelwright's poetry, says that in it "what is usually fragmentary, disjunct, and irreconcilable is given the impact of mass; the result is a tough, squirming, gnostic verse, modified and exhilarated by New England wit and New England eccentricity, and the unique heresy of New England Anglo-Catholicism—and the whole qualified by New England political radicalism."

The continuing interest in this "recalcitrant" poetry led, thirty years later, to the publication of Wheelwright's *Collected Poems*, edited by Alvin H. Rosenfeld. It assembled the work that had already been collected in earlier volumes and some that had not, including *Dusk to Dawn*, a volume which had been ready for publication at the time of the author's death. John Ashbery, discussing it in the *New York Review of Books*, thought it the poetry of a "major crank" who seemed destined "to end up, albeit kicking and struggling, as classic American." The difficulty of these poems, Ashbery suggested, "proceeds less from arcane allusions than from Wheelwright's peculiarly elliptical turn of mind which convolutes and compresses clarities to the point of opacity. . . . Wheelwright demands that we follow a logic perceptible to him but only intermittently so to us, and that we be prepared to abandon it without warning for another kind of poetic logic. If Crane's poetry presents a baroque façade, Wheelwright's is the architectural underpinnings and calculations that would support such a façade, which we glimpse only rarely in his calmer, lyrical moments." In time, no doubt, scholarship will reveal more of this remarkable structure; meanwhile, as Ashbery says, "the feats of engineering that we can take in are almost enough in themselves."

Wheelwright awakened a fierce loyalty among his friends and admirers, many of whom were themselves poets. Winfield Townley Scott left this description of him: "John Wheelwright was the only American poet who looked as though he might be a member of the Sitwell family. His slenderness made him look taller than he was, a little under six feet. He was long-fingered, nervous in movement; the hair a darkening blond receding from a high forehead; large nose and mouth but small, light-colored eyes which gave his otherwise impressive face an embarrassed attentiveness, shy or sly. 'Cat-eyed, slit-eyed,' Robert Fitzgerald once wrote of him. His grin, his quick habit of blushing, were rather silly and endearing. He could be stern and snappish, like a righteous schoolmarm, the definitive chin setting hard. But he was often amused because basically he was serious, and I recall him as bubbling, gay, easily excited; he would go off in a rapture of whinnying giggle, talking right along through it. He spoke the struck-pie-tin, unresonant nasalities of Boston's upper class." Kenneth Rexroth wrote: "No one has ever taken the place of this dynamic, inexhaustible and lovable mind and completely original talent. Had he written in French, he would have died loaded with honors. As it is, few people have ever heard of him." Austin Warren called him "a serious, meticulous poet; not a minor wit but a master of metaphysical poetry."

PRINCIPAL WORKS: Rock and Shell: Poems, 1923–1933, 1934; Mirrors of Venus: A Novel in Sonnets, 1914–1938, 1938; Political Self-Portrait, 1919–1939, 1940; Selected Poems, 1941; Collected Poems, 1972.

ABOUT: Blackmur, R. P. *prefatory note to* Wheelwright, J. Selected Poems, 1941; Cowley, M. Exile's Return, 1935; Deutsch, B. Poetry in Our Time (2nd ed. rev.), 1963; Gregory, H. and Zaturenska, M. History of American Poetry, 1900–1940, 1946; Rexroth, K. Assays, 1961; Scott, W. T. Exiles and Fabrications, 1961; Warren, A. New England Saints, 1956. *Periodicals*—New York Review of Books February 22, 1973; Southern Review Spring 1972.

WHITE, ANTONIA (March 31, 1899–), English novelist, translator, and journalist, was born in London, the only child of Cecil and Christine (White) Botting. Her father was senior classics master at St. Paul's, the noted London school. He and his wife became converts to Roman Catholicism when Antonia White was seven, and she was then baptized into that faith. She "read voraciously" from the age of four, began to write stories not much later, and was soon "publishing" her own newspaper, which included enthusiastic reviews of her own (imaginary) books.

At nine she went as a boarder to the Convent of the Sacred Heart at Roehampton, Surrey, where she consistently won prizes for her work in languages, literature, and Christian doctrine. When she was fifteen she wrote a Ouidaesque novel which was discovered and caused her expulsion from the convent school, an experience which, she says, left her permanently "burdened by guilt and anxiety about the writing of anything in which I am free to choose my own subject."

From 1914 to 1916 Miss White attended St. Paul's Girls' School, leaving against her father's wishes to become first a governess, then (at seventeen) a teacher in a boys' school, then a civil servant, eking out her income by writing magazine stories and advertising copy as a precocious freelance. In 1919 she went to what is now the Royal Academy of Dramatic Art, and the following year toured the provinces in ingenue roles.

Antonia White's first marriage, in 1921, was a "disaster" and was annulled in 1924 after she had had a mental breakdown and spent nine months in an asylum. Her second marriage (1924) was "a meeting of minds" which lasted until 1929. During these years Miss White became head woman copywriter in an advertising agency, and then

ANTONIA WHITE

spent six months as assistant to Desmond MacCarthy when he was editor of *Life and Letters*. In 1930 she married the journalist Tom Hopkinson. She continued her own journalism and copywriting and also, with her husband's encouragement, completed her first novel, *Frost in May*. The same year, 1933, she became fashion editor of the mass circulation *Daily Mirror* and drama critic of *Time and Tide*.

Mental illness recurred in 1934 and eventually cost her the *Daily Mirror* post. Gradually, however, thanks to a long and "remarkably successful" Freudian analysis, she began to recover, and by 1937 she was a highly paid copywriter for J. Walter Thompson. In that year she was divorced from Tom Hopkinson, and in the following one became fashion editor of the *Sunday Pictorial*. During World War II Miss White worked first for the BBC (1940–1943), then for the Political Intelligence Department of the Foreign Office (1943–1945). Since the war she has supported herself as a writer, journalist, and translator.

Although Miss White lapsed from the Roman Catholic Church in 1926 and returned to it, still full of doubts, only in 1940, Catholicism has never ceased to be her "native language." She is, she says, "incurably religious, by temperament." Her work has been said to draw its tension from the conflict between her rational doubts and instinctive faith. *Frost in May* is a fictionalized account of her life at and expulsion from the convent school, a "neat accomplished" story which became a best seller and remains her best-known book.

It was followed after a long interval by three novels about a young woman, Clara Batchelor, whose life story in many respects parallels Miss White's own. In *The Lost Traveller* Clara leaves school, becomes a governess, and is involved in the accidental death of her pupil. *The Sugar House* carries Clara, now an actress, through a damaging love affair and an unconsummated marriage. *Beyond the Glass* is an account of Clara's collapse into insanity in which Miss White's "exact, realistic and uncharged prose" achieves "not simply a clinical dissection of madness but a most moving evocation of a spirit still suffering though loosed from its controls." Reassessing Miss White's work in the *Times Literary Supplement* (July 3, 1969), Samuel Hynes called these three novels "truth-telling works of art" whose "one, terrible theme [is] the inevitability of the closed heart." The short stories collected in *Strangers* were less highly regarded by most reviewers.

The Hound and the Falcon is a collection of letters written in 1940 and 1941 to a fellow Catholic in which Antonia White discusses her reconversion and gives some account of herself and her life up to those years. Malcolm Muggeridge, praising the book, wrote that its author "is a writer of great talent, and is blessed with a mind of singular, almost terrifying honesty." Another critic has found in her work evidence of "a curiously divided literary personality which expresses itself in one aspect in . . . exact realism and in the other in a sentimentality of the most naïve kind." She is unquestionably one of the most accomplished Catholic women writers of her generation in Britain. Since 1950, when she won the Denyse Clairouin prize for her first translation (of Maupassant's *La Vie*), Miss White has established a new reputation as the extremely distinguished translator of more than thirty books, including a number by Colette.

Antonia White has two daughters, Susan and Lyndall. In 1959 she went as a visiting lecturer in English to St. Mary's College, Notre Dame, Indiana. She received Arts Council grants in 1966 and 1969 and is a Fellow of the Royal Society of Literature. An interviewer described her in 1966 as still "pretty and petite," living with "a bossy Siamese cat in a neat third-floor flat in Kensington." In recent years Miss White has added to her long-standing enthusiasm for cats, conversation, and clothes a "passionate" devotion to cricket.

PRINCIPAL WORKS: Frost in May (novel), 1933; Three in a Room (play), 1947; The Lost Traveller (novel), 1950; The Sugar House (novel), 1952; Beyond the Glass (novel), 1954; Strangers (stories), 1954; Minka and Curdy (for children), 1957; The Hound and the Falcon: The Story of a Reconversion to the Catholic Faith, 1965; Life With Minka and Curdy (for children), 1970.

ABOUT: Catholic Authors, 1952; Vinson, J. (ed.) Contemporary Novelists, 1972; White, A. The Hound and the Falcon, 1965; Who's Who, 1973. *Periodicals*—Observer December 4, 1966; Times Literary Supplement July 3, 1969.

WHITE, THEODORE H(AROLD) (May 6, 1915–), American journalist, historian, and novelist, writes: "I was born in Boston, Massachusetts, a lovely russet-brown city, on May 6, 1915. That is a long time ago but I still find it difficult to think of myself as a writer. I have written novels, histories, journalism, television and movie material; yet it has always seemed to me that I have been more provoked by what was happening outside and around me than by any inner conviction of my own wisdom, authority, or skills. What is happening in the *now* excites me—and if people have been willing to listen to what I have to say then this has been quite simply good fortune.

"The bare bones of my career are simple: I graduated from the Boston Public Latin School in 1932; graduated from Harvard College in 1938, *summa cum laude*; planned to be an academic historian, but received a traveling fellowship which carried me to China-at-war in 1939. The bombs were falling on Chungking; I wrote about the raids; and to my astonishment, found myself a war correspondent; and thus left academia forever.

"I was with the war in Asia until 1945; had a fling at magazine editing after the war; then, from 1948 on, spent five and a half years in Europe reporting its recovery. Thereafter, I returned to the United States (in 1953), had a try at reporting American politics and another at editing magazines until, in 1956, my last magazine, *Collier's*, vanished. Thereafter, novels engaged my energies until, in 1960, I went back to reporting politics in book form. My particular fascination was, and remains, the way of leaders with their people, how they evoke loyalties and capture command in a democracy. The precise focus of such ruminations has been for me the American presidency, and continues to be so, although occasionally, in off years, I try my hand at plays (unproduced), poems (unpublished) and consultancies to various publishing or broadcasting firms (unheeded).

"Out of all this have come a number of books. Two histories—*Thunder Out of China* (1946) and *Fire in the Ashes* (1953) (both Book-of-the-Month Club choices). One collection of memoirs, *The Stilwell Papers* (1948); two novels, *The Mountain Road* (1958) (Book-of-the-Month) and *The View From the Fortieth Floor* (1960) (Literary Guild). To which must be added, finally, two studies of the American presidency: *The Making of the President—1960* and *The Making of the President—1964*. In between have been many articles for American magazines and newspapers, some of which make me proud and others of which are best forgotten; plus three television documentaries—two based on the Making-of-the-President books, and one (*China: The Roots of Madness*) based on my experience in Asia.

THEODORE H. WHITE

"Out of this thirty-year output has come a number of honors. Among them: the Air Medal of the United States Air Corps; the Pulitzer Prize; the Benjamin Franklin Award; the Emmy Award; the Sidney Hillman Award; the Overseas Press Club Award; the Secondary School Board Award (three times); the Sigma Delta Chi Award. The list could stretch longer but, in short, I have been more than adequately rewarded and recognized for what talent I have.

"It is common, I am told, in such efforts as this to attempt a literary self-assessment or analysis. I find this rather awkward. Looking back, I suppose my '*formation*,' as the French call it, was forbiddingly classical. Years of Latin at the Boston Latin School; years of Hebrew at the Hebrew schools of Boston; years of classical Chinese at Harvard and the Harvard Yenching Institute. To which was added the brisk editorial influence of *Time* magazine, my first employers, with their insistence on anecdote, quote, and embellishment. Too much rhetoric, ancient and journalistic, has been pounded into me to retain much taste for rhetoric. Such influences I suppose still linger in my writing and surface in embarrassing patches of purple. But mostly I try hard to be clear; for the best style, it seems to me, is that the reader should be unconscious of style. The reader should be able to peer through the writer's words as if they were transparent. I must admit I sometimes admire the stylists whose artistry can give words a life of their own; as for me, I try to make the words as simple and unobtrusive as possible.

"I find the writing of novels the most difficult of forms; to write a really good novel must be the most gratifying of all achievements. Though my novels have been successful in popular terms I have never written a really good one. I find semi-history the easiest and altogether the pleasantest form of writing. And there is a peculiar thrill in the writing of TV documentaries: words must drape themselves across pictures at precisely the proper points in an exercise of craftsmanship akin to engraving.

"I live in New York City with my wife Nancy Bean White (married 1947) whom I cherish. We have two children—a girl, Ariana van der Heyden White (born 1949) and a son, David Fairbank White (born 1951)."

Theodore H. White, the son of a lawyer, had what he thinks of as "a normal Boston boyhood—placid, penurious, hopeful." Harvard taught him Chinese and his Sheldon Traveling Fellowship took him to China, where in 1939 he joined the Far Eastern staff of *Time* magazine. During the next six years he reported the Sino-Japanese War with an accuracy and insight that made him the youthful "dean of the Chunking correspondents." White resigned as chief of *Time*'s China bureau in 1946, and the same year, in collaboration with Annalee Jacoby, wrote *Thunder Out of China*. Its criticisms of the Nationalist Government made it a highly controversial work, but most reviewers found it "the clearest, frankest and most combatively readable key to an understanding of [China's] current tragedy."

In 1947 White served for a time as a senior editor of the *New Republic* and in 1948, after a year's free-lancing, began his long tour of duty in Europe, first as chief correspondent of the Overseas News Agency, then as European correspondent of the *Reporter* magazine. *Fire in the Ashes* was a study of the postwar regeneration of Europe and of America's contribution to it, "the sanest and most specific appraisal . . . of the pluses and minuses of United States postwar policies toward Europe." Two novels followed, *The Mountain Road*, set in China, and *The View From the Fortieth Floor*, about the Manhattan publishing world. Authentic in background, and sharply observed, both were thought to have the considerable but limited virtues of good journalism.

With *The Making of the President—1960*, White won the Pulitzer Prize and invented a new kind of American political literature. He had spent a year following the seven serious presidential candidates across the United States, from the first primaries to Kennedy's inauguration. The book is a wonderfully detailed account of the contenders' personalities and backgrounds, their supporters and enemies, their strategies and tactics, and the national and often the local issues involved. This mass of data is pointed with countless anecdotes and selected and organized with an unfailing sense of drama.

Some reviewers found occasional gaps in the record, or errors of emphasis; Richard H. Rovere deplored passages of "rhetorical extravagance" and others thought that White's personal admiration for Kennedy here and there overcame his generally successful struggle for objectivity. But these were minor complaints in an almost unanimous chorus of critical enthusiasm for "one of the classic records of American politics." Erwin D. Canham said that "never has there been as competent, penetrating, and complete an account of an American presidential election" and other reviewers spoke of it as the most significant political study of the decade, the work of a "Breughel of the contemporary political scene." It numbered among its four million readers such professionals as Charles de Gaulle and Harold Wilson, and was avidly studied by the candidates in the 1964 presidential election. It has inspired a vogue for massively detailed "inside" stories in newspapers and magazines all over the world.

White has since produced equally comprehensive chronicles of the presidential election campaigns of 1964, 1968, and 1972. None has been received with quite so much excitement as the first (if only because the campaigns themselves have been less dramatic and clear-cut), but all have been welcomed, and studied, and admired: the series has become an American institution.

Long before Watergate, White had expressed his disquiet at the declining quality of American political life. In his play *Caesar at the Rubicon* he proposes that Caesar destroyed the Roman Republic when the power it had given him induced paranoia, "the occupational disease of leaders." The play was received with considerable interest and admiration, but found rather lacking in true theatricality.

According to *Newsweek*, White combines "the eagerness of a little boy, the persistence of an inchworm and an absolute refusal to be bored by anything or anyone in the world. His face is round and cherubic; it doesn't quite match his body, which is muscular, barrel-chested and has a room-filling vitality." His hobbies include "household tinkering and mechanics," swimming, hiking, painting, and reading. He regards himself as "an old-fashioned liberal" who has been forced to see that "goodwill and money" alone are not going to achieve utopia. "So what should a liberal like me think?" he asks. "The forerunner of action is ideas, but we've run out of ideas. The governing ideas of America no longer fit the reality of American life. . . . Before the politicians can work they need new ideas."

PRINCIPAL WORKS: (with Annalee Jacoby) Thunder Out of China, 1946; Fire in the Ashes: Europe in Mid-century,

1953; The Mountain Road (novel), 1958; The View From the Fortieth Floor (novel), 1960; The Making of the President—1960, 1961; The Making of the President—1964, 1965; Caesar at the Rubicon (play), 1968; China: The Roots of Madness (based on television documentary), 1968; The Making of the President—1968, 1969; The Making of the President—1972, 1973. *As editor*—The Stilwell Papers, 1948.

ABOUT: Current Biography, 1955; Who's Who in America, 1972–1973. *Periodicals*—Atlantic Monthly November 1953; National Review July 28, 1966; New York Review of Books August 5, 1965; November 21, 1968; New York Times Book Review May 22, 1960; July 9, 1961; July 11, 1965; July 27, 1969; Newsweek May 12, 1958; July 12, 1965; Publishers Weekly June 11, 1973; Saturday Review May 10, 1958; May 21, 1960; Time May 3, 1968; Vogue October 1, 1959.

WHITING, JOHN (ROBERT) (November 15, 1917–June 16, 1963), English dramatist, was a precursor in the early 1950s of the "new wave" in the British theatre. Writing for an audience not quite ready to hear him, he received a critical mauling which, by curbing his output and perhaps his originality, cost the theatre dearly.

Whiting was born in Salisbury, Wiltshire, the son of Charles Whiting, a solicitor, and the former Dorothy Herring, and educated at Taunton School. Drawn to the theatre from the beginning, he studied at the Royal Academy of Dramatic Art (1935–37) and had started an acting career in repertory when World War II began. As a young man he was a fervent socialist and, like most of his generation, was deeply affected by the Spanish Civil War. Whiting served during World War II in the Royal Artillery and afterwards returned to the stage, spending three years in the York repertory theatre, and playing small parts in Gielgud seasons in London. It was then that he began to write.

His first play, *Conditions of Agreement* (1946), found no producer during his lifetime. *Saint's Day*, written in 1947, at first fared no better. In 1951, however, *A Penny for a Song* achieved the London equivalent of a Broadway production. Written, Whiting said, at a time of intense personal happiness, it is a historical fantasy of great charm, set in Dorset during the Napoleonic wars. It was received with interest by the critics, who found in it a lyricism reminiscent of Christopher Fry, but had only a short run. The same year *Saint's Day* was produced at the Arts Theatre, winning a Festival of Britain play contest, and in the process setting off a bitter and prolonged debate.

Saint's Day is a morality play (and for Whiting a sadly prophetic one), concerned, at the most literal level, with a great writer, Southman, who has been savaged into silence by his critics. Near senility, the old iconoclast is belatedly to be honored as a literary giant. A smooth young critic-poet arrives to escort him to his apotheosis in London, and then rational development is abandoned. The "point of deviation" has been reached and the play lurches off into an apocalyptic vision of anarchy and self-destruction.

The London critics, bewildered by the play's tangled religious symbolism, and irritated by its immaturity, gave it "the worst press in English dramatic criticism." Practicing theatre people protested violently, insisting that "its passion and its unbroken tension" were "the products of a new and extraordinary theatrical mind." Indeed, a 1965 revival elicited an infinitely more respectful response from a generation of critics which, conditioned to private symbolism by Beckett and Pinter, was ready to acknowledge the play's disturbing poetic power. Peter Hall believes that the play "at one blow had changed the post-war theatre," restoring to it its radical function.

Whiting returned in *Marching Song* (1954) to the theme of self-destruction, but this time with a tightly controlled lucidity which chilled the critics as it impressed them. Forster is a general who has massacred a swarm of children blocking the advance of his tanks and then, appalled by what he has done, has in effect relinquished the war to the enemy. The government asks him to kill himself as a scapegoat for his nation's humiliation, and the play turns on his decision. It is a theme that recurs in Whiting's plays: a flawed but heroic figure is forced to weigh the demands of his ego against the claims of humanity, and is obliged by what he learns to accept the destruction of self.

Whiting himself called the play "anti-theatrical" and commercially it failed. For seven years after that London saw no new play by Whiting, though he made some excellent Anouilh translations and wrote a "bitter comedy" called *The Gates of Summer* which closed on tour in 1956. The same play had a considerable success on the Continent where, especially in Germany, Whiting had quickly found an audience.

Just when it seemed that he might be lost altogether to the British theatre, Whiting was commissioned by Peter Hall to write a play for the Royal Shakespeare Company. The result was *The Devils* (1961), derived from Aldous Huxley's *The Devils of Loudon*, about a case of mass demoniacal possession in a French nunnery in the seventeenth century. It was Whiting's last, and in its agonized way, his most hopeful variation on the theme of self-destruction.

Its hero is a libertine priest, Grandier, who inspires the jealous lust of the nunnery's prioress. The nuns pretend possession by the devil and blame Grandier. He is tortured but refuses to confess and, before his horrible death, his lecherous pride in ruins, undergoes a conversion; it is an ambiguous conversion however, to Humanity, it would seem, rather than to the Christian God.

The play offended many Catholics and struck some critics, for all "its rapid mosaic construction and its sharply economical dialogue," as less deeply felt and less original than its predecessors. But to most reviewers, *The Devils* seemed close to a masterpiece, its "dark theatrical eloquence" reminding them of Webster and the greater Jacobeans. The play, later filmed by Ken Russell, brought Whiting his first and, in the event, his only commercial success. He died of cancer in 1963, at the age of forty-five.

Whiting left unfinished a second play for the Royal Shakespeare Company. He had written several unremarkable films, some dramatic criticism (reprinted in two posthumous collections), a drastically revised television version of *Conditions of Agreement*, a one-act play called *No Why*, and a number of short stories. A slight, dark man, Whiting was shy and withdrawn, though with "enormous reserves of emotion." Peter Hall says that his "vision was proud, arrogant, skeptical, yet it was also facetious, sentimental, naïve. Like all misanthropes, he was a great idealist." He had abandoned the socialism of his youth in favor of a belief in the "private man," and he considered that "art is not an efficient means of propaganda." He was survived by his wife, the former Asthore Lloyd Mawson, and four children.

Whiting is now generally recognized to have been a tragically underrated dramatist who died just as he was about to receive the acclaim due to him. But it is not easy to blame the critics and audiences who failed to appreciate Whiting's early plays. In a postwar period, when the British theatre was dominated by a general hunger for undemanding entertainment, he offered nihilistic and nonrealistic plays, their plots dense with philosophical themes, their dialogue moving disturbingly from the colloquial to the poetic, their imagery often obscure. It is not surprising that their large virtues were overlooked. Ronald Hayman has described those virtues in his study of Whiting, and seizes in particular on his ability, "partly because of the poetry in his prose, partly because of the poetry in his situations," to create tragic heroes of the caliber of Southman in *Saint's Day* and Forster in *Marching Song*; "in a period when tragedy was thought to be dead . . . Whiting has quietly revived the corpse."

PRINCIPAL WORKS: *Plays*—The Plays of John Whiting (Saint's Day, A Penny for a Song, Marching Song), 1957; The Devils, 1961; No Why, 1961; The Collected Plays of John Whiting (2 vols.), 1969. *Criticism*—John Whiting on Theatre, 1966; The Art of the Dramatist, 1970.

ABOUT: Armstrong, W. A. (ed.) Experimental Drama, 1963; Hayman, R. John Whiting, 1969; International Theatre Annual, 1956; Lumley, F. New Trends in Twentieth Century Drama, 1960; Taylor, J. R. Anger and After, 1962; Trussler, S. The Plays of John Whiting, 1972. *Periodicals*—Drama Spring 1956, Autumn 1963; Encore November–December 1957, January–February 1960, July–August 1964; Modern Drama Spring 1965, December 1968; New Statesman October 13, 1951; October 20, 1951; April 17, 1954; February 24, 1961; May 14, 1965; New York Times June 17, 1963; November 14, 1965; Nimbus Autumn 1954; Spectator March 10, 1961; August 10, 1962; Times June 17, 1963; Tulane Drama Review Winter 1966; World Theatre 4 1955.

WHITTEMORE, (EDWARD) REED (September 11, 1919–), American poet, short story writer, essayist, critic, and editor, writes: "My father was a doctor in New Haven, Connecticut, my mother a young schoolteacher from North Adams, Massachusetts. I was born in 1919 on East Rock Road in New Haven, and when I was still a baby my parents moved up the street to live in the large—and for my mother forbidding—house of my paternal grandmother. I had electric trains and bikes and a private room and all—we seem to have been fairly rich until the Crash—and I went to private schools after the fourth and fifth grade (first Hopkins Grammar School in New Haven, then Phillips Academy, Andover) and spent summers at camp or with friends on Cape Cod. I first got interested in writing at Andover. In my senior year there I won a prize for a misty essay entitled 'On Being Disinterested,' and from then on I was stuck. I went to Yale and immediately became a literary entrepreneur. I started several novels (all, as I remember, single-spaced), wrote poems and stories, was elected *to* the Yale Lit and became disillusioned *by* the Yale Lit, all in one year. Then late in my sophomore year I began with my roommate, Jim Angleton, a non-campus or off-campus literary magazine called *Furioso*. Yale went on. I graduated in 1941 and was drafted. When Pearl Harbor came I had completed basic training and was in line for OCS. I became a second lieutenant in the Infantry in the middle of 1942, and found myself in the Air Force abroad by fall. I stayed overseas in the Mediterranean with the Twelfth Air Force for three years, emerging as a captain—a non-flying, headquarters officer who earned a Bronze Star for writing fine memoranda and keeping records of one-hundred octane gas consumption.

"Back home I didn't know what to do with myself, so went to Princeton graduate school for a year, concentrating in history. Offered a temporary teaching job at Carleton College in Minnesota, I took it and stayed on, abandoning graduate work. I started up *Furioso* again, first with an editorial board of writer friends, then with a board of Carleton English teachers. The magazine went on until 1953, then was resumed under college auspices (*The Carleton Miscellany*) in 1960. During all this postwar time I was writing, mostly in the summers, mostly poems and essays. I had given up novels. I had decided that my talent, whatever it was, was a short-term recurrent thing suited for lots of starts, few long-range continuances (I even contemplated a book of poems once which was to consist entirely of prefaces). But one can get tired of that too. By the time I reached forty my real interest was in extended discursive statements in prose and verse, and I was persuaded that poems of mine like 'The Self-Made Man' or 'The Seven Days' were probably the kind in which I was most at home (after a fling with some Pope-like mock epics I had decided that I really had little interest in narrative, in prose or verse). And this is where I am now.

"As I write this I have been teaching, off and on, at Carleton for nearly twenty years, and have settled in as an academic husband with three children for somewhat less than that (my wife's maiden name: Helen Lundoon). In 1964–1965 I was Consultant in Poetry at the Library of Congress. As a director of the Association of Literary Magazines of America I still have my finger in the little-magazine pie, and as an ex-chairman of the Carleton English Department I can frequently be heard pontificating about how to teach freshman composition, or how to modify, no, rebuild graduate training in English. Perhaps I will end being thought of as an administrator poet, but I hope not. The books to relieve me of that title, if only they will, are listed below."

Heroes and Heroines contained poems written between 1941 and 1946, most of them witty verse portraits of figures from life, literature, or legend. Reviewers were reminded of Auden's early work and praised "a talent that is lyric, critical and dramatic." Similarly amusing and bookish poems, including some revised from the first book, made up *An American Takes a Walk*, which was generally enjoyed, though some reviewers wondered if Whittemore should not be making more serious use of his "very obvious" gifts.

Poems and essays written between 1957 and 1962 were collected in *The Boy from Iowa*, and *The Fascination of the Abomination* was another selection of prose (including short stories as well as essays) and verse. Both volumes lament or satirize the inadequacies of contemporary American society and the absurdity of the artist in it—"the insufficiences of his own meditations, his own art, his own rhetoric." It was the essays which fared best in reviews of these two works. The verse seemed to most critics uneven in tone and quality, reminiscent now of Byron, now of Ogden Nash, and for the most part "sturdy anti-romantic verse put together at relatively low temperatures." The stories were even less warmly received, but were thought most successful in the creation of a particular mood or feeling—most often nostalgic. But for

REED WHITTEMORE

the essays and reviews there was little but praise. X. J. Kennedy called them "bitter-witted harangues by an engaging egoist," presented in "what may be at the moment one of the lithest prose styles going." Julian Moynihan said that in this form Whittemore "writes like a person; that is, with humor, toughmindedly, tentatively and with genuine personal involvement."

Howard Nemerov believes that Whittemore's verse, because it is "often funny" and "often literary," has been unjustly neglected. *Poems: New and Selected*, however, renewed critical interest in Whittemore's verse. Lewis Turco thought he had showed "that the best qualities of prose may be a fit vehicle for a new poetry. Not that Whittemore's are prose-poems, exactly. Still, many of these poems, particularly the recent ones, make more use of grammatical constructions . . . than of the cadences-based units traditional in Anglo-American verse." Laurence Lieberman, rather similarly, admired the "knotty, gymnastic rhythms" he found in the later poems and, even though he thought them at times gratuitously difficult, welcomed "a fresh and promising tone frequency that could lead to a strangely alive new scale in Whittemore's art."

"To find one's self, to know one's self": these, Whittemore believes, "are perhaps the major quests of most poetic meditation." He thinks of poetry as "a thing of the mind" and tends to judge it "by the qualities of mind it displays." He joined the faculty of Carleton College in 1947 and was professor of English there from 1962 to 1967, chairman of his department from 1962 to 1964. In 1967–1968 he was at Princeton University as the

Bain-Swiggert Lecturer and since then he has been professor of English at the University of Maryland. In 1969 he became literary editor of the *New Republic*. The most notable of the honors accorded him is the Harriet Monroe Prize, awarded by *Poetry* in 1954.

PRINCIPAL WORKS: Heroes and Heroines: Poems, 1946; An American Takes a Walk, and Other Poems, 1956; The Self-Made Man, and Other Poems, 1959; The Boy from Iowa: Poems and Essays, 1962; The Fascination of the Abomination: Poems, Stories, Essays, 1963; Poems: New and Selected, 1967; From Zero to the Absolute (essays), 1967; Fifty Poems Fifty, 1970.

ABOUT: Contemporary Authors 9–10, 1964; Murphy, R. (ed.) Contemporary Poets of the English Language, 1970; Nemerov, H. Poetry and Fiction, 1963; Whittemore, R. Poetry As Discovery, *in* Nemerov, H. (ed.) Poets on Poetry, 1966; Who's Who in America, 1972–1973.

WHYTE, LANCELOT LAW (November 4, 1896-September 14, 1972), British philosopher of science, wrote: "In my parents' home in Edinburgh everything was viewed against a universal and international background, above the sectarian divisions that separate man from man. The key to my work is expressed in the words of Henry Drummond (which my mother read to me when I was a child and have remained with me ever since): "*The Law of Continuity*: if nature is a harmony, all aspects of man (physical, mental, moral, and spiritual) fall within the circle of nature, and are inseparable from one another. There are no discontinuities between the physical, organic, mental, and spiritual." That sense of a comprehensive unity is the underlying theme of eleven books in which I have sought help to develop a '*unitary*' way of thinking appropriate to the twentieth century.

"Eight happy years at Bedales (J. H. Badley's co-educational school in England) were followed by three on the Western Front, 1916–1918, as an artillery officer, and then by three at Cambridge, studying mathematics and physics. But the war had left me restless, and as I was interested in physical *ideas*, while support was then given mainly to experiment and mathematics, I left Cambridge. During the two decades 1924–1945, I was in turn scientist in industry, Rockefeller Fellow (physics, in Berlin), with an investment bank, and during the Second World War in the Ministry of Supply in London. In October 1935 I met Frank Whittle, the creator of the British jet engine, and had no doubt that he was one of the great inventor engineers of our time. As my own ideas developed very slowly I was glad to earn a living by helping to develop the ideas of others, and from 1936 to 1941 I was managing director of Power Jets Limited, the company which brought Whittle's engine from the drawing board to the first successful flight in 1941.

"From 1930 onwards I had watched with growing horror the progressive collapse of the old Europe under Hitler. The murderous Battle of the Somme (1916) represented for me the end of the classical European idealism, and the 1930s proved that this interpretation was right. The tragedies of 1933–1940 affected me deeply because my second wife Lotte (who died in 1941) was born in Vienna. Hence I was led to write, 1939–1943, *The Next Development in Man*, in which I sought to interpret the decline of a noble but inadequate European ideal and to foretell the emergence of a new 'unitary man.'

"Since 1945 I have devoted myself to writing on various aspects of 'unitary thought,' such as the importance of 'form' and of 'formative processes' in the inorganic world, organic nature, and man; the formative power of the unconscious mind; the role of internal factors in evolution; and the transformation of 'atomic' ideas towards a future theory of *ordered structures* at many levels of the inorganic and organic realms.

"This work has been made possible by the generous response of individuals and institutions in the U.S.A., where I have lectured frequently. My future books will probably be concerned with one major theme: the advance towards a comprehensive unification and simplification of scientific knowledge (in spite of everything I still believe this possible!), so that everyone can, in some degree, *feel* its truth in their own experience. Scientific knowledge must become human understanding. That is, I believe, the only way in which humanity can acquire the moral strength to control technology.

"In 1947 I married Eva Korner, born Czech."

The author's father, who was sixty when Whyte was born, was senior minister of the United Free Church of St. George in Edinburgh. On the ground floor of their house was a gymnasium where the minister's assistants taught sexual sublimation through physical training. All this Scottish Calvinism was ameliorated, however, by the religious eclecticism of Whyte's mother, who had a passion for Buddhism and a variety of other faiths, and by his sister's Christian Science. Whyte's education in a succession of experimental schools in England also did much to free him from the rigid sexual attitudes of this eccentric, scholarly household.

At Bedales (1906–1915) Whyte read widely, discovering through such works as Bertrand Russell's *Problems of Philosophy* (1912) that his prime interest was in the constitution of matter. The direction his work was to take was already established when World War I intervened. That war, in which Whyte won the Military Cross, can scarcely have been conducive to the development of a philosophy of "comprehensive unity" and, as Whyte said in his note above, Cambridge did little to help.

Frustrated, threatened by the onset of a severe neurosis and the end of his early first marriage, Whyte left the university in 1922 feeling that his life and his ambitions were in ruins. For three years he wandered about the world, building up contacts in European academic and industrial circles, and becoming particularly attached to Vienna. There he met his second wife, Lotte Heller, whom he married on Christmas Day, 1926. This relationship, together with other stabilizing factors, enabled Whyte to order and clarify his ideas.

His first book, *Archimedes: or, The Future of Physics*, appeared in 1928. It suggests ways in which a universal science might be approached by linking recent advances in physics to the problems of matter, life, and mind. He developed these ideas in *Critique of Physics* (1931), and still further in his first important book, *The Next Development in Man* (1944), in which he attempted to formulate his new system of thought, based on the "unitary postulate."

Whyte went on to outline two of the elements in this unitary system in *The Unitary Principle in Physics and Biology*, and examined the idea of a characteristic formal pattern as the basis of matter in *Accent on Form*. He saw in the history of the universe a developing, pulsating system of organisms from which our world has gradually built up: " 'Life' may be regarded as the spreading of a pattern as it pulsates."

Whyte was profoundly influenced by the work of Freud and Jung, and by a general appreciation of the importance of the subconscious in the development of thought processes as well as in character development. *The Unconscious Before Freud* is both an account of pre-Freudian theories of the unconscious and an application of Whyte's unitary theories to the development of mind. Even in his autobiography, *Focus and Diversions*, he found a vehicle for this theory, constructing the book as a sequence of "tales" about various episodes in his life in such a way as to emphasize the inseparability of life and thought. *Internal Factors in Evolution* proposes an evolutionary theory in keeping with his views.

Scientists tend to complain that Whyte's ideas are difficult to grasp, often closer to metaphysics than to science, and supported by too little experimental evidence. Others, however, even when they do not accept his arguments, are stimulated by the "brilliance and daring" of his thought, his willingness to grapple with really fundamental questions. A writer in the *Times Literary Supplement*,

LANCELOT LAW WHYTE

reviewing Whyte's autobiography, acknowledged that his unitary theory has not so far been found convincing but adds: "Who knows that some future historian may not . . . say, 'It's all in Whyte!' "

PRINCIPAL WORKS: Archimedes: or, The Future of Physics, 1928; Critique of Physics, 1931; The Next Development in Man, 1944; Everyman Looks Forward, 1946; The Unitary Principle in Physics and Biology, 1949; (as ed.) Aspects of Form, 1951; Accent on Form, 1954; The Unconscious Before Freud, 1960; The Atomic Problem, 1961; Essay on Atomism, 1961; Focus and Diversions (autobiography), 1963; Internal Factors in Evolution, 1965; (ed., with others) Hierarchical Structures, 1969.

ABOUT: Contemporary Authors 15–16, 1966. *Periodicals*—New Statesman September 5, 1931; New York Herald Tribune Book Review April 25, 1948; January 1, 1961; Saturday Review April 24, 1948; Time March 8, 1948; Times (London) September 19, 1972; Times Literary Supplement August 17, 1951; January 2, 1964.

WIBBERLEY, LEONARD (PATRICK O'CONNOR) (April 9, 1915–), Anglo-Irish writer for children and adults, was born in Dublin. He is one of the six children of Thomas Wibberley, a professor of agriculture who was influential during the 1920s in the modernization of Irish agriculture, and the former Sinaid O'Connor, a teacher. He had his early education in Gaelic and learned English only after the family moved to London when he was eight. Wibberley says that he is "three parts Irish, one part English," and his literary background was similarly divided between the Irish legends and folktales he absorbed from his parents and his nurse as a small boy and the English books he encountered at Cardinal Vaughan's School in London—notably *Treasure Island*, still

LEONARD WIBBERLEY

his favorite work of fiction, and the one that first stirred his own literary ambitions.

His father died when Wibberley was fifteen, and he was obliged to leave school and set about earning his living. He wanted to be a journalist and began in the traditional manner, as a copy boy on the London *Sunday Express*. He had graduated to a reporter's job on the *Daily Mirror* when the Depression put him out of work. After a stint as an itinerant street musician he returned to Fleet Street as assistant London editor of two Malayan newspapers. In 1936 he went to Trinidad, where he worked as an editor and in other capacities, and served for two years at the beginning of World War II with the Trinidad Artillery Volunteers. In 1943 Wibberley settled in the United States, where he worked for the Associated Press, as American correspondent for the London *Evening News*, on the Los Angeles *Times*, and at various other jobs until 1954. By then he had published several books and grown tired of selling his life, as he puts it, for the money to feed himself. He has earned his living ever since as a remarkably prolific and versatile freelance writer.

Wibberley does not consider that he works very hard, but finds it easy to turn out five or ten pages a day. This has very quickly added up to a great many books—something like seventy of them by 1968. About two thirds of these have been for teenagers and children, and this aspect of his work is discussed in his own note in *More Junior Authors* and in Ted Hines's profile of Wibberley in the *Wilson Library Bulletin* (June 1963). Some of Wibberley's books for young people are published as by "Patrick O'Connor."

Of his books for adults, the best known are no doubt his amiable satirical fantasies, especially *The Mouse That Roared*, *The Mouse on the Moon*, and *The Mouse on Wall Street*, about the adventures of a minute and run-down European principality which involves itself with hilarious results in the cold war power struggle. Both books were praised for their sound and pleasant style, the skill and humor with which Wibberley wins the reader's "enchanted suspension of disbelief," and the satirical touches, which add up to a telling "plea for sanity." Wibberley's gift for fantasy is also evident in his lyrical novels of the Galway coast, like *The Hands of Cormac Joyce* and *Stranger at Killknock*, which have some of the quality of the folktales he learned as a child. As "Leonard Holton," Wibberley writes mystery stories set in Los Angeles, with a Roman Catholic priest as his resident detective.

Wibberley's adult nonfiction shares the characteristics of his fiction—much gusto, goodwill, and common sense, a generally light touch, and a smooth-running if undistinguished prose style. He often writes best when his own engaging personality becomes part of the narrative, as it does for example in such travel books as *No Garlic in the Soup*, an anecdotal account of a family visit to Portugal, and his Irish adventures, *The Land That Isn't There* and *The Shannon Sailors*.

Leonard Wibberley is a slim, blue-eyed man somewhat above average height, who wears spectacles and a very considerable beard. He is married to the former Katherine Holton, has six children, and lives in California. He describes himself as a liberal and a Christian, and enjoys music and painting.

PRINCIPAL WORKS: *Fiction*—Mrs. Searwood's Secret Weapon, 1954; The Mouse That Roared, 1954; The Hands of Cormac Joyce, 1960; Stranger at Killknock, 1961; The Mouse on the Moon, 1962; A Feast of Freedom, 1964; The Road from Toomi, 1968; The Mouse on Wall Street, 1969; Meeting with a Great Beast, 1971; The Testament of Theophilus: A Novel of Christ and Caesar, 1973. *Nonfiction*—Epics of Everest, 1954; Trouble with the Irish, 1956; The Coming of the Green, 1958; No Garlic in the Soup, 1959; The Land That Isn't There, 1960; Yesterday's Land, 1961; Ventures into the Deep: The Thrill of Scuba Diving, 1962; Toward a Distant Island, 1966; Something to Read (essays), 1967; Hound of the Sea, 1969; Voyage by Bus, 1971; The Shannon Sailors, 1972.

ABOUT: Contemporary Authors 7–8, 1963; More Junior Authors, 1963; Ward, M. E. and Marquardt, D. A. Authors of Books for Young People, 1964. *Periodicals*—Wilson Library Bulletin June 1963.

***WIESEL, ELIE(ZER)** (September 30, 1928–), American novelist and journalist, writes: "Born in Sighet, a small Transylvanian town somewhere in the Carpathian mountains, where most people didn't know whether they were Hungarian or

* vē zel′

Rumanian nationals, I am now (1966) an American citizen who writes Jewish-inspired novels in French.

"As far as I can recall my first name has always been a source of confusion to me and to others as well; it still is.

"I was given the Hebrew name—Eliezer—of my father's father who died for the Kaiser in the first world war. But for some bureaucratic reason it was transcribed as Lazare on my birth certificate. At home I was nicknamed Liczu, while at school everybody seemed to prefer me as Leizer. Present-day friends call me Elie. And I do not like to be addressed by my last name alone which anyway is inevitably more often than not misspelled or mispronounced—or both.

"And I was too timid to correct mistakes of this kind. I still am. For years I used to blush whenever I heard myself pronouncing my own name.

"My father owned a grocery store and his dream had been to make me go to renowned universities and then return home as a doctor of philosophy. As for my mother, she was devotedly religious and she saw in me a future Hasidic Rabbi. Both died before realizing that I would become neither.

"Sighet chased out its Jews in 1944. One night we arrived in Auschwitz. I saw my mother and younger sister go into darkness before turning the clouds ablaze. That was the last time I saw them. I did not know where they were going. Now there is little that I do not know.

"My father remained with me to the end—his end. I lost him early in 1945 in Buchenwald. I watched him losing ground. He was saying something unintelligible and often I like to think that the words I write are his unspoken ones.

"After liberation I refused to be repatriated and find strangers in my home. I went to France instead, with a transport of refugee children. One news magazine covered our arrival and for the first time in my life my picture appeared in print. One copy fell into the hands of my oldest sister. That's how she discovered that I was alive. That's how I learned that another sister survived as well. This may explain why I have been for many years associated with newspapers—although there must have been more prosaic reasons too.

"It was in Paris that I became a journalist, but my first writings were done while still a child. At the age of twelve or thirteen I filled hundreds of pages: not stories or fiction, but commentaries to the Bible and Talmud. Some were found by a friend who did not return to Sighet. Thanks to his generosity and indulgence, they are now in my possession again—but unfit for publication.

"That I was going to try and do some 'serious' writing—that became clear to me during the months immediately following the liberation. But secretly I was afraid of the word 'serious.' Thus I made a vow to wait ten full years before I was to tell my first tale, and that was 'Night.'

ELIE WIESEL

"I still work for newspapers—though less than before—and between one tale and the other I wonder whether they can at all be told."

Elie Wiesel is the son of Shlomo and Sarah (Feig) Wiesel. He was fifteen when he and his family entered Auschwitz, not yet seventeen when he emerged alone from Buchenwald. He began his journalistic career in 1948, when he went to Israel as a nineteen-year-old war correspondent for a French newspaper. From 1948 to 1951 he studied at the Sorbonne, earning his living as a choir director and as a teacher of the Bible, and paying a visit to India. He subsequently became chief foreign correspondent of the Tel Aviv daily *Yedioth Ahronot*, and in 1956 was in New York to report on the United Nations when he was struck and seriously injured by a taxicab in Times Square. Despite this painful initiation, while recovering in a New York hospital he decided to settle in the United States. Since 1957 he has been on the staff of the New York Yiddish-language newspaper the *Jewish Daily Forward*.

The first of the books that Wiesel calls his "serious work" was *La Nuit* (1958, translated by Stella Rodway as *Night*). It is a "spare, unblinking" record of what had happened to him and to his family in the German concentration camps and of the destruction of his faith in God. The book had first appeared in Yiddish in Buenos Aires as *Un di Velt Hot Geshvign* (And the World Has Remained Silent, 1956), and had been written at the urging of François Mauriac, whom Wiesel had interviewed in 1954 and who had become a close friend. A reviewer in the *New Yorker* wrote: "The concentration camp appears to be one of the distinctive institutions of the twentieth century; Mr. Wiesel's book has conveyed its essence, and Mauriac's foreword succinctly states the appalling metaphysical question it poses to the Christian."

There followed a series of brief mythopoeic novels in which Wiesel explores the fate and role of such survivors as himself. *L'Aube* (1960, translated by Anne Borchardt as *Dawn*) studies a young Israeli terrorist schooling himself to hate his enemy. *Le Jour* (1961, translated by Anne Borchardt as *The Accident*) is a strongly autobiographical novel about another death camp survivor, recovering from an automobile accident in New York, who comes to realize that his failure to die with his fellows in Auschwitz had become a stigma that was driving him to self-destruction. *La Ville de la chance* (1964, translated by Stephen Becker as *The Town Beyond the Wall*), a painful parable about the world's indifference to cruelty and injustice, was called "a legend of an ascent from purgatory to possibility."

An altogether more complex novel, *Les Portes de la fôret* (1966), also has the quality of a folk legend or parable. Translated by Frances Frenaye as *The Gates of the Forest*, it tells the story of a young Hungarian Jew who survives the German occupation because of the self-sacrifice of other men. "It ends," as one critic wrote, "with an identification between the Messiah and Everyman, and an insistence on the creation of joy from despair." Denser in texture than Wiesel's earlier books, "its moral action is also translated precisely and forcefully into dramatic action."

Wiesel visited the Soviet Union in 1965, and in *The Jews of Silence* pleads urgently for the world's Jews to speak out against the oppression of Soviet Jewry: "What torments me most is not the Jews of silence I met in Russia; but the silence of the Jews I live among today." *Legends of Our Time* is a collection of stories, reportage, and autobiographical fragments seeking to provide a moral perspective from which to view the horrors of the Nazi regime. It draws its strength, Robert Alter suggested, from its "blurring of conventional distinctions between fact and fiction, observation and invention." In Wiesel's own words, "some events do take place, but are not true; and others are—although they never occurred."

This blend of fact and invention is maintained in *Le Mendiant de Jérusalem* (1968, translated by Lily Edelman and the author as *A Beggar in Jerusalem*). Wiesel had returned to Israel at the outbreak of the Six-Day War in June 1967. The war is represented in this ambitious novel as a turning point in the tormented history of the Jews—a coming of age of an entire people. This is symbolized in the experiences of David, another of Wiesel's survivor figures who, in the course of a long night at the Wailing Wall in Jerusalem, after the victory, is freed from the burden of his past. V. S. Pritchett found the reporting of the war out of key with the rest, and wrote that "Wiesel is at his best when his impulse is poetic and almost saintly, when he is snatching the spirit of the Jewish tale, in his power to move us with sharp fragments of Jewish history." But David Stern called the book "a spiritual adventure so profound that it demands to be judged in terms of major world literature." It received the Prix Médicis in France, and was a best seller there and in the United States.

Entre deux soleils (1970) is a collection of essays, prose poems, and stories translated by Lily Edelman and the author as *One Generation After*. Wiesel said that it would be his last book about the Holocaust—that in future he would address himself to some of the more affirmative aspects of the Jewish tradition. This he does in *Souls on Fire*, a book which grew out of his lectures on Hasidism at the Sorbonne and at the New York YMHA. It retells Hasidic tales and legends and blends these with portraits of some of the Hasidic masters and an account of the movement. The contemporary relevance of Hasidism, Wiesel suggests, is that it offers not answers to the great questions which haunt mankind, but a way to live—even to live joyously—in a world without answers; it advocates the "laughter that springs from lucid and desperate awareness . . . a laughter of revolt against a universe where man, whatever he may do, is condemned in advance." Charles E. Silberman thought that scholars might quarrel with Wiesel's version of Hasidism, but argued that the book is not intended as a work of historical scholarship: "It is a work of genius and of art—an extraordinary man's extraordinary effort 'to humanize fate.' "

Wiesel's concerns are fundamentally religious: a passionate attempt to forgive God for his betrayal of man; a passionate affirmation, in the teeth of the evidence, of faith in man. Irving Wardle called *The Gates of the Forest* "less a novel than a prayer," and whether Wiesel is an artist or simply a witness is a matter of opinion. Emile Capouya has found his writing close to sentimentality and undistinguished in style, and R. M. Elman says that some of his "existentialist parables are deeply flawed by an opacity of language and construction." But critical admiration for his work has always outweighed such complaints, and does so increasingly. Daniel Stern has said that "not since Albert Camus has there been such an eloquent spokesman for man," and Silberman thinks him "one of the great writers of this generation."

Wiesel was married in 1969 to Marion Erster

Rose, by whom he has a son, Shlomo Elisha. He lives in New York City, where he often visits members of the Hasidic community in the Williamsburg section of Brooklyn. He also spends much time in Paris and in Israel. He writes mostly in French, but also knows Hebrew and Yiddish, English, Hungarian, and German. In 1972–1973 he was a visiting professor at the City University of New York, teaching courses in Hasidism and Jewish literature, and in 1973 he joined the university's faculty as a Distinguished Professor. He holds several honorary degrees.

The author, slight in build, short in stature, is said to speak softly, "as though he is thinking aloud," and to have "the dark, somber intensity of a Dante or a Savonarola." His annual fall lectures at the Ninety-Second Street YMHA in New York are sold out months in advance and, according to an article in the New York *Times*, "no major Jewish organization feels it has arrived until it has had Elie Wiesel address a meeting." Indeed he has become something of a spiritual phenomenon —a symbol of those who survived the holocaust and yet can conceive of the possibility of hope. Wiesel himself has sometimes confessed to a sense of impotence as a post-Holocaust writer: "the words lag behind reality." But he believes that "some writing can sometimes, in moments of grace, attain the quality of deeds," creating meaning where no meaning can be.

PRINCIPAL WORKS IN ENGLISH TRANSLATION: Night, 1960; Dawn, 1961; The Accident, 1962; The Town Beyond the Wall, 1964; The Gates of the Forest, 1966; The Jews of Silence: A Personal Report on Soviet Jewry, 1966; Legends of Our Time, 1968; Zalem, or, The Madness of God (play), 1968; A Beggar in Jerusalem, 1970; One Generation After, 1970; Souls on Fire, 1972; The Oath, 1973.

ABOUT: Alter, R. After the Tradition, 1969; Contemporary Authors, 1st revision 5–8, 1969; Current Biography, 1970; Kahn, L. Mirrors of the Jewish Mind, 1968; Who's Who in America, 1972–1973; Who's Who in World Jewry, 1972. *Periodicals*—Book Week May 29, 1966; Book World October 20, 1968; Commonweal May 12, 1967; April 28, 1972; Figaro Littéraire June 1966, December 1968; Nation October 17, 1968; New York Review of Books March 23, 1967; January 2, 1969; New York Times January 31, 1973; New York Times Book Review June 12, 1966; January 21, 1969; January 25, 1970; March 5, 1972; Nouvelles Littéraires November 1968; Saturday Review October 19, 1968; January 31, 1970.

WILLIAMS, JAY (May 31, 1914–), American novelist, was born in Buffalo, New York, the son of Max and Lillian (Weinstein) Jacobson. He spent his childhood in Buffalo and Rochester and still has vivid memories of the imaginative games he played as a boy "in the woods of Rochester and in and about the Barge Canal, which became, by turns, Sherwood Forest, Caerleon, the African jungles, or the Amazon River." Williams attended De Witt Clinton High School in New York City; at the University of Pennsylvania (1932–1933) and at Columbia University (1933–1934) he majored in English and took part in university theatricals.

JAY WILLIAMS

Williams emerged from college into the Depression, and at first drifted from one job to another. For a while he studied at the Art Students League and then, following in his father's path, worked as a comedian and as a master of ceremonies on the "borscht circuit" in the Catskills. For two years he was a general stage manager in the Federal Theatre Project, and from 1937 to 1941 he was a theatrical press agent for the Group Theatre, Jed Harris, and others. He served in the army during World War II, and saw action in Germany, where he earned a Purple Heart.

It was during the war that Williams' first book appeared, a historical mystery for boys called *The Stolen Oracle*. Set in Augustan Rome, it was praised for the authenticity of its background, and generally well received. *The Counterfeit African*, another book for boys, followed in 1944. When Williams was discharged from the army in 1945 he settled down to full-time writing, and since then has produced a great many admirable books, factual as well as fictional, for children and teen-agers.

The Good Yeomen, Williams' first historical novel for adults, was published in 1948. It is a highly original interpretation of the Robin Hood story, in which the folk hero is seen as merely a "conservative" bandit leader, and Little John is presented as the true champion of the oppressed peasantry. The critics liked the book, finding in it the pace, the concern for accuracy, and the solid characterization which distinguish Williams' stories for children. One reviewer described the author's use of fourteenth century language as "a little self-conscious" but concluded that "he tells a lively, often bawdy, and very reasonable version of the familiar story."

In 1949 Williams received a Guggenheim Fellowship which enabled him to travel in Europe, gathering material for new historical novels. Perhaps the most notable of these has been *Tomorrow's Fire*, set in the twelfth century during the Third Crusade. The novel purports to quote from and comment upon the journal of Denys de Courtebarbe, a poet and God-seeker in the service of Richard Cœur de Lion. This device, as Mary Renault wrote, takes the reader "right inside the age" but also allows him "most effectively to look from the outside too. Above all, Richard I has been prized free at last from the dead hand of romancers and brilliantly interpreted as Richard Yea-and-Nay, the strange, complex, magnetic Angevin that he really was. The great panorama shines like a cleaned picture, vivid and real." The antiromantic gusto of Williams' historical novels reflects the influence of his acknowledged master, François Rabelais.

The Forger, Williams' first contemporary novel, is set in the New York art world, where an ambitious young painter becomes two kinds of forger—in his work and in his attempt to remold his girl's personality. Edmund Fuller thought the book had "shallows with its depths," that it was a little too neat and smart and flippant, but he called it "distinctly a good book, lively and highly readable," an opinion shared by most reviewers. The author's other contemporary fiction includes several civilized and exciting suspense novels, published as by "Michael Delving," and dealing with the adventures of a Connecticut rare book dealer in the remoter parts of rural Britain. Notable among Williams' nonfiction books are *Fall of the Sparrow*, a wryly humorous survey of animal species that have become extinct in the past two thousand years and others that will soon disappear if man does not mend his ways, and *Change of Climate*, an account of the author's travels abroad.

Jay Williams was married in 1941 to Barbara Girsdansky. They have two children and live in West Redding, Connecticut, where Williams is very active in community affairs. The author is five feet ten inches in height and has blue eyes. He is a keen amateur naturalist, and enjoys travel, archery, and fencing. In 1953 he played a featured role in the movie *Little Fugitive*.

PRINCIPAL WORKS: The Good Yeomen (novel), 1948; Fall of the Sparrow (ecology), 1951; The Rogue from Padua (novel), 1952; The Siege (novel), 1955; Change of Climate (travel), 1956; The Witches (novel), 1957; Solomon and Sheba (novel), 1959; The Forger (novel), 1961; Tomorrow's Fire (novel), 1964; Uniad (novel), 1968. *As "Michael Delving"*—Smiling the Boy Fell Dead (novel), 1967; The Devil Finds Work (novel), 1969; Die Like a Man (novel), 1970; A Shadow of Himself, 1972.

ABOUT: Contemporary Authors 2, 1963; Current Biography, 1955; Ward, M. E. and Marquardt, D. A. Authors of Books for Young People, 1964.

WILLIAMS, JOHN A(LFRED) (December 5, 1925-), American novelist, poet, and journalist, writes: "I was born to John Henry Williams and Ola Mae Jones in Hinds County, Mississippi, not far from Jackson, on my grandfather's eighty-eight-acre farm. My mother had already left the South and met my father in Syracuse, New York. They married there and returned South for my birth, as was customary. I remained in the South with them for one year, then we returned to Syracuse where I spent my boyhood.

"I grew up in what might be called an integrated ghetto. But the houses were of good quality and the neighbors friendly. Among my friends were Negroes, Jews, Irish, Greeks and Italians. I, of course, attended the public schools where I was a mediocre student, preferring athletics to studies. I was a Boy Scout, rising to the rank of Life Scout.

"I joined the U.S. Navy in 1943, became a Hospital Corpsman and served in the Pacific with several units. Discharged in 1946, I returned to Syracuse and completed my high school education, graduating when I was twenty-one. That same year, I entered Syracuse University, after an abortive enrollment at Morris Brown College in Atlanta, Georgia. I had met enough Southerners in the Navy. While attending college and working part time, I married Carolyn Clopton, and Gregory Darrell was born to us the following year.

"I had begun writing while in the Navy, but, while in the University, I published a number of poems as well as several vignettes. I graduated in 1950 and went on to graduate school. Our second son, Dennis Alfred, was born in 1951. We divorced in 1953 and I moved to California, then moved back to New York in 1955 where I held a number of jobs. I completed my first novel in 1956, but it was not published until 1960, as *The Angry Ones*, a paperback original.

"I was thirty-five when the book was published, and that was my deadline to myself; if I hadn't published by then, I would have quit writing. I suppose in some way I've always wanted to be a writer; people at home tell me that when I visit Syracuse. I've always liked books and spent all my early Saturdays in the Syracuse Public Library at the corner of Montgomery and Jefferson Streets. In ten years I've produced many books and articles, all without help from the literary foundations except the National Institute of Arts and Letters, which gave me a grant after some small furor back in 1962.

"I write easily enough. I think like a proletarian, which means that for me writer's blocks cannot exist; they are luxuries I cannot afford. And most of the time I enjoy what I am writing about.

"I've done some piddling television work, which I enjoyed, but the people in television apparently don't like me, which is no big thing. It will come, and I am interested in the visual.

"In 1965 I married Lorrain Isaac and in 1967 Adam Jeremy was born to us. Gregory is now a teacher in the Syracuse, New York, public school system, having graduated from Syracuse University in 1969. Dennis is a student at Cornell University. I met the second Mrs. Williams when we were both working for a publishing house, and I still find her to be the most perceptive and sensitive editor I've ever worked with. It is rather nice having a great editor and wife rolled into one.

"I like to travel, although not as much as I did when I was younger. I've visited about thirty countries, many of them two and three times. I consider myself to be a radical, both politically and in a literary sense; it goes without saying that my writing is realistic, or has been. I believe my most important work to date has been *The Man Who Cried I Am* (1967), my fourth novel."

Williams' first novel, the paperback *The Angry Ones*, was not much noticed, but *Night Song* was received with a great deal of interest. Set in the Greenwich Village night world of jazz, it centers upon a black café owner, Keel Robinson, and Richie Stokes, a great saxophonist destroyed by heroin. Most reviewers found the story contrived and overwritten and the characterization, especially of white people, only sporadically convincing; nevertheless they recognized in the book signs of an authentic "raw power" and promise.

Sissie, a portrait of an old black woman's hard life and times, was followed by a factual book about Africa, and then by Williams' report (originally published in *Holiday* magazine) on an eight-month journey through the United States in 1963–1964, *This Is My Country Too*. It was a reasonable, moderate, and sometimes poetic account of the prejudice and hostility he encountered—his inability to travel in his own country without constant fear of insult or physical attack.

The work which finally established Williams as a writer of unquestioned ability and originality was *The Man Who Cried I Am*. Max Reddick is a black American writer dying of cancer. He has left the hospital and gone to Holland to say goodbye to his Dutch wife. In the course of twenty-four hours in Amsterdam, Reddick comes to terms with his bitter past and dwindling future. This long book encompasses his recollections of his career as a soldier, journalist, and writer; his love affairs and

JOHN A. WILLIAMS

his marriage; bitter vignettes of his experiences in United Nations, civil rights, and literary circles in New York and Washington, and the sterile life of black expatriates in Europe. Reddick's pilgrimage to Amsterdam leads to a final and shattering disillusionment, when he uncovers there details of the "King Alfred Contingency Plan," a Washington scheme for the extermination of American blacks "in the event of widespread and continuing and coordinated racial disturbances." In the face of all this, and in a sense because of it, Reddick is able in the end to make the assertion expressed in the book's title.

The novel is to some extent a *roman à clef*, containing recognizable and sometimes savage portraits of prominent writers, politicians, and civil rights workers, white and black. Beyond that, as Eric Moon wrote, "it tells the story of a decade or more of hope repeatedly offered and repeatedly extinguished for the black man, and it shows, perhaps better than any academic exercise in social history, what this period has done to the Negro's attitudes." It was warmly and almost unanimously praised for its controlled anger, its sardonic humor, and "cool honesty."

Sons of Darkness, Sons of Light is set in New York City during one long hot summer in the immediate future. The killing of a black boy by a white policeman sets off a chain reaction leading to a massive outbreak of black terrorism which draws in both Jewish and Mafia elements. Henrietta Buckmaster, though she thought the book raised profound moral questions that it failed adequately to answer, called it "a blueprint for now, seen from the dark side of despair and betrayal."

It was followed by *Captain Blackman*, in which a black officer, wounded in Vietnam, is presented as a kind of black Everyman. Drifting in and out of consciousness on the way to the hospital, he also drifts back and forth in history, becoming the black American soldier who has fought in every war since the Revolution, bearing the full brunt of racial prejudice throughout. One reviewer wrote: "It is a dramatically sound and exciting retelling of history, and even though the format begins to seem a bit too predictable, the character of the captain is quirky and individual enough to keep you wondering what will happen next. The reward comes in the surprise ending, and a lovely one it is."

Williams' success has been slow in coming. Over the years, as he told an interviewer in the New York *Times Book Review* (October 29, 1967), he had supported himself and his family in the "usual" assortment of jobs: "foundry worker, vegetable clerk, welfare investigator. A miserable year in California; I starved." After he went to New York he promoted books for a vanity publisher, launched his own short-lived business newsletter, worked for an advertising agency and for the American Committee on Africa—"and there were long gaps of unemployment." He is the compiler of *Beyond the Angry Black*, a much admired collection of essays, poems, and stories about contemporary problems, and the author of a rather ambiguous and sometimes cruel study of the life and work of Martin Luther King, *The King God Didn't Save*. In 1970 Williams became co-editor with Charles F. Harris of *Amistad*, a new magazine of black culture.

PRINCIPAL WORKS: *Fiction*—The Angry Ones, 1960; Night Song, 1961; Sissie, 1963 (England, Journey Out of Anger); The Man Who Cried I Am, 1967; Sons of Darkness, Sons of Light, 1969; Captain Blackman, 1972. *Nonfiction*—Africa: Her History, Lands, and People, 1963; This Is My Country Too, 1965; The Most Native of Sons: A Biography of Richard Wright (for children), 1970; The King God Didn't Save, 1970; Flashbacks (articles and essays), 1973. *As editor*—Beyond the Angry Black, 1962 (rev. and enlarged 1968).

ABOUT: O'Brien, J. (ed.) Interviews With Black Writers, 1973; Who's Who in America, 1972–1973; Williams, J. A. Flashbacks, 1973. *Periodicals*—Book World June 2, 1968; Chicago Sunday Tribune April 8, 1962; New York Times Book Review October 29, 1967; March 30, 1969; June 29, 1969; March 21, 1972; Publishers' Weekly March 25, 1968; Saturday Review October 6, 1962.

WILLIAMS, RAYMOND (HENRY) (August 31, 1921–), Welsh novelist, social critic, and cultural historian, writes: "I was born in the Welsh border village of Pandy, where my father, who before his service in the war had been a farmworker and a porter, was one of the three railway signalmen. My mother came from a farmworking family in the same region, between the Black Mountains and the Malvern Hills. My growing-up was closely affected by this sense of place and change, though there was now available, as there had not been to my father, a process of extended formal education, which has affected my whole adult life. I attended the local church school, and in 1932 won a scholarship to the Abergavenny Grammar School. I enjoyed my years there, and was glad to be guided by my headmaster, and by my masters in English, History and Latin, to go on a state scholarship to Trinity College, Cambridge, in 1939. I joined the army in 1941, and became an anti-tank captain in the Guards Armoured Division in the campaign in North-West Europe. I returned to Cambridge in 1945, but in 1946 turned down an opportunity to do academic research, and took a job in adult education with Oxford University. I stayed in that work, teaching evening classes, until 1961, when I was invited to come back to Cambridge as a Lecturer in English and Fellow of Jesus College. I married Joy Dalling in 1942, and we have three children, born between 1944 and 1950.

"I began to write while at school: a novel and a play. I published short stories at Cambridge and during the war. In 1946 I started again on the unpublished novel, and it went through about seven rewritings until it was finally published, now in a wholly different form, as *Border Country* in 1960. During that period, I also wrote three other novels, still unpublished. Writing the kind of novel in which I was interested was a long process, full of errors, and the delay meant that I became first known as a writer in other fields. I published *Drama From Ibsen to Eliot* in 1952: a continuation of my work at Cambridge. It was followed by *Drama in Performance* (1954) and *Modern Tragedy* (1966). Meanwhile, in the late forties I had begun work on the cultural history and social criticism which were eventually published as *Culture and Society* and *The Long Revolution*. My second novel, *Second Generation*, was published in 1964, and I am now working on a third which will complete what is intended as a trilogy. I have also continued to write plays: *Koba* (in *Modern Tragedy*), and *A Letter From the Country*, for television.

"I am mainly interested in the realist tradition in the novel, and especially in the unique combination of that change in experience and in ideas which has been both my personal history and a general history of my generation. I have been glad to be able to write about this change in critical and historical ways, for the cultural tradition I encountered in Cambridge seems to me deeply inadequate and needing challenge in its own terms. At the same time, the whole point of these general arguments was a stress on a new kind of connection between social, personal, and intellectual experience (which have all been diminished by being separated), and I am still excited by the challenge of learning to express this connection in novels, difficult as this continues to be. I see this as my main work in the future."

The elements that make up Raymond Williams' literary personality stem from his deep attachment to the patterns of working-class life, his dedication to the ideals of democratic socialism, and his training in English under F. R. Leavis. All of these elements were apparent in *Politics and Letters* (1946–1948), the periodical he founded with Clifford Collins and Wolf Mankowitz.

Politics and Letters set out to inquire into the origins (during the Industrial Revolution) of the word "culture" in its modern sense, and to reinterpret the tradition thus revealed in terms of modern British experience. *Culture and Society*, the first of his books to attract widespread attention, continues the same inquiry, with a view to discovering the roots of a *common* English culture—one in which the working class might participate. It begins with an able description of a central tradition in nineteenth century English thought: the attempt by men of letters to engage themselves with the major forces acting on and through their society. Williams traces the tradition from Burke and Cobbett to Coleridge, through to the industrial novelists, to Carlyle, Ruskin, and Morris, and up to Eliot and Lawrence and Leavis. *The Long Revolution* includes essays on the theory of culture, a historical examination of some institutions which have influenced the English cultural tradition, and a discussion of the process of change in modern Britain.

Many critics of these books found Williams' theories muddled and his definition of culture unsatisfactory. They regretted his precommitment to a socialist and a literary view of society, and his lack of interest in the religious and scientific aspects of the social revolution he described. Nevertheless most readers were impressed and some were moved by these "serious, original, stimulating" books, and their pursuit of what Richard Wollheim called "the English Dream: the ideal of the collective, unalienated folk society, where honest men work together and create together." And there was much praise for Williams' sympathetic elucidation of the views of other writers, especially in *Culture and Society*. Frank Kermode called it a "magnificent" book, of "quite radical importance," and it established Williams as an important influence in English intellectual life.

Reviewers of both books commented on the author's often abstract and clumsy prose. This graceless style seems to arise, not from an incapacity with language, but from Williams' dour and earnest temperament, and a mistrust of the kind of literary amenity that could be associated with the world of the English establishment. It

RAYMOND WILLIAMS

may, in fact, reflect his perpetual consciousness of the tension between his working-class origins and the later course of his public career.

This tension is quite overt in his novels, which, however, are much better written than his critical books. *Border Country*, the first and best of them, is about a university lecturer called home from London to Wales for his father's last illness, and forced to examine his own equivocal position in the "border country" between two ways of life. It was widely admired, though it presses hard on Williams' central thesis: the necessity for the individual and the community to exist in a creative relationship with each other. Significantly, the book is most alive when it is most nostalgic, when it recreates the hopes briefly aroused in the working class—here, Welsh railwaymen—by the General Strike of 1926.

Williams' survey of modern drama since Ibsen reflects his view that a play is primarily a work of literature, not a blueprint to be realized only in production. This approach, and the preference it implies for the naturalistic theatre, displeased some critics, but the book (completely revised in 1968) was generally welcomed as a thoughtful, judicious, and "coherent account of the extraordinarily diverse trends and manifestations of the modern drama." *Drama in Performance*, to some extent a complementary work, examines a dozen plays not only textually but in relation to the historical and social conditions of the period and the nature of the audience.

Modern Tragedy brings together the two sides of Williams' work. It begins with a historical account of the idea of tragedy, and leads via an analysis of the relationship between tragedy and history into a discussion of the contemporary relationship between tragedy and revolution. This is followed by a series of essays on tragedy in modern literature from Ibsen to Sartre. The intention is to examine the connection between tragedy in literature "and the kinds of experience that in our lives and times we ordinarily call tragic." Thus it continues the themes of *Drama From Ibsen to Eliot* and also of *Culture and Society* and *The Long Revolution*, and was praised and condemned in the same terms as those books. It was felt that Williams had ignored some contemporary writers whose experience of tragedy was outside the scope of his social views, and had in other ways failed to press his arguments beyond "the near edge of vital complication, of originality, of abrasive judgement." The *Economist* called it an "important and sincere statement of [Williams'] beliefs," but thought that in its discussion of contemporary literature "the socialist constricts the critic: the writer's intense social commitment produces a flattened and over-systematised reading of twentieth century literature." Much the same sort of thing was said about *The English Novel From Dickens to Lawrence*, which argues that the novel became the dominant form it was in the middle of the nineteenth century because it expressed a new consciousness, brought about as the English became "the first predominantly urban people in the long history of human societies." Williams' study of Orwell in the Fontana Modern Masters series also seemed to some reviewers less a critical estimate than a polemic, seeking to present Orwell as a pioneer of the New Left—the Left which opposes both socialism and communism as well as "democratic capitalism."

In *The Country and the City*, Williams examines the ways in which writers have dealt with these contrasting themes, beginning as far back as the Greek bucolic poets, but concentrating on post-Renaissance English literature. The survey seeks to expose the exploitation and degradation of the English peasantry which gave the lie to lyrical celebrations of the pastoral ideal, but does so without concealing his own deep love of the country. The book was on the whole very warmly received, and Marshall Berman thought it Williams' best, in which "the intellectual power and the ideological passion and the personal integrity come together more convincingly than ever before."

Raymond Williams has lectured throughout England for the British Council and gives occasional radio talks. From 1962 to 1970 he served as general editor of the New Thinkers Library. He still teaches at Cambridge, where since 1967 he has been University Reader in Drama, but in 1973 went to the United States as visiting professor of political science at Stanford University. He gives his recreations as gardening and camping. His play *Koba* appears only in the English edition of *Modern Tragedy*.

PRINCIPAL WORKS: *Fiction*—Border Country, 1960; Second Generation, 1964. *Nonfiction*—Reading and Criticism, 1950; Drama From Ibsen to Eliot, 1952 (rev. as Drama From Ibsen to Brecht, 1968); (with Michael Orrom) Preface to Film, 1954; Drama in Performance, 1954 (rev. 1968); Culture and Society, 1780–1950, 1958; The Long Revolution, 1961; Britain in the Sixties: Communications, 1962 (rev. as Communications, 1966); Modern Tragedy, 1966; The English Novel From Dickens to Lawrence, 1970; Orwell, 1971; The Country and the City, 1973. *As editor*—May Day Manifesto, 1968; (with Roger Sharrock) Pelican Book of English Prose, 1970. *Plays*—Koba *in* Modern Tragedy, 1966; A Letter From the Country *in* Stand 2, 1971.

ABOUT: Kazin, A. Contemporaries, 1962; Macdonald, D. Against the American Grain, 1963; Vinson, J. (ed.) Contemporary Novelists, 1972; Who's Who, 1973; Wollheim, R. Socialism and Culture, 1961. *Periodicals*—Anglo-Welsh Review Spring 1967; Book Week August 28, 1966; Critical Quarterly Summer 1961; Encounter August 1966; Nation February 7, 1959; New Left Review Summer, Autumn 1961; New Republic February 2, 9, 1959; May 15, 1965; New Statesman September 27, 1958; March 10, 1961; May 4, 1962; July 19, 1966; New York Times Book Review July 15, 1973; Reporter July 23, 1959; Spectator March 10, 1961; April 27, 1962; Times Literary Supplement August 11, 1966; September 7, 1973; Universities and Left Review Spring 1959; Views Summer 1965.

WILSON, COLIN (HENRY) (June 26, 1931–), English novelist and writer on philosophy, sociology, music, literature, and the occult, writes: "I was born in Leicester, a Midlands engineering town, in 1931. My father was a boot and shoe operative. As far as I know, no one in our family has ever had the slightest literary or artistic bent, although my maternal grandparents were on the variety stage before they married. (But as they married young, this couldn't have been for long.)

"I showed no particular aptitudes at school, and couldn't read until I was eight. I managed to win a scholarship to a Secondary School at the age of eleven. By this time I'd taken a definite interest in chemistry, due to a chemistry set someone had bought me, and to a science fiction magazine given to me by my grandfather. Until I was sixteen I thought of nothing but science and hoped to become an atomic physicist. Unfortunately, there was never the slightest encouragement of any kind, and no suggestion that I should even try for a university scholarship, so I left school at the age of sixteen (although I returned some months later as a laboratory assistant). By this time the feeling of frustration had become so intense that I spent most of my time reading poetry, and the plays of Shaw, which had been a strong influence on me since I was thirteen. I had been scribbling stories since I was about ten, and now I tried writing plays. The result of all this literary activity—and the consequent neglect of my lab. duties—was that I was sacked from the laboratory when I was seventeen. I then went into the civil service—taxes—having no better ideas—and continued to write voluminously. (Everything was promptly returned by editors.) I spent six months in the RAF and managed to get out by claiming to be homosexual (I am not) and then decided to become a tramp for a period. I married when I was twenty and moved to London—a son arrived very quickly—and took various factory jobs. Separated from my wife eighteen months later, having been on the dole for several months, and had six lodgings in the short period of our marriage (landladies objected to babies). A second period in Paris (which I'd visited in my 'tramping' year) and the beginning of my novel *Ritual in the Dark*.

"On returning to London I decided to sleep out on Hampstead Heath, to save rent, and spend my days in the British Museum writing *Ritual*. It was at this time I decided to dash off my first published book, *The Outsider*, while the first part of *Ritual* was being read by Angus Wilson (whom I'd met in the British Museum). This I did in a few months of 1955, while working in a coffee house as dish washer. The book appeared in 1956, and to everyone's amazement, became a best seller—I believe the only example of a heavy philosophical book becoming an overnight best seller in literary history. I was labelled the first of the 'Angry Young Men' (John Osborne being another) and the publicity machine ground at a full tilt for two years or so, while the book went into sixteen languages.

"The inevitable reaction nauseated me, and it became very clear that the publicity was the worst possible method of being taken seriously as a philosopher in the tradition of European existentialism. (It was my ambition to create a new 'optimistic' existentialism to replace Sartre's.) I moved to a remote cottage in Cornwall with my second wife, and settled down to my main business, writing. Since 1957 I have written twenty books, seven of them novels. I have two children with my second wife.

"In effect, I have been going through an extremely long period of doldrums since 1957. My second philosophical book probably achieved a record of its own in being more violently slaughtered by every kind of critic than any book since the war. The attitude to my work could be summed up by a sneer in *Encounter* to the effect that I was an 'intellectual Tommy Steele.' Since I still believe that I have more to contribute than any other European thinker, this has made the attacks on—or contemptuous dismissals of—my books since 1957 rather hard to swallow. At the time of writing (1965) I believe I am gaining ground slowly, but at this rate it will take another fifty years for my

COLIN WILSON

'new existentialism' to gain widespread acceptance. I am at present writing a play—my sixth—about Strindberg."

———

Colin Wilson is the eldest son of Arthur and Anetta (Jones) Wilson. The sole hereditary source of his literary enthusiasm seems to be his mother's appetite for books of all kinds. His first wife was Dorothy Betty Troop; his second is Pamela Stewart, a librarian, with whom he lives in Gorran Haven, Cornwall, and by whom he now has three children. He is reported by all who meet him, including those who disapprove of his intellectual attitudes, to be of an unusually likable and gentle personality. His recreations are mathematics and collecting phonograph records (mainly opera).

The enthusiastic reception by the literary establishment of Wilson's first work, *The Outsider*, was irresponsible and—in the long term—cruel. The book is an oversimplified popularization of the views of Kierkegaard, Sartre, and others about the position of the man who "sees too deep and too much"; its literary examples, from Camus, T. E. Lawrence, Hemingway, Kafka, Nietzsche, *et al.*, are often inept. Nevertheless, the vigor and sense of excitement which Wilson brought to his presentation, and the fact that it had been written by a self-educated vagrant in his early twenties, made it a literary phenomenon. The British critics outdid each other in their praise and Philip Toynbee called it "an exhaustive and luminously intelligent study of a representative theme of our time." It became an international best seller, and its youthful author (who showed a Shavian talent for self-advertisement) basked in the full glare of publicity.

The reaction set in with the publication of *Religion and the Rebel*, a companion volume to *The Outsider*, no better but no worse than its predecessor. The *Times Literary Supplement* condemned the sloppiness of its language and thought, and concluded that Wilson was no more than a popular journalist, out of his depth in his chosen field. Other critics echoed or extended this judgment and Philip Toynbee not only attacked the book but went on to temper his praise of *The Outsider*. This turnabout must be regarded as an exposure of the shortcomings of literary journalism no less than of Colin Wilson himself.

Wilson has continued to develop his philosophical views in half a dozen books which draw on literature, sociology, and psychology in pursuit of his optimistic "new existentialism." His theories have not been taken very seriously, partly because of his obvious lack of training and his grandiloquent valuation of himself. Nevertheless, reactions to some of the later works in his "Outsider cycle" have been relatively encouraging. A reviewer of *Beyond the Outsider* praised its account of the views of Kierkegaard, Husserl, and Heidegger, and went on: "His new book offers an argument which, if it is not quite adequately sustained, is yet almost consistently referred back to and sometimes carried forward and which is both tenable and heartening." Colin Wilson remains a writer whose capacity to communicate his own sense of excitement about the books he has read might yet be modified into something cogent and original.

It is in fiction that Wilson has so far enjoyed his most solid success. His themes are crude, leaning heavily on a preoccupation with sexual crimes as an expression of the outsider's alienation from society; but he writes with brilliant lucidity and can hold the reader's attention with an ease that must be the envy of many more "serious" novelists. Indeed he is the kind of natural writer who could succeed in being readable in almost any genre. His musical essays, while not profound in a technical sense, show this. It is clear that he has the talent and the energy he needs to retrieve his reputation and there is some evidence of success in the fact that in recent years he has been invited to teach as a visiting professor at Hollins College, Virginia, at the University of Washington in Seattle, and at Dowling College, Majorca.

PRINCIPAL WORKS: *"Outsider cycle"*—The Outsider, 1956; Religion and the Rebel, 1957; The Age of Defeat (U.S., The Stature of Man), 1959; The Strength to Dream, 1962; Origins of the Sexual Impulse, 1963; Beyond the Outsider, 1965; Introduction to the New Existentialism, 1966. *Fiction*—Ritual in the Dark, 1960 (also pub. as screenplay, 1967); Adrift in Soho, 1961; The Man Without a Shadow (U.S., The Sex Diary of Gerard Sorme), 1963; The World of Violence (U.S., The Violent World of Hugh Greene), 1963; Necessary Doubt, 1964; The Glass Cage, 1966; The Mind Parasites, 1967; The Philosopher's Stone, 1969; The Killer, 1970 (U.S. Lingard); The Black Room, 1971; The God of the Labyrinth, 1971 (U.S. The Hedonists). *Miscellaneous*—(with Patricia Pitman) Encyclopedia of Murder, 1961; Rasputin and the Fall of the Romanovs, 1964; The Brandy of the Damned (musical essays), 1964 (U.S., Chords and Discords); Eagle and Earwig (literary essays), 1965; Sex and the Intelligent Teenager, 1966; Bernard Shaw: A Reassessment, 1969; Voyage to a Beginning: An Intellectual Autobiography, 1969; Poetry and Mysticism, 1970; A Casebook of Murder, 1970; Strindberg (play), 1970; The Occult, 1971; New Pathways in Psychology: Maslow and the Post-Freudian Revolution, 1972; Order of Assassins: The Psychology of Murder, 1972.

ABOUT: Allsop, K. The Angry Decade, 1959; Campion, S. The World of Colin Wilson, 1962; Current Biography, 1963; Gindin, J. J. Postwar British Fiction, 1962; Priestley, J. B. Thoughts in the Wilderness, 1957; Vinson, J. (ed.) Contemporary Novelists, 1972; Who's Who, 1973; Who's Who in America, 1972–1973; Wiegel, J. A. Colin Wilson, 1971. *Periodicals*—Month March 1960; Nation August 25, 1956; New York Times Book Review July 1, 1956; November 15, 1959; March 6, 1960; Times Literary Supplement October 25, 1957; January 28, 1965.

WILSON, JOHN ANTHONY BURGESS. *See* "BURGESS, ANTHONY"

WILSON, SLOAN (May 8, 1920–), American novelist, writes: "I was born in a rather lavishly remodeled farmhouse in Norwalk, Connecticut. My father was the son of a New England schoolmaster and a daughter of German immigrants. He had worked his way through the University of Virginia, and had worked as an editor of the old *Literary Digest*. He wrote a book of verse, helped to start the School of Journalism at NYU, and was lecturing there when I came along.

"My mother was the daughter of a naval officer who had been on a disastrous polar expedition, and who died tragically when she was an infant. Her brother too was a regular naval officer. She had inherited a lot of money from her grandfather, who had been a banker in upstate New York, and after graduating from Vassar, she was trying to work as a journalist, a task which was made somewhat difficult by her mother, who believed it wrong for a lady of quality to be alone with a man in any circumstances.

"My father had a bad heart and when I was about four years old, he retired from teaching. We acquired a large house in northern Florida and a lavish layout in the Adirondacks. We had everything money could buy, but the household was a gloomy one because both my parents were in poor health much of the time, and both were unable to achieve the recognition they wanted as writers.

"They gave me more than even rich kids usually have. When I was eighteen, I had an eighty-seven-foot schooner which I tried to make into a sort of business, cruising with college friends from Cuba to Nova Scotia.

"It makes me feel ungrateful and very peculiar to realize that in the midst of all this splendor, I was just another tense, miserable kid. When I was nineteen, my father died and my mother's health deteriorated, and my youth came to an abrupt halt.

"One of the things I discovered was that I was simply unable to live alone. At the age of twenty I married a girl with a background as fortunate and as unfortunate as my own.

"Then there was the war. I had it in my mind to become a great naval hero, but I had no technical education, and was constantly seasick. It seemed to me to be a great triumph when in Greenland at the age of twenty-three, I was given command of a trawler used by the Coast Guard. After that I commanded a tiny freighter and a small gas tanker in the South Pacific. I hated everything about military service, and my only boast is that no one on my ships ever got killed.

"While I was in New Guinea in 1944, I wrote some verse that the *New Yorker* bought. Before I got home, I also sold some short stories to good magazines. It seemed to me that I must be a writer, since obviously I was never going to be the kind of naval officer I had dreamt of being.

"When I got home in 1946, I was rather surprised to find that I had to make a living. Perhaps wisely, my family felt that money belongs only in the hands of the oldest generation, and everyone else should fend for himself. My family loved writing, but would have been shocked at the thought of anyone going bohemian. I, as much as my wife, could not imagine living anywhere except in a white house in the suburbs.

"I could not sell enough short pieces to buy that house, and when I wrote a novel, *Voyage to Somewhere*, it sold only sixteen hundred copies. I got various jobs, first as a newspaper reporter, then as a minor factotum at *Time*, and finally as a public relations man for schools and colleges. This allowed me to acquire one suburban house after another while I worked on short stories and books during the evenings and weekends. This went on for nine years.

"In 1955, *The Man in the Gray Flannel Suit* made me a full-time writer and increased the size of all those suburban houses. I followed it with *A Summer Place*, *A Sense of Values*, and *Georgie Winthrop*. I do not think it accurate to say that success went to my head, but it gave me freedom to express my congenital desperation. I hired a lawyer to handle taxes and investments for me, and his judgment combined with mine soon rid me of all money problems, along with all the money. I got psychoanalyzed, divorced, and became an expert on fine liquors.

"All this stopped about four years ago, and since then, things have been looking up. I have a new wife, a new daughter, and an apartment in the city. I'm not at all sure what I want to write yet, and for better or for worse, writing frankly seems less important to me than it used to. One has to learn how to live before one can write anything that means much. I've busted out of one framework and I have to build another before I can make any sense on paper.

"At the age of forty-five, I feel damn lucky to be alive and to be capable of enjoying my breakfasts."

SLOAN WILSON

Sloan Wilson is the son of Albert and Ruth (Danenhower) Wilson. He was educated by "a succession of small country day schools, tutors and boarding schools," and at Harvard, where he received his B.A. in 1944. *Voyage to Somewhere* was a novel about life during World War II on a small Navy supply ship. It was warmly praised for its sincerity and restraint, but, as he says sold poorly. Wilson's first novel might have fared better if it had not faced the competition of a more remarkable book on the same theme, Thomas Heggen's *Mister Roberts*, published the same year.

As it was, Wilson had a long wait for success, which was provided bountifully by his second novel, *The Man in the Gray Flannel Suit*. It tells the ordinary story of an ordinary middle-class American husband and father, who sometimes remembers more romantic and exciting times, but who mostly just gets on with his job and with his life. Some reviewers thought this "biography of the commuter" shallow and slick, but most found its prose literate and witty, its characterizations "sure, bright and alive," its observation exact and convincing. And this time the public agreed. *The Man in the*

Gray Flannel Suit was a major best seller, gave a new term to the language, and was filmed.

None of Wilson's subsequent novels has quite equaled this success, at least with the reviewers. They have tended to focus on middle-aged, middle-class people whose emotional crises reflect in some way upon the breakdown of American values. They have all demonstrated a "painstaking, Marquand-like care for narrative structure and life-like detail," and an excellent sense of place, but have all seemed to many critics too smooth, predictable, and hollow. In Arthur Mizener's opinion, "the trouble is that his craftsmanship serves a conception of life that will not stand examination. . . . All these characters are implausible; they are the oversimplified fantasy images of what are, apparently, the dominant values of the present American middle class. Because Mr. Wilson describes them earnestly and thoroughly, they have their fascination, though it is a fascination different from the one Mr. Wilson intended, and not without its own kind of horror."

Wilson faces such attacks with a mixture of humility and defiance. "I'd like to learn to write better," he says. "I come by plots easily—I know that—but my danger is that I'll dash along with the plot and not hover over characters." He has repudiated his third novel, *A Summer Place*, as "badly written." But he maintains nevertheless that he has something valid to say. "I describe what I am and see as honestly as I can," he says, "and happily a few critics think that I understand a little about the American middle class, an important subject which most writers duck."

Sloan Wilson's first wife was Elise Pickhardt; in 1962 he married Betty Joan Stephens. They have spent some time living aboard his yacht *Pretty Betty*, cruising in the Bahamas and elsewhere, and Wilson has written an extremely readable account of their travels in *Away from It All*. The author has four children, three of them by his first marriage.

PRINCIPAL WORKS: *Fiction*—Voyage to Somewhere, 1946; The Man in the Gray Flannel Suit, 1955; A Summer Place, 1958; A Sense of Values, 1960; Georgie Winthrop, 1963; Janus Island, 1967; All the Best People, 1970. *Travel*—Away from It All, 1969.

ABOUT: Celebrity Register, 1963; Vinson, J. (ed.) Contemporary Novelists, 1972; Who's Who in America, 1972–1973.

WIMSATT, W(ILLIAM) K(URTZ), JR. (November 17, 1907–), American critic and scholar, writes: "I am a university professor, scholar, and theorist of literature, and nearly all my writing comes out of and relates to my activities in these roles. In 1958 my friend George Winchester Stone, then executive secretary of the Modern Language Association of America, wrote a 'vignette' of me for the publication of the Association (*PMLA*) on the occasion of my finishing a term as a member of the Executive Council (1955–1958). This is the only account of myself that I can or am willing to produce—or work from, as follows. (A good deal more about my ideas on literature can be found in the articles in *Comparative Literature*, the London *Times Literary Supplement*, and *Belfagor*, which I list below.) I was born in Washington, D.C. My father, and my grandfather, William A. Wimsatt, were wholesale lumber dealers on the old Washington waterfront (now obliterated by the Federal Redevelopment). My mother was Bertha Stuart McSherry of Frederick, Maryland, and my maternal grandfather was Judge James McSherry, of the Maryland Court of Appeals. I went to Georgetown University and graduated A.B. *summa cum laude*, 1928, and stayed another year for an A.M., 1929. I got my Ph.D. in English at Yale University in 1939. Meanwhile I had been head of the English department and a teacher of Latin at the Portsmouth Priory School, in Portsmouth, Rhode Island, 1930–1935, and had studied and taught at the Catholic University of America in 1935–1936. I have been a member of the English Department at Yale since 1939. I am now Frederick Clifford Ford Professor of Literature, and a Fellow of Silliman College. In 1944 I married Margaret Elizabeth Hecht, of Chicago. We have had two sons, of whom one survives, James Christopher, aged seventeen. I have honorary degrees from Villanova (1962), Notre Dame (1963), St. Louis (1964), and Le Moyne College, Syracuse (1965). I have been a chairman of the English Institute Supervising Committee, 1954, and of the Catholic Commission on Intellectual and Cultural Affairs, 1964. I am a member of the American Academy of Arts and Sciences, 1965– . I happen to stand about six feet, nine inches (seven feet at my maximum, as a boy of seventeen), and Stone says that at MLA meetings I have thus been an 'easy focus for eighteenth-century scholars as well as for those interested in poetics and literary criticism.' Stone records, accurately, that I 'collect Indian artifacts, rocks and minerals, and old American stamped envelopes,' and that I take a 'considerable interest in events of the Civil War. (The surrender papers at Appomattox were signed on a great-grand-uncle's dining room table.)' His name was Wilmer McLean, and he had retreated to Appomattox from a farm at Manassas, Virginia, after the first battle there, when his house was used as Beauregard's headquarters. Stone goes on to mention my boyhood interest in golf, which we played together during the 1930s at George Washington University Professor R. W. Bolwell's course in the woods near White Oak, Maryland. He adds, what is correct, that I maintain that I 'have played better chess than golf,' and in my time have 'published a number of original chess problems.' Add a strong interest, developed during the past fifteen years, in English portrait-painting. Stone says that my 'standards of student accomplishment are high.' He records a somewhat exaggerated story that at Yale I 'once had a class of a single registered student and thirteen auditors.' He concludes with a remark that I value, that my 'influence has been strong in making critical studies, as opposed to scholarly diggings, respectable activity for English graduate students.' "

W. K. Wimsatt, wrote a critic in the *Times Literary Supplement* in 1965, "is known throughout the English departments of the world as the most lucid theorist in the United States of cognitive criticism." His first important statement of his position was made in *The Verbal Icon*, a volume of essays, learned and difficult, which persuaded Austin Warren that Wimsatt was "one of the two or three best literary theorists we have in the English-writing world."

W. K. WIMSATT

Literary Criticism, which Wimsatt wrote with Cleanth Brooks, is called "a short history" but is in fact another polemical work from the cognitive point of view. As the authors said, the book might more properly have been called an "Argumentative History of Literary Argument in the West." Wimsatt and Brooks had set out to inquire into "the kind of knowledge which a criticism of a poem, or a poem itself, can lay claim to." They had studied the answers to this question offered by many theorists of literature, from Plato to the present. The most satisfying solutions, in their opinion, were offered by I. A. Richards's poetics of tension and irony, by the "impersonal" theory of Eliot and Pound, and by the religious speculations of some of the "New Critics." They looked with far less favor on the trend to myth and archetype criticism.

In his "epilogue" to the book, Wimsatt urges "a double or paradoxical theory," operating through metaphor. He believes that metaphor provides the "most radically and relevantly fused union of the detail and the universal idea," and can achieve a truth of "coherence" rather than "correspondence." Wimsatt opposes the reduction of aesthetic values to either sensory qualities or "conceptualized ethical and religious" ones. Nevertheless, as a Christian, he favors a kind of literary theory compatible with "the vision of suffering, the optimism, the mystery which are embraced in the religious doctrine of the Incarnation." Murray Krieger commended Brooks and Wimsatt for "the humane and witty quality of their writing, their acute responsiveness to actual poems, and their professional awareness and depth of understanding . . . in all matters of philosophy."

Wimsatt develops and defends his position in the essays in *Hateful Contraries*, stressing in particular the danger of regarding literature as a source of direct lessons in morality. He considers in turn four kinds of literary criticism and, concluding that no method is adequate alone, calls for a "tensional" approach. This means, according to one reviewer, "holding the poem as a concrete object between the tugs of these four abstract poles." The book also contains interesting and frequently witty articles on symbolism, on meter, and on other subjects. The *Times Literary Supplement* called it "a first-rate book of criticism, the work of a cool, formidable, commanding but humane mind."

Wimsatt is the author also of monographs on the prose style of Samuel Johnson and on the portraits of Alexander Pope. He received a Guggenheim Fellowship in 1946–1947, a Fund for the Advancement of Education Fellowship in 1953–1954, and a Yale senior faculty fellowship in 1960–1961.

PRINCIPAL WORKS: The Prose Style of Samuel Johnson, 1941; Philosophic Words: A Study of Style and Meaning in the Rambler and Dictionary of Samuel Johnson, 1948; The Verbal Icon: Studies in the Meaning of Poetry, and Two Preliminary Essays written in collaboration with Monroe C. Beardsley, 1954; (with Cleanth Brooks) Literary Criticism: A Short History, 1957; (ed. with F. A. Pottle) Boswell for the Defence 1769–1774, 1959; Hateful Contraries: Studies in Literature and Criticism, with an Essay on English Meter written in collaboration with Monroe C. Beardsley, 1965; The Portraits of Alexander Pope, 1965; (ed.) The Idea of Comedy, 1969.

ABOUT: Contemporary Authors 1–4 1st rev., 1967; Hoehn, M. Catholic Authors, 1948; Krieger, M. The Play and Place of Criticism, 1967; Sutton, W. Modern American Criticism, 1963; Vivas, E. The Artistic Transaction, 1963; White, A. and others, A Sketchbook of American Chess Problematists, 1942; Who's Who in America, 1972–1973; Wimsatt, W. K. How to Compose Chess Problems and Why (autobiographical booklet printed by the author), 1966. *Periodicals*—Archaeology Summer 1958; Arion

Winter 1964; Belfagor November 1966; Comparative Literature Fall 1955; PMLA December 1958; Times Literary Supplement February 20, 1959; December 9, 1965.

WINDHAM, DONALD (July 2, 1920–), American novelist, short story writer, memoirist, and dramatist, writes: "I was born in Atlanta, Georgia, of Scotch, Irish, French, and English ancestry. My early life centered on my mother. She and my father, both native Georgians, were divorced when I was six years old and by then she had returned with me and my brother to live in her parents' fourteen-room house where she had grown up, at Peachtree Street and Thirteenth Street. For nearly a decade, my world did not extend far from there and those years developed in me a strong sense of place and love of my surroundings. Then the income my mother received from her parents' estate vanished; the homeplace was torn down; she went to work, and we lived in a series of three-room apartments. Mother became receptionist in the home office of the Coca-Cola Company, and the day after I was graduated from high school, shortly before my eighteenth birthday, I was given a job in the company's barrel factory. During my adolescence, I had come to dislike the possibilities of myself that I saw reflected around me in Atlanta, and a little over a year after I started to work, when I was given my first, one-week, vacation, I left by Greyhound bus for New York, where I have lived on and off ever since. My life through this departure is described in detail in *Emblems of Conduct: An Autobiography of Childhood.* New York bestowed upon me a longed-for anonymity, but jobs were hard to find and after a few joyous but impecunious months I found myself working for the Coca-Cola Company again, selling drinks in a stand at the 1940 World's Fair. I had started writing before I left Atlanta; the first year that I was in New York Tennessee Williams and I became friends, and in 1942–1943 we wrote together a play, *You Touched Me*, but it was not produced in New York until 1945, after the success of his *The Glass Menagerie.* (This is a good place to point out that the events of those years, as portrayed in a recent biography of Tennessee Williams and his friends, are, as far as I am concerned, remarkably inaccurate.) In the meantime, among other jobs, I worked as editor of a small magazine, *Dance Index*, in an office pleasantly situated amidst the classrooms of the American School of Ballet. After *You Touched Me* was produced on Broadway I had enough money to quit work and finish the novel I had started. *The Dog Star* was completed during my first trip to Italy in 1948, but publishers rejected it for nine months after I returned to New York and the book did not appear until the spring of 1950, by which time I was back in Europe. Italy, where I stayed almost a year this time, bestowed various blessings on me, but it did not prevent my next decade from being one of hard work and no success. Back in New York, I completed and discarded a second novel; wrote a play, *The Starless Air*, which was tried out in Texas (directed by Williams) and optioned by the Theatre Guild for New York, but never produced there; adapted a French movie and a Danish novel for the stage, with equally involved and unprofitable results; and worked on short stories. I had been submitting fiction to American magazines since 1940, and a number of my stories had appeared in Cyril Connolly's *Horizon* in England, in the *Paris Review* in France, and in *Botteghe Oscure* in Italy. No magazine in the United States, however, was willing to buy my work (with the exception of a single story that was turned down by a fiction editor, then bought by the head editor of the same magazine when she saw it in the BBC publication, *The Listener*), until the end of 1959 when William Maxwell of the *New Yorker* accepted a group of childhood reminiscences that, from his encouragement, later developed into *Emblems of Conduct.* His interest seemed to change my fortune. I completed, and the next year published, *The Hero Continues*, a novel I had been working on for seven years (stubborn persistence is perhaps my strongest trait), as well as a volume of short stories, *The Warm Country*, for which E. M. Forster wrote an introduction. (Both books appeared in England before the United States.) Also, in 1960 I was granted a Guggenheim Fellowship for creative writing in fiction. My receiving the grant coincided with the tearing down of the brownstone I had lived in for seventeen years at Madison Avenue and Sixty-fifth Street, so I put my possessions into a friend's cellar and went to Europe for a year and a half, staying several months each in Greece, Denmark, and England before returning to Italy.

"I am unmarried but not unsettled. My attachment to people is even stronger than my attachment to places and to work. For a writer of my slow acceptance, friends are audience as well as family. (They love and praise our aspiration rather than our performance, Thoreau says; but a little of this is needed.) I enjoy cooking and dislike eating alone. I am attached to possessions, too; to books and to paintings, collages, and constructions given me by friends. I like clothes better the longer I have them, hate ever to throw away anything, and discovered myself in Lord Byron's letters: 'Mr. Windham with his coat *twice* turned.' My hair, completely gray by thirty, was white by forty; in Italy I am asked if I am the father of friends my own age, whereas in New York I have been called —by the customers of the store where I worked delivering liquor to supplement my income in the mid-1950s—'the boy with white hair.'

"I disagree with the advice 'write about what you know'; write about what you *need* to know, in an effort to understand.

"Since the end of 1961 I have been living in New York again and have recently published another novel, *Two People*, set in Rome."

Windham's parents were Fred Windham, whom he saw only twice after he was six, and the former Louise Donaldson. Growing up in Atlanta (to quote Eleanor Perry's summary of *Emblems of Conduct*), "he went to movies on Saturday, he was given a coin with a hole in it by a tramp, he read books (Saroyan and Joyce and Proust, not Dickens and Cooper and Irving), he watched his grandfather's Victorian house being torn down, he saw the family furniture on the sidewalk after a dispossess notice, he went for Sunday rides with a family friend, he longed for a square jaw, and at eighteen he took a bus to New York City." At that time, according to Gilbert Maxwell, Windham was "a modest youngster with a fresh-skinned, boyish face, curly dark hair, clear shortsighted eyes behind rimless glasses, and a laugh which usually doubled high up with glee at the sheer exultant joy of being alive." (It is Maxwell's *Tennessee Williams and Friends* that Windham rejects above as inaccurate in its account of events of those years.) *You Touched Me*, the play which Williams and Windham adapted from a D. H. Lawrence short story, opened in 1945 and was rather coolly received.

The first of Windham's books to attract much attention was *The Hero Continues*, a short episodic novel about the plight of the artist in America, and specifically about a gifted young dramatist seduced by success on Broadway. The reviewers, who found the novel interesting but imperfect, responded with far more enthusiasm to *The Warm Country*, which contains fourteen short stories, many of them set in Georgia, one or two in Italy. Plotless and rather shapeless, these stories, it was said, show us "human beings as displaced persons, pushing out their horns like timid snails in a world at once remote and familiar and then sharply withdrawing them again as the contact made proves harsh or unfriendly or startling." E. M. Forster, in his introduction to the volume, wrote that Windham's stories "are simply written, they do not shout or fuss, they do not contain too much alcohol, and above all they are completely free from the slickness that comes from attending courses in Creative Literature." Several stories in *The Warm Country* are drawn from autobiographical incidents recounted in *Emblems of Conduct*, "a childhood written with such integrity and a feeling of fidelity to time and place that not merely Southerners will feel a sense of recognition."

DONALD WINDHAM

Windham's third published novel, *Two People*, is set in Italy and explores a brief homosexual affair between a young American businessman whose marriage has disintegrated and a Roman boy. For both of them, their relationship proves a step toward self-knowledge and the capacity to love wholly (and heterosexually). Some reviewers thought that it dealt too much with surface behavior and left "too many questions unanswered" (a criticism made also of *The Hero Continues*). It was nevertheless warmly praised for its restraint and sensitivity, its "stylistic and realistic brilliance, humor, and intelligence." The Italian writer Mario Soldati particularly admired its characterization, and thought it had a special appeal for Italians—"that of suddenly discovering our own images, which seem all the more real in the limpid mirror of the prose of a foreign writer who sees us as we are, even though he loves us and judges us with the greatest charity." It has been said that Windham's "is the art of the small incident scrupulously explored in precise, grave and cultivated prose," a kind of "literary chamber music."

PRINCIPAL WORKS: *Fiction*—The Dog Star, 1950; The Hero Continues, 1960; The Warm Country (stories), 1960; Two People, 1965; Tanaquil, 1972. *Play*—(with Tennessee Williams) You Touched Me, 1947. *Autobiography*—Emblems of Conduct, 1964.

ABOUT: Contemporary Authors 2, 1965; Forster, E. M. *introduction to* The Warm Country, 1960; Maxwell, G. Tennessee Williams and Friends, 1965; Tischler, N. M. Tennessee Williams, 1961; Vinson, J. (ed.) Contemporary Novelists, 1972. *Periodicals*—Book Week February 16, 1964; Book Week August 8, 1965; Il Giorno July 13, 1965; Village Voice March 26, 1964.

PAUL WINTERTON

WINTERTON, PAUL (February 12, 1908–), English mystery story writer and journalist, is best known as "Andrew Garve," but has published also under his own name and as "Roger Bax" and "Paul Somers." He was born in Leicester, England, the son of Ernest Winterton, also a journalist, and for a time a Member of Parliament. Paul Winterton attended a succession of schools, including Purley County School, in Surrey, and went on from there to the London School of Economics, receiving his B.Sc. in economics in 1928.

He joined the staff of *The Economist* in 1929, moving to a London daily, the *News Chronicle*, in 1933. Winterton worked for the *News Chronicle* for thirteen years as reporter, editorial writer, and foreign correspondent, and represented his newspaper in Moscow from 1942 to 1945. He had made his first visit to Russia immediately after his graduation, in the winter of 1928–1929, and this trip was the subject of his first book, *A Student in Russia* (1931). He published two more books and a number of articles on the Soviet Union at the end of World War II, but since the late 1940s he has written only fiction.

In 1938 Winterton had written the first of several ingenious mysteries published under the pseudonym "Roger Bax," all of which were well received by the reviewers. "Andrew Garve" became Winterton's pseudonym in *No Tears for Hilda* (1950), a "splendid portrait of a murderee," and it is in this manifestation that he has made his mark as one of the most literate, likable, and satisfying of contemporary mystery writers.

There are no conventional detectives in the Garve stories, and if it is difficult to define their special quality it is because their salient characteristic is their variety. In form they range from the "classic" detection of *The Cuckoo Line Affair* to the chase themes of *End of the Track* and other books; in *The Narrow Search* there is no murder at all. Their backgrounds, always admirably observed and full of interest, are equally varied: *Byline for Murder* and *Murder Through the Looking Glass* draw on the author's knowledge of journalism, and several stories reflect his liking for sailing and the sea; *The Narrow Search* is set on a canal boat, and *A Hole in the Ground* mixes politics and potholing (cavern exploration) and is equally well informed about both subjects. Garve has set his books in the West Indies and the Scilly Isles, in the English countryside and in London, in Russia and in Ireland. As Lenore Glen Offord says, "He never writes two books alike."

Garve's ironical view of life is reflected in his choice of heroes, usually ordinary men caught up in extraordinary events. Sometimes indeed they are so ordinary—so venal, or so cowardly—as scarcely to qualify as heroes at all. It is one of his special talents that he is able to enlist the reader's concern for such people. His plots are notably and invariably ingenious, if sometimes rather slight, usually beginning with "an unusual and powerful premise" from which all that happens, however unlikely, proceeds logically and acceptably. He is regularly praised for his "fine, direct, unselfconscious narrative" style, and has been commended for his unfashionable reticence about sex. As "Paul Somers" he has produced some lighthearted detective stories with a journalistic background.

Many of Paul Winterton's books have been translated into other languages. Some have been adapted for radio and television in Britain and the United States, and several have been filmed.

PRINCIPAL WORKS: A Student in Russia, 1931; Russia With Open Eyes, 1937; Report on Russia, 1945; Inquest on an Ally, 1948. *As "Roger Bax"*—Death Beneath Jerusalem, 1938; Red Escapade, 1940; Disposing of Henry, 1947; Blueprint for Murder (U.S., The Trouble With Murder), 1948; Came the Dawn (U.S., Two if by Sea), 1949; A Grave Case of Murder, 1951. *As "Andrew Garve"*—No Tears for Hilda, 1950; No Mask for Murder (U.S., Fontego's Folly), 1950; Press of Suspects (U.S., Byline for Murder), 1951; Murder in Moscow (U.S., Murder Through the Looking Glass), 1951; Hole in the Ground, 1952; The Cuckoo Line Affair, 1953; Death and the Sky Above, 1953; The Riddle of Samson, 1954; End of the Track, 1956; The Megstone Plot, 1956; The Narrow Search, 1957; The Galloway Case, 1958; A Hero for Leanda, 1959; The Far Sands, 1960; The Golden Deed, 1960; House of Soldiers, 1961; Prisoner's Friend, 1962; The Sea Monks, 1963; Frame Up, 1964; Ashes of Loda, 1965; Murderer's Fen (U.S., Hide and Go Seek), 1966; A Very Quiet Place, 1967; The Long Short Cut, 1968; The Ascent of D-13, 1968; Boomerang, 1970; The Late Bill Smith, 1971; The Case of Robert Quarry, 1972. *As "Paul Somers"*—Beginner's Luck, 1958; Operation Piracy, 1958; The Shivering Mountain, 1959; The Broken Jigsaw, 1961.

ABOUT: Contemporary Authors 5–6, 1963.

***WITTGENSTEIN, LUDWIG (JOSEF JOHANN)** (April 26, 1889–April 29, 1951), Austrian-born British philosopher, had Protestant, Catholic, and Jewish elements in his ancestry. His father, Karl Wittgenstein, was an engineer who made a fortune in the steel industry, a man of exceptional intelligence and determination. His mother was a highly cultivated woman who numbered Brahms among her friends. Their house in Vienna was a kind of salon, a center of cultural and intellectual discussion. Wittgenstein had his early education at home, learning mathematics and the clarinet and developing a burning ambition to be a conductor. It is clear that he would have had a brilliant career in music if he had persisted; he was a genius whose immense ability had several possible outlets. His brother Paul (there were eight children) in fact became a distinguished concert pianist, who lost an arm in World War I and for whom Ravel wrote his *Concerto for the Left Hand.*

At fourteen Wittgenstein went to school in Linz and at seventeen he entered the engineering course at the Technische Hochschule in Berlin. In 1908 he went to England for three years of intermittent study in aeronautical engineering at Manchester University. His interest in this subject led him to mathematics and then to the philosophy of mathematics as expounded in the writings of Gottlob Frege and Bertrand Russell. He went to Jena to visit Frege, who advised him to study with Russell. In 1912 Wittgenstein entered Trinity College, Cambridge, and was quickly recognized by Russell and G. E. Moore as their best pupil.

All the same, Wittgenstein could not settle at Cambridge. Three of his brothers committed suicide, and he was often tempted to follow their example, driven by an extremity of self-disgust that was sometimes not far from madness. (W. W. Bartley has suggested that Wittgenstein was "a homosexual given to bouts of extravagant and almost uncontrollable promiscuity," and that this was the source of his intense guilt and suffering; others have found Bartley's evidence inconclusive.) One prolonged bout of melancholia, induced when his father died of cancer in 1912, apparently reached some sort of crisis in 1913, when he left Cambridge and went to Norway. He settled near Skjolden in complete seclusion, a retreat which was ended by the outbreak of World War I in 1914. He returned to Vienna, enlisted in the Austrian army and served as an artillery officer on the Eastern Front.

One day in the trenches, reading a newspaper, Wittgenstein noticed a diagram of a possible sequence of events in an automobile accident. It struck him that language functioned rather as the diagram did, and he developed the analogy, identifying a verbal proposition as a kind of picture, depicting a possible combination of elements in reality. This notion, imposed on the work he had done in logic with Russell, and what he had learnt from Schopenhauer and Kant, provided the basis for *Tractatus Logico-Philosophicus,* the manuscript of which was in his rucksack when he was captured by the Italians in 1918.

* vit′gen shtīn

The *Tractatus* was smuggled out, with the aid of John Maynard Keynes, to Russell, who published it with an uncomprehending introduction that has encouraged much misunderstanding. It appeared in Germany in 1921 and in England in 1922. It sets out to investigate the limits of language as a vehicle of logical thought, and its governing idea is that the structure of language is determined, fundamentally, by the structure of reality. A meaningful sentence—one capable of representing facts—will be based upon a number of elementary "fact-picturing propositions." In such elementary propositions there will be names, each a verbal picture of some simple constituent of the world, some irreducible object. Any statement which cannot be related in this direct way to reality is meaningless. For example, most arguments about aesthetic, moral, and metaphysical problems are meaningless—statements of opinion, or examples of wishful thinking (when they are not statements of the obvious). Indeed, "most propositions and questions that have been written about philosophical matters are not false, but nonsensical. We cannot therefore answer questions of this kind at all, but only state their senselessness." However, by analyzing statements into their constituent propositions, philosophers should be able to define the structure and limits of factual discourse and stop talking nonsense: "The object of philosophy is the logical clarification of thoughts."

These ideas were by no means wholly original; Russell for one had already said some similar things. But Wittgenstein's arguments were based on an apparently faultless logical framework of the greatest possible technical brilliance. The dignity and beauty of the book's language, and the brevity and elegance of its organization, were also profoundly admired. It consists of numbered propositions, beginning with "1. The world is all that is the case." This is followed by "1.1. The world is the totality of facts, not of things." Then "1.11. The world is determined by the facts, and by their being *all* the facts." Then "1.12. For the totality of facts determines what is the case, and also whatever is not the case." The argument develops in this way until it reaches the famous penultimate proposition, 6.54, in which Wittgenstein points out that his own book is an example of the kind of abstract, speculative philosophy it attacks—a ladder to be climbed and then discarded. Then, "7. What we cannot speak about we must consign to silence."

The *Tractatus* was widely recognized as a work of genius and greatly impressed many leading philosophers, including Bertrand Russell and the philosophers of the Vienna Circle. It was an important work in the development of logical positivism, and it is easy to see why. All the same, as has been increasingly clear from the writings published since Wittgenstein's death, he was not himself a positivist—certainly not a destructive one like Russell. Wittgenstein wanted to end philosophizing about ethical and metaphysical questions, but not because he considered these nonlogical matters valueless, as Russell believed. On the contrary, as Stephen Toulmin and others have explained, he always insisted that "the unsayable alone has genuine value." Spiritual truths should be "shown," not spoken, for "the higher" can only be damaged and distorted by so gross a tool as language. As his friend Paul Engelmann wrote, "Wittgenstein passionately believed that all that really matters in human life is precisely what, in his view, we must be silent about."

Having, as he (and many others) thought, demolished most of the problems of philosophy, and shown how the rest could be solved, Wittgenstein turned his attention to more important matters. He gave away the large fortune left him by his father and enrolled in a Vienna teachers' college. Beginning in 1920 he taught in schools in Lower Austria, moving from one remote village to another. This was a less eccentric choice than it seems; in fact hundreds of newly trained and often very talented young people, many of them returned veterans, joined in the socialist school reform program initiated during the first years of the Republic. The reformers were not always welcomed by the peasants. Wittgenstein himself was apparently an extremely imaginative and ingenious teacher, but provoked hostility by his exaggeratedly austere life-style, and became increasingly frustrated. In 1926 he was accused of cruelty to the children he taught and, though he was acquitted in the subsequent court case, the incident left him completely disillusioned with teaching. He became a gardener, worked in monasteries, and thought of joining a religious order. Instead he returned to Vienna and spent two years designing and constructing a house for one of his sisters, a brilliant modern building that showed another aspect of his genius. For a time after that he was a sculptor.

Meanwhile, in 1927, he had been persuaded to enlarge on some of the more cryptic propositions in the *Tractatus* in conversations with members of the Vienna Circle. Wittgenstein was so far from being the doctrinaire positivist they had expected that, after his initial meeting with Moritz Schlick, Wittgenstein said that "each of us must have thought that the other was crazy." These discussions led Wittgenstein to believe that his work as a philosopher was not finished. He returned as a research student to Trinity College, Cambridge (presenting the *Tractatus* as a doctoral thesis). He became a fellow of Trinity in 1930, and in 1939 succeeded G. E. Moore as the university's professor of philosophy. He had become a British citizen a year earlier, when Hitler annexed Austria.

During his years at Cambridge, Wittgenstein lived in two almost completely bare rooms, without a single book, painting, photograph, or reading lamp. He sat on a cheap wooden chair and did his writing at a card table. He also possessed a fireproof safe for his manuscripts, two canvas chairs, some empty flowerpots, and a bed. It was in these surroundings that he received his students, who were expected to carry in their own chairs. According to Iris Murdoch, Wittgenstein "was very good-looking. . . . Rather small, and with a very, very intelligent, shortish face and piercing eyes —a sharpish, intelligent, alert face and those very piercing eyes. He had a trampish sort of appearance. . . . Both he and his setting were very unnerving. His extraordinary directness of approach and the absence of any sort of paraphernalia were the things that unnerved people. . . . [With most people] there isn't a naked confrontation of personalities. But Wittgenstein always imposed this confrontation on all his relationships." This was true even of his lectures, during which, according to Norman Malcolm, he "carried on a visible struggle with his thoughts" in which his students were encouraged to participate.

He had come to believe that the linguistic theory he had advanced in the *Tractatus* was wrong, and he now sought a new philosophy through an empirical investigation of language. In his thoughts and discussions there was a constant struggle against the attractions of abstract theorizing, a constant reference back to actual linguistic practices. Wittgenstein would not publish his new work during his lifetime and so an extraordinary situation developed —a man considered by many to be the greatest living philosopher was known to have radically altered his opinions, but his new ideas were known only through his students' notes and through rumors.

During World War II, from 1941 to 1944, Wittgenstein worked as a porter in Guy's Hospital and then in a medical laboratory in Newcastle. In 1944 he resumed his chair at Cambridge. But academic life became intolerable to him, and in 1947 he resigned. He settled in a lonely guest house two hours by bus from Dublin, without friends and in a state of nervous instability, working slowly and painfully at his new book. After five months he moved to the west coast of Ireland, where he became a legend among the fishermen for his power to tame birds. Then he went to Vienna, to Cambridge, to Dublin, to Vienna, to America—returning from there to Cambridge with an undiagnosed illness, eventually found to be cancer. He went back to Austria, then Oxford, then Norway, then Cambridge. For the last two years of his life he believed that he had lost his philosophical talent. He died in April 1951.

"When I think of his profound pessimism," wrote Norman Malcolm, "the intensity of his mental and moral suffering, the relentless way in which he drove his intellect, his need for love together with the harshness that repelled love, I am inclined to believe that his life was fiercely unhappy. Yet at the end he himself exclaimed that it had been 'wonderful!' To me this seemed a mysterious and strangely moving utterance."

Philosophical Investigations appeared two years after Wittgenstein's death, in 1953. Like the *Tractatus*, it is set out in numbered paragraphs, but the paragraphs are less charged and taut—less like a kind of abstract prose poetry—and are numbered consecutively, not according to a master plan. Compared to the *Tractatus*, the book is prolix, circuitous, and colloquial, with no clear line of development and no settled conclusions. But this was in accordance with Wittgenstein's new philosophy, and *Philosophical Investigations* is not less original and important than the earlier book.

Wittgenstein had believed that all languages have a uniform logical structure, which at a basic level reflects the structure of reality. His later studies convinced him that, on the contrary, language is a form of social behavior—that the way in which we use language reflects not some absolute reality but our own attitudes and assumptions. To understand some part of language is merely to be a party to the prevailing conventions for its use, to know the rules of a particular "language-game." Even a linguistic practice like logical inference has no independent foundation in reality; it is an acceptable "language-game" only because people have agreed to think and speak in accordance with its rules. (This would seem to demolish the difference between factual and nonfactual discourse, the sayable and the unsayable. It suggests that metaphysical philosophizing of the sort dismissed in the *Tractatus* is after all a legitimate "language-game." But Wittgenstein is not clear on this.)

Philosophical Investigations, like the *Tractatus*, is an investigation of the limits of language. But Wittgenstein now asks not how language relates to reality but (as Stephen Toulmin says) "by what procedures do men *establish* links between language and the real world?" *Philosophical Investigations*, therefore, scrupulously avoids abstractions and generalizations, and consists of careful descriptions of the actual or possible use of words, selected and arranged not in order to prove a theory, but to illustrate the great variety of ways in which a given word can be used.

Russell, who had been so deeply impressed by the *Tractatus*, thought *Philosophical Investigations* by comparison a trivial investigation of language which had nothing to do with philosophy and led to completely unsystematic results. Others thought it a work of seminal importance, and its technique has been widely applied, most notably in the philosophy of mind. Moreover, it has been argued that, although Wittgenstein consistently moves from philosophical generalizations to the particular facts that falsify them, these facts may nevertheless imply truer (though more complex) generalizations, and perhaps were not so completely unsystematic as Wittgenstein himself meant them to be. David Pears believes that Wittgenstein in *Philosophical Investigations* avoided the triviality of which Russell accused him, "and possibly he avoided it more conspicuously and more consistently than any other philosopher. But he avoided it by genius, and not by relying on his own later method."

Several more works have been published posthumously, and have helped to clarify Wittgenstein's views. These include *Notebooks, 1914–1916*, and *Prototractatus*, both preliminary studies for the *Tractatus*; *The Blue and Brown Books* (preliminary studies for *Philosophical Investigations*, dictated to students in 1933–1934 and 1934–1935); *Über Gewissheit* (translated as *On Certainty*), an important late work on the theory of knowledge; fragments collected as *Zettel*; and such items as Wittgenstein's letters to Paul Engelmann.

PRINCIPAL WORKS IN ENGLISH TRANSLATION: Tractatus Logico-Philosophicus (tr. by C. K. Ogden and F. P. Ramsey, 1922; tr. by D. F. Pears and B. F. McGuinness, 1961); Philosophical Investigations (tr. by G. E. M. Anscombe), 1953; Remarks on the Foundations of Mathematics (tr. by G. E. M. Anscombe), 1956; The Blue and Brown Books, 1958; Notebooks, 1914–1916 (tr. by G. E. M. Anscombe), 1961; Lectures and Conversations on Aesthetics, Psychology, and Religious Belief (ed. by Cyril Barrett), 1966; Letters from Ludwig Wittgenstein: With a Memoir by Paul Engelmann (tr. by L. Furtmüller, ed. by B. F. McGuinness), 1967; Zettel (tr. by G. E. M. Anscombe), 1967; On Certainty (tr. by Denis Paul and G. E. M. Anscombe, ed. by G. E. M. Anscombe and G. H. von Wright), 1969; Prototractatus (tr. by D. F. Pears and B. F. McGuinness, ed. by B. F. McGuinness and others), 1971; Letters to C. K. Ogden (ed. by G. H. von Wright), 1973.

ABOUT: Ambrose, A. and Lazerowitz, M. (eds.) Ludwig Wittgenstein: Philosophy and Language, 1972; Anscombe, G. E. M. An Introduction to Wittgenstein's Tractatus, 1959; Bartley, W. W. Wittgenstein, 1973; Black, M. A Companion to Wittgenstein's Tractatus, 1964; Copi, I. M. and Beard, R. W. (eds.) Essays on Wittgenstein's Tractatus, 1961; Fann, K. T. Ludwig Wittgenstein, the Man and His Philosophy, 1967; Fann, K. T. Wittgenstein's Conception of Philosophy, 1969; Griffin, J. Wittgenstein's Logical Atomism, 1964; Janik, A. and Toulmin, S. Wittgenstein's Vienna, 1973;

Malcolm, N. Ludwig Wittgenstein: A Memoir, 1958; Maslow, A. A Study in Wittgenstein's Tractatus, 1961; Mehta, V. Fly and the Fly Bottle, 1962; Moore, G. E. Philosophical Papers, 1959; Pears, D. F. Ludwig Wittgenstein, 1971; Pitcher, G. The Philosophy of Wittgenstein, 1964; Pitcher, G. (ed.) Wittgenstein: The Philosophical Investigations, 1966; Pole, D. The Later Philosophy of Wittgenstein, 1958; Rhees, R. Discussions of Wittgenstein, 1970; Stenius, E. Wittgenstein's Tractatus, 1960; Waismann, F. Wittgenstein und der Wiener Kreis, 1967; Winch, P. (ed.) Studies in the Philosophy of Ludwig Wittgenstein, 1969. *Periodicals*—Encounter January 1969; Mind July 1951, April 1952; Philosophical Review October 1955.

WOLFE, BERTRAM D(AVID) (January 19, 1896–), American historian and biographer, writes: "I was born in Brooklyn. Mother scraped and saved to keep us fed, clothed, and self-respecting. Father earned what he could, was an easy mark for touches, gave me his habit of jesting and shrugging off troubles. I selected library books for my mother, censoring them even as a little boy as she was prudish.

"The third of four children, I went to work early, after school and during vacations, contributing my earnings intact to the family exchequer. But my school record being exceptional, I was permitted (the first of my family) to continue beyond elementary school, with the understanding that I would earn what I could and never flunk any course.

"Only the fact that C.C.N.Y. was tuition-free and that I worked after hours in the Post Office enabled me to go on to college. When the going got hard I would take sick leave, being careful to get well when the Post Office needed me most as during the Christmas rush. I graduated in February 1916 Phi Beta Kappa, *cum laude*, majoring in English as the best road to writing, and silently modifying the college's ephebic oath concerning the City into a vow to leave the English language not worse than I found it. I think I have kept that vow.

"My M.A. was earned twice in Romance languages (University of Mexico, 1925, Columbia, 1931). In 1962 the University of California gave me an LL.D. for 'notable contributions to historical literature.' I have had three Guggenheim Fellowships, two Senior Fellowships in Slavic Studies in the Hoover Institution on War, Revolution, and Peace, where I am now a Senior Research Associate, and in the Russian Institute of Columbia University.

"I began by teaching English in Boys High School, Brooklyn, in 1916–1917, and married Ella Goldberg, Brooklyn school teacher, who has shared my vicissitudes to this day. I became head of the foreign language department of the Miguel Lordo de Tejada High School of Mexico City from 1922 to 1925, was Visiting Instructor in Hispanic Culture at Stanford University in 1950, and 'Distinguished Visiting Professor of Russian History' at the University of California in 1961–1962.

"In 1917, at twenty-one, I was stirred by the fact that the United States entered the First World War and Russia left the war the same year. My interest in Russia began at that moment, with one of my few successful prophecies. When the February 1917 Revolution destroyed the old apparatus of command, and obedience, I predicted that no one could keep Russia in the war and an attempt to do so would lead to a second revolution within the year. I opened up too large a credit to the second revolution, believing that it was intended to abolish war, an evil which I had been taught was no longer possible in the 'civilized twentieth century.'

"A close-up view of the new regime in Russia in 1929 and a prolonged argument with Joseph Stalin, who had not yet perfected his technique for cutting short discussion, caused me to write off the spiritual investment of a decade as a total loss. Russia was too painful a topic for me ever to think of again.

"During the thirties I wrote on Mexico, Latin America, Spain, on the life of Diego Rivera, and other subjects far removed from Russia.

"But when Stalin and Hitler signed a pact in 1939, I signed a contract to write a history of the Russian Revolution. Nine years in the writing, it taught me the unreliability of witnesses and even documents, the need to master the Russian tongue and thought and culture, to search for the truths of the defeated, check them against the truths of the victorious, the available documentary records, and the inherent probabilities in the evaluation of each person and event. The result after nine years was *Three Who Made a Revolution* (1948). Having published a history, I found that I was accounted a historian. I abandoned any pretense at Latin American expertise, for I was henceforth doomed to be bogged down in the Pripet Marshes like any other invader of Russia.

"On June 4, 1950, a study of the Russian press led me to predict that South Korea would be invaded on June 25, 1950, a fact I sent to the Department of State, which duly ignored it. After the invasion, on schedule, the Department enlisted my services to set up its Ideological Advisory Staff, recruit its personnel, and become its chief. I built so solidly that when I resigned in 1954, my organization collapsed and my subordinates were reassigned.

"Since 1939 I have limited my work to studies of Russian history, literature, politics, culture, social organization, traditions, the Soviet regime, its methods and leaders, publishing my studies in the *Slavic Review*, the *Russian Review*, *Foreign Affairs*, etc. and in the books, *Khrushchev and Stalin's Ghost*,

1957; *Communist Totalitarianism*, 1961; *Marxism: 100 Years in the Life of a Doctrine*, 1965; *Strange Communists I Have Known*, 1965; and *The Bridge and the Abyss* (*The Troubled Friendship of V. I. Lenin and Maxim Gorky*)."

———

Bertram D. Wolfe is the son of William and Rachel (Samter) Wolfe. During his years as a member of the United States Communist party he came to know the American leaders of the movement, among them John Reed, Jim Larkin, and Sam Putnam, and in the course of three disillusioning visits to the Soviet Union met Molotov, Bukharin, and Stalin. After he left the party in 1929 he talked to Kerensky, Chernov, and other exiled Russian leaders. Wolfe continued his researches into Soviet affairs as a senior Fellow in Slavic Studies at the Hoover Library and at Columbia's Russian Institute, and in his work as director of the Ideological Advisory Staff to the State Department and the Voice of America (1950–1954).

In the 1930s, as he says, Wolfe confined himself, in the bitterness of his disenchantment with Soviet communism, to writings about Mexico (*Portrait of Mexico*, 1937); Spain (*Civil War in Spain*, 1937); and Latin America. The first of his two biographies of Diego Rivera, whom he had met as a young teacher in Mexico City in 1922, appeared in 1939.

During the following decade Wolfe turned once more to Soviet affairs and began to publish the articles which soon established him as an eminent authority on Russia. After nine years of research he published *Three Who Made a Revolution*, his first and still his best-known book in this field. This volume, containing studies of Lenin, Trotsky, and Stalin, rich in new material, masterly in its organization, and brilliantly written, seemed to many critics "the best book in its field in any language." Edmund Wilson called Wolfe "the first responsible writer who has tried to tell the whole story" and said he had scrutinized his material with "an objective critical intelligence" uncommon in such works. The book established Wolfe as America's leading authority on the early years of the Soviet Revolution. It has been widely translated and in this and other ways has justified Wilson's belief that "the whole work may well be a classic."

Wolfe's subsequent books have added to his reputation. *Khrushchev and Stalin's Ghost* provided the first full text in English of Khrushchev's 1956 attack on Stalin, supporting this with information essential to an understanding of the event, and earning the author universal praise for his "mordant rhetoric and massive knowledge." *Six Keys to the Soviet System* collected a half-dozen of Wolfe's "most brilliant essays," charting Communist strategy and tactics. *Marxism*, the most ambitious and wide-ranging of Wolfe's books, traces the mutations in the evolution of Marx's thought which have occurred at the hands of his followers and of history. Most reviewers found it a lesser book than *Three Who Made a Revolution*, though Wolfe "presents the fantastically complicated story with admirable precision and clarity, keeping his own strong views under strict control until the later chapters, where he gives free rein to his deep hatred of the totalitarianism . . . so widely accepted as the sole Marxist orthodoxy."

BERTRAM D. WOLFE

The three books which followed, all largely biographical in their concerns, include a new and generally well received study of Diego Rivera; a gallery of portraits of ten "strange Communists"—among them Reed, Larkin, Putnam, Rosa Luxemburg, and Trotsky—known to Wolfe personally or through research; and *The Bridge and the Abyss*, a "graphic and absorbing" study of the quarrelsome friendship between Lenin and Maxim Gorky.

A reviewer in the *Times Literary Supplement* has suggested that in matters of theory, Wolfe "is not outstandingly subtle or percipient; he also lacks that degree of sympathy with his subject which would seem to be a qualification for reaching the highest levels of understanding." Not all critics would accept this reservation, and even the one who makes it finds Wolfe compulsively readable, speaks of his immense knowledge, and says that he excels "as a historian with a penchant for detective-type investigations." Those who know him best say that Wolfe exhibits in his private life all of the integrity, wit, and wisdom which distinguish his books.

PRINCIPAL WORKS: Portrait of Mexico, 1937; Civil War in Spain, 1937; Diego Rivera: His Life and Times, 1939;

Three Who Made a Revolution, 1948; Six Keys to the Soviet System, 1956 (rev. as Communist Totalitarianism, 1961); Khrushchev and Stalin's Ghost, 1956; The Fabulous Life of Diego Rivera, 1963; Marxism: 100 Years in the Life of a Doctrine, 1965; Strange Communists I Have Known, 1965; The Bridge and the Abyss: The Troubled Friendship of Maxim Gorky and V. I. Lenin, 1967; An Ideology in Power: Reflections on the Russian Revolution (essays), 1969.

ABOUT: Contemporary Authors 7–8, 1963; Who's Who in America, 1972–1973. *Periodicals*—American Heritage February 1960; New York Times Book Review October 3, 1948; New Yorker December 18, 1948; Reporter March 3, 1960; Times Literary Supplement September 8, 1966; April 27, 1967.

WRIGHT, DAVID (JOHN MURRAY) (February 23, 1920–), British poet, born in South Africa, writes: "My father was descended on both sides from the first British emigrants to South Africa, the 1820 Settlers. One of his forebears came from Cork in Ireland; another was from Newcastle on Tyne, and is said to have been a musician. A feeling for music seems to have run in the family—my father and his two sisters were given a musical education at Dresden just before the Kaiser's war. In that war my father fought in South West Africa and at Passchendaele. At the end of it he had a foot amputated at Guy's Hospital in London, and thus met my mother, who was one of the nursing sisters. She same from Annan in Scotland. Her father, John Murray, a builder and quarrymaster, had been born in Ayrshire during the reign of George IV (that side of my family had a habit of marrying late.) According to family tradition, cousins of ours were neighbours of Robert Burns at Alloway, and one of them, it is said, as a boy 'held the plough' for the poet.

"I was born in Johannesburg, where my father was then a stockbroker (the firm crashed in 1929). At the age of seven I became totally deaf after contracting scarlet fever. When I was fourteen I was sent to a deaf school at Northampton, England. At that time it was the only establishment to provide secondary education for deaf pupils. When in 1939 I won a place at Oriel College, Oxford, I was, I believe, only the fourth or fifth deaf man ever to enter a university.

"At Oxford most of my friends were intramural biochemists and extramural ballet-dancers; but in my last year I came to know the poet Sidney Keyes through the accident of our taking digs at the same house in High Street. Through Keyes I met Drummond Allison (also killed in the war) and John Heath-Stubbs. I left Oxford in 1942 with a moderate second-class honours degree in English, and came to live in London.

"In London, in the public-houses north of Oxford Street, I continued my education; for it was there I met, and listened to, poets like Roy Campbell, Dylan Thomas, George Barker, W. S. Graham, and, later, Patrick Kavanagh and Hugh MacDiarmid. About 1948 I got tired of London and for a year lived on the moors near Zennor in Cornwall, in a series of five-bob-a-week cottages (one of them had sheltered Katharine Mansfield).

DAVID WRIGHT

"My first and let us hope worst book of poems was published in 1949, after so many delays that by the time it came out the volume no longer represented the kind of thing I was doing. In 1950 I was given one of the last Atlantic Awards for Literature and went to Italy, where for the first time I was introduced to the idea of civilization. The following year I met and married the actress Phillipa Reid, a colonial like myself (she was born in New Zealand). For some years she acted in the famous self-contained mobile theatre unit, the Century Theatre; which resulted for me in an intimate knowledge of the north of England, and visits to Dublin and Edinburgh for the festivals. I have always liked travelling. As a boy, and on visits to my parents in 1937 and 1951, I managed to see a large part of Africa. Whenever I could I travelled in Europe: to France, Italy, Greece, Spain, and Portugal.

"I began writing verse the year after I became deaf. I may have begun reading and enjoying poetry because I found in it a substitute for music. I do not know. When I was twenty I made up my mind that poetry was what I could do best (or what I would rather do) and from then on allowed events to arrange themselves round that proposition. I had no ambition for a career or indeed any notion what I could do to earn a living (translating, anthologies, and windfalls like the Atlantic Award and Guinness

Poetry Prizes turned out to be part of the answer). Most of my poems are in praise of the miracle of the visible world; those which are satiric are the obverse of the same coin."

Although he can lip read, Wright's deafness cut him off from many of the ordinary experiences of childhood and adolescence. At Oxford, he says, "my main preoccupation lay in nerving myself to approach people, to talk to them, to find out, in fact, how life was lived." He taught himself to row, became a highly successful Captain of Boats, and in this and other ways made many friends. After he left the university he was, according to *Contemporary Authors*, a staff member of the London *Sunday Times* from 1942 to 1947.

Wright's poetry is vividly visual. He has been called a word-juggler, but one more powerful than graceful. At times he seems to some readers uncertain of his aims or the best way to achieve them. He is most successful in long poems, like "A Voyage to Africa," which are written out of his special experience as an expatriate or as a deaf man. Then "he can sustain a theme without recourse to verbal sleight-of-hand, he can move without self-pity, and he can relate a series of brilliant visual images to the wider context of the poem."

Wright held the Gregory Fellowship in Poetry at the University of Leeds in 1965–1967. He has collaborated with Patrick Swift on three notable travel books about Portugal, and is the author of *Deafness: A Personal Account*. The latter, according to Paul West, is both an "articulate and relentless" autobiography and a history of deafness and the education of the deaf. West called the book "a triumph of style in expressing a lifelong struggle . . . a celebration and an exercise of gifts inexplicably given in the place of one commonplace-seeming faculty just as inexplicably denied."

PRINCIPAL WORKS: *Poetry*—Poems, 1949; Moral Stories, 1954; Monologue of a Deaf Man, 1958; Adam at Evening, 1965; Nerve Ends, 1969. *Nonfiction*—Roy Campbell, 1960; (with Patrick Swift) Algarve, 1965; (with Patrick Swift) Minho and North Portugal, 1968; Deafness: A Personal Account, 1969; (with Patrick Swift) Lisbon, 1971. *As translator*—Beowulf, 1957; The Canterbury Tales, 1964. *As editor*—(with John Heath-Stubbs) The Forsaken Garden: An Anthology of Poetry, 1824–1909, 1950; Seven Victorian Poets, 1964; (with John Heath-Stubbs) The Faber Book of Twentieth Century Verse, revised ed., 1965; The Mid-Century: English Poetry, 1940–1960, 1965; Longer Contemporary Poems, 1966; The Penguin Book of English Romantic Verse, 1968.

ABOUT: Abse, D. (ed.) Modern Poets in Focus 1, 1973; Contemporary Authors 9-10, 1964; Murphy R. (ed.) Contemporary Poets of the English Language, 1970; Who's Who in America, 1972–1973; Wright D. Deafness, 1969. *Periodicals*—London Magazine April 1965; Times Literary Supplement March 7, 1958.

JAMES WRIGHT

WRIGHT, JAMES (ARLINGTON) (December 13, 1927–), is an American poet whose work has a very wide readership and great influence upon younger poets; he received the Pulitzer Prize in 1972. He was born in the overindustrialized steel mill area along the Ohio River, at Martins Ferry, Ohio. His father was himself a steelworker. The devastated and hopeless landscape of his Midwest birthplace—blast furnaces, squalid shacks, the poisoned river—is often evoked in his poetry.

After four years in the United States Army, Wright went to Kenyon College while John Crowe Ransom was teaching there, and graduated in 1952. In 1952–1953 he studied at the University of Vienna on a Fulbright grant, and in 1953 he went to the University of Washington in Seattle where he received his M.A. in 1954 and his doctorate in 1959, and where he studied with Theodore Roethke. Wright taught at the University of Minnesota and Macalester College in St. Paul, Minnesota, until 1966, when he joined the Department of English at Hunter College of the City University of New York—he refuses to teach "creative writing."

In 1955 Wright received the Eunice Tietjens Memorial Prize for three poems published in *Poetry*. His first book, *The Green Wall*, appeared two years later in the Yale Series of Younger Poets, and his second, *Saint Judas*, in 1959. These early poems were welcomed as the work of a "new Frost," with a rare talent for distilling in his poetry "the common in experience." His principal master at this time however was not Frost but Edwin Arlington Robinson. This is very evident in "Saint Judas," though the poem is much more aggressively unconventional than anything that Robinson wrote: "Then I remembered bread my flesh had eaten, / The kiss that ate my flesh. Flayed without hope, / I held the man for nothing in my arms."

Many of the poems in these first two books show a debt to Robinson in both manner and content—in their fondness for colloquies with the dead, in their concern with the difficulty of achieving self-identity, in a heavily pessimistic tone challenged only by astonishment. It is not difficult to see why Glauco Cambon should speak of Wright as an existentialist poet; Wright himself once described the modern poet's task as that of "stating and examining and evaluating truth. I have tried . . . to ask some moral questions: exactly what *is* a good and humane action? And, even if one knows what such an action is, then exactly why should he perform it?" There was much praise for Wright's uncompromising but not unsympathetic honesty in these "harshly eloquent" poems, and Joseph P. Clancy said that he "leaves me haunted with his work, compelled to read it again and again."

"Whatever I write from now on will be entirely different," Wright said after *Saint Judas*. "I don't know what it will be, but I am finished with what I was doing in that book." The nature of his change of direction was determined initially by his association with Robert Bly and the other "programmatic surrealists" who contribute to Bly's magazine *The Seventies*. These poets attach great importance to the making of verse translations, as an enlarging technical and emotional discipline, and Wright has been very much affected by what he has learned in preparing English versions of Georg Trakl, César Vallejo, and Pablo Neruda.

The result is to be seen in *The Branch Will Not Break*. Here the iambics of Wright's earlier work have given way to rhythms based on those of ordinary American speech, and there is a far greater freedom of form. His plain strong diction now evokes images which, if they are wholly American and even midwestern in inspiration, are often surrealist in their juxtapositions. Some critics regretted this development, and George Garrett complained that "the triumph of Bly is all too obvious in the 'new' James Wright." But many others disagreed, and Michael Hamburger wrote that "this medium dispenses with argument and rhetoric, and presents the pure substance of poetry, images which are the 'objective correlative' of emotion and feeling."

It would be wrong to make too much of the change in Wright's poetry, which is still fundamentally concerned with the problems of identity and self-realization. Certainly, however, it has gained fresh momentum from a new delight in nature and landscape, and from a political commitment to humane and liberal values. The Spanish influence is easily seen in one of the most highly praised poems in the book, "Lying in a Hammock at William Duffy's Farm in Pine Island, Minnesota": "Over my head, I see the bronze butterfly, / Asleep on the black trunk, / Blowing like a leaf in green shadow. / Down the ravine behind the empty house, / The cowbells follow one another / Into the distances of the afternoon. / To my right, / In a field of sunlight between two pines, / The droppings of last year's horses / Blaze up into golden stones. / I lean back, as the evening darkens and comes on. / A chicken hawk floats over, looking for home. / I have wasted my life."

This is poetry—though some might say minor poetry—of the finest quality. But in other poems, especially some of those in his next book *Shall We Gather at the River*, Wright appears for the moment to have overreached himself: "The soul of a cop's eyes / Is an eternity of Sunday daybreak in the suburbs / of Juárez, Mexico." Martin Dodsworth has pointed out the weakness and pretentiousness of these lines as evidence that Wright has cultivated a style, "obscure yet suggestive, that reduces tension instead of increasing it." Some of the best poems in *Shall We Gather at the River* are about vagrants, symbols of America's free-ranging hobo past, brought to despair and death beside the polluted Ohio. Here, and in Wright's moving poems about his resigned, exploited father, he achieves, as David Ignatow says, "a metaphor of our land." Another reviewer, in the *Times Literary Supplement*, said that "he has begun to voice a degree of pathos that shatters his own dignity but is profoundly touching." It is an uneven collection, but seemed to many readers to represent a painful but crucial advance.

This advance is continued in the new poems and translations that appear, with almost all of his earlier work, in his *Collected Poems*. In their openness to the "deep" image, in the passion and sweetness of their vision of brotherly love, and their devotion to what Wright calls "the pure clear word," his new poems seemed to many critics to place him among the best American poets of his generation. The volume brought Wright both the Pulitzer Prize and the 1972 Fellowship of the Academy of American Poets. He has also received a *Kenyon Review* fellowship (1958), the Robert Frost Prize (1962), a grant from the National Institute of Arts and Letters (1963), and the Brandeis University Creative Arts Award (1971), among other honors. He lives in Manhattan with his second wife, the former Edith Anne Runk, and has two sons.

PRINCIPAL WORKS: *Poetry*—The Green Wall, 1957; Saint Judas, 1959; (with William Duffy and Robert Bly) The Lion's Tail and Eyes: Poems Written Out of Laziness and Silence, 1962 (*Wright's poems from this collection appear also in* The Branch Will Not Break); The Branch Will Not Break, 1963; Shall We Gather at the River, 1968; Collected Poems, 1971; Two Citizens, 1973. *As translator*—(with Robert Bly) Twenty Poems of Georg Trakl,

1962; Twenty Poems of César Vallejo, 1964; The Rider on the White Horse, by Theodor Storm, 1964; (with Robert Bly) Twenty Poems of Pablo Neruda, 1967.

ABOUT: Cambon, G. Recent American Poetry, 1962; Garrett, G. American Poetry, 1965; Kostelanetz, R. (ed.) The New American Arts, 1965; Murphy, R. (ed.) Contemporary Poets of the English Language, 1970; Rosenthal, M. L. The New Poets, 1967; Stepanchev, S. American Poetry Since 1945, 1965. *Periodicals*—Chicago Review February 1967; New York Times Book Review March 9, 1969; Paris Review Fall 1966; Poetry June 1960, September 1963; Times Literary Supplement November 28, 1963; October 17, 1968; November 14, 1968.

WRIGHT, JUDITH (ARUNDELL) (May 31, 1915–), Australian poet, critic, and biographer, writes: "I was born near Armidale, a country town in the New England district of New South Wales, then, and for that matter still, a district of pastoralists with a town of some educational fame; and I suppose this background explains a good deal of what I have done. Both my mother's and father's families were well-off pastoral settlers with a tradition of English country houses behind them; both had come early to Australia and made their living from the land, but remained vaguely bookish even in their new surroundings, though the books they bought were the usual mixture of nineteenth-century 'classics' and the day's best sellers, and radicalism or experiment were far from their ambit. The lives of the houses I remember as a child centred round sheep, cattle and horses, and much of my childhood was spent on horseback behind mobs of sheep or Herefords (not wholly to my own pleasure, since it was books I preferred); at any rate, the country was deep in my bones, and I loved to look at it.

"I was lucky in having a paternal grandmother who had, as a fairly young widow, taken over the responsibility of running the station her husband had died too early to set entirely on its feet, and made a huge success of it; this matriarchal background meant that the capacities of women were respected in my family as they were not always in others. So when I showed signs of wanting to be a writer I was encouraged; especially since I was no beauty and obviously impractical. Until I was thirteen I did not go to school; correspondence lessons and governesses took care of my own and my brothers' early education. Boarding-school when it descended on me was therefore more unpleasant even than usual, though I was lucky in having a delightfully intelligent English teacher, whose knowledge and understanding of poetry helped me much. Hopeless at mathematics, I did not matriculate, but with the help of money left me by my grandmother, was nevertheless allowed to go on to the University of Sydney for the usual three-year Arts degree course—most of which I spent reading outside the English stipulations, with

JUDITH WRIGHT

Ezra Pound's *Guide to Kulchur* as my mentor—far more valuable to a writer than the English Honours course in Anglo-Saxon which I abandoned after one year—and equally usefully falling in and out of love. By this time I had manuscript books full of poetry and occasional short stories, none of which satisfied me. A year in England and on the Continent, and a business-college course, seemed to qualify me for nothing much except teaching or secretarial work, and rejecting the first, I took jobs in Sydney—an oil-company, an advertising firm, a university secretaryship, living in a King's Cross flat with university friends. These matters, and the varied miseries of mismanaged love affairs, occupied me until 1942. Then I returned to the country, since my brothers were in the Army and my father needed help; and here for the first time, under the influence of a well-remembered countryside and the threat of the Japanese war, I began to produce poetry that seemed worth writing. This enormously encouraged my by now battered ego (I had, in the last two years, also begun to go deaf); and in 1944 I went to Brisbane to work at the University of Queensland as a clerk, and to help in spare time with the production of a literary magazine, *Meanjin*. I was publishing poetry in the *Sydney Bulletin* and in the numerous small literary magazines which sprang up like mushrooms in Australia under the influence of war and the temporary difficulty in importing books; I began to feel myself a poet rather more than *manqué*.

"My first book of poems was published in 1946, and the reviews helped to repair my self-esteem; in 1949 I applied for a Commonwealth Literary Fund grant to work on the diaries of my grandfather, and to my surprise got it. I left my university job and set up as a writer. The book I produced that year, *The Generations of Men*, did not find a publisher for several years after that, but by now I had tasted freedom, and took no more nine-to-five jobs.

"Since then, I have produced a number of books of verse, some short stories, books for children, some criticism, as well as the usual hotchpotch of anthologies, school broadcasts, reviews and lectures which boil a modest pot. With my husband, J. P. McKinney, and my daughter, I now live fifty miles from Brisbane, a distance which allows for privacy and the country kind of living which I prefer; but lately I have been a good deal involved in the rather more public job of helping to administer a society concerned with the problems of wildlife conservation and the production of its magazine on a national basis. This, I suppose, ties in with my outlook as a poet too; I have always been painfully aware of belonging to an exploitive economy which has had far too little interest in and respect for the land it has been raping, and of the inevitable effects on mind and feeling of living in a society which regards its environment as something given it to exploit; regardless of aesthetic responsibility or the fact that ugly attitudes mean ugly living. I am thoroughly scared by the notion of a country, settled for less than two hundred years, which seems bent on wiping out all its original inhabitants in favour of a shoddy and temporary prosperity and a ruined and eroded countryside, and by the hideous proliferation of suburbia, barbed-wire fences and treeless poisoned landscapes on which Australians seem determined. Fighting this losing battle takes a great deal of time and irritating detail, but since to any poet in this world losing battles are the only ones worth fighting, and since in engaging in it I am paying a human and poetic debt and associating myself with people equally simple and quixotic, I shall probably go on with it."

As a critic has said in the *Times Literary Supplement*, Judith Wright is "unquestionably the most accomplished woman poet in Australia today," and "one of the best known anywhere in the literary world." Her stature is truly international. She is the universally acknowledged ambassador of Australian poetry, both as a balanced and skillful anthologist and as a trenchant and informative critic. Her intelligent awareness of European and American traditions, together with her determination to be a validly Australian poet, helps to explain the high degree of her achievement. Her biohistorical researches, which in poetic terms represent research into her own origins, are also extremely relevant.

Her first book, *The Moving Image* (1946), introduced the main perennial features of her verse. These graceful lyrics, traditional in their forms and rather bare in their diction, are packed with memorable visual images. In their themes they reveal a specifically non-Christian preoccupation with death and decay, balanced by images of birth and renewal. And like all her work they reflect her consciousness of her national heritage. A well-known poem from this collection, "Bullocky," celebrates the work of the bullock-driver: "Beside his heavy-shouldered teams, / thirsty with drought and chilled with rain, / he weathered all the striding years / till they ran widdershins in his brain." Using this poem as an illustration, Vincent Buckley has written that "Judith Wright surpasses all other Australian poets in the extent to which she mediates the pressure, and reveals the contours, of Australia as a place, an atmosphere, a separate being."

Woman to Man, which followed in 1949, is thought by some critics to contain Judith Wright's best work, in poems which accept, but define (and even solemnize) woman's domesticity and her sexuality. This passage from the title poem, in which the woman speaks of her unborn child, gives some idea of its quality: "This is no child with a child's face, / this has no name to name it by: / yet you and I have known it well. / This is our hunter and our chase, / the third who lay in our embrace." Cecil Hadgraft has said that "with its press and urgency it is in its kind probably the greatest lyric in Australian poetry."

In *The Gateway* (1953) and subsequent collections, Judith Wright has widened the scope of her poetry. Most critics regret the relatively abstract and intellectual nature of her later work. They argue that some of the lyrics in her first two books achieve in their most particular and concrete passages a powerful, almost mystical, sense of the universality of human experience; and that nothing of the sort happens when she addresses herself consciously to philosophical problems which she is not equipped to solve. Instead, according to her critics, her verse has tended to lose its immediacy and control, to descend at times to intellectual and even verbal clichés. Her champions argue that a serious artist cannot and must not stand still, and welcome in some of her later poems a new "ruthlessness both of style and mind."

As a biographer Judith Wright is lucid, scrupulous, and unsentimental. *The Generations of Men*, her fictionalized account of the life in Australia of her immigrant grandparents, contrives, it was said, "to purify and distil emotions more commonly owned than she may realize"—which is, after all "the proper function of a poet." In her criticism she is lively but objective, as is shown in her excellent study of Shaw Neilson's work in *Quadrant* (Spring, 1959). With Buckley's *Essays in Poetry*, her *Preoccupations in Australian Poetry* is the most revealing and informative book on its subject. It is free from the parochialism and self-assertiveness that mar much Australian criticism. "No reader of this serious and well-proportioned book," wrote a reviewer in the *Times Literary Supplement*, "will feel disposed in future to dismiss the Australian poetic experience as provincial." Her short stories are slight and graceful and deal forthrightly with feminine situations and problems.

Judith Wright was educated at the New England Girls' School at Armidale. She was the recipient of Sydney University's Literary Fund Scholarship in 1949 and again in 1962. She holds two honorary doctorates and in 1964 won the Britannica Award for Literature. She is a Fellow of the Australian Academy of the Humanities. Now a widow, she lives at North Tamborine, Queensland, and is an Honours Tutor in English at the University of Queensland.

PRINCIPAL WORKS: *Poetry*—The Moving Image, 1946; Woman to Man, 1949; The Gateway, 1953; The Two Fires, 1955; Birds, 1962; Five Senses, 1963; The Other Half, 1966; Collected Poems 1942–1970, 1972; Alive: Poems 1971–1972, 1973. *Nonfiction*—Charles Harpur (biography), 1963; Preoccupations in Australian Poetry (criticism), 1965; Henry Lawson, 1967. *Fiction*—The Generations of Men, 1959; The Nature of Love, 1966. *For children*—Kings of the Dingoes, 1958; Range the Mountains High, 1963; The Day the Mountains Played, 1963; The River and the Road, 1966. *As editor*—A Book of Australian Verse, 1956; New Land, New Language, 1957; Selections from John Shaw Neilson, 1963.

ABOUT: Buckley, V. Essays in Poetry, 1957; Green, H. M. A History of Australian Literature, 1960; International Who's Who, 1973–74; Murphy, R. (ed.) Contemporary Poets of the English Language, 1970; Stewart, D. The Flesh and the Spirit, 1948; Thomson, A. K. (ed.) Critical Essays on Judith Wright, 1968; Wesson, A. The Poetry of Judith Wright, 1963; Who's Who, 1973; Who's Who in Australia, 1971. *Periodicals*—Australian Letters March 1958, July 1960; Australian Literary Studies June 1, 1963; Australian Quarterly March 1964; Australian Studies October 1966; Journal of Commonwealth Literature June 1971; London Magazine February 1962, November 1964; Meanjin 1953; Opinion August 1963; Quadrant Winter 1961; Southerly 1956, 1965; Times Literary Supplement September 5, 1958; October 2, 1959; June 30, 1966.

"WYNDHAM, JOHN" (pseudonym of John Wyndham Parkes Lucas Beynon Harris) (July 10, 1903–March 11, 1969), English science fiction writer, wrote also as John Beynon Harris, "John Beynon," and "Lucas Parkes." He was born in the village of Knowle, in Warwickshire. His father, George Beynon Harris, was a barrister of Welsh descent; his mother, the former Gertrude Parkes, was the daughter of a Birmingham ironmaster. They separated when Wyndham was eight years old, and after that he and his brother had no settled home. His mother moved from place to place, living in hotels, and he grew up mostly in a series

JOHN WYNDHAM

of boarding schools, staying longest at Bedales, an advanced co-educational school which he left at eighteen. According to his brother, the writer Vivian Beynon Harris, this was however by no means a rootless or unhappy childhood: "we loved our mother and each other and we were as close as it is possible for a family to be. . . . He had a wonderful childhood and teen-age time." After Bedales, Wyndham studied farming for a while, then "crammed" to enter Oxford University, then changed his mind again and tried advertising. He wrote a great many short stories without much success and lived mostly on a small allowance from his parents.

Always fascinated by the speculative fiction of H. G. Wells, Wyndham discovered his métier in 1929, when he came across a copy of *Amazing Stories* and began to write for the American science fiction pulp magazines. His first success was "Worlds to Barter," published in *Wonder Stories* in 1931. It was an ingenious time story about earthlings of the future who, seeking an undespoiled planet, return to an earlier period in the earth's history and set about ousting their ancestors. A series of other popular and much-emulated stories was published during the 1930s in the American pulps, where the author's name appeared as John Beynon Harris. From the beginning they showed a degree of literacy and stylistic grace uncommon in the field, and hints of an equally rare concern with moral and philosophical values. Some of these early stories were published in book form (as by "John Beynon"), beginning with *The Secret People* (193[illegible]). In 1937 an English science fiction critic said that "judged from the standpoint of literary ability,

[Harris] is probably the best of our modern science fiction writers." Sam Moskowitz has said that "though his early work possesses the strong element of action then preferred by the science-fiction magazines, they are, nevertheless, grimly serious social and religious satires and turn on philosophic and psychological pivots."

During the late 1930s Wyndham contributed a great deal to the British science fiction magazines launched at that time. This market soon collapsed, and he published little during the war, though he tried his hand at poetry and translated some French plays. Wyndham was a civil servant from 1940 to 1943, working in censorship, but went into the army in time to participate in the Normandy invasion. He was a corporal cipher operator in the Royal Signal Corps.

After the war Wyndham found that the tone and content of science fiction had changed—instead of the old reliance on scientific fantasy and hectic action there was a more sophisticated demand for psychological insight and plausibility; the "willing suspension of disbelief" had to be worked for. For two years this new mode eluded him, and the many short stories he wrote at this time were for the most part rejected.

He found his way when he returned to the novel with *The Day of the Triffids* (1951). A spectacular explosion in space causes mass blindness on earth. At the same time an agricultural experiment goes wrong and armies of giant carnivorous plants emerge, threatening the very existence of mankind. The chaos that follows draws much of its horror from the fact that no one, including the still sighted narrator, fully understands what is happening as civilization collapses and gives way to nightmare and anarchy. The well-realized character of the narrator, and the tone of the writing—calm, practical, and intelligent—add greatly to the authenticity and power of the story. The novel was immensely popular and established the Wyndham pen name. E. F. Walbridge called it "the most terrifying as well as the best-written science fiction novel of the year, or for several years." An English reviewer thought it "one of the best exercises in the Wells manner I have read." It was later filmed.

The Kraken Wakes, published in America as *Out of the Deeps*, is another study of human personality and institutions under hideous stress, narrated by an intelligent and likable participant. Some critics complained that the plotting is a little arbitrary, but the poet John Betjeman wrote that Wyndham "has all the imagination necessary for his theme: the terrifying attacks of this great creature [the Kraken] . . . are told with mounting intensity: the final phase with the flooding of London is finely described."

Wyndham's subsequent novels can all be read as allegorical criticisms of society. *The Chrysalids*, for example, called *Rebirth* in America, is a harsh attack on conformism in which the remnants of a shattered civilization, blindly clinging to old religions, destroy anyone, child or adult, who deviates physically or emotionally from the established norm. *The Midwich Cuckoos*, filmed as *Village of the Damned*, about an alien colony of children implanted in a quiet English village, speculates about the likely human reaction to a community of superior beings and the technical and moral problems involved in its destruction. A similar theme is explored in *Chocky*, while *Trouble with Lichen* is concerned with the social effects of the discovery of a life-extending drug. In the latter book, Wyndham's philosophical preoccupations tend to slow the action. In other novels his plotting has been found weak, and he was seldom able to contrive a really satisfactory climax. These reservations apart he was, as one critic said, "a storyteller nearly perfect in every respect."

Wyndham was married in 1963 to Grace Wilson. He lived the life of a country gentleman in a secluded country house near Petersfield, in Hampshire, just outside the grounds of Bedales school—which, according to Vivian Beynon Harris, was the strongest influence on his brother's life. A passionate lover of the countryside (as his books show), Wyndham was extremely skillful at all kinds of handicrafts, especially leatherwork and bookbinding. He was a shy man who disliked personal publicity and said: "My life has been practically devoid of interest to anyone but myself—though I have quite enjoyed it, of course, in those moments when I did not seem to have been sent to occupy a largely lunatic world."

PRINCIPAL WORKS: *As "John Beynon"*—The Secret People, 1935; Foul Play Suspected, 1935; The Planet Plane, 1936. *As "John Wyndham"*—The Day of the Triffids, 1951; The Kraken Wakes (U.S., Out of the Deeps), 1953; Jizzle, and Other Stories, 1954; The Chrysalids (U.S., Rebirth), 1955; The Seeds of Time (stories), 1956; Tales of Gooseflesh and Laughter, 1956; (with Lucas Parkes) The Outward Urge, 1959; The Midwich Cuckoos, 1957; Trouble with Lichen, 1960; Consider Her Ways (stories), 1961; The Infinite Moment, 1961; The John Wyndham Omnibus, 1964; Chocky, 1968.

ABOUT: Moskowitz, S. Seekers of Tomorrow, 1966. *Periodicals*—Times (London) March 16, 1968; March 12, 1969.

YATES, RICHARD (February 3, 1926–), American short story writer and novelist, was born in Yonkers, New York, the son of Vincent M. Yates, a sales executive, and Ruth (Maurer) Yates. He grew up in various parts of New York City and its suburbs. Yates began his career in 1943 as a copyboy on the old New York *Sun*. He served from 1944 to 1946 in the army—for part of the time as an infantry private in Europe. After the war he worked on a grocery trade journal, a trade union newspaper, as a United Press rewrite man, and as a publicity writer for a business machines company. In 1951 he went to Europe and devoted himself to fiction writing for two and a half years.

Yates had begun to write stories when he was fifteen, and after he left the army submitted many to magazines. It was not until 1953 however that he had his first success, when his story "Jody Rolled the Bones" was accepted by the *Atlantic Monthly* and won first prize in the year's Atlantic "First" awards. Thereafter many short stories appeared in such magazines as *Esquire*, the *Paris Review*, and *Cosmopolitan*, and a group of four stories were published in a 1958 Scribner's collection called *Short Story, 1*. From 1953 to 1959, while he was building his reputation as a story writer, Yates supported himself and his family as a freelance industrial journalist and as a ghostwriter.

Revolutionary Road, a novel on which Yates had worked for five years, appeared in 1961. Frank Wheeler is a businessman who believes that he should be doing something more rewarding and exotic; his wife, April, is a would-be actress. Trapped in the Connecticut suburbs, convinced that they are meant for higher things, their marriage disintegrating, they plan a fresh start in Paris. This escape is threatened when April becomes pregnant. Her attempt at self-induced abortion causes her death.

The novel attracted a great deal of attention. It was read variously as an indictment of the emptiness of American life and as a study of the dangers of self-delusion (though Yates said "it was just supposed to be a story about a couple of people"). Some few critics found it an unimpressive addition to a long line of complaints from suburbia, but the majority thought it uniquely powerful and perceptive, compelling in its characterization and "uncanny" in the precision of its dialogue. "Perhaps all this has been said before," wrote David Boroff, "but rarely with such precise notation of feeling, such mordant, unsentimental perception." Tennessee Williams went so far as to call it a masterpiece.

The first collection of Yates's stories was published a year later as *Eleven Kinds of Loneliness*, and was also generally admired. According to Hollis Alpert, Yates "depends on our recognizing his characters, and many of his stories gain strength not because they are unique, but because he has thrown a searchlight on the lives of the more or less anonymous ones." There was at the same time a feeling, expressed by several reviewers, that Yates's range was rather narrow.

A Special Providence, Yates's second novel, appeared after a long silence in 1969, and had a quieter but generally respectful reception. It describes the mother-dominated childhood of its hero, Robert J. Prentice, and his coming to maturity in the latter part of World War II, in army training camp and in battle in Belgium. He learns that the best one can do, in a world where there is "no settling of accounts, no resolution, no proof," is simply to survive. Robert Phillips called the novel "a triumph of lucidity—utterly lacking in stylistic gymnastics or self-conscious mannerisms," though "within the limits of quotidian detail [Yates] is especially skillful at devising symbolic acts that reverberate with meaning."

RICHARD YATES

Richard Yates has been married twice—to Sheila Bryant in 1948 and to Martha Speer in 1968. He has two children. He has taught creative writing at New York's New School (1959–1962) and at Columbia University (1961–1962), and since 1966 has been assistant professor of English at the University of Iowa. In 1971–1972 he was writer-in-residence at Wichita State University, Kansas. He wrote the screenplay based on William Styron's *Lie Down in Darkness*. Yates was a Guggenheim Fellow in 1962, and has received grants from the National Institute of Arts and Letters (1963), the National Foundation on the Arts (1966), and the Rockefeller Foundation (1967). In 1963 he served as a speechwriter for Attorney General Robert F. Kennedy.

PRINCIPAL WORKS: Revolutionary Road (novel), 1961; Eleven Kinds of Loneliness (short stories), 1962; (ed.) Stories for the Sixties, 1963; A Special Providence, 1969.

ABOUT: Contemporary Authors 7–8, 1963; Solotaroff, T. The Red-Hot Vacuum, 1970; Vinson, J. (ed.) Contemporary Novelists, 1972; Who's Who in America, 1972–1973. *Periodicals*—L'Express October 17, 1963; New York Times Book Review March 5, 1961.

SERGEI YESENIN

*YESENIN, SERGEI (ALEKSANDROVICH) (September 21 [old style, i.e., October 3], 1895–December 27, 1925), Russian poet, was born in Ryazan province in the town of Konstantinovo, now renamed Yesenino. He has left several vivid autobiographical accounts of his childhood in introductions to his various books of verse. He came from a peasant family, but his parents moved to the city when he was two, while he was brought up in his native village by his peasant grandfather, who belonged to an Old Believer sect. He grew up in a deeply religious atmosphere, his first memories going back to a walk with his grandmother to the Radovetsky Monastery, some forty versts away. Images that stayed with the poet all his life came from his grandfather's weekend recitations of passages from the Bible and "Sacred Chronicle," and the visits of blind old men who wandered from village to village singing sacred chants about the saints and the glories of paradise.

In contrast to this was the adventurous outdoor life that he led with his young uncles, who stuck him onto a saddleless horse at the age of three and put it at once to a gallop, taught him to swim by tossing him naked into the water, and then used him as a retriever when they went duck shooting. He attended the village school until he was twelve, when he was sent to an ecclesiastical teachers' training school. His family wanted him to become a teacher, but after reading Pushkin he had decided to become a poet, and he had begun to write verse at the age of nine.

When he was eighteen he went to Moscow, where he worked as proofreader in a printing shop, and for a year (1912–1913) attended lectures on history, literature, and philosophy at the Shanyavski People's University. He was sending his poetry to various St. Petersburg magazines, without result, until in 1914 he himself went to the capital, which at the time was the center for the rival poetic movements of symbolism, acmeism, and futurism. Under the patronage of Blok and Gorodetsky, Yesenin here became one of the "peasant poets," a group led by Nikolai Klyuev, who became his friend and teacher.

Yesenin always remained the poet of "wooden and vegetable Russia": the best of his spontaneous and lyrical poetry describes the Russian countryside in simple melodious verse, evoking its tranquil beauty and peaceful simplicity and lamenting with gentle melancholy and nostalgia the gradual disappearance of traditional village and peasant life under the impact of industrialization. His first book was *Radunitsa* (1916), whose untranslatable title refers to the day on which feasts are held in memory of deceased parents, a surviving pagan Slavonic ritual. It is in two sections: "Rus," which begins with the life story of a Christian saint, the wanderer Mikola; and "Makovye pobaski" (Poppy Tales), which begins with a secular love lyric. This reflects his own divided experience as a boy, which he had come to see as characteristic of Russian national life; he said: "The Russian lives his days in double fashion—churchwise, and in the daily round."

The good-looking golden-haired young man was a sensational success in the literary salons of St. Petersburg (then called Petrograd) as he chanted his poems, dressed in cap, top boots, and an embroidered peasant blouse. Certainly there was a degree of artificiality in Yesenin's performance as a simple country lad, but his attachment to peasant values was genuine, and he brought vitality and spontaneity to Russian verse at a time when it was hidebound and anemic.

In 1916 Yesenin was drafted into the army, and was at the front at the time of the 1917 Revolution. Like millions of other soldiers he deserted, returning to Petersburg. There he married Zinaida Reich, an actress at the Kamerny Theatre, but separated from her the following year. He enthusiastically welcomed the Revolution, but as a religious rather than a political event—a great spiritual cataclysm which he identified with a new mystical Christianity. It gave his poetry a new impetus, and he entered a period of intense productivity, while at the same time wandering all over Russia, from the Arctic to Turkestan, reciting his poems.

Like Bely and Blok he fell at this time under the influence of Ivanov-Razumnik's national messianic philosophy of Scythianism. His revolutionary poetry in this apocalyptic vein appears in *Preo-*

* yi sā′ nyin

brazheniye (Transfiguration, 1918) and *Inonia* (1918) —the title is a coined word meaning "Other-Land." He exalts the Revolution as a kind of cosmic rebirth, which will bring a rustic democratic utopia where life will be in complete accord with nature. He celebrated the new life in poems that echo the religious chants of his childhood, though his religious mysticism sometimes veers into heresy and blasphemy, into a parody of Christian hopes and beliefs. These poems are usually regarded as his weakest, but the romantic appeal of revolution and his passionate sympathy for the enslaved peasants did inspire some excellent poetry in the verse-play *Pugachev* (1921), based on the heroic life of the eighteenth century rebel leader, which was brilliantly staged in the 1960s at the Taganka Theatre by the director Yury Lyubimov.

But instead of the transformation of Russia into the earthly paradise of the peasant, the Revolution brought the agonies of the Civil War. Yesenin's passionate enthusiasm gave way to progressive disillusionment as he realized that the industrial and materialistic nature of the Bolshevik system meant the triumph of the Iron Age that he feared and hated. In a rapidly changing world he was unable to find the security he longed for, and from about 1919 a new note of tortured self-examination entered his work. His confessional verses became a vehicle for dramatizing his personal plight—that of "the last village poet," crushed by the inexorable demands of the time, and torn between nostalgia for the pastoral innocence he had lost and the febrile attractions of the city, with its taverns and prostitutes.

For a time he was a leader of the short-lived literary movement of imaginism, which stressed the importance of vivid imagery as the "primary pigment of poetry." Yesenin had always had a bent for colorful, somewhat bizarre imagery that stemmed from folklore, in which there is a continuous identification between men, animals, plants, and stars: the moon is at one time a bear, then a frog, then "that ruddy goose," then "a curly lamb strolling through blue grass." In works such as *Treryadnitsa* (1919) his imagery became strained and farfetched, reaching its most extreme in *Pugachev*, in which "the pliers of sunrise yank the stars like teeth from the jaw of darkness." But his involvement with imaginist theories was not profound (according to Gorodetsky it was "a way out of his pastoralness, out of his role of a country lad clad in homespun and playing an accordion"), and his later poetry is characterized by the unforced simplicity and genuineness of its lyrical diction, for which Pushkin was the model.

It was at this time that he entered irretrievably upon a rowdy *vie de bohème* in the taverns and cafés of Moscow, where he became the reprehensible hero of youthful Soviet intellectuals. His pyschological experiences during these years are forcefully conveyed in *Ispoved khuligana* (Confessions of a Hooligan, 1921) and *Moskva kabatskaya* (Moscow of the Taverns, 1922). They showed how enthusiastically Yesenin had adopted the mystique of the *poète maudit*, and boasted that if he had not been born a poet he would have been a thief and cutthroat. Soviet critics have condemned these poems as full of filth and vice, with nothing to recommend them, and his anarchic peasant ways led to the name *Yeseninshchina*, or Yeseninism, being coined for his kind of hooliganism. But in fact it is clear from these verses that the poet, as Marc Slonim observes, "actually bore within himself a constant sense of guilt and the wistful yearning of a prodigal son: what he wanted above all things was to return to the village, to the peaceful kindliness of his mother, to the healing bosom of nature, and in order to drown his feminine sensitivity and his nostalgic drives, he drank, took drugs, indulged in cynicism, changed wives and mistresses, and made all sorts of mischief."

The culmination of this period of profoundly self-destructive debauchery and scandal came with Yesenin's disastrous marriage in 1922 to the famous American dancer Isadora Duncan, who was then already middle-aged, some fifteen years older than the poet. Neither could speak the other's language, and their only real bond was a taste for drinking and high living. Yesenin accompanied her on a long tour through Western Europe and the United States. He was particularly repelled by America, the epitome of everything that he most disliked about the modern world, but he was out of place everywhere, and drunk most of the time. Their quarrelsome odyssey filled the world's scandal sheets with stories of such exploits as Yesenin's appearance in the hall of the Hotel Crillon in Paris wearing nothing but a top hat. When he returned to Russia his marriage was finished and his mental and physical health were fatally impaired.

In 1924, worn out and frustrated, Yesenin returned to his native village. He found it changed out of all recognition, and he poignantly lamented the loss of his youth and of the rural Russia in which he had grown up. In the title poem in *Rus sovetskaya* (Soviet Russia, 1925) he declares: "I live an alien in my own land." He protests against the invasion of the countryside by the technological monsters of modern civilization, the telegraph poles and electric cables and locomotives, contrasting them with the beauty and naturalness of the horse. And he writes with an equal sense of loss about his plight as a man and artist, and his forebodings of death.

A relatively serene interlude of travel in Persia in 1924 led to the poems in *Persidskie motivy* (Persian

Themes, 1925). In 1925 he sought refuge in a third marriage, this time to a granddaughter of Leo Tolstoy. But the disintegration of his personality continued, and he was writing such poems as "Cherny chelovek" (The Black Man, 1925), a morbid alcoholic nightmare that is also a horrifying self-indictment, in which a demon confesses all his sins and failings, until the poet strikes him with a stick and finds that he has broken his own mirror. The same year Yesenin had a nervous breakdown and spent a short time in a mental hospital. At the end of the year, in the Hotel Angleterre in Leningrad, he slit his wrist and wrote in his own blood the deeply touching farewell poem "Do svidanya, drug moy, do svidanya" (Good-bye, my friend, good-bye), which ends: "In this life there's nothing new in dying, but, of course, there is as little novelty in living." Then he hanged himself.

Renato Poggioli wrote that "the most genuine of Yesenin's masterpieces are to be found among his shortest, least ambitious lyrics, written in the pure and simple modes of the elegy and the idyll, devoid of any rhetorical and anecdotal structure, and lightly woven as a cobweb of transparent words around the cluster of a few bright and striking images. Each one of these songs may be reduced to a landscape and to the mood it evokes within the soul of the poet. Although the narrative element is lacking, or hardly present, such poems partake of the magic aura of the legend and the fairy tale. They recreate a private and intimate universe, domestic and rustic, where all things are humanized by a naïve animism, by a pathetic anthropomorphism." Increasingly, his poems reflected his hunger for the lost Eden of his childhood—the conflict between his desire for a new order and his nostalgia for the old one—perfectly expressing the dilemma of the Russian people as a whole. The popular appeal of his work has never waned, and he has been one of the most widely read of modern Russian poets, both at home and abroad. During the 1930s official critics deplored his popularity with Soviet youth but without effect. His poetry is now regularly reprinted in very large editions of two hundred thousand or three hundred thousand copies which are quickly sold out. Only Mayakovsky rivals him in this respect, and the two poets, in many ways so different, the one rural and looking nostalgically to the past, the other urban and with his eyes on the future, resemble each other profoundly in other ways, especially in their self-destructive tendencies and spectacular suicides, and in the intimate connection between their work and their lives.

PRINCIPAL WORKS IN ENGLISH TRANSLATION: Confessions of a Hooligan, tr. by Geoffrey Thurley, 1973. *Poems in* Barnstone, W. (ed.) Modern European Poetry, 1966; Blake, P. and Hayward, M. (eds.) Dissonant Voices in Soviet Literature, 1964; Bowra, C. M. (ed.) A Book of Russian Verse, 1943; Bowra, C. M. (ed.) A Second Book of Russian Verse, 1948; Guerney, B. G. (ed.) Anthology of Russian Literature in the Soviet Period, 1960; Hughes, T. and Weissbort, D. Modern Poetry in Translation 6, 1970; Lindsay, J. (tr. and ed.) Russian Poetry 1917–1955, 1957; Markov, V. and Sparks, M. (eds.) Modern Russian Poetry, 1966; Obolensky, D. Penguin Book of Russian Verse, 1962; Reavey, G. Modern European Poetry, 1966.
ABOUT: Alexandrova, V. A History of Soviet Literature, 1963; De Graaff, F. Sergei Yesenin: A Biographical Sketch, 1966; Eastman, M. Artists in Uniform, 1934; Ehrenburg, I. First Years of Revolution 1918–1921, 1962; Erlich, V. The Double Image: Concepts of the Poet in Slavic Literatures, 1964; Kaun, A. S. Soviet Poets and Poetry, 1943; Lavrin, J. Aspects of Modernism from Wilde to Pirandello, 1935; Lavrin, J. Russian Writers: Their Lives and Literature, 1954; Milner-Gulland, R. Soviet Russian Verse, 1961; Penguin Companion to Literature 2, 1969; Peterkiewicz, J. The Other Side of Silence: The Poet at the Limits of Language, 1970; Poggioli, R. The Poets of Russia, 1890–1930, 1960; Schneider, I. Isadora Duncan: The Russian Years, 1968; Seroff, V. The Real Isadora, 1971; Slonim, M. Modern Russian Literature, 1953; Slonim, M. Soviet Russian Literature: Writers and Problems, 1964; Smith, H. (ed.) Columbia Dictionary of Modern European Literature, 1947; Struve, G. 25 Years of Soviet Russian Literature, 1944; Zavalishin, V. Early Soviet Writers, 1958. *Periodicals*—Living Age November 15, 1927; Russian Review April 1967; Slavonic Review March 1929.

***YEVTUSHENKO, YEVGENY (ALEKSANDROVICH)** (July 18, 1933–), Russian poet, was born in Zima, a small junction on the Trans-Siberian Railway near Lake Baikal. His grandfather, Yermolai Yevtushenko, who came from a peasant family of Ukrainian origin deported to Siberia under the Czars, rose to be a commander in the revolutionary army, but he was a victim of Stalin's purges, as was Yevtushenko's other grandfather, the Latvian mathematician Rudolf Gangnus. Both his parents were geologists who had met while studying at the Geological Institute; but according to Yevtushenko's autobiography they were psychological opposites, and they were divorced in the late 1930s. Thanks to them, he has said, "I will always be half an intellectual and half a peasant." The young Yevtushenko went with his mother to live in Moscow, but after the German invasion they were evacuated in 1941 back to Zima, returning to Moscow in 1944. Yevtushenko himself says that his work at school was exceedingly bad, and at the age of fifteen he was expelled after being falsely accused of breaking into the headmaster's study. He traveled on the roof of a train to join his father's geological expedition in Kazakhstan, working as a laborer, and wrote a long narrative poem about another expedition to the Altai mountains two years later.

He had been writing verse all through his school years, but preferred football; he abandoned his intention of becoming a full-time soccer player

* yef to͞o shen′ kō

only after his first published poems appeared in a sporting journal in 1949. Between 1951 and 1954 he attended the Gorky Institute of Literature in Moscow but achieved little success there, for he was very slow to mature as a poet, and his first book, *Razvedchiki gryadushchego* (Prospectors of the Future, 1952), like the numerous poems he published in magazines at this time, neither received nor merited much critical attention.

It was only after the death of Stalin in 1953 that he emerged as spokesman for the younger generation; he published three books in rapid succession—*Trety sneg* (The Third Snow, 1955), *Chaussé Entuziastov* (1956), and *Obeshchanie* (The Promise, 1957)—which made him a famous and controversial figure. All his poetry is autobiographical, but two kinds of theme can be distinguished in it, the personal and the public, though he moves readily from one to the other, and sometimes combines them in a single poem. As Andrei Sinyavsky has put it, his work is like "a fascinating novel in verse with a vividly expressed hero—the poet—in the center."

His public poetry is topical and journalistic, as in his early masterpiece, the long poem "Stantsiya Zima" (1956) translated as "Zima Junction." This is an account of his visit in the summer of 1953 to Zima, of the relatives and other people he meets there, and of his attempts to resolve both private self-doubts and the public moral problems raised by Stalin's death and the revelations that followed. The poem drew an enthusiastic response because it tackled subjects that had hitherto been avoided; but this, along with the poet's youth and personal flamboyance, also provoked much criticism in the press, and he had to withdraw temporarily from the Komsomol. In 1954 Yevtushenko married the poet Bella Akhmadulina, who inspired some notable love lyrics. His next collection, *Luk i Lira* (Longbow and Lyre, 1959), was the result of a stay in Gruzia (Georgia), and besides original poetry contains many translations of Georgian poetry. This youthful phase of Yevtushenko's work ended with a selection from all his previous volumes, under the title *Stikhi raznykh let* (Poems of Several Years, 1959).

In 1960 he began the travels and poetry readings abroad, in France, Britain, Africa, America, and Cuba, which by 1962 had made him an international figure. It was at this time that his famous poem "Babi Yar" appeared in the periodical *Literaturnaya gazeta*. Babi Yar is the name of a ravine near Kiev where ninety-six thousand Jews were murdered by the Nazis during the German occupation. Yevtushenko's poem provoked a storm of controversy because it attacked Russian as well as German anti-Semitism. Nevertheless, it became immensely popular at the public poetry recitals to

YEVGENY YEVTUSHENKO

which readings by Yevtushenko, Voznesensky, and others were drawing vast crowds of young people. At this point in his career Yevtushenko was described by Olga Carlisle as a "very tall and slender" young man with "transparent blue eyes. . . . He is fair and has high cheek bones, his eyes are narrow and shrewd. His manner has a kind of winning candidness, yet it seemed a little calculated, as that of a flirtatious child."

There followed one of Yevtushenko's most notable collections, *Vzmakh ruki* (1962, A Wave of the Hand). Besides twenty-eight poems about the foreign countries he had been visiting there were also fifty-seven new poems which are more concentrated than his earlier work and show a deepening of his thought. These include political poems like "Karera" (A Career), dealing with Galileo's fight for truth against the authority of the church, and "Yumor" (Humor), in which the power of laughter emerges triumphant over despotism. Both of these, with "Babi Yar," were among the five Yevtushenko poems which Shostakovich set for bass and male chorus as his *Thirteenth Symphony*.

Nezhnost (Tenderness) appeared later the same year. The poems in the first section include many on the nature and character of women; in one of them he bluntly enumerates the stresses and strains which led to his divorce from Bella Akhmadulina. (Since then he has married Galina Semenovna, a fellow Siberian well known as a translator from English.) The last section of the book consists of twenty-two poems on Cuba, which he had visited for the second time in the summer of 1962.

Yevtushenko is a natural revolutionary, and in this respect has often been compared to Mayakovsky, a much greater poet but one with the same hatred of hypocrisy and stagnation and a similarly direct, declamatory style. Yevtushenko measures contemporary Russia by the standards of pure idealism he associates with the early years of the Revolution, and he finds the whole Stalin era and its legacy hopelessly corrupt, a crime against the guiltless Russian people. Cuba was important to him as a younger and purer expression of the revolutionary ideal. His Cuban cycle was welcomed even by many conservative critics as evidence of Yevtushenko's new "civic-mindedness" though, as Burton Rubin has pointed out, "the fact is that politically he has more in common with the young Western radicals of the 'New Left' than he does with these self-styled 'Communist' critics." And the latter were soon to be disillusioned by Yevtushenko's poem "Nasledniki Stalina" (The Heirs of Stalin), which appeared in *Pravda* in October 1962. Stalin's coffin is carried from the mausoleum which it had briefly shared with Lenin. Inside it Stalin, only pretending to be dead, is peering through the cracks, telephone to hand. His followers prune their roses and await his call.

In the early months of 1963 Yevtushenko, along with Voznesensky and Aksenov, was subjected to a barrage of criticism. Yevtushenko was attacked with particular violence because, during a poetry-reading tour of Western Europe, he had allowed his "Notes for an Autobiography" to be serialized without official permission in the French newspaper *L'Express*. This work subsequently appeared as a book, the English version of which was published as *A Precocious Autobiography* (1963). Yevtushenko has frequently been accused of "self-admiration" and the justice of this charge is very evident in this colorful and uninhibited book. It attacks the betrayal of the Revolution, but welcomes a new, post-Stalinist, spiritual revolution, a struggle for the Soviet future in which the poet is proud to participate.

In 1965 Yevtushenko published his long poem *Bratskaya GES* (translated as *The Bratsk Station*). As Andrei Sinyavsky wrote: "It seeks to communicate the experience of the modern age and to connect this with the experience of the past, with Russian history. A panorama unfolds of varied human destinies and ordeals, of labor and struggle. . . . What holds it together is the dispute between two themes: 'unbelief' comprised in the soliloquies of an Egyptian pyramid—and 'faith,' expressed in those of a hydroelectric station and through figures, episodes, and lyrical meditations connected with its building. We have before us the outlines of a vast monumental scheme." Most Western critics agreed with Sinyavsky that Yevtushenko "falls short of his own demands, and is concerned with developing his theme in breadth when he ought to have gone deep." The work was later adapted and performed as a play. Yevtushenko has continued to publish much new poetry, but recently he has turned increasingly to prose and to the theatre. His first important stage piece was *Under the Skin of the Statue of Liberty*. It is a series of revue sketches about America, attacking its violence but celebrating the idealism of its young people. Produced in 1972 by Yuri Lyubimov, a leader of the Soviet avant-garde much influenced by Brecht, it was a huge success, especially with young people. Earlier that year, his international popularity as a public performer continued to rise. On January 28, he topped the bill at the most successful poetry reading ever held in the United States, when he, with Stanley Kunitz, James Dickey, Richard Wilbur, and former Senator Eugene J. McCarthy filled the five-thousand-seat Felt Forum of Madison Square Garden twice in a single evening.

"The hostile image of Yevtushenko," comments Max Hayward, "whether in its Eastern or Western version, is not to be taken very seriously. . . . Those who are well acquainted with his work will be struck by his humility and his acute awareness of his own limitations. With quite unaffected modesty, he has often publicly pointed to Voznesensky as a greater poet than himself. He has spoken of his own failure to elaborate a real style of his own and regards his poetic manner as an eclectic one derived from Blok, Mayakovsky and Pasternak."

And indeed the sensational rise of his reputation, and its subsequent decline, are related to his role as a public figure rather than to the literary merit of his poetry. The basic theme of his poetry is a search for the self, but Sinyavsky argues that "Yevtushenko, prone though he is to self-display, lacks the stamp of an exclusive personality, the idea of a vocation, of a great and terrible fate." Unlike Voznesensky he is not a stylistic innovator and, to quote Katherine Hunter Blair, his "importance lies above all in his consistent expression of the feelings of his generation." It is true, no doubt, that Yevtushenko's work lacks depth, but his best poems show him to be an authentic lyricist of considerable technical accomplishment and linguistic resource.

Yevtushenko's reputation as a liberal has declined in recent years, and some of his former friends have expressed their contempt for his willingness to act as a spokesman of the literary establishment. However, in February 1974, when the novelist Aleksandr Solzhenitsyn was arrested by the KGB (and before it was known that he was about to be expelled from the Soviet Union), Yevtushenko found the courage to send a telegram to Leonid Brezhnev, the Communist party leader, expressing his fears for Solzhenitsyn's safety and for the damage that would be done to Soviet prestige. This was followed by the international publication of an open letter in which Yevtushenko protested against the punishment he had received for sending the telegram—the abrupt cancellation of an important recital of his poems.

PRINCIPAL WORKS IN ENGLISH TRANSLATION: Selected Poems (tr. by Robin Milner-Gulland and Peter Levi), 1962; A Precocious Autobiography (tr. by A. W. MacAndrew), 1963; Winter Station (tr. by O. J. Frederiksen), 1965 (Munich); The Poetry of Yevgeny Yevtushenko, 1953–1965 (tr. by George Reavey), 1965; Yevgeny Yevtushenko: Poems Chosen by the Author (tr. by Peter Levi and Robin Milner-Gulland), 1966; Yevtushenko: Poems (tr. by Herbert Marshall), 1966; The Bratsk Station and Other Poems (tr. by Tina Tupikina-Glaessner and others), 1966; Stolen Apples (tr. by James Dickey and others), 1971. *Poems in numerous anthologies.*

ABOUT: Alexandrova, V. History of Soviet Literature, 1963; Blair, K. H. A Review of Soviet Literature, 1966; Brown, E. J. Russian Literature Since the Revolution, 1963; Carlisle, O. Voices in the Snow, 1962; Carlisle, O. Poets on Street Corners, 1969; Current Biography, 1963; Hayward, M. and Labedz, L. (eds.) Literature and Revolution in Soviet Russia, 1963; Hayward, M. and Crowley, E. L. (eds.) Soviet Literature in the Sixties, 1965; Simmonds, G. W. (ed.) Soviet Literature, 1967; Slonim, M. Soviet Russian Literature, 1964; Who's Who in America, 1972–1973. *Periodicals*—Encounter April 1967; Listener January 5, 1967; Nation November 21, 1966; New York Times January 29, 1972; June 3, 1973; New York Times Book Review December 26, 1965; New York Times Magazine September 30, 1973; New Yorker September 4, 1965; Observer May 27, 1962; Playboy December 1972; Times (London) February 19, 1974; Times Literary Supplement August 10, 1967.

YOUD, SAMUEL ("John Christopher") (1922–), English novelist writes: "I was born not far from Liverpool, on the border-line between the two villages (as they were then) of Huyton and Knowsley, and lived in Lancashire until my family moved to Hampshire when I was ten years old. I was educated at Peter Symonds School, Winchester.

"On being demobilized from the Army in 1946, I was given a grant by the Rockefeller Foundation which enabled me to write full-time for a year. Subsequently, I wrote in my spare time, but since 1958 have been a professional novelist in the strictest sense of the term: apart from a very occasional short story, the income on which my family and I must live derives from novels alone.

"This is a hazardous way of making a living, particularly for someone who is married and has five children of school age. There have been occasional strokes of good fortune, but in between there are years in which income remains well below essential outgoings. I have written novels under several names, and of several different kinds, including light comedy, detective thrillers, even two with cricket backgrounds. My early novels were more serious in intent and published under my own name. I continued to write these until a couple of years ago, and they were published, though with little success. I have had to abandon them since my American publisher understandably refused to go on with a course that was even more financially disastrous to him than it was to me. As a result of his decision, the last of these books, published in 1963, netted me two hundred and twenty-five pounds after deduction of agent's commission: scarcely adequate to keep a family of seven for half a year.

"The relatively more successful Christopher novels began as science fiction and are commonly given that label. They are, in fact, adventure stories involving a study of human reactions to severe environmental stresses. Thus, while in some action has taken place in a world denuded of grasses, or against the menace of extra-terrestrial entities capable of taking over the minds and personalities of their victims, others have dealt with people trapped in underground caves, or forced to trek across the Greenland ice-pack from an ice-bound ship. *The Long Winter*, starting from the premiss of a new ice age, was in fact concerned with the ironic possibilities of the whites of northern Europe fleeing as refugees to an arrogant and rich Black Africa.

"I live now in Guernsey, in the Channel Isles."

By the late 1930s, according to Sam Moskowitz, Samuel Youd was sufficiently interested in science fiction to edit and publish an amateur magazine—*The Fantast*, whose inaugural issue appeared in April 1939. After World War II, Youd worked as an assistant editor (or editorial assistant) on a technical journal in the field of industrial diamonds, selling an occasional short story written in his spare time. His first novel, *The Winter Swan*, was published in 1949.

For some years after that, Youd seems to have concentrated on the more or less traditional novels he writes under his own name. Among the more notable of these are *Giant's Arrow*, a story of business rivalry and the problems of marriage, which impressed Riley Hughes as a "brilliant short novel, exquisitely written, which opposes a Catholic view of life to the secularist view," and *Messages of Love*, "a long, quiet book filled with well-realized characters," praised for its "sharp vignettes of upper-middle-class social life," and said to resemble the work of John Galsworthy.

In spite of their encouraging critical reception, the Youd books had, as their author says, no commercial success, and since the mid-1950s he has experimented with almost every conceivable novelistic genre, preserving a different literary identity in each. His detective stories are attributed to "Peter Graaf" and "Peter S. Nichols," his cricketing books to "William Godfrey," and as "Hilary Ford" he has written several extremely gay and funny Wodehousian farces about the tribulations of an Angry Young novelist on his way to the top.

It is however as "John Christopher" that this prolific and versatile writer has had his greatest success. In all of the Christopher books (and to some extent in his other fiction as well) Youd is, as he explains, primarily concerned with the way human behavior patterns alter under stress. In *Caves of Night* the environment that produces the pressure is simply a cave in Austria; in other books the situation is far less ordinary. But even when Christopher borrows his situation from science fiction, his real concern is with character rather than with scientific speculation, and purists deny that he is a science fiction writer at all.

A very good and characteristic example is *The Death of Grass*, the book which, serialized in *Saturday Evening Post* in 1957 as "No Blade of Grass," established Christopher's reputation. As usual, the author starts with a single acceptable premise—the development of a virus which attacks rice and grain crops—and then unrolls an appalling but entirely logical chain of consequences. As the vital crops fail, civilization begins to break down all over the world. The novel focuses on one small band of English refugees who fight their way across country to a valley which promises food and security. As order disintegrates, the carefully nurtured middle-class values of the travelers crumble. Roles and allegiances change, submerged impulses are released, a meek little man becomes a cold killer. It is a book which reveals as dark a view of humanity as William Golding's *Lord of the Flies*, though it is probable that Christopher owes his large and growing audience less to his moral attitudes than to the pace and suspense of his stories. "Christopher's invention is appallingly plausible," one critic wrote of *The Long Winter*, and he is "adept at hooking in the unobtrusively poisonous detail which lodges in the memory until the time comes to rip open the horrors."

Most of the recent Christopher books have been for teen-agers. They include the "Tripods" trilogy, in which the earth has been enslaved by aliens from another planet, and the "Prince in Waiting" trilogy, set in an England converted by some disaster into a collection of warring city states. Another story, the "uncomfortably authentic prophetic novel" *The Guardians*, received the 1971 *Guardian* Award for Children's Fiction.

Youd lives in comparative isolation with his family on the island of Guernsey and avoids personal publicity.

PRINCIPAL WORKS: *As Christopher Youd*—The Winter Swan, 1949. *As Samuel Youd*—Babel Itself, 1951; The Brave Conquerors, 1952; Crown and Anchor, 1953; Palace of Strangers, 1954; Holly Ash (U.S., The Opportunist), 1955; The Choice, 1961; Messages of Love, 1961; The Summers at Accorn, 1963. *As "John Christopher"*—The Twenty-second Century, 1954; The Year of the Comet, 1955; The Death of Grass, 1956 (U.S., No Blade of Grass); The Caves of Night, 1958; A Scent of White Poppies, 1959; The Long Voyage, 1960 (U.S., The White Voyage); The World in Winter (U.S., The Long Winter), 1962; Cloud on Silver (U.S., Sweeney's Island), 1964; The Possessors, 1965; A Wrinkle in the Skin, 1965 (U.S., The Ragged Edge); The Little People, 1967; The "Tripods" Trilogy (for children): The White Mountains, 1967; The City of Gold and Lead, 1967; The Pool of Fire, 1968; Pendulum, 1968; The Lotus Caves, 1969; The Guardians (for children), 1970; The "Prince in Waiting" Triology (for children): The Prince in Waiting, 1970; Beyond the Burning Lands, 1971; The Sword of the Spirits, 1972; Dom and Va (for children), 1973. *As "Anthony Rye"*—Giant's Arrow, 1956 (U.S., published under his own name, 1960). *As "William Godfrey"*—Malleson at Melbourne, 1956; The Friendly Game, 1957. *As "Peter Graaf"*—Dust and the Curious Boy (U.S., Give the Devil His Due), 1957; Daughter Fair, 1958; The Sapphire Conference, 1959; The Gull's Kiss, 1962. *As "Hilary Ford"*—Felix Walking, 1958; Felix Running, 1959; Bella on the Roof, 1965. *As "Peter S. Nichols"*—Patchwork of Death, 1965.

ABOUT: Amis, K. New Maps of Hell, 1960; Moskowitz, S. Seekers of Tomorrow, 1965. *Periodicals*—Books and Bookmen February 1965; Saturday Evening Post April 27, 1957.

YOUNG, ANDREW (JOHN) (April 29, 1885–November 26, 1971), Scottish-born poet, wrote: "My birthplace was Elgin, county town of Moray, Scotland, but when I was two years old the family moved to Edinburgh. My education began at the age of four, my father teaching me Latin. After attending two schools I gained a scholarship to the famous Royal High School of Edinburgh. This scholarship was taken from me a few years later for playing truant, but I gained another scholarship before the end of the term. I continued to play truant occasionally, and it had far-reaching results. It took me out into the country where, having to spend long hours with nothing much to do, I began to take an interest in wild plants. This interest became the main hobby of my life. I have written two books about British plants, not botanical but, I hope, not unbotanical. But there was more to it than that; my hobby led me to explore the country and when I developed a desire to write poetry, it was natural that I should write about the things there that I saw and heard. Hence my short poems, which may be called nature poems and form the main part of *Collected Poems*.

"At the age of eighteen I went to Edinburgh University where I spent five leisurely years in what usually takes three years, the Arts Course. I took little interest in my work, though, of course, I graduated as M.A. From the University I went to New College, a Presbyterian theological college in Edinburgh. There I took an interest in my work, for I was naturally religious; theology and Biblical study with a background of philosophy became and have continued to be to me of the greatest interest. Another interest was in the writings of the mystics from Plotinus to St. John of the Cross and later; to these I still attach great importance.

"On leaving the college I became assistant minister in a Presbyterian church in Berwick-on-Tweed, and two years later had a church of my own at Temple, Midlothian. I married Janet Green, a lecturer in English Literature; we have had two children, and we celebrated our golden wedding in 1964. The first Great War had begun, and during part of it I worked with the Y.M.C.A. in France, an experience which led me to become a pacifist. Even in my student days I had been drawn to England, partly because of my interest in Gothic architecture, and in 1920 I became minister of the Presbyterian Church of Hove, Sussex, now St. Cuthbert's.

"At college a small book of verse, *Songs of Night*, had been published at my father's expense. Other small books of verse followed, then in 1933 the Nonesuch Press, noted for its finely produced books, published a collection of my poems, *Winter Harvest*. This was so well reviewed that it gave me an established position among contemporary poets. In 1936 appeared *Collected Poems*; this was republished several times till the final edition, which included a play, frequently produced in this country and also abroad, *Nicodemus*. It has music by Imogen Holst.

"For some time I had been drawn to the Anglican Church, partly by its ritual, and just before the second Great War I was confirmed. I attended a theological college at Wells, but that was mere form for one trained in the Scottish Presbyterian Church. After being priest in charge for a short time at Plaistow in Sussex, I became Vicar of Stonegate in the same county in 1941. I resigned in 1959 and came to live in retirement at Yapton, partly to be near Chichester Cathedral. I had become a Canon of the Cathedral a few years after my confirmation. Such an experience must be almost unique.

"As I was interested more in religion than in anything else, it was natural my poetical efforts should turn in a new direction. I wrote what might be called an eschatological poem, for it begins with my funeral at Stonegate, 'Into Hades.' It was republished along with another poem, 'A Traveller in Time,' under the title *Out of the World and Back*. To these poems I attach a greater importance than to the short nature poems. They do not appear in *Collected Poems*.

"My chief awards have been the Queen's Gold Medal for Poetry, the Royal Society of Literature's Silver Medal and the Duff Cooper Award."

According to John Arlott, Canon Young was "a shy man, in some respects austere, and of conscious simplicity and strict routine," who "never pressed any claim for himself or his work . . . barely even made any effort towards publication." His output was small, he belonged to no literary movement, and had little taste for modernism. It was not until he was nearly fifty that the publication of *Winter Harvest* brought him a measure of recognition, and not until 1952 that his stature was acknowledged by the award of the Queen's Medal. He had an honorary LL.D. from Edinburgh University.

ANDREW YOUNG

Most of Young's poems are about English or Scottish scenes, flowers, birds, or animals, observed with the clinical exactness and strangeness of vision which a microscope can bring to familiar things. Young has been compared to the metaphysical poets in the felicity of his conceits, and was said to share with Herrick "the same Japanese eye, the same separateness and the same unexpected moments of self-confrontation." According to a note in *The Concise Encyclopedia of Modern World Literature*, his poems are traditional in form, and seldom exceed twenty lines in length, and yet when each is written "nothing in it could be altered, and no more could be said. . . . In a sense all of his brief poems collect into an immense single poem, about nature and death and the religious man in the midst of nature and death." It is his fate and meaning "in the midst of death" that Young contemplates in "Into Hades," which Leonard Clark calls "a poem of a bracing, beginning-of-the-world, dawn chilliness." Among modern poets, Young learned most from Hardy, whose verse in its entirety he read through every year.

Canon Young was an authority on English wild flowers, and indeed *A Prospect of Flowers* and *A Retrospect of Flowers* have had a wider public than his poetry. These books, which complement the poems, discuss not only flowers, but Young's travels in search of them, and are full of quotations, wry anecdotes, and strange information reflecting an erudition extending beyond botany to archaeology, literature, history, and folklore. *The Poet and the Landscape* deals in the same incomparable way with English pastoral poets and their habitats, and *The New Poly-Olbion*, a similar work, includes "an introductory account of the poet's early days." *The Poetic Jesus*, published shortly after Young's death, is a prose poem of which one reviewer wrote that it "might, without exaggeration, be called a fifth Gospel."

PRINCIPAL WORKS: *Poetry*—Songs of Night, 1910; Boaz and Ruth, 1920; The Death of Eli, 1921; Thirty-one Poems, 1922; The Bird-Cage, 1926; The Cuckoo-Clock, 1929; The New Shepherd, 1931; Winter Harvest (selected poems), 1933; The White Blackbird, 1935; Collected Poems, 1936 (rev. 1950, 1960); Speak to the Earth, 1939; The Green Man, 1947; Into Hades, 1952; Out of the World and Back, 1958; Quiet as Moss (selected poems), 1959; Burning as Light (further selection), 1967. *Plays*—The Adversary, 1923; Nicodemus, 1937. *Prose*—A Prospect of Flowers, 1945; A Retrospect of Flowers, 1950; A Prospect of Britain, 1956; The Poet and the Landscape, 1962; The New Poly-Olbion, 1967; The Poetic Jesus, 1972.

ABOUT: Clark, L. Andrew Young, 1964; Clark, L. (ed.) Andrew Young: A Prospect of a Poet, 1958; Grigson, G. (ed.) The Concise Encyclopedia of Modern World Literature, 1963; Murphy, R. (ed.) Contemporary Poets of the English Language, 1970; Who's Who, 1971; Who's Who in America, 1972–1973. *Periodical*—Spectator December 18, 1953.

YOUNG, MARGUERITE (VIVIAN) (1909–), American novelist, prose writer, and poet, writes: "A native of Indiana, I have lived in New York City since 1943, with a few years away as a resident of Italy and as Visiting Lecturer in Creative Writing at the University of Iowa.

"I attended Indiana and Butler universities, majoring in English and French. I have my master's degree from the University of Chicago, where I wanted desperately to be a student of Oriental religions but where, as then in my early twenties I thought I was too old to embark upon Sanskrit and other Eastern tongues, I did my graduate work in the English department. My special field was John Milton, with particular emphasis upon the rival cosmologies and various epics of the Fall of Man which entered into the writing of *Paradise Lost*. The subject of my thesis was not, however, Milton—I preferred to enlarge upon my field by a study of the poetic prose of the Elizabethan and Jacobean writers and their symbolic uses of birds and beasts of the emblem literature and ancient bestiaries. I analyzed the various moral and social meanings of the birds and beasts in John Lyly's *Euphues* and related works and traced these figures to their multiple sources in poetry and in a quasi-mythological zoology. I was also a student of the eighteenth century novel with the great aesthetician in that field, Ronald Salmon Crane—studying Fielding, Sterne, Richardson, all of whom, along with Cervantes and Joyce, remain my most beloved novelists. Later, at the University of Iowa, I wrote, for René Wellek, an essay upon the philosophic backgrounds of *Tristram Shandy*. At the University of Iowa, where I was a candidate for the doctorate, my field was a combination of philosophy and literature. Studying with the philosopher Gustav Bergmann, I became deeply interested in Locke, Berkeley, Hume, William James—a greater influence upon my writing than brother Henry whom, however, I also love and who often visits me in my dreams and talks of the literary arts.

"I am a collateral descendant upon my father's side of Brigham Young. Upon my mother's side, I am a direct descendant of John Knox, who had the grace to marry a Stewart, and from whom are descended so many of the marvelous writers of our language—James Boswell, Lord Byron, Herman Melville, among others. I spent my childhood with my very brilliant grandmother, Marguerite Herron Knight, who sensed by the time I was four or five years old that I would become a writer and who gave to me what she believed to be the very best preparation for this, an intimate acquaintance with biblical literature. I learned verses of the Bible every day—a fact for which I am extremely grateful—there is no more sonorous, more beautiful language than the English Bible.

"I have always been a close reader of poetry. That novel which interests me most is the novel which may be considered the lyric or the epic poem. The epic novel may contain ten thousand poems—each sentence, musical and imagistic, is a poem. This is surely one of the oldest traditions in English literature—I am always surprised by those who have apparently no such complex orientation toward their cultural past and judge furiously that the plain school is the only school. Those of this bias, based as much on ignorance as temperament, may wish to forbid also investigation into the psychological mysteries and dimensions which lie just beneath the surface of ordinary life—and, indeed, at the surface.

"I have written two books of poems—*Prismatic Ground* and *Moderate Fable*. The first was a teen-age book which I believe may claim no particular distinction. The second is still highly regarded by poets—and was greatly influenced by Darwin's imagery of birds and beasts, coral islands, formations of continents. My first prose was the epic nonfiction *Angel in the Forest: A Fairy Tale of Two Utopias*—that of the German Scriptural Communists of married celibates at New Harmony, Indiana, where the angel Gabriel appeared in a hop field, and that of Robert Owen, a community of free lovers and agnostics which followed immediately after in the same place. Robert Owen was to become the father of the British labor movement. This book explores the illusions, hallucinations, errors of judgment which may take place for good or evil in conflicting Utopias.

"My first novel was the epic *Miss MacIntosh, My Darling*, an exploration of the illusions, hallucinations, errors of judgment in individual lives, the central scene of the novel being an opium addict's paradise. Although the novel is about drug addiction, I myself have never taken a drug to induce dreams—I need none. I did live for a while in my youth, however, in the home of a beautiful opium lady in the city of Chicago—so that what I write is based upon experience—upon close observation of a fabulosity which was real."

MARGUERITE YOUNG

W. R. Benét claimed a certain distinction for *Prismatic Ground*, if its author does not, welcoming "a fresh and fragile talent," and a simplicity which seemed to some other critics excessive. Miss Young's next book of verse, *Moderate Fable*, was something quite different. J. F. Nims said she had "taken a complete change of direction.... Her technique ... has worked toward greater subtlety and complexity, longer lines, more diffused and varied rhythms. She is concerned with such weighty themes as perfection, flaw, time, probability, reality and illusion." Nims found it a difficult book; "little is direct or passionate; always the whimsy and the indirection, the delicate evasion, the escape into fancy." It was nevertheless, he thought, the work of "a fine and important poet."

Angel in the Forest was called "a kind of poetic brooding upon the history" of the two utopian experiments at New Harmony—one an exercise in sexual deprivation that produced marvelous hallucinations, one an attempt at total rationality that led to assorted aberrations, including alcoholic delusions. The book is among other things a consideration of the difference and the similarity between appearance and reality. It calls on many aspects of Miss Young's learning, not least on her studies of the floral and animal symbolism of the Elizabethans and Jacobeans. Some critics were quite defeated by so much erudition and "fruitcake" prose, but Mark Van Doren recognized that the book was "conceived as great poems are conceived, and composed with the same exciting, inexhaustible energy." Martin Lebowitz wrote that it was "repetitive, obscure, diffuse, overwritten, tiresomely obsessed with copulation and with analogical images of flowers, insects, and birds, scornful at many points of coherence, continuity, and form; yet it is a book of astonishing subtlety and brilliance, a genuine work of art, and together with her two previous volumes of verse it should establish its author as one of the truly notable writers of her generation."

In 1947 Miss Young embarked on a novel which was to occupy her for about two years. In fact it took over seventeen. During this time she supported herself by teaching creative writing—at the New School for Social Research in New York, and at the universities of Iowa, Indiana, Columbia, Fairleigh Dickinson, and Fordham. She has also received awards from the National Institute of Arts and Letters (1946), the Guggenheim Foundation (1948), the Newberry Library (1951), and the Rockefeller Foundation (1954). In all these years she never put the book aside, but worked on it all day, every day that her teaching allowed. She says "It was always a joy, a joy to wake up knowing what was going to happen next."

Miss MacIntosh, My Darling, eleven hundred and ninety-seven pages long, was published in 1965 by Scribner's, who had waited for it patiently ever since Maxwell Perkins signed the contract with Miss Young in 1947. The novel is Vera Cartwheel's account of her pilgrimage in search of her old nurse. Vera's mother is the "beautiful opium lady," who lives among dreams in New England and rejects the very idea of certainty; everyone else that Vera recalls or encounters is possessed by illusion. Miss MacIntosh, long lost and presumed drowned, represents by contrast the very principle of commonsense reality, and it is this reality Vera pursues from New England to the Middle West. But Miss MacIntosh, when discovered, is discovered to be hairless, incomplete, false, and life is seen to be "imagination even to the last tenth." The book, A. S. Byatt wrote, like *Angel in the Forest*, is "a novel about the nature of reality. But it is, more importantly, a myth about the nature of myth and the nature of the image-forming consciousness." To quote Vera Cartwheel: "What is man but a series of competing mythologies, most fearful and wonderful?"

Many critics thought *Miss MacIntosh* a masterpiece and many thought it a failure, self-indulgent in its language, amorphous in its proliferation of interwoven metaphors. Melvin Maddocks called the author "a poet celebrating sheer uncertainty, a lyrical lover of blur. She has started with a valid insight, that life is often a deception.... But she has made the insight so central, so explicit, so systematic that the insight has devoured her." For William Goyen on the other hand, "Marguerite Young has found . . . her grand metaphor; and it glistens and radiates and *exists* in this colossal shape as hard and as concrete as truth itself. It is a masterwork."

Marguerite Young is a small woman, friendly, voluble, and enthusiastic. She lives on Bleecker Street in Greenwich Village, in a building on the site where Herman Melville was born. Her two-room apartment is crammed with sculptures and paintings, many of them of angels. She is said to be working on a biography of James Whitcomb Riley.

PRINCIPAL WORKS: Prismatic Ground, 1937; Moderate Fable, 1944; Angel in the Forest: A Fairy Tale of Two Utopias, 1945 (England, 1967); Miss MacIntosh, My Darling, 1965.

ABOUT: Contemporary Authors 15–16, 1966; Vinson, J. (ed.) Contemporary Novelists, 1972; Who's Who in America, 1972–1973. *Periodicals*—Book Week September 12, 1965; Encounter September 1966; Mademoiselle September 1965; New York Review of Books November 25, 1965; New York Times Book Review September 12, 1965; Times Literary Supplement March 16, 1967.

***"YOURCENAR, MARGUERITE" (pseudonym of Marguerite de Crayencour)** (June 8, 1903–), French-American novelist, poet, dramatist, essayist, and translator, writes: "Although resident in the United States, and a citizen of this country since 1947, I write only in my native language, which is French. My family home was Mont Noir, one of those hills of French Flanders near Lille; I merely happened to be born in Brussels, of a Belgian mother, Fernande de Cartier de Marchienne (who died a few days after my birth), and a French father, Michel de Crayencour. Education entirely at home, first under a governess, later under tutors as I requested them, and always, from an early age, by extensive reading aloud with my father, in French, English, Latin, and Greek. Winters were spent in Paris or in Southern France. In September, 1914, we escaped the German invasion by sailing from Ostend in my father's small yacht, taking with us our household of the time and other refugees, and landing with difficulty in England, there to remain for a year before regaining Paris. Meanwhile Mont Noir was occupied by the British High Command in Flanders, and was therefore soon destroyed by German bombardment. When Paris was bombarded by the first German long-range guns we left for the Riviera, where we lived in a succession of modest villas until 1927, with the exception of a few visits to Italy and Switzerland.

* yo͞or sə när′

"First literary productions: two small books of verse, published in 1921 and 1922, but composed from the age of fourteen on. The first of these efforts, a dramatic version of the legend of Icarus, had the virtue of childish simplicity, and in subject matter and themes was anticipatory of much of my later work. The second, though more varied in content, was feebly imitative of poets in vogue at the time whose techniques I was seriously studying. Also at this early period I launched upon at least two great projects, composing what were to be mere first versions of works not finally achieved until very much later on, namely, a first *Hadrian* in third person and another in dialogue (both wisely committed thereafter to the flames) and a novel, fragments of which I published as the three short stories of *La Mort conduit l'attelage* (1934). The first of these stories, in its turn, was recently developed into the long work, *L'Œuvre au noir*.

"From 1927 to 1930 I was much in Switzerland, and revisited Belgium and Holland which I had known as a child. From 1930 to 1939, I went regularly between Paris and Italy, then Paris and Greece, each year, with long stops in Switzerland and Austria en route. From about 1927 or 1928, I had begun to contribute poems and essays to the literary periodicals of the time. My first novel, published in 1929, met with praise from substantial critics; the second, less good, was followed by an essay on Pindar and a novel set in the Italy of Mussolini, *Denier du rêve* (1934), republished later in more developed form. *Feux*, a volume of personal interpretations of ancient Greek stories, and *Nouvelles orientales*, recounting both ancient and contemporary tales of the Near and Far East, reflects the preoccupations and experiences of my life in the Eastern Mediterranean. *Les Songes et les sortes* (1938) treats of the individual mythology and aesthetic of dream, quite apart from contemporary psychoanalytic trends. On a return to Italy in 1938, I wrote *Le Coup de grâce*, almost at a single "sitting" (of some weeks' duration!), after having heard the actual story from a friend some short time before.

Translations from Virginia Woolf, Henry James, and the modern Greek poet Cavafy, the latter in collaboration with a friend in Athens, date from this second period.

"After a first visit to a friend in the United States in 1937, I planned to return for a lecture tour in 1939. Delayed by the war, and uncertain about further publication in a divided France, I prolonged my stay here and became, while continuing to write, a part-time instructor in French Literature and History of Art for nearly ten years. As for every expatriate, these years were filled with anxieties and stress, but also with new and ultimately valuable experience. Three plays on classical Greek themes date from this period, as do most of my translations of Negro spirituals, although these were not assembled in volume form until much later.

"The account of my resumption of the *Hadrian* in 1948 is given in 'Notebooks on the Writing of Memoirs of Hadrian,' now published with that novel in the illustrated edition. While completing the *Hadrian* during a leave of absence in 1950 I purchased, in common with a friend, a small house on Mount Desert Island which continues to be my home between travels ranging from Scandinavia and Poland to Portugal and Spain, and from Newfoundland to the Gulf of Mexico and New Mexico. Apart from continuous study and writing, my particular absorption in recent years has been in the problem of conservation of natural resources and wild life."

With the publication of *Mémoires d'Hadrien* (1951) and its English translation, *Memoirs of Hadrian*, Marguerite Yourcenar joined the select band of historical novelists who are read by historians. The external events of Hadrian's life are well documented, and the novel testifies to a scrupulous use of the impressive list of sources published with it. The emperor's attitude to these events is the result of a different type of reconstruction, based on anecdotes about him, fragments of his writing, and those of his contemporaries, brought together and synthesized by Miss Yourcenar's instinctive sympathy for the man. She says in her "Notebooks on the Writing of Memoirs of Hadrian" that she wrote the book with "one foot in scholarship, the other in magic, or more exactly and without metaphor, in that sympathetic magic which consists of projecting oneself mentally into the mind of someone else."

As she says, the novel matured very slowly in her mind. There is a poem about a statue of Hadrian's beloved Antinoüs in *Les Dieux ne sont pas morts* (1922), and the first of several versions of the novel was begun in 1924. The project was nearly abandoned in 1940, when the latest manuscript was

MARGUERITE YOURCENAR

temporarily lost. Then, on a train journey to the American Midwest, came the inspiration to complete the work in its present form, as a letter written by Hadrian shortly before his death to his grandson, Marcus Aurelius. She wrote the first fifty pages on the train; a friend says: "She couldn't stop, she couldn't hear the train wheels, she just kept on writing and writing and writing."

Hadrian's lifetime (76–138 A.D.) was not superficially an exciting period in Roman history—a time of consolidation rather than of conquest. And the *Memoirs*, supposedly written during his last long illness, "bear an unmistakable sickbed stamp of dreamlike, classic detachment," the battles of his early years "stilled and scaled down to the reverent silence about the Imperial couch." The Hadrian who writes is enlightened in his government and eclectic in his philosophy, mildly self-indulgent, with a weakness for mysticism, astrologers, and magicians. "Above everything," wrote a critic in the *Times Literary Supplement*, "permeating all his memories, rises the beautiful sad face of Antinoüs; and it is [Marguerite] Yourcenar's greatest achievement to have restored to this relationship of Roman Emperor and Bithynian youth the classic eternal quality towards which so many sculptors have strived in vain."

Miss Yourcenar is also widely respected as a scholar, as a translator (of Henry James and Virginia Woolf among others), as a dramatist, and as the author of several other novels. Of these the most notable is *L'Œuvre au noir* (The Black Work, 1968), about the life and death of a Flemish doctor, alchemist, and philosopher during the Renaissance. It was warmly admired for its evocation of the sublime curiosity of a savage, turbulent, and brilliant age, written with "a pictorial vividness and sharpness worthy of Bosch and Brueghel." It brought its author the Prix Fémina in France, and it is reported that the Fémina jury was unanimous on the first ballot, an almost unique occurrence.

PRINCIPAL WORKS IN ENGLISH TRANSLATION: Memoirs of Hadrian, 1954; Coup de Grâce, 1957.
ABOUT: Moore, H. T. French Literature Since World War II, 1966; Peyre, H. French Novelists of Today, 1967; Who's Who in America, 1972–1973. *Periodicals*—New York Times Book Review December 26, 1954; August 25, 1968; Saturday Review November 27, 1954; Times Literary Supplement July 1, 1955; November 22, 1957; December 15, 1968.

***ZABOLOTSKY, NIKOLAI (ALEKSEYEVICH)** (May 7, 1903–October 14, 1958), Russian poet, was born in Kazan, the son of an agricultural expert. At the age of seventeen he went to Leningrad, where he worked in children's publishing as one of the group of brilliant young writers which Samuil Marshak had gathered around himself. His debt to children's literature, which was his livelihood during the 1920s and 1930s, has never been sufficiently examined, though he did himself write some very interesting children's verse.

Many influences have been seen in his work, but one of the most important was the iconoclastic and dada-like literary circle to which he belonged at this time, the *Obereuty* (a contraction of the words for "Association of Real Creativity"). This represented the last phase of futurism, and his extraordinary first collection of poems, *Stolbtsy* (Columns), which made his reputation when it was published in 1929, is strongly influenced by the futurism of Khlebnikov.

The poems in this book make up a series of satirical sketches of the coarsest and most futile aspects of daily life in Leningrad, such as brothels and beer halls, described in realistic though often grotesquely distorted detail mixed with unexpected poetic metaphor, word play, and fantasy. Ghosts and speaking animals rub shoulders with fishmongers, thieves, and clowns, while "Above them the sky was riddled / By a cheerful, double-barrelled oath, / And life gave a hearty crack / Like an upside-down flying trough." One well-known poem in *Stolbtsy*, "Ivanovy" (The Ivanovs), ends with the world reduced to a small room where one of the young country-bred Ivanovs is in the arms of a whore; but on the way there the city has opened out to become a sea, and the tram on which the Ivanovs travel becomes a steamer, from which they watch the prostitutes as sirens gliding along the waves of the roadway. The long poem *Torzhestvo zemledeliya* (The Triumph of Agriculture, 1933) takes a similarly satirical view of the countryside and introduces the main theme of Zabolotsky's later poetry, man's place in nature.

* za bo lot′ ski

NIKOLAI ZABOLOTSKY

Like hundreds of other writers and artists he was a victim of Stalin's purges, and from 1938 to 1946 he was in exile; but he was one of the few writers lucky enough to survive and ultimately to return, so that by 1947 he was back in Moscow and able to publish again. His later poems are more traditional and less experimental in both style and subject matter, but it is not clear how far this was the result of political pressures and how far it was due to his own poetic development. Certainly the change is not an abrupt one, but is apparent if one examines the odes he wrote during the mid-1930s. Several critics have regarded these as among his best works because they have something of the virtues of both manners, combining formal perfection with a startling originality of imagery and perception. Like Pasternak he moved increasingly towards poetry which was rooted in the heritage of nineteenth century poets such as Pushkin and Tyutchev; and his later poetry has also been found reminiscent of Nekrasov in its poignant note of human sympathy and pity.

Zabolotsky has come to be seen as an important philosophical poet whose ideas link his earlier satires on the soulless materialism of city life with the later explorations of the relationship between man and nature. His quasi-religious philosophy extends his early vision of the tragicomic chaos of city life to the whole of nature, where all life undergoes constant metamorphosis through death. Typical of the shorter poems in his later rural elegiac mode are the last two in the *Penguin Book of Russian Verse*, affirmations of the beauty of life as mirrored in the rapture of spring or, as in *Detstvo* (Childhood), seen through the eyes of a young girl.

His early futuristic work was strongly criticized by Marxists within the Soviet Union and attacked even more vigorously in the West by Khodasevich, a leading émigré poet living in France who detested futurism. Zabolotsky fell into obscurity during his exile, but after his return he did once again manage to achieve some recognition in Russia, especially in the literary revival which followed the death of Stalin. In the West he still tended to be dismissed with such judgments as that of Renato Poggioli: "There resounded for a while the mischievous and whimsical voice of Nikolaj Zabolotsky, who was, however, first reprimanded into silence, and then tamed into that parrotry which seems to be the supreme law of Soviet art." It is only since his death, with the publication of larger editions of his work both in America and in Russia, that he has come to be recognized as a really major poet, a far more significant figure than the well-publicized young poets of the post-Stalin thaw. A volume of selected poems was published in English in 1971 as *Scrolls*, but the translations seemed to one reviewer quite inadequate.

The first three decades of the twentieth century constituted one of the great periods of Russian poetry, but the important writers of the time had already been active before the Revolution; Zabolotsky is the most important poet to have begun his literary career after the Revolution. "Political persecutions prevented Zabolotsky from receiving the recognition his original talent deserved," says Marc Slonim, but adds, "there is no doubt that his stature will grow with the years." His life embraced all the major experiences which Soviet writers have undergone, and a writer in the *Times Literary Supplement* suggests that Zabolotsky may be accepted as *the* Soviet poet (or even *the* Soviet writer) in a sense that Mayakovsky, who died in 1930, or the older though longer-lived Pasternak, or the young poets of the "thaw" generation cannot be, and concludes: "He is perhaps the only major poet—on a European scale—to have grown up under Soviet rule."

PRINCIPAL WORKS IN ENGLISH TRANSLATION: Scrolls: Selected Poems, tr. by Daniel Weissbort, 1971. *Poems in* Carlisle, O. Poets on Street Corners, 1969; Markov, V. and Sparks, M. (eds.) Modern Russian Poetry, 1966; Obolensky, D. (ed.) Penguin Book of Russian Verse, 1962; Penguin Russian Review July 1960.

ABOUT: Cohen, J. M. Poetry of This Age, 1966; Gulland, R. M. Soviet Russian Verse, 1961; Penguin Companion to Literature 2, 1969; Slonim, M. Soviet Russian Literature, 1964; Struve, G. P. and Filipoff, B. A. (eds.) Nikolai Zabolotski: Poems, 1965. *Periodicals*—Times Literary Supplement May 11, 1967.

MIKHAIL ZOSHCHENKO

*__ZOSHCHENKO, MIKHAIL (MIKHAILOVICH)__ (August 10, 1895–July 22, 1958), Russian humorist, was born probably in Poltava, Ukraine, though St. Petersburg is given in some accounts. His mother was a Russian actress and his father a Ukrainian landowner belonging to the minor nobility, a socialist sympathizer and a painter of historical subjects who was a member of the artistic group known as the *Peredvizhniki* (Wanderers) because of the traveling exhibitions they organized. The family, cultivated and comfortably off, soon moved to Petersburg, where the boy was educated and where he was to spend most of his life.

Small, nervous, and sensitive, he was not a success at school and suffered from recurrent bouts of depression, leading after one examination failure to attempted suicide. In 1913 he entered Petersburg University to study law, but spent most of his time listening to the physics professor instead, and was expelled. During the summer of 1914 he worked as a railway guard in the Caucasus and on his return to Petersburg in the fall, just after the outbreak of World War I, he volunteered for the army. He did so, he said, not out of patriotism but because "I simply couldn't stay in one place on account of hypochondria and melancholia." Zoshchenko was rapidly promoted to the rank of major, but after being wounded and gassed in 1916, suffering permanent damage to his heart and liver, he was invalided out.

By the time of the February Revolution in 1917 he was back in Petersburg, and was sent by the Kerensky government to administer a military post

* zôsh′ chin ko

office in Arkhangelsk. During the following three years his restlessness and melancholy led him to wander through Russia taking up a variety of unlikely jobs in a dozen cities: professional gambler, telephonist in the frontier guards, officer in the Red Army in action on the Narva front, detective, instructor in rabbit and poultry breeding in Smolensk province, shoemaker, and finally clerk-typist.

He had already written some short stories, though without success, and in 1921 he joined the Serapion Brothers, an informal literary group, including Zamyatin, Fedin, Vsevolod Ivanov, and Tikhonov, which believed that art must remain independent of politics and that every writer should express his own personality in the way most suited to him. Zoshchenko's first collection of stories, *Rasskazy Nazara Il'icha, gospodina Sinebryukhova* (Stories of Nazar Ilyich, Mr. Bluebelly, 1922), became an immediate success, and he enjoyed enormous popularity throughout the rest of his literary career, despite increasing official disapproval. Marc Slonim gives this description of him: "Like many humorists, he had a sad countenance, was afflicted by fits of anxiety, and wandered around as if he were running away from his own shadow. Despite his reserved manners and slow, controlled speech, this small young man with regular features and dark thoughtful eyes was extremely nervous and impressionable."

Zoshchenko quickly evolved a style and manner of his own which make his writings instantly recognizable. The form he most favored is a very short story describing incidents from the everyday life of the Soviet lower middle classes. The technique he uses is that of *skaz*, the oral tale which derives from Gogol and Leskov, told by an absurd narrator who is himself a character and becomes a colorful intermediary between the ridiculous situation he narrates and the reader. Zoshchenko's spokesman is the Russian man-in-the-street, and much of the stories' untranslatable humor lies in the highly personal voice of this narrator—a rich mixture of peasant idiom, slang, current journalese, rhetorical flourishes, and ludicrously garbled Marxist jargon.

As Zoshchenko's narrators speak, what they reveal above all is *themselves*, their own stupidity and pettiness, their absurd pretensions; they moralize and philosophize, unaware that the stories they offer in support of their views totally contradict their pompous pronouncements. Zoshchenko's stories satirize not so much the postrevolutionary decline of standards as the perennial philistinism and vulgarity of human nature. But his situations are those characteristic of the Soviet Union in his own day, so that his stories give a picture of Russian life in the 1920s and 1930s which, though satirically exaggerated, vividly captures the flavor of this period of hardship.

"Having your own apartment is a very bourgeois thing to do," says one smug narrator, who resides in a bathroom that he must vacate every time someone comes to use it. In "Banya" (The Bathhouse), the little man who uses the public bath is frustrated at every turn: he needs tickets to reclaim his clothes, but "where is a naked man going to put tickets?" Zoshchenko wrote hundreds of such short sketches about everyday incidents, published in numerous collections such as *Rasskazy* (Stories, 1923), *Uvazhaemye grazhdane* (Respected Citizens, 1926), *Nervnie lyudi* (Nervous People, 1927) which were immensely popular with the reading public and went through countless editions. In them men's lives are farcical, ruled by absurdity and frustration, but he also wrote longer stories in which an undercurrent of tragedy can be sensed beneath the comedy, as in the long stories and parodies collected under the title *Sentimentalnye povesti* (Sentimental Tales, 1927).

Zoshchenko always aspired to longer literary forms, and in 1933 he published the short novel *Vozvrashchennaya molodost* (Youth Restored). The elderly professor of astronomy Volosatov deludes himself that his youth is restored, leaves his stupid wife for a Black Sea vacation with nineteen-year-old Tulya, and has a stroke when he finds her in the arms of a younger lover, though he is finally cured and returns to his family to take up his rejuvenatory exercises again.

At the end of the book the author expresses the pious hope that by encouraging the workers to look after their health, his work will "be useful in the struggle for socialism which our country is carrying on." His actual intentions in this work have been much discussed. It certainly reflects and satirizes his own hypochondria, but some Soviet critics rather amazingly treated it as a serious attempt to introduce science into literature, in accordance with the socialist realist emphasis on technology. Western critics, however, have usually seen the book as another variation on Zoshchenko's usual theme: that the imperfections of human nature are pretty much a constant, so that though the professor seeks Tulya and his youth, just as the Communist party was seeking the regeneration of man, life follows its own inexorable laws.

Zoshchenko was a master of ambiguity, and his mockery of the solemn hypocrisies of the Soviet regime could always be presented as criticism of "capitalist survivals." Nevertheless, as socialist realism increasingly became the orthodoxy of the 1930s, disapproval of his work mounted, and in response to criticism he tried to write on new themes and broaden the range of his satire. Such works as his biographical sketch of Kerensky, *Besslavny konets* (Inglorious End, 1937), though it allowed free play for his irony, are not usually considered very successful.

Golubaya kniga (The Blue Book, 1934–1935), a sort of satirical history of human relations, uses fictional material within an apparently factual framework. During World War II Zoshchenko began the autobiographical *Pered voskhodom solntsa* (1943, translated in part by J. Richardson as *Before Sunrise*), in which he recalls various episodes of his life in an attempt to answer the question he poses at the beginning: "Why am I such a melancholy man?" It includes brief sketches of Blok, Yesenin, Gorky, Mayakovsky, and other writers he had known. The last part has still not appeared, for its publication was stopped after vicious attacks against him for producing such a subjective work.

After the war Stalin's cultural bully Zhdanov singled out Zoshchenko for special attack, along with the poet Anna Akhmatova, and both were expelled from the Writers' Union in 1946. After Stalin's death he published only a few more stories before his own death in 1958 from the heart disease he had developed in the 1914 war. The new editions of his works which have appeared in the Soviet Union since his death have sold out immediately, and his popularity remains undiminished. There have been signs of a more positive critical revaluation of his work, and Kornei Chukovsky looked beyond the satirist to the man whose intensity of spiritual growth led him to explore ever-new fields of creativity. Ilf and Petrov are the only other Soviet humorists who approached his achievement, but their work is more directly satirical. As Professor Edward J. Brown has said, Zoshchenko "feels neither anger nor scorn as he observes his contemporaries, but only perverse pity and baffled amusement both at them and at himself."

PRINCIPAL WORKS IN ENGLISH TRANSLATION: Russia Laughs (short stories) (tr. by Helena Clayton), 1935; The Woman Who Could Not Read, and Other Tales (tr. by Elisaveta Fen), 1940; The Wonderful Dog, and Other Tales (tr. by Elisaveta Fen), 1942); Scenes from the Bathhouse, and Other Stories of Communist Russia (tr. by Sidney Monas), 1961; Nervous People and Other Satires (tr. by Maria Gordon and Hugh McLean), 1963. *Stories in* Blake, P. and Hayward, M. (eds.) Dissonant Voices in Soviet Literature, 1964; Fen, E. Modern Russian Stories, 1943; Graham, S. (ed.) Great Russian Short Stories, 1959; Guerney, B. G. A Treasury of Russian Literature, 1948; Konovalov, S. Bonfire, Stories of Soviet Russia, 1934; Kunitz, J. (ed.) and Robbins, J. J. (tr.) Azure Cities, 1929; Montagu, I. and Marshall, H. (eds.) Soviet Short Stories, 1942; Rodker, J. (ed.) Soviet Anthology, 1943; Reddaway, P. Soviet Short Stories 2, 1968; Slonim, M. and Reavey, G. Soviet Literature, 1933; Struve, G. (ed.) Russian Stories, 1961; Yarmolinsky, A. Soviet Short Stories, 1960; Partisan Review 3–4, 1961; Slavonic Review March 1929; Soviet Literature 4, 1967.

ABOUT: Alexandrova, V. A History of Soviet Literature 1917–1963, 1963; Blair, H. and Greene, M. *English introduction to* Lyudi, 1967; Brown, E. J. Russian Literature Since the Revolution, 1963; Gibian, G. and Samilov, M. (eds.) Modern Russian Short Stories, 1965; Murphy, A. B. *English introduction to* Stories of the 1920s, 1969; Reavey, G. Soviet Literature Today, 1946; Simmons, E. J. (ed.) Through the Glass of Soviet Literature, 1953; Slonim, M. Modern Russian Literature, 1953; Slonim, M. Soviet Russian Literature, 1964; Swayze, H. Political Control of Literature in the USSR 1946–1959, 1962; Zavalishin, V. Early Soviet Writers, 1958. *Periodicals*—Books Abroad Winter 1969; London Magazine October 1964; Russian Review October 1962; Soviet Literature 4, 1969; Survey April–June 1961; Times (London) July 25, 1958.

ZUKOFSKY, LOUIS (January 23, 1904–), American poet, critic, and translator, writes: "As a poet I have always felt that the work says all there needs to be said of one's life. But the bare facts are: I was born in Manhattan, January 23, 1904, the year Henry James returned to the American scene to look at the lower East Side. The contingency appeals to me as a forecast of the first-generation American infusion into twentieth century literature. At one time or another I have lived in all the boroughs of New York City—for over thirty years in Brooklyn Heights not far from the house on Cranberry Street where Whitman's *Leaves of Grass* was first printed.

"My first exposure to letters at the age of four was thru the Yiddish theatres, most memorably the Thalia on the Bowery. By the age of nine I had seen a good deal of Shakespeare, Ibsen, Strindberg and Tolstoy performed—all in Yiddish. Even Longfellow's *Hiawatha* was to begin with read by me in Yiddish, as was Aeschylus' *Prometheus Bound*. My first exposure to English was, to be exact, P.S. 7 on Chrystie and Hester Streets. By eleven I was writing poetry in English, as yet not 'American English,' tho I found Keats rather difficult as compared with Shelley's 'Men of England' and Burns' 'Scots, wha hae.'

"My poems first appeared in print in 1920 and continued to appear in more than one hundred 'little' magazines, national and international. The appearances led to friendship with Ezra Pound and William Carlos Williams beginning in 1927. I wrote the first extended essay on Pound's *Cantos 1–30*, which appeared in French in *Échanges* (Paris) 1930. It was thru Pound's efforts that Harriet Monroe invited me to edit the February 1931 issue of *Poetry* (Chicago). But it was not until 1965 that an easily accessible volume of my poetry appeared on the American scene. My thanks for this fact are due to W. W. Norton and Company.

"As for subsistence I can only quote with affection e.e. cummings: 'no thanks.'

"My wife Celia and son Paul have been the only reason for the poet's persistence. She has collaborated with me in my work on Shakespeare and Catullus. Paul is a violinist and composer. I trust considering his gifts that his art will be welcomed sooner than mine."

Louis Zukofsky is the son of Russian immigrants, Paul Zukofsky, a presser, and Chana (Pruss)

LOUIS ZUKOFSKY

Zukofsky. He grew up on New York's Lower East Side when "new blood was being pumped into the traditional elements and there was more willingness . . . to examine and learn." Zukofsky was evidently a remarkably good learner. His first poems were published when he was sixteen and Columbia gave him his M.A. when he was twenty. Thereafter he earned his living mostly as a teacher. He was at the University of Wisconsin and Queens College in the 1930s (with a year of travel in 1933 in France, Hungary, and Italy). In 1939 he married the poet Celia Thaew. After World War II (in which he tried without success to enlist), he went to Colgate University (1947) and then to the Polytechnic Institute of Brooklyn, where he remained until his retirement in 1966. There have been further periods of travel—in Europe, Mexico, and Canada. In 1958 he was poet-in-residence at San Francisco State College.

Zukofsky was associated with William Carlos Williams, George Oppen, and Charles Reznikoff in the "objectivist" movement of the early 1930s, and for many subsequent years was thought of, if at all, as a disciple of Williams and of Ezra Pound. Until recently all his books were published by small presses, sometimes privately. In 1965 and 1966 Norton brought out all of his shorter poems in two volumes, thus confirming his belated "discovery." Credit for this belongs principally to the "Black Mountain" poets—Charles Olson, Robert Duncan, and Robert Creeley—who have learned from Zukofsky's work as they have from that of Pound and Williams. Even now opinions are sharply divided as to the value of his achievement, and he is reviled as well as revered.

The indifference of former years has never driven Zukofsky to compromise, and he is a difficult poet to appreciate. His melodies, however rewarding, are not easy to hear and, as he says, he "moves faster *between* the words than most people." Denis Donoghue, in a discussion of Zukofsky in the *New York Review of Books* (April 25, 1968), begins by illustrating his commitment to "organic form"—"This is my face / This is my form. / Faces and forms, I would write you down / In a style of leaves growing." For Zukofsky, Donoghue says, "the form starts from the object, apprehended with love."

In 1931, writing in *The Criterion* about Ezra Pound, Zukofsky said that the *Cantos* "are directed towards inclusiveness, which sets down one's extant world and all other worlds existing within one, and interrelates them in a general scheme of people, each speaking the speech accordant with the musical measure, or having it spoken as song about them." Zukofsky's poems are similarly directed, with a willingness to include in a poem *every* pun and analogy that occurs to him as he writes it. So Marx is allowed to suggest larks, a praying mantis the praying poor, Homer's Argos Handel's *Largo*, and Senator Wayne Morse remorse. These things are, of course, not metaphors for each other but entities connected by the poem, which becomes a microcosm of the larger world in which everything is connected: "The order that rules music, the same / controls the placing of the stars and the feathers / in a bird's wing."

So, in a way that sometimes resembles surrealism, and is resembled by the "open field" poetry of the Black Mountaineers, the content of a poem is decided by the ideal or merely verbal associations that the initial object sparks in the poet's mind. There remains the problem of form. William Carlos Williams accused Zukofsky in 1938 of "placing sentences, paragraphs, slices of speech in a line, without sequence, without 'swing,' without consecutiveness." Denis Donoghue agrees that Zukofsky's early poetry was like this, made jerky and unmelodic by a tendency to suppress transitions, to jump-cut from one image or one voice to another. Later, he believes, Zukofsky learned "that the richest cadence comes from the imagination when nothing is suppressed," achieving "verse in a style of leaves growing, the extant world and all the minor worlds certified by the propriety of the voice." Donoghue turns for evidence to the twelfth section of "A," the long autobiographical poem, still unfinished, which Zukofsky began in 1927: "There are places out of sight / Filled with voices. / What the mind sees / And the eyes see—the / Shape of their ground, the same. / Dreaming kings storm towns / Cry aloud, murdered, / Without moving."

Zukofsky has attempted to apply his poetic

method to translation. For example, in the homophonic version he and his wife have made of the poems of Catullus, "Pedicabo ego vos et irrumabo" becomes "Piping, beans, I'll go *whoosh* and I'll rumble you." This bewildered and affronted most reviewers. A typically gnomic and intensely personal approach also characterizes his criticism, collected in *Prepositions*, and he is perhaps most easily approached through his fiction, collected in *It Was* (published in Japan in 1961) but more readily available, in selection, in *Ferdinand*. It is here that Zukofsky's concerns are most directly expressed, and his own modest and kindly personality most accessible.

PRINCIPAL WORKS: All the Collected Short Poems, 1923–1958, 1965; All the Collected Short Poems, 1956–1964, 1966; A 1–12, 1967; A 13–21, 1969; Autobiography (fifteen poems, set to music by Celia Zukofsky), 1970. *Fiction*—It Was, 1961; Ferdinand, 1968. *Nonfiction*—Le Style Apollinaire, 1934; A Test of Poetry, 1948; Five Statements for Poetry, 1958; Bottom: On Shakespeare, 1963; Prepositions, 1967; The Gas Age, 1969. *As translator*—(with Celia Zukofsky) Catullus: Gai Valeri Catulli Veronensis, 1969. *As editor*—An "Objectivists" Anthology, 1932.

ABOUT: Corman, C. At: Bottom, 1966; Leary, P. and Kelly, R. (eds.) A Controversy of Poets, 1965; Murphy, R. (ed.) Contemporary Poets of the English Language, 1970; Penguin Companion to Literature 3, 1971; Pound, E. Polite Essays, 1937; Zukofsky, C. A Bibliography of Louis Zukofsky, 1969. *Periodicals*—Agenda December 1964; The Critic February–March, 1967; Extra Verse Spring 1965; Guardian May 14, 1969; Kulchur Winter 1963; Summer 1964; National Review October 6, 1964; New Quarterly of Poetry Winter 1947–1948; New York Review of Books April 25, 1968; New York Times Book Review November 28, 1948; January 23, 1966; December 6, 1970; Poetry October 1965; The Review January 1964; Sunday Times (London) July 2, 1967; Times Literary Supplement October 24, 1952; August 6, 1964; November 25, 1965; June 16, 1966; July 17, 1969.

PICTURE CREDITS

Abrahams, Ron Spillman, Black Star. *Achebe*, Mark Gerson. *Ackerley*, Syndication International. *Acton*, Cecil Beaton. *Akhmadulina*, Ardis Publishers. *Albee*, Alex Jeffry. *Alfred*, Frederick Rolf. *Allen*, Mark Gerson. *Almedingen*, Phillips City Studio. *Alsop*, Philippe Charpentier. *Alterman*, Genazim. *Alvarez*, Jill Krementz. *Amado*, Sascha Harnisch. *Andrzeyevski*, Marek Holzman. *Annan*, Angus Dunn. *Antoninus*, Allen Say. *Arendt*, Alfred Bernheim. *Arguedas*, Cultura y Pueblo. *Armstrong*, Pat Willson Studio. *Arrowsmith*, University of Texas. *Ashton-Warner*, R. Hutchins. *Asimov*, Jay K. Klein. *Asturias*, Jesse A. Fernandez. *Auchincloss*, Nancy Sirkis. *Axelrod*, Joan Engels. *Ayer*, Paul Popper Ltd. *Bachmann*, R. Piper & Co. *Baldwin*, Martha Holmes. *Bandeira*, Manchete—Pictorial. *Banti*, G. Lotti. *Barnett*, Richard Borst. *Barraclough*, Bassano & Vandyk. *Barth*, Alex Gotfryd. *Barthes*, Lütfi Özkök. *Barzini*, Publifoto. *Bassani*, Jerry Bauer. *Bate*, Harvard University. *Bateson*, Lafayette, Ltd. *Bedford*, Tony Armstrong Jones. *Behan*, Dennis Hughes-Gilbey. *Berger*, Robert Morton. *Bergman*, Albert Bonniers. *Bialik*, Yivo Institute for Jewish Research. *Bissell*, Dale Stierman. *Blackburn*, Ida Kar. *Blais*, Consuelo Kanaga. *Blish*, Jay K. Klein. *Bloch-Michel*, Jacques Sassier. *Booth*, Rollie McKenna. *Borges*, Harold Mantell. *Borland*, E. W. Hutchinson. *Bosco*, A. Laugier. *Bourjaily*, William Hubbell. *Braine*, Jack Hickes. *Brancati*, Archivio Fotografico Bompiani. *Brée*, University of Wisconsin, Dept. of Photography-Cinema. *Broud*, Edward Leigh. *Brodsky*, Ardis Publishers. *Bronowski*, David Farrell. *Brooke-Rose*, Ida Kar. *Brophy*, Jerry Bauer. *Brustein*, Judy Feiffer. *Bultmann*, Dähn Foto. *Burgess*, Jerry Bauer. *Burnshaw*, John King. *Burroughs*, Charles Henri Ford. *Calder-Marshall*, Mike Peters. *Calisher*, Louis d'Almeida. *Campbell, D.*, Australian News & Information Bureau. *Campbell, J. W.*, Jay K. Klein. *Canaday*, New York Times. *Canetti*, Helen Craig. *Carnap*, UCLA Library. *Carruth*, Pat Orviss. *Cash*, Alfred A. Knopf. *Cassill*, Elspeth Vevers. *Cassola*, Jerry Bauer. *Cau*, Rafael Cubiles. *Causley*, Parkers. *Celan*, A. von Mangoldt. *Céspedes*, Alain Cerf. *Chambers*, Lida Moser. *Chang*, Warolin. *Char*, Irisson. *Charles*, Mark Gerson. *Charteris*, Fay Godwin. *Chayefsky*, NBC. *Cheever*, Warren Inglese. *Chukovskaya*, Russian Literature Triquarterly. *Cockburn*, Universal Pictorial. *Condon*, David Bailey. *Connell*, Seymour Linden. *Conquest*, Mark Gerson. *Conrad*, Fred Lyon. *Coon*, Ralph Solecki. *Cooper*, Mark Gerson. *Cotterell*, Mark Gerson. *Cottrell*, Jerry Bauer. *Coxe, G. H.*, Fabian Bachrach. *Creasey*, Mark Gerson. *Creeley*, Horace Coleman. *Creighton*, Ashley & Crippen. *Crispin*, Nicholas Horne Ltd. *Crossman*, Central Office of Information, London. *Cunningham*, Brandeis University. *Curnow*, Rita Hammond. *Dahl*, Elliott Erwitt. *Daninos*, Almasy. *Davidson*, James Holt. *Davies, H. S.*, Mark Gerson. *Davies, R.*, McKague. *Davis*, Vytas Valaitis. *Deighton*, Adrian Flowers. *Del Castillo*, René Saint-Paul. *De Lima*, Neva Powell. *Dermoût*, Netherlands Information Service. *Deutscher*, Angus McBean. *Devlin*, Irish Times. *De Vries*, Bernard Gotfryd. *Djilas*, International News Photos. *Dodge*, Joy Griffin West. *Dolci*, André Martin. *Donald*, Elliott Erwitt. *Donleavy*, Jerry Bauer. *Dugan*, E. W. Holden. *Dumitriu*, Gerd Sietzen. *Duncan*, Nata Piaskowski. *Duras*, Jerry Bauer. *Durrell*, W. Suschitzky. *Dürrenmatt*, B. Herbold. *Eastlake*, William Ptaszynski. *Edel*, Pach Bros. *Edelman*, Mark Gerson. *Eiseley*, Henrik Boudakian. *Ekelöf*, Lütfi Özkök. *Eliade*, Archie Lieberman. *Elliott*, Dorothea Lange. *Ellison*, Chris Corpus. *Engle*, Conrad Knickerbocker. *Enright*, Australian Broadcasting Commission. *Enzensberger*, Lütfi Özkök. *Fairburn*, Pegasus Press. *Falkner*, Dean and Chapter of Durham. *Fall*, Newsweek—François Sully. *Feydeau*, Photo Benque. *Fielding*, Howard Coster. *Finlay*, Jonathan Williams. *Fitzgibbon*, Harsch. *Flanner*, Jerry Bauer. *Fleming*, Douglas Glass. *Fowles*, Jerry Bauer. *Fraser*, Edward Lucie-Smith. *Frayn*, Flair Photography Ltd. *Freeling*, J. de Srebnicki. *Freyre*, Alfred A. Knopf. *Fried*, BBC Copyright Photograph. *Friedman*, Seymour Linden. *Frye*, F. Roy Kemp. *Fuentes*, Lola Alvarez Bravo. *Fuller, E.*, Chris Corpus. *Furnas*, Rappaport Studios, Inc. *Gaddis*, Martin S. Dworkin. *Gaiser*, Carl Hanser Verlag. *Gallant*, Julius Szelei. *Gann*, Harry Stearns. *Gardner, H.*, Walter Bird. *Gardner, I. S.*, Robert Gardner. *Garrett*, Richard Griffith. *Gascar*, Marc Foucault. *Gascoyne*, Berg Collection, New York Public Library. *Gelber*, Paul Fusco. *Genet*, Jerry Bauer. *Ghelderode*, Charles Leirens. *Gilbert*, Mark Gerson. *Gilboa*, Encyclopaedia Judaica. *Ginsberg*, Fred McDarrah. *Gipson*, Lehigh University. *Godden*,

Mark Gerson. *Gold, H. L.*, Sanford Gold. *Golden*, Tom Walters. *Golding*, Howard Coster. *Gombrowicz*, Bogdan Paczowski. *González Martínez*, Instituto Nacional de Bellas Artes, Mexico. *Gorter*, University of Amsterdam. *Gover*, R. Bramms. *Gowers*, Lenare. *Grau*, John Howard. *Green, F. C.*, Mrs. M. B. Green. *Green, G.*, Sandra Roome. *Guillén, N.*, Monthly Review Press. *Güiraldes*, photo from Ramachandra Gowda. *Gunn*, Ander Gunn. *Hagiwara*, Heibonsha—Orion Press. *Hamburger*, James Wood. *Hampshire*, Orren Jack Turner. *Harrod*, Macmillan Press Ltd. *Hassall*, Howard Coster. *Hawkes*, Edward D. Winter. *Hearne*, Fine Art Engravers, Ltd. *Hecht*, Lotte Jacobi. *Heiberg*, Royal Norwegian Embassy. *Heller*, Seymour Linden. *Henson*, Dean and Chapter of Durham. *Herlihy*, Stanley Mills Haggart. *Hernández*, Spanish Institute. *Highsmith*, Alexandra Lawrence. *Hochhuth*, Jerry Bauer. *Hochwälder*, Lütfi Özkök. *Hodgins*, Time Magazine. *Hoffman, F. J.*, Blackstone—Shelburne N.Y. *Hofstadter*, Alfred A. Knopf. *Holbrook*, Pejstrup. *Hollander*, David Rumsey. *Holmes*, Joan Liffring. *Holthusen*, Hilde Zemann. *Hope*, Coward of Canberra. *Hostovsky*, Jan Lukas. *Hough*, Popperfoto. *House*, Elliott & Fry, Ltd. *Howard, R.*, Rollie McKenna. *Howes*, Gregory Jay Smith. *Hoyle*, The Times. *Hughes*, Fay Godwin. *Humphrey*, Stan Wayman. *Humphreys*, BBC Copyright Photograph. *Hunter*, Gene Federico. *Illyés*, Hunyady József. *Innes*, Fayer. *Ionesco*, Jerry Bauer. *Jacobson*, Syracuse University. *Jellicoe*, Roger Mayne. *Jenkins, E.*, Joanna Spence Associates. *Jenkins, Roy*, Vivienne. *Jennings*, Ramsey & Muspratt. *Jiménez*, University of Puerto Rico. *Jones, D.*, Welsh Arts Council. *Jouhandeau*, Daniel Faunières. *József*, G. D. Hackett. *Juhász*, G. D. Hackett. *Kanin*, Cecil Beaton. *Kauffmann*, New York Times. *Kelley*, Edward N. Barnett. *Kemal*, BBC Copyright Photograph. *Kempton*, Jill Krementz. *Kennan*, Blackstone Studio. *Kennedy*, Christopher Longyear. *Kenner*, Mary Anne Kenner. *Kermode*, Jill Krementz. *Kerr, J.*, Shirley Zeiberg. *Kerr, W.*, New York Herald Tribune. *Khodasevich*, Russian Literature Triquarterly. *Kirk*, G. W. Harvey. *Kizer*, John Palmer. *Knight*, Ed Emsh. *Knowles, D.*, Cambridge University Press. *Knowles, J.*, Leni Iselin. *Koch*, Frank Lima. *Koningsberger*, David Gahr. *Kopit*, Jack Mitchell. *Körmendi*, Binder & Duffy. *Kott*, Express-Roustan. *Kunitz*, Lenscraft Studio, Inc. *Lanham*, Bruce Cunningham. *Leduc*, Jerry Bauer. *Lee, H.*, G. D. Hackett. *Lehmann*, Ingrid Lockemann. *Lessing*, Michael Rabider. *Levertov*, Chris Corpus. *Levi*, Sandra Lousada. *Lévi-Strauss*, Ruth Steinberg. *Lind*, Fred Stein. *Link*, Orren Jack Turner. *Lins do Rêgo*, Manchete. *Livings*, Sefton Samuels. *Logue*, Mark Gerson. *Lord*, Philippe Halsman. *Lukács*, Vattay Elemér. *MacDonald, J. D.*, Tram Pickett. *MacInnes*, Ida Kar. *Macken*, Yann Studios. *MacLean*, Clayton Evans. *McLuhan*, Ashley & Crippen. *Malgonkar*, Marilyn Silverstone. *Malleson*, Ellis Sykes. *Mallet-Joris*, Jerry Bauer. *Mandelstam*, Ardis Publishers. *Mankowitz*, Gered Mankowitz. *Mannes*, Frances McLaughlin-Gill. *Manning, O.*, Ida Kar. *Marceau*, Giselle Freund. *Marek*, Walter Boie. *Markfield*, James P. Armstrong. *Marshall*, Jerry Dempnock. *Martinson*, Albert Bonniers. *Matthiessen*, Luisa Gilardenghi. *Mattingly*, Werner J. Kuhn. *Mayer*, Conway. *Megged*, Prior. *Mehta*, Arnold Newman. *Merrill*, Rollie McKenna. *Merritt*, Liveright. *Merwin*, Dido Merwin. *Meyerstein*, English Faculty Library, Oxford. *Millar, K.*, Alfred A. Knopf. *Millar, M.*, Hal Boucher. *Miller, W.*, Eileen Kimmel. *Milosz*, Gordon Mueller. *Mishima*, Y. Hayata. *Mitford*, Romaine Studio. *Montagu*, John Vickers. *Montale*, Jerry Bauer. *Moore, B.*, Kershner. *Moore, J.*, Mark Gerson. *Moore, W.*, Brooke Elgie. *Morante*, Homolka. *Mori*, Orion Press. *Móricz*, G. D. Hackett. *Morton, F.*, Jerry Bauer. *Morton, J. B.*, London Express. *Muggeridge*, BBC Copyright Photograph. *Munk*, The Danish Institute. *Murdoch*, Jerry Bauer. *Murphy*, Irish Times. *Myrdal*, Sven-Gösta Johansson. *Nagai*, Orion Press. *Naipaul*, Roger Mayne. *Nairn*, BBC Copyright Photograph. *Natsume*, Orion Press. *Needham*, Cambridge News. *Norton*, Fred Daniel. *O'Connor, E.*, Hans Namuth. *Ogden*, James Wood. *Olson*, Fabian Bachrach. *Oman*, Lenare. *Osborne*, International News Photos. *Otero*, F. Catalá Roca. *Owen*, Roy Baxendale. *Pack*, Enid Rubin. *Packard*, Marvin Koner. *Pagnol*, Gerald Bauer. *Painter*, Vina Rogers. *Pargeter*, Mark Gerson. *Paz*, New Directions Publishing Corp. *Peyrefitte*, Claude Magelhaes. *Pinget*, Photo Pic. *Pinter*, The Sunday Times. *Pohl*, Jay K. Klein. *Pope-Hennessy*, John Murphy. *Powell, L. C.*, Robert Eisenbach. *Powell, R.*, Gus Pasquarella. *Press*, Mark Gerson. *Price*, Joel Arrington. *Purdy*, Fabian Bachrach. *Quasimodo*, Wide World Photo. *Quine*, Harvard University. *Raja Rao*, Hans Beacham. *Rattigan*, Evening Standard. *Raymond*, Universal Pictorial. *Read*, Ramsey & Muspratt. *Redgrove*, Nicholas Elder. *Reid*, Susan Greenburg Wood. *Reyes*, Alberto Dallal. *Rich*, Sissy Krook. *Richler*, Jack Clayton. *Robbe-Grillet*, Jerry Bauer. *Rolo*, Helen Merrill. *Rosa*, Editora Abril. *Rosenthal*, Paul Berg. *Ross*, Henry Grossman. *Roth, P.*, Nancy Crampton. *Roussel*, Éditions Jean-Jacques Pauvert. *Runciman*, J. Russell & Sons. *Salisbury*, New York Times. *Samuels*, Northwestern University. *Sargeson*, Dennis McEldowney. *Schary*, Friedman-Abeles. *Scott, G.*, New York Public Library, Astor, Lenox and Tilden Foundations. *Scott, P.*, Mark Gerson. *Selvon*, Longman Group Ltd. *Senghor*, Ambassade de la République du Sénégal. *Settle*, Lewis Raines. *Sewell*, R. E. George. *Sexton*, Rollie McKenna. *Shadbolt*, Raymond Barlin. *Shaw*, Columbia Pictures Industries, Inc. *Shiga*, Kodansha Ltd. *Shneour*, Leo Baeck Institute. *Sigal*, Peter Keen. *Sillitoe*, Terence Harjula. *Simon, C.*, Leon Herschtritt. *Simpson, L.*, Marianne Zittau. *Simpson, N. F.*, Roger Mayne. *Sinclair*, Lewis Morley. *Singer, I. B.*, Alfred Sundel. *Skelton*, P. W. Jarrett. *Slonim*, Gary Gladstone. *Smith, S. G.*, G. Wright. *Smith, W. J.*, Laurence B. Fink. *Snow*, The Hartford Courant. *Sontag*, Peter Hujar. *Spark*, Mark Gerson. *Sperber*, Hertz Grosbard. *Stadler*, Goethe House. *Steiner*, Benjamin Hertzberg. *Stephan*, Maryette Charlton. *Stern, J.*, Charles Leirens. *Stewart, D.*, Rembrandt Studios. *Stewart, M.*, E. R. Yerbury & Son. *Storey*, John Haynes. *Streeter*, G. D. Hackett. *Sturgeon*, Jay K. Klein. *Sturt*, George Sturt Memorial Fund. *Styron*, A. Blakelee Hine. *Swados*, Bernard Gotfryd. *Swanberg*, Christopher Lukas. *Swenson*, Henry Carlisle. *Sykes*, Janet Stone. *Tamási*, Mrs. Irén ÁCS. *Tardieu*, Jacques Sassier. *Taylor, R. L.*, George Cserna. *Tchernichovski*, Zionist Archives and Library. *Thomas, H.*, Niki Ekstrom. *Thomas, R. S.*, BBC Copyright Photograph. *Thorp*, Clearose Studio. *Tillotson*, Lotte Meitner-Graf. *Tolkien*, John Wyatt. *Tolson*, Polks Studio. *Toomer*, Marjorie Content Toomer. *Troyat*, Jerry Bauer. *Tucci*, Seymour Linden. *Tuchman*, Blackstone—Shelburne N.Y. *Turnell*, K. J. R. Godfrey. *Tynan*, Godfrey MacDomnic. *Tzara*, Sketch by Paul Eluard. *Updike*, Ivan Massar. *Ustinov*, Halsman. *Vailland*, Gupier-Garanger. *Vansittart*, Helen Craig. *Verwey*, Nederlands Letterkundig Museum en Documentatiecentrum. *Vesaas*, Johan Brun. *Vestdijk*, Nijgh & Van Ditmar. *Vonnegut*, Bossi. *Voznesensky*, Arkady Hershman. *Wagoner*, Paul V. Thomas. *Wain*, Mark Gerson. *Walcott*, Paul Rupp Associates. *Wallant*, Harcourt Brace Jovanovich. *Walser*, Hugo Jehle. *Waterhouse*, Mayne Studios Ltd. *Watts*, Louis Yates. *Wedgwood*, Douglas Glass. *Weinbaum*, Christine E. Haycock, M.D. *Weiss, P.*, Zollna. *Weiss, T.*, Dorothy Humphrey. *Welch*, University of Texas. *Wellek*, Blackstone-Shelburne N.Y. *West, P.*, Art Soll. *White, A.*, Yvonne. *White, T. H.*, Ted Russell. *Williams, Jay*, Steve Schapiro. *Wilson, C.*, H. L. C. Coode-Adams. *Wilson, S.*, Philippe Halsman. *Windham*, Sandy Campbell. *Winterton*, Elliott & Fry Ltd. *Yates*, John Paul Lowens. *Yevtushenko*, Alex Gotfryd.

Among the institutions and agencies that have been particularly helpful are the following: Austrian Information Service, Deutsche Presse-Agentur, French Cultural Services, French Embassy Press & Information Division—NYC, German Information Center, Ministry of Culture and Sciences—Athens, Italian Cultural Institute, and Sovfoto.

NECROLOGY

Aleixandre, V. Dec. 13, 1984
Alterman, N. Mar. 28, 1970
Andrić, I. Mar. 13, 1975
Andrzeyevski, G. Apr. 20, 1983
Arendt, H. Dec. 4, 1975
Arnow, H. S. Mar. 22(?), 1986
Aron, R. Oct. 17, 1983
Ashton-Warner, S. Apr. 28, 1984
Asturias, M. A. June 9, 1974
Bacchelli, R. Oct. 8, 1985
Bachmann, I. Oct. 17, 1973
Baker, C. Apr. 18, 1987
Baldwin, J. Dec. 1, 1987
Barnett, L. Sept. 8, 1979
Barraclough, G. Dec. 26, 1984
Barthes, R. Mar. 25, 1980
Barzini, L. Mar. 30, 1984
Bateson, F. W. Oct. 16, 1978
Benchley, N. Dec. 14, 1981
Bissell, R. May 4, 1977
Blish, J. July 30, 1975
Böll, H. July 16, 1985
Borges, J. L. June 14, 1986
Borland, H. Feb. 22, 1978
Bosco, H. May 4, 1976
Braine, J. Oct. 28, 1986
Bronowski, J. Aug. 22, 1974
Buckmaster, H. Apr. 26, 1983
Bultmann, R. July 30, 1976
Bunting, B. Apr. 16, 1985
Calvino, I. Sept. 19, 1985
Canaday, J. July 19, 1985
Carpentier, A. Apr. 24, 1980
Cassola, C. Jan. 29, 1987
Chapin, K. G. Dec. 30, 1977
Char, René Feb. 19, 1988
Chayefsky, "P." Aug. 1, 1981
Cheever, J. June 18, 1982
Cockburn, C. Dec. 15, 1981
Coon, C. S. June 3, 1981
Cortázar, J. Feb. 12, 1984
Cottrell, L. Oct. 6, 1974
Crommelynck, F. Mar. 17, 1970
Crossman, R. Apr. 5, 1974
Cunningham, J. V. Mar. 30, 1985
Dangerfield, G. Dec. 27, 1986
Déry, T. Aug. 18, 1977
Duncan, R. Feb. 3, 1988
Edelman, M. Dec. 14, 1975
Eiseley, L. July 9, 1977
Eliade, M. Apr. 22, 1986
Ellin, S. July 31, 1986
Elliott, G. P. May 3, 1980
Ellmann, R. May 13, 1987
Evans-Pritchard, E. E. Sept. 11, 1973
Fedin, K. July 15, 1977
"Fielding, G." Nov. 27, 1986
FitzGibbon, C. Mar. 23, 1983
Flanner, J. Nov. 7, 1978
Freyre, G. July 18, 1987
Gardner, I. S. July 7, 1981
Gary, R. Dec. 2, 1980
Genet, J. Apr. 15, 1986
Golden, H. Oct. 2, 1981
Goyen, W. Aug. 30, 1983
Griffin, J. H. Sept. 9, 1980
"Halliday, B." Feb. 4, 1977
Harrod, R. Mar. 9, 1978
Himes, C. Nov. 12, 1984
Hoffer, E. May 21, 1983
Johnson, U. Mar. 1984
Jones, D. Oct. 28, 1974
Jouhandeau, M. Apr. 7, 1979
Kästner, E. July 29, 1974
Kendrick, B. Mar. 22, 1977
Kessel, J. July 23, 1979
Knowles, D. Nov. 21, 1974
Lanham, E. July 24, 1979
Larkin, P. Dec. 2, 1985
Laye, C. Feb. 4, 1980
Leyda, J. Feb. 15, 1988
Logan, J. Nov. 6, 1987
Macdonald, D. Dec. 19, 1982
MacDonald, J. D. Dec. 28, 1986
MacInnes, C. Apr. 22, 1976
MacLean, A. Feb. 2, 1987
Malamud, B. Mar. 18, 1986
Malleson, L. B. Dec. 9, 1973
Manning, O. July 23, 1980
Manzini, G. Aug. 31, 1974
Marcel, G. Oct. 8, 1973
Marcuse, H. July 29, 1979
Marshall, S. L. A. Dec. 17, 1977
Martinson, H. Feb. 11, 1978
McGivern, W. P. Nov. 18, 1982
McLuhan, M. Dec. 31, 1980
Mehring, W. Oct. 3, 1981
Millar, K. July 11, 1983
Miller, M. June 10, 1986
Montale, E. Sept. 12, 1981
Moore, H. T. Apr. 11, 1981
Morante, E. Nov. 25, 1985
Moss, H. Sept. 16, 1987
Myrdal, G. May 17, 1987
Nekrasov, V. Sept. 3, 1987
Ostroff, A. Apr. 9, 1978
Pagnol, M. Apr. 18, 1974

Pasolini, P. P. Nov. 2, 1975
Pevsner, N. Aug. 18, 1983
Piovene, G. Nov. 12, 1974
Polanyi, M. Feb. 22, 1976
Pope-Hennessy, J. Jan. 25, 1974
Prévert, J. Apr. 11, 1977
Rattigan, T. Nov. 30, 1977
Raymond, E. May 14, 1974
"Renault, M." Dec. 13, 1983
Rhys, J. May 14, 1979
Ritchie-Calder Jan 31, 1982
Rolo, C. J. Oct. 26, 1982
Rosenberg, H. July 11, 1978
Ryle, G. Oct. 6, 1976
Schary, D. July 7, 1980
Scott, P. Mar. 1, 1978
Seton-Watson, H. Dec. 19, 1984
Sexton, A. Oct. 4, 1974
Shaw, R. Aug. 28, 1978
Slonim, M. May 8, 1976
Smith, R. P. Jan. 30, 1977
Smith, S. G. Jan. 16, 1975
Snow, W. Sept. 28, 1977
Streeter, E. Mar. 31, 1976
Sturgeon, T. May 8, 1985
Tanner, E. E., 3d Nov. 6, 1976
Tarsis, V. Mar. 3, 1983
Thomas, G. Apr. 14, 1981
Tynan, K. July 26, 1980
Weiss, P. May 10, 1982
Wheeler, H. July 27, 1987
White, T. H. May 15, 1986
Wibberley, L. Nov. 22, 1983
Williams, Jay July 12, 1978
Williams, R. Jan. 26, 1988
Wimsatt, W. K., Jr. Dec. 17, 1975
Wolfe, B. D. Feb. 21, 1977
Wright, James Mar. 25, 1980
"Yourcenar, M." Dec. 17, 1987
Zukofsky, L. May 19, 1978